International Dictionary of Films and Filmmakers-3
ACTORS and ACTRESSES

International Dictionary of Films and Filmmakers

Volume 1
FILMS

Volume 2
DIRECTORS

Volume 3
ACTORS and ACTRESSES

Volume 4
WRITERS and PRODUCTION ARTISTS

International Dictionary of Films and Filmmakers-3
ACTORS and ACTRESSES
THIRD EDITION

EDITOR

AMY L. UNTERBURGER

PICTURE EDITOR

CLAIRE LOFTING

ST. JAMES PRESS
AN IMPRINT OF GALE

Detroit • New York • Toronto • London

Amy L. Unterburger, *Editor*
David E. Salamie, *Contributing Editor*

ST. JAMES PRESS STAFF

Nicolet V. Elert, *Project Coordinator*
Laura Standley Berger, Peg Bessette, Joann Cerrito, David Collins, Miranda H. Ferrara,
Janice Jorgensen, Margaret Mazurkiewicz, Michael J. Tyrkus, *Contributing Editors*
Peter M. Gareffa, *Managing Editor, St. James Press*

Mary Beth Trimper, *Production Director*
Shanna Heilveil, *Production Assistant*

Cynthia Baldwin, *Art Director*
C. J. Jonik, *Desktop Publisher*
Pamela A. Hayes, *Photography Coordinator*
Randy Bassett, *Image Database Supervisor*
Mikal Ansari, Robert Duncan, *Imaging Specialists*

Victoria B. Cariappa, *Research Manager*
Jennifer Lund, *Research Specialist*
Julia C. Daniel, *Research Associate*

∞™ The paper used in this publication meets the minimum
requirements of American National Standard for Information Sciences—
Permanence Paper for Printed Library Materials, ANSI Z39.48-1984.

♾ This book is printed on recycled paper that meets Environmental Protection Agency Standards.

International dictionary of films and filmmakers. — 3rd ed.
    p. cm.
    Includes bibliographical references and indexes.
    Contents: v. 1. Films / editors, Nicolet V. Elert, Aruna Vasudevan — v. 2. Directors / editor, Laurie Collier Hillstrom — v. 3. Actors and actresses / editor, Amy Unterburger — v. 4. Writers and production artists / editor, Grace Jeromski.
    ISBN 1-55862-300-0 (v. 1 : alk. paper). — ISBN 1-55862-301-9 (v. 2 : alk. paper). — ISBN 1-55862-302-7 (v. 3 : alk. paper). — ISBN 1-55862-303-5 (v. 4 : alk. paper)
    1. Motion pictures—Plots, themes, etc. 2. Motion picture producers and directors—Biography—Dictionaries. 3. Motion picture actors and actresses—Biography—Dictionaries.
PN1997.8.I58 1996
791.43'03—dc20
                                                                                96-31536
                                                                                CIP

Printed in the United States of America

St. James Press is an imprint of Gale

Cover photograph—Norma Talmadge courtesy Kobal Collection

10 9 8 7 6 5 4 3 2 1

P75848

CONTENTS

EDITOR'S NOTE

This is a revised edition of the third volume of the *International Dictionary of Films and Filmmakers* series which also includes Volume 1, *Films*, Volume 2, *Directors*, and Volume 4, *Writers and Production Artists*. This book has 652 entries (86 new to this edition), each consisting of a brief biography, a complete filmography, a selected bibliography of works on and by the entrant, and an expository essay by a specialist in the field. The majority of the entries from the previous edition have been retained here, with most being thoroughly updated. A few of the new entrants are people who are also listed in either the *Directors* or *Writers* volumes, but their entries in this volume are completely new and have been written from the standpoint of their work as actors. As film is primarily a visual medium, the majority of entries are illustrated, either by a portrait or by a representative still from the entrant's *oeuvre*.

The selection of entrants is a difficult process, and it is once again based on the recommendations of the advisers listed on page xiii. The book is intended to represent the wide range of interests within North American, British, and European film scholarship and criticism. The actors and actresses selected were deemed to be of interest based on popularity as well as critical acclaim. The eclecticism in both the list of entrants and the critical stances of the different writers emphasizes the multifarious notions of the cinema.

Thanks are due to the following: the staff of St. James Press, especially Nicolet Elert; all the advisers and contributors for their cooperation; and finally, my predecessors on this series, whose achievements I am proud and fortunate to build on.

A NOTE ON THE ENTRIES

Boldface rubrics have been added to the biographical section to make the various types of information (e.g., birth date, awards, agent's address) easier to locate. Non-English-language film titles are ordinarily given in the original language or a transliteration of it. Alternate release titles in the original language(s) are found within parentheses in italic, followed by release titles in English (American then British if there is a difference) and translations. The date of a film is understood to refer to its year of release in its country of origin unless stated otherwise.

In the list of films in each entry, a name in parentheses following a film title is that of the director(s). Information within the parentheses following the director's name, modifies, if necessary, then adds to the subject's principal function(s). The most common abbreviations used are:

assoc	associate
asst	assistant
d	director
ed	editor
exec pr	executive producer
mus	music
ph	cinematographer or director of photography
pr	producer
ro	role
sc	scenarist or scriptwriter

"Co-" preceding a function indicates collaboration with one or more persons. Other abbreviations that may be used to clarify the nature of an individual film are "doc"—documentary, and "ep"—episode. Finally, it should be noted that film titles in bold denote an entry on that film in Volume 1, *Films*.

PICTURE ACKNOWLEDGEMENTS

We are grateful to the following for supplying photographs, and granting permission to reproduce them in this volume.

Allaris Cooks-Erato-Films Inc./Recorded Releasing (courtesy Kobal Collection) (Helen Mirren)

Argos Films (Peter Falk, Bruno Ganz, Eiji Okada)

Artificial Eye - Mayfair Films (Anthony Hopkins, Emma Thompson)

Artificial Eye Film Company Ltd (Irene Papas, Michel Simon, Oleg Yankovsky)

BBC Picture Archives (Miranda Richardson)

BFI/Film on Four International/Sankofa Film & Video (courtesy Kobal Collection) (Kathy Bates)

British Film Institute, Department of Stills, Posters and Designs

Cannon (courtesy Kobal Collection) (Kim Basinger)

Carolco (courtesy Kobal Collection) (Arnold Schwarzenegger, Sharon Stone)

Carson-Sundance Institute/Columbia (courtesy Kobal Collection) (Ellen Barkin)

Castle Rock/Nelson/Columbia (courtesy Kobal Collection) (Meg Ryan)

Ciby 2000/Recorded Picture Company (courtesy Kobal Collection) (Keanu Reeves)

Le Cinémathèque Française, droits réservés (Gaston Modot)

Cinematograph AB (Liv Ullmann)

Cinergi Pictures (courtesy Kobal Collection) (Bruce Willis)

Columbia Pictures Industries Inc. (Ernest Borgnine, Marlon Brando, Charles Bronson, Richard Burton, Geraldine Chaplin, Montgomery Clift, Glenn Close, Charles Coburn, Claudette Colbert, Robert De Niro, Gérard Depardieu, Richard Dreyfuss, Faye Dunaway, Glenn Ford, Jodie Foster, John Garfield, Gloria Grahame, Cary Grant, Jean Harlow, Sterling Hayden, Rita Hayworth, Katharine Hepburn, William Holden, Gene Kelly, Jack Lemmon, Fred MacMurray, Karl Malden, Lee Marvin, Walter Matthau, Steve McQueen, Peter O'Toole, Julia Roberts, Eva Marie Saint, George C. Scott, Randolph Scott, Jean Seberg, Omar Sharif, Terence Stamp, James Stewart, Meryl Streep, Margaret Sullavan, Elizabeth Taylor, Eli Wallach)

Contemporary Films Limited (Elisabeth Bergner, Marcel Dalio, Klaus Kinski, Fernando Rey, Hanna Schygulla, Jean-Louis Trintignant)

CTE (Carlton) Limited (Leslie Howard, Charles Laughton, Vivien Leigh, Merle Oberon)

Daiei Co., Ltd. (Machiko Kyo, Toshiro Mifune)

De Laurentiis (courtesy Kobal Collection) (Isabella Rossellini)

El Desea-Lauren (courtesy Kobal Collection) (Carmen Maura)

Embassy (courtesy Kobal Collection) (Ralph Richardson)

EMI (courtesy Kobal Collection) (Mary Steenburgen)

Era Films (HK) Ltd. (Gong Li)

Erre Productions/Sovereign/ReteItalia (courtesy Kobal Collection) (Christopher Walken)

Film Booking Offices Ltd. (Claire Bloom, John Gielgud)

Les Films du Carrosse (Jean-Pierre Léaud, Oskar Werner)

Friedrich-Wilhelm-Murnau-Stiftung/Transit-Film-GmbH (Lil Dagover, Gustav Fröhlich, Werner Krauss, Conrad Veidt)

Gala Film Distributors Limited (Stéphane Audran, Dirk Bogarde)

Greenwich (courtesy Kobal Collection) (Jean-Pierre Cassel)

Hammer (courtesy Kobal Collection) (Raquel Welch)

Hulton Deutsch Collection (Jean Gabin, Clark Gable, Pola Negri, Mary Pickford, Norma Shearer, Barbara Stanwyck, Gloria Swanson)

Image Organisation (courtesy Kobal Collection) (Laurence Fishburne)

Island (courtesy Kobal Collection) (Roberto Benigni)

Island Alive (courtesy Kobal Collection) (Sonia Braga, William Hurt, Raul Julia)

The Kobal Collection (Bibi Andersson, Lew Ayres, James Cagney, Kevin Costner, James Dean, Michael Douglas, W.C. Fields, Errol Flynn, Paulette Goddard, John Huston, Ben Kingsley, Laurel and Hardy, Spike Lee, Jayne Mansfield, The Marx Brothers, Robert Mitchum, Winona Ryder, Sylvester Stallone, Norma Talmadge, Kathleen Turner)

The Kobal Collection, photographer: Virgil Apger (Ava Gardner)

Ladd Company/Warner Bros (courtesy Kobal Collection) (Ed Harris, James Woods)

Live Entertainment (courtesy Kobal Collection) (Harvey Keitel)

London Films/British Lion (courtesy Kobal Collection) (Trevor Howard)

Lucas Film Ltd/Paramount (courtesy Kobal Collection) (Harrison Ford)

Lumiere Pictures Limited (Julie Christie, Joseph Cotten, Diana Dors, Robert Duvall, Gracie Fields, Joan Greenwood, Jack Hawkins, Michael Redgrave, Vanessa Redgrave, Paul Robeson, Donald Sutherland, Terry-Thomas, Googie Withers)

MacFilm/Entertainment (courtesy Kobal Collection) (John Turturro)

Merchant Ivory (courtesy Kobal Collection) (Greta Scacchi)

Merchant Ivory/Goldcrest (courtesy Kobal Collection) (Helena Bonham-Carter)

MGM (courtesy Kobal Collection) (Wallace Beery, Sidney Poitier)

MGM/Pathe (courtesy Kobal Collection) (Geena Davis)

MGM/United Artists (courtesy Kobal Collection) (Susan Sarandon)

Miramax/Buena Vista (courtesy Kobal Collection) (Samuel L. Jackson)

Mosfilm International (Sergei Bondarchuk, Vera Maretskaya)

NSW Film Corporation (courtesy Kobal Collection) (Judy Davis)

Orion (courtesy Kobal Collection) (Dudley Moore, Sean Penn, Dianne Wiest)

Orion/Paramount (courtesy Kobal Collection) (Anjelica Huston)

Paragon Entertainment Corporation, courtesy of HandMade Films Limited (John Cleese, Bob Hoskins, Maggie Smith)

Paramount (courtesy Kobal Collection) (Woody Allen, Kevin Bacon, Andy García, Richard Gere, Tom Hanks, Steve Martin, Demi Moore, Eddie Murphy, Bill Murray, Kim Novak, Anthony Perkins, Debra Winger)

Pathe (courtesy Kobal Collection) (Jean-Louis Barrault, Pierre Brasseur)

PolyGram Filmed Entertainment (Nicolas Cage, Hugh Grant, Barbara Hershey, Jennifer Jason Leigh, Tim Robbins)

Propaganda/Polygram/Viacom (courtesy Kobal Collection) (Juliette Lewis, Brad Pitt)

The Rank Organisation Plc (Michael Caine, Madeleine Carroll, Cyril Cusack, Edith Evans, Richard Harris, Oscar Homolka, Jeremy Irons, Celia Johnson, Kay Kendall, Deborah Kerr, James Mason, John Mills, Margaret Rutherford, Anton Walbrook, Norman Wisdom)

Renaissance Films/BBC/Curzon Films (courtesy Kobal Collection) (Kenneth Branagh)

Renn/Burrill/SFP (courtesy Kobal Collection) (Nastassja Kinski)

RKO (courtesy Kobal Collection) (Agnes Moorehead)

Romulus Films Ltd (Humphrey Bogart, Leslie Caron, Simone Signoret)

The Samuel Goldwyn Company (Dana Andrews, Walter Brennan, Eddie Cantor, Frances Farmer, Miriam Hopkins, Walter Huston, Danny Kaye, Myrna Loy, Laurence Olivier, Frank Sinatra)

The Saul Zaentz Company (courtesy Kobal Collection) (Juliette Binoche)

Selznick/United Artists (courtesy Kobal Collection) (Joan Fontaine)

Shochiku Co., Ltd. (Setsuko Hara, Kyoko Kagawa, Chishu Ryu, So Yamamura)

Silver Pictures (courtesy Kobal Collection) (Antonio Banderas)

AB Svensk Filmindustri (Max Von Sydow)

Touchstone Pictures (courtesy Kobal Collection) (Warren Beatty, Danny DeVito, Martin Landau, Sam Shepard)

Touchstone/Warner Bros (courtesy Kobal Collection) (Robin Williams)

Tri Star (courtesy Kobal Collection) (Denzel Washington)

Twentieth Century Fox (courtesy Kobal Collection) (Don Ameche, Julie Andrews, Angela Bassett, Anne Baxter, Mel Brooks, Johnny Depp, Melanie Griffith, Charlton Heston, Holly Hunter, Bette Midler, Paul Newman, Gregory Peck, Joe Pesci, Harry Dean Stanton)

United Artists (courtesy Kobal Collection) (Sean Connery, Peter Finch, Dustin Hoffman, Diane Keaton, Shirley MacLaine)

United Artists/Fantasy Films (courtesy Kobal Collection) (Jack Nicholson)

Universal (courtesy Kobal Collection) (Abbott and Costello, Danny Aiello, Willem Dafoe, Deanna Durbin, Dennis Hopper, Jessica Lange, Lena Olin, Uma Thurman, Jean-Claude Van Damme)

Universal, photographer: James David (courtesy Kobal Collection) (Ralph Fiennes, Liam Neeson)

Vestron/MGM/United Artists (courtesy Kobal Collection) (Jamie Lee Curtis)

Vic/Appia (courtesy Kobal Collection) (Alan Bates)

Vog/Sigma photographer: Raymond Voinquel (courtesy Kobal Collection) (Jules Berry)

Warner Bros (courtesy Kobal Collection) (John Candy, Morgan Freeman, Whoopi Goldberg, Tommy Lee Jones, Michael Keaton, Kevin Kline, John Malkovich, Malcolm McDowall, Sam Neill, Kate Nelligan, Edward James Olmos, Michelle Pfeiffer, Sissy Spacek, Sigourney Weaver, Forest Whitaker)

Warner Bros/Silver Pictures (courtesy Kobal Collection) (Wesley Snipes)

Zoetrope/United Artists (courtesy Kobal Collection) (Martin Sheen)

ADVISERS

Jeanine Basinger
Rhona Berenstein
Rui Santana Brito
Robert Burgoyne
Michel Ciment
Douglas Gomery
Gina Marchetti

Ib Monty
Susan Oka
P. Adams Sitney
Anthony Slide
Robin Wood
Carole Zucker

CONTRIBUTORS

Joanne Abrams
Charles Affron
Anthony Ambrogio
Joseph Arkins
Cynthia Baron
Jeanine Basinger
John Baxter
Ronald Bowers
Pat H. Broeske
Constance Clark
William M. Clements
Elizabeth Coffman
Allen Cohen
Samantha Cook
R. F. Cousins
Corey K. Creekmur
Ramona Curry
Alan Dale
Jerome Delamater
Charles Derry
Maria DiBattista
Jay Dickson
Susan M. Doll
Raymond Durgnat
Rob Edelman
Mark W. Estrin
Quentin Falk
Greg S. Faller
Mario Falsetto
Rodney Farnsworth
Howard Feinstein
Cynthia Felando
M. S. Fonseca
Alexa L. Foreman
Anita Gabrosek
John A. Gallagher
Behroze Gandhy
Frances Gateward
Alan Gevinson
H. M. Glancy
Ilene S. Goldman

Douglas Gomery
Vcroslav Hába
Patricia King Hanson
Stephen L. Hanson
Matthew Hays
Catherine Henry
Steven Higgins
Kyoko Hirano
Guo-Juin Hong
Daniel Humphrey
Peter Hutchings
Curtis Hutchinson
Stuart M. Kaminsky
Virginia Keller
Philip Kemp
Susan Knobloch
Audrey E. Kupferberg
Philip Leibfried
Donald Liebenson
Roy Liebman
Richard Lippe
Janet E. Lorenz
Judah Löwe
G. C. Macnab
Frances M. Malpezzi
Elaine Mancini
Roger Manvell
Gina Marchetti
Donald W. McCaffrey
John McCarty
Joe McElhaney
Andy Medhurst
Vacláv Merhaut
Joseph Milicia
Ib Monty
John Mraz
Robert Murphy
Ray Narducy
Kim Newman
Arthur Nolletti Jr.
Linda J. Obalil

Daniel O'Brien
Margaret O'Connor
Liam O'Leary
Maryann Oshana
Kelly Otter
R. Barton Palmer
Robert Pardi
Sylvia Paskin
Julian Petley
Maria Racheva
Nancy Jane Richards
David E. Salamie
Richard Sater
H. Wayne Schuth
Ella Shochat
Don M. Short
Ulrike Sieglohr
Charles L. P. Silet
Anthony Slide
Edward S. Small
Claudia Springer
Jeff Stafford
Linda J. Stewart
Christina Stoyanova

Karel Tabery
Nicholas Thomas
Frank Thompson
Doug Tomlinson
Lee Tsiantis
Andrew Tudor
Frank Uhle
Blažena Urgošíková
Fiona Valentine
Ravi Vasudevan
Usha Venkatachallam
Mark Walker
George Walsh
Graham Webb
James M. Welsh
Dennis West
James D. Wilson
Richard Wilson
Bill Wine
Rob Winning
Robin Wood
Joanne L. Yeck
Carole Zucker

International Dictionary of Films and Filmmakers-3
ACTORS and ACTRESSES

LIST OF ENTRANTS

Bud Abbott and Lou Costello
Victoria Abril
Isabelle Adjani
Danny Aiello
Anouk Aimée
Woody Allen
Don Ameche
Dev Anand
Bibi Andersson
Harriet Andersson
Dana Andrews
Julie Andrews
Ann-Margret
Roscoe ("Fatty") Arbuckle
Alan Arkin
Arletty
Pedro Armendáriz
Antonin Artaud
Jean Arthur
Fred Astaire
Mary Astor
Richard Attenborough
Stéphane Audran
Gene Autry
Lew Ayres
Shabana Azmi

Lauren Bacall
Kevin Bacon
Stanley Baker
Lucille Ball
Anne Bancroft
Antonio Banderas
Vilma Banky
Theda Bara
Brigitte Bardot
Ellen Barkin
Jean-Louis Barrault
Ethel Barrymore
John Barrymore
Lionel Barrymore
Richard Barthelmess
Kim Basinger
Angela Bassett
Alan Bates
Kathy Bates
Anne Baxter
Nathalie Baye
Warren Beatty
Wallace Beery
Ralph Bellamy
Jean-Paul Belmondo
John Belushi
Roberto Benigni

Joan Bennett
Ingrid Bergman
Elisabeth Bergner
Jules Berry
Francesca Bertini
Juliette Binoche
Gunnar Björnstrand
Bernard Blier
Joan Blondell
Claire Bloom
Dirk Bogarde
Humphrey Bogart
Ward Bond
Sergei Bondarchuk
Helena Bonham-Carter
Ernest Borgnine
Clara Bow
Charles Boyer
Sonia Braga
Kenneth Branagh
Klaus Maria Brandauer
Marlon Brando
Pierre Brasseur
Rossano Brazzi
Walter Brennan
Jeff Bridges
Vlastimil Brodský
Charles Bronson
Louise Brooks
Mel Brooks
Joe E. Brown
Yul Brynner
Jack Buchanan
Geneviève Bujold
Ellen Burstyn
Richard Burton

James Caan
Nicolas Cage
James Cagney
Michael Caine
Louis Calhern
John Candy
Cantinflas
Eddie Cantor
Claudia Cardinale
Harry Carey
Leslie Caron
John Carradine
Madeleine Carroll
Jean-Pierre Cassel
Gino Cervi
Jackie Chan
Lon Chaney

Charles Chaplin
Geraldine Chaplin
Cyd Charisse
Soumitra Chatterjee
Cher
Nikolai Cherkassov
Maurice Chevalier
Julie Christie
John Cleese
Montgomery Clift
Glenn Close
Lee J. Cobb
Charles Coburn
James Coburn
Claudette Colbert
Ronald Colman
Scan Connery
Eddie Constantine
Gary Cooper
Jackie Cooper
Kevin Costner
Joseph Cotten
Broderick Crawford
Joan Crawford
Donald Crisp
Bing Crosby
Tom Cruise
Alain Cuny
Jamie Lee Curtis
Tony Curtis
Cyril Cusack
Peter Cushing

Willem Dafoe
Lil Dagover
Eva Dahlbeck
Marcel Dalio
Linda Darnell
Danielle Darrieux
Marion Davies
Bette Davis
Geena Davis
Judy Davis
Doris Day
Daniel Day-Lewis
James Dean
Olivia de Havilland
Alain Delon
Dolores Del Rio
Cathérine Deneuve
Robert De Niro
Gérard Depardieu
Johnny Depp
Bruce Dern

Danny DeVito
Angie Dickinson
Marlene Dietrich
Matt Dillon
Robert Donat
Diana Dors
Kirk Douglas
Melvyn Douglas
Michael Douglas
Marie Dressler
Richard Dreyfuss
Margaret Dumont
Faye Dunaway
Irene Dunne
Jimmy Durante
Deanna Durbin
Dan Duryea
Robert Duvall

Clint Eastwood
Nelson Eddy
Denholm Elliott
Edith Evans

Aldo Fabrizi
Douglas Fairbanks
Peter Falk
Frances Farmer
Mia Farrow
Alice Faye
María Félix
Fernandel
José Ferrer
Edwige Feuillère
Sally Field
Gracie Fields
W. C. Fields
Ralph Fiennes
Peter Finch
Albert Finney
Laurence Fishburne
Barry Fitzgerald
Errol Flynn
Henry Fonda
Jane Fonda
Joan Fontaine
Glenn Ford
Harrison Ford
Jodie Foster
Kay Francis
Morgan Freeman
Pierre Fresnay
Gustav Fröhlich

Jean Gabin
Clark Gable
Bruno Ganz
Greta Garbo
Andy García
Ava Gardner
John Garfield

Judy Garland
James Garner
Greer Garson
Vittorio Gassman
Janet Gaynor
Daniel Gélin
Richard Gere
Giancarlo Giannini
Mel Gibson
John Gielgud
John Gilbert
Annie Girardot
Lillian Gish
Paulette Goddard
Whoopi Goldberg
Gong Li
Ruth Gordon
Elliott Gould
Betty Grable
Gloria Grahame
Stewart Granger
Cary Grant
Hugh Grant
Lee Grant
Sydney Greenstreet
Joan Greenwood
Melanie Griffith
Alec Guinness

Gene Hackman
Tom Hanks
Setsuko Hara
Jean Harlow
Ed Harris
Richard Harris
Rex Harrison
William S. Hart
Kazuo Hasegawa
Jack Hawkins
Goldie Hawn
Sessue Hayakawa
Sterling Hayden
Susan Hayward
Rita Hayworth
Sonja Henie
Paul Henreid
Audrey Hepburn
Katharine Hepburn
Barbara Hershey
Charlton Heston
Dustin Hoffman
William Holden
Judy Holliday
Oscar Homolka
Bob Hope
Anthony Hopkins
Miriam Hopkins
Dennis Hopper
Edward Everett Horton
Bob Hoskins
Leslie Howard

Trevor Howard
Rock Hudson
Holly Hunter
Isabelle Huppert
John Hurt
William Hurt
Anjelica Huston
John Huston
Walter Huston

Pedro Infante
Jeremy Irons

Glenda Jackson
Samuel L. Jackson
Sam Jaffe
Emil Jannings
Celia Johnson
Al Jolson
James Earl Jones
Jennifer Jones
Tommy Lee Jones
Erland Josephson
Louis Jourdan
Louis Jouvet
Raul Julia

Kyoko Kagawa
Anna Karina
Boris Karloff
Danny Kaye
Buster Keaton
Diane Keaton
Michael Keaton
Ruby Keeler
Harvey Keitel
Gene Kelly
Grace Kelly
Kay Kendall
Arthur Kennedy
Deborah Kerr
Ben Kingsley
Klaus Kinski
Nastassja Kinski
Kevin Kline
Fritz Kortner
Werner Krauss
Dilip Kumar
Machiko Kyo

Alan Ladd
Veronica Lake
Hedy Lamarr
Dorothy Lamour
Burt Lancaster
Elsa Lanchester
Martin Landau
Harry Langdon
Jessica Lange
Angela Lansbury
Charles Laughton

Stan Laurel and Oliver Hardy
Jean-Pierre Léaud
Bruce Lee
Christopher Lee
Spike Lee
Janet Leigh
Jennifer Jason Leigh
Vivien Leigh
Jack Lemmon
Jerry Lewis
Juliette Lewis
Max Linder
Harold Lloyd
Margaret Lockwood
Gina Lollobrigida
Herbert Lom
Carole Lombard
Tadeusz Łomnicki
Sophia Loren
Peter Lorre
Myrna Loy
Bela Lugosi
Paul Lukas
Ida Lupino

Jeanette MacDonald
Shirley MacLaine
Fred MacMurray
Harald Madsen and Carl Schenstrøm
Anna Magnani
Karl Malden
John Malkovich
Dorothy Malone
Silvana Mangano
Jayne Mansfield
Jean Marais
Fredric March
Vera Maretskaya
Mae Marsh
Herbert Marshall
Dean Martin
Steve Martin
Lee Marvin
The Marx Brothers
Giulietta Masina
James Mason
Raymond Massey
Marcello Mastroianni
Walter Matthau
Victor Mature
Carmen Maura
Joel McCrea
Hattie McDaniel
Roddy McDowall
Malcolm McDowell
Victor McLaglen
Steve McQueen
Adolphe Menjou
Melina Mercouri
Burgess Meredith
Bette Midler

Toshiro Mifune
Ray Milland
Ann Miller
John Mills
Sal Mineo
Liza Minnelli
Carmen Miranda
Helen Mirren
Robert Mitchum
Tom Mix
Gaston Modot
Marilyn Monroe
Yves Montand
Robert Montgomery
Demi Moore
Dudley Moore
Agnes Moorehead
Jeanne Moreau
Michèle Morgan
Masayuki Mori
Ivan Mozhukin
Armin Mueller-Stahl
Paul Muni
Eddie Murphy
Bill Murray

Alla Nazimova
Anna Neagle
Patricia Neal
Liam Neeson
Pola Negri
Sam Neill
Kate Nelligan
Paul Newman
Jack Nicholson
Asta Nielsen
David Niven
Philippe Noiret
Nick Nolte
Mabel Normand
Kim Novak
Ramon Novarro
Ivor Novello
Jan Nowicki

Warren Oates
Merle Oberon
Edmond O'Brien
Margaret O'Brien
Donald O'Connor
Maureen O'Hara
Eiji Okada
Daniel Olbrychski
Gary Oldman
Lena Olin
Laurence Olivier
Edward James Olmos
Maureen O'Sullivan
Peter O'Toole

Al Pacino
Geraldine Page

Jack Palance
Irene Papas
Smita Patil
Gregory Peck
Sean Penn
Anthony Perkins
Joe Pesci
Michelle Pfeiffer
Gérard Philipe
Michel Piccoli
Mary Pickford
Walter Pidgeon
Brad Pitt
Donald Pleasence
Sidney Poitier
Dick Powell
Eleanor Powell
William Powell
Tyrone Power
Micheline Presle
Elvis Presley
Robert Preston
Vincent Price
Richard Pryor
Edna Purviance

Dennis Quaid
Anthony Quayle
Anthony Quinn

George Raft
Raimu
Luise Rainer
Claude Rains
Fritz Rasp
Basil Rathbone
Ronald Reagan
Robert Redford
Michael Redgrave
Vanessa Redgrave
Oliver Reed
Keanu Reeves
Serge Reggiani
Lee Remick
Fernando Rey
Burt Reynolds
Debbie Reynolds
Miranda Richardson
Ralph Richardson
Thelma Ritter
Jason Robards
Tim Robbins
Julia Roberts
Rachel Roberts
Cliff Robertson
Paul Robeson
Bill ("Bojangles") Robinson
Edward G. Robinson
Ginger Rogers
Roy Rogers

Will Rogers
Mickey Rooney
Françoise Rosay
Isabella Rossellini
Mickey Rourke
Gena Rowlands
Jane Russell
Rosalind Russell
Margaret Rutherford
Meg Ryan
Robert Ryan
Winona Ryder
Chishu Ryu

Eva Marie Saint
Dominique Sanda
George Sanders
Susan Sarandon
Greta Scacchi
Roy Scheider
Maria Schell
Maximilian Schell
Romy Schneider
Arnold Schwarzenegger
Hanna Schygulla
George C. Scott
Randolph Scott
Jean Seberg
George Segal
Peter Sellers
Delphine Seyrig
Omar Sharif
Robert Shaw
Norma Shearer
Martin Sheen
Sam Shepard
Takashi Shimura
Sylvia Sidney
Simone Signoret
Jean Simmons
Michel Simon
Simone Simon
Frank Sinatra
Everett Sloane
Maggie Smith
Wesley Snipes
Alberto Sordi
Sissy Spacek
Sylvester Stallone
Terence Stamp

Harry Dean Stanton
Barbara Stanwyck
Mary Steenburgen
Rod Steiger
James Stewart
Sharon Stone
Meryl Streep
Barbra Streisand
Margaret Sullavan
Donald Sutherland
Gloria Swanson
Blanche Sweet

Hideko Takamine
Norma Talmadge
Kinuyo Tanaka
Jacques Tati
Elizabeth Taylor
Robert Taylor
Shirley Temple
Terry-Thomas
Emma Thompson
The Three Stooges
Ingrid Thulin
Uma Thurman
Gene Tierney
Topol
Spencer Tracy
John Travolta
Claire Trevor
Jean-Louis Trintignant
Yoko Tsukasa
Kathleen Turner
Lana Turner
John Turturro
Beata Tyszkiewicz

Liv Ullmann
Peter Ustinov

Rudolph Valentino
Alida Valli
Lee Van Cleef
Jean-Claude Van Damme
Charles Vanel
Conrad Veidt
Nelson Villagra
Monica Vitti
Rüdiger Vogler

Jon Voight
Gian Maria Volonté
Max Von Sydow

Anton Walbrook
Christopher Walken
Robert Walker
Eli Wallach
Denzel Washington
John Wayne
Sigourney Weaver
Clifton Webb
Paul Wegener
Johnny Weissmuller
Raquel Welch
Tuesday Weld
Orson Welles
Oskar Werner
Mae West
Forest Whitaker
Pearl White
Richard Widmark
Dianne Wiest
Cornel Wilde
Gene Wilder
Esther Williams
Robin Williams
Bruce Willis
Debra Winger
Angela Winkler
Shelley Winters
Norman Wisdom
Googie Withers
Anna May Wong
Natalie Wood
James Woods
Joanne Woodward
Fay Wray
Jane Wyman

Isuzu Yamada
So Yamamura
Oleg Yankovsky
Susannah York
Loretta Young
Robert Young

Mai Zetterling
Zhao Dan

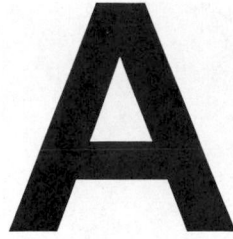

ABBOTT, Bud, and Lou COSTELLO

ABBOTT. Nationality: American. **Born:** William Abbott in Asbury Park, New Jersey, 2 October 1895. **Education:** Dropped out of school in 1909. **Family:** Married Betty Smith, 1918, 2 adopted children. **Career:** During childhood worked in carnivals, then assistant treasurer of Casino Theater in Brooklyn, treasurer or manager of various theaters throughout the United States; while manager at the National Theater in Detroit, worked vaudeville as straight man to performers such as Harry Steppe and Harry Evanson; 1931—while working as a cashier in a Brooklyn theater, asked to substitute for Costello's sick straight man, became a comic team; 1960s—unsuccessfully attempted to revive act with new partner Candy Candido; 1966—provided voiceover for cartoon version of *The Abbott and Costello Show*. **Died:** 26 February 1959.

COSTELLO. Nationality: American. **Born:** Louis Francis Cristillo in Paterson, New Jersey, 6 March 1906. **Education:** Finished high school. **Family:** Married the dancer Anne Battlers, 1934, children: Carole, Patricia, and Lou Jr. **Career:** Late 1920s—carpenter at MGM and Warners, later became stunt man, then comic in vaudeville; 1931—began working with Abbott; 1959—appeared on his own in a film and on television. **Died:** *24 April 1974.*

From 1931—worked as a team in burlesque (including Minsky's), minstrel shows, vaudeville and movie houses; 1938—team became known nationally from radio appearances on *The Kate Smith Hour*; 1939—starred in Broadway review *The Streets of Paris*, and signed by Universal for first film, *One Night in the Tropics*; 1941-49—starred in radio show *The Abbott and Costello Program* for ABC (1941-46) and NBC (1946-49); 1952-53—TV series *The Abbott and Costello Show*; 1957—both went broke, the team split up.

Films as Actors:

1940 *One Night in the Tropics* (Sutherland)
1941 *Buck Privates* (*Rookies*) (Lubin); *In the Navy* (Lubin); *Hold That Ghost* (Lubin); *Keep 'Em Flying* (Lubin); *Meet the Stars No. 4*
1942 *Who Done It?* (Kenton); *Ride 'Em Cowboy* (Lubin); *Rio Rita* (Simon); *Pardon My Sarong* (Kenton)
1943 *It Ain't Hay* (*Money for Jam*) (Kenton); *Hit the Ice* (Lamont)
1944 *In Society* (Yarbrough); *Lost in a Harem* (Riesner)
1945 *Here Come the Co-eds* (Yarbrough); *The Naughty Nineties* (Yarbrough); *Abbott and Costello in Hollywood* (Simon)
1946 *Little Giant* (*On the Carpet*) (Seiter); *The Time of Their Lives* (Barton); *The Ghost Steps Out* (Barton) (Abbott only)
1947 *Buck Privates Come Home* (*Rookies Come Home*) (Barton); *The Wistful Widow of Wagon Gap* (*The Wistful Widow*) (Barton)
1948 *The Noose Hangs High* (Barton); *Abbott and Costello Meet Frankenstein* (*Abbott and Costello Meet the Ghosts*) (Barton); *Mexican Hayride* (Barton)
1949 *Abbott and Costello Meet the Killer, Boris Karloff* (Barton); *Africa Screams* (Barton)
1950 *Abbott and Costello in the Foreign Legion* (Lamont); *The Real McCoy* (Abbott only)
1951 *Abbott and Costello Meet the Invisible Man* (Lamont); *Comin' Round the Mountain* (Lamont)
1952 *Jack and the Beanstalk* (Yarbrough); *Abbott and Costello Meet Captain Kidd* (Lamont); *Lost in Alaska* (Yarbrough)
1953 *Abbott and Costello Go to Mars* (Lamont)
1954 *Abbott and Costello Meet Dr. Jekyll and Mr. Hyde* (Lamont); *Screen Snapshots No. 225*
1955 *Abbott and Costello Meet the Keystone Cops* (Lamont); *Abbott and Costello Meet the Mummy* (Lamont)
1956 *Dance with Me, Henry* (Barton)
1959 *The 30 Foot Bride of Candy Rock* (Miller) (Costello only)
1965 *The World of Abbott and Costello* (compilation produced by Max Rosenberg and Milton Subotsky)

Publications

On ABBOTT and COSTELLO: books—

Anobile, Richard J., *Who's on First? Verbal and Visual Gems from the Films of Abbott and Costello*, New York, 1973.
Mulholland, Jim, *The Abbott and Costello Book*, New York, 1975.
Thomas, Bob, *Bud and Lou: The Abbott and Costello Story*, Philadelphia, 1977.
Costello, Chris, and Raymond Strait, *Lou's on First: A Biography*, New York, 1981.
Cox, Stephen, and John Lofflin, *The Official Abbott and Costello Scrapbook*, Chicago, 1990.
Furmanek, Bob, and Ron Palumbo, *Abbott and Costello in Hollywood*, New York, 1991.

On ABBOTT and COSTELLO: articles—

Barton, Charles, "Abbott and Costello: Wacky Camaraderie," in *Close-Ups: The Movie Star Book*, edited by Danny Peary, New York, 1978.
Shipman, David, in *The Great Movie Stars: The Golden Years*, rev. ed., London, 1979.
Article on Costello, in *Classic Images* (Indiana, Pennsylvania), May 1982.
Gifford, Denis, "Abbott and Costello," in *Films and Filming* (London), June 1984.

On ABBOTT and COSTELLO: film—

Bud and Lou, television movie directed by Robert C. Thompson, 1978.

* * *

Bud Abbott was the tall, mustached straight man; Lou Costello was the short, roly-poly clown. From 1941 to 1951 they reigned as Hollywood's top comedy team. Signed by Universal in 1939, the team was eventually thrown into a war comedy with the Andrews sisters, *Buck Privates*. Reportedly this film grossed a then-corporate record of

Bud Abbott (right) and Lou Costello with Jackie Loughery in *Abbott and Costello Go to Mars*

$10 million, and helped vault this pair of burlesque-trained comics onto the list of the top stars in Hollywood. In 1942 Abbott and Costello finished first in the poll, ahead of the likes of Clark Gable, Gary Cooper, Bob Hope, Betty Grable, and Spencer Tracy.

When they were discovered by Hollywood in 1939, the pair had already been working together for nearly a decade. They tried and perfected their verbal slapstick routines on thousands of burlesque and vaudeville audiences, taking the best of their material and performing it first to the nation as a whole on radio, and then in the movies. Even on Broadway in *Street of Paris*, they were "Abbott and Costello" exchanging funny dialogue in long-established routines. Their films, consequently, represent almost archival recordings of the long-lost art of burlesque comedy.

During World War II, they made an average of two films per year using a formula from which they rarely varied. The duo invariably were placed in a specific but familiar setting (often the military service) and left to wreak havoc, only interrupted for the required subplot involving a romance between two now long-forgotten Universal contract players. Only rarely did they have much help at the box office. Notable exceptions were the aforementioned Andrews sisters and in *Keep 'em Flying*, Martha Raye playing twin sisters.

But the box-office returns throughout the World War II era always stayed high; during that period the duo needed little help. As soon as the war was over, however, the pair began a steady decline. Universal tried a new formula featuring the pair confronted by a ghost or other force of evil. *Abbott and Costello Meet Frankenstein* set off a new seven-year cycle which included the duo dueling with Boris Karloff, the Invisible Man, Captain Kidd (portrayed by none other than Charles Laughton), Mr. Hyde, and the Mummy. During this run Abbott and Costello alternatively journeyed to exotic locales to romp: twice to Africa, and once each to rural Kentucky, Alaska, and the planet Mars.

All these filmic efforts only served to underscore the declining popularity of the comic pair, and so it was not surprising that they turned to the new medium of television in 1951. That year, they made their debut on NBC's *Colgate Comedy Hour* simply repeating an old radio routine. Then they decided to create their own half-hour series, *The Abbott and Costello Show* for the 1952-53 season. Although the series lasted only one year in prime time, the 52 episodes were then rerun constantly during the rest of 1950s. Once the package moved to independent stations it became a staple; one New York City station is said to have run each episode at least 200 times.

The residuals from the television series helped settle the duo's final public performance—a bout with the Internal Revenue Service over back taxes. After Costello's death, Abbott tried to revive the act with a new partner, Candy Candido, a Costello look-alike. This failed, but Abbott and Costello live on in their glory through the constant repetition of their movies and television shows on cable television.

—Douglas Gomery

ABRIL, Victoria

Nationality: Spanish. **Born:** Victoria Merida Rojas in Madrid, 14 July 1959. **Education:** Began studying dance at age eight, focused on ballet at Conservatory of Madrid until age 14. **Family:** Married Gustavo Lauve, 1976 (divorced 1981); two sons by current companion the cinematographer Gerard de Battista. **Career:** 1974—host of Spanish TV game show at age 15; 1976—English-language debut in *Robin and Marian*; 1978—in TV mini-series *The Bastard*; 1980s—top box-office attraction in Spain; 1990-93—international stardom via Almodóvar films; 1994—Hollywood debut in *Jimmy Hollywood*. Lives in France. **Awards:** San Sebastian Film Festival, Best Actress, for *El Lute: Camina o Revienta*, 1987; Berlin Film Festival, Best Actress, for *Amantes*, 1991; San Sebastian Film Festival, Best Actress, for *Nadie Hablara de Nosotras Cuando Hayamos Muerto*, 1995. **Agent:** Sandy Bresler, 15760 Ventura Boulevard, #1730, Encino, CA 91436, U.S.A.

Films as Actress:

1975 *Obsession*
1976 *Cambio de Sexo* (Aranda) (as José María/María José); *Robin and Marian* (Lester); *El Puente (The Lost Weekend)* (Bardem) (as Lolita)
1977 *Doña Perfecta* (Ardavin)
1979 *Mater Amatisima* (Salgot)
1980 *The Girl with the Golden Panties* (Aranda) (as Mariana)
1981 *Comin' at Ya!* (Baldi) (as Abilene)
1982 *Asesinato en el Comite Central (Murder in the Central Committee)* (Aranda); *J'ai Espouse une Ombre (I Married a Dead Man; I Married a Shadow)* (Robin Davis) (as Fifo); *La Colmena (The Beehive)* (M. Camus)
1983 *Le Batard* (van Effenterre) (as Betty); *Las Bicicletas Son Para el Verano (Bicycles Are for the Summer)* (Chavarri); *La Lune dans le Caniveau (The Moon in the Gutter)* (Beineix) (as Bella)
1984 *L'Addition* (Amar) (as Patty); *Le Voyage* (Andrieu) (as Veronique); *La Noche Mas Hermosa (The Most Beautiful Night)* (Gutiérrez Aragón) (as Elena); *Rio Abajo (On the Line)* (Borau) (as Engracia); *Padre Nuestro (Our Father)* (Regueiro) (as Cardenala)
1985 *L'Addition (The Bill)* (Amar) (as Patty); *After Darkness* (Othenin-Girard) (as Pascale); *Rouge Gorge* (Zucca); *La Hora Bruja* (De Arminan) (as Saga)
1986 *Tiempo de Silencio (Time of Silence)* (Aranda) (as Dorita); *Max Mon Amour (Max My Love)* (Oshima) (as Maria); *Ternosecco* (Giancarlo Giannini)
1987 *El Lute: Camina o Revienta (Lute: Forge on or Die)* (Aranda) (as Consuelo); *El Juego Mas Divertido* (Martínez-Lazardo) (as Ada Lasa/Sara); *El Placer de Matar (The Pleasure of Killing)* (Rotaeta); *Barrios Altos* (García Berlanga)
1988 *Baton Rouge* (Moleon) (as Ana Alonso); *Ada dans La Jungle* (Zingg) (as Carmen); *Sans Peur et Sans Reproche (Without Fear or Blame)* (Jugnot) (as Jeanne)

1989 *Si Te Dicen Que Caí (If They Tell You That I Fell)* (Aranda) (as Menchu/Ramona/Aurora Nin)
1990 *¡Atame! (Tie Me Up! Tie Me Down!)* (Almodóvar) (as Marina Osorio); *Sandino* (Littin); *A Solas Contigo* (Campoy); *Amantes (Lovers: A True Story)* (Aranda) (as Luisa)
1991 *Une Epoque Formidable (Wonderful Times)* (Jugnot) (as Juliette); *Tacones Lejanos (High Heels; Talons Lejanos)* (Almodóvar) (as Rebecca)
1992 *Demasiado Corazon* (Campoy)
1993 *Intruso (Intruder)* (Aranda) (as Luisa)
1994 *Kika* (Almodóvar) (as Andrea Scarface); *Jimmy Hollywood* (Levinson) (as Lorraine); *Casque Bleu (Blue Helmet)* (Jugnot) (as Alicia)
1995 *Gazon Maudit (French Twist)* (Balasko) (as Loli); *Nadie Hablara de Nosotras Cuando Hayamos Muerto (Nobody Will Talk about Us When We're Dead)* (Díaz Janes) (as Gloria)
1996 *Libertarias* (Aranda) (as Aura); *Trois Vies et Une Seule Mort* (Raúl Ruiz)

Publications

By ABRIL: articles—

"The Pain in Spain," interview with D. Wells, in *Time Out* (London), 4 May 1992.
"Queen Victoria," interview with Pedro Almodóvar, in *Interview* (New York), April 1994.

On ABRIL: books—

Besas, Peter, *Behind the Spanish Lens*, Denver, 1985.
Schwartz, Ronald, *The Great Spanish Films*, Metuchen, New Jersey, 1991.
Kinder, Marsha, *Blood Cinema*, London, 1993.
Deveny, Thomas G., *Cain on Screen: Contemporary Spanish Cinema*, Metuchen, New Jersey, 1993.
Monterde, José Enrique, *Veinte Años de Cine Español (1973-1992)*, Barcelona, 1993.

On ABRIL: articles—

Marinero, F., and V. Ciompi, "Victoria Por Si Misma," in *Casablanca* (Madrid), February 1984.
"Victoria Abril, Varier Les Roles de Composition," in *Revue du Cinéma* (Paris), June 1984.
"El Cine Como Pasion," in *Semana Internacional de Cine Valladolid* (Valladolid), 1991.
Millea, Holly, "Victor, Victoria," in *Premiere* (New York), May, 1994.

* * *

For those who only know Victoria Abril from her stunning Almodóvar troika, it may come as a shock that the classically trained dancer has been a working cinema actress since the age of 15. Unsurprisingly, given her background, her physicality and wanton body language are essential components of all her roles. She moves like a panther prowling to a flamenco beat. Burning up the international cinema with a sensuality that is not the by-product of cosmetic enhancement or Hollywood glamour, Abril possesses an animal magnetism that will deepen with the years like the appeal of Moreau, Magnani, or Ava Gardner. Abril attacks her parts with the same natural abandon with which she often sheds her clothes on screen; it is as if she wants no barrier between the reality of her characterization and the audience. You do not just watch an Abril performance, you experience it through your pores.

When you consider her wide range of roles, you realize that her sexuality is a gift of personality, a force of nature that she savvily uses to communicate as an actress. From her first English-language film appearance as the woodsy diversion for the King of England in *Robin and Marian*, she has made love to the camera as well as to her on-screen partners. From the mid-seventies, Spanish directors clamored for her services until she became that nation's top box-office attraction long before Almodóvar tied her up or down. In *Cambio de Sexo*, she portrayed a transsexual with a virtuosity well beyond the capabilities associated with a 16-year-old actress. In *Mater Amatisima*, she heartbreakingly enacted the mother of an 8-year-old autistic child despite being only 20 at the time. Despite her ebullient persona, her eyes suggest a familiarity with pain that has enabled her to tackle mature roles from her teenhood. During her ascent to superstardom espagnole, she played a free spirit inadvertently entangled in an incestuous affair in *The Girl with the Golden Panties*, subtly shaded three different whore roles in *If They Tell You That I Fell*, and limned another prostitute part with uncommon power in *On the Line*. Moving to France with her lover, cinematographer Gerard de Battista (with whom she has two sons), she spent her Abril in Paris years escaping the scathing reviews meted out for *The Moon in the Gutter* and impressing American audiences as one of the few causes for celebration in the star-deficient nineties. In the orgasmic film noir, *Lovers: A True Story*, she unleashed the sexual licentiousness that Hollywood femmes fatales of yesteryear could only intimate. Although the controversial *Tie Me Up! Tie Me Down!* played like an awkward blind date between director Almodóvar and his game-for-anything star, *High Heels*, their next collaboration, showcased Abril's unique blend of reckless vulnerability and murderously intense passion to dazzling effect. In this combination salute to Lana Turner's real-life excesses and acidic parody of women's films, Abril sent up all those resentful daughters of Melodrama who are content to pillory their mothers for their own frustrations. Following up her delicious roast of a television reality-show hostess who would sell her own soul (if she had one) for a scoop in *Kika*, Abril played sexy second banana to Joe Pesci in Barry Levinson's unwieldy show biz satire *Jimmy Hollywood*. Lighting up a gimmicky script with refreshing candor, she stole the film.

Although Levinson changed his mind about using her as the defense attorney in *Disclosure*, one hopes American moviemakers will divine the combustibility she could bring to Lotus Land and that her assets will be used more wisely than those of other emigrée casualties such as Lena Olin and Emmanuelle Béart. Whether in drama or comedy, what sets this off-the-wall temptress apart from other Euro-goddesses is that she takes Passion seriously, but not herself. Far beyond her awesome pliability as a screen presence, there is an Abrilian life force that rattles viewers out of complacency and makes every Abril performance seem as if you are discovering her for the very first time.

—Robert J. Pardi

Victoria Abril

Isabelle Adjani

ADJANI, Isabelle

Nationality: French. **Born:** Paris, 27 June 1955. **Education:** Attended Courbevoie public school. **Family:** Son, Barnabe, with film director Bruno Nuytten; son with actor Daniel Day Lewis. **Career:** 1969—debut in first film, *Le Petit Bougnat*, during school holiday; 1970—stage debut in Lorca's *The House of Bernada Alba* at Reims; 1973—became member of Comédie Française, Paris. **Awards:** Prix Suzanne Bianchetti, 1974; Best Actress, New York Film Critics, for *The Story of Adèle H.*, 1975; Best Actress, Cannes Festival, for *Possession* and *Quartet*, 1981; César Awards for Best Actress, for *Possession*, 1981, *L'Été meutrier*, 1983, and *Camille Claudel*, 1988.

Films as Actress:

1969   *Le Petit Bougnat* (Michel) (as Rose)
1972   *Faustine et le bel été* (*Faustine and the Beautiful Summer*) (Companeez) (as Camille); *L'Ecole des femmes* (Rouleau—for TV) (as Agnes)
1974   *La Gifle* (*The Slap*) (Pinoteau) (as Isabelle Doulean)

1975   *L'Histoire d'Adèle H.* (*The Story of Adèle H.*) (Truffaut) (title role)
1976   *Le Locataire* (*The Tenant*) (Polanski) (as Stella); *Barocco* (Téchiné) (as Laure)
1977   *Violette et François* (Rouffio) (as Violette)
1978   *The Driver* (Walter Hill) (as the Player)
1979   *Nosferatu—Phantom der Nacht* (*Nosferatu—The Vampire*) (Herzog) (as Lucy Harker); *Les Soeurs Brontë* (*The Brontë Sisters*) (Téchiné) (as Emily)
1980   *Clara et les chics types* (*Clara and the Nice Guys*) (Monnet) (as Clara)
1981   *Quartet* (Ivory) (as Marya Zelli); *Possession* (Zulawski) (as Anna/Helen); *L'Année prochaine si tout va bien* (*Next Year If All Goes Well*) (Hubert) (as Isabelle)
1982   *Antonieta* (Saura) (title role); *Tout feu tout flamme* (*All Fired Up*) (Rappeneau) (as Pauline Valance)
1983   *L'Été meurtrier* (*One Deadly Summer*) (Jean Becker) (as Eliane/Elle); *Mortelle randonnée* (*Deadly Circuit*) (Claude Miller) (as Catherine Leiris/Lucie "Marie")
1985   *Subway* (Besson) (as Helena)
1987   *Ishtar* (Elaine May) (as Shirra Assel)
1988   *Camille Claudel* (Nuytten) (title role, + co-pr)

1990 *Favorita Del Re* (Corti); *Fleur de Rubis* (Mocky); *Lung Ta:*
      Les cavaliers du vent (De Poncheville) (as narrator)
1993 *Toxic Affair* (Esposito) (as Penelope)
1994 *La Reine Margot* (*Queen Margot*) (Chéreau) (title role)
1996 *Diabolique* (Chechik) (as Mia)

Publications

By ADJANI: articles—

Interview with Guy Braucourt, in *Ecran* (Paris), November 1975.
Interview in *Interview* (New York), March 1976.
Interview with D. Maillet, in *Cinématographe* (Paris), January 1977.
"Une image filante," interview with André Philippon, in *Cahiers du Cinéma* (Paris), May 1983.
Interview with D. Maillet, in *Cinématographe* (Paris), December 1984.
Interview with Claire Devarrieux, in *Les Acteurs au travail*, Rennes, France, 1986.
Interview in *Première* (Paris), December 1988.
"The Story of Isabelle A," interview with Marilyn Goldin, in *Interview* (New York), January 1990.
Interview with Holly Milea, in *Premiere* (New York), March 1996.

On ADJANI: book—

Roques-Briscard, Christian, *Le Passion d'Adjani*, Paris, 1987.

On ADJANI: articles—

Truffaut, François, "Non conosco Isabelle Adjani," in *Filmcritica* (Rome), January/February 1976.
Ciné Revue (Paris), 22 April 1981 and 3 November 1983.
Séquences (Montreal), January 1984.
Toubiana, Serge, "Chére Isabelle Adjani," in *Cahiers du Cinéma* (Paris), December 1988.
Current Biography 1990, New York, 1990.
Rosen, Miriam, "Isabelle Adjani: The Actress as Political Activist," in *Cineaste* (New York), vol. 17, no. 4, 1990.
Bishop, Kathy, "Isabelle Stops at Nothing," in *American Film* (Hollywood), January 1990.
Collins, G., "The 'Hounding' of Isabelle Adjani," in *New York Times*, 6 January 1990.
Simmons, Judy, "Isabelle Adjani's Passion for Camille Claudel," in *Ms. Magazine* (New York), July/August 1990.

*   *   *

Isabelle Adjani is an intelligent and dedicated actress who chooses her roles with care and works on them with single-minded application. Unfortunately she has yet to achieve stardom outside France due to the mostly forgettable films in which she has so far elected to appear.

Truffaut, who gave her her first significant screen part in *L'Histoire d'Adèle H.*, observed that "she acts as though her life depended on it." Intensity, the fierce wounded stare of a woman at once independent and painfully vulnerable, is the essence of her screen persona, and, on all the evidence, of Adjani herself. "One acts nothing but oneself," she concedes, "no matter how fiercely one denies it." The film set the pattern for her career in more ways than one. In casting Adjani as Victor Hugo's daughter Adèle, who pursued an unrequited love beyond the brink of madness, it foreshadowed her frequent later roles as solitary obsessives, alienated and victimized by a punitive society.

In some ways, Adjani's exceptional beauty has worked against her. Small and delicate, with large, deep-blue eyes set in an oval face, she

has on occasion been reduced to little more than a decorative role—the errant socialite of Luc Besson's modish *Subway*, or the sexy friend of the dead woman the paranoid title character becomes involved with in Polanski's *Le Locataire*. Adjani's fragile looks have also landed her roles as emotionally or physically exploited women.

Her ambiguous combination of tenacity, even toughness, behind an air of childlike vulnerability underlies much of Adjani's best work. She has never lacked courage, professional or personal, and in a 1986 interview, disgusted by the rise of Le Pen's racist National Front, proclaimed her own non-French origins (she was born to a German mother and an Algerian father). Public reaction was swift and malicious: a rumor swept the country that she was dying of AIDS. Even her appearance on television, alive and in furious health, failed to still the whispers completely.

This ordeal fed powerfully into her playing of *Camille Claudel*. The film was a cherished personal project; she closely identified with the brilliant sculptress, destroyed by her affair with the egocentric Rodin and incarcerated for her last 30 years in an asylum. The urgency and fervor of her performance persistently burst through the film, her best in years. The follow-up epic *La Reine Margot*, from a novel by Alexandre Dumas, provided her with another meaty role, although her relatively one-note character is fairly overwhelmed by the substantial political intrigues which are the film's main subject. As the Catholic royal forced by her scheming mother Catherine de Médicis (Virna Lisi) to marry a Protestant royal to forge a political alliance, even though she loves another, she is constantly upstaged by the villainous Lisi, who has the much meatier role.

Her first two American movies—Walter Hill's Melvillesque thriller *The Driver* and Elaine May's megabuck disaster *Ishtar* were less than satisfactory attempts at launching the Hollywood career Adjani's considerable talents and beauty warrant. The more recent *Diabolique*, a botched updated remake of the classic Clouzot chiller that takes a panderingly feminist slant at the end which sinks the entire enterprise, will probably not do the trick, either.

—Philip Kemp, updated by John McCarty

AIELLO, Danny

Nationality: American. **Born:** New York City, 20 June 1933. **Education:** Attended James Monroe High School (two weeks). **Military Service:** U.S. Army. **Family:** Married Sandy Cohen, 1955, sons: Rick, Danny III, and Jaime, daughter: Stacey. **Career:** 1972—film debut in *The Godmother* (unreleased); 1973—first released film *Bang the Drum Slowly*; 1975—stage debut in *Lampost Reunion*, Little Theatre, New York City; 1985-86—in TV series *Lady Blue*. **Awards:** Theatre World Award, for *Lampost Reunion*, Little Theatre, New York City, 1975; Faberge Award, Straw Hat Award, Theatre World Award, Theatre of Reunion Award, for *That Championship Season*, Chicago production, 1975; Best Actor Award, L.A. Drama Critics Circle, for *Hurly Burly*, Los Angeles production, 1985; Los Angeles, Boston, and Chicago Film Critics Awards, for *Do the Right Thing*, 1989. **Agent:** William Morris Agency, 151 El Camino Drive, Beverly Hills, CA 90212, U.S.A. **Address:** 4 Thornhill Drive, Ramsey, NJ 07446, U.S.A.

Films as Actor:

1972 *The Godmother* (Russo—unreleased)
1973 *Bang the Drum Slowly* (Hancock) (as Horse)

Danny Aiello (right) with Spike Lee in *Do the Right Thing*

1974   ***The Godfather, Part II*** (Francis Ford Coppola) (as Tony Rosato)

1976   *The Front* (Ritt) (as Danny La Gattuta); *Hooch* (Edward Mann); *Kojak: Black Thorn* (Dubin—for TV)

1978   *Bloodbrothers* (*A Father's Love*) (Mulligan) (as Artie); *Fingers* (Toback) (as Butch); *The Last Tenant* (Jud Taylor—for TV) (as Carl); *Lovey: A Circle of Children, Part II* (Jud Taylor—for TV) (as Bernie Serino)

1980   *Defiance* (Flynn) (as Carmine); *Hide in Plain Sight* (Caan) (as Sal Carvello)

1981   *Chu Chu and the Philly Flash* (Rich) (as Johnson); *Fort Apache, the Bronx* (Petrie) (as Morgan)

1982   *Amityville II: The Possession* (Damiana); *A Question of Honor* (Jud Taylor—for TV) (as Martelli)

1983   *Blood Feud* (Newell—for TV) (as Randy Powers)

1984   *Deathmask* (Friedman) (as Mike Gress); *Old Enough* (Marisa Silver) (as Mr. Bruckner); ***Once upon a Time in America*** (Leone) (as Police Chief Aiello)

1985   *Key Exchange* (Kellman) (as Carabello); *The Protector* (Glickenhaus) (as Danny Garoni); *The Purple Rose of Cairo* (Woody Allen) (as Monk); *The Stuff* (Cohen) (as Vickers)

1986   *Tales from the Darkside: The Odds* (John Strysik—for TV) (as Tommy Vale)

1987   *Man on Fire* (*Absinthe*) (Chouraqui) (as Conti); *Moonstruck* (Jewison) (as Johnny Cammareri); *The Pick-Up Artist* (Toback) (as Phil); *Radio Days* (Woody Allen) (as Rocco); *Daddy* (Herzfeld—for TV) (as Coach Jacobs); *Russicum* (*The Third Solution*; *Russicum I Giorni del Diavolo*) (Squitieri) (as George Sherman)

1988   *White Hot* (Benson) (as Charlie Buick); *Alone in the Neon Jungle* (*Command in Hell*) (Georg Stanford Brown—for TV) (as Chief of Police)

1989   *The January Man* (O'Connor) (as Capt. Vincent Alcoa); *Crack in the Mirror* (*Do It Up*) (Benson) (as Charlie); *Do the Right Thing* (Spike Lee) (as Sal Frangoni); *Making of* Do the Right Thing (Bourne—doc) (as himself); *Harlem Nights* (Eddie Murphy) (as Phil Cantone); *The Preppie Murder* (Herzfeld—for TV) (as Detective Mike Sheehan)

1990   *Jacob's Ladder* (*Dante's Inferno*) (Lyne) (as Louis); *Lost Idol* (*Shock Troop*) (Chalong) (as John Cunningham)

1991   *The Closer* (Logothetis) (as Chester Grant); *29th Street* (Gallo) (as Frank Pesce Sr.); *Hudson Hawk* (Lehmann) (as Tommy Five-Tone); *Once Around* (Hallström) (as Joe Bella)

1992   *Mistress* (Primus) (as Carmine Rasso); *Ruby* (Mackenzie) (title role)

1993   *The Cemetery Club* (Duke) (as Ben Katz); *Me and the Kid* (Dan Curtis) (as Harry); *The Pickle* (Mazursky) (as Harry Stone)

1994   *Leon* (*The Cleaner*; *The Professional*) (Besson) (as Tony, + co-pr); *Ready to Wear* (*Prêt-a-Porter*) (Altman) (as Major Hamilton)

1995   *Lieberman in Love* (Lahti) (as Joe Lieberman); *The Road Home* (*He Ain't Heavy*) (Hamilton); *Power of Attorney* (Himelstein) (as Joe Scassi)

1996   *City Hall* (Harold Becker) (as Frank Anselmo); *Two Much* (Trueba) (as Gene Paletto); *2 Days in the Valley* (Herzfeld); *Mojave Moon* (Dowling); *Long Road Home*

Publications

By AIELLO: articles—

"*Harlem Nights*: Danny Aiello Is a Crooked Cop on the Take," interview with Charles Fleming, in *American Film*, November 1989.
"Case Study: Danny Aiello," interview with Kevin Koffler, in *Hollywood Reporter*, 8 May 1990.
"Danny Aiello: Hard Times to High Times," interview with Rod Lurie, in *West Side Spirit* (New York), 4 February 1991.
"Broadway Danny Aiello," interview with Gavin Smith, in *Film Comment* (New York), July/August 1991.

On AIELLO: articles—

Decker, John, "Call Him the Great Danny," in *Soho Weekly News* (New York), 14 June 1979.
Chase, Chris, "Danny Aiello, the Actor, Still a Working Man," in *New York Times*, 8 May 1981
Loeser, Deborah, "Forget the Screen Image—Danny Aiello Is More Cream Puff than Hard Roll," in *Chicago Tribune*, 24 March 1985.
Tajima, Renee, "Say the Right Thing," in *Village Voice* (New York), 20 June 1989.
Van Gelder, Lawrence, "At the Movies: for Danny Aiello, Life Is Busy and Sal the Pizza Man Is Not a Bigot," in *New York Times*, 7 July 1989.
Goldstein, Patrick, "Beyond the Bronx with Danny Aiello," in *Los Angeles Times Calendar*, 24 September 1989.
Carcaterra, Lorenzo, "Making Room for Danny," in *US* (New York), 11 December 1989.

Norman, Michael, "His Bus Came In," in *New York Times Magazine*, 21 January 1990.
Carcaterra, Lorenzo, "Danny Aiello," in *People Weekly* (New York), 19 February 1990.
Flatow, Sheryl, "I Wanted to Be More," in *Parade Magazine* (New York), 2 December 1990.
Schweiger, Daniel, "Once Around with Danny Aiello," in *Village View* (New York), 18-24 January 1991.
Golden, Tim, "Danny Aiello Travels the Blue-Collar Route to Stardom," in *New York Times*, 16 February 1991.
Smith, Gavin, "Broadway Danny Aiello," in *Film Comment* (New York), 1 July 1991.
Current Biography 1992, New York, 1992.
"Inspirational Actor Danny Aiello. Set to Start 'Breaking Legs' in Cerritos," in *Drama-Logue* (Hollywood), 30 September-6 October 1993.
Mischel, Rick, "Smiling All the Way to Success," in *Entertainment Today* (New York), 11-17 November 1994.

*   *   *

In the Hollywood studio era Danny Aiello would have made a respectable living as a character actor representing the tough urban guy from the school of hard knocks. His urban upbringing has had a definite bearing on his work in the theater and movies. A product of New York who can be considered a New York actor, Aiello has been featured in many films and television productions with a New York setting and theme.

He grew up in a large Italian family, with a father who was missing most of the time; his mother and siblings struggled. He had very little schooling, ran with street gangs, went into the Army, married, and found himself with a family at an early age. During a particularly desperate time in his life he reverted to criminal activity (which he freely admits) in order to pay the rent and feed his family.

He came to acting relatively late, more or less by chance, with virtually no training; even so he was soon working with important directors: Francis Ford Coppola, Martin Ritt, and Woody Allen. Over the course of his career to date, his roles have ranged from the vicious murdering cop in *Fort Apache, the Bronx* to more compassionate cop roles such as in *The Preppie Murder*. He has played small roles in many important films: *The Front*; *Bloodbrothers*, an impressive, underrated New York film; and *Jacob's Ladder*. In more major roles he has shown a distinctive acting ability, such as the crude, insensitive husband of *The Purple Rose of Cairo*; and the Momma's Boy, Johnny Cammareri, in *Moonstruck*, which brought out his comedic abilities. He is quite successful as the lead in *The Pickle*, a film that may be absurd in its concept, but which provides Aiello a showcase for his great comic talent as a Hollywood director with a nasty streak, struggling to overcome a string of flops.

He has also had leading roles as Jack Ruby in *Ruby* and Chester Grant in *The Closer* (a role recreated from the 1976 Broadway play *Wheelbarrow Closers*), but while these parts share the same characteristics—small-time loser and hood and paid FBI informer compared to a hard-driven, bitter, and nasty man alienated from his family—the films themselves are not successful. In many ways this underlines the dilemma in Aiello's acting career. Given good writers and directors, he can shine; if not, he will fall into a characteristic mold: a loud-mouthed and profane persona with a trademark laugh not always pertinent to the action of the film.

His most important film to date, the one that has gained him the most fame and recognition, is Spike Lee's *Do the Right Thing*. He is excellent in this film as the embattled Sal Frangoni, holding on to his pizza parlor in an all-black Bedford-Stuyvesant. Some of his best acting occurs in the interchanges between father and sons, and this type of relationship, both in real life and on the screen, has great importance to him. While vituperative, angry, opinionated and frustrated to the point of violence, he is still able to convey warmth and compassion for the African Americans that he lives with. He says to his bigoted son: "Why is there so much anger in you? I never had trouble with these people. They grew up on my food. I'm very proud of it. Sal's is here to stay. I'm your father and I love you." Aiello claims that there is about 85 percent of himself in the film; his wife in real life claims it is 100 percent.

While this film has been the most important of his career, his most successful films have been the ones in which he portrays a family man, a loving father and husband, working hard to keep his family together. The two films that show him with this wonderful range of acting ability, along with his characteristic hard edges, are *29th Street* and *Once Around*. The essence of Aiello's acting may well be found in these films; his performances show great depth, compassion, sympathy, and humor. The films are moving and successful in large part because of him—probably due to the opportunity they offer Aiello to act out much of what he lacked as a child when his father was not around, and there was not much love and support from his father for his children. Danny Aiello is making up for those hard times, and being quite successful at it.

—Allen Cohen

AIMÉE, Anouk

Nationality: French. **Born:** Françoise Sorya Dreyfus in Paris, 27 April 1932, daughter of the actor Henri Dreyfus (performed as Henri Murray, or simply Murray) and Geneviève Sorya (family name Durand). **Education:** Attended École de la rue Milton, Paris; École de Barbezieux; Pensionnat de Bandol; Institution de Megève; studied dance at Marseilles Opera; studied theater in England, then at Cours Bauer-Therond. **Family:** Married 1) Edouard Zimmermann, 1949 (divorced); 2) the director Nico Papatakis, 1951 (divorced 1954), daughter: Manuela; 3) Pierre Barouh, 1966 (divorced); 4) the actor Albert Finney, 1970 (divorced 1978). **Career:** Began stage acting at age 14; 1946—film debut in *La Maison sous la mer* (as "Anouk"); 1948—first screen success in *Les Amants de Vérone* in role written for her by Jacques Prévert. **Awards:** Best Foreign Actress, British Academy, for *Un Homme et une femme*, 1966; Best Actress, Cannes Festival, for *Salto nel vuoto*, 1979. **Agent:** Artmédia, 10 av George V, 75008 Paris, France.

Films as Actress:

1946   *La Maison sous la mer* (Calef)
1947   *La Fleur de l'âge* (Carné—unfinished)
1948   *Les Amants de Vérone* (*The Lovers of Verona*) (Cayatte) (as Georgia "Juliette" Maglia)
1949   *Golden Salamander* (Neame) (as Anna)
1951   *Conquêtes du froid* (Vidal); *Noche de tormenta* (*Nuit d'orage*) (de Moyora)
1952   *La Bergère et le ramoneur* (Grimault) (as voice); *The Paris Express* (*The Man Who Watched Trains Go By*) (French) (as Jeanne); *Le Rideau cramoisi* (*Les Crimes de l'amour*; *The Crimson Curtain*) (Astruc) (as Albertine)
1953   *Ich suche dich* (Fischer)
1954   *Forever My Heart* (*Happy Birthday*) (Arliss and Knowles)
1955   *Contraband Spain* (Huntington) (as Elena Vargas); *Les Mauvaises Rencontres* (Astruc)
1956   *Nina* (Jugert) (as Nina Iwanowa); *Stresemann* (Braun)

1957   *Tous peuvent me tuer* (*Anyone Can Kill Me*) (Decoin); *Pot-Bouille* (*The House of Lovers*) (Duvivier); *Montparnasse 19* (*Modigliani of Montparnasse*; *The Lovers of Montparnasse*) (Jacques Becker) (as Jeanne Hebuterne)
1958   *La Tête contre les murs* (*The Keepers*) (Franju); *Carve Her Name with Pride* (Gilbert)
1959   *The Journey* (*Some of Us May Die*) (Litvak) (as Eva); *Les Dragueurs* (*The Chasers*; *The Young Have No Morals*) (Mocky)
1960   *La dolce vita* (Fellini) (as Maddalena)
1961   *Lola* (*Donna di vita*) (Demy) (title role); *Le Farceur* (*The Joker*) (de Broca) (as Helene Laroche); *L'imprévisto* (Lattuada); *Quai Notre Dame* (Berthier); *Il giudizio universale* (*The Last Judgment*) (de Sica)
1962   *Sodoma e Gomorra* (*Sodom and Gomorrah*; *The Last Days of Sodom and Gomorrah*) (Aldrich and Leone) (as Queen Bera); *Les Grands Chemins* (*Of Flesh and Blood*; *Il Baro*) (Marquand) (as Anna)
1963   *8½* (*Otto e mezzo*) (Fellini) (as Luisa Anselmi); *Il giorno più corto* (*The Shortest Day*) (Corbucci); *Il terrorista* (de Bosio); *Il successo* (Morassi and Risi) (Blasetti)
1964   *Liolà* (*A Very Handy Man*); *Le voci bianche* (*White Voices*; *Le Sexe des Anges*; *Under Cover Rouge*) (Campanile and Franciosa) (as Lorenza); *La fuga* (Spinola) (as Luisa)
1965   *Il morbidone* (Franciosa); *La stagione del nostro amore* (*A Very Handy Man*; *Liola*) (Vancini) (as Mita)
1966   *Lo scandalo* (Gobbi); *Un Homme et une femme* (*A Man and a Woman*) (Lelouch) (as Anne Gauthier)
1968   *Un Soir, un train* (*One Night, a Train*) (Delvaux) (as Anne)
1969   *The Model Shop* (Demy) (as Lola); *Justine* (Cukor) (title role); *The Appointment* (Lumet) (as Carla)
1976   *Si c'était à refaire* (*If I Had to Do It All over Again*; *A Second Chance*) (Lelouch) (as Sarah Gordon)
1978   *Mon Premier Amour* (*My First Love*) (Chouraqui) (as Jane Romain)
1979   *Salto nel vuoto* (*A Leap in the Dark*; *Leap into the Void*) (Bellocchio) (as Marta Ponticelli); *Une Page d'amour* (Chouraqui—for TV)
1981   *La Tragedia di un uomo ridiculo* (*The Tragedy of a Ridiculous Man*) (Bertolucci) (as Barbara Spaggiari)
1982   *Qu'est-ce qui fait courir David?* (Chouraqui); *Le Général de l'armée morte* (*Il generale dell'armata morta*) (Tovoli)
1984   *Vive la vie* (Lelouch); *Success Is the Best Revenge* (Skolimowski) (as Monique de Fontaine)
1985   *Flagrant Desire* (*A Certain Desire*) (Faraldo)
1986   *Un Homme et une femme: vingt ans déjà* (*A Man and a Woman: 20 Years Later*) (Lelouch) (as Anne Gauthier)
1989   *La Table tournante* (Grimault); *Arrivederce e Grazie* (Capitani)
1990   *There Were Days and Moons*; *Bethune: The Making of a Hero* (*Dr. Bethune*) (Borsos—released in U.S. in 1993) (as Marie-France Coudaire)
1991   *Voices in the Garden* (Bouton); *Das Schicksal des Freiherrn von Leisenbohg* (Molinaro)
1993   *Ruptures* (Citti) (as Marthe); *Les Marmottes* (*The Groundhogs*) (Chouraqui) (as Françoise)
1994   *Ready to Wear* (*Pret-a-Porter*) (Altman) (as Simone Lowenthal)
1995   *Les Cent et une Nuits* (*A Hundred and One Nights*) (Varda) (as Actor for a Day); *Dis-Moi Oui*

Publications

By AIMÉE: book—

Fables de la Fontaine en bandes dessinées, Paris, 1984.

Anouk Aimée

By AIMÉE: article—

Interview in *Télérama* (Paris), 24 May 1980.

On AIMÉE: articles—

Ecran (Paris), November 1979.
Ciné Revue (Paris), 3 April 1980, 26 March 1981, 17 March 1983, and 12 July 1984.

* * *

Anouk Aimée made her film debut in 1946 in a small role in the Calef film *La Maison sous la mer*. Her first starring role was in Marcel Carné's *La Fleur de l'âge*, but that film remained unfinished. In effect, then, her first real success was in Cayatte's love drama *Les Amants de Vérone*, a loose adaptation of Shakespeare's *Romeo and Juliet*. Critics had reservations about the script, but there was no doubt about the obvious talent of the young actress. She went on to play in Astruc's *Le Rideau cramoisi* and *Les Mauvaises Rencontres*. Not only her abilities as an actress but also the photogenic qualities of her face, with its fine lines, expression of elation, and suggestive gaze, were used to particular effect in Duvivier's *Pot-Bouille*, Becker's *Montparnasse 19*, and Franju's *La Tête contre les murs*.

But she was not always lucky. In spite of being known outside France (she made films in Spain, Great Britain, and Germany), she did not always work with directors who knew how to make use of her art. Then in the early 1960s she attracted worldwide attention in the title role of Demy's *Lola* and particularly in the part of the rich, haughty Maddalena in Fellini's *La dolce vita*, in which her aristocratic demeanor provided a telling contrast to the more elemental charms of Anita Ekberg. She appeared again for Fellini in the role of the patient wife in *8½*. Aimée remained in Italy during the first half of the 1960s, and made a variety of films for Italian directors which are of varying qualities and genres— among them, *Liolà*, *Le voci bianche*, and *La stagione del nostro amore*.

The greatest success of her career came in 1966, in a film by the then still relatively unknown French director Claude Lelouch, *Un Homme et une femme*. The young director succeeded in rendering a seemingly banal love story in an unexpected and new way, through his mastery of camera technique and setting the action in the milieu of automobile racing. Yet the tremendous international success it enjoyed (it won both the Grand Prize at the Cannes Film Festival in 1966 and an American Oscar) were undoubtedly due to the excellent performances of the stars, Aimée and Jean-Louis Trintignant.

In her subtle portrayal of the heroine—self-protective, then succumbing to a new love—Aimée seemed to create a new kind of femme fatale and a characterization she would return to in the future: a woman of sensitivity whose emotions are often kept secret. She has continued to play that woman, with the same moderation and tact but within a growing gamut of different emotions. A good example is Belgian director André Delvaux's *Un Soir, un train* in which she plays a Walloon woman who sacrifices herself to her husband, a university professor played by Yves Montand. The complicated relationship between the couple, exacerbated by their different languages and hovering on the boundary between reality and fantasy, ends in painful and tragic misunderstanding. Aimée's interpretation is perfect.

—Karel Tabery

ALLEN, Woody

Nationality: American. **Born:** Allen Stewart Konigsberg in Brooklyn, New York, 1 December 1935. **Education:** Attended Midwood High School, Brooklyn; New York University and City College of New York, 1953. **Family:** Married 1) Harlene Rosen, 1954 (divorced); the actress Louise Lasser, 1965 (divorced); one son and one daughter with the actress Mia Farrow. **Career:** 1952—started writing for Sid Caesar's show *Caesar's Hour*, also wrote for the *Ed Sullivan Show* and the *Tonight Show*; 1961—having been urged by managers Jack Rollins and Charles Joffe to become a stand-up comedian, debuted at The Duplex, a Greenwich Village nightclub; 1964-65—in TV series *That Was the Week That Was*; 1966—first play, *Don't Drink the Water*, opened on Broadway; 1969-70—played the leading role of Allan Felix in his own drama, *Play It Again, Sam* on Broadway; 1965—film acting debut in *What's New, Pussycat?*, his own screenplay; 1969—film directing debut in *Take the Money and Run*. **Awards:** Sylvania Award, for script of an episode of *Caesar's Hour*, 1957; Academy Awards for Best Director and Best Original Screenplay, and National Society of Film Critics Award, for *Annie Hall*, 1977; British Academy Award and New York Film Critics Award, Best Screenplay, for *Manhattan*, 1979; Academy Award for Best Screenplay, Golden Globe Award, and New York Film Critics Award, for *Hannah and Her Sisters*, 1987; D. W. Griffith Lifetime Achievement Award, Directors Guild of America, 1996. **Agent:** Rollins and Joffe, 130 West 57th Street, New York, NY 10019, U.S.A.

Films as Actor:

1965 *What's New, Pussycat?* (Clive Donner) (as Victor Shakapopulis, + sc)
1966 *What's Up, Tiger Lily?* (Tanaguchi—dubbed Japanese film) (as narrator, + pr, co-sc)
1967 *Casino Royale* (Huston and others) (as Jimmy Bond/Dr. Noah)
1972 *Play It Again, Sam* (*Aspirins for Three*) (Ross) (as Allan Felix, + sc)
1976 *The Front* (Ritt) (as Howard Prince)
1987 *King Lear* (Godard) (as Mr. Alien)
1991 *Scenes from a Mall* (Mazursky) (as Nick)

Films as Actor, Director, and Scriptwriter:

1969 *Take the Money and Run* (as Virgil Starkwell, co-sc)
1971 *Bananas* (as Fielding Mellish, co-sc)
1972 *Everything You Always Wanted to Know about Sex but Were Afraid to Ask* (as Victor/Fabrizio/Fool/Sperm)
1973 *Sleeper* (as Miles Monroe, co-sc, + mus)
1975 *Love and Death* (as Boris Dimitrovich Grushenko)
1977 **Annie Hall** (as Alvy Singer, co-sc)
1978 *Interiors* (d, sc only)
1979 **Manhattan** (as Isaac Davis, co-sc)
1980 *Stardust Memories* (as Sandy Bates)
1982 *A Midsummer Night's Sex Comedy* (as Andrew)
1983 **Zelig** (as Leonard Zelig)
1984 *Broadway Danny Rose* (title role)
1985 *The Purple Rose of Cairo* (d, sc only)
1986 *Hannah and Her Sisters* (as Mickey)
1987 *Radio Days* (as narrator); *September* (d, sc only)
1988 *Another Woman* (d, sc only)
1989 "Oedipus Wrecks" ep. of *New York Stories* (as Sheldon Mills); *Crimes and Misdemeanors* (as Cliff Stern)
1990 *Alice* (d, sc only)
1992 *Shadows and Fog* (as Kleinman); *Husbands and Wives* (as Gabe Roth)
1993 *Manhattan Murder Mystery* (as Larry Lipton, co-sc)
1994 *Bullets over Broadway* (d, co-sc only); *Don't Drink the Water* (for TV)
1995 *Mighty Aphrodite* (as Lenny Weinrib)

Other Films:

1969   *Don't Drink the Water* (Morris) (sc)

Publications

By ALLEN: books—

Don't Drink the Water (play), New York, 1967.
Play It Again, Sam (play), New York, 1969.
Getting Even, New York, 1971.
Death (one-act play), New York, 1975.
God (one-act play), New York, 1975.
Without Feathers, New York, 1975.
Non-Being and Somethingness, New York, 1978.
Side Effects, New York, 1980.
The Floating Light Bulb (play), New York, 1982.
Four Films of Woody Allen (*Annie Hall, Interiors, Manhattan, Stardust Memories*), New York, 1983.
Hannah and Her Sisters, New York, 1987.
Three Films of Woody Allen (*Zelig, Broadway Danny Rose, The Purple Rose of Cairo*), New York, 1987.
Central Park West (one-act play), New York, 1995.

By ALLEN: articles—

"How Bogart Made Me the Superb Lover I Am Today," in *Life* (New York), 21 March 1969.
"On Love and Death," in *Esquire* (New York), 19 July 1975.
Inberview with Anthony DeCurtis, in *Rolling Stone* (New York), 16 September 1993.
"So You're the Great Woody Allen . . . ?," interview with Bill Zehme, in *Esquire* (New York), October 1994.

On ALLEN: books—

Lax, Eric, *On Being Funny: Woody Allen and Comedy*, New York, 1975.
Yacowar, Maurice, *Loser Take All: The Comic Art of Woody Allen*, New York, 1979; rev. ed., 1991.
Palmer, M., *Woody Allen*, New York, 1980.
Jacobs, Diane, *. . . But We Need the Eggs: The Magic of Woody Allen*, New York, 1982.
Brode, Douglas, *Woody Allen: His Films and Career*, New York, 1985.
Pogel, Nancy, *Woody Allen*, Boston, 1987.
Sinyard, Neil, *The Films of Woody Allen*, London, 1987.
McCann, Graham, *Woody Allen: New Yorker*, New York, 1990.
Lax, Eric, *Woody Allen*, New York, 1992.
Groteke, Kristi, *Mia & Woody*, New York, 1994.
Björkman, Stig, *Woody Allen on Woody Allen*, New York, 1995.
Blake, Richard Aloysius, *Woody Allen: Profane and Sacred*, Metuchen, New Jersey, 1995.
Perspectives on Woody Allen, edited by Renee R. Curry, New York, 1996.

On ALLEN: articles—

"Comedians: His Own Boswell," in *Time* (New York), 13 February 1963.
Mee, Charles L., "On Stage Woody Allen," in *Horizon* (New York), May 1963.
Zinsser, William K., "Bright New Comic Clowns toward Success: Woody Allen," in *Saturday Evening Post* (New York), 21 September 1963.
Schickel, Richard, "The Basic Woody Allen Joke," in *New York Times Magazine*, 7 January 1973.
Gilliatt, Penelope, "Profiles: Guilty, with an Explanation," in *New Yorker*, 4 February 1974.

Trow, George W. S., "A Film about a Very Funny Man," in *Film Comment* (New York), May/June 1977.
Gelmis, Joseph, "An Allen Overview" (plus critics's evaluations of three of his films), in *National Society of Film Critics on Movie Comedy*, New York, 1977.
Current Biography 1979, New York, 1979.
Gittleson, Natalie, "The Maturing of Woody Allen," in *New York Times Magazine*, 22 April 1979.
Didion, Joan, "Review of *Annie Hall, Interiors*, and *Manhattan*," in *New York Review of Books*, August 1979.
McMurtry, Larry, "Woody Allen: Neighborhood Filmmaker," in *American Film*, September 1979.
Maslin, Janet, "Woody Allen: Shunning Mastery?," in *New York Times*, 16 July 1982.
Liebman, R. L., "Rabbis or Rakes, Schlemiels or Supermen? Jewish Identity in Charles Chaplin, Jerry Lewis, and Woody Allen," in *Literature Film Quarterly* (Salisbury, Maryland), vol. 12, no. 3, July 1984.
Neibaur, James L., "Woody Allen," in *Movie Comedians: The Complete Guide*, Jefferson, North Carolina, 1986.
Zoglin, Richard, "Manhattan's Methuselah," in *Film Comment* (New York), May/June 1986.
Morris, Christopher, "Woody Allen's Comic Irony," in *Literature Film Quarterly* (Salisbury, Maryland), vol. 15, no. 3, 1987.
White, Armond, "Class Clowns," in *Film Comment* (New York), April 1987.
Blansfield, Karen C., "Woody Allen and the Comic Tradition in American," in *Studies in American Humor* (San Marcos, Texas), vol. 6, 1988.
Minowitz, Peter, "Crimes and Controversies: Nihilism from Machiavelli to Woody Allen," in *Literature Film Quarterly* (Salisbury, Maryland), vol. 19, no. 2, 1991.
Gabler, Neal, "Film View: Chaplin Blazed the Trail, Woody Allen Follows," in *New York Times*, 27 September 1992.
Combs, Richard, "Little Man, What Now?," in *Film Comment* (New York), July/August 1993.
Gopnik, Adam, "The Outsider," in *New Yorker*, 25 October 1993.
Siegel, Scott, and Barbara Siegel, "Woody Allen," in *American Film Comedy* (New York), 1994.
McGrath, Douglas, "Woody's World," in *New York*, 17 October 1994.
Jefferson, Margo, "Tapping the Funny Bone of American Comics," in *New York Times*, 14 January 1996.

*   *   *

Approaching his sixties after enacting more than 20 important or leading roles, Woody Allen portrays the middle-aged sports writer Lenny Weinrib in *Mighty Aphrodite*. This 1995 film reveals some characteristics of his part in a minor role playing opposite Peter Sellers and Peter O'Toole in the 1967 *What's New, Pussycat?* The dimension of the character and the maturity of Allen's acting skills, however, proved to be worlds apart from the earlier film. In his first appearance he portrayed a bumbling eccentric, Victor Shakapopulis, a role executed with a narrow range of the comedian's acting skills. Giving an elaborate interview conducted by Stig Björkman for the book, *Woody Allen on Woody Allen*, this writer-director-actor claimed that since he was directed by another person, he was allowed to see the results of his acting but never was allowed to redo scenes to correct the faults he saw in his work. The same he claimed was true of the role of the childishly temperamental, girl-chasing Jimmy Bond, a spoof of the famous Bond secret agent series in a film called *Casino Royale* (1967). Not until he was able to be his own director and writer for the 1969 *Take the Money and Run* would Allen control his own performance.

Woody Allen's *Mighty Aphrodite* still displays the features of the bumbler he created in his initial performance in *What's New, Pussycat?* This is revealed when he meets a prostitute named Linda Ash, enacted

Woody Allen in *Play It Again, Sam*

by Mira Sorvino. Her opening conversation with him produces confusion, frustration, and inadequacy—a typical pattern of reaction that Woody established in many of his film characterizations when faced with an aggressive or independent woman. Her sexual vulgarisms and blunt talk about various forms of physical encounters make him squirm. When he acts in such a scene, the audience can almost visualize an aura of perspiration radiating about his body.

Mighty Aphrodite also displays another variation on Woody's acting talents tied to a stressful situation. As Lenny, the sportswriter in this move, he is threatened by a sadistic thug, Linda Ash's pimp, because Lenny tries to steer Linda away from prostitution. The wimp Allen had played before in so many of his films can be noticed at this point of the movie, but he gives a twist that reveals his maturity as an actor. Faced with a brute who has him by the throat, Allen covers his fear with bravado as he promises the hulk he can get him tickets for a sporting event. Another feature of the comedian's use of character traits emerges. When pressed physically or when he wants to influence someone to take action, this nerd will con people. In *Mighty Aphrodite*, the juxtaposition of a variety of contrasting emotions makes this one of his most deft acting performances.

To understand the acting style of Woody Allen, it should be realized that he was a writer for many television comedians and hosts of talk shows such as Sid Caesar, Art Carney, Carol Channing, Jack Paar, and Garry Moore. His agents urged him to become a performer, and he made his debut as a stand-up comedian in 1961 at the Duplex nightclub in Greenwich Village. After moving to a number of clubs in New York City, he traveled to Chicago and San Francisco. Consequently, his fame as a performer spread throughout the nation. In the early 1960s he continued his writing because he could get more money. According to a *Time* article (15 February 1963): "He now gets $1,500 for supplying a comedian with a five-minute bit." His film writing reveals the stand-up comedy influence: the monologue as narration and the one-liner became an intrinsic part of many of his films.

The monologue-narration also relates directly to Allen's published humorous essays and to his stand-up comedian days and his acting in a number of films. Risible narration exists in *Take the Money and Run* (1969), *Bananas* (1971), *Love and Death* (1975), *Annie Hall* (1977), *Zelig* (1983), and *Radio Days* (1986).Woody Allen's ability as a stand-up comedian has been transferred to the screen as he plays a character in the comic drama. In *Take the Money and Run* Woody describes his own inadequacy as a bank robber in the character of Virgil Starkwell. This offscreen commentary is delivered in an off-hand, dry manner that makes this comedian's acting endearing to his fans. Overstatement and understatement may exist in the script, but Allen gives a

13

matter-of-fact delivery to punctuate the absurdity of the situation. The same can be said for the frame narration—especially in the beginning and ending of the film drama—of the award-winning *Annie Hall*. As Alvy Singer, the comedian rationalizes his struggle in this battle of the sexes.

A more direct use of the stand-up comedian's role is created when Allen plays the role of Court Jester in *Everything You Always Wanted to Know about Sex but Were Afraid to Ask* (1972). Woody portrays an appointed fool for royalty who fails as he tries his jokes on an audience that does not respond. When one of his weak one-liners falls flat, he says, with a breathy, frustrated voice, "I know you're out there: I can hear you breathing."

One-liners are, of course, the stock-in-trade gimmick for the stand-up comedian. In *Mighty Aphrodite*, the protagonist, face to face with a towering, amply endowed prostitute, declares whimsically, "At my age, if I made love to you, they'd have to put me on a respirator."

Even monologues are sprinkled with one- and two-liners. In *Annie Hall*'s opening narrative, Allen as Alvy Singer, faces the camera that uses this device. In a vague attempt to look on the bright side of turning 40 as he develops a bald spot, he uses a set-up line followed by a comic reversal: "I think I'm going to get better as I get older—you know, I think I'm going to be the balding, virile type." Allen's delivery is low-keyed with a clear-cut self-depreciating agony because he has broken up with his lover, Annie. In the closing remarks of *Love and Death*, filmed two years earlier, he faces the camera as he used to face an audience as a stand-up comic, and sums up his philosophy of life: "If it turns out there is a God, I don't think he's evil. The worst you can say is—he's an underachiever."

It should be noted that the quality of these one- and two-liner examples almost stand on their own because of Allen's innovative sense of humor. He received an Oscar nomination for acting in 1977 for *Annie Hall*. In addition, he received two other awards for writing and directing this film. Actresses he has groomed to excel in the cinema art have received kudos from the critics while his talent as an actor seems to be taken for granted. Woody's low-level intensity of acting not only fits his character, it also complements the characters of the other actors and actresses that play opposite him, to benefit the total production. His sharp timing from one joke to another possibly reflects his admiration for the ability of Bob Hope to deliver his lines (from Björkman's *Woody Allen on Woody Allen*).

In spite of this possible influence from another comedian, Woody Allen is no imitator of others. Since he plays a little man plagued by a variety of pretenders and bullies, some evaluators have compared his character and his control of his total work to those qualities of Chaplin's. "I can't tell you what I am, but I can tell you what I'm not: Chaplinesque," he is quoted in an entry for *World Film Directors*. Merely competent as a story teller, Chaplin became a genius as a director and a master filmmaker in a different way: a titan as a writer and director. His acting, as important as it is to many of his films, remains only distinctive and effective. Time will tell if Allen's acting will be considered by critics to be worthy of a higher rank.

—Donald W. McCaffrey

AMECHE, Don

Nationality: American. **Born:** Dominic Felix Amici in Kenosha, Wisconsin, 31 May 1908. **Education:** Attended Columbia Academy, Dubuque, Iowa; Columbia College (Loras College), Dubuque, 1926-28; studied law at Marquette University, Milwaukee, Georgetown University, Washington, D.C., and University of Wisconsin, Madison. **Family:** Married Honore Prendergast, 1932 (died 1978), children: Dominic Felix, Ronald John, Thomas Anthony, Lawrence Michael, Barbara,

and Cornelia (daughters adopted). **Career:** Late 1920s—while student acted with Madison stock company; 1929—brief Broadway appearance in *Jerry-for-Short*; toured briefly with Texas Guinan's vaudeville show; 1930—in radio series *The Empire Builder*, and others; 1936—contract with 20th Century-Fox; 1950—concentrated on TV and stage work; early 1980s—revived film career. **Awards:** Oscar for Best Supporting Actor, for *Cocoon*, 1985. **Died:** Of prostate cancer, in Scottsdale, Arizona, 6 December 1993.

Films as Actor:

1935   *Clive of India* (Boleslawski) (as Black Hole of Calcutta prisoner)
1936   *Sins of Man* (Brower and Ratoff) (as Karl Freyman/Mario Singarelli); *Ramona* (Henry King) (as Alessandro); *Ladies in Love* (Griffith) (as Dr. Rudy Imre)
1937   *One in a Million* (Lanfield) (as Bob Harris); *Love Is News* (Garnett) (as Martin Canavan); *Fifty Roads to Town* (Taurog) (as Peter Nostrand); *You Can't Have Everything* (Taurog) (as George Macrae); *Love under Fire* (George Marshall) (as Tracy Egan)
1938   *In Old Chicago* (King and Webb) (as Jack O'Leary); *Happy Landing* (Del Ruth) (as Jimmy Hall); *Josette* (Dwan) (as David Brossard Jr.); *Alexander's Ragtime Band* (Henry King) (as Charlie Dwyer); *Gateway* (Werker) (as Dick)
1939   *The Three Musketeers* (Dwan) (as D'Artagnan); *Midnight* (Leisen) (as Tibor Czerny); *The Story of Alexander Graham Bell* (Cummings) (title role); *Hollywood Cavalcade* (Cummings) (as Michael Linnett Connors); *Swanee River* (Lanfield) (as Stephen Foster)
1940   *Lillian Russell* (Cummings) (as Edward Solomon); *Four Sons* (Mayo) (as Chris); *Down Argentina Way* (Cummings) (as Ricardo Quintana)
1941   *That Night in Rio* (Cummings) (as Larry Martin/Baron Duarte); *Moon over Miami* (Walter Lang) (as Phil O'Neil); *Kiss the Boys Goodbye* (Schertzinger) (as Lloyd Lloyd); *The Feminine Touch* (Van Dyke) (as John Hathaway); *Confirm or Deny* (Mayo) (as Mitch)
1942   *The Magnificent Dope* (Walter Lang) (as Dawson); *Girl Trouble* (Schuster) (as Don Pedro Sullivan)
1943   *Heaven Can Wait* (Lubitsch) (as Henry Van Cleve); *Happy Land* (Pichel) (as Lew Marsh); *Something to Shout About* (Ratoff) (as Ken Douglas)
1944   *Wing and a Prayer* (Hathaway) (as Flight Cmdr. Bingo Harper); *Greenwich Village* (Walter Lang) (as Kenneth Harvey)
1945   *It's in the Bag* (Wallace); *Guest Wife* (Wood) (as Joe)
1946   *So Goes My Love* (Ryan) (as Hiram Stephen Maxim)
1947   *That's My Man* (*Will Tomorrow Ever Come*) (Borzage) (as Joe Grange)
1948   *Sleep, My Love* (Sirk) (as Richard Courtland)
1949   *Slightly French* (Sirk) (as John Gayle)
1961   *A Fever in the Blood* (Sherman) (as Sen. A. S. Simon)
1966   *Rings around the World* (segments of *International Showtime* TV circus program shown theatrically); *Picture Mommy Dead* (Gordon) (as Edward Shelley)
1970   *Suppose They Gave a War and Nobody Came?* (Averback) (as Col. Flanders); *The Boatniks* (Tikar) (as Cmdr. Taylor)
1983   *Trading Places* (Landis) (as Mortimer Duke)
1985   *Cocoon* (Ron Howard) (as Art Selwyn)
1986   *Masterpiece of Murder* (Dubin—for TV) (as Frank Aherne)
1987   *Harry and the Hendersons* (Dear) (as Dr. Wallace Wrightwood); *Pals* (Antonio—for TV) (as Art Riddle)
1988   *Cocoon: The Return* (Petrie) (as Art Selwyn); *Things Change* (Mamet) (as Gino); *Coming to America* (Landis) (as Mortimer Duke)

1991 *Oscar* (Landis) (as Father Clemente)
1992 *Oddball Hall* (Hunsicker) (as G. Paul Siebriese); *Folks!* (Kotcheff) (as Harry Aldrich)
1993 *Homeward Bound: The Incredible Journey* (Dunham) (voice of Shadow, the golden retriever)
1994 *Corinna, Corinna* (Jessie Nelson) (as Granpa Harry Singer)

Publications

By AMECHE: articles—

"The Reminiscences of Don Ameche," interview with Ronald D. Davis, Southern Methodist University oral history project on the performing arts, no. 3 (microfiche), Sanford, North Carolina, 1978.
Interview with L. Tanner, in *Films in Review* (New York), January 1989.

On AMECHE: articles—

Current Biography 1965, New York, 1965.
Madden, J. C., "Don Ameche," in *Films in Review* (New York), January 1972.
Chase, Chris, "Don Ameche Explains His Absence from Films," in the *New York Times*, 17 June 1983.

Roddick, Nick, "The Don Is Far from Dead," in *Cinema Papers* (Melbourne), November 1985.
Lancourt, B., "L'étonnant comeback de Don Ameche," in *Revue du Cinéma* (Paris), February 1989.
Obituary in *Variety* (New York), 20 December 1993.
Obituary in *New York Times*, 8 December 1993.

* * *

Clean-cut with dark wavy hair and a pencil-thin moustache, Don Ameche was good-looking but not handsome in the conventional movie star manner. Yet in film after film for Twentieth Century-Fox in the late 1930s and 1940s, he successfully held his own while sharing the screen with strong romantic all-American leads Tyrone Power and John Payne and exotic, naughty charmer Cesar Romero. Too soft and gentlemanly to play an effective villain and not leathery enough to play outdoorsmen, Ameche often portrayed the likable "regular guy" whose bland qualities were meant to contrast the allure of the star protagonist.

Even though Ameche's charisma was far more subtle than the likes of Power and Payne, audiences responded well to him and the powers at Fox found a variety of roles to keep him in front of the cameras. In his prime, he managed to have a successful screen career with starring and supporting roles in more than 40 motion pictures running the

Don Ameche in *The Story of Alexander Graham Bell*

gamut of genres. In a musical version of *The Three Musketeers*, he even got to play a singing D'Artagnan.

Ameche's work in *In Old Chicago*, a Fox prestige epic which offered him a featured part in the early stages of his contract, exemplifies his abilities and limitations. Ameche plays Jack O'Leary, an idealistic young lawyer and political reformer who is manipulated by his brother Dion (Tyrone Power), a wheeler-dealer with no scruples and nonstop sex appeal. Ameche is believable in the role, but it only requires him to be sweet and smiling, bland and stiff. Jack O'Leary is a case study in the one-dimensional utility parts Ameche often played. In fact, he continued to replay this type in a string of successful Technicolor musicals, appearing opposite Brazilian bombshell Carmen Miranda, forthright Alice Faye, and beautiful Betty Grable. Because he had such a calm and pleasant way about him in the midst of such vibrant stars, he too often wound up the wallflower of the bunch.

Ameche's finest portrayals at this stage of his career are in *Midnight* and *Heaven Can Wait*. These two films prove that given the right script and proper direction, he could turn in a first-rate performance. In *Midnight* Mitchell Leisen directs Ameche in an exemplary Billy Wilder-Charles Brackett screwball comedy. Here, he finally had a role with gradations and nuances: Tibor Czerny, a Hungarian taxi driver in Paris who comes to the aid of a down-and-out showgirl (Claudette Colbert). This film offers Ameche the rare opportunity to be determined and flirtatious, playful and cunning. For once he is Tyrone Power, John Payne, Cesar Romero—and Don Ameche—all packed into one strong performance. He is absolutely charming.

In the Ernst Lubitsch Technicolor masterpiece *Heaven Can Wait*, Ameche carries the film on his shoulders playing a spoiled rich kid who is seen over several decades, from boyhood to old age. For this role, Ameche loosened his traditionally stiff approach and gave a full-blooded comedy performance.

From the 1950s on, Ameche appeared infrequently on the big screen. His "comeback" came in 1985 in *Cocoon*, for which he won a Best Supporting Actor Oscar playing an energetic, spirited senior citizen; he further proved his acting mettle, drawing upon the gentlemanly quality which so endeared him decades before, for another comedy role. In *Things Change*, he played a humble Italian shoemaker who enjoys one final fling upon agreeing to take a murder rap for a Chicago mobster.

—R. Barton Palmer, updated by Audrey E. Kupferberg

ANAND, Dev

Nationality: Indian. **Born:** Devdutt Pishorimal Anand in Gurdaspur, 26 September 1923; brother of the directors Chetan Anand and Vijay Anand. **Education:** Attended Punjabi University, arts degree. **Family:** Married the actress Kalpana Kartik, two children, including the actor Suneil Anand. **Career:** 1946—film acting debut; 1949—co-founder of Navketan company, for which he has produced more than 20 films; 1970—directed first film, *Prem Pujari*; 1979—unsuccessful candidate for President of the National Party to oppose Indira Gandhi.

Films as Actor:

1946 *Hum Ek Hain* (P. L. Santoshi)
1947 *Aage Badho*; *Mohan*
1948 *Hum Bhi Insaan Hain*; *Ziddi*; *Vidya*
1949 *Jeet*; *Namuna*; *Shaysr*; *Udhaar*
1950 *Afsar* (Chetan Anand) (as Kapur); *Birha Ki Raat*; *Dilruba*;
        Hindustan Hamara; *Khel*; *Madhubala*; *Nili*; *Nirala*
1951 *Aaram*; *Baazi* (*A Game of Chance*) (Dutt) (as Madan, + pr);
        Do Sitare; *Nadaan*; *Sanam*; *Sazaa*; *Stage*

1952 *Aandhiyan* (Chetan Anand) (as Ram Mohan); *Jaal* (*The Net*)
        (Dutt) (as Tony); *Tamasha*; *Zalzala*; *Rahi* (*Two Leaves and
        a Bud*) (K. A. Abbas)
1953 *Armaan*; *Humsafar*; *Patita*
1954 *Baadbaan* (Phani Majumdar) (as Naren); *Feri*; *Taxi Driver*
        (Chetan Anand) (as Mangal); *Kashti*
1955 *Faraar*; *Makan no. 44* (*House No. 44*; *Ghar Number 44*) (M.
        K. Burman) (as Ashok); *Insaniyat* (*Humanity*) (Vasan) (as
        Bhanu); *Milap*; *Munimji* (Subodh Mukherjee) (as Amar)
1956 *C.I.D.* (Khosla) (as Police Inspector Shekhar); *Funtoosh*;
        Pocketmaar
1957 *Baarish*; *Dushman*; *Nau Do Gyarah* (Vijay Anand) (as Madan);
        Paying Guest (S. Mukherjee) (as Ramesh)
1958 *Amar Deep*; *Kala Pani* (Khosla) (as Karan); *Solva Saal*
1959 *Love Marriage*
1960 *Bambai Ka Babu* (Khosla) (Babu); *Ek Ke Baad Ek*; *Jaali Note*
        (Samanta) (as Inspector Dinesh); *Manzil*; *Sarhad*; *Kala
        Bazaar* (Vijay Anand) (as Raghuvir)
1961 *Hum Dono* (*We Two*) (Amarjeet) (as Capt. Anand/Maj. Verma);
        Maya; *Roop Ki Rani Choron Ka Raja*; *Jab Pyar Kisise Hota
        Hai* (Nasir Hussain) (as Sunder)
1962 *Baat Ek Raat Ki*; *Asli Naqli*
1963 *Tere Ghar Ke Saamne* (Vijay Anand) (as Rakesh Kumar); *Kinare
        Kinare*
1964 *Sharabi*
1965 *Teen Deviyan*; *Guide* (*Survival*) (Vijay Anand—Indian version; Danielewski—U.S. version) (as Raju)
1966 *Pyar Mohabbat*
1967 *Jewel Thief* (Vijay Anand) (as Vinay)
1968 *Duniya*; *Kahin Aur Chal*
1969 *Mahal*
1970 *Johnny Mera Naam* (Vijay Anand) (as Sohan)
1971 *Gambler*; *Tere Mere Sapne* (Vijay Anand) (as doctor)
1972 *Yeh Gulistan Hamara*
1973 *Banarasi Babu*; *Chhupa Rustom*; *Joshila*; *Shareef Badmash*
1974 *Amir Garib*; *Prem Shastra*
1975 *Warrant*
1976 *Jaaneman*; *Bullet*
1977 *Kalabaaz*; *Darling Darling*; *Saheb Bahadur*
1980 *Man Pasand*
1989 *Lashkar*
1990 *Aman Ke Farishte*

Films as Actor and Director:

1970 *Prem Pujari* (as Ram)
1971 *Hare Rama Hare Krishna*
1973 *Heera Panna*
1975 *Ishq Ishq Ishq*
1978 *Des Pardes*
1980 *Lootmaar*
1982 *Swami Dada*
1984 *Anand Aur Anand*
1985 *Hum Naujawan*
1989 *Sachche Ka Bol Bala*
1990 *Awwal Number*
1991 *Sau Crore*
1992 *Pyar Ka Tarana* (d only)

Publications

By ANAND: article—

Interviews in *Film World* (India), July 1975, January 1977, and January 1980.

On ANAND: books—

Willemen, Paul, and Behroze Ghandy, *Indian Cinema*, London, 1982.
Ramachandran, T. M., *70 Years of Indian Cinema (1913-1983)*, Bombay, 1985.

On ANAND: articles—

"Bombay Filmmaker Aims to Cut 'Ethnic Barrier' Facing Indian Pix," in *Variety* (New York), 1 November 1978.
"Profile," in *Films and Filming* (London), April 1979.
Film World (India), January 1980.
Filmfare, July 1983.
Khalid, "Golden Era Begins," in *Cinema in India* (Bombay), vol. 4, no. 6, 1990.
Sathe, V. P., "The Three Aces," in *Cinema in India* (Bombay), vol. 4, no. 4, 1993.
Rajadhyaksha, Ashish, and Paul Willemen, in *Encyclopaedia of Indian Cinema*, New Dehli, 1994.

*   *   *

One of the "Big Three" heroes of the 1940s and 1950s, sharing the triumvirate with Raj Kapoor and Dilip Kumar, Dev Anand now produces and directs his own films and still manages to play lead roles, a phenomenon that has earned him a reputation as the "evergreen hero"—the veritable Peter Pan of the Indian film world. He says his personal philosophy is "Don't look back, look forward." That he definitely does, as he proceeds from picture to picture with the same vigor and versatility that he brought with him 50 years ago.

His youthful image, while preserved with painstaking care, has mainly to do with his attitude toward life, rushing in where angels fear to tread and always being involved in new projects that sustain his bubbling enthusiasm. These range from being the first to use Himalayan backgrounds for love stories, to producing a smash hit based on the hippie phenomenon, seen from the point of view of the Indian popular establishment.

He started his film career in 1946 with *Hum Ek Hain*, directed by P. L. Santoshi. His first screen success, however, was *Ziddi* in 1948. Soon he was established as the trendsetter and the rage among the youngsters in India after independence. His production company Navketan, started in 1949, has given an opportunity to many acclaimed directors such as Guru Dutt and Raj Khosla. Though Anand's first directorial venture was *Prem Pujari* (1970), *Hare Rama Hare Krishna* (1971), a story based on the then popular hippie generation, had the viewers swaying to the tunes and the cash registers ringing in response.

The films are conceived more as a vehicle for the latest Anand image, than from sound commercial judgment, but of these perilous ventures *Guide*, the first Indo-American co-production, is of great significance. A collaboration with Pearl Buck, the deal involved two versions, the Indian version being very popular, with Anand playing the role of the guide who redeems his scurrilous image by fasting to death for rain and saving the lives of millions of drought-stricken villagers. His role in *Baazi* helped to launch the career of Guru Dutt, a very fruitful collaboration since Guru Dutt emerged as one of the great masters of Indian cinema.

Standing alone against the tide of the Congress government's recent courtship of film stars, he continues a resistance begun in 1979 when he stood as President of the National Party to oppose Indira Gandhi, though the campaign collapsed in shambles as it merely provoked the ogling response of the masses who came out to see one of their favorite film stars.

His film career is not as unlucky. He still is the hero in his films—raps, fights, and courts the younger heroines—as he did 50 years ago. His stature in Hindi cinema is such that he can now afford to experi-

ment with content and the style of filmmaking without a concern about the box office, an achievement indeed in the commerce-driven Bollywood. As veteran actor Shashi Kapoor said: "Dev Anand is the only star among us. His films may flop. But he goes on and on. We totter at our first flop."

—Behroze Gandhy, updated by Usha Venkatachallam

ANDERSSON, Bibi

Nationality: Swedish. **Born:** Berit Andersson in Stockholm, 11 November 1935. **Education:** Attended the Terserus Drama School; Royal Dramatic Theater School, Stockholm, 1954-56; attended theater school in Malmö. **Family:** Married 1) the director Kjell Grede, 1960 (divorced 1973), daughter: Jenny Matilda; 2) Per Ahlmark, 1978. **Career:** 1949—began working as an extra for the movies; 1955—appeared in *Smiles of a Summer Night*, first of several successful films for Ingmar Bergman; 1973—American stage debut in Erich Maria Remarque's *Full Circle*; 1990—debut as stage director, Stockholm. **Awards:** Best Actress (collectively awarded), Cannes Festival, for *Brink of Life*, 1958; Étoile de Cristal of French Film Academy for Best Actress, for *My Sister, My Love*, 1965; British Academy Award, Best Foreign Actress, for *The Touch*, 1971. **Address:** c/o Royal Dramatic Theatre, Storgatan 1, Stockholm 11444, Sweden.

Films as Actress:

1953   *Dum Bom* (*Stupid Bom*) (Poppe)
1954   *En natt på Glimmingehus* (*A Night at Glimminge Castle*) (Wickman); *Herr Arnes penningar* (*Sir Arne's Treasure*) (Molander)
1955   **Sommarnattens leende** (*Smiles of a Summer Night*) (Bergman) (as actress); *Flickan i regnet* (*Girl in the Rain*) (Kjellin); *Staden vid vattnen* (*Town by the Sea*) (Kjellgren) (as narrator)
1956   *Sista paret ut* (*Last Pair Out*; *Last Couple Out*) (Sjöberg) (as Kerstin); *Egen ingång* (*Private Entrance*) (Ekman)
1957   **Det sjunde inseglet** (*The Seventh Seal*) (Bergman) (as Mia); **Smultronstället** (*Wild Strawberries*) (Bergman) (as Sara); *Sommarnöje sökes* (*A Summer Place Is Wanted*) (Ekman)
1958   *Nära livet* (*Brink of Life*; *So Close to Life*) (Bergman) (as Hjordis Petterson); *Du är mitt äventyr* (*You Are My Adventure*) (Olin); *Ansiktet* (*The Face*; *The Magician*) (Bergman) (as Sara)
1959   *Den kära leken* (*The Love Game*) (Fant)
1960   *Bröllopsdagen* (*The Wedding Day*) (Fant) (as Sylvia Blom); *Djävulens öga* (*The Devil's Eye*) (Bergman) (as Britt-Marie)
1961   *Karneval* (*Carnival*) (Olsson); *Lustgården* (*The Pleasure Garden*) (Kjellin) (as Anna); *Nasilje na Trgu* (*Square of Violence*) (Bercovici) (as Maria)
1962   *Älskarinnan* (*The Swedish Mistress*) (Sjöman) (as girl); *Kort är sommaren* (*Pan*; *Short Is the Summer*) (Henning-Jensen) (as Edvarda Mack)
1964   *För att inte tala om alla dessa kvinnor* (*All These Women*; *Now about All These Women*) (Bergman) (as Humian); *Ön* (*The Island*) (Sjöberg)
1965   *Juninatt* (*June Night*) (Liedholm); *Syskonbädd 1782* (*My Sister, My Love*) (Sjöman)
1966   *Scusi, lei è favorevole o contrario* (*Scusi lei è contrario o favorevole*) (Sordi); **Persona** (*Masks*) (Bergman) (as Nurse Alma); *Duel at Diablo* (Ralph Nelson) (as Ellen Grange)

Bibi Andersson

1967 Le Viol (A Question of Rape; Overgreppet) (Doniol-Valcroze) (as Marianne Pescourt)

1968 Flickorna (The Girls) (Zetterling and Hughes); Svarta palmkronor (Black Palm Trees) (Lindgren)

1969 Storia di una donna (Story of a Woman) (Bercovici) (as Karin Ullman); Una estate in quattro (L'isola) (Vancini); Taenk på ett tal (Think of a Number) (Kjaerulff-Schmidt); En passion (A Passion; The Passion of Anna) (Bergman) (as Eva Vergerus)

1970 The Kremlin Letter (Huston) (as Erika Böck)

1971 Beröringen (The Touch) (Bergman) (as Karin Vergerus); Ingmar Bergman (Bjorkman) (as interviewee)

1972 Chelovek s drugoi storoni (The Man from the Other Side) (Yegorov)

1973 Scener ur ett äktenskap (Scenes from a Marriage) (Bergman— for TV, shortened version shown theatrically) (as Katarina); Afskedens timme (The Hour of Parting) (Holst)

1974 La rivale (The Rival; My Husband, His Mistress and I) (Gobbi)

1975 Il pleut sur Santjago (It Is Raining on Santiago) (Soto); Blondy (Germicide; Vortex) (Gobbi)

1976 En dåres försvarstal (A Madman's Defence) (Grede—for TV)

1977 I Never Promised You a Rose Garden (Ingen dans på rosor) (Page) (as Dr. Fried)

1978 An Enemy of the People (Schaefer) (as Catherine Stockmann); Justices (Cayatte); L'Amour en question (Cayatte) (as Catherine Dumas)

1979 The Concorde—Airport '79 (Airport '80—The Concorde) (Rich) (as Francine); Twee Vrouwen (Two Women; Twice a Woman; Second Touch) (Sluizer) (as Laura); Barnförbjudet (The Elephant Walk; Not for Children; The Elephant) (Bergenstråhle); Quintet (Altman) (as Ambrosia); A Look at Liv (Norway's Liv Ullmann; Liv Ullmann's Norway) (Kaplan—doc)

1980 Marmeladupproret (Marmalade Revolution) (Josephson and Nykvist); Prosperous Times

1981 Jag rödnar (I Blush) (Sjöman)

1982 Berget på månens baksida (Hjalström)

1983 Exposed (Toback) (as Margaret Carlson); Svarte fugler (Black Crows) (Glomm)

1984 Sista leken (The Last Summer) (Lindström)

1985 Wallenberg: A Hero's Story (Lamont Johnson—for TV)

1986 Husmenna (Rosma); Pobre Mariposa (Poor Butterfly) (De La Torre) (as Gertrud)

1987 Dueños del silencio (Lemos) (as Swedish ambassador); Svart Gryning (Lemos); Babette's Gastebud (Babette's Feast) (Axel) (as Lady-in-Waiting)

1988 Remando al Viento (Rowing with the Wind) (Suarez)

1989 Fordringsagare (Creditors) (Bohm) (as Tekla)

1992 Una Estacion de paso (Whistle Stop) (Querejeta) (as Lise)

1994 Dromspel (Dreamplay) (Straume) (as Victoria); Il Sogno della farfalla (The Butterfly's Dream) (Bellocchio) (as Mother)

1996 I rollerna tre (Olofson—doc) (as herself)

Publications

By ANDERSSON: article—

Interview by E. Decaux and B. Villien, in *Cinématographe* (Paris), January 1981.

On ANDERSSON: books—

Björkman, Stig, editor, *Bergman on Bergman,* New York, 1973.

On ANDERSSON: articles—

Burnevich, J., in *Séquences* (Montreal), February 1967.
"Dialogue on Film: Bibi Andersson," seminar in *American Film* (Washington, D.C.), March 1977.
Current Biography 1978, New York, 1978.
"Bibi Andersson," in *Ecran* (Paris), October 1978.
Parra, D., "Bibi Andersson: 'Eviter la nostalgie ...,'" in *Revue du Cinéma* (Paris), June 1990.
Lahr, John, "Ingmar's Woman," in *New Yorker*, 17 May 1993.

*   *   *

While still in her teens, Bibi Andersson began making her rounds of the film studios in Sweden; and her first important role was as an extra in a publicity film made by the man who discovered her, Ingmar Bergman. To further her career she took lessons at the Stockholm Drama School, and made her stage debut in a potato cellar that was the best known avant-garde theater in Stockholm in the early 1950s.

Following her theater training which included study at the Royal Dramatic Theater School from 1954-56, and a series of bit parts in films, Andersson made her first memorable screen appearance in a small role in *Smiles of a Summer Night*, thereby joining the wonderful company of actors who played in Bergman's films of the 1950s and 1960s.

Like other European-trained actors, Andersson's work is not an emotionally cathartic experience, but rather an exercise of knowledge and technique, as her versatility proves. Following her role in *The Seventh Seal*, as the wife in the pair of fairground innocents who survive the destruction of the knight and his family after the apocalypse, she played the hitchhiker in *Wild Strawberries*, again projecting a youthful hopefulness and innocence. Her portrayal of the unmarried mother in *Brink of Life* revealed a broader range and won her an award at Cannes (along with Ingrid Thulin for the same film).

With the exception of a role in *Now about All These Women*, Andersson did not work with Bergman for six years. Their collaboration resumed with her most important film, *Persona*, in which she established herself as an actress of international stature. This masterpiece owes much to Andersson's brilliance and is evidence of her greater emotional experience than was apparent in her earlier work. Playing opposite Liv Ullmann as the mute Elisabeth, Andersson was required to carry the dialogue of the film. A mutual transference of personae occurs, signified by the merging of their images on screen. The film required of Andersson an enormous extension of her talent; her submission to the film's somewhat cruel objectivity attested to Andersson's dedication—not only to the aims of Bergman's films but also to the demands made by a role of extraordinary emotional complexity. The characterization did much to erase the rather condescending view of her as a pleasant, lightweight actress, and elevated her to the first rank of Bergman's ensemble, along with Thulin and Ullmann.

Andersson then made a number of films with other Swedish directors, and worked again with Bergman in a supporting part in *The Passion of Anna*, in a central role opposite Elliott Gould in *The Touch*, and in a brief appearance in one episode of *Scenes from a Marriage*, which would be the last films they made together. In *The Touch* she turned in a performance that established her, according to one critic, as the warmest and most free-spirited of Bergman's women, both robust and compassionate.

Through her connection with Bergman, Andersson has been associated with Sweden's most famous international director, and through her marriage to the director Kjell Grede she has been linked to the New Wave of Swedish film. Interestingly enough she never made a theatrical film with Grede, but did appear in Vilgot Sjöman's *My Sister, My Love*, Lars-Magnus Lindgren's *Black Palm Trees*, and Mai Zetterling's *The Girls*. Like Ullmann and Thulin she has also appeared in a number of international films, usually wasting her talent. In such movies as John Huston's *The Kremlin Letter*, Sergio Gobbi's *Blondy*, Anthony Page's *I Never Promised You a Rose Garden*, George Schaefer's *An Enemy of the People*, and Robert Altman's *Quintet*, Andersson has not been able to achieve the level of performance attained in the finest of her Swedish films.

Andersson has also performed in numerous stage productions, including her 1973 Broadway debut in Otto Preminger's *Full Circle*, *After the Fall*, *Who's Afraid of Virginia Woolf?*, and *The Night of the Tribades*. She performed in Bergman's 1993 production of Ibsen's *Peer Gynt*, and in his 1995 production of Shakespeare's *A Winter's Tale*, both at the Brooklyn Academy of Music. She also directed a play in Stockholm about Strindberg's women, and a production of Sam Shepard's *True West* at the Royal Dramatic Theater of Sweden.

—Charles L. P. Silet, updated by Kelly Otter

ANDERSSON, Harriet

Nationality: Swedish. **Born:** Stockholm, 14 January 1932. **Family:** Married the director Jörn Donner. **Career:** 1949—stage debut in Stockholm revue; 1950—first film released, *Medan staden sover*; 1952—impressed with her performance in *Trots*, Ingmar Bergman wrote film *Monika* for her; 1954—engaged by Bergman for regular stage company, Malmö; later acted with Intiman theater of Stockholm, 1956, and with Hälsingborg town theater, 1961; 1980s—appeared regularly at Kungliga Dramatiska Teatern, Stockholm; **Awards:** German Film Critics Grand Prize, for *Through a Glass Darkly*, 1961; Venice Film Festival, Best Actress Award, for *To Love*, 1964; Swedish Film Association plaque. **Address:** c/o Sandrew Film and Theater AB, Box 5612, 114 86 Stockholm, Sweden.

Films as Actress:

1950   *Medan staden sover* (*While the City Sleeps*) (Kjellgren); *Anderssonskans Kalle* (*Mrs. Andersson's Charlie*) (Husberg) (as Majken); *Motorkavalierer* (*Cavaliers on the Road*) (Ahrle); *Två trappor över gården* (*Backyard*) (Werner)
1951   *Biffen och Bananen* (*Beef and the Banana*) (Husberg); *Puck heter jag* (*My Name Is Puck*) (Bauman); *Dårskapens hus* (*House of Folly*) (Ekman); *Frånskild* (*Divorced*) (Molander) (as applicant)
1952   *Sabotage* (Jonsson); *Ubåt 39* (*U-boat 39*) (Faustman); *Trots* (*Defiance*) (Molander)
1953   *Sommaren med Monika* (*Summer with Monika*) (Bergman) (title role); **Gycklarnas afton** (*Sawdust and Tinsel*; *The Naked Night*) (Bergman) (as Anne)
1954   *En lektion i kärlek* (*A Lesson in Love*) (Bergman) (as Nix)

1955   *Hoppsan!* (Olin); *Kvinnodröm (Dreams; Journey into Au-*
        tumn) (Bergman) (as Doris); ***Sommarnattens leende*** *(Smiles*
        of a Summer Night) (Bergman) (as Petra the Maid)
1956   *Sista paret ut (The Last Couple Out; Last Pair Out)* (Sjöberg)
        (as Anita); *Nattbarn (Children of the Night)* (Hellström)
1957   *Synnöve Solbakken* (Hellström)
1958   *Kvinna i leopard (Woman in Leopardskin; Woman in a*
        Leopardskin Coat) (Jan Molander); *Flottans överman (Com-*
        mander of the Navy) (Olin)
1959   *Brott i Paradiset (Crime in Paradise)* (Kjellgren); *Noc Poslubna*
        (Hääyö; En Brölloppsnatt; Wedding Night) (Blomberg)
1961   *Såsom i en spegel (Through a Glass Darkly)* (Bergman) (as
        Karin, the daughter); *Barbara* (Wisbar)
1962   *Siska* (Kjellin)
1963   *Lyckodrömmen (Dream of Happiness)* (Abramson); *En söndag*
        i september (A Sunday in September) (Jörn Donner)
1964   *För att inte tala om alla dessa kvinnor (All These Women; Now*
        about All These Women) (Bergman) (as Isolde); *Att älska (To*
        Love) (Jörn Donner) (as Louise); *Älskande par (Loving*
        Couples) (Zetterling and Hughes) (as Agda)
1965   *För vänskaps skull (Just Like Friends; For Friendship)*
        (Abramson); *Lianbron (The Vine Bridge; The Vine Garden)*
        (Nykvist); *Här börjar äventyret (Täällä Alkaa Seikkilu;*
        Adventure Starts Here) (Jörn Donner)
1966   *Ormen (The Serpent)* (Abramson)
1967   *The Deadly Affair* (Lumet) (as Ann Dobbs); "Han-hon" ("He-
        She") ep. of *Stimulantia* (Jörn Donner) (as woman in hotel
        room); *Mënniskor modes og sod musik opstår i hjertet*
        (Männeskor mötas och ljuv musik uppstår i hjärtat; People
        Meet and Sweet Music Fills the Air) (Carlsen) (as Sofia
        Petersen); *Tvärbalk (Rooftree; Crossbeams)* (Jörn Donner)
1968   *Jag älskar, du älskar (I Love, You Love)* (Björkman); *Flickorna*
        (The Girls) (Zetterling and Hughes) (as Marianne); *Kampf*
        um Rom (Fight for Rome) (Siodmak)
1969   *Kampf um Rom II (Fight for Rome II)* (Siodmak)
1970   *Anna* (Jörn Donner) (title role)
1971   *I havsbandet (The Sea's Hold; On the Archipelago Boundary)*
        (Lagerkvist—for TV)
1972   ***Viskningar och rop*** *(Cries and Whispers)* (Bergman) (as Agnes)
1973   *Bebek (Baby)* (Barbro and Karabuda—for TV)
1974   *Kallelsen* (Nykvist) (as narrator)
1975   "Den vita väggen" ("The White Wall") ep. of *Två Kvinnor*
        (Two Women) (Björkman—ep. also shown separately);
        Monismanien 1995 (Monismania 1995) (Fant)
1977   *Hempas bar (Triumph Tiger '57; Cry of Triumph)* (Thelestam)
1979   *Linus eller Tegelhusets hemlighet (Linus)* (Sjöman); *La sabina*
        (The Sabina) (Borau) (as Monica)
1982   ***Fanny och Alexander*** *(Fanny and Alexander)* (Bergman) (as
        Justina)
1983   *Raskenstam (Raskenstam—The Casanova of Sweden)*
        (Hellström) (as Cecilia Andersson)
1985   *De Två Saliga (These Blessed Two)* (Bergman—for TV) (as
        Viveka Burman)
1986   *Gösta Berlings Saga* (Lagerkvist)
1987   *Sommarkvåller på Jorden* (Lindblom) (as Magda)
1988   *Himmel og Helvede* (Arnfred) (as Jasmin)
1990   *Blankt Vapen* (Nykvist) (as Mama)
1993   *Hoyere enn Himmelen (Beyond the Sky)* (as Miss Kjaer)
1996   *I rollerna tre* (Olfson—doc) (as herself)

Publications

On ANDERSSON: articles—

Filmography in *Film Dope* (Nottingham, England), December 1972.

"Le vedette de la semaine: Harriet Andersson," in *Ciné Revue* (Brussels), 26 October 1978.

Ecran (Paris), February 1979 and 15 May 1979.

Bjorkman, S., "Harriet Andersson," in *Chaplin* (Stockholm), vol. 39, no. 5, 1993.

*   *   *

Of the many remarkable actresses associated with the work of Ingmar Bergman, Harriet Andersson has been perhaps the most versatile, yet there is a common denominator to all her seemingly diverse characterizations: sensuality (or, in certain cases, its frustration or repression). It is the keynote of the performance that established her as a major Bergman star, in the title role of *Summer with Monika*: apparently sluttish, shallow, and self-centered, the character is redeemed (both for Bergman and for the audience) partly by the film's graphic account of her squalid, miserable background, but more by her spontaneous, animal-like physicality. In the film's privileged moment, Bergman abruptly breaks the predominantly naturalistic, sequence-shot treatment of most of the film to isolate her face in close-up. As the background darkens, she stares straight into the camera, at *us*, defying us to "cast the first stone." Though the characterizations and contexts are quite different, Andersson's portrayals of the circus-owner's mistress in *The Naked Night* and the pert and experienced maidservant in *Smiles of a Summer Night* utilize the same basic trait of unashamed and unrepressed sexuality.

It is this basic premise of Andersson's image (as a Bergman star) that makes so moving the anguish of her more overtly serious roles in later films. In *Through a Glass Darkly* her physicality finds no release, caught as she is between a dull, well-meaning, unimaginative husband and a father who clinically studies her decline into schizophrenia; her ultimate breakdown is provoked by her desperate seduction of her younger brother in the womblike hull of an abandoned boat. The breakdown itself takes a hideously physical form: the hallucination of being violated by God in the form of a monstrous spider.

Andersson's Agnes in *Cries and Whispers* builds on her sensuality in another way: haggard, emaciated, eaten away by cancer, her whole body expresses the physical experience of pain perhaps more vividly than it has ever been expressed in the cinema. The significance of her scene of physical contact with the maid Anna has been much debated: is it maternal or lesbian? As the infant's first erotic experiences involve intimate contact with the mother, it can clearly be both, a reading strongly supported by Andersson's persona. Her most recent appearance in a Bergman theatrical film—as the middle-aged maidservant in the household of the repressive stepfather in *Fanny and Alexander*—again plays on Andersson's physicality: the character's sexual repression (sexuality perverted into mean-spirited aggression) expresses itself in the *physical* symptoms of open sores.

—Robin Wood

ANDREWS, Dana

Nationality: American. **Born:** Carver Dana Andrews in Collins, Mississippi, 1 January 1909 or 1912. **Education:** Attended Sam Houston College. **Family:** Married 1) Janet Murray (died 1935), child: David (deceased); 2) the actress Mary Todd, 1939, children: Katharine, Stephen, and Susan. **Career:** Early 1930s—hitchhiked to California to pursue career in films; 1935—studied to be a singer; 1936-38—worked at Pasadena Playhouse and made the rounds of stage companies and film studios; 1939-50—worked for both Goldwyn's studio and 20th Century-Fox as one of first actors under a split contract; 1958—

began appearing as guest star on various television series; 1969-72—on daytime TV soap opera *Bright Promise*; 1979—in TV mini-series *Ike*. **Died:** Of pneumonia in Los Angeles, California, 17 December 1992.

Films as Actor:

1940 *Lucky Cisco Kid* (Humberstone) (as Sergeant Dunn); *Sailor's Lady* (Dwan) (as Scrappy Wilson); *The Westerner* (Wyler) (as Bart Coble); *Kit Carson* (Seitz) (as Capt. John C. Fremont)

1941 *Tobacco Road* (John Ford) (as Dr. Tim); *Belle Starr* (Cummings) (as Maj. Thomas Crail); *Swamp Water* (*The Man Who Came Back*) (Renoir) (as Ben)

1942 *Ball of Fire* (Hawks) (as Joe Lilac); *Berlin Correspondent* (Forde) (as Bill Roberts)

1943 *Crash Dive* (Mayo) (as Lt. Cdr. Dewey Connors); *The Ox-Bow Incident* (*Strange Incident*) (Wellman) (as Donald Martin); *The North Star* (*Armored Attack*) (Milestone) (as Kolya); *December 7th* (Toland and Ford)

1944 *Up in Arms* (Nugent) (as Joe); *The Purple Heart* (Milestone) (as Capt. Harvey Ross); *Wing and a Prayer* (Hathaway) (as Moulton); *Laura* (Preminger) (as Mark McPherson)

1945 *State Fair* (Walter Lang) (as Pat Gilbert); *Fallen Angel* (Preminger) (as Eric Stanton); *A Walk in the Sun* (Milestone) (as Sergeant Tyne); *Know Your Enemy: Japan* (as narrator)

1946 *Canyon Passage* (Jacques Tourneur) (as Logan Stuart); *The Best Years of Our Lives* (Wyler) (as Fred Derry)

1947 *Boomerang* (Kazan) (as Henry L. Harvey); *Daisy Kenyon* (Preminger) (as Dan O'Mara); *Night Song* (Cromwell) (as Dan)

1948 *The Iron Curtain* (Wellman) (as Igor Gouzenko); *Deep Waters* (King) (as Hod Stilwell); *No Minor Vices* (Milestone) (as Perry Aswell)

1949 *The Forbidden Street* (*Britannia Mews*) (Negulesco) (as Herbert Lambert/Gilbert Lauderdale); *Sword in the Desert* (Sherman) (as Mike Dillon)

1950 *My Foolish Heart* (Robson) (as Walt Dreiser); *Where the Sidewalk Ends* (Preminger) (as Mark Dixon); *Edge of Doom* (*Stronger Than Fear*) (Robson) (as Father Roth)

1951 *Sealed Cargo* (Werker) (as Pat Bannon); *The Frogmen* (Lloyd Bacon) (as Flannigan); *I Want You* (Robson) (as Martin Greer)

1952 *Assignment Paris* (Parrish) (as Jimmy Race)

1954 *Elephant Walk* (Dieterle) (as Dick Carver); *Duel in the Jungle* (George Marshall) (as Scott Walters); *Three Hours to Kill* (Werker) (as Jim Guthrie)

1955 *Smoke Signal* (Jerry Hopper) (as Brett Halliday); *Strange Lady in Town* (LeRoy) (as Rork O'Brien)

1956 *Comanche* (Sherman) (as Read); *While the City Sleeps* (Fritz Lang) (as Ed Mobley); *Beyond a Reasonable Doubt* (Fritz Lang) (as Tom Garrett); *Hollywood Goes A-Fishing*

1957 *Night of the Demon* (*Curse of the Demon*) (Jacques Tourneur) (as John Holden); *Spring Reunion* (Pirosh) (as Fred Davis); *Zero Hour* (Bartlett) (as Ted Stryker)

1958 *The Fearmakers* (Jacques Tourneur); *Enchanted Island* (Dwan)

1960 *The Crowded Sky* (Pevney) (as Dick Barnett)

1962 *Madison Avenue* (Humberstone) (as Clint Lorimer)

1965 *In Harm's Way* (Preminger) (as Admiral Broderick); *The Satan Bug* (John Sturges) (as the General); *Crack in the World* (Marton) (as Stephen Sorensen); *Brainstorm* (Conrad) (as Cort Benson); *Town Tamer* (Selander); *The Loved One* (Richardson) (as Gen. Brinkson); *Battle of the Bulge* (Annakin) (as Col. Pritchard); *Catacombs* (*The Woman Who Wouldn't Die*) (Hessler)

1966 *Appuntamento per le spie* (*Spy in Your Eye*) (Sala) (as Col. Lancaster); *Johnny Reno* (Springsteen) (title role); *Supercolpo da 7 miliard* (*The 1000 Carat Diamond*; *Ten Million Dollar Grab*)

1967 *Il Cobra* (*The Cobra*) (Sequi) (as Kelly); *Hot Rods to Hell* (Brahm) (as Tom Phillips); *The Frozen Dead* (Leder) (as Dr. Norberg)

1968 *I diamanti che nessuno voleva rubare* (*No Diamonds for Ursula*); *The Devil's Brigade* (McLaglen) (as Brig. Gen. Walter Naylor)

1972 *Innocent Bystanders* (Collinson) (as Blake)

1974 *Airport 1975* (Smight) (as Scott Freeman)

1975 *Take a Hard Ride* (Dawson) (as Morgan); *Shadow in the Streets* (Donner—for TV)

1976 *The Last Tycoon* (Kazan) (as Red Ridingwood)

1977 *Good Guys Wear Black* (Post) (as government man)

1978 *The American Girls*; *Born Again* (Rapper) (as Tom Phillips)

1981 *The Pilot* (*Danger in the Skies* (Robertson) (as Randolph Evers)

1984 *Prince Jack* (Lovitt) (as the Cardinal)

Publications

By ANDREWS: articles—

Interview with Allen Eyles, in *Focus on Film* (London), winter, 1976.
Interview by Carol Easton, in *The Search for Sam Goldwyn*, New York, 1976.

On ANDREWS: articles—

Polonsky, Abraham, "*The Best Years of Our Lives*," in *Hollywood Quarterly*, April 1947.
Current Biography 1959, New York, 1959.
Parish, James Robert, with Gregory W. Mank, in *The Hollywood Reliables*, Westport, Connecticut, 1980.
Wegner, H., "From Expressionism to Film Noir: Otto Preminger's *Where the Sidewalk Ends*," in *Journal of Popular Film* (Washington, D.C.), Summer 1983.
Classic Images (Indiana, Pennsylvania), May 1984.
Obituary in *New York Times*, 19 December 1992.
Obituary in *Variety* (New York), 21 December 1992.

*   *   *

Dana Andrews is remembered for his performances in *The Ox Bow Incident, Laura,* and *The Best Years of Our Lives*. Impeccably groomed, and possessing a rich baritone voice, Andrews epitomizes the movie star of 1940s: handsome but rugged, smooth but vulnerable. Andrews looks like the average nice guy, but because of his often inscrutable countenance, he can become a morally ambiguous figure.

Andrews left a secure job as an accountant in Texas to go to Hollywood in the early 1930s. For the next several years, he worked odd jobs and performed at the Pasadena Playhouse. In 1938, he was "discovered" and signed to a contract with Samuel Goldwyn. In 1940, Andrews made his screen debut in *The Westerner*. Fox purchased half of Andrews's contract, and his performance in *Tobacco Road* moved him into A pictures. In 1941, Andrews appeared in Jean Renoir's *Swamp Water,* a simple, atmospheric film Andrews recalled as one of his favorites.

In 1943, Andrews moved closer to star status with his convincing portrayal of Donald Martin, the young rancher hanged by the lynching mob in *The Ox Bow Incident*. His position at Fox improved as well, for that same year two of Zanuck's well-established stars, Tyrone Power and Henry Fonda, joined the armed services. Andrews, in his

Dana Andrews in *The Best Years of Our Lives* © 1946, Samuel Goldwyn

thirties with two children, was ineligible for enlistment, and Fox once again "discovered" Andrews, who looked like a handsome young man in his twenties. He established himself as a star through his solid and appealing performances in a trio of war films: *The North Star, The Purple Heart,* and *Wing and a Prayer.* Goldwyn decided to use Andrews as the romantic lead in *Up in Arms,* and from there, he played romantic leads in a second trio of films: *Laura, Fallen Angel,* and *State Fair.*

In *Laura,* Andrews demonstrates his ability to play troubled or morally ambiguous characters. His tightly controlled portrayal of the detective entranced with the woman whose (apparent) murder he is investigating finds a perfect match in Gene Tierney's masklike elegance, and his performance is charged with sexuality, for his character's interest in the case suggests sensitivity, integrity—and moral deviance. In *The Best Years of Our Lives,* Andrews's portrait of the troubled but admirable young captain draws its power from the distance Andrews maintains from the other characters—and the audience—except in moments of controlled revelation. In *Boomerang,* Andrews's portrayal of the conscience-driven district attorney is compelling because it is so guardedly reserved; an expression that passes through Andrews's eyes when he first interviews the alleged murderer is the only sign we have that the attorney will work to defend the man he is supposed to prosecute.

In the late 1940s, Andrews began looking for small-scale projects to produce independently. The studios had other plans. Throughout the 1950s and 1960s, Andrews was cast in remakes (*I Want You, Brainstorm*), war films (*In Harm's Way, The Battle of the Bulge*), spy melodramas (*Assignment Paris, The Fearmakers*), and mad-scientist thrillers (*Crack in the World, The Frozen Dead*). Rather than playing complex characters in well-directed films, Andrews appeared in a series of humorless, one-dimensional roles, and his reputation became tied to the declining status of Hollywood "studio pictures."

Andrews looked to other venues for work. He had been involved in theater throughout the 1940s and early 1950s as a founding member of the "Eighteen Actors" Company, and in the late 1950s, Andrews returned to theater in earnest. In 1958, he began a two-year run on Broadway in *Two for the Seesaw,* and in the 1960s he appeared in stage productions of *A Man for All Seasons, The Odd Couple,* and *Plaza Suite.* He continued in theater throughout the 1970s. From 1969 to 1972 Andrews appeared in the soap opera *Bright Promise.* Andrews's movie career reactivated in the 1970s. He was part of the star-studded cast that made *Airport 1975* a box-office success. And, as an actor emblematic of Hollywood's golden age, Andrews helped create the portrait of "old Hollywood" in *The Last Tycoon.*

A tough guy and a gentleman, Andrews's most memorable characters are always in perfect control of themselves, but that control is the result of great effort, for Andrews's underplaying conveys characters' attempts *not* to show how deeply situations affect them.

—Cynthia Baron

ANDREWS, Julie

Nationality: British. **Born:** Julie Elizabeth Wells in Walton-on-Thames, England, 1 October 1935. **Family:** Married 1) the art director Tony Walton, 1959 (divorced 1968), daughter: Emma; 2) the director Blake Edwards, 1969, daughters (adopted): Joanne and Amy. **Career:** 1947—first stage appearance in the "Starlight Roof" revue in London; 1954—New York stage debut in *The Boy Friend*; 1964—film debut in Disney's *Mary Poppins*; 1972-73—featured in TV series *The Julie Andrews Hour* on ABC-TV, winner of eight Emmy Awards; 1979—film career revived by appearance in *10*, first of series of comedies directed by husband Blake Edwards; 1992—in TV series

Julie; 1996—on Broadway in *Victor, Victoria.* **Awards:** Best Actress Academy Award, and Most Promising Newcomer, British Academy, for *Mary Poppins*, 1964. **Address:** P.O. Box 666, Beverly Hills, CA 90213, U.S.A.

Films as Actress:

1964   *Mary Poppins* (Stevenson) (title role); *The Americanization of Emily* (Hiller) (title role)
1965   *The Sound of Music* (Wise) (as Maria)
1966   *Torn Curtain* (Hitchcock) (as Sarah Sherman); *Hawaii* (George Roy Hill) (as Jerusha Bromley)
1967   *Thoroughly Modern Millie* (George Roy Hill) (title role); *The Singing Princess* (animation) (as voice of Princess Zeila)
1968   *Star!* (Wise) (as Gertrude Lawrence)
1970   *Darling Lili* (Edwards) (title role)
1974   *The Tamarind Seed* (Edwards) (as Judith Farrow)
1979   *10* (Edwards) (as Sam)
1980   *Little Miss Marker* (Bernstein) (as Amanda)
1981   *S.O.B.* (Edwards) (as Sally Miles)
1982   *Victor/Victoria* (Edwards) (title role)
1983   *The Man Who Loved Women* (Edwards) (as Marianna)
1984   *Hanya: Portrait of a Dance Legend* (Cristofori)
1985   *Pandora's Box* (Heath)
1986   *Duet for One* (Konchalovsky) (as Stephanie Anderson); *That's Life!* (Edwards) (as Gillian Fairchild)
1991   *Our Sons* (Erman—for TV) (as Audrey Grant)
1992   *A Fine Romance* (Tchin-Tchin) (Saks) (as Pamela Picquet)

Publications

By ANDREWS: books—

Mandy (children's fiction), 1973.
The Last of the Really Great Whangdoodles (children's fiction), 1973.

By ANDREWS: articles—

"My Fair Victor/Victoria," interview with John Gruen, in *Dance*, September 1995.
"Victor/Victorious," interview with Jonathan Van Meter, in *Vanity Fair* (New York), October 1995.

On ANDREWS: books—

Cottrell, John, *Julie Andrews*, New York, 1968.
Rosen, Marjorie, *Popcorn Venus*, New York, 1973.
Windeler, Robert, *Julie Andrews: A Biography*, New York, 1983.
Spindle, Les, *Julie Andrews: A Bio-Bibliography*, New York, 1989.
Arntz, James, *Julie Andrews*, Chicago, 1995.

On ANDREWS: articles—

Shipman, David, "The All-Conquering Governess," in *Films and Filming* (London), August 1966.
"The Now and Future Queen" (cover story), in *Time* (New York), 23 December 1966.
Lawrenson, Helen, "Sweet Julie," in *Esquire* (New York), January 1967.
Higham, Charles, "The Rise and Fall—and Rise—of Julie Andrews," in *New York Times*, 21 August 1977.
Gross, Linda, "Julie Andrews: A Talk with a Flickering Star," in *Close-Ups: The Movie Star Book*, edited by Danny Peary, New York, 1978.

Julie Andrews in *The Sound of Music*

Articles in *Ciné Revue* (Paris), 25 June 1981, 2 September 1982, and 27 January 1983.

Bennetts, Leslie, "Julie Andrews: Prim and Improper," in *New York Times*, 14 March 1982.

Szymanski, Michael, "Our Fair Lady: Julie Andrews Discusses Gay Fans, AIDS, and Her TV Movie Debut," *Advocate* (Los Angeles), 21 May 1991.

"Julie Andrews," in *Stars*, March 1992.

Current Biography 1994, New York, 1994.

*   *   *

Julie Andrews's cinematic persona was established with her first appearance on screen as the magical title character in Walt Disney's *Mary Poppins* (one of the top grossing films of all time). Her performance a year later as Maria von Trapp in *The Sound of Music* further reinforced her popular "sweetness and light" image, and the movie was an unprecedented financial success. This, together with her Academy Award for *Mary Poppins*, placed Andrews at the forefront of bankable Hollywood stars of the 1960s. Winning the Oscar for *Mary Poppins* was also a personal coup for Andrews. Just before getting the role, she had lost the movie role of Eliza Doolittle—a character she had brought to life in the Broadway production of *My Fair Lady*—to Audrey Hepburn.

After a while, Andrews became tired of this squeaky clean screen image and like most actors, sought different kinds of roles. Unfortunately, however, a subsequent string of box-office failures, as well as several atypical film roles, failed to alter the picture of Andrews that had become so firmly entrenched in the moviegoing public's mind, and it is only in her more recent films with her husband, director Blake Edwards, that the actress has succeeded (at least partially) in changing the sugary image that has followed her throughout her career. With the exception of *Victor/Victoria*, however, these movies did not really showcase her talent.

The phenomenal impact of Andrews's debut in films coincided with the final days of the traditional movie musical. The decade's increasing desire for realism and relevancy led to an inevitable decline in stories that allowed their characters to express themselves in song and dance. Andrews, however, was a former child star of British revues and a very successful Broadway star (*The Boy Friend, My Fair Lady, Camelot*) and her theatrical training made her ideally suited to the filmmaking style that had had its heyday in the Hollywood musicals of the 1940s and 1950s. Yet the very films that brought her international acclaim, also made it impossible for audiences—and producers—to envision her in realistic, nonmusical roles at just the time that such roles were the only ones available.

Andrews's portrayals of Mary Poppins and Maria von Trapp—roles that so marked and, in effect, pigeonholed her career—are nevertheless separate and distinct performances. She creates in the former a strict but loving figure whose no-nonsense manner hides magical powers and enables her to regard them as commonplace. While Mary Poppins is all-knowing and supremely confident, the young novice Maria is inexperienced, naive, and frequently unsure of herself. Both roles are made memorable by Andrews's fresh, energetic style, a quality which would also color her work in such later films as *Thoroughly Modern Millie, Star!*, and *Victor/Victoria*. Yet her early dramatic parts in *The Americanization of Emily, Torn Curtain*, and *Hawaii* demonstrated Andrews's ability to handle nonsinging characters with quiet assurance, although her reception in these roles was never equal to that accorded her musical work.

In recent years, however, Andrews's films with Blake Edwards have given a new direction in her career. Although their first film together, the box-office disaster *Darling Lili*, proved professionally damaging to both, Edwards has succeeded in broadening his wife's public image by casting her in a series of uncharacteristic roles. In the popular *10*,

Andrews gives a much underrated performance as the intelligent, outspoken woman Dudley Moore forsakes to pursue Bo Derek, while the savagely funny *S.O.B.* finds Andrews's playing a spoof of her own on-screen persona. The latter includes a brief, highly publicized scene in which she appears topless. *Victor/Victoria* dealt the final blow to Andrews's pristine image, presenting her as a woman masquerading as a "male" female impersonator in Edwards's sophisticated examination of sexual lifestyles and stereotypes. (In 1996 Andrews appeared on Broadway in *Victor/Victoria*, once again on stage where she first began her show biz career.) The Academy Award nomination for her performance suggested that Andrews had at last broken free of her "singing governess" image and had embarked on a promising new phase in her career.

—Janet E. Lorenz, updated by Linda J. Stewart

ANN-MARGRET

Nationality: American. **Born:** Ann-Margaret Olsson in Stockholm, Sweden, 28 April 1941; spent her first five years in Valsjobyn; became U.S. citizen 1949. **Education:** Attended New Trier High School, Winnetka, Illinois; Northwestern University, Evanston, Illinois. **Family:** Married the actor Roger Smith, 1967, now also her manager. **Career:** 1946—at age five, emigrated to the United States; 1957—appeared on *Ted Mack's Amateur Hour* on television; 1960—made first appearance on the Las Vegas nightclub circuit; 1961—made film debut as ingenue in *Pocketful of Miracles* with Bette Davis, and in subsequent roles established persona as a sex kitten; 1968—*The Ann-Margret Show*, the first of many prime-time specials in the sixties and seventies, created a sensation on American network television, and Ann-Margret established career as major Las Vegas headliner; 1971—breakthrough performance in *Carnal Knowledge* inaugurated critical reevaluation of her dramatic abilities and garnered Academy award nomination; 1972—suffered near-fatal fall during nightclub performance and recovered, with much publicized plastic surgery; 1983—took lead role in *Who Will Love My Children?*, an acclaimed TV movie, beginning a series of TV films with serious subjects and a collaboration with director John Erman; 1987—in TV mini-series *The Two Mrs. Grenvilles, Alex Haley's Queen*, 1993, and *Scarlett*, 1994. **Awards:** Golden Globe Award for Supporting Actress, for *Carnal Knowledge*, 1971; Golden Globe Award, for *Tommy*, 1975.

Films as Actress:

1961   *Pocketful of Miracles* (Frank Capra) (as Louise)
1962   *State Fair* (José Ferrer) (as Emily Porter)
1963   *Bye-Bye Birdie* (Sidney) (as Kim McAfee)
1964   *Viva Las Vegas* (Sidney) (as Rusty Martin); *Kitten with a Whip* (Heyes) (as Jody Dvorak); *The Pleasure Seekers* (Negulesco) (as Fran Hobson)
1965   *Bus Riley's Back in Town* (Harvey Hart) (as Laurel); *Once a Thief* (Ralph Nelson) (as Kristine Pedak); *The Cincinnati Kid* (Jewison) (as Melba)
1966   *Made in Paris* (Sagal) (as Maggie Scott); *Stagecoach* (Gordon Douglas) (as Dallas); *The Swinger* (Sidney) (as Kelly Olsson); *Murderers' Row* (Henry Levin) (as Suzie Solaris)
1967   *The Criminal Affair*; *Rebus* (Zanchin); *Il Tigre* (*The Tiger and the Pussycat*) (Dino Risi) (as Carolina); *Il Profeta* (*The Prophet*; *Mr. Kinky*) (Dino Risi)
1968   *Sette uomini e un Cervello* (*Criminal Symphony*; *Seven Men and One Brain*) (Edward Ross)

1970   *C.C. and Company* (*Chrome Hearts*) (Robbie) (as Ann McCalley); *R.P.M.* (Stanley Kramer) (as Rhoda)

1971   *Carnal Knowledge* (Mike Nichols) (as Bobbie); *Dames at Sea* (for TV)

1973   *The Train Robbers* (Burt Kennedy) (as Mrs. Lowe); *Un Homme est Mort* (*The Outside Man*; *Funerale a Los Angeles*) (Deray) (as Nancy Robson)

1975   *Tommy* (Ken Russell) (as Nora Walker Hobbs)

1976   *Folies bourgeoises* (*The Twist*) (Chabrol) (as Charlie Minerva)

1977   *Joseph Andrews* (Tony Richardson) (as Lady Booby); *The Last Remake of Beau Geste* (Marty Feldman) (as Lady Flavia Geste)

1978   *The Cheap Detective* (Robert Moore) (as Jezebel Dezire); *Magic* (Attenborough) (as Peggy Ann Snow)

1979   *The Villain* (Needham) (as Charming Jones)

1980   *Middle Age Crazy* (John Trent) (as Sue Ann)

1982   *The Return of the Soldier* (Alan Bridges) (as Jennie Baldry); *I Ought to Be in Pictures* (Herbert Ross) (as Stephanie); *Lookin' to Get Out* (Ashby) (as Patti Warner)

1983   *Who Will Love My Children?* (Erman—for TV) (as Lucile Fray)

1984   *A Streetcar Named Desire* (Erman—for TV) (as Blanche DuBois)

1985   *Twice in a Lifetime* (Yorkin) (as Audrey Minelli)

1986   *52 Pick-Up* (Frankenheimer) (as Barbara Mitchell)

1988   *A Tiger's Tale* (Peter Douglas) (as Rose Butts); *A New Life* (Alda) (as Jackie Giardino)

1991   *Our Sons* (Erman—for TV) (as Luanne Barnes)

1992   *Newsies* (Ortega) (as Medda Larkson)

1993   *Grumpy Old Men* (Donald Petrie) (as Ariel Truax)

1994   *Following Your Heart* (Lee Grant—for TV); *Nobody's Children* (Wheatley—for TV) (as Carol Stevens)

1995   *Grumpier Old Men* (Deutch) (as Ariel Truax Gustafson)

1996   *Seduced by Madness: The Diane Borchardt Story* (John Patterson—for TV) (title role)

Publications

By ANN-MARGRET: book—

Ann-Margret: My Story, with Todd Gold, New York, 1994.

By ANN-MARGRET: articles—

"A Weep in the Deep," interview with Arthur Bell, in *Village Voice* (New York), 31 March 1975.

"Pro-Ann-Margret," interview, in *Films Illustrated*, July 1975.

"Ann-Margret," interview with R. Hartford, in *Ciné Revue* (Paris), 7 August 1975.

"Something to Offer: Ann-Margret," interview with Gordon Gow, in *Films and Filming* (London), January 1976.

Interview with Merrill Shindler, in *Los Angeles Magazine*, July 1988.

"Ann-Margret a Go-Go," interview with Paul Rosenfield, in *Vanity Fair* (New York), October 1991.

On ANN-MARGRET: book—

Peters, Neal, *Ann-Margret: A Photo Extravaganza and Memoir*, New York, 1981.

On ANN-MARGRET: articles—

Current Biography 1975, New York, 1975.

"La vedette de la semaine: Ann-Margret," in *Ciné Review* (Paris), 11 August 1977.

Sarris, Andrew, "Films in Focus: Magic and Ann-Margret: The Alter-Ego Meets the Icon," in *Village Voice* (New York), 13 November 1978.

Veljkovic, M., "Dancebiz: Las Vegas Seen," in *Dance Magazine*, June 1983.

Bulnes, J., "Les immortels du cinema: Ann-Margret," in *Ciné Revue* (Paris), 8 December 1983.

Farber, Stephan, "TV Is Polishing Ann-Margret's Image," in *New York Times*, 17 July 1984.

Canby, Vincent, "Film View: Ann-Margret Produces Yet Another Surprise," in *New York Times*, 17 February 1985.

Robinson, Jeffrey, "Shy and Silent Superstar Ann-Margret," in *McCall's*, October 1988.

Clark, John, "Ann-Margret," in *Premiere* (New York), September 1989.

Oney, Steve, "A Vegas Valkyrie Alights at Radio City," in *New York Times*, 20 October 1991.

"Optimism," in *New Yorker*, 3 February 1992.

Hampton, Howard, "Elvis Dorado: The True Romance of *Viva Las Vegas*," in *Film Comment* (New York), July 1994.

*   *   *

The Swedish-born Ann-Margret began her film career as the ingenue in the Frank Capra film *Pocketful of Miracles*, holding her own opposite luminaries Bette Davis and Glenn Ford, an omen, certainly, of her considerable presence and ability. A more important personal success was achieved with the musical *Bye, Bye, Birdie*, in which Ann-Margret exhibited her abundant skills as a singer and dancer, energizing the film with her powerful sexuality as well as with her innocence and fresh charm.

In *Viva Las Vegas*, one of the most underrated musicals of the American cinema, Ann-Margret played opposite Elvis Presley—providing Presley one of his few memorable co-stars. Indeed, in *Viva Las Vegas*, Ann-Margret exuded an undulating sexuality and unbridled energy so overwhelming that her musical scenes with Presley reflect the *Zeitgeist* of the sexual revolution of the sixties.

Ann-Margret followed *Viva Las Vegas* with a series of films that cemented—rather unfortunately for her—her reputation as a sex kitten. Films such as *Kitten with a Whip* and *Bus Riley's Back in Town* created a rather tawdry image which critics of the time found necessary to ridicule. Not surprisingly, her often sensitive performances—as, for instance, the vulnerable wife in *Once a Thief*, opposite Alain Delon—were ignored. The critical nadir to her career occurred at the end of the sixties, when, after a series of foreign films disrespected by Hollywood, she returned to the United States to star opposite the rather wooden football player, Joe Namath, in a motorcycle melodrama, *C.C. and Company*, produced by her husband Roger Smith; and in Stanley Kramer's *R.P.M.*, an unconvincing Vietnam-era drama about student protest on a college campus. Rather unfairly, Ann-Margret had become a joke.

Her critical comeback occurred in 1971, when Mike Nichols cast her opposite Jack Nicholson in *Carnal Knowledge*. As Nicholson's mistress, Bobbie, Ann-Margret played a woman whose very essence had been defined by her large breasts and sexuality. Nichols's film, based on the script by Jules Feiffer, showed persuasively how that simplistic definition was forced upon Bobbie by a sexist, male-dominated culture which refused to acknowledge or value other possibilities for a woman. That there was a certain autobiographical resonance to the role could not but help Ann-Margret to deliver what has been considered her greatest, most subtle, performance: vulnerable, hard-edged, pathetic, direct, emotional, brutally honest—a breakthrough Academy award-nominated performance which has prevented critics since from denigrating Ann-Margret's talents or seeing her only in terms of her considerable sensuousness.

In fact, so rehabilitated was her reputation that Ann-Margret could afford to take the music and sex-oriented role of Tommy's mother in

Ann-Margret

Ken Russell's version of the rock opera *Tommy*—in which a key scene had a sensuously clad Ann-Margret writhing in perhaps tons of baked beans. Her knockout performance was again nominated for an Academy Award.

Ann-Margret's career since has alternated between her high-powered live Las Vegas shows spotlighting her singing and dancing with film and television roles generally requiring her to provide more subdued characterizations in serious drama. Her much-lauded performance in *Who Will Love My Children?* as a dying Iowa farm woman attempting to find homes for her ten children was heartbreakingly expressive—and indeed, was publicly praised by Barbara Stanwyk at an Emmy Awards ceremony as one of the best performances ever in the American cinema, as Stanwyck disparaged her own award for a competing performance. And as Blanche du Bois in a television version of Tennessee Williams' *A Streetcar Named Desire*, Ann-Margret again received critical accolades, holding her own against the sacred memory of Vivien Leigh. Moving and honest performances can be found as well in *The Return of the Soldier* (playing an old maid opposite acting heavyweights Glenda Jackson and Julie Christie and comparing well), *Twice in a Lifetime*, *The Two Mrs. Grenvilles*, and the AIDS drama *Our Sons*.

Indeed, Ann-Margret's confluence of sexuality with innocence and vulnerability is even more appealing as she moves through her mature middle-age. Yet if other performers who have drawn upon sexual personas or aggressive femininity have tended to display a coyness or self-consciousness (if they have not self-destructed, like Marilyn Monroe), Ann-Margret must be seen as always projecting a natural grace and intelligence, coupled with a sincerity and honesty so straightforward and unapologetic as to be almost unnerving.

Certainly, one must note that only a remarkably unselfconscious performer could take on so many roles which so shamelessly commented upon or exploited her own image—her comic turn in *The Swinger*, for instance, in which she plays a character with her own real last name (Olsson), who only pretends to be promiscuous to garner success; or roles that lampoon her own physical attributes—such as Lady Booby in *Joseph Andrews*, or Charming Jones in *The Villain* (which crosses Road Runner cartoons with Al Capp caricatures). Other elements also present in her trouper image—which have undoubtedly helped Ann-Margret sustain her popularity over the decades—are a certain coarseness; a connection to the blue-collar world; a populist appeal to women as well as men, straights as well as gays; and a lack of taste sometimes so outrageous as to itself become classy, if not camp.

—Charles Derry

ARBUCKLE, Roscoe ("Fatty")

Nationality: American. **Born:** Roscoe Conklin Arbuckle in Smith Center, Kansas, 24 March 1887; family moved to Santa Ana, California, in 1888. **Family:** Married 1) the actress Minta Durfee, 1908 (divorced 1925); 2) Doris Deane, 1925 (divorced 1929); 3) Addie Oakley Dukes McPhail, 1932. **Career:** 1895—stage debut in Frank Bacon's stock company; 1902-08—toured in stock companies, and on vaudeville and burlesque circuits; 1908—worked as an extra for Colonel Selig's Polyscope Company while continuing to perform in vaudeville; 1909—film debut in *Ben's Kid* for Boggs; 1913—hired by Mack Sennett to replace Fred Mace in Keystone film comedies; later that year, he appeared with Mabel Normand in the first of a successful series of shorts starring the pair; 1914—allowed to devise and direct his own films; 1917—joined producer Joseph Schenk and headed his own studio, the Comique Film Company, in New York; Buster Keaton joined Arbuckle's film company; later that year, the company moved to Long Beach, California; 1920—his first feature-length film released through Paramount; 1921—as a result of the scandal involving his arrest for the rape or manslaughter of a starlet, his films were banished from many theaters across the country though he was later acquitted; 1923—attempted comeback in Chicago nightclub; 1924—returned to vaudeville; 1925-32—directed films for Sennett's Educational film company under the name William B. Goodrich while continuing to headline in vaudeville under his own name; 1932-33—in a series of talking shorts for Vitaphone Division of Warner Brothers. **Died:** In New York, 29 June 1933.

Films as Actor:

(shorts unless otherwise noted; contribution as director indicated where known):

1909   *Ben's Kid* (Boggs); *Mrs. Jones' Birthday*; *Making It Pleasant for Him*

1910   *The Sanitarium* (*The Clinic*) (Santschi)

1913   *Alas! Poor Yorick* (Colin Campbell) (as player in female costume); *The Gangsters* (Lehrman); *Passions, He Had Three* (Lehrman); *Help! Help!, Hydrophobia!* (Lehrman); *The Waiters' Picnic* (Sennett); *The Bandit* (Sennett); *Peeping Pete* (Sennett); *For the Love of Mabel* (Lehrman); *The Tell Tale Light* (Sennett); *A Noise from the Deep* (Sennett); *Love and Courage* (Lehrman); *Professor Bean's Removal* (Lehrman); *The Riot* (Sennett); *Mabel's New Hero* (Sennett); *Fatty's Day Off* (Wilfred Lucas); *Mabel's Dramatic Career* (Sennett); *The Gypsy Queen* (Sennett); *Mother's Boy* (Lehrman); *The Fatal Taxicab* (Sennett); *When Dreams Come True* (Sennett); *Two Old Tars* (Lehrman); *A Quiet Little Wedding* (Wilfred Lucas); *The Speed Kings* (Wilfred Lucas); *Fatty at San Diego* (George Nichols); *Wine* (George Nichols); *Fatty Joins the Forces* (George Nichols); *The Woman Haters* (Lehrman); *Fatty's Flirtation* (George Nichols); *His Sister's Kids* (George Nichols); *He Would a Hunting Go* (George Nichols); *Ride for a Bride* (George Nichols)

1914   *A Misplaced Foot* (Wilfred Lucas); *The Under Sheriff* (George Nichols); *A Flirt's Mistake* (George Nichols); *In the Clutches of the Gang* (George Nichols); *A Rebecca's Wedding Day* (George Nichols); *A Robust Romeo* (George Nichols); *Twixt Love and Fire* (George Nichols); *A Film Johnnie* (George Nichols); *Tango Tangles* (Sennett); *His Favorite Pastime* (George Nichols) (as fellow drunk); *A Rural Dream* (*A Rival Demon*) (Sennett and Lehrman); *Barnyard Flirtations* (*A Barnyard Flirtation*); *Chicken Chaser* (+ d); *A Bath House Beauty* (+ d); *Where Hazel Met the Villain* (+ d); *A Suspended Ordeal* (+ d); *The Water Dog* (+ d); *The Alarm* (+ co-d); *The Knockout* (Avery); *Fatty and the Heiress* (+ co-d); *Fatty's Finish* (+ d); *Love and Bullets* (+ d); *A Rowboat Romance* (+ d); *The Sky Pirate* (+ co-d); *Those Happy Days* (+ d); *That Minstrel Man* (+ d); *Those Country Kids* (+ d); *Fatty's Gift* (+ co-d); *The Masquerader* (*The Masquerade*) (Chaplin); *A Brand New Hero* (+ co-d); *The Rounders* (Chaplin); *Lover's Luck* (+ d); *Fatty's Debut* (+ co-d); *Fatty Again* (+ d); *Their Ups and Downs* (+ d); *Zip, the Dodger* (+ d); *Lovers' Post Office* (+ d); *An Incompetent Hero* (+ d); *Fatty's Jonah Day* (+ co-d); *Fatty's Wine Party* (+ co-d); *The Sea Nymphs* (+ d); *Leading Lizzie Astray* (+ co-d); *Shotguns that Kick* (+ d); *Fatty's Magic Pants* (*Fatty's Magic Party*; *Fatty's Suitless Day*) (+ co-d); *Fatty and Minnie He-Haw* (*Fatty's Minnie-He-Haw*) (+ co-d); *Our Country Cousin*;

Caught in a Flue; The Baggage Smasher; Tillie's Punctured Romance (Sennett); *Killing Horace; The Bowery Boys; Lover's Post Office; How Hiram Won Out; The Peddler*

1915 *Mabel and Fatty's Wash Day* (+ d); *Mabel and Fatty's Simple Life (Fatty and Mabel's Simple Life)* (+ d); *Fatty and Mabel at the San Diego Exposition* (+ d); *Mabel, Fatty, and the Law* (+ d); *Fatty's New Role* (+ co-d); *Mabel and Fatty's Married Life (Fatty and Mabel's Married Life)* (+ d); *Fatty's Reckless Fling* (+ d); *Fatty's Chance Acquaintance* (+ d); *Love in Armor* (+ d); *That Little Band of Gold* (+ co-d); *Fatty's Faithful Fido* (+ co-d); *When Love Took Wings* (+ d); *Wished on Mabel* (+ d); *Mabel and Fatty Viewing the World's Fair at San Francisco, California* (+ d); *Mabel's Wilful Way* (+ d); *Miss Fatty's Seaside Lovers* (+ d); *The Little Teacher (Small Town Bully)* (Sennett); *Fatty's Plucky Pup* (+ d); *Fatty's Tintype Tangle* (+ d); *Fickle Fatty's Fall* (+ d); *The Village Scandal* (+ d); *Fatty and the Broadway Stars* (+ co-d); *Rum and Wallpaper; Colored Villainy; Among the Mourners*

1916 *Fatty and Mabel Adrift* (+ d); *He Did and He Didn't (Love and Lobsters)* (+ d); *The Bright Lights (The Lure of Broadway)* (as cook, + d); *His Wife's Mistake* (as janitor, + d); *The Other Man* (+ d); *The Waiters' Ball* (+ d); *His Alibi* (+ d); *A Cream Puff Romance (A Reckless Romeo)* (+ d)

1917 *The Butcher Boy* (+ d, sc); *The Rough House* (+ d, sc); *His Wedding Night* (+ d, sc); *Oh, Doctor!* (+ d, sc); *Fatty at Coney Island* (+ d, sc); *A Country Hero* (+ d, sc)

1918 *Out West* (+ d, sc); *The Bell Boy* (title role, + d, sc); *Moonshine* (as Chief Revenue Officer, + d, sc); *Good Night, Nurse!* (+ d, sc); *The Cook* (+ d, sc); *The Sheriff* (title role, + d, sc)

1919 *Camping* (+ d, sc); *The Pullman Porter* (+ d, sc); *Love* (+ d, sc) (as farm boy); *The Bank Clerk* (+d, sc); *A Desert Hero* (+ d, sc); *Back Stage* (+ d, sc); *The Hayseed* (+ d, sc); *The Garage* (as fire chief, + d, sc)

1920 *The Round-Up* (Melford—feature) (as Sheriff Slim Hoover); *The Life of the Party* (Henabery) (as Algernon Leary)

1921 *Brewster's Millions* (Henabery—feature) (as Montgomery "Monty" Brewster); *The Dollar-a-Year Man* (Cruze—feature) (as Franklin Pinney); *The Traveling Salesman* (Henabery—feature) (as Bob Blake); *Gasoline Gus* (Cruze—feature) (title role); *Crazy to Marry* (Cruze—feature) (as Dr. Hobart Hupp)

1922 *Leap Year* (Cruze—not released in U.S.) (as Stanley Piper); *Freight Prepaid* (Cruze—feature, not released in U.S.) (as Erastus Berry)

1923 *Hollywood* (Cruze—feature) (as man in casting office)

1925 *Go West* (Buster Keaton—feature) (as fat woman in department store)

1932 *Hey, Pop!*

1933 *How've You Been?* (feature); *Buzzin' Around; Close Relations; Tomalio* (Ray McCarey); *In the Dough*

Films as Director Only:

1916 *The Moonshiners* (directed under name William B. Goodrich)
1924 *Sherlock, Jr.* (co-d with Buster Keaton)
1925 *The Movies; The Tourist*
1926 *Cleaning Up; The Fighting Dude; Home Cured; My Stars; His Private Life; Fool's Luck; One Sunday Morning*
1927 *Peaceful Oscar; The Red Mill* (feature); *Special Delivery*
1930 *Won by a Neck; Three Hollywood Girls; Si Si Senor; Up a Tree*
1931 *Crashing Hollywood; The Lure of Hollywood; Windy Riley Goes Hollywood; Queenie of Hollywood; Honeymoon Trio; Ex-Plumber; Peat and Repeat; Marriage Rows; The Back*

Page; That's My Line; Up Pops the Duke; Beach Pajamas; Take 'em and Shake 'em; That's My Meat; One Quiet Night; Once a Hero; The Tamale Vendor; Smart Work; Idle Roomers

1932 *Hollywood Luck; Anybody's Goat; Moonlight and Cactus; Keep Laughing; Bridge Wives; Mother's Holiday; Niagara Falls; Hollywood Lights; Gigolettes; It's a Cinch*

Publications

On ARBUCKLE: books—

Keaton, Buster, with Charles Samuels, *My Wonderful World of Slapstick*, New York, 1960.
Durgnat, Raymond, *The Crazy Mirror: Hollywood Comedy and the American Image*, New York, 1966.
Yallop, David A., *The Day the Laughter Stopped: The True Story of Fatty Arbuckle*, London, 1976.
Parish, James Robert, *The Funsters*, New Rochelle, New York, 1979.
Edmonds, Andy, *Frame-up: The Untold Story of Roscoe "Fatty" Arbuckle*, New York, 1991.
Oderman, Stuart, *Roscoe "Fatty" Arbuckle: A Biography of the Silent Film Comedian, 1887-1933*, Jefferson, North Carolina, 1994.
Young, Robert Jr., *Roscoe "Fatty" Arbuckle: A Bio-Bibliography*. Westport, Connecticut, 1994.

On ARBUCKLE: articles—

Obituary in *New York Times*, 30 June 1933.
Durgnat, Raymond, "World of Comedy," in *Films and Filming* (London), July, August, September, October, November, and December 1965, and January 1966.
Peeples, S. A., "Films on 8 & 16," in *Films in Review* (New York), February 1973.
Zito, S., "Hollywood Versus the Press," in *American Film* (Washington, D.C.), May 1978.
Oderman, Stuart, "Fatty's First," in *Classic Film/Video Images*, in 15 parts, beginning with no. 64, July 1979 (note: publication changed title to *Classic Images* in 1980).
Oderman, Stuart, "The Abduction of Minta Arbuckle," in *Films in Review* (New York), August/September 1985.
Kobal, John, "Silent Laughs," in *Films and Filming* (London), December 1987.
Le Fanu, Mark, "Vitagraph and the Great Arbuckle," in *Sight and Sound* (London), Winter 1987/88.
Telotte, J. P., "Arbuckle Escapes: The Pattern of Fatty Arbuckle's Comedy," in *Journal of Popular Film and Television* (Washington, D.C.), Winter 1988.

*   *   *

Among the many shorts created by the Mack Sennett comedy mill, Roscoe "Fatty" Arbuckle's movies remain significant contributions to the pioneer period of the one- and two-reel humorous cinema. After an apprenticeship in vaudeville and in short films for the Selig Polyscope Company as early as 1908, Arbuckle went on to such renown that eventually he was supervising his own films for Keystone. In 1913 he starred (often with Mabel Normand) in 47 films. As an actor, he enjoyed a fame second only to that of Chaplin, who began directing and playing leading roles in 1914, the same year that Sennett gave Arbuckle charge of a unit at Keystone.

Arbuckle had the right combination of obesity and agility to become a member of Sennett's company. He was fleet-footed enough to dash about in the many chase scenes, and he could execute the frequent pratfalls that occurred in the frantic comedy of the Sennett

Roscoe "Fatty" Arbuckle

studio. Early in his career he developed a charisma (the fat man as leading comic figure) that was almost as appealing as that projected by the much-loved John Bunny, a skillful actor who played middle-aged roles in genteel comedies. Arbuckle could play a variety of types: a likable country oaf, a lovesick suitor, a philandering husband. Eventually he moved away from the more primitive Keystone caricatures to a more solid comic creation: the young man next door trying to succeed.

Arbuckle developed a more independent style when he left Sennett to work for the Comique Film Corporation. There he created many effective two-reelers and introduced Buster Keaton to the screen as his supporting comedian. He left directing when he graduated to features in the early 1920s starring in *Brewster's Millions* and *Traveling Salesman*.

Forced from the screen as a result of his involvement in one of Hollywood's great sex scandals, Arbuckle became a filmmaker for Educational under the assumed name of William Goodrich. Such two-reelers as *Cleaning Up* in 1926 were minor efforts, but in 1927 he directed his first feature, *The Red Mill* (adapted from the musical by Victor Herbert). As an actor, the scandal that plagued him allowed him a chance at only bit parts. In the second period he created shorts for Educational and made a modest comeback by starring in some of them. Warner Brothers, under the subsidiary corporation Vitaphone, starred him in *Hey, Pop!*, *Buzzin' Around*, *How've You Been?*, and *Tomalio* in the early 1930s. The latter film was a broad farce set in South America. Director Ray McCarey, creator of Hal Roach shorts and a Laurel and Hardy feature, *Pack Up Your Troubles*, did little to help Arbuckle in what might have been a comeback. There were other problems too. A poverty of gag invention plagued this cheaply made two-reeler. Also, the comedian lacked the vocal skills necessary for the sound medium. In the climatic sequence, an obese man engaging in a foot race, the humor is crude. With such weak films Arbuckle did not have much of a chance, but had he been able to move on from such ventures to better parts in better films, he might have been a star again. Unfortunately, he died in 1933.

Arbuckle made a real contribution to the comedy film in his Keystone and Comique days. Also, he taught Buster Keaton all phases of filmmaking, and his student became one of the most important comedians the screen has known.

—Donald McCaffrey

ARKIN, Alan

Nationality: American. **Born:** Alan Wolf Arkin in New York City, 26 March 1934. **Education:** Attended Los Angeles City College. **Family:** Married Barbara Dana, 1964; sons: the actor Adam and Matthew from previous marriage, and Anthony. **Career:** Late 1950s—member of folk singing group the Tarriers; early 1960s—member of Chicago improvisational acting company Second City, a group including Mike Nichols and Elaine May; 1963—Broadway debut in *Enter Laughing* received much critical attention; mid-1960s—stage directing career began with off-Broadway production of *Little Murders*; 1966—feature film debut in *The Russians Are Coming, the Russians Are Coming*; 1971—directed first feature film, *Little Murders*; 1987—in TV series *Harry*. **Awards:** Best Actor, New York Film Critics, for *The Heart Is a Lonely Hunter*, 1968; Best Supporting Actor, New York Film Critics, for *Hearts of the West*, 1975; Golden Globe for Comedy Performance, for *The Russians Are Coming*, 1966; Canadian Genies, for Best Actor for *Improper Channels*, 1981, and for Best Supporting Actor for *Joshua Then and Now*, 1985. **Address:** c/o William Morris Agency, 151 El Camino, Beverly Hills, CA 90212.

Films as Actor:

1962   *That's Me* (short)
1963   *The Last Mohican* (short)
1966   *The Russians Are Coming, the Russians Are Coming* (Jewison) (as Rosanov)
1967   *Wait until Dark* (Young) (as Roat); "The Suicides" ep. of *Woman Times Seven* (De Sica) (as Fred)
1968   *The Heart Is a Lonely Hunter* (Miller) (as John Singer); *Inspector Clouseau* (Yorkin) (as title role)
1969   *Popi* (Hiller) (title role); *The Monitors* (Shea) (cameo)
1970   *Catch-22* (Nichols) (as Yossarian)
1972   *The Last of the Red Hot Lovers* (Saks) (as Barney Cashman); *Deadhead Miles* (Zimmerman)
1974   *Freebie and the Bean* (Rush) (as Bean); *It Couldn't Happen to a Nicer Guy* (Cy Howard—for TV)
1975   *Rafferty and the Gold Dust Twins* (Richards) (as Rafferty); *Hearts of the West* (Zieff) (as Kessler)
1976   *The Seven-Per-Cent Solution* (Ross) (as Freud)
1978   *The Defection of Simon Kudirka* (Rich—for TV) (title role)
1979   *The Magician of Lublin* (Golan) (as Yasha); *The In-Laws* (Hiller) (as Sheldon Kornpett, + exec pr)
1980   *Simon* (Brickman) (as Simon Mendelssohn)
1981   *Chu Chu and the Philly Flash* (Rich); *Improper Channels* (Till) (as Jeffrey)
1982   *The Last Unicorn* (Rankin and Bass) (as voice of Schmendrick, the Magician)
1983   *The Return of Captain Invincible* (*Legend in Leotards*) (Mora) (title role)
1984   *A Matter of Principle* (Arner)
1985   *Big Trouble* (Cassavetes) (as Leonard Hoffman); *Bad Medicine* (Miller) (as Dr. Madera); *Joshua Then and Now* (Kotcheff) (as Reuben Shapiro); *The Fourth Wise Man* (Michael Ray Rhodes—for TV)
1986   *A Deadly Business* (Korty—for TV)
1987   *Escape from Sobibor* (Gold—for TV) (as Feldhendler); *Necessary Parties* (Arner—for TV) (+ sc)
1990   *Coupe de Ville* (Roth) (as Fred Libner); *Too Much Sun* (Downey); *Edward Scissorhands* (Burton) (as Bill Boggs); *Havana* (Pollack) (as Joe Volpi); *The Rocketeer* (Johnston) (as Peevy)
1992   *Glengarry Glen Ross* (Foley) (as George Aaronow)
1993   *So I Married an Axe Murderer* (Schlamme); *Indian Summer* (Binder) (as Uncle Lou); *Taking the Heat* (Tom Mankiewicz—for TV) (as Tommy Canard); *Cooperstown* (Haid—for TV) (as Harry Willette)
1994   *North* (Rob Reiner) (as Judge Buckle); *The Jerky Boys* (Melkonian) (as Lazarro); *Doomsday Gun* (Robert M. Young—for TV)
1995   *Steal Big, Steal Little* (Andrew Davis) (as Lou Perilli)

Films as Director:

1967   *T.G.I.F.* (short) (+ sc)
1969   *People Soup* (short) (+ sc)
1971   *Little Murders* (+ ro as detective)
1977   *Fire Sale* (+ ro as Ezra Fikus)
1987   *The Visit*
1993   *Samuel Beckett Is Coming Soon* (+ ro as the director)

Publications

By ARKIN: books—

Tony's Hard Work Day (for children), 1972.

Halfway through the Door: An Actor's Journey Towards the Self, New York, 1979.
The Clearing (for children), New York, 1986.
The Lemming Condition (for children), New York, 1989.
Some Fine Grampa (for children), New York, 1995.

By ARKIN: article—

Interview in *Films and Filming* (London), November 1967.

On ARKIN: article—

Current Biography 1967, New York, 1967.

*   *   *

Alan Arkin is the poor man's Jack Lemmon. Think of Lemmon's major film roles, from *It Should Happen to You* to *The Apartment*, *Save the Tiger* to *Missing*. Arkin could have played any one of these parts effectively. Both actors can play comical bumblers with serious sides, and both excel as sensitive characters whose nervous temperaments are hair-triggered. Considering Arkin's solid talent and his proven versatility, it is regrettable that this actor has not had Lemmon's opportunities to shine on the silver screen.

Arkin was no novice to acting when he made his feature film debut in the popular satirical comedy *The Russians Are Coming, the Russians Are Coming*. Three years prior to that, he had won a Tony Award for his much acclaimed starring role in the Broadway production of Carl Reiner's autobiographical seriocomedy *Enter Laughing*. In *Russians*, Arkin, co-starring with Reiner and a large star cast, won an Oscar nomination playing a zany Russian squad leader who steps off a Soviet submarine which accidentally has been grounded near an island off the Massachusetts coastline. As he communicated with the startled natives, Arkin spoke a blend of strange Russian lingo and broken Russian-English, which left a bizarre, but very comical, impression.

His next effort, *Wait until Dark*, was a very showy role for the newcomer. In this taut suspense film, he played a psychotic who dresses up as three different people in order to retrieve a cache of drugs unwittingly in the possession of a blind woman (Audrey Hepburn). His menacing leap at the helpless woman's ankles and the unrelieved wickedness of his character even in his death throes gave audiences the dark and dramatic side of the actor's repertoire. After his appearance the following year in *The Heart Is a Lonely Hunter*, as a lonesome deaf-mute who befriends a young girl, it seemed as though Arkin's new status as a major movie star was cemented. So moving was his portrayal that he received his second Academy Award nomination.

Since then, only a handful of important screen roles have come his way. The most significant of these was in *Catch-22*, where he played Captain Yossarian in Joseph Heller's scathing satire of U.S. Army life during World War II, which was presented in a surreal and absurdist style. He also gave outstanding comic performances in *The Last of the Red Hot Lovers* and *The In-Laws*, and made an interesting and credible Freud in *The Seven-Per-Cent Solution*. In fact, Arkin never has done poorly in a film, even when the material was flawed or forgettable. Yet he has been unable to sustain the stardom and attention he obtained so early; the multidimensional, extraordinary roles with which he began his film acting career inexplicably dried up.

Arkin turned to directing in the late 1960s, and in 1971 did a credible job bringing Jules Feiffer's *Little Murders* to the screen. In the 1970s, he also wrote several books, including an autobiographical work about his involvement with yoga. In the past few years, Arkin has been appearing in films on a steady basis, sometimes enriching mediocre movies with brief but sparkling appearances. His two most significant recent roles have been as the camp director in *Indian Summer* and a real estate salesman in *Glengarry Glen Ross*, the film

version of David Mamet's Pulitzer Prize-winning play, in which he shares screen time with Jack Lemmon. Nevertheless, it is a shame that an actor of Arkin's caliber has not, over the years, been offered more and better lead roles, and been allowed to fulfill the promise he exhibited in his earliest films.

—Doug Tomlinson, updated by Audrey E. Kupferberg

ARLETTY

Nationality: French. **Born:** Léonie Bathiat in Courbevoie, 15 May 1898. **Education:** Attended Institution Edith Barbier, Puteaux. **Career:** 1917—employed as factory worker at Darracq Ltd.; later worked as secretary for offices of Schneider du Creusot; 1918—worked as model; 1919—debut at Théâtre des Capucines; 1920s—appeared in music hall revues, plays, and operettas; 1930—film debut; 1936—major stage success in *Fric-Frac*; 1938—in *Hôtel du Nord*, first of several appearances in films of Marcel Carné; c.1946—jailed for two months for collaboration with the Nazis as a consequence of an affair with a German officer during the occupation; 1949—resumed acting on both stage and screen. **Awards:** Special César, 1982. **Died:** In Paris, 24 July 1992.

Films as Actress:

1930 *La Douceur d'aimer* (Hervil)
1931 *Un Chien qui rapporte* (Choux) (as Josyane)
1932 *Das schöne Abenteuer* (*La Belle Aventure*) (Schünzel) (as Mme. des Mignieres); *Enlevez-moi* (Perret) (as Lulu); *Une Idée folle* (Natanson) (as Anita)
1933 *Walzerkrieg* (*La Guerre des valses*) (Berger) (as Ilonka); *Un Soir de réveillon* (Anton) (as Viviane); *Je te confie ma femme* (Guissart) (as Totoche); *Le Voyage de Monsieur Perrichon* (Tarride) (as Anita)
1934 *Le Vertige* (Schiller) (as Emma)
1935 *Pension Mimosas* (Feyder) (as Parasol); *La Fille de Madame Angot* (Bernard-Derosne) (as Mlle Delaunay); *Amants et voleurs* (Bernard) (as Agatha)
1936 *La Garçonne* (de Limur) (as Niquette); *Aventure à Paris* (Marc Allégret) (as Rose de Saint-Leu); *Le Mari rêve* (Capellani) (as Eve Roland); *Feu la mère de madame* (Fried—short) (as Yvonne); *Mais n'te promène donc pas toute nue* (Joannon—short) (as Clarisse)
1937 *Désiré* (Guitry) (as Madeleine Crapicheau); *Les Perles de la couronne* (*Pearls of the Crown*) (Guitry and Christian-Jaque) (as Queen of Ethiopia); *Faisons un rêve* (Guitry); *Si tu m'aimes* (*Mirages*) (Ryder) (as Arlette); *Aloha ou Le Chant des îles* (Mathot) (as Ginette Gina)
1938 *Hôtel du Nord* (Carné) (as Madame Raymonde); *Le Petit Chose* (Cloche) (as Irma Borel); *La Chaleur du sein* (Boyer) (as Bernadette)
1939 *Le Jour se lève* (*Daybreak*) (Carné) (as Clara); *Fric-Frac* (Lehmann and Autant-Lara) (as LouLou); *Circonstances atténuantes* (*Extenuating Circumstances*) (Boyer) (as Marie Qu'a d'ça)
1940 *Tempête* (Bernard-Deschamps) (as Ida Maulaincourt)
1941 *Madame Sans-Gêne* (Richebé) (title role); *Boléro* (Boyer) (as Catherine)
1942 *Les Visiteurs du soir* (*The Devil's Envoys*; *The Devil's Own Envoy*) (Carné) (as Dominique); *La Femme que j'ai le plus aimée* (Vernay) (as La Divette); *L'Amant de Bornéo* (Feydeau) (as Stella Losange); *La Loi du 21 juin 1907* (Guitry—short)

Arletty

1945 *Les Enfants du paradis* (*Children of Paradise*) (Carné) (as Garance)

1949 *Portrait d'un assassin* (Roland) (as Martha)

1951 *L'Amour, madame . . .* (Grangier) (as herself); *Gibier de potence* (Richebé) (as Mme. Alice)

1953 *Le Père de mademoiselle* (L'Herbier and Dagan) (as Edith Mars)

1954 *Le Grand Jeu* (*Flesh and the Woman*; *Il grande giuoco*; *The Big Game*) (Siodmak) (as Mme. Blanche); *Huis clos* (*No Exit*) (Audry) (as Inès); *L'Air de Paris* (Carné) (as Blanche Le Garrec)

1956 *Mor Curé chez les pauvres* (Diamant-Berger) (as L'epouseuse); *Vacances explosives* (Stengel) (as Arlette Bernard)

1957 *Le Passager clandestin* (Habib) (as friend)

1958 *Maxime* (Verneuil) (as Gazelle); *Un Drôle de dimanche* (Marc Allégret) (as Juliette Harmier); *Et ta soeur* (Delbez) (as Lucrèce du Boccage)

1959 *Paris la belle* (Prevert—short) (as narrator)

1960 *Les Primitifs du XIIIe* (Guilbaud—short) (as narrator)

1961 *La Gamberge* (Carbonnaux) (as Mother); *Les Petits Matins* (Audry)

1962 *The Longest Day* (Annakin, Marton, Wicki and Oswald) (as Mme. Barrault); *La Loi des hommes* (Gerard) (as La Comtesse); *Temp di Roma* (de la Patellière) (as Cri-Cri); *Le Voyage à Biarritz* (Grangier) (as Fernande)

1967 *Dina chez les lois* (Delouche—short) (as narrator)

Publications

By ARLETTY: books—

La Défense, Paris, 1971.
Je suis comme je suis . . . , with Michel Souvais, Paris, 1987.
Les Mots d'Arletty, edited by Claudine Brecourt-Villars, Paris, 1988.

By ARLETTY: articles—

"Strictly *Entre Nous*," in *Penguin Film Review* (London), September 1948.
Interview with Edward Baron Turk, in *American Film* (New York), November 1981.
Interview with E. Decaux and Bruno Villien, in *Cinématographe* (Paris), March 1985.

On ARLETTY: books—

Perrin, Michel, *Arletty*, Paris, 1952.
Ariotti, Philippe, and Philippe de Comes, *Arletty*, Paris, 1978.
Monnier, Pierre, *Arletty*, Paris, 1984.
Gilles, Christian, *Arletty: ou la liberté d'être*, Paris, 1988.

On ARLETTY: articles—

Ecran (Paris), June 1978.
Siclier, Jacques, "The Great Arletty," in *Rediscovering French Film*, edited by M. L. Bandy, New York, 1983.
Beylie, C., "Arletty et ses peaux-rouges," in *Cinéma* (Paris), 18-24 March 1987.
Lacombe, A., "La Chaussee des geants," in *L'Avant-Scène Cinéma*, March 1988.
Barbry, F.-R., "Arletty: la revanche de la mémoire et du talent," in *Cinéma* (Paris), 4 May 1988.
Cartier, J. "Tous les taxis du monde l'adorent . . . ," in *Cine-Tele-Revue*, 5 May 1988.

"La Vedette de la semaine," in *Cine-Tele-Revue*, 12 May 1988.
Stars (Mariembourg, Belgium), September 1990.
"Je m'appelle Garance . . . C'est un nom de fleur," in *Cahiers du Cinéma* (Paris), supplement, May 1991.
Obituary in *New York Times*, 25 July 1992.
Obituary in *Variety* (New York), 3 August 1992.
"The End," in *Skoop* (Amsterdam), September 1992.
Berrier, H., and I. Champion, "L'Humain peut m'epater," in *Positif* (Paris), December 1992.
"Une fleur nommée Arletty," in *La Revue de la Cinématheque*, January/February 1993.

* * *

Arletty, the legendary and captivating actress was a major star during France's "Golden Age" of cinema in the 1930s and 1940s. As women's film roles during this period tended to lack complexity and left only a marginal space for women, Arletty is indeed quite an important and still treasured figure.

Well-known for her working-class origins, the beautiful and sublime Arletty was as famous for her work on the music hall stage as for her film performances. Her successful collaboration with the esteemed director Marcel Carné, especially in the films *Hôtel du Nord*, *Le Jour se lève*, *Les Visiteurs du soir*, and *Les Enfants du paradis*, brought both recognition and the opportunity to develop a "mysterious femininity"—and they are among the most popular and critically acclaimed films in the history of French cinema. Prior to her appearance in Carné's *Hôtel du Nord*, Arletty's film career was limited to supporting roles—most often she played prostitutes and, not surprisingly, music hall performers in which she capitalized on her working-class Parisian accent and gestures. In *Pension Mimosas*, for example, she played a street-smart woman of questionable virtue.

Despite her early inauspicious film roles and a certain constraint based upon typecasting, as her career evolved it was noteworthy for its diversity. Indeed, her performances in the somber "poetic realist" *Le Jour se lève*, the medieval fable *Les Visiteurs du soir*, and the epic study of the early 19th-century stage, *Les Enfants du paradis*, each demonstrate an extraordinary range and depth, and importantly, her characters exude a remarkably honest, complex, and unconventional sexuality, as well as a singular self-awareness and independence. In *Le Jour se lève* she quits her job and her lover, and in *Les Visiteurs du soir* she is an androgynous, shrewd, and seductive emissary of the devil posing as a traveling performer. But it was her characterization of the beautiful, ethereally elegant, and sexually desiring courtesan Garance who is loved by four different men in *Les Enfants du paradis* for which she is best remembered—and whose uncommon individuality became synonymous with Arletty's own persona.

Unlike many other French stars, Arletty remained in France during the German occupation of the 1940s; thus her work helped contribute to a partial sense of continuity in French cinema during this period. For a time, Arletty was discussed primarily in terms of her well-known love affair with a German officer and for her brief imprisonment after the liberation than for her work on-screen. She returned to the screen after 1949 in several films, the most notable of which was an adaptation of Sartre's play *Huis clos*. She continued to work on the stage, including as Blanche in the French version of Tennessee Williams's *A Streetcar Named Desire*. Her only appearance in an American film was in an episode of *The Longest Day*. Then in the 1960s, her work as an actress was seriously hindered by an accident that badly affected her sight. In 1984, Arletty's legendary status was confirmed when a cinema opened in the Pompidou Centre in Paris that was named after her most famous character, Salle Garance.

—Cynthia Felando

ARMENDÁRIZ, Pedro

Nationality: Mexican. **Born:** Churubusco, 9 May 1912. **Education:** San Antonio, Texas, public schools; graduated from University of California at Los Angeles, 1928. **Family:** Married Carmen Pardo, 1939, children: son Pedro, two daughters. **Career:** Following graduation from college, moved to Mexico, and considered it his home throughout career; early 1930s—brief stage career in Mexico; 1935—Mexican film debut; 1935-44—in 44 Mexican films: called "the Mexican Clark Gable" (or "John Wayne" or "James Mason"); 1947—American film debut in John Ford's *The Fugitive*; 1963—admitted to UCLA Medical Center with advanced cancer. **Died:** Of self-inflicted gunshot at UCLA Medical Center, 17 June 1963.

Films as Actor:

1935   *Maria Elena*; *Rosario*; *Bordertown*

1937   *Las cuatro milpas*; *Amapola del Camino*; *La adelita*; *Jalisco nunca pierde*

1938   *Canto a mi tierra*; *Mi candidato*; *Los millones de Chafian*

1939   *Con los dorados de Pancho Villa*; *El Indio*; *La China hilaria*; *Borrasca humana*

1940   *Los olvidados de dios*; *La reina del Rio*; *Malahierra*; *El torro de falisco*; *El charro negro*; *Pobre diablo*; *El jefe maximo*

1941   *El secret del Sacerdote*; *La e ropeya del camino*; *Del ranco a la capital*; *La isla de la pasion* (*Passion Island*) (Fernández); *Ni sangre ni arena*; *Alía en el bajia*

1942   *Soy puro mexicano* (Fernández)

1943   *Las calaveras del terror, Guadalajara*; *Flor Silvestre* (Fernández); *Konga roja*; *The Life of Simon Bolivar* (*Simon Bolivar*); *Distinto amanecer* (Bracho) (as Octavio); **María Candelaria** (*Xochimilco*; *Portrait of Maria*) (Fernández) (as Lorenzo Rafael); *La guerra de los pasteles*

1944   *El corsario negro*; *Tierra de pasiónes*; *Alma de bronce*; *La campana de mi pueblo*; *Las abandonadas* (Fernández); *El Capitan Malacara*; *Entre Hermanos*; *Bugambilia* (Fernández)

1945   *Rayando el sol*; *La perla* (*The Pearl*) (Fernández)

1946   *Enamorada* (Fernández)

1947   *La casa colorado*; *Juan Charrasqueado*; *Albur de amor*; *The Fugitive* (John Ford)

1948   *Maclovia* (Fernández); *En la hacienda de la flor*; *Al caer de la tarde*; *Three Godfathers* (John Ford); *Fort Apache* (John Ford)

Pedro Armendáriz (left) in *María Candelaria*

1949   *Tulsa* (Heisler); *La lalquerida*; *Villa vuelve*; *La masquerada*; *El abandonado*; *We Were Strangers* (Huston); *The Outlaw and the Lady*; *Pancho Villa*; *Bodas de Fuego*

1950   *Camino de infierno*; *Del odio nace el amor* (*The Torch*; *Bandit General*) (Fernández); *Rosauro Castro*; *Tierra baja*; *La loga de la casa*; *Puerta falsa*; *Nos Veremos en el cielo*

1951   *Elly y yo*; *Por querer a una mujer*; *La noche avanza*

1952   *Carne de presidio*; *El rebozo de la soledad*; *El Bruto*

1953   *Les Amants de Tolède* (*The Lovers of Toledo*; *Tyrant of Toledo*) (Decoin); *Lucrèce Borgia* (*Lucrezia Borgia*; *Sins of the Borgias*; *Lucretia Borgia*) (Christian-Jaque); *Reportaje* (Fernández); *Mate a la vida*; *Mulata*

1954   *Dos mundos y un amor*; *La rebelion de los Colgados*; *El diablo del desierto* (Borderia); *Border River* (Sherman)

1955   *The Littlest Outlaw* (Gavaldón); *Les amants du tage*; *Tam Tam Mayumba* (*Native Drums*; *Tom Toms of Mayumba*); *El pequeno proscrito*; *La escondida* (*The Hidden Woman*) (Gavaldón)

1956   *Uomini e lupi* (*Men and Wolves*) (De Santis); *The Conqueror* (Dick Powell); *Diane* (David Miller); *Canasta de cuentos mexicanos*; *La major que no tuvo infancia*; *El Impostor* (Fernández); *Viva revolución*

1957   *Flor de mayo* (*A Mexican Affair*; *Beyond All Limits*) (Gavaldón); *The Big Boodle* (Wilson); *Ando volando bajo*; *La pandilla del soborno*; *El Zarco* (*El Zarco—The Bandit*); *Asi era Pancho Villa*; *Affair in Havana* (Benedek); *Manuela* (*Stowaway Girl*) (Hamilton)

1958   *Pancho Villa y la valentina*; *Cuando viva villa es la muerte*; *Café Colón de la Cerna*; *Las Senoritas Vivanco* (Blake); *Los desarraigados*; *La cucaracha* (*The Bandit*) (Alazraki)

1959   *Yo Pecador* (Rodríguez); *El hombre nuestro de Cada Dia*; *Calibre 44*; *The Wonderful Country* (Parrish); *El pequeno salvaje*

1960   *La cárcel de Cananca*; *El induito*; *800 Leguas por el Amazona*; *Dos hijos desobedientes*

1961   *Los valientes no mueren*; *El rejedor de Milagros*; *Arrivani i titani* (*Sons of Thunder*; *The Titans*); *Francis of Assisi* (Curtiz)

1962   *La Bandida*

1963   *Los hermanos del hierro* (*My Son, the Hero*) (Tessari); *Captain Sinbad* (Michelet); *From Russia with Love* (Young)

Publications

On ARMENDÁRIZ: books—

Mora, Carl J., *Mexican Cinema: Reflections of a Society 1896-1980*, Berkeley, 1982.

Riera, Emilio Garcia, and Fernando Macotela, *La guia del cine mexicano: De la pantella grande a la television 1919-1987*, Mexico City, 1984.

*   *   *

Pedro Armendáriz was Mexico's major movie star of the 1940s, frequently appearing in films of that country's leading director Emilio Fernández, whose work gained international recognition, ushering in a period of critical attention and acclaim for Mexican filmmaking. As a part of this new Mexican cinema, Armendáriz too gained some degree of recognition and began acting in American films around 1947, and later in some European films. He continued to work both at home and abroad until his death in 1963.

A key role in Armendáriz's early career was the lead in Julio Bracho's *Distinto amanecer*, in which he played Octavio, an idealistic labor leader fleeing the gunmen of a corrupt governor. The film was noted for depicting the tensions of contemporary Mexican society.

Armendáriz was often cast as the romantic lead in his Mexican films. Perhaps his best-known role was as Lorenzo, the Indian peasant, in Fernández's *Mariá Candelaria*. In the film, Lorenzo loves Maria, but finally cannot save her from being stoned to death by the villagers because of a tragic misunderstanding. Though the film was internationally acclaimed, it was also criticized by Mexican intellectuals for depicting Mexican Indians in terms of idealized stereotypes. However, Fernández's approach and Armendáriz's portrayal of Lorenzo presented a positive view of Indians—a group that had often been negatively stereotyped and made the butt of jokes.

His first role in an English-language film was in John Ford's *The Fugitive*. He worked on three subsequent films by Ford, including *Three Godfathers*, in which he co-starred with John Wayne. Though Armendáriz's move into American and international films can be seen as a career advance, he never appeared as a romantic leading man in American films, but in character parts that called for a Mexican ethnic actor.

—Susan M. Doll

ARTAUD, Antonin

Nationality: French. **Born:** Antoine-Marie-Joseph Artaud in Marseilles, 4 September 1896. **Military Service:** 1914-15—served 9 months with military; medical discharge: addicted to drugs with first period of hospitalization. **Career:** 1901—stricken with meningitis and nearly dies; subsequently suffered from severe headaches and neurological pain; 1916-20—hospitalized frequently; 1921-24—worked as actor and designer for theater companies of Charles Dullin and George Pitöeff; 1924-26—associated with Surrealist movement; 1924-35—actor in films by Gance, Dreyer, and others; 1926—co-founder, Théâtre Alfred Jarry in Paris with Roger Vitrac and Robert Aron; 1928, 1931 and 1933—lecturer on theater at the Sorbonne, Paris; 1937-46—confined in various asylums; 1946—final release from asylum. **Awards:** Prix Sainte-Beuve for extended essay *Van Gogh, le suicidé de la société*, 1948. **Died:** 4 March 1948.

Films as Actor:

1917   *Mater Dolorosa* (Gance)

1923   *Faits divers* (Autant-Lara)

1924   film for Yvan Goll's "Mathusalem" (Painlevé); *Surcouf* (Morat)

1925   *Graziella* (Vandal)

1926   *Le Juif errant* (Morat)

1927   **Napoléon** (Gance) (as Marat)

1928   **La Passion de Jeanne d'Arc** (Dreyer) (as Massieu); *Verdun, visions d'histoire* (Poirier) (sound version released 1931)

1929   *L'Argent* (L'Herbier) (as Mazaud); *Tarakanova* (Bernard)

1931   **Die Dreigroschenoper** (Pabst) (member of Mackie's gang); *Faubourg Montmartre* (Bernard); *La Femme d'un nuit* (L'Herbier)

1932   *Les croix de Bois* (Bernard); *Coups de feu à l'aube* (de Poligny); *L'Enfant de ma soeur* (Wullschleger)

1933   *Mater Dolorosa* (Gance)

1934   *Liliom* (Lang); *Sidonie Panache* (Wullschleger)

1935   *Lucrèce Borgia* (Gance) (as Savonarola); *Koenigsmark* (Maurice Tourneur) (as Cyrus Beck)

Other Films:

1926   **L'Etoile de mer** (Man Ray) (sc)

1927 *La Coquille et le clergyman* (*The Seashell and the Clergyman*) (Dulac) (sc, role)

Publications

By ARTAUD: books—

Tric-trac du ciel (poems), Paris, 1923.
Le Théâtre Alfred Jarry et l'hostilité du publique, with Roger Vitrac, Paris, 1930.
Le Théâtre de la cruauté, Paris, 1933.
Le Théâtre de Séraphin, Paris, 1936.
Le Théâtre et son double, Paris, 1938; as *The Theater and Its Double*, New York, 1958.
Artaud le mômo (poems), Paris, 1947; as *Artaud the Momo*, Santa Barbara, California, 1976.
Supplement aux Lettres de Rodez suivi de Coleridge le traître, Paris, 1949.
Lettres d'Antonin Artaud à Jean-Louis Barrault, Paris, 1952.
La Vie et mort de Satan le feu, Paris, 1953; as *The Death of Satan and Other Mystical Writings*, London, 1974.
Galapagos, les îles du bout du monde, Paris, 1955.
Autre chose que l'enfant beau, Paris, 1957.
Voici un endroit, Paris, 1958.
Artaud Anthology, edited by Jack Hirschman, San Francisco, 1965.
Oeuvres complète, 16 vols., Paris, 1956-81.
Collected Works, 4 vols., London, 1968-75.
Selected Writings, edited by Susan Sontag, New York, 1976.
Nouvelles écrits de Rodez, Paris, 1977.
Lettres à Anie Besnard, Paris, 1978.
Watchfiends & Rack Screams: Works from the Final Period, edited and translated by Clayton Eshleman, with Bernard Bador, 1995.

On ARTAUD: books—

Knapp, Bettina, *Antonin Artaud: Man of Vision*, New York, 1969.
Greene, Naomi, *Antonin Artaud: Poet without Words*, New York, 1970.
Brau, Jean-Louis, *Antonin Artaud*, Paris, 1971.
Sollers, Philippe, editor, *Artaud*, Paris, 1973.
Hayman, Ronald, *Artaud and After*, London, 1977.
Esslin, Martin, *Antonin Artaud*, New York, 1977.
White, Kenneth, *Le monde d'Antonin Artaud, ou, Pour une culture cosmopoetique*, Brussels, 1989.
Percival, *Artaud, Beckett, Blake: essaer och tolkningar*, Stockholm, 1992.
Prevel, Jacques, *En compagnie d' Antonin Artuad; suivi de, Poems*, Paris, 1994.

On ARTAUD: articles—

Blanchot, Maurice, "Artaud," in *La Nouvelle Revue Française* (Paris), November 1956.
Koch, Stephen, "On Artaud," in *Tri-Quarterly* (Evanston, Illinois), Spring 1966.
Virmaux, A., "Artaud and Film," in *Tulane Drama Review* (New York), Fall 1966.
Derrida, Jacques, "La Parole soufflée," and "Le Théâtre de la Cruauté et la clôture de représentation," in *L'Ecriture et la différence*, Paris, 1967.
Kestner, J. A., "Stevenson and Artaud: The Master of Ballantrae," in *Film Heritage* (Dayton, Ohio), Summer 1972.
Amengual, Barthélémy, "Un Disciple inattendu d'Eisenstein: Antonin Artaud," in *Ecran* (Paris), September/October 1973.
Sontag, Susan, "Approaching Artaud," in the *New Yorker*, 19 May 1973.

Dozoretz, Wendy, "Dulac vs. Artaud," in *Wide Angle* (Athens, Ohio), no. 1, 1979.
Greene, Naomi, "Artaud and Film: A Reconsideration," in *Cinema Journal* (Champaign, Illinois), Summer 1984.
Virmaux, A., and O. Virmaux, "L'Affaire: Antonin Artaud acteur raté," in *Cinématographe* (Paris), May 1986.

*   *   *

It is difficult to assess Antonin Artaud on the mere strength of his acting. His collected writings run to many volumes. He was a poet, theater director, stage and screen actor, theorist on theater and cinema, and a considerable influence on modern drama. That he was also a madman recording the shadowy world between life and death gave to his existence a unique poignancy. He burned with the insanity of genius and was a visionary and mystic, yet he won many devoted friends and followers, one of whom was Anaïs Nin.

Coming from Marseilles where he was born in 1896 to the exciting Paris of 1920, he found it rife with experiment and the promotion of new ideas in all the arts. In the cinema Gance and L'Herbier spearheaded the avant-garde, but it was to the theater he first turned and came under the influence of the great directors Firmin Gemier and Charles Dullin. Artaud sought another outlet in poetry, which he attempted to apply to the cinema. He wrote: "The first degree of filmic thought seems to me to lie in the utilization of existing objects and forms which one can cause to express anything, for the arrangements of nature are profound and infinite."

He wrote seven scenarios, one of which was filmed by Germaine Dulac. This was *La Coquille et le clergyman*. It was presented as a dream and overloaded with technical virtuosity, an interpretation rejected bitterly by Artaud. He was received with open arms by the Surrealists but this association did not last long. He was able to make a major contribution to cinema as an actor, though many of his film appearances were necessitated by his financial difficulties. He appeared in both silent and sound versions of Gance's *Mater Dolorosa* and in the same director's epic *Napoléon*, in an incisive and highly individual portrayal of Marat. In contrast, his angelic young monk in Dreyer's *La Passion de Jeanne d'Arc* created an image of spirituality and compassion. He was in L'Herbier's *L'Argent*, Poirier's *Verdun* (as the young intellectual), and in the French version of Pabst's *Die Dreigroschenoper*. He played in popular films such as Luitz Morat's *Surcouf* and *Le Juif errant*. Perhaps more congenial to him was the early *Faits divers* by Autant-Lara.

By 1936 his eccentricities reflected the inroads of insanity. His journeys to Mexico to visit the land of the Tarahumaras and his visit to Ireland where he was arrested and returned to a mental home in France were characteristic actions. His last days were spent in asylums wasting away from the dread disease that hung over his whole life. He was eventually removed from the Rodez Asylum and spent his last days with a kind doctor at Ivry-sur-Seine where he died of cancer in 1948. The images he brought to the screen live on. His "Theatre of Cruelty" inspired a whole new generation of actors and playwrights; a vast body of writing has grown up around him; and he has become a major cult figure of the theater.

—Liam O'Leary

ARTHUR, Jean

Nationality: American. **Born:** Gladys Georgianna Greene in New York City, 17 October 1905 (other sources say 1900, 1901 or 1909). **Family:** Married 1) the photographer Julian Anker (divorced); 2) the

Jean Arthur

producer Frank J. Ross Jr., 1932 (divorced 1949). **Career:** 1920—quit school to become a model; 1923—film debut in bit role in John Ford's *Cameo Kirby*; 1932-34—actress on New York stage; mid-1940s—released from Columbia contract; 1955—played Peter Pan on Broadway; 1966—in own TV series *The Jean Arthur Show*; 1970s—taught drama at Vassar and other colleges. **Died:** In Carmel, California, 19 June 1991.

Films as Actress:

1923   *Cameo Kirby* (Ford)
1924   *Biff Bang Buddy* (Ingraham); *Bringin' Home the Bacon* (Thorpe); *Travelin' Fast*; *Fast and Fearless* (Thorpe); *Thundering Romance* (Thorpe); *Spring Fever*; *Case Dismissed*; *The Powerful Eye*; *The Temple of Venus*
1925   *The Drugstore Cowboy* (Frame); *The Hurricane Horseman* (Eddy); *Seven Chances* (Buster Keaton) (as receptionist); *Tearin' Loose* (Thorpe); *The Fighting Smile* (Marchant); *A Man of Nerve* (Chaudet); *Thundering Through* (Bain)
1926   *The Block Signal* (O'Connor); *Born to Battle* (De Lacey); *The College Boob* (Garson); *The Cowboy Cop* (De Lacey); *Double Daring* (Thorpe); *The Fighting Cheat* (Thorpe); *Lightning Bill* (Chaudet); *Twisted Triggers* (Thorpe); *Under Fire* (Elfelt); *The Mad Racer* (Stoloff); *Eight Cylinder Bull* (Leys); *Hello Lafayette (Lafayette, Where Are We?)* (Gold and Davis)
1927   *The Broken Gate* (McKay); *Flying Luck* (Raymaker); *Horse Shoes* (Bruckman); *Husband Hunters* (Adolfi); *The Poor Nut* (Wallace); *The Masked Menace* (Heath—serial); *Bigger and Better Blondes* (Parrott)
1928   *Brotherly Love* (Reisner); *Sins of the Fathers* (Berger) (as Mary Spengler); *Wallflowers* (Meehan); *Warming Up* (Newmeyer); *Easy Come, Easy Go* (Tuttle)
1929   *The Canary Murder Case* (St. Clair) (as Alice LaFosse); *The Greene Murder Case* (Tuttle) (as Ada Greene); *Half Way to Heaven* (Abbott) (as Greta Nelson); *The Mysterious Dr. Fu Manchu* (Rowland V. Lee) (as Lila Eltham); *The Saturday Night Kid* (Sutherland) (as Janie); *Stairs of Sand* (Brower); *Sins of the Fathers* (Berger)
1930   *Danger Lights* (Seitz) (as Mary Ryan); "Dream Girl" ep. of *Paramount on Parade* (Arzner and others); *The Return of Dr. Fu Manchu* (Rowland V. Lee) (as Lila Eltham); *The Silver Horde* (Archainbaud) (as Mildred Wayland); *Street of Chance* (Cromwell) (as Judith Marsden); *Young Eagles* (Wellman) (as Mary Gordon)
1931   *The Gang Buster* (Sutherland) (as Sylvia Martine); *Virtuous Husband* (Moore) (as Barbara Olwell); *The Lawyer's Secret* (Gasnier and Marcin) (as Beatrice Stevens); *Ex-Bad Boy* (Moore) (as Ethel Simmons)
1933   *Get That Venus* (Grover Lee); *The Past of Mary Holmes* (Thompson and Vorkapich) (as Joan Hoyt)
1934   *Whirlpool* (Neill) (as Sandra Morrison); *The Defense Rests* (Hillyer) (as Joan Hayes); *Most Precious Thing in Life* (Hillyer)
1935   *The Whole Town's Talking (Passport to Fame)* (Ford) (as Wilhelmina "Bill" Clark); *Public Hero Number One* (Ruben) (as Theresa O'Reilly); *Party Wire* (Kenton) (as Marge Oliver); *Diamond Jim* (Sutherland); *Public Menace* (Kenton) (as Cassie); *If You Could Only Cook* (Seiter) (as Joan Hawthorne)
1936   *Mr. Deeds Goes to Town* (Capra) (as Babe Bennett); *The Ex-Mrs. Bradford* (Roberts) (as Paula Bradford); *Adventure in Manhattan (Manhattan Madness)* (Ludwig) (as Claire Peyton); *The Plainsman* (Cecil B. DeMille) (as Calamity Jane); *More Than a Secretary* (Alfred E. Green) (as Carol Baldwin)

1937   *History Is Made at Night* (Borzage) (as Irene Vail); *Easy Living* (Leisen) (as Mary Smith)
1938   *You Can't Take It with You* (Capra) (as Alice Sycamore)
1939   *Only Angels Have Wings* (Hawks) (as Bonnie Lee); ***Mr. Smith Goes to Washington*** (Capra) (as Saunders)
1940   *Too Many Husbands* (Ruggles) (as Vicky Lowndes); *Arizona* (Ruggles) (as Phoebe Titus)
1941   *The Devil and Miss Jones* (Wood) (as Mary Jones)
1942   *The Talk of the Town* (Stevens) (as Nora Shelley)
1943   *The More the Merrier* (Stevens) (as Connie Milligan); *A Lady Takes a Chance* (Seiter) (as Mollie Truesdale)
1944   *The Impatient Years* (Cummings) (as Janie Anderson)
1948   *A Foreign Affair* (Wilder) (as Phoebe Frost)
1953   ***Shane*** (Stevens) (as Marion Starrett)

Publications

By ARTHUR: article—

"Jean Arthur, Great Star as Great Lady," interview with J. Springer and others, in *Inter/View* (New York), June 1972.

On ARTHUR: books—

Rosen, Marjorie, *Popcorn Venus*, New York, 1973.
Pierce, Arthur, and Douglas Swarthout, *Jean Arthur: A Bio-Bibliography*, New York, 1990.

On ARTHUR: articles—

Current Biography 1945, New York, 1945.
Vermilye, Jerry, "Jean Arthur," in *Films in Review* (New York), June-July 1966.
Harvey, Stephen, "Jean Arthur: Passionate Primrose," in *Close-Ups: The Movie Star Book*, edited by Danny Peary, New York, 1978.
Shipman, David, in *The Great Movie Stars: The Golden Years*, rev. ed., London, 1979.
Classic Images (Indiana, Pennsylvania), September 1981, and March and April 1984.
Bauer, Steven L., "A Star of the Golden Era: Remembering Jean Arthur," and Ralph Haven Wolfe, "For Jean Arthur: In Appreciation," in *Journal of Popular Film and Television* (Washington, D.C.), vol. 17, no. 1, 1989.
Obituary in *New York Times*, 20 June 1991.
Obituary in *The Times* (London), 22 June 1991.

*   *   *

Jean Arthur began her film career in John Ford's *Cameo Kirby*, which she followed with a series of ingenue and other lead parts in some 20 silent, low-budget Westerns and comedy shorts, graduating to a wider variety of roles for bigger studios by the coming of sound. In 1932, feeling that she needed to improve her acting skills, she left Hollywood and worked on the stage, both in New York and in summer stock, for the next two years. She played a variety of parts, even touring as Kalonica in a production of *Lysistrata*. In 1934 she returned to California to appear in *Whirlpool*, but received her first real break the next year, once again under John Ford's direction, in *The Whole Town's Talking*. In this movie she created the light-comedy character of a good-natured, sentimental girl-next-door, a character she later transformed into the vivacious, often oddball heroine most fully realized in the comedies of Frank Capra, who described her as his favorite actress.

Capra's *Mr. Deeds Goes to Town* and *Mr. Smith Goes to Washington* provided Arthur with her most memorable roles. In both films she played a somewhat hard-boiled urbanite who is at first appalled and later smitten by the honest country boys: Gary Cooper, as Deeds, and James Stewart, as Smith. Capra made fine use of the femininity just beneath the toughness expressed by her distinctive husky, cracked voice, a voice which became her trademark though it initially kept her out of roles in early talkies.

She was very active in films from the later 1930s to the mid-1940s. She played Calamity Jane opposite Gary Cooper in Cecil B. DeMille's *The Plainsman*, and starred in various other adventure films as well, including Wesley Ruggles's *Arizona* and Howard Hawks's *Only Angels Have Wings* with Cary Grant, turning in one of her best performances as his sentimental sidekick. She was at her peak in a number of classic Hollywood comedies, including Mitchell Leisen's *Easy Living* (with a Preston Sturges script) and Sam Wood's *The Devil and Miss Jones*, in the latter as the spunky shopgirl who reforms her crotchety boss, working incognito in his own department store. She also appeared in two romantic comedies directed by George Stevens, *The Talk of the Town* and *The More the Merrier*, the latter written specially for her by Garson Kanin. She received her only Oscar nomination for the second of these, but lost to Jennifer Jones.

After being released from her Columbia contract following a long dispute with Harry Cohn, the studio's boss, she appeared in only two productions, Billy Wilder's *A Foreign Affair* and Stevens's *Shane*. Though she stopped making films, she appeared occasionally on the stage (winning critical acclaim for her part in *Peter Pan* on Broadway) and on television, in both guest spots and in a short-lived *The Jean Arthur Show*.

—Charles L. P. Silet, updated by Frank Uhle

ASTAIRE, Fred

Nationality: American. **Born:** Fred Austerlitz in Omaha, Nebraska, 10 May 1899. **Education:** Attended Alvienne School of the Dance, New York; Ned Wayburn Studio of Stage Dancing. **Family:** Married 1) Phyllis Baxter Potter, 1933 (died 1954), children: two sons, one daughter; 2) the jockey Robyn Smith, 1980. **Career:** 1906—began dancing professionally with sister Adele: worked vaudeville circuits, according to some sources appeared in Mary Pickford's film *Fanchon the Cricket*, 1915, the Broadway musical *Over the Top*, 1917, and *The Passing Show of 1918*, first major success; 1918-31—several successful stage musicals on Broadway and in London; c.1931—partnership with sister ended when she married Lord Charles Cavendish; 1933—film acting debut in *Dancing Lady*; appeared in *Flying Down to Rio*, first of ten films with Ginger Rogers as dancing partner; 1948—in *Easter Parade*, replacing ailing Gene Kelly; 1959—first dramatic film role in Stanley Kramer's *On the Beach*; 1961-63—host of dramatic anthology TV series *Alcoa Premiere*; 1967-70—appeared occasionally in TV series *It Takes a Thief*. **Awards:** Honorary Academy Award, for "his unique artistry and his contributions to the technique of musical pictures," 1949; Best Supporting Actor, British Academy, for *The Towering Inferno*, 1974; Life Achievement Award, American Film Institute, 1981. **Died:** Of pneumonia, in Los Angeles, 22 June 1987.

Films as Actor:

1931   *Municipal Bandwagon* (short)
1933   *Dancing Lady* (Leonard) (as himself); *Flying Down to Rio* (Freeland) (as Fred Ayres)
1934   *The Gay Divorcee* (Sandrich) (as Guy Holden); **Top Hat** (Sandrich) (as Jerry Travers)

1935   *Roberta* (Seiter) (as Huck Haines, + choreographer)
1936   *Follow the Fleet* (Sandrich) (as Bake Baker); *Swing Time* (Stevens) (as John "Lucky" Garnett)
1937   *Shall We Dance* (Sandrich) (as Pete Peters); *A Damsel in Distress* (Stevens) (as Jerry Halliday)
1938   *Carefree* (Sandrich) (as Tony Flagg)
1939   *The Story of Vernon and Irene Castle* (Potter) (as Vernon Castle)
1940   *Broadway Melody of 1940* (Taurog) (as Johnny Brett); *Second Chorus* (Potter) (as Danny O'Neill)
1941   *You'll Never Get Rich* (Lanfield) (as Robert Curtis)
1942   *Holiday Inn* (Sandrich) (as Ted Hanover); *You Were Never Lovelier* (Seiter) (as Robert Davis, + choreographer)
1943   *The Sky's the Limit* (Edward H. Griffith) (as Fred Atwell/Fred Burton, + choreographer)
1945   *Yolanda and the Thief* (Minnelli) (as Johnny Riggs)
1946   *Ziegfeld Follies* (Minnelli) (as himself/Raffles/Tai Long); *Blue Skies* (Heisler) (as Jed Potter)
1948   *Easter Parade* (Walters) (as Don Hewes, + co-choreographer)
1949   *The Barkleys of Broadway* (Walters) (as Josh Barkley)
1950   *Three Little Words* (Thorpe) (as Bert Kalmar, + co-choreographer); *Let's Dance* (McLeod) (as Don Elwood)
1951   *Royal Wedding* (*Wedding Bells*) (Donen) (as Tom Bowen)
1952   *The Belle of New York* (Walters) (as Charles Hall)
1953   **The Band Wagon** (Minnelli) (as Tony Hunter)
1954   *Deep in My Heart* (Donen) (as guest)
1955   *Daddy Long Legs* (Negulesco) (as Jervis Pendleton)
1957   *Funny Face* (Donen) (as Dick Avery, + co-choreographer); *Silk Stockings* (Mamoulian) (as Steve Canfield)
1959   *On the Beach* (Kramer) (as Julian Osborn)
1961   *The Pleasure of His Company* (Seaton) (as Pogo Poole)
1962   *The Notorious Landlady* (Quine) (as Franklyn Armbruster)
1964   *Paris When It Sizzles* (Quine) (as voice)
1968   *Finian's Rainbow* (Francis Ford Coppola) (as Finian McLonergan)
1969   *Midas Run* (*A Run on Gold*) (Kjellin) (as John Pedley)
1970   *The Over-the-Hill Gang Rides Again* (McGowan—for TV); *Santa Claus Is Comin' to Town* (for TV, animation) (as voice of mailman)
1973   *Imagine*
1974   *The Towering Inferno* (Guillermin and Irwin Allen) (as Charles Claiborne); *That's Entertainment!* (Haley Jr.—compilation) (as host)
1976   *That's Entertainment, Part 2* (Kelly) (as host); *The Amazing Dobermans* (David and Byron Chudnow) (as Daniel Hughes)
1977   *Un Taxi mauve* (*The Purple Taxi*) (Boisset) (as Doctor Scully); *The Easter Bunny Is Comin' to Town* (for TV, animation) (as voice of mailman)
1978   *A Family Upside Down* (Rich—for TV); *Battleship Gallactica* (Colla—for TV)
1979   *The Man in the Santa Claus Suit* (Corey Allen—for TV)
1981   *Ghost Story* (Irvin) (as Ricky Hawthorne)
1984   *George Stevens: A Filmmaker's Journey* (George Stevens Jr.—doc) (as himself)

Publications

By ASTAIRE: book—

Steps in Time, New York, 1959; rev. ed., 1981.

By ASTAIRE: article—

"The Modest Mr. Astaire Talks with Carol Saltus," in *Interview* (New York), June 1973.

Fred Astaire

On ASTAIRE: books—

Springer, John, *All Talking, All Singing, All Dancing*, New York, 1966.
Hackl, Alfons, *Fred Astaire and His Work*, Vienna, 1970.
Kobal, John, *Gotta Sing, Gotta Dance*, New York, 1970.
Thompson, Howard, *Fred Astaire: A Pictorial Treasury of His Films*, New York, 1970.
Green, Stanley, *Ring Bells! Sing Songs!*, New Rochelle, New York, 1971.
Croce, Arlene, *The Fred Astaire and Ginger Rogers Book*, New York, 1972.
Thomas, Lawrence B., *The MGM Years*, New Rochelle, New York, 1972.
Green, Stanley, and Burt Goldblatt, *Starring Fred Astaire*, New York, 1973.
Harvey, Stephen, *Fred Astaire*, New York, 1975.
Freedland, Michael, *Fred Astaire*, London, 1976.
Green, Benny, *Fred Astaire*, London, 1979.
Delameter, James, *Dance in the Hollywood Musical*, Ann Arbor, Michigan, 1981.
Thomas, Bob, *Astaire: The Man, the Dancer*, New York, 1984.
Mueller, John, *Astaire Dancing: The Musical Films*, New York, 1985.
Drouin, Frédérique, *Fred Astaire*, Paris, 1986.
Adler, Bill, *Fred Astaire: A Wonderful Life*, New York, 1987.
Mast, Gerald, *Can't Help Singin': The American Musical on Stage and Screen*, Woodstock, New York, 1987.

Satchell, Tim, *Astaire: The Biography*, London, 1987.
Giles, Sarah, editor, *Fred Astaire: His Friends Talk*, New York, 1988.
Altman, Rick, *The American Film Musical*, London, 1989.
Kaminsky, Stuart M., *Dancing in the Dark* (fiction), New York, 1996.

On ASTAIRE: articles—

Eustis, M., "Actor-Dancer Attacks His Part: Fred Astaire," in *Theater Arts* (New York), May 1937.
Pratley, Gerald, "Fred Astaire's Film Career," in *Films in Review* (New York), January 1957.
O'Hara, John, "There's No One Quite Like Astaire," in *Show* (New York), October 1962.
Current Biography 1964, New York, 1964.
Benayoun, Robert, "Freddy, Old Boy," in *Positif* (Paris), April 1970.
Spiegel, Ellen, "Fred and Ginger Meet Van Nest Polglase," in *Velvet Light Trap* (Madison, Wisconsin), Autumn 1973.
Lydon, Susan, "My Affaire with Fred Astaire," in *Rolling Stone* (New York), 6 December 1973.
Yorkin, Bud, "Fred Astaire: A Touch of Class," in *Close-Up: The Movie Star Book*, edited by Danny Peary, New York, 1978.
Mueller, John, "Films: Fred Astaire's 'Dancing in the Dark,'" in *Dance Magazine* (New York), May 1979.
Wood, Robin, "Never, Never Change, Always Gonna Dance," in *Film Comment* (New York), September/October 1979.

Telotte, J. P., "Dancing the Depression: Narrative Strategy in the Astaire-Rogers Films," in *Journal of Popular Film* (Washington, D.C.), Fall 1980.

Harvey, Stephen, "Fred Astaire," in *The Movie Star*, edited by Elisabeth Weis, New York, 1981.

Mueller, John, "The Filmed Dances of Fred Astaire," in *Quarterly Review of Film Studies* (Pleasantville, New York), Spring 1981.

Green, A., "The Magic of Fred Astaire," in *American Film* (New York), April 1981.

Georgakas, Dan, "The Man behind Fred and Ginger: An Interview with Hermes Pan," in *Cineaste* (New York), vol. 12, no. 4, 1983.

Mueller, John, "Fred Astaire and the Integrated Musical," in *Cinema Journal* (Champaign, Illinois), Fall 1984.

Obituary in *New York Times*, 23 June 1987.

Obituary in *Variety* (New York), 24 June 1987.

Meyerson, H., "Astaire Way to Heaven," in *Film Comment* (New York), September/October 1987.

Comuzio, Ermanno, "Fred Astaire: al di la del mito, la tecnica," in *Bianco e Nero* (Rome), October/December 1987.

Kemp, P., "Degrees of Radiance," in *Cinema Papers* (Melbourne), March 1988.

Meisel, J., "Some Enchanted Evenings," in *American Film* (Hollywood), May 1988.

Davis, Francis, "Astaire's Other Talent," in *Connoisseur*, March 1991.

*   *   *

Fred Astaire is in a class by himself. Of all the movie legends of the golden era in Hollywood, he is perhaps the most universally accepted as unquestionably great. His film career encompassed more than 50 years as a top star, and his theater, recording, and television work have also been recognized as outstanding. The name "Fred Astaire" not only means "dance on film," it also represents quality, longevity, and that most elusive characteristic of an artist—a true personal style.

Astaire is one of a small group of actors who have been able to shape their own movies and make a distinct contribution to film history beyond the level of entertainment or personality. Known to be a perfectionist, his insistence on control of his own dance work expanded his influence on films. Not only did he create his own choreography in most films, he also participated in the decision-making process of how his dances would be photographed, scored, and edited; generally the camera frames his entire body, moves only in response to his lead, and keeps running in order to preserve the integrity of the dance. The careful matching of dance, image, and rhythm (both of sound and cutting) seen in his best numbers was a direct result of his desire for the best in every aspect of his work. Astaire pioneered the serious presentation of dance in motion pictures, both by his on-screen influence and his behind-the-scenes collaboration (most importantly with his alter ego at RKO, choreographer Hermes Pan).

Astaire's film debut, after a successful 25-year stage career dancing with his sister Adele, was in a minor role as himself in an MGM Joan Crawford-Clark Gable film, *Dancing Lady*. His first real success came when he was paired with Ginger Rogers for a series of elegant RKO musicals in the 1930s. Astaire and Rogers were not the leads in their first film, *Flying Down to Rio*, but their enormous appeal and talent were immediately apparent, and their next eight films solidified their status as one of the cinema's great teams. (The pair was reunited later at MGM for their last film, *The Barkleys of Broadway*.) The RKO films, with their charmingly complicated plots, excellent music, art deco decor, and remarkable dances, represent the high point of the 1930s musical genre. Although Astaire was paired thereafter with many beautiful women who were also fine dancers—Rita Hayworth, Vera-Ellen, Lucille Bremer, and Cyd Charisse—most critics agree that his most compatible partner in film was Rogers, whose looks and personality made a perfect contrast and complement to his own. Besides their exquisite dancing, they share a wonderful comic rapport; while many of his later co-stars such as Rita Hayworth and Eleanor Powell were possibly more accomplished dancers, none could deflate Astaire's comic vanity with a well-timed wisecrack like Rogers.

During the 1940s and 1950s Astaire appeared in several outstanding musical films produced by the celebrated Freed unit at Metro-Goldwyn-Mayer, including the highly self-reflexive *The Band Wagon* (the title of the last show Fred and Adele starred in on Broadway in 1931), constructed as a stirring reassertion of Astaire's value as an entertainer in a world losing its glamour. He continued his career past his dancing years, playing light comedy and dramatic roles in both television and film with equal success, earning an Oscar nomination for his supporting role in *The Towering Inferno*. He also "co-hosted" the first two *That's Entertainment* compilations, introducing the Hollywood musical to a younger generation, and providing a strong shot of nostalgia for his original fans.

Although Astaire is associated with a certain European elegance of casual dress, his personality on film is actually that of a brash American who cracks wise and cons his way forward toward his true moment of deep expression: the dance. Astaire's typical film character was saved from banality and the brink of unpleasantness by the joy, the tenderness, and the sexual tension of his dancing. The easy way in which he moved seemed to suggest to viewers that we could all be dancers, that music and dancing could and should be natural parts of self-expression. As critic Gerald Mast noted, for Astaire, singing and dancing are direct extensions of talking and walking; musical performance is a fundamental part of everyday life for Astaire, though perhaps no one ever walked, sat, or smoked on-screen quite as artfully.

Although less obviously skilled as a singer, Astaire was frequently recognized as an ideal interpreter of the songs of America's greatest popular songwriters; Irving Berlin, the Gershwins, and Jerome Kern delighted in providing material for Astaire, and consistently praised his precise phrasing as an exact interpretation of their intentions. Although most of the songs he introduced were subsequently recorded by more powerful or versatile vocalists, his subtle renditions of such classics as Kern and Fields's "A Fine Romance" or the Gershwins' "Let's Call the Whole Thing Off" remain the definitive versions.

Astaire's screen work involved all kinds of dancing—tap, ballet, acrobatic, and jazz. Many of his routines were simple and elegant, and the photography was designed to match that quality. In some later films, however, he executed tricky routines that might be called experimental—dancing on the ceiling in *Royal Wedding*, in slow motion in *Easter Parade*, dancing on air in *The Belle of New York*, and with empty shoes in a shoe repair shop in *The Barkleys of Broadway*. But simple or experimental, Astaire's routines were always perfectly danced and perfectly presented on film. His command of cinema was as great as his command of dance; he has been rightly compared to Buster Keaton, another artist for whom body and cinema act in tandem. As a result, he constitutes a major revolutionary force in the development of musical films. (In the 1930s his only conceptual rival was Busby Berkeley, who brilliantly choreographed large groups of anonymous dancers, whereas Astaire's art always emphasizes the individual or the couple.)

Astaire won a special Academy Award in 1949, and the American Film Institute Life Achievement Award in 1981. His place in film history is not just assured. It is cemented. There is no one to equal him, but his own assessment of his contribution is reflective of his personal modesty, simplicity, and elegance: "I have no desire to prove anything by it," he wrote in his autobiography, *Steps in Time*. "I just dance."

—Jeanine Basinger, updated by Corey K. Creekmur

ASTOR, Mary

Nationality: American. **Born:** Lucille Langhanke in Quincy, Illinois, 3 May 1906. **Education:** Attended Kenwood-Loring School for Girls, Chicago. **Family:** Married 1) Ken Hawks, 1928 (died 1930); 2) Dr. Franklyn Thorpe, 1931 (divorced 1935), daughter Marylyn; 3) Manuel del Campo, 1937 (divorced 1941), son: Antonio; 4) Thomas Wheelock, 1945 (divorced 1955). **Career:** 1917-20—father entered her in various beauty contests grooming her for career in movies; 1920—signed 6-month contract with Famous Players-Lasky in New York; early 1920s—acted for independent movie company producing 2-reelers about famous paintings; 1923—under contract again to Famous Players-Lasky of New York; 1924—became star after *Beau Brummel* with John Barrymore; 1926—appeared in *Don Juan*, first use of synchronized musical soundtrack via sound on disc; 1929—began freelancing; also some stagework; 1931—contract with RKO; 1934—her parents, who had guided her career until 1928, sued her for nonsupport; mid-1930s—contract with Columbia; 1936—headline-making scandal during custody battle over daughter involved her diaries which allegedly listed the names of men with whom she had had affairs; 1940s—first appearance on Broadway in *Many Happy Returns*; 1951—reported suicide attempt after bouts with alcoholism; 1953—turned to Motion Picture Relief Fund for financial help; 1960s—began writing novels while making infrequent film appearances. **Awards:** Best Supporting Actress Academy Award, for *The Great Lie*, 1941. **Died:** Of respiratory failure, in Woodland Hills, California, 25 September 1987.

Films as Actress:

1921 *The Beggar Maid* (Blaché); *Bullets or Ballots* (Tuttle and Woolley); *Brother of the Bear* (Carle); *The Lady o' the Pines* (Carle); *The Bashful Suitor* (Blaché)

1922 *The Young Painter* (Blaché); *Hope* (Le Jaren à Hiller); *The Scarecrow* (Blaché and Le Jaren à Hiller); *The Angelus* (Blaché and Le Jaren à Hiller); *John Smith* (Heerman); *The Man Who Played God* (Weight); *The Rapids* (Hartford)

1923 *The Bright Shawl* (Robertson); *Hollywood* (Cruze); *To the Ladies* (Cruze); *The Marriage Maker* (William DeMille); *Puritan Passions* (Tuttle); *Second Fiddle* (Tuttle); *Success* (Ralph Ince); *Woman-Proof* (Green)

1924 *Beau Brummel* (Beaumont); *The Fighting American* (Forman); *The Fighting Coward* (Cruze); *Inez from Hollywood* (*The Good Bad Girl*) (Green); *The Price of a Party* (Giblyn); *Unguarded Woman* (Crossland)

1925 *Don Q, Son of Zorro* (Crisp); *Enticement* (Archainbaud); *Oh, Doctor!* (Pollard); *The Pace That Thrills* (Campbell); *Playing with Souls* (Ralph Ince); *Scarlet Saint* (Archainbaud)

1926 *Don Juan* (Crosland); *Forever After* (Weight); *High Steppers* (Carewe); *The Wise Guy* (Lloyd)

1927 *No Place to Go* (LeRoy); *Rose of the Golden West* (Fitzmaurice); *The Rough Riders* (Fleming); *The Sea Tiger* (Dillon); *The Sunset Derby* (Rogell); *Two Arabian Knights* (Milestone)

1928 *Dressed to Kill* (Cummings); *Dry Martini* (D'Arrast); *Heart to Heart* (Beaudine); *Romance of the Underworld* (Cummings); *Sailors' Wives* (Henabery); *Three-Ring Marriage* (Neilan)

1929 *New Year's Eve* (Lehrman); *The Woman from Hell* (Erickson)

1930 *Ladies Love Brutes* (Rowland V. Lee) (as Mimi Howell); *The Runaway Bride* (Crisp) (as Mary); *Holiday* (Edward H. Griffith) (as Julia Seton); *The Lash* (*Adios*) (Frank Lloyd) (as Rosita Garcia); *The Royal Bed* (*The Queen's Husband*) (Sherman) (as Princess Anne)

1931 *Steel Highway* (*Other Men's Women*) (Wellman) (as Lily); *Behind Office Doors* (Brown) (as Mary Linden); *The Sin Ship* (Wolheim) (as Kitty); *White Shoulders* (Melville Brown) (as Norma Selbee); *Smart Woman* (La Cava) (as Nancy Gibson); *Men of Chance* (Archainbaud) (as Marthe)

1932 *The Lost Squadron* (Archainbaud) (as Follette Marsh); *Those We Love* (Florey) (as May); *A Successful Calamity* (Adolfi) (as Emmie Wilton); *Red Dust* (Fleming) (as Barbara Willis)

1933 *The Little Giant* (Del Ruth) (as Ruth Wayburn); *Jennie Gerhardt* (Gering) (as Letty Pace); *The World Changes* (LeRoy) (as Virginia); *The Kennel Murder Case* (Curtiz) (as Hilda Lake); *Convention City* (Mayo) (as Arlene Dale)

1934 *Easy to Love* (Keighley) (as Charlotte); *Upperworld* (Del Ruth) (as Mrs. Hettie Stream); *Return of the Terror* (Bretherton) (as Olga Morgan); *The Man with Two Faces* (Mayo) (as Jessica Wells); *The Case of the Howling Dog* (Crosland) (as Bessie Foley); *The Hollywood Gad-About*

1935 *I Am a Thief* (Florey) (as Odette Mauclair); *Straight from the Heart* (Beal) (as Marian Henshaw); *Red Hot Tires* (*Racing Luck*) (Lederman) (as Patricia Sanford); *Dinky* (Lederman and Bretherton) (as Mrs. Daniels); *Page Miss Glory* (LeRoy) (as Gladys Russell); *Man of Iron* (McGann) (as Vida)

1936 *The Murder of Dr. Harrigan* (McDonald) (as Lillian Ash); *And So They Were Married* (Nugent) (as Edith Farnham); *Trapped by Television* (*Caught by Television*) (Lord) (as Bobby Blake); *Dodsworth* (Wyler) (as Edith Coatright); *Lady from Nowhere* (Wiles) (as Polly)

1937 *The Prisoner of Zenda* (Cromwell) (as Antoinette De Mauban); *The Hurricane* (Ford) (as Madame Germaine De Laage)

1938 *No Time to Marry* (Lachman) (as Kay McGowan); *Paradise for Three* (*Romance for Three*) (Buzzell) (as Mrs. Mallebre); *There's Always a Woman* (Hall) (as Lola Fraser); *Woman against Woman* (Sinclair) (as Cynthia Holland); *Listen, Darling* (Marin) (as Dottie Wingate)

1939 *Midnight* (Leisen) (as Helene Flammarion)

1940 *Turnabout* (Roach) (as Marion Manning); *Brigham Young—Frontiersman* (*Brigham Young*) (Hathaway) (as Mary Ann Young)

1941 *The Great Lie* (Goulding) (as Sandra Kovak); **The Maltese Falcon** (Huston) (as Brigid O'Shaughnessy)

1942 *In This Our Life* (Huston) (unbilled cameo); *Across the Pacific* (Huston) (as Alberta Marlow); *The Palm Beach Story* (Preston Sturges) (as Princess Centimillia)

1943 *Thousands Cheer* (Sidney) (as Hyllary Jones); *Young Ideas* (Dassin) (as Jo Evans)

1944 **Meet Me in St. Louis** (Minnelli) (as Mrs. Anne Smith); *Blonde Fever* (Whorf) (as Delilah Donay)

1946 *Claudia and David* (Walter Lang) (as Elizabeth Van Doren)

1947 *Desert Fury* (Lewis Allen) (as Fritzie Haller); *Cynthia* (*The Rich, Full Life*) (Leonard) (as Louise Bishop); *Fiesta* (Thorpe) (as Senora Morales); *Cass Timberlane* (Sidney) (as Queenie Havock)

1949 *Act of Violence* (Zinnemann) (as Pat); *Little Women* (LeRoy) (as Marmee March); *Any Number Can Play* (LeRoy) (as Ada)

1956 *The Power and the Prize* (Koster) (as Mrs. George Salt); *A Kiss before Dying* (Oswald) (as Mrs. Corliss)

1957 *The Devil's Hairpin* (Wilde) (as Mrs. Jargin)

1958 *This Happy Feeling* (Edwards) (as Mrs. Tremaine)

1959 *Stranger in My Arms* (Kautner) (as Mrs. Beasley)

1961 *Return to Peyton Place* (Ferrer) (as Roberta Carter)

1964 *Youngblood Hawke* (Daves) (as Irene Perry); *Hush . . . Hush, Sweet Charlotte* (Aldrich) (as Jewel Mayhew)

Mary Astor

Publications

By ASTOR: books—

My Story, New York, 1959.
The Incredible Charlie Carewe, New York, 1960.
A Place Called Saturday, New York, 1968.
A Life on Film, New York, 1971.

On ASTOR: articles—

Current Biography 1961, New York, 1961.
Higham, Charles, "Meeting Mary Astor," in *Sight and Sound* (London), Spring 1964.
Shipman, David, in *The Great Movie Stars: The Golden Years*, rev. ed., London, 1979.
Ciné Revue (Paris), 13 March 1980.
Obituary in *Variety* (New York), 30 September 1987.
Obituary in *Films and Filming* (London), November 1987.
Anderson, Lindsay, "Mary Astor," in *Sight and Sound* (London), Autumn 1990.

*   *   *

Mary Astor is best known for her performance as Brigid O'Shaughnessy in *The Maltese Falcon*. One of film's most versatile actresses, Astor played everything from ingenues to mothers in a career that lasted almost 45 years and included more than 100 films, including *The Great Lie* for which she won an Oscar for her portrayal of temperamental pianist, Sandra Kovak. One of Astor's best performances is as the easygoing heiress in *The Palm Beach Story*. Another, and the actress's personal favorite, is *Dodsworth*, which casts her as the widow who brings happiness into the life of a downtrodden businessman. It contains one of the more memorable introductory lines in American cinema: on board ship Dodsworth asks the steward to bring him a drink to steady his nerves; from the dark reaches of a deck chair comes the voice of Mary Astor, "Why don't you try stout, Mr. Dodsworth?"

Astor made her screen debut at 15, a hauntingly innocent presence in *The Beggar Maid*. When John Barrymore cast her in *Beau Brummel*, Astor became established as a leading actress. Even in this early, silent film, Astor's performance is expressive but not histrionic, her concentrated intensity an ideal match for Barrymore's bravura performance. Astor's delicate beauty and graceful carriage made her particularly suited to historical melodramas such as *Don Q, Son of Zorro* and *Don Juan*. It was an image that lasted into the 1930s when she made her last historical drama, *The Prisoner of Zenda*.

Almost a has-been at 23, Fox executives told Astor they were not impressed with the way her voice recorded. But her performance in a hit play led to several studio offers, and she ably made the transition to sound. The coolly confident Astor image first emerges in *Holiday* where Astor proves more than a match for the film's star, Broadway-trained Ann Harding. Astor's career again looked as if it was in trouble when the scandal associated with her infamous diaries erupted. Some critics feel that the publicity surrounding her divorce and custody battle in 1936 has dulled recognition of her as work as an actress. Yet it appears that the scandal, and her "fortitude under stress" actually boosted her career, and helped reshape her star image, from ingenue to lovely but knowing woman-of-the-world, a transformation that allowed her to play the roles for which she is best remembered.

Critics often discuss Astor's performances in *The Great Lie* and *The Maltese Falcon* in terms of her marvelous bitchiness. Yet what is remarkable is Astor's ability to play women who were charming, clever, perfectly manicured, but who also had an intensity, a candor, and an appetite for life that made them undeniably real. With her performances in the late 1930s and 1940s, Astor became a woman with a style and class unto herself. In 1948 the British magazine *Sequence* observed that "in *Dodsworth* she was intelligently lovely, in *Hurricane* intelligently conventional, in *The Palm Beach Story* intelligently crazy, in *The Maltese Falcon* intelligently depraved."

Astor's image changed again when she began to accept mother roles, notably in *Meet Me in St. Louis* and *Little Women*, where she displayed a maternal charm almost symbolic of the American mother. Mother roles continued to come her way in the 1950s and 1960s, although in *Stranger in My Arms* and *Return to Peyton Place* she was not quite as nice as she had been a decade earlier. Astor ended her career with a cameo in *Hush . . . Hush, Sweet Charlotte* where her piercing eyes, expressive voice, and keen sense of dramatic timing give a succinct portrait of a Southern lady whose recognition of her "ruined finery" only enhances her elegance.

In 1965 Astor turned to writing full time. She said that she never really cared for the industry of which she was so long a part, but that she is proud of the work of the actress called Mary Astor.

—Anthony Slide, updated by Cynthia Baron

ATTENBOROUGH, (Lord) Richard

Nationality: British. **Born:** Richard Samuel Attenborough in Cambridge, England, 29 August 1923. **Education:** Attended Wyggeston Grammar School, Leicester; Leverhulme Scholarship, Royal Academy of Dramatic Art, London. **Military Service:** Royal Air Force, 1943-46 (assigned to RAF Film Unit, 1944). **Family:** Married the actress Sheila Sim, 1945, one son and two daughters. **Career:** 1941—first stage appearance as Richard Miller in *Ah, Wilderness*, Palmers Green, London; 1942—film debut in Noël Coward's *In Which We Serve*; 1949-59—active as stage actor; 1959—formed Beaver Films with actor-director Bryan Forbes; 1960—formed Allied Filmmakers; 1970—appointed chairman of Royal Academy of Dramatic Art; 1971—vice-president of British Academy of Film and Television (Fellowship 1982); chairman, British Film Institute. **Awards:** Best Actor, British Academy, for *Guns at Batasi* and *Séance on a Wet Afternoon*, 1964; Golden Globes for Best Supporting Actor, for *The Sand Pebbles*, 1966, and *Doctor Dolittle*, 1967; Golden Globe for Best Director, British Academy of Film and Television Arts Award for Best Director, Directors Guild Award for Outstanding Directorial Achievement, and Academy Award for Best Film, for *Gandhi*, 1982; Berlinale Kamera, for *Cry Freedom*, 1987; Lifetime Achievement Award, Cinema Expo International, 1995. Commander, Order of the British Empire, 1967; knighted, 1976; Jean Renoir Humanitarian Award, 1987. **Address:** c/o Richard Attenborough Productions Ltd., Beaver Lodge, Richmond Green, Surrey TW9 1NQ, England.

Films as Actor:

1942   *In Which We Serve* (Lean and Coward) (as young Stoker)
1943   *The Hundred Pound Window* (Hurst) (as Tommy Draper); *Schweik's New Adventures* (Lamac) (as railway worker)
1945   *Journey Together* (John Boulting) (as David Wilton)
1946   *A Matter of Life and Death* (*Stairway to Heaven*) (Powell and Pressburger) (as English pilot); *Secret Flight* (*School for Secrets*) (Ustinov) (as Jack Arnold)
1947   *The Man Within* (*The Smugglers*) (Knowles) (as Francis Andrews); *Dancing with Crime* (Carstairs) (as Ted Peters); *Brighton Rock* (*Young Scarface*) (John Boulting) (as Pinky Brown)

1948   *London Belongs to Me* (*Dulcimer Street*) (Gilliat) (as Percy Boon); *The Guinea Pig* (*The Outsider*) (Roy Boulting) (as Jack Read)
1949   *The Boys in Brown* (Tully) (as Jackie Knowles)
1950   *The Lost People* (Knowles) (as Jan); *Morning Departure* (*Operation Disaster*) (Baker) (as Stoker Snipe)
1951   *Hell Is Sold Out* (Anderson) (as Pierre Bonnet); *The Magic Box* (John Boulting) (as Jack Carter)
1952   *The Gift Horse* (*Glory at Sea*) (Bennett) (as Dripper Daniels); *Father's Doing Fine* (Cass) (as Dougal)
1953   *Eight O'Clock Walk* (Comfort) (as Tom Manning)
1955   *Private's Progress* (John Boulting) (as Pvt. Cox); *The Ship that Died of Shame* (Dearden and Relph) (as George Hoskins)
1956   *The Baby and the Battleship* (Jay Lewis) (as Knocker White)
1957   *Brothers in Law* (Roy Boulting) (as Henry Marshall); *The Scamp* (*Strange Affection*) (Rilla) (as Stephen Leigh)
1958   *Dunkirk* (Norman) (as John Holden); *The Man Upstairs* (Chaffey) (as Peter Watson); *Sea of Sand* (*The Desert Patrol*) (Guy Green) (as Trooper Brody)
1959   *I'm All Right, Jack* (Roy Boulting) (as Sidney de Vere Cox); *Jet Storm* (Endfield) (as Ernest Tilley); *S.O.S. Pacific* (Guy Green) (as Whitey); *The League of Gentlemen* (Dearden) (as Edward Lexy); *Danger Within* (*Breakout*) (Chaffey) (as Captain "Bunter" Phillips)
1960   *The Angry Silence* (Guy Green) (as Tom Curtis, + co-pr)
1961   *All Night Long* (Relph and Dearden) (as Rod Hamilton)
1962   *Only Two Can Play* (Gilliat) (as Probert); *The Dock Brief* (*Trial and Error*) (Hill) (as Fowle)
1963   *The Great Escape* (John Sturges) (as Big "X" Bartlett)
1964   *Seance on a Wet Afternoon* (Forbes) (as Billy Savage, + co-pr); *The Third Secret* (Charles Crichton) (as Alfred Price-Gorham); *Guns at Batasi* (Guillermin) (as RSM Lauderdale)
1965   *The Flight of the Phoenix* (Aldrich) (as Lew Moran)
1966   *The Sand Pebbles* (Wise) (as Frenchy)
1967   *Doctor Dolittle* (Fleischer) (as Albert Blossom)
1968   *The Bliss of Mrs. Blossom* (McGrath) (as Robert Blossom); *Only When I Larf* (Dearden) (as Silas)
1970   *The Last Grenade* (Flemying) (as General Charles Whiteley); *The Magic Christian* (McGrath) (as Oxford Coach); *David Copperfield* (Delbert Mann—for TV) (as Mr. Tungay); *A Severed Head* (Dick Clement) (as Palmer Anderson); *Loot* (Narizzano) (as Truscott)
1971   *10 Rillington Place* (Fleischer) (as John Reginald Halliday Christie)
1975   *And Then There Were None* (*Ten Little Indians*) (Collinson) (as Judge); *Brannigan* (*Joe Battle*) (Hickox) (as Commander Swann); *Rosebud* (Preminger) (as Sloat); *Conduct Unbecoming* (Anderson) (as Major Lionel Roach)
1978   *Shatranj Ke Khilari* (*The Chess Players*) (Satyajit Ray) (as Gen. Outram)
1986   *Mother Teresa* (Ann Petrie and Jeanette Petrie—doc) (as narrator)
1979   *The Human Factor* (Preminger) (as Colonel John Daintrey)
1993   *Jurassic Park* (Spielberg) (as Dr. John Hammond)
1994   *Miracle on 34th Street* (Columbus) (as Kris Kringle)

Other Films:

1961   *Whistle Down the Wind* (Forbes) (pr)
1962   *The L-Shaped Room* (Forbes) (co-pr)
1969   *Oh! What a Lovely War* (d, co-pr)
1972   *Young Winston* (d, co-pr)
1977   *A Bridge Too Far* (d)

1978   *Magic* (d)
1982   *Gandhi* (d, pr)
1985   *A Chorus Line* (d)
1987   *Cry Freedom* (d, co-pr)
1992   *Chaplin* (d, co-pr)
1993   *Shadowlands* (d, co-pr)
1996   *In Love and War* (d)

Publications

By ATTENBOROUGH: books—

In Search of Gandhi, London, 1982.
Richard Attenborough's Chorus Line, with Diana Carter, 1986.
Cry Freedom: A Pictorial Record, 1987.

By ATTENBOROUGH: articles—

"An Actor's Actor," interview with C. Hanson, in *Cinema* (Beverly Hills), March 1966.
"Why I Became a Director," in *Action* (Los Angeles), January/February 1969.
"Elements of Truth," in *Films and Filming* (London), June 1969.
Interview with K. Freund, in *American Film* (New York), vol. 14, no. 7, 1972.
"Dialogue on Film: Richard Attenborough," in *American Film* (New York), March 1983.
Interview with M. Buckley, in *Films in Review* (New York), December 1987.
Interview in *Revue du Cinéma* (Paris), March and April 1988.
"Sir Richard Replies . . . ," in *Eyepiece* (Greenford, Middlesex), vol. 11, no. 6, 1990.
Interview with David Robinson, in *Times* (London), 22 March 1990.
"Attenborough on Ray," in *Sight and Sound* (London), August 1992.
"Les faits plus que la fiction," interview with J. Lefebvre, in *Jeune Cinéma* (Paris), April/May 1993.

On ATTENBOROUGH: books—

Castell, David, *Richard Attenborough: A Pictorial Film Biography*, London, 1984.
Woods, Donald, *Filming with Attenborough: The Making of* Cry Freedom, New York, 1987.
Eberts, Jake, and Terry Ilott, *My Indecision Is Final: The Rise and Fall of Goldcrest Films*, London, 1990.
Dougan, Andy, *The Actors' Director: Richard Attenborough behind the Camera*, Edinburgh, 1994.

On ATTENBOROUGH: articles—

Ratcliffe, Michael, "The Public Image and the Private Eye of Richard Attenborough," in *Films and Filming* (London), August 1963.
Castell, D., "His 10-Year Obsession," in *Films Illustrated* (London), September 1974.
A Bridge Too Far Section of *American Cinematographer* (Hollywood), April 1977.
Screen International (London), 17 October and 4 December 1981, 22 January and 14 May 1983.
National Film Theatre Booklet (London), October/November 1983.
Current Biography 1984, New York, 1984.
Tanner, L., "Sir Richard Attenborough," in *Films in Review* (New York), January 1986.
Houston, Penelope, "Parker, Attenborough, Anderson," in *Sight and Sound* (London), Summer 1986.

Richard Attenborough in *Brighton Rock*

Hacker, Jonathan, and David Price, "Richard Attenborough," in *Take 10: Contemporary British Film Directors*, London, 1991.

Stivers, C., "Trampled," in *Premiere* (New York), January 1993.

*   *   *

Today, Richard Attenborough is primarily recognized as the director of prestigious, large-scale message pictures and historical epics (*Gandhi, Cry Freedom, A Bridge Too Far*), and biographies (*Young Winston, Chaplin*). Prior to his directorial debut in 1969 with *Oh! What a Lovely War*, however, he enjoyed a quarter-century-long career in front of the camera. His on-screen debut came in the kind of film he might have directed himself: Noël Coward's *In Which We Serve*, a World War II drama set aboard a British destroyer. He portrayed a coward and, unfortunately, found himself typecast as characters who at least start out as fainthearted and indecisive before (occasionally) redeeming themselves: the RAF pilot trainee in *Journey Together*; the young seaman in *The Man Within*; the gutless submarine crew member in *Morning Departure*.

Physically, Attenborough was stocky and boyish; he lacked the required good looks to become a leading man. And so, early in his career, he also was cast as characters far younger than his real years: most incredibly, as a schoolboy in *The Guinea Pig* (released when he was 25 years old); the thief who is sent to a borstal in *The Boys in Brown*; the South London boardinghouse resident convicted of murder in *London Belongs to Me*; and, most memorably, as Pinky Brown, the ill-fated adolescent killer, in *Brighton Rock* (in which he gives his foremost early career performance).

Eventually, Attenborough was able to transcend this typecasting, becoming a solid and reliable character actor who won supporting and occasional lead roles in a variety of films. He had the ability to convey considerable shadiness behind genial bluster, particularly in the Boulting comedies *I'm All Right, Jack* and *Brothers in Law* and the Basil Dearden-directed dramas *The Ship that Died of Shame* and *The League of Gentlemen*. Still, some of his best characters remained submissive ones, such as the compliant mate of deranged medium Kim Stanley in *Seance on a Wet Afternoon*. Additionally, he was perfectly cast as unbending intellectuals (the soldier who concocts a breakout from a German POW camp in *The Great Escape*) and characters of unyielding integrity (the victimized factory worker in *The Angry Silence*). In the latter two films, he offers appropriately intense performances which are among the best of his career.

By the late 1950s and early 1960s, Attenborough was envisioning a career behind the cameras. In 1959, he formed Beaver Films, his own production company, with Bryan Forbes and Guy Green, and began producing or co-producing films in which he appeared (*The Angry Silence, Seance on a Wet Afternoon*) and others in which he did not (*Whistle Down the Wind, The L-Shaped Room*). A segue into directing was part of his natural progression.

By the time he directed *Gandhi* in 1982, Attenborough already had established himself as a filmmaker. He had desired to tell the story of Mohandas K. Gandhi since the 1960s; "This is what I've wanted to do more than anything else I've been involved with," he explained. "Everything I've directed was a sort of training. I didn't want to direct per se, I wanted to make *Gandhi*." The film was a multi-Academy Award winner; included in its honors was a Best Director statue for Attenborough. Nevertheless, in recent years *Gandhi* (as well as Attenborough's other big-budget projects) has come to be regarded as ponderous: a stuffy, overblown epic which did not extend on the stylistic innovation he displayed in *Oh! What a Lovely War*. Perhaps his best film, which harks back to his more intimate stints as an actor, remains the thriller *Magic*, which showed that Attenborough the director, without the benefit of a cast of thousands and a huge backdrop, could spin a compelling yarn.

—Quentin Falk, updated by Rob Edelman

AUDRAN, Stéphane

Nationality: French. **Born:** Colette Suzanne Jeannine Dacheville in Versailles, 2 or 8 November 1932. **Education:** Attended Lycée Lamartine, Paris; studied drama with Tania Balachova and Michel Vitold. **Family:** Married 1) the actor Jean-Louis Trintignant (divorced); 2) the director Claude Chabrol, 1964 (divorced), son: Thomas. **Career:** 1959—appeared in Chabrol's *Les Cousins*, beginning long personal and professional relationship; work for TV includes *Orient-Express*, for French TV, 1979, and *Brideshead Revisited* for BBC TV, 1981, mini-series *Mistral's Daughter*, 1984. **Awards:** Best Actress, Berlin Festival, for *Les Biches*, 1968; Best Actress, British Academy, for *The Discreet Charm of the Bourgeoisie* and *Juste avant la nuit*, 1973; César Award for Best Actress, for *Violette Nozière*, 1978; Best Actress Award (UK Critics Circle) and Robert Award (Danish Film Academy), for *Babette's Feast*, 1988. **Address:** 95 rue de Chézy, 92200 Neuilly, France.

Films as Actress:

1959   *Les Cousins* (*The Cousins*) (Chabrol) (as Françoise); *Le Signe de lion* (Rohmer)

1960   *Les Bonnes Femmes* (Chabrol) (as Ginette); *Saint-Tropez Blues* (Moussy)

1961   *Les Godelureaux* (Chabrol)

1962   *L'Oeil du malin* (*The Third Lover*) (Chabrol) (as Hélène Hartmann)

1963   *Landru* (*Bluebeard*) (Chabrol) (as Fernande Segret)

1964   *Le Tigre aime la chair fraîche* (*The Tiger Loves Fresh Blood*) (Chabrol); *Les Durs à cuire* (Pinoteau)

1965   "La Muette" ep. of *Paris vu par . . .* (*6 in Paris*) (Chabrol) (as wife); *Marie-Chantal contre le Docteur Kha* (Chabrol)

1966   *La Ligne de démarcation* (*Line of Demarcation*) (Chabrol)

1967   *Le Scandale* (*The Champagne Murders*) (Chabrol) (as Jacqueline/Lydia)

1968   *Les Biches* (*The Does; The Girlfriends*) (Chabrol) (as Frederique)

1969   *La Peau de torpédo* (Delannoy); ***La Femme infidèle*** (*Unfaithful Wife*) (Chabrol) (as Hélène Desvallées)

1970   *La Dame dans l'auto avec des lunettes et un fusil* (*The Lady in the Car with Glasses and a Gun*) (Litvak) (as Anita Caldwell); ***Le Boucher*** (*The Butcher*) (Chabrol) (as Hélène Marcoux); *La Rupture* (*The Breakup*) (Chabrol) (as Hélène)

1971   *Juste avant la nuit* (*Just before Nightfall*) (Chabrol (as Helen); *Sans mobile apparent* (*Without Apparent Motive*) (Labro) (as Hélène Vallee); *Aussi loin que l'amour* (Rossif)

1972   *Un Meurtre est un meurtre* (Périer); *Dead Pigeon on Beethoven Street* (Fuller); ***Le Charme discrèt de la bourgeoisie*** (*The Discreet Charm of the Bourgeoisie*) (Buñuel) (as Mme. Alice Sénéchal)

1973   *Les Noces rouges* (*Wedding in Blood*) (Chabrol); *Hay que matar a B.* (*B. Must Die*) (Borau)

1974   *And Then There Were None* (*Ten Little Niggers; Ten Little Indians*) (Collinson) (as Ilona); *Comment reussir dans la vie quand on est con et pleurnichard* (Audiard); *Le Cri du coeur* (Lallemand); *Vincent, François, Paul, et les autres* (*Vincent, François, Paul, and the Others*) (Sautet)

1975   *The Black Bird* (Giler) (as Anna Kemidon); one ep. of *Chi dice donna dice . . . donna* (Cervi)

1976   *Folies bourgeoises* (*The Twist*) (Chabrol) (as wife)

1977   *Mort d'un pourri* (Lautner); *Des Teufels Advokat* (*The Devil's Advocate*) (Green)

Stéphane Audran with Michel Bouquet in *La Femme infidèle*

1978   *Silver Bears* (Passer) (as Shireen Firdausi); *Les Liens du sang*
        (*Blood Relatives*) (Chabrol) (as Mother); *Violette Nozière*
        (*Violette*) (Chabrol) (as Germaine Nozière); *Eagle's Wing*
        (Harvey) (as the widow)

1979   *Le Gagnant* (Gion); *Le Soleil en face* (Kast)

1980   *The Big Red One* (Fuller) (as Walloon)

1982   *Boulevard des assassins*; *Le Choc*; *Le paradis pour tous* (Jessua);
        Coup de torchon (*Clean Slate*) (Tavernier) (as Huguette)
        (Cordier)

1984   *Le Sang des autres* (*The Blood of Others*) (Chabrol); *The Bay
        Boy* (Petrie) (as Blanche); *The Sun Also Rises* (for TV)

1985   *Poulet au vinaigre* (*Cop au Vin*) (Chabrol) (as Mme. Cuno);
        La Cage aux Folles 3: The Wedding (Lautner) (as
        Matrimonia); *La Scarlatine* (Aghion) (as Minon Palazzi);
        Les Plouffe (Carle) (as Mme. Boucher); *Night Magic* (Furey)
        (as Janice)

1986   *L'Isola* (Lizzani); *La Gitane* (De Broca) (as Brigitte); *Suivez
        Mon Regard* (Curtelin)

1987   *Babette's Gastebud* (*Babette's Feast*) (Axel) (as Babette); *Les
        Saisons du Plaisir* (Mocky) (as Bernadette); *Poor Little
        Rich Girl: The Barbara Hutton Story* (Jarrott—for TV) (as
        Pauline); *Les Predateurs de la Nuit*; *Corps źa Corps* (Halimi)
        (as Edna Chabert)

1988   *Manika, une vie plus tard* (François Villiers) (as Ananda)

1989   *Sons* (Rockwell); *Champagne Charlie* (Allan Eastman—for
        TV)

1990   *Jours tranquilles à Clichy* (*Quiet Days in Clichy*) (Chabrol)

1992   *The Turn of the Screw* (Lemorande) (as Mrs. Gross)

1993   *Betty* (Chabrol) (as Laure)

1995   *Au petit Marguery* (Benegui) (as Josephine)

Publications

By AUDRAN: articles—

Interview with Guy Braucourt, in *Ecran* (Paris), November 1972.
Interview with Karl Lagerfeld, in *Inter/View* (New York), April 1975.
Interview in *Ciné Revue* (Paris), 29 September 1983.

On AUDRAN: books—

Wood, Robin, and Michael Walker, *Claude Chabrol*, New York, 1970.
Fassbinder, Rainer Werner, and others, *Reihe Film 5: Claude Chabrol*,
    Munich, 1975.
Magny, Joel, *Claude Chabrol*, Paris, 1987.
Derry, Charles, *The Suspense Thriller: Films in the Shadow of Alfred
    Hitchcock*, Jefferson, North Carolina, 1988.

On AUDRAN: articles—

"Chabrol Issue" of *Image et Son* (Paris), December 1973.
Walker, Michael, "Claude Chabrol into the '70s," in *Movie* (London),
    Spring 1975.

"I Fell in Love with Violette Nozière," interview with Claude Chabrol, in *Monthly Film Bulletin* (London), April 1979.
Ciné Revue (Paris), 26 August 1982, 1 March and 8 November 1984.

*   *   *

Stéphane Audran's career is intimately connected to the emerging New Wave in France as well as to the career of her husband, Claude Chabrol, who directed Audran in her most acclaimed performances. Her beauty is remarkable: the luminous eyes, the exquisitely high cheekbones, the long neck, the grace with which she moves—her hand cocked at a slight angle. What makes Audran different from Garbo or Dietrich (whom she in some ways evokes) is that one never feels that an Audran film has been constructed as a vehicle for her, but rather that her performance, though central, remains subservient to the film's overall conception. Audran has perfected her portrayal of the bourgeois French woman—elegant, aloof, reserved, and yet often compassionate—who becomes embroiled in a murderous conflict. Her major performances are all related; indeed, in at least five instances, the character Audran plays is named "Hélène," although each Hélène demonstrates a subtly different psychological makeup. Minor, early Audran performances in Chabrol's films include the salesgirl who yearns for success on the stage in *Les Bonnes Femmes*, the first incarnation as Hélène in the triangular tale of jealousy and murder, *L'Oeil du malin*, and a double role—as a mousy secretary and a femme fatale—in *Le Scandale*.

At least four later performances stand out as extraordinary. In *La Femme infidèle* Audran plays, with the most incredible subtlety and economy, an unfaithful wife: when her lover is killed by her husband in a moment of passion, Hélène lies flat on her bed and emits three tiny sobs. One remembers Audran's mysterious and wondrous expression of approval as she rediscovers her husband's passion; one remembers, too, the delicacy of her posture at the moment she burns the picture. Although *La Femme infidèle* takes the emotional conflict between husband and wife as its psychological subject, it is significant to note that not one word passes between them on the subject of their relationship or her infidelity: the conflict is all in the subtext, and Audran makes the subtext dominant through her considerable nuance and skill. In *Le Boucher* Audran plays a schoolteacher (again, Hélène) who sublimates her sexual desire into her work, but who nevertheless becomes involved with a homicidal maniac who falls in love with her. Here again, as in *La Femme infidèle*, Audran's performance seems so extraordinarily integrated into the fabric of the film that one can hardly tell where actress Audran leaves off and director Chabrol begins. Certain images of Audran in *Le Boucher* are difficult to forget: her elegant walk through town, sustained in a very long tracking shot; her yoga posture, formal and self-absorbing, as she attempts to shut out the world and her problems; her scene of breakdown and tears while eating cherries in her kitchen; and her ultimate isolation—serene and yet desolate—by film's end. In *La Rupture*, Audran's Hélène is this time of a somewhat lower class, but here absolutely virtuous: a strong and prepossessed woman who is unaware of the horrible plot being spun against her. Here one is drawn to the generosity and innocence of her portrayal. Again, certain scenes stand out: her heartrending monologue about her troubled past delivered on a streetcar in a scene recalling Murnau's *Sunrise*; her triumphant speech as it appears she will finally vanquish her enemies ("I am a woman, and I have all my strength!"); her regression to childhood and subsequent release in a drug-induced fantasy at film's climax. In *Violette Nozière*, Audran surprised many with her portrayal, drawn from a historical character, of a lower-class, almost slatternly mother who is poisoned by her daughter. Although her earlier Chabrol performances are arguably more significant, Audran's playing against type in a narrative that gave the leading role to the younger Isabelle Huppert, finally brought Audran the official acclaim of the French "Oscar," the César. And yet certainly, virtually all of Audran's leading performances for Chabrol have been extraordinary, even if they have been judged by some as too many variations on the same theme to be accorded great acclaim—including her upper-class lesbian in a bisexual love triangle in *Les Biches*; her adulterous, murderous wife in *Les Noces rouges*; and again her status-conscious Hélène in *Juste avant la nuit*.

At least two other directors have managed to use Audran as skillfully as Chabrol: Luis Buñuel in *The Discreet Charm of the Bourgeoisie* and Gabriel Axel in *Babette's Feast*. In Buñuel's film, Audran with great wit plays an archetypal bourgeoisie, mistress of the manor, totally and comically unflappable in her designer gowns as she oversees huge dinner parties, is visited by terrorists, climbs down garden ivy for a quickie with her husband, and listens politely to strangers who insist on telling her their violent dreams; as well, Buñuel's recurring cutaways to images of his rich protagonists, including Audran, walking down the road (of life?) to an unclear destination, are surprisingly moving. *Babette's Feast* represents an even more impressive personal achievement for Audran, not only because she was working outside the French industry, but because she plays a role far from the bourgeois, glacial persona which has become her trademark. Although Audran enters the film late, once she does, she totally dominates it with the understated warmth of her sincere, if discreet, working woman, a cook whose earthy meals ultimately reveal her to be the most luminous and sensuous artist. Audran deservedly received several acting awards, and the film reaped huge international box office virtually everywhere except for its native Denmark.

Nevertheless, true international fame has eluded Audran. By the time of *Brideshead Revisited*, Audran's English had improved enough to play Laurence Olivier's Italian mistress, but the role attracted little attention. Despite a variety of opportunities in English-language roles (in *The Black Bird*, *The Silver Bears*, and the television films *Mistral's Daughter*, *The Sun Also Rises*, and *Poor Little Rich Girl*), American stardom also has continued to elude Audran—in part because her demonstrated inability to speak English without a heavy, sometimes impenetrable accent renders many performances phonetic and rigid. Audran's charisma is subtle, certainly, and perhaps inherently French; and too, one must consider the failure of the French mystique to travel well to American culture—the number of French stars (Bardot, Deneuve, Moreau) who have failed spectacularly in the American market is numerous. More recently, Audran has been taking supporting roles—even in Chabrol's work—which, to her fans, must be seen as somewhat of a disappointment. That most of these supporting roles are in films that have had virtually no release outside of France makes it particularly difficult for an American commentator to generalize. But many of the performances that have been marginally available—for instance, her alcoholic, older woman in Chabrol's *Betty*—do not seem especially interesting or notable. It is clear that as Audran ages further and loses that particular confluence of beauty and charisma that marked the period of her greatest performances for Chabrol, her challenges will be to find other roles worthy of her talents and to find directors—like Axel—who will spur her to complex, rich, inventive work.

—Charles Derry

AUTRY, Gene

Nationality: American. **Born:** Orvon Gene Autry on a ranch near Tioga, Texas, 29 September 1907. **Military Service:** Served as flight officer with Air Transport Command, 1942-46. **Family:** Married 1) Ina Mae Spivey, 1932 (died 1980); 2) Jacqueline Ellam, 1981. **Career:** Following high school, worked as freight handler and roustabout for St. Louis and San Francisco Railroad in Oklahoma; became a telegrapher; 1928—began singing on local radio show; 1931—in own radio show and made first recordings; 1933—awarded the first gold record for *That Golden-Haired Daddy of Mine*; 1934—first film appearance; 1935—starring role in 13-chapter serial *Phantom Empire*, contract with Republic Pictures; late 1940s—contract with Columbia Pictures (produced 32 films for Columbia); formed own company, Gene Autry Productions; early 1950s—his Flying A Pictures production company began producing TV series such as *The Gene Autry Show* (1950-54), *The Adventures of Champion*, and *Annie Oakley*; by 1960—ceased acting, business interests in hotels, real estate, radio and TV stations, and as co-owner of Los Angeles Angels baseball team (later sole owner after team changed name to California Angels); 1988—opened the Autry Museum of Western Heritage, Los Angeles; 1989—hosted *Melody Ranch Theatre* for TV; 1994—TV special *Gene Autry—The Singing Cowboy*; 1995—TV special *Gene Autry—Melody of the West*. **Awards:** D. W. Griffith Career Award, 1990.

Films as Actor:

1934   *In Old Santa Fe* (David Howard); *Mystery Mountain* (Brower and Eason)

1935   *The Phantom Empire* (Brower and Eason—serial); *Tumbling Tumbleweeds* (Kane); *Melody Trail* (Kane); *The Sagebrush Troubadour* (Kane); *The Singing Vagabond* (Pierson)

1936   *Red River Valley* (Eason); *Comin' Round the Mountain* (Wright); *The Singing Cowboy* (Wright); *Guns and Guitars* (Kane); *Oh! Susanna* (Kane); *Ride, Ranger, Ride* (Kane); *The Big Show* (Wright); *The Old Corral* (Kane)

1937   *Round-Up Time in Texas* (Kane); *Git along Little Dogies* (Kane); *Rootin' Tootin' Rhythm* (Wright); *Yodelin' Kid from Pine Ridge* (Kane); *Public Cowboy Number One* (Kane); *Boots and Saddles* (Kane); *Manhattan Merry-Go-Round* (Riesner); *Springtime in the Rockies* (Kane)

1938   *The Old Barn Dance* (Kane); *Gold Mine in the Sky* (Kane); *Man from Music Mountain* (Kane); *Prairie Moon* (Staub); *Rhythm of the Saddle* (Sherman); *Western Jamboree* (Staub)

1939   *Home on the Prairie* (Townley); *Mexicali Rose* (Sherman); *Blue Montana Skies* (Eason); *Mountain Rhythm* (Eason); *Colorado Sunset* (Sherman); *In Old Monterey* (Kane); *Rovin' Tumbleweeds* (*Washington Cowboy*) (Sherman); *South of the Border* (Sherman)

1940   *Rancho Grande* (McDonald); *Shooting High* (Green); *Gaucho Serenade* (McDonald); *Carolina Moon* (McDonald); *Ride, Tenderfoot, Ride* (McDonald); *Melody Ranch* (Stantley)

1941   *Ridin' a Rainbow* (Landers); *Back in the Saddle* (Landers); *The Singing Hill* (Landers); *Sunset in Wyoming* (Morgan); *Under Fiesta Stars* (McDonald); *Down Mexico Way* (Santley); *Sierra Sue* (Morgan)

1942   *Cowboy Serenade* (Morgan); *Heart of the Rio Grande* (Morgan); *Home in Wyomin'* (Morgan); *Stardust on the Sage* (Morgan); *Call of the Canyon* (Santley); *Bells of Capistrano* (Morgan)

1946   *Sioux City Sue* (McDonald)

1947   *Trail to San Antone* (English); *Twilight on the Rio Grande* (McDonald); *Saddle Pals* (Selander); *Robin Hood of Texas* (Selander); *The Last Roundup* (English)

1948   *The Strawberry Roan* (English)

1949   *Loaded Pistols* (English); *The Big Sombrero* (McDonald); *Riders of the Whistling Pines* (English); *Rim of the Canyon* (English); *The Cowboy and the Indians* (English); *Riders in the Sky* (English)

1950   *Sons of New Mexico* (English); *Mule Train* (English); *Cow Town* (English); *Beyond the Purple Hills* (English); *Indian Territory* (English); *The Blazing Sun* (English)

1951   *Gene Autry and the Mounties* (English); *Texans Never Cry* (McDonald); *Whirlwind* (English); *Silver Canyon* (English); *Hills of Utah* (English); *Valley of Fire* (English)

1952   *The Old West* (Archainbaud); *Night Train to Galveston* (Archainbaud); *Apache Country* (Archainbaud); *Barbed Wire* (Archainbaud); *Wagon Team* (Archainbaud); *Blue Canadian Rockies* (Archainbaud)

1953   *Winning of the West* (Archainbaud); *On Top of Old Smoky* (Archainbaud); *Goldtown Ghost Raiders* (Archainbaud); *Pack Train* (Archainbaud); *Saginaw Trail* (Archainbaud); *Last of the Pony Riders* (Archainbaud)

1959   *Alias Jesse James* (Farrow) (as himself)

Publications

By AUTRY: book—

Back in the Saddle Again, with Mickey Herskowitz, Garden City, New Jersey, 1978.

On AUTRY: books—

Fenin, George, and William K. Everson, *The Westerns, from Silents to Cinerama*, New York, 1962.

Barbour, Alan G., *Days of Thrills and Adventure*, New York, 1970.

Harmon, Jim, and Donald Glut, *The Great Movie Serials: Their Sound and Fury*, New York, 1972.

Horwitz, James, *They Went Thataway*, New York, 1976.

Barbour, Alan G., *Cliffhangers: A Pictorial History of the Motion Picture Serial*, New York, 1977.

Rothel, David, *The Gene Autry Book*, Waynesville, North Carolina, 1986.

McDonald, Archie P., editor, *Shooting Stars: Heroes and Heroines of Western Film*, Bloomington, Indiana, 1987.

Buscombe, Ed, editor, *BFI Companion to the Western*, London, 1988.

On AUTRY: articles—

Kahn, Gordon, "Lay That Pistol Down," in *Atlantic Monthly* (Greenwich, Connecticut), April 1944.

Current Biography 1947, New York, 1947.

Skylite, November/December 1982.

Hample, Henry S., "Gene Autry," in *Premiere*, March 1994.

*   *   *

In no small way Gene Autry popularized and defined the low-budget B Western of the 1930s and 1940s. From a base at Republic Pictures, Autry established himself as *the* most famous of the singing cowboys. He even made it onto the list of the top ten most popular Hollywood stars for 1940, 1941, and 1942. During those extraordinary years before he entered the U.S. Army Air Force, Autry ranked ahead of the likes of Tyrone Power, James Cagney, Bette Davis, and Judy Garland, all under contract with major studios.

With the 57-minute *Tumbling Tumbleweeds*, Autry established a formula that would remain virtually unchanged for 25 years. Along with his horse, Champion, and sidekick, Smiley Burnette, Autry would in less than an hour—in Frank Capraesque fashion—save an innocent victim, usually female, from some evil exploitative businessman. All this action took place in a modern West, complete with automobiles, radios, and airplanes. From five to eight times during one of these films, Autry would break into song, often regardless of narrative logic. These B low-budget programmers for Republic cost between $50,000 and $100,000, and more often than not grossed well in excess of $500,000.

Gene Autry with Champion

No critics found much in Autry's persona or acting style that could have predicted his enormous popularity. One probable explanation lay with his Bing Crosby-like singing voice. Autry wrote more than 200 songs, and sold millions of records, including seven million discs alone with his 1949 "Rudolph the Red-Nosed Reindeer."

Yet Autry probably had his greatest success in the business world. One of the first important stars to enter television, he realized that the new medium would consume the B Western. So, under the banner of his Flying A productions, Autry turned producer and developed several early televison series, including *Range Rider*, *The Adventures of Champion*, *Buffalo Bill, Jr.*, and *Annie Oakley*.

By 1960, Gene Autry was completely out of acting, and long away from the movie business. He had taken his riches and plowed them into interests in building hotels, buying television and radio stations, and securing California real estate. By the end of the twentieth century he had become one of the richest persons in the United States, and probably best known to younger Americans for his popular Western museum.

—Douglas Gomery

AYRES, Lew

Nationality: American. **Born:** Lewis Frederick Ayres III in Minneapolis, Minnesota, 28 December 1908. **Education:** Attended Lake Harriet Grammar School and West High School, Minneapolis; high school in San Diego, California. **Military Service:** During World War II, assigned to conscientious objector camp at Cascade Locks, Oregon, then served in U.S. Army Medical Corps; participated in beachhead landings in South Pacific. **Family:** Married 1) the actress Lola Lane, 1931 (divorced 1933); 2) the actress Ginger Rogers, 1934 (divorced 1941); 3) Diana (Ayres), 1964, son: Justin Bret. **Career:** Mid-1920s—following high school, formed band with friends, briefly toured Mexico; joined Henry Halstead band; 1928—spotted in Hollywood nightclub by agent Ivan Kahn, signed with Pathe Studios, 1929; 1929—role in *The Kiss* opposite Garbo for MGM followed by role of Paul Baumer in *All Quiet on the Western Front*; early 1930s—under contract to Universal; 1935—moved to Paramount; 1936—directing debut with *Hearts in Bondage*; 1938—given title role in *Young Doctor Kildare*; Kildare series continues through 1941; 1942—following decision not to fight in World War II, his films banned in many theaters; 1945—after considering the ministry, returned to Hollywood; early 1950s—began producing religious documentaries; 1958—host of TV series *Frontier Justice*; 1973-76—produced documentary *Altars of the World*; 1985—in TV series *Lime Street*.

Films as Actor:

1929 *The Sophomore* (McCarey); *The Kiss* (Feyder); *Big News* (La Cava) (as copyboy)

1930 **All Quiet on the Western Front** (Milestone) (as Paul Baumer); *Common Clay* (Fleming) (as Hugh Fullerton); *Doorway to Hell* (*A Handful of Clouds*) (Mayo) (as Louie); *East Is West* (Bell) (as Billy Benson)

1931 *Many a Slip* (Moore) (as Jerry Brooks); *The Iron Man* (Browning) (as Kid Mason); *Up for Murder* (*Fires of Youth*) (Bell) (as Robert Marshall); *The Spirit of Notre Dame* (*Vigour of Youth*) (Mack) (as Bucky O'Brien); *Heaven on Earth* (Mack) (as States)

1932 *The Impatient Maiden* (Whale) (as Dr. Myron Brown); *Cohens and Kellys in Hollywood* (Dillon); *Night World* (Henley) (as Michael Rand); *Okay America* (*Penalty of Fame*) (Garnett) (as Larry Wayne)

1933 *State Fair* (Henry King) (as reporter Pat Gilbert); *Don't Bet on Love* (Roth) (as Bill McCaffrey); *My Weakness* (David Butler) (as Ronnie Gregory)

1934 *Cross Country Cruise* (Buzzell) (as Norman); *Let's Be Ritzy* (Ludwig) (as Jimmie); *She Learned about Sailors* (George Marshall) (as Larry Wilson); *Servants' Entrance* (Lloyd) (as Eric Landstrom)

1935 *Lottery Lover* (Thiele) (as Cadet Frank Harrington); *Spring Tonic* (Bruckman); *Silk Hat Kid* (Humberstone) (as Eddie Howard)

1936 *The Leathernecks Have Landed* (Bretherton) (as Woody Davis); *Panic on the Air* (Lederman) (as Jerry); *Shakedown* (Selman) (as Bob Sanderson); *Lady Be Careful* (Reed) (as Dud "Dynamite"); *Murder with Pictures* (Burton) (as Kent Murdock)

1937 *The Crime Nobody Saw* (Barton) (as Nicholas Carter); *The Last Train from Madrid* (Hogan) (as Bill Dexter); *Hold 'em Navy!* (Neumann) (as Tommy Gorham)

1938 *Scandal Street* (Hogan) (as Joe McKnight); *King of the Newsboys* (Vorhaus) (as Jerry Flynn); *Holiday* (*Free to Live*; *Unconventional Linda*) (Cukor) (as Ned Seton); *Rich Man, Poor Girl* (Schunzel) (as Henry Thayer); *Young Doctor Kildare* (Bucquet) (title role); *Spring Madness* (Simon) (as Sam Thatcher)

1939 *The Ice Follies of 1939* (Schunzel) (as Eddie Burgess); *Broadway Serenade* (Leonard) (as James Geoffrey Seymour); *Calling Dr. Kildare* (Bucquet) (title role); *These Glamour Girls* (Simon) (as Philip S. Griswold); *Remember?* (McLeod) (as Sky Ames); *Secret of Dr. Kildare* (Bucquet) (title role)

1940 *Dr. Kildare's Strange Case* (Bucquet) (title role); *The Golden Fleecing* (Fenton) (as Henry Twinkle); *Dr. Kildare Goes Home* (Bucquet) (title role); *Dr. Kildare's Crisis* (Bucquet) (title role)

1941 *Maisie Was a Lady* (Marin) (as Bob Rawlston); *The People vs. Dr. Kildare* (*My Life Is Yours*) (Bucquet) (title role); *Dr. Kildare's Wedding Day* (*Mary Names the Day*) (Bucquet) (title role); *Dr. Kildare's Victory* (*The Doctor and the Debutante*) (Van Dyke) (title role)

1942 *Fingers at the Window* (Lederer) (as Oliver Duffy)

1946 *The Dark Mirror* (Siodmak) (as Dr. Scott Elliott)

1947 *The Unfaithful* (Sherman) (as Larry Hannaford)

1948 *Johnny Belinda* (Negulesco) (as Dr. Robert Richardson)

1950 *The Capture* (John Sturges) (as Vanner)

1951 *New Mexico* (Reiss) (as Capt. Hunt)

1953 *No Escape* (Bennett) (as John Tracy); *Donovan's Brain* (Feist) (as Dr. Patrick J. Cory)

1962 *Advise and Consent* (Preminger) (as the vice president)

1964 *The Carpetbaggers* (Dmytryk) (as McAllister)

1968 *Hawaii Five-O* (Wendkos—for TV) (as Governor)

1969 *Marcus Welby, M.D.* (David Lowell Rich—for TV)

1971 *Earth II* (Gries—for TV); *She Waits* (Delbert Mann—for TV)

1972 *The Biscuit Eater* (McEveety) (as Mr. Ames); *The Man* (Sargent) (as Harley)

1973 *Battle for the Planet of the Apes* (J. Lee Thompson) (as Mandemus); *The Questor Tapes* (Colla—for TV) (as Vaslovik); *The Stranger* (Katzin—for TV)

1974 *Heat Wave!* (Jameson—for TV)

1976 *Francis Gary Powers: The True Story of the U-2 Spy Incident* (Delbert Mann—for TV)

1978 *Damien—Omen II* (Taylor) (as Bill Atherton); *End of the World* (Grilo and Hayes); *Battlestar Gallactica* (Colla) (as President Adar); *Suddenly, Love* (Margolin—for TV)

1979 *Salem's Lot* (Hooper—for TV); *Letters from Frank* (Parone—for TV)

1980 *Reunion* (Mayberry—for TV)

125

Lew Ayres

1981 *Of Mice and Men* (Badiyi—for TV)
1983 *Don Camillo* (Hill)
1986 *Under Siege* (Roger Young—for TV) (as John Pace)
1989 *Cast the First Stone* (*Cast the First Stone: The Diane Martin Story*) (Korty—for TV) (as Mr. Martin)
1994 *Hart to Hart: Crimes of the Hart* (Hunt—for TV) (as Professor Kamen)

Film as Director:

1936 *Hearts in Bondage*

Films as Producer:

1955 *Altars of the East* (doc) (+ sc, ro as narrator)
1976 *Altars of the World* (ed-doc) (+ d, ph)

Publications

On AYRES: articles—

Cutts, John, "Classics Revisited: *All Quiet on the Western Front*," in *Films and Filming* (London), April 1963.

Luft, H. G., "Lew Ayres," in *Films in Review* (New York), June-July 1978.

Shipman, David, in *The Great Movie Stars: The Golden Years*, rev. ed., London, 1979.

"Lew Ayres," in *Classic Images* (Indiana, Pennsylvania), December 1986.

*   *   *

"Many things come together to create a man's outlook on life," Lew Ayres once remarked. But nothing quite had the impact on both his life *and* career as did *All Quiet on the Western Front*. From a "bit" actor and supporting player (to Garbo) in *The Kiss*, Ayres became a star thanks to his performance as Paul Baumer in *All Quiet on the Western Front*. He is quick to credit his success to the dialogue director, George Cukor, who carefully coached the actors in the use of "neutral" accents and quiet underplaying. The film also instilled in Ayres a pacifist outlook on life, which eventually was to cause controversy for him as a member of the Hollywood community.

In the early 1930s Ayres starred in a string of minor features, the perfect leading man for every actress from Janet Gaynor to Jean Harlow. His career was failing rapidly, however, and he was turning up more and more frequently in B pictures (and even directing one film, *Hearts in Bondage*) when he accepted a co-starring role in *Holiday*, playing the alcoholic brother of Katharine Hepburn. Louis B. Mayer liked his performance and signed him for the title role in the *Dr. Kildare* series. He was now a success. Then came World War II.

Ayres declared himself a conscientious objector, and Hollywood was quick to denounce him. While the industry hailed the stars who, with maximum publicity, entered the armed forces yet never saw active service, Lew Ayres quietly went about his work as a medical orderly at the South Pacific battlefront. There is a haunting photograph of the actor taping up the wounds of a Japanese prisoner in the Philippines, which appeared in *Life* magazine (25 December 1944).

On his return from the war, Ayres had aged. He looked more assured, more dignified, less a pretty face and more a figure with character and personality. A new phase of his career began, as he immediately appeared in *The Dark Mirror* (as a doctor), *The Unfaithful* (as an attorney), and *Johnny Belinda* (in one of his all-time-best roles, as a

compassionate small-town doctor). From the 1950s, his film work has been sporadic, with his most notable credits being *Advise and Consent* and *The Carpetbaggers*. And his commitment to a spiritualist philosophy remained a constant, as evidenced by his involvement in the documentaries *Altars of the East* and *Altars of the World*.

—Anthony Slide, updated by Audrey E. Kupferberg

AZMI, Shabana

Nationality: Indian. **Born:** 1950; daughter of the poet Kaifi Azmi and the actress Shaukat. **Education:** Attended Indian Film Institute, Poona. **Family:** Married to the screenwriter Javed Akhtar. **Career:** 1974—film debut in *The Seedling*, the first film of Shyam Benegal; 1980—on stage in *Safed Kundali*, the Hindi version of *The Caucasian Chalk Circle*; 1994—on stage in *Tumhari Amrita*, the Hindi/Urdu version of *Love Letters*; member of the UN Human Rights Commission. **Awards:** Best Actress, Indian National Film Awards, for *The Seedling*, 1974; *The Meaning*, 1982; *Ruins*, 1983; and *The Crossing*, 1984.

Films as Actress:

1973 *The December Evening* (short); *Munshiji* (short); *Ankur* (*The Seedling*) (Benegal)
1974 *Parinay*; *Ishq, Ishq, Ishq* (Dev Anand); *Faslah* (Abbas)
1975 *Sewak*; *Kadamberi*; *Nishant* (Benegal)
1976 *Fakira*; *Shaque*; *Vishwasghaat*
1977 *Aadha din aadhi raat*; *Hira aur Patthar*; *Amar Akbar Anthony* (Desai); *Chor Sipahi*; *Ek hi rasta*; *Parvarish*; *Khel Khiladi ka*; *Kissa Kursi Ka*; *Karm*; *Swami*; *Kanneshwara Rama*; *Zamanat*
1978 *Devata*; *Atithee*; *Swarg narak*; *Khoon ki pukar*; *Toote Khilone*; *Junoon* (*Obsession*) (Benegal); *Shatranj Ke Khilari* (*The Chess Players*) (Satyajit Ray) (as Mirza's wife)
1979 *Bagula bhagat*; *Amar deep*; *Lahu ke do rang*; *Sparsh* (Paranjapye); *Jeena yahan*
1980 *Jwalamukhi*; *Albert Pinto ko gussa kyon aata hai* (*Why Albert Pinto Is Angry*) (Mirza); *Ek baar kaho*; *Apne paraye*; *Thodisi bewafai*; *Yeh kaisa insaaf*; *Hum paanch*
1981 *Ek hi bhool*; *Shama*; *Sameera* (Shulka); *Raaste pyare ke*
1982 *Namkeen*; *Ashanti*; *Anokha bandhan*; *Suraag*; *Yeh Nazdeekiyan*; *Arth* (Mahash Bhatt); *Log kya kahenge*; *Masoom* (*Innocent*) (Shekhar Kapur)
1983 *Doosri Doolhan*; *Sweekar kiya maine*; *Avtaar*; *Mandi* (*Market Place*) (Benegal); *Khandahar* (*The Ruins*) (Mrinal Sen) (as Jamila); *Pyaasi Aankhen*
1984 *Aaj ka M.L.A. Ram Avtaar*; *Bhavna*; *Kamla*; *Itihaas*; *Lorie*; *Libaas*; *Sparsh* (Paranjapye); *Kamyaab*; *Paar* (Goutam Ghose); *Gangvaa*; *Hum Rahe Na Hum*; *Yaadon K.I. Zanjeer*; *Mr. X*; *Ram Tera Desh*
1985 *Rahi Badal Gaye*; *Uttarayan*; *Khamosh* (Vidhu Vinod Chopra) (as herself); *Shart*
1986 *Anjuman* (Muzaffar Ali); *Ek Pal*; *Samay Ki Dhara*; *Nasihat*; *Susman* (*The Essence*) (Benegal); *Genesis* (Mrinal Sen) (as the woman)
1987 *Itihaas*; *Jallianwala Bagh*; *Pestonjee* (Vijaya Mehta)
1988 *Mardon Wali Baat*; *Madame Sousatzka* (Schlesinger) (as Sushila Sen); *Ek Din Achanak* (*Suddenly, One Day*) (Mrinal Sen); *Nuit Bengali* (*Bengali Night*) (Klotz) (as Indira Sen)
1989 *Oonch Neech Beech*; *Libaas*; *Jhoothi Sharm*; *Rakhwala*; *Main Azaad Hoon* (Tinnu Anand); *Sati* (Aparna Sen)

1990 *Disha* (Paranjapye); *Picnic* (Aparna Sen—for TV); *Amba*;
      Muqaddar Ka Badshah; *Ek Doctor Ki Maut*
1991 *Immaculate Conception* (Jamil Dehlavi) (as Samira); *Dharavi*
      (*City of Dreams*) (Sudhir Mishra) (as Kumud)
1992 *Adharm*; *Jhoothi Shaan*; *City of Joy* (Joffé) (as Kamla Pal);
      Antarnaad
1993 *Son of the Pink Panther* (Edwards) (as the Queen)
1994 *Patang* (*The Kite*) (Goutam Ghose) (as Jitni); *In Custody*
      (*Hifazaat*) (Merchant) (as Imtiaz Begum)
1996 *Fire* (Deepa Mehta)

Publications

By AZMI: articles—

"Tsentr pritiazheniia," interview with A. Solodov, in *Ishkusstvo Kino*
   (Moscow), no. 5, 1986.
Interview with M. Sen, in *Cinema in India* (Bombay), vol. 3, no. 1,
   1992.

On AZMI: articles—

Gahlot, D., "Great Expectations," in *Cinema in India* (Bombay), vol.
   4, no. 7, 1990.
Rajadhyaksha, Ashish, and Paul Willemen, in *Encyclopaedia of Indian
   Cinema*, New Dehli, 1994.

*   *   *

Shabana Azmi shares with Smita Patil her position as the most
important contemporary actress in Indian cinema (though not necessarily the most popular with the public) because of her unusual ability
to successfully straddle the two worlds of commercial and art cinema.
Many themes of the new cinema revolve around the personalities of
women, providing opportunities for actresses to demonstrate their
histrionic abilities. Azmi, like Patil, was not a conventional glamour
girl, but through sheer personal magnetism found herself cast in Shyam
Benegal's first film *Ankur*, a landmark in India's new cinema, after
being turned down by him for a modeling assignment.

Azmi had always hoped to succeed in commercial films in order to
cultivate a following for her art films. Her career was undoubtedly
aided by the box-office success of her first big-budget movie, *Fakira*,
which succeeded in spite of her. After several years and 60-odd films,

making a dent in all kinds of cinema—from the lowest budget to the
most crassly commercial—it is remarkable that she has been consistently shrewd enough to know which roles would suit her and yet
impress the public with her versatility as an actress. From such roles as
the madam of a brothel in Shyam Benegal's *Mandi*, a bellicose part for
which she had to gain considerable weight, or the subdued Jamila in
Mrinal Sen's *Khandahar*, where the camera lovingly explores her
beauty amongst decaying ruins, she can switch to the tear-jerking
melodramas which have won her a wider following.

Her secret lies in an ability to throw herself completely into the
part, not worrying about what her friends think about a "dancing
around the trees" routine. As she has said, "After a while, I realized
that even such scenes needed a measure of talent to carry off convincingly and decided to throw myself into it wholeheartedly."

Azmi's multifaceted talents bring a three-dimensionality, depth,
and freshness to every character she takes on. She is the child prodigy's
grasping mother in *Madame Sousatzka*, the poet-pretender second
wife of the aging poet Nur in *In Custody*, the unwedded tough mother
Jitni in the Bengali film *Patang*, and the scheming queen in *Son of the
Pink Panther*. Whether she is engaged in a war of wills with her son's
teacher, or trying to push her own poetry above her husband's, or
trying to bridge the gap between her son and lover, or planning the
kidnaping of her stepdaughter, there is one common characteristic:
she is vivacious.

More recently, Azmi tried her hand at stage acting in *Tumhari
Amrita*, an adaptation of A. K. Gurney's *Love Letters*. Azmi and Farouque
Shaikh, who formed the duo cast, sat on the stage just reading letters
and pouring their hearts out in the process. The play was critically
acclaimed and had rave responses from audiences, adding another to
Azmi's impressive forte of talents.

Azmi's commitment not only to the portrayal of the weaker sections of the society, but also to their upliftment has been manifested
in many of her activities. Staging a hunger strike to stop the evacua-
tion of slum dwellers, protesting the killing of noted playwright Safdar
Hashmi, organizing the film industry to help the Bombay riot victims—her convictions earn credit to her as a concerned human being,
as much as her histrionics bring her acclaim as an actress.

Azmi, called the activist actress, is a member of the United Nations
Human Rights Commission, and presented their Peace Award to South
African President Nelson Mandela in 1994. She was also honored at
the General State of Human Rights Conference at Paris in 1989.

—Behroze Gandhy, updated by Usha Venkatachallam

BACALL, Lauren

Nationality: American. **Born:** Betty Joan Perske in the Bronx, New York, 16 September 1924. **Education:** Attended Julia Richman High School; American Academy of Dramatic Arts, New York. **Family:** Married 1) the actor Humphrey Bogart, 1945 (died 1957), children: Stephen Humphrey and Leslie Howard; 2) the actor Jason Robards, 1961 (divorced 1973), son: Sam Prideaux. **Career:** Early 1940s—began modeling, also theater-related odd jobs; 1942—New York stage debut as walk-on in *Johnny Two-by-Four*; 1943—appeared on *Harper's Bazaar* cover and attracted attention of director Howard Hawks; personal contract with Hawks who changed her name to Lauren Bacall; 1944—film debut in Hawks's *To Have and Have Not* with Humphrey Bogart; mid-1940s—contract sold to Warners; 1947—protested against HUAC in Washington with Bogart and other celebrities; late 1940s—fined and suspended by Warners for failing to accept roles; 1959—first Broadway starring role in *Goodbye Charlie*; from 1960s—periodic film roles combined with highly successful Broadway appearances. **Address:** c/o Johnnie Planco, William Morris Agency, 1350 Avenue of the Americas, New York, NY 10019, U.S.A.

Films as Actress:

1944 *To Have and Have Not* (Hawks) (as Marie Browning)
1945 *Confidential Agent* (Shumlin) (as Rose Cullen)
1946 *Two Guys from Milwaukee* (*Royal Flush*) (Butler) (as herself); **The Big Sleep** (Hawks) (as Vivian Sternwood Rutledge)
1947 *The Dark Passage* (Daves) (as Irene Jansen)
1948 *Key Largo* (Huston) (as Nora Temple)
1950 *Young Man with a Horn* (*Young Man of Music*) (Curtiz) (as Amy North); *Bright Leaf* (Curtiz) (as Sonia Kovac)
1953 *How to Marry a Millionaire* (Negulesco) (as Schatze Page)
1954 *Woman's World* (Negulesco) (as Elizabeth)
1955 *The Cobweb* (Minnelli) (as Meg Paversen Rinehart); *Blood Alley* (Wellman) (as Cathy)
1956 **Written on the Wind** (Sirk) (as Lucy Moore Hadley)
1957 *Designing Woman* (Minnelli) (as Marilla Hagen)
1958 *The Gift of Love* (Negulesco) (as Julie Beck)
1959 *Flame over India* (*Northwest Frontier*) (Thompson) (as Catherine Wyatt)
1964 *Shock Treatment* (Denis Sanders) (as Dr. Edwina Beighley); *Sex and the Single Girl* (Quine) (as Sylvia)
1966 *Harper* (*The Moving Target*) (Smight) (as Mrs. Elaine Sampson)
1974 *Murder on the Orient Express* (Lumet) (as Mrs. Hubbard)
1976 *The Shootist* (Siegel) (as Bond Rogers)
1978 *Perfect Gentlemen* (Cooper—for TV) (as Lizzie Martin)
1980 *Health* (Altman) (as Esther Brill)
1981 *The Fan* (Bianchi) (as Sally Ross); *The Great Muppet Caper* (Henson)
1988 *In from the Cold* (Palmer—doc); *Mr. North* (Danny Huston) (as Mrs. Amelia Cranston); *Appointment with Death* (Winner) (as Lady Westholme)

1989 *Dinner at Eight* (Lagomarsino—for TV) (as Carlotta Vance)
1990 *The Tree of Hands* (*Innocent Victims*) (Foster) (as Marsha Archdale); *Misery* (Rob Reiner) (as Marcia Sindell); *Ed Murrow: This Reporter* (Steinberg); *A Star for Two* (Kaufman); *A Little Piece of Sunshine* (James Clellan Jones—for TV) (as Beatrix Coltrane)
1991 *All I Want for Christmas* (Lieberman) (as Lillian Brooks)
1993 *The Portrait* (Arthur Penn—for TV) (as Fanny Church); *A Foreign Field* (Sturridge—for TV) (as Lisa); *The Parallax Garden* (David Trainer—for TV)
1994 *Ready to Wear* (*Pret-a-Porter*) (Altman) (as Slim Chrysler)
1995 *From the Mixed-Up Files of Mrs. Basil E. Frankweiler* (Marcus Cole—for TV) (title role)

Publications

By BACALL: books—

Lauren Bacall by Myself, New York, 1979.
Now, New York, 1994.

By BACALL: articles—

"No Chicken for Bacall," interview with P. Ast, in *Inter/View* (New York), November 1972.
"Brève recontre avec Lauren Bacall," interview with A. Lacombe, in *Ecran* (Paris), June/July 1975.
"All about Betty," interview with Kevin P. Buckley, in *Interview* (New York), March 1988.
"What Becomes a Legend Most," interview with James Kaplan, in *New York*, 10 October 1994.

On BACALL: books—

Goodman, Ezra, *Bogey: The Good-Bad Guy*, New York, 1965.
Huston, John, *An Open Book*, New York, 1972.
Hyams, Joe, *Bogart and Bacall: A Love Story*, New York, 1975.
Greenberger, Howard, *Bogey's Baby*, London, 1976.
Parish, James, *The Forties Gals*, Westport, Connecticut, 1980.
Quirk, Lawrence J., *Lauren Bacall: Her Films and Career*, Secaucus, New Jersey, 1986.
Royce, Brenda Scott, *Lauren Bacall: A Bio-Bibliography*, New York, 1992.

On BACALL: articles—

Hagen, Ray, "Lauren Bacall," in *Films in Review* (New York), April 1964.
Current Biography 1970, New York, 1970.
Thomson, David, "Lauren Bacall: A Look and a Voice," in *Close-Ups: The Movie Star Book*, edited by Danny Peary, New York, 1978.
Buckley, M., "Lauren Bacall," in *Films in Review* (New York), May/June 1992.

Lauren Bacall

Morris, Bob, "Just Shooting the Breeze," in *New York Times*, 19 September 1993.

Haskell, Molly, "To Have and Have Not: The Paradox of the Female Star," in *American Imago*, Winter 1993.

The Advocate, 27 December 1994.

* * *

Lauren Bacall's rise to fame as a Hollywood star was meteoric. Soon after Mrs. Howard Hawks noticed her on the March 1943 cover of *Harper's Bazaar*, the 19-year-old model was quickly signed by producer-director Hawks to a seven-year studio contract.

For her first film, *To Have and Have Not*, Hawks molded the as yet untried actress into the ideal woman of many men of that period—insolent and provocative, yet one who, underneath her femme fatale exterior, really was a "regular Joe." In her first autobiography, Bacall writes that Hawks "wanted to be a Svengali." He created her voice, her manner, her persona, and quite by accident—because in her nervousness she could not keep her head from shaking—"The Look." Her chin was kept low. Her eyes stared up at a curious and fascinated Humphrey Bogart. When Bacall told Bogart her now famous line—"You know how to whistle, don't you Steve? You just put your lips together and blow"—she emerged an overnight sensation.

Her seductive portrayal of Slim in *To Have and Have Not* captivated audiences—especially male viewers. Her glamour and apparent sophistication were imitated by the women in the audience. Yet writer Moss Hart cautioned the burgeoning star, "You realize, of course, from here on you have nowhere to go but down."

Hart's words proved prophetic. Bacall's phenomenal success was immediately followed by a crashing critical and box-office failure, *Confidential Agent*. Miscast as a British upper-class ingenue and lacking Hawks's strong directorial support, Bacall floundered. Jack Warner (who had bought her contract from Hawks) attempted to boost her career by building up her role in the already completed *The Big Sleep* (in which she was again directed by Hawks). Retakes and new scenes were added to this most confusing film, injecting the qualities that had made her famous—primarily her aloof bearing and on-screen chemistry with Bogart (who by that time she had married). Despite its narrative flaws, *The Big Sleep* was a box-office success, and Bacall was back on top.

During her tenure at Warner Brothers she starred in only seven films—four of them with Bogart. The fan magazines reveled in the Bogart-Bacall relationship, which only added to their growing popularity as a screen team. Nevertheless, Bacall continually fought with Jack Warner over her assignments, rejecting properties she did not feel would advance her career. This resulted in a series of contract suspensions. One disagreement in particular made headlines when the actress announced she could not be cast in the frothy comedy *The Girl from Jones Beach* because it required her to appear in a bathing suit.

After leaving Warners in 1950, Bacall experimented with a wider range of material, succeeding at both comedy (*How to Marry a Millionaire*) and high drama (*Written on the Wind*). Her beloved Bogie died in 1957; four years later, she married Jason Robards Jr., and her screen appearances became even less frequent. It was not until the 1970s, when Bacall made the transition to character actress, that her work in films took on a new direction. While not incapable of offering solid performances (as she did in the John Wayne Western *The Shootist*), Bacall too often has come to play herself—a sophisticated, cosmopolitan woman of taste—in such films as *Mr. North* and *Ready to Wear*.

Concurrent with her film career, Bacall has appeared in series television (*The Rockford Files*) and television movies (*Perfect Gentlemen, Dinner at Eight*), and has lent her distinctive voice to many commercials. Her work on stage is noteworthy—particularly her performances in the comedy *Cactus Flower* and the musicals *Applause* and *Woman of the Year*. Today, she remains one of few surviving major stars of the 1940s, having worked in Hollywood's Golden Age with such luminaries as Bogart, Hawks, John Huston, Gary Cooper, Lionel Barrymore, Edward G. Robinson, and Vincente Minnelli. Her two autobiographies have served as the finishing touches to her career.

—Joanne L. Yeck, updated by Audrey E. Kupferberg

BACON, Kevin

Nationality: American. **Born:** Philadelphia, Pennsylvania, 8 July 1958. **Education:** Studied at Circle in the Square Theatre School; Manning Street Actor's Theatre. **Family:** Married the actress Kyra Sedgwick, son: Travis, and daughter: Sosie Ruth. **Career:** Appeared in daytime TV series *Search for Tomorrow* and *The Guiding Light*; 1978—off-Broadway debut in *Getting Out*; film debut in *National Lampoon's Animal House*; 1983—Broadway debut in *Slab Boys*; 1984—appeared in live TV special *Mr. Roberts*, as Ensign Pulver; 1996—film directorial debut with *Losing Chase* (for Showtime). **Awards:** Obie Award for Distinguished Performance, for *Forty Deuce*, 1981; Best Actor, Broadcast Critics Association, for *Murder in the First*, 1995. **Agent:** Creative Artists Agency, 9830 Wilshire Boulevard, Beverly Hills, CA 90212, U.S.A.

Films as Actor:

1978 *National Lampoon's Animal House* (Landis) (as Chip Diller)
1979 *Starting Over* (Pakula); *The Gift* (Don Taylor—for TV) (as Teddy)
1980 *Hero at Large* (Davidson) (as 2nd teenager); *Friday the 13th* (Cunningham) (as Jack)
1981 *Only When I Laugh* (*It Hurts Only When I Laugh*) (Glenn Jordan) (as Don)
1982 *Forty Deuce* (Morrissey) (as Rickey); *Diner* (Levinson) (as Fenwick)
1983 *The Demon Murder Case* (*The Rhode Island Murders*) (Hale—for TV) (as Kenny Miller); "Alexandra's Story" ep. of *Enormous Changes at the Last Minute* (*Trumps*) (Bank—for TV, re-released theatrically in 1985) (as Dennis)
1984 *Footloose* (Ross) (as Ren MacCormack)
1986 *Quicksilver* (Donnelly) (as Jack Casey)
1987 *White Water Summer* (*Rites of Summer*) (Bleckner) (as Vic); *Planes, Trains and Automobiles* (Hughes) (as Taxi Racer); *Lemon Sky* (Egleson—for TV) (as Alan)
1988 *End of the Line* (Jay Russell) (as Everett); *She's Having a Baby* (Hughes) (as Jefferson "Jake" Briggs)
1989 *Criminal Law* (Campbell) (as Martin Thiel); *The Big Picture* (Christopher Guest) (as Nick Chapman)
1990 *Tremors* (Underwood) (as Valentine McKee); *Flatliners* (Schumacher) (as David Labraccio)
1991 *Queens Logic* (Rash) (as Dennis); *He Said, She Said* (Kwapis and Marisa Silver) (as Dan Hanson); *Pyrates* (Noah Stern—released direct to video) (as Sam); *J.F.K.* (Oliver Stone) (as Willie O'Keefe)
1992 *A Few Good Men* (Rob Reiner) (as Capt. Jack Ross)
1994 *The Air Up There* (Glaser) (as Jimmy Dolan); *The River Wild* (Hanson) (as Wade)
1995 *Murder in the First* (Rocco) (as Henri Young); *Apollo 13* (Ron Howard) (as Jack Swigert); *Balto* (Wells—animation) (as voice of Balto)
1996 *Sleepers* (Levinson) (as Nokes)

Kevin Bacon in *Footloose*

Film as Director:

1996   *Losing Chase* (for TV)

Publications

By BACON: articles—

"Totally Candid Kevin Bacon," interview with Chris Chase, in *Cosmo-politan* (New York), September 1994.
"25 Helpings of Kevin Bacon," interview with Ray Rogers, in *Interview* (New York), October 1994.
"Kevin Bacon Wants to Be the Guy," interview with Holly Sorensen, in *Premiere* (New York), March 1995.
Interview with Mark Salisbury, in *Empire* (London), no. 79, 1996.

On BACON: articles—

Lubow, Arthur, "Footloose Fever," in *People Weekly* (New York), 2 April 1984.
Saban, S., "Bacon Bounces Back," in *Movieline* (Escondido, California), December 1992.
"Making Waves," in *Film Review* (London), March 1995.

*   *   *

The good-looking, WASPish Kevin Bacon has had a shaky but generally respected acting career, both in the American cinema and on the New York stage. For a time in the mid-eighties, Bacon was considered a major star, but because of a number of poor project choices and a certain stiffness the actor displays on camera he has not quite maintained his major rank. In the 1990s Bacon reestablished himself as something of a character actor playing the kind of sexy, dangerous roles he began his career with and he seems poised to follow many of his colleagues into directing.

By the time Herbert Ross's *Footloose* came out in 1984, vaulting Bacon to stardom, he had already made an impression on critics with his drugged-out gay hustler Ricky in the off-Broadway production *Forty Deuce* and as Fenwick in Barry Levinson's 1982 sleeper, *Diner*. While the former is virtually unknown outside the New York Village scene (the Paul Morrissey film adaptation starring Bacon and Orson Bean was barely released), Bacon's performance in it exemplifies his appeal to directors looking for attractive young actors willing to throw vanity aside and play unglamorous, unlikable people. (Ricky was a character Bacon would recreate, to a certain extent, for Oliver Stone's *J.F.K.*) Bacon's praised work as the intelligent but foolish and self-destructive Fenwick in *Diner* is also part of this actors' tradition Bacon still subscribes to.

It almost seems an anomaly that Bacon wound up in *Footloose*, one of the shallower films in his credits (and a role he did not seem quite comfortable with), but the film was a major blockbuster and it seemed to increase anticipations that the 25-year-old actor would become a major star. Expectations were suddenly very high, but Bacon tellingly chose to claim a kinship with the stage in a live television performance of the play *Mr. Roberts* (as Ensign Pulver) a month after *Footloose*'s record-breaking run had begun.

While Bacon might have done well to swing back and forth from "acting" on stage (and in independent cinema) and "starring" in major studio films, the choices offered him in these realms were often second-rank. *Quicksilver* was Bacon's *Footloose* follow-up, but critics and audiences ignored the formulaic picture. *Lemon Sky* was an actorly realization of a Lanford Wilson script for American Playhouse, but, aside from giving Bacon an opportunity to act with his future wife Kyra Sedgwick, it did little to further his career. Some of Bacon's best work in the late eighties was either in poor films (his brilliant psychopath Martin Thiel, opposite Gary Oldman, in *Criminal Law*) or in fine, but little-seen pictures (such as the winsome sci-fi pastiche *Tremors*). Bacon enjoyed moderate success in *She's Having a Baby* as an expectant father opposite Elizabeth McGovern but his next major comedy *The Big Picture*, a satire of Hollywood, was barely released. By the nineties, Bacon seemed to star only in critical and box-office disappointments such as *He Said, She Said* and *The Air Up There*.

Bacon did regain some cachet in such ensemble films as *Queens Logic* and *Apollo 13* (as a touchingly portrayed Jack Swigert) but it was in character roles that he most impressed nineties audiences. Bacon returned to hustling, distinguishing himself in a cast of heavy-hitters, in *J.F.K.*; played a convincingly menacing military lawyer for Rob Reiner in *A Few Good Men*; held his own against Meryl Streep in *The River Wild*; and surprised many observers with his nearly operatic turn as Henri Young, an inmate driven mad by the conditions of Alcatraz in *Murder in the First*. As the nineties continued, Bacon reteamed with Barry Levinson for the ensemble film *Sleepers*, co-starring Robert De Niro, Brad Pitt, and Jason Patric but his future may place him more often behind the camera. Bacon's directorial debut, the Showtime film *Losing Chase*, premiered at Sundance in 1996 to enthusiastic responses. While the project was hampered by a contrived script, its surefooted style and uniform acting excellence indicates that Bacon may harbor considerable talents as a director.

—Daniel Humphrey

BAKER, (Sir) Stanley

Nationality: British. **Born:** Ferndale, Rhondda Valley, Wales, 8 February 1928. **Education:** Schools in Ferndale. **Military Service:** 1946-48—served in Royal Army Service Corps. **Family:** Married Ellen Martin, 1950, three sons, one daughter. **Career:** 1943—film debut in *Underground*; 1943-49—concentrated on stage acting in repertory work in Birmingham and London; 1953—critical attention for role in film *The Cruel Sea*; 1960—with Joseph Losey and Alun Owen formed Cambria Films; c.1963—formed Diamond Productions with Cy Endfield, began co-producing some of his films; 1967—formed Oakhurst Productions with Michael Deeley; 1968-76—Director, Harlech TV; 1972-76—in TV series *How Green Was My Valley*. Knighted 1976. **Died:** In Malaga, Spain, 28 June 1976.

Films as Actor:

1943   *Undercover* (*Underground*) (Nolbandov) (as Peter)
1948   *Obsession* (*The Hidden Room*) (Dmytryk)

1949   *All over the Town* (Twist) (as Barnes)
1950   *Your Witness* (*Eye Witness*) (Montgomery) (as Sgt. Bannoch); *Lilli Marlene* (Crabtree) (as Evans)
1951   *The Rossiter Case* (Searle) (as Joe); *Cloudburst* (Searle) (as Milkman); *Home to Danger* (Fisher) (as Willie Dougan); *Captain Horatio Hornblower R.N.* (Walsh) (as Mr. Harrison)
1952   *Whispering Smith Hits London* (*Whispering Smith vs. Scotland Yard*) (Searle) (as reporter)
1953   *The Cruel Sea* (Frend) (as First Officer Bennett); *The Red Beret* (*The Paratrooper*) (Young) (as Breton); *The Tell-Tale Heart* (Williams) (as Edgar Allan Poe); *Hell Below Zero* (Robson) (as Erik Bland)
1954   *The Good Die Young* (Gilbert) (as Mike); *The Beautiful Stranger* (*Twist of Fate*) (Miller) (as Louis Galt); *Knights of the Round Table* (Thorpe) (as Mordred)
1955   *Helen of Troy* (Wise) (as Achilles); *Richard III* (Olivier) (as Henry Tudor)
1956   *Alexander the Great* (Rossen) (as Attalus); *Child in the House* (De Lautour and Endfield) (as Stephen Lorimer); *A Hill in Korea* (*Hell in Korea*) (Amyes) (as Corporal Ryker); *Checkpoint* (Thomas) (as O'Donovan)
1957   *Hell Drivers* (Endfield) (as Tom Yatley); *Campbell's Kingdom* (Thomas) (as Owen Morgan); *Violent Playground* (Dearden) (as Sgt. Truman)
1958   *Sea Fury* (Endfield) (as Abel Hewson)
1959   *The Angry Hills* (Aldrich) (as Konrad Heisler); *Yesterday's Enemy* (Guest) (as Captain Langford); *Jet Storm* (Endfield) (as Captain Bardow); *Blind Date* (*Chance Meeting*) (Losey) (as Inspector Morgan)
1960   *Hell Is a City* (Guest) (as Inspector Martineau); *The Criminal* (*The Concrete Jungle*) (Losey) (as Johnny Bannion)
1961   *The Guns of Navarone* (Thompson) (as C.P.O. Brown)
1962   *Sodoma e Gomorra* (*Sodom and Gomorrah*; *The Last Days of Sodom and Gomorrah*) (Aldrich and Leone) (as Astaroth); *Eva* (*Eve*) (Losey) (as Tyvian Jones); *In the French Style* (Parrish) (as Walter Beddoes); *A Prize of Arms* (Owen) (as Turpin); *The Man Who Finally Died* (Lawrence) (as Joe Newman)
1963   *Zulu* (Endfield) (as Lt. John Chard) (+ co-pr)
1965   *Dingaka* (Uys) (as Tom Davis); *Sands of the Kalahari* (Endfield) (as Bain) (+ co-pr); *One of Them Is Named Brett* (Graef) (as narrator); *Who Has Seen the Wind?* (Sidney—for TV):
1967   *Accident* (Losey) (as Charley); *Robbery* (Yates) (as Paul Clifton) (+ co-pr); *Code Name Heraclitus* (for TV)
1968   *La ragazza con la pistola* (*The Girl with the Pistol*) (Monicelli) (as Dr Osborne)
1969   *Where's Jack* (Clavell) (as Jonathan Wild) (+ co-pr); *The Games* (Winner) (as Bill Oliver)
1970   *Perfect Friday* (Hall) (as Mr. Graham); *The Last Grenade* (Flemyng) (as Major Harry Grigsby); *Popsy Pop* (*The 21 Carat Snatch*) (Herman) (as Inspector Silva)
1971   *Una lucertola con la pelle di donna* (*A Lizard with a Woman's Skin*; *Schizoid*) (Fulci) (as Inspector Corvin)
1972   *Innocent Bystanders* (Collinson) (as John Craig)
1975   *Zorro* (Tessari) (as Huerta); *Orzowei* (Yves Allégret)
1976   *Petita Jimenez* (*Bride to Be*) (Alba) (as Pedro de Vargas)

Films as co-producer:

1969   *The Italian Job* (Collinson)
1970   *Colosseum and Juicy Lucy* (Palmer)

Stanley Baker

Publications

By BAKER: article—

"Playing the Game," in *Films and Filming* (London), August 1970.

On BAKER: book—

Storey, Anthony, *Stanley Baker: Portrait of an Actor*, London, 1977.

On BAKER: article—

"Stanley Baker," in *Ecran* (Paris), September 1978.

*   *   *

Almost alone in the British postwar cinema, Stanley Baker embodied the essence of working-class ability to command. A Welsh-miner chunkiness put aristocratic roles beyond him, a deficiency on which he capitalized by playing the self-motivated man in charge—minor military officer, professional criminal, cop—who gets a dirty job done.

Years of servitude as an unsympathetic support performer in British programme films (notably as a gluttonous officer in *The Cruel Sea*) ended with Robert Wise's *Helen of Troy*: his strutting Achilles radiated power and arrogance. Thereafter, a shrewd association with exiled left-wing Hollywood directors Joseph Losey and Cy Endfield led to his gaining highly effective roles in three Endfield thrillers and as a sadistic professional thug or equally ruthless cop in Losey's *The Criminal* and *Blind Date*, Val Guest's *Hell Is a City*, and Cliff Owen's *A Prize of Arms*.

In association with the South African-born Endfield, Baker co-produced and starred in *Zulu* and *Sands of the Kalahari*. In *Zulu*, as a pragmatic Lieutenant of Engineers, struggling to fortify Rorke's Drift against Cetewayo's imminent hordes and the more pressing pomposity of an aristocratic Michael Caine, Baker showed a maturing talent for finely shaded performance. He sustained it in *Robbery* as the criminal mastermind of the so-called Great Train Robbery. But Baker's most improbable acting success was in the Losey/Pinter *Accident*: he offered a brilliantly offhand portrait of an academic-turned-media-hero, narcissistic, petulant, languid, effortlessly agile in argument but helpless in anything requiring a trace of humanity.

Baker's five years in a variety of Italian and French thrillers before his premature death in 1976 did little justice to a powerful and distinguished performer.

—John Baxter

BALL, Lucille

Nationality: American. **Born:** Lucille Desirée Ball in Jamestown, New York, 6 August 1911; also used names Lucy Montana and Diane Belmont. **Education:** Attended John Murray Anderson-Robert Milton drama school, New York. **Family:** Married 1) singer/bandleader Desi Arnaz, 1940 (divorced 1960), children: Lucie Desirée and Desi Jr.; 2) Gary Morton, 1961. **Career:** 1927—on stage in New York as chorus girl; also in the road company of *Rio Rita*; late 1920s—worked as model under the name Diane Belmont; 1933—appearance on Chesterfield cigarette poster led to small role in film *Broadway thru a Keyhole*; picked as one of "Goldwyn Girls" imported to Hollywood to appear in *Roman Scandals*; 1934—signed player contract with Columbia; 1935—dropped by Columbia but joined RKO where she attended the acting classes of Lela Rogers (Ginger's mother); 1943-46—contract with MGM; 1947-51—in radio series *My Favorite Husband* while freelancing in films; 1951—with Arnaz, formed Desilu Productions which created and produced *I Love Lucy* TV series; 1957—with Arnaz, purchased the RKO studios and lot; Desilu began producing several other TV series including *Our Miss Brooks*, *The Ann Sothern Show*, and *The Untouchables*; 1960—debut on Broadway in *Wildcat*, but collapsed on stage from exhaustion after four months; 1962—bought Arnaz's share of Desilu and returned to TV in series *The Lucy Show*; 1966-74—in TV series *Here's Lucy*; 1967—sold Desilu to Gulf & Western. **Awards:** Friar's Club Life Achievement Award, 1977. **Died:** In Los Angeles, of a heart attack, 26 April 1989.

Films as Actress:

1929   *Bulldog Drummond* (Jones)

1933   *Broadway Thru a Keyhole* (Sherman); *Blood Money* (Rowland Brown); *Roman Scandals* (Tuttle) (as slave girl); *The Bowery* (Walsh)

1934   *Moulin Rouge* (Landfield); *Nana* (Arzner) (as chorus girl); *Bottoms Up* (Butler); *Hold That Girl* (MacFadden); *Jealousy* (Neill) (as girl); *Men of the Night* (Hillyer) (as Peggy); *Fugitive Lady* (Rogell) (as beauty operator); *Bulldog Drummond Strikes Back* (Del Ruth) (as girl); *The Affairs of Cellini* (La Cava); *Kid Millions* (Del Ruth); *Broadway Bill* (Capra)

1935   *Carnival* (Walter Lang) (as nurse); *The Whole Town's Talking* (*Passport to Fame*) (John Ford) (as girl); *Roberta* (Seiter); *Old Man Rhythm* (Ludwig) (as college girl); *The Three Musketeers* (Rowland V. Lee); *Top Hat* (Sandrich) (as flower clerk); *I Dream Too Much* (Cromwell) (as Gwendolyn Dilley)

1936   *The Farmer in the Dell* (Holmes) (as Gloria); *Chatterbox* (Nicholls) (as Lillian Temple); *Follow the Fleet* (Sandrich) (as Kitty Collins); *Bunker Bean* (*His Majesty Bunker Bean*) (Hamilton and Killy) (as Miss Kelly); *That Girl from Paris* (Jason) (as Claire Williams); *Winterset* (Santell) (as girl)

1937   *Don't Tell the Wife* (Cabanne) (as Ann Howell); *Stage Door* (La Cava) (as Judy Canfield)

1938   *Go Chase Yourself* (Kline) (as Carol Meely); *Joy of Living* (Garnett) (as Salina); *Having Wonderful Time* (Santell) (as Miriam); *The Affairs of Annabel* (Landers) (title role); *Room Service* (Seiter) (as Christine); *The Next Time I Marry* (Kanin) (as Nancy Fleming)

1939   *Beauty for the Asking* (Tryon) (as Jean Russell); *Twelve Crowded Hours* (Landers) (as Paula Sanders); *Panama Lady* (Hively) (as Lucy); *Five Came Back* (Farrow) (as Peggy Nolan); *That's Right, You're Wrong* (Butler) (as Sandra Sand); *Annabel Takes a Tour* (Landers) (as Annabel Allison)

1940   *You Can't Fool Your Wife* (McCarey) (as Clara Hinklin/Mercedes Vasquez); *The Marines Fly High* (Nicholls and Stoloff) (as Joan Grant); ***Dance, Girl, Dance*** (Arzner) (as Bubbles); *Too Many Girls* (Abbott) (as Connie Casey)

1941   *A Girl, a Guy, and a Gob* (*The Navy Steps Out*) (Wallace) (as Dot Duncan); *Look Who's Laughing* (Dwan) (as Julie Patterson)

1942   *Valley of the Sun* (George Marshall) (as Christine Larson); *The Big Street* (Reis) (as Gloria); *Seven Days' Leave* (Whelan) (as Terry)

1943   *DuBarry Was a Lady* (Del Ruth) (as May Daly/Mme. DuBarry); *Best Foot Forward* (Buzzell) (as herself); *Thousands Cheer* (Sidney) (as herself)

1944   *Meet the People* (Riesner) (as Julie Hampton)

1945   *Without Love* (Bucquet) (as Kitty Trimble); *Abbott and Costello in Hollywood* (Simon)

1946   *Ziegfeld Follies* (Minnelli); *The Dark Corner* (Hathaway) (as Kathleen); *Easy to Wed* (Buzzell) (as Gladys Benton); *Two Smart People* (Dassin) (as Ricki Woodner); *Lover Come Back* (Seiter) (as Kay Williams)

1947   *Lured* (*Personal Column*) (Sirk) (as Sandra Carpenter); *Her Husband's Affairs* (Simon) (as Margaret Weldon)

1949   *Sorrowful Jones* (Lanfield) (as Gladys O'Neill); *Easy Living* (Jacques Tourneur) (as Anne); *Miss Grant Takes Richmond* (*Innocence Is Bliss*) (Lloyd Bacon) (as Ellen Grant)

1950   *A Woman of Distinction* (Buzzell) (as guest); *Fancy Pants* (George Marshall) (as Agatha Floud); *The Fuller Brush Girl* (Lloyd Bacon) (as Sally Elliot)

1951   *The Magic Carpet* (Landers) (as Narah)

1954   *The Long, Long Trailer* (Minnelli) (as Tracy Collini)

1956   *Forever, Darling* (Hall) (as Susan Vega)

1960   *The Facts of Life* (Frank) (as Kitty Weaver)

1963   *Critics Choice* (Weis) (as Angela Ballantine)

1967   *A Guide for the Married Man* (Kelly) (as cameo)

1968   *Yours, Mine and Ours* (Shavelson) (as Helen North)

1974   *Mame* (Saks) (title role)

1985   *Stone Pillow* (Schaefer—for TV)

Publications

By BALL: article—

"Lucille Ball," interview in *Dialogue on Film* (Beverly Hills, California), May-June 1974.

On BALL: books—

Morella, Joe, and Edward Epstein, *Lucy: The Bittersweet Life of Lucille Ball*, Secaucus, New Jersey, 1973; as *Forever Lucy: The Life of Lucille Ball*, 1986.

Arnaz, Desi, *A Book*, New York, 1976.

Parish, James Robert, *The Funsters*, New Rochelle, New York, 1979.

Higham, Charles, *Lucy: The Life of Lucille Ball*, New York, 1986.

Turck, Mary, *Lucille Ball*, Mankato, Minnesota, 1989.

Brochu, Jim, *Lucy in the Afternoon: An Intimate Memoir of Lucille Ball*, Sevenoaks, England, 1990.

Harris, Warren G., *Lucy & Desi: The Legendary Love Story of Television's Most Famous Couple*, New York, 1991.

Krohn, Katherine E., *Lucille Ball: Pioneer of Comedy*, Minneapolis, 1992.

Sanders, Coyne Steven, *Desilu: The Story of Lucille Ball and Desi Arnaz*, New York, 1993.

Brady, Kathleen, *Lucille: The Life of Lucille Ball*, New York, 1994.

Wyman, Ric B., *For the Love of Lucy: The Complete Guide for Collectors and Fans*, New York, 1995.

Lucille Ball

On BALL: articles—

Nugent, Frank, "The Bouncing Ball," in *Photoplay* (New York), September 1946.
Dinter, Charlotte, "I Just Couldn't Take Any More," in *Photoplay* (New York), June 1960.
Bowers, Ronald, in *Films in Review* (New York), June-July 1971, additions and corrections in August-September 1971.
Current Biography 1978, New York, 1978.
Shipman, David, in *The Great Movie Stars: The Golden Years*, rev. ed., London, 1979.
Films in Review (New York), June-July 1984.
Obituary in *Variety* (New York), 3 May 1989.

*   *   *

For too many years in the early part of her career, Lucille Ball appeared in low-budget, second-rate RKO features in which her dramatic and comic talents were sorely squandered. In an irony of ironies, after her overwhelming popular success in the infant days of television, she—with her husband and *I Love Lucy* co-star, Desi Arnaz—was able to purchase the studio. Ball thus had her revenge on the Hollywood system, for in the new medium (to which, in some important ways, the old industry has become subordinate) she became, unquestionably, the most watched and appreciated female performer of her time. On the small screen, her gift for Keatonesque physical comedy and her talent for kooky screwball antics finally were adequately showcased. By virtue of her television work, Ball's place among the entertainment industry's great comedians had finally been assured.

After leaving home as a teenager, Ball studied with John Murray Anderson in New York and worked at various jobs in the hope of beginning a stage career. Never achieving recognition on Broadway, she moved to Hollywood to attempt to break into film. During the early 1930s she appeared in a great number of films—most notably as a bit player and "Goldwyn Girl," seen on a chorus line of statuesque starlets—before signing with RKO. There, unfortunately, she was overshadowed by Ginger Rogers. Although Ball appeared in some good productions, she was never given much opportunity to come into her own. Her roles in *Follow the Fleet* and *Stage Door* exemplify the kind of work she did during this period. In both films (paired with Eve Arden in the second) she functioned as a wisecracking female chorus. Later at RKO she was given leading parts, most memorably in *Five Came Back*, *That's Right, You're Wrong*, *The Affairs of Annabel*, and *Annabel Takes a Tour*. Nevertheless, her gifts for physical comedy were hardly exploited.

During the early 1940s Ball's talents were wasted in more one-dimensional roles, particularly in light comedy and musical productions. One notable exception was Dorothy Arzner's *Dance, Girl, Dance*, a film with a feminist theme, in which Ball and Maureen O'Hara portray working girls trying to succeed in a male-dominated world. In this film her brash, in-your-face energy markedly contrasts with O'Hara's reserved charm. Ball also had a solid role in the drama *The Big Street*, a competent but hardly striking production in which her embodiment of a self-centered and anxiety-ridden cripple far outshines Henry Fonda's uninspired hero. Another of her better RKO credits is *Too Many Girls*, an entertaining Rodgers and Hart college musical in which she plays a footloose coed.

In the mid-1940s Ball signed on with MGM. She had leading roles in Vincente Minnelli's *Ziegfeld Follies* and Jules Dassin's *Two Smart People*, but, yet again, these films hardly exploited her comic gifts. After several years as a freelancer (and some interesting work with Bob Hope) she signed on with Columbia, where she made two films, *Miss Grant Takes Richmond* and *The Fuller Brush Girl*, in which she further developed the character of the overly eager working woman determined to be a success in a man's world.

In 1951, after a 20-year film career, Ball began *I Love Lucy* with then-husband Desi Arnaz. With this show, she became an overnight and lasting success as the irrepressibly enterprising wife of band leader Ricky Ricardo. The crux of the comedy focused on Lucy's scatter-brained schemes, leading to minor domestic catastrophes and inevitable happy endings. Three successful television shows followed: *The Lucy-Desi Comedy Hour*, *The Lucy Show*, and *Here's Lucy*. Her cinematic swan song came in an ill-cast adaptation of the Jerry Herman musical *Mame*. Ball was far too old to play the part, and her performance is awkward and stiff.

—R. Barton Palmer, updated by Audrey E. Kupferberg

BANCROFT, Anne

Nationality: American. **Born:** Anna Maria Luisa Italiano in the Bronx, New York, 17 September 1931. **Education:** Attended Public School 12 and Christopher Columbus High School, the Bronx; studied at American Academy of Dramatic Arts, New York, 1948-50, with Herbert Berghof, 1957, and at the Actors Studio, New York, 1958. **Family:** Married 1) Martin A. May, 1953 (divorced 1957); 2) the director Mel Brooks, 1964, son: Maximilian. **Career:** 1950—first TV appearance (as Ann Italiano) in Turgenev's *The Torrents of Spring*; 1951—contract with 20th Century-Fox; chose name "Anne Bancroft" from list submitted to her by Darryl Zanuck; 1952—film debut in *Don't Bother to Knock*; 1953—resumed TV work; 1955—two-picture contract with Columbia; 1958-59—Broadway appearances in *Two for the Seesaw* and *The Miracle Worker*; 1970s—Broadway appearances in *The Devils* and *Golda*; mid-1970s—attended American Film Institute's Woman's Directing Workshop and directs first film, *The August* (never released); 1980—wrote and directed *Fatso* for 20th Century-Fox; 1994—in TV mini-series *The Oldest Living Confederate Widow Tells All*. **Awards:** Best Actress Academy Award and Best Foreign Actress, British Academy, for *The Miracle Worker*, 1962; co-recipient: Best Actress, Cannes Festival, and Best Foreign Actress, British Academy, for *The Pumpkin Eater*, 1964; Best Actress, British Academy, for *84 Charing Cross Road*, 1988. **Address:** c/o Toni Howard, William Morris Agency, 151 EL Camino Drive, Beverly Hills, CA 90212, U.S.A.

Films as Actress:

1952 *Don't Bother to Knock* (Baker) (as Lyn Leslie)
1953 *Treasure of the Golden Condor* (Daves) (as Marie); *Tonight We Sing* (Leisen) (as Mrs. Sol Hurok); *The Kid from Left Field* (Jones) (as Marian)
1954 *Demetrius and the Gladiators* (Daves) (as Paula); *The Raid* (Fregonese) (as Katy Bishop); *Gorilla at Large* (Jones) (as Laverne Miller); *A Life in the Balance* (Horner) (as Maria Ibinia); *New York Confidential* (Rouse) (as Kathy Lupo)
1955 *The Naked Street* (Shane) (as Rosalie Regalzyk); *The Last Frontier* (Mann) (as Corinna Marston)
1956 *Walk the Proud Land* (Hibbs) (as Tianay); *The Girl in Black Stockings* (Koch) (as Beth Dixon); *Nightfall* (Tourneur) (as Marie Gardner); *The Restless Breed* (Dwan) (as Angelita)
1962 *The Miracle Worker* (Penn) (as Annie Sullivan)
1963 *The Pumpkin Eater* (Clayton) (as Jo Armitage)
1965 *The Slender Thread* (Pollack) (as Inga Dyson); *Seven Women* (Ford) (as Dr. D. R. Cartwright)
1967 **The Graduate** (Nichols) (as Mrs. Robinson)
1970 *Arthur Penn* (Hughes—doc) (as an interviewee)
1972 *Young Winston* (Attenborough) (as Lady Randolph Churchill)

1975   *The Prisoner of Second Avenue* (Frank) (as Edna); *The Hindenburg* (Wise) (as the Countess)
1976   *Lipstick* (Johnson) (as Carla Bondi); *Silent Movie* (Mel Brooks)
1977   *The Turning Point* (Ross) (as Emma Jacklin)
1979   *Jesus of Nazareth* (Zeffirelli) (as Mary Magdalene)
1980   *The Elephant Man* (Lynch) (as Mrs. Kendal)
1983   *To Be or Not to Be* (Mel Brooks) (as Anna Bronski)
1984   *Garbo Talks* (Lumet) (as Estelle Rolfe)
1985   *Agnes of God* (Jewison) (as Sister Miriam Ruth)
1986   *'night, Mother* (Moore) (as Thelma Cates); *84 Charing Cross Road* (Jones) (as Helene Hanff)
1988   *Torch Song Trilogy* (Bogart) (as Ma)
1989   *Bert Rigby, You're a Fool* (Carl Reiner) (as Meredith Perlestein)
1992   *Broadway Bound* (Bogart); *Love Potion No. 9* (Launer) (as Madame Ruth); *Honeymoon in Vegas* (Bergman) (as Bea Singer); *Mrs. Cage* (for TV)
1993   *Point of No Return* (Badham) (as Amanda); *Mr. Jones* (Figgis) (as Dr. Catherine Holland); *Malice* (Becker) (as Claire Kennsinger)
1995   *How to Make an American Quilt* (Moorhouse); *Home for the Holidays* (Foster) (as Adele Larson)

Film as Director and Scriptwriter:

1980   *Fatso* (+ ro as Antoinette)

Publications

By BANCROFT: article—

Interview with Allan Hunter, in *Films and Filming* (London), May 1987.

On BANCROFT: book—

Holtzman, Will, *Seesaw, A Dual Biography of Anne Bancroft and Mel Brooks*, New York, 1979.

On BANCROFT: articles—

Current Biography 1960, New York, 1960.
Arthur, Karen, "Anne Bancroft: She Paid Her Dues," in *Close-Up: The Movie Star Book*, edited by Danny Peary, New York, 1978.
"Anne Bancroft," in *Ecran* (Paris), September 1978.
Haspiel, J. R., "Anne Bancroft: The Odyssey of Ruby Pepper," in *Films in Review* (New York), January 1980.

* * *

There is not a more commanding actress captured on celluloid than Bancroft, yet there are occasions (*Bert Rigby, You're a Fool, Torch Song Trilogy*) when aficionados want to lecture her reprovingly. Why survive being manhandled by a gorilla in 3-D, silence your naysayers by winning two Tony awards, an Emmy, and an Oscar, only to specialize in irascibly cute character roles (*Home for the Holidays*)? And yet, how can one censure her for playing the steady work game when Hollywood cavalierly wastes the most gifted actresses of her era (Julie Harris, Gena Rowlands, and others).

Never garnering less than laudatory notices (*Don't Bother to Knock, A Life in the Balance*) during her starlet period, Bancroft showed her moxie by fleeing the twilight time of contractual stardom and resurrecting her career with two consecutive Broadway smashes. Although *Two for the Seesaw* disintegrated on-screen with Shirley MacLaine's gamine overload, director Arthur Penn fought for his original theater stars to shine in his trenchant visualization of *The Miracle Worker*. After her Oscar victory, Bancroft won universal acclaim as a housewife imprisoned by her own maternal instinct (*The Pumpkin Eater*), then reversed this victim image and became a sixties icon as *The Graduate*'s Mrs. Robinson, a suburban mom manqué who might have died laughing at Stella Dallas's nobility. Occasionally recharging herself with Broadway stints (*The Devils, Golda*), Bancroft's finest hour in the seventies was a still-cherished TV variety special, *Annie: The Women in the Life of a Man*, which showcased a dazzling musical comedy brio (that briefly resurfaced in her husband's *To Be or Not to Be* remake where Bancroft's tomfoolery bore favorable comparison with Carole Lombard's).

Although *The Turning Point* restored melodrama to transitory box-office glory, Bancroft's Daughter-of-Bette-Davis thesping barely tapped her resources. And if *84 Charing Cross Road* was stagebound and *Garbo Talks* was gimmicky, Bancroft evidenced enough magnetism to transform medium and long shots into personal close-ups. In addition to wasting her time with great lady stints in *Young Winston* and *Elephant Man*, she sugarcoated otherwise perceptive interpretations of vinegary characters (*Agnes of God, 'night, Mother*) with her own desire to be liked. Through all the years of compromised performances, however, Bancroft rebounded again and again. In virtual cameos in *Malice* and *Point of No Return*, she electrified stalled escapism with mini tours de force in which a lifetime of training pulsed through every gesture.

Television has been particularly stimulating for Bancroft who spilled an entire Crayola box of colors over her elegist role in *The Oldest Living Confederate Widow Tells All*. As the apparently motiveless avenger in *Mrs. Cage* and as the careworn homemaker railing against obsolescence in *'night, Mother*, Bancroft was a virtuoso clearly deserving of the epithet, great actress. When she attacks her roles cleanly without fussbudget mannerisms or a conspiratorial wink, she is surpassingly effective. The only question remaining is whether she will ever infuse an old-fashioned musical with her volcanic energy—she would have made the ideal movie *Mame*, a character in sync with Bancroft's own dynamo nature and sophisticated style.

—Robert Pardi

BANDERAS, Antonio

Nationality: Spanish. **Born:** José Antonio Dominguez Banderas in Malaga, 10 August 1960. **Family:** Married the actress Ana Leza (separated). **Education:** Began four-year course of studies in classics at Malaga's School of Dramatic Art, 1974. **Career:** 1980—moved to Madrid in search of professional career as actor; 1981—stage debut with Spain's National Theatre in *Los Trantos*; 1982—film debut in *Laberinto de Pasiones*, the first of five films for director Pedro Almodóvar; 1992—U.S. film debut in *The Mambo Kings*. **Agent:** Creative Artists Agency, 9830 Wilshire Boulevard, Beverly Hills, CA 90212, U.S.A.

Films as Actor:

1982   *Laberinto de Pasiones* (*Labyrinth of Passion*) (Almodóvar) (as Sadec); *Pestañas Postizas* (*False Eyelashes*) (Belloch); *Y Del Seguro, Libranos Señor* (*And Surely Set Us Free Lord*) (del Real)
1983   *El Señor Galindez* (*Mr. Galindez*) (Khun) (as Eduardo)

Antonio Banderas in *Assassins*

1984   *El Caso Almería* (*The Almería Case*) (Costa); *Los Zancos* (*The Stilts*) (Saura) (as Alberto)

1985   *Caso Cerrado* (*Closed Case*) (Arecha); *Réquiem por un Campsino Español* (*Requiem for a Spanish Peasant*) (Betriu) (as Paco); *La Corte de Faraon* (*The Court of the Pharaoh*) (Sánchez) (as Friar José)

1986   *27 Horas* (*27 Hours*) (Armendáriz); *Puzzle* (Comeron); *Matador* (*Bullfighter*) (Almodóvar) (as Angel Giménez)

1987   *Así Como Habían Sido* (*The Way They Were*) (Linares) (as Damian); *La Ley del Deseo* (*The Law of Desire*) (Almodóvar) (as Antonio Benitez)

1988   *El Placer de Matar* (*The Pleasure of Killing*) (Rotaeta); *Baton Rouge* (Moleón) (as Antonio); **Mujeres al Borde de un Ataque de Nervios** (*Women on the Verge of a Nervous Breakdown*) (Almodóvar) (as Carlos); *Bajarse al Moro* (*Going South Shopping*) (Colomo) (as Alberto)

1989   *Si Te Dicen Que Caí* (*If They Tell You That I Fell*) (Aranda) (as Marcos); *La Blanca Paloma* (*The White Dove*) (Minon) (as Mario)

1990   *¡Atame!* (*Tie Me Up! Tie Me Down!*) (Almodóvar) (as Ricki); *Contra el Viento* (*Against the Wind*) (Perinan) (as Juan)

1991   *Terra Nova* (*New Land*) (Salvo); *Truth or Dare* (*In Bed with Madonna*) (Keshishian) (as himself); *Cuentos de Borges I* (*Borges Tales Part I*) (Vera) (as Rosendo Juárez)

1992   *The Mambo Kings* (Glimcher) (as Nestor Castillo); *Una Mujer Bajo la Lluvia* (*A Woman in the Rain*) (Vera) (as Miguel)

1993   *¡Dispara!* (*Outrage*; *Shoot!*) (Saura) (as Marcos); **Philadelphia** (Jonathan Demme) (as Miguel Alvarez); *The House of the Spirits* (August) (as Pedro)

1994   *Interview with the Vampire* (Neil Jordan) (as Armand); *Of Love and Shadows* (Kaplan) (as Francisco)

1995   *Miami Rhapsody* (Frankel) (as Antonio); *Never Talk to Strangers* (Hall) (as Tony Ramírez); *Assassins* (Richard Donner) (as Miguel Bain); *Desperado* (*El Mariachi 2*) (Rodríguez) (as El Mariachi); "The Misbehavers" ep. of *Four Rooms* (as the Father)

1996   *Two Much* (Trueba) (as Art and Bart Dodge); *Zorro* (Rodríguez) (title role); *Evita* (Alan Parker) (as Che Guevara)

Publications

By BANDERAS: article—

Interview with Frederick Kaufman, in *Interview* (New York), May 1990.

On BANDERAS: articles—

Bethany, Marilyn, "Banderas Plays On," in *Premiere* (New York), March 1994.

Ryan, James, "Antonio's Secret," in *Vogue* (New York), January 1995.

Johnson, Hillary, "My Antonio," in *Harper's Bazaar* (New York), August 1995.

Ansen, David, "A Neo-Latin Lover," in *Newsweek* (New York), 4 September 1995.

Gelman-Waxner, Libby, "My Antonio," in *Premiere* (New York), November 1995.

*   *   *

In the tradition of Rudolph Valentino, whom the actor was to have portrayed in Nagisa Oshima's abortive 1992 film, *Hollywood Zen*, Antonio Banderas, with his sensuous, seductive charm and his black, curly hair, has become the Latin Lover for the 1980s and 1990s. "Is that man beautiful or what?" asks Madonna in *Truth or Dare*, and through his ambivalent on-screen attitude towards both gay and straight sex, Banderas has been able to persuade women and men to endorse Madonna's opinion. He must be the only actor to have graced the covers of the national gay publication, *The Advocate* (8 February 1994) and *GQ* (December 1995).

Banderas made "an irrational decision" to become an actor after seeing the performers appear nude in a 1974 Spanish production of *Hair*. And that same openness in regard to sex and nudity has been a prevailing factor in his career. He made his debut in Pedro Almodóvar's *Labyrinth of Passion*, playing a gay terrorist who French kisses and fondles the genitals of leading man Imanol Arias. In Almodóvar's *The Law of Desire*, which helped make Banderas an international star, the actor gives an extraordinary performance as a young man losing his virginity to a director with whom he is besotted and whom he later dominates to the point of obsession. The seduction sequence in which the Banderas character is anally penetrated with the camera fixed in close up on the actor's face is remarkable not only for the thoughts that the viewer perceives as passing through his mind but also for the physical position in which Almodóvar has placed his performer. In that *The Law of Desire* is, apparently, semiautobiographical, one can only agree with the critics who suggested that Banderas had become Jose Dallesandro to Almodóvar's Warhol.

It is Almodóvar who nurtured Banderas's career, casting him as a bullfighting student who faints at the sight of blood in *Matador*, and as the former psychiatric patient whose obsession with a porno actress leads to S&M and bondage in *Tie Me Up! Tie Me Down!* The professional relationship with Almodóvar obviously led to the actor's casting in a gay role in his second feature, *False Eyelashes*, but his later Spanish films gave Banderas wider scope for his talents. At least three, *Requiem for a Spanish Peasant*, *If They Tell You That I Fell*, and *The Court of Pharaoh*, deal with Spain's fascist era. His willingness to experiment on screen with any role led Banderas to accept leading roles in the first films of directors Enrique Belloch, Pedro Costa, Juan Caño Arecha, Andrés Linares, Felix Rotaeta, and Rafael Moleón.

The American films are not the equal of those from Spain. Banderas's casting as a Cuban in *The Mambo Kings* was ill-conceived, as have been efforts to present him as an action hero in *Assassins* and *Desperado*. He was wasted in the small role of Tom Hanks's lover in *Philadelphia*. All that Banderas's American work has done is advance his image as a sex symbol. In 1992, *People* magazine named him one of the 50 Most Beautiful People in the World, and that same year, at the Academy Awards presentation, Billy Crystal described the actor as "the sexiest man alive," as Banderas presented an award with Sharon Stone (with whom he co-starred in a Freixenet champagne advertisement, directed by Bigas Luna). Unfortunately, as Caryn James wrote in the *New York Times* (21 October 1995), reviewing *Never Talk to Strangers*, Banderas and a mediocre script is "not an odd situation these days," and as the actor begins to look haggard and show signs of aging, it is obvious that a major career reevaluation is needed.

—Anthony Slide

BANKY, Vilma

Nationality: Hungarian/American. **Born:** Vilma Lonchit in Nagyrodog, Hungary, 9 January 1898. **Education:** Attended Budapest Film School. **Family:** Married the actor Rod La Rocque, 1927 (died 1969). **Career:** 1920-25—appeared in Hungarian, Austrian, and French films; 1925—signed by Samuel Goldwyn in Budapest, moved to Hollywood; billed as "The Hungarian Rhapsody"; 1929—first talking film, *This Is Heaven*; 1930-31—with husband Rod La Rocque toured U.S. with *Cherries Are Ripe*; 1932—with La Rocque, went to Germany and made last film. **Died:** 18 March 1991.

Films as Actress:

(European listings incomplete)

1920   *Im letzten Augenblick* (Boese)
1921   *Galathea* (Balogh); *Tavaszni szerelem* (von Bolvary); *Veszelyban a pokol* (Balogh)
1922   *Kauft Mariett-Aktien* (von Antalffy); *Das Auge des Toten* (Boese); *Schattenkinder des Glücks* (Osten)
1924   *Hotel Potemkin (Die letzte Stunde)* (Neufeld); *Das verbotene Land (Die Liebe des Dalai Lama)* (Feher); *Das schöne Abenteuer (The Lady from Paris)* (Noa)
1925   *Das Bildnis (L'Image)* (Feyder); *Soll man heiraten? (Intermezzo einer Ehe in sieben Tagen)* (Noa); *Der Zirkuskönig (Klown aus Liebe; Le Roi du cirque)* (Violet and Linder); *The Dark Angel* (Fitzmaurice) (as Kitty Vane); *The Eagle* (Brown) (as Mascha Troekouroff)
1926   *Son of the Sheik* (Fitzmaurice) (as Yasmin); *The Winning of Barbara Worth* (Henry King) (as Barbara Worth and her mother)
1927   *The Night of Love* (Fitzmaurice) (as Princess Marie); *The Magic Flame* (Henry King) (as Bianca, the aerial artist)
1928   *Two Lovers* (Niblo) (as Donna Leonora de Vargas); *The Awakening* (Fleming) (as Marie Ducrot)
1929   *This Is Heaven* (Santell) (as Eva Petrie)
1930   *A Lady to Love* (Seastrom) (as Lena Shultz); *Die Sehnsucht jeder Frau* (Seastrom—German version of *A Lady to Love*) (as Mizzi)
1932   *The Rebel* (Trenker and Knopf—English-language version of German film, *Der Rebell*) (as Erika Riederer)

Publications

By BANKY: articles—

"Marry? I Zink Ya!," interview with Mildred Kenworthy, in *Photoplay* (New York), April 1927.

Interview with R. Biery, in *Photoplay* (New York), March 1928.

On BANKY: articles—

Chute, Margaret, "With Vilma Banky on Location," in *Pictures and Picturegoer*, May 1929.

Lewis, G., letter in *Films in Review* (New York), February 1973.

Films in Review (New York), May 1974.

Bodeen, DeWitt, "Rod La Rocque and Vilma Banky," in *Films in Review* (New York), August/September 1977.

Ankerich, M., "Reel Stars: Vilma Banky: Gone But Not Forgotten," in *Classic Images* (Muscatine, Iowa), October 1992.

Obituary in *Variety* (New York), 19 October 1992.

Vilma Banky with Rudolph Valentino in *The Son of the Sheik*

Obituary in *New York Times*, 12 December 1992.

Ankerich, M., "Pondering the Banky Story," in *Classic Images* (Muscatine, Iowa), February 1993.

*　　*　　*

Her film career may have spanned more than a decade and two continents, but Vilma Banky is remembered for a handful of Hollywood silents made in the mid-to-late 1920s. Samuel Goldwyn discovered the blond beauty with the striking violet eyes (something the black-and-white film stock could never appreciate!) while visiting Budapest in January 1925. He instructed her to lose ten pounds and then started a media blitz to sell her to the Hollywood influentials and the public at large as "The Hungarian Rhapsody." That spring she was cast opposite Ronald Colman in *The Dark Angel* as the fiancée rejected by self-sacrificing Colman after he loses his sight in battle. Goldwyn's publicity campaign may have proven unnecessary, because Banky's looks and acting were so effective that she became a Hollywood star on her own merits. So impressive was her debut that screen heartthrob Rudolph Valentino asked Joe Schenck to cast her as his romantic leading lady in *The Eagle*. She played with Valentino one more time in his final film, *Son of the Sheik*, cast as the exotic Yasmin, the role for which she is best-remembered. So successful were these films that she began to receive $50,000 per picture from Goldwyn.

In retrospect, Banky's acting style was rather undemonstrative. She was neither melodramatic in the grand European manner of Pola Negri nor overresponsive in the American style of playing best exemplified by Gloria Swanson. But her soft, wavy blond hair and refined good looks endowed her with an undated beauty, much like Dolores Costello. Both actresses had a timeless quality which led them to play in historic epics and literary adaptations. Two of Banky's strongest performances came in a Western, *The Winning of Barbara Worth*, cast in the dual role of mother and daughter, and *A Lady to Love*, an early sound film based on Sidney Howard's *They Knew What They Wanted*, playing a mail-order bride.

Talking pictures unraveled Banky's career. Critics belabored descriptions of her thick accent. By 1930, she and Goldwyn argued about who would pay the $50 per week required for her speech lessons. Age also may have been a factor in the demise of her career, as Banky already was past her 30th birthday in youth-conscious Hollywood. In 1932, she traveled to Germany to appear in Louis Trenker's English-language production of *The Rebel*, a Mountain-style film about a brave Tyrolean's struggle to stop Napoleon from conquering his land. The film was touted as Banky's return to the silver screen. The critics, however, still harped on her Hungarian accent. It was to be her final screen appearance.

Their many fans considered Banky and her handsome movie star husband Rod La Rocque one of Hollywood's happiest couples, and it is a disappointment that they never appeared together on screen. She spent many of her post-movie years pursuing her favorite sport, golf, and died at age 93.

—-Anthony Slide, updated by Audrey E. Kupferberg

BARA, Theda

Nationality: American. **Born:** Theodosia Goodman in Cincinnati, Ohio, 29 July 1890 (year approximate). **Family:** Married the director Charles Brabin, 1921. **Career:** 1908—on Broadway in production of *The Devil* acting as Theodosia de Coppet; about 1914—met director Frank Powell, cast as "The Vampire" in his *A Fool There Was;* imaginary biography given out by press agents establishing her "Egyptian" background; created much-imitated character of "the vamp," woman who entices, then debases men; 1919—on stage in *The Blue Flame*; 1921-24—inactive during first years of marriage; 1925—resumed film acting briefly; also appeared in several stage and vaudeville productions before retiring altogether. **Died:** 7 April 1955.

Films as Actress:

1915　*A Fool There Was* (Powell) (as "The Vampire"); *The Kreutzer Sonata* (Brenon); *The Clemenceau Case* (Brenon); *The Devil's Daughter* (Powell) (as "La Gioconda"); *Lady Audley's Secret* (Farnum) (as Lady Audley); *The Two Orphans* (Brenon) (as Henriette); *Sin* (Brenon); *Carmen* (Walsh) (title role); *The Galley Slave* (Edwards)

1916　*Destruction* (Davis); *The Serpent* (Walsh); *Gold and the Woman* (Vincent); *The Eternal Sappho* (Bracken); *East Lynne* (Bracken) (as Lady Isabel); *Under Two Flags* (Edwards); *Her Double Life* (Edwards); *Romeo and Juliet* (Edwards) (as Juliet); *The Vixen* (Edwards)

1917　*The Darling of Paris* (Edwards) (as Esmeralda); *The Tiger Woman* (Edwards) (as Princess Petrovich); *Her Greatest Love* (Edwards); *Heart and Soul* (Edwards) (as Jess); *Camille* (Edwards) (as Marguerite Gauthier); *Cleopatra* (Edwards) (title role); *The Rose of Blood* (Edwards)

1918　*The Forbidden Path* (Edwards); *Madame DuBarry* (Edwards) (title role); *The Soul of Buddha* (Edwards) (+ story); *Under the Yoke* (Edwards); *When a Woman Sins* (Edwards); *Salome* (Edwards) (title role)

1919　*The She-Devil* (Edwards); *The Light* (Edwards); *When Men Desire* (Edwards); *The Siren's Song* (Edwards); *A Woman There Was* (Edwards); *Kathleen Mavourneen* (Brabin) (title role); *La Belle Russe* (Brabin); *The Lure of Ambition* (Lawrence)

1925　*The Unchastened Woman* (Young)

1926　*Madame Mystery* (Wallace and Laurel)

Publications

By BARA: articles—

"How I Became a Vampire," in *Forum*, June-July 1919.

Interview with Olga Petrova in *Shadowland*, March-April 1920.

Interview with Gladys Hall and Adele Fletcher in *Motion Picture Magazine*, November 1922.

On BARA: books—

Parish, James Robert, *The Fox Girls*, New Rochelle, New York, 1971.

Lahue, Kalton C., *Ladies in Distress*, South Brunswick, New Jersey, 1971.

Rosen, Marjorie, *Popcorn Venus*, New York, 1973.

Bodeen, DeWitt, *From Hollywood: The Careers of 15 Great American Stars*, South Brunswick, New Jersey, 1976.

On BARA: articles—

Smith, Agnes, "The Confessions of Theda Bara," in *Photoplay*, (New York), June 1920.

Bara, Pauline, "My Theda Bara II," in *Motion Picture Classic*, (Brooklyn), January 1921.

Bodeen, DeWitt, "Theda Bara," in *Films in Review* (New York), May 1968.

Theda Bara

Shipman, David, in *The Great Movie Stars: The Golden Years*, revised edition, London, 1979.
Filmography in *Ciné Revue* (Paris), 30 July 1981.

*   *   *

Theda Bara is the archetypical case of the entirely artificial screen personality; even her "background" was entirely fictitious. The actuality was that Theda Bara was Theodosia Goodman, daughter of a tailor in Cincinnati, who went on the stage in stock and, reaching Hollywood at the age of 20, worked there as an extra. She dyed her hair black and concentrated on looking thoroughly exotic. Then in 1915 she was starred by the Fox studios in a film called *A Fool There Was* derived from a novel and play inspired by Rudyard Kipling's poem "The Vampire." She became at the age of 25 an overnight sensation as a wholly artificial character type—the primitive silent film's version of the hypnotically evil femme fatale. Parallel with the release of the film came one of the most effective of the earlier forms of absurdist publicity campaign: Theodosia Goodman (her real name totally suppressed) was "Theda Bara," the name composed from anagrams for "Death" and "Arab"; she had been born in the Sahara, daughter of a French artist and his Egyptian mistress, an Arab princess, and possessed mysterious, supernatural powers. In 1917 Theda Bara became the actress's legal name.

The real nature of her appeal to mass audiences could be readily discerned: she was the kind of woman who seduced her men—normally middle-aged, well-established members of the professional or executive classes—sapping their waning sexual energies and reducing them to enervated slaves, crawling helpless at her feet. In the film that launched this absurd character, the famous line (which became another publicity slogan) was, "Kiss me, my fool." This macho-in-reverse image of the sinister female devouring men through the exploitation of their baser sexual desires seemed to fascinate audiences, women especially, since respectable (if unsophisticated) wives and mothers have always loathed and dreaded the antisocial mistress/whore, tending to see her projected in the form of such extreme fantasy.

The films in which Bara appeared were at once exploitations of sexual fantasy and moral tracts exposing the fearful consequences of such sinful goings-on. In publicity photographs Bara sat, her eyes peering through the blackened frame of her eye makeup, her features pallid, her arms twisted about her in would-be Egyptian-like postures—the very epitome of the vampire woman. In some photographs the skeleton of a man whose flesh she had devoured lay at her feet. The irony of it all was that the actress herself was apparently an entirely respectable lady who disliked the screen image with which fate had endowed her, though it brought her fame and financial reward. She eased her conscience by indulging in spiritualism.

She was to appear in a seemingly ceaseless run of more than 40 sexual melodramas (mostly period pieces) during a strictly limited period, 1915-19; she was a husband-stealer in *The Kreutzer Sonata*, a lustful gypsy in *Carmen*, "the champion vampire of the season" in *The Tiger Woman*. She starred as Camille, Cleopatra, Salome. But the bonanza was only too soon to collapse for her and her producers. By 1920 the postwar public at last saw through the image and laughed it off the screen, and although Bara continued working for a while, her final attempt to return to the screen took the form of a comedy short that Stan Laurel helped direct, *Madame Mystery* (1926), in which she was invited to parody her past self. The moral of this can be spelled out in her own words, "To understand those days, you must consider that people believed what they saw on the screen. . . . They thought that the stars of the screen were the way they saw them. Now they know it is all make-believe."

—Roger Manvell

BARDOT, Brigitte

Nationality: French. **Born:** Paris, 28 September 1934. **Education:** Studied ballet as a child. **Family:** Married 1) the director Roger Vadim, 1952 (divorced 1957); 2) the actor Jacques Charrier, 1959 (divorced), son: Nicholas Jacques; 3) Gunther Sachs, 1966 (marriage dissolved 1969); 4) Bernard d'Ormale, 1992. **Career:** 1948—a "dancing model" for fashion show in mother's shop; established as popular model by 1949: appeared on cover of *Elle* as "BB" or "Bébé"; 1952—film debut; 1955—refused offer by Warners of seven-year contract; 1957—New York premiere of *And . . . God Created Woman* established U.S. stardom; 1957—three-picture deal with Columbia for French productions featuring Bardot; 1976—formed the Foundation for the Protection of Distressed Animals; 1978—speaks before the Council of Europe against the slaughter of baby seals. **Awards:** Crystal Star of L'Acádemie du cinema, 1966; Chevalier dans l'ordre national de la légion d'honneur, 1985.

Films as Actress:

1952   *Le Trou normand* (*Crazy for Love*) (Boyer) (as Javotte Lemoine); *Manina, la fille sans voiles* (*The Lighthouse Keeper's Daughter*; *The Girl in the Bikini*) (Rozier) (as Manina); *Les Dents longues* (Gélin)

1953   *Act of Love* (Litvak) (as Mimi); *Le Portrait de son père* (Berthomieu) (as Domino); *Si Versailles m'était conté* (*Affairs in Versailles*; *Royal Affairs in Versailles*) (Guitry) (as Mlle. de Rosille)

1954   *Tradita* (*La Notte del nozze*; *Night of Love*) (Bonnard) (as Anna); *Futures vedettes* (*Sweet Sixteen*) (Marc Allégret); *Le Fils de Caroline chérie* (Devaivre)

1955   *Helen of Troy* (Wise) (as Andraste); *Doctor at Sea* (Thomas) (as Helene Colbert); *La Lumière d'en face* (*The Light across the Street*; *The Female and the Flesh*) (Lacombe) (as Olivia Marceau); *Les Grandes Manoeuvres* (*Summer Manoeuvres*; *The Grand Maneuver*) (Clair) (as Lucie); *Cette Sacrée gamine* (*Mam'zell Pigalle*) (Boisrond)

1956   *Mio figlio Nerone* (*Nero's Mistress*; *Nero's Weekend*) (Steno) (as Poppaea); *En effeuillant la Marguerite* (*Mam'selle Striptease*; *Please, Mr. Balzac*; *While Plucking the Daisy*) (Marc Allégret); ***Et . . . Dieu créa la femme*** (*And . . . God Created Woman*) (Vadim) (as Juliette Hardy); *La Mariée est trop belle* (*The Bride Is Much Too Beautiful*) (Gaspard-Huit) (as Chouchou)

1957   *Une Parisienne* (*La Parisienne*) (Boisrond) (as Brigitte Laurier); *Les Bijoutiers du clair de lune* (*The Night Heaven Fell*; *Heaven Fell that Night*) (Vadim) (as Ursula Desfontaines)

1958   *En cas de malheur* (*Love Is My Profession*; *In Case of Adversity*) (Autant-Lara) (as Yvette); *La Femme et le pantin* (*A Woman Like Satan*; *The Female*; *The Woman and the Puppet*) (Duvivier) (as Eva)

1959   *Babette s'en va-t-en guerre* (*Babette Goes to War*) (Christian-Jaque) (title role); *Voulez-vous danser avec moi?* (*Come Dance with Me*) (Boisrond) (as Virginia); *Le Testament d'Orphée* (*The Testament of Orpheus*) (Cocteau) (as herself)

1960   *La Vérité* (*The Truth*) (Clouzot) (as Dominique Marceau); *L'Affaire d'une nuit* (*It Happened at Night*) (Verneuil)

1961   *La Bride sur le cou* (*Please, Not Now!*) (Vadim and Aurel) (as Sophie); "Agnès Bernauer" ep. of *Amours célèbres* (Boisrond)

Brigitte Bardot

1962 *Le Repos du guerrier* (*Il Riposo del guerriero*; *Warrior's Rest*;
      Love on a Pillow) (Vadim) (as Genevieve Le Theil); *La Vie*
      privée (*A Very Private Affair*) (Malle) (as Jill)

1963 *Tentazioni proibite* (Civirani); *Le Mépris* (*Contempt*) (Godard)
      (as Camille Javal)

1964 *Paparazzi* (Rozier—doc); *Marie Soleil* (Bourseiller); *Une*
      ravissante idiote (*A Ravishing Idiot*; *Adorable Idiot*; *Agent*
      38-24-36; *The Warm-Blooded Spy*) (Molinaro) (as Penelope
      Light Feather)

1965 *Viva Maria* (Malle) (as Maria Fitzgerald O'Malley/Maria II);
      Dear Brigitte (Koster) (as herself)

1966 *Masculin-féminin* (*Masculine-Feminine*) (Godard) (as woman
      in a couple)

1967 *A coeur joie* (*Two Weeks in September*) (Bourguignon) (as
      Cecile)

1968 *Shalako* (Dmytryk) (as Countess Irina Lazaar); "William
      Wilson" ep. of *Histoires extraordinaires* (*Tales of Mystery*;
      Spirits of the Dead) (Malle) (as Giuseppina)

1969 *Les Femmes* (Aurel) (as Clara); *L'Ours et la poupée* (*The Bear*
      and the Doll) (Deville) (as Felicia)

1970 *Les Novices* (*The Novices*) (Casaril)

1971 *Les Pétroleuses* (*The Legend of Frenchie King*; *The Petroleum*
      Girls) (Christian-Jaque) (as Frenchie); *Boulevard du rhum*
      (*Rum Runner*) (Enrico)

1973 *Don Juan 1973 ou Si Don Juan était une femme* (*Ms. Don*
      Juan; *Don Juan, or if Don Juan Were a Woman*) (Vadim);
      L'Histoire très bonne et très joyeuse de Colinot Trousse-
      Chemise (*The Happy and Joyous Story of Colinot, the Man*
      Who Pulls Up Skirts; *Colinot*) (Companeez); *Il soriso del*
      grande tentatore (*The Tempter*; *The Devil Is a Woman*)
      (Damiani)

Publications

By BARDOT: article—

"And God Created an Animal Lover," interview with Alan Riding, in
New York Times, 30 March 1994.

On BARDOT: books—

Carpozi, George, *The Brigitte Bardot Story*, New York, 1961.
de Beauvoir, Simone, *Brigitte Bardot and the Lolita Syndrome*, London, 1961.
Evans, Peter, *Bardot: Eternal Sex Goddess*, New York, 1973.
Rosen, Marjorie, *Popcorn Venus*, New York, 1973.
Crawley, Tony, *Bebe: The Films of Brigitte Bardot*, London, 1975; rev.
ed., Secaucus, New Jersey, 1994.
Frischauer, Willi, *Bardot: An Intimate Biography*, London, 1978.
Roberts, Glenys, *Bardot: A Personal Biography*, London, 1984.
Rihoit, Catherine, *Brigitte Bardot: un mythe français*, Paris, 1986.
Vadim, Roger, *Bardot, Deneuve and Fonda: The Memoirs of Roger*
Vadim, New York, 1986.
Alion, Yves, *Brigitte Bardot*, Paris, 1989.
Choko, Stanislas, *Brigitte Bardot à l'affiche*, Paris, 1992.
French, Sean, *Bardot*, London, 1994.
Robinson, Jeffrey, *Bardot: An Intimate Portrait*, New York, 1994.

On BARDOT: articles—

Current Biography 1960, New York, 1960.
Silke, J., "The Tragic Mask of Bardolatry," in *Cinema*, (Beverly Hills),
no. 2, 1962.
Durgnat, Rayond, "B. B.," in *Films and Filming* (London), January 1963.
Maurois, A., "B. B.: The Sex Kitten Grows Up," in *Playboy*, (Chicago),
July 1964.
"B. B. Mythe ou femme?," in *Cinéma* (Paris), May 1973.
Beylie, C., and G. Braucourt, "Seven Women and Seven Women," in
Ecran (Paris), August-September 1974.
Grant, J., "Une Femme et des pantins," in *Cinéma* (Paris), May 1977.
Sarne, M., "A Definition of Stardom," in *Films and Filming* (London),
October 1978.
Williamson, Bruce, "Brigitte Bardot," in *The Movie Star*, edited by
Elisabeth Weis, New York, 1981.
Izzo, J.-C., "Bardot: bonheur perdu," in *Cinéma* (Paris), 17 February
1988.

* * *

Jeanne Moreau is rare among filmmakers in giving serious attention to the career of Brigitte Bardot. "Brigitte was the real modern revolutionary character for women," she says. "And Vadim, as a man and a lover and a director, felt that. What was true in the New Wave is that suddenly what was important was vitality, emotion, energy, love, and passion. One has to remember it was Vadim who started everything, with Bardot." It was veteran director Marc Allégret who noticed the teenage Brigitte Bardot modeling for the cover of *Elle* magazine, and later found her some minor film roles. But his friend and assistant Vadim married her, and directed her in *Et . . . Dieu créa la femme*, the film that cemented her fame and triggered the *nascent nouvelle vague*.

Vadim did not share Moreau's unstinting admiration for Bardot. "She could portray a character in any situation—as long as that character was herself." No more than a competent actress (just as Vadim is at best an average director) Bardot, like all true stars, projected one quality that survived even the most tawdry material. Posing and pouting in suntanned nudity for *Et . . . Dieu créa la femme*, Bardot epitomized what Simone de Beauvoir was later to isolate as "the Lolita syndrome"—an infantile, almost animal sexuality that freed her from all the inhibitions of adulthood. The innocent daughter or wife, eager for sexual awakening, was a role she had already played half a dozen times in such films as *Manina, la fille sans voiles* and *La Lumière d'en face*, but Vadim's Riviera melodrama offered the character Eastmancolor and CinemaScope, which made the film more than acceptable to foreign audiences.

Along with the film went Bardot's increasingly sensational reputation. More than any other actress of the 1960s (and certainly more than any French performer thrown up by the youth boom) she fulfilled, on-screen and off, the expectations of her mainly middle-aged audience. Shrewdly, Vadim placed her opposite not only the virile young Trintignant and Marquand, but matched her too with a subsidiary *homme de moyen âge* in Curt Jurgens. In *Une Parisienne*, she becomes romantically entangled with visiting prince Charles Boyer (a transparent imitation of the Duke of Edinburgh) to win back her younger husband's interest, and she teased improbably with Jean Gabin in *En cas de malheur*.

For a decade, newspapers made gleeful capital of Bardot, transparently incognito in dark glasses, sojourning with her latest boyfriend. On film, she appeared in Godard's *Le Mépris* and *Masculin-féminin*, and as herself in Cocteau's *Le Testament d'Orphée*, and the American comedy *Dear Brigitte*, where she is the love object of a lovable (but pointedly prepubescent) little boy. She even made a much-publicized stab at serious acting in Clouzot's *La Vérité*, a courtroom drama which presents the conflicting evidence in a murder case and the tangled motives that lead a lazy, sexy Parisienne to steal her sister's lover, then kill him. Once again more sinned against than sinning, Bardot pleads the case of the hedonist too sensitive to live by social rules, but even Clouzot could not induce in audiences the pity needed to hammer this point home.

Louis Malle, who later directed her opposite Moreau in the western romp *Viva Maria*, exploited these parallels more effectively than anyone in *La Vie privée*. Bardot the star moons about the Spoleto festival, frustrated in both love and career, and ponders the Kleist play being produced by lover Marcello Mastroianni until despair sends her toppling in slow motion from the heights of the medieval town.

Bardot's last screen appearances came in 1973. One of her final films, *Don Juan 1973 ou Si Don Juan était une femme*, serves as a pointed demonstration that, even in her forties, she still could play nude scenes and captivate an audience. It appears unlikely that she ever will make any sort of celluloid comeback. She has isolated herself with her causes, focusing on the animals that she was once thought so much to resemble. Nevertheless, Bardot still remains a popular figure in the news for her animal-rights activism. Soon after her exit from movies she founded the Foundation for the Protection of Distressed Animals, and eventually auctioned her jewels to help fund the organization; she has been the subject of almost as many "intimate" and "personal" biographies as her American counterpart as prefeminist sex icon, Marilyn Monroe.

—John Baxter, updated by Rob Edelman

BARKIN, Ellen

Nationality: American. **Born:** The Bronx, New York, 16 April 1954. **Family:** Married the actor Gabriel Byrne, 1988 (separated), son: Jack Daniel, daughter: Romy Marian. **Education:** Attended High School of the Performing Arts, Manhattan; Hunter College; studied acting with Lloyd Richards, Marcia Haufrecht, and Wynn Handman. **Career:** Worked as a waitress in downtown New York; off-Broadway debut in *Irish Coffee*; several appearances on daytime soap opera *Search for Tomorrow*; gained notice in play *Shout across the River*, Phoenix Repertory Company; also appeared off Broadway in *Extremities*, *Eden Court*, and *Killings on the Last Line*; 1982—theatrical film debut in *Diner*. **Agent:** Rick Nicita, Creative Artists Agency, 9830 Wilshire Boulevard, Beverly Hills, CA 90212, U.S.A.

Films as Actress:

1981 *Kent State* (James Goldstone—for TV); *We're Fighting Back* (Antonio—for TV)
1982 *Diner* (Barry Levinson) (as Beth); *Parole* (Tuchner—for TV)
1983 *Tender Mercies* (Bruce Beresford) (as Sue Anne); *Eddie and the Cruisers* (Martin Davidson) (as Maggie Foley); *Daniel* (Lumet) (as Phyllis Isaacson)
1984 *The Adventures of Buckaroo Banzai across the 8th Dimension* (W. D. Richter) (as Penny Priddy); *Harry and Son* (Paul Newman) (as Katie); *Terrible Joe Moran* (Joseph Sargent—for TV) (as Ronnie)
1985 "Virginia's Story" ep. of *Enormous Changes at the Last Minute* (*Trumps*) (Bank—produced in 1982) (as Virginia); *Terminal Choice* (*Critical List*; *Death List*; *Deathbed*; *Trauma*) (Larry—produced in 1982) (as Mary O'Connor)
1986 *Desert Bloom* (Corr) (as Aunt Starr); *Down by Law* (Jarmusch) (as Laurette); *Act of Vengeance* (John Mackenzie—for TV) (as Annette Gilly)
1987 *The Big Easy* (McBride) (as Anne Osborne); *Siesta* (Mary Lambert) (as Claire); *Made in Heaven* (Alan Rudolph) (as Lucille, unbilled)
1988 *Clinton and Nadine* (*Blood Money*) (Schatzberg—for TV) (as Nadine Powers)

1989 *Sea of Love* (Harold Becker) (as Helen)
1991 *Johnny Handsome* (Walter Hill) (as Sunny Boyd); *Switch* (Edwards) (as Amanda Brooks)
1992 *Man Trouble* (Rafelson) (as Joan Spruance); *Mac* (Turturro) (as Oona)
1993 *This Boy's Life* (Caton-Jones) (as Caroline Wolff); *Into the West* (Newell) (as Kathleen)
1995 *Bad Company* (Damian Harris) (as Margaret Wells); *Wild Bill* (Walter Hill) (as Calamity Jane)
1996 *The Fan* (Tony Scott)

Publications

By BARKIN: articles—

"Ellen Barkin, Face to Face," interview with Joe Klein, in *New York*, 13 June 1983.
"Ellen Barkin: Hot Ticket," interview with Stacy Title, in *New York Woman*, January 1988.
"Barkin's Bite," interview with James Wolcott, in *Vanity Fair* (New York), February 1990.
"Ellen Barkin Goes Mano a Mano," interview with Philip Weiss, in *Esquire* (New York), April 1991.
"Barkin Back," interview with Julia Reed, in *Vogue*, May 1993.

On BARKIN: article—

Hoffman, Jan, "Ellen Barkin: Is She Difficult or Just Straight Outta Queens?," in *New York Times*, 4 April 1993.

*   *   *

Ellen Barkin caught the attention of critics from her first screen appearance, as Beth in *Diner*, a young married girl baffled by her record-collecting husband's inability to let go of his adolescent male pals and turn toward her. What stood out was that Barkin played this wife, who was treated as an inessential appendage, without the usual appeals to sentimentality; Beth seems trapped but not helpless. Barkin has the natural advantage of a great, ambivalent movie face: bright eyes with a built-in wince and an amazing propeller mouth—when she smiles the right side curves up and the left side curves down. Her face can register pain without pathos, and with her tough chick manner, developed on the streets of Queens, she manages to project her characters' feelings without hedging her bets as an actress by flirting with the audience. In her best dramatic roles she brings an almost objective tragicomic gallantry to ordinary women's battles.

Once she began getting larger roles, Barkin combined self-protection with a susceptibility to women's woes in a way that recalled Barbara Stanwyck. This tough-tender duality is remarkably adaptable. It works for her in the naturalistic omnibus *Enormous Changes at the Last Minute*, in the soap opera *Desert Bloom* (a soap opera despite its nostalgic-political coming-of-age sensitivity), and in the melodramatic thriller *Sea of Love*. Furthermore, for a critical favorite she has an unusually potent physicality. In *Desert Bloom* in particular she shines with the lacquered glamour of an earlier era of Hollywood moviemaking, but it was after *The Big Easy* and *Sea of Love* that audiences caught on to her sexual presence. A conscientious actress, she has in fact used her strapping physique with an eye to variety of character and tone. As Starr in *Desert Bloom*, Barkin show us how her endowments represent a temptation to Starr herself to use what nature bestowed no matter how counterproductive it might prove. (It was as if Marilyn Monroe had showed up instead of Blanche at Stella and Stanley's.) In *Sea of Love* Barkin's heroic scale serves to magnify Helen's frank desire for experience. The Blake Edwards comedy *Switch*,

Ellen Barkin in *Desert Bloom*

in which Barkin plausibly draws on the butch edge of her manner to play a skirt-chaser punitively reincarnated in the body of a gorgeous blond babe, was a game attempt to lighten her recently acquired image as a sheet-scorcher. In this rowdy farce, as in *The Adventures of Buckaroo Banzai*, *Down by Law*, and *Wild Bill*, Barkin uses her scale to intensify the comedy of her character's discomposure. She is not afraid of physical gags, so it is particularly unfortunate that in *Switch* Edwards lacks the story sense to build the material to a satisfying finish (the heavenly maternity ending is definitely not for anyone who has been desperately trying to enjoy the first three-quarters of the movie). Toppling off her pumps Barkin is clearly ready for some classic slapstick, but Edwards's touch is numb—the chaos is repetitive. Barkin's role as Calamity Jane in *Wild Bill* is smaller, and requires too much nagging, but its comic liveliness fits neatly in a more consistent work. Barkin gives Jane a squeaky voice with a boondocks twang and plays it off her unwavering ruggedness. Her Jane is in the position of Jean Arthur dogging Cary Grant's heel in *Only Angels Have Wings*, but she is also a believably independent frontier gal. Wild Bill is Jane's *only* weakness, and Barkin and Hill have the comic sense to give Jane's teary frustration in love the same muscularity as her horsewhipping of two black hats.

In the 1980s Barkin was the favorite private stock of movie lovers. She now plays leads, but has never been able to get on a roll of major parts. She has had the bad luck to be miscast as a fearful, hankie-waving opera singer in *Man Trouble* opposite Jack Nicholson and to be teamed with Robert De Niro in *This Boy's Life* in which Leonardo DiCaprio as her son had all the good material—his bottle rocket flash dimmed our perception of Barkin. Her movies are always worth seeing, but no one in Hollywood has had the sense to offer her the kind of vehicle that she could really take somewhere.

—Alan Dale

BARRAULT, Jean-Louis

Nationality: French. **Born:** Le Vésinet, 8 September 1910. **Education:** Attended Collège Chaptal and École du Louvre, Paris, received bachelor's degree; studied theater with Charles Dullin and pantomime with Ètienne Decroux. **Family:** Married the actress Madeleine Renaud, 1940. **Career:** Late 1920s—worked as apprentice bookkeeper, flower salesman, and assistant master at Collège Chaptal; 1931—stage debut in Paris in *Volpone* at Charles Dullin's workshop; 1935—stage directorial debut of *Autour d'une mère*; film debut in *Les Beaux Jours*; 1936—founded own theater-workshop, Le Granier des Augustins; 1940-46—acted and directed with Comédie Française; from late 1940s—with various stage companies, including the Théâtre Marigny and the Théâtre de l'Odéon; formed own stage company, Compagnie Renaud-Barrault, in partnership with wife; 1959—named director of Théâtre de France at the Théâtre de l'Odéon; produced *Woyzeck* for Paris Opera, 1963, and *Faust* for Metropolitan Opera, New York, 1965; 1965-67—director of Théâtre des Nations; 1968—removed as director of Théâtre de France for siding with students and workers during May 1968 riots; 1972-74—again served as director of Théâtre des Nations; 1974-81—director of Théâtre d'Orsay. **Died:** In Paris, 22 January 1994.

Films as Actor:

1935   *Les Beaux Jours* (Marc Allégret)
1936   *Sous les yeux d'Occident* (Marc Allégret); *A nous deux, Madame la vie* (Mirande); *Un Grand Amour de Beethoven* (*Beethoven, le voleur de femmes*; *The Life and Loves of Beethoven*) (Gance) (as Karl); *Hélène* (Benoît-Levy and Epstein); *Jenny* (Carné)
1937   *Mademoiselle Docteur* (Pabst); *Police mondaine* (Chamborant and Bernheim); *Le Puritain* (Musso); *Les Perles de la couronne* (*Pearls of the Crown*) (Guitry and Christian-Jaque) (as Gen. Bonaparte); *Mirages* (Ryder); *Drôle de drame* (*Bizarre Bizarre*) (Carné); *Altitude 3200* (Benoît-Levy and Epstein)
1938   *Nous les jeunes* (Benoît-Levy and Epstein); *Orage* (Marc Allégret); *La Piste du Sud* (Billon)
1939   *Farinet oder das falsche Geld* (*Farinet ou l'or dans la montagne*) (Haufler)
1941   *Parade en sept nuits* (Marc Allégret); *Le Destin fabuleux de Desirée Clary* (Guitry); *Montmartre-sur-Seine* (Lacombe)
1942   *La Symphonie fantastique* (Christian-Jaque) (as Hector Berlioz)
1943   *Lumière d'été* (Grémillon); *L'Ange de la nuit* (Berthomieu)
1945   **Les Enfants du paradis** (*Children of Paradise*) (Carné) (as Baptiste Debureau); *La Part de l'ombre* (Delannoy)
1946   *Le Cocu magnifique* (de Meyst)
1947   *La Rose et le réséda* (Michel) (as narrator)
1948   *D'homme à hommes* (Christian-Jaque)
1949   *Le Bateau ivre* (Chaumel) (as narrator)
1950   **La Ronde** (*Circle of Love*) (Max Ophüls) (as Robert Kuhlenkampf)
1951   *Paul Claudel* (Gillet) (as narrator)
1953   *Si Versailles m'était conté* (*Affairs in Versailles*; *Royal Affairs in Versailles*) (Guitry) (as François Fenelon)
1959   *Le Testament du Docteur Cordelier* (Renoir)
1960   *Le Dialogue des Carmélites* (Bruckberger and Agostini)
1961   *Le Miracle des loups* (Hunebelle); *Architecture, art de l'espace* (Haesaerts) (as narrator)
1962   *The Longest Day* (Annakin, Marton, Wicki, and Oswald) (as Fr. Roulland)
1964   *Répétition chez Jean-Louis Barrault* (Hessens); *La Grande frousse* (*La Cité de l'indiciblepeur*) (Mocky)
1966   *Chappaqua* (Rooks) (as doctor)
1967   *La Route d'un homme* (Hacquard) (as narrator)
1968   *Je tire chemin* (Lesage) (as narrator)
1981   *La Nuit de Varennes* (*That Night in Varennes*; *The New World*) (Scola) (as Nicolas Edme Restif de la Bretonne)
1988   *La Lumière du lac* (Comencini)

Publications

By BARRAULT: books—

Le Procès (play), with André Gide, Paris, 1947; as *The Trial*, London, 1950.
A propos de Shakespeare et du théâtre, Paris, 1949.
Refléxions sur le théâtre, Paris, 1949; as *Reflections on the Theatre*, London, 1951.
Un Troupe et ses auteurs, Paris, 1950.
Je suis homme de théâtre, Paris, 1955.
Nouvelles refléxions sur le théâtre, Paris, 1959; as *The Theatre of Jean-Louis Barrault*, London, 1961.
Journal de bord, Paris, 1961.
Portrait de La Fontaine (play), Paris, 1964.
Portrait de Molière (play), Paris, 1964.
Odéon Théâtre de France, with Simone Benmussa, Paris, 1965.
Saint-Exupéry (play), Paris, 1967.
Rabelais (play), Paris, 1969; as *Rabelais*, London, 1971.
Jarry sur la butte (play), Paris, 1970.
Textes, edited by André Frank, Paris, 1971.

Jean-Louis Barrault (right) with Gaston Modot in *Les Enfants du paradis*

Mise en scène de Phèdre, Paris, 1972.
Souvenirs pour demain, Paris, 1972; as *Memories for Tomorrow*, New York, 1974.
Correspondence with Paul Claudel, edited by Michel Lioure, Paris, 1974.
Ainsi parlait Zarathustra (play), Paris, 1975.
Comme je le pense, Paris, 1975.
Joël Le Bon, with Madeleine Renaud, Paris, 1982.
Saiser le présent, Paris, 1984.

On BARRAULT: books—

Germain, Anne, *Renaud-Barrault: les faux de la rampe et de l'amour*, Paris, 1992.
Lorda Mur, Clara Ubaldina, *Jean-Louis Barrault: teatre i humanisme*, Barcelona, 1992.

On BARRAULT: articles—

Current Biography 1953, New York, 1953.
Obituary in *New York Times*, 23 January 1994.
Obituary in *Time* (New York), 31 January 1994.

*   *   *

Though Jean-Louis Barrault made his greatest contribution to French theater, his performance in *Les Enfants du paradis* is frequently cited as a singular illustration of pantomimic art on film.

After studying with Charles Dullin and the famous mime Ètienne Decroux, Barrault made his Paris debut in a 1931 production of *Volpone*. His first screen appearance four years later in *Les Beaux Jours* marked the first of a series of films for Marc Allégret, but it was for Marcel Carné, in films written by Jacques Prévert, that Barrault created his two most memorable roles, in *Drôle de drame*, and as Baptiste Debureau in *Les Enfants du paradis*. It was Barrault who had suggested to Carné and Prévert a story about Debureau, France's greatest pantomimist of the 19th century, whose fate is intertwined with those of the great romantic actor Frederick Lemaître (Pierre Brasseur), and the famous actress Garance (played by Arletty).

But the film was, in the words of its director, "a tribute to the theatre," which Barrault had firmly embraced when he joined the Comédie Française in 1940 where, in addition to acting, he directed a series of notable productions including *Phaedra* and *Antony and Cleopatra*. After leaving the Comédie Française in 1946, Barrault and his wife, the actress Madeleine Renaud, founded a now-famous acting company. They profoundly influenced the postwar development of theater in France through such productions as Barrault's adaptation of Kafka's *The Trial*.

Barrault appeared in several films after the war, including Delannoy's *La Part de l'ombre*, and *D'homme à hommes* directed by Christian-Jaque for whom Barrault had already created the role of the composer Berlioz in *La Symphonie fantastique* during the war. He was part of the brilliant cast assembled by Max Ophüls for *La Ronde* in 1950, but subsequently devoted his energies entirely to theater.

In 1959 Barrault played the double title role in Jean Renoir's *Le Testament du Docteur Cordelier*, but Barrault was not again offered a major film role until 1981 when Ettore Scola engaged him for *La Nuit de Varennes*, in which Barrault plays the writer Restif de la Bretonne, witness to the French Revolution.

—Karel Tabery

BARRYMORE, Ethel

Nationality: American. **Born:** Ethel Mae Blythe in Philadelphia, Pennsylvania, 15 August 1879; sister of the actors Lionel and John Barrymore. **Education:** Attended Academy of Notre Dame, Philadelphia. **Family:** Married Russell Colt, 1909 (divorced 1923), one daughter, two sons. **Career:** 1894—stage debut in Canada in *The Rivals*; 1901—critical and popular success on Broadway in *Captain Jinks of the Horse Marines*; 1914—film debut in Augustus Thomas's *The Nightingale*; 1919—headed actors' strike (including bit players) against Broadway management; 1944—having concentrated on stage work, returned to films in *None but the Lonely Heart*; 1949—five-year contract with MGM; 1953—host of series *The Ethel Barrymore Theater*. **Awards:** Best Supporting Actress Academy Award, for *None but the Lonely Heart*, 1944. **Died:** In Beverly Hills, California, 18 June 1959.

Films as Actress:

1914   *The Nightingale* (Thomas)
1915   *The Final Judgment* (Carewe)
1916   *The Kiss of Hate* (Night); *The Awakening of Helen Ritchie* (Noble)
1917   *The White Raven* (Baker); *The Call of Her People* (Noble); *The Greatest Power* (Carewe); *The Lifted Veil* (Baker); *Life's Whirlpool* (Lionel Barrymore); *The Eternal Mother* (Reicher); *An American Widow* (Reicher)
1918   *Our Mrs. McChesney* (Ralph Ince); *The Divorcee* (Blaché)
1919   *The Spender* (Swickard)
1932   *Rasputin and the Empress* (*Rasputin—The Mad Monk*) (Boleslawski) (as Empress Alexandra)
1944   *None but the Lonely Heart* (Odets) (as Ma Mott)
1946   *The Spiral Staircase* (Siodmak)
1947   *The Paradine Case* (Hitchcock) (as Lady Sophie Horfield); *The Farmer's Daughter* (Potter) (as Mrs. Morley); *Moss Rose* (Ratoff) (as Lady Sterling); *Night Song* (Cromwell) (as Miss Willey)
1948   *Moonrise* (Borzage) (as Grandma); *Portrait of Jennie* (*Jennie*) (Dieterle) (as Miss Spinney)
1949   *The Great Sinner* (Siodmak) (as Granny); *That Midnight Kiss* (Taurog) (as Abigail Budell); *The Red Danube* (Sidney) (as Mother Superior); *Pinky* (Kazan) (as Miss Em)
1951   *Kind Lady* (John Sturges) (as Mary Herries); *Daphne, the Virgin of the Golden Laurels* (Hoyningen-Huene) (as narrator); *It's a Big Country* (one ep.) (Brown and others) (as Mrs. Brian Patrick Riordon); *The Secret of Convict Lake* (Gordon) (as Granny)

1952   *Deadline—U.S.A.* (*Deadline*) (Richard Brooks) (as Mrs. Garrison); *Just for You* (Nugent) (as Allida de Bronkhart)
1953   "Mademoiselle" ep. of *The Story of Three Loves* (*Equilibrium*; *Three Stories of Love*) (Minnelli and Reinhardt) (as Mrs. Pennicott); *Main Street to Broadway* (Garnett) (as herself)
1954   *Young at Heart* (Gordon Douglas) (as Aunt Jessie)
1957   *Johnny Trouble* (Auer) (as Mrs. Chandler)

Publications

By BARRYMORE: book—

Memories, an Autobiography, New York, 1955.

By BARRYMORE: articles—

"How Can I Be a Great Actress?," in *Ladies' Home Journal* (New York), 15 March 1911.
"My Reminiscences," in *Delineator*, September 1923 through February 1924.

On BARRYMORE: books—

Barrymore, John, *We Three: Ethel—Lionel—John*, Akron, Ohio, 1935.
Barrymore, Lionel, *We Barrymores*, as told to Cameron Shipp, London, 1951.
Alpert, Hollis, *The Barrymores*, New York, 1969.
Fox, Mary Virginia, *Ethel Barrymore: A Portrait*, Chicago, 1970.
Kotsilibas-Davis, James, *The Barrymores: The Royal Family in Hollywood*, New York, 1981.
Thorleifson, Alex, *Ethel Barrymore*, New York, 1991.

On BARRYMORE: articles—

Barrymore, John, "Lionel, Ethel, and I," in *American Magazine*, February, March, April, and May 1933.
Woolf, S. J., "Miss Barrymore Refuses to Mourn the 'Good Old Days,'" in *New York Times Magazine*, 13 August 1939.
Current Biography 1941, New York, 1941.
"Ethel Barrymore, a Star for Forty-two Years," in *Vogue* (New York), 1 April 1943.
Wilson, John S., "Queen of the American Stage," in *Theatre Arts* (New York), December 1954.
Obituary in *New York Times*, 19 June 1959.
Downing, Robert, "Ethel Barrymore, 1879-1959," in *Films in Review* (New York), August-September 1959.
Gray, B., "An Ethel Barrymore Index," in *Films in Review* (New York), June-July 1963.
Classic Images (Indiana, Pennsylvania), July 1982.
Ciné Revue (Paris), 31 March 1983.

*   *   *

Ethel Barrymore came late to the movies after two false starts, and it is a pity that there is little footage of the actress in her prime left to us today. While her brothers Lionel and John embraced motion pictures early on, Ethel stayed on Broadway and lived up to her reputation as Queen of the Great White Way.

Although she recognized the cinema's burgeoning importance and transition from nickelodeon peep show to middle-class entertainment, she made her film debut for financial reasons. She was paid $15,000 to play in *The Nightingale*, written for her by Augustus Thomas, and starred in a number of pictures made at Metro's New York City studios. Interestingly, brother Lionel directed her in *Life's Whirlpool*, from his own story.

One of her early works that does survive is *The White Raven*, in which she plays a financially ruined Wall Street stockbroker's daughter who winds up singing in an Alaskan saloon. Although the melodrama is trite and her performance is humdrum, it is exciting to see Barrymore moving about as a young woman. In fact, she disliked all her early pictures (with the exception of *The Awakening of Helen Ritchie*), and remained away from films until her fortunes were reduced by the Great Depression. She accepted the role of Empress Czarina Alexandra in MGM's *Rasputin and the Empress*, with Lionel as the mad monk and John as Prince Chegodieff. The picture was fraught with difficulty (the original director Charles Brabin was replaced by Richard Boleslawski); today, it is best-known as the lone film in which the three Barrymores appeared.

However, Ethel did not like Hollywood. She returned to New York, and did not make another film for a dozen years. Even though her financial ills continued, she ignored acting offers from the studios, and made a stage comeback in 1940 as Miss Moffat in *The Corn Is Green*. When Clifford Odets saw her do the play in Los Angeles, he persuaded her to take the part of Ma Mott, Cockney Cary Grant's mother, in *None but the Lonely Heart*. Under Odets's direction, she toned down the excesses that marred her previous film work, and won a Best Supporting Actress Oscar.

This time she stayed on in Hollywood, and moved from film to film in supporting parts. Her roles did not vary, and she was pigeonholed as a grande dame, more than occasionally a bit brittle but with a warm and womanly core, lending regal presence and authority to top-grade melodramas such as *The Spiral Staircase*, *The Paradine Case*, *Moonrise*, and *Portrait of Jennie*, and lesser soap operas such as *Young at Heart* and *Johnny Trouble*, in which she eloquently essayed the part of a lonely old woman.

She and Lionel enjoyed a double cameo in Tay Garnett's *Main Street to Broadway*, and though her screen time is minimal, one is afforded an inside look at Ethel and Lionel's natural rapport, much more so than in the more theatrical *Rasputin and the Empress*. She outlived both her brothers, and continued to hold court and preserve the legacy of the family name.

—John A. Gallagher, updated by Audrey E. Kupferberg

BARRYMORE, John

Nationality: American. **Born:** John Sidney Blythe in Philadelphia, 15 February 1882; brother of the actor Lionel and the actress Ethel Barrymore. **Education:** Attended Georgetown Academy; Seton Hall, New Jersey; King's College, Wimbledon, England. **Family:** Married 1) Katharine Harris, 1910 (divorced 1917); 2) Michael Strange (Blanche Oelrichs), 1920 (divorced 1928), daughter: Diana; 3) the actress Dolores Costello, 1928 (divorced 1935), one daughter, son: the actor John Jr.; 4) Elaine Barrie, 1936 (divorced 1940); also son, born 1915, to unknown mother: the actor Eugene Barrymore. **Career:** Early 1900s—cartoonist for New York newspaper, also illustrated poems for popular journal; 1903—stage debut in Cleveland; New York stage debut in comedy *Glad of It*; 1913—contract with Adolph Zukor's Famous Players film company to make comedies; 1921—contract with First National: series of roles as romantic hero; 1922—huge stage success in *Hamlet*; contract with Warners; 1926—contract with United Artists; appeared in *Don Juan*, first use of sychronized musical soundtrack via sound on disc; 1929—returned to Warners for one million dollars per year; 1932—lured from Warners to MGM by Irving Thalberg for $150,000 per picture; in *Rasputin and the Empress* with brother Lionel and sister Ethel; early 1930s—health deteriorated in part due to alcoholism, began periodical treatment in sanitariums; 1937—began working regularly on radio, often with Rudy Vallee. **Died:** In Los Angeles, 29 May 1942.

Films as Actor:

1914   *An American Citizen* (Dawley); *The Man from Mexico* (Heffron)
1915   *Are You a Mason?* (Heffron); *The Director* (Heffron); *The Incorrigible Dukane* (Durkin)
1916   *Nearly a King* (Thompson) (as Prince of Bulwana); *The Lost Bridegroom* (Kirkwood); *The Red Widow* (Durkin) (as Cicero Hannibal Butts)
1917   *Raffles, the Amateur Cracksman* (Irving); *The Empress*
1918   *On the Quiet* (Withey)
1919   *Here Comes the Bride* (Robertson); *The Test of Honor* (Robertson)
1920   *Dr. Jekyll and Mr. Hyde* (Robertson) (title roles)
1921   *The Lotus Eater* (Neilan)
1922   *Sherlock Holmes* (*Moriarty*) (Parker) (as Sherlock Holmes)
1924   *Beau Brummell* (Beaumont) (as George Bryan Brummell)
1926   *The Sea Beast* (Webb) (as Captain Ahab); *Don Juan* (Crosland) (as Don Jose/Don Juan)
1927   *When a Man Loves* (*His Lady*) (Crosland); *The Beloved Rogue* (Crosland) (as François Villon); *Twenty Minutes at Warner Brothers Studios*
1928   *Tempest* (Taylor)
1929   *Eternal Love* (Lubitsch); *The Show of Shows* (Adolfi) (as Richard II); *General Crack* (Crosland) (as Prince Christian/Gen. Crack/Duke of Kent)
1930   *The Man from Blankley's* (Alfred E. Green) (as Lord Strathpeffer); *Moby Dick* (Lloyd Bacon) (as Captain Ahab); *Handsome Gigolo, Poor Gigolo*
1931   *Svengali* (Mayo) (title role); *The Mad Genius* (Curtiz) (as Ivan Tzarakov)
1932   *Arsène Lupin* (Conway) (as Duke of Charmerace); *Grand Hotel* (Goulding) (as Baron Felix von Gaigern); *State's Attorney* (*Cardigan's Last Case*) (Archainbaud) (as Tom Cardigan); *A Bill of Divorcement* (Cukor) (as Hillary Fairfield); *Rasputin and the Empress* (*Rasputin—The Mad Monk*) (Boleslawski) (as Prince Paul Chegodieff)
1933   *Topaze* (D'Arrast) (as Auguste Topaze); *Reunion in Vienna* (Franklin) (as Rudolf); *Dinner at Eight* (Cukor) (as Larry Renault); *Night Flight* (Brown) (as Riviere); *Counsellor-at-Law* (Wyler) (as George Simon)
1934   *Long Lost Father* (Schoedsack) (as Carl Bellaire); *Twentieth Century* (Hawks) (as Oscar Jaffe); *This Side of Heaven* (William K. Howard)
1936   *Romeo and Juliet* (Cukor) (as Mercutio)
1937   *Maytime* (Leonard) (as Nicolai Nazaroff); *Bulldog Drummond Comes Back* (Louis King) (as Col. Nielson); *Night Club Scandal* (Murphy) (as Dr. Ernest S. Tindal); *Bulldog Drummond's Revenge* (Louis King) (as Col. Nielson); *True Confession* (Ruggles) (as Charley)
1938   *Romance in the Dark* (Potter) (as Zolton Jason); *Bulldog Drummond's Peril* (Hogan) (as Col. Nielson); *Marie Antoinette* (Van Dyke) (as King Louis XV); *Spawn of the North* (Hathaway) (as Windy); *Hold That Co-ed* (*Hold That Gal*) (George Marshall) (as governor)
1939   *The Great Man Votes* (Kanin) (as Vance); *Midnight* (Leisen) (as George Flammarion); *Jesse James* (Henry King)
1940   *The Great Profile* (Walter Lang) (as Evans Garrick)
1941   *The Invisible Woman* (A. Edward Sutherland) (as Prof. Gibbs); *World Premiere* (Tetzlaff) (as Duncan DeGrasse); *Playmates* (David Butler) (as himself)
1942   *Screen Snapshots No. 107*

Publications

By BARRYMORE: books—

Confessions of an Actor, Indianapolis, 1926.
We Three: Ethel—Lionel—John, Akron, Ohio, 1935.

By BARRYMORE: articles—

"John Barrymore Writes on the Movies," in *Ladies' Home Journal* (New York), August 1922.
"Hamlet in Hollywood," in *Ladies' Home Journal* (New York), June and July 1927.
"Up Against It in Hollywood," in *Ladies' Home Journal* (New York), January 1928.
"Lionel, Ethel, and I," in *American Magazine*, February, March, April, and May 1933.

On BARRYMORE: books—

Power-Waters, Alma, *John Barrymore, the Legend and the Man*, New York, 1941.
Barrymore, Lionel, *We Barrymores*, as told to Cameron Shipp, London, 1951.
Barrymore, Diana, and Gerald Frank, *Too Much, Too Soon*, New York, 1957.
Barrymore, Elaine, and Sanford Dody, *All My Sins Remembered*, New York, 1964.
Alpert, Hollis, *The Barrymores*, New York, 1969.
Card, James, *The Films of John Barrymore*, Rochester, New York, 1969.
Fowler, Gene, *Good Night, Sweet Prince: The Life and Times of John Barrymore*, New York, 1971.
Thomas, Tony, *Cads and Cavaliers: The Gentleman Adventurers of the Movies*, New York, 1973.
Kobler, John, *Damned in Paradise: The Life of John Barrymore*, New York, 1977.
Rosen, Sheldon, *Ned and Jack*, Toronto, 1978.
Garten, Joseph W., *The Film Acting of John Barrymore*, New York, 1980.
Kotsilibas-Davis, James, *The Barrymores: The Royal Family in Hollywood*, New York, 1981.
Norden, Martin F., *John Barrymore: A Bio-Bibliography*, Westport, Connecticut, 1995.

On BARRYMORE: articles—

Smith, Rex, "John Barrymore: An Amazing Personality," in *Theatre* (New York), April 1928.
Lardner, Ring, "Onward and Upward—Or, Jack Barrymore's Revenge," in *Collier's* (New York), 16 February 1929.
Obituary in *New York Times*, 30 May 1942.
Berger, S., "The Film Career of John Barrymore," in *Films in Review* (New York), December 1952.
Hecht, Ben, "A Last Performance," in *Theatre Arts* (New York), June 1954.
Bodeen, DeWitt, "John Barrymore and Dolores Costello," in *Focus on Film* (London), Winter 1972.
"John Barrymore: Profile of a Royal Performer," by Herman G. Weinberg, and "John Carradine Remembers," in *Close-Ups: The Movie Star Book*, edited by Danny Peary, New York, 1978.
Schickel, Richard, "John Barrymore," in *The Movie Star*, edited by Elisabeth Weis, New York, 1981.
Mank, G., "Marian Marsh Recalls Filming *Svengali* with John Barrymore," in *Films in Review* (New York), December 1985.
Abbe, J. B., in *Vanity Fair* (New York), October 1992 (reprint of August 1925 article).

* * *

John Barrymore was a member of an illustrious theatrical family: his father, Maurice Barrymore, and mother, the comedienne Georgia Drew, were regarded as among the greatest actors of their day, and his brother and sister, Lionel and Ethel, had built substantial reputations of their own. The Barrymores became so popular that the media dubbed them "The Royal Family of Broadway."

After a brief period illustrating poems for a popular journal (he had initially decided that unlike the rest of his family, he did not wish to be an actor), Barrymore got the acting bug when, at the age of 20, he replaced an actor in a play in Cleveland in which his sister was appearing. A year later, he made his New York debut, and soon became one of Broadway's most popular comedy actors.

Ten years later, in 1913, he signed his first film contract—with Famous Players—and soon thereafter appeared in an adaptation of his stage success *An American Citizen*. (Purportedly, he had earlier been cast in several Lubin films.) For a number of years Barrymore continued to divide his time between the stage and film. In 1916 he appeared on stage in a role that was to become a classic, the bank clerk driven to suicide, in a stage adaptation of Galsworthy's *Justice*. There were other stage triumphs, most notably in the title roles in Shakespeare's *Richard III* and *Hamlet*.

Meanwhile, he had become a successful screen actor, one of the matinee idols of silent films, popular with audiences for his handsome face (the "Great Profile") and skill in romantic comedies and swashbuckling melodramas, films mainly distinguished for his performances. Barrymore himself preferred parts with more meat: he achieved international acclaim in 1920 in *Dr. Jekyll and Mr. Hyde* (making the transformation from one character to the other without benefit of makeup or sophisticated camera tricks), and it remained one of his favorite roles.

In 1922 Barrymore moved to Warners. His best work during this period came in *The Sea Beast*, *The Beloved Rogue*, and *Don Juan* (notable as the first feature to have a synchronized soundtrack). During this period, he was at the height of his physical prowess and beauty, which is evident in his screen appearances. In 1932 he was enticed away by Irving Thalberg and a lucrative, more exclusive contract at MGM, worth $150,000 per picture. At the advent of the sound film, he had been able to add his compelling and resonant voice to his portrayals, and at MGM he appeared in a series of varied and distinguished films: *Arsène Lupin*, *Grand Hotel*, *A Bill of Divorcement*, *Topaze*, *Counsellor-at-Law*, *Dinner at Eight*, *Reunion in Vienna*, and *Twentieth Century*.

By this time, however, Barrymore was beginning to show his age, as the ravages of drink had puffed out his features. He had been a notoriously heavy drinker since before his first stage appearance; the bad habits of a lifetime, including a series of rocky marriages and love affairs, were beginning to destroy the actor, his appearance, and his ability to act. During the filming of *Romeo and Juliet* in 1936, Thalberg suggested that Barrymore enter a nearby sanitarium. After *Romeo*, in which he gave a stirring performance as Mercutio, Barrymore continued to get sicker and more desperate, and, having proven unfit to star opposite Greta Garbo in *Camille*, he again entered a sanitarium for treatment.

From this point on, his acting and the kind of parts he was offered—from leading man to member of the supporting cast—varied, it seemed, according to his ability, at any given period, to perform. Some of his parts sadly involved self-parody; at times, he was reduced to playing hammy comedy, and to acting as Rudy Vallee's stooge on radio. He died at the age of 60 while rehearsing for one of these broadcasts.

But even during this latter period, there still were some brilliant Barrymore performances, in particular in *The Great Man Votes* and *Midnight*. Today, Barrymore is best-remembered as a dramatic actor, but in these two films (as well as his earliest silent films and the likes of *Topaze*, *Reunion in Vienna*, and *Twentieth Century*), he proved to be a deft comic performer.

Barrymore's career ranged from the brilliant to the abysmal, but he will always be recalled for that period between the 1920s and mid-1930s when his triumphs on the screen far outshone his later failures.

—Graham Webb, updated by Audrey E. Kupferberg

BARRYMORE, Lionel

Nationality: American. **Born:** Lionel Blythe in Philadelphia, 28 April 1878; brother of the actress Ethel and the actor John Barrymore. **Education:** Attended Gilmore School, London; St. Vincent's Academy, New York; Seton Hall, New Jersey; Arts Students League, New York. **Family:** Married 1) Doris Rankin, 1904 (divorced 1922); 2) Irene Fenwick, 1923 (died 1936). **Career:** 1900—Broadway debut in *Sag Harbor*; 1904—critical and public attention for performances on Broadway in *The Mummy and the Hummingbird* and *The Other Girl*; 1906-09—moved to Paris to study painting; 1909—returned to Broadway in *Fines of Fate*; employed at Biograph as actor and writer, and worked with D. W. Griffith; 1911—starring roles in Griffith's films, as well as those of other directors, while continuing to write scripts; mid-'teens—began to do some directing; 1920s—began to play mainly character roles; 1925—abandoned theater completely for film acting; 1926—contract with MGM where he remained for the rest of his career; 1928—appeared in talking film for first time; 1932—in *Rasputin and the Empress* with brother John and sister Ethel; 1938—role as Dr. Gillespie, first in series of 15 Dr. Kildare films; partially paralyzed by a combination of arthritis and a leg injury, and confined to a wheelchair, but continued acting; 1942—composed tone poem "In Memoriam" for brother John; performed by the Philadelphia Symphony. **Awards:** Best Actor Academy Award, for *A Free Soul*, 1930/31. **Died:** In Van Nuys, California, 15 November 1954.

Films as Actor:

(in films directed or supervised by D. W. Griffith, unless otherwise noted)

1911   *The Battle*; *Fighting Blood*
1912   *Friends*; *So Near, Yet So Far*; *The Chief's Blanket*; *The One She Loved*; *Gold and Glitter*; *My Baby*; *The Informer*; *Brutality*; *The New York Hat*; *The Burglar's Dilemma*; *A Cry for Help*; *The God Within*; *Home Folks*; *Love in an Apartment Hotel*
1913   *Three Friends*; *The Telephone Girl and the Lady*; *An Adventure in the Autumn Woods*; *Oil and Water*; *Near to Earth*; *Fate*; *The Sheriff's Baby*; *The Perfidy of Mary*; *A Misunderstood Boy*; *The Lady and the Mouse* (+ sc); *The Wanderer*; *House of Darkness*; *The Yaqui Cur*; *Just Gold*; *The Power of the Press*; *A Timely Interception*; *The Well*; *Death's Marathon*; *The Switch Tower*; *A Girl's Stratagem*; *Classmates* (Kirkwood); *House of Discord* (Kirkwood); *Death's Marathon*; *The Rancher's Revenge*; *Her Father's Silent Partner*; *Pa Says*; *The Fatal Wedding*; *Father's Lesson*; *His Inspiration*; *A Welcome Intruder*; *Mister Jefferson Green*; *So Runs the Way*; *The Suffragette Minstrels*

1914   *The Massacre*; *Strongheart* (Kirkwood); *Men and Women* (Kirkwood); *Judith of Bethulia* (as extra); *Brute Force*; *Under the Gaslight*
1915   *Wildfire* (Middleton); *A Modern Magdalen* (Davis); *The Curious Conduct of Judge Legarde*; *The Romance of Elaine* (Seitz—serial); *The Flaming Sword* (Middleton); *Dora Thorne*; *A Yellow Streak* (Nigh); *The Exploits of Elaine* (Seitz—serial)
1916   *Dorian's Divorce* (Lund); *The Quitter* (Horan); *The Upheaval* (Horan); *The Brand of Cowardice* (Noble)
1917   *The End of the Tour* (Baker); *His Father's Son*; *The Millionaire's Double* (Davenport)
1919   *The Valley of Night*
1920   *The Copperhead* (Maigne); *The Mastermind* (Webb); *The Devil's Garden* (Webb)
1921   *The Great Adventure* (Webb); *Jim the Penman*
1922   *Boomerang Bill* (Terriss); *The Face in the Fog* (Crosland) (as Boston Blackie)
1923   *Enemies of Women* (Crosland) (as Prince Lubimoff); *Unseeing Eyes* (E. H. Griffith); *The Eternal City* (Fitzmaurice)
1924   *Decameron Nights* (Wilcox); *America* (*Love and Sacrifice*) (as Capt. Walter Butler); *Meddling Women* (Abramson); *I Am the Man* (Abramson)
1925   *Die Frau mit dem schelechten Ruf*; *The Iron Road* (*A Man of Iron*) (Bennett); *Fifty Fifty* (Diamiant); *The Girl Who Wouldn't Work* (DeSano); *Children of the Whirlwind* (Bennett); *The Splendid Road* (Lloyd); *The Wrongdoers* (Dierker)
1926   *The Barrier* (Hill); *Brooding Eyes* (Le Saint); *Paris at Midnight* (Hopper); *The Lucky Lady* (Walsh); *The Temptress* (Niblo); *The Bells* (Young); *Wife Tamers* (Roach)
1927   *The Show* (Browning); *Women Love Diamonds* (Goulding); *Body and Soul* (Barker); *The Thirteenth Hour* (Franklin)
1928   *Drums of Love*; *Sadie Thompson* (Walsh) (as Alfred Atkinson); *The Lion and the Mouse* (Lloyd Bacon) (as John "Ready Money" Ryder); *Love* (*Anna Karenina*) (Goulding); *The River Woman* (Henabery) (as Bill Lefty); *West of Zanzibar* (Browning) (as Crane)
1929   *Alias Jimmy Valentine* (Conway) (as Doyle); *The Hollywood Review* (Riesner); *The Mysterious Island* (Hubbard) (as Count Andre Dakkar)
1930   *Free and Easy* (*Easy Go*) (Sedgwick) (as himself, in bedroom scene); *The Love Parade* (Lubitsch) (as Prime Minister)
1931   *A Free Soul* (Brown) (as Stephen Ashe); *Guilty Hands* (Van Dyke) (as Richard Grant); *The Yellow Ticket* (*The Yellow Passport*) (Walsh) (as Baron Igor Andrey); *Mata Hari* (Fitzmaurice) (as Gen. Serge Shubin)
1932   *Broken Lullaby* (*The Man I Killed*) (Lubitsch) (as Dr. Holderlin); *Arsène Lupin* (Conway) (as Guerchard); *Grand Hotel* (Goulding) (as Otto Kringelein); *Washington Masquerade* (*Mad Masquerade*) (Brabin) (as Jeff Keane); *Rasputin and the Empress* (*Rasputin—The Mad Monk*) (Boleslawski) (as Rasputin)
1933   *Sweepings* (Cromwell) (as Daniel Pardway); *Looking Forward* (*The New Deal*) (Brown) (as Michael Benton); *The Stranger's Return* (King Vidor) (as Grandpa Storr); *Dinner at Eight* (Cukor) (as Oliver Jordan); *One Man's Journey* (Robertson) (as Dr. Eli Watt); *Night Flight* (Brown) (as Rabineau); *Christopher Bean* (*Her Sweetheart*) (Wood) (as doctor); *Should Ladies Behave?* (Beaumont) (as Augustus Merrick); *Berkeley Square* (Frank Lloyd) (as innkeeper); *La ciudad de carton* (*Cardboard City*)
1934   *This Side of Heaven* (William K. Howard) (as Martin Turner); *Carolina* (*The House of Connelly*) (Henry King) (as Bob

Lionel Barrymore

Connelly); *The Girl from Missouri (One Hundred Percent Pure)* (Conway) (as T. B. Paige); *Treasure Island* (Fleming) (as Billy Bones)

1935 *David Copperfield* (Cukor) (as Dan Peggotty); *Mark of the Vampire* (Browning) (as Prof. Zelen); *The Little Colonel* (David Butler) (as Col. Lloyd); *Public Hero Number One* (Ruben) (as Dr. Josiah Glass); *The Return of Peter Grimm* (Nicholls Jr.) (title role); *Ah, Wilderness* (Brown) (as Nat Miller)

1936 *The Voice of Bugle Ann* (Thorpe) (as Springfield Davis); *The Road to Glory* (Hawks) (as Papa LaRoche); *The Devil Doll* (Browning) (as Paul Lavond); *The Gorgeous Hussy* (Brown) (as Andrew Jackson)

1937 *Camille* (Cukor) (as Monsieur Duval); *Captains Courageous* (Fleming) (as Disko); *A Family Affair* (Seitz) (as Judge Hardy); *Saratoga* (Conway) (as Grandpa Clayton); *Navy Blue and Gold* (Wood) (as Capt. "Skinny" Dawes)

1938 *A Yank at Oxford* (Conway) (as Dan Sheridan); *Test Pilot* (Fleming) (as Howard B. Drake); *You Can't Take It with You* (Capra) (as Martin Vanderhof); *Young Dr. Kildare* (Bucquet) (as Dr. Leonard Gillespie)

1939 *Let Freedom Ring* (Conway) (as Thomas Logan); *Calling Dr. Kildare* (Bucquet) (as Dr. Leonard Gillespie); *On Borrowed Time* (Bucquet) (as Julian Northup, "Gramps"); *The Secret of Dr. Kildare* (Bucquet) (as Dr. Leonard Gillespie)

1940 *Dr. Kildare's Strange Case* (Bucquet) (as Dr. Leonard Gillespie); *Dr. Kildare Goes Home* (Bucquet) (as Dr. Leonard Gillespie); *Dr. Kildare's Crisis* (Bucquet) (as Dr. Leonard Gillespie)

1941 *The Penalty* (Bucquet) (as "Grandpop" Logan); *The Bad Man (Two-Gun Cupid)* (Thorpe) (as Uncle Henry Jones); *Cavalcade of the Academy Awards*; *The People vs. Dr. Kildare (My Life Is Yours)* (Bucquet) (as Dr. Leonard Gillespie); *Lady Be Good* (McLeod) (as Judge Murdock); *Dr. Kildare's Wedding Day (Mary Names the Day)* (Bucquet) (as Dr. Leonard Gillespie); *Dr. Kildare's Victory (The Doctor and the Debutante)* (Van Dyke) (as Dr. Leonard Gillespie)

1942 *Calling Dr. Gillespie* (Bucquet) (as Dr. Leonard Gillespie); *Dr. Gillespie's New Assistant* (Goldbeck) (as Dr. Leonard Gillespie); *Tennessee Johnson (The Man on America's Conscience)* (Dieterle) (as Congressman Thaddeus Stevens)

1943 *Dr. Gillespie's Criminal Case (Crazy to Kill)* (Goldbeck) (as Dr. Leonard Gillespie); *The Last Will and Testament of Tom Smith* (Bucquet) (as Gramps); *A Guy Named Joe* (Fleming) (as the General); *Thousands Cheer* (Sidney) (as announcer)

1944 *Three Men in White* (Goldbeck) (as Dr. Leonard Gillespie); *Dragon Seed* (Conway and Bucquet) (as narrator); *Since You Went Away* (Cromwell) (as clergyman); *Between Two Women* (Goldbeck) (as Dr. Leonard Gillespie)

1945 *The Valley of Decision* (Garnett) (as Pat Rafferty)

1946 *Three Wise Fools* (Buzzell) (as Dr. Richard Gaunght); *The Secret Heart* (Leonard) (as Dr. Rossiger); *It's a Wonderful Life* (Capra) (as Mr. Potter); *Duel in the Sun* (King Vidor and Dieterle) (as Sen. McCanles)

1947 *Dark Delusion (Cynthia's Secret)* (Goldbeck) (as Dr. Gillespie)

1948 *Key Largo* (Huston) (as James Temple)

1949 *Some of the Best* (Whitbeck) (as narrator); *Down to the Sea in Ships* (Hathaway) (as Capt. Bering Joy)

1950 *Malaya (East of the Rising Sun; Alien Orders)* (Thorpe) (as John Manchester); *Right Cross* (John Sturges) (as Sean O'Malley)

1951 *The M-G-M Story* (as narrator); *Bannerline* (Weis) (as Hugo Trimble)

1952 *Lone Star* (Sherman) (as Andrew Jackson)

1953 *Main Street to Broadway* (Garnett) (as himself)

Films as Director:

1917 *Life's Whirlpool*
1929 *Confession; Madame X (Absinthe); His Glorious Night* (+ pr, mus); *The Unholy Night (The Green Ghost)*
1930 *The Rogue Song* (+ pr)
1931 *Ten Cents a Dance*

Films as Scriptwriter:

1911 *Fighting Blood* (Griffith)
1912 *My Hero* (Griffith); *The Musketeers of Pig Alley* (Griffith); *The Tender-Hearted Boy* (Griffith)
1913 *The Vengeance of Galora*
1914 *The Battle of Elderbush Gulch* (Griffith); date uncertain: *The Woman in Black*; *The Span of Life*; *The Seats of the Mighty*

Publications

By BARRYMORE: book—

We Barrymores, as told to Cameron Shipp, London, 1951.

By BARRYMORE: articles—

"The Present State of the Movies," in *Ladies' Home Journal* (New York), September 1926.
"Introduction," in *A Christmas Carol in Prose, Being a Ghost Story of Christmas*, by Charles Dickens, Philadelphia and Chicago, 1938.

On BARRYMORE: books—

Barrymore, John, *We Three: Ethel—Lionel—John*, Akron, Ohio, 1935.
Alpert, Hollis, *The Barrymores*, New York, 1969.
Kotsilibas-Davis, James, *The Barrymores: The Royal Family in Hollywood*, New York, 1981.

On BARRYMORE: articles—

Mullet, Mary, "Lionel Barrymore Tells How People Show Their Age," in *American Magazine*, February 1922.
Pringle, Henry F., "Late-Blooming Barrymore," in *Collier's* (New York), 1 October 1932.
Barrymore, John, "Lionel, Ethel, and I," in *American Magazine*, February, March, April, and May 1933.
Current Biography 1943, New York, 1943.
Crichton, Kyle, "Barrymore, the Lion-hearted," in *Collier's* (New York), March 1949.
Obituary in *New York Times*, 16 November 1954.
"Lionel Barrymore," in *Image* (Rochester, New York), December 1954.
Downing, R., "Lionel Barrymore 1878-1954," in *Films in Review* (New York), January 1955.
Gray, B., "A Lionel Barrymore Index," in *Films in Review* (New York), April 1962.
Classic Images (Indiana, Pennsylvania), June 1982.

*   *   *

Lionel Barrymore, the oldest of the three Barrymore siblings who comprised probably the greatest acting family of the American theater and cinema, began his career in films shortly before 1910. He started out acting in Biograph shorts, and was soon starring in and occasionally writing and directing a wide variety of films for various studios. His roles were characterized by their diversity, from romantic leads and villains to character parts, in films such as D. W. Griffith's *The New York Hat*, *Wildfire*, and *Just Gold*.

In the 1920s Barrymore appeared in dozens of films, among them *America*, also directed by Griffith, *Sadie Thompson*, in which he played a self-righteous reformer, and *Alias Jimmy Valentine*, as the detective Doyle. The 1920s were a turning point in his career, for he began more and more to play character parts and older men, something he was to do for the rest of his life. Although in his younger days Lionel had resembled his younger brother John in his good looks, his jowlishness in middle age necessitated a switch to character parts when he was still relatively young. By the early 1930s Lionel usually appeared as a father-type or as a heavily made-up character, as in *Rasputin and the Empress*. That film marked the only time that Lionel, John, and Ethel Barrymore all played together in the same film.

Lionel Barrymore won an Oscar in 1931 as Best Actor (tying with Wallace Beery for *The Champ*) for *A Free Soul*, in which he played Norma Shearer's drunken father. His performance stands up well, as do many of his others of the period, such as *Grand Hotel* (in which he is memorably cast as the dying accountant attempting to squeeze every last drop of life). Barrymore is equally remembered, however, for his role as Dr. Leonard Gillespie in the long-running MGM series of Dr. Kildare films produced in the 1930s and 1940s. Barrymore appeared in all 15 of the films, more than anyone else connected with the series. His first Dr. Kildare film, *Young Dr. Kildare*, opened in late 1938 and seemed ideally suited to Barrymore because he was by then afflicted with severe arthritis and could act only on crutches or while sitting down. The series accommodated his illness by allowing him to remain in a wheelchair yet be vital in his characterization. Dr. Gillespie was the definitive Barrymore combination of exaggerated moves, intensity, and emotional vacillation. He could be calm and tender with patients yet extremely agitated with everyone else.

A short time before the Dr. Kildare series began, Barrymore had appeared in the first of MGM's Andy Hardy films as Judge Hardy in *A Family Affair*. Barrymore gave an excellent, calm performance which in retrospect seems more realistic than the wise and overtly patient characterization given by Lewis Stone in the subsequent films.

Apart from the Dr. Gillespie role, Barrymore continued to act in dozens of films throughout the final years of his life, usually in a wheelchair or deskbound yet still dominating his scenes. His screen persona in the latter years was often the butt of nightclub impressionists who copied his unusually pitched and timed voice and grandiose hand gestures. Yet Barrymore's career was a diverse one with as many calmly serious roles as flamboyant ones. It is unfortunate that the lasting impression he left is more that of Mr. Potter in Frank Capra's *It's a Wonderful Life* than the worried businessman in *Dinner at Eight* or the smart detective in *Arsène Lupin*. He was a consummate actor who worked hard and gave almost 300 screen performances of wide diversity, a great accomplishment by any standard.

—Patricia King Hanson, updated by Audrey E. Kupferberg

BARTHELMESS, Richard

Nationality: American. **Born:** Richard Semler Barthelmess in New York City, 9 May 1895. **Education:** Trinity College, Hartford, Connecticut, 1913-16. **Military Service:** 1942-45—served in Navy, eventually attaining rank of Commander. **Family:** Married 1) the actress Mary Hay, 1920 (divorced 1927), daughter: Mary; 2) Jessica Stewart Sargeant, 1928. **Career:** Early 1910s—during summers while in college acted in stock companies, and, briefly, for Hartford Film Corpo-

ration; 1916—as extra in Billie Burke serial; contract with Herbert Brenon, on recommendation of actress Nazimova; 1918—hired by Griffith to appear in Dorothy Gish comedy, then given 3-year contract; 1919—role in *Broken Blossoms* established star status; 1921—incorporated Inspiration Pictures as part of financing deal to produce *Tol'able David*; 1927—contract with first National; 1936—Broadway debut in *The Postman Always Rings Twice*; retired from filmmaking after war. **Died:** In Southampton, New York, 18 August 1963.

Films as Actor:

1916 *Gloria's Romance* (Kline); *War Brides* (Brenon); *Snow White* (Searle)
1917 *The Moral Code* (Miller); *The Eternal Sin* (Brenon); *The Valentine Girl* (Dawley); *The Soul of Magdalen* (King); *The Streets of Illusion*; *Bab's Diary* (Dawley); *Bab's Burglar* (Dawley); *For Valour* (Parker); *Nearly Married* (Withey); *The Seven Swans* (Dawley)
1918 *Sunshine Nan* (Giblyn); *Rich Man, Poor Man* (Dawley); *Hit the Trail Holiday* (Neilan); *The Hope Chest* (Clifton)
1919 *The Girl Who Stayed at Home* (Griffith); ***Broken Blossoms*** (Griffith) (as Cheng Huan); *Boots* (Clifton); *Three Men and a Girl* (Neilan); *Peppy Polly* (Clifton); *I'll Get Him Yet* (Clifton)
1920 *Scarlet Days* (Griffith); *The Idol Dancer* (Griffith); *The Love Flower* (Griffith); *Way Down East* (Griffith) (as David Bartlett)
1921 *Experience* (Fitzmaurice); *Tol'able David* (King) (as David Kinemon)
1922 *The Seventh Day* (King); *Just a Song at Twilight* (Carlton King); *Sonny* (King); *The Bond Boy* (King); *Fury* (Goulding)
1923 *The Bright Shawl* (Robertson); *The Fighting Blade* (Robertson); *Twenty One* (Robertson)
1924 *The Enchanted Cottage* (Robertson); *Classmates* (Robertson)
1925 *New Toys* (Robertson); *Soulfire* (Robertson); *Shore Leave* (Robertson); *The Beautiful City* (Webb)
1926 *Just Suppose* (Webb); *Ranson's Folly* (Olcott); *The Amateur Gentleman* (Olcott); *The White Black Sheep* (Olcott)
1927 *The Dropkick* (Santell); *The Patent Leather Kid* (Santell)
1928 *The Noose* (Dillon); *The Little Shepherd of Kingdom Come* (Santell); *The Wheels of Chance* (Santell); *Out of the Ruins* (Santell); *Scarlet Seas* (Dillon)
1929 *Weary River* (Lloyd); *Drag* (Lloyd); *Young Nowheres* (Lloyd); *The Show of Shows* (Adolfi)
1930 *Son of the Gods* (Lloyd); *The Dawn Patrol* (Hawks); *The Lash* (Lloyd)
1931 *The Finger Points* (Dillon); *The Last Flight* (Dieterle)
1932 *Alias the Doctor* (Curtiz); *Cabin in the Cotton* (Curtiz)
1933 *Central Airport* (Wellman); *Heroes for Sale* (Wellman)
1934 *Massacre* (Crosland); *A Modern Hero* (Pabst); *Midnight Alibi* (Crosland)
1935 *Four Hours to Kill* (Leisen)
1936 *Spy of Napoleon* (Elvey)
1939 *Only Angels Have Wings* (Hawks)
1940 *The Man Who Talked Too Much* (Sherman)
1942 *The Mayor of Forty-Fourth St.* (Green); *The Spoilers* (Enright)

Publications

By BARTHELMESS: articles—

"A La William Tell," in *Photo-Play Journal*, June 1919.
"15 Years of Fame," in *Pictures and Picturegoer*, June 1929.

Richard Barthelmess

On BARTHELMESS: articles—

Weitzel, Edward, "The Rise of Richard Barthelmess," in *Moving Picture World*, 26 July 1919.

Hall, Gladys, "Richard the Tenth," in *Motion Picture Magazine*, April 1921.

Wilson, B. F., "A Terribly Intimate Portrait," in *Motion Picture Classic* (Brooklyn), August 1924.

Collier, Lionel, "The Idol Richard," in *Pictures and Picturegoer*, June 1929.

Jacobs, J., "Richard Barthelmess," in *Films in Revue* (New York), January 1958.

Pickard, Roy, "The Tough Race," in *Films and Filming* (London), September 1971.

Fox, J., "The Country Boys, an aspect of Rural America in the Age of Innocence," in *Films and Filming* (London), May 1972.

Shipman, David, in *The Great Movie Stars: The Golden Years*, revised edition, London, 1979.

* * *

Some actors achieve a place in the filmic hall of fame by the totality of their performances. Others, like Richard Barthelmess, are known for one or two outstanding roles that overshadow all their other work.

His mother was the great Nazimova's English teacher, and when the Russian actress made her film debut in Herbert Brenon's *War Brides*, young Richard shared her honors. Several performances helped establish Barthelmess as a star before D. W. Griffith engaged him to play opposite Lillian Gish in *Broken Blossoms*. His interpretation of a poetic Chinese boy from the London docks who falls in love with a battered waif of the streets is one of the most remarkable examples of screen acting. The following year Griffith again used Barthelmess and Gish in *Way Down East*, an old melodrama brought to life by the master. Griffith also directed him in four other films.

Forming his own company, Inspiration Pictures, in cooperation with the director Henry King, he again gave an outstanding performance in the film masterpiece *Tol'able David* based on a Joseph Hergesheimer story of a country boy's courage when a gang of ruffians threaten his family. King's direction and Barthelmess's playing make this a classic of the cinema which influenced many directors, including the great Russian Pudovkin.

The Bright Shawl, again based on Hergesheimer and starring Dorothy Gish, and *The Enchanted Cottage* with May McAvoy, added to his laurels, and his popularity continued to the end of the silent period. His career was by no means finished with the coming of sound, and he had leading roles in Howard Hawks's *The Dawn Patrol* and *Only Angels Have Wings*, Michael Curtiz's *Cabin in the Cotton* with the young Bette Davis, and Pabst's only American film, *A Modern Hero*. As Barthelmess grew older he undertook minor character roles but left Hollywood forever after joining the navy in 1942. He enjoyed a comfortable retirement until his death at his Long Island home in 1963.

—Liam O'Leary

BASINGER, Kim

Nationality: American. **Born:** Athens, Georgia, 8 December 1953. **Education:** Attended University of Georgia. **Family:** Married 1) Ron Britton, 1982 (divorced 1990); 2) Alec Baldwin, 1993, one child: Ireland. **Career:** 1969—Breck Shampoo girl; 1976-77—episodic appearances in TV series, *Charlie's Angels*, *The Six-Million Dollar Man*; 1977—in TV series, *Dog and Cat*; 1978—first leading role in TV movie *Katie: Portrait of a Centerfold*; 1979—in TV mini-series *From Here to Eternity*; 1981—film debut in *Hard Country*; 1989—bought town of Braselton, Georgia, for future development; 1993—sued by Main Line Pictures for reneging on agreement to do *Boxing Helena*; forced to declare bankruptcy; decision against Basinger later reversed by California Court of Appeals. **Agent:** William Morrow Agency, 151 El Camino Drive, Beverly Hills, CA 90212, U.S.A.

Films as Actress:

1977 *Dog and Cat* (Kelljan—for TV) (as Officer J. Z. Kane)
1978 *Katie: Portrait of a Centerfold* (Greenwald—for TV) (as Katie); *The Ghost of Flight 401* (Steven Hilliard Stern—for TV) (as Prissy Frasier)
1981 *Killjoy* (*Who Murdered Joy Morgan?*) (Moxey—for TV) (as Laury Medford); *Hard Country* (David Greene) (as Jodie Lynn Palmer)
1982 *Mother Lode* (Charlton Heston and Joe Canutt) (as Andrea Spalding)
1983 *Never Say Never Again* (Kershner) (as Domino Petachi); *The Man Who Loved Women* (Edwards) (as Louise)
1984 *The Natural* (Levinson) (as Memo Paris)
1985 *Fool for Love* (Altman) (as May)
1986 *No Mercy* (Pearce) (as Michel Duval); *9½ Weeks* (Lyne) (as Elizabeth)
1987 *Blind Date* (Edwards) (as Nadia Gates); *Nadine* (Benton) (title role)
1988 *My Stepmother Is an Alien* (Richard Benjamin) (as Celeste Martin)
1989 *Batman* (Burton) (as Vicki Vale)
1991 *The Marrying Man* (*Too Hot to Handle*) (Rees) (as Vicki Anderson)
1992 *Final Analysis* (Joanou) (as Heather Evans); *Cool World* (Bakshi) (as Holli Would)
1993 *Wayne's World 2* (Surjik) (as Honey Horne); *The Real McCoy* (Mulcahy) (as Karen McCoy)
1994 *The Getaway* (Donaldson) (as Carol McCoy); *Ready to Wear* (*Prêt-a-Porter*) (Altman) (as Kitty Potter)

Publications

By BASINGER: articles—

"Kim Basinger," interview with Ivor Davis, in *Los Angeles Magazine*, December 1988.

"Kim Basinger Talks," interview with Brendan Lemon, in *Interview* (New York), December 1994.

On BASINGER: articles—

Stivers, Cyndi, "Blond Ambition," in *Premiere* (New York), September 1989.

Current Biography 1990, New York, 1990.

Masters, Kim, "Princess," in *Premiere* (New York), March 1990.

Fleming, Michael, "*Boxing* K.O. Spurs Bout with Basinger," in *Variety* (New York), 24 June 1991.

* * *

Her beauty is the subject of regular comment in her films but Jack Nicholson's Joker in *Batman*, gives us the most accurate, if sardonic appraisal of her eye-catching looks: "You're beautiful, in an old-fashioned kind of way." A Breck girl at the age of 16 and a Playboy

Kim Basinger in *Fool for Love*

model a year later, Kim Basinger, with her full lips, glowing skin, and wayward honeyed locks, was the most sultry but also the most conventional of the sex symbols of the eighties. Although capable of conveying sexual menace, her specialty has been to mimic the sexual availability and emotional vulnerability patented by Marilyn Monroe, whose breathy style she acknowledges as influencing her own in *Cool World.*

Her first star turn in *Katie: Portrait of a Centerfold* already contained the home recipe for Basinger's trademark sexual confection—a melting Southern sweetness, a soft center, a girlish and confiding, often nervous laugh. Even when dressed in the height of fashion, Basinger hardly strikes the eye as modern, either in her looks or attitudes. She typically belongs to a society in which, as a character in *No Mercy* observes, it is pleasurable to be a man. Basinger is generally cast as the sexual trophy trying to escape from such a world, which is why flight and the chase figure so prominently in her films, sometimes to deliriously happy effect, as in the boisterous *Nadine,* in which she gives her most endearing comic performance, but more often as a dangerous game of erotic pursuit. Films such as *No Mercy* and the soft-pornographic *9½ Weeks* as well as the film she famously did *not* make—*Boxing Helena*—cast her in elaborate scenarios of sexual bondage. Even in the more elegantly appointed thrillers, such as *Final Analysis,* she inhabits what appear to be exhibition cases for human display. Her films often present her as handicapped for anything resembling self-reliant womanhood—twice by alcohol disorders, once by illiteracy, once (arguably more than once) by masochistic sex addiction.

Basinger has tried to maneuver within the narrow confines of her sexpot image by parodying her heartstopper reputation. Like Kathleen Turner, she enjoys lampooning the hypnotic power of her own sexuality, although her Holli Would in the nightmarish *Cool World* is the diabolic double of Turner's "good blond" in *Who Framed Roger Rabbit?* Basinger's attempts at self-parody spoof rather than reinvent the Blond Bombshell: Honey Horne incarnates adolescent sex fantasies in *Wayne's World 2,* itself a spoof on the icons of media culture; and her Celeste in *My Stepmother Is an Alien* is a woman so good-looking that sex with her is treated as a cosmic event. Still in that film and in more earthbound, but equally frenetic vehicles, such as the witless *Blind Date,* Basinger displays a goofiness and slapstick limberness deserving of better stunts.

It remains to be seen whether Basinger can modernize her screen persona, which while glamorous, lacks the independence, drive, and determination that characterize the screen's most "modern" women from Bette Davis to Sharon Stone. *Final Analysis* suggests she might, with the right vehicle, shed the mannerisms that have kept her in relative subjection to men. In this unapologetic remake of *Vertigo,* Basinger brings a murderous resolve to her role as Heather Evans, a more sinister and cunning descendent of Kim Novak's compliant, zombified Madeleine. When she falls to her death from atop a lighthouse tower, it is after having rejected the new age masculinity offered to her by her hapless lover and dupe, Richard Gere. The man on the tower remains standing, in command of the scene, but the phallic structure supporting him is much in need of repairs.

The entire question of role choice ceased to be academic when Basinger was sued by Main Line Pictures for backing out of an oral agreement to star in Jennifer Lynch's *Boxing Helena.* The initial judgment against her sent Basinger into bankruptcy although it was later reversed by the California Court of Appeals. Despite the setback, Basinger is in top comic form in Robert Altman's *Ready to Wear,* enlivening the fairly drab and mean-spirited satire on the fashion industry as Kitty Potter, an undismayable commentator for FADTV. Altman's sly joke is to give this luminous beauty, defined by image culture all her professional life, the final clear-eyed pronouncement on the mystique of the female body beautiful.

—Maria DiBattista

BASSETT, Angela

Nationality: American. **Born:** Harlem, New York, 16 August 1958. **Education:** Attended Yale University, B.A., 1980; Yale School of Drama, M.F.A., 1982. **Career:** 1980s—appeared on Broadway in *Ma Rainey's Black Bottom* and *Joe Turner's Come and Gone*; TV appearances include *A Man Called Hawk, The Cosby Show, Guiding Light, Tour of Duty*; 1986—first on-screen film credit in *F/X*; 1992—in TV mini-series *The Jacksons: An American Dream.* **Awards:** Golden Globe Award, for *What's Love Got to Do with It,* 1994; Black Women of Achievement Key Honoree, NAACP Legal Defense and Educational Fund, 1994. **Agent:** ICM Artists Ltd., 40 West 57th Street, New York, NY 10019-4001, U.S.A.

Films as Actress:

1985   *Doubletake* (Jud Taylor—for TV)
1986   *F/X* (Mandel) (as TV reporter)
1990   *Kindergarten Cop* (Reitman) (as stewardess); *Perry Mason: The Case of the Silenced Singer* (Satlof—for TV) (as Carla Peters); *In the Best Interest of the Child* (David Greene—for TV) (as Lori); *Family of Spies* (Gyllenhaal—for TV); *Challenger* (Glenn Jordan—for TV) (as Cheryl McNair)
1991   *Boyz N the Hood* (Singleton) (as Reva Styles); *City of Hope* (Sayles) (as Reesha); *One Special Victory* (Stuart Cooper—for TV); *Line of Fire: The Morris Dees Story* (Korty—for TV) (as Pat); *Fire! Trapped on the 37th Floor* (Robert Day—for TV) (as Allison)
1992   *Innocent Blood* (Landis) (as U.S. Attorney Sinclair); *Malcolm X* (Spike Lee) (as Betty Shabazz); *Passion Fish* (Sayles) (as Dawn/Rhonda); *Critters 4* (Harvey) (as Fran); *Locked Up: A Mother's Rage* (Rooney—for TV) (as Willie); *The Heroes of Desert Storm* (Ohlmeyer—for TV) (as Lt. Jeter)
1993   *What's Love Got to Do with It* (Brian Gibson) (as Tina Turner)
1995   *Panther* (Van Peebles) (cameo as Betty Shabazz); *Vampire in Brooklyn* (Craven) (as Rita); *Strange Days* (Bigelow) (as Mace Mason); *Waiting to Exhale* (Whitaker) (as Bernadine)

Publications

By BASSETT: articles—

"Angela Bassett Takes on Tina Turner," interview with Theresa Sturley, in *Interview* (New York), June 1993.
Interview with James Ryan, in *GQ* (New York), September 1995.
"Angela Bassett Is *Not* a Diva!," interview with Karen Grigsby Bates, in *Essence* (New York), December 1995.

On BASSETT: articles—

Zoglin, Richard, "Out of the Shadows at Last," in *Time* (New York), 21 June 1993.
Collier, Aldore, "*What's Love Got to Do with It*: Larry Fishburne and Angela Bassett Portray Ike and Tina Turner in New Movie," in *Ebony* (Chicago), July 1993.
Testino, Mario, "Just You Wait," in *Harper's Bazaar* (New York), October 1995.
Webster, Andy, filmography in *Premiere* (New York), December 1995.

*   *   *

Angela Bassett in *Waiting to Exhale*

When Angela Bassett was 15 years old, she went on a field trip to the Kennedy Center in Washington, D.C., with the Upward Bound program for gifted students. It was here that she saw James Earl Jones in a production of the play *Of Mice and Men*, and she knew that she wanted to act. In talking about the performance, she said, "I just wept. I thought, if I could make someone feel the way I feel right now. . . ."

Bassett grew up in a single-parent household in St. Petersburg, Florida, with her sister D'Nette and her mother Betty, where she was the first African-American student accepted in her high school's National Honor Society. She credits her mother with instilling in her a strict work ethic, a firm grounding, and a strong sense of self. These traits are evident in the roles she has chosen—many of which are strong mothers—and in the intensity and commitment she brings to the acting process.

Her acting career began on the stage for which she was trained at the prestigious Yale School of Drama under the tutelage of veteran director Lloyd Richards. She acted in two August Wilson plays on Broadway before making her foray onto the screen. Her first screen credit is an unmemorable small part with one line of dialogue in the thriller *F/X*. Shortly after, she migrated to California, and while guesting on numerous television shows, she also began making screen appearances. The first role that got her noticed was as Reva, the driven mother of the film's protagonist Tre, in *Boyz N the Hood*. Bassett obviously identified with the strong-willed mother who sends her son to live with his father so he has an adult male role model. She forged

a friendship with co-star Laurence Fishburne on the set, and this bond would prove to serve her well later.

Bassett had supporting roles in two of John Sayles's small-budget, but well-regarded films, *City of Hope* and *Passion Fish*. The next role that garnered her attention, however, was as Betty Shabazz, the wife of Malcolm X, in Spike Lee's film about the widely known activist. She brought a sense of dignity to the role, and in the process helped the film transcend a script calling mainly for large doses of humbleness. Bassett played a legendary figure again when she took on the role of Katherine Jackson in the television mini-series *The Jacksons: An American Dream*. The drama spans Jackson's life from age 15 to 55. Bassett received mainly positive notices for her performance, but her next role is the one that catapulted her to fame.

She won the coveted star role of Tina Turner in the biopic *What's Love Got to Do with It* over numerous other popular actresses. To prepare for the role, Bassett physically trained for more than a month. She worked with dialect coaches, and studied hours of videotape of Turner's performances. Bassett's rigorous work ethic paid off. She won the Golden Globe for her riveting portrayal, and was nominated for an Academy Award. Once again, Bassett was able to bring a sense of dignity, vulnerability, and mercy to a character who could have been seen purely as a victim of domestic abuse. It was of utmost importance that the audience understand why Turner—through years of violence—would stay with Ike (played by Fishburne, who accepted the role in large part because Bassett was playing Turner). Bassett accomplished this by showing Turner's sense of loyalty and grace.

Bassett seems to have an uncanny knack at showing opposite emotions in her characters, a skill essential to good acting. It is also to her credit that the film is never about an actress playing Tina Turner. Bassett seemed to become Turner. This is most evident at the end of the film when Turner herself appears in a stage number, and the illusion of reality of the film is not broken.

In 1995, Bassett was seen in two major films in very different roles. She was cast opposite Ralph Fiennes in the action-adventure *Strange Days*, set at the end of the millennium amidst racial wars. Her heroic character—another single parent—carries equal emotional heft to Fiennes's lead role. Her most recent film is *Waiting to Exhale*, which has been strongly criticized for male bashing. Bassett has said, however, that was not her or the director Forest Whitaker's intention. The film also received praise for its strong, black female roles. In a time when there are more, but still too few good, female roles, Bassett seems to find them, and to be able to cross racial boundaries.

—Anita Gabrosek

BATES, Alan

Nationality: British. **Born:** Arthur Bates in Allestree, Derbyshire, 19 February 1934. **Education:** Attended Herbert Strutt Grammar School, Belper, Derbyshire; Royal Academy of Dramatic Art, London. **Military Service:** early 1950s—served with the Royal Air Force. **Family:** Married Victoria Ward, 1970, twin sons. **Career:** 1945—stage acting debut; 1955-60—acted primarily on stage including roles in *Look Back in Anger* and *The Caretaker*; worked occasionally on television; 1960—film debut in Tony Richardson's *The Entertainer*; 1972—co-produced short *Second Best*, directed by Steven Dartnell; 1977—in TV mini-series *The Mayor of Casterbridge*. **Agent:** Michael Linnit, Globe Theatre, Shaftesbury Avenue, London W1, England.

Films as Actor:

1960   *The Entertainer* (Richardson) (as Frank Rice)
1961   *Whistle Down the Wind* (Forbes) (as Arthur Blakey)
1962   *A Kind of Loving* (Schlesinger) (as Vic Brown)
1963   *The Running Man* (Reed) (as Stephen Maddox); *The Caretaker* (*The Guest*) (Clive Donner) (as Mick)
1964   *Nothing but the Best* (Clive Donner) (as Jimmy Brewster); **Zorba the Greek** (Cacoyannis) (as Basil)
1965   *Insh' Allah* (Hudson) (as narrator)
1966   *Georgy Girl* (Narizzano) (as Jos); *King of Hearts* (*Le Roi de coeur*) (de Broca) (as Pvt. Charles Plumpick)
1967   *Far from the Madding Crowd* (Schlesinger) (as Gabriel Oak); *Rece do gory* (*Hands Up!*) (Skolimowski)
1968   *The Fixer* (Frankenheimer) (as Yakov Bok)
1969   *Women in Love* (Russell) (as Rupert Birkin)
1970   *Three Sisters* (Olivier) (as Vershinin)
1971   *The Go-Between* (Losey) (as Ted Burgess); *A Day in the Death of Joe Egg* (Medak) (as Brian)
1972   *Second Best* (Dartnell) (+ co-pr)
1973   *L'Impossible objet* (*The Impossible Object*) (Frankenheimer) (as Harry)
1974   *Mikis Theodorakis: A Profile of Greatness*; *Butley* (Pinter) (title role); *The Story of Jacob and Joseph* (Cacoyannis—for TV) (as narrator)
1975   *In Celebration* (Lindsay Anderson) (as Andrew Shaw)
1976   *Royal Flash* (Lester) (as Rudi von Starnberg); *Where Adam Stood* (Brian Gibson—for TV)

1977   *An Unmarried Woman* (Mazursky) (as Keplan)
1978   *The Shout* (Skolimowski) (as Charles Crossley)
1979   *The Rose* (Rydell) (as Rudge)
1980   *Nijinsky* (Ross) (as Sergei Diaghilev)
1981   *Quartet* (Ivory) (as H. J. Heidler)
1982   *The Return of the Soldier* (A. Bridges) (as Capt. Chris Baldry); *A Voyage Round My Father* (Rakoff—for TV) (as the son); *Britannia Hospital* (Lindsay Anderson)
1983   *The Wicked Lady* (Winner) (as Capt. Jerry Jackson); *Separate Tables* (Schlesinger—for TV) (as Mr. Malcolm/Maj. Pollock)
1984   *Dr. Fischer of Geneva* (Lindsay-Hogg—for TV) (as Jones)
1985   *An Englishman Abroad* (Schlesinger—for TV) (as Guy Burgess)
1986   *Duet for One* (Konchalovsky) (as David Cornwallis)
1987   *Pack of Lies* (Page—for TV) (as Stewart); *A Prayer for the Dying* (Hodges) (as Jack Meehan)
1988   *We Think the World of You* (Gregg) (as Frank); *The Dog It Was That Died* (Wood—for TV) (as Blair)
1989   *Force majeure*(*Uncontrollable Circumstances*) (Jolivet) (as Malcolm Forrest); *Club Extinction* (*Dr. M*) (Chabrol) (as Dr. Marsfeldt/Guru)
1990   *Hamlet* (Zeffirelli) (as Claudius); *Mister Frost* (Setbon) (as Felix Detweiller); *102 Boulevard Haussmann* (Prassad—for TV) (as Marcel Proust); *Shuttlecock* (Piddington) (as James Prentis)
1991   *Unnatural Pursuits* (for TV) (as Hamish Partt)
1992   *Secret Friends* (Potter) (as John); *Silent Tongue* (Shepard) (as Eamon McCree)
1994   *Hard Times* (Peter Barnes—for TV) (as Bounderby)
1995   *The Grotesque* (J. P. Davidson) (as Sir Hugo Coal)

Publications

By BATES: articles—

Interview in *Time Out* (London), 30 May 1985.
Interview with Simon Banner, in *Times* (London), 22 September 1989.

On BATES: articles—

Cowie, Peter, "The Face of '63—Great Britain," in *Films and Filming* (London), no. 5, 1963.
Current Biography 1969, New York, 1969.
Leslie, Ian, "Women in Love," in *Sight and Sound* (London), Winter 1969-70.
Ciné Revue (Paris), 26 February 1981.
Screen International, 31 March 1984.
Slodowski, J., "Grek Zorba," *Filmowy Serwis Prasowy*, vol. 36, no. 5/6, 1990.

* * *

Alan Bates has distinguished himself in a number of important realistic and romantic films made by several of Britain's best directors of the postwar generation, including Tony Richardson (*The Entertainer*), Bryan Forbes (*Whistle Down the Wind*), Ken Russell (*Women in Love*), and John Schlesinger (*A Kind of Loving* and *Far from the Madding Crowd*).

Bates made his acting debut in 1955 on the stage. He created the role of Cliff in John Osborne's *Look Back in Anger*, the quintessential Angry Young Man drama, and also starred in Harold Pinter's *The Caretaker*, a role that he later brought to the screen. Once he had made the transition from stage to screen, his talents were soon widely recognized and his reputation became an international one. He held

Alan Bates in *Far from the Madding Crowd*

his own opposite Anthony Quinn's flamboyant portrayal of the title character in Michael Cacoyannis's *Zorba the Greek*, and his performance as an unfairly incarcerated Jewish handyman in turn-of-the-century Russia in John Frankenheimer's *The Fixer* earned him an Academy Award nomination. He went on to do splendid work for Joseph Losey in *The Go-Between*, Paul Mazursky in *An Unmarried Woman*, and Jerzy Skolimowski in *The Shout*.

Bates is an actor of impressive range and flexibility. In *Far from the Madding Crowd* he played Thomas Hardy's Gabriel Oak as a pillar of stability: the actor's purposefully wooden exterior was ideal for playing a simple character who is defined by patience, dedication, and loyalty. (Bates also appeared in Hardy's *The Mayor of Casterbridge* for BBC-TV.) In sharp contrast to Gabriel Oak is his role in *The Go-Between* as Ted Burgess, another strong peasant type, also infatuated with a striking woman who, like Bathsheba Everdene in *Far from the Madding Crowd*, breaks his heart. But in *The Go-Between*, his character's response is much different. As the plot moves towards its climax, Bates must suggest that Burgess's spirit has been broken. He very effectively portrays the inner turbulence of the character, but even more challenging is the mystical enigma of Charles Crossley in *The Shout*, adapted from a strange and disturbing short story by Rob-

ert Graves concerning an intruder with shamanic powers who disrupts the lives of a staid English couple. Roles such as these make his performance as the romantic lead in *An Unmarried Woman* seem rather conventional (though decidedly entertaining) by comparison.

Bates has had his best later-career role in *The Grotesque*, giving a picture-stealing performance as Sir Hugo Coal, a crusty, aristocratic English squire who is fascinated by dinosaurs to the point of reproducing a full-scale model of one. Of course, he himself, as a representative of the stuffy upper classes, is a dinosaur. Sir Hugo no longer sleeps with his wife, and prefers physically tussling with men. As a member of a repressed class, however, he can only fantasize or act out the kind of sexuality in which his amoral new servant (played by Sting) revels. The character of Sir Hugo makes for a telling contrast to Bates's earthy Rupert Birkin in *Women in Love*: in the latter, he raised eyebrows with his nude wrestling scene with Oliver Reed.

In the first part of *The Grotesque*, Bates seems to be parodying Nigel Bruce's Dr. Watson, but as the story progresses he also gets to be seriously dramatic. His performance is superb, and one hopes that, in the future, he will be offered similar, equally challenging roles.

—James M. Welsh, updated by Rob Edelman

BATES, Kathy

Nationality: American. **Born:** Kathleen Doyle Bates in Memphis, Tennessee, 28 June 1948. **Family:** Married the actor Tom Campisi. **Education:** B.F.A., Southern Methodist University. **Career:** Late 1960s—worked in regional theater in Washington, D.C., and at the Actors Theater in Louisville; 1970—moved to New York to pursue acting career; early 1970s—worked as a singing waitress in a Catskill Mountain resort; 1971—made screen debut in a bit role in *Taking Off*; 1976—had first off-Broadway role in *Vanities*; 1977—began appearing in roles on TV series, and had recurring role on daytime soap *All My Children*; 1980—made Broadway debut in *Goodbye Fidel*; 1990—had first important screen role in *Misery*; 1994—in TV mini-series *The Stand*. **Awards:** Best Actress Academy Award, Golden Globe Award, and Chicago Film Critics Award, for *Misery*, 1990. **Agent:** Susan Smith and Associates, 121 North Vicente Boulevard., Beverly Hills, CA 90211, U.S.A.

Films as Actress:

1971   *Taking Off* (Forman) (bit role as a singer)

1978   *Straight Time* (Grosbard) (as Selma Darin)

1982   *Come Back to the 5 and Dime, Jimmy Dean, Jimmy Dean* (Altman) (as Stella Mae)

1983   *Two of a Kind* (Herzfeld) (as Furniture Man's Wife)

1986   *Johnny Bull* (Weill—for TV) (as Katrine Kovacs); *The Morning After* (Lumet) (as woman on Mateo Street)

1987   *Summer Heat* (Gleason) (as Ruth); *Murder Ordained* (Mike Robe—for TV) (as Bobbi Bank)

1988   *Arthur 2: On the Rocks* (Yorkin) (as Mrs. Canby)

1989   *Signs of Life* (Coles) (as Mary Beth); *High Stakes (Melanie Rose)* (Kollek) (as Jill); *Roe vs. Wade* (Hoblit—for TV) (as Jessie); *No Place Like Home (Homeless)* (Grant—for TV) (as Bonnie Cooper)

1990   *Misery* (Rob Reiner) (as Annie Wilkes); *Men Don't Leave* (Brickman) (as Lisa Coleman); *Dick Tracy* (Beatty) (as Mrs. Green); *White Palace* (Mandoki) (as Rosemary Powers)

1991   *At Play in the Fields of the Lord* (Babenco) (as Hazel Quarrier); *Fried Green Tomatoes* (Avnet) (as Evelyn); *The Road to Mecca* (Fugard and Goldsmid) (as Elsa Barlow)

1992   *Shadows and Fog* (Woody Allen) (as prostitute); *Prelude to a Kiss* (Rene) (as Leah Blier); *Used People* (Kidron) (as Bibby)

1993   *Hostages* (Wheatley—for TV) (as Peggy Say); *A Home of Our Own* (Bill) (as Frances Lacey)

1994   *North* (Rob Reiner) (as Alaskan Mom); *Curse of the Starving Class* (McClary) (as Ella)

1995   *Dolores Claiborne* (Hackford) (title role); *Angus* (Johnson) (as Meg)

1996   *Diabolique* (Chechik) (as the detective); *The Late Shift* (Betty Thomas—for TV) (as Helen Kushnick); *The War at Home*

Publications

By BATES: articles—

Interview with Sonia Taitz, in *New York Times*, 21 August 1988.

"I Was Never an Ingenue," interview with David Sacks, in *New York Times*, 22 January 1991.

Interview with Nikki Finke, in *New York Newsday* (Melville, New York), 28 March 1991.

Interview with Michael Lassell and Timothy Greenfield-Sanders, in *Interview* (New York), August 1991.

On BATES: articles—

Farrell, Mary, and Craig Thomashoff, "Wallowing in *Misery*, Kathy Bates Bludgeons Her Way to Stardom," in *People Weekly* (New York), 24 December 1990.

Current Biography 1991, New York, 1991.

Ferguson, K., "Kathy Bates: The Unlikely Star," in *Film Monthly* (Berkhamsted, England), June 1992.

Gelman-Waxner, Libby, "She Ain't Heavy," in *Premiere* (New York), July 1995.

*   *   *

Kathy Bates is a fine actress with a natural, straightforward style, who for years had impressed discerning viewers and critics with her stage work. But despite this recognition, she failed to break through the boundaries of regional and New York-based theater into the mainstream of the motion picture industry. Indeed, between 1979 and 1987 she originated roles in three hit stage plays: *Crimes of the Heart*, *'night, Mother*, and *Frankie and Johnny in the Clair de Lune*—the latter a part written especially for her. Yet when it came time to cast each property for the big screen, Bates was replaced by, respectively, Diane Keaton, Sissy Spacek, and Michelle Pfeiffer. The reasons were twofold: Not only was Bates an unknown celluloid commodity, but at 5' 4" with a square build she lacked the inborn glamour of standard Hollywood leading ladies. In the late 1980s, Bates offered an explanation for Hollywood's hesitation to cast her when she declared, "I do lose roles because I'm not slender and glamorous."

When not appearing on stage, Bates earned a living in guest spots on prime-time television series and made-for-television films. She even had a regular role in the popular daytime soap opera *All My Children*. Feature film roles were infrequent and, for the most part, forgettable. Bates was past her 40th birthday when Rob Reiner became the first Hollywood director to recognize her screen power. He cast her in what was to be an Academy Award-winning performance in Stephen King's *Misery*, playing Annie Wilkes, the "Number One Fan" of a famous romance novelist (James Caan), whom she nurses after he is injured in a car accident. Annie is significantly psychotic, and the bedridden writer soon becomes her prisoner. Bates's bravura performance is nothing short of extraordinary. She unveils an astonishingly wide range of emotions as she befriends and then suddenly taunts her captive.

This breakthrough performance was proof that Bates could be a dynamo in character roles. *Misery*, however, was not her first interesting screen role. In the little-seen *The Road to Mecca*, based on a play by Athol Fugard, she was cast as a Capetown, South Africa, teacher—a part she earlier had played on the stage, but which was not considered significant enough for her to have lost it to a more well-known performer.

The year following the release of *Misery*, Bates created the pivotal role of Evelyn in *Fried Green Tomatoes*, the screen version of Fannie Flagg's offbeat novel. Bates plays a repressed Southern housewife who meets an elderly but spirited woman (Jessica Tandy) who resides in a nursing home. The old woman's intricate yarns of people and events of the 1920s have a decided influence on Evelyn's own lifestyle. Bates's power-packed portrayal of Evelyn works in tandem with Tandy's more delicate but equally forthright performance. The vigor of the pair (who appeared together one more time in *Used People*) represents a collaboration of the best of two generations of actresses.

Two other pivotal Bates performances came in *A Home of Our Own*, in which she is cast as a spirited single mother who settles with her children in a small Idaho town; and especially *Dolores Claiborne*, also based on a Stephen King story and her best role since *Misery*. In *Dolores Claiborne*, she offers an award-caliber tour de force as the title character, a Down East Maine woman accused of killing her boss—and who years earlier may have done in her abusive husband—and who is reunited with her long-estranged daughter (Jennifer Jason

Kathy Bates (left) with Jessica Tandy in *Fried Green Tomatoes*

Leigh). Here, Bates and Leigh, cast as characters who share a deeply complex and involved personal history, play opposite each other just as impressively as Bates and Tandy had in *Fried Green Tomatoes*.

Character actresses traditionally have benefited from age in the film industry. In middle age, Kathy Bates finally and deservedly was able to attain stardom as a reliable and occasionally riveting motion picture character performer. Her success is proof that there is room in Hollywood for both the slender "glamour girl" and the commanding character actress.

—Audrey E. Kupferberg

BAXTER, Anne

Nationality: American. **Born:** Michigan City, Indiana, 7 May 1923. **Education:** Attended Theodora Irvine's School of Theatre, 1934-36; Lenox School, 1937-38; Brearly School, 1938-39; studied acting with Maria Ouspenskaya, 1936-40. **Family:** Married 1) the actor John Hodiak, 1946 (divorced 1953), daughter: Katrina; 2) Randolph Galt, 1960 (divorced 1970), daughters: Melissa Ann and Maginel; 3) David Klee, 1977 (died 1977). **Career:** 1936—Broadway debut in *Seen but Not Heard*; 1940—film debut in *20 Mule Team*; 1957—TV debut as guest star on *General Electric Theater*; appeared in numerous TV productions over remainder of life; 1961—moved with husband to cattle station in the Australian outback where she lived for several years; 1969-70—in TV series *Marcus Welby*; 1971—return to Broadway in *Applause*, musical version of *All about Eve*, taking over role of Margo Channing from Lauren Bacall; 1976—in TV miniseries *The Moneychangers*, and *East of Eden*, 1982; 1982—final stage appearance as Queen Gertrude in *Hamlet*, American Shakespeare Theatre, Stratford, Connecticut; 1983-85—in TV series *Hotel*. **Awards:** Best Supporting Actress Academy Award, for *The Razor's Edge*, 1946. **Died:** Of stroke, in New York City, 12 December 1985.

Films as Actress:

1940 *20 Mule Team* (Thorpe) (as Jean Johnson); *The Great Profile* (Walter Lang) (as Mary Maxwell)

1941 *Charley's Aunt* (*Charley's American Aunt*) (Mayo) (as Amy Spettigue); *Swamp Water* (*The Man Who Came Back*) (Renoir) (as Julie)

1942 **The Magnificent Ambersons** (Welles) (as Lucy Morgan); *The Pied Piper* (Pichel) (as Nicole Rougeron)

1943 *Crash Dive* (Mayo) (as Jean Hewlett); *Five Graves to Cairo* (Wilder) (as Mouche); *The North Star* (*Armored Attack*) (Milestone) (as Marina)

1944 *The Eve of St. Mark* (Stahl) (as Janet Feller); *Guest in the House* (Brahm) (as Evelyn Heath); *The Sullivans* (*The Fighting Sullivans*) (Lloyd Bacon) (as Katherine Mary); *Sunday Dinner for a Soldier* (Lloyd Bacon) (as Tessa Osborne); *The Purple Heart* (Milestone) (as voice)

1945 *A Royal Scandal* (*Czarina*) (Preminger) (as Countess Anna Jaschikoff)

1946 *Smoky* (Louis King) (as Julie Richards); *Angel on My Shoulder* (Mayo) (as Barbara Foster); *The Razor's Edge* (Edmund Goulding) (as Sophie MacDonald)

1947 *Mother Wore Tights* (Walter Lang) (as narrator); *Blaze of Noon* (Farrow) (as Lucille Stewart)

1948 *Homecoming* (LeRoy) (as Penny Johnson); *The Luck of the Irish* (Koster) (as Nora); *The Walls of Jericho* (Stahl) (as Julia Norman); *Yellow Sky* (Wellman) (as Mike)

1949 *You're My Everything* (Walter Lang) (as Hannah Adams)

1950 *A Ticket to Tomahawk* (Sale) (as Kit Dodge Jr.); **All about Eve** (Joseph L. Mankiewicz) (as Eve Harrington)

1951 *Follow the Sun* (Lanfield) (as Valerie Hogan)

1952 *Screen Snapshots No. 206*; *My Wife's Best Friend* (Sale) (as Virginia Mason); "The Last Leaf" ep. of *O. Henry's Full House* (*Full House*) (Negulesco) (as Joanna); *The Outcasts of Poker Flat* (Joseph M. Newman) (as Cal)

1953 *I Confess* (Hitchcock) (as Ruth Grandfort); *The Blue Gardenia* (Fritz Lang) (as Norah Larkin)

1954 *Carnival Story* (Neumann) (as Willie)

1955 *Bedevilled* (Leisen) (as Monica Johnson); *One Desire* (Jerry Hopper) (as Tacey Cromwell); *The Spoilers* (Hibbs) (as Cherry Malotte)

1956 *The Come-On* (Birdwell) (as Rita Kendrick); *The Ten Commandments* (Cecil B. DeMille) (as Princess Nefretiri); *Three Violent People* (Maté) (as Lorna Hunter Saunders)

1958 *Chase a Crooked Shadow* (Anderson) (as Kimberley)

1960 *Cimarron* (Anthony Mann) (as Dixie)

1961 *Season of Passion* (*Summer of the 17th Doll*) (Norman) (as Olive)

1962 *Mix Me a Person* (Norman) (as Dr. Anne Dyson); *Walk on the Wild Side* (Dmytryk) (as Teresina Vidarverri)

1965 *The Family Jewels* (Jerry Lewis) (cameo)

1966 *Frauen, die durch die Hölle gehen* (*The Tall Women*; *Donna alla frontiera*; *Sette donne per una strage*) (Grooper or Zehetgruber, Parolini, and Pink) (as Mary Ann)

1967 *The Busy Body* (Castle) (as Margo Foster); *Stranger on the Run* (Siegel—for TV) (as Valvera Johnson)

1968 *Companions in Nightmare* (Norman Lloyd—for TV) (as Carlotta Mauridge)

1969 *Marcus Welby, M.D.* (Rich—for TV) (as Myra Sherwood)

1970 *The Challengers* (Martinson—for TV, produced in 1968) (as Stephanie York); *Ritual of Evil* (Day—for TV) (as Jolene Wiley)

1971 *Fools' Parade* (*Dynamite Man from Glory Jail*) (McLaglen) (as Cleo); *If Tomorrow Comes* (McCowan—for TV) (as Miss Cramer); *The Late Liz* (Dick Ross) (as Liz Addams Hatch)

1972 *Lapin 360* (Lewis—unreleased); *The Catcher* (Miner—for TV) (as Kate)

1973 *Lisa, Bright and Dark* (Swarc—for TV) (as Margaret Schilling)

1978 *Little Mo* (Webb—for TV) (as Jess Connolly)

1979 *Nero Wolfe* (Gilroy—for TV) (as Rachel Bruner)

1980 *Jane Austen in Manhattan* (Ivory) (as Liliana Zorska)

1983 *The Architecture of Frank Lloyd Wright* (Grigor—doc) (as narrator)

1984 *Sherlock Holmes and the Masks of Death* (*Masks of Death*) (Roy Ward Baker—for TV)

Publications

By BAXTER: book—

Intermission: A True Story, New York, 1976.

On BAXTER: books—

Parish, James Robert, *The Fox Girls*, New Rochelle, New York, 1971.
Fowler, Karin J., *Anne Baxter: A Bio-Bibliography*, New York, 1991.

On BAXTER: articles—

"All about Anne Baxter," in *Photoplay* (New York), September 1943.
Graham, Sheila, "As You Were, Annie," in *Photoplay* (New York), April 1953.
Pollock, L., "Between Heaven and H . . .," in *Photoplay* (New York), April and May 1957.
Current Biography 1972, New York, 1972.
Bawden, J., "Anne Baxter," in *Films in Review* (New York), October 1977.
Ciné Revue (Paris), 19 March 1981.
Photoplay (London), November 1981 and November 1984.
Obituary in *New York Times*, 13 December 1985.
Obituary in *Variety* (New York), 18 December 1985.

*   *   *

Given the creative legacy of Anne Baxter's family—she was Frank Lloyd Wright's granddaughter—her artistic accomplishments were scripted from childhood. She was from the age of ten determined to become an actress after seeing a stage production starring Helen Hayes in New York; her aspirations were encouraged by her parents and grandfather.

There was an air of duplicity about Baxter that she and her directors used to diverse effect throughout her career. Her steely-eyed, intelligent beauty was composed of elements disparate enough to hint at complex or contradictory aspects of a character. Few of Baxter's roles were straightforward interpretations; her characters, more often than not, play *other* characters. The masks that Baxter's women wear may depict treachery (*All about Eve*), mental unbalance (*Guest in the*

Anne Baxter with George Sanders in *All about Eve*

House), or a rugged, no nonsense exterior that disguises a vulnerable, tentative personality (*Yellow Sky*). Many of Hollywood's best directors found Baxter a surprisingly intense performer and she did first-rate work for Hitchcock, Welles, Wellman, Edmund Goulding, Negulesco, Milestone, and Joseph L. Mankiewicz.

Without establishing a dominant screen persona, she made several good films from the time she was only a teenager. At the age of 16 she tested for the title role in Hitchcock's *Rebecca*, but her youth prevented her from being cast; she had to settle for an ingenue part in *20 Mule Team*. From the beginning, though, her assignments and her performances were varied and interesting; she was earnest in *The Great Profile*, earthy in *Swamp Water*, and a coquette in *Charley's Aunt*. *The Magnificent Ambersons* gave her the best role of her early career and her performance is subtle and thoughtfully shaded. She won an Academy Award for her tragic dipsomaniac in *The Razor's Edge* and was again nominated for her Eve Harrington in *All about Eve*, which she played, as *The New York Times* put it, with "an icy calm."

Her career peaked sooner than seems just. While she continued to give good, sometimes inspired performances in *I Confess*, *O. Henry's Full House* (in Negulesco's "The Last Leaf" episode), *The Blue Gardenia*, and *The Ten Commandments*, eventually she found herself

slogging through forgettable programmers. *Walk on the Wild Side* and *Fools' Parade* gave her a few shining moments, but she soon had to turn to television and the stage for sustenance. In 1971, she took over Lauren Bacall's role of Margo Channing in *Applause*, a stage musical based on *All about Eve*, and found herself in the intriguing position of playing the established star at odds with the young upstart, Eve, whom Baxter herself had played so memorably on film.

Though she never achieved the status of superstar, she did achieve longevity, diversity, and popularity throughout a very stable career. In her final role, Baxter portrayed Victoria Cabot on the television series *Hotel* from 1983 until her death, caused by a massive stroke in 1985.

—Frank Thompson, updated by Kelly Otter

BAYE, Nathalie

Nationality: French. **Born:** Mainneville, 6 July 1948. **Education:** Trained as a dancer; studied acting in Cours (René) Simon; attended

Paris Conservatory of Dramatic Art, graduated 1972. **Family:** One child. **Career:** At 17, studied classical and modern dance in New York, and toured with dance company; returned to France for vacation, decided to stay and study acting; 1971—film debut in *Faustine and the Beautiful Summer*; 1974—in Pirandello's *Liolla* at Théâtre de la Commune; also TV work; 1978-79—stage appearance in *Three Sisters*, directed by Lucian Pintillé. **Awards:** Best Supporting Actress César Award, for *Sauve qui peut*, 1980; Best Supporting Actress César Award, for *Une Étrange Affaire*, 1981; Best Actress César Award, for *La Balance*, 1982. **Agent:** Artmédia, 10 av Georges V, Paris 75008, France.

Films as Actress:

1971	*Faustine et le belété* (*Faustine and the Beautiful Summer*) (Companeez) (as Giselle)
1972	*Two People* (Wise) (bit role)
1973	*La Nuit américaine* (*Day for Night*) (Truffaut) (as Joëlle)
1974	*La Gueule ouverte* (*The Mouth Agape*) (Pialat); *Un Jour de fête* (Sisser); *La Gifle* (*The Slap*) (Pinoteau) (as Christine)
1975	*Le Voyage des noces* (*Honeymoons*) (Trintignant); *La Jalousie* (Trintignant)
1976	*Mado* (Sautet) (as Catherine); *Le Plein de super* (*Fill It Up, Premium!*) (Cavalier); *L'ultima donna* (*The Last Woman*) (Ferreri); *La Communion solonnelle* (Féret)
1977	*L'Homme qui aimait les femmes* (*The Man Who Loved Women*) (Truffaut) (as Martine Desdoits); *Monsieur Papa* (Monnier) (as Janine)
1978	*La Chambre verte* (*The Green Room*) (Truffaut) (as Cecilia Mandel); *Mon Premier Amour* (*My First Love*) (Chouraqui) (as Fabienne); *La Mémoire courte* (*Short Memory*) (de Gregorio)
1979	*Je vais craquer* (*The Rat Race*) (Leterrier)
1980	*Sauve qui peut* (*La Vie; Slow Motion; Every Man for Himself*) (Godard) (as Denise Rimbaud); *Une Semaine de vacances* (*A Week's Vacation*) (Tavernier) (as Laurence); *La Provinciale* (*The Girl from Lorraine*) (Goretta) (as Christine)
1981	*Beau-Père* (Blier) (as Charlotte); *Une Étrange Affaire* (Granier-Deferre); *L'Ombre rouge* (Comolli); *Le Retour de Martin Guerre* (*The Return of Martin Guerre*) (Vigne) (as Bertrande de Roi)
1982	*La Balance* (*The Nark*) (Swaim) (as Nicole); *J'ai épousé une ombre* (*I Married a Dead Man; I Married a Shadow*) (Robin Davis) (as Hélène/Patricia)
1984	*Rive droit, rive gauche* (*Right Bank, Left Bank*) (Labro) (as Sacha Vernakis); *Madame Sourdis* (Huppert)
1985	*Notre histoire* (*Our Story; Separate Rooms*) (Blier) (as Donatienne Pouget/Marie-Therese Chatelard/Genevieve Avranche); *Le Neveu de Beethoven* (*Beethoven's Nephew*) (Morrissey) (as Leonore); *Lune di miel* (*Honeymoon*) (Jamain) (as Cecile Carline); *Détective* (Godard) (as Françoise Chenal)
1987	*En Toute Innocence* (Jessua) (as Catherine)
1988	*Guerre Lasse* (Enrico)
1989	*Gioco al massacro* (Damiani)
1990	*The Man Inside* (Roth) (as Christine); *Un Weekend sur deux* (*Every Other Weekend*) (Garcia) (as Camille Valmont); *La Baule-les-pins* (*C'est la vie*) (Kurys) (as Lena)
1992	*Mensonge* (*Lie*) (François Margolin) (as Emma)
1993	*And the Band Played On* (Spottiswoode—for TV)
1994	*La Machine* (*The Machine*) (Dupeyron) (as Marie)
1995	*François Truffaut: Portraits Voles* (*François Truffaut: Stolen Portraits*) (Toubiana and Pascal—doc)
1996	*Enfants de salaud* (Tonie Marshall) (as Sophie)

Publications

By BAYE: articles—

"Nathalie Baye: Portrait," in *Cinéma Français* (Paris), no. 18, 1977.
Interviews in *Cinéma Français* (Paris), June and July 1980.
Ciné Revue (Paris), 6 May 1982, 17 February 1983, and 8 March 1984.
Interview with Gaston Haustrate, in *Cinéma* (Paris), June 1982.
Interview with F. Mauro, in *Cahiers du Cinéma* (Paris), May 1985.

On BAYE: articles—

Films and Filming (London), December 1981.
Truffaut, François, in *Ciné Revue* (Paris), 3 March 1983.

*   *   *

"I could leave a man for a film, but never a film for a man." The comment is that of Joëlle, the continuity girl played by Nathalie Baye in Truffaut's *La Nuit américaine*, and more than 20 years later it is still one of the actress's best-remembered lines. Though such total devotion to the movies may not be true of Baye herself—"If I only lived for the cinema, I don't think I would be able to act," she once observed—it fairly sums up a strong aspect of her on-screen persona: level-headed, professional, dedicated to the task in hand. It is hard to imagine her staging a tantrum and storming off the set.

Though *La Nuit américaine* was one of Baye's first films, her inexperience was hardly evident. The conviction with which she inhabited her role led some people—including, apparently, Billy Wilder—to imagine she really was Truffaut's continuity girl. (Irritated at the time, Baye later realized what an involuntary compliment she had been paid.) Truffaut, whom she found sympathetic and supportive ("He's not just in love with the movies, he loves actors"), subsequently used her in two more films—but neither the episodic *L'Homme qui aimait les femmes* nor the gloom of *La Chambre verte* offered much scope to her growing talent.

It was Bertrand Tavernier who established her on the international scene. As the Lyonnaise schoolteacher in *Une Semaine de vacances*, troubled by the urge to step back and take stock of her too well-ordered existence, Baye conveyed a sense of lived emotion in a performance subtly detailed without ever seeming self-conscious. Tavernier paid tribute to her "quivering inwardness . . . she confronts a scene head-on, with neither fear nor tricks." She herself speaks of "le déclic essentiel," the moment when identification with a part clicks into place, no longer studied but felt.

She was now ranked among the "nouvelle actrices" of French cinema, along with Isabelle Huppert, Isabelle Adjani and Miou-Miou—players for whom personal considerations of looks or prestige were subordinated to the demands of the role. Baye in any case has never aspired to glamour, or even to conventional notions of prettiness. She can look plain, at times almost ugly, then at once—as a shaft of thought or passion lights up the eyes—unexpectedly beautiful. She moves with an unobtrusive grace, her dancer's training standing her in good stead. "Her every gesture is musical," Tavernier noted.

Such understated qualities can invite typecasting in dutiful or victimized roles—as in undemanding material such as Goretta's *La Provinciale*—and Baye in turn has sometimes tended to fall back on certain well-tried mannerisms: the tremulous smile, the hurt look in the eyes. To counter these tendencies she has consistently aimed to widen her range, favoring directors who will cast her against type and "make me do things that weren't immediately obvious for me."

Two films of the early 1980s helped her shatter the nice-girl image. In Daniel Vigne's period drama *Le Retour de Martin Guerre*, she brought an unleashed sensuality to her scenes with Gérard Depardieu—evidently indifferent, in the joy of her rekindled passion, as to whether he is or is not her long-lost husband. Even more against type was her hooker in *La Balance*, Bob Swaim's slick *policier*, crude and aggressive in her street-life, direct and tender in her devotion to her boyfriend as the trap closes around them both. Baye's performance won her first César as Best Actress.

Her talent for comedy has perhaps been underused. As the enigmatic focus of Bertrand Blier's surreal farce *Notre histoire*, she deftly switched personae under the bemused gaze of Alain Delon. She also emerged with credit from the labyrinthine comedy of Godard's *Détective*, playing the apex of an erotic triangle with Claude Brasseur and her offscreen lover at that period, the pop-singer Johnny Hallyday. Godard remains one of her favorite directors. "There's often stuff in his films that irritates me, but he saw things in me that nobody had seen before. He knew how to look at me. And it's invaluable for an actor to feel that you're being really looked at."

Between 1985 and 1987 Baye made no films, concentrating instead—with considerable success—on the theater. On her return to the cinema her career seemed for a time to hang fire, but picked up again with two films directed by women: *La Baule-les-pins*, the third in Diane Kurys's autobiographical trilogy, and Nicole Garcia's *Un Weekend sur deux*. For Kurys, as the woman juggling the demands of daughters, a collapsing marriage, and her own love life, Baye presented a more sophisticated figure than her predecessors in the two previous films—poised and determined, though still vulnerable.

If for Kurys she was playing close to her known strengths, Garcia offered her a challenging contrast: the role of a failed actress chaotically prey to her own emotions, denied custody of her children, who on an impulse kidnaps them for a wild flight across country. Baye's Camille, with her abrupt, nervy reactions and slightly off-focus gaze, suggested a woman sliding helplessly out of touch with reality. It was a brave, risky performance—but then, risks have always brought out the best in Nathalie Baye.

—Philip Kemp

BEATTY, Warren

Nationality: American. **Born:** Warren Beaty in Richmond, Virginia, 30 March 1938; brother of the actress Shirley MacLaine. **Education:** Attended Northwestern University, Evanston, Illinois; studied drama at Stella Adler Acting School. **Family:** Married the actress Annette Bening, 1992, two children. **Career:** 1959-60—role in TV series *The Many Loves of Dobie Gillis*; abortive contract with MGM; 1960-61—lead role in *Compulsion* in stock, and on Broadway in William Inge's *A Loss of Roses*; 1961—film debut in Elia Kazan's *Splendor in the Grass*; 1967—produced first film, *Bonnie and Clyde*; 1975—first scriptwriting effort with *Shampoo*, co-scripted with Robert Towne; 1978—first directorial effort with *Heaven Can Wait*, co-directed with Buck Henry; 1981—wrote, produced, directed, and acted in award-winning film *Reds*. **Awards:** Oscar for Best Director, D. W. Griffith Award for Best Director, and Directors Guild of America Award, for *Reds*, 1981. **Address:** JRS Productions, 555 Melrose Avenue, Los Angeles, CA 90038, U.S.A.

Films as Actor:

1961   *Splendor in the Grass* (Kazan) (as Bud Stamper); *The Roman Spring of Mrs. Stone* (Quintero) (as Pablo di Leo)
1962   *All Fall Down* (Frankenheimer) (as Berry-Berry Willart)
1964   *Lilith* (Rossen) (as Vincent Bruce)

1965   *Mickey One* (Arthur Penn) (title role)
1966   *Promise Her Anything* (Hiller) (as Harley Rummel); *Kaleido-scope* (Smight) (as Barney Lincoln)
1967   **Bonnie and Clyde** (Arthur Penn) (as Clyde Barrow, + pr)
1969   *The Only Game in Town* (Stevens) (as Joe Grady)
1971   *McCabe and Mrs. Miller* (Altman) (as McCabe); *$* (*Dollars*; *The Heist*) (Richard Brooks) (as Joe Collins)
1973   *Year of the Woman* (Hochman—doc)
1974   *The Parallax View* (Pakula) (as Joseph Frady)
1975   *Shampoo* (Ashby) (as George, + co-pr, co-sc); *The Fortune* (Nichols) (as Nicky)
1987   *Ishtar* (May) (as Lyle Rogers, + pr)
1991   *Bugsy* (Levinson) (title role, + co-pr); *Truth or Dare* (Keshishian—doc) (as himself)
1993   *Taking the Heat* (for TV)
1994   *Love Affair* (Caron) (as Mike Gambril, + pr, co-sc)
1995   *Falling for You* (for TV) (as reporter)

Films as Director:

1978   *Heaven Can Wait* (co-d with Buck Henry, + pr, co-sc, ro as Joe Pendleton)
1981   *Reds* (+ pr, co-sc, ro as John Reed)
1990   *Dick Tracy* (+ pr, title role)

Film as Producer:

1987   *The Pick-up Artist* (Toback)

Publications

By BEATTY: articles—

Interview with Curtis Lee Hanson, in *Cinema* (Beverly Hills), Summer 1967.
"Anything but Passive," interview with Gordon Gow, in *Films and Filming* (London), August 1975.
Interview with Philip Thomas and others, in *Empire* (London), September 1990.
"The Warren Report," interview with Norman Mailer, in *Vanity Fair* (New York), November 1991.
"A Conversation with Warren Beatty," interview with S. Royal, in *American Premiere*, vol. 12, no. 1, 1992.
"A Question of Control," interview with Gavin Smith, in *Film Comment*, January/February 1992.
"Warren Beatty," interview with Bill Zehme, in *Rolling Stone*, 11 June 1992 and 31 May 1990.
"Love Story," interview with Dominick Dunne, in *Vanity Fair* (New York), September 1994.

On BEATTY: books—

Wake, Sandra, and Nicola Hayden, *The Bonnie and Clyde Book*, New York, 1972.
Focus on Bonnie and Clyde, edited by John Cawelti, Englewood Cliffs, New Jersey, 1973.
Munshower, Suzanne, *Warren Beatty: Lovemaker Extraordinary*, London, 1976.
Kercher, John, *Warren Beatty*, London, 1984.
Spada, James, *Shirley and Warren*, New York, 1985.
Thomson, David, *Warren Beatty: A Life and a Story*, London, 1987.
Quirk, Lawrence J., *The Films of Warren Beatty*, New York, 1990.

Warren Beatty in *Dick Tracy*

Parker, John, *Warren Beatty: The Last Great Lover of Hollywood*, London, 1993.

On BEATTY: articles—

Wilmington, Michael, "Warren Beatty: Unlucky Seducer," in *Close-Ups: The Movie Star Book*, edited by Danny Peary, New York, 1978.
Rich, Frank, "Warren Beatty," in *The Movie Star*, edited by Elisabeth Weis, New York, 1981.
Screen International, 13 March and 31 July 1982.
Camy, G., "Warren Beatty, un homme de cinéma des anneés soixante et soixante-dix," in *Jeune Cinéma* (Paris), September 1982.
Current Biography 1988, New York, 1988.
Biskind, Peter, "Warren and Me," in *Premiere* (New York), July 1990.
Biskind, Peter, "Chronicle of a Life Untold," in *Premiere* (New York), January 1992.
Bailey, E., and B. Hirsch, "The Six Million Dollar+ Men," in *Movieline*, July 1992.

*   *   *

Warren Beatty is one of the wealthiest and most respected men in Hollywood. He has been a leading player since his screen debut in 1961, and a combination producer/writer/director since 1975. He is the only person to have been nominated for an Academy Award in four categories—director, actor, producer, and writer—on two occasions (*Heaven Can Wait* and *Reds*). With such multiple credit success, Beatty has served as an inspiration for actors wishing to extend their talents to other aspects of moviemaking.

His older sister Shirley MacLaine was already a star when Beatty arrived in Hollywood. Playwright William Inge, however, discovered Beatty and arranged for him to play opposite Natalie Wood in Elia Kazan's film version of Inge's *Splendor in the Grass*. With his exceptional looks, Beatty made an impressive debut as the son of a wealthy family who is forced to abandon his girlfriend of lower social standing. Fitting into the post-James Dean wounded youth syndrome, he immediately was earmarked for success and given the highly sought-after role of gigolo to Vivien Leigh's fading, middle-aged actress in Tennessee Williams's *The Roman Spring of Mrs. Stone*. His alienated youth period continued with another William Inge story, *All Fall Down*, in which he is a narcissistic pretty boy. In *Lilith*, he plays a psychiatric worker who becomes fixated upon a patient and eventually needs psychiatric help himself. Both performances are studies of brooding instability, and they displayed his ability to convey a mixture of boyish innocence and world-weary cynicism.

Beatty's antihero persona lead him to the part of the troubled nightclub comedian in *Mickey One*, directed by Arthur Penn. The quirks of this character may have been too offbeat, and the film failed at the box office. Beatty reteamed with Penn for the most important role of his career: ruthless, psychotic killer Clyde Barrow in *Bonnie and Clyde*, which was also his first producing venture. The film was a blockbuster, one which had an immense impact on filmmaking styles, not to mention fashion. With its stylized violence, *Bonnie and Clyde* was on the cutting edge of its time. Its success opened up career possibilities for Beatty both in front of and behind the camera. The film made him a millionaire, and from that point onward he chose his projects slowly and with caution—but not always wisely. In *McCabe and Mrs. Miller*, directed by Robert Altman, he played an itinerant gambler who builds a whorehouse for his girlfriend. The moody, rambling Western was considered jumbled and sluggish by many critics and hardly was considered at all by ticket buyers, although, today, its reputation has improved.

As early as 1973, announcements appeared in the press concerning Beatty's development of a project about American leftist writer John Reed, but that film, *Reds*, did not reach screens until 1981. Meanwhile, he co-produced, co-wrote, and starred in 1975's *Shampoo*, a stinging satire on Southern California lifestyles, in which he is a hairstylist who tries to achieve financial security through sexual opportunism. The character also had a blend of the boy/man Beatty seems destined to play again and again. Some understood his hairdresser to be an autobiographical rumination on his own Casanova reputation.

In 1978 Beatty was producer, co-director, co-writer, and star of *Heaven Can Wait*, a successful remodeling of the classic romantic comedy *Here Comes Mr. Jordan*. Popular with the public and lauded by critics, *Heaven Can Wait* was followed by *Reds*, which turned out to be a sprawling romantic epic with political overtones, taking John Reed (Beatty) into communism and through the Russian Revolution, as well as into a relationship with a freethinking woman. *Reds* allowed Beatty an opportunity to create a larger-than-life romantic character, and place that character into a setting of sociological significance—an indication of Beatty's own inclination toward liberal politics.

Then came *Ishtar*. An out-of-control budget and costly delays resulted in Hollywood's worst financial disaster since *Heaven's Gate*. The flat comedy follows two untalented singer-songwriters (Beatty and Dustin Hoffman) into desert intrigue. The film was only a temporary embarrassment for Beatty, who regained box-office success three years later as *Dick Tracy*. By then, Beatty's handsome face had lost some of its allure and he seems too old for the part—his yellow Burberry raincoat has more luster than he does in his role as the crime-fighting comic-strip hero. Beatty is much more effective as real-life gangster Benjamin "Bugsy" Siegel in *Bugsy*. Here is a serious, gritty character role, one which is a maturation of the troubled youths and gangsters he played so well in the 1960s.

Beatty the movie idol has not aged well. At the opening of *Love Affair*, Gary Shandling (playing the lawyer of Beatty's character, football star turned television sports commentator Mike Gambril) comments on how good Gambril looks on television. This bit of script maneuvering seems meant to telegraph the idea to the viewer that, contrary to opinion, Beatty himself remains a hunk. Gambril might be a clone of Beatty, a continent-hopping celebrity who has "been with a lot of women" and whom the paparazzi are eager to photograph. In the course of the story Gambril meets *the* woman, played by Beatty's wife Annette Bening, who will intrigue and then domesticate him—just as Bening did to Beatty in real life.

In *Bugsy* and *Love Affair*, Beatty and Bening trade quips, which are the basis of their attraction. In *Bugsy* the actors work with an intelligent script, while in *Love Affair* the conversation is vapid. Beatty no longer can get by on-screen only with charm and good looks. He is far better off playing character roles, as he did so well in *Bugsy*.

—Doug Tomlinson, updated by Audrey E. Kupferberg

BEERY, Wallace

Nationality: American. **Born:** Kansas City, Missouri, 1 April 1885. **Education:** Kansas City public schools. **Military Service:** 1933—

commissioned a Lt. Commander in U.S. Naval Reserve Aviation Corps. **Family:** Married 1) the actress Gloria Swanson, 1916 (divorced 1918); 2) Rita Gilman, adopted daughter: Carol Ann. **Career:** 1901—worked briefly on railroad and in blacksmith shop; 1902—joined Forepaugh-Sells circus, became "elephant man," in charge of leading elephants; soon in charge of Ringling Bros. circus elephants; 1904—began stage career in chorus of *Babes in Toyland*; 1908—first film appearances as extra in New Rochelle, N.Y., studio; 1910-12—in road shows of musicals; 1913—began acting in Essanay film comedies produced in Chicago; played female roles (e.g., Sweedie) and worked on technical staff; 1915—moved to Essanay studio at Niles, California, near San Francisco; also studio manager and "second-string" director; joined Keystone company; 1925-29—under contract with Paramount; then signed by MGM. **Awards:** Best Actor Academy Award (co-recipient) for *The Champ*, 1931/32; Best Actor, Venice Festival, for *Viva Villa!*, 1934. **Died:** In Beverly Hills, 15 April 1949.

Films as Actor:

(in one-reelers):

1913   *His Athletic Wife*; *Mr. Dippy Dipped*; *A Successful Failure*; *The Usual Way*; *Day by Day*; *Sweet Revenge*; *Hello Trouble*; *Smithy's Grandma's Party*; *At the Old Maid's Ball*

1914   *A Foot of Romance*; *Looking for Trouble*; *One-Two-Three*; *Oh, Doctor*; *Mrs. Manley's Baby*; *A Queer Quarantine*; *Three Little Powders*; *This Is the Life*; *Bargain Hunters*; *The Winner*; *The Ups and Downs*; *Actor Finney's Finish* (Hopper); *The Fable of the Brash Drummer and the Nectarine* (Ade); *Grass Country Goes Dry*; *Curing a Husband*; *The Fable of Napoleon and the Bumpkin* (Ade); *The Prevailing Craze*; *The Fable of the Coming Champion Who Was Delayed* (Ade); *In and Out*; *The Epidemic*; *Sweedie, the Swatter* (title role); *Sweedie and the Lord* (title role); *Topsy-Turvy Sweedie* (title role); *Sweedie and the Double Exposure* (title role); *Sweedie Springs a Surprise* (title role); *Love and Soda* (Hopper); *Sweedie's Skate* (title role); *Sweedie's Clean-Up* (title role); *The Fickleness of Sweedie* (title role); *The Fable of the Business Boy and the Droppers-in*; *Sweedie Learns to Swim* (title role); *She Landed a Big One*; *Rivalry and War*; *The Laundress*; *Sweedie and the Trouble Maker* (title role); *Countess Sweedie* (title role); *Sweedie at the Fair* (title role); *A Maid of War*; *Cheering a Husband*; *Madame Double X*; *Golf Link Champion "Chick" Evans Links with Sweedie* (title role); *The Fable of the Bushleague Lover Who Failed to Qualify* (Ade); *Two Dinky Dramas of a Non-Serious Kind* (Ade—no. 1: "Another Sidetrack," no. 2: "The Fatal Album"); *Sweedie and the Hypnotist* (title role); *Their Cheap Vacation*

1915   *Sweedie Collects for Charity* (title role); *Sweedie and the Sultan's Present* (title role); *Sweedie's Suicide* (title role); *Sweedie and Her Dog* (title role); *Two Hearts that Beat as Ten*; *The New Teacher*; *Sweedie Goes to College* (Baker) (title role); *The Victor*; *A Pound for a Pound*; *Ain't It the Truth*; *Sweedie's Hopeless Love* (title role); *Father's New Maid*; *Love and Trouble*; *Sweedie Learns to Ride* (title role); *The Bouquet*; *Done in Wax*; *Sweedie in Vaudeville* (title role); *Sweedie's Hero* (title role); *Sweedie's Finish* (title role); *The Broken Pledge*; *The Slim Princess* (Cole—4 reels); *Education*; *The Fable of the Roystering Blades* (Baker)

(in two-reel films):

1916   *A Dash of Courage* (Chase)
1917   *Maggie's First False Step* (Griffith); *Teddy at the Throttle*
       (Badger); *Cactus Nell* (Fishback); *A Clever Dummy*
       (Raymaker); *That Night* (Cline); *Patria* (Jaccard—serial in
       15 chapters)

(in feature-length films):

1917   *The Little American* (DeMille)
1918   *Johanna Enlists* (Taylor)
1919   *The Love Burglar* (Cruze); *The Unpardonable Sin* (Neilan);
       Life Life (Tourneur); *Soldiers of Fortune* (Dwan) (as
       Mendoza); *Victory* (Tourneur) (as Schomberg); *Behind the
       Door* (Willat) (as Lt. Brandt)
1920   *The Virgin of Stamboul* (Browning) (as Achmed Hamid); *The
       Mollycoddle* (Fleming) (as Henry Von Holkar); *The Last of
       the Mohicans* (Tourneur) (as Magua); *The Roundup*
       (Melford) (as Buck McKee); *Eight-Thirteen* (Sidney) (as
       Major Parbury/Ribiera)
1921   *A Tale of Two Worlds* (Lloyd) (as Ling Jo); *The Golden Snare*
       (Hartford) (as Bram Johnson); **The Four Horsemen of the
       Apocalypse** (Ingram) (as Lt.-Col. Von Richthoffen); *The
       Last Trail* (Flynn) (as William Kirk); *The Rookie's Return*
       (Nelson) (as Francois Dupont)
1922   *Wild Honey* (Ruggles) (as "Buck" Roper); *Hurricane's Girl*
       (Holubar) (as Chris Borg); *I Am the Law* (Carewe) (as Fu
       Chang); *The Rosary* (Storm) (as Kenwood Wright); *The Man
       from Hell's River* (Cummings) (as Gaspard); *Trouble* (Aus-
       tin) (as Ed Lee); *Only a Shop Girl* (LeSaint) (as Jim Brennan);
       Robin Hood (Dwan) (as King Richard the Lion-Hearted);
       The Sagebrush Trail (Thornby) (as José Fagaro)
1923   *Bavu* (Paton) (as Felix Bavu); *The Drums of Jeopardy* (Dillon)
       (as Gregor Karlov); *The Flame of Life* (Henley) (as Don
       Lowrie); *Stormswept* (Thornby) (as William McCabe); *Three
       Ages* (Keaton and Cline) (as The Villain); *White Tiger* (Brown-
       ing) (as Count Donelli/Hawkes); *Ashes of Vengeance* (Lloyd)
       (as Duc de Tours); *Drifting* (Browning) (as Jules Repin); *The
       Spanish Dancer* (Brecon) (as King Philip IV); *The Eternal
       Struggle* (Barker) (as Barode Dukane); *King Richard the
       Lion-Hearted* (Withey) (title role)
1924   *Unseen Hands* (Jaccard) (as Jean Scholast); *Another Man's
       Wife* (Mitchell) (as Capt. Wolf); *The Sea Hawk* (Lloyd) (as
       Jasper Leigh); *Dynamite Smith* (Ralph Ince) (as "Slugger"
       Rourke); *The Signal Tower* (Brown) (as Joe Standish); *Ma-
       donna of the Streets* (Carewe) (as Bill Smythe); *The Red Lily*
       (Niblo) (as Bobo); *So Big* (Brabin) (as Klass Poole)
1925   *Coming Through* (Sutherland) (as Joe Lawler); *The Devil's
       Cargo* (Fleming) (as Ben); *In the Name of Love* (Higgin) (as
       M. Glavis); *Let Women Alone* (Powell) (as Cap Bullwinkle);
       The Lost World (Hoyt) (as Prof. Challenger); *The Great
       Divide* (Barker) (as Dutch); *Adventure* (Fleming) (as Mor-
       gan); *The Pony Express* (Cruze) (as "Rhode Island" Red);
       Rugged Water (Willat) (as Capt. Bartlett)
1926   *The Wanderer* (Walsh) (as Pharis); *Behind the Front*
       (Sutherland) (as Riff Swanson); *Volcano* (Howard) (as
       Quembo); *We're in the Navy Now* (Sutherland) (as Knockout
       Hansen); *Old Ironsides* (Cruze) (as Bos'n)
1927   *Casey at the Bat* (Brice) (as Casey); *Fireman, Save My Child*
       (Sutherland) (as Elmer); *Now We're in the Air* (Strayer) (as
       Wally)
1928   *Wife Savers* (Cedar) (as Louis Hozenozzle); *Partners in Crime*
       (Strayer) (as Mike Doolan); *The Big Killing* (Jones) (as Pow-
       der-Horn Pete); *Beggars of Life* (Wellman) (as Oklahoma Red)

1929   *Chinatown Nights* (Wellman) (as Chuck Riley); *The River of
       Romance* (Wallace) (as Gen. Orlando Jackson); *Stairs of
       Sand* (Brower) (as Guard Larey)
1930   *The Big House* (Hill) (as Butch); *Billy the Kid* (Vidor) (as
       Garrett); *A Lady's Morals* (Franklin) (as P. T. Barnum); *Min
       and Bill* (Hill) (as Bill); *Way for a Sailor* (Wood) (as Tripod)
1931   *The Stolen Jools* (*The Lost Jools*; *The Slippery Pearls*)
       (Heerman and McGann—short); *The Secret Six* (Hill) (as
       Louis Scorpio); *The Champ* (Vidor) (as Andy Purcell); *Hell
       Divers* (Hill) (as Windy)
1932   *Grand Hotel* (Goulding) (as Preysing); *Flesh* (Ford) (as Polikai)
1933   *Tugboat Annie* (LeRoy) (as Terry Brennan); *Dinner at Eight*
       (Cukor) (as Dan Packard); *The Bowery* (Walsh) (as Chuck
       Connors)
1934   *Viva Villa!* (Conway) (as Pancho Villa); *Treasure Island*
       (Fleming) (as Long John Silver); *The Mighty Barnum* (Walter
       Lang) (as P. T. Barnum)
1935   *West Point of the Air* (Rosson) (as Big Mike); *China Seas* (Garnett)
       (as Jamesay MacArdle); *O'Shaughnessy's Boy* (Boleslawsky)
       (as Windy); *Ah, Wilderness!* (Brown) (as Sid Miller)
1936   *A Message to Garcia* (Marshall) (as Sgt. Dory); *Old Hutch*
       (Ruben) (as Hutch)
1937   *Good Old Soak* (Ruben) (as Clem Holly); *Slave Ship* (Garnett)
       (as Jack Thompson)
1938   *The Bad Man of Brimstone* (Ruben) (as Trigger Bill); *Port of
       Seven Seas* (Whale) (as Cesar); *Stablemates* (Wood) (as
       Tom Terry)
1939   *Stand Up and Fight* (Van Dyke) (as Capt. Starkey); *Sergeant
       Madden* (Sternberg) (as Shawn Madden); *Thunder Afloat*
       (Seitz) (as John Thorson)
1940   *The Man from Dakota* (*Arouse and Beware*) (Fenton) (as Sgt.
       Barstow); *20-Mule Team* (Thorpe) (as Bill Bragg); *Wyo-
       ming* (*Bad Man of Wyoming*) (Thorpe) (as Reb Harkness)
1941   *The Bad Man* (*Two Gun Cupid*) (Thorpe) (as Lopez); *Bar-
       nacle Bill* (Thorpe) (as Bill Johansen)
1942   *The Bugle Sounds* (Simon) (as Hap Doan); *Jackass Mail*
       (Macleod) (as Marmaduke "Just" Baggott)
1943   *Salute to the Marines* (Simon) (as Sgt. Maj. William Bailey)
1944   *Rationing* (Goldbeck) (as Ben Barton); *Barbary Coast Gent*
       (Del Ruth) (as Honest Plush Brannon)
1945   *This Man's Navy* (Wellman) (as Ned Trumpett)
1946   *Bad Bascomb* (Simon) (as Zeb Bascomb)
1947   *The Mighty McGurk* (Waters) (as "Slag" Morgan)
1948   *Alias a Gentleman* (Beaumont) (as Jim Breedin); *A Date with
       Judy* (Thorpe) (as Melvin R. Foster)
1949   *Big Jack* (Thorpe) (as Big Jack Horner)

Films as director of and principal actor in one-reelers:

1916   *The Janitor* (+ sc); *Just a Few Little Things* (+ sc); *The Janitor's
       Vacation* (+ sc); *A Capable Lady Cook* (+ pr); *Timothy Dobbs,
       That's Me* (+ pr—series of 10 one-reel films); *Sweedie and the
       Janitor* (+ sc); *Bombs and Banknotes* (+ pr)
1918   *The Bathhouse Scandal* (+ pr)
1919   *Only a Janitor* (+ pr); *A Beach Nut* (+ sc)

Publications

By BEERY: articles—

"Her," in *Motion Picture Magazine* (New York), April 1931.
"My Life until Now," as told to Eric Ergenbright, in *The New Movie
Magazine*, April 1934.

Wallace Beery in *The Big House*

On BEERY: book—

Moore, Dick, *Twinkle, Twinkle, Little Star*, New York, 1984.

On BEERY: articles—

Dressler, Marie, "Him," in *Motion Picture Magazine* (New York), April 1931.
Johnston, A., "Wallace Beery," in *New Yorker*, 9 November 1935.
Article in *Films in Review* (New York), June/July and August/September 1973.
Shipman, David, in *The Great Movie Stars: The Golden Years*, revised edition, London, 1979.
Parish, James, and Gregory Mank, in *The Hollywood Reliables*, Westport, Connecticut, 1980.

* * *

One of the unlikeliest movie stars in Hollywood history, Wallace Beery possessed a last name that seemed to personify his on-screen persona of a blustery, rubber-faced, ham-fisted palooka. Although his style of eye-rolling, eyebrow-contorting histrionics died with burlesque, Beery succeeded in creating a rogues gallery of memorable performances while maintaining a popularity with moviegoers that lasted 25 years.

Oddly enough, Beery entered motion pictures in drag, playing a Swedish maid named Sweedie in a series of comedies. (His private life was just as incongruous, with a brief marriage to starlet Gloria Swanson.) He quickly gravitated towards roles as a "heavy," playing a marvelously malevolent Magua in *The Last of the Mohicans*, and appearing as Henry Van Holkar, Douglas Fairbanks's wealthy nemesis, in *The Mollycoddle*. As a suave international diamond smuggler, Beery drew critical praise and engaged in a spectacular undoubled brawl with Fairbanks for the film's finale.

At first glance, Beery's career seems to be built on roles of menace, but he won attention as a leading character actor with his King Richard in the Fairbanks version of *Robin Hood*, and repeated the role a year later in *King Richard the Lion-Hearted*. He also had an atypical part as Professor Challenger in *The Lost World* and co-starred in a series of raucous comedies teamed with Raymond Hatton, including *Behind the Front*, *Fireman, Save My Child*, and *Now We're in the Air*.

It was in William Wellman's excellent *Beggars of Life* that Beery perfected his stock character of the scoundrel with a heart of gold. As Oklahoma Red, the King of the Hoboes, Beery had perhaps his best role of the 1920s, antagonizing the lovers Louise Brooks and Richard Arlen before sacrificing his life for them at fade-out.

Two events helped transform Beery into a major star—the coming of sound and a contract with MGM. His gravel voice became an integral part of his screen persona, and Metro cast him in important pictures with strong production values. He was at his peak as an actor from 1930 to roughly 1937, with his best pictures and performances. Beery was nominated for an Oscar for his hard-boiled convict Butch Schmidt in *The Big House*, and received one for the title role in the well-crafted King Vidor soaper *The Champ* (an honor he shared with Fredric March in *Dr. Jekyll and Mr. Hyde*). Metro teamed him with blowzy Marie Dressler in *Min and Bill* and *Tugboat Annie*, both immensely successful with Depression audiences, tired perhaps of Hollywood glitz, and reveling in the simple patter between Dressler and Beery. He also found an ideal child star complement in Jackie Cooper, with whom he made *The Champ*, *The Bowery* (on loan to Darryl Zanuck's Twentieth Century Pictures), *Treasure Island* and *O'Shaughnessy's Boy*. The Beery-Cooper team likewise found mass acceptance with their blend of toughness and sentimentality.

Metro kept Beery busy in a succession of quality pictures, ogling Joan Crawford and speaking with a German accent in *Grand Hotel*; as a boorish businessman married to Jean Harlow in *Dinner at Eight*; as a decidedly

non-Hispanic Pancho Villa in *Viva Villa!*; camping it up as Long John Silver in the quintessential Beery role in *Treasure Island*; battling Gable and Harlow in *China Seas* as a modern pirate; and portraying showman P. T. Barnum in *A Lady's Morals* and *The Mighty Barnum*. Beery could also turn in a sensitive, atypical role as in *Ah, Wilderness!*

The key to Beery's success lies in his good fortune with directors, and he worked with an impressive roster, as his filmography reveals. After he turned fifty, Beery settled into a formula groove at Metro, enacting his familiar character in a string of low-budget programmers. Frequently he was teamed with Marjorie Main in a vain attempt to duplicate the popularity of Beery and Dressler.

—John A. Gallagher

BELLAMY, Ralph

Nationality: American. **Born:** Chicago, Illinois, 17 June 1904. **Education:** New Trier High School, Wilmette, Illinois. **Family:** Married 1) Alice Delbridge, 1922 (divorced 1931); 2) Catherine Willard, 1931 (divorced 1945), children: Lynn and Willard; 3) Ethel Smith, 1945 (divorced); 4) Alice Murphy, 1949. **Career:** 1922—formed own troupe of actors "The North Shore Players" in Chicago area; later toured midwest stage circuit; 1922-24—stage manager for the Madison Stock Company; later with various stock companies in Indiana and Iowa; 1927—own stock company in Des Moines, the Ralph Bellamy Players, which he later moved to Nashville; 1929—on Broadway in *Town Boy*; 1930—film contract with Joseph Schenk; 1930s—involved with organizing the Screen Actors Guild; 1940s—worked in films, stage, and radio; 1949-54—in live TV series *Man against Crime*; 1957-59—panelist on TV series *To Tell the Truth*; 1961—host on TV series *Frontier Justice*, and in series *Eleventh Hour*, 1963-64, *The Survivors*, 1969, *The Most Deadly Game*, 1970-71, *Hunter*, 1977, and mini-series *The Winds of War*, 1983. **Awards:** New York Drama Critics Award for *Sunrise at Campobello*, 1958; Tony Award for *Sunrise at Campobello*, 1959; Honorary Academy Award for "his unique artistry and his distinguished service to the profession of acting," 1986. **Died:** 29 November 1991.

Films as Actor:

1931   *The Secret Six* (Hill); *The Magnificent Lie* (Viertel); *Surrender* (Howard); *West of Broadway* (Beaumont)
1932   *Forbidden* (Capra); *Disorderly Conduct* (Considine); *Young America* (*We Humans*) (Borzage); *Rebecca of Sunnybrook Farm* (Santell); *The Woman in Room Thirteen* (Henry King); *Wild Girl* (*Salomy Jane*) (Walsh); *Almost Married* (Menzies); *Air Mail* (Ford)
1933   *Second Hand Wife* (MacFadden); *Parole Girl* (Cline); *Destination Unknown* (Garnett); *Picture Snatcher* (Bacon); *Narrow Corner* (Green); *Below the Sea* (Rogell); *Headline Shooter* (Brower); *Blind Adventure* (Schoedsack); *Ever in My Heart* (Mayo); *Flying Devils* (Birdwell); *Ace of Aces* (Ruben)
1934   *Once to Every Woman* (Hillyer); *One Is Guilty* (Hillyer); *Spitfire* (Cromwell); *This Man Is Mine* (Cromwell); *Before Midnight* (Hillyer); *The Crime of Helen Stanley* (Lederman); *Girl in Danger* (Lederman); *Woman in the Dark* (Rosen)
1935   *Helldorado* (Cruze); *Air Hawks* (Rogell); *Eight Bells* (Neill); *The Healer* (Barker); *Gigolette* (Lamont); *Beauty's Daughter* (*Navy Wife*) (Dwan); *The Wedding Night* (King Vidor); *Rendezvous at Midnight* (Cabanne); *Hands across the Table* (Cabanne)

1936   *Dangerous Intrigue* (Selman); *The Final Hour* (Lederman);
        Roaming Lady (Rogell); *Straight from the Shoulder* (Heisler);
        Wild Brian Kent (Bretherton)

1937   *Counterfeit Lady* (Lederman); *Let's Get Married* (Green); *The
        Man Who Lived Twice* (Lachman); *The Awful Truth*
        (McCarey)

1938   *The Crime of Dr. Hallet* (Simon); *Fools for Scandal* (LeRoy);
        Boy Meets Girl (Bacon); *Carefree* (Sandrich); *Girl's School*
        (Brahm); *Trade Winds* (Garnett)

1939   *Let Us Live* (Brahm); *Blind Alley* (Charles Vidor); *Smashing
        the Spy Ring* (Cabanne); *Coast Guard* (Ludwig)

1940   **His Girl Friday** (Hawks) (as Bruce Baldwin); *Flight Angels*
        (Seiler); *Brother Orchid* (Bacon); *Queen of the Mob* (Hogan);
        Dance, Girl, Dance (Arzner) (as Steve Adams); *Public Deb
        Number One* (Ratoff); *Ellery Queen, Master Detective*
        (Neumann); *Meet the Wildcat* (Lubin)

1941   *Ellery Queen's Penthouse Mystery* (Hogan); *Footsteps in the
        Dark* (Bacon); *Affectionately Yours* (Bacon); *Ellery Queen
        and the Perfect Crime* (Hogan); *Dive Bomber* (Curtiz); *Ellery
        Queen and the Murder Ring* (Hogan); *The Wolf Man*
        (Waggner)

1942   *The Ghost of Frankenstein* (Kenton); *Lady in a Jam* (La Cava);
        Men of Texas (*Men of Destiny*) (Enright); *The Great Imper-
        sonation* (Rawlings)

1943   *Stage Door Canteen* (Borzage)

1944   *Guest in the House* (Brahm)

1945   *Delightfully Dangerous* (Lubin); *Lady on a Train* (David)

1955   *The Court Martial of Billy Mitchell* (Preminger)

1960   *Sunrise at Campobello* (Donehue)

1966   *The Professionals* (Richard Brooks)

1967   *Wings of Fire* (Rich—for TV)

1968   **Rosemary's Baby** (Polanski) (as Dr. Sapirstein)

1969   *The Immortal* (Sargent—for TV)

1971   *Doctors' Wives* (Schaefer)

1972   *Something Evil* (Spielberg—for TV); *Cancel My Reservation*
        (Bogart)

1974   *Log of the Black Pearl* (McLaglen—for TV) .

1975   *Murder on Flight 502* (McGowan—for TV); *Adventures of the
        Queen* (Rich—for TV); *Search for the Gods* (Taylor—for TV)

1976   *McNaughton's Daughter* (London—for TV); *Nightmare in
        Badham County* (Moxey—for TV); *Return to Earth* (Tay-
        lor—for TV); *The Boy in the Plastic Bubble* (Kleiser—for
        TV)

1977   *Charlie Cobb: Nice Night for a Hanging* (Michaels—for TV);
        Oh, God! (Reiner)

1978   *The Clone Master* (Medford—for TV); *The Millionaire* (Weis—
        for TV)

1979   *Condominium* (Hayers—for TV); *The Billion Dollar Threat*
        (Shear)

1980   *The Memory of Eva Ryker* (Grauman—for TV); *Power* (Shear—
        for TV)

1983   *Trading Places* (Landis) (as Randolph Duke)

1985   *Fourth Wise Man* (Rhodes—for TV)

1987   *Amazon Women on the Moon* (Dante) (as Mr. Gower);
        Disorderlies (Schultz) (as Albert Dennison)

1988   *The Good Mother* (Nimoy) (as Grandfather); *Coming to
        America* (Landis) (as Randolph Duke)

1990   *Pretty Woman* (Marshall) (as James Morse)

Publications

By BELLAMY: book—

When the Smoke Hit the Fan, New York, 1979.

By BELLAMY: articles—

Interview in *American Classic Screen* (Shawnee Mission, Kansas), Janu-
    ary—February 1983.
Classic Images (Indiana, Pennsylvania), June 1984.

On BELLAMY: articles—

Parish, James Robert, and William T. Leonard, *Hollywood Players: The
    Thirties*, New Rochelle, New York, 1976.
Films in Review (New York), January 1984.

                    *   *   *

Ralph Bellamy's talents were formidable and his range great. He
played detective Ellery Queen in a series of comedy-mysteries for
Columbia, appeared as a conventional leading man (*Dance, Girl,
Dance*), and could be effectively villainous (*The Wedding Night* and
The Professionals). Still, Bellamy was never able completely to escape
being typecast as a bumbling, dopey, good-natured "other man" who
repeatedly loses the girl to Cary Grant, Fred Astaire, or even Robert
Young.

Bellamy came to films after a decade on the stage, a period of
apprenticeship that included his own company, The Ralph Bellamy
Players. He never achieved true star status in motion pictures, though
his easy charm and natural performances kept him busy throughout
the 1930s and 1940s. He won an Academy Award nomination for his
naive, good-hearted, slow-witted Texan who woos Irene Dunne in *The
Awful Truth*, and thereafter was featured in film after film playing
variations on the same role.

Bellamy's triumph is that he never coasted through these parts.
Indeed, each of them is well-considered and subtle. Bellamy took these
caricatures and filled them with a humanity and poignance that made
them likable and realistic. His best "other man" appears in Hawks's
His Girl Friday, a fast, cynical, hard-edged feature in which Bellamy
comes off as the most sympathetic character.

After 1945, Bellamy devoted much of his time to the stage. His
Franklin Delano Roosevelt in *Sunrise at Campobello* won him Tony
and New York Drama Critics awards, and in 1960 he recreated the role
on film in a performance that is thoughtful and beautifully modulated.
He worked infrequently in motion pictures thereafter, though relatively minor parts in *The Professionals* and *Rosemary's Baby* still
display his command of the craft. His appearance with Don Ameche
in the box-office smash *Trading Places* proved that Bellamy still had
a way with a comic line as well.

Bellamy remains undervalued as a performer, but his remarkable
sense of comedy and his perplexed and affable presence have redeemed many a poor film and have made more than one great film a
bit greater.

                                                —Frank Thompson

BELMONDO, Jean-Paul

Nationality: French. **Born:** Neuilly sur Seine, 9 April 1933. **Education:** Attended Collège Pascal, Paris; National Conservatory of Dramatic Art, Paris. **Family:** Married Elodie (Belmondo), 1952 (divorced 1967), children: Patricia, Florence, and Paul. **Career:** 1949—
short-lived attempt at boxing career; 1950—stage debut; c. 1956-
57—founder, with Annie Girardot and Guy Bedos, of traveling stage
company to play Parisian suburbs and the provinces; 1956-58—in
comic and character roles on French stage and screen; 1959—interna-

Jean-Paul Belmondo

tional stardom for role of antihero in Godard's *A bout de souffle*; 1960—first starring role on French TV in production of *The Three Musketeers*; 1963-66—president of Syndicat Français des Acteurs; late 1960s—formed production company Cerito Films; 1990—acted title role in *Cyrano de Bergerac*, Paris. **Awards:** Chevalier de la Légion d'honneur; L'Ordre national du Mérite et des Arts et des Lettres; César for Best Actor, for *L'Itinéraire d'un enfant gâté*, 1987. **Address:** 9 rue des St. Peres, 75007 Paris, France.

Films as Actor:

1955   *Molière* (Tildian)
1956   *Dimanche nous volerons*
1957   *A pied, à cheval et en voiture* (Delbez) (as Venin)
1958   *Sois belle et tais-toi* (*Blonde for Danger*; *Just Another Pretty Face*) (Marc Allégret) (as Pierrot); *Drôle de dimanche* (Marc Allégret) (as Patrick); *Les Tricheurs* (*Youthful Sinners*; *The Cheaters*) (Carné) (as Lou); *Charlotte et son Jules* (Godard) (as Jean, the old boyfriend); *Les Copains du dimanche* (Aisner) (as Trebois)

1959   *Mademoiselle Ange* (*Ein Engel auf Erden*; *Angel on Earth*) (von Radvanyi); ***A bout de souffle*** (*Breathless*) (Godard) (as Michel Poiccard); *A double tour* (*Web of Passion*; *Leda*; *A Doppia mandata*) (Chabrol) (as Laszlo Kovacs)
1960   *Classe tous risques* (*The Big Risk*) (Sautet) (as Eric Stark); *Les Distractions* (*Trapped by Fear*) (Dupont) (as Paul); "L'Adultère" ("Adultery") ep. of *La Française et l'amour* (*Love and the Frenchwoman*) (Verneuil) (as Gil); *Lettere di una novizia* (*Letter from a Novice*; *Rita*) (Lattuada) (as Giuliano Verdi); *Moderato cantabile* (*Seven Days . . . Seven Nights*) (Brook) (as Chauvin)
1961   *La ciociara* (*Two Women*) (de Sica) (as Michele); *La viaccia* (*The Love Makers*) (Bolognini) (as Amerigo Casamonti); *Léon Morin, prêtre* (*Leon Morin, Priest*; *The Forgiven Sinner*) (Melville); *Une Femme est une femme* (*A Woman Is a Woman*) (Godard) (as Alfred Lubitsch); "Lauzun" ep. of *Amours célèbres* (Boisrond); *Un Nommé La Rocca* (Jean Becker)
1962   *Cartouche* (*Swords of Blood*) (de Broca) (title role); *Un Singe en hiver* (*It's Hot in Hell*; *A Monkey in Winter*) (Verneuil) (as Gabriel Fouquet); *I Don Giovanni della Costa Azzurra* (Sala);

L'Aîné des Ferchaux (*Magnet of Doom*) (Melville) (as Michel Maudet); *Un Couer gros comme ca* (*The Winner*) (Reichenbach)

1963 *Le Doulos* (*The Fingerman*; *Doulos—The Fingerman*) (Melville) (as Silien); *Mare matto* (Castellani); *Il giorno più corto* (*The Shortest Day*) (Corbucci); *Dragées au poivre* (*Sweet and Sour*) (Baratier) (as Raymond); *Cent mille dollars au soleil* (*Greed in the Sun*) (Verneuil) (as Rocco)

1964 *Peau de banane* (*Banana Peel*) (Marcel Ophüls) (as Michel); *L'Homme de Rio* (*That Man from Rio*) (de Broca) (as Adrien Dufourquet); *Enchappement libre* (*Backfire*) (Jean Becker); *La Chasse à l'homme* (*The Gentle Art of Seduction*; *Male Hunt*; *Scappamento Aperto*) (Molinaro) (as Fernand); *Weekend à Zuydcoote* (*Weekend at Dunkirk*) (Verneuil) (as Sgt. Julien Maillat)

1965 *Par un beau matin d'été* (*Crime on a Summer Morning*) (Deray); *Les Tribulations d'un chinois en Chine* (*Up to His Ears*; *Chinese Adventures in China*) (de Broca) (as Arthur Lempereur); *Pierrot le fou* (*Peter the Crazy*) (Godard) (as Ferdinand Griffon, "Pierrot")

1966 *Paris brûle-t-il* (*Is Paris Burning?*) (Clément) (as Morandat); *Tendre voyou* (*Tender Scoundrel*) (Jean Becker) (as Tony Marechal)

1967 *Le Voleur* (*The Thief of Paris*) (Malle) (as Georges Randal); *La Bande à Bébel* (Gérard); *Casino Royale* (Huston and others) (as French Legionnaire)

1968 *Ho!* (Enrico) (title role)

1969 *Le Cerveau* (*The Brain*) (Oury) (as Arthur); *La Sirène du Mississippi* (*Mississippi Mermaid*) (Truffaut) (as Louis Mahe); *Un Homme qui me plait* (*Love Is a Funny Thing*; *Again a Love Story*; *Un Tipo chi mi place*) (Lelouch) (as Henri); *Dieu a choisi Paris* (Prouteau and Arthuys)

1970 *Borsalino* (Deray) (as François Capella)

1971 *Les Mariés de l'an II* (*The Scoundrel*) (Rappeneau) (as Nicholas Philabert); *Le Casse* (*The Burglars*) (Verneuil) (as Asad)

1972 *Docteur Popaul* (*Scoundrel in White*; *High Heels*) (Chabrol) (as Paul Simay); *La Scoumoune* (Giovanni) (as Borgo)

1973 *L'Héritier* (*The Inheritor*) (Labro) (as Barthelemy Cordell)

1974 *Le Magnifique* (*How to Destroy the Reputation of the Greatest Secret Agent . . . . The Magnificent One*) (de Broca) (as Bob Saint-Clair/François Merlin); *Stavisky* (Resnais) (title role)

1975 *Peur sur la ville* (*The Night Caller*; *Fear over the City*) (Verneuil) (as Commissioner Jean Letellier); *L'Incorrigible* (*The Incorrigible*) (de Broca) (as Victor)

1976 *Le corps de mon ennemi* (Verneuil) (as François Leclerc, + pr, co-sc); *L'Alpagueur* (Labro) (as Roger Pilard/l'Alpagueur)

1977 *L'Animal* (*The Animal*; *Stuntwoman*) (Zidi) (as Mike Gaucher/Bruno Ferrari)

1979 *Flic ou voyou* (Lautner) (as Commissioner Stanislas Borowitz/Angelo Crutti)

1980 *Le Guignolo* (Lautner) (as Alain Dupre); *I piccioni di Piazza San Marco*; *The Hunter* (*Will Get You*) (Labro) (title role)

1981 *Le Professionnel* (Lautner) (as Joss Baumont)

1982 *L'As des as* (*Ace of Aces*; *The Super Ace*) (Oury) (as Joe Cavalier, + pr)

1983 *Les Morfalous* (*The Vultures*) (Verneuil) (as Pierre Augagneur); *Le Marginal* (*The Outsider*) (Deray) (as Commissioner Philippe Jordan)

1984 *Joyeuses Pâques* (*Happy Easter*) (Lautner) (as Stephane Margelle); *The Swashbuckler* (*The Scarlet Buccaneer*) (Rappeneau)

1985 *Hold-Up* (Arcady) (as Grimm)

1987 *Le Solitaire* (Deray) (as Commissioner Stan Jalard); *L'Itinéraire d'un enfant gâté* (Lelouch) (as Sam Lion)

1990 *Fleur de Rubis* (Mocky)

1992 *L'Inconnu dans al Maison* (*Stranger in the House*) (Lautner) (as Loursat, + pr)

1995 *Les Misérables* (Lelouch) (as Jean Valjean/Roger Fortin/Henri Fortin); *Les Cent et une nuits* (*A Hundred and One Nights*) (Varda) (as Actor for a Day)

1996 *Desire* (Murat) (title role)

Publications

By BELMONDO: book—

Trente ans et vingt-cinq films, Paris, 1963.

By BELMONDO: articles—

Interview with Joseph Barry, in *New York Times*, 21 June 1964.
Interview with Rex Reed, in *Herald Tribune* (New York), 17 October 1965.
Unifrance Film (Paris), no. 6, 1981.

On BELMONDO: books—

Chazal, Robert, *Jean-Paul Belmondo*, Paris, 1971.
Gúerif, François, and Stéphane Levy-Klein, *Belmondo*, Paris, 1976.
Turroni, Giuseppe, *Jean-Paul Belmondo*, Milan, 1979.
Zana, Jean-Claude, *Jean-Paul Belmondo*, Paris, 1981.
Durant, Philippe, *Jean-Paul Belmondo*, Paris, 1984.
Grenier, Alexandre, *Jean-Paul Belmondo*, Paris, 1985.
Durant, Philippe, *Belmondo*, Paris, 1993.

On BELMONDO: articles—

Baby, Yvonne, "Mon Film est un documentaire sur Jean Seberg et J.-P. Belmondo," in *Le Monde* (Paris), 18 March 1960.
"Two Actors," and "Jean-Paul Belmondo," in *Films and Filming* (London), October 1960.
Time (New York), 10 July 1964.
Shipman, David, "Belmondo," in *Films and Filming* (London), September 1964.
Current Biography 1965, New York, 1965.
Towne, Robert, "Bogart and Belmondo," in *Cinema* (Beverly Hills), December 1965.
Grenier, R., "Son of Bogie," in *Esquire* (New York), January 1966.
Barr, Charles, "*A bout de souffle*," in *The Films of Jean-Luc Godard*, edited by Ian Cameron, New York, 1970.
"Jean-Paul Belmondo," in *Ecran* (Paris), February 1978.
Articles in *Ciné Revue* (Paris), 2 October and 4 December 1980, 14 May and 23 July 1981, and 24 December 1982.
Sarris, Andrew, "Jean-Paul Belmondo," in *The Movie Star*, edited by Elisabeth Weis, New York, 1981.
Unifrance Film (Paris), No. 10, 1982.
Film Français (Paris), 5 and 26 November 1982.
Privat, Pascal, "France's War of the Noses; Dueling Cyranos of Stage and Screen," in *Newsweek* (New York), 7 May 1990.

*   *   *

When Jean-Paul Belmondo entered films in the mid-1950s, his expressive face, with thick lips, the broken nose of a boxer, and the mocking gaze of a rascal, did not correspond to the conception of the traditional young film hero/lover. He received his first real on-screen opportunity only with the coming of the French New Wave, when he began playing defiant and discontented young men who instinctively rebelled against their environment and society's status quo. Such was his role in Chabrol's *A double tour* (in which he substituted for an ailing Jean-Claude Brialy), but this film did not receive a great deal of attention. However, it was his role in Godard's *A bout de souffle*, made in the same year—1959, a watershed for the French New Wave— which won him unexpected success from the public and the critics and made him famous all over the world. The hero of the film, Michel Poiccard, is a car thief, living from hand to mouth, who finally becomes a murderer and pays with his life for his recklessness and irresponsibility. The success of *A bout de souffle* even resulted in a wave of "Belmondism" in the hipper circles of Paris, manifesting itself in a particular style of behavior, clothing, and expression.

Previously, Godard had directed Belmondo in an interesting short-length study, *Charlotte et son Jules*, and they worked together again in *Une Femme est une femme* and, more importantly, *Pierrot le fou*. To express his anarchistic conception of modern life, Godard, rejecting everything conventional and static, had found in Belmondo the ideal screen hero. In several other films, the actor replayed this type of rough, isolated (and ultimately ill-fated) character. He had similarly motivated roles in Becker's *Un Nommé La Rocca*, while in Verneuil's *Un Singe en hiver*, where Belmondo partnered with Jean Gabin, the dramatic situations were alternated with comic elements. He gathered further experience in Italy where he made films under the direction of Lattuada (*Lettere di una novizia*), de Sica (*La ciociara*), and Bolognini (*La viaccia*). Almost as consequential to his work with Godard were the films he made with Jean-Pierre Melville, including *Léon Morin, prêtre*, *Le Doulos*, and *L'Aîné des Ferchaux*.

But thereafter, Belmondo began breaking off his connection to the authors of the New Wave. After the Louis Malle black comedy *Le Voleur*, and especially after the ambitious but unsuccessful attempt by Alain Resnais to revive in film the character of a famous speculator and crook from the 1930s—*Stavisky*—Belmondo began appearing almost exclusively in commercially oriented features. His films offered few artistic demands, but nevertheless were widely popular and filled the cinemas. Among these early commercial pictures were de Broca's *L'Homme de Rio* and *Les Tribulations d'un chinois en Chine*, films in which Belmondo proved not only his dramatic talent but also his physical dexterity. He followed up these successful works with roles as a dauntless secret agent in *Le Magnifique* and a brilliant crook in *L'Incorrigible*, also directed by de Broca.

Belmondo appeared in a series of eight films made with Verneuil, most of which were written with him in mind. The director's ambition was, above all, to entertain audiences, offering up a combination of spectacle and charismatic star performances. A typical Verneuil-Belmondo feature is the adventure story of truck drivers in the Sahara, *Cent mille dollars au soleil*, in which he plays the role of Rocco, a criminal who attempts to double-cross his colleagues. This picture won the Cannes Prize of Golden Ticket *ex aequo*, awarded for the first time by the Union of the French Cinema Owners. The film *Weekend à Zuydcoote* followed, adapted from the novel of Robert Merle, in which the tragic events near Dunkirk from the beginning of World War II are mirrored via the fate of several French soldiers. Belmondo played one of them, a fighter who is at once easygoing and resolute. He co-starred with Omar Sharif in the next film by Verneuil, *Le Casse*, as a member of a gang of jewel thieves. As a commissar-in-chief of the Paris police in *Peur sur la ville*, he again had the opportunity to give an athletic and acrobatic performance. Another noteworthy Belmondo-Verneuil collaboration is *Les Morfalous*, an adventure story of death and greed during the war in Tunisia.

Belmondo has also worked with other directors in recent years. In Lautner's *Flic ou voyou*, he appeared in the role of a nonconformist policeman who sets out to rid Nice of gangsterism and corruption. In this case, however, the dialogue and humor were more prominent than the action. He played a charming, aging adventurer in subsequent films by Lautner, *Le Guignolo* and *Le Professionnel*, and another police commissar in Deray's *Le Marginal*.

After decades of appearing in such genre fare, Belmondo had his most challenging, highest-profile role since the 1960s in Lelouch's *Les Misérables*, a provocative drama inspired by the Victor Hugo classic. He played Henri Fortin, an uneducated ex-pugilist who befriends an intellectual Jewish family escaping the Nazis during World War II. Through them, he learns the story of Jean Valjean, with the film eventually becoming a meditation on the essence of Hugo's story. One only can ponder the course of Belmondo's career had he, earlier on, chosen to accept roles in films as ambitious as *Les Misérables*.

—Karel Tabery, updated by Rob Edelman

BELUSHI, John

Nationality: American. **Born:** Chicago, Illinois, 24 January 1949. **Education:** Attended Wheaton High School, Chicago; studied theater arts at Michigan State University and the University of Illinois. **Family:** Married Judith Jacklin, 1967. **Career:** 1969—began as comedian in a Chicago coffee house; 1972—joined Del Close's improvisational troupe, Second City; cast in National Lampoon's *Lemmings* revue; 1975-79—performer on *Saturday Night Live* for NBC; 1978—first role in significant film, *Goin' South*. **Died:** Of a drug overdose, in West Hollywood, 5 March 1982.

Films as Actor:

1975   *Shame of the Jungle* (Picha and Szulzinger—animation) (as voice)
1977   *Things We Did Last Summer* (Weis)
1978   *Goin' South* (Nicholson) (as Hector); *National Lampoon's Animal House* (Landis) (as John "Bluto" Blutarsky); *All You Need Is Cash* (*The Rutles*) (Idle and Weis—for TV) (as Ron Decline)
1979   *Old Boyfriends* (Tewkesbury) (as Eric Katz); *1941* (Spielberg) (as Captain Wild Bill Kelso)
1980   *The Blues Brothers* (Landis) (as Joliet Jake Blues)
1981   *Neighbors* (Avildsen) (as Earl Keese); *Continental Divide* (Apted) (as Souchak)
1993   *The Best of the Blues Brothers* (compilation, released direct to video) (as Joliet Jake Blues)

Publications

On BELUSHI: books—

Woodward, Bob, *Wired: The Short Life and Fast Times of John Belushi*, New York, 1984.
Belushi, Judith Jacklin, *Samurai Widow*, New York, 1990.

On BELUSHI: articles—

Current Biography 1980, New York, 1980.
Obituary in *Hollywood Reporter*, 8 March 1982.
Obituary in *Films and Filming* (London), May 1982.
Spielberg, Steven, in *Film Comment* (New York), May/June 1982.
"Wired," in *Time Out* (London), 6 December 1984.
Milligan, P. M., "Slob Story," in *Film Directions* (Belfast), January/ February 1986.

Interview with Judy Jacklin Belushi, in *Interview* (New York), August 1986.

Young, Charles M., "Son of Samurai," in *Rolling Stone* (New York), 11 June 1992.

On BELUSHI: film—

Wired, film biography directed by Larry Peerce, 1989.

*   *   *

After his brilliant work with the *Saturday Night Live* troupe, John Belushi went on to a somewhat disappointing, and very brief, movie career. Belushi made seven feature films in four years and fits uneasily into a line of weighty comic entertainers stretching from Fatty Arbuckle to Oliver Hardy to Jackie Gleason to John Candy. Ironically, he was at his funniest when taking on a "wild man" screen persona: one which permeated his off-camera life, and led to his premature death by drug overdose. His early film work, including *Goin' South*, *Old Boyfriends*, *1941*, *The Blues Brothers*, and most famously, *Animal House*, falls into this category. Later, *Continental Divide* and *Neighbors* have him playing very uncomfortably against this type.

Belushi's "wild man" persona is the defining feature of his character in *Goin' South*, his feature film debut. In it, he plays a sort of bandido in an over-the-top, "we don't got to show you no stinking badges" performance. In all these films—most notably *Animal House*, as the toga-clad, human food-vacuum, food-fight-loving John "Bluto" Blutarsky; *1941*, as the maniacal Captain Wild Bill Kelso in a scenery (and cigar) chewing performance; and *The Blues Brothers*, as Joliet Jake Blues—Belushi's body is wonderfully expressive. There is a quintessential image of Belushi in motion near the end of *Animal House*: after a stirring speech about the Germans bombing Pearl Harbor, he runs out of the frat house intending to lead his brothers to battle. He jumps to get a running start, puts his arms out, and then hops a few times to slow down, disappearing around a corner, last seen tilting like a dangerously overloaded cargo plane. In this sequence, Belushi is as graceful and light-on-his-feet as he is a furiously anarchic cartoon character come to life.

In these and many other gestures and movements, Belushi seems indebted to the comic style of Jackie Gleason. His marvelously expressive eyes and eyebrows were totally his own, however, and he was able to raise mugging to a comic art form when allowed to perform in a no-holds-barred atmosphere. Had he lived—and continued creating the type of comical characters found in the likes of *Goin' South* and *Animal House*—he might have become as legendary and enduring as Gleason.

But as his film career progressed, Belushi was either instigator or victim of bad decisions. This was the case regarding his last two films, one of which tried to position him as a romantic lead, the other as a nebbish. *Continental Divide* comes closer to being a success, and Belushi's crusading newspaperman, who chain-smokes and favors pork-pie hats, is at times charming and romantic. Still, had Belushi lived, his career as a leading man would have proven severely limited. And in *Neighbors*, in which he tries to play Laurel to Dan Aykroyd's Hardy, the result is most disappointing. In his suit, horn-rims, and powdered sideburns, he looks extremely uncomfortable. His hair appears thinner, his lips prissier; he is generally more stiff and pasty. He does, however, get off one great double-take as his neighbor's car rolls into a swamp.

It is hard to avoid wondering about the projects, mentioned in *Wired*, Bob Woodward's best-selling biography, which Belushi reportedly was interested in just before he died. One of these was *The Joy of Sex*, supposedly being tailored for him as a return to his earlier work and seemingly a natural for a "wild man" comeback. More intriguing was *Noble Rot*, his script about the misadventures of a wine maker, the title of which perhaps offers some clue to his mind-set near the end of his life. Unfortunately, in 1989, the Woodward book was made into a film, also titled *Wired*. It starred Michael Chiklis as Belushi, and is a mess of a movie which failed abysmally to capture the comic's talent and appeal.

Belushi's first line in *Animal House* is "Grab a brew, it don't cost nothing." But, truly living the wild-man life, John Belushi did not stick to beer, a choice that eventually led to his young demise.

—Mark Walker, updated by Rob Edelman

BENIGNI, Roberto

Nationality: Italian. **Born:** Arrezo, Tuscany, 27 October 1952. **Family:** Married the actress Nicoletta Braschi, 1991. **Career:** At age 10 or 11, member of troubadour act in rural Tuscany that improvised songs and poetry; also was a circus clown for a short time; late 1960s—moved to Rome and acted in underground experimental theater there; 1976—film debut in adaptation of "Cioni Mario" monologue, *Berlinguer ti volgio bene*; 1982—directing debut with *Tu mi turbi*; live TV monologue critical of Pope John Paul II brought widespread notoriety; 1984—met Jim Jarmusch at a film festival near Parma, leading to American debut in *Down by Law*, 1986, and appearance in second Jarmusch film, *Night on Earth*, 1991; 1993—first major Hollywood studio role in the box-office failure *Son of the Pink Panther*; 1995-96—toured Italy in one-man show, a mock political rally, drawing overall attendance of more than one million. **Awards:** Italian Golden Grail for Best Actor, for *Il minestrone*, 1980; Nastri d'Argento Award for Best Actor, for *Down by Law*, 1986; David Di Donatello Award for Best Actor, for *Il piccolo diavolo*, 1988. **Address:** Via Traversa 44, Vergaglio, Prato, Italy.

Films as Actor:

1976   *Berlinguer ti volgio bene* (*I Love You, Berlinguer*) (Giuseppe Bertolucci) (as Cioni Mario, + co-sc)
1979   *Chiedo asilo* (Marco Ferreri) (as Roberto, + co-sc); *Clair de femme* (*Womanlight*) (Costa-Gavras); *La Luna* (*Luna*) (Bernardo Bertolucci) (as upholsterer)
1980   *Il minestrone* (*Minestrone*)
1981   *Il Pap'Occhio* (*In the Pope's Eye*) (Arbore)
1985   *Tuttobenigni* (*All Benigni*) (Giuseppe Bertolucci)
1986   *Down by Law* (Jarmusch) (as Roberto)
1989   *La Voce della Luna* (*The Voice of the Moon*) (Fellini) (as Ivo Salvini)
1991   "Rome" ep. of *Night on Earth* (Jarmusch) (as Gino, the taxi driver)
1993   *Son of the Pink Panther* (Edwards) (as Jacques Gambrini/Jacques Clouseau, Jr.)

Films as Actor and Director:

1982   *Tu mi turbi* (*You Disturb Me*)
1984   *Non ci resta che piangere* (*There's Nothing Left but Crying*) (as Saverio, co-d with Massimo Troisi)
1988   *Il piccolo diavolo* (*The Little Devil*) (as Giuditta, + co-sc)
1991   *Johnny Stecchino* (*Johnny Toothpick*) (as Dante/Johnny Stecchino, + co-sc)
1994   *Il mostro* (*The Monster*) (as Loris, + co-sc, co-pr)

Roberto Benigni in *Down by Law*

Publications

By BENIGNI: books—

Johnny Stecchino, with Vincenzo Cerami, Rome, 1991.
Il mostro: romanzo, with Vincenzo Cerami, Milan, 1994.

By BENIGNI: articles—

Interview with J. Rood, in *Skoop* (Amsterdam), June/July 1980.
"Eloge du bouffon," interview with F. Sabouraud, in *Cahiers du Cinéma* (Paris), March 1987.
"Roberto Benigni Is a True Maestro among Clowns, a Fool as Fine Artist," interview with Robert Gerber, in *Interview* (New York), April 1990.
Interview with A. Samueli, in *Cahiers du Cinéma* (Paris), May 1990.
"Mille et une emotions," in *Positif* (Paris), May 1990.
"Een harlekijn uit Toscanie," interview with F. Sartor, in *Film en Televisie + Video* (Brussels), May/June and July/August 1992.
Interview with Tom Waits, in *Interview* (New York), January 1993.

On BENIGNI: articles—

Darnton, Nina, "*Down by Law* Star: A Pinocchio, by Way of Chico Marx," in *New York Times*, 19 November 1986.

Buffa, M., "Benigni esorcista di se," in *Filmcritica* (Rome), January/February 1989.
Saada, N., and T. Jousse, "Roberto Benigni," in *Cahiers du Cinéma* (Paris), June 1989.
Filmography in *Segnocinema* (Vincenza, Italy), January/February 1992.
Brennan, Judy, "A Benigni Press Conference Baedeker," in *Variety* (New York), 18 May 1992.
Cowell, Alan, "Roberto Benigni Readies More Laughs for Export," in *New York Times*, 19 July 1992.
Randall, Frederika, "Italy's Comic Savior," in *Wall Street Journal*, 10 April 1996.

*   *   *

Screen comedians seem to be overly burdened with comparisons to past comedic giants. In a relatively short career to date, Roberto Benigni—the most popular comic talent in Italy in the late 20th century—has been compared to more than his share, with the list ranging from the inevitable (Toto) to the obvious (Chaplin, Keaton, Laurel and Hardy, Harpo and Chico Marx) to the seriously misguided (Woody Allen, Lenny Bruce, Jim Carrey). Cliché though it may be, Benigni is a unique comic genius whose variety of talents stem from a most unusual apprenticeship into entertainment, and conjure up such a wellspring of comparisons.

Benigni was born and raised in poverty in a small Tuscan village. His gift for improvisation was nurtured early on (age 10 or 11) with his immersion into the Italian tradition of improvised song and poetry through a sort of troubadour act that traveled rural Tuscany. After another formative experience during the several months he spent as a circus clown, Benigni's vocation was cemented when at about age 16 he leaped up on a platform in the town square of Prado (in Tuscany, near Florence) and, pretending to be a political candidate, gave a "speech" that was greeted with hearty laughter from the crowd that filled the square. In the audience was the director of an avant-garde theater company, who persuaded Benigni to move to Rome and join his company.

In Rome, Benigni worked in the theater, television, and film throughout the 1970s and early 1980s, achieving initial success through monologues, particularly one called "Cioni Mario" about a sex-obsessed man from his hometown who never has sex, but thinks and talks of nothing else. This was adapted by Giuseppe Bertolucci in 1976 as *Berlinguer ti volgio bene*, Benigni's film debut; later Bertolucci would adapt another smash stage show, *Tuttobenigni*. Benigni's initial appearances in features were in minor roles but for major directors: Marco Ferreri's *Chiedo asilo*, Costa-Gavras's *Clair de femme*, and Bernardo Bertolucci's *La Luna*. He made a very early move into directing—forced to, he says, because of the lack of Italian directors able to do comedy—debuting in 1982 with *Tu mi turbi*, but received accolades for his second directing effort, *Non ci resta che piangere*. Co-directed with co-star Massimo Troisi, this delightful film has the two stars time-traveling to 1492 Italy where they attempt to cash in on their 20th century foreknowledge with comic results.

During this period, Benigni developed his signature persona, building off a body well-suited to physical comedy—wild hair, receding, creating a halo head; tall with gangling limbs accentuated by plain suits, worn one size too large, flopping about; and a most expressive comic face, highlighted by an impish grin. His characters are generally down-to-earth urban survivors, relying on their wits, motormouths, and low-level scams to get by, often remaining amazingly ignorant of the mayhem around them caused either directly or indirectly by their actions or inactions.

A chance meeting at an Italian film festival led Jim Jarmusch to cast Benigni in 1986's *Down by Law*, his U.S. debut. The comic nearly stole the film as an Italian tourist—thrown into a New Orleans jail cell occupied by two deadbeats (John Lurie and Tom Waits)—who knows little English but tries to engage the others in conversation (Benigni himself knew little English at the beginning of the film's production). Even better was his second film for Jarmusch, *Night on Earth*, where his gifts for monologue and improvisation shine as the taxi driver in the "Rome" episode who confesses his sex life to a priest—pumpkins, sheep, and sister-in-law, all. The initial scene in the episode where Benigni drives around Rome keeping himself (and the audience) amused with his banter is classic.

In Italy he achieved superstardom in the late 1980s and early 1990s through three consecutive box-office blockbusters: *Il piccolo diavolo*, with co-star Walter Matthau as a priest whose life is made chaotic by Benigni's devil; *Johnny Stecchino*, where a bus driver is mistaken for a Mafiaso to comic effect, with Benigni enacting both roles, the former much more effectively than the latter; and *Il mostro*, his best film to date, another case of mistaken identity in which Benigni's witless errand boy Loris is suspected, through a hilarious sequence of misinterpreted police videotape, of being a mass murderer.

Along the way, Benigni was cast against type in Federico Fellini's final film, *La Voce della Luna*, which has yet to be released in the United States. Benigni has, however, become a favorite of the American art-house crowd through his Jarmusch films and his self-directed efforts. Such successes led to his ill-fated debut in a major U.S. film as Jacques Clouseau's son in the box-office failure, *Son of the Pink Panther*, where his best efforts are undermined by an inferior script (his "Wasn't that fun!" at the end is a truly embarrassing line).

Benigni remains immensely popular in Italy, evidenced by the huge crowds that attended his mock political rallies in 1995 and 1996, where he skewered one of his favorite targets—politicians. One would hope that in the future his great talent could be exposed to a larger North American audience—perhaps through a collaboration with an American director, given Benigni's self-acknowledged limitations in that area. In any event, there is no doubt that Benigni will in the not-too-distant future be added to the pantheon of comedic giants to which rising film comedians are compared.

—David E. Salamie

BENNETT, Joan

Nationality: American. **Born:** Joan Geraldine Bennett in Palisades, New Jersey, 27 February 1910; daughter of the actor Richard Bennett; sister of the actress Constance Bennett. **Education:** Attended St. Margaret's, Waterbury, Connecticut; Le Lierre, Paris, finishing school, 1925. **Family:** Married 1) John Marion Fox, 1926 (divorced 1928), daughter: Adrienne; 2) the screenwriter Gene Markey, 1932 (divorced 1937), daughter: Melinda; 3) the director Walter Wanger, 1940 (divorced 1965), daughters: Stephanie and Shelley; 4) the critic David Wilde, 1978. **Career:** 1914—stage debut in Chicago in *Damaged Goods*, directed by and starring father Richard Bennett; 1915—film debut, with sister Constance Bennett, in father's *The Valley of Decision*; 1928—Broadway debut in father's production *Jarnegan*; 1929—five-year contract with United Artists; released from contract after two films; 1930—two-year contract at Fox; 1933—success in *Little Women*: personal contract with Walter Wanger; 1941—contract with Columbia and 20th Century-Fox; made first of four pictures with Fritz Lang; 1945—with Fritz Lang formed Diana Productions; 1951—agent Jennings Lang shot and wounded by jealous husband Walter Wanger; Wanger served four-month sentence; scandal temporarily ended Bennett's film acting career; 1959—in TV series *Too Young to Go Steady*; 1966-70—in daytime TV series *Dark Shadows*. **Died:** In Scarsdale, New York, 7 December 1990.

Films as Actress:

1915   *The Valley of Decision* (Berger) (as an "unborn soul")
1923   *The Eternal City* (Fitzmaurice) (bit role)
1928   *Power* (Higgin) (as waitress)
1929   *The Divine Lady* (Lloyd) (as an extra); *Bulldog Drummond* (F. Richard Jones) (as Phyllis Benton); *Three Live Ghosts* (Freeland) (as Rose Gordon); *Disraeli* (Alfred E. Green) (as Lady Clarissa Pevensey); *The Mississippi Gambler* (Barker) (as Lucy Blackburn)
1930   *Puttin' on the Ritz* (Sloman) (as Dolores Fenton); *Crazy That Way* (MacFadden) (as Ann Jordan); *Moby Dick* (Lloyd Bacon) (as Faith); *Maybe It's Love* (Wellman) (as Nan Sheffield); *Scotland Yard* (*Detective Clive, Bart*) (William K. Howard) (as Xandra)
1931   *Many a Slip* (Vin Moore) (as Pat Coster); *Doctors' Wives* (Borzage) (as Nina Wyndram); *Hush Money* (Lanfield) (as Janet Gordon)
1932   *She Wanted a Millionaire* (Blystone) (as Jane Miller); *Careless Lady* (MacKenna) (as Sally Brown/Mrs. Illington); *The Trial of Vivienne Ware* (William K. Howard) (title role); *Weekends Only* (Crosland) (as Venetia Carr); *Wild Girl* (*Salomy Jane*) (Walsh) (as Salomy Jane Clay); *Me and My Gal* (*Pier 13*) (Walsh) (as Helen Riley)

1933   *Arizona to Broadway* (Tinling) (as Lynn Martin); *Little Women* (Cukor) (as Amy)

1934   *The Pursuit of Happiness* (Hall) (as Prudence Kirkland)

1935   *The Man Who Reclaimed His Head* (Ludwig) (as Adele Verin); *Mississippi* (A. Edward Sutherland) (as Lucy Rumford); *Private Worlds* (La Cava) (as Sally MacGregor); *Two for Tonight* (Tuttle) (as Bobbie Lockwood); *She Couldn't Take It* (*Woman Tamer*) (Garnett) (as Carol Van Dyke); *The Man Who Broke the Bank at Monte Carlo* (Roberts) (as Helen Berkeley)

1936   *Thirteen Hours by Air* (Leisen) (as Felice Rollins); *Big Brown Eyes* (Walsh) (as Eve Fallon); *Two in a Crowd* (Alfred E. Green) (as Julia Wayne); *Wedding Present* (Wallace) (as Monica "Rusty" Fleming)

1937   *Vogues of 1938* (*Walter Wanger's Vogues of 1938*; *All This and Glamour Too*) (Cummings) (as Wendy Van Klettering)

1938   *I Met My Love Again* (Ripley, Logan, and Cukor) (as Julie); *The Texans* (Hogan) (as Ivy Preston); *Trade Winds* (Garnett) (as Kay Kerrigan); *Artists and Models Abroad* (*Stranded in Paris*) (Leisen) (as Patricia Harper)

1939   *The Man in the Iron Mask* (Whale) (as Maria Theresa); *The Housekeeper's Daughter* (Roach) (as Hilda)

1940   *Green Hell* (Whale) (as Stephanie Richardson); *The House across the Bay* (Mayo) (as Brenda "Lucky" Bentley); *The Man I Married* (Pichel) (as Carol); *The Son of Monte Cristo* (Rowland V. Lee) (as Grand Duchess Zona)

1941   *Confirm or Deny* (Mayo) (as Jennifer Carson); *Man Hunt* (Fritz Lang) (as Jerry); *She Knew All the Answers* (Wallace) (as Gloria Winters); *Wild Geese Calling* (Brahm) (as Sally)

1942   *Girl Trouble* (Schuster) (as June Delaney); *Twin Beds* (Whelan) (as Julie Abbott); *The Wife Takes a Flyer* (*A Yank in Dutch*) (Wallace) (as Anita Woverman); *Hedda Hopper's Hollywood No. 6* (doc, short) (as herself)

1943   *Margin for Error* (Preminger) (as Sophie Baumer)

1945   *The Woman in the Window* (Fritz Lang) (as Alice Reed); *Colonel Effingham's Raid* (*Man of the Hour*) (Pichel) (as Ella Sue Dozier); *Nob Hill* (Hathaway) (as Harriet Carruthers); *Scarlet Street* (Fritz Lang) (as Kitty March)

1947   *The Macomber Affair* (Z. Korda) (as Margaret Macomber); *The Woman on the Beach* (Renoir) (as Peggy Butler)

1948   *Secret beyond the Door* (Fritz Lang) (as Celia Lamphere); *Hollow Triumph* (*The Scar*) (Sekely) (as Evelyn Nash)

1949   *The Reckless Moment* (Max Ophüls) (as Lucia Harper)

1950   *Father of the Bride* (Minnelli) (as Ellie Banks); *For Heaven's Sake* (Seaton) (as Lydia)

1951   *Father's Little Dividend* (Minnelli) (as Ellie Banks); *The Guy Who Came Back* (Joseph M. Newman) (as Kathy Joplin)

1954   *Highway Dragnet* (Juran) (as Mrs. Cunningham); *We're No Angels* (Curtiz) (as Amelie Ducotel)

1956   *Navy Wife* (*Mother—Sir!*) (Bernds) (as Peg Blain); *There's Always Tomorrow* (Sirk) (as Marion Groves)

1960   *Desire in the Dust* (Claxton) (as Mrs. Marquand)

1970   *House of Dark Shadows* (Curtis) (as Elizabeth Collins Stoddard)

1972   *Gidget Gets Married* (Swackhamer—for TV); *The Eyes of Charles Sand* (Badiyi—for TV)

1974   *Inn of the Damned* (Burke—unreleased)

1977   *Suspiria* (Argento) (as Madame Blank, the school head)

1978   *Suddenly, Love* (Margolin—for TV)

1981   *This House Possessed* (Wiard—for TV)

1982   *Divorce Wars: A Love Story* (Wrye—for TV)

Joan Bennett

Publications

By BENNETT: books—

How to Be Attractive, New York, 1943.
The Bennett Playbill, with Lois Kibbee, New York, 1970.

On BENNETT: articles—

Bowers, Ron, "Joan Bennett," in *Films in Review* (New York), June/July 1977.

Shipman, David, in *The Great Movie Stars: The Golden Years*, rev. ed., London, 1979.

Obituary in *New York Times*, 9 December 1990.

Obituary in *Times* (London), 10 December 1990.

Obituary in *Variety* (New York), 17 December 1990.

Thomson, David, "Lazy Legs," in *Film Comment* (New York), March/April 1991.

Viviani, C., "Joan Bennett, la 'chose enrobee de cellophane,'" in *Positif* (Paris), July/August 1991.

*   *   *

Joan Bennett, the youngest of the three acting daughters of prominent stage and screen star Richard Bennett, was the last of the sisters to enter films seriously, but she had the longest and, in retrospect, the most meaningful career of any of her family. Joan, like Constance and Barbara, was a gorgeous woman, slender and blond, with dramatic eyes. She acted in numerous films during the 1930s, many of which were important, such as *Disraeli* and *Little Women*, but none of them was particularly noteworthy for her participation. It was not until the late 1930s when she dyed her hair dark brown that Bennett became more than just another beautiful Hollywood blond and began to have significant impact on films. She frequently played a sultry femme fatale in her new image, outstandingly beautiful but destructive. In her two most highly regarded films, *The Woman in the Window* and *Scarlet Street*, both directed by Fritz Lang, she displayed a cool, pernicious character, the antithesis of the mild-mannered, unsophisticated common man played by Edward G. Robinson in each film.

In these two films, as well as others such as Jean Renoir's *The Woman on the Beach*, Bennett was able to appear beautifully innocent and vulnerable on the surface, while hiding a stony evilness on the inside. Lang, and others, have expressed great admiration for Bennett's contributions to her films of this period, and some critics have called her the epitome of the film noir heroine.

Yet, despite her success in dramatic roles, Bennett also acted successfully in more sympathetic comedy roles. At age 40, and still a very beautiful, young-looking woman, she was very charming in the box-office success *Father of the Bride*, portraying Spencer Tracy's wife and Elizabeth Taylor's mother. Unlike many other beautiful actresses, Bennett decided to begin playing "mothers" and older parts before she actually needed to. She also took chances in her career and varied her roles, dividing her time among costume epics, melodramas, and tearjerkers such as Max Ophüls's *The Reckless Moment* and Douglas Sirk's *There's Always Tomorrow*. In the latter film, Bennett played a boring housewife married to Fred MacMurray who feels stifled by her presence and that of their children and contemplates leaving them for a former sweetheart.

Bennett's career flourished in the 1940s not only because of her change of hair color but also because of her marriage to the prominent producer Walter Wanger. Wanger guided her career and can take much of the credit for the powerful roles which she accepted. He produced many of the films in which she appeared during their marriage, and provided her with some of the outstanding European directors who were working in Hollywood during that period. They divorced relatively quietly in 1965, but their relationship created international headlines in 1951 when Wanger shot Bennett's agent Jennings Lang, purportedly out of jealousy; Wanger went briefly to prison. By 1956 Bennett had virtually retired from films and thereafter confined herself to occasional theater and television work. From the mid-1950s on, her most prominent role was as one of the main characters of the very popular supernatural television soap opera, *Dark Shadows*, the only long-running daytime serial in history to spawn both a film, *House of Dark Shadows* (which Bennett also starred in), and successful rerun engagement (as well as a short-lived 1991 prime-time reprisal, also called *Dark Shadows*, which debuted on January 13, a little over one month after Bennett died).

—Patricia King Hanson

BERGMAN, Ingrid

Nationality: Swedish. **Born:** Stockholm, 29 August 1915. **Education:** Royal Dramatic Theater School, Stockholm. **Family:** Married 1) Peter Lindstrom, 1937 (divorced 1950), daughter: Pia; 2) the di-

rector Roberto Rossellini, 1950 (annulled 1957), children: Robertino Ingmar and twins Isotta and Isabella; 3) Lars Schmidt, 1958 (divorced 1975). **Career:** 1933—stage debut in Stockholm; 1934—film debut in Svensk Filmindustri's *Munkbrogreven*; 1935—contract with director Gustav Molander; 1939—attracted attention of David O. Selznick who offered her role in American remake of *Intermezzo*; moved to America after outbreak of World War II in Europe; 1941—American stage debut in Eugene O'Neill's *Anna Christie* produced by the Selznick Company; 1949—traveled to Italy to work on Roberto Rossellini's *Stromboli*; scandal involving affair with Rossellini and subsequent pregnancy without marriage disrupted her career in Hollywood for 7 years; 1956—successful return to Hollywood films with *Anastasia*; 1959—star of TV adaptation of Henry James's *Turn of the Screw* directed by John Frankenheimer; stage roles in *Captain Brassbound's Conversion*, 1971, *The Constant Wife*, 1973, and *Waters of the Moon*, 1977; 1982—star of TV mini-series *Golda* based on life of Golda Meir. **Awards:** Best Actress Academy Award for *Gaslight*, 1944; Best Actress, New York Film Critics, for *Spellbound* and *The Bells of St. Mary's*, 1945; Best Actress Academy Award, and Best Actress, New York Film Critics, for *Anastasia*, 1956; Best Supporting Actress Academy Award, and Best Supporting Actress, British Academy, for *Murder on the Orient Express*, 1974; Best Actress, New York Film Critics, for *Autumn Sonata*, 1978. **Died:** In London 29 August 1982.

Films as Actress:

1934 *Munkbrogreven (The Count of Monk's Bridge)* (Adolphson and Wallen) (as Elsa)
1935 *Brannigar (Ocean Breakers; The Surf)* (Johansson) (as Karin Ingman); *Swedenhielms (The Family Swedenhielms)* (Molander) (as Astrid); *Valborgsmassoafton (Walpurgis Night)* (Edgren) (as Lena Bergstrom)
1936 *Pa solsidan (On the Sunny Side)* (Molander) (as Eva Bergh); *Intermezzo* (Molander) (as Anita Hoffman)
1938 *Dollar* (Molander) (as Julia Balzar); *En kvinnas ansikte (A Woman's Face)* (Molander) (as Anna Holm); *Die vier gesellen (The Four Companions)* (Frölich) (as Marianne)
1939 *En enda natt (Only One Night)* (Molander) (as Eva); *Intermezzo (A Love Story)* (Ratoff) (as Anita Hoffman)
1940 *Juninatten (A Night in June)* (Lindberg)
1941 *Adam Had Four Sons* (Ratoff) (as Emilie Gallatin); *Rage in Heaven* (W. S. Van Dyke) (as Stella Bergen); *Dr. Jekyll and Mr. Hyde* (Fleming) (as Ivy Peterson)
1942 *Casablanca* (Curtiz) (as Ilsa)
1943 *For Whom the Bell Tolls* (Wood) (as Maria); *Swedes in America* (Lerner)
1944 *Gaslight* (Cukor) (as Paula Alquist)
1945 *Saratoga Trunk* (Wood) (as Clio Dulaine); *Spellbound* (Hitchcock) (as Dr. Constance Peterson); *The Bells of St. Mary's* (McCarey) (as Sister Benedict)
1946 *Notorious* (Hitchcock) (as Alicia Huberman)
1948 *Arch of Triumph* (Milestone) (as Joan Madou); *Joan of Arc* (Fleming) (title role)
1949 *Under Capricorn* (Hitchcock) (as Lady Henrietta Considine)
1950 *Stromboli* (Rossellini) (as Karin)
1951 *Europa '51 (The Greatest Love)* (Rossellini) (as Irene Girard)
1953 *Siamo donne (We, the Women)* (Rossellini)
1954 *Giovanna d'Arco al rogo (Joan at the Stake)* (Rossellini); *Viaggio in Italia (Journey to Italy; The Lonely Woman)* (Rossellini) (as Katherine Joyce)
1955 *Angst (La Paura; Fear)* (Rossellini)
1956 *Anastasia* (Litvak) (title role)
1957 *Elena et les hommes (Paris Does Strange Things)* (Renoir) (title role)

1958   *Indiscreet* (Donen) (as Ann Kalman); *Inn of the Sixth Happi-ness* (Robson) (as Gladys Aylward)
1961   *Aimez-vous Brahms?* (*Goodbye Again*) (Litvak) (as Paula Tessier)
1964   *Der Besuch* (*The Visit*) (Wicki) (as Karla Zachanassian)
1965   *The Yellow Rolls-Royce* (Asquith) (as Mrs. Gerda Millett)
1967   *Stimulantia* ("Smycket" or "The Necklace" ep.) (Molander)
1969   *Cactus Flower* (Saks) (as Stephanie Dickinson)
1970   *A Walk in the Spring Rain* (Green) (as Cissy Meredith); *Henri Langlois* (Hershon and Guerra)
1973   *From the Mixed-Up Files of Mrs. Basil E. Frankweiler* (Cook)
1974   *Murder on the Orient Express* (Lumet)
1976   *A Matter of Time* (Minnelli)
1978   *Autumn Sonata* (Ingmar Bergman) (as Charlotte)

Publications

By BERGMAN: book—

Ingrid Bergman: My Story, with Alan Burgess, New York, 1980.

By BERGMAN: articles—

"Ingrid Bergman on Rossellini," interview by Robin Wood in *Film Comment* (New York), July-August 1974.
Interview with Ingrid Bergman in *Michael Curtiz's "Casablanca"*, by Richard Anobile, New York, 1975.

On BERGMAN: books—

Steele, Joseph Henry, *Ingrid Bergman*, 1959.
Brown, Curtis F., *Ingrid Bergman*, New York, 1973.
Rosen, Marjorie, *Popcorn Venus*, New York, 1973.
Taylor, John Russell, *Ingrid Bergman*, London, 1983.
Leamer, Laurence, *As Time Goes By: The Life of Ingrid Bergman*, New York, 1986.
Quirk, Lawrence J., *The Complete Films of Ingrid Bergman*, New York, 1989.

On BERGMAN: articles—

Tynan, K., "The Abundant Miss Bergman," in *Films and Filming* (London), December 1958.
Vermilye, J., "An Ingrid Bergman Index," in *Films in Review* (New York), May 1961.
Ross, Lillian, "Ingrid Bergman," in *The New Yorker*, 21 October 1961.
Bowers, R., "Ingrid Bergman," in *Films in Review* (New York), February 1968.
Bourget, J.-L., "Romantic Dramas of the Forties," in *Film Comment* (New York), January-February 1974.
Damico, J., "Ingrid from Lorraine to Stromboli: Analyzing the Public's Perception of a Film Star," in *Journal of Popular Film* (Bowling Green, Ohio), v. 4, no. 1, 1975.
Waldman, Diane, "Ingrid Bergman: An Outcast Returns" and "A Nun Does Not Fall in Love with an Italian" in *Close-Ups: The Movie Star Book*, edited by Danny Peary, New York, 1978.
"Ingrid Bergman," in *Ecran* (Paris), April 1978.
"Rossellini's *Stromboli* and Ingrid Bergman's Face," in *Movietone News* (Seattle), December 1979.
Films in Review (New York), March 1980.
Harvey, Stephen, "Ingrid Bergman" in *The Movie Star*, edited by Elisabeth Weis, New York, 1981.
Amiel, M., obituary, in *Cinéma* (Paris), October 1982.
In *The Annual Obituary 1982*, New York, 1983.

*   *   *

The complexity of Ingrid Bergman's career (with its notorious vicissitudes), and of the image that is its product, raises a number of important issues about stars: the perennial one (but here in a peculiarly acute form) of the tensions between acting and presence; the efforts of Hollywood to construct a star according to a specific prescription and the actress's rebellion against that construction; the diverse and sometimes contradictory ways in which a "star image," once constructed, can be inflected in the work of different directors.

The use for which Hollywood initially intended her is clear enough: she was the new Swedish import, the new Garbo, and yet, emphatically, *not* Garbo, the public appearing to be rejecting Garbo's image of an aloof Goddess. Instead of aloofness, mystery, and glamour, what was stressed above all (both on screen and in publicity) was naturalness. Two publicity handouts epitomized this quality: the widely broadcast decision *not* to remold her features in the interests of glamour; and the "secret" of how she maintained her flawless complexion (by going for walks in the rain). The naturalness was, however, immediately qualified by a second layer of signification that already introduced into the image a potential tension: Bergman was natural but she was also a lady, in a sense in which Dietrich was decidedly not, and a sense quite incompatible with Garbo's "mystery"; a "lady" might be expected to end up with a "gentleman" (such as the George Sanders of *Rage in Heaven*) and settle down to a stable respectability. (Certain of the early films—*Intermezzo* and *Adam Had Four Sons*—play upon this possibility by frustrating it.)

Bergman's partial rebellion against this image-construction was motivated by a desire to prove that she could *act*, and was not merely a star. When in the 1941 *Dr. Jekyll and Mr. Hyde* MGM cast her as Jekyll's high society fiancée and Lana Turner as Hyde's low-life mistress and victim, it was Bergman who took the initiative (enlisting Turner's cooperation) in demanding that they exchange roles. A somewhat curious accent aside, her promiscuous cockney barmaid was extremely successful (though the critics, predictably, said she was miscast).

Two of Bergman's finest performances in two of her finest films draw directly upon the natural/lady opposition: the persecuted wife of Cukor's *Gaslight* and the energetic and forthright nun of McCarey's *The Bells of St. Mary's*. The latter, too easily dismissed by embarrassed sophisticates for its alleged sentimentality, is among other things, a complex and delicate study of gender roles, allowing Bergman a wide range of expression within the apparent confines of her nun's habit. Bergman's notions of being an actress (centered on a striving after obviously big acting roles such as Maria in *For Whom the Bell Tolls* and, above all, Joan of Arc in the disastrous Fleming film of that name) were always somewhat naive; her richest and most complex performances arose not out of "big" roles but out of collaborations with directors such as Cukor and McCarey who were particularly sensitive and sympathetic to *performers*, collapsing the usual distinction between presence and acting ability. One may also note that, for all her efforts to establish a wider range, Bergman was quite incapable of playing a bad woman convincingly; the irreducible beauty of her character partly undermines the dismally reactionary project of Ingmar Bergman's *Autumn Sonata*, the chastisement of a great pianist for failing to be a great mother.

The core of Bergman's achievement is in her work for two of the cinema's greatest filmmakers: the three films for Hitchcock, the five for Rossellini. Both, again, drew on the persona, inflecting it in quite different ways. *Spellbound* (the least interesting Hitchcock) reconstructs the natural Bergman out of the repressed psychiatrist. Both *Notorious* and *Under Capricorn* achieve great resonance by playing upon the possibility of the persona's irreparable degradation (through heavy drinking and promiscuity in the former, alcoholism and potential insanity in the latter) and its eventual, triumphant rehabilitation.

The Rossellini films are still disgracefully underrated, even largely unknown, outside small circles of initiates; they are essentially films

Ingrid Bergman

about Bergman (though they are also about much else besides), obliquely relating to her personal situation. *Stromboli* places the lady, as a displaced person, among the physical and emotional brutalities of a primitive community and explores her reactions; *Europa '51* begins by abruptly demolishing the facade of elegance and sophistication that represents one aspect of the woman and proceeds to release the natural side of the woman and develop it towards sainthood; *Viaggio in Italia* reunites the lady with George Sanders in all the sterility of a respectable bourgeois marriage and proceeds to show her reaching out to make contact with eroticism, death, and the terror of emptiness, as a necessary movement towards the discovery of meaning. Bergman herself did not greatly value her work in these films: she didn't "act," she "walked through them." Yet they constitute the essence of her own meaning, as star, presence, actress, image.

—Robin Wood

BERGNER, Elisabeth

Nationality: British. **Born:** Elisabeth Ettel in Drohobyez, Poland (now Drohobych, Ukraine), 22 August 1897; became citizen of Great Britain, 1938. **Education:** Vienna Conservatory, c. 1915-19. **Family:** Married director Paul Czinner, 1931 or 1933 (died 1972). **Career:** 1919—stage debut in Zurich; 1923—film debut in *Der Evangelimann*; late 1920s-early 1930s—international reputation for stage work, particularly in Max Reinhardt productions *Peer Gynt* and *St. Joan*; 1933—moved to England with Czinner; successful London stage debut in *Escape Me Never*, and on Broadway in 1935; late 1930s—5-year contract with United Artists stipulating that the films be made in England; 1940—moved to U.S.; 1950—resettled in England 1950s-1960s—worked intermittently in Germany and Austria; 1962—returned to film acting after 20-year absence. **Awards:** Best Actress Academy Award for *Escape Me Never*, 1935. **Died:** In London, 12 May 1986.

Films as Actress:

1923	*Der Evangelimann* (Holger-Madsen)
1924	*Nju* (*Husbands or Lovers*) (Czinner)
1926	*Der Geiger von Florenz* (*Impetuous Youth*; *The Violinist of Florence*) (Czinner); *Liebe* (Czinner)
1927	*Dona Juana* (Czinner)
1928	*Queen Louise* (*Königin Luise*) (Grune)
1929	*Fräulein Else* (*Miss Else*) (Czinner)
1931	*Ariane* (*The Loves of Ariane*) (Czinner) (title role)
1932	*Der traümende Mund* (*Dreaming Lips*) (Czinner)
1934	*Catherine the Great* (Czinner) (title role)
1935	*Escape Me Never* (Czinner) (as Gemma Jones)
1936	*As You Like It* (Czinner) (as Rosalind)
1937	*Dreaming Lips* (Czinner and Garmes) (as Gaby Lawrence)
1938	*Stolen Life* (Czinner) (as Sylvia/Martina Lawrence)
1941	*Paris Calling* (Marin)
1962	*Die glücklichen Jahre der Thorwalds* (Staudte)
1968	*Strogoff* (*Courier to the Tsar*) (E. Visconti)
1970	*Cry of the Banshee* (Hessler) (as Oona)
1973	*Der Füssgänger* (*The Pedestrian*) (Schell)
1978	*Der Pfingstausflug* (*The Pentecost Outing*; *The Whitsun Outing*) (Gunther)
1982	*Feine Gesellschaft—Beschränkte Haftung* (Runze)
1985	*Der Garten* (Liebeneiner)

Publications

By BERGNER: book—

Bewundert viel und viel gescholten . . . : unordentliche Erinnerungen, Munich, 1978.

By BERGNER: articles—

Interviews in *Picturegoer* (London), 6 January and 18 August 1934.
Interview by Eva Orbanz in *Exil—Sechse Schauspieler aus Deutschland*, Berlin, 1938.
Filmecho/woche (Germany), 11 December 1981.

On BERGNER: book—

Völker, Klaus, *Elisabeth Bergner: das Leben einer Schauspielerin*, Berlin, 1990.

On BERGNER: articles—

Close Up (London), December 1932.
Film Weekly (London), 10 November 1933, 24 August and 14 December 1934.
Picturegoer (London), 2 February 1935, and 1 April 1939.
"Elisabeth Bergner," in *Films in Review* (New York), April 1973, additions to filmography in November 1974 and January 1976 issues.
Shipman, David, in *The Great Movie Stars: The Golden Years*, revised edition, London, 1979.
Ciné Revue (Paris), 9 October 1980.
Kino, Spring 1981, Spring 1983, and Summer 1983.
Obituary in *Variety* (New York), 21 May 1985.

* * *

The dramatic art of Elisabeth Bergner was nourished on stage first in Zurich and then in various Austrian and German cities. When she came to Berlin her popularity was soon established as she captivated spectators and critics with strongly emotive portrayals in such stage productions as *Romeo and Juliet*, *Queen Christine*, and *Camille*. She subsequently began to specialize in playing women with childlike or boyish traits. Her stage and film career is closely related to the work of Hungarian director Paul Czinner who had come to Germany from Budapest via Vienna. He became both her artistic partner and her husband.

Their film collaboration began with *Nju* and continued with *Der Geiger von Florenz*, *Liebe*, *Dona Juana*, and *Fräulein Else*. Her co-stars included the great German film actors Emil Jannings, Conrad Veidt, and Albert Bassermann. The bisexual type that she portrayed in *Der Geiger von Florenz* and in other film and stage roles reflected a contemporary German taste derived, according to Kracauer in *From Caligari to Hitler*, from an "inner laxity of manners."

With the coming of sound, Bergner began to portray a more sentimental and delicate woman. Soon critics labeled her characters as fragile, emotional, or nervous. Bergner acted her roles in such a manner as to charm her audience in an almost hypnotic way. Czinner allowed her to play the whole gamut of emotional experience in a series of films made in Germany, and then in Great Britain to which both of them fled after the rise to power of the Nazis.

The peak of her career is represented by her work in two films. In the first, *Ariane*, an adaptation of a novel by the French author Claude Anet, Bergner played a girl who plunges into adventure with an older, more experienced man. The second is the drama *Der traümende Mund*, an adaptation of a play by Henri Bernstein. Here Bergner played a sensitive, pure woman who cannot escape her passion for a musical

Elisabeth Bergner in *Ariane*

virtuoso, but does not want to hurt her loving husband. This film was remade by Czinner as *Dreaming Lips*, with Bergner again in the leading role. None of her later films achieved such critical popular success. After having made a few films in England, Bergner again dedicated herself to the theater, both as an actress and director. Her profoundly sensitive acting, which influenced the German cinema of the 1920s and 1930s, is, fortunately, preserved on film for future generations.

—Karel Tabery

BERRY, Jules

Nationality: French. **Born:** Jule Paufichet in Poitiers, 9 February 1883. **Education:** Studied architecture at Lycée Louis-le-Grand, Paris. **Military Service:** 1914-19—awarded Croix de Guerre. **Career:** 1903—auditioned for Théâtre Antoine on a whim, and hired for company; 1907—success in Feydeau's *La Duchesse des Folies-Bergères* in Lyons; engagement by Théâtre des Galeries-Saint-Hubert, Brussels; 1908-20—pursued career in Brussels; 1911—in "films d'art" produc-

tion *Cromwell*; 1920s—established reputation as front rank comedic actor in Paris; 1928—induced to take small role in L'Herbier's *L'Argent*; early 1930s—worked in film studios in Stockholm, Berlin, and Budapest; 1933—temporarily ceased stage acting; 1940—last stage appearance, Paris. **Died:** 23 April 1951.

Films as Actor:

1908   *Tirez s'il vous plait* (Gasnier)
1911   *Cromwell* (Desfontaines)
1928   **L'Argent** (L'Herbier)
1931   *Mon Coeur et ses millions* (Arveyres) (as Frank Creighton)
1932   *Quick* (Siodmak) (title role); *Le Roi des palaces* (Gallone) (as Claude Decourcy)
1933   *Arlette et ses papas* (Roussel) (as Pierre)
1934   *Une Femme chipée* (Colombier) (as Germont); *Un Petit Trou pas cher* (Ducis—short)
1935   *Baccara* (Mirande) (as André Leclerc); *Et moi j'te dis qu'elle t'a fait de l'oeil* (Forrester) (as André Courvalin); *Jeunes Filles à marier* (Vallée) (as Perret); *Le Crime de Monsieur Pégotte* (Ducis—short) (as M. Pégotte); *Touche à tout* (Dréville) (as Comte de Bressac); *Monsieur Personne* (Christian-Jaque) (as Comte de Trégunc)

1936   *Le Disque 413* (Pottier); *Les Loups entre eux* (Mathot) (as Commissaire Raucourt); *Cargaison blanche* (*Le Chemin de Rio*) (Siodmak) (as Moreno); *La Bête aux sept manteaux* (*L'Homme à la cagoule noire*) (de Limur) (as Pierre Arnal); *Un Colpo di vento* (Tavano); *Adventure à Paris* (Marc Allégret) (as Michel Levasseur); *Le Mort en fuite* (Berthomieu) (as Trignol); *Rigolboche* (Christian-Jaque) (as Bobby); *Une Poule sur un mur* (Gleize); *27, Rue de la Paix* (Pottier) (as Denis Grand); *Le Voleur de Femmes* (Gance); **Le Crime de Monsieur Lange** (Renoir) (as Batala)

1937   *Rendez-vous aux Champs-Elysées* (Houssin) (as Maxime Germont); *Le Club des aristocrates* (Colombier) (as Serge de Montbreuse); *Les Rois du sport* (Colombier) (as Burette); *L'Habit vert* (Richebé) (as Parmeline); *Les Deux Combinards* (*Le System bouboule*) (Houssin) (as Barisart); *Arsène Lupin Detective* (Diamant-Berger) (title role); *L'Occident* (Fescourt); *L'Homme à abattre* (*Ceux du deuxième bureau*) (Mathot) (as Commissaire Raucourt); *Un Déjeuner de soleil* (Cohen) (as Pierre Haguet)

1938   *L'Inconnue de Monte-Carlo* (Berthomieu) (as Messirian); *Café de Paris* (Lacombe) (as Louis Fleury); *Mon Père et mon papa* (Schoukens) (as La Vaillant); *Eusebe depute* (Berthomieu); *L'Avion de minuit* (Kirsanoff) (as Carlos); *Hercule* (Esway) (as Vasco); *Clodoche* (*Sous les ponts de Paris*) (Lamy) (as Prince Berky); *Carrefour* (Bernhardt) (as Lucien Sarroux); *Balthazar* (Colombier) (title role)

1939   *Cas de conscience* (Kapps) (as Laurent Arnoux); *Accord final* (Bay) (as Baron Larzac); *Son Oncle de Normandie* (*La Fugue de Jim Baxter*) (Dréville) (as Joseph); *Derrière la façade* (Mirande and Lacombe) (as Alfredo); **Le Jour se lève** (*Daybreak*) (Carné) (as Valentin); *Retour au bonheur* (*L'Enfant de la tourmente*) (Jayet); *La Famille duraton* (Stengel) (as Samy); *Paris—New York* (Mirande and Heymann) (as the manager)

1940   *L'Héritier des Mondésir* (Valentin) (as Waldemar); *L'An quarante* (Mirande); *Soyez les bienvenus* (de Baroncelli)

1941   *L'Embuscade* (Rivers—produced 1939); *Face au destin* (Fescourt—produced 1939) (as Claude); *Parade en sept nuits* (Marc Allégret); *Les Petit riens* (Leboursier)

1942   *Après l'orage* (Ducis) (as Alex Krakow); *La Symphonie fantastique* (Christian-Jaque) (as Schlesinger); *La Troisième Dalle* (Dulud) (as Stéphane Barbaroux); *L'Assassin a peur la nuit* (Delannoy) (as Jérôme); *Les Visiteurs du soir* (Carné) (as le Diable); *Le Grand Combat* (Roland) (as Charlie)

1943   *Des jeunes filles dans la nuit* (Hénaff and Mirande); *Le Camion blanc* (Joannon) (as Shabbas); *Le Voyageur de la Toussaint* (Daquin) (as Plantel); *Marie-Martine* (Valentin) (as Loïc Limousin); *Le Soleil de minuit* (Roland) (as Forestier); *L'Homme de Londres* (Decoin) (as Brown); *Tristi amori* (Gallone); *T'amero sempre* (Camerini)

1944   *Le Mort ne reçoit plus* (Tarride); *Beatrice devant le désir* (de Marguenat)

1945   *Dorothée cherche l'amour* (Gréville) (as Monsieur Pascal)

1946   *Monsieur Gregoire s'evade* (Daniel-Norman) (as Charles Tuffal); *Messieurs Ludovic* (Le Chanois) (as Guillaume Maréchal); *Etoiles sans lumière* (Blistène); *L'Assassin n'est pas coupable* (Delacroix) (as himself); *Desarroi* (Dagan) (as Frontenac)

1947   *Rêves d'amour* (Stengel) (as Belloni); *La Taverne du poisson couronne* (Chanas) (as Fléo)

1948   *Si jeunesse savait* (Cerf) (as Charles Vigne)

1949   *Portrait d'un assassin* (Roland) (as Pfeiffer); *Histoires extraordinaires* (Faurez) (as Fortunato)

1950   *Pas de week-end pour notre amour* (Montazel) (as Baron Richard); *Tête blonde* (Cam) (as Frédéric Truche); *Sans tambour ni trompette* (Blanc); *Le Gang des tractions-arrière* (Loubignac) (as Baron Dupuy de la Margelle); *Les Maitres-Nageurs* (Lepage) (as Chamboise)

Publications

On BERRY: book—

Marc, Henri, *Jules Berry: Le Jouer*, Paris, 1988.

On BERRY: article—

Barrot, O., "Jules Berry," in *Anthologie du Cinéma*, vol. 8, Paris, 1972.

                *   *   *

After graduating from secondary school Jules Berry began training to become an architect, but took a job as an apprentice in a theater company and therefore his fate was sealed. He appeared in various minor roles, then attracted attention during the visit of his theater company to Lyons and was engaged by a company in Brussels where he was to remain for many years. He appeared in Paris on tour in 1910 and 1913, and during those years he occasionally played a small part in a film. After the First World War Berry returned to Paris and appeared in a series of vaudevilles and light comedies that were not particularly challenging but did give him the opportunity to play a great variety of parts and to refine his talent. In his private life, he was a ladies' man and a gambler (he gambled away much of what he earned in his life), and something of the aura of the dandy pervaded his performances: he became noted for his elegant appearance, vivid temperament, timing, and his ease at portraying both lovers and seducers—roles he was to be equally adept at playing in films.

Berry made his first important film appearance in 1928 in L'Herbier's *L'Argent*, an adaptation of the work by Zola. In the early 1930s, like many of his fellow stage actors, he made films abroad, in Sweden, Hungary, and Germany (he appeared in Siodmak's *Quick* in Berlin). After returning to Paris he got a part in Roussell's *Arlette et ses papas*, returned briefly to the stage, then left the theater entirely for a time and accepted any film offers that came his way without much concern for the quality of the script or the director. From 1933 until his death in 1951 Berry appeared in almost 100 films, often as many as 10 a year, his reputation in the theater often serving as a guarantee for many adaptations on plays, talky efforts that had little to do with the expressionistic techniques available to film. These unpretentious products were popular with French audiences of the early 1930s, and Berry was the ideal representative of the usual hero—high society sophisticate, aristocrat, successful industrialist, cynical Don Juan. He played yet another variant on his usual range of characters in *Le Crime de Monsieur Lange* in 1935, but this was a film written by Prévert and directed by Jean Renoir, and here Berry achieved a greater conciseness and dramatic tension in performance than in his other films. As the entrepreneur Batala, whose interests are dictated by his egoism, who not only mercilessly exploits his employees but also tries to dupe them, he gave a performance that was universally admired.

Berry had some success in the part of the police commissioner Raucourt in films made by Mathot in 1936-37, and he returned to detective films in 1938-40. He worked with such directors as Pottier, Allégret, Mirande and others, but none of his films of the late 1930s in notable. The exception is *Le Jour se lève*, with a script by Prévert and directed by Carné, in which Berry had one of his most important roles—the artist Valentin, a demonic incarnation of evil who obstructs the love of two young people. Berry gives a masterful perfor-

Jules Berry with Arletty in *Le Jour se lève*

mance of rich nuance, expressing a series of contradictory states of mind: a charlatan who sneers at human goodness and weakness, abuses his power, dissimulates, torments others with his cruelty, then tries to evoke pity for himself. He created yet another incarnation of evil in the 1942 Carné film, *Les Visiteurs du soir*. The film was highly praised, and it marks a high point in Berry's career as a film actor.

From then on, however, Berry's career seemed to go into eclipse. He made more detective films and played yet another unsympathetic character in Daguin's *Le Voyageur de la Toussaint*. But Berry was not really offered the opportunities in the 1940s that his talent and reputation should have commanded. An exception in André Cerf's *Si jeunesse savait* (reminiscent in many ways of the style of Clair, whose assistant Cerf had been). Berry plays a billionaire in this brilliant comedy, and provides additional evidence, if any were needed, of the exceptional range, technique, and mature interpretational style he had developed.

—Karel Tabery

BERTINI, Francesca

Nationality: Italian. **Born:** Elena Seracini Vitiello in Florence, 11 April 1888 (some sources state 6 February 1892). **Family:** Married Count Paul Cartier, 1921, one son. **Career:** c. 1903—stage debut at Teatro Nuovo in Naples; member of troupe of dialect players under Gennaro Pantalena; about 1907—film debut in Neapolitan film *La dea del mare*; acted for Film d'Arte Italiana Pathé, 1910-11, for Cine production company, 1912, for Celio production company, 1912-14; 1914—began acting for Caeser and Bertini Film; 1915—international star after role in *Assunta spina*; 1918—co-directed *La Tosca*, first and only attempt at film direction; 1920—contract with 20th Century-Fox; 1921—broke contract with Fox to retire from acting after marriage to Count Cartier; late 1920s—appeared in a few sound films in Germany and France; 1930-76—made occasional special appearance in various films. **Died:** October 1985.

Films as Actress:

c.1907 *La dea del mare*
1910 *Il trovatore* (Gasnier)
1911 *Ernani*; *Guilietta e Romeo*; *Tristano e Isotta*; *Francesca da Rimini*; *La contessa di Challant*; *Re Lear*; *Folchetto di Narbonne*; *Lorenzo il Magnifico*; *Pia De' Tolomei*
1912 *La morte civile*; *Il ritratto dell'amata*; *Il mercante di Venezia*; *La suonatrice ambulante*; *La rosa di Tebe*; *Il Pappagallo della zia Berta* (Negroni); *Idillio tragico* (Negroni); *Lagrime e sorrisi* (Negroni)
1913 *La gloria* (Negroni); *L'avvoltoio nero*; *L'arma dei vigliacchi*; *Terra promessa*; *La maestrina* (Negroni); *La bufera* (Negroni); *Tramonte*; *L'Histoire d'un Pierrot* (Negroni); *Idolo infranto*; *L'anima del demi-monde* (Negroni); *L'arrivista*; *La cricca dorata*; *In faccia al destino* (Negroni); *La madre* (Negroni); *La vigilia di natale*; *Salome*; *Per la sua gioia*
1914 *Eroismo d'amore* (Ravà); *L'onesta che uccide*; *L'amazzone mascherata*; *La canzone di Werner*; *Sangue bleu* (Ravà); *Nelly la gigolette* (Ghione); *Une donna!*; *Per il blasone*; *La principessa straniera*; *Rose e spine*; *Il veleno della parole*; *Colpa altrui*
1915 *Assunta spina* (Serena); *La signora dalle camelie* (Serena); *Nella fornace* (Oxilia); *Ivonne* (Serena); *Diana l'affascinatrice* (De Antoni); *Il capestro degli Asburgo*

1916 *La perla del cinema* (De Liguoro or Serena or De Antoni); *Fedora* (De Liguoro or De Antoni); *Odette* (De Liguoro); *My Little Baby* (*Baby l'indiavolate*) (De Liguoro); *Ferréol* (De Antoni); *Oberdan* (Serena); *Vittima dell'ideale* (Serena)
1917 *Don Pietro Caruso* (Bracco); *Lacrimae rerum* (*Nel gorgo della vita*) (Del Liguoro); *Andreina* (Roberti or Serena); *L'alba*; *Anima redenta*
1918 *La Tosca* (+ co-d with De Antoni or Serena); *L'affaire Clémenceau* (De Antoni); *Piccolo Fonte* (Roberti); *Frou Frou* (Roberti or De Antoni); *La piovra* (Roberti); *Malia* (De Antoni); *Anima allegra* (Roberti); *La donna nuda* (Roberti); *Mariute* (Bencivenga); *Saracinesca* (Roberti)
1919 *Oltre le legge*; *L'ombra* (Roberti); *Principessa Giorgio* (Roberti); *La contessa Sarah* (Roberti); *Lise Fleron* (Roberti); *Spiritismo* (Roberti); *La serpe* (Roberti); *Beatrice* (De Riso); *La sfinnge* (Roberti)
1920 *I sette piccata capitali* (series of 7 films) (Roberti, De Riso, Bencivenga, De Antoni, and possibly d'Ambra); *Anima selvaggia*
1921 *Maddalena Ferat* (Roberti); *Le blessure* (Roberti); *Marion* (Roberti); *La giovinezza del diavolo* (D'Annunzio); *La fanciulla di Amalfi*; *Amore vince amore*; *La donna, il diavolo, il tempo*; *Fama* (Roberti); *La Ferita* (Roberti); *Ultimo sogno* (Roberti)
1922 *Consuelita* (Roberti)
1928 *Monte Carlo* (*La fine di Montecarlo*); *Odette* (*Mein Leben fur das deine*) (Morat)
1929 *Possession* (Perret); *Tu m'appartiens* (Glieze)
1930 *La donna di una notte* (Palermi); *La Femme d'une nuit* (L'Herbier) (French version of previous film)
1943 *Dora*
1956 *A sud niente di nuovo* (Simonelli)
1976 *1900* (*Novecento*) (Bertolucci)

Publications

By BERTINI: book—

Il resto non conta, Pisa, 1969.

On BERTINI: books—

Bianchi, Pietro, *Francesca Bertini e le dive del cinema muto*, Torino, 1969.
Costantini, Costanzo, *La diva imperiale: ritratto di Francesca Bertini*, Milano, 1982.

On BERTINI: articles—

Mariátegui, J. C., "La ultima pelicula de Francesca Bertini," in *Hablemos de cine* (Lima), January/March 1972.
Filmography in *Bianco e nero* (Rome), May 1978.
Cahiers de la Cinématheque (Paris), nos. 26-27, 1979.
Cinema nuovo (Turin), August 1981.

On BERTINI: film—

The Last Diva, Gianfranco Mingozzi, 1983.

*   *   *

A type of film star grew up in the early Italian cinema: sophisticated, glamorous, highly temperamental, and a trendsetter in fashion and romance. The film divas were highly competitive and jealously

Francesca Bertini

guarded their status in the cinema; they were also highly paid. Lyda Borelli and Hesperia were two of them, but Francesca Bertini was to become the most famous.

After having begun her career in Naples, Bertini came to Rome and played with Celio films, where she was groomed for stardom. In 1913 she scored a great success in Baldassare Negroni's *L'Histoire d'un Pierrot*. Apart from her performance, the film showed a mastery of screen language and attracted wide audiences outside of Italy. Her repertoire included popular Italian and French plays such as those of Sardou. In 1915 she made her best film, *Assunta spina*, a break with the torrid society dramas to which her public was accustomed. Her *Nelly la gigolette*, intelligently directed by Emilio Ghione the previous year, was also a more down-to-earth creation. *Assunta spina* was the story of a working-class girl who is a slave of circumstance, attracting men whose loves, jealousies, and selfishness lead her to a tragic end. A faithful depiction of its setting (it was shot in the streets of Naples), it anticipates the neorealism of the 1940s. Its director, Gustave Serena, played the lead.

For great roles such as *La Tosca*, *Fedora*, and *La signora dalle camelie*, she rose to the occasion. The latter was rushed through to challenge her rival Hesperia, then appearing in the same role. Bertini's output was prolific, encompassing all kinds of subjects; she possessed both a photogenic beauty, and an expressive personality.

In 1921 she married Count Paul Cartier and retired from films. But she did return to filmmaking in Germany and Spain at the beginning of the sound period and thereafter made special appearances, as Burt Lancaster's sister, for example, in Bertolucci's *1900*. When the London Film Festival of 1983 presented a film about her by Gianfranco Mingozzi she was planning to attend the showing, though she was then in her nineties. The title of the film was *The Last Diva*. Louis Delluc, an admirer of hers, said: "One does not know till too late that it is necessary to study all the work of Francesca Bertini."

—Liam O'Leary

BINOCHE, Juliette

Nationality: French. **Born:** Paris, France, 9 March 1965. **Education:** Attended acting school in the late 1970s and later took classes at the Paris Conservatoire. **Family:** Son with André Halle: Raphael. **Career:** 1983—film debut in *Liberty Belle*; 1988—international success with *The Unbearable Lightness of Being*; on stage in Paris in Chekhov's *The Seagull*; mid-1990s—Lancôme model for the fragrance Pôeme. **Awards:** Best Actress Award, Venice Film Festival, for *Blue*, 1993. **Agent:** Intertalent Agency, 131 South Rodeo Drive, Suite 300, Beverly Hills, CA 90212, U.S.A.

Films as Actress:

1983 *Liberty Belle* (Kane)
1984 *Les Nanas* (*The Women*) (Lanoe)
1985 *Je vous salue, Marie* (*Hail Mary*) (Godard) (as Juliette); *La Vie de famille* (*Family Life*) (as Natacha); *Rendez-vous* (Téchiné) (as Nina Larrieu)
1986 *Mauvais Sang* (*The Night Is Young; Bad Blood*) (Carax) (as Anna); *Mon Beau-frère a tué ma soeur* (*My Brother-in-Law Has Killed My Sister*) (as Esther)
1988 *The Unbearable Lightness of Being* (Kaufman) (as Tereza)
1989 *Un Tour de manège* (*Roundabout*) (as Elsa)
1991 *Les Amants du Pont Neuf* (*The Lovers on the Pont-Neuf*) (Carax) (as Michele); *Women & Men II* (*Women & Men: In Love There Are No Rules*) (Bernstein, Figgis, and Zea—for TV) (as Mara)

1992 *Wuthering Heights* (Kosminsky—not released in U.S.) (as Catherine Earnshaw); *Fatale* (*Damage*) (Malle) (as Anna Barton)
1993 *Trois Couleurs: Bleu* (*Three Colours: Blue*) (Kieślowski) (as Julie); *Trois Couleurs: Blanc* (*Three Colours: White*) (Kieślowski) (cameo as Julie)
1994 *Trois Couleurs: Rouge* (*Three Colours: Red*) (Kieślowski) (cameo as Julie)
1995 *Le Hussard sur le toit* (*The Horseman on the Roof*) (as Pauline de Theus)
1996 *The English Patient* (Minghella) (as Hanna); *Lucie Aubrac* (Berri); *Un Divan a New York* (*A Couch in New York*) (Akerman) (as Beatrice Saulnier)

Publications

By BINOCHE: articles—

Interview with Josephine Hart, in *Interview* (New York), December 1992.
"Juliette Speaks . . .," interview with Maro Sorrenti, in *Harper's Bazaar* (New York), November 1995.

Juliette Binoche in *The Unbearable Lightness of Being*

On BINOCHE: articles—

Kavanagh, Julie, and Nick Briggs, "Binoche, by Gosh," in *Vanity Fair* (New York), May 1992.
Riding, Alan, "Juliette Binoche Plays a Riddle without a Solution," in *New York Times*, 20 December 1992.
Sight and Sound (London), September 1993.
Reilly, Anthony, "Bluebelle," in *Premiere* (New York), January 1994.
London Observer, 31 December 1995.

*   *   *

Juliette Binoche was introduced to French theater at the age of 12 by her actress-writer mother, with whom her acting studies began. Her father is a former mime who creates masks for the theater. Her parents separated when she was two years old, and she believes she was drawn into the theater because it represented a family. While better known for her film roles, Binoche remains tied to the theater where she began her career (she appeared on stage in Paris in 1988 in Chekov's *The Seagull*, directed by Andrei Konchalovsky).

Binoche was urged to audition for films when she was 18 by a casting director who helped her get some bit parts. Despite her success at an early age, Binoche did not emerge overnight. After studying acting for several years she performed in stage productions in the early 1980s and in some television films. Her first film roles followed: in Pascal Kane's *Liberty Belle*; a small part in Jean-Luc Godard's *Hail Mary*, with her youthful innocence as her selling point; and a more substantial role in Annick Lanoe's *Les Nanas*.

She met the director Léos Carax in 1985, starred in his thriller *Mauvais Sang*, and began to undergo a transformation. They moved in together and this relationship dominated her professional and emotional life for four years. Carax molded Binoche for the role of Anna in *Mauvais Sang*, requiring her to adopt a gamin look and to lose weight. She studied dance and voice, read Balzac, and even changed her laugh. (Later Carax would cast Binoche as the one-eyed, gun-toting painter, Michele, in *Les Amants du Pont Neuf*, an unsuccessful, $30 million film which proved to be the most expensive thus far in French history.)

Later in the 1980s she reached international fame with her English-language debut, *The Unbearable Lightness of Being*, based on the Milan Kundera novel, playing a sexual free spirit. In her next two widely seen roles—in Louis Malle's *Damage* and *Blue*, the first film of Krzysztof Kieślowski's *Trzy Kolory* trilogy—Binoche was not free spirited at all, but rather gave exceptionally passive and solemn portrayals, too detached for many observers. Binoche had turned down the female lead in Steven Spielberg's *Jurassic Park* (played by Laura Dern), to star in *Blue*—likely a smart move given how difficult it is to imagine her in such an action-filled thriller at this stage of her career.

In her latest film to date, *A Couch in New York*, the first major film of Belgian director Chantal Akerman, Binoche changed her image again—away from the serious, sad beauty—toward a lighter character sans the once-in-vogue anguish that pervaded her earlier characters. Whether this welcome transformation is successful will go a long way toward determining the future direction of a still young career.

—Kelly Otter

BJÖRNSTRAND, Gunnar

Nationality: Swedish. **Born:** Stockholm, 13 November 1909. **Education:** Royal Dramatic Theatre School, Stockholm. **Family:** Married Lillie Lundahl, 1935, three daughters. **Career:** 1931—film debut in *Pour mon coeur et ses millions*; 1936-38—acted at the Swedish Theater in Helsinki; after stint at Swedish Theater, continued stage acting mainly in Stockholm; 1946—first film with Ingmar Bergman, *Det regnar på vår kärlek*, which began long professional association; 1948—guest artist at Royal Dramatic Theater, Stockholm; 1966—in film *Pälsen (The Overcoat)* for Swedish television. **Awards:** Swedish Film Society's Gösta Ekman Prize, 1953. **Died:** 24 May 1986.

Films as Actor:

1931   *Pour mon coeur et ses millions (The False Millionaire)* (Berthomieu)
1938   *Vi som går scenvägen (We from the Theatre)* (Wahlberg); *Juninatten (Night in June)* (Lindberg)
1939   *Panik (Panic)* (Willoughby); *Vi två (We Two)* (Bauman); *Mot nya tider (Towards New Times)* (Wallén)
1940   *Hjältar i gult och blått (Heroes in Yellow and Blue)* (Bauman); *Karl för sin hatt (An Able Man)* (Bauman); *Hennes melodi (Her Melody)* (Thor Brooks); *Alle man på post (Everybody at His Station)* (Henrikson)
1942   *Snapphanar (Scanian Guerilla)* (Ohberg); *En äventyrare (Adventurer)* (Olsson); *General von Döbeln* (Molander)
1943   *Natt ihamn (Night in the Harbour)* (Faustman); *Jag dräpte (I Killed)* (Olof Molander)
1944   *Appassionata* (Olof Molander); *Lev farlight (Live Dangerously)* (Falk); *Mitt folk är icke ditt (My People Are Not Yours)* (Hildebrand); *Nyordning på Sjögårda (New Order at Sjögårda)* (Hildebrand); *Hets (Frenzy)* (Sjöberg)
1945   *Sussie* (Mattsson); *I som här inträden . . . (You Who Are about to Enter . . .)* (Mattsson)
1946   *Peggy på vift (Peggy on a Spree)* (Mattsson); *Kristin Kommenderar (Kristin Commands)* (Edgren); *Rötägg (Bad Eggs)* (Mattsson); *Det regnar på vår kärlek (It Rains on Our Love; The Man with an Umbrella)* (Bergman); *Medan porten var stängd (While the Door Was Locked)* (Ekman); *Midvinterblot (Midwinter Blood)* (Werner)
1947   *Bruden kom genom taket (Bride Came through the Ceiling)* (Palm); *Pappa sökes (Daddy Wanted)* (Mattsson); *Krigsmans erinran (Soldier's Duties)* (Faustman); *En fluga gör ingen sommar (One Swallow Doesn't Make a Summer)* (Ekman); *Här kommer vi (Here We Come)* (Lagerwall and Zacharias); *Två kvinnor (Two Women)* (Sjöstrand)
1948   *Musik i mörker (Music in Darkness; Night Is My Future)* (Bergman); *Var sin väg (Each to His Own Way)* (Ekman); *En svensk tiger (A Swedish Tiger)* (Edgren); *Lilla Märta kommer tilbaka (Little Märta Returns)* (Ekman); *Soldat Bom (Private Bom)* (Kjellgren)
1949   *Skola skolen (Playing Truant)* (Bauman); *Flickan från tredje raden (Girl from the Third Row)* (Ekman); *Pappa Bom (Father Bom)* (Kjellgren)
1950   *Min syster och jag (My Sister and I)* (Bauman); *Fästmö uthyres (Fiancée for Hire)* (Gustaf Molander); *Kyssen på kryssen (Kiss on the Cruise)* (Mattsson); *Den vita katten (The White Cat)* (Ekman); *Kvartetten som sprängdes (The Quartet That Was Split Up)* (Gustaf Molander)
1951   *Tull-Bom (Customs Officer Bom)* (Kjellgren)
1952   *Säg det med blommer (Say It with Flowers)* (Kjellgren); *En fästman i taget (One Fiancé at a Time)* (Bauman); *Kvinnors väntan (Secrets of Women; Waiting Women)* (Bergman); *Flyg-Bom (Bom the Flyer)* (Kjellgren); *Oppåt med gröna hissen (Up with the Green Lift)* (Larsson)
1953   *Dansa min docka (Dance with My Doll)* (Söderhjelm); *Vi tre debutera (We Three Debutantes)* (Ekman); **Gycklarnas afton** *(The Naked Night; Sawdust and Tinsel)* (Bergman); *Glasberget (Unmarried)* (Gustaf Molander)

1954 *Flottans glada gossar* (*Happy Lads of the Fleet*) (Husberg); *Seger i mörker* (*Victory in the Dark*) (Folke); *En lektion i kärlek* (*A lesson in Love*) (Bergman); *Gabrielle* (Ekman)

1955 *Stampen* (*Pawn Shop*) (Lagerkvist); *Kvinnodröm* (*Dreams*; *Journey into Autumn*) (Bergman); **Sommarnattens leende** (*Smiles of a Summer Night*) (Bergman)

1956 *Det är aldrig för sent* (*It's Never Too Late*) (Boman); *Sjunde himlen* (*Seventh Heaven*) (Ekman)

1957 *Skorpan* (*The Rusk*) (Lagerkvist); **Det sjunde inseglet** (*The Seventh Seal*) (Bergman); *Natten ljus* (*Night Light*) (Kjellgren); *Sommarnöje sökes* (*Summer Place Wanted*) (Ekman); **Smultronstället** (*Wild Strawberries*) (Bergman)

1958 *Du är mitt äventyr* (*You Are My Adventure*) (Olin); *Fröken April* (*Miss April*) (Gentele); *Ansiktet* (*The Magician*; *The Face*) (Bergman)

1959 *Det svänger på slottet* (*Swinging at the Castle*) (Kjellin); *Brott i paradiset* (*Crime in Paradise*) (Kjellgren); *Himmel och pannkaka* (*Heaven and Pancakes*) (Ekman); *Mälarpirater* (*Pirates on the Malaren*) (Holmgren)

1960 *Djävulens öga* (*The Devil's Eye*) (Bergman)

1961 *Såsom i en spegel* (*Through a Glass Darkly*) (Bergman); *Lustgården* (*The Pleasure Garden*) (Kjellin)

1963 *Nattvardsgästerna* (*Winter Light*) (Bergman); *Lyckodrömmen* (*Dream of Happiness*) (Abramson); *Min kära är en ros* (*My Love Is Like a Rose*) (Ekman)

1964 *Klänningen* (*The Dress*) (Sjöman); *Aktenskapabrottaren* (*Marriage Wrestler*) (Ekman); *Allskande par* (*Loving Couples*) (Zetterling)

1965 *Syskonbädd 1782* (*My Sister, My Love*) (Sjöman)

1966 *Träfracken* (*The Sadist*) (Lindgren); **Persona** (Bergman); *Här har du ditt liv* (*Here Is Your Life*) (Troell)

1967 *Den rode kappe* (*The Red Mantle*) (Axel); *Stimulantia* ("Smycket" or "The Necklace" ep.) (Gustaf Molander); *Tofflan-en lycklig komedi* (*Slipper*) (Anderberg)

1968 *Flickorna* (*The Girls*) (Zetterling); *Skammen* (*Shame*) (Bergman)

1969 *Pappa, varför är du arg? Du gjorde likadant själv när du var ung* (*Daddy, Why Are You Angry? You Did the Same When You Were Young*) (Stivell); *Riten* (*The Rite*) (Bergman—for TV); *Una estate in quattro* (*L'isola*) (Vancini)

1971 *Lockfågeln* (*The Birdcall*) (Wickman)

1973 *Pistolen* (*The Pistol*) (Tirl)

1976 *Ansikte mot ansikte* (*Face to face*) (Bergman—for TV)

1977 *Tabu* (*Taboo*) (Sjöman)

1978 *Herbstsonate* (*Autumn Sonata*; *Höstsonaten*) (Bergman)

1982 **Fanny och Alexander** (*Fanny and Alexander*) (Bergman)

Publications

On BJÖRNSTRAND: article—

Obituary in *Variety* (New York), 28 May 1986.

*   *   *

Gunnar Björnstrand made a career portraying morally upright figures plagued by doubt and temptation. A courtly actor who seemed equally at home in comedy and melodrama, he came to the attention of non-Swedish film audiences in the dozen or so films of Ingmar Bergman in which he appeared.

Björnstrand made his first film for Bergman in 1946, *It Rains on Our Love*, and rose to international prominence in a series of films beginning with *Sawdust and Tinsel*, and culminating with *Winter Light*. His role in this last film was a tour de force for Björnstrand who played

a man of God who had lost his faith and, although he searched for meaning in the modern world, could provide little guidance for himself or his parishioners. The elegance of Björnstrand's bearing provided a vivid contrast to the inner torment caused by his religious uncertainty. For *The Seventh Seal*, on the other hand, where he played the cynical Sancho Panza-like companion to Max von Sydow's questing knight, he was cast against type and provided a shrewd foil to his Quixotic master.

Björnstrand continued to play roles in other Swedish productions including Vilgot Sjöman's *The Dress* and the same director's controversial *My Sister, My Love*, Jan Troell's first feature, *Here Is Your Life*, and Mai Zetterling's *Loving Couples* and *The Girls*. He also appeared in Bergman's more recent films such as *Shame*, *Face to Face*, and the international success, *Autumn Sonata*.

—Charles L. P. Silet

BLIER, Bernard

Nationality: French. **Born:** Buenos Aires, Argentina, of French parents, 11 January 1916. **Education:** Lycée Condorcet; studied drama with Raymond Rouleau, and at Paris Conservatory under Louis Jouvet. **Family:** Married; son: film director Bertrand Blier; daughter: Brigitte. **Career:** 1936—stage debut at Théâtre de l'Etoile, Paris; 1937—film debut in *Troix-six-neuf*; 1940—mobilized at beginning of war, taken prisoner by Germans; 1942—resumed stage appearances; after war—leading player in "boulevard comedies" on Parisian stage. **Awards:** Brussels Prize, 1949; Prix Feminin de Cinéma, 1950; Prix Balzac, 1973; Chevalier de la Legion d'honneur; Special César, 1988. **Died:** In Paris, 29 March 1989.

Films as Actor:

1937 *Trois-six-neuf* (Rouleau); *Gribouille* (*Heart of Paris*) (M. Allégret); *Le Messager* (Rouleau); *La Dame de Malacca* (M. Allégret); *L'Habit vert* (Richebé)

1938 *Altitude 3200* (*Youth in Revolt*) (Benoît-Lévy); *Entrée des artistes* (*The Curtain Rises*) (M. Allégret); *Hôtel du Nord* (Carné); *Grisou* (de Canonge); *Double Crime sur la Ligne Maginot* (*Treachery Within*) (Candera); *Place de la Concorde* (Lamac); *Accord final* (Bay)

1939 **Le Jour se lève** (*Daybreak*) (Carné); *L'Enfer des anges* (Christian-Jaque); *Quartier Latin* (Colombier); *Nuit de Décembre* (*Heure exquise*) (Bernhardt); *Tourelle 3* (Christian-Jaque—unfinished due to outbreak of war)

1941 *L'Assassinat du Père Nöel* (*Who Killed Santa Claus?*) (Christian-Jaque); *Le Pavillon Brûle* (de Baroncelli); *Premier bal* (Christian-Jaque); *Caprices* (Joannon)

1942 *La Symphonie fantastique* (Christian-Jaque); *La Femme que j'ai le plus aimée* (Vernay); *Romance à trois* (Richebé); *La Nuit fantastique* (L'Herbier); *Le Journal tombe à cinq heures* (Lacombe); *Le Mariage de chiffon* (Autant-Lara); *Marie Martine* (Valentin)

1943 *Les Petites du quai aux Fleurs* (M. Allégret); *Je suis avec toi* (Decoin); *Domino* (Richebé)

1944 *Farandolle* (Zwoboda)

1945 *Seul dans la nuit* (Stengel); *Monsieur Gregoire s'évadé* (Daniel-Norman)

1946 *Messieurs Ludovic* (Le Chanois); *Le Café du Cadran* (Gehret)

1947 *Quai des Orfèvres* (Clouzot)

1948   *Dédée d'Anvers* (*Dédée*) (Y. Allégret); *D'homme à hommes* (*Man to Men*) (Christian-Jaque); *Les Casse-pieds* (*The Spice of Life*) (Dreville)

1949   *L'Ecole buissonière* (*Passion for Life*; *I Have a New Master*) (Le Chanois); *Monseigneur* (Richebé); *Retour à la vie* ("Tante Emma" ep.) (Cayatte); *L'Invité du Mardi* (Deval)

1950   *La Souricière* (Calef); *Manèges* (*The Cheat*; *Riding for a Fall*) (Y. Allégret); *Les Anciens de Saint-Loup* (Lampin); *Souvenirs perdus* (Christian-Jaque)

1951   *Sans laisser d'adresse* (Le Chanois); *La Maison Bonnadieu* (Rim)

1952   *Agence matrimoniale* (Le Chanois); *Je l'ai été trois fois* (Guitry)

1953   *Secrets d'alcôve* ("Le Lit de la Pompadour" ep.) (*The Bed*) (Delannoy); *Suivez cet homme!* (Lampin)

1954   *Avant le déluge* (Cayatte); *Scènes de ménage* (Berthomieu)

1955   *Le Dossier noir* (Cayatte); *Les Hussards* (Joffe)

1956   *Crime et châtiment* (*Crime and Punishment*) (Lampin); *Prigionieri del male* (Costa); *Rivelazione*

1957   *L'Homme à l'imperméable* (*The Man in the Raincoat*) (Duvivier); *Retour de Manivelle* (*There's Always a Price Tag*) (de la Patellière); *Quand la femme s'en mêle* (Y. Allégret); *La Bonne Tisane* (Bromberger)

1958   *Les Misérables* (Le Chanois) (as Javert); *La Chatte* (*The Cat*) (Decoin); *Les Grandes Familles* (*The Possessors*) (de la Patellière); *Sans famille* (Michel); *En légitime défense* (Berthomieu); *Le Joueur* (Autant-Lara); *L'Ecole des cocottes* (Audry)

1959   *Marie-Octobre* (Duvivier); *La grande querra* (*La Grande Guerre*; *The Great War*) (Monicelli) (as Captain Castelli); *Marche ou crève* (Lautner); *Archimède, le clochard* (*The Magnificent Tramp*) (Grangier) (as Pichon); *Les Yeux de l'amour* (de la Patellière)

1960   *Il Gobbo* (*Le Bossu de Rome*; *The Hunchback of Rome*) (Lizzani) (title role); *Crimen* (. . . *and Suddenly It's Murder*) (Camerini) (as police commissioner); *Vive Henri IV, vive l'amour!* (Autant-Lara); *Le Secret du Chevalier d'Eon* (Audry); *Le Président* (Verneuil)

1961   *Le Cave se rebiffe* (*The Counterfeiters of Paris*; *Money, Money, Money*) (Grangier) (as Charles); *Arrêtez les tambours* (*Women and War*) (Lautner) (as Mayor Leproux); *I briganti italiani* (*Les Guerilleros*) (Camerini); *Les Petits Matins* (Audry); *Le Monocle noir* (Gerard)

1962   *Mathias Sandorff* (Lampin); *Le Septième Juré* (*The Seventh Juror*) (Lautner) (as Grégoire Duval); *Pourquoi Paris?* (de la Patellière); *Les Saintes Nitouches* (Montazel)

1963   *I compagni* (*The Organizer*) (Monicelli) (as Martinetti); *Il magnifico avventuriero* (Freda); *Germinal* (Y. Allégret); *Cent Mille Dollars au Soleil* (*Greed in the Sun*) (Verneuil) (as Mitch-Mitch)

1964   *La Bonne Soupe* (*Careless Love*) (Thomas) (as Monsieur Joseph); "Gente modern" ("Modern People") ep. of *Alta infedeltà* (*High Infidelity*) (Monicelli) (as Reguzzoni); *Il magnifico cornuto* (*The Magnificent Cuckold*) (Pietrangeli) (as Corna d'Oro); *La Chasse à l'homme* (*Male Hunt*) (Molinaro) (as Monsieur Heurtin); *Les Barbouzes* (*The Great Spy Chase*) (Lautner) (as Cafarelli); "Une Chance explosive" or "Le Jeu de la chance" ep. of *La Chance et l'amour* (Tavernier)

1965   "La Fermeture" ep. of *Les Bons Vivants* (Grangier); *Una questione d'onore* (*A Question of Honor*) (Zampa); *Quand passent les faisans* (Molinaro)

1966   *Du mou dans la gachette* (Grospierre); *Duello nel mundo* (Scott); *Delitto quasi perfetto* (Camerini); *Le Grand Restaurant* (Besnard); *Un Idiot à Paris* (Korber)

1967   *Lo straniero* (*The Stranger*) (Visconti) (as defense counsel); *Peau d'espion* (*To Commit a Murder*) (Molinaro) (as Rhome); *Le fou du Labo 4* (Besnard); *Caroline chérie* (de la Patellière); *Copain suavé sa peau* (Boisset); *Si j'étais un espion* (*Breakdown*; *If I Were a Spy*) (Bertrand Blier)

1968   *Faut pas prendre les enfants du bon Dieu pour les canards sauvages* (*Operation Leontine*) (Audiard); *Riusciranno i nostri eroi a trovare il loro amico misteriosamente scomparso in Africa?* (Scola); *Elle boit pas, elle fume pas, elle drogue pas, mais elle cause* (Audiard); *Appelez-moi Mathilde* (Mondy)

1969   *Mon Oncle Benjamin* (Molinaro)

1970   *Le Cri du cormoran le soir au-dessus des jonques* (Audiard); *Le Distrait* (Richard); *Laisse aller, c'est une valse* (Lautner)

1971   *Catch Me a Spy* (Clement); *Homo eroticus* (*Man of the Year*) (Vicario) (as Dr. Mezzini); *Il furto e l'anima del commercio* (Corbucci); *Quarta parete* (Bolzoni); *Le Tueur* (de la Patellière); *Jo* (Girault)

1972   *Le Grand Blond avec une chaussure noire* (*The Tall Blond Man with One Black Shoe*) (Robert) (as Milan); *Tout le monde il est beau, tout le monde il est gentil* (Yanne); *Elle cause plus, elle flinque* (Audiard); *Boccaccio* (Corbucci)

1973   *Moi y'en a vouloir des sous* (Yanne); *Je sais rien, mais je dirai tout* (Richard); *Par le sang des autres* (Simenon); *Les Tontons flingueurs* (Lautner)

1974   *. . . la main à couper* (Perier); *Les Chinois à Paris* (Yanne) (as President); *C'est pas parce qu'on a rien à dire qu'il fermer sa gueule* (Besnard); *Bons baisers à lundi* (Audiard); *Il piatto piange* (Nuzzi); *Processo per direttissima* (de Caro)

1975   *Ce cher Victor* (Davis); *Amici miei* (*My Friends*) (Germi and Monicelli); *C'est dur pour tout le monde* (Gion); *Le Faux-Cul* (Hanin); *Calmos* (*Femmes fatales*) (Bertrand Blier)

1976   *Le Corps de mon ennemi* (Verneuil); *La Nuit d'or* (Moatti)

1977   *Le Témoin* (Mocky)

1978   *Le Compromis* (Zerbib)

1979   *Il malato imaginario* (*La malade imaginaire*; *The Hypochondriac*) (Cervi); *Série noire* (Corneau) (as Staplin); *Buffet froid* (Bertrand Blier) (as police inspector)

1980   *Voltati Eugenio* (Comencini)

1981   *Passione d'amore* (Scola) (as Major Tarasso); *Pétrole, pétrole* (Gion)

1985   *Le due vite di Mattia Pascal* (*The Two Lives of Mattia Pascal*) (Monicelli) (as Paleari); *Ca n'arrive qu'a moi* (Perrin); *Sceno di querra* (Risi); *Amici miei atto III* (Loy)

1986   *Je hais les acteurs* (*I Hate Actors*) (Krawczyk) (as J. B. Cobb); *Spaggia privata* (Bozzetto); *Twist Again à Moscou* (Poure) (as Minister); *Speriamo che sia femmina* (*Let's Hope It's a Girl*) (Monicelli) (as Uncle Gughi)

1987   *Sotto il ristorante cinese* (Bozzetto) (as Eva's father); *I Picari* (Monicelli)

1988   *Mangeclous* (Mizrahi); *Ada dans la jungle* (Zingy)

1989   *Una botta di vita* (Oldaini); *Paganini* (Kinski)

Publications

By BLIER: article—

Interview by B. Villien and P. Carcassone in *Cinématographe* (Paris), January 1980.

On BLIER: book—

Blier, Annette, and Claude Dufresne, *Bernard Blier*, Paris, 1989.

On BLIER: articles—

"Bernard Blier," in *Ecran* (Paris), July 1978.
Obituary in *Variety* (New York), 5 April 1989.
Beylie, Claude, "L'Ami Blier," in *Avant-Scène du Cinéma* (Paris), May 1989.

* * *

Although Bernard Blier made his film debut at the age of 21 in films by Marc Allégret and Rouleau (two films by each director in 1937), and worked regularly in films during the next few years, he began to get good roles only after the war. He had played ordinary workers in different settings quite convincingly, but was able to show his many-sided dramatic abilities in *Dédée d'Anvers* (Yves Allégret) and, particularly, in *Quai des Orfèvres* (Clouzot), a classic film of the criminal genre, in which he appeared with Jouvet and Dullin. His performance as a country teacher in *L'Ecole buissonière* (Le Chanois) solidified his reputation, and he won several prizes for his acting in it.

From that time he regularly appeared in French and foreign films as a leading character actor. Audiences have been particularly fond of his roles as police inspectors, his most notable performances in this vein being Javert in Le Chanois's version of Hugo's *Les Misérables* and in Cayatte's *Le Dossier noir*. But he also appeared in such works as Zola's *Germinal* (Yves Allégret), Camus's *Lo straniero* (Visconti), and many comic films.

His filmography, containing some 200 film roles, is evidence of the intensity of his work. He earned the reputation of an excellent and many-sided interpreter due to his discipline and exactingness, and he continued to occupy a prominent place in French film.

His work on the stage, begun slightly before his work in films, was also outstanding. His work in boulevard comedies climaxed in his success in Roussin's comedy *Le Marie, la femme, et la mort* which ran almost three years. He also appeared with Isabelle Adjani in the Comédie Française production of *L'Ecole des femmes* for the 300th anniversary celebration of Molière's death in 1973.

—Karel Tabery

BLONDELL, Joan

Nationality: American. **Born:** New York City, 30 August 1909. **Family:** Married 1) the cameraman George Barnes, 1933 (divorced 1935), son: Norman Scott; 2) the actor Dick Powell, 1936 (divorced 1945), daughter: Ellen; 3) the producer Michael Todd, 1947 (divorced 1950). **Career:** 1910—born into vaudeville family; stage debut at age 14 months; 1919—incorporated into family vaudeville act; toured U.S., Europe, China, and Australia; 1926—joined stock company in Dallas; won "Miss Dallas" beauty contest; on Broadway in *Tarnished* and *The Trial of Mary Dugan*; also in the *Ziegfeld Follies*; 1929—played lead in Broadway musical *Maggie the Magnificent*; 1930—signed with Warners to star in *Sinners' Holiday*; 1938—left Warners and begins to freelance; 1940s—began working in radio and making USO appearances; 1951-56—worked on stage and television only; 1963—in TV series *The Real McCoys*; 1968-70—in TV series *Here Come the Brides*; 1972-73—in TV series *Banyon*. **Died:** Of leukemia in Santa Monica, California, 25 December 1979.

Films as Actress:

1930 *The Office Wife* (Bacon) (as Catherine Murdock); *Sinners' Holiday* (Adolfi) (as Myrtle); *Broadway's Like That* (Roth)

1931 *Illicit* (Mayo) (as Helen "Duckie" Childers); *Millie* (Dillon) (as Angie); *My Past* (Del Ruth) (as Marion Moore); *God's Gift to Women* (Curtiz) (as Fifi); **The Public Enemy** (Wellman) (as Mamie); *Other Men's Women* (Wellman) (as Marie); *Big Business Girl* (Seiter) (as Pearl); *Night Nurse* (Wellman) (as Maloney); *The Reckless Hour* (Dillon) (as Myrtle Nicholas); *Blonde Crazy* (Del Ruth) (as Anne Roberts)

1932 *Make Me a Star* (Beaudine) (as Flips Montague); *Union Depot* (Green) (as Ruth); *The Greeks Had a Word for It* (Sherman) (as Schatze); *The Crowd Roars* (Hawks) (as Anne); *The Famous Ferguson Case* (Bacon) (as Maizie Dickson); *Miss Pinkerton* (Bacon) (as Miss Adams/Miss Pinkerton); *Big City Blues* (LeRoy) (as Vida); *Three on a Match* (LeRoy) (as Mary Keaton); *Central Park* (Adolfi) (as Dot); *Lawyer Man* (Dieterle) (as Olga)

1933 *Blondie Johnson* (Enright) (title role); *Broadway Bad* (Lanfield) (as Tony Landers); *Gold Diggers of 1933* (LeRoy) (as Carol King); *Goodbye Again* (Curtiz) (as Anne); *Footlight Parade* (Bacon) (as Nan Prescott); *Havana Widows* (Enright) (as Mae Knight); *Convention City* (Mayo) (as Nancy Lorraine)

1934 *I've Got Your Number* (Enright) (as Maria Lawson); *Smarty* (Florey) (as Vicki Wallace Thorpe); *He Was Her Man* (Bacon) (as Rose Lawrence); *Dames* (Enright) (as Mabel Anderson); *Kansas City Princess* (Keighley) (as Rosy)

1935 *Traveling Saleslady* (Enright) (as Angela Twitchell); *Broadway Gondolier* (Bacon) (as Alice Hughes); *We're in the Money* (Enright) (as Ginger Stewart); *Miss Pacific Fleet* (Enright) (as Gloria Fay)

1936 *Colleen* (Green) (as Minnie Mawkins); *Sons O'Guns* (Bacon) (as Yvonne); *Bullets or Ballots* (Keighley) (as Lee Morgan); *Stagestruck* (Berkeley) (as Peggy Revere); *Three Men on a Horse* (LeRoy) (as Mabel); *Gold Diggers of 1937* (Bacon) (as Norma Parry)

1937 *The King and the Chorus Girl* (LeRoy) (as Dorothy); *Back in Circulation* (Enright) (as Timothea Blake); *The Perfect Specimen* (Curtiz) (as Mona Carter); *Stand-In* (Garnett) (as Lester Plum)

1938 *There's Always a Woman* (Hall) (as Sally Reardon)

1939 *Off the Record* (Flood) (as Jane Morgan); *East Side of Heaven* (Butler) (as Mary); *The Kid from Kokomo* (Seiler) (as Doris Harvey); *Good Girls Go to Paris* (Hall) (as Jenny); *The Amazing Mr. Williams* (Hall) (as Maxine Carroll)

1940 *Two Girls on Broadway* (Simon) (as Molly Mahoney); *I Want a Divorce* (Murphy) (as Geraldine "Jerry" Brokaw)

1941 *Topper Returns* (Del Ruth) (as Gail Richards); *Model Wife* (Jason) (as Joan Keating Chambers); *Three Girls about Town* (Jason) (as Hope Banner); *Lady for a Night* (Jason) (as Jenny Blake)

1943 *Cry Havoc* (Thorpe) (as Grace)

1945 *A Tree Grows in Brooklyn* (Kazan) (as Aunt Sissy); *Don Juan Quilligan* (Tuttle) (as Marjorie Mossrock); *Adventure* (Fleming) (as Helen Molohn)

1947 *The Corpse Came C.O.D.* (Levin) (as Rosemary Durant); *Nightmare Alley* (Goulding) (as Zeena)

1950 *For Heaven's Sake* (Seaton) (as Lydia)

1951 *The Blue Veil* (Bernhardt) (as Annie Rawlings)

1956 *The Opposite Sex* (Miller) (as Crystal)

1957 *Lizzie* (Haas) (as Aunt Morgan); *Desk Set* (Walter Lang) (as Peg Costello); *Will Success Spoil Rock Hunter?* (Tashlin) (as Violet)

1961 *Angel Baby* (Wendkos) (as Mollie Hays)

1964 *Advance to the Rear* (Marshall) (as Easy Jenny)

1965 *The Cincinnati Kid* (Jewison) (as Lady Fingers)

Joan Blondell

1966   *Ride beyond Vengeance* (McEveety) (as Mrs. Lavender);
        Waterhole Number Three (Graham) (as Lavinia); *Winchester*
        '73 (Daugherty) (as Larouge)
1968   *Stay Away, Joe* (Tewksbury) (as Glenda Callahan); *Kona Coast*
        (Johnson) (as Kittibelle Lightfoot)
1970   *The Phynx* (Katzin) (as Ruby)
1971   *Support Your Local Gunfighter* (Kennedy) (as Jenny)
1975   *The Dead Don't Scream* (Harrington—for TV) (as Levenia);
        Winner Take All (Bogart—for TV) (as Beverly Craig)
1976   *Won Ton Ton, the Dog Who Saved Hollywood* (Winner) (as
        landlady); *Death at Love House* (Swackhamer—for TV) (as
        Marcella Geffenhart)
1977   *Opening Night* (Cassavetes) (as Sarah Goode)
1978   *Grease* (Kleiser); *Battered* (Werner—for TV); *The Glove*
        (Hagen) (as Mrs. Fitzgerald)
1979   *The Champ* (Zeffirelli) (as Dolly Kenyon); *Family Secrets* (for TV)
1981   *The Woman Inside* (Van Winkle) (as Aunt Coll)

Publications

By BLONDELL: book—

Center Door Fancy, 1972.

By BLONDELL: article—

"Joan Blondell, The Great Golddigger Still Digging Hollywood," interview with M. Koch in *Inter/View* (New York), August 1972.

On BLONDELL: book—

Parish, James, and Don Stanke, *The Leading Ladies*, New York,
1977.

On BLONDELL: articles—

Bowers, Ron, "Joan Blondell," in *Films in Review* (New York), April
1972.
Shipman, David, in *The Great Movie Stars: The Golden Years*, revised
edition, London, 1979.
Obituary in *Cinéma* (Paris), March 1980.

*   *   *

Joan Blondell's career spanned a half-century and her output numbered nearly a hundred films, not to mention innumerable television
appearances, yet she was never less than vivid, bright, and appealing;
often she is the single saving grace of an otherwise tepid work.

She played roles of every description, but specialized in a specific type; the brassy, blowzy, blonde golddigger with a kind heart and legs that won't quit. She could trade quips, crack wise, wring tears, and generally meet any challenge a scriptwriter could throw her way. Though she wasn't much of a musical performer, she was so thoroughly a trooper that Warner Brothers felt no compunction in featuring her prominently in most of the popular and influential Busby Berkeley musicals; as often as not, she remains more vividly in the memory than the more accomplished singers and dancers in the films. "Remember My Forgotten Man" from *Gold Diggers of 1933* and "The Girl at the Ironing Board" from *Dames* are but two examples of the impressive emotional range of which her rather ordinary voice was capable. Her versatility and professionalism made her invaluable to her employers (a little *too* valuable since, more than once, Blondell was worked to the point of exhaustion) but the public responded to her round, expressive face, Art Deco eyes, and brilliant (though friendly and familiar) smile.

She came to Hollywood with James Cagney in 1930 to appear in *Sinners' Holiday*, the movie of a hit play in which they had co-starred. They both signed long-term contracts with Warner Brothers on the same day and were immediately put on the treadmill. Cagney's star ignited with more intensity than that of his co-star, and Blondell never quite escaped the supporting player category. Nevertheless she regularly eclipsed the "stars" of her pictures and built a loyal following and an impressive, diverse body of work.

She made over 50 films at Warners during her first decade in films and this pace must have contributed to the frenetic edge which characterizes her style. Her beauty, optimism, quick wit, and unpretentious bearing made her the archetypical 1930s woman. For a workhorse, it is surprising how many facets of herself she exposed to the public gaze: she is wistful and sentimental in that otherwise hard-edged *The Public Enemy*; in *Night Nurse* she and Barbara Stanwyck spend an inordinate amount of time in their underwear. Her delightful way with snappy patter illuminates *Blonde Crazy, The Crowd Roars, The Greeks Had a Word for It*, and the hilarious and unjustly neglected *Convention City*.

After her exhausting stint at Warners, Blondell began to slow down and choose her films with more care. As she became more matronly, her character roles took on a different, but equally interesting character. *A Tree Grows in Brooklyn* gave her a rich part which she played brilliantly. She was nominated for an Academy Award for *The Blue Veil* and proved that her sense of comedy was as keen as ever in *The Desk Set, Will Success Spoil Rock Hunter?*, and *Advance to the Rear*.

A more dramatic part came her way in the tense and dramatic *Cincinnati Kid*, in which she plays a tough cardsharp, but her roles thereafter lack punch. She remains dependable and bright in the otherwise tepid *Support Your Local Gunfighter, Grease* and *The Champ*, but *The Woman Inside* was a poor swan-song: low budget, sleazy, and poorly done in every way.

Still, over the whole of her career, there is an astonishingly high level of quality and a reevaluation of her work is called for. Three years before her death she said, "I don't have any regrets about my career, though I'm sensible enough to know that if I'd taken myself more seriously and fought for better roles I might have been a damn good dramatic actress." Those willing to do as she did not and take her career seriously, will find a talent as open and generous as that beaming, malleable face of hers.

—Frank Thompson

BLOOM, Claire

Nationality: British. **Born:** Patricia Claire Bloom in North Finchley, London, England, 15 February 1931. **Education:** Attended school in Cardiff; Badminton School; Fern Hill Manor School New Milton; Dora Russel's school, London; Guildhall School of Music and Drama, London, 1944-45; Central School of Speech and Drama, London, 1945-46. **Family:** Married 1) the actor Rod Steiger, 1959 (divorced 1969), daughter: Anna; 2) Hillard Elkins, 1969 (divorced 1976); 3) the writer Philip Roth, 1990. **Career:** 1940-43—in the United States as evacuee: child singer and actress on radio; 1946—radio debut in England in dramatization of *Confessions of an Opium Eater*; stage debut at Oxford Playhouse; 1947—West End debut in *The White Devil*; short film contract with J. Arthur Rank; 1948—with the Royal Shakespeare Company, Stratford-upon-Avon; 1951—cast by Charlie Chaplin in *Limelight*; 1952—debut at Old Vic in *Romeo and Juliet*; toured with the same play in the United States, 1956; later stage appearances include *The Trojan Women* in Spoleto, 1963, *A Doll's House* in New York, 1970, and *A Streetcar Named Desire* in London, 1974; work for TV includes the mini-series *Backstairs at the White House*, 1979, *Brideshead Revisited*, 1981, *Ellis Island*, 1984, *Queenie*, 1988, and *Camomile Lawn*, 1992. **Awards:** Most Promising Newcomer, British Academy, for *Limelight*, 1952. **Agent:** Marion Rosenberg Agency, 8428 Melrose Place, Suite C, Los Angeles, CA 90069, U.S.A.

Films as Actress:

1948   *The Blind Goddess* (French) (as Mary Dearing)
1952   ***Limelight*** (Chaplin) (as Terry)
1953   *Innocents in Paris* (Parry) (as Susan Robbins); *The Man Between* (Reed) (as Susanne Mallinson)
1955   *Richard III* (Olivier) (as Lady Anne)
1956   *Alexander the Great* (Rossen) (as Barsine)
1958   *The Brothers Karamazov* (Richard Brooks) (as Katya); *The Buccaneer* (Quinn)
1959   ***Look Back in Anger*** (Richardson) (as Helena Charles)
1960   *Die Schachnovelle* (*Brainwashed*; *The Royal Game*; *Three Moves to Freedom*) (Oswald) (as Irene Andreny)
1962   *The Wonderful World of the Brothers Grimm* (Levin) (as Dorothea Grimm); *The Chapman Report* (Cukor) (as Naomi Shields)
1963   *The Haunting* (Wise) (as Theodosia); *Il maestro di Vigevano* (Petri); *80,000 Suspects* (Guest) (as Julie Monks)
1964   "Peccato nel pommeriggio" ("Sin in the Afternoon") ep. of *Alta infideltà* (*High Infidelity*) (Petri) (as Laura); *The Outrage* (Ritt) (as Wife)
1965   *The Spy Who Came in from the Cold* (Ritt) (as Nan Perry)
1967   *Soldier in Love* (Schaefer—for TV)
1968   *Charly* (Nelson) (as Alice Kinian)
1969   *Three into Two Won't Go* (Hall) (as Frances Howard); *The Illustrated Man* (Smight) (as Felicia)
1970   *A Severed Head* (Dick Clement) (as Honor Klein)
1971   *Red Sky at Morning* (Goldstone) (as Ann Arnold); *The Going Up of David Lev* (Collier—for TV)
1973   *A Doll's House* (Garland) (as Nora Helmer)
1977   *Islands in the Stream* (Schaffner) (as Audrey)
1980   *Hamlet, Prince of Denmark* (Rodney Bennett—for TV) (as Gertrude)
1981   *Clash of the Titans* (Desmond Davis) (as Hera)
1982   *Cymbeline* (Moshinsky—for TV) (as Queen)
1983   *Separate Tables* (Schlesinger—for TV) (as Miss Cooper)
1984   *Memories of Monet* (Martindale) (as narrator); *Oedipus the King* (Don Taylor—for TV) (as Jocasta); *The Ghost Writer* (Tristam Powell—for TV)
1985   *Déjà Vu* (Richmond) (as Eleanor Harvey); *Florence Nightingale* (Duke—for TV) (as Fanny Nightingale); *Promises to Keep* (Black) (as Sally); *Shadowlands* (Norman Stone—

Claire Bloom with Laurence Olivier in *Richard III*

for TV) (as Joy Gresham); *This Lightning Always Strikes Twice* (for TV)

1986 *Anastasia: The Mystery of Anna* (Chomsky—for TV) (as Czarina Alexandra); *Hold the Dream* (Don Sharp—for TV) (as Edwina); *Liberty* (Sarafian—for TV)

1987 *Sammy and Rosie Get Laid* (Frears) (as Alice); *Intimate Contact* (Hussein—for TV) (as Ruth)

1988 *Beryl Markham: A Shadow on the Sun* (*Shadow on the Sun*) (Richardson—for TV) (as Lady Florence Delamere)

1989 *Crimes and Misdemeanors* (Woody Allen) (as Miriam Rosenthal); *The Lady and the Highwayman* (Hough—for TV) (as Lady Emma Darlington)

1993 *A Hercegnoe es a Kobold* (*The Princess and the Goblin*) (Gemes—animation) (as voice of Fairy Godmother); ***The Age of Innocence*** (Scorsese) (uncredited role); *Miss Marple: The Mirror Crack'd* (*The Mirror Crack'd from Side to Side*) (Norman Stone—for TV) (as Marina Gregg); *It's Nothing Personal* (Bradford May—for TV) (as Evelyn Whitloff); *Barbara Taylor Bradford's Remember* (Herzfeld—for TV) (as Anne)

1995 *Mighty Aphrodite* (Woody Allen) (as Amanda's mother); *Mad Dogs and Englishmen* (Henry Cole) (as Stringer's wife)

Publications

By BLOOM: book—

Limelight and After: The Education of an Actress, London, 1982.

By BLOOM: articles—

"A Star without the Limelight," interview with P. Baker, in *Films and Filming* (London), March 1956.

"The Year of the Steigers," interview in *Cinema* (Beverly Hills), March 1966.

"Charles the Great" (remembering Charles Chaplin), in *Vogue* (New York), December 1992.

On BLOOM: articles—

Cover story in *Time* (New York), 17 November 1952.
Current Biography 1956, New York, 1956.
Films and Filming (London), February 1956.
Ciné Revue (Paris), 20 December 1979.
Photoplay (London), January 1982.

Bohlen, C., "New Voices for Two Silenced Russian Poets," in *New York Times*, 24 January 1993.

* * *

The screen persona of Claire Bloom has most often emerged as a blend of regality and vulnerability. This combination of traits manifested itself in the role of Terry, the ballerina heroine of Charles Chaplin's *Limelight*. Although the 1952 film did not mark her film debut (she had appeared in *The Blind Goddess* four years earlier), *Limelight* earned Bloom an international reputation. That she perceives this film as the real beginning of her career is evident from the title of her autobiography published in 1982, *Limelight and After: The Education of an Actress*.

Bloom's regality has characterized her performances in films ranging from *Richard III*, in which she played opposite Laurence Olivier, to *Clash of the Titans*, a Ray Harryhausen fantasy in which, as the goddess Hera, she again appeared opposite Olivier as Zeus. Vulnerability is the dominant trait of Bloom's parts in such films as *The Outrage*, Martin Ritt's Old West remake of *Rashomon*, Akira Kurosawa's study of shared guilt in feudal Japan. Perhaps Bloom has been at her most effective when a role allows her to merge the two traits. The *Limelight* part benefited from such an amalgam as did her characterization of Theodosia, the lesbian psychic in *The Haunting*. Based on a horror novel by Shirley Jackson, Robert Wise's film required Bloom to dominate such characters as Julie Harris's neurotic spinster while maintaining a somewhat subservient stance in relation to the mysterious—and, at times, frustratingly unseen—force that pervades the film's Val Lewton-ish milieu.

Bloom's continuing appearance in classical stage roles has definitely contributed to her screen presence. She has acted such Shakespearean parts as Juliet and Ophelia as well as modern roles such as Blanche DuBois in *A Streetcar Named Desire*.

Still in demand for screen work by important contemporary directors, she has appeared recently for Stephen Frears's in *Sammy and Rose Get Laid* and for Woody Allen in the ensemble cast of the seriocomic *Crimes and Misdemeanors*, as well as in Allen's *Mighty Aphrodite*. Earlier, she essayed the role of the American divorcée who captures the heart of British writer C. S. Lewis (Joss Ackland) in a television version of William Nicholson's stage drama *Shadowlands*— but for Richard Attenborough's 1993 film of the play, the role was taken by Debra Winger.

Bloom's most memorable on-screen partner, however, was Richard Burton, with whom she made three films: *Alexander the Great*, *Look Back in Anger*, and, most enduringly, *The Spy Who Came in from the Cold*, based on John Le Carré's gloomy tale of love doomed by the duplicities of East-West espionage.

—William M. Clements, updated by John McCarty

BOGARDE, (Sir) Dirk

Nationality: British. **Born:** Derek Jules Gaspard Ulric Niven van den Bogaerde in Hampstead, London, England, 29 March 1921. **Education:** Attended University College School and Allan Glen's School, Scotland. **Military Service:** In Far East, 1940-45: lieutenant; **Career:** 1939—acting debut; 1947—appeared in West End production of *Power without Glory*; signed seven-year contract with J. Arthur Rank Organisation; 1960s—moved to France; 1977—published first volume of memoirs, *A Postillion Struck by Lightning*; 1980s—worked in TV, in France and Britain; 1990—returned to England. **Awards:** Best British Actor, British Academy, for *The Servant*, 1963; Best British Actor, British Academy, for *Darling*, 1965; Honorary D. Litt, St. Andrews University, 1985; BFI Fellowship, 1987; British Academy of Film and Televison Arts Award for "outstanding contribution to world cinema," 1990; knighted, 1992.

Films as Actor:

1947 *Dancing with Crime* (Carstairs) (as policeman)

1948 *Esther Waters* (Dalrymple and Proud) (as William Latch); "Alien Corn" ep. of *Quartet* (French) (as George Bland); *Once a Jolly Swagman* (*Maniacs on Wheels*) (Jack Lee and McNaughton) (as Bill Fox)

1949 *Dear Mr. Prohack* (Freeland) (as Charles Prohack); *Boys in Brown* (Tully) (as Alfie Rawlins)

1950 *The Blue Lamp* (Dearden) (as Tom Riley); *So Long at the Fair* (Fisher and Darnborough) (as George Hathaway); *The Woman in Question* (*Five Angles on Murder*) (Asquith) (as Bob Baker)

1951 *Blackmailed* (Marc Allégret) (as Stephen Mundy); *Penny Princess* (Guest) (as Tony Craig)

1952 *Hunted* (*The Stranger in Between*) (Charles Crichton) (as Chris Lloyd); *The Gentle Gunman* (Dearden) (as Matt Sullivan)

1953 *Desperate Moment* (Bennett) (as Simon von Halder); *Appointment in London* (Leacock) (as Wing Commander Tim Mason)

1954 *They Who Dare* (Milestone) (as Lt. Graham); *Doctor in the House* (Thomas) (as Dr. Simon Sparrow); *The Sleeping Tiger* (Joseph Losey under pseudonym "Victor Hanbury") (as Frank Clements); *For Better, for Worse* (*Cocktails in the Kitchen*) (J. Lee Thompson) (as Tony Howard)

1955 *The Sea Shall Not Have Them* (Lewis Gilbert) (as Flight Sgt. Mackay); *Simba* (*Simba—Mark of Mau Mau*) (Hurst) (as Alan Howard); *Doctor at Sea* (Thomas) (as Dr. Simon Sparrow); *Cast a Dark Shadow* (Lewis Gilbert) (as Edward Bare)

1956 *The Spanish Gardener* (Leacock) (as Jose)

1957 *Ill Met by Moonlight* (*Night Ambush*; *Intelligence Service*) (Powell and Pressburger) (as Major Patrick Leigh Fermor); *Doctor at Large* (Thomas) (as Dr. Simon Sparrow); *Campbell's Kingdom* (Thomas) (as Bruce Campbell)

1958 *The Wind Cannot Read* (Thomas) (as Flight Lt. Michael Quinn); *A Tale of Two Cities* (Thomas) (as Sydney Carton); *The Doctor's Dilemma* (Asquith) (as Louis Dubedat)

1959 *Libel* (Asquith) (as Sir Mark Lodder/Number 15/Frank Welney)

1960 *The Angel Wore Red* (Johnson) (as Arturo Carrera); *Song without End* (Charles Vidor) (as Franz Liszt)

1961 *The Singer Not the Song* (Baker) (as Anacleto); *Victim* (Dearden) (as Melville Farr)

1962 *H.M.S. Defiant* (*Damn the Defiant!*) (Lewis Gilbert) (as First Lt. Scott-Padget); *The Password Is Courage* (Andrew L. Stone) (as Sergeant Major Charles Coward); *We Are in the Navy Now* (*We Joined the Navy*) (Toye) (as Dr. Simon Sparrow); *The Mind Benders* (Dearden) (as Dr. Henry Longman)

1963 *I Could Go On Singing* (Neame) (as David Donne); *Doctor in Distress* (Thomas) (as Dr. Simon Sparrow); *The Servant* (Losey) (as Hugo Barrett); *Hot Enough for June* (*Agent 8 3/4*) (Thomas) (as Nicholas Whistler); *The Epic that Never Was* (doc for TV)

1964 *King and Country* (Losey) (as Captain Hargreaves); *The High Bright Sun* (*McGuire Go Home!*) (Thomas) (as Major McGuire)

1965 *Darling* (Schlesinger) (as Robert Gold); *Little Moon of Alban* (for TV)

1966 *Modesty Blaise* (Losey) (as Gabriel); *Blithe Spirit* (for TV)

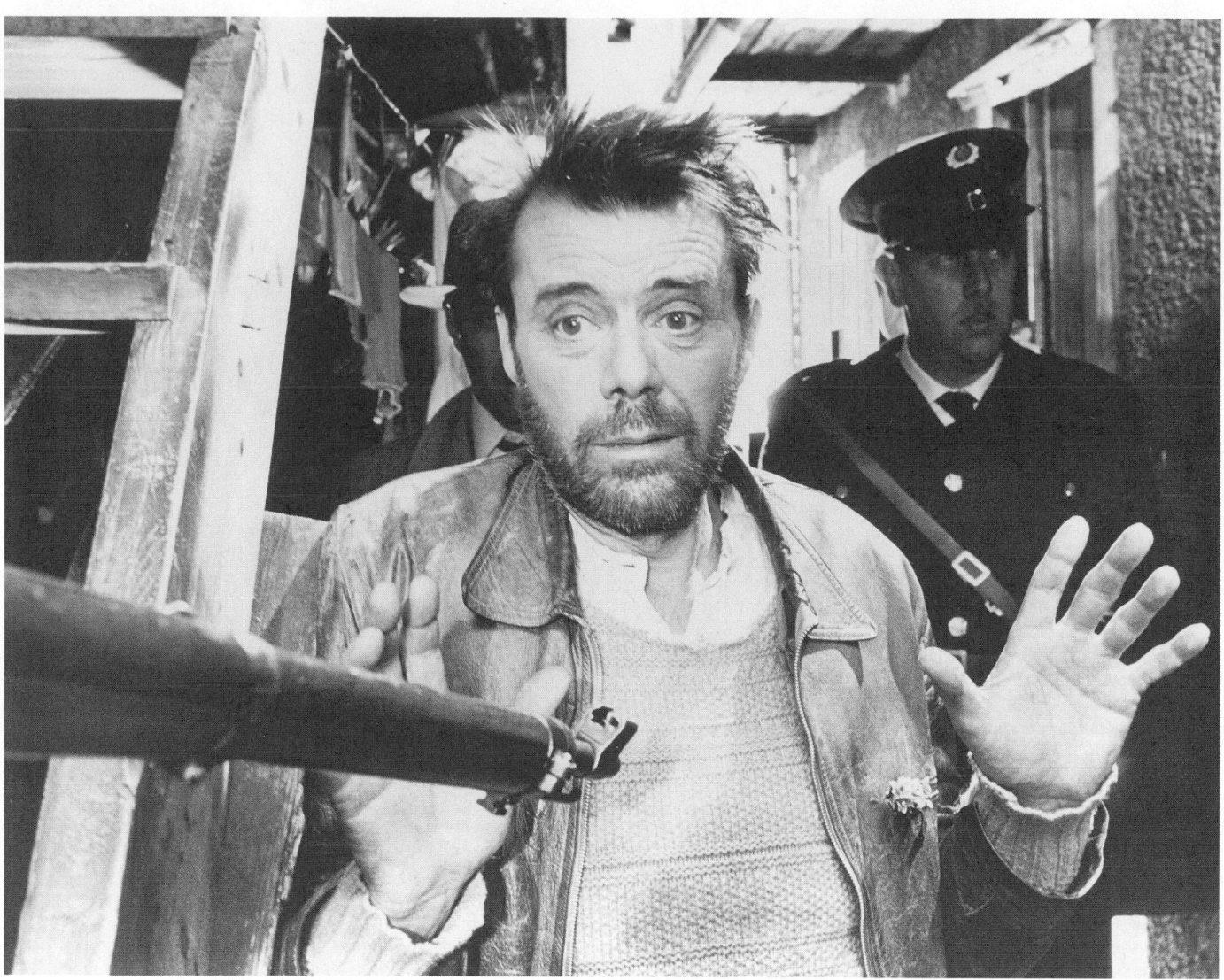

Dirk Bogarde in *Despair*

1967   *Our Mother's House* (Clayton) (as Charlie Hook); *Accident*
        (Losey) (as Stephen)
1968   *Mr. Sebastian* (*Sebastian*) (David Greene) (title role); *The*
        Fixer (Frankenheimer) (as Bibikov)
1969   *Oh! What a Lovely War* (Attenborough) (as Stephen); *Justine*
        (Cukor) (as Pursewarden); *La caduta degli dei* (*The Damned*)
        (Visconti) (as Freidrich Bruckman); *Upon This Rock* (doc
        for TV) (as Bonnie Prince Charlie)
1971   *Morte a Venezia* (*Death in Venice*) (Visconti) (as Gustav von
        Aschenbach)
1973   *Le Serpent* (*The Serpent*; *Night Flight from Moscow*) (Verneuil)
        (as Philip Boyle); *The Night Porter* (Cavani) (as Maximilian
        Theo Aldorfer)
1975   *Permission to Kill* (Frankel) (as Alan Curtis)
1977   *Providence* (Resnais) (as Claude Langham); *A Bridge Too*
        Far (Attenborough) (as Lt. Gen. Frederick "Boy" Brown-
        ing); *Eine Reise ins Licht* (*Despair*) (Fassbinder) (as
        Hermann Karlovich); *To See Such Fun* (Scofield—
        compilation)
1981   *Act of Love* (*The Patricia Neal Story*) (Harvey and Page—for
        TV) (as Roald Dahl)

1986   *May We Borrow Your Husband?* (Mahoney—for TV) (as Wil-
        liam Harris, + sc)
1987   *The Vision* (Norman Stone—for TV) (as James Marriner)
1990   *Daddy Nostalgie* (*Daddy Nostalgia*; *These Foolish Things*)
        (Tavernier) (as Tommy "Daddy" Russell)

Publications

By BOGARDE: books—

A Postillion Struck by Lightning, London, 1977.
Snakes and Ladders, London, 1978.
A Gentle Occupation (novel), London, 1980.
Voices in the Garden (novel), London, 1981.
An Orderly Man, London, 1983.
West of Sunset (novel), London, 1984.
Backcloth, London, 1986.
A Particular Friendship, London, 1989.
Great Meadow, London, 1992.
Jericho (novel), London, 1992.
A Short Walk from Harrods, London, 1993.

By BOGARDE: articles—

Interview with G. Gow, in *Films and Filming* (London), May 1971.
"2 Heures avec Dirk Bogarde," interview with A. Garel, in *Ecran* (Paris), 1974.
"Dirk Bogarde," interview with Bruno Villien, in *Cinématographe* (Paris), March 1977.
Interview with Quentin Falk, in *Guardian* (London), 20 July 1986.
"A Half-Life in World's End," in *Independent* (London), 19 September 1988.
"You Used to Be Dirk Bogarde," in *Independent on Sunday* (London), 30 September 1990.
Interview with Gary Indiana, in *Interview* (New York), January 1991.
"Bogarde redux," interview with John Heilpern, in *Vogue* (New York), March 1991.

On BOGARDE: books—

Hinxman, Margaret, and Susan d'Arcy, *The Films of Dirk Bogarde*, London, 1974.
Tanitch, Robert, *Dirk Bogarde: The Complete Career Illustrated*, New York, 1988.

On BOGARDE: articles—

"Dirk Bogarde," in *Films and Filming* (London), August 1955.
Whitehall, R., "Dirk Bogarde," in *Films and Filming* (London), November 1963.
Current Biography 1967, New York, 1967.
Tessier, M., "Dirk Bogarde," in *Ecran* (Paris), May 1974, corrections in June 1974 issue.
"Dirk Bogarde," in *Ecran* (Paris), February 1978.
Bodeen, DeWitt, "Dirk Bogarde," in *Films in Review* (New York), November 1980 and February 1981.
Medhurst, Andy, "Dirk Bogarde," in *All Our Yesterdays*, edited by Charles Barr, London, 1986.
Gray, M., "Dirk Bogarde," in *Film Monthly* (Berkhamsted, England), October 1990.
Parra, D., "Dirk Bogarde: rester au sommet," in *Revue du Cinéma* (Paris), December 1990.
Davies, Terence, in *National Film Theatre Programme* (London), January 1991.
Billington, M. "Dirk Bogarde Journeys into 'Nostalgia'," in *New York Times*, 7 April 1991.

*   *   *

Dirk Bogarde's career is a classic case of a gradual rise from light matinee idol roles to ones requiring depth and maturity—the latter eventually earning him a knighthood for his contribution to British and world cinema.

A quiet and retiring person in private life, Bogarde started his acting career in 1939 on the stage, only to have it interrupted by war service. After the war, the British Rank Organisation gave him a contract (they were grooming young and promising actors and actresses), and from 1947 to 1961 Bogarde appeared in more than 30 British films. Assuming the *nom de screen* "Dirk," a sort of Continental variation on the Hollywood "Rock," "Troy," and "Tab," he starred in a succession of featherweight movies designed to launch him as a teen heartthrob image—which, for years, caused him to be perceived by most critics as a glamour boy of minor talent. He became one of the team of young actors who appeared and reappeared in the highly successful *Doctor* series of comedies—*Doctor in the House, Doctor at Sea, Doctor at Large*, and, later, *Doctor in Distress*. Like most actors who had seen war service, he was in demand for a seemingly endless turnover of war

films from *Desperate Moment, They Who Dare*, and *The Sea Shall Not Have Them* to *Ill Met by Moonlight, H.M.S. Defiant*, and *The Password Is Courage*. He did further service in another action genre, the British crime film—which American audiences tended to find tepid and dull in comparison with American films in a similar vein.

Approaching his forties, Bogarde began to show his maturing capacity to handle more complex and demanding characters in Anthony Asquith's adaptation of Bernard Shaw's *The Doctor's Dilemma* and Basil Dearden's *Victim*, the first British film to deal seriously with the problems of a homosexual in public life. Public recognition of his excellence as an actor was really to come, however, when he teamed up with Joseph Losey to play the key role in *The Servant*, a part into which he injected a new, dark vein of subtle, insinuating evil as the manservant who secures a Mephistophelian hold over the rich young man he serves. The performance won him a British Academy Award as Best Actor. Now in his forties and independent, Bogarde embarked on a series of singular performances. He was the defending officer in a court martial in Losey's *Paths of Glory* variation, *King and Country*—and the Oxford academic with complex professional and emotional problems in Losey's *Accident*. As well, he appeared effectively in such notable films as John Schlesinger's *Darling*—for which he won his second British Best Actor award—Losey's *Modesty Blaise*, Jack Clayton's *Our Mother's House*, Richard Attenborough's *Oh! What a Lovely War*, and Alain Resnais's impressive film *Providence*. Widening his scope still further, Bogarde appeared in a series of arty and experimental films made abroad: Visconti's controversial *The Damned*, about the impact of Nazism on a vicious upper-class family; the same director's exquisite version of Thomas Mann's *Death in Venice*; Liliana Cavani's *The Night Porter*, as a former Nazi SS concentration camp officer; and, in marked contrast, Fassbinder's extraordinary film *Despair*, as a survivor of the Holocaust.

Although Bogarde continues to act from time to time, he has turned increasingly and successfully to writing. Besides novels, he has written four volumes of memoirs, *A Postillion Struck by Lightning, Snakes and Ladders, An Orderly Man*, and *Backcloth*, the second volume covering his film career up to *Death in Venice* (with fascinating details in particular of working with Losey and Visconti) and the third including accounts of the making of *Night Porter, Providence*, and *Despair*.

—Roger Manvell, updated by John McCarty

BOGART, Humphrey

Nationality: American. **Born:** Humphrey DeForest Bogart in New York City, 23 January 1899. **Education:** Attended Trinity School, New York; expelled from Philips Academy, Andover, Massachussetts. **Family:** Married 1) Helen Menken, 1926 (divorced 1927); 2) Mary Philips, 1928 (divorced 1938); 3) Mayo Methot, 1938 (divorced 1945); 4) the actress Lauren Bacall, 1945, son: Stephen Humphrey, daughter: Leslie Howard. **Career:** 1918-19—served in U.S. Navy; 1920-22—managed stage company owned by William S. Brady; performed various chores at Brady's New York film studio; 1922—began acting regularly on stage; 1930—film debut in short *Broadway's Like That*; 1930-35—minor film roles for various studios while continuing to work on stage; 1936—success of film version of *The Petrified Forest* led to long-term contract with Warner Brothers; 1947—protested against HUAC activities with actress wife Lauren Bacall and other celebrities. **Awards:** Best Actor Academy Award, for *The African Queen*, 1951. **Died:** Of cancer, in Hollywood, California, 14 January 1957.

Films as Actor:

1930 *Broadway's Like That* (Roth—short); *Up the River* (John Ford) (as Steve); *A Devil with Women* (Cummings) (as Tom Standish)

1931 *Body and Soul* (Santell) (as Jim Watson); *Bad Sister* (Henley) (as Valentine Corliss); *A Holy Terror* (Cummings) (as Steve Nash); *Women of All Nations* (Walsh) (as Stone)

1932 *Love Affair* (Freeland) (as Jim Leonard); *Big City Blues* (LeRoy) (as Adkins); *Three on a Match* (LeRoy) (as Ace)

1934 *Midnight* (Erskine) (as Garboni)

1936 *The Petrified Forest* (Mayo) (as Duke Mantee); *Bullets or Ballots* (Keighley) (as Bugs Fenner); *Two against the World* (McGann) (as Sherry Scott); *China Clipper* (Enright) (as Hap Stuart); *Isle of Fury* (McDonald) (as Val Stevens)

1937 *Black Legion* (Mayo) (as Frank Taylor); *The Great O'Malley* (Dieterle) (as John Phillips); *Marked Woman* (Lloyd Bacon) (as David Graham); *Kid Galahad* (Curtiz) (as Turkey Morgan); *San Quentin* (Lloyd Bacon) (as Joe "Red" Kennedy); *Dead End* (Wyler) (as Baby Face Martin); *Stand-In* (Garnett) (as Quintain)

1938 *Swing Your Lady* (Enright) (as Ed Hatch); *Crime School* (Seiler) (as Mark Braden); *Men Are Such Fools* (Berkeley) (as Harry Galleon); *The Amazing Dr. Clitterhouse* (Litvak) (as Rock Valentine); *Racket Busters* (Lloyd Bacon) (as Martin); *Angels with Dirty Faces* (Curtiz) (as James Frazier)

1939 *King of the Underworld* (Seiler) (as Joe Gurney); *The Oklahoma Kid* (Lloyd Bacon) (as Whip McCord); *You Can't Get Away with Murder* (Seiler) (as Frank Wilson); *Dark Victory* (Goulding) (as Michael O'Lery); **The Roaring Twenties** (Walsh) (as George Hally); *The Return of Doctor X* (Sherman) (as Dr. Marshall Cane)

1940 *Invisible Stripes* (Lloyd Bacon) (as Chuck Martin); *Virginia City* (Curtiz) (as John Murrell); *It All Came True* (Seiler) (as Grasselli); *Brother Orchid* (Lloyd Bacon) (as Jack Buck); *They Drive By Night* (*The Road to Frisco*) (Walsh) (as Paul Fabrini)

1941 **The Maltese Falcon** (Huston) (as Sam Spade); **High Sierra** (Walsh) (as Roy Earle); *The Wagons Roll at Night* (Enright) (as Nick Coster)

1942 *All Through the Night* (Sherman) (as Gloves Donahue); *In This Our Life* (Huston); *The Big Shot* (Seiler) (as Duke Berne); *Across the Pacific* (Huston) (as Rick Leland); **Casablanca** (Curtiz) (as Rick Blaine)

1943 *Action in the North Atlantic* (Lloyd Bacon) (as Joe Rossi); *Thank Your Lucky Stars* (David Butler); *Sahara* (Zoltan Korda) (as Sgt. Joe Gunn)

1944 *Passage to Marseilles* (Curtiz) (as Martac); *To Have and Have Not* (Hawks) (as Harry Morgan)

1945 *Conflict* (Bernhardt) (as Richard Mason)

1946 *Two Guys from Milwaukee* (David Butler); **The Big Sleep** (Hawks) (as Philip Marlowe)

1947 *Dead Reckoning* (Cromwell) (as Rip Murdock); *The Two Mrs. Carrolls* (Godfrey) (as Geoffrey Carroll); *Dark Passage* (Daves) (as Vincent Parry); *Always Together* (de Cordova)

1948 **The Treasure of the Sierra Madre** (Huston) (as Fred C. Dobbs); *Key Largo* (Huston) (as Frank McCloud)

1949 *Knock on Any Door* (Nicholas Ray) (as Andrew Martin); *Tokyo Joe* (Heisler) (as Joe Barrett)

1950 *Chain Lightning* (Heisler) (as Matt Brennan); **In a Lonely Place** (Nicholas Ray) (as Dixon Steele)

1951 *The Enforcer* (Windust, uncredited Raoul Walsh) (as Martin Ferguson); *Sirocco* (Bernhardt) (as Harry Smith)

1952 **The African Queen** (Huston) (as Charlie Allnut); *Deadline—U.S.A.* (Richard Brooks) (as Ed Hutcheson); *The Road to Bali* (Walker) (as himself)

1953 *Battle Circus* (Richard Brooks) (as Major Jeb Webbe); *Beat the Devil* (Huston) (as Billy Danreuther)

1954 *The Love Lottery* (Charles Crichton); *The Caine Mutiny* (Dmytryk) (as Captain Queeg); *A Star Is Born* (Cukor) (voice only); *Sabrina* (Wilder) (as Linus Larabee); *The Barefoot Contessa* (Joseph L. Mankiewicz) (as Harry Dawes)

1955 *We're No Angels* (Curtiz) (as Joseph); *The Left Hand of God* (Dymytryk) (as Jim Carmady); *The Desperate Hours* (Wyler) (as Glen Griffin)

1956 *The Harder They Fall* (Robson) (as Eddie Willis)

Publications

On BOGART: books—

Gehman, Richard, *Bogart*, Greenwich, Connecticut, 1965.

Goodman, Ezra, *Bogey: The Good-Bad Guy*, New York, 1965.

McCarty, Clifford, *Bogey: The Films of Humphrey Bogart*, New York, 1965.

Michael, Paul, *Humphrey Bogart: The Man and His Films*, Indianapolis, 1965.

Ruddy, Jonah, and Jonathan Hill, *The Bogey Man: Portrait of a Legend*, London, 1965.

Hyams, John, *Bogie*, New York, 1966.

Huston, John, *An Open Book*, New York, 1972.

Barbour, Alan, *Humphrey Bogart*, New York, 1973.

Benchley, Nathaniel, *Humphrey Bogart*, Boston, 1975.

Eyles, Allen, *Bogart*, New York, 1975.

Hyams, Joe, *Bogart and Bacall*, New York, 1975.

Bacall, Lauren, *Lauren Bacall by Myself*, New York, 1978.

Screen Greats, Volume III: Bogart, New York, 1980.

Cutterland, Frank, *Humphrey Bogart*, Paris, 1981.

Pettigrew, Terence, *Bogart: A Definitive Study of His Film Career*, London, 1981.

Brooks, Louise, *Lulu in Hollywood*, New York, 1982.

Winkler, Willi, *Humphrey Bogart und Hollywoods Schwarze Serie*, Munich, 1985.

Fuchs, Wolfgang J., *Humphrey Bogart: Cult-Star: A Documentation*, Berlin, 1987.

Coe, Jonathan, *Humphrey Bogart: Take It & Like It*, New York, 1991.

Sklar, Robert, *City Boys: Cagney, Bogart, Garfield*, Princeton, New Jersey, 1992.

Stuart, Gloria, *Boating with Bogart*, Los Angeles, 1993.

Bogart, Stephen Humphrey, with Gary Provost, *Bogart: In Search of My Father*, New York, 1995.

On BOGART: articles—

Current Biography 1942, New York, 1942.

Obituary in *New York Times*, 15 January 1957.

McCarty, Clifford, "Humphrey Bogart 1899-1957," in *Films in Review* (New York), May 1957.

Cooke, Alistair, "Epitaph for a Tough Guy," in *Atlantic* (Greenwich, Connecticut), May 1957.

Towne, Robert, "Bogart and Belmondo," in *Cinema* (Beverly Hills), December 1965.

Brooks, Louise, "Humphrey and Bogey," in *Sight and Sound* (London), Winter 1966-67.

Davis, Paxton, "Bogart, Hawks, and *The Big Sleep* Revisited—Frequently," in *Film Journal* (New York), Summer 1971.

"Humphrey Bogart," in *Lumière du cinéma* (Paris), March 1977.

Mellen, Joan, "Humphrey Bogart: Moral Tough Guy," in *Close-Ups: The Movie Star Book*, edited by Danny Peary, New York, 1978.

Humphrey Bogart in *The African Queen*

Sarris, Andrew, "Humphrey Bogart," in *The Movie Star*, edited by Elisabeth Weis, New York, 1981.

Schickel, Richard, "Bogart," in *Film Comment* (New York), May/June 1986.

Talty, Stephen, "Young Bogart," in *American Film* (Washington, D.C.), April 1991.

*   *   *

Humphrey Bogart had a privileged upbringing in Manhattan, the son of a noted surgeon; later, he had to leave college for disciplinary reasons. He served during World War I in the Navy, and suffered an injury during shelling which slightly paralyzed his upper lip, giving him the tight-lipped appearance and the suggestion of hesitancy in his speech that became the hallmark of his screen persona. After the war, he worked in the theater, first as a junior in stage management and later as a performer in youthful, romantic parts. A celebrated review by Alexander Woolcott in 1922 described him in a play called *Swiftly* as "inadequate." Nevertheless, during the 1920s he remained in employment, and he had the pertinacity to go to Hollywood when sound required the participation of new, stage-trained performers from Broadway. He constantly returned to the stage when he was dissatisfied with the supporting roles he was given in such films as *A Devil with Women*, *Body and Soul*, and *Love Affair*. The first role characteristic of his future image was in the theater production of Robert E. Sherwood's semipoetic play *The Petrified Forest* (1935), which the following year was made into a film by Warner Brothers. Warners intended to give Bogart's part—the gangster, Duke Mantee—to Edward G. Robinson. That Bogart got the part had to do with the intervention of Leslie Howard, who played the lead in both the play and the film; Howard insisted that Bogart reappear as Duke Mantee. 1936, therefore, marked the first appearance in film of the gaunt, sinister, slow-speaking Bogart persona. Fortunately, the film was successful and drew favorable critical attention.

Bogart was not, however, to become a charismatic star immediately, though he appeared, normally in a gangster role, in an endless flow of films during the next five years, from *San Quentin*, *Crime School*, and *Racket Busters* to *Angels with Dirty Faces*, *King of the Underworld*, and *The Roaring Twenties*. The Bogart image was very marked in William Wyler's *Dead End* in which he played a ruthless, cynical gangster rejected alike by his mother and his former girlfriend on his return to the New York slums in which he had been raised. This was followed in 1941 by Raoul Walsh's *High Sierra* with an exceptional script by John Huston and performance by Bogart as the aging, disillusioned gangster who has a change of heart. The devotion to "Bogey" was born of such later films as Huston's *The Maltese Falcon*, with Bogart as the ruthless but basically human Sam Spade; Michael Curtiz's Oscar-winning *Casablanca*, again with Bogart as the rough-surfaced but vulnerable dark horse; and Howard Hawks's two films *To Have and Have Not*—Lauren Bacall's film debut—and *The Big Sleep*, also with Bacall and with Bogart playing a private eye with a heart. Bogart's celebrated romance with Bacall led to her becoming his fourth wife.

Bogart's widening range of characters (which added to his stature as an actor, while increasing the impact of his always recognizable personal style and image) expanded notably under Huston in *The Treasure of the Sierra Madre*, *Key Largo*, and *The African Queen* (the latter gaining him an Oscar); in Nicholas Ray's *In a Lonely Place*; in Richard Brooks's serious story with a newspaper setting, *Deadline*; and Edward Dmytryk's *The Caine Mutiny*, in which he gave one of his finest performances as the paranoid Captain Queeg. He returned to his former gangster role in William Wyler's *The Desperate Hours*, and in his last appearance before his premature death in 1957, in Mark Robson's *The Harder They Fall*, he played a worn-out sportswriter in the more cynical mood of earlier films.

As Joan Mellen calls Bogart the epitome of a "moral tough guy," his stardom, considerably shorter than actors such as Cary Grant and Gary Cooper, also presents an irony that none of the other stars of his generation "remains such a lively presence in our imaginations." Indeed, as Richard Schickel continues to remind us "it is worth lingering at that crossroads and contemplating the evidence about who he was and what he was that was left there in plain sight." Throughout his career till his death and onward for almost four decades now, the Bogart image and the sense of integrity and courage that image carries prevail at the center of American film history.

—Roger Manvell, updated by Guo-Juin Hong

BOND, Ward

Nationality: American. **Born:** Denver, Colorado, 9 April 1905. **Education:** University of Southern California, Los Angeles. **Family:** Married 1) Doris Sellers, 1936 (divorced 1944); 2) Mary Lou (Bond), 1954. **Career:** 1929—while attending USC, selected, along with John Wayne, by John Ford to appear in film *Salute*, which resulted in lifelong friendship and professional association between Bond, Ford, and Wayne; 1929-59—in supporting roles in some 200 films for several major directors including Ford, Hawks, Fleming, etc.; 1957-61—star of TV series *Wagon Train*. **Died:** In Dallas, Texas, 5 November 1960.

Films as Actor:

1929   *Salute* (Ford); *Words and Music* (Tinling)

1930   *Born Reckless* (Ford); *The Big Trail* (Walsh)

1932   *High Speed* (Lederman); *White Eagles* (Hillyer); *Rackety Rax* (Werker); *Hello, Trouble* (Hillyer); *Virtue* (Buzzell)

1933   *When Strangers Meet* (Badger); *Heroes for Sale* (Wellman); *Wild Boys of the Road* (Wellman); *The Wrecker* (Rogell); *Unknown Valley* (Hillyer); *Police Car Seventeen* (Hillyer); *Obey the Law* (Stoloff); *The Sundown Rider* (Hillyer)

1934   *Whirlpool* (Neill); *Most Precious Thing in Life* (Hillyer); *Straightaway* (Brower); *The Poor Rich* (Sedgwick); *Frontier Marshal* (Seiler); *Broadway Bill* (*Strictly Confidential*) (Capra); *It Happened One Night* (Capra); *The Defense Rests* (Hillyer); *Fighting Rangers* (Seitz); *Here Comes the Groom* (Sedgwick); *The Fighting Code* (Hillyer); *The Voice in the Night* (Coleman); *A Man's Game* (Lederman); *The Crime of Helen Stanley* (Lederman); *Girl in Danger* (Lederman); *The Human Side* (Buzzell); *Kid Millions* (Del Ruth); *Against the Law* (Hillyer)

1935   *Devil Dogs of the Air* (Bacon); *Little Big Shot* (Bischoff); *The Informer* (Ford); *The Crimson Trail* (Raboch); *She Gets Her Man* (Nigh); *His Night Out* (Nigh); *Black Fury* (Curtiz); *Western Courage* (Bennett); *Fighting Shadows* (Selman); *Guard That Girl* (Hillyer); *Murder in the Fleet* (Sedgwick); *The Headline Woman* (Nigh); *Waterfront Lady* (Santley); *Men of the Night* (Hillyer); *Justice of the Range* (Selman); *Too Tough to Kill* (Lederman)

1936   *Cattle Thief* (Bennett); *Muss 'em Up* (*House of Fate*) (Charles Vidor); *The Bride Walks Out* (Jason); *Second Wife* (Killy); *Without Orders* (Landers); *Crash Donovan* (Nigh); *Conflict* (Howard); *They Met in a Taxi* (Green); *The Man Who Lived Twice* (Lachman); *The Legion of Terror* (Coleman); *The Leathernecks Have Landed* (*The Marines Have Landed*) (Bretherton); *Pride of the Marines* (Lederman); *Avenging Waters* (Bennett)

Ward Bond

1937   *You Only Live Once* (Fritz Lang); *Dead End* (Wyler); *Park Avenue Logger (Tall Timber; Millionaire Playboy)* (Howard); *The Devil's Playground* (Kenton); *23½ Hours Leave* (Blystone); *Night Key* (Corrigan); *Escape by Night* (McFadden); *The Wildcatter* (Collins); *A Fight to the Finish* (Coleman)

1938   *Born to Be Wild* (Kane); *Flight into Nowhere* (Collins); *Hawaii Calls* (Cline); *Reformatory* (Collins); *Gun Law* (Howard); *The Law West of Tombstone* (Tryon); *Professor Beware* (Nugent); *Mr. Moto's Gamble* (Tinling); *Submarine Patrol* (Ford); *Prison Break* (Lubin); *Numbered Woman* (Karl Brown); *Over the Wall* (MacDonald); *The Amazing Dr. Clitterhouse* (Litvak)

1939   *They Made Me a Criminal* (Berkeley); *Made for Each Other* (Bean); *Dodge City* (Curtiz); *Waterfront* (Morse); **Gone with the Wind** (Fleming); *Trouble in Sundown* (Howard); *Return of the Cisco Kid* (Leeds); **Young Mr. Lincoln** (John Ford); *Frontier Marshal* (Dwan); *The Girl from Mexico* (Goodwins); *The Kid from Kokomo (The Orphan of the Ring)* (Seiler); *Drums along the Mohawk* (John Ford); *Dust Be My Destiny* (Seiler); *The Oklahoma Kid* (Bacon); *Heaven with a Barbed Wire Fence* (Cortez); *Mr. Moto in Danger Island* (Leeds)

1940   *Virginia City* (Curtiz); *The Cisco Kid and the Lady* (Leeds); **The Grapes of Wrath** (John Ford); *Little Old New York* (King); *Santa Fe Trail* (Curtiz); *Buck Benny Rides Again* (Sandrich); *The Mortal Storm* (Borzage); *Kit Carson* (Seitz); *The Long Voyage Home* (John Ford)

1941   *Tobacco Road* (John Ford); *A Man Betrayed* (Auer); *The Shepherd of the Hills* (Hathaway); *Swamp Water (The Man Who Came Back)* (Renoir); *Sergeant York* (Hawks); *Manpower* (Walsh); *Doctors Don't Tell* (Tourneur); *Wild Bill Hickok Rides* (Enright); **The Maltese Falcon** (Huston)

1942   *The Falcon Takes Over* (Reis); *In This Our Life* (Huston); *Ten Gentlemen from West Point* (Hathaway); *Gentleman Jim* (Walsh); *Sin Town* (Enright)

1943   *Hello Frisco, Hello* (Humberstone); *A Guy Named Joe* (Fleming); *Hitler—Dead or Alive* (Grinde); *Slightly Dangerous* (Ruggles); *They Came to Blow Up America* (Ludwig); *Cowboy Commandos* (Luby)

1944   *Home in Indiana* (Hathaway); *The Sullivans* (Bacon); *Tall in the Saddle* (Marin)

1945   *Dakota* (Kane); *They Were Expendable* (John Ford)

1946   *Canyon Passage* (Jacques Tourneur); **It's a Wonderful Life** (Capra); **My Darling Clementine** (John Ford)

1947   *The Fugitive* (John Ford); *Unconquered* (DeMille)

1948   *Fort Apache* (John Ford); *The Time of Your Life* (Potter); *Tap Roots* (Marshall); *Joan of Arc* (Fleming); *Three Godfathers* (John Ford)

1950   *Riding High* (Marshall); *Wagonmaster* (John Ford); *Singing Guns* (Springsteen); *The Great Missouri Raid* (Douglas); *Kiss Tomorrow Goodbye* (Douglas)

1951   *Operation Pacific* (Waggner); *Only the Valiant* (Douglas); *On Dangerous Ground* (Nicholas Ray)

1952   *Hellgate* (Warren); *Thunderbirds* (Auer); **The Quiet Man** (John Ford)

1953   *Blowing Wild* (Fregonese); *The Moonlighter* (Rowland); *Hondo* (Farrow)

1954   *Gypsy Colt* (Marton); **Johnny Guitar** (Nicholas Ray); *The Bob Mathias Story (The Flaming Torch)* (Lyon)

1955   *The Long Gray Line* (John Ford); *Mr. Roberts* (John Ford); *A Man Alone* (Milland)

1956   **The Searchers** (John Ford); *Dakota Incident* (Foster); *Pillars of the Sky* (Marshall)

1957   *The Wings of Eagles* (John Ford); *The Halliday Brand* (Lewis)

1958   *China Doll* (Borzage)

1959   **Rio Bravo** (Hawks); *Alias Jesse James* (McLeod)

Publications

On BOND: books—

See entry on John Ford in *International Dictionary of Films and Filmmakers, Volume 2: Directors.*

*   *   *

Ward Bond acted best what he was in reality: a dyed-in-the-wool social and political conservative, a perfect expression of the American west. He proudly displayed his extreme right-wing views during the 1940s and 1950s when he worked for the still relatively liberal John Ford, and he set himself up for some merciless kidding from his mentor. In fact, Ford went beyond mere "kidding." His papers at the Lilly Library at Indiana University again and again exhibit a contempt for Bond, and that attitude had something to do with the kinds of roles that Ford, from among his company of stock players, chose Bond to play.

In the early films the conservative Bond is usually cast by Ford as an unimaginative and stolid foil to a rebellious John Wayne—the Wayne persona, if not the man himself. In the later films Wayne himself assumes the role of the inflexible man: there is no need for a Bond figure in, say, *The Man Who Shot Liberty Valance.*

There are a number of films in which Ford achieves his "balance" in this way. In *The Three Godfathers* the bank robber (played by Wayne) is set in opposition to the conventional lawman-in-pursuit (played by Bond). The two even fight over the unusual name given the lawman's grandchild, who has been christened and adopted by the bank robber. Again, it is a fight between the supporter of social order (Bond) against the disrupter from the desert (Wayne). As sheriff, Bond is, at once, the gravel-voiced commander and the always-joking upholder of the status quo.

In *The Quiet Man* Bond plays a priest. Set as he is against the fiery personalities of Wayne and Victor McLagen, Bond is nothing more than the stuffy representative of an anachronistic Irish Catholicism. The demands of this particular part, however, seem to be beyond him. The stiffness with which he plays the part of an intriguer demonstrates not only his limitations as an actor, but also his inability as a person to play, even for a moment, the social Other. Only in pious poses and (as the film's narrator) in priestly tones is Bond at ease.

In *Wagonmaster* Ford fully exploits the dominant aspect of Bond's persona—the organization man. He portrays a Mormon elder, the intractable punisher of sin—sin in the form of a young sinner who has joined the wagon train to Zion—and here the portrayal is completely successful. In this unsettling film Bond becomes the pivotal emblem for all that is reactionary in our society—the American Patriarch. This figure represents only one part of Ford's vision of America. But it was a part—one piece among many others—that Bond embodied to perfection.

—Rodney Farnsworth

BONDARCHUK, Sergei

Nationality: Russian. **Born:** Sergei Fedorovich Bondarchuk in Belozersk, Ukraine, 25 September 1920. **Education:** Attended Rostov Theatrical Institute (studies interrupted by World War II); studied under Sergei Gerasimov at All Union State Institute of Cinematography. **Military Service:** served in army during World War II. **Family:** Married Irina Skobtseva, 1959, children: Aljona and Fiodr. **Career:** Began acting with army unit; 1946-48—member of Actor's Faculty, Moscow Film Institute; 1948—cast by Sergei Gerasimov in first film, *The Young Guard*; 1960s—spent six years preparing and filming *War and Peace*. **Awards:** People's Artist of the Soviet Union, 1952; Hero of Soviet Labor, 1980; Order of Red Banner; Order of Lenin (twice). **Died:** Of blood disease, in Moscow, Russia, 20 October 1994.

Films as Actor:

1948 *The Young Guard* (Gerasimov) (as Valko); *The Story of a Real Man* (Stolper) (as Gvozdev); *Michurin* (Dovzhenko)
1949 *The Path of Glory* (Buneev, Rybakov, and Shveitser) (as District Party Secretary)
1950 *A Knight of the Gold Star* (*The Bearer of the Golden Star*) (Raizman) (as Tutarinov)
1951 *Taras Shevchenko* (Savchenko) (title role)
1953 *Admiral Ushakov* and *The Ships Are Storming the Bastions* (*Attack from the Sea*) (Romm) (as Tikhon Prokoviev)
1954 *It Mustn't Be Forgotten* (*This Must Not Be Forgotten*) (Lukov) (as Garmash)
1955 *Poprigunya* (*The Gadfly*; *The Grasshopper*) (Samsonov) (as Dr. Dymov); *Neokonchennaya povest* (*The Unfinished Tale*; *Unfinished Story*) (Ermler) (as Yershov)
1956 *Othello* (Yutkevich) (title role); *Ivan Franko* (Levchuk) (title role)
1957 *Two from the Same Block* (*Two from One Housing Block*) (Gurin and Ibragimov); *Pages from the Story* (Kryzhanovsky) (as Stage reader)
1958 *Shli soldaty* (*The Soldier Marched*) (Trauberg) (as Matvei Krylov)
1959 *A Spring Wind on Venaya* (as narrator)
1960 *Seryozha* (*A Summer to Remember*) ((Danelia and Talankin) (as Korostelyov); *Era notte a Roma* (*It Was Night in Rome*) (Rossellini) (as Fyodor)
1961 *Povest plamennykh* (*Story of the Turbulent Years*; *The Flaming Years*; *Chronicle of Flaming Years*) (Solntseva) (as narrator)
1969 *Bitka na Neretvi* (*Battle of Neretva*) (Bulajic) (as Martin)
1970 *Dyadya Vanya* (*Uncle Vanya*) (Mikhalkov-Konchalovsky) (as Dr. Astrov)
1973 *Molchaniye Doktoraivens* (*The Silence of Dr. Evans*) (Metalnikov) (as Dr. Evans)
1974 *Such High Mountains* (Solntseva) (as Ivan Nikolayevich)
1975 *The Choice of a Goal* (Talankin) (as Kurchatov)
1989 *La Bataille des trois rois* (Barka)

Films as Director:

1959 *Sudba cheloveka* (*Destiny of a Man*; *Fate of a Man*) (+ ro as Andrei Sokolov)
1965-7 *Voina i mir* (*War and Peace*) (+ sc, ro as Pierre Bezukhov)
1970 *Waterloo* (+ co-sc)
1975 *Oni srazhalis za rodinu* (*They Fought for the Country*) (+ co-sc, ro as Zvyagintsev)
1976 *The Peaks of Zelengore*
1977 *The Steppe* (+ sc)
1982 *Mexico in Flames*; *Krasnye Kolakola*; *October*
1983 *Red Bells: I've Seen the Birth of the New World* (*I Saw the New World Born*)
1986 *Boris Godunov* (for TV) (+ sc)

Publications

By BONDARCHUK: books—

Za druzheskie disskussie, Moscow, 1959.
Zhelanie chuda, Moscow, 1984.

By BONDARCHUK: articles—

Interview in *Film a doba* (Prague), October 1972.
"Dolgi i pravo hudožnika," in *Iskusstvo Kino* (Moscow), August 1973.
Interview with S. Tschertok, in *Film und Fernsehen* (Berlin), April 1975.
"Ot serdca k serduc," in *Iskusstvo Kino* (Moscow), May 1980.

On BONDARCHUK: books—

Shalunovsky, V., *Sergei Bondarchuk*, Moscow, 1959.
Khaniutin, I., *Sergei Bondarchuk*, Moscow, 1961.
Ignateva, N. *Sergei Bondarchuk*, Moscow, 1961.

On BONDARCHUK: articles—

"Director of the Year," in *International Film Guide*, London, 1969.
Zolotussky, Igor, "*War and Peace*: A Soviet View," in *London Magazine*, March 1969.
Gillett, John, "Thinking Big," in *Sight and Sound* (London), Summer 1970.
Guralnik, Uran, "Vast as an Ocean," in *Films and Filming* (London), September-October 1970.
Lind, John, "The Road to *Waterloo*," in *Focus on Film* (London), September-October 1970.
"The Coming of the Russians," in *Action* (Los Angeles), June 1971.
Zubkov, J., "Akter-avtor obraza," in *Iskusstvo Kino* (Moscow), February 1972.
Citrinjak, G., "Zarkie dni ijulja," in *Iskusstvo Kino* (Moscow), January 1975.
Tolcenova, N., "Pora Cehova," in *Iskusstvo Kino* (Moscow), July 1977.
Gerasimov, Sergei, "Soviet Cinema: Films, Personalities, Problems," in *Soviet Film* (Moscow), no. 271, 1979.
Karaganov, A., and others, "Poesija pravdy," in *Iskusstvo Kino* (Moscow), September 1980.
"Profile," in *Soviet Film* (Moscow), no. 5, 1986.
Obituary in *New York Times*, 21 October 1994.

*　　*　　*

Sergei Bondarchuk made his film acting debut as a stock company player while still attending film school in Moscow. One of his earliest important roles was in Gerasimov's *The Young Guard*. But Bondarchuk's undisputed talent only became evident in his seventh feature, *Taras Shevchenko*, in which he played the great Ukrainian poet of that name who also wrote the script. The deficiencies of Shevchenko's imperfect screenplay made Bondarchuk's introductory scenes seem cold and rhetorical, but in the scenes from the close of the author's life on through the final exile episode, showing the inhumanity of the czar's soldiers, Bondarchuk succeeded on his own in raising the film to a truly tragic level.

Bondarchuk's acclaim in this role, and his being given the title of State Artist in 1952, made him one of the most prominent actors in the Soviet Union. Yet with the exception of Samsonov's *The Grasshopper*, in which he starred as a physician locked in a marriage with a

Sergei Bondarchuk in *Voina i mir*

woman unimpressed by his devotion to duty and achievements for the common folk, most of his films of the 1950s were not as impressive as his early success had promised—even though he was given important parts in films by most of the country's best directors, including Yutkevich's *Othello*, one of the first Soviet filmings of a Shakespeare play.

Bondarchuk's interest in Sholokhov's story "The Destiny of Man," about the struggles of people to maintain some vestige of their former lives while surrounded by war, pushed him to direct as well as star in the film version. The result was a successful blending of Bondarchuk's already-recognized thespian talents with—for an actor *and* first-time director—a stunningly cinematic visual style. This led to the Lenin Prize and a succession of films as actor and director in both the Soviet Union and abroad.

The overall result of these personal triumphs led Bondarchuk to attempt a definitive film version of Tolstoy's massive work *War and Peace*. One of the most expensive (estimates reach as high as $100 million) and exquisitely staged Soviet films, the ambitious undertaking took two years to reach the screen. The immense scope of the film, which ran more than eight hours in its original version and was shown in Soviet cinemas over several nights, was amply balanced by Bondarchuk's poetic vision of the broad spaces of the Russian landscape. For sheer spectacle, its battle scenes have yet to be surpassed. Bondarchuk himself played the key role of Pierre Bezukhov, Tolstoy's intellectual hero and mouthpiece. Though some critics felt him too old for the part, Bondarchuk won the Moscow Festival Prize for his performance. The film itself, released abroad in a slightly scaled down six-hour version, also shown over several nights, captured the 1968 Oscar for best foreign film.

Bondarchuk followed *War and Peace* with another epic, *Waterloo*, for Dino DeLaurentiis, in which he took only a small role. It too was highlighted by battles scenes of bravura size and spectacle, and caused him to be compared with Orson Welles, who also had a small role in the film, because of their both being actor/directors, their robust appearance, and their grandiosity of purpose.

The film was not a hit, however. Moreover, Bondarchuk had been unable to control the volcanic temperament of his scenery-chewing star, Rod Steiger (as Napoleon). Thereafter, he retreated to his native industry where his autonomy was assured; most of his subsequent films received little exposure elsewhere. They included smaller scale projects inspired by Chekhov and Sholokhov, and a return to the epic format with the two-part *Mexico in Flames*, a film based on the career of the journalist John Reed, the only American to be honored with burial in the Kremlin. A Soviet counterpart and response to Warren Beatty's Hollywoodized *Reds*, the film chronicles the maverick Reed's exploits covering and participating in both the Russian and Mexican revolutions.

Bondarchuk's work as both actor and director typically focuses on sturdy characters full of mental stamina and patriotic pathos with a credo that is indomitably optimistic. At the time of his death in 1994, Bondarchuk had become a living monument in Soviet film, and arguably its most important figure since that earlier Sergei named Eisenstein.

—Karel Tabery, updated by John McCarty

BONHAM-CARTER, Helena

Nationality: British. **Born:** London, England, 26 May 1966; great-granddaughter of Liberal Prime Minister Lord Herbert Asquith, granddaughter of socialite Lady Violet Bonham Carter and grand-niece of the director Anthony Asquith. **Education:** Attended South Hampstead High School; Westminster School. **Career:** 1986—made screen debut when chosen by director Trevor Nunn for the title role in *Lady Jane*; began association with director James Ivory when cast in *A Room with a View*; 1988—made London stage debut in *The Woman in White*. **Agent:** Adam Isaacs, United Talent Agency, 9560 Wilshire Boulevard, Beverly Hills, CA 90212, U.S.A.

Films as Actress:

1983   *A Pattern of Roses* (for TV) (as Netty)
1986   *Lady Jane* (Nunn) (title role); ***A Room with a View*** (Ivory) (as Lucy Honeychurch)
1987   *Maurice* (Ivory) (as young lady at cricket match); *The Vision* (Norman Stone—for TV) (as Jo Marriner); *A Hazard of Hearts* (John Hough—for TV) (as Serena Staverley)
1988   *La Maschera* (*The Mask*) (Infascelli) (as Iris)
1989   *Francesco* (Caviani) (as Chiara); *Getting It Right* (Kleiser) (as Lady Minerva Munday)
1990   *Hamlet* (Zeffirelli) (as Ophelia)
1991   *Where Angels Fear to Tread* (Sturridge) (as Caroline Abbott)
1992   ***Howards End*** (Ivory) (as Helen Schlegel)
1993   *Fatal Deception: Mrs. Lee Harvey Oswald* (*Marina's Story*) (Dornhelm—for TV) (as Marina Oswald)
1994   *Mary Shelley's Frankenstein* (Branagh) (as Elizabeth); *A Dark-Adapted Eye* (Fywell—for TV) (as adult Faith)
1995   *Mighty Aphrodite* (Woody Allen) (as Amanda); *Margaret's Museum* (Ransen) (as Margaret MacNeil)
1996   *Twelfth Night* (Trevor Nunn) (as Olivia); *Portraits chinois* (Dugowson)

Publications

By BONHAM-CARTER: articles—

"From School to Stardom: A Teen-ager's Lark for Helena Bonham-Carter," interview with Nina Darnton, in *New York Times*, 2 March 1986.
"Helena Bonham-Carter; Cary Elwes," interview with Louise Tanner, in *Films in Review* (New York), April 1986.

On BONHAM-CARTER: articles—

Amberson, M., "Helena's Niche," in *Movieline* (Los Angeles), June 1991.
Mundy, C., "She's Leaving Home. Really," in *Premiere* (New York), November 1994.

*   *   *

When one thinks of Merchant/Ivory/Jhabvala and E. M. Forster, one also thinks of Helena Bonham-Carter. Other actors, including Emma Thompson, Anthony Hopkins, James Wilby, and Hugh Grant have appeared in more than one James Ivory-directed feature during the past decade. But it seems as if Bonham-Carter had been in them all—and this perception has been the actress's undoing.

Bonham-Carter most often has acted on screen in period costume. This was the case in her first starring film, *Lady Jane*, directed by Trevor Nunn and set in sixteenth-century England. She is well-cast as Lady Jane Grey, daughter of the Duke and Duchess of Suffolk: the ill-equipped, ill-fated adolescent who, as the result of political intrigue, is forced into marriage with Guilford Dudley (Cary Elwes), son of the Duke of Northumberland; and ends up on the throne of England for barely a week before being executed. Bonham-Carter adequately expresses Lady Jane's initial shyness and naïveté, and her transformation as she discovers her sexuality and embraces youthful idealism while coming to envision a far more equitable world. At this point in her career, one can see Bonham-Carter cast as Juliet in Franco Zeffirelli's *Romeo and Juliet*.

In Forster's *A Room with a View*, her first film with Ivory, Bonham-Carter gives a thoughtful performance as Lucy Honeychurch, a wealthy, detached young woman who has traveled to Florence in the company of her fastidious aunt (Maggie Smith). As in *Lady Jane*, Bonham-Carter's character undergoes an emancipation as she becomes involved in a romantic relationship. After this promising start, however, Bonham-Carter faltered. In Ivory and Forster's *Howards End* she is just one of an ensemble, with her fellow actors—including Hopkins, Thompson, Vanessa Redgrave and Samuel West—cast in the juicier roles. As a result, Bonham-Carter registers on screen as little more than a kewpie doll presence. The actress especially suffers when cast opposite strong, naturalistic performers. This is most apparent in Kenneth Branagh's *Mary Shelley's Frankenstein*, in which she is Dr. Frankenstein's love interest, whom he turns into a monster reminiscent of Elsa Lanchester in *The Bride of Frankenstein*. She is the weak link in a cast headed by Branagh (as Dr. Frankenstein) and Robert De Niro (as the Frankenstein monster). After *Lady Jane* and *A Room with a View*, Bonham-Carter's best period-film performance came in *Where Angels Fear to Tread* (based on an E. M. Forster novel but directed by Charles Sturridge rather than Ivory). Here, she is cast as another repressed young Englishwoman who gets in touch with her emotions when she becomes involved romantically.

Bonham-Carter on occasion has appeared in contemporary settings, most successfully in *Getting It Right*, in which she plays a quirky, unstable young Lady. But in Woody Allen's *Mighty Aphrodite*, she has the far less interesting of the two leading female roles. She is a Manhattan art gallery owner, married to Allen's sportswriter, with the scenario set in motion when the couple decides to adopt a baby. The film's showcase role is played by Mira Sorvino, cast as the loopy prostitute who is the child's birth mother.

As Bonham-Carter's career progresses, she might be best advised to avoid period films and scenarios in which she plays the ingenue, and seek out characters who are earthier and have, at the story's outset, experienced more of life. She did just that in *Margaret's Museum*, a low-profile Canadian film in which she plays an embittered small-

Helena Bonham-Carter in *A Room with a View*

town woman who despises the local mines, and is wooed and won by a former miner.

—Rob Edelman

BORGNINE, Ernest

Nationality: American. **Born:** Ermes Effron Borgnino in Hamden, Connecticut, 24 January 1917 (some sources say 1915 or 1918). **Education:** Attended New Haven Public Schools; studied acting at Randall School of Dramatic Art, Hartford, Connecticut. **Military Service:** 1935-45—served in U.S. Navy, mainly as gunner's mate on destroyers. **Family:** Married 1) Rhoda Kemins, 1948 (divorced 1959), daughter: Nancy; 2) the actress Katy Jurado, 1959 (divorced 1963); 3) the singer Ethel Merman, 1964 (divorced 1964); 4) Donna Rancourt, 1964 (divorced 1972), children: Sharon and Christopher; 5) Tova Traesnaes Newman, 1972. **Career:** After graduation from high school worked as truck driver for short time; 1946-50—in repertory at Barber Theater, Abingdon, Virginia; 1951—film debut in *China Corsair*; 1952—Broadway debut in *Mrs. McThing*; active on television from 1950s; 1962-66—in TV comedy series *McHale's Navy*; 1984—in TV mini-series *Last Days of Pompeii*; 1984-85—in TV series *Airwolf*; 1995-96—in TV series *The Single Guy*. **Awards:** Best Actor, Cannes Festival, Best Actor Academy Award, Best Actor, New York Film Critics, and Best Foreign Actor, British Academy, for *Marty*, 1955. **Address:** c/o Harry Flynn, The Flynn Company, 1110 Hortense Street, North Hollywood, CA 91602, U.S.A.

Films as Actor:

1951 *China Corsair* (Nazzaro) (as Hu Chang); *The Whistle at Eaton Falls* (Siodmak) (as Bill Street); *The Mob* (Parrish) (as Joe Castro)
1953 *The Stranger Wore a Gun* (de Toth) (as Bull Slager); *From Here to Eternity* (Zinnemann) (as Fatso)
1954 *Johnny Guitar* (Nicholas Ray) (as Bart Lonergan); *Demetrius and the Gladiators* (Daves) (as Strabo); *The Bounty Hunter* (de Toth) (as Rachin); *Vera Cruz* (Aldrich) (as Donnegan)
1955 *Bad Day at Black Rock* (John Sturges) (as Coley Trimble); *Marty* (Delbert Mann) (title role); *Run for Cover* (Nicholas Ray) (as Morgan); *Violent Saturday* (Fleischer) (as Stadt); *The Last Command* (Lloyd) (as Mike Radin); *The Square Jungle* (Jerry Hopper) (as Bernie Browne)
1956 *Jubal* (Daves) (as Shep Horgan); *The Catered Affair* (Richard Brooks) (as Tom Hurley); *The Best Things in Life Are Free* (Curtiz) (as Lew Brown)
1957 *Three Brave Men* (Dunne) (as Bernie Goldsmith)
1958 *The Vikings* (Fleischer) (as King Ragnar); *The Badlanders* (Daves) (as John McBain); *Torpedo Run* (Pevney) (as Lt. Archer Sloan)
1959 *The Rabbit Trap* (Leacock) (as Eddie Colt)
1960 *Man on a String* (de Toth) (as Boris Mitrov); *Pay or Die* (Wilson) (as Lt. Joseph Petrosino)
1961 *Go Naked in the World* (MacDougall) (as Pete Stratton); *Il re di Poggioreale* (Coletti); *Il giudizio universale* (*The Last Judgment*) (De Sica); *Barabba* (*Barabbas*) (Fleischer) (as Lucius); *Season of Passion* (Norman) (as Roo); *I briganti italiani* (*Les Guerilleros*) (Camerini)
1964 *McHale's Navy* (Montagne) (as Lt. Cdr. Quinton McHale)
1966 *Flight of the Phoenix* (Aldrich) (as Tuucker Cobb); *The Oscar* (Rouse) (as Barney Yale)

1967 *The Dirty Dozen* (Aldrich) (as Gen. Worden); *Chuka* (Douglas) (as Sgt. Otto Hahnsbach)
1968 *The Legend of Lylah Clare* (Aldrich) (as Barney Sheean); *The Split* (Flemyng) (as Bert Clinger); *Ice Station Zebra* (John Sturges) (as Boris Vaslov)
1969 *The Wild Bunch* (Peckinpah) (as Dutch Engstrom); *Vengeance Is Mine* (Buchs)
1970 *Los desperados* (*A Bullet for Sandoval*) (Buchs) (as Don Pedro Sandoval); *The Adventurers* (Gilbert) (as Fat Cat); *Suppose They Gave a War and Nobody Came?* (*War Games*) (Averback) (as Sheriff Harve)
1971 *Willard* (Daniel Mann) (as Al Martin); *Rain for a Dusty Summer* (Lubin) (as dictator); *Hannie Caulder* (Kennedy) (as Emmett Clemens); *Un uomo dalla pelle dura* (*Ripped-Off*; *The Boxer*) (Prosperi)
1972 *The Revengers* (Daniel Mann) (as Hoop); *The Poseidon Adventure* (Neame) (as Mike Rogo); *Bunny O'Hare* (Oswald) (as Bill Green)
1973 *The Neptune Factor* (*An Underwater Odyssey*; *The Neptune Disaster*) (Petrie) (as Don "Mack" MacKay); *Emperor of the North Pole* (*Emperor of the North*) (Aldrich) (as Shack)
1974 *Law and Disorder* (Passer) (as Cy)
1975 *Sunday in the Country* (Trent) (as Adam Smith); *The Devil's Rain* (Fuest) (as Corbis); *Hustle* (Aldrich) (as Santoro)
1976 *Natale in Casa di Appuntamento* (*Christmas at the Brothel*) (Nannuzzi); *Won Ton Ton, the Dog Who Saved Hollywood* (Winner); *Shoot* (Hart) (as Lou)
1977 *The Prince and the Pauper* (*Crossed Swords*) (Fleischer) (as John Canty); *The Greatest* (Gries) (as Angelo Dundee)
1978 *The Cops and Robin* (Reisner—for TV); *Convoy* (Peckinpah) (as Lyle Wallace)
1979 *The Black Hole* (Nelson) (as Harry Booth); *Ravagers* (Compton) (as Rann); *The Double McGuffin* (Camp) (as Firat)
1980 *When Time Ran Out* (*Earth's Final Fury*) (Goldstone) (as Tom Conti)
1981 *Escape from New York* (Carpenter) (as Cabbie); *Deadly Blessing* (Craven) (as Isaiah); *High Risk* (Raffill) (as Clint); *Super Fuzz* (*Supersnooper*) (Corbucci) (as Willy Dunlop)
1983 *Young Warriors* (Foldes) (as Lt. Bob Carrigan); *Blood Feud* (Newell—for TV); *Carpool* (Swackhamer—for TV) (as Mickey Doyle)
1984 *The White Stallion* (Fournier); *Codename Wildgeese* (Dawson) (as Fletcher); *Love Leads the Way* (Delbert Mann)
1985 *The Dirty Dozen: The Next Mission* (McLaglen—for TV) (as Gen. Worden); *Alice in Wonderland* (Harry Harris) (as Lion)
1986 *Manhunt* (Ludman) (as Ben Robeson); *Isola del tesoro* (Dawson)
1987 *Skeleton Coast* (*Coast of Skeletons*) (Cardos) (as Col. Smith); *The Dirty Dozen: The Deadly Mission* (Katzin—for TV) (as Gen. Worden)
1988 *The Dirty Dozen: The Fatal Mission* (Katzin—for TV) (as Gen. Worden); *Spike of Bensonhurst* (Morrissey) (as Baldo Cacetti); *Jake Spanner, Private Eye* (Katzin—for TV)
1989 *Ociano* (Deodato—for TV); *Turnaround*
1990 *Laser Mission* (*Soldier of Fortune*) (Davis) (as Prof. Braun); *Any Man's Death* (Clegg—for TV) (as Gantz); *Last Match* (Ludman); *The Opponent* (Martino) (as Victor); *Appearances* (Phelps—for TV) (as Emil Danzig); *Moving Target* (Mattei) (as Captain Morrison); *Tides of War* (Rossati)
1992 *Mistress* (Primus) (as himself)
1993 *Tieraerztin Christine* (Retzer—for TV) (as Dr. Gruber); *Der Blaue Diamant* (Retzer—for TV) (as Hans Kroger)
1995 *The Legend of O. B. Taggert*; *Tieraerztin Christine II* (Retzer—for TV) (as Dr. Gruber); *Captiva Island* (Biffar)

Ernest Borgnine in *From Here to Eternity*

Publications

On BORGNINE: articles—

Current Biography 1956, New York, 1956.
Ecran (Paris), July 1978.
Ciné Revue (Paris), 14 May 1981 and 14 October 1982.
Films Illustrated (London), June 1981.
Jacobs, A. J., "Borgnine's Lives," in *Entertainment Weekly*, 6 October 1995.

*   *   *

Ernest Borgnine, best known as a supporting player, has one of the most familiar faces in movies and television. It is a difficult one to forget; burly, gap-toothed, and pug-ugly, with bushy black eyebrows, and a smile that can suggest warmhearted affability or gleeful sadism. Borgnine has won acclaim playing roles appropriate to both smiles.

Portrayals in two Academy Award-winning films display these sides of his screen persona. In 1953, he co-starred as the brutal sergeant "Fatso" Judson who got his kicks treading on Frank Sinatra in *From Here to Eternity*. But two years later Borgnine, usually associated with villainous roles, especially in Westerns, did an about-face and won the Best Actor award as the lonely, gentle butcher in the title role of *Marty*, a part he got by default when Rod Steiger, the actor who originated the character of Marty in Paddy Chayefsky's award-winning television drama, was unable to do the film version because he was busy making the film version of the hit Broadway musical *Oklahoma!*

Borgnine's familiarity with audiences stems in part from his stint on the long-running television sitcom *McHale's Navy* (1962-66), in which he starred as the scheming but good-hearted Captain McHale, playing mother hen to a wacky crew of misfits. Borgnine returned to series television in 1995, playing opposite comic Jonathan Silverman in the NBC sitcom *The Single Guy*.

In films, however, Borgnine's commanding presence has been put to its best use in menacing or villainous roles. One of his most memorable performances was as a weary member of a doomed gang of outlaws in a changing West in the Sam Peckinpah classic *The Wild Bunch*, which underwent a major restoration and theatrical rerelease in 1995 to mark the film's 25th anniversary. Whether in Westerns, disaster films, or biblical epics, Borgnine is at his most sublime when in a lumbering, blustering rage.

—Donald Liebenson, updated by John McCarty

BOW, Clara

Nationality: American. **Born:** Brooklyn, New York, 29 July 1905. **Education:** P.S. 98, Sheepshead Bay, New York; left school in 8th grade. **Family:** Married the cowboy actor and rancher Rex Bell (George F. Beldam), 1931 (died 1962), children: Rex and George. **Career:** 1921—won movie fan magazine photo contest and given screen test; 1922—first film appearance in *Beyond the Rainbow*; 1923—contract with Preferred Pictures; 1925—contract sold to Paramount; 1927—role in Elinor Glyn's production of *It* established reputation as "the 'It' girl"; 1930-31—negative publicity and scandal resulting from revelations by former secretary Daisy De Voe, brought to trial for embezzling funds from Bow, accompanied decline in popularity; 1931—mental breakdown; 1932—comeback attempt with *Call Her Savage*; 1933—retired. **Died:** 26 September 1965.

Films as Actress:

1922 *Beyond the Rainbow* (Cabanne)
1923 *Down to the Sea in Ships* (Clifton); *Enemies of Women* (Crosland); *Maytime* (Gasnier) (as Alice Tremaine); *Daring Years* (Webb)
1924 *Grit* (Tuttle); *Black Oxen* (Lloyd); *Poisoned Paradise* (Gasnier); *Daughters of Pleasure* (Beaudine); *Wine* (Gasnier); *Empty Hearts* (Santell); *This Woman* (Rosen); *Black Lightning* (Hogan)
1925 *Capital Punishment* (Hogan); *Helen's Babies* (Seiter); *The Adventurous Sex* (Giblyn); *My Lady's Lips* (Hogan); *Parisian Love* (Gasnier); *Eve's Lover* (Del Ruth); *Kiss Me Again* (Lubitsch); *The Scarlet West* (Adolfi); *The Primrose Path* (Hoyt); *The Plastic Age* (Ruggles); *Keeper of the Bees* (Meehan); *Free to Love* (O'Connor); *Best Bad Men* (Blystone); *Lawful Cheaters* (O'Connor)
1926 *Ancient Mariner* (Bennett); *My Lady of Whims* (Fitzgerald); *Dancing Mothers* (Brenon); *Shadow of the Law* (Worsley); *Two Can Play* (Ross); *The Runaway* (DeMille); *Mantrap* (Fleming); *Kid Boots* (Tuttle)
1927 *It* (Badger); *Children of Divorce* (Lloyd); *Rough House Rosie* (Strayer); *Wings* (Wellman); *Hula* (Fleming); *Get Your Man* (Arzner)
1928 *Red Hair* (Badger); *Ladies of the Mob* (Wellman); *The Fleet's In* (St. Clair); *Three Weekends* (Badger)
1929 *The Wild Party* (Arzner); *Dangerous Curves* (Mendes); *Saturday Night Kid* (Sutherland)
1930 *Paramount on Parade* (various directors); *True to the Navy* (Tuttle); *Love among the Millionaires* (Tuttle); *Her Wedding Night* (Tuttle)
1931 *No Limit* (Tuttle); *Kick In* (Wallace)
1932 *Call Her Savage* (Dillon)
1933 *Hoopla* (Lloyd)

Publications

By BOW: articles—

"Evoking Emotions Is No Child's Play," in *Theatre World* (New York), November 1927.
"My Life Story," as told to Adela Rogers St. Johns in *Photoplay* (New York), February through April 1928.
"Quit Pickin' on Me," in *Photoplay* (New York), January 1931.
"My Second Career," in *Pictures and Picturegoer*, 3 December 1932.

On BOW: books—

Rosen, Marjorie, *Popcorn Venus*, New York, 1973.
Morella, Joe, and Edward Epstein, *The "It" Girl: The Incredible Story of Clara Bow*, New York, 1976.
Stenn, David, *Clara Bow: Runnin' Wild*, New York, 1988.

On BOW: articles—

Alton, Maxine, "Clara's First Train Ride," in *Photoplay* (New York), January 1930.
Fletcher, Adele, "Beauty—Brains—Or Luck?" in *Photoplay* (New York), September 1930.
Behlmer, Rudy, "Clara Bow," in *Films in Review* (New York), October 1963 (see also November issue).
Robinson, David, and others, "Twenties Show People," in *Sight and Sound* (London), Autumn 1968.

Clara Bow

Shipman, David, in *The Great Movie Stars: The Golden Years*, revised edition, London, 1979.

* * *

Clara Bow was one of the outstanding "flapper" stars of the 1920s silent cinema in America. Flappers were the "liberated" girls of the so-termed jazz age, the youthful generation of the postwar Prohibition era, the "bright young things" who broke away from the outright innocence that had been represented in films most notably by Mary Pickford, and totally rejected the repressed lives led by their mothers. They smoked, drank (illegally), and lived it up alongside their male peers; they danced all night and often slept around promiscuously. They were characterized by their neurotic energy, their slickly bobbed hair, their pallid features, and their lips neatly made up into narrow cupids bows. Their breasts were flattened boyishly, and their skirts were above the knees.

Clara Bow had the appropriate looks and energy. Born in Brooklyn of a mentally disturbed mother, she had been reared in poverty. Her good fortune came when at 16 she won a beauty contest which, as part of the prize, gave her the chance to make a momentary appearance in a film. Her undoubted good looks and sparkling manner secured her a contract with the independent producer B. P. Schulberg; between 1923 and 1925 she appeared in more than 20 films with such titles as *Poisoned Paradise* and *Daughters of Pleasure*. She was seen in *Grit* (scripted by F. Scott Fitzgerald) and in Lubitsch's *Kiss Me Again*. Schulberg rejoined Paramount as producer in 1925 and introduced her to this major studio. In 1925 she appeared in no less than 14 films, followed by eight in 1926; many of these films had titles no less provocative: *This Plastic Age, Dancing Mothers, My Lady's Lips, Paradise Love, The Primrose Path, Free to Love, Mantrap*. She was promoted by the studio as the archetypical jazz age girl; the *New York Times* referred to her "elfin sensuousness" (she was only 5' 3½" tall).

Clara Bow finally accomplished international stardom in the film *It* (1927; one of six for that year). The film was adapted by the then popular, though matronly, Elinor Glyn from her best selling novel. The "It" girl was one who possesses qualities that went beyond basic sex appeal; they included an irresistibly scintillating personality. It was more important to be attractive than pretty.

After 1927 (when her salary reached $2,700 weekly), Clara Bow appeared in a diminishing number of films. The coming of sound affected her career somewhat, but she weathered it for a while. Her first sound film was *The Wild Party*, about a girl student who seduces her professor (Fredric March). Off screen she lived freely; her manners were rough, her speech lower class, her language fruity. Matching her way of life to her screen image, the kind of scandal she excited only contributed to the growing public criticism of Hollywood in a period that was about to see the introduction of film censorship through the Hays Office and the Production Code; it certainly did not favor films with titles such as *Ladies of the Mob, Dangerous Curves*, and *No Limit*.

In 1931 she married the wealthy cowboy star Rex Bell, who took her to his ranch in Nevada. She made an attempt at a comeback in 1932-33, but the films failed, and she retired to live on Bell's ranch when she was not receiving psychiatric treatment elsewhere.

—Roger Manvell

BOYER, Charles

Nationality: French American. **Born:** Figeac, France, 28 August 1897; became citizen of the United States. **Education:** The Sorbonne in philosophy; studied drama at the Paris Conservatory. **Family:** Married Patricia Patterson, 1934 (died 1978), son: Michael (died 1965). **Career:** 1920—made both stage and film debut in Paris; 1920s—worked primarily on Parisian stage becoming matinee idol; from 1931—Hollywood film career as one of the screen's "greatest lovers"; during World War II—involved in promoting Franco-American cultural relations; early 1950s—returned to acting in European films while continuing to make films in Hollywood; made occasional stage appearances; 1951—co-founder, with Dick Powell and David Niven, Four Star Television, and actor in several productions: *Four Star Playhouse*, 1952-56, *Alcoa Theatre*, 1957-58, and *The Rogues*, 1964-65. **Awards:** Special Academy Award for establishment of French Research Foundation in Los Angeles; Best Supporting Actor, New York Film Critics, for *Stavisky*, 1974. **Died:** Of drug overdose in Phoenix, Arizona, 26 August 1978.

Films as Actor:

1920 *L'Homme du Large* (L'Herbier)
1921 *Chantelouve* (Monca)
1923 *L'Esclave* (Monca); *Le Grillon du foyer* (Manoussi)
1927 *Le Capitaine Fracassé* (Cavalcanti)
1928 *La Ronde infernale* (Morat)
1929 *La Barcarolle d'amour* (Trotz); *Le Procès du Mary Dugan* (Chautin)
1930 *Revolte dans la prison* (Fejos)
1931 *Tumultes* (Trotz); *The Magnificent Lie* (Viertel)
1932 *F.P. ne répond plus* (Hartl); *The Man from Yesterday* (Viertel); *Red Headed Woman* (Conway)
1933 *Moi et l'impératrice* (Hollander); *The Only Girl* (Hollander); *L'Epervier* (L'Herbier); *Le Bonheur* (L'Herbier); *La Bataille* (Farkas)
1934 *The Battle* (*Thunder in the East*) (Farkas) (English-language version of *La Bataille*); *Liliom* (Fritz Lang); *Caravan* (Charell)
1935 *Private Worlds* (La Cava); *Break of Hearts* (Moeller); *Shanghai* (Flood)
1936 *Mayerling* (Litvak); *The Garden of Allah* (Boleslawsky)
1937 *History Is Made at Night* (Borzage); *Conquest* (Brown); *Tovarich* (Litvak)
1938 *Orage* (Marc Allégret); *Algiers* (Cromwell)
1939 *Love Affair* (McCarey); *When Tomorrow Comes* (Stahl)
1940 *All This and Heaven Too* (Litvak)
1941 *Back Street* (Stevenson); *Hold Back the Dawn* (Leisen); *Appointment for Love* (Seiter)
1942 *Tales of Manhattan* (Duvivier)
1943 *The Constant Nymph* (Goulding); *Flesh and Fantasy* (Duvivier)
1944 *Gaslight* (Cukor); *Together Again* (Charles Vidor)
1945 *Confidential Agent* (Shumlin)
1946 *Cluny Brown* (Lubitsch)
1947 *A Woman's Vengeance* (Zoltan Korda)
1948 *Arch of Triumph* (Milestone)
1951 *The Thirteenth Letter* (Preminger); *The First Legion* (Sirk)
1952 *The Happy Time* (Fleischer)
1953 *Madame de . . .* (*The Earrings of Madame De*) (Ophüls); *Thunder in the East* (Charles Vidor)
1954 *Nana* (Christian-Jaque)
1955 *La fortuna di Essere Donna* (Blasetti); *The Cobweb* (Minnelli)
1956 *Paris-Palace Hôtel* (Verneuil); *Around the World in Eighty Days* (Anderson)
1957 *Une Parisienne* (Boisrond)
1958 *Maxime* (Verneuil); *The Buccaneer* (Quinn)
1961 *Les Démons de minuit* (Allégret); *Fanny* (Logan)
1962 *Adorable Julia* (Weidenmann); *The Four Horsemen of the Apocalypse* (Minnelli)
1963 *Love Is a Ball* (Swift)

1965   *A Very Special Favor* (Gordon)
1966   *How to Steal a Million* (Wyler); *Paris brûle-t-il?* (*Is Paris Burning?*) (Clément)
1967   *Casino Royale* (Huston and others); *Barefoot in the Park* (Saks)
1969   *The April Fools* (Rosenberg); *The Madwoman of Chaillot* (Forbes); *The Day the Hot Line Got Hot* (Perler)
1973   *Lost Horizon* (Jarrott)
1974   *Stavisky* (Resnais)
1976   *A Matter of Time* (Minnelli)

Publications

On BOYER: book—

Swindell, Larry, *The Reluctant Lover: Charles Boyer*, New York, 1983.

On BOYER: articles—

Higham, Charles, "Charles Boyer: French Charmer" in *Close-Ups: The Movie Star Book*, edited by Danny Peary, New York, 1978.
Passek, J.-L., "Charles Boyer," in *Cinéma* (Paris), November 1978.
Shipman, David, in *The Great Movie Stars: The Golden Years*, revised edition, London, 1979.
"Charles Boyer," in *Ecran* (Paris), February 1979.
Article in *Classic Images* (Indiana, Pennsylvania), July 1982.

* * *

Charles Boyer's stardom is exceptional on several counts: his success was more durable, by far, than that of any other French performer in American cinema; during the period in which the major studios exerted their greatest power, he was able both to maintain his position as an independent and to command a top salary; before and after World War II he worked consistently on both sides of the Atlantic; and, although publicized as "the great lover," he was equally adept at comedy and character roles.

The "great lover" label is both misleading and accurate. It gives an erroneously narrow impression of Boyer's range, but it does locate the center of his screen presence, the utter concentration and focus with which he relates to his co-stars. That presence, centered in his large, dark eyes, conveys depths of feeling and emotions that are unquestionably sincere, that provide the visual proof of love and commitment so often lacking in "romantic" dialogue. Eyes, and also voice. The unmistakable French accent and the rich bass timbre serve a delivery of infinite variety and inflection. We remember Boyer for his "duets" with the great stars of the 1930s and 1940s, with the serious Claudette Colbert in *Private Worlds* and the comic one in *Tovarich*, dancing the tango in an empty restaurant with Jean Arthur in *History Is Made at Night*, trading sophisticated chatter and sentiment with Irene Dunne in *Love Affair*, "speaking" the love with his eyes that he must not express in words to Bette Davis in *All This and Heaven Too*, dying during the agonizing phone call to Margaret Sullavan in *Back Street*, nearly driving Ingrid Bergman crazy with his malevolent shifts of tone in *Gaslight*. His films with Dietrich (*The Garden of Allah*) and Garbo (*Conquest*) are frustrating because his roles in them are, by far, the more interesting, and thus we are denied the promise of those particularly alluring sympathies.

The extent of Boyer's ability to respond to his co-stars most clearly emerges by the pairing of two films he made with Danielle Darrieux. As Crown Prince Rudolph in *Mayerling*, the intensity of his gaze is an invitation to his young lover to share his death; more than 15 years later, in *Madame de . . .*, in one fleeting moment, the world-weary husband looks at his unfaithful wife with all the love he has revealed to us in his long career.

—Charles Affron

BRAGA, Sonia

Nationality: Brazilian. **Born:** Maringá, Paraná, Brazil 16 (or 8) June 1951. **Education:** Left school at the age of 14. **Career:** 1968—television debut in *Gardin encatado* (*The Enchanted Garden*), a Brazilian telenovela (soap opera); also in telenovela *The Girl of the Blue Sailboat*; 1969—stage debut in *Jorge Danin*; first principal stage role in *Hair*; 1970—feature film debut in *A Moreninha*; 1974—in telenovela *Gabriela*; 1977—gained international attention as Doña Flor in *Doña Flor and Her Two Husbands*; 1985—U.S. film debut in *Kiss of the Spider Woman*; 1986—two episodes as Anna María Westlake on TV series *The Cosby Show*; 1992—in "This'll Kill Ya" episode of television anthology series *Tales from the Crypt*; 1995—in TV mini-series *Streets of Laredo*. Jury member, Cannes International Film Festival, Cannes, France. **Agent:** Michael Black, International Creative Management, 8899 Beverly Boulevard, Los Angeles, CA 90048, U.S.A.

Films as Actress:

1970   *A Moreninha* (*The Little Brunette*) (Laurelli) (title role); *Captain Bandeira vs. Dr. Moura*
1973   *Mestice: A Escrava Indomavel* (*Mestiza, the Indomitable Slave*) (Perroy) (title role)
1974   *O Casal* (*The Couple*) (Filho)
1977   **Doña Flor e Seus Dois Maridos** (*Doña Flor and Her Two Husbands*) (Barreto) (as Doña Flor)
1978   *A Dama do Lotacdao* (*Lady on the Bus*) (Neville D'Almeida); *Dancin' Days* (telenovela for TV Globo)
1981   *Eu Te Amo* (*I Love You*) (Arnaldo Jabor) (as Woman)
1983   *Gabriela* (Barreto) (title role)
1985   *Kiss of the Spider Woman* (*O Beijo Da Mulher Aranha*) (Hector Babenco) (as Leni Lamaison/Marta/Spider Woman)
1988   *The Milagro Beanfield War* (Redford) (as Ruby Archuleta); *Moon over Parador* (Mazursky) (as Madonna); *The Man Who Broke 1,000 Chains* (Daniel Mann—for TV) (as Emily)
1990   *The Rookie* (Eastwood) (as Liesel)
1991   *The Last Prostitute* (Antonio—for TV) (as Loah)
1993   *Roosters* (Robert M. Young) (as Juana)
1994   *The Burning Season* (Frankenheimer—for TV) (as Regina de Carvalho)
1996   *Two Deaths* (Roeg) (as Ana Puscasu); *Money Plays* (Gilroy—for TV)
1997   *Tieta de Agreste* (Diegues)

Publications

On BRAGA: articles—

Wolf, William, "Flying Up from Rio," in *New York*, 17 May 1982.
Konder, Rodolfo, "Ordinary Woman Turned Sex Symbol," in *Américas* (Washington, D.C.), March/April 1983.

* * *

In *Kiss of the Spider Woman*, prison inmates William Hurt and Raul Julia spin tales inhabited by a raven-haired sensual beauty. Alternately a 1940s film star, Julia's revolutionary girlfriend, and the mysterious Spider Woman, she embodies for both men the promise and elusiveness of freedom. Playing all three female roles, Sonia Braga captured international attention in her first English-language film. An immediate star, Braga was sought after by Hollywood studios and was invited to be a jury member at the Cannes International Film Festival.

Sonia Braga with Herson Capri in *Kiss of the Spider Woman*

Braga's "overnight success" actually followed 15 years of stage, film, and television acting in Brazil. At the age of 18 Braga caused a sensation when she appeared naked in a São Paulo production of *Hair*. She then debuted on television, appearing in several telenovelas and on *Vila Sésamo* (*Sesame Street*). In the telenovelas Braga cultivated the glamour, sexuality, and dramatic power for which she would become known.

Her performance in TV Globo's *Gabriela*, based on Jorge Amado's novel, raised Braga to the level of "legend." *Gabriela* marked a radical change in Braga's personal and professional life. Although she still describes herself as pale, ugly, plain, and buck-toothed, Braga realized that when she stepped into the role of a woman determined to be beautiful, she too started being pretty. Braga, offscreen an unremarkable yet not unattractive woman, has come to personify the desire to loosen social standards of beauty, to be attractive on one's own terms.

Of her early films, only *A Moreninha* had relative box-office success. These first film roles, however, did establish Braga as a Brazilian femme fatale, a dangerously sensual screen presence who bewitches men with her searing gaze and her lovely smile.

The release of *Doña Flor and Her Two Husbands* in 1977 garnered Braga's first international success. In this film, Braga plays a young villager, widowed by the untimely death of her woman- and drink-loving husband. Remarried to a serious, kind, but unexciting pharmacist, Doña Flor craves the steamy satisfying sex of her first marriage. Her womb cries out to her dead husband whose ghost returns to sate her sexual appetite. The rest of the film narrates her hilarious attempt to balance her two husbands and to have both the stability of her second marriage and the sexual excitement and perversity of the first.

After 1979, Braga retired from television. The success of her films in the late seventies made a film career seem attainable, and inevitable. *Doña Flor* led to Braga's being cast opposite Marcelo Mastroianni in the film version of *Gabriela*. And in 1985, after *Kiss of the Spider Woman*, Braga looked poised to conquer Brazilian cinema, Hollywood, and the world. *Spider Woman* seems, however, to have been the pinnacle of Braga's career. Only after her U.S. television appearances in 1986 on *The Cosby Show* did Braga return to the big screen. As Ruby Archuleta in the ill-fated *The Milagro Beanfield War* and as Madonna in *Moon over Parador,* Braga delivered competent but uninspired performances.

Indeed, Braga's post-*Spider Woman* career has been rather disappointing. Although she declared her intentions to *not* become a Hollywood actress, the largely moribund Brazilian film industry has prevented Braga from revisiting her "hometown" glory. Recent attempts to return to Brazilian television have proven disastrous. In 1995, Braga returned to U.S. television in the mini-series *Streets of Laredo* and in an episode of HBO's popular creep show, *Tales from the Crypt*.

Braga's 1996 appearance in Nicolas Roeg's *Two Deaths* was likely intended as her triumphant return to film. Braga plays a striking but silent, shuffling housekeeper, Ana Puscau, who is the object of her employer's sexual obsession. Steven Holden of the *New York Times* noted the "grave, pensive sensuality" with which Braga infuses the film. *Two Deaths* may ultimately seal Braga's fate as an actress typecast for her burning sensuality and her "different" look—more pensive perhaps, but no deeper.

—Ilene S. Goldman

BRANAGH, Kenneth

Nationality: British. **Born:** Kenneth Charles Branagh in Belfast, Northern Ireland, 10 December 1960; moved to Reading, England, at age nine. **Family:** Married the actress Emma Thompson 1989 (separated 1995). **Education:** Was graduated from the Royal Academy of Dramatic Art, London. **Career:** 1982—acted on the British stage, gaining attention for his performance in *Another Country*; 1984—joined the Royal Shakespeare Company; in TV mini-series *Boys in the Bush*; 1987—co-founded the Renaissance Theatre Company, for which he writes and directs; in TV mini-series *Fortunes of War*; 1988—in TV series *Thompson*; 1989—wrote biography, *Beginning*, in order to raise money for the Renaissance Theatre Company; earned international acclaim as director, adapter, and star of *Henry V*. **Awards:** Bancroft Gold Medal, Royal Academy of Dramatic Art, 1982; Society of West End Theatres' Award, Most Promising Newcomer, and Plays and Players Award, for *Another Country*, 1982; Best Director, National Board of Review, Best New Director, New York Film Critics Circle, Best Actor and Young European Film of the Year, European Film Awards, British Academy of Film and Television Arts Award for Best Director, and Evening Standard Award, Best Film, for *Henry V*, 1989; Evening Standard Peter Sellers Award for Comedy, for *Peter's Friends*, 1992; BAFTA Michael Balcon Award, Outstanding Contribution to the Cinema, 1993. **Agent:** Clifford Stevens, STE Representation, Beverly Hills, CA, U.S.A. **Address:** 83 Berwick Street, London W1V 3PJ, England.

Films as Actor:

1982   *Too Late to Talk to Billy* (Paul Seed—for TV)
1983   *To the Lighthouse* (Colin Gregg—for TV) (as Charles Tansley)
1985   *Coming Through* (Barber-Fleming—for TV) (as D. H. "Bert" Lawrence)
1986   *Ghosts* (Moshinsky—for TV) (as Oswald)
1987   *High Season* (Peploe) (as Rick Lamb); *A Month in the Country* (O'Connor) (as Charles Moon); *Strange Interlude* (Herbert Wise—for TV) (as Gordon Evans); *The Lady's Not for Burning* (Julian Amyes—for TV) (as Thomas Mendip)
1989   *Look Back in Anger* (Judi Dench—for TV) (as Jimmy Porter)
1992   *Swing Kids* (Carter) (as SS official, unbilled)
1995   *Anne Frank Remembered* (Blair—doc) (as narrator)
1996   *Othello* (Alan Parker) (as Iago)

Films as Director:

1989   *Henry V* (+ title role, sc)
1991   *Dead Again* (+ ro as Roman Strauss/Mike Church)

1992   *Peter's Friends* (+ ro as Andrew, pr); *Swan Song* (short)
1993   *Much Ado about Nothing* (+ ro as Benedick, co-pr, sc)
1994   *Mary Shelley's Frankenstein* (+ ro as Dr. Frankenstein, co-pr)
1995   *A Midwinter's Tale* (*In the Bleak Midwinter*) (+ sc)
1996   *Hamlet* (+ title role)

Publications

By BRANAGH: books—

Beginning, London, 1989.
Henry V, London, 1989.
Much Ado about Nothing, London, 1993.
Mary Shelley's Frankenstein: The Classic Tale of Terror Reborn on Film, New York, 1994.
In the Bleak Midwinter: The Shooting Script, New York, 1995.

By BRANAGH: articles—

"Formidible Force," interview with Michael Billington, in *Interview* (New York), October 1989.
"Kenneth Branagh," interview in *Premiere* (New York), February 1993.
"It's a Monster: Kenneth Branagh Unveils His Biggest Creation Yet— *Mary Shelley's Frankenstein*," interview with Graham Fuller, in *Interview* (New York), November 1994.

On BRANAGH: book—

Shuttleworth, Ian, *Ken & Em*, New York, 1995.

On BRANAGH: articles—

Haskell, Molly, "People Are Talking about . . . Slow Idyll," in *Vogue* (New York), January 1988.
Billington, Michael, "Stage Sprite," in *Vanity Fair* (New York), March 1988.
Billington, Michael, "A New Olivier Is Taking on *Henry V* on the Screen," in *New York Times*, 8 January 1989.
Corliss, Richard, "King Ken Comes to Conquer," in *Time* (New York), 13 November 1989.
Fuller, Graham, "Kenneth," in *Film Comment* (New York), November-December 1989.
Stuart, Cynthia, "Man Power: Modern British Explorers," in *Esquire* (New York), January 1990.
Turnbull, Robert, "Much Ado about Something," in *Harper's Bazaar* (New York), February 1990.
DeCurtis, Anthony, "Hail to the New King on the Block," in *Rolling Stone* (New York), 8 February 1990.
Stanfill, Francesca, "To the Mantle Born?," in *New York*, 12 February 1990.
Weber, B., "From Shakespeare to Hollywood," in *New York Times*, 18 August 1991.
Johnson, Brian D., "Big-Screen Theatre," in *Maclean's* (Toronto), 26 August 1991.
Booe, M., "Ken Again," in *Premiere* (New York), September 1991.
Lantos, J., "Beyond the Bard," in *Movieline* (Hollywood), September 1991.
Perret, E., "L.A. Bard," in *Esquire* (New York), September 1991.
Feeney, F. X., "Vaulting Ambition," in *American Film* (New York), September/October 1991.
Wilson, P., "Kenneth Branagh," in *Film Monthly* (Berkhamsted, England), November 1991.
Miller, R., "Emma Thompson's Family Business," in *New York Times*, 28 March 1993.

Kenneth Branagh (left) with Brian Blessed in *Henry V*

James, Caryn, "Why Branagh's Bard Glows on the Screen," in *New York Times*, 16 May 1993.

Smith, Dinitia, "Much Ado about Branagh," in *New York*, 24 May 1993.

Stuart, O., "Mold of Fashion," in *Village Voice* (New York), 25 May 1993.

Light, A., "The Importance of Being Ordinary," in *Sight & Sound* (London), September 1993.

"Much Ado about Shakespeare," in *Economist* (New York), 2 October 1993.

Witchel, Alex, "How *Frankenstein* Has Created a Hunk," in *New York Times*, 9 November 1994.

* * *

When *Henry V* was released, Kenneth Branagh was little-known in America. He had appeared in several films and British made-for-television movies, acted on the stage and co-founded his own theater troupe, the Renaissance Theatre Company. But the 28-year-old film-maker-phenomenon immediately was hailed as the "new Olivier" for both directing and starring as Shakespeare's warrior-king. *Henry V* is stirring filmmaking, and a tour de force which instantly thrust Branagh into the front ranks of international film personalities. As British critic Alexander Walker observed, the film "confirmed that all Laurence Olivier taught us about filming Shakespeare has not been forgotten—only boldly revised to fit a crueller world of kingship and power, mercifully one still tempered by magnificently spoken poetry." With an emphasis on Henry's exploration of his inner self, Branagh had produced a coming-of-age film that appealed to a broad contemporary audience. Although his battle scenes are bloodier than Olivier's and his wounded warriors are more ghastly, Branagh's view clearly is antiwar, a philosophy which touched modern viewers. As a critics' favorite and darling of the art film crowd, Branagh signed a lucrative contract to write his autobiography, a witty anecdotal ramble aptly called *Beginnings*, which was published while he still was in his twenties.

Branagh's other major go at cinematizing Shakespeare is the almost-equally successful *Much Ado about Nothing*, a delightfully airy, inventive version of the Shakespeare comedy adapted by Branagh. He and his then-wife, Emma Thompson, are cast as Benedick and Beatrice. They are especially charming when pitching cleverly written, risqué puns and slurs at each other. The same year, he found time to appear unbilled as a Nazi in *Swing Kids*, an unusual World War II story about the Nazi persecution of German adolescents who enjoyed American popular music.

Between his robust interpretations of the Bard, Branagh again won praise for directing and starring in two films which are very different in nature. In the British-made comedy-drama *Peter's Friends*, he is the husband of a flamboyant and ill-tempered Hollywood television star. In the Hollywood-produced film noir thriller *Dead Again*, he audaciously plays two roles, a fast-talking gumshoe and a sophisticated European composer who has emigrated to Los Angeles (in flashbacks to the 1940s). In both films, his co-star is Thompson.

It seemed Branagh the wunderkind could do no wrong until he was hired by Francis Ford Coppola to direct and star in the lavish, $40-million production, *Mary Shelley's Frankenstein*. The briskly-paced, stylized attempt to bring the classic novel to the screen with authenticity resulted in a bizarre, out-of-control disaster. Critics turned thumbs down, audiences shied away, and Branagh encountered the first major setback of what had seemed a charmed career.

Since that debacle marred his remarkable record, Branagh has scaled back the extent of his involvement in film projects. What followed was *A Midwinter's Tale*, the first film he directed (and wrote) in which he did not appear before the cameras. The black-and-white British production offers a somewhat coy, comical take on the "Let's put on a show in the barn" theme. At the time the film was released, another blow fell when the announcement was made that he and Thompson had separated. At that time, Branagh's immediate plans included starring as Iago in Oliver Parker's upcoming film of *Othello* and directing and playing the lead in *Hamlet*.

—Audrey E. Kupferberg

BRANDAUER, Klaus Maria

Nationality: Austrian. **Born:** Altaussee, Austria, 22 June 1944. **Education:** Studied at the Stuttgart Academy of Music and Dramatic Art, graduated 1963. **Family:** Married Karen Mueller, son: Christian. **Career:** From 1970—actor and director with the Burgtheater (the National Theater of Austria), Vienna; 1972—film debut in *The Salzburg Connection*; unhappy with film, returned to stage work; 1981—international success with *Mephisto*; 1989—debut as film director with *The Artisan*. **Awards:** Deutscher Filmpreis, for *Colonel Redl*, 1985; Golden Globe, D. W. Griffith Award, and New York Film Critics Award for Best Supporting Actor, for *Out of Africa*, 1985; Golden Ciak Award, Venice Festival, for *Burning Secret*, 1988. **Address:** Bartensteingasse 8/9, A-1010 Vienna, Austria.

Films as Actor:

1972   *The Salzburg Connection* (Katzin) (as Johann Kronsteiner)
1974   *Der Widerspenstigen Zaehmung* (Schenk—for TV) (as Petruccio)
1975   *Das Konzert* (Haugk—for TV)
1976   *Die Babenberger in Oesterreich* (Umgelter—for TV); *Darf ich mitspielen?* (Davy—for TV)
1981   ***Mephisto*** (Szabó) (as Hendrik Höfgen)
1983   *Never Say Never Again* (Kershner) (as Maximilian Largo); *Der Weg ins Freie* (Karen Brandauer—for TV)
1984   *Kindergarten* (Yevtushenko); *Der Snob* (Staudte—for TV)
1985   *Redl Ezredes* (*Oberst Redl*; *Colonel Redl*) (Szabó) (as Alfred Redl); *Out of Africa* (Pollack) (as Baron Bror Blixen-Finecke); *Quo Vadis* (Rossi—for TV) (as Nero)
1986   *Streets of Gold* (Roth) (as Alek Neuman); *The Lightship* (Skolimowski) (as Capt. Miller)
1988   *Burning Secret* (Birkin) (as Baron)
1989   *Hanussen* (Szabó) (title role); *Das Spinnennetz* (*Spider's Web*) (as Lenz); *La Revolution Française* (*The French Revolution*) (Enrico and Heffron) (as Georges Jacques Danton)
1990   *The Russia House* (Schepisi) (as Savelev, "Dante")
1991   *White Fang* (Kleiser) (as Alex)
1992   *Becoming Colette* (*Colette*) (Danny Huston) (as Henri Gauthier-Villars)
1994   *Felidae* (Schaack—animation) (as voices of Pascal and Claudandus)

Films as Director:

1989   *The Artisan*
1990   *Georg Elser—Einer aus Deutschland* (*Georg Elser; Seven Minutes*) (+ title role)
1994   *Mario und der Zauberer* (*Mario and the Magician*) (as Cipolla) (+ ro as Cipolla, sc)
1995   *Die Wand*

Publications

By BRANDAUER: articles—

"Out of Austria," interview with Karen Jaehne, in *Stills* (London), March 1986.
Interview in *Interview* (New York), June 1986.
Interview in *Hollywood Reporter*, 30 December 1986.
Interview with Lynne Tillman, in *Interview* (New York), February 1991.

On BRANDAUER: book—

Lanz, Peter, *Klaus Maria Brandauer: Ein Portrait des berühmten Schauspielerin*, Munich, 1986.

On BRANDAUER: articles—

Cinema (Germany), July 1987.
Current Biography 1990, New York, 1990.
Kurdriavtsev, S., in *Iskusstvo Kino* (Moscow), no. 11, 1990.

*   *   *

Klaus Maria Brandauer is an actor who actually has two very different and distinct careers. One is as a star in his native Europe. The other came out of his emergence during the mid-1980s as a supporting player in American films. Brandauer generally has received his greatest acclaim as an actor in Europe. The three films that are central to this aspect of his career are *Mephisto*, which won a Best Foreign Film Academy Award in 1981; *Colonel Redl*, released in 1985; and *Hanussen*, which came out in 1989. All are directed by Istvan Szabó, and are set in Europe before or during World War I or leading to the rise of Hitler. In each, Brandauer creates a character who, though not necessarily sympathetic to the existing power structure or "new order," compromises himself as he resigns himself to the reality of the time. Thus, a crisis of conscience is created, with each characterization becoming a skillful study in turmoil hidden beneath bravado and supreme egotism. The Brandauer characters in these films are an egocentric actor who sells out to the Nazis upon Hitler's coming to power (in *Mephisto*); a determined career soldier of modest background who achieves a lofty position in the Austro-Hungarian military prior to World War I (in *Colonel Redl*); and an Austrian soldier in World War I who is wounded in battle, and who attains the ability to foresee the future (in *Hanussen*).

His American films include *The Lightship*, in which he is an ex-German naval officer who captains the title craft; *Never Say Never Again*, in which he plays a diabolical West German terrorist; *The Russia House*, portraying a mysterious, charismatic Russian physicist; and *Streets of Gold*, as a champion Russian fighter who coaches two young Americans for the Olympics. As in his films with Szabó, these characters feel obligated to an inflexible code. Thus, the commander of the lightship is bound by his responsibility to his ship, even after it is boarded by ruthless gangsters, while the obsessive boxing coach in *Streets of Gold* lives rigidly by the notion that all must be sacrificed to the will-to-win.

For the most part, Brandauer's roles in American films have been supporting ones. The sole exception is *Streets of Gold*, which did not succeed either critically or commercially in making him a force in the American cinema. Supporting roles have, however, by his own admission, allowed him the freedom to create deeper, psychologically motivated character studies. The prime example of this is his Academy Award-nominated role as Meryl Streep's unfaithful husband in Sydney Pollack's *Out of Africa*—easily his highest-profile English-language performance to date. It is characters such as this one—subtle, idiosyncratic, seemingly unequivocal in their motivations—which are the real hallmarks of Brandauer's career.

—Rob Winning, updated by Rob Edelman

BRANDO, Marlon

Nationality: American. **Born:** Omaha, Nebraska, 3 April 1924. **Education:** Attended Shattuck Military Academy, Faribault, Minnesota; studied acting with Stella Adler, New School for Social Research, New York. **Family:** Married 1) Anna Kashfi, 1957 (divorced 1959), son: Christian Devil; 2) Maria Castaneda, 1960, children: Miko and Rebecca; children by Tarita Teriipaia: Teihotu and Tarita Zumi "Cheyenne" (deceased). **Career:** 1944—Broadway debut in role of Nels in *I Remember Mama*; 1947—stage stardom established by performance in *A Streetcar Named Desire*; 1950—film debut in *The Men*; 1959—founded Pennebaker Productions to produce *One-Eyed Jacks*; 1972—declined Academy Award for role in *The Godfather*, delegated Indian actress, Sasheen Littlefeather, to read statement accusing film industry of misrepresenting the American Indian; 1979—in TV mini-series *Roots: The Next Generation*. **Awards:** Best Actor, Cannes Festival, and Best Foreign Actor, British Academy, for *Viva Zapata!*, 1952; Best Foreign Actor, British Academy, for *Julius Caesar*, 1953; Best Actor Academy Award, Best Actor, New York Film Critics, and Best Foreign Actor, British Academy, for *On the Waterfront*, 1954; Best Actor Academy Award (declined), for *The Godfather*, 1972; Best Actor, New York Film Critics, for *Last Tango in Paris*, 1973. **Address:** Home: Tetiaroa Island, Tahiti.

Films as Actor:

1950 *The Men* (Zinneman) (as Ken)
1951 *A Streetcar Named Desire* (Kazan) (as Stanley Kowalski)
1952 *Viva Zapata!* (Kazan) (as Emiliano Zapata)
1953 *Julius Caesar* (Joseph L. Mankiewicz) (as Mark Antony)
1954 *The Wild One* (Benedek) (as Johnny); ***On the Waterfront*** (Kazan) (as Terry Malloy); *Desiree* (Koster) (as Napoleon Bonaparte)
1955 *Guys and Dolls* (Joseph L. Mankiewicz) (as Sky Masterton)
1956 *The Teahouse of the August Moon* (Daniel Mann) (as Sakini)
1957 *Sayonara* (Logan) (as Major Lloyd Gruver)
1958 *The Young Lions* (Dmytryk) (as Christian Diestl)
1960 *The Fugitive Kind* (Lumet) (as Val Xavier)
1962 *Mutiny on the Bounty* (Milestone) (as Fletcher Christian)
1963 *The Ugly American* (Englund) (as Harrison Carter MacWhite)
1964 *Bedtime Story* (Levy) (as Freddy)
1965 *The Saboteur—Code Name Morituri* (*Morituri*) (Wicki) (as Robert Crain)
1966 *The Chase* (Arthur Penn) (as Sheriff Calder); *The Appaloosa* (*Southwest to Sonora*) (Furie) (as Matt Fletcher)
1967 *A Countess from Hong Kong* (Chaplin) (as Ogden Mears); *Reflections in a Golden Eye* (Huston) (as Major Weldon Penderton)

1968 *Candy* (Marquand) (as Grindl)
1969 *The Night of the Following Day* (Cornfield) (as Bud); *Burn!* (*Queimada!*) (Pontecorvo) (as Sir William Walker)
1971 *The Nightcomers* (Winner) (as Peter Quint)
1972 ***The Godfather*** (Francis Ford Coppola) (as Don Vito Corleone)
1973 ***L'ultimo tango a Parigi*** (*Last Tango in Paris*) (Bertolucci) (as Paul)
1976 *The Missouri Breaks* (Arthur Penn) (as Robert E. Lee Clayton)
1978 *Superman* (Richard Donner) (as Jor-El, father of Superman)
1979 ***Apocalypse Now*** (Francis Ford Coppola) (as Colonel Kurtz)
1980 *The Formula* (Avildsen) (as Adam Steiffel)
1989 *A Dry White Season* (Palcy) (as Ian McKenzie)
1990 *The Freshman* (Andrew Bergman) (as Carmine Sabatina)
1992 *Christopher Columbus: The Discovery* (Glen) (as Tomas de Torquemada)
1995 *Don Juan DeMarco* (Leven) (as Dr. Jack Mickler)
1996 *The Island of Dr. Moreau* (Frankenheimer) (title role, + co-sc)

Film as Director:

1961 *One-Eyed Jacks* (+ ro as Rio)

Publications

By BRANDO: books—

Conversations with Brando, with Lawrence Grobel, New York, 1991.
Brando: Songs My Mother Taught Me, with Robert Lindsey, New York, 1994.

By BRANDO: articles—

"Brando's Oscar Speech," in *Cineaste* (New York), vol. 5, no. 4, 1973.
"The Complete Transcript of Brando's Speech at the First American Gala," in *Interview* (New York), January 1975.
Interview in *Ciné Revue* (Paris), 27 March 1980.

On BRANDO: books—

Zuckerman, Ira, *The Godfather Journal*, New York, 1972.
Carey, Gary, *Brando*, New York, 1973.
Jordan, René, *Marlon Brando*, New York, 1973.
Morella, Joe, *Brando: The Unauthorized Bioraphy*, New York, 1973.
Puzo, Mario, *The Making of the Godfather*, Greenwich, Connecticut, 1973.
Thomas, Bob, *Marlon: Portrait of the Rebel as Artist*, New York, 1973.
Thomas, Tony, *The Films of Marlon Brando*, Secaucus, New Jersey, 1973.
Shipman, David, *Brando*, London, 1974; rev. ed., as *Marlon Brando*, London, 1989.
Braithwaite, Bruce, *The Films of Marlon Brando*, 1977.
Brando, Anna Kashfi, and E. P. Stein, *Brando for Breakfast*, New York, 1979.
Downing, David, *Marlon Brando*, New York, 1984.
Carey, Gary, *Marlon Brando: The Only Contender*, New York, 1985.
Higham, Charles, *Brando: The Unauthorized Biography*, London and New York, 1987.
Nickens, Christopher, *Brando: A Biography in Photographs*, New Yori, 1987.
Fauser, Jorg, *Marlon-Brando-Biographie*, Hamburg, 1990.
Schickel, Richard, *Brando: A Life in Our Times*, New York, 1990.
McCann, Graham, *Rebel Males: Clift, Brando, and Dean*, London, 1991.

Marlon Brando in *On the Waterfront*

Mourousi, Yves, *Le destin Brando*, Paris, 1991.

Ryan, Paul, *Marlon Brando: A Portrait*, New York, 1991.

Bly, Nellie, *Marlon Brando: Larger than Life*, New York, 1994.

Manso, Peter, *Brando: The Biography*, New York, 1994.

Tanitch, Robert, *Brando*, 1995.

On BRANDO: articles—

Current Biography 1952, New York, 1952.

Houseman, John, "Filming *Julius Caesar*," in *Films in Review* (New York), April 1953 and *Sight and Sound* (London), July/September 1953.

Brinson, P., "The Brooder," in *Films and Filming* (London), October 1954.

Capote, Truman, "Marlon Brando," in *Newsweek* (New York), 9 November 1957.

Rush, B., "Brando—The Young Lion," in *Films and Filming* (London), March 1958.

Malden, Karl, "The 2 Faces of Brando," in *Films and Filming* (London), August 1959.

McVay, Douglas, "The Brando Mutiny," in *Films and Filming* (London), December 1962.

Steele, R., "Meet Marlon Brando," in *Film Heritage* (Dayton, Ohio), Fall 1966.

McGillivray, D., "Marlon Brando," in *Focus on Film* (London), Autumn 1972.

Haskell, Molly, articles on Brando in *Village Voice* (New York), 14 June 1973 through 30 August 1973.

Sarris, A., "A Tribute to Marlon Brando," in *Film Comment* (New York), May/June 1974.

Gow, G., "The Brando Boom," in *Films and Filming* (London), November 1974.

Bodeen, DeWitt, "Marlon Brando," in *Films in Review* (New York), December 1980.

Kael, Pauline, "Marlon Brando and James Dean," in *The Movie Star*, edited by Elisabeth Weis, New York, 1981.

Schickel, Richard, "Celebrity," in *Film Comment* (New York), January/February 1985.

Peary, Gerald, "The Wild One," in *American Film* (New York), June 1986.

Kram, Mark, "Brando," in *Esquire* (New York), November 1989.

Webster, Andy, filmography in *Premiere* (New York), October 1994.

Brodkey, Harold, "Translating Brando," in *New Yorker*, 24 October 1994.

Naremore, James, "*Brando: Songs My Mother Taught Me, Brando: The Biography*," in *Cineaste* (New York), vol. 21, no. 1-2, Winter/Spring 1995.

* * *

Marlon Brando is the preeminent actor of American postwar cinema. In the early 1950s, he received Academy Award nominations for Best Actor in four successive years, and in 1954 won the Oscar for Best Actor for his performance in *On the Waterfront*. His portrayal of the leather-jacketed biker in *The Wild One* established an integral connection between rebellion, defiance, and sexual prowess, and made Brando a generation's symbol of masculinity. Brando himself studied the work of actors such as Spencer Tracy, Paul Muni, and Cary Grant, but for actors of his generation and beyond, it has been Brando who has served as the model.

Often considered America's greatest actor, Brando has, throughout his career, demonstrated a remarkable ability to reveal characters' contradictions. His portrayals of rebels such as Stanley Kowalski (*A Streetcar Named Desire*) and Terry Malloy (*On the Waterfront*) present us with brutish characters who possess an innate intelligence and fundamental nobility; his characterizations of figures such as Major Penderton (*Reflections in a Golden Eye*) and Sir William Walker (*Burn!*), men who understand and live by the rules of "civilized" society, become studies of personal disintegration and the devastating effects of power. Brando's skill in representing complex characters creates compelling and contradictory points of contact for spectators: in *The Young Lions*, Brando's portrayal of the young Nazi officer is disturbing for he is, at times, a sympathetic and attractive figure; in *The Godfather*, Brando's Don Corleone is both ruthless and kindhearted; in *The Last Tango in Paris*, Brando's representation of Paul mobilizes *and* lays siege to the image of masculinity Brando's early film roles helped to establish.

Brando studied with Stella Adler and came to Hollywood from Broadway after his performance in *A Streetcar Named Desire* caught the attention of the critics and the public. In an interview with Truman Capote in 1957, Brando explained that he intended to remain a film actor because "movies have the greatest potential. You can say important things to a lot of people. About discrimination and hatred and prejudice." Brando's work with Adler had instilled in him the belief that actors should have a point of view toward society, and we can get a sense of that view by looking at the parts he has chosen to play throughout his career (e.g., the Mexican revolutionary in *Viva Zapata!*), and the specific coloring he has given many of his characters (e.g., his portrayal of Fletcher Christian in *Mutiny on the Bounty* who, because of the forces of class and commerce, cannot live inside or outside the law).

The conventional wisdom is that Brando wasted his talents in the period between his auspicious beginning in the 1950s and his commercial and critical comeback in the 1970s (in films such as *The Godfather* and *Last Tango in Paris*). A more comprehensive consideration of his work suggests that is not the case. For example, in 1961, Brando directed and starred in *One-Eyed Jacks*, an effective ensemble piece and, in its reworking of Western formulas, an interesting (Hamlet-like) study of revenge. In 1970's *Burn!*, playing the part of the agent of imperial and capitalist aggression, Brando gave what he sees as his best performance. This role is especially illustrative of the actor's authorial control and ideological concerns, for in portraying Sir William, Brando candidly articulates why the British imperial forces will defeat the island's guerrilla army in a way that echoes, almost word for word, the speech he gives as Major Penderton when lecturing on military strategy in *Reflections in a Golden Eye*. Brando's performances in the late seventies, eighties, and nineties—for example, as Colonel Kurtz in *Apocalypse Now*, as Ian McKenzie in *A Dry White Season*, and as Tomas de Torquemada in *Christopher Columbus*—reveal his signature reshaping of material and his abiding (social) concerns.

Like other stars, Brando's work as an actor has been understood through and in terms of certain roles and highly publicized moments of his private life. Yet rather than focusing on the rebel roles of his early career or incidents that have provided fuel for gossip columnists, Brando's work should be considered as a whole, for as James Naremore points out, Brando's achievements are remarkable, and his performances reveal a negotiation between the contradictions of not only his own personality, but those of the culture as well. What is significant is that Brando has not simply continued to play the rebel throughout his career, but instead has put together a body of work that examines the exercise of power in all its troubling aspects.

—Cynthia Baron

BRASSEUR, Pierre

Nationality: French. **Born:** Pierre-Albert Espinasse in Paris, 22 December 1903 or 1905. **Education:** Studied acting at the Paris Conservatory; later studied with Harry Baur. **Military Service:** 1924-25—served in French Army. **Family:** Married 1) the actress Odette

Joyeux (divorced), son: the actor Claude Brasseur; 2) Lina Magrini, 1947 (divorced). **Career:** c.1920—stage acting debut; 1924—film debut in *La Fille de l'Eau*; 1925—his play *L'Ancre noire* produced at the Théâtre de l'Oeuvre; early 1930s—popular attention for appearing in series of villainous roles in several French versions of German films; 1934—in Hollywood film *Caravan*; 1940—directed Marcel Achard's play *Domino*; 1940s-50s—continued to act both on stage and in films. **Died:** In Brunico, Italy, 14 August 1972.

Films as Actor:

1924 *La Fille de l'Eau*
1925 *Madame Sans Gêne* (Pérret) (as walk-on)
1928 *Feu!* (de Baroncelli) (as sailor)
1930 *Je suis un as* (Tzipine—short); *Ce qu'on dit, ce qu'on pense* (short); *Etoile filant* (Bouquet—short); *Une Heure de rêve* (Tzipine—short); *Un Trou dans le mur* (Barberis) (as Anatole)
1931 *Circulez!* (de Limur) (as Jean Dupont-Desroches); *Papa sans le savoir* (R. Wyler—short); *Une Rêve blond* (Martin) (as Maurice)
1932 *Mon ami Victor* (Berthomieu); *Quick* (Siodmak) (as Maxime); *Moi et l'impératrice* (Martin and Holländer) (as Didier); *Voyage de noces* (Schmidt) (as Rudi); *La Chanson d'une nuit* (Litvak) (as Koretzky); *F.P.1 ne répond plus* (Hartl) (as Georges); *Une Faim de loup* (Fried and Morskoi—short)
1933 *Le Sexe faible* (Siodmak) (as Jimmie); *Incognito* (Gerron) (as Marcel); *L'Oncle de Pekin* (Darmont) (as Philippe); *Le Médécin de service* (Cerf—short); *Vacances conjugales* (Greville) (as Pierre)
1934 *Caravane* (*Caravan*) (Charell) (as Le Lieutenant de Tokay); *La Garnison amoureuse* (Vaucorbeil) (as Pierre); *Johnny haute-couture* (de Poligny) (as Johnny); *Le Miroir aux alouettes* (Le Bon) (as Jean Forestier); *Quadrille d'amour* (Fried) (as Robert Lancelot)
1935 *Le Bébé de l'escadron* (*Quand la vie était belle*) (Sti) (as Georges); *Bout-de-chou* (Wulschléger); *Jeunesse d'abord* (Stelli) (as Stéphane Minot); *Un Oiseau rare* (Pottier) (as Jean Berthier)
1936 *Pattes de mouche* (Grémillon) (as Michel); *Vous n'avez rien à déclarer?* (Joannon) (as Edmond de Trivelin); *Une Femme qui se partage* (Cammage) (as Cornette); *Le Mari rêve* (Capellani) (as René Doray/Achille Leroy); *Passé à vendre* (Pujol) (as Bob); *Prête-moi ta femme* (Cammage) (as Gontran); *La Reine des resquilleuses* (Glass); *La Valse eternelle* (Neufeld) (as Le Prince Georges)
1937 *Mademoiselle ma mère* (Decoin) (as Georges); *La Schpountz* (Pagnol) (as Cousine)
1938 *Claudine à l'école* (*Claudine*) (de Poligny) (as Le Docteur Dubois); *Giuseppe Verdi* (Gallone) (as Alexandre Dumas); **Quai des brumes** (*Port of Shadows*) (Carné) (as Lucien); *Goose de riche* (de Canonge) (as Pierre Mougins); *Café de Paris* (Lacombe) (as Le Rec); *Hercule ou l'incorruptible* (Esway) (as Bastien); *Grisou* (de Canonge) (as Henri Hagnauer, + sc)
1939 *Visages de femmes* (Guissart) (as Fred); *Les Frères corses* (*The Corsican Brothers*) (Kelber); *Dernière jeunesse* (*Last Desire*) (Musso) (as M. de Gilhooley); *La Père Lebonnard* (de Limur) (as Freddy); *Le Chemin de l'honneur* (Paulin) (as Lt. Philippe Drierminoff); *Frères d'Afrique* (Navarra); *Sixième étage* (Cloche) (as Jonval); *Trois Argentines à Montmartre* (Hugon) (as Toninett)
1941 *Le Soleil a toujours raison* (Billon) (as Gabriel)

1942 *Les Deux Timides* (Y. Allégret) (as Thibaudier); *Promesse à l'inconnue* (Berthomieu) (as Lussac); *Le Croisée des chemins* (Berthomieu) (as Hubert Epervans)
1943 *Adieu Léonard* (Prevert) (as Bonenfant); *Lumière d'été* (Grémillon) (as Roland Maillard)
1945 *Le Pays sans étoiles* (Lacombe) (as Jean-Pierre/Francois-Charles); **Les Enfants du paradis** (*The Children of Paradise*) (Carné) (as Frédérick Lemaître); *La Femme fatale* (Boyer) (as Jean Pleyard)
1946 *Jéricho* (Calef) (as "Marche Noir"); *Les Portes de la nuit* (*Gates of the Night*; *Ports of the Night*) (Carné) (as Georges); *Pétrus* (M. Allégret) (as Rodriguez); *L'Arche de Noë* (*Noah's Ark*) (Jacques) (as Bitru); *L'Amour autour de la maison* (de Hérain) (as Douze-Apôtres); *Rocambole* (2 parts: *Rocambole* and *La Revanche de Baccarat*) (de Baroncelli)
1947 *Croisière pour l'inconnu* (Montazel) (as Emile Fréchisse)
1948 *Les Amants de Vérone* (*The Lovers of Verona*) (Cayatte) (as Raffaele); *La Nuit blanche* (Pottier) (as Pierre); *Le Secret de Monte-Cristo* (Valentin) (as Francois Picard)
1949 *Portrait d'un assassin* (Roland) (as Fabius); *Millionnaires d'un jour* (Hunebelle) (as Francis)
1950 *Souvenirs perdus* ("La Statuette" ep.) (Christian-Jaque) (as Philippe); *Maître après Dieu* (*Skipper Next to God*) (Daquin) (as Capitaine Joris); *L'Homme de la Jamaique* (de Canonge) (as Jacques Marel); *Julie de Carneilhan* (Manuel) (as Herbert Espivant); *De Renoir à Picasso* (Haesaerts) (as narrator)
1951 *Barbe-Bleue* (*Bluebeard*) (Christian-Jaque) (as Amadée de Salfère); *Les Mains sales* (*Dirty Hands*) (Rivers) (as Hoederer)
1952 *Le Plaisir* (*House of Pleasure*) ("La Maison Tellier" ep.) (Max Ophüls) (as Julien Le Dentu); *La Pocharde* (Combret) (as Renneville); *Le Rideau rouge* (Barsacq) (as Ludovic Arns); *Saint-Tropez, devoir de vacances* (Paviot—short); *Torticola contre Frankensberg* (Paviot—short); *Jouens le jeu* ("L'Impatience" ep.) (Gillois)
1953 *La Bergère et le ramoneur* (Grimault) (as voice of the bird); *Vestire gli ignudi* (Pagliero) (as Gorlier)
1954 *Raspoutine* (Combret) (title role); *Les Soliloques du pauvre* (Drach—short) (as narrator)
1955 *La Tour de Nèsle* (Gance) (as Buridan); *Napoléon* (Guitry) (as Barras)
1957 *Porte de Lilas* (*Gates of Paris*) (Clair) (as Juju)
1958 *Sans famille* (Michel) (as Jeroboam Driscoll); *Les Grandes Familles* (*The Possessors*) (de la Patellière) (as Maublanc); *La Vie à deux* (Duhour) (as Pierre Carreau)
1959 *La Loi* (*Where the Hot Wind Blows*) (Dassin) (as Don Cesare); *La Tête contre les murs* (Franju) (as Docteur Varmont); *Messieurs les ronds-de-cuir* (Diamant-Berger) (as Docteur Nègre)
1960 **Les Yeux sans visages** (*Eyes without a Face*) (Franju) (as Genessier); *Cartagine in fiamme* (*Carthage in Flames*) (Gallone) (as Sidone); *Il bell'Antonio* (Bolognini) (as Alfio Magnano); *Candide* (Carbonnaux) (as Pangloss); *Le Dialogue des Carmélites* (Agostini) (as commissioner of the people); *Les Ennemis* (Molinaro)
1961 *Les Amours célèbre* ("Agnès Bernauer" ep.) (Boisrond) (as Le Grand-Duc Ernest de Wittelsbach); *Pleins feux sur l'assassin* (Franju) (as Comte Hervé de Keraudren); *Vive Henri IV, Vive l'amour* (Autant-Lara) (as Montmorency); *Le Bateau d'Emile* (de la Patellière) (as François Larmentiel); *Les Petits Matins* (Audry) (as Achille Pipermint); *Rencontres* (Agostino) (as Carl Krasner)
1962 *Le Crime ne paie pas* (*Crime Does Not Pay*) ("L'Affaire Fenayrou" ep.) (Oury) (as Martin Fenayrou); *L'Abominable Hommes des douanes* (M. Allégret) (as Le Tueur Russe)

Pierre Brasseur with Arletty in *Les Enfants du paradis*

1963   *Les Bonnes Causes* (*Don't Tempt the Devil*) (Christian-Jaque) (as Cassidi)

1964   *Liola* (*A Very Handy Man*) (Blasetti) (as Simone Palumbo); *Le Magot de Joséfa* (Autant-Lara) (as the Mayor); *Humour noir* ("La Bestoile" ep.) (Autant-Lara); *Un Soir . . . par hasard* (Govar) (as Charles); *Le Grain de sable* (Kast) (as Georges Richter); *Lucky Joe* (Deville) (as chief commissioner); *Les Comédians* (Thierry—short)

1965   *La Métamorphose des cloportes* (Granier-Deferre) (as Tonton); *Deux Heures à tuer* (Govar) (as Laurent); *L'Or du duc* (Baratier) (as uncle); *Pas de caviar pour tante Olga* (Becker) (as Patache); *Pas de panique* (Gobbi) (as Toussaint)

1966   *La Vie de château* (*A Matter of Resistance*) (Rappeneau) (as Dimanche); *Un mondo nuovo* (*A Young World*) (de Sica) (as boss); *La Fille de la mer morte* (Golan); *King of Hearts* (*Le Roi de coeur*) (de Broca) (as Général Géranium)

1967   *Le Fou de Labo 4* (Besnard) (as Father Ballanchon); *La Petite Vertu* (Korber) (as Polnik)

1968   *Les Oiseaux vont mourir aux Pérou* (*Birds in Peru*) (Gary) (as husband); *Goto, île d'amour* (Borowczyk) (as Goto); *Sous la signe de Monte-Cristo* (Hunebelle) (as Faria)

1970   *Macédoine* (Scandelari) (as Bloch-Dupond)

1971   *Les Mariés de l'an deux* (Rappeneau) (as Gosselin)

1972   *La più bella serata della mia vita* (Scola) (as Comte la Brunetière)

Film as screenwriter:

1957   *Les Amants de demain* (Blistène)

Publications

By BRASSEUR: books—

Aile est morte (verse), with Dede Sunbeam, Paris, 1926.
La Guerre de mines (play), Paris, 1939.
Tobie est un ange (script for film never completed), Paris, 1941.
Un Ange passe (play), Paris, 1947.
Le Mascaret (play), Paris, 1947.
L'Enfant du dimanche (play), Paris, 1959.
Ma Vie en vrac, Paris, 1972.

By BRASSEUR: articles—

"Vous m'avez appris mon métier," in *Les Lettres Françaises* (Paris), 20 November 1958.
Interview in *Cinémonde* (Paris), 4 July 1961.

On BRASSEUR: articles—

Cinémonde (Paris), 10 October and 19 December 1952, and September 1971.
Beylie, Claude, "Mort d'un bateleur," in *Ecran* (Paris), November 1972.
Barrot, Oliver, and Philippe Ariotti, "Pierre Brasseur" in *Anthologie du cinéma*, Vol. VIII, No. 76, Paris, 1974.
Ecran (Paris), January 1978, updated 15 December 1979.

*   *   *

Pierre Brasseur once wrote, "There exist three kinds of actors, the good, the bad, and the great." As a participant in practically every major development in the French cinema after 1920, he proved himself to be one of that final category. His early involvement with the Parisian avant-garde in the 1920s was followed by his first leading roles in French-German co-productions of the early 1930s. He found his best roles during the grand epoch of poetic realism, and survived the desert of the 1950s French filmmaking to find himself stranded in the 1960s: an actor's actor in a director's cinema.

His stage work was always central to his career, and in the mid-1920s the charming young comedian was adopted by the intelligentsia. He first worked with Jean Cocteau in 1924, and was soon associated with the Surrealist group, having contact with André Breton and others, and contributing poems and texts to *La Révolution Surréaliste*. In 1925 his first play, *L'Ancre noire*, was produced, and he continued to write or collaborate on play and film scripts, notably with Marcel Dalio.

After military service, the first major phase of his acting career began at UFA studios in Berlin in films made for German and French release. "To be employed at UFA was, for me, more important than going to Hollywood," he wrote, and he remained in Berlin for a year and a half, establishing himself as a leading comedian in a series of romantic farces. He did briefly visit Hollywood in 1934, where Erik Charell was directing *Caravan* for Fox in English and French versions. Brasseur played the Philip Holmes role in the French one, opposite Charles Boyer who starred in both.

On his return to France, Brasseur lent his presence to a series of quickly made and undistinguished films, although one of these, *Un Oiseau rare*, marked the first of 11 films he made which were written by Jacques Prévert. Among his films of this period were a number of bawdy comedies, a genre then accounting for a significant proportion of French production. Perhaps not untypical of his mid-1930s work is his appearance, along with such comedians as Raimu and Saturnin Fabre, in Joannon's extremely vulgar *Vous n'avez rien à déclarer?*, in which Brasseur appears as a timid young man who is temporarily impotent.

In 1936 he first worked with Jean Grémillon, in the minor and commercially unsuccessful *Pattes de mouche*, but it was his brief appearance opposite Jean Gabin in Carné's *Quai des brumes* in 1938 that revealed another Brasseur, one capable of infinitely more subtle and complex characterization. He nevertheless continued to play the cynical Don Juan and various playboys until the war, taking over that specialty from the aging Jules Berry.

It was during the war that Brasseur left his mark. After working with Yves Allégret on *Tobie est un ange*, which Brasseur co-scripted (the film's negatives were destroyed in a fire before its release), and on *Les Deux Timides*, he collaborated once again with Grémillon in *Lumière d'été*. Brasseur starred as the brilliant, decadent painter Roland Maillard,

in a celebrated performance detailing the disintegration of an artistic career.

He soon followed this with his greatest role, as the famous nineteenth-century actor Frederick Lemaître in *Les Enfants du Paradis*. The film brought together two performers at the summit of their art: Jean-Louis Barrault and Brasseur, the mime and the comedian. Brasseur's performance, requiring him to create roles such as Othello within the role of Lemaître, is an example of a complex character thought over in every detail.

After the war, theatrical work increasingly occupied Brasseur. In 1948 he joined the renowned company of Barrault and Madeleine Renaud, appearing in plays of Camus, Claudel, and others. He worked in films between theatrical engagements, and these films were often adaptations of stage plays, such as Sartre's *Les Mains sales* or *Vestire gli ignudi* from Pirandello.

After the success of his humorous and pathetic Juju in Clair's *Porte de Lilas*, Brasseur was cast mainly in supporting roles. Though he made interesting film appearances, especially in a series of three films for Georges Franju, and in Bolognini's *Il bell'Antonio*, his work in theater was more notable, for example his acclaimed performance in a 1967 Paris production of Harold Pinter's *The Homecoming*.

—Judah Löwe

BRAZZI, Rossano

Nationality: Italian. **Born:** Bologna, 18 September 1916; brother of the director Oscar Brazzi. **Education:** Attended schools in Florence. **Family:** Married 1) the actress Lydia Bertolini, 1940 (died 1981); 2) Isle Fischer. **Career:** Mid-1930s—began three-year period as apprentice lawyer, Rome; 1939—three-year contract with Scalera Film; international star in 1950s; 1969-70—in TV series *The Survivors*; 1984—arrested for involvement in an arms smuggling conspiracy; 1990—in TV series *Ruth Rendell Mysteries*. **Died:** In Rome, 24 December 1994.

Films as Actor:

1940   *Il ponto di Vetro* (Alessandrini); *Ritorno* (von Bolvary); *La forza bruta* (Bragaglia); *È caduta una donna* (Guarini); *Provesso e morte di Socrate* (D'Errico); *La Tosca* (*The Story of Tosca*) (Koch) (as Mario Cavardossi); *Kean* (Brignole)

1941   *Il re si diverte* (*The King's Jester*) (Bonnard) (as Francesco I); *Il bravo di Venezia* (Campogalliani)

1942   *Noi vivi—addio Kira* (*We the Living*) (Alessandrini) (as Leo Kovalensky); *Damals* (Hansen); *Una signora dell'ovest* (Koch); *I due Foscari* (Fulchignoni); *La gorgona* (Brignone); *Treno crociato* (Campogalliani)

1943   *Baruffe chiozzotte* (Menardi); *Silenzio, si gira* (Campogalliani)

1945   *Malia* (Amato); *La resa di Titi* (*The Merry Chase*) (Bianchi); *I dieci commandamenti* (*The Ten Commandments*)

1946   *La grande aurora* (*The Great Dawn*) (Scotese) (as Renzo Gamba); *Aquila Nera* (*The Black Eagle*; *Return of the Black Eagle*) (Freda) (as Vladimir Dubrowsky)

1947   *Furia* (Alessandrini) (as Antonio); *Il corriere del re* (Righelli); *Eleanora Duse* (Ratti); *La monaca di Monza* (Pacini); *Il passatore* (*A Bullet for Stefano*; *The Ferryman*) (Coletti) (as Stefano Pelloni); *Il diavolo bianco* (Malasomma) (as Prince Mdwani/title role)

1948   *I contrabbandieri del mare* (Montero)

1949 *Vulcano* (*Volcano*) (Dieterle) (as Donato); *Little Women* (LeRoy) (as Professor Bhaer)

1950 *Romanza d'amore* (Toselli); *Gli enesorabilia* (Mastrocinque); *La corona negra* (Saslavski) (as Andres)

1951 *La leggenda de Genofeffa* (Rabenalt); *La vendetta di Aquila Nera* (Freda); *Incantesimo tragico* (*Hechizo tragico*; *Oliva*) (Segui) (as Pietro)

1952 *L'ingiusta condanna* (*Guilt Is Not Mine*) (Masini) (as Carlo Rocchi); *La prigionera della torre dell cuoco* (Chili); *La donna che inventà l'amore* (Carlo); *Il boia di Lilla* (Cottafavi); *Eran trecento* (Callegari); *Il figlio di Lagardere* (Cerchio)

1953 *Il fuco nelle vene* (*La Chair et le diable*; *Flesh and Desire*) (Josipovici); *La barriera delle legge* (Costa); *C'era una volta Angelo Musco* (Chili)

1954 *La Castiglione* (Combret); *Carne de horca* (*Il terrore dell 'Andalusia*) (Vajda); *Three Coins in the Fountain* (Negulesco) (as Georgio Bianchi); *The Barefoot Contessa* (Joseph L. Mankiewicz) (as Vincenzo Torlato-Favrini)

1955 *Angela* (Anton) (as Nino); *Summertime* (*Summer Madness*) (Lean) (as Renato Di Rossi); *Gli ultima cinque minuti* (Amato)

1956 *Loser Takes All* (Annakin) (as Bertrand)

1957 *Legend of the Lost* (Hathaway) (as Paul Bonnard); *Interlude* (Sirk) (as Tonio Fischer); *The Story of Esther Costello* (*Golden Virgin*) (Miller) (as Carlo Landi)

1958 *South Pacific* (Logan) (as Émile de Becque); *A Certain Smile* (Negulesco) (as Luc)

1959 *Count Your Blessings* (Negulesco) (as Charles-Edouard de Valhubert)

1960 *L'assedio di Siracusa* (*Siege of Syracuse*) (Francisci) (as Archimedes); *Austerlitz* (*The Battle of Austerlitz*) (Gance) (as Lucien Bonaparte)

1962 *Light in the Piazza* (Guy Green) (as Signor Naccarelli); *Rome Adventure* (*Lovers Must Learn*) (Daves) (as Roberto Orlandi); "Le Lièvre et la tortue" ("The Tortoise and the Hare") ep. of *Les Quatres Vérités* (*Three Fables of Love*) (Blasetti) (as Leo)

1964 *Dark Purpose* (*L'Intrigue*) (George Marshall) (as Count Paolo Barbarelli)

1965 *Un amore* (Vernuccio); *La ragazza in prestito* (*Engagement Italiano*) (Giannetti) (as Mario); *The Battle of the Villa Fiorita* (Daves) (as Lorenzo)

1966 *La ragazzo del bersagliere* (Blasetti); *Per amore . . . per magia* (*For Love . . . For Magic*) (Tessari)

1967 *The Bobo* (Parrish) (as Carlos Matabosch); "Amateur Night" ep. of *Woman Times Seven* (*Sette volta donna*; *Sept fois femme*) (de Sica) (as Giorgio); *La schiava del paradiso*

1968 *One Step to Hell* (*Rey de Africa*; *King of Africa*) (Sandy Howard) (as Dr. Hamilton)

1969 *Krakatoa, East of Java* (*Volcano*) (Kowalski) (as Giovanni Borghese); *The Italian Job* (Collinson) (as Beckerman)

1970 *The Adventurers* (Lewis Gilbert) (as Baron de Coyne); *Intimita proibite di una giovane sposa* (Oscar Brazzi); *Il sesso di diavolo* (Oscar Brazzi)

1971 *Mr. Kingstreet's War* (Rubens); *Il giorno del guidizio* (Gariazzo)

1972 *Detras de esa puerta* (*Political Asylum*) (Dreguez) (as Ambassador Lara); *The Great Waltz* (Andrew L. Stone) (as Baron Tedesco); *De aire y fuego*; *Il castello di paura*

1973 *House of Freaks* (*Frankenstein's Castle of Freaks*; *Il Castello delle donne maledotti*; *Terror*; *Terror Castle*) (Oliver) (as Count Frankenstein)

1974 *Storia del pugliato degli antichi ad oggi*; *Drummer of Vengeance* (Paget)

1975 *Il cavaliere Costante Nicosia indemontiato ovvero Dracula in Brianza* (*Dracula in the Provinces*) (Fulci); *Il tempo degli assassino* (Andrei); *Gil angeli dalle mani bendate* (Oscar Brazzi); *La farina del diavolo* (Valenzano)

1976 *I telefoni bianchi* (*White Telephones*) (Risi)

1977 *Maestro d'amore* (*Master of Love*) (Rondi)

1980 *A Time for Miracles* (O'Herlihy—for TV) (as Fillipo Fillici)

1981 *The Final Conflict* (Graham Baker) (as Decarlo); *Io e Caterina* (*Catherine and I*) (Sordi) (as Arthur)

1982 *La voce* (Oscar Brazzi—for TV)

1984 *Fear City* (*Ripper*) (Ferrara); *The Far Pavilions* (Duffell—for TV) (as Rana of Bhithor)

1985 *Formula for Murder* (*Formula for a Murder*) (De Martino [Martin Herbert]) (as Dr. Sernich); *Cristoforo Colombo* (*Christopher Columbus*) (Lattuada—for TV) (as Diego Ortiz De Vilhegas); *Final Justice* (Nicholas von Sternberg) (as Don La Manna)

1987 *Russicum* (*The Third Solution*) (Squitieri) (as Marini)

1988 *Ticket to Ride* (Franklin—for TV)

Films as Director:

1966 *Il natale che quasi non fu* (*The Christmas that Almost Wasn't*) (+ ro as Phineas T. Prune)

1968 *Sette uomini e un cervello* (d as "Edward Ross," + ro)

1969 *Salvare la faccia* (*Psychout for Murder*) (co-d as "Edward Ross" with Ted Kneeland, + ro as Brigoli)

1972 *Cappucetto rosso, Cenerentola . . . et voi ci credete* (+ ro)

Publications

On BRAZZI: articles—

Current Biography 1961, New York, 1961.
Ciné Revue (Paris), 14 February 1980 and 24 June 1984.
Obituary in *New York Times*, 27 December 1994.
Obituary in *Time* (New York), 9 January 1995.

* * *

Rossano Brazzi was one of the busiest Italian screen actors from the 1940s through the early 1980s. Although he never achieved major stardom outside Italy, he appeared in dozens of films made elsewhere in Europe and in the United States, often in starring roles.

Despite the fact that his parents were killed by Fascists before World War II and his participation in the anti-Fascist movement, Brazzi entered the Italian film industry in 1939 and appeared in numerous films throughout the war. His dark handsome looks made him a screen idol in Italy, and accounted for his first role in an American film, *Little Women*, for MGM. Unfortunately, Brazzi had a small, lackluster part which obscured his potential as a romantic leading man, so he returned to Italy. His first successful American ventures were *The Barefoot Contessa* and *Three Coins in the Fountain*, in which his secondary roles brought him significant recognition. But it was his next film, *Summertime*, directed by David Lean, that brought him international stardom. He played opposite Katharine Hepburn, perfecting a part he frequently repeated, that of a handsome Italian who appears to be something of a cad, but who is actually sincere.

Although Brazzi never achieved the star status of Marcello Mastroianni or Vittorio De Sica, he was certainly one of the most recognizable Italian male stars. He never seemed to surpass his *Summertime* role, but was successful in a series of light romantic films, including *Rome Adventure* and *The Battle of the Villa Fiorita*. He was particularly effective in *South Pacific*, even though his singing voice had to be dubbed. From the late 1960s until his death in 1994, Brazzi appeared in many international productions and several television movies, including the highly touted *The Far Pavilions*.

—Patricia King Hanson

BRENNAN, Walter

Nationality: American. **Born:** Swampscott, Massachusetts, 25 July 1894. **Education:** Studied engineering. **Military Service:** 1917—enlisted in service during World War I. **Family:** Married Ruth Wells, 1920, children: Arthur, Walter, and Ruth. **Career:** Mid-'teens—worked at various jobs including lumberjack and bank clerk; appeared in vaudeville and stock; 1923—began career in Hollywood as extra and stuntman; 1927—first film role in *The Ridin' Rowdy*; 1957-63—in TV series *The Real McCoys*; 1964-65—in TV series *Tycoon*; 1967-69—title role in TV series *The Guns of Will Sonnett*; 1970-71—TV series *To Rome, with Love*. **Awards:** Best Supporting Actor Academy Award for *Come and Get It*, 1936; Best Supporting Actor Academy Award for *Kentucky*, 1938; Best Supporting Actor Academy Award for *The Westerner*, 1940. **Died:** In Oxnard, California, 21 September 1974.

Films as Actor:

1927   *The Ridin' Rowdy* (Thorpe); *Tearin' into Trouble* (Thorpe)
1928   *Silks and Saddles* (*Thoroughbreds*); *The Ballyhoo Buster* (Thorpe)
1929   *The Long Trail* (Robson); *The Lariat Kid* (Eason); *One Hysterical Night* (Craft); *The Shannons of Broadway* (Flynn); *Smilin' Guns* (MacRae)
1930   *Scratch as Scratch Can*; *The King of Jazz* (Anderson)
1931   *Neck and Neck* (Thorpe); *Dancing Dynamite* (Mason)
1932   *Law and Order* (Cahn); *The Iceman's Ball*; *The Texas Cyclone* (Lederman); *Two Fisted Law* (Lederman); *The All-American* (*Sport of a Nation*) (Mack)
1933   *Man of Action* (Melford); *Fighting for Justice* (Brower); *The Keyhole* (Curtiz); *Lilly Turner* (Wellman); *Baby Face* (*Baby Face Harrington*) (Green); *Female* (Curtiz); *From Headquarters* (Dieterle); *Sing, Sinner, Sing* (Christy); *One Year Later* (Hopper); *Strange People* (Thorpe); *Parachute Jumper* (Green)
1934   *Woman Haters*; *Housewife* (Green); *Desirable* (Mayo); *Half a Sinner* (Newman); *Riptide* (Goulding); *Stamboul Quest* (Wood); *The Painted Veil* (Boleslawski); *Good Dame* (Gering)
1935   *Man on a Flying Trapeze* (*The Memory Expert*) (Bruckman); *Barbary Coast* (Hawks) (as Old Atrocity); *Restless Knights*; *Metropolitan* (Boleslawski); *Bric-a-Brac*; *Seven Keys to Baldpate* (Hamilton); *The Bride of Frankenstein* (Whale); *Lady Tubbs* (Crosland); *Northern Frontier* (Newfield); *The Wedding Night* (King Vidor); *Law beyond the Range* (Beebe)
1936   *These Three* (Wyler); *The Three Godfathers* (Boleslawski); **Fury** (Fritz Lang) (as Bugs Meyers); *Come and Get It* (Hawks and Wyler); *Banjo on My Knee* (Cromwell); *The Moon's Our Home* (Seiter); *The Prescott Kid* (Selman)
1937   *When Love Is Young* (Seiter); *Wild and Wooly* (Werker); *She's Dangerous* (Foster and Carruth); *The Affairs of Cappy Ricks* (Staub)

1938   *Kentucky* (Butler); *The Buccaneer* (DeMille); *The Texans* (Hogan); *The Adventures of Tom Sawyer* (Taurog); *Mother Carey's Chickens* (Rowland V. Lee); *The Cowboy and the Lady* (Potter)
1939   *The Story of Irene and Vernon Castle* (Potter); *Stanley and Livingston* (King); *They Shall Have Music* (Mayo); *Joe and Ethel Turp Call on the President* (Sinclair)
1940   *Northwest Passage* (King Vidor); *The Westerner* (Wyler) (as Judge Roy Bean); *Maryland* (King)
1941   *Meet John Doe* (Capra) (as the "Colonel"); *Swamp Water* (*The Man Who Came Back*) (Renoir); *Sergeant York* (Hawks); *Rise and Shine* (Dwan); *Nice Girl?* (Seiter); *This Woman Is Mine* (Lloyd)
1942   *Pride of the Yankees* (Wood); *Stand by for Action* (*Cargo of Innocents*) (Leonard)
1943   *Hangmen Also Die* (Fritz Lang); *The North Star* (Milestone); *The Last Will and Testament of Tom Smith*; *Slightly Dangerous* (Ruggles); *Home in Indiana* (Hathaway); *The Princess and the Pirate* (Butler); *To Have and Have Not* (Hawks) (as Eddy)
1945   *Dakota* (Kane)
1946   *A Stolen Life* (Bernhardt); *Centennial Summer* (Preminger); **My Darling Clementine** (John Ford) (as Old Man Clanton); *Nobody Lives Forever* (Negulesco)
1947   *Driftwood* (Dwan)
1948   **Red River** (Hawks) (as Groot); *Scudda Hoo! Scudda Hay!* (*Summer Lightning*) (F. Hugh Herbert); *Blood on the Moon* (Wise)
1949   *Task Force* (Daves); *The Great Dan Patch* (Newman); *The Green Promise* (*Raging Waters*) (Russell); *Brimstone* (Kane)
1950   *Surrender* (Dwan); *Curtain Call at Cactus Creek* (*Take the Stage*) (Lamont); *A Ticket to Tomahawk* (Sale); *Singing Guns* (Springsteen); *The Showdown* (Darrel and Stuart McGowan)
1951   *Along the Great Divide* (Walsh); *The Wide Blue Yonder* (*Thunder across the Pacific*) (Dwan); *Best of the Bad Men* (Russell)
1952   *Lure of the Wilderness* (Negulesco); *Return of the Texan* (Daves)
1953   *The Sea of Lost Ships* (Kane)
1954   *Drums across the River* (Juran); *Four Guns to the Border* (Carlson); *Bad Day at Black Rock* (John Sturges) (as Doc Velie)
1955   *The Far Country* (Anthony Mann); *At Gunpoint!* (*Gunpoint!*) (Werker)
1956   *The Proud Ones* (Webb); *Glory* (Butler); *Come Next Spring* (Springsteen); *Goodbye, My Lady* (Wellman)
1957   *Tammy and the Bachelor* (*Tammy*) (Pevney); *God Is My Partner* (Claxton); *The Way to the Gold* (Webb)
1959   **Rio Bravo** (Hawks) (as Stumpy)
1962   *How the West Was Won* (Hathaway, Ford, Marshall)
1965   *Those Calloways* (Tokar)
1966   *The Oscar* (Rouse)
1967   *Who's Minding the Mint?* (Morris); *The Gnome-Mobile* (Stevenson)
1968   *The One and Only Genuine Original Family Band* (O'Herlihy)
1969   *Support Your Local Sheriff* (Kennedy); *The Over-the-Hill Gang* (Yarbrough—for TV)
1970   *The Over-the-Hill Gang Rides Again* (McGowan—for TV); *The Young Country* (Huggins—for TV)
1971   *Smoke in the Wind* (Kane); *Two for the Money* (Kowalski—for TV)
1972   *Home for the Holidays* (Moxey—for TV)

Walter Brennan in *The Westerner* © 1940, Samuel Goldwyn

Publications

On BRENNAN: articles—

"Nécrologie: Walter Brennan," in *Cinéma* (Paris), November
    1974.
Ciné Revue (Paris), 15 January 1981.

*   *   *

From the 1930s through the 1950s Walter Brennan was the definitive character actor—a colorful, memorable supporting player and an essential ingredient in scores of fine films for an array of top directors. If he had a particular specialty among his wide range of sidekicks, employees, buddies, colleagues, and antagonists, it was in playing crusty old-timers—well before he was one himself.

After serving in World War I, Brennan began working in movies in 1923 as an extra and a stuntman. He had his teeth knocked out in an accident in 1932, providing him with a natural toothlessness—as well as removable false teeth—that he would occasionally use for comic value.

He won the Academy Award for Best Supporting Actor an astonishing and unprecedented three times in the space of five years—as a lumberjack in the Howard Hawks-William Wyler *Come and Get It*, as a horse-racing colonel in David Butler's *Kentucky*, and as the ornery Judge Roy Bean in William Wyler's *The Westerner*, the last role in support of Gary Cooper. Brennan was again nominated for the Oscar the following year for his role as the pastor in Howard Hawks's *Sergeant York*—again in support of Gary Cooper, who won that year's Best Actor Award for his performance.

Brennan's first substantial screen assignment came when he had well over 20 features under his belt. It was for Howard Hawks in *Barbary Coast*, playing a character called "Old Atrocity." He would eventually work in Hawks films no fewer than six times: he performed in the World War II drama *To Have and Have Not* as Humphrey Bogart's rummy pal, in the Western *Red River* as the quarrelsome Groot, and, perhaps most memorably, in another Western, *Rio Bravo*, as the loyal, cantankerous Stumpy, guarding the jailhouse with a shotgun for sheriff John Wayne.

Among the other famous directors who found Brennan's colorful persona both useful and effective, were John Ford (*My Darling Clementine*), King Vidor (*The Wedding Night*), Fritz Lang (*Fury*), Frank Capra (*Meet John Doe*), Jean Renoir (*Swamp Water*), Lewis Milestone (*The North Star*), Raoul Walsh (*Along the Great Divide*), and John Sturges (*Bad Day at Black Rock*). Although he performed in a wide variety of genres, it was the Western with which he became most strongly associated.

With the television series *The Real McCoys*, a countrified situation comedy in which Brennan played Grandpappy Amos McCoy (a flat-out comic version of the blustery but lovable screen character he had been essaying for years), Brennan became, during the program's six-year tenure, something of a television icon. Bringing the same skill to his television work that he had given to the cinema for decades, he kept nightclub impressionists and the general public busy imitating everything about his character—from his cornpone accent to his axle-grease-squeaky voice to his coming-apart-at-the-seams limp. Moreover, his characterization on television was so strong that it nearly obliterated the public's memory of his fruitful movie career, which he ended in a series of theatrical family films and several made-for-television movies, staying productive right up to the time of his death, at the age of eighty, in 1974.

—Bill Wine

BRIDGES, Jeff

Nationality: American. **Born:** Los Angeles, 4 December 1949; son of the actor Lloyd Bridges; brother of the actor Beau Bridges. **Education:** Attended University High School, Los Angeles; studied acting at Berghoff Studios, New York. **Family:** Married Susan (Bridges), three daughters: Isabelle, Jessica, and Hayley. **Career:** 1951—in film *The Company She Keeps*; early 1950s—acting debut in father Lloyd Bridges's television series *Sea Hunt*; 1969—composed and sang "Lost in Space" on soundtrack of film *John and Mary*; continued to be active as songwriter; 1970—feature film debut in *Halls of Anger*. **Agent:** c/o Creative Artists Agency, 9830 Wilshire Boulevard, Beverly Hills, CA 90212, U.S.A.

Films as Actor:

1951	*The Company She Keeps* (Cromwell)

1951   *The Company She Keeps* (Cromwell)
1969   *Silent Night, Lonely Night* (Petrie—for TV)
1970   *Halls of Anger* (Bogart) (as Douglas); *In Search of America* (Bogart—for TV); *The Yin and Yang of Mr. Go* (Meredith)
1971   ***The Last Picture Show*** (Bogdanovich) (as Duane Jackson)
1972   *Fat City* (Huston) (as Ernie); *Bad Company* (Benton) (as Jake Ramsey)
1973   *Lolly Madonna XXX* (*The Lolly-Madonna War*) (Sarafian) (as Zack Feather); *The Last American Hero* (Johnson) (as Elroy Jackson Jr.); *The Iceman Cometh* (Frankenheimer) (as Don Parritt)
1974   *Thunderbolt and Lightfoot* (Cimino) (as Lightfoot); *Rancho Deluxe* (Perry) (as Jack McKee)
1975   *Hearts of the West* (*Hollywood Cowboy*) (Zieff) (as Lewis Tater)
1976   *King Kong* (Guillermin) (as Jack Prescott); *Stay Hungry* (Rafelson) (as Craig Blake)
1978   *Somebody Killed Her Husband* (Johnson) (as Jerry Green)
1979   *Winter Kills* (Richert—produced in 1977) (as Nick Kegan)
1980   ***Heaven's Gate*** (Cimino) (as John H. Bridges); *The American Success Company* (*Success*) (Richert) (as Harry)
1981   *Cutter and Bone* (*Cutter's Way*) (Passer) (as Richard Bone); *The Last Unicorn* (Rankin Jr. and Bass—animation) (as voice of Prince Lir)
1982   *Tron* (Lisberger) (as Kevin Flynn/Clu); *Kiss Me Goodbye* (Mulligan) (as Rupert)
1984   *Against All Odds* (Hackford) (as Terry Brogan); *Starman* (Carpenter) (as Alien)
1985   *Jagged Edge* (Marquand) (as Jack Forrester)
1986   *8 Million Ways to Die* (Ashby) (as Matthew Scudder); *The Morning After* (Lumet) (as Turner Kendall); *The Thanksgiving Promise* (Beau Bridges—for TV) (as neighbor, uncredited)
1987   *Nadine* (Benton) (as Vernon Hightower)
1988   *Tucker* (*Tucker: The Man and His Dream*) (Coppola) (as Preston Tucker); *See You in the Morning* (Pakula) (as Larry Livingston)
1989   *The Fabulous Baker Boys* (Kloves) (as Jack Baker)
1990   *Texasville* (Bogdanovich) (as Duane Jackson); *Quarter Time* (Bogayevicz); *Cold Feet* (Dornhelm) (as bartender)
1991   *The Fisher King* (Gilliam) (as Jack Lucas)
1993   *The Vanishing* (Sluizer) (as Barney); *Fearless* (Weir) (as Max Klein); *American Heart* (Bell) (as Jack Keely, + co-pr)
1994   *Blown Away* (Hopkins) (as Jimmy Dove)
1995   *Wild Bill* (Walter Hill) (title role)
1996   *White Squall* (Ridley Scott) (as Christopher "Skipper" Sheldon)

Publications

By BRIDGES: articles—

"Jeff Bridges," interview with S. Munshower, in *Inter/View* (New York), February 1975.
Interview with B. Lewis and Brian Baxter, in *Films and Filming* (London), November/December 1988.
"American Heart," interview with Sheila Benson, in *Interview* (New York), October 1992.
"Building Bridges," interview with M. Frankel, in *Movieline*, September 1993.

On BRIDGES: articles—

Brown, Barry, "Jeff Bridges: Popular Non-Actor," in *Close-Ups: The Movie Star Book*, edited by Danny Peary, New York, 1978.
Rolling Stone (New York), 19 August 1982.
Andrew, Geoff, "Bridges' Way," in *National Film Theatre Programme* (London), December 1988.
Frankel, Martha, "Lone Star Bridges," in *American Film* (Washington, D.C.), October 1990.
Current Biography 1991, New York, 1991.
Natahnson, Richard, "The Two Jeffs," in *Premiere* (New York), April 1992.
Maslin, Janet, "The Reluctant Star," in *New York Times Magazine*, 17 October 1993.
Svetkey, Benjamin, "Blast Action Hero: Jeff Bridges Hits Pyrotechnic Pay Dirt with Explosive *Blown Away*," in *Entertainment Weekly*, 15 July 1994.

* * *

"Inexplicably underrated" are the words that best describe Jeff Bridges. In 1971, his role as 1950s Texas teenager Duane Jackson in Peter Bogdanovich's *The Last Picture Show* earned him an Oscar nomination. Over the next quarter century, he offered an impressive array of performances, and he continues growing and maturing as an actor. Throughout the years, he has been a consistent critics' favorite, yet he has never been considered among the front rank of movie stars—perhaps because he has never had that one blockbuster film to thrust him into the epicenter of media attention and public adoration.

Son of Lloyd and brother of Beau, Bridges began acting when he was four months old, appearing alongside Jane Greer in *The Company She Keeps*; he also was a child actor on *Sea Hunt*, his father's television series. He had just graduated high school when he appeared in *The Last Picture Show*. In his role as the teenaged Duane Jackson, he projected an instinctive ease, which he continued to put forth over the next few years in roles as boyish types in *Fat City* (playing a boxer), *The Last American Hero* (as stock-car driver Junior Jackson), and *Bad Company*; he was especially fine in the latter, a bleak anti-Western, playing a Civil War draft dodger. Still, despite earning critical acclaim, Bridges admitted that self-doubts about his abilities did not allow him to take acting seriously. His attitude changed in 1973, after appearing in the film version of Eugene O'Neill's *The Iceman Cometh*. As Don Parritt, another boyish character to be sure, but one with levels of psychological depth (courtesy of O'Neill), Bridges gives his first fully mature screen performance. A critic in *Variety*, in describing Bridges's acting, perfectly summed up the essence of his most typical roles by calling his performance "a brilliant mixture of innocence, guilt, despair, and hope. His vulnerability and yearning . . . seem almost physically evident from the beginning." At the time, Pauline Kael characterized Bridges as being "so fresh and talented that just about every movie director with a good role wants him for it."

Over the next several years, Bridges's roles were diversified. His generous screen presence allowed his co-stars ample space without detracting from the power of his own performances. His second-fiddle roles—to John Heard's crazed Vietnam veteran in *Cutter's Way*, for example, or to leading man Clint Eastwood in the tragic homoerotic buddy movie *Thunderbolt and Lightfoot*—are deceptively passive. In the old-fashioned way of a Gary Cooper or James Stewart, his dreamy boyishness ended up leaving a profound impression on the viewer.

Bridges's first important starring role came as the naive, noirish hero in *Against All Odds*, a remake of *Out of the Past*. He was superb in his next film, *Starman*, an offbeat, bittersweet science fiction romance, in which he plays a vulnerable, birdlike extraterrestrial. His intense research into the difficult role—watching the movements of children and animals, and videotaping himself writhing naked on the floor in an attempt to capture the essence of his embryo-hatching scene—demonstrated that Bridges's commitment to his craft is no less than that of a Dustin Hoffman or Robert De Niro.

Bridges continued playing dreamers and likably flawed heroes, as he did so effectively as visionary automobile manufacturer Preston Tucker in *Tucker: The Man and His Dream* and the artistically frustrated cocktail lounge piano player opposite brother Beau and Michelle Pfeiffer in *The Fabulous Baker Boys*. But he also toyed with his outward appearance of innocence. In *Jagged Edge*, he plays a high-powered newspaper publisher accused of killing his wife, and who wholeheartedly proclaims his guiltlessness. As the story unfolds, the question remains: Did he, or did he not, do it? In this film, Bridges effectively pivots on the ambiguity of his lovableness, flinging the audience between adoring trust and uneasy suspicion.

In 1990, it seemed that his career had come full circle when he played an older, wiser, more portly Duane Jackson in *Texasville*, a sequel to *The Last Picture Show*. But at the same time, as he has aged, Bridges has gone on to diversify his career even more, taking on challenging roles that are anything but boyish—and which the younger Jeff Bridges never would have been called on to play. In *The Vanishing*, George Sluizer's American remake of his Dutch thriller, Bridges gives a forceful performance as a crafty kidnapper who reveals himself to the boyfriend of the woman he abducted. In *Fearless* and *The Fisher King*, he is cast as two very different characters whose lives are thrown into major crises. In the former, he conveys levels of emotion as a deeply troubled plane crash survivor. In the latter, he starts out as a hard-hearted, egotistical radio talk show host who undergoes a transformation after one of his listeners, whom he has just crudely dismissed, goes on a murder spree. As the story progresses, Bridges effectively communicates the confusion within a man whose outward characteristic is pomposity. But Bridges is at his best in one of his least-known films: *American Heart*, a staunch, at times daring drama about love and redemption, which depicts the pain and promise of its two key characters. Bridges offers a fierce, heartrending performance as an ex-con who has just been paroled from prison. His plans for continuing his life are sidetracked upon the arrival of his lonely, 14-year-old son whom he had abandoned, and who is determined to establish a relationship with him.

At this juncture of his career, it seems less likely that Jeff Bridges ever will earn superstardom. But he is still respected, still taking intelligent risks, and still a pleasure to watch on screen.

—Samantha Cook, updated by Rob Edelman

BRODSKÝ, Vlastimil

Nationality: Czech. **Born:** 1920. **Education:** Attended E. F. Burian School. **Family:** Married the actress Jana Brejchová. **Career:** Member of the Na Vinohradech Theatre, Prague. **Awards:** Best Actor, Berlin Festival, for *Jacob der Lügner*, 1975; Artist of Merit, Czechoslovakia.

Vlastimil Brodský (left) in *Jakob der Lugner*

Films as Actor:

1947   *Uloupená hranice* (*The Stolen Frontier*) (Weiss)

1953   *Tajemství krve* (*The Secret of Blood*; *The Mystery of Blood*) (Frič)

1957   *Zářijové noci* (Jasný)

1958   *Mezi nebem a zemi* (*Between Heaven and Earth*) (Podskalský)

1959   *Pět z milionů* (Brynych)

1963   *Až přijde kocour* (*That Cat*) (Jasný); *Transport z rje* (*Transport from Paradise*) (Brynych)

1964   *Každý den odvahu* (*Everyday Courage*; *Courage for Everyday*) (Schorm)

1965   *Povídky z prvń republiky* (Krejčík); *Ztracena tvar* (*The Lost Face*) (Hobl)

1966   *Lidé z maringotek* (*People on Wheels*) (Frič); ***Ostře sledované vlaky*** (*Closely Watched Trains*; *Closely Observed Trains*) (Menzel) (as Councilor Zedniček); *Spadla s měsice* (*The Girl from the Moon*; *Never Strike a Woman with a Flower*) (Podskalský)

1968   *Rozmarné léto* (*Capricious Summer*) (Menzel) (as Major Hugo); *Zločin v šantánu* (*Crime in a Night Club*) (Menzel) (as Minister of the Interior); *Farářuv konec* (*End of a Priest*) (Schorm) (as Sexton); *Vsichni dobri rodaci* (*All My Good Countrymen*) (Jasný); *Skrivanci na niti* (*Larks on a String*) (Menzel) (as professor for literature)

1970   *Kam čert nemuže* (*Where the Devil Cannot Get*; *A Devilish Honeymoon*) (Podskalský)

1975   *Jakob der Lügner* (*Jacob the Liar*) (Beyer) (title role); *Tak laska Zacina* (Bocan)

1976   *At ziji duchove* (Lipsky); *Smrt nacerno* (Toman)

1977   *Talíre nad Velkym Malikovem* (*Flying Saucers Coming!*; *Flying Saucers over Our Town*) (Jireš); *Zitra vstanu a oparim se cajem* (Polak)

1979   *Od zitrka necaruji* (Polak); *Poplach v oblacich* (Polak); *Tchan* (Mika)

1981   *Tajemny hrad v Karpatech* (*Mystery Castle in the Carpathians*) (Lipsky) (as Ignac)

1982   *Pocitani ovecek* (Kachyna)

1983   *A csoda vege* (Veszi)

1984   *Oci pro plac* (Mika)

1986   *Neni Sirotek Jako Sirotek* (Strnad)

1987   *Sasek a kralovna* (Chytilová) (as Vaclav); *Smich se lepi na paty* (Bocan); *Chobotnice Z II. Patra* (Polak) (as Grandfather Holan)

1992   *The Flying Sneaker* (Pojar) (as Dr. Renc); *Labyrinth* (Jireš)

Publications

By BRODSKÝ: book—

Tidbits from a Soul Hock Shop (autobiography), 1995.

On BRODSKÝ: article—

Film a doba (Prague), no. 11, 1975.

* * *

A multitalented actor who performs in the theater and on film, television, and radio, Vlastimil Brodský is closely linked with the entire postwar development of Czech filmmaking, in which he began to work after some stage experience following the end of World War II. He has made more than 90 films, in which he portrayed the most diverse human characters, good and evil, tragic and comic, within an extraordinary rich expressive range. Despite the universality of his characterizations, we can discern prevalent features of his acting. He imbues his characters with a deeply human quality, and has therefore become identified first and foremost with the unsentimental, average man, the everyday hero.

At the outset of his acting career Brodský appeared only as youthful characters in brief scenes. From the theater he brought to the screen fine diction and a particular gift for movement (originally he had wanted to be a dancer). His first great success came in 1953, when he performed in Martin Frič's *The Mystery of Blood*. Here for the first time he created the type of role that would assert itself in his work more and more strongly—a hero of everyday life. The critics were enthusiastic about his performance, but in the years that followed, the cinema was unable to offer him roles that matched the level of his talent. In 1958 he met the director Zdeněk Podskalský during their work on the film *Between Heaven and Earth*. Brodský conceived the story and also played the leading role, that of a pretty clerk who is given the courage to stand up to injustice only by the anticipation of impending death. Here Podskalský, a specialist in film humor, gives Brodský his first opportunity to use the comic side of his genius. Brodský went on to develop this talent in collaborations with Podskalský on subsequent films, including *Where the Devil Cannot Get*, *The Girl from the Moon*, *The White Lady*, and *Night at Karlštejn*.

Brodský's unique comedic talent has been put to good use by many directors in dozens of minor and major parts. But the best acting opportunities were offered to him by the directors of the Czech New Wave in the sixties—Vojtěch Jasný in *That Cat*, Evald Schorm in *Courage for Everyday* and *End of a Priest*, and Jiří Menzel in *Capricious Summer* and *Larks on a String*. These directors made it possible for Brodský to develop another talent, one that would eventually become predominant: the ability to express, under a veneer of seeming lightness, sadness caused by the external contrast between ideals and their realization in life and the irreversible flow of time. Brodský then applied the whole range of his mature acting in varying degrees in films—for the last time in *Too Noisy Solitude after Bohumil Hrabal*—on television, and in the theater, although he had already stopped appearing regularly on stage. In his inimitable noblesse he tells us his experience as an actor, his life story, and his declaration of humanity in his autobiography, *Tidbits from a Soul Hock Shop*, published in 1995.

—Blažena Urgošiková

BRONSON, Charles

Nationality: American. **Born:** Charles Buchinsky in Ehrenfield, Pennsylvania, 3 November 1920 (some sources list 1921). **Education:** Attended Pasadena Community Playhouse school. **Military Service:** U.S. Army, 1943-45: gunner. **Family:** Married 1) Harriet Tendler, 1949 (divorced 1965); two children; 2) the actress Jill Ireland 1968 (died 1990), one daughter Zuleika and three stepchildren. **Career:** 1935—worked in coal mine in Pennsylvania; after World War II— studied art and joined Philadelphia Play and Players Troupe as set designer; 1947—began acting in and around New York; 1949—enrolled at Pasadena Community Playhouse; 1951—began playing small roles in Hollywood films; 1954—changed name to "Bronson"; 1958-60—in TV series *Man with a Camera*; 1963-64—in TV series *Empire* and *The Travels of Jamie McPheeters*; 1968—left Hollywood to make films in Europe; 1971-72—returned to acting in Hollywood films. **Address:** 3210 Retreat Court, Malibu, CA 90263. **Agent:** c/o Paul Kohner, Michael Levy Agency, 9169 Sunset Boulevard, Los Angeles, CA 90069, U.S.A.

Films as Actor:

(as Charles Buchinsky)

1951 *You're in the Navy Now* (*U.S.S. Teakettle*) (Hathaway) (as Wascylewski); *The People against O'Hara* (John Sturges) (as Angelo Korvac); *The Mob* (*Remember That Face*) (Parrish) (as Jack)

1952 *Red Skies of Montana* (*Smoke Jumpers*) (Joseph M. Newman) (as Neff); *My Six Convicts* (Fregonese) (as Jocko); *The Marrying Kind* (Cukor) (as Eddie); *Pat and Mike* (Cukor) (as Hank Tasling); *Diplomatic Courier* (Hathaway) (as Bronson); *Bloodhounds of Broadway* (Harmon Jones)

1953 *House of Wax* (de Toth) (as Igor); *Miss Sadie Thompson* (Bernhardt) (as Pvt. Edwards); *The Clown* (Leonard) (as Eddie)

1954 *Crime Wave* (*The City Is Dark*) (de Toth) (as Hastings); *Tennessee Champ* (Wilcox) (as Sixty Jubel); *Riding Shotgun* (de Toth) (as Pinto); *Apache* (Aldrich) (as Hondo); *Vera Cruz* (Aldrich) (as Pittsburgh)

(as Charles Bronson)

1954 *Drum Beat* (Daves) (as Capt. Jack)

1955 *Big House, U.S.A.* (Koch) (as Benny Kelly); *Target Zero* (Harmon Jones) (as Sgt. Vince Gaspari)

1956 *Jubal* (Daves) (as Reb Haislipp)

1957 *Run of the Arrow* (*Hot Lead*) (Fuller) (as Blue Buffalo)

1958 *Machine Gun Kelly* (Corman) (title role); *Gang War* (Fowler Jr.) (as Alan Avery); *Showdown at Boot Hill* (Fowler Jr.) (as Luke Welsh); *When Hell Broke Loose* (Crane) (as Steve Boland); *Ten North Frederick* (Dunne)

1959 *Never So Few* (John Sturges) (as Sgt. John Danforth)

1960 *The Magnificent Seven* (John Sturges) (as O'Reilly)

1961 *Master of the World* (Witney) (as Strock); *A Thunder of Drums* (Joseph M. Newman) (as Trooper Hanna); *X-15* (Richard Donner) (as Lt. Col. Lee Brandon)

1962 *This Rugged Land* (Hiller); *Kid Galahad* (Karlson) (as Lew Nyack); *The Meanest Men in the West* (Fuller) (as Harge Talbot Jr.)

1963 *The Great Escape* (John Sturges) (as Danny Velinski); *Four for Texas* (Aldrich) (as Matson)

1964 *Guns of Diablo* (Sagal) (as Linc Murdock)

1965 *The Sandpiper* (Minnelli) (as Cos Erickson); *Battle of the Bulge* (Annakin) (as Major Wolenski)

1966 *This Property Is Condemned* (Pollack) (as J. J. Nichols)

1967 *The Dirty Dozen* (Aldrich) (as Joseph Wladislaw); *La Bataille de San Sébastian* (*Guns for San Sebastian*) (Verneuil) (as Teclo)

1968 *Adieu l'ami* (*Farewell Friend*; *Honor among Thieves*) (Herman) (as Franz Propp); *Villa Rides* (Kulik) (as Fierro); *C'era una volta il West* (*Once upon a Time in the West*) (Leone) (as the Man "Harmonica")

Charles Bronson in *Hard Times*

1969 *Twinky* (*Lola*) (Richard Donner) (as Scott Wardman); *Le Passager de la pluie* (*Rider on the Rain*) (Clément) (as Col. Harry Dobbs)

1970 *You Can't Win 'em All* (Collinson) (as Josh Corey); *Città violenta* (*Violent City*; *The Family*) (Solima) (as Jeff)

1971 *Soleil rouge* (*Red Sun*) (Terence Young) (as Link); *Quelqu'un derriére la porte* (*Two Minds for Murder*; *Someone behind the Door*) (Gessner) (as the stranger); *Chato's Land* (Winner) (as Chato); *L'uomo dalle due ombre* (*De la part des copains*; *Cold Sweat*) (Terence Young) (as Joe Martin)

1972 *The Valachi Papers* (*Joe Valachi: I segretti di Cosa Nostra*) (Terence Young) (as Joseph Valachi); *The Mechanic* (Winner) (as Arthur Bishop)

1973 *The Stone Killer* (Winner) (as Det. Lou Torrey); *Valdez il mezzosanque* (*The Valdez Horses*; *Valdez, the Halfbreed*; *Chino*) (John Sturges and Coletti) (as Chino Valdez)

1974 *Mr. Majestyk* (Fleischer) (title role); *Death Wish* (Winner) (as Paul Kersey)

1975 *Breakout* (Gries) (as Nick Colton); *Hard Times* (*The Streetfighter*) (Walter Hill) (as Chaney); *Breakheart Pass* (Gries) (as John Deakin)

1976 *From Noon Till Three* (Gilroy) (as Graham Dorsey); *St. Ives* (J. Lee Thompson) (as Raymond St. Ives)

1977 *Raid on Entebbe* (Kershner—for TV) (as General Dan Shomron); *Telefon* (Siegel) (as Grigori Borzov); *The White Buffalo* (*Hunt to Kill*) (J. Lee Thompson) (as Wild Bill Hickok/James Otis)

1978 *Love and Bullets* (Rosenberg) (as Charlie Congers)

1979 *Caboblanco* (J. Lee Thompson) (as Giff Hoyt)

1980 *Borderline* (Freedman) (as Jeb Maynard)

1981 *Death Hunt* (Hunt) (as Johnson); *Death Wish II* (Winner) (as Paul Kersey)

1982 *10 to Midnight* (J. Lee Thompson) (as Leo Kessler)

1984 *The Evil that Men Do* (J. Lee Thompson) (as Holland)

1985 *Death Wish III* (Winner) (as Paul Kersey)

1986 *Murphy's Law* (J. Lee Thompson) (as Jack Murphy); *Act of Vengeance* (Mackenzie—for TV) (as Jock Yablonski)

1987 *Assassination* (Hunt) (as Jay Killian); *Death Wish IV: The Crackdown* (J. Lee Thompson) (as Paul Kersey); *Wild West* (compilation)

1988 *Messenger of Death* (*Avenging Angels*) (J. Lee Thompson) (as Garrett Smith)

1989 *Kinjite: Forbidden Subjects* (J. Lee Thompson) (as Lt. Crowe); *Act of Vengeance . . . A True Story* (Mackenzie—for TV)

1991 *The Indian Runner* (Sean Penn) (as Father); *Yes, Virginia, There Is a Santa Claus* (Jarrott—for TV) (as Francis Church)

1993   *The Sea Wolf* (Michael Anderson—for TV) (as Capt. Wolf
        Larsen); *Donato and Daughter* (Holcomb—for TV) (as Sgt.
        Mike Donato)
1994   *Death Wish V: The Face of Death* (Goldstein) (as Paul Kersey)

Publications

By BRONSON: articles—

"A Conversation with Charles Bronson," by C. L. Hanson in *Cinema*
(Beverly Hills), December 1965.
Interview in *Cinéma 71* (Paris), January 1971.
"Yes, Virginia, There Is a Charles Bronson," interview with Mary
Murphy, in *TV Guide* (Radnor, Pennsylvania), 7 December 1991.

On BRONSON: books—

Harbinson, William A., *Bronson! A Biographical Portrait*, London,
1976.
Vermilye, Jerry, *The Films of Charles Bronson*, Secaucus, New Jersey,
1980.
Downing, David, *Charles Bronson*, New York, 1983.
Setbon, Philippe, *Bronson*, Paris, 1983.

On BRONSON: articles—

"Here Comes Charlie," in *Newsweek* (New York), 29 May 1972.
Ebert, Roger, "Bronson Speak! You Listen!," in *Esquire* (New York),
August 1974.
Kauffman, Stanley, "World's Most Popular Actor," in *New Republic*
(New York), 10 August 1974.
Current Biography 1975, New York, 1975.
Dickey, James, "Charles Bronson: Silence under the First," in *Close-
Ups: The Movie Star Book*, edited by Danny Peary, New York, 1978.
Classic Images (Indiana, Pennsylvania), July and August 1982.

*   *   *

The French call Charles Bronson "the sacred monster." That quality and the characteristics suggested by the "man of few words" and
"man of action" are the main reasons Bronson became one of the "big
three" of film macho-men of the 1970s. He is often compared with
Clint Eastwood or Burt Reynolds, but Bronson's masculinity is
unglamorized, distant, and often brutal in a fashion that previously
had not been particularly successful with American audiences until
Eastwood himself paved the way with his series of Sergio Leone revenge Westerns in the 1960s. Unlike Eastwood, Bronson had appeared in major roles in many Hollywood films by then, but his ascendancy to stardom, like Eastwood's, evolved in Europe.

Burt Reynolds has said of Bronson that there is an "undercurrent of
danger" in his characterizations. The subtle explosiveness is the element of his acting style that is most exploited in his major roles in
Europe. The first real example is Sergio Leone's *Once upon a Time in
the West* in which Bronson plays a ruthless gunfighter seeking revenge.
The vengeance scenario has in fact always been the ideal one for
Bronson's volatile and seemingly ruthless personality on screen—
most notably in the series of *Death Wish* films he made after his
stardom in Europe transitioned to America. For the director Michael
Winner, Bronson brought these qualities to his portrayal of a betrayed
hitman in *The Mechanic* and to that of a Mafia driver whose past
becomes a threat to him in *Cold Sweat*. In both films Bronson's
character at first glimpse seems to be resigned and calm, but ultimately
he explodes violently against those who threaten him. Early on in his
career, he satirized his already evolving tough-guy screen image as the

outwardly macho but inwardly gutless real-life title character in Roger
Corman's *Machine Gun Kelly*.

Bronson began in films in 1951, billing himself under his real name,
Charles Buchinsky, until 1954 in the Western *Drum Beat* opposite
Alan Ladd. From the beginning, his rugged persona lent itself mostly
to action films, gangster films and Westerns, in which he was often
cast as an Indian or Mexican. He specialized in action films, except
for occasional anomalies such as the 3-D horror thriller *House of Wax*,
the torrid *Miss Sadie Thompson*, and the Red Skelton comedy-
tearjerker, *The Clown*.

The action films in which Bronson has appeared in America are far
less cynical than his European films, and he benefited from working
with some of the great masters of the action genre: John Sturges in
The Magnificent Seven and *The Great Escape*; Robert Aldrich in
Apache, Vera Cruz, Four for Texas, and *The Dirty Dozen*; and Don
Siegel in *Telefon*. His greatest commercial success in America has been
Death Wish, in which he plays an unassuming architect who becomes
an obsessed urban vigilante after his wife and daughter are brutalized by
street punks. The film was followed by four sequels. His virtually
nonstop activity as a major screen tough guy slacked off a bit following the death of his wife Jill Ireland, with whom he often co-starred; he
has appeared in only two big screen films since—Sean Penn's *The
Indian Runner*, and the latest (to date) installment in the long-running *Death Wish* series, titled *Death Wish V: The Face of Death*. In
1986, he had a memorable turn as the murdered United Mine Workers
official Jock Yablonski in the made-for-cable docudrama *Act of Vengeance*, one of Bronson's few forays into television since his own,
now almost forgotten, TV series *Man with a Camera* disappeared
from the airwaves in the 1950s.

Although in the past the Bronson persona has always seemed to
work best in roles in which he plays the bad guy or the madman, a
degree of variation has been involved in some of his more recent
films, such as the offbeat Frank D. Gilroy Western *From Noon Till
Three*, in which Bronson again kidded his image, and *10 to Midnight*,
where he played a police detective who, to get his man, uses the same
means as the psycho he is tracking—in "the name of the law." The
role seemed to marry the role of the brutal man of action which made
him a star in Europe to that of the righteous avenger, which made him
a star in America.

—Rob Winning, updated by John McCarty

BROOKS, Louise

Nationality: American. **Born:** Cherryvale, Kansas, 14 November
1906. **Family:** Married 1) the director Edward Sutherland, 1926 (divorced 1928); 2) Deering Davis (divorced 1933). **Career:** With mother
as accompanist, performed as a child at fairs and other public gather-
ings in southeast Kansas; 1919—family moved to Wichita, Kansas;
1922—joined the Denishawn Dancers; 1924—dismissed from Dancers; began dancing in chorus of *George White's Scandals* on Broadway;
1924-25—briefly danced in London, returned to New York and cast
by Florenz Ziegfeld in *Louie the 14th* 1925—film debut in *The Street
of Forgotten Men* 1925-26—last Broadway appearances in *Ziegfeld
Follies* of 1925/26; late 1925—contract with Paramount; 1927—
Paramount Astoria studios closed, sent to Hollywood; 1928—in Berlin at request of G. W. Pabst, for lead in *Pandora's Box*; 1930—first
talkie, *Prix de beauté*; 1930—returned to Hollywood, promised (but
not given) contract by Columbia; 1931—small roles in pre-Broadway
run of *Louder Please*; early 1930s—in nightclub dance act; 1936-
38—returned briefly to Hollywood in small roles; 1940-43—ran dance
studios in Wichita; 1943—moved to New York City, worked in radio

soap serials, publicity agencies, and as saleslady at Saks Fifth Avenue store; 1948—quit job at Saks, "kept" by rich men for several years; 1955—work is featured by Henry Langlois in Paris exhibition "60 Years of Cinema"; group of friends provide annuity; 1956—moved to Rochester, New York, at suggestion of archivist James Card at Eastman House; began writing about film history and personalities for *Sight and Sound*, *Film Culture*, and other publications. **Died:** 8 August 1985.

Films as Actress:

1925   *The Street of Forgotten Men* (Brenon) (bit role)
1926   *The American Venus* (Tuttle) (as Miss Bayport); *A Social Celebrity* (St. Clair); *It's the Old Army Game* (Sutherland) (as Mildred Marshall); *The Show-Off* (St. Clair) (as Clara); *Just Another Blonde* (Santell) (as Dian O'Sullivan); *Love 'em and Leave 'em* (Tuttle) (as Janie Walsh)
1927   *Evening Clothes* (Reed) (as Fox Trot); *Rolled Stockings* (Rosson) (as Carol Fleming); *The City Gone Wild* (Cruze) (as Snuggles Joy); *Now We're in the Air* (Strayer) (as Grisette Chelaine)
1928   *A Girl in Every Port* (Hawks) (as Marie); *Beggars of Life* (Wellman) (as Nancy); *Die Büchse der Pandora* (*Pandora's Box*) (Pabst) (as Lulu)
1929   *The Canary Murder Case* (St. Clair) (as Margaret O'Dell); *Das Tagebuch einer Verlorenen* (*The Diary of a Lost Girl*) (Pabst)
1930   *Prix de beauté* (*Miss Europe*; *Beauty Prize*) (Genina)
1931   *Windy Reilly Goes to Hollywood* ("William Goodrich," i.e. Roscoe Arbuckle—short); *It Pays to Advertise* (Tuttle); *God's Gift to Women* (*Too Many Women*) (Curtiz)
1936   *Empty Saddles* (Selander)
1937   *King of Gamblers* (Florey) (bit role); *When You're in Love* (*For You Alone*) (Riskin) (bit role)
1938   *Overland Stage Raiders* (Sherman)

Publications

By BROOKS: book—

Lulu in Hollywood, New York, 1982.

By BROOKS: articles—

"Pabst and Lulu," in *Sight and Sound* (London), Summer 1965.
"Humphrey Bogart," in *Sight and Sound* (London), Winter 1966/67.
"On Location with William Wellman," in *Positif* (Paris), March 1970.
"The Other Face of W. C. Fields," in *Sight and Sound* (London), Spring 1971.
"Beggars of Life," in *Focus on Film* (London), Winter 1972.
"Why I Shall Never Write My Memoirs," in *Positif* (Paris), December 1977/January 1978.

On BROOKS: books—

Atwell, Lee, *G. W. Pabst*, Boston, 1977.
Tynan, Kenneth, *Show People*, New York, 1980.
Jaccard, Roland, editor, *Louise Brooks: Portrait of an Anti-Star*, London, 1987.
Paris, Barry, *Louise Brooks*, New York, 1989.

On BROOKS: articles—

Card, James, "The 'Intense Isolation' of Louise Brooks," in *Sight and Sound* (London), Summer 1958.

Tynan, Kenneth, "The Girl Who Was Lulu," in the *Observer Magazine* (London), 11 November 1979.
"Loulou," special issue of *Avant-Scène du Cinéma* (Paris), 1 December 1980.
American Film (Washington, D.C.), October 1982.
Classic Images (Indiana, Pennsylvania), February, April, and May 1983, with additions in issue for October 1983.
Elsaesser, Thomas, "Lulu and the Meter Man," in *Screen* (London), vol. 24, nos 4-5, July/October 1983.
Sarris, Andrew, in *Village Voice* (New York), 27 September 1983.
Brooks issue of *Filmcritica* (Rome), July 1984.
Obituary in *Variety* (New York), 14 August 1985.
Louise Brooks Section of *Positif* (Paris), November 1985.
Everson, William K., "Remembering Louise Brooks," in *Films in Review* (New York), November 1985.
Herrmann, L., "Louise Brooks," in *Frauen und Film* (Frankfurt), December 1985.
Paris, Barry, "Lulu in Rochester," in *American Film* (New York), September 1986.
Paris, Barry, "Our Wild Miss Brooks," in *American Film* (Hollywood), vol. 15, no. 2, 1989.
Yusuf, Nilgin, "The Girl in the Black Helmet," in the *Guardian* (London), 2 April 1990.

* * *

Louise Brooks is one of those rare personalities in the screen acting profession who make a sudden, sensational rise to fame as a unique artist and then in effect disappear from public view—not, however, in her case with quite the archetypical suddenness of a Falconetti; nevertheless, she made a similar mark in film history as a great actress with a permanent and, happily, a faithfully recorded place. She was, in a way, for a period in the 1930s, betrayed by her own particular kind of success and by the very role with which she was identified and in which she proved so remarkably potent. "I was possessed by the tramp essence of Lulu," she told Kenneth Tynan in her old age.

Dark, petite, bob-haired, with an excellent figure and a face (especially the eyes) of striking beauty and vivacity, she appeared at first as yet another lively, loose-living "flapper," pacesetting the jazz-age. By 15 she was a dancer (*George White's Scandals*, *The Ziegfeld Follies*) with Martha Graham as companion. After a brief, patchy, self-indulgent career, during which she acquired such friends as Humphrey Bogart and W. C. Fields, by the mid-1920s she was under contract in Hollywood for routine appearances in films with such titles as *The American Venus*, *Love 'em and Leave 'em* and *Rolled Stockings*. She learned how to project her personality in comedy until directors of caliber, Howard Hawks and William Wellman, starred her and developed her amoral talents in two films of 1928 that are now forgotten, *A Girl in Every Port* and *Beggars of Life*. She had never trained as an actress, "I was simply playing myself," she said. But she was also creating an image that was to attract attention abroad.

It was G. W. Pabst, the distinguished Austrian director of fatalistic, psychological silent films made in German studios, who raised her in 1929, when she was still only 23, to the rank of a great actress in two of his finest and most demanding silent films—*Die Büchse der Pandora* and *Das Tagebuch einer Verlorenen*. In the first (adapted, like Berg's opera *Lulu*, from Frank Wederkind's two highly erotic plays *Erdgeist* and *Die Büchse der Pandora*) she brought to the part of Lulu an intense vivacity and an almost childlike charm along with a kind of innocently immoral depravity. Throughout the prolonged action, in which she plays with such highly established actors as Fritz Kortner and Gustav Diessl (Jack the Ripper), Brooks holds the film together by sheer screen personality, and the final scene with the Ripper has detail of action and understanding of psychotic sexuality unmatched for its period.

Louise Brooks

Brooks went on to act with similar subtlety and beauty in *Das Tagebuch einer Verlorenen* (with Fritz Rasp), which is in many respects a better constructed, less episodic film than its predecessor. After giving another excellent performance in a somewhat cliché-ridden French film, *Prix de beauté*, directed by the Italian Augusto Genina, she returned to Hollywood the same year and to virtual obscurity, performing bit parts and working in cabaret. She ultimately retired in 1938, working modestly outside the industry and eventually, when still little more than 40, becoming a recluse; she lived alone in Rochester, New York, after 1956. Kenneth Tynan's celebrated interview with her (in his book *Show People*) gives a portrait of her when she was 71; this was to be supplemented by her own *Lulu in Hollywood*.

A woman of considerable intellectual ability and independence of judgment, Brooks began during the 1950s to write occasionally for the more thoughtful film journals after the revival of interest in Pabst's silent films, and she appeared at one or two film festivals, notably in Paris in 1958.

—Roger Manvell

BROOKS, Mel

Nationality: American. **Born:** Melvin Kaminsky in Brooklyn, New York, 28 June 1926. **Education:** Attended Virginia Military Institute, 1944, and Brooklyn College. **Family:** Married 1) Florence Baum (divorced), one son, two daughters; 2) the actress Anne Bancroft, one son. **Career:** 1944-46—combat engineer, U.S. Army; late 1940s—jazz drummer, stand-up comedian, and social director, Grossinger's resorts; 1950-58—writer and occasional performer for Sid Caesar's TV show; 1963—conceived, wrote, and narrated cartoon short *The Critic*; 1965—co-creator (with Buck Henry) of *Get Smart* TV show (ran 1965-69); 1968—directed first feature, *The Producers*; 1975—creator and producer of TV series *When Things Were Rotten*; 1980—founder, Brooksfilms. **Awards:** Academy Award for Best Short Subject, for *The Critic*, 1963; Academy Award for Best Story and Screenplay, and Writers Guild Award for Best Written Screenplay, for *The Producers*, 1969; American Comedy Awards Lifetime Achievement Award, 1987. **Address:** 2301 La Mesa, Santa Monica, CA 90405, U.S.A.

Films as Actor:

1969 *Putney Swope* (Downey) (as Mr. Forget It)
1979 *The Muppet Movie* (Frawley) (as Professor Max Krassman)
1983 *To Be or Not to Be* (Alan Johnson) (as Frederick Bronski, + pr, co-sc)
1990 *Look Who's Talking, Too!* (Heckerling) (as voice of Mr. Toilet Man)
1994 *Il silenzio dei prosciutti* (*The Silence of the Hams*) (Greggio); *The Little Rascals* (Spheeris) (as Mr. Welling)

Films as Actor, Director, and Scriptwriter:

1963 *The Critic* (animated) (as narrator)
1968 *The Producers* (as narrator)
1970 *The Twelve Chairs* (as Tikon, + mus)
1974 *Blazing Saddles* (as Governor Lepetomane/Indian Chief, co-sc, + mus); *Young Frankenstein* (*Frankenstein Jr.*) (co-sc)
1976 *Silent Movie* (as Mel Funn, co-sc)

1977 *High Anxiety* (as Dr. Richard Thorndyke, co-sc, + pr, mus)
1981 *History of the World, Part I* (as Moses/Comicus/Torquemada/Jacques/King Louis XVI, co-sc, + pr, mus)
1987 *Spaceballs* (as President Skroob/Yogurt, co-sc, + pr)
1991 *Life Stinks!* (as Goddard Bolt, co-sc, + pr)
1993 *Robin Hood: Men in Tights* (as Rabbi Tuckman, co-sc, + pr)
1995 *Dracula: Dead and Loving It* (as Dr. Abraham Van Helsing, co-sc, + pr)

Films as Executive Producer:

1980 *The Elephant Man* (David Lynch)
1985 *The Doctor and the Devils* (Francis)
1986 *The Fly* (Cronenberg); *Solarbabies* (Johnson)
1987 *84 Charing Cross Road* (David Jones)
1992 *The Vagrant* (Walas)

Publications

By BROOKS: books—

Silent Movie, New York, 1976.
History of the World, Part I, New York, 1981.
The 2000 Year Old Man, with Carl Reiner, New York, 1981.

By BROOKS: articles—

"Confessions of an Auteur," in *Action* (Los Angeles), November/December 1971.
Interview with James Atlas, in *Film Comment* (New York), March/April 1975.
"Fond Salutes and Naked Hate," interview with Gordon Gow, in *Films and Filming* (London), July 1975.
Interview with A. Remond, in *Ecran* (Paris), November 1976.
"Comedy Directors: Interview with Mel Brooks," interview with R. Rivlin, in *Millimeter* (New York), October and December 1977.
Interview with Alan Yentob, in *Listener* (London), 8 October 1981.
Interview in *Time Out* (London), 16 February 1984.
Interview in *Screen International*, 3 March 1984.
Interview in *Hollywood Reporter*, 27 October 1986.
Interview with L. Stegel, in *Playboy* (Chicago), January 1989.
"Mel Brooks: Of Woody, the Great Caesar, Flop Sweat and Cigar Smoke," in *People Weekly* (New York), Summer 1989 (special issue).

On BROOKS: books—

Adler, Bill, and Jeffrey Fineman, *Mel Brooks: The Irreverent Funnyman*, Chicago, 1976.
Bendazzi, G., *Mel Brooks: l'ultima follia di Hollywood*, Milan, 1977.
Holtzman, William, *Seesaw: A Dual Biography of Anne Bancroft and Mel Brooks*, New York, 1979.
Allen, Steve, *Funny People*, New York, 1981.
Yacowar, Maurice, *Method in Madness: The Comic Art of Mel Brooks*, New York, 1981.
Smurthwaite, Nick, and Paul Gelder, *Mel Brooks and the Spoof Movie*, London, 1982.
Squire, Jason E., *The Movie Business Book*, Englewood Cliffs, New Jersey, 1983.

On BROOKS: articles—

"Two Thousand Year Old Man," in *Newsweek* (New York), 4 October 1965.

Mel Brooks in *High Anxiety*

Current Biography 1974, New York, 1974.

Diehl, D., "Mel Brooks," in *Action* (Los Angeles), January/February 1975.

Lees, G., "The Mel Brooks Memos," in *American Film* (Washington, D.C.), October 1977.

Carcassonne, P., "Dossier: Hollywood 79: Mel Brooks," in *Cinématographe* (Paris), March 1979.

Karoubi, N., "Mel Brooks Follies," in *Cinéma* (Paris), February 1982.

Dictionary of Literary Biography, Vol. 26: American Screenwriters, Detroit, 1984.

Erens, Patricia, "You Could Die Laughing: Jewish Humor and Film," in *East-West Film Journal* (Honolulu), no.1, 1987.

Frank, A., "Mel's Crazy Movie World," in *Photoplay Movies & Video* (London), January 1988.

Goldstein, T., "A History of Mel Brooks: Part I," in *Video* (New York), March 1988.

Stauth, C., "Mel and Me," in *American Film* (Los Angeles), April 1990.

* * *

Mel Brooks has said that the funniest man in the world is Harry Ritz of The Ritz Brothers, the successful sibling comic act of the 1930s and 1940s. Harry and his brothers had a Catskill Mountain style of Jewish humor, the basis of which is snappy patter, quick and graceful moves, funny faces, and meticulous comic timing. For the past 25 years, Brooks has been trying to fit Harry Ritz's comedy style into his own film acting roles. As a young man in the 1940s he worked as a stand-up comic in the Borscht Belt, and it was there that he fine-tuned his comic delivery.

Brooks's first major film role came in his production of the Russian story *The Twelve Chairs*. He plays Tikon, an elderly janitor at an old-age home which used to be the wealthy mansion of a nobleman for whom he was manservant. Tikon appears only at the start of the film, and is on screen for a relatively short time. But Tikon becomes a star turn for Brooks, as he is given the chance to play a wildly funny drunk.

Brooks's next acting job came in *Blazing Saddles*, in which he cast himself in two roles: Governor Lepetomane and an Indian Chief, both of which are parodies rather than full-fledged characterizations. One of the biggest laughs in a film crammed with belly laughs comes when the Chief suddenly starts talking Yiddish. It is not so much Brooks's acting ability as it is his comic timing and the surprise gag that leave audiences teary-eyed with delight. In later endeavors, perhaps because many in his audience did not understand the source of the humor, Brooks stopped emphasizing comedy that relies on a Jewish ethnic identity and pursued more mainstream themes.

In *Silent Movie* he plays a has-been director. Since the movie actually is almost completely without dialog, Brooks gives a more physically expressive performance than usual, but the part is more silly than artful. *High Anxiety*, a spoof of Alfred Hitchcock's thrillers, saw him as a Harvard professor/psychiatrist, suffering from a fear of heights, who is invited to be Director of The Psycho-Neurotic Institute for the Very, Very Nervous. As in his previous roles, Brooks presents a skillful, polished—though at times manic—comic performance.

Two performances stand out for Brooks, the screen actor. The first is his starring part as famed Polish stage star Frederick Bronski in his remake of Ernst Lubitsch's black comedy *To Be or Not To Be*. In this satire about a group of Warsaw thespians facing Nazi extermination at the beginning of World War II, Brooks plays the first full-bodied role of his career. Bronski first appears singing and dancing a hilarious Polish-language version of "Sweet Georgia Brown" with Anne Bancroft, playing his wife and partner Anna Bronski. The duet is a milestone in movie comedy, the sort of clip one might choose to take to a desert island. But the character of Bronski does more than sing and dance. Brooks is called upon to show Bronski as a man who tries to be brave and funny while in danger of losing his house, his theater, the lives of his colleagues and wife, and his own life. Brooks also spends much of the film as Bronski posing as other characters, particularly a bearded Nazi-scientist who has an eye for his wife. Brooks has scenes where he expresses fear and sadness very convincingly, although the script is structured so that each of these emotional moments is followed by a comical line. A final note about Brooks in *To Be or Not to Be*: He is the first and only comedy actor to play Hamlet and Hitler in the same film!

The second fully developed Brooks character appears in *Life Stinks!*, an otherwise disappointing attempt at a comedy involving the lives of homeless people. In what might be deemed Brooks's least funny film, he gives his most serious, naturalistic performance to date. He is Goddard Bolt, a heartless billionaire who agrees to live without money (or wig) for 30 days in a Los Angeles slum area in order to win a lucrative bet. On the streets for a couple of days, lacking food and shelter, he adopts more humane values and concerns. The film is slower-paced than his previous works, allowing Brooks to offer a more thoughtful and sensitive portrayal.

Many comedians—Jerry Lewis, Charlie Chaplin, Milton Berle, Bert Lahr, and Danny Kaye are just a few—have given outstanding dramatic performances on stage, screen and television. Now that Mel Brooks, master of comedy, has disclosed a talent for portraying man's serious side, perhaps he will execute a straight dramatic characterization in the future.

—Audrey E. Kupferberg

BROWN, Joe E.

Nationality: American. **Born:** Joseph Evan Brown in Holgate, Ohio, 28 July 1892. **Family:** Married Frances McGraw, 24 December 1915, children: Donald Evan, Joe LeRoy, adopted daughters Mary Elizabeth Ann and Kathryn Frances. **Career:** 1902—joined tumbling act The Five Marvelous Ashtons and toured with Sells and Downs Circus, then the John Robinson Circus, and later vaudeville; 1906—joined acrobatic act the Bell-Prevost Trio; later played burlesque circuit as The Prevost Brothers, and then Prevost and Brown with Brown nicknamed The Corkscrew Kid; mid-'teens—played semipro baseball during summer layoffs from vaudeville and burlesque; c. 1918—following first "single" act in burlesque show *Sporting Widows*, offered lead in *Listen Lester* on Broadway; 1918-28—in several musicals on and off Broadway; mid-1920s—in Vitaphone one-reeler *Don't Be Jealous*; 1928—signed for film *Crooks Can't Win* after director Ralph Ince saw him on Broadway in *Twinkle Twinkle*; 1930—long-term contract with Warners after success of *Hold Everything*; 1930s-40s—worked frequently on radio; 1939—began freelancing for various studios including RKO, MGM, and Columbia; 1941-45—entertained troops during World War II; Bronze Star; 1950s—frequent television appearances; 1964—last media appearance in *The Greatest Show on Earth* for ABC-TV. **Died:** In Brentwood, California, 6 July 1973.

Films as Actor:

1928 *Crooks Can't Win* (Ralph Ince); *Me, Gangster* (Walsh); *Road House* (Rosson or McGuinness); *Dressed to Kill* (Cummings); *Burlesque*; *Don't Be Jealous* (produced mid-1920s); *Hit of the Show* (Ralph Ince); *The Circus Kid* (Seitz) (as King Kruger); *Take Me Home* (Neilan)

1929 *On with the Show* (Crosland) (as Ike); *The Dancing Instructor*; *In Old Arizona* (Walsh) (as bartender); *Sunny Side Up* (David Butler) (as Joe Vitto); *The Cock Eyed-World* (Walsh) (as

Brownie); *The Ghost Talks* (Seiler) (as Peter Accardi); *Protection* (Stoloff); *Molly and Me* (Albert Ray) (as Jim Wilson); *My Lady's Past* (Ray); *Sally* (Dillon) (as Connie); *Painted Faces* (Rogell) (as Hermann/Beppo)

1930   *Screen Snapshots No. Five*; *Up the River* (Ford) (as Deputy Warden); *Born Reckless* (Ford) (as Needle Beer Grogan); *City Girl* (Murnau); *Song of the West* (Enright) (as Hasty); *Hold Everything* (Del Ruth) (as Gink Schiner); *Top Speed* (LeRoy) (as Elmer Peters); *The Lottery Bride* (Stein) (as Hoke Curtis); *Maybe It's Love* (Wellman) (as Speed Hanson)

1931   *Screen Snapshots No. Eight*; *Going Wild* (Seiter) (as Rollo Smith); *Sit Tight* (Lloyd Bacon) (as Jojo); *Broad Minded* (LeRoy) (as Ossie Simpson); *Local Boy Makes Good* (LeRoy) (as John Miller)

1932   *The Tenderfoot* (Enright) (as Peter Jones); *The Putter*; *The Stolen Jools* (*The Slippery Pearls*) (McGann and others—short); *Fireman, Save My Child* (Lloyd Bacon) (as Joe Grant); *You Said a Mouthful* (Lloyd Bacon) (as Joe Holt)

1933   *Hollywood on Parade No. Eight*; *Elmer the Great* (LeRoy) (as Elmer); *Son of a Sailor* (Lloyd Bacon) (as Handsome Callahan)

1934   *A Very Honorable Guy* (Lloyd Bacon) (as Feet Samuels); *The Circus Clown* (Enright) (as Happy Howard/his father); *Six-Day Bike Rider* (Lloyd Bacon) (as Wilfred Simpson)

1935   *Alibi Ike* (Enright) (as Frank X. Farrell); *Bright Lights* (Berkeley) (as Joe Wilson); *A Midsummer Night's Dream* (Reinhardt and Dieterle) (as Flute)

1936   *Sons o' Guns* (Lloyd Bacon) (as Jimmy Canfield); *Earthworm Tractors* (*Natural Born Salesman*) (Enright) (as Alexander Botts); *Polo Joe* (McGann) (as Joe Bolton)

1937   *When's Your Birthday?* (Beaumont) (as Dustin Willoughby); *Riding on Air* (*All Is Confusion*) (Sedgwick) (as Elmer Lane); *Fit for a King* (Sedgwick) (as Virgil Jones)

1938   *Wide Open Faces* (Neumann) (as Wilbur Meeks); *The Gladiator* (Sedgwick) (as Hugo Kipp); *Flirting with Fate* (McDonald) (as Dixon)

1939   *$1,000 a Touchdown* (Hogan) (as Marlowe Mansfield Booth); *Beware Spooks!* (Sedgwick) (as Roy Gifford)

1940   *So You Won't Talk* (Sedgwick) (as Whiskers/Brute Hanson)

1942   *The Daring Young Man* (*Brownie*) (Strayer); *Shut My Big Mouth* (Barton) (as Wellington Holmes); *Joan of Ozark* (*Queen of Spies*) (Santley) (as Cliff Little)

1943   *Chatterbox* (Santley) (as Rex Vane)

1944   *Casanova in Burlesque* (Goodwins) (as Joseph M. Kelly Jr./Casanova); *Pin-Up Girl* (Humberstone) (as Eddie); *Hollywood Canteen* (Daves) (as himself)

1947   *The Tender Years* (Schuster) (as the Rev. Will Norris)

1951   *Show Boat* (Sidney) (as Capt. Andy Hawks)

1952   *Memories of Famous Hollywood Comedians* (as narrator)

1954   *Hollywood Fathers*

1956   *Around the World in Eighty Days* (Anderson) (as stationmaster)

1959   **Some Like It Hot** (Wilder) (as Osgood E. Fielding III)

1963   *It's a Mad, Mad, Mad, Mad World* (Kramer) (as union official)

1964   *The Comedy of Terrors* (*The Graveside Story*; *Comedy of Horrors*) (Jacques Tourneur) (as cemetery keeper)

Publications

By BROWN: books—

Your Kids and Mine, New York, 1944.

Laughter Is a Wonderful Thing, as told to Ralph Hancock, New York, 1956.

On BROWN: book—

Parish, James Robert, *The Funsters*, New Rochelle, 1979.

On BROWN: articles—

Current Biography 1945, New York, 1945.
Obituary in *New York Times*, 7 July 1973.
Phelps, Donald, "Golden Boy: The Life, Times, and Comedic Genius of Joe E. Brown," in *Film Comment* (New York), November/December 1994.

*   *   *

In *Fireman, Save My Child*, *Elmer the Great*, and *Alibi Ike*, Joe E. Brown plays a bush-league baseball player with phenomenal talents as a pitcher or hitter. He is egotistical about those skills, but he has all the naivety of a country bumpkin. Arriving in the big city to play on a major league team, the rube appears to be easy prey for crooks and a shady lady. But he not only defeats, by pluck and luck, the villains who plague him, he also wins the game and the hand of the little girl back home.

In many of his films Brown plays the eager young-man-next-door—a direct descendant of the "go-getters" of the 1920s, of whom Harold Lloyd was the most successful. In fact, Brown's 1931 college picture, *Local Boy Makes Good*, has many of the characteristics of Lloyd's 1925 *The Freshman*. Written by Elliot Nugent, *Local Boy* has Brown portraying a meek social outcast who tries to become popular by becoming an athlete. The shy little fellow struggles and wins out in the end, in a climatic track race.

In the three baseball pictures, Brown fully developed this comic portrait. *Elmer the Great*, one of his best films, was originally written by Ring Lardner and George M. Cohan as a stage play. Brown found the lack of immediate audience reaction in films to be adversely affecting the development of his comic skills, and he returned to the stage in this play to hone his talents and boost his morale. Because he had also played professional baseball himself, and continued to be involved with many of the colorful personalities in that sport, he was able to sketch a convincing Elmer—a sleepy-eyed, naive, small-town ballplayer who has superhuman talent on the diamond. He used audience response to refine his portrayal. The character—and the film, which could be seen by a much larger audience—obviously profited from Brown's decision to play the role on the stage first.

In *Earthworm Tractors* Brown portrays not an athlete but a struggling salesman; it is the outstanding comedy film of his career. Once more, the film is essentially in the vein of the Horatio Alger rags-to-riches saga. By 1936, when the film was made, the triumphant athlete story had been rather overworked, and the eager young man selling tractors offered a certain freshness. The director Ray Enright, a former gagman for Mack Sennett, proved that a comic writer can sometimes prove an inspired director. *Earthworm Tractors* contains excellent gags—the best in any of Brown's pictures—and Enright seemed to understand how to handle the comedian to get a lively, spontaneous performance.

Some of Brown's later films demonstrate just how important the lack of a good director could be, for there were basic problems with Brown's comic style. His ability to control the level of comic overstatement was faulty, at times he overacted a scene, not knowing when to stop. The "success story," of which his films are variants, is in fact from a genteel comic tradition: Brown sometimes used a style that was too broad, that suggested that more farcical events were about to transpire.

But, at his best, when his talent as a comedian was properly controlled, Brown could be very good indeed; he displayed a charm and magnetism that only great comedians possess. Although he never achieved the critical acclaim accorded such comic actors as W. C. Fields or the Marx Brothers, Brown enjoyed great popularity in the 1930s, almost as great as that of Laurel and Hardy.

—Donald McCaffrey

BRYNNER, Yul

Nationality: Swiss. **Born:** Taidje Kahn on Sakhalin Island, 12 July 1915; became citizen of Switzerland, late 1960s. **Family:** Married 1) the actress Virginia Gilmore, 1944 (divorced 1960), son: Yul Brynner II; 2) Doris Kleiner, 1960 (divorced), daughter: Victoria; 3) Jacqueline de Croisset, 1972, two daughters. **Career:** 1940—came to U.S. with actor Michael Chekhov's Shakespeare company; 1942—recruited by U.S. Office of War information as radio commentator in French; 1946—Broadway debut in *Lute Song*; late 1940s—began directing for CBS-TV on series *Danger* and *Studio One*; 1949—film acting debut in *Port of New York*; 1950—director, *Life with Snarky Parker*, children's television puppet show; 1951—critical and popular attention for role of King of Siam in *The King and I* on Broadway, and in film version, 1956; 1956—formed Alciona Productions; 1958—formed Alby Productions with Anatole Litvak; 1959-62—narrated documentaries for United Nations on refugee children; late 1960s—moved to Switzerland; 1972—in U.S. TV series *The King and I*; 1972—returned to acting in Hollywood films; 1975—returned to Broadway in unsuccessful *Home Sweet Homer* 1977—in successful revival of *The King and I* on Broadway; 1981-85—on tour in revival of *The King and I*. **Awards:** Best Actor Academy Award for *The King and I*, 1956. **Died:** 10 October 1985.

Films as Actor:

1949   *Port of New York* (Benedek)

1956   *The King and I* (Walter Lang); *The Ten Commandments* (DeMille); *Anastasia* (Litvak)

1958   *The Brothers Karamazov* (Brooks); *The Buccaneer* (Quinn)

1959   *The Journey* (Litvak); *The Sound and the Fury* (Ritt); *Solomon and Sheba* (King Vidor); *Le Testament d'Orphée* (*The Testament of Orpheus*) (Cocteau); *Mission to No Man's Land* (Pessis) (as narrator)

1960   *Once More, with Feeling!* (Donen); *Profile of a Miracle* (as narrator); *Surprise Package* (Donen); *The Magnificent Seven* (John Sturges)

1961   *Goodbye Again* (*Aimez-vous Brahms?*) (Litvak); *My Friend Nicholas* (Raymond) (as narrator)

1962   *Escape from Zahrain* (Neame); *Taras Balba* (Thompson); *Man Is to Man . . .* (Wright) (as narrator)

1963   *Kings of the Sun* (Thompson)

1964   *Flight from Ashiya* (Anderson); *Invitation to a Gunfighter* (Wilson)

1965   *Morituri* (*The Saboteur Code Name "Morituri"*) (Wicki)

1966   *Paris brûle-t-il?* (*Is Paris Burning?*) (Clément); *Cast a Giant Shadow* (Shavelson); *Return of the Seven* (Kennedy); *Danger Grows Wild* (*The Poppy Is Also a Flower*) (Young); *Triple Cross* (Young)

1967   *The Long Duel* (Annakin); *The Double Man* (Schaffner)

1968   *Villa Rides* (Kulik)

1969   *Bitka na Neretvi* (*The Battle of Neretva*) (Bulajic); *The File of the Golden Goose* (Wanamaker); *The Magic Christian* (McGrath); *The Madwoman of Chaillot* (Forbes)

1970   *Indio Black, sai che ti dico: sei un gran figlio di . . .* (*Adios Sabata*; *The Bounty Hunters*) (Frank Kramer, i.e. Gianfranco Parolini)

1971   *Romance of a Horsethief* (Polonsky); *Catlow* (Wanamaker); *La Luz del fin del mundo* (*The Light at the Edge of the World*) (Billington)

1972   *The Picasso Summer* (Salin); *Fuzz* (Colla)

1973   *Le Serpent* (*Night Flight from Moscow*) (Verneuil); *Westworld* (Crichton)

1975   *The Ultimate Warrior* (Clouse)

1976   *Futureworld* (Heffron); *Con la rabbia agli occhi* (*Death Rage*; *Anger in His Eyes*) (Anthony Dawson, i.e. Antonio Margheriti)

Publications

By BRYNNER: book—

Bring Forth the Children, New York, 1960.

By BRYNNER: articles—

Interview in *Ciné Revue* (Paris), 4 September 1980.
Interview by Rocky Brynner in *Inter/View* (New York), March 1981.

On BRYNNER: books—

Robbins, Jhan, *Yul Brynner: The Inscrutable King*, New York, 1987.
Brynner, Rock, *Yul: The Man Who Would Be King*, New York, 1989.

On BRYNNER: articles—

"Head of Hair for a Head of Skin," in *Life* (New York), 18 March 1957.
"Yul Brynner—Golden Egghead," in *Newsweek* (New York), 19 May 1958.
Shipman, David, "Yul Brynner" in *The Great Movie Stars: The International Years*, New York, 1972.
Homage to Brynner, with filmography, in 1980 Deauville Film Festival Programme Booklet.
Obituary in *Variety* (New York), 16 October 1985.

*   *   *

Yul Brynner's trademark—his baldness—was obviously the actor's most identifiable feature. On a deeper level, his bald pate signified the type he has played in films and on stage through most of his career. His image—exotic, often sinister, and foreign, yet virile, masculine, and authoritative—was undeniably linked to his physique, his Eurasian facial features, but most especially his bald head.

Early in his career, most of the publicity surrounding Brynner centered on his baldness. During the production of his early films such as *The Ten Commandments* and *The King and I*, articles in popular magazines were quick to equate his baldness with sexual attractiveness. A career article in *Newsweek*, for example, quoted several female fans at length on the subject of Brynner's appearance. One declared him to be "ugly magnetic" while another thought him "the most attractive man alive even if he grew grass on his head." Interestingly, in publicity for later films in which Brynner often donned hairpieces, attention was still directed to his baldness, as photography sessions were arranged by the studios to record the fitting of various wigs.

Brynner had originally shaved his head for his part as the King of Siam in the stage production of *The King and I*, a role which both made him a star and first presented him as exotic and erotic. Screen roles such as the Pharaoh in *The Ten Commandments*, the King in the

Yul Brynner

filmed version of *The King and I*, and Jean Lafitte in *The Buccaneer*, reinforced this image—an image in stark contrast to that of other box office stars of the 1950s, including John Wayne, Rock Hudson, Jimmy Stewart, and Alan Ladd, who were masculine, yet distinctly American, and were rarely presented in such a sinister or seemingly negative manner.

Brynner himself added to the exotic aspects of his image by inventing several versions of his childhood for various publications. He declared himself to be either a gypsy or the illegitimate son of a gypsy and a wealthy Russian. Often he stated that he studied philosophy at the Sorbonne in Paris, alternating this story with those about working as a gypsy singer in Parisian night spots or as a trapeze artist in a circus.

The peak of his film career was perhaps his role as the black-clad leader of a gang of cutthroats and outlaws in John Sturges's *The Magnificent Seven*. The film emphasized his authoritarian air, while playing down his more exotic side, depicting him as "the gunfighter," an outsider who by the nature of his profession can never be civilized. Brynner would reprise this character type again in later Westerns including *Invitation to a Gunfighter*, *Return of the Seven* (a sequel to *The Magnificent Seven*), *Indio Black*, and *Westworld*.

Unfortunately, by the late 1960s too many roles with too little variation had him hopelessly stereotyped as foreign heads of state or doomed gunfighters. In 1968 *Variety* actually listed him as a liability to producers because his films were consistent financial and critical flops. A move to Switzerland and roles in several European films did little to change his box office status. His most outrageous role, and one that purposely played against his image, was a cameo as a transvestite in *The Magic Christian*.

Brynner died of lung cancer in 1985. His last "performance" was by far his most dramatic and perhaps his most courageous. Shortly before his death, Brynner filmed a public service announcement for the American Cancer Society in which he warned viewers about the dangers of cigarette smoking. Brynner makes clear to the audience in his monologue that by the time they see the commercial, he will already have died from the result of smoking. It was a truly memorable exit from a dynamic film star who had always shrouded himself in drama and mystery.

—Susan M. Doll

BUCHANAN, Jack

Nationality: British. **Born:** Helensburgh, Scotland, 2 April 1890. **Education:** Larchfield School, Helensburgh; Glasgow Academy. **Family:** Married 1) Saffro Arnau, 1915; 2) Suzie Bussett, 1949. **Career:** Amateur stage appearances while an office worker; 1911—professional debut in variety theater; 1915-17—toured in successful play *Tonight's the Night*; 1917—film debut in *Auld Lang Syne*; 1921—critical and popular acclaim for role in Charlot's *A—Z* musical revue in London; later on Broadway; 1920s—series of leading roles in minor British films; 1929-30—appeared in a few Hollywood films; 1931—built Leicester Square Theatre in London; 1932—directed (with Herbert Wilcox) first film, *Yes Mr. Brown*; late 1930s—began producing his own films; entertained troops during World War II; 1953—sagging career restored by role in Minnelli's *The Band Wagon*. **Died:** In London, 21 October 1957.

Films as Actor:

1917   *Auld Lang Syne* (Morgan) (as Vane)
1919   *Her Heritage* (Merwin) (as Bob Hales)

1923   *The Audacious Mr. Squire* (Greenwood) (as Tom Squire)
1924   *The Happy Ending* (Cooper) (as Capt. Dale Conway)
1925   *Settled Out of Court* (*Evidence Enclosed*) (Cooper) (as husband); *Stage Stars Off Screen* (short); *A Typical Budget* (Brunel—short); *Bulldog Drummond's Third Round* (Morgan) (as Capt. Hugh Drummond)
1927   *Confetti* (Cutts) (as Count Andrea Zorro)
1928   *Toni* (Maude) (as Toni Marr/Marini)
1929   *Paris* (Badger) (as Guy Pennell); *Show of Shows* (Adolfi)
1930   *Monte Carlo* (Lubitsch) (as Count Rudolph Fallière); *The Glee Quartette* (short)
1931   *The Invisible Enemy* (charity appeal short); *Man of Mayfair* (Mercanton) (as Lord William)
1932   *Goodnight Vienna* (*Magic Night*) (Wilcox) (as Capt. Max Schlettof); *Yes Mr. Brown* (*Geschaft nit Amerika*) (as Nicholas Baumann, + co-d with Herbert Wilcox); *That's a Good Girl* (as Jack Barrow, + d, co-sc)
1935   *Brewster's Millions* (Freeland) (as Jack Brewster); *Come Out of the Pantry* (Raymond) (as Lord Robert Brent)
1936   *When Knights Were Bold* (Raymond) (as Sir Guy de Vere); *This'll Make You Whistle* (Wilcox) (as Bill Hopping); *Limelight* (*Backstage*) (Wilcox) (as himself)
1937   *Smash and Grab* (Whelan) (as Jack Forrest, + pr); *The Sky's the Limit* (as Dave Harber, + co-d with Lee Garmes, pr)
1938   *Cavalcade of Stars* (short); *Break the News* (*Le Mort en fuite*) (Clair) (as Teddy Fenton, + pr)
1939   *The Middle Watch* (Bentley) (as Capt. Maitland); *The Gang's All Here* (*The Amazing Mr. Forrest*) (Freeland) (as Forrest, + co-pr)
1940   *Bulldog Sees It Through* (Huth) (as Bill Watson)
1944   *Some Like It Rough* (short) (as narrator)
1951   *A Boy and a Bike* (short)
1952   *Giselle* (short) (as narrator)
1953   **The Band Wagon** (Minnelli) (as Jeffrey Cordova)
1955   *As Long as They're Happy* (Thompson) (as John Bentley); *Josephine and Men* (Boulting) (as Charles Luton)
1956   *The French They Are a Funny Race* (*The Diary of Major Thompson*) (Preston Sturges)

Other Films:

1938   *Sweet Devil* (*Quelle drole de gosse*) (Guissart) (pr only)
1943   *Happidrome* (Brandon) (co-pr only)

Publications

On BUCHANAN: books—

Leonard, William, and James Robert Parish, *Hollywood Players: The Thirties*, New York, 1976.
Marshall, Michael, *Top Hat and Tails: The Story of Jack Buchanan*, London, 1978.
Shipman, David, *The Great Movie Stars: The Golden Years*, revised edition, London, 1979.

*   *   *

Jack Buchanan typified the suave, debonair (almost bland) English gentleman of stage and screen; he could sing and dance hardly more than adequately, but there was something about his personality ("something about you that's different," as one of his songs put it) that was very charming and attractive. Usually attired in top hat and tails, Buchanan was hailed by many critics as the British Fred Astaire, and although his dancing style was far more simplistic than Astaire's, Buchanan did possess the same relaxed manner.

Jack Buchanan with Anna Neagle in *Goodnight Vienna*

Buchanan made his film debut as a leading man in the silent era; the films were all second-rate, and Buchanan was hopelessly miscast in them. He made his debut in "talkies" in America in leading roles opposite Irene Bordoni in *Paris* and Jeanette MacDonald in *Monte Carlo.* Somehow he lacked the natural charm of MacDonald's other leading man from this period, Maurice Chevalier; he returned to England to continue his film career there. (Interestingly Buchanan and Chevalier were later co-starred in one film, René Clair's *Break the News.*)

In England Buchanan's leading ladies included the American Fay Wray (*When Knights Were Bold*) and the French-born American star Lili Damita (*Brewster's Millions*). His best British films, however, are those with Anna Neagle and Elsie Randolph; both ladies possessed just the right middle-class quality to complement Buchanan's aristocratic air. *Goodnight Vienna/Magic Night* is probably his best film with Neagle, in which he charmingly sings the title song to her over the telephone, while *This'll Make You Whistle,* his best work with Randolph, introduces the delightful "I'm in a Dancing Mood."

The Buchanan charm was still apparent, despite the ravages of age and cancer, in his return-to-Hollywood feature, *The Band Wagon.* It was missing from his last film, Preston Sturges's depressingly unfunny *The French They Are a Funny Race.*

—Anthony Slide

BUJOLD, Geneviève

Nationality: Canadian. **Born:** Montreal, 1 July 1942. **Education:** Studied at a convent and at the Quebec Conservatory of Drama. **Family:** Married the director Paul Almond, 1967 (divorced 1973), sons: Matthew and Emmanuel. **Career:** 1962—joined Théâtre du Gesù's production of *The Barber of Seville;* 1963—became member of Le Théâtre du Rideau Vert; 1963-64—acted in some 60 TV and radio shows; 1964—first role in Canadian-French co-production *La Fleur de l'age;* 1965—toured Europe and the Soviet Union with Rideau Vert company; 1966—while in Paris, chosen by Alain Resnais to play opposite Yves Montand in *Le Guerre est finie;* on return to Canada appeared in stage and film productions directed by husband Paul Almond; 1969—international fame after starring role in *Anne of the Thousand Days*. **Awards:** Best Actress, Canadian Film Awards, for *Isabel*, 1968; Best Actress, Canadian Film Awards, for *Acte de coeur*, 1970; Best Actress Award, LA Film Critics, 1988. **Address:** c/o Trauber and Flynn, 2029 Century Park East, Suite 300, Los Angeles, CA 90027, U.S.A.

Films as Actress:

1963   *Amantia Pestilens* (Bonnière)

1964   "Geneviève" ep. of *La Fleur de l'age* (*Les Adolescents*; *The Adolescents*) (Brault) (as Geneviève)

1966   *La Guerre est finie* (*The War Is Over*) (Resnais) (as Nadine Sallanches); *Le Roi de coeur* (*King of Hearts*) (de Broca) (as Coquelicot)

1967   *Le Velour* (*The Thief of Paris*) (Malle) (as Charlotte); *Entre la mer et l'eau douce* (Brault)

1968   *Isabel* (Almond) (title role)

1969   *Anne of the Thousand Days* (Jarrott) (as Anne Boleyn)

1970   *Acte du coeur* (*Act of the Heart*) (Almond) (as Martha Hayes); *Marie-Christine* (short)

1971   *The Trojan Women* (Cacoyannis) (as Cassandra)

1972   *Journey* (Almond) (as Saguenay)

1973   *Kamouraska* (Jutra) (as Elisabeth)

1974   *Earthquake* (Robson) (as Denise)

1975   *L'Incorrigible* (*The Incorrigible*) (de Broca) (as Marie-Charlotte)

1976   *Swashbuckler* (*The Scarlet Buccaneer*) (Goldstone) (as Janet Barnet); *Obsession* (De Palma) (as Elizabeth Courtland); *Alex and the Gypsy* (*Love and Other Crimes*) (Korty) (as Maritza)

1977   *Un Autre Homme, une autre chance* (*Another Man, Another Chance*) (Lelouch) (as Jeanne Leroy)

1978   *Coma* (Crichton) (as Dr. Susan Wheeler); *Mistress of Paradise* (Medal—for TV) (as Elizabeth Beaufort)

1979   *Murder by Decree* (Clark) (as Annie Crook); *Final Assignment* (Almond) (as Nicole Thomson)

1980   *The Last Flight of Noah's Ark* (Jarrott) (as Bernadette Laffeur)

1982   *Monsignor* (Perry) (as Clara)

1984   *Tightrope* (Tuggle) (as Beryl Thibodeaux); *Choose Me* (Rudolph) (as Dr. Nancy Love)

1985   *Trouble in Mind* (Rudolph) (as Wanda)

1988   **Dead Ringers** (Cronenberg) (as Claire Niveau); *The Moderns* (Rudolph) (as Libby Valentin)

1989   *Les Noces de papier* (*A Paper Wedding*) (Brault—for TV) (as Claire); *Secret Places of the Heart* (Bridges); *Red Earth, White Earth* (Greene—for TV) (as Madeline)

1990   *False Identity* (Keach) (as Rachel Roux); *Une Certaine Charme* (Aghian); *And the Dance Goes On* (Almond) (as Rick and James's mother)

1991   *Rue du Bac* (as Marie Aubriac)

1992   *Oh, What a Night* (Till) (as Eva)

1993   *Spending Time with Family* (Barron); *An Ambush of Ghosts* (Lewis) (as Irene Betts)

1994   *Mon Ami Max* (*My Friend Max*) (as Marie-Alexandrine Brabant)

1995   *Pinocchio*

Publications

By BUJOLD: articles—

Interview by M. Euvrard, in *Cinéma Québec* (Montreal), March-April 1973.

"Kamouraska: Geneviève Bujold," interview by Kiss/Koler and A. Ibrányi-Kiss, in *Cinema Canada* (Montreal), April-May 1973.

On BUJOLD: articles—

"Geneviève Bujold: The Flame Within," in *Time* (New York), 28 September 1970.

Almond, Paul, "Geneviève Bujold: In Transition," in *Close-Ups: The Movie Star Book*, edited by Danny Peary, New York, 1978.

Ciné Revue (Paris), 12 June 1980.

Schupp, P., "Geneviève Bujold: l'indépendance et la volonté," in *Séquences* (Montreal), October 1987.

*   *   *

Surely few film actresses so distinguished as Geneviève Bujold have appeared in so few distinguished films. Bujold began her career strongly with memorable supporting roles as the provocative, lissome admirer of Yves Montand in Alain Resnais's *La Guerre est finie* and the wistfully fey inmate in Philippe de Broca's *King of Hearts*. Shortly thereafter she took on a starring role as Anne Boleyn in *Anne of the Thousand Days*.

Three years later she met the challenge of Greek tragedy on film, as Cassandra in Michael Cacoyannis's *The Trojan Women*, holding her own against Katharine Hepburn, Vanessa Redgrave, and Irene Papas. Many must have felt, with Pauline Kael, that "this performance is a leap in her career; her ambitiousness in tackling a role like this suggests prodigies ahead."

As it turned out, most of her American films in the next 12 years were to be glossy, unimaginative genre exercises: *Earthquake*, *Swashbuckler*, *Monsignor*, and *Coma* (in which she at least brought an air of authority to her starring role as a doctor in a gothic dilemma). In between, there were some little-seen (in the United States, at least) French-Canadian films directed by her husband, Paul Almond—*Isabel*, *Acte du coeur*, *Journey*, *Final Assignment*—and a few offbeat projects such as John Korty's *Alex and the Gypsy* and Claude Lelouch's underrated *Another Man, Another Chance*.

Following good notices for her role as a rape victim therapist in the thriller *Tightrope* in 1984, Bujold has appeared in some extremely varied and distinctive character parts, notably in a trio of films by Alan Rudolph and in David Cronenberg's *Dead Ringers*. *Choose Me*, the first of the Rudolph films, provided her a most unusual deadpan comic role, as a radio "Love Doctor" who gives brilliant advice to her listeners but is a psychological mess outside the studio. Her first scene, establishing her cool, self-assured radio persona, using her deep voice to superb effect, is contrasted later by her tour-de-force dialogue with Keith Carradine, in which, under a false name, she admiringly describes the radio star with a sort of daffy abandon, totally absorbed in herself. In *Dead Ringers*, Bujold, playing a jaded actress, manages to make the character neither ludicrous nor villainous—a considerable achievement, since the plot calls for her to be having an affair with twin brothers without realizing there is more than one man, and later, after a denunciation and reconciliation, carelessly leading one of them into drug addiction.

Bujold brings to nearly all her roles a striking combination of qualities: both toughness and vulnerability (a copywriter's hackneyed pairing, but truly pertinent here), and both an air of poised, experienced, unexaggerated sensuality and a convent-girlish or hurt-child innocence. These qualities have worked together most perfectly perhaps in a television production of Jean Anouilh's *Antigone*, an adaptation of Sophocles that retains the original plot but uses deliberately anachronistic modern speech. The force and conviction of Bujold's performance eliminated potentially ludicrous clashes of style and lapses into sentimentality, while keeping the pride and pathos.

Of her English-language motion pictures, perhaps *Obsession* has used her best: for her haunting (and distinctly French) facial features, again a combination of soft and firm elements, which obsess the hero, as well as for her conflicting emotional qualities. Bujold projects the air of a remote yet intense and (for the man) seemingly attainable sensuality; of kindly, intelligent concern (both feigned and real, as it turns out); while underneath she is a determined avenger, and underneath that, a hurt, unloved child pleading for help.

Bujold's screen presence is so strong that she can be a major part of the success of a film in which she has only one scene: such is the case in the Sherlock Holmes drama *Murder by Decree*, in which she plays the pivotal role of a madwoman who not only reveals the information necessary for Holmes to solve the case but who is so vitally appealing that Holmes makes an emotional commitment to her that carries him to a climatic denunciation.

In recent years Bujold has pursued a private life more than a film career, though she was briefly notorious for abandoning her role as the captain in the *Star Trek: Voyager* television series. She has continued to work mainly in French-Canadian productions, and occasionally in such American independent projects as *An Ambush of Ghosts*, where she plays a woman driven mad by guilt, receiving excellent notices as always but little public renown.

—Joseph Milicia

BURSTYN, Ellen

Nationality: American. **Born:** Edna Rae Gillooly in Detroit, Michigan, 7 December 1932. **Education:** Attended Cass Tech High School, Detroit. **Family:** Married 1) William C. Alexander; 2) Paul Roberts; 3) Neil Burstyn, son: Jefferson. **Career:** 1951-57—model in New York and Texas as Edna Rae; dancer in Montreal club as Keri Flynn; "Glee Girl" on *The Jackie Gleason Show* (as Erica Dean); 1957—on Broadway in *Fair Game* (as Ellen McRae); early 1970s—studied at Actors Studio; 1973—bought script of *Alice Doesn't Live Here Anymore*, and chose Martin Scorsese as director; 1975—returned to Broadway in *Same Time Next Year*; other New York stage work includes *The Three Sisters* (1977) and *84 Charing Cross Road* (1982); 1979—named co-artist director, with Al Pacino, of the Actors Studio following death of Lee Strasberg; president, Actors' Equity Association, 1982-85. **Awards:** Best Supporting Actress, New York Film Critics, for *The Last Picture Show*, 1971; Best Actress Academy Award, and Best Actress, British Academy, for *Alice Doesn't Live Here Anymore*, 1975; honorary doctorates from Dowling College, 1983, and School of Visual Arts, New York City, 1983. **Address:** c/o Todd Smith, Creative Artists Agency, 1888 Century Park E., Suite 1400, Los Angeles, CA 90067, U.S.A.

Films as Actress:

(as Ellen McRae)

1964 *For Those Who Think Young* (Martinson) (as Dr. Pauline Thayer); *Goodbye Charlie* (Minnelli) (as Franny)
1969 *Pit Stop* (Hill) (as Ellen McLeod)

(as Ellen Burstyn)

1970 *Alex in Wonderland* (Mazursky) (as Beth); *Tropic of Cancer* (Strick) (as Mona)
1971 **The Last Picture Show** (Bogdanovich) (as Lois)

1972 *The King of Marvin Gardens* (Rafelson) (as Sally)
1973 *The Exorcist* (Friedkin) (as Chris)
1974 *Harry and Tonto* (Mazursky) (as Shirley); *Alice Doesn't Live Here Anymore* (Scorsese) (as Alice Hyatt); *Thursday's Game* (Moore—for TV)
1977 *Providence* (Resnais) (as Sonia)
1978 *A Dream of Passion* (Dassin) (as Brenda); *Same Time Next Year* (Mulligan) (as Doris)
1980 *Resurrection* (Petrie) (as Edna Mae McCauley)
1981 *The Silence of the North* (King) (as Olive Fredrickson)
1984 *The Ambassador* (Thompson) (as Alex Hacker)
1985 *Twice in a Lifetime* (Yorkin) (as Kate MacKenzie); *Surviving* (Hussein—for TV); *Into Thin Air* (Young—for TV)
1986 *Something in Common* (Glenn Jordan—for TV)
1987 *Pack of Lies* (Page—for TV); *Hello Actors Studio* (Tresgot—doc); *Look Away* (Seidelman); *Dear America* (*Letters Home from Vietnam*) (doc—for TV) (voice)
1988 *Hanna's War* (Golan) (as Katarina Senesh)
1989 *Act of Vengeance ... A True Story* (Mackenzie—for TV)
1990 *The Color of Evening* (Stafford); *When You Remember Me* (Winer—for TV) (as Nurse Cooder)
1991 *Dying Young* (Schumacher) (as Mrs. O'Neil); *Mrs. Lambert Remembers Love* (for TV) (as Lil Lambert)
1992 *Taking Back My Life* (for TV) (as Wilma); *Grand Isle* (Lambert—for TV) (as Mademoiselle Reisz)
1993 *Shattered Trust: The Shari Karney Story* (for TV) (as Joan Delvecchio); *The Cemetery Club* (Duke) (as Esther Moskowitz)
1994 *Getting Gotti* (Young—for TV) (as Jo Giacalone); *Trick of the Eye* (for TV) (as Frances Griffin); *When a Man Loves a Woman* (Mandoki) (as Emily); *Getting Out* (for TV) (as Arlie's mother)
1995 *The Baby-Sitter's Club* (as Mrs. Haberman); *Roommates* (Yates) (as Judith); *How to Make an American Quilt* (Moorhouse) (as Hy); *My Brother's Keeper* (for TV) (as Helen); *Follow the River* (for TV) (as Gretel)
1996 *The Spitfire Grill* (Zlotoff)

Publications

By BURSTYN: article—

Interview, in *Take One* (Montreal), March 1977.

On BURSTYN: articles—

Current Biography 1975, New York, 1975.
Glaessner, Verina, "*Alice Doesn't Live Here Anymore*," in *Focus on Film* (London), Summer 1975.
Bell, Arthur, "Burstyn without Masks," in *Village Voice* (New York), 5 November 1980.
Berkvist, Robert, "The Miracle of Ellen Burstyn," in *Cosmopolitan* (New York), February 1982.

*   *   *

Ellen Burstyn is an unparalleled re-inventress. While many actresses transmute their image after stardom wanes, Burstyn tried on different identities prior to Hollywood glory. It is her inbred survivability and desire to refashion adversity in a favorable image that informs her finest work. Having been christened Edna Rae Gillooly, and having danced as Keri Flynn, Ellen "Erica Dean" Burstyn then promenaded as one of Jackie Gleason's television Glee Girls, snared a fling at Broadway ingenuedom as Ellen McRae, and paid her dues as

Ellen McLeod in such drive-in filler as *Pit Stop*. Before she chucked her marginal screen-acting progress to hone her craft at the Actors Studio, Burstyn had already gone through more name changes than Joan Crawford. If great actresses should be chameleons, then Burstyn returned to film work in 1970 as well-prepared by her own catch-as-catch-can life as by Strasberg's Method. Playing vitally attractive women with some mileage on them, Burstyn sent critics scrambling for superlatives by shifting from supportive but insecure mom in *The Last Picture Show* to the destructively paranoid stepmother in *King of Marvin Gardens*. At an age when most female stars have accumulated the bulk of their above-title credits, Burstyn was just hitting her stride. Maintaining dignity amidst the pea soup-spitting hysteria of the box-office avalanche, *The Exorcist*, Burstyn slyly demonstrated the chutzpah that nourished her slow-burning career. Negotiating a deal for a project she rescued from television, Burstyn starred in the finest flowering of feminism for the masses, *Alice Doesn't Live Here Anymore* and won the Oscar. Chronicling a minor lounge singer's embattled insistence on not sacrificing rewarding work for a Prince Charming, she fueled the film with the rage she must have felt waiting so long for stardom herself.

Having hit this unexpected height in her forties, Burstyn repeated her Tony-award triumph in *Same Time, Next Year*, but on-screen, the shenanigans seemed better suited to Doris Day's Ross Hunter period. As a conventional movie star, Burstyn registered as too unyielding. More challenged by varying her range with misguided art films such as Resnais's stuffy chat-fest *Providence* and Dassin's *A Dream of Passion* (an attempt to do for *Medea* what Bergman did for *Persona*), Burstyn's star power experienced a *Resurrection*, in which she filtered her tensile fortitude through her most translucent performance as a widow transformed into a psychic healer by personal tragedy. Sadly, this perfect mesh of actress and role led only to claptrap (*Silence of the North*), post-stardom supporting crumbs (*Twice in a Lifetime*) and the welcoming vista of television where she suffered to stunning effect in *Pack of Lies* and *Into Thin Air*, and wreaked emotional chaos in *Getting Out*. Having briefly sampled Hollywood immortality, Burstyn seemed content to cast herself as working actress, returning to Broadway as a female priest in *Sacrilege* or gracing ensemble films such as *How to Make an American Quilt* and *Cemetery Club*. Sometimes faltering in grande dame parts (e.g., television's *Primal Secret*), the still-radiantly sexy Burstyn needs to display her many facets in something other than retreads of Fay Bainter roles. Appearing briefly in younger actresses' Oscar-pandering vehicles (Julia Roberts's *Dying Young* and Meg Ryan's *When a Man Loves a Woman*), Burstyn wipes the little darlings off the screen. A talent educated in the school of hard knocks is likely to endure.

—Robert Pardi

BURTON, Richard

Nationality: British. **Born:** Richard Walter Jenkins Jr. in Pontrhydyfen, Wales, 10 November 1925. **Education:** Attended Exeter College, Oxford. **Military Service:** Royal Air Force, 1944-47. **Family:** Married 1) the actress Sybil Williams, 1949 (divorced), daughters: Kate and Jessica; 2) the actress Elizabeth Taylor, 1964 (divorced 1974; remarried 1975, divorced 1976), child: adopted daughter Maria; 3) Susan Hunt, 1976 (divorced 1982); 4) Sally Hay, 1983. **Career:** 1943—changed name to Richard Burton, after schoolmaster Philip Burton who encouraged his acting career; stage debut in Liverpool in *Druid's Rest*; 1948—following military service, returned to stage in London; film debut in *The Last Days of Dolwyn*; 1949—Broadway

debut in *The Lady's Not for Burning*; 1952—appeared in first American film, *My Cousin Rachel*; 1961-62—while making film *Cleopatra*, met and fell in love with Elizabeth Taylor; 1962-73—acted in series of films with Taylor; 1983—with Taylor on Broadway in revival of Nöel Coward's *Private Lives*; 1984—in TV mini-series *Ellis Island*. **Awards:** Best Actor, British Academy, for *The Spy Who Came in from the Cold* and *Who's Afraid of Virginia Woolf?*, 1966; Commander of the British Empire, 1970; Fellow of St. Peter's College, Oxford, 1975. **Died:** Of a stroke, in Geneva, Switzerland, 5 August 1984.

Films as Actor:

1948   *The Last Days of Dolwyn* (*Dolwyn*) (Williams) (as Gareth)

1949   *Now Barabbas Was a Robber . . .* (*Which Will You Have?*) (Parry) (as Paddy)

1950   *Waterfront* (*Waterfront Women*) (Anderson) (as Ben Satterthwaite); *The Woman with No Name* (*Her Panelled Door*) (Vajda and O'Ferrall) (as Nick Chamerd)

1951   *Green Grow the Rushes* (*Brandy Ashore*) (Twist) (as Robert "Bob" Hammond)

1952   *My Cousin Rachel* (Koster) (as Philip Ashley)

1953   *The Desert Rats* (Wise) (as Capt. MacRoberts); *The Robe* (Koster) (as Marcellus Gallio); *Thursday's Children* (Anderson and Brenton) (as narrator)

1954   *Demetrius and the Gladiators* (Daves) (in film clip from *The Robe*); *Prince of Players* (Dunne) (as Edwin Booth)

1955   *The Rains of Ranchipur* (Negulesco) (as Dr. Safti); *Alexander the Great* (Rossen) (title role)

1957   *Sea Wyf and Biscuit* (*Sea Wyf*) (McNaught) (as Biscuit); *Amère victoire* (*Bitter Victory*) (Nicholas Ray) (as Capt. Leith)

1958   *March to Aldermaston* (as narrator)

1959   **Look Back in Anger** (Richardson) (as Jimmy Porter)

1960   *The Bramble Bush* (Petrie) (as Guy); *Ice Palace* (Vincent Sherman) (as Zeb Kennedy)

1961   *Dylan Thomas* (Howells—short); *A Midsummer Night's Dream* (Sackler); *Sen noci svatojánské* (Jiří Trnka) (as narrator of English-language version)

1962   *The Longest Day* (Annakin, Marton, Wicki, and Oswald) (as RAF pilot)

1963   *Cleopatra* (Joseph L. Mankiewicz) (as Mark Antony); *The V.I.P.s* (Asquith) (as Paul Andros); *Zulu* (Endfield) (as narrator); *Inheritance* (Irvin—short) (as narrator)

1964   *Becket* (Glenville) (title role); *The Night of the Iguana* (Huston) (as the Rev. T. Lawrence Shannon); *Hamlet* (Colleran—for TV, filmed record of Gielgud's New York theater production) (title role)

1965   *The Sandpiper* (Minnelli) (as Dr. Edward Hewitt); *What's New, Pussycat?* (Clive Donner) (as man in bar); *The Spy Who Came in from the Cold* (Ritt) (as Alec Leamas); *Eulogy to 5.02* (Herschensohn—short) (as narrator); *The Days of Wilfred Owen* (produced by Lewine and Bach) (as narrator)

1966   *Who's Afraid of Virginia Woolf?* (Mike Nichols) (as George); *La Bisbetica Domata* (*The Taming of the Shrew*) (Zeffirelli) (as Petruchio, + co-pr)

1967   *The Comedians* (Glenville) (as Brown); *The Comedians in Africa* (short)

1968   *Boom!* (Losey) (as Chris Flanders); *Candy* (Marquand) (as McPhisto); *Where Eagles Dare* (Hutton) (as John Smith); *The Rime of the Ancient Mariner* (Queenan) (as narrator)

1969   *Anne of the Thousand Days* (Jarrott) (as King Henry VIII); *Staircase* (Donen) (as Harry Leeds)

1971   *Villain* (Tuchner) (as Vic Dakin); *Raid on Rommel* (Hathaway) (as Capt. Alec Foster)

Richard Burton with Elizabeth Taylor in *The Taming of the Shrew*

1972   *The Assassination of Trotsky* (Losey) (title role); *Hammersmith Is Out* (Ustinov) (title role); *Barbe-Bleue* (*Bluebeard*) (Dmytryk) (as Baron Von Sepper/title role); *A Wall in Jerusalem* (Knobler and Rossif—English-language version of *Un Mur à Jérusalem*) (as narrator); *Sutjeska* (*The Fifth Offensive*) (Delic) (as Josip Broz Tito)

1973   *Il viaggio* (*The Voyage*; *The Journey*) (de Sica) (as Cesar Braggi); *Under Milk Wood* (Sinclair) (as narrator); *Divorce: His/Divorce: Hers* (*Divorce*) (Hussein—for TV); *Rappresaglia* (*Massacre in Rome*) (Cosmatos) (as Col. Kappler)

1974   *The Klansman* (Terence Young) (as Breck Stancill); *Gathering Storm* (Wise) (as Winston Churchill); *Brief Encounter* (Alan Bridges—for TV)

1976   *Volcano* (Brittain) (as narrator); *Resistance* (McMullen)

1977   *Exorcist II: The Heretic* (Boorman) (as Father Lamont); *Equus* (Lumet) (as Dr. Martin Dysart)

1978   *The Wild Geese* (McLaglen) (as Col. Allen Faulkner); *Stars' War: The Flight of the Wild Geese* (Johnstone—short); *The Medusa Touch* (Gold) (as John Morlar)

1979   *Breakthrough* (*Sergeant Steiner*) (McLaglen) (as Sgt. Steiner); *Love Spell* (Donovan)

1980   *Circle of Two* (Dassin) (as Ashley St. Clair)
1981   *Absolution* (Anthony Page) (as Fr. Goddard)
1983   *Wagner* (Palmer—for TV) (title role)
1984   *1984* (Radford) (as O'Brien)

Film as Director:

1967   *Doctor Faustus* (co-d with Nevill Coghill, + title role, co-pr)

Publications

By BURTON: book—

A Christmas Story (novel), New York, 1964.

By BURTON: article—

Interview in *Playboy* (Chicago), September 1963.

On BURTON: books—

Cottrell, John, and Fergis Cashin, *Richard Burton, Very Close Up*, Englewood Cliffs, New Jersey, 1972.

Ferris, Paul, *Richard Burton*, New York, 1981.

Junor, Penny, *Burton: The Man behind the Myth*, London, 1985.

Alpert, Hollis, *Burton*, New York, 1986.

Bragg, Melvyn, *Rich: A Biography of Richard Burton*, London, 1988; as *Richard Burton: A Life*, New York, 1989.

Jenkins, Graham, with Barry Turner, *Richard Burton: My Brother*, London, 1988.

Bradanyi, Ivan, *Richard es Elizabeth: Richard Burton es Elizabeth Taylor elete*, Budapest, 1992.

Steverson, Tyrone, *Richard Burton: A Bio-Bibliography*, Westport, Connecticut, 1992.

On BURTON: articles—

Brinson, P., "Prince from Wales," in *Films and Filming* (London), May 1955.

Current Biography 1960, New York, 1960.

Dunne, Philip, "Richard Burton: A True Prince of Players," in *Close-Up: The Movie Star Book*, edited by Danny Peary, New York, 1978.

"Richard Burton," in *Ecran* (Paris), February 1978.

Obituary in *New York Times*, 6 August 1984.

Obituary in *Variety* (New York), 8 August 1984.

Baxter, Brian, "Richard Burton," in *Films and Filming* (London), October 1984.

Guérif, F., "Richard Burton," in *Revue du Cinéma* (Paris), November 1984.

Merkin, D., obituary in *Film Comment* (New York), November/December 1984.

Denby, David, "Requiem for a Heavyweight," in *Premiere* (New York), February 1991.

"Richard Burton & Elizabeth Taylor," in *People Weekly* (New York), 12 February 1996.

*   *   *

Richard Burton's turbulent life overwhelmed the public perception of his vast talent. Born Richard Jenkins, the twelfth child of a hard-drinking Welsh miner, he was raised from the age of two by his eldest sister following the death of their mother. Love of language (exclusively Welsh until the age of five) and gift of gab influenced an early plan to enter the ministry, a notion extinguished in his teens when, anticipating his role as the minister defrocked for dallying with his underage parishioners in *The Night of the Iguana*, he realized he lacked all religious feeling. He turned instead to acting under the eventual tutelage of a secondary school teacher, Philip Henry Burton, who coached him to develop his remarkably resonant voice and, equally, to erase traces of his rough-hewn upbringing; he became Burton's ward at 18 and permanently assumed his name. Richard Burton made his film debut in *The Last Days of Dolwyn* opposite fellow Welshman Emlyn Williams, whose early life, as fictionalized in Williams's *The Corn Is Green*, remarkably mirrored Burton's own.

English stage and screen roles in the late 1940s and early 1950s led to plum Shakespearean parts with the Old Vic, most notably Hamlet in 1953, and a contract with Twentieth Century-Fox, for whom he played the brooding hero of Daphne du Maurier's *My Cousin Rachel*, his American film debut; the Roman officer Marcellus in *The Robe*, the first CinemaScope film; actor Edwin Booth in *Prince of Players*; and—forever changing his life and career—Mark Antony, opposite Elizabeth Taylor, in *Cleopatra*.

Burton and Taylor: each married to another when they co-starred in *Cleopatra* in 1963, their names became permanently linked, from initial banner-headlined scandal, through marriage, divorce, remarriage, and redivorce, to photographs of a grieving, feebly disguised Taylor retreating from the press near Burton's Swiss gravesite a week after his death in 1984. On the screen as well as off they wooed each other in a series of films usually featuring warring but emotionally bonded couples, roles calculated to obliterate any separation between life and art in the mind of the viewer. Of the 11 films they made together, 2 will stand the test of time—the superb *Who's Afraid of Virginia Woolf?* in which the staged-trained Burton delivered one of his best film performances (though Taylor took home the Oscar), and Franco Zeffirelli's colorfully raucous adaptation of Shakespeare's *The Taming of the Shrew*.

It is commonplace to maintain that Burton squandered his talent, that he chose, in words attributed to Laurence Olivier, to become a "household word" instead of the great Shakespearean actor he promised to become. His unfulfilled plan to return to the theater as King Lear following a successful Broadway run in *Equus* was thwarted by intermittent bouts with the bottle and a serious spinal ailment that forced him out of a praised *Camelot* revival in 1980. His final stage appearance occurred in a Broadway revival of *Private Lives*, Nöel Coward's stylish comedy of divorce and reassignation, an attempt to resurrect the glitter of past associations with Elizabeth Taylor, who co-starred.

As revealed in Melvyn Bragg's 1988 biography *Rich*, cobbled together largely from Burton's own private diaries and letters, Burton was a highly intelligent, articulate man. He was at his best on screen capturing dispirited men at the end of their tether, cynical world-weary men such as Leamas in John le Carré's *The Spy Who Came in from the Cold* and George in Edward Albee's *Who's Afraid of Virginia Woolf?*; burnt-out, self-destructive men such as the defrocked minister at war with his lack of faith, T. Lawrence Shannon, in John Huston's now-legendary adaptation of Tennessee Williams's *Night of the Iguana*; angry young men such as John Osborne's Jimmy Porter in *Look Back in Anger*; and—still overwhelmingly—Shakespeare's tortured Danish prince in the 1964 Broadway production of *Hamlet* (directed by John Gielgud), which was photographed for posterity in a now elusive film transcription, and recorded on vinyl, as well.

—Mark W. Estrin, updated by John McCarty

CAAN, James

Nationality: American. **Born:** Queens, New York, 26 March 1939.
Education: Attended Rhodes High School, Manhattan; Michigan State
University; Hofstra College, Long Island; studied acting with Wynn
Handman of the Neighborhood Playhouse, New York. **Family:** Married 1) Dee Jay Mattis, 1961 (divorced 1966), daughter: Tara; 2)
Sheila Ryan, 1976, son: Scott Andrew; 3) Ingrid Hajek, 1990; also
son: Alexander. **Career:** 1960—began acting at the Neighborhood
Playhouse; 1963—film debut in unbilled bit role in Wilder's *Irma La
Douce*; early 1960s—on Broadway in *Mandingo* and *Blood, Sweat
and Stanley Poole*; 1970—gained public attention in role of Brian
Piccolo in TV film *Brian's Song*; 1972—critical acclaim for role in
The Godfather. **Address:** 1435 Stone Canyon, Los Angeles, CA 90077,
U.S.A.

Films as Actor:

1963 *Irma La Douce* (Wilder)
1964 *Lady in a Cage* (Grauman) (as Randall)
1965 *The Glory Guys* (Laven) (as Pvt. Anthony Dugan); *Red Line
       7000* (Hawks) (as Mike Marsh)
1967 *El Dorado* (Hawks) (as Alan "Mississippi" Bourdillon
       Traherne); *Games* (Harrington) (as Paul)
1968 *Countdown* (*Moonshot*) (Altman) (as Lee); *Journey to Shiloh*
       (Hale) (as Buck Burnett); *Submarine X-1* (Graham) (as Lt.
       Cmdr. Bolton)
1969 *The Rain People* (Francis Ford Coppola) (as Jimmie "Killer"
       Kilgannon)
1970 *Rabbit, Run* (Smight) (as Rabbit Angstrom); *Brian's Song*
       (Kulik—for TV) (as Brian Piccolo)
1971 *T. R. Baskin* (*Date with a Lonely Girl*) (Ross) (as Larry Moore)
1972 **The Godfather** (Francis Ford Coppola) (as Sonny Corleone)
1973 *Slither* (Zieff) (as Dick Kanipsia); *Cinderella Liberty* (Rydell)
       (as John Baggs Jr.)
1974 *Freebie and the Bean* (Rush) (as Freebie); *The Gambler* (Reisz)
       (as Axel Freed); **The Godfather, Part II** (Francis Ford
       Coppola) (as Sonny Corleone)
1975 *Gone with the West* (*Man without Mercy*; *Bronco Busters*; *Little
       Moon and Jud McGraw*) (Girard); *Funny Lady* (Ross) (as
       Billy Rose); *Rollerball* (Jewison) (as Jonathan E.); *Killer
       Elite* (Peckinpah) (as Mike Locken)
1976 *Harry and Walter Go to New York* (Rydell) (as Harry Dighby);
       Silent Movie (Mel Brooks) (as himself)
1977 *A Bridge Too Far* (Attenborough and Hayers) (as Sgt. Dohun);
       Un autre Homme, une autre Chance (*Another Man, Another Chance*; *Another Man, Another Woman*) (Lelouch)
       (as David Williams)
1978 *Comes a Horseman* (Pakula) (as Frank)
1979 *Chapter Two* (Moore) (as George Schneider)
1981 *Thief* (*Violent Streets*) (Michael Mann) (as Frank); *Les Uns et
       les autres* (*Bolero*; *Within Memory*) (Lelouch) (as Glenn Sr./
       Glenn Jr.)

1982 *Kiss Me Goodbye* (Mulligan) (as Jolly Villano)
1987 *Gardens of Stone* (Francis Ford Coppola) (as Sgt. Clell Hazard)
1988 *Alien Nation* (*Outer Heat*) (Baker) (as Matthew Sykes)
1990 *Misery* (Rob Reiner) (as Paul Sheldon); *Dick Tracy* (Beatty) (as
       Spaldoni)
1991 *For the Boys* (Rydell) (as Eddie Sparks); *The Dark Backward*
       (Rifkin) (as Dr. Scurvy)
1992 *Honeymoon in Vegas* (Andrew Bergman) (as Tommy Korman)
1993 *The Program* (Ward) (as Coach Sam Winters); *Flesh and Bone*
       (Kloves) (as Roy Sweeney); *Earth and the American Dream*
       (Couturie—doc) (as voice)
1995 *A Boy Called Hate* (Marcus); *Tashunga* (*Grand nord*; *North
       Star*) (Gaup)
1996 *Bottle Rocket* (Wes Anderson) (as Mr. Henry); *Bulletproof*
       (Dickerson); *Eraser* (Chuck Russell)

Film as Director:

1979 *Hide in Plain Sight* (+ ro as Thomas Hacklin)

Publications

By CAAN: articles—

"James Caan: His Godfather's Son," interview with R. Feiden, in *Inter/
View* (New York), May 1972.
"James Caan: Off Set," interview with V. Fremont, in *Interview* (New
York), January 1974.
Interview in *Photoplay* (London), October 1982.

On CAAN: books—

Zuckerman, Ira, *The Godfather Journal*, New York, 1972.
Puzo, Mario, *The Making of the Godfather*, Greenwich, Connecticut,
1973.

On CAAN: articles—

McGillivray, D., "James Caan," in *Focus on Film* (London), Autumn
1972.
Current Biography 1976, New York, 1976.
Ciné Revue (Paris), 23 April 1981, and 24 March 1983.
Weinraub, Bernard, "James Caan Rises from the Ashes of His Career,"
in *New York Times*, 17 November 1991.
Reinert, Al, "Raising Caan," in *Premiere* (New York), December 1991.
Rebello, S., "The Ultimate Caan Game," in *Movieline*, October 1993.

*   *   *

Back in the late 1960s and early 1970s, James Caan was one of the
most promising and interesting young actors in Hollywood. Clearly,
he was multitalented. As the young punk who terrorizes Olivia de

Havilland in *Lady in a Cage*, his first featured movie role, he showcased his skill at playing a sadistic thug who could rattle your spine—an aspect of his range he would expand on less than a decade later as Sonny Corleone in *The Godfather*. He further demonstrated his talent, offering a likable, star-making performance in Howard Hawks's *El Dorado*. In his role as the young drifter Mississippi (aka Alan Bourdillon Traherne), Caan is showcased opposite John Wayne's hero-gunfighter Cole Thornton and Robert Mitchum's drunken sheriff J. P. Harrah. In this part, the young actor was able to put across macho and swagger while at the same time remaining likably boyish.

Caan added to his expanding reputation with a sensitive performance as the ill-fated pro football player Brian Piccolo opposite Billy Dee Williams's Gale Sayers in *Brian's Song*, one of the best-ever made-for-television movies. Another key (but often overlooked) early Caan performance which adds yet another dimension to his career came in *The Rain People*, the story of a pregnant housewife (Shirley Knight) who abandons her husband and commences a cross-country journey of self-discovery. Along the way, she picks up a deeply vulnerable, brain-damaged ex-college football player (Caan). The film is ahead of its time in its depiction of a woman struggling for an independent identity; while Knight is outstanding, Caan matches her with his deeply sensitive and keenly insightful performance in a role which easily might have defeated a less-talented actor.

The penultimate accomplishment of Caan's career remains Sonny Corleone: a performance that announced his arrival as one of his generation's major movie stars. Caan's acting is galvanizing, as he inhabits the role of the psychotic, trigger-happy heir to the Corleone throne, who (predictably but appropriately) meets a violent and bloody end. The film depicts organized crime as an extension of American capitalism; the Corleones essentially are a family of prosperous businessmen, a corporate entity whose powers comprehend all too well that ruthlessness and treachery are accepted means to success. Sonny, however, more than any other character, represents the true nature of the clan Corleone: thoroughly remorseless in its out-of-control violence. If you so much as stare at Sonny Corleone, let alone attempt to defy him, he will challenge you, and then promptly blow you away. Sonny, as played by Caan, is the family enforcer, the reality behind the facade of respectability, in a business which relies on employing guns or fists instead of telephone calls or memos as a means of communication.

Since the release of *The Godfather* in 1972, Caan has, unfortunately, found it impossible to top himself and extend his filmography. Unlike his *Godfather* co-star Al Pacino, he has not had great roles in memorable films; none of his subsequent work matches the overall quality of *Serpico* and *Dog Day Afternoon*, Pacino's *Godfather* follow-ups. And so Caan (who also lacks Pacino's Actors Studio pedigree) does not enjoy a reputation similar to Pacino as an actor's actor.

He has, however, done substantial work in a number of films, which have allowed him to display his range. He has played nice guys (the kindhearted sailor in *Cinderella Liberty* and the widowed writer in *Chapter Two*, both opposite Marsha Mason); a cerebral lawbreaker (the title character in *Thief*); a career soldier/war veteran who has come to oppose America's involvement in Vietnam, in *Gardens of Stone* (which, as *The Rain People* and *The Godfather*, was directed by Francis Ford Coppola); and, most memorably, the pitifully addicted college professor/title character in *The Gambler*. Caan also directed as well as starred in *Hide in Plain Sight*, playing a divorced man in search of his children.

Chapter Two (at least on screen) is second-tier Neil Simon, while *Gardens of Stone* is a secondary Vietnam-related title. *The Gambler* is obscured by the similar *California Split*, which also came to movie theaters in 1974. And far too many of Caan's films simply have been third rate, if not outright disasters: *Freebie and the Bean*, *Funny Lady*, *Rollerball*, *Killer Elite*, *Harry and Walter Go to New York*, and *Kiss Me Goodbye*. In the case of *Misery* and *For the Boys*, he has been overshadowed by his co-star: Kathy Bates in the former, giving an Oscar-winning performance as a psycho fan opposite Caan's romance novelist; and Bette Midler in the latter, in an Oscar-nominated performance as a star singer opposite Caan's star comedian.

In his best later-career films—*Misery* and *Honeymoon in Vegas*, in which he plays a comical mobster—Caan has emerged as a solid character actor. But for the most part, he remains a misused and too-often untapped talent.

—Rob Edelman

CAGE, Nicolas

Nationality: American. **Born:** Nicolas Coppola in Long Beach, California, 7 January 1964; nephew of the director Francis Ford Coppola. **Family:** Married the actress Patricia Arquette, 1995; son, Weston Coppola Cage, by former girlfriend, the actress Kristina Fulton. **Education:** Attended Beverly Hills High School, left in 11th grade with an equivalency degree; studied at the American Conservatory Theatre, San Francisco; studied acting with Peggy Feury. **Career:** 1981—appeared in TV movie *The Best of Times*; 1982—made theatrical film debut as Nicolas Coppola in *Fast Times at Ridgemont High*; 1983—changed last name to avoid being rated as Francis Ford Coppola's nephew, choosing Cage in double homage to composer John Cage and comic book superhero Luke Cage; 1989—gained notoriety for eating a live cockroach in *Vampire's Kiss*. **Awards:** Best Actor, New York Film Critics, Golden Globe for best drama actor, Screen Actors Guild Award, National Society of Film Critics, and Academy Award, for *Leaving Las Vegas*, 1995. **Agent:** Brillstein/Grey, 9200 Sunset Boulevard, #428, Los Angeles, CA 90069, U.S.A.

Films as Actor:

(as Nicolas Coppola)

1981   *The Best of Times* (for TV)
1982   *Fast Times at Ridgemont High* (Heckerling) (as Brad's bud)

(as Nicolas Cage)

1983   *Valley Girl* (Coolidge) (as Randy); *Rumble Fish* (Francis Ford Coppola) (as Smokey)
1984   *Racing with the Moon* (Richard Benjamin) (as Nicky); *The Cotton Club* (Francis Ford Coppola) (as Vincent Dwyer); *Birdy* (Alan Parker) (as Al Columbato)
1986   *The Boy in Blue* (Jarrott) (as Ned Hanlan); *Peggy Sue Got Married* (Francis Ford Coppola) (as Charlie Bodell)
1987   *Raising Arizona* (Coen) (as Hi); *Moonstruck* (Jewison) (as Ronny Cammareri)
1988   *Never on Tuesday* (Rifkin) (as man in red sports car, uncredited)
1989   *Vampire's Kiss* (Bierman) (as Peter Loew)
1990   *Fire Birds* (David Green) (as Jake Preston); *Wild at Heart* (David Lynch) (as Sailor Ripley); *Tempo di Uccidere* (*Time to Kill*; *The Short Cut*) (Montaldo) (as Enrico Silvestri); *Industrial Symphony No. 1: The Dream of the Broken Hearted* (Lynch) (as Heartbreaking Man)
1991   *Zandalee* (Pillsbury) (as Johnny Collins)
1992   *Honeymoon in Vegas* (Andrew Bergman) (as Jack Singer)
1993   *Amos & Andrew* (Frye) (as Amos Odell); *Deadfall* (Christopher Coppola) (as Eddie); *Red Rock West* (Dahl) (as Michael Williams)

Nicolas Cage in *Wild at Heart*

1994   *Guarding Tess* (Hugh Wilson) (as Doug Chesnic); *It Could Happen to You* (Andrew Bergman) (as Charlie Lang); *Trapped in Paradise* (George Gallo) (as Bill Firpo)

1995   *Kiss of Death* (Schroeder) (as Little Junior Brown); *Leaving Las Vegas* (Figgis) (as Ben Sanderson)

1996   *The Rock* (Bay)

Publications

By CAGE: articles—

Interview with Robert Crane, in *Playboy* (Chicago), June 1989.

"The Beasts within . . . Nicolas Cage," interview with Mark Rowland, in *American Film* (Washington, D.C.), June 1990.

"Nicolas Cage, the Sunshine Man," interview with Ellen Pall, in *New York Times*, 24 July 1994.

"Nicolas Cage," interview with Mark Marvel, in *Interview* (New York), August 1994.

"Dangerous, Dedicated, and Wild at Heart, Nicolas Cage Is a Hollywood Samurai," interview with Fred Schruers, in *Rolling Stone* (New York), 16 November 1995.

On CAGE: articles—

Hirschfeld, Neal, "A New Face in the Crowd," in *New York Daily News Magazine*, 3 February 1985.

Clark, John, "Nicolas Cage," in *Premiere* (New York), September 1990.

Current Biography 1994, New York, 1994.

Babitz, Eve, "Nicolas Cage," *Harper's Bazaar* (New York), July 1994.

Daly, Steve, "High Spirits," in *Entertainment Weekly* (New York), 8 March 1996.

* * *

In his early screen appearances Nicolas Cage came across as a bit of a blowhard. But when he turned himself into a cartoon, as the gentle thief Hi in *Raising Arizona*, his all-out style became emphatically pleasurable. Cage plays wild hare comedy off his lanky-hunky body, his air of eternal devotion, and a glimmer of Old World honor in his round, dark-lidded eyes. A berserkly anomalous courtliness gives him a romantic air even in the looniest slapstick. He furthered his comic style in the more sophisticated *Moonstruck* as Ronny, a young butcher in love with his estranged older brother's fiancée. Ronny's brooding perfectly matches the dormancy of Cher's good daughter Loretta; when he proclaims his love for her and she smacks him and tells him to "Snap out of it!," they seem to jolt each other to life. Romantic comedy pairings rarely carry such a richly sensual charge.

Cage then outdid himself in his starring role in *Vampire's Kiss* as a yuppie editor who thinks he is turning into a vampire; he makes too much seem like just the right amount. His Peter Lowe is at once grotesque and bounding, both a heavily florid comedian such as the young Charles Laughton and a leaping calorie-burner such as Douglas Fairbanks. He keeps falling prey to obsessions and topping one tantrum with another, and getting more and more amusing. Cage achieves transformations as alarmingly funny as Jim Carrey's in *The Mask*, but without the special effects. (Like Carrey, Cage shows the influence of Jerry Lewis, whom he claims to have idolized as a child.)

Cage was less successful in David Lynch's *Wild at Heart* as a junkie sailor on the run with his girlfriend, because his craziness has too much competition from the murky swirl of the story and visuals; Lynch was straining. Cage was more impressive in a series of light comedies in the early 1990s, working especially well with Andrew Bergman. As Jack Singer in *Honeymoon in Vegas* he plays a man who overcomes his fear of marriage when he loses his girlfriend in a poker game. Jack has vacillated too long; by the time he acts the situation requires more than ordinary effort. Jack quickly becomes hilariously exasperated, and Cage gives classic accelerating delivery to such lines as, "He lives in a SHACK!" Cage shows his peerless ability to engage in the most frantic complications of romantic comedy and remain not only funny but sexy.

He was also good in the calmer role of the married cop who leaves a winning lottery ticket as a tip to a waitress in Bergman's *It Could Happen to You*, and in a straight performance in John Dahl's film noir *Red Rock West*. Cage is fresh and convincing in both pictures in which he has to be more essentially stable than the way his life is turning out. However, you miss his earmark outbursts. He does not seem actory in *Red Rock West*, but he does not seem like himself either. He has matured on screen, getting continually manlier and handsomer, and he may be incapable of a bum performance, but he needs to have his composure cracked to work at his most imaginative.

Finally with *Leaving Las Vegas* he got a chance to really plumb his comic skill. He plays Ben Sanderson, an alcoholic writer who leaves Hollywood for Vegas with the stated goal of drinking himself to death. The script lets us know that Cage's goofiness is the character's; when Ben tape records a pornographic-alcoholic fantasy while waiting in line at the bank, it is the showy misbehavior of a writer, a man emulating Henry Miller and Charles Bukowski. Cage's mugging and flashily affected readings stem from Ben's self-destructive perversity, and the writer-director Mike Figgis enables Cage to push his one-man-band inventiveness to a level of expressiveness that could not be reached any other way. There is no other approach to Ben; he is too smart and too self-conscious to *emote*. Ben's spaced-out put-on is an extraordinary invention—it is how a man who needs human interaction to the very end keeps in touch with people without letting them intervene in his determination to get to the end. Cage, by showing us how to see through Ben's evasiveness without violating Ben's terms of play, pulls off what Quentin Tarantino could not in *Pulp Fiction* when at the closing he went sincere with Samuel L. Jackson's freaky takeoff on black Baptist oratory. (Tarantino is a great joker, but he had not provided himself with a fleck of emotional fiber to spin.) Cage has long been the most exciting young actor in American movies; with *Leaving Las Vegas* he became the most stirring as well.

—Alan Dale

CAGNEY, James

Nationality: American. **Born:** James Francis Cagney Jr. in New York City, 17 July 1899; brother of the actress Jeanne Cagney. **Education:** Attended Stuyvesant High School, New York; briefly attended Columbia University. **Family:** Married Frances Willard (Willie) Vernon, 1922, adopted children: James and Cathleen. **Career:** Acted in productions staged by Lenox Hill Settlement House during childhood; 1919—worked in vaudeville as chorus dancer and female impersonator; 1920—in chorus of Broadway musical *Pitter-Patter*; 1925—began playing leads on Broadway; 1927-28—opened the Cagney School

of Dancing with wife; 1929—following success in Broadway musical *Penny Arcade*, contracted by Warners to appear in film version, retitled *Sinner's Holiday*; 1930—long-term contract with Warners; early 1930s—involved in Screen Actors Guild, later serving as vice president (1934-39) and president (1942-43); 1936—sued Warners over breach of contract and won; 1936-38—in two films for small Grand National Pictures; 1938—re-signed with Warners; 1943—formed William Cagney Productions with brother; 1953—final independent Cagney production *A Lion Is in the Streets*; 1957—directed film *Short Cut to Hell*; 1961—retired from acting; 1981—came out of retirement for role in Forman's *Ragtime*. **Awards:** Best Actor, New York Film Critics, for *Angels with Dirty Faces*, 1938; Best Actor Academy Award, and Best Actor, New York Film Critics, for *Yankee Doodle Dandy*, 1942; Life Achievement Award, American Film Institute, 1974; Honored for "Lifetime Achievement in the Performing Arts" by the Kennedy Center, 1980. **Died:** In Stansfordville, New York, 30 March 1986.

Films as Actor:

1930   *Sinner's Holiday* (Adolfi) (as Harry Delano); *Doorway to Hell* (*A Handful of Clouds*) (Mayo) (as Steve Mileaway); *Intimate Interview* (Elliott)

1931   *Other Men's Women* (Wellman) (as Ed); *The Millionaire* (Adolfi) (as Schofield); **The Public Enemy** (Wellman) (as Tom Powers); *Smart Money* (Alfred E. Green) (as Jack); *Blonde Crazy* (*Larceny Lane*) (Del Ruth) (as Bert Harris); *How I Play Golf* (Marshall)

1932   *Taxi!* (Del Ruth) (as Matt Nolan); *The Crowd Roars* (Hawks) (as Joe Greer); *Winner Take All* (Del Ruth) (as Jim Kane)

1933   *Hard to Handle* (LeRoy) (as Lefty Merrill); *Picture Snatcher* (Lloyd Bacon) (as Danny Kean); *The Mayor of Hell* (Mayo) (as Patsy Gargan); *Footlight Parade* (Lloyd Bacon) (as Chester Kent); *Lady Killer* (Del Ruth) (as Dan Quigley); *Hollywood on Parade*

1934   *Jimmy the Gent* (Curtiz) (as Jimmy Corrigan); *He Was Her Man* (Lloyd Bacon) (as Flicker Hayes); *Here Comes the Navy* (Lloyd Bacon) (as Chesty O'Connor); *The St. Louis Kid* (*A Perfect Weekend*) (Enright) (as Eddie Kennedy); *Hollywood Gad-About*; *Screen Snapshots One*

1935   *Devil Dogs of the Air* (Lloyd Bacon) (as Tommy O'Toole); *G-Men* (Keighley) (as James "Brick" Davis); *The Irish in Us* (Lloyd Bacon) (as Danny O'Hara); *A Midsummer Night's Dream* (Reinhardt and Dieterle) (as Bottom); *Frisco Kid* (Lloyd Bacon) (as Bat Morgan); *Ceiling Zero* (Hawks) (as Dizzy Davis); *A Trip through a Hollywood Studio*; *Mutiny on the Bounty* (Lloyd) (as extra)

1936   *Great Guy* (*Pluck of the Irish*) (Blystone) (as Johnny Cave)

1937   *Something to Sing About* (Schertzinger) (as Terry Rooney)

1938   *Boy Meets Girl* (Lloyd Bacon) (as Robert Law); *Angels with Dirty Faces* (Curtiz) (as Rocky Sullivan); *For Auld Lang Syne* (Bilson)

1939   *The Oklahoma Kid* (Lloyd Bacon) (as Jim Kincaid); *Each Dawn I Die* (Keighley) (as Frank Ross); **The Roaring Twenties** (Walsh) (as Eddie Bartlett)

1940   *The Fighting 69th* (Keighley) (as Jerry Plunkett); *Torrid Zone* (Keighley) (as Nick Butler); *City for Conquest* (Litvak) (as Danny Kenny)

1941   *The Strawberry Blonde* (Walsh) (as Biff Grimes); *The Bride Came C.O.D.* (Keighley) (as Steve Collins)

1942   *Captains of the Clouds* (Curtiz) (as Brian MacLean); **Yankee Doodle Dandy** (Curtiz) (as George M. Cohan)

1943   *Johnny Come Lately* (*Johnny Vagabond*) (William K. Howard) (as Tom Richards); *Show Business at War* (*March of Time*); *You, John Jones* (LeRoy) (as Air Raid Warden)

James Cagney

1944   *Battle Stations* (as narrator)
1945   *Blood on the Sun* (Lloyd) (as Nick Condon)
1946   *13 Rue Madeleine* (Hathaway) (as Bob Sharkey)
1948   *The Time of Your Life* (Potter) (as Joe)
1949   ***White Heat*** (Walsh) (as Cody Jarrett)
1950   *The West Point Story* (Del Ruth) (as Elwin Bixby); *Kiss Tomorrow Goodbye* (Gordon Douglas) (as Ralph Cotter)
1951   *Come Fill the Cup* (Gordon Douglas) (as Lew Marsh); *Starlift* (Del Ruth) (as himself)
1952   *What Price Glory?* (John Ford) (as Captain Flagg)
1953   *A Lion Is in the Streets* (*A Lion in the Streets*) (Walsh) (as Hank Martin)
1955   *Run for Cover* (Nicholas Ray) (as Matt Dow); *Love Me or Leave Me* (Charles Vidor) (as Martin "Gimp" Snyder); *Mister Roberts* (John Ford and LeRoy) (as Captain); *The Seven Little Foys* (Shavelson) (as George M. Cohan)
1956   *Tribute to a Bad Man* (Wise) (as Jeremy Rodock); *These Wilder Years* (Rowland) (as Steve Bradford)
1957   *Man of a Thousand Faces* (Pevney) (as Lon Chaney Sr.)
1959   *Never Steal Anything Small* (Lederer) (as Jake MacIllaney); *Shake Hands with the Devil* (Anderson) (as Sean Lenihan)
1960   *The Gallant Hours* (Montgomery) (as Adm. William F. "Bull" Halsey, + pr)
1961   *One, Two, Three* (Wilder) (as C. P. MacNamara)
1962   *Road to the Wall* (doc) (as narrator)
1966   *Ballad of Smokey the Bear* (voice only)
1968   *Arizona Bushwhackers* (Selander) (as narrator)
1975   *Brother, Can You Spare a Dime?* (Mora—doc) (as voice of Everyman)
1981   *Ragtime* (Forman) (as Police Commissioner Rhinelander Waldo)
1984   *Terrible Joe Moran* (Sargent—for TV) (title role)

Film as Director:

1957   *Short Cut to Hell*

Publications

By CAGNEY: book—

Cagney by Cagney, New York, 1976.

By CAGNEY: articles—

"How I Got This Way," as told to Pete Martin in *The Saturday Evening Post* (Philadelphia), 7, 14, and 21 January 1956.
"Interview with James Cagney," by Philip Oakes in *Sight and Sound* (London), Winter 1958-59.
"James Cagney Talking . . . ," in *Films and Filming* (London), March 1959.

On CAGNEY: books—

O'Brien, Pat, *The Wind at My Back*, New York, 1964.
Sennett, Ted, *Warner Brothers Presents*, New Rochelle, New York, 1971.
Dickens, Homer, *The Films of James Cagney*, Secaucus, New Jersey, 1972.
Offen, Ron, *Cagney*, Chicago, 1972.
Bergman, Andrew, *Cagney*, New York, 1973.
Freedland, Michael, *James Cagney*, London, 1974.
Wallis, Hal, and Charles Higham, *Starmaker*, New York, 1980.
James Cagney dans l'objectif, Paris, 1981.

Clinch, Minty, *Cagney: The Story of His Film Career*, London, 1982.
McGilligan, Patrick, *Cagney: The Actor as Auteur*, San Diego, 1982.
Warren, Doug, *James Cagney: The Authorized Biography*, London, 1983; rev. ed., 1986.
Schickel, Richard, *James Cagney: A Celebration*, London, 1985.
Sklar, Robert, *City Boys: Cagney, Bogart, Garfield*, Princeton, New Jersey, 1992.

On CAGNEY: articles—

Kirstein, Lincoln, "Cagney and the American Hero," in *Hound and Horn* (New York), April 1932.
Potamkin, H. A., "The Personality of the Player: A Phase of Unity," in *Close-Up* (London), March 1933.
Durant, John, "Tough on and Off," in *Collier's* (New York), 31 August 1940.
Current Biography 1942, New York, 1942.
Cole, Lester, "Unhappy Ending," in *Hollywood Quarterly*, October 1945.
Brown, John Mason, "Cagney Rides Again," in *Saturday Review* (New York), 1 October 1949.
Tynan, Kenneth, "Cagney and the Mob," in *Sight and Sound* (London), May 1951.
Parsons, Louella, "Cagney's Year," in *Cosmopolitan* (New York), June 1955.
Miller, Don, "James Cagney," in *Films in Review* (New York), August/September 1958.
"Yankee Doodle Dandy," in *Newsweek* (New York), 22 April 1968.
Haskell, Molly, "Partners in Crime and Conversation," in *The Village Voice* (New York), 7 December 1972.
Lawrence, K. G., "Homage to James Cagney," in *Films in Review* (New York), May 1974.
McGilligan, Patrick, "Just a Dancer Gone Wrong: The Complication of James Cagney," in *Take One* (Montreal), September 1974.
Kandel, Abel, "James Cagney: Man of Principle" in *Close-Ups: The Movie Star Book*, edited by Danny Peary, New York, 1978.
"The Conversation: Studs Terkel and James Cagney," in *Esquire* (New York), October 1981.
Kroll, Jack, "James Cagney" and "Cagney vs. Allen vs. Brooks" by William S. Pechter, in *The Movie Star*, edited by Elisabeth Weis, New York, 1981.
Buckley, M., "James Cagney," in *Films in Review* (New York), March 1982.
Cieutat, M., "Tribute to a Good Man: James Cagney ou l'ambivalence de l'Amérique," in *Positif* (Paris), April 1982.
Sklar, Robert, "L'Acteur en lutte: James Cagney contre Warner Bros.," in *Filméchange* (Paris), Summer 1983.
Hagopian, Kevin, "Declarations of Independence: A History of Cagney Productions," in *Velvet Light Trap* (Madison, Wisconsin), no. 22, 1986.
Obituary in *New York Times*, 31 March 1986.
"James Cagney Succumbs at 86: Quintessential Film Tough Guy," obituary in *Variety* (New York), 2 April 1986.
Buckley, M., obituary in *Films in Review* (New York), June/July 1986.
McGilligan, Patrick, "Yankee Doodle Diary," in *Film Comment* (New York), July/August 1986.

*   *   *

Jimmy Cagney was a natural actor with an astonishing range. As Bottom in Reinhardt and Dieterle's *A Midsummer Night's Dream*, he demonstrated that he could play comedy effectively. He was Lon Chaney in *Man of a Thousand Faces*, and twice played George M. Cohan, winning an Academy Award for *Yankee Doodle Dandy*, and repeating the role in 1955 for *The Seven Little Foys*. But his specialty was Irish tough guys: prizefighters, gangsters, bootleggers, and racketeers.

In 1931, a year after his film career began, Cagney created the definitive portrait of a tough, swaggering movie gangster in Wellman's *The Public Enemy*. Fifty years later, and in failing health, he gave Milos Forman an equally memorable portrayal as New York police commissioner Rhinelander Waldo in the film version of E. L. Doctorow's *Ragtime*. The swagger was still there, and the charisma. As early as 1939, critic Otis Ferguson paid tribute to Cagney by noting that it would be "hard to say what our impression of the total American character would have been without him."

Cagney learned the American character on the streets of New York. When he played Irish tough guys on the screen, he was able to draw on his own youthful experiences. Cagney began his performing career as a hoofer in a show called *Every Sailor* at Keith's 86th Street Theatre, then, in 1920, he landed a specialty dance in the show *Pitter-Patter*. His future wife, Frances Willard Vernon, was in the chorus line and after *Pitter-Patter* closed, they joined to form a dance team called "Vernon and Nye." His first important acting assignment came in 1925 when he was cast with Charles Bickford in the Maxwell Anderson play *Outside Looking In*.

In 1929 he played opposite Joan Blondell in *Maggie the Magnificent*, and subsequently in *Penny Arcade*. Al Jolson procured the rights for this play and then sold it to Warner Brothers. Cagney and Blondell were part of the package, and so Cagney went to Hollywood, where *Penny Arcade* became *Sinner's Holiday*. A year later he had the lead in *The Public Enemy* and was on his way to becoming a star.

His great talent was confined by the apparently stereotyped roles he often played over the next 25 years, but no one could do them better than Cagney. He perfectly understood the characters of the punks he portrayed, from the raw and brutal ambition of Tom Powers to the psychotic complexity of Cody Jarrett in *White Heat*, 18 years later.

In his portrayal of "Gimp" Snyder for Charles Vidor in *Love Me or Leave Me*, Cagney drew upon all the vitality and charisma of his old gangster roles to present the melancholy figure of a man who loves and respects a woman, Doris Day's Ruth Etting, whose sense of decency he is incapable of understanding. Cagney takes a modest melodrama and gives it an almost tragic dimension as Snyder attempts to reform but is finally driven crazy by his jealousy and shoots the piano player (Cameron Mitchell), who is his rival.

Rat-a-tat-tating those famous feet like machine gun fire in his musicals, Cagney was a whirling dervish whose finest performances, even in nonmusicals, seem choreographed. Both his upbringing in Hell's Kitchen and his vaudeville trouping inform every step this *sui generis* takes. Unlike other male superstars of Hollywood's Golden Age, Cagney was unafraid of returning to his gangster roots throughout his long, kinetic career. Only an actor unconstrained by image considerations could deliver as chilling a portrait of psychopathy as his migraine-plagued Mama's boy, Cody Jarrett. By contrast, think of the roles Gable, Stewart, Tracy, and Grant chose after their mass appeal hardened around their personas. Bringing humanity to his criminals and moral uncertainty to his good guys, Cagney created the myth of the streetwise cynic, who could just as fatefully be recruited to walk the straight and narrow or stride through a police lineup with attitude to burn. The only characterizational common ground was an energy-level unknown to the rest of us. In *One, Two, Three*, a virtuoso collaboration with Billy Wilder (then intended as Cagney's retirement film), the performer propels the Cold War farce forward and flies past topical references that date the film, as if his acting were independent of tired plot mechanics, as if his personality could simply burn through familiar gags until the audience is left only with the distilled essence of Cagney. One wishes this vital actor had accepted Jack Warner's offer to play Alfred P. Doolittle in *My Fair Lady*, a museum piece that would have benefited from his irreverent cock-of-the-walk strut.

Whether tackling bad guys on-screen or battling the Brothers Warner offscreen in his heyday, Cagney always placed his convictions in the forefront. Going independent at a time in the forties when such ven-

tures were considered suicidal, Cagney's production company created some lovely films, such as *Johnny Come Lately*, before going down fighting. But bucking the odds has always been a signature move on Cagney's part, whether knocking himself out to put on a show in *Footlight Parade* or sizing up Ann Sheridan on a rubber plantation in *Torrid Zone*. Not only could he jump in the job pool from G-Man to America's most wanted but he could also enliven Shakespeare or impersonate Adm. "Bull" Halsey in *The Gallant Hours* with the same self-confident *droit du seigneur*. Whereas less versatile stars played storybook versions of heroism, Cagney always scrapped for his honor because he was not a to-the-manner-born savior like John Wayne but a conflicted hero who had to arrive at virtue by sometimes battling his own instincts. Jimmy Cagney embodied the personal charisma of star acting during Hollywood's Golden Era. His abilities were unique, and his classic films are forever marked by his personal brilliance.

—James M. Welsh, updated by Robert Pardi

CAINE, Michael

Nationality: British. **Born:** Maurice Micklewhite in London, 14 March 1933. **Military Service:** 1951-53—served in Korea with Royal Fusiliers. **Family:** Married 1) Patricia Haines, 1954 (divorced 1956), one daughter; 2) Shakira Khatoon Baksh, 1973, one daughter. **Career:** Late 1940s-early 1950s—acted with amateur groups while working as a laborer; 1954-56—played small parts in provincial theaters and Joan Littlewood's Theatre Workshop; appeared frequently on British television; 1956—began appearing in bit roles in feature films; 1964—critical attention for role in *Zulu*; 1965—played role of Harry Palmer in first of series of films, *The Ipcress File*; early 1970s—involved with Klinger-Caine-Hodges Productions; 1980s—much work for TV, including *Jack the Ripper*, 1988, and *Jekyll and Hyde*, 1990. **Awards:** British Academy Award for Best Actor, for *Educating Rita*, 1983; Best Supporting Actor Academy Award, for *Hannah and Her Sisters*, 1986; CBE, 1993. **Address:** c/o Dennis Selinger, International Creative Management, Oxford House, 76 Oxford Street, London W1N OAX, England.

Films as Actor:

1956   *A Hill in Korea* (*Hell in Korea*) (Amyes) (bit role as Pvt. Lockyer)
1957   *How to Murder a Rich Uncle* (Patrick) (as Gilrony)
1958   *The Key* (Reed) (bit role); *Blind Spot* (Maxwell) (bit role); *The Two Headed Spy* (de Toth) (bit role as 2nd Gestapo agent); *Carve Her Name with Pride* (Gilbert)
1959   *Passport to Shame* (*Room 43*) (Rakoff) (bit role); *Danger Within* (*Breakout*) (Chaffey) (bit role)
1960   *Foxhole in Cairo* (Moxey) (as Weber); *The Bulldog Breed* (Asher) (bit role)
1961   *The Day the Earth Caught Fire* (Guest) (bit role)
1962   *Solo for Sparrow* (Flemyng) (as Mooney); *The Wrong Arm of the Law* (Owen) (bit role)
1964   *Zulu* (Endfield) (as Lt. Granville Bromhead)
1965   *The Ipcress File* (Furie) (as Harry Palmer)
1966   *Alfie* (Gilbert) (title role); *The Wrong Box* (Forbes) (as Michael); *Gambit* (Neame) (as Harry); *Funeral in Berlin* (Hamilton) (as Harry Palmer); *Hurry Sundown* (Preminger) (as Henry Warren)
1967   *Billion Dollar Brain* (Russell) (as Harry Palmer); "Snow" ep. of *Woman Times Seven* (De Sica) (as handsome stranger)

Michael Caine in *The Ipcress File* courtesy of The Rank Organisation Plc

1968   *Deadfall* (Forbes) (as Henry Clarke); *Play Dirty* (de Toth) (as Capt. Douglas); *The Magus* (Green) (as Nicholas Urfe)

1969   *The Italian Job* (Collinson) (as Charlie Croker); *Battle of Britain* (Hamilton) (as Sqdn. Leader Canfield); *Too Late the Hero* (Aldrich) (as Tosh)

1970   *The Last Valley* (Clavell) (as Captain); *Get Carter* (Hodges) (as Jack Carter); *Simon, Simon* (short)

1971   *Kidnapped* (Delbert Mann) (as Alan Breck); *Zee and Company* (*X, Y, and Zee*) (Hutton) (as Robert)

1972   *Pulp* (Hodges) (as Mickey King); *Sleuth* (Mankiewicz) (as Milo Tindle)

1974   *The Black Windmill* (Siegel) (as Major John Tarrant); *The Marseilles Contract* (*The Destructors*) (Parrish) (as Deray)

1975   *The Wilby Conspiracy* (Nelson) (as Keogh); *The Romantic Englishwoman* (Losey) (as Lewis Fielding); *The Man Who Would Be King* (Huston) (as Peachy Carnehan)

1976   *Peeper* (Hyams) (as Leslie Tucker); *The Eagle Has Landed* (John Sturges) (as Col. Kurt Steiner)

1977   *A Bridge Too Far* (Attenborough) (as Lt. Col. Joe Vandeleur); *Harry and Walter Go to New York* (Rydell) (as Adam Worth)

1978   *California Suite* (Ross) (as Sidney Cochran); *Ashanti* (Fleischer) (as Dr. David Lenderby); *Silver Bears* (Passer) (as Doc Fletcher)

1979   *The Swarm* (Irwin Allen) (as Brad Crane); *The Island* (Ritchie) (as Maynard); *Beyond the Poseidon Adventure* (Irwin Allen) (as Mike Turner)

1980   *Dressed to Kill* (De Palma) (as Dr. Robert Elliott)

1981   *Victory* (*Escape to Victory*) (Huston) (as Colby); *The Hand* (Stone) (as Jon Landsdale)

1982   *Deathtrap* (Lumet) (as Sidney Bruhl)

1983   *The Honorary Consul* (*Beyond the Limit*) (Mackenzie) (as Charlie Fortnum); *Educating Rita* (Gilbert) (as Professor)

1984   *The Jigsaw Man* (Young) (as Sir Philip Kimberly/Sergei Kuzminsky); *Blame It on Rio* (Donen) (as Matthew Hollis)

1985   *The Holcroft Convention* (Frankenheimer) (as Noel Holcroft); *Water* (Clement) (as Baxter)

1986   *Half Moon Street* (Swaim) (as Lord Bulbeck); *Hannah and Her Sisters* (Woody Allen) (as Elliot); ***Mona Lisa*** (Neil Jordan) (as Mortwell); *Sweet Liberty* (Alda) (as Elliott James)

1987   *The Fourth Protocol* (Mackenzie) (as John Preston, + exec pr); *Jaws—the Revenge* (Sargent) (as Hoagie); *Surrender* (Belson) (as Sean Stein, mystery novelist); *The Whistle Blower* (Langton) (as Frank Jones)

1988   *Dirty Rotten Scoundrels* (Oz) (as Lawrence Jamieson); *Without a Clue* (Eberhardt) (as Sherlock Holmes); *Jack the Ripper* (Wickes) (as Frederick Abberline—for TV)

1989   *Movie Life of George* (Brand—for TV); *The Trouble with Michael Caine* (Macmilan—for TV)

1990   *A Shock to the System* (Egleson) (as Graham Marshall); *Bullseye!* (Winner) (as Sidney Lipton/Dr. Daniel Hicklar); *Mr. Destiny* (Orr) (as Mike); *Jekyll & Hyde* (Wickes—for TV) (title role)

1991   *Noises Off* (Bogdanovich) (as Lloyd Fellowes)

1992   *The Muppet Christmas Carol* (Henson) (as Scrooge); *Death Becomes Her* (Zemeckis); *Blue Ice* (Mulcahy—for TV) (as Harry Anders, + pr)
1994   *On Deadly Ground* (Seagal) (as Michael Jennings); *World War II: When Lions Roared* (Joseph Sargent—for TV) (as Joseph Stalin)
1995   *Len Deighton's Bullet to Beijing* (Mihalka) (as Harry Palmer)

Publications

By CAINE: books—

Not Many People Know That, London, 1985.
Not Many People Know This Either, London, 1986.
Acting in Films: An Actor's Take on Movie Making, New York, 1990.
What's It All About?, New York, 1992.

By CAINE: articles—

"Interview: Michael Caine," in *Playboy* (Chicago), July 1967.
"Playing Dirty," interview in *Films and Filming* (London), April and May 1969.
"The Man Who Would Be Caine," interview with M. Rosen, in *Film Comment* (New York), July/August 1980.
Interview with Nick Roddick, in *Stills* (London), October 1984.
Interview with John Kobal, in *Films and Filming* (London), January 1985.

On CAINE: books—

Andrews, Emma, *The Films of Michael Caine*, London, 1977.
Hall, William, *Raising Caine: The Authorized Biography*, Englewood Cliffs, New Jersey, 1982.
Judge, Philip, *Michael Caine*, New York, 1985.
Gallagher, Elaine, *Candidly Caine*, London, 1990.

On CAINE: articles—

Farber, Stephen, "Alfie," in *Film Quarterly* (Berkeley), Spring 1967.
"Michael Caine," in *Focus on Film* (London), Spring 1973.
Films (London), October 1982.
Ciné Revue (Paris), 27 January 1983 and 12 April 1984 (both with filmography).
Photoplay (London), June 1983 and February 1984.
Current Biography 1988, New York, 1988.

*   *   *

Michael Caine belonged in the Cockney contingent (Anthony Newley, Terence Stamp, Twiggy) that rose to stardom soon after kitchen-sink Northerners such as Albert Finney and Tom Courtenay. While Stamp came on as the smart tough mod, and Newley led with his pathos, Caine's basic persona was the upwardly mobile Cockney, with 1960s executive specs and crispy well-groomed wavy hair, who yet retains, without inverted snobbery and in a naturally neat voice, his Cockney accent. He was laid-back, too—tall, amiable, almost lordly—and his cool blue eyes, bespoke calm calculation, bedroom sensitivity, and/or deep dark scheming. This balance of easy sociability and private purpose is of the essence.

Son of a fish porter and a charwoman, Caine rose through rep to television, which he alternated with innumerable bit and supporting parts. Auditioning for a grumbling Cockney soldier in *Zulu*, he was surprised to be offered a lead role, and as an aristocratic young officer,

whose authority must be overthrown by toughly professional Stanley Baker. Caine revamped his stereotypically effete character, so that his languid air proved deceptive.

While Caine's performance in *Zulu* drew considerable critical attention, he languished for almost a year without film offers after the picture's release. Then Harry Saltzman, co-producer of the fabulously successful James Bond films, tapped him for the lead in the screen version of Len Deighton's espionage novel *The Ipcress File*. As the insolent, working-class secret agent Harry Palmer, Caine was a complete antithesis to James Bond. The long, improvised, supermarket scene in the film embellishes the everyday melancholy that extended Caine's rapport with audiences. The subsequent Palmer films, *Funeral in Berlin* and *Billion Dollar Brain*, the latter directed by Ken Russell, Caine's handpicked choice, neglected that intimate rapport with audiences, and failed. In *Alfie* Caine's Cockney chauffeur, a smoothly relentless Casanova, with his insidiously cynical chats direct to the audience, stirred a deep uneasiness about permissiveness. It was a role shunned by almost every eligible star; Caine won his first Oscar nomination, and the film was the biggest-ever British money-earner in the United States. It made him the star he is today.

Caine contributed polished performances to many lesser films, although his very Englishness, as domestic production flagged, set him adrift in productions of "ersatz internationalism," as he called it. Of various war action films in exotic locales, the most interesting were two toughly ironic meditations on idealism and power: *The Last Valley*, written and directed by the late novelist James Clavell of *Shogun* and *Noble House* fame, with Caine as a thoughtful German mercenary in the Thirty Years' War; and John Huston's long-aborning *The Man Who Would Be King*, with Caine as the feet-on-the-ground adventurer Peachy Carnehan, opposite Sean Connery's upstart title character. In both films, settings and trimmings somehow eclipsed stars and themes intrinsically as powerful as *The Bridge on the River Kwai* or *Apocalypse Now*. Caine's long line of affable scoundrels and conmen extended to chillingly calm London gangsters in *Get Carter*, a pet project of Caine's directed by Mike Hodges, and *Mona Lisa*, for which Caine took substantially less than his usual astronomical fee in order to get the film made. In *Kidnapped* his sword-fencing worked in well with his airily long-limbed command of personal space.

Caine's sharply blue, yet softly bulbous, eyes suggested quietly devious, complicated, or creative characters. *Pulp*, *Sleuth*, and *Deathtrap* were dialogue comedies involving writers in murder-plot-and-counterplot; they were near two-handers, Caine "duetting" with, respectively, Mickey Rooney, Laurence Olivier (Caine plucking an Oscar nomination from under the knightly nose), and Christopher Reeve. A fourth variation on writer/reality games, *The Romantic Englishwoman*, with Caine as a writer fantasizing his wife's adultery, promised greater depth, but the eagerly awaited collaboration between Caine and director Joseph Losey seemed short-circuited by a tricksy script.

Caine's air of mischievous sensuality explains his three gay roles: in *Deathtrap* (where he and Reeve kiss), *Dressed to Kill* (as a psychiatrist who is also a transvestite homicidal maniac), and *California Suite* (with Maggie Smith as sexually ambiguous Hollywood marrieds doubly nervy while awaiting the Oscar announcements).

By 1979 Caine's career again risked losing direction, with a run of parts in mediocre spy, horror, and disaster films. *Educating Rita* was a "return to roots," to the director of *Alfie*, and to Oscar nomination. Caine played an extinct poet turned university lecturer, disillusioned by the grooves of academe, and vacillating between his textbooks and his whiskey bottle; but revivified by the cheek and eager optimism of working-class housewife Julie Walters. Alan Alda's *Sweet Liberty* and Woody Allen's *Hannah and Her Sisters* brought Caine into fully American comedy of manners. In Alda's film he sketches a film star surely based on himself. A gregarious Cockney now King of Hollywood, he good-naturedly jollies Alda, as a history professor, out of his misery about moviemakers travestying his serious book. In Allen's slightly sad comedy, Caine, a business manager for rock stars, is torn by guilt about loving two sisters, and ends up prey to the nervousness with which the Allen character began; an intriguing role reversal. Though every character but Allen's was dissatisfyingly foreshortened, Caine won a Supporting Actor Oscar.

He continues a highly popular star, though he is frequently criticized for being less than selective about the projects he takes on. He played the real inspector Frederick Abberline, the working-class chief detective on the trail of the infamous serial killer Jack the Ripper in writer-director David Wickes's two-part telefilm produced for the Ripper's centenary. The film proposed a final solution to the century-old mystery, naming the Queen's royal physician as the legendary killer, a solution offered by the 1979 Ripper film, *Murder by Decree*, as well. For Wickes also, Caine played the title roles in *Jekyll and Hyde*, the umpteenth version of the durable Robert Louis Stevenson barnstormer, this one produced for British and American television.

He returned to comedy with *Noises Off*, Peter Bogdanovich's film adaptation of playwright Michael Frayn's takeoff on British sex farces, appearing opposite his old *Deathtrap* flame Christopher Reeve. In *The Muppet Christmas Carol*, he played Scrooge opposite a bevy of Jim Henson's puppet creatures in Dickensian garb. 1992's *Blue Ice*, a film he also produced, found Caine once again embroiled in secret agentry. And he was a villainous oil baron whom Steven Seagal prevents from destroying the Alaskan landscape in *On Deadly Ground*. The busy star somehow managed to find the time find to write his autobiography, published in 1992 under the title *What's It All About?*, Caine's famous refrain from *Alfie*.

—Raymond Durgnat, updated by John McCarty

CALHERN, Louis

Nationality: American. **Born:** Carl Henry Vogt in New York City, 19 (or 16) February 1895. **Family:** Married 1) the actress and writer Ilka Chase, 1926 (divorced 1926); 2) Julia Hoyt, 1927 (divorced 1932); 3) Natalie Schafer, 1933 (divorced); 4) Marianne Stewart, 1946 (divorced). **Career:** Late 1910s-early 1920s—worked on Broadway stage; 1921—film debut in *The Blot*; followed by romantic leading man roles in silent films; 1931—talking film debut in *Stolen Heaven*; 1938—on stage in *Golden Boy* in London; later stage roles include *Life with Father*, 1942, *The Magnificent Yankee* (and film version), and *King Lear*, 1950; after 1949—worked exclusively for MGM, mainly in supporting roles. **Died:** In Tokyo, Japan, 12 May 1956.

Films as Actor:

1921 *The Blot* (Weber) (as Phil West); *Too Wise Wives* (Weber); *What's Worth While?* (Weber)
1922 *Woman, Wake Up!* (Harrison)
1923 *The Last Moment* (Read)
1931 *Blonde Crazy* (*Larceny Lane*) (Del Ruth) (as Dapper Dan Barker); *Stolen Heaven* (Abbott) (as Steve Perry); *The Road to Singapore* (Alfred E. Green) (as Dr. George March)
1932 *Okay America* (*Penalty of Fame*) (Garnett) (as Mileaway Rosso); *They Call It Sin* (Freeland) (as Ford Humphries); *Night after Night* (Mayo) (as Dick Bolton); *Afraid to Talk* (Cahn) (as Wade)
1933 *20,000 Years in Sing Sing* (Curtiz) (as Joe Finn); *The Woman Accused* (Sloane) (as Leo Young); *Duck Soup* (McCarey) (as Ambassador Trentino); *Frisco Jenny* (Wellman) (as Steve

Dutton); *Strictly Personal* (Murphy) (as Magruder); *The World Gone Mad* (*The Public Be Hanged*) (Cabanne) (as Christopher Bruno); *Diplomaniacs* (Seiter) (as Winklereid)
1934 *The Count of Monte Cristo* (Rowland V. Lee) (as Raymond de Villefort Jr.); *The Affairs of Cellini* (La Cava) (as Ottaviano); *The Man with Two Faces* (Mayo) (as Stanley Vance)
1935 *The Arizonian* (Charles Vidor) (as Jake Mannen); *The Last Days of Pompeii* (Cooper) (as prefect); *Sweet Adeline* (LeRoy) (as Maj. Jim Day); *Woman Wanted* (Seitz) (as Smiley)
1936 *The Gorgeous Hussy* (Brown) (as Sunderland)
1937 *The Life of Emile Zola* (Dieterle) (as Maj. Dort); *Her Husband Lies* (Ludwig) (as Sordoni)
1938 *Fast Company* (*The Rare Book Murder*) (Buzzell) (as Elias Z. Bannerman)
1939 *Juarez* (Dieterle) (as LeMarc); *Fifth Avenue Girl* (La Cava) (as Dr. Kessler); *Charlie McCarthy, Detective* (Tuttle) (as Arthur Aldrich); *The Story of Dr. Ehrlich's Magic Bullet* (*Dr. Ehrlich's Magic Bullet*) (Dieterle) (as Dr. Brockdorf); *I Take This Woman* (Van Dyke) (as Dr. Duveen)
1943 *Heaven Can Wait* (Lubitsch) (as Randolph Van Cleve); *Nobody's Darling* (Anthony Mann)
1944 *The Bridge of San Luis Rey* (Rowland V. Lee) (as viceroy); *Up in Arms* (Nugent) (as Col. Ashley)
1946 *Notorious* (Hitchcock) (as Paul Prescott)
1948 *Arch of Triumph* (Milestone) (as Morosow)
1949 *The Red Danube* (Sidney) (as Col. Piniev); *The Red Pony* (Milestone) (as Grandpa)
1950 *Nancy Goes to Rio* (Leonard) (as Gregory Elliott); *Two Weeks with Love* (Rowland) (as Horatio Robinson); *The Magnificent Yankee* (*The Man with Thirty Sons*) (John Sturges) (as Oliver Wendell Holmes Jr.); *The Devil's Doorway* (Anthony Mann) (as Verne Coolan); *A Life of Her Own* (Cukor) (as Jim Leversoe); *The Asphalt Jungle* (Huston) (as Alonzo D. Emmerich); *Annie Get Your Gun* (Sidney) (as Buffalo Bill)
1951 *The Man with a Cloak* (Markle) (as Thevenet); *It's a Big Country* (Thorpe and others) (as narrator)
1952 *Invitation* (Reinhardt) (as Simon Bowker); *The Bad and the Beautiful* (Minnelli) (as voice on the recording); *We're Not Married* (Goulding) (as Freddie Melrose); *The Prisoner of Zenda* (Thorpe) (as Col. Zapt); *Washington Story* (*Target for Scandal*) (Pirosh) (as Charles W. Birch)
1953 *Confidentially Connie* (Buzzell) (as Opie Bedloe); *Julius Caesar* (Joseph L. Mankiewicz) (title role); *Remains to Be Seen* (Weis) (as Benjamin Goodwin); *Main Street to Broadway* (Garnett) (as himself); *Latin Lovers* (LeRoy) (as Grandfather Santos)
1954 *Rhapsody* (Charles Vidor) (as Nicholas Durant); *Executive Suite* (Wise) (as George Nyle Caswell); *The Student Prince* (Thorpe) (as King of Karlsburg); *Men of the Fighting Lady* (Marton) (as James A. Michener); *Betrayed* (Reinhardt) (as Gen. Ten Eyck); *Athena* (Thorpe) (as Grandpa Ulysses Mulvain)
1955 *The Blackboard Jungle* (Richard Brooks) (as Jim Murdock); *The Prodigal* (Thorpe) (as Nahreeb)
1956 *Forever, Darling* (Hall) (as Charles Y. Bewell); *High Society* (Walters) (as Uncle Willie)

Publications

On CALHERN: articles—

Current Biography 1951, New York, 1951.

Houseman, John, "Filming *Julius Caesar*," in *Films in Review* (New York), April 1953 and *Sight and Sound* (London), July/September 1953.
Obituary in *New York Times*, 13 May 1956.

* * *

In the first half of the 1950s it seemed as if Louis Calhern was in every other MGM picture released. He had signed with that studio in 1949 and immediately began creating character roles that were always interesting and occasionally more. One of his first portrayals was Buffalo Bill, long white hair flowing, in the musical *Annie Get Your Gun*.

In 1950 Calhern recreated for the cinema his acclaimed stage role in *The Magnificent Yankee*, in which he had definitively impersonated—or perhaps reincarnated—Justice Oliver Wendell Holmes. The previous year he had returned to Broadway to play the role he had prepared himself for most of his professional life: the great mad King Lear.

Despite the actor's gray-haired and dignified mien he was not always cast as a rock of probity. It was John Huston's crime drama *The Asphalt Jungle* that gave Calhern one of his few truly memorable film parts. With an inexperienced but plainly nubile Marilyn Monroe in a supporting role as his decades-younger mistress, he brought both understated menace and a sad world-weariness to his sleazy, crooked lawyer Emmerich. To her he euphemistically may have been "Uncle Lon" but he was far from avuncular.

This was somewhat of a return to Calhern's film roots. He began his sound film career in 1931 and throughout the decade he played villains or at least men with morality in various shades of gray. When he wasn't plotting dirty work in melodramas he was sometimes found doing it in such comedies as Paramount's *Duck Soup* in which the formidable Groucho Marx was his adversary.

Calhern was also subjected to indignities by the comedy team of Wheeler and Woolsey in *Diplomaniacs* and by Danny Kaye in *Up in Arms*. In viewing those films one is led to wonder whether Calhern really had much sense of humor. He seems to have a puzzled look on his face that may or may not have been called for in the script. Either he wittingly played against his persona in comedies or it was played against without his complicity.

Calhern usually essayed authoritative characters, helped by a powerful physical presence with a height in the 6'2" to 6'3" range. This imposing physique was topped by a face like that on some ancient coin. His was a Roman nose incarnate and indeed it was seen at least twice above a Roman toga in *The Last Days of Pompeii* and the title role in the all-star *Julius Caesar*.

Calhern had begun his illustrious career humbly enough trouping in a Bronx stock company about 1912. He gradually made his way upward through vaudeville and repertory, eventually joining a stock company in Los Angeles. He was discovered for the cinema in the very lair of the movie industry and taken under the wing of director Lois Weber.

It was in 1921 that Louis Calhern made the first three of his five silent movies. He partnered the beauteous Weber star Claire Windsor who got far more mileage out of their pictures together than he did. With such unprepossessing titles as *What's Worth While?*, *Woman, Wake Up!*, and *Too Wise Wives* to his dubious credit, he soon headed east again. This time it was to a career as a Broadway matinee idol.

With the success of *The Song and Dance Man* in 1923 and the romantic lead in the next year's even more popular *The Cobra*, the decade of the Roaring Twenties was Calhern's. His reappearance in movies during the 1930s did not necessarily bring him greater fame but aging theater idols do not have great job security. He certainly did not give up the theater; a road company of *Life with Father* later provided him with another born-to-play role.

Louis Calhern's film career had its ups and downs but he proved himself to be a distinguished character actor. If he had to endure *Charlie McCarthy, Detective* and *The Gorgeous Hussy* there were also the rewards of *The Life of Emile Zola* and *Heaven Can Wait*. Indeed, as fine wines do, Calhern got better as he aged. His once arrogant screen persona softened and grew more likable. Good roles still came, such as that of the once great actor George Lorison in *The Bad and the Beautiful, Executive Suite* and *High Society*, his last completed film, also provided him with worthy assignments. He was, as he wanted to be, still in harness and still in demand when he died in Japan during the making of what would have been his 73rd film, *The Teahouse of the August Moon*.

—Roy Liebman

CANDY, John

Nationality: Canadian. **Born:** John Franklin Candy in Toronto, 31 October 1950. **Education:** Attended Holy Cross Separate School; Neil McNeil High School; Centennial Community College, Toronto. **Family:** Married Rosemary Margaret Hober, 1979, daughter: Jennifer, son: Christopher. **Career:** 1969—roles in Toronto underground theater and children's theater; 1971—feature film debut in *Face-Off*; 1972—moved to Chicago to join the Second City comedy troupe; 1974—moved back to Toronto to help establish a Second City troupe there; 1975—had first important movie comic role in Canadian film *It Seemed Like a Good Idea at the Time*; 1977-81—with Second City (Toronto) troupe, in syndicated TV series *Second City TV* (*SCTV*); 1981-83—in successor to *SCTV*, *SCTV Network 90* (later *SCTV Network*) which followed *The Tonight Show* on Friday nights; 1991—appeared in two serious roles in *JFK* and *Only the Lonely*. **Awards:** Emmy Awards for writing, for *SCTV Network* episodes, 1982 and 1983. **Died:** Of heart attack, in Chupaderos, Mexico, 4 March 1994.

Films as Actor:

1971 *Face-Off*
1973 *Class of '44* (Bogart)
1975 *It Seemed Like a Good Idea at the Time* (*Good Idea!*) (Trent) (as Kopek)
1976 *Find the Lady* (*Kopek and Broom*; *Call the Cops!*) (Trent) (as Kopek); *Tunnelvision* (Israel and Swirnoff) (as Agent Cooper); *The Clown Murders* (Burke) (as Ollie)
1978 *The Silent Partner* (Duke) (as Simonsen)
1979 *Lost and Found* (Melvin Frank) (as Carpentier); *1941* (Spielberg) (as Foley)
1980 *The Blues Brothers* (Landis) (as Burton Mercer); *Double Negative* (Bloomfield); *The Courage of Kavik, the Wolf Dog* (Kavik, the Wolf Dog) (Peter Carter—for TV)
1981 *Heavy Metal* (Potterton—animation) (as voice of Desk Sergeant/Dan/Den/Robot); *Stripes* (Reitman) (as Ox)
1982 *It Came from Hollywood* (Leo and Solt—compilation) (as narrator)
1983 *National Lampoon's Vacation* (Ramis) (as Lasky); *Going Berserk* (Steinberg) (as John Bourgignon)
1984 *Splash* (Ron Howard) (as Freddie Bauer); *The Last Polka* (Blanchard—for TV) (as Yosh Schmenge)
1985 *Volunteers* (Nicholas Meyer) (as Tom Tuttle from Tacoma); *Sesame Street Presents: Follow that Bird* (Kwapis) (as state trooper); *Brewster's Millions* (Walter Hill) (as Spike Nolan); *Summer Rental* (Carl Reiner) (as Jack Chester); *Tears Are Not Enough*

1986   *The Canadian Conspiracy*; *Little Shop of Horrors* (Oz) (as Wink Wilkinson); *Armed and Dangerous* (Lester) (as Frank Dooley)

1987   *Planes, Trains and Automobiles* (Hughes) (as Del Griffith); *Spaceballs* (Mel Brooks) (as Barf the Mawg, copilot); *Really Weird Tales* (Paul Lynch and McBrearty—for TV)

1988   *Hot to Trot* (Dinner) (as voice of Don); *The Great Outdoors* (Deutch) (as Chet Ripley); *She's Having a Baby* (Hughes) (uncredited cameo)

1989   *Uncle Buck* (Hughes) (title role); *Who's Harry Crumb?* (Flaherty) (title role, + exec pr); *Speed Zone!* (*Cannonball Fever*) (Drake) (as Charlie Cronyn)

1990   *The Rescuers Down Under* (Butoy and Gabriel—animation) (as voice of Wilbur); *Home Alone* (Columbus) (as Gus Polinski); *Masters of Menace* (Raskov) (cameo)

1991   *Delirious* (Tom Mankiewicz) (as Jack Gable); *Nothing but Trouble* (Aykroyd) (as Dennis/Eldona); *JFK* (Oliver Stone) (as Dean Andrews); *Only the Lonely* (Columbus) (as Danny Muldoon); *Career Opportunities* (*One Wild Night*) (Bryan Gordon) (as C. D. Marsh, uncredited); *Boris and Natasha* (Simoneau and Charles Martin Smith—for TV) (as Kallishak)

1992   *Once upon a Crime* (*Criminals*) (Levy) (as Augie Morosco)

1993   *Cool Runnings* (Turtletaub) (as Irv Blitzer); *Rookie of the Year* (Daniel Stern) (as announcer, uncredited)

1994   *Canadian Bacon* (Michael Moore) (as Bud B. Boomer); *Wagons East!* (Markle) (as James Harlow)

Film as Director:

1994   *Hostage for a Day* (for TV) (+ uncredited role)

Publications

By CANDY: articles—

Interview with Cutler Durkee, in *People Weekly* (New York), 13 July 1981.
Interview with Robert Crane, in *Playboy* (Chicago), August 1989.

On CANDY: books—

Sweet, Jeffrey, *Something Wonderful Right Away*, New York, 1978.
McCrohan, Donna, *The Second City: A Backstage History of Comedy's Hottest Troupe*, New York, 1987.

On CANDY: articles—

Seeff, Norman, and Cyndi Stivers, "Buffoons: SCTV Is Vidiot's Delight with Bite," in *Life* (New York), October 1982.

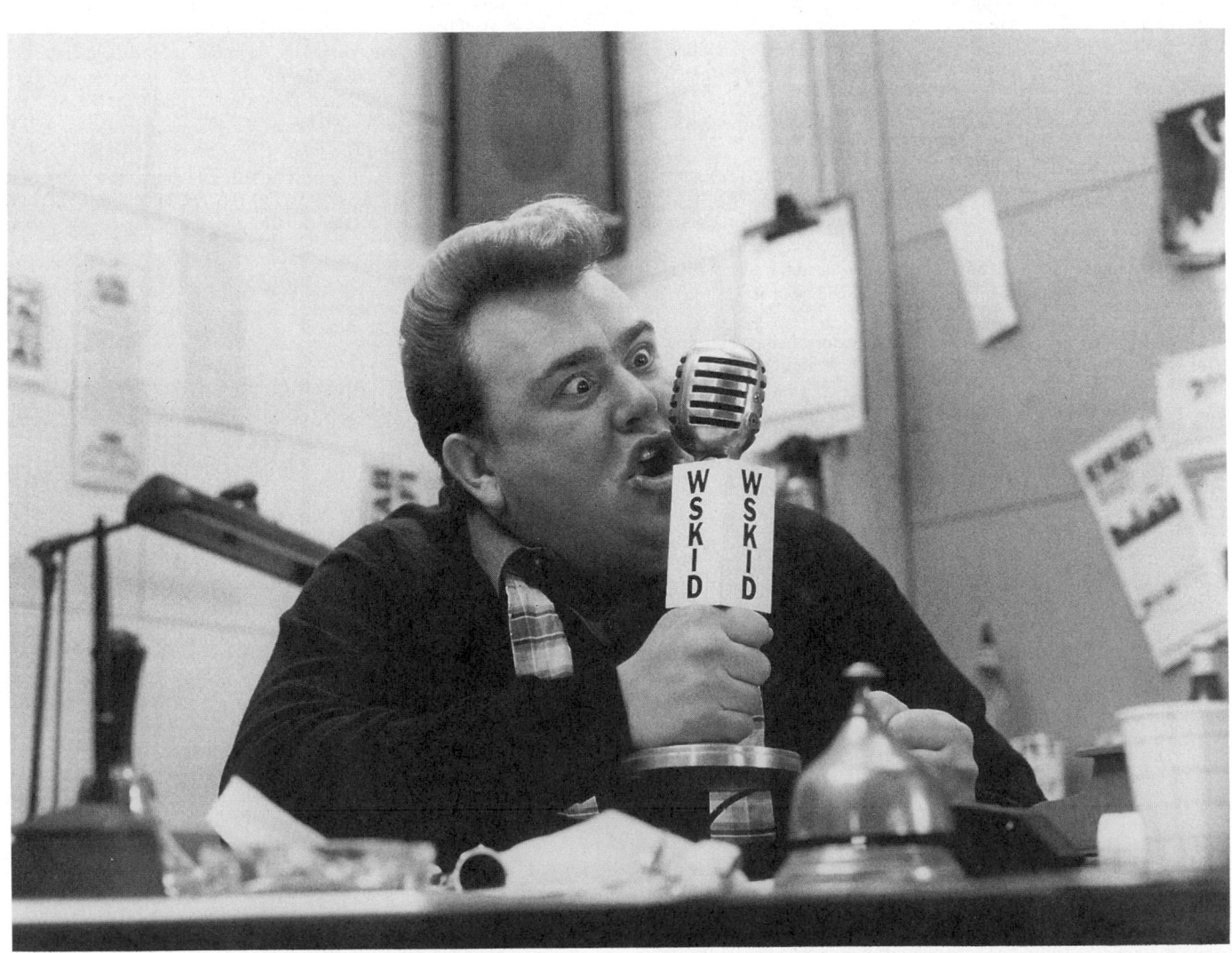

John Candy in *Little Shop of Horrors*

Brown, Ian, "The Comic Triumph of SCTV," in *Maclean's* (Toronto), 27 December 1982.

McGuigan, Cathleen, and David Ansen, "Hollywood's Silly Season," in *Newsweek* (New York), 26 August 1985.

Johnson, Brian D., "From Gags to Riches," in *Maclean's* (Toronto), 9 June 1986.

Current Biography 1990, New York, 1990.

Siegel, Scott, and Barbara Siegel, "John Candy," in *American Film Comedy: From Abbott and Costello to Jerry Zucker*, New York, 1994.

Cox, Dan, obituary in *Variety* (New York), 7 March 1994.

Johnson, Brian D., "Candy's Sweet Legacy: Canadian Comic King John Candy Was One of the Best-Loved Stars," in *Maclean's* (Toronto), 14 March 1994.

Hajari, Nisid, "Life Was Sweet," in *Entertainment Weekly* (New York), 18 March 1994.

Schneider, Karen S., "Exit Laughing," in *People Weekly* (New York), 21 March 1994.

Golfman, Noreen, "Canadian Candy," in *Canadian Forum*, May 1994.

Housley, John, filmography in *Premiere* (New York), May 1994.

*   *   *

In the Hollywood tendency to redo a popular novel such as *Brewster's Millions*, director Walter Hill made a mistake in retaining Richard Pryor in the lead role of Monty Brewster and John Candy as his sidekick, Spike Nolan. In hindsight the casting director should have switched the parts. Vincent Canby, in a *New York Times* review (2 June 1985), noted that the supporting role of Spike was "played far more energetically by the rotund John Candy." The headline for this evaluation was "Richard Pryor in Search of His Comic Genius." Maybe the slipping career of Pryor in the mid-eighties was not apparent nor was the emerging popularity of Candy recognized clearly. Nevertheless, we now understand that the obese actor (reminiscent of Roscoe "Fatty" Arbuckle, who played the role of Brewster in the 1921 version of *Brewster's Millions*) would have endowed the role with enthusiasm and warmth. Viewed today we can see Pryor as lackluster—he appeared to be perplexed with the role that required him to give away millions of dollars to obtain a much larger inheritance.

The next year, 1986, Candy began to show his mettle in *Armed and Dangerous*. He enacted the lead role of Frank Dooley, a private security officer, with another comedian, Eugene Levy, as his sidekick, Norman. Candy's part becomes the focus of the entire plot. Furthermore, his character has more intelligence than characters he played in previous films, such as the police officer in 1975's *It Seemed Like a Good Idea at the Time*. As a security officer with a past as a police officer in *Armed and Dangerous*, he retains the savvy of his former job: shooting skills and investigative abilities to fight and expose a crooked union leader. At one point in the film he dreams up disguises to escape the hit men chasing him. In drag he employs a Medusa-like feathered wig, a brilliant orange dress, and high heels, while his partner Norman dons all-leather apparel. When Frank encounters one of the pursuing thugs, he repulses him with a proposition: "What are you doing later on tonight?" Candy executes this cross-dresser disguise with finesse by lightening his voice—avoiding the usual cliché of the falsetto overstatement, resulting in a subtle comic incident in the movie.

With some help from scripts by John Hughes, the comedian furthered the scope of his acting with *Planes, Trains and Automobiles* (1987) and *Uncle Buck* (1989). Co-starring with Steve Martin in the former film that has two men trying to travel home for a Thanksgiving holiday, Candy presents a portrait of a boisterous, obnoxious, hail-fellow-unfortunately-met. His performance is one of his classical, blow-hard, amiable con men. Candy plays the slob to Martin's fastidious character; as a result the audience may be reminded of Neil Simon's *The Odd Couple*. With extensive stage and television experience in improvisational, lampoon comedy, Candy's acting talent ranged from a type of broad comedy, evident in his earlier films, to more genteel, character-based, comedies. Del Griffith, his salesman character in *Planes, Trains and Automobiles*, proves to be more in line with the latter. Any scene that allows the actor to show the likable side of his portrait is one that Candy executes with a wink and a laugh; and the comedian's laugh is so disarming and welcome—so believable—it becomes a natural part of his character. As Buck Russell, the unconventional, ne'er-do-well uncle in *Uncle Buck*, Candy again allows the positive side of his character to dominate the movie.

In the same year of *Uncle Buck*'s release, however, the comedian switches back to the earlier mode of farcical, broad comedy. In the title role of *Who's Harry Crumb?*, Candy reveals more clearly his background in television burlesque sketches from 1970s work for *Second City TV*. A *Variety* critic wrote: "Candy finds a fertile vehicle in this [work], easily carrying every scene and getting laughs in a bizarre array of disguises and plenty of wild, physical stunts, made funnier by his ample girth." As a private detective on surveillance for his client, Harry Crumb tries to hide his identity. This sleuthing, of course, reveals a very awkward, dim-witted character. But there is another side to Crumb. An overload of trivia fills his brain so that he sometimes appears to be brilliant to a naive client. Also, the flood of useless knowledge pushes him to self-delusion and pride. Nevertheless, this farcical portrait becomes likable because of Crumb's innocent and good-spirited demeanor. Some of the disguises the detective uses are those of foreigners from India and Europe, plus incredibly absurd depictions of a jockey and a drag queen. Candy's height and breadth create overstatement humor which promotes the laughter in the film.

Toward the end of his career Candy proved he could act with restraint in developing two characters: Danny Muldoon in *Only the Lonely* (1991) and Irv Blitzer in *Cool Runnings* (1993). Both of these enactments have been classified as straight roles and like some of the best comedians, Candy switches to a lower intensity and a more realistic tone in his acting. Irv Blitzer can be considered a pure straight part as a bobsled coach in the Canadian Winter Olympics of 1988. Comedy is created by Jamaican blacks who make up an unusual bobsled team. Only one line delivered by Candy suggests his mainstay was humorous roles. To an official who doubts Blitzer's team can make the time of a qualifying run, Blitzer replies with a Jamaican accent and word choice: "No problem, man."

His performance of a Chicago policeman, Danny Muldoon, in *Only the Lonely* might be the best of his 51 films because of the range and subtlety of his acting. Candy plays a milder version of some parts he handled earlier. Danny is portrayed as a talkative amicable bachelor of 38 who has had little success with women, although the character has insight into some of his problems. He apologizes: "I'm a motor-mouth." He later realizes he is too tied to his mother. Scripted by John Hughes, the plot is a retread of the award-winning *Marty* of 1955. Candy's portrait, however, shows his own spin and has little resemblance to the Ernest Borgnine enactment of the earlier movie. Candy's portrayal rings true as a realistic simple, honest soul with both faults and virtues.

Candy's last two films before his death were not his best, but illustrate how he, all through his 23-year film career, did the best he could with what was given him. *Canadian Bacon* and *Wagons East!* were entertaining because of this most likable comedian, an actor who brought joy to many audiences.

—Don McCaffrey

CANTINFLAS

Nationality: Mexican. **Born:** Mario Moreno Reyes in Ciudad de los Palacios, 12 August 1911. **Education:** Studied at the Universidad Nacional Autonoma de Mexico in the school of medicine. **Family:**

Married Valentina Zubareff, 1937 (died 1966), son: Mario Arturo Moreno Ivanova. **Career:** 1930—began working in variety theaters, using name Cantinflas to hide identity from family; 1936—first film role as comic in *No te engañes corazón*; 1940—became leading comic figure of Spanish-language cinema with lead role in *Ahí está el detalle*; 1941—founded Posa Films production company and produced *Ni sangre ni arena*; began lifelong professional relationship with the director Miguel M. Delgado after first film together, *El gendarme desconocido*; 1956—became known internationally after role as Passepartout in *Around the World in Eighty Days*; 1960—commercial and critical failure of *Pepe* led to his departure from Hollywood and return to Mexico; 1981—final feature film, after which he concentrated on philanthropic interests. **Awards:** Special Prize, Ariel Awards, Mexico, for "work on behalf of the Mexican cinema," 1950-51; Golden Globe for Best Actor, for *Around the World in Eighty Days*, 1956; Special Award, Golden Globes, 1960; Special Prize, Mexican Silver Goddesses, 1969; named "symbol of peace and happiness of the Americas," by the Organization of American States, 1983; Diploma of Honor, Inter-American Council of Music, 1983; honored for lifelong contribution to Mexican cinema, by the Mexican Academy of Cinemagraphic Arts and Sciences, 1988. **Died:** Of lung cancer, in Mexico City, 20 April 1993.

Films as Actor:

1936   *No te engañes corazón* (*Don't Deceive Yourself, My Heart*) (Torres)
1937   *Así es mi tierra!* (Boytler); *Aguila o sol* (Boytler)
1939   *Siempre listo en las tinieblas* (Rivero—short); *Jengibre contra dinamita* (Rivero—short); *El signo de la muerte* (Urueta)
1940   *Ahí está el detalle* (*There Is the Detail*; *Here's the Point*) (Oro) (as himself); *Cantiflas y su prima* (Toussain—short); *Cantinflas boxeador* (*Cantinflas the Boxer*) (Rivero—short); *Cantinflas ruletero* (Rivero—short)
1941   *Ni sangre ni arena* (*Neither Blood Nor Sand*) (Galindo) (+ pr); *El gendarme desconocido* (Delgado) (as 77)
1942   *Los tres mosqueteros* (*The Three Musketeers*) (Delgado) (as D'Artagnan); *El circo* (Delgado)
1943   *Romeo y Julieta* (*Romeo and Juliet*) (Delgado) (as Romeo)
1944   *Gran hotel* (Delgado)
1945   *Un día con el diablo* (Delgado)
1946   *Soy un prófugo* (Delgado)
1948   *El supersabio* (Delgado)
1949   *Puerta . . . joven* (Delgado); *El mago*
1950   *El siete machos* (Delgado); *El bombero atómico* (*The Atomic Fireman*) (Delgado)
1951   *Si yo fuera diputado* (Delgado)
1952   *El señor fotógrafo* (Delgado)
1953   *Caballero a la medida* (Delgado)
1954   *Abajo el telón* (Delgado)
1956   *El bolero de Raquel* (Delgado); *Around the World in Eighty Days* (Anderson) (as Passepartout)
1957   *Les Bijoutiers du clair de lune* (*The Night Heaven Fell*; *Heaven Fell that Night*) (Vadim) (as Alfonso)
1958   *Ama a tu prójimo* (Demicheli); *Sube y bajo* (Delgado); *Agguato a Tangeri* (*Trapped in Tangiers*) (Freda)
1960   *Pepe* (Sidney) (title role); *El analfabeto* (Delgado) (as Inocencio Prieto y Calvo)
1962   *El extra* (Delgado) (Rogaciano)
1963   *Entrega immediata* (Delgado) (as Feliciano)
1964   *El padrecito* (Delgado) (as Padre Sebas)
1965   *El señor doctor* (Delgado) (as Dr. Medina)
1966   *Su exelencia* (Delgado)
1968   *Por mis pistolas* (Delgado) (as Fidenco)
1969   *Don Quijote sin mancha* (Delgado)
1970   *El profe* (Delgado)
1972   *Don Quijote cabalga de nuevo* (Delgado) (as Sancho Panza)
1976   *El ministro y Yo* (Delgado)
1978   *El patrullero 777* (*Patrol Car 777*) (Delgado)
1981   *El Barrendero* (Delgado)
1985   *Mexico . . . Estamos Contigo* (for TV)

Publications

By CANTINFLAS: book—

Cantiflas: Apología de un humilde, Mexico, n.d.

On CANTINFLAS: books—

García Riera, Emilio, *Historia documental del cine mexicano*, vols. 1-9, Mexico, 1969-78.
Ayala Blanco, Jorge, *La aventura del cine mexicano*, Mexico, 1979.
Mora, Carl J., *Mexican Cinema: Reflections of a Society 1896-1980*, Berkeley, 1982.
Reachi, Santiago, *La Revolución, Cantinflas y JoLoPo*, Mexico City, 1982.
Ayala Blanco, Jorge, *La búsqueda del cine mexicano*, Mexico City, 1986.
Ayala Blanco, Jorge, *La condición del cine mexicano*, Mexico City, 1986.
De los Reyes, Aurelia, *Medio siglo de cine mexicano (1896-1947)*, Mexico City, 1987.

On CANTINFLAS: articles—

Time (New York), 26 August 1940.
Oliver, M. R., "Cantinflas," in *Hollywood Quarterly*, April 1947.
Ross, B., "Mexico's Chaplin," in *Sight and Sound* (London), Summer 1948.
Current Biography 1953, New York, 1953.
"The Comedy of Cantinflas," in *Films in Review* (New York), January 1958.
Zunser, J., "Mexico's Millionaire Mirthquake," in *Cue*, 23 August 1958.
Butler, Ron, "Cantinflas: Mexico's Prince of Comedy," in *Américas*, April 1981.
Mejias-Rentas, Antonio, "Cantinflas Given D.C. Tribute," in *Nuestro*, June/July 1983.
García Marruz, Fina, "Cantinflas," in *Cine Cubano* (Havana), no. 111, 1985.
Obituary in *New York Times*, 22 April 1993.
Obituary in *Variety* (New York), 26 April 1993.
"OAS Bids Farewell to Cantinflas," in *Américas*, May/June 1993.
Stavans, Ilan, "The Riddle of Cantinflas," in *Transition*, no. 67, 1995.

*   *   *

The best-known figure of Spanish-language cinema, Cantinflas gained international recognition through his rendering of a purely local character. The *Pelado* is native to Mexico City's slums—a lumpen-proletarian created by rapid, unplanned, and uncontrollable urbanization, the clash of classes in a dependent and underdeveloped society, and the racial mixing and antagonism of Indians and Europeans. Streetwise as only the powerless learn to become, the *pelado* relies on wit and guile in dealing with the state apparatus—law, for instance—which oppresses rather than protects him. Cantinflas's *peladito* was a comic variant of this character but the actor's lack of a critical class consciousness led in the end to his acceptance of the very forces that he had built his career on attacking.

Literally, *pelado* means stripped clean, broke. Cantinflas himself defined his "prototype of the humble people from the urban *barrio*" in this way: "superficially educated and practically non-existent socially, but with a highly developed ingenuity (a Mexican characteristic), a formidable astuteness—and a large, gentle, and open heart." Confronted with the rich and powerful, Cantinflas's *peladito* delights in turning the tables and confusing them with their own tools of domination.

Language—the instrument of the educated—is one of the ways the privileged classes maintain their position, but it is also a front on which the *peladito* excels. Cantinflas's enormous gift for impromptu verbal invention was the very essence of his comedy—requiring, for example, that he be allowed to improvise fully on scripts. In Mexico, to *cantinflear* has come to mean to talk a lot and say nothing, while the noun *cantinflas* means lovable clown. As Cantinflas put it, when an explanation is demanded "by the policeman whose hat you stepped on or the boss whose shirt you just spilled catsup down, the *pelado's* defense is to talk, talk, talk."

In Cantinflas's early films this nonsensical double-talk was used to criticize forms of social control—for example, when he confused a courtroom full of lawyers, infecting them with his incoherent verbiage in *Ahí está el detalle*. In the later works, however, this critical attitude toward the use and abuse of language was replaced with word games which essentially denied the existence of social problems. In his last several movies Cantinflas became openly reactionary, taking on social roles he had earlier criticized, such as priest, doctor, and politician. Under the guise of being nonideological, Cantinflas spouted a rabid and simplistic anticommunism while calling fervidly for free enterprise—and offering himself as the most cogent and apparent example of what hard work can do for one.

Even if on one hand Cantinflas lost touch with his slum roots as he became a multimillionaire with five homes, a thousand-acre ranch, and his own airplane, he at the same time freely donated his time and money to philanthropic causes, appearing at numerous benefits each year and, notably, at one time financially supporting more than 250 poor families in a Mexico City slum. In the end Cantinflas was, justifiably or not, a hero to the Mexican masses, evidenced by the thousands of people who gathered outside the funeral home where his body lay, in tribute to his great talent for making people laugh as well as his enormous generosity.

—John Mraz, updated by David E. Salamie

CANTOR, Eddie

Nationality: American. **Born:** Edward Israel Iskowitch in New York City, 31 January 1892. **Family:** Married Ida Tobias, 1914, five daughters. **Career:** 1907—debut at the Clinton Music Hall; later joined Gus Edwards's "Kid Kabaret"; 1914-15—with Lily Lee, performed as Cantor and Lee; 1916—moved to the West Coast, performed with the "Canary Cottage" company; 1917-19—in the Ziegfeld "Follies"; 1920—debut as star in *The Midnight Rounders*; 1926—film debut in filmed version of stage success, *Kid Boots*; 1930s—president of Jewish Theatrical Guild of America, and of the American Federation of Radio Artists (1937); 1950-54—host of *The Colgate Comedy Hour*; 1955—host of *Eddie Cantor Comedy Theatre*. **Awards:** Honorary Oscar, for "distinguished service to the film industry," 1956. **Died:** 10 October 1964.

Films as Actor:

1926   *Kid Boots* (Tuttle) (title role)
1927   *The Speed Hound* (short); *Follies*; *Special Delivery* (Goodrich) (as Eddie, the mail carrier, + story)

1929   *Glorifying the American Girl* (Webb) (as himself, performing in revue); *That Party in Person* (short); *Getting a Ticket* (Blumenstock—short) (as himself)
1930   *Whoopee!* (Freeland) (as Henry Williams); *Insurance* (short) (as Sidney B. Sweiback)
1931   *Mr. Lemon of Orange* (co-sc only); *Palmy Days* (A. Edward Sutherland) (as Eddy Simpson, + co-story, co-sc)
1932   *The Kid from Spain* (McCarey) (as Eddie Williams)
1933   *Roman Scandals* (Tuttle) (as Eddie)
1934   *Kid Millions* (del Ruth) (as Eddie Wilson Jr.); *Hollywood Cavalcade* (short); *Screen Snapshots No. 11* (short)
1936   *Strike Me Pink* (Taurog) (as Eddie Pink)
1937   *Ali Baba Goes to Town* (David Butler) (title role)
1940   *Forty Little Mothers* (Berkeley) (as Gilbert J. Thompson)
1943   *Thank Your Lucky Stars* (David Butler) (as Joe Sampson/himself)
1944   *Hollywood Canteen* (Daves) (as himself); *Show Business* (Marin) (as Eddie Martin, + pr)
1945   *Rhapsody in Blue* (Rapper)
1948   *If You Knew Susie* (Gordon Douglas) (as Sam Parker, + pr)
1952   *The Story of Will Rogers* (Curtiz) (as himself)
1953   *The Eddie Cantor Story* (Alfred E. Green) (appearance)
1956   *Seidman and Son* (for TV)

Publications

By CANTOR: books—

My Life Is in Your Hands, as told to David Freedman, New York, 1928.
Caught Short: A Saga of Wailing Wall Street, New York, 1929.
World's Book of Best Jokes, editor, Cleveland and New York, 1943.
Take My Life, with Jane Kesner, New York, 1957.
The Way I See It, edited by Phyllis Rosenteur, New York, 1959.
As I Remember Them, New York, 1963.

By CANTOR: articles—

Photoplay (New York), November 1926.
Film Weekly (London), 8 December 1933.

On CANTOR: books—

Altman, Rick, *The American Film Musical*, Bloomington, Indiana, 1989.
Koseluk, Gregory, *Eddie Cantor: A Life in Show Business*, Jefferson, North Carolina, 1995.

On CANTOR: articles—

Belfrage, Cedric, in *Film Weekly* (London), 25 October 1930.
Forde, Walter, in *Film Weekly* (London), 2 January 1932.
Current Biography 1954, New York, 1954.
Obituary in *New York Times*, 11 October 1964.
Obituary in *Hollywood Reporter*, 12 October 1964.
Films in Review (New York), November and December 1971; also January 1972 and January 1973.

On CANTOR: film—

The Eddie Cantor Story, musical biography directed by Alfred E. Green, 1955.

*   *   *

With the exception of the Marx Brothers team no other comedian has brought from the stage to the screen so much of the vigor of

Eddie Cantor with Eleanor Hunt in *Whoopee!* © 1930, Samuel Goldwyn

vaudeville and the musical comedy as Eddie Cantor. A stand-up comic with the skills of a song and dance man, he possessed the charisma to dominate a theater or film skit. During the transition to sound in 1929 and 1930 his one-reel films such as *Getting a Ticket* were refurbished vaudeville sketches. As an actor who obviously had developed a kinetic comic style that matched the lively pace of the musical comedy, Cantor then starred in a series of films in the early 1930s that equalled such well-known musicals as *Forty-Second Street* and *Footlight Parade*. His *Roman Scandals*, produced the same year as these works, remains one of the best examples of his contribution. One of the achievements in this film is a manic portrait that bursts with energy; consequently, when his character switches from straight dialogue to a musical number, it seems quite logical. Cantor also developed a working method similar to that of Charles Chaplin and Buster Keaton. He created a persona who exists on the edge of society, a tramp-child character, who nevertheless possesses a mind which works differently than those of his social superiors, creating the anomalous "wise fool." Comic ingenuity reigns as his oddball mind produces a tactic to escape the wrath of his enemies.

In *Roman Scandals* many facets of Cantor's skill evolved. He exhibits comic cowardice, a con man's ability to bilk authority, and a childlike spirit of play when faced with each new situation. Visually, the actor becomes as adroit as he does verbally. Many of his reactions, the rolling of his large eyes, the gaiety of movement, the charming

smile, and the overall warmth of a little fellow struggling against odds and escaping are intriguing. His aggression is distinctive, but he never becomes the brash confidence man in the vein of his contemporary, Groucho Marx. In this 1933 musical, for example, his wisecracks have a more flippant tone. But while Eddie's invective humor may not prove to be a match for Groucho's, his deftness as a song and dance man left the leader of the Marx team far behind. In his films Cantor could sell a song such as "Making Whoopee," "Keep Young and Beautiful," and "My Honey Said Yes, Yes." Of course, it could have been partly a case of the public preferring allusions to the high life over the social cynicism of Groucho.

In these early 1930s musicals the comedian retained the lion's share of the focus even when he was flanked by a Busby Berkeley battalion of beauties dancing in swirling, kaleidoscopic patterns. Eddie does not merely hold his own; he dominates. With his strutting patter routine, he hops about in an eccentric dance, pressing palms together and clapping with delight, his huge eyes revolving. He is a standout figure as his vaudeville "blackface" dance and song routines keep him in the center of the action—among the circling, scantily costumed blonds.

Like many top comedians, Cantor had a number of impersonations up his sleeve. In *Palmy Days*, he skillfully handles three roles: he impersonates a woman to escape his adversaries, a phony French spiritualist to con a quack medium, and a wacky efficiency expert recruited by a bakery tycoon through a mistaken identity plot development in the film. Another farcical twist shows the comedian acting out the role of a toreador in *The Kid from Spain*, an effort that wins the approval of the crowd because of his supposed innovative deviations from the art of bullfighting. In all of these contrivances the comedian portrays the coward on the run who achieves safety and even fame by pluck and luck.

In the musical with a strong comedy emphasis, Eddie Cantor can be rated as king of them all. By 1933 he was the highest-paid comedian in the country; not merely through his films but also as America's leading radio comedian. In fact, his success in that medium cut into the number of films he created in the 1930s, and consequently, his influence on the musical began to wane. His ability to turn a line, even a mediocre one, was an asset that made him a successful radio comedian, but he was skilled in visual comedy as well. It was a pity that, with his success in radio, he did not concentrate on films. Even a second-rate Cantor work was better than most of the musical comedy movies of the 1930s. It is, however, only conjecture that he might have changed the face of the musical. *Roman Scandals* may have been a fortunate combination of writing, directing, and production talents which could not be equalled in a later picture, such as *Kid Millions*. If the quality of his work in film had continued, he might now be ranked with the best laugh getters of the period—the Marx Brothers, W. C. Fields, and Laurel and Hardy. As a comedian in the musical comedy, however, Eddie Cantor had no equal.

—Donald McCaffrey

CARDINALE, Claudia

Nationality: Italian. **Born:** Tunis, Tunisia, 15 April 1939. **Education:** Attended acting classes at Centro Sperimentale film school, Rome. **Family:** Married the producer Franco Cristaldi. **Career:** 1956—appeared in small part in short film *Anneaux d'or*; 1957—contract with Cristaldi; 1958—began appearing in secondary roles in Italian films; early 1960s—international stardom, particularly with Fellini's *8½*; 1977—in TV mini-series *Jesus of Nazareth*. **Awards:** Silver Ribbons, Italy, for Best Actress, for *La ragazza di Bube*, 1963, and *Claretta*, 1984-85, and for Best Supporting Actress, for *La pelle*, 1981-82. **Address:** Via Flamina Km.17,200, 1-0018 Rome, Italy.

Films as Actress:

1956   *Anneaux d'or* (*Chaines d'or*) (Vautier)
1957   *Goha* (Baratier)
1958   *I soliti ignoti* (*Big Deal on Madonna Street*; *Persons Unknown*) (Monicelli) (as Carmelina); *Tre straniere a Roma* (Gora); *La prima notte* (Cavalcanti); *Totò e Marcellino* (Masa)
1959   *Il magistrato* (Zampa); *Un maledetto imbroglio* (*The Facts of Murder*) (Germi); *Audace colpo dei soliti ignoti* (*Fiasco in Milan*; *Hold-up á la Milanaise*) (Loy); *Vento del sud* (Provenzale); *Upstairs and Downstairs* (Thomas) (as Maria)
1960   *Austerlitz* (*The Battle of Austerlitz*) (Gance) (as Pauline); *Il bell'Antonio* (Bolognini) (as Barbara Puglisi); *I delfini* (Maselli); *Rocco e i suoi fratelli* (*Rocco and His Brothers*; *Rocco et ses freres*) (Visconti) (as Ginetta)
1961   *La ragazza con la valigia* (*Girl with a Suitcase*; *Pleasure Girl*) (Zurlini) (as Aida Zepponi); *Les lions sont lâchés* (Verneuil); *Senilità* (Bolognini) (as Angiolina); *La viaccia* (*The Love Makers*) (Bolognini)
1962   *Cartouche* (*Swords of Blood*) (de Broca) (as Venus)

1963   *Il gattopardo* (*The Leopard*) (Visconti) (as Angelica Sedara/Bertiana); *8½* (*Otto e mezzo*) (Fellini) (as Claudia); *La ragazza di Bube* (*Bebo's Girl*) (Comencini) (as Mara)
1964   *Circus World* (*The Magnificent Showman*) (Hathaway) (as Toni Alfredo); *The Pink Panther* (Edwards) (as Princess Dala); *Il magnifico cornuto* (*The Magnificent Cuckold*) (Pietrangeli) (as Maria Grazia Artusi); *Gli indifferenti* (*A Time of Indifference*) (Maselli) (as Carla Ardengo)
1965   *Vaghe stelle dell'Orsa* (*Sandra*; *Of a Thousand Delights*) (Visconti) (as Sandra)
1966   *Blindfold* (Dunne) (as Vicky Vincenti); *Una rosa per tutti* (*A Rose for Everyone*; *Every Man's Woman*) (Rossi) (as Rosa); "Fata Armenia" ("Queen Armenia") ep. of *Le fate* (*The Queens*; *Sex Quartet*) (Monicelli) (as Armenia); *Lost Command* (*Not for Honor and Glory*) (Robson) (as Aicha); *The Professionals* (Richard Brooks) (as Maria Grant)
1967   *Don't Make Waves* (Mackendrick) (as Laura Califatti); *Piero Gherardi* (Werba)
1968   *The Hell with Heroes* (Sargent) (as Elena); *C'era una volta il West* (*Once upon a Time in the West*) (Leone) (as Jill McBain); *Il giorno della civetta* (*The Day of the Owl*; *La Maffia fait la loi*; *Mafia*) (Damiani) (as Rosa Nicolosi)
1969   *La tenda rossa* (*Krasnaya palatka*; *The Red Tent*) (Kalatozov) (as Nurse Valeria); *Nell'anno del signore* (Magni) (as Giuditta Di Castro); *Ruba al prossimo tuo* (*Una coppia tranquilla*; *A Fine Pair*) (Maselli) (as Esmeralda Marini)
1970   *The Adventures of Gerard* (Skolimowski) (as Countess Teresa); *Certo, certissimo . . . anzi probabile* (*Certain, Very Certain, as a Matter of Fact . . . Probable*) (Fondato) (as Marta)
1971   *Popsy Pop* (*The Butterfly Affair*; *The 21 Carat Snatch*; *Queen of Diamonds*) (Herman) (as Popsy); *Les Pétroleuses* (*The Legend of Frenchie King*; *The Petroleum Girls*) (Christian-Jaque) (as Maria); *L'udienza* (*Tee Audience*; *The Papal Audience*) (Ferreri); *Bello, onesto, emigrato Australia sposerebbe compaesana illibata* (Zampa)
1972   *La scoumoune* (Giovanni) (as Genevieve Saratov)
1973   *Libera, amore mio* (*Libera, My Love*) (Giovanni); *I guappi* (*Blood Brothers*) (Squitieri); *Il giorno del furore* (*Days of Fury*; *One Russian Summer*) (Calenda) (as Anya)
1974   *Gruppo di famiglia in un interno* (*Conversation Piece*; *Violence et Passion*) (Visconti) (as wife)
1975   *A mezzanotte va la ronda del piacere* (*The Immortal Bachelor*; *Midnight Pleasures*; *Qui comincia l'avventura*) (Fondato) (as Gabriella Sansoni)
1976   One ep. of *Il communo senso del pudore* (*A Common Sense of Modesty*) (Sordi); *The Pink Panther Strikes Again* (Edwards)
1977   *Blonde in Black Leather* (Di Palma); *Un jour peut-être à San Pedro ou ailleurs*; *Il prefetto di ferro* (Squitieri); *La part du feu* (Périer); *Goodbye e Amen* (*Goodbye and Amen*) (Damiani) (as Aliki)
1978   *Cocktails for Three*; *L'arma* (*The Gun*) (Squitieri) (as Marta Campagna); *La petite fille en velours bleu* (*The Little Girl in Blue Velvet*) (Bridges); *Corleone* (*Father of the Godfather*) (Squitieri) (as Rosa Accordino)
1979   *L'ingorgo* (*Traffic Jam*) (Comencini); *Escape to Athena* (Cosmatos) (as Eleana)
1980   *Si salvi chi vuole* (Faenza)
1981   *La pelle* (Cavani); *The Salamander* (Zinner) (as Elena)
1982   *Le Cadeau* (*The Gift*) (Michel Lang) (as Antonella); *Fitzcarraldo* (Herzog) (as Molly); *Burden of Dreams* (Blank—doc)
1983   *Le Ruffian* (*The Ruffian*) (Giovanni) (as la "baronne"); *Princess Daisy* (Hussein—for TV); *Stelle emigranti* (Mazeni—for TV)
1984   *Claretta* (Squitieri); *Enrico IV* (*Henry IV*) (Bellochio) (as Matilda)

Claudia Cardinale in *Rocco e i suoi fratelli*

1985 *La storia (History)* (Comencini) (as Ida); *Donna delle meraviglie (The Woman of Wonders)* (Beraviglie)
1986 *L'Été prochain (Next Summer)* (Trintignant) (as Jeanne)
1987 *Un Homme amoureux (A Man in Love)* (Kurys) (as Julia Steiner); *Sniper* (Jameson)
1988 *Blu Elettrico (Electric Blue)* (Gaeng) (as Tata)
1989 *La bataille des trois rois (The Battle of Three Kings; Tambores de duego; Drums of Fire)* (Barka); *La Revolution Française (The French Revolution)* (Enrico and Heffron) (as the Countess); *Ben Webster: The Brute and the Beautiful* (Jeremy—doc)
1990 *Hiver 54, l'Abbé Pierre* (Amar); *Atto di dolore* (Squitieri); *Money* (Stern)
1991 *Mayrig* (as Araxi/Mayrig); *Act of Contrition* (Squitieri)
1992 *588 Rue Paradis (Mother)* (as Araxi/Mayrig)
1993 *Son of the Pink Panther* (Edwards) (as Maria)
1994 *Elles ne pensent qu'a ca (Women Have Only One Thing on Their Minds)* (as Margaux)

Publications

By CARDINALE: book—

Io, Claudia, tu, Claudia, with Anna Maria Mori, Milan, 1995.

On CARDINALE: articles—

Lane, John Francis, in *Films and Filming* (London), January 1963.
Ecran (Paris), January 1978.
"Claudia Cardinale in *Claretta*," in *Cinema Nuovo* (Turin), June 1984.

* * *

Claudia Cardinale, the Italian actress famous for her husky, almost raspy voice, began her career by winning a contest for "the most beautiful Italian girl in Tunisia." As the winner, she was granted a trip to the Venice Film Festival, and eventually attended acting classes at the Centro Sperimentale in Rome. She was promoted by producer Franco Cristaldi, who carefully guided her every move in regard to the cinema, and later married her.

Cardinale was discovered during the era when Brigitte Bardot created one sensation after another both on screen and off. Cardinale could merely have become "the Italian Bardot," and, indeed comparisons have been drawn between the two actresses. But a number of factors helped lead Cardinale's career in a different direction. The publicity surrounding both Cardinale's films and her personal life was not nearly as sensational as that concerning Bardot. More importantly, Cardinale soon began appearing in the films of the major Italian auteurs. Minor, and later more substantial, roles in the films of Mario Monicelli, Mauro Bolognini, Luchino Visconti, and Federico Fellini made her a star in Italy and abroad.

While many of Bardot's films are now known simply because she is in them, Cardinale's films are often important works in the careers of their respective directors. For example, she appeared in Monicelli's best-known comedy (*Big Deal on Madonna Street*), co-starred in a fine series of films for Bolognini (*Il bell'Antonio, La viaccia*, and *Senilità*), and gained critical and popular recognition for her role as the fiancée of the eldest brother in Visconti's *Rocco and His Brothers*. She appeared in multiple roles in Fellini's *8½*, one of her most memorable films.

In these films, Cardinale's characters were, more often than not, portrayed as glamorous sex objects, not unlike Bardot. The variations each director introduced in the presentation of Cardinale in this type of character, however, prove interesting. In *8½* she plays Claudia,

herself, as well as the ideal woman of Guido's dreams. Outside the immediate narrative context of the film, her character becomes a symbol for Fellini of unspoiled, yet unattainable, innocence. Though beautiful and sensuous, she is not crassly sexual.

Later, in Leone's *Once upon a Time in the West*, Cardinale portrays Jill McBain, the new bride of murdered settler Brett McBain. Again, her character could be described as the object desired by the male figures in the film, but Jill McBain signifies much more within the context of the film's complex narrative, and within the genre of the Western itself. She represents the forces of civilization, as female characters often do in Westerns. The final scene depicts Jill providing water to the thirsty workers building the railroad (that other symbol of the taming of the west), implying that Jill will fulfill her husband's dream of running a railroad station. Her past life as a prostitute in New Orleans, however, recalls the less than desirable elements of civilization, which will inevitably follow the settlers. In this film, as in *8½*, Cardinale's character carries symbolic, almost mythic connotations.

Cardinale made her American film debut in Blake Edwards's very popular *The Pink Panther*, securing her international star status. Other American films, such as *The Professionals*, followed. During the 1970s and 1980s, however, Cardinale made most of her films in Italy and Europe. Many were not distributed in America or suffered from limited distribution, thereby reducing Cardinale's international exposure. Three 1980's roles, in Liliana Cavani's *La pelle* (well-received at Cannes), in Werner Herzog's *Fitzcarraldo*, and Diane Kurys's *A Man in Love*, have again focused attention on her as she enters a more mature phase of her life and career.

—Susan M. Doll

CAREY, Harry

Nationality: American. **Born:** Henry DeWitt Carey II in the Bronx, New York, 16 January 1878 (some sources list 1880). **Education:** Attended New York University. **Family:** Married 1) Alma Fern (divorced); 2) Olive Fuller Gordon, children: the actor Harry Jr. and Ellen. **Career:** Pre-1909—worked at various occupations including writing melodramas; 1909—began acting in films for Biograph, working in many early Griffith productions; 1917—emerged as star of Westerns by such directors as John Ford; 1928—left films to seek voice training for the coming of sound; 1931—returned to films with role in *Trader Horn*. **Died:** In Brentwood, California, 21 September 1947.

Films as Actor:

c.1909 *Bill Sharkley's Last Game*
1911 *Riding de Trail*
1912 *An Unseen Enemy* (D. W. Griffith); *A Cry for Help* (D. W. Griffith); *The Musketeers of Pig Alley* (D. W. Griffith); *In the Aisles of the Wild* (D. W. Griffith); *Friends* (D. W. Griffith); *Heredity* (D. W. Griffith); *The Unwelcome Guest* (D. W. Griffith); *An Adventure in the Autumn Woods* (D. W. Griffith); *My Hero* (D. W. Griffith); *Love in an Apartment Hotel* (D. W. Griffith); *The Informer* (D. W. Griffith); *Three Friends* (D. W. Griffith); *Brothers* (D. W. Griffith)
1913 *Broken Ways* (D. W. Griffith); *The Ranchero's Revenge* (D. W. Griffith); *The Left-Handed Man* (D. W. Griffith); *The Hero of Little Italy* (D. W. Griffith); *Olaf—An Atom* (D. W. Griffith); *The Sheriff's Baby* (D. W. Griffith); *Two Men of the Desert* (D. W. Griffith)

1914   *Judith of Bethulia* (D. W. Griffith); *McVeagh of the South Seas* (*Brute Island*; *Brute Force*; *Wars of the Primal Tribes*) (D. W. Griffith); *Travellin' On*; *The Master Cracksman* (as Gentleman Joe, the Cracksman)

1915   *Graft*

1917   *Beloved Jim*; *The Fighting Gringo*; *The Secret Man* (Ford); *A Marked Man* (Ford); *Bucking Broadway* (Ford); *Two Guns*; *Straight Shooting* (*The Cattle War*; *Joan of the Cattle Country*) (Ford) (as Cheyenne Harry)

1918   *Thieves' Gold* (Ford); *Wild Women* (Ford); *Three Mounted Men* (Ford); *A Woman's Fool* (Ford); *The Scarlet Drop* (Ford); *The Phantom Riders* (Ford); *Hell Bent* (Ford)

1919   *By Indian Post* (Ford); *The Rustlers* (Ford); *Gun Law* (Ford); *The Gun Packer* (*The Gun Pusher*) (Ford); *The Last Outlaw* (Ford); *The Fighting Brothers* (Ford); *Blind Husbands* (von Stroheim); *A Fight for Love* (Ford); *Bare Fists* (Ford); *Riders of Vengeance* (Ford); *The Outcasts of Poker Flat* (Ford); *The Ace in the Saddle* (Ford); *A Gun Fightin' Gentleman* (Ford); *The Rider of the Law* (Ford); *Marked Men* (Ford); *Sure Shot Morgan*

1920   *Hitchin' Posts* (Ford); *Overland Red*; *West Is West*; *Sundown Slim*; *Human Stuff*; *Bullet Proof*; *Blue Streak McCoy*

1921   *"If Only" Jim* (Jaccard); *The Freeze Out* (Ford); *Hearts Up*; *Desperate Trails* (Ford); *The Fox* (Thornby); *The Wallop* (Ford)

1922   *Man to Man* (Paton); *The Kick Back* (Paul); *Good Men and True* (Neitz)

1923   *Canyon of the Fools* (Paul); *Crushin' Thru* (Paul); *Desert Driven* (Paul); *The Miracle Baby* (Paul)

1924   *The Night Hawk* (Paton); *The Man from Texas*; *Tiger Thompson* (Eason); *The Lightning Rider* (Ingraham); *Roaring Rails* (Forman); *The Flaming Forties* (Forman)

1925   *Soft Shoes* (Ingraham); *Beyond the Border* (Dunlap); *Silent Sanderson* (Dunlap); *The Texas Trail* (Dunlap); *Wanderer*; *The Bad Lands* (Henderson); *The Prairie Pirate* (Mortimer); *The Man from Red Gulch* (Mortimer)

1926   *Driftin' Thru* (Dunlap); *The Seventh Bandit* (Dunlap); *The Frontier Trail* (Dunlap); *Satan Town* (Mortimer)

1927   *A Little Journey* (Leonard); *Slide, Kelly, Slide* (Sedgwick)

1928   *The Trail of '98* (Brown); *The Border Patrol* (Hogan); *Burning Bridges* (Hogan)

1931   *Trader Horn* (Van Dyke) (title role); *Bad Company* (Garnett) (as McBaine); *The Vanishing Legion* (Eason—serial); *Across the Line*; *Double Sixes*; *Horse Hoofs*; *The Hurricane Rider*; *Cavalier of the West* (McCarthy)

1932   *Border Devils* (Nigh); *Without Honors* (Nigh); *Law and Order* (*Guns A' Blazing*) (Cahn) (as Ed Brant); *Last of the Mohicans* (Beebe—serial); *The Devil Horse* (Brower—serial); *The Night Rider* (Nigh)

1933   *Man of the Forest* (Hathaway) (as Jim Gaynor); *Sunset Pass* (Hathaway) (as John Hesbitt)

1934   *The Thundering Herd* (*In the Days of the Thundering Herd*) (Hathaway) (as Clark Sprague)

1935   *The Last of the Clintons* (Fraser) (as Trigger Carson); *Rustlers' Paradise* (Fraser) (as Cheyenne Kincaid); *Powdersmoke Range* (Fox) (as Tucson Smith); *Barbary Coast* (Hawks) (as Slocum); *Wagon Trail* (Fraser) (as Sheriff Hartley); *Wild Mustang* (Fraser) (as Norton)

1936   *The Prisoner of Shark Island* (Ford) (as Commandant of Fort Jefferson "Shark Island"); *Little Miss Nobody* (Blystone) (as John Russell); *The Last Outlaw* (*Last of the Outlaws*) (Cabanne) (as Dean Payton); *Sutter's Gold* (Cruze) (as Kit Carson); *Valiant Is the Word for Carrie* (Ruggles) (as Phil Yonne); *The Accusing Finger* (Hogan) (as Sen. Nash); *The Three Mesquiteers* (Saylor); *Man behind the Mask* (Powell)

1937   *Racing Lady* (Fox) (as Tom Martin); *Born Reckless* (St. Clair) (as Dad Martin); *Kid Galahad* (Curtiz) (as Silver Jackson); *Souls at Sea* (Hathaway) (as Captain of the *William Brown*); *Ghost Town* (Fraser) (as Cheyenne Harry); *Border Cafe* (Landers) (as Tex); *Annapolis Salute* (*Salute to Romance*) (Cabanne) (as Chief Martin); *Aces Wild* (Fraser); *Danger Patrol* (Landers) (as "Easy" Street)

1938   *You and Me* (Fritz Lang) (as Mr. Morris); *Sky Giant* (Landers) (as Col. Stockton); *The Law West of Tombstone* (Tryon) (as Bill Barker); *Gateway* (Werker) (as Commissioner Nelson); *Port of Missing Girls* (Karl Brown) (as Capt. Storm); *King of Alcatraz* (Florey) (as Capt. Glennan); *Code of the Streets* (Harold Young) (as Lt. Lewis)

1939   *Burn 'em Up O'Connor* (Sedgwick) (as P. G. Delano); *Inside Information* (Lamont) (as Capt. Bill Dugan); **Mr. Smith Goes to Washington** (Capra) (as President of the Senate); *Street of Missing Men* (Salkow) (as Putnam); *My Son Is Guilty* (Barton) (as Tim Kerry)

1940   *Outside the 3-Mile Limit* (*Mutiny on the Seas*) (Collins) (as Capt. Bailey); *Beyond Tomorrow* (A. Edward Sutherland) (as George Melton); *They Knew What They Wanted* (Kanin) (as doctor)

1941   *Among the Living* (Heisler) (as Dr. Ben Saunders); *The Shepherd of the Hills* (Hathaway) (as Daniel Howitt); *Parachute Battalion* (Goodwins) (as Bill Richards); *Sundown* (Hathaway) (as Dewey)

1942   *The Spoilers* (Enright) (as Al Dextry)

1943   *Air Force* (Hawks) (as Sgt. Robby White); *Happy Land* (Pichel) (as Gramp)

1945   *The Great Moment* (Preston Sturges) (as Prof. Warren); *China's Little Devils* (Bell)

1946   *Duel in the Sun* (King Vidor and others) (as Lem Smoot)

1947   *Angel and the Badman* (Grant) (as Wistful McClintock); *The Sea of Grass* (Kazan) (as Doc Reid)

1948   **Red River** (Hawks) (as Mr. Millville)

1949   *So Dear to My Heart* (Schuster) (as judge at county fair)

Publications

By CAREY: articles—

Interviews with M. Cheatham, in *Motion Picture Classic* (Brooklyn), February 1921 and November 1921.

On CAREY: books—

Fenin, George, and William K. Everson, *The Western, from Silents to Cinerama*, New York, 1962.

On CAREY: article—

Obituary in *New York Times*, 22 September 1947.

*   *   *

When John Ford dedicated *Three Godfathers* "to the memory of Harry Carey—bright Star of the early Western sky" he acknowledged more than the death of an old friend and colleague. Carey, like Ford himself, was an Easterner who fell in love with the West, adopted its ethos, and came to feel himself, as did William S. Hart, a custodian of its ethics and principles.

With Ford and others, Carey for many years lived a communal Western-style existence on a small ranch near Newhall, California, counterfeiting a life that, as the son of a New York judge, he had never

Harry Carey

known. Distrusting Griffith's sentimental view of the frontier, and the
antics of such stars as Tom Mix and Hoot Gibson whose comedy/
action Westerns reflected their rodeo and traveling show backgrounds,
Carey and Ford, in 26 silents together, often co-written and co-directed, combined myth and truth to construct a legendary West more
consistent with their own intellect and morality.

Carey's lined, impassive face with its turned-down mouth epitomized the Russell/Remington vision of frontier life—violent, grinding, dirty. As Henry Nash Smith wrote in *Virgin Land*, the hero of this
West, "even after his reformation, could not easily be distinguished
from the criminals opposing him." Most Americans soon unquestion-
ingly accepted the West of Carey's Cheyenne Harry films as literal
truth.

Carey survived the move to sound better than many of his colleagues. Playing the white scout Hawkeye in a serial version of *Last of
the Mohicans*, he introduced his stern face and growling voice to new
audiences. He was excellent in the underrated Earp/Holliday film
Law and Order, and transferred his frontier rectitude to Africa for
Trader Horn. Few character actors could have rallied the force to
face down Lionel Barrymore so effectively in *Duel in the Sun*.
When Hitchcock, with characteristic malice, suggested him for the
Nazi spy in *Saboteur*, Carey's wife advised him indignantly that he
now occupied the position in the American pantheon vacated by
Will Rogers. Her claim was exaggerated, but not without its justifi-
cation.

—John Baxter

CARON, Leslie

Nationality: French. **Born:** Leslie Claire Margaret Caron in
Boulogne-Billancourt, near Paris, 1 July 1931. **Education:** Attended
the Convent of the Assumption, Paris; studied dance at the
Conservatoire de Paris, 1944-46. **Family:** Married 1) George Hormel,
1951 (divorced 1954); 2) the director Peter Hall, 1956 (divorced
1965), one son, one daughter; 3) the producer Michael Laughlin,
1969 (marriage dissolved). **Career:** 1946-47—dancer with Ballet des
Champs-Elysées; 1949—head ballerina for Ballet des Champs-Elysées;
1951—discovered by Gene Kelly and chosen for role in *An American
in Paris*, beginning her film career in MGM musicals; 1954-55—
toured with Ballet de Paris; 1955—stage debut in Jean Renoir's *Orvet*;
1955-on—continued to appear on stage in London, Paris, and on
Broadway between films; 1972—began acting mostly in European
films; 1974—in TV mini-series *QB VII*; 1980—in French TV series
Docteur Erica Werner; 1984—in TV mini-series *Master of the Game*,
and *The Man Who Lived at the Ritz*, 1988. **Awards:** Best Foreign
Actress, British Academy, for *Lili*, 1953; Best British Actress, British
Academy, for *The L-Shaped Room*, 1962.

Films as Actress:

1951   *An American in Paris* (Minnelli) (as Lise Bouvier); *The Man
        with a Cloak* (Markle) (as Madeline Minot)
1952   *Glory Alley* (Walsh) (as Angela)
1953   "Mademoiselle" ep. of *The Story of Three Loves* (Minnelli) (as
        Mademoiselle); *Lili* (Walters) (title role)
1955   *The Glass Slipper* (Walters) (as Ella); *Daddy Long Legs*
        (Negulesco) (as Julie Andre)
1956   *Gaby* (Bernhardt) (title role)
1958   *Gigi* (Minnelli) (title role); *The Doctor's Dilemma* (Asquith)
        (as Mrs. Dubedat)

1959   *The Man Who Understood Women* (Johnson) (as Ann
        Garantier); *Austerlitz* (*The Battle of Austerlitz*) (Gance) (as
        Mlle. de Vaudey)
1960   *The Subterraneans* (MacDougal) (as Mardou Fox); *Fanny*
        (Logan) (title role)
1962   "Les Deux Pigeons" ("Two Pigeons") ep. of *Les Quatres Vérités*
        (*Three Fables of Love*) (Clair); *Guns of Darkness* (Asquith) (as
        Claire Jordan); *The L-Shaped Room* (Forbes) (as Jane Fosset)
1964   *Father Goose* (Nelson) (as Catherine Freneau)
1965   *A Very Special Favor* (Gordon) (as Lauren Boullard)
1966   *Promise Her Anything* (Hiller) (as Michele O'Brien); *Paris
        brûle-t-il?* (*Is Paris Burning?*) (Clément) (as Françoise Labe)
1967   *Il padre di famiglia* (*The Head of the Family*; *Jeux D'adultes*)
        (Loy) (as Paola)
1970   *Madron* (Jerry Hopper) (as Sister Mary)
1971   *Chandler* (Magwood) (as Katherine)
1972   *Nicole* (Ventilla); *Purple Night* (film not listed in most sources)
1975   *James Dean, the First American Teenager* (Connolly—doc)
        (as herself); *Carola* (Lloyd—for TV)
1976   *Sérail* (de Gregorio)
1977   *L'Homme qui aimait les femmes* (*The Man Who Loved Women*)
        (Truffaut) (as Vera); *Valentino* (Ken Russell) (as Alla
        Nazimova)
1978   *The Contract* (Hui)
1979   *Goldengirl* (Sargent) (as Dr. Sammy Lee); *Tous vedettes* (Michel
        Lang)
1981   *Kontrakt* (*The Contract*) (Zanussi) (as Penelope); *Chanel soli-
        taire* (Kaczender)
1982   *Imperative* (Zanussi) (as Mother); *Die unerreichbare* (*The
        Unapproachable*) (Zanussi)
1984   *La Diagonale du fou* (*Dangerous Moves*) (Dembo) (as Henia
        Liebskind)
1987   *The Sealed Train* (for TV)
1989   *Guerriers et captives* (*Warriors and Prisoners*) (Cozarinsky);
        Courage Mountain (Leitch) (as Jane Hillary)
1990   *Blue Notte* (Serafini)
1992   *Damage* (*Fatale*) (Malle) (as Elizabeth Prideaux)
1993   *The Genius* (Joe Gibbons); *Jean Renoir* (David Thompson—doc)
1994   *That's Entertainment! III* (Friedgen and Sheridan—compila-
        tion)
1995   *Funny Bones* (Chelsom) (as Katie Parker); *Let It Be Me*
        (Bergstein)

Publications

By CARON: articles—

Interview with J. Fieschi and B. Villien, in *Cinématographe* (Paris),
    October 1980.
"Polonaises," in *Cinématographe* (Paris), April 1982.
"Enfin Star!," in *Cinématographe* (Paris), November 1983.
"Un Ami: Truffaut," in *Cinématographe* (Paris), December 1984.

On CARON: books—

Springer, John, *All Talking, All Singing, All Dancing*, New York, 1966.
Kobal, John, *Gotta Sing, Gotta Dance*, New York, 1970.
Knox, Donald, *The Magic Factory*, New York, 1973.

On CARON: article—

Current Biography 1954, New York, 1954.

*   *   *

Leslie Caron in *The L-Shaped Room*

Originally a Gallic twinkletoes and all-purpose gamine for MGM, Leslie Caron became the only dancing star of her day to transpose brilliance en pointe to pointedly dramatic performance. While Cyd Charisse, Ann Miller, Ginger Rogers, and Vera-Ellen remain symbols of a glamorous yesterday, Caron (who had never intended to be a thespian, let alone a movie star) has matured into a working actress keenly aware of contemporary trends. Disparaging her early MGM work in the book, *The Magic Factory*, she has lately softened those ungenerous remarks. Never a happy camper within the studio system, outspoken Caron need not play down her escapist past in order to emphasize her present seriousness.

If *An American in Paris* now registers as a rather puffed-up sacrifice to the Art of Dance, that musical does have its saving graces including the moonstruck pas de deux that Kelly and Caron dance to "Our Love Is Here to Stay." In all her MGM diversions (although it is least evident in *Lili*), there is a disdainful chilliness about Caron as if she is hiding her feelings from the camera. (In retrospect, it may be that she simply was not comfortable making these films.) While her reserve melts whenever she moves to music, the Roland Petit choreography is not much of a godsend to her in the second-rate *The Glass Slipper* and *Daddy Long Legs*. Still, an ebullient delight, *Lili* characterizes the actress's reticence as diffidence and her cool composure as innocence

vanquishing the hard heart of sophistication. Bringing immense conviction to the scenes where she converses with *poupées*, Caron speaks to the inner child in us all—no mean feat since some of the human actors she contends with such as Mel Ferrer are more wooden than the puppets.

In her nonmusicals, Caron was forced to be a one-woman Gallic goodwill ambassador, and you can feel her resentment at having to typify all things French. Since MGM already limited her range, she was probably wise to nix *Les Girls*, just one more nail in the coffin of the movie musical. Salvation was at hand when the cinema' premiere continental charmer Audrey Hepburn rejected *Gigi*, for which Caron was ideally suited. Enchanting as the child raised to be a courtesan, she was bewitching as the adult who scandalizes her instructors by preferring *l'amour* to family traditions of impropriety. At the other end of the soignée scale came the box-office smash *Fanny* which scuttled the gorgeous Harold Rome score except for the rapturous title theme, failed to come within hailing distance of the Pagnol original, and straitjacketed Caron into embodying the soul of France for one final occasion. Since then, her forays into art films have been as unrewarding as sporadic returns to Hollywood, where her strenuous comedy technique went down for the count with *A Very Special Favor* and *Promise Her Anything*. The one bright note of the post-MGM period came with the kitchen-sink soap opera, *The L-Shaped Room*, for which she earned an Oscar bid for conveying the anguish of an unwed mother. This film, which could be dubbed, "The Death of Innocence" benefited greatly from a supporting cast of consummate British players and from Caron's insight into the plight of an abandoned foreigner.

One wishes late-career highlights such as *Il padre di famiglia* and *Dangerous Moves* had offset pretentious misfires and commercial duds. Fortunately, in 1995, Caron graced a little-seen masterwork *Funny Bones*. It is exactly the kind of personal, offbeat film that she had always championed. Protecting her psychologically damaged son from the unkindness of strangers or vanquishing a crooked cop who mistakes her womanliness for softness, Caron contributed significantly to the film's impact. Looking more lovely than ever, Caron can confidently expect further adventures in cinematic artistry, foreshadowed by her variegated and supremely confident work in *Funny Bones*.

—Robert Pardi

CARRADINE, John

Nationality: American. **Born:** Richmond Reed Carradine in New York City, 5 February 1906. **Education:** Christ Church School, Kingston, New York; Graphic Art School; Episcopal Academy, Philadelphia. **Family:** Married 1) Ardanelle Cosner, 1935 (divorced 1944), sons: Bruce John and the actor John Arthur (David); 2) Sonia Sorel, 1945 (divorced 1955), sons: Christopher, John, and the actors Keith Ian and Robert Reed; 3) Doris Rich, 1957 (died 1971); 4) Emily Cisneros, 1975. **Career:** Pre-1925—traveled throughout the South working as sketch artist; 1925—stage debut in *Camille* in New Orleans; then joined Shakespearean stock company; 1927-30—appeared in stage productions in Los Angeles; 1930—film debut using professional name Peter Richmond in *Tol'able David*; also appeared as John Peter Richmond until 1935; 1936—changed name to John Carradine after signing contract with 20th Century-Fox; c. 1930s-60s—acted on stage between film assignments; 1940s—began freelancing for various studios; 1950—host of TV series *The Trap*; 1953-54—in TV series *My Friend Irma*; 1964-66—appeared occasionally as Mr. Gateman on TV series *The Munsters*; 1978—in TV mini-series *Greatest Heroes of the Bible*. **Died:** In Milan, 27 November 1988.

Films as Actor:

1930   *Tol'able David* (Blystone) (as Buzzard)
1931   *Heaven on Earth* (Mack) (as Chicken Sam); *Bright Lights* (Curtiz)
1932   *The Sign of the Cross* (DeMille); *Forgotten Commandments* (Gasnier and Schorr)
1933   *The Invisible Man* (Whale); *This Day and Age* (DeMille); *The Story of Temple Drake* (Roberts) (as trial spectator); *To the Last Man* (Hathaway) (as Pete Garon)
1934   *The Black Cat* (Ulmer) (as member of cult); *Cleopatra* (DeMille) (as Roman citizen); *The Meanest Gal in Town* (Mack)
1935   *The Man Who Broke the Bank at Monte Carlo* (Roberts); *Alias Mary Dow* (Neumann); *Les Miserables* (Boleslawski); *The Crusades* (DeMille); ***The Bride of Frankenstein*** (Whale) (as Woodsman); *Clive of India* (Boleslawski); *She Gets Her Man* (Nigh); *Cardinal Richelieu* (Lee); *Bad Boy* (Blystone); *Transient Lady* (*False Witness*) (Buzzell)

1936   *Anything Goes* (*Tops Is the Limit*) (Milestone); *Captain January* (Butler); *The Prisoner of Shark Island* (John Ford) (as Sgt. Rankin); *Under Two Flags* (Lloyd) (as Cafard); *White Fang* (Butler) (as Beauty Smith); *Ramona* (King) (as Jim Farrar); *Dimples* (Seiter) (as Richards); *Mary of Scotland* (John Ford) (as David Rizzio); *Daniel Boone* (Howard) (as Simon Girty); *Winterset* (Santell) (as Romagna); *The Garden of Allah* (Boleslawski); *A Message to Garcia* (Marshall) (as voice of President McKinley); *Half Angel* (Lanfield); *Laughing at Trouble* (*Laughing at Death*) (Strayer)
1937   *Nancy Steele Is Missing* (Marshall) (as Harry Wilkins); *Danger—Love at Work* (Preminger) (as Herbert Pemberton); *This Is My Affair* (*His Affair*) (Seiter) (as Ed); *Love under Fire* (Marshall) (as Captain Delmar); *Thank You, Mr. Moto* (Foster) (as Pereira); *Captains Courageous* (Fleming) (as Long Jack); *The Last Gangster* (Ludwig) (as Caspar); *The Hurricane* (John Ford); *Ali Baba Goes to Town* (Butler) (as Ishak)
1938   *International Settlement* (Forde) (as Murdock); *Four Men and a Prayer* (John Ford) (as Gen. Adolfo Arturo Sebastian); *I'll Give a Million* (Walter Lang) (as Kopelpeck); *Kentucky Moonshine* (*Four Men and a Girl*) (Butler) (as Reef Hatfield); *Kidnapped* (Werker) (as Gordon); *Alexander's Ragtime Band* (King) (as cabbie); *Gateway* (Werker); *Submarine Patrol* (Ford) (as McAllison); *Of Human Hearts* (Brown) (as Abraham Lincoln)
1939   *Jesse James* (King) (as Bob Ford); *The Hound of the Baskervilles* (Lanfield) (as Barryman); *Frontier Marshal* (Dwan) (as Ben Carter); *Drums along the Mohawk* (John Ford) (as Caldwell); *The Three Musketeers* (*The Singing Musketeer*) (Dwan) (as Naveau); ***Stagecoach*** (John Ford) (as Hatfield); *Captain Fury* (Roach) (as Coughy); *Five Came Back* (Farrow) (as Crimp); *Mr. Moto's Last Warning* (Foster) (as Danforth)
1940   ***The Grapes of Wrath*** (John Ford) (as Jim Casey); *The Return of Frank James* (Fritz Lang) (as Bob Ford); *Brigham Young—Frontiersman* (*Brigham Young*) (Hathaway) (as Porter Rockwell); *Chad Hanna* (King) (as Bisbee)
1941   *Western Union* (Fritz Lang) (as Murdoch); *Blood and Sand* (Mamoulian) (as El Nacional); *Man Hunt* (Fritz Lang) (as Mr. Jones); *Swamp Water* (*The Man Who Came Back*) (Renoir) (as Jesse Wick)
1942   *Whispering Ghosts* (Werker) (as "Long Jack"/"Norbert"); *Son of Fury* (Cromwell) (as Caleb Green); *Northwest Rangers* (Newman) (as Martin Caswell); *Reunion* (*Reunion in France*; *Mademoiselle France*) (Dassin) (as Ulrich Windler); *Information Please* no. 5 (short) (as guest panelist)
1943   *Silver Spurs* (Kane); *Captive Wild Woman* (Dmytryk) (as Dr. Walters); *Hitler's Madman* (*Hitler's Hangman*) (Sirk) (as Heydrich); *I Escaped from the Gestapo* (*No Escape*) (Young); *The Isle of Forgotten Sins* (Ulmer)
1944   *The Mummy's Ghost* (LeBorg); *Barbary Coast Gent* (Del Ruth) (as Duke Cleat); *The Adventures of Mark Twain* (Rapper) (as Bret Harte); *The Black Parachute* (Landers); *The Invisible Man's Revenge* (Beebe) (as Dr. Drury); *The Return of the Ape Man* (Rosen); *Voodoo Man* (Beaudine) (as Job); *Alaska* (Archainbaud); *House of Frankenstein* (Kenton) (as Dracula); *Waterfront* (Sekely); *Gangway for Tomorrow* (Auer); *Revenge of the Zombies* (*The Corpse Vanished*) (Sekely); *Bluebeard* (Ulmer) (title role)
1945   *House of Dracula* (Kenton) (as Dracula); *Fallen Angel* (Preminger); *Captain Kidd* (Lee) (as Orange Povey); *It's in the Bag* (*The Fifth Chair*) (Wallace) (as Pike)
1946   *Down Missouri Way* (Berne) (as Thorndyke Dunning); *The Face of Marble* (Beaudine)
1947   *The Private Affairs of Bel Ami* (Lewin) (as Charles Forestier)
1949   *C-Man* (Lerner) (as Doc Spencer)

1954 *Thunder Pass* (McDonald) (as Bergstron); *Casanova's Big Night* (McLeod) (as Foressi); **Johnny Guitar** (Nicholas Ray) (as Old Tom); *The Egyptian* (Curtiz)

1955 *Stranger on Horseback* (Jacques Tourneur); *Desert Sands* (Selander) (as Arab Jala); *The Kentuckian* (Lancaster) (as Fletcher)

1956 *The Female Jungle* (Ve Sota); *The Black Sheep* (*Dr. Cadman's Secret*) (LeBorg) (as Borg); *The Ten Commandments* (DeMille) (as Aaron); *Around the World in Eighty Days* (Anderson) (as Col. Proctor Stamp); *Hidden Guns* (Gannaway) (as Snipe Harding); *The Court Jester* (Panama and Frank); *Dark Venture* (Trevlac, i.e. John Calvert)

1957 *The Unearthly* (Peters); *Half Human* (*Jujin Yukiotoko*) (Honda and Crane); *Hell Ship Mutiny* (Sholem and Williams) (as Malone); *The True Story of Jesse James* (Nicholas Ray) (as Rev. Bailey); *The Story of Mankind* (Allen) (as Pharaoh Khufu)

1958 *The Proud Rebel* (Curtiz); *The Last Hurrah* (Ford) (as Amos Force); *Showdown at Boot Hill* (Fowler, Jr.) (as Doc Weber)

1959 *The Oregon Trail* (Fowler, Jr.) (as Zachariah); *The Cosmic Man* (Greene); *Invisible Invaders* (Cahn)

1960 *The Adventures of Huckleberry Finn* (Curtiz); *Tarzan the Magnificent* (Day); *Sex Kittens Go to College* (Zugsmith); *The Incredible Petrified World* (Warren)

1962 *Invasion of the Animal People* (*Terror in the Midnight Sun*) (Vogel and Warren); **The Man Who Shot Liberty Valance** (Ford) (as Major Cassius Starbuckle)

1964 *The Patsy* (Lewis) (as Bruce Alden); *Cheyenne Autumn* (John Ford) (as Major Jeff Blair); *Curse of the Stone Hand* (Warren and Schlieppe)

1965 *House of the Black Death* (*Blood of the Man Devil*; *Night of the Beast*) (Daniels and LeBorg); *The Wizard of Mars* (Hewitt); *Something for Mrs. Gibbs* (Van Praag—advertising short)

1966 *Billy the Kid vs. Dracula* (Beaudine) (as Dracula); *Night Train to Mundo Fine* (Francis); *Broken Sabre* (McEveety); *Munster, Go Home!* (Bellamy) (as Cruikshank); *The Emperor's New Clothes* (Clark—unreleased)

1967 *The Hostage* (Doughten) (as Otis Lovelace); *Hillbillys in a Haunted House* (Yarbrough); *Dr. Terror's Gallery of Horrors* (*The Blood Suckers*; *Gallery of Horror*; *Return from the Past*) (Hewitt) (as narrator and warlock in one ep.); *La Senora Muerte* (*Mrs. Death*; *The Death Woman*) (Salvador)

1968 *They Ran for Their Lives* (Payne) (as Laslow); *Pacto diabolico* (*Pact with the Devil*) (Salvador); *The Astro-Zombies* (Mikels); *Autopsia de un fantasma* (*Autopsy on a Ghost*) (Rodriguez) (as Satan); *The Helicopter Spies* (Sagal—for TV); *Genesis* (*Genesis I*) (organized by R. B. Childs—compilation film) (as narrator)

1969 *Blood of Dracula's Castle* (Adamson and Hewitt) (as George); *The Good Guys and the Bad Guys* (Kennedy); *The Trouble with Girls* (Tewksbury); *Daughter of the Mind* (Grauman—for TV); *Dracula vs. Frankenstein* (*The Blood Seekers*; *Blood of Frankenstein*) (Adamson); *Las vampiras* (*The Vampires*) (Curiel)

1970 *The McMasters* (Kjellin); *Myra Breckinridge* (Sarne); *Hell's Bloody Devils* (*The Fakers*; *Swastika Savages*; *Operation M*; *Smashing the Crime Syndicate*) (Adamson); *Crowhaven Farm* (Grauman—for TV); *Cain's Cutthroats* (*Cain's Way*; *Justice Cain*) (Osborne) (as Preacher Sims); *Blood of the Iron Maiden* (*Trip to Terror*; *Is This Trip Really Necessary?*) (Benoit); *Horror of the Blood Monsters* (*The Flesh Creatures*; *Flesh Creatures of the Red Planet*; *Creatures of the Prehistoric Planet*; *Creatures of the Red Planet*; *Vampire Men of the Lost Planet*) (Adamson); *Five Bloody Graves* (*The Lonely Man*; *Five Bloody Days to Tombstone*; *Gun Riders*) (Adamson)

1971 *Shinbone Alley* (Wilson and Detiege—animated feature) (as voice); *The Seven Minutes* (Meyer)

1972 *Richard* (Yerby and Hurwitz); *Boxcar Bertha* (Scorsese); *Everything You Always Wanted to Know about Sex but Were Afraid to Ask* (Allen); *Blood of Ghastly Horror* (*The Fiend with the Electronic Brain*; *Psycho a Go-Go!*; *The Love Maniac*; *Man with the Synthetic Brain*) (Adamson—produced 1969); *Portnoy's Complaint* (Lehman) (as voice of judge); *Shadow House* (short); *Decisions! Decisions!* (Segal—TV pilot); *The Legend of Sleepy Hollow* (animated short) (as narrator)

1973 *Silent Night, Bloody Night* (*Zora*; *Night of the Full Dark Moon*) (Gershuny); *Terror in the Wax Museum* (Fenady); *Bad Charleston Charlie* (Nagy); *Hex* (Garen); *Superchick* (Forsyth) (as Igor Smith); *House of Dracula's Daughter* (Hessler); *One Million A.D.* (Baron—unreleased); *The Cat Creature* (Harrington—for TV); *The Night Strangler* (Curtis—for TV); *Legacy of Blood* (Monson); *The Gatling Gun* (Gordon—produced 1969 as *King Gun*); *Bigfoot* (Slatzer)

1974 *The House of the Seven Corpses* (Harrison); *Moonchild* (Gadney—produced 1972) (as "The Walker")

1975 *Mary, Mary, Bloody Mary* (Moctezuma); *Stowaway to the Moon* (McLaglen—for TV) (as Jacob Avril)

1976 *Won Ton Ton, the Dog Who Saved Hollywood* (Winner); *Crash* (Band); *The Killer Inside Me* (Kennedy); *The Shootist* (Siegel) (as Hezekiah Beckum); *The Last Tycoon* (Kazan) (as studio tour guide); *Death at Love House* (*The Shrine of Lorna Love*) (Swackhamer—for TV) (as Conan Carroll)

1977 *The Sentinel* (Winner); *Shock Waves* (*Death Corps*; *Almost Human*) (Weiderhorn); *The White Buffalo* (Thompson) (as Amos Briggs); *Golden Rendezvous* (Lazarus); *Tail Gunner Joe* (Taylor—for TV); *The Christmas Coal Mine Miracle* (*Christmas Miracle in Caufield, U.S.A.*) (Taylor—for TV); *Satan's Cheerleaders* (Clark); *Journey into the Beyond* (Olsen) (as narrator); *The Lady and the Lynchings*; *Frankenstein Island* (Warren) (as Dr. Frankenstein)

1978 *Sunset Cove* (*Save Our Beach*) (Adamson) (as Judge Winslow); *Vampire Hookers* (Santiago); *The Bees* (Zacharias) (as Dr. Sigmund Hummel)

1979 *Monster* (*Monster: The Legend That Became a Terror*) (Hartford); *The Seekers* (Hayers—for TV); *Teheran Incident* (*Missile X*; *The Neutron Bomb Incident*; *Cruise Missile*) (Martinson); *Phobia* (*The Nesting*) (Weston); *Nocturna* (*Granddaughter of Dracula*) (Tampa, i.e. Harry Hurwitz) (as Dracula); *The Mandate of Heaven*

1980 *Carradines in Concert* (doc); *The Monster Club* (Baker); *The Howling* (Dante) (as Kenton); *The Boogey Man* (Lommel)

1982 *The Secret of NIMH* (Bluth) (as voice of Great Owl); *The Scarecrow* (Pillsbury)

1983 *House of Long Shadows* (Walker); *The Ice Pirates* (Raffill) (as Emperor)

1985 *Evils of the Night* (Rustam) (as Dr. Kozmar); *The Vals* (Polakof) (as Mr. Stanton)

1986 *Peggy Sue Got Married* (Coppola) (as Leo); *Revenge* (Lewis) (as Sen. Bradford); *The Tomb* (Olen Ray) (as Mr. Androheb)

1987 *Evil Spawn* (*Deadly Sting*; *Alive by Night*) (Hall) (as Dr. Zeitman); *Monster in the Closet* (Dahlin) (as Old Joe)

1988 *Star Slammer* (*Prison Ship*) (Olen Ray) (as The Justice)

Publications

By CARRADINE: article—

Interview by S. Eyman in *Films and Filming* (London), December 1981.

On CARRADINE: book—

Young, Jordan R., *Reel Characters: Great Movie Character Actors*, Beverly Hills, 1986.

On CARRADINE: articles—

Bühler, W.-E., "John Carradine," in *Filmkritik* (Munich), January 1972.
Parrish, J. R., and M. R. Pitts, "The Good, the Bad, and the Most," in *Focus on Film* (London), Summer 1973.
Films in Review (New York), October 1979, corrections and additions to filmography in January 1980 issue.
L'Ecran Fantastique, no. 15, 1980 and nos. 45 and 46, 1984.

* * *

The film career of John Carradine was one of the longest and most prolific in Hollywood. He claimed to have appeared in over 400 films and the range of his roles varies widely. Although he made a successful career for himself in films, Carradine's first love was always the theater, particularly Shakespeare. His training in theater is apparent in his film work, creating "larger than life" characters with exaggerated gestures and a booming voice.

Carradine began acting in films in the early 1930s using the name John Peter Richmond. He found fairly steady work as a bit player with such directors as Cecil B. DeMille (*The Sign of the Cross*, *This Day and Age*, *Cleopatra*) and James Whale (*The Bride of Frankenstein*, *The Invisible Man*). In 1936, using the name John Carradine, he became a Fox contract player. That same year Carradine appeared in John Ford's *The Prisoner of Shark Island*. (Carradine eventually appeared in ten films directed by John Ford, including *Stagecoach*, *The Grapes of Wrath*, and *The Man Who Shot Liberty Valance*.) Carradine received excellent notices for his performance as a prison guard in *The Prisoner of Shark Island*, which led to villainous roles in other films.

In addition to his reputation as a film "bad guy" Carradine also became known for his roles in cheap horror pictures. These films were produced very quickly and so there are many of them among Carradine's credits. In 1945 he appeared in two low-budget films for Universal, *House of Frankenstein* and *House of Dracula*, which marked the first times that Carradine played a vampire. His subsequent horror films, with titles like *The Incredible Petrified World* and *Billy the Kid vs. Dracula*, did not carry much credibility, but this kind of film kept Carradine employed for a good number of years. Carradine became so well known for playing the "mad scientist" in low-budget horror films that he was enlisted to do a parody of himself in a segment of Woody Allen's *Everything You Always Wanted to Know about Sex but Were Afraid to Ask*. With such an amazingly diverse list of film credits, it is not greatly surprising that John Carradine became one of the most recognizable character actors on the American screen.

—Linda J. Obalil

CARROLL, Madeleine

Nationality: British American. **Born:** Marie Madeleine Bernadette O'Carroll in West Bromwich, Warwickshire, England, 26 February 1906; became United States citizen, 1943. **Education:** Attended Birmingham University, B.A. in French. **Family:** Married 1) Philip Astley, 1931 (divorced 1939); 2) the actor Sterling Hayden, 1942 (divorced 1946); 3) the producer Henri Lavorel, 1946 (divorced 1949); 4) Andrew Heiskell, 1950 (divorced 1965): one daughter. **Career:** French teacher in girls' school in Hove, Sussex; 1927—stage debut in *The*

Lash, London; 1928—film debut in *The Guns of Loos*; 1936—film contract with Walter Wanger: made films in Hollywood; during World War II—worked with refugee orphans, then entertainment director for merchant seamen in New York; 1943-45—worked with the Red Cross in France and Italy, and subsequently with UNESCO (made documentary films for the United Nations and others: e.g., *Children's Republic* and *The Eternal Fight*); 1948—on Broadway in *Goodbye, My Fancy*. **Awards:** Legion of Honor (France); United States Medal of Freedom. **Died:** In Marbella, Spain, 2 October 1987.

Films as Actress:

1928 *The Guns of Loos* (Hill) (as Diana Cheswick); *What Money Can Buy* (Greenwood) (as Rhoda Pearson); *The First Born* (Mander) (as Lady Madeleine Boycott)
1929 *The Crooked Billet* (Brunel) (as Joan Easton); *The American Prisoner* (Bentley) (as Grace Malherb); *Atlantic* (Dupont) (as Monica)
1930 *The "W" Plan* (Saville) (as Rosa Hartmann); *Young Woodley* (Bentley) (as Laura Simmons); *French Leave* (Raymond) (as Dorothy Glenister); *Escape* (Dean) (as Dora); *The School for Scandal* (Elvey) (as Lady Teazle); *Kissing Cup's Race* (Knight) (as Lady Molly Adair)
1931 *Madame Guillotine* (Fogwell) (as Lucille de Choisigne); *Fascination* (Mander) (as Gwenda Farrell); *The Written Law* (Fogwell) (as Lady Margaret Rochester)
1933 *Sleeping Car* (Litvak) (as Anne); *I Was a Spy* (Saville) (as Marthe Cnockhaert)
1934 *The World Moves On* (Ford)
1935 *The Dictator* (*The Love Affair of the Dictator*; *The Loves of a Dictator*; *For Love of a Queen*) (Saville and Santell) (as Caroline Struensee); *The 39 Steps* (Hitchcock) (as Pamela)
1936 *The Story of Papworth* (charity appeal) (as guest); *The Secret Agent* (Hitchcock) (as Elsa); *The Case against Mrs. Ames* (Seiter); *The General Died at Dawn* (Milestone); *Lloyds of London* (King)
1937 *On the Avenue* (Del Ruth); *It's All Yours* (Nugent); *The Prisoner of Zenda* (Cromwell)
1938 *Blockade* (Dieterle)
1939 *Cafe Society* (Griffith); *Honeymoon in Bali* (*Husbands or Lovers*) (Griffith)
1940 *My Son, My Son!* (Charles Vidor); *Safari* (Griffith); *Northwest Mounted Police* (DeMille)
1941 *Virginia* (Griffith); *One Night in Lisbon* (Griffith); *Bahama Passage* (Griffith)
1942 *My Favorite Blonde* (Lanfield)
1946 *La Petite Republique* (Vicas)
1947 *White Cradle Inn* (*High Fury*) (French) (as Magda)
1948 *Don't Trust Your Husband* (*An Innocent Affair*) (Bacon)
1949 *The Fan* (*Lady Windermere's Fan*) (Preminger)

Publications

On CARROLL: articles—

"Madeleine Carroll" in *Current Biography 1949*, New York, 1949.
Obituary in *Films and Filming* (London), November 1987.

* * *

Although her primary fame was for her unusually refined blonde good looks, Madeleine Carroll was nonetheless a capable film actress. Her current reputation is based on her work with Alfred Hitchcock (notably in *The 39 Steps* and *The Secret Agent*). These were by no means the only worthwhile films she made; she was one Hollywood import who thrived on its soil. The highlights of her Hollywood years were *The General Died at Dawn* and the fanciful romantic epic *The Prisoner of Zenda* in which she played opposite Ronald Colman.

She began in the theater after attending the University of Birmingham, and entered the British film scene in the late 1920s. Gaumont British traded her for Warner Baxter, in an arrangement with 20th Century-Fox, and it was thus that she made her first American film, *The World Moves On* (John Ford, 1934). She returned to England for her work with Hitchcock, and finally returned to America under contract to Walter Wanger. She ended up at Paramount, and found her niche as a comedienne. Although her films were rather lackluster, her restrained and subtle performances won her a loyal following, and she remained active until the late 1940s. Her later films included a version of Oscar Wilde's *Lady Windermere's Fan* (*The Fan*) and a string of comedies in which she was teamed with Fred MacMurray. She also had a huge stage success in the early 1950s with Garson Kanin's *Goodbye, My Fancy*.

As a film actress, Carroll was notable for her underplaying, her lack of posturing or reliance on mannerism. This was unusual in an era when such qualities were more common than they are now, and perhaps explains her enduring popularity among film enthusiasts.

—Joseph Arkins

CASSEL, Jean-Pierre

Nationality: French. **Born:** Jean-Pierre Crochon in Paris, 27 October 1932. **Education:** Attended Lycées Rollin and Condorcet, Paris; studied drama with René Simon. **Family:** Married 1) Sabine Litique (divorced), children: Vincent, Olivia (deceased), and Mathias; 2) Anne Célérier, daughter: Cécile. **Career:** Early 1950s—stage acting debut in *L'Amour toujours l'amour*; film debut in *Pigalle-Saint-Germain-des-Prés*; 1961-1980s—appeared periodically on French television; 1966-74—president of L'Union des artistes; in TV miniseries *Se un giorno busseri alla mia porta*, 1986, *The Secret of the Sahara*, 1989, and *Fantaghiro*, 1991. **Awards:** Chevalier de l'ordre national du Mérite et des Arts et des Lettres. **Agent:** International Creative Management, 388/396 Oxford Street, London W1, England.

Films as Actor:

1950   *Pigalle-Saint-Germain-des-Prés* (Berthomieu)
1956   *The Happy Road* (Kelly)
1957   *A pied, à cheval, et en voiture* (Delbez) (as Mariel); *La Peau de l'ours* (Boissol); *Les Surmenés* (Doniol-Valcroze)

Madeleine Carroll with Robert Donat in *The 39 Steps* courtesy of The Rank Organisation Plc

Jean-Pierre Cassel (center) with **Fernando Rey** (left) and **Paul Frankeur** in *Le Charme discret de la bourgeoisie*

1958   *Le Désordre et la nuit* (Grangier); *En case de malheur* (Autant-Lara); *Et ta soeur* (Delbez); *Sacrée jeunesse* (Berthomieu)

1959   *La Marraine de Charley* (Chevalier); *Les Jeux de l'amour* (*The Love Game*) (de Broca) (as Victor)

1960   *Candide* (Carbonnaux) (title role)

1961   *Le Farceur* (*The Joker*) (de Broca) (as Edouard Berlon); *La Gamberge* (Carbonnaux); *Napoléon II, l'aiglon* (Boissol)

1962   *L'Amant de cinq jours* (de Broca); "L'Avarice" ep. of *Les Sept Péchés capitaux* (*The Seven Capital Sins*) (Chabrol); *Le Caporal épinglé* (*The Elusive Corporal*) (Renoir) (title role); *Arsène Lupin contre Arsène Lupin* (Molinaro)

1963   *Cyrano et D'Artagnan* (Gance); *Nunca pasa nada* (*Une Femme est passée*) (Bardem)

1964   "L'Homme qui vendit la Tour Eiffel" ep. of *Les Plus Belles Escroqueries du monde* (*The Beautiful Swindlers*; *World's Greatest Swindlers*) (Chabrol); "La sospirosa" ("The Victim") ep. of *Alta infedeltà* (*High Infidelity*) (Salce) (as Tonino); *Un Monsieur de compagnie* (*Male Companion*) (de Broca) (as Antoine)

1965   *Those Magnificent Men in Their Flying Machines* (Annakin) (as Pierre Dubois); *Les Fêtes galantes* (Clair) (as Joliecoeur)

1966   *Paris brûle-t-il?* (*Is Paris Burning?*) (Clément) (as Lt. Henri Karcher)

1967   *Jeu de massacre* (*The Killing Game*; *All Weekend Lovers*) (Jessua) (as Pierre Meyrand); *Le dolci signore* (*Anyone Can Play*) (Zampa) (as Aldo)

1969   *Oh! What a Lovely War* (Attenborough) (as French colonel); *L'Armée des ombres* (*The Shadow Army*) (Melville) (as Jean François); *L'Ours et la poupée* (*The Bear and the Doll*) (Deville) (as Gaspard)

1970   *La Rupture* (*The Break Up*) (Chabrol)

1971   *Le Bateau sur l'herbe* (Brach)

1972   *Malpertuis* (Kumel) (as Lampernisse); ***Le Charme discret de la bourgeoisie*** (*The Discreet Charm of the Bourgeoisie*) (Buñuel) (as M. Henri Senechal)

1973   *Baxter* (Jeffries) (as Roger Tunnell); *Il magnate* (Grimaldi); *The Three Musketeers* (*The Queen's Diamonds*) (Lester) (as Louis XIII)

1974   *Le Mouton enragé* (*The French Way*; *Love at the Top*) (Deville) (as Fabre); *The Four Musketeers* (*The Revenge of Milady*) (Lester) (as Louis XIII); *Murder on the Orient Express* (Lumet) (as Pierre Paul Michel)

1975 *Docteur Françoise Gailland* (*No Time for Breakfast*) (Bertucelli) (as Daniel Letessier); *Le Veinard* (*That Lucky Touch*) (Miles) (as Leo Devivia); *Les Oeufs brouillés* (Santini)

1976 *Folies bourgeoises* (*The Twist*) (Chabrol) (as Jacques)

1978 *Who Is Killing the Great Chefs of Europe?* (*Too Many Chefs*) (Kotcheff) (as Kohner); *Les Rendez-vous d'Anna* (Akerman)

1979 *La Ville de silences* (Marboeuf); *Le Maestro*; *Le Soleil en face* (Kast); *5% des risques* (Pourtale); *Alicja* (*Alice*) (Grusa and Bromski); *Da Dunkerque all vittoria* (*From Hell to Victory*) (Milestone [Lenzi]) (as Bick Sanders)

1982 *La Vie continue* (Mizrahi) (as Pierre); *La Truite* (*The Trout*) (Losey Rambert); *La Guérillera* (Kast); *Ehrengard* (Greco)

1983 *Nudo di donna* (Manfredi); *Desir* (Scarpitta); *Vive la sociale* (Mordillat)

1984 *Tenero Tramonto* (Del Bazo)

1985 *Tranches de vie* (Leterrier)

1986 *Ehrengard* (Greco); *Liberty* (Sarafian—for TV)

1987 *Vado a riprendermi il gatto* (Biagetti); *A Matter of Convenience* (Lewis—for TV) (as Alphonse Toronto); *Sentimental Journey* (Patzak—for TV); *Casanova* (Langton—for TV) (as Louis XV)

1988 *Chouans* (de Broca) (as Baron de Tiffauges); *The Return of the Musketeers* (Lester) (as Cyrano de Bergerac); *Mangeclous* (Mizrahi)

1990 *Mister Frost* (Setbon) (as Inspector Corelli); *Vincent et Theo* (*Vincent and Theo*) (Altman) (as Dr. Paul Gachet); *Amor e Dedinhos de Pe* (*Amor y deditos del pie*) (Rocha) (as Goncalo Bothelo); *The Fatal Image* (Wright—for TV) (as Vandelle); *Phantom of the Opera* (Richardson—for TV) (as Inspector Ledoux)

1991 *The Favor, the Watch, and the Very Big Fish* (Lewin) (as Zalman); *Aqui d'el Rei!* (Vasconcelos)

1992 *The Maid* (Toynton) (as C. P. Oliver); *Petain* (Marboeuf) (as Hans Roberto); *Noir au citron* (de Macedo); *L'oeil ecarlate* (Roulet); *Coub de jeune* (Gélin); *Notorious* (Bucksey—for TV) (as Alex Sebastian)

1993 *Entre el cielo y la tierre* (*Between Heaven and Earth*; *Sur la terre comme au ciel*; *In Heaven as on Earth*) (Hansel) (as the Editor-in-Chief); *Das Geheimnis des 13. Wagen* (Bonnot) (as Charles de Malasset); *Metisse* (*Cafe au lait*) (Kassovitz)

1994 *Casque Bleu* (*Blue Helmet*) (Jugnot) (as Nicolas); *L'Enfer* (*Hell*; *Jealousy*) (Chabrol) (as M. Vernon); *Ready to Wear* (*Pret-a-Porter*) (Altman) (as Olivier de la Fontaine)

1995 *La Ceremonie* (*A Judgment in Stone*) (Chabrol) (as Georges Lelievre); *Tatort—Eine todsichere Falle* (Blumenberg—for TV) (as Dupeyron)

Publications

By CASSEL: articles—

"*Le Crime de l'Orient Express*," interview with H. Béhar, in *Image et Son* (Paris), May 1975.

Interviews in *Ciné Revue* (Paris), 26 November 1981 and 10 February 1983.

On CASSEL: articles—

"Discreet Charm, in the French Style," in *Films Illustrated* (London), April 1973.

Ciné Revue (Paris), 13 January 1980 and 6 September 1984.

* * *

Jean-Pierre Cassel, after acting on stage (including a notable success in Marcel Achard's *L'Idiot*) and appearing in several films (including the comedy *The Happy Road*, directed by Gene Kelly), achieved his first real success in films in Philippe de Broca's first feature, *Les Jeux de l'amour*. This love story of a woman caught between two men was made with wit, grace, and poetry, and was dominated by the central pair of actors, Geneviève Cluny and Cassel. It was seen by critics as the first comedy of the "new wave," and the type of young man created by Cassel, a careless but likable and successful conqueror of girls' hearts, remained for some time his established role in subsequent films. By his appearance, elegance, and charm, he was as if predestined to embody such a characteristic example of the French male. In both *Le Farceur* and *L'Amant de cinq jours* (both also directed by de Broca), he continued this characterization.

Since the early 1960s, he has extended his range greatly. He played a prisoner of war in Jean Renoir's *Le Caporal épinglé*, and he has appeared in several detective films (*Arsène Lupin contre Arsène Lupin*, *Murder on the Orient Express*). He has appeared in international productions (*Oh! What a Lovely War*, *The Three Musketeers*, *The Four Musketeers*, and *Ready to Wear*), and in the war films *Paris brûle-t-il?* and *L'Armée des ombres*. But the films that best display his expanded dramatic range are Buñuel's *Le Charme discret de la bourgeoisie*, Kast's *Le Soleil en face*, Akerman's *Les Rendez-vous d'Anna*, and Mizrahi's *La Vie continue*. His role in Losey's *La Truite* confirmed his position as one of the leading contemporary French actors.

—Karel Tabery

CERVI, Gino

Nationality: Italian. **Born:** Luigi Cervi in Bologna, 3 May 1901. **Family:** Married the actress Nini Gordini, son: the producer Tonino Cervi. **Career:** 1924—stage debut with Aldo Borelli's troupe; later performed with Pirandello's acting troupe as well as other theater groups; 1932—screen debut in patriotic air force epic *L'armata assura*; late 1950s—began appearing frequently on TV, notably as Inspector Maigret in series based on Simenon novels. **Died:** In Punta Alta, Italy, 3 January 1974.

Films as Actor:

1932 *L'armata assura* (Righelli)

1933 *T'amerò sempre* (Camerini)

1934 *Frontiere* (Meano and Caraphi)

1935 *Aldebaran* (Blasetti) (as Camado Valeri); *Amore* (Bragaglia) (as Paolo)

1936 *I due sergenti* (Guazzoni)

1937 *Ettore Fieramosca* (Blasetti); *Gli uomini non sono ingrati* (Brignone); *L'argine* (d'Errico) (as Zugni)

1938 *I figli del marchese Lucera* (Palermi); *Inventiamo l'amore* (Mastrocinque) (as Carlo); *Voglio vivere con Letizia* (Mastrocinque)

1940 *La peccatrice* (Palermi) (as Alberto); *Un'avventura di Salvator Rosa* (Blasetti) (as Salvator Rosa); *Melodie eterne* (*Eternal Melodies*) (Gallone) (as Mozart); *Une romantica avventura* (Camerini); *La corona di ferro* (*The Iron Crown*) (Blasetti) (as King Sedemondo)

1941 *I promessi sposi* (*Father Christopher's Prayer*; *The Spirit and the Flesh*) (Camerini) (as Renzo); *La regina di Navarra* (Gallone) (as Charles V); *Il sogno di tutti* (Biancoli and Kisch)

1942   *L'ultimo addio* (Cerio) (as Paolo); *Acque di primavera* (Malasomma); *Don Cesare di Bazan* (Freda) (as Don Cesare); *Gente dell'aria* (Pratelli); *Quattro passi fra le nuvole* (*Four Steps in the Clouds*) (Blasetti); *Quarta pagina* (Manzari)

1943   *Tristi amori* (Gallone); *Che distinta famiglia* (M. Bonnard); *T'amero sempre* (Camerini); *La locandiera* (Chiarini) (as the Poet); *Nessuno torna indietro* (Blasetti)

1944   *Quartetto Pazzo* (Salvini); *Sensa famiglia* (Ferroni); *Vivere ancora* (Gianini)

1945   *Lo sbaglio di essere vivo* (*My Widow and I*) (Bragaglia); *Le miserie del signor Travet* (*His Young Wife*) (Soldati)

1946   *Malia* (Amato); *Umanità* (Bragaglia); *Un uomo ritorna* (*Revenge*) (Neufeld); *Aquila nera* (Freda)

1947   *L'angelo e il diavolo* (Camerini); *Cronaca nera* (Bianchi); *Daniele Cortis* (Soldati); *Furia* (Alessandrini)

1948   *I miserabili* (*Les Miserables*) (Freda) (as Jean Valjean); *La signora della camelie* (Bernard); *Anna Karenina* (Duvivier) (as Enrico)

1949   *Guglielmo Tell* (*William Tell*) (Pastino); *Yvonne la nuit* (Amato); *La fiamma che no si spegne* (Cottafavi); *Fabiola* (Blasetti); *La passione secondo San Matteo* (Marischka); *La sposa non puo attendere* (Franciolini)

1950   *Donne senza nome* (*Women without Names*) (Radvanyi); *Il cielo è rosso* (Gora); *La scolgiera del peccato* (Montero); *Sigillo rosso* (Calzavaro); *Il caimano del Piave* (Bianchi)

1951   *Cristo proibito* (*Forbidden Christ*; *Strange Deception*) (Malaparte); *Cameriera bella presenza offrersi* (Pastini); *O.K. Nerone* (*O.K. Nero*) (Soldati) (as Nero)

1952   *Le Petit Monde de Don Camillo* (*The Little World of Don Camillo*) (Duvivier) (as Peppone); *Tre storie proibite* (*Three Forbidden Stories*) (Genina); *Moglie per una notte* (*Wife for a Night*) (Camerini); *La regina di Saba* (*The Queen of Sheba*) (Francisci) (as Solomon); *La Dame aux camélias* (Bernard)

1953   *Stazioni termini* (*Indiscretion of an American Wife*) (De Sica); *Le Retour de Don Camillo* (*The Return of Don Camillo*) (Duvivier) (as Peppone); *La signora senza camelie* (*Camille without Camelias*) (Antonioni); *Les Trois Mousquetaires* (Hunebelle); *Si Versailles m'était conté* (Guitry); *Nerone a Messalina* (Zeglio); *Maddalena* (Genina); *Addio mia bella signora* (Cerchio); *Fate largo ai moschettieri* (Hunebelle); *La grande avventura*; *Cavallina storna* (Morelli); *Una donna libera* (Cottafavi); *Napoléon* (Guitry)

1955   *Il cardinale Lambertini* (Pastini); *Frou frou* (Genina); *Non c'è amore piu grande* (Bianchi); *Don Camillo e l'onorevole Peppone* (Gallone) (as Peppone); *Gli innamorati* (*Wild Love*) (Bolognini); *Il coraggio* (Paolella)

1956   *Guardia, guardia scelta, brigadiere e maresciallo* (Bolognini); *Beatrice Cenci* (Freda); *Moglie e buoi . . .* (de Mitri); *Amanti del deserto* (*Le Fils du chiek*; *The Desert Warrior*) (Cerchio)

1957   *Amore e chiacchiere* (Blasetti); *Ragazze delle nuvole* (Costa)

1958   *Agguato a Tangeri* (Freda); *Le belle dell'aria* (Costa); *La maja desnuda* (*The Naked Maja*) (Koster) (as King Carlos of Spain); *Sans Famille* (Michel)

1959   *Nel segno di Roma* (Brignone); *Noi gangsters*; *Brevi amori a Palma di Majorca* (Bianchi); *Cartagine in fiamme*; *Le grand chef* (*The Big Chief*) (Verneuil)

1960   *La lunga notte del '43* (Vancini); *I sicari di Hitler*; *L'assedio di Siracusa* (*Siege of Syracuse*) (Francisci) (as Gerone); *Le olimpiadi dei mariti* (Bianchi); *Femmine di lusso* (*Love the Italian Way*) (White) (as Lemeni); *La rivolta degli schiavi* (*The Revolt of the Slaves*) (Malasomma); *Herrin der Welt* (Dieterle)

1961   *Che gioia vivere* (*Quelle joie de vivre*) (Clément); *Un figlio d'oggi* (Girolami and Graziano); *Don Camillo, monsignore . . . ma non troppo* (Gallone) (as Peppone); *Gli attendenti* (Bianchi); *Geheimaktion schwarze Kapelle* (Habib)

1962   *Le Crime ne paie pas* (*Crime Does Not Pay*) ("La Masque" ep.) (Oury); *Dieci italiani per un Tedesco* (*La Furie des S.S.*) (Ratti); *La monaca di Monza* (Gallone); *Gli anni ruggenti* (Zampa); *Il cambio della guardia* (Bianchi); *Avanti la musica* (Bianchi); *Il fiorno piu'corto* (Corbucci)

1963   *La smania addosso* (*Eye of the Needle*) (Andrei) (as D'Angelo); *Gli onorevoli* (Corbucci); *Le Bon Roi Dagobert* (Chevalier)

1964   *Becket* (Glenville) (as Cardinal Zambelli); *Volles Herz und leere Tashcen* (Mastrocinque)

1965   *Il compagno Don Camillo* (Comencini) (as Peppone)

1967   *Maigret a Pigalle* (Landi)

1972   *Don Camillo e i giovani d'oggi* (as Peppone); *Uccidere in silenzio* (Rolando); *I racconti romani di Pietro l'Aretino* (Tosini)

Publications

On CERVI: article—

"Gino Cervi," letter from V. Martinelli in *Films in Review* (New York), June-July 1975.

*   *   *

For several decades, Gino Cervi was the leading character actor in Italy and certainly one of the pillars of the industry. He began as a stage actor in 1924; a few years later he made his screen debut in a film on the Air Force. Immediately demonstrating his versatility, he starred in Camerini's melancholic love story *T'amerò sempre*. He was one of Alessandro Blasetti's favorite actors, providing a commanding presence in the historical epics *Ettore Fieramosca*, *Un'avventura di Salvator Rosa*, and *La corona di ferro*. Blasctti recognized Cervi's range and cast him in the role of the plain, downtrodden traveling salesman who aids an unwed mother in *Four Steps in the Clouds*, the first of Cervi's films to be shown widely outside Italy.

His performance in one scene of a little-known film, *La Peccatrice*, is a tour de force that represents Cervi's combination of technical virtuosity and naturalness. He plays a cad living in a small town; a person he has victimized, the "sinner" of the title, has returned to the town after several years and watches him eating alone in a restaurant. In this scene he must express the cad's entire character—his disregard for others, his lack of conscience, his pomposity—simply by eating his meal.

After the war, he continued to give credence to Italian costume dramas and historical epics but reached an international audience through his portrayal of Peppone, the Communist mayor in Giovanni Guareschi's series of novels about Don Camillo. Cervi played the role in Duvivier's first version of the story in 1952 and in the many sequels. His resonant voice enabled him to work as a dubber (he dubbed Olivier's voice for the Italian versions of his Shakespeare films) and achieve considerable success on stage. For Italian television, he played Georges Simenon's Inspector Maigret in a series of productions.

—Elaine Mancini

CHAN, Jackie

Pseudonym: Known to Chinese audiences as Sing Lung, meaning "to become a dragon." **Nationality:** Hong Kong. **Born:** Chan Kong-Sang in Hong Kong, 7 April 1954. **Education:** Studied at Peking Opera School, Hong Kong, 1961-71. **Career:** 1962—screen debut in the Cantonese film *Huang Tian Ba*, subsequently appeared as child actor in more than 20 films; 1972-73—worked as film stuntman and martial artist; 1976—contracted as lead actor by Lo Wei Film Company; 1978—first real success with two films for Ng See-Yuen's Seasonal Film Corporation; 1979—directed himself for the first time in *The Fearless Hyena*; 1980—made first film for major Golden Harvest company; mid-1980s—co-founder, Golden Way production company; 1995—received first widespread North American attention with *Rumble in the Bronx*.

Films as Actor:

(films as child actor not included)

1971 *Little Tiger from Canton*
1973 *Enter the Dragon* (*The Deadly Three*) (Clouse)
1975 *Countdown in Kung Fu* (*Hand of Death*) (Woo)
1976 *Xin Ching-Wu Men* (*New Fist of Fury*) (Lo Wei) (as Ai Long); *Shaolin Wooden Men* (*36 Wooden Men*; *Shaolin Chamber of Death*) (Ch'en Chih-Hua and Lo Wei); *The Killer Meteors* (Lo Wei)
1977 *Snake and Crane Arts of Shaolin* (Ch'en Chih-Hua)
1978 *To Kill with Intrigue* (Lo Wei); *Magnificent Bodyguards* (Lo Wei); *Snake in the Eagle's Shadow* (*The Eagle's Shadow*) (Yuen Woo-ping); *Spiritual Kung-Fu* (*Karate Ghostbuster*) (Lo Wei)
1979 *Dragon Fist* (*In Eagle Dragon Fist*) (Lo Wei); *Drunken Master* (*Drunken Monkey in a Tiger's Eye*; *The Story of Drunken Master*) (Yuen Woo-ping) (as Huang Fei-hong)
1980 *The Big Brawl* (*Battle Creek Brawl*) (Clouse) (as Jerry); *Half a Loaf of Kung Fu* (Ch'en Chi-Hua) (+ martial arts director)
1981 *The Cannonball Run* (Needham) (as Subaru driver no. 1); *Snake Fist Fighter*
1983 *Winners and Sinners* (Samo Hung); *The Fearless Hyena: Part 2* (Chuen Chan)
1984 *Cannonball Run 2* (Needham) (as Jackie); *Meals on Wheels* (Samo Hung); *Eagle's Shadow* (Yuen Woo-ping)
1985 *My Lucky Stars* (Samo Hung) (as Muscles); *Twinkle, Twinkle, Lucky Stars* (Samo Hung); *First Mission*; *The Protector* (Glickenhaus) (as Billy Wong); *Ninja Thunderbolt* (Ho)
1986 *Heart of the Dragon* (*The First Mission*) (Samo Hung)
1987 *Dragons Forever* (Samo Hung); *Fist of Death*
1990 *The Deadliest Art: The Best of the Martial Arts Films* (Weintraub—compilation)
1992 *City Hunter* (Jing Wong) (as Ryu Saeba); *Supercop: Police Story III* (Stanley Tong) (as Chan Chia-chu); *Twin Dragons* (Ringo Lam and Hark Tsui) (as John Ma/Boomer)
1993 *Police Story 4: Project S* (*Once a Cop*; *Project S*; *Supercop 2*) (Stanley Tong); *Crime Story* (Kirk Wong) (as Inspector Eddie Chan)
1995 *Hong Faan Kui* (*Rumble in the Bronx*) (Stanley Tong) (as Ah Keung, + martial arts director); *Thunderbolt*

Films as Actor and Director:

1979 *Siukun gwaitsiu* (*The Fearless Hyena*) (co-d)
1980 *Sidai cheutma* (*The Young Master*) (+ co-sc)
1982 *Lung siuye* (*Dragon Lord*; *Young Master in Love*) (+ co-sc, martial arts choreographer)
1983 *A gaiwak* (*Project A*) (as Dragon Ma, + co-sc)
1985 *Gingchat gusi* (*Police Story*; *Police Force*; *Jackie Chan's Police Story*; *Jackie Chan's Police Force*) (+ co-sc)
1986 *Lunghing fudai* (*The Armour of God*) (+ co-sc)
1987 *A gaiwatsuktsap* (*Project A: Part II*) (+ co-sc)
1988 *Gingchat gusi tsuktsap* (*Police Story Part II*) (+ co-sc)

1989 *Keitsik* (*Miracle*; *Black Dragon*; *Miracles: The Canton Godfather*; *Mr. Canton and Lady Rose*) (as Kuo Cheng-wah/Mr. Canton, + co-sc)
1990 *Lunghing fudai tsuktsap* (*The Armour of God II: Operation Condor*) (as Jackie/"Condor," + sc); *Island on Fire* (*Island of Fire*; *The Prisoner*)
1994 *Tsui Kun II* (*Drunken Master II*) (as Huang Fei-hong)

Publications

By CHAN: articles—

Interview with Tony Rayns and C. Tesson, in *Cahiers du Cinéma* (Paris), September 1984.
"Jackie Chan, American Action Hero?," interview with Jaime Wolf, in *New York Times Magazine*, 21 January 1996.

On CHAN: book—

Rayns, Tony, *The Mind Is a Muscle: An Appreciation of Jackie Chan*, London, 1987.

On CHAN: articles—

Film Review (London), November 1980.
Ciné Revue (Paris), November 1987.
Kehr, Dave, "Chan Can Do," in *Film Comment* (New York), May/June 1988.
"Jackie Chan's Big Dilemma: How Long Can He Keep It Up?," in *Variety* (New York), 1 February 1989.
"Hong Kong Focus," in *London Film Festival Programme*, 1990.
Ingram, Bruce, "Fast-Moving Jackie Chan's Slow on the Set," in *Variety* (New York), 18 March 1991.
Elley, Derek, "More Than 'The Next Bruce Lee'," *Variety* (New York), 23 January 1995.
Corliss, Richard, "Jackie Can!," in *Time* (New York), 13 February 1995.
Dannen, Fredric, "Hong Kong Babylon," in *New Yorker*, 7 August 1995.
Straus, Neil, "Higher Style from Hong Kong's Masters," in *New York Times*, 18 February 1996.

* * *

Jackie Chan emerged out of the ranks of martial arts stuntmen and bit players in the mid-1970s as the most talented of those hoping for the international megastardom Bruce Lee had achieved before his death in 1973. In 1976, Lo Wei introduced Chan in a sequel to one of Lee's more popular films, *Fist of Fury* (*The Chinese Connection*), called *New Fist of Fury*, in which Chan imitates Lee's fighting style for the most part. Throughout his career, Chan has been haunted by comparisons with Lee. Despite his huge popularity in Asia, evidenced by the box-office records films such as *Police Story* and *Project A: Part II* have broken, Chan still aspires to break into the European and American market the way Lee was able to with his *Enter the Dragon*. To date, Chan's English-language vehicles, *The Big Brawl* and *The Protector*, have failed to appeal to most audiences in the West, and Chan is perhaps still most often recognized outside of Asia from his cameo role as the comic Chinese racer in *The Cannonball Run* series. In 1995, he makes another attempt at winning the American audience with *Rumble in the Bronx*, filmed "on location" in Vancouver. Although Chan has enjoyed a certain amount of critical attention since his films have been hailed at several international festivals as artistic "masterpieces," popular appeal, outside the Asian community, eludes him.

Comparisons to Lee and failure to win over the Western mass audience are both understandable and unfortunate. Although publicized as a "new Bruce Lee" and encouraged to imitate Lee very early in his film career, Chan, in fact, can best be appreciated as Lee's polar opposite in terms of performance persona and martial arts style. Whereas Lee was fascinated by Western boxing, Philippine stick fighting, and European fencing, which all became part of his very eclectic style, Chan has stuck more to the acrobatic movements associated with the traditional Chinese opera he studied as a young man. A significant part of this involves comic pantomime, and, unlike the more serious and intense Lee, who only occasionally threw in a humorous bit for comic relief, Chan excels at the lighter aspects of the operatic tradition in which his martial skills are rooted. This gift for both acrobatics and comedy has led some critics to compare Chan to Harold Lloyd or Buster Keaton. Conscious of the comparison, Chan has recreated Lloyd's daredevil clock tower stunt and Keaton's infamous falling house stunt in his own films (*Project A: Parts I* and *II*). Like his silent Hollywood film heroes, Chan prides himself on doing his own stunts, and he has had a number of brushes with death as a result (the most serious a head injury when filming *Armour of God*). In the closing credits of his more recent films, outtakes show the bloody results of failed stunts, adding an element of machismo to his star persona missing from the insouciant characters he typically portrays.

With his wide, almost bulbous nose, sparkling eyes and mischievous smile, Chan's boyish ebullience and remarkable physical prowess seem best put to use in the costume martial arts comedies he made in the late 1970s and early 1980s. During this phase of his career, Chan began to choreograph his own fighting, act as martial arts instructor, and, eventually, direct his own features. As a result, a characteristic Chan star persona really began to emerge, displaying Chan's acrobatic and martial skills to their best advantage.

In most of these films, Chan plays reluctant students who excel at kung fu in spite of themselves. With the exception of *Dragon Lord*, they all feature scenes that display Chan's physical prowess in training as well as combat. The Chan character is repeatedly tortured by eccentric masters (exemplified by the "drunken master" played by Simon Yuen in *Drunken Master* and *Snake in the Eagle's Shadow*), who casually drink or smoke while Chan sweats blood and plots to escape from kung-fu practice. Set in the past, all these films make use of traditional costumes and weaponry as well as such Chinese arts as lion dancing and calligraphy, and allude to (indeed mildly satirize) established Chinese customs and institutions. In *Drunken Master*, for example, Chan portrays a young, impudent and impulsive Huang Fei-hong, in sharp contrast to Jet Li's more sober portrayal of the same folk hero in the *Once upon a Time in China* series. Scenes with expressly Chinese content, however, might explain the cool reception Chan has been given outside the Asian community in the West.

Chan's most recent films mark a significant break with his earlier successes. These later films are set in the present or the more recent past. Unlike the earlier films which delight in Chinese traditions, archaic weaponry, and the arcane aspects of Chinese kung fu, these films have a more Western orientation with gun play, automobile chases, shopping malls, cops, and gangsters replacing rival kung-fu schools, drunken masters, and operatic swordplay. Although Chan continues to play an affable hero, more attention is given to the action-adventure aspects of the plot and to the spectacular, often noncombative stunts than to Chinese martial artistry or acrobatics. No longer the troublesome pupil, Chan has matured into Asia's best-loved comic action hero.

With his own production unit at Hong Kong's Golden Harvest studios, Chan has artistic and a great deal of economic control over his current projects. More than just a kung-fu superstar, Chan has also become a shrewd film producer and promoter. As 1997 (when Hong Kong returns to the governance of the People's Republic of China) approaches, however, Chan's future career remains uncertain. His recent films place Hong Kong and its citizens on the world stage, as players in their own right, with an identity separate from mainland China. In *City Hunter,* Chan plays a Japanese detective, partly as a tribute to his loyal Japanese fans and partly as a means of looking beyond the confines of Hong Kong. As *Rumble in the Bronx* brings him back to North America, Chan embodies the fantasy of the Chinese global citizen, acting outside the strictures of a vacillating national identity. In addition to solidifying his appeal outside of Chinese circles, this transnational persona has a particular poignancy for many in Hong Kong who feel the pressures associated with 1997.

—Gina Marchetti

CHANEY, Lon

Nationality: American. **Born:** Alonzo Chaney in Colorado Springs, Colorado, 1 April 1883. **Family:** Married 1) Cleva Creighton, 1905 (divorced 1914), son: Creighton Tull Chaney (i.e., the actor Lon Chaney Jr.); 2) Hazel Bennett Hastings, 1915. **Career:** 1895—prop boy and scene painter in local theater in Colorado Springs; 1901—toured with brother John's stock company; remained with company after John sold his interest to Denver showman; c.1906-07—moved to California and became song and dance man in variety musicals; c.1909—joined San Francisco company of the comedians Kolb and Dill; 1912—began appearing in one- and two-reel slapstick films; 1914-17—began experimenting with unusual makeup for roles in off-beat films directed by Joseph DeGrasse or Ida May Park (Mrs. DeGrasse); 1915—regular member of Universal's stock company; directed series of one- and two-reelers, also contributed to the scripts; 1918—began freelancing; role in highly successful film *Riddle Gawne* attracted attention of other directors and producers; 1919—became popular star after role in *The Miracle Man*; appeared in Tod Browning's *The Wicked Darling*, the first of ten films with that director; 1930—in sound remake of *The Unholy Three*, his only talking film. **Died:** 26 August 1930.

Films as Actor:

1913   *Poor Jake's Demise* (Curtis); *The Sea Urchin* (August); *The Trap* (August); *Almost an Actress*; *Back to Life* (Dwan); *Red Margaret-Moonshiner* (Dwan); *Bloodhounds of the North* (Dwan)

1914   *The Lie*; *The Honor of the Mounted* (Dwan); *Remember Mary Magdalene* (Dwan); *Discord and Harmony* (Dwan); *The Menace to Carlotta* (Dwan); *The Embezzler* (Dwan); *The Lamb, The Woman, The Wolf* (Dwan); *The End of the Feud* (Dwan); *The Tragedy of Whispering Creek* (Dwan); *The Unlawful Trade* (Dwan); *The Forbidden Room* (Dwan); *The Old Cobbler* (MacQuarrie); *A Ranch Romance*; *Her Grave Mistake*; *By the Sun's Rays*; "The Oubliette" (Part I of *The Adventures of François Villon* series) (Giblyn); *A Miner's Romance*; *Her Bounty* (Dwan); *Richelieu* (Dwan); *The Pipes of Pan* (DeGrasse); *Virtue Is Its Own Reward* (DeGrasse); *Her Life's Story* (DeGrasse); *Lights and Shadows* (DeGrasse); *The Lion, The Lamb, The Man* (DeGrasse); *A Night of Thrills* (DeGrasse); *Her Escape* (DeGrasse)

1915   *The Sin of Olga Brandt* (DeGrasse); *Star of the Sea* (DeGrasse); *Threads of Fate* (DeGrasse); *The Measure of a Man* (DeGrasse); *When the Gods Played a Badger Game* (DeGrasse); *Such Is Life* (DeGrasse); *Where the Forest Ends* (DeGrasse); *All for Peggy* (DeGrasse); *The Desert Breed* (DeGrasse); *Outside the Gates* (DeGrasse); *The Grind* (DeGrasse); *Maid of the Mist* (DeGrasse); *The Girl of the*

Lon Chaney

Night (DeGrasse); *An Idyll of the Hills* (DeGrasse); *The Stronger Mind* (DeGrasse); *Steady Company* (DeGrasse); *Bound on the Wheel* (DeGrasse); *Mountain Justice* (DeGrasse); *Quits* (DeGrasse); *The Pine's Revenge* (DeGrasse); *The Fascination of the Fleur de Lis* (DeGrasse); *Alas and Alack* (DeGrasse); *A Mother's Atonement* (DeGrasse); *Lon of the Lone Mountain* (DeGrasse); *The Millionaire Paupers* (DeGrasse); *Father and the Boys* (DeGrasse); *Under a Shadow* (DeGrasse); *Stronger Than Death* (DeGrasse)

1916 *The Grip of Jealousy* (DeGrasse); *Dolly's Scoop* (DeGrasse); *Tangled Hearts* (Park); *The Gilded Spider* (DeGrasse); *Bobbie of the Ballet* (DeGrasse); *Grasp of Greed* (DeGrasse); *The Mark of Cain* (DeGrasse); *If My Country Should Call* (DeGrasse); *Place beyond the Winds* (DeGrasse); *Felix on the Job* (Felix); *The Price of Silence* (DeGrasse); *The Piper's Price* (DeGrasse); *Hell Morgan's Girl* (DeGrasse); *The Mask of Love* (DeGrasse); *The Girl in the Checkered Coat* (DeGrasse); *The Flashlight Girl* (Park); *A Doll's House* (DeGrasse); *Fires of Rebellion* (Park); *Vengeance of the West* (DeGrasse); *The Rescue* (Park); *Triumph* (DeGrasse); *Pay Me* (DeGrasse)

1917 *The Empty Gun* (DeGrasse); *Anything Once* (DeGrasse); *Bondage* (Park); *The Scarlet Car* (DeGrasse)

1918 *The Grand Passion* (Park) (as Argos); *Broadway Love* (Park) (as Elmer Watkins); *The Kaiser, The Beast of Berlin* (Julian) (as Admiral Von Tirpitz); *Fast Company* (Reynolds) (as Dan McCarty); *A Broadway Scandal* (DeGrasse) (as Kink Colby); *That Devil Bateese* (Wobert) (as Louis Courteau); *The Talk of the Town* (Holubar) (as Jack Lanchome); *Riddle Gawne* (Hillyer) (as Hame Bozzam); *Danger—Go Slow* (Leonard) (as Bud)

1919 *The Wicked Darling* (Browning) (as Stoop Connors); *The False Faces* (Willet) (as Karl Eckstrom); *A Man's Country* (Kolker) (as Three Card Duncan); *Paid in Advance* (Holubar) (as Bateese Le Blanc); *The Miracle Man* (Tucker) (as the Frog); *When Bearcat Went Dry* (Sellers) (as Kindard Powers); *Victory* (Maurice Tourneur) (as Ricardo)

1920 *Daredevil Jack* (W. S. Van Dyke); *Treasure Island* (Maurice Tourneur) (as Pew); *The Gift Supreme* (Sellers) (as Merney Stagg); *Nomads of the North* (Hartford) (as Raoul Challoner); *The Penalty* (Worsely) (as Blizzard)

1921 *Outside the Law* (Browning) (as Black Mike Silva and Joe Wang); *For Those We Love* (as Trix Ulner); *Bits of Life* (Neilan, Flood, and Scully); *Ace of Hearts* (Worsley) (as Farralone)

1922 *The Trap* (Thornby) (as Gaspard); *Flesh and Blood* (Cummings) (as David Webster); *Voices of the City* (Worsley) (as O'Rourke); *The Light in the Dark* (Brown) (as Tony Pantelli); *Shadows* (Forman) (as Yen Sin); *Oliver Twist* (Lloyd) (as Fagin); *Quincy Adams Sawyer* (Badger) (as Obadiah Strout); *The Blind Bargain* (Worsley) (as Dr. Lamb)

1923 *All the Brothers Were Valiant* (Willat) (as Mark Shore); *While Paris Sleeps* (Maurice Tourneur) (as Henri Santados); *The Shock* (Hillyer) (as Wilse Dilling); *The Hunchback of Notre Dame* (Worsley) (as Quasimodo)

1924 *The Next Corner* (Wood) (as Juan Serafin); **The Phantom of the Opera** (Julian) (as Erik, the Phantom); *He Who Gets Slapped* (Seastrom) (as "He")

1925 *The Monster* (West) (as Dr. Ziska); *The Unholy Three* (Browning) (as Echo); *The Tower of Lies* (Seastrom) (as Jan)

1926 *The Blackbird* (Browning) (as Blackbird/Bishop); *The Road to Mandalay* (Browning) (as Singapore Joe); *Tell It to the Marines* (Hill) (as Sgt. O'Hara)

1927 *Mr. Wu* (Nigh) (title role); *The Unknown* (Browning) (as Alonzo); *Mockery* (Christensen) (as Sergei); *London after Midnight* (Browning) (as Burke)

1928 *The Big City* (Browning) (as Chuck Collins); *Laugh, Clown, Laugh* (Brenon) (as Tito); *While the City Sleeps* (Conway) (as Dan); *West of Zanzibar* (Browning) (as Phroso)

1929 *Where East Is East* (Browning) (as Tiger Haynes); *Thunder* (Nigh) (as Grumpy Anderson)

1930 *The Unholy Three* (Conway) (as Echo)

Films as Director and Actor:

1915 *The Stool Pigeon*; *For Cash*; *The Oyster Dredger* (+ sc); *The Violin Maker*; *The Chimney's Secret* (+ sc); *The Trust*

Publications

By CHANEY: article—

Interview, in *Motion Picture Magazine* (New York), December 1922.

On CHANEY: books—

Clemens, Carlos, *An Illustrated History of the Horror Film*, New York, 1967.

Bull, Clarence Sinclair, and Raymond Lee, *The Faces of Hollywood*, New York, 1969.

Anderson, Robert G., *Faces, Forms, Films: The Artistry of Lon Chaney*, South Brunswick, New Jersey, 1971.

Bodeen, DeWitt, *From Hollywood: The Careers of Fifteen Great American Stars*, South Brunswick, New Jersey, 1976.

Ross, Nathaniel Lester, *Lon Chaney: Master Craftsman of Make-Believe*, New York, 1987.

Blake, Michael F., *Lon Chaney: The Man behind the Thousand Faces*, Vestal, New York, 1993.

Blake, Michael F., *A Thousand Faces: Lon Chaney's Unique Artistry in Motion Pictures*, Vestal, New York, 1995.

On CHANEY: articles—

Howe, Herbert, "A Miracle Man of Make-Up," in *Picture Play*, March 1920.

Ussher, Kathleen, "Chaney the Chameleon," in *Pictures and Picturegoer*, March 1926; also December 1927.

Obituary, in *New York Times*, 27 August 1930.

Mitchell, George, "Lon Chaney," in *Films in Review* (New York), December 1953.

Braff, R., "A New Lon Chaney Index," in *Films in Review* (New York), April 1970.

Bodeen, DeWitt, "Lon Chaney: Man of a Thousand Faces," in *Focus on Film* (London), May/August 1970.

Viviani, C., "Lon Chaney ou la politique de l'acteur," in *Positif* (Paris), July-August 1978.

Shipman, David, *The Great Movie Stars: The Golden Years*, rev. ed., London, 1979.

Meth, S., "Reflections in a Cinema Eye: Lon Chaney," in *Classic Film Collector* (Indiana, Pennsylvania), July 1979.

Dempsey, Michael, "Lon Chaney: A Thousand and One Faces," in *Film Comment* (New York), May/June 1995.

On CHANEY: film—

Man of a Thousand Faces, directed by Joseph Pevney, 1957.

* * *

During the 1920s one of the biggest names at the box office was that of Lon Chaney, who specialized in playing bizarre characters often bordering on the macabre. His mastery at creating so many different kinds of characters (he even played multiple roles in some of his films) earned him the title "The Man of a Thousand Faces." Chaney is often considered to be the first horror star and the first actor to develop makeup in film as an art.

Chaney's use of makeup was both unique and innovative. In some cases it was also extremely painful. For example, in *The Penalty* Chaney plays a man whose legs were amputated by an evil surgeon. To create a realistic amputee, Chaney bound his legs up behind him in a harness and walked about on his knees. The makeup for his *The Hunchback of Notre Dame* took four-and-a-half hours to prepare and included over 70 pounds of weight on his back to create the hump. For *The Phantom of the Opera* Chaney placed wires inside his nose to tilt his nostrils upwards so that his face would more closely resemble a skull.

While these makeup techniques were very effective, it was Chaney's acting ability that gave his roles a psychological dimension. He played these ugly and deformed characters with a pathetic intensity, elevating them above the stereotypical "monster."

Chaney's film career started with work as an extra and bit player in shorts (he also occasionally worked as a director and screenwriter). He soon was appearing in a wide variety of roles, from playboys to aristocrats, and often as villains. Some of his early films were directed by Tod Browning, who later would direct Chaney in some of his most successful films. He became a star with the success of Paramount's *The Miracle Man* in 1919, portraying a phony cripple. While continuing to play a variety of roles after this, Chaney began to veer toward parts that were distinctly macabre and sometimes physically challenging.

Chaney's portrayals of the leads in *The Hunchback of Notre Dame* and *The Phantom of the Opera* (with its horrific unmasking scene) cemented his reputation as the silent screen's greatest horror star. He continued to have success when he and director Browning were both signed to MGM, in films such as *The Unknown* (as an armless circus knife thrower) and *London after Midnight* (portraying both a policeman and a vampire).

At the height of Chaney's popularity, sound pictures were introduced. He was against sound; he preferred the art of pantomime, of which he was a master. Under pressure from the studio, however, Chaney made *The Unholy Three*, an almost shot-for-shot remake of his 1925 Browning-directed hit. Just as he had altered his appearance to play multiple roles in silent films, Chaney altered his voice to play different characters. *The Unholy Three* proved to be very popular and plans were made for other Chaney sound pictures. His sudden death (of bronchial cancer) shocked the film industry and ended a promising new career in sound.

—Linda J. Obalil, updated by Frank Uhle

CHAPLIN, (Sir) Charles (Charlie)

Nationality: British. **Born:** Charles Spencer Chaplin in London, England, 16 April 1889. **Family:** Married 1) Mildred Harris, 1918 (divorced 1920); 2) Lita Grey, 1924 (divorced 1927), two sons; 3) Paulette Goddard, 1936 (divorced 1941); 4) Oona O'Neill, 1943, eight children. **Career:** At age nine, followed the careers of his parents, Charles and Hannah Chaplin, as a music hall performer; 1903-06—appeared as the youth Billy in the stage play *Sherlock Holmes*; 1907—hired for the Fred Karno troupe; 1913—signed by Mack Sennett for Keystone studios after second Karno tour of the United States; moved to Hollywood; 1914—first film, *Making a Living*, followed by

34 more films that same year; 1915—left Keystone to write, direct, and act in 14 films for Essanay Films; 1916—moved to Mutual Films to create 12 films through 1917; 1918-23—produced seven shorts and one feature, *The Kid* (1921), for First National; 1919—co-founder with D. W. Griffith, Mary Pickford, and Douglas Fairbanks of United Artists; 1923—first film for United Artists, *A Woman of Paris*; 1952—visited London; political pressure forced cancellation of his reentry permit to return to the United States; 1953—moved to Vevey, on Lake Geneva, Switzerland. **Awards:** Best Actor, New York Film Critics, for *The Great Dictator*, 1940; Foreign Language Press Critics designate *Limelight* as best film, 1953; Honorary Oscar, "for the incalcuable effect he has had in making motion pictures the art form of this century," 1971; Academy Award for Best Original Dramatic Score (shared), for *Limelight*, 1972 (film first released in 1952, but had not been shown in Los Angeles until 1972); Golden Lion, Venice Film Festival, 1972; Knighted, 1975. **Died:** In Vevey, Switzerland, 25 December 1977.

Films as Actor:

(shorts for Keystone Film Company; role as Charlie unless otherwise noted)

1914 *Making a Living* (*A Busted Johnny*; *Troubles*; *Doing His Best*) (Lehrman) (as reporter); *Kid Auto Races at Venice* (*The Kid Auto Race*) (Lehrman); *Mabel's Strange Predicament* (*Hotel Mixup*) (Lehrman and Sennett); *Between Showers* (*The Flirts*; *Charlie and the Umbrella*; *In Wrong*) (Lehrman); *A Film Johnnie* (*Movie Nut*; *Million Dollar Job*; *Charlie at the Studio*) (Sennett); *Tango Tangles* (*Charlie's Recreation*; *Music Hall*) (Sennett); *His Favorite Pastime* (*The Bonehead*; *His Reckless Fling*) (Nichols); *Cruel, Cruel Love* (Sennett); *The Star Boarder* (*The Hash-House Hero*) (Sennett); *Mabel at the Wheel* (*His Daredevil Queen*; *Hot Finish*) (Norman and Sennett); *Twenty Minutes of Love* (*He Loved Her So*; *Cops and Watches*) (Sennett) (as Charlie, + sc); *The Knockout* (*Counted Out*; *The Pugilist*) (Arbuckle); *Tillie's Punctured Romance* (*Tillie's Nightmare*; *For the Love of Tillie*; *Marie's Millions*) (Sennett—feature)

(other films)

1914 *His Regeneration* (Anderson) (guest appearance)
1921 *The Nut* (Reed) (guest appearance)
1923 *Souls for Sale* (Hughes) (guest appearance)
1928 *Show People* (King Vidor) (guest appearance)

Films as Actor, Director, and Scriptwriter:

(shorts for Keystone Film Company)

1914 *Caught in a Cabaret* (*Jazz Waiter*; *Faking with Society*) (co-d, co-sc); *Caught in the Rain* (*At It Again*; *Who Got Stung?*); *A Busy Day* (*Lady Charlie*; *Militant Suffragette*); *The Fatal Mallet* (*The Pile Driver*; *The Rival Suitors*; *Hit Him Again*) (co-d, co-sc); *Her Friend the Bandit* (*Mabel's Flirtation*; *A Thief Catcher*) (co-d with Normand, co-sc); *Mabel's Busy Day* (*Charlie and the Sausages*; *Love and Lunch*; *Hot Dogs*) (co-d with Normand, co-sc); *Mabel's Married Life* (*When You're Married*; *The Squarehead*) (co-d with Normand); *Laughing Gas* (*Tuning His Ivories*; *The Dentist*); *The Property Man* (*Getting His Goat*; *The Roustabout*; *Vamping Venus*); *The Face on the Bar-Room Floor* (*The Ham Artist*);

Recreation (Spring Fever); The Masquerader (Putting One Over; The Female Impersonator); His New Profession (The Good-for-Nothing; Helping Himself); The Rounder (Two of a Kind; The Love Thief; Oh, What a Night!); The New Janitor (The Porter; The Blundering Boob); Those Love Pangs (The Rival Mashers; Busted Hearts); Dough and Dynamite (The Doughnut Designer; The Cook); Gentlemen of Nerve (Some Nerve; Charlie at the Races); His Musical Career (The Piano Movers; Musical Tramps); His Trysting Place (Family Home); Getting Acquainted (A Fair Exchange; Hullo Everybody); His Prehistoric Past (A Dream; King Charlie; The Caveman)

(shorts, two-reelers unless noted otherwise, for Essanay Company)

1915 *His New Job; A Night Out (Champagne Charlie); The Champion (Battling Charlie); In the Park (Charlie on the Spree) (one reel); A Jitney Elopement (Married in Haste); The Tramp (Charlie the Hobo); By the Sea (Charlie's Day Out) (one reel); Work (The Paper Hanger; The Plumber); A Woman (The Perfect Lady); The Bank; Shanghaied (Charlie the Sailor; Charlie on the Ocean); A Night in the Show*
1916 *Carmen (Charlie Chaplin's Burlesque on Carmen); Police! (Charlie the Burglar)*

(two-reelers for Mutual Films)

1916 *The Floorwalker (The Store); The Fireman; The Vagabond; One A.M.; The Count; The Pawnshop; Behind the Screen; The Rink*
1917 **Easy Street**; *The Cure; The Immigrant; The Adventurer*
1918 *Triple Trouble (an Essanay compilation release of 1915 Chaplin footage plus non-Chaplin footage)*

(for First National Film Company)

1918 *A Dog's Life (three reels); The Bond (half-reel for Liberty Loan Committee); Shoulder Arms (three reels)*
1919 *Sunnyside (three reels); A Day's Pleasure (two reels)*
1921 **The Kid** (+ pr); *The Idle Class (two reels) (+ pr)*
1922 *Pay Day (two reels) (+ pr); Nice and Friendly (+ pr) (made privately and unreleased)*
1923 *The Pilgrim (four reels) (+ pr)*

(features for United Artists Company)

1923 *A Woman of Paris* (+ pr)
1925 **The Gold Rush** (+ pr, narration, mus for sound reissue)
1928 *The Circus* (+ pr, mus, song for sound reissue)
1931 **City Lights** (+ pr, mus)
1936 **Modern Times** (+ pr, mus)
1940 **The Great Dictator** (+ pr, mus)
1947 *Monsieur Verdoux* (+ pr, mus)
1952 **Limelight** (+ pr, co-mus, co-choreographer)

(feature for Attic-Archway Company)

1957 *A King in New York* (+ pr, mus)

(feature for Universal)

1967 *A Countess from Hong Kong* (+ mus)

Publications

By CHAPLIN: books—

Charlie Chaplin's Own Story, Indianapolis, 1916.

My Trip Abroad, New York, 1922.
A Comedian Sees the World, New York, 1933.
My Autobiography, London, 1964.
My Life in Pictures, London, 1974.

By CHAPLIN: articles—

"How I Made My Success," in *The Theatre* (New York), September 1915.
"What People Laugh At," in *American Magazine* (New York), 1918.
"In Defense of Myself," in *Colliers* (New York), 11 November 1922.
"Pantomime and Comedy," in *New York Times*, 25 January 1931.
Interview with Margaret Hinxman, in *Sight and Sound* (London), Autumn 1957.
Interview with Richard Merryman, in *Life* (New York), 10 March 1967.
"The INS Interview with Chaplin," edited by Charles J. Maland, in *Cineaste* (New York), vol. 14, no. 4, 1986.

On CHAPLIN: books—

Delluc, Louis, *Charlie Chaplin*, Paris, 1921; translation by Hamish Miles, London, 1922.
Tyler, Parker, *Chaplin, the Last of the Clowns*, New York, 1947.
Cotes, Peter, and Thelma Niklaus, *The Little Fellow: The Life and Works of Charles Spencer Chaplin*, London, 1951, reprinted, New York, 1965.
Huff, Theodore, *Charlie Chaplin*, New York, 1951.
Payne, Robert, *The Great God Pan: A Biography of the Tramp Played by Charlie Chaplin*, New York, 1952.
Minney, R. J., *Chaplin, the Immortal Tramp*, London, 1954.
McDonald, Gerald D., Michael Conway, and Mark Ricci, editors, *The Films of Charlie Chaplin*, New York, 1965.
Martin, Marcel, *Charlie Chaplin*, Paris, 1966; 3rd ed., Paris, 1983.
McCaffrey, Donald W., *Four Great Comedians: Chaplin, Lloyd, Keaton, Langdon*, New York, 1968.
Quigley, Isabel, *Charlie Chaplin: Early Comedies*, London, 1968.
Leprohon, Pierre, *Charles Chaplin*, Paris, 1970.
McCaffrey, Donald W., editor, *Focus on Chaplin*, Englewood Cliffs, New Jersey, 1971.
Manvell, Roger, *Chaplin*, Boston, 1974.
Lyons, T. J., compiler, *Charles Chaplin—A Guide to References and Resources*, Boston, 1977.
Sobel, Raoul, and David Francis, *Chaplin, Genesis of a Clown*, London, 1977.
McCabe, John, *Charlie Chaplin*, New York, 1978.
Gehring, Wes D., *Charlie Chaplin: A Bio-Bibliography*, Westport, Connecticut, 1983.
Kamin, Dan, *Charlie Chaplin's One-Man Show*, Metuchen, New Jersey, 1984.
Smith, Julian, *Chaplin*, Boston, 1984.
Robinson, David, *Chaplin: His Life and Art*, London, 1985.
Geduld, Harry W., *Chapliniana I: The Keystone Films*, Bloomington, Indiana, 1987.
Epstein, Jerry, *Remembering Charlie: A Pictorial Biography*, Garden City, New York, 1989.
MacCann, Richard Dyer, editor, *The Silent Comedians* (vol. 4 of *American Movies: The First Thirty Years*), Metuchen, New Jersey, 1993.
Hale, Georgia, *Charlie Chaplin: Intimate Close-Ups*, edited by Heather Kierman, Metuchen, New Jersey, 1995.
Milton, Joyce, *Tramp: The Life of Charlie Chaplin*, New York, 1996.

On CHAPLIN: articles—

Ramsaye, Terry, "Chaplin—And How He Does It," in *Photoplay* (New York), September 1917.

Hilbert, James E., "A Day with Charlie Chaplin on Location," in *Motion Picture Classic* (New York), November 1917.

Young, Stark, "Dear Mr. Chaplin," in *New Republic* (New York), 23 August 1922.

Carr, Harry, "Chaplin vs. Lloyd, a Comparison," in *Motion Picture Magazine* (New York), November 1922.

Seldes, Gilbert, "'I Am Here Today': Charlie Chaplin," in *The 7 Lively Arts*, New York, 1924; reprinted, 1957.

Cooke, Alistair, "Charlie Chaplin," in *Atlantic Monthly* (New York), August 1939.

Agee, James, "Comedy's Greatest Era," in *Life* (New York), 5 September 1949.

"Chaplin at Work: He Reveals His Movie-Making Secrets," in *Life* (New York), 17 March 1952.

Montgomery, John, "Chaplin—The Perfect Clown," in *Comedy Films*, London, 1954.

Spears, Jack, "Chaplin Collaborators," in *Films in Review* (New York), January 1962.

Brownlow, Kevin, "Chaplin," in *The Parade's Gone By . . .*, New York, 1968.

"Chaplin" issue of *Film Comment* (New York), September/October 1972.

Mast, Gerald, "Chaplin and Keaton" (part III), in *The Comic Mind: Comedy and the Movies*, New York, 1973.

Schickel, Richard, "A Chaplin Overview," in *The National Society of Film Critics on Movie Comedy*, edited by Stuart Byron and Elisabeth Weis, New York, 1977.

Obituary in *New York Times*, 26 December 1977.

Canby, Vincent, "He Took Pains to Make Us Laugh," in *New York Times*, 1 January 1978.

Corliss, Richard, "Chaplin," in *Film Comment* (New York), March/April 1978.

"Chaplin" issue of *University Film Association Journal* (Houston), no. 1, 1979.

Everson, William K., "Rediscovery: 'New' Chaplin Films," in *Films in Review* (New York), November 1981.

Millar, Gavin, "The Unknown Chaplin," in *Sight and Sound* (London), Spring 1983.

"Chaplin" section of *American Film* (Washington, D.C.), September 1984.

Winokur, Mark, "*Modern Times* and the Comedy of Transformation," in *Film/Literature Quarterly* (Salisbury, Maryland), vol. 15, no. 3, 1987.

Maland, Charles J., "From *The Kid* to *The Gold Rush*," in *Chaplin and American Culture: The Evolution of the Star Image*, Princeton, New Jersey, 1989.

Jones, Chuck, "Journal" (on Chaplin), in *Film Comment* (New York), March/April 1989.

Kerr, Walter, "Spinning Reels of Memory on a Master's Centenary," in *New York Times*, 9 April 1989.

Canby, Vincent, "The Charlie Chaplin Centennial: A Genius Revisited," in *New York Times*, 14 April 1989.

Nightingale, Benedict, "The Melancholy that Forged a Comic Genius," in *New York Times*, 22 March 1992.

Gabler, Neal, "Film View: Chaplin Blazed the Trail, Woody Allen Follows," in *New York Times*, 27 September 1992.

Siegel, Scott, and Barbara Siegel, "Charlie Chaplin," in *American Film Comedy*, New York, 1994.

Frumkes, Roy, "Chaplin on Laser Disc," in *Films in Review* (New York), February 1994.

Miller, Blair, "Charles Spencer 'Charlie' Chaplin," in *American Silent Film Comedies: An Illustrated Encyclopedia of Persons, Studios, and Terminology*, Jefferson, North Carolina, 1995.

Codelli, Lorenzo, editor, "Forgotten Laughter: A Symposium on American Silent Comedy," in *The Journal of Film History: Griffithiana* (Italy/United States), May 1995.

On CHAPLIN: films—

Chaplinesque, My Life and Hard Times, documentary directed by Harry Hurwitz, 1972.

Unknown Chaplin, television documentary directed by Kevin Brownlow and David Gill, 1983.

Young Charlie Chaplin, television film biography directed by Baz Taylor, 1989.

Chaplin, film biography directed by Richard Attenborough, 1992.

* * *

It took only a very busy year of acting and directing short films for Charles Chaplin to launch his own career and alter the format of the Mack Sennett comic film. While the famous comedian owed much to the Sennett tradition—the story material and plotting, the techniques of the medium, and the comic vigor—he had his own contribution to make to the comic film. The more subtle humor of this English music hall entertainer was thwarted by the fast pace and farcical plotting of many of the Sennett one- and two-reel comedies.

Chaplin's fame emerged with the development of the little tramp character as early as 1914 when he co-starred with Mabel Normand for Keystone studio and producer Mack Sennett. When he left Sennett's company to work for Essanay and Mutual studios he added finishing touches to the tramp character so that it became a marvelous comic portrait for all times. At the same time, from 1915 to 1917 Chaplin came very close to perfection in the construction of the two-reel humorous film, especially with *The Cure* and *Easy Street* in 1917. But the most important aspect of his work was not structure, it was the heights he brought to his acting skills.

The quality of Chaplin's acting as it relates to the total work and his fellow players surfaced in these early works. *The Cure* and *Easy Street*, for example, illustrate how he achieved a balanced enactment with his casts. Although he is the leading figure, there are convincing performances by all of the supporting players so that the works display theatrical unity. From the documentary on the working method of Chaplin, 1983's *Unknown Chaplin*, featuring a number of outtakes from the comedian's *The Cure*, we now know he often acted out a number of roles which would later be played by other members of his cast. From the evidence in this documentary, extensive rehearsal by all cast members proved Chaplin demanded the devotion of those who worked with him on his films. With all the repetition of one scene it is a wonder the acting did not become stale, flat, and mechanical. But the comedian's portraits emerged fresh, providing a first-time illusion. Especially noteworthy in *The Cure* is Chaplin's portrayal of an alcoholic who has arrived at a mineral springs hotel for a cure. Gone from his portrayal is the broad, staggering stereotype of the Sennett comedies. He teeters and leans aslant as his locomotion becomes comically askew. And, of course, his mind also reveals it is askew. When he is pushed into gym to receive physical therapy he sees the masseur as an attacker and strikes the pose of a wrestler. He then begins a series of moves to avoid what he thinks is an opponent. The comedian handles this pantomime adroitly with the grace of a dancer. It is little wonder then that W. C. Fields is reported to have declared in a fit of jealousy: "The son of a bitch is a ballet dancer!"

When Chaplin moved to the feature length film with *The Kid* in 1921, the richness of his character and acting sprang forth. A greater range of humor was finally achieved because the feature allowed the actor the total dimension of the little tramp. While his two-reelers often moved in the rapid, farcical, slapstick style of Mack Sennett, his full-length films explored the spectrum of his little man-child clown. The quiet, personal moments of the social outcast blossomed, and what critics called "Chaplin's pathos" was born. The little tramp raises a foundling to have many of the awry social values of a social outcast—providing the viewer with some understanding of survival

Charlie Chaplin

necessities. The kid breaks windows with a pocketful of rocks as the little tramp follows behind as a glazer who repairs the damage for a fee. When an orphanage official takes the kid away in a truck, the tramp pursues and stops the abduction. In an emotional embrace of his adopted son, Chaplin underplays the joy of the moment in a powerful shot of the scene. It may not be what has been called "pathos"—more like sympathy—nevertheless, this shows the essence of a subtle tone without moving to sentimentality.

Other examples of the range of Chaplin's acting deftness display his skill. Critics often point to turns of Chaplin's innovation, such as the oceanic roll dance when he entertains a guest with a routine that shows his head hovering over rolls on forks executing a ballet—an unusual bit in *The Gold Rush*. There are also more subtle scenes such as one when the little fellow is starving in a remote cabin in Alaska. With delicate, facile pantomime the hollow-eyed, comic hero eyes the stub of a candle. Sadly, the little tramp picks it up and nibbles it with rabbit bites—as if the candle were a piece of carrot or celery. And with a deft touch that again shows Chaplin's genius, he sprinkles salt on the morsel of wax, finds that it tastes better, and pops it into his mouth. With such actions a new depth in comic character was added, a dimension that was to make Chaplin the darling of the critics.

Evaluators of the comedian's work have been most generous in the hundreds of articles published and more than 25 major books solely devoted to his life and films. Sometimes critics believe comedy films do not receive recognition for social significance and employ sweeping symbols and allusions to elevate them. Theodore Huff, usually detached and low-key in his 1951 work, *Charlie Chaplin*, writes that the comedian has become "a symbol of the age, the twentieth-century Everyman." In *The Little Fellow*, Peter Cotes and Thelma Niklaus try to give the comedian the position of the champion of the poor and oppressed by stating: "He and Dickens are of the same stock, filled with the same humanism, the same passionate pity for the underdog, the same blaze of anger against persecution, exploitation, and injustice." Such statements strain credulity because the majority of evaluators see *Modern Times* and *The Great Dictator* as designed or intended to be satires but end up being lampoons. By far the most rhapsodic commentary comes from Robert Payne who uses the pretentious title *The Great God Pan* for a biography of Chaplin. He writes: "Far more than Sir Galahad, he [Chaplin] represents the heroic figure of the man pure and undefiled."

These three statements by writers of major works in the early 1950s use allusions that touch upon themes and not the acting, which was the major quality that places Chaplin as the leading king of comedy of the 1920s. For subtle nuances in humor he is the champion. Both Harold Lloyd and Buster Keaton were his equal in the broad, athletic comic moments, but only in a few flickering moments in their features did these two rival the master. Much of this early affection for Chaplin resulted from the continued showing of his films and the fact that much of the work of Keaton did not see the light until the 1960s. Since then, 8 studies of Lloyd and 11 evaluations of Keaton focused on the life and films of these two comedians.

One of the most neglected of the kings of silent screen comedy, Harry Langdon, was the one actor most often compared with Chaplin's character—because Langdon employed a tramplike and child-man person. Nevertheless, Langdon's character falls into the class of "dumb" clowns—low mental ability. Most of the humor of his best films, *The Strong Man* and *Long Pants*, directed by Frank Capra, springs from a childlike man who is lost in a sophisticated world. Much of the complicated world is a wonder to this wide-eyed person who tries to figure out things that baffle him, like a four year old. Also, Langdon's character does not have the joy and enthusiasm that Chaplin exhibits in his relationship with another person, as in *The Kid* with his child and in *Modern Times* with a girlfriend waif.

The type of enthusiasm and joy Chaplin gave to his character is another distinguishing feature. Granted, Harold Lloyd possessed it—like the boy-next-door—but Chaplin had it in the manner of the child in slums who finds a quarter. As critics have pointed out, Chaplin followed in the tradition of the *commedia dell'arte*. He combined many characteristics of the sad and joyful clowns as he acted in various scenes of his movies. He almost seemed to be the reincarnation of the famous nineteenth-century French clown, Jean-Gaspard Debureau, a renowned Pierrot, blended with all the rollicking good spirit of the Clown created by the English music hall's favorite comedian, Grimaldi.

—Donald W. McCaffrey

CHAPLIN, Geraldine

Nationality: American. **Born:** Santa Monica, California, 31 July 1944; daughter of the actor Charlie Chaplin. **Education:** Attended Swiss schools; Royal Ballet School, London, 1961. **Family:** Lived with the director Carlos Saura, son: Shane Saura Chaplin O'Neill. **Career:** 1952—screen debut as street urchin in father Charlie's *Limelight*; 1963—professional engagement as dancer in chorus of *Cinderella* in London; 1964—first major screen role in French film *Par un beau matin d'été*; 1966-67—appeared in some episodes of Spanish TV series *La familia Colón*; 1967—on Broadway under Mike Nichols's direction in *The Little Foxes*; in *Peppermint frappé*, first film with Carlos Saura; 1969—collaborated on script of *La madriguera* with Saura and Rafael Azcona; 1975—in *Nashville*, first of several films for Robert Altman; 1978—in TV mini-series *The Word* and *My Cousin Rachel*, 1983. **Agent:** William Morris Agency, 1350 Avenue of the Americas, New York, NY 10019, U.S.A.

Films as Actress:

1952 *Limelight* (Chaplin) (as street urchin)
1964 *Dernier soir* (Pourtale); *Par un beau matin d'été* (Deray)
1965 *Doctor Zhivago* (Lean) (as Tonia)
1966 *Andremo in città* (Nelo Risi)
1967 *A Countess from Hong Kong* (Chaplin) (as girl at dance); *J'ai tué Raspoutine* (*I Killed Rasputin*) (Hossein); *Stranger in the House* (*Cop-Out*) (Rouve) (as Angela Sawyer); *Peppermint frappé* (Saura) (as Elena)
1968 *Stress es tres tres* (Saura)
1969 *La madriguera* (*The Honeycomb*) (Saura) (as Teresa, + co-sc)
1970 *El jardin de las delicias* (Saura); *The Hawaiians* (*Master of the Islands*) (Gries) (as Purity Hoxworth)
1971 *Sur un arbre perché* (Korber); *Carlos* (Geissendörfer)
1972 *Innocent Bystanders* (Collinson); *La casa sin fronteras* (Olea); *Z.P.G.* (*Zero Population Growth*) (Campus) (as Carole McNeil)
1973 *Ana y los lobos* (*Ana and the Wolves*) (Saura) (as Ana); *The Three Musketeers* (*The Queen's Diamonds*) (Lester) (as Anne of Austria); *Y el projimo?* (del Pozo); *Verflucht dies Amerika* (*La banda de Jaider*) (Vogeler) (as Kate Elder)
1974 *Le mariage à la mode* (Mardore); *Sommerfuglene* (*Summer of Silence*) (Boger); *The Four Musketeers* (*The Revenge of Milady*) (Lester) (as Queen Anne of Austria)
1975 *Nashville* (Altman) (as Opal); *The Gentlemen Tramp* (Patterson—doc)
1976 *Cria Cuervos* (*The Secret of Anna*; *Raise Ravens*; *Cria!*) (Saura) (as Ana as an adult/her mother Maria); *Buffalo Bill and the Indians, or Sitting Bull's History Lesson* (Altman) (as Annie Oakley); *Noroît* (*Scènes de la vie parallèle: 3 Noroît*; *Une Vengeance*) (Rivette); *Welcome to L.A.* (Rudolph) (as Karen Hood); *Scrim* (Bijl)

Geraldine Chaplin in *Remember My Name*

1977 *Elisa, vida mía (Elisa, My Life)* (Saura) (as Elisa); "The Hustle" ep. of *Roseland* (Ivory) (as Marilyn); *In Memoriam* (Brasó) (as Paulina Arevalo); *Une page d'amour* (Rabinowicz)

1978 *Los ajos vandados* (Saura); *A Wedding* (Altman) (as Rita Billingsley); *Remember My Name* (Rudolph) (as Emily); *L'Adoption (The Adoption)* (Grunebaum) (as wife); *The Masked Bride; Mais où et donc ornicar?* (van Effenterre) (as Isabelle)

1979 *Tout est à nous; Mama cumple cien años (Mama Turns 100)* (Saura) (as Ana)

1980 *La Viuda de Montiel* (Littin); *The Mirror Crack'd* (Hamilton) (as Ella Zielinsky)

1981 *Les Uns et les autres (Bolero; Within Memory)* (Lelouch) (as Suzan/Sara Glenn); *Voyage en douce* (Deville) (as Lucie)

1984 *L'Amour par terre (Love on the Ground)* (Rivette) (as Charlotte); *La Vie est un roman (Life Is a Bed of Roses)* (Resnais) (as Nora)

1985 *The Corsican Brothers* (Sharp—for TV); *Gentile Alouette* (Castilla) (as Angela Duverger)

1988 *White Mischief* (Radford) (as Nina Soames); *The Moderns* (Rudolph) (as Nathalie de Ville)

1989 *The Return of the Musketeers* (Lester) (as Queen Anne of Austria); *Je veux rentrer à la maison (I Want to Go Home)* (Resnais) (as Terry Armstrong)

1990 *The Children* (Tony Palmer) (as Joyce Wheater); *Buster's Bedroom* (Horn) (as Diana Daniels); *Duel of Hearts* (Hough—for TV) (as Mrs. Miller)

1992 *Chaplin* (Attenborough) (as Hannah Chaplin); *Zwischensaison (Hors Saison; Off Season)* (Schmid) (as anarchist)

1993 ***The Age of Innocence*** (Scorsese) (as Mrs. Welland); *A Foreign Field* (Sturridge—for TV) (as Beverley)

1994 *Words upon the Window Pane* (McGuckian) (as Miss MacKenna)

1995 *Para recibir el canto de los pajaros (The Bird's Singing)* (Sanjines) (as Catherine); *Home for the Holidays* (Jodie Foster) (as Aunt Glady)

1996 *Jane Eyre* (Zeffirelli) (as Miss Scatcherd); *Gulliver's Travels* (Sturridge—for TV) (as Empress Munodi)

Publications

By CHAPLIN: articles—

Interview with Jonathan Rosenbaum, in *Film Comment* (New York), September/October 1975.

"Geraldine Chaplin: el recuerdo de su padre," interview with M. Pereira, in *Cine Cubano* (Havana), no. 99, 1981; see also no. 106, 1983.

"Entretien avec Geraldine Chaplin," interview with J. Lefebvre, in *Jeune Cinema*, April/May 1993.

On CHAPLIN: articles—

Ecran (Paris), October 1978.

Current Biography 1979, New York, 1979.

Michiels, D., "Geraldine Chaplin," in *Film en Televisie* (Brussels), July-August 1981.

Télérama (Paris), 20 October 1984.

Francke, Linda Bird, "Life with Charlie," in *Interview* (New York), September 1989.

Guerin, N., "Geraldine Chaplin et la Camera d'Or," in *Cinema 91*, July/August 1991.

On CHAPLIN: film—

Féminin singulier: Geraldine Chaplin, directed by Jean Kerchbron in France, 1965.

*   *   *

As the oldest daughter of the legendary Charlie Chaplin, Geraldine Chaplin's career in films would doubtless have attracted a considerable degree of attention regardless of her own merits as an actress. In the years since her portrayal of Tonia in *Doctor Zhivago*, however, Chaplin has established herself as a talented—if somewhat limited—performer with an intriguing on-screen appeal. Her dark, waiflike beauty, reminiscent of her mother, Oona O'Neill Chaplin, and her graceful, enigmatic qualities have made her a favorite of directors Robert Altman, Alan Rudolph, and Carlos Saura, while her facility for languages has enabled her to move with ease between American and European films.

It is perhaps ironic that, as the child of one of the world's greatest comedians, Chaplin has worked primarily in the realm of serious drama. Even her performance as the affected journalist in Altman's *Nashville* falls into the area of satire rather than straightforward comedy, and her particular strength as an actress has been the combination of dramatic intensity and a certain ethereal quality that she brings to her characters. Much of her best work has resulted from her collaboration with Saura, her longtime companion and one of Spain's leading filmmakers. Under his direction in such films as *Cria*, *Aña y los lobos*, and *Elisa, vida mía*, Chaplin gives sensitively drawn performances of depth and feeling.

Chaplin's vulnerable physical appearance also can work to her advantage when contrasted with a strong inner character. In Alan Rudolph's disturbing *Remember My Name*, she plays a revenge-obsessed woman whose seeming delicacy belies her ruthless, street-smart nature. It is one of her finest performances, and a startling departure from her usual screen roles.

Chaplin has had the good fortune throughout her career to work with directors who have utilized her unique talents and provided her with roles which complement her striking personal style. With strong films to display her abilities, she has created a professional identity apart from her early one as "Charlie Chaplin's daughter." Yet at the same time, in *Chaplin*, Richard Attenborough's celluloid biography of the Little Tramp, she was called upon to portray her own intensely, tragically disturbed grandmother. No actress in the world would have been a more logical and appropriate choice for the role.

—Janet E. Lorenz, updated by Rob Edelman

CHARISSE, Cyd

Nationality: American. **Born:** Tula Ellice Finklea in Amarillo, Texas, 8 March 1921 (some sources list 1922). **Family:** Married 1) the dancer Nico Charisse, 1939 (divorced 1947); 2) the singer Tony Martin, 1948. **Career:** 1934—joined Ballet Russe; late 1930s-early 1940s—European tour with Ballet Russe interrupted by World War II; 1943—began working in films as bit player under the name Lily Norwood; 1946—contract with MGM as Cyd Charisse; 1960s—begins appearing in European films; appeared in nightclub revue with husband Tony Martin; 1972—in Australian stage production of *No, No Nanette*; 1992—Broadway debut in *Grand Hotel*. **Address:** 10390 Wilshire Boulevard #1507, Los Angeles, CA 90024, U.S.A.

Films as Actress:

1943   *Something to Shout About* (Ratoff) (as Lily, credited as Lily Norwood); *Mission to Moscow* (Curtiz) (as specialty dancer); *Thousands Cheer* (Sidney)

1946   *The Harvey Girls* (Sidney) (as Deborah); "Meet the Ladies" ep. of *Ziegfeld Follies* (Minnelli or Sidney) (as ballet dancer); *Three Wise Fools* (Buzzell) (as Rena Fairchild); *Till the Clouds Roll By* (Whorf)

1947   *Fiesta* (Thorpe) (as Conchita); *The Unfinished Dance* (Koster) (as Mlle. Ariane Bouchet)

1948   *On an Island with You* (Thorpe) (as Yvonne Torro); *The Kissing Bandit* (Benedek) (as fiesta dancer); *Words and Music* (Taurog) (as Margo Grant)

1949   *Tension* (Berry) (as Mary Chanler); *East Side, West Side* (LeRoy) (as Rosa Senta)

1951   *Mark of the Renegade* (Fregonese) (as Manuella)

1952   **Singin' in the Rain** (Kelly and Donen) (as dancer); *The Wild North* (Marton) (as Indian girl)

1953   *Sombrero* (Norman Foster) (as Lola de Torrano); **The Band Wagon** (Minnelli) (as Gaby Gerard); *Easy to Love* (Walters)

1954   *Deep in My Heart* (Donen); *Brigadoon* (Minnelli) (as Fiona Campbell)

1955   *It's Always Fair Weather* (Kelly and Donen) (as Jackie Leighton)

1956   *Meet Me in Las Vegas* (*Viva Las Vegas*) (Rowland) (as Maria Corvier)

1957   *Silk Stockings* (Mamoulian) (as Ninotchka); *Invitation to the Dance* (Kelly)

1958   *Twilight for the Gods* (Pevney) (as Chaarlotte King); *Party Girl* (Nicholas Ray) (as Vicki Gaye)

1960   "Deuil en 24 heures" ("A Merry Mourning") ep. of *Les Collants noirs* (*Un, deux, trois, quatre?*; *Black Tights*) (Terence Young)

1961   *Five Golden Hours* (Zampi) (as Baronessa Sandra)

1962   *Two Weeks in Another Town* (Minnelli) (as Carlotta)

1963   *Il segreto del vestito rosso* (*Assassinio Made in Italy*; *Murderer Made in Italy*) (Amadio)

1966   *The Silencers* (Karlson) (as Sarita)

1967   *Maroc 7* (O'Hara) (as Louise Henderson)

1971   *Call Her Mom* (Paris—for TV)

1976   *Won Ton Ton, the Dog Who Saved Hollywood* (Winner)

1978   *Warlords of Atlantis* (Connor) (as Atsil)

1980   *Portrait of an Escort* (Stern—for TV)

1984   *That's Dancing* (Haley Jr.—doc)

1989   *Swimsuit* (Thomson—for TV) (as Mrs. Allison)

1990   *Visioni Privati* (*Private Screening*)

1994   *That's Entertainment! III* (Friedgen and Sheridan) (as host)

Publications

By CHARISSE: book—

The Two of Us, with Tony Martin, New York, 1976.

Cyd Charisse

On CHARISSE: books—

Kobal, John, *Gotta Sing, Gotta Dance*, New York, 1970.
Thomas, Lawrence B., *The MGM Years*, New Rochelle, New York, 1972.
Stern, Lee Edward, *The Movie Musical*, New York, 1974.
Missiaen, Jean Claude, *Cyd Charisse: du ballet classique a la comedie musicale*, Paris, 1978.
Thomas, Tony, *That's Dancing!*, New York, 1985.
Altman, Rick, *The American Film Musical*, Bloomington, Indiana, 1989.

On CHARISSE: articles—

Current Biography 1954, New York, 1954.
Ecran (Paris), March 1978.
Wolf, W. R., "Making *Singin' in the Rain*," in *Film en Televisie* (Brussels), March 1979.
Leahy, N., "Cyd Charisse," in *Films and Filming* (London), April 1987.
Briggs, C., "Cyd Charisse - at Last on Broadway!," in *Hollywood: Then and Now*, vol. 25, no. 5, 1992.
Kisselgoff, A., "Cyd Charisse's Dance Card Is Full Once More," in *New York Times*, 5 April 1992.

*   *   *

A dancer of formidable talent, Cyd Charisse was a major presence in several important musicals of the 1950s. At MGM she worked within the Arthur Freed unit where her special abilities were successfully exploited. Classically trained, Charisse always played characters tailored to her natural elegance and sophistication. Since her background was in ballet rather than in the dance forms of musical comedy, her roles often drew on the conventional associations of ballet in film, such as high art, dreaminess, and aloofness. Her work in five films—*Singin' in the Rain*, *The Band Wagon*, *Brigadoon*, *It's Always Fair Weather*, and *Silk Stockings*—epitomized her contribution to the genre.

As Gene Kelly's unapproachable femme fatale in the "Broadway Melody" sequence in *Singin' in the Rain*, Charisse establishes an image continued through the other four films, although in the course of each her character is modified—and she usually becomes a less balletic performer as well. In *Singin' in the Rain* she does not play a character, but rather is a torrid stage image who dances with Kelly.

In the other films she plays characters who are part of the plots; in each, she must lose her distance and stiffness before becoming an impassioned dancer and suitable romantic partner. Playing a ballet star in *The Band Wagon*, she cannot fall in love with Fred Astaire until she abandons her high art pretensions. In *Brigadoon* she is the woman Kelly loves, but she lives (and dances) in a town that comes to life only once every hundred years. She has an encyclopedic memory in *It's Always Fair Weather* and uses it at first to intimidate Kelly. And in *Silk Stockings* she is the remote Russian Ninotchka, the anticapitalist who ultimately capitulates to Fred Astaire's dancing. Charisse could not sing and her vocals were always dubbed, but this does not diminish her performances since their emphasis is on dancing—and she participated in the richest period of musical production in film history.

After her screen career waned in the early 1960s, Charisse and her second husband, Tony Martin, appeared together on the nightclub circuit. She also has starred in musical stage productions that draw on nostalgia for the era with which she was such an integral part.

—Jerome Delamater, updated by Audrey E. Kupferberg

CHATTERJEE, Soumitra

Nationality: Indian. **Born:** 1934. **Education:** Studied acting with Ahindra Choudhury. **Career:** Amateur actor with Sisir Kumar Bahaduri; 1954—entered films; 1959—first film for the director Satyajit Ray, *Apur Sansar*; 1962—co-editor of literary magazine *Eksham*.

Films as Actor:

1959   *Apur Sansar* (*The World of Apu*) (Satyajit Ray) (as Apurba Kumar Roy)
1960   *Devi* (*The Goddess*) (Satyajit Ray) (as Uma Prasad); *Kshudista Pashan* (Tapan Sinha)
1961   "Samapti" ep. of *Teen Kanya* (*Two Daughters*) (Satyajit Ray) (as Amulya); *Swaralipi*; *Swayambara*; *Jhinder Bandi*; *Punashcha*
1962   *Abhijan* (*The Expedition*) (Satyajit Ray) (as Narsingh); *Shasti*; *Atal Jaler Ahwan*; *Agun*; *Banarasi*
1963   *Saat Pake Bandha* (Ajoy Kar); *Shesh Prahar*; *Barnali*
1964   *Charulata* (*The Lonely Wife*) (Satyajit Ray) (as Amal); *Pratinidhi*; *Kinu Goyalar Gali*; *Ayananta*
1965   *Baksha Badal*; *Ek Tuku Basa*; *Raj Kanya*; *Kapurush-o-Mahapurush* (*The Coward and the Holy Man*) (Satyajit Ray) (as Amitabha Roy); *Akash Kusum* (Mrinal Sen); *Eki Ange Eto Rup*

1966   *Joradighir Choudhury Paribar*; *Kanch Kata Hirey* (Ajoy Kar); *Manihar*
1967   *Ajana Shapath*; *Hathat Dekha*; *Mahashweta*; *Prastar Swakshar*
1968   *Baghini*; *Parishodh*
1969   *Aparichita*; *Chena Achena*; *Parineeta*; *Teen Bhubhaner Parey*
1970   *Aranyar din Ratri* (*Days and Nights in the Forest*) (Satyajit Ray) (as Ashim); *Aleyar Alo*; *Padmagolap*; *Pratham Kadam Phool*
1971   *Khunje Berai*; *Malayadaan*; *Sansar*
1972   *Jiban Saikate*; *Natun Diner Alo*; *Stree*; *Basanta Bilap*; *Bilet Pherat*
1973   *Ashani Sanket* (*Distant Thunder*) (Satyajit Ray) (as Gamgacharan Chakravarti); *Epar Opar*; *Nishi Kanya*; *Shesh Pristhay Dekhun*; *Agni Bhraman*
1974   *Sonar Kella* (*The Golden Fortress*) (Satyajit Ray) (as Felu); *Asati*; *Jadi Jantem*; *Sangini*; *Chhutir Phande*
1975   *Nishi Mrigaya*; *Sansar Simantey* (Majumdar); *Sudur Niharika*
1976   *Datta*; *Nandita*
1977   *Babu Moshai*; *Mantramugdha*; *Pratima*
1978   *Joi Baba Felunath* (*The Elephant God*) (Satyajit Ray) (as Felu); *Nadi Theke Sagare*; *Ganadevata* (Majumdar); *Job Charnaker Bibi*; *Pronoy Pasha*
1979   *Devdas*; *Nauka Dubi*
1980   *Darpachurna*; *Gharer Baire Ghar*; *Hirak Rajar Deshe* (*The Kingdom of Diamonds*) (Satyajit Ray—for TV) (as Pandit Moshai); *Pankhiraj*
1981   *Father*; *Nyay Anyay*; *Khelar Putul*

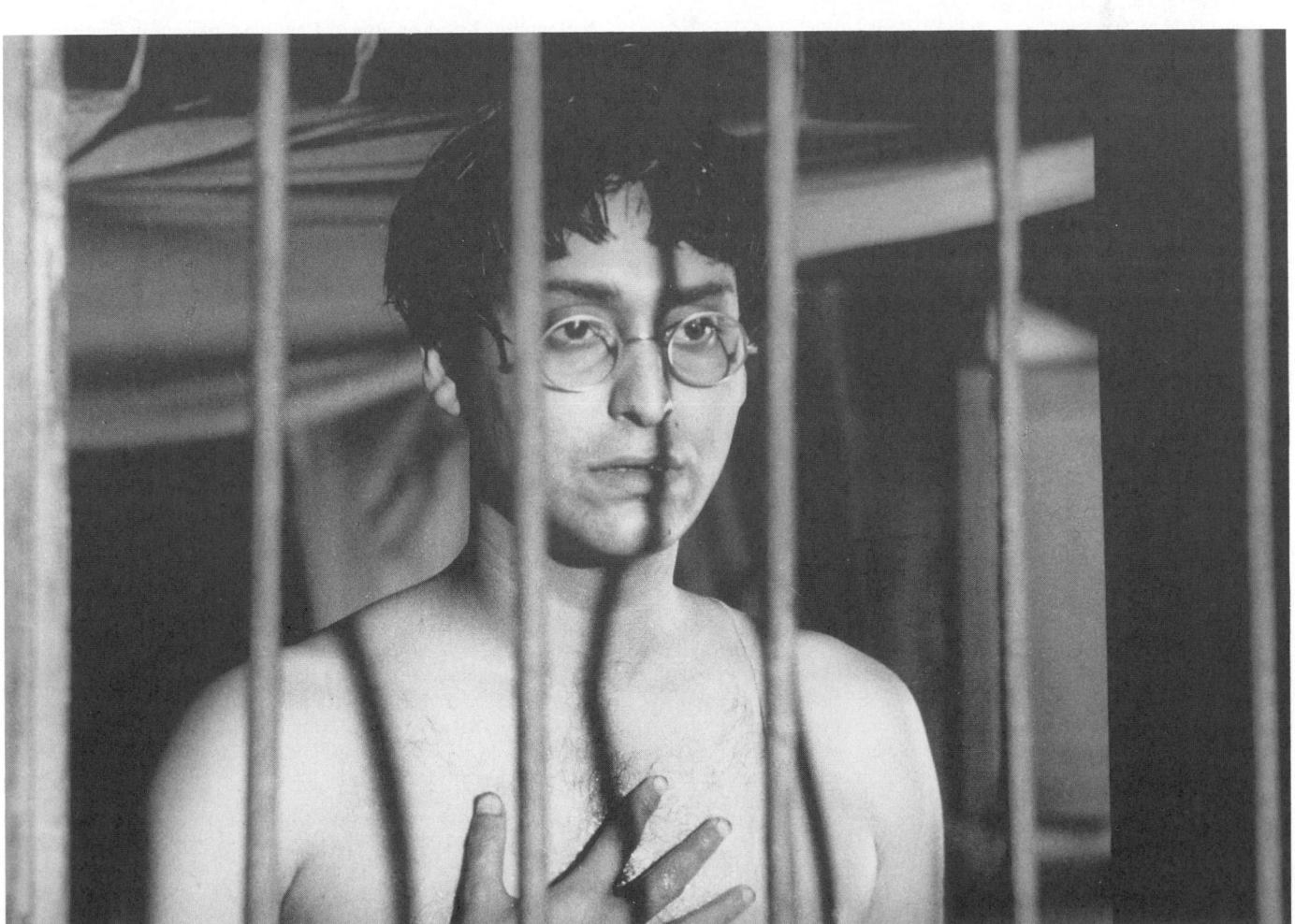

Soumitra Chatterjee in *Teen Kanya*

1982   *Preyasi*; *Matir Swarga*; *Agradani*; *Simanta Raag*
1983   *Indira*; *Chena Achena*; *Amar Geeti*
1984   *Achena Mukh*; *Kony*; *Lal Golap*; *Ghare Baire* (*The Home and
         the World*) (Satyajit Ray) (as Sandip Mukherjee); *Vasundhara*
         (Sekhar Chatterjee)
1985   *Baikunther Will*; *Tagori*; *Sandhya Pradeep*
1986   *Urbashe*; *Shyam Saheb*
1987   *Atanka* (Sinha); *Raj Purush*; *Nyay Adhikar*; *Sukumar Ray*
1988   *Ekti Jiban* (Mitra) (as Gurudas); *Nuit Bengali* (*Bengali Night*)
         (Klotz) (as Narendra Sen); *Channachara*; *Agaman*; *Agni
         Sanket*; *Agun*; *Debibaran*; *Anjali*; *Pratik*
1989   *Ganashatru* (*An Enemy of the People*) (Satyajit Ray) (as Dr.
         Ashok Gupta); *Maryada*; *Jankar*; *Amar Shapath*
1990   *Shakha Proshakha* (*Branches of the Tree*) (Satyajit Ray) (as
         Proshanto); *Manasi*; *Ekhane Amar Swarga*; *Apon Amar Apon*
1992   *Mahaprithivi* (as Father)
1994   *Uttoran* (*The Broken Journey*) (Sandip Ray) (as Dr. Sengupta)

Publications

By CHATTERJEE: articles—

Interview in "Satyajit Ray Issue" of *Montage* (Bombay).
"Soumitra Chatterjee et Sandip Ray," interview with E. Decaux and
    others, in *Cinématographe* (Paris), June 1985.
"A Joining of Ways," interview with D. Chaterji, in *Cinema in India*
    (Bombay), vol. 3, no. 2, 1989.
Interview with B. Datta, in *Cinema in India* (Bombay), vol. 3, no. 1, 1992.

On CHATTERJEE: articles—

Valot, J., "Soumitra Chatterjee: apu et les autres . . . ," in *Revue du
    Cinéma* (Paris), December 1988.
Rajadhyaksha, Ashish, and Paul Willemen, in *Encyclopaedia of Indian
    Cinema*, New Dehli, 1994.

* * *

Soumitra Chatterjee's name as an actor cannot be evoked without
recalling the films of Satyajit Ray, almost as if Chatterjee were synonymous with the Apu trilogy, although he appeared in his first film
role only in the final part of the trilogy, as the grown Apu in *Apu
Sansar*. Ray is renowned for being a consistently sensitive director of
actors, and Chatterjee became a particular favorite, his chief asset
undoubtedly being a naturally sensitive appearance. Robin Wood, in
his book on the Apu Trilogy, says that his beauty, which is "at once
physical and spiritual, seems an ideal incarnation of Ray's belief in
human potential."

Chatterjee had some theatrical experience before his first film role,
and subsequently became a star in numerous films made by other
directors, mainly in the Bengali cinema. While the memory of his
performances in those films has faded, the roles he has played in Ray's
films—as the husband in *Devi*, the suitor with tartan socks in *Teen
Kanya*, the thinly veiled portrait of Rabindranath Tagore in *Charulata*,
the arrogant leader in *Aranyar din Ratri*, or the revolutionary in the
more recent *Ghare Baire*—have left a lasting impression. Chatterjee's
last collaborations with Ray have also been impressive, such as in
Ganashatru, where Chatterjee, as Dr. Ashok Gupta, emotionalizes the
conflicting pulls of the beliefs of the orthodox society, and the mechanics of modern science, where eventually no one is the winner.
And in *Uttoran*, the last script penned by Satyajit Ray and directed by
his son Sandip Ray, the talents of Soumitra Chatterjee are showcased,
again. He brings a new depth to the character of Dr. Sengupta, the
cardiologist, who is cosmopolitan in living and outlook. Satyajit Ray's

intention of making a commentary on modern medicine losing the
values of humaneness, was realized by the complexity that Chatterjee
brought to the portrayal. When the doctor is stuck in a village due to
a flat tire, his experiences change his outlook. Drawn irrevocably into
the life of a sick peasant and his family, the doctor decides it is time
for him to do a good deed. It is Chatterjee's talents that makes us question
if this conventional climax is an end at all, or only a beginning.

Indian actors and actresses have often been accused of one-dimensional performance, either heroic or villainous, with no subtlety of
nuance or gesture. It is a tradition inherited from the theatrical origins
of Indian cinema, whereas Ray's cinema, imbibing the values of his
colonial overlords and firmly rooted within the tradition of Western
humanism, set out to create psychologically rounded characters and
thus changed the whole style of cinema acting in India. According to
Chatterjee, "Ray's films brought about a real change from the acting
point of view—actors began trying to be cinema actors. I didn't know
what to do when Mr. Ray first asked me. I didn't know the real
difference between stage and screen acting." He seemed to have quickly
mastered the difference, for Ray regularly returned to Chatterjee with
more and more challenging roles.

—Behroze Gandhy, updated by Usha Venkatachallam

CHER

Nationality: American. **Born:** Cherilyn Sarkisian in Southern California, 20 May 1946. **Education:** Trained for the stage with Jeff
Corey. **Family:** Married 1) Sonny Bono, 1964 (some sources say
1969) (divorced 1974), daughter: Chastity; 2) Gregg Allman, 1975
(divorced), son: Elijah Blue. **Career:** 1965—with husband, as Sonny
and Cher, had first U.S. hit, *Baby Don't Go*; 1971-74—co-host, *The
Sonny and Cher Comedy Hour* for CBS (also *Cher*, 1975-76, and *The
Sonny and Cher Show*, 1976-77); 1982—appeared on stage (then on
film) in *Come Back to the Five and Dime, Jimmy Dean, Jimmy Dean*;
late 1980s—international success as actress and recording artist. **Awards:**
Cannes Film Festival, Best Actress, for *Mask*, 1985; Best Actress Academy Award, for *Moonstruck*, 1987. **Address:** c/o Creative Artists Agency,
9830 Wilshire Boulevard, Beverly Hills, CA 90212, U.S.A.

Films as Actress:

1967   *Good Times* (Friedkin) (as herself)
1969   *Chastity* (De Paola) (title role)
1982   *Come Back to the Five and Dime, Jimmy Dean, Jimmy Dean*
         (Altman) (as Sissy)
1983   *Silkwood* (Nichols) (as Dolly Pelliker)
1985   *Mask* (Bogdanovich) (as Rusty Dennis)
1987   *The Witches of Eastwick* (Miller) (as Alexandra Medford); *Sus-
         pect* (Yates) (as Kathleen Riley, Public Defender); *Moon-
         struck* (Jewison) (as Loretta Castorini)
1990   *Mermaids* (Benjamin) (as Mrs. Flax)
1992   *The Player* (Altman) (as herself)
1994   *Ready to Wear* (*Pret-a-Porter*) (Altman) (as herself)
1996   *Faithful* (Mazursky)

Publications

By CHER: book—

Cher in Her Own Words, compiled by Nigel Goodall, London, 1992.

By CHER: articles—

Interview with Allan Hunter, in *Films and Filming* (London), August 1985.
Interview in *Time Out* (London), 21 October 1987.
Interview with A. Kass, in *Films and Filming* (London), December 1987.
"Cher: Chez la femme," interview with Harlan Jacobson, in *Film Comment* (New York), January/February 1988.
Interview with Eugenie Ross-Leming and David Standish, interview in *Playboy* (Chicago), December 1988.
Interview with Bruce Roberts, in *Interview* (New York), October 1994.

On CHER: books—

Taraborelli, J. Randy, *Cher: A Biography*, New York, 1986.
Quirk, Lawrence J., *Totally Uninhibited: The Life and Wild Times of Cher*, New York, 1991.
St. Michael, Mick, *Cher: The Visual Documentary*, London, 1993.

On CHER: articles—

Connelly, Christophe, "Uncommon Women," in *Premiere* (New York), November 1990.
Current Biography 1991, New York, 1991.

*   *   *

Cher is an unpredictable woman, a talented entertainer who seems to enjoy sampling various show business venues without getting attached to any one. It might be unfair to categorize her as a film star, since her active film career may be limited to a few films in the 1980s. One is on more secure ground calling Cher a celebrity.

Her emergence as a critically acclaimed screen actress in the 1980s is surprising not only because few would have guessed she could be a talented actress, but also because the roles she has taken are so different from her celebrity image. In most of her films, she plays distinctly unglamorous women, a far cry from the glittery persona associated with her long-standing fame.

For a decade, 1965-74, she was the overtly talented half of the singing duo Sonny and Cher. After several hit singles and a popular television show, the marriage ended and so the act folded. Cher continued her singing career and had a number of hits ("Gypsies, Tramps and Thieves," "Half Breed," "Dark Lady") which alluded to a difficult and impoverished upbringing as the daughter of a part Cherokee Indian mother who was married eight times. Aside from buying her records, the public craved information about her love affairs with younger men, her provocative—and quite tacky—scanty clothing, and her face and figure. The tabloids were quick to supply any and all information they could run down or make up. She cashed in on her celebrity in the late 1970s with a solo act in Las Vegas for which she was paid $300,000 per week.

Few performers have made the leap from Las Vegas to art cinema, but Cher managed to do just that when she took the role of Sissy, a good-natured but hard-drinking and rough-talking waitress, in Robert Altman's screen version of the stage play *Come Back to the Five and Dime, Jimmy Dean, Jimmy Dean*, whose plot involves the 1975 reunion of the James Dean Fan Club, a group of forlorn women who share the events of their unfulfilled lives. The genesis of her film career occurred the year before the film was made when she moved to New York City to seek work in the theater, and Altman hired her for a Broadway run of the play.

Mike Nichols was so impressed with Cher's stage performance as Sissy that he cast her in *Silkwood* as the blue-collar, frumpy lesbian roommate of Karen Silkwood (Meryl Streep). This was a much more mainstream movie than *Jimmy Dean*, and Cher's praised performance paved the way for her to play unglamorous leads in other Hollywood

films. All of a sudden, baby boomers who had grown to maturity alongside Cher were realizing that Sonny was not the only member of the duo with brains. Scratch Cher's sequined exterior and you find an intelligent and insightful actress.

She next starred in *Mask* as a drug-addicted, foul-mouthed motorcycle mama who is a loving mother to a son suffering from craniodiaphyseal dysplasia, a disease that causes enlargement of the head and disfigurement of the facial features. It was the sort of down-and-dirty role that many stars would refuse. Cher relished the part and became friendly with real-life disease victim Rusty Dennis, and has since raised funds to support victims of this disease. Cher fought with director Peter Bogdanovich throughout the production, insisting on playing the character in her own instinctual way. For her determined efforts, she wound up winning the 1985 Cannes Film Festival Best Actress Award.

In the late 1980s, Cher continued to record hit tunes and appear in a variety of films. *The Witches of Eastwick* is an entertaining black comedy about three New England sex-starved females who conjure up a charming devil of a man (Jack Nicholson). She also played a public defender in *Suspect*, a film which did little to further her career. But in *Moonstruck*, Cher found an outstanding opportunity in the plain-Jane role of Loretta Castorini, who is 37 going on 50. Loretta dresses like a frump. Her frizzy black hair has more than a touch of gray. A widow of seven years, she is a dutiful daughter who lives with her very ethnic Italian-American parents in a very ethnic Italian neighborhood in Brooklyn. She has been dating Johnny Cammareri (Danny Aiello), a respectable but boring fellow. When Johnny proposes marriage, she readily accepts. But Loretta has yet to meet Johnny's estranged brother Ronny (Nicolas Cage), who causes her to bloom like the cherry blossoms in the Brooklyn Botanic Garden on a sunny spring afternoon. Loretta's catharsis is the thrust of *Moonstruck*; by the time she played Loretta, Cher had developed into a solid screen actress. Her performance in the film ranks with her roles in *Silkwood* and *Mask* as her best work on celluloid, but this time she earned a Best Actress Academy Award.

Mermaids allowed Cher to play a sexy single mom to Winona Ryder, and was a solid comedy hit. Cher put in a fine performance (and had enough creative leverage to have director Frank Oz replaced by Richard Benjamin), but the role was not in the same league as *Moonstruck*. Perhaps that sense of anticlimax is the reason Cher has not been in a film since 1990, with the exception of cameo appearances in *The Player* and *Ready to Wear*. She has starred in exercise videos that show off the fabulous body she claims comes from workouts rather than nips and tucks, and occasionally appears on infomercials; seemingly, she has decided to rest on her acting laurels.

—H. M. Glancy, updated by Audrey E. Kupferberg

CHERKASSOV, Nikolai

Nationality: Russian. **Born:** Nikolai Konstantinovich Cherkassovin in St. Petersburg, 27 July 1903; name sometimes transliterated as Cherkasov. **Education:** Attended the Leningrad Theatre Institute, 1923-26. **Career:** 1926-33—actor for Leningrad Youth theater; 1927—film debut in *Poet i tsar*; 1933—member of Pushkin Theatre, Leningrad; 1938—elected Deputy for Kuibyshev district of Leningrad. **Awards:** Order of Lenin, 1939; People's Artist of the USSR, 1947. **Died:** In Leningrad, 14 September 1966.

Films as Actor:

1927   *Poet i tsar* (*The Poet and the Czar*) (Gardin) (as Sharl); *Ego prevoskhoditelstvo* (*His Excellency*) (Roshal)

1928   *Moi syn* (*My Son*) (Chervyakov); *Luna sleva* (*The Moon Is to the Left*) (Ivanov) (as Kalugin)
1929   *Rodnoi brat* (*Blood Brother*) (Krol)
1930   *Vsadniki vetra* (*Horsemen of the Wind*) (Zhemchuzhnikov)
1932   *Schastye* (*Happiness*) (Fainzimmer and Soloviev) (as police agent)
1933   *Pervaya lyubov* (*First Love*) (Shreiber)
1934   *Zhenitba Jana Knukke* (*Jan Knukke's Wedding*) (Ivanov) (as Pfal); *Lyubliu tebya?* (*Do I Love You?*) (Gerasimov) (as student)
1935   *Granitsa* (*Staroye Dudino; Old Dudino*) (Dubson) (as Gaidul); *Podrugi* (*Girl Friends*) (Arnstam) (as Belyi); *Goryachie dyenechki* (*Hectic Days*) (Zarkhi and Heifitz) (as Kolka Loshak)
1936   *Deputat Baltiki* (*Baltic Deputy*) (Zarkhi and Heifitz) (as Prof. Polezhaev); *Deti kapitana Granta* (*Captain Grant's Children*) (Vainshtok) (as Paganel)
1937   *Ostrov sokrovishch* (*Treasure Island*) (Vainshtok) (as Billy Bones); *Ka sovetskuyu rodinu* (*For the Soviet Homeland*) (Muzkant)
1937-9 *Piotr Pervyi* (*Peter the Great*) (Petrov—in 2 parts) (as Tsarevich Alexei)
1938   *Druzya* (*Friends*) (Arnstam); *Chelovek s ruzhyom* (*Man with a Gun*) (Yutkevich) (as general); **Alexander Nevsky** (Eisenstein) (title role)
1939   *Koncert na ekrane* (*Film Concert No. One*) (Timoshenko); *Lenin i 1918 godu* (*Lenin in 1918*) (Kozintsev and Trauberg) (as Maxim Gorky)
1942   *Ego zovut Sukhe-Bator* (*His Name Is Sukhe-Bator*) (Zarkhi and Heifitz) (as Baron Ungern)
1943   *Shestdesyat dnei* (*Sixty Days*) (Shapiro) (as Antonov)
1944   **Ivan Groznyi** (*Ivan the Terrible*) (Eisenstein) (title role)
1946   *Vo imya zhizni* (*In the Name of Life*) (Zarkhi and Heifitz) (as Lukich)
1947   *Pirogov* (Kozintsev) (as Liadov); *Novyi dom* (*New House*) (Korsh-Sablin); *Vesna* (*Spring*) (Alexandrov) (as Gromov)
1949   *Schastlivogo plavaniya* (*Bon Voyage*) (Lebedev) (as Levashov); *Akademik Ivan Pavlov* (*Academician Ivan Pavlov*) (Roshal) (as Maxim Gorky); *Alexander Popov* (Rappoport and Eisimont) (title role); *Stalingradskaya bitva* (*The Battle of Stalingrad*) (Petrov) (as President Roosevelt)
1950   *Mussorgsky* (Roshal) (as Stasov)
1952   *Rimsky-Korsakov* (Roshal and Kozansky) (title role)
1955   *Oni znali Mayakovsky* (*They Knew Mayakovsky*) (Petrov) (as Mayakovsky)
1957   *Don Kikhot* (*Don Quixote*) (Kozintsev) (title role)
1958   **Ivan Groznyi II: Boyarsky zagovor** (*Ivan the Terrible, Part II: The Boyars' Plot*) (Eisenstein—completed 1946) (title role)
1963   *Vse ostaetsia lyudyam* (*Everything Remains for the People*; *Legacy*) (Natanson) (as Dronov)
1965   *La Nuit des adieux* (Petipa) (Dréville)

Publications

By CHERKASSOV: books—

Iz zapisok aktera, Moscow, 1951, translated as *Notes of a Soviet Actor*, Moscow, 1957.
Chertvertyi Don Kikhot, Leningrad, 1958.

By CHERKASSOV: articles—

"Lyubimyi obraz" in *Deputat Baltiki*, Moscow, 1937.
"Rabota nad istoricheskoi roliu" in *Sovetsky istorichesky film*, Moscow, 1939.

"Cherkassov's Don Quixote," (selections from article in *Iskusstvo Kino*) and review of *Notes of a Soviet Actor*, in *Sight and Sound* (London), Autumn 1958.
Soviet Film (Moscow), October and November 1958.

On CHERKASSOV: books—

Dreiden, C., *Nikolai Cherkassov*, Moscow, 1939.
Slaventatov, D., *Nikolai Cherkassov*, Moscow, 1939.
Baili, A., *Narodnyi artist SSSR. N.K. Cherkassov*, Moscow, 1951.
Benyash, R., *Nikolai Konstantinovich Cherkassov*, Moscow, 1952.
Gerasimov, Yuri, *Cherkassov*, Moscow, 1976.

On CHERKASSOV: articles—

On film *Everything Remains for the People* in *Soviet Film* (Moscow), January 1964.
Cahiers du Cinéma (Paris), February 1967.
Iskusstvo Kino (Moscow), July 1973.
Soviet Film (Moscow), August 1973.

On CHERKASSOV: film—

Riadom a drugon (*Our Friend Is with Us*) about Cherkassov, directed by Alexander Abramov, 1970.

*   *   *

Nikolai Cherkassov, a graduate of the Leningrad Theatre Institute, began his professional career on stage in 1920, developing his skill in burlesque, and subsequently making his first film appearance in 1927 in *The Poet and the Czar*. Although his basic training had been in ballet, opera, and even the circus as well as the theater, he concentrated in the mid-1920s on legitimate acting and joined the Leningrad Pushkin Theatre, working for much of his career in both theater and film. His international reputation in the cinema was made in the character of Professor Polezhaev in the celebrated film that established "historic realism" in the Soviet Union of the 1930s, Josef Heifitz and Alexander Zarkhi's *Baltic Deputy*, in which at the age of only 32 he played a man of 75; of the part Cherkassov said, "He was so young in spirit that only a young actor could play him." As he described it, the film presented the attitude of the "progressive, democratic intelligentsia in the early stages of the Revolution." This part (for which he had so much longed) came at approximately the same time as his interpretation of the Tsarevich Alexei in the first part of Vladimir Petrov's magnificent, two-part historical spectacle, *Peter the Great*, and it was for this latter part that he received his first official decoration the same year. In his roster of well-known character parts, he was to appear much later as Franklin D. Roosevelt in Petrov's *The Battle of Stalingrad* and in the title role of Grigori Kozintsev's *Don Quixote* in 1957.

Cherkassov is primarily known internationally for his magnificent portrayals in the title roles of Eisenstein's *Alexander Nevsky* and *Ivan the Terrible*. These were heavily stylized performances in the heroic mold of historical figures idealized in order to fulfil Soviet reinterpretation of Russian history and legend. Cherkassov had, however, been trained in the traditional mode of Russian realist acting. Once he had submitted himself to the special disciplines of performance imposed by Eisenstein on his players, which tended to turn the actors into a mobile part of the total pictorial design of each shot, Cherkassov gave both Nevsky and Ivan a grandeur on the screen which was as much due to his deep, reverberant voice as it was to his magnificent appearance.

In spite of the difficulties and severe physical trials Cherkassov and his fellow players endured while working on *Alexander Nevsky* and *Ivan the Terrible*, he became a close friend of Eisenstein. When invited to play Ivan late in 1941, the year of the Nazi invasion of Russia, Cherkassov had been evacuated with the Pushkin Theatre from besieged Leningrad to Novo Sibirsk in Siberia, from which he had to travel in the winter of early 1942 to the studios of Alma Ata in Central Asia where Eisenstein and his production team had been sent from Moscow. Cherkassov complained that Eisenstein treated his actors "like wax dummies," and that he was forced to "practice long and tiringly to produce the tragic bend of Tsar Ivan's figure." In his *Notes of a Soviet Actor* he wrote further, "the general custom is to try to make the historical personage 'accessible,' to portray him as an ordinary person sharing the ordinary, human traits of other people. . . . But with Ivan we wanted a different tone. In him we wished chiefly to convey a sense of majesty, and this led us to adopt majestic forms." His makeup was so brilliantly constructed by the makeup artist V. Goryunov that the composer for the film, Sergei Prokofiev, failed to recognize him when they were seated close together at the premiere. When *Ivan the Terrible, Part II* incurred Stalin's hostility and the film was banned on ideological grounds, it was Cherkassov who accompanied Eisenstein (then in declining health) to a meeting with Stalin in 1947 at which, after considerable modifications were introduced, permission was granted to resume work. This was never to be, but in February 1948 when Eisenstein died, one of his last notes was a message penned to Cherkassov.

During the period he worked with Eisenstein, Cherkassov became a deputy of the Supreme Soviet, giving him a political as well as acting career. (Note: Nikolai Cherkassov should not be confused with his namesake, the actor Nikolai P. Cherkasov, who starred in many Russian films, most notably Pudovkin's wartime biographical film, *General Suvorov*.)

—Roger Manvell

CHEVALIER, Maurice

Nationality: French. **Born:** Maurice Auguste Chevalier in Ménilmontant, Paris, 12 September 1888. **Education:** Attended the École des Frères, Paris. **Military Service:** Began military service, 1913, wounded and taken prisoner, 1914, spent two years in German prisoner-of-war camp at Alten Grabow. **Family:** Married the dancer Yvonne Vallée, 1926 (divorced 1935). **Career:** 1901—began performing in Paris cafés as "Le Petit Chevalier"; three-season contract with Folies Bergères; in second season chosen by star Mistinguett as partner in act, and began ten-year association with her; 1910—beginning of film career, though appeared in bit part in 1908; 1919—in London with Elsie Janis in revue *Hullo, America*; 1920—suffered breakdown, recuperated at Saujon; 1923-26—at Empire Theatre, Paris; 1928—contract with Paramount; 1929—after release of *The Love Parade*, salary tripled; 1933—contract with MGM; 1936-39—made films in France and Britain; 1940-45—in seclusion, performing rarely; performance in Germany for French prisoners gave rise to rumors of collaboration; exonerated after war; 1947—resumed touring in one-man recitals; 1951—refused entry into U.S. for having signed Stockholm Appeal for banning of nuclear weapons; from mid-1950s—numerous TV appearances; 1968—last performance, at Théâtre des Champs-Elysées, Paris. **Awards:** Croix de Guerre, 1917; Légion d'honneur, 1938; Order of Leopold, Belgium, 1943; Special Academy Award, "for his contributions to the world of entertainment for more than half a century," 1958; Ordre merite national, France, 1964. **Died:** 1 January 1972.

Films as Actor:

1908 *Trop crédules* (Durand)
1910 *Un Marie qui se fait attendre* (Gasnier)

1911 *La Mariée recalcitrante* (Gasnier)
1914 *Par habitude* (Linder); *La Valse renversante* (Monca)
1917 *Une Soirée mondaine* (Diamant-Berger)
1922 *Le Match Criqui-Ledoux* (Diamant-Berger); *Le Mauvais Garçon* (Diamant-Berger)
1923 *Gonzague* (Diamant-Berger); *L'Affaire de la Rue de Lourcine* (Diamant-Berger); *Par habitude* (Diamant-Berger); *Jim Bougne, boxeur* (Diamant-Berger)
1928 *Bonjour New York!* (Florey)
1929 *Innocents of Paris* (Wallace) (as Maurice Marny); *The Love Parade* (Lubitsch) (as Count Alfred Renard)
1930 *Paramount on Parade* (Lubitsch) (as guest star); *The Big Pond* (Henley) (as Pierre Mirande); *La Grande Mare* (Henley and Bataille-Henri—French version of *The Big Pond*); *Playboy of Paris* (Berger) (as Albert Loriflan); *Le Petit Café* (Diamant-Berger—French version of *Playboy of Paris*)
1931 *The Smiling Lieutenant* (Lubitsch) (as Niki); *El cliente seductor* (Rey and Blumenthal—short)
1932 *One Hour with You* (Lubitsch and Cukor) (as Dr. André Bertier); *Make Me a Star* (Beaudine) (guest appearance); *The Stolen Jools* (*The Slippery Pearls*) (McGann and others—short); *Love Me Tonight* (*Marez-moi ce soir*) (Mamoulian) (as Maurice Courtelin); *Stopping the Show* (Fleischer) (as voice)
1933 *A Bedtime Story* (*Monsieur Bébé*) (Taurog) (as René); *The Way to Love* (Taurog) (as François)
1934 *The Merry Widow* (*The Lady Dances*) (Lubitsch) (as Prince Danilo)
1935 *Folies Bergère* (*The Man from the Folies Bergère*) (Del Ruth) (as Eugene Charlier/Fernard, the Baron Cassini)
1936 *The Beloved Vagabond* (Bernhardt) (as Paragot); *L'Homme du jour* (*The Man of the Hour*) (Duvivier) (as himself/Alfred Boulard); *Avec le sourire* (*With a Smile*) (Maurice Tourneur) (as Victor Larnois)
1937 *Break the News* (Clair) (as François Verrier)
1939 *Pièges* (*Personal Column*) (Siodmak) (as Robert Fleury)
1947 *Le Silence est d'or* (*Man about Town*; *Silence Is Golden*) (Clair) (as Emile)
1949 *Le Roi* (*A Royal Affair*; *The King*) (Sauvajon) (as the King)
1950 *Ma Pomme* (*Just Me*; *My Apple*) (Sauvajon) (title role)
1952 *Jouons le jeu . . . L'Avarice* (Gillois) (as interviewee)
1953 "Amore 1954" ep. of *Cento anni d'amore* (De Felice); *Schlagerparade* (Ode); *Chevalier de Ménilmontant* (Baratier)
1954 *Caf' Conc 1954* (Barthomieu—short); *Sur toute la gamme* (Régamey—short); *Visite à Maurice Chevalier* (Lucot and Folgoas—for TV)
1955 *J'avais sept filles* (*My Seven Little Sins*; *I Have Seven Daughters*) (Boyer) (as Count Andre)
1956 *The Happy Road* (Kelly) (title song)
1957 *Rendez-vous avec Maurice Chevalier* (Régamey—6 shorts); *Love in the Afternoon* (Wilder) (as Claude Chavasse); *The Heart of Show Business* (Staub) (as guest)
1958 *Gigi* (Minnelli) (as Honoré Lachaille)
1959 *Count Your Blessings* (Negulesco) (as Duc de St. Cloud)
1960 *Can-Can* (Walter Lang) (as Paul Barriere); *Un, deux, trois, quatre?* (*Les Collants noirs*; *Black Tights*) (Terence Young) (as narrator); *A Breath of Scandal* (Curtiz) (as Prince Philip); *Pepe* (Sidney) (as himself)
1961 *Fanny* (Logan) (as Panisse)
1962 *Jessica* (*La Sage-femme, le curé, et le bon Dieu*) (Negulesco) (as Father Antonio); *In Search of the Castaways* (Stevenson) (as Prof. Jacques Paganel)
1963 *A New Kind of Love* (Shavelson) (as himself)

Maurice Chevalier

1964   *Panic Button* (Sherman) (as Philippe Fontaine); *I'd Rather be Rich* (Smight) (as Philip Dulaine); linking sequence of *La Chance et l'amour* (Chabrol) (as interviewee)
1967   *Monkeys, Go Home!* (McLaglen) (as Father Sylvain)
1970   *The Aristocats* (Reitherman—animation) (as voice only—singer of title song)
1971   **Le Chagrin et la pitié** (*The Sorrow and the Pity*) (Marcel Ophüls) (songs)

Publications

By CHEVALIER: books—

Ma route et mes chansons, 8 vols., Paris, 1946-63.
The Man in the Straw Hat, New York, 1949.
C'est l'amour, Paris, 1959; as *With Love*, Boston, 1960.
Mome à cheveux blancs, Paris, 1969; as *I Remember It Well*, Boston, 1970.
Les Pensées de Momo, Paris, 1970.
My Paris, New York, 1972.
Bravo Maurice!, London, 1973.

On CHEVALIER: books—

Ringgold, Gene, and DeWitt Bodeen, *Chevalier: The Films and Career of Maurice Chevalier*, Secaucus, New Jersey, 1973.

Colin, Gerty, *Maurice Chevalier: Une Route semée d'étoiles*, Paris, 1981.
Freedland, Michael, *Maurice Chevalier*, New York, 1981.
Maurice Chevalier 1888-1972, photo album chosen by André Fildier, Paris, 1981.
Sabates, Fabien, *Maurice Chevalier*, Paris, 1981.
Harding, James, *Maurice Chevalier: His Life, 1888-1972*, London, 1982.
Berruer, Pierre, *Maurice Chevalier*, Paris, 1988.
Kirgener, Claudine, *Maurice Chevalier: itinéraire d'un inconne célèbre*, Paris, 1988.
Behr, Edward, *Thank Heaven for Little Girls: The True Story of Maurice Chevalier's Life and Times*, New York, 1993.

On CHEVALIER: articles—

"Maurice Chevalier" issue of *Visages* (Paris), October 1936.
"The Mature Chevalier," in *Newsweek* (New York), 3 November 1947.
Current Biography 1969, New York, 1969.
Obituary in *New York Times*, 2 January 1972.
Morin, J., "Maurice Chevalier: Un Coup de canotier," in *Cinéma* (Paris), February 1972.
Beylie, Claude, "Le Chevalier de carton," in *Ecran* (Paris), March 1972.

Monsees, R. A., "Maurice Chevalier 1888-1972," in *Films in Review* (New York), May 1972.
Ciné Revue (Paris), 8 April 1982.

*   *   *

After performing in French cafés as he struggled to establish his career, mixing clown capers with coarse song and dance routines, Maurice Chevalier gradually evolved the sophisticated man-about-town character which was to make him famous and loved by stage and screen audiences. His charismatic presence was enhanced by the attire that became his trademark: a formal or semiformal suit, straw hat, and sometimes a cane. His jaw extended, and sporting an engaging smile, he deftly cocked the hat and swung his cane as he strutted through song and dance numbers. While he did appear in 13 silent films, 5 of them created by his own production company, the full range of his debonair character could not be realized until the arrival of sound movies.

In 1929 the famous Parisian music hall star was fortunate to have Ernst Lubitsch direct his second American film, *The Love Parade*. Chevalier was teamed with Jeanette MacDonald in one of the most sophisticated movie musicals made in Hollywood. The breezy Gallic charm of the French singer proved so successful that, as the New York film critic Mordaunt Hall noted, the audience clapped for some scenes at the premiere of the film as if they were witnessing a stage performance. Some of the memorable Chevalier numbers were "Louise," "My Ideal," "You Brought a New Love to Me," and "One Hour with You"—songs that became part of the singer's repertoire. The director Rouben Mamoulian also assisted the development of the French actor's international reputation by once more using the Chevalier and MacDonald team in *Love Me Tonight*. Lubitsch's adaptation of the Franz Lehar operetta, *The Merry Widow*, is the final entry in the trio of best films from the actor's first Hollywood period.

Disenchanted with what he considered an endless repetition of the same screen character, Chevalier abandoned Hollywood and attempted to continue his career in France. His 1930s and 1940s films, such as *L'Homme du jour* and *Pièges*, reveal a wider range of acting ability because of the variety of his roles. In René Clair's *Le Silence est d'or* he played the type of charming, older character role that would be typical of his final film successes in the United States.

As he turned 70, Chavalier had a second career in Hollywood with late 1950s films such as Billy Wilder's *Love in the Afternoon*, and the memorable *Gigi*, a Lerner and Loewe musical. The highlight of *Gigi* was his beguiling rendition of the song "Thank Heaven for Little Girls." The energy the actor projected in his early musicals was absent, but the warmth of his portrayal of Honoré Lachaille in *Gigi* revealed an acting talent that had matured. For years Chevalier was a favorite subject of entertainers doing impressions, who imitated his distinctive style as a singer, though they could never capture his charm.

—Donald McCaffrey

CHRISTIE, Julie

Nationality: British. **Born:** Julie Frances Christie in Chukua, Assam, India, 14 April 1941. **Education:** Studied art in France, attended Brighton Technical College and Central School for Music and Drama, London. **Career:** 1957—acting debut on stage with Frinton Repertory Company, Essex; early 1960s—on British TV, including title role in serial *A for Andromeda*; 1962—film debut in small part in *Crooks Anonymous*; 1963—first lead role in Schlesinger's *Billy Liar*; 1984—

in TV mini-series *Entscheidung am Kap Horn*. **Awards:** Best Actress Academy Award, Best Actress, New York Film Critics, and Best British Actress, British Academy, for *Darling*, 1965. **Agent:** International Creative Management, 40 West 57th Street, New York, NY 10019, U.S.A.

Films as Actress:

1962   *Crooks Anonymous* (Annakin) (as Babette La Vern)
1963   *The Fast Lady* (Annakin) (as Claire Chingford); *Billy Liar* (Schlesinger) (as Liz)

1965   *Young Cassidy* (Cardiff and Ford) (as Daisy Battles); *Darling* (Schlesinger) (as Diana Scott); *Doctor Zhivago* (Lean) (as Lara)
1966   *Fahrenheit 451* (Truffaut) (as Linda/Clarisse)
1967   *Far from the Madding Crowd* (Schlesinger) (as Bathsheba Everdene); *Tonite Let's All Make Love in London* (Whitehead—doc)
1968   *Petulia* (Lester) (title role)
1970   *In Search of Gregory* (Peter Wood) (as Catherine)
1971   *The Go-Between* (Losey) (as Marian Maudsley); *McCabe and Mrs. Miller* (Altman) (as Mrs. Miller)
1973   **Don't Look Now** (Roeg) (as Laura Baxter)
1975   *Shampoo* (Ashby) (as Jackie Shawn); **Nashville** (Altman) (as herself)
1977   *The Demon Seed* (Cammell) (as Susan Harris)
1978   *Heaven Can Wait* (Beatty and Henry) (as Betty Logan)
1981   *Memoirs of a Survivor* (Gladwell) (as "D"); *The Animals Film* (Schonfeld and Alaux) (as narrator)
1982   *The Return of the Soldier* (Bridges) (as Kirry Baldry); *Les Quarantièmes Rugissants* (de Chalonges)
1983   *Heat and Dust* (Ivory) (as Anne)
1984   *The Gold Diggers* (*Women Make Movies*) (Potter) (as Ruby); *Separate Tables* (Schlesinger—for TV) (as Mrs. Shankland/Miss Railton-Bell); *Broadside: Taking on the Bomb* (doc for TV) (as narrator); *Why Their News Is Bad News* (for TV) (as narrator)
1985   *Champagne amer* (Vert)
1986   *Miss Mary* (Bemberg) (as Mary Mulligan); *Power* (Lumet) (as Ellen Freeman)
1987   *Agent Orange: Policy of Poison* (Iverson—doc) (as narrator); *Yilmaz Güney: His Life, His Films* (Cousins-Mills—for TV) (as narrator); *Secret Obsession* (Vart)
1988   *La Memoire Tatouée* (Behi) (as Betty); *Dadah Is Death* (*Deadly Decision*) (London—for TV) (as Barbara Barlow); *Vater und Sonhe* (*Fathers and Sons*; *Sins of the Fathers*) (Sinkel—for TV)
1990   *Fools of Fortune* (O'Connor) (as Mrs. Quinton)
1991   *Short Step* (Babenco)
1992   *The Railway Station Man* (Whyte—for TV) (as Helen Cuffe)
1996   *Hamlet* (Branagh) (as Gertrude); *Dragonheart* (Cohen)

Publications

By CHRISTIE: articles—

Interview in *Photoplay* (New York), September 1971.
Interview with B. R. Rich, in *American Film* (New York), May 1983.
Interview with Karen Jaehne, in *Cineaste* (New York), vol. 15, no. 2, 1986.
Interview with A. Cockburn, in *American Film* (New York), January/February 1986.

Julie Christie in *Don't Look Now*

On CHRISTIE: books—

Callan, Michael Feeney, *Julie Christie*, London, 1984.
Murphy, Robert, *Sixties British Cinema*, London, 1992.

On CHRISTIE: articles—

Focus on Film (London), Autumn 1973.
McCreadie, M., "Valuelessness and Vacillation in the Films of Julie Christie," in *Journal of Popular Film* (Bowling Green, Ohio), vol. 6, no. 3, 1978.
Ciné Revue (Paris), 30 August 1979 and 2 July 1981.
Klein, Andy, filmography in *American Film*, February 1990.

On CHRISTIE: film—

Star, short directed by Alan Lovell, 1966.

*   *   *

Julie Christie became an international star in the decade her performances seemed to celebrate. (And a lot of Christie's star appeal was tied into her youth and associated with the rebellious youth of the 1960s.) Her characters defied convention, joyfully reveling in zoom-lensed sensuality in *Billy Liar*, selfishly courting the high life in *Darling*, impetuously pursuing dangerous whims in *Petulia*. But in the morally schizoid world of 1960s cinema, screenwriters often exacted a high price for their characters' sexual liberation. For such films—epitomized by her Oscar-winning *Darling*—Julie Christie was the perfect actress.

Her particular talent appeared double-edged. Her model's beauty and the slick style in which she was photographed (especially by John Schlesinger), invited the viewer to admire her characters and to covet the glossy worlds they inhabited. But as *Darling* and later *The Go-Between* strikingly confirm, numerous Christie performances gradually reveal the enigmatic frost initially concealed by her characters' husky-voiced charm, thus permitting the viewer to accept, even enjoy, their eventual comeuppance.

Starring roles in three prestigious but overproduced adaptations of novels—two historical (Boris Pasternak's *Doctor Zhivago* and Thomas Hardy's *Far from the Madding Crowd*), the third futuristic (Ray Bradbury's *Fahrenheit 451*)—reflect Christie's career-long resistance to typecasting. Dual performances as Oskar Werner's dreadful, book-hating wife and his magnificent, book-loving mistress in *Fahrenheit 451* might have broadened public perception of her acting range, but fade into the film's pretentious moralizing, and are smothered by Truffaut's apparent discomfort with an English-language film.

Three roles in early 1970s pictures underline more vividly her rejection of glamorous roles in favor of challenging, literate scripts filmed by brilliantly quirky directors. All three movies—Altman's *McCabe and Mrs. Miller*, Losey's *The Go-Between*, and Roeg's *Don't Look Now*—thrive on narrative ambiguity, and rebel against the filmic genres from which they are derived—Western, English romance, and gothic thriller, respectively—through consistent frustration of audience expectations. In all three, her identity as a star is submerged. In *The Go-Between* and *McCabe and Mrs. Miller* (a second Oscar nomination), Christie disappears from view for considerable stretches of time; in *Don't Look Now* she is offscreen for more than a quarter of the film. In the movie *The Go-Between*, adapted by Harold Pinter from L. P. Hartley's complex novel, her performance is integrated with the remarkable ensemble playing of its all-British cast. Yet in all three films, Christie dominates the frame when she is in it, and she displays a depth and range of acting skill, that in her 1960s work, seemed almost secondary to her beauty.

With enviable control, inner torment pokes through to disclose the characteristic Christie embodiment of the clash between illusion and reality in all three women: frizzy-headed prostitute Mrs. Miller (opposite Warren Beatty's McCabe) in the eccentric, elliptical world of Robert Altman; radiant aristocrat Marian Maudsley who, by *The Go-Between*'s end, reveals unforgivable streaks of cruelty; and Laura Baxter, haunted by her husband's and daughter's deaths in the terrifying, fractured universe of *Don't Look Now*, but regal as she musters her emotional resources. More recently, Christie played a mother in the 1988 television movie *Dadah Is Death*. It was a part most would not identify with her early screen persona. She starred in this fact-based story about an Australian woman's efforts to clear her son of drug charges in Malaysia. It was not a glamorous or offbeat role, but Christie played it with the same kind of intensity.

Christie is committed to political and social causes which, since *Heaven Can Wait*, have increasingly determined the roles she accepts: nuclear disarmament (*Memoirs of a Survivor*; *Broadside: Taking on the Bomb*, a television documentary); animal experimentation (*The Animals Film*); and feminism (*The Gold Diggers*, directed by Sally Potter and produced by a crew comprised entirely of women). The specialized, uncommercial nature of the films she tends to select, and her conscious shedding of the star image, have combined in recent years to limit Christie's audience to that of art houses and cinema societies. The single exception is *Heat and Dust*, in which the actress portrays a young woman searching for clues to her great-aunt's life in India, where Christie herself was born. Like *The Go-Between*, it uses the past to reflect upon the present; as in the three films of the early 1970s, Christie is offscreen for long periods. And like other Christie films, its source is a rich literary text, Ruth Prawer Jhabvala's novel of the same name, a further example of the actress's discriminating taste.

—Mark W. Estrin, updated by Linda J. Stewart

CLEESE, John

Nationality: British. **Born:** John Marwood Cleese in Weston-Super-Mare, 27 October 1939. **Education:** Attended Clifton College; studied law at Downing College, Cambridge, graduated 1963. **Family:** Married 1) Connie Booth, 1968 (divorced 1978), daughter: Cynthia; 2) Barbara Trentham, 1981 (divorced 1990), daughter: Camilla; 3) Alyce Faye Eichelberger, 1992. **Career:** 1963—appeared on stage in West End as a cast member of Cambridge Footlights Revue (same show given on Broadway in 1964); 1965—in *Half a Sixpence* on Broadway; 1966-67—wrote with Graham Chapman for and appeared on *The Frost Report* and *At Last the 1948 Show* for TV; 1969—in the first series of *Monty Python's Flying Circus* for BBC TV, developed with Chapman, Terry Jones, Michael Palin, Eric Idle, and Terry Gilliam; 1971—appears in first *Monty Python* film, *And Now for Something Completely Different*; founded a company for industrial training films, Video Arts Ltd.; 1975—co-writer and co-actor with Connie Booth, *Fawlty Towers* TV series; 1982—in TV series *Whoops Apocalypse*. **Awards:** Honorary LLD, St. Andrew's University, 1971; Emmy Award for best performance in comedy for guest appearance, for *Cheers* episode, "Simon Says," 1987; British Academy of Film and Television Arts Award for Best Actor, for *A Fish Called Wanda*, 1988; Jack Oakie Award for comedy in motion pictures, Screen Actors Guild in the United States, 1994. **Agent:** David Wilkinson Associates, 115 Hazlebury Road, London SW6 2LX, England. **Address:** c/o 8 Clarendon Road, London W11 3AA, England.

Films as Actor:

1968 *Interlude* (Billington) (as TV publicist); *The Best House in London* (Savile); *The Bliss of Mrs. Blossom* (McGrath)

1970 *The Rise and Rise of Michael Rimmer* (Billington) (as Plumer, + co-sc); *The Magic Christian* (McGrath) (as director in Sotheby's, + co-sc); *The Statue* (Amateau) (as Harry)

1971 *And Now for Something Completely Different* (Macnaughton) (+ co-sc)

1972 *It's a 2'6" above the Ground World* (*The Love Ban*) (Thomas)

1974 *Romance with a Double Bass* (Robert Young) (as Musician Smychkov, + co-sc)

1975 *Monty Python and the Holy Grail* (Gilliam and Terry Jones) (as Sir Lancelot/minor roles, + co-sc)

1977 *The Strange Case of the End of Civilisation as We Know It* (McGrath—for TV) (as Arthur Sherlock Holmes, + co-sc)

1979 *Monty Python's Life of Brian* (*Life of Brian*) (Terry Jones) (as Reg/minor roles, + co-sc); *The Secret Policeman's Ball* (Graef)

1980 *The Taming of the Shrew* (Jonathan Miller—for TV) (as Petruchio)

1981 *Time Bandits* (Gilliam) (as Robin Hood); *The Great Muppet Caper* (Henson) (as Neville)

1982 *The Secret Policeman's Other Ball* (Temple); *Monty Python Live at the Hollywood Bowl* (Terry Hughes and Ian MacNaughton) (various roles, + co-sc); *Privates on Parade* (Blakemore) (as Major Giles Flack)

1983 *Monty Python's the Meaning of Life* (Terry Jones) (as Second Fish/Grim, + co-sc, co-mus); *Yellowbeard* (Damski) (as Blind Pew)

1985 *Silverado* (Kasdan) (as Sheriff Langston)

1986 *Clockwise* (Morahan) (as Brian Stimpson)

1987 *The Secret Policeman's Third Ball*

1988 *A Fish Called Wanda* (Charles Crichton) (as Archie Leach, + exec pr, sc)

1989 *The Big Picture* (Guest) (as bartender); *Erik the Viking* (Terry Jones) (as Halfdan the Black)

1990 *Bullseye!* (Winner) (as man on the beach in Barbados who . . .)

1991 *An American Tail: Fievel Goes West* (Nibbelink and Wells—animation) (as voice of Cat R. Waul)

1993 *Splitting Heirs* (Robert M. Young) (as Raoul P. Shadgrind)

1994 *Mary Shelley's Frankenstein* (Branagh) (as Prof. Waldman); *Rudyard Kipling's the Jungle Book* (*The Jungle Book*) (Sommers) (as Dr. Plumford); *The Swan Princess* (Richard Rich—animation) (as voice of Jean-Bob)

1996 *Fierce Creatures* (Robert M. Young) (as Rollo Lee, + co-sc, co-pr)

Other Film:

1972 *Rentadick* (Jim Clark) (co-sc)

Publications

By CLEESE: books—

The Strange Case of the End of Civilisation as We Know It, with Jack Hobbs and Joe McGrath, London, 1970.
Fawlty Towers, with Connie Booth, Volume I, London, 1977; Volume II, 1979.
Families and How to Survive Them, with Robin Skynner, London, 1983.
The Golden Skits of Wing-Commander Muriel Volestrangler, FRHS and Bar, London, 1984.

The Complete Fawlty Towers, with Connie Booth, London, 1988.
A Fish Called Wanda: The Screenplay, New York, 1988.
Life and How to Survive It, with Robin Skynner, London, 1993.

By CLEESE: articles—

Interview in *Time Out* (London), 5 November 1982.
Interview in *Interview* (New York), April 1985.
Interview with Quentin Falk, in *Sight and Sound* (London), Spring 1988.
Interview with Allan Hunter and Philip Strick, in *Films and Filming* (London), October 1988.
Interview with Robert Benayoun and others, in *Positif* (Paris), February 1989.

On CLEESE: books—

Perry, George, *Life of Python*, London, 1983.
Johnson, Kim "Howard," *The First 200 Years of Monty Python*, New York, 1989.
Margolis, Jonathan, *Cleese Encounters*, New York, 1992.

On CLEESE: articles:

Current Biography 1984, New York, 1984.
Castro, Janice, "Monty Python in the Boardroom: Comic John Cleese Gets Laughs with Corporate Training Films," in *Time* (New York), 20 October 1986.
Gilliatt, Penelope, "Height's Delight," in *New Yorker*, 2 May 1988.
"This Man Is Not Fishing for Compliments," in *Life* (New York), September 1988.
Voss, Bristol, "John Cleese Gets Serious about Training," in *Sales & Marketing Management*, March 1991.
Dwyer, Paula, "John Cleese's Flying Business Circus: He's a One-Man Conglomerate and Playing It Straight—Sort Of," in *Business Week*, 21 June 1993.

*   *   *

The bulk of John Cleese's acting career featured his work as a comedian and ranged from an occasional sophisticated stage comedy to surreal, odd humor typical of British comedy linked to the radio *Goon Show*, the college revue, and the variety stage. Critics lauded as superior his Petruchio in the BBC TV version of *The Taming of the Shrew*. However, most of the actor's portraits were in original comedies, some of which he had a hand in writing. Cleese's most popular and critically successful solo performance—at least in the United States—appeared in 1988 with *A Fish Called Wanda*. He was the lead actor, writer, and executive producer of this movie in which he played a role close to that of the light, sophisticated male comedian of the thirties—a character with romantic possibilities with the female comedienne. As Archie Leach, a lawyer, the actor played the role of a person who realized he led a staid existence and wanted to break away from such a stuffy life.

The premise of *A Fish Called Wanda* tends to follow that which was sometimes used by writer-director Preston Sturges who created such witty comedies as *Easy Living* (1937), as a writer, and *The Lady Eve* (1941), as a writer-director. This Cleese vehicle uses the kind of picaresque characters that Sturges used for a broader type of comedy. The 1988 comedy features two American con-artist-robbers, Wanda, played by Jamie Lee Curtis, and Otto, enacted by Kevin Kline. These two free-spirited oddballs provide comic contrast with the conservative lawyer, Archie.

As Wanda moves in to seduce Archie, he says, before they kiss, "Sorry if I seem pompous." Cleese handles the line with even more

John Cleese in *Monty Python's Life of Brian* © 1979 Paragon Entertainment Corporation/Courtesy of HandMade Films

effective understatement than he employed in all the stuffy English gentlemen he portrayed in the broad comic *Monty Python* and *Fawlty Towers* shows.

When confronted by the other con artist, Otto, the lawyer is, once more, no match when intimidated. Expansive, high-intensity comedy evolves when Otto stalks Archie to thwart any sexual encounter with Wanda. Kevin Kline, who received an Academy Award for the supporting role of Otto, enacts a foil diametrically the opposite of the lawyer. This volatile, comically explosive cross between a neo-Nazi and Mafia hit man, provides a counterpoint to Cleese's humorously impotent personality. Pushing Archie backwards on a window sill so that he dangles upside down, held only by Otto leaning on his legs, the temperamental, jealous madman demands an apology for trying to seduce Wanda. Cleese, as Archie, responds in lawyer type terms: "All right. All right. I apologize. I'm, really, really sorry—unreservedly. . . . I offer a complete and utter retraction. The imputation was totally without basis."

Less than a decade earlier, broader portraits of the upper-class Englishman show Cleese as a master of depicting this type of comic figure. Critic Anthony Slide lauds the actor's enactment of a minor role in *Time Bandits* (1981) and view it as a lampoon of royalty: "Cleese is unquestionably the funniest man in the film, and one can

only wish that his sequence had been longer. As Robin Hood, Cleese appears to have based his characterization on the present British Royal Family, patronizingly distributing wealth to the poor. 'Have you met the poor? Charming people,' he says." (Essay on *Time Bandits* in *Magill's Cinema Annual 1982.*)

A few more examples of the variety of roles and the range of John Cleese's acting deserve a concluding survey. In *Monty Python and the Holy Grail* (1975) as Lancelot he botches a heroic rescue from the tower of a person he believes is a fair damsel. After he has hacked his way through a crowd of wedding guests, killing a multitude with his sword, he finds out that the prisoner in the tower is the groom who does not want to get married. His discovery is capped with a meek, "Sorry." As a con man and informer named Blind Pew in a swashbuckling pirate movie, *Yellowbeard* (1983) Cleese enacts one of his most picaresque parts. With an exaggerated claim that he has such acute hearing he can detect the pirate Yellowbeard from the rustling of his beard, he gives his pronouncements in a harsh voice, using the accent of a growling, low-class cockney. Three years later, in the 1986 *Clockwise*, Cleese is back playing the would-be cultured gentleman as a headmaster who is a tyrant and an unreasonable disciplinarian, barking reprimands over a public address system as he views questionable activities on a school playground. In his physical demeanor and voice this character that Cleese portrays is another authority figure lampoon. Then, ten years later the actor creates another picaresque character. As an insane lawyer in *Splitting Heirs* (1993) the comedian kills a number of people "to clear the path" for the rightful heir to achieve the title of duke. When the heir finds the lawyer is responsible for the deaths, he declares, "You're mad!" With aplomb the killer jovially replies, "Well, we are all a bit mad."

While the inventory of humor in the actor's craft proves to be his vocal intonations, phrasings, and timing of responses, Cleese has a definite, unusual physical side to his comedy. In his *Monty Python* period he was noted for his silly walks—exaggerated, eccentric movements of his long legs. A 6' 4" man, he also created funny movements when frustrated or angry by odd jumps and twists or, when playing an eccentric character, by just walking away with an erratic gait. The former was most often displayed when he portrayed Basil Fawlty in the situation comedy series *Fawlty Towers*. The latter is evident in *Splitting Heirs*, with his creation of a quirky, deranged lawyer.

John Cleese has enjoyed a rich and varied career as both a writer and actor for stage, television, and movies. His innovation as a writer obviously makes it possible for him to design parts with which he can exhibit a variety of roles and a range of acting skills. This combination of writing and acting to best show his talent was, of course, most evident in the 12 *Fawlty Towers* television shows and the feature movie *A Fish Called Wanda*.

—Donald W. McCaffrey

CLIFT, Montgomery

Nationality: American. **Born:** Edward Montgomery Clift in Omaha, Nebraska, 17 October 1920. **Career:** 1933-34—first stage experience for amateur theatrical group in Sarasota, Florida; 1935—Broadway debut in *Fly Away Home*; 1942—joined the Group Theater in New York; 1945—first starring role on Broadway in *Foxhole in the Parlor*; 1947—co-founder, Actors Studio in New York; 1948—release of first two films *Red River* and *The Search*; three-film contract with Paramount; 1949—refusal of role in *Sunset Boulevard* resulted in cancellation of contract by Paramount; 1953—starring role on Broadway in *The Sea Gull*; 1956—three-film contract with MGM; 1957—face permanently scarred as a result of automobile accident; 1960s—progressive emotional and physical decline. **Died:** In New York City, 23 July 1966.

Films as Actor:

1948   *The Search* (Zinnemann) (as Ralph Stevenson); ***Red River*** (Hawks) (as Matthew Garth)
1949   *The Heiress* (Wyler) (as Morris Townsend)
1950   *The Big Lift* (Seaton) (as Danny MacCullough)
1951   *A Place in the Sun* (Stevens) (as George Eastman)
1953   *I Confess* (Hitchcock) (as Father Michael William Logan); ***From Here to Eternity*** (Zinnemann) (as Robert E. Lee "Prew" Prewitt); *Stazione termini* (*Indiscretion of an American Wife*; *Terminal Station*; *Indiscretion*) (de Sica) (as Giovanni Doria)
1957   *Raintree County* (Dmytryk) (as John Wickliff Shawnessy)
1958   *The Young Lions* (Dmytryk) (as Noah Ackerman); *Lonelyhearts* (Donehue) (as Adam White)
1959   *Suddenly Last Summer* (Joseph L. Mankiewicz) (as Dr. John Cukrowicz)
1960   *Wild River* (Kazan) (as Chuck Glover)

1961   ***The Misfits*** (Huston) (as Perce Howland); *Judgment at Nuremberg* (Kramer) (as Rudolph Petersen)
1962   *Freud* (*Freud—The Secret Passion*) (Huston) (as Sigmond Freud)
1966   *The Defector* (*L'Espion*; *Lautlose Waffen*) (Levy) (as Prof. James Bower)

Publications

On CLIFT: books—

Huston, John, *An Open Book*, New York, 1972.
LaGuardia, Robert, *Monty: A Biography of Montgomery Clift*, New York, 1977.
Bosworth, Patricia, *Montgomery Clift: A Biography*, New York, 1978.
Kass, Judith, *The Films of Montgomery Clift*, Secaucus, New Jersey, 1981.
Fernandez, Lluis, *Monty Clift: Pasion Secreta*, Barcelona, 1989.
Hoskyns, Barney, *Montgomery Clift: Beautiful Loser*, London, 1991.
McCann, Graham, *Rebel Males: Clift, Brando, and Dean*, London, 1991.
Parker, John, *Five for Hollywood*, Secaucus, New Jersey, 1991.
Kalfatovic, Mary C., *Montgomery Clift: A Bio-Bibliography*, Westport, Connecticut, 1994.

On CLIFT: articles—

Hamilton, J., "Montgomery Clift," in *Look* (New York), July 1949.
Current Biography 1954, New York, 1954.
Cole, C., "Eyes that Say More than Words," in *Films and Filming* (London), September 1956.
Obituary in *New York Times*, 24 July 1966.
Zinnemann, Fred, "Montgomery Clift," in *Sight and Sound* (London), Autumn 1966.
Roman, Robert C., "Montgomery Clift," in *Films in Review* (New York), November 1966.
Gow, Gordon, "Closer to Life," in *Films and Filming* (London), April 1975.
Bosworth, Patricia, "Montgomery Clift: First of a New Breed," in *Close-Ups: The Movie Star Book*, edited by Danny Peary, New York, 1978.
"Montgomery Clift," in *Ecran* (Paris), March 1978.
Reed, Rex, "Montgomery Clift," in *The Movie Star*, edited by Elisabeth Weis, New York, 1981.
Lippe, Richard, "Montgomery Clift: A Critical Disturbance," in *CineAction!* (Toronto), no. 17, 1989.
Purtell, Tim, "No Place in the Sun," in *Entertainment Weekly* (New York), 23 July 1993.

*   *   *

Among the 17 films that Montgomery Clift appeared in, it is impossible to point to any one role as "defining" Clift's image on screen, in the way that *A Streetcar Named Desire* and *Rebel without a Cause* established Brando's and James Dean's personalities in the public's mind. Yet Clift was one of the first actors of his generation to capture the attention of moviegoing audiences with performances that were sensitive, complex, and deeply introspective in nature. The combination of intensity and vulnerability that he brought to his characters—qualities magnified in later years by the car accident that destroyed his matinee-idol good looks and compounded the problems of an already troubled personality—was unique in 1948, when Clift was catapulted to stardom by the release of his first two films, *The Search* (for which he received an Oscar nomination) and *Red River*.

Red River in particular represents an important juncture in film history, pairing Clift with John Wayne in a genre usually defined by its

Montgomery Clift in *From Here to Eternity*

rigid codes of male behavior. The central conflict in Howard Hawks's film, however, is between Wayne's brand of brutal, bullying masculinity and Clift's quiet blend of toughness and compassion. Theirs is a clash of reason and brute strength, and although their reconciliation takes the form of a violent physical confrontation, the role of Matthew Garth clearly presents Clift as an alternative to the rugged, unyielding protagonists of traditional Westerns. It was a part that heralded a shift in the characteristics that would define screen heroes in the decade to come.

Clift portrayed another man challenging stereotypical views of masculinity—this time in the U.S. military—in *From Here to Eternity*. As Prewitt, the bugler and former boxer who silently stands up to the harassment of his fellow soldiers when he refuses to reenter the ring after blinding a man, Clift gives one of his strongest performances. In the role that brought him his third Oscar nomination (the second was for *A Place in the Sun*), he conveys both the courage and the inner torment of a man whose unshakable moral convictions form the heart of his sense of self-worth, yet cause him to be labeled a coward. The complexity that Clift brings to the character is a trait that marks his work as a whole, charging his performances with an underlying pain that few actors of his day dared to reveal.

These qualities were a central part of Clift's relationships with women in films. Clift never overwhelms women in the manner of Gable or Flynn but attracts them instead with an almost hypnotic emotional power that often seems to arise from some deep inner need. This is especially true of his films with Elizabeth Taylor, whose dark beauty made her an ideal physical match for Clift on the screen. In both *A Place in the Sun* and *Raintree County*, the similarity between the two is so striking that they might almost be brother and sister, and there is an erotic tension in their work together that reaches its climax in the former film's extraordinary close-ups of the couple's romantic scenes. Clift's vulnerability is also a factor in his relationship with Donna Reed in *From Here to Eternity* and, on a platonic level, in the understanding and friendship between his character and that of Marilyn Monroe in *The Misfits*.

The tension and internal conflict in Clift's screen persona form the basis for his portrayals of the priest in Hitchcock's *I Confess* and Noah Ackerman, the Jewish soldier battling anti-Semitism, in *The Young Lions*. Each man is placed at odds with society by his religious convictions, and Clift conveys the hidden pain of both Father Michael's struggle with his conscience and Ackerman's scrappy refusal to tolerate religious slurs. Clift's intensity took on an increasingly unsettling quality in the films following his accident (which occurred during the filming of *Raintree County*), and in *Suddenly Last Summer*, *The Misfits*, and *Freud*, in which he played the title role, there is a tightly wound, neurotic edge to the characters that is both compelling and disturbing. In Stanley Kramer's *Judgment at Nuremberg* this quality reaches its peak in Clift's brief supporting role as a mildly retarded man testifying against Nazi war criminals. It is a riveting performance, jarringly real and often painful to watch, and it brought Clift his fourth Academy Award nomination. It is this sense of emotional risk-taking that makes Clift a magnetic presence in even his less effective roles and which places his best work next to that of the finest actors of his generation.

With the recent revelation of the fact of Clift's bisexuality, one is able to see more into the correlation between his star personality (that of vulnerability, sensitivity, and almost effeminate masculinity closer to androgyny) and the real-life Clift (whose swinging sexuality and unsettling dissatisfaction throughout life mirrors and projects a troubled soul onto the big screen). Clift's own claim regarding this uncertainty in him reveals more than a touch of stubbornness and pride: "I don't want to be labeled as either a pansy or a heterosexual. Labeling is so self-limiting" (quoted by Graham McCann in *Rebel Males*). Throughout Clift's career, one sees a wide range of roles

played, each of them nothing short of constant erotic tensions coming not only from the dramatic characters or his *acting* but also from a lifelong *felt* and *lived* conflict of an unsettled sexuality.

—Janet E. Lorenz, updated by Guo-Juin Hong

CLOSE, Glenn

Nationality: American. **Born:** Greenwich, Connecticut, 19 March 1947. **Education:** Attended William and Mary College, Williamsburg, Virginia, graduated 1974. **Family:** Married 1) Cabot Wade; 2) James Marlas, 1984 (divorced 1986); one daughter with John Starke: Annie Maude. **Career:** 1974—debut on Broadway in *Love for Love*; 1982—film debut in *The World According to Garp*. **Awards:** Two Tony Awards; Emmy Award, Actress in Mini-series or Special, for *Serving in Silence: The Margarethe Cammermeyer Story*, 1995. **Address:** c/o Fred Specktor, Creative Artists Agency, 9830 Wilshire Boulevard, Beverly Hills, CA 90212, U.S.A.

Films as Actress:

1979   *The Orphan Train* (William A. Graham—for TV) (as Jessica); *Too Far to Go* (Fielder Cook—for TV) (as Rebecca Kuehn)
1982   *The World According to Garp* (George Roy Hill) (as Jenny Fields)
1983   *The Big Chill* (Kasdan) (as Sarah Cooper)
1984   *The Stone Boy* (Cain) (as Ruth Hillerman); *The Natural* (Levinson) (as Iris Raines); *Something about Amelia* (Haines—for TV) (as Gail Bennett); *Greystoke: The Legend of Tarzan, Lord of the Apes* (Hudson) (voice only, dubbed Andie MacDowell's voice)
1985   *Jagged Edge* (Marquand) (as Teddie Barnes); *Maxie* (*Free Spirit*) (Aaron) (as Jan/Maxie)
1987   *Fatal Attraction* (Lyne) (as Alex Forrest); *Gandahar* (*Light Years*) (Wernstein—animation) (voice only)
1988   *Stones for Ibarra* (Gold—for TV) (as Sara Everton); *Dangerous Liaisons* (Frears) (as Marquise de Merteuil)
1989   *Immediate Family* (*Parental Guidance*) (Kaplan) (as Linda Spector)
1990   *Hamlet* (Zeffirelli) (as Gertrude); *Reversal of Fortune* (Schroeder) (as Martha "Sunny" von Bulow); *I'll Take Romance* (Haggard—for TV)
1991   *Sarah, Plain and Tall* (Glenn Jordan—for TV) (title role, + co-exec pr); *Meeting Venus* (Szabo) (as Karin Anderson); *Hook* (Spielberg) (as pirate); *Brooklyn Laundry* (as Birdie)
1992   *Lincoln* (Kunhardt—TV doc) (as voice of Mary Todd Lincoln)
1993   *Skylark* (Sargent—for TV) (as Sarah Wittig, + exec pr)
1993   *The House of the Spirits* (August) (as Ferula)
1994   *The Paper* (Ron Howard) (as Alicia Clark)
1995   *Serving in Silence: The Margarethe Cammermeyer Story* (Bleckner—for TV) (title role, + exec pr)
1996   *Mary Reilly* (Frears) (as Mrs. Farraday); *101 Dalmations* (as Cruella De Vil); *Mars Attacks!* (Tim Burton) (as First Lady Martha Dale)

Other Film:

1987   *Do You Mean There Are Still Real Cowboys?* (Blair—doc) (pr)

Publications

By CLOSE: articles—

Interview with J. Hurley, in *Films in Review* (New York), February 1983.
"Too Close for Comfort," interview with Ross Wetzsteon, in *American Film* (New York), May 1984.
Interview in *Time Out* (London), 1 March 1989.
Interview with B. Hadleigh, in *Film Monthly*, July 1990.
Interview with Frank Spotnik, in *American Film*, November/December 1991.
"Glenn Close, Opera Queen: The Diva of *Meeting Venus* Is Game for Anything Gay," in *Advocate* (Los Angeles), 3 December 1991.
"Playing the Diva," interview with Stephen Schiff, in *New Yorker*, 14 November 1994.

On CLOSE: book—

Newcomer, Ron, *The Films of Glenn Close*, Secaucus, New Jersey, 1996.

On CLOSE: articles—

Current Biography 1984, New York, 1984.
Allenman, Richard, "Getting Close," in *Vogue*, November 1994.

*   *   *

1992 witnessed the explosion of three dramatic actresses who enjoyed great popularity and critical accolades throughout the eighties: Meryl Streep, Jessica Lange, and Glenn Close. In the Academy Awards of 1982, Streep competed against Lange for Best Actress honors, which Streep won. Lange's "consolation" prize was winning the Best Supporting Actress award over Glenn Close. This "third place" position seems to offer a defining characteristic of much of Close's career. Nominated for five Oscars between 1982 and 1988 (three nominations out of her first four films), she never won an award. Even when Close's fourth nomination honored her lead role in the third most popular film of 1987 (*Fatal Attraction*) and marked her as the top female box-office attraction she failed to win. Close's Oscar curse notwithstanding, her superior acting skills mark her as one of Hollywood's most distinguished actresses and as an acclaimed television and theatrical performer.

Close's early films established an image of conservative femininity: a nurturing, virtuous, attractive, and vulnerable woman. She plays an overly protective mother in *The World According to Garp*, a serene and coolly informal wife in *The Big Chill*, and a deified muse in *The Natural*. This stereotype (which won Close her first three Academy Award nominations) also underscores the dilemma of women's roles during a decade that championed masculine heroism. Actresses found themselves playing one-dimensional characters who merely supported the male lead in his endeavors. When this stereotype of the feminine

Glenn Close in *Jagged Edge*

ideal becomes threatened in *The World According to Garp* (Jenny Fields's mothering leads her to a radical feminism) or questioned in *Jagged Edge* (Teddie Barnes improperly uses the legal system to protect her lover, the killer), the character is punished by assassination or physical and emotional trauma.

Jagged Edge introduced the opposite side of Close's stardom: the feminine threat. Her next two roles, Alex in *Fatal Attraction* and the Marquise de Merteuil in *Dangerous Liaisons*, unleashed characters who follow the tradition of the femme fatale; women who are sexy, independent, manipulative, and duplicitous. Alex is a successful businesswoman, but unmarried and childless. Her desire to achieve a "traditional" family initiates a perverse drive to replace the legitimate wife. Her unsuccessful attempt results in Alex's death (at the hands of the legitimate wife), the punishment of the adulterous husband, and the reestablishment of the nuclear family. The Marquise's social and sexual machinations, based upon contempt for love and masculine power, destroy everyone including herself. Utterly alone, she recognizes her contempt has denied her any chance of happiness. This second stereotype (which won Close her next two Academy Award nominations) again underscores the dilemma of women's roles in contemporary Hollywood. Actresses found themselves playing one-dimensional characters who threatened the male lead and deserved punishment for their aggression. Her stunningly psychotic performance as Norma Desmond in the stage version of *Sunset Boulevard*, although masterfully controlled, still reinforces and continues this aspect of her film stardom.

The tension between these two stereotypes reached its apex in *Maxie*. Close plays a character who literally manifests the notion of feminine duality. Portraying a dedicated wife possessed by the spirit of a freewheeling "flapper," Close must synthesize the contradictions of these two characters to achieve peace and emerge as an ideal figure of womanhood.

Close's difficulty in finding films that do not perpetuate the two extremes of the feminine stereotype (or treat it superficially as in *Maxie*) links her to Bette Davis, whom she admits emulating. Davis always played a strong woman inflected in two ways: a self-sacrificing and maternal figure or a manipulative and destructive one. Close continues this tradition. In *Immediate Family, Hamlet, Sarah, Plain and Tall, Skylark,* and *The House of the Spirits* she plays strong, nurturing, virtuous, and yet vulnerable women. Each character offers a different facet of this model, from altruistic mother to repressed spinster, but the result is the same. In *Reversal of Fortune, Meeting Venus,* and *The Paper* she plays strong, sexy, independent, and manipulative women who are punished in some way for the problems they create. In *Reversal of Fortune* she plays "Sunny" von Bulow whose "failure" to be a traditional mother offers another explanation why her husband attempts to kill her. In *Meeting Venus* she plays Karin Anderson, an opera diva whose affair with a conductor destroys the conductor's marriage. In *The Paper*, she plays Alicia Clark, the managing editor of a New York daily newspaper. She engages in a surprisingly physical brawl with Michael Keaton; an altercation she ultimately wins. Yet when accidentally shot, parallel editing equates her helplessness to Michael Keaton's wife's emergency C-section.

And like Davis, Close demonstrates superb acting techniques. More an actress than a star, Close disappears into her roles finding a new mannerism and vocal quality to make each character memorable. Her most interesting films include *Reversal of Fortune, Meeting Venus,* and the Hallmark Hall of Fame's *Sarah, Plain and Tall* and its sequel, *Skylark*. In *Reversal of Fortune,* playing a comatose Sunny von Bulow, Close appears in flashbacks as a woman who suffers emotionally and physically from a diffident husband, coolly detached children, diabetes, alcoholism, and an upper class ennui. In *Meeting Venus,* Close portrays a celebrated artist confident with her career but less certain about her romantic relationships. The film parallels *Fatal Attraction* except it is not a thriller and no one dies. In *Sarah, Plain and Tall* and *Skylark,* she creates her most complex character; an obdurate New

England spinster who answers a mail-order wife ad and moves to Kansas to raise her stoic husband's two children. Ostensibly a Western, the film allows Close that rare opportunity to play a woman who embodies the characteristics of both a nurturing mother and a fiercely independent woman without lapsing into either stereotype.

—Greg S. Faller

COBB, Lee J.

Nationality: American. **Born:** Leo Jacoby in New York City, 8 December 1911 (some sources list 9 December). **Education:** Attended accounting classes at City College of New York (CCNY). **Family:** Married 1) Helen Beverly, 1940 (divorced 1952), children: Vincent and Julie; 2) Mary Hirsch, 1957, sons: Tony and Jerry. **Career:** 1920s—trained as a violinist, but broken wrist ended musical career; 1928—ran away from home to Hollywood, but failed to secure work in film industry as actor; 1928-31—returned to New York City and acted in radio dramas to pay for classes at CCNY; 1931—stage debut at Pasadena Playhouse, California; 1934—film debut in serial *Vanishing Shadow*; 1935—joined Group Theater in New York; 1949—role as Willie Loman in Arthur Miller's *Death of a Salesman* on Broadway; early 1950s—forced to testify before the House Un-American Activities Committee; 1962-66—starred as Judge Henry Garth in TV series *The Virginian*; 1970-71—in TV series *The Young Lawyers*. **Died:** In Woodland Hills, California, 11 February 1976.

Films as Actor:

1934   *Vanishing Shadow* (serial)
1937   *North of the Rio Grande* (Watt) (as Goodwin); *Rustler's Valley* (Watt) (as Cal Howard); *Ali Baba Goes to Town* (David Butler)
1938   *Danger on the Air* (Garrett) (as Tony)
1939   *Golden Boy* (Mamoulian) (as Mr. Bonaparte); *The Phantom Creeps* (serial)
1941   *This Thing Called Love* (*Married but Single*) (Hall) (as Julio Diestro); *Men of Boys Town* (Taurog) (as Dave Morris); *Paris Calling* (Marin) (as Schwabe)
1943   *The Moon Is Down* (Pichel) (as Dr. Winter); *Tonight We Raid Calais* (Brahm) (as Bonnard); *The Song of Bernadette* (Henry King) (as Dr. Dozous); *Buckskin Frontier* (*The Iron Road*) (Selander) (as Jeptha Marr)
1944   *Winged Victory* (Cukor) (as doctor)
1946   *Anna and the King of Siam* (Cromwell) (as Kralahome)
1947   *Boomerang* (Kazan) (as Chief Robinson); *Captain from Castile* (Henry King) (as Juan Garcia); *Johnny O'Clock* (Rossen) (as Inspector Koch); *Carnival in Costa Rica* (Ratoff)
1948   *The Miracle of the Bells* (Pichel) (as Marcus Harris); *Call Northside 777* (Hathaway) (as Brian Kelly); *The Luck of the Irish* (Koster) (as D. C. Augur)
1949   *The Dark Past* (Maté) (as Dr. Andrew Collins); *Thieves' Highway* (Dassin) (as Mike Figlia)
1950   *The Man Who Cheated Himself* (Feist) (as Ed Cullen)
1951   *Sirocco* (Bernhardt) (as Col. Feroud); *The Family Secret* (Levin) (as Howard Clark)
1952   *The Fighter* (Kline) (as Durango)
1953   *The Tall Texan* (Williams) (as Capt. Theodore Bess)
1954   *Yankee Pasha* (Pevney) (as Sultan); *Gorilla at Large* (Harmon Jones) (as Det. Sgt. Garrison); *On the Waterfront* (Kazan) (as Johnny Friendly); *Day of Triumph* (Pichel and Coyle) (as Zadok)

1955 *The Racers (Such Men Are Dangerous)* (Hathaway) (as Maglio); *The Road to Denver* (Kane) (as Jim Donovan); *The Left Hand of God* (Dmytryk) (as Mieh Yang)

1956 *The Man in the Gray Flannel Suit* (Johnson) (as Judge Bernstein); *Miami Exposé* (Sears) (as Bart Scott)

1957 *Twelve Angry Men* (Lumet) (as Juror no. 3); *The Three Faces of Eve* (Johnson) (as Dr. Luther); *The Garment Jungle* (Aldrich and Vincent Sherman) (as Walter Mitchell)

1958 *The Brothers Karamazov* (Richard Brooks) (as Fyodor Karamazov); *Man of the West* (Anthony Mann) (as Dock Tobin); *Party Girl* (Nicholas Ray) (as Rico Angelo)

1959 *But Not for Me* (Walter Lang) (as Jeremiah MacDonald); *The Trap (The Baited Trap)* (Panama) (as Victor Massonetti); *Green Mansions* (Mel Ferrer) (as Nuflo)

1960 *Exodus* (Preminger) (as Barak Ben Canaan)

1962 *The Brazen Bell* (Sheldon—for TV); *The Four Horsemen of the Apocalypse* (Minnelli) (as Julio Madariaga)

1963 "The Outlaws" ep. of *How the West Was Won* (Hathaway) (as Lou Ramsey); *Come Blow Your Horn* (Yorkin) (as Mr. Baker)

1966 *Our Man Flint* (Daniel Mann) (as Cramden)

1967 *In Like Flint* (Gordon Douglas) (as Cramden)

1968 *Las Vegas 500 milliones (They Came to Rob Las Vegas; Les Hommes de Las Vegas)* (Isasi) (as Skorsky); *Il giorno della civetta (The Day of the Owl; La Maffia fait la loi; Mafia)* (Damiani) (as Don Mariano Arena); *MacKenna's Gold* (J. Lee Thompson) (as the editor); *Coogan's Bluff* (Siegel) (as Sheriff McElroy)

1970 *The Liberation of L. B. Jones* (Wyler) (as Oman Hedgepath); *Macho Callahan* (Kowalski) (as Duffy)

1971 *Heat of Anger* (Taylor—for TV); *Lawman* (Winner) (as Vincent Bronson)

1973 *Double Indemnity* (Smight—for TV); *The Man Who Loved Cat Dancing* (Sarafian) (as Lapchance); *La polizia sta a guardare* (Infascelli); *The Exorcist* (Friedkin) (as Lt. Kinderman)

1974 *Dr. Max* (Goldstone—for TV) (title role); *The Great Ice Ripoff* (Curtis—for TV); *Trapped beneath the Sea* (Graham—for TV) (as Victor Bateman); *Venditore di palloncini (The Last Circus Show; The Balloon Vendor.; Last Moments)* (Gariazzo)

1975 *Mark il poliziotta (Blood, Sweat and Fear)* (Massi); *Ultimatum alla città (Ultimatum)*; *That Lucky Touch* (Miles) (as Lt. Gen. Henry Steedman)

1976 *I Amici di Nick Nezard (Nick the Sting)* (Di Leo); *Cross Shot (La legge violenta della squadra anticrimine)* (Massi)

1979 *Arthur Miller on Home Ground* (Rasky)

Publications

On COBB: articles—

Current Biography 1960, New York, 1960.

Obituary in *New York Times*, 12 February 1976.

Pickard, Roy, "Lee J. Cobb," in *Films in Review* (New York), November 1977.

Cobb, Julie, "Lee J. Cobb: My Father," in *Close-Ups: The Movie Star Book*, edited by Danny Peary, New York, 1978.

Ecran (Paris), April 1978.

* * *

Lee J. Cobb died while preparing to repeat in *Exorcist II: The Heretic* the role of investigating detective he played in the original film. It was an ironic end for an actor whose impeccable credentials would, on any European stage, have earned him fame and honor. Unfortunately, this fine character actor, who appeared in the early plays of Odets for the Group Theatre and created Willy Loman in Arthur Miller's *Death of a Salesman*, spent most of a long screen career in distinctive but undemanding work.

On occasion, Cobb would play thoughtful, supportive characters, such as the psychiatrist who attempts to cure Joanne Woodward of her psychological disorder in *The Three Faces of Eve*. But in his best screen roles, he was effectively cast as an urban predator paradoxically tormented by twentieth-century anxieties: a wolf with an ulcer. Cobb redeemed a score of routine roles as gang boss, cop, or rancher with his capacity for conveying disquiet or a residual sensitivity. Behind his snarl lurked a weakness that already had betrayed him or would do so in the last reel. Gang-boss Rico Angelo in *Party Girl* is softened by a fugitive sentimentality toward Robert Taylor's tame cultivated attorney, while loneliness for the son he terrorized away from him racks the bigot in *Twelve Angry Men*.

In comedy Cobb seldom convinced. His Jewish father in *Come Blow Your Horn* is a performance anyone might have given. But in Don Siegel's *Coogan's Bluff* he played a weary and impatient New York detective to some effect against Eastwood's Arizona cowboy cop.

Sensitive or not, Cobb had the crooked mouth that allowed him to play pure evil. Pouring acid over a paper party decoration in *Party Girl* to demonstrate what might happen to Cyd Charisse's face, blustering himself into exhausted acquiescence to Henry Fonda's intelligence and logic in *Twelve Angry Men* or, most memorably, as union racketeer Johnny Friendly, ranting at the longshoremen whom Marlon Brando leads back to work in *On the Waterfront*, he defined for all time a sector in the outer limits of urban desperation.

From an acting standpoint, *On the Waterfront* is most fondly recalled for the legendary "I coulda been a contender" taxicab scene between Marlon Brando and Rod Steiger. But Cobb's electrifying performance as Friendly—a bully destined to crumble and fall when one man becomes determined to defy him—remains every bit as impressive as those of Brando and Steiger.

—John Baxter, updated by Rob Edelman

COBURN, Charles

Nationality: American. **Born:** Savannah, Georgia, 19 June 1877. **Family:** Married 1) Ivah Wilks, 1906 (died 1937); 2) Winifred Natzka, 1939. **Career:** 1891—program boy at theater in Savannah, then manager, 1894; 1901—Broadway acting debut; 1906—organized Coburn Shakespeare Players with wife; 1933—film debut in *Boss Tweed*; 1934—supporting role in *Say It with Flowers* began long career as character actor in films. **Awards:** Best Supporting Actor Academy Award for *The More the Merrier*, 1943. **Died:** In New York City, 30 August 1961.

Films as Actor:

1933 *Boss Tweed* (title role)

1934 *Say It with Flowers*

1935 *The People's Enemy* (Wilbur)

1938 *Of Human Hearts* (Clarence Brown); *Yellow Jack* (Seitz); *Lord Jeff (The Boy from Barnado's)* (Wood); *Vivacious Lady* (Stevens)

1939 *Idiot's Delight* (Clarence Brown); *Made for Each Other* (Cromwell); *The Story of Alexander Graham Bell (The Modern Miracle)* (Cummings); *Stanley and Livingstone* (Henry King); *Bachelor Mother* (Kanin); *In Name Only* (Cromwell)

Charles Coburn (right) with Joel McCrea in *The More the Merrier*

1940　*The Road to Singapore* (Schertzinger); *Three Faces West* (*The Refugee*) (Vorhaus); *Florian* (Marin); *Edison the Man* (Clarence Brown); *The Captain Is a Lady* (Sinclair)

1941　*The Devil and Miss Jones* (Wood); **The Lady Eve** (Preston Sturges); *H.M. Pulham, Esq.* (King Vidor); *King's Row* (Wood); *Our Wife* (Stahl); *Unexpected Uncle* (Godfrey)

1942　*In This Our Life* (Huston); *George Washington Slept Here* (Keighley)

1943　*The Constant Nymph* (Dean); *The More the Merrier* (Stevens); *Heaven Can Wait* (Lubitsch); *Princess O'Rourke* (Krasna); *My Kingdom for a Cook* (Wallace)

1944　*Knickerbocker Holiday* (Harry Brown); *Wilson* (Henry King); *The Impatient Years* (Cummings); *Together Again* (Charles Vidor)

1945　*A Royal Scandal* (*Czarina*) (Preminger); *Colonel Effingham's Raid* (*Man of the Hour*) (Pichel); *Shady Lady* (Waggner); *Over Twenty-One* (Hall); *Rhapsody in Blue* (Rapper)

1946　*The Green Years* (Saville)

1947　*Lured* (*Personal Column*) (Sirk); *The Paradine Case* (Hitchcock)

1948　*B. F.'s Daughter* (*Polly Fulton*) (Leonard); *Green Grass of Wyoming* (Louis King)

1949　*Everybody Does It* (Goulding); *The Doctor and the Girl* (Bernhardt); *Yes Sir, That's My Baby* (Sherman); *The Gal Who Took the West* (de Cordova); *Peggy* (de Cordova); *Impact* (Lubin)

1950　*Mr. Music* (Haydn); *Louisa* (Hall)

1951　*Oh Money, Money*; *The Highwayman* (Selander)

1952　*Has Anybody Seen My Gal?* (Sirk); *Monkey Business* (Hawks)

1953　*Trouble along the Way* (Curtiz); *Gentlemen Prefer Blondes* (Hawks)

1954　*The Rocket Man* (Rudolph); *The Long Wait* (Saville)

1955　*How to Be Very, Very Popular* (Johnson)

1956　*Around the World in Eighty Days* (Anderson); *The Power and the Prize* (Koster)

1957　*Town on Trial* (Guillermin); *The Story of Mankind* (Allen)

1958　*How to Murder a Rich Uncle* (Patrick)

1959　*Stranger in My Arms* (Kautner); *The Remarkable Mr. Pennypacker* (Levin); *John Paul Jones* (Farrow)

1960　*Pepe* (Sidney)

Publications

On COBURN: article—

Hicks, Jimmie, "Charles Coburn," in *Films in Review* (New York), May 1987.

*　　*　　*

A character can be the backbone of a motion picture, providing the familiar face we recognize even if we forget the name. Charles Coburn's portly body, with his jowly, thick-lipped face usually sporting a monocle and cigar, lent itself well to various film characterizations. Because of Coburn's physical appearance and gravelly voice one got the impression that he was a hard, overbearing personality, a person to be disliked. But this was not the case. Whether he was playing a hard-nosed businessman with a heart of gold, or a romantic, sophisticated elder gentleman, by the time the film was finished he had won the audience's heart. Coburn's characters could be gentle or stern, wise, worldly, perceptive, and romantic.

If one were to view all of Coburn's films the similarities would become quite evident. He was the stern but gentle father figure in *Together Again*, *Bachelor Mother*, and *Vivacious Lady*; he was the businessman with the heart of gold in *The Devil and Miss Jones* and *Has Anybody Seen My Gal*; he was the cynical businessman in *Made for Each Other* and *Louisa*. Though he typically played careermen, he could be a priest or politician or a college professor. In his characterizations there was a common thread: he was a manipulator—whether with good or bad motives he managed to take control of other people's lives. For instance, in *King's Row* he was a self-serving doctor who enjoyed playing God by controlling the lives of his family and their friends, taking this to the limits of selfishness by needlessly amputating the legs of his daughter's love interest, so she would no longer have the desire to marry the man. On the other hand, in *The More the Merrier* his manipulations were all well intended, as he played Cupid for Jean Arthur and Joel McCrea, not satisfied until the two were happily married. This Academy-Award-winning performance was a typical Coburn characterization.

—Maryann Oshana

COBURN, James

Nationality: American. **Born:** Laurel, Nebraska, 31 August 1928. **Education:** Studied acting at Los Angeles City College and University of Southern California; studied acting with Stella Adler in New York. **Military Service:** U.S. Army during World War II, served as radio operator. **Family:** Married Beverly Kelly, 1959, children: James IV and Lisa. **Career:** 1940s—stage debut at La Jolla Playhouse in *Billy Budd*; early 1950s—in television commercials and various live drama series including *Studio One*; 1959—film debut in *Ride Lonesome*; 1960s-1980s—formed production companies Panpiper, and later Armageddon Productions; 1960-61—in TV series *Klondike*, and *Acapulco*, 1961; 1977—began directing with episode of TV series *The Rockford Files*; 1978—in TV mini-series *The Dain Curse*; 1981-82— host of TV series *Darkroom*; 1992—in TV series *The Fifth Corner*. **Agent:** Special Artists, 335 North Maple Drive, #360, Beverly Hills, CA 90210, U.S.A.

Films as Actor:

1959　*Ride Lonesome* (Boetticher) (as Wid); *Face of a Fugitive* (Wendkos) (as Purdy)

1960　*The Magnificent Seven* (John Sturges) (as Britt)

1962　*Hell Is for Heroes* (Siegel) (as Cpl. Henshaw); *The Murder Men* (Peyser—for TV)

1963　*The Great Escape* (John Sturges) (as "The Manufacturer" Sedgwick); *Charade* (Donen) (as Tex Panthollow); *The Man from Galveston* (Conrad) (as Boyd Palmer)

1964　*The Americanization of Emily* (Hiller) (as Lt. Cmdr. "Bus" Cummings)

1965　*Major Dundee* (Peckinpah) (as Samuel Potts); *A High Wind in Jamaica* (Mackendrick) (as Zac); *The Loved One* (Richardson) (as immigration officer)

1966　*Our Man Flint* (Daniel Mann) (as Derek Flint); *What Did You Do in the War, Daddy?* (Edwards) (as Lt. Christian); *Dead Heat on a Merry-Go-Round* (Girard) (as Eli Kotch)

1967　*In Like Flint* (Gordon Douglas) (as Derek Flint); *Waterhole #3* (Graham) (as Lewton Cole); *The President's Analyst* (Flicker) (as Dr. Sidney Schaefer)

1968　*Duffy* (Parrish) (title role); *Candy* (Marquand) (as Dr. Krankeit)

1969　*Hard Contract* (Pogostin) (as John Cunningham); *Blood Kin* (*The Last of the Mobile Hot-Shots*) (Lumet)

1972   *Giù la testa* (*Duck, You Sucker!*; *A Fistful of Dynamite*) (Leone)
        (as Sean Mallory); *The Honkers* (Ihnat) (as Lew Lathrop);
        The Carey Treatment (Edwards) (as Peter Carey)

1973   *The Last of Sheila* (Ross) (as Clinton); *Pat Garrett and Billy
        the Kid* (Peckinpah) (as Pat Garrett); *Harry in Your Pocket*
        (*Harry Never Holds*) (Geller) (title role); *Una ragione per
        vivere e una per morire* (*A Reason to Live, a Reason to Die*;
        Massacre at Fort Holman) (Valerii) (as Col. Pembroke)

1974   *The Internecine Project* (Ken Hughes) (as Robert Elliot)

1975   *Bite the Bullet* (Richard Brooks) (as Luke Matthews); *Hard Times*
        (*The Streetfighter*) (Walter Hill) (as Spencer "Speed" Weed)

1976   *Sky Riders* (Hickox) (as Jim McCabe); *Midway* (*The Battle of
        Midway*) (Smight) (as Capt. Vinton Maddox); *The Last Hard
        Men* (McLagen) (as Zach Provo); *White Rock* (Maylam) (as
        narrator); *A Fast Drive in the Country: The Heydays of Le
        Mans* (Maylam) (as narrator)

1977   *Cross of Iron* (Peckinpah) (as Steiner)

1979   *Firepower* (Winner) (as Jerry Fanon/Eddie); *The Muppet Movie*
        (Frawley) (as El Sleezo Cafe Owner); *Goldengirl* (Sargent)
        (as Jack Dryden)

1980   *Mr. Patman* (Guillermin) (title role); *Loving Couples* (Smight)
        (as Walter); *The Baltimore Bullet* (Robert Ellis Miller) (as
        Nick Casey)

1981   *High Risk* (Raffill) (as Serrano); *Looker* (Michael Crichton)
        (as John Reston); *Jacqueline Susann's Valley of the Dolls*
        (*Valley of the Dolls*) (Grauman—for TV) (as Henry Bellamy)

1983   *Malibu* (Swackhamer—for TV); *Digital Dreams* (Dornhelm)

1984   *Draw!* (Steven Hilliard Stern—for TV) (as Sam Starret)

1985   *Martin's Day* (Alan Gibson) (as Lt. Lardner); *Sins of the Fa-
        ther* (Sinkel—for TV) (as Frank Murchison)

1986   *Death of a Soldier* (Mora) (as Maj. Patrick Danneberg);
        Mackendrick (Quarrie—for TV)

1988   *Walking after Midnight* (Kay)

1989   *Place of Skulls* (Logan—for TV); *Tag till Himlen* (Anderberg);
        Call from Space (Fleischer)

1990   *Young Guns II* (Murphy) (as John Chisum)

1991   *Hudson Hawk* (Lehmann) (as George Kaplan); *Helicon* (Eng)

1992   **The Player** (Altman) (as himself); *Hugh Hefner: Once upon a
        Time* (Heath—doc) (as narrator); *Crash Landing: The Res-
        cue of Flight 232* (*A Thousand Heroes*) (Lamont Johnson—
        for TV) (as Jim Hathaway)

1993   *Sister Act 2: Back in the Habit* (Duke) (as Mr. Crisp); *Deadfall*
        (Christopher Coppola) (as Mike Donan); *The Hit List*
        (Webb—for TV) (as Peter Mayhew)

1994   *Ray Alexander: A Taste for Justice* (Gary Nelson—for TV) (as
        Jeffrey Winslow); *Greyhounds* (Manners—for TV) (as John
        Dolan); *A Christmas Reunion* (as Santa Claus); *Maverick*
        (Richard Donner) (as Commodore)

1995   *The Set Up* (as Jeremia Cole); *The Avenging Angel* (Baxley—
        for TV) (as Porter Rockwell); *Ray Alexander: A Menu for
        Murder* (Gary Nelson—for TV) (as Jeffrey Winslow)

1996   *Eraser* (Chuck Russell)

Other Films:

1978   *Convoy* (Peckinpah) (second unit d)
1979   *Circle of Iron* (*The Silent Flute*) (Richard Moore) (co-story)

Publications

By COBURN: articles—

"James Coburn on Acting, Directors, Hollywood, and the Movies," inter-
    view with C. L. Hanson, in *Cinema* (Beverly Hills), December 1965.

"James Coburn: His Life and *Hard Times*," interview with J. Leydon,
    in *Take One* (Montreal), December 1975.
"Becoming Involved," interview with G. Gow, in *Films and Filming*
    (London), November 1978.

On COBURN: articles—

"Cool Killer," in *Films Illustrated* (London), September 1974.
Ecran (Paris), May 1978.
Ciné Revue (Paris), 10 November 1983.
Goodman, Mark, "Return of Our Man Flint," in *People Weekly* (New
    York), 17 June 1991.
"Silver Fox," in *Variety* (New York), 15 July 1991.

*   *   *

As the movies of the 1960s became more sexually explicit and
graphically violent, they required different types of stars than the
glamorously good-looking ones of the old studio system. In particular,
male stars had to look convincing and comfortable in rugged situations, and actors such as James Coburn, Clint Eastwood, Steve McQueen,
and Lee Marvin gained popularity during this period.

Coburn began his film career with supporting roles in that most
American genre, the Western, and found much success playing quiet
and usually deadly gunslingers. His poised, laconic knife thrower in
The Magnificent Seven brought him much attention. His later role as
the scout in Sam Peckinpah's *Major Dundee* and the sheriff in the
same director's *Pat Garrett and Billy the Kid* are refined and more
mature versions of his early Western roles for such directors as Budd
Boetticher. As Garrett, Coburn is still quiet, but his face is worn and his
whole manner suggests wearily gained experience. He brought the
same qualities to his performance as the battle-hardened Steiner in
Peckinpah's grim World War II opus *Cross of Iron*. Coburn's association with Peckinpah, a close friend as well as a filmmaker the actor
particularly admired, extended to Coburn's taking over some of the
directorial chores on Peckinpah's modern day Western *Convoy* when
Peckinpah's alcoholism, drug taking, and other eccentricities rendered
him incapable of carrying on.

Coburn branched out from the Western action film by playing an
American hero different from the strong silent type. His roles in
Dead Heat on a Merry-Go-Round, *Harry in Your Pocket*, and *Hard
Times* were as talkative con men and hustlers. Coburn's pace, so restrained and controlled in the Westerns, is in high gear in these films.
Words fly out of his mouth at such speed that one can barely keep
up, let alone understand the plans, logic, or details being given. The
gangster film *Hard Contract*, in which Coburn appeared as a hit
man, made use of these same qualities, but the film turned out a
pretentious talkathon, rather than the intellectual thriller it was
intended to be.

Coburn is not limited to these basic types. Audiences have accepted
him in roles that placed him in operating rooms, gambling casinos,
and even a boxing gym. His versatility has allowed him to resist being
typecast as an action hero, and Coburn's career is noteworthy for
balancing lead and character parts. The common denominator of his
roles is the character's air of confidence, often coupled with sophistication. This characteristic combination is probably at the root of his
success in comic roles which are often parodies of his serious ones.
Much like Marvin in *Cat Ballou*, Coburn can reprise the serious types
he has successfully portrayed, playing them for laughs. One of his
most popular films, *In Like Flint*, displays this ability. Derek Flint, ace
of spies, deftly conquers every obstacle and villain. His victories are
achieved so easily that the battles become humorous. This effortlessness must be accepted by the audience, and it is here that the confidence and sophistication come into play, as Coburn makes saving the
world look like a relaxed weekend romp in the tropics.

Of late, the actor has appeared mostly on television. But as the Western began to make another of its short-lived comebacks following the success of Costner's *Dances with Wolves* and Eastwood's *Unforgiven*, Coburn returned to the big screen—and to the genre in which he had made his name—in Donner's *Maverick*, a bloated homage to the classic television series, appearing along with many other movie and television Western stars of the past in a cameo role.

—Ray Narducy, updated by John McCarty

COLBERT, Claudette

Nationality: American. **Born:** Claudette Lily Chauchoin in Paris, France, 13 September 1903. **Education:** Attended Washington Irving High School, New York, graduated 1923; studied briefly at Art Students League, New York. **Family:** Married 1) the actor Norman Foster, 1928 (divorced 1935); 2) Dr. Joel J. Pressman, 1935 (died 1968). **Career:** 1912—family moved to New York; 1923—met playwright Anne Morrison, offered bit part in her *The Wild Westcotts*; changed name to Colbert; 1925-26—on Broadway in *A Kiss in a Taxi*; 1927—first film role, for Paramount at Astoria studios; 1929—first talkie, *The Hole in the Wall*; Paramount contract; 1944—terminated Paramount contract; 1952-55—worked in European films and theater; 1956—replaced Margaret Sullavan in Broadway production of *Janus*; occasional stage appearances: with Rex Harrison on Broadway in *The Kingfisher*, 1978, and in London and New York in *Aren't We All?*, 1984-85; 1984—tribute staged by Film Society of Lincoln Center; 1987—in TV mini-series *The Two Mrs. Grenvilles*. **Awards:** Best Actress Academy Award, for *It Happened One Night*, 1934. **Died:** In Barbados, 30 July 1996.

Films as Actress:

1927 *For the Love of Mike* (Capra) (as Mary)
1929 *The Hole in the Wall* (Florey) (as Jean Oliver); *The Lady Lies* (Henley) (as Joyce Roamer)
1930 *The Big Pond* (Henley) (as Barbara Billings); *La Grande Mare* (Henley—French version of *The Big Pond*); *Young Man of Manhattan* (Bell) (as Ann Vaughn); *Manslaughter* (Abbott) (as Lydia Thorne); *L'Enigmatique Monsieur Parkes* (Gasnier—French version of *Slightly Scarlet*) (as Lucy de Stavrin)
1931 *Honor among Lovers* (Arzner) (as Julia Traynor); *The Smiling Lieutenant* (Lubitsch) (as Franzi); *Le Lieutenant souriant* (Lubitsch—French version of *The Smiling Lieutenant*); *Secrets of a Secretary* (Abbott) (as Helen Blake); *His Woman* (Sloman) (as Sally Clark)
1932 *The Wiser Sex* (Viertel) (as Margaret Hughes); *The Misleading Lady* (Walker) (as Helen Steele); *The Man from Yesterday* (Viertel) (as Sylvia Suffolk); *Phantom President* (Taurog) (as Felicia Hammond); *The Sign of the Cross* (Cecil B. DeMille) (as Empress Poppaea); *Make Me a Star* (Beaudine) (as guest star)
1933 *Tonight Is Ours* (Walker) (as Princess Nadja); *I Cover the Waterfront* (Cruze) (as Julie Kirk); *Three-Cornered Moon* (Nugent) (as Elizabeth Rimplegar); *Torch Singer* (*Broadway Singer*) (Hall and Somnes) (as Sally Trent/Mimi Barton)
1934 *Four Frightened People* (Cecil B. DeMille) (as Judy Cavendish); **It Happened One Night** (Capra) (as Ellie Andrews); *Cleopatra* (Cecil B. DeMille) (title role); *Imitation of Life* (Stahl) (as Beatrice Pullman)

1935 *The Gilded Lily* (Ruggles) (as Lillian David); *Private Worlds* (La Cava) (as Dr. Jane Everest); *She Married Her Boss* (La Cava) (as Julia Scott); *The Bride Comes Home* (Ruggles) (as Jeanette Desmereau)
1936 *Under Two Flags* (Lloyd) (as Cigarette)
1937 *Maid of Salem* (Lloyd) (as Barbara Clarke); *I Met Him in Paris* (Ruggles) (as Kay Denham); *Tovarich* (Litvak) (as Grand Duchess Tatiana Petrovna)
1938 *Bluebeard's Eighth Wife* (Lubitsch) (as Nicole de Loiselle)
1939 *Zaza* (Cukor) (title role); *Midnight* (Leisen) (as Eve Peabody/ "Baroness Czerny"); *It's a Wonderful World* (Van Dyke) (as Edwina Corday); *Drums along the Mohawk* (Ford) (as Lana "Magdelana" Martin)
1940 *Boom Town* (Conway) (as Betsy Bartlett); *Arise My Love* (Leisen) (as Augusta Nash)
1941 *Skylark* (Sandrich) (as Lydia Kenyon); *Remember the Day* (Henry King) (as Nora Trinell)
1942 *The Palm Beach Story* (Preston Sturges) (as Gerry Jeffers); *Hedda Hopper's Hollywood No. 6*
1943 *So Proudly We Hail* (Sandrich) (as Lt. Janet Davidson); *No Time for Love* (Leisen) (as Katherine Grant)
1944 *Since You Went Away* (Cromwell) (as Anne Hilton); *Practically Yours* (Leisen) (as Peggy Martin)
1945 *Guest Wife* (Wood) (as Mary)
1946 *Tomorrow Is Forever* (Pichel) (as Elizabeth MacDonald Hamilton); *Without Reservations* (LeRoy) (as Christopher "Kit" Madden); *The Secret Heart* (Leonard) (as Lee Addams)
1947 *The Egg and I* (Erskine) (as Betty MacDonald)
1948 *Sleep, My Love* (Sirk) (as Alison Courtland); *Family Honeymoon* (Binyon) (as Katie Armstrong Jordan)
1949 *Bride for Sale* (William D. Russell) (as Nora Shelly)
1950 *Three Came Home* (Negulesco) (as Agnes Keith); *The Secret Fury* (Mel Ferrer) (as Ellen)
1951 *Thunder on the Hill* (*Bonaventure*) (Sirk) (as Sister Mary Bonaventure); *Let's Make It Legal* (Sale) (as Miriam Halsworth)
1952 *The Planter's Wife* (*Outpost in Malaya*) (Annakin) (as Liz Frazer)
1953 *Si Versailles m'était conté* (*Affairs in Versailles*; *Royal Affairs in Versailles*) (Guitry) (as Mme. de Montespan)
1954 "Elizabeth" ep. of *Destinées* (*Daughters of Destiny*; *Love, Soldiers and Women*; *Lysistrata*) (Pagliero) (as Elizabeth I)
1955 *Texas Lady* (Whelan) (as Prudence Webb)
1960 *Parrish* (Daves) (as Ellen McLean)
1986 *Three Came Home* (Negulesco—for TV)

Publications

By COLBERT: article—

Interview in *Films* (London), August 1984.

On COLBERT: books—

Everson, William K., *Claudette Colbert*, New York, 1976.
Quirk, Lawrence J., *Claudette Colbert: An Illustrated Biography*, New York, 1985.

On COLBERT: articles—

Pacheco, Joseph B., Jr., "Claudette Colbert," in *Films in Review* (New York), May 1970.
Scott, Allan, "Claudette Colbert: Broadway Belle," in *Close-Ups: The Movie Star Book*, edited by Danny Peary, New York, 1978.

Claudette Colbert with Clark Gable in *It Happened One Night*

Shipman, David, in *The Great Movie Stars: The Golden Years*, rev. ed., London, 1979.

Harvey, S., "Legs," in *Film Comment* (New York), March/April 1984.

Sigal, Clancy, "Claudette in Control," in *Listener* (London), 26 April 1984.

National Film Theatre Booklet (London), July 1984.

Denby, David, "A Tale of Two Sillies," in *Premiere* (New York), June 1990.

Dudar, H., "Claudette Colbert Revels in a Happy, Starry Past," in *New York Times*, 27 October 1991.

"90th Birthday for Claudette Colbert," in *New York Times*, 15 September 1993.

Cohen, Meg, "*It Happened One Night*: Actress Claudette Colbert Reminisces on Film with Clark Gable," in *Harper's Bazaar* (New York), January 1994.

* * *

Claudette Colbert is the epitome of Hollywood glamour, but not the glamour that comes bolstered by furs and feathers like Dietrich's or by mystery and aloneness like Garbo's. Colbert's glamour is the sort that women attain for themselves by using their intelligence to create a timeless personal style. It is an attainable kind of glamour, but only if one has the natural gifts of brains and beauty associated with Colbert.

Colbert is most often remembered for her expert comic timing, which was displayed in a series of screwball comedies she made throughout the 1930s and 1940s, chief among them her Academy Award-winning performance in Frank Capra's *It Happened One Night*. In that film, Colbert took out a patent on the runaway heiress character, and anyone else who played such a role did so in her shadow. All her comedies present her as a well-dressed modern woman who can handle any situation. *Midnight* opens on a rainy night in which a train pulls into a Paris station, bearing Colbert, asleep, in a third-class coach. She is without funds, without luggage, and without contacts, but she is nevertheless wearing a fabulous silver lamé evening gown. She wakes up, picks the straw out of her hair, and steps confidently out into the lousy weather, her wits sharp and her wardrobe up to whatever social advantage she can promote. This illustrates a typical Colbert comedy character—the woman of resource, humor, style, and, above all else, confidence.

Despite her association with comedy, Colbert played a wide range of roles. Her versatility is seldom commented on, but it is reflected in her other two Oscar nominations: for her role as a psychiatrist in *Private Worlds*, and as a wartime wife in *Since You Went Away*. She appeared in mysteries, costume dramas, melodramas, musicals, and epics. She portrayed everyone from Cleopatra to a modern egg farmer, a villainess to a maid of Salem, an authoress to a nun. Whatever the role, her grace and timing always prevented her from seeming to be humiliated or defeated. Thus, she could endure a prison camp, as in *Three Came Home*, go out of control on a bobsled in *I Met Him in Paris*, or fall about in a ship's galley while trying to fry a fish in *Skylark*, without ever seeming to lose her ladylike grace. This quality, coupled with her delicate features, might have doomed her to stuffy roles had she not also projected a genuine warmth, enhanced by an unforgettable laugh, a delicious speaking voice, and a sparkling quality that humanized her.

At first Colbert planned to become a fashion designer, but a growing interest in dramatics led her to Broadway. She became respected and popular primarily as a result of her 1927 performance as a carnival snake charmer in *The Barker*, a success which led inevitably to a film career. Her first big hit was as the seductress, Empress Poppaea, in Cecil B. DeMille's *The Sign of the Cross*, and she might have become typed as a villainess had she not been assigned to *It Happened One Night*.

Colbert became known in Hollywood for her shrewd business sense, and the successful direction of her career is said to be largely due to her own good instincts. She left the comforts of a Paramount contract after appearing in *Practically Yours* in 1944, and spent the rest of her Hollywood years as a freelance artist. Her one big career disappointment was due to an illness which forced her to step out of the leading role in *All about Eve*, which then went to Bette Davis. Otherwise Colbert maintained a steady pace until she chose to retire after playing a mother in *Parrish*. Although that remains her last feature film, she found continuing popularity and acceptance in the theater, having returned to leading roles in New York and London. After a 25-year hiatus from movies, she gave a heralded performance in the television mini-series *The Two Mrs. Grenvilles*, playing the matriarch of a socially prominent family.

Claudette Colbert is the sort of actress whose best qualities were those that the passage of time could not date or diminish: a sense of wit, a core of strength, and, above all, a strong projection of intelligence. Had she been only a clotheshorse, or a model of whatever glamorous style was currently in fashion, she would not have lasted. Yet her good looks, slim figure, and timeless chic endured over seven decades of work in film and theater. She herself said it best, "I don't need that awful artificial glamour that Hollywood devises for people who don't have any personalities." Colbert's ability to create her own brand of glamour helped her outlast many of her less self-sufficient contemporaries.

—Jeanine Basinger, updated by Audrey E. Kupferberg

COLMAN, Ronald

Nationality: British. **Born:** Richmond, Surrey, 9 February 1891. **Education:** Attended London University. **Family:** Married 1) the actress Thelma Victoria Maud, 1918 (divorced 1935); 2) the actress Benita Hume, 1938, daughter: Julia Benita Colman. **Military Service:** Served with London Scottish during World War I; wounded at Messines and decorated with Mons medal, invalided out of service. **Career:** 1908—office boy with British Steamship Company while performing with Bancroft Amateur Dramatic Society; 1916-20—on London stage; 1919—feature film debut in *The Toilers*; 1920—emigrated to America and appeared in various stage roles, including small part with George Arliss in *The Green Goddess*; 1923—chosen by Lillian Gish as leading man in film *The White Sister*; 1924—invited to Hollywood by Samuel Goldwyn; early 1930s—star status acknowledged when Goldwyn allows him luxury of making only one film per year; 1933—sued Goldwyn for false publicity concerning rumors of his drinking on set of *The Masquerader*; 1940s—began working on radio, including regular guest spots with wife Benita Hume on Jack Benny's program; 1950-52—starred with Benita Hume in radio series *The Halls of Ivy*, and in TV series, 1954-55. **Awards:** Best Actor Academy Award, for *A Double Life*, 1947. **Died:** In Santa Barbara, California, 19 May 1958.

Films as Actor:

1917   *The Live Wire* (Dewhurst—short, never released)
1919   *The Toilers* (Watts) (as Bob); *A Daughter of Eve* (Walter West); *Sheba* (Hepworth); *Snow in the Desert* (Walter West) (as Rupert Sylvester)
1920   *A Son of David* (Plumb) (as Maurice Phillips); *Anna the Adventuress* (Hepworth) (as Walter Brendan); *The Black Spider* (Humphrey) (as Vicomte de Beauvais)
1921   *Handcuffs or Kisses?* (Archainbaud) (as Lodyard)

1923   *The White Sister* (Henry King) (as Capt. Giovanni Severi); *The Eternal City* (Fitzmaurice)

1924   *$20 a Week* (Weight) (as Chester Reeves); *Tarnish* (Fitzmaurice) (as Emmet Carr); *Romola* (Henry King) (as Carlo Bucellini)

1925   *Her Night of Romance* (Franklin) (as Paul Menford); *A Thief in Paradise* (Fitzmaurice) (as Maurice Blake); *The Sporting Venus* (Neilan) (as Donald MacAllan); *His Supreme Moment* (Fitzmaurice) (as John Douglas); *Her Sister from Paris* (Franklin) (as Joseph Weyringer); *The Dark Angel* (Fitzmaurice) (as Capt. Alan Trent); *Stella Dallas* (Henry King) (as Stephen Dallas); *Lady Windermere's Fan* (Lubitsch) (as Lord Darlington)

1926   *Kiki* (Clarence Brown) (as Victor Renal); *Beau Geste* (Brenon) (as Michael "Beau" Geste); *The Winning of Barbara Worth* (Henry King) (as Willard Holmes)

1927   *The Night of Love* (Fitzmaurice) (as Montero); *The Magic Flame* (Henry King) (as Tito the Clown/Cassati the Count)

1928   *Two Lovers* (Niblo) (as Mark Van Rycke)

1929   *The Rescue* (Brenon) (as Tom Lingard); *Bulldog Drummond* (F. Richard Jones) (title role); *Condemned!* (Ruggles) (as Michel Auban)

1930   *Raffles* (Fitzmaurice and d'Arrast) (as A. J. Raffles); *The Devil to Pay* (Fitzmaurice) (as Willie Hale)

1931   *The Unholy Garden* (Fitzmaurice) (as Barrington Hunt); *Arrowsmith* (John Ford) (as Dr. Martin Arrowsmith)

1932   *Cynara* (*I Was Faithless*) (King Vidor) (as Jim Warlock)

1933   *The Masquerader* (Wallace) (as Sir John Chilcote/John Loder)

1934   *Bulldog Drummond Strikes Back* (Del Ruth) (as Hugh Drummond)

1935   *Clive of India* (Boleslawski) (as Robert Clive); *The Man Who Broke the Bank at Monte Carlo* (Roberts) (as Paul Gallard); *A Tale of Two Cities* (Conway) (as Sydney Carton)

1936   *Under Two Flags* (Lloyd) (as Sgt. Victor)

1937   *Lost Horizon* (Capra) (as Robert Conway); *The Prisoner of Zenda* (Cromwell) (as Rudolf Rassendyll/King Rudolph V)

1938   *If I Were King* (Lloyd) (as François Villon)

1939   *The Light that Failed* (Wellman) (as Dick Heldar)

1940   *Lucky Partners* (Milestone) (as David Grant/Paul Knight Somerset)

1941   *My Life with Caroline* (Milestone) (as Anthony Mason)

1942   *The Talk of the Town* (Stevens) (as Michael Lightcap); *Random Harvest* (LeRoy) (as Charles Rainier/John "Smithy" Smith)

1944   *Kismet* (*Oriental Dream*) (Dieterle) (as Hafiz)

1947   *The Late George Apley* (Joseph L. Mankiewicz) (title role); *A Double Life* (Cukor) (as Anthony John)

1950   *Champagne for Caesar* (Whorf) (as Beauregard Bottomley); *Shakespeare's Theater: The Globe Playhouse* (W. and M. Jordan) (as narrator)

1956   *Around the World in Eighty Days* (Anderson) (as railway official)

1957   *The Story of Mankind* (Irwin Allen) (as Spirit of Man)

Publications

On COLMAN: books—

Griffith, Richard, *Samuel Goldwyn: The Producer and His Films*, New York, 1956.

Colman, Juliet Benita, *Ronald Colman: A Very Private Person*, New York, 1975.

Quirk, Lawrence J., *The Films of Ronald Colman*, Secaucus, New Jersey, 1977.

Smith, R. Dixon, *Ronald Colman, Gentleman of the Cinema: A Biography and Filmography*, Jefferson, North Carolina, 1991.

On COLMAN: articles—

Current Biography 1943, New York, 1943.

Jacobs, Jack, "Ronald Colman," in *Films in Review* (New York), April 1958.

Obituary in *New York Times*, 20 May 1958.

Richards, Jeffrey, "Ronald Colman and the Cinema of Empire," in *Focus on Film* (London), September/October 1970.

Fox, Julian, in *Films and Filming* (London), March and April 1972.

Wyatt, Jane, "Ronald Colman: Elegant Englishman," in *Close-Ups: The Movie Star Book*, edited by Danny Peary, New York, 1978.

Films and Filming (London), April 1983.

The Listener (London), 15 March 1984.

*   *   *

Suave, debonair, a gentleman hero with dashing good looks, Ronald Colman is the quintessential Hollywood-Englishman. One of the few stars of the silent era to maintain and even increase their popularity after the transition to sound, Colman was a leading man for more than 20 years, for in addition to his handsome grace, Colman possessed a beautifully cultured and modulated voice. Colman is known for roles where he is above all polite and well-mannered, but the source of his success may lie beyond his ability to portray characters who are refined but sentimental, mysterious but thoughtful. As Sheridan Morley points out, Colman's sense of humor made him stand out from other good-looking Englishmen. Moreover, Colman was a consummate craftsman; director George Cukor explains that Colman knew more about acting for the camera than any actor he had worked with.

Colman began with small parts in the theater. His (silent) film career received its greatest impetus in the two films he made with Lillian Gish, *The White Sister* and *Romola*. Handsome, graceful, exuding good nature, he complemented Gish, and demonstrated the magnetism that captured the public in subsequent starring vehicles such as *The Dark Angel* and *Beau Geste*. Reviewers of the time noted that Colman was stepping into the shoes of Rudolph Valentino and John Gilbert.

Colman's first sound film, *Bulldog Drummond*, for which he received an Academy Award nomination, might be a surprise to viewers who know the actor primarily for his later films, because he races through this rather madcap detective story with a verve and athleticism that recall Douglas Fairbanks, and his dialogue delivery matches the humor and panache of his physical presence. That same vibrant intensity informs his portrayal of Robert Clive's rise from office boy to British officer in *Clive of India*.

By the mid-1930s, Colman's performances in such films as *Clive of India*, *Arrowsmith*, *A Tale of Two Cities*, *Lost Horizon*, *The Prisoner of Zenda* had made him one of the most popular male stars in Hollywood. Sought after for "important" pictures, Colman played the selfless hero and the noble Englishman in film after film. In *A Tale of Two Cities*, Colman comforts Elizabeth Allan on the way to the guillotine, richly atoning, "It is a far, far better thing I do"; in *Lost Horizon* he incarnates the idealism of author James Hilton and director Frank Capra.

There was no diminution of Colman's romantic appeal in the 1940s. Exemplary of MGM's Anglophilia, *Random Harvest* proved to be one of the most popular films of the war years, and it united Colman with a particularly congenial co-star, Greer Garson. Colman's star image, in part that of the Englishman who is reserved to the point of shyness, contributes to the film, as do his intelligent choices in representing Smithy/Rainier—Colman conveys the profound impact of finally, suddenly recognizing Paula's voice as the voice of his long-lost love in one simple move: with his back to us, he simply raises his head.

A Double Life, the film for which Colman received an Academy Award, is an intriguing commentary on acting, and, in particular, the performances of a star such as Colman, a "movie" actor par excellence, who in this film plays a "legitimate" actor who becomes so immersed in the role of Othello that he is pushed to murder. Here, Colman, the dashing romantic lead, is measured against one of the great tragic roles in the Western tradition. Our sense of Colman having a go at Shakespeare is fully tested twice in the film: on opening night, when his style is conventionally theatrical, and near the end, when he replays the same scene, prey to guilt and madness, in rhythms and tones that are decidedly cinematic. The film suggests that Colman, and others like him, depend on their charm, wit, grace, but that they labor, sometimes even to their own detriment to be "good actors." The film not only plays on Colman's star image, it also provides an occasion for us to see the actor at the height of his craft, for Colman's meticulous preparation and execution is apparent even in small scenes. Early in the film, as the character recalls how he had already come a long way with his ambition, Colman caricatures the juvenile in tennis shorts "he" used to be, then performs a remembered scene with "his father," then comes back to "himself" as he remembers having to teach himself how to talk, how to move, how to think. Like so many scenes in Colman's career, it is a passage of seamless virtuosity.

In the 1950s, Colman turned in a marvelously funny portrayal of a television quiz show sensation in *Champagne for Caesar*, co-starred in a radio series, "Halls of Ivy," the Best New Radio Show for 1950, and moved to television with the series which was named Best New Television Show for 1954.

—Charles Affron, updated by Cynthia Baron

CONNERY, Sean

Nationality: British. **Born:** Thomas Connery in Edinburgh, Scotland, 25 August 1930. **Education:** Attended Edinburgh School of Art. **Family:** Married 1) the actress Diane Cilento, 1962 (divorced 1973), children: Jason and Giovana; 2) Micheline Roquebrun, 1975, stepson: Stefan. **Career:** 1945—in Royal Navy but discharged because of ulcers; late 1940s-early 1950s—bodybuilder and model; 1951-53—toured in chorus of *South Pacific*; mid-1950s—gained acting experience in repertory theater; 1955—first film, *Lilacs in the Spring*; contract with 20th Century-Fox the following year; 1957-62—in small and featured roles in non-Fox productions; 1962—first appearance as James Bond; 1969—directed unreleased documentary film *The Bowler and the Bonnet*; 1972—formed production company Tantallon Productions. **Awards:** Academy Award for Best Supporting Actor, and D. W. Griffith Award, for *The Untouchables*, 1987; British Academy of Film and Television Arts Award for Best Actor, for *The Name of the Rose*, 1986; Légion d'honneur (France); Cecil B. DeMille Lifetime Achievement Award, Hollywood Foreign Press Association, 1995. **Agent:** Creative Artists Agency, 9830 Wilshire Boulevard, Beverly Hills, CA 90212, U.S.A.

Films as Actor:

1955   *Lilacs in the Spring* (*Let's Make Up*) (Wilcox) (bit part)
1956   *No Road Back* (Tully) (as Spike)
1957   *Hell Drivers* (Endfield) (as Johnny); *Time Lock* (Thomas) (as welder); *Action of the Tiger* (Terence Young) (as Mike)
1958   *Another Time, Another Place* (Lewis Allen) (as Mark Trevor); *A Night to Remember* (Baker)
1959   *Darby O'Gill and the Little People* (Stevenson) (as Michael McBride); *Tarzan's Greatest Adventure* (Guillermin) (as O'Bannion)

1961   *The Frightened City* (Lemont) (as Paddy Damion); *On the Fiddle* (*Operation Snafu*) (Frankel) (as Pedlar Pascoe)
1962   *The Longest Day* (Annakin, Marton, Wicki, and Zanuck) (as Pvt. Flanagan); *Dr. No* (Terence Young) (as James Bond)
1963   *From Russia with Love* (Terence Young) (as James Bond)
1964   *Woman of Straw* (Dearden) (as Anthony Richmond); **Marnie** (Hitchcock) (as Mark Rutland); *Goldfinger* (Hamilton) (as James Bond)
1965   *The Hill* (Lumet) (as Joe Roberts); *Thunderball* (Terence Young) (as James Bond)
1966   *A Fine Madness* (Kershner) (as Samson Shillitoe)
1967   *You Only Live Twice* (Lewis Gilbert) (as James Bond)
1968   *Shalako* (Dmytryk) (title role)
1969   *The Molly McGuires* (Ritt) (as Jack Kehoe); *La tenda rossa* (*The Red Tent*) (Kalatozov) (as Amundsen)
1971   *The Anderson Tapes* (Lumet) (as Duke Anderson); *Diamonds Are Forever* (Hamilton) (as James Bond)
1972   *The Offence* (Lumet) (as Johnson)
1973   *Zardoz* (Boorman) (as Zed)
1974   *The Terrorists* (*Ransom*) (Wrede) (as Nils Tahlvik); *Murder on the Orient Express* (Lumet) (as Col. Arbuthnott)
1975   *The Wind and the Lion* (Milius) (as Mulay El Raisuli); *The Man Who Would Be King* (Huston) (as Daniel Dravot)
1976   *Robin and Marian* (Lester) (as Robin Hood); *The Next Man* (Serafian) (as Khalif Abdul-Muhsen)
1977   *A Bridge Too Far* (Attenborough) (as Maj. Gen. Urquhart)
1978   *The Great Train Robbery* (*The First Great Train Robbery*) (Michael Crichton) (as Edward Pierce)
1979   *Meteor* (Neame) (as Bradley); *Cuba* (Lester) (as Robert Dapes)
1981   *Time Bandits* (Gilliam) (as King Agamemnon); *Outland* (Hyams) (as O'Neil)
1982   *Wrong Is Right* (*The Man with the Deadly Lens*) (Richard Brooks) (as Patrick Hale); *Five Days One Summer* (Zinnemann—re-edited version released 1988) (as Douglas)
1983   *Never Say Never Again* (Kershner) (as James Bond); *Sword of the Valiant* (Weeks) (as the Green Knight)
1986   *Highlander* (Mulcahy) (as Ramirez); *The Name of the Rose* (*Rosa dei nomi*) (Annaud) (as William of Baskerville)
1987   *The Untouchables* (De Palma) (as James Malone)
1988   *The Presidio* (Hyams) (as Lt. Col. Alan Caldwell); *Memories of Me* (Henry Winkler) (as himself)
1989   *Family Business* (Lumet) (as Jessie McMullen); *Indiana Jones and the Last Crusade* (Spielberg) (as Professor Henry Jones)
1990   *The Russia House* (Schepisi) (as Barley Blair); *The Hunt for Red October* (McTiernan) (as Marko Ramius)
1991   *Robin Hood: Prince of Thieves* (Kevin Reynolds) (as King Richard); *Highlander II* (Mulcahy) (as Ramirez)
1992   *Medicine Man* (McTiernan) (as Dr. Robert Campbell, + exec pr)
1993   *Rising Sun* (Kaufman) (as John Connor, + exec pr)
1994   *A Good Man in Africa* (Beresford) (as Dr. Alex Murray)
1995   *Just Cause* (Glimcher) (as Paul Armstrong, + exec pr); *First Knight* (Zucker) (as King Arthur)
1996   *Dragonheart* (Cohen) (as voice of Draco); *The Rock* (Bay)

Publications

By CONNERY: articles—

Interview in *Playboy* (Chicago), November 1965.
"A Secretive Person," interview with G. Gow, in *Films and Filming* (London), March 1974.
Interviews in *Ciné Revue* (Paris), 3 September 1981 and 24 November 1983.

Interview with Ben Fong-Torres, in *American Film* (Hollywood), May 1989.

"Leading Man," interview with Robert Walsh, in *Interview* (New York), July 1989.

"Back in the USSR," interview with Robert Scheer, in *Premiere* (New York), April 1990.

"Straight Talk," interview with John H. Richardson, in *Premiere* (New York), February 1992.

"Great Scot," interview with Zoe Heller, in *Vanity Fair* (New York), June 1993.

On CONNERY: books—

Andrews, Emma, *The Films of Sean Connery*, Farncombe, Surrey, 1977.

Brosnan, John, *James Bond in the Cinema*, San Diego, 1981.

Rubin, Steven Jay, *The James Bond Films*, Westport, Connecticut, 1981.

Callan, Michael Feeney, *Sean Connery*, New York, 1983; rev. ed., 1993.

Passingham, Kenneth, *Sean Connery: A Biography*, London, 1983.

Durant, Philippe, *Sean Connery*, Paris, 1985.

Dupuis, Jean-Jacques, *Sean Connery*, Paris, 1986.

Sellers, Robert, *The Films of Sean Connery*, London, 1990.

Tanitch, Robert, *Sean Connery*, London, 1992.

Yule, Andrew, *Sean Connery: From 007 to Hollywood Icon*, New York, 1992.

Hunter, John, *Great Scot: The Life of Sean Connery*, London, 1993.

Parker, John, *Sean Connery*, Chicago, 1993.

Pfeiffer, Lee, and Philip Lisa, *The Films of Sean Connery*, Secaucus, New Jersey, 1993.

Freedland, Michael, *Sean Connery: A Biography*, London, 1994.

On CONNERY: articles—

Houston, Penelope, "007," in *Sight and Sound* (London), Winter 1964-65.

Crichton, Michael, "Sean Connery: A Propensity for Stylish Mayhem," in *Close-Ups: The Movie Star Book*, edited by Danny Peary, New York, 1978.

Films Illustrated (London), October 1981.

Photoplay (London), January 1984.

"Sean Connery," in *From Limelight to Satellite: A Scottish Film Book*, edited by Eddie Dick, London, 1990.

Jones, A., "Sean Connery's Superstar Clout," in *Cinefantastique* (Oak Park, Illinois), vol. 21, no. 5, 1991.

Current Biography 1993, New York, 1993.

Curreri, J., "Older, Sexier Sean Connery," in *Classic Images* (Muscatine, Iowa), January 1993.

*   *   *

"When asked what he would like as an epitaph," Lee Pfeiffer and Philip Lisa state, "Connery replied, 'I'd like to be an old man with a good face—like Picasso or Hitchcock.' " Indeed, Connery's striking good looks seem to increase as he ages. So does his fame and fortune. Most remembered as "James Bond, 007," and bringing to the screen a physical toughness (he was once a Mr. Universe contestant) oddly coupled with savvy, upper-class refinement and confident, sexual appeal, Connery as star has never been short of labels such as "the sexiest man in the world." It is hardly believable now that he once was mockingly referred to by some American film executives when first chosen to star in *Dr. No* as "the truck driver." Steven Jay Rubin atttributes Connery's transformation from an impoverished youth growing up in the slum of Edinburgh to the "serious, sexy, deadly, and unbeatable" Bond to director Terrence Young's tailoring. But accord-

ing to Connery, an unknown American stage actor, Brian Henderson, changed his life by encouraging and training him in the early 1950s to pursue an acting career. Through gradually increasing appearances on television, particularly a live production about the rise and fall of a professional boxer, he landed a contract with Twentieth Century-Fox and started to play parts in low-budget films until he was cast by producers Albert Broccoli and Harry Saltzman in 1961 to be the first Agent 007 on the big screen. Connery's Bond moved with a tensile grace, a feral virility touched with a disturbing edge of danger. Yet the suggestion of cruelty was set off—and made all the more attractive—by a glint of sardonic complicity, inviting the audience in on the joke. The balance was finely gauged. A straighter performance would have made the comic-strip violence distasteful; a more flippant one would have defused the menace.

Agent 007 not only brought Connery fame and fortune but also inhibited his screen persona for years to come. In a conscious effort to define himself as capable of a much broader range of characters, Connery took up roles that would establish himself to be a serious actor, be it the predatory sadist in *Marnie*, the sweaty imprisoned NCO in Sidney Lumet's *The Hill*, or the boozy, disreputable poet in *A Fine Madness*. Only with the Bond period (barring his late comeback) safely behind him did a distinct cinematic identity, inherent rather than willed, start to emerge. And in many ways it was the antithesis of everything Bond had stood for.

Upon leaving the role of James Bond after *Diamonds are Forever*, Connery seemed unable to uphold his fame and descended into a long period of down time. The 1979 big-budgeted flop *Meteor*, though it did not crash on him, can be seen as a perfect example of his dilemma. Deprived from substantial commercial success yet lacking any recognition for his acting, Connery was overshadowed by the mixed and often conflicted expectations of the audience and himself. Though his portrayal of Professor Bradley in *Meteor* was a decent performance, the film itself was so disastrous that even the all-star cast, high budget, and the then trendy disaster film genre could not save it. Coming not as a total surprise, *Never Say Never Again*, another 007 flick, starred Connery again.

It seems that only after having proved himself once again to be a big enough box-office draw was he able to revitalize his career both commercially and artistically. Amidst a string of blockbusters, such as *Highlander*, *Indiana Jones and the Last Crusade*, and *The Hunt for Red October*, Connery also rendered two of his most memorable performances in *The Name of the Rose* as William of Baskerville and, most notably, as James Malone in Brian De Palma's *The Untouchables*. The latter also won him a long-awaited Academy Award as Best Supporting Actor, among other professional recognitions. Indeed, as Pfeiffer and Lisa put it, "at an age when most men are looking forward to retirement, Sean Connery is at the peak of his career." The confidence that can only come with age is seen mostly vividly in the fact that, perhaps along with Clint Eastwood and Anthony Hopkins, Connery is not interested in maintaining any illusion of youth but is capable of emitting the brilliance of a star at every phase of his career.

Yet Connery is in some ways an unlikely star, a down-to-earth and unpretentious actor notoriously resistant to the glamour of the movie world. "There's nothing special about being an actor," he once remarked. "It's a job, like being a carpenter or a bricklayer, and I've never stopped being amazed at the mystique people attach to my business." One, however, should also understand that the glamour, the fame, and fortune—for Connery and any other people in his trade—are the point of this business and exactly what distinguish it from carpentry. It is also why he was able to found the Scottish Education Trust (and later donated to it $1 million in 1971) to help deprived Scottish children, as few bricklayers could ever have done.

—Philip Kemp, updated by Guo-Juin Hong

Sean Connery in *From Russia with Love*

CONSTANTINE, Eddie

Nationality: American/French. **Born:** Los Angeles, 29 October 1917; became French citizen. **Education:** Vienna Conservatory. **Family:** Married 1) the ballet dancer Helene Mussel; 3) Maja Faber-Janssen, children: Tania, Barbara, Lemmy, and Mia Bella Marie. **Career:** 1936—taken to Vienna by singing teacher Igor Gorin; while studying at Vienna Conservatory earned tuition by singing in cafes; 1938—worked in New York City and Newark at odd jobs; singing debut in Bayonne, New Jersey, theater in trio; trio joined by two others to form "The 5 Musketeers," performed in burlesque theaters and with swing bands; 1939—single dates in nightclubs; 1940—worked in Los Angeles singing and as movie extra; early 1940s—worked in radio in New York; 1949—first big success in Rio de Janeiro, nightclub dates and recordings in Paris after moving to France with first wife; 1952—signed to do gangster film by producer Victor Stoloff, *Egypt by Three*; 1953—cast by director Bernard Borderie in breakthrough role as Detective Lemmy Caution in first of series of low-budget films; 1956—formed Belmont Productions; 1967—formed Panda Films with Robert Kronenberg and James Henaghan; 1970s—revived career with roles in films by new generation of German filmmakers, such as

Fassbinder's *Beware of a Holy Whore*; 1978—moved to Weisbaden, West Germany, to live with third wife; 1986—in TV series *Roncalli*; 1990s—subject of a film retrospective in Germany shortly before his death. **Died:** Of heart attack, in Weisbaden, Germany, 25 February 1993.

Films as Actor:

1953 *Egypt by Three* (Stoloff) (as Nick); *La Môme vert-de-gris (Poison Ivy)* (Borderie) (as Lemmy Caution); *Cet homme est dangereux (This Man Is Dangerous)* (Sacha) (as Lemmy Caution)

1954 *Les Femmes s'en balancent* (Borderie) (as Lemmy Caution); *Votre Devoue, Blake* (Laviron) (as Captain Blake)

1955 *Ça va barder!* (Berry); *Avanzi di galera* (Cottafavi); *Je suis un sentimental (Headlines of Destruction)* (Berry)

1956 *Vous pigez?* (Chevalier) (as Lemmy Caution); *Les Truands* (Rim); "Paris after Dark" ep. of *Around the World with Orson Welles* (as himself); *L'Homme et l'enfant* (Andre)

1957 *Folies-Bergère* (Decoin) (as Bob Hardie); *Le Grand Bluff* (Dally)

1958   *Ces dames preferent le Mambo* (*Dishonorable Discharge*) (Borderie); *Incognito* (Dally); *Hoppla, jetzt kommt Eddie!* (Kingler) (as Eddie Petersen)

1959   *Passport to Shame* (*Room 43*; *The Girl in Room 43*) (Rakoff) (as Johnny); *Du Rififi chez les femmes* (*Riff Raff Girls*) (Joffé) (as Williams); *S.O.S. Pacific* (Guy Green) (as Mark); *The Treasure of San Teresa* (*Hot Money Girl*; *Rhapsodie in Blei*) (Rakoff) (as Larry Brennan)

1960   *Bomben auf Monte Carlo* (Jacoby); *Comment qu'elle est!* (Borderie) (as Lemmy Caution); *Le Chien de pique* (Yves Allégret)

1961   *Ca va etre ta fête* (*Tout feu, tout flamme*; *It's Your Birthday*) (Montazel); *Me faire ca à moi!* (Grimblat); *En pleine bagarre* (*Haut les mains!*; *Destination Fury*) (Bianchi); *Cause toujours, mon lapin* (LeFranc)

1962   "La Paresse" ("Laziness") ep. of *Les Sept Péchés capitaux* (*The Seven Capital Sins*) (Godard) (as himself); *Lemmy pour les dames* (Borderie) (as Lemmy Caution); **Cléo de cinq à sept** (*Cleo from 5 to 7*) (Varda); *Une Grosse Tête* (*La Guerre des karts*) (de Givray); *Bonne Chance, Charlie* (*De la poudre et des balles*) (Richard); *L'Empire de la nuit* (*The Empire of Night*) (Grimblat) (as Eddie); *Nous irons à Deauville* (Rigaud) (bit role)

1963   *Les Femmes d'abord* (Andre) (as Bobby Caro); *Comme s'il en pleuvait* (*If It Were Raining*) (Monter); *A toi de faire, Mignonne* (*Your Turn, Darling*) (Borderie) (as Lemmy Caution)

1964   *Des frissons partout* (Andre) (as Jeff Gordon); *Nick Carter va tout casser* (*Nick Carter casse tout*; *License to Kill*) (Decoin) (as Nick Carter); *Laissez tirer les tireurs* (LeFranc) (as Jeff Gordon); *Lucky Jo* (Deville) (title role)

1965   *Ces Dames s'en melent* (Andre) (as Jeff Gordon); **Alphaville** (*Une étrange aventure de Lemmy Caution*; *Alphaville: A Strange Adventure of Lemmy Caution*; *Tarzan versus I.B.M.*) (Godard) (as Lemmy Caution); *Feu à volonte* (*Faites vos jeux, mesdames*) (Marcel Ophüls) (as Mike Warner); *Je vous salue, Mafia* (*Hail, Mafia*) (Lévy) (as Rudy); *Nick Carter et le trefle rouge* (Savignac) (as Nick Carter); *Cartes sur table* (*Attack of the Robots*) (Franco) (as Al Pereira)

1967   *Residencia para espias* (*Dan chez les gentlemen*) (Franco) (as Dan Layton)

1968   *Le Consortium* (*Spara per primo vivrai di più*; *A tout casser*) (Berry)

1969   *Lion's Love* (Varda)

1970   *Malatesta* (Lilienthal); *Eine Rose für Jane* (Geissendörfer—for TV)

1971   *Warnung vor einer heiligen Nutte* (*Beware of a Holy Whore*) (Fassbinder)

1973   *Welt am Draht* (Fassbinder—for TV) (as man in Rolls Royce)

1975   *Der Zweite Frühling* (Lommel) (as Frank Cabot); *Souvenir de Gibralter*

1977   *Le Couple témoin* (Klein); *Raid on Entebbe* (Kershner—for TV) (as Capt. Michel Bacos)

1978   *It Lives Again* (*It's Alive II*) (Cohen) (as Dr. Forrest)

1979   *Die dritte Generation* (*The Third Generation*) (Fassbinder) (as Lenz); *Bestellt—Geklaut—Geliefert* (*Car-napping*) (Wicker) (as Lauroux, police officer)

1980   *The Long Good Friday* (Mackenzie) (as Charlie); *Exit . . . nur Keine Panik* (Novotny); *Panische Zeiten* (Fratzscher and Lindenberg)

1982   *Rote Liebe* (Von Prauheim); *Boxoffice* (Josef Bogdanovich) (as Hugh Barren)

1983   *Der Schnüffler* (Runze); *La Bête noire* (Chaput)

1984   *Fluchtpunkt Berlin* (*Flight to Berlin*) (Petit); *J'ai bien l'honneur* (Ruffio); *Dorian Grey im Spiegel del Boulevardpresse* (Ottinger)

1985   *Tiger—Fruhling in Wien* (Partzak); *Paul Chevrolet en de ultieme hallucinatie* (*Paul Chevrolet and the Ultimate Hallucination*) (de la Parra) (as Boy Pappa, a gangster)

1986   *Elanprostekt nr. 4* (*Macaroni Blues*) (Csepcsanyi) (as a bootlegger); *Frankenstein's Aunt*

1987   *Nouvelle brigades du tigre* (Vieds); *Helsinki Napoli: All Night Long* (Mika Kaurismäki) (as old gangster)

1988   *Pehavy Max a Strasilda* (Jakubisco)

1989   *Europa Abends* (Schroder)

1991   *Allemagne annee 90 neuf zero* (*Germany Year 90 Nine Zero*) (Godard) (as Lemmy Caution)

1992   *Zentropa* (*Europa*) (von Trier) (as Col. Harris)

Publications

By CONSTANTINE: book—

The Godplayer, New York, 1976 (English-language translation of novel *La Proprietaire*).

By CONSTANTINE: articles—

Interview with M. Lindsay, in *Cinema* (Beverly Hills), no. 4, 1968.
"On aime Eddie Constantine," interview with V. Berthommier and M. C. Questerbert, in *Cahiers du Cinéma* (Paris), February 1980.
Interview with A. Le Guay, in *Cinématographe* (Paris), December 1980.
Interview in *Time Out* (London), March 1984.

On CONSTANTINE: books—

Hasemann, Dieter, and Michael Dittmar, *Hoppla: hier kommt Eddie! Eddie Constantine und seine Filme*, Berlin, 1986.
Thissen, Rolf, *Eddie Constantine: seine Filme, sein Leben*, Munich, 1991.

On CONSTANTINE: articles—

"The Star Who Didn't Come Home," in *Show* (Hollywood), May 1962.
Roud, Richard, "Anguish: *Alphaville*," in *Sight and Sound* (London), Autumn 1965.
Nolan, Jack Edmund, "Eddie Constantine," in *Films in Review* (New York), August-September 1968.
Ciné Revue (Paris), 22 July 1982.
Tuliara, P., "Eddie Constantine!," in *Filmihullu* (Helsinki), no. 4, 1989.
Seesslen, G., "Eddie Constantine," in *EPD Film* (Frankfurt), September 1991.
Sauvaget, D., "Eddie Constantine," in *Revue du Cinéma* (Paris), November 1991.
Obituary in *New York Times*, 2 March 1993.
Obituary in *Variety* (New York), 8 March 1993.
Stars (Mariembourg, Belgium), Spring 1993; see also Autumn 1993.
Obituary in *Classic Images* (Muscatine, Iowa), April 1993.
Obituary in *EPD Film* (Frankfurt), April 1993.

*   *   *

Eddie Constantine's film roles are primarily in one of two categories: two-dimensional, hard-boiled American detectives in fast-paced French action thrillers or variations on these sleuths in politically and aesthetically provocative films by French new wave and new German filmmakers. There are exceptions—such as his down-and-out American loser in *Lucky Jo*—but the exceptions prove the rule.

Constantine was born in Los Angeles. As a young man he studied opera in Vienna, but on his return to America he achieved nothing more exalted than the chorus at the Radio City Music Hall in New York. He went back to Europe in 1947, settled in Paris, began singing in nightclubs there, became a protégé of Edith Piaf, and before long had become a popular French recording star. The French director Bernard Borderie gave him his first real opportunity in films in 1953, not as a musical performer but as Lemmy Caution, the hero of *La Môme vert-de-gris*, derived from Peter Cheyney's mystery novels. Constantine went on to play Lemmy—sometimes as a private eye, sometimes as an instrument of the FBI—in several other films by Borderie (the importance of the role to the actor is evidenced by the naming of Constantine's son Lemmy). The popularity of his screen persona determined the roles he played in films by other directors such as Yves Allégret, Henri Decoin, and Marcel Ophüls.

In the late 1960s various of the more "cerebral" directors began to use the Constantine persona, well known to European audiences, to make their avant-garde political films more accessible. This easily recognized actor played an actor in several self-reflexive films, such as Agnes Varda's *Cleo from 5 to 7*, Godard's "Laziness" episode of *The Seven Capital Sins*, and Fassbinder's *Beware of a Holy Whore*. These films are far removed from the transparent genre films for which Constantine had become famous.

He once again played Lemmy Caution—or rather a parody of Lemmy—in Godard's *Alphaville*, an aggressive political parody of the science-fiction and detective genres. He portrays the quiet but firm anarchist leader in Peter Lilienthal's conventional but politically charged *Malatesta*. Fassbinder goes further in *The Third Generation*. He uses the Constantine screen persona in this instance as a wealthy industrialist who arranges his own kidnapping by leftist terrorists in order to consolidate his own power. There is method in the transposition: Constantine had moved in his film career from the individualistic private eye or FBI operative to the omnipotent head of a multinational corporation.

In one of Constantine's last films before his death in 1993, however, he was able to bring a more explicit, and perhaps more fitting, culmination to his career through one last reprise of Lemmy Caution in another Godard film, 1991's *Germany Year 90 Nine Zero*. Here, Caution is "the last spy" lost in a post-Cold War Germany bereft of conflict, yes, but also bereft of any meaning beyond that of commerce. With this transition, the easily recognized Constantine image is effectively shown to be obsolete and irrelevant, climaxing with Constantine/Caution's epigrammic cry of "The bastards!" at film's end.

—Howard Feinstein, updated by David E. Salamie

COOPER, Gary

Nationality: American. **Born:** Frank James Cooper in Helena, Montana, 7 May 1901. **Education:** Dunstable College, England, until WWI; Wesleyan College, Bozeman, Montana; Grinnell College, Iowa. **Family:** Married Veronica Balfe, 1933, daughter: Maria. **Career:** 1924—worked as political cartoonist for newspapers in Los Angeles; began working as extra and stunt rider in Westerns; 1925—appeared as villain in Marilyn Mills's Western shorts; 1926—first major featured role in *The Winning of Barbara Worth*; contract with Paramount; 1928—first appearance in sound film, *The Shopworn Angel*; 1937—named by *New York Times* as highest paid entertainer; contract with Samuel Goldwyn; 1944—formed own production company, International Pictures; 1947—testified before House Un-American Activities Committee, but named no names; contract with Warners; 1952—critical comeback in *High Noon* after several unsuccessful films; formed production company, Baroda Productions; 1961—narrated "The Real

West" episode of *Project 20* for television, his last media appearance. **Awards:** Best Actor Academy Award, and Best Actor, New York Film Critics, for *Sergeant York*, 1941; Best Actor Academy Award for *High Noon*, 1952; Special Academy Award 1961. **Died:** 13 May 1961.

Films as Actor:

(also appeared as extra in about 30 films during 1925-26 including: *Dick Turpin*; *The Thundering Herd*; *Wild Horse Mesa*; *The Lucky Horseshoe*; *The Vanishing American*; *The Eagle*; *The Enchanted Hill*; *Watch Your Wife*)

1926   *Tricks* (Mitchell); *Three Pals* (Mitchell); *Lightnin' Wins* (Tiesler); *The Winning of Barbara Worth* (King) (as Abe Lee)

1927   *It* (Badger) (as reporter); *Children of Divorce* (Lloyd) (as Ted Larrabee); *Arizona Bound* (Waters) (as the Cowboy); *Wings* (Wellman) (as Cadet White); *Nevada* (Waters) (as Jim Lacy); *The Last Outlaw* (Rossen) (as Sheriff Buddy Hale)

1928   *Beau Sabreur* (Waters) (as Major Henri de Beaujolais); *Legion of the Condemned* (Wellman) (as Gale Price); *Doomsday* (Rowland V. Lee) (as Arnold Furze); *Half a Bride* (La Cava) (as Captain Edmunds); *Lilac Time* (Fitzmaurice) (as Captain Philip Blythe); *The First Kiss* (Rowland V. Lee) (as Mulligan Talbot); *The Shopworn Angel* (Wallace) (as William Tyler)

1929   *Wolf Song* (Fleming) (as Sam Lash); *Betrayal* (Milestone) (as Andre Frey); *The Virginian* (Fleming) (title role)

1930   *Only the Brave* (Tuttle) (as Captain James Braydon); *Paramount on Parade* (Arzner and others) (as himself); *The Texan* (Cromwell) (as Enrique "Quico"); *Seven Days Leave* (Wallace) (as Kenneth Dowey); *The Man from Wyoming* (Rowland V. Lee) (as Jim Baker); *The Spoilers* (Carewe) (as Glenister); *Morocco* (von Sternberg) (as Tom Brown)

1931   *Fighting Caravans* (Brower and Burton) (as Clint Belmet); *City Streets* (Mamoulian) (as The Kid); *I Take This Woman* (Gering) (as Tom McNair); *His Woman* (Sloman) (as Captain Sam Whalan)

1932   *Make Me a Star* (Beaudine) (as himself); *The Devil and the Deep* (Gering) (as Lieutenant Sempter); *If I Had a Million* (Lubitsch and others) (as Gallagher); *A Farewell to Arms* (Borzage) (as Frederic Henry); *The Slippery Pearls* (short); *Voice of Hollywood* (short) (as himself)

1933   *Today We Live* (Hawks) (as Bogard); *One Sunday Afternoon* (Roberts) (as Biff Grimes); *Design for Living* (Lubitsch) (as George Curtis); *Alice in Wonderland* (McLeod) (as The White Knight); *Operator Thirteen* (Boleslawsky) (as Captain Jack Gailliard)

1934   *Now and Forever* (Hathaway) (as Jerry Day)

1935   *The Lives of a Bengal Lancer* (Hathaway) (as Lieutenant McGregor); *The Wedding Night* (Vidor) (as Tony Barrett); *Peter Ibbetson* (Hathaway) (title role); *Star Night at the Coconut Grove* (short) (as himself)

1936   *Desire* (Borzage) (as Tom Bradley); *Mr. Deeds Goes to Town* (Capra) (as Longfellow Deeds); *Hollywood Boulevard* (Florey) (as guest at bar); *The General Died at Dawn* (Milestone) (as O'Hara); *The Plainsman* (DeMille) (as Wild Bill Hickok); *La Fiesta De Santa Barbara* (short)

1937   *Souls at Sea* (Hathaway) (as "Nuggin" Taylor); *Lest We Forget* (short) (as himself)

1938   *The Adventures of Marco Polo* (Mayo) (as Marco Polo); *Bluebeard's Eighth Wife* (Lubitsch) (as Michael Brandon); *The Cowboy and the Lady* (Potter) (as Stretch)

1939   *Beau Geste* (Wellman) (title role); *The Real Glory* (Hathaway) (as Dr. Bill Canavan)

Gary Cooper

1940   *The Westerner* (Wyler) (as Cole Hardin); *Northwest Mounted Police* (DeMille) (as Dusty Rivers); *Meet John Doe* (Capra) (as John Doe or Long John Willoughby)

1941   *Sergeant York* (Hawks) (title role); *Ball of Fire* (Hawks) (as Prof. Bertram Potts)

1942   *The Pride of the Yankees* (Wood) (as Lou Gehrig)

1943   *For Whom the Bell Tolls* (Wood) (as Robert Jordan)

1944   *Memo for Joe* (Richard Fleischer) (as himself); *The Story of Dr. Wassell* (DeMille) (as Dr. Corydon M. Wassell); *Casanova Brown* (Wood) (title role)

1945   *Along Came Jones* (Heisler) (as Melody Jones, + pr); *Saratoga Trunk* (Wood) (as Col. Clint Maroon)

1946   *Cloak and Dagger* (Fritz Lang) (as Prof. Alvah Jesper)

1947   *Unconquered* (DeMille) (as Captain Christopher Holden); *Variety Girl* (Marshall) (as himself)

1948   *Good Sam* (McCarey) (as Sam Clayton); *The Fountainhead* (King Vidor) (as Howard Roark)

1949   *It's a Great Feeling* (Butler) (as himself); *Task Force* (Daves) (as Jonathon L. Scott); *Snow Carnival* (short) (as narrator, + pr); *Bright Leaf* (Curtiz) (as Brant Royle); *Dallas* (Heisler) (as Blayde "Reb" Hollister)

1951   *You're in the Navy Now* (Hathaway) (as Lt. John Harkness); *Starlift* (Del Ruth) (as guest star); *It's a Big Country* (Thorpe and others) (as Texas); *Distant Drums* (Walsh) (as Capt. Quincy Wyatt)

1952   **High Noon** (Zinnemann) (as Will Kane); *Springfield Rifle* (deToth) (as Major Alex Kearney)

1953   *Return to Paradise* (Robson) (as Mr. Morgan); *Blowing Wild* (Fregonese) (as Jeff Dawson)

1954   *Garden of Evil* (Hathaway) (as Hooker); *Vera Cruz* (Aldrich) (as Benjamin Trane)

1955   *The Court-Martial of Billy Mitchell* (Preminger) (as Billy Mitchell)

1956   *Friendly Persuasion* (Wyler) (as Jess Birdwell)

1957   *Love in the Afternoon* (Wilder) (as Frank Flanagan)

1958   *Ten North Frederick* (Dunne) (as Joe Chapin); *Man of the West* (Anthony Mann) (as Link Jones)

1959   *The Hanging Tree* (Daves) (as Doc Joseph Frail); *Alias Jesse James* (McLeod) (as himself); *The Wreck of the Mary Deare* (Anderson) (as Gideon Patch); *They Came to Cordura* (Rossen) (as Major Thomas Thorn)

1961   *The Naked Edge* (Anderson) (as George Ratcliffe)

Publications

By COOPER: articles—

"The Big Boy Tells His Story," in *Photoplay* (New York), April and May 1929.

"The Role I Liked Best," in the *Saturday Evening Post* (Philadelphia), 6 May 1950.

"Well It Was This Way," in the *Saturday Evening Post* (Philadelphia), 18 and 25 February, 3, 10, 17, 24 and 31 March, and 7 April 1956.

On COOPER: books—

Schickel, Richard, *The Stars*, New York, 1962.

Fenin, George, and William K. Everson, *The Western, From Silents to Cinerama*, New York, 1962.

Gehman, Richard, *The Tall American: The Story of Gary Cooper*, New York, 1963.

Escoubé, Lucienne, *Gary Cooper: Le Cavalier de l'ouest*, Paris, 1965.

Dickens, Homer, *The Films of Gary Cooper*, New York, 1970.

Carpozi, George Jr., *The Gary Cooper Story*, New Rochelle, N.Y., 1970.

Jordan, René, *Gary Cooper*, New York, 1974.

Arce, Hectore, *Gary Cooper, An Intimate Biography*, New York, 1979.

Kaminsky, Stuart, *Coop: The Life and Legend of Gary Cooper*, New York, 1980.

Swindell, Larry, *The Last Hero: A Biography of Gary Cooper*, New York, 1980.

Chardair, N., *Gary Cooper*, Paris, 1981.

McDonald, Archie P., editor, *Shooting Stars: Heroes and Heroines of Western Film*, Bloomington, Indiana, 1987.

Wayne, Jane Ellen, *Cooper's Women*, New York, 1988.

On COOPER: articles—

Busby, Marquis, "The New Two-Gun Man," in *Photoplay* (New York), April 1930.

Wood, Tom, "Gary Cooper," in *Look* (New York), 16 May 1944.

Goodman, Ezra, "Average Guy: Gary Cooper Reflects on Twenty Years in Film," in the *New York Times*, 19 December 1948.

Clarens, Carlos, "Gary Cooper," in *Films in Review* (New York), December 1959.

Guy, Rory, "Gary Cooper Was a Great Actor, No, He Was Not! He Was...," in *Cinema* (Beverly Hills), October-November 1964.

Carle, Teet, "Gary Cooper: The Man Who Seemed Eternal," in *Hollywood Studio*, May 1972.

Schwartz, W., "Gary Cooper," in *Films in Review* (New York), January 1973, + filmo added to 1959 article.

Corey, Jeff, "Gary Cooper: Natural Talent" in *Close-Ups: The Movie Star Book*, edited by Danny Peary, New York, 1978.

Schickel, Richard, "Gary Cooper" in *The Movie Star*, edited by Elisabeth Weis, New York, 1981.

*   *   *

The film career of Gary Cooper seems to fall into six distinct periods:

1926-30: *The Naive Young Hero*. In this four-year period Cooper made 23 films, an average of five a year from *The Winning of Barbara Worth* to *The Spoilers*. More than half of them are Westerns or military pictures, films in which Cooper appeared as the tentative, shy young man, loose and limber of body, sure of the moral position he shared with the world. In this pre-Depression era, Cooper represented the young American who believed in the triumph of simple virtues and his commitment to them. In his own life, Cooper was, in fact, developing more and more confidence, was at the peak of his physical appearance and health, and was by the conclusion of this period not a tentative, shy man at all.

1930-36: *Cynicism and Disillusion*. In this six-year period Cooper made 19 films, an average of about three a year, from *Morocco* to *Desire*. Only one of these films is a Western. The Western image of affirmation was submerged by the Depression. In these films Cooper emerges as a tense and cautious figure, one who distrusts others or is loath to commit himself to others, though he can be touched.

1936-41: *Altruism and Dedication*. In this four-year period Cooper made 14 films, from *Mr. Deeds Goes to Town* to *Sergeant York*. Cooper's character is now that of a determined man, a man who sees hope in the future and is willing to sacrifice himself for the future of mankind. Many of these films are set in the past.

1942-47: *Intellect and Purpose*. In this five-year period Cooper made eight films, from *Ball of Fire* through *Unconquered*. In these films made during and immediately after World War II Cooper is a man out of his natural environment, a man who must deal with the riddles of an unfamiliar world and triumph by his native wit and determination, even when others distrust him. The only exceptions to this pattern are the two films his production company or Cooper himself produced, *Casanova Brown* and *Along Came Jones*, both of which represent an earlier Cooper image, an attempt to create a variation on what he had done before. It seems that the public image of Cooper changed slowly, even though he himself wanted to try broader variations on that image. It was surely a source of unhappiness to him that whenever he strayed from his accepted image in a particular period, the public failed to respond.

1948-56: *The Man Alone*. In this eight-year period Cooper made 16 films, from *The Fountainhead* to *The Court-Martial of Billy Mitchell*. It is significant that half of the films he made in this period are Westerns, often harking back to the period of his tentative shyness. Now however, Cooper was a rapidly aging man who stood resolutely against the world. That *The Virginian* should be the culmination of his earlier Western period and *High Noon* the peak of his second Western period is not a coincidence. Cooper as well as others saw the similarity of the two films. The differences between them are equally striking. Will Kane in *High Noon* seeks help from his society; the Virginian wanted to be on his own. Will Kane learns the bitter lesson of having to be alone; the Virginian never has to face this problem. Throughout this period, the Cooper character is faced with defeat and indecision—a character alone by choice, as in *The Fountainhead*, or because his society rejects him, as in *The Court-Martial of Billy Mitchell*. It is the time of the Cold War, in which the Cooper character's old values were rejected.

1956-61: *Questioning the Past*. In this five-year period Cooper made eight films, from *Love in the Afternoon* through *The Naked Edge*. This period is ushered in by a transition film, *Friendly Persuasion*, a film in which Cooper's character discarded his guns and rejected the violence that characters in the other periods had accepted with little question. This questioning of the past continues to the end of Cooper's life. It is significant that this is the period in which Cooper had the most control of his parts, was producing his own films, but felt he had let his public down. He was now trying to extend his range as an actor and was willing to do so by questioning his image in the past. His role as the lover in *Love in the Afternoon* is an ironic comment on his past comedy images. In his Westerns of this period, he is a self-sufficient but highly reluctant, somber man. His final films constantly question his past. In *They Came to Cordura* the very essence of filmic courage that Cooper had represented is questioned, and in his final film, *The Naked Edge*, the possibility of Cooper being a vicious murderer is proposed. It is true that in all these films the Cooper character is ultimately heroic, but the films play with the image, toy with the possibilities of that image. Cooper's work is certainly no less good in this period. What was reacted to by critics and public was what Cooper now represented, the weary questioner of the American mythic past.

It is perhaps appropriate that Cooper's two Academy Awards (for *Sergeant York* and *High Noon*) should be for two separate periods, one in which he was the optimistic hero of the past and the other in which he was the pessimistic retainer of the past. In fact, more than 60 of Cooper's films were set in the past. It may well have been that it was what he represented in American history and culture as well as his performances in these films for which he was honored.

As one critic said, Gary Cooper's face was the map of America. In it, we read our past. We liked it or did not like it, but we could not turn away from the compelling man who represented it.

—Stuart M. Kaminsky

COOPER, Jackie

Nationality: American. **Born:** John Cooper, Jr. in Los Angeles, California, 15 September 1921; nephew of the director Norman Taurog. **Education:** Attended Notre Dame University, Indiana. **Military**

Service: U.S. Navy during World War II. **Family:** Married 1) June Horne, son: John; 2) Hildy Parks; 3) Barbara Kraus, children: Russell, Julie, and Christina. **Career:** At age three acted in comedies with Bobby Clark and Lloyd Hamilton; 1929—in eight episodes of the *Our Gang* comedies; 1931—in series of successful films with Wallace Beery, beginning with *The Champ*; mid-1930s—contract with MGM; late-1940s—on Broadway in *Magnolia Alley*; then national tour as Ensign Pulver in *Mister Roberts*; 1954—star of Broadway play *King of Hearts*; 1955-58—in TV series *The People's Choice*, and in *Hennesey*, 1959-62; 1963-72—in charge of television production for Columbia Pictures Television; 1970s—regular appearances on TV series *Columbo* and *Police Story*, and host of *The Dean Martin Comedy World*, 1974, and in series *Mobile One*, 1975; also director of episodes of *M*A*S*H*, *The Rockford Files*, *Kojak*, and *Quincy*. **Awards:** Emmy Awards for direction, for *M*A*S*H* episode, "Carry on Hawkeye," 1973, and for the pilot of *The White Shadow*, 1978. **Address:** 9621 Royalton Drive, Beverly Hills, CA 90210, U.S.A.

Films as Actor:

1929   8 *Our Gang* comedy shorts; *Fox Movietone Follies of 1929* (Butler); *Sunny Side Up* (David Butler) (as tenement boy); *Boxing Gloves* (Mack and McGowan—short) (as Jackie)

1931   *Skippy* (Taurog) (title role); *Donovan's Kid* (*Young Donovan's Kid*) (Niblo) (as Midge Murray); *The Champ* (King Vidor) (as Dink); *Sooky* (Taurog) (as Skippy Skinner)

1932   *When a Feller Needs a Friend* (Pollard) (as Eddie Randall); *Divorce in the Family* (Reisner) (as Terry Parker)

1933   *Broadway to Hollywood* (*Ring Up the Curtain*) (Mack) (as Ted Hackett Jr. as child); *The Bowery* (Walsh) (as Swipes McGurk)

1934   *Lone Cowboy* (Sloane) (as Scooter O'Neal); *Treasure Island* (Fleming) (as Jim Hawkins); *Peck's Bad Boy* (Cline) (as Bill Peck)

1935   *Dinky* (Bretherton and Lederman) (title role); *O'Shaughnessy's Boy* (Boleslawski) (as Stubby); *Tough Guy* (Franklin) (as Freddie)

1936   *The Devil Is a Sissy* (*The Devil Takes the Count*) (Van Dyke) (as "Buck" Murphy)

1937   *Boy of the Streets* (Nigh) (as Chuck)

1938   *White Banners* (Goulding) (as Peter Trimble); *Gangster's Boy* (Nigh) (as Larry Kelly); *That Certain Age* (Ludwig) (as Ken); *Newsboys' Home* (Harold Young) (as "Rifle" Edwards)

1939   *Scouts to the Rescue* (Taylor and James—serial); *The Spirit of Culver* (*Man's Heritage*) (Taurog) (as Tom Allen); *Streets of New York* (*The Abe Lincoln of Ninth Avenue*) (Nigh) (as Jimmy); *Two Bright Boys* (Santley) (as Roy O'Donnell); *The Big Guy* (Lubin) (as Timmy Hutchins); *What a Life!* (Reed) (as Henry Aldrich)

1940   *Gallant Sons* (Seitz) (as Byron "By" Newbold); *The Return of Frank James* (Fritz Lang) (as Clem/Tom Grayson); *Seventeen* (Louis King) (as William Sylvanus Baxter)

1941   *Ziegfeld Girl* (Leonard) (as Jerry Regan); *Her First Beau* (Reed) (as Chuck Harris); *Glamour Boy* (*Hearts in Springtime*) (Murphy) (as Tiny Barlow); *Life with Henry* (Reed) (as Henry Aldrich)

1942   *Syncopation* (Dieterle) (as Johnnie); *Men of Texas* (*Men of Destiny*) (Enright) (as Robert Houston Scott); *The Navy Comes Through* (A. Edward Sutherland) (as Babe)

1943   *Where Are Your Children?* (Nigh) (as Danny)

1947   *Stork Bites Man* (Endfield) (as Ernie); *Kilroy Was Here* (Karlson) (as John J. Kilroy)

1948   *French Leave* (*Kilroy on Deck*) (McDonald) (as Skitch)

1961   *Everything's Ducky* (Don Taylor) (as Lt. Parnell)

Jackie Cooper

1968   *Shadow on the Land* (Sarafian—for TV)
1971   *The Love Machine* (Haley) (as Danton Miller); *Maybe I'll Come Home in the Spring* (*Deadly Desire*) (Sargent—for TV)
1972   *The Astronaut* (Robert Michael Lewis—for TV)
1974   *Chosen Survivors* (Roley) (as Raymond Couzins); *The Day the Earth Moved* (Robert Michael Lewis—for TV)
1975   *The Invisible Man* (Robert Michael Lewis—for TV)
1976   *The Pink Panther Strikes Again* (Edwards) (as service repairman)
1977   *Operation Petticoat* (Astin—for TV)
1978   *Superman* (Richard Donner) (as Perry White)

1980   *Superman II* (Lester) (as Perry White)
1983   *Superman III* (Lester) (as Perry White)
1987   *Superman IV: The Quest for Peace* (Furie) (as Perry White); *Surrender* (Belson) (as Ace Morgan)

Films as Director:

1972   *Stand Up and Be Counted*
1978   *Having Babies III* (for TV); *Perfect Gentlemen* (for TV) (+ pr); *Rainbow* (for TV)
1979   *Sex and the Single Parent* (for TV)

255

1980   *Marathon* (for TV); *Rodeo Girl* (for TV); *White Mama* (for TV)
1981   *Leave 'em Laughing* (for TV)
1982   *Rosie: The Rosemary Clooney Story* (for TV)
1984   *The Ladies* (for TV); *The Night They Saved Christmas* (for TV)
1985   *Izzy and Moe* (for TV)

Publications

By COOPER: book—

Please Don't Shoot My Dog (autobiography), with Dick Kleiner, New York, 1981.

By COOPER: article—

"That Old 'Gang' of Theirs," interview with Frank Lovece, in *Entertainment Weekly* (New York), 19 August 1994.

On COOPER: articles—

De Roos, Robert, "When the Wise Guys Were Wrong," and "How Did Jackie Cooper Escape the Classic Child-Star Fate?," in *TV Guide* (New York), 6 and 13 October 1968.
Ciné Revue (Paris), 31 October 1979.
"And We Thought He Hated Cleo," in *Los Angeles Magazine*, March 1981.
Films in Review (New York), October 1981.
Screen International (London), 23 July 1983.

*   *   *

Child actors as stars and protagonists in features had become an important part of movie fare by the mid-1930s. Jackie Cooper, a boy who had gained audience approval in the "Our Gang" comedies when this series switched to sound in 1929, became a star in 1931 with the full-length films *Skippy* and *The Champ*, well before such moppet actors as Shirley Temple, Mickey Rooney, and Judy Garland were cast in leading roles.

In *Skippy* Cooper plays an enterprising boy able to manipulate his middle-class parents, who do not always approve of his adventures with boys from the "wrong side of the tracks." Cooper's skills were even more evident in *The Champ* in which he portrays the son of a prizefighter on the skids. Although this work lapses into sentimentality, the combined talents of Wallace Beery ("The Champ") and Cooper helped to make this work an important film of the early 1930s. Because their names were similar, Cooper was sometimes confused with Jackie Coogan. In fact there was another connection: in 1934 Jackie Cooper played the lead in the film *Peck's Bad Boy*, a role that Coogan had created in a silent version 13 years earlier.

Cooper went on to play Jim Hawkins to Beery's Long John Silver in the screen adaptation of Robert Louis Stevenson's *Treasure Island*. At the age of 17 he played opposite Deanna Durbin in *That Certain Age*, the kind of film that Mickey Rooney and Judy Garland were handling more successfully in the "Andy Hardy" series. As Cooper grew older, his acting became less fresh and natural.

After establishing himself as an actor and director in television, Cooper returned to the medium that had made him a star when he released his *Stand Up and Be Counted* in 1972, his debut as a film director. Still active today as both an actor and director, Cooper remains best known for the roles he created as a child star in the early 1930s.

—Donald McCaffrey

COSTELLO, Lou. *See* ABBOTT, Bud, and Lou COSTELLO.

———

COSTNER, Kevin

Nationality: American. **Born:** Compton, near Los Angeles, 18 January 1955. **Education:** Studied business at the University of California, Fullerton; studied acting at the South Coast Actors Co-op. **Family:** Married Cindy Silva (divorced 1994), three children: Annie, Lily, and Joe. **Career:** Worked in marketing for six weeks, left and became stage manager at Raleigh Movie Studios; 1981—film debut in small nonunion picture, *Stacey's Knights*; late 1980s—set up own production company, TIG; 1995—executive producer and narrator of TV series *500 Nations*. **Awards:** Oscar for Best Director, for *Dances with Wolves*, 1990.

Films as Actor:

1981   *Stacey's Knights* (*Winning Steak*) (Wilson) (as Will Bonner); *Shadows Run Black* (Heard) (as Jimmy Scott); *Chasing Dreams* (Roche and Conte)
1982   *Frances* (Clifford); *Night Shift* (Ron Howard) (as Frat Boy #1)
1983   **The Big Chill** (Kasdan) (as Alex); *Testament* (Littman) (as Phil Pitkin); *Table for Five* (Lieberman) (as newlywed)
1984   *American Flyers* (Badham) (as Marcus Sommers)
1985   *Silverado* (Kasdan) (as Jake); *Fandango* (Kevin Reynolds) (as Gardner Barnes)
1986   *Sizzle Beach* (Brander—produced in 1974) (as John Logan)
1987   *The Untouchables* (De Palma) (as Eliot Ness); *No Way Out* (Donaldson) (as Lt. Cmdr. Tom Farrell)
1988   *Bull Durham* (Shelton) (as Crash Davis)
1989   *Field of Dreams* (Robinson) (as Ray Kinsella); *The Gunrunner* (Castillo—produced in 1983) (as Ted Beaubien)
1990   *Revenge* (Scott) (as Cochran, + co-pr)
1991   *Robin Hood: Prince of Thieves* (Kevin Reynolds) (title role, + co-pr); *JFK* (Stone) (as Jim Garrison); *Truth or Dare* (Keshishian—doc) (appearance)
1992   *The Bodyguard* (Jackson) (as Frank Farmer, + co-pr)
1993   *A Perfect World* (Eastwood) (as Butch Haynes)
1994   *The War* (Avnet) (as Stephen); *Wyatt Earp* (Kasdan) (title role, + pr)
1995   *Waterworld* (Kevin Reynolds) (as the Mariner, + co-pr)
1996   *Tin Cup* (Ron Shelton)

Film as Director:

1990   *Dances with Wolves* (+ pr, ro as Lt. John J. Dunbar)

Films as Producer:

1993   *Rapa Nui* (Kevin Reynolds)
1996   *Head above Water* (Jim Wilson) (co-pr)

Publications

By COSTNER: book—

Dances with Wolves: The Illustrated Story of the Epic Film, with Michael Blake and Jim Wilson, New York, 1990.

By COSTNER: articles—

Biskind, Peter, "Kevin Costner: *The Untouchables*' New Ness," in *American Film* (Hollywood), vol. 12, no. 8, 1987.
Interview in *Time Out* (London), 6 January 1988.

On COSTNER: books—

Hamilton, Sue L., *Kevin Costner: Award-Winning Actor/Director*, Edina, Minnesota, 1991.
Keith, Todd, *Kevin Costner: The Unauthorized Biography*, London, 1991.
Wright, Adrian, *Kevin Costner: A Life on Film*, London, 1992.
Caddies, Kelvin, *Kevin Costner: Prince of Hollywood*, 1994.
Fournier, Roland, *Kevin Costner*, Monaco, 1995.

On COSTNER: articles—

McGillivray, David, "Kevin Costner," in *Films and Filming* (London), July 1987.
"Pursuing the Dream," in *Time* (New York), 26 August 1989.
Current Biography 1990, New York, 1990.
Morais, R. C., "Kevin Costner Journeys to a New Frontier," in *New York Times*, 4 November 1990.
Schruers, Fred, "Kevin Costner," in *Rolling Stone* (New York), 29 November 1990.
Hubler, Eric, "The Way You Were," in *Premiere* (New York), January 1991.
Deitch, Mark, "Kevin Costner: Screen of Dreams," in National Film *Theatre Booklet* (London), February 1991.
Pearce, Garth, "*Robin Hood: Prince of Thieves*," in *Empire* (London), August 1991.
Mills, Bart, "Kevin Costner: A Modest Superstar," in *Saturday Evening Post*, September/October 1991.
Klein, Edward, "Costner in Control," in *Vanity Fair* (New York), January 1992.
Janos, Leo, "Kevin Costner: The Prince Who Would Be King (of Hollywood)," in *Cosmopolitan*, March 1992.
Weinraub, Bernard, "The Name Costner Acquires a Question Mark," in *New York Times*, 21 February 1995.

* * *

At the beginning of his career, Kevin Costner spent several years knocking around the edges of the film industry. Some of his roles were so small that his presence was barely noticed. Others were bigger parts in dreadful low-budget potboilers which later came back to haunt him when they ingloriously appeared in video stores. He caught the attention of critics and audiences with his scene-stealing, star-making supporting performance as Jake, a roguish gunslinging cowboy, in the Lawrence Kasdan Western *Silverado*. The plum role was a payback of sorts from Kasdan; Costner earlier had played Alex, whose suicide sparks the chain of events which unfolds in *The Big Chill*, but the director decided to cut the character from the film's final edit. All that remains of Costner in *The Big Chill* are his feet in the opening sequence, as Alex is being prepared for his funeral. Costner similarly had been cut from *Frances*, a biography of Frances Farmer, appearing on-screen ever so briefly, in a scene in an alley in which he has one line.

Costner was to solidify his stardom playing square-jawed, true-blue all-American heroes. He specialized in such character types early on, playing Eliot Ness in *The Untouchables*, a remake of the classic television series, and a stalwart naval officer who uncovers corruption in *No Way Out*. Both these characters are generic Hollywood good guys, who remain uncorrupted as they take on the scenario's villains. Around this time, Costner expressed his desire to be linked to the Frank

Capra-Jimmy Stewart tradition, playing boyish and stable leads, and he did just that in the baseball films *Bull Durham* and *Field of Dreams*. In the former, he is aging catcher Crash Davis, a ballyard purist who understands and loves the game, but whose limited talent has kept him in the minor leagues for most of his career, with only brief appearances in "The Show." In the latter, by far his most Capraesque film, he is Ray Kinsella, a Midwest farmer who is told by a divine voice to replace his corn stalks with a baseball field. Both these heroes are in the classic Hollywood tradition. In an earlier era, each might have been played by Stewart; indeed, during its publicity tour, Costner touted *Field of Dreams* as "our generation's *It's a Wonderful Life*." Furthermore, Costner's Jim Garrison in *JFK* may lack the outright innocence of Stewart's Jefferson Smith in *Mr. Smith Goes to Washington*, but they remain linked in their idealism and vigor. As Costner orates in court on how the facts of the assassination of President John F. Kennedy have been concealed from the American public, he becomes reminiscent of Stewart filibustering on the Senate floor and exposing venal Washington politicians.

Nevertheless, the appealing boyishness of Costner's characters was not always Capraesque. It may be in *Field of Dreams*, where Ray Kinsella's true-blue idealism becomes one of the scenario's overriding factors. But in *Silverado*, that innocence is portrayed as outright immaturity, as his character acts recklessly (and easily might have come to be known as "Jake the Kid"). At the same time, Costner has more than adequately played the contemporary male sex symbol. His characters are anything but boyish when tangling with their female counterparts. In *No Way Out*, he and Sean Young share a headline-making rendezvous in the back seat of a limousine, and his between-the-sheets antics with Susan Sarandon in *Bull Durham* are no less erotically charged.

Costner's heroes also are contemporary in that they are alienated souls who occasionally take on subversive edges. His Lt. John Dunbar, the Civil War soldier in *Dances with Wolves*, is anything but the traditional American Western hero in that he is as deeply troubled as highly principled, and he goes on to renounce western civilization and join (rather than fight) a Lakota Sioux Indian tribe. Overall, in the first section of his career, Costner embodied the traditional Hollywood hero. The actors surrounding him may be cast in the juicier and more colorful roles: Robert De Niro and Sean Connery in *The Untouchables*; Gene Hackman in *No Way Out*; Tim Robbins in *Bull Durham*; Graham Greene and Rodney A. Grant in *Dances with Wolves*; and, later on, Alan Rickman and Morgan Freeman in *Robin Hood: Prince of Thieves*. But Costner's presence in each film is essential, as it serves as a consistent calming and stabilizing force at the scenario's center.

Dances with Wolves is to date the summit of Costner's career, if only because he directed as well as starred in the film—and won Oscars for Best Picture and Best Director. As a film, it is deeply flawed. With the exception of Dunbar, the whites all are depicted as grungy, crazy, sadistic, or (in the case of the Civil War general who travels with his own personal surgeon) products of a class system. Meanwhile, the Lakota Sioux are, to a person, attractive, squeaky-clean models of reason. *Dances with Wolves* is almost laughable in its superficial political correctness. And why so much graphic, stomach-churning violence? Perhaps Costner was trying to contrast the harsh reality of life on the American frontier with its breathtaking natural beauty. This could have been accomplished in one poignant, cleverly directed sequence. In *Dances with Wolves*, there is a distasteful overdose of blood and pain.

Costner has slipped somewhat in his post-*Dances with Wolves* career, in that he has been unable to find an interesting role in a commercially successful film. By far his two best parts have come in *A Perfect World* and *The War*. In each, he plays a character with a deeply troubled past who attempts to be a positive role model to children. Costner may have given an excellent performance—arguably the best

Kevin Costner in *No Way Out*

of his career—in *A Perfect World*, playing Butch Haynes, a sympathetic prison escapee who takes a young boy hostage. The film's director, Clint Eastwood, has the standard hero role, that of the Texas Ranger who sets out on Haynes's trail. But audiences rejected Costner in *A Perfect World*, and the film was a financial failure. He also is fine in *The War*, playing an unstable but well-intentioned Vietnam veteran. But moviegoers did not flock to see the film, preferring him instead in *The Bodyguard*, in which he stars as an icy-cold professional bodyguard who falls for the superstar singer he has been hired to protect. Aside from its wide popularity, however, *The Bodyguard* is an overripe exercise in Hollywood corn.

In spite of the prominence of his role in *JFK*, that film is a star vehicle for its director, Oliver Stone, rather than any of the actors in its cast. *Robin Hood: Prince of Thieves* (despite a delightfully campy performance from Alan Rickman as the Sheriff of Nottingham) pales in comparison to similar films of an earlier era; the same might be said for *Wyatt Earp*, featuring Costner in the title role, in which he is reteamed with *Silverado* director Kasdan.

In *Waterworld*, Costner attempted to enter Stallone-Schwarzenegger territory as a cartoon hero in a special effects-laden action movie extravaganza. But the film will be remembered not for its entertainment value but for the reams of negative publicity it earned as the costliest movie ever made. While not the fiasco of a *Heaven's Gate* or *Ishtar*, *Waterworld* did nothing to enhance Costner's career.

If he is to remain a bankable movie star, Costner would be advised to seek out roles which are aging, more mature versions of the ones that firmed up his stardom a decade earlier.

—Mark Walker, updated by Rob Edelman

COTTEN, Joseph

Nationality: American. **Born:** Joseph Cheshire Cotten in Petersburg, Virginia, 15 May 1905. **Education:** Studied at Hickman School of Expression, Washington, D.C. **Family:** Married 1) Lenore Kipp Lamont, 1931 (died 1960), one stepdaughter; 2) the actress Patricia Medina, 1960. **Career:** 1929—occasional drama critic for Miami *Herald* while selling paint and later advertising space in Miami; 1930—engaged by Belasco Theatre as understudy and assistant stage manager in New York; 1931—actor with Copley Square Theatre; worked in summer stock; 1932—Broadway debut with small screen role in *Absent Father*; 1936—joined Orson Welles's Federal Theater project; 1938—joined Welles and John Houseman's Mercury Theater; 1939—critical acclaim for role opposite Katharine Hepburn in *The Philadelphia Story* on Broadway; 1941—film debut in *Citizen Kane*; 1942—seven-year contract with David O. Selznick after Mercury players forced to leave RKO; 1948—contract sold to Warners; 1949—began to freelance for other studios; 1950-53—contract with 20th Century-Fox; 1953-54—returned to Broadway for starring role in *Sabrina Fair*; 1955-56—host on TV series *The 20th Century-Fox Hour*; 1956-57—host and occasional actor on TV series *On Trial*, later *The Joseph Cotten Show*, produced by his own company, Fordyce Productions; 1963-64—host on TV series *Hollywood and the Stars*, and appeared in TV mini-series *Aspen*, 1977. **Awards:** Best Actor, Venice Festival, for *Portrait of Jennie*, 1949. **Died:** In Westwood, California, 6 February 1994.

Films as Actor:

1941   *Citizen Kane* (Welles) (as Jed Leland); *Lydia* (Duvivier) (as Michael Fitzpatrick)

1942   *The Magnificent Ambersons* (Welles) (as Eugene Morgan); *Journey into Fear* (Norman Foster) (as Graham, + co-sc)

1943   *Shadow of a Doubt* (Hitchcock) (as Uncle Charlie); *Hers to Hold* (Ryan) (as Bill Morley)

1944   *Gaslight* (*The Murder in Thornton Square*) (Cukor) (as Brian Cameron); *Since You Went Away* (Cromwell) (as Lt. Anthony Willett); *I'll Be Seeing You* (Dieterle) (as Zachary Morgan)

1945   *Love Letters* (Dieterle) (as Alan Quinton)

1946   *Duel in the Sun* (King Vidor and others) (as Jesse McCanles)

1947   *The Farmer's Daughter* (Potter) (as Glenn Morley)

1948   *Portrait of Jennie* (*Jennie*) (Dieterle) (as Eben Adams)

1949   *The Third Man* (Reed) (as Holly Martins); *Under Capricorn* (Hitchcock) (as Sam Flusky); *Beyond the Forest* (King Vidor) (as Dr. Lewis Moline)

1950   *Walk Softly, Stranger* (Stevenson) (as Chris Hale); *Two Flags West* (Wise) (as Col. Clay Tucker); *September Affair* (Dieterle) (as David Lawrence)

1951   *Half Angel* (Sale) (as John Raymond); *Peking Express* (Dieterle) (as Michael Bachlin); *The Man with a Cloak* (Markle) (as Dupin)

1952   *Untamed Frontier* (Fregonese) (as Kirk Denbow); *Gone to Earth* (Powell) (as narrator); *The Wild Heart* (Powell and Pressburger—revised version of *Gone to Earth*, shortened) (as narrator); *The Steel Trap* (Andrew L. Stone) (as Jim Osborne); *Othello* (Welles) (as Senator)

1953   *Niagara* (Hathaway) (as George Loomis); *A Blueprint for Murder* (Andrew L. Stone) (as Whitney Cameron); *Egypt by Three* (Stoloff) (as narrator)

1955   *Special Delivery* (*Von Himmel gefallen*) (Brahm) (as Jonathan Adams)

1956   *The Killer Is Loose* (Boetticher) (as Sam Wagner); *The Bottom of the Bottle* (*Beyond the River*) (Hathaway) (as P. M.); *Nobody Runs Away* (Parker—short)

1957   *The Halliday Brand* (Joseph H. Lewis) (as Daniel)

1958   *Touch of Evil* (Welles) (as Detective); *From the Earth to the Moon* (Haskin) (as Victor Barbicane)

1960   *The Angel Wore Red* (Nunnally Johnson) (as Hawthorne)

1961   *The Last Sunset* (Aldrich) (as John Breckenridge); *The Karma* (for U.S. Dept. of Health, Education and Welfare) (as narrator)

1964   *Hush . . . Hush, Sweet Charlotte* (Aldrich) (as Drew)

1965   *The Great Sioux Massacre* (Salkow) (as Maj. Reno); *Krakatoa* (Izard) (re-edited version of 1933 film) (as narrator)

1966   *The Oscar* (Rouse) (as Kenneth H. Regan); *The Money Trap* (Kennedy) (as Dr. Horace Van Tilden); *Gli uomini dal passo pesante* (*The Tramplers*) (Sequi and Antonini, English-language copies: Band) (as Temple Cordeen)

1967   *Some May Live* (*In Saigon, Some May Live*) (Sewell) (as Col. Woodward); *Brighty of the Grand Canyon* (Norman Foster) (as Jim Owen); *Jack of Diamonds* (Taylor) (as Ace of Diamonds); *I crudeli* (*The Hellbenders*) (Corbucci) (as Jonas); *Comancho blanco* (*White Comanche; Rio Hondo*) (Briz, English-language copies: Kay)

1968   *Petulia* (Lester) (as Mr. Danner); *Split Second to an Epitaph* (Horn—for TV); *Gangster '70* (Guerrini)

1969   *The Lonely Profession* (Heyes—for TV); *Cutter's Trail* (McEveety—for TV); *Keene*

1970   *The Grasshopper* (Paris) (as Richard Morgan); *E venne l'ora della vendetta*; *Do You Take This Stranger?* (Heffron—for TV); *Assault on the Wayne* (Chomsky—for TV) (as Admiral); *Ido zero daisakusen* (*Latitude Zero*) (Honda) (as Capt. Craig McKenzie); *Tora! Tora! Tora!* (Fleischer) (as Henry Stimson); *City beneath the Sea* (*One Hour to Doomsday*) (Irwin Allen—for TV)

1971 *The Abominable Dr. Phibes* (Fuest) (as Dr. Vesalius); *La figlia di Frankenstein* (*Lady Frankenstein*) (Mel Welles) (as Baron)

1972 *The Devil's Daughter* (Szwarc—for TV) (as Judge Wetherby); *The Screaming Woman* (Smight—for TV); *Lo scopone scientifico* (*The Scientific Cardplayer*) (Comencini) (as George); *Gli orrori del castello di Norimberga* (*Baron Blood*) (Bava) (as Becker/the Baron); *Doomsday Voyage* (Vidette) (as Capt. Jason)

1973 *Soylent Green* (Fleischer) (as William Simonson); *A Delicate Balance* (Richardson) (as Harry)

1975 *Timber Tramps* (Garnett); *F for Fake* (*Vérités et mensonges*; *About Fakes*; *Nothing but the Truth*) (Welles); *Il giustiziere sfida la citta* (Lenzi)

1976 *The Lindbergh Kidnapping Case* (Kulik—for TV); *Un sussurro nel buio* (*A Whisper in the Dark*) (Aliprandi)

1977 *Twilight's Last Gleaming* (Aldrich) (as Arthur Renfrew); *Airport '77* (Jameson) (as Nicholas St. Downs II)

1978 *Screamers* (*The Island of the Fish Men*; *L'isola degli uomini Pesci*) (Martino and Miller) (as Prof. Marvin); *L'Ordre et la sécurité du monde* (Martino and Miller); *Caravans* (Fargo) (as Crandall); *Return to Fantasy Island* (McGowan—for TV)

1979 *Trauma* (Beattie); *Churchill and the Generals* (Gibson—for TV); *Concorde affaire* (*S.O.S. Concorde*) (Desdato)

1980 *Guyana: Cult of the Damned* (*Guyana: Crime of the Century*) (Cardona Jr.) (as Richard Gable); **Heaven's Gate** (Cimino) (as the Reverend Doctor); *The Hearse* (Bowers) (as Walter Pritchard); *Survivor* (Hemmings) (as priest); *Casino* (Chaffey—for TV) (as Ed Booker)

1984 *Delusion* (*The House Where Death Lives*) (Beattie—produced in 1980)

Publications

By COTTEN: book—

Vanity Will Get You Somewhere, New York, 1987.

By COTTEN: articles—

Interview in *The Hollywood Reporter*, 19 February 1980.
Interview with Allan Hunter, in *Films and Filming* (London), October 1987.

On COTTEN: books—

Higham, Charles, *The Films of Orson Welles*, Berkeley, 1971.
Kael, Pauline, *The Citizen Kane Book*, New York, 1971.

Joseph Cotten in *The Third Man*

McBride, Joseph, *Orson Welles*, London, 1972.
Memo from: David O. Selznick, edited by Rudy Behlmer, New York, 1972.
Bowers, Ronald, *The Selznick Players*, New York, 1976.

On COTTEN: articles—

Current Biography 1943, New York, 1943.
Obituary in *New York Times*, 7 February 1994.

*   *   *

Self-effacing to the point of never drawing attention away from his healthy-egoed leading ladies, Joseph Cotten was an indispensable part of forties romantic hagiography. When Cotten stared soulfully at a woman, his eyes revealed a man consumed by his feelings—not to the point of traditional derring-do or fancy declarations of love, but to the level of psychological breakdown. The term lovesick could have been coined for him. With the burgeoning fascination with psychoanalysis (given impetus by *Spellbound*), Freudians could study Cotten as the era's prime symbol of emotional defeat and sublimation. If only one of his roles (*I'll Be Seeing You*) featured an actual victim of shell-shock, many of his other opuses (*Love Letters, Since You Went Away, The Magnificent Ambersons, Portrait of Jennie*) could be considered studies of a love-shocked martyr in thrall to elusive women on pedestals. That above list includes some of the period's most winsome classics and one masterpiece, Welles's studio-mauled *Ambersons*, in which Cotten loses his lady fair while regretting the progress he has implemented, aware that his mechanical forward-strides have destroyed his beloved Isabelle's family. Even in his debut film, *Citizen Kane*, always complaisant Cotten is a fence-sitting wag content to criticize and conjecture regarding someone else, but not forcefully pursuing his own goals. In the mythology of Hollywood, the reactive Cotten is a Cupid-struck Sisyphus forever pushing his own heart up that hill. Usually proving that the good guy finishes, if not last, at least lovelorn, Cotten spends World War II waiting for Claudette Colbert to have a weak adulterous moment in *Since You Went Away* but surrender never comes. In *Portrait of Jennie* (a movie immeasurably enhanced by its dreamy score and iridescent black and white cinematography), the unrequited suitor Cotten does not have a ghost of a chance with his spectral love object. But real or otherwise, all this leading man's dream girls turn out to be figurative if not literal phantoms.

The downside of Cotten's ineffectuality is that his innate decency is never backed up by action. Thus, while typifying all the cherished virtues of modern times in the adult sagebrusher *Duel in the Sun*, Cotten is helpless to save his heart's desire, Pearl, from the call of the wild represented by his compunction-free brother, Lewt. Complexly, the scenario of this Western epic makes it crystal clear that Cotten is a catalyst in the film's tragic ending. Hawking the necessity of goodness is not enough when villains run helter-skelter in the devil's employ.

After his peak period, watch-and-wait Cotten's lack of willfulness takes on a more pejorative coloration. In two fifties classics of cuckoldry, he is cast as the middle-aged good provider who is less slow-burning than burned out. Unable to curb his wife's infantile pining for a flashy lifestyle in *Beyond the Forest*, Cotten is Stoicism incarnate but playing second banana to Bette Davis's mood shifts ends up being a career misstep into character roles. Visibly older by the time he visits *Niagara* to punish the bombshell wife he craves but cannot satisfy, Cotten's screen alter ego finally takes steps, but homicide brings the spineless spouse no vengeful joy.

On one previous occasion—the high point of Cotten's acting career—Hitchcock divined the underside to Cotten's sober nobility and cast him, atypically, as a man of confident action. In *Shadow of a Doubt*, Cotten's Uncle Charlie pursues women not for their beauty but for their pocketbooks. Contemptuous of humanity in general, this terminator of wealthy widows kills for fun and profit. Pitilessly zeroing in on the killer's self-loathing, Hitchcock and Cotten characterize cold-blooded Uncle Charlie's strangleholds as a reaction to his basic impotence. It is as if each killing was a shameful admittance of lack of character.

Sadly, for a career that includes the superb postwar thriller *The Third Man* and roles or cameos in five Welles classics, Cotten seemed to give up on stardom with the same lack of coyness his characters suffered from. He was lucky to average two good movies a decade from the fifties onward. In addition to a memorable appearance as the Reverend Doctor failing to inspire a graduating class in *Heaven's Gate*, Cotten was supremely swinish as a greedy plotter in *Hush . . . Hush, Sweet Charlotte*, and stomach-churningly class conscious as an overprotective father in *Petulia*. Perhaps it is merciful to overlook those decades of perfectly intoned line deliveries that he palmed off as performances and concentrate on his glory days as a luckless Lothario forever reaching for the unattainable woman. Falling short or pulling fatefully back, Cotten is remembered as the hero-in-stasis, a man whose goodness ultimately proved ineffective in his pursuit of happiness.

—Robert Pardi

CRAWFORD, Broderick

Nationality: American. **Born:** William Broderick Crawford in Philadelphia, 9 December 1911. Son of the actress Helen Broderick. **Education:** Dean Academy, Franklin, Massachusetts, 1924-28. **Military Service:** 1942-45—served as sergeant in U.S. Army Air Force. **Family:** Married 1) the actress Joan Tabor (divorced), son: Kim; 2) the actress Kay Griffith, 1940, children: Lauren and Kelly; two later marriages. **Career:** 1928-30—after high school, joined parents in Max Gordon's vaudeville unit; c. 1932-36—appeared occasionally on radio; c. 1934—legitimate stage debut in London production of *She Loves Me Not*; 1935—Broadway debut in *Point Valaine*; 1937—contract with MGM: film debut in *Woman Chases Man*; 1949—starring role in *All the King's Men*; contract with Columbia; 1955-59—starred in syndicated TV series *Highway Patrol*; 1960s—in many Italian and Spanish Westerns and adventure films; 1961-62—in syndicated TV series *King of Diamonds*; 1970-71—in TV series *The Interns*; 1974—on Broadway in *That Championship Season*; late 1970s—guest host of *Saturday Night Live*. **Awards:** Best Actor Academy Award, and Best Actor, New York Film Critics, for *All the King's Men*, 1949. **Died:** In Rancho Mirage, California, 26 April 1986.

Films as Actor:

1937 *Woman Chases Man* (Blystone); *Submarine D-1* (Bacon)
1938 *Start Cheering* (Rogell)
1939 *Ambush* (Neumann); *Sudden Money* (Grinde); *Undercover Doctor* (Louis King); *Island of Lost Men* (Neumann); *Beau Geste* (Wellman); *The Real Glory* (Hathaway); *Eternally Yours* (Garnett)
1940 *Slightly Honorable* (Garnett); *I Can't Give You Anything but Love, Baby* (Rogell); *When the Daltons Rode* (Marshall); *Seven Sinners* (Garnett); *Trail of the Vigilantes* (Dwan); *The Texas Rangers Ride Again* (Hogan)
1941 *The Black Cat* (Rogell); *Tight Shoes* (Rogell) (as Speedy Miller); *Badlands of Dakota* (Green); *South of Tahiti* (Waggner)

1942 *North to the Klondike* (Kenton); *Butch Minds the Baby* (Rogell)
(as Aloysius "Butch" Grogan); *Larceny, Inc.* (Bacon); *Broadway* (Seiter); *Men of Texas* (*Men of Destiny*) (Enright); *Sin Town* (Enright); *Keeping Fit* (Lubin—short)
1946 *The Runaround* (Lamont); *The Black Angel* (Neill)
1947 *Slave Girl* (Lamont); *The Flame* (Auer)
1948 *The Time of Your Life* (Potter); *Sealed Verdict* (Allen); *Bad Men of Tombstone* (Neumann)
1949 *Night unto Night* (Siegel); *A Kiss in the Dark* (Daves); *Anna Lucasta* (Rapper); ***All the King's Men*** (Rossen) (as Willie Stark)
1950 *Cargo to Capetown* (McEvoy); *Convicted* (Levin); *Born Yesterday* (Cukor) (as Harry Brock)
1951 *The Mob* (*Remember That Face*) (Parrish)
1952 *Lone Star* (Sherman); *Scandal Sheet* (*The Dark Page*) (Karlson); *Last of the Comanches* (*The Sabre and the Arrow*) (de Toth); *Stop, You're Killing Me* (Del Ruth)
1953 *The Last Posse* (Werker)
1954 *Night People* (Johnson); *Human Desire* (Fritz Lang); *Down Three Dark Streets* (Laven)
1955 *Big House, U.S.A.* (Koch); *New York Confidential* (Rouse); *Not as a Stranger* (Kramer); *Il bidone* (*The Swindlers*) (Fellini); *Man on a Bus* (Lewis—for United Jewish Appeal Fund)
1956 *The Fastest Gun Alive* (Rouse); *Between Heaven and Hell* (Fleischer)
1958 *The Decks Ran Red* (Stone)
1960 *La vendetta di Ercole* (*Goliath and the Dragon*; *The Revenge of Hercules*) (Cottafavi)
1961 *Nasilje na trgu* (*Square of Violence*) (Bercovici)
1962 *Convicts Four* (*Reprieve*) (Kaufman); *The Castilian* (Setó)
1964 *A House Is Not a Home* (Rouse)
1965 *Up from the Beach* (Parrish); *Kid Rodelo* (Carlson)
1966 *The Oscar* (Rouse); *El escuadró de la muerte* (*Per un dollaro di gloria*; *Mutiny at Fort Sharp*) (Cerchio); *The Texican* (Selander); *The Vulture* (Huntington)
1967 *Red Tomahawk* (Springsteen)
1970 *Wie kommt ein so reizendes Mädchen zu diesem Gewerbe?* (*How Did a Nice Girl Like You Get into This Business?*) (Tremper); *Maharlika* (Hopper); *The Challenge* (Smithee—for TV)
1971 *A Tattered Web* (Wendkos—for TV)
1972 *Embassy* (Hessler); *House of Dracula's Daughter* (Hessler); *The Candidate* (Ritchie) (as voice)
1973 *Hell's Bloody Devils* (*Smashing the Crime Syndicate*) (Adamson); *Terror in the Wax Museum* (Fenady); *The Adventures of Nick Carter* (Krasny—for TV)
1974 *The Phantom of Hollywood* (Levitt—for TV)
1976 *Won Ton Ton, the Dog Who Saved Hollywood* (Winner); *Mayday at Forty Thousand Feet* (Butler—for TV); *Look What's Happened to Rosemary's Baby* (O'Steen—for TV)
1977 *The Private Files of J. Edgar Hoover* (*J. Edgar Hoover*) (Cohen) (title role); *Ningen no shomei* (*Proof of the Man*) (Sato)
1979 *A Little Romance* (George Roy Hill) (as Brod); *Supertrain* (Curtis—for TV)
1980 *Harlequin* (Wincer); *There Goes the Bride* (Marcel)
1981 *The Upper Crust* (Patzak)
1982 *Liar's Moon* (Fisher)

Publications

On CRAWFORD: articles—

Herald Tribune (New York), 28 November 1937.
"Broderick Crawford" in *Current Biography*, New York, 1950.

*   *   *

During the Eisenhower era, Broderick Crawford was everyone's favorite "authority figure" on television. With his bulldog face and barking voice, he roared down the highway after lawbreakers as Chief Dan Matthews in *Highway Patrol*. Prior to his television success, however, it was Crawford's performance as Willie Stark in the film *All the King's Men* that had established his reputation as an actor. As the honest country lawyer who becomes a ruthless demagogue, Crawford is frighteningly convincing in his transformation of character. His physical gifts as an actor—the beefy physique, the aggressive stance, the gruff voice—were never more perfectly exploited than in his portrayal of the dichotomous nature of Stark. Crawford's intelligent performance will always stand as a model interpretation of how power can corrupt the individual. He was later to draw on this same persona in his perversely sympathetic portrayal of J. Edgar Hoover in Larry Cohen's *The Private Files of J. Edgar Hoover*, a comic book-style fantasy that depicts Hoover as a sexually repressed neurotic who freely violated the law.

After his screen debut in 1937 Crawford appeared in supporting roles and as an occasional lead in "B" pictures such as *Sin Town* and *The Runaround*. It was his experience in vaudeville and on Broadway that prepared him for his success in his first lead roles, as Speedy Miller in *Tight Shoes* and Aloysius "Butch" Grogan in *Butch Minds the Baby*. In these two broad theatrical comedies by Damon Runyon, Crawford established himself as the quintessential Runyon hero—the soft-hearted, streetwise mobster. His familiarity with the underworld personality, the result of his portrayal of these amiable rogues, served him well when he gave a brilliant comic performance as Harry Brock, the arrogant self-made tycoon in *Born Yesterday*.

Crawford is never more likable than when he plays against type, as in *The Time of Your Life* (a melancholy policeman), *Not as a Stranger* (a cynical doctor), and *The Real Glory* (an officer who loves orchids). The subtlety of his performance in these offbeat roles tends to be overshadowed by his more familiar image as a screen heavy, the raging psychopath, as in *The Scandal Sheet*, *New York Confidential*, *Big House, U.S.A.*, and *The Fastest Gun Alive*, in which he plays a trigger-happy desperado who must compulsively and continually prove his manhood with a gun.

Apart from his acclaimed performances in *All the King's Men*, *Born Yesterday*, and *The Mob* (in which he plays a tough undercover cop), however, most of Crawford's fine work has been ignored by critics. Two of his most memorable performances are in this category: Fritz Lang's *Human Desire* and Federico Fellini's *Il bidone*. In the Lang film, Crawford commands pity and fear as the tormented railway engineer driven to insane jealousy and murder by his unfaithful wife. In the Fellini film, he is eloquent and moving as the petty thief who attempts to redeem himself for the sake of his adoring daughter. The tragic final image of *Il bidone*, Crawford alone and dying on a deserted mountain road, is one of the most heartrending in the history of the cinema.

—Jeff Stafford

CRAWFORD, Joan

Nationality: American. **Born:** Lucille LeSueur in San Antonio, Texas, 23 March 1908; adopted name of stepfather, Cassin, as a child. **Education:** Attended St. Agnes School and Rockingham; Stephens College, Columbia, Missouri, for about three months. **Family:** Married 1) the actor Douglas Fairbanks Jr., 1929 (divorced 1933); 2) the actor Franchot Tone, 1935 (divorced 1939); 3) Phillip Terry, 1942 (divorced 1946), adopted children: Christina, Christopher, Cynthia, and Cathy; 4) Alfred N. Steele, 1955 (died 1959). **Career:** Took dancing lessons as a child, and became a dancer; 1923—dancer at Oriole Terrace club, Detroit; 1924—in chorus of Broadway revue *Innocent Eyes* and *The Passing Show of 1924*; spotted by MGM talent scout; 1925—contract with MGM, and given name "Joan Crawford," prize-winning name in movie magazine contest; 1928—dancer in film *Our Dancing Daughters*; 1929—first talkie, *Untamed*; 1943—left MGM, signed with Warner Brothers; occasional TV appearances from 1953; 1955—after marriage to Alfred Steele, chairman of Pepsi-Cola Company, began making promotional appearances for company; 1959—following death of Steele, became first woman member of company's board of directors, and later became company's official hostess and vice president; 1964—suffered pneumonia while working on *Hush . . . Hush, Sweet Charlotte*, replaced by Olivia de Havilland. **Awards:** Best Actress Academy Award, for *Mildred Pierce*, 1945. **Died:** In New York City, 13 May 1977.

Films as Actress:

(as Lucille LeSueur)

1925   *Lady of the Night* (Bell) (as double for Norma Shearer); *Proud Flesh* (King Vidor) (as party guest); *Pretty Ladies* (Bell) (as Bobby)

(as Joan Crawford)

1925   *The Circle* (Borzage) (as young Lady Catharine); *Old Clothes* (Cline) (as Mary Riley); *Sally, Irene, and Mary* (Goulding) (as Irene)

1926   *The Boob* (Wellman) (as Jane); *Tramp, Tramp, Tramp* (Edwards and Capra) (as Betty Burton); *Paris* (Goulding) (as the Girl)

1927   *The Taxi Dancer* (Millarde) (as Joslyn Poe); *Winners of the Wilderness* (Van Dyke) (as Renee Contrecoeur); *The Understanding Heart* (Conway) (as Monica Dale); *The Unknown* (Browning) (as Estrellita); *Twelve Miles Out* (Conway) (as Jane); *Spring Fever* (Sedgwick) (as Allie Monte)

1928   *West Point* (Sedgwick) (as Betty Channing); *Rose-Marie* (Hubbard) (title role); *Across to Singapore* (Nigh) (as Priscilla Crowninshield); *The Law of the Range* (Nigh) (as Betty Dallas); *Four Walls* (Nigh) (as Frieda); *Our Dancing Daughters* (Beaumont) (as Diana Medford); *Dream of Love* (Niblo) (as Adrienne)

1929   *The Duke Steps Out* (Cruze) (as Susie); *Hollywood Revue of 1929* (Riesner); *Our Modern Maidens* (Conway) (as Billie Brown); *Untamed* (Conway) (as Bingo)

1930   *Montana Moon* (St. Clair) (as Joan); *Our Blushing Brides* (Beaumont) (as Jerry Marsh); *Paid* (Wood) (as Mary Turner)

1931   *Dance, Fools, Dance* (Beaumont) (as Bonnie Jordan); *Laughing Sinners* (Beaumont) (as Ivy Stevens); *This Modern Age* (Grinde) (as Valentine Winters); *Possessed* (Brown) (as Marian Martin)

1932   *Grand Hotel* (Goulding) (as Flaemmchen); *Letty Lynton* (Browning) (title role); *Rain* (Milestone) (as Sadie Thompson)

1933   *Today We Live* (Hawks) (as Diana Boyce-Smith); *Dancing Lady* (Leonard) (as Janie Barlow)

1934   *Sadie McKee* (Brown) (title role); *Chained* (Brown) (as Diane Lovering)

1935   *Forsaking All Others* (Van Dyke) (as Mary Clay); *No More Ladies* (Edward H. Griffith and Cukor) (as Marcia Townsend); *I Live My Life* (Van Dyke) (as Kay)

1936   *The Gorgeous Hussy* (Brown) (as Peggy O'Neal Eaton); *Love on the Run* (Van Dyke) (as Sally Parker)

1937   *The Last of Mrs. Cheyney* (Boleslawski) (as Fay Cheyney); *The Bride Wore Red* (Arzner) (as Annie Palowitz/Signorina Vivaldi); *Mannequin* (Borzage) (as Jessie Cassidy)

1938   *The Shining Hour* (Borzage) (as Olivia Riley)

1939   *Ice Follies of 1939* (Schunzel) (as Mary McKay); ***The Women*** (Cukor) (as Crystal Allen)

1940   *Strange Cargo* (Borzage) (as Julie); *Susan and God* (Cukor) (as Susan Trexel)

1941   *A Woman's Face* (Cukor) (as Anna Holm); *When Ladies Meet* (Leonard) (as Mary Howard)

1942   *They All Kissed the Bride* (Hall) (as Margaret J. Drew); *Reunion in France* (Dassin) (as Michele de la Becque)

1943   *Above Suspicion* (Thorpe) (as Frances Myles)

1944   *Hollywood Canteen* (Daves)

1945   ***Mildred Pierce*** (Curtiz) (title role)

1946   *Humoresque* (Negulesco) (as Helen Wright)

1947   *Possessed* (Bernhardt) (as Louise Howell); *Daisy Kenyon* (Preminger) (title role)

1949   *Flamingo Road* (Curtiz) (as Lane Bellamy); *It's a Great Feeling* (David Butler) (as guest)

1950   *The Damned Don't Cry* (Sherman) (as Ethel Whitehead/Lorna Hansen Forbes); *Harriet Craig* (Sherman) (title role)

1951   *Goodbye, My Fancy* (Sherman) (as Agatha Reed)

1952   *This Man Is Dangerous* (Feist) (as Beth Austin); *Sudden Fear* (Miller) (as Myra Hudson)

1953   *Torch Song* (Walters) (as Jenny Stewart)

1954   ***Johnny Guitar*** (Nicholas Ray) (as Vienna)

1955   *Female on the Beach* (Pevney) (as Lynn Markham); *Queen Bee* (MacDougall) (as Eva Phillips)

1956   *Autumn Leaves* (Aldrich) (as Milly)

1957   *The Golden Virgin* (Miller); *The Story of Esther Costello* (Miller) (as Margaret Landi)

1959   *The Best of Everything* (Negulesco) (as Amanda Farrow)

1962   *Whatever Happened to Baby Jane?* (Aldrich) (as Blanche Hudson)

1963   *The Caretakers* (Bartlett) (as Lucretia Terry)

1964   *Strait-Jacket* (Castle) (as Lucy Harbin)

1965   *I Saw What You Did* (Castle) (as Amy Nelson); *Della* (Gist) (title role)

1967   *The Karate Killers* (Shear—compilation of *The Man from U.N.C.L.E.* eps.) (as Amanda True)

1968   *Berserk!* (O'Connolly) (as Monica Rivers)

1969   "Eyes" segment of *Night Gallery* (Spielberg—for TV) (as Miss Menlo)

1970   *Trog* (Francis) (as Dr. Brockton)

Publications

By CRAWFORD: books—

A Portrait of Joan: The Autobiography of Joan Crawford, with Jane Kesner, New York, 1962.
My Way of Life, New York, 1971.
Conversations with Joan Crawford, by Roy Newquist, New York, 1981.

By CRAWFORD: article—

"The Job of Keeping at the Top," in *Saturday Evening Post* (Philadelphia), 17 June 1933.

On CRAWFORD: books—

Quirk, Lawrence J., *The Films of Joan Crawford*, New York, 1968.
Carr, Larry, *Four Fabulous Faces*, New Rochelle, New York, 1971.
Rosen, Marjorie, *Popcorn Venus*, New York, 1973.
Harvey, Stephen, *Joan Crawford*, New York, 1974.
Crawford, Christina, *Mommie Dearest*, New York, 1978.

Joan Crawford

Thomas, Bob, *Joan Crawford: A Biography*, New York, 1978.

Walker, Alexander, *Joan Crawford, The Ultimate Star*, New York, 1983.

Kobal, John, editor, *Joan Crawford: Legend*, London, 1985.

Crawford, Christina, *Survivor*, New York, 1988.

Wayne, Jane Ellen, *Crawford's Men*, New York, 1988.

Considine, Shaun, *Bette and Joan: The Divine Feud*, New York, 1989.

Guiles, Fred Lawrence, *Joan Crawford: The Last Word*, Secaucus, New Jersey, 1995.

Robertson, Pamela, *Guilty Pleasures: Feminist Camp from Mae West to Madonna*, Durham, North Carolina, 1996.

On CRAWFORD: articles—

St. Johns, Ivan, "She Doesn't Use Lipstick in Public," in *Photoplay* (New York), May 1927.

Biery, Ruth, "The Story of the Dancing Girl," in *Photoplay* (New York), September through November 1928.

"Adela Rogers St. Johns Presents Joan Crawford Starring in the Dramatic Rise of a Self-Made Star," in *Photoplay* (New York), October through December 1937.

"Joan Crawford," in *Sight and Sound* (London), April-June 1952.

Card, J., "The Film Career of Joan Crawford," in *Image* (Rochester, New York), January 1956.

Braun, E., "Forty Years a Queen," in *Films and Filming* (London), May 1965.

Quirk, Lawrence J., "Joan Crawford," in *Films in Review* (New York), December 1965.

Current Biography 1966, New York, 1966.

Bowers, Ronald, "Joan Crawford: Latest Decade," in *Films in Review* (New York), June-July 1966 (see also August-September issue).

Bowers, Ronald, "Joan Crawford's Fiftieth Anniversary," in *Films in Review* (New York), January 1975.

Obituary in *New York Times*, 14 May 1977.

Bowers, Ronald, "Hors d'oeuvre," in *Films in Review* (New York), April 1977; see also August-September 1977 issue.

Harvey, S., "In Memoriam: Joan Crawford," in *Film Comment* (New York), July-August 1977.

Passek, J.-L., "Joan Crawford," in *Cinéma* (Paris), August-September 1977.

Bourget, J.-L., "Faces of the American Melodrama: Joan Crawford," and "Afterword Note to Jean-Louis Bourget's Article," by B. Horrigan, in *Film Reader 3*, 1978.

Bagh, P., "Visages de Joan Crawford," in *Ecran* (Paris), January 1978.

Harvey, Stephen, "Joan Crawford," in *The Movie Star*, edited by Elisabeth Weis, New York, 1981.

Thomson, D., "All Our Joan Crawfords," in *Sight and Sound* (London), Winter 1981-82.

Herzog, C. C., and J. M. Gaines, "Puffed Sleeves before Teatime: Joan Crawford, Adrian and Women Audiences," in *Wide Angle* (Baltimore, Maryland), vol. 6, no. 4, 1985.

Clark, John, filmography in *Premiere* (New York), November 1989.

Sorel, Edward, "Joan Crawfod and Bette Davis," in *Atlantic* (New York), September 1991.

Carroll, Kathleen, "Hostess Dearest," in *Premiere* (New York), Winter 1994.

*   *   *

Dismissed by Bette Davis as a Star (rather than an Actress like Bette), taken for granted by MGM, ignored as an aging legend, and trashed in a tell-all bio by her daughter (who claims Joan was an Actress rather than a Mother), Joan Crawford survives the contumely of others. This controversial patron saint of fan magazines, who has been labeled everything from a porn-star to child-beater to spitefully jealous co-star to closet alcoholic, is undisputably one thing, a great film star. Whatever Crawford was offscreen, she is our most representative American film icon because she wanted it more than all the others.

Free-spiriting her way through the silent era in true flapper fashion, Crawford thought nothing of altering her look or jumping on a promising trend whenever she needed to pump plasma into an anemic career. Directors are on record as stating she needed careful reining because she lacked the technique to control her emotions; critics point to her forties performances as evidence of the musty staleness of the studio system. But the woman who never let a fan letter go unanswered always respected her public and tried to give them what they wanted. When they tired of Joan, the Blue-Collar Goddess, she gave them Joan, the Domestic Martyr, and when that image ran out of vim, Crawford restyled herself as the Untamable Shrew. What the many faces of Crawford had in common is glamour; it is a quality that is missing in modern films which kow-tow to naturalism and have little to do with theatrical notions of acting but a lot to do with great screen acting in which the star must communicate her intense belief in her own make-believe image to the movie public. In big hits such as *Possessed* (1931) and *Mannequin* (1937), she offered the shop girl's fantasy of herself, with upward mobility in a good man's arms—the ultimate prize. Later in her career, while still exuding that movie star *je ne sais quoi,* she became a menopausal everywoman living out the worst fears of an audience that had aged with her. Naturally, the gloved hand choking back Crawford's tears was encircled in a haul from Harry Winston's.

Yet, the number one Hurrell-photographed drone in the Tinseltown film factory could step out of her Joan-ness with stunning results (a fiery Sadie Thompson in *Rain*, a performance which the passage of time has vindicated). Even her acting triumphs in offbeat roles capitalized on her trademark stoic chic—a poised demeanor whose formidableness is softened by those mascara-lashed eyes widening in apprehension about what emotional dark woods attractive scoundrels might lead her into. In the forties especially, the Crawford visage was a study in face-saving willfulness—expansive lips for quivering, lighthouse eyes for staring unfathomably, luxurious eyebrows for arching disdainfully; these features seldom acted in concert but were often immobile as if her face was on strike against appearing vulnerable. When emotions finally galvanized that paralyzed pan, all histrionic hell broke loose. More than any other screen icon, Crawford made suffering attractive. Comfortable with being the Queen of masochism, versatile Joan could also be spikily funny as the other woman in *The Women*, convincingly hard-as-nails as a symbolic mouthpiece in *Strange Cargo*, hypnotically ambivalent in *A Woman's Face* as a scarred con woman, alluringly vexatious in *Humoresque* as a social pillar whose cigarette roomfuls of swains rush to light, deservedly Oscared for completing her ten-step program in how to bake pies and spoil a child while wearing a halo of face powder and pastry flour in *Mildred Pierce*, sufficiently unhinged as a schizophrenic in *Possessed* (1947) to impress the intransigent James Agee, taken for granted in her seething-with-suppressed-rage tour de force in *Baby Jane* and chillingly brittle as a *Night Gallery* control-freak who treats everyone as potential toadies.

Admittedly, the long arm of camp was reaching out for Crawford long before *Night Gallery* or William Castle got mileage out of her waning stardom. From *Flamingo Road* onward, Crawford was not only prepared to do battle with sexist roadblocks but with her own feminity. What that cockeyed wonder of a film version of *Mommie Dearest* suggests is that the price of succeeding in a world dominated by men is to end up a quasi man oneself. In what emerged not as a hatchet job but as an empathetic analysis by interpreter Dunaway, *Mommie Dearest* portrays Crawford's life as a series of great moments from films such as *Torch Song*, *Queen Bee*, etc. When Dunaway's Crawford tells Pepsi executives that she fought bigger monsters than them in Hollywood and won, cinephiles laugh and then they cry, at the sacrifices this warrior-star made in a fool's quest to stay a star at the top.

Throughout the fifties in her mannish period, Crawford became a bitch-on-wheels forever at the mercy of a gigolo (*Female on the Beach*) or disturbed younger man (*Autumn Leaves*) or even a repressed lesbian (*Johnny Guitar*) but the constant in all these films is the ongoing punishment of Joan Crawford who seemed to be a female Christ-figure paying for the sins of every love-starved fan in the audience. Glamorous to the end, Crawford still had those massive shoulders for bearing such a burden.

What shines through all these bizarre melodramas is Crawford's unchecked fever for adulation; what the teary-eyed spectators accepted as Joan's desire for fade-out surrender to a man was actually Joan's love affair with her own career. Those who still respond to Crawford's icy soap operas regard *Harriet Craig* as her most characteristic role. Substitute a movie career for the symbolic dream house and you can appreciate the essence of The Joan Crawford Story. Although lovers were fickle and friends had the effrontery to snag better roles, only a legendary film career could bring the joy few mortals know, or so Joan thought. Rejected by the industry in the last years of her life, Crawford had too much spare time to contemplate the drawbacks of the choice she had made.

—Robert Pardi

CRISP, Donald

Nationality: British. **Born:** Aberfeldy, Perthshire, Scotland, 27 July 1880. **Education:** Eton College and Oxford University. **Military Service:** 1899-1902—trooper in Boer War; wounded; during World War I—served as British Intelligence Officer, providing information on conditions in Russia. **Family:** Married 1) Marie Stark (divorced 1919); 2) the screenwriter Jane Murfin, 1932 (divorced 1944). **Career:** 1906—moved to U.S.; hired for musical *Floradora*; also sang for Fisher-Reilly Opera Company; 1906-09—produced and appeared in some Mutascopes in New York; c. 1909—joined Biograph as actor; 1910s—became part of D. W. Griffith's stock company and later served as Griffith's assistant director on several films. 1914-30—worked as both director and actor; 1922—supervised Famous-Lasky studios in Bombay, India; 1920s-1950s—served as loan adviser to film companies for Bank of Italy. **Awards:** Best Supporting Actor Academy Award for *How Green Was My Valley*, 1941. **Died:** In Van Nuys, California, 25 May 1974.

Films as Actor:

1907 *The French Maid*
1910 *Sunshine Sue* (Griffith); *Winning Back His Love* (Griffith)
1911 *The Two Paths* (Griffith); *Fate's Turning* (Griffith); *A Wreath of Orange Blossoms* (Griffith); *What Shall We Do with Our Old* (Griffith); *The Primal Call* (Griffith); *Out from the Shadow* (Griffith); *The Diving Girl*; *The Adventures of Billy* (Griffith); *The Battle* (Griffith); *The Failure* (Griffith)
1912 *When Kings Were the Law* (Griffith)
1913 *The Best Man Wins* (Cabanne); *Drink's Lure* (Cabanne); *The Daylight Burglar* (Cabanne); *Two Men of the Desert* (Griffith); *Intolerance* (Griffith)
1914 *The Battle of the Sexes* (Griffith); *The Avenging Conscience*; *The Escape* (Griffith); *Home, Sweet Home* (Griffith); *The Great Leap* (Cabanne); *The Different Man*; *The Mountain Rat* (Kirkwood); *The Sisters* (Davis); *A Question of Courage* (Cabanne)
1915 *The Birth of a Nation* (Griffith); *Bred in the Bone* (Powell); *Such a Little Queen* (Hugh Ford); *The Love Route* (Dwan);

The Commanding Officer (Dwan); *May Blossom* (Dwan); *A Girl of Yesterday* (Dwan); *The Foundling* (Dwan); *Joan the Woman* (DeMille) (+ uncredited 2nd unit d)
1918 *One More American* (DeMille)
1919 **Broken Blossoms** (Griffith)
1926 *The Black Pirate* (Parker)
1928 *The River Pirate* (Howard)
1929 *Trent's Last Case* (Hawks); *The Pagan* (W. S. Van Dyke); *The Viking* (Neill); *The Return of Sherlock Holmes* (Dean)
1930 *Scotland Yard* (*Detective Clive, Bart*) (Howard)
1931 *Svengali* (Mayo); *Kick In* (Wallace)
1932 *A Passport to Hell* (*Burnt Offering*) (Lloyd); *Red Dust* (Fleming)
1933 *Broadway Bad* (*Her Reputation*) (Lanfield)
1934 *The Crime Doctor* (Robertson); *The Key* (Curtiz); *The Life of Vergie Winters* (Santell); *What Every Woman Knows* (La Cava); *The Little Minister* (Wallace)
1935 *Vanessa, Her Love Story* (Howard); *Laddie* (Stevens); *Oil for the Lamps of China* (LeRoy); *Mutiny on the Bounty* (Lloyd)
1936 *The White Angel* (Dieterle); *Mary of Scotland* (John Ford); *A Woman Rebels* (Sandrich); *The Charge of the Light Brigade* (Curtiz); *The Great O'Malley* (Dieterle); *Beloved Enemy* (Potter)
1937 *Parnell* (Stahl); *The Life of Emile Zola* (Dieterle); *That Certain Woman* (Goulding); *Confession* (May); *Sergeant Murphy* (Eason)
1938 *Jezebel* (Wyler); *The Beloved Brat* (*A Dangerous Age*) (Lubin); *The Amazing Dr. Clitterhouse* (Litvak); *Valley of the Giants* (Keighley); *The Sisters* (Litvak); *The Dawn Patrol* (Goulding); *Comet over Broadway* (Berkeley)
1939 *The Oklahoma Kid* (Bacon); *Wuthering Heights* (Wyler); *Juarez* (Dieterle); *Daughters Courageous* (Curtiz); *The Old Maid* (Goulding); *The Private Lives of Elizabeth and Essex* (Curtiz)
1940 *The Story of Dr. Ehrlich's Magic Bullet* (*Dr. Ehrlich's Magic Bullet*) (Dieterle); *Brother Orchid* (Bacon); *City for Conquest* (Litvak); *The Sea Hawk* (Curtiz); *Knute Rockne—All American* (Bacon)
1941 *Shining Victory* (Rapper); *Dr. Jekyll and Mr. Hyde* (Fleming); *How Green Was My Valley* (John Ford)
1942 *The Battle of Midway* (John Ford—short) (as narrator); *The Gay Sisters* (Rapper)
1943 *Forever and a Day* (Clair and others); *Lassie Come Home* (Wilcox)
1944 *The Uninvited* (Allen); *The Adventure of Mark Twain* (Rapper); *National Velvet* (Brown)
1945 *Son of Lassie* (Simon); *The Valley of Decision* (Garnett)
1947 *Ramrod* (De Toth)
1948 *Hills of Home* (*Master of Lassie*) (Wilcox); *Whispering Smith* (Fenton)
1949 *Challenge to Lassie* (Thorpe)
1950 *Bright Leaf* (Curtiz)
1951 *Home Town Story* (Pierson)
1954 *Prince Valiant* (Hathaway); *The Long Gray Line* (John Ford)
1955 *The Man from Laramie* (Anthony Mann)
1957 *Drango* (Bartlett)
1958 *Saddle the Wind* (Parrish); *The Last Hurrah* (John Ford)
1959 *A Dog of Flanders* (Clark)
1960 *Pollyanna* (Swift)
1961 *Greyfriar's Bobby* (Chaffey)
1963 *Spencer's Mountain* (Daves)

Films as Director:

1914 *Her Father's Silent Partner*; *The Dawn*; *The Mysterious Shot* (+ ro); *The Newer Woman* (+ ro); *Her Birthday Present*;

Their First Acquaintance; *The Idiot*; *The Tavern of Tragedy*; *Her Mother's Necklace*; *Frenchy*; *The Milkfed Boy*; *Down the Hill to Creditville*; *The Warning* (+ ro); *His Mother's Trust*; *Sands of Fate*; *The Availing Prayer*; *His Lesson*

1915 *An Old Fashioned Girl*; *How Hazel Got Even* (uncredited direction)

1916 *Ramona* (+ ro under pseudonym James Needham)

1917 *His Sweetheart*; *The Bond Between*; *The Marcellini Millions*; *The Cook of Canyon Camp* (+ co-sc); *Lost in Transit*; *The Countess Charming* (+ ro); *The Clever Mrs. Carfax*; *A Roadside Impressario*

1918 *Jules of the Strong Heart*; *Rimrock Jones*; *The House of Silence*; *Believe Me Xant(h)ippe*; *The Firefly of France*; *Less Than Kin*; *The Goat*; *The Way of a Man with a Maid*; *Under the Top*; *Venus in the East*

1919 *Johnny Get Your Gun*; *Poor Boob*; *Something to Do*; *Putting It Over*; *A Very Good Young Man*; *Love Insurance*; *Why Smith Left Home*; *It Pays to Advertise*; *Too Much Johnson*

1920 *The Six Best Cellars*; *Miss Hobbs*; *Held by the Enemy*

1921 *The Barbarian*; *Appearances*; *The Princess of New York*; *Beside the Bonnie Brier Bush* (*The Bonnie Brier Bush*) (+ ro)

1923 *Ponjola*

1924 ***The Navigator*** (co-d only, with Buster Keaton); *Tell Your Children*

1925 *Don Q of Zorro* (+ ro)

1926 *Sunny Side Up* (*Footlights*); *Young April*; *Man Bait*

1927 *Nobody's Widow*; *Vanity*; *The Fighting Eagle* (*Brigadier Gerard*); *Dress Parade*

1928 *Stand and Deliver*; *The Cop*

1930 *The Runaway Bride*

Publications

By CRISP: article—

"We Lost So Much Dignity as We Came of Age," interview in *Films and Filming* (London), December 1960.

On CRISP: articles—

Moret, H., "D'autres ... ," in *Ecran* (Paris), July 1974.
Slide, Anthony, "The Other Griffith Actors," in *Films in Review* (New York), October 1975.

* * *

One of the unassuming pillars of the industry, Donald Crisp had a very long and successful career in motion pictures. A Scot who was educated at Oxford and served as a soldier in the Boer War, he emigrated to New York and appeared in opera as a leading tenor in 1906. He also acted in stage plays before joining the Biograph Company as an extra in 1909. He moved with D. W. Griffith to Majestic as a director, and made 35 one- and two-reelers in a little over one year. He never stopped working; he also acted in several of these films and served as assistant director to Griffith on *The Birth of a Nation* and *Broken Blossoms*. His performance as Lillian Gish's brutal father in the latter brought him much acclaim.

Throughout the 1920s, Crisp continued his hectic schedule, directing a few films in Britain; serving on the board of directors of the Bank of Italy (later Bank of America) which approved loans for film productions; acting in several dozen more films opposite Vilma Banky, Douglas Fairbanks, and other major stars; and serving as Buster Keaton's co-director.

Because of his sonorous voice and long experience in film, Crisp adapted easily to sound and became one of the favorite character actors of the 1930s and 1940s. For a while he was under contract to Warner Brothers, appearing in *Jezebel*, playing Francis Bacon in *The Private Lives of Elizabeth and Essex*, and playing the kindly doctor in *The Old Maid*. He was equally good in adventure stories such as *Mutiny on the Bounty* and action films such as *The Dawn Patrol* and *Juarez*, but his personal amiability, to which everyone attested, communicated itself superbly on-screen, and he evolved as the character actor perfectly suited to play wise doctors, good friends, and loyal confidants. He is especially remembered as the kindly, benevolent father in the Lassie films of the 1940s and in *National Velvet*.

Although the type remained the same, Crisp brought a freshness to each role, never falling into repetitive portrayals and always inventing original gestures. Perhaps the best example is his performance in *How Green Was My Valley* for which he received the Academy Award for Best Supporting Actor at the age of 61. Retirement was far from his mind, and he continued to act in a few dozen more films in the 1950s and 1960s. He was lovable and understanding in *Pollyanna*, in a minor role, and gave a performance full of pathos as the leading role of the old man in *Greyfriar's Bobby*. He died in California at the age of 93, a respected and well-liked veteran of more than 400 productions spanning 55 years in the film industry.

—Elaine Mancini

CROSBY, Bing

Nationality: American. **Born:** Harry Lillis Crosby in Tacoma, Washington, 2 May 1901 (year of birth also given as 1903 and 1904 in various sources); nickname "Bing" acquired in grade school through avid reading of comic strip "The Bingville Bugle." **Education:** Attended Gonzaga High School; Gonzaga University, 1920-22. **Family:** Married 1) Wilma Winnifred Wyatt ("Dixie Lee"), 1930 (died 1952), sons: Gary, Philip and Dennis (twins), and Lindsay; 2) Kathryn Grant, 1957, children: Harry Jr., Mary, and Nathaniel. **Career:** 1922—drummer and vocalist with band "The Musicaladers"; 1926—singer with Paul Whiteman band; 1927—dropped from Whiteman show reportedly due to heavy drinking; teamed with Al Rinker and Harry Barris as "Paul Whiteman's Rhythm Boys" appearing on Keith circuit; 1929—initial film work in Hollywood at Pathe and for Sennett; 1930—solo singer on nightly broadcasts from Cocoanut Grove in Los Angeles; 1931—began broadcasting for CBS; five-picture Paramount contract: association with Paramount lasted until 1956; 1932—debut as featured actor in *The Big Broadcast*; 1934—signed with Decca Record Co.; 1935—coast-to-coast broadcast for Kraft Music Hall; 1936-46—host of Kraft program; 1945—two films produced by Bing Crosby Productions do poorly at box office; 1964-65—actor in TV series *The Bing Crosby Show*. **Awards:** Best Actor, Academy Award for *Going My Way*, 1944. **Died:** 14 October 1977.

Films as Actor:

1930 *Two Plus Fours* (Ray McCarey—short); *Ripstitch the Tailor* (Ray McCarey—short, unreleased); *King of Jazz* (Anderson); *Check and Double Check* (Brown) (cameo role); *Reaching for the Moon* (Goulding)

1931 *Confessions of a Co-ed* (*Her Dilemma*) (Burton and Murphy) (as voice); *I Surrender Dear* (Sennett—short); *One More Chance* (Sennett—short)

1932   *Dream House* (Lord—short); *Billboard Girl* (Pearce—short); *The Big Broadcast* (Tuttle)

1933   *Blue of the Night* (Pearce—short); *Sing, Bing, Sing* (Stafford—short); *College Humor* (Ruggles); *Too Much Harmony* (Sutherland); *Please* (Gillstrom—short); *Going Hollywood* (Walsh)

1934   *Just an Echo* (Gillstrom—short); *We're Not Dressing* (Taurog); *She Loves Me Not* (Nugent); *Here Is My Heart* (Tuttle)

1935   *Star Night at the Cocoanut Grove* (Lewyn—short); *Mississippi* (Sutherland); *Two for Tonight* (Tuttle); *The Big Broadcast of 1936* (Taurog)

1936   *Anything Goes* (Milestone); *Rhythm on the Range* (Taurog); *Pennies from Heaven* (McLeod)

1937   *Waikiki Wedding* (Tuttle); *Double or Nothing* (Reed)

1938   *Doctor Rhythm* (Tuttle); *Sing You Sinners* (Ruggles); *Don't Hook Now* (Short)

1939   *Paris Honeymoon* (Tuttle); *East Side of Heaven* (Butler); *The Star Maker* (Del Ruth)

1940   *Road to Singapore* (Schertzinger); *If I Had My Way* (Butler); *Swing with Bing* (Polesie—short); *Rhythm on the River* (Schertzinger)

1941   *Road to Zanzibar* (Schertzinger); *Birth of the Blues* (Schertzinger)

1942   *Angels of Mercy* (short); *My Favorite Blonde* (Lanfield) (as guest); *Holiday Inn* (Sandrich); *Road to Morocco* (Butler); *Star Spangled Rhythm* (Marshall) (as guest)

1943   *Dixie* (Sutherland)

1944   *Going My Way* (McCarey) (as Father O'Malley); *The Road to Victory* (Prinz—short); *The Princess and the Pirate* (Butler) (as guest); *Here Come the Waves* (Sandrich); *The Shining Future* (Prinz—short)

1945   *All Star Bond Rally* (Audley—short); *Hollywood Victory Caravan* (Russell—short); *Out of this World* (Walker) (as voice); *Duffy's Tavern* (Walker) (as guest); *The Bells of St. Mary's* (McCarey) (as Father O'Malley); *Road to Utopia* (Walker)

1946   *Monsieur Beaucaire* (Marshall) (as guest); *Blue Skies* (Heisler); *The Road to Hollywood* (compilation of early Crosby shorts)

1947   *My Favorite Brunette* (Nugent) (as guest); *Welcome Stranger* (Nugent); *Road to Rio* (McLeod); *Variety Girl* (Marshall) (as guest)

1948   *The Emperor Waltz* (Wilder)

1949   *A Connecticut Yankee* (*A Connecticut Yankee in King Arthur's Court*; *A Yankee in King Arthur's Court*) (Garnett); "Ichabod Crane" ep. of *The Adventures of Ichabod and Mr. Toad* (Geronimi and Algar) (as narrator); *Top o' the Morning* (Miller); *The Road to Peace* (Webb—short); *You Can Change the World* (McCarey) (as guest)

1950   *Riding High* (Capra); *Mr. Music* (Haydn)

1951   *Angels in the Outfield* (*Angels and the Pirates*) (Brown) (as guest); *Here Comes the Groom* (Capra); *A Millionaire for Christy* (Marshall) (as voice)

1952   *The Greatest Show on Earth* (DeMille) (as guest); *Son of Paleface* (Tashlin) (as guest); *Just for You* (Nugent); *Off Limits* (*Military Policemen*) (Marshall) (as guest)

1953   *Scared Stiff* (Marshall) (as guest); *Little Boy Lost* (Seaton); *Faith, Hope and Hogan* (Denove—short) (as guest)

1954   *White Christmas* (Curtiz); *The Country Girl* (Seaton)

1955   *Bing Presents Oreste* (Dmytryk—short)

1956   *High Society* (Walters); *Anything Goes* (Lewis—not a remake of 1936 film)

1957   *Man on Fire* (MacDougall); *The Heart of Show Business* (Staub) (as narrator)

1958   *Showdown at Ulcer Gulch* (Culhane—short)

1959   *Alias Jesse James* (McLeod) (as guest); *Say One for Me* (Tashlin)

1960   *Let's Make Love* (Cukor) (as guest); *High Time* (Edwards); *Pepe* (Sidney) (as guest)

1961   *The Road to Hong Kong* (Panama)

1964   *Robin and the Seven Hoods* (Douglas)

1965   *Cinerama's Russian Adventure* (*Bing Crosby in Cinerama's Russian Adventure*) (doc) (as narrator)

1966   *Stagecoach* (Douglas)

1968   *Bing Crosby's Washington State* (Gardner—short) (as narrator)

1970   *Golf's Golden Years* (Evans—short) (as narrator)

1971   *Dr. Cook's Garden* (Post—for TV) (title role)

1972   *Cancel My Reservation* (Bogart) (as guest); *The World of Sport Fishing* (Morgan—for TV)

1974   *That's Entertainment!* (Haley Jr.) (as narrator)

Publications

By CROSBY: book—

Call Me Lucky, as told to Pete Martin, New York, 1953.

By CROSBY: article—

"The Bing Crosby Experience," interview by R. Kent, in *Inter/View* (New York), September 1973.

On CROSBY: books—

Crosby, Kathryn, *Bing and Other Things*, New York, 1967.

Pleasants, Henry, *The Great American Popular Singers*, New York, 1974.

Thompson, Charles, *Bing: The Authorized Biography*, London, 1975.

Barnes, Ken, *The Crosby Years*, New York, 1980.

Shepard, Donald, and Robert Slatzer, *Bing Crosby*, New York, 1981.

Crosby, Gary, and Ross Firestone, *Going My Own Way*, New York, 1983.

Crosby, Kathryn, *My Life with Bing*, London, 1983.

Morgereth, Timothy A., *Bing Crosby: A Discography, Radio Program List, and Filmography*, Jefferson, North Carolina, 1987.

Osterholm, J. Roger, *Bing Crosby: A Bio-Bibliography*, Westport, Connecticut, 1994.

On CROSBY: articles—

Marill, A. H., "Bing Crosby," in *Films in Review* (New York), June-July 1968.

Passek, J.-L., "Bing Crosby," in *Cinéma* (Paris), December 1977.

Warner, A., "The Gold of His Day," and letter from M. Kreuger in *Films in Review* (New York), January 1978.

Shipman, David, in *The Great Movie Stars: The Golden Years*, rev. ed., London, 1979.

*   *   *

Although Bing Crosby had made films for Paramount Pictures from the early 1930s to the mid-1950s, it was during the 1940s with his "Road" films that he achieved major box-office status. In 1944 he reached the acme of star ranking in Hollywood and remained there for five consecutive years. All his "Road" films with Bob Hope ranked among the top grossers for their respective years. But so did *Going My Way*, *Here Come the Waves*, *Blue Skies*, *Welcome Strangers*, and *A Connecticut Yankee in King Arthur's Court*, all Crosby films sans Hope. Indeed, in 1944 Crosby stood as the American film industry's number one star, earned an Academy Award, and recorded "Swinging on a Star," a record that sold a million copies.

Bing Crosby

Bing Crosby retained his ranking as a top movie star until 1954. Throughout the early 1950s, he continued to win awards and generate millions for Paramount, the studio for which he had labored so long. In 1954, for example, he earned an Academy Award nomination for *The Country Girl* and starred in *White Christmas*, the highest grossing film of the year. It was in 1956, with *Anything Goes*, that he terminated a 24-year association with Paramount, and began to freelance as a movie actor working for Twentieth Century-Fox, Columbia, United Artists, and Warner Brothers. In the mid-1960s he ended his movie career, and turned to full-time work in television with his second wife and new brood of children.

Surprisingly, his success in the new visual medium of television never matched his popularity in films. There were the annual specials featuring family and guest star, Bob Hope. But his only weekly television series, a domestic situation comedy for ABC entitled *The Bing Crosby Show*, proved a major disappointment, and was canceled in 1964 after only one season. In the long run, Crosby's greatest success in television came through his production company with such popular series hits as *Ben Casey*, *The Wild, Wild West*, and *Hogan's Heroes*.

Crosby first achieved national popularity on the radio, and would never forget these origins: he continued with a weekly radio show well into the 1950s. His popularity on radio during the Great Depression ignited his career as a phonograph recording star. It was in this sector of American show business that Crosby's impact was truly staggering. He sold 22 million single records; he recorded more than 2,600 different songs; he sold 400 million records total (by 1975). And one recording, "White Christmas," went on to sell more than 30 million copies alone.

His radio, record, movie, and television activities made Bing Crosby one of the richest persons in the history of American show business. He was one of the first stars of any media to incorporate himself—in 1936. Once his show business success was assured, he began to invest in real estate, mines, oil wells, cattle ranches, race horses, music publishing, baseball teams, and the aforementioned television production company. But his greatest wealth probably did not even come from his extraordinary movie and singing career but from his financing of what later became the Minute Maid Orange Juice Corporation. This investment alone made him a multimillionaire.

Crosby's successes as a movie star should best be thought of as an extension of his enormous popularity as a singer and radio star. Through hundreds and hundreds of "performances," he was able to project an image as the unexceptional, even lazy character who sang effortlessly, always playing himself. He became an extension of the icon of the "bashful hero." Along with Jimmy Stewart and Gary Cooper he represented the "average American male," who always seemed to stumble toward success. With his stable, solid image in a world of depressions, world wars, and cold wars, Bing Crosby more than any star became a symbol for his generation.

—Douglas Gomery

CRUISE, Tom

Nationality: American. **Born:** Thomas Cruise Mapother IV in Syracuse, New York, 3 July 1962. **Education:** Attended high school in Glen Ridge, New Jersey. **Family:** Married 1) the actress Mimi Rogers, 1987 (divorced 1990); 2) the actress Nicole Kidman, 1990, son: Connor, daughter: Isabella. **Career:** 1981—film debut in *Endless Love*; 1993—directed an episode of TV series *Fallen Angels*. **Agent:** Creative Artists Agency, 9830 Wilshire Boulevard, Beverly Hills, CA 90212, U.S.A.

Films as Actor:

1981 *Endless Love* (Zeffirelli) (as Billy); *Taps* (Becker) (as David Shawn)
1983 *Losin' It* (Hanson) (as Woody); *The Outsiders* (Francis Ford Coppola) (as Steven Randall); *Risky Business* (Brickman) (as Joel Goodson); *All the Right Moves* (Chapman) (as Stef Djordevic)
1985 *Legend* (Ridley Scott) (as Jack)
1986 *Top Gun* (Tony Scott) (as Lt. Pete Mitchell); *The Color of Money* (Scorsese) (as Vincent)
1988 *Cocktail* (Donaldson) (as Doug Coughlin); *Rain Man* (Levinson) (as Charlie Babbitt)
1989 *Born on the Fourth of July* (Oliver Stone) (as Ron Kovic)
1990 *Days of Thunder* (Tony Scott) (as Cole Trickle)
1992 *A Few Good Men* (Rob Reiner) (as Lt. J. G. Daniel Kaffe); *Far and Away* (Ron Howard) (as Joseph Donelly)
1993 *The Firm* (Pollack) (as Mitch McDeere)
1994 *Interview with the Vampire* (as Lestat de Lioncourt)
1996 *Mission: Impossible* (DePalma) (as Ethan, + pr)
1997 *Eyes Wide Shut* (Kubrick); *Jerry Maguire* (Crowe)

Publications

By CRUISE: articles—

Interview in *Ecran Fantastique* (Paris), August 1985.
Interview in *Interview* (New York), May 1986.
Interview with Robert Scheer, in *Playboy* (Chicago), January 1990.
Interview with Patrick Goldstein, in *Rolling Stone* (New York), 28 May 1992.
"60 Minutes with Tom Cruise," interview with S. Rebello, in *Movieline*, December 1992.
"The Interview, the Vampire, the Actor," interview with Ingrid Sischy, in *Interview* (New York), November 1994.

On CRUISE: books—

Anthony, Jolene M., *Tom Cruise*, New York, 1988.
Netter, Susan, *Cruise Control: The Unauthorized Biography*, New York, 1988.
Cross, Edward, *Top Gun: The Films of Tom Cruise*, Las Vegas, 1990.
Clarkson, Wensley, *Tom Cruise: Inside Story*, 1994.
Sanello, Frank, *Tom Cruise: The Strictly Unauthorised Biography*, London, 1994.
Sellers, Robert, *Tom Cruise: Biography*, 1995.

On CRUISE: articles—

Current Biography 1987, New York, 1987.
"Tom Cruise," in *Films and Filming* (London), April 1987.
Gabriel, Trip, "Cruise at the Crossroads," in *Rolling Stone* (New York), 11 January 1990.
Pye, Michael, "Boy Wonder with a Stain of Anger," in *Independent on Sunday* (London), 18 March 1990.
Richardson, J. H., "Catch a Rising Star," in *Premiere* (New York), September 1993.
Lurie, Rod, "No More Mr. Nice Guy," in *Los Angeles Magazine*, October 1993.

* * *

Despite his male model features and proven box-office clout, there is something thin and underdeveloped about Tom Cruise's screen image. Has any leading man gotten so much mileage out of playing variations on the same theme in such a relatively short time span? Immensely likable, Cruise calculatedly plays the cocky all-American overachiever who is ultimately humbled by life-lessons learned at the knee of an older male mentor and eventually humanized by the love of the proverbial good woman. Capable of bending the law slightly on occasion, this self-assured locker room antihero gets knocked down a few pegs in formulaic fashion; it is a neatly stage-managed persona that has served Cruise well in *Risky Business*, *Cocktail*, *Top Gun*, *The Color of Money*, *Rain Man*, *Days of Thunder*, *A Few Good Men*, *Far and Away*, and *The Firm*. Incredibly, the only clinker marring this track record is the meandering fairy tale, *Legend*. When required to stretch, Cruise can perform with sleek assuredness matching Paul Newman shot for shot in *The Color of Money* and outclassing the contemporary cinema's Paul Muni—Dustin Hoffman—in the sappy *Rain Man*.

If Cruise's career seems less the by-product of a thespic drive than the inspiration of well-connected business managers, Cruise has tried to stretch himself although not with any of the daring moves associated with Richard Gere, for example. Still, in *Born on the Fourth of July*, the Vietnam War film based on Ron Kovic's book of the same name, Cruise convincingly and effectively portrays a Ron Kovic who moves from naive recruit to angry, wheelchair-bound paraplegic. Although the movie version of *Interview with the Vampire* guts the homoerotic content of the novel (a Cruise movie always has both eyes on the box office), this profitable bloodbath was a bold move on Cruise's part, and he rises to the challenge with an atypically flamboyant turn as a hedonist bloodsucker for whom no standard Cruise-ian redemption awaits. Modulating his usually strained vocal resources, Cruise, for the first time in his career, etches an eerily believable characterization far removed from his heel-reborn-as hero image. Although this *Interview* is too glumly serious, deficient in mystery, and sadistic to be scarily entertaining, Cruise does pump it full of vampiric glee.

Still young and shrewdly determined to keep the machinery of his success oiled, Cruise carries out a *Mission Impossible* in order to upgrade his stature as a film star who can play with the big boys (Ford, Schwarzenegger) in the action flick arena. Having caught the public's eye as a cynical youth, Cruise will no doubt broaden his range and modify his appeal as he approaches 40. Thus far, his mainstream success stands as a monument to the never-ending adolescence of men who enjoy exercising their braggadocio, treating women like trophies, and egotistically excelling at various sports. Whether flying MIGs, racing cars, playing pool, boxing bare-knuckled, footballing for a scholarship, or shaking a cocktail, Cruise taps into the American male's unconscious desires. What this really amounts to is Peter Pan with a sex drive or Huckleberry Finn discovering puberty. It is a juvenile conception, and fans to the contrary, it is an image which Cruise cannot go on revamping. That crooked grin could become as obsolete as Mary Pickford's sausage curls. A jock among stars, Cruise plays shallow hunks defined less by sportsmanship than by their love of toys. The high-tech hardware and sports equipment can start to weigh a ton as the years go by and the formula gets flabby; to stay in shape as a superstar, charismatic Cruise must find ways to move beyond his immature persona.

—Robert Pardi

CUNY, Alain

Nationality: French. **Born:** René Xavier Marie in Saint-Malo, 12 July 1908. **Education:** Attended Insitut Libre de Saint-Lô and the Collège Locroy-Saint-León; studied architecture at École Nationale Supérieure des Beaux-Arts, Paris; studied drama with Charles Dullin. **Family:** Married Marie-Blanche Guidicelli, 1962. **Career:** Began career in film as costume and set designer for Cavalcanti, Feyder, and Renoir; late 1930s—began acting on stage; 1941—film debut in Jean Grémillon's *Remorques*; early 1950s—began starring in Italian in addition to French films; 1960—international recognition for role of Steiner in Fellini's *La dolce vita*. **Died:** In Paris, 16 May 1994.

Films as Actor:

1941   *Remorques (Stormy Waters)* (Grémillon)

1942   *Les Visiteurs du soir (The Devil's Envoys; The Devil's Own Envoy)* (Carné) (as Giles)

1943   *Le Baron fantôme (The Phantom Baron)* (de Poligny); *Madame Sans-Gêne* (Richebé)

1946   *Solita de Cordoue* (Koster)

1951   *Il Cristo proibito (Forbidden Christ; Strange Deception)* (Malaparte) (as Mastro Antonio); *Camicie rosse (Anita Garibaldi; Red Shirts)* (Rosi and Alessandrini) (as Bueno)

1952   *Les Conquérants solitaires* (Vermoral); "Minna de Vanghel" ep. of *Le Rideau carmoisi (Les Crimes de l'amour; The Crimson Curtain)* (Astruc)

1953   *La signora senza camelie (The Lady without Camelias)* (Antonioni—released in U.S. in 1981) (as Lodi)

1956   *Notre Dame de Paris (The Hunchback of Notre Dame)* (Delannoy) (as Claude Frollo)

1958   *Les Amants (The Lovers)* (Malle) (as Henri Tournier)

1960   ***La dolce vita*** (Fellini) (as Steiner)

1961   *Scano boa* (Dall'Ar) (as Cavarazan)

1962   *La Croix de vivants (Cross of the Living)* (Govar) (as Count)

1963   *La corruzione (Corruption)* (Bolognini) (as Leonardo)

1964   *Peau de banane (Banana Peel)* (Marcel Ophüls) (as Bontemps)

1965   *Le Festin des mots* (Dansereau)

1969   *La Voie lactée (The Milky Way; La Via Lattea)* (Buñuel) (as man with cape); *Fellini Satyricon (Satyricon)* (Fellini) (as Lichas)

1970   *Uomini contro* (Rosi) (as General Leone)

1971   *Valparaiso, Valparaiso* (Aubier)

1972   *L'udienza* (Ferreri); *La grande scrofa nera* (Ottoni); *Il maestro i Margarita* (Petrovic)

1973   *La rosa rossa* (Giraldi)

1974   *Emmanuelle* (Jaeckin) (as Marco); *Touche pas la femme blanche (Don't Touch White Women)* (Ferreri)

1975   *El recurso del metedo* (Littin); *Il contesto* (Rosi); *I prosseneti* (Rondi)

1976   *Cadaveri eccellenti (Illustrious Corpses)* (Rosi); *Irene, Irene* (Del Monte)

1978   *La Chanson de Roland* (Cassenti)

1979   ***Cristo si è fermato a Eboli*** *(Christ Stopped at Eboli)* (Rosi) (as Baron Rotundo)

1980   *Les Jeux de la comtesse*; *Semmelweis* (Bettettini)

1984   *Basileus Quartet* (Carpi) (as Finkel)

1985   *Détective* (Godard) (as Old Mafioso)

1987   *Cronaca di una morte annunciata (Chronicle of a Death Foretold)* (Rosi) (as Widower)

1989   *Camille Claudel* (Nuytten) (as Louis-Prosper Claudel)

1992   *Uova di Garofano (Farewell Sweet War)* (Agosti) (as Crimen); *Le Retour de Casanova (Casanova's Return)* (Niermans) (as Marquis)

Film as Director:

1991   *L'announce faite a Mariei*

Alain Cuny

Publications

By CUNY: articles—

Interview in *Ciné Revue* (Paris), 4 December 1975.
"La photographie nous aveugle," in *Cahiers du Cinéma* (Paris), December 1991.
Interview with A. Eichenberger, in *Ciné & Media* (Brussels), no. 1/2, 1992.
"La bellezza salvera il mondo," in *Rivista del Cinemotografo* (Rome), April 1992.
Interview with M. Bernink and P. Pisters, in *Skrien* (Amsterdam), February/March 1993.
"Alain Cuny Is de Naam," interview in *Film en Televisie + Video* (Brussels), April 1993.

On CUNY: book—

Germain-Thomas, Olivier, *Agora: "les aventuriers de l'esprit,"* Besancon, France, 1991.

On CUNY: articles—

Ciné Revue (Paris), 10 March 1977.
Lauwaert, D., "De Gekwelde commandeur," in *Skrien* (Amsterdam), February/March 1993.
Obituary in *New York Times*, 19 May 1994.

* * *

After working as an assistant director to Alberto Cavalcanti, and as set and costume designer for Cavalcanti, Feyder, and Renoir, Alain Cuny made his film acting debut in an insignificant role in Grémillon's *Remorques* in 1941. During the war, he was active in the theater, but he first received serious attention in two film roles that made him instantly famous.

The first was a lively performance as the strolling minstrel and Devil's assistant, Gilles, in Marcel Carné's *Les Visiteurs du soir*, and the second the role of Hervé in Serge de Poligny's *Le Baron fantôme*, for which Cuny also collaborated on the script. Opposite Jean Cocteau, as the Baron, Cuny, the Baron's son and heir, created an unusual version of the romantic hero, reflecting the film's fantastic and legendary quality.

Thereafter, Cuny played increasingly realistic roles, and his performances became deeper and more psychologically complex. This gradual change was probably due to the influence of his theatrical work, especially after he began to appear at the Théâtre National Populaire under Jean Vilar. Cuny's first major stage success came at the 1947 Avignon Festival in Paul Claudel's *L'Histoire de Tobie et de Sarah*, and he also appeared in Vilar's subsequent production of *Macbeth*. In the mid-1950s he became a member of Madeleine Renaud and Jean-Louis Barrault's company; his appearance in their production of *Tête d'or* confirmed Cuny's standing as a great tragedian.

In the early 1950s he pursued a film career mainly in Italy, notably in an early Antonioni film, *La signora senza camelie*. Delannoy's *Notre Dame de Paris*, with Cuny opposite Gina Lollobrigida, was an Italian co-production. The emerging New Wave made good use of his capabilities, through his appearance in Louis Malle's *Les Amants*, but Cuny continued to make his most significant impact in Italian films.

His remarkable performance as the philosophizing author Steiner in Fellini's *La dolce vita* presented a seemingly quiet and even-tempered man, living happily with a beautiful and intelligent wife, who yields to a sudden, mysterious attack of folly and commits suicide. Cuny subsequently worked with Fellini in *Satyricon*. Equally important was the beginning of his collaboration with Francesco Rosi in *Uomini contro*, as General Leone, followed by performances in Rosi's *Cadaveri eccellenti*, *Cristo si è fermato a Eboli*, and *Cronaca di una*

morte annunciata, which continued to demonstrate Cuny's skill and dramatic sophistication.

—Karel Tabery

CURTIS, Jamie Lee

Nationality: American. **Born:** Los Angeles, California, 22 November 1958; daughter of the actor Tony Curtis and the actress Janet Leigh. **Education:** Studied at Choate School, Connecticut; University of the Pacific, California. **Family:** Married the actor/director Christopher Guest, 1984, daughter: Annie, son: Thomas Haden. **Career:** 1970s—actress for TV, including *Operation Petticoat*, 1977-78; 1978—film debut in *Halloween*; 1989-92—in TV series *Anything but Love*. **Awards:** British Academy of Film and Television Arts Award for Best Supporting Actress, for *Trading Places*, 1983. **Address:** 10573 West Pico Boulevard #242, Los Angeles, CA 90064-2348, U.S.A.

Films as Actress:

1978 *Halloween* (Carpenter) (as Laurie Strode)
1980 *The Fog* (Carpenter) (as Elizabeth Solley); *Prom Night* (Lynch) (as Kim); *Terror Train* (Spottiswoode) (as Alana)
1981 *Road Games* (Franklin) (as Pamela Rushworth); *Halloween II* (Carpenter) (as Laurie Strode); *Escape from New York* (Carpenter) (as opening narrator/voice of computer); *Death of a Centerfold: The Dorothy Stratten Story* (Beaumont—for TV) (title role); *She's in the Army Now* (Averback—for TV) (as Rita Jennings)
1982 *Money on the Side* (Robert E. Collins—for TV) (as Michelle Jamison)
1983 *Trading Places* (Landis) (as Ophelia); *Love Letters* (*My Love Letters*) (Amy Jones) (as Anna Winter)
1984 *The Adventures of Buckaroo Banzai: Across the Eighth Dimension* (Richter) (as Dr. Sandra Banzai); *Grandview, U.S.A.* (Kleiser) (as Michelle "Mike" Cody)
1985 *Perfect* (Bridges) (as Jessica Wilson); *8 Million Ways to Die* (Ashby); *Annie Oakley* (*Shelley Duvall's Tall Tales and Legends: Annie Oakley*) (Lindsay-Hogg—for TV)
1986 *As Summer Dies* (Tramont—for TV) (as Whitsey Loftin)
1987 *Amazing Grace and Chuck* (*Silent Voice*) (Newell) (as Lynn Taylor); *A Man in Love* (*Un Homme amoureux*) (Kurys) (as Susan Elliot)
1988 *Dominick and Eugene* (Robert M. Young) (as Jennifer Reston); *A Fish Called Wanda* (Charles Crichton) (as Wanda Gershwitz)
1990 *Blue Steel* (Bigelow) (as Megan Turner)
1991 *Queens Logic* (Rash) (as Grace); *My Girl* (Zieff) (as Shelly DeVoto)
1992 *Forever Young* (Miner) (as Claire)
1994 *My Girl 2* (Zieff) (as Shelly Sultenfuss); *Mother's Boys* (Simoneau) (as Jude); *True Lies* (Cameron) (as Helen Tasker)
1995 *The Heidi Chronicles* (for TV) (as Heidi Holland)
1996 *Fierce Creatures* (Robert M. Young) (as Willa Weston); *House Arrest*

Publications

By CURTIS: books—

When I Was Little: A Four-Year-Old's Memoir of Her Youth, New York, 1993.
Tell Me Again: About the Night I Was Born, New York, 1995.

Jamie Lee Curtis in *Blue Steel*

By CURTIS: articles—

Interviews in *Interview* (New York), September 1983 and August 1989.
Interview with C. Krista, in *Films in Review* (New York), August/September 1985.
Interview in *Time Out* (London), 3 January 1990.
Interview in *Premiere* (New York), February/March 1990.
"Tuff Enough," interview with Rod Lurie, in *Los Angeles Magazine*, July 1994.

On CURTIS: articles—

Photoplay (London), May 1979.
Thomson, David, "Class of 1985," in *Film Comment* (New York), March/April 1985.
Hibbin, S., "Jamie Lee Curtis," in *Films and Filming* (London), August 1985.
"Blue Steel," in *American Cinematographer* (Hollywood), May 1989.
Lerner, Michael, "Zany Jamie," in *Interview* (New York), August 1989.
Clark, John, filmography in *Premiere* (New York), September 1989.
Boyd, Blanche McCrary, "The Rules of the Jamie Game," in *Premiere* (New York), November 1991.
Diamond, J., "Jamie Lee Curtis Faces Up to Her Image," in *New York Times*, 27 December 1992.

*   *   *

Like many a cinematic ingenue, Jamie Lee Curtis started out as a heroine of horror/terror films: John Carpenter's *Halloween*, *The Fog*, and *Halloween II*; Paul Lynch's *Prom Night*; and Roger Spottiswoode's *Terror Train*. But unlike scores of attractive but inexperienced young actresses, she was never forced to make films which were strictly cheesy, Grade D exploitation. Similarly, unlike scores of other young actresses whose careers never transcend their roots, she has been able to secure a series of showy supporting and starring roles in an impressive range of films. Perhaps her career progressed in this direction because of her lineage: her parents are, of course, Tony Curtis and Janet Leigh. Keeping in mind her parents, Curtis's casting in horror films may be linked to the shower her mother took in *Psycho*; prior to debuting in *Halloween*, Curtis appeared in a television series based on the film *Operation Petticoat*, the original of which had starred her father.

But this is not to imply that Curtis simply inherited her fame. Early in her career, she "paid her dues" in television movies which were variously stupid (*She's in the Army Now*, a tepid reworking of *Private Benjamin*),exploitative (*Death of a Centerfold: The Dorothy Stratten Story*), or stupid and exploitative (*Money on the Side*, playing a suburban housewife who becomes a prostitute—a film which would never be confused with Buñuel's *Belle du jour*). In all these films, Curtis imbued her characters with an intelligence far greater than that supplied by the scriptwriters.

Having the proper connections may have helped her early on, but Curtis's acting ability and on-screen appeal, coupled with her undeniable sexiness, are what have sustained her. In *Halloween*, for instance, her talent is showcased to good advantage. As the likable, partnerless member of a trio of young women, she manages to convey her character's repressed sexuality—an irony, considering the in-your-face eroticism inherent in so many of her future roles. Indeed, in some of Curtis's biggest box-office hits, she has traded on a combination of her natural effervescence and sex appeal. In *Trading Places*, one of her earlier films, she is memorable in her supporting role as a Bronx-accented hooker-with-a-heart-of-gold. It was here where she first displayed her flair for comedy. In *A Fish Called Wanda*, she blends seamlessly with a choice cast (John Cleese, Kevin Kline, Michael Palin) as a sexy con woman. Her instant-classic striptease scene in *True Lies* (in which she is cast as Arnold Schwarzenegger's wife) is as eye-popping as any of the film's special effects.

While she was taking showy roles in such films as *Trading Places*, *A Fish Called Wanda*, and *True Lies*, however, Curtis was also tackling parts that stretched her as an actress—most successfully, as the young woman who comes upon her late mother's romantic correspondence with a married man in *Love Letters*; and the title role in the television adaptation of Wendy Wasserstein's *The Heidi Chronicles*. She also has played characters of integrity in films that were simply unsuccessful: the aerobics instructor in the inane *Perfect* and the cop in the muddled *Blue Steel*. And she has taken supporting roles in projects she has believed in: *A Man in Love*, *Dominick and Eugene*, and *Amazing Grace and Chuck*.

Because her highest-profile roles have been supporting ones (*Trading Places*, *True Lies*) or as a part of an ensemble (*A Fish Called Wanda*), Curtis never has won a place in the inner circle of actress-stars, alongside the likes of Demi Moore and Julia Roberts. This is unfortunate, as she is every bit as attractive as (and, in some ways, far more charismatic than) Moore and Roberts. Curtis's full-bodied performance in *The Heidi Chronicles* serves as evidence that she has matured as an actress, and is quite capable of playing characters whose intelligence and vulnerability transcend their sexuality.

—Rob Edelman

CURTIS, Tony

Nationality: American. **Born:** Bernard Schwartz in the Bronx, New York, 3 June 1925; known as James Curtis and Anthony Curtis during early career. **Education:** Attended Seward Park High School, New York; City College of New York; acting classes at New York's Dramatic Workshop. **Military Service:** World War II—served with U.S. Navy. **Family:** Married 1) the actress Janet Leigh, 1951 (divorced 1962), daughters: the actresses Kelly Lee and Jamie Lee Curtis; 2) the actress Christine Kaufmann, 1963 (divorced 1967), daughters: Alexandra, Allegra; 3) Leslie Allen, 1968 (divorced 1981), sons: Nicholas, Benjamin. **Career:** Mid-1940s—started Empire Players theater in Newark, New Jersey; later joined the Dramatic Workshop of the Cherry Lane Theater and Drama Workshop of Walt Whitman; late 1940s—began acting professionally with Stanley Woolf Players which toured "Borscht Circuit" in Catskills; appeared briefly off-Broadway; 1948—film debut in bit role in *Criss Cross*; 1949—contract with Universal; late 1950s—formed Curtleigh Productions with wife Janet Leigh; early 1960s—formed production company Curtis Enterprises; later formed Reynard production company; 1971-72—in the TV series *The Persuaders*; 1975-76—in TV series *McCoy*; 1978-82—semi-regular on ABC-TV series *Vegas*. **Address:** c/o Jerry Zeitman, The Agency, 10351 Santa Monica Blvd., Suite 211, Los Angeles, CA 90025, U.S.A.

Films as Actor:

1948   *Criss Cross* (Siodmak) (as gigolo)
1949   *City across the River* (Shane) (as Mitch); *The Lady Gambles* (Gordon) (as bellboy); *Johnny Stool Pigeon* (Castle) (as Joey Hyatt); *Francis* (Lubin) (as Capt. Jones)

1950   *Sierra* (Green) (as Brent Coulter); *I Was a Shoplifter* (Lamont) (as Pepe); *Winchester '73* (Anthony Mann) (as Doan); *Kansas Raiders* (Enright) (as Kit Dalton)
1951   *The Prince Who Was a Thief* (Maté) (as Julna); *Flesh and Fury* (Pevney) (as Paul Callan)
1952   *No Room for the Groom* (Sirk) (as Alvah Morrell); *Son of Ali Baba* (Newmann) (as Kashma Baba)
1953   *Houdini* (George Marshall) (title role); *The All-American* (*The Winning Way*) (Hibbs) (as Nick Bonelli); *Forbidden* (Maté) (as Eddie Darrow)
1954   *Beachhead* (Heisler) (as Burke); *Johnny Dark* (Sherman) (title role); *The Black Shield of Falworth* (Maté) (as Myles Falworth); *So This Is Paris* (Quine) (as Joe Maxwell)
1955   *Six Bridges to Cross* (Pevney) (as Jerry Florea); *The Purple Mask* (Humberstone) (as René); *The Square Jungle* (Jerry Hopper) (as Eddie Quaid)
1956   *The Rawhide Years* (Maté) (as Ben Matthews); *Trapeze* (Reed) (as Tino Orsini)
1957   *Mister Cory* (Edwards) (title role); **The Sweet Smell of Success** (Mackendrick) (as Sidney Falco); *The Midnight Story* (*Appointment with a Shadow*) (Pevney) (as Joe Martini)
1958   *The Vikings* (Fleischer) (as Eric); *Kings Go Forth* (Daves) (as Britt Harris); *The Defiant Ones* (Kramer) (as John Jackson); *The Perfect Furlough* (*Strictly for Pleasure*) (Edwards) (as Cpl. Paul Hodges)
1959   **Some Like It Hot** (Wilder) (as Joe/Josephine); *Operation Petticoat* (Edwards) (as Lt. Nick Holden); *Who Was That Lady?* (Sidney) (as David Wilson)
1960   *The Rat Race* (Mulligan) (as Pete Hammond Jr.); *Spartacus* (Kubrick) (as Antoninus); *The Great Impostor* (Mulligan) (as Ferdinand Waldo Demara Jr.); *Pepe* (Sidney) (as guest)
1961   *The Outsider* (Delbert Mann) (as Ira Hamilton Hayes)
1962   *Forty Pounds of Trouble* (Jewison) (as Steve McCluskey); *Taras Bulba* (Thompson) (as Andrei Bulba)
1963   *The List of Adrian Messenger* (Huston) (as Italian); *Captain Newman, M.D.* (Miller) (as Cpl. Jackson Laibowitz); *Paris When It Sizzles* (Quine) (as second policeman)
1964   *Wild and Wonderful* (Anderson) (as Terry Williams); *Goodbye Charlie* (Minnelli) (as George Tracy); *Sex and the Single Girl* (Quine) (as Bob Weston)
1965   *The Great Race* (Edwards) (as The Great Leslie); *Boeing-Boeing* (Rich) (as Bernard Lawrence)
1966   *Not with My Wife, You Don't* (Panama) (as Tom Ferris); *Chamber of Horrors* (Averback) (as Mr. Julian); *Arrivederci, Baby* (*Drop Dead, Darling*) (Hughes) (as Nick)
1967   *La cintura di castita* (*A Funny Thing Happened on the Way to the Crusades*; *The Chastity Belt*) (Campanile) (as Guerrando da Montone); *Don't Make Waves* (Mackendrick) (as Carlo Cofield)
1968   **Rosemary's Baby** (Polanski) (as voice of Donald Baumgart); *The Boston Strangler* (Fleischer) (as Albert de Salvo)
1969   *Quei temerari sulle loro pazze, scatenate, scalcinate carriole* (*Those Daring Young Men in Their Jaunty Jalopies*; *Monte Carlo or Bust!*) (Annakin) (as Chester Schofield)
1970   *Suppose They Gave a War and Nobody Came?* (Averback) (as Shannon Gambroni); *You Can't Win 'em All* (Collinson) (as Adam Dyer)
1973   *The Third Girl from the Left* (Medak—for TV)
1974   *Lepke* (Golan) (title role)
1975   *The Count of Monte Cristo* (Greene—for TV) (as Mondego); *The Big Rip-Off* (Hardgrove—for TV)
1976   *The Last Tycoon* (Kazan) (as Rodriguez)

1977   *Casanova & Co.* (*The Rise and Rise of Casanova*; *Some Like It Cool*) (Legrand, i.e., Franz Antel) (title role); *The Manitou* (Girdler) (as Harry Erskine)

1978   *Sextette* (Hughes) (as Alexei); *The Bad News Bears Go to Japan* (Berry) (as Marvin); *The Users* (Hardy—for TV); *Vegas* (Richard Lang—for TV) (as Phillip Roth)

1979   *It Rained All Night the Day I Left* (Gessner) (as Robert Talbot); *Title Shot* (Rose) (as Frank Renzetti)

1980   *Little Miss Marker* (Bernstein) (as Blackie); *The Mirror Crack'd* (Hamilton) (as Marty N. Fenn); *Moviola: The Scarlett O'Hara War* (Erman—for TV)

1981   *The Million Dollar Face* (O'Herlihy—for TV); *Inmates: A Love Story* (Green—for TV)

1982   *Brainwaves* (Lommel) (as Dr. Clavius); *Portrait of a Showgirl* (Stern—for TV); *Othello—The Black Commando* (Boulois) (as Iago); *Balboa* (Polakof) (as Ernie Stoddard)

1984   *Where Is Parsifal?* (Helman) (as Parsifal Katzenellenbogen)

1985   *Insignificance* (Roeg) (as the Senator)

1986   *The Last of Philip Banter* (Hachuel) (as Charles Foster); *Mafia Princess* (Collins—for TV) (as Salvatore "Sam" Giancana); *Balbao* (Polakof) (as Ernie Stoddard)

1987   *Club Life* (Vane) (as Hector)

1988   *Pascsagier—Welcome to Germany* (Brasch) (as Cornfield)

1989   *Lobster Man from Mars* (Sheff) (as J. P. Shelldrake); *Midnight* (Vane); *Walter & Carlo i Amerika* (Friis-Mikkelsen) (as Wally La Rouge)

1990   *Tarzan in Manhattan* (Schultz—for TV) (as Archimedes Porter); *Bloodlaw* (Heavener); *Thanksgiving Day* (Tanasescu—for TV) (as Max Schloss)

1991   *Prime Target* (Heavener) (as Marrietta Copella)

1992   *Center of the Web* (Prior) (as Stephen Moore); *Christmas in Connecticut* (Schwarzenegger—for TV) (as Alex Yardley)

1994   *The Mummy Lives* (Gerry O'Hara) (as Aziru/Dr. Mohassid); *Bandit: Beauty and The Bandit* (Needham—for TV) (as Lucky Bergstrom); *A Perry Mason Mystery: The Case of the Grimacing Governor* (Tash—for TV) (as Johnny Steele); *Naked in New York* (Algrant) (as Carl Fisher)

1995   *The Immortals* (for TV); *The Celluoid Closet* (Epstein and Friedman—doc) (as interviewee)

Publications

By CURTIS: books—

Kid Andrew Cody and Julie Sparrow (novel), 1977.
Tony Curtis: The Autobiography, with Barry Paris, New York, 1993.

By CURTIS: articles—

Interview with Brian Baxter, in *Films and Filming* (London), August 1985.
Interview with G. Fuller, in *Interview*, June 1991.

On CURTIS: books—

Richards, Jeffrey, *Swordsmen of the Screen: From Douglas Fairbanks to Michael York*, London, 1977.
Farber, Stephen, and Marc Green, *Hollywood Dynasties*, New York, 1984.
Leigh, Janet, *There Really Was a Hollywood*, 1984.
Munn, Michael, *The Kid from the Bronx: A Biography of Tony Curtis*, London, 1984.
Hunter, Allan, *Tony Curtis: The Man and His Movies*, Edinburgh, 1985.

On CURTIS: articles—

Cassa, A., "Tony Curtis," letter, in *Films in Review* (New York), January 1973.
Letter from K. Canham in *Films in Review* (New York), May 1974.
Ecran (Paris), September 1978.
Root, Steve, "Tony Curtis," *Los Angeles Magazine*, March 1989.

*   *   *

Ironically, Tony Curtis is today best known as the father of actress Jamie Lee Curtis. But in a career that spans more than five dozen films and a panorama of genres, he has proved to be an engaging light comedian—particularly when guided by Blake Edwards or Billy Wilder; he has also startled critics with a smattering of sharp-edged dramatic portrayals. Sadly, his acting reputation has long been eclipsed by that of his personal life, most notably his marriages (which proved fodder for fan magazines during their heyday). Even his physical qualities, his "pretty-boy" looks, which initially propelled him to stardom during the glamour-obsessed late 1950s and early 1960s, have worked against him.

Certainly, he was badly miscast early in his career: with his Bronx accent, the former Bernard Schwartz stuck out like the proverbial sore thumb in a string of Westerns, swashbucklers, and Arabian Nights-induced flights of fancy, wherein he uttered such immortal lines as "Yonda is the castle uv my fodda."

The critical sniggering that dogged those early performances came to a halt in 1957 with Curtis's stunning portrayal of oily press agent Sidney Falco in the gritty film noir *The Sweet Smell of Success*. Incomprehensibly, Curtis was not nominated for an Oscar in that performance. A year later, however, he was Best Actor nominee for *The Defiant Ones*, a chase film about racial prejudice directed by Stanley Kramer. Armed with critical acclaim, Curtis gave confident performances (sans Bronx accent) in the memorable period spectacles, *The Vikings* and *Spartacus*.

It was the back-to-back release in 1959 of two frantic comedies—*Some Like It Hot*, directed by Wilder, and *Operation Petticoat*, one of his many collaborations with Edwards (they also teamed up for such films as *Mister Cory* and *The Great Race*)—that displayed his impeccable comic timing. At his most convincing when cast opposite strong (or, at the very least, ingratiating) performers, Curtis proved a deft foil for Jack Lemmon and a charming romantic lead opposite Marilyn Monroe in the Wilder comedy. In *Operation Petticoat* he more than held his own with Cary Grant (whose distinctive voice he successfully parodied in *Some Like It Hot*).

Curtis went on to breezy work in so-called sophisticated comedies such as *Sex and the Single Girl*, then reinforced his dramatic reputation with his chilling portrayal of Albert de Salvo in *The Boston Strangler* (1968). Curtis campaigned long and hard to win the role, knowing it was a long shot; he gained almost 30 pounds and had his face rebuilt with a false nose to look like de Salvo. His perseverance earned him the role and good reviews, but not the Oscar nomination he sought and expected. The academy did not like serial killers, regardless of how persuasively they were played on the screen; it had previously ignored Anthony Perkins's now-classic performance in *Psycho*. Not until Anthony Hopkins's Hannibal the Cannibal in *Silence of the Lambs* in 1991 would such an honor be bestowed—not only was Hopkins nominated, he won.

The Boston Strangler proved to be Curtis's last major film role. He has since appeared mostly in low-budget and foreign films and in various television productions, often playing aging Sicilian godfathers and other Mafioso types.

—Pat H. Broeske, updated by John McCarty

Tony Curtis

CUSACK, Cyril

Nationality: Irish. **Born:** Cyril James Cusack in Durban, South Africa, 26 November 1910. **Education:** Attended Dominican College, Newburgh, Ireland; University College, Dublin. **Family:** Married 1) Mary Margaret Kiely, 1945 (died in the 1970s), sons: Paul and Padraig, daughters: the actresses Sinead, Sorcha, Niamh, and Catherine; 2) Mary. **Career:** 1916—stage debut as Little Willie Carlyle in *East Lynne*; 1918—film debut as Young O'Brien in *Knocknagow*; acted on stage during childhood in family touring company (with mother Alice Violet [Cole] and stepfather Brefni O'Rourke); 1928-32—member of Norwich Repertory Co., Norfolk, England; 1932-35—member, Abbey Theatre, Dublin (also acted in many Abbey Theatre productions during lifetime); 1935—began appearing in films regularly; 1935-36—producer of the Gaelic Players; 1936—London stage debut as Richard in *Ah, Wilderness*; 1942—production of his play in Gaelic *Tar eis an aifrinn (After Mass)*; 1944—manager of the Gaiety Theatre; 1944-61—managing director of Cyril Cusack Productions; 1948—began appearing in television plays regularly; 1957—Broadway debut as Phil Hogan in *A Moon for the Misbegotten*; 1961—in TV miniseries *The Power and the Glory*; 1966—associate and stockholder of the National Theatre, Dublin; 1972—in TV miniseries *The Golden Bowl*, as narrator, and in *Jesus of Nazareth*, 1977; 1990—appeared with his three daughters, Sinead, Sorcha, and Niamh in the London stage production of *The Three Sisters*. **Awards:** English Tatler Radio Critics Award, for *The Dark Tower*, 1954; Sylvania Television Citation, for *The Moon and Sixpence*, 1959; International Critics Award, for *Arms and the Man* and *Krapp's Last Tape*, 1961; Best Actor, Irish Television Critics' Award, 1963; Honorary LL.D, Honoris Causa, National University of Ireland, 1977; Honorary Degree, Litt., University of Ulster, Northern Ireland, 1982. **Died:** In London, 7 October 1993.

Films as Actor:

1918   *Knocknagow (Homes of Tipperary)* (O'Donovan) (as Young O'Brien)

1935   *Guests of the Nation* (Johnston); *Late Extra* (Albert Parker) (as Jules); *The Man without a Face* (G. King) (as Billy Desmond)

1936   *Servants All* (Bryce) (as Billy)

1938   *The Shadow of the Glen* (for TV)

1941   *Inspector Hornleigh Goes to It (Mail Train)* (Forde); *Once a Crook* (Mason) (as Bill Hopkins)

1947   **Odd Man Out** (*Gang War*) (Reed) (as Pat)

Cyril Cusack in *Odd Man Out* courtesy of The Rank Organisation Plc

1948   *Esther Waters* (Dalrymple) (as Fred Parsons); *Escape* (Joseph L. Mankiewicz) (as Rogers); *Once a Jolly Swagman* (*Maniacs on Wheels*) (Jack Lee and McNaughton) (as Duggie Lewis); *Highland Fling* (for TV); *Ship Day*

1949   *The Small Back Room* (*Hour of Glory*) (Powell and Pressburger) (as Cpl. Taylor); *The Blue Lagoon* (Launder) (as James Carter); *All over the Town* (Twist) (as Gerald Vane); *Christopher Columbus* (McDonald); *The Sensible Man* (for TV)

1950   *Gone to Earth* (Powell) (as Edward Marston); *The Wild Heart* (Powell and Pressburger—revised version of *Gone to Earth*, shortened); *The Elusive Pimpernel* (*The Fighting Pimpernel*) (Powell and Pressburger) (as Chauvelin); *W. B. Yeats—A Tribute* (Fleischmann—doc) (as narrator, with others)

1951   *The Blue Veil* (Bernhardt) (as Frank Hutchins); *The Secret of Convict Lake* (Michael Gordon) (as Limey); *Soldiers Three* (Garnett) (as Pvt. Dennis Malloy)

1953   *Oedipus Complex* (for TV)

1954   *Destination Milan* (Huntington) (as Paddy O'Clafferty); *The Last Moment* (Comfort) (as Daniel O'Driscoll); *Saadia* (Lewin) (as Khadir)

1955   *Passage Home* (Roy Ward Baker) (as Bohannon); *The Thoroughbred* (Huth—for TV)

1956   *Jacqueline* (Roy Ward Baker) (as Mr. Flannagan); *The Man in the Road* (Comfort) (as Dr. Kelly); *The Man Who Never Was* (Neame) (as taxi driver); *The March Hare* (*Gamblers Sometimes Win*) (O'Ferrall) (as Lazy Mangan); *The Spanish Gardener* (Leacock) (as Garcia); *Deidre* (for TV)

1957   *Ill Met by Moonlight* (*Night Ambush*) (Powell and Pressburger) (as Sandy); *Miracle in Soho* (Aymes) (as Sam Bishop); "The Majesty of the Law" ep. of *The Rising of the Moon* (Ford) (as Inspector Michael Dillon); *The Moon and Sixpence* (Mulligan—for TV) (as Dr. Coutras)

1958   *Cradle of Genius* (Rotha—doc) (as himself)

1959   *Floods of Fear* (Charles Crichton) (as Peebles); *Gideon's Day* (*Gideon of Scotland Yard*) (Ford) (as Herbert "Birdy" Sparrow); *Shake Hands with the Devil* (Anderson) (as Chris Noonan); *The Enchanted* (for TV); *What Every Woman Knows* (Mulligan—for TV)

1960   *Johnny Nobody* (Patrick—released in U.S. in 1965) (as Prosecuting Counsel); *Once upon a Tram* (Sarsfield and Maguire—doc) (as narrator); *A Terrible Beauty* (*The Night Fighters*) (Garnett) (as Jimmy Hannafin)

1962   *I Thank a Fool* (Stevens) (as Capt. Ferris); *Waltz of the Toreadors* (*The Amorous General*) (Guillermin) (as Dr. Grogan); *The Chairs* (for TV); *Don Juan in Hell* (for TV); *The Dummy* (for TV); *The Lotus Eater* (for TV); *The Wedding Dress* (for TV)

1963   *80,000 Suspects* (Guest) (as Father Maguire); *Accidental Death* (for TV); *In the Train* (for TV); *Krapp's Last Tape* (for TV) (as Krapp); *Tryptych* (for TV); *The Workhouse Ward* (for TV) (as Michael McInerney)

1964   *The Big Toe* (for TV) (as Petley; *Murder in the Cathedral* (Foa—for TV) (as Thomas à Becket); *Six Characters in Search of an Author* (for TV) (as the father)

1965   *The Spy Who Came in from the Cold* (Ritt) (as Control); *Passage to India* (Hussein—for TV); *Where the Spies Are* (*Passport to Oblivion*; *One Spy Too Many*) (Guest) (as Peter Rosser); *I Was Happy Here* (*Time Lost and Time Remembered*; *Passage of Love*) (Desmond Davis) (as Hogan)

1966   *Fahrenheit 451* (Truffaut) (as Captain)

1967   *Jonathan Swift* (Hickey—doc) (as narrator, with others); *The Taming of the Shrew* (*La Bisbetica Domata*) (Zeffirelli) (as Grumio); *Dial M for Murder* (Moxey—for TV) (as Inspector Hubbard); *Oedipus the King* (*Oedipus Rex*) (Saville) (as Messenger)

1968   *Galileo* (Cavani) (title role); *Stage Irishman* (Hickey—doc) (as himself)

1969   *Country Dance* (*Brotherly Love*) (J. Lee Thompson) (as Dr. Maitland)

1970   *David Copperfield* (Delbert Mann—for TV) (as Barkis)

1971   *Harold and Maude* (Ashby) (as sculptor); *King Lear* (Peter Brook) (as Duke of Albany); *Sacco e Vanzetti* (*Sacco and Vanzetti*) (Montaldo) (as Frederick Katzmann); *Tam Lin* (*The Devil's Widow*) (McDowall) (as Vicar Julian Ainsley)

1972   *La polizia ringrazia* (*From the Police, with Thanks*; *The Law Enforcers*; *Execution Squad*) (Steno) (as Stolfi); *Piu forte ragazzi!* (*All the Way, Boys*) (Colizzi) (as Matto); *Clochmerle* (Mills—for TV); *The Hands of Cormac Joyce* (Cook—for TV) (as Mr. Reese)

1973   *The Day of the Jackal* (Zinnemann) (as Gozzi the gunsmith); *The Homecoming* (Hall) (as Sam); *La "mala" ordina* (*Manhunt*; *Manhunt in Milan*; *The Italian Connection*) (Di Leo) (as Corso); *Tristan et Iseult* (*Tristan and Isolde*) (Legrange); *Catholics, a Fable for the Future* (Gold—for TV) (as Father Manus); *The Reunion* (for TV)

1974   *The Abdication* (Harvey) (as Chancellor Oxenstierna); *Arrivano Joe e Margherito* (*Joe y Margherito*; *Run, Run, Joe*) (Colizzi); *Juggernaut* (Lester) (as Maj. O'Neill); *Venditore di palloncini* (*The Last Circus Show*; *The Balloon Vendor*; *Last Moments*) (Gariazzo) (as balloon vender); *The Good and Faithful Servant* (for TV)

1975   *Children of Rage* (Arthur Alan Seidelman) (as David's father); *Crystal and Fox* (for TV)

1976   *Lo mano spietata della legge* (*The Bloody Hands of the Law*; *Execution Squad*) (Gariazzo); *Paura in città* (*Hot Stuff*; *Fear in the City*; *Street War*) (Rosati); *Portrait of a Library* (Hickey—doc) (as narrator)

1978   *Les Misérables* (Glenn Jordan—for TV) (as Fauchelevent); *Cry of the Innocent* (O'Herlihy—for TV)

1979   *Poitin* (*Poteen*) (Quinn) (as a poteen maker); *Love Spell* (*Tristan and Isolt*) (Donovan) (as Gorman of Ireland); *The Hitchhiker* (Reid—for TV)

1980   *Cry of the Innocent* (O'Herlihy) (as Detective Inspector Tom Moloney); *Strumpet City* (for TV)

1981   *True Confessions* (Grosbard) (as Cardinal Danaher); *Andrina* (Forsyth—for TV) (as retired sea captain); *No Country for Old Men* (Powell—for TV)

1982   *The Ballroom of Romance* (O'Connor—for TV) (as Mr. Dwyer); *The Ghost Downstairs* (*The Neighbour Downstairs*) (Gosling—for TV); *The Plough and the Stars* (for TV); *The Search for Shaw* (Cash—doc for TV) (as the voice of Bernard Shaw)

1983   *Don Camillo* (Hill); *Comedy of Errors* (James Cellan Jones—for TV) (as Aegeon); *Death of an Expert Witness* (Wise—for TV) (as Mr. Lorrimer); *One of Ourselves* (O'Connor—for TV) (as Quigley); *Wagner* (Tony Palmer—for TV) (as Sulzer); *The Kingfisher* (James Cellan Jones—for TV)

1984   *1984* (Radford) (as Charrington); *At the Cinema Palace—Liam O'Leary* (Taylor—doc) (as himself); *2 x Forsyth* (*No Comebacks*): *A Careful Man* (O'Herlihy—for TV) (as Martin Pound); *Dr. Fischer of Geneva* (Lindsay-Hogg—for TV) (as Steiner); *Introduction to English Poetry, 1384-Present* (doc for TV) (poetry read by Cusack and others); *Rainy Day Women* (Bolt—for TV) (as Reed); *Restoration and Augustan Poetry* (Mervyn—doc for TV) (poetry read by Cusack and others)

1986   *The Theban Plays: Oedipus the King* (Don Taylor—for TV) (as the priest)

1987   *Little Dorrit* (Part I: *Nobody's Fault* and Part II: *Little Dorrit's Story*) (Edzard) (as Frederick Dorrit); *Cusack by Cusack* (doc for TV)

1988   *Menace Unseen* (for TV); *The Tenth Man* (Gold—for TV) (as the parish priest)
1989   *My Left Foot* (Sheridan) (as Lord Castlewelland); *Danny, the Champion of the World* (Millar—for TV) (as Doc Spencer)
1990   *The Fool* (Edzard) (as the Ballad Seller)
1991   *The Company: Inigo and His Jesuits* (Fenton) (as host)
1992   *Far and Away* (Ron Howard) (as Danty Duff); *As You Like It* (Edzard) (as Adam); *Memento Mori* (Clayton and Hubbard—for TV) (as the poet Percy Mannering)
1993   *Young Indiana Jones Chronicles: Paris, May 1919* (Hare—for TV) (as Georges Clemenceau)

Publications

By CUSACK: books—

Timepieces (verse), Dublin, 1970.
Tar eis an aifrinn: drama aonghnimh, Baile Atha Cliath, 1989.
Between the Acts and Other Poems, Gerrards Cross, England, 1990.

By CUSACK: articles—

Focus (London), March 1953.
Interview with Elliot Norton, in *Boston Record*, 14 May 1957.
"A Player's Reflections on *Playboy*," in *Twentieth Century Interpretations of* The Playboy of the Western World, *A Collection of Critical Essays*, edited by Thomas R. Whitaker, Englewood Cliffs, New Jersey, 1969.
"Cusack: Every Week a Different School," in *Flight from the Celtic Twilight*, by Des Hickey and Gus Smith, Indianapolis, 1973.
"That Angelic Devilment," interview with Clive Hodgson, in *Radio Times* (London), 19-25 November 1983.
"The Ideal Theater of Playwright and Player," in *Irish Traditions*, edited by Kathleen Jo Ryan and Bernard Share, New York, 1985.
"Interview with Cyril Cusack," in *World Cinema 4: Ireland*, by Brian McIlroy, Trowbridge, England, 1988.
"A Childhood: Cyril Cusack Talks to Paddy Burt: 'I'm a Listener, Not a Talker,'" in *Times* (London), 28 July 1990.

On CUSACK: articles—

Today's Cinema, 11 March 1953.
Thomson, David, "Featuring . . . Cyril Cusack," in *Film Comment* (New York), November/December 1989.
Obituary in *Irish Independent* (Dublin), 8 October 1993.
Obituary in *New York Times*, 8 October 1993.
Obituary in *Times* (London), 8 October 1993.
Obituary in *Variety* (New York), 18 October 1993.

*   *   *

In a life of almost 83 years Cyril Cusack spent 77 of those years active in the theater, film, radio, television, recordings, and publishing, with well over 100 theatrical productions, 90 films, and 75 television productions to his credit.

After his birth in Durban, Natal, South Africa, his actress mother brought him to Ireland at any early age. He was a devoted Irishman—as actor and nationalist—and in many ways his theatrical and film work reflects this. In an incident recounted in *Cinema and Ireland* (1988), Cusack and a group of fellow actors and students, offended by what they considered to be a stereotypical depiction of the Irish shouted down a screening of the American film *Smiling Irish Eyes* (1929) in a Dublin theater. He was fluent in the Irish language, sent his children to Irish language schools, and wrote a play in Gaelic, *Tar eis*

an aifrinn, which was staged in 1942. At the age of eight he was cast in the early silent Irish film *Knocknagow* which dealt with the Irish famine. In 1979 he starred as a poteen maker in *Poitin (Poteen)*, which is considered the first Irish feature film in Gaelic. Many of the films in which he appeared are about the Irish fight for independence: *Guests of the Nation*, *Odd Man Out*, *The Rising of the Moon*, and *Shake Hands with the Devil*.

He often said that his movie career supported his primary interest of mounting theatrical productions. While long associated with the Abbey Theatre he also ran his own company, Cyril Cusack Productions. His theatrical contributions included the major Irish figures of the stage from Boucicault to Beckett. His favorite roles included The Covey in O'Casey's *The Plough and the Stars* and Christy Mahon in Synge's *The Playboy of the Western World*. The full extent of his abilities as a stage actor are not always captured on film. But his long association with Caedmon Records provides one with an opportunity to at least hear him in some of his important Shakespearean and Irish roles, and the plays of Genet and Ionesco. (He also recorded the poetry and writings of Hopkins, Yeats, Joyce, and Beckett). One of Cusack's proudest moments was the production of *The Three Sisters* (Royal Court Theatre, London, 1990) in which he acted with his three actress daughters, who through their active stage and screen careers have extended the Cusack acting dynasty into its fourth generation.

While Cusack's film career has included some major roles: Chauvelin in *The Elusive Pimpernel*, the title role in *Galileo*, and as Frederick Katzmann in *Sacco and Vanzetti*, virtually his whole body of film work has been devoted to the portrayal of character roles. In a way this is a pity, because Cusack was a major actor, of great talent, who had honed his craft through long years of experience. (He had great confidence in his acting abilities and did not particularly appreciate directors who wanted to tell him how to act the parts.) On the other hand one has the opportunity of experiencing this great talent in relatively short, concentrated scenes. Some of these are gems of acting skill. The two short scenes as Control with Richard Burton in *The Spy Who Came in from the Cold* underline the subtlety of his acting. In the theme and plot of this wonderfully complex film, his role is extremely important to the action. There is subtlety of interpretation, an almost "minimalist" approach of expression, movement, speech, and body language that projects the depth of character. Here is Cusack as a prissy, meticulous, almost insufferable bore, irritated because the "office girl" did not warm the teapot. He was able to project an exterior of extreme propriety, a person meticulously dressed, while underneath it there is a ruthless schemer. Other movies in which this ability to flesh out the role of a minor character who often has an impact on the plot of the film are: *Odd Man Out*, *The Passage Home*, *Fahrenheit 451*, *Day of the Jackal*, *Juggernaut*, *True Confessions*, "A Careful Man" sequence in *2 x Forsyth*, and *The Tenth Man*.

—Allen Cohen

CUSHING, Peter

Nationality: British. **Born:** Kenley, Surrey, 26 May 1913. **Education:** Attended Purley Secondary School; Guildhall School of Music and Drama, London. **Family:** Married Helen Beck, 1940 (died 1971). **Career:** Early 1930s—assistant stage manager of Worthing Repertory Company in Sussex; 1935—stage debut in *The Middle Watch* in Worthing; 1939—film debut in *The Man in the Iron Mask*; 1940—Hollywood film debut in *Vigil in the Night*; 1941—New York stage debut in *The Seventh Trumpet*; 1943—London stage debut in *War and Peace*; 1948—toured Australia and New Zealand with Old Vic Company; 1954—critical and popular acclaim for role in *1984* for British television; 1957—began acting in long series of horror films produced by Hammer Films and directed by Terence Fisher; 1968—in British TV series *Sherlock Holmes*. **Awards:** Officer, Order of the British Empire, 1989. **Died:** Of cancer, in Canterbury, England, 11 August 1994.

Films as Actor:

1939   *The Man in the Iron Mask* (Whale)
1940   *Hidden Master* (short); *Dreams* (short); *Laddie* (Hively) (as Robert Pryor); *Women in War* (Auer) (as Capt. Evans); *A Chump at Oxford* (Goulding) (as student); *Vigil in the Night* (Stevens) (as Joe Shand)
1941   *They Dare Not Love* (Whale); *We All Help* (short); *The New Teacher* (short); *Safety First* (short)
1947   *It Might Be You* (short)
1948   *Hamlet* (Olivier) (as Osric)
1952   *Moulin Rouge* (Huston) (as Marcel de la Voisier)
1954   *The Black Knight* (Garnett) (as Sir Palamides)
1955   *The End of the Affair* (Dmytryk) (as Henry Miles)
1956   *Magic Fire* (Dieterle) (as Otto Wesendonk); *Alexander the Great* (Rossen) (as Memnon); *Time without Pity* (Losey) (as Jeremy Clayton)
1957   *The Abominable Snowman* (*The Abominable Snowman of the Himalayas*) (Guest) (as Dr. John Rollason); *The Curse of Frankenstein* (Fisher) (as Victor Frankenstein)
1958   *Violent Playground* (Dearden) (as priest); **Dracula** (*The Horror of Dracula*) (Fisher) (as Dr. Van Helsing)
1959   *The Mummy* (Fisher) (as John Banning); *The Hound of the Baskervilles* (Fisher) (as Sherlock Holmes); *John Paul Jones* (Farrow) (as Capt. Pearson)
1960   *The Flesh and the Fiends* (*Mania*; *Psycho Killers*; *The Fiendish Ghouls*) (Gilling) (as Dr. Robert Knox); *Code of Silence* (*Trouble in the Sky*) (Frend) (as Captain Clive Judd); *Suspect* (*The Risk*) (Boulting) (as Prof. Sewell); *The Brides of Dracula* (Fisher) (as Dr. Van Helsing); *Sword of Sherwood Forest* (Fisher) (as Sheriff of Nottingham)
1961   *Fury at Smuggler's Bay* (Gilling) (as Squire Trevenyan); *The Naked Edge* (Anderson) (as Wrack); *The Hellfire Club* (Baker) (as Merryweather); *Cash on Demand* (Lawrence) (as Fordyce)
1962   *The Devil's Agent* (Carstairs); *Captain Clegg* (*Night Creatures*) (Scott) (as Dr. Blyss/Capt. Nathaniel Clegg); *The Man Who Finally Died* (Fisher) (as Dr. von Brecht)
1964   *The Evil of Frankenstein* (Fisher) (as Baron Frankenstein); *Dr. Terror's House of Horrors* (Francis) (as Dr. Sandor Schreck); *The Gorgon* (Fisher) (as Dr. Namaroff)
1965   *She* (Day) (as Major Horace Holly); *The Skull* (Francis) (as Prof. Christopher Maitland); *Dr. Who and the Daleks* (Fleming) (as Dr. Who)
1966   *Island of Terror* (Fisher) (as Dr. Brian Stanley); *Daleks—Invasion Earth A.D. 2150* (Fleming) (as Dr. Who)
1967   *Frankenstein Created Woman* (Fisher) (as Baron Frankenstein); *Torture Garden* (Francis) (as Canning); *The Mummy's Shroud* (Gilling) (as narrator); *Some May Live* (*They Also Kill*) (Sewell—for TV) (as John Meredith); *Night of the Big Heat* (*Island of the Burning Damned*) (Fisher) (as Dr. Stone); *Caves of Steel*
1968   *The Blood Beast Terror* (*The Vampire Beast Craves Blood*) (Sewell) (as Inspector Quennell); *Corruption* (Hartford-Davis) (as Sir John Brown)
1969   *Frankenstein Must Be Destroyed* (Fisher) (as Baron Frankenstein); *Scream and Scream Again* (Hessler) (as Major Heinrich); *One More Time* (Lewis) (as Frankenstein)

1970   *The Vampire Lovers* (Baker) (as General Spielsdorf); *The House That Dripped Blood* (Duffell) (as Philip Grayson); *Incense for the Damned* (*Bloodsuckers*) (Hartford-Davis) (as Dr. Goodrich)
1971   *Twins of Evil* (Hough) (as Gustav Weil)
1972   *I, Monster* (Weeks) (as Utterson); "Poetic Justice" ep. of *Tales from the Crypt* (Francis) (as Mr. Grimsdyke); *Nothing but the Night* (Sasdy) (as Sir Mark Ashley); *Michael Carmichael* (*Fear in the Night*) (Sangster); *Asylum* (Baker) (as Smith); *Dr. Phibes Rises Again* (Fuest) (as Captain); *Dracula A.D. 1972* (Gibson) (as Van Helsing); *Panico en el Transiberiano* (*Horror Express*) (Martin) (as Dr. Wells)
1973   *The Satanic Rites of Dracula* (*Count Dracula and His Vampire Bride*) (Gibson) (as Van Helsing); *Frankenstein and the Monster from Hell* (Fisher) (as Dr. Frankenstein); *The Creeping Flesh* (Francis) (as Emmanuel Hildern); *And Now the Screaming Starts* (Baker) (as Dr. Pope); *From Beyond the Grave* (Connor) (as shopkeeper)
1974   *Legend of the Werewolf* (Francis) (as Paul Cataflangue); *The Golden Vampire* (*The Seven Brothers Meet Dracula*; *The Legend of the Seven Golden Vampires*) (Baker) (as Van Helsing); *Madhouse* (Clark) (as Herbert Flay); *La Grande Trouille* (*Tendre Dracula*) (Grunstein) (as voice); *The Beast Must Die* (Annett) (as Dr. Lungren)
1975   *Call Him Mr. Shatter* (*Shatter*) (Carreras); *The Ghoul* (Francis) (as Dr. Lawrence); *Shock Waves* (*Almost Human*; *Death Corps*) (Wiederhorn) (as Scar)
1976   *The Devil's Men* (*Land of the Minotaur*) (Carayiannis) (as Baron Corofax); *Trial by Combat* (*Choice of Weapons*; *Dirty Knight's Work*) (Connor) (as Sir Edward Gifford); *At the Earth's Core* (Connor) (as Dr. Abner Perry); *The Great Houdinis* (Shavelson—for TV)
1977   *The Uncanny* (Herous) (as Wilbur Gray); *Die Standarte* (*Battle Flag*) (Runze) (as Maj. von Hackenberg); **Star Wars** (Lucas) (as Grand Moff Tarkin)
1978   *Hitler's Son* (Amateau) (as Heinrich Hussner); *The Detour*
1979   *Touch of the Sun* (Curran) (as Commissioner Potts); *Arabian Adventure* (Connor) (as Wazir Al Wurzara)
1980   *A Tale of Two Cities* (Jim Goddard—for TV) (as Dr. Manette); *Misterio en la isla de los monstruos* (*Monster Island*; *Mystery of Monster Island*) (Piquer) (as Colderup); *Black Jack* (Boulois)
1982   *House of the Long Shadows* (Walker) (as Sebastian)
1983   *Sword of the Valiant* (Weeks) (as Seneschal)
1984   *Top Secret!* (Abrahams, Zucker, and Zucker) (as Sven Jorgensen); *The Silent Scream* (Alan Gibson); *Sherlock Holmes and the Masks of Death* (*Masks of Death*) (Roy Ward Baker—for TV); *Helen Keller: The Miracle Continues* (Alan Gibson—for TV) (as Prof. Charles Copeland)
1985   *Biggles: Adventures in Time* (*Biggles*) (Hough) (as Colonel Raymond)

Publications

By CUSHING: books—

Tales of a Monster Hunter (horror tales selected by Peter Cushing), London, 1977.
Peter Cushing: An Autobiography, London, 1986.
Past Forgetting: Memoirs of the Hammer Years, London, 1988.

By CUSHING: articles—

Interviews in *Cinéma* (Paris), July-August 1972.

Peter Cushing as Van Helsing in *Brides of Dracula*

Film Review, September 1976.
Films Illustrated (London), December 1980.

On CUSHING: books—

McCarty, John, *Splatter Movies: Breaking the Last Taboo of the Screen*, New York, 1984.
McCarty, John, *The Modern Horror Film*, New York, 1990.
Del Vecchio, Deborah, and Tom Johnson, *Peter Cushing: The Gentle Man of Horror and His 91 Films*, Jefferson, North Carolina, 1992.
McCarty, John, *Movie Psychos and Madmen*, New York, 1993.
McCarty, John, *The Fearmakers*, New York, 1994.
Miller, Mark A., *Christopher Lee and Peter Cushing and Horror Cinema*, Jefferson, North Carolina, 1994.

On CUSHING: articles—

Films Illustrated (London), December 1971.
Article about Peter Cushing and Christopher Lee in *Photoplay* (New York), June 1972.
Ringel, H., "The Horrible Hammer Films of Terence Fisher," in *Take One* (Montreal), May 1973.
Transcript of John Player lecture on "Frankenstein and Others," in *Films Illustrated* (London), October 1973.
Carrère, E., "Prométhée délivré (sur les 'Frankenstein' de Terence Fisher)," in *Positif* (Paris), July-August 1977.
Photoplay (New York), October 1980.
Ecran Fantastique (Paris), no. 19, 1981.
Obituary in *New York Times*, 12 August 1994.
"The Arm of God," obituary in *Film Comment* (New York), November/December 1994.

*   *   *

Peter Cushing was identifiable by his noble air and refined manner, by all appearances a gentleman. Yet he is best remembered for those moments in film where he plunges the stake, without reservation or mercy, into the waiting chest of the sleeping vampire, amid deafening screams from the dying and a pool of blood to reassure us that the deed is done. For Cushing was one of the mainstays of the British horror film, as defined by Hammer Films. His frequent pairing with Christopher Lee in dozens of horror films over several decades was the most famous "scream team" since Boris Karloff and Bela Lugosi went to their great rewards.

Beginning in the late 1950s, Hammer began turning out loose remakes, in color, of the classic Universal horror films of the 1930s under the guidance of house directors such as Terence Fisher and Freddie Francis. In these films Hammer created a fairy tale gothic atmosphere distinctively its own. It combined this with unprecedentedly graphic violence and sexual exploitation which contributed much to breaking down the walls of screen censorship in Britain and elsewhere. Cushing brought to the title character of *The Curse of Frankenstein*—the first of Hammer's gothic horrors—a touch of nastiness that audiences weaned on Colin Clive's portrayal in the 1931 original had never seen before. No mere mad scientist, Cushing's Baron von Frankenstein was the ultimate narcissist: cold, ruthless, remorseless, and a murderer to boot—the true monster of the film. He played the part, with which he is most identified by horror fans, in five Hammer sequels, the last of which, *Frankenstein and the Monster from Hell*, found him the chief lunatic in charge of his private asylum.

Cushing's other famous role was that of Dracula's arch nemesis, the vampire destroyer Dr. Abraham Van Helsing. Cushing injected the character with a degree of neurotic obsession barely hinted at in Bram Stoker's novel. He first played the role in Hammer's *Horror of Dracula*, the studio's smash hit follow-up to *The Curse of Frankenstein*. It remains the studio's most celebrated film. Cushing played Van Helsing (as well as Van Helsing's nephew, Lorimar) in five Hammer sequels, the oddest of which was 1974's *The Legend of the Seven Golden Vampires* produced by the Shaw brothers in Hong Kong. Here, the martial arts meet the black arts, as Cushing allies himself with sibling martial artists to fight a horde of kung-fu vampires created by Dracula.

Cushing also made an indelible mark as Sherlock Holmes in Hammer's *The Hound of the Baskervilles*, one of the best screen versions of Conan Doyle's oft-filmed tale. Cushing's Holmes was an intellectual neurotic whose obsession with solving the mystery almost leads to his client's death. The screen had never presented Holmes in such a light, but this was precisely as Conan Doyle had written the character; thus, Cushing's Holmes, like his Baron Frankenstein and Van Helsing before it, was a groundbreaker, paving the way for a host of similarly authentic Holmes interpretations, culminating with the late Jeremy Brett's even more neurotic (and obsessive) incarnation a quarter of a century later on television. Cushing also played the character on television in a series of 16 Holmes adventures produced for the BBC in the 1960s, one of them yet another remake of *The Hound of the Baskervilles*, trimmed to an hour-long format.

In addition to Lee, Cushing teamed with another icon of modern horror cinema, Vincent Price, in several films, most notably *House of the Long Shadows*, an homage to the gothic "old dark house" genre of horror films based on the oft-filmed Earl Derr Bigger's thriller *Seven Keys to Baldpate*.

Cushing and Lee's final teaming was a documentary on Hammer Films, *Flesh and Blood*, which they hosted and narrated for producer-director Ted Newsom. The documentary aired in two parts on the BBC in August 1994. Ill at the time, Cushing's spirits were buoyed by the arrival of thousands of fan letters after the first episode aired. His death (from cancer) on 11 August 1994, before the second episode reached the airwaves, marked the end of an era for horror fans, young and old, around the world.

—Rob Winning, updated by John McCarty

DAFOE, Willem

Nationality: American. **Born:** William Dafoe in Appleton, Wisconsin, 22 July 1955. **Family:** Son with Elizabeth LeCompte: Jack. **Education:** Attended University of Wisconsin, Milwaukee. **Career:** 1975—Member of Theatre X experimental theatrical company; 1977—joined Wooster Group theatrical company; 1980—film debut in *Heaven's Gate*. **Agent:** Creative Artists Agency, 9830 Wilshire Boulevard, Beverly Hills, CA 90212, U.S.A.

Films as Actor:

1980 *Heaven's Gate* (Cimino)
1982 *The Loveless* (Bigelow) (as Vance)
1984 *The Hunger* (Tony Scott) (as phone booth youth); *New York Nights* (Nuchtern) (as punk boyfriend); *Roadhouse 66* (John Mark Robinson) (as Johnny Harte); *Streets of Fire* (Walter Hill) (as Raven)
1985 *To Live and Die in L.A.* (Friedkin) (as Eric Masters); *The Communists Are Comfortable* (Kobland)
1986 *Platoon* (Oliver Stone) (as Sgt. Elias)
1987 *Dear America: Letters Home from Vietnam* (Couturie—doc, for TV) (as co-narrator); *Hitchhiker 3* (for TV)
1988 *The Last Temptation of Christ* (Scorsese) (as Jesus Christ); *Mississippi Burning* (Alan Parker) (as Alan Ward); *Off Limits* (*Saigon*) (as Buck McGriff) (Crowe)
1989 *Born on the Fourth of July* (Oliver Stone) (as Charlie); *Triumph of the Spirit* (Robert M. Young) (as Salamo Arouch)
1990 *Cry-Baby* (Waters) (as hateful guard); *Wild at Heart* (Lynch) (as Bobby Peru)
1991 *Flight of the Intruder* (Milius) (as Lt. Commander Virgil Cole)
1992 *Light Sleeper* (Schrader) (as John LeTour); *White Sands* (Donaldson) (as Ray Dolezal)
1993 *Body of Evidence* (Edel) (as Frank Dulaney); *Faraway, So Close* (*In Weiter Ferne, So Nah!*) (Wenders) (as Emit Flesti)
1994 *Clear and Present Danger* (Noyce) (as Clark); *The Night and the Moment* (Tato) (as the writer); *Tom & Viv* (Brian Gilbert) (as T. S. Eliot)
1995 *The English Patient* (Minghella) (as Caravaggio); *Victory* (Peploe)
1996 *Basquiat* (*Build a Fort, Set It on Fire*) (Schnabel); *The Foolish Heart* (Babenco)

Publications

By DAFOE: articles—

"In Search of Dafoe," interview with James Leverett and Kevin Sessums, in *Interview* (New York), June 1988.
"Willem Dafoe and John Lurie," interview with Lori J. Smith, in *Interview* (New York), October 1988.
"Willem Dafoe: Center Stage," in *American Film* (Washington, D.C.), May 1990.
"Willem Dafoe: Bigger than Life," interview with Michael Lassiter, in *Advocate* (Los Angeles), 13 August 1992.
Cover story, interview with Russell Banks, in *Interview* (New York), January 1993.

On DAFOE: articles—

Rochlin, Mary, "Lords of the Ring," in *Harper's Bazaar* (New York), December 1989.
Current Biography 1990, New York, 1990.
Woodward, Richard B., "The Wild One," in *New York*, 27 August 1990.

* * *

Although one has a vivid mental image of Willem Dafoe, and the impression of a strong and striking presence, the more one thinks about his performances and the range of his roles (from demonic biker to Jesus Christ, with many variables in between), the more complex the persona appears, the more difficult to fix upon a stable core. Certain pattern form, but they are often contradictory.

One may begin by defining him negatively, by what he *does not* do. Aside from the grotesquerie of his small roles in *Cry-Baby* and *Wild at Heart*, he never plays comedy; he is seldom permitted a happy ending, especially the traditional one of lovers united; he is only slightly more frequently involved in love stories; although he has played in "action" movies he is far from a typical "action" hero. He is the kind of actor, in fact, that Hollywood needs but does not quite know what to do with when it gets one. There is his unusual and expressive face, far from the conventional good looks that get inferior actors cast as romantic leads, which can be at times incredibly beautiful (*Off Limits*), intensely malevolent (*Streets of Fire*), or intriguingly decadent (*To Live and Die in L.A.*).

He has appeared most frequently in "dark" movies: contemporary variants on film noir (*White Sands*, *Light Sleeper*) or films of notably grim subject matter (*Platoon*, *Triumph of the Spirit*). His roles in these, however, have been extremely varied, running the gamut from villainy and evil to heroism and Christlike martyrdom. The first films in which he made a strong impression established the former. *Streets of Fire* is a misguided, deliriously stylized, homage to/parody of bad fifties B movies, that ends being at least as empty as what it parodies. The two leads, Michael Paré (doing a Sylvester Stallone imitation) and Diane Lane (looking sulky), form an ideal context in which Dafoe's demon biker can shine: he looks like a juvenile Frankenstein's monster gone berserk, and easily steals the film. The far more interesting *To Live and Die in L.A.* gives him a richer context and a much more complex role. His murderous counterfeiter, associated with art and (in the film's strangest moment) sexual ambiguity, is only ambiguously the villain in a film in which the nominally good/moral can easily (as in certain other Friedkin movies, notably *Cruising*) switch places with the nominally evil/immoral, within a world where everyone is implicated in corruption.

Willem Dafoe in *The Last Temptation of Christ*

Only one year later Oliver Stone cast him in *Platoon*, initiating the series of "Christ" roles, as Stone's treatment of his death scene makes quite explicit. This is followed by two more "hero" roles: his purification through experience and the love of a good nun in *Off Limits*, his naive and idealistic young civil rights worker from the North coming South to teach the helpless blacks how to take a stand in Alan Parker's *Mississippi Burning*, an eloquent example of those good intentions to which the road to hell is said to be paved. These in turn are followed by the culmination of this particular career trajectory, his selection by Scorsese to play Jesus himself in *The Last Temptation of Christ*. Despite the evident commitment and the all-too-obviously strenuous effort, this seems to me Scorsese's one serious failure. But how *do* you present Christ on the screen? What course to steer between the human and the divine, between skepticism and belief? Significantly it is Dafoe's least memorable performance in a major role. *Triumph of the Spirit*, a year later, offered him more practicable opportunities in a variation on the "savior" role: a concentration camp inmate who both survives, and helps others to survive, through his prowess as a boxer, driving himself to ever greater exertions in order to stay alive.

Three years later, after a period in which it appeared that Dafoe had been relegated to the status of supporting player, taking variously grotesque roles in films ranging from the distinguished but compromised *Born on the Fourth of July* to the relentlessly atrocious *Wild at Heart*, his great moment arrived, in that unpredictable way in which such things occasionally happen in Hollywood: the central roles, and two of his best performances, in two films of considerable distinction,

both released in 1992: *White Sands* and *Light Sleeper*. Unfortunately (as far as Dafoe's future career is concerned), the former performed at the box office indifferently, the latter disastrously.

All the negatives by which I defined Dafoe at the outset are contradicted in *White Sands*. This critically underrated film is among the most interesting of contemporary attempts to revive (by updating) film noir: it exceeds expectations in one direction while negating them in others. The image of America as a nation characterized by all-pervasive corruption and the resulting paranoia was a given of classical film noir but is here pushed further: the FBI are as criminal as the nominal criminals, and the ultimate figure of evil (Mickey Rourke) is finally revealed as a representative of the CIA. On the other hand, the apparent femme fatale (Mary Elizabeth Mastroantonio) emerges as (although not uncontaminated—as she says, "It's a fine line") one of the film's most admirable characters, and the hero (Dafoe), whom we constantly expect to be sucked into the seemingly inescapable corruption, emerges intact (even if guilty of brief marital infidelity). Dafoe navigates the film's quicksands with splendid assurance, often as bewildered as the traditional noir protagonist (not to mention the audience) by the web of intrigue and double-dealing, but through a combination of pragmatism and integrity managing (just) to survive its pitfalls and temptations, his self-respect intact.

Light Sleeper (more central to the noir tradition with its urban setting, criminal underworld, and fallible and corrupt protagonist), offers him even greater opportunities to develop a complex character, here a drug dealer, tired and beginning to feel his age, attempting to extricate himself from a life he has come to find oppressive, but the forces of which, set in motion, are all-but-impossible to combat. Specifically, he is an apparently lost soul struggling upward toward salvation. The two films in juxtaposition might be taken as summing up two sides of the Dafoe persona, the innocent and the corrupt, striving for life within a dark, menacing, and hostile world.

Unfortunately, the following year (after a brief, indecisive venture into international co-production for Wenders's *Faraway, So Close*) marked the nadir of Dafoe's career so far: *Body of Evidence*, in which his ignominious function was to "support" the insupportable. Doubtless it seemed a good career move at the time, but it rebounded disastrously, as such things tend to do. Since then, and up to the time of writing, Dafoe's only exposure to general audiences has been in an unrewarding supporting role in *Clear and Present Danger*.

—Robin Wood

DAGOVER, Lil

Nationality: Dutch. **Born:** Marie Antonia Siegelinde Marta Liletts in Madiven, Java (now Djawa), 30 September 1897 (or 1894). **Education:** Boarding schools in Baden-Baden and Weimar, Germany, Lausanne and Geneva, Switzerland. **Family:** Married 1) the actor Fritz Daghofer, 1917 (divorced 1919), daughter: Eva Marie; 2) the producer George Witt, 1936. **Career:** 1919—film debut in Fritz Lang's *Harakiri*; 1925—stage debut under the direction of Max Reinhardt in Salzburg; 1926-27—appeared in a few Swedish films; 1927—visited Hollywood; 1928-29—appeared in several French films; 1932—in only U.S. film, *The Woman from Monte Carlo*; 1940s-1979—acted occasionally on stage and television, and in films. **Awards:** State Actress, Germany, 1937; Bundesfilmpreis, 1962; Cross of Merit, Federal Republic of Germany, 1967. **Died:** In Munich, 23 January 1980.

Films as Actress:

1919   *Harakiri* (Lang) (as Butterfly); *Die Spinnen, Part 1: Der goldene See* (*The Spiders, Part 1: The Golden Lake*) (Lang)

1920   ***Das Kabinett des Dr. Caligari*** (*The Cabinet of Dr. Caligari*) (Wiene) (as Jane); *Die Spinnen, Part 2: Das Brillantenschiff* (*The Spiders, Part 2: The Diamond Ship*) (Lang); *Das Blut der Ahnen* (Gerhardt); *Die Jagd nach dem Tode* (Gerhardt); *Das Geheimnis von Bombay* (Holz); *Spiritismus* (Zelnik); *Die Toteninsel* (Froelich)

1921   *Der müde Tod* (*Destiny; Between Two Worlds; Beyond the Wall*) (Lang); *Der Richter von Zalamea* (Berger); *Das Medium* (Rosenfeld)

1922   *Phantom* (Murnau); *Luise Millerin* (*Kabale und Liebe*) (Froelich) (title role); ***Dr. Mabuse, der Spieler*** (*Dr. Mabuse, The Gambler*) (Lang); *Tiefland* (Licho); *Macht der Versuchung* (Stein)

1923   *Seine Frau, die Unbekannte* (*Wilbur Crawfords wundersames Abenteuer*) (Christensen); *Liebe macht Blind* (*Love Makes Us Blind*) (Mendes); *Die Prinzessin Sawarin* (Guter)

1924   *Komödie des Herzens* (Gliese)

1925   *Tartüff* (*Tartuffe*) (Murnau) (as Elmira); *Zur Chronik von Grieshuus* (*Chronicles of the Grey House; At the Grey House*) (von Gerlach); *Die Doppelgängerin*; *Der Demütiger und die Sängerin* (Dupont)

1926   *Der geheime Kurier* (*Red and the Black*) (Righelli); *Die Brüder Schellenberg* (*The Two Brothers*) (Grüne); *Der Veilchenfresser* (Zelnik); *Hans engelska fru* (*His English Wife; Discord*) (Molander)

1927   *Bara en danserska* (*Only a Dancing Girl*) (Morel); *Der Anwalt des Herzens* (Thiele); *Ein moderner Don Juan*; *Orient-Express* (Thiele)

1928   *Der Ungarische Rhapsodie* (*Hungarian Rhapsody*) (Schwarz); *Monte Cristo* (Fescourt); *Le Tourbillon de Paris* (Duvivier)

1929   *La Grande Passion* (*The Grand Passion*) (Hugon); *Der Günstling von Schönbrunn* (Waschneck); *Spielereien einer Kaiserin* (Strijewski); *Die Ehe* (Frowein); *Es flüstert die Nacht* (*Hungarian Nights*) (Janson); *Melodie des Herzens* (*Melody of the Heart*) (Schwarz); *Der weisse Teufel* (*The White Devil*) (Volkoff)

1930   *Der grosse Sehnsucht* (Szekely); *Das alte Lied* (*Zu jedem kommt einmal die Liebe*) (Waschneck); *Boykott* (*Primanerehe*) (Land); *Es gibt eine Frau, die Dich niemals vergisst* (Mittler); *Va bangue* (Waschneck)

1931   *Der Fall des Generalstabsoberst Redl* (*The Case of Colonel Redl*) (Anton); *Elisabeth von Osterreich* (*Elizabeth of Austria*) (Trotz); *Der Kongress tanzt* (*The Congress Dances*) (Charell)

1932   *The Woman from Monte Carlo* (Curtiz); *Die letzte Illusion* (Waschneck); *Das Schicksal einer schönen Frau* (Conrad Wiene) (as Madame Blaubart)

1933   *Johannisnacht* (Reiber); *Die Tänzerin von Sanssouci* (*Barberina, die Tänzerin von Sanssouci; The King's Dancer*) (Zelnik); *Der Storch hat uns getraut* (*Married by the Stork*); *Das Abenteuer der Thea Roland* (*Das Abenteuer einer schönen Frau*) (Kösterlitz)

1934   *Ich heirate meine Frau* (Riemann); *Einer Frau, die weiss, was sie will* (Janson); *Der Flüchtling aus Chicago* (*The Fugitive from Chicago*) (Meyer)

1935   *Der höhere Befehl* (Lamprecht); *Der Vogelhändler* (Emo); *Lady Windermeres Fächer* (*Lady Windermere's Fan*) (Hilpert)

1936   *Schlussakkord* (*Final Accord*) (Sierck, i.e., Sirk); *Fridericus* (Meyer); *August der Starke* (Wegener); *Das Mädchen Irene* (Schünzel)

1937   *Streit um den Knaben Jo* (*Strife over the Boy Jo*) (Waschneck); *Das Schönheit-spflästerchen* (*The Beauty Shop*) (Hansen); *Die Kreutzersonate* (*The Kreutzer Sonata*) (Harlan)

1938   *Dreiklang* (Hinrich); *Maja zwischen zwei Ehen* (Kirchhoff); *Rätsel um Beate* (Meyer)

1939   *Umwege zum Glück* (Buch)

1940   *Friedrich Schiller* (*Der Triumph eines Genies*) (Maisch); *Bismarck* (Liebeneiner)

1942   *Wien 1910* (Emo); *Kleine Residenz* (Zerlett)

1944   *Musik in Salzburg* (Maisch)

1948   *Die Söhne des Herrn Gaspary* (Meyer)

1949   *Man spielt nicht mit der Liebe* (Deppe)

1950   *Das Geheimnis von Bergsee*; *Es kommt ein Tag* (*A Day Will Come*) (Jugert); *Vom Teufel gejagt* (Tourjansky)

1953   *Rote Rosen, rote Lippen, roter Wein* (Martin); *Königliche Hoheit* (Braun)

1955   *Schloss Hubertus: Der Fischer von Heiligensee* (*The Big Barrier*) (Weiss); *Die Barrings* (Thiele); *Ich wiess, wofür ich lebe* (Verhoeven); *Rosen im Herbst* (*Effi Briest*) (Jugert); *Meine 16 Söhne* (Domnick)

1956   *Kronprinz Rudolfs letzte Liebe* (Jugert); *Verwegene Musikanten* (Domnick)

1957   *Unter Palmen am blauen Meer* (Deppe); *Bekenntnisse des Hochstaplers Felix Krull* (*The Confessions of Felix Krull*) (Hoffmann)

1959   *Buddenbrooks* (Weidenmann—for TV)

1961   *Die seltsame Gräfin* (von Baky)

1974   *Karl May* (Syberberg); *Der Fussgänger* (*The Pedestrian*) (Schell)

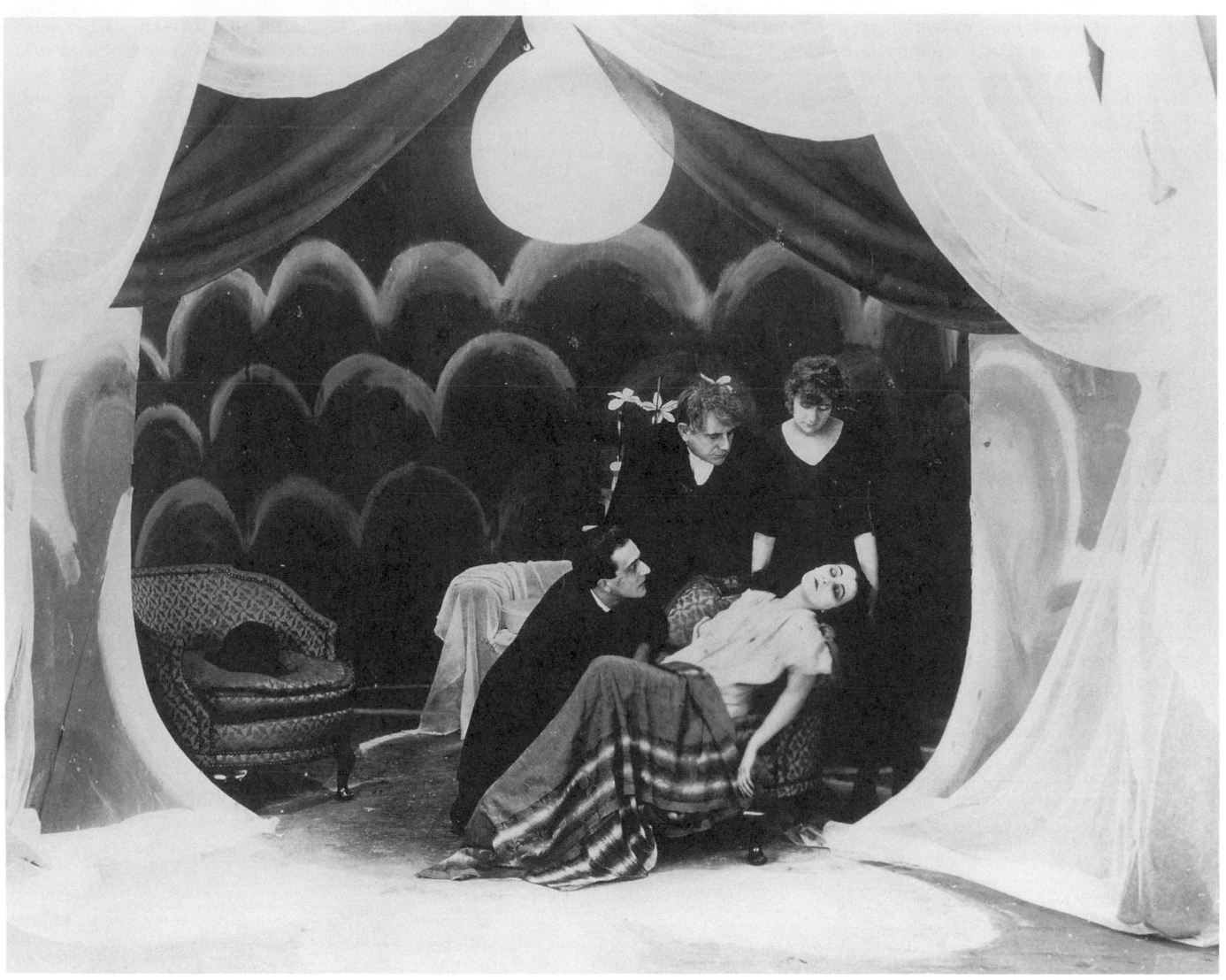

Lil Dagover (seated) in *Das Kabinett des Dr. Caligari*

1975   *Der Richter und sein Henker* (*End of the Game*; *Deception*;
       Murder on the Bridge; *The Judge and His Hangman*) (Schell)
1977   *Die Standarte* (*Battle Flag*) (Runze)
1979   *Geschichten aus den Wienerwald* (*Tales from the Vienna Woods*)
       (Schell)

Publications

By DAGOVER: book—

Ich war die Dame, Rastatt, West Germany, 1980.

By DAGOVER: article

Interview with John Kobal, in *Films and Filming* (London), September 1983.

On DAGOVER: book—

Romani, Cinzia, *Le dive del Terzo Reich*, Rome, 1981.

On DAGOVER: article—

The Annual Obituary 1980, New York, 1981.

*   *   *

Lil Dagover's dark beauty, heavily outlined by makeup, featured prominently during the so-called golden age of the German silent cinema after World War I. The daughter of a Dutchman working in Java, she was educated in Germany and was introduced to films after marrying, at age 20, the well-established actor Fritz Daghofer, a man more than twice her age whom she divorced in 1919, before starring in the celebrated German expressionist film, Robert Wiene's *The Cabinet of Dr. Caligari*. In this film, her jet-black hair, parted in the middle and flattened to the shape of her head, her long, white face, and her huge, expressive eyes all served to create the archetypical, victimized heroine of the expressionist melodramas of the early 1920s.

Dagover was most often employed by Fritz Lang at this stage in her career (she had appeared in his *Harakiri* just before *Caligari*): for Lang she went on to repeat the same, semi-idealized, artificial feminine image in a succession of stylized films, *Die Spinnen*, *Der müde Tod*, and *Dr. Mabuse, The Gambler*. After these films, among a wide range of parts in German, Swedish, and French films, she appeared in two outstanding productions of the German cinema of the mid-1920s: Murnau's *Tartuffe* (with Emil Jannings) and Arthur von Gerlach's *Zur Chronik von Grieshuus*.

Lil Dagover survived professionally both the coming of sound and the period of the Third Reich, appearing mostly in costume, period films such as *The Congress Dances, Lady Windermere's Fan, Fridericus, Friedrich Schiller*, and *Bismarck* and, after World War II, in *The Confessions of Felix Krull* and *Buddenbrooks*. Her career in film lasted over half a century from 1919 to 1979, during which she appeared in only one American film, *The Woman from Monte Carlo*.

—Roger Manvell

DAHLBECK, Eva

Nationality: Swedish. **Born:** Saltsjö-Duvnäs, 8 March 1920. **Education:** Attended Royal Dramatic Theatre School, Stockholm. **Family:** Married Col. Sven Lampell, 1944, two sons. **Career:** 1941—stage acting debut; 1942—stage role in *Rid i natt* at Theatre Royal, Stockholm, then first film appearance in Gustaf Molander's film adaptation of that play; extensive stage career included singing roles, e.g., Jenny in *Die Dreigoschenoper* (1950); 1952-55—in European-filmed U.S. TV series *Foreign Intrigue*; 1970s—career predominantly devoted to writing. **Awards:** Aftontidningen's Film Trophy, 1946; Medal of Honour, Swedish Filmassociation, 1951; Mauritz Stiller Award, 1956; Best Actress (collectively awarded), Cannes Festival, for *Brink of Life*, 1958; Golden Beetle for Outstanding Performance, for *The Cats*, 1965. **Address:** c/o Svenska Filminstitutet, Kungsgatan 48, Stockholm C, Sweden; or, Rödklöverägen 39 S-16573 Hässelby, Sweden.

Films as Actress:

1942 *Rid i natt* (*Ride Tonight!*) (Gustaf Molander)
1944 *Räkna de lyckliga stunderna blott* (*Only Count the Happy Moments*) (Carlsten)
1945 *Oss tjuvar emellan eller En burk ananas* (*Between Us Thieves*) (Olaf Molander); *Svarta rosor* (*Black Roses*) (Carlsten); *Den allvarsamma leken* (*The Serious Game*) (Carlsten)
1946 *Pengar—en tragikomisk saga* (*Money—a Tragicomedy*) (Poppe); *Brita i grosshandlarhuset* (*Brita in the Wholesaler's House*) (Ohberg); *Kärlek och störtlopp* (*Love and Downhill Skiing*) (Husberg); *Möte i natten* (*Meeting in the Night*) (Ekman) (as Marit Rylander)
1947 *Nyckeln och ringen* (*Key and the Ring*) (Henrikson); *Två kvinnor* (*Two Women*) (Sjöstrand); *Folket i Simlångsdalen* (*People of the Simlången Valley*) (Ohberg)
1948 *Var sin väg* (*Each to His Own Way*) (Ekman); *Lars Hård* (Faustman); *Eva* (Gustaf Molander) (as Susanne); *Flickan från fjällbyn* (*Girl from the Mountain Village*) (Henrikson)
1949 *Kvinna i vitt* (*Woman in White*) (Mattsson); *Bara en mor* (*Only a Mother*) (Sjöberg) (as Rya-Rya)
1950 *Hjärter Knekt* (*Jack of Hearts*) (Ekman); *Kastrullresan* (*Saucepan Journey*) (Mattsson)
1951 *Sköna Helena* (*Helen of Troy*) (Edgren); *Bärande hav* (*Rolling Sea*) (Mattsson); *Fästmö uthyres* (*Fiancée for Hire*) (Gustaf Molander)
1952 *Sabotage* (Jonsson); *Ubåt 39* (*U-Boat 39*) (Faustman); *Trots* (*Defiance*) (Gustaf Molander); *Kvinnors väntan* (*Secrets of*

Women; Waiting Women) (Bergman) (as Karin); *Kinder in Gottes Hand* (Lindtberg)
1953 *Das Pestalozzidorf* (*The Village*) (Lindtberg) (as Wanda Piwonska); *Skuggan* (*Shadow*) (Fant); *Barabbas* (Sjöberg); *Kvinnohuset* (*House of Women*) (Faustman); *Göingehövdingen* (*The Chief from Göinge*) (Ohberg)
1954 *En lektion i kärlek* (*A Lesson in Love*) (Bergman) (as Marianne Erneman)
1955 *Resa i natten* (*Night Journey*) (Faustman); *Kvinnodröm* (*Dreams; Journey into Autumn*) (Bergman) (as Susanne); *Paradiset* (*Paradise*) (Ragneborn); *Sommarnattens leende* (*Smiles of a Summer Night*) (Bergman) (as Desirée Armfeldt)
1956 *Sista paret ut* (*Last Pair Out; Last Couple Out*) (Sjöberg) (as Susanna Dahlin); *Tarps Elin* (Fant)
1957 *Möten i skymningen* (*Twilight Meetings*) (Kjellin); *Sommarnöje sökes* (*Summer Place Wanted*) (Ekman)
1958 *Nära livet* (*Brink of Life; So Close to Life*) (Bergman) (as Stina Andersson)
1960 *Kärlekens decimaler* (*Decimals of Love*) (Ekman); *Tre önskningar* (*Three Wishes*) (Ekman)
1961 *De sista stegen* (*A Matter of Morals*) (Cromwell) (as Eva Walderman)
1962 *The Counterfeit Traitor* (Seaton) (as Ingrid Erickson); *Biljett till paradiset* (*Ticket to Paradise*) (Mattsson)
1964 *För att inte tala om alla dessa kvinnor* (*All These Women; Now about All These Women*) (Bergman) (as Adelaide); *Älskande par* (*Loving Couples*) (Zetterling) (as Mrs. Landborg)
1965 *Kattorna* (*The Cats*) (Carlsen); *Morianerna* (*Morianna; I, the Body*) (Mattsson) (as Anna Vade)
1966 *Les Créatures* (*Varelserna*) (Varda) (as Michele Quellec)
1967 *Den rode kappe* (*The Red Mantle; Hagbard and Signe*) (Axel) (as the Queen); *Mënniskor modes og sod musik opstår i hjertet* (*Männeskor mötas och ljuv musik uppstår i hjärtat; People Meet and Sweet Music Fills the Air*) (Carlsen) (as Devah Sorensen)
1968 *Markurells i Wadköping* (*Markurells of Wadköping*) (Dahlin—for TV)
1970 *Tintomara* (Abramson)

Film as Scriptwriter:

1966 *Yngsjömordet* (*Woman of Darkness*) (Mattsson)

Publications

By DAHLBECK: books—

Dessa mina minsta [My Smallest Ones] (play), 1955.
Föräves Abisag [In Vain Abisag] (play), 1957.
Genom fönstren [Through the Windows] (poems), under pseudonym Lis Edvardson, Stockholm, 1963.
Hem till kaos [Home to Chaos] (novel), Stockholm, 1964.
Sista spegeln [The Last Mirror] (novel), Stockholm, 1965.
Dem sjunde natten [The Seventh Night] (novel), Stockholm, 1966.
Domen [The Judgment] (novel), Stockholm, 1967.
Med seende ögon [With Seeing Eyes] (novel), Stockholm, 1972.
Hjärtslagen [The Heart Beats] (novel), Stockholm, 1974.
Saknadens dal [The Valley of Want] (novel), Stockholm, 1976.
Maktspråket [The Dictatorial Language] (novel), Stockholm, 1978.
I våra tomma rum [In Our Empty Rooms] (novel), Stockholm, 1980.
Serveto och den criga elden [Serveto and the Eternal Fire] (historic documentary), Stockholm, 1988.
Vapenhandlarens död [The Death of an Arms Dealer] (novel), Stockholm, 1991.

By DAHLBECK: articles—

"Framför filmkameran [In Front of the Camera]," in *Filmboken/The Film Book*, Stockholm, 1951-57.
Interview in *Cinéma* (Paris), July/August 1958.

On DAHLBECK: articles—

Chaplin (Stockholm), December 1965.
Ecran (Paris), November 1979.

*　　*　　*

Eva Dahlbeck was a major figure in Ingmar Bergman's films of the 1950s, from *Waiting Women* to *Brink of Life*. It is significant that her only subsequent appearance for him was in his only late comedy, *Now about All These Women*. It is essentially as a comic presence—aware, ironic, sophisticated—that Dahlbeck functions in Bergman's work, and the path he chose at the end of the 1950s led to the virtual abandonment of comedy.

In *Waiting Women*, *A Lesson in Love*, and *Smiles of a Summer Night* Dahlbeck played opposite Gunnar Björnstrand, and they formed a team one might compare without absurdity to the great couples of Hollywood comedy, such as Cary Grant and Katharine Hepburn, playing to each other with extraordinarily refined precision and nuance. Their episode of the three-story *Waiting Women* takes place almost entirely in an elevator stuck between floors in which, as a couple whose marriage has become stale and routine, they work their way through a series of mutual recriminations to discover a new basis for their relationship; the entire episode is built essentially on the actors' comic gifts for facial expression, timing, and body language. All three Björnstrand-Dahlbeck films are concerned with the humiliation of the male, exposing the vulnerability and childishness behind a complacent exterior; in all three Dahlbeck represents poise and maturity, with strong overtones of motherliness. (No doubt part of the sense of frustration one experiences with the curious, unsatisfactory *Journey into Autumn* derives from the fact that, although Björnstrand and Dahlbeck are both in it, they are never together.)

Bergman's most telling use of Dahlbeck, and arguably her finest performance, is in *Brink of Life*. The film draws upon the motherliness more explicitly than before: as one of three women sharing a room in a maternity ward, Dahlbeck exudes health, self-confidence, lovingness, warmth, and pride in her imminent motherhood, to a degree that, while remaining extremely sympathetic, continually threatens to become cloying. But this is central to the film's theme: the gulf between the images of ourselves we project (and believe in) and the reality that our consciousness can never quite control and that our bodies eventually express. In labor (in the film's most harrowing sequence) her body refuses to release the baby, finally killing it. Afterwards, her earth-mother image irreparably shattered, her entire comportment has changed: the moment when she viciously slaps the hand of the young woman (Bibi Andersson) who offers her water is among the most unforgettable in Bergman's cinema.

—Robin Wood

DALIO, Marcel

Nationality: French. **Born:** Israel Moshe Blauschild in Paris, 17 July 1900. **Education:** Attended the Paris Conservatoire, 1916-18. **Family:** Married twice, second marriage to Madeleine Lebeau. **Military Service:** Served in armed forces during World War I. **Career:** 1920s— appeared in cabarets, revues, and some plays; stage name taken from character Prince Danilo in *The Merry Widow*; 1933—feature film debut in *Mon Chapeau*; 1930s—acted in both films and the theater; 1937—author, with Pierre Brasseur, of play *Grisou*, seen in Paris, and basis of film by Maurice de Canonge; 1939—at outbreak of World War II, forced to flee France; escaped to Canada and then to Hollywood; 1941—began appearing in Hollywood films; after the war returned to France; 1950s—appeared mostly in Hollywood films; 1955-56—in TV series *Casablanca*; 1960s-1970s—acted in both American and French films, eventually returning to Paris to live. **Died:** In Paris, 20 November 1983.

Films as Actor:

1932 *Les Quatres Jambes* (Marc Allégret—short)
1933 *Mon Chapeau* (Guissart)
1934 *Turandot, princesse de Chine* (Lamprecht); *Une Nuit à l'hôtel* (Mittler); *Les Affaires publiques* (Bresson)
1936 *Quand minuit sonnera* (Joannon); *L'Or* (de Poligny); *Un Grand Amour de Beethoven* (*Beethoven, le voleur de femmes*; *The Life and Loves of Beethoven*) (Gance) (as Steiner)
1937 *Cargaison blanche* (*Le Chemin de Rio*; *French White Cargo*; *Traffic in Souls*; *Woman Racket*) (Siodmak); *Naples au baiser de feu* (*The Kiss of Fire*) (Genina) (as the photographer); *Les Perles de la couronne* (*The Pearls of the Crown*) (Guitry and Christian-Jaque); *L'Homme à abattre* (Mathot); *Marthe Richard* (Bernard); *Sarati le terrible* (Hugon); *Miarka la fille à l'ours* (Choux); *Gribouille* (*Heart of Paris*) (Marc Allégret); *Troîka sur la piste blanche* (Dréville); **La Grande Illusion** (*Grand Illusion*) (Renoir) (as Rosenthal); **Pépé-le-Moko** (Duvivier) (as L'Arbi); *L'Affaire Lafarge* (Chenal)
1938 *Chéri-Bibi* (Mathot); *Mollenard* (*Capitaine Mollenard*; *Capitaine Corsaire*; *Hatred*) (Siodmak); *L'Alibi* (Chenal); *La Maison du Maltais* (*Sirocco*) (Chenal); *Les Pirates du rail* (Christian-Jaque); *Entrée des artistes* (*The Curtain Rises*) (Marc Allégret); *Conflit* (*The Affair Lafont*; *Conflict*) (Moguy); *Les Courtes Jambes* (short)
1939 **La Règle du jeu** (*Rules of the Game*) (Renoir) (as Marquis Robert de la Chesnave); *Le Bois sacré* (Mathot); *L'Esclave blanche* (*The Pasha's Wives*) (Sorkin); *La Tradition de minuit* (Richebé); *Le Corsaire* (Marc Allégret—not completed)
1940 *Tempête sur Paris* (Deschamps)
1941 *The Shanghai Gesture* (*Shanghai*) (von Sternberg) (as croupier); *Unholy Partners* (LeRoy) (as Molyneaux); *One Night in Lisbon* (Edward H. Griffith) (as concierge)
1942 **Casablanca** (Curtiz) (as Emil, the croupier); *The Pied Piper* (Pichel) (as Foquet); *Flight Lieutenant* (*Le Pilote de la morte*) (Salkow) (as Faulet); *Joan of Paris* (Stevenson)
1943 *Tonight We Raid Calais* (Brahm) (as Jacques Grandet); *The Desert Song* (*Le Chant du départ*) (Florey) (as Tarbouch); *The Song of Bernadette* (Henry King) (as Callet); *Paris after Dark* (*The Night Is Ending*) (Moguy) (as Michel); *Flesh and Fantasy* (Duvivier) (as clown); *The Constant Nymph* (Edmund Goulding) (as Georges)
1944 *Pin Up Girl* (Humberstone) (as headwaiter); *The Conspirators* (Negulesco) (as croupier); *Action in Arabia* (Moguy) (as Chakka); *To Have and Have Not* (Hawks) (as Gerard); *Passage to Marseilles* (Curtiz); *Wilson* (Henry King) (as Georges Clemenceau)
1945 *A Bell for Adano* (Henry King) (as Zito)
1946 *Petrus* (Marc Allégret); *Son Dernier Rôle* (Gourguet); *Le Bataillon du ciel* (Billon)

Marcel Dalio in *La Grande Illusion*

1947   *Temptation Harbour* (*Le Port de la tentation*) (Comfort) (as Inspector Dupre); *Les Maudits* (*The Damned*) (Clément) (as Larga); *Erreur judiciaire* (de Canonge); *Snowbound* (McDonald) (as Stefan Valdini)

1948   *Hans le Marin* (*Hans the Sailor*; *Wicked City*) (Villiers) (as Aime); *Sombre dimanche* (Loubignac); *Dédée d'Anvers* (*Dédée*; *Woman of Antwerp*) (Yves Allégret) (as Marco); *Les Amants de Vérone* (*The Lovers of Verona*) (Cayatte) (as Amadeo Maglia)

1949   *Maya* (Bernard); *Captain Blackjack* (*Black Jack*) (Duvivier) (as Capt. Nikarescu); *Portrait d'un assassin* (Rolland); *Menace de mort* (Leboursier); *Aventure à Pigalle* (Leboursier)

1950   *Porte d'Orient* (Deray)

1951   *On the Riviera* (Walter Lang) (as Philippe Lebrix); *Rich, Young, and Pretty* (Taurog) (as Claude Duval); *Nous irons à Monte Carlo* (Boyer) (as Poulos)

1952   *The Happy Time* (Fleischer) (as Grandpere Bonnard); *The Snows of Kilimanjaro* (Henry King) (as Emile); *The Merry Widow* (Bernhardt) (as police sergeant); *Lovely to Look At* (LeRoy) (as Pierre)

1953   *Gentlemen Prefer Blondes* (Hawks) (as Judge); *Flight to Tangier* (Warren) (as Gogo); *M. Scrupule, gangster* (Deray)

1954   *Sabrina* (*Sabrina Fair*) (Wilder) (as Baron); *La Patrouille des sables* (Chanas); *Lucky Me* (*Mademoiselle Porte-bonheur*) (Donohue) (as Anton)

1955   *Jump into Hell* (*L'Enfer de Dien Bien Phu*) (David Butler) (as Sgt. Taite); *Les Amants du Tage* (*Lover's Net*; *Port of Shame*; *Lovers of Lisbon*) (Verneuil) (as Porfirio); *Razzia sur la chnouff* (*Razzia*) (Decoin)

1956   *Miracle in the Rain* (*L'Immortel Amour*) (Maté) (as waiter)

1957   *The Sun Also Rises* (Henry King) (as Zizi); *Ten Thousand Bedrooms* (Thorpe) (as Vittorio Cisini); *Lafayette Escadrille* (*Hell Bent for Glory*) (Wellman) (as drillmaster); *Tip on a Dead Jockey* (*Time for Action*) (Thorpe) (as Toto del Aro); *China Gate* (Fuller) (as Father Paul)

1958   *Classe tous risques* (*The Big Risk*) (Sautet) (as Gibelin); *The Perfect Furlough* (*Strictly for Pleasure*) (Edwards) (as Henri)

1959   *Pillow Talk* (Michael Gordon) (as Pierot); *The Man Who Understood Women* (Johnson) (as Le Marne)

1960   *Le Diable et les dix commandements* (*The Devil and the Ten Commandments*) (Duvivier); *Can-Can* (Walter Lang) (as headwaiter); *Song without End* (Charles Vidor and Cukor, uncredited) (as Chelard)

1961   *Le Petit Garcon de l'ascenseur* (Granier-Deferre); *The Devil at Four O'Clock* (LeRoy) (as Gaston); *La Loi des hommes* (Gérard)

1962   *Jessica* (*La Sage-femme, le curé et le bon dieu*) (Negulesco) (as Luigi Tuffi); *A couteaux tirés* (Gérard); *Cartouche* (*Swords of Blood*) (de Broca) (as Malichot)

1963   *L'Abominable Homme des douanes* (Marc Allégret); *Donovan's Reef* (Ford) (as Father Cluzeot); *The List of Adrian Messenger* (Huston) (as Anton Karoudjian)

1964   *Wild and Wonderful* (*Monsieur Cognac*) (Anderson) (as Dr. Reynard); *Le Monocle rit Jaune* (Lautner); *Un Monsieur de compagnie* (*Male Companion*) (de Broca) (as Krieg von Spiel)

1965   *Made in Paris* (Sagal) (as Georges); *Lady L* (Ustinov) (as Sapper)

1966   *Tendre voyou* (*Tender Scoundrel*) (Jean Becker) (as Veronique's father); *Le 17e ciel* (Bernard); *How to Steal a Million* (Wyler) (as Señor Paravideo)

1967   *La 25e Heure* (*The 25th Hour*; *La Vingt-cinquième Heure*) (Verneuil) (as Strul); "Aujourd'hui" ("Paris Today") ep. of *Le Plus Vieux Métier du monde* (*The Oldest Profession*) (Autant-Lara) (as Older Man)

1968   *L'Amour c'est gai, l'amour c'est triste* (Pollet); *How Sweet It Is!* (Paris) (as Louis)

1969   *Le Blé en liasses* (Brunet); *Justine* (Cukor) (as French Consul General)

1970   *Catch-22* (Mike Nichols) (as Old Man); *The Great White Hope* (Ritt) (as French promoter)

1971   *Aussi loin que l'amour* (Rossif); *Papa les petits bateaux* (Kaplan); *Les Yeux fermés* (Santoni)

1972   *Dédé la tendresse* (van Belle)

1973   *La Punition* (Jolivet); *Les Aventures de Rabbi Jacob* (*The Mad Adventures of Rabbi Jacob*; *The Adventures of Rabbi Jacob*) (Oury) (title role); *Ursule et Grelu* (Korber)

1974   *La Bête* (*The Beast*) (Borowczyk) (as Duc du Balo); *Hommage irrespectueux comme tous les hommages* (Rochefort—short); *La Chatte sur un doigt brûlant* (Chardon)

1975   *Trop c'est trop* (Kaminka); *Le Faux cul* (Hanin); *Que la fête commence* (*Let Joy Reign Supreme*) (Tavernier)

1976   *La Communion solennelle* (Féret); *L'Aile ou la cuisse* (Zidi); *L'Ombre des châteaux* (Duval); *Madame Claude* (Jaeckin)

1977   *Une Page d'amour* (Rabinowicz); *Le Paradis des riches* (Barge)

1978   *Chausette surprise* (Davy); *L'Honorable Société* (Weinberger)

1980   *Brigade mondaine, vaudou aux Caraîbes* (Monier)

Publications

By DALIO: book—

Mes années folles, Paris, 1976.

By DALIO: article—

Interview with E. Decaux, in *Cinématographe* (Paris), April 1979.

On DALIO: articles—

Gauteur, Claude, "Flash back sur Dalio," in *Image et Son* (Paris), December 1975.

Ecran (Paris), April 1978, additions in November 1978, and January, April, and 15 December 1979.

Cinéma Français (Paris), November 1980.

Villien, Bruno, obituary in *Cinématographe* (Paris), December 1983.

Gauteur, Claude, "Dalio Marcel: métèques en tous genres," in *Avant-Scène du Cinéma* (Paris), January 1984.

Obituary in *Cinéma* (Paris), January 1984.

*   *   *

The art in playing waiters on screen lies, as in life, in giving the impression that you are doing the customer a favor. During a long Hollywood career impersonating waiters, Marcel Dalio, previously one of the most refined character performers of the prewar French cinema (a distinction confirmed by the simple use of his surname alone in the credits), conveyed with unfailing good taste the hauteur of a man who served others from a position of power.

Dalio had earned his air of casual superiority. For Renoir, first in *La Grande Illusion* as the wealthy and likable Jewish prisoner-of-war on whose largesse his companions depend for the comforts of good food and wine, then as the equally rich and cultivated host of the house party in *La Règle du jeu*, the diminutive Dalio embodied noblesse oblige. In the Renoir films and also in Duvivier's *Pépé-le-Moko*, he trod with wit, taste, and delicacy the narrow line between character and caricature. His nobleman in *La Règle du jeu* is his masterpiece. A childlike delight in his collection of music machines does not make his pain at the infidelity of his wife or the party's dislocation by her tormented lover any less poignant.

Despite this success in a leading role, Dalio was destined to remain mainly a character actor. World War II broke out shortly after the completion of *La Règle du jeu*, and Dalio's face was used by Nazi propagandists on posters displayed in Paris captioned "the typical Jew." Forced to flee the country, Dalio eventually arrived in Hollywood, which at first could find nothing for him to do. Dorothy Parker is said to have connived at his salvation by pointing him out at a party as "the great French actor Dalio." Unfortunately, the parts that came his way were those of waiters and domestics, leavened with the occasional curé or military officer, the sort of roles handed out to most accented émigrés.

With better material he was commensurately more memorable. As the croupier in *Casablanca*, handing his winnings to a Claude Rains who has just closed down Rick's Cafe Américain because gambling is taking place there, he made a good enough impression to play the Rains role in a later television series. His one scene in *Sabrina*, as the baron returning to cooking school to take a refresher course in soufflés, is a delight. In general, however, his Hollywood career is a monument to the unimaginativeness of casting directors.

—John Baxter

DARNELL, Linda

Nationality: American. **Born:** Monetta Eloyse Darnell in Dallas, Texas, 16 October 1923. **Family:** Married 1) the cameraman Peverell J. Marley, 1943 (divorced 1951), adopted daughter: Charlotte Mildred; 2) Philip Liebman, 1954 (divorced 1955); 3) Merle Roy Robertson, 1957 (divorced 1963). **Career:** Dancer as a child; then worked as model; talent competitions from age 11; at age 16, won "Gateway to Hollywood" competition; 1939-51—under contract with 20th Century-Fox: film debut in *Hotel for Women*; 1940—first of several films with Tyrone Power, *Star Dust*; worked in television from the mid-1950s; 1956—on Broadway in *Harbor Lights*; 1964-65—toured with the play *Janus*. **Died:** Of burns in house fire, 10 April 1965.

Films as Actress:

1939   *Hotel for Women* (Ratoff); *Day-Time Wife* (Ratoff)

1940   *Star Dust* (Walter Lang); *Brigham Young—Frontiersman* (Hathaway); *The Mark of Zorro* (Mamoulian); *Chad Hanna* (King)

1941   *Blood and Sand* (Mamoulian); *Rise and Shine* (Dwan)

Linda Darnell

1942 *The Loves of Edgar Allan Poe* (Lachman) (as Virginia Clemm)
1943 *City without Men* (Salkow); *The Song of Bernadette* (King) (as face of the virgin); *It Happened Tomorrow* (Clair)
1944 *Buffalo Bill* (Wellman); *Summer Storm* (Sirk); *Hangover Square* (Brahm); *The Great John L. (A Man Called Sullivan)* (Tuttle); *Sweet and Lowdown* (Mayo); *Fallen Angel* (Preminger)
1945 *All-Star Bond Rally* (short)
1946 *Anna and the King of Siam* (Cromwell) (as Tuptim); *Centennial Summer* (Preminger); **My Darling Clementine** (Ford) (as Chihuahua)
1947 *Forever Amber* (Preminger) (as Amber)
1948 *The Walls of Jericho* (Stahl); *Unfaithfully Yours* (Preston Sturges)
1949 *A Letter to Three Wives* (Mankiewicz); *Slattery's Hurricane* (de Toth); *Everybody Does It* (Goulding)
1950 *No Way Out* (Mankiewicz); *Two Flags West* (Wise)
1951 *The Thirteenth Letter* (Preminger); *The Guy Who Came Back* (Newman); *The Lady Pays Off* (Sirk)
1952 *Island of Desire (Saturday Island)* (Heisler); *Night without Sleep* (Baker); *Blackbeard the Pirate* (Walsh)
1953 *Second Chance* (Maté); *Donne proibite (Angels of Darkness; Forbidden Women)* (Amato)
1954 *This Is My Love* (Heisler)
1955 *Gli ultimi cinque minuti (The Last Five Minutes)* (Amato)
1956 *Dakota Incident* (Foster)
1957 *Zero Hour!* (Bartlett)
1964 *Black Spurs* (Springsteen)

Publications

On DARNELL: book—

Davis, Ronald L., *Hollywood Beauty: Linda Darnell and the American Dream*, Norman, Oklahoma, 1991.

On DARNELL: articles—

Obituary, in *New York Times*, 11 April 1965.
Obituary, in *Times* (London), 12 April 1965.
Roman, Robert C., in *Films in Review* (New York), October 1966.

*   *   *

Acting brilliance has rarely been prerequisite to movie stardom; exotic-looking all-American Linda Darnell is an example of studio-groomed competence transformed by luscious good looks and a personality charged by restless energy. While most Hollywood sex symbols grow more mythic in our own glamour-deficient contemporary cinema, only a handful merit reevaluation as actresses. Some like Darnell were so awesomely lovely that their beauty, while perpetuating stardom, may have blinded the studios to their range. The tart delivery and bemusement about men Linda brought to late-career hits such as *Everybody Does It* seem astonishing only if one undervalues her dewy-eyed starlet period when breathtaking beauty swept all else before it.

Still in her teens, she left Texas in the late 1930s and won a contract at Twentieth Century-Fox, where she co-starred immediately with such established actors as Tyrone Power and Henry Fonda. Although cast as the Blessed Mother herself (*Song of Bernadette*), Darnell did not register as a star in the spirited pure heroine roles of *Mark of Zorro* or *Blood and Sand*, but as a smart cookie well aware of the teasing value of décolletage. From the mid-1940s and into the next decade, she played looser and far more interesting characters—tramps,

wise girls, prima donnas—with trademark flounce. Sadly betrayed by the seventeenth-century claptrap of the bodice ripper *Forever Amber*, Darnell did not soar to the Lana Turner-Rita Hayworth pantheon, but she was a savvier actress than either.

Ultimately, it is the Mankiewicz classics (*A Letter to Three Wives*, *No Way Out*) and Sturges's icy black comedy (*Unfaithfully Yours*) for which she will be remembered: rare occasions when her extraordinarily sumptuous exterior meshed with her worldly-wise, who're-you-kiddin' interior. After Fox dropped her contract, her striking stage work on tour in *Janus* and *Tea and Sympathy* might have heralded a comeback as the character actress who was always hiding underneath her Love Goddess camouflage.

Her death—resulting from a house fire—earns her an ironic footnote. Earlier that evening she had been poking fun at *Star Dust*, one of her old movies on television.

A more durable image of Darnell would be *A Letter to Three Wives*' cynical gold digger Lorna Mae, trading quips with her older husband whom she mistakenly believes moved her from the wrong side of the tracks strictly for her beauty. A similar dissatisfaction—the nagging suspicion that men embraced her sleek packaging without appreciating her fiery spirit—fueled Darnell's finest performances.

—Richard Sater, updated by Robert Pardi

DARRIEUX, Danielle

Nationality: French. **Born:** Bordeaux, 1 May 1917. **Education:** Studied the cello at the Paris Conservatory. **Family:** Married 1) the director Henri Decoin, 1934 (divorced 1940); 2) Porfirio Rubirosa, 1942 (divorced 1947); 3) the author Georges Mitsinkides, 1948. **Career:** 1931—film acting debut in *Le Bal*; 1936—international recognition for role in *Mayerling*; 1937—stage debut in Paris; 1950s-1975—made films in a number of countries; 1960s—began making concert appearances and recordings; 1970—replaced Katharine Hepburn in Broadway musical *Coco*; 1971—on London stage in *The Ambassadors*. **Awards:** Chevalier de la legion d'honneur, 1962; Officier de la legion d'honneur, 1977. **Address:** 1 rue Alfred de Vingnu, 75008 Paris, France.

Films as Actress:

1931 *Le Bal* (Thiele)
1932 *Coquecigrole* (Berthomieu); *Panurge* (Bernheim); *Le Coffret de laque* (Kemm)
1933 *Château de rêve* (Bolvary and Clouzot)
1934 *Mauvaise graine (Bad Blood)* (Wilder and Esway) (as Jeanette); *Volga en flammes* (Tourjansky); *La Crise est finie* (Siodmak); *Dédée* (Guissart); *L'Or dans la rue* (Bernhardt); *Mon Coeur t'appelle* (Gallone and Veber)
1935 *Le Contrôleur des wagon-lits* (Eichberg); *Quelle drôle de gosse!* (Joannon); *J'aime toutes les femmes* (Lamac); *Le Domino vert* (Decoin and Selpin); *Mademoiselle Mozart* (Noé)
1936 *Mayerling* (Litvak) (as Marie Vetsera); *Tarass Boulba* (Granowski) (as Marina); *Port-Arthur* (Farkas); *Club de femmes* (Deval); *Un Mauvais Garçon* (Boyer)
1937 *Mademoiselle ma mère* (Decoin); *Abus de confiance (Abused Confidence)* (Decoin) (as Lydia)
1938 *Katia* (Maurice Tourneur); *Retour à l'aube* (Decoin); *The Rage of Paris* (Koster) (as Nicole de Cortillon); *Avocate D'amour (Counsel for Romance)* (Ploquin) (as Jacqueline Serval)

1939   *Battements de coeur* (Decoin)

1941   *Premier rendez-vous* (*Her First Affair*) (Decoin) (as Micheline Chevassu); *Caprices* (Joannon)

1942   *La Fausse Maîtresse* (Cayatte)

1945   *Adieu Chérie* (Bernard)

1946   *Au petit bonheur* (L'Herbier)

1947   *Bethsabée* (Moguy); *Ruy Blas* (Billon) (as Queen)

1948   *Jean de la lune* (Achard)

1949   *Occupe-toi d'Amélie* (Autant-Lara) (as Amélie d'Avranches)

1950   **La Ronde** (*Circle of Love*) (Max Ophüls) (as Emma Breitkopf); *Romanzo d'amore* (Toselli) (Coletti)

1951   *Rich, Young, and Pretty* (Taurog) (as Marie Deverone); *La Maison Bonnadieu* (Rim); "La Maison Tellier" ("The House of Madame Tellier") ep. of *Le Plaisir* (*House of Pleasure*) (Max Ophüls) (as Rosa); *La Vérité sur Bébé Donge* (Decoin)

1952   *Five Fingers* (*Operation Cicero*) (Joseph L. Mankiewicz) (as Anna); *Adorables créatures* (*Adorable Creatures*) (Christian-Jaque) (as Christians)

1953   *Le Bon Dieu sans confession* (Autant-Lara); **Madame de . . .** (*The Earrings of Madame De . . .*; *The Diamond Earrings*) (Max Ophüls) (as Countess Louise de); *Châteaux en Espagne* (Wheeler)

1954   *Escalier de service* (Rim); *Napoléon* (Guitry) (as Eleonore Denuelle); *Bonnes à tuer* (Decoin); *Le Rouge et le noir* (*The Red and the Black*) (Autant-Lara) (as Mme. Louise de Rênal)

1955   *L'Affaire des poisons?* (*One Step to Eternity*) (Decoin) (as Mme. de Montespan); *L'Amant de Lady Chatterley* (*Lady Chatterley's Lover*) (Marc Allégret) (as Constance Chatterley)

1956   *Si Paris nous était conté* (*If Paris Were Told to Us*) (Guitry) (as Agnes Sorel); *Alexander the Great* (Rossen) (as Olympias); *Typhon sur Nagasaki* (*Typhoon over Nagasaki*) (Ciampi); *Le Salaire du péché* (de la Patellière)

1957   *Pot-Bouille* (*The House of Lovers*) (Duvivier)

1958   *Le Septième Ciel* (Bernard); *Le Désordre et la nuit* (*Night Affair*) (Grangier) (as Therese Marken); *La Vie à deux* (*Life as a Couple*) (Duhour); *Un Drôle de dimanche* (Marc Allègret) (as Catherine)

1959   *Marie-Octobre* (Duvivier); *Les Yeux de l'amour* (de la Patellière)

1960   *Meurtre en 45 tours* (*Death at 45 RPM*; *Murder at 45 RPM*) (Périer) (as Eve Faugeres); *L'Homme à femmes* (Cornu)

1961   *The Greengage Summer* (*Loss of Innocence*) (Lewis Gilbert) (as Mme. Zisi); *Les Lions sont lâchés* (Verneuil); *Les Bras de la nuit* (Guymont); *Vive Henri IV, Vive l'Amour* (Autant-Lara)

1962   "L'Homme de l'avenue" ("The Man on the Avenue") ep. of *Le Crime ne paie pas* (*Crime Does Not Pay*; *The Gentle Art of Murder*) (Oury); "L'Inceste" ep. of *Le Diable et les dix commandements* (*The Devil and the Ten Commandments*) (Duvivier) (as Clarisse Ardant); *Pourqoui Paris?* (de la Patellière)

1963   *Landru* (*Bluebeard*) (Chabrol) (as Berthe Heon); *Du grabuge chez les veuves* (Poitrenaud); *Méfiez-vous, mesdames!* (Hunebelle)

1964   *Patate* (*Friend of the Family*) (Thomas) (as Edith Rollo)

1965   *Le Coup de grâce* (Cayrol and Durand); *L'Or du Duc* (Baratier); *Le Dimanche de la vie* (Herman)

1967   *Les Demoiselles de Rochefort* (*The Young Girls of Rochefort*) (Demy) (as Yvonne); *L'Homme à la Buick* (Grangier)

1968   *Les Oiseaux vont mourir au Pérou* (*Birds Come to Die in Peru*; *Birds Do It*) (Gary) (as Fernande); *Vingt-quatre heures de la vie d'une femme* (*24 Hours in a Woman's Life*) (Delouche) (as Alice)

1969   *La Maison de campagne* (Girault)

1972   *No encontre rosas para mi madre* (*Roses rouges et piments verts*) (Beleta)

1975   *Divine* (Delouche)

1976   *L'Année sainte* (Girault) (as Christina)

1978   *Le Cavaleur* (*Practice Makes Perfect*; *The Skirt Chaser*) (de Broca) (as Suzanne Taylor)

1980   *Mort en sautoir* (Goutas)

1982   *Une Chambre en ville* (*A Room in Town*) (Demy) (as Baroness de Neuville)

1983   *En Haut des marches* (Vecchichi) (as Françoise Canavaggia); *Dame aux milles et une vies* (Gautas)

1984   *L'Age vermeil* (Kahane—for TV); *Marie, Marie* (Chatel—for TV)

1986   *Le Lieu du crime* (*The Scene of the Crime*) (Téchiné) (as Grandmother); *Corps et biens* (Jacquot) (as Mme. Krantz)

1987   *Lawyers* (de la Patellière); *Quelques jours avec moi* (*A Few Days with Me*) (Sautet) (as Mme. Pasquier)

1988   *La Tête dans la nuages* (Vecchiali)

1989   *Bille en tête* (*Headstrong*) (Cotti) (as L'Arquebuse)

1991   *Le Jour des Rois* (as Armande)

1996   *Les Mille et une recettes du cuisinier a moureux* (Djorddjadze)

Publications

By DARRIEUX: articles—

Interview in *Ciné Revue* (Paris), 5 February 1981.
Interview with N. Angel, in *Cinématographe* (Paris), October 1983.

On DARRIEUX: articles—

Billard, G., "But Darrieux Seeks New Horizons," in *Films and Filming* (London), October 1955.
Whitehall, Richard, "Danielle Darrieux," in *Films and Filming* (London), December 1961.
Ecran (Paris), April 1978.
Ciné Revue (Paris), 24 September 1981.
Cinéma (Paris), January 1983.
Chirat, R., "Le temps de Danielle," in *L'Avant-Scene Cinema* (Paris), February 1991.
Stars (Mariembourg, Belgium), Spring 1993.

*   *   *

In a career extending over seven decades and more than 100 films Danielle Darrieux has deployed her considerable talents in an impressive diversity of roles. Though most readily associated with sophisticated comedy or romantic drama, she has also brought depth to melodrama and graced musicals with her fine voice.

After her debut at the age of 14 in *Le Bal* as a willful adolescent, she was frequently cast during the 1930s as the fractious, wayward teenager who eventually succeeds despite misfortune or social handicap. Her burgeoning vocal talents were heard in musicals such as *La Crise est finie*, and her innate vitality and sense of timing enlivened lighthearted comedies such as *Un Mauvais Garçon*, while a controlled passivity in her playing conveyed a tragic quality to period melodramas such as *Port-Arthur*. International acclaim came with *Mayerling* in which, as the beautiful and tragic Marie Vetsera, she achieved a deeply moving and seemingly intuitive characterization.

Stardom brought her contracts with many filmmakers in several countries, but Darrieux's major performances are associated with three directors in particular: Henri Decoin, Claude Autant-Lara, and Max Ophüls. During the 1930s Decoin, then her husband, developed her talents in a variety of films that reflected the different styles of the period. Following her tragic debut in *Le Domino vert* as the heroine

Danielle Darrieux in *Madame de ...*

under emotional and financial stress, she appeared in *Mademoiselle ma mère*, a film of dark poetic realism, in which as a headstrong daughter rejecting parental advice she marries a middle-aged man and then has an affair with his son. The mood is brighter in *Abus de confiance* where she portrays an orphan who cheerfully dupes her benefactor. In *Battements de coeur* she confirmed her range by playing an unruly delinquent who is transformed into a sophisticated woman of the world.

Her performances for Decoin, impressive in their variety alone, were never less than convincing, but it was with Autant-Lara in the late 1940s and early 1950s that Darrieux distinguished her film career as a brilliant romantic actress. In *Occupe-toi d'Amélie*, an unashamedly theatrical Feydeau farce, she played with sparkling vivacity and considerable elegance the beautifully enticing but outrageously self-centered Amélie d'Avranches who delights in teasing her many suitors. In complete contrast was her later role as Madame de Rênal in *Le Rouge et le noir*. Now as a bored provincial falling selflessly in love with a proud and insecure young man, she gave a performance of great tenderness, maturity, and restraint, conveying with tremulous delicacy the powerful but guilty emotion she feels. In films directed by Max Ophüls her interpretation of romantic roles was further extended. In *La Ronde* her performance as the understanding married woman in bed with her lover beset by temporary impotence is exquisitely subtle in tone and timing. As Rosa, the prostitute of *Le Plaisir*, she again excelled in a more robust and wickedly ironic part, but perhaps her finest acting came in *Madame de . . .* , in which, as the elegant aristocrat, she suffers deeply and is ultimately destroyed when a casual affair develops into an impossible passion. To this tragic role she lent a fragile dignity and a sense of resignation which crystallized in unsurpassed romantic acting.

Films made outside France also mark Darrieux's career, notably those produced in America. Before the war she appeared in a Hollywood star vehicle, *The Rage of Paris*, as a vulnerable French girl alone in New York seeking a husband. In the 1950s she returned to play and sing as Marie Deverone, a French cabaret artist, in the MGM musical *Rich, Young, and Pretty*. She appeared as a double-crossing countess in *Five Fingers*, and in the epic *Alexander the Great* was a commendable Olympias. During the late 1950s and 1960s her range did not diminish: she played comic parts opposite Bourvil in *Un Drôle de dimanche* and Fernandel in *L'Homme à la Buick*, tragic parts in Resistance dramas such as *Marie-Octobre* and *Le Coup de grâce*, now a poised elegant widow in *Pot-Bouille*, now a hard lesbian madame in *Les Oiseaux vont mourir au Pérou*, and in a delightful though nostalgic role she was the slightly eccentric mother of *Les Demoiselles de Rochefort*.

During the late 1970s Darrieux increasingly turned her attention to television work and the theater. The 1980s, however, brought a welcome return to the screen with memorable parts that confirmed the undiminished breadth and depth of her talents. In Vecchiali's *En Haut des marches*, a demanding emotional range was required as Françoise Canavaggia, a French woman intent on revenging her husband's wartime death at the hands of collaborators; in *Corps et biens* she was the alcoholic Mme. Krantz doggedly investigating her friend's death; in Demy's musical comedy *Une Chambre en ville* she excelled as the lonely alcoholic industrialist Baronness de Neuville, determined to break a strike.

—R. F. Cousins

DAVIES, Marion

Nationality: American. **Born:** Marion Cecilia Douras in Brooklyn, New York, 3 January 1897. **Education:** Convent of the Sacred Heart.

Hastings, N.Y., 1910-16; Theodore Kosloff's Ballet School, Manhattan; Wayburn School; Sargent School; Empire School of Acting. **Family:** Married Horace Brown, 1951. **Career:** 1913—began appearing in revues and musicals as dancer; 1914—received billing as "Marion Davis" in Jerome Kern musical *Nobody Home*; 1916—featured role in the *Ziegfeld Follies of 1916*; 1917—film debut; contract with William Randolph Hearst; 1918—began starring in films of Hearst-owned Cosmopolitan Pictures; Hearst papers began intensive promotion of Davies films; 1920—last stage appearance; 1922—first film hit, *When Knighthood Was in Flower*; 1924—Cosmopolitan joined Metro-Goldwyn merger; 1929—first sound picture, *The Broadway Melody*; 1929-33—president of Motion Picture Relief Fund; 1934—Cosmopolitan severed connection with MGM in favor of Warners; 1937—retired from film; 1951—Hearst died. **Died:** Of cancer, 23 September 1961.

Films as Actress:

1917   *Runaway Romany* (Lederer) (as Romany, + sc); *Cecilia of the Pink Roses* (Steger and King) (as Cecilia); *The Burden of Proof* (Steger) (as Elaine Brooks)

1919   *The Belle of New York* (Steger) (as Violet Gray); *Getting Mary Married* (Dwan) (as Mary); *The Dark Star* (Dwan) (as Rue Carew); *The Cinema Murder* (Baker) (as Elizabeth Dalston)

1920   *April Folly* (Leonard) (as April Poole); *The Restless Sex* (Leonard and D'Usseau) (as Stephanie Cleland)

1921   *Buried Treasure* (Baker); *Enchantment* (Vignola)

1922   *Beauty's Worth* (Vignola) (as Prudence Cole); *When Knighthood Was in Flower* (Vignola) (as Mary Tudor); *The Bride's Play* (Terwilliger); *The Young Diana* (Capellani and Vignola); *Adam and Eva* (Vignola)

1923   *Little Old New York* (Olcott) (as Patricia O'Day)

1924   *Yolanda* (Vignola) (as Princess Mary of Burgundy/Yolanda); *Janice Meredith* (*The Beautiful Rebel*) (Hopper) (title role)

1925   *Lights of Old Broadway* (*Merry Wives of Gotham*) (Bell) (as Fely/Anne); *Zander the Great* (Hill) (as Mamie Smith)

1926   *Beverly of Graustark* (Franklin) (as Beverly Calhoun)

1927   *The Red Mill* (Goodrich, i.e. Roscoe Arbuckle) (as Tina); *Tillie the Toiler* (Henley) (as Tillie Jones); *The Fair Co-ed* (*The Varsity Girl*) (Wood) (as Marion); *Quality Street* (Franklin) (as Phoebe Throssel)

1928   *The Patsy* (*The Politic Flapper*) (Vidor) (as Patricia Harrington); *Her Cardboard Lover* (Leonard) (as Sally); *Show People* (Vidor) (as Peggy Pepper)

1929   *The Hollywood Revue of 1929* (Reisner); *Marianne* (Leonard) (title role); *The Five O'Clock Girl* (Green—unreleased)

1930   *Not So Dumb* (*Dulcy*) (Vidor) (as Dulcy); *The Floradora Girl* (*The Gay Nineties*) (Beaumont) (as Daisy)

1931   *The Bachelor Father* (Leonard) (as Tony); *It's a Wise Child* (Leonard) (as Joyce); *Five and Ten* (*Daughter of Luxury*) (Leonard) (as Jennifer Rarick); *The Christmas Party* (*Jackie Cooper's Christmas*) (Reisner—short) (as guest)

1932   *Polly of the Circus* (Santell) (as Polly); *Blondie of the Follies* (Goulding) (as Blondie McClune)

1933   *Peg o' My Heart* (Leonard) (as Peg); *Going Hollywood* (Walsh) (as Sylvia Bruce)

1934   *Operator Thirteen* (*Spy Thirteen*) (Boleslawsky) (as Gale Loveless)

1935   *Page Miss Glory* (LeRoy) (as Loretta)

1936   *Hearts Divided* (Borzage) (as Betsy Patterson); *Cain and Mabel* (Bacon) (as Mabel O'Dare); *Pirate Party on Catalina Isle* (Lewyn—short)

1937   *Ever since Eve* (Bacon) (as Marge Winton)

Marion Davies

Publications

By DAVIES: book—

The Times We Had: Life with William Randolph Hearst, edited by Pamela Pfau and Kenneth Marx, Indianapolis, 1975.

By DAVIES: article—

"How I Keep in Condition," in *Photoplay* (New York), January 1922.

On DAVIES: books—

Swanberg, W. A., *Citizen Hearst*, New York, 1969.
Guiles, Fred, *Marion Davies: A Biography*, New York, 1972.
Wallis, Hal, and Charles Higham, *Starmaker*, New York, 1980.
Chaney, Lindsay, and Michael Cieply, *The Hearsts: Family and Empire—The Later Years*, New York, 1981.

On DAVIES: articles—

Montayne, Lilian, "Marion of the Golden Hair," in *Motion Picture Classic* (Brooklyn), September 1919.
Evans, Delight, "Galatea on Riverside Drive," in *Photoplay* (New York), October 1919.
St. Johns, Adela Rogers, "An Impression of Marion Davies," in *Photoplay* (New York), January 1925.
York, Cal, "The Girl on the Cover," in *Photoplay* (New York), September 1926.
Gaines, William, "Davies' Secret of Success," in *Photoplay* (New York), February 1935.
Milne, Tom, "Marion Davies," in *Sight and Sound* (London), Autumn 1968.
Kendall, P., "Marion Davies," in *Silent Picture* (London), Summer 1970.
Anderson, E., "Marion Davies," in *Films in Review* (New York), June-July 1972.
Classic Images (Indiana, Pennsylvania), November and December 1982.

* * *

Citizen Kane may have been wickedly accurate in its lampooning of newspaper tycoon William Randolph Hearst, but Dorothy Comingore's portrayal of Susan Alexander Kane has tended to cast an unfortunate pall on posterity's view of Marion Davies, Hearst's mistress. Film scholarship is rife with those who—without benefit of actually having seen any of Davies's films—are content to dismiss her as a vapid, talent-free beauty who lucked into an association with the biggest Stage-Door Johnny of them all.

In fact, Davies has been unfairly maligned. She was a delightful talent with a fine comedic sense, a flair for mimicry, and a natural, agreeable personality. Her liaison with Hearst may have paid the rent at San Simeon (where she reigned as the ultimate Hollywood hostess) but his overbearing attentions effectively stifled the development of her true gifts. Hearst's relentless publicity machine made Davies a star but it lost her the respect of the industry and the patience of the public who felt that a truly talented performer would have no need of such a constant media blitz.

If not for the Hearst connection, Davies would almost certainly be regarded more highly now. Few of her films were very bad and there are a surprising number of real gems in her filmography. She shines in comedies such as King Vidor's *The Patsy* and *Show People* (of the former, Vidor wrote that it "even got some good reviews outside of the Hearst Press"). But Hearst's ideas of her capabilities seldom matched with reality; he saw her as another Lillian Gish: noble, delicate, vir-

ginal. Costume spectacles such as *Janice Meredith* and *When Knighthood Was in Flower* feature the Davies that Hearst sought to showcase: prim, doll-like, a little dull. Unpretentious comedies such as *Tillie the Toiler*, *Her Cardboard Lover*, and *Not So Dumb* display the bounce and wit that were among Davies's most obvious attractions.

Her career started to wind down by the time sound pictures came along, but she managed to put her best foot forward in *Blondie of the Follies*, *Going Hollywood*, and *Page Miss Glory*. After the dopey and plodding *Ever since Eve*, Davies retired from the screen. Her professional reputation has since fallen into neglect. Her career is due for reexamination, though; it remains a classic case of too-often misdirected talent. Hearst was an empire builder. He wanted Marion Davies to be a magnificent cathedral when all she was was a simple country church.

—Frank Thompson

DAVIS, Bette

Nationality: American. **Born:** Ruth Elizabeth Davis in Lowell, Massachusetts, 5 April 1908. **Education:** Attended Cushing Academy, Ashburnham, Massachusetts; Mariarden School of Dancing; studied acting at Robert Milton-John Murray Anderson School of the Theatre, New York. **Family:** Married 1) Harmon Nelson, 1932 (divorced 1938); 2) Arthur Farnsworth, 1941 (divorced 1943); 3) William Grant Sherry, 1945 (divorced), daughter: Barbara Davis Sherry; 4) the actor Gary Merrill, 1950 (divorced 1960). **Career:** 1928—professional stage debut in George Cukor's stock production of *Broadway* in Rochester, New York; 1929—acted with Blanche Yurka Company in stock productions; Broadway debut in *The Lady from the Sea*; 1930—contract with Universal; 1931—film debut in *Bad Sister*; 1932—after series of unsuccessful films, dropped by Universal; long-term contract with Warners; 1934—critical acclaim for role in *Of Human Bondage*; 1936—refused to appear in poor quality films and suspended without pay from Warners; attempt to act in Alexander Korda film thwarted by Warners; sued Warners over situation but lost long court battle; 1941—president of The Academy of Motion Pictures Arts and Sciences; co-founder and president of Hollywood Canteen; 1946—formed production company B.D., Inc.; 1949—terminated contract with Warners with Jack Warner's approval after series of unsuccessful films; 1952—returned to stage in musical revue *Two's Company*; 1956—television debut; early 1960s—change in direction of career occurs after appearances in low-budget horror films; 1978—in TV miniseries *The Dark Secret of Harvest Home*, and, briefly, in the TV series *Hotel*, 1983. **Awards:** Best Actress Academy Award, for *Dangerous*, 1935; Best Actress, Venice Festival, for *Marked Woman* and *Kid Galahad*, 1937; Best Actress Academy Award, for *Jezebel*, 1938; Best Actress, New York Film Critics, and Best Actress, Cannes Festival, for *All about Eve*, 1951; Life Achievement Award, American Film Institute, 1977. **Died:** In Neuilly sur Seine, France, 6 October 1989.

Films as Actress:

1931   *Bad Sister* (Henley) (as Laura Madison); *Seed* (Stahl) (as Margaret Carter); *Waterloo Bridge* (Whale) (as Janet)
1932   *Way Back Home* (*Old Greatheart*) (Seiter) (as Mary Lucy); *The Menace* (Neill) (as Peggy); *Hell's House* (Higgin) (as Peggy Gardner); *The Man Who Played God* (Adolfi) (as Grace Blair); *So Big* (Wellman) (as Dallas O'Mara); *The Rich Are Always with Us* (Alfred E. Green) (as Malbro); *The Dark Horse* (Alfred E. Green) (as Kay Russell); *The Cabin in

the Cotton (Curtiz) (as Madge Norwood); *Three on a Match* (LeRoy) (as Ruth Westcott)

1933 *20,000 Years in Sing Sing* (Curtiz) (as Fay); *Parachute Jumper* (Alfred E. Green) (as Alabama); *The Working Man* (Adolfi) (as Jenny Hartland); *Ex-Lady* (Florey) (as Helen Bauer); *Bureau of Missing Persons* (Del Ruth) (as Norma Phillips)

1934 *Fashions of 1934* (Dieterle) (as Lynn Mason); *The Big Shakedown* (Dillon) (as Norma Frank); *Jimmy the Gent* (Curtiz) (as Joan Martin); *Fog over Frisco* (Dieterle) (as Arlene Bradford); *Of Human Bondage* (Cromwell) (as Mildred Rogers); *Housewife* (Alfred E. Green) (as Patricia Barclay/Ruth Smith)

1935 *Bordertown* (Mayo) (as Marie Roark); *The Girl from Tenth Avenue* (Alfred E. Green) (as Miriam Brady); *Front Page Woman* (Curtiz) (as Ellen Garfield); *Special Agent* (Keighley) (as Julie Carston)

1936 *Dangerous* (Alfred E. Green) (as Joyce Heath); *The Petrified Forest* (Mayo) (as Gabrielle Maple); *The Golden Arrow* (Alfred E. Green) (as Daisy Appleby); *Satan Met a Lady* (Dieterle) (as Valerie Purvis)

1937 *Marked Woman* (Lloyd Bacon) (as Mary Dwight/Strauber); *Kid Galahad* (Curtiz) (as Louise "Fluff" Phillips); *That Certain Woman* (Goulding) (as Mary Donnell); *It's Love I'm After* (Mayo) (as Joyce Arden)

1938 *Jezebel* (Wyler) (as Julie Marsden); *The Sisters* (Litvak) (as Louise Elliot)

1939 *Dark Victory* (Goulding) (as Judith Traherne); *Juarez* (Dieterle) (as Empress Carlotta von Habsburg); *The Old Maid* (Goulding) (as Charlotte Lovell); *The Private Lives of Elizabeth and Essex* (Curtiz) (as Queen Elizabeth)

1940 *All This and Heaven Too* (Litvak) (as Henriette Deluzy Desportes); *The Letter* (Wyler) (as Leslie Crosbie)

1941 *The Great Lie* (Goulding) (as Maggie Patterson); *The Bride Came C.O.D.* (Keighley) (as Joan Winfield); *Shining Victory* (Rapper) (as nurse); **The Little Foxes** (Wyler) (as Regina Hubbard Giddens)

1942 *In This Our Life* (Huston) (as Stanley Timberlake); **Now, Voyager** (Rapper) (as Charlotte Vale); *The Man Who Came to Dinner* (Keighley) (as Maggie Cutler)

1943 *Watch on the Rhine* (Shumlin) (as Sara Muller); *Thank Your Lucky Stars* (David Butler) (as herself); *Old Acquaintance* (Vincent Sherman) (as Kitty Marlowe); *Stars on Horseback* (Swartz—doc, short); *A Present with a Future* (Swartz—short)

1944 *Mr. Skeffington* (Vincent Sherman) (as Fanny Tellis Skeffington); *Hollywood Canteen* (Daves) (as herself)

1945 *The Corn Is Green* (Rapper) (as Miss Lilly Moffat); *Second Victory Loan Campaign Fund* (Vincent Sherman—short)

1946 *A Stolen Life* (Bernhardt) (as Kate Bosworth/Pat Bosworth, + pr); *Deception* (Rapper) (as Christine Radcliffe)

1948 *Winter Meeting* (Windust) (as Susan Grieve); *June Bride* (Windust) (as Linda Gilman)

1949 *Beyond the Forest* (King Vidor) (as Rosa Moline)

1950 **All about Eve** (Mankiewicz) (as Margo Channing)

1951 *Payment on Demand* (Bernhardt) (as Joyce Ramsey)

1952 *Another Man's Poison* (Rapper) (as Janet Frobisher); *Phone Call from a Stranger* (Negulesco) (as Marie Hoke); *The Star* (Heisler) (as Margaret Elliot)

1955 *The Virgin Queen* (Koster) (as Queen Elizabeth)

1956 *Storm Center* (Taradash) (as Alicia Hull); *The Catered Affair* (*Wedding Breakfast*) (Richard Brooks) (as Aggie Conlon Hurley)

1959 *John Paul Jones* (Farrow) (as Catherine the Great); *The Scapegoat* (Hamer) (as the Countess)

1961 *Pocketful of Miracles* (Capra) (as Apple Annie)

1962 *Whatever Happened to Baby Jane?* (Aldrich) (as Jane Hudson)

1964 *Dead Ringer* (Henreid) (as Margaret de Lorca/Edith Philips); *La noia* (*The Empty Canvas*) (Damiani) (as Dino's mother); *Where Love Has Gone* (Dmytryk) (as Mrs. Gerald Hayden); *Hush . . . Hush, Sweet Charlotte* (Aldrich) (as Charlotte Hollis)

1965 *The Nanny* (Holt) (title role)

1968 *The Anniversary* (Baker) (as Mrs. Taggart)

1971 *Connecting Rooms* (Gollings) (as Wanda Fleming)

1972 *Bunny O'Hare* (Oswald) (title role); *Madame Sin* (David Greene—for TV) (title role); *Lo scopone scientifico* (*The Scientific Cardplayer*) (Comencini) (as Millionairess); *The Judge and Jake Wyler* (Rich—for TV) (as Judge Meredith)

1973 *Scream, Pretty Peggy* (Hessler—for TV) (as Mrs. Elliott)

1976 *Burnt Offerings* (Curtis) (as Aunt Elizabeth); *The Disappearance of Aimee* (Harvey—for TV) (as Aimee's mother)

1978 *Return from Witch Mountain* (Hough) (as Letha); *The Children of Sanchez* (Bartlett); *Death on the Nile* (Guillermin) (as Mrs. Van Schuyler); *Dark Secret of Harvest Home* (Leo Penn—for TV) (as Widow Fortune)

1979 *Strangers* (Katselas—for TV)

1980 *The Watcher in the Woods* (Hough) (as Mrs. Aylwood); *White Mama* (Cooper—for TV) (as Adele Malone)

1981 *Skyward* (Ron Howard—for TV); *Family Reunion* (Cook—for TV) (as Elizabeth Winfield)

1982 *A Piano for Mrs. Cimino* (Schaefer—for TV) (as Esther Cimino); *Little Gloria . . . Happy at Last* (Hussein—for TV) (as Alice Vanderbilt)

1983 *Right of Way* (Schaefer—for TV)

1985 *Murder with Mirrors* (Lowry—for TV) (as Carrie Louise Serrocold)

1986 *As Summers Die* (Tramont—for TV) (as Hannah Loftin); *Directed by William Wyler* (Slesin—doc) (as herself)

1987 *The Whales of August* (Lindsay Anderson) (as Libby Strong)

1989 *Wicked Stepmother* (Cohen) (as Miranda); *As Summer Dies* (Tramont—for TV)

1991 *Here's Looking at You, Warner Bros.* (Guenette—doc for TV) (as herself)

Publications

By DAVIS: books—

The Lonely Life: An Autobiography, New York, 1962.
This 'n' That, with Michael Herskowitz, New York, 1987.
I'd Love to Kiss You: Conversations with Bette Davis, with Whitney Stine, New York, 1990.
Bette Davis Speaks (interviews), by Boze Hadleigh, New York, 1996.

By DAVIS: articles—

"I Was Not Found on a Soda Fountain Stool," interview with C. Cole, in *Films and Filming* (London), May 1956.
"I Think . . . ," in *Films and Filming* (London), May 1959.
"Meeting Baby Jane," interview with P. J. Dyer, in *Sight and Sound* (London), Summer 1963.
"What Is a Star?," in *Films and Filming* (London), September 1965.
"Bette," interview with Margaret Hinxman in *Sight and Sound* (London), Winter 1971-72.
"Sincerely, Bette Davis," interview with R. C. Hay, in *Inter/View* (New York), December 1972.
"Bette Davis: A Star Views Directors," interview with P. Gardner, in *Action* (Los Angeles), September-October 1974.
Interview with M. Henry and C. Viviani, in *Positif* (Paris), March 1988.

On DAVIS: books—

Noble, Peter, *Bette Davis: A Biography*, London, 1948.
Ringgold, Gene, *The Films of Bette Davis*, New York, 1966.
Mankiewicz, Joseph L., with Gary Carey, *More about "All about Eve,"* New York, 1972.
Rosen, Marjorie, *Popcorn Venus*, New York, 1973.
Vermilye, Jerry, *Bette Davis*, New York, 1973.
Stine, Whitney, *Mother Goddam: The Story of the Career of Bette Davis*, with commentary by Bette Davis, New York, 1974.
Affron, Charles, *Star Acting: Gish, Garbo, Davis*, New York, 1977.
Wallis, Hal, and Charles Higham, *Starmaker*, New York, 1980.
Higham, Charles, *Bette: The Life of Bette Davis*, New York, 1981.
Robinson, Jeffrey, *Bette Davis: Her Stage and Film Career*, London, 1982.
Hyman, B. D., *My Mother's Keeper*, New York, 1985.
Champion, Isabelle, *Bette Davis*, Paris, 1986.
Walker, Alexander, *Bette Davis: A Celebration*, London, 1986.
Hyman, B. D., with Jeremy Hyman, *Narrow Is the Way*, New York, 1987.
Merrill, Gary, *Bette, Rita, and the Rest of My Life*, Augusta, Maine, 1988.
Baker, Roger, *Bette Davis: A Tribute 1908-89*, New York, 1989.
Considine, Shaun, *Bette and Joan: The Divine Feud*, New York, 1989.
Moseley, Roy, *Bette Davis: An Intimate Memoir*, New York, 1989.
Brown, Gene, *Bette Davis, Film Star*, New York, 1990.
Quirk, Lawrence J., *Fasten Your Seat Belts: The Passionate Life of Bette Davis*, New York, 1990.
Ringgold, Gene, *The Complete Films of Bette Davis*, New York, 1990.
Leaming, Barbara, *Bette Davis*, New York, 1992.
Riese, Randall, *All about Bette: Her Life from A to Z*, Chicago, 1993.
Spada, James, *More than a Woman: An Intimate Biography of Bette Davis*, New York, 1993.
Baxt, George, *The Bette Davis Murder Case* (fiction), New York, 1994.

On DAVIS: articles—

Flanner, Janet, "Bette Davis," in *New Yorker*, February 1943.
"Bette Davis," in *Look* (New York), August 1946.
Lambert, G., "Portrait of an Actress: Bette Davis," in *Sight and Sound* (London), August-September 1951.
Current Biography 1953, New York, 1953.
Baker, Peter, "All about Bette," in *Films and Filming* (London), May 1956.
Shipman, David, "Whatever Happened to Bette Davis," in *Films and Filming* (London), April 1963.
Quirk, Lawrence J., "Bette Davis," in *Films in Review* (New York), December 1965.
Reed, Rex, "Bette Davis," in *Conversations in the Raw*, New York, 1969.
Carey, Gary, "The Lady and the Director: Bette Davis and William Wyler," in *Film Comment* (New York), Fall 1970.
Guerin, Ann, "Bette Davis," in *Show* (Hollywood), April 1971 and May 1972.
Cook, P., "The Sound Track," in *Films in Review* (New York), November 1973; also December 1984.
"A Toast to Bette Davis!," in *American Film* (Washington, D.C.), March 1977.
Bessie, Alvah, "Bette Davis: A Lifelong Love Affair," in *Close-Ups: The Movie Star Book*, edited by Danny Peary, New York, 1978.
McCourt, J., "Davis," in *Film Comment* (New York), March-April 1978.
Marill, A. H., "An Evening with Bette Davis," in *Films in Review* (New York), December 1979.
Arnold, Gary, "Bette Davis," in *The Movie Star*, edited by Elisabeth Weis, New York, 1981.
LaPlace, M., "Bette Davis and the Ideal of Consumption," in *Wide Angle* (Baltimore, Maryland), vol. 6, no. 4, 1985.

Schatz, Thomas, "A Triumph of Bitchery: Warner Bros., Bette Davis and *Jezebel*," in *Wide Angle* (Baltimore, Maryland), vol. 10, no. 1, 1988.
Schickel, Richard, "Bette," in *Film Comment* (New York), March/April 1989.
Poe, Gregory, "Restless Legend," in *Interview* (New York), April 1989.
Obituary in *Variety* (New York), 11 October 1989.
"Freedom Fighter," in *Economist* (London), 14 October 1989.
Clark, John, filmography in *Premiere* (New York), November 1989.
O'Toole, Lawrence, "Whatever Happened to Bette Davis," in *Sight and Sound* (London), Summer 1990.

* * *

If Warner Brothers's commitment in the 1930s to films based on "spot news" had any historical justification, it was the creation of Bette Davis as America's most influential female star. After a generation of desuetude, the working-class heroine became not an occasional feature of American film but the role model by which the women of a new generation could measure themselves. Above all Davis exhibited resilience and resource, taking nothing for granted, accepting no statement without its due degree of scepticism. She typified the kind of woman we now think of as a mid-century standard—tough, ambitious, competent, laconic, yet vulnerable, retaining her feminity even as she competed with men. Both in films and in her dealings with the studios she controlled her environment and the people in it to achieve her ends, always reaffirming her strength and independence.

During the 1930s Davis made a dozen minor pictures which established her as a fighter and a survivor, a type in contradistinction to the other female stars then at Warner Brothers: in *Three on a Match* Ann Dvorak is the socialite who comes to a bad end, Joan Blondell the showgirl who rises in her place, and Davis the stenographer who is simply lucky to be alive at the end. Davis would always survive. She may suffer as Spencer Tracy's self-sacrificing mistress in *20,000 Years in Sing Sing*, but it is Tracy who goes gallantly to the electric chair for the crime she had committed in an attempt to save him. And in *Dangerous*, the unjustly excoriated melodrama for which Davis won her first Oscar, Franchot Tone willingly toys with destruction to rescue her, however embittered and suicidal she might be.

As her range of roles expanded, her technique and style also developed until by 1939 she could play with conviction a queen in *The Private Lives of Elizabeth and Essex*. Davis made three films with William Wyler, a director with a meticulous, exhausting style who changed what had become mannerisms into new and adaptable techniques. Resource became calculation, and determination became command.

In *Jezebel*, Warner Brothers's hurried answer to the threatening success of *Gone with the Wind*, Davis schemed and sacrificed with a new and potent sensuality. As a coldly dissembling tropical murderess in *The Letter*, she enmeshes husband Herbert Marshall and solicitous policemen in a net as intricate as the lace she wears mantilla-like around her face. And in *The Little Foxes* as ruthless, self-regarding Regina Giddens, she shows a precisely perfected seductive skill. The final annihilating confession of *The Letter*, "I still love the man I killed," and the moment in *The Little Foxes* where she withholds from her husband the medicine that will prevent his heart attack, are insights into a type of character almost unknown in American movies of the time.

The gallery of classic Davis performances is unmatched by any other screen actress because Bette is impossible to dismiss even in the most wretched circumstances. Garbo had more allure; Stanwyck could play comedy with greater ease; the ageless Kate Hepburn perceptively chose better written vehicles from the fifties onward, but none of these titans bears watching in their bombs. In the campy bitterness of *Beyond the Forest* (in a Morticia Addams wig, Davis induces a miscarriage and blasts a mealy mouthed caretaker to death) or the souped-up melodrama of *In This Our Life* (rolling her eyes like a human slot machine, seductive Davis plays an incestuously inclined uncle for a sap), Davis is at her most mesmerizing, like a thespic warrior sumo-wrestling with flawed material. A valiant actress, temperamental Davis broke with the convention of her time and prided herself on sacrificing her looks for the honesty of a characterization; an intuitive grasp of building a role through externals infused her work from *Of Human Bondage* through *Mr. Skeffington* all the way up to *Whatever Happened to Baby Jane?* and beyond. Although Davis's numerous home runs, such as Empress Carlotta going mad in *Juarez* or Judith Traherne self-sufficiently facing her *Dark Victory* are as well-documented as her comeback in the quintessential Davis part of Margo Channing in *All about Eve*, it is more instructive to examine how the celluloid Duse handled what the industry grudgingly handed her after the title First Lady of the Screen had purely retrospective value. After her unjustly neglected Southern scenery-mastication in *Hush . . . Hush, Sweet Charlotte* (Kenneth Tynan called hers a great performance), Davis's silver-screen opportunities evaporated except for being brilliantly restrained in *The Nanny* and hilariously out of sorts in *Death on the Nile*. Having had checkered success on Broadway over the years and having struck out repeatedly in launching her own television series, Davis also chickened out of a stage musical Lazarus-act with *Miss Moffat*, a·Dixie transplant of *The Corn Is Green*. From the 1970s onwards, Davis retreated to the Land of TV Movies, where she was superbly imperious in a tiny role in *Little Gloria . . . Happy at Last* and heartbreakingly truculent paired opposite Gena Rowlands in *Strangers*, for which Davis won an Emmy.

A born scrapper, after surviving the traumas of mastectomies, strokes, cancer, inferior television fodder, and a vicious tell-all book by her ungrateful daughter, Bette was a haunting shell of her former self in *The Whales of August* which would have been a fine artistic capstone to her career. Then, despite a troubled production history and Davis's unhealthy appearance, *The Wicked Stepmother* provided a few final rumblings from that Davis volcano. Displeased with the rushes and terminally ill, Davis bowed out of a project that writer-director Larry Cohen had created in response to the movie business's neglect of her. Against the wishes of the actress, Cohen reshot around Davis's existing footage in a manner not seen since Ed Wood Jr.'s heyday. If this legend did not triumph artistically in her swansong, at least willful Davis went out battling a producer/director; that combativeness was the essence of her character and her unassailable artistry.

—John Baxter, updated by Robert Pardi

DAVIS, Geena

Nationality: American. **Born:** Virginia Davis in Wareham, Massachusetts, 21 January 1957. **Family:** Married 1) Richard Emmolo (divorced); 2) the actor Jeff Goldblum (divorced); 3) the director Renny Harlin, 1993. **Education:** Attended Boston University, BFA, 1979. **Career:** Late 1970s—began acting on stage with the Mount Washington Repertory Company in New Hampshire; 1979—moved to New York to break into theater; early 1980s worked as a model; 1982—screen debut in *Tootsie*; 1983-84—in TV sitcom *Buffalo Bill*; 1985—title role in TV sitcom *Sara*; 1988—breakthrough screen roles in *Beetlejuice* and *The Accidental Tourist*; 1990s—established her own production company, Genial Pictures. **Awards:** Best Supporting Actress Academy Award, for *The Accidental Tourist*, 1988. **Agent:** Paramount Communications, 15 Columbus Circle, New York, NY 10019, U.S.A.

Films as Actress:

1982   *Tootsie* (Pollack) (as April)
1985   *Fletch* (Ritchie) (as Larry); *Transylvania 6-5000* (DeLuca) (as Odette); *Secret Weapons* (*Secrets of the Red Bedroom*; *Sexpionage*) (Don Taylor—for TV) (as Tamara Reshevsky)
1986   *The Fly* (Cronenberg) (as Veronica "Ronnie" Quaife)
1988   *Beetlejuice* (Burton) (as Barbara Maitland); *The Accidental Tourist* (Kasdan) (as Muriel Pritchett)
1989   *Earth Girls Are Easy* (Temple) (as Valerie Dale)
1990   *Quick Change* (Howard Franklin and Bill Murray) (as Phyllis)
1991   **Thelma & Louise** (Ridley Scott) (as Thelma Dickinson)
1992   *Hero* (*Accidental Hero*) (Frears) (as Gale Gayley); *A League of Their Own* (Penny Marshall) (as Dottie Hinson)
1994   *Angie* (Coolidge) (as Angie Scacciapensieri); *Speechless* (Underwood) (as Julia, + co-pr)
1995   *Cutthroat Island* (Harlin) (as Morgan Adams)

Publications

By DAVIS: articles—

"Accidental Ingenue," interview with Michael Musto and Dan Lepard, in *Interview* (New York), December 1988.
Interview with Martha Sherrill, in *Washington Post*, 12 May 1989.
Interview with Johanna Schneller, in *GQ* (New York), June 1989.
"20 Questions," interview with David Rensin, in *Playboy* (Chicago), October 1989.
"An Interview with Geena Davis," interview with S. Royal, in *Premiere* (Los Angeles), no. 3, 1991.
"An Interview with Geena Davis," interview with Tom Hanks, in *Interview* (New York), March 1992.
"The Brainy Bombshell," interview with George Kalogerakis, in *Vogue* (New York), May 1994.

On DAVIS: articles—

DiNicolo, David, "People Are Talking About: Movies," in *Vogue* (New York), April 1988.
Sherman, Jeffrey, "Tour Divorce," in *Vogue* (New York), November 1988.
Rasenberger, Jim, "Dreams of Geena," in *Vanity Fair* (New York), January 1989.
Handy, Bruce, "What's So Strange about Geena Davis?," in *Rolling Stone* (New York), 23 March 1989.
Ferguson, K., "Geena Davis," in *Film Monthly* (Hemel,England), June 1989.
"Women We Love," in *Esquire* (New York), August 1989.
Current Biography 1991, New York, 1991.
Jerome, Jim, "Riding Shotgun," in *People Weekly* (New York), 24 June 1991.
Schickel, Richard, "Gender Bender," in *Time* (New York), 24 June 1991.
Diamond, Jamie, "Geena: The Goddess Next Door," in *Vogue* (New York), September 1992.
Sessums, Kevin, "Geena's Sheen," in *Vanity Fair* (New York), September 1992.

*   *   *

If Paula Prentiss were working in movies today, she would be up for the same roles as Geena Davis. The two talented actresses have similar lanky, long-legged good looks and the ability to project appealing,

Geena Davis in *Thelma and Louise*

offbeat personalities. Because neither was mistaken for Marilyn Monroe or Michelle Pfeiffer during her early career, the ingenue roles in which the young actresses were cast suggested capricious types. Prentiss's film career lost steam in the early 1970s as she entered her mid-thirties; however, the increase in solid, three-dimensional film roles for women in the 1990s allowed Davis's career to thrive at the same age.

Her screen debut came in an eye-opening supporting role in *Tootsie*, playing a soap opera actress who shares a dressing room with Michael Dorsey (Dustin Hoffman), an unemployable character actor secretly taking on a woman's identity in order to work. After ongoing roles in two television series, Davis returned to making movies. She co-starred with then-husband Jeff Goldblum in three films. The first was *Transylvania 6-5000*, an unfunny Dracula-themed picture in which she appeared as a sex-crazed vampiress. But her talent was apparent. According to *New York Times* critic Janet Maslin, Davis "appears to have wandered in from another, much better movie." In *The Fly* she is underutilized as a journalist who has an affair with the fly/man played by Goldblum. And in the imaginative *Earth Girls Are Easy* she is a harebrained Valley-girl manicurist who falls for a space alien.

The films with Goldblum proved Davis could be credible in fantasy-world films. The most outstanding and appealing of her fantasy cycle is Tim Burton's *Beetlejuice*, the now-classic horror tale of a recently deceased couple who attempt to haunt-out a dysfunctional family from the house that had been theirs. Davis is completely at home in Burton's fanciful, surreal after-death world. An actor has to have a special sense of the absurd in order to evoke emotions while wearing rubber monster masks and prancing around in a sheet (even if it is a designer sheet).

Lawrence Kasdan's *The Accidental Tourist* provided Davis with a more substantial role, one which allowed her an opportunity to develop a personality of full measure. From the pages of Kasdan's adaptation of Anne Tyler's best-selling novel, Davis brings to life the character of an ingenuous dog trainer whose free-flowing personality unlocks the emotions of a pent-up travel writer she comes to love. The clarity and feeling she applied to the role earned her an Oscar for Best Supporting Actress.

The outstanding role in Davis's career to date is that of Thelma, an Arkansas housewife who takes to the road with her waitress friend (Susan Sarandon) in the highly-touted female buddy film *Thelma & Louise*. Callie Khouri's original script presents the full-blooded character of an unhappy ditzy housewife who develops into a determined criminal. Feminist viewers were enthralled as they watched the two women characters travel across the Southwest in their '66 T-bird. In Paula Prentiss's 20-year career, she never once had such a solid role.

The year after *Thelma & Louise*, Davis gave a well-rounded performance in *A League of Their Own* as a farm girl who becomes a star baseball player in a women's league during World War II. Here, her rangy build gave credibility to the character's athletic prowess. Her most recent portrayals are of independent women who face romance and marriage with some amount of trepidation. She has the title role in *Angie*, playing an independent Brooklyn woman facing marriage and motherhood. In *Speechless*, she is seen in the timely comedy of a political speech writer who falls for a man who writes speeches for opposing candidates. Critics noted the strength of her performances in both these films.

With the support of several above-average scripts, Davis has gone from playing zany but one-dimensional roles to multifaceted star turns in motion pictures that are both critical and box-office successes. So powerfully does Davis carry off well-written roles that she has been able to create a new and different look for female film stars.

—Audrey E. Kupferberg

DAVIS, Judy

Nationality: Australian. **Born:** Perth, Australia, 23 April 1955. **Family:** Married the actor Colin Friels, 1984, son: Jack. **Education:** Attended the West Australia Institute of Technology; National Institute of Dramatic Art, Sydney. **Career:** Joined the South Australia Theatre Company; 1977—film debut in *High Rolling*. **Awards:** Sammy Award (Australia), and British Film Academy, Best Actress Award, for *My Brilliant Career*, 1979. **Agent:** Shanahan Management Proprietary Ltd., P.O. Box 478, Kings Cross, NSW 2011 Australia. **Address:** c/o Colin Friels, 129 Bourke Street, Woollomooloo, Sydney, NSW 2011, Australia.

Films as Actress:

1977   *High Rolling (High Rolling in a Hot Corvette)* (Auzins) (as Lynn)

1979   ***My Brilliant Career*** (Gillian Armstrong) (as Sybylla Melvyn)

1981   *Hoodwink* (Whatham) (as Sarah)

1982   *The Final Option (Who Dares Win)* (Ian Sharp) (as Frankie Leith); *Winter of Our Dreams* (Duigan) (as Lou); *The Merry Wives of Windsor* (David Jones—for TV) (as Mistress Ford); *A Woman Called Golda* (Alan Gibson—for TV) (as the young Golda Meir)

1983   *Heatwave* (Noyce) (as Kate Dean)

1984   ***A Passage to India*** (Lean) (as Adela Quested)

1986   *Kangaroo* (Burstall) (as Harriet Somers); *Rocket to the Moon* (John Jacobs—for TV) (as Cleo)

1987   *Georgia* (Lewin) (as Nina Bailey/Georgia); *High Tide* (Gillian Armstrong) (as Lilli)

1990   *Alice* (Woody Allen) (as Vicki); *Impromptu* (Lapine) (as George Sand)

1991   ***Barton Fink*** (Coen) (as Audrey Taylor); *Naked Lunch* (Cronenberg) (as Joan Frost/Joan Lee); *One against the Wind* (Elikann—for TV) (as Mary Lindell)

1992   *Husbands and Wives* (Woody Allen) (as Sally); *Where Angels Fear to Tread* (Sturridge) (as Harriet Herriton); *On My Own* (Tibaldi) (as Mother)

1994   *The New Age* (Tolkin) (as Katherine Witner); *The Ref* (Ted Demme) (as Caroline)

1995   *Serving in Silence: The Margarethe Cammermeyer Story* (Bleckner—for TV) (as Diane)

1996   *Children of the Revolution* (Peter Duncan)

Publications

By DAVIS: articles—

"Judy Davis: An Actress of Raw Nerve," interview with Graham Fuller, in *Interview* (New York), October 1992.

"Judy, Judy, Judy," interview with Leslie Bennetts, in *Harper's Bazaar* (New York), October 1992.

"'I Go to the Core,'" interview with Gavin Smith, in *Film Comment* (New York), November/December 1992.

On DAVIS: articles—

Clark, John, filmography in *Premiere* (New York), February 1992.
Current Biography 1993, New York, 1993.
Biskind, Peter, "Punchin' Judy," in *Premiere* (New York), October 1994.

*   *   *

Judy Davis in *My Brilliant Career*

Judy Davis's intermittently brilliant career effectively began with *My Brilliant Career*, her first film after drama school and her first starring role, which won her immediate international attention, establishing her as among Australia's leading stars and opening up prospects beyond. Critics compared her to the young Katharine Hepburn, and although the resemblance has proved transitory (it was a resemblance of role as much as personality) the comparison suggests certain characteristics basic to Davis's persona: a strength, activeness and determination conventionally perceived as "masculine," a resistance to domination (especially by men), and a refusal of conformity to social convention. The film itself was overrated, the kind of "safe" feminist movie that threatens no one: Davis's own comment, though perhaps overly harsh, is accurate enough ("I thought it was a children's film, it was so simplistic"). The characteristics have remained fairly stable, but Davis has (rather surprisingly) had few opportunities to develop the positive, Hepburn-like aspects of this early role, its exuberance and untrammeled energy. Increasingly, in both the Australian and American films, the strength and nonconformity have been complicated, at times canceled out, by other factors: neurosis, desperation, defeat. It is interesting that, two years after *My Brilliant Career*, she was chosen to play the young Ingrid Bergman (as Golda Meir) in *A Woman Called Golda*—her subsequent roles have been, in general, closer to Bergman's than to Hepburn's.

It is sometimes the case that an appearance in a bad film can reveal more of an actor's essence than many performances in better ones; a case in point, in *The Final Option*. The film's project is clear: a simpleminded, blatantly right-wing drama about good guys vs. evil terrorists. Davis's remarkable performance almost turns this on its head: in the context of the colorless and boring spokespersons for law and order and the status quo, she gives such force, conviction, and passion to the leading terrorist that the film comes close to being dangerously subversive.

The most obvious, and least interesting, of her "neurotic" or "desperate" roles are her two appearances in E. M. Forster adaptations (*A Passage to India* and *Where Angels Fear to Tread*), where the character is warped by sexual repression. Far more interesting, because they allow her greater range of expression and opportunities to express her energy, are her recent roles in three consecutive films of some distinction: Woody Allen's *Husbands and Wives*, Ted Demme's *The Ref*, and above all, Michael Tolkin's *The New Age*. Allen's film gives her the chance to "let rip" as a frustrated wife going increasingly out of control: energy expressed as hysteria. *The Ref*, in which her role is a comic variant on this, allows her a rare opportunity to display a quite wonderful gift for comedy, her impeccable timing matched by that of her two male co-stars. *The New Age* is very closely related to Tolkin's previous (and even more remarkable) film *The Rapture*, which drew from Mimi Rogers one of the greatest performances in all of Hollywood cinema. Davis's character in *The New Age* closely resembles that of Rogers, but without allowing the actress to push things quite as far; nevertheless, Davis matches it as far as the film's relative limitations allow, emerging gradually as its true emotional center, revealing an authenticity in a character defined initially as incorrigibly inauthentic. Both of Tolkin's films are driven by their characters' sense of the meaninglessness and emptiness of their lives and the desperate search for meaning in a world that seems to have abandoned its very possibility: a theme that perfectly suits Davis's persona and abilities.

Davis has frequently played women from real life; since her casting as the young Golda Meir she has taken on two particularly celebrated or notorious historical figures, Frieda Lawrence in *Kangaroo* (thinly disguised as "Harriet Somers"), and George Sand in *Impromptu*, on both occasions with conspicuous success. *Kangaroo* is not a satisfactory film; though, to be fair, its weaknesses derive from D. H. Lawrence's inferior novel, and the filmmakers have made some halfhearted attempts to mitigate them. The subject is Lawrence's brief flirtation with, and eventual—if perhaps only temporary—repudiation of, fascism (as dramatized in an imaginary Australian political movement). He did not live to witness fascism's worst consequences, and it might have been possible to regard the flirtation more sympathetically in the 1920s; today it is difficult not to feel very impatient with the time it takes Somers/Lawrence to see through its spurious attractions, and extremely dissatisfied with his grounds for rejecting it. In the novel (as in certain of his others) Lawrence seems to make a determined effort to give his representation of Frieda an effective "voice," but as usual it tends to be shouted down by his own. In the film—thanks largely to Davis at her most mesmerizing—Harriet/Frieda's challenge to her husband becomes so strong that our impatience with his obtuseness is intensified. Though she is absent through many of the later episodes, and though Colin Friels (her real-life husband) gives a very intelligent performance as Lawrence, it becomes very much Davis's film, the triumph of a brilliant actress over dubious material and even more dubious ideology.

Davis's George Sand is another splendid assumption. Striding through most of the film in men's clothes and asserting her right to the kinds of recognition that men take for granted, her Mme. Sand falls hopelessly in love with Chopin (Hugh Grant)—clearly because he is gentle, passive, "feminine," and probably gay. Although the film does not suggest that Sand was other than heterosexual, the gender ambiguity is fascinating in relation to the Davis persona, and it is interesting that Davis eventually played a lesbian (as Glenn Close's lover in the television move *Serving in Silence: The Margarethe Cammermeyer Story*).

Richard Lippe has suggested that there is a fairly consistent difference between Davis's status in the Australian films and in her Hollywood ones: in the latter she is usually part of an ensemble (if often a dominant member), whereas the former seem conceived as star vehicles that she is expected essentially to carry. Several of the American films may be superior to any of the Australian, but to fully appreciate Davis's strength one must certainly take into account *Heatwave* and what are to date her last two Australian movies: *High Tide*, which reunites her with Gillian Armstrong for the first time since *My Brilliant Career*, a powerful melodrama about intergenerational conflicts among women; and the intriguing but ultimately disappointing *Georgia*, in which she plays both mother (in the past) and daughter (in the present).

—Robin Wood

DAY, Doris

Nationality: American. **Born:** Doris von Kappelhoff in Cincinnati, Ohio, 3 April 1924. **Education:** Attended Withrow High School, Cincinnati; Fanchon and Marco Dance School, Los Angeles, 1937. **Family:** Married 1) Al Jorden, 1941 (divorced 1942), son Terry; 2) George Weidlen, 1947; 3) Martin Melcher, 1951 (died 1968); 4) Barry Comden, 1976. **Career:** 1940—singer with Bob Crosby's band in Chicago; 1940-46—singer in Les Brown's band; also became successful recording star; 1947-48—under personal contract to director Michael Curtiz, made film acting debut in *Romance on the High Seas*; contract with Warners; 1948—appeared with Bob Hope on weekly radio shows and concert tours; 1955—contract with Warner Brothers expired; formed Arwin Productions; 1968—discovered life earnings had been mismanaged and embezzled after death of manager-husband Melcher, sued former lawyer for $22 million; won suit, 1974; 1968-73—star of TV series *The Doris Day Show*; late 1960s-1970s—involved in animal causes; 1985—host of TV show *Doris Day and Friends*.

Films as Actress:

1948 *Romance on the High Seas* (Curtiz) (as Georgia Garrett)
1949 *My Dream Is Yours* (Curtiz) (as Martha Gibson); *It's a Great Feeling* (Butler) (as Judy Adams)
1950 *Young Man with a Horn* (*Young Man of Music*) (Curtiz) (as Jo Jordan); *Tea for Two* (Butler) (as Nanette Carter); *The West Point Story* (Del Ruth) (as Jan Wilson); *Storm Warning* (Heisler) (as Lucy Rice)
1951 *The Lullaby of Broadway* (Butler) (as Melinda Howard); *On Moonlight Bay* (Del Ruth) (as Marjorie Winfield); *I'll See You in My Dreams* (Curtiz) (as Grace LeBoy Kahn); *Starlift* (Del Ruth) (as Herself)
1952 *The Winning Team* (Seiler) (as Aimee); *April in Paris* (Butler) (as Ethel "Dynamite" Jackson)
1953 *By the Light of the Silvery Moon* (Butler) (as Marjorie Winfield); *Calamity Jane* (Butler) (title role)
1954 *Lucky Me* (Donohue) (as Candy)
1955 *Young at Heart* (Douglas) (as Laurie Tuttle); *Love Me or Leave Me* (Charles Vidor) (as Ruth Etting)
1956 *The Man Who Knew Too Much* (Hitchcock) (as Jo McKenna); *Julie* (Stone) (as Julie Benton)
1957 *The Pajama Game* (Abbott and Donen) (as Katie "Babe" Williams)
1958 *Teacher's Pet* (Seaton) (as Erica Stone); *The Tunnel of Love* (Kelly) (as Isolde Poole)
1959 *It Happened to Jane* (Quine) (as Jane Osgood); *Pillow Talk* (Gordon) (as Jan Morrow)
1960 *Please Don't Eat the Daisies* (Walters) (as Kate Mackay); *Midnight Lace* (Miller) (as Kit Preston)
1962 *Lover Come Back* (Delbert Mann) (as Carol Templeton); *That Touch of Mink* (Delbert Mann) (as Cathy Timberlake); *Billy Rose's Jumbo* (Walters) (as Kitty Wonder)
1963 *The Thrill of It All* (Jewison) (as Beverly Boyer); *Move Over, Darling* (Gordon) (as Ellen Wagstaff Arden)
1964 *Send Me No Flowers* (Jewison) (as Judy)
1965 *Do Not Disturb* (Levy) (as Janet Harper)
1966 *The Glass Bottom Boat* (Tashlin) (as Jennifer Nelson)
1967 *Caprice* (Tashlin) (as Patricia Fowler); *The Ballad of Josie* (McLaglen) (as Josie Minick)
1968 *Where Were You When the Lights Went Out?* (Averback) (as Margaret Garrison); *With Six You Get Egg Roll* (Morris) (as Abby McClure)
1994 *That's Entertainment! III* (Friedgen and Sheridan)

Publications

By DAY: book—

Doris Day: Her Own Story, with A. E. Hotchner, New York, 1976; rev. ed., 1985.

On DAY: books—

Rosen, Marjorie, *Popcorn Venus*, New York, 1973.
Haskell, Molly, *From Reverence to Rape: The Treatment of Women in the Movies*, New York, 1974.
Morris, George, *Doris Day*, 1976.
Young, Christopher, *The Films of Doris Day*, Secaucus, New Jersey, 1977.
Gelb, Alan, *The Doris Day Scrapbook*, New York, 1977.
Clarke, Jane, and Diana Simmons, *Move over Misconceptions: Doris Day Reappraised*, London, 1980.
Braun, Eric, *Doris Day*, London, 1991.

On DAY: articles—

Current Biography 1954, New York, 1954.
Shipman, D., "Doris Day," in *Films and Filming* (London), August 1962.
Capp, Al, "The Day Dream," in *Show* (Hollywood), December 1962.
Morris, George, "Doris Day: No Pollyanna," in *Close-Ups: The Movie Star Book*, edited by Danny Peary, New York, 1978.
Haskell, Molly, "Doris Day," in *The Movie Star*, edited by Elisabeth Weis, New York, 1981.
Williamson, Judith, in *Consuming Passions* (London), 1986.
Casablanca, T., "The Awful Truth," in *Premiere*, February 1993.

* * *

Having at various times been ridiculed as the vacuous heroine of not very distinguished Warner Brothers musical comedies in the 1950s or as the perpetual virgin of Universal's sex comedies in the 1960s, Doris Day now finds herself the victim of a critical change of heart; it now appears that she may have been a gifted and unappreciated actress as well as remaining, for most of her career, one of the top two or three attractions at the American box office.

Most of the snide criticism of her work in fact came at the end of it, when from the perspective of the late 1960s and early 1970s Day's girl next door seemed an affront to the less romance-centric lifestyles of the sexual revolution. No such taint affected her career during the years when she was actually acting, when a Doris Day film was consistent with, and a kind of vindication of, 1950s and early 1960s versions of the ideal woman. By any standard, she was one of the great popular singers of her generation, and that talent at times threatened to overwhelm her work as an actress. Her breath control was exact, her diction was flawless, and her tone was beautiful, but her unique talent was that she could evoke great emotion (and in the process spellbind her audience) without obvious histrionics. No one who has seen her first film, *Romance on the High Seas*, can ever forget the moment when Doris Day first sings "It's Magic." Improving with age, several Day musicals have emerged as the most enjoyable of that genre: a bouncy Broadway transplant (*Pajama Game*), an energized photocopy of *Annie Get Your Gun* (*Calamity Jane*), a surprisingly hard-edged if falsified biopic about Ruth Etting (*Love Me or Leave Me*), and the splashy MGM musical swansong (*Jumbo*).

She began her career as a big band singer in the early 1940s; though she now modestly denies it, she was also a fine dancer; most importantly, however, she created a "character"—the American girl, bright, carefree, resilient, honest, caring, tough when she had to be, nobody's fool, unfailingly optimistic. Day's personal life throughout the 1940s and 1950s was far from pleasant; the character she portrayed on screen was indeed just that—a persona, the work of an actress, achieved with great cunning. It was an accomplishment of and for its time, perhaps, but it proved more durable than the exotic showgirls of her predecessor, Betty Grable, or the eccentrics of her successor, Julie Andrews.

That persona was so effectively developed and so convincing that her directors were able to "use" Day in opposition to herself (*The Pajama Game*) or to inject the "character" into other, mildly inappropriate contexts (Hitchcock in *The Man Who Knew Too Much*) to achieve a subtle resonance. The great transition in Day's career—from musical star to light comedy performer—is "odd," in retrospect, only if one forgets that persona. At the time of her first great comedy success—*Pillow Talk* in 1959—Doris Day was already 35 years old, too old for continued success in musical comedies, a form that was dying anyway; her career ought to have ended. Yet the Day persona was so much established in the moviegoer's consciousness, so much what the American woman was then, rightly or wrongly, imagined to be, that Day's transition to another genre was, in fact, both painless

Doris Day

and successful; the American girl next door of 20 became the American career girl of 30. The new Day was more popular with the audiences than she had ever been.

Stretching her versatility to extremes may have prolonged her stardom, but whereas Day is irreplaceable in musicals and endearing in comedies, she is often uncomfortable in melodrama. One senses her flinging her emotions haphazardly at the camera. Yet, even caught up in the hysteria of *Midnight Lace* (whimpering while fleeing in her high heels on skyscraper girders from a gaslighting husband) or choking back tears in *Julie* (while crash-coursing in flying a plane after her deranged spouse shoots the pilot), Day arouses our protective instincts.

Today, armed with deconstructive works such as *Rock Hudson's Home Movies*, buffs approach the Day-Hudson comedies with smirking knowingness, as if awareness of Rock's homosexuality somehow invalidated these romantic trifles. While it is doubtful that *Pillow Talk* or *Lover Come Back* would ever have had the enduring appeal of Lubitsch's or Sturges's escapist wish-fulfilment, it is time to accept these films not as mislabeled sophisticated farces but as double-standard sex romps illuminated by Day's perky savoir faire. With her bubble-domed coiffure and enviably sleek wardrobe, Day's career gal was as key an identification figure in the sixties as TV's Mary Richards was in the seventies. Playing an independent working woman, Day single-handedly removed the stigma from the word "unmarried."

Contractually bound to repeat herself in films handpicked by her husband (who also obligated her to a TV series without her knowledge, a fact she discovered after his death), Day did not end her film career on a high note. As her beloved image faded due to repetition, in *Caprice*, and other late sixties films, the soft-focus, time-erasing filters seemed to blur her unsinkable spirit; she became a Doris Day impersonator.

Transcending her late spouse's shady business deals, Day recovered her fortune from an unscrupulous lawyer and now devotes herself to animal rights. Still smashing-looking, she declines comeback offers from Hollywood power brokers and an offer to sleuth in a TV detective series with the same finality with which she once nixed the Mrs. Robinson role in *The Graduate*. Having conquered every field but Broadway, Day inspires a new generation of devotees who respond to this strong-willed star who outgrew being the girl next door, the career girl next door, and the mature-but-ageless-looking married girl next door.

Doris Day was one of cinema's most popular stars because she synthesized for millions of people a particular kind of dream, but in those moments when she sang, she was something more. In those moments, she was an artist who could take us beyond ourselves.

—George Walsh, updated by Robert Pardi

DAY-LEWIS, Daniel

(Sometimes Day Lewis). **Nationality:** British. **Born:** London, England, 29 April 1957; son of the poet laureate Cecil Day Lewis and the actress Jill Balcon. **Family:** Son with the actress Isabelle Adjani. **Education:** Attended Bedales School and at Bristol Old Vic Theatre School. **Career:** 1971—film debut as teenager in *Sunday, Bloody Sunday*; stage work includes *Another Country*, 1982, *Romeo and Juliet* for the Royal Shakespeare Company, 1983-84, and *Hamlet* at the National Theatre, 1989; TV work includes *The Insurance Man*, 1985. **Awards:** Best Supporting Actor Award, New York Film Critics, for *My Beautiful Laundrette* and *A Room with a View*; Oscar for Best Actor, British Academy of Film and Television Arts, Best Actor Award, and Best Actor Award, New York Film Critics and Los Angeles Film Crit-

ics, for *My Left Foot*, 1989. **Agent:** c/o William Morris, 151 El Camino Drive, Beverly Hills, CA 90210, U.S.A.

Films as Actor:

1971 *Sunday, Bloody Sunday* (Schlesinger)
1982 *Gandhi* (Attenborough) (as Colin)
1984 *The Bounty* (Donaldson) (as Fryer)
1985 ***My Beautiful Laundrette*** (Frears) (as Johnny); *The Insurance Man* (Eyre—for TV) (as Mr. Kafka)
1986 ***A Room with a View*** (Ivory) (as Cecil Vyse); *Nanou* (Templeman) (as Max)
1988 *Stars and Bars* (O'Connor) (as Henderson Dores); *The Unbearable Lightness of Being* (Kaufman) (as Tomas)
1989 *My Left Foot* (Sheridan) (as Christy Brown); *Eversmile, New Jersey* (Sorin) (as Dr. Fergus O'Connell)
1992 *The Last of the Mohicans* (Michael Mann) (as Nathaniel Poe/Hawkeye)
1993 *In the Name of the Father* (Sheridan) (as Gerald Conlon); ***The Age of Innocence*** (Scorsese) (as Newland Archer)
1996 *The Crucible* (Hytner) (as John Proctor)

Publications

By DAY-LEWIS: articles—

Interviews in *City Limits* (London), 10 April and 13 November 1986, and 7 April 1988.
Interview with Graham Fuller, in *American Film* (New York), January/February 1988.
Interview in *Interview* (New York), April 1988.
Interview with Allan Hunter, in *Films and Filming* (London), April 1988.
Interview in *American Film* (Los Angeles), December 1989.

On DAY-LEWIS: books—

Jenkins, Garry, *Daniel Day-Lewis: The Fire Within*, London, 1994.
Jackson, Laura, *Daniel Day-Lewis: Biography*, 1995.

On DAY-LEWIS: articles—

McGillivray, David, "Daniel Day Lewis," in *Films and Filming* (London), August 1986.
Kennedy, Harlan, "Brit Pack," in *Film Comment* (New York), January/February 1988.
Mayne, Richard, "Framed: Daniel Day Lewis," in *Sight and Sound* (London), Autumn 1989.
Gurewitsch, Matthew, "Risk Taker Supreme: Is Daniel Day Lewis Too Good to Be a Movie Star?," in *Connoisseur*, December 1989.
Current Biography 1990, New York, 1990.
De Vries, Hilary, "Acting Up," in *Rolling Stone* (New York), 8 February 1990.
Woodward, Richard B., "The Intensely Imagined Life of Daniel Day-Lewis," in *New York Times Magazine*, 5 July 1992.
Buck, Joan Juliet, "Actor from the Shadows," in *New Yorker*, 12 October 1992.
Corliss, Richard, "Dashing Daniel," in *Time* (New York), 21 March 1994.

*   *   *

Daniel Day-Lewis's instinctive, fiery power is unusual for a stage-trained British actor (something Gary Oldman and David Thewlis can only fake). Day-Lewis's repertory theater skills allow him to play men of disparate eras, nationalities, and tendencies with more surface fidelity than, say, De Niro. But at the same time he will go passionately freestyle in voice and movement in order to get at his character's motivation, a deliberate expense of effort that would have seemed superfluous to Olivier.

Day-Lewis came to moviegoers' attention with his smashing performance as Johnny in Stephen Frears's *My Beautiful Laundrette*, based on Hanif Kureishi's script. As a fascistic punk tired of his violent, pointless life, Day-Lewis brings fresh comic impulses to the naturalistic view of hopeless English kids and immigrant Pakistanis in depressed South London. When the Pakistani Omar recognizes his old schoolfriend Johnny in a threatening street gang, Johnny does not attack Omar, he falls for him (and for the economic advantage of associating with Omar's enterprising family). Like *Sunday, Bloody Sunday*, *Laundrette* does not load its gay characters with the pathos of unrecognized nobility; but unlike Peter Finch, Day-Lewis is movie-star sexy. His foxy eyes and quiet-confident body language help make Johnny one of the few characters in movie history with sexual imagination. When Johnny spits champagne from his mouth into Omar's, Day-Lewis creates a gay character more to be envied than censured.

Playing the Irish painter and writer Christy Brown, afflicted from childhood with cerebral palsy, in *My Left Foot* made Day-Lewis an international star. In such roles actors usually cannot help begging for sympathy. The playwright-director Jim Sheridan enabled Day-Lewis to shoot past pity to get at primal emotions about mother-son love and the rage for expression. Without coordinated movements and barely speaking comprehensibly Day-Lewis gave a performance about not swallowing nature's insults, about living fully with severe limitations, that had the vulcanized intensity of Robert De Niro's in *Taxi Driver*.

Day-Lewis scored again with Sheridan in *In the Name of the Father*, as Gerry Conlon, a Northern Irishman in London whose false imprisonment on charges of IRA terrorism tears his family apart. The English zealously fabricate evidence of a terror network within Gerry's family; this adolescent, semicriminal dork, living out a parody of his own futurelessness, ends up sharing a prison cell with his father. In *My Left Foot* Christy Brown scrawls the word "Mother" on the floor with chalk clenched in his toes. *In the Name of the Father* is about a young man face-to-face with an unassuming father who never impressed him. The movie comes from headlines, but Sheridan and Day-Lewis push it to a symbolic level: Gerry's being locked up with his father is a metaphor for how all young men feel locked in the prison upstairs with their dads. In Day-Lewis's finest speeches he relives his frustration over his father's weakness. But Gerry comes to appreciate the older man's nonviolent forbearance; he grows up by witnessing the virtues of the "model" he has been trying to reject.

Before working with Sheridan, Day-Lewis had starred impressively in Philip Kaufman's adaptation of Milan Kundera's *The Unbearable Lightness of Being*, making Tomas's skirt-chasing seem an existential defiance of a politically dead culture. Day-Lewis played opposite two very different leading ladies, the almost impersonally provocative Lena Olin and Juliette Binoche with her needy hot-baby flesh. Working for Kaufman they brought an experienced tragicomic sensibility to a novel that was a trifle oversketched.

Day-Lewis was also a fine athletic lead in Michael Mann's handsome, large-scale Harlequinized *The Last of the Mohicans*. But it did not call on his special skills—he was not inauthentic as Tom Cruise would have been, but there was not anything to be authentic about. He was less interesting in Martin Scorsese's too well-mannered adaptation of Edith Wharton's *Age of Innocence*, but the fault lies with the source. We never understand what makes Newland Archer superior to his surroundings, and when he does nothing to avoid marriage to a woman he does not love, it is hard to share the movie's concern for him. Thin roles can expose the calculations behind Day-Lewis's act-

ing, most notably in his stiff performance as Cecil Vyse in *A Room with a View*. But he has a hot-spring of inspiration that usually keeps him running high, despite or perhaps because of the hiatuses between pictures. We await his new releases the way we looked forward to De Niro's in the 1970s.

—Alan Dale

DEAN, James

Nationality: American. **Born:** James Byron Dean in Marion, Ohio, 8 February 1931. **Education:** Attended Santa Monica Junior College; acting classes, University of California, Los Angeles; studied at the Actors Studio, New York. **Career:** 1950—appeared in TV commercial for Pepsi Cola; 1950-51—member of James Whitmore's acting workshop; 1951—began playing bit roles in films; 1952—entered Actors Studio in New York and began playing small roles on television; 1953—critical recognition for role on Broadway in *The Immoralist*; 1955—cast by Elia Kazan in film *East of Eden*; contract with Warners; killed in auto accident just before gaining international critical and public acclaim. **Died:** 30 September 1955.

Films as Actor:

1951 *Fixed Bayonets* (Fuller) (as soldier)
1952 *Sailor, Beware!* (Walker) (bit role as sailor); *Has Anybody Seen My Gal?* (Sirk) (bit role)
1955 *East of Eden* (Kazan) (as Cal Trask); *Rebel without a Cause* (Nicholas Ray) (as Jim Stark)
1956 *Giant* (Stevens) (as Jett Rink)

Publications

By DEAN: book—

James Dean in His Own Words, London, 1991.

On DEAN: books—

Bast, William, *James Dean: A Biography*, New York, 1956.
Myerson, Peter, editor, *The Official James Dean Anniversary Book*, New York, 1956.
Salgues, Yves, *James Dean ou le mal de vivre*, Paris, 1957.
Thomas, T. T., *I, James Dean*, New York, 1957.
Ellis, Royston, *Rebel*, London, 1962.
DeVillers, Marceau, *James Dean*, Paris, 1966; Paris, 1984; London, 1985.
Ciment, Michel, *Kazan on Kazan*, London, 1973.
Dalton, David, *James Dean: The Mutant King*, San Francisco, 1974.
Herndon, Venable, *James Dean: A Short Life*, New York, 1974.
Howlett, John, *James Dean: A Biography*, New York, 1975.
Stock, Dennis, *James Dean Revisited*, New York, 1978.
Whitman, Mark, *The Films of James Dean*, St. Paul, Minnesota, 1978.
Dutton, Gerald, *James Dean*, Paris, 1981.
McGee, Mark Thomas, and R. J. Robertson, *The JD Films: Juvenile Delinquency in the Movies*, Jefferson, North Carolina, 1982.
Bourget, Jean-Loup, *James Dean*, Paris, 1983.
Morrissey, Steven, *James Dean Is Not Dead*, Manchester, 1983.
Dalton, David, and Ron Cayen, *James Dean: American Icon*, London, 1984.

James Dean

Beath, Warren Newton, *The Death of James Dean*, London, 1986.
Hoskyns, Barney, *James Dean: Shooting Star*, London, 1989.
St. Michael, Mick, *James Dean in His Own Words*, London, 1989.
Dean, D., *James Dean: Behind the Scenes*, Secaucus, New Jersey, 1990.
Parker, John, *Five for Hollywood*, Secaucus, New Jersey, 1991.
Riese, Randall, *The Unabridged James Dean: His Life and Legacy from A to Z*, Chicago, 1991.
Hyams, Joe, *James Dean: Little Boy Lost*, New York, 1992.
McCann, Graham, *Rebel Males: Clift, Brando, and Dean*, New Brunswick, New Jersey, 1993.
Alexander, Paul, *Boulevard of Broken Dreams: The Life, Times, and Legend of James Dean*, New York, 1994.
Schroeder, Alan, *James Dean*, New York, 1994.
Holley, Val, *James Dean: The Biography*, New York, 1995.
Martinetti, Ronald, *The James Dean Story: A Myth-Shattering Biography of an Icon*, Secaucus, New Jersey, 1995.
Hofstede, David, *James Dean: A Bio-Bibliography*, Westport, Connecticut, 1996.
Spoto, Donald, *Rebel: The Life and Legend of James Dean*, New York, 1996.

On DEAN: articles—

"Portrait de l'acteur en jeune homme," in *Cahiers du Cinéma* (Paris), no. 66, 1956.
Cole, Clayton, "The Dean Myth," in *Films and Filming* (London), January 1957.
Bean, Robin, "Dean—Ten Years After," in *Films and Filming* (London), October 1965.
Truffaut, François, "James Dean est mort," in *L'Avant-Scène du Cinéma* (Paris), November 1975.
Thomson, David, "James Dean: Youth in Bold Rebellion," in *Close-Ups: The Movie Star Book*, edited by Danny Peary, New York, 1978.
Kael, Pauline, "Marlon Brando and James Dean," in *The Movie Star*, edited by Elisabeth Weis, New York, 1981.
Pettigrew, Terence, "James Dean, the Rebel Saint, 30 Years On," in *Films and Filming* (London), September 1985.
Ebert, Roger, "The Myth and Mystery of James Dean," in *Denver Post*, 30 September 1995.

On DEAN: films—

The James Dean Story, documentary, directed by Robert Altman and George W. George, 1957.
James Dean, the First American Teenager, documentary, directed by Ray Connolly, 1975.
James Dean, television movie, directed by Robert Butler, 1976.
9-30-55, feature film based on effect of Dean's death on American teens, directed by James Bridges, 1977.
James Dean: A Portrait, television documentary, directed by Gary Legon, 1996.

*   *   *

On 30 September 1955, a barely known, 24-year-old actor wove a Porsche Spyder through the Southern California countryside toward a Paso Robles road race. At the intersection of highways 466 and 41, James Dean collided with a commonplace Ford driven by a college student named Donald Turnupseed. Dean's only passenger, mechanic Rolf Wentherich, survived the crash—as did Turnupseed. Dean himself died at the wheel. Yet that crash began, rather than ended, a legend which each decade has affirmed to be anything but commonplace, and which may prove to be as immortal as any conferred and preserved by the cinema.

James Dean lives through the somewhat faded colors of three Warner Brothers features made during the last 15 months of his life—two of them released posthumously; one of them, *Giant*, was still in postproduction when its young star was killed, requiring director George Stevens to bring in actor Nick Adams, a friend of Dean's, to mimic Dean's voice for some last-minute looping of dialogue. His two stage productions are without record beyond publicity stills. His bit parts in films are brief and mute. His television kinescopes lack the resolution required to recall his subtle performance, that nuance of eye, hand, or mouth often more clearly preserved in the various still photos that have become such a commodity since his death.

It remains difficult to explain the why of an enduring appeal based upon but some two to three hundred minutes of screen time. We only know that he was singular, and we can only point to some aspects of that singularity. James Whitmore's Los Angeles workshops probably provided Dean's introduction to method acting. He received formal instruction in the Stanislavsky method from Lee Strasberg at the New York Actors Studio in 1952, while doing radio and television work. Actual influence is difficult to assess. Dean's performances have been compared to those of the young Montgomery Clift and to Brando's Strasberg-influenced style. But one may see an equally clear prototype in some of Gary Cooper's early work. Dean would have been about 12 years old when Cooper's portrayal of Lou Gehrig in *Pride of the Yankees* appeared in Indiana movie houses. To watch Cooper's performance with Dean in mind is striking. The often taut corners of the mouth, the awkward, shy gesture of hand-combing the hair, the hunched shoulders and downcast eye, the sometimes stumbling hesitation of speech—all seem to have been absorbed (and transformed) by Dean.

Dean's three major characters—Cal Trask in *East of Eden*, Jim Stark in *Rebel without a Cause*, and Jett Rink in *Giant*—are more than shy, of course. They are sly and clever, desperately trying to balance cynicism and idealism. They stumble in speech or gesture partly from adolescent awkwardness, but also from mature ambivalence, from a desire to love and communicate conflicting with an almost certain expectation that no one will understand.

Dean's personae are volatile amalgams of rage and compassion alternating within the barest fraction of a beat. This is neither Brando's inarticulate working man nor Cooper's kindly Mr. Deeds. His numerous biographers maintain that these archetypal emblems for troubled youth were actually an extension of the actor's own character—and this may have been the case. It may suggest why the legend of James Dean, the "Mutant King" as biographer David Dalton calls him, has not just endured from generation to generation but grown to proportions matched only by the legend of the late "King" himself, Elvis Presley.

In 1995 alone, the 30th anniversary of Dean's death, two new Dean books arrived on the shelves, with more announced for publication. One television movie, starring Stephen McHattie, has already been made about Dean's life, from a script by Dean's one-time roommate William Bast. At least two theatrical biopics have been on the dockets at major studios for years, just waiting for the right young new heartthrob, from Brad Pitt to Luke Perry, to accept the near-impossible challenge of playing the iconographic rebel without a cause—whose indelible image still haunts us, from television and movie screens everywhere.

—Edward S. Small, updated by John McCarty

DE HAVILLAND, Olivia

Nationality: American. **Born:** Olivia Mary de Havilland in Tokyo, Japan, to English parents, 1 July 1916; sister of the actress Joan Fontaine; became U.S. citizen, 1941. **Education:** Attended Notre Dame Convent, Belmont, California. **Family:** Married 1) Marcus

Goodrich, 1946 (divorced 1953), son: Benjamin; 2) Pierre Galante, 1955 (divorced 1979), daughter: Gisele. **Career:** 1933—stage debut in *Alice in Wonderland* with Saratoga Community Players; 1934—in Max Reinhardt's Los Angeles production of *A Midsummer Night's Dream*, and in film version, 1935; seven-year contract with Warners; 1943-45—made no films due to legal difficulties and contract disputes with Warners but performed with USO and on radio; 1945—freed from Warners' contract in landmark court decision; two-film deal with Paramount; 1951—New York stage debut in *Romeo and Juliet*; late 1950s—began living in France on semipermanent basis; late 1960s-1970s—occasional film and TV work (e.g., in mini-series *Roots: The Next Generation*, 1979, *North and South II*, 1986). **Awards:** Best Actress Academy Award, for *To Each His Own*, 1946; Best Actress, New York Film Critics, for *The Snake Pit*, 1948; Best Actress Academy Award, and Best Actress, New York Film Critics, for *The Heiress*, 1949; Best Actress, Venice Festival, for *The Snake Pit*, 1949. **Address:** B.P. 156, 75764 Paris Cedex 16, France.

Films as Actress:

1935 *Alibi Ike* (Enright) (as Dolly); *The Irish in Us* (Lloyd Bacon) (as Lucille Jackson); *A Midsummer Night's Dream* (Reinhardt and Dieterle) (as Hermia); *Captain Blood* (Curtiz) (as Arabella Bishop)

1936 *Anthony Adverse* (LeRoy) (as Angela Guisseppi); *The Charge of the Light Brigade* (Curtiz) (as Elsa Campbell); *A Day at Santa Anita* (short)

1937 *Call It a Day* (Mayo) (as Catherine Hilton); *The Great Garrick* (Whale) (as Germaine De Le Corbe); *It's Love I'm After* (Mayo) (as Marcia West)

1938 *Gold Is Where You Find It* (Curtiz) (as Serena Ferris); ***The Adventures of Robin Hood*** (Curtiz and Keighley) (as Maid Marian); *Four's a Crowd* (Curtiz) (as Lorri Dillingwell); *Hard to Get* (Enright) (as Margaret Richards)

1939 *Wings of the Navy* (Lloyd Bacon) (as Irene Dale); *Dodge City* (Curtiz) (as Abbie Irving); *The Private Lives of Elizabeth and Essex* (Curtiz) (as Lady Penelope Gray); ***Gone with the Wind*** (Fleming—additional scenes directed by Cukor, Wood, Menzies, and David O. Selznick) (as Melanie Hamilton)

1940 *Raffles* (Wood) (as Gwen); *My Love Came Back* (Bernhardt) (as Amelia Cullen); *Santa Fe Trail* (Curtiz) (as Kit Carson Halliday)

1941 *The Strawberry Blonde* (Walsh) (as Amy Lind); *Hold Back the Dawn* (Leisen) (as Emmy Brown); *They Died with Their Boots On* (Walsh) (as Elizabeth Brown Custer)

1942 *The Male Animal* (Nugent) (as Ellen Turner); *In This Our Life* (Huston) (as Roy Timberlake)

1943 *Thank Your Lucky Stars* (David Butler) (as herself); *Princess O'Rourke* (Krasna) (as Maria); *Government Girl* (Dudley Nichols) (as Smokey)

1946 *The Well-Groomed Bride* (Lanfield) (as Margie); *To Each His Own* (Leisen) (as Josephine Norris); *Devotion* (Bernhardt) (as Charlotte Brontë); *The Dark Mirror* (Siodmak) (as Terry Collins/Ruth Collins)

1948 *The Snake Pit* (Litvak) (as Virginia Cunningham)

1949 *The Heiress* (Wyler) (as Catherine Sloper)

1952 *My Cousin Rachel* (Koster) (as Rachel)

1955 *That Lady* (Terence Young) (as Ana de Mendoza); *Not as a Stranger* (Kramer) (as Kristina Hedvigson)

1956 *The Ambassador's Daughter* (Krasna) (as Joan)

1958 *The Proud Rebel* (Curtiz) (as Linnett Moore)

1959 *Libel* (Asquith) (as Lady Maggie Loddon)

1962 *Light in the Piazza* (Guy Green) (as Margaret Johnson)

1964 *Lady in a Cage* (Grauman) (as Mrs. Hilyard); *Hush . . . Hush, Sweet Charlotte* (Aldrich) (as Miriam Deering)

1970 *The Adventurers* (Lewis Gilbert) (as Deborah Hadley)

1972 *The Screaming Woman* (Smight—for TV) (as Laura Wynant); *Pope Joan* (Michael Anderson) (as Mother Superior)

1977 *Airport '77* (Jameson) (as Emily Livingston); *Behind the Iron Mask (The Fifth Musketeer)* (Annakin) (as Queen Anne)

1978 *The Swarm* (Irwin Allen) (as Maureen)

1982 *Murder Is Easy* (Whatham—for TV) (as Honoria Waynflete); *The Royal Romance of Charles and Diana* (Levin—for TV) (as the Queen Mother)

1986 *Anastasia: The Mystery of Anna* (Chomsky—for TV) (as Dowager Emperess Maria)

1988 *The Woman He Loved* (Jarrott—for TV) (as Bessie Merryman)

Publications

By DE HAVILLAND: book—

Every Frenchman Has One, New York, 1962.

By DE HAVILLAND: articles—

"Dream That Never Died," in *Look* (New York), 12 December 1967.
"Olivia de Havilland Seminar," interview in *Dialogue on Film* (Beverly Hills), December 1974.
Interview in *Classic Images* (Indiana, Pennsylvania), March 1983.

On DE HAVILLAND: books—

Parish, James, and Don Stanke, *The Leading Ladies*, New Rochelle, New York, 1971.
Memo from: David O. Selznick, edited by Rudy Behlmer, New York, 1972.
Flamini, Roland, *Scarlett, Rhett, and a Cast of Thousands: The Filming of* Gone with the Wind, New York, 1975.
Thomas, Tony, *The Films of Olivia de Havilland*, Secaucus, New Jersey, 1983.
Higham, Charles, *Sisters: The Story of Olivia de Havilland and Joan Fontaine*, New York, 1984.

On DE HAVILLAND: articles—

Doyle, Neil, "Olivia de Havilland," in *Films in Review* (New York), February 1962; also April 1982.
Current Biography 1966, New York, 1966.
Shipman, David, in *The Great Movie Stars: The Golden Years*, rev. ed., London, 1979.
Ciné Revue (Paris), 27 August 1981.
Niderost, E., "Olivia de Havilland—The Bright-Eyed Ingenue Who Became a Star," in *Classic Images*, (Muscatine, Iowa) November 1992.

*   *   *

Almost immediately after making her screen debut, Olivia de Havilland was established as a popular actress through her presence in *Captain Blood*. The film's pairing of de Havilland and Errol Flynn was a great success, and Warner Brothers, during the next six years, reteamed the two in seven films. Although these films gave de Havilland a leading lady status, her function was essentially that of supporting and adoring the male. The function was carried over into *Gone with the Wind*, yet this key role gave her at last an opportunity to display her potential as a skillful actress. The assignment was particularly chal-

Olivia de Havilland

lenging in that Melanie, in contrast to Scarlett O'Hara, is bland and two-dimensional; yet, arguably, de Havilland's performance is superior to Vivien Leigh's in conception, modulation, and emotional resonance, convincingly communicating the strength beneath Melanie's shy and timid outer self.

The characterization, in addition to establishing de Havilland as a major actress, also, to an extent, gave shape to her 1940s screen persona. During the decade, two of de Havilland's most highly regarded performances are built around seemingly simple women who, unexpectedly, prove to be compelling presences when engaged in emotional interaction. Structurally, both *Hold Back the Dawn* and *The Heiress* are centered on narratives in which physically plain and unimaginative women are courted by handsome men who have no interest in what they have to offer—sincerity and virtuousness. De Havilland imparts a forcefulness to the characterizations by making the women self-conscious about their ordinariness so that the characters' emotional vulnerability become a crucial factor in these portrayals. In *The Heiress* in particular, the effectiveness of de Havilland's performance hinges on the emotional exploitation she willingly submits to and her ultimate response to it.

Essentially, the same persona is the basis of de Havilland's characterization in the less caustic *To Each His Own* in which she enacts various stages in the life of a woman who must deny herself the fulfillment of motherhood because her child was illegitimate. While the film's flashbacks allow de Havilland a greater range (glamour, sophistication) than the above-mentioned films, in the present-day sequences she has a severe physical plainness and projects an intense emotionalism which is held in check through sheer will power.

During the 1940s de Havilland gave two other notable performances in films that can be seen as functioning as implicit commentary on her filmic persona. In *The Dark Mirror* de Havilland plays identical twins who are opposing embodiments of "good" and "evil." The film, in effect, splits the character she plays to expose the end result of the oppressions and repressions the de Havilland persona, in part, represents. In the follow-up film, *The Snake Pit*, she is cast as another ordinary woman who undergoes a mental breakdown because she is not able to fully express her identity.

At the height of her powers, de Havilland seemed to have lost the fighting spirit that enabled her to bring the dreaded seven-year studio contract system to its knees, a court battle previously lost by the redoubtable Bette Davis. Prissily concerned with her star image like Melanie guarding Southern traditions in *Gone with the Wind*, de Havilland rejected the chance to play Blanche Dubois. Considering her icy brilliance in *Snake Pit*, it is interesting to contemplate what dimensions she would have brought to the most challenging role ever written for an actress. Throughout the fifties, she tackled Broadway to a lukewarm reception (*Romeo and Juliet*, *Candida*) and worked less frequently on-screen—hypnotically ambiguous in *My Cousin Rachel* and authoritatively embodying pioneer spirit in *Proud Rebel*, but ludicrously sporting an eye patch and saccharine airs for the period costumer, *That Lady*, and ladling on a thick Swedish meatball accent for *Not as a Stranger*. Almost all the rest is disappointing with de Havilland making great lady appearances rather than flexing her acting muscles (on televised awards ceremonies, she gushes as if impressed with her own place in film history). If she mainly played it safe as part of all-star disaster ensembles (*The Swarm*, *Airport '77*), her latter-day career is marked with two striking returns to form. In an ABC-TV Stage 67 production of Katherine Anne Porter's *Noon Wine*, de Havilland is gravely beautiful as a careworn Texas landowner. Although she had to be coaxed to star after Bette Davis drove rival Joan Crawford to nervous illness while shooting *Hush . . . Hush, Sweet Charlotte*, de Havilland is superb in that juicy Southern Gothic hysteria. Counterbalancing Davis's campy splendor, she builds suspense by undermining her pristine screen image for a change. Whereas Crawford would have telegraphed her duplicity, de Havilland sneaks up on the audience with betrayal up her sleeve. This film demonstrates that de Havilland could have pursued acting in a more complex vein if she had not preferred typecasting herself as the good twin from *The Dark Mirror*.

—Richard Lippe, updated by Robert Pardi

DELON, Alain

Nationality: French. **Born:** Sceaux, 8 November 1935 (or 1936). **Education:** Attended a Catholic boarding school in Bagneux (expelled); St. Nicholas d'Issy and St. Nicholas d'Igny. **Military Service:** French Marines, 1952-53: parachutist in Indochina. **Family:** Married 1) the actress Nathalie Barthelemy (born Canovas), 1964 (divorced 1969), one son; 2) Rosalie, son: Alain-Fabien, daughter: Anouchka. **Career:** Mid-1950s—worked at various odd jobs, including waiter, salesman, and porter in Les Halles market; 1957—film debut in Yves Allégret's *Quand la femme s'en mêle*; declined contract with Selznick studios; 1960—international critical recognition for role in Visconti's *Rocco e i suoi fratelli*; 1961—stage role in *Tis Pity She's a Whore*, directed by Visconti, Paris; 1964—formed film company Delbeau Productions; produced short film *Journal d'un combat* directed by Guy Gilles; 1968—involved in murder, drug, and sex scandal that indirectly implicated major politicians and show business personalities; eventually cleared of charges; late 1960s—formed film company Adel-Film; 1970—began producing feature films; 1981—directed first film *Pour la peau d'un flic*; 1988—in TV mini-series *Cinema*. **Address:** c/o Leda Productions, 4 rue Chambiges, Paris 75800, France.

Films as Actor:

1957 *Quand la femme s'en mêle* (*Send a Woman When the Devil Fails*; *When the Woman Gets Confused*) (Yves Allégret) (as Jo)
1958 *Sois belle et tais-toi* (*Blonde for Danger*; *Just Another Pretty Face*) (Marc Allégret); *Christine* (Gaspard-Huit) (as Franz)
1959 *Faibles femmes* (*Women Are Weak*; *Three Murderesses*) (Boisrand) (as Julien); *Le Chemin des écoliers* (Boisrand) (as Antoine Michaud); *Plein soleil* (*Purple Noon*; *Lust for Evil*) (Clément) (as Tom Ripley)
1960 *Rocco e i suoi fratelli* (*Rocco and His Brothers*; *Rocco et ses freres*) (Visconti) (as Rocco Parondi)
1961 *Che gioia vivere* (*Quelle joie de vivre*) (Clément) (as Ulysse Cecconato); "Agnès Bernauer" ep. of *Amours célèbres* (Boisrand)
1962 *L'eclisse* (*The Eclipse*) (Antonioni) (as Piero); "L'Inceste" ep. of *Le Diable et les dix commandements* (*The Devil and the Ten Commandments*) (Duvivier) (as Pierre Messager); *Mélodie en sous-sol* (*The Big Snatch*; *Any Number Can Play*; *Big Grab*) (Verneuil); *Carambolages* (Bluwal)
1963 *Il gattopardo* (*The Leopard*) (Visconti) (as Tancredi); *La Tulipe noire* (*The Black Tulip*) (Christian-Jaque) (as Julien de Saint-Preux)
1964 *Les Félins* (*Joy House*; *The Love Cage*) (Clément) (as Marc); *L'Insoumis* (Cavalier) (as Thomas); 2nd ep. of *The Yellow Rolls-Royce* (Asquith) (as Stefano); *L'Amour à la mer* (Gilles)
1965 *Once a Thief* (Ralph Nelson) (as Eddie Pedak)
1966 *Lost Command* (*Not for Honor and Glory*) (Robson) (as Capt. Philippe Escavier); *Paris brûle-t-il?* (*Is Paris Burning?*) (Clément) (as Jacques Chaban-Delmas); *Texas across the River* (Michael Gordon) (as Don Andrea Baldasar)

315

1967 *Les Aventuriers* (*The Last Adventure*) (Enrico) (as Manu); *Le Samourai* (*The Godson*) (Melville) (as Jef Costello); *Diaboliquement vôtre* (*Diabolically Yours*) (Duvivier) (as Pierre)

1968 "William Wilson" ep. of *Histoires extraordinaires* (*Tales of Mystery*; *Spirits of the Dead*) (Malle) (as Wilson); *The Girl on a Motorcycle* (*La Motocyclette*; *Naked under Leather*) (Cardiff) (as Daniel); *Adieu l'ami* (*Farewell Friend*; *Honor among Thieves*) (Herman) (as Dino Barran); *La Piscine* (*The Sinners*) (Deray); *Le Clan des Siciliens* (*The Sicilian Clan*) (Verneuil) (as Roger Sartet)

1969 *Jeff* (Herman); *Le Cercle rouge* (Melville); *Madly* (*The Love Mates*) (Kahane)

1970 *Borsalino* (Deray) (as Roch Siffredi, + pr)

1971 *Doucement les basses!* (Deray); *Fantasia chez les ploucs* (Pirès); *Soleil rouge* (*Red Sun*) (Terence Young) (as Gauche); *La veuve Couderc* (Granier-Deferre)

1972 *L'Assassinat de Trotsky* (*The Assassination of Trotsky*) (Losey) (as Frank Jacson); *Un flic* (*Dirty Money*; *A Cop*) (Melville) (as Coleman); *La prima notte di quiete* (*Le Professeur*) (Zurlini); *Traitement du choc* (*Shock Treatment*) (Jessu) (as Devilers); *Il était une fois un flic* (Lautner); *Big Guns* (*No Way Out*; *Tony Arzenta*) (Tessari)

1973 *Scorpio* (Winner) (as Laurier); *Deux hommes dans la ville* (*Two Men in Town*; *Two against the City*) (Giovanni) (as Gino, + pr); *Les Granges brûlées* (Chapot)

1974 *La Race des "Seigneurs"* (Granier-Deferre); *Les Seins de glace* (Lautner); *Borsalino & Co.* (Deray) (as Roch Siffredi, + pr)

1975 *Flic Story* (Deray) (as Roger Borniche, + pr); *Zorro* (Tessari); *Le Gitan* (Giovanni) (title role, + co-pr)

1976 *Mr. Klein* (Losey) (title role, + pr); *Comme un boomerang* (Giovanni) (+ co-sc); *Le Gang* (Deray)

1977 *America at the Movies* (as narrator); *L'Homme presse* (Molinaro); *Armageddon* (Jessua); *Mort d'un pourri* (Lautner); *Attention, les enfants regardent* (*Attention, the Kids Are Watching*) (Leroy) (as Man)

1978 *Indian Summer* (Zurlini) (as Professor)

1979 *Le Toubib* (*The Medic*) (Granier-Deferre); *The Concorde—Airport '79* (*Airport '80—The Concorde*) (Rich) (as Metrand); *Teheran Incident* (*Teheran 1943*; *The Eliminator*) (Alov and Naumov)

1980 *Trois Hommes à abattre* (*Three Men to Destroy*) (Deray) (as Michel Gerfaut)

1982 *Le Choc* (*The Shock*) (Davis)

1984 *Swann in Love* (*Un Amour de Swann*) (Schlöndorff) (as Baron De Charlus)

1985 *Notre histoire* (*Our Story*) (Blier); *Parole de flic* (Pinheiro) (as Daniel Pratt, + co-sc)

1986 *Le Passage* (Manzor) (as Jean Diaz, + co-pr)

1988 *Ne Reveillez pas un flic qui dort* (Pinheiro) (as Eugene Grindel, + co-sc)

1990 *Nouvelle Vague* (Godard) (as Roger Lennox/Richard Lennox); *Dancing Machine* (Behat) (as Alan Wolf)

1992 *Le Retour de Casanova* (*Casanova's Return*) (Niermans) (title role, + co-exec pr); *Un Crime* (Deray)

1993 *L'ours en Peluche* (*The Teddy Bear*) (Deray) (as Jean Riviere)

1995 *Les Cent et une Nuits* (*A Hundred and One Nights*) (Varda) (as Actor for a Day)

Films as Producer:

1964 *Journal d'un combat* (Gilles—short)
1970 *Sortie de secours* (Kahane)

Films as Actor and Director:

1970 *Pour la peau d'un flic* (*For a Cop's Hide*; *Whirlpool*)
1982 *Le Battant* (*The Cache*) (as Darnay, + co-sc)

Publications

By DELON: articles—

"Creating with a Passion," interview in *Films and Filming* (London), June 1970.
Interview in *Cinéma Français* (Paris), October 1980.
Interviews in *Ciné Revue* (Paris), 27 August 1981 and 27 January 1983.

On DELON: books—

Warfield, Nancy, *Alain Delon and Borsalino; An Essay on the Actor and the Film*, New York, 1973.
Rode, Henri, *Alain Delon*, Paris, 1977.
Alain Delon: Films/Portraits, Paris, 1979.
Zana, Jean-Claude, *Alain Delon*, Paris, 1981.
Barbier, Philippe, *Alain Delon*, Paris, 1983.
Zondergeld, Rein A., *Alain Delon: seine Filme, sein Leben*, Munich, 1984.
Dazat, Olivier, *Alain Delon*, Paris, 1988.

On DELON: articles—

Current Biography 1964, New York, 1964.
Bean, R., "Reaching for the World," in *Films and Filming* (London), February 1965.
Ecran (Paris), January 1978.
Film Français (Paris), 7 January 1983.
"Dossier: Alain Delon," in *Cinématographe* (Paris), September/October 1984.

* * *

Alain Delon is, with Jean-Paul Belmondo, the most popular male star of the contemporary French film. Without previous professional preparation, he came to embody the young, energetic, often morally corrupted man. With his attractive appearance, he was also predestined to play tender lovers and romantic heroes, and for many he was in the beginning a French embodiment of the type created in America by James Dean.

His first outstanding success came with the role of the parasite Tom Ripley in Clément's *Plein soleil*. Delon presented a psychological portrait of a murderous young cynic who attempts to take on the identity of his victim. A totally different role was offered him by Visconti in *Rocco e i suoi fratelli*. In this film, Delon plays the devoted Rocco, who accepts the greatest sacrifices to save his characterless brother Simon. After several other films in Italy, he returned to the criminal genre, with Jean Gabin, in *Melodie en sous-sol* (Verneuil). This work, a classic example of the genre, was distinguished not only by a soundly worked-out screenplay, but also by the careful production and the excellent performances of both Delon and Gabin. Several other films about gangsters or thieves followed, including a historical bandit in *La Tulipe noire* (Christian-Jaque).

Since 1968, Delon has often participated in his films as a producer. Though he has continued to make crime and thriller films, he has also undoubtedly attempted to extend his range. Two interesting psychological roles—as a judge in *Les Granges brulées* (Chapot) and as the self-assured doctor in a luxurious sanatorium in *Traitement du choc* (Jessu)—were followed by his role in Joseph Losey's pretentious re-

Alain Delon in *Plein soleil*

construction of the murder of the revolutionary in exile, *The Assassination of Trotsky*. In *Mr. Klein* he took on the ambitious role of an Aryan merchant who throws in his lot with the Jews in occupied France. A serious attempt to consider the imperfect judicial system of contemporary society is made in the film *Deux hommes dans la ville*, in which he plays a thief who tries in vain to participate in ordinary life after his release from prison. His most unusual role has been in Schlöndorff's *Un Amour de Swann*, based on the Proust novel, continued evidence of his genuine acting talent and attempts to seek new expressive opportunities.

—Karel Tabery

DEL RIO, Dolores

Nationality: Mexican. **Born:** Lolita Dolores Martínez Asunsolo López Negrette in Durango, 3 August 1905. **Education:** Convent of St. Joseph, Mexico City. **Family:** Married 1) Jaime Del Rio, 1920 (died 1928); 2) the designer Cedric Gibbons, 1930 or 1932 (divorced 1941); 3) Lewis Riley, 1959. **Career:** 1925—personal contract with the director Edwin Carewe; film debut in *Joanna*; 1926—selected as WAMPAS (Western Association of Motion Picture Advertisers) baby star; 1928—critical and public recognition for role in *Ramona*; worked with United Artists, 1929-31, RKO, 1932-33, Warners, 1934-36, Columbia, 1937, and 20th Century-Fox, 1937-38; 1943—left Hollywood to seek more rewarding career in Mexico; in *Flor Silvestre*, first of several successful films for director Emilio Fernández. **Awards:** Ariele Awards for Best Actress, for *Las abandonados*, 1944, *Doña Perfecta*, 1951, and *The Boy and the Fog*, 1953; Special Ariele Award, 1974. **Died:** In Newport Beach, California, 11 April 1983.

Films as Actress:

1925   *Joanna* (Carewe) (as Carlotta de Silva)
1926   *High Steppers* (Carewe) (as Evelyn Iffield); *Pals First* (Carewe) (as Jeanne Lamont); *The Whole Town's Talking* (Edward Laemmle) (as Rita Renault); *What Price Glory?* (Walsh) (as Charmaine de la Cognac)
1927   *Resurrection* (Carewe) (as Katusha Maslova); *The Loves of Carmen* (Walsh) (as Carmen)
1928   *The Gateway of the Moon* (Wray) (as Chela "Toni"); *The Trail of '98* (Brown) (as Berna); *Ramona* (Carewe) (title role); *The Red Dance* (Walsh) (as Tasia); *No Other Woman* (Tellegen) (as Carmelita Desano); *Revenge* (Carewe) (as Rascha)
1929   *Evangeline* (Carewe) (title role)
1930   *The Bad One* (Fitzmaurice) (as Lita)
1932   *Girl of the Rio* (Brenon) (as Dolores); *Bird of Paradise* (King Vidor) (as Luana)
1933   *Flying Down to Rio* (Freeland) (as Belinha de Rezende)
1934   *Hollywood on Parade, No. 13* (short); *Wonder Bar* (Lloyd Bacon) (as Inez); *Madame DuBarry* (Dieterle) (title role)
1935   *A Trip thru a Hollywood Studio* (short); *In Caliente* (Lloyd Bacon) (as Rita Gomez); *I Live for Love* (Berkeley) (as Donna Alvares)
1936   *The Widow from Monte Carlo* (Collins) (as Inez); *Accused* (Freeland) (as Gaby Seymour)
1937   *Devil's Playground* (Kenton) (as Carmen); *Ali Baba Goes to Town* (David Butler) (as herself); *Lancer Spy* (Ratoff) (as Dolores Daria)
1938   *International Settlement* (Forde) (as Leonore)

1940   *The Man from Dakota* (Fenton) (as Eugenia)
1942   *Journey into Fear* (Norman Foster and Welles) (as Josette Martel)
1943   *Flor Silvestre* (Fernández) (as Esperanza)
1944   ***María Candelaria*** (*Xochimilco*; *Portrait of Maria*) (Fernández) (title role); *Bugambilia* (Fernández) (as Amalia de los Robles); *Las abandonados* (Fernández) (as Margarita Perez)
1945   *La selva de fuego* (de Fuentes)
1946   *Lo otra* (Gavaldón) (as Magdalena Mendez/María Mendez)
1947   *The Fugitive* (John Ford) (as María Dolores)
1948   *Historia de una mala mujer* (Saslavsky)
1949   *La malquerida* (Fernández) (as Raimunda)
1950   *La casa chica* (Gavaldón) (as Amalia)
1951   *Deseada* (Gavaldón); *Doña Perfecta* (Galindo) (as Perfecta)
1953   *Reportaje* (Fernández) (as María Enriqueta); *El nino y la niebla* (*The Boy and the Fog*) (Gavaldón) (as Marta)
1954   *Señora Ama* (Bracho) (as Dominica)
1957   *Torero* (Velo)
1958   *A donde van nuestros hijos* (*Media tono*) (Alazraki) (as Rosa); *La cucaracha* (*The Soldiers of Pancho Villa*; *The Bandit*) (Rodríguez) (as Chabela)
1960   *Flaming Star* (Siegel) (as Neddy Burton); *El pecado de una madre* (Blake)
1964   *Cheyenne Autumn* (John Ford) (as Spanish woman)
1966   *La dama del Alba* (Beleta); *Casa de mujeres* (Soler)
1967   *C'era una volta* (*More than a Miracle*; *Cinderella, Italian Style*; *Happily Ever After*) (Rosi) (as Princess Mother); *Rio Blanco* (Gavaldón)
1978   *The Children of Sanchez* (Bartlett)

Publications

By DEL RIO: article—

"Achieving Stardom," in *Breaking into the Movies*, edited by Charles Reed, New York, 1927.

On DEL RIO: books—

Nevares, Beatrice, *The Mexican Cinema Interviews*, 1976.
Bodeen, DeWitt, *From Hollywood: The Careers of 15 Great American Stars*, South Brunswick, New Jersey, 1976.
Parish, James, with Gregory Mank and Don Stanke, *The Hollywood Beauties*, New York, 1978.
Woll, Allen L., *The Films of Dolores Del Rio*, New York, 1978.
Mora, Carl J., *Mexican Cinema: Reflections of a Society: 1896-1980*, Berkeley, 1982.
Monsivais, Carlos, *Dolores Del Rio*, Huelva, Spain, 1983.

On DEL RIO: articles—

Askenazy, Natalia, "Two Kinds of Mexican Movies," in *Films in Review* (New York), May 1951.
Manuel, Michel, "Mexican Cinema: A Panoramic View," in *Film Quarterly* (Berkeley), Summer 1965.
Bodeen, DeWitt, "Dolores Del Rio," in *Films in Review* (New York), May 1967.
Gómez-Sicre, J., "Dolores Del Rio," in *Américas*, November 1967.
Braun, Eric, "Queen of Mexico," in *Films and Filming* (London), July 1972.
Shipman, David, *The Great Movie Stars: The Golden Years*, rev. ed., 1979.
Obituary in *New York Times*, 13 April 1983.
Obituary in *Variety* (New York), 13 April 1983.

Obituary, in *Cinéma* (Paris) September 1983.
The Annual Obituary 1983, Chicago, 1984.

* * *

Dolores Del Rio, born into an aristocratic Mexican family, was the daughter of a banker, and also second cousin to the actor Ramon Novarro. In 1925 she came to the United States to begin an acting career that continued into the 1970s. She worked in American and Mexican films (she won four Arieles, Mexico's equivalent to the Oscar), and international productions, with such major directors as Edwin Carewe (who discovered her at a Mexico City tea party, brought her to Hollywood, and was instrumental in helping her career), Busby Berkeley, Clarence Brown, Emilio Fernández, Roberto Gavaldón, Francesco Rosi, Don Siegel, Raoul Walsh, and Orson Welles.

Among the reasons for her remarkable staying power were her skill in creating believable characters and a beauty that transcended age—she was as lovely at 65 as she had been at 25. Most importantly, she never allowed herself to be typed as the sexy Mexican spitfire who fractures the English language. She brought dignity to both leading and character parts, portraying with ease women of all social classes.

Silent films had allowed Del Rio great flexibility in the roles she could play, with nationalities ranging from American Indian to Russian, Acadian, Brazilian, French, Spanish, and, of course, Mexican. In sound films she was more often cast as a woman of Mexican or Spanish descent because of her accent. Some of her most memorable roles in American films were as Charmaine in the World War I classic *What Price Glory?,* the Acadian woman who searches the bayous of Louisiana for her lost love in *Evangeline*, the stunning Brazilian heiress in *Flying Down to Rio*, a beautiful Polynesian native in *Bird of Paradise*, the title role in *Madame Du Barry*, the dancer Josette in *Journey into Fear*, María Dolores in *The Fugitive*, and a Kiowa Indian married to a white settler in *Flaming Star*.

The first American phase of her career lasted from Edwin Carewe's *Joanna* in 1925 to Orson Welles's 1942 *Journey into Fear*, after which she returned to Mexico. She may have seen new opportunities in her native land: by brilliantly assembling a top director, Emilio Fernández, a top cinematographer, Gabriel Figueroa, and a top leading actor, Pedro Armendáriz, Del Rio shortly became one of Mexico's leading box-office attractions. She continued to appear occasionally in some American films and television programs (for example, John Ford's *Cheyenne Autumn* and an episode of *Marcus Welby, M.D.*). By the 1970s she was devoting less time to performing and more to charity work in Mexico.

In her article "Achieving Stardom" in *Breaking into the Movies*, Del Rio wrote, "my conception of a great success is . . . being capable of reflecting and impersonating all the beauty and cleverness of every different type of woman." In her long and varied career, she conveyed both the inner and outer beauty of her characters, and she did so with authenticity and dignity.

—H. Wayne Schuth

DENEUVE, Cathérine

Nationality: French. **Born:** Cathérine Dorléac in Paris, 22 October 1943; sister of the actress Françoise Dorléac. **Education:** Attended École Lamazou and Lycée La Fontaine. **Family:** Married the photographer David Bailey, 1965 (divorced 1970); son with the director Roger Vadim; daughter with the actor Marcello Mastroianni: the actress Chiara Mastroianni. **Career:** 1956—film debut in bit role in *Les Collégiennes*; 1960—began personal and professional relationship with director Roger Vadim; 1964—in Polanski's *Repulsion*, first role in English-language film; 1969—American film debut in Stuart Rosenberg's *The April Fools*; 1971—formed production company Films de la Citrouille. **Awards:** César Award (France), Best Actress, for *Indochine*, 1992. **Address:** c/o Place St. Sulpice 76, Rue Bonaparte, Paris 75006, France.

Films as Actress:

1956   *Les Collégiennes* (*The Twilight Girls*) (Hunebelle)

1959   *Les Petits Chats* (*Wild Roots of Love*) (Villa)

1960   *Les Portes claquent* (*The Doors Slam*) (Poitrenaud and Fermaud); *L'Homme à femmes* (Cornu)

1961   "Sophie" ep. of *Les Parisiennes* (*Tales of Paris*; *Of Beds and Broads*) (Marc Allégret) (as Sophie)

1962   *. . . et Satan conduit le bal* (*Satan Leads the Dance*) (Dabat); *Le Vice et la vertu* (*Vice and Virtue*) (Vadim) (as Justine); *Vacances portugaises* (Kast)

1964   "L'Homme qui vendit la tour Eiffel" ("Paris") ep. of *Les Plus Belles Escroqueries du monde* (*The Beautiful Swindlers*; *World's Greatest Swindlers*) (Chabrol); *Les Parapluies de Cherbourg* (*The Umbrellas of Cherbourg*) (Demy) (as Genevieve Emery); *La Chasse à l'homme* (*The Gentle Art of Seduction*; *Male Hunt*) (Molinaro) (as Denise); *Un Monsieur de compagnie* (*Male Companion*) (de Broca) (as Isabelle); *La costanza della ragione* (*Avec amour et avec rage*) (Campanile); **Repulsion** (Polanski) (as Carol Ledoux)

1965   *Le Chant du monde* (Camus); "Der Somnabule" ep. of *Das Liebeskarussell* (*Who Wants to Sleep?*) (Thiele)

1966   *Les Créatures* (*Varelserna*) (Varda) (as Mylene); *La Vie de Château* (*A Matter of Resistance*) (Rappeneau) (as Marie)

1967   **Belle de jour** (Luis Buñuel) (as Severine Sevigny); *Les Demoiselles de Rochefort* (*The Young Girls of Rochefort*) (Demy) (as Delphine Garnier)

1968   *Benjamin ou Les mémoires d'un puceau* (*Benjamin*; *The Diary of an Innocent Boy*) (Deville) (as Anne de Clecy); *Manon 70* (Aurel) (title role); *La Chamade* (Cavalier); *Mayerling* (Terence Young) (as Baroness Maria Vetscra)

1969   *The April Fools* (Rosenberg) (as Cathérine Gunther); *La Sirène du Mississippi* (*Mississippi Mermaid*) (Truffaut) (as Julie Roussel/Marion); *Tout peut arriver* (*Don't Be Blue*) (Labro)

1970   *Tristana* (Luis Buñuel) (title role); *Peau d'âne* (*The Magic Donkey*; *Donkey Skin*) (Demy) (title role/Blue Queen); *Henri Langlois* (Hershon and Guerra)

1971   *Ça n'arrive qu'aux autres* (*It Only Happens to Others*) (Trintignant) (as Cathérine)

1972   *La cagna* (*Liza*) (Ferreri) (as Liza); *Un flic* (*Dirty Money*; *A Cop*) (Melville) (as Cathy)

1973   *L'Evènement le plus important depuis que l'homme a marché sur la lune* (*The Slightly Pregnant Man*) (Demy); *Touche pas à la femme blanche* (*Don't Touch White Women*) (Ferreri) (as Marie-Elene)

1974   *Fatti di gente perbene* (*La Grande Bourgeoise*; *The Murri Affair*; *Drama of the Rich*) (Bolognini) (as Linda Murri); *La Femme aux bottes rouges* (*The Lady with the Red Boots*; *The Woman with the Red Boots*) (Juan Buñuel) (as Françoise); *Zig-zag* (Szabó) (as Marie)

1975   *L'Agression* (*Act of Aggression*) (Pirès); *Hustle* (Aldrich) (as Nicole Britton); *Le Sauvage* (*Lovers Like Us*; *The Savage*) (Rappeneau) (as Nelly)

Cathérine Deneuve in *Tristana*

1976   *Si c'était à refaire* (*Second Chance*) (Lelouch) (as Cathérine); *Anima persa* (*Lost Soul; The Forbidden Room*) (Risi)

1977   *March or Die* (Richards) (as Simone Picard); *Coup de foudre* (Enrico); *Il Casotto* (*The Beach Hut*) (Citti) (as woman in the dream)

1978   *L'Argent des autres* (*Dirty Money*) (de Chalonge); *Si je suis comme ça, c'est la faute de papa* (*When I Was a Kid, I Didn't Dare*); *Ecoute voir . . .* (*Look See . . .*) (Santiago) (as Alphanol)

1979   *Ils sont grands ces petits* (*These Kids Are Grown-ups*) (Santoni) (as Louise); *À Nous deux* (*Adventure for Two*) (Lelouch)

1980   *Courage, fuyons* (Robert) (as Eva); *Le Dernier Métro* (*The Last Metro*) (Truffaut) (as Marion Steiner); *Je vous aime* (*I Love All of You*) (Berri); *Abattre*

1981   *Le Choix des Armes* (*Choice of Arms*) (Corneau) (as Nicole Durieux); *A Second Chance* (Lelouch) (as Cathérine Berger); *Reporters* (Depardon)

1982   *Le Choc* (*The Shock*) (Robin Davis); *Hotel des Amériques* (*Hotel of the Americas*) (Téchiné) (as Hélène)

1983   *L'Africain* (*The African*) (de Broca) (as Charlotte); *Fort Saganne* (Corneau) (as Louise); *Le Bon Plaisir* (Girod) (as Clair Despres)

1984   *The Hunger* (Tony Scott) (as Miriam); *Paroles et musique* (*Love Songs*) (Chouraqui) (as Margaux)

1985   *Speriamo che sia femmina* (*Let's Hope It's a Girl*) (Monicelli) (as Aunt Claudia)

1986   *Le Lieu du crime* (*The Scene of the Crime*) (Téchiné) (as Lili)

1987   *Agent Trouble* (Mocky) (as Amanda Weber)

1988   *Drole d'endroit pour une rencontre* (*A Strange Place to Meet*) (Dupeyron) (as France, + pr); *Fréquence meurtre* (Rappeneau) (as Jeanne Quester)

1989   *Terres jaunes* (Wargnier); *Helmut Newton: Frames from the Edge* (doc) (as herself)

1990   *Fleur de Rubis* (Mocky)

1991   *La Reine Blanche* (Hubert) (as Liliane Ripoche)

1992   *Indochine* (Wargnier) (as Eliane Devries); *Contre l'oubli* (*Against Oblivion*) (Akerman and others) (as herself)

1993   *Ma Saison Préférée* (*My Perfect Season*) (Téchiné) (as Emilie); *Les Demoiselles ont eu 25 Ans* (*The Young Girls Turn 25*) (Varda—doc)

1994   *La Partie d'echecs* (*The Chess Game*) (Hanchar) (as Marquise); *Petits heures du matin*

1995   *Les Cent et une nuits* (*A Hundred and One Nights*) (Varda) (as Actor for a Day); *O Convento* (*The Convent*) (de Oliviera) (as Hélène)

1996   *L'Enfant de la nuit* (*The Child of the Night*) (Téchiné); *Place Vendome* (Nicole Garcia)

Publications

By DENEUVE: articles—

"Une Créature du Cinéma," interview with M. Most, in *Cinema* (Beverly Hills), no. 1, 1965.
Interview with Nadine Liber, in *Life* (New York), 24 January 1969.
"Cathérine Deneuve," interview with P. Carcassone, in *Cinématographe* (Paris), April 1977.
Interview with G. Haustrate and J.-P. Le Pavec, in *Cinéma* (Paris), July-August 1981.
"Les Jeux de l'instinct et du hasard," interview with M. Chevrie and D. Dubroux, in *Cahiers du Cinéma* (Paris), December 1984.
Interview with Serge Toubiana, in *Cahiers du Cinéma* (Paris), May 1986.
"A Conversation with Cathérine Deneuve," interview with Bill Grantham, in *Interview* (New York), January 1993.
"Deneuve," interview with Judy Wieder, in *Advocate* (Los Angeles), 25 July 1995.

On DENEUVE: books—

Vadim, Roger, *Memoirs of the Devil*, New York, 1977.
Neuhoff, Eric, *Cathérine Deneuve*, Paris, 1980.
Gerber, François, *Cathérine Deneuve*, Paris, 1981.
Barbier, Philippe, and Jacques Moreau, *Cathérine Deneuve*, Paris, 1984.
D'une etoile l'autre, Paris, 1986.
Vadim, Roger, *Bardot, Deneuve, Fonda: The Memoirs of Roger Vadim*, London, 1986.
Cathérine Deneuve: portraits chosis, Paris, 1993.

On DENEUVE: articles—

Current Biography 1978, New York, 1978.
Ecran (Paris), January 1978.
Canby, Vincent, "The Performer vs. the Role: Cathérine Deneuve and James Mason," in *The Movie Star*, edited by Elisabeth Weis, New York, 1981.
Hotchner, A. E., "Cathérine Deneuve: A Vulnerable Dream Girl in Paris," in *Choice People*, 1984.
DeNicolo, D., "Eternally French. She's Deneuve," in *New York Times*, 20 December 1992.

*   *   *

The wit who mistranslated "*La Belle Dame sans merci*" as "The Beautiful Lady Who Never Says 'Thank You'" achieved by chance a perfect encapsulation of France's two most potent female stars of the 1960s. On an axis with Jeanne Moreau at one pole and Cathérine Deneuve at the other, that cinema can be seen to revolve—an industry and art, paradoxically for a nation united under de Gaulle in its respect for family, social formality, and *la gloire*, which preoccupied itself with the *demi-mondaine*: gamblers, criminals, soldiers of fortune, and, most of all, its destructive, beguiling, but always unbeholden feminine adventurers.

Of the actresses who played these soiled heroines, none succeeded more stylishly than Deneuve. Moreau's pouting sourness led her, via an association with the nouvelle vague, to the epicene baroque of late Fassbinder. Deneuve, almost preternaturally beautiful, a confection of peach skin and gold hair, offered little to stimulate the new directors, with the exception of Roger Vadim. She survived two routine films with him (as well as the obligatory domestic entanglement) to become one of France's most successful star exports, a symbol of lustful purity for forces as disparate as Luis Buñuel and Chanel perfume.

The title of an otherwise unremarkable film, *Touche pas á la femme blanche,* might be her emblem. Deneuve's most potent stock in trade

has always been a beguiling and complaisant innocence, combined with an ingrained seriousness, even solemnity, that her most unbuttoned action cannot dislodge. To see Deneuve laughing is to see her naked, yet physical nudity reveals no more of this remarkable woman than it would of the young Garbo.

Whether playing a high-priced Los Angeles call girl in Aldrich's *Hustle*, a psychopath in Polanski's *Repulsion*, the bisexual private eye of *Ecoute voir . . .*, or a second-rate chanteuse in the trivial farce *Courage, fuyons*, she remains apparently remote, calm, moving to a private rhythm, occupied with thoughts uniquely her own. As Jacques Siclier wrote of her role as the compromised political wife in *Le Bon Plaisir*, "Here, where artifice covers everything, Cathérine Deneuve remains honest, natural and disinterested."

An actress capable of playing, on the one hand, the sentimental provincial heroines of Demy's musical fantasies *Les Parapluies de Cherbourg* and *Les Demoiselles de Rochefort* and the fairy story *Peau d'âne*, and on the other the calculating lovers of *Benjamin ou Les mémoires d'un puceau*, *Manon 70*, *Mayerling*, and Truffaut's *La Sirène du Mississippi*, as well as the insouciant anti-Nazi schemer of his *Le Dernier Métro*, would clearly attract Buñuel. But it was the disinterest Siclier mentions which gave Buñuel the material for *Belle de jour* and *Tristana*.

Buñuel distilled the essence of Deneuve's appeal. Calm but never placid, distant but always touchable, subtly or, as the amputee of *Tristana*, grossly mutilated but confident in her essential concept of self, she epitomized his vision of woman as destroying angel—a whore with a heart, not of gold, but of glass. In particular in *Belle de jour*, Deneuve's sexuality is self-contained; she is the detached yet eternally sexual (as opposed to romantic) creature. In this film, she was never more beautiful in the role of Severine, a virginal upper-class lady of leisure who has everything a woman who has not embraced feminism could ask for: porcelain good looks, a handsome and successful husband, servants and good clothes, and all the time to spend money she has had no part in earning. But Severine is despondent. She begins having erotic fantasies. And soon, she takes part-time work in a brothel: a job she eventually comes to relish. Severine does not know why she is so attracted to her double life. "But without this I could not live," she eventually remarks, of her employment. One cannot imagine any actress other than Deneuve in the role of Severine.

As she has aged, Deneuve has continued to play the sexual creature, in films ranging in quality (from the low of *Paroles et musique*, in which she has a relationship with an ambitious young rock singer, to the high of *Indochine*, in which she and her adopted Vietnamese daughter fall for a navy officer). And like Moreau, Deneuve has decorated her middle years with portraits of surpassing decadence, but characteristically the crumbling exterior of Moreau's raddled madam in *Querelle* hid a girlish romantic, while Deneuve as the vampire in Tony Scott's *The Hunger*, though outwardly unmarked by age, has decayed to the core with centuries of lust and self-regard. Yet her innocence remains, almost to the end, unsullied, her tenderness for her dying partner David Bowie sincere and touching, her seduction of Susan Sarandon no mere acquisition of fresh meat but an act of carnal and spiritual love. *La Belle Dame sans merci*, certainly, but also, as so often with this remarkable actress, *sans peur et sans reproche*.

—John Baxter, updated by Rob Edelman

DE NIRO, Robert

Nationality: American. **Born:** New York City, 17 August 1943. **Education:** Attended Rhodes School, New York; High School of Music and Art, New York; studied acting with Stella Adler at the Actors

Studio, New York. **Family:** Married the actress Diahnne Abbott, 1976 (divorced 1979), children: Drena and Raphael; twin boys with Toukie Smith. **Career:** 1960s—appeared in workshop and off-off-Broadway theater productions; 1969—film debut in *The Wedding Party*; 1969-70—with the Theatre Company of Boston for one season; 1973—first film with director Martin Scorsese, *Mean Streets*; late 1980s—set up TriBeCa project, New York. **Awards:** Best Supporting Actor, New York Film Critics, for *Mean Streets*, 1973; Oscar for Best Supporting Actor, for *The Godfather, Part II*, 1974; Best Actor, New York Film Critics, for *Taxi Driver*, 1976; Oscar for Best Actor, and Best Actor Award, New York Film Critics, for *Raging Bull*, 1980; Best Actor, New York Film Critics, for *Awakenings* and *Goodfellas*, 1990; D. W. Griffith Award for Best Actor (with Robin Williams), for *Awakenings*, 1990. **Agent:** Jay Julien, 1501 Broadway, New York, NY 10036, U.S.A.

Films as Actor:

1969   *The Wedding Party* (De Palma) (as Cecil); *Greetings* (De Palma) (as Jon Rubin)

1970   *Hi, Mom!* (De Palma) (as Jon Rubin); *Bloody Mama* (Corman) (as Lloyd Barker)

1971   *Jennifer on My Mind* (Black) (as gypsy cab driver); *The Gang That Couldn't Shoot Straight* (Goldstone) (as Mario); *Born to Win* (Passer) (as Danny)

1973   *Bang the Drum Slowly* (Hancock) (as Bruce Pearson); ***Mean Streets*** (Scorsese) (as Johnny Boy)

1974   ***The Godfather, Part II*** (Coppola) (as Vito Corleone)

1976   ***Taxi Driver*** (Scorsese) (as Travis Bickle); *Novecento* (*1900*) (Bertolucci) (as Alfredo); *The Last Tycoon* (Kazan) (as Monroe Stahr)

1977   *New York, New York* (Scorsese) (as Jimmy); ***The Deer Hunter*** (Cimino) (as Mike)

1980   ***Raging Bull*** (Scorsese) (as Jake LaMotta); *The Swap* (Shade) (as Sammy)

1981   *True Confessions* (Grosbard) (as Des Spellacy)

1982   ***The King of Comedy*** (Scorsese) (as Rupert Pupkin)

1984   ***Once Upon a Time in America*** (Leone) (as Noodles); *Falling in Love* (Grosbard) (as Frank)

1985   ***Brazil*** (Gilliam) (as Tuttle)

1986   *The Mission* (Joffe) (as Mendoza)

1987   *Angel Heart* (Parker) (as Louis Cyphre); *The Untouchables* (De Palma) (as Al Capone); *Dear America: Letters Home from Vietnam* (Coutaurié—doc for TV)

1988   *Jacknife* (David Jones) (as Joseph "Megs" Megessey); *Midnight Run* (Brest) (as Jack Walsh)

1989   *Stanley and Iris* (Ritt) (as Stanley Cox); *We're No Angels* (Neil Jordan) (as Ned/Fr. Reilly, + exec pr)

1990   ***Goodfellas*** (Scorsese) (as James Conway); *Awakenings* (Penny Marshall) (as Leonard Love)

1991   *Guilty by Suspicion* (Irwin Winkler) (as David Merrill); *Backdraft* (Ron Howard) (as Donald Rimgale); *Cape Fear* (Scorsese) (as Max Cady)

1992   *Night and the City* (Winkler) (as Harry Fabian); *Mistress* (Primus) (as Evan M. Wright, + co-pr)

1993   *This Boy's Life* (Caton-Jones) (as Dwight); *Mad Dog and Glory* (McNaughton) (as Wayne "Mad Dog" Dobie)

1994   *Mary Shelley's Frankenstein* (Branagh) (as The Creature/Sharp, + assoc pr)

1995   *Casino* (Scorsese) (as Sam "Ace" Rothstein); *Heat* (Michael Mann) (as Neil McCauley); *Les Cent et une Nuits* (*A Hundred and One Nights*) (Varda) (as Actor for a Day)

1996   *Affirmative Action*; *The Fan* (Tony Scott); *Marvin's Room* (Zaks) (+ pr); *Sleepers* (Barry Levinson)

Film as Director:

1993   *A Bronx Tale* (+ co-pr, ro as Lorenzo Anello)

Film as Co-Producer:

1992   *Thunderheart* (Apted)

Publications

By DE NIRO: articles—

"Dialogue on Film: Robert De Niro," interview in *American Film* (Washington, D.C.), March 1981.

Interview with Barry Paris, in *American Film* (Hollywood), October 1989.

Interview with Steve Grant, in *Time Out* (London), 22 May 1991.

"A Walk and a Talk with Robert De Niro," interview with Peter Brant and Ingrid Sischym, in *Interview* (New York), November 1993.

"De Niro on De Niro," in *Vogue*, January 1995.

On DE NIRO: books—

Cameron-Wilson, James, *The Cinema of Robert De Niro*, London, 1986.

McKay, Keith, *Robert De Niro: The Hero behind the Masks*, New York, 1986.

Zurhorst, Meinolf, *Robert De Niro: Seine Filme, sein Leben*, Munich, 1987.

Agan, Patrick, *Robert De Niro: The Man, the Myth and the Movies*, London, 1989.

Scorsese, Martin, *Scorsese on Scorsese*, edited by Ian Christie and David Thompson, London, 1989.

Brode, Douglas, *The Films of Robert De Niro*, Secaucus, New Jersey, 1993.

On DE NIRO: articles—

Cieutat, M., "Robert De Niro ou les contraires inséparables," in *Positif* (Paris), November 1977.

Harris, Mark, "Robert De Niro/Michael Moriarty: Obedience to Self," in *Close-Ups: The Movie Star Book*, edited by Danny Peary, New York, 1978.

Kroll, Jack, "Robert De Niro," in *The Movie Star*, edited by Elisabeth Weis, New York, 1981.

Goldsmith, Barbara, "The Incredible Talent of Robert De Niro," in *Parade*, 2 December 1984.

Le Fanu, Mark, "Looking for Mr. De Niro," in *Sight and Sound* (London), Winter 1985/86.

Cooke, L., "*New York, New York*: Looking at De Niro," in *Movie* (London), no. 31/32, Winter 1986.

Pulleine, Tim, "Defining De Niro," in *Films and Filming* (London), October 1988.

Schruers, Fred, "Awake and Sing," in *Premiere* (New York), January 1991.

Current Biography 1993, New York, 1993.

Stromberg, R., "De Niros hemlighet," in *Chaplin*, vol. 35, no. 3, 1993.

"Courting a Monster Star in Hopes of a Monster Film," in *New York Times*, 28 February 1993.

Kaye, Elizabeth, "Robert De Niro," in *New York Times Magazine*, 14 November 1993.

*   *   *

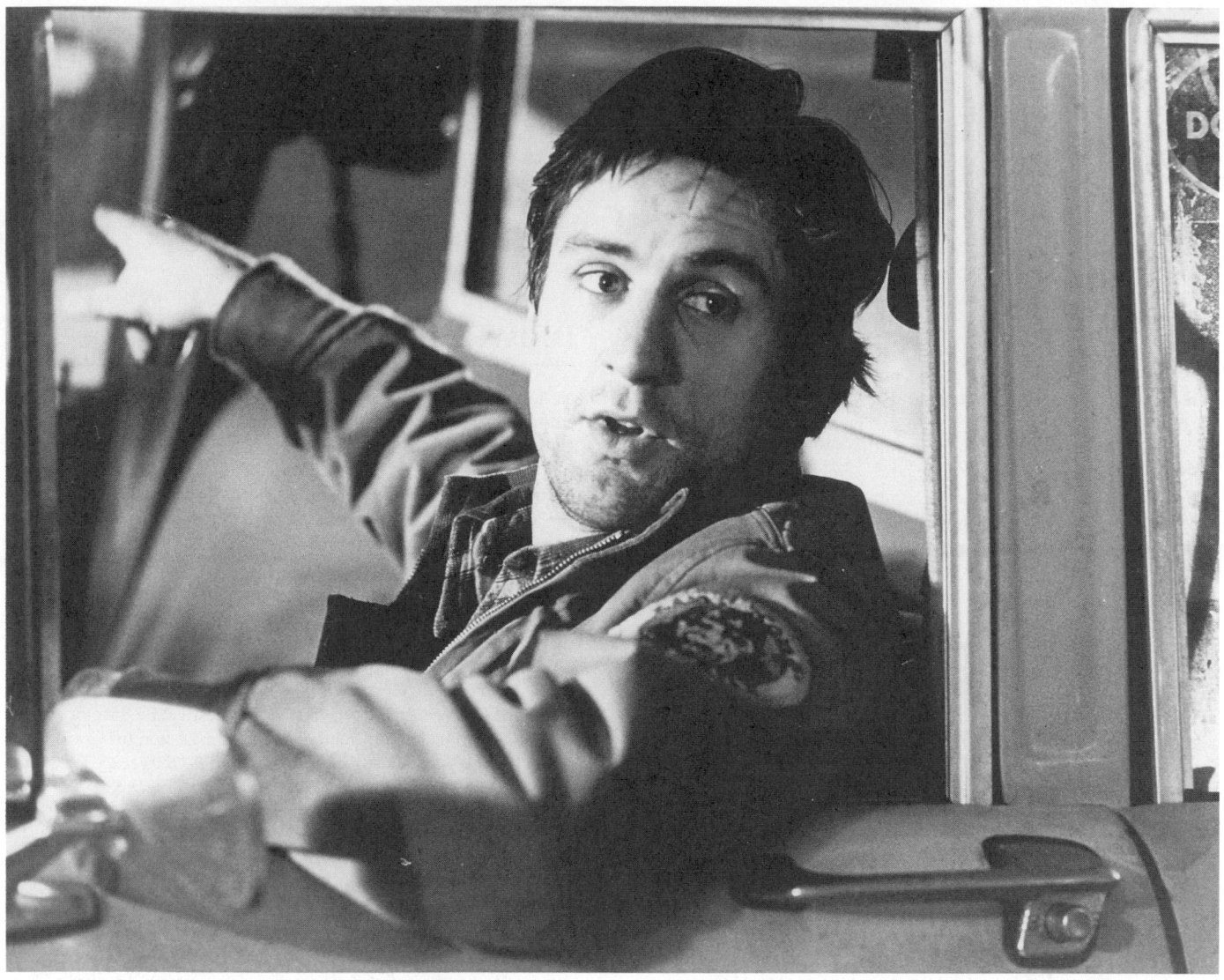

Robert De Niro in *Taxi Driver*

Robert De Niro is nearly incapable of a thoughtless performance. Early in his career, he radiated appeal in several carefully devised, vividly realistic supporting roles, notably as the none-too-bright, fatally ill baseball player in *Bang the Drum Slowly* and young Vito Corleone in *The Godfather, Part II*, even winning an Oscar for the latter. Still, this stage of his career is best exemplified by the film in which he first gained prominence, Martin Scorsese's *Mean Streets*, in which he plays Johnny Boy, a reckless young hood who roams—and invariably finds trouble on—the byways of New York's Little Italy.

In the tradition of Marlon Brando—who originated the role of Vito Corleone in the first *Godfather* film—De Niro eschews the Method approach in creating a role. Reportedly, he drove a cab before playing the title character in *Taxi Driver*, spent hours hitting baseballs prior to *Bang the Drum Slowly*, and even gained the excess poundage required for his appearance as the aging Jake LaMotta in *Raging Bull*. His casting as the younger Vito symbolizes the passing of the mantle from one generation of Method actors to the next. Unlike Brando, however, De Niro did not dissipate his talent, ultimately showing up infrequently on-screen and mumbling his way through his roles. If anything, De Niro has been a prolific screen actor, appearing in an aston-

ishing variety of roles both starring and supporting, and playing each with equal aplomb.

Yet De Niro's career remains most associated with that of Scorsese. In the annals of screen history, the Scorsese-De Niro union rates right alongside the collaboration of von Sternberg and Dietrich. Their director-actor relationship is even visualized on-screen in *Taxi Driver*, in which Scorsese, in a cameo role as a frenzied passenger in De Niro's cab, verbalizes the paranoia that motivates the De Niro character and the subsequent, violent bloodbath he will instigate.

In *The King of Comedy* and *Taxi Driver*, De Niro superbly plays a classic Scorsese character: the social misfit-psychotic who is transformed into a weirdo-celebrity by a society ever willing to elevate oddballs to pop-culture status. In *The King of Comedy*, the actor perfectly captures the superficial and destructive amiability of Rupert Pupkin, a fame-obsessed nonentity who yearns to be a guest on a late night talk show hosted by a Johnny Carson-like celebrity. While Pupkin does have some talent as a stand-up comic, he really does not want to work at his craft. All he wants is stardom and fame. It is the idea of being a celebrity that appeals to him, not the creative work involved in honing his craft. He eventually wins that celebrity, but only after kidnapping the talk show host. In *Taxi Driver*, De Niro gives a now-legendary performance as Travis Bickle, an ex-Marine and pill-popping loner from some nameless spot in the Midwest who has come to New York and taken a job driving a cab. The semiarticulate Bickle is an outsider even to the prostitutes, deadbeats, and castoffs who inhabit the Manhattan terrain like rats in a ghetto hovel. There is a void in his brain; although he earnestly tries to communicate with others, he comes off with the charm and coherence of an airplane glue freak. He sets out to assassinate a presidential hopeful—which would link him to the Lee Harvey Oswalds and James Earl Rays of history—but instead kills a vicious pimp who has enslaved a 12-year-old runaway-prostitute, so he is lionized by the media.

In *Raging Bull*, De Niro's second Oscar-winning performance, he plays a deeply flawed character who did earn fame based on legitimate merit: real-life boxer Jake LaMotta, the Bronx Bull, who in 1949 copped the middleweight title from Marcel Cerdan. LaMotta is depicted as an inarticulate, insanely jealous man who does not use his mind and cannot control his temper. He starts out as a cocky and confident young fighter and ends up fat, punchdrunk, and pathetic, separated and alienated from the people he loves. As LaMotta, De Niro is nothing short of extraordinary. He simply chews into the role, digests it, and spits it out across the screen.

The actor's other screen characterizations for Scorsese, all of them fully realized, have placed him within the milieu of gangsters and wiseguys. In *GoodFellas*, he is a career hoodlum; in *Cape Fear*, he is a vengeful psychopath; in *Casino*, he is a bookie-gambler who becomes a Las Vegas casino manager, leaving the muscle to others. Another superlative criminal role came in *Heat*, directed by Michael Mann, in which he is a cool, disciplined gang boss who is the prey of a determined cop (Al Pacino, whose acting style and city boy charisma inexorably link him to De Niro). These parts can be contrasted to his ingratiatingly comical bounty hunter in *Midnight Run*; sensitive intellectual in *Guilty by Suspicion*; patient who awakens from a three-decades-long coma in *Awakenings*; and, most tellingly, his small town Ukrainian-American steelworker with a firmly rooted sense of honor and duty, who heads off to Vietnam in *The Deer Hunter*. De Niro even has played the Frankenstein monster (in *Mary Shelley's Frankenstein*), adding an impressive level of depth and feeling to the character. In *A Bronx Tale* (playing a bus driver), *Falling in Love* (cast as a suburbanite), and *Mad Dog and Glory* (playing a cop), the actor showed that he can act average, essentially colorless, and even retiring characters with the same verve and believability as his Al Capone in *The Untouchables*. Only rarely does De Niro miscalculate a performance. Such a case is *We're No Angels*, in which he hams it up in his role as a none-too-bright escaped convict.

De Niro made his directorial debut with *A Bronx Tale*, expanded from Chazz Palminteri's one-character play. It is a story of the coming-of-age of a young Italian-American on the Bronx streets during the early 1960s, and his relationship to two very different men. They are Lorenzo (played by De Niro), his honest, hard-working bus driver father; and Sonny (played by Palminteri), a macho gangster who is feared by all in the neighborhood and who thinks that working men like Lorenzo are suckers. For a young boy attempting to define his identity, Sonny is a much more appealing role model than Lorenzo. In this regard, the scenario contrasts these two characters: the flashy guy who "pulls the trigger," and the less glamorous, more anonymous man who actually is the real "tough guy" in that he gets up each morning, goes to work, and supports his family. Additionally, *A Bronx Tale* examines the roots and meaning of racism as it depicts the changing face of urban America. As the years pass, the turf of the Italian-American Bronx neighborhood in which the film is set is encroached upon by an African-American community. The residents of each are culturally disparate, and their mistrust of each other borders on blind hatred.

Not surprisingly, *A Bronx Tale* is a New York City drama which, in its best moments, seethes with the same raw emotion found in the De

Niro-Scorsese collaborations. "I'm not crazy about directing myself in a film, because for me it takes the joy out of acting," De Niro declared, at the 1993 Toronto Film Festival. "But I would like to direct more movies. It takes a lot of work and energy to direct. But it's worth it, if you are able to make something that is good and special." This last sentiment might also apply to De Niro's body of work in front of the camera, which ranks among the best of any late twentieth-century American actor.

—Robin Wood, updated by Rob Edelman

DEPARDIEU, Gérard

Nationality: French. **Born:** Châteauroux, 27 December 1948. **Education:** Attended École communale; Cours d'art dramatique de Charles Dullin; École d'art dramatique de Jean Laurent Cochet. **Family:** Married Elisabeth Guignot, 1970, children: Guillaume and Julie. **Career:** Early 1960s—spent early teens as petty thief; prison psychologist suggested dramatics as possible therapy; 1965—film debut at 16 in Leenhardt's *Le Beatnik et le minet*; 1966-1970s—in occasional drama on French television; 1968-1970s—in a number of plays in Paris; 1974—in French TV series *L'Inconnu*; early 1980s—international critical and popular recognition for roles in films *Le Retour de Martin Guerre* and *Danton*; 1983—co-producer of *Les Compères*; 1984—directed first film, *Tartuffe*; 1990—first English-language film, *Green Card*. **Awards:** Prix Gérard Philipe, France, 1973; César Award, Best Actor, for *Le Dernier Métro* 1980; Venice Festival Best Actor Award, for *Police*, 1985; Golden Globe Award for Best Actor, for *Green Card*, 1990; César Award, Best Actor, for *Cyrano de Bergerac*, 1990. **Address:** Artmédia, 10 av George V, 75008 Paris, France.

Films as Actor:

1965 *Le Beatnik et le minet* (Leenhardt—short); *Christmas Carol* (Varda)
1970 *Le Cri du cormoran, le soir au-dessus des jonques* (Audiard)
1971 *Un peu de soleil dans l'eau froide* (Deray); *Le Tueur* (de la Patellière)
1972 *Nathalie Granger* (Duras) (as salesman); *La Scoumoune* (Giovanni) (as burglar); *Au rendez-vous de la mort joyeuse* (Juan Buñuel); *L'Affaire Dominici* (Bernardt-Aubert); *Le Viager* (Tchernia)
1973 *Deux hommes dans la ville* (*Two against the Law*) (Giovanni); *Rude journée pour la reine* (*Rough Day for the Queen*) (Allio); *Les Gaspards* (*The Holes*) (Tchernia); *Les Valseuses* (*Going Places*) (Blier) (as Jean-Claude); *Stavisky* (Resnais); *La Femme du Ganges* (Duras)
1974 *Vincent, François, Paul, et les autres* (Sautet); *Pas si méchant que ça* (*The Wonderful Crook*) (Goretta) (as Pierre)
1975 *Maîtresse* (Schroeder) (as Olivier); *7 Morts sur ordonnance* (Rouffio); *Je t'aime, moi non plus* (Gainsbourg) (as René la Canne); *Bertolucci secondo il cinema* (Amelia—doc); *L'ultima donna* (*La Dernière Femme*) (Ferreri)
1976 *1900* (*Novecento*) (Bertolucci) (as Olmo Dalco); *Barocco* (Téchiné) (as Samson); *Baxter—Vera Baxter* (Duras); *René la Canne* (Girod)
1977 *Le Camion* (Duras); *Violanta* (Schmid); *La Nuit tous les chats sont gris* (Zingg); *Dites-lui que je l'aime* (*This Sweet Sickness*) (Miller); *Die linkshändige Frau* (*The Left-Handed Woman*) (Handke) (as man with T-shirt); *Préparez vos mouchoirs* (*Get Out Your Handkerchiefs*) (Blier) (as Raoul)

1978 *Ciao maschio* (*Bye Bye Monkey*; *Reve de Singe*) (Ferreri) (as Gérard Lafayette); *Le Sucre* (Rouffio); *Les Chiens* (Jessua)

1979 *L'Ingorgo* (*Traffic Jam*) (Comencini) (as Franco); *Temporale Rosy* (Monicelli) (as Raoul); *Buffet froid* (Blier) (as Alphonse Tram)

1980 *Mon Oncle d'Amerique* (Resnais) (as Rene Ragueneau); *Le Dernier Métro* (*The Last Metro*) (Truffaut) (as Bernard Granger); *Inspecteur La Bavure* (Zidi) (as Roger Morzini); *Je vous aime* (*I Love All of You*) (Berri); *Loulou* (Pialat) (title role)

1981 *Le Chèvre* (*The Goat*) (Veber—released in U.S. in 1985) (as Campana); *La Femme d'à côte* (*The Woman Next Door*) (Truffaut) (as Bernard Coudray); *Le Choix des armes* (*Choice of Arms*) (Corneau) (as Mickey); *Le Retour de Martin Guerre* (*The Return of Martin Guerre*) (Vigne) (title role)

1982 *Danton* (Wajda) (title role); *Le Grand Frère* (Girod) (as Gérard Berger/Bernard Vigo)

1983 *La Lune dans le caniveau* (*The Moon in the Gutter*) (Beineix) (as Gérard); *Les Compères* (Veber) (as Jean Lucas, + co-pr); *Fort Saganne* (Corneau) (as Charles Saganne)

1984 *Rive droite, rive gauche* (*Right Bank, Left Bank*) (Labro) (as Paul Senznques)

1985 *Police* (Pialat) (as Mangin); *Une Femme ou deux* (*One Woman or Two*; *A Woman or Two*) (Vigne) (as Julien Chayssac)

1986 *Les Fugitifs* (Veber) (as Jean Lucas); **Jean de Florette** (Berri) (as Cadoret/title role); *Rue du départ* (Gatlif) (as Dr. Lombart); *Tenue de soirée* (*Menage*) (Blier) (as Bob); *Je hais les acteurs* (*I Hate Actors*) (Krawczyk) (as prisoner in police station)

1987 *Sous le soleil de Satan* (*Under Satan's Sun*) (Pialat) (as Father Donissan)

1988 *Camille Claudel* (Nuytten) (as Auguste Rodin); *Drole d'endroit pour une rencontre* (*A Strange Place to Meet*) (Dupeyron) (as Charles)

1989 *Je veux rentrer à la maison* (*I Want to Go Home*) (Resnais) (as Christian Gauthier); *Deux* (*Two*) (Zidi); *Trop belle pour toi* (*Too Beautiful for You*) (Blier) (as Bernard Barthélémy)

1990 **Cyrano de Bergerac** (Rappeneau) (title role); *Green Card* (Weir) (as Georges Fauré); *Shakha Proshakha* (*Branches of the Tree*) (Satyajit Ray)

1991 *Uranus* (Berri) (as Leopold); *Merci la vie* (*Thanks for Life*) (Blier) (as Dr. Worms); *Mon Pere ce heros* (Lauzier) (as André)

1992 *1492: The Conquest of Paradise* (Ridley Scott) (as Christopher Columbus); *Tous les matins du monde* (*All the Mornings of the World*) (Corneau) (as Marin Marias)

1993 *Hélas pour moi* (*Oh, Woe Is Me*) (Godard) (as Simon Donnadieu); *My Father, the Hero* (Miner) (as André); *Germinal* (Berri) (as Maheu)

1994 *Une Pure Formalité* (*A Pure Formality*) (Tornatore) (as Onoff); *La Machine* (*The Machine*) (Dupeyron) (as Marc); *Elisa* (Jean Becker) (as Jacques Desmoulins); *Le Garcu* (Pialat) (as Gérard)

1995 *Colonel Chabert* (Angelo) (title role); *Les Cent et une Nuits* (*A Hundred and One Nights*) (Varda) (as Actor for a Day); *François Truffaut: Portraits Voles* (*François Truffaut: Stolen Portraits*) (Toubiana and Pascal—doc)

1996 *Les Anges Gardiens* (Poiré) (as Antoine Carco); *Bogus* (Jewison); *Le Gaulois*; *Hamlet* (Branagh) (as Reynaldo); *The Secret Agent* (Hampton) (as Ossipon); *Unhook the Stars* (Nick Cassavetes)

Other Films:

1984 *Tartuffe* (d, title role)
1991 *Agantuk* (*The Stranger*; *The Visitor*) (Satyajit Ray) (co-exec pr)

Publications

By DEPARDIEU: book—

Lettres volées, Paris, 1988.

By DEPARDIEU: articles—

Interviews in *Ciné Revue* (Paris), 13 November 1975, 14 July 1977, 16 March 1978, 5 May 1981, and 13 January 1983.

Interview in *Cahiers du Cinéma* (Paris), May 1981.

"Gérard Depardieu: 'Hunk? Moi?,'" interview with Marcia Froelke Coburn, in *American Film* (New York), October 1983.

Interview with I. Ginsburg, in *Interview* (New York), January 1986.

"Gérard Depardieu en liberte," interview with O. Dazat, in *Cinématographe* (Paris), July/August 1986.

Interview with Serge Toubiana, in *Cahiers du Cinéma* (Paris), December 1986.

"France's Leading Man," interview with J. Dupont, in *New York Times*, 14 January 1987.

"Entretien avec Gérard Depardieu: l'exercise de la passion," interview with Serge Toubiana and I. Katsahnias, in *Cahiers du Cinéma* (Paris), May 1989.

Interview with Stephen O'Shea, in *Interview* (New York), December 1990.

On DEPARDIEU: books—

Chazal, Robert, *Gérard Depardieu: l'autodidacte inspiré*, Paris, 1982.
Gonzalez, Christian, *Gérard Depardieu*, Paris, 1985.
Dazat, Olivier, *Gérard Depardieu*, Paris, 1988.
Gray, Marianne, *Depardieu: A Biography*, London, 1991.
Chutkow, Paul, *Depardieu*, New York, 1994.

On DEPARDIEU: articles—

Stein, H., "Depardieu: French Primitive," and "You Gérard, Me Jane," by M. Haskell, in *Film Comment* (New York), March/April 1978.

Benhamou, A.-Fr., "Deux Monstres naissants," in *Cinématographe* (Paris), October 1980.

Ehrenstein, David, "French Active," in *Advocate* (Los Angeles,) 3 November 1982.

"La Vedette de la semaine: Gérard Depardieu," in *Ecran* (Paris), 1 March 1984.

Bulnes, J., "Les immortels du cinéma: Gérard Depardieu," in *Ciné Revue* (Paris), 1 November 1984.

Dazat, Olivier, and D. Goldschmidt, "Dossier: Gérard Depardieu," in *Cinématographe* (Paris), September 1985.

Deriex, M., "Gérard Depardieu, l'homme-passion!," in *Ciné Revue* (Paris), 15 May 1986.

Schupp, P., "Gérard Depardieu," in *Séquences* (Montreal), October 1986.

Current Biography 1987, New York, 1987.

Chutkow, P., "Gérard Depardieu Stokes the Creative Fires with Passion," in *New York Times*, 4 March 1990.

Privat, Pascal, "France's War of the Noses: Dueling Cyranos Stage and Screen," in *Newsweek* (New York), 7 May 1990.

Stars (Mariembourg, Belgium), June 1990.

Collins, G., "Depardieu Mystery: Gentleness of Heart in Boxer's Physique," in *New York Times*, 4 June 1990.

Clark, John, filmography in *Premiere* (New York), February 1991.

Hearty, K. B., "French Connection," in *Premiere* (New York), February 1991.

Corliss, Richard, "Life in a Big Glass: Gérard Depardieu Has an Appetite for Wine, Words, and Stardom," in *Time* (New York), 4 February 1991.

Gérard Depardieu in *L'ultima donna*

Conroy, Tom, "Gérard Depardieu Is the Hardest Working Man in Le Show Business," in *Rolling Stone* (New York), 7 March 1991.

Gray, Marianne, "Depardieu," in *Film Monthly* (Berkhamsted, England), May 1991.

Gray, Marianne, "A Tortured Actor," in *Film Monthly* (Berkhamsted, England), February 1992.

Williams, Michael, "Le Cinema c'est moi, dit Gérard," in *Variety* (New York), 7 February 1994.

*   *   *

Simply put, Gérard Depardieu is both a consummate actor and his generation's premier European-born screen star. Like Marcello Mastroianni before him, he has been able to outshine his fellow European leading men and become a respected and valued international star: one of the few actors who primarily appears in non-English language films, but who has name recognition even among those who dismiss "art house" fare in favor of the most commercial Hollywood product.

Also like Mastroianni, Depardieu is an actor with smoldering intensity and a riveting screen presence who is as equally adept in dramas and comedies, serious films and strictly entertaining ones, and both period and contemporary scenarios. In them, he has brilliantly played a rainbow of characters: from peasant to politico; average working- or middle-class hero who finds himself in extraordinary situations to brooding, alienated antihero; idealistic romantic to bullying macho man and despicable, antisocial villain. A glance at Depardieu's eye-poppingly lengthy filmography serves as a reminder that he has appeared in an extraordinary number of the most praiseworthy motion pictures released since the mid-1970s.

Unlike Mastroianni, however, Depardieu lacks a more traditional movie-star handsomeness. He is a burly man who is inclined to put on weight, and whose facial characteristics might be described as common; his physical presence is closer to that of a Jean Gabin than a Mastroianni. As a type, he is more closely related to Gabin, Lino Ventura, and Harry Baur than suave Charles Boyer and Louis Jourdan, two Frenchmen who went on to become Hollywood personalities.

Among Depardieu's noteworthy early career roles—those that helped solidify his stardom—were ones in which his characters are seethingly sexual, and fashioned to shock middle-class complacency: the amoral hooligan who uses and abuses (sexually and otherwise) everyone he meets, in *Going Places*; the carefree but brutal working class lout who is more appealing to a bourgeois young woman than her well-bred lover, in *Loulou*; and the male chauvinist of classic proportion who is confused by the changing role of women, in *The Last Woman*. In the latter, he mostly parades about in the nude and, at the finale, cuts off his sex organ. Depardieu's talent for portraying brute force and vulnerability, in part through the contrast between his massive body and tender voice, has coincided with a feminist-oriented interest in questioning traditional gender roles and identity. And so he has played the sexually-oriented male whose actions are, to say the least, unconventional: the husband who willing finds his sexually unresponsive wife a lover, in *Get Out Your Handkerchiefs*; the devil-may-care homosexual crook, in *Menage*; and the businessman who rejects his beautiful wife for his otherwise plain, ordinary-looking temporary office worker, in *Too Beautiful for You*. Like *Going Places*, these three films were directed by Bertrand Blier; Depardieu has, over the years, consistently worked with the most respected French auteurs, including François Truffaut, Alain Resnais, Marguerite Duras, Maurice Pialat, and Claude Berri.

Perhaps the most striking aspect of Depardieu's talent is his ability to make believable completely disparate characters. He is perfectly cast as the simple blue-collar Everyman who is the victim of injustice (most especially as the hunchback farmer in *Jean de Florette*); yet he is as equally mesmerizing as characters who are uncompromisingly hard-boiled (the sexist, racist lawman in *Police*) and brilliantly idealistic (the title characters in *Danton* and *Cyrano de Bergerac*, arguably his two greatest screen roles to date).

Despite his heady list of intense and serious characterizations, Depardieu's versatility is further evidenced by his appearances in such undemanding, popular comedies as *Les Compères* and *Les Fugitifs*. In a similar vein, he has given charming performances in two English-language comedies, *Green Card* and *My Father, the Hero* (a remake of his 1991 French feature *Mon Pere ce heros*). In each, his charisma manages to transcend the thinness of the material.

As Depardieu approaches the half-century mark, his on-screen output remains as diverse, challenging, and compelling as ever, and there is no indication that he will forfeit his superstar status either at home or abroad.

—Rob Edelman

DEPP, Johnny

Nationality: American. **Born:** John Christopher Depp, Owensboro, Kentucky, 9 June 1963; raised in Miramar, Florida. **Family:** Married Lori Anne Allison (divorced). **Education:** Dropped out of high school in Miramar, Florida, at age 16. **Career:** 1976—at 13 started his own rock group, Flame; later played lead guitar with band, The Kids, who opened shows for the B-52s, Talking Heads, and Iggy Pop; subsequently with the Rock City Angels; 1980—film debut in *Friday the 13th*; 1987-90—as Tom Hanson in TV series *21 Jump Street*. **Agent:** International Creative Management, 8942 Wilshire Boulevard, Beverly Hills, CA 90211, U.S.A.

Films as Actor:

1980   *Friday the 13th* (Sean S. Cunningham)
1984   *A Nightmare on Elm Street* (Craven) (as Glen Lantz)
1985   *Private Resort* (George Bowers) (as Jack Marshall)
1986   *Platoon* (Oliver Stone) (as Lerner); *Slow Burn* (Matthew Chapman—for TV)
1990   *Cry-Baby* (Waters) (title role); *Edward Scissorhands* (Tim Burton) (title role)
1991   *Freddy's Dead: The Final Nightmare* (Talalay) (cameo)

1992   *Arizona Dream* (Kusturica) (as Axel Blackmar)
1993   *Benny & Joon* (Chechik) (as Sam); *What's Eating Gilbert Grape* (Hallström) (title role)
1994   *Ed Wood* (Tim Burton) (title role)
1995   *Nick of Time* (Badham) (as Gene Watson); *Don Juan DeMarco* (Jeremy Leven) (title role)
1996   *Donnie Brasco* (Newell); *Dead Man* (Jarmusch) (as William Blake)

Publications

By DEPP: articles—

Interview in *Interview* (New York), July 1987.
Interview with John Waters, in *Interview* (New York), April 1990.
Interview with Jamie Diamond, in *Cosmopolitan* (New York), November 1993.
Interview with Brendan Lemon, in *Interview* (New York), December 1995.
Interview with Kevin Cook, in *Playboy* (Chicago), January 1996.

On DEPP: book—

Reisfeld, Randi, *Johnny Depp*, New York, 1989.

On DEPP: articles—

Zehme, Bill, "Sweet Sensation," in *Rolling Stone* (New York), 10 January 1991.
Morgan, Susan, "Depp Perception," in *Harper's Bazaar* (New York), May 1993.
Schneller, Johanna, "Johnny Angel," in *GQ* (New York), October 1993.
"Beat Poet Alan Ginsberg and Actor-on-the-Beat Johnny Depp in a Conversation that Spans the Nation and the Generations," in *Interview* (New York), June 1994.
Beller, Thomas, "Fame Is a Four-Letter Word," in *Harper's Bazaar* (New York), December 1995

*   *   *

In watching Johnny Depp in his early movies, one may have been charmed by his performances, such as that in *Cry-Baby*, but few would have claimed the young man was destined to become one of the finest actors/stars/presences of his generation. One could not, back then, be aware of his potential range—both emotional range and range of characterization. A mere five years after *Cry-Baby*, we find him in *Don Juan DeMarco*, paired with Marlon Brando, no less, and elegantly holding his own. He is perhaps, in his way, Brando's equal—though an equal as different as can be imagined, Depp's performance style being far removed from Method-derived acting.

In many respects he seems a strange anomaly in contemporary Hollywood, with its preoccupation with violent action or special effects in movies characterized by the hysterical overvaluation of masculinity in the persons of stars such as Stallone and Schwarzenegger (an obvious response to feminism, and already disintegrating into self-parody). While his image has been consistently rooted in male heterosexuality (even when he cross-dresses in *Ed Wood*), he is surely the least aggressively masculine of all currently popular stars. His persona is centered upon gentleness, sensitivity, vulnerability, and an emotional as well as physical delicacy. This was already evident in *Cry-Baby* (and to be capable of expressing delicacy in a John Waters movie is already an achievement), but received its definitive formulation in *Edward Scissorhands*, made the same year, which is a somewhat dis-

Johnny Depp in *Edward Scissorhands*

appointing film, but Depp's pathetic, sweet, and lovable freak, whose inventor (Vincent Price) dies before he could give him "real" hands, is unforgettably poignant and touching. Indeed, the irreducible sweetness is already there in a film Depp would doubtless not care to be reminded of: the 1985 *Private Resort*, a typically mindless boys-trying-to-get-laid comedy in which he looks about 15 years old and is rather charmingly miscast as a frantic pursuer of tits-and-ass.

The much more textured "Scissorhands" persona was developed further in the two films of 1993, *Benny & Joon* and *What's Eating Gilbert Grape*. The former—a little movie rendered almost irresistible by its three stars—gave Depp's comedic talents their full expression, especially in his celebrated Buster Keaton routine; like Keaton (and unlike, for example, Jim Carrey), Depp knows that you can only be *really* funny if you never, never suggest that you know you are being funny. In *What's Eating Gilbert Grape* he found, perhaps, his most sympathetic director aside from Tim Burton, Lasse Hallström, a filmmaker with a sensibility of a delicacy to match Depp's. Any other actor in the role wold surely have been upstaged by Leonardo di Caprio's extraordinary performance in a far more showy role; Depp and Hallström have understood that quietness and understatement can make an equally telling and indelible impression.

Three films released in 1994 and 1995 contain marvelous performances that show a broadening of his range without ever betraying the qualities and values of his basic persona. The most recent of the three, *Nick of Time*, a silly, gimmicky movie unworthy of Depp's talents, demands little attention, but Depp gives it what distinction it has in his portrayal of a very ordinary, unimaginative young bureaucrat spurred into activity and inventiveness by the threat to his little daughter's life—Depp's first "ordinary" character. *Ed Wood* and *Don Juan DeMarco* are another matter; they are, with *Gilbert Grape*, the most distinguished films in which Depp has appeared so far, and are both (not to belittle the quite marvelous support he gets) essentially carried on his own apparently slender shoulders.

Ed Wood reunites him with Tim Burton, and they have collaborated to develop a character (does anyone *really* care whether it is factually accurate?) that both takes up and extends the "Scissorhands" persona. Like the earlier Edward, Depp's Edward D. Wood, Jr. is at once a "freak" and an artist: an artist so caught up in his delight in creation that he is never able to recognize that his products are worthless, and will in fact end up being celebrated as the "worst films ever made." Yet it is doubtful whether anyone—not even Kirk Douglas's van Gogh—has been able more convincingly to communicate on screen the sheer joy of creativity. The Burton-Depp Ed Wood is at once funny, touching, and pathetic, yet oddly inspirational; the suggestion is that the delight in creation is sufficient unto itself, irrespective of the value posterity places upon the works. After all, one of our culture's greatest artists, Schubert, composed a number of his supreme works without the least guarantee or even expectation that they would ever be performed. This is not to collapse Schubert's great intelligence with Edward D. Wood's virtually insane delusions of grandeur—we are concerned here with personal pleasure and satisfaction, not objective value.

Depp's Don Juan DeMarco is an equally remarkable assumption, in certain ways closely paralleling his Ed Wood. Here, creativity is recast in sexual terms, in which the character's fantasy is no longer that he produces great art, but that he brings a transitory happiness to frustrated women. Depp's Don Juan can best be defined by juxtaposition with Mozart's Don Giovanni. Mozart's Don is an extraordinarily—almost bafflingly—complex figure: a social/sexual revolutionary who breaks all the restrictive conventions of the culture, yet always at the expense of those (especially women) in a socially inferior and vulnerable position. He is at once the hero and the villain of the opera. Against Don Giovanni's exploitation of women we have Don Juan DeMarco's total identification with them, his assumed role as "great lover" built less upon personal gratification than on empathy and compassion. Depp's Don Juan is unlike Ed Wood in that he is not entirely the victim of delusion; he really *does* change people's lives. The film clarifies most beautifully the very basis of the persona, its fascination and complexity—strong and unambiguous heterosexual appeal, combined with an extreme and potentially revolutionary femininity.

—Robin Wood

DERN, Bruce

Nationality: American. **Born:** Bruce MacLeish Dern in Winnetka, Illinois, 4 June 1936. **Education:** Attended Choate Preparatory School, Connecticut, and New Trier Township High School, Winnetka; University of Pennsylvania; studied acting at the American Foundation of Dramatic Art, Philadelphia, and Actors Studio, New York. **Family:** Married 1) actress Diane Ladd (divorced), daughter: actress Laura Elizabeth; 2) Andrea Beckett, 1969. **Career:** 1958—bit part in stage play *Shadow of a Gunman*; 1959—in Kazan's production of *Sweet Bird of Youth*; 1960—film debut in Kazan's *Wild River*; 1962-63—regular on TV series *Stoney Burke*. **Awards:** Best Supporting Actor Award, U.S. National Society of Film Critics, for *Drive, He Said*, 1971. **Address:** c/o K. J. Sparkman, P.O. Box 327, Troy, MT 59935, U.S.A.

Films as Actor:

1960   *Wild River* (Kazan) (as Jack Roper)
1961   *The Crimebusters* (Sagal—for TV)
1963   *Bedtime Story* (Levy)
1964   *Marnie* (Hitchcock) (as sailor); *Hush . . . Hush, Sweet Charlotte* (Aldrich) (as John Mayhew)
1966   *The Wild Angels* (Corman) (as Loser/Joey Kerns)
1967   *The War Wagon* (Kennedy) (as Hammond); *The St. Valentine's Day Massacre* (Corman) (as John May); *Waterhole Number Three* (Graham) (as deputy); *Will Penny* (Gries) (as Rafe Quint); *The Trip* (Corman) (as John); *Hang 'em High* (Post) (as Miller)
1968   *Support Your Local Sheriff* (Kennedy) (as Joe Danby); *Psych-Out* (Rush) (as Steve Davis)
1969   *Rebel Rousers* (Cohen) (as "J. J."); *Castle Keep* (Pollack) (as Lt. Billy Byron Bix); *Number One* (Gries) (as Richie Fowler); *They Shoot Horses, Don't They?* (Pollack) (as James)
1970   *Bloody Mama* (Corman) (as Kevin Kirkman); *Drive, He Said* (Nicholson) (as Coach Bullion); *The Incredible Two-Headed Transplant* (Lanza) (as Roger); *Cycle Savages* (Brame) (as Keeg)
1971   *The Cowboys* (Rydell) (as Long Hair); *Sam Hill: Who Killed the Mysterious Mr. Foster?* (Cook—for TV); *Silent Running* (Trumbull) (as Freeman Lowell)
1972   *Thumb Tripping* (Masters) (as Smitty); *The King of Marvin Gardens* (Rafelson) (as Jason Staebler)
1974   *The Laughing Policeman* (*An Investigation of Murder*) (Rosenberg) (as Leo Larsen); *The Great Gatsby* (Clayton) (as Tom Buchanan); *Smile* (Ritchie) (as "Big Bob" Freelander)
1975   *Posse* (Kirk Douglas) (as Jack Strawhorn)
1976   *Won Ton Ton, the Dog Who Saved Hollywood* (Winner) (as Grayson Potchuck); *Family Plot* (Hitchcock) (as Lumley); *Folies Bourgeoises* (*The Twist*) (Chabrol) (as writer)
1977   *Black Sunday* (Frankenheimer) (as Lander)

329

1978 *Coming Home* (Ashby) (as Capt. Bob Hyde); *The Driver* (Walter Hill) (as detective)
1980 *Middle Age Crazy* (Trent) (as Bobby Lee)
1981 *Tattoo* (Bob Brooks) (as Karl)
1982 *That Championship Season* (Jason Miller) (as George Sitkowski); *Harry Tracy* (Graham) (title role)
1985 *Toughlove* (Glenn Jordan—for TV) (as Rob Charters); *On the Edge* (Nilsson) (as Wes Holman)
1987 *Big Town* (Bolt) (as Mr. Edwards); *Roses Are for the Rich* (Michael Miller—for TV); *Uncle Tom's Cabin* (Lathan)
1988 *1969* (Thompson) (as Cliff); *World Gone Wild* (Katzin) (as Ethan); *The 'Burbs* (Dante) (as Mark Rumsfield)
1989 *Trenchcoat in Paradise* (Coolidge—for TV) (as John Hollander)
1990 *After Dark, My Sweet* (Foley) (as Uncle Bud); *The Court-Martial of Jackie Robinson* (Peerce—for TV) (as Scout Ed Higgins)
1991 *Into the Badlands* (for TV) (as T L Barston); *Carolina Skeletons* (for TV) (as Junior Stoker)
1992 *Diggstown* (*Midnight Sting*) (Ritchie) (as John Gillon)
1993 *It's Nothing Personal* (Bradford May—for TV) (as Billy Archer)
1994 *Dead Man's Revenge* (for TV) (as Payton McCay); *Amelia Earhart: The Final Flight* (Simoneau—for TV) (as George Putnam)
1995 *A Mother's Prayer* (for TV) (as John Walker)
1996 *Down Periscope* (David S. Ward) (as Admiral Yancy Graham)

Publications

By DERN: article—

"Bruce Dern," interview by J. Delson, in *Take One* (Montreal), July 1973.

On DERN: articles—

Actors on Acting, edited by Joanmarie Kalter, 1979.
"Bruce Dern: On-Set Interview," by N. M. Stoop in *Films in Review* (New York), October 1980.
Crane, W., "Creative Conflict: Bruce Dern and the Making of *Coming Home*," in *Post Script* (Jacksonville, Florida), Winter 1982.
Singer, M., "That Dern Cat," in *Movieline*, July 1992.
Diamond, Jamie, "Bruce Dern's Career of Con Men and Killers," in *New York Times*, 23 August 1992.

*   *   *

Bruce Dern seems to have been around forever, but it is impossible to come up with a single film by which to center a portrait of a distinguished career. There were plenty of good roles in the career of this Roger Corman-school-trained actor, with the best still being the lead in Alfred Hitchcock's final tongue-in-cheek thriller, *Family Plot*. But with a brief moment in the Oscar sun (for a nomination for *Coming Home*), Dern's time as a leading actor passed, although he continued to be steadily employed as a character actor.

Still Dern's career is dotted with memorable moments. He made his debut in Elia Kazan's *Wild River*, singled out for his portrait of a country hoodlum. His roles for Roger Corman in *The Wild Angels*, and for Alfred Hitchcock in *Marnie* will long be remembered by those lucky enough to have seen those films during their original theatrical screenings. But sadly these two films seemed to set a trend; Dern has never been able to harness himself out of the image of an unbalanced, frighteningly disturbed man. This is due in part to his high, midwestern

twang (he hails from an upper-class suburb of Chicago), narrow, almost gaunt face, and wild, unruly curly hair.

But at one point in the late 1960s and into the early 1970s Dern seemed to become a public favorite as "Mr. Demented." He played a deranged dancer in Sydney Pollack's *They Shoot Horses, Don't They?*, and a wild-eyed basketball coach in *Drive, He Said*, directed by Jack Nicholson. This led to his finest roles in Bob Rafelson's *The King of Marvin Gardens*, Alfred Hitchcock's *Family Plot*, and Michael Ritchie's *Smile*. In the latter, Dern proved his ability at comedy in the underrated send-up of American-style beauty pageants.

Through the 1980s Dern worked regularly, but in small parts, too often for secondary studios. In 1988, for instance, he appeared as a father in *1969*, a low-budget affair for Atlantic Films in which college classmates go through the times Dern was so much a part of—the late 1960s: dodging the draft, dropping out of school and society alike, splitting apart families. That year he took the lead in *World Gone Wild*, a low-budget film about a hippie survivor of the apocalypse who brings peace and love to those in a desert community that was blessed with the only water supply left in the world. Dern played the establishment figure who turns violent to repel the evildoers, led by a character played by teen idol Adam Ant. By the end of the twentieth century, roles were fewer and fewer and so sadly, younger fans only knew Bruce Dern as the father of actress Laura Dern.

—Douglas Gomery

DeVITO, Danny

Nationality: American. **Born:** Neptune, New Jersey, 17 November 1944. **Education:** Attended parochial school in Asbury Park, New Jersey; Oratory Prep School in Summit, New Jersey; Wilfred Academy of Hair and Beauty Culture; the American Academy of Dramatic Arts, New York City, graduated 1966. **Family:** Married the actress Rhea Perlman, 1982, daughters: Lucy Chet and Gracie, son: Jake. **Career:** 1968—stage debut, off-Broadway, in a program of Pirandello one-acts; 1969—film debut in *Dreams of Glass*; 1978-83—starred in the TV series *Taxi* (as Louie DePalma); 1984—directed *The Ratings Game*, a cable TV movie; 1985—directed and starred in "The Wedding Ring" episode of Steven Spielberg's *Amazing Stories* (TV anthology); has directed numerous shorts and TV shows in addition to feature films; 1987—directorial feature debut with *Throw Momma from the Train*; starting 1988—provided voice of Herbert Powell for several episodes of the cartoon TV series *The Simpsons*. Performed in several TV specials for children; has an active production company, Jersey Films; produced *Reality Bites* and *Pulp Fiction*, 1994; and *Feeling Minnesota*, 1996. **Awards:** Best Supporting Actor Emmy Award, for *Taxi*, 1981. **Agent:** Fred Specktor, Creative Artists Agency, 9830 Wilshire Boulevard, Beverly Hills, CA 90212, U.S.A.

Films as Actor:

1969 *Dreams of Glass* (Klouse)
1971 *Bananas* (Woody Allen) (as subway hood); *La Mortadella* (*Lady Liberty*) (Monicelli) (as Fred Mancuso)
1973 *Hurry Up, or I'll Be 30* (Jacoby) (as Petey); *Scalawag* (Kirk Douglas) (as Fly Speck)
1975 ***One Flew over the Cuckoo's Nest*** (Forman) (as Martini); *The Money* (Workman)
1976 *Car Wash* (Schultz); *Deadly Hero* (Nagy); *The Van* (Grossman) (as Andy)

Danny DeVito in *Tin Men*

1977   *The World's Greatest Lover* (Gene Wilder) (as the assistant
        director)
1978   *Goin' South* (Nicholson) (as Hog)
1979   *Valentine* (Philips—for TV)
1981   *Going Ape!* (Kronsberg) (as Lazlo)
1983   *Terms of Endearment* (James L. Brooks) (as Vernon
        Dahlart)
1984   *Johnny Dangerously* (Heckerling) (as Burr); *Romancing the
        Stone* (Zemeckis) (as Ralph)
1985   *The Jewel of the Nile* (Teague) (as Ralph); *Happily Ever After*
        (Melendez—for TV) (as voice)
1986   *Head Office* (Finkleman) (as Stedman); *My Little Pony* (Joens)
        (as voice of Grundle King); *Ruthless People* (Abrahams,
        Zucker, and Zucker) (as Sam Stone); *Wise Guys* (DePalma)
        (as Harry Valentini)
1987   *Tin Men* (Levinson) (as Ernest Tilley)
1988   *Twins* (Reitman) (as Vincent Benedict)
1991   *Other People's Money* (Jewison) (as Lawrence Garfield)
1992   *Batman Returns* (Burton) (as Penguin/Oswald Cobblepot)
1993   *Last Action Hero* (McTiernan) (as voice of Whiskers,
        uncredited); *Look Who's Talking Now* (Ropelewski) (as
        voice of Rocks); *Jack the Bear* (Herskovitz) (as John
        Leary)
1994   *Junior* (Reitman) (as Dr. Larry Arbogast); *Renaissance Man*
        (*Army Intelligence*) (Penny Marshall) (as Bill Rago)
1995   *Get Shorty* (Sonnenfeld) (as Martin Weir, + pr)

Films as Actor and Director:

1984   *The Ratings Game* (for TV) (as Vic De Salvo)
1987   *Throw Momma from the Train* (as Owen Lift)
1989   *The War of the Roses* (as Gavin D'Amato)
1992   *Hoffa* (as Bobby Ciaro, + co-pr)
1996   *Matilda*

Other Films:

1994   *Reality Bites* (Stiller) (co-pr); ***Pulp Fiction*** (Tarantino) (co-
        exec pr)
1995   *Get Shorty* (Sonnenfeld) (co-pr)

Publications

By DeVITO: article—

Interview in *Playboy* (Chicago), February 1993.

On DeVITO: articles—

Current Biography 1988, New York, 1988.
Seidenberg, Robert, "Funny as Hell," in *American Film* (New York),
September 1989.

"Little Boss Man," in *Rolling Stone* (New York), 16 November 1989.

Corman, Avery, "Danny DeVito, This Year's Redford," in *New York Times*, 8 September 1991.

Clark, John, "Danny DeVito," in *Interview* (New York), July 1992.

Reed, Julia. "DeVito Raises Hoffa," in *Vogue* (New York), December 1992.

Young, Josh, "Danny DeVito: Center of the Universe?," in *New York Times*, 6 November 1994.

*   *   *

An actor seemingly proscribed from leading man status by his physical instrument—his five-foot, 150-pound body, his dark-haired, dark-eyed "ethnic" features, and his flat, fast, New Jersey-rooted speech—Danny DeVito over the past decade has established himself as one of the defining screen comics of his generation. Like most recent movie comedians, DeVito first achieved fame in television and continued to work with creative television personnel as he moved into film. But his persona is marked as a product of his times even more by his central theme: the journey of a formerly antiauthoritarian, "freaky"—post-1960s—entrepreneur toward his slice of the American pie. DeVito's life story and those of his characters neatly cohere around this subject.

While also working on-stage, DeVito spent the 1970s playing background roles in mostly unremarkable films and television shows. Unshakably dedicated, he also produced and directed several short films. DeVito's biggest movie role of the 1970s was as one of the inmates who take over the asylum in *One Flew over the Cuckoo's Nest*. That film's sympathy for the socially maladjusted persisted into DeVito's breakthrough role, as Louie DePalma in the 1978-83 television situation comedy *Taxi*. With Louie, however, DeVito moved from portraying the odd and exploited to portraying the odd and exploited exploiter—the type to which most of his subsequent movie characters adhere.

The dispatcher in a taxi company full of nice fallout victims from the 1960s (a recovering addict, a divorced mother, a Vietnam veteran), Louie is unfettered capitalism embodied—grasping, volatile, and rude. Stamped by the late 1970s, however, *Taxi* made Louie less a figure of unmitigated scorn than, for instance, its generic predecessor *M*A*S*H* made the moneygrubbing Frank Burns in the decade's early years. DeVito's performances play to this softening, employing his ability to slide between naturalism and cartoonish excess. DeVito conveys not only Louie's gratingly innocent delight in his gratuitous abusiveness but his fear and loneliness. As he does throughout his career, DeVito in *Taxi* often treats his own body as a prop; he sparks fresh ideas from the ensemble's other players; and he fully exploits his voice. DeVito's thoughtful choices among a subtly wide range of (mostly) East Coast accents, pitches, and volumes individuate his various characters even as they ground these men in the everyday and the middle class.

DeVito's first showcase supporting movie role came from *Taxi* producer James Brooks, who cast him in a subdued key in 1983's *Terms of Endearment*. (People who work with DeVito once seem inclined to repeat the experience.) The next year DeVito directed his first feature-length project, the made-for-cable *The Ratings Game*: all his evolving persona's key traits are present in his leading role as a mob-linked executive from New Jersey who becomes a television star and marries a good woman, played by DeVito's wife and frequent collaborator, Rhea Perlman. For the well-grossing feature *Romancing the Stone* and its sequel *Jewel of the Nile*, DeVito's crooked small-time businessman type metamorphosed into a true crook, in a supporting role as a goofily unhappy, drug-smuggling kidnapper. DeVito got glowing reviews, and the chance to star in two big-screen vehicles—the organized crime spoof *Wise Guys*, and the black comedy of big business and marriage, *Ruthless People*.

With *Ruthless People* DeVito attained movie stardom. He then moved between sour and soft comedies, acting in and directing the former with *Throw Momma from the Train*, his theatrical film debut as director, and *The War of the Roses*; and starring in the latter with *Tin Men* (as a crazed salesman), *Twins* (as a gangster), and *Other People's Money* (as a corporate raider). Almost all of DeVito's post-*Taxi* characters are criminals, either organized, white collar, or both. They are ambivalent figures of mixed pathos and satire, their unlawfulness sometimes standing in for their outsider's natures, but their ill will more often entwining with their situations as capitalist cogs.

In 1992, DeVito played the supporting role of comic-book villain Penguin in *Batman Returns*, while also turning his directorial hand to drama with *Hoffa*, starring his old friend Jack Nicholson; the first was a huge success, though the second fizzled. *Jack the Bear*, a rare noncrime drama (directed by Marshall Herskovitz, a television veteran), did not receive either critical or commercial recognition. DeVito continued to move away from the criminal type and to work with television-bred comic talent in *Renaissance Man* (directed by television star Penny Marshall) and *Get Shorty* (starring television star John Travolta). Both succeeded at the box office, as did *Junior*, his second pairing with Arnold Schwarzenegger. In 1996 DeVito will release *Matilda*, based on Roald Dahl's children's story of a young girl working past her venial and grotesque parents (DeVito and Perlman). As the era's Hollywood dean of corrupt but salvageable authority, DeVito thus pursues his great theme.

—Susan Knobloch

DICKINSON, Angie

Nationality: American. **Born:** Angeline Brown in Kulm, North Dakota, 30 September 1931. **Education:** Attended parochial schools; Immaculate Heart College; Glendale College, California. **Family:** Married 1) Gene Dickinson (divorced 1959); 2) the composer Burt Bacharach, 1965 (divorced 1980), daughter: Nikki. **Career:** Early 1950s—secretary at aircraft company while taking bit parts in TV and acting lessons; 1954—film debut in *Lucky Me*; 1962—Broadway appearance in *The Perfect Setup*; 1974—guest in episode of TV series *Police Story*; asked to star in spin-off series *Police Woman*, 1974-78; 1978—in TV mini-series *Pearl*; 1982—in TV series *Cassie & Company*; 1985—in TV mini-series *Hollywood Wives*, and *Wild Palms*, 1993; also former Mayor of Universal City, California. **Address:** c/o Dorothy Howe, 1524 Walgrove Avenue, Mar Vista, CA 90066, U.S.A.

Films as Actress:

1954   *Lucky Me* (Donahue) (as party guest)

1955   *Man with the Gun* (*Man without a Gun*; *The Trouble Shooter*) (Wilson) (as Kitty); *Tennessee's Partner* (Dwan) (as girl); *The Return of Jack Slade* (*Texas Rose*) (Schuster) (as Polly Logan)

1956   *Hidden Guns* (Gannaway) (as Becky Carter); *Tension at Table Rock* (Warren) (as Cathy); *Gun the Man Down* (*Arizona Mission*) (McLaglen) (as Janice); *The Black Whip* (Warren) (as Sally)

1957   *Run of the Arrow* (*Hot Lead*) (Fuller) (as dubbed voice of Yellow Moccasin, played by Sarita Montiel); *Shoot-Out at Medicine Bend* (Bare) (as Priscilla); *China Gate* (Fuller) (as Lucky Legs); *Calypso Joe* (Dein)

1958   *Cry Terror* (Andrew L. Stone) (as Eileen Kelly); *I Married a
        Woman* (Kanter) (as wife of John Wayne character in film-
        within-film)
1959   ***Rio Bravo*** (Hawks) (as Feathers); *I'll Give My Life* (Claxton);
        Frontier Rangers (Jacques Tourneur—for TV)
1960   *Ocean's Eleven* (Milestone) (as Beatrice Ocean); *The Sins of
        Rachel Cade* (*Rachel Cade*) (Gordon Douglas) (title role);
        The Bramble Bush (Petrie) (as Fran)
1961   *A Fever in the Blood* (Sherman) (as Cathy Simon)
1962   *Rome Adventure* (*Lovers Must Learn*) (Daves) (as Lyda); *Jes-
        sica* (*La Sage-femme, le curé et le bon Dieu*) (Negulesco)
        (title role)
1963   *Captain Newman, M.D.* (David Miller) (as Lt. Francie
        Corum)
1964   *The Killers* (*Ernest Hemingway's The Killers*) (Siegel) (as Sheila
        Farr)
1965   *The Art of Love* (Jewison) (as Laurie)
1966   *Cast a Giant Shadow* (Shavelson) (as Emma Marcus); *Danger
        Grows Wild* (*The Poppy Is Also a Flower*) (Terence Young)
        (as Linda Benson); *The Chase* (Arthur Penn) (as Ruby
        Calder)
1967   *Point Blank* (Boorman) (as Chris); *The Last Challenge*
        (*Pistolero of Red River*) (Thorpe) (as Lisa Denton)
1969   *Some Kind of a Nut* (Kanin) (as Rachel Amidon); *Sam
        Whiskey* (Laven) (as Laura Breckinridge); *Young Billy
        Young* (*Who Rides with Kane*) (Kennedy) (as Lily
        Beloit)
1970   *The Love War* (McCowan—for TV)
1971   *Pretty Maids All in a Row* (Vadim) (as Miss Smith); *The Resur-
        rection of Zachary Wheeler* (Wynn) (as Dr. Johnson); *Thief*
        (Graham—for TV) (as Jean Melville); *See the Man Run*
        (Corey Allen—for TV)
1973   *Un Homme est morte* (*Funerale a Los Angeles*; *The Outside
        Man*) (Deray) (as Jackie Kovacs); *The Norliss Tapes* (Curtis—
        for TV)
1974   *Big Bad Mama* (Carver) (as Wilma McClatchie); *Pray for the
        Wildcats* (Robert Michael Lewis—for TV)
1977   *A Sensitive, Passionate Man* (Newland—for TV); *Le Labyrinthe*
        (*Labyrinths*)
1978   *Overboard* (Newland—for TV)
1979   *L'Homme en colère* (*The Angry Man*) (Pinoteau) (as Karen);
        The Suicide's Wife (*A New Life*) (Newland—for TV) (title
        role)
1980   *Klondike Fever* (*Jack London's Klondike Fever*) (Carter)
        (as Belinda McNair); *Dressed to Kill* (De Palma) (as Kate
        Miller)
1981   *Death Hunt* (Hunt) (as Vanessa); *Charlie Chan and the
        Curse of the Dragon Queen* (Clive Donner) (as Dragon
        Queen); *Dial M for Murder* (Segal—for TV) (as Margot
        Wendice)
1982   *One Shoe Makes It Murder* (William Hale—for TV)
1984   *A Touch of Scandal* (Nagy—for TV) (as Katherine Gilvay);
        Jealousy (Bloom—for TV) (as Georgia/Laura/Ginny)
1987   *Big Bad Momma II* (Wynorski) (as Wilma McClatchie);
        Police Story: The Freeway Killings (Graham—for TV)
        (as Off. Anne Cavanaugh); *Stillwatch* (Holcomb—for
        TV)
1988   *Once upon a Texas Train* (Kennedy—for TV) (as Maggie)
1989   *Fire and Rain* (Jameson—for TV) (as Beth Mancini); *Prime
        Target* (Robert Collins—for TV)
1992   *Treacherous Crossing* (Wharmby—for TV) (as Beverly Tho-
        mas)
1994   *Even Cowgirls Get the Blues* (Van Sant) (as Miss Adrian)
1995   *The Crossing Guard* (Sean Penn); *The Maddening* (Danny
        Huston); *Sabrina* (Pollack) (as Ingrid Tyson)

Publications

By DICKINSON: articles—

Interview in *Photoplay* (London), January 1985.
Interview in *Los Angeles Magazine*, April 1985.
"Surrogate," interview in *New Yorker*, 9 December 1991.
"Angie Dickinson Nearly Bares It All," interview with Alan Carter, in
    Entertainment Weekly (New York), 14 May 1993.
"Thoroughly Modern Angie," interview with George Wayne, in *Vanity
    Fair* (New York), April 1995.

On DICKINSON: book—

Zenka, Lorraine, *Angie Dickinson*, New York, 1992.

On DICKINSON: articles—

Lester, Peter, "Redress or Undress? Feminists Fume While Angie Scores
    in Sexy Thriller," in *People Weekly* (New York), 15 September 1980.
Ciné Revue (Paris), 9 October 1980 and 22 June 1984.
Current Biography 1981, New York, 1981.
Haller, Scot, "Sex and the Single Star," in *People Weekly* (New York),
    25 February 1985.
Reed, J. D., "Still Sexy After All These Years," in *People Weekly* (New
    York), 24 May 1993.

*   *   *

Like James Caan, Angie Dickinson has never equaled, let alone
surpassed, the impression she made early in her career in a Howard
Hawks movie, in her case *Rio Bravo*, though she has given numerous
sympathetic performances for other directors. It is a striking phenomenon that many stars have given their most vivid, most definitive performances under Hawks's direction. That is not to suggest that
Dickinson's "Feathers" was somehow Hawks's creation, yet one must
lament the fact that Dickinson, one of the most potentially (and, in
Rio Bravo, actually) vibrant presences of Hollywood cinema since the
late 1950s, has so seldom worked with good directors, or directors
responsive to her very distinctive personality. Hawks was never interested in what is commonly known as "great acting," and that is not
the issue here. The knack he had with actors was that of eliciting an
aliveness of response, not simply to his direction but in mutual interplay. Hence, in *Rio Bravo* one cannot really talk of Dickinson's
performance in isolation. The inexhaustible delight of her scenes with
John Wayne derives, not from "acting," but from the way they play
off each other to create one of the quintessential Hawksian male/
female relationships: his silence, stoicism, stiffness, apparent impreg-
nability, set against her continuous nervous talk, emotionalism, spontaneity, vulnerability. Her characterization becomes one of the strategies in the film for developing an affectionate and ironic critique of
the Wayne character and the Wayne persona.

It is sad that, with Dickinson yet again, Hawks adhered to his weird
principle of never using the same female star twice in a leading role
(Lauren Bacall the solitary exception, perhaps because of her partnership with Bogart). Dickinson made a strong impression both before
Rio Bravo (Samuel Fuller's *China Gate*) and after (Arthur Penn's *The
Chase*, where her presence transforms what is basically a very conventional role); even reduced to the ignominy of playing a decadent
femme fatale bent on seducing Troy Donahue (*Rome Adventure*), she
is not negligible; and her presence added an extra dimension to the
complex (or confused) sexual politics of De Palma's *Dressed to Kill*.
But the magic of her "Feathers" has never quite been recaptured: if she
never appeared again, she would deserve a niche in cinema history for
that alone.

—Robin Wood

DIETRICH, Marlene

Nationality: American. **Born:** Marie Magdalene Dietrich in Berlin, Germany, 27 December 1901 (some sources list 1904); became citizen of United States, 1939. **Education:** Attended the Augusta Victoria School, Berlin, and boarding schools in Weimar; Hochschule für Musik. **Family:** Married Rudolf Sieber, 1924 (separated 1939), daughter: Maria. **Career:** Early 1920s—chorus girl in revue circuit in Germany; 1922—accepted into Max Reinhardt's Deutsche Theaterschule; began appearing in films for Ufa, debut in *So sind die Männer*; 1928—first starring film role in *Prinzessin Olala*; 1930—in the first German talking film, *Der blaue Engel*, beginning long personal and professional relationship with director Josef von Sternberg; contract with Paramount and moved to Hollywood; 1935—in last film for von Sternberg, *The Devil Is a Woman*; 1936—walked out on Paramount contract and began freelancing for other studios; 1937—approached by Nazi agents with offer to return to German films but refused, resulting in the banning of her films in Germany; 1943-46—entertained American troops, participating in war bond drives, and made anti-Nazi broadcasts in German; 1950s—recording and cabaret performer; in radio series *Cafe Istanbul* and *Time for Love*; 1967—Broadway debut in one-woman cabaret act. **Awards:** Medal of Freedom, for entertaining American troops and working against Nazi Germany, 1947; Chevalier de la Légion d'Honneur, 1951. **Died:** In Paris, 6 May 1992.

Films as Actress:

1922   *So sind die Männer* (*Napoleons kleiner Brüder*; *Der kleine Napoleon*; *Men Are Like This*; *Napoleon's Little Brother*; *The Little Napoleon*) (Jacoby) (as Kathrin)

1923   *Tragödie der Liebe* (*Tragedy of Love*) (Joe May) (as Lucie); *Der Mensch am Wege* (*Man by the Roadside*) (Dieterle)

1924   *Der Sprung ins Leben* (*They Leap into Life*) (Guter)

1925   *Die freudlose Gasse* (*Joyless Street*; *The Street of Sorrow*) (Pabst) (as extra)

1926   *Manon Lescaut* (Robison) (as Micheline); *Eine DuBarry von Heute* (*A Modern DuBarry*) (Korda); *Kopf hoch, Charly!* (*Heads Up, Charly*) (Wolff) (as Edmée Marchand); *Madame wünscht keine Kinder* (*Madame Wants No Children*) (Wolff) (bit part)

1927   *Seine grösster Bluff* (*Er oder Dich*; *His Greatest Bluff*) (Piel) (as Yvette); *Café Electric* (*Wenn ein Weib den Weg verliert*; *When a Woman Loses Her Way*) (Ucicky) (as Erni); *Der Juxbaron* (*The Imaginary Baron*) (Wolff) (as Sophie)

1928   *Prinzessin Olala* (*Princess Olala*; *Art of Love*) (Land) (as Chicotte de Gastoné); *Die glückliche Mutter* (Sieber—short)

1929   *Ich küsse Ihre Hand, Madame* (*I Kiss Your Hand, Madame*) (Land) (as Laurene Gerard); *Die Frau, nach der Man sich sehnt* (*The Woman One Longs For*; *Three Loves*) (Bernhardt) (as Stascha); *Das Schiff der verlorenen Menschen* (*Le Navire des hommes perdus*; *The Ship of Lost Souls*) (Maurice Tourneur) (as Miss Ethel); *Liebesnächte* (*Gefahren der Brautzeit*; *Aus dem Tagebuch eines Verführers*; *Eine Nacht der Liebe*; *Liebesbriefe*; *Nights of Love*; *Love Letters*) (Sauer) (as Evelyn)

1930   *Der blaue Engel* (*The Blue Angel*) (von Sternberg) (as Lola Frohlich); *Morocco* (von Sternberg) (as Amy Jolly)

1931   *Dishonored* (von Sternberg) (as X-27)

1932   *Shanghai Express* (von Sternberg) (as Shanghai Lilly); *Blonde Venus* (von Sternberg) (as Helen Faraday)

1933   *Song of Songs* (Mamoulian) (as Lily Czepanek)

1934   *The Scarlet Empress* (von Sternberg) (as Catherine II)

1935   *The Devil Is a Woman* (von Sternberg) (as Concha Perez)

1936   *Desire* (Borzage) (as Madeleine de Beaupré); *I Loved a Soldier* (Hathaway); *The Garden of Allah* (Boleslawski) (as Domini Enfilden)

1937   *Knight without Armor* (Feyder) (as Alexandra Vladinoff); *Angel* (Lubitsch) (as Maria Barker)

1939   *Destry Rides Again* (George Marshall) (as Frenchy)

1940   *Seven Sinners* (Garnett) (as Bijou)

1941   *The Flame of New Orleans* (Clair) (as Claire Ledeux); *Manpower* (Walsh) (as Fay Duval)

1942   *The Lady Is Willing* (Leisen) (as Elizabeth Madden); *The Spoilers* (Enright) (as Cherry Mallotte); *Pittsburgh* (Seiler) (as Josie Winters)

1943   *Screen Snapshots No. 103* (short)

1944   *Follow the Boys* (A. Edward Sutherland); *Kismet* (Dieterle) (as Jamilla)

1946   *Martin Roumagnac* (*The Room Upstairs*) (Lacombe) (as Blanche Ferrand)

1947   *Golden Earrings* (Leisen) (as Lydia)

1948   *A Foreign Affair* (Wilder) (as Erika von Schluetow)

1949   *Jigsaw* (Markle) (as nightclub patron)

1950   *Stage Fright* (Hitchcock) (as Charlotte Inwood)

1951   *No Highway in the Sky* (*No Highway*) (Koster) (as Monica Teasdale)

1952   *Rancho Notorious* (Fritz Lang) (as Altar Keane)

1956   *Around the World in Eighty Days* (Anderson) (as hostess)

1957   *The Monte Carlo Story* (Taylor) (as Marquise Maria de Crevecoeur); *Witness for the Prosecution* (Wilder) (as Christine Vole)

1958   *Touch of Evil* (Welles) (as Tanya)

1961   *Judgment at Nuremberg* (Kramer) (as Mme. Bertholt)

1962   *The Black Fox* (Stoumen) (as narrator)

1963   *Paris When It Sizzles* (Quine)

1979   *Schöner Gigolo—armer Gigolo* (*Just a Gigolo*) (Hemmings) (as Baroness von Semering)

Publications

By DIETRICH: books—

Marlene's ABC, 1961.
My Life Story, New York, 1979.
Ich bin, Gott sei dank, Berlinerin, Frankfurt, 1987; as *My Life*, London, 1989.

On DIETRICH: books—

Talky, Jean, *Marlène Dietrich, femme énigme*, Paris, 1932.
Griffith, Richard, *Marlene Dietrich—Image and Legend*, New York, 1959.
von Sternberg, Josef, *Fun in a Chinese Laundry*, New York, 1965.
Frewin, Leslie, *Dietrich: The Story of a Star*, New York, 1967.
Dickens, Homer, *The Films of Marlene Dietrich*, New York, 1968; as *The Complete Films of Marlene Dietrich*, revised and updated by Jerry Vermilye, New York, 1992.
Kobal, John, *Marlene Dietrich*, New York, 1968.
Baxter, John, *The Cinema of Josef von Sternberg*, New York, 1971.
Rosen, Marjorie, *Popcorn Venus*, New York, 1973.
Silver, Charles, *Marlene Dietrich*, New York, 1974.
Kracauer, Siegfried, *From Caligari to Hitler: A Psychological History of the German Film*, Princeton, New Jersey, 1974.
Morley, Sheridan, *Marlene Dietrich*, London, 1976
Higham, Charles, *Marlene: The Life of Marlene Dietrich*, New York, 1977.

Marlene Dietrich

Hampton, Joe, *Marlène Dietrich*, Paris, 1981.

De Navacelle, Thierry, *Sublime Marlene*, London, 1984.

Seydel, Renate, *Marlene Dietrich: Eine Chronik ihres Lebens in Bilden und Dokumenten*, Berlin, 1984.

Walker, Alexander, *Dietrich*, London, 1984.

Spoto, Donald, *Falling in Love Again: Marlene Dietrich*, Boston, 1985.

Studlar, Gaylene, *In the Realm of Pleasure: Von Sternberg, Dietrich, and the Masochistic Aesthetic*, Chicago, 1988.

Zucker, Carole, *The Idea of the Image: Josef von Sternberg's Dietrich Films*, Cranbury, New Jersey, 1988.

O'Connor, Patrick, *Dietrich: Style and Substance*, New York, 1991.

Bach, Steven, *Marlene Dietrich: Life and Legend*, New York, 1992.

Bosquet, Alain, *Marlene Dietrich: un amour par telephone*, Paris, 1992.

Bozon, Louis, *Marlene: la femme de ma vie*, Paris, 1992.

Lieberman, Alexander, *Marlene: An Intimate Photographic Memoir*, New York, 1992.

Spoto, Donald, *Blue Angel: The Life of Marlene Dietrich*, New York, 1992.

Baxt, George, *The Marlene Dietrich Murder Case* (fiction), New York, 1993.

Hofmann, Barbara, *Marlene Dietrich, die Privatsammlung*, Frankfurt, 1993.

Riva, Maria, *Marlene Dietrich*, New York, 1993.

Mentele, Richard, *Auf Liebe eingestellt: Marlene Dietrich's schone Kunst*, Bensheim, 1993.

Martin, W. K., *Marlene Dietrich*, New York, 1995.

Hanut, Eryk, *I Wish You Love: Conversations with Marlene Dietrich*, Berkeley, California, 1996.

On DIETRICH: articles—

George, Manfred, "Marlene Dietrich's Beginning," in *Films in Review* (New York), February 1952.

Sargeant, W., "Dietrich and Her Magic Myth," and "Tribute to Mamma from Papa Hemingway," by Ernest Hemingway, in *Life* (New York), 18 August 1952.

Knight, Arthur, "Marlene Dietrich," in *Films in Review* (New York), December 1954.

Lane, J. F., "Give Her Dirt—and Hard Work," in *Films and Filming* (London), December 1956.

Kyrou, Ado, "Sternberg et Marlène," in *Le Surrealism au Cinéma* (Paris), 1963.

Higham, Charles, "Dietrich in Sydney," in *Sight and Sound* (London), Winter 1965-66.

Current Biography 1968, New York, 1968.

Calendo, J., "Dietrich and the Devil," in *Inter/View* (New York), October and November 1972.

Rheuban, Joyce, "Josef von Sternberg: The Scientist and the Vamp," in *Sight and Sound* (London), Autumn 1972-73.

Gow, Gordon, "Alchemy: Dietrich + Sternberg," in *Films and Filming* (London), June 1974.

Flinn, T., "Joe Where Are You?," in *Velvet Light Trap* (Madison, Wisconsin), Winter 1977.

von Sternberg, J., and A. Kerr, "Marlene wird geschaffen," in *Film und Fernsehen* (Berlin), October 1977.

Baxter, P., "On the Naked Thighs of Miss Dietrich," in *Wide Angle* (Athens, Ohio), no. 2, 1978.

Lewis, W. W., "Marlene Dietrich: From Devil to Angel . . . and Back" and "Sam Jaffe on Dietrich and Sternberg," in *Close-Ups: The Movie Star Book*, edited by Danny Peary, New York, 1978.

Zucker, C., "Some Observations on Sternberg and Dietrich," in *Cinema Journal* (Evanston), Spring 1980.

"Marlene Dietrich—Stationen eines Lebens," in *Film und Fernsehen* (Berlin), December 1980.

Rheinsberg, A., "Hommage," in *Frauen und Film* (Frankfurt), February 1984.

Marlene Dietrich Section of *Positif* (Paris), September 1984.

Sorel, Nancy Caldwell, "Alexander Fleming and Marlene Dietrich," in *Atlantic* (New York), March 1991.

Obituary in *New York Times*, 7 May 1992.

McBride, Joseph, obituary in *Variety* (New York), 11 May 1992.

On DIETRICH: film—

Marlene, documentary directed by Maximilian Schell, Germany, 1984.

* * *

For decades, filmgoers have clustered to her like moths around a flame, to paraphrase her signature tune "Falling in Love Again." That eternal flame burned brightest from the thirties onward, but Dietrich had toiled in the silent cinema for nearly ten years before her discovery as Teuton siren, Garbo-threat, and sphinxlike beauty of the international cinema.

The standard critical line is that without cine-magician von Sternberg, there would be no Dietrich; the less supportable exaggeration of this contention is that only the seven Dietrich-von Sternberg collaborations merit serious discussion. If von Sternberg deserves credit for sculpting her image and breathing life into this goddess, then let us applaud implacable Marlene with variations on a theme of mysterious enticement after *The Devil Is a Woman* and until *Just a Gigolo*. Even as a contentious old woman (who refused to appear on camera) in Maximilian Schell's riveting documentary, *Marlene* (1984), her mystique was untouched by time, and as someone once said, "her voice alone could break your heart." Forty years of image maintenance suggests that the provenance of Dietrich's legend was not the vision of her Svengali but could be found in her own steel will.

Certainly, the von Sternberg/Dietrich combination represents a singular symbiosis of visually oriented auteur and perfect camera subject. If Garbo drew the camera to her like a magnet, Dietrich not only fascinated viewers with her sultry glare but transfixed every other aspect of the mise-en-scène, a smoky world of sequined nets, exotic feathers, and glistening surfaces masked by shadows. It is a cinema in which style is the substance. Whether a plump temptress in *The Blue Angel*, foreign-legion groupie in *Morocco*, a fallen angel in *Shanghai Express*, or Czarina of Russia in *The Scarlet Empress*, Dietrich the great illusionist helped von Sternberg fabricate a fabulistic ambience where people lived and died for love. Whether impulsively stealing a kiss from a young woman in *Morocco* or defiantly reapplying her lipstick before the firing squad guns her down in *Dishonored*, the one constant in Dietrich's persona was her supreme control, a guarded willfulness she only relinquished for the one lover of her dreams. And if some of her less than dynamic co-stars (Clive Brook, Herbert Marshall) seemed hidden in her shadow, they were only props anyway. Dietrich's sacrificial gestures, however, were in no way lessened by the unworthiness of their recipients. No man could measure up to a divinity (although *Morocco*'s Gary Cooper is a step in the right direction).

After the peak of the von Sternberg/Dietrich teamwork, the ravishingly decadent *The Devil Is a Woman* (Dietrich's favorite movie), the movie's ultimate apotheosis of the femme fatale, Dietrich floundered a bit, but did not, as some suggest, survive as a mere impersonator of her former exalted self. Are cinephiles supposed to credit von Sternberg with the streak of wit Lubitsch helped unearth in the delicious romantic comedy, *Desire*? And if the raucous comeback of *Destry Rides Again* represents a coarsening of her unapproachable allure, Dietrich's decision to prevail as a more democratic love goddess is completely defensible. What Dietrich cleverly did, while delightfully exploiting a freewheeling side to her nature, was to Americanize herself for the mass audience no matter what nationality she was supposed to be playing in *Seven Sinners* or *The Flame of New Orleans*. Converted to American attitudes, she became a one-woman emigrant experience on display. Rather than her beauty, her largesse made her a citizen of the world.

Repudiating Nazi Germany and touring for Yankee troops further endeared her to Americans and helped sustain her eminence through the difficult middle portion of her career. In a petulant biography, however, Dietrich's spiteful daughter Maria Riva implies that the khaki pinup girl simply used World War II for her own convenience and played the patriot as another acting assignment. In shortchanging her mother's sacrifices, Riva only conclusively establishes her own jealousy; obviously Dietrich's nurturing of her image was murder on child-rearing.

Rigidly taking care of her beauty, the way champions train their muscles for prize fights, Dietrich cheated time in her postwar film work and in the wildly successful cabaret act that kept her legend alive in an environment of husky-voiced song styling and perfectly positioned stage lighting that burned years off the fabulous face. On-screen, she was still surpassingly lovely as double-crossing dames in *Witness for the Prosecution*, *Stage Fright*, and *A Foreign Affair*. Somehow, the good-time gal of the forties was the aloof temptress of the thirties once more. In our contemporary cinema in which glamour seems to dissolve as soon as it is revealed on-screen, Dietrich remains the movies' most durable symbol of the power of artifice. Like Swanson and Crawford, her enemy was time but she did not go down without a long fight. When we stare at her perfection even in the gauze-lensed *Just a Gigolo*, we look into the face of our dreams—nostalgic dreams of a time when stars offered an escape from the commonplace not just a reaffirmation of it.

—Robert Pardi

DILLON, Matt

Nationality: American. **Born:** New Rochelle, New York, 18 February 1964. **Education:** Attended high school in New Rochelle; studied acting at the Lee Strasberg School. **Career:** 1979—film debut in *Over the Edge* after being spotted by casting director Vic Ramos. **Awards:** U.S. Independent Spirit Award for Best Actor, for *Drugstore Cowboy*, 1989. **Agent:** Ed Limato, William Morris Agency, 151 El Camino Drive, Beverly Hills, CA 90212, U.S.A.

Matt Dillon in *Target*

Films as Actor:

1979   *Over the Edge* (Kaplan) (as Richie)
1980   *Little Darlings* (Maxwell) (as Randy); *My Bodyguard* (Bill) (as Moody)
1982   *Liar's Moon* (Fisher) (as Jack Duncan); *Tex* (Hunter) (as Tex McCormick); *The Great American Fourth of July and Other Disasters* (Bartlett—for TV)
1983   *The Outsiders* (Francis Ford Coppola) (as Dallas Winston); *Rumble Fish* (Francis Ford Coppola) (as Rusty James)
1984   *The Flamingo Kid* (Garry Marshall) (as Jeffrey Willis)
1985   *Rebel* (Jenkins) (title role); *Target* (Arthur Penn) (as Chris Lloyd)
1986   *Native Son* (Freedland) (as Jan)
1987   *The Big Town* (Bolt) (as J. C. Cullen); *Dear America: Letters Home from Vietnam* (Couturie—doc)
1988   *Kansas* (David Stevens) (as Doyle Kennedy)
1989   *Drugstore Cowboy* (Van Sant) (as Bob Hughes); *Bloodhounds of Broadway* (Brookner) (as Regret); *When He's Not a Stranger* (John Gray—for TV)
1991   *A Kiss before Dying* (Dearden) (as Jonathan Corliss); "Return to Kansas City" ep. of *Women & Men II* (*Women & Men: In Love There Are No Rules*) (Bernstein, Figgis, and Zea—for TV) (as Eddie Megeffin)
1992   *Singles* (Crowe) (as Cliff Poncier); **Malcolm X** (Spike Lee) (as DJ at the Harlem "Y" Dance)
1993   *The Saint of Fort Washington* (Hunter) (as Matthew); *Mr. Wonderful* (Minghella) (as Gus DeMarco)
1994   *Golden Gate* (Madden) (as Kevin Walker)
1995   *To Die For* (Van Sant) (as Larry Maretto); *Frankie Starlight* (Lindsay-Hogg) (as Terry Klout)
1996   *Beautiful Girls* (Ted Demme) (as Tommy "Birdman" Rowland); *Albino Alligator* (Spacey) (as Dova)

Publications

By DILLON: articles—

Interview in *Interview* (New York), December 1983.
Interviews in *Ciné Revue* (Paris), 29 March 1984 and 28 May 1987.
Interview in *Time Out* (London), 27 October 1985 and 22 November 1989.
Interview with Brendan Lemon, in *Interview* (New York), April 1991.

On DILLON: book—

Mead, Cheryl L., *The Matt Dillon Scrapbook*, New York, 1984.

On DILLON: articles—

Seale, Jim, "Marshaling Dillon Tex," in *Film Comment* (New York), July/August 1982.
Scott, Jay, "Susie Loves Matt," in *American Film* (New York), April 1983.
Hibbin, S., "Matt Dillon," in *Films and Filming* (London), October 1984.
Current Biography 1985, New York, 1985.
Yakir, Dan, "Rebels with a Cause," in *Horizon* (New York), July/August 1985.
Arrington, Carl Wayne, "Mighty Matt," *Rolling Stone* (New York), 30 November 1989.
Ellis, Bret Easton, "The Dillon Papers," in *American Film*, February 1991.
Brantley, Ben, "Strange Love," in *Vanity Fair* (New York), April 1991.
Hoban, Phoebe, "Rough Boy," in *Premiere* (New York), May 1991.

*   *   *

Early in his career, Matt Dillon came to personify the alienated celluloid teen, adept at conveying adolescent angst (if not outright menace). Sometimes, his characters were thoroughly amoral and anti-social, such as Richie, the nihilistic young punk, in his debut feature, Jonathan Kaplan's much-underrated *Over the Edge*. As a depiction of disarray among suburban (as opposed to urban) teenagers, *Over the Edge* may be linked to the classic of the genre, *Rebel without a Cause*. Dillon's presence in the film served as a solid launching pad to screen stardom.

From *Over the Edge*, he segued into secondary roles as the stereo-typical teen bully in *Little Darlings* and *My Bodyguard*. In what were his most highly publicized early films, *The Outsiders* and *Rumble Fish* (both directed by Francis Coppola, and based on the writings of S. E. Hinton), Dillon played troubled teens who were more complexly drawn. Unfortunately, both films were far from the definitive views of youthful angst intended by the director. Dillon earlier had played a variation of his *Outsiders/Rumble Fish* characters in Tim Hunter's *Tex*, a far more cohesive adaptation of an S. E. Hinton story, in which he effectively conveys his character's insecurity and vulnerability. But easily the most congenial of his early performances came in *The Flamingo Kid*. Here, Dillon winningly plays a young man who is an outsider because of class, and who is anything but surly and antisocial. He is the child of a Brooklyn blue-collar family whose upwardly mobile instincts take root when he hires on as a cabana boy at a country club.

The Flamingo Kid might have been a career breakthrough. But what followed for Dillon was a spate of roles in films that were essentially minor in nature (*Rebel*, *The Big Town*, and *Kansas*), or those with higher pedigrees which were outright misfires (*Target*). During the second half of the 1980s, it appeared as if Dillon's career was in the process of self-destructing; furthermore, he already had entered his twenties, and could not forever play troubled or rebellious (or even likable) young antiheroes.

His celluloid salvation came when he was cast as Bob Hughes, the junkie-thief, in Gus Van Sant's *Drugstore Cowboy*. The film is a vivid depiction of life and survival within a drug subculture, and for Dillon it was a transitional role. Upon its release, many critics expressed surprise at the excellence of his performance. But he always had been a fine actor. This misconception regarding his talent was fostered by the fact that too many of his films had been undistinguished, and were quickly forgotten. His films with Coppola were disappointments; *Over the Edge* was barely seen. So *Tex* and *The Flamingo Kid* seemed to be deviations in a lackluster career. Additionally, Dillon may have suffered, in terms of the critical estimate of his acting ability, from having such a handsome face. He was victimized by the widespread prejudice that if you are beautiful you cannot act, and if you can act you cannot be beautiful.

In *Drugstore Cowboy*, however, Dillon proved that he indeed knew how to act. Since then, he has done nicely in a variety of roles, notably the ill-fated homeless camera buff befriended by Danny Glover in the unfortunately overlooked *The Saint of Fort Washington*; the ex-husband who tries to avoid paying alimony by marrying off former wife Annabella Sciorra in *Mr. Wonderful*; and the ill-fated husband of Nicole Kidman in *To Die For*. The latter role is especially interesting, given the roots of Dillon's screen persona. His Larry Maretto, a loving and well-adjusted nice guy who is satisfied with his small-town American life and only wants to start a family with his wife, is the antithesis of his early roles. Rather than being the cause of (or conduit for) chaos, Larry is the victim, as his murder is instigated by his wife—and he is bumped off by the type of characters he might have played a decade earlier.

The careers of so many of the young actors who, along with Dillon, came to fame in the 1980s have evaporated. In the mid-1990s, they nearly are absent from movie screens; whatever roles they secure are in films that are of the direct-to-video variety. Topping the list are Rob Lowe, Judd Nelson, Molly Ringwald, Ally Sheedy, C. Thomas

Howell, and Anthony Michael Hall; Dillon joins Demi Moore as exceptions to this scenario. Unlike Moore, Dillon may never become a star who commands a multimillion dollar salary. But his solidly reliable presence in such films as *The Saint of Fort Washington*, *Mr. Wonderful*, and *To Die For* portends his professional survival.

—Rob Edelman

DONAT, Robert

Nationality: British. **Born:** Withington, near Manchester, 18 March 1905. **Family:** Married 1) the dancer Ella Annesey Voysey, 1930 (divorced 1948), three children; 2) the actress Renée Asherson. **Career:** Left school at 14; toured with elocution teacher James Barnard giving Bible readings and Shakespearian recitals; 1921—joined Henry Baynton touring company as actor, stage manager, assistant director; 1924—toured with Sir Frank Benson company as featured actor, directed occasionally; 1928—joined Liverpool Repertory Co. 1930—first West End appearance as Gideon Sarn in *Precious Bane*; 1932—contract with Alexander Korda; continued to perform on stage throughout film career; 1934—starring role in *The Count of Monte Cristo* established film career; ill health due to chronic asthma caused cancellation of several projects during career; 1939—acted with Old Vic company; 1940s—active as stage producer in addition to acting; 1953—last theatrical appearance in *Murder in the Cathedral*. **Awards:** Best Actor Academy Award for *Goodbye, Mr. Chips*, 1939; Special Citation, D. W. Griffith Awards, for "the valor of his last performance in *The Inn of the Sixth Happiness*," 1958. **Died:** 9 June 1958.

Films as Actor:

1933   *Men of Tomorrow* (Sagan) (as Julian Angell); *That Night in London* (*Overnight*) (Lee) (as Dick Warren); *Cash* (*For Love or Money*) (Zoltan Korda) (as Paul Martin); *The Private Life of Henry VIII* (Alexander Korda) (as Thomas Culpepper)

1934   *The Count of Monte Cristo* (Lee) (as Edmond Dantes)

1935   *The 39 Steps* (Hitchcock) (as Richard Hannay)

1936   *The Ghost Goes West* (Clair) (as Murdoch Glourie/Donald Glourie)

1937   *Knight without Armour* (Feyder) (as A. J. Fothergill)

1938   *The Citadel* (Vidor) (as Dr. Andrew Manson)

1939   *Goodbye, Mr. Chips* (Wood) (as Charles Edward Chipping)

1942   *Young Mr. Pitt* (Reed) (as William Pitt)

1943   *The Adventures of Tartu* (*Tartu*) (Bucquet) (as Terrance Stevenson)

1946   *Perfect Strangers* (*Vacation from Marriage*) (Korda) (as Robert Wilson)

Robert Donat in *The Count of Monte Cristo*

1947   *Captain Boycott* (Launder) (as Charles Stewart Parnell); *The British—Are They Artistic?* (*This Modern Age, Number Sixteen*) (pr: Nolbandov—short) (as interviewee)
1948   *The Winslow Boy* (Asquith) (as Sir Robert Morton)
1951   *The Magic Box* (Boulton) (as William Friese-Greene)
1954   *Lease of Life* (Frend) (as Rev. William Thorne)
1956   *The Stained Glass at Fairford* (Wright—doc) (as narrator)
1958   *The Inn of the Sixth Happiness* (Robson) (as Chinese mandarin)

Film as Producer and Director:

1949   *The Cure for Love* (+ co-sc, ro as Sgt Jack Hardacre)

Publications

On DONAT: books—

Richards, Jeffrey, *The Age of the Dream Palace: Cinema and Society 1930-1939*, London, 1984.
Barrow, Kenneth, *Mr. Chips: The Life of Robert Donat*, London, 1985.

On DONAT: article—

Bodeen, DeWitt, "Robert Donat," in *Films in Review* (New York), December 1981; additions to filmography in issue for March 1982.

*   *   *

Robert Donat was one of the martyrs of the acting profession, a potentially great actor hampered by ill-health, which he resolutely strove to overcome throughout his career. Though favored with romantic, even dashing good looks and a richly beautiful voice, he had initially to cope in childhood with a serious stutter. Training in elocution gradually controlled this nervous impediment, with the result that, once established as an actor, he became famous alike for his voice and his sensitivity of expression. However, he also suffered from chronic asthma throughout his life.

Before his London debut in 1930, he had had virtually a decade of experience as a youthful actor in repertory and touring companies, performing in a wide range of plays, including those of Shakespeare. He developed a particular gift for reciting verse, which he was later to consolidate through his recordings. After rejecting an offer from Irving Thalberg—he had a particular dread of going to Hollywood—he accepted a contract with Alexander Korda and, like Merle Oberon as Anne Boleyn, achieved stardom in *The Private Life of Henry VIII*, in which he played her ill-fated lover. After that he played Edmond Dantes successfully in an American version of *The Count of Monte Cristo*, but this single experience only confirmed him in his view that he must remain in England, where until his death in 1958 he was always the much admired star of stage and screen.

He appeared in one of Hitchcock's best, and most romantic, British films, *The 39 Steps*, and brought charm and distinction to René Clair's English film made for Korda, *The Ghost Goes West*. After working with Marlene Dietrich in *Knight without Armour* and playing the doctor in the film version of A. J. Cronin's novel *The Citadel*, he won an Academy Award for his remarkable achievement spanning youth to extreme old age as the beloved schoolmaster in *Goodbye, Mr. Chips*. Later roles included the title role in *The Young Mr. Pitt*, the dedicated lawyer in the film of Rattigan's play *The Winslow Boy*, and the British film pioneer William Friese-Greene in *The Magic Box*.

Donat's health finally gave way during the filming of *The Inn of the Sixth Happiness*, which he only managed to complete with the help of oxygen. The last line he spoke in the film became famous for its tragic appositeness: "We shall not see each other again, I think. Farewell." He died before the picture was released.

—Roger Manvell

DORS, Diana

Nationality: British. **Born:** Diana Fluck in Swindon, Wiltshire, England, 23 October 1931. **Education:** London Academy of Dramatic Art. **Family:** Married 1) Denis Hamilton, 1951 (divorced 1957); 2) Richard Dawson, 1959 (divorced 1967), two sons; 3) Alan Lake, 1968, one son. **Career:** 1944—won beauty contest; 1946—film debut in *The Shop at Sly Corner*; late 1940s—signed 10-year contract (later abandoned) with J. Arthur Rank, became member of Rank's "Charm School"; 1952—set up production company, Diana Dors Ltd.; 1959—moved to Beverly Hills with new husband, signed contract with RKO pictures, ended when company broke up; 1970—declared bankrupt; 1974—appeared on stage as Queen Iocasta in *Oedipus*, Chichester Festival; late 1970s—in *Just William*, on TV, as Mrs. Bott; 1983—TV agony aunt on *Good Morning Britain*. **Died:** Of cancer, 4 May 1984.

Films as Actress:

1946   *The Shop at Sly Corner* (King); *Dancing with Crime* (Carstairs)
1947   *Holiday Camp* (Annakin)
1948   *Good Time Girl* (Macdonald); *Penny and the Pownall Case* (Hand); *The Calendar* (Crabtree); *My Sister and I* (Huth); *Oliver Twist* (Lean); *Here Comes the Huggetts* (Annakin) (as Diana)
1949   *It's Not Cricket* (Roome); *Vote for Huggett* (Annakin) (as Diana); *Diamond City* (Macdonald); *A Boy, a Girl and a Bike* (Smart)
1950   *Dance Hall* (Crichton)
1951   *Lady Godiva Rides Again* (Launder); *Worm's Eye View* (Raymond) (as Saucy Maid)
1952   *The Last Page* (*Manbait*) (Fisher) (as Ruby); *My Wife's Lodger* (Elvey); *The Great Game* (Elvey)
1953   *Is Your Honeymoon Really Necessary?* (Elvey); *It's a Grand Life* (Blakeley); *The Weak and the Wicked* (*Young and Willing*) (Thompson) (as Betty)
1955   *As Long as They're Happy* (Thompson); *A Kid for Two Farthings* (Reed) (as Sonia); *Miss Tulip Stays the Night* (Arliss) (as Kate Dax); *Value for Money* (Annakin) (as Ruthine); *An Alligator Named Daisy* (Thompson) (as Vanessa)
1956   *Yield to the Night* (*Blonde Sinner*) (Thompson) (as Mary)
1957   *The Unholy Wife* (Farrow); *The Long Haul* (Hughes)
1958   *Tread Softly Stranger* (Parry) (as Calico); *I Married a Woman* (Kanter) (as Janice Briggs)
1959   *Passport to Shame* (*Room 43*) (Rakoff) (as Vicki); *Scent of Mystery* (*Holidays in Spain*) (Cardiff); *La ragazza del Palio* (*The Love Specialist*) (Zampa) (as Diana Wilson)
1961   *On the Double* (Shavelson); *King of the Roaring Twenties* (*The Big Bankroll*) (Newman)
1962   *Mrs. Gibbons' Boys* (Max Varnel); *Encontra a Mallorca*
1963   *West 11* (Winner)
1966   *Allez France* (*The Counterfeit Constable*) (Dhery) (as herself); *The Sandwich Man* (Hartford-Davis)

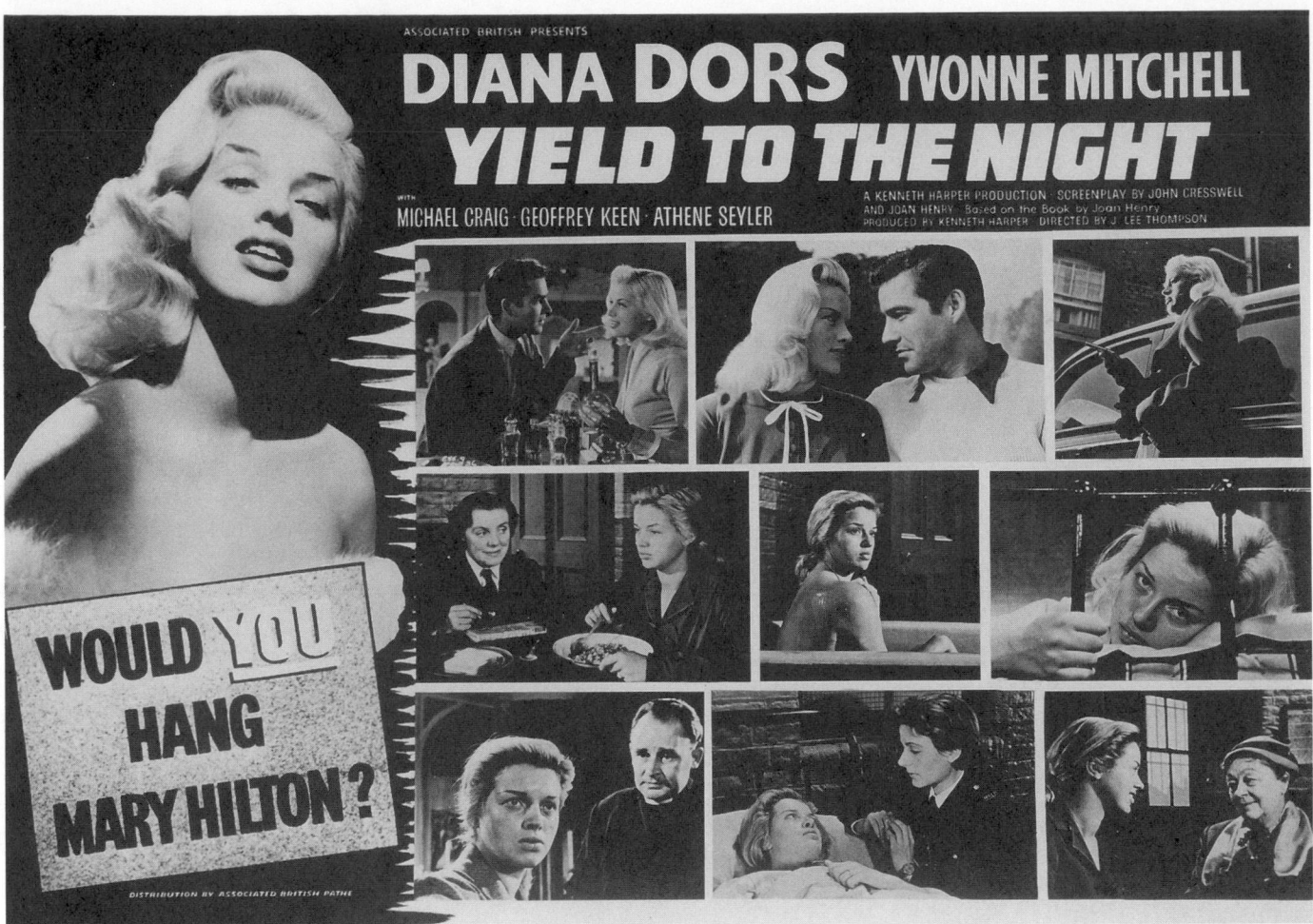

Diana Dors: poster for *Yield to the Night*

1967   *Berserk!* (O'Connolly); *Danger Route* (Holt)
1968   *Hammerhead* (Miller); *Baby Love* (Reid)
1970   *There's a Girl in My Soup* (Boulting); *Deep End* (Skolimowski)
1971   *Hannie Caulder* (Kennedy); *Pied Piper* (Demy)
1972   *The Amazing Mr. Blunden* (Jeffries); *Nothing but the Night* (Sasdy)
1973   *Theatre of Blood* (Hickox); *From beyond the Grave* (Connor); *Steptoe and Son Ride Again* (Sykes); *Craze* (Francis)
1974   *The Groove Room* (*Swedish Wildcats*; *What the Swedish Butler Saw*) (Becker); *Bedtime with Rosie* (Rilla); *Three for All*
1975   *Confessions of a Driving Instructor*
1976   *Keep It Up Downstairs*
1977   *Adventures of a Private Eye*
1979   *Confessions from the David Galaxy Affair*
1981   *Dick Turpin* (for TV)
1984   *Steaming* (Losey) (as Violet)

Publications

By DORS: books—

Swingin' Dors, London, 1960.
For Adults Only, London, 1978.
Behind Closed Dors, London, 1979.
Dors by Dors, London, 1981.

By DORS: articles—

"Diana Dors: On Her Own Terms," in *Films and Filming* (London), February 1973; also May issue.
Interview in *TV Times* (London), 22 February 1979.
Interview with Allan Hunter, in *Films and Filming* (London), July 1984.

On DORS: books—

Hill, John, *Sex, Class and Realism: British Cinema 1956-63*, London, 1986.
Flory, Joan, and Damien Walne, *Diana Dors: Only a Whisper Away*, London, 1987.
Murphy, Robert, *Realism and Tinsel*, London, 1989.

On DORS: articles—

Picturegoer (London), 7 October 1950.
"A Window on Dors," in *Films and Filming* (London), April 1955.
Films and Filming (London), January 1963.
Film Review (London), November 1972.
Ciné Revue (Paris), 11 November 1976.
Braun, Eric, in *Films and Filming* (London), July 1979.
Jones, D. A. N., in the *Listener* (London), 6 August 1981.
Obituary in *Variety* (New York), 9 May 1984.

Tribute in *Films* (London), June 1984.

TV Times (London), 13, 20, and 27 October 1984.

"Diana Dors," in *All Our Yesterdays: 90 Years of British Cinema*, edited by Charles Barr, London, 1986.

"Diana Dors," in *Ciné Revue* (Paris), 12 November 1987.

*   *   *

Everyone knows that Diana Dors is Britain's only fully-fledged sex symbol but it would be difficult to deduce this from her films. Admittedly as a teenager she looked a likely successor to Jean Kent as the bad girl of British cinema—pouting and flouncing in *The Shop at Sly Corner*, jitterbugging in *Holiday Camp*, sultrily sulking in *Good Time Girl*. But these were little more than walk-on parts and ironically her first substantial role was as the grubbily unglamorous coffin-maker's maid in *Oliver Twist*. Enjoyable cameos were found in films such as *Vote for Huggett* and *Dance Hall* but, except for the ill-fated *Diamond City*, the first film that could properly be seen as providing her with a starring role was J. Lee Thompson's *Yield to the Night*. The year before she had launched herself on the Venice Film Festival in a mink bikini, but here as a convicted murderess (closely modeled on the recently executed Ruth Ellis) she spent most of the film dressed in a drab prison overall.

Yield to the Night was a critical and popular success and provided Dors with her long coveted ticket to Hollywood. Unfortunately a combination of mediocre films and the increasingly irrational antics of her syphilitic husband Denis Hamilton sank any chance of her career taking off. When she returned to England it was to play in low-budget melodramas such as *Passport to Shame* and *Tread Softly Stranger*.

Apart from another brief foray into the Hollywood jungle at the end of the 1950s, her career as a sex symbol was over as far as the film industry was concerned. In the meager selection of roles she was offered in the 1960s she tended to play blowzy women with a gone-to-seed sexuality of marginal attraction to men. In Seth Holt's *Danger Route* she is given enough space to develop a sympathetic and convincing character (the housekeeper seduced by brush salesman/secret agent Richard Johnson) but more typical is her role in *There's a Girl in My Soup* where—like the fat ladies in seaside postcards—she provides an awful contrast to the lissome young women who trip through Peter Sellers's bedroom.

This sort of treatment, and the punishing routine of cabaret appearances in working men's clubs she put herself through in order to maintain her lavish lifestyle, might be seen as vengeance exacted by British society on this small town girl who dared to flaunt her sexuality. But despite her disastrous marriages, her running battles with the tax man, her disappointing film career, and her tussles with illness, Dors was never a victim. By the time she died—of cancer in 1984—she had become a popular television personality and agony aunt, and when Joseph Losey's *Steaming* was released after her death, her restrained, finely-judged performance confirmed that underneath the mane of peroxide blonde hair she was, after all, a fine actress.

—Robert Murphy

DOUGLAS, Kirk

Nationality: American. **Born:** Issur Danielovitch in Amsterdam, New York, 9 December 1916. **Education:** Attended St. Lawrence University, 1935-39, B.A.; American Academy of Dramatic Art, 1939-41. **Military Service:** 1943-44—served as lieutenant in U.S. Navy. **Family:** Married 1) Diana Dill, 1943 (divorced 1951), sons: Joel and the actor-producer Michael Douglas; 2) Anne Budyens, 1954, sons:

Peter and Eric. **Career:** 1939-41—acted in summer stock in New York and Pennsylvania; also served as drama coach for Greenwich House Settlement in New York City; 1941—Broadway acting debut in *Spring Again*; 1942—in Broadway play *Three Sisters* under pseudonym George Spelvin Jr.; 1946—screen acting debut in *The Strange Love of Martha Ivers*; five-year contract with Wallis; 1947—contract with Wallis terminated, began to freelance as actor; 1949—contract with Warner Brothers; 1952—left Warners to form own film production company, Bryna Productions; 1957—TV acting debut; 1960—producer for first time on *Spartacus*; 1962—formed Joel Productions, an offshoot of Bryna; 1973—directed first film *Scalawag*; 1976—in TV mini-series *The Moneychangers*; 1987—in TV mini-series *Queenie;* 1988—published autobiography, *The Ragman's Son.* **Awards:** Best Actor, New York Film Critics, for *Lust for Life*, 1956; Cecil B. DeMille Prize, U.S. Golden Globe Awards, 1967; U.S. Presidential Medal of Freedom, 1981; elected to the Cowboy Hall of Fame, 1984; Knight, Legion of Honor, France, 1985; Life Achievement Award, American Film Institute, 1991; Honorary Academy Award, 1996. **Address:** c/o Bryna Company, 141 El Camino, Beverly Hills, CA 90212, U.S.A.

Films as Actor:

1946   *The Strange Love of Martha Ivers* (Milestone) (as Walter O'Neil)

1947   *Mourning Becomes Electra* (Nichols) (as Peter Niles); **Out of the Past** (*Build My Gallows High*) (J. Tourncur) (as Whit); *I Walk Alone* (Haskin) (as Noll Turner)

1948   *The Walls of Jericho* (Stahl) (as Tucker Wedge); *My Dear Secretary* (Martin) (as Owen Waterbury); *A Letter to Three Wives* (Mankiewicz) (as George Phipps)

1949   *Champion* (Robson) (as Midge Kelly)

1950   *Young Man with a Horn* (*Young Man of Music*) (Curtiz) (as Rick Martin); *The Glass Menagerie* (Rapper) (as Jim O'Connor)

1951   *Along the Great Divide* (Walsh) (as U.S. Marshal Clint Merrick); *The Big Carnival* (*Ace in the Hole*) (Wilder) (as Charles Tatum); *Detective Story* (Wyler) (as Jim McLeod)

1952   *The Big Trees* (Feist) (as Jim Fallon); *The Big Sky* (Hawks) (as Deakins); *The Bad and the Beautiful* (Minnelli) (as Jonathan Shields)

1953   "Equilibrium" ep. of *The Story of Three Loves* (G. Reinhardt) (as Pierre Narval); *The Juggler* (Dmytryk) (as Hans Muller); *Act of Love* (*Un Acte d'amour*) (Litvak) (as Robert Teller)

1954   *Twenty Thousand Leagues under the Sea* (Fleischer) (as Ned Land); *Ulisse* (*Ulysses*) (Camerini) (title role)

1955   *The Racers* (*Such Men Are Dangerous*) (Hathaway) (as Gino); *Man without a Star* (King Vidor) (as Dempsey Rae); *The Indian Fighter* (de Toth) (as Johnny Hawks)

1956   *Lust for Life* (Minnelli) (as Vincent Van Gogh)

1957   *Top Secret Affair* (*Their Secret Affair*) (Potter) (as Major General Melville Goodwin); *Gunfight at the O.K. Corral* (John Sturges) (as Doc Holliday); **Paths of Glory** (Kubrick) (as Colonel Dax)

1958   *The Vikings* (Fleischer) (as Einer)

1959   *Last Train from Gun Hill* (John Sturges) (as Matt Morgan); *The Devil's Disciple* (Hamilton) (as Richard Dudgeon)

1960   *Strangers When We Meet* (Quine) (as Larry Coe); *Spartacus* (Kubrick) (title role, + exec pr)

1961   *The Last Sunset* (Aldrich) (as Brendan O'Malley); *Town without Pity* (G. Reinhardt) (as Major Steve Garrett)

1962   *Lonely Are the Brave* (D. Miller) (as Jack Burns); *Two Weeks in Another Town* (Minnelli) (as Jack Andrus)

Kirk Douglas

1963   *The Hook* (Seaton) (as First Sergeant P. J. Briscoe); *For Love or Money* (Gordon) (as Deke Gentry); *The List of Adrian Messenger* (Huston) (as George Brougham)

1964   *Seven Days in May* (Frankenheimer) (as Colonel Martin "Jiggs" Casey)

1965   *In Harm's Way* (Preminger) (as Commander Paul Eddington); *The Heroes of Telemark* (Anthony Mann) (as Dr. Rolf Pedersen)

1966   *Cast a Giant Shadow* (Shavelson) (as David "Mickey" Marcus); *Paris brûle-t-il?* (*Is Paris Burning?*) (Clément) (as General George Patton)

1967   *The Way West* (McLagen) (as Senator William J. Tadlock); *The War Wagon* (Kennedy) (as Lomax)

1968   *A Lovely Way to Die* (*A Lovely Way to Go*) (Rich) (as Jim Schuyler)

1969   *The Brotherhood* (Ritt) (as Frank Ginetta, + pr); *The Arrangement* (Kazan) (as Eddie Anderson); *French Lunch* (Cox—short)

1970   *There Was a Crooked Man* (Mankiewicz) (as Paris Pitman Jr.)

1971   *A Gunfight* (Johnson) (as Will Tenneray); *La luz del fin del mondo* (*The Light at the Edge of the World*) (Billington) (as Denton, + pr); *Catch Me a Spy* (D. Clement) (as Andre)

1974   *Un uomo da rispettare* (*The Master Touch*; *Hearts and Minds*; *A Man to Respect*) (Lupo) (as Wallace); *Mousey* (*Cat and Mouse*) (Petrie) (as George Anderson)

1975   *Once Is Not Enough* (Green) (as Mike Wayne)

1976   *Victory at Entebbe* (Chomsky—for TV) (as Hershel Vilnovsky)

1978   *The Fury* (De Palma) (as Peter); *The Chosen* (De Martino) (as Caine)

1979   *The Villain* (Needham) (as Cactus Jack)

1980   *The Final Countdown* (Don Taylor) (as Capt. Matthew Yelland); *Saturn Three* (Donen) (as Adam); *Home Movies* (De Palma) (as Dr. Tuttle)

1981   *La Luz del Fin del Mundo* (Billington) (+ pr)

1982   *Remembrance of Love* (Smight—for TV); *The Man from Snowy River* (George Miller) (as Spur)

1983   *Eddie Macon's Run* (Haley and Rauch) (as Marzack)

1984   *Draw!* (Stern—for TV) (as Harry H. Holland)

1985   *Amos* (Tuchner—for TV) (as Amos Lacher)

1986   *Tough Guys* (Kanew) (as Archie Long)

1988   *Inherit the Wind* (Greene—for TV) (as William Jennings Bryan)

1990   *Money* (Stern)

1991   *Oscar* (Landis) (as Snaps's father); *Bienvenido a Veraz* (*Welcome to Veraz*) (Xavier Castano) (as Quentin)

1992   *The Secret* (Arthur—for TV) (as Mike Dunmore)

1994   *Greedy* (Lynn) (as Uncle Joe McTeague); *Take Me Home Again* (for TV) (as Ed Reece)

1996   *A Song for David*

Films as Director:

1973   *Scalawag* (+ ro)

1975   *Posse* (+ ro, pr)

Other Film:

1971   *Summertree* (Newley and Record) (pr)

Publications

By DOUGLAS: books—

The Ragman's Son: An Autobiography, New York, 1988.
Dance with the Devil (novel), New York, 1990.

The Gift (novel), New York, 1992.
Last Tango in Brooklyn (novel), New York, 1994.

By DOUGLAS: articles—

Interview in *Films and Filming* (London), September 1972.
"Kirk Douglas: All American Boy," interview with K. Kelly, in *Inter/View* (New York), January 1974.
Interviews in *Ciné Revue* (Paris), 12 July and 27 September 1984.

On DOUGLAS: books—

McBride, Joseph, *Kirk Douglas*, New York, 1976.
Parish, James, *The Tough Guys*, New Rochelle, New York, 1976.
Lacourbe, Roland, *Kirk Douglas*, Paris, 1980.
Farber, Stephen, and Marc Green, *Hollywood Dynasties*, New York, 1984.
Munn, Michael, *Kirk Douglas*, New York, 1985.
Kaye, Annene, and Jim Sclavunos, *Michael Douglas and the Douglas Clan*, London, 1989.
Thomas, Tony, *The Films of Kirk Douglas*, New York, 1991.
Press, Skip, *Michael and Kirk Douglas*, New York, 1995.

On DOUGLAS: articles—

Current Biography 1952, New York, 1952.
Meisel, Myron, "Kirk Douglas: Last Angry Man" in *Close-Ups: The Movie Star Book*, edited by Danny Peary, New York, 1978.
Ebert, Robert, "Kirk Douglas," in *The Movie Star*, edited by Elisabeth Weis, New York, 1981.
Lantos, J., "The Last Waltz," in *American Film* (New York), October 1986.
Hibbin, S., "Tough Guy," in *Films and Filming* (London), April 1987.
Buckley, Michael, "Kirk Douglas" (in 2 parts), in *Films in Review* (New York), vol. 40, nos. 8/9 and 10, 1989.
Thompson, F., "A Man Cut for the Screen," in *American Film* (Washington, D.C.), March 1991.

*   *   *

Now approaching his sixth decade of movie stardom, Kirk Douglas has played lead roles in the vast majority of the 70-odd films he has made. His screen persona has been characterized by resoluteness and ferocity, the typical ingredients of his steadfast, driven heroes, and occasionally the psychological foundation for his formidable and relentless villains. These variations on a theme of perseverance have pleased audiences who have come to know the Douglas face as a movie icon—eyes blazing with anger or resistance, teeth clenched in determination, a distinctive cleft in his firmly planted chin.

Following a brief Broadway career and Navy service during World War II, Douglas made his movie debut in a supporting role as the ineffectual district attorney husband of Barbara Stanwyck in Lewis Milestone's melodrama *The Strange Love of Martha Ivers*. After appearing in another half-dozen features, Douglas earned major stardom as an unscrupulous boxer who punches and claws his way to the top in Mark Robson's *Champion*, a performance which earned him an Oscar nomination for Best Actor.

The next few years saw him star in a series of exceptional films by front-rank directors, including Michael Curtiz's *Young Man with a Horn*, Raoul Walsh's *Along the Great Divide*, Billy Wilder's *The Big Carnival*, William Wyler's *Detective Story*, Howard Hawks's *The Big Sky*, Vincente Minnelli's *The Bad and the Beautiful*, and King Vidor's *Man without a Star*. This series of memorable, strong-willed protagonists fixed the Douglas image firmly in the public's consciousness.

The actor's intense portrayal of the tormented Vincent van Gogh in Minnelli's *Lust for Life* was followed by that of an idealistic French officer fighting a corrupt military bureaucracy during World War I in Stanley Kubrick's powerful antiwar film *Paths of Glory*. Three years later, he again starred for Kubrick in the historical epic *Spartacus* as a slave who leads an insurrection against the powerful and oppressive leaders of Imperial Rome. In both Kubrick films, Douglas plays a strong-willed, noble leader who suffers an unjust defeat.

Although the 1950s was his most accomplished decade, Douglas continued to star as a rugged individual in respectable, entertaining movies in the 1960s, including David Miller's *Lonely Are the Brave*, Minnelli's *Two Weeks in Another Town*, and John Frankenheimer's *Seven Days in May*. Nevertheless, many of his film projects of that era—including some through the auspices of Bryna Productions, his own production company—were of mediocre quality.

At the end of the 1960s, Douglas starred in what he has referred to as a trilogy: Martin Ritt's *The Brotherhood* (as a Mafia leader), Elia Kazan's *The Arrangement* (as an advertising executive), and Joseph L. Mankiewicz's *There Was a Crooked Man* (as a prison inmate obsessed with escaping). The films were of wildly uneven quality, to be sure, but they served as evidence that Douglas, fast approaching 60, remained a sturdy, effective leading man.

None of his theatrical films since then has made such a strong impact, although as a canny veteran actor Douglas remains a convincing and watchable presence, effortlessly communicating resolve and urgency. Among his better late-career credits are *Tough Guys*, in which he was cast one final time with longtime friend and frequent co-star Burt Lancaster; the television movie *Remembrance of Love*, portraying a concentration camp survivor who has an emotional reunion with a woman he had loved decades earlier, in the Warsaw Ghetto; and another television movie, *Amos*, in which he played an elderly man living against his will in a nursing home.

Finally, in his seventies, Douglas has launched a new career as a writer. In 1988, he published his autobiography, *The Ragman's Son*, and since has written several novels.

—Bill Wine, updated by Audrey E. Kupferberg

DOUGLAS, Melvyn

Nationality: American. **Born:** Melvyn Edouard Hesselberg in Macon, Georgia, 5 April 1901. **Military Service:** 1918—served in U.S. Army; enlisted in Army as private, rose to rank of major, serving in India-China-Burma theater. **Family:** Married the actress (and later politician) Helen Gahagan, 1931 (died 1980), children: Peter and Mary; son Gregory by previous marriage. **Career:** 1919—joined Owens repertory company, acting debut in Chicago in *The Merchant of Venice*; changed surname to Douglas; 1920s—toured Midwest with Owens and Jessie Bonstelle companies; 1928—in Broadway production of *A Free Soul*; 1931—film debut under contract to Goldwyn in *Tonight or Never*; 1933—requested release from contract and returned to Broadway; 1935—7-year contract with Columbia; late 1930s—with wife became increasingly involved in support of liberal political causes; 1940—delegate to Democratic Convention; signs contract with MGM; 1942—appointed director of the Arts Council of the Office of Civilian Defense; 1946—produced successful musical revue *Call Me Mister*; 1950s—television work, including *Steve Randall* series, 1952-53, and *Blind Date*, 1953; host, *Frontier Justice* series, 1959; 1951—moved to New York, stage acting successes in *Inherit the Wind* (1955), *The Waltz of the Toreadors* (1957), and *The Best Man* (1960); 1962—resumed film acting. **Awards:** Best Supporting Actor Academy Award for *Hud*, 1963; Best Supporting Actor Academy Award and Best Supporting Actor, New York Film Critics, for *Being There*, 1979. **Died:** 4 August 1981.

Films as Actor:

1931 *Tonight or Never* (LeRoy) (as Fletcher)

1932 *As You Desire Me* (Fitzmaurice) (as Count Bruno Varelli); *Prestige* (Garnett) (as Lieutenant Andre Verlaine); *The Wiser Sex* (Viertel) (as David Rolfe); *The Broken Wing* (Corrigan) (as Philip Marvin); *The Old Dark House* (Whale) (as Roger Penderel)

1933 *The Vampire Bat* (Strayer) (as Karl Brettschneider); *Nagana* (Frank) (as Dr. Walt Radnor); *Counsellor-at-Law* (Wyler) (as Roy Darwin)

1934 *Dangerous Corner* (Rosen) (as Charles); *Woman in the Dark* (Rosen) (as Robson)

1935 *The People's Enemy* (Wilbur) (as Traps); *She Married Her Boss* (La Cava) (as Richard Barclay); *Annie Oakley* (Stevens) (as Jeff Hogarth); *Mary Burns, Fugitive* (Howard) (as Barton Powell); *The Lone Wolf Returns* (Neill) (as Michael Lanyard)

1936 *And So They Were Married* (Nugent) (as Stephen Blake); *Theodora Goes Wild* (Boleslawski) (as Michael Grant)

1937 *Women of Glamour* (Wiles) (as Richard Stark); *I'll Take Romance* (Griffith) (as James Guthrie); *I Met Him in Paris* (Ruggles) (as George Potter); *Angel* (Lubitsch) (as Anthony Halton); *Captains Courageous* (Fleming)

1938 *Arsene Lupin Returns* (Fitzmaurice) (as Arsene Lupin); *Fast Company* (Buzzell) (as Joel Sloane); *The Toy Wife* (Thorpe) (as George Sartoris); *There's Always a Woman* (Hall) (as William Reardon); *The Shining Hour* (Borzage) (as Henry Linden); *That Certain Age* (Ludwig) (as Vincent Bulitt)

1939 *There's That Woman Again* (Hall) (as William Reardon); *Tell No Tales* (Fenton) (as Michael Cassidy); **Ninotchka** (Lubitsch) (as Count Leon Dalga); *Good Girls Go to Paris* (Hall) (as Ronald Brooke); *The Amazing Mr. Williams* (Hall) (as Kenny Williams)

1940 *Too Many Husbands* (Ruggles) (as Henry Lowndes); *He Stayed for Breakfast* (Hall) (as Paul Boliet); *Third Finger Left Hand* (Leonard) (as Jeff Thompson)

1941 *This Thing Called Love* (Hall) (as Tice Collins); *That Uncertain Feeling* (Lubitsch) (as Larry Baker); *A Woman's Face* (Cukor) (as Dr. Gustaf Segert); *Our Wife* (Stahl) (as Jerry Marvin); *Two-Faced Woman* (Cukor) (as Larry Blake)

1942 *We Were Dancing* (Leonard) (as Nicki Prax); *They All Kissed the Bride* (Hall) (as Michael Holmes)

1943 *Three Hearts for Julia* (Thorpe) (as Jeff Seabrook)

1947 *Sea of Grass* (Kazan) (as Bruce Chamberlain); *The Guilt of Janet Ames* (Levin) (as Smithfield Cobb)

1948 *Mr. Blandings Builds His Dream House* (Potter) (as Bill Cole); *My Own True Love* (Bennett) (as Clive Heath)

1949 *A Woman's Secret* (Ray) (as Luke Jordan); *The Great Sinner* (Siodmak) (as Armand de Glasse)

1951 *My Forbidden Past* (Stevenson) (as Paul Beaurevel); *On the Loose* (Lederer) (as Frank Bradley)

1962 *Billy Budd* (Ustinov) (as The Dansker)

1963 *Hud* (Ritt) (as Homer Bannon)

1964 *Advance to the Rear* (Marshall) (as Col. Brackenby); *The Americanization of Emily* (Hiller) (as Adm. William Jessup)

1965 *Rapture* (Guillerman) (as Larbaud)

1967   *Hotel* (Quine) (as Warren Trent)
1968   *Companions in Nightmare* (Lloyd—for TV)
1970   *I Never Sang for My Father* (Cates) (as Tony Garrison); *Hunters Are for Killing* (Girard—for TV)
1971   *Death Takes a Holiday* (Larkin—for TV)
1972   *One Is a Lonely Number* (Stuart) (as Joseph Provo); *The Candidate* (Ritchie) (as John J. McCay)
1974   *The Death Squad* (Falk—for TV); *Murder or Mercy* (Hart—for TV)
1976   *The Tenant* (Polanski) (as Monsieur Zy)
1977   *Intimate Strangers* (*Battered!*) (Moxey—for TV); *Twilight's Last Gleaming* (Aldrich) (as Zachariah Guthrie)
1979   *The Seduction of Joe Tynan* (Schatzberg) (as Senator Birney); *Being There* (Ashby) (as Benjamin Rand); *The Changeling* (Medak) (as Senator Joseph Carmichael)
1980   *Tell Me a Riddle* (Grant) (as David)
1981   *French Kiss* (*Act of Deceit*) (Vadim) (as Max); *Ghost Story* (Irvin) (as John Kaffrey)

Publications

By DOUGLAS: book—

See You at the Movies: The Autobiography of Melvyn Douglas, Lanham, Maryland, 1986.

By DOUGLAS: article—

"How Do You Like Pictures?" in *Stage*, December 1936.

On DOUGLAS: book—

Parish, James Robert, and Don E. Stanke, *The Debonairs*, New Rochelle, New York, 1975.

On DOUGLAS: articles—

Spensley, Dorothy, "Hollywood's Most Civilized Marriage," in *Motion Picture Magazine* (New York), November 1936.
Millstein, Gilbert, "Melvyn Douglas," in *Theatre Arts* (New York), January 1960.
Lewis, K., "The Two Careers of Melvyn Douglas," and "Melvyn Douglas: A Filmography," in *Films in Review* (New York), October and November 1981; additions to filmography in issues for February, March, and August-September 1982.
The Annual Obituary 1981, New York, 1982.

*   *   *

Melvyn Douglas's career may be divided into two major periods, each of which earned him a considerable reputation as a skillful performer. Although Douglas began as a dramatic actor and played numerous serious roles during the 1930s, he was most effective in sophisticated comedy. In the latter half of the decade, beginning with *She Married Her Boss*, Douglas appeared in a series of films in which his suaveness functioned as both a source of romantic appeal and the means by which he became, in reaction to humorous circumstances, the heroine's foil.

Theodora Goes Wild, an early screwball comedy, confirmed Douglas's ability, which he shared with Cary Grant, to maintain the credibility of a leading man while having his masculine ego deflated through increasingly foolish behavior. This ability is most fully realized in *Ninotchka* which, in a way, concerns Douglas's persona as much as Garbo's. Lubitsch, in particular, is attuned to the class and gender implications

Douglas's presence carries. In *Ninotchka* Lubitsch subtly undermines Douglas's debonair manner through a number of witty verbal exchanges in which Garbo, who, from Douglas's viewpoint, lacks humor and sophistication, gets the upper hand and then crowns this strategy, in the famous moment when "Garbo laughs," by having Douglas take a very undignified pratfall. Although Douglas appeared in other successful comedies in the late 1940s, this film remains the highlight of this period of his career.

In the early 1950s, Douglas abandoned Hollywood to devote himself to the theater; after more than 10 years, he returned to filmmaking as a character actor in *Billy Budd*. In the interim, Douglas had developed into a distinguished dramatic actor and his Academy Award-winning performance in *Hud* was followed by a series of memorable roles. Of his late films, *Tell Me a Riddle*, in addition to being a stunning film, contains one of Douglas's most sensitive, humane, and touching portrayals as an elderly, conservative man, who, on the brink of his wife's death, is compelled to grapple with her feminist and socialist principles.

—Richard Lippe

DOUGLAS, Michael

Nationality: American. **Born:** New Brunswick, New Jersey, 25 September 1944; son of the actor Kirk Douglas. **Education:** Attended Choate preparatory school, Wallingford, Connecticut; University of California at Santa Barbara, graduated in drama 1968; studied acting with Wynn Handman at the American Place Theatre in New York City. **Family:** Married Diandra Luker, 1977, son: Cameron. **Career:** 1965—assistant director on film starring father, *The Heroes of Telemark*; also acted at the O'Neill Center's Playwrights' Conference during university vacations; 1969—screen debut in *Hail, Hero!*; 1972-76—appeared as Inspector Steve Keller in *The Streets of San Francisco* for TV; 1975—co-producer of Oscar-winning *One Flew over the Cuckoo's Nest*; 1988—signed three-year production deal with Columbia Pictures. **Awards:** Oscar for Best Actor, for *Wall Street*, 1987. **Address:** c/o Creative Artists Agency, 9830 Wilshire Boulevard, Beverly Hills, CA 90212, U.S.A.

Films as Actor:

1969   *Hail, Hero!* (Miller) (as Carl Dixon)
1970   *Adam at 6 A.M.* (Scheerer) (as Adam Gaines)
1971   *Summertree* (Newley) (as Jerry McAdams); *When Michael Calls* (*Shattered Silence*) (Leacock—for TV)
1972   *Napoleon and Samantha* (McEveety) (as Danny); *The Streets of San Francisco* (Grauman—for TV)
1978   *Coma* (Crichton) (as Mark Bellows)
1979   *The China Syndrome* (Bridges) (as Richard Adams, + pr); *Running* (Steyn) (as Michael Andropolis)
1980   *It's My Turn* (Weill) (as Ben Lewin)
1983   *The Star Chamber* (Hyams) (as Steven Hardin)
1984   *Romancing the Stone* (Zemeckis) (as Jack C. Colton, + pr)
1985   *A Chorus Line* (Attenborough) (as Zach); *The Jewel of the Nile* (Teague) (as Jack C. Colton, + pr)
1987   *Fatal Attraction* (Lyne) (as Dan Gallagher); *Wall Street* (Stone) (as Gordon Gekko)
1989   *Black Rain* (Scott) (as Nick Conklin); *The War of the Roses* (DeVito) (as Oliver Rose)

Michael Douglas

1992   *Shining Through* (Seltzer) (as Ed Leland); *Basic Instinct* (Verhoeven) (as Detective Nick Curran)
1993   *Falling Down* (Schumacher) (as D-Fens)
1994   *Disclosure* (Levinson) (as Tom Sanders)
1995   *The American President* (Rob Reiner) (as President Andrew Shepherd)
1996   *A Song for David* (+ pr); *The Ghost and the Darkness* (Stephen Hopkins)

Other Films:

1962   *Lonely Are the Brave* (Miller) (asst d)
1965   *The Heroes of Telemark* (Anthony Mann) (asst d)
1966   *Cast a Giant Shadow* (Shavelson) (asst d)
1975   *One Flew over the Cuckoo's Nest* (Forman) (co-pr)
1984   *Starman* (Carpenter) (exec pr)
1990   *Flatliners* (Schumacher) (co-pr)
1991   *Eyes of an Angel* (Harmon) (exec pr)
1992   *Radio Flyer* (Richard Donner) (exec pr)
1993   *Made in America* (Benjamin) (co-pr)

Publications

By DOUGLAS: articles—

Interview in *Photoplay Film Monthly* (London), May 1976.
"Dialogue on Film: Michael Douglas," in *American Film* (Washington, D.C.), July/August 1979.
Interview in *Films Illustrated* (London), September 1979.
Interview in *Ciné Revue* (Paris), 5 February 1981.
Interviews in *Time Out* (London), 23 August 1984 and 20 January 1988.
Interview in *Films and Filming* (London), December 1989.
Interview with Fred Schruers in *Rolling Stone* (New York), 14 January 1988.
"Business as Usual," interview with David Thomson, in *Film Comment* (New York), January/February 1990.
"Angry Everyman with a Reason to Smile," interview with Janet Maslin, in *New York Times*, 11 March 1993.
"Michael's Full Disclosure," interview with Nancy Collins, in *Vanity Fair* (New York), January 1995.

On DOUGLAS: books—

Douglas, Kirk, *The Ragman's Son*, New York, 1988.
Kaye, Annene, and Jim Sclavunos, *Michael Douglas and the Douglas Clan*, London, 1989.
Stresau, Norbert, *Michael Douglas: Seine Filme, sein Leben*, Munich, 1990.
Press, Skip, *Michael and Kirk Douglas*, Parsippany, New Jersey, 1995.

On DOUGLAS: articles—

Current Biography 1987, New York, 1987.
Thompson, Anne, "The Art of the Hollywood Deal: Michael Douglas's Mini Movie Studio Moves Ahead with Four Films," in *Entertainment Weekly*, 29 September 1995.

* * *

Son of the equally famous male movie icon, Kirk Douglas, Michael Douglas has come to personify the contemporary, Caucasian middle-to-upper-class American male who finds himself the brunt of female anger because of real or imagined sexual slights. To this harried representative of his gender, any kind of sexual contact with someone other than his mate and the mother of his children is destined to come at a costly price.

In *Fatal Attraction*, he is an otherwise happily married man whose one-night stand with a seductress-from-Hell (Glenn Close) transforms his—and his family's—existence into a seemingly never-ending horror movie. In *Basic Instinct*—a title that purposefully features the same cadence as *Fatal Attraction*—he is a cop whose sense of professionalism disappears when he becomes involved with a sexy murder suspect (Sharon Stone). *Disclosure* is a drama of sexual harassment in the workplace, only the tables are turned: the boss, the sexually aggressive harasser (Demi Moore), is a woman, while the underling, the happily-married nice-guy harassee (Douglas), is a man. The female characters in *Fatal Attraction*, *Basic Instinct*, and *Disclosure* are cut-throat villainesses, an antifeminist's fantasy of a man-eating monster. Poor Michael Douglas is the Everyman who must contend with, and be victimized by, these women and their raging, psychotic sexuality.

A fourth Douglas film to add to the above trio is *The War of the Roses*, only here Douglas's tormentor is his wife (Kathleen Turner), with whom he is in the throes of divorce and cannot agree on a property settlement. *The War of the Roses* extends the Douglas Everyman in that Douglas's tormentor does not come from outside the family circle. Douglas literally digs into the trenches and goes to war with the woman whom he once loved.

Falling Down is a natural extension of Douglas's character in *The War of the Roses*. D-Fens is an alienated powder keg who has lost his job and is estranged from his wife. All of his humanity has been stripped away by an uncaring society. One day, he explodes internally while his car is stuck in a traffic jam on a Los Angeles freeway, and he sets off on a violent odyssey across the urban landscape of Southern California.

Conversely, in *Wall Street*, Douglas for once gets to play the victimizer rather than the victim. Gordon Gekko is his most fascinating character of all: the heaviest of the heavy hitters, a stock and real estate speculator whose face adorns the cover of *Fortune* magazine. To Gekko, $800,000 is just another day's profit. Ambitious young stockbroker Bud Fox (Charlie Sheen) pursues Gekko, and soon becomes the master's protege. With this position comes a price: Involvement with the ruthless, passionless Gekko means twisting the rules, using insider information to trade stocks and artificially manipulate the market.

If Gekko is no nice guy lost in a maze of aggressive females, he is the other modern American male: the greedy yuppie personification of the Me generation, a white-collar criminal from skin to soul who is convinced that "greed is good," and who is a fitting corporate villain for the Reagan years, played by Douglas with just the right touch of menace and swagger.

Upon Douglas's earning major screen stardom in the mid-1980s with his delightful performance as an idealistic soldier of fortune in *Romancing the Stone* and its sequel, *The Jewel of the Nile*, it became easy to forget that he previously had enjoyed a successful career both in front of and behind the camera. In the 1970s, he co-starred with Karl Malden in the long-running television series, *The Streets of San Francisco*. He was the Academy Award-winning co-producer of *One Flew over the Cuckoo's Nest*. He had a nice supporting role in *The China Syndrome* (which he also produced), a first-rate drama about the attempted cover-up of a nuclear power plant accident, and one of the most intelligent Hollywood films of the 1970s. In 1983 he had an interesting starring role in *The Star Chamber*, a provocative drama about a judge who has come to regard as inadequate the legal system with which he is such an integral part, and who becomes involved with a diabolical vigilante group. After scoring in *Fatal Attraction* and *Wall Street*, Douglas proved he could play a Stallone-like action hero in his role as a New York cop in *Black Rain*.

—Rob Edelman

DRESSLER, Marie

Nationality: Canadian. **Born:** Leila Marie Koerber in Cobourg (or Coburg), 9 November 1869. **Family:** Married George Hoppert (also spelled Huppert or Hoeppert), 1899 (or 1900); possibly married manager James Dalton, 1914 (died 1921). **Career:** 1886—stage debut as Cigarette in *Under Two Flags* in Saginaw, Michigan, adopted name of Marie Dressler; played for 3 years with George Baker Opera Company; 1892—Broadway debut in Maurice Barrymore musical *The Robber of the Rhine*; performed in New York music halls; 1896—first stage hit as Flo Honeydew in *The Lady Slavey*; by 1900—vaudeville headliner in sketch with Adele Farrington; 1907—London stage debut in *Palace Music Hall*; 1910—biggest stage success, *Tillie's Nightmare*; 1914—accepted offer from Mack Sennett to appear in feature-length film version of *Tillie's Nightmare* (*Tillie's Punctured Romance*); about 1916—formed short-lived Marie Dressler Motion Picture Company; late 'teens—toured country selling Liberty bonds; early 1920s—stage career declined, worked as hostess at Ritz Supper Club, New York; 1926—cast by Alan Dwan in *The Joy Girl*; scriptwriter Frances Marion arranged for role in *The Callahans and the Murphys*; career revived with series of subsequent supporting roles; 1929—stock contract by MGM; 1933—seriously ill with cancer while completing last 3 films. **Awards:** Best Actress Academy Award for *Min and Bill*, 1930/31. **Died:** In Santa Barbara, California, 28 July 1934.

Films as Actress:

(in feature-length films—as Tillie Blobbs through *Tillie's Tomato Surprise*, 1917):

1914   *Tillie's Punctured Romance* (Sennett)
1915   *Tillie Wakes Up* (Davenport)

(in two-reelers)

1916   *Tillie's Day Off*; *Tillie's Divorce Case*; *Tillie's Love Affair*; *Elopement*; *Night Out*

Marie Dressler in *Tillie's Punctured Romance*

1917   *Tillie's Tomato Surprise* (Hansel—feature length); *The Scrublady*

1918   *The Agonies of Agnes*; *Fired*; *The Cross Red Nurse*

(in feature-length films)

1927   *The Joy Girl* (Dwan) (as Mrs. Heath); *The Callahans and the Murphys* (Hill) (as Mrs. Callahan); *Breakfast at Sunrise* (St. Clair) (as Queen)

1928   *Bringing Up Father* (Conway) (as Annie Moore); *The Patsy* (Vidor) (as Ma Harrington); *The Divine Lady* (Lloyd) (as Mrs. Hart)

1929   *The Hollywood Revue of 1929* (Reisner); *The Vagabond Lover* (Neilan) (as Mrs. Whitehall); *Dangerous Females* (Christie—two-reeler)

1930   *Chasing Rainbows* (*The Road Show*) (Reisner) (as Bonnie); *Anna Christie* (Brown) (as Marthy Owen); *The Girl Said No* (Wood) (as Hettie Brown); *One Romantic Night* (Stein) (as Princess Beatrice); *Caught Short* (Reisner) (as Marie Jones); *Let Us Be Gay* (Leonard) (as Mrs. Boucicault); *Min and Bill* (Hill) (as Min); *The Voice of Hollywood* (short); *Call of the Flesh* (Brabin)

1931   *Reducing* (Reisner); *Politics* (Reisner) (as Hattie Burns); *The Christmas Party* (*Jackie Cooper's Christmas*) (Reisner—short)

1932   *Emma* (Brown); *Prosperity* (Wood)

1933   *Tugboat Annie* (LeRoy) (title role); *Dinner at Eight* (Cukor) (as Carlotta Vance); *Christopher Bean* (Wood) (as Abby)

1934   *Hollywood on Parade, Number Thirteen* (short)

Publications

By DRESSLER: books—

The Eminent American Comedienne Marie Dressler in the Life Story of an Ugly Duckling ... , New York, 1924.

My Own Story, as told to Mildred Harrington, New York edition, 1936.

By DRESSLER: articles—

Interview in *Photoplay* (New York), July 1928.

"Him," in *Motion Picture Magazine* (New York), April 1931.

Interview in *Film Weekly* (London), 30 May 1931.

"Confessions," in *Picturegoer* (London), in five parts, weekly from 12 September to 17 October 1931.

Her own story "as told to" Adela Rogers St. Johns in *Photoplay* (New York), September 1932.

Interview in *Picturegoer* (London), 25 November 1933.

On DRESSLER: books—

Harding, Alfred, *The Revolt of the Actors*, New York, 1929.
Blum, Daniel, *Great Stars of the Stage*, New York, 1952.
Crowther, Bosley, *The Lion's Share: The Story of an Entertainment Empire*, New York, 1957.
Parish, James Robert, and Ronald Bowers, *The MGM Stock Company*, New Rochelle, New York, 1973.

On DRESSLER: articles—

Ruth, Jay, "Marie Dressler—A Venture in Coming Back," in *Theatre* (New York), October 1930.
Beery, Wallace, "Her," in *Motion Picture Magazine* (New York), April 1931.
Photoplay (New York), February and September 1931.
Spensley, Dorothy, "Marie Dressler—Grand Old Fire Horse," in *Motion Picture Magazine* (New York), April 1932.
Storm, Lesley, in *Film Weekly* (London), 13 January 1933.
"Tugboat Annie," cover story in *Time* (New York), 7 August 1933.
Turner, Z., "Marie Dressler, 1869-1934," in *Films in Review* (New York), August-September 1975.
Focus on Film (London), Spring 1976.
Ciné Revue (Paris), 11 December 1980.

*   *   *

Marie Dressler had none of the qualities associated with a Hollywood star. She was a large woman with a build like an opera singer. Her face was reminiscent of a Saint Bernard dog with low-hanging jowls and dark circles under sad eyes. The stage veteran did not even begin her screen career until she was 45 years old. Yet at one time she was the highest-paid actress at MGM.

Dressler made her screen debut in *Tillie's Punctured Romance*, usually considered America's first feature-length comedy. She played the title role, being teamed with Charlie Chaplin as an unscrupulous city slicker. As Tillie "the pride of Yokeltown and apple of her papa's eye," Dressler was costumed in huge dresses and outrageous bonnets designed in the manner of clothing for little girls. She could be funny without moving a muscle, but standing still was not part of Dressler's technique. In her initial meeting with the city slicker, who is more interested in Tillie's money than in Tillie herself, the shy but overbearing country lass flirts timidly, smiling and biting her apron. After her first sample of alcohol, however, Tillie becomes a wild woman, waving her arms, dancing with abandon, and nearly falling to the barroom floor. Countless victims are hurled to the ground with one thrust of her great derrière. Luckily, there are six men handy to steady her.

Following a career decline, Dressler made a comeback with the aid of screenwriter Frances Marion, and was teamed successfully with Polly Moran (*The Callahans and the Murphys*, *Bringing Up Father*, *Dangerous Females*, *Reducing*, *Politics*) and Wallace Beery (*Min and Bill*, *Tugboat Annie*). With *Min and Bill*, she won the Academy Award for best actress. Though Dressler had made her reputation as a comedienne, she was given the chance to try her hand at drama. In *Anna Christie*, supporting Garbo, and in the underrated *Emma*, she proved that she was quite good with serious roles.

Considering her background in opera, theater and silent comedy, and her sheer size, it is not surprising that Dressler was never understated in her acting. Her stumbling reaction to Jean Harlow's "I was reading a book the other day," in *Dinner at Eight*, is a subtle as a horse tripping. Though exaggerated, the gesture is funny and not unlike Tillie's reaction 20 years before. In fact, this woman is Tillie, older, dressed in evening clothes, and feigning sophistication. Inside, however, she is still the innocent from Yokeltown, wide-eyed in disbelief.

—Alexa L. Foreman

DREYFUSS, Richard

Nationality: American. **Born:** Richard Stephan Dreyfuss in Brooklyn, New York, 29 October 1947. **Education:** Beverly Hills High School; enrolled briefly at San Fernando State College, California. **Military Service:** 1967-69—conscientious objector: alternative service as file clerk at Los Angeles County General Hospital. **Family:** Married Jeramie Rain (Susan Davis) (divorced), two sons, one daughter. **Career:** First stage appearance at age 10 playing Theodor Herzl at West Side Jewish Center; mid-1960s—while high school student acted at Gallery Theatre, Los Angeles; 1964-65—in TV series *Karen*; 1966—joined The Session, an improvisational comedy group working in San Francisco; late 1960s—acted occasionally on TV; 1969—first Broadway appearance in *But Seriously*; 1969-70—with stage company New Theater for Now, Los Angeles; 1971—in several off-Broadway shows, New York; 1972—with Center Theater Group, Los Angeles; toured in national company of *The Time of Your Life* with Henry Fonda; 1973—appearance in *American Graffiti* launched screen career; 1984—in Mark Medoff's play *The Hands of Its Enemy* in Los Angeles; 1992—on Broadway in *Death and the Maiden*. **Awards:** Best Actor Academy Award and Best Actor, British Academy, for *The Goodbye Girl*, 1977. **Address:** c/o Richard Grant and Associates, 8500 Wilshire Boulevard, Suite 520, Beverly Hills, CA 90211, U.S.A.

Films as Actor:

1967   ***The Graduate*** (Nichols) (bit role as Berkeley student); *Valley of the Dolls* (Robson) (bit role)
1968   *The Young Runaways* (Dreifuss) (as Terry); *Hello Down There (Sub-A-Dub-Dub)* (Arnold) (as Harold Webster)
1972   *Two for the Money* (Kowalski—for TV)
1973   *Dillinger* (Milius) (as Baby Face Nelson); ***American Graffiti*** (Lucas) (as Curt Henderson)
1974   *The Second Coming of Suzanne* (Barry) (as Clavius); *The Apprenticeship of Duddy Kravitz* (Kotcheff) (title role)
1975   ***Jaws*** (Spielberg) (as Matt Hooper); *Inserts* (Byrum) (as Boy Wonder, + assoc pr)
1976   *Victory at Entebbe* (Chomsky—for TV) (as Col. Netanyahu)
1977   ***Close Encounters of the Third Kind*** (Spielberg) (as Roy Neary); *The Goodbye Girl* (Ross) (as Elliott Garfield)
1978   *The Big Fix* (Kagan) (as Moses Wine, + co-pr)
1980   *The Competition* (Oliansky) (as Paul Dietrich)
1981   *Whose Life Is It Anyway?* (Badham) (as Ken Harrison); *Jacqueline Susann's Valley of the Dolls* (*Valley of the Dolls*) (Grauman—for TV)
1982   *SPFX 1140* (Balaban)
1983   *The Buddy System* (Glenn Jordan) (as Joe)
1986   *Down and Out in Beverly Hills* (Mazursky) (as Dave Whiteman); *Stand by Me* (Rob Reiner) (as The Writer)
1987   *Stakeout* (Badham) (as Chris Leece); *Tin Men* (Levinson) (as Bill "BB" Babowsky); *Nuts* (Ritt) (as Aaron Levinsky); *Funny, You Don't Look 200* (Michener) (presenter, + sc, pr)
1988   *Moon over Parador* (Mazursky) (as Jack Noah)
1989   *Let It Ride* (Pytka) (as Jay Trotter); *Always* (Spielberg) (as Pete Sandich)
1990   *Postcards from the Edge* (Nichols) (as Dr. Frankenthal)
1991   *Rosencrantz and Guildenstern Are Dead* (Stoppard) (as The Player); *Once Around* (Hallstrom) (as Sam Sharpe); *What about Bob?* (Oz) (as Dr. Leo Marvin); *Prisoner of Honor* (Russell—for TV) (as George Piquart, + exec pr)
1992   *Lincoln* (Kunhardt—TV doc) (as voice of William T. Sherman)
1993   *Lost in Yonkers* (Coolidge) (as Louie); *Another Stakeout* (Badham) (as Chris Leece)

Richard Dreyfuss in *Close Encounters of the Third Kind*

1994   *Silent Fall* (Beresford) (as Jake Reiner)
1995   *The Last Word* (Spiridakis—for TV) (as Larry); *The American President* (Rob Reiner) (as Sen. Bob Rumson)
1996   *Mr. Holland's Opus* (Herek) (as Glenn Holland); *Night Falls on Manhattan*; *James and the Giant Peach* (Selick) (as voice of the Centipede)

Other Film:

1994   *Quiz Show* (Redford) (exec pr)

Publications

By DREYFUSS: book—

The Two Georges (science fiction), with Harry Turtledove, New York, 1996.

By DREYFUSS: articles—

"Richard Dreyfuss . . . So Much More Than Duddy," interview with L. Hartt, in *Cinema Canada* (Montreal), June-July 1974.

Interview with Judy Klemesrud, in *New York Times*, 27 October 1974.
Hunter, Allan, "Rich Time," in *Films and Filming* (London), March 1988.
"Richard Dreyfuss," interview with Claudia Dreifus, in *Progressive* (Madison, Wisconsin), May 1993.

On DREYFUSS: articles—

Rogers, Michael, in *Rolling Stone* (Boulder, Colorado), 31 July 1975.
Current Biography 1976, New York, 1976.
Gottlieb, Carl, "Richard Dreyfuss: Forceful Intellect," in *Close-Ups: The Movie Star Book*, edited by Danny Peary, New York, 1978.
Photoplay (London), April 1982.
Diehl, Digby, "Richard Dreyfuss: Fast, Funny, . . . and Finally, Fearless," in *Cosmopolitan*, November 1990.
Elia, M., "Richard Dreyfuss," in *Sequences*, June 1991.

*   *   *

Richard Dreyfuss's great success as a film actor can be attributed to a basic, and archetypal need he fulfills in society. He is the representative of the little guy, who lives out the fantasies of the everyman for adventure, love, and heroic action. Dreyfuss does not have movie-star good looks—he is short, chunky, and appealing rather than handsome—yet he makes it possible to believe that the dreams of the ordinary person are accessible and even possible.

Dreyfuss began his career in films, apart from bit or insignificant parts, as Baby Face Nelson in John Milius's low-budget version of *Dillinger* (1973), in which he impressively erupted with psychotic energy and rage. But it was his next part, as the thoughtful, nerdy Curt in the surprise hit *American Graffiti*, filmed the same year and directed by George Lucas, that boosted Dreyfuss to international prominence. His affiliation with Lucas also initiated Dreyfuss's association with the "New Hollywood," or "The Movie Brats," most especially with Steven Spielberg, with whom Dreyfuss achieved his most memorable and enduring fame. The year following *Graffiti*, Dreyfuss starred in the Canadian/U.S. co-production of *The Apprenticeship of Duddy Kravitz*, in which he gives an exuberant and desperate portrait of Mordecai Richler's eponymous Montreal hustler. The following year, Dreyfuss consolidated his international success, starring as ichthyologist Matt Hooper in Spielberg's instant classic, *Jaws*. Much of the fun in *Jaws* is generated by witnessing smart-ass, university-trained, small-statured Dreyfuss more than holds his own against the manly "life-is-my-teacher" Robert Shaw. 1977 is perhaps the apogee of what might roughly be called the first part of Dreyfuss's professional life. In that year he portrayed Roy Neary, the ordinary guy, consumed with trying to articulate his otherworldly experiences in *Close Encounters of the Third Kind*. This film perfectly captures the qualities Dreyfuss embodied at this stage of his career. When Neary builds and rebuilds the site of his alien encounter first with mashed potatoes, then with dirt and foliage from his landscaped garden—to the astonishment and then distress of his family—Dreyfuss is the personification of obsession, intensity, and concentration. The same year, Dreyfuss won an Academy Award for his role as Elliott, the determined actor in the Neil Simon-scripted *The Goodbye Girl*. Again he gets to play a character who seeks to fulfill his aspirations against all obstacles and naysayers. *The Big Fix* saw Dreyfuss not only starring, but also co-producing the film, his first foray into producing a major industry film. The roles Dreyfuss played in the 1970s—and into the early 1980s, with such films as *The Competition* and *Whose Life Is it Anyway?*—are remarkable for the actor's almost manic energy, a driven quality leavened by copious quantities of charisma and talent.

The early to mid-1980s saw Dreyfuss sidelined by personal crises, some of which may have accounted for his surplus of energy. After resolving these difficulties, Dreyfuss starred in 1986 in what was considered his comeback role, as coat hanger manufacturer Dave Whiteman in *Down and Out in Beverly Hills*, a lighthearted, by far less interesting remake of Jean Renoir's classic *Boudu sauvé des eaux*. During this period, in such films as *Stakeout*, *Nuts*, and *Tin Men*, one witnesses a more mature, contemplative actor. Although still vigorous, Dreyfuss had by now lost some of his trademark intensity. While a strong sense of commitment and truth was present in earlier works, it was sometimes masked by a frenetic level of intensity. Dreyfuss is still capable of immense passion, as in his characterization of Pete, the doomed aviator, in Spielberg's unjustly maligned 1989 film *Always*. It is not coincidental that this film was a remake of *A Guy Named Joe*, which starred Dreyfuss's idol, Spencer Tracy. Like Tracy, Dreyfuss displays breezy charm as well as no-nonsense, no frills honesty. In one of the film's key scenes, the dead Pete, returned temporarily to earth as a ghost, watches his beloved and bereaved, Holly Hunter, as she begins to let go of Pete's memory and fall in love again. The emotion Dreyfuss conveys in this scene as he must watch the lovers, but do and say nothing, is deeply touching and sorrowful, in a way perhaps unavailable to Dreyfuss before.

1991 was another exceptional year for Dreyfuss, allowing him to display a full range of talents in such diverse items as *Rosencrantz and Guildenstern Are Dead*, where he plays the declaiming Player King; *Once Around*, in his role as the incredibly boorish, but ultimately

sympathetic Sam Sharpe (who once again woos Holly Hunter); the beleaguered psychiatrist pestered by patient Bill Murray in *What about Bob?*; and a lawyer in the infamous Dreyfus case, in *Prisoner of Honor*, yet another Ken Russell misfire, executive-produced by the actor. Lately, Dreyfuss has divided his abilities among producing projects (with his own company, Dreyfuss-James), acting in films such as *Silent Fall* and *Mr. Holland's Opus*, and engaging in a host of liberal political causes.

—Carole Zucker

DUMONT, Margaret

Nationality: American. **Born:** Margaret Baker in Brooklyn, New York, 20 December 1889. **Career:** Singer; made stage debut at age 18 in a play by George M. Cohan; 1925—first appeared with the Marx Brothers in stage play *The Cocoanuts*, and appeared in a series of their films from 1929; 1952-53—in TV series *My Friend Irma*; later appeared on TV with Bob Hope, Dean Martin, and Groucho Marx. **Died:** Of heart attack in Hollywood, 6 March 1965.

Films as Actress:

1917   *A Tale of Two Cities* (Bacon) (as prisoner)
1929   *The Cocoanuts* (Florey and Santley) (as Mrs. Potter)
1930   *Animal Crackers* (Heerman) (as Mrs. Rittenhouse)
1932   *The Girl Habit* (Cline) (as Mrs. Ledyard)
1933   **Duck Soup** (McCarey) (as Mrs. Teasdale)
1934   *Kentucky Kernels* (*Triple Trouble*) (Stevens)
1935   *Fifteen Wives* (*The Man with the Electric Voice*) (Strayer) (as Sybilla Crum); *Gridiron Flash* (*Luck of the Game*) (Tryon) (as Mrs. Fields); **A Night at the Opera** (Wood) (as Mrs. Claypool); *Orchids to You* (Seiter); *Rendezvous* (Howard)
1936   *Anything Goes* (*Tops Is the Limit*) (Milestone) (as Mrs. Wentworth); *The Song and Dance Man* (Brenon) (as Mrs. Whitney)
1937   *A Day at the Races* (Wood) (as Mrs. Emily Upjohn)
1938   *The Life of the Party* (Seiter) (as Mrs. Penner); *High Flyers* (Cline); *Wise Girl* (Jason) (as Mrs. Bell-Rivington); *Youth on Parole* (Rosen) (as Landlady)
1939   *Dramatic School* (Sinclair) (as Pantomimic teacher); *At the Circus* (Buzzell) (as Mrs. Dukesbury); *The Women* (Cukor)
1941   *For Beauty's Sake* (Traube); *The Big Store* (Reisner) (as Martha Phelps)
1942   *Never Give a Sucker an Even Break* (Cline) (as Mrs. Hemoglobin); *Born to Sing* (Ludwig) (as Mrs. E. V. Lawson); *Sing Your Worries Away* (Sutherland) (as Flo Faulkener); *About Face* (Neuman) (as Mrs. Culpepper)
1943   *Rhythm Parade* (Sutherland) (as Ophelia); *Dancing Masters* (St. Clair) (as Mrs. Harron)
1944   *Up in Arms* (Nugent) (as Mrs. Willoughby); *Bathing Beauty* (Sidney) (as Mrs. Allenwood); *Seven Days Ashore* (Auer) (as Mrs. Croxton-Lynch)
1945   *The Horn Blows at Midnight* (Walsh) (as Mrs. Rodholder); *Billy Rose's Diamond Horseshoe* (*Diamond Horseshoe*) (Seaton) (as Mrs. Sand Standish); *Sunset in El Dorado* (McDonald)
1946   *Little Giant* (*On the Carpet*) (Seiter) (as Mrs Hendrickson); *Susie Steps Out* (Le Borg) (as Mrs. Starr)
1952   *Stop, You're Killing Me* (Del Ruth) (as Mrs. Whitelaw); *Three for Bedroom C* (Bren) (as Mrs. Hawthorne)

1956 *Shake, Rattle and Rock* (Cahn) (as Georgina); *Auntie Mame* (DaCosta)
1962 *Zotz!* (Castle) (as Persephone Updike)
1965 *What a Way to Go!* (Lee Thompson) (as Mrs. Foster)

Publications

On DUMONT: books—

Crichton, Kyle, *The Marx Brothers*, New York, 1951.
Marx, Groucho, *Groucho and Me*, New York, 1959.
Zimmerman, Paul D., and Burt Goldblatt, *The Marx Brothers and the Movies*, New York, 1968.
Eayles, Allen, *The Marx Brothers: Their World of Comedy*, New York, 1969 + biblio.
Adamson, Joseph, *Groucho, Harpo, Chico and Sometimes Zeppo: A History of the Marx Brothers and a Satire on the Rest of the World*, New York, 1973.
Chandler, Charlotte, *Hello, I Must Be Going: Groucho and His Friends*, Garden City, N.Y., 1978.

On DUMONT: article—

Monthly Film Bulletin (London), June 1971.

* * *

Margaret Dumont's career was initially intended to be that of a professional singer, but opportunity put her on the Broadway stage at the age of 18, and an inspired choice later led her to be featured as the tall, well-built, dignified, but utterly humorless matron who played foil to the Marx Brothers in their madcap burlesque stage shows, beginning with *The Cocoanuts*, which achieved its success on Broadway late in 1925. It was with them that she made her name and won a permanent place in American film comedy history, although (if we are to believe Groucho Marx) she "was the same off-stage as she was on" and, he claimed, "she didn't really understand the jokes."

She appeared in seven of their films, which were initially based on their stage shows, starting with *The Cocoanuts* in 1929 (when she was around 40) and running through *Animal Crackers*, *Duck Soup*, *A Night at the Opera*, *A Day at the Races*, *At the Circus*, and *The Big Store*. She was normally the foil in particular of Groucho, who pretended violent passion for her while conning her for all he could get. She stood much rough treatment as he leaped into her arms or up on her knees, her stately, statuesque, dowager-like frame more than a match for his grotesquely volatile agility.

She was by no means exclusively a member of the Marx Brothers troupe. She became a hardy, enduring veteran. She worked with W. C. Fields in *Never Give a Sucker an Even Break*, with Laurel and Hardy in *Dancing Masters*, with Danny Kaye in *Up in Arms*, and with Jack Benny in *The Horn Blows at Midnight*. Her last film appearance was made when she was in her mid-seventies, in *What a Way to Go!* A week or so before her death she had just completed a television sketch with Groucho.

—Roger Manvell

DUNAWAY, Faye

Nationality: American. **Born:** Dorothy Faye Dunaway in Bascom, Florida, 14 January 1941. **Education:** Attended U.S. Army schools in Texas, Arkansas, Utah, and Mannheim, Germany; completed high school at Tallahassee, Florida; Florida State University, University of Florida, and Boston University School of Fine and Applied Arts, graduated 1962; studied in training program of Lincoln Center Repertory Theatre. **Family:** Married 1) the rock musician Peter Wolf, 1974; 2) the photographer Terry O'Neill, one son. **Career:** 1962—replaced Olga Bellin as Margaret in Broadway production of *A Man for All Seasons*; 1964—with Lincoln Center company in *After the Fall* and *But for Whom Charlie*; 1966—first film role in *The Happening*; contract with Otto Preminger; 1971—in summer stock production of *Candida* and TV adaptation of *Hogan's Goat*; 1993—in TV series *It Had to Be You*. **Awards:** Most Promising Newcomer, British Academy, for *Bonnie and Clyde*, 1967; Best Actress, Academy Award for *Network*, 1976. **Agent:** Sam Cohn, ICM, 40 W. 57th Street, New York, NY 10019, U.S.A.

Films as Actress:

1966 *The Happening* (Silverstein) (as Sandy); *Hurry Sundown* (Preminger) (as Lou McDowell)
1967 ***Bonnie and Clyde*** (Penn) (as Bonnie Parker)
1968 *The Extraordinary Seaman* (Frankenheimer) (as Jennifer Winslow); *The Thomas Crown Affair* (Jewison) (as Vicky Anderson); *Amanti* (*A Place for Lovers*) (De Sica) (as Julia)
1969 *The Arrangement* (Kazan) (as Gwen)
1970 *Little Big Man* (Penn) (as Mrs. Pendrake); *Puzzle of a Downfall Child* (Schatzberg) (as Lou Andreas Sand)
1971 *Doc* (Perry) (as Kate Elder); *La Maison sous les arbres* (*The Deadly Trap*) (Clément) (as Jill); *The Woman I Love* (Wendkos—for TV) (as Mrs. Wallis Simpson)
1973 *Oklahoma Crude* (Kramer) (as Lena Doyle); *The Three Musketeers* (*The Queen's Diamonds*) (Lester) (as Lady de Winter)
1974 *After the Fall* (Cates—for TV); *The Four Musketeers* (*The Revenge of Milady*) (Lester) (as Lady de Winter); ***Chinatown*** (Polanski) (as Evelyn Mulwray); *The Towering Inferno* (Guillermin) (as Susan Franklin)
1975 *Three Days of the Condor* (Pollack) (as Kathy Hale)
1976 *The Disappearance of Aimée* (Harvey—for TV); *Network* (Lumet) (as Diana Christensen); *Voyage of the Damned* (Rosenberg) (as Denise Kreisler)
1978 *The Eyes of Laura Mars* (Kershner) (title role)
1979 *Arthur Miller—on Home Ground* (Rasky—doc); *The Champ* (Zeffirelli) (as Annie)
1980 *The First Deadly Sin* (Hutton) (as Barbara Delaney)
1981 *Mommie Dearest* (Perry) (as Joan Crawford); *Evita Peron* (Chomsky—for TV) (title role)
1983 *The Wicked Lady* (Winner) (as Lady Barbara Skelton)
1984 *Supergirl* (Szwarc) (as Selena); *Ellis Island* (London—for TV)
1985 *13 at Dinner* (Antonio—for TV); *Cristoforo Colombo* (Lattuada—for TV)
1986 *Beverly Hills Madam* (Hart—for TV); *Cowgirls* (Walker—for TV)
1987 *Barfly* (Shroeder) (as Wanda Wilcox); *Casanova* (Langton—for TV); *Midnight Crossing* (Holzberg) (as Helen Barton)
1988 *Raspberry Ripple* (Finch—for TV); *Burning Secret* (Birkin) (as Sonya Tuchman)
1989 *Wait until Spring, Bandini* (Deruddere) (as Mme. Effie Hildegarde); *Up to Date* (Wertmüller); *Cold Sassy Tree* (Tewkesbury—for TV)
1990 *The Handmaid's Tale* (Schlöndorff) (as Serena Joy); *The Two Jakes* (Nicholson) (voice of Evelyn Mulwray); *Silhouette* (Schenkel—for TV) (as Samantha Kimball)
1992 *Scorchers* (Beaird) (as Thais); *Double Edge* (Kollek) (as Faye Milano); *Arizona Dream* (Kusturica) (as Elaine Stalker)

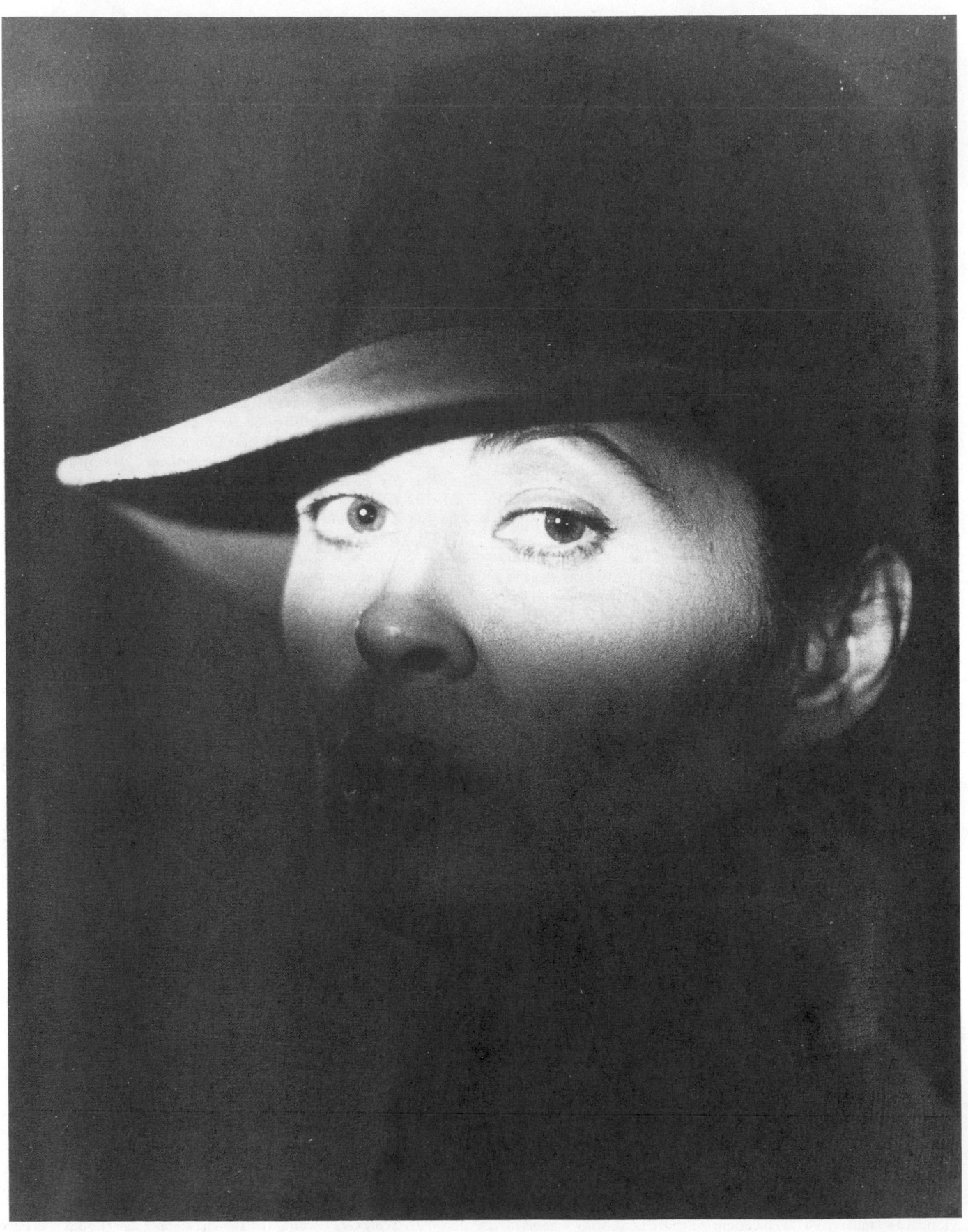

Faye Dunaway in *The Eyes of Laura Mars*

1993   *The Temp* (Holland) (as Charlene Towne); *Columbo: It's All in the Game* (for TV) (as Lauren Black)
1995   *Don Juan DeMarco* (Leven) (as Marilyn Mickler); *A Family Divided* (for TV) (as Karen Billingsly)
1996   *Dunston Checks In* (Kwapis) (as Mrs. Dubrow)

Publications

By DUNAWAY: book—

Looking for Gatsby: My Life, with Betsy Sharkey, New York, 1995.

By DUNAWAY: articles—

Interviews, in *Newsweek* (New York), 4 March 1968.
Photoplay (London), September 1983.
Interview with Allan Hunter, in *Films and Filming* (London), September 1986.
"Playing against Type and Time," interview with Betsy Sharkey, in *New York Times*, 11 October 1992.
Interview with Graham Fuller, in *Interview*, February 1993.

On DUNAWAY: books—

Wake, Sandra, and Nicola Hayden, *The Bonnie and Clyde Book*, New York, 1972.
Hunter, Allan, *Faye Dunaway*, New York, 1986.

On DUNAWAY: articles—

Wiley, Mason, "Faye Dunaway: Breaking the Ice," in *Close-Ups: The Movie Star Book*, edited by Danny Peary, New York, 1978.
Dunning, Jennifer, "Faye Dunaway as Hollywood Terror," in *New York Times*, 13 September 1981.
Bell, Arthur, "Faye Loves Joan," in *The Village Voice* (New York), 16-22 September 1981.
Article on TV career, in *Films in Review* (New York), August-September 1982.
Cieutat, M., "Portrait d'une etoile errante," in *Positif*, February 1993.
Schneider, Karen S., "Tough Act to Follow," in *People Weekly*, 8 May 1995.

*   *   *

From the moment Faye Dunaway suggestively sized up Warren Beatty as a one-way ticket out of Smalltown, U.S.A. in *Bonnie and Clyde*, she has dominated movie screens with a relentless drive and soigné sex appeal. When she launched a fashion frenzy with *Bonnie and Clyde*'s slick sixties take on thirties clothes for the well-dressed bandit, her stardom was clinched. After a brief period with the fledgling Lincoln Center Repertory Theater and several critically acclaimed off-Broadway appearances, she achieved international recognition in this, her third film; the odd conundrum about Dunaway's career is that this diva has miscast herself as a studio-era movie star. Blessed with a firm director and a role that ignites her trademark turbulent angst, Dunaway is overpowering, a star by virtue of her instinctual talent. Unfortunately, such inspired occasions (*Bonnie and Clyde*, *Chinatown*, *Network*, *Mommie Dearest*, *Barfly*) are outnumbered by clotheshorse vehicles (*Thomas Crown Affair*, *Puzzle of a Downfall Child*), premature camp outings (*Supergirl*, *Wicked Lady*), or indifferent television forays (*Disappearance of Aimée*, *Beverly Hills Madam*).

Whereas stars often make concessions to unrewarding box-office gigs (e.g., Dustin Hoffman in *Outbreak*) to maintain the muscle to acquire dream roles, Dunaway sleepwalks through such compromises (*Towering Inferno*, *Three Days of the Condor*) as though in some low-key artistic rebellion. At times, she lets her cheekbones do her acting for her (*Eyes of Laura Mars*) but, fortunately, the acting triumphs are too impressive to ignore.

In a role earmarked for the totally unsuitable Ali McGraw, Dunaway employed her distancing haughtiness to suggest unfathomable mystery in *Chinatown*. Perhaps the reported vicious disagreements on the set pushed her to transfer her distaste for director Polanski into disgust for her vile parent in the movie. As her carefully rehearsed illusions crumbled, *Chinatown*'s Evelyn Mulwray preserved a front of composure (prefiguring Dunaway's Joan Crawford image-maintenance in *Mommie Dearest*). Subverting this facade, Dunaway subtly conveyed the trauma behind the Evelyn Mulwray mask her character wore to conceal her secrets.

Next, Oscar came calling with a stunning evocation of the soullessness of *Network* TV. In Chayefsky's sour grapes diatribe, Dunaway's barnstorming was in sync with the hyperbolic proselytizing and the actor-dominated mise-en-scène. In all her memorable roles, there is an element of playacting, of sizing up what men want from her and then jockeying for power once she has satisfied the fools. Nowhere was that practiced insincerity more chilling than when used to inhabit Diana Christensen, the ratings-mad media shark who circles her rivals for the scent of blood.

The touchstone of Dunaway's career, *Mommie Dearest*, a ferocious tribute to fellow warrior-star Joan Crawford, brought Faye celluloid immortality of sorts, a cool reception from Hollywood's old guard, and a persistent case of role reverberation. Like that other victim of identification with one characterization—Tony Perkins/Norman Bates—Dunaway has been handicapped by a diabolically acute impersonation that cemented her screen image: in her case, as a souped-up virago conversant with obscenities and psychologically shackled to deranged Norman Vincent Pealisms. Dunaway's star-freak emerged as an avatar of hostility. Although the film is alternately silly and searing, Dunaway eyebrow-penciled the greatest caricature in film history since Chaplin's comic-kaze assault on Hitler.

Having played a monster, Dunaway found it difficult to assume the mantle of just plain folks. By the time we spotted her as a conventional mortal in *Don Juan DeMarco*, one felt one was witnessing a tornado consigned to do a breeze's work. After working with directors unable to control her idiosyncrasies, Dunaway redeemed herself in *Barfly* by self-effacingly portraying a washed-out woman whose prime pleasure derives from the bottle. Unforgettably tagging Wanda as a loner who is damaged but who will not be messed with, Dunaway conveyed how this dipso was so pathologically fearful of being alone that she would go with any man who had a fifth of whiskey.

Stymied by *Mommie Dearest* identification syndrome, Dunaway survived a sitcom fiasco, *It Had to Be You*, in high style, only to be ignominiously fired from the Los Angeles company of *Sunset Boulevard* for singing deficiencies one would assume Andrew Lloyd Webber might have gauged in advance. Cursed by Joan Crawford and Norma Desmond, lesser stars might have capitulated, but brittle, compulsively watchable Dunaway will rise again. Too unique to craft smaller-than-life interpretations, and too gifted to toil in the graveyard shift of Camp Cinema, Dunaway feeds off flamboyant characters poised on the risky brink of self-destruction.

—Robert Pardi

DUNNE, Irene

Nationality: American. **Born:** Irene Marie Dunn in Louisville, Kentucky, 20 December 1898. **Education:** Attended Chicago Musical College, diploma 1919. **Family:** Married Francis J. Griffin, 1928

Irene Dunne

(died 1965). **Career:** 1920—stage debut in touring company of *Irene*, Chicago; 1922—Broadway debut in *The Clinging Vine*; 1929—as Magnolia in *Show Boat* road show company; last Broadway appearance in *Luckee Girl*; 1930—film debut in *Leathernecking*; 1940-51—re-created various screen roles for Lux Radio Theatre; 1952—retired from films; hostess for *Schlitz Playhouse of Stars*, and made TV appearances on *Ford Theatre*, *The Loretta Young Show*, *The June Allyson Show*, and *General Electric Theater*; 1957-58—alternative delegate to the 12th General Assembly of the United Nations; 1965—elected to Board of Directors, Technicolor Inc. **Awards:** Kennedy Center Award, for achievement in the performing arts, 1985. **Died:** In Los Angeles, 4 September 1990.

Films as Actress:

1930 *Leathernecking (Present Arms)* (Cline) (as Delphine); *Cimarron* (Ruggles) (as Sabra Cravat)

1931 *Bachelor Apartment* (Sherman) (as Helene Andrews); *Consolation Marriage (Married in Haste)* (Sloane) (as Mary); *The Great Lover* (Beaumont) (as Diana Page)

1932 *The Stolen Jools (The Slippery Pearls)* (McGann and others—short) (as guest); *Symphony of Six Million (Melody of Life)* (La Cava) (as Jessica); *Back Street* (Stahl) (as Ray Schmidt); *Thirteen Women* (Archainbaud) (as Laura Stanhope)

1933 *No Other Woman* (Ruben) (as Anna Stanley); *The Secret of Madame Blanche* (Brabin) (as Sally); *The Silver Cord* (Cromwell) (as Christina Phelps); *Ann Vickers* (Cromwell) (title role); *If I Were Free (Behold We Live)* (Nugent) (as Sarah Cazenove)

1934 *This Man Is Mine* (Cromwell) (as Toni Dunlap); *Stingaree* (Wellman) (as Hilda Bouverie); *The Age of Innocence* (Moeller) (as Countess Ellen Olenska)

1935 *Sweet Adeline* (LeRoy) (as Adeline Schmidt); *Roberta* (Seiter) (as Stephanie); *Magnificent Obsession* (Stahl) (as Helen Hudson)

1936 *Show Boat* (Whale) (as Magnolia Hawks); *Theodora Goes Wild* (Boleslawski) (as Theodora Lynn)

1937 *High, Wide, and Handsome* (Mamoulian) (as Sally Watterson); *The Awful Truth* (McCarey) (as Lucy Warriner)

1938 *Joy of Living* (Garnett) (as Margaret "Maggie" Garret)

1939 *Love Affair* (McCarey) (as Terry McKay); *Invitation to Happiness* (Ruggles) (as Eleanor Wayne); *When Tomorrow Comes* (Stahl) (as Helen)

1940 *My Favorite Wife* (Kanin) (as Ellen Arden)

1941 *Penny Serenade* (Stevens) (as Julia Gardiner Adams); *Unfinished Business* (La Cava) (as Nancy Andrews)

1942 *Lady in a Jam* (La Cava) (as Jane Palmer)

1943 *A Guy Named Joe* (Fleming) (as Dorinda Durston)

1944 *The White Cliffs of Dover* (Clarence Brown) (as Susan Dunn Ashwood); *Together Again* (Charles Vidor) (as Anne Crandall)

1945 *Over 21* (Charles Vidor) (as Paula Wharton)

1946 *Anna and the King of Siam* (Cromwell) (as Anna)

1947 *Life with Father* (Curtiz) (as Vinnie Day)

1948 *I Remember Mama* (Stevens) (as Mama)

1950 *Never a Dull Moment* (George Marshall) (as Kay); *The Mudlark* (Negulesco) (as Queen Victoria)

1952 *It Grows on Trees* (Lubin) (as Polly Baxter)

Publications

By DUNNE: articles—

"Irene Dunne," interview with John Kobal, in *Focus on Film* (London), no. 28, 1977.

Interview with J. Harvey, in *Film Comment* (New York), January-February 1980.

On DUNNE: books—

Cavell, Stanley, *Pursuits of Happiness*, Cambridge, Massachusetts, 1981.
Kendall, Elizabeth, *The Runaway Bride: Hollywood Romantic Comedy of the 1930s*, New York, 1990.
Schultz, Margie, *Irene Dunne: A Bio-Bibliography*, New York, 1991.

On DUNNE: articles—

Current Biography 1945, New York, 1945.
Madden, J. C., "Irene Dunne," in *Films in Review* (New York), December 1969.
Bodeen, DeWitt, "Irene Dunne: Native Treasure," in *Close-Ups: The Movie Star Book*, edited by Danny Peary, New York, 1978.
McCourt, James, "Irene Dunne: The Awesome Truth," in *Film Comment* (New York), January-February 1980.

* * *

Irene Dunne is one of the most durable and delightful stars of Hollywood's golden period. Although she is most often associated with a series of excellent screwball comedies she made in the 1930s, she starred with equal success in melodramas and musicals. Her five Oscar nominations indicate her versatility across a range of genres: *Cimarron*, *Theodora Goes Wild*, *The Awful Truth*, *Love Affair*, and *I Remember Mama*.

Dunne originally studied to be an opera singer, but a failed audition at the Metropolitan Opera resulted in her choosing a musical comedy career instead. She toured in *Irene*, played several roles on Broadway (both musical and nonmusical), and joined the Chicago company of *Show Boat* as Magnolia in 1929. Her enormous success in that Jerome Kern-Oscar Hammerstein II favorite led to a Hollywood contract with RKO. From her film debut in *Leathernecking* to her retirement following *It Grows on Trees*, she played with equal grace and skill in musicals (the film version of *Show Boat* in 1936, *High, Wide, and Handsome*, *Sweet Adeline*, *Roberta*), comedies (*Joy of Living*, *My Favorite Wife*), and serious drama (*Back Street*, *Magnificent Obsession*, *When Tomorrow Comes*).

Dunne began freelancing early in her career, picking her roles with care, alternating between drama and comedy, and searching for as many chances to sing on film as she could find. Some of her musical performances are indelible: the ethereal "Smoke Gets in Your Eyes" from *Roberta* with Dunne in white fur, and the achingly sweet "Make Believe" or crowd-rousing "After the Ball" from *Show Boat* are highlights. Her persona was that of the lady, but always the modern lady, with a sharp wit, imagination, and independence. She could combine and make believable a remarkable range of behavior and seemingly contradictory characteristics. She wore clothes with grace and style, but was never considered an actress who was merely a clotheshorse. She looked fragile and delicate, with a truly feminine beauty, but she was never weak or trivial. She played women with virtue, but she was never a prig and she projected feeling and passion in great love stories; her performances in *Back Street* and *Love Affair* make them the most haunting versions of these oft-filmed stories. She had dignity on screen, yet could be incredibly funny in slapstick sequences, displaying impeccable timing and excellent physical control; her outrageous impersonation of a "vulgar" nightclub performer in *The Awful Truth* is one of screwball comedy's funniest moments. Her screen personality has often been described by the word "captivating," as she charmed male and female viewers alike with her beauty, unusual speaking voice, and personal style.

After Dunne retired from the screen in 1952, she appeared on television, on *Ford Theatre* and the *Schlitz Playhouse of Stars*. In 1957, she was appointed by President Eisenhower (Dunne was a lifelong Republican) as an alternate delegate to the United Nations 12th General Assembly, and remained active in Catholic charities, for which she was awarded Notre Dame's Laetare Medal. In retrospect, Irene Dunne may be seen as an example of a type of actress that has almost disappeared from movies—a woman of intelligence and versatility who, no matter what the pressure, be it comic or tragic, keeps going with humor, elegance, and dignity.

—Jeanine Basinger, updated by Corey K. Creekmur

DURANTE, Jimmy

Nationality: American. **Born:** James Francis Durante in New York City, 10 February 1893. **Education:** Attended Public School 114, New York, dropped out in seventh grade. **Family:** Married 1) Maud Jeanne Olson, 1921 (died 1943); 2) Margie Little, 1960, adopted daughter: Cecilia Alicia, 1961. **Career:** Piano player and singer from c.1908; c.1913-21—organized the Durante Original Jazz Novelty Band and alternated between playing the Alamo in Harlem and the Coney Island College Inn; early 1920s—own nightclub in Manhattan, Club Durante; formed singing and dancing trio with Eddie Jackson and Lou Clayton; 1923—Club Durante closed down for Prohibition violations; trio worked for several Manhattan clubs managed by organized crime members; vaudeville theaters in New York City, in Florenz Ziegfeld's production of *Show Girl*, 1929, and in film *Roadhouse Nights*; 1930—five-year solo contract with MGM; 1934—on *Chase and Sanborn's Radio Coffee Hour*; 1935—returned to musical comedy theater in Billy Rose's extravaganza *Jumbo*; late 1930s-1940s—in films, musical comedies on Broadway, and nightclubs and on radio; 1944—"rediscovered" by critics and new generation of audiences after record-breaking appearance in New York nightclub; 1950s-1960s—frequent guest-star appearances on television variety programs; 1954-56—host of *The Jimmy Durante Show* on NBC-TV, based on nightclub act from 1920s and featuring former partners Clayton and Jackson. **Awards:** Peabody Award for Entertainment, 1950. **Died:** In Santa Monica, California, 29 January 1980.

Films as Actor:

1929 *Roadhouse Nights* (Henley) (as Daffy)
1931 *The New Adventures of Get-Rich-Quick Wallingford* (*Get-Rich-Quick Wallingford*) (Wood) (as Schnozzle); *The Cuban Love Song* (Van Dyke) (as O. O. Jones)
1932 *The Passionate Plumber* (Sedgwick) (as McCracken); *The Wet Parade* (Fleming) (as Abe Schilling); *Speak Easily* (Sedgwick) (as James); *The Phantom President* (Taurog) (as Curly Cooney); *Blondie of the Follies* (Edmund Goulding) (as Jimmy)
1933 *What! No Beer?* (Sedgwick) (as Jimmy Potts); *Hell Below* (Conway) (as Ptomaine); *Broadway to Hollywood* (*Ring Up the Curtain*) (Mack); *Meet the Baron* (Walter Lang) (as Joe McGoo)
1934 *Palooka* (*The Great Schnozzle*; *Joe Palooka*) (Stoloff) (as Knobby Walsh); *George White's Scandals* (*George White's Scandals of 1934*) (White) (as Happy McGillicuddy); *Hollywood Party* (Boleslawski, Dwan, and Rowland [uncredited]); *Strictly Dynamite* (Nugent) (as Moxie Slaight); *Student Tour* (Riesner) (as Hank)

1935 *Carnival* (Walter Lang) (as Fingers)
1936 *Land without Music* (*Forbidden Music*) (Forde) (as Jonah J. Whistler)
1938 *Start Cheering* (Rogell) (as Willie Gumbatz); *Sally, Irene and Mary* (Seiter) (as Jefferson Twitchell); *Little Miss Broadway* (Cummings) (as Jimmy Clayton)
1940 *Melody Ranch* (Santley and Mackay) (as Cornelius J. Courtney)
1941 *You're in the Army Now* (Seiler) (as Jeeper Smith); *The Man Who Came to Dinner* (Keighley) (as Banjo)
1944 *Two Girls and a Sailor* (Thorpe) (as Billy Kipp); *Music for Millions* (Koster) (as Andrews)
1946 *Two Sisters from Boston* (Koster) (as "Spike")
1947 *It Happened in Brooklyn* (Whorf) (as Nick Lombardi); *This Time for Keeps* (Thorpe) (as Ferdi Farro)
1948 *On an Island with You* (Thorpe) (as Buckley)
1950 *The Great Rupert* (Pichel) (as Mr. Amendola); *The Milkman* (Barton) (as Breezy Albright)
1957 *Beau James* (Shavelson) (as guest)
1960 *Pepe* (Sidney) (as himself)
1961 *Il giudizio universale* (*The Last Judgment*) (De Sica)
1962 *Jumbo* (*Billy Rose's Jumbo*) (Walters) (as Pop Wonder)
1963 *It's a Mad, Mad, Mad, Mad World* (Kramer) (as Smiler Grogan)
1966 *Alice through the Looking Glass* (Handley—for TV) (as Humpty-Dumpty)

Publications

By DURANTE: books—

Night Clubs, with Jack Kofoed, 1931.
The Candidate (humor), 1952.

On DURANTE: books—

Cahn, William, *Good Night, Mrs. Calabash: The Secret of Jimmy Durante*, New York, 1963.
Parish, James Robert, *The Funsters*, New Rochelle, New York, 1979.
Adler, Irene, *I Remember Jimmy: The Life and Times of Jimmy Durante*, Westport, Connecticut, 1980.
Robbins, Jhan, *Inka Dinka Doo: The Life of Jimmy Durante*, New York, 1991.
Bakish, David, *Jimmy Durante: His Show Business Career*, Jefferson, North Carolina, 1995.

On DURANTE: articles—

Time (New York), 24 January 1944.
Variety (New York), 5 June 1946.
The Annual Obituary 1980, New York, 1981.
Holden, Stephen, "Pals on the Comeback Trail: Frank Sinatra, Jimmy Durante and Meat Loaf," in *New York Times*, 26 December 1993.

*   *   *

One of the most lovable of the eccentric comic actors, Jimmy Durante was paired with Buster Keaton in the early 1930s. This combination would appear to have given Keaton some hope of making a smoother transition to sound pictures; as a team their talents could have been complementary. Durante, however, had a role in *What! No Beer?* that pushed the famous silent screen comedian into the background. Urging Keaton to invest in a brewery just as Prohibition is about to be repealed, this lad with the Cyrano de Bergerac profile played the manic character with gusto, shouting the type of malapropism and mixed metaphor that would become typical of his characters: "A hundred-twenty million cracked lips are straining at the *leach*. Where's your *patronism?* Here's a chance to do something for your country."

Though Durante appeared to be headed for star billings in the early 1930s, he remained a likable eccentric who was more often the second banana. The most durable of old-timers, he provided excellent support for Donald O'Connor in *The Milkman*. When you look at this slight, contrived work today, you realize Durante stole the show from O'Connor without effort. The young comedian "knocked himself out" while the "Schnozzola," as Durante was nicknamed, sailed through his own part with all the charm of an old pro (he was 60 when he made this film) who knew how to make the best of each comic situation. Appearing in movies, vaudeville, nightclubs, and radio at the time of his greatest popularity in the 1930s, Durante may have spread his talent too thin. Unfortunately, the comedian does not have a single movie to his credit that has the quality to be ranked with the best comedies. As it failed to utilize the comedy skills of Bert Lahr (now known only for his portrait of the Cowardly Lion in *The Wizard of Oz*), Hollywood never exploited Durante's potential.

—Donald McCaffrey

DURBIN, Deanna

Nationality: American. **Born:** Edna Mae Durbin in Winnipeg, Manitoba, Canada, 4 December 1921; family moved to southern California in 1923. **Education:** Studied singing with Andres de Segurola. **Family:** Married 1) Vaughn Paul 1941 (divorced 1943); 2) Felix Jackson, 1945 (divorced 1948); 3) the director Charles David, 1950. **Career:** 1936—appeared in *Every Sunday*, musical short for MGM with Judy Garland; upon seeing it, the head of the studio, Louis B. Mayer, decided to keep both youngsters, but through a misunderstanding, Durbin was dropped; she then signed with Universal Studios where she made her first feature film *Three Smart Girls*, and signed a radio contract with Eddie Cantor; 1948—retired from screen acting; 1950—moved to France. **Awards:** Special Academy Award (with Mickey Rooney), "for their significant contribution in bringing to the screen the spirit and personification of youth and as juvenile players setting a high standard of ability and achievement," 1938.

Films as Actress:

1936   *Every Sunday* (*Every Sunday Afternoon*) (Feist—short); *Three Smart Girls* (Koster) (as Penny Craig)
1937   *100 Men and a Girl* (Koster) (as Patricia Cardwell)
1938   *Mad about Music* (Taurog) (as Gloria Harkinson); *That Certain Age* (Ludwig) (as Alice Fullerton)
1939   *Three Smart Girls Grow Up* (Koster) (as Penny "Mouse" Craig); *First Love* (Koster) (as Constance Harding)
1940   *It's a Date* (Seiter) (as Pamela Drake); *Spring Parade* (Koster) (as Ilonka Tolnay)

Deanna Durbin in *Lady on a Train*

1941   *Nice Girl?* (Seiter) (as Jane Dana); *It Started with Eve* (Koster)
(as Anne Terry)

1943   *The Amazing Mrs. Holliday* (Manning) (as Ruth); *Hers to Hold*
(Ryan) (as Penelope Craig); *His Butler's Sister* (Borzage) (as
Ann Carter); *Show Business at War* (De Rochemont—doc,
short) (as herself)

1944   *Christmas Holiday* (Siodmak) (as Jackie Lamont/Abigail Martin); *Can't Help Singing* (Ryan) (as Caroline)

1945   *Lady on a Train* (David) (as Nikki Collins)

1946   *Because of Him* (Wallace) (as Kim Walker)

1947   *I'll Be Yours* (Seiter) (as Louise Ginglebusher); *Something in
the Wind* (Pichel) (as Mary Collins)

1948   *Up in Central Park* (Seiter) (as Rosie Moore); *For the Love of
Mary* (de Cordova) (as Mary Peppertree)

Publications

By DURBIN: articles—

Interview with J. H. Seidelman, in *Film Weekly* (London), 9 April 1938.
Interviews in *Photoplay* (New York), 11 November 1938.
Films and Filming (London), December 1983.

On DURBIN: articles—

Picturegoer (London), 6 March 1937 and 2 April 1938.
"Bringing Up a Breadwinner," in *Picturegoer* (London), 4 February
1939.
Universal Outlook, Spring, Summer, Autumn, and Winter 1940, and
Summer 1941, "the magazine for all interested in Deanna Durbin."
Current Biography 1941, New York, 1941.
Photoplay Film Monthly (New York), May 1971.
"Deanna Durbin," in *Films in Review* (New York), November 1976;
letter in February 1977 and April 1978 issues.
Shipman, David, "Nostalgia—Deanna Durbin," in *Films and Filming*
(London), December 1983.
Everson, William K., "Deanna Durbin and Jean Renoir," in *Films in
Review* (New York), August/September 1986; see also October 1987.
Sesonske, Alexander, "*The Amazing Mrs. Holliday*," in *Films in Review*
(New York), June/July 1987.

*   *   *

Deanna Durbin's appearance in an MGM short with Judy Garland is
a precious document, highlighting two remarkable talents. (Louis B.
Mayer was apparently furious when, after putting Garland but not
Durbin under contract, Durbin became such a huge success so quickly,
for another studio.) Garland went on to become a legend, her films
frequently revived; Durbin, who when she grew up suffered from a
weight problem, as did Garland, retired from the movies—from performing altogether—in her mid-twenties, and has none of the cult
following of her teenage rival. Contemporary viewers are often puzzled
to learn that Deanna Durbin is credited with having saved Universal
from bankruptcy with her feisty adolescent nature and her sweet voice.
In a series of films directed by Henry Koster, she was indeed sensationally popular in the United States and England.

Durbin's sweet voice and sound musical instincts take on particular
value when she is compared to her 1940s counterparts, the "legit"
sopranos Jane Powell and Kathryn Grayson. Like Garland, Durbin was
also a very talented actress with an individual, recognizable style.
That style, related to her musical discipline, is perceived in her fluent,
rapid-fire, but utterly clear delivery of dialogue, in a diction with
irresistible impetus and energy, in irony that never smacks of
brattishness but rather, of real intelligence, and in a warmth of person-

ality that echoes her singing/speaking voice. One of her first "grown-
up" roles, in *It Started with Eve*, pits her against the formidable Charles
Laughton, and the modulations of their relationship is one of the joys
of this romantic comedy. Her dramatic roles in *Christmas Holiday* and
Lady on a Train suggest that at a different studio—and perhaps with a
different level of ambition on her part—Durbin's career would not
have been truncated so abruptly. Her pluckiness remains a significant
image of America in the late 1930s.

—Charles Affron

DURYEA, Dan

Nationality: American. **Born:** White Plains, New York, 23 January
1907. **Education:** Cornell University, Ithaca, New York. **Family:**
Married Helen (Duryea) (died 1976), sons: Peter and Richard. **Career:** Early 1930s—worked in advertising, quit after heart attack;
1935—debut on Broadway in Sidney Kingsley's *Dead End*; 1939—
critical acclaim for role of Leo in Lillian Hellman's *The Little Foxes*
on Broadway, and in film version, 1941; mid-1940s—contract with
Universal; 1952-55—in TV series *China Smith*; 1967-68—in TV series *Peyton Place* as Eddie Jacks. **Died:** Of cancer in Hollywood, 8
June 1968.

Films as Actor:

1941   *The Little Foxes* (Wyler) (as Leo Hubbard); *Ball of Fire* (Hawks)

1942   *The Pride of the Yankees* (Wood); *That Other Woman* (Ray
McCarey)

1943   *Sahara* (Zoltan Korda); *Ministry of Fear* (Lang)

1944   *Man from Frisco* (Florey); *The Woman in the Window* (Lang);
Mrs. Parkington (Garnett); *None but the Lonely Heart*
(Odets); *Main Street after Dark* (Cahn)

1945   *The Great Flamarion* (Mann); *The Valley of Decision* (Garnett);
Along Came Jones (Heisler); *Lady on a Train* (David); *Scarlet
Street* (Lang)

1946   *The Black Angel* (Neill); *White Tie and Tails* (Barton)

1948   *Black Bart* (*Black Bart, Highwayman*) (Sherman); *Another
Part of the Forest* (Gordon); *River Lady* (Sherman); *Larceny*
(Sherman); *Criss Cross* (Siodmak)

1949   *Manhandled* (Foster); *Too Late for Tears* (Haskin); *Johnny
Stool Pigeon* (Castle)

1950   *One Way Street* (Fregonese); *Winchester '73* (Mann); *The Underworld Story* (*The Whipped*) (Endfield)

1951   *Al Jennings of Oklahoma* (Nazzaro); *Chicago Calling*
(Reinhardt)

1953   *Thunder Bay* (Mann); *Sky Commando* (Sears); *Thirty-Six Hours*
(*Terror Street*) (Tully); *Ride Clear of Diablo* (Hibbs)

1954   *World for Ransom* (Aldrich); *Rails into Laramie* (Hibbs); *Silver Lode* (Dwan); *This Is My Love* (Heisler)

1955   *Foxfire* (Pevney); *The Marauders* (Mayer); *Storm Fear* (Wilde)

1957   *The Burglar* (Wendkos); *Battle Hymn* (Sirk); *Kathy O'* (Sher);
Night Passage (Neilson); *Slaughter on Tenth Avenue* (Laven)

1959   *Gunfight at Sandoval* (Keller—for TV); *Platinum High School*
(*Rich, Young, and Deadly*) (Haas)

1961   *Six Black Horses* (Keller)

1963   *He Rides Tall* (Springsteen); *Do You Know This Voice?* (Nesbitt);
Walk a Tightrope (Nesbitt)

1964   *Taggart* (Springsteen)

1965   *The Bounty Killer* (Bennet); *The Flight of the Phoenix* (Aldrich);
Incident at Phantom Hill (Bellamy)

1966 *Un fiume di dollari* (*The Hills Run Red*) (Beaver, i.e. Carlo Lizzani)
1967 *Winchester '73* (Daugherty—for TV); *Five Golden Dragons* (Summers); *Stranger on the Run* (Siegel—for TV)
1968 *The Bamboo Saucer* (Telford)

Publications

On DURYEA: articles—

Classic Images (Indiana, Pennsylvania), March 1981.
Michelson, Leon M., "Dan Duryea: Playing Villains Pays Well," in *Video Movies* (Skokie, Illinois), October 1984.

*   *   *

Dan Duryea's fate as a film actor was sealed with his first role as Leo Hubbard in *The Little Foxes*. The tall, almost emaciated actor with the slicked-back blond hair and the ready smirk became the 1940s' premier louse. Duryea made an art of selfish cynical opportunism. He developed a repertoire of understated shoulder shrugs, slight raisings of the eyebrow, a twitch of the mouth, and an almost imperceptible "suit-yourself, take-it-or-leave-it" movement of the hand. He became a master of the small signs of character that the camera could pick up, and he wielded his reedy, high voice like an irritating, cutting scimitar.

While his best known roles as the petty thief and blackmailer in Fritz Lang's *The Woman in the Window* and *Scarlet Street* allowed him to display his skill, his presence is as memorable in his portrayal of the reporter in *Pride of the Yankees*. As the evil counterpart for the lanky heroes of the 1940s, particularly Gary Cooper in *Along Came Jones*, Duryea brought out the emerging attitude of disillusionment toward the end of World War II and in the years after. In the 1950s Duryea's mocking image became less one to be faced and overcome by the hero than one which had to be accepted as part of the postwar world. As the neurotic, tubercular brother to Cornel Wilde in *Storm Fear*, Duryea was an uncomfortable alternative to the villain. As the tough sergeant in *Battle Hymn*, he portrayed a heroic cynic, and contributed to the character of the 1960s anti-hero. By 1965, Duryea's persona had developed its final twist. In *The Flight of the Phoenix*, he played a bespectacled passenger on a crashed plane who nervously supports rather than mirrors the lanky hero played by Jimmy Stewart. However, Duryea's mastery of the uncomfortable, deceitful, mocking and cynical villain had pioneered a new type of villainy carried on briefly by Richard Widmark, and finally turned to filmic art by Lee Marvin.

—Stuart Kaminsky

DUVALL, Robert

Nationality: American. **Born:** Robert Selden Duvall in San Diego, California, 5 January 1931. **Education:** Attended Principia College, Illinois. **Military Service:** U.S. Army, in Korea, early 1950s. **Family:** Married 1) Barbara Benjamin, 1964 (divorced); 2) Gail Youngs, 1982; 3) Sharon Brophy, 1991. **Career:** Studied acting with Sanford Meisner at Neighborhood Playhouse in New York; acted in Horton Foote's *The Midnight Caller*; 1957—cast by stage director Ulu Grosbard in studio production of *A View from the Bridge*, beginning long professional relationship; late 1950s—began acting on television; 1962— cast in first film, *To Kill a Mockingbird*, at Horton Foote's insistence; 1965—critical acclaim for role in Grosbard's off-Broadway produc-

tion of *A View from the Bridge*, and for role in *Wait until Dark* on Broadway; 1977—on Broadway in *American Buffalo* directed by Grosbard; first directorial effort, *We're Not the Jet Set*; 1979—played title role in TV mini-series *Ike*; 1989—in TV mini-series *Lonesome Dove*. **Awards:** Best Supporting Actor, New York Film Critics, for *The Godfather*, 1972; Best Supporting Actor, British Academy, for *Apocalypse Now*, 1979; Academy Award for Best Actor, for *Tender Mercies*, 1983. **Agent:** Arnold Rifkin, William Morris Agency, 151 El Camino Drive, Beverly Hills, CA 90212, U.S.A.

Films as Actor:

1962 *To Kill a Mockingbird* (Mulligan) (as Boo Radley)
1963 *Nightmare in the Sun* (Lawrence) (as motorcyclist); *Captain Newman, M.D.* (David Miller) (as Capt. Paul Cabot Winston)
1966 *Fame Is the Name of the Game* (Rosenberg—for TV); *The Chase* (Arthur Penn) (as Edwin Stewart)
1967 *Cosa Nostra: An Arch Enemy of the FBI* (Medford—for TV)
1968 *Countdown* (*Moonshot*) (Altman) (as Chiz); *The Detective* (Gordon Douglas) (as Nestor); *Bullitt* (Yates) (as Weissberg)
1969 *True Grit* (Hathaway) (as Ned Pepper); *The Rain People* (Francis Ford Coppola) (as Gordon)
1970 *M*A*S*H* (Altman) (as Major Frank Burns); *The Revolutionary* (Williams) (as Despard)
1971 *Lawman* (Winner) (as Vernon Adams); *THX-1138* (Lucas) (title role)
1972 ***The Godfather*** (Francis Ford Coppola) (as Tom Hagen); *The Great Northfield, Minnesota Raid* (Kaufman) (as Jesse James); *Joe Kidd* (John Sturges) (as Frank Harlan); *Tomorrow* (Anthony) (as Jackson Fentry)
1973 *Badge 373* (Koch) (as Eddie Ryan); *Lady Ice* (Gries) (as Ford Pierce); *The Outfit* (Flynn) (as Earl Macklin)
1974 *The Conversation* (Francis Ford Coppola); ***The Godfather, Part II*** (Francis Ford Coppola) (as Tom Hagen)
1975 *Breakout* (Gries) (as Jay Wagner); *The Killer Elite* (Peckinpah) (as George Hansen)
1976 *Network* (Lumet) (as Frank Hackett); *The Seven-Per-Cent Solution* (Ross) (as Dr. Watson); *The Eagle Has Landed* (John Sturges) (as Col. Max Radl)
1977 *The Greatest* (Gries) (as Bill McDonald)
1978 *The Betsy* (Petrie) (as Loren Hardeman III); *Invasion of the Body Snatchers* (Kaufman) (as guest)
1979 ***Apocalypse Now*** (Francis Ford Coppola) (as Lt. Col. Bill Kilgore); *The Great Santini* (*The Ace*) (Carlino) (as Bull Meechum)
1981 *True Confessions* (Grosbard) (as Tom Spellacy); *The Pursuit of D. B. Cooper* (Spottiswoode) (as Bob Gruen)
1983 *Tender Mercies* (Beresford) (as Max Sledge, + co-pr); *The Terry Fox Story* (Thomas—for TV)
1984 *The Stone Boy* (Cain) (as Joe Hillerman); *The Natural* (Levin) (as Max Mercy)
1986 *Belizaire the Cajun* (Pitre) (as Preacher); *The Lightship* (Skolimowski) (as Caspary)
1987 *Hotel Colonial* (Torrini) (as Carrasco); *Let's Get Harry* (Smithee [Stuart Rosenberg]) (as Norman Shrike)
1988 *Colors* (Dennis Hopper) (as Bob Hodges); *Convicts* (Masterson); *Roots in a Parched Ground* (Masterson)
1990 *The Handmaid's Tale* (Schlöndorff) (as Commander); *A Show of Force* (Barreto) (as Howard Baslin); *Days of Thunder* (Tony Scott) (as Harry Hogge)
1991 *Rambling Rose* (Coolidge) (as Daddy Hillyer); *Convicts* (Masterson) (as Soll Gautier)

Robert Duvall in *Tender Mercies*

1992 *Newsies* (Ortega) (as Joseph Pulitzer); *The Plague* (*La peste*) (Puenzo) (as Joseph Grand); *Stalin* (Passer—for TV) (title role)

1993 *Wrestling Ernest Hemingway* (Haines) (as Walt); *Falling Down* (Schumacher) (as Prendergast); *Geronimo: An American Legend* (Walter Hill) (as Al Sieber); *Cachao . . . como su ritmo no hay dos* (*Like His Rhythm There Is No Other*) (García—doc) (as himself)

1994 *The Paper* (Ron Howard) (as Bernie White)

1995 *The Scarlet Letter* (Joffé) (as Roger Chillingworth); *Something to Talk About* (Hallstrom) (as Wyly King); *The Stars Fell on Henrietta* (Keach) (as Mr. Cox)

1996 *A Family Thing* (Richard Pearce) (as Earl, + co-pr); *The Man Who Captured Eichmann* (for TV) (as Adolf Eichmann/ Ricardo Clement, + co-pr); *Phenomenon* (Turteltaub)

Films as Director:

1977 *We're Not the Jet Set* (doc)

1983 *Angelo, My Love* (+ co-pr, sc)

Publications

By DUVALL: articles—

Interview in *Interview* (New York), September 1977.

Interviews in *Time Out* (London), 27 March 1981 and 8 July 1983.

"Robert Duvall: America's Hard-Boiled Olivier," interview with L. McCormick, in *American Film* (Washington, D.C.), September 1981.

Interview with K. M. Chanko, in *Films in Review* (New York), May 1983.

Interview with T. Ryan, in *Cinema Papers* (Melbourne), July 1984.

Interview with Laura Dern, in *Interview* (New York), October 1991.

On DUVALL: book—

Slawson, Judith, *Robert Duvall: Hollywood Maverick*, New York, 1985.

On DUVALL: articles—

Current Biography 1977, New York, 1977.

Foote, Horton, "Robert Duvall: No Limits," in *Close-Ups: The Movie Star Book*, edited by Danny Peary, New York, 1978.

Bogre, M., "The Filming of *Angelo My Love*," in *American Cinematographer* (Los Angeles), July 1981.

"Robert Duvall," in *Films in Review* (New York), May 1983.

Robert Duvall Section of *Positif* (Paris), April 1984.

Hibbin, S., "Robert Duvall," in *Films and Filming* (London), May 1986.

Weinraub, Bernard, "Playing Stalin the Man Not Stalin the Monster," in *New York Times*, 5 November 1992.

*   *   *

From his screen debut as silently staring Boo Radley, the antithesis of a childhood bogeyman, the skull-faced Duvall has often acted like the eye of a hurricane, unleashing his power upon spectators when they least expect it. His specialty is submerged violence that overheats and then steams out of simple souls, and he is an expert at playing self-controlled men who should not be pushed too far. Throughout his steady career as a character star on a par with Gene Hackman, Duvall has (until recently) never given a less than multifaceted performance in even the smallest roles.

With just a glance, he sums up Boo Radley's entire solitary life as a child-man cut off from normal human experience in *To Kill a Mockingbird*. Psychologically damaged in *Captain Newman, M.D.*, way too sure of himself in *True Grit*, and disastrously clueless about Shirley Knight's needs in *The Rain People*, Duvall never seemed like the same actor in any of these movies, and that invisible adaptability may have prevented him from coming to prominence sooner. Although he is a drolly funny born-again phony in *M*A*S*H*, and touchingly overwhelmed as a futuristic man in *THX-1138*, Duvall's key role is Tom Hagen, the buttoned-down Mafia facilitator in the *Godfather* movies. Always weighing his options and always loyally cleaning up after his colorful masters, Duvall's outsider is a fully realized characterization, the compromised man blinded by forever looking the other way. If one has read the original script for *The Godfather, Part III*, in which Tom Hagen played a key role in the Mafia-Vatican chicanery, one realizes that Coppola made a big mistake in not meeting Duvall's salary demands. Underestimating Duvall's essentialness to his trilogy, Coppola gave birth to a watered-down conclusion to his epic; with company-man Duvall aboard to play Mr. Fix-it, the third mezza-mezza installment might have consequently attained the stature of the first two masterworks.

Over the years, Duvall continued painting his one-man gallery of regional types—luminous portraits of faceless Americans living lives of quiet desperation. Instead of repeating himself, Duvall broadened his artistry and reworked his stage performance as the hapless Jackson Fentry in a grim *Tomorrow* with an intuitive grasp of how to scale down the performance for the cinema. As vital a presence when gearing up for bombast as he is with harkening attention with an actor's silences, Duvall can be insinuatingly sinister while running a *Network*, appallingly macho while badgering his family with Marine mentality in *The Great Santini* or hilariously psychotic as a lieutenant colonel treating Vietnam like a vacation spot in *Apocalypse Now*. Even in junk such as *The Betsy*, he does not abdicate his responsibility to the audience. Although he beat four acclaimed Brits to win his best actor Oscar for *Tender Mercies*, his redemption-seeking country-western singer does not have the full-bodied richness of his detective eaten up by the acid of departmental corruption in *True Confessions*, or his rock-solid street cop in *Colors* or his loving family man in *Rambling Rose*. Perhaps that is because he is playing a symbolic force in the dry-as-dust *Tender Mercies* and can develop the characters in these other films along less pretentious lines.

Lately, Duvall has been stretching himself with roles outside his safe Yankee territory. Despite his wavering accent, he is touching as a straight-laced Cuban gentleman in the geriatric soap opera, *Wrestling Ernest Hemingway*. If he appears to be home on the world-weary prairies of *Lonesome Dove*, he seems bogusly out of place in Russia as *Stalin*. As versatile as he is, his uncluttered directness is more compatible with interpreting such American figureheads as *Ike* than foreign despots.

Floundering in the Harlequin Romancing of Hawthorne's *The Scarlet Letter*, Duvall is betrayed by the insipid writing and composition-conscious director into botching a part that he is temperamentally attuned to, the demented Roger Chillingworth, an avenging angel hiding behind a bible. Future performances will be molded by Duvall with his unsparing honesty and spare methods. (After all, he cannot be blamed for playing second-fiddle to Demi Moore's buffed body. He exudes more star-chemistry opposite James Earl Jones in the engaging comedy, *A Family Thing*.) The Man of a Thousand Nuances, Duvall is an exemplary actor who feeds every characterization with the accidental discoveries gifted by his insight. Because he is so forceful when he holds your gaze sans words, when Duvall finally chooses to speak, everyone listens.

—Robert Pardi

EASTWOOD, Clint

Nationality: American. **Born:** Clinton Eastwood Jr. in San Francisco, California, 31 May 1930 (some sources give 30 or 31 May 1931). **Education:** Attended Oakland Technical High School; studied business administration, Los Angeles City College, 1953-54. **Military Service:** 1950—U.S. Army; served as swimming instructor at Fort Ord, California. **Family:** Married 1) Maggie Johnson, 1953 (divorced in mid-1980s), children: Kyle Clinton and Alison; 2) Dina Ruiz, 1996; daughter with Roxanne Tunis: Kimber; daughter with actress Frances Fisher: Francesca Ruth. **Career:** 1954-55—contract with Universal; 1955—screen debut in *Francis in the Navy*; late 1950s—worked sporadically in films, and as lifeguard and for swimming pool contractor; 1959-66—second lead as Rowdy Yates in TV series *Rawhide* (took over lead as trail boss, autumn 1965); 1964—*A Fistful of Dollars* for Sergio Leone, first of series of three, was big hit in Europe and, in 1967, in U.S.; 1967—first starring role in U.S. film, *Hang 'em High*; formed Malpaso production company; 1971—directed first film, *Play Misty for Me*; 1982—first effort at producing, on *Firefox*; 1986-88—mayor of Carmel, California. **Awards:** Chevalier des Lettres, France, 1985; Academy Awards for Best Direction and Best Picture, for *The Unforgiven*, 1992; Fellowship of the British Film Institute, 1993; Irving G. Thalberg Memorial Award, 1995. **Address:** c/o Malpaso Productions, 4000 Warner Boulevard, Burbank, CA 91522, U.S.A.

Films as Actor:

1955   *Francis in the Navy* (Lubin) (as Jonesy); *Revenge of the Creature* (Arnold) (as technician); *Lady Godiva* (Lubin) (as Saxon); *Tarantula* (Arnold) (as Air Force pilot)
1956   *Never Say Goodbye* (Jerry Hopper) (as lab assistant); *The First Traveling Saleslady* (Lubin) (as Jack Rice); *Star in the Dust* (Haas) (bit role)
1957   *Escapade in Japan* (Lubin) (as Dumbo); *Ambush at Cimarron Pass* (Copeland) (as Keith Williams); *Lafayette Escadrille* (*Hell Bent for Glory*) (Wellman) (as George Moseley)
1964   *A Fistful of Dollars* (*Per un pugno di dollari*) (Leone) (as The Stranger)
1965   *For a Few Dollars More* (*Per qualche dollari in piu*) (Leone) (as The Stranger); "Civic Sense" ep. of *Le streghe* (*The Witches*) (Visconti, Pasolini, Bolognini, Rossi, and de Sica) (as husband)
1966   *Il buono, il brutto, il cattivo* (*The Good, the Bad, and the Ugly*) (Leone) (as Joe)
1967   *Hang 'em High* (Post) (as Jed Cooper)
1968   *Coogan's Bluff* (Siegel) (as Walt Coogan)
1969   *Paint Your Wagon* (Logan) (as Pardner)
1970   *Kelly's Heroes* (Hutton) (as Kelly); *Two Mules for Sister Sara* (Siegel) (as Hogan)
1971   *The Beguiled* (Siegel) (as John McBurney); *Dirty Harry* (Siegel) (as Harry Callahan)
1972   *Joe Kidd* (John Sturges) (title role)
1973   *Magnum Force* (Post) (as Harry Callahan)
1974   *Thunderbolt and Lightfoot* (Cimino) (as John "Thunderbolt" Doherty)
1976   *The Enforcer* (Fargo) (as Harry Callahan)
1977   *Every Which Way but Loose* (Fargo) (as Philo Beddoe)
1978   *Escape from Alcatraz* (Siegel) (as Frank Morris)
1980   *Any Which Way You Can* (Van Horn) (as Philo Beddoe)
1984   *Tightrope* (Tuggle) (as Wes Block, + co-pr); *City Heat* (Benjamin)
1988   *The Dead Pool* (Van Horn) (as Harry Callahan)
1989   *Pink Cadillac* (Van Horn) (as Tommy Mowak)
1993   *In the Line of Fire* (Petersen) (as Frank Horrigan)
1994   *Don't Pave Main Street: Carmel's Heritage* (Cartwright and Ludwig—doc) (as narrator)
1995   *Casper* (Silberling) (uncredited cameo)

Films as Director:

1971   *Play Misty for Me* (+ ro as Dave Garland)
1973   *High Plains Drifter* (+ ro as the stranger); *Breezy*
1975   *The Eiger Sanction* (+ ro as Jonathan Hemlock)
1976   *The Outlaw Josey Wales* (+ title role)
1977   *The Gauntlet* (+ ro as Ben Shockley)
1980   *Bronco Billy* (+ ro as Bronco Billy McCoy)
1982   *Honkytonk Man* (+ pr, ro as Red); *Firefox* (+ pr, ro as Mitchell Gant)
1983   *Sudden Impact* (+ pr, ro as Harry Callahan)
1985   *Pale Rider* (+ pr, ro as Preacher)
1986   *Heartbreak Ridge* (+ pr, ro as Tom Highway)
1988   *Bird* (+ pr)
1990   *White Hunter, Black Heart* (+ pr, ro as John Wilson); *The Rookie* (+ ro as Nick Pulovski)
1992   *Unforgiven* (+ pr, ro as William Munny)
1993   *A Perfect World* (+ pr, ro as Red Garnett)
1995   *The Bridges of Madison County* (+ pr, ro as Robert Kincaid)

Other Films:

1989   *Thelonious Monk: Straight No Chaser* (Zwerin—doc) (exec pr)
1995   *The Stars Fell on Henrietta* (Keach) (pr)

Publications

By EASTWOOD: articles—

Interview with Arthur Knight, in *Playboy* (Chicago), February 1974.
"Clint Eastwood, Auteur," by R. Thompson and T. Hunter, in *Film Comment* (New York), January-February 1978.
"Conversation with Clint Eastwood," by Larry Cole, in *Oui* (Chicago), June 1978.
Interview with R. Gentry, in *Millimeter* (New York), December 1980.

Clint Eastwood

Interview with David Thomson, in *Film Comment* (New York), September/October 1984.

Interview with C. Tesson and O. Assayas, in *Cahiers du Cinéma* (Paris), February 1985.

Rayns, Tony, "Clint at Claridges," in *Sight and Sound* (London), Spring 1985.

Interview with Michel Ciment and Hubert Niogret, in *Positif* (Paris), July/August 1988.

"Flight of Fancy," interview with Nat Hentoff, in *American Film* (Los Angeles), September 1988.

Interview with Allan Hunter, in *Films and Filming* (London), November/December 1988.

Interview with R. Gentry, in *Film Quarterly*, vol. 42, no. 3, 1989.

Interview with Michel Ciment, in *Positif* (Paris), no. 351, 1990.

"The Man Who Would Be Huston," interview with Graham Fuller, in *Interview* (New York), October 1990.

"The Padron" (Don Siegel), in *Film Comment* (New York), September/October 1991.

Interview with M. Henry in *Positif* (Paris), no. 380, 1992.

Interview with David Breskin, in *Rolling Stone* (New York), 17 September 1992.

Interview in *Reel West*, October/November 1992.

Interview with David Wild, in *Rolling Stone* (New York), 24 August 1995.

On EASTWOOD: books—

Douglas, Peter, *Clint Eastwood: Movin' On*, Chicago, 1974.

Kaminsky, Stuart, *American Film Genres*, New York, 1974.

Kaminsky, Stuart, *Clint Eastwood*, New York, 1974.

Agan, Patrick, *Clint Eastwood: The Man Behind the Myth*, New York, 1975.

Staig, Lawrence, and Tony Williams, *Italian Westerns: The Opera of Violence*, London, 1975.

Downing, David, with Gary Herman, *Clint Eastwood, All-American Anti-Hero: A Critical Appraisal of the World's Top Box Office Star and His Films*, London, 1977.

Ferrari, Philippe, *Clint Eastwood*, Paris, 1980.

Johnstone, Iain, *The Man with No Name: Clint Eastwood*, London, 1981; rev. ed., 1988.

Zmijewsky, Boris, and Lee Pfeiffer, *The Films of Clint Eastwood*, Secaucus, New Jersey, 1982; rev. ed., 1988.

Cole, Gerald, and Peter Williams, *Clint Eastwood*, London, 1983.

Guerif, François, *Clint Eastwood*, Paris, 1983; New York, 1986.

Ryder, Jeffrey, *Clint Eastwood*, New York, 1987.

Lagarde, Hélène, *Clint Eastwood*, Paris, 1988.

Weinberger, Michèle, *Clint Eastwood*, Paris, 1989.

Plaza, Fuensanta, *Clint Eastwood/Malpaso*, Carmel Valley, California, 1991.

Frayling, Christopher, *Clint Eastwood*, London, 1992.

Munn, Michael, *Clint Eastwood: Hollywood's Loner*, London, 1992.

Thompson, Douglas, *Clint Eastwood: Riding High*, Chicago, 1992.

Smith, Paul, *Clint Eastwood: A Cultural Production*, Minneapolis, 1993.

Zmijewsky, Boris, and Lee Pfeiffer, *The Films of Clint Eastwood*, New York, 1993.

Bingham, Dennis, *Acting Male: Masculinities in the Films of James Stewart, Jack Nicholson and Clint Eastwood*, New Brunswick, New Jersey, 1994.

Clinch, Minty, *Clint Eastwood*, London, 1994.

Gallafent, Edward, *Clint Eastwood: Filmmaker and Star*, New York, 1994.

Ortoli, Philippe, *Clint Eastwood: la figure du guerrier*, Paris, 1994.

Tanitch, Robert, *Clint Eastwood*, 1995.

On EASTWOOD: articles—

Bodeen, DeWitt, "Clint Eastwood," in *Focus on Film* (London), Spring 1972.

Kael, Pauline, "Current Cinema," in *New Yorker*, 14 January 1974.

Shadoian, J., "Dirty Harry: A Defense," in *Western Humanities Review* (Salt Lake City), Spring 1974.

Vallely, J., "Pumping Gold with Clint Eastwood, Hollywood's Richest Actor," in *Esquire* (New York), 14 March 1978.

Alpert, Robert, "Clint Eastwood Plays Dumb Cop," in *Jump Cut* (Chicago), May 1979.

Kehr, Dave, "Clint Eastwood," in *The Movie Star*, edited by Elisabeth Weis, New York, 1981.

Patterson, E., "Every Which Way but Lucid: The Critique of Authority in Clint Eastwood's Police Films," in *Journal of Popular Film* (Washington, D.C.), Fall 1982.

Mailer, Norman, "All the Pirates and People," in *Parade Magazine*, 23 October 1983.

Clint Eastwood section of *Positif* (Paris), January 1985.

Kehr, Dave, "A Fistful of Eastwood," in *American Film* (Washington, D.C.), March 1985.

Holmlund, C., "Sexuality and Power in Male Doppelganger Cinema: The Case of Clint Eastwood and *Tightrope*," in *Cinema Journal*, vol. 26, no. 1, 1986.

Chevrie, M., and D. J. Wiener, "Le Dernier des cow-boys," in *Cahiers du Cinéma* (Paris), March 1987.

Current Biography 1989, New York, 1989.

Bingham, D., "Men with No Names: Clint Eastwood, the Stranger Persona, Identification and the Impenetrable Gaze," in *Journal of Film and Video*, vol. 42, no. 4, 1990.

Sheehan, Henry, "Scraps of Hope: Clint Eastwood and the Western," in *Film Comment* (New York), September/October 1992.

Combs, Richard, "Shadowing the Hero," in *Sight and Sound* (London), October 1992.

Tibbetts, J. C., "Clint Eastwood and the Machinery of Violence," in *Literature Film Quarterly*, vol. 21, no. 1, 1993.

Biskind, Peter, "Any Which Way He Can," in *Premiere* (New York), April 1993; see also August 1992.

Grenier, Richard, "Clint Eastwood Goes PC," in *Commentary*, March 1994.

*   *   *

It would be difficult to sustain a case for Clint Eastwood as a great actor. Competent, certainly, even polished within a limited range, but hardly a Marlon Brando or even a James Stewart. If comparisons have to be made, the obvious one is with John Wayne, another movie figure whose emblematic significance far outweighed his conventional thespian talents. Both, of course, owed their initial breakthrough to the Western, and both built cleverly on the generic image with which they were furnished.

Eastwood (then taking small parts in Hollywood) first came to public attention in the late 1950s, playing Rowdy Yates in the television Western series *Rawhide*. Lean, weather-beaten, and a man of few words but much integrity, he epitomized one strand in the classic image of the Westerner. It was this tradition which was to be extended almost into parody in the three massively successful Westerns that Eastwood made with director Sergio Leone: *A Fistful of Dollars*, *For a Few Dollars More*, and *The Good, the Bad, and the Ugly*. In all three films he had little to say, and what little there was only just escaped in the wake of the cheroot that he continually rolled from one side of his mouth to the other. The Man with No Name (as the character came to be known) was founded on that mannerism, on Eastwood's distinctive physical appearance, and on his role as the poncho-clad gunfighter who rides into town bringing vengeance and death. Like Leone's films themselves, the Man with No Name was a distillation of a Western myth, and it turned Eastwood into top box-office.

It was a happy conjunction of man and image, and, recognizing that his talents lay here, Eastwood set about constructing a career that made the most of them. Simple variations upon the Man with No Name have served well in the likes of *Hang 'em High*, *Two Mules for Sister Sara*, *Joe Kidd*, *High Plains Drifter*, and *Pale Rider*. A modern urban counterpart turned up in *Coogan's Bluff* in the guise of a policeman from out West blundering none too appealingly through New York, and emerged fully fledged in another film made for Don Siegel, the controversial and highly successful *Dirty Harry*. Its central character, Harry Callahan, an obsessive, ruthless, and violent cop, became even more ruthlessly violent in its immediate sequels, *Magnum Force* and *The Enforcer*, rapidly joining the Man with No Name as a permanent fixture in the modern cinema's chamber of action heroes.

It is on these two interrelated personae that Eastwood's acting style has been built. Only rarely has he had the opportunity to stretch himself beyond these limits (in, for example, *The Beguiled*, *Play Misty for Me*, *Tightrope*, and *The Bridges of Madison County*) and when he does so he generally produces performances even more understated than those he gives when fully in persona. To put it glibly, he does not so much rise to such parts as allow himself to lapse into them. As an actor, then, Eastwood is a product of his image. His success is based on recognizing that fact and ensuring that every performance uses it in some way. Thus, much of the apparent power of his performance in *In the Line of Fire* is a consequence of the skillfully wrought contrast (mostly achieved in the editing since they do not play scenes together directly) between Malkovich's actorly intensity and Eastwood's laid-back evocation of that familiar screen persona.

That said, it is important to note that the sheer strength of the Eastwood image can be used to create distance as well as to encapsulate characters. Although most of his roles have been fairly straightforward expressions of his established screen personae, on a few occasions he has sought to open up some space between character and myth. Sometimes that edges close to pastiche, as it does in the cause of heightened effects in the two likably overwrought Westerns, *High Plains Drifter* and *Pale Rider*. Sometimes it is more openly humorous, as in the wilder excesses of *The Gauntlet*, the good natured self-mockery of *Bronco Billy*, or the rather knowing evocation of the Harry Callahan cycle in *The Dead Pool*. Just occasionally Eastwood has found some balance between evoking the image and using it as a kind of comment upon itself. One such film is *The Outlaw Josey Wales* where he plays Josey Wales without the usual superhuman overtones, thus trading on the tension between persona-based expectations and the character's actual behavior. Another case is *Heartbreak Ridge*, where the assertive masculinity of the Eastwood persona (here in a military version) is to some degree rendered insecure. And yet another instance is *Unforgiven* which works by allowing the classic persona to emerge slowly in the course of the film. William Munny, former gunman turned responsible single parent, is to be found at the film's opening covered in mud and struggling with his hogs. By its culminating sequence he has recovered his classic guise as Western avenging angel, in the process turning the movie into a formidable expression of the genre's romantic individualism.

These films, of course, are as much the products of Eastwood the director as Eastwood the actor, which may explain both their ambition and the fact that they do not quite pull it off. As a director Eastwood clearly learned well from both Leone and Siegel, the two filmmakers most responsible for his on-screen persona. It is a pity, therefore, that however well he has learned (and he *is* a good director), the Eastwood image that they conjointly created is now probably too strong to be overcome.

—Andrew Tudor

EDDY, Nelson

Nationality: American. **Born:** Providence, Rhode Island, 29 June 1901. **Education:** Attended grade schools, Providence, New Bedford, Connecticut, and Pawtucket, Rhode Island. **Family:** Married Ann Denitz Franklin, 1939. **Career:** 1921—copywriting job with N. W. Ayer & Son; 1922—debut in musical *The Marriage Tax* at Academy of Music, Philadelphia; joined local Gilbert and Sullivan group; 1924—debut with Philadelphia Civic Opera as Amonasro in *Aida*; studied in Dresden and Paris for several months; 1924-28—sang extensively in United States, and toured from 1928; 1931—appeared at Metropolitan Opera in Berg's *Wozzeck*; 1933—sang at Los Angeles Philharmonic Auditorium; contract with MGM; 1935—teamed for first time with Jeanette MacDonald in *Naughty Marietta*; made concert tours and radio appearances; 1942—released from MGM contract; 1947—last film; continued to work in radio, give concerts, and appear in light opera; 1952—in TV version of operetta *The Desert Song*; from mid-1950s concentrated on nightclub appearances and recording. **Died:** Of stroke in Miami Beach, 6 March 1967.

Films as Actor:

1933   *Broadway to Hollywood* (*Ring Up the Curtain*) (Mack); *Dancing Lady* (Leonard) (as himself)
1934   *Student Tour* (Reisner) (as himself)
1935   *Naughty Marietta* (Van Dyke) (as Capt. Dick Warrington)
1936   *Rose Marie* (*Indian Love Call*) (Van Dyke) (as Sgt. Bruce)
1937   *Maytime* (Leonard) (as Paul Allison); *Rosalie* (Van Dyke) (as Dick Thorpe)
1938   *The Girl of the Golden West* (Leonard) (as Ramerez/Lt. Johnson); *Sweethearts* (Van Dyke) (as Ernest Lane)
1939   *Let Freedom Ring* (Conway) (as Steve Logan); *Balalaika* (Schunzel) (as Prince Peter Karagin)
1940   *New Moon* (Leonard) (as Charles Mission); *Bitter Sweet* (Van Dyke) (as Carl Linden)
1941   *The Chocolate Soldier* (Del Ruth) (as Karl Lang)
1942   *I Married an Angel* (Van Dyke) (as Count Willie Palaffi)
1943   *Phantom of the Opera* (Lubin) (as Anatole Garron)
1944   *Knickerbocker Holiday* (Harry Joe Brown) (as Brom Broeck)
1946   *Make Mine Music* (Kinney and others—animation) (as voice of Willie the Singing Whale)
1947   *Northwest Outpost* (*End of the Rainbow*) (Dwan) (as Capt. James Laurence)

Publications

On EDDY: books—

Knowles, Eleanor, *The Films of Jeanette MacDonald & Nelson Eddy*, South Brunswick, New Jersey, 1975.
Goodrich, Diane, and S. Rich, *Farewell to Dreams*, Los Angeles, 1979.
Castanza, Philip, *The Films of Jeanette MacDonald and Nelson Eddy*, Secaucus, New Jersey, 1981.
Kiner, Larry F., *Nelson Eddy: A Bio-Discography*, Metuchen, New Jersey, 1992.
Rich, Sharon, *Sweethearts: The Timeless Love Affair—On-screen and Off—Between Jeanette MacDonald and Nelson Eddy*, New York, 1994.

On EDDY: articles—

Current Biography 1943, New York, 1943.
Obituary in *New York Times*, 7 March 1967.

Brossard, J.-P., "Nelson Eddy 1901-1965," in *Films in Review* (New York), 1974.

On EDDY: film—

Nelson and Jeanette, televison documentary directed by Michael Lorentz, 1992.

* * *

As half of America's "Singing Sweethearts" in the 1930s, Nelson Eddy—along with his better half (in terms of acting ability, at any rate), Jeanette MacDonald—starred in a series of schmaltzy screen operettas that featured him as a singer with a strong, baritone voice.

Eddy signed a movie contract with MGM in the early 1930s, appearing in a singing part in Willard Mack's musical *Broadway to Hollywood*, followed by a more prominent role in the finale of Robert Z. Leonard's musical *Dancing Lady*, in support of Joan Crawford and Clark Gable.

In his fourth film, the Victor Herbert operetta *Naughty Marietta*, directed by W. S. Van Dyke, he was teamed with Jeanette MacDonald for the first of eight times. He played an Indian scout, she a runaway French princess, and musical numbers include the oft-parodied "Ah, Sweet Mystery of Life." The film almost single-handedly restored the popularity of the filmed operetta. Over the next seven years, Eddy and MacDonald starred in an enormously popular group of musical films: *Rose Marie* (singing "Indian Love Call," which the film subsequently came to be retitled), *Maytime*, *The Girl of the Golden West*, *Sweethearts*, *New Moon*, *Bitter Sweet*, and *I Married an Angel*.

Along the way, Eddy also starred opposite Eleanor Powell in *Rosalie*, Virginia Bruce in *Let Freedom Ring*, Ilona Massey in *Balalaika*, and Rise Stevens in *The Chocolate Soldier*. After the on-screen collaboration with MacDonald ended, Eddy starred in a sound remake of *Phantom of the Opera*, the film version of the Kurt Weill-Maxwell Anderson musical *Knickerbocker Holiday*, and the film of the Rudolf Friml operetta *Northwest Outpost*. He also served as the operatic voice of Willie the Singing Whale in the animated Disney feature, *Make Mine Music*, lending his familiar tones to the film's final climactic sequence— a chance to demonstrate his impressively larger-than-life baritone without his distressingly stiffer-than-life histrionics.

—Bill Wine

ELLIOTT, Denholm

Nationality: British. **Born:** Denholm Mitchell Elliott in London, England, 31 May 1922. **Education:** Attended Malvern College; studied at the Royal Academy of Dramatic Art, London, 1939. **Military Service:** Royal Air Force, Bomber Command, 1940-45; held as prisoner of war in Germany, 1940-43. **Family:** Married 1) the actress Virginia McKenna, 1954 (divorced 1957); 2) Susan Robinson, 1962, two children. **Career:** 1946—West End stage debut in *The Guinea-Pig*; 1949—film debut in *Dear Mr. Prohack*; 1950—New York stage debut in *Ring around the Moon*; from 1970s—much work on TV, including mini-series *Marco Polo*, 1982, *Bleak House*, 1985, *Noble House*, 1988, and *Bankok Hilton*, 1992. **Awards:** British Academy of Film and Television Arts Awards for Best Supporting Actor, for *Trading Places*, 1983, *A Private Function* and *Defence of the Realm*, 1985; Commander, Order of the British Empire, 1988. **Died:** In Ibiza, Spain, 6 October 1992.

Films as Actor:

1949   *Dear Mr. Prohack* (Freeland) (as Ozzie Morfrey)
1952   *The Sound Barrier* (*Breaking the Sound Barrier*) (Lean) (as Christopher Ridgefield); *The Holly and the Ivy* (O'Ferrall) (as Mick Gregory); *The Ringer* (Hamilton) (as John Lenley)
1953   *The Cruel Sea* (Frend) (as Morrell); *The Heart of the Matter* (O'Ferrall) (as Wilson)
1954   *They Who Dare* (Milestone) (as Sgt. Corcoran); *Lease of Life* (Frend) (as Martin Blake); *The Man Who Loved the Redheads* (French) (as Denis)
1955   *The Night My Number Came Up* (Norman) (as Flight Lt. McKenzie)
1956   *Pacific Destiny* (Rilla) (as Arthur Grimble)
1960   *Scent of Mystery* (*Holidays in Spain*) (Cardiff) (as Oliver Larker)
1962   *Station Six-Sahara* (Holt) (as Macey)
1963   *Nothing but the Best* (Clive Donner) (as Charlie Prince); *The Leather Boys* (Furie)
1964   *The High Bright Sun* (*McGuire Go Home!*) (Thomas) (as Baker)
1965   *King Rat* (Forbes) (as Lt. Col. Denholm Larkin); *You Must Be Joking!* (Winner) (as Capt. Tabasco)
1966   *Alfie* (Lewis Gilbert) (as abortionist); *The Spy with a Cold Nose* (Petrie) (as Pond-Jones)
1967   *Maroc 7* (O'Hara) (as Inspector Barrada); *Here We Go 'Round the Mulberry Bush* (Clive Donner) (as Mr. Beauchamp)
1968   *The Night They Raided Minsky's* (Friedkin) (as Vance Fowler); *The Sea Gull* (Lumet) (as Dorn)
1969   *Too Late the Hero* (*Suicide Run*) (Aldrich) (as Capt. Hornsby)
1970   *The Rise and Rise of Michael Rimmer* (Billington) (as Peter Niss); *The House that Dripped Blood* (Duffel) (as Charles)
1971   *Percy* (Thomas) (as Emmanuel Whitbread); *Quest for Love* (Thomas) (as Tom Lewis)
1972   *Madame Sin* (David Greene)
1973   *A Doll's House* (Losey) (as Krogstad); "Drawn and Quartered" ep. of *The Vault of Horror* (Roy Ward Baker) (as Diltant)
1974   *Percy's Progress* (*It's Not the Size that Counts*) (Thomas) (as Emmanuel Whitbread); *The Apprenticeship of Duddy Kravitz* (Kotcheff) (as Friar)
1975   *Russian Roulette* (Lombardo) (as Commander Petapiece)
1976   *Voyage of the Damned* (Rosenberg) (as Admiral Canaris); *Robin and Marian* (Lester) (as Will Scarlett); *To the Devil a Daughter* (Sykes) (as Henry Beddows); *Partners* (Don Owen) (as John Grey); *The Signalman* (Lawrence Gordon Clark—for TV) (title role)
1977   *A Bridge Too Far* (Attenborough) (as RAF meteorological officer); *The Hound of the Baskervilles* (Morrissey) (as Stapleton); *The Strange Case of the End of Civilisation as We Know It* (McGrath—for TV) (as English delegate)
1978   *The Sweeney II* (Clegg) (as Jupp); *Watership Down* (Rosen— animation) (as voice of Cowslip); *The Boys from Brazil* (Schaffner) (as Sidney Beynon)
1979   *Saint Jack* (Bogdanovich) (as William Leigh); *A Game for Vultures* (Fargo) (as Raglan Thistle); *Cuba* (Lester) (as Skinner); *Zulu Dawn* (Hickox) (as Lt. Col. Pulleine)
1980   *Rising Damp* (McGrath) (as Seymour); "An Englishman's Home" ep. of *Sunday Lovers* (*Les Séducteurs*) (Forbes and others) (as Parker); *Bad Timing* (*A Sensual Obsession*) (Roeg) (as Stefan Vognic); *Blade on the Feather* (*Deep Cover*) (Loncraine)
1981   ***Raiders of the Lost Ark*** (Spielberg) (as Marcus Brody)
1982   *The Missionary* (Loncraine) (as the Bishop of London); *Brimstone and Treacle* (Loncraine) (as Thomas Bates)

Denholm Elliott

1983   *Trading Places* (Landis) (as Coleman); *The Wicked Lady* (Winner) (as Sir Ralph Skelton); *The Hound of the Baskervilles* (Hickox) (as Dr. Mortimer)

1984   *The Razor's Edge* (Byrum) (as Elliott Templeton); *Camille* (Desmond Davis—for TV) (as Count de Nolly)

1985   *A Private Function* (Mowbray) (as Dr. Swaby); *Defence of the Realm* (Drury) (as Vernon Bayliss); *Past Caring* (Eyre)

1986   ***A Room with a View*** (Ivory) (as Mr. Emerson); *The Whoopee Boys* (Byrum) (as Col. Hugh Phelps); *Underworld* (*Transmutations*) (Pavlou) (as Dr. Savary); *Hotel du Lac* (Giles Foster—for TV) (as Philip Neville); *Mrs. Delafield Wants to Marry* (Schaefer—for TV) (as George Parker)

1987   *Maurice* (Ivory) (as Dr. Barry); *September* (Woody Allen) (as Howard); *Overindulgence* (Devenish); *Scoop* (Millar—for TV) (as Mr. Salter)

1988   *Hanna's War* (Golan); *Keys to Freedom* (Feke); *Return from the River Kwai* (McLaglen); *The Bourne Identity* (Roger Young—for TV) (as Washburn); *Codename: Kyril* (Ian Sharp—for TV)

1989   *Indiana Jones and the Last Crusade* (Spielberg) (as Marcus Brody); *Stealing Heaven* (Clive Donner) (as Fulbert); *Killing Dad* (Austin) (as Monty Berg); *Rude Awakening* (Greenwalt and Russo); *The Strange Case of Dr. Jekyll and Mr. Hyde* (Lindsay-Hogg—for TV)

1990   *The Love She Sought* (*A Green Journey*) (Sargent—for TV) (as James O'Hannon)

1991   *Toy Soldiers* (Petrie) (as the Headmaster); *One against the Wind* (Elikann—for TV) (as Father LeBlanc); *Murder of Quality* (Millar—for TV) (as George Smiley)

1992   *Scorchers* (Beaird) (as Howler); *Noises Off* (Bogdanovich) (as Selsdon Mowbray/the Burglar)

Publications

By ELLIOTT: articles—

Interview in *Film Review* (London), December 1979.
Interview in *Radio Times* (London), 26 November 1983.
"Our Island Story," interview in *Stills* (London), December 1984/January 1985.

On ELLIOTT: articles—

Ciné Revue (Paris), 10 November 1988.
Obituary in *New York Times*, 7 October 1992.
Obituary in *Variety* (New York), 12 October 1992.
Obituary in *Classic Images* (Muscatine, Iowa), November 1992.
Obituary in *Film en Televisie + Video* (Brussels), December 1992.

*   *   *

Denholm Elliott is one of those British supporting/character actors whose presence in a film automatically guarantees that, if not of the highest quality, it at least will be watchable and well-acted. In this regard, Elliott may be categorized with the likes of John Mills, Trevor Howard, and Jack Hawkins as dependable British character players who appeared in both English and American-made films, small-scale dramas which emphasized character development, and occasional glitzy big-budget spectaculars.

In his look and demeanor, Elliott had the air of coming from the lower levels of the British gentleman classes; he would fit snugly into the role of a clergyman's son struggling to keep his head above the murky waters of the "shabby genteel." Whatever his character's trappings, he never truly could be classy, but rather would seem a poseur.

This is effectively communicated in one of his best early roles: Morrell, the young naval officer/barrister turned barrack-room lawyer, in *The Cruel Sea*. At one point in the film, Morrell (whose wife is a bitchy actress) is on leave, and he answers her telephone only to hear a jovial caller ask if "that clot of a husband" is away.

With his quick nail-biter's grin, Elliott could be corruptible. He was expert at playing the complainer, the clever loser, the resentful schemer, the failed gentleman pulled down by his own inherent pretension, who ends up conniving and clawing his way through shabby schemes and deals. His range also extends, however, to brave, despairing—and, ultimately, ill-fated—victims of duty.

Elliott was cast in some of the finer British films of the 1950s. In addition to *The Cruel Sea*, he was the doomed aviator forced to test-fly airplanes by his heartless airplane factory owner father (Ralph Richardson) in *Breaking the Sound Barrier*; the covetous clerk dogging Trevor Howard in *The Heart of the Matter*; and Michael Redgrave's assistant in *The Night My Number Came Up*. Many of his earlier films were linked to World War II-related themes of sacrifice, but the increased affluence and social mobility of the 1960s (along with the arrival of John Osborne's Angry Young Man) restored to the British cinema a certain cynicism, or worldly wisdom, about snobberies, one-upmanship, the rat race, and unabashed unworthiness. Elliott was suited to such films, and his knowing performance as Charlie Prince, the debased character who teaches manners to an ambitious, social climbing clerk (Alan Bates) in *Nothing but the Best*, closes off the first phase of his career and serves as a prelude to his future. A perfect follow-up was his distasteful, unorthodox abortionist in *Alfie*.

Elliott's highest-profile roles were to come in the 1970s and 1980s. He was never better as Friar, the inebriated, unscrupulous filmmaker who creates the garish bar mitzvah movie, in *The Apprenticeship of Duddy Kravitz*; and Mr. Emerson, the eccentric up-by-the-bootstraps businessman, in *A Room with a View*. He was a solid addition to the cast of *Robin and Marian*, playing the role of Will Scarlett. All the while, he still gave exemplary performances in lesser-known films: *Defence of the Realm*, playing a veteran journalist whose mysterious death sets a Fleet Street tabloid reporter (Gabriel Byrne) on a quest for truth; and *Bad Timing*, as Theresa Russell's wearily resigned Czech husband.

In his later years, Elliott's international visibility increased as he began appearing in popular American films. In *Raiders of the Lost Ark* and *Indiana Jones and the Last Crusade*, he is Harrison Ford's professional associate. In *Trading Places*, he is Coleman, Dan Aykroyd's valet, who ends up ministering to Eddie Murphy; his presence is a fine counterpose to John Gielgud's waspish loftiness as another gentleman's gentleman in *Arthur*.

Elliott's roots are in middle-class Englishness, and he fashioned his characters with sympathy and without complacency. He may have been deprived of full-length, in-depth celluloid stardom, but this loss only enhances the importance of the gallery of types and attitudes he brought to the films in which he did appear.

—Raymond Durgnat, updated by Rob Edelman

EVANS, (Dame) Edith

Nationality: British. **Born:** Edith Mary Evans in London, England, 8 February 1888. **Education:** Attended St Michael's School, Chester Square, London. **Family:** Married George Booth, 1925 (died 1935). **Career:** Worked as a milliner, and studied acting with Miss E. C. Massey; 1912—stage debut in *Troilus and Cressida*; 1915—film debut in *A Welsh Singer*; 1918—toured with the actress Ellen Terry; 1925-26—season at the Old Vic Theatre, London, then many classical and modern roles, including roles in *Antony and Cleopatra*, *The Way of the*

Edith Evans in *The Importance of Being Earnest* **courtesy of The Rank Organisation Plc**

World, The Cherry Orchard, The Chalk Garden (and film version), and *The Chinese Prime Minister*; 1948—first sound film, *The Queen of Spades*; 1952—reprised her most famous stage role, Lady Bracknell, in the film *The Importance of Being Earnest*; acted on television from the 1950s; 1971—in the TV mini-series *The Gambler*, and *QB VII*, 1974. **Awards:** Best Actress, Berlin Festival, Best Actress, British Academy, and Best Actress, New York Film Critics, for *The Whisperers*, 1967; Dame Commander, Order of the British Empire, 1946. **Died:** In Cranbrook, England, 14 October 1976.

Films as Actress:

1915	*A Welsh Singer* (Edwards); *A Honeymoon for Three* (Elvey)
1916	*East Is East* (Edwards)
1948	*The Queen of Spades* (Dickinson) (as Countess Raevskaya); *The Last Days of Dolwyn* (*Dolwyn*) (Emlyn Williams) (as Merri)
1952	*The Importance of Being Earnest* (Asquith) (as Lady Bracknell)
1959	*The Nun's Story* (Zinnemann) (as Mother Emmanuel Superior General); *Look Back in Anger* (Richardson) (as Mrs. Tanner)
1963	*Tom Jones* (Richardson) (as Miss Western)
1964	*The Chalk Garden* (Neame) (as Mrs. St. Maugham)
1965	*Young Cassidy* (Cardiff and Ford) (as Lady Gregory)
1967	*The Whisperers* (Forbes) (as Mrs. Margaret "Maggie" Ross); *Norman Conquests in the Bayeux Tapestry* (Brown—short); *Fitzwilly* (*Fitzwilly Strikes Back*) (Delbert Mann) (as Victoria Woodworth)
1968	*Prudence and the Pill* (Cook and Neame) (as Lady Roberta Bates)
1969	*The Madwoman of Chaillot* (Forbes) (as Josephine, the Madwoman of La Concorde); *Crooks and Coronets* (*Sophie's Place*) (O'Connolly) (as Lady Sophie Fitzmore)
1970	*Scrooge* (Neame) (as Ghost of Christmas Past); *David Copperfield* (Delbert Mann—for TV) (as Betsy Trotwood); *Upon This Rock* (Rasky)
1973	*A Doll's House* (Garland) (as Anne-Marie)
1974	*Craze* (*The Infernal Idol*) (Francis) (as Aunt Louise)
1976	*The Slipper and the Rose* (*The Story of Cinderella*) (Forbes) (as Dowager Queen); *Nasty Habits* (*The Abbess*) (Lindsay-Hogg) (as Hildegarde)

Publications

By EVANS: article—

"Nothing Like a Dame," interview with M. Tierney, in *Plays & Players*, April 1971.

On EVANS: books—

Batters, Jean, *Edith Evans: A Personal Memoir*, London, 1977.
Forbes, Bryan, *Ned's Girl: The Authorised Biography of Dame Edith Evans*, London, 1977.

On EVANS: articles—

Current Biography 1956, New York, 1956.
Goodwin, I., "Grand Dame," in *Newsweek* (New York), 1 April 1968.
Obituary in *New York Times*, 15 October 1976.

*   *   *

Film theory may insist that the medium is far more important than merely a recording device, but the capacity to capture on celluloid remains an important function. Without it, how could future generations study and enjoy such exotic sights and sounds as the pomp of a royal coronation, the mating rituals of the mountain gorilla, or the acting of Edith Evans? For watching Evans in a film is rarely anything more than passively witnessing a spectacle. If the greatness of her stage career is a legend that scarcely needs repeating, then the truth about her film career badly needs stating. Her place in British cinema history is at best marginal.

Entering films (brief silent performances aside) in the late 1940s, her reputation and age combined to ensure her institutionalization as a Great British Eccentric. The film that irrevocably sealed that fate is the film that immortalized her style, especially that unforgettable voice—*The Importance of Being Earnest*. That film is a classic demonstration of the meretriciousness of film-as-record, resembling, in its Technicolor clutter, some lurid display in a museum of British character acting.

The same must be said about *Tom Jones*, although here, thanks to Tony Richardson's flashy arrogance, we are swept through the museum on a switchback. Evans is one of a procession of caricatures, and does little new except dress Lady Bracknell in the clothes of the previous century.

Two films are exceptions in her career, two attempts to present her as a film actress rather than an institution filmed. *The Whisperers* fails, because it tries too hard in such an endeavor, because it is too obviously a tribute to her theatrical gifts, and because it too readily indulges her mannerisms, different though this set are from the quivering-necked indignation of all those Bracknells. But *The Queen of Spades* succeeds, because it finds a subject, setting, and style to match the baroque contours of her performance, and because it uses and shapes her excesses for a specific cinematic purpose rather than simply being content to record them from a respectful, reverent distance.

—Andy Medhurst

FABRIZI, Aldo

Nationality: Italian. **Born:** Rome, 1 November 1905. **Family:** Married Beatrice Rocchi, two children (twins). **Career:** 1931—began stage work as comedian in variety theater; 1930s—dialect comedy on radio and in music halls; 1942—film debut in *Avanti c'è posto*; 1949—directed the film *Emigrantes*. **Died:** In Rome, 2 April 1990.

Films as Actor:

1942 *Avanti c'è posto* (Zampa) (as Cesare, + co-story)
1943 *Campo dei fiori* (*The Peddlar and the Lady*) (Bonnard) (as Peppino); *L'ultima carrozzella* (Mattoli) (as Toto)
1944 *Circo equestre* Za-Bum (Mattolli)
1945 **Roma, città aperta** (*Rome, Open City*; *Open City*) (Rossellini) (as Don Pietro)
1946 *Mio figlio professore* (*Professor My Son*) (Castellani); *Vivere in pace* (*To Live in Peace*) (Zampa) (+ co-sc)
1947 *Il delitto di Giovanni Episcopo* (*Flesh Will Surrender*) (Lattuada) (+ co-sc); *Tombola, paradiso nero* (Ferroni)
1948 *Natale al campo 119* (*Escape into Dreams*) (Francisci) (+ co-sc)
1949 *Antonio di Padova* (*Anthony of Padua*) (Francisci)
1950 *Prima comunione* (*Father's Dilemma*) (Blasetti); *Francesco—giullare di Dio* (*Flowers of St. Francis*) (Rossellini) (as Nikolai); *Vita di cani* (*It's a Dog's Life*) (Monicelli and Steno)
1951 *Guardie e ladri* (*Cops and Robbers*) (Monicelli and Steno) (+ sc); *Parigi è sempre Parigi* (Emmer); *Signori in carrozzo* (Zampa) (+ sc); *Tre passi a nord* (*Three Steps North*) (W. L. Wilder); *Cameriera bella presenza offresi* (Pastina)
1952 "Il carrettino dei libri vecchi," ep. of *Altri tempi* (*Times Gone By*; *In Olden Days*; *Infidelity*) (Blasetti); *Cinque poveri in automobile* (*The Lucky Five*) (Mattoli); *La voce del silenzio* (Pabst)
1953 *L'età dell'amore* (De Felice); *Siamo tutti inquilini* (Mattoli); *Cose da pazzi* (Pabst)
1954 "Garibaldina" ep. of *Cento anni d'amore* (De Felice)
1955 *Accadde al penitenziario* (Bianchi); *Carosello di varietà*; *I due compari* (Borghesio); *Io piaccio* (Bianchi)
1956 *Donatella* (Monicelli); *Guardia, guardia scelta, brigadiere e maresciallo* (Bolognini); *Mi permette, babbo?* (Bonnard); *I pappagalli* (Paolinelli); *Un po' di cielo* (Moser)
1957 *Festa di maggio* (*Premier May*) (Saslavsky)
1958 *I prepotenti* (Mattoli)
1959 *Fernando I, re di Napoli* (Franciolini); *Prepotenti più di prima* (Mattoli); *I tartassati* (*The Overtaxed*) (Steno); *La sposa bella* (*The Angel Wore Red*) (Johnson)
1960 *Un militare e mezzo* (Steno); *Totó, Fabrizi e i giovani d'oggi* (Mattoli)
1962 *Gerarchi si muore* (Simonelli); *Le meraviglie di Aladino* (*The Wonders of Aladdin*) (Levin) (as Sultan); *Orazi e Curiazi* (*Duel of Champions*) (Young and Baldi); *I quattro monaci*; *Twist, ninfette e vitelloni* (Firolami)

1963 *I quattro moschettieri* (Bragaglia); *Totò contro i quattro* (Vanzina)
1964 *Fra Manisco cerca quai* (Tamburella); "I quattro tassisti" ep. of *La donna è una cosa meravigliosa* (Bolognini)
1965 *Made in Italy* (Loy)
1966 *Sette monaci d'oro* (Rossi)
1967 *Three Bites of the Apple* (Ganzer) (as Doctor)
1971 *Cose di Cosa Nostra* (*The Godson*) (Steno)
1973 *La Tosca* (Magni); *Non toccate la donna bianca* (*Touche pas la femme blanche*) (Ferreri)
1974 *Permettete che ami vostre figlia?* (*Madam, Permit Me to Love Your Daughter*; *Claretta and Ben*) (Polidoro); *C'eravamo tanti amati* (*We All Loved Each Other So Much*; *Those Were the Years*) (Scola); *I baroni* (Lomi)
1977 *Il ginecologo della mutua* (*Ladies Doctor*) (D'Amato)
1986 *Giovanni Senzapensieri* (Colli)

Films as Director:

1949 *Emigrantes* (+ sc, ro)
1950 *Benvenuto reverendo!* (+ sc, ro)
1951 *La famiglia Passaguai* (+ sc, ro)
1952 *La Famiglia Passaguai fa fortuna* (+ sc, ro); *Papa diventa Mamma* (+ sc, ro)
1953 *Una di quelle* (+ sc, ro)
1954 "Marsini stretta" ep. of *Questa è la vita* (*Of Life and Love*) (+ sc, ro)
1955 *Hanno rubato un tram* (+ sc, ro)
1958 *Il maestro* (*The Teacher and the Miracle*) (+ pr, co-sc, ro as Giovanni Merino)

Publications

By FABRIZI: article—

Interview in *Cinémonde* (Paris), 19 September 1952.

On FABRIZI: article—

"Aldo Fabrizi: L'amoureux parfait de Rome," in *Ciné Revue* (Paris), 24 May 1990.

* * *

Aldo Fabrizi started out as a comedian in the variety theater in the 1930s. On radio and in the music hall, he specialized in dialect comedy, and this led to his first film efforts. These films, such as *Avanti c'è posto*, *Campo dei fiori*, and *L'ultima carrozzella*, were all comedies devoted to the everyday life of poor but honest folk. Fabrizi's portrayal of a bus conductor, a market vendor, and a coachman, respectively, brought his sanguine persona and his ability at comic mugging to the attention of the public.

Aldo Fabrizi in *Roma, città aperta*

The potential danger of becoming stereotyped by such roles was overcome by his dramatic and heartrending portrayal of Don Pietro in *Open City*. He plays a Catholic priest who fights in the Resistance and who displays unshakable faith, immense courage, and compassion towards both his companions and his torturers even until his execution. Not only was it a brilliant performance, the best of his career, but the film inaugurated the critical success of neorealism around the world, and broke box-office records.

Fabrizi continued to exert an enormous influence over the development of Italian neorealist acting in *Professor My Son* and *To Live in Peace*, another international success. Alessandro Blasetti used him as the harried, inept father in *Father's Dilemma* while, in the same year, Rossellini used Fabrizi's corpulence and grotesque qualities for the tribal chieftain Nikolai in *Flowers of St. Francis*.

In the 1950s, Fabrizi began directing and continued his scriptwriting career although films written or directed by him have not received much critical attention in Italy. Even his acting roles in the 1950s and 1960s were in films that were rarely distributed internationally. More recently, Fabrizi allowed himself to lose control over his delivery and often deteriorated into cheap and vulgar humor. Because of his enormous body, he tended to be cast as exaggeratedly grotesque characters. Ettore Scola paid homage to Fabrizi's contribution to the Italian cinema in *We All Loved Each Other So Much*.

—Elaine Mancini

FAIRBANKS, Douglas

Nationality: American. **Born:** Douglas Elton Ulman in Denver, Colorado, 23 May 1883; mother reassumed the name of her first husband, Fairbanks, after divorcing Douglas's father. **Education:** Attended Colorado School of Mines, until 1900; special student at Harvard University, 5 months. **Family:** Married 1) Anna Beth Sully, 1907 (divorced 1918), son: the actor Douglas Fairbanks, Jr.; 2) the actress Mary Pickford, 1920 (divorced 1936); 3) Sylvia Ashley, 1936. **Career:** Made first stage appearance with Denver theatrical troupe at age 12; 1900—toured with Frederick Warde theatrical company; after traveling company failed, studied briefly at Harvard and worked at various jobs including Wall Street clerk; 1902—Broadway debut in *Her Lord and Master*; 1905—featured stage role in *A Case of Frenzied Finance*; 1906—first stage hit, *The Man of the Hour*; 1907—left stage briefly after marrying Anna Beth Sully to work in her family's soap company; 1913—established as stage star with *He Comes Up Smiling*; 1915—last stage appearance in *The Show Shop*; 3-year contract with D. W. Griffith's Triangle Film Corporation; film debut in *The Lamb*; 1916—first screen success in *His Picture in the Papers*; 1917—formed Douglas Fairbanks Pictures Corp., releasing through Artcraft, a subsidiary of Famous Players-Lasky (later Paramount); 1919—with Mary Pickford, Charles Chaplin, and D. W. Griffith, formed United Artists distribution company; 1927—first president of the Academy of Motion Picture Arts and Sciences; 1929—first sound film, *The Taming of the Shrew*, opposite Mary Pickford; 1936—announced retirement from acting; 1938—formed Fairbanks International production company. **Died:** 12 December 1939.

Films as Actor:

1915   *The Lamb* (Cabanne) (as Gerald); *Double Trouble* (Cabanne) (as Mr. Amidon/Mr. Brassfield)

1916   *His Picture in the Papers* (Emerson) (as Pete Prindle); *The Habit of Happiness* (*Laugh and the World Laughs*) (Dwan) (as "Sunny" Wiggins); *The Good Bad Man* (*Passing Through*) (Dwan) (as "Passin' Thru," + sc); *Reggie Mixes In* (*Mysteries of New York*) (Cabanne) (as Reginald Morton); *Firting with Fate* (Cabanne) (as "Augy" Holliday); *The Mystery of the Leaping Fish* (Emerson—two reels) (as Coke Anneyday); *The Half Breed* (Dwan—rereleased in abridged version as *Flames of '49*) (as Lo Dorman); *Manhattan Madness* (Dwan) (as Stever O'Dare); *American Aristocracy* (Ingraham) (as Cassius Lee); *The Matrimaniac* (Powell) (as Jimmy Conroy); *The Americano* (Emerson) (title role); *Intolerance* (Griffith) (as extra)

1917   *In Again, Out Again* (Emerson) (as Teddy Rutherford); *Wild and Wooly* (Emerson) (as Jeff Hillington); *Down to Earth* (Emerson) (as Bill Gaynor, + story); *The Man from Painted Post* (Henabery) (as Fancy Jim Sherwood, + sc); *Reaching for the Moon* (Emerson) (as Alexis Caesar Napoleon Brown); *War Relief* (short)

1918   *A Modern Musketeer* (Dwan) (as Ned Thacker); *Headin' South* (Rosson) (as "Headin' South"); *Mr. Fix-It* (Dwan) (title role); *Say! Young Fellow* (Henabery) (as "Young Fellow"); *Bound in Morocco* (Dwan) (as The Boy); *He Comes Up Smiling* (Dwan) (as Jerry Martin); *Sic 'em Sam!* (Parker—short); *Fire the Kaiser* (Henabery—short)

1919   *The Knickerbocker Buckaroo* (Parker) (as Teddy Drake, + sc); *His Majesty, the American* (*One of the Blood*) (Henabery) (as William Brooks, + co-sc as "Elton Banks"); *When the Clouds Roll By* (Fleming) (as Daniel Boone Brown, + co-sc); *Arizona* (Parker) (as Lt. Danton, + sc)

1920   *The Mollycoddle* (Fleming) (as Richard Marshall, + co-sc); *The Mark of Zorro* (Niblo) (as Don Diego/Zorro, + sc as "Elton Thomas")

1921   *The Nut* (Reed) (as Charlie Jackson, + co-sc as "Elton Thomas"); *The Three Musketeers* (Niblo) (as D'Artagnan, + co-sc as "Elton Thomas")

1922   *Robin Hood* (Dwan) (as The Earl of Huntingdon/Robin Hood, + sc as "Elton Thomas")

1924   *The Thief of Bagdad* (Walsh) (as The Thief, + sc as "Elton Thomas")

1925   *Don Q, Son of Zorro* (Crisp) (as Don César de Vega/Zorro)

1926   *The Black Pirate* (Parker) (as Michel, the Black Pirate)

1928   *The Gaucho* (Jones) (title role)

1929   *The Iron Mask* (Dwan) (as D'Artagnan, + sc as "Elton Thomas"); *The Taming of the Shrew* (Taylor) (as Petruchio)

1931   *Reaching for the Moon* (Goulding) (as Larry Dacy); *Around the World in 80 Minutes* (*Around the World with Douglas Fairbanks*) (Fleming) (as himself, + sc)

1932   *Mr. Robinson Crusoe* (Sutherland) (as Steve Drexel, + story as "Elton Thomas")

1934   *The Private Life of Don Juan* (Korda) (title role)

Publications

By FAIRBANKS: books—

Laugh and Live, New York, 1917.
Making Life Worth While, New York, 1918.
My Secret Success, Los Angeles, 1922.
Youth Points the Way, New York, 1924.

By FAIRBANKS: articles—

"Combining Play with Work," in *American* (New York), July 1917.
"The Development of the Screen," in *Moving Picture World* (New York), 21 July 1917.
"Roping Doug Fairbanks into an Interview," by Frederick Smith in *Motion Picture Classic* (Brooklyn), September 1917.
"A Photo Interview with Douglas Fairbanks," by Alfred Cohn in *Photoplay* (New York), October 1917.
"Douglas Fairbanks' Own Page," in *Photoplay* (New York), November 1917-April 1918.
"Why Big Pictures?" in *Ladies Home Journal* (New York), April 1924; also May and September issues.
"What Is Love?" in *Photoplay* (New York), February 1925.
"The Magic Carpet of My Life as Told to Stuart Jackson," in *Pictures and Picturegoer*, 18 March 1933-1 April 1933.

On FAIRBANKS: books—

Florey, Robert, *Douglas Fairbanks*, Paris, 1926.
Talmey, Allene, *Doug and Mary, and Others*, New York, 1927.
Leloir, Maurice, *Cinq Mois à Hollywood avec Douglas Fairbanks*, Paris, 1929.
Cooke, Alistair, *Douglas Fairbanks: The Making of a Screen Character*, New York, 1940.
Hancock, Ralph, and Letitia Fairbanks, *Douglas Fairbanks—The Fourth Musketeer*, New York, 1953.
Eisenschitz, Bernard, *Douglas Fairbanks*, Paris, 1969.
Carrol, David, *The Matinee Idols*, New York, 1972.
Lahue, Kalton C., *Gentlemen to the Rescue: The Heroes of the Silent Screen*, New York, 1972.
Schickel, Richard, *His Picture in the Papers*, New York, 1973.
Thomas, Tony, *Cads and Cavaliers—The Film Adventurers*, New York, 1973.
Fairbanks, Douglas, Jr., *The Fairbanks Album*, introduction and narrative by Richard Schickel, Boston, 1975.
Carey, Gary, *Doug and Mary: A Biography of Douglas Fairbanks and Mary Pickford*, New York, 1977.
Tibbetts, John, and James Welsh, *His Majesty the American: The Cinema of Douglas Fairbanks, Sr.*, New Brunswick, N.J., 1977.
Herndon, B., *Mary Pickford and Douglas Fairbanks: The Most Popular Couple the World Has Ever Known*, New York, 1977.
Richards, Jeffrey, *Swordsmen of the Screen: From Douglas Fairbanks to Michael York*, London, 1977.
Ford, Charles, *Douglas Fairbanks ou La Nostalgie de Hollywood*, Paris, 1980.
Fairbanks, Douglas, Jr., *The Salad Days*, New York, 1988.

On FAIRBANKS: articles—

Hornblow, Arthur, Jr., "Douglas Fairbanks, Dramatic Dynamo," in *Motion Picture Classic* (Brooklyn), March 1917.
Zeidman, Bennie, "Trailing Dynamic Douglas Fairbanks," in *Photoplay* (New York), May 1917.
Naylor, Hazel, "The Fairbanks Scale of Americanism," in *Motion Picture Magazine*, February 1919.

Douglas Fairbanks in *The Thief of Bagdad*

Bates, Billy, "The Pickford-Fairbanks Wooing," in *Photoplay* (New York), June 1920.

St. Johns, Adela Rogers, "The Married Life of Doug and Mary," in *Photoplay* (New York), February 1927.

Mercer, Janet, "The Fairbanks' Social War Is On," in *Photoplay* (New York), August 1936.

Lambert, Gavin, "Fairbanks and Valentino: The Last Heroes," in *Sequence* (London), Summer 1949.

Behlmer, Rudy, "Swordplay on the Screen," in *Films in Review* (New York), June-July 1965.

Beresford, Bruce, "Swashbuckling Movies," in *Granta*, 3 May 1967.

Bodeen, DeWitt, "Douglas Fairbanks," in *Focus on Film* (London), Winter 1970.

Gow, G., "Doug," in *Films and Filming* (London), May 1973.

Schickel, Richard, "Douglas Fairbanks" in *The Movie Star*, edited by Elisabeth Weis, New York, 1981.

Carbonnier, A., "Douglas Fairbanks," in *Cinéma* (Paris), January 1982.

Podheiser, J., "Pep on the Range, or Douglas Fairbanks and the World War 1 era Western," in *Journal of Popular Film* (Washington, D.C.), Fall 1983.

Oakes, Philip, "That Fairbanks," in *Listener* (London), 26 January 1984.

On FAIRBANKS: film—

Birth of a Legend, produced and directed by Matty Kemp, released 1966 to accompany widescreen, rerecorded, and rescored version of *The Taming of the Shrew*.

*   *   *

The significance of Douglas Fairbanks is linked to the development of early screen comedy and the later development of the star system in the American film industry. His early career parallels Chaplin's—both began as silent comedians at approximately the same time and both succeeded in developing popular and distinctive screen personas. In 1919 they were both celebrities with sufficient autonomy to enter into a partnership with Mary Pickford and D. W. Griffith to form the United Artists Association, a very important precedent for movie stars, since its adjunct operation, the United Artists Corporation, was to give them control over the distribution of their films. No longer would stars of their rank necessarily be salaried employees. Of the "artists" involved, only Fairbanks was not bound by a long-term contract, and he was the first to complete films distributed by the new corporation, *His Majesty, the American* and *When* the Clouds Roll By, both in 1919. The following year would see a major shift in his style and his image, guaranteeing him continued popular success for the following decade.

Fairbanks had held a conventional desk job for a while before turning to Broadway and a serious theatrical career. By 1914 he was a popular success and under contract to make films for the Triangle Film Corporation, which offered him $2,000 per week for his services. By 1916 he had become one of Triangle's top stars at double his original salary, after having made 13 films in 18 months. When Triangle balked at his demand for a $15,000 weekly salary, Fairbanks offered to form his own corporation that would produce eight features yearly to be purchased for $200,000 each. By March of 1917 the Douglas Fairbanks Pictures Corporation, centered in New York, had been set up, with the movies to be distributed by the Artcraft Corporation.

The first Fairbanks screen persona emerged out of his theatrical roles: a cheerful young man of natural good humor, capable of integrating rural and urban values, often a rich idler wrenched from the city and rejuvenated through being challenged by the American wilderness. His early comedies tapped popular interests—the "social gospel" of Billy Sunday, for example, and the rugged individualism of Teddy Roosevelt. In The Mollycoddle, a picture that drew its title from a word Roosevelt had coined, the Fairbanks character is costumed to resemble Roosevelt. Both Fairbanks and Roosevelt were obsessed with physical culture and the "gospel of strenuosity." The typical Fairbanks character of this period attempts to integrate the values of the east and the American west.

The great redefinition of the Fairbanks character came in 1920 with The Mark of Zorro, the first of his extremely popular costume films, but here and subsequently Fairbanks remained primarily a comedian in costume, a satirical swashbuckler inclined to laugh in the face of danger. Fairbanks managed to cover his popularity from several angles. He married Mary Pickford in 1920, making a business connection into a family tie, and the matinee idol was to reign over Hollywood with "America's Sweetheart" from the palatial estate of Pickfair for about ten years. Singly, each was tremendously popular; together they were unbeatable, the very embodiment in the popular mind of "Hollywood happiness." Fairbanks certainly knew how to attract and sustain the attention of the American public.

Oddly enough, however, Fairbanks and Pickford did not star in a picture together until 1929, when their marriage was on the verge of breaking up. The picture, Shakespeare's Taming of the Shrew (with "additional dialogue by Sam Taylor"), was itself strangely ironic, with Fairbanks as Petruchio playing against Pickford's Kate. By this time, however, Fairbanks had already peaked. No picture made after The Taming of the Shrew would match the artistry or popularity of his great costume films—The Black Pirate, The Thief of Bagdad, Robin Hood, or The Three Musketeers, though some very interesting work was also done towards the latter end of the decade in The Gaucho and The Iron Mask. None of the post-Pickford films—Reaching for the Moon, Around the World in 80 Minutes, Mr. Robinson Crusoe, or The Private Life of Don Juan—worked well for him. After his divorce from Pickford in 1936 (they had separated, finally, in 1933), and his third marriage to Lady Sylvia Ashley, his film career was in fact over, but he had managed to sustain a youthful and energetic image far longer than most men could have done.

—James M. Welsh

FALK, Peter

Nationality: American. **Born:** Peter Michael Falk in New York City, 16 September 1927. **Education:** Attended Ossining High School, New York, graduated 1945; Hamilton College, Clinton, New York; New School for Social Research, New York, B.A. 1951; Syracuse University, M.A. in public administration, 1953. **Military Service:** Merchant marine, 1945-46: cook. **Family:** Married Alice Mayo, 1960, daughters: Katherine and Jackie. **Career:** At age three, right eye removed during surgery for malignant tumor; 1953-55—management analyst (efficiency expert) with Connecticut State Budget Bureau, Hartford; began acting with Mark Twain Maskers, Hartford; studied under Eva Le Gallienne, White Barn Theatre, Westport, Connecticut; 1955—moved to New York to pursue theatrical career; 1956—professional stage debut in Molière's Don Juan, New York; studied acting with Jack Landau and Sanford Meisner; 1958—film acting debut in Wind across the Everglades; considered for Columbia contract but rejected because of glass eye; 1965-66—in TV series The Trials of O'Brien; mid-1960s—formed Mayo Productions; 1968—created character of Lieutenant Columbo in made-for-TV movie Prescription: Murder and starred in the TV series Columbo, 1971-77, also directed some of the episodes; 1970—co-financed and acted in John Cassavetes film Husbands (also helped finance A Woman under the Influence); late 1980s—Columbo character revived for TV movies. **Awards:** Five Emmy Awards for Outstanding Lead Actor, for Columbo; Chevalier of Arts and Letters, 1996. **Address:** 1004 North Roxbury Drive, Beverly Hills, CA 90210, U.S.A.

Films as Actor:

1958   Wind across the Everglades (Nicholas Ray) (as writer)
1959   The Bloody Brood (Roffman) (as Nico)
1960   Pretty Boy Floyd (Leder) (as Shorty Walters); Murder, Inc. (Rosenberg and Burt Balaban) (as Abe "Kid Twist" Reles); The Secret of the Purple Reef (Witney)
1961   Pocketful of Miracles (Capra) (as Joy Boy)
1962   Pressure Point (Cornfield) (as young psychiatrist)
1963   It's a Mad, Mad, Mad, Mad World (Kramer) (as second cab driver); The Balcony (Strick) (as police chief)
1964   Robin and the Seven Hoods (Gordon Douglas) (as Guy Gisborne); Italiani brava gente (Italiano brava gente; Attack and Retreat) (De Santis) (as medic captain)
1965   The Great Race (Edwards) (as Max)
1966   Too Many Thieves (Biberman—for TV, two Trials of O'Brien eps.); Penelope (Hiller)
1967   Luv (Clive Donner) (as Milt Manville)
1968   Lo sbarco di Anzio (Anzio; The Battle for Anzio) (Dmytryk) (as Cpl. Rabinoff); Gli intoccabili (Machine Gun McCain) (Montaldo) (as Charles Adamo); Prescription: Murder (Irving—for TV) (as Columbo)
1969   Castle Keep (Pollack) (as Sgt. Orlando Rossi)
1970   Husbands (Cassavetes) (as Archie); Operation Snafu (Situation Normal All Fouled Up; Rosolino paternò, soldato . . .) (Loy); Step Out of Line (McEveety—for TV)
1971   Ransom for a Dead Man (Irving—for TV) (as Columbo)
1972   The Politics Film (Miller—short) (as narrator)
1974   A Woman under the Influence (Cassavetes) (as Nick Longhetti)
1976   Mikey and Nicky (Elaine May) (as Mikey); Murder by Death (Robert Moore) (as Sam Diamond); Griffin and Phoenix: A Love Story (Today Is Forever) (Duke—for TV) (as Geoffrey Griffin)
1977   Opening Night (Cassavetes) (as guest)
1978   The Cheap Detective (Robert Moore) (as Lou Peckinpaugh); The Brink's Job (Friedkin) (as Tony Pino)
1979   The In-Laws (Hiller) (as Vince Ricardo)
1981   The Great Muppet Caper (Henson) (as a tramp); . . . All the Marbles (The California Dolls) (Aldrich) (as Harry Sears)
1984   Sanford Meisner: The Theatre's Best Kept Secret (Doob—doc)
1986   Big Trouble (Cassavetes) (as Steve Rickey)

Peter Falk in *Der Himmel über Berlin* Argos Films and Road Movies for Wings of Desire

1987   *Happy New Year* (Avildsen) (as Nick); *Duenos del silencio* (Lemos); *Der Himmel über Berlin* (*Wings of Desire*) (Wenders) (as himself); *The Princess Bride* (Rob Reiner) (as the Grandfather)

1988   *Rattornas Vinter* (Hellberg); *Vibes* (Kwapis) (as Harry Buscafusco)

1989   *Cookie* (Susan Seidelman) (as Dino Capisco); *Columbo Goes to the Guillotine* (for TV) (title role)

1990   *In the Spirit* (Seacat) (as Roger Flan); *Motion and Emotion* (Paul Joyce); *Columbo Goes to College* (for TV) (title role); *Columbo: Grand Deception* (for TV) (title role); *Tune in Tomorrow* (*Aunt Julia and the Scriptwriter*) (Amiel) (as Pedro Carmichael); *Plates* (for TV) (as Columbo)

1991   *My Dog Stupid* (Berri); *Columbo and the Murder of a Rock Star* (for TV) (title role, + co-exec pr); *Columbo: Murder Can Be Hazardous to Your Health* (for TV) (title role, + co-exec pr); *Death Hits the Jackpot* (for TV)

1992   *The Player* (Altman); *No Time to Die* (for TV) (as Columbo, + exec pr); *Columbo: A Bird in the Hand* (for TV) (title role, + exec pr)

1993   *In Weiter Ferne, So Nah!* (*Faraway, So Close*) (Wenders) (as himself); *Columbo: It's All in the Game* (McEveety—for TV) (title role, + exec pr, sc)

1994   *Columbo: Undercover* (for TV) (title role, + sc); *Columbo: Butterflies in Shades of Grey* (for TV) (title role, + exec pr)

1995   *Roommates* (Yates) (as Rocky); *Columbo: Strange Bedfellows* (for TV) (title role, + exec pr)

Publications

By FALK: articles—

Interview in *Kaleidoscope*, vol. 2, no. 3, 1967.
"Peter Falk," in *Conversations*, by Don Shay, New York, 1969.
Interview in *Photoplay* (London), January 1979.
Interview with Simon Kinnersly, in *TV Times* (London), 23 February 1991.

On FALK: articles—

Current Bigraphy 1972, New York, 1972.
Hobson, Dick, in *TV Guide* (New York), 25 March 1972.
Marill, Alvin H., in *Films in Review* (New York), January 1975.
"Peter Falk," in *Film Dope* (London), September 1978.
Ciné Revue (Paris), 30 April 1987.
Simms, Paul, "Back in the Raincoat Again," in *Rolling Stone* (New York), 9 March 1989.
Collins, G. "Falk's Career Strategy: Who Needs a Strategy?," in *New York Times*, 28 November 1990.

Leahy, Michael, "Raincoat Man," in *TV Guide* (Radnor, Pennsylvania), 14 December 1991.

Allis, Tim, and Robin Mitchell, "A Wrinkle in Time," in *People Weekly* (New York), 16 December 1991.

* * *

Everything about the on-screen Peter Falk bespeaks lived-in disarray—his raspy voice, slumping posture, ill-fitting clothes, even his squinty, slightly cockeyed look (the result of losing an eye as a child). In combination with an ingratiatingly ironic style of delivery, Falk's physiognomy makes him especially effective in comedies and in dramas with strong comedic undercurrents.

Bored with his career as an efficiency expert, Falk turned to stage acting in the 1950s, gaining valuable experience in several off-Broadway productions, including Eugene O'Neill's *The Iceman Cometh*. Television and film work followed quickly, his feature debut coming in Nicholas Ray's *Wind across the Everglades*. For his fourth film role, that of Abe Reles, the mob assassin who blew the whistle on the Organization's professional hit squad *Murder, Inc.* only to become a victim of it himself before he could take the stand, he deftly combined the two aspects of his acting persona by making the weaselish Reles a confused and slightly comic figure who is nevertheless chilling given the nature of his job. Falk earned an Academy Award nomination as Best Supporting Actor for his standout performance in the otherwise undistinguished gangland docudrama. Years later, he showed similar acting dexterity in Friedkin's gangland comedy-drama *The Brink's Job* as the goofball mastermind behind the "crime of the century" who is done in by a pathetic, losing nature.

Falk's hilarious performance as a Damon Runyon character in Frank Capra's *Pocketful of Miracles* unwrapped his gift for comedy and paved the way for a string of farcical roles, many of which crossed over into slapstick—in Stanley Kramer's *It's a Mad, Mad, Mad, Mad World*, as a taxi driver; Gordon Douglas's *Robin and the Seven Hoods*, as another Runyonesque hoodlum; Blake Edwards's *The Great Race*, as the riotously inept assistant to frustrated villain Jack Lemmon; and *The Cheap Detective*, as a bumbling, Bogart-like gumshoe named "Peckinpaugh."

By the 1970s Falk was elevated to starring or co-starring roles in such dramas as *Husbands* and *A Woman under the Influence*, written and directed by his close friend John Cassavetes, as well as various comedies. But he achieved actual stardom with the popular television series *Columbo*, the vehicle with which he is most closely associated. As the disheveled, dumb-like-a-fox police lieutenant of the title, a character the show's creators Levinson and Link patterned after Charles Vanel's detective in the classic Clouzot chiller *Diabolique*, he brought a sly, rumpled, earthy charm which was chiefly responsible for the series' success and which remains its trademark. Falk continues to play the part in occasional made-for-television *Columbo* movies and shows up on the big screen now and then either in cameos or substantive character parts such as that of the irascible old guy who raises his orphaned grandson in Yates's sentimental *Roommates*.

—Bill Wine, updated by John McCarty

FARMER, Frances

Nationality: American. **Born:** Seattle, Washington, 19 September 1913 (some sources give 1914). **Education:** University of Washington, Seattle, majoring in journalism and then drama, entered 1931. **Family:** Married 1) the actor Leif Erickson, 1936 (divorced 1942); 2) Alfred Lobley, 1953 (divorced 1958); 3) Leland Mikesell, 1958.

Career: 1935—personal contract with Shepard Traube, then with Paramount; 1936—feature film debut in *Too Many Parents*; 1937—on Lux Radio Theatre with Spencer Tracy in *Men in White* and with Errol Flynn in *British Agent*; 1937—stage appearance in *At Mrs. Beams*, Westchester Playhouse; obtained release from Paramount contract, in Group Theatre production of Clifford Odets' *Golden Boy* in New York and on tour, 1938; 1939—in Irwin Shaw's *Quiet City* on Broadway, and in Group Theatre production of *Thunder Rock*; early 1940s—returned to Hollywood; 1942—alcoholism forced her retirement; spent the next few years in and out of mental institutions; 1957—appeared on Ed Sullivan Show, followed by work in summer stock and on television; 1958—began 6-year run of Indianapolis TV show *Frances Farmer Presents*, nightly movie program; mid 1960s—actress-in-residence at Purdue University; 1972—autobiography published; 1981—film biography *Frances*, starring Jessica Lange. **Died:** In Indianapolis, Indiana, 1 August 1970.

Films as Actress:

1936   *Too Many Parents* (McGowan); *Border Flight* (Lovering); *Rhythm on the Range* (Taurog); *Come and Get It* (Wyler and Hawks) (as Lotta Bostrom/Lotta's daughter)

1937   *Exclusive* (Hall); *The Toast of New York* (Lee) (as Josie Mansfield); *Ebb Tide* (Hogan) (as Faith Wishart)

1938   *Ride a Crooked Mile* (Green)

1940   *South of Pago-Pago* (Green); *Flowing Gold* (Green)

1941   *World Premiere* (Tetzlaff); *Badlands of Dakota* (Green) (as Calamity Jane); *Among the Living* (Heisler)

1942   *Son of Fury* (Cromwell) (as Isobel)

1958   *The Party Crashers* (Girard)

Publications

By FARMER: book—

Will There Really Be a Morning? An Autobiography, New York, 1972.

On FARMER: books—

Arnold, William, *Shadowland*, New York, 1978.
Elliot, Edith Farmer, *Look Back in Love*, Sequim, Washington, 1978.

On FARMER: articles—

Photoplay (New York), February 1937.
Focus on Film (London), Winter 1975-76.
Films in Review (New York), August-September 1979.
Films Illustrated (London), January 1982.
Films in Review (New York), May 1983.
Classic Images (Indiana, Pennsylvania), July 1983.

On FARMER: films—

Frances, directed by Graeme Clifford, 1982.
Will There Really Be a Morning?, for TV, 1982.
Committed, directed by Sheila McLaughlin and Lynne Tillman, 1984.

* * *

Some 50 years after her best work, Frances Farmer remains contemporary. A screen actress whose performances transcend her own time is rare; Farmer had that quality. No one seeing her on-screen will forget her deep voice and lovely eyes and no one learning of her life

Frances Farmer with Joel McCrea in *Come and Get It* © 1936, Samuel Goldwyn

can dismiss her tragic story easily. Yet renewed interest in the actress's life has drawn attention from her remarkable talent.

Farmer had a beauty and grace that the camera loved and she quickly gained box-office popularity. Whether costumed in sarongs (*Ebb Tide, South of Pago-Pago*), period clothes (*Come and Get It, The Toast of New York, Son of Fury*), or covered in mud (*Flowing Gold*), she exuded intelligence and honesty. Farmer's talent, however, could not salvage inferior films that appeared designed to punish her for outspokenness and a preference for the stage. In *World Premiere*, for example, Farmer, a long black wig covering her blond hair, plays a loud egotistical actress. In one scene she is called upon to crawl on her knees down a train aisle. The result is unwatchable.

The climax of Frances Farmer's brief career was *Come and Get It* in which she portrayed two characters: Lotta, a husky-voiced saloon singer, and Lotta's daughter, a high-voiced delicate innocent. Though only 22 years old, Farmer is relaxed and confident, changing her voice pitch, the look in her eyes, and modifying her gestures for the two roles. While Lotta is sarcastic, knowing, and slow to reveal emotion or trust, her daughter is polite, with bright eyes that register each emotion without hesitation. The indestructible blood tie between the past and the present is represented by the song "Aura Lee" which both sing, but in their own individual styles.

Under Howard Hawks's direction and care, Farmer blossoms and gives her best performance. It was typical of the curious circumstances of Farmer's career that the one director who was attentive to the actress and her talent was replaced during production. Farmer's performance, however, will be rediscovered by each successive generation, for it is as true as the day it was recorded on film.

—Alexa L. Foreman

FARROW, Mia

Nationality: American. **Born:** Maria de Lourdes Villiers Farrow in Los Angeles, California, 9 February 1945; daughter of the film director John Farrow and the actress Maureen O'Sullivan. **Education:** Attended convent schools in Madrid, Spain, and in London; Marymount School, Los Angeles; Cygnet School, near London, through 1962. **Family:** Married 1) the singer Frank Sinatra, 1966 (divorced 1968); 2) the conductor André Previn, 1970 (divorced 1979), twin boys; two children with director Woody Allen; also six adopted children. **Career:** 1963—off-Broadway debut as Cecily in *The Importance of Being Earnest*; performed with stock company in Warren, Ohio; 1964-66—in TV series *Peyton Place*; 1968—breakthrough film performance in Roman Polanski's *Rosemary's Baby* as the young New Yorker raped by the devil; 1971—on London stage in Arthur Honegger's *Jeanne d'Arc*, directed by Previn; 1970s—continued theatrical career in London, including appearances in 1975 and 1976 with Royal Shakespeare Company; 1981—began personal and professional relationship (both ended in 1992) with Woody Allen with production of *A Midsummer Night's Sex Comedy*. **Awards:** Etoile de Cristal (France), for *Secret Ceremony*, 1969; David Di Donatello award (Italy) 1968/69, for *Rosemary's Baby*; D. W. Griffith Award for Best Actress, for *Alice*, 1990. **Agent:** Lionel Larner Ltd., 130 W. 57th Street, New York, NY 10019, U.S.A.

Films as Actress:

1959 *John Paul Jones* (Farrow) (bit role)
1963 *The Age of Curiosity* (short)
1964 *Guns at Batasi* (Guillermin) (as Karen Ericksson)

1967 *Johnny Belinda* (Bogart—for TV) (title role)
1968 *A Dandy in Aspic* (Anthony Mann) (as Caroline); *Secret Ceremony* (Losey) (as Cenci); ***Rosemary's Baby*** (Polanski) (as Rosemary)
1969 *John and Mary* (Yates) (as Mary)
1971 *Goodbye Raggedy Ann* (Cook—for TV); *Blind Terror* (*See No Evil*) (Fleischer) (as Sarah); *Follow Me!* (*The Public Eye*) (Reed) (as Belinda Sidley)
1972 *Docteur Popaul* (*Scoundrel in White*; *High Heels*) (Chabrol) (as Christine)
1974 *The Great Gatsby* (Clayton) (as Daisy)
1976 *Peter Pan* (Hemion—for TV); *Full Circle* (Loncraine)
1978 *Avalanche* (Corey Allen) (as Caroline Brace); *Death on the Nile* (Guillermin) (as Jacqueline de Bellefort); *A Wedding* (Altman) (as Buffy)
1979 *Hurricane* (Troell) (as Charlotte Bruckner)
1981 *The Haunting of Julia* (Loncraine) (title role)
1982 *A Midsummer Night's Sex Comedy* (Woody Allen) (as Ariel); *The Last Unicorn* (Rankin Jr. and Bass—animation) (as voice of Last Unicorn/Lady Amalthea)
1983 *Zelig* (Woody Allen) (as Dr. Eudora Fletcher)
1984 *Broadway Danny Rose* (Woody Allen) (as Tina Vitale); *Sarah and the Squirrel* (part animation); *Supergirl* (Szwarc) (as Alura Zor-El)
1985 *The Purple Rose of Cairo* (Woody Allen) (as Cecilia); *Hannah and Her Sisters* (Woody Allen) (as Hannah)
1986 *Radio Days* (Woody Allen) (as Sally White)
1987 *September* (Woody Allen) (as Lane)
1988 *Another Woman* (Woody Allen) (as Hope)
1989 "Oedipus Wrecks" ep. of *New York Stories* (Woody Allen) (as Lisa); *Crimes and Misdemeanors* (Woody Allen) (as Halley Reed)
1990 *Alice* (Woody Allen) (as Alice)
1992 *Shadows and Fog* (Woody Allen) (as Irmy); *Husbands and Wives* (Woody Allen) (as Judy Roth)
1994 *Widows' Peak* (Irvin) (as Catherine O'Hare)
1995 *Miami Rhapsody* (Frankel) (as Nina); *Reckless* (René) (as Rachel)

Publications

By FARROW: articles—

Interview in *Films and Filming* (London), June 1986.
Interview with Christine Haas, in *Première* (Paris), February 1990.
Interview in *Time Out* (London), 18 July 1990.
"Mia's Story," interview with Maureen Orth, in *Vanity Fair* (New York), November 1992.
Interview with Ingrid Sischy, in *Interview* (New York), April 1994.

On FARROW: books—

Romero, J., *Sinatra's Women*, New York, 1976.
Rubin, Sam, and Richard Taylor, *Mia Farrow: Flowerchild, Madonna, Muse*, New York, 1989.
Epstein, Edward Z., and Joe Morella, *Mia: The Life of Mia Farrow*, New York, 1991.
Groteke, Kristi, and Marjorie Rosen, *Mia and Woody: Love and Betrayal*, New York, 1994.

On FARROW: articles—

"The Moonchild and the Fifth Beatle," in *Time* (New York), 7 February 1969.

Current Biography 1970, New York, 1970.

Shipman, David, in *The Great Movie Stars: The International Years*, London, 1972.

"Mia Farrow," in *Film Dope* (London), September 1978.

Photoplay (London), September 1984.

Ciné Revue (Paris), 23 October 1986.

Brown, Georgia A., "Much Ado about Mia," in *American Film* (Washington, D.C.), March 1987.

On FARROW: film—

Love and Betrayal: The Mia Farrow Story, for television, 1995.

*   *   *

Mia Farrow began her career in the successful television series *Peyton Place* playing Allison Mackenzie, a type of role that would become standard in her repertoire: the virginal and innocent waif—sensitive, vulnerable, and intelligent. Admired for her long Alice-in-Wonderland hair, Farrow shocked Hollywood one day by cutting it all off, an independent act which, odd as it may seem now, made headlines across the country, and characterized Farrow as not just another pretty face content to follow the instructions of her male Hollywood bosses.

That Farrow's boyish charm was a significant part of her attractiveness is clear; her slightly enigmatic grin, those fetching and luminous eyes, the short hair that sets off her features, and the thin body, recalling Audrey Hepburn. "Victim" roles followed: in a television adaptation of *Johnny Belinda*, in which she played a deaf mute who is raped; and in *Rosemary's Baby*, in which she plays a contemporary New York City woman who is raped by the devil and subsequently gives birth to Satan's son. Directed by Roman Polanski, *Rosemary's Baby* was an incredible box-office and critical success. Farrow's slight physical presence and vulnerability made her a believable victim. It seems ironic that at a time of emerging women's liberation, an actress should appear whose persona was that of a woman apparently so in need of being taken care of.

Despite the popularity of *Rosemary's Baby*, Farrow has never been especially admired by the critics or popular at the box office; that she failed to win an Academy Award nomination for this or any other film seems to reflect her lack of general appeal. *John and Mary*, Farrow's first film after *Rosemary's Baby*, was widely ridiculed, although today, while still rarely screened, it seems to be among the earliest American films of the 1960s to deal with sexual relationships in a relatively honest way. Another underrated performance was as Daisy in *The Great Gatsby*, a multimillion dollar film which cast her opposite Robert Redford. Here director Jack Clayton revealed Farrow's innocence and beauty as a corrupt facade in a film that looks increasingly praiseworthy, as does her performance in it. Other Farrow roles seem either to perpetuate the waif/victim persona (such as *See No Evil*, in which she plays a blind woman who is terrorized by a killer, or in her theatrical and television performances as *Peter Pan*), or to manipulate and subvert the waif/victim persona by countering audience expectations (as in the Agatha Christie adaptation *Death on the Nile*, Robert Altman's *A Wedding*, or Claude Chabrol's *Docteur Popaul*). Yet if Farrow's persona is often vulnerable, her offscreen image has about it a considerable element of independence: one thinks of her interest in social issues, her adoption of Vietnamese children, her visits to the Maharishi Mahesh Yogi in the 1960s, and her highly publicized relationships with a variety of famous and talented men such as Frank Sinatra, André Previn, and Woody Allen.

Certainly the period of Farrow's career with the highest profile comprises her numerous performances for director Woody Allen. While generally thought of as an instinctual, if mannered, actress, Farrow reveals herself in Allen's films to be an actress of substantial technical skill; and before its termination, their collaboration acquired the stat-

ure of a Chabrol and Audran, a Fellini and Masina, a Bergman and Ullmann. Farrow played a liberated freethinker in *A Midsummer Night's Sex Comedy*, a psychiatrist in the pseudodocumentary *Zelig*, and—most surprisingly—a vulgar Italian woman in *Broadway Danny Rose*, a key Allen film in which Farrow played *il bruto* to Allen's Gelsomina in a contemporary comedy evoking Fellini's *La Strada*. Her excellent work for Woody Allen has been judged surprising particularly by those critics who had already tended to underrate or dismiss her. Her totally luminous and sensitive performance as the forlorn movie fan in the 1985 *The Purple Rose of Cairo* seems already to be a key performance in the American cinema: the performance and film both extraordinary achievements largely ignored at their release, pushed aside by the Spielberg-inspired, special-effects spectaculars of the Reagan era. As the daughter in *September* (based loosely on Lana Turner's relationship with her daughter in the aftermath of the Johnny Stompanato murder), Farrow shows the ability to eradicate her own charismatic personality within an intimate chamber drama in a way that recalls and rivals Liv Ullmann in *Autumn Sonata*, with which the film bears comparison: Farrow's sniffling, whiny protagonist is both terrifyingly vulnerable and pitiable, as well as the temperamental opposite to Farrow's spunky cigarette girl who becomes a star in *Radio Days*, in which Farrow offers a deft, comic turn.

Perhaps unfortunately, one cannot comprehensively discuss Farrow in the mid-1990s without some consideration of the extraordinary scandal that gripped tabloid America for over a year. The Allen-Farrow breakup, which included dismissed charges against Allen of child sexual abuse and revelations of an acknowledged affair between Allen and Farrow's then teenaged adopted daughter, Soon-Yi, put the Farrow-Allen collaboration under a microscope. A reevaluation of Allen's use of Farrow reveals, perhaps surprisingly to some, that Farrow's persona in Allen's films (with the exception, perhaps, of *Alice*, which emphasizes the Roman Catholic, giving component of Farrow's identity) was by no means a heroic or valorized one. In *Hannah and Her Sisters*, one of Allen's most sustained works, shot largely in Farrow's Manhattan apartment, Farrow played a role patterned upon her own life, allowing the spectator a kind of voyeuristic entrance into Farrow's life with Allen. And yet, if barely commented upon at the time of the film's release, Farrow's Hannah—only apparently the stable, expressive center in Allen's world—is relatively smug, and it is clear that the filmmaker expends much more narrative time and interest on her sisters, as Allen's surrogate (Hannah's husband, played by Michael Caine) falls in love with a sister-in-law—an incestual precursor to Allen's later disenchantment. In *Crimes and Misdemeanors* (arguably Woody Allen's finest work), Farrow plays an archetype for our time: the amoral smiler—smart, attractive, talented, and sensitive, yet ultimately ambitious and pragmatic in ways which are all too recognizable. In retrospect it is clearer that in *The Purple Rose of Cairo*, *September*, and *Another Woman* (in which a very pregnant Farrow spends most of the film in therapy and tears), there is a profound element of masochism implicit in Farrow's suffering, and sadism on the part of the director and/or the narrative. *Husbands and Wives*, the Allen masterwork representing the last of their collaboration, in production while the scandal was unfolding, has Farrow and Allen playing a married couple whose marriage traumatically unravels, with Farrow presented as a woman who subtly uses her charm and passivity to manipulate those around her. In this film of vertiginous style and emotion, Farrow's heartrending performance, for many, was so persuasive, that the film was greeted (though to disappointing box office) as psychodrama in the Cassavetes style, too painful to watch. Even in the "Oedipus Wrecks" segment of *New York Stories*, the character played by Woody Allen ultimately rejects as his perfect match the fantasy of Mia Farrow in favor of the reality of Julie Kavner. Is any more evidence necessary that Allen has been no Sternberg elevating his Dietrich? As a last curious footnote to the scandal, one notes that even in non-Allen films, major roles in

Rosemary's Baby, *Death on the Nile*, *Docteur Popaul*, and *The Great Gatsby* (among others) put Farrow in a sexual triangle that ends in tragic sensation.

Since the breakup with Allen, Farrow has managed to acquit herself professionally in fine, interesting, idiosyncratic work. Returning to her Irish roots in *Widows' Peak*, a gentle and surprising comedy, Farrow again played a victim more apparent than real. Especially interesting is *Miami Rhapsody*, a comedy directed by David Frankel explicitly in the style of Woody Allen, in which Farrow plays a woman whose daughter is given the opportunity to sleep with her mother's lover, but *refuses* out of moral principle—a sly, cinematic rebuke to Allen, if ever there was one. One expects Farrow to continue to provide unusual work, such as 1995's *Reckless*, within a career that will probably always be too fine and subtle for either contemporary public acclaim or extraordinary critical reward.

—Charles Derry

FAYE, Alice

Nationality: American. **Born:** Alice Jeanne Leppert in New York City, 5 May 1912. **Family:** Married 1) the singer Tony Martin, 1937 (divorced 1940); 2) the bandleader Phil Harris, 1941 (died 1995), two daughters. **Career:** At age 14 began dancing with Chester Hale Dance Group; 1931—Broadway debut in chorus of *George White's Scandals*; singer with Rudy Vallee's orchestra and on radio show; 1934—cast in film version of *George White's Scandals of 1934*; signed to contract by 20th Century-Fox; 1940s—increased friction with studio head Darryl Zanuck; 1945—retired from films; mid-1940s-mid-1950s—in radio situation comedy, spin-off of Jack Benny show, with husband Phil Harris; 1962—returned to screen for remake of *State Fair*; mid-1970s—toured with John Payne in revival of musical *Good News*.

Films as Actress:

1934   *George White's Scandals* (*George White's Scandals of 1934*) (White, Freeland, and Lachman) (as Kitty Donnelly); *Now I'll Tell* (Burke) (as Peggy Warren); *She Learned about Sailors* (George Marshall) (as Jean Legoi); *365 Nights in Hollywood* (George Marshall) (as Alice Perkins)

1935   *George White's Scandals* (*George White's 1935 Scandals*) (White) (as Honey Walters); *Every Night at Eight* (Walsh) (as Dixie Dean); *Music Is Magic* (George Marshall) (as Peggy Harper)

1936   *King of Burlesque* (Lanfield) (as Pat Doran); *Poor Little Rich Girl* (Cummings) (as Jerry Dolan); *Sing, Baby, Sing* (Lanfield) (as Joan Warren); *Stowaway* (Seiter) (as Susan Parker)

1937   *On the Avenue* (Del Ruth) (as Mona Merrick); *Wake Up and Live* (Lanfield) (as Alice Huntley); *You Can't Have Everything* (Taurog) (as Judith Poe Wells); *You're a Sweetheart* (David Butler) (as Betty Bradley)

1938   *Sally, Irene, and Mary* (Seiter) (as Sally Day); *In Old Chicago* (Henry King) (as Belle Fawcett); *Alexander's Ragtime Band* (Henry King) (as Stella Kirby)

1939   *Tail Spin* (Del Ruth) (as Trixie Lee); *Rose of Washington Square* (Ratoff) (title role); *Hollywood Cavalcade* (Cummings) (as Molly Adair); *Barricade* (Ratoff) (as Emmy Jordan)

1940   *Little Old New York* (Henry King) (as Pat O'Day); *Lillian Russell* (Cummings) (title role); *Tin Pan Alley* (Walter Lang) (as Katie Blane)

1941   *That Night in Rio* (Cummings) (as Baroness Cecilia Duarte); *The Great American Broadcast* (Mayo) (as Vicki Adams); *Weekend in Havana* (Walter Lang) (as Nan Spencer)

1943   *Hello, Frisco, Hello* (Humberstone) (as Judy Evans); *The Gang's All Here* (*The Girl He Left Behind*) (Berkeley) (as Eadie Allen)

1944   *Four Jills in a Jeep* (Seiter) (as herself)

1945   *Fallen Angel* (Preminger) (as June Mills)

1962   *State Fair* (Ferrer) (as Melissa Drake)

1976   *Won Ton Ton, the Dog Who Saved Hollywood* (Winner) (cameo as secretary at gate)

1978   *Every Girl Should Have One* (Hyatt); *The Magic of Lassie* (Chaffey) (as waitress)

1986   *Irving Berlin's America* (Dubose—for TV)

1994   *Carmen Miranda: Bananas Is My Business* (Soldberg—doc) (as herself)

Publications

By FAYE: book—

Growing Older, Staying Younger, with Dick Kleiner, New York, 1990.

By FAYE: articles—

Interview with M. Buckley, in *Films in Review* (New York), November 1982; see also issue for March 1983.

On FAYE: books—

Moshier, W. Franklyn, *The Films of Alice Faye*, San Francisco, 1972.
Moshier, W. Franklyn, *The Alice Faye Movie Book*, Harrisburg, Pennsylvania, 1974.
Rivadue, Barry, *Alice Faye: A Bio-Bibliography*, Westport, Connecticut, 1990.

On FAYE: articles—

Terry, Clifford, "Lots of 'Oomph' Left in Alice Faye," in *Chicago Tribune*, 26 September 1984.
Screen International, 5 January 1985.
Ovens, D., "Alice Faye!," in *Hollywood: Then and Now*, vol. 24, no. 12, 1991.

*   *   *

George White's Scandals of 1934 began Alice Faye's exclusive 12-year contract with Twentieth Century-Fox. Appearing in 31 musicals, she became one of Hollywood's top female stars during the late 1930s and early 1940s. An excellent singer with a smooth and emotional contralto voice ("husky and honey-coated" according to Michael Buckley), Faye introduced a string of popular hits. Many of these became standards and some, such as "That's What I Like about the South," "All Alone," "I've Got My Love to Keep Me Warm," and "You'll Never Know" (the Oscar winning song from *Hello, Frisco, Hello*), are still closely associated with her. In 1937, when George Gershwin, Cole Porter, and Irving Berlin named her the best female singer in Hollywood, Porter said "There's something about the way Alice projects a song that spells immediate success for it." Faye's success kept her trapped in the (highly profitable) Technicolor romantic escapism known as the Twentieth Century-Fox style.

Faye represented the idealized patriarchal fantasy of femininity. Initially modeled as a clone of Jean Harlow, Fox eventually removed the hard-edged brassiness of her early screen image and initiated the

Alice Faye

emergence of the classic Faye persona in 1936. She was beautiful, warm, honest, talented, championed love above all else, and willingly submitted to masculine power. Jack Kroll defined her quality as "ripeness," radiating "the double promise of sumptuous sexuality and good fellowship." Faye resolved the cultural contradictions between marital and sexual partner by merging the socially sanctioned role of protectable wife/mother with the potential of aggressive and fleshy carnal abandonment. Her roles were constructed so that she embodied the submissive female perfectly. She most frequently portrayed a character who allowed external events to rule her life. Consequently, she was usually unhappy, yet rarely attempted to actively remedy her romantic dilemma. As David Shipman states in *The Great Movie Stars*: "When men crossed her, she didn't start throwing things but quietly left the room, her eyes welling with tears." She most often cried over Don Ameche (in six films), John Payne (in four films), and Tyrone Power (in three films).

Contrary to the musical genre's custom of granting the female lead a central position of visual power during routines that exhibit performance capabilities, Alice Faye's compositional placement during her songs failed to allow any suggestion of strength. She sang in medium shot with a high camera angle that isolated her in a corner or side of the frame. Leaning against something or sitting, she gazed upward with wide, moist eyes and sang, predominantly, ballads or torch songs. Her performance positioning reinforced her narrative placement as gentle and easily controlled. She is one of the few female song and dance stars depicted as "helpless" in both the narrative and performance discourses of the musical.

This fact was not lost on Faye; she referred to Twentieth Century-Fox as "Penitentiary Fox"; she stated that all her films used the same script; and described her never-changing character as a "painted doll-like dummy." When she attempted the transition into drama, in Otto Preminger's *Fallen Angel*, the studio undercut her work by reducing her role. Frustrated, she retired from Hollywood.

During the height of her popularity, Faye provided an alternative (and more conservative) female image to that of the self-sufficient, aggressive, and pragmatic woman who frequently emerged from the Hollywood system during the 1930s and 1940s. Faye's retirement allowed Fox's other major musical star, Betty Grable, to fully dominate the post-World War II musical.

—Greg S. Faller

FÉLIX, María

Nationality: Mexican. **Born:** María de los Angeles Félix Guereña in Alamos, Sonora, Mexico, 4 May 1914. **Family:** Married 1) the singer Raúl Prado (divorced); 2) Enrique Alvarez (divorced), son: Enrique Alvarez Félix; 3) the composer and singer Agustín Lara (divorced); 4) the actor Jorge Negrete, 1952 (died 1953); 5) Alexander Berger, 1956 (died 1974). **Career:** 1942—film debut in *El peñon de las ánimas*; international reputation enabled her to make films in Argentina, Spain, Italy, and France; 1970—in TV series *La Constitucion*. **Awards:** Ariele Awards for Best Actress, for *A Woman in Love*, 1945; *Hidden River*, 1946-47; and *Doña Diabla*, 1949-50; Ariele Life Achievement Award, 1985; Mexico City Prize, 1985.

Films as Actress:

1942   *El peñon de las ánimas* (*The Crag of the Spirits*) (Zacarías) (as María Angela Valdivia); *María Eugenia* (Castillo) (title role)

1943   *Doña Barbara* (de Fuentes) (title role); *La mujer sin alma* (*Woman without a Soul*) (de Fuentas); *La china poblana* (Palacios) (as Catarina de San Juan)

1944   *Amok* (Momplet) (as Señora Trevis/Señora Belmont); *La monja alférez* (Gómez Muriel) (as Catalina Erauso/Don Alfonso)

1945   *El monje blanco* (Bracho) (as Galata Orsina); *Vértigo* (Momplet) (as Mercedes Mallea); *La mujer de todos* (*Everybody's Woman*) (Bracho) (as Maria Romano)

1946   *La devoradora* (*The Devourer*) (de Fuentes) (as Diana de Arellano); *Enamorada* (*A Woman in Love*) (Fernández) (as Beatriz Peñafiel)

1947   *Rio escondido* (*Hidden River*) (Fernández) (as Rosaura Salazar); *La diosa arrodillada* (Gavaldón) (as Raquel Serrano); *Que Dios me perdone* (Tito Davison) (as Sofia/Lena Kovach)

1948   *Mare Nostrum* (Gil) (as Freya); *Maclovia* (Fernández) (title role)

1949   *Doña Diabla* (Tito Davison) (as Angela); *Una mujer cualquiera* (Gil) (as Nieves Blanco)

1950   *La noche de sabado* (Gil) (as Imperia); *La corona negra* (Saslavsky) (as Mara)

1951   *Messalina* (*The Affairs of Messalina*) (Gallone) (title role); *Incantesimo tragico* (*Hechizo tragico*; *Oliva*) (Segui) (as Oliva)

1953   *Camelia* (Gavaldón) (title role); *La pasión desnuda* (*Naked Passion*) (Amadori) (as Malva Rey); *Reportaje* (Fernández) (as María); *El rapto* (Fernández) (as Aurora Campos y Campos)

1954   *La Belle Otéro* (*La bella Otéro*) (Pottier) (title role); *French Cancan* (*Only the French Can*) (Renoir) (as Margot "La Belle Abbesse")

1955   *Les Héros sont fatigués* (*Heroes and Sinners*; *The Heroes Are Tired*) (Ciampi) (as Gabriela); *La escondida* (*The Hidden Woman*) (Gavaldón) (as Gabriela); *Canasta de cuentos mexicanos* (Bracho) (as Luisa Bravo)

1956   *Tizoc* (*Amor Indio*) (Rodríguez) (as Maria); *Faustina* (de Heredia) (title role)

1957   *Flor de mayo* (*Beyond All Limits*) (Gavaldón) (as Magdalena)

1958   *Miércoles de ceniza* (Gavaldón) (as Victoria Rivas); *La cucaracha* (*The Soldiers of Pancho Villa*) (Ismael Rodríguez) (title role); *La estrella vacia* (*The Empty Star*) (Gómez Muriel) (as Olga Lang); *Café Colón* (Alazraki) (as Mónica); *Razzia sur la chnouf* (Decoin)

1959   *Sonatas* (Bardem) (as La Niña Chole); *Juana Gallo* (Zacarías) (as Angela Ramos/Juana Gallo)

1960   *La Fièvre monte à El Pao* (*Los ambiciosos*; *Republic of Sin*) (Buñuel) (as Inés Rojas)

1962   *La bandida* (*The Bandit*) (Roberto Rodríguez) (as María Mendoza/title role); *Si yo fuera millionario* (Soler) (as herself)

1963   *Amor y sexo* (Alcoriza) (as Diana)

1965   *La Valentina* (González) (as Valentina Zuñiga)

1970   *Le generala* (Ibañez) (as Mariana San Pedro/title role)

Publications

By FÉLIX: book—

Todas mis guerras, Mexico, 1993.

On FÉLIX: books—

García Riera, Emilio, *Historia documental del cine mexicano*, vols. 1-9, Mexico City, 1969-78.
Ramon, David, *80 años de cine en México*, Mexico City, 1977.

María Félix

Ayala Blanco, Jorge, *La aventura del cine mexicano*, Mexico City, 1979.

Mora, Carl J., *Mexican Cinema: Reflections of a Society 1896-1980*, Berkeley, 1982.

Taibo, Paco Ignacio, *María Félix: 47 Pasos por el cine*, Mexico City, 1985.

Ayala Blanco, Jorge, *La búsqueda del cine mexicano*, Mexico City, 1986.

De los Reyes, Aurelio, *Medio siglo de cine mexicano (1896-1947)*, Mexico City, 1987.

Barajas Sandoval, Carmen, *Una mujer llamada María Félix: historia no autorizadada*, Mexico City, 1993.

* * *

María Félix reportedly remarked, "Don't call me a legend because it sounds to me like the past." Yet, Félix was, in fact, one of the brightest of stars of the Mexican cinema's "Golden Age," appearing in more than 45 Mexican and European films. And despite rumors in the early 1980s of an imminent return to the screen, Félix the "legend" is part of the Mexican cinema's rich past. Her celebrity caused her personal life and physical beauty to be fetishized: she was painted by artists such as Diego Rivera, Leonora Carrington, and Jean Cocteau; Agustín Lara wrote songs for his "María Bonita" (as she came to be known); poems about her beauty were composed by Efraín Huerta and Renato Leduc; Dior designed her gowns; and even a master such as Jean Renoir rendered homage to her pulchritude by filming her differently—in "Matisse's style"—from the other actors in *French Can-can*.

In the title role of *Doña Barbara*, Fernando de Fuentes's screen adaptation of the Rómulo Gallegos novel, Félix won a place as one of the primary figures in Mexican cinema and earned her lifelong nickname, "La Doña." But it was in *La mujer sin alma* that Félix concretized the archetypal woman with whom she would be identified throughout her career—a strong woman, driven by love, whose independence and sexual appetite challenge the code of Mexican *machismo*.

"The most beautiful face in the history of Mexican cinema," said one Mexican critic of Félix; but this star is also an example of the underdevelopment endemic to that nation's films. Despite working with several of Mexico's most renowned directors, Félix never really rose above her role of the vamp. She was a mediocre actress with atrocious diction, whose dramatic range was limited to raising an eyebrow or staring fixedly ahead. These "techniques" drew attention to her large, luminous eyes, while obscuring her thespian shortcomings.

From early in her career, the theme of a María Félix film was Félix herself, and her movies elevated her public image at the expense of story line or acting. The interest of *El rapto*, for example, lay in the recent marriage of its co-stars, Félix and Jorge Negrete, and in the fact that it was completed shortly before Negrete died. The title of other Félix vehicles bespeak her femme fatale character: *Doña Diabla* (*Mrs. Devil*), *La mujer de todos* (*Everybody's Woman*), *La mujer sin alma* (*Woman without a Soul*), and—in her preeminent characterization—*La devoradora* (*The Devourer*), promoted with this advertising pitch: "Three men burned in this woman's flame, this devourer of lives."

Félix's consumption of men, however, must be seen in the context of Mexican *machismo*. Her beauty threatened social convention and stability for, as one of her suitors says in *Doña Diabla*, "A beautiful woman can't be the property of just one man." Buffeted by the storms unleashed by her smoldering sexuality, the Félix character developed the *image* of a strong woman; for example, as recently as 1980 she argued, "They want to portray the Mexican woman as docile, stupid and obedient. We aren't like that; we're strong and brave and dare to struggle." As if to prove the force of her character, her later screen appearances were in the roles usually considered to be masculine. Thus, in a series of lavishly produced paeans to the Mexican Revolu-

tion—*La cucaracha, Juana Gallo, La bandida, La Valentina*—she represents powerful personifications of that process, culminating in *La generela*. Nonetheless, Félix's cinematic combativeness functions essentially to make more appetizing her eventual subjugation. The role she played time and again was nothing more than that of the "shrew tamed." In *Enamorada, El rapto, La tigresa*, and *La Valentina*, Félix begins as a willful and independent woman, sure of herself and of the direction in which she is guiding her life. By the end of these films, Félix trails along after her man, obedient to his wishes and attendant to his needs. Félix's screen rebellions finally served only to prove the futility of such resistance.

—John Mraz, updated by Ilene S. Goldman

FERNANDEL

Nationality: French. **Born:** Fernand Joseph Désiré Contandin in Marseilles, 8 May 1903. **Military Service:** Compulsory military service in the 1920s; French army, 1939-40. **Family:** Married Henriette Manse, 1925, children: Josette, Janine, Franck, and Gérard. **Career:** Stage debut at age five in melodrama, Théâtre Chave; while attending school, appeared at night with father and brother in Marseilles music halls; 1914—left school and worked in various jobs while continuing to perform; 1922—contract by Eldorado Theatre, Nice; contract on Paramount vaudeville circuit; 1930—offered first film role by director Marc Allégret; through 1930s continued to appear on stage in Marseille and Paris; 1934—first substantial film role as Saturnin in Marcel Pagnol's *Angèle*; 1942—directed children's film *Simplet*; 1948—first tour of United States and Canada; 1950—began appearing in serious roles, in Sacha Guitry's *Tu m'as sauvé la vie*; 1967—in TV series *L'Amateur*. **Awards:** Chevalier of the Légion d'Honneur. **Died:** In Paris, 26 February 1971.

Films as Actor:

1930   *La Meilleure Bobonne* (Marc Allégret and Heymann) (as Lucien Pivoine); *J'ai quelque chose à vous dire* (Marc Allégret); *Le Blanc et le noir* (Florey) (as Le Groom)

1931   *Attaque nocturne* (Marc Allégret and de Marguenat); *On purge bébé* (Renoir) (as Horace Truchet); *Vive la classe* (Cammage); *Coeur de Lilas* (Litvak—French version of his *The Mad Genius*) (as le garçon d'honneur); *La Fine combine* (Chotin—short) (as valet); *Pas un mot à ma femme* (Chotin); *Bric a Brac et Cie* (Chotin); *Paris-Beguin* (Génina) (as Ficelle)

1932   *Cunegonde* (short—filmed song); *Elle disait non* (short—filmed song); *Le Rosier de Madame Husson* (*He*) (Deschamps) (as Isidore); *Maruche* (Péguy); *Un Homme sans nom* (*L'Homme sans nom*) (Ucicky—French version of *Mensch ohne Namen*) (as Julot); *Les Gaités de l'escadron* (Maurice Tourneur) (as Venderague); *La Claque* (Péguy—short); *Par habitude* (Cammage—short); *Quand tu nous tiens, amour* (Cammage—short); *Le Jugement de minuit* (Esway and Charlot) (as Sam); *Une Brune piquante* (de Poligny); *Ordonnance malgré lui* (Cammage) (as chauffeur); *Un Beau Jour de noces* (Cammage—short); *La Terreur de la Pampa* (Cammage); *Comme une carpe* (Heymann—short); *L'Idoire* (Maurice Tourneur—short) (title role)

1933   *Ça colle* (Christian-Jaque—short); *Le Coq du regiment* (Cammage); *Le Gros Lot* (*La Veine d'Anatole*) (Cammage); *L'Ordonnance* (*The Orderly*) (Tourjansky); *D'amour et

389

Fernandel in *Le Petit monde de Don Camillo*

d'eau fraîche (Gandéra); *Adéma i aviateur* (Tarride) (as Michelet); *La Garnison amoureuse* (de Vaucorbeil); *Restez diner* (short)

1934 *Une Nuit de folies* (Cammage); *Le Cheri de sa concierge* (Glavanti); *Le Train de 8 h 47* (Wulschleger) (as Croquebol); *L'Hôtel du libre échange* (Marc Allégret); *Angèle* (Pagnol) (as Saturnin); *Les Bleus de la marine* (Cammage) (as Lafraise); *Le Cavalier Lafleur* (Ducis) (as Lafleur en activité); *La Porteuse de pain* (Sti)

1935 *Ferdinand le noceur* (Sti) (as Ferdinand); *Jim la houlette* (Berthomieu) (as Moluchet); *Les Gaités de la finance* (Forrester)

1936 *Un de la Légion* (Christian-Jaque) (as Fernand Espitalion); *Josette* (Christian-Jaque)

1937 *François Ier* (*Francis the First*) (Christian-Jaque) (as Honorin); *Les Degourdis de la onzième* (Christian-Jaque); *Ignace* (Colombier) (as Ignace Boitaclou); *Regain* (*Harvest*) (Pagnol) (as Urbain Gédémus); *Le Schpountz* (*Heartbeat*) (Pagnol) (as Irené Fabre); *Les Rois du sport* (Colombier) (as Fernand); *Un Carnet de bal* (*Life Dances on, Christine*) (Duvivier) (as Fabien Coutissol); *Hercule* (*L'Incorruptible*) (Esway) (title role)

1938 *Barnabé* (Esway) (title role); *Raphael et Cacolet* (Colombier) (as Modeste Manosque); *Ernest le rebelle* (Christian-Jaque); *Les Cinq sous de Lavarède* (Cammage) (as Armand Lavarède)

1939 *Berlingot et Cie* (Rivers) (as François); *Fric-Frac* (Lehmann and Autant-Lara) (as Marcel); *L'Héritier des Mondésir* (Valentin)

1940 *L'Acrobate* (Boyer) (as Ernest Sauce); *Monsieur Hector* (Cammage) (as Hector); *Un Chapeau de paille d'Italie* (*The Italian Straw Hat*) (Cammage) (as Fadinard); *La nuit merveilleuse* (Paulin); *La Fille du puisatier* (*The Well-Digger's Daughter*) (Pagnol) (as Felipe Rambert)

1941 *Une Vie de chien* (Cammage) (as Gustave Bourdillon); *Les Petits Riens* (Leboursier); *Le Club des soupirants* (Gleize) (as Antoine Valoisir)

1942 *La Bonne Étoile* (Boyer) (as Auguste); *Ne le criez pas sur les toits* (Norman) (as Vincent Fleuret)

1943 *La Cavalcade des heures* (Noé) (as Antonin); *Guignol, marionnette de France* (short)

1945 *La Mystère Saint-Val* (Le Hénaff); *Irma la voyante* (short); *Naïs* (Pagnol) (as Tione); *Les Gueux au paradis* (*Hoboes in Paradise*) (Le Hénaff) (as Pons)

1946 *Pétrus* (Marc Allégret) (title role); *L'Aventure de Cabassou* (Grangier); *La Caissière du Grand Cafe* (short); *Comediens ambulants* (short); *Coeur de coq* (Cloche) (as Tulipe Barbaroux)

1947 *Escale au soleil* (Verneuil); *Emile l'africain* (Vernay) (as Emile)

1948 *Si ça peut vous faire plaisir* (Norman) (as Martial Gonfaron); *L'Armoire volante* (*The Cupboard Was Bare*) (Rim) (as Alfred Puc)

1949 *L'Héroique Monsieur Boniface* (Labro) (as Boniface); *On démande un assassin* (Neubach) (as Bob Laurent); *Botta e risposta* (*Je suis de la revue*) (Soldati)

1950 *Casimir* (Pottier) (title role); *Muertres* (*Three Sinners*) (Pottier) (as Noël Annaquin); *Tu m'as sauvé la vie* (Guitry) (as Fortuné Richard); *Uniformes et grandes manoeuvres* (Le Hénaff) (as Luc); *Topaze* (Pagnol) (title role); *Boniface somnambule* (Labro) (as Boniface)

1951 *L'Auberge rouge* (*The Red Inn*) (Autant-Lara) (as Le Capucin); *La Table aux crèves* (Verneuil) (as Urbain Coindet)

1952 *Le Petit monde de Don Camillo* (*The Little World of Don Camillo*) (Duvivier) (title role); *Coiffeur pour dames* (*The French Touch*) (Boyer) (as Mario); *Le Fruit défendu* (*Forbidden Fruit*) (Verneuil) (as Charles Pellegrin); *Le Boulanger de Valorgue* (Verneuil) (as Félicien)

1953 *Le Retour de Don Camillo* (*The Return of Don Camillo*) (Duvivier) (title role); *L'Ennemi public No. 1* (*The Most Wanted Man*) (Verneuil) (as Joé Calvet); *Carnaval* (*Carnival*) (Verneuil) (as Dardamelle); *Mam'zelle Nitouche* (Yves Allégret) (as Célestin-Floridor); *Le Mouton à cinq pattes* (*The Sheep Has Five Legs*) (Verneuil) (as Saint Forget/Alain/Bernard/Charles/Désiré/Étienne); *Ali Baba et les quarante voleurs* (*Ali Baba*) (Jacques Becker) (as Ali Baba); *Le Printemps, l'automne et l'amour* (Grangier) (as Noël Sarrazin)

1955 *Don Camillo e l'onorevole Peppone* (*La Grande Bagarre de Don Camillo*) (Gallone) (title role); *Don Juan* (*Pantaloons*) (Berry) (as Sagnarelle)

1956 *Le Couturier de ces dames* (*Fernandel the Dressmaker*) (Boyer) (as Fernand); *Sous le ciel de Provence* (*The Virtuous Bigamist*) (Soldati) (as Paul Verdier); *Le Telephone* (Régamey— short); *Honoré de Marseilles* (Régamey) (as Honoré); *L'Homme à l'impermeable* (*The Man in the Raincoat*) (Duvivier) (as Albert Constantine); *L'Art d'etre Papa* (short—for TV); *Around the World in Eighty Days* (Anderson) (as Parisian coachman)

1957 *Sénéchal le magnifique* (*Senechal the Magnificent*) (Boyer) (as Sénéchal); *Le Chômeur de Clochemerle* (*The Easiest Profession*) (Boyer); *A Paris tous les deux* (Oswald); *La Loi, c'est la loi* (*The Law Is the Law*) (Christian-Jaque)

1958 *La Vie à deux* (Duhour); *Les Vignes du seigneur* (Boyer) (as Henri); *Le Grand Chef* (*The Big Chief*) (Verneuil) (as Antoine)

1959 *Le Confident de ces dames* (Boyer); *La Vache et le prisonnier* (*The Cow and I*) (Verneuil) (as Charles Bailly)

1960 *Cresus* (Giono) (as Jules); *Le Caïd* (Borderie); *Cocagne* (Cloche) (as Marc-Antoine); *Dynamite Jack* (Bastia)

1961 *Don Camillo, monsignore . . . ma non troppo* (*Don Camillo Monseigneur*) (Gallone) (as Don Camillo); *L'Assassin est dans l'annuaire* (Joannon); *Il giudizio universale* (De Sica)

1962 *Le Diable et les dix commandements* (*The Devil and the Ten Commandments*) (Duvivier) (as God); *En avant la musique* (*Avanti la musica*) (Bianchi); *Le Voyage à Biarritz* (Grangier) (as Guillaume Dodut)

1963 *Blague dans le coin* (Labro); *Le Bon Roi Dagobert* (Chevalier) (as Dagobert); *La Cuisine au beurre* (*My Wife's Husband*) (Grangier)

1964 *Relaxe-toi, cheri* (Boyer); *L'Age ingrat* (Grangier) (+ co-pr)

1965 *Il compagno Don Camillo* (*Don Camillo en Russie*; *Don Camillo à Moscou*) (Comencini) (title role); *La Bourse et la vie* (Mocky) (as Migue)

1966 *Le Voyage du père* (de la Patellière) (as Quantin)

1967 *L'Homme à la Buick* (Grangier) (as Monsieur Jo)

1968 *Palmares des chansons* (Pradines—for TV)

1969 *Heureux qui comme Ulysse* (Colpi) (as Antonin)

Films as Actor and Director:

1942 *Simplet* (title role, co-d with Carlo Rim)

1943 *Adrien* (title role)

1951 *Adhémar* (*Le Jouet de la fatalité*) (title role)

Publications

By FERNANDEL: article—

"I'm an Actor, Not a Comedian," in *Films and Filming* (London), October 1960.

On FERNANDEL: books—

Rim, Carlo, *Fernandel*, Paris, 1952.

Castans, Ramond, *Fernandel m'a raconte*, Paris, 1976.

Plume, Christian, *Fernandel*, Paris, 1976.

Fernandel 1903-1971, photo album chosen by André Fildier, Paris, 1981.

Jelot-Blanc, Jean-Jacques, *Fernandel: Quand le cinéma parlait provençal*, Nice, 1981.

Lorcey, Jacques, *Fernandel*, Paris, 1981.

Fernandel, Franck, *Fernandel de peres en fils*, Paris, 1991.

On FERNANDEL: articles—

"Fernandel," issue of *Visages* (Paris), July 1938.

Current Biography 1955, New York, 1955.

"Fernandel," in *Films and Filming* (London), May 1955.

Hume, R., "French Face Man," in *Films and Filming* (London), February 1956.

Gerald, Y., "Fernandel's Comic Style," in *Films in Review* (New York), March 1960.

Obituary in *New York Times*, 28 February 1971.

Lorcey, Jacques, "Fernandel," in *Anthologie du cinéma*, vol. 9, Paris, 1973.

Domke, G., "Fernandel," letter, in *Films in Review* (New York), April 1973, and corrections in August/September 1973.

Ecran (Paris), February 1978.

Ciné Revue (Paris), 8 November 1984.

*   *   *

Attending so-called art movie theaters during the late 1940s and early 1950s, American audiences discovered the comic genius of Fernandel in such films as *The Well-Digger's Daughter*, *The Little World of Don Camillo*, and *The Sheep Has Five Legs*. His physical features were pure caricature, as if a cartoonist had designed him, with an unusually long, hang-dog face, big eyes and thick lips, and a broad, horse-toothed smile. His head was set on a thick, short frame with arms and legs that moved awkwardly, as if attached to a much taller man.

Despite this nearly grotesque figure he was one of the most captivating international comic personalities. Usually an innocent, a "fall guy" for those much wiser than he, Fernandel projected a childlike warmth and high spirits that would cause a beautiful, young country girl to want him for a husband. Playing a suitor who Is easily manipulated by the father of a wronged girl in *The Well-Digger's Daughter*, the comedian achieved critical and popular attention. As a guileless country lad Fernandel was marvelously suited to play opposite the more seasoned Raimu. Fernandel's fame increased in the 1950s when he appeared in the title role of *The Little World of Don Camillo* and its four sequels. The squabbles of a communist mayor and a mild village priest provided a strong comic base for the film as Fernandel blended seriousness with comedy. *The Sheep Has Five Legs* illustrated the comedian's deftness in handling multiple roles, a feat comparable to that of Alec Guinness in *Kind Hearts and Coronets*. The French comedian played six roles, a father and his five sons, providing a study in all the types of characters this talented actor portrayed throughout his long career.

—Donald McCaffrey

FERRER, José

Nationality: American. **Born:** José Vicente Ferrer Otero y Cintron in Santurce, Puerto Rico, 8 January 1912. **Education:** Studied architecture at Princeton University, graduated 1934; postgraduate work in Romance languages, Columbia University, 1934-35. **Family:** Married 1) the actress Uta Hagen, 1938 (divorced 1948), daughter Leticia; 2) Phyllis Hill, 1948 (divorced 1953); 3) the singer Rosemary Clooney, 1953 (divorced 1967, five children; 4) Stella Magee. **Career:** Moved with family to U.S. at age 6; acted with Princeton Triangle Club, with James Stewart and Joshua Logan; 1935—assistant stage manager for Joshua Logan's stock company in Suffern, New York; Broadway debut in walk-on role in *A Slight Case of Murder*; 1940—engaged to direct summer stock at Westchester Playhouse, New York; played lead in successful Broadway revival of *Charley's Aunt*; 1943—with Hagen as Desdemona, played Iago to Paul Robeson's Othello in long-running Broadway production of *Othello*; 1946—on Broadway in title role of *Cyrano de Bergerac*; 1948—screen debut as Dauphin in *Joan of Arc*; 1955—screen directing debut with *The Shrike*; mid-1950s—made several successful recordings with third wife Rosemary Clooney; from mid-1960s—active in TV; 1983-85—artistic adviser, Coconut Grove Playhouse. **Awards:** Best Actor Academy Award for *Cyrano de Bergerac*, 1950. **Died:** In Miami, Florida, 26 January 1992.

Films as Actor:

1946   *Bolivia* (short) (as narrator)
1948   *Joan of Arc* (Fleming) (as Dauphin)
1949   *The Sydenham Plan* (short) (as narrator); *Whirlpool* (Preminger)
1950   *Crisis* (Brooks); *Cyrano de Bergerac* (Gordon) (title role)
1951   *Anything Can Happen* (Seaton)
1952   *Moulin Rouge* (Huston) (as Toulouse-Lautrec); *Article Fifty-Five* (Seltzer—short) (as narrator)
1953   *Miss Sadie Thompson* (Bernhardt)
1954   *The Caine Mutiny* (Dmytryk) (as Barney Greenwald); *Deep in My Heart* (Donen) (as Sigmund Romberg)
1961   *Forbid Them Not* (Kimble) (as narrator)
1962   ***Lawrence of Arabia*** (Lean); *Nine Hours to Rama* (Robson); *Progress for Freedom* (Seltzer—short) (as narrator)

1963   *Verspätung in Marienborn* (*Stop Train 349*) (Haedrich); *Cyrano et d'Artagnan* (Gance)
1965   *The Greatest Story Ever Told* (Stevens); *Ship of Fools* (Kramer)
1966   *Enter Laughing* (Reiner)
1968   *Le Avventure e gli amori di Miguel Cervantes* (*The Young Rebel*; *Cervantes*) (Sherman)
1969   *The Little Drummer Boy* (short)
1970   *The Aquarians* (McDougall—for TV)
1971   *Cross Current* (*The Cable Car Murders*) (Thorpe—for TV); *Banyon* (Day—for TV)
1973   *El clan de los immorales* (*Order to Kill*) (Maessa); *The Marcus-Nelson Murders* (*Kojak and the Marcus-Nelson Murders*) (Sargent—for TV)
1975   *E' Lollipop* (*Forever Young, Forever Free*) (Lazarus); *Paco* (O'Neill); *The Missing Are Deadly* (McDougall—for TV); *Medical Story* (Nelson—for TV); *The Art of Crime* (Roman Grey) (Irving—for TV)
1976   *The Sentinel* (Winner); *The Big Bus* (Frawley); *Voyage of the Damned* (Rosenberg)
1977   *Zoltan . . . Hound of Dracula* (*Dracula's Dog*) (Band); *Who Has Seen the Wind?* (King) (as Ben); *Crash* (Band—for TV); *Exo-Man* (Irving—for TV)
1978   *The Swarm* (Allen) (as Dr. Andrews); *The Amazing Captain Nemo* (March—for TV); *Fedora* (Wilder) (as Dr. Vando); *The Private Files of J. Edgar Hoover* (Cohen) (as Lionel McCoy)
1979   *The Fifth Musketeer* (*Behind the Iron Mask*) (Annakin) (as Athos); *Natural Enemies* (Kanew)
1980   *The Big Brawl* (Clouse) (as Dominici); *Pleasure Palace* (Grauman—for TV); *The Murder That Wouldn't Die* (Satlof—for TV)
1981   *Evita Peron* (Chomsky—for TV); *Berlin Tunnel Twenty-One* (Michaels—for TV)
1982   *A Midsummer Night's Sex Comedy* (Woody Allen) (as Leopold); *Blood Tide* (Jeffries)
1983   *The Being* (Kong); *This Girl for Hire* (Jameson—for TV); *To Be or Not to Be* (Mel Brooks) (as Professor Siletski); *Blood Feud* (*Bad Blood*) (Newell)
1984   *The Evil That Men Do* (Thompson); *Dune* (Lynch); *George Washington* (Kulik—for TV); *Samson and Delilah* (Philips—for TV)
1985   *Seduced* (Freedman—for TV); *Jacques Cousteau—The First 75 Years* (for TV) (as narrator); *Hitler's SS: Portrait in Evil* (for TV)
1986   *Bloody Birthday* (Hunt) (as Doctor); *The Violins Came with the Americans* (Conway)
1988   *Strange Interlude* (Wise—for TV)
1989   *Hired to Kill* (Mastovakis)
1990   *Old Explorers* (Pohlad)

Film as Composer:

1953   *The Beautiful Stranger* (*Twist of Fate*) (Miller) (music for song "Love Is a Beautiful Stranger")

Films as Director:

1955   *The Shrike* (+ ro); *Cockleshell Heroes* (+ ro)
1956   *The Great Man* (+ co-sc, ro)
1957   *I Accuse* (+ ro as Dreyfus)
1958   *The High Cost of Loving* (+ ro)
1961   *Return to Peyton Place*
1962   *State Fair*

Publications

By FERRER: article—

"Cyrano and Others," in *Films and Filming* (London), July 1962.

On FERRER: articles—

London, Julie, "The Two Faces of Ferrer," in *Films and Filming* (London), June 1958.
Ciné Revue (Paris), 6 August 1981.
Buckley, Michael, "Jose Ferrer," in *Films in Review* (New York), February and March 1987.

* * *

It may be said of José Ferrer's career in films that his prestige outweighs his success. While considered a major actor, and associated with many important films, some of them innovative milestones, others "message" films, Ferrer never enjoyed a consistently satisfying or secure career.

Far from denying the decline in his film work since his heyday in the early 1950s, Ferrer later commented, "My entire film career has been dominated by *Cyrano de Bergerac* and *Moulin Rouge*. I have learned to live with the situation, but I regret the form my career has taken." In both films the character actor portrayed sensitive souls who had physical deformities. Cyrano was a complex interpretation of a hapless, ugly, unrequited lover who was also a brave iconoclast and sensitive poet. As Toulouse Lautrec, the brilliant Parisian painter who was a dwarf, Ferrer literally went on his knees. *Cyrano* earned Ferrer an Academy Award, yet some years later he mused that the honor was no assurance of success. He stated bluntly in 1961, "For three years there has been no call for my services as a film actor."

Ferrer always preferred to have a strong hand in any production with which he was involved, and naturally turned to directing. He cast himself as the lead in films which he also directed, such as *I Accuse*, in which he played the persecuted French Jewish Officer, Dreyfus, and *The Shrike*, starring as the victimized husband. He was always attracted to films with a social message, and objected to the soft-pedaling of the Jewish issue in *The Caine Mutiny*, in which he was cast as naval lawyer Barney Greenwald. In *Ship of Fools* he portrayed the Nazi antagonist.

Ferrer's quality on film has been perceived as serious, even dour, and he was usually typecast as a "heavy." In the 1970s and into the 1980s Ferrer made several TV films. What others might term supporting roles, or at least "cameos," Ferrer sarcastically called "bit parts, to earn a fast buck . . . the roles where I play the villain or I go up in flames in the end."

Ferrer remained active in the theater, acting on and off Broadway and on the road in a broad range of roles; he also did musicals. He directed in New York, in stock and regional theaters, and even returned to work in his native Puerto Rico. Yet, in a 1983 interview he complained that he was reduced to doing TV voice-overs. Ironically, Ferrer's voice and diction were so distinctive and so well known as to render anonymity an impossibility.

—Constance Clark

FEUILLÈRE, Edwige

Nationality: French. **Born:** Edwige Caroline Cunati-Koenig (or Caroline Edwige Cunati) in Vésoul, Haute-Saone, 29 October 1907. **Education:** Attended Dijon Lyceum; studied acting with George Le Roy at Paris Conservatory from 1928. **Family:** Married the actor Pierre Feuillère, 1929 (divorced 1933). **Career:** 1930—began acting on stage using name Cora Lynn; 1931-33—member of Comédie Française, debut in *Le Mariage de Figaro*; film debut, also using name Cora Lynn, in short *La Fine combine* opposite Fernandel; from mid-1930s—active on Paris stage; 1947—created role of the Queen in *The Eagle with Two Heads*, written for her by Jean Cocteau; 1951—first London stage appearance with Jean-Louis Barrault company in *Partage de midi*; 1957—London season with own company in *La Dame aux Camélias* and other plays; also performed in TV adaptations of stage plays, and in TV series *Le Chef de famille*. **Awards:** Honorary César award, French Academy, 1984; Commandeur des Arts et Lettres; Grand Officier de la Légion d'Honneur, 1993. **Address:** 19 rue Eugène-Manuel, 75016 Paris, France.

Films as Actress:

1931 *La Fine combine* (Chotin—short); *Cordon-bleu* (Anton)
1932 *La Perle* (Guissart); *Monsieur Albert* (Anton); *Une Petite Femme dans le train* (Anton); *Maquillage* (Anton)
1933 *Topaze* (Gasnier) (as Coco); *Les Aventures du Roi Pausole* (Granowsky); *Toi que j'adore* (von Bolvary and Valentin—French-language version of von Bolvary's *Ich kenn' dich nicht und liebe dich*); *Matricule 33* (Anton); *Ces messieurs de la santé* (Colombier)
1934 *Le Miroir aux alouettes* (Steinhoff and Le Bon—French-language version of Steinhoff's *Lockvogel*)
1935 *Lucrèce Borgia* (Gance) (title role); *Golgotha* (Duvivier) (as Claudia); *Barcarolle* (Lamprecht and Le Bon—French-language version of Lamprecht's *Barcarole*); *Stradivarius* (von Bolvary and Valentin—French-language version of von Bolvary's *Stradivari*); *Amore* (Bragaglia); *La Route heureuse* (Lacombe—French-language version of *Amore*)
1936 *Mister Flow* (*Compliments of Mister Flow*) (Siodmak) (as Lady Helena Scarlett)
1937 *Marthe Richard au service de la France* (*Marthe Richard, l'espionne au service de la France*) (Bernard); *Feu!* (de Baroncelli); *La Dame de Malacca* (Marc Allégret)
1938 *J'étais une aventurière* (Bernard)
1939 *L'Émigrante* (Joannon)
1940 *Sans lendemain* (Max Ophüls); *De Mayerling à Sarajevo* (*Mayerling to Sarajevo*) (Max Ophüls) (as Sophie Chotkova)
1941 *Mam'zelle Bonaparte* (Maurice Tourneur); *L'Honorable Catherine* (L'Herbier); *La Duchesse de Langeais* (de Baroncelli)
1943 *Lucrèce* (Joannon)
1945 *La Part de l'ombre* (*Blind Desire*) (Delannoy) (as Agnes Noblet); *Tant que je vivrai* (de Baroncelli)
1946 *L'Idiot* (Lampin) (as Nastasia Filipovna); *Il suffit d'une fois* (Feix)
1947 *L'Aigle à deux têtes* (*The Eagle with Two Heads*) (Cocteau) (as the Queen)
1948 *Woman Hater* (Terence Young) (as Colette Marly)
1949 *Julie de Carneilhan* (Manuel)
1950 "La Statuette" ep. of *Souvenirs perdus* (Christian-Jaque); *Olivia* (Audry)
1951 *Le Cap de l'Espérance* (Bernard)
1952 *Adorables Créatures* (*Adorable Creatures*) (Christian-Jaque) (as Denise)
1953 *Le Blé en herbe* (*The Game of Love*) (Autant-Lara) (as Mme. Dalleray)
1954 *Les Fruits de l'été* (Bernard)
1957 *Quand la femme s'en mêle* (*Send a Woman When the Devil Fails*; *When the Woman Gets Confused*) (Yves Allégret); *Le Septième Commandement* (Bernard)

Edwige Feuillère

1958   *En cas de malheur* (*Love Is My Profession*; *In Case of Adversity*) (Autant-Lara) (as Viviane Gobillot); *La Vie à deux* (*Life as a Couple*) (Duhour)

1961   "Les Comédiennes" ep. of *Amours célèbres* (Boisrond)

1962   "Le Masque" ("The Mask") ep. of *Le Crime ne paie pas* (*Crime Does Not Pay*; *The Gentle Art of Murder*) (Oury) (as Dona Lucrezia)

1964   *Aimez-vous les femmes?* (*A Taste for Women*) (Léon) (as Aunt Flo)

1967   *La Route d'un homme* (Hacquard—short) (as narrator)

1968   *Scusi, facciamo l'amore* (*Et si on faisait l'amour?*; *Listen, Let's Make Love*) (Caprioli) (as Giuditta Passani)

1970   *Le Clair de terre* (Gilles)

1974   *La Chair de l'orchidée* (*Flesh and the Orchid*; *Flesh of the Orchid*) (Chéreau) (as Madame Bastier-Wagener)

1981   *Chef de famille* (Companeez)

1984   *Dames de la côte* (Companeez); *La Tueur triste* (Gessner—for TV)

1987   *Un château au soleil*

1988   *Cinéma*

1993   *La Dame de Lieu-dit*

Publications

By FEUILLÈRE: books—

Les Feux de la mémoire, Paris, 1977.
Moi, la Clairon, Paris, 1984.

By FEUILLÈRE: articles—

Interviews in *Ciné Revue* (Paris), 10 May 1979 and 16 April 1981.

On FEUILLÈRE: books—

Kemp, Robert, *Edwige Feuillère*, Paris, 1951.
Feydeau, Alain, *Edwige Feuillère*, Paris, 1983.

On FEUILLÈRE: articles—

Cinémonde (Paris), 25 May 1948 and 9 February 1956.
Films and Filming (London), December 1960.
Ecran (Paris), October 1978, additions in issue for February 1979.

Cahiers du Cinéma (Paris), March 1981.

Curtiss, T. Q., "Veteran Film Stars Brighten a Season of Theater in Paris," in *New York Times*, 15 April 1990.

Stars (Mariembourg, Belgium), December 1990.

* * *

Edwige Feuillère is more famous as a stage actress than as a screen actress, but her many film roles in the 1930s and 1940s almost made her the acknowledged leading lady of French cinema.

Her first film and her acceptance into the Comédie Française in the early 1930s brought her attention from film producers, and Louis Gasnier cast her in the first film version of *Topaze*, based on the play by Marcel Pagnol; her charm and elegance opposite Louis Jouvet were widely appreciated. The role of Lucrezia Borgia in Abel Gance's 1935 version solidified her popularity. Over the next few years her roles as elegant and often heartless women were displayed in *Marthe Richard au service de la France* (as a charming spy opposite Erich von Stroheim), *J'étais une aventurière*, *La Dame de Malacca*, and *De Mayerling à Sarajevo* (as the young Sophia Chotkova).

Her triumph as Nastasia Filipovna in *L'Idiot* notwithstanding, she tended to make fewer films after the war, though her stage performances made her even more appreciated in films when she made them. She played in both the stage and film versions of *Lucrèce*, and her successful stage role in *The Eagle with Two Heads* (written for her by Cocteau) was also translated to the screen. Her role as the older woman introducing an adolescent to love in *The Game of Love*, based on Colette's novel, was a scandal, even though Feuillère was brilliant in the role and the writer kept out any suggestion of prurience. She appeared later in the 1950s with Jean Gabin and Brigitte Bardot in *Love Is My Profession*.

—Karel Tabery

FIELD, Sally

Nationality: American. **Born:** Pasadena, California, 6 November 1946. **Education:** Attended Birmingham High School, California; Actors Studio, New York, 1968 and 1973-75; studied acting with David Craig. **Family:** Married 1) Steve Craig, 1968 (divorced 1973), sons: Peter and Elijah; 2) the producer Alan Greisman, 1984 (divorced 1995), son: Sam. **Career:** 1964—enrolled in Columbia Pictures Workshop, a branch of Columbia Studios; 1965-66—in title role of TV series *Gidget* and *The Flying Nun*, 1967-70; 1971-73—role as Clementine Hale in TV series *Alias Smith and Jones*; 1973-74—in title role of TV series *The Girl with Something Extra*; mid-1970s—studied acting and appeared in summer stock; 1984—formed Fogwood Films Ltd. production company; starred in and co-executive produced TV mini-series *A Woman of Independent Means*. **Awards:** Emmy Award, for *Sybil*, 1976; Academy Award for Best Actress, Best Actress, Cannes Festival, and Best Actress, New York Film Critics, for *Norma Rae*, 1979; Academy Award for Best Actress, for *Places in the Heart*, 1984. **Agent:** Creative Artists Agency, 9830 Wilshire Boulevard, Beverly Hills, CA 90212, U.S.A.

Films as Actress:

1967   *The Way West* (McLaglen) (as Mercy McBee)

1970   *Marriage: Year One* (Graham—for TV); *Maybe I'll Come Home in the Spring* (*Deadly Desire*) (Sargent—for TV) (as Denise)

1971   *Hitched* (*Westward the Wagon*) (Sagal—for TV); *Mongo's Back in Town* (Chomsky—for TV) (as Vikki)

1972   *Home for the Holidays* (Moxey—for TV)

1976   *Stay Hungry* (Rafelson) (as Mary Tate Farnsworth); *Bridger* (Rich—for TV); *Sybil* (Petrie—for TV) (title role)

1977   *Smokey and the Bandit* (Needham) (as Carrie); *Heroes* (Kagan) (as Carol)

1978   *Hooper* (Needham) (as Gwen); *The End* (Burt Reynolds) (as Mary Ellen)

1979   *Norma Rae* (Ritt) (title role); *Beyond the Poseidon Adventure* (Irwin Allen) (as Celeste Whitman)

1980   *Smokey and the Bandit II* (*Smokey and the Bandit Ride Again*) (Needham) (as Carrie)

1981   *Back Roads* (Ritt) (as Amy Post); *Absence of Malice* (Pollack) (as Megan)

1982   *Kiss Me Goodbye* (Mulligan) (as Kay Villano)

1984   *Places in the Heart* (Benton) (as Edna Spalding)

1985   *Murphy's Romance* (Ritt) (as Emma Moriarty, + exec pr)

1987   *Surrender* (Belson) (as Daisy Morgan, Artist)

1988   *Punchline* (Seltzer) (as Lilah Krytsik)

1989   *Steel Magnolias* (Ross) (as M'Lynn Eatenton)

1990   *Not without My Daughter* (Brian Gilbert) (as Betty Mahmoody)

1991   *Soapdish* (Hoffman) (as Celeste Talbert)

1993   *Mrs. Doubtfire* (Columbus) (as Miranda Hillard); *Homeward Bound: The Incredible Journey* (Dunham) (as voice of Sassy the cat)

1994   *Forrest Gump* (Zemeckis) (as Forrest's mother)

1996   *Eye for an Eye* (Schlesinger) (as Karen McCann); *Homeward Bound II: Lost in San Francisco* (David R. Ellis) (as voice of Sassy the cat)

Other Films:

1991   *Dying Young* (co-pr)

Publications

By FIELD: articles—

Interview in *Films Illustrated* (London), August 1979.

"Teleperforming vs. Screen Acting," in *The Movie Star*, edited by Elisabeth Weis, New York, 1981.

"Table Talk," interview with Nancy Griffin, in *Premiere* (New York), Winter 1993.

On FIELD: books—

Bonderoff, Jason, *Sally Field*, New York, 1987.

Goldstein, Toby, *Sally Field*, New York, 1988.

On FIELD: articles—

Klemesrud, Judy, in *New York Times*, 27 December 1977.

Current Biography 1979, New York, 1979.

Ciné Revue (Paris), 31 July 1980.

Revue du Cinéma (Paris), January 1983.

Hibbin, S., "Sally Field," in *Films and Filming* (London), June 1985.

Shindler, Merrill, "Hollywood's Greatest Survivor," in *Los Angeles Magazine*, November 1989.

Webster, Ann, "Sally Field," in *Premiere* (New York), August 1994.

* * *

Gritty, plucky, feisty—and other adjectives that have fallen out of favor—spring to mind when contemplating the essence of Sally Field's appeal. Her limitations (including a regrettably thin voice, a failing that puts her in good company with Elizabeth Taylor and Natalie Wood) are as immediately apparent as her virtues (a translucent honesty which rescues her from the precipice of seeming too actressy). A specialist in regional scrappers, Field has not shown a yen for foreign accents or idiosyncratic filmmakers, but, within her self-prescribed range as the steamrolling American flattening injustices like so much roadkill, she is in a league of her own. What is most remarkable about her stimulating performances is that she willed herself into the position to create them, despite the campy backlash in the wake of *The Flying Nun* and *Gidget*. How many other troupers could have not only survived being a cutie-pie in such fluff as *The Girl with Something Extra* but also have gone on to silence her detractors with two Oscars on her mantlepiece.

Even during her humble starlet origins, there must have been dozens of characters this pop-culture princess yearned to give birth to; in a sense, she unleashed them all with her breakthrough role in *Sybil*. Playing a multiple personality, she gave a knockout performance that has stood the test of time; it was so stunning in its clarity and so terrifying in its chameleon shifts of mood, that even her critics had to clam up. A hard act to follow, *Sybil* did not open any eyes at the film studios, so Field slipped into movies by the rear door of Burt Reynolds's speeding car (*Smokey and the Bandit*). Proving she could breezily peel rubber through America's back roads, Field again amazed the industry with a heartfelt performance as a Southern factory worker whose low self-esteem gets a shot in the arm from her awakened social conscience. Turned down by many big stars, the *Norma Rae* role provided a perfect outlet for Field's native intelligence and fired-up passion. It was a much more creditable and credible glimpse into the blue-collar soul than Meryl Streep's similar but phonily twangy *Silkwood*.

Aside from these high points, Field was believably contentious as a parasitic journalist making amends in *Absence of Malice* and was engaging as an eager-to-please housewife balancing career and home in that stand-up comedy cavalcade, *Punchline*. Often cast in mother roles, she tended to repeat standard renditions of resoluteness in the terminal-illness crowd-pleaser *Steel Magnolias* and that heartland ode *Places in the Heart*, a beloved movie that reduces all its interesting conflicts into tests of cornpone indomitability. Is it any wonder Field was pegged to play a further reduction of a Hallmark Hall of Fame-type mommy in the megagrosser *Forrest Gump* which not only revisits Field's little-people roots but also applauds the dumb luck of the mentally challenged? Nor was she wise to cast herself as an avenging vigilante-mom battling male prerogatives in *Not without My Daughter* and *Eye for an Eye*. Gussied up as feminist tracts, these thrillers were Charlotte Bronson odysseys which almost parodied Field's spirit of rage. Rather than contribute further to the stupidization of American films, Field could put her grassroots valor to better use in vehicles such as her mini-series, *A Woman of Independent Means*. In one of her classiest roles, Field illuminates a feminist soap opera by making her wife-mother's journey to self-realization painfully moving. Like Norma Rae, and Sybil, this typical Field character digs deep to find a courage that is new to her. A master at revealing how everyday people shock themselves with such discoveries, Field is really the role-model next door.

—Robert Pardi

FIELDS, Gracie

Nationality: British. **Born:** Grace Stansfield in Rochdale, Lancashire, 9 January 1898. **Education:** Public primary school. **Family:** Married

1) the comedian Archie Pitt, 1923 (divorced 1940); 2) the director Monty Banks, 1940 (died 1950); 3) Boris Alperovici, 1952. **Career:** Child singer in music halls; 1913-15—worked 2 years in cotton mill; 1915—joined revue *Yes, I Think So*, Manchester; first London appearance at Middlesex Music Hall; 1918—began touring in hugely successful *Mr. Tower of London*; 1928—made first recording, soon became major recording star; 1931—film debut in *Sally in Our Alley*; popular radio star during 1930s; 1935—contract with Associated Talking Pictures; 1937—brought to U.S. by Darryl Zanuck, under contract for short time; during World War II lived in U.S.; after 1952—lived in Italy. **Awards:** Commander, Order of the British Empire, 1938; Honorary M.A., Victoria University, Manchester, 1940; Dame Commander, Order of the British Empire, 1979. **Died:** 27 September 1979.

Films as Actress:

1931   *Sally in Our Alley* (Elvey) (as Sally Winch)
1932   *Looking on the Bright Side* (Dean and Cutts) (as Gracie)
1933   *This Week of Grace* (Elvey) (as Grace Milroy)
1934   *Love, Life, and Laughter* (Elvey) (as Nellie Gwynn); *Sing as We Go* (Dean) (as Gracie Platt)
1935   *Look Up and Laugh* (Dean) (as Grace Pearson)
1936   *Queen of Hearts* (Banks) (as Grace Perkins)
1937   *The Show Goes On* (Dean) (as Sally Lee)
1938   *We're Going to Be Rich* (Banks) (as Kit Dobson); *Keep Smiling* (*Smiling Along*) (Banks) (as Gracie Gray)
1939   *Shipyard Sally* (Banks) (as Sally Fitzgerald)
1943   *Stage Door Canteen* (Borzage); *Holy Matrimony* (Stahl) (as Alice Challice)
1945   *Molly and Me* (Seiler) (as Molly Barry); *Paris Underground* (*Madame Pimpernel*) (Ratoff) (as Emmeline Quayle)

Publications

By FIELDS: book—

Sing as We Go, London, 1960.

By FIELDS: articles—

Interviews in *Film Weekly* (London), 18 April 1931 and 13 October 1933. *Picturegoer* (London), 4 August 1934.

On FIELDS: books—

Our Gracie (Rochdale Arts and Entertainment Services), Rochdale, England, 1978.
Moules, Joan, *Our Gracie: The Life of Dame Gracie Fields*, London, 1983.
Richards, Jeffrey, *The Age of the Dream Palace: Cinema and Society 1930-1939*, London, 1984.
Hudson, Peter, *Gracie Fields: Her Life in Pictures*, London, 1989.

On FIELDS: articles—

Loder, John, in *Film Weekly* (London), 20 April 1934.
Macfadyen, Joanna, "Gracie's Artistry Reflects Psychology of the Masses," in *World Film News*, June 1936.
Banks, Monty, in *Film Weekly* (London), 2 May 1936.
Picturegoer (London), 24 April 1937.
Newnham, John, in *Film Weekly* (London), 8 May 1937.
Time (New York), 28 February 1938 and 19 August 1940.
Film Weekly (London), 7 January 1939.

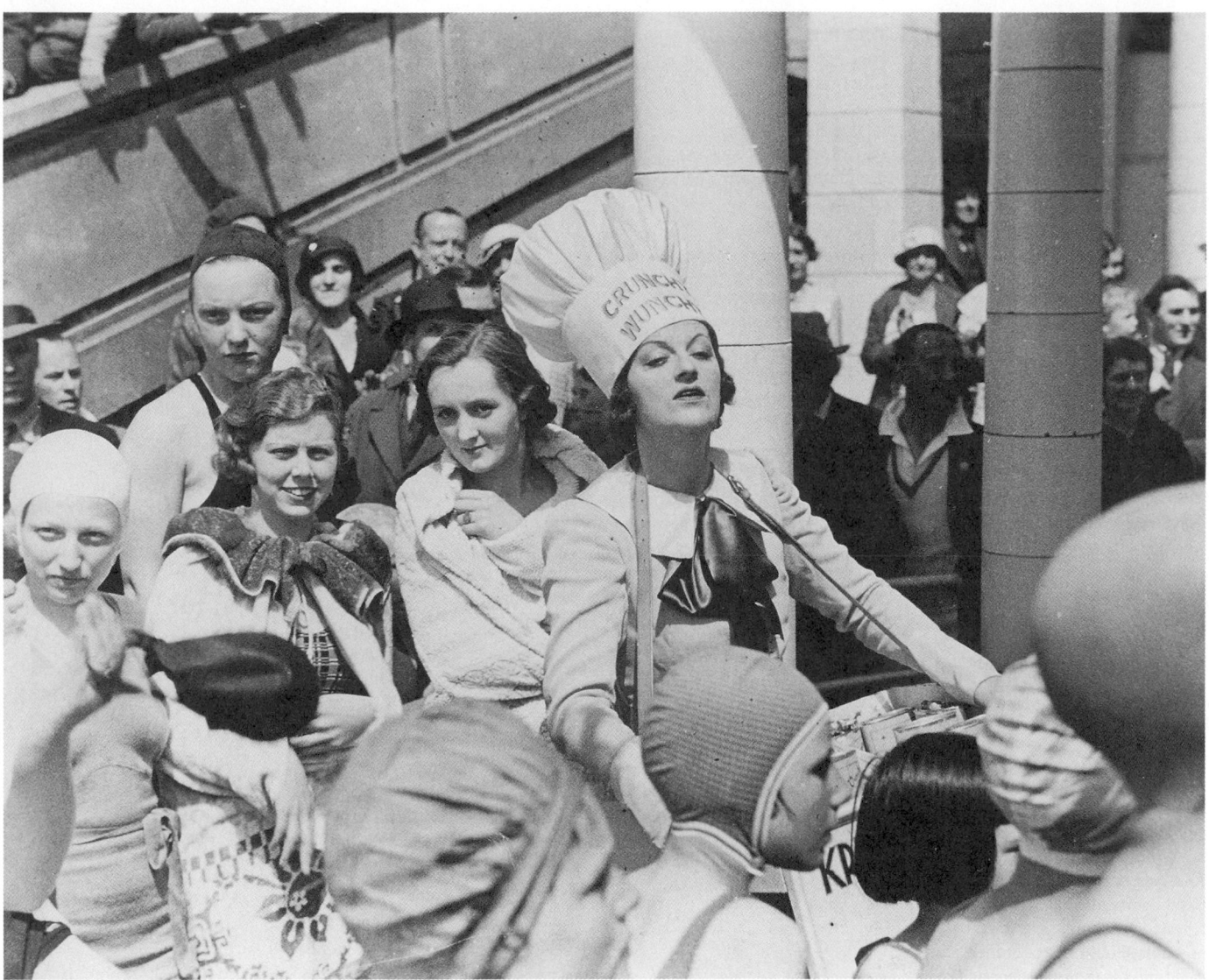

Gracie Fields in *Sing as We Go*

"Gracie in America," in *Picturegoer* (London), 1 March 1941.

"Gracie—Forty-Eight Years Young," in *Picturegoer* (London), 5 January 1946.

Richards, Jeffrey, "Gracie Fields: 'The Lancashire Britannia'," in two parts, in *Focus on Film* (London), August and December 1979.

*   *   *

As with a number of British stars of the period, Gracie Fields's successful film career was closely tied to her stage performances and recording career. Her status as a music hall performer was well established before entering the film industry and the tireless touring of manufacturing towns and seaside resorts continued throughout her British film career. Quoted in the popular film magazine *Picturegoer* in 1934, Grace declared "I'd like to step off the screen and say 'Hullo!' in every town and city in England where the people have been kind to me. And that's nearly everywhere." This expressed desire to reach out to everyone in the land is an important aspect of the Gracie Fields persona. The establishment of her widespread and universal appeal is the key to understanding the enormity of Gracie Fields's success.

During the 1930s Gracie Fields became the number one box office star in Britain. Her distinctive brand of brash Northern comedy, cheerful self-reliance and never-say-die spirit combined with pathos and romance in spirited tales in which "Our Gracie" would overcome adversity in her role as heroine of the people. Her remarkable singing voice was also a central feature of her performances and a key aspect of the Gracie phenomenon.

The basis for Gracie Fields's appeal was a combination of her "ordinariness" (undisguised origins and lack of glamour) and her "extraordinariness" (her talent as a singer and comic). While the early films express this in terms of class, her character later developed to serve a more universal role as symbol of the nation. The idea that Grace was just being herself in the films added to the intensity of this symbolic role. Notions of honesty, straightforwardness and reliability imbue the screen persona and were confirmed by offscreen appearances.

In the early 1930s Gracie Fields is often cast as a working class girl in films that show a sharp awareness of class differences. The later films tend to be far more patriotic, associating her qualities with nation rather than class. Her rise to the status of a national heroine, minimizing class difference and promoting a common consciousness, is charted in some detail by Jeffrey Richards in two articles for *Focus on Film* in which he quotes from a *Times* review of *Look Up and Laugh* (1935) to indicate the nature of this transformation.

> Mr. Basil Dean has skillfully designed the film . . . to bring out the most interesting aspects of Miss Gracie Fields' character, her gusto and good temper, her candid sentimentality, her readiness to defend herself and her friends against all pomp and privilege, and, in fact, all those qualities which make her so excellent a representative of the people. For it is as a representative of the people that she now appears . . . the sentiment is richly plebeian; there is a strong flavour of liberty, of equality, and, what is even more remarkable, of fraternity. But it is emphatically an indigenous sense of freedom that we are invited to admire; these true born English men of the market are almost absurdly native, as indeed, is the whole film.

Writing in retrospect of *Sing as We Go* (released one year before *Look Up and Laugh*), David Robinson commented in the *Financial Times* in 1964,

> Admittedly, this fairy tale of factory life is no documentary about the depression period; but the film at least acknowledges unemployment, and back-to-back housing, and its location shooting in Blackpool has a gusto which evokes more of a Northern working class life than many a GPO documentary.

While it might not be possible to claim *Sing as We Go* as a radical film on the basis of its narrative, Robinson does touch upon an important aspect of the film's relationship to class difference. These ambiguities and pleasures are less apparent in later films where Gracie is more often cast as petite bourgeoisie—*Look Up And Laugh*, for example, is the first time she is not a working class girl.

While the development of Fields's film career might be seen as a subversion of a powerful working class symbol to the service of the Establishment, the extent of her popularity and the mere fact that a talented working class woman from Rochdale could achieve such a position should not be underestimated.

At the close of the decade the situation suddenly changed. Having overcome serious illness, Gracie Fields left for Canada in 1939 with her husband, Italian-born director Monty Banks, to avoid his internment at the outbreak of war. The British public in many ways felt betrayed by this departure, seeing it as a desertion of her country at a time of danger, and her popularity was seriously undermined. Consequently she failed to become the symbol of the nation for the war years and never regained the level of popularity achieved during the 1930s.

—Margaret O'Connor

FIELDS, W. C.

Nationality: American. **Born:** William Claude Dukenfield in Philadelphia, 10 February 1879 or 29 January 1880. **Family:** Married Harriet "Hattie" Hughes, 1900. **Career:** 1893—hired as juggler at Pennsylvania amusement park, then worked as "comic juggler" and "silent humorist" in vaudeville; 1901—toured Europe for first time; top billed at Folies Bergère, Paris, and in London, command performance at Buckingham Palace; 1905—first appearance in Broadway play, *The Ham Tree*; 1906-24—worked consistently on Broadway and in various revues, including, from 1915, Ziegfeld Follies; 1914—on Broadway in Irving Berlin's *Watch Your Step*; 1915—first film, *Pool Sharks*, based on vaudeville act; 1916—began to introduce dialogue into act; 1923—created role of Eustace McGargle in successful Broadway show *Poppy*; 1925—in *Sally of the Sawdust*, film version of *Poppy*, directed by D. W. Griffith; 1930—first sound film, two-reeler *The Golf Specialist*; 1932-33—made series of shorts for Mack Sennett; 1935—only straight dramatic role, Mr. Micawber in *David Copperfield*; from 1937—on radio, often with ventriloquist Edgar Bergen. **Died:** In Pasadena, California, 25 December 1946.

Films as Actor:

1915 *Pool Sharks* (Middleton); *His Lordship's Dilemma* (Haddock—short)

1924 *Janice Meredith* (*The Beautiful Rebel*) (E. Mason Hopper) (as British sergeant)

1925 *Sally of the Sawdust* (D. W. Griffith) (as Prof. Eustace McGargle); *That Royle Girl* (D. W. Griffith) (as father)

1926 *It's the Old Army Game* (A. Edward Sutherland) (as Elmer Prettywillie); *So's Your Old Man* (La Cava) (as Samuel Bisbee)

1927 *The Potters* (Newmeyer) (as Pa Potter); *Running Wild* (La Cava) (as Elmer Finch); *Two Flaming Youths* (*The Side Show*) (Waters) (as Gabby Gilfoil)

1928 *Tillie's Punctured Romance* (*Marie's Millions*) (A. Edward Sutherland) (as Ringmaster); *Fools for Luck* (Reisner) (as Richard Whitehead)

1930 *The Golf Specialist* (Brice—short) (+ story, uncredited)

1931 *Her Majesty Love* (Dieterle) (as Lia's father)

1932 *Million Dollar Legs* (Cline) (as the President of Klopstokia); *If I Had a Million* (Taurog or Humberstone) (as Rollo); *The Dentist* (Pearce—short) (title role, + story, uncredited)

1933 *The Fatal Glass of Beer* (Bruckman—short) (as Mr. Snavely, + story, uncredited); *The Pharmacist* (Ripley—short) (+ story); *International House* (A. Edward Sutherland) (as Prof. Quail); *The Barber Shop* (Ripley—short) (+ story); *Hip Action* (Marshall—no. 3 of series *How to Break Ninety*); *Tillie and Gus* (Francis Martin) (as Augustus Q. Winterbottom); *Alice in Wonderland* (McLeod) (as Humpty Dumpty)

1934 *Six of a Kind* (McCarey) (as Sheriff "Honest John" Hoxley); *You're Telling Me!* (Kenton) (as Sam Bisbee); *The Old-Fashioned Way* (Beaudine) (as the Great McGonigle, + story); *Mrs. Wiggs of the Cabbage Patch* (Taurog) (as Mr. C. Ensworth Stubbins); *It's a Gift* (McLeod) (as Harold Bissonette, + story as "Charles Bogle")

1935 *David Copperfield* (Cukor) (as Mr. Micawber); *Mississippi* (A. Edward Sutherland) (as Commodore Jackson); *The Man on the Flying Trapeze* (*The Memory Expert*) (Bruckman) (as Ambrose Wolfinger, + co-story as "Charles Bogle")

1936 *Poppy* (A. Edward Sutherland) (as Prof. Eustace McGargle)

1938 *The Big Broadcast of 1938* (Leisen) (as T. Frothingill/S. B. Bellows)

1939 *You Can't Cheat an Honest Man* (George Marshall; Fields sequences directed by Cline, uncredited) (as Larson E. Whipsnade, + story as "Charles Bogle")

1940 *My Little Chickadee* (Cline) (as Cuthbert J. Twillie, + co-story); *The Bank Dick* (*The Bank Detective*) (Cline) (as Egbert Souse, + story as "Mahatma Kane Jeeves")

1941 *Never Give a Sucker an Even Break* (*What a Man*) (Cline) (as the Great Man, + story as "Otis Criblecoblis")

1943 *Show Business at War* (*March of Time* series) (De Rochemont)

1944 *Follow the Boys* (A. Edward Sutherland) (as guest); *Song of the Open Road* (Simon) (as himself); *Sensations of 1945* (*Sensations*) (Andrew L. Stone) (as guest)

1949 "The Dentist" ep. of *Down Memory Lane* (Karlson—compilation)

W. C. Fields

Publications

By FIELDS: books—

Drat! Being the Encapsulated View of Life by W. C. Fields in His Own Words, edited by Richard J. Anobile, New York, 1969.
Fields for President, introduction and commentary by Michael Taylor, New York, 1971.
W. C. Fields by Himself: His Intended Autobiography, commentary by Ronald Fields, Englewood Cliffs, New Jersey, 1973.

On FIELDS: books—

Taylor, Robert Lewis, *W. C. Fields: His Follies and Fortunes*, New York, 1949.
Everson, William K., *The Art of W. C. Fields*, Indianapolis, 1967.
Deschner, Donald, *The Films of W. C. Fields*, New York, 1969.
Monti, Carlotta, with Cy Rice, *W. C. Fields and Me*, Englewood Cliffs, New Jersey, 1971.
W. C. Fields in Never Give a Sucker an Even Break *and* Tillie and Gus (scripts), London, 1973.
Parish, James Robert, and William T. Leonard, *The Funsters*, New Rochelle, New York, 1979.
Fields, Ronald J., *W. C. Fields: A Life on Film*, New York, 1984.
Gehring, Wes D., *W. C. Fields: A Bio-Bibliography*, Westport, Connecticut, 1984.

Rocks, David T., *W. C. Fields—An Annotated Guide*, Jefferson, North Carolina, 1993.
Gehring, Wes D., *Groucho and W. C. Fields: Huckster Comedians*, Jackson, Mississippi, 1994.

On FIELDS: articles—

Johnston, Alva, "W. C. Fields," in *New Yorker*, 2-16 February 1935.
Obituary in *New York Times*, 26 December 1946.
Tynan, Kenneth, "Toby Jug and Bottle," in *Sight and Sound* (London), February 1951.
Robinson, David, "Dukinfield Meets McGargle," in *Sight and Sound* (London), Summer 1967.
McVay, D., "Elysian Fields," in *Film* (London), Winter 1967.
Gilliat, Penelope, "W. C. Fields," in *The Movie Star*, edited by Elisabeth Weis, New York, 1981.
Millar, Gavin, "No Children or Dogs," in *Listener* (London), 18 August 1983; see also 29 September 1983.
Gehring, Wes D., "W. C. Fields: The Copyrighted Sketches," in *Journal of Popular Film and Television* (Washington, D.C.), Summer 1986.
Freeman, Everett, "Close Encounters with W. C. Fields," in *Saturday Evening Post*, December 1987.
Denby, David, "Diary of a Mean Man," in *Premiere* (New York), September 1989.
Hamburger, Philip, "On the Whole," in *New Yorker*, 8 March 1993.

Mazzocco, Robert, "Milking an Elk," in *New York Review of Books*, 30 November 1995.

*   *   *

A successful vaudeville juggler, W. C. Fields underwent a slow metamorphosis to become one of the outstanding comedians of the sound film. He seems a reincarnation of an ancient comic type: there is something of the braggart soldier from Roman comedy, the strutting capitano of the commedia dell'arte, or Shakespeare's Falstaff. He is also the bungling husband, harassed by his wife—a comic type common to the classical Greek stage, the medieval tale, Restoration and 18th-century comedy, and modern times.

Fields's introduction to the sound film proved to be a humble one. He had had prominent roles in 11 mediocre silent screen comedies, and a 20-minute two-reeler made in 1930, *The Golf Specialist*, merely lifted material from one of his vaudeville routines, a sketch about giving golf lessons to a beautiful girl. The full potentiality of Fields's talent was not realized until he made four shorts for Mack Sennett in 1932 and 1933. He scripted them himself, and at least one film, *The Barber Shop*, containing a catalog of Fieldsian humor, paved the way for better things.

Fields began to gain more control of his material in the mid-1930s with such works as *The Old-Fashioned Way*, *It's a Gift*, and *The Man on the Flying Trapeze*. These last two works featured the comedian as a dominated husband struggling against great odds to achieve peace of mind and modest success in a humble business venture. *The Old-Fashioned Way*, on the other hand, was a portrait of the con man trying his best not to give the sucker an even break. The pompous charlatan who quickly retreated when exposed is sometimes considered to be the most amusing character the comedian created, and is subsequently seen in *Poppy* (a remake of his 1925 silent film, *Sally of the Sawdust*), *You Can't Cheat an Honest Man*, and *My Little Chickadee*. The bungling, harassed husband would continue to appear in such films as *The Bank Dick*.

The genius of Fields lies in his ability to effectively combine verbal and visual traits in his comic character. His three masterpieces, *It's a Gift*, *The Bank Dick*, and *The Man on the Flying Trapeze* display this fusion at its best. Along with this he evolved a fully developed comic portrait of a mature man, and this creation proved to be unique not only for the golden age of sound comedy in the 1930s, but also for the great preceding decade of silent comedy. Most prominent in both these periods was the young man with traits of dumbness and naivety. Fields was the only actor to create comic middle-aged characters of enduring greatness.

Critics have long considered Fields the comic king of the 1930s because of his uniqueness, innovation, and many-faceted character. At the core of his personality there is the warmth and charm of a Falstaff even though he snarls and mutters insults. Even in weak films the power of his acting comes through. As with Chaplin, we have begun to associate the man with the character, and when that happens, the artist's work becomes a permanent creation.

—Donald McCaffrey

FIENNES, Ralph

Nationality: British. **Born:** Suffolk, 22 December 1962; brother of the director Martha Fiennes. **Family:** Married the actress Alex Kingston (separated 1995). **Education:** Attended Bishop Woodsworth Boys' School; Chelsea College of Art & Design; was graduated from the Royal Academy of Dramatic Art, London. **Career:** 1987—joined National Theatre, London; 1989—joined Royal Shakespeare Company, became leading actor there; 1991—in TV mini-series *Prime Suspect*; 1993—earned international acclaim for role in *Schindler's List*; 1995—American stage debut in *Hamlet*. **Awards:** New York Film Critics Circle and Golden Globe Awards, Best Supporting Actor, for *Schindler's List*, 1993; Tony Award, Best Actor, for *Hamlet*, 1995. **Agent:** Bryan Lourd, Creative Artists Agency, 9830 Wilshire Boulevard, Beverly Hills, CA 90212, U.S.A.

Films as Actor:

1991   *A Dangerous Man: Lawrence after Arabia* (Menaul—for TV) (as T. E. Lawrence)
1992   *Wuthering Heights* (Kosminsky—for TV) (as Heathcliff)
1993   **Schindler's List** (Spielberg) (as Amon Goeth); *The Baby of Macon* (Greenaway) (as the Bishop's son); *The Cormorant* (Markham—for TV) (as John Talbot)
1994   *Quiz Show* (Redford) (as Charles Van Doren)
1995   *Strange Days* (Bigelow) (as Lenny Nero)
1996   *The English Patient* (Minghella) (title role); *Eugene Onegin* (Martha Fiennes)

Publications

By FIENNES: articles—

"Self-Made Monster: An Actor's Creation," interview with John Darnton, in *New York Times*, 14 February 1994.
"A Fiennes Madness," interview with Leslie Bennetts, in *Vanity Fair* (New York), November 1995.

On FIENNES: articles—

Corliss, Richard, "The Man behind the Monster," in *Time* (New York), 21 February 1994.
Millea, Holly, "Quiz Kid," in *Premiere* (New York), September 1994.
Lane, Anthony, "The Play's the Thing," in *New Yorker*, 17 April 1995.
Koestenbaum, W., "The New Prince of Broadway," in *Harper's Bazaar* (New York), May 1995.

*   *   *

In 1993, Ralph Fiennes burst upon the international film scene with his riveting—and almost picture-stealing—performance as SS Commandant Amon Goeth in Steven Spielberg's Holocaust drama, *Schindler's List*. Certainly, Goeth was not the first despicably evil Nazi ever depicted on screen—just as *Schindler's List* was not the first Hollywood film to portray the heroic actions of individuals caught up in the Nazi scourge.

But Fiennes made Goeth far more than the stereotypical stock Nazi villain found in scores of World War II films. His Goeth is a fascinatingly complex personality, a man of subtle, intrinsic evil. At one point in the story, as he is being driven through the Krakow Jewish ghetto, Goeth complains that he is freezing. He has no comment on the humanity around him. It is as if the Jews are non-human beings, incapable of feeling hunger or pain (let alone of being inconvenienced by inclement weather). In his eyes, they already are a mass of cadavers. As the *Variety* critic so aptly observed, "The extraordinary Fiennes creates an indelible character in Goeth. With paunch hanging out and eyes filled with disgust both for his victims and himself, he's like a minor-league Roman emperor gone sour with excess, a man in whom too much power and debauchery have crushed anything that might once have been good."

Ralph Fiennes in *Schindler's List*

While unfamiliar to movie audiences at the release of *Schindler's List*, Fiennes was a known quantity in the acting world. For several years, he had been impressing London audiences in a variety of roles at the National Theatre and with the Royal Shakespeare Company. His performance as T. E. Lawrence in the television movie *A Dangerous Man: Lawrence after Arabia* led to Spielberg's casting him in *Schindler's List*.

In order to display his versatility as an actor and avoid typecasting as clones of Goeth, Fiennes chose for his follow-up screen role an altogether different character. In Robert Redford's *Quiz Show*, he is Charles Van Doren, clean-cut all-American prince and offspring of a wealthy, renowned intellectual family, who compromises his ideals by cheating when he appears on the television quiz show *Twenty-One*. If *Schindler's List* was overly hyped as a Holocaust film, *Quiz Show*, too, was highly overrated. The film is, in essence, a far-too obvious exercise in self-righteousness.

But Fiennes's performance transcends the film's faults. His Charles Van Doren is an entirely believable character, as contemplative and compromised as Amon Goeth is psychotic and compromised. If Goeth is the victimizer of others, Van Doren is victimized by his own ingenuousness.

For his third screen role, Fiennes selected a part completely different from Goeth and Van Doren. Kathryn Bigelow's *Strange Days* is an in-your-face combination sci-fi fantasy/mystery/police drama, set in the final days of the year 1999. Fiennes plays Lenny Nero, ex-Los Angeles vice cop who is the dealer of a new and altogether different kind of illegal drug: high-tech, state-of-the-art "virtual reality" tapes, on which are recorded real-life events. Those who "wire-trip" get to re-experience those events. In essence, Lenny—who is described as "the Santa Claus of the subconscious"—peddles pieces of other peoples' lives, with his customers "using the wire" and "getting off on tape."

Lenny also is a schemer who in his own way is strung out, as he lives from one score to the next. The core of the story focuses on what happens when he comes into possession of tapes on which are recorded horrible events, including the rape and murder of a prostitute and the murder of a rap artist who is one of the most powerful and controversial black men in America. Fiennes's performance as Lenny is every bit as impressive as his work in *Schindler's List* and *Quiz Show*. It is appropriately edgy, with the actor vividly expressing his character's pain, confusion, and yearning.

Despite his celluloid success, Fiennes remains as much a stage actor as a budding movie star. In 1995, he brought his *Hamlet* from London to Broadway, earning respectful (and in some cases, superlative) reviews. Wrote John Lahr, "Fiennes radiates an elegance of spirit that rivets the audience with its sense of unspoken mystery. His performance is a stylish event." Added Vincent Canby, "Mr. Fiennes . . . is in command at the Belasco from beginning to end. He's a charismatic stage actor. He has a fine strong voice (and complete control of it) that never becomes monotonously distinctive."

On screen, Fiennes has gone from playing characters out of the recent past (in *Schindler's List* and *Quiz Show*) to characters in the near future (in *Strange Days*). One wonders how he would do in a more conventional contemporary role.

—Rob Edelman

FINCH, Peter

Nationality: British. **Born:** Peter Ingle-Finch in Kensington, London, England, 28 September 1916. **Education:** Attended French primary schools until age ten; North Sydney Inter High School, Australia. **Military Service:** Australian First Army antiaircraft battalion, organized troop entertainments during World War II. **Family:** Married 1) the dancer Tamara Tchinarova, 1943 (divorced 1958), daughter: Anita; 2) the actress Yolande Turner, 1959 (divorced 1966), children: Samantha and Charles; also daughter Diana by Eletha Barrett. **Career:** After leaving high school, reporter-trainee on Sydney *Sun* newspaper, and traveled around Australia as hobo; 1935—toured New South Wales and Queensland in *While Parents Sleep*; began working in Australian radio; 1945—formed stage company, Mercury Players, named after Orson Welles's Mercury Theater; 1948—under personal contract by Olivier; 1949—London debut; featured role in first British film, *Train of Events*; early 1950s—active on London stage, including Old Vic: roles include Iago to Orson Welles's Othello in 1951 production of *Othello*; 1954—first starring film role, opposite Elizabeth Taylor, in *Elephant Walk*; 1955—contract with J. Arthur Rank Organisation; 1961—with wife Yolande Turner, wrote, produced, and directed low-budget short *The Day*. **Awards:** Best British Actor, British Academy, for *A Town Like Alice*, 1956; Best British Actor, British Academy, for *The Trials of Oscar Wilde*, 1960; Best Actor, Berlin Festival, and Best Actor, British Academy, for *No Love for Johnnie*, 1961; Best Actor, British Academy, for *Sunday, Bloody Sunday*, 1971; Best Actor Academy Award, and Best Actor, British Academy, for

Network, 1976. **Died:** Of heart attack, in Beverly Hills, California, 14 January 1977.

Films as Actor:

1935   *Magic Shoes* (Fleming—unreleased)
1938   *Dad and Dave Come to Town* (*The Rudd Family Goes to Town*) (Hall) (as Bill Ryan)
1939   *Mr. Chedworth Steps Out* (Hall); *Ants in His Pants* (Freshman)
1941   *The Power and the Glory* (Monkman)
1944   *The Rats of Tobruk* (*The Fighting Rats of Tobruk*) (Chauvel) (as Peter Linton); *South West Pacific* (Hall—Finch may appear only in footage taken from *The Rats of Tobruk*); *Jungle Patrol* (Gurr—short) (as narrator)
1945   *Red Sky at Morning* (*Escape at Dawn*) (Arthur) (as Michael)
1946   *A Son Is Born* (Porter) (as Paul Graham); *Indonesia Calling* (Ivens—short) (as narrator); *Native Earth* (Heyer—short) (as narrator)
1949   *Eureka Stockade* (*Massacre Hill*) (Watt) (as John Humffray); "The Actor" ep. of *Train of Events* (Dearden) (as Philip Mason); *Primitive Peoples: Australian Aborigines* (Heath—in three parts) (as narrator, + asst d)
1950   *The Wooden Horse* (Jack Lee) (as the Australian); *The Miniver Story* (Potter) (as Polish officer)
1952   *The Story of Robin Hood and His Merrie Men* (Annakin) (as Sheriff of Nottingham)
1953   *The Story of Gilbert and Sullivan* (*Gilbert and Sullivan; The Great Gilbert and Sullivan*) (Gilliat) (as Rupert D'Oyly Carte); *The Heart of the Matter* (O'Ferrall) (as Father Rank)
1954   *Elephant Walk* (Dieterle) (as John Wiley); *Father Brown* (*The Detective*) (Hamer) (as Flambeau); *Make Me an Offer!* (Frankel) (as Charlie)
1955   *The Dark Avenger* (*The Warriors*) (Levin) (as Count De Ville); *Passage Home* (Baker) (as Captain "Lucky" Ryland); *Josephine and Men* (Boulting, Harvey, and Balchin) (as David Hewer); *Simon and Laura* (Box) (as Simon Foster); *The Queen in Australia* (Hawes—short) (as narrator); *Melbourne—Olympic City* (pr: Hawes) (as narrator)
1956   *A Town Like Alice* (*Rape of Malaya*) (Jack Lee) (as Joe Harman); *The Battle of the River Plate* (*Pursuit of the Graf Spee*) (Powell and Pressburger) (as Captain Langsdorff); *The Royal Tour of New South Wales* (short) (as narrator)
1957   *The Shiralee* (Norman) (as Jim Macauley); *Robbery under Arms* (Jack Lee) (as Captain Starlight); *Windom's Way* (Neame) (as Alec Windom)
1959   *The Nun's Story* (Zinnemann) (as Dr. Fortunati); *Operation Amsterdam* (McCarthy) (as Jan Smit); *A Far Cry* (Peet) (as narrator)
1960   *Kidnapped* (Stevenson) (as Alan Breck Stewart); *The Sins of Rachel Cade* (*Rachel Cade*) (Gordon Douglas) (as Colonel Henri Derode); *The Trials of Oscar Wilde* (*The Man with the Green Carnation; The Green Carnation*) (Hughes) (title role)
1961   *No Love for Johnnie* (Thomas) (as Johnnie Byrne)
1962   *I Thank a Fool* (Robert Stevens) (as Stephen Dane)
1963   *Girl with Green Eyes* (Desmond Davis) (as Eugene Gaillard); *In the Cool of the Day* (Robert Stevens) (as Murray Logan)
1964   *First Men in the Moon* (Juran) (as guest); *The Pumpkin Eater* (Clayton) (as Jake Armitage)
1965   *Judith* (Daniel Mann) (as Aaron Stein); *The Flight of the Phoenix* (Aldrich) (as Captain Harris)
1966   *10:30 P.M. Summer* (Dassin) (as Paul)
1967   *Far from the Madding Crowd* (Schlesinger) (as William Boldwood)

Peter Finch (left) with Glenda Jackson and Murray Head in *Sunday, Bloody Sunday*

1968   *The Legend of Lylah Clare* (Aldrich) (as Lewis Zarkan)
1969   *La tenda rossa* (*Krasnaya palatka*; *The Red Tent*) (Kalatozov) (as General Umberto Nobile)
1971   ***Sunday, Bloody Sunday*** (Schlesinger) (as Dr. Daniel Hirsch)
1972   *Something to Hide* (*Shattered*) (Reid) (as Harry Field)
1973   *Lost Horizon* (Jarrott) (as Richard Conway); *A Bequest to the Nation* (*The Nelson Affair*) (James Cellan Jones) (as Lord Horatio Nelson); *England Made Me* (Duffell) (as Erich Krogh)
1974   *The Abdication* (Harvey) (as Cardinal Azzolino)
1976   *Network* (Lumet) (as Howard Beale)
1977   *Raid on Entebbe* (Kirshner—for TV) (as Yitzhak Rabin)
1979   *A Look at Liv* (Kaplan—doc) (as himself)

Film as Director:

1961   *Antonito* (*The Day*) (short) (+ pr, sc)

Publications

By FINCH: articles—

"How I Learnt to Laugh at Myself," in *Films and Filming* (London), September 1958.

"Peter, Peter, Pumpkin Eater," in *Films and Filming* (London), June 1964.
"The Mind's Eye," in *Films and Filming* (London), August 1970.

On FINCH: books—

Faulkner, Trader, *Peter Finch: A Biography*, London, 1979.
Dundy, Elaine, *Finch, Bloody Finch: A Life of Peter Finch*, New York, 1980.
Finch, Yolanda, *Finchy*, New York, 1981.

On FINCH: articles—

Nemy, Enid, in *The New York Times*, 22 September 1968.
Current Biography 1972, New York, 1972.
Obituary in *New York Times*, 15 January 1977.
"Peter Finch," in *Cinéma* (Paris), March 1977.
Ecran (Paris), April 1978.
Norman, Barry, in *Radio Times* (London), 26 July 1980.

*   *   *

Dead at 61 of a heart attack induced by a life of drink, sex, and hard living, Peter Finch belongs on the roster of stars who were expert at projecting insecurity on screen. A confident Finch is indeed a contradiction: indecision, sexual confusion, the drag of ambition or the demands of good manners undermined his most memorable screen characters. The high, sloping brow would wrinkle and the sensitive eyes would narrow as he contemplated yet another painful choice in which no one would suffer more than himself.

The product of a broken Australian/English marriage, Finch initially was thrown into the desert of the prewar Australian film industry. He alternated featured film roles for Cinesound as scapegrace sons with stage work and radio acting that exploited his distinctive and resonant voice. The independent director Noel Monkman wrote *The Power and the Glory* for the man he called "the finest film actor in Australia," but the story—about a Nazi saboteur down under—was too clichéd to win overseas interest.

It was Finch's stage work that attracted the attention of Laurence Olivier and Vivien Leigh during their 1948 Australian tour, and Olivier subsequently put him under personal contract. This was the beginning, Olivier was to claim, of the end of his marriage to Leigh, with whom Finch had one of his many calamitous affairs, culminating in her nervous breakdown while on Sri Lankan location with Finch for *Elephant Walk*. The film, however, earned Finch star status. He was an effective aristocratic thief pursued by Alec Guinness's *Father Brown*, a percipient antique dealer in *Make Me an Offer!*, and the captain of the German battleship *Graf Spee* who elects to scuttle the boat in Michael Powell's *The Battle of the River Plate*. British companies' increased use of Australia as an exotic location drew Finch back for *Robbery under Arms*, *A Town Like Alice*, and *The Shiralee*. His respective roles as a period bandit, an Australian soldier tortured by the Japanese for helping refugee Englishwomen, and an itinerant on the Australian roads forced to take along his young daughter like a "shiralee," or blanket roll, helped Finch to define his screen persona.

It was evident his future lay with the international roles such as that in the Powell film rather than with the then-limping Australian industry. *The Trials of Oscar Wilde* is emblematic of this new stage of his career, with Finch building a vivid portrait of the homosexual playwright destroyed by hubris. His portrayal of a politician in *No Love for Johnnie*, choosing ambition over love, and films such as *The Pumpkin Eater* and *Girl with Green Eyes*, further established him with American studios as a compelling leading man. During this period, he was dividing his time between Europe and the United States, appearing opposite Audrey Hepburn in *The Nun's Story* as an idealistic doctor, with Sophia Loren in the Israeli drama *Judith*, and for Robert Aldrich in the embarrassing flop *The Legend of Lylah Clare* as a film director reminiscent of Josef von Sternberg. Finch also tackled period dramas, with varying success. As the cuckolded farmer in Thomas Hardy's *Far from the Madding Crowd*, he was superbly distraught, the model of wounded British rectitude. He played opposite Liv Ullmann in *The Abdication*, a gloomy account of the Queen Christina story, and was Nelson to Glenda Jackson's Emma Hamilton in *A Bequest to the Nation*.

Sunday, Bloody Sunday and especially *Network* are the two films for which Finch is best-remembered. In the first, he is the model of world-weariness, with his Jewish homosexual doctor in love with a feckless bisexual boy a brilliantly credible portrait of well-mannered urban desperation. In the second, he is the model of outrageous anger. In *Network*, Paddy Chayefsky's caustic satire of television, Finch deservedly won a posthumous Best Actor Oscar for his performance as Howard Beale, the frenzied television anchorman turned "mad prophet of the airwaves." His classic pronunciation—"I'm mad as hell, and I'm not going to take it anymore"—has become a symbolic rallying cry of those exasperated by the inanity of television programming (which serves to mirror the superficiality of contemporary materialist society).

—John Baxter, updated by Rob Edelman

FINNEY, Albert

Nationality: British. **Born:** Salford, Lancashire, England, 9 May 1936. **Education:** Attended Salford Grammar School; Royal Academy of Dramatic Art, London, graduated 1955. **Family:** Married 1) the actress Jane Wenham, 1957 (divorced 1961), son: Simon; 2) the actress Anouk Aimée, 1970 (divorced 1978). **Career:** 1955—joined Birmingham Repertory Theatre: stage debut as Decius Brutus in *Julius Caesar*, 1956; 1958—London debut in *The Party*; 1959—season with Stratford Shakespeare company; 1960—film debut in *The Entertainer*; 1963—opens on Broadway in *Luther*; 1965—joined National Theatre Company; formed stage and television production company Memorial Enterprises Ltd. with Michael Medwin; 1967—directed first film, *Charlie Bubbles*; 1972-75—associate artistic director, Royal Court Theatre; 1976—played Hamlet in opening production of Lyttelton Theatre; 1990—in TV mini-series *The Green Man*. **Awards:** Most Promising Newcomer, British Academy, for *Saturday Night and Sunday Morning*, 1960; Best Actor, New York Film Critics, and Best Actor, Venice Festival, for *Tom Jones*, 1963; Acting Award, UK Film Critics' Circle, for *Under the Volcano*, 1984. **Agent:** International Creative Management, 388-396 Oxford Street, London W1N 9HE, England.

Films as Actor:

1960   *The Entertainer* (Richardson) (as Mick Rice); ***Saturday Night and Sunday Morning*** (Reisz) (as Arthur Seaton)
1963   ***Tom Jones*** (Richardson) (title role); *The Victors* (Foreman) (as Russian soldier)
1964   *Night Must Fall* (Reisz) (as Danny, + co-pr)
1966   *Two for the Road* (Donen) (as Mark Wallace)
1970   *The Picasso Summer* (Dallin—unreleased); *Scrooge* (Neame) (title role)
1971   *Gumshoe* (Frears) (as Eddie Ginley)
1972   *Alpha Beta* (Page—for TV)
1974   *Murder on the Orient Express* (Lumet) (as Hercule Poirot)
1975   *The Adventure of Sherlock Holmes' Smarter Brother* (Gene Wilder) (as guest)
1977   *The Duellists* (Ridley Scott) (as Fouche)
1980   *Loophole* (Quested) (as Mike Daniels)
1981   *Wolfen* (Wadleigh) (as N. York); *Looker* (Crichton) (as Dr. Larry Rogers)
1982   *Shoot the Moon* (Parker) (as George); *Annie* (Huston) (as Daddy Warbucks)
1983   *The Dresser* (Yates) (as Sir)
1984   *Under the Volcano* (Huston) (as Geoffrey Firmin); *Pope John Paul II* (Wise—for TV) (title role)
1986   *Looker* (Crichton) (Dr. Larry Roberts)
1987   *Orphans* (Pakula) (as Harold)
1989   *The Endless Game* (Forbes—for TV) (as Alec Hillsden)
1990   *Miller's Crossing* (Coen) (as Leo); *The Image* (Werner—for TV) (as Jason Cromwell)
1991   *The Green Man* (Moshinsky—for TV) (as Maurice Allington)
1992   *The Playboys* (MacKinnon) (as Constable Hegarty)
1993   *Rich in Love* (Beresford) (as Warren Odom)
1994   *The Browning Version* (Figgis) (as Andrew Crocker-Harris); *A Man of No Importance* (Krishnamma) (as Alfie Byrne)
1995   *The Run of the Country* (Yates) (as Father)

Films as Director:

1967   *Charlie Bubbles* (+ title role)
1984   *The Biko Inquest* (co-d with Graham Evans—for TV, + ro as Kentridge)

Albert Finney in *Saturday Night and Sunday Morning*

Publications

By FINNEY: articles—

"Talking about Acting," in *Sight and Sound* (London), Spring 1961.
Interview in *Positif* (Paris), June 1969.
Interviews in *Photoplay* (London), October 1980 and August 1982.
Interview in *Time Out* (London), 4 November 1987.

On FINNEY: book—

Falk, Quentin, *Albert Finney in Character: A Biography*, London, 1992.

On FINNEY: articles—

Current Biography 1963, New York, 1963.
Shipman, David, in *The Great Movie Stars: The International Years*, London, 1972.
Films Illustrated (London), October 1977.
National Film Theatre Booklet (London), June 1982.

Radio Times (London), 14 July and 27 October 1990.
Time Out (London), 29 August 1990.
Baldinger, Scott, "Mercurial Master," in *Harper's Bazaar*, April 1991.

*   *   *

In the late 1950s and early 1960s Britain's angry young men began appearing with increasing frequency on stage and screen, and Albert Finney was the perfect actor to embody the soulful working-class loner. He himself was the son of a bookie, and his combination of charm, energy, and roguish good looks enabled him to personify the angry young man and become one of Britain's rising young talents. His first angry young man characterization came on stage in *Billy Liar*. But it was his casting in Karel Reisz's *Saturday Night and Sunday Morning* which earned him his first attention among moviegoers. Finney's Arthur Seaton is an alienated Nottingham factory worker who strikes out against his dreary working-class plight. He may defiantly declare, "Don't let the bastards grind you down," but he is destined to make no holes in the invisible wall separating the classes in England. The actor's gritty performance remains as vital and touching today as in 1960.

Finney next peppered the rebellion of the angry young man with a delightful bawdiness in Tony Richardson's *Tom Jones*, based on the Henry Fielding novel about a young man's randy adventures in eighteenth-century England. Released in 1963, the film is more than just an entertaining, Oscar-winner. It is a landmark as a forerunner of the sexual revolution of the late 1960s. Finney's performance is crammed with moxie, and is a major star turn. If *Saturday Night and Sunday Morning* had made him a name among more discerning filmgoers, *Tom Jones* secured his reputation as a popular movie star.

But Finney is a serious actor, and he chose not to exploit this fame. For the most part, he has carefully selected his screen projects. More often than not, he has given his most interesting performances as unhappy (if not deeply troubled) men whose lives are in a state of crisis. They may have attained a certain degree of material success, but their marriages have failed and their lives are characterized by boredom and indifference. He directed as well as starred in *Charlie Bubbles*, playing a fabulously successful but otherwise dead-to-the-world writer. In *Shoot the Moon*, he again is a famous writer whose marriage breaks up. In *Two for the Road*, he is one-half of a troubled couple who look back on their 12 years of marriage. In *Under the Volcano*, based on Malcolm Lowry's autobiographical novel, he is especially fine in the complex and demanding role of a self-destructive former British consul, guilt-ridden over his life, who has been abandoned by his wife and is slowly drinking himself into oblivion. Finney also has played character parts: Ebenezer Scrooge in *Scrooge*, Hercule Poirot in *Murder on the Orient Express*, and Daddy Warbucks in *Annie*. Other important roles came in *Gumshoe*, in which he gave a cleverly funny performance as a Liverpool bingo caller who finds himself playing detective in a murder case, and *Miller's Crossing*, cast as a mobster and political boss.

In the latter stages of his career, Finney's most poignant performances have come as deluded older men whose inner repressions have not allowed them to fully develop their potential as human beings. He is the entire show in *The Browning Version*, a middling updating of the Terence Rattigan play, which previously had been filmed in 1951 with Michael Redgrave. Finney offers an emotionally rich performance as Andrew Crocker-Harris, professor of languages at a staid British boys school. After almost two decades on the job, he is resigning because of ill health. It quickly becomes apparent, however, that he has been forced out of his job. He is held in disdain by his wife, who has been cheating on him, and he also is unloved by his students. He has never been an inspiring, caring teacher but rather is a stuffy, efficient bureaucrat who has never learned how to communicate his love of Latin and the classics. *The Browning Version* is worth seeing for Finney's beautifully modulated performance, as he brings just the right amount of sadness and eloquence to Crocker-Harris.

Finney is equally superb as Alfie Byrne, a friendly, middle-aged bus conductor in *A Man of No Importance*, set in early 1960s Dublin. Alfie, a bachelor, is obsessed with Oscar Wilde, and is intent upon mounting an amateur theatrical production of *Salome*. The key to the character is that he is a closeted homosexual, and has a crush on the young driver of his bus. Alfie lives in a society in which homosexuality is an "unspeakable sin." For this reason he not only has kept his sexual preference hidden but also has never dared become involved in a sexual or romantic relationship of any kind. Finney is a joy to watch, especially as he confronts his feelings and laments that his "hands are innocent of affection." His Alfie is a gentle, poetic soul who, unfortunately, was destined to be born at the wrong time and in the wrong place.

With *The Browning Version* and *A Man of No Importance*, Finney has effortlessly segued his career into middle-aged character roles. One senses that some of his best screen work is ahead of him.

—Rob Edelman

FISHBURNE, Laurence (Larry)

Nationality: American. **Born:** Laurence Fishburne III in Augusta, Georgia, 30 July 1961. **Family:** Married Majna Fishburne, children: Langston Issa, Montana Isis. **Career:** Early 1970s—acted on the daytime soap opera *One Life to Live* while not yet in his teens; 1975—screen debut in *Cornbread, Earl and Me*; 1979—lied about his age in order to be cast in *Apocalypse Now*; 1980s—played the role of Cowboy Curtis on the TV show *Pee-wee's Playhouse*, and made guest appearances on TV series *M*A*S*H*, *Trapper John, M.D.*, and others; 1993—altered billing from Larry to Laurence; in the TV mini-series *The Wild West*. **Awards:** Tony Award, for *Two Trains Running*, 1992; Emmy Award, for guest starring role in TV series *Tribeca*, 1993. **Agent:** Paradigm Talent Agency, 10100 Santa Monica Boulevard, 25th Floor, Los Angeles, CA 90067, U.S.A.

Films as Actor:

(as Laurence Fishburne III)

1975   *Cornbread, Earl and Me* (Manduke) (as Wilford Robinson)
1979   *Fast Break* (Smight) (as street kid)

(as Larry Fishburne)

1979   *Apocalypse Now* (Francis Ford Coppola) (as Clean)
1980   *A Rumor of War* (Heffron—for TV) (as Lightbulb); *Willie and Phil* (Mazursky) (as Wilson)
1982   *Death Wish II* (Winner) (as Cutter)
1983   *I Take These Men* (Peerce—for TV) (as Hank Johnson); *Rumble Fish* (Francis Ford Coppola) (as Midget); *For Us, the Living* (Schultz—for TV)
1984   *The Cotton Club* (Francis Ford Coppola) (as Bumpy Rhodes)
1985   *The Color Purple* (Spielberg) (as Swain)
1986   *Quicksilver* (Donnelly) (as Voodoo); *Band of the Hand* (Glaser) (as Cream)
1987   *A Nightmare on Elm Street 3: Dream Warriors* (Chuck Russell) (as Max); *Gardens of Stone* (Francis Ford Coppola) (as Cpl. Flanagan)
1988   *School Daze* (Spike Lee) (as Vaughn "Dap" Dunlap); *Red Heat* (Walter Hill) (as Lt. Stobbs); *Cherry 2000* (De Jarnatt) (as Glu Glu Lawyer)
1989   *Cadence* (*Stockade*) (Sheen) (as Stokes)
1990   *King of New York* (Ferrara) (as Jimmy Jump); *Decoration Day* (Markowitz—for TV) (as Michael Waring)
1991   *Class Action* (Apted) (as Nick Holbrook); ***Boyz N the Hood*** (Singleton) (as Furious Styles); *Hearts of Darkness: A Filmmaker's Apocalypse* (Bahr and Hickenlooper—doc) (appearance)
1992   *Deep Cover* (Duke) (as Russell Stevens Jr./John Q. Hull)

(as Laurence Fishburne)

1993   *What's Love Got to Do with It?* (Gibson) (as Ike Turner); *Searching for Bobby Fischer* (*Innocent Moves*) (Zaillian) (as Vinnie)
1995   *Higher Learning* (Singleton) (as Professor Maurice Phipps); *Bad Company* (Harris) (as Nelson Crowe); *Just Cause* (Glimcher) (as Tanny Brown); *The Tuskegee Airmen* (Markowitz—for TV) (as Hannibal Lee)
1996   *Othello* (Alan Parker) (title role); *Fled* (Kevin Hooks)

Laurence Fishburne in *Deep Cover*

Publications

By FISHBURNE: articles—

"Getting Serious," interview with B. Coleman, in *Village Voice* (New York), 19 May 1992.
Interview in *Playboy* (Chicago), April 1994.
"Laurence Fishburne: The Actor Who Puts Risk before Reputation—and Proves Why That Matters So Much," interview with Sheila Benson, in *Interview* (New York), January 1995.
"Catching Fishburne," interview with Leslie Bennetts, in *Vanity Fair* (New York), December 1995.

On FISHBURNE: articles—

Smith, Gavin, "Nobody Rides for Free," in *Film Comment* (New York), July/August 1990.
Smith, C., "Men and Boyz," in *New York*, 22 July 1991.
Weinraub, Bernard, "Teetering on the Brink of Stardom," in *New York Times*, 18 November 1991.
Ryan, J., "Deep Actor," in *Premiere* (New York), May 1992.
Giles, Jeff, "Searching for Larry Fishburne," in *Newsweek* (New York), 26 July 1993.
Edwards, Audrey, "A Man Called Fish," in *Essence* (New York), November 1994.
Smith, Chris, "Home Again," in *New York*, 6 November 1995.

*   *   *

Laurence Fishburne is a quietly powerful actor with a commanding screen presence who brings an earnestness and deep intensity to his roles. Essentially, he has played two character-types on screen. The first is analogous to a brutally psychotic timebomb ticking down and waiting to explode. Fishburne is an expert in such parts: witness his Oscar-nominated work as the physically and psychologically abusive Ike Turner, opposite Angela Bassett's Tina in *What's Love Got to Do with It?* Fishburne's scenes opposite Bassett are nothing short of electrifying as he controls her like a puppeteer manipulating a puppet, shrewdly exploiting her personality flaws while transforming her into his virtual prisoner.

One example of a variation on this character is in *Just Cause*, in which Fishburne is cast as Tanny Brown, a character who first comes off as a black redneck: a cocksure, chillingly ruthless small-town cop in the New South, where blacks in power can be as corrupt as whites. Brown has brutalized a young black man, accused of raping and murdering a child, into confessing to the crime. As the scenario unfolds, Brown is softened somewhat as he is proven to have been correct in his instincts. Still, this cop's methods can in no way be condoned, and Fishburne's performance is far more interesting at the beginning of the film, when he is menacing. When playing such roles Fishburne beautifully acts out his characters' intimidating nature, delivering threats in a soft, low voice. The characters he is browbeating—and the viewer—know he means business, know he is a dangerous man.

The other Fishburne screen persona is the streetwise good guy, a thoughtful, soulful sort who has seen too much of the ugly side of life (most usually in urban America). His consummate performance in this role has been in *Boyz N the Hood*, the first feature directed by 23-year-old John Singleton. Fishburne plays Furious Styles, a black man desperately attempting to be a positive role model for his son Tre (Cuba Gooding, Jr.) in violence-laden South Central Los Angeles. Furious lectures Tre on living a responsible life, and not allowing himself to be seduced by the seamier aspects of the streets. The actor's performance in *Boyz N the Hood* is every bit as impressive, and as equally award-worthy, as his Ike Turner.

Fishburne rehashes Furious Styles in Steven Zaillian's *Searching for Bobby Fischer*, in which he also plays an adult who acts as role model to a boy. His Vinnie is a chess hustler who hangs out in New York's Washington Square Park and becomes the mentor of a seven-year-old chess genius. Vinnie prefers that the boy play the game using his instinct, his gut, and his heart—exactly the qualities Fishburne brings to his roles. Yet another "good guy" character is the no-nonsense political science professor in *Higher Learning*, also directed by John Singleton, in which he is thoroughly believable as a teacher who attempts to motivate his students by massaging their minds and getting them to think for themselves.

In *Deep Cover*, Fishburne plays variations on both "good" and "bad" characters. He starts out the contemplative good guy: Russell Stevens Jr., a cop who agrees to go undercover to ferret out some major-league drug dealers. Stevens, who as a child had seen his father shot to death while committing a robbery, has become a cop because of his desire to "make a difference." Here, too, he plays role model to a boy, a next-door-neighbor whose mother is an irresponsible parent. But as the story develops and Stevens sees he is being lied to by his superiors, he goes over the edge, becoming a renegade—and in essence, becoming the other Fishburne character.

One of Fishburne's first roles was in Francis Coppola's *Apocalypse Now*, in which he was cast as Clean, a young GI serving in Vietnam. The actor was not of legal age when hired for the film; reportedly, he lied about his age so that he could win the role and go on location in the Philippines. Additionally, he has been cast in roles which, scant years earlier, a black actor never could have played in Hollywood movies: the lover of a white woman (Ellen Barkin) in *Bad Company*, for example, and the Southern sheriff in *Just Cause*.

—Rob Edelman

FITZGERALD, Barry

Nationality: Irish. **Born:** William Joseph Shields in Dublin, 10 March 1888; brother of the actor Arthur Shields. **Education:** Attended Merchant Taylor School, Dublin; Skerrys College, Dublin; Civil Service College. **Career:** 1909-29—civil servant in Unemployment Insurance Division, Dublin; began acting at the Abbey Theatre, Dublin, 1915; 1929—became professional actor: *The Silver Tassie* written for him by Sean O'Casey; film debut in *Juno and the Paycock* in role he'd played at Abbey Theatre; 1932—visited the United States with the Abbey Theatre; 1936—U.S. film debut in *When Knights Were Bold*; continued to work on stage; 1945—in radio series *His Honor, The Barber*. **Awards:** Best Supporting Actor Academy Award for *Going My Way*, 1944 (also nominated for Best Actor in same film). **Died:** In Dublin, 4 January 1961.

Films as Actor:

1929   *Juno and the Paycock* (Hitchcock) (as Orator)
1936   *When Knights Were Bold* (Raymond) (as Barker)
1937   *The Plough and the Stars* (Ford); *Ebb Tide* (Rossen)
1938   **Bringing Up Baby** (Hawks); *Marie Antoinette* (Van Dyke); *Four Men and a Prayer* (Ford); *The Dawn Patrol* (Goulding)
1939   *The Saint Strikes Back* (Farrow); *Pacific Liner* (Landers); *Full Confession* (Farrow)
1940   *The Long Voyage Home* (Ford)
1941   *San Francisco Docks* (Lubin); *The Sea Wolf* (Curtiz); *How Green Was My Valley* (Ford); *Tarzan's Secret Treasure* (Thorpe)
1943   *The Amazing Mrs. Holliday* (Manning); *Two Tickets to London* (Marin); *Corvette K-225* (Rossen)

1944   *Going My Way* (McCarey); *I Love a Soldier* (Sandrich); *None but the Lovely Heart* (Odets)

1945   *Incendiary Blonde* (Marshall); *Duffy's Tavern* (Walker); *And Then There Were None* (Clair); *The Stork Club* (Walker)

1946   *Two Years before the Mast* (Farrow)

1947   *California* (Farrow); *Easy Come, Easy Go* (Farrow); *Welcome Stranger* (Nugent); *Variety Girl* (Marshall)

1948   **The Naked City** (Dassin) (as Lt. Muldoon); *The Sainted Sisters* (Russell); *Miss Tatlock's Millions* (Hayden)

1949   *Top o' the Morning* (Miller); *The Story of Seabiscuit* (Butler)

1950   *Union Square* (Maté)

1951   *Silver City* (Haskin)

1952   **The Quiet Man** (Ford); *Il filo d'erba (A da veni . . . Don Calogero)* (Vassarotti)

1954   *Happy Ever After (Tonight's the Night)* (Zampi) (as Thady O'Heggarty)

1956   *The Catered Affair* (Brooks)

1958   *Rooney* (Pollock) (as Grandfather O'Flynn)

1959   *Broth of a Boy* (Pollock) (as Patrick Farrell); *Cradle of Genius* (Rotha—doc)

Publications

On FITZGERALD: articles—

Picturegoer (London), 3 February 1945.

Ecran (Paris), January 1978, additions in issues for September 1978 and January and May 1979.

Ciné Revue (Paris), 22 June 1980.

*   *   *

If Sara Allgood was the stereotypical Irish stage mother then Barry Fitzgerald was the stereotypical Irishman, a whimsical character with a thick Irish brogue and a succession of quaint expressions that were closer to Hollywood in origin than to Dublin. Fitzgerald was the quintessential Irish character actor whose mere presence was guaranteed to steal any scene from a film's star; indeed this subtle self-promotion from supporting player to star is best exemplified by Fitzgerald's being nominated for Oscars for both Best Actor *and* Best Supporting Actor for his work in *Going My Way*.

When John Ford first brought Barry Fitzgerald over from Dublin's Abbey Theatre to recreate the role of Fluther Good in Ford's screen version of O'Casey's *The Plough and the Stars*, Fitzgerald was still more an actor than a personality. He was quite a good actor, and as late as 1940 and 1941 Fitzgerald gave fine performances, under John Ford's direction, as the nasty steward in *The Long Voyage Home* and even as a Welshman in *How Green Was My Valley*.

The Irish blarney took over with *Going My Way*, and Fitzgerald was permanently typecast. As he once remarked, "I have always said that no matter what nationality of character I am given to play, he turns out to be an Irishman." However, Fitzgerald was not always cast as a lovable character; as he had demonstrated in *The Long Voyage Home* there could be a decidedly unpleasant side to his screen personality, a side on display in *And Then There Were None* and *The Naked City* among other films.

—Anthony Slide

FLYNN, Errol

Nationality: American. **Born:** Errol Leslie Thomson Flynn in Hobart, Tasmania, Australia, 20 June 1909; became U.S. citizen, 1942. **Edu-**cation: Attended Sydney Church of England Grammar School; Northshire School, Sydney; South London College at Barnes (expelled). **Family:** Married 1) the actress Lili Damita, 1935 (divorced 1942); 2) Nora Eddington, 1943 (divorced 1949); 3) the actress Patrice Wymore, 1950 (separated 1957), children: Sean, Deirdre, Rory, and Annella Roma. **Career:** 1926—clerk for Sydney shipping company; 1927—government cadet in New Guinea; worked on copra plantation; gold miner in New Guinea, and guide for documentary filmmakers in New Guinea (film released 1932 as *Dr. H. Erben's New Guinea Expedition*); 1930—bought schooner *Sirocco*, wrote articles for *Sydney Bulletin*; 1933—first film role in Australian semi-documentary *In the Wake of the Bounty*; studied acting in England, joined Northampton Repertory Co. 1934—given contract by Warners, moved to Hollywood; 1935—became star for Warners in *Captain Blood*; 1951—produced *The Bargain*; 1952—broke Warners contract; 1954—formed Errol Flynn Enterprises production company; 1956—TV debut in *Playhouse 90*; 1957-58—host of TV series *The Errol Flynn Theater (Goodyear Theater)*; 1958—in play *The Master of Thornfield* in Detroit and Cincinnati. **Died:** 14 October 1959.

Films as Actor:

1933   *In the Wake of the Bounty* (Chauvel) (as Fletcher Christian)

1935   *Murder at Monte Carlo* (Ince) (as Dyter, newspaper reporter); *The Case of the Curious Bride* (Curtiz) (as Moxley); *Don't Bet on Blondes* (Florey) (as David Van Dusen); *Captain Blood* (Curtiz) (as Peter Blood)

1936   *The Charge of the Light Brigade* (Curtiz) (as Maj. Geoffrey Vickers); *Pirate Party on Catalina Island* (short)

1937   *The Green Light* (Borzage) (as Dr. Newell Paige); *The Prince and the Pauper* (Keighley) (as Miles Hendon); *Another Dawn* (Dieterle) (as Capt. Denny Roark); *The Perfect Specimen* (Curtiz) (as Gerald Beresford Wicks)

1938   **The Adventures of Robin Hood** (Curtiz and Keighley) (title role); *Four's a Crowd* (Curtiz); *The Sisters* (Litvak) (as Frank Medlin); *The Dawn Patrol* (Goulding) (as Courtney)

1939   *Dodge City* (Curtiz) (as Wade Hatton); *The Private Lives of Elizabeth and Essex* (Curtiz) (as Robert Devereaux, Earl of Essex)

1940   *Virginia City* (Curtiz) (as Kerry Bradford); *The Sea Hawk* (Curtiz) (as Capt. Geoffrey Thorpe); *Santa Fe Trail* (Curtiz) (as Jeb Stuart)

1941   *Footsteps in the Dark* (Lloyd Bacon) (as Francis Warren); *Dive Bomber* (Curtiz) (as Lt. Doug Lee); *They Died with Their Boots On* (Walsh) (as Gen. George Armstrong Custer)

1942   *Desperate Journey* (Walsh) (as Flight Lt. Terrence Forbes); *Gentleman Jim* (Walsh) (as James J. Corbett)

1943   *Edge of Darkness* (Milestone) (as Gunnar Brogge); *Thank Your Lucky Stars* (David Butler); *Northern Pursuit* (Walsh) (as Steve Wagner)

1944   *Uncertain Glory* (Walsh) (as Jean Picard)

1945   *Objective, Burma!* (Walsh) (as Maj. Nelson); *San Antonio* (David Butler) (as Clay Hardin); *Peeks at Hollywood* (Applebaum—short) (appearance)

1946   *Never Say Goodbye* (Kern) (as Phil Gayley)

1947   *Cry Wolf* (Godfrey) (as Mark Caldwell); *Escape Me Never* (Godfrey) (as Sebastian Dubrok); *Always Together* (de Cordova) (as guest)

1948   *Silver River* (Walsh) (as Capt. Mike McCombs)

1949   *The Adventures of Don Juan* (Sherman) (title role); *That Forsyte Woman (The Forsyte Saga)* (Bennett) (as Soames Forsyte); *It's a Great Feeling* (David Butler) (as Jerry Bushfinkle)

1950   *Montana* (Enright) (as Morgan Lane); *Rocky Mountain* (Keighley) (as Lafe Barstow); *Kim* (Saville) (as Mahub Ali)

1951 *The Adventures of Captain Fabian* (William Marshall) (title role)

1952 *Mara Maru* (Gordon Douglas) (as Gregory Mason); *Against All Flags* (Sherman) (as Brian Hawke)

1953 *The Master of Ballantrae* (Keighley) (as James Durrisdeer); *Il maestro di Don Giovanni* (*Crossed Swords*) (Krims) (as Renzo)

1955 *Lilacs in the Spring* (*Let's Make Up*) (Wilcox) (as John Beaumont); *The Dark Avenger* (*The Warriors*) (Levin) (as Prince Edward); *King's Rhapsody* (Wilcox) (as King Richard of Laurentic)

1957 *The Big Boodle* (*Night in Havana*) (Wilson) (as Ned Sherwood); *Istanbul* (Pevney) (as Jim Brennan); *The Sun Also Rises* (Henry King) (as Mike Campbell)

1958 *Too Much, Too Soon* (Napoleon) (as John Barrymore); *The Roots of Heaven* (Huston) (as Major Forsythe); *Hello God* (William Marshall—produced in 1951) (as man on Anzio beach)

1959 *Cuban Rebel Girls* (*Assualt of the Rebel Girls*) (Mahon) (as himself/narrator, + sc, co-pr)

Films as Director:

1952 *Cruise of the Zaca* (short) (+ appearance); *Deep Sea Fishing* (short) (+ appearance)

Publications

By FLYNN: books—

Beam Ends, New York, 1937.
Showdown, New York, 1946.
My Wicked, Wicked Ways, New York, 1959.
From a Life of Adventure: The Writings of Errol Flynn, edited by Tony Thomas, Secaucus, New Jersey, 1980.

On FLYNN: books—

Devilliers, Gerard and Marceau, *Errol Flynn*, Paris, 1969.
Parish, James Robert, editor, *Errol Flynn*, New York, 1969.
Thomas, Tony, Rudy Behlmer, and Clifford McCarty, *The Films of Errol Flynn*, New York, 1969.
Thomas, Tony, *Cads and Cavaliers: The Gentlemen Adventurers of the Movies*, South Brunswick, New Jersey, 1973.
Godfrey, Lionel, *The Life and Crimes of Errol Flynn*, New York, 1977.
Richards, Jeffrey, *Swordsmen of the Screen: From Douglas Fairbanks to Michael York*, London, 1977.
Freedland, Michael, *The Two Lives of Errol Flynn*, New York, 1979.
Higham, Charles, *Errol Flynn: The Untold Story*, New York, 1980.
Leguèbe, Eric, *Errol Flynn*, Paris, 1981.
Norman, Don, *Errol Flynn: The Tasmanian Story*, Hobart, 1981.
Valenti, Peter, *Errol Flynn: A Bio-Bibliography*, Westport, Connecticut, 1984.
Wiles, Buster, *My Days with Errol Flynn*, Santa Monica, 1988.
Thomas, Tony, *Errol Flynn: The Spy Who Never Was*, New York, 1990.
McDonald, Roger, *Flynn: A Novelisation*, New York, 1992.
Nicholson, Geoff, *The Errol Flynn Novel*, London, 1994.

On FLYNN: articles—

Obituary in *New York Times*, 15 October 1959.
Thomas, Anthony, "Errol Flynn," in *Films in Review* (New York), January 1960.

Behlmer, Rudy, "Robin Hood on the Screen," in *Films in Review* (New York), February 1965.
Behlmer, Rudy, "Swordplay on the Screen," in *Films in Review* (New York), June/July 1965.
Beresford, Bruce, "Swashbuckling Movies," in *Granta*, 3 May 1967.
Cutts, J., "Requiem for a Swashbuckler," in *Films and Filming* (London), Summer 1967.
Davis, John, "Captain Blood," in the *Velvet Light Trap* (Madison, Wisconsin), June 1971.
"Deirdre Flynn: Looking Down on Daddy," interview with D. Galligan, in *Interview* (New York), February 1975.
Viviani, C., "Errol Flynn: une romanticisme souriante," in *Positif* (Paris), April 1978.
Morris, George, "Errol Flynn," in *The Movie Star*, edited by Elisabeth Weis, New York, 1981.
Valenti, P., "The Many Lives of Errol Flynn," in *Journal of Popular Film* (Washington, D.C.), Winter 1982.
Webb, T., letter, in *Films in Review* (New York), October 1986.
Beuselink, James, "Errol Flynn," in *Films in Review* (New York), vol. 38, no. 4, 1987.

On FLYNN: film—

My Wicked, Wicked Ways . . . The Legend of Errol Flynn, film biography directed by Don Taylor, 1985.

*   *   *

It has been said of Errol Flynn that, although he played a variety of roles, he ultimately always portrayed himself. Like Douglas Fairbanks before him, he excelled in depictions of swashbuckling, virile heroes which seemed virtual prototypes of the idealized American male. The typical Flynn character as defined by his two favorite directors, Michael Curtiz and Raoul Walsh, embodied such qualities as moral courage, exuberance, and, above all, outstanding athletic ability.

Yet, as exemplified by the fact that he was turned down for service in World War II due to a combination of heart trouble, recurrent malaria, and a degree of tuberculosis, the image that he portrayed on the screen was based more than a little on solid acting ability and a desire to compensate for his physical maladies. His offscreen personality often seemed to be afflicted by a desire actually to become his larger-than-life persona, and his personal life was marred by excess: brawls, amorous adventures, and other assorted hedonistic activities. Like the author Ernest Hemingway, he seemed to wish to elevate the artistic self to the mythical status of his fictional creations. In the end, his private life was viewed by filmgoers as virtually inseparable from his screen appearances, and added considerable believability to his performances, even when played "tongue in cheek" as in *The Adventures of Don Juan*.

In what many people consider his best performance, *Gentleman Jim*, Flynn delivered a complex performance that relied less upon acting for its great impact than on the subtle nuances of character the actor brought to the role. Projecting both high spirits and charm, Flynn turned James J. Corbett into a charismatic figure with a gift of the gab that, along with a good left jab, carried him to the top of San Francisco society. Although Flynn was purportedly no slouch with his fists, he worked hard to capture exactly Corbett's style in the ring. He even worked out with boxer Mushy Callahan and did his own fighting in the film. The result is an energetic performance that reflects the amount of effort the actor expended to achieve his screen image.

In the late 1940s, the strain on his personal life took its toll on his craft and he became increasingly less careful in preparing for his roles. By the 1950s, he had become tired of swashbuckling, and aspired to more serious parts. But with the exception of *Mara Maru*, which invites comparison with his earlier achievements, he did not find

Errol Flynn

himself much in demand in Hollywood, even for adventure films. He tried to resurrect his career in Europe with little success and lost most of his money on an ill-fated production of *William Tell*.

After his return to Hollywood in 1956, Flynn played in three films of a relatively serious nature: *The Sun Also Rises*, an adaptation of Ernest Hemingway's first novel, *Too Much, Too Soon*, the story of Diana Barrymore in which he played John Barrymore, and *The Roots of Heaven*. Again Flynn's personal adventures detracted from the critical regard accorded these films. Though he had a reputation as a drunk and all three films featured heavy drinking, Flynn's portrayals, particularly that in *The Sun Also Rises*, were finely delineated and deserve to be taken more seriously. His better films are part of an adventure genre that has all but disappeared, and no recent actor has been able to assume his mantle as one of the screen's preeminent swashbuckling heroes.

Flynn still fascinates. His action films and swashbucklers continue to play to large audiences on television and remain top sellers in video stores. But it is his sometimes scandalous private life upon which most biographers have focused in recent years.

Especially scurrilous was Charles Higham's *Errol Flynn: The Untold Story*. In addition to suggesting that the virile Flynn carried on affairs with men as well as women—the kind of shocking, albeit unsubstantiated, revelation which has become such a must in new biographies of deceased, former Hollywood sex symbols that it virtually borders on cliché—Higham posits the theory that the actor who won World War II singlehandedly on-screen was actually a Nazi sympathizer and spy offscreen. Perhaps Higham felt he needed another shocker to sell copies of his book, as rumors of homosexuality were no longer enough. The accusation generated considerable ink—as well as a strong rebuttal to the author's less than weighty "evidence" of Flynn's treasonous activities from film scholar Tony Thomas in a follow-up tome, *Errol Flynn: The Spy Who Never Was*.

—Stephen L. Hanson, updated by John McCarty

FONDA, Henry

Nationality: American. **Born:** Henry Jaynes Fonda in Grand Island, Nebraska, 16 May 1905. **Education:** Attended Omaha Central High School, graduated 1923; studied journalism, University of Minnesota (dropped out after second year). **Military Service:** U.S. Navy, 1942-45: lieutenant; Bronze Star and Presidential citation. **Family:** Married 1) the actress Margaret Sullavan, 1931 (divorced 1933); 2) Frances Seymour Brokaw, 1936 (died 1950); children: the actress Jane and the actor Peter; 3) Susan Blanchard, 1950 (divorced 1956), daughter: Amy (adopted); 4) Countess Afdera Franchetti, 1957 (divorced 1962), 5) Shirlee Adams, 1965. **Career:** 1925-27—performed at Omaha Community Playhouse, and worked at menial jobs; 1927—toured vaudeville with George Billings; assistant director at Omaha Playhouse; 1928—moved to New York; played summer stock at Cape Cod; 1928-32—appeared with University Players Guild, Falmouth, Massachusetts; 1929—Broadway debut in *The Game of Love and Death*; 1929-31—associated with National Junior Theatre, Washington, D.C.; 1934—revue appearance in *New Faces*; film contract with Walter Wanger; created character of Dan Harrow in *The Farmer Takes a Wife* on Broadway, repeated it in film debut; 1939—began association with John Ford on *Young Mr. Lincoln*; to obtain role of Tom Joad in *The Grapes of Wrath*, required to sign seven-year contract with 20th Century-Fox; 1948—returned to Broadway in acclaimed performance as *Mister Roberts*; early 1950s—concentrated on stage appearances, culminating in portrayal of defense lawyer in *The Caine Mutiny Court Martial*; 1959-60—in TV series *The Deputy* (also co-producer); 1971-

72—in TV series *The Smith Family*; 1974—toured and appeared on Broadway in one-man show *Clarence Darrow*; 1976—in TV miniseries *Captains and the Kings*, and *Roots: The Next Generation*, 1979. **Awards:** Best Foreign Actor, British Academy, for *Twelve Angry Men*, 1957; Life Achievement Award, American Film Institute, 1978; Honorary Oscar, "in recognition of his brilliant accomplishments and enduring contribution to the art of motion pictures," 1980; Best Actor Academy Award, for *On Golden Pond*, 1981. **Died:** In Los Angeles, 12 August 1982.

Films as Actor:

1935 *The Farmer Takes a Wife* (Fleming) (as Daniel Harrow); *Way Down East* (Henry King) (as David Bartlett); *I Dream Too Much* (Cromwell) (as Jonathan Street)
1936 *Trail of the Lonesome Pine* (Hathaway) (as Dave Tolliver); *The Moon's Our Home* (Seiter) (as Anthony Amberton); *Spendthrift* (Walsh) (as Townsend Middleton)
1937 *You Only Live Once* (Fritz Lang) (as Eddie Taylor); *Wings of the Morning* (Schuster) (as Kerry); *Slim* (Enright) (title role); *That Certain Woman* (Goulding) (as Jack Merrick)
1938 *I Met My Love Again* (Ripley, Logan [uncredited], and Cukor) (as Ives); *Jezebel* (Wyler) (as Preston Dillard); *Blockade* (Dieterle) (as Marco); *Spawn of the North* (Hathaway) (as Jim Kimmerlee); *The Mad Miss Manton* (Jason) (as Peter Ames)
1939 *Jesse James* (Henry King) (as Frank James); *Let Us Live* (Brahm) (as "Brick" Tennant); *The Story of Alexander Graham Bell* (*The Modern Miracle*) (Cummings) (as Tom Watson); *Young Mr. Lincoln* (Ford) (as Abraham Lincoln); *Drums along the Mohawk* (Ford) (as Gil Martin)
1940 *The Grapes of Wrath* (Ford) (as Tom Joad); *Lillian Russell* (Cummings) (as Alexander Moore); *The Return of Frank James* (Fritz Lang) (as Frank James/Ben Woodson); *Chad Hanna* (Henry King) (title role)
1941 *The Lady Eve* (Preston Sturges) (as Charles Pike); *Wild Geese Calling* (Brahm) (as John); *You Belong to Me* (*Good Morning Doctor*) (Ruggles) (as Peter Kirk)
1942 *The Male Animal* (Nugent) (as Tommy Turner); *Rings on Her Fingers* (Mamoulian) (as John Wheeler); *The Magnificent Dope* (Walter Lang) (as Tad); Sequence B of *Tales of Manhattan* (Duvivier) (as George); *The Big Street* (Irving Reis) (as Little Pinks); *The Ox-Bow Incident* (*Strange Incident*) (Wellman) (as Gil Carter)
1943 *The Immortal Sergeant* (Stahl) (as Colin)
1946 *My Darling Clementine* (Ford) (as Wyatt Earp)
1947 *The Long Night* (Litvak) (as Joe Adams); *The Fugitive* (Ford) (title role); *Daisy Kenyon* (Preminger) (as Peter)
1948 *On Our Merry Way* (*A Miracle Can Happen*) (King Vidor and Fenton) (as Hank); *Fort Apache* (Ford) (as Colonel Owen Thursday)
1949 *Jigsaw* (Markle) (as nightclub waiter)
1950 *Grant Wood* (Sorkin/Kipnis—short: included in compilation film *Pictura*, 1952) (as narrator); *Home of the Hopeless* (short) (as narrator)
1951 *The Growing Years* (Resnick—short, for Girl Scouts) (as narrator); *Benjy* (Zinnermann—short) (as narrator)
1952 *The Impressionable Years* (Elgar) (as narrator); *Pictura* (Dupont, Emmer, Hessens, and Resnais—doc) (as narrator)
1955 *Mister Roberts* (Ford and LeRoy) (as Lieutenant Roberts)
1956 *War and Peace* (King Vidor) (as Pierre); *The Wrong Man* (Hitchcock) (as Manny Balestrero)
1957 *The Tin Star* (Anthony Mann) (as Morg Hickman); *Twelve Angry Men* (Lumet) (as Juror Number Eight, + co-pr)

1958   *Stage Struck* (Lumet) (as Lewis Easton); *Reach for Tomorrow* (Weissman—short) (as narrator)

1959   *Warlock* (Dmytryk) (as Clay Blaisdell); *The Man Who Understood Women* (Johnson) (as Willie Bauche)

1962   *Advise and Consent* (Preminger) (as Robert Leffingwell); *The Longest Day* (Annakin, Marton, Wicki, and Oswald) (as Brig. Gen. Theodore Roosevelt Jr.)

1963   "The Railroad" ep. of *How the West Was Won* (George Marshall) (as Jethro Stuart); *Spencer's Mountain* (Daves) (as Clay Spencer); *Rangers of Yellowstone* (short) (as narrator)

1964   *The Best Man* (Schaffner) (as William Russell); *Fail Safe* (Lumet) (as the President); *Sex and the Single Girl* (Quine) (as Frank)

1965   *The Rounders* (Kennedy) (as Howdy Lewis); *In Harm's Way* (Preminger) (as CINCPAC Admiral); *Battle of the Bulge* (Annakin) (as Lieutenant Colonel Kiley)

1966   One ep. of *La Guerre secrète* (*La guerra segreta*; *Spione unter sich*; *The Dirty Game*; *The Dirty Agents*) (Terence Young, Christian-Jaque, and Lizzani) (as Kourlov); *A Big Hand for the Little Lady* (*Big Deal at Dodge City*) (Cook) (as Meredith)

1967   *Welcome to Hard Times* (*Killer on a Horse*) (Kennedy) (as Will Blue); *Stranger on the Run* (Siegel—for TV) (as Ben Chamberlin); *The Golden Flame* (Brown) (as narrator); *All about People* (for United Jewish Welfare Fund—doc)

1968   *Firecreek* (McEveety) (as Larkin); *Yours, Mine and Ours* (Shavelson) (as Frank Beardsley); *Madigan* (Siegel) (as Commissioner Anthony X. Russell); *The Boston Strangler* (Fleischer) (as John S. Bottomly); *Born to Buck* (Tibbs) (as narrator); ***C'era una volta il West*** (*Once upon a Time in the West*) (Sergio Leone) (as Frank)

1969   *An Impression of John Steinbeck—Writer* (Wrye—short) (as narrator)

1970   *Too Late the Hero* (Aldrich) (as Captain Nolan); *There Was a Crooked Man* (Joseph L. Mankiewicz) (as Woodward Lopeman); *The Cheyenne Social Club* (Kelly) (as Harley Sullivan)

1971   *Sometimes a Great Notion* (*Never Give an Inch*) (Paul Newman) (as Henry Stamper); *Directed by John Ford* (Bogdanovich—doc) (as interviewee)

1973   *The Red Pony* (Totten—for TV) (as Carl Tiffin); *Ash Wednesday* (Peerce) (as Mark Sawyer); *The Alpha Caper* (*Inside Job*) (Robert Michael Lewis—for TV) (as Mark Forbes); *Le Serpent* (*The Serpent*) (Verneuil) (as Allan Davies); *Film Making Techniques: Acting* (Barr—doc) (as interviewee)

1974   *Mussolini—ultimo atto* (*The Last Four Days*; *Last Days of Mussolini*) (Lizzani) (as Cardinal Schuster); *Il mio nome e nessuno* (*My Name Is Nobody*) (Valeril) (as Jack Beauregard); *Valley Forge* (as narrator)

1975   *Collision Course* (Page—for TV)

1976   *Midway* (*Battle of Midway*) (Smight) (as Admiral Chester W. Nimitz); *The Displaced Person* (Glenn Jordan—for TV)

1977   *Tentacles* (*Tentacoli*) (Hellman, i.e., Sonia Assonitis)

1977   *Rollercoaster* (Goldstone) (as Simon Davenport); *Il grande attaco* (*The Great Battle*; *The Biggest Battle*; *Battle Force*; *La battaglia di Mareth*; *The Battle of Mareth*) (Lenzi) (as "Gen. Foster"); *The World of Andrew Wyeth* (Schwartz and Wallace—for TV) (introductory appearance); *Alcohol Abuse: The Early Warning Signs* (short) (as narrator)

1978   *The Great Smokey Roadblock* (*The Last of the Cowboys*; *Elegant John and His Ladies*) (John Leone) (as Elegant John); *Fedora* (Wilder) (as himself); *Big Yellow Schooner to Byzantium* (Stouffer—short) (as narrator); *Home to Stay* (Delbert Mann—for TV); *The Swarm* (Irwin Allen) (as Dr. Krim); *America's Sweetheart: The Mary Pickford Story* (Edwards—for TV) (as narrator)

1979   *Meteor* (Neame) (as President of the United States); *Wanda Nevada* (Peter Fonda) (as Prospector); *City on Fire* (Rakoff) (as Fire Chief Albert Risley)

1980   *Gideon's Trumpet* (Robert E. Collins—for TV) (as Clarence Earl Gideon); *The Jilting of Granny Weatherall* (Haines—for TV); *The Oldest Living Graduate* (Hofsiss—for TV)

1981   *On Golden Pond* (Rydell) (as Norman Thayer Jr.); *Summer Solstice* (Rosenblum—for TV)

Publications

By FONDA: book—

My Life, as told to Howard Teichman, New York, 1981.

By FONDA: articles—

"Fonda on Fonda," in *Films and Filming* (London), February 1963.
"Reflections on Forty Years of Make-Believe," interview with C. L. Hanson, in *Cinema* (Beverly Hills), December 1966.
Interview with Roberta Ostroff, in *Take One* (Montreal), March-April 1972.
"Fonda on Fonda," interview with R. Nogueira, in *Sight and Sound* (London), Spring 1973.

On FONDA: books—

Springer, John, *The Fondas: The Films and Careers of Henry, Jane, and Peter Fonda*, New York, 1970.
Kerbel, Michael, *Henry Fonda*, New York, 1975.
Goldstein, Norm, *Henry Fonda: His Life and Work*, London, 1982.
Thomas, Tony, *The Films of Henry Fonda*, Secaucus, New Jersey, 1983.
Cole, Gerald, and Wes Farrell, *The Fondas*, London, 1984.
Roberts, Allen, and Max Goldstein, *Henry Fonda: A Biography*, Jefferson, North Carolina, 1984.
Fonda, Afdera, *Never before Noon: An Autobiography*, with Clifford Thurlow, New York, 1986.
Piton, Jean-Pierre, *Henry Fonda*, Paris, 1986.
Tiratova, Evgeniia, *Genri Fonda*, Moscow, 1989.
Collier, Peter, *The Fondas: A Hollywood Dynasty*, London, 1991.
Sweeney, Kevin, *Henry Fonda: A Bio-Bibliography*, New York, 1992.

On FONDA: articles—

Springer, John, "Henry Fonda," in *Films in Review* (New York), November 1960.
Ross, Lillian, "Henry Fonda," in *New Yorker*, 28 October 1961.
Cowie, Peter, "Fonda," in *Films and Filming* (London), April 1962.
Hagen, R., "Fonda: Without a Method," in *Films and Filming* (London), June 1966.
Logan, Joshua, "Fonda Memories," in *Show* (Hollywood), April 1970.
Current Biography 1974, New York, 1974.
"Dialogue on Film: Henry Fonda," seminar in *American Film* (Washington, D.C.), May 1977.
Morris, George, "Henry Fonda," in *The Movie Star*, edited by Elisabeth Weis, New York, 1981.
Rosterman, R., "Henry Fonda Omaha Tribute," in *Films in Review* (New York), April 1981.
Corliss, Richard, "Two Who Get It Right," in *Time* (New York), 16 November 1981.
Buckley, M., "Henry Fonda," in *Films in Review* (New York), January 1982.
Sarris, Andrew, "Henry Fonda: An Appreciation," in *American Film* (Washington, D.C.), January/February 1982.

Schickel, Richard, "The Making of a Legend—From Abe Lincoln to Norman Thayer," in *People Weekly* (New York), 12 April 1982.

Obituary in *New York Times*, 13 August 1982.

Schickel, Richard, "A Palpable, Homespun Integrity," in *Time* (New York), 23 August 1982.

Obituary in *Cinéma* (Paris), October 1982.

Cieutat, M., "Henry Fonda ou l'Amérique des certitudes," in *Positif* (Paris), March 1983.

Fonda, Jane, "Remembering Dad," in *TV Guide* (Radnor, Pennsylvania), 11 January 1992.

*   *   *

If one actor could be taken as the personification of liberal America, it would have to be Henry Fonda. In contrast to the two-fisted, redneck persona of John Ford's other favorite protagonist, John Wayne, Fonda stood for a quiet, troubled decency. His was a figure of reasoned integrity, slow to anger, aiming always to overcome his opponents by persuasion rather than force, if humanly possible. Dreamy idealism emanated from his shy, gangling lope. Four years into his film career he played *Young Mr. Lincoln*; his Tom Joad aside, this portrait of Lincoln as a struggling, truth-seeking young lawyer is the definitive early Fonda performance.

Fonda's acting, like his screen image, was built around an unpretentious honesty, a seemingly artless naturalism which concealed a good deal of hard work. "My goal," he once remarked, "is that the audience must never see the wheels go round, not see the work that goes into this. It must seem effortless and real." His achievement was to make goodness appear both likable and credible, even if on occasion a touch priggish. There was a darker side to his character, which rarely appeared on screen, although he was now and again cast in unsympathetic roles and even, late in his career, as villains. Fonda himself was well aware of this less amiable aspect. "I don't really like myself. Never have. People mix me up with the characters I play." Perhaps for that reason, he was only really happy while working. "I was damn lucky I became an actor. . . . Acting to me is putting on a mask. The worst torture that can happen to me is not having a mask to get in back of."

John Ford supplied Fonda with several of his best masks. In addition to his Abe Lincoln, he was a serenely heroic Wyatt Earp in the mythopoetic *My Darling Clementine*, and the emotional power of his Tom Joad in *The Grapes of Wrath*—building skillfully on his own Midwest rural background—lent validity to that film's populism. Ford also made shrewd use of Fonda's stuffier side, casting him against type as the stiff-necked martinet to John Wayne's easygoing subordinate in *Fort Apache*.

With his air of melancholy determination, Fonda was ideally fitted for those films in which a lone individual reluctantly but doggedly resists the consensus: the protestor against a lynching in Wellman's *The Ox-Bow Incident*, the dissenting conscience in Lumet's archetypal jury-drama *Twelve Angry Men*. The downbeat, claustrophobic impact of Hitchcock's *The Wrong Man* derived in great part from the intensity of Fonda's central performance. He could also play comedy, though the roles that came his way were far from his best. Sturges's *The Lady Eve* provided a sparkling exception, Fonda preserving an engaging solemnity in the face of Stanwyck's protean and wily adventuress.

Integrity can become boring, and so at times could Fonda—especially in a bad film, of which he was cast in far too many. Twice in his career he fled from Hollywood entirely: into the Navy during the war, and then from 1948 to 1955 returning to his first and lasting love, the theater. Only Ford's insistence lured him back for the film of his Broadway hit, *Mr. Roberts*. Ironically, the two men then disagreed vehemently over interpretation, eventually coming to blows, and never worked together again.

Parts were never lacking, but the films got duller, with Fonda filling stolid cameos as authority figures. Sergio Leone, though, offered him the blackest role of his career, in *Once upon a Time in the West*. Fonda played it to the hilt, gunning down defenseless nine-year-olds with evident relish. His last feature film, *On Golden Pond*, brought his long-delayed Best Actor Oscar, and his first good role in years. The dignity of his performance, and that of Katharine Hepburn, rescued the movie from gross sentimentality, and turned it into a moving valedictory.

Fonda also is the senior member of one of Hollywood's most celebrated acting families. Daughter Jane became a preeminent (and highly controversial) movie star of the 1960s and 1970s; son Peter's participation in *Easy Rider* alone earns him more than an asterisk in the Hollywood history books; and commencing in the late 1980s, granddaughter Bridget (the daughter of Peter) became a star of Hollywood films. And since his death, Fonda (along with his family) has been the subject of several biographies.

—Philip Kemp, updated by Rob Edelman

FONDA, Jane

Nationality: American. **Born:** Jane Seymour Fonda in New York City, 21 December 1937; daughter of the actor Henry Fonda; sister of the actor Peter Fonda. **Education:** Attended Greenwich Academy, Connecticut; Emma Willard School, Troy, New York; Vassar College, Poughkeepsie, New York. **Family:** Married 1) the director Roger Vadim, 1965 (divorced 1970), one daughter; 2) Tom Hayden, 1973 (divorced 1989), one son; 3) Ted Turner, 1991. **Career:** 1955—stage debut with her father in *The Country Girl* in Omaha; late 1950s—joined the Actors Studio, New York; 1960—Broadway debut in *There Was a Little Girl*; film debut in *Tall Story*; 1965—French film debut in *La Ronde*, directed by Vadim; 1971—toured Southeast Asia with Anti-War Troupe, and visited North Vietnam, 1972; 1976—formed own production company, IPC Films: series of commercial and critical film successes followed; 1981—marketed popular exercise program on record and videotape and in book; 1980s on—has made numerous aerobic and exercise videotapes. **Awards:** Best Actress, New York Film Critics, for *They Shoot Horses, Don't They?*, 1969; Oscar for Best Actress, and Best Actress, New York Film Critics, for *Klute*, 1971; Oscar for Best Actress, for *Coming Home*, 1978; Best Actress, British Academy, for *Julia*, 1978; Best Actress, British Academy, for *The China Syndrome*, 1979. **Address:** c/o Fonda Films, Inc., P.O. Box 491355, Los Angeles, CA 90049-9355, U.S.A.

Films as Actress:

1960   *Tall Story* (Logan) (as June Ryder)

1962   *Walk on the Wild Side* (Dmytryk) (as Kitty Twist); *The Chapman Report* (Cukor) (as Kathleen Barclay); *Period of Adjustment* (Hill) (as Isabel Haverstick)

1963   *In the Cool of the Day* (Stevens) (as Christine Bonner); *Sunday in New York* (Tewksbury) (as Eileen Tyler)

1964   *Les Félins (Joy House; The Love Cage)* (Clément) (as Melinda)

1965   *La Ronde (Circle of Love)* (Vadim) (as the married woman); *Cat Ballou* (Silverstein) (title role)

1966   *The Chase* (Arthur Penn) (as Anna Reeves); *Any Wednesday (Bachelor Girl Apartment)* (as Ellen Gordon); *La Curée (The Game Is Over)* (Vadim) (as Renee Saccard)

1967   *Hurry Sundown* (Preminger) (as Julie Ann Warren); *Barefoot in the Park* (Saks) (as Corie Bratter)

1968   *Barbarella* (Vadim) (title role)
1969   "Metzengerstein" ep. of *Histoires extraordinaires* (*Spirits of the Dead*) (Vadim) (as Countess Frederica); *They Shoot Horses, Don't They?* (Pollack) (as Gloria)
1971   ***Klute*** (Pakula) (as Bree Daniels)
1972   *F.T.A.* (*Foxtrot Tango Alpha*; *Free the Army*; *Fuck the Army*) (Parker) (+ co-pr, co-sc); *Steelyard Blues* (Myerson) (as Iris)
1973   ***Tout va bien*** (Godard and Gorin) (as She); *A Doll's House* (Losey—for TV) (as Nora)
1974   *Introduction to the Enemy* (doc) (appearance)
1976   *The Bluebird* (Cukor) (as Night)
1977   *Julia* (Zinnemann) (as Lillian Hellman); *Fun with Dick and Jane* (Kotcheff) (as Jane)
1978   *Coming Home* (Ashby) (as Sally Hyde); *Comes a Horseman* (Pakula) (as Ella Connors); *California Suite* (Ross) (as Hannah)
1979   *The China Syndrome* (Bridges) (as Kimberley Wells); *The Electric Horseman* (Pollack) (as Hallie Martin)
1980   *Nine to Five* (Higgins) (as Judy Barnly)
1981   *On Golden Pond* (Rydell) (as Chelsea Thayer Wayne); *Rollover* (Pakula) (as Lee Winters)
1982   *The Dollmaker* (Petrie—for TV) (as Gertie Knells, + co-pr)
1985   *Agnes of God* (Jewison) (as Dr. Martha Livingston)
1987   *The Morning After* (Lumet) (as Alex Sternbergen); *Leonard Part 6* (Weiland) (as herself)
1989   *Old Gringo* (Puenzo) (as Harriet Winslow, + pr)
1990   *Stanley and Iris* (Ritt) (as Iris King)

Publications

By FONDA: books—

Jane Fonda's Workout Book, New York, 1981.
Jane Fonda's Year of Fitness and Health, New York, 1984.
Women Coming of Age, with Mignon McCarthy, New York, 1984.

By FONDA: articles—

"'I Prefer Films That Strengthen People': An Interview with Jane Fonda," in *Cineaste* (New York), v. 6, no. 4, 1975.
"*Julia*—Jane Fonda zu den Dreharbeiten," interview with D. Seyrig, in *Frauen und Film* (Berlin), December 1978.
"Never Play It Safe," interview in *Films* (London), March 1981.
"Jane Raw: An Emotionally Candid Fonda Opens up on Her Separation, Her Recovery, Her Lost Night in the Woods, God, and Death," interview with Sally Ogle Davis, in *Los Angeles Magazine*, October 1989.
"Remembering Dad," *TV Guide*, 11 January 1992.

On FONDA: books—

Springer, John, *The Fondas: The Films and Careers of Henry, Jane, and Peter Fonda*, New York, 1970.
Kiernan, Thomas, *Jane: An Intimate Biography of Jane Fonda*, New York, 1977.
Erlanger, Ellen, *Jane Fonda*, Minneapolis, 1981.
Haddad, G. G., *The Films of Jane Fonda*, Secaucus, New Jersey, 1981.
Guiles, Fred, *Jane Fonda, The Actress in Her Time*, New York, 1982.
Cole, Gerald, and Wes Farrell, *The Fondas*, London, 1984.
Spada, James, *Fonda: Her Life in Pictures*, London, 1985.
Vadim, Roger, *Bardo, Deneuve and Fonda: The Memoirs of Roger Vadim*, London, 1986.
Freedland, Michael, *Jane Fonda: A Biography*, London, 1988.

Anderson, Christopher, *Citizen Jane: The Turbulent Life of Jane Fonda*, London, 1990; rev. ed., London, 1993.
Davidson, Bill, *Jane Fonda: An Intimate Biography*, New York, 1990.
Collier, Peter, *The Fondas: A Hollywood Dynasty*, London, 1991.
Shorto, Russell, *Jane Fonda: Political Activism*, Brookfield, Connecticut, 1991.

On FONDA: articles—

Peary, G., "Jane Fonda on Tour: Answering 'Letter to Jane'," in *Take One* (Montreal), July 1974.
Young, T., "Fonda Jane," in *Film Comment* (New York), March-April 1978.
Kroll, Jack, "Jane Fonda," in *The Movie Star Book*, edited by Elisabeth Weis, New York, 1981.
Bygrave, Mike, and Joan Goodman, "Jane Fonda: Banking on Message Movies," in *American Film* (Washington, D.C.), November 1981.
Pally, M., "Choice Parts," in *Film Comment* (New York), September/October 1985.
Current Biography 1986, New York, 1986.
Posner, C., "Jane Fonda's Most Important Part," in *Films in Review* (New York), March 1987.
Davis, Sally Ogle, "Jane Fonda Bounces Back," in *Cosmopolitan*, January 1990.
Adler, Jerry, "Jane and Ted's Excellent Adventure," in *Esquire* (New York), February 1991.

* * *

Jane Fonda's career has reflected her personal values and the political turmoil of her times. On the issue of Vietnam she acted in defiance of government constraints, risking surveillance and blacklisting, and at the expense of alienating her public. Years later, in 1984, conservative protesters picketed Marshall Field's department store in Chicago when she appeared there to promote a new line of exercise clothing. In September 1984, on the other hand, she was honored by earning an Emmy for her role in *The Dollmaker*, an ABC television presentation which she had attempted for 12 years to get on the air. Because of her celebrity and her outspokenness, her life became a public affair, fully documented in the popular press.

Fonda was born to a life of wealth and privilege. Her father, Henry Fonda, was a successful movie star, her mother an heiress of substantial means. After studying art, she had pursued a successful modeling career (twice featured on the cover of *Vogue*), before taking up studies with Lee Strasberg at the Actors Studio. Her first movie contract was with her father's friend, the director Josh Logan, for *Tall Story* in 1960, followed by *Walk on the Wild Side* and *The Chapman Report*. On the basis of these early films, the critic Stanley Kauffmann was among the first to acknowledge her talent in "performances that are not only fundamentally different from one another but are conceived without acting cliché and executed with skill." Ahead, however, were the consequences of her developing a political consciousness that would cause her to be variously described by others as a "late-blooming flower child" and an "all-American antiheroine." (Notably, her father once commented with disdain on her tendency to champion every social issue imaginable, calling her "Jane of Arc.")

In the next phase of her acting career the French director Roger Vadim transformed Fonda, after marrying her, into the sex goddess of his cartoonish *Barbarella*. About the same time, during the late 1960s, she became a social and political activist, dedicated to antiestablishment causes. A new seriousness was also reflected in her films, particularly *They Shoot Horses, Don't They?* and *Klute*. Her political instincts drew her to the radical French director Jean-Luc Godard, who featured her in *Tout va bien* in 1973. Protesting the Vietnam War she founded in 1971 an antiwar troupe (Entertainment Industry for Truth and

Jane Fonda

Justice) which toured Southeast Asia and went on to produce a film entitled *F.T.A.* (*Foxtrot Tango Alpha, Free the Army, Fuck the Army*).

Her well-intentioned opposition to the war characterized her as a radical in the minds of many Americans and alienated her from viewers who were political conservatives, as did her marriage to Tom Hayden, an antiwar militant who had been a highly visible spokesperson for the radical Left. In movies her political commitment continued to surface in *Coming Home* (about the physical and psychological effects of the Vietnam experience), *Julia* (in which she portrayed Lillian Hellman), and *The China Syndrome* (concerning the danger of a meltdown at a nuclear plant, released, by coincidence, just before the near meltdown at the Three Mile Island plant in Pennsylvania, conservative critics of the film having foolishly judged the plot to be preposterous). Other films in her later career have also shown a continuing and genuine concern for important and timely issues. *Nine to Five*, for example, was a satire on the male-dominated world of business, which, despite its box-office success, was by no means a trivial picture. *On Golden Pond* was also a huge popular success, mainly because it offered nostalgic appeal by casting Henry Fonda (in his last film) opposite Katharine Hepburn; but it provided, at the same time, a thoughtful examination of the problems of old age.

By the mid-1980s the Fonda image had mellowed, though the actress still seemed seriously interested in the problems of women and in liberal causes. "I believe it's important to make responsible films," Fonda remarked at the time *The China Syndrome* was released. The marketing success of her exercise program indicated a degree of mainstream acceptance, and the Motion Picture Academy was surely impressed by the achievement of *On Golden Pond*, a film project that involved a substantial personal commitment for her in a production she had instigated. Winning the Emmy Award in 1984 was another demonstration of popular appeal, newly extended to television. In *The Dollmaker* she presented the struggle of a poor woman from the South, attempting to hold her family together through a unique dispute in a northern industrial city where her husband had gone to find work. *The Dollmaker* seemed more sincere than brilliant, but it was certainly superior to the usual television fare.

The later stage of Fonda's career indicates a kind of withdrawal from the controversy that had marked much of her work. After her divorce from Hayden, she chose films that addressed social issues, but decidedly safe ones. *The Morning After*, for example, dealt with the issue of substance abuse, as Fonda portrayed an aging alcoholic. In *Stanley and Iris*, she dealt with an illiterate Robert De Niro, helping him learn to read. The issues here were safe and a far cry from Vietnam (who could possibly be in favor of illiteracy or alcoholism?). Many have seen Fonda's mellowing and her apparent embracing of capitalism (with her fitness empire estimated to be worth tens of millions of dollars and her marriage to media mogul Ted Turner) as a sign of hypocrisy; nevertheless, her melding of a political consciousness with an acting career has been hugely influential. Sadly, in the early 1990s the woman many consider to be the most important American actress of her generation announced her retirement from acting. Taking care of husband Turner, she explained, was a full-time job.

—James M. Welsh, updated by Matthew Hays

FONTAINE, Joan

Nationality: American. **Born:** Joan de Beauvoir de Havilland in Tokyo, Japan, to English parents, 22 October 1917; sister of the actress Olivia de Havilland; took name of stepfather, Fontaine; grew up in Saratoga, California; became U.S. citizen, 1943. **Education:** Attended Los Gatos High School in California; American School in

Kami-Meguro, Japan; Max Reinhardt Drama School. **Family:** Married 1) the actor Brian Aherne, 1939 (divorced 1944); 2) the producer William Dozier, 1946 (divorced 1951), daughter: Deborah Leslie; 3) the film producer Collier Hudson Young, 1952 (divorced 1961); 4) Alfred Wright Jr., 1964 (divorced 1969). **Career:** 1935—stage debut in *Kind Lady*; film debut in *No More Ladies*, billed as Joan Burfield; 1936—briefly used name Joan St. John before settling on Joan Fontaine; signed seven-year contract with Jesse Lasky, who soon sold it to RKO; 1938—RKO drops contract; 1939—signed seven-year contract with David O. Selznick; 1947—formed Rampart Productions with husband William Dozier; 1954—on Broadway in *Tea and Sympathy*; 1981—host of syndicated TV talk show *Joan Fontaine*; 1986—in TV miniseries *Crossings*. **Awards:** Canadian Film Critics Award, for *Rebecca*, 1940; Best Actress Academy Award, and Best Actress, New York Film Critics, for *Suspicion*, 1941.

Films as Actress:

1935   *No More Ladies* (Edward H. Griffith and Cukor) (as Caroline Rumsey, billed as Joan Burfield)

1937   *Quality Street* (Stevens) (as Charlotte Parratt); *The Man Who Found Himself* (Landers) (as Doris King); *You Can't Beat Love* (Cabanne) (as Trudy Olson); *Music for Madame* (Blystone) (as Jean Clemens); *A Damsel in Distress* (Stevens) (as Lady Alyce Marshmorton)

1938   *Maid's Night Out* (Holmes) (as Sheila Harrison); *A Million to One* (Shores) (as Joan Stevens); *Blond Cheat* (Santley) (as Julie); *Sky Giant* (Landers) (as Meg); *The Duke of West Point* (Alfred E. Green) (as Ann Porter)

1939   *Gunga Din* (Stevens) (as Emmy Stebbins); *Man of Conquest* (Nicholls Jr.) (as Eliza Allen); ***The Women*** (Cukor) (as Peggy Day)

1940   *Rebecca* (Hitchcock) (as Mrs. de Winter)

1941   *Suspicion* (Hitchcock) (as Lina McLaidlaw)

1942   *This Above All* (Litvak) (as Prudence Cathaway)

1943   *The Constant Nymph* (Goulding) (as Teresa "Tessa" Sanger)

1944   *Jane Eyre* (Stevenson) (title role); *Frenchman's Creek* (Leisen) (as Lady Dona St. Columb)

1945   *The Affairs of Susan* (Seiter) (as Susan Darell)

1946   *From This Day Forward* (Berry) (as Susan)

1947   *Ivy* (Wood) (title role)

1948   ***Letter from an Unknown Woman*** (Max Ophüls) (as Lisa Berndle); *The Emperor Waltz* (Wilder) (as Johanna Augusta Franziska von Stultzenberg); *Kiss the Blood off My Hands* (*Blood on My Hands*) (Norman Foster) (as Jane Wharton); *You Gotta Stay Happy* (Potter) (as Dee Dee Dillwood)

1950   *Born to be Bad* (Nicholas Ray) (as Christabel Caine); *September Affair* (Dieterle) (as Manina Stuart)

1951   *Darling, How Could You!* (*Rendezvous*) (Leisen) (as Alice Grey)

1952   *Something to Live For* (Stevens) (as Jenny Carey); *Ivanhoe* (Thorpe) (as Rowena); *Othello* (Welles) (as page)

1953   *Decameron Nights* (Fregonese) (as Fiametta/Bartolomea/Ginevra/Isabella); *Flight to Tangier* (Warren) (as Susan); *The Bigamist* (Lupino) (as Eve Graham)

1954   *Casanova's Big Night* (McLeod) (as Francesca Bruni)

1956   *Serenade* (Anthony Mann) (as Kendall Hale); *Beyond a Reasonable Doubt* (Fritz Lang) (as Susan Spencer)

1957   *Island in the Sun* (Rossen) (as Mavis Norman); *Until They Sail* (Wise) (as Anne Leslie)

1958   *A Certain Smile* (Negulesco) (as Françoise Ferrand); *South Pacific* (Logan) (cameo)

1961   *Voyage to the Bottom of the Sea* (Irwin Allen) (as Dr. Susan Hiller)

Joan Fontaine in *Rebecca*

1962 *Tender Is the Night* (Henry King) (as Baby Warren)
1966 *The Witches* (*The Devil's Own*) (Frankel) (as Gwen Mayfield, + co-pr)
1978 *The Users* (Hardy—for TV) (as Grace St. George)
1985 *Hitchcock: il brivido del genio* (*The Thrill of Genius*) (Bortolini and Masenza)
1986 *Dark Mansions* (London—for TV) (as Margaret Drake)
1994 *Good King Wenceslas* (*The Good King*) (Tuchner—for TV) (as Queen Ludmilla)

Publications

By FONTAINE: book—

No Bed of Roses, New York, 1978.

By FONTAINE: articles—

Interview with Carol Craig, in *Motion Picture Magazine* (New York), August 1937.
"This Must Be It," interview with Bosley Crowther, in *New York Times*, 11 February 1940.
"Hollywood at Home," interview with Adele Whitely Fletcher, in *Photoplay* (New York), July 1940.
"These Above All," interview with Lean Surmelian, in *Photoplay* (New York), April 1942.
"A Mistake I Wouldn't Make Again," in *Photoplay* (New York), May 1943.
"Fontaine's Fling," interview with Adele Whitely Fletcher, in *Photoplay* (New York), December 1944.
"Come into the Kitchen, Darling," in *Photoplay* (New York), May 1946.
"Till Work Do Us Part," interview with Sheilah Graham, in *Photoplay* (New York), September 1947.
"Joan Fontaine Casts a Vote for Independence," interview with Thomas M. Pryor, in *New York Times*, 16 November 1947.
"Miss Dozier's Bank Account," in *Photoplay* (New York), April 1949.
Interview with P. Anthony, in *Photoplay* (New York), March 1962.
"Olivia and I," in *Good Housekeeping*, August 1978.
Interview with C. P. Andersen, in *People* (New York), 20 November 1978.
Interview with Brian McFarlane, in *Cinema Papers* (Melbourne), June 1982.
Interview in *Cinématographe* (Paris), November 1983.
Interview with Gregory Speck, in *Interview* (New York), February 1987.

On FONTAINE: books—

Memo from: David O. Selznick, edited by Rudy Behlmer, New York, 1972.
Higham, Charles, *Sisters: The Story of Olivia de Havilland and Joan Fontaine*, New York, 1984.
Beeman, Marsha Lynn, *Joan Fontaine: A Bio-Bibliography*, Westport, Connecticut, 1994.

On FONTAINE: articles—

Fletcher, Adele Whitely, "Sister Act," in *Photoplay* (New York), September 1941.
Baskette, Kirtley, "Olivia's Little Sister," in *American Magazine*, April 1942.
Waterbury, Ruth, "Personal Conquest," in *Photoplay* (New York), June 1942 and July 1942.
Current Biography 1944, New York, 1944.
Graham, Sheilah, "Is There a Man in the House?," in *Photoplay* (New York), August 1949.

Carlyle, John, "Joan Fontaine: Is as Believable as a Sophisticate as She Was as an Ingenue," in *Films in Review* (New York), March 1963.
Bourget, Jean-Loup, "The Coming of Age of Joan Fontaine," in *Film Comment* (New York), January-February 1974.
Ciné Revue (Paris), 1 September 1983.

*   *   *

Joan Fontaine established her screen persona in the early 1940s in Alfred Hitchcock's *Rebecca* and *Suspicion*. In both films, she plays young Englishwomen but, interestingly, while the two characters are from opposite economic and social backgrounds, Fontaine projects a similar "passive" identity in each film—a quality she also brought to her title role in the non-Hitchcock *Jane Eyre*. In these and other films, Fontaine evidenced skill at playing characters who, because of the restrictions society places on the woman's role, depend on the construction of romantic fantasies which they project onto an "active" male. In our society, since passivity is considered a feminine trait, it is best exemplified through a corresponding demeanor which reflects, as Fontaine's screen persona does, such qualities as patrician beauty, elegance, and refinement. In the Hollywood cinema passivity is particularly associated with European female characters and, not surprisingly, Fontaine has most often appeared in such roles, as she does in Max Ophüls's *Letter from an Unknown Woman*, Arguably, the film contains her finest screen performance and, even more so than *Rebecca*, *Suspicion*, and *Jane Eyre*, the film depends on Fontaine's persona to elaborate its thematic concerns.

Fontaine was best used in the 1940s romance melodramas mentioned above which have directors who are sensitive to the social and sexual tensions these characterizations embody. Undoubtedly Fontaine was conscious of being typecast but her most notable attempt to expand her image by playing an assertive woman, in Mitchell Leisen's *Frenchman's Creek*, was an unfortunate choice. In particular, Leisen's direction lacks the necessary delicacy and nuance that Fontaine's persona demands. Another change of pace film (if not quite role) in the noir thriller *Kiss the Blood off My Hands* opposite producer-star Burt Lancaster failed to expand her image much either.

In the 1950s Fontaine was no longer contemporary in a cinema which distilled the images of woman into either Doris Day or Marilyn Monroe. Increasingly, under the circumstances, Fontaine had no recourse but to exploit her feminine demeanor by playing worldly and, by extension, self-centered women (characters anticipated in Sam Wood's *Ivy*). The "bitch" implications of this persona are most fully realized in Anthony Mann's *Serenade*, but are more interestingly employed in Fritz Lang's *Beyond a Reasonable Doubt* and Henry King's *Tender Is the Night*.

Unlike some of her contemporaries from Hollywood's Golden Age—Bette Davis, Joan Crawford, and even her sister, Olivia de Havilland—Fontaine did not take advantage of her age and latter-day "bitch" persona to fashion a new career for herself by appearing in horror films, although she did make one for England's Hammer Productions—*The Witches*; in it she played, not the harridan villain, but a patrician doctor of elegance and refinement in the vein of her earlier Hollywood roles. She also co-produced the film.

—Richard Lippe, updated by John McCarty

FORD, Glenn

Nationality: American. **Born:** Gwyllyn Samuel Newton Ford in Quebec, Canada, 1 May 1916; grew up in Santa Monica, California. **Education:** Attended Santa Monica High School, graduated 1934. **Mili-**

tary Service: U.S. Marine Corps, 1942-45; served in marine unit in Vietnam, 1967-68: colonel. **Family:** Married 1) the actress Eleanor Powell, 1943 (divorced 1959), son: the actor Peter Ford; 2) the actress Kathryn Hays, 1966 (divorced 1968); 3) the actress Cynthia Hayward, 1977; 4) Jeanne Baus, 1993. **Career:** Worked with Wilshire Theatre, Los Angeles; 1935—stage debut in *The Children's Hour*; 1939—film debut in *Heaven with a Barbed Wire Fence*; contract with Columbia; 1971-72—in TV series *Cade's County*, and series *The Family Holvak*, 1975; 1976—in TV mini-series *Once an Eagle*, and *Evening in Byzantium*, 1978. **Agent:** c/o Artists Group, 9200 Sunset Boulevard, Suite 318, Los Angeles, CA 90069, U.S.A.

Films as Actor:

1939 *Heaven with a Barbed Wire Fence* (Cortez) (as Joe); *My Son Is Guilty* (*Crime's End*) (Barton) (as Barney)

1940 *Convicted Woman* (Grinde) (as Jim Brent); *Men without Souls* (Grinde) (as Johnny Adams); *Babies for Sale* (Barton) (as Steve Burton); *The Lady in Question* (*It Happened in Paris*) (Charles Vidor) (as Pierre Morestan); *Blondie Plays Cupid* (Strayer) (as Charlie)

1941 *So Ends Our Night* (Cromwell) (as Ludwig Kern); *Texas* (George Marshall) (as Tod Ramsey); *Go West, Young Lady* (Strayer) (as Tex Miller)

1942 *The Adventures of Martin Eden* (Salkow) (title role); *Flight Lieutenant* (Salkow) (as Danny Doyle)

1943 *The Desperadoes* (Charles Vidor) (as Cheyenne Rogers); *Destroyer* (Seiter) (as Mickey Donohue); *Hollywood in Uniform* (appearance)

1946 *Gilda* (Charles Vidor) (as Johnny Farrell); *A Stolen Life* (Bernhardt) (as Bill Emerson); *Gallant Journey* (Wellman) (as John Montgomery)

1947 *Framed* (*Paula*) (Wallace) (as Mike Lambert)

1948 *The Mating of Millie* (Levin) (as Doug Andrews); *The Man from Colorado* (Levin) (as Col. Owen Devereaux); *The Loves of Carmen* (Charles Vidor) (as Don José); *The Return of October* (*Date with Destiny*) (Joseph H. Lewis) (as Prof. Bassett); *Make It Real* (short for United Jewish Appeal) (as narrator)

1949 *Undercover Man* (Joseph H. Lewis) (as Frank Warren); *Lust for Gold* (*For Those Who Dare*) (Simon) (as Jacob Walz); *Mr. Soft Touch* (*House of Settlement*) (Douglas and Levin) (as Joe Miracle); *The Doctor and the Girl* (Bernhardt) (as Dr. Michael Corday); *Hollywood Goes to Church* (Staub—short)

1950 *The White Tower* (Tetzlaff) (as Martin Ordway); *Convicted* (*One Way Out*) (Levin) (as Joe Hufford); *The Flying Missile* (Levin) (as Cmdr. Bill Talbot); *The Redhead and the Cowboy* (Fenton) (as Gil Kyle)

1951 *Follow the Sun* (Lanfield) (as Ben Hogan); *The Secret of Convict Lake* (Michael Gordon) (as Canfield); *Young Man with Ideas* (Leisen) (as Maxwell Webster); *The Green Glove* (*Le Gantelet vert*) (Maté) (as Michael Blake)

1952 *Affair in Trinidad* (Sherman) (as Steve Emery); *Time Bomb* (*Terror on a Train*) (Tetzlaff) (as Peter Lyncourt)

1953 *The Man from the Alamo* (Boetticher) (as John Stoud); *Plunder of the Sun* (Farrow) (as Al Colby); ***The Big Heat*** (Fritz Lang) (as David Bannion); *Appointment in Honduras* (Jacques Tourneur) (as Steve Corbett)

1954 *Human Desire* (Fritz Lang) (as Jeff Warren); *The Violent Men* (*Rough Company*) (Maté) (as John Parrish); *City Story* (Beaudine) (as narrator)

1955 *The Americano* (Castle) (as Sam Dent); *Blackboard Jungle* (Richard Brooks) (as Richard Dadier); *Interrupted Melody* (Bernhardt) (as Dr. Thomas King); *Trial* (Robson) (as David Blake)

1956 *Ransom!* (Segal) (as David G. Stannard); *Jubal* (Daves) (as Jubal Troop); *The Fastest Gun Alive* (Rouse) (as George Temple); *The Teahouse of the August Moon* (Daniel Mann) (as Capt. Fisby)

1957 *3:10 to Yuma* (Daves) (as Ben Wade); *Don't Go Near the Water* (Walters) (as Lt. Max Siegel)

1958 *The Sheepman* (George Marshall) (as Jason Sweet); *Cowboy* (Daves) (as Tom Reece); *Imitation General* (George Marshall) (as M/Sgt. Murphy Savage); *Torpedo Run* (Pevney) (as Lt. Cmdr. Barney Doyle)

1959 *It Started with a Kiss* (George Marshall) (as Sgt. Joe Fitzpatrick)

1960 *Cimarron* (Anthony Mann) (as Yancey Cravet); *The Gazebo* (George Marshall) (as Elliott Nash); *Cry for Happy* (George Marshall) (as Andy Cyphers)

1961 *Pocketful of Miracles* (Capra) (as Dave "the Dude" Conway, + co-pr)

1962 *Experiment in Terror* (*The Grip of Fear*) (Edwards) (as John Ripley); *The Four Horsemen of the Apocalypse* (Minnelli) (as Julio Desnoyers)

1963 *The Courtship of Eddie's Father* (Minnelli) (as Tom Corbett); *Love Is a Ball* (*All This and Money Too*) (Swift) (as John Davis)

1964 *Advance to the Rear* (*Company of Cowards?*) (George Marshall) (as Capt. Jared Heath); *Fate Is the Hunter* (Ralph Nelson) (as McBane); *Dear Heart* (Delbert Mann) (as Harry Mork)

1965 *The Rounders* (Kennedy) (as Ben Jones); *Seapower* (as narrator)

1966 *The Money Trap* (Kennedy) (as Joe Baron); *Rage* (*El mal*) (Gazcon) (as Reuben); *Paris brûle-t-il?* (*Is Paris Burning?*) (Clément) (as Gen. Omar Bradley)

1967 *The Last Challenge* (*Pistolero of Red River*) (Thorpe) (as Marshal Don Blaine); *A Time for Killing* (*The Long Ride Home*) (Karlson) (as Maj. Charles Wolcott)

1968 *Day of the Evil Gun* (Thorpe) (as Warfield)

1969 *Heaven with a Gun* (Katzin) (as Jim Killian); *Smith!* (O'Herlihy) (title role)

1970 *The Brotherhood of the Bell* (Wendkos—for TV); *The Gold Diggers* (for TV)

1972 *Santee* (Gary Nelson) (title role)

1973 *Jarrett* (Shear—for TV)

1974 *The Disappearance of Flight 412* (Jud Taylor—for TV); *The Greatest Gift* (Sagal—for TV) (as Rev. Holvak); *Punch and Jody* (Shear—for TV)

1976 *Midway* (*Battle of Midway*) (Smight) (as Rear Adm. Raymond A. Spruance)

1977 *The Three Thousand Mile Chase* (Mayberry—for TV) (as Dvorak/Staveck)

1978 *Superman* (Richard Donner) (as Jonathan Kent)

1979 *The Gift* (Don Taylor—for TV) (as Billy Devlin); *The Sacketts* (Totten—for TV); *Beggarman, Thief* (Doheny—for TV)

1980 *Fukkatsu no hi* (*The Virus*) (Fukasaku) (as Richardson); *Il Visitatore* (*The Visitor*) (Paradisi) (as Detective)

1981 *Happy Birthday to Me* (J. Lee Thompson) (as Dr. David Faraday); *Day of the Assassin* (Trenchard-Smith) (as Christakis)

1989 *Casablanca Express* (Martino) (as Sheriff John Danahar)

1990 *Border Shootout* (McIntyre)

1991 *Raw Nerve* (Prior) (as Captain Gavin); *The Final Verdict* (Fisk—for TV) (as the Reverend Lowell Rogers)

1992 *Our Hollywood Education* (Beltrami—doc)

Publications

By FORD: book—

Glenn Ford, R.F.D. Beverly Hills, with Margaret Redfield, Old Tappan, New Jersey, 1970.

Glenn Ford (right) with Gloria Grahame and Broderick Crawford in *Human Desire*

By FORD: articles—

Interview in *TV Times* (London), 11 August 1977.
Interview in *Ciné Revue* (Paris), 9 April 1987.

On FORD: articles—

Current Biography 1959, New York, 1959.
Shipman, David, in *The Great Movie Stars: The International Years*, London, 1972.
"Glenn Ford in His House," in *Photoplay Film Monthly*, May 1972.
"The Many Loves of Glenn Ford," in *Photoplay Film Monthly*, December 1972; see also January 1976.
Marill, Alvin H., in *Films in Review* (New York), March 1978.
Ciné Revue (Paris), 4 September 1980, 1 October 1981, and 26 July 1984.
Hollywood Reporter, 20 November 1981.

* * *

Glenn Ford's mouth is a scar of suffering, his eyes dim lights of introspection, and his voice expresses the cool, contemplative restraint of masculinity under control. In effect, he is somewhat drier than the heroes America wanted from the movies, and this may explain his secondary star status behind Gary Cooper, John Wayne, James Stewart, and others. His popularity took off with *Gilda* in the late 1940s, playing opposite Rita Hayworth—although it was George Macready to whom Ford observed, "I was born the night you met me." Ford mainly stayed within the melodrama/film noir tradition and did his best work in these genres. His most successful portrayals were in two films by Fritz Lang, *Human Desire* and *The Big Heat*, because it is in these films that Ford came closest to portraying the type of role he was usually denied—the antihero, the tarnished hero, the role so much associated with Humphrey Bogart.

In *Human Desire*, Lang's remake of Renoir's *La Bête humaine*, Ford portrayed a man whose lust nearly leads him to commit murder. He steals for Gloria Grahame, and only the unexpected presence of a passerby prevents him from committing the act of murder—there is little moral choice involved. Ford is even more interesting in *The Big Heat*. Using his influence as a police officer and hiding behind the moral camouflage of a husband out to revenge the murder of his wife, Ford is responsible for more corpses than any of the film's "real" criminals. In a brilliant piece of plotting, Ford persuades Gloria

Grahame to kill Jeanette Nolan, neatly sidestepping the act of murder himself.

Unfortunately, after these efforts, Ford generally made what seemed to be bids for broader appeal and acceptance—*The Americano*, *Cowboy*, and *The Gazebo* with Debbie Reynolds. His appearances in a number of 1950s and 1960s Westerns bear some notice, though. In Delmer Daves's *3:10 to Yuma* Ford is effective as an outlaw playing mind games with captor Van Heflin, while both await the title train. He is also interesting in Richard Brooks's *The Blackboard Jungle*, as a high school teacher in a tough New York classroom, and as a widower in *The Courtship of Eddie's Father*, with Vincente Minnelli in charge. Pictures such as these, and the Lang films, make it easier for us to forgive a career otherwise dedicated to an overeagerness to make banal statements on the American situation.

—Don M. Short, updated by Frank Uhle

FORD, Harrison

Nationality: American. **Born:** Chicago, Illinois, 13 July 1942. **Education:** Attended Ripon College, Wisconsin. **Family:** Married 1) Mary (Ford), sons: Willard, Benjamin; 2) the screenwriter Melissa Mathison, 1983, son: Malcolm. **Career:** Actor in summer stock, Wisconsin, and in Laguna Beach Playhouse, 1963; 1964—signed contract with Columbia; 1966—film debut in *Dead Heat on a Merry-Go-Round*; fired by Columbia; late 1960s—signed contract with Universal; 1970s—worked as carpenter between roles; 1977—role in *Star Wars* brings international fame. **Address:** c/o Pat McQueeney, McQueeney Management, 146 North Almont Drive, Suite 8, Los Angeles, CA 90048, U.S.A.

Films as Actor:

1966   *Dead Heat on a Merry-Go-Round* (Girard) (as bellboy)
1967   *A Time for Killing* (*The Long Ride Home*) (Karlson) (as Lt. Shaffer); *Luv* (Clive Donner)
1968   *Journey to Shiloh* (Hale) (as Willie Bill Beardon)
1970   *Getting Straight* (Rush) (as Jake); *Zabriskie Point* (Antonioni) (role edited out of final version); *The Intruders* (Graham—for TV) (as Carl)
1973   *American Graffiti* (Lucas) (as Bob Falfa)
1974   *The Conversation* (Francis Ford Coppola) (as Martin Stett)
1976   *Dynasty* (Philips—for TV) (as Mark Blackwood)
1977   *The Possessed* (Thorpe—for TV) (as Paul Winjam); *Star Wars* (Lucas) (as Han Solo); *Heroes* (Kagan) (as Kenny Boyd)
1978   *Force 10 from Navarone* (Hamilton) (as Lt. Col. Mike Barnsby)
1979   *Hanover Street* (Hyams) (as David Halloran); *The Frisco Kid* (Aldrich) (as Tommy Lillard); *Apocalypse Now* (Francis Ford Coppola) (as Colonel); *More American Graffiti* (Norton) (as motocycle cop, unbilled cameo)
1980   *The Empire Strikes Back* (Kershner) (as Han Solo)
1981   *Raiders of the Lost Ark* (Spielberg) (as Indiana Jones)
1982   *Blade Runner* (Ridley Scott) (as Rick Deckard)
1983   *Return of the Jedi* (Marquand) (as Han Solo)
1984   *Indiana Jones and the Temple of Doom* (Spielberg) (title role)
1985   *Witness* (Weir) (as John Book)
1986   *The Mosquito Coast* (Weir) (as Allie Fox)
1988   *Frantic* (Polanski) (as Dr. Richard Walker); *Working Girl* (Mike Nichols) (as Jack Trainer)
1989   *Indiana Jones and the Last Crusade* (Spielberg) (title role)
1990   *Presumed Innocent* (Pakula) (as Rusty Sabich)

1991   *Regarding Henry* (Mike Nichols) (as Henry Turner)
1992   *Patriot Games* (Noyce) (as Jack Ryan); *L'Envers du Decor: Portrait de Pierre Guffroy* (*Behind the Scenes: A Portrait of Pierre Guffroy*) (Salis—doc)
1993   *The Fugitive* (Andrew Davis) (as Dr. Richard Kimble); *Earth and the American Dream* (Couturie—doc) (as voice)
1994   *Clear and Present Danger* (Noyce) (as Jack Ryan); *Jimmy Hollywood* (Levinson) (as himself); *Mustang: The Hidden Kingdom* (Tony Miller—doc) (as narrator)
1995   *Les Cent et une nuits* (*A Hundred and One Nights*) (Varda) (as Actor for a Day); *Sabrina* (Pollack) (as Linus Larrabee)
1996   *Devil's Own* (Pakula)
1997   *Air Force One*

Publications

By FORD: articles—

Interview with R. Appelbaum, in *Films* (London), September 1981.
Interview with P. H. Broeske, in *Cinema Papers* (Melbourne), May 1985.
"An Innocent Man," interview with Dan Yakir, in *Empire* (London), October 1990.
"Off Camera," interview with Lawrence Grobel, in *Playboy* (Chicago), September 1993.
"Facing His Biggest Risk of All, Romantic Comedy," interview with Trip Gabriel, in *New York Times*, 10 December 1995.

On FORD: books—

Clinch, Minty, *Harrison Ford: A Biography*, London, 1984.
McKenzie, Alan, *The Harrison Ford Story*, New York, 1984.
Honeyford, Paul, *Harrison Ford: A Biography*, London, 1986.
Jelot-Blanc, Jean Jacques, *Harrison Ford*, Paris, 1987.
Sellers, Robert, *Harrison Ford: A Biography*, London, 1993.
Pfeiffer, Lee, *The Films of Harrison Ford*, Secaucus, New Jersey, 1995.

On FORD: articles—

Crawley, T., "*Wars* Star: How Harrison Ford Flew Solo and Won His Wings," in *Films Illustrated* (London), April 1978.
Rickey, Carrie, and Artie West, "The Return of the Wasp Hero," in *American Film* (Washington, D.C.), November 1981.
Current Biography 1984, New York, 1984.
Hibbin, S., "Harrison Ford," in *Films and Filming* (London), January 1984.
Clarke, Gerald, "Stardom Time for a Bag of Bones," in *Time* (New York), 25 February 1985.
Martin, Guy, "The American Leading Man Is Strong, Sexy and Stranger than Ever: Harrison Ford and the Jungle of Gloom," in *Esquire* (New York), October 1986.
Hunter, Allan, "Harrison Ford," in *Films and Filming* (London), February 1987.
Hoban, Phoebe, "Court and Spark," in *Premiere* (New York), August 1990.
Halberstam, David, "The Fugitive Star," in *Vanity Fair* (New York), July 1993.
Hearty, Kitty Bowe, "Born to Run," in *Premiere* (New York), September 1993.
Halberstam, David, "The Code of Harrison Ford," in *Reader's Digest* (Canadian), December 1993; see also issue of October 1993.

*   *   *

Harrison Ford in *Raiders of the Lost Ark*

Shying away from the Hollywood limelight has not hurt maverick superstar Harrison Ford's career one iota. For a man who once cut back on making the acting rounds to concentrate on his carpentry sideline, the ever-practical Ford is now one of filmdom's bona fide bankable stars. The same pragmatic bent that encouraged Ford to maintain a backup career informs his work as an actor. Reliable and forthright, Ford is a man's man determined to do a good job and not about to suffer fools or slackers gladly. If a certain solemnity mars his dramatic work, he is a freewheeling force of nature in his rugged adventures and a champagne-class laugh-getter in his comedies.

After uncertain beginnings, Ford hit his stride with the megahit, *Star Wars* as his wise-guy persona blasted into space. Han Solo is a reluctant hero, but, once coerced or tricked into a galactic war, he out-battles the most accustomed saviors in orbit. Armed with a sarcastic wit, as well as space blasters or a bullwhip, Ford's leading men zip beyond the legacy of Flynn and Power as this modern star ridicules the feats of derring-do expected of him, particularly as repackaged by Lucas and Spielberg to the nth power. Nudging his fans in the ribs, Ford seems to be saying, "How am I getting away with this?," but a task's daunting impossibility never actually stops him from accomplishing it. If Ford's Han Solo and Indiana Jones have a true progenitor, it is not so much the macho myth-makers of yesteryear but Burt Lancaster's tongue-in-cheek daredevil in *The Crimson Pirate*. Taking into account the crushing weight of all the megabudgeted special effects in his movies, Ford's light touch prevents the Lucas and Spielberg oeuvre from collapsing into tiresome, revisionist aging boys' adven-

tures. With jocular Ford at the center of these expensive diversions, the audience cares about how each of the cliffhangers laced through the films will turn out; he is indispensable to their success.

Forever kidding the image of the resolute American redemptor in the *Star Wars* and *Indiana Jones* trilogies, Ford also expanded his dramatic range. In the thought-provoking futuristic noir, *Blade Runner*, he brings gravity to the part of an android-hunting Philip Marlowe type in a movie dismissed in its time, but now esteemed as a classic melding of the detective and sci-fi genres. Winning an Oscar nomination as the big city cop in awe of the Amish people he choose to protect (*Witness*), Ford followed this breakthrough performance with the flawed *The Mosquito Coast*, an acting challenge about an antisocial man who subjects his family to his own ramshackle Shangri-La in the jungles of Central America; unfortunately the box-office disappointment of this ambitious film may have caused Ford to retrench artistically. Increasingly, since *Frantic*, Ford has been more and more dramatically clenched in his performances in serious fare. Particularly in *Presumed Innocent*, his face is a mask of pain underlined by one expression of resigned perplexity. At least in the Jack Ryan espionage thrillers and in that update of *Les Misérables*, *The Fugitive*, Ford's histrionic liabilities are camouflaged by a plethora of stunt-men heroics and unceasing physical action. Ford is much better when humor is part of the equation, and he can triumph wittily over his own wavering, save-your-own-skin philosophy. In prestige dramas, he deliberately holds back as if some refrigerator light in his soul had been turned off.

423

In comedies such as *Working Girl* and *Sabrina*, Ford's humanity shines through unabashed, and he is never as sexy in his he-man gambols as he is in these effervescent romances. If he could bring just a bit of this casualness to his serious endeavors, he might develop into something finer than the most personable action star on the contemporary scene. He might blast through his rigidity and emerge as the actor he left behind on *The Mosquito Coast*. As charismatic as Gibson and handsomer than Cruise, Ford is a superstar in the classic mold; it may be unfair to demand more from someone who has given moviegoers so much pleasure. His ruffled dignity makes him a perfect foil in comedies, and he carries on the bloodline of an elegant tradition by doing his own modification of Gary Cooper in *Working Girl* and finding nuances in *Sabrina* left untouched by Bogart.

But the suspicion persists that Ford has tapped but a portion of his talent thus far. In interviews, he stresses the importance of script texture in the films he chooses to make and insists that all his projects must tell a good story. As an interpreter of the escapism he selects for production, Ford can already be considered a master storyteller.

—Robert Pardi

FOSTER, Jodie

Nationality: American. **Born:** Alicia Christian Foster in Los Angeles, California, 19 November 1962. **Education:** Attended Lycée Français, Los Angeles; Yale University, B.A. 1985. **Career:** Actress in TV commercials from the age of three, original "Coppertone Girl" character in suntan lotion ads; 1969—acting debut on TV in *Mayberry, R.F.D.*; 1972—film debut in *Napoleon and Samantha* for Disney; 1970s—much work for TV, including TV series *Bob & Carol & Ted & Alice*, 1973, and *Paper Moon*, 1974-75; 1991—directed first film, *Little Man Tate*. **Awards:** U.S. National Film Critics Award, and Los Angeles Film Critics Award, for *Taxi Driver*, 1976; British Academy of Film and Television Arts Awards for Best Supporting Actress and Most Promising Newcomer, for *Taxi Driver* and *Bugsy Malone*, 1976; Academy Award for Best Actress, for *The Accused*, 1988; Chevalier dans l'Orde des Arts et de Lettres, 1995; Governors Award, American Society of Cinematographers, 1996. **Agent:** ICM, 8942 Beverly Boulevard, Beverly Hills, CA 90211, U.S.A.

Films as Actress:

1970 *Menace on the Mountain* (McEveety—for TV) (as Suellen McIver)
1972 *Napoleon and Samantha* (McEveety) (as Samantha); *Kansas City Bomber* (Freedman) (as Rita)
1973 *Tom Sawyer* (Taylor) (as Becky Thatcher); *One Little Indian* (McEveety) (as Martha); *Rookie of the Year* (Elikann—for TV)
1974 *Alice Doesn't Live Here Anymore* (Scorsese) (as Audrey); *Smile Jenny, You're Dead* (Thorpe—for TV) (as Liberty)
1976 *Echoes of a Summer* (*The Last Castle*) (Taylor) (as Deirdre Striden); *Freaky Friday* (Nelson) (as Annabel Andrews); *Bugsy Malone* (Alan Parker) (as Tallulah); *Taxi Driver* (Scorsese) (as Iris Steensman)
1977 *The Little Girl Who Lives down the Lane* (Gessner) (as Rynn Jacobs); *Candleshoe* (Tokar) (as Casey Brown); *Il casotto* (*The Beach House*) (Citti) (as Teresina)
1978 *Moi, Fleur Bleue* (*Stop Calling Me Baby!*) (as Fleur Bleue)
1980 *Foxes* (Lyne) (as Jeanie); *Carny* (Kaylor) (as Donna)

1983 *O'Hara's Wife* (Bartman) (as Barbara O'Hara); *Le Sang des autres* (*The Blood of Others*) (Chabrol) (as Hélène); *Svengali* (Harvey—for TV) (as Zoe Alexander)
1984 *The Hotel New Hampshire* (Richardson) (as Franny Berry)
1986 *Mesmerized* (*Shocked*) (Laughlin) (as Victoria, + co-pr)
1987 *Siesta* (Lambert) (as Nancy)
1988 *Five Corners* (Bill) (as Linda); *The Accused* (Kaplan) (as Sarah Tobias); *Stealing Home* (Kampmann) (as Katie Chandler)
1989 *Backtrack* (*Catchfire*) (Dennis Hopper—released in U.S. in 1991) (as Anne Benton)
1991 *The Silence of the Lambs* (Jonathan Demme) (as Clarice Starling)
1992 *Shadows and Fog* (Woody Allen) (as prostitute)
1993 *Sommersby* (Amiel) (as Laurel); *It Was a Wonderful Life* (Ohayon—doc) (as narrator)
1994 *Maverick* (Richard Donner) (as Annabelle Bransford); *Nell* (Apted) (title role, + co-pr)
1996 *Contact* (Zemeckis)

Films as Director:

1991 *Little Man Tate* (+ ro as Dede Tate)
1995 *Home for the Holidays* (+ co-pr)

Publications

By FOSTER: articles—

Interview in *Ciné Revue* (Paris), 1 July 1976.
Interview in *Screen International* (London), 8 October 1977.
Interview with Andy Warhol, in *Interview* (New York), June 1980.
Interview, by Foster, with Nastassia Kinski, in *Film Comment* (New York), September/October 1982.
"Why Me?," in *Esquire* (New York), December 1982.
Interview, by Foster, with Rob Lowe, in *Interview* (New York), May 1984.
Interview in *Time Out* (London), 8 November 1984.
Interview in *Interview* (New York), August 1987.
Interview with Linda R. Miller, in *American Film* (Los Angeles), October 1988.
"American Original," interview with Michael A. Lerner, in *Interview* (New York), September 1989.
Interview with Rod Lurie, in *Empire* (London), June 1991.
Interview with Ingrid Sischy, in *Interview* (New York), October 1991.
"Wunderkind," interview with Arion Berger, in *Harper's Bazaar* (New York), November 1991.

On FOSTER: books—

Sinclair, Marian, *Hollywood Lolita: The Nymphet Syndrome in the Movies*, London, 1988.
Chunovic, Louis, *Jodie: A Biography*, Chicago, 1995.
Kennedy, Philippa, *Jodie Foster: A Life on Screen*, New York, 1996.
Smolen, Diane, *The Films of Jodie Foster*, Secaucus, New Jersey, 1996.

On FOSTER: articles—

Van Meter, Jonathan, "Child of the Movies," in *New York Times Magazine*, 6 January 1991.
Clark, John, filmography in *Premiere* (New York), March 1991.
Hirshey, Geari, "Jodie Foster," in *Rolling Stone* (New York), 21 March 1991.

Jodie Foster in *Taxi Driver*

Cameron, Julie, "Burden of the Gift," in *American Film*, November/
  December 1991.
Current Biography 1992, New York, 1992.
Schnayerson, Michael, "Pure Jody," in *Vanity Fair* (New York), May
  1994.
Abramowitz, Rachel, "Fearless," in *Premiere* (New York), January
  1995.

                              *   *   *

Foster is so versatile and invests her star-power into so many different film genres, it is difficult to find a tidy critical pigeonhole for
her. Elusive in interviews, the intensely private Foster has turned her
attention to directing as a natural offshoot of her precise acting; her
style-in-progress is pristine, liberal-minded, and nonthreateningly offbeat.

There has been something strikingly quirky about Foster from the
start—or at least from her fifth film appearance as the tomboyish
Audrey in *Alice Doesn't Live Her Anymore*. Since that cherished feminist road show, Foster has taken acting risks but has steered clear of
the androgyny that was so arresting in her early films as a child.
Certainly, it was brave of this young actress to explore adult psycho-
sexuality by impersonating a teen streetwalker in *Taxi Driver*. That
she succeeded so uncondescendingly in evoking this callow runaway's
unblinking acceptance of hooking is a testament to Foster's innate
talent. Too original a presence as a youngster, Foster simply did not
have it in her to become America's sweetheart, although Disney tried.
The subversiveness of her brand of innocence (corrupted in *Taxi Driver*;
turned homicidal in *The Little Girl Who Lives down the Lane*), found
fuller expression in the teenaged angst of *Foxes*, an underappreciated
examination of drifting adolescents turned off by parental hypocrisy
and societal pressures. At this point, Foster might have become fossil-
ized as a symbol of teen anomie, but she broadened her horizons by
attending Yale and expanded the intelligence that had informed her
work since childhood. Surviving the terrifying public ordeal of being
stalked by John Hinckley, who shot President Reagan to impress her,
she exhibited grace under fire, graduated with honors from school, and
resumed her career with honors, too.

Before her breakout role in *The Accused*, nothing Foster chose was
conventional, and, even in such pretentious misfires as *Five Corners*
and *Carny* and in bombs such as *Siesta* and *The Hotel New Hampshire*,
she infused the roles with keen self-awareness, a quality that stamped
her as much too independent a presence to be at home in standard
girlfriend roles. If *The Accused* is really a politically correct television
movie at heart, Foster was a revelation as the trailer-trash hedonist
filing rape charges in order to regain the self-respect stolen in the
assault. A female buddy-buddy movie to boot, *The Accused* stands or
falls on Foster's performance as a survivor who refused to be further
victimized by the courts or by the caveman ideology of her attackers.
Winning an Oscar for this and for a second less flashy role in *The
Silence of the Lambs*, Foster found her niche as a feminist role model
with a specialty in playing against-all-odds heroines. Battling her own
psychological demons in *Silence of the Lambs* (a film turned down by
several Hollywood names including Michelle Pfeiffer), Foster's Clarice
Starling not only proved she was just as good as the FBI's male professionals but also outwitted two men, Buffalo Bill and Hannibal Lechter,
who happen to be serial killing monsters. Since starring in a movie
that ranks among the scariest of modern times, Foster has bewitch-
ingly acquitted herself in period costumes as the staunch widow in
Sommersby and played the Hollywood shell game deftly in the big-
budgeted *Maverick*, in which she tantalizingly reveals a glib, subtly
sexy movie star presence.

Confident enough to breeze through *Maverick* on charm, she won
another Oscar nomination as the wild child adjusting to civilization in
Nell, a film that would have seemed preposterous without her convic-

tion. Sensitively piloting her debut film *Little Man Tate*, she directed
with focus and sincerity but was less successful with her second feature,
Home for the Holidays, in which she failed to filter a light sense of
abandon through proceedings that were more frenetic than funny.
Foster is a powerhouse communicator who puts up no barriers between
her uncluttered interpretations of characters and the audience's embrace of her performances. There is a purity about her work that
makes the audience feel secure, as if their faith will never be betrayed
by false histrionics. Many film stars gain their public's adoration; only
a few such as Jodie Foster gain their trust.

—Robert Pardi

FRANCIS, Kay

Nationality: American. **Born:** Katherine Edwina Gibbs in Oklahoma
City, Oklahoma, 13 January 1899 (some sources give 1905). **Education:** Attended Miss Fuller's Girls Academy, Ossining, New York;
Cathedral School of St. Mary, Garden City, New York. **Family:** Married 1) James Dwight Francis, 1922 (divorced); 2) William A. Gaston;
3) the screenwriter John Meehan (sources differ about this marriage);
4) the actor Kenneth McKenna, 1931 (divorced 1934); 5) Erik
Barnekow. **Career:** 1925—Broadway debut as understudy in *The Green
Hut*; first billed role in modern dress version of *Hamlet*; 1926—member of Stuart Walker stock company; 1929—film debut in *Gentleman
of the Press*; contract with Paramount; 1932—contract with Warner
Brothers; 1945-46—producer/star in three Monogram feature films;
1946-48—on Broadway and tour of *State of the Union*; 1948-52—in
summer stock; then retired from acting. **Died:** In New York City, 26
August 1968.

Films as Actress:

(as Katherine Francis)

1929   *Gentlemen of the Press* (Webb) (as Myra May); *The Cocoanuts*
         (Florey and Santley) (as Penelope)

(as Kay Francis)

1929   *Illusion* (Mendes) (as Zelda Paxton); *Dangerous Curves*
         (Mendes) (as Zara Flynn); *The Marriage Playground*
         (Mendes) (as Zinnie la Crosse)
1930   *Behind the Make-Up* (Milton) (as Kitty Parker); *Street of
         Chance* (Cromwell) (as Alma Marsden); *Paramount on
         Parade* (Arzner and others); *A Notorious Affair* (Bacon) (as
         Countess Balakireff); *Raffles* (D'Arrast and Fitzmaurice)
         (as Lady Gwen); *For the Defense* (Cromwell) (as Irene Man-
         ners); *Let's Go Native* (McCarey) (as Constance Cook); *The
         Virtuous Sin* (*Cast Iron*) (Cukor and Gasnier) (as Marya
         Ivanovna); *Passion Flower* (William C. DeMille) (as Dulce
         Morado)
1931   *Scandal Sheet* (Cromwell) (as Mrs. Flint); *Ladies' Man*
         (Mendes) (as Norma Page); *The Vice Squad* (Cromwell) (as
         Alice Morrison); *Transgression* (Brenon) (as Elsie Maury);
         Guilty Hands (Van Dyke) (as Marjorie West); *Twenty-Four
         Hours* (*The Hours Between*) (Gering) (as Fanny Towner);
         Girls about Town (Cukor) (as Wanda Howard)
1932   *The False Madonna* (*The False Idol*) (Walker) (as Tina);
         Strangers in Love (Mendes) (as Diana Merrow); *Man Wanted*
         (Dieterle) (as Lois Ames); *Street of Women* (Mayo) (as

Natalie Upton); *Jewel Robbery* (Dieterle) (as Baroness Teri von Horhenfels); *One Way Passage* (Garnett) (as Joan Ames); **Trouble in Paradise** (Lubitsch) (as Mariette Colet); *Cynara* (King Vidor) (as Clemency Warlock)

1933 *The Keyhole* (Curtiz) (as Anne Valee Brooks); *Storm at Daybreak* (Boleslawski) (as Irina Dushan); *Mary Stevens, M.D.* (Bacon) (title role); *I Loved a Woman* (Green) (as Laura McDonald); *The House on Fifty-Sixth Street* (Florey) (as Peggy)

1934 *Mandalay* (Curtiz) (as Tanya); *Wonder Bar* (Bacon) (as Liane Renaud); *Dr. Monica* (Keighley) (as Dr. Monica Braden); *British Agent* (Curtiz) (as Elena)

1935 *Living on Velvet* (Borzage) (as Amy Prentiss); *Stranded* (Borzage) (as Lynn Palmer); *The Goose and the Gander* (Green) (as Georgiana Summers); *I Found Stella Parish* (LeRoy) (as Stella Parish)

1936 *The White Angel* (Dieterle) (as Florence Nightingale); *Give Me Your Heart* (*Sweet Aloes*) (Mayo) (as Linda Warren); *Stolen Holiday* (Curtiz) (as Nicole Picot)

1937 *Confession* (May) (as Vera); *Another Dawn* (Dieterle) (as Julia Ashton); *First Lady* (Logan) (as Lucy Chase Wayne)

1938 *Women Are Like That* (Logan) (as Claire Landin); *My Bill* (Farrow) (as Mark Colbrook); *Secrets of an Actress* (Keighley) (as Fay Carter); *Comet over Broadway* (Berkeley) (as Eve Appleton)

1939 *King of the Underworld* (Seiler) (as Carole Nelson); *Women in the Wind* (Farrow) (as Janet Steele); *In Name Only* (Cromwell) (as Maida Walker)

1940 *It's a Date* (Seiter) (as Georgia Drake); *When the Daltons Rode* (Marshall) (as Julie King); *Little Men* (McLeod) (as Jo); *Play Girl* (Woodruff) (as Grace Herbert)

1941 *The Man Who Lost Himself* (Ludwig) (as Adrienne Scott); *Charley's Aunt* (*Charley's American Aunt*) (Mayo) (as Donna Lucia); *The Feminine Touch* (Van Dyke) (as Nellie Woods)

1942 *Always in My Heart* (Graham) (as Marjorie Scott); *Between Us Girls* (Koster) (as Christine Bishop)

1944 *Four Jills in a Jeep* (Seiter) (as herself)

1945 *Divorce* (Nigh) (as Dianne Hunter Carter, + co-pr); *Allotment Wives* (*Woman in the Case*) (Nigh) (as Sheila Seymour, + co-pr)

1946 *Wife Wanted* (*Shadow of Blackmail*) (Karlson) (as Carole Raymond, + co-pr)

Publications

By FRANCIS: article—

"Acting in a Business Way," interview with K. Roberts in *Collier's* (New York), 16 March 1935.

On FRANCIS: articles—

Parish, J., and G. Ringgold, "Kay Francis," in *Films in Review* (New York), February 1964.
Classic Images (Indiana, Pennsylvania), September 1984.

* * *

Kay Francis belongs to the 1930s. Her moist eyes, dark, doelike features, and statuesque beauty were natural resources of the "women's picture"—her niche. Opposite Ronald Colman, Errol Flynn, or Leslie Howard, Francis remained glamorous, feminine, and aloof.

Francis signed with Paramount in 1929 after a brief stage career. Her elegance caused some impact in supporting roles, and she graduated to leads, teaming effectively with William Powell for six pictures, beginning

with *Behind the Make-Up*. Both performers transferred to Warners in 1932. Francis hit her stride with the romantic *One Way Passage*; she, terminally ill, and Powell, a criminal sentenced to death, share love aboard ship; they appeared as the innocent victims of jewel thieves in Ernst Lubitsch's sparkling *Trouble in Paradise*.

She co-starred with George Brent in *Living on Velvet*; the studio made them a team, but their material—syrupy melodrama—grew progressively weaker. Bette Davis competed for top roles with Francis, whose popularity by the middle 1930s was in decline; Davis won out, and Francis worked out her contract mostly in B pictures. *In Name Only*, as Cary Grant's selfish wife, and *Charley's Aunt*—as the aunt—offered good opportunities, but by the 1940s, Francis had virtually retired, resurfacing only at low-budget Monogram Studios for a trio of barely released vehicles. A conscientious actress, Francis was hampered by her own limitations as well as her material. She was affected with a slight lisp; reviewers of her films commented that the Rs in her dialogue sometimes became Ws. But Francis epitomized chic in the depression era. She possessed a light comic touch and, equally, a light dramatic touch, serving as little more than a fashion plate in many of her films. Undeniably a box-office attraction, she figured prominently on best-dressed lists. At her best, Kay Francis and her regal attire provided decorative escapist romance.

—Richard Sater

FREEMAN, Morgan

Nationality: American. **Born:** Memphis, Tennessee, 1 June 1937; grew up in Greenwood, Mississippi. **Family:** Married 1) Jeanette Adair Bradshaw (divorced), daughter: Morgana, adopted Bradshaw's daughter, Deena; 2) the costume designer Myrna Colley-Lee; has two sons, Alphonso and Saifoulaye, from other relationships. **Education:** Attended Los Angeles City College. **Career:** 1955—joined Air Force, beginning a four-year stint; 1960—took up acting while at college; 1960s—had small role in touring company of *The Royal Hunt of the Sun* and worked with the Opera Ring, a San Francisco musical-theater troupe; 1964—worked as dancer at the New York World's Fair; 1967—made off-Broadway debut in *The Niggerlovers* and Broadway debut in all-black-cast production of *Hello, Dolly!*, with Pearl Bailey; 1971—made film debut in small role in *Who Says I Can't Ride a Rainbow?*; 1971-76—played role of "Easy Reader" on PBS TV series *The Electric Company*; 1970s—continued acting on stage; 1978—first came to prominence with stage role in *The Mighty Gents*; 1987—had first important screen role in *Street Smart*; 1991—returned to the stage as Petruchio opposite Tracey Ullman in *The Taming of the Shrew*; 1993—made directorial debut with *Bopha!* **Awards:** Obie Award, for *Coriolanus*, 1979; Obie Award, for *Mother Courage and Her Children*, 1980; Obie Award, for *The Gospel at Colonus*, 1984; Obie Award, for *Driving Miss Daisy*, 1987; Clarence Derwent and Drama Desk Awards, for *The Mighty Gents*, 1978; New York Critics Circle, Los Angeles Film Critics, National Society of Film Critics, Best Supporting Actor awards, for *Street Smart*, 1987; Golden Globe Award, National Board of Review Award, for *Driving Miss Daisy*, 1989. **Agent:** William Morris Agency, 151 El Camino Drive, Beverly Hills, CA 90210, U.S.A.

Films as Actor:

1965 *The Pawnbroker* (Lumet) (extra)

1971 *Who Says I Can't Ride a Rainbow?* (*Barney*) (Edward Mann) (as Afro)

1978 *Roll of Thunder, Hear My Cry* (Smight—for TV)
1979 *Hollow Image* (Chomsky—for TV) (as Sweet Talk)
1980 *Brubaker* (Rosenberg) (as Walter); *Attica* (Chomsky—for TV)
      (as Hap Richards)
1981 *Eyewitness* (*The Janitor*) (Yates) (as Lt. Black); *The Marva
      Collins Story* (Levin—for TV) (as Clarence Collins); *Death
      of a Prophet* (King Jr.)
1984 *Teachers* (Hiller) (as Lewis); *Harry & Son* (Paul Newman) (as
      Siemanowski)
1985 *Marie* (Donaldson) (as Charles Traughber); *That Was Then . . .
      This Is Now* (Cain) (as Charlie Woods); *The Atlanta Child
      Murders* (Erman—for TV) (as Ben Shelter)
1986 *Resting Place* (Korty—for TV) (as Luther Johnson)
1987 *Street Smart* (Schatzberg) (as Fast Black); *Fight for Life*
      (Silverstein—for TV) (as Dr. Sherard)
1988 *Clean and Sober* (Caron) (as Craig); *Clinton and Nadine* (*Blood
      Money*) (Schatzberg—for TV) (as Dorsey Pratt)
1989 *Glory* (Zwick) (as John Rawlins); *Lean on Me* (Avildsen) (as
      Joe Clark); *Driving Miss Daisy* (Beresford) (as Hoke
      Colburn); *Johnny Handsome* (Walter Hill) (as Lt. A. Z.
      Drones); *The Execution of Raymond Graham* (Petrie—for
      TV)
1990 *The Bonfire of the Vanities* (DePalma) (as Judge Leonard White)
1991 *Robin Hood: Prince of Thieves* (Kevin Reynolds) (as Azeem)
1992 **Unforgiven** (Eastwood) (as Ned Logan); *The Power of One*
      (Avildsen) (as Geel Piet)
1994 *The Shawshank Redemption* (Darabont) (as Ellis "Red"
      Redding)
1995 *Outbreak* (Petersen) (as Gen. Billy Ford); *Seven* (Fincher) (as
      William Sommerset)
1996 *Moll Flanders* (Densham) (as Jemmy); *Chain Reaction* (An-
      drew Davis)

Film as Director:

1993 *Bopha!*

Publications

By FREEMAN: articles—

Interview with Robert Berkvist, in *New York Times*, 21 April 1978.
"Morgan Freeman Takes Off," interview with Ross Wetzsteon, in *New
    York*, 14 March 1988.
"Quiet Cool," interview with Anthony DeCurtis, in *Rolling Stone* (New
    York), 5 May 1988.
Interview with Richard Harrington, in *Washington Post*, 3 March 1989.
"Two for the Road," interview with H. Alford, in *Interview* (New York),
    November 1989.
"For Morgan Freeman, Stardom Wasn't Sudden," interview with Helen
    Dudar, in *New York Times*, 10 December 1989.
Interview with Lynn Darling, in *New York Newsday* (Melville, New
    York), 10 December 1989.

On FREEMAN: articles—

Lombardi, John, "Morgan Freeman," in *Esquire* (New York), June
    1988.
Southgate, Martha, "Star Quality," in *Essence* (New York), December 1988.
Meises, Stanley, "Street Smart," in *Premiere* (New York), December
    1989.
Lombardi, Fred, "Focus on an Actor: Morgan Freeman," in *Interna-
    tional Film Guide* (London, Hollywood), 1990.

Schiff, Stephen, "Freeman's Freeway," in *Vanity Fair* (New York), Janu-
    ary 1990.
Whitaker, Charles, "Is Morgan Freeman America's Greatest Actor?,"
    in *Ebony* (Chicago), April 1990.
Current Biography 1991, New York, 1991.
Webster, Andy, "Morgan Freeman," in *Premiere* (New York), March
    1995.

                              *   *   *

For years, Morgan Freeman was an award-winning stage actor who
occasionally would appear in supporting roles in movies. While he
may have been a known quantity to discerning theatergoers, he was
barely a name (if not a face) to the public at large: His greatest mass
exposure had come during the 1970s, when he played "Easy Reader"
on the PBS children's series *The Electric Company*. As late as 1983—
even after winning two Obie Awards, Clarence Derwent and Drama
Desk awards, and a Tony nomination—he seriously considered abandoning acting and becoming a taxi driver.

Freeman's career went on the permanent upswing in 1987 when he
riveted audiences as Fast Black, a vicious, slyly evil pimp, in the grade-
B urban crime drama *Street Smart*. He was especially effective as his
character segued from relaxed cordiality to menacing, frightening
evil. Not all moviegoers immediately became aware of Freeman, because *Street Smart* is a genre film that appealed only to a limited
viewership. Nevertheless, critics who otherwise might pass by such a
film were taken by his memorable acting. Pauline Kael, one of the
most influential of all American critics, asked point-blank in her
review, "Is Morgan Freeman the greatest American actor?" As a result, Freeman earned a Best Supporting Actor Oscar nomination, a
rare feat for a performance in a film like *Street Smart*.

In the past decade, Freeman has showcased his manifold abilities in
a wide variety of parts. Perhaps his most memorable performance
came in a film that is strikingly dissimilar to *Street Smart*: *Driving
Miss Daisy*, set in the preintegration South, in which he plays Hoke
Colburn, a modest, unpretentious black man hired as chauffeur to a
petulant white lady (Jessica Tandy). Freeman, who also played the
role on stage, makes Hoke a likable and deeply sympathetic character.
His subtle performance also allows the viewer a peek into the soul of
a black man who not only had come of age but had grown to maturity
in a segregated Southern society. Freeman and Tandy's performances
blend beautifully together, and both actors earned Oscar nominations.
She, and not he, won the statuette, but his performance as Hoke
nonetheless served as testimony that the actor was no Oscar nominee
one-shot.

Freeman is capable of creating a wide range of characters. If he
played a bad guy who was tough and satanic in *Street Smart*, he also
could play good guys who are tough and dynamic (real-life high school
principal Joe Clark in *Lean on Me*); tough and thoughtful (the grave
digger who becomes a Civil War infantry recruit in *Glory*, the ex-addict
who conducts a therapy group in *Clean and Sober*); and tough and
world-weary (the veteran cop on the trail of a serial killer in *Seven*). In
Driving Miss Daisy, he shined in a starring role; yet he also had sense
to accept quality roles in quality films even if those parts are satellites
of the scenario's main character. This was the case in *Unforgiven*, in
which Freeman plays Clint Eastwood's cowboy buddy, and *The
Shawshank Redemption*, in which he is cast as the wizened veteran
convict who befriends falsely convicted Tim Robbins. For the latter
film, Freeman netted his third Oscar nomination. He has emerged
unscathed from his few unwise career choices, most notoriously his
casting as the judge in the mega-bomb *The Bonfire of the Vanities*.

In 1993, Freeman made his directorial debut with *Bopha!*, a tense,
politically savvy drama about Master Sergeant Micah Mangena (Danny
Glover), a black policeman in a South African township. Mangena
teaches his class of new recruits that their job is to "uphold the law,

Morgan Freeman with Jessica Tandy in *Driving Miss Daisy*

and maintain the peace." To many, in particular South Africa's political radicals, Mangena is little more than an Uncle Tom, a tool of the white ruling class, a cog in a system in which blacks are oppressed. His world is destined to crumble, and he will undergo a crisis of conscience, when his son, whom he expects to follow in his footsteps by becoming a police officer, takes part in a rebellion against the discipline and curriculum of the local white-run school. This choice of projects serves as evidence that Freeman is not unaware of his role as an African-American artist, and that he is concerned with examining black characters in all their flaws and contradictions.

—Rob Edelman

FRESNAY, Pierre

Nationality: French. **Born:** Pierre-Jules Laudenbach in Paris, 4 April 1897. **Education:** Lycée Montaigne and Lycée Henri-IV, Paris; studied with George Berr at Conservatoire National d'Art Dramatique, Paris. **Military Service:** 1916-19—service in army; 2nd lieutenant. **Family:** Married 1) Rachel Berendt (divorced); 2) the actress Berthe Bovy (divorced); 3) the actress Yvonne Printemps, 1934. **Career:** 1912—stage debut at Théâtre Réjane in *L'Aigrette*; 1915—debut with Comédie Française in *Le Jeu de l'amour et du hasard*; film debut in *France d'abord*; 1920—first London stage role, with Comédie Française, in *Le Misanthrope*; 1926—resigned from Comédie Française; 1931-36—co-starred with Raimu in Marcel Pagnol film trilogy *Marius, Fanny, and César*; 1934—replaced Noël Coward in *Conversation Piece*, came to New York with show; 1937—co-manager with wife Yvonne Printemps, and lead actor of Théâtre de la Michodière, Paris; 1972—last stage play, Roussin's *La Claque*. **Awards:** Best Actor, Venice Festival, for *Monsieur Vincent*, 1947; Prix Féminin du Cinéma, 1949. **Died:** In Neuilly-sur-Seine, France, 9 January 1975.

Films as Actor:

1915   *France d'abord* (Pouctal)
1916   *Quand même* (Pouctal)
1920   *L'Essor* (Burguet)
1922   *Les Mystères de Paris* (Burguet) (as Prince Rodolphe); *Le Diamant noir* (Hugon); *La Bâillonnée* (Burguet); *Les Premiéres Armes de Rocambole* (Maudru and de Marsan); *Le Petit Jacques*
1928   *La Vierge folle* (Morat)
1930   *Ça aussi c'est Paris* (Mourne)
1931   *Marius* (Korda) (title role)
1932   *Fanny* (Allégret) (as Marius)
1933   *Ame de clown* (Noé and Didier) (as Jack)
1934   *La Dame aux camélias* (*Camille*) (Gance) (as Armand Duvall); *The Man Who Knew Too Much* (Hitchcock) (as Louis Bernard)
1935   *Le Roman d'un jeune homme pauvre* (Gance) (as le jeune homme pauvre)
1936   *Koenigsmark* (Tourneur) (as Raoul Vignerte); *Sous les yeux d'occident* (*Razumov*) (Allégret) (as Razumov); *César* (Pagnol) (as Marius); *Mademoiselle Docteur* (*Salonique*; *Nid d'espions*; *Street of Shadows*) (Pabst) (as Capitaine Carrière)
1937   **La Grande Illusion** (*Grand Illusion*) (Renoir) (as Capitaine de Boeldieu); *La Bataille silencieuse* (Billon) (as René Bordier); *Le Puritain* (Musso) (as Le Commissaire de police); *Chéri-Bibi* (Mathot) (title role)

1938   *Adrienne Lecouvreur* (L'Herbier) (as Maurice de Saxe); *Alerte en Méditerranée* (*SOS Mediterranean*) (Joannon) (as Le Commandant Lestailleur); *Trois Valses* (*Three Waltzes*) (Berger) (three roles)
1939   *La Charrette fantôme* (Duvivier) (as David Holm)
1941   *Le Dernier des six* (Lacombe) (as L'Inspecteur Wens); *Les Inconnus dans la maison* (Decoin) (as narrator); *Le Briseur de chaînes* (*Mamouret*) (Norman) (as Le Dompteur)
1942   *Le Journal tombe à cing heures* (Lacombe) (as Le Reporter); *L'Assassin habite au 21* (*The Murderer Lives at Number 21*) (Clouzot) (as Commissaire Wens); *La Main du diable* (*Carnival of Sinners*) (Tourneur) (as Le Peintre)
1943   *Le Corbeau* (*The Raven*) (Clouzot) (as Docteur Germain); *Je suis avec toi* (Decoin) (as François); *Le Voyageur sans baggage* (Anouilh) (as Gaston); *L'Escalier sans fin* (Lacombe) (as Le Mauvais Garçon)
1945   *La Fille du diable* (*The Devil's Daughter*) (Decoin) (as Ludovic Mercier-Saget)
1946   *Le Visiteur* (*Tainted*) (Dréville) (as M. Sauval)
1947   *Monsieur Vincent* (Cloche) (title role); *Les Condamnés* (Lacombe) (as Jean Séverac)
1948   *Barry* (Pottier) (as Le Moine Théotime); *Combourg, visage de pierre* (de Casembroot—short) (as narrator)
1949   *Au grand balcon* (Decoin) (as Didier Daurat); *Vient de paraître* (Houssin) (as L'Editor Moscat); *La Valse de Paris* (*The Paris Waltz*) (Achard) (as Offenbach); *Gisants* (Noël—short) (as narrator)
1950   *Ce siècle a cinquante ans* (Tual) (as narrator); *Dieu a besoin des hommes* (*God Needs Men*) (Delannoy) (as Thomas Gourvennec); *Justice est faite* (Cayatte) (as voice); *Vezelay* (Zimmer—short) (as narrator); *Le Pèlerin de la beauce* (Chuteau—short) (as narrator)
1951   *Un Grand Patron* (*The Perfectionist*) (Ciampi) (as Louis Delage); *Monsieur Fabre* (*The Amazing Monsieur Fabre*) (Diamant-Berger) (as Jean Henri Fabre); *Voyage en Amérique* (*Voyage to America*) (Lavorel) (as Gaston Fournier)
1952   *Il est minuit, Docteur Schweitzer* (Haguet)
1953   *Le Défroqué* (Joannon) (as Morand); *La Route Napoléon* (Delannoy) (as Édouard Martel)
1954   *Les Évadés* (Le Chanois) (as Le Lieutenant Pierre)
1955   *Les Aristocrates* (de la Patellière) (as Marquis de Maubrun)
1956   *L'Homme aux clefs d'or* (Joannon) (title role); *Fleuve Dieu* (Jallaud—short) (as narrator)
1957   *Les Fanatiques* (*A Bomb for a Dictator*) (Joffé) (as Luis); *Les Oeufs de l'autruche* (*The Ostrich Has Two Eggs*) (de la Patelliére) (as Hippolyte Barjus)
1958   *Et ta soeur?* (Delbez); *Tant d'amour perdu* (Joannon) (as le père faible)
1959   *La Millième Fenêtre* (Menegoz) (as Armand Vallin); *Les Affreux* (Allégret) (as César); *Sont morts les bâtisseurs* (Berne—short) (as narrator)
1960   *Les Vieux de la vieille* (Grangier) (as Baptiste Talon)
1963   *Malmaison* (de Casembroot—short) (as narrator)
1966   *La Vallée aux loups* (de Casembroot—short) (as narrator); *Ecce homo* (Saury—short) (as narrator)
1968   *Le Neveu de Rameau* (Lucot—for TV); *L'Idée fixe* (Hubert—for TV)
1969   *Tête d'horloge* (Sassy—for TV); *Mon Faust* (Georgot—for TV)
1971   *Père* (Hubert—for TV)
1973   *Le Jardinier* (Léonard—for TV)
1974   *Le Savant* (Olivier—for TV); *Le K* (Buzzati—for TV)

Film as Director:

1939   *Le Duel* (+ ro as l'abbé Daniel)

Pierre Fresnay with Orane Demazis in *Marius*

Publications

By FRESNAY: books—

Je suis comédien, interviews with Albert Dubeux, Paris, 1954.
Pierre Fresnay, with François Possot, Paris, 1976 + biblio.

On FRESNAY: books—

Dubeux, Albert, *Pierre Fresnay*, Paris, 1950.
Ford, Charles, *Pierre Fresnay: Gentilhomme de l'ecran*, Paris, 1981 + biblio.

On FRESNAY: articles—

Beylie, C., "Pierre Fresnay," in *Ecran* (Paris), March 1975.
Passek, J.-L., "Nécrologie: Pierre Fresnay," in *Cinéma* (Paris), April 1975.
Ford, Charles, "Pierre Fresnay (1897-1975)," in *Anthologie du Cinéma* (Paris), October 1976 + biblio.
Ecran (Paris), May 1978.

*   *   *

Pierre Fresnay was interested in being an actor from an early age, and was helped in his ambitions by his uncle, the actor Jules Dietz, a member of the Comédie Française (and a film actor under the name of Claude Garry). Fresnay made recitations on family occasions from the age of five, performed in a vaudeville of Jean Cocteau, and made his stage debut at 14 in a small part with the actress Réjane at her own theater. With his uncle's help, and because of the mobilization of several actors during the war, Fresnay was able to make his debut at the Comédie Française at the age of 18, and to keep his position there after the war was over. Though he resigned from the Comédie Française in 1926 over its preferential treatment practices, and was fined for breaching his contract, his years there had confirmed his interest in stage acting. He continued to act on the stage, and from 1937 to co-manage his own company, until the end of his life.

Fresnay's 60-year-long film acting career began with small parts in the 1910s and 1920s. His film "break" came with the arrival of sound, and his being cast in the title role of *Marius*. He had played the role in the stage version, though his co-star, Raimu, and even the author, Maurice Pagnol, had expressed doubts concerning Fresnay's temperament and his over-distinguished theatrical demeanor. Yet the apprehensions proved unfounded, the play was a popular and critical success (reaching a record number of performances), and the film was also highly acclaimed. The sequels, *Fanny* and *César* (directed by Pagnol himself), were equally well-received.

Fresnay's versatility was proved by the different roles he played in *Ame de Clown*, *The Man Who Knew Too Much* (a French spy), *Sous les yeux d'occident* (the counter-revolutionary Rasputin), and *Cheri-Bibi* (a convict). But what really solidified his film career was his role as a French officer in Renoir's *La Grande Illusion*. He and von Stroheim represent two mutually antagonistic countries at war, yet they find mutual sympathy for one another on the basis of a common social class. In another group of films, Fresnay portrayed detectives: *Puritain*, *Dernier des six*, and *L'Assassin habite au 21* (in the last two of which he played Inspector Wens, created by Georges Simenon). Another group of films, in which he was cast in historical biographies, began with *Monsieur Vincent*, in which he played Saint Vincent de Paul; he played the pioneer flyer Didier Daurat in *Au grand balcon*, the composer Offenbach in *La Valse de Paris*, Schweitzer in *Il est minuit, Docteur Schweitzer*, and the scientist Henri Fabre in *Monsieur Fabre*.

His film work in the 1950s and after is generally thought to be outdated, but he made such interesting films as *Le Défroqué* and *Les Évadés*, and continued to work on television until his death.

—Karel Tabery

FRÖHLICH, Gustav

Nationality: German. **Born:** Gustav Fredrich Fröhlich in Hanover, 21 March 1902. **Education:** Attended gymnasium in Berlin. **Family:** Married 1) the actress Gitta Alpar (divorced); 2) Maria Hajek. **Career:** Stage actor: at Heilbronn Theatre, then Volksbühne, Berlin; 1925—film debut in *Die Frau mit dem schlechten Ruf*; 1934—co-directed the film *Rakoczy-Marsch*, and directed *Abenteuer eines jungen Herrn in Polen*, 1935; 1930s—evidently lived with Lida Baarová, a Czech actress working in Berlin; Goebbels's interest in her caused a high-level scandal, and she left Germany; continued to act in and direct films after World War II; after 1960—actor for TV, including *The Laurents* series, 1982. **Awards:** Deutscher Filmpreis for career, 1973. **Died:** In Lugano, Switzerland, 22 December 1987.

Films as Actor:

1925   *Die Frau mit dem schlechten Ruf* (Christensen); *Friesenblut* (Sauer); *Schiff in Not* (Sauer)

1926   *Die Frau, die nicht "nein" sagan kann* (Sauer); **Metropolis** (Fritz Lang) (as Freder)

1927   *Die elf Teufel* (Zoltan Korda); *Gehetzte Frauen* (Oswald); *Ich hierate meine Frau* (Reichmann); *Jahrmarkt des Lebens* (von Balogh); *Jugendrausch (Eva and the Grasshopper)* (Asagaroff); *Der Miester von Nürnberg (The Meistersinger of Nuremberg)* (Berger); *Die leichte Isabell* (Busch and Wellin); *Die Pflicht zu schweigen* (Wilhelm); *Schwere Jungens—Leichte Mädchen* (Boese)

1928   *Angst* (Steinhoff); *Die Rothausgasse* (Oswald); *Wenn die Schwalben heimwärts ziehn (Fremdenlegionär)* (Bauer); *Heimkehr (Homecoming)* (May); *Hurrah! Ich lebe! (Hurrah I'm Alive)* (Thiele)

1929   *Asphalt* (May); *Das Brennende Herz (The Burning Heart)* (Berger); *Hochverrat (High Treason)* (Meyer)

1930   *Der unsterbliche Lump (The Immortal Vagabond)* (Ucicky); *Brand in der Oper (Fire in the Opera House)* (Froelich); *Zwei Menschen* (Waschneck)

1931   *Voruntersuchung (Inquest)* (Siodmak); *Die heilige Flamme* (Viertel); *Kismet* (Dieterle); *Gloria* (Behrendt); *Liebeslied* (David); *Mein Leopold* (Steinhoff); *So lang noch ein Walzer von Strauss erklingt* (Wiene) (as Johann Strauss, Jr.); *Liebeskommando (Love's Command)* (von Bolvary)

1932   *Unter falscher Flagge* (Meyer); *Kaiserwalzer (Johann Strauss, K und I. Hofballmusikdirektor)* (Wiene); *Gitta entdeckt ihr Herz* (Froelich); *Eine Mann mit Herz* (von Bolvary); *Ein Lied, ein Kuss, ein Mädel* (von Bolvary); *Die verliebte Firma* (Ophüls)

1933   *Sonnenstrahl* (Fejos); *Die Nacht der grossen Liebe (The Night of the Great Love)* (von Bolvary); *Rund um eine Million* (Neufeld); *Was Frauen träumen (What Women Dream)* (von Bolvary)

1934   *Der Flüchtling aus Chikago* (Meyer)

1935   *Stradivari* (von Bolvary); *Barcarole* (Lamprecht); *Liebesleute (Hermann und Dorothea von heute)* (Waschneck); *Oberwachtmeister Schwenek* (Froelich); *Ein Teufelskerl (A Devil of a Fellow)* (Jacoby); *Es flüstert die liebe* (von Bolvary); *Nacht der Verwandlung (Demaskierung)* (Deppe)

1936   *Die Stunde der Versuchung* (Wegener); *Die Entführung* (von Bolvary); *Stadt Anatol* (Tourjansky); *Gleisdreieck (Alarm auf Gleis B)* (Stemmle); *Inkognito* (Schneider-Edenkoben); *Die unmögliche Frau* (Meyer)

1937   *Gabriele ein, zwei, drei* (Hansen); *Alarm in Peking* (Selpin)

1938   *Frau Sixta* (Ucicky); *Die kleine und die grosse Liebe (Minor Love and the Real Thing)* (von Baky); *In geheimer Mission* (von Alten)

1939   *Renate im Quartett* (Verhoeven); *Alarm aus Station III* (Mayring)

1940   *Herz modern möbliert* (Lingen); *Ihr Privatsekretär* (Klein); *Herz geht vor Anker* (Stöckel); *Alles Schwindel* (Hoffmann)

1941   *Sechs Tage Heimaturlaub* (von Alten); *Clarissa* (Lamprecht)

1942   *Der grosse König* (Harlan); *Mit den Augen einer Frau* (Külb)

1943   *Tolle Nacht* (Lingen)

1944   *Das Konzert* (Verhoeven); *Familie Buchholz (Neigungsehe)* (Froelich); *Der grosse Fall (Ihr grosse Fall)* (Anton); *Eine alltägliche Geschichte* (Rittau)

1946   *Sag' die Wahrheit* (Weiss)

1948   *Des verlorene Gesicht (Secrets of a Soul)* (Hoffmann)

1949   *Diese Nacht vergess' ich nie* (Meyer)

1950   *Diese Mann gehört mir* (Verhoeven); *Die Sünderin (The Sinner)* (Forst)

1951   *Stips* (Froelich)

1952   *Haus des Lebens* (Hartl)

1953   *Gefährliches Abenteuer (Abenteuer in Wien)* (Reinert); *Ehe für eine Nacht* (Tourjansky); *Von der Liebe reden wir später* (Anton)

1954   *Die kleine Stadt will schlafen gehen* (König); *Rosen aus dem Süden* (Antel); *Ball der Nationen* (Ritter)

1956   *Der erste Frühlingstag* (Weiss); *Vergiss, wenn Du kannst* (König)

1960   *. . . und keiner schämte sich (. . . and Nobody Was Ashamed)* (Schott-Schöbinger)

Films as Director:

1933   *Rakoczy-Marsch* (co-d; + ro)

1934   *Abenteuer eines jungen Herrn in Polen (Liebe und Trompetenklang)* (+ ro)

1945   *Leb' wohl Christina* (+ co-sc)

1948   *Wege im Zwielicht* (+ ro)

1949   *Der Bagnosträfling* (+ sc)

1950   *Die Lüge* (+ sc)

Gustav Fröhlich in *Metropolis*

1951   *Torreani* (+ ro)
1955   *Seine Tochter ist der Peter*

Publications

By FRÖHLICH: book—

Das waren Zeiten: Ein deutsches Filmheldenleben, Munich, 1983.

On FRÖHLICH: books—

Holl, W., *Gustav Frölich, Kunstler und Mensch*, Berlin, 1936.
Kracauer, Siegfried, *From Caligari to Hitler: A Psychological History of the German Film*, Princeton, New Jersey, 1974.

On FRÖHLICH: articles—

Picturegoer (London), September 1929.
Mein Film, 3 July 1953.
Retro, May-June 1981.
Obituary in *Variety* (New York), 6 January 1988.

*   *   *

At an early age Gustav Fröhlich was attracted to the theater and was helped in his career by a German industrialist. From the Heilbronn Theatre he went to the Volksbühne in Berlin. When Fritz Lang cast him as the juvenile lead in the sensational *Metropolis* his career in films was assured. His good looks and youthful earnestness were assets, and his acting ability was further tested in Joe May's *Heimkehr* with Lara Hanson and Dita Parlo, and *Asphalt* with Betty Amann. He also played in Ludwig Berger's *Der Meister von Nürnberg*. In this film one of the players was Veit Harlan, later to become an important director, for whom Fröhlich was to act. He gave an outstanding performance in Johannes Meyer's *Hochverrat* and in Benjamin Christensen's curious *Die Frau mit dem schlechten Ruf* which featured Lionel Barrymore. Fröhlich also played in three pictures by Fred Sauer, a sensitive director of films about the problems of young people.

His early sound film *Der unsterbliche Lump* by Gustav Ucicky had an international success in an English version. Fröhlich increased his status as an actor in such films as Waschneck's *Zwei Menschen*, Hans Behrendt's *Gloria* opposite Brigitte Helm, Lamprecht's German version of *Barcarole*, and the German version of *Kismet* directed by Wilhelm Dieterle. For Max Ophüls he played in *Die verliebte Firma* and for Paul Fejos in *Sonnenstrahl*. In 1942 he was in Viet Harlan's *Der grosse König* which had a checkered career under the Goebbels censorship. This was a most elaborate production which for a time was shelved and later issued with drastic alterations.

Fröhlich directed several films in the sound period, including— *Rakoczy-Marsch* and *Abenteuer eines jungen Herrn in Polen* with Olga Tschechowa. He survived the war and appeared in many films, notably *Die Sünderin* with Hildegard Knef directed by Willi Forst.

—Liam O'Leary

GABIN, Jean

Nationality: French. **Born:** Jean-Alexis Moncorgé in Paris, 17 May 1904; some sources give surname as Monçorge and Morcorge; father a cafe entertainer who performed using the name Gabin. **Military Service:** Joined Free French, 1943; participated in Normandy invasion, 1944; received Croix de Guerre and Médaille Militaire; **Family:** Married 1) Gaby Basset, 1928 (divorced 1931); 2) Jeanne Susanne Mauchin, 1932 (divorced 1942); 3) Dominique Fournier, 1949, children: Florence, Valerie, and Mathias. **Career:** 1919—apprenticed to construction company, Chapelle; also worked as auto mechanic; 1920—through father's friendship with impresario Fréjol, engaged at Folies Bergère; 1924-25—military service in French navy; 1926—performed in theater, cabaret, and vaudeville; 1930—contract with Pathé-Nathan; majority of earliest films shot in Germany; 1934—began collaboration with director Julien Duvivier on *Maria Chapdelaine*; 1939-40—served in French navy; 1941—moved to U.S., began working for 20th Century-Fox; 1954—career revived with *Touchez pas au grisbi*; in series of films as Inspector Maigret beginning with *Maigret tend un piège*. **Awards:** Best Actor, Venice Festival, for *La Nuit est mon royaume*, 1951; Best Actor, Venice Festival, for *Touchez pas au grisbi* and *The Air of Paris*, 1954; Best Actor, Berlin Festival, for *Archimède le clochard*, 1959; Best Actor, Berlin Festival, for *Le Chat*, 1971. **Died:** Of heart attack at Neuilly, 15 November 1976.

Films as Actor:

1931   *Chacun sa chance (La Chute dans le bonheur)* (Steinhoff and Pujol—French version of Steinhoff's *Kopfüber ins Glück*); *Mephisto* (Debain and Winter—serial); *Paris-béguin* (Genina); *Gloria* (Behrendt and Noé—French version of Behrendt's *Gloria*); *Tout ça ne vaut pas l'amour* (Jacques Tourneur); *Coeur de Lilas* (Litvak); *Coeur joyeux* (Schwartz and de Vaucorbeil)

1932   *La Belle Marinière* (Lachman); *Les Gaités de l'Escadron* (Maurice Tourneur); *La Foule hurle* (Daumery and Hawks—French version of Hawks's *The Crowd Roars*)

1933   *L'Etoile de Valencia* (de Poligny—French version of Zeisler's *Stern von Valencia*); *Adieu les beaux jours* (Meyer and Beucler—French version of Meyer's *Die schönen Tagen von Aranjuez*); *Le Tunnel* (Bernhardt—French version of *Der Tunnel*); *Du haut en bas* (Pabst); *Au bout de monde* (Ucicky)

1934   *Zouzou* (Allégret); *Maria Chapdelaine* (Duvivier)

1935   *Golgotha* (Duvivier) (as Pontius Pilate); *La Bandéra* (Duvivier); *Variétés* (Farkas)

1936   *La Belle Équipe* (Duvivier) (as Jean); *Les Bas-fonds* (Renoir) (as Pepel); ***Pépé le Moko*** (Duvivier) (title role)

1937   ***La Grande Illusion** (Grand Illusion)* (Renoir) (as Maréchal); *Le Messager* (Rouleau); *Gueule d'amour* (Grémillon)

1938   ***Le Quai des brumes*** (Carné); ***La Bête humaine*** (Renoir) (as Lantier)

1939   *Le Récif de corail* (Gleize); ***Le Jour se lève*** (Carné) (as François)

1941   *Remorques* (Grémillon)

1942   *Moontide* (Mayo)

1944   *The Imposter (Strange Confession)* (Duvivier)

1946   *Martin Roumagnac (The Room Upstairs)* (Lacombe) (title role)

1947   *Miroir* (Lamy)

1949   *Au-delà des grilles (Le mura di Malapaga; The Walls of Malapaga)* (Clément); *La Marie du port* (Carné)

1950   *E più facile che un cammello . . . (Pour l'amour du ciel)* (Zampa)

1951   *Victor* (Heymann); *La Nuit est mon royaume (The Night Is My Kingdom)* (Lacombe); "La Maison Tellier" ep. of *Le Plaisir* (Ophüls); *La Vérité sur Bébé Donge* (Decoin)

1952   *La Minute de vérité* (Delannoy); *Bufere (Fille dangereuse)* (Brignone); *Echos de plateau* (Knapp and Barrère—short)

1953   *Leur Dernière Nuit* (Lacombe); *La Vierge du Rhin* (Grangier); *Touchez pas au grisbi* (Becker) (as Max le menteur)

1954   *L'Air de Paris* (Carné); *Napoléon* (Guitry); *Le Port du désir* (Gréville); *French Cancan* (Renoir); *Razzia sur la chnouf* (Decoin)

1955   *Chiens perdus sans collier* (Delannoy); *Gas-oil* (Grangier); *Des gens sans importance* (Verneuil); *Voici le temps des assassins (Murder à la Carte)* (Duvivier); *Le Sang à la tête* (Grangier)

1956   *La Traversée de Paris (Four Bags Full)* (Autant-Lara); *Crime et châtiment (The Most Dangerous Sin)* (Lampin); *Le Cas du docteur Laurent* (Le Chanois)

1957   *Le Rouge est mis* (Grangier); *Maigret tend un piège* (Delannoy) (title role); *Les Misérables* (Le Chanois)

1958   *Le Désordre et la nuit* (Grangier); *En cas de malheur* (Autant-Lara); *Les Grandes Familles* (de la Patellière); *Archimède le clochard* (Grangier) (+ story); *Maigret et l'affaire Saint-Fiacre* (Delannoy) (title role)

1959   *Rue des prairies* (de la Patellière); *Le Baron de l'écluse* (Delannoy); *Les Vieux de la vieille* (Grangier)

1961   *Le Président* (Verneuil); *Le Cave se rebiffe* (Grangier)

1962   *Un Singe en hiver (Monkey in Winter)* (Verneuil); *Le Gentleman d'Epsom (Les Grands Seigneurs; Le Roi de tiercé)* (Grangier); *Mélodie en sous-sol* (Verneuil)

1963   *Maigret voit rouge* (Grangier) (title role)

1964   *Monsieur* (Le Chanois); *L'Âge ingrat* (Grangier)

1965   *Le Tonnerre de Dieu* (de la Patellière)

1966   *Du Rififi à Paname (The Upper Hand; Rififi in Paris)* (de la Patellière); *Le Jardinier d'Argenteuil* (Le Chanois)

1967   *Le Soleil des voyous (Action Man)* (Delannoy); *Le Pacha* (Lautner)

1968   *Le Tatoué* (de la Patellière); *Le Clan des Siciliens* (Verneuil)

1969   *Sous le signe du taureau* (Grangier)

1970   *La Horse* (Granier-Deferre)

1971   *Le Chat* (Granier-Deferre); *De Drapeau noir flotte sur le marmite* (Audiard)

1972   *Le Tueur* (de la Patellière); *L'Affaire Dominici* (Bernard-Aubert)

1973   *Deux Hommes dans la ville* (Giovanni)

1974   *Verdict* (Cayatte)

1975   *L'Année sainte* (Girault)

Jean Gabin

Publications

By GABIN: article—

"Jean Renoir de *Nana à La Grande Illusion*," interview by C. Gauteur in *Image et Son* (Paris), May 1975.

On GABIN: books—

Gauteur, Claude, and Andre Bernard, *Gabin, ou, Les Avatars d'un mythe*, Paris, 1976 + biblio.
Missiaen, Jean-Claude, and Jacques Siclier, *Jean Gabin*, Paris, 1977.
Betti, Jean-Michel, *Salut, Gabin!*, Paris, 1977.
Millhaud, Sylvie, *Jean Gabin*, Paris, 1981.
Barbier, Philippe, and Jacques Moreau, *Jean Gabin: Album Photos*, Paris, 1983.
Colin, Gerty, *Jean Gabin*, Paris, 1983.
Brunelin, André, *Gabin*, Paris, 1987.

On GABIN: articles—

Duvillars, Pierre, "Jean Gabin's Instinctual Man," in *Films in Review* (New York), March 1951.
Nolan, Jack E., "Jean Gabin," in *Films in Review* (New York), April 1963.
Cowie, Peter, "Jean Gabin," in *Films and Filming* (London), February 1964.
Bazin, André, "The Destiny of Jean Gabin," in *What Is Cinema*, Berkeley, 1971.
Gauteur, Claude, "Pages d'histoire: Gabin sur les planches," in *Ecran* (Paris), June 1974.
"Jean Gabin: sa vie, ses films," in *Cinéma Français* (Paris), no. 7, 1976.
Magny, Joel, "Gabin, miroir de la France," in *Téléciné* (Paris), May 1976.
Fieschi, J., "Gabin dans *Le Jour se lève*," in *Cinématographe* (Paris), January 1977.
Doneux, M., "Hommage à Jean Gabin. La Fin d'un monstre sacré," in *APEC-Revue belge du cinéma* (Brussels), January 1977.
Gévaudan, F., "Jean Gabin," in *Cinéma* (Paris), January 1977.
Minish, G., "Paris Letter: 'Gabin Le Magnifique,'" in *Take One* (Montreal), March 1977.
Sarris, Andrew, "Jean Gabin" in *The Movie Book*, edited by Elisabeth Weis, New York, 1981.
Interview with Florence Moncorgé Gabin in *Ciné Revue* (Paris), 9 August 1984.
Vincendeau, Ginette, "Community, Nostalgia and the Spectacle of Masculinity," in *Screen* (London), November/December 1985.
Nacache, J., "Jean Gabin," in *Cinéma* (Paris), 25 March 1987.
Vincendeau, Ginette, "The Beauty of the Beast," in *Sight and Sound* (London), July 1991.

* * *

Although rarely an actor of great inspiration or subtlety, Jean Gabin was never less than a dedicated, conscientious performer who brought to his roles a measured but compelling authority. Whether as the doomed romantic figure of his 1930s films or the embodiment of stoic calm and worldly wisdom in his later parts, Gabin possessed an extraordinarily powerful screen presence which successive directors, notably Carné, Duvivier, Grémillon, and Renoir, exploited.

After an invaluable if reluctant apprenticeship, Gabin established himself in films as the engaging, noble, and principled hero of humble origins (*La Bandéra*, *La Belle Équipe*, *La Grande Illusion*) and confirmed his popular image in a succession of darkly fatalistic roles that encapsulated the pessimistic mood prevalent in the France of the late 1930s. In *Pépé le Moko* Gabin played a hunted criminal trapped in the Casbah. Infatuated with a socially superior woman, he is tempted to leave his safe hiding place only to be gunned down as she sails for France. *Quai des brumes* reveals him as a cynical army deserter falling in love with a romantically idealistic young girl who is dominated by her vicious guardian. Impetuously he murders this tyrant before falling victim to violence himself. In *La Bête humaine*, based on Zola's novel, he assumed the role of the train driver with a flawed heredity who commits suicide after impulsively killing his mistress. In *Le Jour se lève* he again takes his own life after murdering the despicable seducer of an innocent flower seller. Central to these highly commercial and artistically successful roles was Gabin's cultivated image as the taciturn, uncompromising working-class male who, though well intentioned and possessing clear moral integrity, finds himself on the wrong side of society's laws. Strong and resilient, yet revealing hidden depths of gentleness and generosity, he remains faithful to his ideals despite the adversity of circumstance. With his simple, honest, direct approach, Gabin embodied values which appealed to contemporary audiences: he was a hero of their stature, unassuming, vulnerable, essentially pure and noble, and facing a dark and menacing world.

In the postwar mood of optimism, Gabin's image as the doomed proletarian hero was no longer fashionable. Although his performance as a blind tramp in *La Nuit est mon royaume* was well received, it was not until his role in *Touchez pas au grisbi* that he again captured the public imagination. Now cast as a retired gangster lured back to Paris for a final spectacular coup, he evolved a new image as the experienced, assured male firmly in control of his destiny and no longer vulnerable to female charms. In subsequent roles he combined a practical wisdom with the inherent humanity of his screen personality to uphold the notion that virtue and justice are rewarded. The former criminal, social outcast, and working-class hero of the 1930s became the respectable middle-class professional of the 1950s in the guise of doctor (*La Minute de vérité*), powerful industrialist (*Le Sang à la tête*), banker (*Les Grandes Familles*), lawyer (*En cas de malheur*), detective (*Maigret tend un piège*), and judge (*Chiens perdus sans collier*). These roles projected a new set of values and dispositions: pragmatism and intelligence rather than idealism and physical courage; mature reflection rather than impetuous commitment; serenity rather than a tortured soul.

In a period of renewed self-confidence and self-sufficiency Gabin once again reflected national attitudes. Comic roles were added to his repertoire as the anarchistic tramp in *Archimède le clochard*, the wily politician with a wicked sense of fun in *Le Président*, and the disruptive inmate of a retirement home in *Les Vieux de la vieille* (here co-starring with two long established film comedians, Bourvil and Funès). Co-starring became an important feature of Gabin's later screen career, either appearing with his contemporaries, or in association with the younger generation of rising stars such as Brigitte Bardot in *En cas de malheur* and Jean-Paul Belmondo in *Un Singe en hiver*. Such was Gabin's continuing popular appeal that his presence in a film was a virtual guarantee of commercial success and, apart from the temporary eclipse in the late 1940s, he is acknowledged as one of the enduring mainstays of the French film industry over a period of 30 years.

—R. F. Cousins

GABLE, Clark

Nationality: American. **Born:** William Clark Gable in Cadiz, Ohio, 1 February 1901. **Education:** Attended school in Hopedale, Ohio; Akron University in evening classes. **Military Service:** 1942-45—U.S. Army Air Corps: narrated several Air Corps films; discharged as ma-

Clark Gable

jor. **Family:** Married 1) Josephine Dillon, 1924 (divorced 1930); 2) Ria Langham, 1931 (divorced 1939); 3) the actress Carole Lombard, 1939 (died 1942); 4) Lady Sylvia Ashley, 1949 (divorced 1951); 5) Kay Speckles, 1955, son: John Clark. **Career:** Factory worker in Akron; 1919—callboy in Broadway theaters (for John and Lionel Barrymore in *The Jest*); worked in oil fields in Oklahoma for a year; 1920-22—utility man and actor with Jewell Players, a tent show repertory company; then joined theater group in Portland, Oregon; 1924—film debut in bit part in *Forbidden Paradise*; on Los Angeles stage in *Romeo and Juliet* and *What Price Glory*, and with a Texas stock company; 1928—Broadway debut in *Machinal*; then other stage work in New York; 1931—debut in sound films, *The Painted Desert*; 1934—MGM contract; 1945—returned to films with *Adventure*; 1956—co-founder, Russ-Field Gabco production company. **Awards:** Oscar for Best Actor, for *It Happened One Night*, 1934. **Died:** Of heart attack, 16 November 1960.

Films as Actor:

1924   *Forbidden Paradise* (Lubitsch) (bit role); *White Man* (Gasnier)

1925   *The Merry Widow* (von Stroheim) (bit role); *The Pacemakers* (Ruggles—serial); *Declassée* (*The Social Exile*) (Vignola) (bit role); *The Plastic Age* (Ruggles) (bit role); *North Star* (Powell)

1926   *The Johnstown Flood* (*The Flood*) (Cummings) (bit role); *The Collegians* (serial)

1931   *The Painted Desert* (Higgins) (as Brett); *The Easiest Way* (Conway) (as Nick); *The Secret Six* (Hill) (as Carl); *The Finger Points* (Dillon) (as Louis Blanco); *Laughing Sinners* (Beaumont) (as Carl Loomis); *A Free Soul* (Brown) (as Ace Wilfong); *The Christmas Party* (*Jackie Cooper's Christmas*) (Reisner—short) (as himself); *Night Nurse* (Wellman) (as Nick); *Sporting Blood* (Brabin) (as Tip Scanlon); *Dance, Fools, Dance* (Beaumont) (as Jake Luva); *Susan Lenox, Her Fall and Rise* (*The Rise of Helga*) (Leonard) (as Rodney Spencer); *Possessed* (Brown) (as Mark Whitney); *Hell Divers* (Hill) (as Steve)

1932   *Polly of the Circus* (Santell) (as the Reverend John Hartley); *Strange Interlude* (*Strange Interval*) (Leonard) (as Ned Darrell); *Red Dust* (Fleming) (as Denis Carson); *No Man of Her Own* (Ruggles) (as Babe Stewart)

1933   *The White Sister* (Fleming) (as Giovanni Severi); *Hold Your Man* (Wood) (as Eddie Nugent); *Night Flight* (Brown) (as Fabian); *Dancing Lady* (Leonard) (as Patch Gallegher)

1934   ***It Happened One Night*** (Capra) (as Peter Warne); *Men in White* (Boleslawski) (as Dr. George Ferguson); *Manhattan Melodrama* (Van Dyke) (as Blackie Gallagher); *Chained* (Brown) (as Mike Bradley)

1935   *Forsaking All Others* (Van Dyke) (as Jeff Williams); *After Office Hours* (Leonard) (as Jim Branch); *The Call of the Wild* (Wellman) (as Jake Thorton); *China Seas* (Garnett) (as Alan Gaskell); *Mutiny on the Bounty* (Lloyd) (as Fletcher Christian)

1936   *Wife versus Secretary* (Brown) (as Dan Sanford); *San Francisco* (Van Dyke) (as Blackie Norton); *Cain and Mabel* (Bacon) (as Larry Cain); *Love on the Run* (Van Dyke) (as Michael Anthony); *Parnell* (Stahl) (title role)

1937   *Saratoga* (Conway) (as Duke Bradley)

1938   *Test Pilot* (Fleming) (as Jim Lane); *Too Hot to Handle* (Conway) (as Chris Hunter)

1939   *Idiot's Delight* (Brown) (as Harry Van); ***Gone with the Wind*** (Fleming) (as Rhett Butler)

1940   *Strange Cargo* (Borzage) (as Verne); *Boomtown* (Conway) (as John "Big John" McMasters); *Comrade X* (King Vidor) (as McKinley Thompson)

1941   *They Met in Bombay* (Brown) (as Gerald Meldrick); *Honky Tonk* (Conway) (as Candy Johnson)

1942   *Somewhere I'll Find You* (Ruggles) (as Johnny Davis); *March of Dimes* (Whitebeck—short)

1943   *Hollywood in Uniform* (short) (as himself)

1944   *Aerial Gunner* (Air Corp—short) (as narrator); *Be Careful!* (Air Corps—short) (as narrator); *Wings Up* (Air Corps—short) (as narrator); *Combat America* (Air Corps—short) (as narrator)

1945   *Adventure* (Fleming) (as Henry Patterson)

1947   *The Hucksters* (Conway) (as Vic Norman); *Homecoming* (LeRoy) (as Dr. Ulysses Johnson)

1948   *Command Decision* (Wood) (as Brigadier General K. C. Dennis)

1949   *Any Number Can Play* (LeRoy) (as Charley King)

1950   *Key to the City* (Sidney) (as Steve Fisk); *To Please a Lady* (Brown) (as Mike Brannon)

1951   *Across the Wide Missouri* (Wellman) (as Flint Mitchell); *Callaway Went Thataway* (*The Star Said No*) (Panama and Frank) (as himself)

1952   *Lone Star* (Sherman) (as Devereaux Burke)

1953   *Never Let Me Go* (Daves) (as Philip Sutherland)

1954   *Mogambo* (John Ford) (as Victor Marswell); *Betrayed* (Reinhardt) (as Colonel Pieter Deventer)

1955   *Soldier of Fortune* (Dmytryk) (as Hank Lee); *The Tall Men* (Walsh) (as Ben Allison)

1956   *King and Four Queens* (Walsh) (as Dan Kehoe)

1957   *Band of Angels* (Walsh) (as Hamish Bond)

1958   *Run Silent, Run Deep* (Wise) (as Commander "Rich" Richardson); *Teacher's Pet* (Seaton) (as James Gannon)

1959   *But Not for Me* (Walter Lang) (as Russel Ward)

1960   *It Started in Naples* (Shavelson) (as Mike Hamilton)

1961   ***The Misfits*** (Huston) (as Gay Langland)

Publications

On GABLE: books—

Carpozzi, George Jr., *Clark Gable*, New York, 1961.

Gable, Kathleen, *Clark Gable: A Personal Portrait*, Englewood Cliffs, New Jersey, 1961.

Garceau, Jean, and Inez Cooke, *"Dear Mr. G"—The Biography of Clark Gable*, Boston, 1961.

Samuels, Charles, *The King: A Biography of Clark Gable*, New York, 1961.

Gable: A Complete Gallery of His Screen Portraits, compiled by Gabe Essoe and Ray Lee, Los Angeles, 1967.

Morella, Joe, and Edward Epstein, *Gable & Lombard & Powell & Harlow*, London, 1971.

Behlmer, Rudy, editor, *Memo from: David O. Selznick*, New York, 1972.

Rosen, Marjorie, *Popcorn Venus*, New York, 1973.

Tornabene, Lyn, *Long Live the King: A Biography of Clark Gable*, New York, 1976.

Garceau, Jean, with Inez Cooke, *Gable: A Pictorial Biography*, New York, 1977.

Fearfar, R., *Clark Gable*, Paris, 1981.

Card, James, *Clark Gable*, London, 1986.

Wayne, Jane Ellen, *Gable's Women*, London, 1987.

Wayne, Jane Ellen, *Clark Gable: Portrait of a Misfit*, New York, 1993.

Lewis, Judy, *Uncommon Knowledge*, New York, 1994.

On GABLE: articles—

Current Biography 1945, New York, 1945.

Fowler, D. C., "Clark Gable," in *Look* (New York), 8 July 1947.

Clarens, Carlos, "Clark Gable," in *Films in Review* (New York), December 1960.

McVay, D., "Eternal Images. Part Two: Clark Gable," in *Films and Filming* (London), July 1977.

Champlin, Charles, "Clark Gable," in *The Movie Star*, edited by Elisabeth Weis, New York, 1981.

*   *   *

Crowned King of Hollywood in 1937, Clark Gable remains unchallenged American royalty. He is remembered as the man who made the pencil mustache de rigueur and crippled the undershirt business when he bared his chest in *It Happened One Night*. For many, Gable still represents the ultimate in American masculinity—a man's man and a woman's ideal. The consummate product of the studio system, Gable's screen image was created by MGM publicity executive Howard Strickling who capitalized on Gable's natural assets and his actual background as a laborer. He was to become a symbol of the uncommon common man.

Gable's impressive size projected an enormous physical strength; he could challenge any man and dominate any woman. The ever present wink in his eye transmitted a roguish charm, a casual self-confidence, and an innate sense of humor. But it was what Joan Crawford described as his "sheer animal magic," his magnetic and overt virility, which separated him from the rest, even offscreen; a recent tell-all by Judy Lewis, the daughter of Loretta Young, revealed the long-kept secret of a Gable/Young love affair that spawned Lewis herself. Gable's only acknowledged child, John Clark Gable, the result of his union with Kay Speckles, was born shortly after Gable died.

Hailed as Valentino with a voice, Clark Gable embodied sex appeal. It was his "you'll take it and like it" attitude towards Norma Shearer in *A Free Soul* that catapulted the 30-year-old actor into stardom and kept him among the top ten box-office stars for the next 12 years (1932-43); by 1939 he was earning $5,000 per week.

Gable signed the first in a series of long-term contracts with MGM in December 1930 and worked for the studio until he began freelancing in 1954. The vast majority of his Metro assignments were star vehicles (*Chained*, *Saratoga*, *Test Pilot*, and *Honky Tonk*). These were pictures whose commercial success depended almost entirely on his name and that of the studio's top leading ladies, particularly Joan Crawford, Jean Harlow, Myrna Loy, and Lana Turner. In these films, Gable played the same role time and time again—a roué with a heart of gold.

During the 1930s his occasional opportunities to do something beyond formula material were more often fortuitous than calculated. His casting in a comedy on "Poverty Row" (Columbia's *It Happened One Night*) was designed as a punishment for uncooperative behavior; *Call of the Wild* was another loan-out; *Mutiny on the Bounty* and *San Francisco* were both films Gable himself resisted doing.

The undisputed pinnacle of his career was his role as Rhett Butler in *Gone with the Wind*, another part he initially resisted. Assisted by one of his favorite directors, Victor Fleming, Gable created perhaps the most popular romantic figure of the twentieth century. Offscreen, Gable lived out the myth of the great lover by marrying actress Carole Lombard. Her unexpected death in 1942 drastically changed the actor's attitude towards his life and his work. He turned his back on Hollywood and joined the Army Air Corps. After a two-year absence from the screen, Gable returned with a new seriousness. Personal grief and depression, combined with the onset of middle age, deeply affected his on-screen persona. For many, the motion picture business seemed frivolous after the war; Gable concurred. Even the now-famous slogan for his first postwar film (*Adventure*), "Gable's Back and Garson's Got Him!," struck the actor as frivolous.

Despite the relative infrequency of his screen appearances, Gable reclaimed his top ten box-office status in 1947, 1948, and 1949. His enormous popularity began to wane only in the last decade of his life, although he continued to remain a star, his name well above the title in such pictures as *The Tall Men*, *Band of Angels*, and *The King and Four Queens*, a title obviously geared towards him.

His career culminated with an impressive tour-de-force performance as the mustanger Gay Langland in John Huston's *The Misfits*, which he considered the best of his career, even though he never lived to see the completed film. Three days after the picture wrapped, he died of a heart attack, which, some maintained, was brought on by the strain of doing his own stunt work at Huston's urging during the film's climactic mustang roundup. It was Gable himself who insisted on doing many of his own stunts for the required close-ups. But, contrary to rumor, the real rough-and-tumble action was carried out in long shot by Gable's double, a professional stuntman. This final performance, delivered with remarkable sensitivity and conviction, stands as a tribute, not only to a great star but to the accomplished actor Gable was not always given credit for being.

—Joanne L. Yeck, updated by John McCarty

GANZ, Bruno

Nationality: Swiss. **Born:** Zurich, 22 March 1941. **Military Service:** Served in military. **Family:** Married in 1965; one son. **Career:** After military service, joined the Student Theatre in West Germany; also acted in other theaters in Germany; 1961—film debut in *Chikita*; 1970—co-founder, Schaubühne, Berlin, and acted in productions there for the next six years, and later in title role of Hamlet, 1982; after 1978—lived in Zurich; 1982—co-directed the film *Gedächtnis*. **Awards:** Deutscher Filmpreis for Acting, for *The Marquise of O*, 1976.

Films as Actor:

1961   *Chikita (Wenn Männer Schlange stehen)* (Suter)
1962   *Es Dach überem Chopf* (Früh)
1967   *Der sanfte Lauf* (Senft) (as Bernard Kral)
1975   *Sommergäste (Summer Guests)* (Stein) (as Yakov Schalimov); *Die Marquise von O (The Marquise of O)* (Rohmer) (as the Russian count)
1976   *Lumière* (Moreau) (as Heinrich Grun); *Die Wildente (The Wild Duck)* (Geissendörfer) (as Gregor)
1977   ***Der Amerikanische Freund** (The American Friend)* (Wenders) (as Jonathan Zimmermann); *Die linkshändige Frau (The Left-Handed Woman)* (Handke) (as Bruno)
1978   *Retour à la bienaimée* (Adam); *Schwarz und Weiss wie Tage und Nächte (Black and White Like Day and Night)* (Petersen) (as Thomas Rosenmund); *Messer im Kopf (Knife in the Head)* (Hauff) (as Berthold Hoffmann); *The Boys from Brazil* (Schaffner) (as Prof. Bruckner)
1979   *Nosferatu—Phantom der Nacht (Nosferatu—The Vampire)* (Herzog) (as Jonathan Harker); *5% de risque* (Pourtale); *Oggetti smarriti* (G. Bertolucci)
1980   *La Provinciale (The Girl from Lorraine)* (Goretta) (as Remy); *La Dame aux camélias* (Bolognini); *Polenta* (Simon); *Der Erfinder (The Inventor)* (Gloor) (as Jokob Nüssli)
1981   *Die Fälschung (Circle of Deceit)* (Schlöndorff) (as Georg Laschen); *Etwas wird sichtbar* (Farocki); *Fermata Etna* (Grüber); *Geschichte einer Liebe* (Damek—for TV)
1982   *Logik des Gefühls* (Kratisch) (as himself)

Bruno Ganz in *Der Himmel über Berlin* Argos Films and Road Movies for Wings of Desire

1983   *Krieg und frieden* (*War and Peace*) (Schlöndorff and others—
        doc); *Dans la Ville Blanche* (*In the White City*) (Tanner) (as
        Paul); *System ohne Schatten* (*Closed Circuit*) (Thome) (as
        Faber); *Killer aus Florida* (Schaffhauser)
1985   *De Ijsallon* (Frank)
1986   *El Rio del oro* (*Golden River*) (Chavarri) (as Peter); *Der Pendler*
        (Giger) (as Steiner)
1987   *Der Himmel über Berlin* (*Wings of Desire*) (Wenders) (as Damiel)
1988   *Strapless* (Hare) (as Raymond Forbes); *Vater und Sonhe* (*Fa-
        thers and Sons*) (Sinkel—for TV)
1989   *Bankomatt* (Mermann) (as Bruno)
1991   *Prague* (Sellars) (as Josef); *The Architecture of Doom*
        (*Untergangens Arkitektur*) (Cohen) (as narrator); *Erfolg* (as
        Jacques Tuverlin); *Born Natturunna* (as Engeler)
1992   *Last Days of Chez Nous* (Armstrong) (as J. P.); *Brandnacht* (as
        Peter Keller)
1993   *Especially on Sunday* (*Specialmente la Domenica*)
        (Tornatore) (as Vittorio); *The Absence* (Handke) (as Gam-
        bler); *Faraway, So Close* (*In Weiter Ferne, So Nah!*)
        (Wenders) (as Damiel)
1994   *Bright Day* (as Georg); *Il Grande Fausto* (as Cavanna)

Film as Co-Director:

1982   *Gedächtnis: Ein Film für Curt Bois und Bernhard Minetti*
        (doc) (+ co-ed, ro)

Publications

By GANZ: articles—

Interview with D. Overby, in *Cinema* (Paris), December 1979.
Interview with Walt R. Vian, in *Filmbulletin*, December 1980.

On GANZ: articles—

Dawson, Jan, "A Proper Raincoat Man," in *Sight and Sound* (London),
    Summer 1979.
Premiere, January 1980.
Retro, August-September 1983.

*   *   *

    There is a small scene in Wim Wenders's film *The American Friend*,
which reveals some of the particular talents of Swiss-German actor,
Bruno Ganz. Ganz plays a picture framer; he is seated at a desk in his
shop, and absentmindedly takes a sheet of gold leaf and carefully blows
it into the palm of his hand so that it adheres completely to the
surface. He then slams his palm onto a telephone receiver and makes
a call. That moment—like all great moments in film acting—is a
piece of behavior that reveals Ganz's character. The action embraces
both the delicacy and meticulous nature of Jonathan, the artisan, as
well as his latent violence—by the film's end Jonathan is responsible

for the murder of several men. Ganz does not call attention to his activity—it is simple, subtle, and low-key. Ganz's performance style is distinguished by an eloquence and precision of physical expression, as well as a bruised sensitivity that haunts his best work.

Ganz is one of the few actors to come to prominence in the heyday of the New German Cinema in the mid-1960s to late 1970s to make a successful and sustained leap to the international art cinema circuit. Before beginning his film career in earnest, Ganz was a mainstay of the West German stage, and a founding member of the Schaubühne, one of Germany's most celebrated and vital theater companies. While still performing on stage in the mid-1970s, Ganz starred in *Die Marquise von O*, directed by Eric Rohmer, which brought him to prominence among art-house audiences. The following year he acted in the Jeanne Moreau-directed *Lumière*, as well as playing a leading role in Hans Geissendörfer's film of Ibsen's *The Wild Duck*. *The American Friend* featured a trilingual cast (French, German, English), and catapulted both Wim Wenders and Ganz to worldwide recognition. The actor's next crucial role was as the mild-mannered scientist, Berthold Hoffmann, shot in the head by police, who mistake him for a radical activist. The film, *Messer Im Kopf*, was made at the height of left-wing paranoia and police surveillance in post-Baader-Meinhoff Germany. The part required Ganz to play a man who must completely relearn his cognition, speech, and motor skills. This physically and psychologically demanding portrayal is the result of arduous research combined with the observation and execution of myriad small details of behavior; it is a true, astonishing, and moving feat. Through the constraint of severe expressive limitations, the audience must feel the character's growing anger, frustration, and finally, despair. Ganz, with his usual blend of precision and invention, beautifully delineates a life that is broken, and thrown off course forever. Even as the character's capacity for violence develops in tandem with his faculties, Ganz manages to make his rendition of Hoffmann entirely sympathetic.

Ganz's next interesting role was as Jonathan Harker in Werner Herzog's perverse and beautiful version of *Nosferatu—Phantom der Nacht*. Although somewhat eclipsed by the delicious eccentricities of Klaus Kinski's eponymous demon, Ganz brings depth and subtlety to Harker's transformation from steadfast paramour to lunatic incarnation of evil, as he assumes Kinski's role of *über*-vampire at the film's end.

Although he continued to work with such directors as Claude Goretta (*La Provinciale*), Volker Schlöndorff (*Circle of Deceit*), and Alain Tanner (*Dans la Ville Blanche*), the 1980s proved less than exciting for Ganz's career until he reteamed with Wenders for *Wings of Desire* in 1987, playing the angel, Damiel. As Damiel, one senses a quality of grace and peacefulness that tempers Ganz's earlier angst-filled characterizations. Playing Damiel allows Ganz to deal some of his trump cards—vulnerability, tenderness, and an underlying sadness. When Damiel begins to fall in love with the earthbound trapeze artist, played by Solveig Dommartin, he touches the objects in her room that she has touched, and places his hand on her back. She cannot see or feel him, and the sense of longing that resonates from Ganz in this scene is painful, and deeply felt. When Damiel comes to earth and experiences the pleasures of the material world, the role gives Ganz the opportunity to relish his new physical sensations—drinking hot coffee, feeling cold, hunger, pain—an actor's dream. Ganz returned as Damiel, now a secondary character, in Wenders less successful sequel to *Wings of Desire*, *Faraway, So Close*.

Ganz has remained on the international scene through the mid-1990s, continuing his policy of choosing interesting, if uncommercial projects. In Gillian Armstrong's film, *Last Days of Chez Nous*, Ganz—with German accent intact—plays a homesick Frenchman enmeshed in a failing marriage in Australia. The part gives Ganz a chance to cut loose and display his humor—he has several scenes where he clumsily and delightfully joins in his family's wacky free-form dances. His character is in full midlife crisis, yearning for "more life" in the

company of younger women. Ganz's distinctive mix of vulnerability, gentleness, and quiet longing mark this as one of his most fully realized recent performances.

—Carole Zucker

GARBO, Greta

Nationality: American. **Born:** Greta Lovisa Gustafsson in Stockholm, Sweden, 18 September 1905; became U.S. citizen, 1951. **Education:** Attended Catherine Elementary School; Royal Dramatic Theatre School, Stockholm, 1922-24. **Career:** Worked as latherer in barber shop, clerk in Bergstrom's department store, and model; appeared in advertising films for PUB and Cooperative Society of Stockholm; 1921—film debut as extra in *A Fortune Hunter*; 1923—cast by the director Mauritz Stiller in *Gösta Berlings Saga*; appeared in several other films by him, and went with him to Hollywood; 1925-41—contract with MGM, becoming leading Hollywood film actress, first in silent films, then, following *Anna Christie*, 1930, in sound films; 1941—last film, *Two-Faced Woman*. **Awards:** Best Actress, New York Film Critics, for *Anna Karenina*, 1935, for *Camille*, 1937; Honorary Academy Award, "for her unforgettable screen performances," 1954. **Died:** In New York, 15 April 1990.

Films as Actress:

1921 *En lyckoriddare* (*A Fortune Hunter*) (Brunius) (as extra); *Herr och fru Stockholm* (*Mr. and Mrs. Stockholm*; *How Not to Dress*) (Ring—short) (bit role); *Our Daily Bread* (Ring—short) (bit role)
1922 *Luffar-Petter* (*Peter the Tramp*) (Petschler) (as Greta Nordberg)
1924 **Gösta Berlings Saga** (*The Atonement of Gösta Berling*) (Stiller) (as Countess Elisabeth Dohna)
1925 *Die Freudlose Gasse* (*The Joyless Street*) (Pabst) (as Greta Rumfort)
1926 *The Torrent* (*Ibañez' Torrent*) (Bell) (as Leonora); *The Temptress* (Stiller and Niblo) (as Elena); *Flesh and the Devil* (Brown) (as Felicitas von Kletzingk)
1927 *Love* (*Anna Karenina*) (Goulding) (as Anna Karenina)
1928 *The Divine Woman* (Seastrom) (as Marianne); *The Mysterious Lady* (Niblo) (as Tania); *A Woman of Affairs* (Brown) (as Diana Merrick)
1929 *Wild Orchids* (Franklin) (as Lillie Sterling); *A Man's Man* (Cruze) (as guest); *The Single Standard* (Robertson) (as Arden Stuart); *The Kiss* (Feyder) (as Madame Irène Guarry)
1930 *Anna Christie* (Brown—German and Swedish versions directed by Jacques Feyder) (title role); *Romance* (Brown) (as Rita Cavallini)
1931 *Inspiration* (Brown) (as Yvonne); *Susan Lenox: Her Fall and Rise* (*The Rise of Helga*) (Leonard) (title role)
1932 *Mata Hari* (Fitzmaurice) (title role); *Grand Hotel* (Goulding) (as Grusinskaya); *As You Desire Me* (Fitzmaurice) (as Zara)
1933 *Queen Christina* (Mamoulian) (title role)
1934 *The Painted Veil* (Boleslawski) (as Katrin)
1935 *Anna Karenina* (Brown) (title role)
1937 **Camille** (Cukor) (as Marguerite Gautier); *Conquest* (*Marie Walewska*) (Brown) (as Marie Walewska)
1939 **Ninotchka** (Lubitsch) (title role)
1941 *Two-Faced Woman* (Cukor) (as Karin Borg Blake/Katherine Borg)

Publications

By GARBO: articles—

"What the Public Wants," in *Saturday Review* (New York), 13 June 1931.
Article by Greta Garbo and Ernst Lubitsch, in *New York Times*, 22 October 1939.
"Garbo," interview with A. Gronowicz, in *Journal of Popular Culture*, Summer 1968.
"Ma vie d'artiste," reprinted from 1930 *Ciné-Magazine*, in *Avant-Scène du Cinéma* (Paris), 15 March 1981.
Portion of memoirs, in *Avant-Scène du Cinéma* (Paris), 15 March 1981.

On GARBO: books—

Palmborg, Rilla Page, *The Private Life of Greta Garbo*, New York, 1931.
Wild, Roland, *Greta Garbo*, London, 1933.
Laing, E. E., *Greta Garbo: The Story of a Specialist*, London, 1946.
Bainbridge, John, *Garbo*, New York, 1955.
Wallin, John, *Garbo en stjärnas väg*, Stockholm, 1955.
Billquist, Fritiof, *Garbo: A Biography*, New York, 1960.
Conway, Michael, Dion McGregor, and Marc Ricci, *The Films of Greta Garbo*, New York, 1963.
Durgnat, Raymond, and John Kobal, *Greta Garbo*, New York, 1965.
Zierold, Norman, *Garbo*, New York, 1969.
Ture, Sjolander, *Garbo*, New York, 1971.
Rosen, Marjorie, *Popcorn Venus*, New York, 1973.
Corliss, Richard, *Greta Garbo*, New York, 1974.
Affron, Charles, *Star Acting: Gish, Garbo, Davis*, New York, 1977.
Sands, Frederick, and Sven Broman, *The Divine Garbo*, New York, 1979.
Walker, Alexander, *Greta Garbo: A Portrait*, New York, 1980.
Linton, George, *Greta Garbo*, Paris, 1981.
Brion, Patrick, *Garbo*, Paris, 1985.
Agel, Henri, *Greta Garbo*, Paris, 1990.
Broman, Sven, *Greta Garbo berattar*, Stockholm, 1990; published as *Conversations with Greta Garbo*, New York, 1992.
Gronowicz, Antoni, *Garbo: Her Story*, New York, 1990.
Haining, Peter, *The Legend of Garbo*, London, 1990.
Bunsch, Iris, *Three Female Myths of the 20th Century: Garbo, Callas, Navratilova*, New York, 1991.
Krutzen, Michaela, *The Most Beautiful Woman on the Screen: The Fabrication of the Star Greta Garbo*, Frankfurt, 1992.
Paris, Barry, *Garbo: A Biography*, New York, 1993.
Souhami, Diana, *Greta and Cecil*, San Francisco, 1994.
Vickers, Hugo, *Loving Garbo: The Story of Greta Garbo, Cecil Beaton, and Mercedes de Acosta*, New York, 1994.

On GARBO: articles—

Tully, Jim, "Greta Garbo," in *Vanity Fair* (New York), June 1928.
Virgilia, S., "Greta Garbo," in *New Yorker*, 7 March 1931.
Booth, Clare, "The Great Garbo," in *Vanity Fair* (New York), February 1932.
Maxwell, Virginia, "The Amazing Story behind Garbo's Choice of Gilbert," in *Photoplay* (New York), January 1934.
Canfield, M. C., "Letter to Garbo," in *Theatre Arts* (New York), December 1937.
Huff, Theodore, "The Career of Greta Garbo," in *Films in Review* (New York), December 1951.
Tynan, Kenneth, "Garbo," in *Sight and Sound* (London), Spring 1954.
Current Biography 1955, New York, 1955.
Idestam-Almquist, Bengt, "The Man Who Found Garbo," in *Films and Filming* (London), August 1956.
Fleet, S., "Garbo: The Lost Star," in *Films and Filming* (London), December 1956.
Barthes, Roland, "The Face of Garbo," in *Mythologies*, Paris, 1957; London, 1972.
Brooks, Louise, "Gish and Garbo—The Executive War on Stars," in *Sight and Sound* (London), Winter 1958-59.
Whitehall, Richard, "Garbo—How Good Was She?," in *Films and Filming* (London), September 1963.
Nordberg, Carl Eric, "Greta Garbo's Secret," in *Film Comment* (New York), Summer 1970.
Culff, Robert, "Greta Garbo's Hollywood Silents," in *Silent Picture* (London), Autumn 1972.
Thomson, D., "Waiting for Garbo," in *American Film* (Washington, D.C.), October 1980.
Corliss, Richard, "Greta Garbo," in *The Movie Star*, edited by Elisabeth Weis, New York, 1981.
Lloyd, A., "Stars Oscar Forgot: Greta Garbo," in *Films and Filming* (London), May 1984.
Lubitsch, Ernst, "Mon travail avec Greta Garbo," in *Positif* (Paris), June 1985.
Matthews, Peter, "Garbo and Phallic Motherhood: A 'Homosexual' Visual Economy," in *Screen* (London), vol. 29, no. 3, Summer 1988.
Cohn, Lawrence, "Garbo, Screen's Classiest Siren, Dies at 84," obituary in *Variety* (New York), 18 April 1990.
"Garbo Dies," obituary in *New Republic*, 7 May 1990.
Kauffman, Stanley, "Greta Garbo," in *New Republic*, 21 May 1990.
Horton, Robert, "The Mysterious Lady," in *Film Comment* (New York), July/August 1990.

*   *   *

Peter Matthews describes, in "Garbo and Phallic Motherhood: A 'Homosexual' Visual Economy," that a photograph reproduced in *Photoplay* in the early 1930s shows "Garbo's face in enormous close-up, a white oval emerging from a field of undifferentiated blackness, disembodied . . . as a kind of iconic mask, an eerily suspended object of desire." Her mystique, her unknowability, prevalent both on screen and in real life, daunts and haunts movie viewers long after her early retirement into absolute seclusion.

George Cukor recalled that Irving Thalberg visited the set of *Camille* during the first days of shooting, glanced around, and expressed himself as well satisfied with the young director's skill in handling MGM's premier star. "How could you know?" Cukor asked, and Thalberg, indicating the actress sitting silent and alone between takes, said "Look at her. She's unguarded."

Garbo unguarded was a rare commodity. For a decade, MGM strip-teased the star that her admirers saw as the epitome of restraint, dignity, and private emotion, selling *Anna Christie* with the slogan "Garbo Talks!" and *Ninotchka* with "Garbo Laughs!" When, years later, a publicist confessed his authorship of the latter slogan to her, she said moodily, "How can you forgive yourself?"

It is debatable as to what extent the Garbo taciturnity was a pose; she may have had nothing to say. She never married, and her relationships were limited and private. That she was, like most stars, a woman to whom sexual appetite was less important than fame, is clear enough. But long before the solipsism of meditation and the "Me Decade," Garbo, a fanatic for health foods and ascetic living, found contentment in restraint.

Her strong following in Europe—always greater than in the United States—encouraged MGM to cast her in period roles. They obscure her standing as the first great modern of the cinema—the emancipated woman, surrendering to passion by choice, but resigned always to repentance at leisure. Her best films are set in this century. *Wild Orchids*, with its silky shadowed textures of a fantasy Asia, is a film of

Greta Garbo

immediate eroticism, a living sculpture in Art Deco, and so successful that MGM tried to repeat the effect in *The Painted Veil* five years later.

Feyder's courtroom melodrama *The Kiss*, and the splintered realism of *Anna Christie*, with Garbo's burred drawl successfully evoking the Strindbergian squalor of O'Neill's original, perfectly express their time. Even seducing Ramon Navarro (in *Mata Hari*) into blowing out the votive candle that will signify his surrender, or prowling the nightclub stage, crop-haired and draped in black, for the travesty of Pirandello's *As You Desire Me*, Garbo is as contemporary as Brando or Streep.

Of the period films, few stand the test of repeated viewing. Under the influence of New York stage directors such as Cukor, and emigrés such as Lubitsch and Garbo's tame writer Salka Viertel, Garbo declined into a parody of the Continental heroine. *Camille* and *Conquest* offer little but elaborate *tableaux morts*, triumphs for decorators and the close-up director who scrutinized each shot for inappropriate indications of modernity or emotion. Garbo among the bibelots of *Camille* is a stranded fish gasping for life. In *Conquest* she faces Boyer's Napoleon with an upper lip no less stiff than Clive Brook's in *Shanghai Express*. Surrounded in these films by waxworks such as Henry Stephenson, an aging Lewis Stone, and the Prussian correctness of Basil Rathbone, the vivid, living Garbo was overshadowed, extinguished. She is better in the least of her modern films: despite being physically unsuited to the role as a ballerina in *Grand Hotel*, she achieves the poignancy of a woman betrayed at her most vulnerable.

Among the great absurdities of Garbo's career is its ending. Allegedly horrified by poor notices for Cukor's *Two-Faced Woman*, she retreated, never to return, not even at the prospect of starring in Proust's *À La Recherche du Temps Perdu*. Ironic, then, that the film from which she retreats is at once her most modern, and, of all her contemporary performances, the least inhibited. To watch this stringy lady in her mid-thirties bluff her way through a nightclub slanging session, then, gaining confidence, lead the floor in a frenzied dance of her own devising, is to see acting no less skilled than that of such stars as Cagney and Davis who persisted into the 1980s with productive work. But if "Garbo Talks!" and "Garbo Laughs!" were unforgivable, "Garbo Dances!" is surely the last straw. As so often with Garbo in the films, one laments the loss but respects the impulse. Nothing so much became her career as the leaving of it.

But, "we love it, the mystery," exhilarates Robert Horton about his bewilderment of Garbo in an almost cheerfully dazed tone after the screen goddess's demise in 1990. It is only fitting that she received an honorary Oscar in 1954 for her "unforgettable screen performances." Coming 13 years after she left the big screen, this recognition served not only as a token of her lasting presence immortalized on film, but also as a prophecy foretelling the ongoing fascination surrounding the hereafter all the more invisible actress. Garbo, an ultimate movie icon, as the disembodied face forever suspended larger than life, epitomizes an unreality that perhaps only exists in the world of cinema.

—John Baxter, updated by Guo-Juin Hong

GARCÍA, Andy

Nationality: American. **Born:** Arturo García-Menedez in Havana, Cuba, 12 April 1956; moved to Miami Beach, 1961. **Family:** Married Marivi García, daughters: Dominique, Daniela, Alessandra. **Education:** Attended Florida International University, Miami. **Career:** 1970s—grew up in Florida, where he played in regional theater; late 1970s—moved to Los Angeles, where he played small roles on TV and acted with an improvisational theater; 1983—film debut in small role in *Blue Skies Again*; 1993—

directed and produced documentary *Cachao . . . como su ritmo no hay dos.* **Agent:** Paradigm Talent Agency, 10100 Santa Monica Boulevard, 25th Floor, Los Angeles, CA 90067, U.S.A.

Films as Actor:

1983   *Blue Skies Again* (Michaels) (as Ken); *A Night in Heaven* (Avildsen) (as T. J.)
1985   *The Mean Season* (Borsos) (as Ray Martínez)
1986   *8 Million Ways to Die* (Ashby) (as Angel Maldonado)
1987   *The Untouchables* (DePalma) (as George Stone)
1988   *American Roulette* (Hatton) (as Carlos Quintas); *Stand and Deliver* (Menendez) (as Ramírez); *Clinton and Nadine (Blood Money)* (Schatzberg—for TV) (as Clinton Earl Dillard)
1989   *Black Rain* (Ridley Scott) (as Charlie Vincent)
1990   *Internal Affairs* (Figgis) (as Sgt. Raymond Avila); *The Godfather, Part III* (Francis Ford Coppola) (as Vincent Mancini); *A Show of Force* (Barretto) (as Luis Angel Mora)
1991   *Dead Again* (Branagh) (as Gary Baker)
1992   *Jennifer Eight* (Robinson) (as John Berlin); *Hero (Accidental Hero)* (Frears) (as John Bubber)
1994   *When a Man Loves a Woman* (Mandoki) (as Michael Green)
1995   *Things to Do in Denver When You're Dead* (Fleder) (as Jimmy the Saint); *Steal Big, Steal Little* (Davis) (as Ruben Partida Martínez/Robby Martin)
1996   *Night Falls on Manhattan* (Lumet) (as Sean Casey)

Film as Director and Producer:

1993   *Cachao . . . como su ritmo no hay dos (Like His Rhythm There Is No Other)* (doc) (+ ro as himself)

Publications

On GARCÍA: articles—

Blau, E., "New Face: Andy García, a Fervor for Film Pays Off," in *New York Times*, 24 July 1987.
Honeycutt, Kirk, "Andy García," in *Premiere* (New York), September 1987.
Ferguson, K., "Andy García," in *Film Monthly* (Hemel, England), March 1990.
García, Guy, "The Next Don?," in *American Film* (New York), December 1990.
Clark, John, filmography in *Premiere* (New York), January 1991.
Diamond, Jamie, "Andy García, an Enigma Wrapped Inside Charisma," in *New York Times*, 22 November 1992.
Kellner, Elena, "Private Passion," in *Hispanic* (Austin, Texas), January-February 1994.
Kaylin, Lucy, "Andy García Is a Macho Softy," in *GQ* (New York), July 1994.
Cabrera Infante, G., "The Private Passions of Andy García," in *Harper's Bazaar* (New York), January 1996.

*   *   *

Andy García is a versatile actor who has played a wide range of roles, from stalwart good guy to sadistic villain. He can act light or heavy, and can play the leading man or the character part. Plus, he is blessed with dark, sharp eyes and finely sculptured features, and he looks great on-camera. For years, major stardom has been predicted for him. While being cast in prestige projects, and never offering a sour performance, García somehow never has managed to join the A-list of movie stars.

Andy García in *Internal Affairs*

One explanation is that García has not always selected the kinds of flashy roles guaranteed to capture the media's fancy. He often will play against his physical attributes; he is most concerned with the process of acting, rather than the result, and he will accept a role if it interests him, if he likes the film's point of view, and if he will enjoy working with the director and his fellow cast members.

García first came to critical and audience attention playing a heavy: Angel Maldonado, an impeccably garbed, cocaine-sniffing drug lord, in *8 Million Ways to Die*. Since then, he more often than not has played criminals or cops. He was the former almost a decade later in *Things to Do in Denver When You're Dead*, cast as a Tarantinoesque hood, a retired mob fixer who agrees to perform one final job. In between, he was in *The Godfather, Part III*, offering a showcase performance (and earning an Oscar nomination) as the illegitimate nephew of Michael Corleone. García's Vincent Mancini is as irrationally hot-tempered as his father, Sonny Corleone. Much to his uncle's disapproval, he becomes involved in an affair with Michael's beloved daughter, Mary. *The Godfather, Part III* was a major disappointment, an inferior third installment in the *Godfather* series, but García's performance transcended the film's flaws. Observed the *Variety* critic, "Andy García brings much-needed youth and juice to the ballsy Vincent, heir apparent to the Corleone tradition, much as James Caan sparked the first film and Robert De Niro invigorated the second." If Francis Coppola ever decides to direct *Godfather IV*, he would be well-advised to make García his first casting choice.

García played lawmen in *The Untouchables* (as one of Eliot Ness's "untouchables"); *Black Rain* (as the partner of a New York cop,

played by Michael Douglas); *Internal Affairs* (his first starring role, as an internal affairs detective who investigates a diabolically corrupt cop played by Richard Gere); and *Jennifer Eight* (cast as a burnt-out Los Angeles cop who moves to a small Northern California town and sets out to nab a serial killer of young women). He is especially potent when his characters, whether good guy or bad, explode in dramatic outbursts of rage or frustration.

Not all of García's roles, however, have been cops and robbers. In *Dead Again*, he gave a likable character performance as a shabby journalist. In *When a Man Loves a Woman*, he offered a nuanced one as an outwardly supportive but subtly insensitive husband, who is out of touch with the severe drinking problem of his wife (Meg Ryan). In *Hero*, he was fine as a fraud who takes false credit for saving lives in the aftermath of a plane crash. And in *Steal Big, Steal Little*, he got to play two characters, one good and the other bad: twin brothers Ruben Martínez and Robby Martin, who were orphaned in childhood and separated. One has become a socially committed citizen, while the other has grown into a greedy creep.

Finally, the Cuban-born, Miami-bred actor has not forgotten his roots and his culture. In 1993 he directed a documentary-concert film, *Cachao: Rhythm Like Nobody Else*, about Cuban musician Israel "Cachao" Lopez. It is the filmed record of a concert García organized in honor of Cachao, the long-forgotten father of the mambo.

—Rob Edelman

GARDNER, Ava

Nationality: American. **Born:** Ava Lavinnia Gardner near Smithfield, North Carolina, 24 December 1922. **Education:** Attended Smithfield High School; Atlantic Christian College, Wilson, North Carolina. **Family:** Married 1) the actor Mickey Rooney, 1942 (divorced 1943); 2) the musician Artie Shaw, 1945 (divorced 1946); 3) the singer/actor Frank Sinatra, 1951 (divorced 1957). **Career:** 1941—contract with MGM; 1946-47—roles in *The Killers* and *The Hucksters* established her as a leading sex symbol; 1958—contract with MGM expired; freelance actress; lived for many years in Spain and, from 1968, in London; 1985—in TV mini-series *The Long Hot Summer* and *A.D.*; in TV series *Knots Landing*. **Died:** In London, England, 25 January 1990.

Films as Actress:

1941   *Fancy Answers* (Wrangell—short); *H. M. Pulham, Esquire* (King Vidor) (as girl); *Maisie Was a Lady* (Marin)

1942   *Joe Smith, American* (*Highway to Freedom*) (Thorpe) (as girl); *We Were Dancing* (Leonard) (as girl); *This Time for Keeps* (Reisner) (as girl in car); *Kid Glove Killer* (Zinnemann) (as carhop); *Sunday Punch* (Miller) (as ringsider); *Calling Dr. Gillespie* (Bucquet) (as girl); *Mighty Lak a Goat* (Glazer—short); *Reunion in France* (*Reunion*; *Mademoiselle France*) (Dassin)

1943   *Pilot No. 5* (Sidney) (as girl); *DuBarry Was a Lady* (Del Ruth) (as girl); *Ghosts on the Loose* (*Ghosts in the Night*) (Beaudine) (as Betty); *Hitler's Madman* (Sirk) (as Katy Chotnik); *Young Ideas* (Dassin) (as girl); *Swing Fever* (Whelan) (as girl)

1944   *Lost Angel* (Rowland) (as hatcheck girl); *Three Men in White* (Goldbeck) (as Jean Brown); *Two Girls and a Sailor* (Thorpe) (as Rockette girl); *Maisie Goes to Reno* (*You Can't Do That to Me*) (Beaumont) (as Gloria Fullerton); *Music for Millions* (Koster); *Blonde Fever* (Whorf)

1945   *She Went to the Races* (Goldbeck) (as Hilda Spotts)

1946   *Whistle Stop* (Moguy) (as Mary); **The Killers** (Siodmak) (as Kitty Collins)

1947   *The Hucksters* (Conway) (as Jean Ogilvie); *Singapore* (Brahm) (as Linda)

1948   *One Touch of Venus* (Seiter) (title role)

1949   *The Great Sinner* (Siodmak) (as Pauline Ostrovski); *The Bribe* (Leonard) (as Elizabeth Hinton); *East Side, West Side* (LeRoy) (as Isabel Lorrison)

1951   *My Forbidden Past* (Stevenson) (as Barbara Beaurevel); *Pandora and the Flying Dutchman* (Lewin) (as Pandora Reynolds); *Showboat* (Sidney) (as Julie Laverne)

1952   *Lone Star* (Sherman) (as Martha Ronda); *The Snows of Kilimanjaro* (Henry King) (as Cynthia)

1953   *Ride, Vaquero!* (Farrow) (as Cordelia Cameron); **The Bandwagon** (Minnelli) (as the Movie Star); *Mogambo* (Ford) (as Eloise Kelly); *Knights of the Round Table* (Thorpe) (as Guinevere)

1954   *The Barefoot Contessa* (Joseph L. Mankiewicz) (as Maria Vargas)

1955   *Bhowani Junction* (Cukor) (as Victoria Jones)

1956   *The Little Hut* (Robson) (as Lady Susan Ashlow); *Around the World in Eighty Days* (Anderson) (as spectator)

1957   *The Sun Also Rises* (Henry King) (as Lady Brett Ashley)

1958   *La maja desnuda* (*The Naked Maja*) (Koster, Italian version directed by Mario Russo) (as Duchess of Alba)

1959   *On the Beach* (Kramer) (as Moira Davidson)

1960   *The Angel Wore Red* (*La sposa bella*) (Johnson) (as Soledad)

1962   *55 Days in Peking* (Nicholas Ray) (as Baroness Natalie Ivanoff)

1964   *Seven Days in May* (Frankenheimer) (as Eleanor Holbrook); *The Night of the Iguana* (Huston) (as Maxine Faulk)

1966   *La Bibbia* (*The Bible . . . in the Beginning*; *The Bible*) (Huston) (as Sarah)

1968   *Mayerling* (Terence Young) (as Empress Elizabeth)

1971   *Tam Lin* (*The Devil's Widow*) (McDowall) (as Michaela)

1972   *The Life and Times of Judge Roy Bean* (Huston) (as Lillie Langtry)

1974   *Earthquake* (Robson) (as Remy Graff)

1975   *Permission to Kill* (Frankel) (as Katina Peterson)

1976   *The Bluebird* (Cukor) (as Luxury)

1977   *The Cassandra Crossing* (Cosmatos) (as Nicole); *The Sentinel* (Winner) (as Miss Logan)

1979   *City on Fire* (Rakoff) (as Maggie Garyson)

1980   *The Kidnapping of the President* (Mendeluk) (as Beth Richards)

1981   *Priest of Love* (Miles) (as Mabel Dodge Luhan)

1982   *Regina* (*Roma*) (Prate)

1985   *The Long Hot Summer* (Cooper—for TV) (as Minnie)

1986   *Harem* (Hale—for TV) (as Kadin); *Maggie* (Hussein—for TV)

Publications

By GARDNER: book—

Ava: My Story, New York, 1990.

On GARDNER: books—

Higham, Charles, *Ava: A Life Story*, New York, 1974.
Bernard, Andre, *Ava Gardner*, Paris, 1976.
Romero, J., *Sinatra's Women*, New York, 1976.
Parish, James, with Gregory Mank and Don Stanke, *The Hollywood Beauties*, New York, 1978.
Kass, Judith M., *Ava Gardner*, New York, 1979.
Rampling, Matthew, *Ava Gardner*, Paris, 1981.
Daniell, John, *Ava Gardner*, New York, 1982.
Flamini, Roland, *Ava: A Biography*, New York, 1983.
Dagneau, Gilles, *Ava Gardner*, Paris, 1984.
Fowler, Karin J., *Ava Gardner, A Bio-Bibliography*, New York, 1990.
Wayne, Jane Ellen, *Ava's Men: The Private Life of Ava Gardner*, New York, 1990.

On GARDNER: articles—

Current Biography 1965, New York, 1965.
Vincent, Mal, "Ava Gardner," in *Films in Review* (New York), June/July 1965.
Domarchi, J., "Pour Ava, beau monstre touché par la grâce," in *Cinéma aujourd'hui* (Paris), May/June 1976.
Hauptfuhrer, Fred, "Ava Gardner Is Back and Beautiful at 59—But All She Wants Is Peace and Quiet," in *People Weekly* (New York), 11 January 1982.
Shipman, David, in *Radio Times*, 27 March 1982.
Ciné Revue (Paris), 26 August 1982, and 30 August 1984.
Kobal, John, "Heavenly Bodies: Worshipping at the Shrine of Hollywood's Goddesses," in *American Film*, July/August 1986.
Obituary in *New York Times*, 26 January 1990.
McBridge, Joseph, obituary in *Variety* (New York), 31 January 1990.
Thomas, Walter, "Amorous Ava," in *Harper's Bazaar* (New York), February 1990.
Murphy, Kathleen, "Farewell My Lovelies," in *Film Comment* (New York), July/August 1990.

*   *   *

Ava Gardner

Although Ava Gardner appeared in more than 25 films during the 1940s, her screen identity did not really emerge until the 1950s. A product of the studio system, Gardner was put under long-term contract at MGM in the early 1940s. After playing small roles in mostly minor films, she won acclaim in Robert Siodmak's *The Killers*, emerging (along with Burt Lancaster) as a star, and she is a radiant presence in *The Hucksters*, *Singapore*, *Pandora and the Flying Dutchman*, and *Showboat*, among others. To an extent, the studio succeeded in promoting her as a sex goddess because of her extraordinary beauty and sensuality. Gardner, however, never fulfilled the expectation that she would become a sex symbol.

In fact, during the 1950s, Gardner undermined this status, specifically by not exploiting her physicality or attempting to develop identification with a cinematic stereotype that would make her accessible to the male audience. The feminist critic Marjorie Rosen (*Popcorn Venus*) asserts that Gardner embodied the "ideal fantasy creature" in several films, including Joseph L. Mankiewicz's *The Barefoot Contessa*; but, on the contrary, Gardner refutes this concept of objectification in the film. The film's tensions are produced through her sensitive characterization of a woman who insists in having a right to a subjective identity. She plays a similar "rebel" character in George Cukor's *Bhowani Junction*. Cukor, aware that her potential had been undeveloped because she was treated by the studio as a beautiful object to be featured in mediocre films, encouraged Gardner to explore her emotional range through this challenging assignment. Her other outstanding performance is in John Ford's *Mogambo*, which has the feel of a Hawks film in the construction of the central heterosexual relationship and the sense of ease in the narrative's flow. In the film, Gardner, like the Hawksian heroine, displays "masculine" strength without losing her feminine appeal.

Unfortunately, by the end of the decade, Gardner already was appearing in films that required her to be a star presence projecting an image of ravaged beauty. When given a substantial role, however, she could offer a performance to match her character. Such was the case in *The Night of the Iguana*, in which she played a lusty hotel proprietor opposite Richard Burton's defrocked minister. Her last substantial portrayal came in Roddy McDowall's *Tam Lin* (*The Devil's Widow*), an interesting, but unsuccessful, attempt to explore a woman's fear of aging.

As a star of the 1950s, Gardner's screen identity was uncharacteristic of a period that attempted to equate women's sexual desirability with the size of their physical endowments. Still, no more sublimely beautiful woman ever appeared on a movie screen. Like a number of her characters (such as Pandora Reynolds in *Pandora and the Flying Dutchman* and Lady Brett Ashley in *The Sun Also Rises*), Gardner became an American expatriate, living for many years in London. She died there of pneumonia after having completed her autobiography, which was published posthumously.

—Richard Lippe, updated by Rob Edelman

GARFIELD, John

Nationality: American. **Born:** Jacob Julius Garfinkel in New York City, 4 March 1913; used name Jules Garfield for early stage work. **Education:** Attended Angelo Patri's school, New York; Heckscher Foundation dramatic school; Roosevelt High School; also studied at the American Laboratory School under Maria Ouspenskaya. **Family:** Married the actress Roberta Seidman, 1932, son: David Patton, actor under name John Garfield Jr., daughters: the actress Julia Patton Garfield and Katherine. **Career:** 1932—member of Eva Le Gallienne's Civic Repertory Group: Broadway debut in small part in *Lost Boy*; 1933—

film debut in *Footlight Parade*; 1934-37—member of the Group Theater, and acted in *Waiting for Lefty*, 1935, *Awake and Sing*, 1935, and *Golden Boy*, 1937; 1938—first billed film part in *Four Daughters*; contract with Warner Brothers, 1938-46—acted in radio series *Lux Radio Theatre*; entertained troops during World War II; 1946—formed company Enterprise Productions; 1951—unfriendly witness before the House Un-American Committee; 1951—on stage in *King Lear*. **Awards:** D. W. Griffith Award for Acting, for *Four Daughters*, 1938. **Died:** 21 May 1952.

Films as Actor:

1933   *Footlight Parade* (Lloyd Bacon, Keighley, and Berkeley) (bit role)
1938   *Four Daughters* (Curtiz) (as Mickey Borden)
1939   *They Made Me a Criminal* (Berkeley) (as Johnnie); *Blackwell's Island* (McGann) (as Tim Hayden); *Juarez* (Dieterle) (as Porfirio Diaz); *Daughters Courageous* (*Family Reunion*) (Curtiz) (as Gabriel Lopez); *Dust Be My Destiny* (Seiler) (as Joe Bell); *Saturday's Children* (Sherman) (as Rims O'Neill); *Flowing Gold* (Alfred E. Green) (as Johnny Blake); *Four Wives* (Curtiz) (as ghost of Mickey Borden)
1940   *Castle on the Hudson* (*Years without Days*) (Litvak) (as Tommy Gordon); *East of the River* (Alfred E. Green) (as Joe Lorenzo)
1941   *The Sea Wolf* (Curtiz) (as George Leach); *Out of the Fog* (Litvak) (as Harold Goff)
1942   *Dangerously They Live* (Florey) (as Dr. Michael Lewis); *Tortilla Flat* (Fleming) (as Danny)
1943   *Air Force* (Hawks) (as Sgt. Winocke); *The Fallen Sparrow* (Wallace) (as Kit); *Thank Your Lucky Stars* (David Butler) (as himself)
1944   *Destination Tokyo* (Daves) (as Wolf); *Between Two Worlds* (Blatt) (as Tom Prior); *Hollywood Canteen* (Daves) (as himself)
1945   *Pride of the Marines* (*Forever in Love*) (Daves) (as Al Schmid)
1946   *The Postman Always Rings Twice* (Garnett) (as Frank Chambers); *Nobody Lives Forever* (Negulesco) (as Nick Blake); *Humoresque* (Negulesco) (as Paul Boray)
1947   *Body and Soul* (Rossen) (as Charley Davis); *Gentleman's Agreement* (Kazan) (as Dave); *Daisy Kenyon* (Preminger) (as man in Stork Club)
1948   *Force of Evil* (Polonsky) (as Joe Morse)
1949   *Jigsaw* (*Gun Moll*) (Markle) (bit role as street loiterer); *We Were Strangers* (Huston) (as Tony Fenner)
1950   *Under My Skin* (*La Belle de Paris*) (Negulesco) (as Dan Butler); *The Difficult Years* (Zampa—English-language version of *Anni difficile*) (as narrator); *The Breaking Point* (Curtiz) (as Harry Morgan)
1951   *He Ran All the Way* (Berry) (as Nick Robey)

Publications

On GARFIELD: books—

Gelman, Howard, *The Films of John Garfield*, Secaucus, New Jersey, 1975.
Swindell, Larry, *Body and Soul: The Story of John Garfield*, New York, 1975.
Morris, George, *John Garfield*, New York, 1977.
Beaver, James N., *John Garfield: His Life and Films*, South Brunswick, New Jersey, 1978.

John Garfield in *We Were Strangers*

Sklar, Robert, *City Boys: Cagney, Bogart, Garfield*, Princeton, New Jersey, 1992.

McGrath, Patrick J., *John Garfield: The Illustrated Career in Films and on Stage*, Jefferson, North Carolina, 1993.

Crowdus, Gary, editor, *A Political Companion to American Film,* Chicago, Illinois, 1994.

On GARFIELD: articles—

Current Biography 1948, New York, 1948.

Obituary in *New York Times*, 22 May 1952.

Roman, R., "John Garfield," in *Films in Review* (New York), June/July 1960.

*   *   *

Before Marlon Brando, before James Dean, and before Paul Newman, Robert De Niro, and Al Pacino there was John Garfield, an actor of intensity and sensitivity who embodied the rebel/antihero character. In fact, he was the first actor to consistently play such roles on screen, beginning his career over a decade before Brando. For Garfield the rebel/antihero role was more than a method of acting: he was a New York City street kid who keenly understood his characters' motivation. While no profound political thinker, he was a man of deep emotion and intense loyalty, and his progressive/left-wing contacts made him a target of the Hollywood witch-hunts of the McCarthy era. In his films Garfield represented the socially underprivileged, the common man who clashed with the system. He showed ambition and hard work; he was sensual and strong and exhibited a certain vulnerability. He portrayed a good boy who got all the wrong breaks, but whose rebellious spirit enabled him to battle back against the inequities of his society.

The authenticity of Garfield's alleged initial screen appearance, as an extra in the "Shanghai Lil" sequence of the Warner Brothers musical *Footlight Parade*, is debated to this day. More significantly, in the early 1930s, the playwright Clifford Odets recommended him for membership in the newly formed Group Theater, the legendary and influential theater company/collective whose members included Elia Kazan, Lee Strasberg, and Harold Clurman. After losing the lead role in Odets's *Golden Boy*—a part the writer penned with Garfield in mind—to Luther Adler, Garfield left the theater for Hollywood.

He signed a seven-year Warner Brothers contract and his first role, a supporting turn in Michael Curtiz's *Four Daughters*, made him a star. His character, streetwise pianist/composer Mickey Borden, utters such lines as "Talking about my tough luck is the only fun I get" and "I guess when you're used to standing on the outside looking in, you can see things that other people can't." In *Four Daughters*, Garfield offered his definitive portrayal of the sympathetic iconoclast: a role that was to sustain him throughout his career. Another significant aspect of this film was Garfield's unique acting style, with his moody, soulful sexuality standing out among the more conventional actors of the period.

Upon the success of *Four Daughters*, Warner Brothers chose to recast Garfield in inferior films that recycled the Mickey Borden character. And so the actor found himself playing moody poor boys, if not outright criminals, in such generically titled features as *They Made Me a Criminal*, *Dust Be My Destiny*, and *Nobody Lives Forever*. Garfield's most significant films while under contract were *Pride of the Marines*, a fact-based drama in which he played a soldier blinded while fighting at Guadalcanal; *Humoresque*, cast as a poor but determined violinist; and James M. Cain's *The Postman Always Rings Twice* (made on loan to MGM), in the role of a drifter who falls for a married woman and plots to murder her husband.

After choosing not to renew his studio contract, Garfield formed his own production company. His first independent feature arguably is the best of his career: *Body and Soul*, in which he played an up-from-the-slums prizefighter who is misled by his own ego, forgetting his family and friends for material possessions and a fast lifestyle. Between 1947 and 1950 Garfield did some of his finest screen acting in some of his most interesting films. He had a small but significant part in *Gentleman's Agreement*, a film about anti-Semitism. In the highly regarded film noir *Force of Evil*, the lone film directed by Abraham Polonsky prior to being blacklisted, he played a crooked lawyer. In *We Were Strangers*, he was an American fighting on the side of Cuban revolutionaries. In *The Breaking Point*, based on Hemingway's *To Have and Have Not*, he was a troubled, financially strapped fishing boat captain. His final feature is *He Ran All the Way*, in which he played a doomed criminal who takes a working-class family hostage.

In 1951 Garfield was subpoenaed by the U.S. Congressional Committee on Un-American Activities. He answered all questions, describing himself as a Democratic Party member and political liberal. He told the committee, "I have always hated communism. It is a tyranny which threatens our country and the peace of the world. Of course, then I have never been a member of the Communist party, or a sympathizer with any of its doctrines. I will be pleased to cooperate with the committee." But he would not "name any names," as his street boy's sense of honor would not allow him to rat on his friends. The committee was unhappy with his testimony. An FBI investigation of Garfield was ordered, and the actor found himself blacklisted. In early 1952, Garfield appeared on Broadway in a revival of *Golden Boy*. But he was destroyed by his committee ordeal, and subsequent expulsion from Hollywood. He died of a heart attack that spring, having not reached his 40th birthday.

An actor undoubtedly ahead of his time, Garfield not only played antiheroes but thoroughly immersed himself in his characters. If he was a prizefighter, as in *Body and Soul*, he would train in the ring; for *Tortilla Flat*, he learned how to fish; for *Air Force*, he learned how to operate a machine gun; and for *Humoresque*, he learned how to play the violin. While not as famous as the actors who followed him, Garfield was the prototype of the celluloid antihero. One only can imagine the stage and screen roles he might have created had his life not been cut so tragically short.

—Maryann Oshana, updated by Rob Edelman

GARLAND, Judy

Nationality: American. **Born:** Frances Ethel Gumm in Grand Rapids, Minnesota, 10 June 1922. **Education:** Attended elementary school in Los Angeles; Lawler's Professional School, 1929-31; Bancroft Junior High School and University High School, Los Angeles. **Family:** Married 1) the musician David Rose, 1941 (divorced 1942); 2) the director Vincente Minnelli, 1945 (divorced 1952), daughter: the actress Liza Minnelli; 3) the producer Sid Luft, 1952 (divorced 1965), daughter: the singer Lorna Luft; 4) Mark Herron, 1965 (divorced 1969); 5) Mickey Deans. **Career:** 1929—film debut as a child singer, with her sisters, as The Gumm Sisters, in the *Meglin Kiddie Revue*; also toured with the act, later called The Garland Sisters; 1935—contract with MGM; followed by a series of musical films; 1938—roles in the Andy Hardy series and in *The Wizard of Oz* brought her wide popularity; also acted and sang on radio, and made recordings; 1945—straight dramatic role in *The Clock*; 1950—health problems led to MGM not renewing her contract; 1951—great success in cabaret performances at the London Palladium and the Palace Theatre in New York; later film successes in *A Star Is Born*, 1954, and *Judgment at Nuremberg*, 1961; also continued touring in cabaret and recording; 1963-64—star of *The Judy Garland Show* on television. **Awards:** Special Academy Award, "for her outstanding performance as a screen juvenile during the past year," 1939. **Died:** In London, England, 22 June 1969.

Films as Actress:

1929   *The Meglin Kiddie Revue* (one of the Gumm sisters)

1930   *A Holiday in Storyland* (one of the Gumm sisters); *The Wedding of Jack and Jill* (one of the Gumm sisters)

1936   *La fiesta de Santa Barbara* (one of the Gumm sisters); *Pigskin Parade* (*The Harmony Parade*) (David Butler) (as Sairy Dodd); *Every Sunday* (Feist—short)

1937   *Broadway Melody of 1938* (Del Ruth) (as Betty Clayton); *Thoroughbreds Don't Cry* (Alfred E. Green) (as Cricket West)

1938   *Everybody Sing* (Marin) (as Judy Bellaire); *Love Finds Andy Hardy* (Seitz) (as Betsy Booth); *Listen, Darling* (Marin) (as Pinkie Wingate)

1939   ***The Wizard of Oz*** (Fleming) (as Dorothy Gale); *Babes in Arms* (Berkeley) (as Patsy Barton)

1940   *Andy Hardy Meets Debutante* (Seitz) (as Betsy Booth); *Strike Up the Band* (Berkeley) (as Mary Holden); *Little Nellie Kelly* (Taurog) (title role)

1941   *Ziegfeld Girl* (Leonard) (as Susan Gallagher); *Life Begins for Andy Hardy* (Seitz) (as Betsy); *We Must Have Music* (short—unused sequence from Leonard's *Ziegfeld Girl*, part of series *A Romance of Celluloid*); *Babes on Broadway* (Berkeley) (as Penny Morris)

1942   *For Me and My Gal* (Berkeley) (as Jo Hayden)

1943   *Presenting Lily Mars* (Taurog) (title role); *Girl Crazy* (Taurog) (as Ginger Gray); *Thousands Cheer* (Sidney) (as guest)

1944   ***Meet Me in St. Louis*** (Minnelli) (as Esther Smith)

1945   *The Clock* (*Under the Clock*) (Minnelli) (as Alice Mayberry)

1946   *The Harvey Girls* (Sidney) (as Susan Bradley); *Ziegfeld Follies* (Minnelli); *Till the Clouds Roll By* (Whorf; Garland sequences directed by Minnelli) (as Marilyn Miller)

1948   *The Pirate* (Minnelli) (as Manuela); *Easter Parade* (Walters) (as Hannah Brown); *Words and Music* (Taurog) (as guest)

1949   *In the Good Old Summertime* (Leonard) (as Veronica Fisher)

1950   *Summer Stock* (*If You Feel Like Singing*) (Walters) (as Jane Falbury)

1954   ***A Star Is Born*** (Cukor) (as Esther Blodgett/Vicki Lester)

1960   *Pepe* (Sidney) (as voice)

1961　*Judgment at Nuremberg* (Kramer) (as Irene Hoffman)
1962　*Gay Purr-ee* (Levitow—animation) (as voice of Mewsette)
1963　*A Child Is Waiting* (Cassavetes) (as Jean Hansen); *I Could Go on Singing* (Neame) (as Jenny Bowman)

Publications

On GARLAND: books—

Zierold, Norman, *The Child Stars*, New York, 1965.
Morella, Joe, and Edward Epstein, *Judy: The Films and Career of Judy Garland*, New York, 1969.
Steiger, Brad, *Judy Garland*, New York, 1969.
Tormé, Mel, *The Other Side of the Rainbow with Judy Garland on the Dawn Patrol*, New York, 1970.
Deans, Mickey, and Ann Pinchot, *Weep No More My Lady*, New York, 1972.
Melton, David, *Judy: A Remembrance*, Hollywood, 1972.
Di Orio, Al Jr., *Little Girl Lost—The Life and Hard Times of Judy Garland*, New Rochelle, New York, 1973.
Juneau, James, *Judy Garland*, New York, 1974.
Minnelli, Vincente, with Hector Arce, *I Remember It Well*, New York, 1974.
Edwards, Anne, *Judy Garland: A Biography*, New York, 1975.
Finch, Christopher, *Rainbow: The Stormy Life of Judy Garland*, New York, 1975.
Frank, Gerald, *Judy*, New York, 1975.
Smith, Lorna, *Judy, with Love: The Story of Miss Show Business*, London, 1975.
Baxter, Brian, *The Films of Judy Garland*, Farncombe, Surrey, 1977.
Glickmann, Serge, *Judy Garland*, Paris, 1981.
Kepler, M., *Judy Garland*, Paris, 1981.
Spada, James, with Karen Swenson, *Judy and Liza*, London, 1983.
Dyer, Richard, *Heavenly Bodies: Film Stars and Society*, London, 1987.
Csengery, Judit, *Judy es Liza*, Budapest, 1988.
Harmitz, Aljean, *The Making of* The Wizard of Oz, London, 1989.
Haver, Ronald, A Star Is Born: *The Making of the 1954 Movie and Its 1983 Restoration*, London, 1989.
Coleman, Emily R., *The Complete Judy Garland*, New York, 1990.
Fricke, John, *Judy Garland: World's Greatest Entertainer*, New York, 1992.
Shipman, David, *Judy Garland: The Secret Life of an American Legend*, New York, 1993.

On GARLAND: articles—

St. Johns, Adela Rogers, "His Engagement to Judy Garland," in *Photoplay* (New York), April 1945.
"Star Turn: Judy Garland," in *Sight and Sound* (London), June 1951.
Current Biography 1952, New York, 1952.
Rosterman, Robert, "Judy Garland," in *Films in Review* (New York), April 1952.
McVay, Douglas, "Judy Garland," in *Films and Filming* (London), October 1961.
Obituary in *New York Times*, 24 June 1969.
Pérez, M., "Judy Garland," in *Positif* (Paris), November-December 1972.
Jennings, W., "Nova: Garland in *A Star Is Born*," in *Quarterly Review of Film Studies* (Pleasantville, New York), no. 3, 1979.
Crist, Judith, "Judy Garland," in *The Movie Star*, edited by Elisabeth Weis, New York, 1981.
Mordden, Ethan, "I Got a Song," in *New Yorker*, 22 October 1990.

*　*　*

In his book *Heavenly Bodies: Film Stars and Society*, Richard Dyer offers both an insightful discussion of Judy Garland's star image and an in-depth account of why gay men were so strongly attracted to Garland and particularly her post-1950 image. Yet, as Dyer points out, Garland's image and persona are open to other readings since her appeal was not limited to a subculture and Garland had mass appeal that embraced devoted female fans. Since Garland's death, well-researched books such as *Judy Garland: The Secret Life of an American Legend* have come out of the closet about Garland's bisexuality; how much light these revelations shed on her genius is open to question. Certainly, Garland toyed with sexual ambiguity throughout her career—the tramp number from *Easter Parade*, the newsboy number "Lose that Long Face" and boyish run-through of "Somewhere There's a Someone" in *A Star Is Born*, and the tuxedoed finale of *Summer Stock* which was resurrected for her concert appearances. What revisionist critics cannot lose sight of is that whether Garland was trucking down the Yellow Brick Road or looking for the Man that Got Away, her appeal was universal.

In his discussion of Garland's image, Dyer emphasizes the change that occurs in the perception of her image after 1950, the year in which she was fired by MGM and allegedly attempted suicide. If the MGM studio image celebrating her girl-next-doorness contrasts strongly with her post-1950s image as androgynous camp avatar, the one constant in Garland's persona is an overwhelming psychological need for affection that audiences always wanted to fill. *Summer Stock*, *Meet Me in St. Louis*, *The Clock*, and *The Pirate* draw strength from scenes in which vulnerable Judy becomes very emotional, frequently in response to a man's assertion of dominance. In many of her MGM films, Garland is on the brink of womanhood but nevertheless acts in a refreshingly direct and immediate manner; while her outbursts suggest the childlike, it challenges her co-stars to consider a greater equality of the sexes. In a complex manner, Garland plays off aspects of what are deemed feminine characteristics, but contrary to expectations, her transparent honesty does not make her appear helpless nor does it resort to a masculinizing of her image or a denial of heterosexual desire. Perhaps in the heady intensity of the movie musical, Garland did not have to play games. But unlike other American sweethearts such as Durbin, Allyson, and Powell, Garland grew into a heart-on-her-sleeve star with a persona more complex than the peaches-and-cream MGM image could support.

As Dyer says: "Garland works in an emotional register of great intensity which seems to bespeak equally suffering and survival, vulnerability and strength, theatricality and authenticity, passion and irony." Although these components emerge most forcefully in *A Star Is Born*, it is arguably Garland's emotional complexity that always distinguishes her work from that of more conventional musical comedy performers—in a standard backstage musical such as *Summer Stock*, Garland brings a raw dramatic depth to aspects of her characterization which threatens to unbalance the movie and take it in another generic direction, toward melodrama. In the later stages of her career, she blurred the division between personal and professional identity, which led to criticism regarding her willingness to exploit herself and her audience. Yet, Garland's insistence on being intimately emotional in public had a liberating effect on spectators, as occurs at times with melodramas and the experience they offer. Each Garland concert became a soap opera in song.

What else but the burned-out attitudes of the 1990s could explain why this dynamic entertainer has yet to be rediscovered after her death; in a climate where audiences seem determined to feel nothing but superficial sensation, she has not become an icon like the flashier but infinitely less talented Monroe, Dean, or Presley, three Hollywood legends whose victimhoods are both more accessible and less resonant than Garland's. Perhaps this greatest talent of the twentieth century will undergo a slow renaissance in the pop culture even as she remains the poster girl of the gay cognoscenti. Enjoying videos of her televi-

Judy Garland

sion show (which CBS foolishly slotted opposite *Bonanza*), one is struck with the notion of Judy as a variety show subversive, way too supercharged and neurotic for the nation's living rooms unless they contained a therapist's couch. Moviegoers who bristled at Garland's wholesomeness at MGM respond to this latter-day show biz martyr who offers the audience the challenge of measuring up to her own life of pain.

It is that tremulous quality of radiant endurance which informs Garland's last three film appearances. After winning an Oscar nomination as one of the all-star Nazi survivors in *Judgment at Nuremberg*, she gave a full-bodied performance as a fledgling teacher of the mentally retarded in the unfairly ignored *A Child Is Waiting*, which illustrates the delicate balance of internal and external forces in Garland's persona. Laced with telling dialogue she wrote herself, *I Could Go on Singing* is a proper cinematic swansong in that Garland sings, dances, and acts a fan magazine version of her own trouble-plagued, the show-must-go-on-to-pay-the-bills lifestyle. Socking across paeans to survivability, Garland sings her heart out as if tapping into the frustrated longing of every audience member in thrall to her. Fearfully locking herself in her dressing room, she panicked her way out of *Valley of the Dolls* and a monster role unsuited to her trademark sensitivity. Of course, one wishes there had been one more on-screen comeback before the final disintegration of the Garland rainbow. As Garland entered her last phase of entertaining, the personal and the professional were increasingly conflated in the realm of keeping alive the myth of the Little Girl Lost; she pumped up her concert crowds on a high of snappy-pattered Hollywood horror stories and a frozen repertoire of torch songs functioning as mini-biographies. A performance artist before that term was coined, Garland may have sustained her career by taking advantage of her audiences' ongoing desire to fly with her over the rainbow while their own lives seemed mundanely stuck in the mud. No other singer enjoyed this sort of transcendent transference with devotees. Fittingly, she died in the midst of a concert tour—and what other performer can claim to have sung in a voice which millions felt was a dubbed-in expression of their own inner torment.

In recent years, there has been a concentration of critical writing on stars who defiantly challenged gender dictates (Dietrich, Davis, Hepburn, and others), but their accomplishments should not be lionized at the expense of the irreplaceable Garland whose image as star was highly complicated and deserving of recognition as such.

—Richard Lippe, updated by Robert Pardi

GARNER, James

Nationality: American. **Born:** James Scott Baumgarner in Norman, Oklahoma, 7 April 1928. **Education:** Attended the University of Oklahoma; studied acting at the Herbert Berghof Studios, New York. **Military Service:** Served with U.S. Merchant Marines in Korean War; awarded Purple Heart. **Family:** Married Lois Clarke, 1956, two daughters: Kimberly and Greta Scott. **Career:** Early 1950s—acted in *The Caine Mutiny Court Martial*, in U.S. and on tour; 1955—offered contract with Warner Brothers; 1956—film debut in *Toward the Unknown*; 1957-62—title role in TV series *Maverick*; 1963—founder, Cherokee productions; 1971-72—title role in *Nichols*, for NBC TV; 1974-80—as Jim Rockford in *The Rockford Files*, for NBC TV; 1985—in TV mini-series *Space*; 1991—in TV series *Man of the People*; 1995—in TV mini-series *Streets of Laredo*, a sequel to *Lonesome Dove*. **Agent:** Robinson, Lutrell, and Assoc., 141 El Camino Drive, Suite 110, Beverly Hills, CA 90212, U.S.A.

Films as Actor:

1956   *Toward the Unknown* (LeRoy) (as Maj. Joe Craven); *The Girl He Left Behind* (Butler) (as Preston)

1957   *Shoot-Out at Medicine Bend* (Bare) (as Maitland); *Sayonara* (Logan) (as Capt. Mike Bailey)

1958   *Darby's Rangers* (Wellman) (as Maj. William Darby)

1959   *Up Periscope* (Gordon Douglas) (as Ken)

1960   *Cash McCall* (Pevney) (title role)

1961   *The Children's Hour* (Wyler) (as Dr. Joe Cardin)

1962   *Boys' Night Out* (Gordon) (as Fred Williams)

1963   *The Great Escape* (John Sturges) (as "The Scrounger" Hendley); *The Thrill of It All* (Jewison); *The Wheeler Dealers* (Hiller) (as Henry Tyroon); *Move over Darling* (Gordon) (as Nicholas Arden)

1964   *The Americanization of Emily* (Hiller) (as Lt. Comdr. Charles Madison)

1965   *36 Hours* (Seaton) (as Maj. Jefferson Pike); *The Art of Love* (Jewison) (as Casey)

1966   *A Man Could Get Killed* (Neame) (as William Beddoes); *Duel at Diablo* (Nelson) (as Jess Remsberg); *Mister Buddwing* (*Woman without a Face*) (Delbert Mann) (title role); *Grand Prix* (Frankenheimer) (as Pete Aron)

1967   *Hour of the Gun* (John Sturges) (as Wyatt Earp)

1968   *How Sweet It Is* (Paris) (as Grif Henderson); *The Pink Jungle* (Delbert Mann) (as Ben Morris)

1969   *Marlowe* (Bogart) (as Philip Marlowe); *Support Your Local Sheriff* (Kennedy) (as Jason McCullough)

1971   *A Man Called Sledge* (Morrow) (as Luther Sledge); *Support Your Local Gunfighter* (Kennedy) (as Latigo Smith); *Skin Game* (Kennedy) (as Quincy Drew)

1972   *They Only Kill Their Masters* (Goldstone) (as Police Chief Abel Marsh)

1973   *One Little Indian* (Bernard McEveety) (as Clint Keyes)

1974   *The Rockford Files* (Heffron—for TV) (as Jim Rockford); *The Castaway Cowboys* (Vincent McEveety) (as Lincoln Costain)

1978   *The New Maverick* (Averback—for TV) (as Bret Maverick)

1979   *Health* (Altman) (as Harry Wolff)

1981   *The Fan* (Bianchi) (as Jake Berman)

1982   *Victor/Victoria* (Edwards) (as King); *The Long Summer of George Adams* (Stuart Margolin—for TV)

1984   *Tank* (Chomsky) (as Zack); *Heartsounds* (Glenn Jordan—for TV) (as Harold Lear)

1985   *Murphy's Romance* (Ritt) (as Murphy Jones); *The Glitter Dome* (Stuart Margolin—for TV) (as Al Mackey)

1986   *The Promise* (Glenn Jordan—for TV) (+ co-pr)

1988   *Sunset* (Edwards) (as Wyatt Earp)

1989   *My Name Is Bill W.* (Petrie—for TV) (as Dr. Robert Smith)

1990   *Decoration Day* (Markowitz—for TV) (as Judge Albert Sidney Finch)

1992   *The Distinguished Gentleman* (Lynn) (as Jeff Johnson)

1993   *Fire in the Sky* (Lieberman) (as Lt. Frank Watters); *Barbarians at the Gate* (Glenn Jordan—for TV) (as F. Ross Johnson)

1994   *The Rockford Files: I Still Love L.A.* (James Whitmore Jr.—for TV) (as Jim Rockford, + exec pr); *Maverick* (Donner) (as Zane Cooper); *Breathing Lessons* (Erman—for TV) (as Ira Moran)

1995   *The Rockford Files: A Blessing in Disguise* (Szwarc—for TV) (as Jim Rockford, + exec pr)

1996   *The Rockford Files: If the Frame Fits . . .* (Szwarc—for TV) (as Jim Rockford); *The Rockford Files: Godfather Knows Best* (Wharmby—for TV) (as Jim Rockford); *The Rockford Files: Friends and Foul Play* (Margolin—for TV) (as Jim Rockford, + co-exec pr)

Publications

By GARNER: articles—

Interview in *Photoplay* (London), December 1979.
Interview in *Hollywood Reporter*, 27 December 1985.
Interview with Michele Willens, in *TV Guide*, 20 March 1993.

On GARNER: book—

Strait, Raymond, *James Garner*, New York, 1985.

On GARNER: articles—

Current Biography 1966, New York, 1966.
Shipman, David, "James Garner," in *The Great Movie Stars: The International Years*, London, 1972.
Films in Review (New York), January 1976.
Film Dope (London), September 1979.
Wicking, Chris, in *Time Out* (London), 7 December 1979.
Ciné Revue (Paris), 27 May 1982.
Pond, S., "So You Think It's Easy Being James Garner?," in *New York Times*, 14 March 1993.
Pond, Steve, "The Garner Files," *TV Guide*, 26 November 1994.

* * *

James Garner's strongest work has been done in television, where, with considerable personal behind-the-scenes input, he has been able to use his charming, exasperated con-man persona effectively to reshape, extend, subvert, and epitomize the apparently rigid forms of the Western and private eye series. Whereas the traditional television series hero—cowboy Clint Walker in *Cheyenne*, PI Mike Connors in *Mannix*—is two-fisted and righteous, unconcerned with financial reward, bulling ahead and interfering whenever wrongs need righting and people need help, the Garner character would do anything for an easy life, is stuck with the need to make a living somehow, and has to be prodded out of his slothfulness to turn his slightly shady talents to a good cause.

Signed on as a contract player with Warner Brothers in 1956, Garner entered series television the following year as the star of the studio's tongue-in-cheek Western *Maverick*. As the title character, a duded-up gambler named Bret Maverick, he roamed the Old West trying to stay as far away as possible from guns and horses and as near as possible to cards and money. When production fell drastically behind schedule, actor Jack Kelly was brought in to co-star in alternate episodes as Garner's equally cardsharp brother, Bart. Later Roger Moore and Robert Colbert joined the cast as additional members of the growing Maverick clan. Garner used his clout as the series's most popular brother to begin winning substantial film roles, notably in *Sayonara*, where he played Marlon Brando's buddy. He had his first starring role in Wellman's war film *Darby's Rangers*. Several more starring parts followed and he left the series in 1963 to appear among the large international cast of John Sturges's epic World War II POW film, *The Great Escape*, playing a gun-shy, fast-talking, and devious "scrounger" not dissimilar from his *Maverick* persona.

He would continue to play variations on this persona in *The Americanization of Emily*, as the Bilko-style fixer whom Julie Andrews and the army want to be the first hero to die on the beaches at D-Day; *A Man Could Get Killed*, as an innocent mixed up in a dangerous but unbelievable spy plot; and lazily likable Westerns such as *Support Your Local Sheriff*, *Skin Game*, and *Support Your Local Gunfighter*, in which he is the only man West of the Pecos with the brains not to want to get killed. Meanwhile, he was also bringing his charm, exasperation, and gift for well-heeled comedy to such glossy confections

as *The Thrill of It All*, *The Wheeler Dealers*, *Move Over, Darling*, and *How Sweet It Is*, playing Cary Grant to Doris Day, Lee Remick and Debbie Reynolds with slightly more confidence than Rock Hudson, or even the 1960s Cary Grant, could manage. All of these films find him being driven to the end of his rope by the Barbie-doll heroine, but finally exploding into comic wrath (asked in a bar about his CND amulet in *How Sweet It Is*, he snaps "it's a universal symbol of peace and understanding, want to make anything of it?").

Meanwhile he had taken the role of a suntanned 1960s Philip Marlowe in *Marlowe*, from *The Little Sister*, which was less an adaptation of Raymond Chandler's novel than an unofficial pilot for *The Rockford Files*, and had been lost amid the cars and effects of *Grand Prix*. His best "serious" work came in the late 1960s in a trio of interesting, cynical, revisionist Westerns which found the American genre reaching away from Mann and Boetticher towards Leone and Peckinpah—as an Indian scout in Ralph Nelson's unstressed, cleverly complex *Duel at Diablo*; as an unbending Wyatt Earp gradually becoming a vengeful psychotic in John Sturges's rewrite of his *Gunfight at the OK Corral*, *Hour of the Gun*; and, best of all, as the leader of an efficient but troubled group of outlaws in Vic Morrow's still unjustly unknown *A Man Called Sledge*.

Returning to the small screen, Garner starred in the short-lived *Nichols* and *Bret Maverick* series, the latter a failed attempt at reprising his old hit show in color for a new generation, then the hit *The Rockford Files*, which absorbed most of his energies in the 1970s. In an attempt to reestablish himself as a movie star after *Rockford* went off the air, he appeared in several dead-loss disasters—including Robert Altman's *Health* and Blake Edwards's *Sunset* (in which he reprised Wyatt Earp)—plus the cross-dressing comedy *Victor/Victoria*, the dotty *Murphy's Romance* for which he received an Oscar nomination, and the quirkily unsuccessful *Tank*.

Garner has kept his model good looks as he has aged, even becoming more craggily interesting. Of late, television again has provided him with meatier sustenance than films: in the biting satire of 1980s greed, *Barbarians at the Gate*, where he gave a deftly comic performance as the overreaching buyout king, F. Ross Johnson; *The Promise*, which he co-produced as well as starred in, as a middle-aged man who assumes the responsibility of caring for his mentally ill brother (James Woods) after their mother dies; and the elegiac road movie *Breathing Lessons*, based on Anne Tyler's Pulitzer Prize-winning novel.

Garner has not ignored the big screen, though, and is still much in demand. The Eddie Murphy comedy of Washingtonian con games, *The Distinguished Gentleman*, marked his return after a four-year absence. He has since had roles as a skeptical lawman in the alien abduction thriller *Fire in the Sky*, based on the Travis Walton case, and in *Maverick*, an overblown update of his classic television series in which Garner revealed himself at the top of his game as the father of the character he originated, played by an annoyingly mugging Mel Gibson.

—Kim Newman, updated by John McCarty

GARSON, Greer

Nationality: American. **Born:** County Down, Northern Ireland, 29 September 1903; became U.S. citizen. **Education:** Attended University of London, B.A. with Honors; graduate study at University of Grenoble, France. **Family:** Married 1) Edward Snelson, 1933 (separated 1933, divorced 1941); 2) the actor Richard Ney, 1943 (divorced 1947); 3) Elijah E. "Buddy" Fogelson, 1949 (died 1987). **Career:** Worked in London advertising firm; 1932-34—with Birmingham company for two seasons: debut in *Street Scene*; 1934—London stage

Greer Garson

debut in *The Tempest*; 1938—seen by Louis B. Meyer in *Old Music*, signed for MGM; 1939—film debut in *Goodbye, Mr. Chips*; appeared in very early BBC television production of Shaw's *How He Lied to Her Husband*; 1940s—numerous radio performances; 1954—*Her Twelve Men* last film for MGM; 1955—began appearing in TV dramas, in *Reunion in Vienna* on *Producers' Showcase*; 1958—replaced Rosalind Russell in *Auntie Mame* on Broadway; 1990—completion of Greer Garson Communications Center and Studio, College of Santa Fe, New Mexico, part of her charitable legacy. **Awards:** Best Actress Academy Award for *Mrs. Miniver*, 1942; Commander of the Order of the British Empire, 1993; honorary doctorate of arts, Southern Methodist University. **Died:** Of congestive heart failure, in Dallas, 6 April 1996.

Films as Actress:

1939   *Goodbye, Mr. Chips* (Wood) (as Katherine Ellis); *Remember?* (McLeod) (as Linda Bronson)

1940   *Pride and Prejudice* (Leonard) (as Elizabeth Bennet)

1941   *Blossoms in the Dust* (LeRoy) (as Mrs. Edna Gladney); *When Ladies Meet* (Leonard) (as Claire Woodruff)

1942   ***Mrs. Miniver*** (Wyler) (title role); *Random Harvest* (LeRoy) (as Paula)

1943   *Madame Curie* (LeRoy) (title role); *The Youngest Profession* (Buzzell) (as guest); *A Report from Miss Greer Garson* (Whitebeck—short for March of Dimes)

1944   *Mrs. Parkinton* (Garnett) (title role); *The Miracle of Hickory* (short for March of Dimes)

1945   *The Valley of Decision* (Garnett) (as Mary Rafferty); *Adventure* (Fleming) (as Emily Sears)

1947   *Desire Me* (Cukor and others, all uncredited) (as Marise Aubert)

1948   *Julia Misbehaves* (Conway) (as Julia Packett)

1949   *That Forsyte Woman* (*The Forsyte Saga*) (Bennett) (as Irene Forsyte)

1950   *The Miniver Story* (Potter) (as Mrs. Miniver)

1951   *The Law and the Lady* (Knopf) (as Jane Hoskins)

1953   *Scandal at Scourie* (Negulesco) (as Mrs. Patrick McChesney); *Julius Caesar* (Joseph L. Mankiewicz) (as Calpurnia)

1954   *Her Twelve Men* (Leonard) (as Jan Stewart)

1955   *Strange Lady in Town* (LeRoy) (as Dr. Julia Winslow Garth)

1960   *Pepe* (Sidney) (as guest); *Sunrise at Campobello* (Donehue) (as Eleanor Roosevelt)

1963   *The Invincible Mr. Disraeli* (Schaefer—for TV)

1966   *The Singing Nun* (Koster) (as Mother Prioress)

1967   *The Happiest Millionaire* (Tokar) (as Mrs. Cordelia Biddle)

1968   *The Little Drummer Boy* (Nakamura—animation for TV) (as voice)

1968   *The Little Drummer Boy Book II* (Bass and Rankin Jr.—animation for TV) (as voice of Our Story Teller)

1978   *Little Women* (Rich—for TV) (as Kathryn March)

1986   *Directed by William Wyler* (Slesin—doc) (as herself)

Publications

On GARSON: articles—

Current Biography 1942, New York, 1942.

Luft, H. G., "Greer Garson," in *Films in Review* (New York), March 1961.

Wald, Malvin, "Greer Garson: Blue-Ribbon Winner," in *Close-Ups: The Movie Star Book*, edited by Danny Peary, New York, 1978.

Obituary in *New York Times*, 7 April 1996.

*   *   *

The personification of Louis B. Mayer's ideal of British refinement and beauty, Greer Garson was the queen of MGM during the World War II years. She inherited the mantles of Garbo and Norma Shearer and therefore starred in the most prestigious films produced by the most prestigious studio in Hollywood.

Having had mild success in the English theater, Garson was spotted by Mayer and given an impressive cameo debut in MGM's very popular *Goodbye, Mr. Chips*, produced in England. This role established her screen personality of warmth, good sense, and good humor. If these qualities were appropriate to the heroine of *Pride and Prejudice*, they emerged with particular impact to define Garson's ultimate persona, at just the right moment, in the film that brought her the ultimate honor of Hollywood, the Oscar. *Mrs. Miniver* seemed to sum up the bourgeois nobility of the English in the face of the war and the blitz, and that sum was reflected in the unflappable spirit (and luminous complexion) of Garson, a woman able to cope with a Nazi flier in her kitchen, the fears of her children in a bomb shelter, and the death of her daughter-in-law during a raid. Her next great success, *Random Harvest*, made a bit of fun of Garson's dignity by having her perform a music hall number, but for the body of the film, she reverts to her pristine, classy identity.

The importance of Garson at MGM can be seen in the memorable slogan publicizing Clark Gable's first postwar film, *Adventure*—"Gable's Back and Garson's Got Him." A disappointment to everyone, this marks the beginning of the decline of Garson's popularity, which seemed to fade as quickly as it materialized. The title of *Julia Misbehaves* shows the effort to alter her image. In one of her last films, *Sunrise at Campobello*, she portrays Eleanor Roosevelt, and there, her beautiful face deformed by buck teeth, her mellifluous voice distorted into a semblance of Mrs. Roosevelt's speech impediment, Garson sheds her persona with a virtuosity not always apparent during her years of stardom.

—Charles Affron, updated by Kelly Otter

GASSMAN, Vittorio

Nationality: Italian. **Born:** Genoa, 1 September 1922. **Education:** Attended law school; then studied acting under Silvio D'Amico at the National Academy of Dramatic Art, Rome. **Family:** Second marriage to the actress Shelley Winters, 1952 (divorced 1954), one daughter. **Career:** 1943—joined the Elsa Mellini Company and made stage debut; 1946—film debut in *Preludio d'amore*; 1952—contract with MGM: made several films in Hollywood; 1956—directed the film *Kean*; 1958-59—in TV series *Il mattatore* (and wrote some episodes); 1960—founded his own theater company Teatro Popolare Italiano; has also acted in his own one-man show; 1982—acted in his own Italian version of *Othello*. **Awards:** Best Actor, Cannes Festival, for *Profumo di donna* , 1974; Nastro d'argento Award for Best Actor, for *Lo zio indegno*, 1989. **Address:** Via Flaminia 497, 00191 Rome, Italy.

Films as Actor:

1946   *Preludio d'amore* (Paolucci) (as Davide); *Daniele Cortis* (Soldati) (title role)

1947   *La figlia del capitano* (Camerini) (as Svabrin); *Le avventure di Pinocchio* (Guardone); *L'Ebreo errante* (*The Wandering Jew*) (Alessandrini) (as Mathieu Blumenthal)

1948   *Il cavaliere misterioso* (Freda) (as Casanova); *Riso amaro* (*Bitter Rice*) (De Santis) (as Walter)

1949   *Il lupo della Sila* (Coletti) (as Pietro); *Una voce nel tuo cuore*
         (A Voice in Your Heart) (d'Aversa) (as Paolo Baldini); *I*
         fuorilegge (Vergano) (as Turi); *Ho sognato il paradiso*
         (Pastina) (as Giorgio); *Lo sparviero del Nilo* (Gentilomo)
         (as Yusef)

1950   *Il leone di Amalfi* (Francisci) (as Mauro)

1951   *Il tradimento* (Freda) (as Renato Salvi); *Anna* (Lattuada) (as
         Vittorio); *Il sogno di Zorro* (Soldati) (as Don Antonio)

1952   *La corona negra (La caronna nera)* (Saslavsky) (as Mauricio);
         La tratta delle bianche (Comencini) (as Michele)

1953   *Sombrero* (Norman Foster) (as Alejandro Castillo); *Cry of the*
         Hunted (Joseph H. Lewis) (as Jory); *The Glass Wall* (Shane)
         (as Peter)

1954   *Rhapsody* (Charles Vidor) (as Paul Bronte); *Mambo* (Rossen)
         (as Mario Rossi)

1955   *La donna più bella del mondo (Beautiful but Dangerous)*
         (Leonard) (as Prince Sergio)

1956   *Difendo il mio amore (Defend My Love; I'll Defend You My*
         Love) (Sherman, Italian version directed by Guilio Macchi)
         (as Giovanni); *Giovanni delle Bande Nere* (Grieco) (as
         Giovanni d'Medici); *War and Peace (Guerra e pace)* (King
         Vidor) (as Anatole Kuragin)

1957   *La ragazza del palio (The Love Specialist)* (Zampa) (as Prince
         Piero)

1958   *I soliti ignoti (Big Deal on Madonna Street; Persons Un-*
         known) (Monicelli) (as Peppe); *La tempesta (The Tempest)*
         (Lattuada) (as Pubblico Accusatore)

1959   *La grande guerra (The Great War)* (Monicelli) (as Giovanni
         Busacca); *La cambiale* (Mastrocinque) (as Michele); *Audace*
         colpo dei soliti ignoti (Fiasco in Milan; Hold-up à la
         Milanaise) (Loy) (as Peppe); *Le sorprese dell'amore*
         (Comencini) (as guest); *The Miracle* (Rapper) (as Guido)

1960   *Il mattatore (Love and Larceny)* (Risi) (as Gerardo); *Fantasmi*
         a Roma (Pietrangeli) (as Caparra); *Crimen (. . . And Sud-*
         denly It's Murder; Killing in Monte Carlo) (Camerini) (as
         Remo)

1961   *I briganti italiani* (Camerini) (as O'Caporale); *Barabba*
         (Barabbas) (Fleischer) (as Sahak); *Il giudizio universale* (de
         Sica) (as Cimino); *Una vita difficile* (Risi) (as guest)

1962   *Anima Nera* (Rossellini) (as Adriano); *La marcia su Roma*
         (Risi) (as Domenico Rocchetti); "L'avaro" ep. of *L'amore*
         difficile (Lucignani) (as L'Avvocato); *Il sorpasso (The Easy*
         Life) (Risi) (as Bruno Cortona)

1963   *Lo smania addosso (Eye of the Needle)* (Andrei) (as Mazzano);
         Il successo (Morassi) (as Giulio Ceriani); *I mostri (Opiate*
         '67; 15 from Rome) (Risi); *Frenesia dell'estate* (Zampa) (as
         Capt. Nardoni)

1964   *Se permettete parliamo di donne (Let's Talk about Women)*
         (Scola) (as Proteiforme Adamo); *Il gaucho* (Risi) (as Mario
         Ravicchio); *La congiuntura (One Million Dollars)* (Scola)
         (as Don Giuliano)

1965   *Slalom* (Salce) (as Luci Ridolfi); *Una vergine per il principe*
         (A Maiden for the Prince; A Maiden for a Prince) (Festa
         Campanile) (as Prince don Vincenzo Gonzaga)

1966   One ep. of *La Guerre secrète (La guerra segreta; Spione unter*
         sich; The Dirty Game; The Dirty Agents) (Lizzani) (as
         Perego); *L'armata Brancaleone* (Monicelli) (as Brancaleone
         da Norcia); *Il diavolo innamorato (The Devil in Love;*
         L'arcidiavolo) (Scola) (as Belfager Arcidiavolo); *Le piacevoli*
         notti (Crispini and Lucignani) (as Bastiano da Sangallo)

1967   *Il tigre (The Tiger and the Pussycat)* (Risi) (as Francesco
         Vincenzini); *Lo scatenato (Catch as Catch Can)* (Indovina)
         (as Bob Chiaramonte); *Questi fantasmi (Ghosts, Italian Style;*
         Three Ghosts) (Castellani) (as Pasquale Lojacono); "Linda"
         and "Two against One" eps. in *Woman Times Seven (Sette*

volta donna; Sept fois femme) (de Sica) (as Cenci); *Il profeta*
         (Risi) (as Pietro Breccia)

1969   *Dove vai tutta nuda?* (Festa Campanile) (as Rafus); *L'arcagelo*
         (Capitani) (as Fulvio Bertuccia); *Una su tredici (Twelve Plus*
         One) (Gessner) (as Mario "Mike" Beretti); *La pecora nera*
         (Salce) (as Filippo/Giulio)

1970   "La bomba alla televisione" ep. in *Contestazione generale*
         (Zampa) (as Riccardo); *Il divorzio* (Guerrieri) (as Leonardo);
         Brancaleone alle Crociate (Monicelli) (title role); *Scipione*
         detto anche l'Africano (Magni) (title role)

1971   *Il nome delle popolo italiano* (Risi) (as Lorenzo Santenocito);
         L'udienza (Ferreri) (as Prince Donati)

1972   *Che c'entriamo noi con la rivoluzione?* (Corbucci) (as Guido
         Guidi)

1973   *La Tosca* (Magni) (as Scarpia)

1974   *C'eravamo tanto amati* (Scola) (as Gianni); *Profumo di donna*
         (Scent of a Woman) (Risi) (as Capt. Fausto Censolo)

1975   *A mezzanotte va la ronda del piacere (The Immortal Bach-*
         elor; Midnight Pleasures; Qui comincia l'avventura)
         (Fondato) (as Andrea Sansani)

1976   *Telefoni bianchi* (Risi) (as Franco Denza); *Come una rosa al*
         naso (Pure as a Rose) (Risi) (as Antonie Mancuso); "La
         bomba" ep. of *Signore e signori, buonanotte* (Monicelli) (as
         Tuttunpezzo); *Le désert des Tartares (Il deserto dei Tartari;*
         The Desert of the Tartars) (Zurlini) (as Filimore); *Anima*
         persa (Risi) (as Fabio Stolz)

1977   "Tantum Ergo," "Like a Queen," and "The Inn" eps. of *I*
         nuovi mostri (Viva Italia!; The New Monsters) (Monicelli,
         Risi, and Scola) (several roles)

1978   *A Wedding* (Altman) (as Luigi Corelli)

1979   *Quintet* (Altman) (as San Cristoforo); *Due pezzi di pane* (Citti)
         (as Pippo Mifa); *Caro papà* (Risi) (as Albino Millozza); *La*
         terrazza (Scola) (as Mario)

1980   *Camera d'albergo* (Monicelli) (as Achille Mengaroni); *The*
         Nude Bomb (Clive Donner) (as Nino Salvatore Sebastiani);
         Sono fotogenico (Risi)

1981   *Il turno* (Ceroi) (as Ciro Coppa); *Sharkey's Machine* (Burt
         Reynolds) (as Victor)

1982   *Tempest* (Mazursky) (as Alonzo)

1983   *Benvenuta* (Delvaux) (as Livio Carpi)

1984   *La Vie est un roman (Life Is a Bed of Roses)* (Resnais) (as Walter)

1985   *Le Pouvoir du mal (The Power of Evil; Paradigma)* (Zanussi)
         (as Gotfried); *I soliti ignoti vent'anni dopo (Big Deal on*
         Madonna Street—Update) (Todini) (as Peppe the Panther)

1987   *La famiglia (The Family)* (Scola) (as Carlo/Carlo's Grandfa-
         ther); *I picari (The Picaros)* (Monicelli) (as Baron)

1989   *Lo zio indegno (The Sleazy Uncle)* (Brusati) (as Uncle Lucca)

1990   *Mille et une nuits (Sheherazade)* (de Broca) (as Sinbad); *Tolgo*
         il disturbo (Risi); *Come un bambino* (Risi)

1991   *Dimenticare Palermo (The Palermo Connection)* (Rosi) (as
         Prince)

1992   *Quando eravmo repressi (When We Were Repressed)* (Quartullo)
         (as the sexologist); *El Largo Invierno (The Long Winter)*
         (Camino) (as Claudio)

1994   *Tutti Gli anni una volta l'anno (Once a Year, Every Year)*
         (Lazotti) (as Giuseppe); *Abraham* (Sargent—for TV)

Films as Actor and Director:

1956   *Kean* (title role, + co-sc)

1969   *L'alibi* (co-d, role as Vittorio, + co-sc)

1972   *Senzo famiglia, nullatenenti, cercano affetto . . .* (as Armando,
         + co-sc)

1982   *Di padre in figlio*

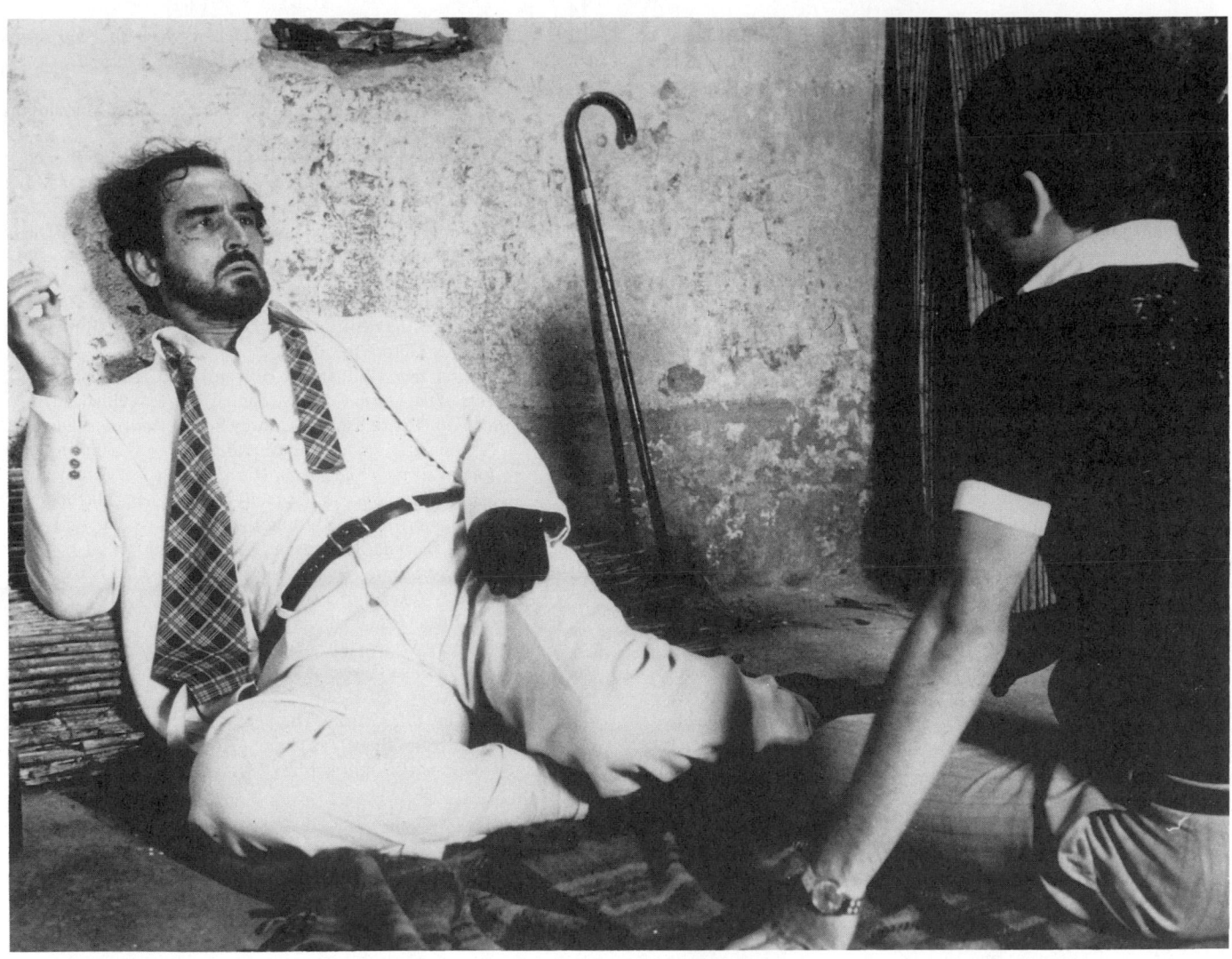

Vittorio Gassman in *Profumo di donna*

Publications

By GASSMAN: books—

Un grande avvenire dietro le spalle, Milan, 1981.
Vocalizzi (poems), Milan, 1988.
Memorie del sottoscala, 1990.
Mal di parola, Milan, 1992.
Camper: farsa edipica in 2 tempi e 10 rounds, Milan 1994.

By GASSMAN: articles—

"Vittorio Gassman, l'homme aux cent visages," interview and article
    by J. A. Gili, in *Ecran* (Paris), October 1975.
Interview with P.-A. Boutang, in *Cinématographe* (Paris), April 1982.
Interview with Dan Yakir, in *Film Comment* (New York), March/April
    1983.

On GASSMAN: books—

Degioanni, Bernard, *Vittorio Gassman*, Paris, 1980.
Cappelletti, Dante, *Vittorio Gassman: solitudine di un mattatore*, Rome
    1988.

Ciro, Rita, *Il mestiere di attore: la pratica artistica e i luoghi di
    formazione: a colloquio con Vittorio Gassman e Bernard Dort*, Citta
    di Castello, Italy, 1992.
Gambetti, Giacomo, *Un attore e la societai Vittorio Gassman*, Urbino,
    Italy, 1994.

On GASSMAN: articles—

Lane, J. F., "Italy's Man of a Thousand Faces," in *Films and Filming*
    (London), April 1959.
Current Biography 1964, New York, 1964.
CinemAction (Conde-sur-Noireau, France), March 1987.
Kudriavtsev, S., "Dos'e 'IK,'" in *Iskusstvo Kino* (Moscow), no. 4, 1991.
Rocco, N., "La 'cattiveria' di Dino Risi," in *Quaderni di Cinema* (Flo-
    rence), April/June 1993.

*   *   *

Of Austrian and Italian parentage, Vittorio Gassman appeared in
dozens of stage plays before making his movie debut in *Preludio
d'amore*. Another of his early films, Giuseppe De Santis's *Riso amaro*,
with Gassman opposite Silvana Mangano in what was considered a
shockingly erotic work, was a box-office success, focusing on Gassman's

considerable international attention. After playing the role of Casanova in *Il cavaliere misterioso*—and while doing intermittent stage roles, many of them classical—he was again teamed with Mangano in Alberto Lattuada's *Anna*, another commercial success.

His handsome looks and casually arrogant manner suggested him as a leading man, and he did eventually become a matinee idol in Italy. After marrying the American actress Shelley Winters, he signed a contract with MGM and made four U.S. films, all at least respectable, though none really caught on. So Gassman returned to Italy, starring in Robert Rossen's *Mambo*, Robert Z. Leonard's *La donna più bella del mondo*, and as Anatole in King Vidor's *War and Peace*.

After acting in and co-directing (with Francesco Rosi) *Kean*, a film about the great English actor, and appearing in Lattuada's *Tempest*, Gassman starred in Mario Monicelli's entertaining caper satire, *I soliti ignoti*, playing a slaphappy ex-boxer and incompetent crook. From that point on, he specialized in comedy, garnering better reviews as a comedian than in roles as a dramatic leading man, for which he had been criticized frequently for overacting.

His favorite director has been Dino Risi, and he has worked in 15 of his films. Other directors he has publicly acknowledged his indebtedness to are Mario Monicelli, who helped Gassman change the direction of his career from strained dramatic lead to deft comedian by offering him his first comic role in *I soliti ignoti* ; and Ettore Scola, who cast him in each of the first four feature films he directed. Gassman also acted in two late-1970s films by American director Robert Altman, *A Wedding* and *Quintet*.

Perhaps his most triumphant performance was in Dino Risi's comedy-drama, *Profumo di donna*, which earned Gassman the Best Actor Award at the 1975 Cannes Film Festival for his performance as a blind rogue forced to rely on his other senses. A comeback of sorts for Gassman—critically, that is, for his career had never floundered commercially—*Profumo di donna* was yet another demonstration that Gassman's forte remains comedy, which brings out his joie de vivre and light touch, and short-circuits his occasional tendency to overact.

—Bill Wine

GAYNOR, Janet

Nationality: American. **Born:** Laura Gainor in Philadelphia, Pennsylvania, 6 October 1906. **Education:** Attended public schools in Chicago and elsewhere; San Francisco Polytechnical High School, graduated 1923. **Family:** Married 1) the film producer Lydell Peck, 1929 (divorced 1933); 2) the costume designer Gilbert Adrian, 1939 (died 1959), son: Robin; 3) the producer Paul Gregory, 1964. **Career:** 1924—began acting as extra at Hal Roach Studio; then female leads in Peewee Holmes and Ben Corbin Westerns at Universal; 1926—contract with Fox; 1927—first film with Charles Farrell, *Seventh Heaven* (last film together in 1934); 1928—contract with Fox; 1939—retired following second marriage; 1951—with Charles Farrell, repeated role in *Seventh Heaven* on Lux Radio Theatre; 1950s—occasional TV appearances; 1959—stage debut in *The Midnight Sun*, Boston and Philadelphia. **Awards:** Best Actress Academy Award, for *Seventh Heaven*, *Street Angel*, and *Sunrise*, 1927/28. **Died:** In Palm Springs, California, 14 September 1984.

Films as Actress:

1926   *The Johnstown Flood* (*The Flood*) (Cummings); *The Shamrock Handicap* (Ford); *The Midnight Kiss* (Cummings); *The Blue Eagle* (Ford); *The Return of Peter Grimm* (Schertzinger)

1927   *Seventh Heaven* (Borzage) (as Diane); **Sunrise** (*Sunrise—A Song of Two Humans*) (Murnau) (as the Wife); *Two Girls Wanted* (Alfred E. Green)

1928   *Street Angel* (Borzage) (as Angela); *Four Devils* (Murnau) (as Marion); *Fox Talent Movietone* (short)

1929   *Christina* (William K. Howard) (title role); *Lucky Star* (Borzage) (as Mary Tucker); *Sunny Side Up* (David Butler) (as Molly Carr)

1930   *Happy Days* (Stoloff) (as guest); *High Society Blues* (David Butler) (as Eleanor Divine); *The Man Who Came Back* (Walsh) (as Angie)

1931   *Daddy Long Legs* (Santell) (as Judy Abbott); *Merely Mary Ann* (Henry King) (title role); *Delicious* (David Butler) (as Heather Gordon)

1932   *The First Year* (William K. Howard) (as Grace Livingston); *Tess of the Storm Country* (Santell) (as Tess Howland)

1933   *State Fair* (Henry King) (as Margy Frake); *Adorable* (Dieterle) (as the Girl); *Paddy, the Next Best Thing* (Lachman) (title role); *La ciudad de carton* (*Cardboard City*) (King)

1934   *Carolina* (*The House of Connelly*) (Henry King) (as Joanna); *Change of Heart* (Blystone) (as Catherine Furness); *Servants' Entrance* (Lloyd) (as Hedda Nilsson)

1935   *One More Spring* (Henry King) (as Elizabeth Cheney); *The Farmer Takes a Wife* (Fleming) (as Molly Larkins)

1936   *Small Town Girl* (Wellman) (as Kay Brannan); *Ladies in Love* (Edward W. Griffith) (as Martha Kerenye)

1937   *A Star Is Born* (Wellman) (as Esther Victoria Blodgett/Vicki Lester)

1938   *Three Loves Has Nancy* (Thorpe) (as Nancy Briggs); *The Young in Heart* (Wallace) (as George-Ann Carleton)

1957   *Bernardine* (Levin) (as Mrs. Wilson)

Publications

By GAYNOR: article—

"My Life—So Far—Told to Dorothy Spensley," in *Photoplay* (New York), December-January 1928-29.

On GAYNOR: book—

Billips, Connie J., *Janet Gaynor: A Bio-Bibliography*, New York, 1992.

On GAYNOR: articles—

Parsons, Harriet, "Janet Goes to War," in *Photoplay* (New York), August 1930.

Albert, Katherine, "Janet Is Back on the Job," in *Photoplay* (New York), November 1930.

Burke, Randolph Carroll, "The Gentle Art of Janet Gaynor," in *Pictures and Picturegoer*, 8 August 1931.

D'Arne, Wilson, "Janet Gaynor's Life Story," in *Pictures and Picturegoer*, 6-20 April 1935.

Bailey, Kent, "A Star Is Born Again," in *Photoplay* (New York), July 1937.

Carr, Chauncey L., "Janet Gaynor," in *Films in Review* (New York), October 1959.

Roud, R., "People We Like: Janet Gaynor," in *Film Comment* (New York), January/February 1974.

Obituary in *Variety* (New York), 19 September 1984.

Nangle, J., obituary in *Films in Review* (New York), November 1984.

*   *   *

Janet Gaynor with Charles Farrell in *Seventh Heaven*

In *Movies in the Age of Innocence*, Edward Wagenknecht writes, "It would be hard to say whether Janet Gaynor is better remembered for her silent or her sound films, but her spirit was that of the silent years, and nobody could possibly have ended them more pleasantly." Gaynor did star for slightly longer in talkies than she did in silent features, but her characterizations were quite definitely formed during the earlier period; she was sweet and sentimental as only a silent ingenue could be, and was a perfect type for Depression-era audiences. She embodied cuteness, but it was never cloying or offensive. Perhaps appropriately, her last screen appearance (after many years of retirement) was in *Bernardine*, which starred the 1950s idea of cuteness in the form of Pat Boone.

Gaynor's persona suggested the child-woman image which Mary Pickford had created, and, indeed, Janet Gaynor remade two of Pickford's silent features as talkies: *Daddy Long Legs* and *Tess of the Storm Country*. Yet Gaynor's characters were a little more sophisticated than Pickford's, a little more worldly-wise. As the director Victor Schertzinger once commented, "She has the maturity of the ages, and yet is singularly youthful."

Under Murnau's direction in *Sunrise*, Gaynor is subdued, very much the German Hausfrau, with a blond wig complementing the harsh makeup she wears. This is perhaps the most untypical Gaynor performance in that Murnau gives the majority of the emotional scenes to her leading man, George O'Brien. The same is not true of Gaynor's films for Frank Borzage, *Seventh Heaven* and *Street Angel*, in which the actress is given free rein for her emotional outbursts.

In *Seventh Heaven* she reaches the height of happiness in the symbolic wedding sequence with Charles Farrell, and the peak of angry emotion as she takes a whip to Gladys Brockwell, running her out of the home she and Farrell have created for themselves. Both *Seventh Heaven* and *Street Angel* illustrate the range of Gaynor's acting ability; in both she grows from a weak, frightened, disillusioned girl into a woman who knows love and experiences an inner strength.

Another key Gaynor-Farrell teaming came in the touching and at times profound part-talkie melodrama, *Lucky Star*, which was rediscovered and theatrically rereleased in the early 1990s. She plays a poor drudge who loves Farrell, who has been paralyzed from the waist down during the war. Gaynor brings to the role a freshness, a hopeful quality in the face of adversity.

Gaynor's first all-talkie, *Sunny Side Up*, is delightful for its songs—"If I Had a Talking Picture of You," "I'm a Dreamer," and the title number—but it is also embarrassing because of the babylike voices emanating from its stars, Gaynor and Farrell. That they were featured together in seven more films is extraordinary, but that Gaynor and Farrell managed to remain so overpoweringly popular is even more remarkable. In fact, Janet Gaynor settled into a comfortable niche as a talkie star. Who else, for example, could have played Will Rogers's daughter in *State Fair*? The actress's last great screen role was as Esther Blodgett in the first version of *A Star Is Born*, and it is curious that she should portray an actress reaching the pinnacle of her fame just as her own career was reaching its end.

—Anthony Slide, updated by Audrey E. Kupferberg

GÉLIN, Daniel

Nationality: French. **Born:** Daniel Yves Gélin in Angers, France, 19 May 1921. **Education:** Attended schools in St. Malo; studied acting with René Simon, and at the Paris Conservatory under Denis d'Ines and Louis Jouvet. **Family:** Married 1) the actress Danièle Delorme, 1945 (divorced 1954), son: the actor-director Xavier Gélin, daughter: the actress Maria Schneider; 2) Sylvie Hirsch, 1954 (divorced), three children; 3) Lydie Zaks, 1973, one daughter. **Career:** 1939—extra in film *Les Surprises de la radio*; 1941—stage debut in *On prend les mêmes*; 1950—important role in *La Ronde*; published first book of verse, *Fatras*; 1952—directed the film *Les Dents longues*; also acted in the TV series *Les Saintes chéries*; directed the play by Sartre, *Les Mains sales*; 1960—in the Théâtre National Populaire production of *Eric XIV*. **Address:** 92 Boulevard Murat, 75016 Paris, France.

Films as Actor:

1939   *Les Surprises de la radio* (Paul) (as extra)
1940   *Miquette et sa mère* (*Miquette*) (Boyer) (as extra); *Soyez les bienvenus* (de Baroncelli) (bit role)
1941   *Premier rendez-vous* (*Her First Affair*) (Decoin); *L'assassin habite... au 21* (Clouzot) (as extra); *Les Cadets de l'océan* (Dréville)
1943   *Les Petites du Quai aux Fleurs* (Marc Allégret)
1944   *L'Enquête sur le 58* (Tedesco—short)
1945   *La Tentation de Barbizon* (Stelli); *Un Ami viendra ce soir* (*A Friend Will Come Tonight*) (Bernard) (as Pierre Ribault)
1946   *La Nuit de Sybille* (Paulin); *Martin Roumagnac* (*The Room Upstairs*) (Lacombe) (as the Lover); *La Femme en rouge* (Cuny)
1947   *Miroir* (Lamy); *Le Mannequin assassiné* (de Hérain)
1948   *Le Paradis des pilotes perdus* (Lampin); *Rendez-vous de Juillet* (Jacques Becker)
1950   ***La Ronde*** (*Circle of Love*) (Max Ophüls) (as Alfred, the young man); *Dieu a besoin des hommes* (*God Needs Men*) (Delannoy); *Chicago-Digest* (*Du sang dans la sciure*) (Paviot—short)
1951   *Edouard et Caroline* (*Edward and Caroline*) (Jacques Becker) (as Edouard Mortier); *Les Mains sales* (*Dirty Hands*) (Rivers) (as Hugo Barine); *Une Histoire d'amour* (Lefranc); "Le Modèle" ("The Model") ep. of *Le Plaisir* (*House of Pleasure*) (Max Ophüls) (as Jean)
1952   *Adorables créatures* (*Adorable Creatures*) (Christian-Jaque) (as André); *Torticola contre Frankensberg* (Paviot—short); *La Minute de vérité* (*The Moment of Truth*) (Delannoy); *Echos de plateau* (Knapp and Berière—short); *La Maison du silence* (*La voce del silenzio*) (Pabst); *Saint-Tropez, devoir de vacances* (Paviot—short)
1953   *Rue de l'Estrapade* (Jacques Becker); *La Neige était sale* (*The Snow Was Black*) (Saslavsky); *L'Esclave* (Ciampi); *Si Versailles m'était conté* (*Affairs in Versailles*; *Royal Affairs in Versailles*) (Guitry) (as Jean Collinet); *Sang et lumières*

(*Love in a Hot Climate*; *Beauty and the Bullfighter*) (Rouquier); *L'Affaire Maurizius* (Duvivier); *Opinione pubblica* (Corgnati)
1954   *Napoléon* (Guitry) (as Bonaparte); *L'allegro squadrone* (Moffa); *La romana* (*Woman of Rome*) (Zampa) (as Mino)
1955   *Les Amants du Tage* (*Lovers' Net*; *Port of Shame*; *Lovers of Lisbon*) (Verneuil) (as Pierre Roubier); *Paris canaille* (*Paris coquin*; *Maid in Paris*) (Gaspard-Huit)
1956   *The Man Who Knew Too Much* (Hitchcock) (as Louis Bernard); *Je reviendrai à Kandara* (Vicas); *En effeuillant la marguerite* (*Mam'selle Striptease*; *Please, Mr. Balzac*; *While Plucking the Daisy*) (Marc Allégret); *Bonsoir Paris, bonjour l'amour* (Baum); *Morte en fraude* (Camus)
1957   *Retour de manivelle* (*There's Always a Price Tag*) (de la Patellière); *Charmants garçons* (Decoin); *Trois jours à vivre* (Grangier); *La Fille de Hambourg* (*Port of Desire*; *The Girl from Hamburg*) (Yves Allégret); *Suivez-moi, jeune homme* (Lefranc); *Ce corps tant désiré* (Saslavsky); *Faisons le point sur les Spoutniks* (Klushantsev—French-language version of Russian film *Doroga k zvezdam*) (as narrator)
1959   *Cartagine in fiamme* (*Carthage in Flames*) (Gallone) (as Phegot); *Julie la Rousse* (*Julie the Redhead*) (Boissol) (as Edouard Lavigne/Jean Lavigne); *Les trois etc... du colonel* (*Le tre eccetera del colonnello*) (Boissol); *Le Testament d'Orphée* (*The Testament of Orpheus*) (Cocteau) (as the intern)
1960   *Austerlitz* (*The Battle of Austerlitz*) (Gance); *La Poie pour l'ombre* (Astruc); *Reveille-toi, chérie* (Magnier)
1961   *La Morte-saison des amours* (*The Season for Love*) (Kast) (as Jacques Saint-Ford); *Les Petits Matins* (Audry)
1962   *Règlements de comptes* (Chevalier); *Vacances portugaises* (Kast); *The Longest Day* (Annakin, Marton, Wicki, and Oswald)
1963   *Tre piger i Paris* (*Trois filles à Paris*) (Axel); *La Bonne Soupe* (*Careless Love*; *The Good Soup*) (Robert Thomas) (as Raymond); *Bolivar 63-29* (d'Artec)
1964   *El niño y el muro* (Rodríguez)
1965   *Zwei Girls vom roten Stern* (Drechsel); *Die Zeugin aus der Hölle* (*Witness Out of Hell*; *Gorge Trave*; *Bitter Grass*) (Mitrovic) (as Petrovid); *Compartiment tueurs* (*The Sleeping Car Murder*) (Costa-Gavras); *Les sultans* (Delannoy)
1966   *Paris brûle-t-il?* (*Is Paris Burning?*) (Clément) (as Yves Bayet); *A belles dents* (Gaspard-Huit); *La Ligne de démarcation* (Chabrol); *Soleil noir* (*Black Sun*) (de la Patellière) (as Guy Rodier); *Eaux vives, eaux mortes* (Renateau—short) (as narrator); *Avec Claude Monet* (Delouche—short) (as narrator)
1967   *Bruegel* (Haesaerts) (as narrator)
1968   *Le Mois le plus beau* (Blanc); *La Trêve* (Guillemot); *La Nature retrouvée* (Renateau—short) (as narrator)
1969   *Slogan* (Grimblat) (as Father); *Hallucinations sadiques* (Korman); *Détruite, dit-elle* (*Destroy, She Said*) (Duras) (as Bernard Alione); *La Servante* (Bertrand); *Israel aujourd'hui* (de la Patellière—short) (as narrator)
1970   *Christa* (*Swedish Fly Girls*) (O'Connell)
1971   ***Le Souffle au coeur*** (*Murmur of the Heart*) (Malle) (as Father)
1972   *Far from Dallas* (Toledano) (as Jean)
1973   *La polizia è al servizio del cittadino* (Guerrieri); *La Gueule de l'emploi* (Rouland)
1974   *Un Linceul n'a pas de poches* (*No Pockets in a Shroud*) (Mocky); *Dialogue d'exilés* (*Dialogo de exilados*) (Ruiz)
1975   *Trop c'est trop* (Kaminka)
1976   *Qu'il est joli garçon, l'assassin de papa* (Caputo)
1977   *Nous irons tous au paradis* (*We Will All Go to Heaven*) (Robert)
1978   *L'Honorable Société* (Weinberger); *Guy de Maupassant* (Drach)

Daniel Gélin in *La voce del silenzio*

1981   *La Nuit de Varennes* (*That Night in Varennes*; *The New World*)
        (Scola) (as De Wendel)
1984   *Delitto* (Nocita)
1985   *Les Enfants* (*The Children*) (Duras) (as father); *Olga e i suoi
        figli* (Nocita)
1986   *Killing Cars* (Michael Verhoeven) (as Kellermann)
1987   *L'Itinéraire d'un enfant gâté* (*Itinerary of a Spoiled Child*)
        (Lelouch) (as Pierre Duvivier); *Via Montenapoleone*
        (Vanzina)
1988   *Dandin* (Planchon) (as M. de Sotenville); *La Vie est un long
        fleuve tranquille* (*Life Is a Long Quiet River*) (Chatiliez) (as
        Dr. Louis Mavial)
1990   *Mister Frost* (Setbon) (as Simon Scolari); *Toutes les femmes se
        ressemblent* (Franc); *Type bien* (Benegui); *Mauvaise Fille*
        (as Fernand)
1991   *Le Candidat*; *Les Secrets professionnels du Docteur Apfelgluck*
        (Capone and others) (as Roland); *Crimes et Jardin* (as
        Lucien); *Un Type Bien* (as Dr. Avril); *Iran: Days of Crisis* (*L'
        Amerique en otage*) (Connor—for TV) (as Shah)
1992   *Coup de jeune* (Xavier Gélin) (as Gaudeamous at 70)
1993   *De force avec d'autres* (*Forced to Be with Others*) (Reggiani);
        La Cité de la peur: une comédie familiale (*Fear City: A
        Family Style Comedy*) (Berberian) (as projectionist); *Les
        Marmottes* (*The Groundhogs*) (Chouraqui) (as Leo); *Roullez
        jeunesse* (Fansten) (as Jean Moulinier)

1994   *Des Feux mal éteints* (*Poorly Extinguished Fires*) (Moati);
        3000 Scenarios contre un virus (*3,000 Scenarios to Com-
        bat a Virus*) (Achache and others); *Pushing the Limits*
        (Donard) (as himself); *Warrior Spirits* (Manzor) (as John
        Ball)
1995   *Une fille galante* (Trintignant)
1996   *Les Bidochoun* (Korber); *Fantôme avec chauffeur* (Oury)

Film as Actor and Director:

1952   *Les Dents longues* (not released in U.S.)

Publications

By GÉLIN: books—

Fatras (verse), Paris, 1950.
Dérives (verse), Paris, 1965.
Poèmes à dire (verse), Paris, 1970.
Deux ou trois vies qui sont les miennes (autobiography), Paris, 1977.
L'orage enseveli, Paris, 1980.
Mon jardin et moi, Paris, 1985.
Cent poètes côté jardin (poetry anthology), n.p., 1990.

By GÉLIN: articles—

Interview with C. Hubert, in *Cinéma* (Paris), 24 February 1988.
"Die Technik dient dem Schauspieler, nicht umgekehrt!," interview with
  G. Midding, in *Filmbulletin* (Winterthur, Switzerland), vol. 33, no.
  3, 1991.

On GÉLIN: book—

Dudognon, Georges, *Comme on s'aimait a Saint-Germain-des-Pres*,
  Paris, 1993.

On GÉLIN: article—

Barbry, F.-R., "Daniel Gélin enfin!," in *Cinéma* (Paris), 9 March 1988.

* * *

Daniel Gélin has specialized in portraying the sensitive and intelligent man who possesses the ability to analyze his own emotions. His dark-haired, modest good looks and sophisticated bearing are reminders of Jean Gabin, who was Gélin's idol. Gélin has acted in films for some of the greatest directors, including Max Ophüls, Sacha Guitry, Julien Duvivier, Abel Gance, and Alfred Hitchcock, but on the whole his films were not the greatest efforts of these formidable practitioners of the cinema.

During the 1940s he had small roles in a number of films including *Martin Roumagnac* directed by Georges Lacombe and starring Gabin. In that film Gélin played the young lover of femme fatale Marlene Dietrich who, after Gabin kills her for being faithless, kills Gabin.

Gélin's best film and best performance was in Ophüls's *La Ronde*, the film in which he achieved stardom. It was his articulate portrayal of Alfred, the young man who attempts to make love to Danielle Darrieux but instead conjures up Stendahl's *De l'amour*, that set the scene for the remainder of his career. In this delightfully ironic merry-go-round about the vicissitudes of love set in Imperial Vienna at the turn of the century, Ophüls was in peak form and Gélin's telling performance later influenced many of France's New Wave directors.

His boyish good looks and sophistication had made him one of France's popular screen actors, and during the 1950s he was quoted as saying he regretted always being cast as a tortured soul and explained that he would prefer to do comedy.

He directed one film, *Les Dents longues*, which starred a young Brigitte Bardot but which was never shown in the United States. He had a few comic turns as an unknown pianist in Jacques Becker's *Edouard et Caroline*, and was outstanding as the war veteran whose wife remarries when she believes him to be dead in Pabst's *La voce del silenzio*.

L'Affaire Maurizius was not up to Julien Duvivier's usual standards and Luigi Zampa's *La romana*, despite being based on Alberto Moravia's novel and providing Gélin with a good role as a neurotic revolutionary, suffered from the limitations of Gina Lollobrigida in the leading role.

Gélin was acceptable as Bonaparte in Sacha Guitry's popular spectacle, *Napoléon*, but much better was his portrayal of Louis Bernard in Alfred Hitchcock's *The Man Who Knew Too Much*. Gélin was perfectly cast as the agent of France's Deuxième Bureau who, after learning there is to be a political assassination in London, is stabbed to death following an exciting chase scene through the bazaar in Marrakesh.

Gélin was properly suave in Marc Allégret's *En effeuillant la marguerite* starring Brigitte Bardot and had small guest shots in Jean Cocteau's *Le Testament d'Orphée*, Abel Gance's *Austerlitz*, and Rene Clement's *Is Paris Burning?* Gélin's "tortured soul" is somewhat anachronistic in today's cinema, but he has remained a familiar face in European films such as *La Nuit de Varennes* directed by Ettore Scola. More recently, he was able to indulge his taste for comedy in a brilliant portrayal of an obstetrician whose life disintegrates at the hands of his revengeful nurse/mistress in 1988's *La Vie est un long fleuve tranquille*, which marked the debut of Etienne Chatiliez in a delightfully satiric look at the differences between the bourgeoisie and the working class.

—Ronald Bowers, updated by David E. Salamie

GERE, Richard

Nationality: American. **Born:** Philadelphia, Pennsylvania, 31 August 1949. **Education:** Attended the University of Massachusetts, Amherst, two years. **Family:** Married the model Cindy Crawford, 1991 (divorced). **Career:** Summer season at Provincetown Playhouse, Massachusetts, at age 19; acted with the Seattle Repertory Theatre, one season; musician and composer; actor in New York: in plays off and on Broadway; in Young Vic production of *The Taming of the Shrew*, London; 1975—film debut in *Report to the Commissioner*; 1980s—involved with environmental groups. **Address:** 26 East 10th Street, Penthouse, New York, NY 10003, U.S.A. **Agent:** Andrea Jaffe Inc., 9229 Sunset Boulevard, Suite 414, Los Angeles, CA 90069, U.S.A.

Films as Actor:

1975   *Report to the Commissioner (Operation Undercover)* (Katselas) (as Billy); *Strike Force* (Shear—for TV)
1976   *Baby Blue Marine* (Hancock) (as marine raider)
1977   *Looking for Mr. Goodbar* (Richard Brooks) (as Tony Lopanto)
1978   ***Days of Heaven*** (Malick) (as Bill); *Bloodbrothers* (Mulligan) (as Thomas Stony DeCoco)
1979   *Yanks* (Schlesinger) (as Matt)
1980   *American Gigolo* (Schrader) (as Julian Kaye)
1981   *Reporters* (Depardon)
1982   *An Officer and a Gentleman* (Hackford) (as Zack Mayo)
1983   *Breathless* (McBride) (as Jesse Lujack); *Beyond the Limit* (Mackenzie) (as Dr. Eduardo Plarr)
1984   *The Cotton Club* (Francis Ford Coppola) (as Dixie Dwyer); *The Honorary Consul* (Mackenzie)
1985   *King David* (Beresford) (title role)
1986   *Power* (Lumet) (as Pete St. John); *No Mercy* (Pearce) (as Eddie Jillette)
1988   *Miles from Home (Farm of the Year)* (Sinese) (as Frank Roberts Jr.)
1990   *Internal Affairs* (Figgis) (as Dennis Peck); *Pretty Woman* (Garry Marshall) (as Edward Lewis)
1991   *Rhapsody in August* (Kurosawa) (as Clark)
1992   *Final Analysis* (Joanou) (as Isaac Barr, + co-exec pr)
1993   *Sommersby* (Amiel) (as Jack, + co-exec pr); *Mr. Jones* (Figgis) (title role, + co-exec pr); *And the Band Played On* (Spottiswoode—for TV) (as choreographer)
1994   *Intersection* (Rydell) (as Vincent Eastman); *Unzipped* (as himself)
1995   *First Knight* (Zucker) (as Lancelot)
1996   *Primal Fear* (Hoblit) (as Martin Vail)

Publications

By GERE: articles—

Interview with B. Riley, in *Film Comment* (New York), March-April 1980.
Interview with Jonathan Cott, in *Rolling Stone* (New York), 25 April 1985.

Richard Gere in *American Gigolo*

"Richard Gere: Derrière le miroir," interview with H. Merrick, in *Revue du Cinéma*, June 1990.

"Top Gere," interview with Leslie Bennetts, in *Vanity Fair* (New York), January 1994.

On GERE: book—

Davis, Judith, *Richard Gere: An Unauthorized Biography*, New York, 1983.

On GERE: articles—

Alpert, H., "The Rise of Richard Gere," in *American Film* (Washington, D.C.), October 1979.
Current Biography 1980, New York, 1980.
"In Camera: Richard Gere," in *Films and Filming* (London), March 1980.
Harvey, S., "Star Quality, Star Power," in *Film Comment* (New York), March-April 1980.
Hibbin, S., "Richard Gere," in *Films and Filming* (London), February 1984.
Elia, M., "Gere," in *Séquences* (Montreal), May 1993.

* * *

Whether raising consciousness about his Buddhist religion or treating an Academy Awards telecast as a political platform for his views, sincere Richard Gere is an adventurous soul open to a wide range of experiences. That is why it is so surprising that many of his screen performances suffer from a certain opaqueness, as if his emotions were something he chose to selectively instill in his work; such rationing does not culminate in memorable screen acting but apparently his followers felt capable of melting the beautiful control freak's reserve. Only since the liberating role of an utter rotter in *Internal Affairs* has Gere begun to flower as film actor rather than superstar.

From the outset, despite his Method Acting fireworks in *Looking for Mr. Goodbar* (where he is clearly outclassed histrionically by the less showy Tom Berenger), Gere became a star because of animal magnetism. Yet, judging from the evidence of his unconventional projects, Gere was never interested in pretty-boy immortality. Whether sublimating his love for Brooke Adams in order to secure a fortune in *Days of Heaven* or abnegating his family's traditions in *Bloodbrothers*, Gere registers as a passionate driving force in offbeat projects, but the audience is never sure exactly what he is driving at. After the dizzying career momentum of *An Officer and a Gentleman* and *American Gigolo*, the rebel continued to thumb his nose at what was expected of him. In *Officer*, he rises above the horrendously dated man's-man stereotypes and beyond Debra Winger's stridency. Having demonstrated the old-fashioned charisma this military soap hungered for, he then replaced John Travolta in the glistening tribute to eighties narcissism, *American Gigolo*, a preposterously arty film in which Gere's sangfroid complemented the movie's sleek superficial surfaces. He seemed to have found a specialty: arctic-blooded social misfits thawed out by man-hungry dames.

Having lulled his fan club into a false sense of security, however, the matinee idol risked his mainstream status by daring to appear ridiculous in a biblical epic, *King David* (just as he had earlier defied conventional wisdom by starring as a gay concentration camp victim in Broadway's *Bent*). Trashed by critics for his next few outings, Gere seemed to sleepwalk through such movies as *The Cotton Club*; in a way he was David Duchovny before there was a David Duchovny, but the Gere deep-freeze started turning people off. After a flawed but wrenchingly well-acted power-to-the people tract called *Miles from Home*, Gere found his footing again as a crooked boy in blue. Matured somewhat by a pepper-gray hair color in *Internal Affairs*, Gere revealed an icy core of self-interest that not only fit the bastard he was playing but also made the actor more seductive than ever.

After penetrating the shell of law-and-order infected by sociopathy, Gere was easy on the eyes in the blockbuster, *Pretty Woman*—ceding the film to the overrated Julia Roberts in a fluffy but retrogressive glamorization of streetwalkers. Risking his neck once again to reactivate the stalled HBO property *And the Band Played On*, Gere was willing to lend his box-office clout to a gentle Kurosawa drama, *Rhapsody in August*. An actor with a conscience, Gere is still a force to be reckoned with as a leading man. He shines with undiminished star-power in both the faux-Hitchcock, *Final Analysis*, and the glossy male

weepie, *Intersection*, a remake of a French film that lost something in translation. Sadly, while these vehicles benefit from his dashing movie star flair, the clumsy *First Knight* returns him to square one with his ludicrous Yankee in King Arthur's Court. As England's Lancelot, he is so contemporary that you expect him to sing a rap ode to Guenevere and then kickbox those responsible for destroying Camelot in a misfired film that has no comprehension of the expansiveness and myth-making of a true epic. Sometimes, Gere's time-travel can be rewarding, however. In a role that takes full advantage of his nineties pliability, a less uptight Gere dazzles in the Civil War revamp of *The Return of Martin Guerre* as a rootless opportunist willing to sacrifice his life to give a false identity credibility. In *Sommersby*, Gere demonstrates the assurance of a star with staying power, breathtakingly breaking down Jodie Foster's resistance in this folktale about regeneration of the soul. Drawn to roles of heroic stature, Gere seems less stingy with his feelings. It is the Richard Gere of *Sommersby*, the romantic truth-seeker, the quixotic lover, that one hopes to see again on-screen.

—Robert Pardi

GIANNINI, Giancarlo

Nationality: Italian. **Born:** Spezia, 1 August 1942. **Education:** Degree in electronics engineering; attended Rome Academy of Drama, diploma 1963. **Family:** Married; sons: Lorenzo and Adriano. **Career:** 1961—stage debut as Puck in *A Midsummer Night's Dream*; 1965—film debut in *Fango sulla metropoli*; 1966—first acted in play by Lina Wertmüller, *Two Plus Two No Longer Make Four* (directed by Franco Zeffirelli), later acted in series of films directed by her; partner in Wertmüller's production company, Liberty Films; 1986—in TV mini-series *Sins*; has also done extensive dubbing of lead roles in American films for the Italian market. **Awards:** Best Actor, Cannes Festival, for *Love and Anarchy*, 1973. **Office:** Julien and Associates, 1501 Broadway, Suite 2600, New York, NY 10036, U.S.A. **Address:** c/o Squillante, Via Della Guiliana, 101, Rome, Italy.

Films as Actor:

1965 *Fango sulla metropoli* (Wilson)
1966 *Rita la zanzara* (*Rita the Mosquito*) (Wertmüller)
1967 *Libido* (Gastaldi); *Non stuzzicate la zanzara* (*Don't Tease the Mosquito*) (Wertmüller); *Stasera mi butto* (Fizzarotti); *Arabella* (Bolognini) (as Saverio)
1968 *Stasera mi butto i due bagnani* (Fizzarotti); *Fräulein Doktor* (*Gospodjica doktor—Spijunka bez imena*) (Lattuada) (as Lt. Hans Ruppert); *Lo sbarco di Anzio* (*Anzio*; *The Battle for Anzio*) (Dmytryk) (as Cellini)
1969 *Le sorelle* (Malenotti); *The Secret of Santa Vittoria* (Kramer) (as Fabio); *Una macchia rosa* (Muzii)
1970 *Dramma della gelosia—Tutti i particolari in cronaca* (*The Pizza Triangle*; *A Drama of Jealousy*; *The Motive Was Jealousy*) (Scola) (as Nello)
1971 *Una prostituta al servizio del pubblico e in regol con le leggi dello stato* (Zingarelli); *Mio Padre Monsignore* (Racioppi); *La tarantol dal ventre nero* (*The Black Belly of the Tarantula*) (Cavara) (as Inspector Tellini); *Mazzabubu . . . quante come stanno quaggiu?* (Laurenti); *Un aller simple* (Giovanni); *Ettore lo fusto* (Castellari)
1972 *Mimi metallurgico ferito nell'onore* (*The Seduction of Mimi*; *Mimi the Metalworker*) (Wertmüller) (as Carmelo "Mimi" Mardocheco); *La prima notte di quiete* (Zurlini) (as Marcello)

1973   *Film d'amore e d'anarchia* (*Love and Anarchy*) (Wertmüller)
        (as Tunin); *Sono stato io* (Lattuada); *Paolo il caldo* (*The
        Sensuous Sicilian*; *The Sensual Man*) (Vicario); *Sesso matto*
        (*How Funny Can Sex Be?*) (Risi)
1974   *Il bestione* (Corbucci); *Fatti di gente per bene* (*La Grande
        Bourgeoise*; *The Murri Affair*; *Drama of the Rich*)
        (Bolognini) (as Tullio Murri); *Travolti da un insolito destino
        nell'azzurro mare d'agosto* (*Swept Away . . . by an Unusual
        Destiny in the Blue Sea of August*; *Swept Away . . .*)
        (Wertmüller) (as Gennarino)
1975   *Pasqualino Settebelleze* (*Seven Beauties*; *Pasqualino: Seven
        Beauties*) (Wertmüller) (as Pasqualino Frafuso, + pr); *A
        mezzanotte va la ronda del piacere* (*The Immortal Bach-
        elor*; *Midnight Pleasures*; *Qui comincia l'avventura*)
        (Fondato) (as Gino Benacio)
1976   *L'innocente* (*The Innocent*) (Visconti) (as Tullio Hermil)
1977   *The End of the World in Our Usual Bed in a Night Full of Rain*
        (*A Night Full of Rain*) (Wertmüller) (as Paolo); *In una notte
        piena di Pioggia* (Wertmüller)
1978   *Indian Summer* (Zurlini) (as narcotics dealer); *Fatto di sangue
        fra due uomini per causa di una vedova* (*Blood Feud*; *Re-
        venge*) (Wertmüller) (as Nick)
1979   *Viaggio con Anita* (*Travels with Anita*; *Lovers and Liars*)
        (Monicelli) (as Guido)
1981   *Lili Marleen* (Fassbinder) (as Robert Mendelsson)
1982   *Bello mia belleza mia* (*My Handsome My Beautiful*) (Corbucci)
1983   *Italia vive* (Turolla)
1984   *American Dreamer* (Rosenthal) (as Victor Marchand); *Blow-
        ing Hot and Cold* (Trenchard-Smith); *Mi manda piccone*
        (*Where's Picone?*) (Loy) (as Salvatore)
1985   *Fever Pitch* (Richard Brooks) (as Charley)
1986   *Saving Grace* (Robert M. Young) (as Abalardi)
1987   *I picari* (Monicelli) (as Guzman)
1988   *Snack Bar Budapest* (Brass)
1989   "Life without Zoe" ep. of *New York Stories* (Francis Ford
        Coppola) (as Claudio); *Ore* (Magni); *Brown Bread Sand-
        wiches* (Liconti) (as Alberto); *Lo zio indegno* (*The Sleazy
        Uncle*) (Brusati) (as Riccardo)
1990   *Tempo di Uccidere* (*Time to Kill*; *The Short Cut*) (Montaldo)
        (as Major); *Il Male oscuro* (*The Obscure Illness*) (Monicelli);
        Blood Red (Masterson) (as Sebastian Collogero); *Scambio*
        (Comencini—for TV); *Il Sole anche di notte* (*Night Sun*)
        (Paolo Tavani and Vittorio Tavani) (as voice of Sergio
        Giuramondo); *Prima di Natale* (*Age of Discretion*; *Before
        Xmas*; *Nel giardino delle rose*; *In the Rose Garden*) (Luciano
        Martino)
1992   *Once upon a Crime* (Levy) (as Inspector Bonnard)
1994   *Jacob* (Peter Hall—for TV) (as Laban); *Come due Coccodrilli*
        (*Like Two Crocodiles*) (Campiotti) (as Father)
1995   *A Walk in the Clouds* (Arau) (as Alberto Aragon); *Celluloid*
        (Lizzani)
1996   *New York Crossing* (Laurenti Mainardi) (as Enzo)

Film as Actor and Director:

1986   *Ternosecco* (*Nino terno-secco*) (+ co-sc)

Publications

By GIANNINI: articles—

"Lina Wertmüller," interview with D. Ratazzi, in *Interview* (New York),
    March 1975.

"Pipistrello della notte," interview with G. Merenda, in *Segnocinema*
    (Vincenza, Italy), March 1990.

On GIANNINI: articles—

Ecran (Paris), July 1978.
Current Biography 1979, New York, 1979.
Reed, Rex, "Giancarlo Giannini," in *The Movie Star*, edited by Elisabeth
    Weis, New York, 1981.

*   *   *

A naturally gifted comic actor, with a slight frame and soulful green
eyes, Giancarlo Giannini has established himself as one of the international cinema's most accomplished seriocomic performers, largely by
way of his extended and fruitful collaboration with the writer-director
Lina Wertmüller. His appearance in a Wertmüller play, *Two Plus Two
No Longer Make Four*, began his association with the director, who
would cast him as the protagonist in virtually all of her successful
films.

Although he also acted in a series of farces not released outside
Italy, and in successful projects for other directors—notably Mauro
Bolognini's *La Grande Bourgeoise*, Mario Monicelli's *Travels with
Anita*, and Luchino Visconti's *The Innocent*—Giannini's reputation
was established through the string of tragicomic Wertmüller films in
which he starred in the 1970s. Typically, Wertmüller cast Giannini as
a Chaplinesque hero flailing against a system that befuddles and mis-
treats him. She photographed his mercurially expressive face lovingly, with a preponderance of scrutinizing close-ups that a less responsive actor would have had difficulty sustaining.

The third Wertmüller film in which Giannini appeared, *The Seduction of Mimi*, established the Wertmüller-Giannini team internationally. In the film, a political sex farce, Giannini plays the title character, a stubborn and none-too-bright metallurgist—opposite Mariangela
Melato as his mistress—who finds himself buffeted about by a
sociopolitical system he does not really understand.

The team's next offering, *Love and Anarchy*, gained for Giannini
the Best Actor Award at the Cannes Film Festival for his dramatic
performance—again opposite Mariangela Melato—as a peasant anarchist who comes to Rome to assassinate Mussolini. By now, the
Wertmüller-Giannini projects were eagerly anticipated and automatically released in the United States. Their next teaming, *Swept Away .
. .*, presented Giannini as a working-class sailor stranded on an island
with his rich female employer in a high-energy parable about sex roles
and their relation to class.

Their most ambitious and successful collaboration was their next
film, *Seven Beauties*, an astonishing mixture of broad comedy and
forbiddingly serious subject matter. In this slapstick tragedy, Giannini
plays a small-time Neapolitan hood who ends up in a Nazi concentration camp, forced to confront the issue of survival at any price. It is
an extraordinary performance—a tour de force that is both hilarious
and oddly touching.

Responding to the commercial success of *Seven Beauties*, Warner
Brothers signed Wertmüller to a four-film contract. Giannini starred
as a Communist journalist in her first English-language project, *The
End of the World in Our Usual Bed in a Night Full of Rain*, opposite
Candice Bergen. The film was both a critical and commercial failure,
Wertmüller's American contract was canceled, and to date this marked
the final Giannini-Wertmüller collaboration.

Although Giannini remained a partner in Wertmüller's production
company, Liberty Films, the 1980s and 1990s saw him work increasingly in Hollywood as well as continuing to star in Italian films and
international co-productions. In his better Hollywood performances
he rose above an inferior screenplay as a Clouseau-like inspector in
Once upon a Crime and was thoroughly convincing in the

oversentimental *A Walk in the Clouds* as the father who is initially suspicious of his daughter's supposed husband (played woodenly by Keanu Reeves) but is eventually won over. In addition to his roles as a boisterous major in the war drama *Time to Kill* and as straight man to Vittorio Gassman's outrageous uncle in *The Sleazy Uncle*, Giannini's co-production work in this period was also highlighted by the little-seen seriocomic *Brown Bread Sandwiches*, about a colorful Italian family who emigrate to mid-1950s Canada and attempt to adjust to their new environment, with Giannini portraying perfectly a middle-aged worker who lives with his brother in the basement of the family's cramped home in Toronto.

—Bill Wine, updated by David E. Salamie

GIBSON, Mel

Nationality: American. **Born:** Peekskill, New York, 3 January 1956. **Education:** Attended National Institute of Dramatic Art, 1977. **Family:** Married Robyn Moore, 1980, six children. **Career:** Moved to Australia in 1968; member of the State Theatre of New South Wales, Sydney; 1977—film debut in *Summer City*; 1983—in stage production of *Death of a Salesman*, Sydney; 1993—directing debut with *The Man without a Face*. **Awards:** Best Actor, Australian Film Award, for *Tim*, 1979, and for *Gallipoli*, 1981; Best Director Academy Award, Best Picture Academy Award (as co-producer), and Golden Globe for Best Director, for *Braveheart*, 1995. **Agent:** Ed Limato, ICM, 8942 Wilshire Boulevard, Beverly Hills, CA 90211, U.S.A.

Films as Actor:

1977   *Summer City* (Fraser) (as Scollop)
1979   *Tim* (Pate) (title role); *Mad Max* (George Miller) (title role)
1980   *Attack Force Z* (Burstall) (as Captain Paul G. Kelly)
1981   *Gallipoli* (Weir) (as Frank Dunne)
1982   *The Road Warrior* (*Mad Max 2*) (George Miller) (title role); *The Year of Living Dangerously* (Weir) (as Guy Hamilton)
1984   *The Bounty* (Donaldson) (as Fletcher Christian); *The River* (Rydell) (as Tom Garvey); *Mrs. Soffel* (*Dear Hearts*) (Gillian Armstrong) (as Ed Biddle)
1985   *Mad Max: Beyond Thunderdome* (*Mad Max 3*) (George Miller and George Ogilvie) (title role)
1987   *Lethal Weapon* (Richard Donner) (as Martin Riggs)
1988   *Tequila Sunrise* (Towne) (as Dale McKussic)
1989   *Lethal Weapon 2* (Richard Donner) (as Martin Riggs)
1990   *Bird on a Wire* (Badham) (as Rick Jarmin); *Hamlet* (Zeffirelli) (title role); *Air America* (Spottiswoode) (as Gene Ryack)
1992   *Lethal Weapon 3* (Richard Donner) (as Martin Riggs); *Forever Young* (Miner) (as Daniel)
1993   *Earth and the American Dream* (Couturie—doc) (as voice)
1994   *Maverick* (Richard Donner) (title role)
1995   *Pocahontas* (Gabriel and Goldberg—animation) (as voice of Captain John Smith); *Casper* (Silberling) (cameo)
1996   *Ransom* (Ron Howard)

Films as Actor and Director:

1993   *The Man without a Face* (as Justin McLeod)
1995   *Braveheart* (as William Wallace, + co-pr)

Publications

By GIBSON: articles—

Interview with M. Smith, in *Cinema Papers* (Melbourne), March 1983.
Interview with Lynn Hirschberg, in *Rolling Stone* (New York), 12 January 1989.
Interview with B. Hadleigh, in *Film Monthly* (Berkhamsted, England), January 1991.
"Thistle Do Nicely," interview with Graham Fuller, in *Interview* (New York), May 1995.
Interview with Lawrence Grobel, in *Playboy* (Chicago), July 1995.

On GIBSON: books—

Ragan, David, *Mel Gibson*, New York, 1985.
Hanrahan, John, *Mel Gibson*, St. Peters, New South Wales, 1986.
McKay, Keith, *Mel Gibson*, Garden City, New York, 1986.
Oram, James, *Reluctant Star: The Mel Gibson Story*, London, 1991.
Clarkson, Wensley, *Mel: The Inside Story*, London, 1993.
Perry, Roland, *Lethal Hero: The Mel Gibson Biography*, New York, 1993.

On GIBSON: articles—

Alberge, D., "Mel Gibson," in *Films and Filming* (London), June 1983.
Current Biography 1984, New York, 1984.
Abramowitz, R., "Mad Mel," in *Premiere* (New York), September 1993.
Mills, Bart, "Mel Gibson: Still Growing Up," in *Saturday Evening Post*, November-December 1993.
Ebert, Roger, "Battle Scenes Stand Out in Gibson's *Braveheart*," in *Denver Post*, 21 May 1995.

*　　*　　*

American-born, Australian-raised, Mel Gibson is a throwback to the chiseled-featured cinema gods of Hollywood's Golden Age. Like Errol Flynn, Tyrone Power, and Robert Taylor, he is comfortable time-traveling through any historical period to save the downtrodden, but this hero-for-all-seasons is a more accomplished actor than any of his predecessors.

After crafting an uncluttered performance as a low IQ youth smitten with an older woman in *Tim*, Gibson reversed sensitivity gears in a series of macho Australian adventures that put him on the international movie public's map (the conventional military rescue mission in *Attack Force Z*, the antiwar soldier boy ode of *Gallipoli*, the apocalyptic survival guide of *Mad Max*). In the *Mad Max* sequel, *The Road Warrior*, Gibson finished construction on the earlier blueprint of his persona: the glowering man-of-action ready with a quip or a fist, as need be. But he savvily broadened his range in *The Year of Living Dangerously* to include a weakness for women and a streak of self-serving practicality. Looking every inch the packaged star whether behind the prow (*The Bounty*) or behind the plow (*The River*), Gibson floundered a bit from trying to fit generic heroic molds until he picked up a *Lethal Weapon*, charged by a newfound affinity for danger which tagged him as not only daring but reckless. When his outlaw restaurateur dreamily wooed Michelle Pfeiffer in atomic-powered charismatic splendor in *Tequila Sunrise*, audiences cheered a rarity who could be accepted as both action maven and matinee idol. Immensely likable, the quick-witted Gibson aimed his own secret weapon, those baby-blue eyes of his, to melt the defenses of Hollywood's reigning female stars, but the *Lethal Weapon* movies revealed something more distinctive than his sex appeal. Out Mad-Maxing Mad Max himself, megastar Gibson sailed past being a dependable righter-of-wrongs and became a rash vigilante who had an intuitive grasp of criminal minds. There but for the grace of God went his Martin Riggs, and that element of surprise (contemplating suicide is practically a hobby), lent these flicks a cutting black-comedy edge before the formula grew stale. As a maestro of drawing moviegoers into theaters, Gibson only misjudged his fans' tolerance levels with *Air America*, a no-brainer comedy about CIA smugglers.

More felicitously, his other crowd-pleasers mesh the character of the brawling loose cannon with the image of poetic connoisseur of women; it is unlikely any of Gibson's contemporaries could have stopped the frozen-in-time romance of *Forever Young* from becoming cloying. In addition to his smooth-as-velvet turn as a confidence man in *Maverick* in which he has to match wits with cardsharps James Garner and Jodie Foster while severely straining his imperturbability, Gibson offered irrefutable evidence that he was more than an extremely pretty face with a multidimensional *Hamlet* that should have won him an Oscar nomination. More than a case of just silencing dumbfounded critics by not tripping over the iambic pentameter, Gibson grasped the Prince of Denmark's moody intransigence fluctuating with angry impatience; Hamlet and Martin Riggs are soulmates.

Acclaimed also as debuting director for his male weepie, *The Man without a Face*, Gibson demonstrated a shrewdness for adding texture to his established image and a true gift for eliciting performances from his cast—even if the film itself was a case of "Mr. Chips Says Goodbye to the Beauty and the Beast." Even more worrisome than the thick sentimentality is a streak of homophobia which snaked through *Man without a Face* (and had earlier reared its ugly head in *Bird on a Wire*, in which Mel tosses off a cruel, dated impersonation of a hairdresser). In his incredibly popular *Braveheart*, the antigay rumblings get lost amidst the power-to-the-people sloganing. Gibson was applauded for starring in and directing this cloddish spectacular because it allegedly revived the Hollywood Epic, but any second-unit director can give you scope and panorama. Tediously surging with self-importance, *Braveheart* lets Mel do his double-dare-you dance in kilts, but as the extras' limbs keep getting lopped off, the film registers less as a historical chronicle than as a medieval slasher film. More noteworthy as an affable player than a moviemaker, Gibson should make certain his movie-star savoir faire is rationed in roles that do not reduce his gallantry to the swelled-headed heroics of a star hogging everything including the camera. And isn't it time to stop legitimizing the vanity of actors-turned-directors such as Gibson and Kevin Costner simply for not getting flustered when confronted with casts of thousands?

—Robert Pardi

GIELGUD, (Sir) John

Nationality: British. **Born:** Arthur John Gielgud in London, England, 14 April 1904; brother of the writer Val Gielgud; grandnephew of the actress Ellen Terry. **Education:** Attended Hillside preparatory school, Godalming; Westminster School, London; studied acting at Lady Benson's School; Royal Academy of Dramatic Art, London, under Claude Rains. **Career:** 1921—super at Old Vic, London; in London production of *The Wheel*; 1922-24—with J. B. Fagan's company in Shakespeare repertory; 1924—film debut in *Who Is the Man?*; 1928—New York debut in *The Patriot*; 1930—in *Hamlet* at the Old Vic, the first of several celebrated productions of the role: in 1936 on Broadway, his *Hamlet* set a Broadway performance record; 1947—directed *The Importance of Being Earnest* in New York, followed by directing and acting in plays; also actor on

television, including the mini-series *QB VII*, 1974, *Edward VII*, 1974, *Brideshead Revisited*, 1981, *War and Remembrance*, 1988-89, *The Strauss Dynasty*, 1991, and *Scarlett*, 1994. **Awards:** Best British Actor, British Academy, for *Julius Caesar*, 1953; Best Supporting Actor, British Academy, for *Murder on the Orient Express*, 1974; Best Actor, New York Film Critics, for *Providence*, 1977; Academy Award for Best Supporting Actor, for *Arthur*, 1981; Best Supporting Actor Award, U.S. National Society of Film Critics, for *Plenty* and *The Shooting Party*, 1985. Knighted, 1953. **Address:** South Pavillion, Wotton Underwood, Aylesbury, HP18, Buckinghamshire, England.

Films as Actor:

1924 *Who Is the Man?* (Summers) (as Daniel)
1929 *The Clue of the New Pin* (Maude) (as Rex Trasmere)
1932 *Insult* (Lachman) (as Henri Dubois)
1933 *The Good Companions* (Saville) (as Inigo Jollifant)
1934 *Full Fathom Five* (Lye—short) (as voice)
1936 *Secret Agent* (Hitchcock) (as Edgar Brodie)
1939 *Hamlet* (Boisen-doc) (title role)
1941 *The Prime Minister* (Dickinson) (as Disraeli); *An Airman's Letter to His Mother* (Powell—short) (as voice)
1943 *Unfinished Journey* (Cekalski—short)
1944 *Shakespeare's Country* (Lawrence—short) (as voice)
1946 *A Diary for Timothy* (Jennings)
1948 *Hamlet* (Olivier) (as voice of Ghost)
1953 *Julius Caesar* (Joseph L. Mankiewicz) (as Cassius)
1954 *Romeo and Juliet* (*Giulietta e Romeo*) (Castellani) (as narrator of prologue)
1955 *Richard III* (Olivier) (as Clarence)
1956 *Around the World in Eighty Days* (Anderson) (as Foster)
1957 *Saint Joan* (Preminger) (as Warwick); *The Barretts of Wimpole Street* (Franklin) (as Mr. Barrett)
1958 *The Immortal Land* (Wright—doc) (as narrator)
1964 *Becket* (Glenville) (as Louis VII); *Hamlet* (Colleran—for TV, filmed record of Gielgud's New York theater production) (as voice of the ghost)
1965 *The Loved One* (Richardson) (as Sir Francis Hinsley)
1966 *Campanadas a Medianoche* (*Chimes at Midnight*; *Falstaff*) (Welles) (as Henry IV)
1967 *Assignment to Kill* (Sheldon Reynolds) (as Curt Valayan); *To Die in Madrid* (English-language version of *Mourir à Madrid*) (Rossif) (as narrator); *October Revolution* (English-language version of *Revolution d'Octobre*) (Rossif) (as narrator)
1968 *Mr. Sebastian* (*Sebastian*) (David Greene) (as Head of British Intelligence); *The Charge of the Light Brigade* (Richardson) (as Lord Raglan); *The Shoes of the Fisherman* (Anderson) (as the Elder Pope)
1969 *Oh! What a Lovely War* (Attenborough) (as Count Berchtold)
1970 *Eagle in a Cage* (Cook) (as Lord Sissal); *Julius Caesar* (Burge) (title role)
1972 *Lost Horizon* (Jarrott) (as Chang); *Probe* (*Search*) (Mayberry—for TV)
1973 *Frankenstein: The True Story* (Smight—for TV)
1974 *11 Harrowhouse* (Avakian) (as Meecham); *Gold* (Hunt) (as Farrell); *Murder on the Orient Express* (Lumet) (as Beddoes); *Galileo* (Losey) (as Cardinal)
1976 *Aces High* (Gold) (as Headmaster); *Joseph Andrews* (Richardson) (as Doctor)
1977 *A Portrait of the Artist as a Young Man* (Strick) (as Preacher); *Providence* (Resnais) (as Clive Langham)

1978   *Murder by Decree* (Clark) (as Lord Salisbury); *Caligula* (*Gore Vidal's Caligula*) (Brass) (as Nerva); *Les Misérables* (Glenn Jordan—for TV) (as Valjean's father)

1979   *The Conductor* (Wajda) (title role); *The Human Factor* (Preminger) (as Brigadier Tomlinson)

1980   *The Elephant Man* (Lynch) (as Carr Gomm); *The Formula* (Avildsen) (as Dr. Esau); *Priest of Love* (Miles) (as Herbert G. Muskett)

1981   *Arthur* (Gordon) (as Hobson); *Sphinx* (Schaffner) (as Abdu); *Lion of the Desert* (*Omar Mukhtar*) (Akkad—produced in 1979) (Akkad) (as Sharif el Gariani); *Chariots of Fire* (Hudson) (as Master of Trinity); *The Hunchback of Notre Dame* (Tuchner—for TV) (as Torturer); *Inside the Third Reich* (Chomsky—for TV) (as Speer's father)

1982   *Gandhi* (Attenborough) (as Lord Irwin); *The Vatican Pimpernel* (as Pope Pacelli)

1983   *The Wicked Lady* (Winner) (as Hogarth); *Wagner* (Palmer—for TV) (as Pfistermeister); *The Scarlet and the Black* (London—for TV)

1984   *Scandalous* (Cohen) (as Uncle Willie); *The Shooting Party* (Bridges) (as Cornelius Cardew); *Buddenbrooks* (Wirth—for TV) (as narrator); *Camille* (Desmond Davis—for TV); *Frankenstein* (Ormerod—for TV); *Ingrid* (Feldman—for TV); *Invitation to the Wedding* (Joseph Brooks) (as the Rev. Clyde Ormiston); *The Far Pavilions* (Duffell—for TV)

1985   *Romance on the Orient Express* (Clark—for TV); *Plenty* (Schepisi) (as Sir Leonard Darwin); *Leave All Fair* (Reid) (as John Middleton Murry); *Time after Time* (Hays) (as Jasper Swift)

1986   *Theban Plays by Sophocles* (for TV); *The Whistle Blower* (Langton) (as Sir Adrian Chapple); *The Canterville Ghost* (Bogart—for TV)

1987   *Quartermaine's Terms* (Hays—for TV); *Barbablu, Barbablu* (*Bluebeard, Bluebeard*) (Carpi)

1988   *Appointment with Death* (Winner) (as Colonel Carbury); *Arthur 2: On the Rocks* (Yorkin) (as Hobson); *A Man for All Seasons* (Charlton Heston—for TV) (as Wolsey)

1989   *Getting It Right* (Kleiser) (as Sir Gordon Munday); *Summer's Lease* (Friend—for TV)

1990   *A TV Dante* (Greenaway and Phillips); *Strike It Rich* (James Scott) (as Herbert Dreuther)

1991   *Prospero's Books* (Greenaway) (as Prospero)

1992   *Shining Through* (Seltzer) (as Konrad Friedrichs, "Sunflower"); *The Power of One* (Avildsen) (as Headmaster St. John); *Swan Song* (Branagh—short) (as Svetlovidov)

1994   *Lovejoy: The Lost Colony* (for TV) (as Wakering); *Hand in Glove* (for TV) (as Percival Pike Period); *The Best of Friends* (for TV) (as Sydney Cockerell)

1995   *First Knight* (Zucker) (as Oswald)

1996   *Gulliver's Travels* (Sturridge—for TV); *Hamlet* (Branagh) (as Priam); *Looking for Richard* (Pacino)

Publications

By GIELGUD: books—

Early Stages, London, 1939; rev. ed., 1987.
Stage Directions, London, 1963.
Distinguished Company, London, 1972.
An Actor and His Time, with John Miller and John Powell, London, 1979; rev. ed., 1989.
Backward Glances: Part One, Times for Reflection; Part Two, Distinguished Company, London, 1989.
Shakespeare: Hit or Miss?, with John Miller, London, 1991; American edition as *Acting Shakespeare*, New York, 1992.

The Mander and Mitchenson Theatre Collection Presents John Gielgud's Notes from the Gods: Playgoing in the Twenties, edited by Richard Morgan, London, 1994.

On GIELGUD: books—

Hayman, Ronald, *John Gielgud*, New York, 1971.
Brandreth, Gyles Daubeney, *John Gielgud: A Celebration*, London, 1984.
Harwood, Ronald, editor, *The Ages of Gielgud: An Actor at 80*, London, 1984.
Tanitch, Robert, *Gielgud*, London, 1988.
Francis, Clive, *Sir John: The Many Faces of Gielgud*, London, 1994.

On GIELGUD: articles—

Ecran (Paris), December 1979.
"Richardson and Gielgud," in *Harper's Bazaar* (New York), April 1983.
Current Biography 1984, New York, 1984.
Classic Images (Indiana, Pennsylvania), April 1984.

*   *   *

Sir John Gielgud belongs to a dynastic acting family that goes back through the nineteenth century, and included his great-aunt Ellen Terry, whose work with Henry Irving illuminated the later nineteenth-century theater in Britain and America. He was therefore destined by family connections to go on the stage, and he was blessed with romantic good looks and a uniquely beautiful voice. Trained at Britain's leading drama school, the Royal Academy of Dramatic Art (RADA), he started his stage career in 1921. By the 1930s, he and Laurence Olivier had become the leading Shakespearean actors of their generation. Indeed, Gielgud, Olivier, and Ralph Richardson are considered by many to be the three best English actors, ever. Gielgud never played romantic leads in movies as a youth, as he registered better on stage. Nevertheless, he has always given his all to whatever role he is cast in. Even playing the butler in *Arthur*, Gielgud brought depth to his character.

The theater was always to remain his principal artistic outlet, as his best film appearances have tended to be in Shakespearean adaptations—as an incisive Cassius in Joseph Mankiewicz's *Julius Caesar*, as a benign Clarence in Olivier's *Richard III*, as a coldly formal Henry IV in Orson Welles's *Chimes at Midnight*, and as a proudly imperious Caesar in Stuart Burge's *Julius Caesar*. His work for the screen dates back to the silent film *Who Is the Man?*, but belongs essentially to sound film. He made an effective young lead in the adaptation of J. B. Priestley's *The Good Companions*, appeared in Hitchcock's *Secret Agent*, played the autocratic father in Sidney Franklin's version of *The Barretts of Wimpole Street*, and was nominated for an Oscar for his Louis VII of France in *Becket*. He has claimed that he learned the hard way to recast his image from the new generation of theater-film directors, notably Lindsay Anderson. "You need a young public to strip your work of its affectations," he said in 1979. As a whole, his later films have scarcely been distinguished, with the exception of cameo appearances in *The Charge of the Light Brigade*, *The Shoes of the Fisherman*, *Murder on the Orient Express*, and Joseph Strick's *A Portrait of the Artist as a Young Man*, but he gave a masterly performance as the elderly and disillusioned writer in Alain Resnais's *Providence*.

In more recent years, Gielgud has made appearances on PBS's *Mystery* series. Even in his advancing age, he has not let his acting lapse into "cruise control"—he gives a brilliant, intense performance every time.

—Roger Manvell, updated by Linda J. Stewart

John Gielgud in *Richard III*

GILBERT, John

Nationality: American. **Born:** John Pringle in Logan, Utah, 10 July 1897 (some sources give 1895); adopted his stepfather's name, Gilbert. **Education:** Attended schools all over the country while his parents traveled with their theater troupe; military school in California. **Family:** Married 1) Olivia Burwell (divorced); 2) the actress Leatrice Joy, 1920 (divorced 1924), daughter: Leatrice Joy Gilbert; 3) the actress Ina Claire, 1929 (divorced 1931); 4) the actress Virginia Bruce, 1932 (divorced 1934), daughter: Susan. **Career:** 1914—assistant stage manager with the Baker Stock Company, Spokane, Washington; 1915—contract with Thomas Ince (Triangle): worked mainly as an extra; 1916—billed film debut in *Bullets and Brown Eyes*; 1917—lead role in *Princess of the Dark*; screenwriting job at Paralta studio; 1919—contract with Maurice Tourneur to write, act, and help direct; 1921-24—contract with Fox, and then with MGM, 1924-29: series of leading roles in films; 1930—sound film *Redemption*; 1933—cast in *Queen Christina* at Garbo's insistence; 1934—MGM released him from his contract. **Died:** Of heart attack, 9 January 1936.

Films as Actor:

1916   *Bullets and Brown Eyes* (Sidney); *The Apostle of Vengeance* (Barker); *The Phantom*; *The Eye of the Night*; *Shell 43* (Barker); *Hell's Hinges* (Swickard)

1917   *The Mother Instinct* (Neill and Hillyer); *The Devil Dodger* (Smith); *Golden Rule Kate* (Barker); *Doing Her Bit*; *Princess of the Dark* (Miller); *The Millionaire Vagrant* (Schertzinger); *Happiness*; *Hater of Men* (Parker)

1918   *Nancy Comes Home* (Dillon); *Sons of Men*; *Three X Gordon* (Warde); *Shackled* (Worsley); *Wedlock* (Worsley); *More Trouble* (Warde); *The Mask (The Mask of Riches)* (Smith); *The Dawn of Understanding* (Smith)

1919   *The White Heather* (Tourneur); *The Busher* (Storm); *Widow by Proxy* (Edwards); *The Red Viper* (Tyrol); *Heart o' the Hills* (Franklin); *Should a Woman Tell?* (John Ince)

1920   *The White Circle* (Tourneur) (+ co-sc); *Deep Waters* (Tourneur) (+ co-sc); *The Great Redeemer* (Brown) (+ co-sc)

1921   *The Servant in the House* (Hugh Ryan Conway and Jack Conway); *Shame* (Flynn) (as William Fidding/David Fidding); *Ladies Must Live* (Tucker) (as gardener)

1922   *Gleam O'Dawn* (Dillon) (title role); *Monte Cristo* (Flynn) (as Edmond Dantes); *Arabian Love* (Storm) (as Norman Stone); *The Yellow Stain* (Dillon) (as Donald Keith); *Honor First* (Storm) (as Jacques Dubois/Honoré Dubois); *Calvert's Valley (Calvert's Folly)* (Dillon) (as Page Emelyn); *The Love Gambler* (Franz) (as Dick Manners); *A California Romance* (Storm) (as Don Patricio Fernando)

1923   *While Paris Sleeps (The Glory of Love)* (Tourneur) (as Dennis O'Keefe); *Truxton King (Truxtonia)* (Storm) (title role); *Madness of Youth* (Storm) (as Jaca Javalie); *St. Elmo (St. Elmo Murray)* (Storm) (as St. Elmo Thornton); *The Exiles* (Mortimer) (as Henry Holcombe); *Cameo Kirby* (Ford) (title role)

1924   *The Wolf Man* (Mortimer) (as Gerald Stanley); *Just Off Broadway* (Mortimer) (as Stephen Moore); *A Man's Mate* (Mortimer) (as Paul); *The Lone Chance* (Mitchell) (as Jack Saunders); *Romance Ranch* (Mitchell) (as Carlos Brent); *His Hour* (Vidor) (as Gritzko); *He Who Gets Slapped* (Seastrom) (as Bezano); *The Snob* (Bell) (as Eugene Curry); *Wife of the Centaur* (Vidor) (as Jeffrey Dwyer)

1925   *The Merry Widow* (von Stroheim) (as Prince Danilo); ***The Big Parade*** (Vidor) (as James Apperson)

1926   *La Bohème* (Vidor) (as Rudolphe); *Bardalys the Magnificent* (Vidor) (title role); *Flesh and the Devil* (Brown) (as Keo von Sellenthin)

1927   *The Show* (Browning) (as Lock Robin); *Twelve Miles Out* (Conway) (as Jerry Fay); *Man, Woman, and Sin* (Bell) (as Al Whitcomb); *Love (Anna Karenina)* (Goulding) (as Vronsky)

1928   *The Cossacks* (Hill) (as Lukashka); *Four Walls* (Nigh) (as Benny); *Show People* (Vidor) (as guest); *The Masks of the Devil* (Seastrom) (as Baron Reiner); *A Woman of Affairs* (Brown) (as Neville); *Voices across the Sea* (short)

1929   *Desert Nights* (Nigh) (as Hugh Rand); *A Man's Man* (Cruze) (as guest); *The Hollywood Revue of 1929* (Reisner); *His Glorious Night* (Barrymore) (as Capt. Kovecs)

1930   *Redemption* (Niblo) (as Feyda); *Way for a Sailor* (Wood) (as Jack)

1931   *Gentleman's Fate* (LeRoy); *The Phantom of Paris* (Robertson); *West of Broadway* (Beaumont)

1932   *Downstairs* (Bell) (+ story)

1933   *Fast Workers* (Browning); *Queen Christina* (Mamoulian)

1934   *The Captain Hates the Sea* (Milestone)

Publications

By GILBERT: article—

"Jack Gilbert Writes His Own Story," in *Photoplay* (New York), June-September 1928.

On GILBERT: books—

Fountain, Leatrice Gilbert, with John R. Maxim, *Dark Star*, London, 1985.

On GILBERT: articles—

Tully, Jim, "John Gilbert," in *Vanity Fair* (New York), May 1928.
Albert, Katherine, "Is Jack Gilbert Through?" in *Photoplay* (New York), February 1930.
Maxwell, Virginia, "The Amazing Story behind Garbo's Choice of Gilbert," in *Photoplay* (New York), January 1934.
St. Johns, Adela Rogers, "What Defeated Jack Gilbert?," in *Photoplay* (New York), June 1935.
St. Johns, Adela Rogers, "The Tragic Truth about John Gilbert's Death," in *Photoplay* (New York), March 1936.
Quirk, Lawrence J., "John Gilbert," in *Films in Review* (New York), March 1956.
Davis, Henry, "A John Gilbert Index," in *Films in Review* (New York), October 1962.
Fox, J., "Casualties of Sound," in *Films and Filming* (London), October 1972.

*   *   *

There is a tendency among film historians to dismiss John Gilbert's career, to label him as Greta Garbo's leading man, a second-rate version of the Latin lover epitomized by Rudolph Valentino. However, Gilbert was more than that. An actor of seemingly effortless grace, he fell prey to his own desire for fame and position before he was able to realize fully his talents. He once claimed that, excepting *The Big Parade*, his entire acting career was worthless, and though a cursory reading of his screen credits shows this judgment to be unduly harsh, the frustration and cynicism exhibited by its severity is telling. The tragedy of Gilbert's life is that he was more talented than he believed himself to be, yet he never measured up to the lofty standards he unrealistically set for himself.

John Gilbert with Renee Adorée in *The Big Parade*

The son of a theatrical family, he entered films following the collapse of a small stock company in which he had been working. A family friend, Herschell Mayall, was at that time a leading player for the New York Motion Picture Company at Inceville, and Gilbert used this connection to launch his screen career. Beginning as an extra, "Jack" Gilbert essayed the roles of cowboy, Indian, gangster, Hindu, hero, and weakling during his two years with Ince, occasionally popping up as a billed player, but more often remaining in the background. From Ince he went on to Paralta, an offshoot of the Ince company established by some of the producer's former employees, working as an actor and a scriptwriter.

Gilbert achieved a certain measure of fame as a leading man in Mary Pickford's *Heart o' the Hills*, but his chronic dissatisfaction with his acting led him to accept a position with Maurice Tourneur as an actor and production assistant. Under Tourneur, Gilbert did everything, or, as he described it for *Photoplay* in 1928, he worked "18 hours a day—writing, co-directing, titling, cutting, and, least of all—acting." He had become the great director's "right hand," and from that position moved to Fox as a star player, making his mark in major productions like Emmet J. Flynn's *Monte Cristo* and John Ford's notable version of the sturdy melodrama *Cameo Kirby*.

Brushing aside his insecurities, Gilbert capitalized upon his reborn acting career and moved to Metro in 1924. There, under such directors as Victor Sjöström and Erich von Stroheim, but most especially for King Vidor, he gave a series of memorable performances that demonstrated his stubborn attention to detail in characterization, as well as revealing his ability to successfully tackle a great variety of roles. Unlike other matinee idols of the day, Gilbert sought to use his popularity with audiences as a bargaining chip, testing his craft and thereby stretching the limits of his fans' loyalty. It was a delicate balancing act which studio pressure and audience demand would eventually force him to abandon in favor of more melodramatic roles.

Gilbert reached his professional peak in 1925 with *The Big Parade*. A naive antiwar tract employing the unbeatable combination of violent spectacle and tender romance, this film was King Vidor's first great popular and critical success. It also gave Gilbert his finest showcase, allowing the actor to abandon his suave image to express the gritty reality of war and its physical and psychic devastation.

At the film's outset, Gilbert is exuberant in his typically American desire to go off to war and experience the thrill of being a hero, but his steady disillusionment in the face of battle's pain and loss graphically illustrates many of his contemporaries' response to the war. There is little in the film or in Gilbert's performance that would be considered subtle, certainly not his coy courtship of the French peasant girl, played to perfection by Renée Adorée, nor his terrifying despair in the midst of battle; yet Vidor keeps in check both his script's sentimentality and his star's penchant for overplaying, creating a vivid representation of an entire generation's emotional trauma. *The Big Parade* was a revelation of its director's sensibilities, but it was also a strong indication of its lead actor's potential when allowed to work on a project suited to his talents. Gilbert would never again find a director so precise and demanding, nor a role so fresh and unencumbered by romantic preconceptions.

In 1927 Gilbert was paired with Greta Garbo in *Flesh and the Devil* and *Love* (followed in 1928 by *A Woman of Affairs*, and thus Gilbert was assured of a dubious immortality. What makes the Gilbert-Garbo films interesting, aside from their obvious value as barometers of popular culture and its ever-changing sexual iconography, is the degree to which these two performers were able to join their divergent acting techniques into a plausible expression of overwrought sensuality. In the midst of filming *Flesh and the Devil*, Gilbert and Garbo's offscreen romance became an open secret, and thus all else in these three films became mere background to the public display of a private passion. One would be foolish to ignore the technical artistry of directors Clarence Brown and Edmund Goulding, or the typically sumptuous art direction of Cedric Gibbons and his MGM colleagues, but these films truly live for the unlikely chemistry of their stars.

Gilbert's flamboyance emphasizes Garbo's passivity, her controlled sexuality complements perfectly his unembarrassed lust, and the resulting tension produced by this highly charged combination still manages to leave audiences limp.

If Gilbert's star rose quickly, it fell ignominiously with the arrival of sound. Talkies made his type of romantic hero foolish and obsolete, at least for a while, and his inability to find a way through the casting difficulties posed by his peculiar talents left him adrift. Lack of studio support, and not the popular myth of an unsuitable speaking voice, caused once devoted fans to question his talent and eventually to abandon him, and he resorted to alcohol as a way out of his despair. After ten poorly received talkies of erratic quality, including one truly fine co-starring performance opposite Garbo in *Queen Christina*, John Gilbert was unemployable. When he died of a heart attack in 1936 he was only 41. Tired and forgotten, his insecurities had overwhelmed him.

—Steven Higgins

GIRARDOT, Annie

Nationality: French. **Born:** Paris, 25 October 1931. **Education:** Studied acting with Henry Bosc and Jean Meyer; then studied at the Paris Conservatory under Henri Collan. **Family:** Married the actor Renato Salvatori, 1962, daughter: Julia. **Career:** 1954-57—member of the Comédie Française; 1955—film debut in *Treize à table*; has also acted on radio and television, and in cabaret; stage work includes Visconti's productions of *Two for the Seesaw* and *After the Fall*; 1960—spoken role in ballet *Persephone*, La Scala, Milan; 1992—in TV miniseries *Delitti Privati*. **Awards:** Best Actress, Venice Film Festival, for *Trois chambres à Manhattan*, 1965; César Award, for *Docteur Françoise Gailland*, 1975. **Address:** 25 place des Vosges, 75003 Paris, France.

Films as Actress:

1955 *Treize à table* (Hunebelle)
1956 *Reproduction interdite* (Grangier); *L'Homme aux clefs d'or* (Joannon)

1957 *Le Rouge est mis* (Grangier); *L'Amour est en jeu* (*Ma femme, mon gosse, et moi*) (Marc Allégret); *Le Désert de Pigalle* (Joannon); *Maigret tend un piège* (*Maigret Lays a Trap*; *Inspector Maigret*) (Delannoy) (as Yvonne Maurin)

1960 *La Corde raide* (*Lovers on a Tightrope*) (Dudremet) (as Cora); *Recours en grâce* (Benedek); "Le Divorce" ep. of *La Française et l'amour* (*Love and the Frenchwoman*) (Christian-Jaque) (as Danielle); *La Proie pour l'ombre* (Astruc) (as Anna); **Rocco e i suoi fratelli** (*Rocco and His Brothers*; *Rocco et ses freres*) (Visconti) (as Nadia)

1961 "Les comédiennes" ep. of *Amours célèbres* (Boisrond); *Le Rendez-vous* (Delannoy)

1962 *Le Bateau d'Emile* (Rossi) (as Fernande); *Pourquoi Paris?* (de la Patellière); *Le Vice et la vertu* (*Vice and Virtue*) (Vadim) (as Juliette); "L'affaire Fenayrou" ("The Fenayrou Case") ep. of *Le Crime ne paie pas* (*Crime Does Not Pay*; *The Gentle Art of Murder*) (Oury) (as Gabrielle Fenayrou); *Il Giorno più corto* (Corbucci) (as guest); *Smog* (Rossi) (as Gabriella)

1963 *La donna scimmia* (*The Ape Woman*) (Ferreri) (as Maria); *I compagni* (*The Organizer*; *The Strikers*; *Les Camarades*) (Monicelli) (as Niobe); *I fuorilegge del matrimonio* (Orsini, Vittorio Taviani, and Paolo Taviani) (as Margherita)

1964 *La Bonne Soupe* (*The Good Soup*) (Thomas) (as young Marie-Paule); *L'Autre Femme* (*La Otra Mujer*; *Quella terribile notte*) (Villiers); *Un Monsieur de compagnie* (*Male Companion*) (de Broca) (as Clara); "Il Principe Azzuro" ep. of *Le Belle famiglie* (Gregoretti)

1965 *La ragazza in prestito* (*Engagement Italiano*) (Giannetti) (as Clara); *Declic et des claques* (Clair); *Trois chambres à Manhattan* (Carné) (as Kay); *L'Or de Duc* (Baratier) (as guest)

1966 "Djibouti" ep. of *La Guerre secrète* (*La guerra segreta*; *Spione unter sich*; *The Dirty Game*; *The Dirty Agents*) (Christian-Jaque) (as Nanette/Monique); *Una voglia da morire* (Tessari); *Zhurnalist* (*Journalist*) (Gerasimov) (as guest)

1967 "La strega bruciate viva" ("The Witch Burned Alive") ep. of *Le streghe* (*The Witches*) (Visconti) (as Valeria); *Vivre pour vivre* (*Live for Life*) (Lelouch) (as Catherine Colomb); *Les Anarchistes ou la Bande à Bonnot* (Fourastié)

1968 *Erotissimo* (Pirès) (as Annie); *Les Gauloises bleues* (Cournot) (as Mother); *Bice skoro propast sveta* (*It Rains in My Village*) (Petrovic); *La Vie, l'amour, la mort* (*Life Love Death*) (Lelouch) (as woman in film); *Dillinger è morto* (*Dillinger Is Dead*) (Ferreri) (as maid)

1969 *Metti, una sera a cena* (*Disons, un soir à dîner*) (Patroni Griffi) (as Giovanna); *Un Homme qui me plaît* (*Love Is a Funny Thing*; *Again a Love Story*; *Un Tipo chi mi place*) (Lelouch) (as Françoise); *Il seme dell'uomo* (*The Seed of Man*) (Ferreri) (as Anna); *Storia di una donna* (*Story of a Woman*) (Bercovici) (as Liliana Cardini)

1970 *Le Clair de terre* (Gilles); *Les Novices* (Casaril) (as Mona Lisa); *Elle boit pas, elle fume pas, elle drague pas . . . mais elle cause* (Audiard); *Mourir d'aimer* (Cayatte)

1971 *Les Feux de la chandeleur* (Korber)

1972 *La Mandarine* (Molinaro) (as Séverine); *La Vieille Fille* (Blanc) (as Muriel Buchon); *Elle cause plus . . . elle flingue* (Audiard) (as Rosemonde); *Traitement de choc* (*Shock Treatment*) (Jessua) (as Hélène); *Il n'y a pas de fumée sans feu* (Cayatte)

1973 *Ursule et Grelu* (Korber) (+ pr); *Juliette et Juliette* (Forlani)

1974 *La Gifle* (*The Slap*) (Pinoteau) (as Hélène Doulean)

1975 *Il sospetto* (Maselli); *D'amour et d'eau fraîche* (Blanc); *Il faut vivre dangereusement* (Makovski); *Le gitan* (Giovanni) (as Ninie); *Il pleut sur Santiago* (Soto); *Docteur Françoise Gailland* (*No Time for Breakfast*) (Bertucelli) (title role)

1976   *Cours après moi que je t'attrape* (Pouret); *A chacun son enfer*
        (*Autopsie d'un monstre*; *Jedem sein Hölle*) (Cayatte)
1977   *Le Dernier Baiser* (Grassian); *Jambon d'Ardenne* (Lamy); *Le*
        Point de mire (Tramont)
1978   *La zizanie* (Zidi); *Vas-y maman* (de Buron); *L'Amour en ques-*
        tion (Cayatte); *La Clé sur la porte* (Boisset); *Le Cavaleur*
        (*Practice Makes Perfect*; *The Skirt Chaser*) (de Broca) (as
        Lucienne); *Tendre Poulet* (*Dear Inspector*; *Dear Detective*)
        (de Broca) (as Lise Tanquerelle)
1979   *Cause toujours . . . tu m'intéresses!* (Molinaro); *L'ingorgo*
        (*Traffic Jam*) (Comencini) (as Irene); *Bobo Jacco* (*Jacko*
        and Lise) (Bal) (as Magda)
1980   *Le Coeur à l'envers* (Apprédéris); *On a volé la cuisse de Jupi-*
        ter (*Jupiter's Thigh*) (de Broca) (as Lise Tanquerelle); *Une*
        Robe noire pour un tueur (Giovanni)
1981   *All Night Long* (Tramont) (as French teacher)
1982   *La Vie continue* (Mizrahi) (as Jeanne)
1983   *Père Noel et fils* (Frederick)
1984   *Souvenirs, souvenirs* (Zeitoun)
1985   *Adieu Blaireau* (Decout) (as Colette); *Partir, revenir* (*Go-*
        ing and Coming Back) (Lelouch) (as Hélène Rivière);
        Olga e i suoi figli (Nocita); *Io e il duce* (*Mussolini and I*)
        (Negrin—for TV); *Liste noire* (*Blacklist*) (Bonnot) (as
        Jeanne Tufour)
1988   *Prisonnières* (Silvera) (as Marthe); *La Tête dans les nuages*
        (Vecchiali)
1989   *Cinq jours en juin* (Legrand) (as Marcelle); *Comedie d'amour*
        (Rawson) (as Le Fleau)
1990   *Il y a des jours . . . et des lunes* (*There Were Days and Moons*)
        (Lelouch) (as woman alone); *Toujours seuls* (Mordillat) (as
        Mme. Chevillard)
1991   *Merci la vie* (*Thanks for Life*) (Blier) (as the Old Mother)
1993   *A Cry in the Night* (Spry) (as Reine)
1994   *Les Braqueuses* (*Girls with Guns*; *The Hold-up Girls*) (Salome)
        (as Mere Cecile)
1995   *Les Misérables* (Lelouch) (as farmer's wife)
1996   *Shangai 1937* (Patzak); *Les Bidochons* (Serge Korber)

Publications

By GIRARDOT: book—

Paroles de femmes, with Marie-Therese Cuny, Paris, 1981.
Vivre d'aimer, Paris, 1989.
Ma vie contre la tienne, Paris, 1993.

By GIRARDOT: articles—

Interview with A. Ignatov, in *Soviet Film* (Moscow), July 1983.
"Nesmotria ni na chto, ia schastliva," interview with A.Braginskii, in
    Iskusstvko Kino (Moscow), no. 8, 1989.

On GIRARDOT: books—

Gilles, Françoise, *D'Annie Girardot*, Paris, 1971.
Merigeau, Pascal, *Annie Girardot*, Paris, 1978.

On GIRARDOT: articles—

Pietzsch, I., "Faszination," in *Film und Fernsehen* (Berlin), Decem-
    ber 1979.
Grandmaire, G., filmography in *Revue du Cinéma* (Paris), June 1991.
Hoffstetter, J., "Annie Girardot: merci la vie," in *Revue du Cinéma*
    (Paris), June 1991.

Stars (Mariembourg, Belgium), Spring 1993, Winter 1993, and Autumn
1993.

*   *   *

Annie Girardot launched her acting career at the Paris Conservatoire
where she studied for stage performance and maintained a successful
apprenticeship in the theater for several years. Brought up in the dark
days of the German occupation, she won a place in the Comédie
Française where Jean Cocteau called her "The finest dramatic temperament of the postwar period." But her inability to contain her need
to take risks and experiment within the rigid dictates of the Comédie
propelled Girardot toward the cinema. She received immediate attention for her performance in *L'Homme aux clefs d'or*, which earned
her the Suzanne Bianchetti prize. It was this role that brought her to
the attention of Luchino Visconti who cast her with Alain Delon and
her future husband, Renato Salvatori, in *Rocco e i suoi fratelli*.

Though the early part of her career was marked by her comedic
performances with the Comédie, her early screen career was circum-
scribed by darker roles when, in the mid-1950s, she was routinely cast
as a woman of dubious morality invariably doomed to a violent end.
After her debut in *Treize à table*, she appeared for Joannon in *L'Homme*
aux clefs d'or as a blackmailing vamp, and in his sentimental *Le Désert*
de Pigalle as a hardened prostitute redeemed by love but stabbed to
death. She performed the role of the prostitute in routine police
dramas *Le Rouge est mis* and *Reproduction interdite*, a deceptive wife
in *Maigret tend un piège*, a scheming adulteress in *Le Crime ne paie*
pas, and a Gestapo general's mistress in *Le Vice et la vertu*. Although
never less than competent in these limited parts, her true potential
was revealed as Nadia, the gangland harlot of Visconti's *Rocco e i suoi*
fratelli. Her depiction of the reformed but sexually abused prostitute
suffering in her humiliation was both poignant and compelling.

In the 1960s and 1970s she continued to work extensively with
Italian directors in both serious and comic roles. In France her perfor-
mances have been associated with the directors Philippe de Broca,
André Cayatte, and Claude Lelouch, and the actor Philippe Noiret.
With de Broca her talent for comedy flourished. After the early *Un*
Monsieur de compagnie, she was Lucienne in the broad sexual farce *Le*
Cavaleur, and her success as the female detective Lise Tanquerelle,
comically caught between personal and professional roles, in *Tendre*
Poulet led to the sequel *On a volé la cuisse de Jupiter*. In the two latter
films she was partnered by Philippe Noiret with whom she has also
appeared in more dramatic roles: in *Le Rendez-vous* as the female
detective; in *La Vieille Fille* as the withdrawn spinster Muriel Buchon
falling in love with an equally shy bachelor; and in *La Mandarine* as
Séverine deserting her boring husband for an attractive teenager. For
Cayatte there were socially, or morally conscious roles, particularly in
Mourir d'aimer as the middle-aged teacher, ostracized and driven to
suicide after an affair with a pupil. Lelouch also drew on her talents for
emotionally charged roles. She gave a reserved, dignified performance
as the deceived but forgiving wife Catherine Colomb in *Vivre pour*
vivre; she was the vivacious Françoise destined to finish unhappily
with Belmondo in the sentimental melodrama *Un Homme qui me*
plaît; and in *Partir, revenir* she was the jealous mother Hélène Rivière,
who commits suicide after denouncing her daughter to the Nazis.

Other more notable roles were as Anna, a career woman torn between her husband and her lover in *La Proie pour l'ombre*; as a vulnerable woman of fading beauty murdering a corrupt, exploitative doctor
in *Traitement de choc*; as the neurotic Kay discovering love in *Trois*
chambres à Manhattan; as a lonely woman finding companionship
with a telephone caller in *Cause toujours . . . tu m'intéresses!*; as
Colette the unhappy mistress of a gangster in *Adieu Blaireau*; and
again as a desperately lonely woman on the point of breakdown in *Il y*
a des jours . . . et des lunes. Maternal roles are found in *Le Coeur à*
l'envers, where she struggles with incestuous desires; in *Liste noire*,

where she seeks to avenge her daughter's death at the hands of gangsters; and in *Souvenirs, souvenirs*, where she has to cope with a difficult teenage daughter.

It is perhaps in her lighter roles as an exuberant comic actress that Annie Girardot has enjoyed most popular appeal. In *Les Novices* she was Mona Lisa, a kindly but cynical prostitute using an ambulance as a traveling brothel; in *La Bonne Soupe* she was Marie-Paule, the irrepressible orphan who seduces her way to the top; and in *Erotissimo* she portrayed the inventive housewife Annie rekindling her husband's flagging sexual interest. Furthermore, her verve and professionalism have frequently rescued indifferent films.

Girardot has appeared in more than 60 films and has become one of France's few box-office stars on a popularity level with Belmondo, Delon, and Montand, and as critically acclaimed as Moreau or Signoret. Equally adept at strong social drama (as evidenced by her work with Cayatte and Visconti) and light distinctive comedy (as in her work for de Broca), she is the epitome of a French star.

—R. F. Cousins, updated by Kelly Otter

GISH, Lillian

Nationality: American. **Born:** Lillian Diana Gish in Springfield, Ohio, 14 October 1896 (some sources say 1893). **Education:** Briefly attended Ursuline Academy, East St. Louis, Illinois. **Career:** About 1902—stage debut in Rising Sun, Ohio, in *The Little Red Schoolhouse*; 1903-04—with mother and sister Dorothy, toured in *Her First False Step*; 1905—danced with Sarah Bernhardt production in New York City; 1908-11—lived with aunt in Massillon, Ohio, and with mother in East St. Louis, and briefly with father in Oklahoma; 1912—film debut as featured player, with sister, in *An Unseen Enemy* for D. W. Griffith; 1913—in Belasco production of *A Good Little Devil* starring Mary Pickford; collapsed during run of play with pernicious anemia; 1920—directed Dorothy Gish in *Remodeling Her Husband*; 1921—last film under Griffith's direction, *Orphans of the Storm*; joined Inspiration Films; 1924—$800,000 contract with MGM; 1930—first talkie, *One Romantic Night*; resumed stage career in *Uncle Vanya*; 1930s—began working in radio; 1948—TV debut in Philco Playhouse production *The Late Christopher Bean*; 1969—began giving film lecture "Lillian Gish and the Movies: The Art of Film, 1900-1928." **Awards:** Honorary Oscar, "for superlative artistry and for distinguished contribution to the progress of motion pictures," 1970; Life Achievement Award, American Film Institute, 1984; D. W. Griffith Award, for "an outstanding career in motion pictures," 1987. **Died:** In New York City, 27 February 1993.

Films as Actress:

1912   *An Unseen Enemy* (Griffith); *Two Daughters of Eve* (Griffith); *In the Aisles of the Wild* (Griffith); *The One She Loved* (Griffith); *The Musketeers of Pig Alley* (Griffith); *My Baby* (Frank Powell); *Gold and Glitter* (Frank Powell); *The New York Hat* (Griffith); *The Burglar's Dilemma* (Griffith); *A Cry for Help* (Griffith)

1913   *Oil and Water* (Griffith); *The Unwelcome Guest* (Griffith); *The Stolen Bride* (O'Sullivan); *A Misunderstood Boy* (Griffith); *The Left-Handed Man* (Griffith); *The Lady and the Mouse* (Griffith); *The House of Darkness* (Griffith); *Just Gold* (Griffith); *A Timely Interception* (Griffith); *Just Kids* (Henderson); *The Mothering Heart* (Griffith); *During the Round Up* (Griffith); *An Indian's Loyalty* (Frank Powell); *A

Woman in the Ultimate (Griffith); *A Modest Hero* (Griffith); *So Runs the Way* (Griffith); *The Madonna of the Storm* (Griffith); *The Blue or the Gray* (Cabanne); *The Conscience of Hassan Bey* (Cabanne); *The Battle at Elderbush Gulch* (Griffith)

1914   *The Green-Eyed Devil* (Kirkwood); *The Battle of the Sexes* (Griffith); *The Hunchback* (Cabanne); *The Quicksands* (Cabanne); *Home, Sweet Home* (Griffith); *Judith of Bethulia* (Griffith) (as the young mother); *Silent Sandy* (Kirkwood); *The Escape* (Griffith); *The Rebellion of Kitty Belle* (Cabanne); *Lord Chumley* (Kirkwood); *Man's Enemy* (Frank Powell); *The Angel of Contention* (O'Brien); *The Wife*; *The Tear that Burned* (O'Brien); *The Folly of Anne* (O'Brien); *The Sisters* (Cabanne); *His Lesson* (Crisp) (as extra)

1915   **The Birth of a Nation** (Griffith) (as Elsie Stoneman); *The Lost House* (Cabanne); *Enoch Arden (As Fate Ordained)* (Cabanne); *Captain Macklin* (O'Brien); *Souls Triumphant* (O'Brien); *The Lily and the Rose* (Paul Powell)

1916   *Daphne and the Pirate* (Cabanne) (as Daphne); *Sold for Marriage* (Cabanne); *An Innocent Magdalene* (Dwan); **Intolerance** (Griffith); *Diane of the Follies* (Cabanne) (title role); *Pathways of Life*; *Flirting with Fate* (Cabanne); *The Children Pay* (Ingraham)

1917   *The House Built upon Sand* (Morrissey)

1918   *Hearts of the World* (Griffith) (as the Girl, Marie Stephenson); *The Great Love* (Griffith); Liberty Bond short (Griffith); *The Greatest Thing in Life* (Griffith); *The Romance of Happy Valley* (Griffith)

1919   **Broken Blossoms** (Griffith) (as Lucy Burrows); *True Heart Susie* (Griffith) (title role); *The Greatest Question* (Griffith)

1920   *Way Down East* (Griffith) (as Anna Moore)

1921   *Orphans of the Storm* (Griffith) (as Henriette Girard)

1923   *The White Sister* (Henry King) (as Angela Chiaromonte)

1924   *Romola* (Henry King) (title role)

1926   *La Bohème* (King Vidor) (as Mimi); *The Scarlet Letter* (Seastrom) (as Hester Prynne)

1927   *Annie Laurie* (Robertson) (title role); *The Enemy* (Niblo)

1928   **The Wind** (Seastrom) (as Letty Mason)

1930   *One Romantic Night* (Stein) (as Alexandra)

1933   *His Double Life* (Hopkins and William B. DeMille) (as Mrs. Alice Hunter)

1942   *The Commandos Strike at Dawn* (Farrow) (as Mrs. Bergesen)

1943   *Top Man (Man of the Family)* (Lamont) (as Beth Warren)

1946   *Miss Susie Slagle's* (Berry) (title role); *Duel in the Sun* (King Vidor) (as Mrs. Laura Belle McCanles)

1948   *Portrait of Jennie (Jennie)* (Dieterle) (as Mother Mary of Mercy)

1955   *The Cobweb* (Minnelli) (as Victoria Inch); **The Night of the Hunter** (Laughton) (as Rachel); *Salute to the Theatres* (supervisor: Loud—short) (appearance)

1958   *Orders to Kill* (Asquith) (as Mrs. Summers)

1960   *The Unforgiven* (Huston) (as Mattilda Zachary)

1963   *The Great Chase* (Killiam—doc)

1966   *Follow Me, Boys!* (Tokar) (as Hetty Seiber)

1967   *Warning Shot* (Kulik) (as Alice Willows); *The Comedians* (Glenville) (as Mrs. Smith); *The Comedians in Africa* (short) (appearance)

1970   *Henri Langlois* (Hershon and Guerra) (as guest)

1976   *Twin Detectives* (Day—for TV)

1978   *A Wedding* (Altman) (as Nettie Sloan)

1981   *Thin Ice* (Aaron—for TV)

1983   *Hobson's Choice* (Cates—for TV)

1984   *Hambone and Hillie* (Watts) (as Hillie)

1986   *Sweet Liberty* (Alda) (as Cecelia Burgess); *The Adventures of Huckleberry Finn* (Hunt)

1987   *The Whales of August* (Lindsay Anderson) (as Sarah Webber)

Lillian Gish

Film as Director:

1920   *Remodeling Her Husband* (+ co-sc with Dorothy Gish as "Dorothy Elizabeth Carter")

Publications

By GISH: books—

Life and Lillian Gish, with Albert Bigelow, New York, 1932.
The Movies, Mr. Griffith, and Me, with Ann Pinchot, Englewood Cliffs, New Jersey, 1969.
Dorothy and Lillian Gish, New York, 1973.
An Actor's Life for Me, as told to Selma Lane, New York, 1987.

By GISH: articles—

"The Gish Girls Talk about Each Other," by Ada Patterson in *Photoplay* (New York), June 1921.
"Dorothy Gish, the Frankest Girl I Know," in *Filmplay Journal*, April 1922.
"We Interview the Two Orphans," by Gladys Hall and Adele Whitely Fletcher, in *Motion Picture Magazine* (New York), May 1922.
"My Sister and I," in *Theatre Magazine* (New York), November 1927.
"Birth of an Era," in *Stage*, January 1937.
"D. W. Griffith: A Great American," in *Harper's Bazaar* (New York), October 1940.
"Silence Was Our Virtue," in *Films and Filming* (London), December 1957.
"Conversation with Lillian Gish," in *Sight and Sound* (London), Winter 1957-58.
"Life and Living," interview in *Films and Filming* (London), January 1970.
"Lillian Gish . . . Director," in *Silent Picture* (London), Spring 1970.
Interview with Y. Lardeau and V. Ostria, in *Cahiers du Cinéma* (Paris), November 1983.
Interview with Allan Hunter, in *Films and Filming* (London), August 1987.

On GISH: books—

Wagenknecht, Edward, *Lillian Gish: An Interpretation*, Seattle, 1927.
Lillian Gish: Actress, compiled by Anthony Slide, London, 1969.
Pratt, George C., *Spellbound in Darkness*, Connecticut, 1973.
Rosen, Marjorie, *Popcorn Venus*, New York, 1973.
Slide, Anthony, *The Griffith Actresses*, New York, 1973.
Affron, Charles, *Star Acting: Gish, Garbo, Davis*, New York, 1977.
Lillian Gish, edited by the Museum of Modern Art, New York, 1980.
Wagenknecht, Edward, *Stars of the Silents*, Metuchen, New Jersey, 1987.

On GISH: articles—

Hall, Gladys, "Lights! Say Lillian!," in *Motion Picture Magazine* (New York), April/May 1920.
Brooks, Louise, "Women in Films," in *Sight and Sound* (London), Winter 1957-58.
Brooks, Louise, "Gish and Garbo. The Executive War on Stars," in *Sight and Sound* (London), Winter 1958-59.
Tozzi, Romano, "Lillian Gish," in *Films in Review* (New York), December 1962, see also issue for April 1964.
Bodeen, DeWitt, "Lillian Gish: The Movies, Mr. Griffith and Me," in *Silent Picture* (London), Autumn 1969.
Morley, Sheridan, "Lillian Gish: Life and Living," in *Films and Filming* (London), January 1970.

Current Biography 1978, New York, 1978.
Curran, T., "Lillian Gish: Tribute to a Great Lady," in *Films in Review* (New York), October 1980.
Kael, Pauline, "Lillian Gish and Mae Marsh," in *The Movie Star*, edited by Elisabeth Weis, New York, 1981.
Naremore, J., "True Heart Susie and the Art of Lillian Gish," in *Quarterly Review of Film Studies* (Pleasantville, New York), Winter 1981.
"Dossier: Lillian Gish," in *Cinématographe* (Paris), October 1983.
Brownlow, Kevin, "Glimpses of a Legend," in *Sight and Sound* (London), Spring 1984.
Brownlow, Kevin, "Lillian Gish," in *American Film* (Washington, D.C.), March 1984.
Slide, Anthony, "Filming Lillian Gish," in *American Cinematographer* (Los Angeles), June 1984.
Obituary in *New York Times*, 1 March 1993.
Obituary in *Variety* (New York), 8 March 1993.

*   *   *

"I was always having bright ideas and suffering for them," Lillian Gish wrote in her memoirs, describing her incredible performance on the ice floes in *Way Down East* (1920). Perhaps the actress who logged more hours of suffering on-screen than any other, Gish brought both dignity and complexity to the genre of silent melodrama. From the very beginning of her 85-year career, Gish dedicated her all to the art of acting, and, as is little-known about her, to writing, editing, and even directing. (Her one directing effort, *Remodeling Her Husband* [1920] is, unfortunately, lost.) The great director, D. W. Griffith, treated Gish as something close to a collaborator in many of their works together; she responded with a loyalty that bordered on devotion. Who else but Gish would write memoirs that are primarily about Griffith rather than herself?

Early in her career Gish demonstrated the restraint and subtlety that adds such depth to her performances. Even before her famous role in *Birth of a Nation* (1915), Gish had developed many of her characteristic poses: in *The Musketeers of Pig Alley* (1912) she cradles her cheek with her hand, a gesture that she later adapts by moving her pinky finger over to her mouth and chewing on her fingernail. Other early poses include the indignant thrust of an elbow as her fist goes to her hip, a head thrown down onto her arms in despair, and the prim pressing of her hands and pursing of her lips as she rebuffs an overzealous lover. Gish, under Griffith's encouragement, often improvised these "details" that came to define her ingenuous style. In *Broken Blossoms* (1919) she created the famous gesture of lifting the corners of her mouth with two fingers when her abusive father berates her for not smiling enough. She also suggested trailing her hair and her hand in the freezing water as she lay collapsed on the ice in *Way Down East*.

Gish studied literature and philosophy, fencing and dancing to prepare her mind and her body for acting. She practiced with the Denishawn Company of Los Angeles, which produced Martha Graham among other famous modern dancers. Similar to Bogart's expressive face, however, Gish's eyes and mouth were her primary instruments of communication. Upon hearing that her lover has been killed, in *The White Sister* (1923), she delivers the gaze that is found in so many of her films: wide-eyed, vulnerable, distant, and tragic. (The intertitle describes her as being in "a trance-like state of dry-eyed despair.") Some of Gish's most powerful moments on film occur when her stoic suffering gives way to an expressive panic. In the climatic scene of *Broken Blossoms*, she flings her body around a tiny room and expresses on her face all of the fear and terror of someone who is about to be beaten brutally. In a similar scene from *The Wind* (1928), Gish is shown clawing at a window pane, eyes wide in horror as she watches the wind uncover the dead body of her rapist.

Too often Gish's acting abilities have been undervalued because they are associated with the stereotype of the "simplistic" moral universe of melodramas. Rarely does Gish express any singular emotion; happiness is tinged with wistfulness, envy with irony, grief with hope. If there is any continuity in her roles it would have to be that her characters are always thoughtful. Gish allows the viewer to watch as her characters progress from one emotion to another, so one can follow as her True Heart Susie first feels disbelief, then horror, then irony touched by hysterical laughter and, finally, a weary acceptance when she discovers her lover plans to wed another; or, again, in *Way Down East*, when Anna baptizes her dying child, the grief, desperation, and loneliness of her character are all discreetly visible in her facial expression and bodily action. Gish's characters are never entirely predictable. Unlike the tableau poses of earlier melodramatic acting, Gish's emotional moments flow together realistically and logically while still retaining an element of surprise.

While Gish's reputation has been established primarily on the basis of her extensive silent film career, she found equal fame on the stage and in sound film and television. After studying voice lessons, her speaking characters appear as natural and as unpretentious as her silent performances. She eased quite gracefully into "older" roles, such as the tough-as-nails, shotgun-toting mother of orphans in *The Night of the Hunter* (1955), or the self-sacrificing sister to a bitter Bette Davis in *The Whales of August* (1987). These final film performances demonstrate Gish's talent for refining and adapting her craft, even as film technology and trends in film acting styles changed radically during her prodigious career.

—Elizabeth Coffman

GODDARD, Paulette

Nationality: American. **Born:** Pauline Marion Goddard Levee in Whitestone Landing, New York, 3 June 1911. **Education:** Attended Mount Saint Dominic's Academy, Caldwell, New Jersey. **Family:** Married 1) Edgar James, 1927 (divorced 1929); 2) the actor Charlie Chaplin, 1936 (divorced 1941); 3) the actor Burgess Meredith, 1944 (divorced 1949); 4) the writer Erich Maria Remarque, 1958 (died 1970). **Career:** 1925—model from age 14; 1926—stage debut in Ziegfeld's *No Fooling*; 1929-32—short contracts with Roach and Goldwyn; 1933-36—studied with Chaplin prior to starring with him in *Modern Times*; 1938—contract with David O. Selznick under special arrangement with Chaplin; 1939—seven-year contract with Paramount; began acting in radio productions; 1944—five-month USO tour of Far East; Paramount renewed contract for seven years; 1947—in *Winterset* at Abbey Theatre, Dublin; 1950s—occasional TV appearances. **Died:** Near Ronco, Switzerland, 23 April 1990.

Films as Actress:

1929   *The Locked Door* (Fitzmaurice); *Berth Marks* (Lewis R. Foster—short) (as train passenger)
1931   *City Streets* (Mamoulian); *The Girl Habit* (Cline) (as lingerie salesgirl)
1932   *The Mouthpiece* (Flood and Nugent) (as girl at party); *Show Business* (White—short); *Young Ironsides* (Parrott—short); *Pack Up Your Troubles* (George Marshall and McCarey); *Girl Grief* (Parrott—short); *The Kid from Spain* (McCarey) (as "Goldwyn" girl)
1933   *Roman Scandals* (Tuttle)
1934   *Kid Millions* (Del Ruth)
1936   **Modern Times** (Chaplin) (as gamine); *The Bohemian Girl* (Horne and Rogers)

1938   *The Young in Heart* (Wallace) (as Leslie Saunders); *Dramatic School* (Sinclair) (as Nana)
1939   *The Women* (Cukor) (as Miriam Aarons); *The Cat and the Canary* (Nugent) (as Joyce Norman)
1940   *The Ghost Breakers* (George Marshall) (as Mary Carter); **The Great Dictator** (Chaplin) (as Hannah); *Northwest Mounted Police* (Cecil B. DeMille) (as Louvette Corbeau); *Second Chorus* (Potter) (as Ellen Miller)
1941   *Pot o' Gold* (*The Golden Hour*) (George Marshall) (as Molly McCorkle); *Hold Back the Dawn* (Leisen) (as Anita Dixon); *Nothing but the Truth* (Nugent) (as Gwen Saunders)
1942   *The Lady Has Plans* (Lanfield) (as Sidney Royce); *Reap the Wild Wind* (Cecil B. DeMille) (as Loxie Claiborne); *The Forest Rangers* (George Marshall) (as Celia Huston); *Star Spangled Rhythm* (George Marshall)
1943   *The Crystal Ball* (Nugent) (as Toni Gerard); *So Proudly We Hail* (Sandrich) (as Lt. Joan O'Doul)
1944   *Standing Room Only* (Lanfield) (as Jane Rogers); *I Love a Soldier* (Sandrich) (as Eva Morgan)
1945   *Duffy's Tavern* (Walker) (as guest); *Kitty* (Leisen) (title role)
1946   *Diary of a Chambermaid* (*Le Journal d'une femme de chambre*) (Renoir) (as Celestine)
1947   *Suddenly It's Spring* (Leisen) (as Mary Morely); *Variety Girl* (George Marshall) (as guest); *Unconquered* (Cecil B. DeMille) (as Abigail Martha "Abby" Hale); *An Ideal Husband* (Korda) (as Mrs. Cheveley)
1948   *On Our Merry Way* (*A Miracle Can Happen*) (King Vidor and Fenton) (as Martha Pease); *Hazard* (George Marshall) (as Ellen Crane)
1949   *Bride of Vengeance* (Leisen) (as Lucretia Borgia); *Anna Lucasta* (Rapper) (title role)
1950   *Del odio nace el amor* (*The Torch*; *Bandit General*) (Fernández) (as María Dolores, + assoc pr)
1952   *Babes in Bagdad* (Ulmer) (as Kyra)
1953   *Vice Squad* (*The Girl in Room 17*) (Laven) (as Mona); *Paris Model* (Alfred E. Green) (as Betty Barnes); *Charge of the Lancers* (Castle) (as Tanya); *Sins of Jezebel* (Le Borg) (title role)
1954   *The Stranger Came Home* (*The Unholy Four*) (Fisher) (as Angie Vickers)
1964   *Gli indifferenti* (*A Time of Indifference*) (Maselli) (as Maria Grazia Ardengo)
1972   *The Snoop Sisters* (*Female Instinct*) (Leonard Stern—for TV) (as Norma Treet)

Publications

On GODDARD: books—

Morella, Joe, and Edward Z. Epstein, *Paulette: The Adventurous Life of Paulette Goddard*, New York, 1985.
Gilbert, Julie Goldsmith, *Opposite Attraction: The Lives of Erich Maria Remarque and Paulette Goddard*, New York, 1995.

On GODDARD: articles—

Current Biography 1946, New York, 1946.
Gorney, J., "Paulette Goddard: Lost Too Many Good Parts," in *Films in Review* (New York), August/September 1974.
Obituary in *New York Times*, 24 April 1990.
Obituary in *Variety* (New York), 25 April 1990.

*   *   *

Paulette Goddard

Paulette Goddard began her career at age 14 as a Ziegfeld girl billed as "Peaches." Although she retired in her teens to wed a timber magnate, Edgar James, she embarked for Hollywood when her marriage failed and moved from bit parts in the 1930s to become one of Paramount's leading ladies in the 1940s. Goddard never allowed herself to be typecast, and variety best characterizes both her choice of roles and of husbands. Her pictures ranged from comedies to musicals and serious drama, and she played everything from the gamine to the frightened heroine and the siren.

After a series of very minor roles, she met Charles Chaplin (whom she eventually married), who gave her the part of the beautiful waif in his last silent release *Modern Times*. Her performance was fresh, seemingly spontaneous, and was widely praised. Her appearance almost netted her the part of Scarlett O'Hara, and she was under contract to Selznick until she was sold to Paramount. With the latter she had her first starring role in *The Cat and the Canary*, opposite Bob Hope. At Paramount and on loan to other studios she was to appear in a wide range of films, including musicals with Fred Astaire (*Second Chorus*) and James Stewart (*Pot o' Gold*), another Hope film (*Nothing but the Truth*) and, with Ray Milland, a spy film (*The Lady Has Plans*), a comedy (*The Crystal Ball*), and a hit costumer (*Kitty*). She received her only Oscar nomination, as best supporting actress, for her performance in a war drama (*So Proudly We Hail*), with Claudette Colbert and Veronica Lake. Goddard also appeared in Chaplin's *The Great Dictator*, their second and last film together (they later divorced).

Of all her roles, critics usually deem one of her best to have been in *Diary of a Chambermaid*, co-produced by Jean Renoir and Goddard's third husband, Burgess Meredith, and directed by Renoir. Goddard starred as an outspoken maid in a 19th-century French household, in what is often regarded as one of Renoir's best American films. Her career was in decline by the 1950s, however, and she appeared in a number of B pictures such as *Babes in Bagdad*, *The Sins of Jezebel*, and *The Charge of the Lancers*. With her marriage to Erich Maria Remarque in 1958, she ceased working, appearing only in the Italian *Gli indifferenti* (based on an Alberto Moravia novel) in 1964 and making a rare television appearance in *The Snoop Sisters* in 1972.

—Frances M. Malpezzi, updated by Frank Uhle

GOLDBERG, Whoopi

Nationality: American. **Born:** Caryn Johnson in New York City, 13 November 1949 (some sources say 1955). **Education:** Attended the New York School for Performing Arts. **Family:** Married 1) (divorced 1974), one daughter: Alexandra; 2) David Claessen, 1986 (divorced 1988); 3) Lyle Trachtenberg, 1994 (separated). **Career:** 1974—moved to California; worked as mortuary beautician; worked in repertory theater with Blake Street Hawkeyes, Berkeley; also co-founder, San Diego Repertory Company, and member, Spontaneous Combustion improvisational group; 1983—*The Spook Show*, one-woman show off-Broadway, seen by Mike Nichols, led to Broadway run, 1984, and film debut in *The Color Purple*, 1985; 1990—in TV series *Bagdad Cafe*; 1988-93—occasional appearances in TV series *Star Trek: The Next Generation*; 1992-93—host of TV talk show *The Whoopi Goldberg Show*; 1994 and 1996—host of the Academy Awards. **Awards:** Oscar for Best Supporting Actress, for *Ghost*, 1990. **Address:** c/o CAA, 9830 Wilshire Boulevard, Beverly Hills, CA 90212, U.S.A.

Films as Actress:

1985   *The Color Purple* (Spielberg) (as Celie)
1986   *Jumpin' Jack Flash* (Penny Marshall) (as Terry Doolittle)

1987   *Burglar* (Wilson) (as Bernice Rhodenbarr); *The Telephone* (Torn) (as Vashti Blue); *Scared Straight: 10 Years Later* (doc) (as host)
1988   *Fatal Beauty* (Holland) (as Rita Rizzoli); *Clara's Heart* (Mulligan) (as Clara Mayfield)
1989   *Homer and Eddie* (Konchalovsky) (as Eddie Cervi); *Beverly Hills Brats* (Sotos); *The Long Walk Home* (Pearce) (as Odessa Cotter); *Kiss Shot* (London)
1990   *Ghost* (Zucker) (as Oda Mae Brown)
1991   *Soapdish* (Hoffman) (as Rose Schwartz); *House Party 2* (Jackson) (as Professor)
1992   *Wisecracks* (Singer—doc); *Sister Act* (Ardolino) (as Deloris Van Cartier/Sister Mary Clarence); *Sarafina!* (Roodt) (as Mary Masembuko); *The Player* (Altman) (as Detective Avery); *The Magical World of Chuck Jones* (Daugherty)
1993   *Sister Act 2: Back in the Habit* (Duke) (as Deloris Van Cartier/Sister Mary Clarence); *National Lampoon's Loaded Weapon 1* (Quintano) (as Sergeant York); *Made in America* (Benjamin) (as Sarah Matthews)
1994   *The Lion King* (Minkoff) (as voice of Shenzi the Hyena); *Naked in New York* (Algrant) (as Tragedy Mask); *Liberation* (Schwartzman—doc) (as narrator); *The Pagemaster* (Hunt and Johnston) (as Fantasy); *Corrina, Corrina* (Jessie Nelson) (title role); *The Little Rascals* (Spheeris) (as Buckwheat's mom); *The Celluloid Closet* (Epstein and Friedman—doc) (as interviewee); *Star Trek: Generations* (David Carson) (as Guinan)
1995   *Moonlight and Valentino* (Anspaugh) (as Sylvie Morrow); *Boys on the Side* (Herbert Ross) (as Jane DeLuca); *T. Rex* (Betuel) (as Kate)
1996   *The Associate* (Petrie); *Bogus* (Jewison); *Eddie*

Publications

By GOLDBERG: book—

Alice (for children), with John Rocco, New York, 1992.

By GOLDBERG: articles—

Interview in *Inter/View* (New York), December 1984.
Interview in *American Film* (Washington, D.C.), December 1985.
Interview with Matthew Modine, in *Interview* (New York), June 1992.
Interview with Rod Lurie, in *Los Angeles Times Magazine*, May 1993.

On GOLDBERG: book—

Adams, Mary Agnes, *Whoopi Goldberg: From Street to Stardom*, New York, 1993.

On GOLDBERG: articles—

Current Biography 1985, New York, 1985.
Erickson, Steve, "Whoopi Goldberg," in *Rolling Stone* (New York), 8 May 1986.
Stone, Laurie, "Goldberg Variations," in *Village Voice* (New York), 17 January 1989.
Randolph, L. B., "The Whoopi Goldberg Nobody Knows," in *Ebony* (Chicago), March 1991.
Dillon, Cathy, "Whooping It Up," in *The Voice* (London), 9 April 1991.
Skow, John, and P. E. Cole, "The Joy of Being Whoopi," in *Time* (New York), 21 September 1992.

*   *   *

Whoopi Goldberg in *The Color Purple*

Whoopi Goldberg is a spunky, likable African-American character actress/comedienne whose many talents have transcended the industry's initially sorely underutilizing her talents.

Her debut performance in *The Color Purple* was proof of Goldberg's celluloid abilities. Based on Alice Walker's acclaimed novel, the film is a stirring ode to African-American sisterhood which was controversial for its depiction of black males as inept, womanizing brutes and its many Academy Award nominations (including one for Goldberg, but excluding one for director Steven Spielberg) without earning a single statue. Goldberg offers a sensitive performance as the passive, much-abused Celie, a deceptively simple, multifaceted character who is "black . . . poor . . . ugly . . . (and) a woman (which means that she's) nothing at all." It is a difficult role, which Goldberg pulls off with the aplomb of a screen veteran.

After this promising debut, Goldberg found herself wasted in a series of uniformly dreadful features: *Jumpin' Jack Flash*, *Burglar*, *Fatal Beauty*, *Clara's Heart*, *The Telephone*, and *Homer and Eddie*. In each, her performance borders on self-caricature, with her character either being poorly defined or an overbearing know-it-all.

Goldberg's screen career was headed for oblivion when it was salvaged by her Oscar-winning turn in *Ghost*, the surprise smash of 1990. Nevertheless, her character—Oda Mae Brown, a storefront medium who conveys messages from a recently deceased Manhattanite (Patrick Swayze) to his grieving widow (Demi Moore)—is a throwback to an ill-informed earlier era. Oda Mae is little more than a slimmed-down Hattie McDaniel: a sassy, bossy contemporary mammy whose role within the scenario is dependent upon those of the hero and heroine. She is an African-American stereotype, an unenlightened picture of a black woman for white moviegoers.

Fortunately for Goldberg, her success in *Ghost* did not lead to her being forever cast as a comical caricature. First she offered a solid performance in *The Long Walk Home* as a domestic in the American South in the 1950s; she later was to play a not-dissimilar role in *Corrina, Corrina*. After a fine turn as a police detective in Robert Altman's *The Player*— she was one of the few stars who appeared in the film playing a character, rather than in a cameo—Goldberg was perfectly cast in the smash-hit comedy *Sister Act* as an on-the-lam lounge singer who hides in a convent after witnessing a murder. The film was so successful that it inspired a sequel, *Sister Act 2: Back in the Habit*, and Goldberg has since had her pick of projects. The most impressive of these are: *The Lion King*, in which she is the voice of Shenzi, and the female buddy movies *Boys on the Side* and *Moonlight and Valentino*. The latter films serve in marked contrast to *Ghost* in that her characters—Jane in *Boys on the Side* and Sylvie Morrow in *Moonlight and Valentino*—are central to, rather than satellites of, the dramatic action, equal to, not subordinates of, her co-stars. Furthermore, they have come full circle from Celie in that they are anything but physically and psychologically beaten down by men; Jane and Sylvie are fully independent, modern, and contemporary—and Jane even is a lesbian.

Offscreen, Goldberg has found herself at the center of controversy. Her recipe for "Jewish American Princess Fried Chicken," published in a book titled *Cooking in Litchfield Hills*, offers instructions to "send a chauffeur to your favorite butcher shop for the chicken," "watch your nails" while shaking the chicken in a brown paper bag, and "have cook prepare rest of meal while you touch up your makeup." During her brief romance with Ted Danson, which began when they co-starred in *Made in America*, he showed up at a Friar's Club function in blackface and delivered an epithet-laden monologue intended, as he explained, "to amuse my dear friend Whoopi." Yet, observed an attendee, "Whoopi was the only one laughing."

But Goldberg has emerged unscathed. Furthermore, while a full-fledged movie star, she is not averse to appearing on the small screen. She has been a regular on the television series *Bagdad Cafe* and *Star Trek: The Next Generation*, appeared on numerous musical and comedy specials, and even hosted her own syndicated talk show.

—Rob Edelman

GONG Li

Nationality: Chinese. **Born:** Shenyang, China, 1965. **Family:** Formerly the constant companion of Zhang Yimou. **Education:** Studied acting at the Central Academy of Drama. **Career:** 1988—discovered by Zhang Yimou while an acting student, and cast in her screen debut, *Red Sorghum*; 1989—remained at the Central Academy of Drama as a teacher after graduation. **Awards:** Best Actress Award, Venice Festival, for *The Story of Qiu Ju*, 1992; Best Supporting Actress, New York Film Critics Circle, for *Farewell, My Concubine*, 1993.

Films as Actress:

1987 *Hong gaoliang* (*Red Sorghum*) (Zhang Yimou) (as Nine, the Grandmother)

1989 *The Empress Dowager* (Li Hanhsiang); *Daihao Meizhoubao* (*Operation Cougar*) (Zhang Yimou); *Qin Yong* (*A Terra-Cotta Warrior*) (Ching Siutung) (as Hon Tong)

1990 *Ju Dou* (Zhang Yimou) (title role)

1991 ***Dahong Denglong Gaogao Guo*** (*Raise the Red Lantern*) (Zhang Yimou) (as Songlian); *Back to Shanghai*; *Haomen Yeyan* (*The Banquet*) (Clifton Ko and Hark Tsui)

1992 *Mungding sifan* (*Mary from Beijing*) (Sylvia Chang) (as Ma Li); ***Qiu Ju Da Guansi*** (*The Story of Qiu Ju*) (Zhang Yimou) (as Wan Qiu Ju)

1993 ***Ba Wang Bie Ji*** (*Farewell My Concubine*) (Chen Kaige) (as Juxian); *The Flirting Scholar* (Richard Lee); *Demi-Gods and Semi-Devils*

1994 *To Live* (Zhang Yimou) (as Jiazhen); *Xi chu bawang* (*The Great Conqueror's Concubine*) (Stephen Shin) (as Lu Zhi); *La Peintre* (*Hua Hun*; *Soul of a Painter*) (Huang Shuquin) (as Pan Yuliang)

1995 *Yao ayao yao dao waipo qiao* (*Shanghai Triad*) (Zhang Yimou) (as Ziao Jingbao); *Temptress Moon* (*Shadow of a Flower*) (Chen Kaige)

Publications

By GONG LI: articles—

"One in a Billion," interview with Philip Lopate, in *Interview* (New York), March 1991.

"Un travail comme un autre," interview with L. Codelli, in *Positif* (Paris), December 1992.

On GONG LI: articles—

Feinstein, Howard, "A Chinese Actress Blossoms on the Screen," in *New York Times*, 11 April 1993.

Reynaud, B., "Gong Li and the Glamour of the Chinese Star," in *Sight and Sound* (London), 15 August 1993.

"China's Screen Siren," in *New Yorker*, 28 November 1994.

Hooper, Joseph, "Raise the Red Curtain," in *Esquire* (New York), December 1994.

* * *

By any standard, Chinese fifth-generation director Zhang Yimou—whose credits include *Ju Dou*, *Raise the Red Lantern*, *The Story of Qiu Ju*, *To Live*, and *Shanghai Triad*—is a world-class filmmaker. And by any standard, Gong Li, his favorite star and leading lady, is a world-class actress. Whether playing simple rural peasants or sophisticated urban temptresses, Gong remains an eminently watchable screen presence. When she is cast in stories set in precommunist China, her roles most often reflect the manner in which women have been treated within traditional Chinese society. When her films are set during or after the 1949 revolution, she plays a woman who suffers, along with her loved ones, at the whims of a callous political state.

Raise the Red Lantern, set in the 1920s, is arguably the best of the actress's "prerevolution" films made with her mentor. Gong plays Songlian, a pretty 19-year-old university student whose father has just died and who is pressured by her stepmother into marrying a rich man. She thus becomes a concubine, the "fourth mistress" in the house of a wealthy feudal nobleman who is addressed by servants and wives alike as "Master." Zhang's primary interest is not this character, but rather Songlian—how she is affected by this marriage, and her relationships with the other mistresses. Gong offers a subtly revealing performance. From the film's opening shot, the various emotions that register on her face speak volumes about her character.

Gong plays a similar role in *Ju Dou*—a young peasant woman coerced into marrying an aged, embittered, and abusive dye mill owner during the 1920s. In *Red Sorghum*, her screen debut, she also is a peasant who is supposed to wed a much older man, this one a winemaker, but ends up as the partner of a man who is closer to her in age.

Shanghai Triad, the most recent Zhang-Gong collaboration, is quite a departure for the pair. Set in the 1930s, it tells the story of a 14-year-old boy who is "fresh from the country," and who is a distant relative of the most powerful gang boss in Shanghai. The teen is brought to the city to work as servant to Ziao Jingbao (Gong), the mobster's glamorous but crass and ill-fated nightclub singer-mistress. *Shanghai Triad* is not Zhang's best film, as it lacks the urgency of his better earlier works. Nevertheless, Gong is ever-resplendent as Ziao Jingbao, a woman who despite her surface toughness is revealed to be a sex object and a victim.

Gong's two "postrevolution" films with Zhang are equally potent. *To Live* is a forceful drama about the fortunes of one Chinese family and how its members become swept up in the events of recent history. Gong plays Jiazhen, wife of the son of a prominent family in a small village. The lives of Jiazhen, her husband, and children undergo much turmoil after the revolution, with the scenario mirroring Zhang's clear and sobering censure of the hypocrisy of life under Mao. Gong is especially fine as she responds with raw emotion to the crises in Jiazhen's life, and in the lives of her children. In *The Story of Qiu Ju*, Gong plays Wang Qiu Ju, an unsophisticated but resolute Chinese farm woman who goes to all lengths to obtain an apology after her husband is brutalized by her village's stubborn leader. This story of a woman's quest for fairness is an adroit examination of government hypocrisy, with Gong a tower of strength.

The sole Zhang-Gong collaboration little known in the West is *Operation Cougar*, the saga of an airline hijacking in which the ac-

Gong Li in *Dahong Denglong Gaogao Guo*

tress has a supporting role as a stewardess. Her one major role in a film not directed by Zhang is Chen Kaige's *Farewell, My Concubine*, an epic that emphasizes the same political concerns found in Zhang's work. *Farewell, My Concubine* features a trio of main characters who share a complex bond. The first two are Chinese opera stars, "stage brothers" who were students at the same acting school and who have become famous for playing the king and his concubine in the title opera. The third is the feisty yet vulnerable prostitute (Gong) who marries one of them.

Farewell, My Concubine was released a scant five years after Gong had made her screen debut in *Red Sorghum*. Yet she had already developed into one of the international cinema's premier actresses.

—Rob Edelman

GORDON, Ruth

Nationality: American. **Born:** Ruth Gordon Jones in Wollaston, Massachusetts, 30 October 1896. **Education:** Attended Wollaston Grammar School and Quincy High School, Wollaston; American Academy of Dramatic Arts, New York. **Family:** Married 1) the actor Gregory Kelly, 1921 (died 1927); 2) the writer Garson Kanin, 1942, son: Jones. **Career:** 1915—Broadway debut in *Peter Pan*; film debut

as extra in *Camille*; 1915-40—on stage, in several plays by Booth Tarkington, opposite Humphrey Bogart in *Saturday's Children*, 1927, in *The Country Wife* in London, 1936, and in Wilder's adaptation of *A Doll's House*, 1937; 1940—billed film debut in *Abe Lincoln in Illinois*; 1944—first of her own plays produced in New York, *Over Twenty-One* (later filmed in her screenwritten version as *The Actress*); 1947—first screenplay, with Kanin, for *A Double Life*; 1955—in stage play *The Matchmaker* in Edinburgh, London and New York; 1965—beginning of a series of film roles in character parts. **Awards:** Best Supporting Actress Academy Award for *Rosemary's Baby*, 1968. **Died:** 28 August 1985.

Films as Actress:

1915   *Camille* (Capellani); *The Whirl of Life* (Bailey)
1940   *Abe Lincoln in Illinois* (*Spirit of the People*) (Cromwell); *The Story of Dr. Ehrlich's Magic Bullet* (*Dr. Ehrlich's Magic Bullet*) (Dieterle); *Information Please* (nos. 2 and 8 of 1940-41 series) (appearances)
1942   *Two-Faced Woman* (Cukor)
1943   *Edge of Darkness* (Milestone); *Action in the North Atlantic* (Bacon)
1965   *Inside Daisy Clover* (Mulligan) (as The Dealer); *Lord Love a Duck* (Axelrod) (as Stella Barnard)
1968   *Rosemary's Baby* (Polanski) (as Minnie Castevet)

1969 *What Ever Happened to Aunt Alice* (Katzin) (as Alice Dimmock)
1970 *Where's Poppa?* (Reiner) (as Mrs. Hocheiser)
1971 *Harold and Maude* (Ashby) (as Maude)
1973 *Isn't It Shocking?* (Badham—for TV)
1976 *The Big Bus* (Frawley); *The Great Houdinis* (Shavelson—for TV); *Look What's Happened to Rosemary's Baby* (*Rosemary's Baby II*) (O'Steen—for TV)
1977 *The Prince of Central Park* (Hart—for TV)
1978 *Perfect Gentlemen* (Cooper—for TV); *Every Which Way but Loose* (Fargo) (as Ma)
1979 *Boardwalk* (Verona) (as Becky Rosen); *Scavenger Hunt* (Schultz—for TV) (as Arvilla)
1980 *My Bodyguard* (Bill) (as Gramma); *Any Which Way You Can* (Van Horn) (as Ma)
1982 *Don't Go to Sleep* (Lang—for TV)
1983 *Jimmy the Kid* (Nelson) (as Bernice)
1984 *Mugsy's Girls* (Brodie)
1985 *Maxie* (Aaron) (as Mrs. Lavin)

Films as Co-Scriptwriter with Garson Kanin:

1947 *A Double Life* (Cukor)
1949 *Adam's Rib* (Cukor)
1952 *The Marrying Kind* (Cukor); *Pat and Mike* (Cukor)
1953 *The Actress* (Gordon only) (Cukor)

Publications

By GORDON: books—

Over Twenty-One (play), New York, 1944.
Years Ago (play), New York, 1947.
The Leading Lady (play), New York, 1949.
A Very Rich Woman (play), New York, 1966.
Myself among Others, New York, 1971.
Adam's Rib (screenplay), with Garson Kanin, New York, 1972.
My Side (autobiography), New York, 1976.
An Open Book, New York, 1980.

By GORDON: articles—

"A Great Lady in the Grand Manner," in *Stage*, January 1937.
"Legitimate Laughton," in *Theatre Arts* (New York), November 1950.
Interview by G. O'Brien, in *Inter/View* (New York), March 1972.

On GORDON: books—

Reed, Rex, *Conversations in the Raw: Dialogues, Monologues, and Selected Short Subjects*, New York, 1969.
Rosen, Marjorie, *Popcorn Venus*, New York, 1973.
Kanin, Garson, *It Takes a Long Time to Become Young . . .* , New York, 1978.

On GORDON: articles—

Young, Stark, "Ruth Gordon Compared with Helen Hayes," in the *New Republic* (New York), 23 December 1931.
Crichton, Kyle, "Gifted Gordon," in *Collier's* (New York), 27 May 1944.
Houghton, Norris, "The Kanins on Broadway," in *Theatre Arts* (New York), December 1946.

Houston, Penelope, "Cukor and the Kanins," in *Sight and Sound* (London), Spring 1955.
Obituary, in *Variety* (New York), 4 September 1985.

*   *   *

The pattern of Ruth Gordon's movie-making career is as bizarre as the parts with which she is now primarily identified. She played brief silent film roles in 1915 and 1916, then did not reappear on the screen until 1940, when she was 44 years old and a firmly established star of the Broadway stage. She made five films in rapid succession, initially appearing as wives to a president (*Abe Lincoln in Illinois*) and to the scientist who discovered a cure for syphilis (*Dr. Ehrlich's Magic Bullet*), then supporting Greta Garbo in her film farewell (*Two-Faced Woman*), directed for MGM by Gordon's friend George Cukor. In 1943 she made two Warner Brothers anti-Nazi pictures starring Errol Flynn (*Edge of Darkness*) and Humphrey Bogart (*Action in the North Atlantic*)—then, for the second time, vanished from the screen for more than 20 years.

Despite a more enduring return to films in 1965, it is strongly arguable that Gordon's most imposing contribution to American cinema occurred during her second long hiatus from screen acting. In this period, with her husband, Garson Kanin, she wrote the screenplays for three classic comedies—Katharine Hepburn and Spencer Tracy's *Adam's Rib* and *Pat and Mike*, and Judy Holliday's *The Marrying Kind*—and for Ronald Colman's Oscar-winning drama, *A Double Life*. Alone, she wrote the screenplay for *The Actress*, based on her autobiographical play *Years Ago* and starring Jean Simmons as the young Ruth Gordon and Spencer Tracy as her father. All five films were directed by George Cukor.

It is difficult to match the literate, wittily sophisticated theater star who wrote Broadway plays, screenplays, and memoirs and played Ibsen, Chekhov, and Shaw alongside frothy comedy with the figure who emerges from the screen and television roles since the mid-1960s. But two Broadway plays—the first a great hit, the second unjustly neglected—accurately prefigure Ruth Gordon's recent screen persona. As the original Dolly Levi in Thornton Wilder's *The Matchmaker* (1955; the source for the musical *Hello, Dolly!*) and as Rona Halpern in Lillian Hellman's *My Mother, My Father and Me* (1963), Gordon played manipulative, money-grasping women in exaggerated, highflying comic style. Both women are cut from the same cloth but Dolly is cute and lovable, embraced by an audience that is, in contrast, utterly repelled by the grotesque Rona.

Gordon's subsequent screen performances replay combinations of Dolly Levi and Rona Halpern. Her comically repulsive old ladies—"elderly" seems a singularly inappropriate term to describe them—sashay into the frame, droppin' their final g's, brandishing their age in implicit defense of their loony hostility. Yet in Gordon's performances these women seem, Dolly-like, to court the viewer's affection with extravagant winks and incessant body flutters. ("As an actress I need to think that the whole audience is just lovin' me," she once said. "It's the only way I can come through.")

At their most sentimental, these screen bag ladies are represented by 80-year-old, life-affirming Maude in the cult film *Harold and Maude*; at their most Oedipally demented, by the senile mother in *Where's Poppa?* who became enshrined in movie-advertising history by biting her 35-year-old son (George Segal) on his bare bottom. After resuming her film career, Gordon also played dotty mothers to Natalie Wood (*Inside Daisy Clover*) and Clint Eastwood (*Every Which Way but Loose*; *Any Which Way You Can*) and, notably, blasphemous midwife to *Rosemary's Baby*, for which she won a Best Supporting Actress Academy Award.

—Mark W. Estrin

GOULD, Elliott

Nationality: American. **Born:** Elliott Goldstein in Brooklyn, New York, 29 August 1938. **Education:** Attended a Brooklyn Hebrew School; Charles Lowe's show business school; Professional Children's School, graduated 1955; Columbia University, briefly. **Family:** Married 1) the singer Barbra Streisand, 1963 (divorced 1971), son: Jason Emanuel; 2) Jennifer Bogart, children: Jennifer, Sam. **Career:** Child actor in vaudeville acts and on television; 1957—Broadway debut as chorus boy in *Rumple*, then roles in *Irma la Douce*, 1960, and *I Can Get It for You Wholesale*, 1962; mid-1960s—began study at Actors Studio, New York; 1964—film debut in *The Confession*; 1969—contract with Columbia; co-founder, with Jack Brodsky, Brodsky-Gould production company; 1984—in TV series *E.R.*; 1986—in TV series *Together We Stand*; has appeared in TV mini-series, including *Act of Betrayal*, 1990, and *Bloodlines: Murder in the Family*, 1993; 1995-96—recurring role on TV series *Friends*. **Agent:** William Morris Agency, 1350 Avenue of the Americas, New York, NY 10019, U.S.A.

Films as Actor:

1964   *The Confession* (*Quick, Let's Get Married*; *Seven Different Ways*) (Dieterle) (as the Mute)

1968   *The Night They Raided Minsky's* (Friedkin) (as Billy Minsky)

1969   *Bob & Carol & Ted & Alice* (Mazursky) (as Ted Henderson)

1970   *M*A*S*H* (Altman) (as Trapper John McIntyre); *Getting Straight* (Rush) (as Henry Bailey); *Move* (Rosenberg) (as Hiram Jaffe); *I Love My Wife* (Stuart) (as Dr. Richard Burrows)

1971   *Beröringen* (*The Touch*) (Bergman) (as David Kovac); *Little Murders* (Arkin) (as Alfred Chamberlain); *Ingmar Bergman* (Björkman) (appearance)

1973   *The Long Goodbye* (Altman) (as Philip Marlowe)

1974   *Busting* (Hyams) (as Keneely); *S*P*Y*S* (Kershner) (as Griff); *California Split* (Altman) (as Charlie Waters); *Who?* (*Man without a Face*) (Gold) (as Sean Rogers)

1975   *Nashville* (Altman) (as guest); *Whiffs* (*C.A.S.H.*) (Post) (as Dudley Frapper); *I Will . . . I Will . . . for Now* (Panama) (as Les Bingham)

1976   *Mean Johnny Barrows* (Williamson) (as the Professor); *Harry and Walter Go to New York* (Rydell) (as Walter Hill)

1977   *A Bridge Too Far* (Attenborough) (as Col. Stout)

1978   *Capricorn One* (Hyams) (as Robert Caulfield); *The Silent Partner* (Duke) (as Miles Cullen); *Matilda* (Daniel Mann) (as Bernie Bonnelli)

1979   *Escape to Athena* (Cosmatos) (as Charlie Dane); *The Lady Vanishes* (Page); *The Muppet Movie* (Frawley) (as guest)

1980   *The Last Flight of Noah's Ark* (Jarrott) (as Noah Dugan); *Falling in Love Again* (Paul) (as Harry Lewis)

1981   *The Devil and Max Devlin* (Steven Hilliard Stern) (as Max Devlin); *Dirty Tricks* (Rakoff) (as Colin)

1983   *Over the Brooklyn Bridge* (Golan) (as Alby Sherman)

1984   *The Naked Face* (Forbes) (as Angeli); *The Muppets Take Manhattan* (Oz)

1986   *Inside Out* (Taicher) (as Jimmy Morgan); *Vanishing Act* (David Greene—for TV) (as Lieut. Rudameyer); *Together We Stand* (Mackenzie—for TV)

1987   *All Tied Up* (Bonerz—for TV); *I miei primi 40 anni* (*My First 40 Years*; *The Story of a Woman*) (Vanzina) (as Editor)

1988   *Dangerous Love* (Ollstein) (as Rick); *The Telephone* (Torn) (as Rodney); *Conspiracy: The Trial of the Chicago 8* (Kagan—for TV) (as Leonard Weinglass); *Lethal Obsession* (*Der Joker*) (Patzak) (as Serge Gart)

1989   *The Big Picture* (Guest) (as an attorney); *Night Visitor* (*Never Cry Devil*) (Hitzig) (as Ron Devereaux); *Gioco al massacra* (Damiani)

1990   *The Lemon Sisters* (Chopra) (as Fred Frank); *Scandalo segreto* (*Act of Betrayal*; *Secret Scandal*) (Vitti—for TV); *Tolgo il disturbo* (Risi); *Stolen: One Husband* (Caitlin Adams—for TV) (as Martin Slade)

1991   *Bugsy* (Levinson) (as Harry Greenberg); *Dead Men Don't Die* (Marmorstein) (as Barry Barron)

1992   **The Player** (Altman) (as himself); *Beyond Justice* (Tessari) (as lawyer); *Hitz* (Sachs); *Somebody's Daughter* (Sargent—for TV) (as Hindeman); *Frogs!* (for TV) (as Bill)

1993   *Wet and Wild Summer* (*Exchange Lifeguards*) (Murphy) (as Mike McCain); *Amore!* (Doumani) (as George Levine); *Hoffman's Hunger* (De Winter) (as Hoffman)

1994   *The Glass Shield* (Burnett) (as Greenwall); *The Feminine Touch* (Janis) (as Sen. George M. Kohn); *Naked Gun 33 1/3: The Final Insult* (Segal) (as himself); *White Man's Burden* (Hines) (as Mr. Baum)

1995   *The Dangerous* (for TV) (as Lips Levine); *A Boy Called Hate* (Marcus); *Let It Be Me* (Bergstein)

1996   *Kicking and Screaming* (Baumbach) (as Grover's dad)

Publications

By GOULD: articles—

Interview in *Playboy* (Chicago), November 1970.

Interview in *Film Review* (London), September 1980.

Interview with Iain F. McAsh, in *Films Illustrated* (London), November 1980.

Films (London), February 1984.

On GOULD: articles—

Cover story in *Time* (New York), 7 September 1970.

Mayer, M., "Elliott Gould as the Entrepreneur," in *Fortune* (New York), October 1970.

Current Biography 1971, New York, 1971.

Cieutat, Michel, "Elliott Gould ou l'argus de la survie," in *Positif* (Paris), February 1975.

Haskell, Molly, "Gould vs. Redford vs. Nicholson," in *The Movie Star*, edited by Elisabeth Weis, New York, 1981.

Hicks, Jack, "Elliott Gould: Trying to Doctor an Ailing Career," in *TV Guide*, 1 December 1984.

*   *   *

Elliott Gould first shot to fame in Paul Mazursky's *Bob & Carol & Ted & Alice* as the nebbishy husband of an unsettlingly provocative wife. Gould's Ted was the one who held up the orgy by lingering in the bathroom. Gould grew up in the era of Jewish assimilation and his Ted is a generalized version of the guy who does not know exactly how to handle having made it in. His cultural confusions could stand for those of all men caught in the upheavals of the late 1960s, and he became a huge star.

Gould next co-starred in Robert Altman's comic sensation *M*A*S*H*, and the superb comic skills he brought to the role of the schlemiel who is late for an orgy enabled him to put across a new style of outsider hipness. As a combat doctor fighting, outraging, or ignoring the government bureaucracy during the Korean War, Gould, with his moustache and sideburns, clearly played to the audience's disillusionment with the government's new Asian conflict. He brought comic fencing skills to the contemporary antiestablishment urge. Thus, in *M*A*S*H*, and even more in his two other starring roles for Altman, *The Long Goodbye* and *California Split*, Gould went beyond the persona of the man raised in a repressed age who stumbles into the greater sexual availability of the 1960s and 1970s, the staple of both square and hip farces in those decades. In *The Long Goodbye* Gould, with the rougher nap of the comic naturalism that Altman brought to American movies, updated Philip Marlowe, who is now a good-boy zhlub whose virtue lies in being out of the game. Mumbling the narration to himself, oddly more festive and certainly less corny than the usual private eye voice-over, Gould becomes the offbeat host for a tour of LA lifestyle decadence, the kind that does not make you envy the rich. Gould's Marlowe may not come out on top, exactly, but he is decent and he has got his own style. A private eye is dragged into a mess not of his making—but in *California Split* Gould's Charlie is not so removed from the action. Paired with a more anxious George Segal, Gould is the gambling demon personified, a man who does not worry as much as he should. And because in *California Split* Charlie tempts fate, Gould's rich, improvisational, comic realism has an edge, even more so than in the murder mystery *The Long Goodbye*.

Gould was not careful with his career. He was everywhere for a few years and then was gone from moviegoers' consciousness, like *that*. As was noted at the time, he embodied what Philip Roth brought to American fiction—the urges of the Jewish boy who feels sexier than his image. (And Gould had much more of a Roth hero's ambivalent horniness than Richard Benjamin, who was cast in *Goodbye, Columbus* and *Portnoy's Complaint*.) But Gould cashed in on Zeitgeist when he was in fact a much more exciting kind of actor than mere synchronicity could have made him. Pictures such as *Harry and Walter Go to New York* in 1976, which return him to the role of the Jewish clown, killed his momentum, as if he had forgotten he was hip-sexy. Some mistakes were more understandable than others. You can certainly appreciate the challenge of appearing opposite Bibi Andersson in Ingmar Bergman's *The Touch*, as an unstable Jewish archaeologist, the child of Holocaust victims, but it is one of his worst performances. Bergman's conception of character is not contemporary, and Gould does not demonstrate the ability to reach the universal through the universal, as Bergman's actors must. Gould's performance in 1991's *Bugsy*, however, as an old friend Warren Beatty has to kill, shows that even in a brief role he can still turn the screen into an actor's party. As he chatted with Beatty and Annette Bening from the backseat of the car on the way to his execution, Gould gives such loopy readings that he cracks the stars up. Gould still clearly has his talent; we can only hope he will get more parts that bring it out.

—Alan Dale

GRABLE, Betty

Nationality: American. **Born:** Ruth Elizabeth Grable in St. Louis, Missouri, 18 December 1916. **Education:** Attended Mary Institute, St. Louis; Hollywood Professional School; Ernest Belcher Academy; Albertina Rasch School. **Family:** Married 1) the actor Jackie Coogan, 1938 (divorced 1941); 2) the musician Harry James, 1943 (divorced 1965), daughters: Victoria, Jessica. **Career:** Child vaudeville singer and dancer; 1929—her mother arranged for her film debut at age 13, in *Let's Go Places*; Fox contract annulled when her age is discovered; 1930-32—contract with Goldwyn; 1932—member of Ted Fiorita's Band as vocalist; worked for RKO and Paramount during the remainder of the 1930s; 1935—toured with Jackie Coogan in vaudeville show; 1940—in featured role on stage in *Du Barry Was a Lady*; 1940-53—contract with 20th Century-Fox; on television in *Twentieth Cen-*

tury; 1960s—on stage in various productions, including *Hello, Dolly!*, 1965-67. **Died:** 2 July 1973.

Films as Actress:

1929 *Let's Go Places (Mirth and Melody)* (Strayer)

1930 *Happy Days* (Stoloff); *Fox Movietone Follies of 1930 (The New Movietone Follies of 1930)* (Stoloff); *Whoopee!* (Freeland) (as chorus girl)

1931 *Kiki* (Taylor); *Palmy Days* (Sutherland) (as chorus girl); *Ex-Sweeties* (Neilan—short); *Crashing Hollywood* (Arbuckle—short)

1932 *The Greeks Had a Word for Them* (Sherman); *Lady! Please!* (Lord—short); *Hollywood Luck* (Arbuckle—short); *Probation (Second Chances)* (Thorpe); *The Flirty Sleepwalker* (Lord—short); *Hollywood Lights* (Arbuckle—short); *Hold 'em Jail* (Taurog); *Over the Counter* (Cummings—short); *The Kid from Spain* (McCarey)

1933 *Cavalcade* (Lloyd); *Sweetheart of Sigma Chi (Girl of My Dreams)* (Marin) (as orchestra member); *Melody Cruise* (Sandrich) (as stewardess); *Child of Manhattan* (Buzzell); *What Price Innocence? (Shall the Children Pay?)* (Mack); *Air Tonic* (White—short)

1934 *Hips, Hips, Hooray!* (Sandrich); *Love Detectives* (Gottler—short); *Business Is a Pleasure* (Cline—short); *The Gay Divorcee (The Gay Divorce)* (Sandrich); *Student Tour* (Reisner) (as Cayenne); *By Your Leave* (Corrigan)

1935 *The Spirit of 1976* (Jason—short); *The Nitwits* (Stevens) (as Mary); *A Night at the Biltmore Bowl* (Goulding—short); *Old Man Rhythm* (Ludwig) (as Sylvia); *A Quiet Fourth* (Guiol—short)

1936 *Collegiate (The Charm School)* (Murphy) (as Dorothy); *Follow the Fleet* (Sandrich); *Don't Turn 'em Loose* (Stoloff); *Pigskin Parade (The Harmony Parade)* (Butler) (as Laura Watson)

1937 *This Way Please* (Florey) (as Jane Morrow); *Thrill of a Lifetime* (Archainbaud) (as Gwen)

1938 *College Swing (Swing, Teacher, Swing)* (Walsh) (as Betty); *Give Me a Sailor* (Nugent) (as Nancy Larkin); *Campus Confession (Fast Play)* (Archainbaud)

1939 *Man about Town* (Sandrich) (as Susan); *Million Dollar Legs* (Grinde); *The Day the Bookies Wept* (Goodwins)

1940 *Down Argentine Way* (Cummings) (as Glenda Crawford); *Tin Pan Alley* (Lang) (as Lily Blane)

1941 *Moon over Miami* (Lang) (as Kay Latimer); *A Yank in the R.A.F.* (King); *Hot Spot (I Wake Up Screaming)* (Humberstone)

1942 *Song of the Islands* (Lang) (as Eileen O'Brien); *Footlight Serenade* (Ratoff) (as Pat Lambert); *Springtime in the Rockies* (Cummings) (as Vicky);

1943 *Coney Island* (Lang) (as Kate Farley); *Sweet Rosie O'Grady* (Cummings) (as Madeleine Marlowe)

1944 *Four Jills in a Jeep* (Seiter) (as guest); *Pin Up Girl* (Humberstone) (as Lorry Jones)

1945 *The All-Star Bond Rally* (Audley—short); *Billy Rose's Diamond Horseshoe (Diamond Horseshoe)* (Seaton) (as Bonnie Collins); *The Dolly Sisters* (Cummings) (as Jenny Dolly)

1946 *Do You Love Me?* (Ratoff) (as guest); *The Shocking Miss Pilgrim* (Seaton) (title role); *Hollywood Park* (short) (as guest)

1947 *Mother Wore Tights* (Lang) (as Myrtle Burt)

1948 *That Lady in Ermine* (Lubitsch) (as Francesca/Angeline); *When My Baby Smiles at Me* (Lang) (as Bonnie Kane)

1949 *The Beautiful Blond from Bashful Bend* (Sturges) (as Freddie Jones)

Betty Grable

1950   *Wabash Avenue* (Koster) (as Ruby Summers); *My Blue Heaven*
           (Koster) (as Molly Moran)
1951   *Call Me Mister* (Bacon) (as Kay Hudson); *Meet Me after the
           Show* (Sale) (as Delilah)
1953   *The Farmer Takes a Wife* (Levin) (as Molly Larkin); *How to
           Marry a Millionaire* (Negulesco)
1954   *Three for the Show* (Potter) (as Julie Lowndes)
1955   *How to Be Very, Very Popular* (Johnson)

Publications

On GRABLE: books—

Rosen, Marjorie, *Popcorn Venus*, New York, 1973.
Warren, Doug, *Betty Grable, The Reluctant Movie Queen*, New York,
    1981.
Pastos, Spero, *Pin-Up: The Tragedy of Betty Grable*, New York, 1986.
Billman, Larry, *Betty Grable: A Bio-Bibliography*, Westport, Connecti-
    cut, 1993.
McGee, Tom, *Betty Grable: The Girl with the Million Dollar Legs*, Vestal,
    New York, 1994.

On GRABLE: articles—

Gorney, J., "Betty Grable 1916-1973," in *Films in Review* (New York),
    August-September 1973.
Film Reader 5 (Evanston, Illinois), 1982.

*   *   *

Betty Grable was truly a potent force in 1940s Hollywood. For 11
consecutive years (1941-51), she ranked among the film industry's
top stars. During the 1940s there was no more popular female movie
star in the world. Grable's most successful films were lavish formulaic
Technicolor musicals, beginning with *Down Argentine Way* in 1940.
In all, she appeared in some 22 of these color spectacles, all for
Twentieth Century-Fox, including *Song of the Islands, Springtime in
the Rockies, Coney Island, Sweet Rosie O'Grady, Diamond Horseshoe,* and *Mother Wore Tights.* All ranked among the most popular
films at the box office for their respective years of release.

One cannot overemphasize the economic importance of Betty
Grable during the 1940s. Except for Tyrone Power in 1940, and
Gregory Peck in 1947, no other Fox player ever made it into the
annual poll of the film industry's top ten stars. Grable's Technicolor
musicals, with their high and consistent revenues, powered Fox from
years in the red in the late 1930s to a position just behind Paramount
Pictures in the film industry's race for profits.

More than any film star of the 1940s, Grable was able to move
beyond her films to become a universally popular icon. Few, even in
this day and age, have not seen her picture in the pose as the attractive
blond in a white bathing suit coyly peeking over her shoulder, flashing
a million-dollar smile. Hers was the image of a woman sexy enough to
satisfy the longings of homesick soldiers, yet wholesome enough not
to cause protest by their fathers and mothers. Grable's face appeared
everywhere: on the covers of *Time* and *Life*, spread across the pages of
countless movie fan magazines, and adorning the sides of B-22 bombers and PT boats.

Twentieth Century-Fox's publicity flacks contributed to and created an image of the girl next door, always struggling to make do. She
was viewed as an actress without much natural talent. Fox always took
the opportunity to point out her limitations—not a very good dancer,
an adequate singer, and even a not-so-classic beauty. But in retrospect,
the talent was always there. She could dance well; see, for example, her
athletic romp with Gwen Verdon in *Meet Me after the Show*. As a

singer, she could sell a song with her small, but clear voice. She generated her share of popular songs, including the classic "I'm Always
Chasing Rainbows." As an actress, she stuck to what she could do well,
avoiding roles that clashed with her image.

In 1945 she ranked among the highest salaried individuals in the
United States; a decade later she was a has-been. In 1951, Twentieth
Century-Fox abandoned her and moved to another sex symbol, Marilyn
Monroe. Grable turned to the dinner theater circuit, only emerging
again into the national spotlight with a replacement role on Broadway
in *Hello Dolly!* during the late 1960s before her tragic death at age 56
of lung cancer.

—Douglas Gomery

GRAHAME, Gloria

Nationality: American. **Born:** Gloria Hallward in Pasadena, California, 28 November 1925. **Education:** Attended Hollywood High School.
Family: Married 1) the actor Stanley Clements, 1945 (divorced 1948);
2) the director Nicholas Ray, 1948 (divorced 1952); 3) the director
Cy Howard, 1954 (divorced 1957); 4) Anthony Ray, 1961. **Career:**
1935—first appeared on stage with Pasadena Community Playhouse;
1943—Broadway debut in *A Highland Fling*; 1944—film contract
with MGM, and debut in *Blonde Fever*; 1960s—returned to stage,
including tour with *The Time of Your Life*; 1976—in TV mini-series
Rich Man, Poor Man; 1978—on London stage. **Awards:** Best Supporting Actress Academy Award for *The Bad and the Beautiful*, 1952.
Died: 5 October 1981.

Films as Actress:

1944   *Blonde Fever* (Whorf)
1945   *Without Love* (Bucquet)
1947   *It's a Wonderful Life* (Capra); *It Happened in Brooklyn*
           (Whorf); *Merton of the Movies* (Alton); *Crossfire*
           (Dmytryk); *Song of the Thin Man* (Buzzell)
1949   *A Woman's Secret* (Ray); *Roughshod* (Robson)
1950   *In a Lonely Place* (Ray)
1952   *The Greatest Show on Earth* (DeMille); *Macao* (von Sternberg);
           Sudden Fear (Miller); *The Bad and the Beautiful* (Minnelli)
1953   *The Glass Wall* (Shane); *Man on a Tightrope* (Kazan); *The Big
           Heat* (Lang); *Prisoners of the Casbah* (Bare)
1954   *The Good Die Young* (Gilbert); *Naked Alibi* (Hopper); *Human
           Desire* (Lang)
1955   *The Cobweb* (Minnelli); *Not as a Stranger* (Kramer); *Okla-
           homa!* (Zinnemann) (as Ado Annie); *The Man Who Never
           Was* (Neame)
1957   *Ride Out for Revenge* (Girard)
1959   *Odds against Tomorrow* (Wise)
1965   *Ride Beyond Vengeance* (McEveety)
1970   *Blood and Lace* (Gilbert); *The Todd Killings* (Shear)
1971   *Escape* (Moxey—for TV); *Black Noon* (Kowalski—for TV);
           Chandler (Magwood) (as guest)
1972   *The Loners* (Roley); *Tarots* (*Angela*) (Forqué)
1974   *Mama's Dirty Girls* (Hayes); *The Girl on the Late Late Show*
           (Nelson—for TV)
1975   *Mansion of the Doomed* (*The Terror of Dr. Chaney*) (Potaki)
1979   *Head over Heels* (*Chilly Scenes of Winter*) (Silver) (as Clara)
1980   *Melvin and Howard* (Demme); *A Nightingale Sang in Berke-
           ley Square* (*The Biggest Bank Robbery*) (Thomas)
1981   *The Nesting* (Weston) (as Florinda)

Gloria Grahame with Humphrey Bogart in *In a Lonely Place*

Publications

On GRAHAME: books—

Turner, Peter, *Film Stars Don't Die in Liverpool*, London, 1986.
Curcio, Vincent, *Suicide Blonde: The Life of Gloria Grahame*, New York, 1989.

On GRAHAME: articles—

Braun, E., "In Camera: Welcome Back Corner," in *Films and Filming* (London), January 1980.
Obituary, in *Films and Filming* (London), December 1981.
Obituary, in *Cinéma* (Paris), April 1982.
Buckley, Michael, "Gloria Grahame," in *Films in Review* (New York), vol. 40, no. 12, 1989.

*   *   *

No American actress epitomizes the Hollywood stereotype of the bad girl better than Gloria Grahame. With her pouting lips, inviting eyes, and seductive physical presence, she played every variation on the fallen woman: the unfaithful wife, the bar tramp, the prostitute with mob connections, the femme fatale. It is the intelligence and depth of characterization that Grahame brings to each of these seem-

ingly clichéd roles that enabled her to transcend a one-dimensional sexual stereotype.

Crossfire was the first of several postwar thrillers that established Grahame as the ideal film noir icon. As Ginny, the pathetic cafe hostess who lives in a night world of bars and casual pick-ups, Grahame embodies the disillusionment and cynicism inherent in this genre. More decadent and sexually aggressive versions of the Ginny character would surface later in dark melodramas such as *Sudden Fear*, *Human Desire*, and *Odds against Tomorrow*. In *Sudden Fear* Grahame goads Jack Palance into a murder scheme and at the same time demands that he crush her when they kiss. In *Human Desire* she taunts her cuckolded husband with sordid details of her sexual exploits until he explodes with murderous rage. In *Odds against Tomorrow*, as a prelude to sex with Robert Ryan, she begs him to describe how it feels to kill someone. In these films, her sexuality is used as a corrupting influence and accents the mood of fatalism.

Possibly her finest work in the film noir cycle is in Fritz Lang's *The Big Heat* and Nicholas Ray's *In a Lonely Place*. In the Lang film, Grahame gives an unforgettable performance as a streetwise prostitute who is disfigured by her hoodlum boyfriend for associating with a policeman. Her transformation from the vain call girl to the horribly scarred mob informer is made all the more moving by her realization that she will never be totally accepted into any social order. Her only salvation is death, thus completing the metamorphosis from whore to martyr and confirming once again the

1950s Hollywood dictum that the only road to respectability for a sexual outlaw is oblivion.

Similar to *The Big Heat* in its harsh, sleazy atmosphere, *In a Lonely Place* also represents a cold and hostile universe where the basic goodness in the main characters is often negated by their destructive impulses. Grahame gives a brilliant performance, alternating between passionate longing and paranoia, as a secretive woman without romantic illusions who finds herself reaching out to a man who may be a murderer (Humphrey Bogart). The unbearable sexual tension that grows between Grahame and Bogart as their romance crumbles into a nightmare of distrust and futility is used to great advantage by director Ray, then her husband. As in most of Ray's films, he was able to find tenderness and love in the midst of alienation and despair but without a victory for the former values.

Apart from Grahame's invaluable contributions to the film noir, she is probably most familiar to filmgoers as the unfaithful wife. Although she played this role to perfection in major films such as *The Greatest Show on Earth* and *Man on a Tightrope*, her best rendition of the married hussy was in Vincente Minnelli's *The Bad and the Beautiful*, for which she won an Academy Award for Best Supporting Actress.

Unfortunately, Grahame's sultry looks proved to be a dubious asset for her Hollywood career. Blessed with the makings of a great actress, she was given few opportunities to broaden her range. It is evident that she had the potential to become a great comedienne, judging from her early work in *Without Love*, *Merton of the Movies*, and particularly Frank Capra's *It's a Wonderful Life*. In the Capra film Grahame shows delightful comic timing and spunk in her few scenes as a small town flirt. It was not until someone had the inspired idea to cast her as Ado Annie in Fred Zinnemann's *Oklahoma!* that Grahame was able to live up to the promise of those early performances and prove that she had a natural affinity for musical comedy.

After 1959 Grahame went through a disappointing 20-year period of accepting roles in low-budget horror films and thrillers; the nadir of her career may have been *Mama's Dirty Girls* in 1974. It was her appearance on television in *Rich Man, Poor Man* in 1976 that revived her screen career. After 1979, Grahame appeared in two critically acclaimed features, *Melvin and Howard* (in which she has an odd nonspeaking role) and *Chilly Scenes of Winter*. Her witty performance in the latter film veers from black comedy to gentle pathos, Grahame flaunting her blond seductress image and intimating that she was capable of more than she was ever allowed to be. As the neurotic, sexy mother of John Heard, Grahame sits fully clothed in a full bathtub, threatening to commit suicide and muttering, "I'm not dead yet!"

—Jeff Stafford

GRANGER, Stewart

Nationality: American. **Born:** James Leblanche Stewart in London, England, 6 May 1913, became U.S. citizen, 1956. **Education:** Attended Epsom College; Webber-Douglas School of Dramatic Art, London. **Military Service:** Served in the British Army, 1949-42; invalided out. **Family:** Married 1) the actress Elspeth March, 1938 (divorced 1948, two children: Jamie and Lindsay; 2) the actress Jean Simmons, 1950 (divorced 1960), one daughter; 3) Viviane Lecerf, 1964 (divorced 1969). **Career:** 1935—stage debut in *The Cardinal* in Hull; 1936-37—acted with Birmingham Repertory Company; 1938—West End debut in *The Sun Never Sets*; successful film roles in the UK during the 1940s led to MGM contract, 1950-57, and series of leading film roles; 1970-71—in TV series *The Men from Shiloh* (continuation of series *The Virginian*); 1986—in TV mini-series *Crossings*; 1989—on New York stage, in *The Circle*. **Died:** Of cancer, in Los Angeles, 16 August 1993.

Films as Actor:

1933   *A Southern Maid* (Hughes) (bit role)
1934   *Give Her a Ring* (Woods) (as diner)
1939   *So This Is London* (Freeland) (as Laurence)
1940   *Convoy* (Tennyson) (as Sutton)
1942   *Secret Mission* (French) (as Lt. Jackson)
1943   *Thursday's Child* (Ackland) (as David Penley); *The Man in Grey* (Arliss) (as Peter Rokeby); *The Lamp Still Burns* (Arliss) (as Larry Rains)
1944   *Fanny by Gaslight* (*Man of Evil*) (Asquith) (as Harry Somerford); *Love Story* (*A Lady Surrenders*) (Arliss) (as Kit Firth); *Madonna of the Seven Moons* (Crabtree) (as Nino Barucci); *Waterloo Road* (Gilliat) (as Ted Purvis); *Caesar and Cleopatra* (Pascal) (as Apollodorus)
1946   *Caravan* (Crabtree) (as Richard Darrel); *The Magic Bow* (Knowles) (as Paganini)
1947   *Captain Boycott* (Launder) (as Hugh Davin); *Blanche Fury* (Marc Allégret) (as Philip Thorn)
1948   *Saraband for Dead Lovers* (*Saraband*) (Dearden) (as Count Philip Koenigsmark); *Woman Hater* (Terence Young) (as Lord Terence Datchett)
1949   *Adam and Evelyne* (*Adam and Evelyn*) (French) (as Adam Black)
1950   *King Solomon's Mines* (Bennett and Marton) (as Allan Quartermain)
1951   *Soldiers Three* (Garnett) (as Pvt. Archibald Ackroyd); *The Light Touch* (Richard Brooks) (as Sam Conride); *The Wild North* (Marton) (as Jules Vincent)
1952   *Scaramouche* (Sidney) (as Andre Moreau/Scaramouche); *The Prisoner of Zenda* (Thorpe) (as Rudolph Rassendyll/King Rudolph V)
1953   *Salome* (Dieterle) (as Commander Claudius); *Young Bess* (Sidney) (as Thomas Seymour); *All the Brothers Were Valiant* (Thorpe) (as Mark Shore)
1954   *Beau Brummell* (Bernhardt) (title role); *Green Fire* (Marton) (as Rian X. Mitchell)
1955   *Moonfleet* (Fritz Lang) (as Jeremy Fox); *Footsteps in the Fog* (Lubin) (as Stephen Lowry); *Bhowani Junction* (Cukor) (as Col. Rodney Savage); *The Last Hunt* (Richard Brooks) (as Sandy McKenzie)
1956   *The Little Hut* (Robson) (as Sir Philip Ashlow)
1957   *Gun Glory* (Rowland) (as Tom Early)
1958   *The Whole Truth* (Guillermin) (as Max Poulton); *Harry Black* (*Harry Black and the Tiger*) (Fregonese) (title role)
1960   *North to Alaska* (Hathaway) (as George Pratt); *The Secret Partner* (Dearden) (as John Brent)
1963   *Sodom e Gomorra* (*Sodom and Gomorrah*) (Aldrich and Leone) (as Lot); *Marcia o crepa* (*Legion's Last Patrol*; *Commando*) (Wisbar) (as Capt. Le Blanc); *Lo spadaccino di Sienna* (*La congiura dei dieci*; *Swordsman of Siena*) (Périer) (as Thomas Stanswood); *Il giorno più corto* (Corbucci) (as guest)
1964   *The Secret Invasion* (Corman) (as Maj. Richard Mace); *The Crooked Road* (Chaffey) (as Duke of Orgagna); *Unter Geiern* (*La dove scenda il sole*; *Among Vultures*; *Frontier Hellcat*) (Vohrer) (as Old Surehand)
1965   *Das Geheimnis der drei Dschunken* (*A 009 Mission to Hong Kong*; *Red Dragon*) (Hofbauer) (as Michael Scott); *Der Ölprinz* (*Rampage at Apache Wells*) (Philipp) (as Old Shatterhand); *Flaming Frontier* (Vohrer) (as Old Surehand)
1966   *Das Geheimnis der gelben Mönche* (*Wie tötet man eine Dame*; *Tiro a segno per uccidere*; *Target for Killing*) (Köhler); *Spie control il mondo* (*Gern hab' ich die Frau'n gekillt*; *Spy against the World*; *Killer's Carnival*) ("Albert Cardiff," i.e., Cardone, Lynn, and Reynolds); *The Trygon Factor* (Frankell) (as Supt. Cooper-Smith)

Stewart Granger with Phyllis Calvert in *Madonna of the Seven Moons*

1967   *Requiem per un agent segreto* (*Consigna: Tanger 67*; *Der Chef schickt seinen besten Mann*; *Requiem for a Secret Agent*) (Sollima) (as John "Bingo" Merrill); *The Last Safari* (Hathaway) (as Gilchrist)

1969   *Any Second Now* (Levitt—for TV) (as Paul Dennison); *The Hound of the Baskervilles* (Crane—for TV) (as Sherlock Holmes)

1978   *The Wild Geese* (McLaglen) (as Sir Edward Malherson)

1982   *The Royal Romance of Charles and Diana* (Levin—for TV) (as Prince Philip)

1987   *A Hazard of Hearts* (Hough—for TV) (as Old Vulcan); *Story of a Recluse* (Reid—for TV); *Code Name Alpha* (Hofbauer)

1988   *Hell Hunters* (Von Theumer) (as Martin Hoffmann)

1989   *Chameleons* (Glen A. Larson—for TV) (as Jason)

1990   *Fine Gold* (D. J. Anthony Loma—for TV) (as Don Miguel)

Publications

By GRANGER: book—

Sparks Fly Upwards, London, 1981.

On GRANGER: article—

Obituary, in *New York Times*, 18 August 1993.

*   *   *

Stewart Granger's reputation as a motion picture actor rests largely on his swashbuckling roles in a series of sumptuous costume epics made for MGM in the 1950s, the waning days of this once very popular film genre. He was a throwback to the 1930s and 1940s hero roles of Errol Flynn, whose mantel he assumed (on screen at least), matching Flynn's athleticism and romantic derring-do, but adding a wry touch of world-weary self-deprecation and cynicism all his own, most notably in *Scaramouche*, the film for which he remains most famous.

Born James Stewart, he left premed school at the bidding of his friend, actor Michael Wilding, who suggested he try working as a film extra. He decided to accept Wilding's advice, and attended the Webber-Douglas school, then worked with the Hull and the Birmingham repertory companies. He achieved matinee idol status with the Old Vic playing opposite Vivien Leigh in *Serena Blandish* in 1939.

He had a number of small parts in films previously but stardom really came with *So This Is London* in 1940. In the hopes that Hollywood would beckon, he decided to change his name at this time to Stewart Granger, so as to avoid confusion with the well-known Hollywood actor James Stewart, the star of numerous MGM films, the studio where Granger was eventually placed under contract as well.

After the war Granger signed a seven-year contract with J. Arthur Rank. His 6' 3" physique and resonant voice at once made him romantic lead material, and he reached box-office stardom in a series of romantic leads, most notably opposite Phyllis Calvert in such films as *The Man in Grey*, in which he was a dashing Cavalier, and in *Madonna of the Seven Moons*, in which he villainously menaced Calvert. He was Apollodorus in Gabriel Pascal's *Caesar and Cleopatra*, from the play by George Bernard Shaw, and the draft-dodging profiteer in *Waterloo Road*. His last film for Rank was *Adam and Evelyne* starring Jean Simmons, whom he later married.

MGM finally beckoned in 1950 and he signed with them to play Allan Quartermain in a remake of *King Solomon's Mines*, shot in color on location in Africa. This expensive Technicolor epic was the first of nearly 20 adventure/costume films for which Granger's physique and handsome features were ready-made. He soon became a favorite of American audiences in such films as *Scaramouche*, *The Prisoner of Zenda* (opposite his *King Solomon's Mines* co-star, Deborah Kerr), *Young Bess* (opposite Jean Simmons), *Beau Brummell* (opposite Elizabeth Taylor), *Moonfleet*, *Bhowani Junction*, and *The Little Hut* (the last two opposite Ava Gardner).

Granger's MGM contract expired in 1957 with a dismal Western called *Gun Glory* directed by Roy Rowland. He moved to Twentieth Century-Fox to make *Harry Black and the Tiger* and *North to Alaska* with John Wayne, then headed to Europe where he appeared in a series of mostly forgettable costume epics throughout the 1960s. Two of the better ones were Robert Aldrich's *Sodom and Gomorrah*, in which he played Lot opposite Pier Angeli's pillar of salt, and *Swordsman of Sienna*, an enjoyable CinemaScope throwback to his halcyon days at MGM.

Granger returned to the United States in Henry Hathaway's *The Last Safari* and, while now white of hair, he was still more physically fit than most of his contemporaries. In 1970 he took the lead in the popular television series, *The Virginian* (renamed *The Men from Shiloh*), but after a one-year stint the series ended. He played a dapper Sherlock Holmes opposite Bernard Fox's Dr. Watson in the television film *The Hound of the Baskervilles* and was Sir Edward Malherson in the worldwide 1978 hit *The Wild Geese*, co-starring Richard Burton, Roger Moore, and Richard Harris. Three years later, he published his autobiography, *Sparks Fly Upwards*, in which he recounted his life up until the year 1960. His memoirs revealed him to be a literate man with a self-deprecating sense of humor much like the romantic heroes he had played on-screen. He maintained that he was not proud of one of his films, always found film acting torture, and if he had been lucky enough to star in just one film like *Inherit the Wind*, he would have immediately retired with pride.

Granger briefly returned to the stage in 1989, making his Broadway debut in a revival of the Somerset Maugham comedy of manners *The Circle* opposite Rex Harrison and Glynis Johns. The play was scheduled to move to London's West End the following year, but closed following its Broadway run when Harrison suffered a stroke and died. Granger followed Harrison in death three years later, never having completed the eagerly awaited volume two of his autobiography.

—Ronald Bowers, updated by John McCarty

GRANT, Cary

Nationality: American. **Born:** Alexander Archibald Leach in Bristol, England, 18 January 1904; early work in vaudeville and on stage as Archie Leach. **Education:** Attended Fairfield Academy, Somerset. **Family:** Married 1) the actress Virginia Cherrill, 1934 (divorced 1935); 2) Barbara Hutton, 1942 (divorced 1945); 3) the actress Betsy Drake, 1949 (divorced 1962); 4) the actress Dyan Cannon, 1965 (divorced 1968), daughter: Jennifer; 5) Barbara Harris, 1981. **Career:** 1919-20—ran away from school to join the Bob Pender Troupe of comedians and acrobats; toured with them to the United States, and decided to stay; then worked as barker on Coney Island, stilt walker at Steeplechase Park, and in vaudeville as straight man; 1927—first role on legitimate stage, *Golden Dawn*; followed by roles in musicals including *Boom, Boom*, 1929, with Jeannette MacDonald, a summer season at the St. Louis Municipal Opera, 1931, and in *Nikki*, 1931, with Fay Wray; 1932-37—contract with Paramount: film debut in *Singapore Sue* (short), 1932; 1937—freelance actor; entertained the armed forces during World War II; 1959—formed his own production company Grantart. **Awards:** Honorary Academy Award, "for his unique mastery of the art of screen acting with the respect and affection of his colleagues," 1969; Life Achievement Award, American Film Institute. **Died:** Of a stroke, in Davenport, Iowa, 29 November 1986.

Films as Actor:

1932   *Singapore Sue* (Robinson—short) (as Archie Leach); *This Is the Night* (Tuttle) (as Stephen); *Sinners in the Sun* (Hall) (as Ridgeway); *Merrily We Go to Hell* (Arzner) (as stage leading man); *Devil and the Deep* (Gering) (as Lt. Jacques); *Blonde Venus* (von Sternberg) (as Nick Townsend); *Hot Saturday* (Seiter) (as Romer Sheffield); *Madame Butterfly* (Gering) (as Lt. Pinkerton)

1933   ***She Done Him Wrong*** (Sherman) (as Capt. Cummings); *The Woman Accused* (Sloane) (as Jeffrey Baxter); *The Eagle and the Hawk* (Walker) (as Henry Crocker); *Gambling Ship* (Gasnier and Marcin) (as Ace Corbin); *I'm No Angel* (Ruggles) (as Jack Clayton); *Alice in Wonderland* (McLeod) (as Mock Turtle)

1934   *Thirty-Day Princess* (Gering) (as Porter Madison); *Born to Be Bad* (Sherman) (as Malcolm Trevor); *Kiss and Make Up* (Thompson) (as Dr. Maurice Lamar); *Ladies Should Listen* (Tuttle) (as Julian de Lussac)

1935   *Wings in the Dark* (Flood) (as Ken Gordon); *The Last Outpost* (Gasnier and Barton) (as Michael Andrews); *Sylvia Scarlett* (Cukor) (as Jimmy Monkley); *Enter Madame* (Nugent) (as Gerald Fitzgerald)

1936   *Pirate Party on Catalina Island* (short); *Big Brown Eyes* (Walsh) (as Danny Bart); *Suzy* (Fitzmaurice) (as Andre); *Wedding Present* (Wallace) (as Charlie); *The Amazing Quest of Ernest Bliss* (*Amazing Adventure*; *Romance and Riches*) (Zeisler) (as Ernest Bliss)

1937   *When You're in Love* (*For You Alone*) (Riskin) (as Jimmy Hudson); *Topper* (McLeod) (as George Kerby); *The Toast of New York* (Rowland V. Lee) (as Nick Boyd); *The Awful Truth* (McCarey) (as Jerry Warriner)

1938   ***Bringing Up Baby*** (Hawks) (as David Huxley); *Holiday* (*Free to Live*; *Unconventional Linda*) (Cukor) (as Johnny Case)

1939   *Gunga Din* (Stevens) (as Sgt. Archibald Cutter); *Only Angels Have Wings* (Hawks) (as Geoff Carter); *In Name Only* (Cromwell) (as Alec Walker); ***His Girl Friday*** (Hawks) (as Walter Burns)

1940   *My Favorite Wife* (Kanin) (as Nick Arden); *The Howards of Virginia* (*The Tree of Liberty*) (Lloyd) (as Matt Howard); ***The Philadelphia Story*** (Cukor) (as C. K. Dexter Haven)

1941   *Penny Serenade* (Stevens) (as Roger Adams); *Suspicion* (Hitchcock) (as Johnnie Aysgarth)

1942   *The Talk of the Town* (Stevens) (as Leopold Dilg); *Once upon
        a Honeymoon* (McCarey) (as Pat O'Toole)
1943   *Mr. Lucky* (Potter) (as Joe Adams)
1944   *Destination Tokyo* (Daves) (as Capt. Cassidy); *Once upon a
        Time* (Hall) (as Jerry Flynn); **Arsenic and Old Lace** (Capra)
        (as Mortimer Brewster); *None but the Lonely Heart* (Odets)
        (as Ernie Mott); *The Road to Victory* (short); *The Shining
        Future* (Prinz—short)
1946   *Without Reservations* (LeRoy) (as guest); *Night and Day*
        (Curtiz) (as Cole Porter); **Notorious** (Hitchcock) (as Devlin)
1947   *The Bachelor and the Bobby-Soxer* (*Bachelor Knight*) (Reis)
        (as Dick Nugent); *The Bishop's Wife* (Koster) (as Dudley)
1948   *Mr. Blandings Builds His Dream House* (Potter) (title role);
        Every Girl Should Be Married (Hartman) (as Dr. Madison
        Brown)
1949   *I Was a Male War Bride* (*You Can't Sleep Here*) (Hawks) (as
        Capt. Henri Rochard); *Polio and Communicable Diseases
        Hospital Trailer* (Hoffman—short)
1950   *Crisis* (Richard Brooks) (as Dr. Eugene Ferguson)
1951   *People Will Talk* (Joseph L. Mankiewicz) (as Dr. Noah
        Praetorius); *Room for One More* (*The Easy Way*) (Taurog)
        (as George "Poppy" Rose)
1952   *Monkey Business* (Hawks) (as Barnaby Fulton)
1953   *Dream Wife* (Sheldon) (as Clemson Reade)
1954   *To Catch a Thief* (Hitchcock) (as John Robie)
1957   *The Pride and the Passion* (Kramer) (as Anthony Trumbull);
        An Affair to Remember (McCarey) (as Nickie Ferrante);
        Kiss Them for Me (Donen) (as Andy Crewson)
1958   *Indiscreet* (Donen) (as Philip Adams); *Houseboat* (Shavelson)
        (as Tom Winston)
1959   **North by Northwest** (Hitchcock) (as Roger Thornhill); *Opera-
        tion Petticoat* (Edwards) (as Matt Sherman)
1960   *The Grass Is Greener* (Donen) (as Victor Rhyall)
1962   *That Touch of Mink* (Delbert Mann) (as Philip Shayne)
1963   *Charade* (Donen) (as Peter Joshua/Alexander Dyle/Adam
        Canfield/Brian Cruickshank)
1964   *Father Goose* (Nelson) (as Walter Eckland)
1965   *Ken Murray's Hollywood* (Murray)
1966   *Walk Don't Run* (Walters) (as William Rutland)
1970   *Elvis: That's the Way It Was* (Sanders—doc)
1977   *Once upon a Time . . . Is Now* (Billington—for TV) (as voice)

Publications

On GRANT: books—

Goldoni, Albert, *Cary Grant, An Unauthorized Biography*, Chicago, 1972.
Rosen, Marjorie, *Popcorn Venus*, New York, 1973.
Vermilye, Jerry, *Cary Grant*, New York, 1973.
Deschner, Donald, *The Films of Cary Grant*, Secaucus, New Jersey,
   1978.
Godfrey, Lionel, *Cary Grant: The Light Touch*, New York, 1981.
Britton, Andrew, *Cary Grant: Comedy and Male Desire*, Newcastle-
   upon-Tyne, 1983.
McIntosh, William Currie, and William Weaver, *The Private Cary
   Grant*, London, 1983; rev. ed., 1987.
Schickel, Richard, *Cary Grant: A Celebration*, London, 1983; rev. ed.,
   1987.
Wansell, Geoffrey, *Cary Grant: Haunted Idol*, London, 1983.
Dupuis, Jean-Jacques, *Cary Grant*, Paris, 1984.
Ashman, Chuck, and Pamela Trescott, *Cary Grant*, London, 1986.
Harris, Warren G., *Cary Grant: A Touch of Elegance*, New York, 1987.
Trescott, Pamela, *Cary Grant: His Movies and His Life*, Washington,
   D.C., 1987.
Donaldson, Maureen, and William Royce, *An Affair to Remember: My
   Life with Cary Grant*, London, 1989.
Higham, Charles, and Ray Moseley, *Cary Grant: The Lonely Heart*, New
   York, 1989.
Buehrer, Beverley Bare, *Cary Grant: A Bio-Bibliography*, New York,
   1990.
Nelson, Nancy, *Evenings with Cary Grant: Recollections in His Own
   Words and by Those Who Knew Him Best*, New York, 1991.
Wansell, Geoffrey, *Haunted Idol: The Story of the Real Cary Grant*, New
   York, 1992.

On GRANT: articles—

Roman, Robert, "Cary Grant," in *Films in Review* (New York), Decem-
   ber 1961.
Current Biography 1965, New York, 1965.
Champlin, Charles, "Cary Grant," in *The Movie Star*, edited by
   Elisabeth Weis, New York, 1981.
McVay, D., "Celebrating Cary Grant," in *Films and Filming* (London),
   January and February 1983.
Thomson, David, "Charms and the Man," in *Film Comment* (New
   York), January/February 1984.
Baxter, Brian, "Cary Grant," in *Films and Filming* (London), June
   1984.
Obituary in *Variety* (New York), 3 December 1986.
Taylor, John Russell, obituary in *Films and Filming* (London), Janu-
   ary 1987.
Corliss, Richard, obituary in *Film Comment* (New York), January/Feb-
   ruary 1987.
Buckley, Michael, obituary in *Films in Review* (New York), February
   1987.
Benayoun, Robert, "L'Image emblématique de Cary Grant," in *Positif*
   (Paris), March 1987.
Kobal, John, "An Affair to Remember," in *American Film* (Washing-
   ton, D.C.), April 1987.
Leahy, J., "Cary on Comedy," in *Films and Filming* (London), Janu-
   ary 1989.
Mattlin, Everett, " . . . And Cary," in *Film Comment* (New York),
   November/December 1989.
Clark, John, filmography in *Premiere* (New York), June 1991.
Buford, Kate, "A Death in the Family," in *Film Comment* (New York),
   May/June 1992.

*   *   *

Cary Grant is one of a handful of actors whose personalities so
captivate the moviegoing public that their names become synonymous with the qualities they embody on the screen. Just as John
Wayne has come to represent a certain brand of rugged masculinity, or Marilyn Monroe a blend of sexuality and childlike innocence, so Cary Grant has become the enduring cinematic personification of elegance, wit, and sophistication. A master of light comic
acting, his much-imitated style is the yardstick by which others
who attempt this difficult technique are measured, yet Grant's seemingly effortless performances remained unequaled. His talent, grace,
and good looks have earned him a place among Hollywood's most
popular male stars.

Grant's polished persona seems the antithesis of his working-class
background, yet his unmistakable style was already much in evidence
in his earliest film roles. His credentials as a traditional leading man
were established with his appearances opposite Marlene Dietrich in
Blonde Venus and Mae West in *She Done Him Wrong* and *I'm No
Angel*, but it was his work with the directors George Cukor, Howard
Hawks, and Leo McCarey which revealed the full measure of his abilities.

Cary Grant with Rosalind Russell in *His Girl Friday*

The fast-paced screwball comedies of the 1930s proved to be the perfect format for displaying Grant's verbal and physical agility. His romantic sparring with Irene Dunne in McCarey's *The Awful Truth*, Rosalind Russell in Hawks's *His Girl Friday*, and Katharine Hepburn in Cukor's *Holiday* and Hawks's *Bringing Up Baby* displayed Grant's deft comic touch in films that served to define the genre. His role as the daredevil flyer in *Only Angels Have Wings*, and his Oscar-nominated performances in *Penny Serenade* and *None but the Lonely Heart* showed him to be a capable dramatic actor as well, but it was in sophisticated comedy that his real strength lay. Grant continued to mine the successful image he had created in these early films throughout his career, and his performance in Stanley Donen's *Charade*—one of his final films—demonstrates the undiminished appeal of his debonair charm.

Although Grant's comedies represent the majority of his best remembered roles, his work with Alfred Hitchcock in several classic films offers a departure from his usual image. As he does with James Stewart in *Rear Window* and *Vertigo*, Hitchcock plays against Grant's familiar persona by incorporating into his characters psychological twists that are in startling contrast to the actor's smooth surface elegance. *To Catch a Thief* is perhaps closest to his characteristic style, with Grant portraying an infamous jewel thief, while *Suspicion* finds him cast as a seemingly loving husband who may or may not be

plotting to murder his wife. In *North by Northwest* Grant's wisecracking character is subtly shown to be a man whose charm hides a basically selfish nature and whose only lasting relationship with a woman is his amusing but obsessive bond with his mother.

It is in *Notorious*, however, that Hitchcock fully utilizes this conflict between Grant's image and his character's personality. As Devlin, a misogynistic, emotionally repressed American agent, he sends the woman he has unwillingly come to love (Ingrid Bergman) into the arms of a Nazi collaborator (Claude Rains). Devlin's struggle against his attraction to the high-living Bergman nearly causes her death when he blindly ignores signs that she may be in danger. The bizarre love triangle in the film hinges on Bergman's attraction to Grant in spite of his consistently callous behavior, and his performance is both fascinating and disturbing.

In David Thomson's essay, "Charms and the Man," he discusses at length the *Notorious* kiss between Grant and his co-star, Ingrid Bergman. The engineered intimacy and the "links between universal voyeurism and filmmaking" are perhaps best expressed by the director in an interview conducted by Truffaut. Hitchcock confesses, "I felt [the kiss] was indispensable that they should not separate, and I also felt that the public, represented by the camera, was the third party to this embrace. The public was given the great privilege of embracing Cary Grant and Ingrid Bergman together. It was a kind of temporary menage à trois" (quoted by Thomson). One sees in this an ultimate working of the Hollywood star system and the ideology manipulated by the machine: if only in illusion do we embrace the unattainable glamour of the stars, so be it *only* in illusion.

Grant's charms and wits may linger larger than life on screen, but it is also his spirit of camp that transcends beyond and steps outside of the frame. If we feel his speech is fast, we are experiencing the thrill of a possibility that his speech is going to be *too* fast to be restrained on film. In his handsome smiles that also hint at a touch of coyness and conceit and the physical as well as mental agility and quickness when "suddenly gone gay," it is tempting to look at Grant not only as a star but also as a star *looking back* at us and, perhaps, at filmmaking itself.

—Janet E. Lorenz, updated by Guo-Juin Hong

GRANT, Hugh

Nationality: British. **Born:** London, England, 9 September 1960. **Education:** Attended Oxford University, BA in English Literature with honors, 1982. **Career:** Appeared with the Oxford University Dramatic Society; 1982—film debut in *Privileged*, student film produced by the Oxford Film Foundation; 1982-85—wrote ad copy for radio commercials; 1985—stage debut at Nottingham Playhouse (repertory work); co-founded comedy troupe Jockeys of Norfolk; in TV mini-series *The Last Place on Earth*; 1986—acted in British TV series *The Demon Lover* and *Ladies in Charge*; 1987—first role in major film, *Maurice*. **Awards:** Best Actor Award, Venice Film Festival, for *Maurice*, 1987. **Agent:** Creative Artists Agency, 9830 Wilshire Boulevard, Beverly Hills, CA 90212, U.S.A.

Films as Actor:

1982   *Privileged* (Hoffman—not released) (as Lord Adrian, billed as Hughie Grant)
1985   *Jenny's War* (Gethers—for TV) (as Peter Baines)
1987   *Maurice* (Ivory) (as Clive Durham); *Lord Elgin and Some Stones of No Value* (for TV) (as William Hamilton); *White Mischief* (Radford) (as Hugh Dickinson)
1988   *The Dawning* (Knights—released in U.S. in 1993) (as Harry); *Nuit Bengali* (*Bengali Night*) (as Allan); *The Lair of the White Worm* (Russell) (as Lord James D'Ampton); *Remando al Viento* (*Rowing with the Wind*) (Suarez) (as Lord Byron)
1989   *Till We Meet Again* (Jarrott—for TV) (as Bruno de Lancel); *The Lady and the Highwayman* (Hough—for TV) (as Lord Lucius Vyne); *Champagne Charlie* (Eastman—for TV) (as Charlie Heidsieck)
1990   *Impromptu* (Lapine) (as Frederic Chopin)
1991   *The Big Man* (*Crossing the Line*) (Leland) (as Gordon); *Our Sons* (*Too Little, Too Late*) (Erman—for TV) (as James)
1992   *Lunes de Fiel* (*Bitter Moon*) (Polanski—released in U.S. in 1994) (as Nigel)
1993   *The Remains of the Day* (Ivory) (as Cardinal); *Night Train to Venice* (Quinterio) (as Martin)
1994   *Sirens* (Duigan) (as the Rev. Anthony Campion); *Four Weddings and a Funeral* (Newell) (as Charles); *The Changeling* (Simon Curtis—for TV) (as Alsemero)
1995   *An Awfully Big Adventure* (Newell) (as Meredith Potter); *The Englishman Who Went Up a Hill but Came Down a Mountain* (Monger) (title role); *Nine Months* (Columbus) (as Samuel Faulkner); *Sense and Sensibility* (Ang Lee) (as Edward Ferrars)

1996   *Restoration* (Michael Hoffman) (cameo as a painter, Elias Finn)

Publications

By GRANT: articles—

Interview, in *Interview* (New York), November 1987.
"Hollywood's Epiphany: Brits Create Hits," interview with Adam Dawltrey, in *Variety* (New York), May 1994

On GRANT: articles—

Farber, Stephen, "Hugh Grant Makes Them Think of Cary Grant," in *New York Times*, 27 February 1994.
Matusik, Angela, "A Subtle Hugh," in *Harper's Bazaar* (New York), April 1994.
Bellafante, Gina, "Not Just Another Pretty Face," in *Time* (New York), 25 April 1994.
Stivers, Cyndi, "Hugh Romance," in *Premiere* (New York), May 1994.
Maslin, Janet, "Even Cannes's Fray Can't Chase Away Hugh Grant's Smile," in *New York Times*, 18 May 1994.
Current Biography 1995, New York, 1995.
Lane, Anthony, "It Had to Be Hugh: The On-Screen and Off-Screen Adventures of a Young British Actor," in *New Yorker*, 24 July 1995.
Millea, Holly, "Hughmongous," in *Premiere* (New York), July 1995.

*   *   *

In the wake of Hugh Grant's big international success with the romantic comedy *Four Weddings and a Funeral*, the press began evoking comparisons between the young British actor and another cinema Grant, the immortal Cary. Like the latter, Hugh Grant's screen persona is that of the intelligent, innately shy, frequently befuddled nice guy masquerading as the charming, always-in-charge sophisticate. And like Cary Grant, Hugh Grant has attracted a large, mostly female following—although Hugh's following is more likely to describe him as "cute and cuddly" than "swooningly handsome" like the elegant Cary.

Stuck (so far) with playing mostly one-note roles as polished but sexually repressed Brits or effete, often homosexual, aristocrats (sometimes both at once), Hugh Grant has yet to demonstrate the range of Cary Grant. He is more akin to Roger Moore—a resemblance the producers of the James Bond series took note of as well when they considered him for the 007 role before settling on Pierce Brosnan. Another Moore role, that of Simon Templar in a big screen version of *The Saint,* had at one time also been offered to Hugh Grant.

He made his screen debut in the student film *Privileged* (1982) made at Oxford, where he was referred to by friends as Hughie Grant, the cute and cuddly name under which he is billed in the unreleased movie. After graduation, he worked in advertising, writing comic radio commercials for which he occasionally supplied the voices as well. He joined the Nottingham Playhouse in 1985 for a season in repertory, but grew dissatisfied with the nondescript roles he was assigned and formed his own comedy troupe shortly thereafter.

Grant left the troupe in 1987 when he won his first role in a major film, the Merchant-Ivory production of E. M. Forster's once-scandalous novel of homosexual awakening among the student upper crust at Cambridge, *Maurice*. As the aristocratic Clive Durham who forsakes his homosexuality for the straight life in order to pursue a career in politics, Grant earned critical raves and a best actor award at the Venice Film Festival which he shared with actor James Whilby, who played Maurice.

Hugh Grant with Andie MacDowell in *Four Weddings and a Funeral*

A slew of roles followed in British television and barely released, independently made movies—the most memorable of which was Ken Russell's horror spoof *The Lair of the White Worm*, based on the last published novel of *Dracula* author Bram Stoker, who was dying of "brain disease" when he wrote the feverish piece. Grant again played the aristocrat, Lord James D'Ampton, whose ancestor dispatched the legendary D'Ampton Worm, a snake god worshiped by the once-pagan Brits of the shire. History repeats itself when the Worm returns thanks to snake goddess Amanda Donohoe, whose beguiling charms Grant almost succumbs to before dispatching both her and the Worm at the film's high-camp conclusion.

Grant segued from the Russell scream and laugh fest to the more serious *Rowing with the Wind*, an Italian-made biopic about the tempestuous relationship between Lord Byron (Grant), Percy and Mary Shelley, and Dr. John Polidori that led to Mary's writing *Frankenstein*. Ironically, the same subject was dealt with by director Ken Russell in the 1986 film *Gothic* with Gabriel Byrne as Byron. Subsequently Grant played in several more biopics and docudramas, including *White Mischief*, a true tale of murder among the British upper crust in Kenya during World War II; the PBS mini-series *The Last Place on Earth* about the ill-fated Scott expedition to beat Amundsen to the Pole; and *Impromptu*, James Lapine's Ken Russell-like chronicle of the love affair between writer George Sand (Judy Davis) and the consumptive composer Chopin (Grant).

The turning point year for Grant was 1994. Three of his films were released concurrently in the United States: *Bitter Moon*, *Sirens*, and *Four Weddings and a Funeral*. The most potent, but least well received commercially and critically, of the trio was Polanski's *Bitter Moon*, which had actually been made in 1992 but did not make its way to U.S. shores until two years later. Grant again played a shy, sexually repressed Brit, Nigel, whose shipboard encounter with a kinky couple (Peter Coyote and Emmanuelle Seigner) spells trouble for his own marriage. Duigan's erotically charged *Sirens* (Grant as sexually repressed cleric) fell in between in terms of popular success, though the critics liked it. But Newell's *Four Weddings and a Funeral* (Grant as cynical, upscale bachelor turned tongue-tied bumbler when he falls for Andie MacDowell) was an unexpected smash hit with everyone. It catapulted Grant to stardom; he had two other small British films virtually in the can to take advantage of his newfound fame—including a follow-up with Newell, *An Awfully Big Adventure* (Grant as manipulative, gay stage manager) and the lengthily titled *The Englishman Who Went Up a Hill but Came Down a Mountain* (Grant as befuddled, sexually repressed Brit). The big time beckoned and Grant made his major Hollywood film debut in the Chris Columbus comedy *Nine Months*, playing a befuddled, soon-to-be-parent, his most Cary Grant-like role (and performance) to date.

Then scandal struck. Grant was pinched in a compromising position with a Sunset Strip hooker by the Los Angeles cops. Many believed the tabloid controversy that ensued would finish him with female fans, and destroy *Nine Months*, then on the eve of release, at the box office. The embarrassed Grant countered by making the rounds of the late night television talk shows in public apology, and succeeded in defusing the situation with ingratiatingly self-deprecating humor. *Nine Months* gained from this and was a minor hit, something studio executives no doubt appreciated and will likely remember. Once the "Hugh-and-cry" simmered down, Grant was back on the screen in the kind of small British film that made him, actress Emma Thompson's adaptation of Jane Austin's comedy of sexual manners, *Sense and Sensibility* (Grant as shy, sexually repressed aristocrat). A second big budget Hollywood movie cannot be far behind.

—John McCarty

GRANT, Lee

Nationality: American. **Born:** Lyova Haskell Rosenthal in New York City, 31 October 1926 (some sources give 1928 or 1931). **Education:** Attended Art Student League; Juilliard School of Music; High School of Music and Art; George Washington High School; Neighborhood Playhouse theater school under Sanford Meisner; Actors Studio, New York. **Family:** Married 1) the writer Arnold Manoff (died 1965), daughter: the actress Dinah Manoff; 2) the producer Joseph Feury, 1967. **Career:** 1933—stage debut as a child in the opera *L'Oracolo*; 1944—professional stage debut on tour in *Oklahoma*; 1948—Broadway debut in *Joy to the World*; 1949—in stage play *Detective Story*, and in film version in 1951; also a stage director; 1965-66—in TV series *Peyton Place*, also the series *Fay*, 1975-76; 1968—in stage play *Plaza Suite*, and the film version, 1971; 1973—co-directed the TV special *The Shape of Things*; 1976—directed *The Stronger*; 1979— in TV mini-series *Backstairs at the White House*, and *Mussolini: The Untold Story*, 1985. **Awards:** Best Actress, Cannes Festival, for *Detective Story*, 1951; Academy Award for Best Supporting Actress, for *Shampoo*, 1975; Academy Award for Best Documentary Feature, for *Down and Out in America*, 1985; Directors Guild Award for Best Dramatic Television Special, for *Nobody's Child*, 1986. **Agent:** Jim Wyatt, ICM, 8899 Beverly Boulevard, Los Angeles, CA 90048, U.S.A.

Films as Actress:

1951   *Detective Story* (Wyler) (as shoplifter)
1955   *Storm Fear* (Wilde) (as Edna)
1959   *Middle of the Night* (Delbert Mann) (as Marilyn)
1962   *The Balcony* (Strick) (as Carmen)
1963   *Terror in the City* (*Pie in the Sky*) (Baron) (as Suzy); *An Affair of the Skin* (Maddow) (as Katherine McCleod)
1967   *Divorce American Style* (Yorkin) (as Dede Murphy); *In the Heat of the Night* (Jewison) (as Mrs. Leslie Colbert); *Valley of the Dolls* (Robson) (as Miriam)
1968   *Buona Sera, Mrs. Campbell* (Frank) (as Fritzie Braddock)
1969   *Marooned* (John Sturges) (as Celia Pruett); *The Big Bounce* (March) (as Joanne)
1970   *The Landlord* (Ashby) (as Mrs. Enders); *There Was a Crooked Man . . .* (Joseph L. Mankiewicz) (as Mrs. Bullard); *Night Slaves* (Post—for TV)
1971   *Plaza Suite* (Hiller) (as Norma Hubley) (as Leslie Williams); *Ransom for a Dead Man* (Irving—for TV); *The Neon Ceiling* (Pierson—for TV)
1972   *Portnoy's Complaint* (Lehman) (as Sophie Portnoy); *Lieutenant Schuster's Wife* (Rich—for TV)

1973   *Partners in Crime* (Smight—for TV); *What Are Best Friends For?* (Sandrich—for TV)
1974   *The Internecine Project* (Hughes) (as Jean Robertson)
1975   *Shampoo* (Ashby) (as Felicia Carr)
1976   *Voyage of the Damned* (Rosenberg) (as Lillian Rosen); *Perilous Voyage* (Graham—for TV, produced 1968)
1977   *Airport '77* (Jameson) (as Karen Wallace); *The Spell* (Philips—for TV); *Once upon a Time . . . Is Now* (Billington—doc for TV)
1978   *Damien: Omen II* (Don Taylor) (as Ann Thorn); *The Swarm* (Irwin Allen) (as Anne MacGregor); *When You Comin' Back, Red Ryder?* (Katselas) (as Clarisse Ethridge); *The Mafu Cage* (*My Sister, My Love*) (Arthur) (as Ellen)
1979   *You Can't Go Home Again* (Nelson—for TV)
1980   *Little Miss Marker* (Bernstein) (as the Judge)
1981   *Charlie Chan and the Curse of the Dragon Queen* (Clive Donner) (as Mrs. Lupowitz); *The Million Dollar Face* (O'Herlihy—for TV); *For Ladies Only* (Damski—for TV) (as Anne Holt)
1982   *Thou Shalt Not Kill* (Rapaport—for TV); *Visiting Hours* (Lord) (as Deborah Ballin); *Bare Essence* (Grauman)
1983   *Will There Really Be a Morning* (Cook—for TV)
1984   *Teachers* (Hillier) (as Dr. Burke); *Trial Run* (Read); *A Billion for Boris* (Grassoff)
1986   *Arriving Tuesday* (Riddiford)
1987   *The Big Town* (Bolt) (as Ferguson Edwards)
1989   *The Hijacking of the Achille Lauro* (Collins—for TV) (as Marilyn Klinghoffer)
1990   *She Said No* (John Patterson—for TV) (as D.A. Doris Cantore)
1991   *Defending Your Life* (Albert Brooks) (as Lena Foster)
1992   *Something to Live For* (McLoughlin—for TV) (as Carol Gertz); *Citizen Cohn* (Pierson—for TV) (as Dora); *In My Daughter's Name* (Jud Taylor—for TV) (as Maureen Leeds)
1993   *Earth and the American Dream* (Couturie—doc) (as voice)
1994   *Under Heat* (Peter Reed) (as Jane)
1996   *It's My Party* (Kleiser) (as Amalia Stark)

Films as Director:

1976   *The Stronger* (short)
1980   *The Wilmar 8* (doc); *Tell Me a Riddle*
1983   *When Women Kill* (+ narrator)
1985   *What Sex Am I?* (*A Matter of Sex*) (doc for TV) (+ ro as narrator); *Cindy Eller: A Modern Fairy Tale*; *Down and Out in America* (doc)
1986   *Nobody's Child* (for TV)
1989   *Staying Together*; *Homeless*; *No Place Like Home* (for TV)
1994   *Seasons of the Heart* (for TV); *Reunion* (for TV); *Following Her Heart* (for TV)

Publications

By GRANT: articles—

"Lee Grant: No Complaints," interview with G. Oberon, in *Inter/View* (New York), August 1972.
"Actress Lee Grant Directs Her First Film," interview with Larry Gross, in *Millimeter* (New York), April 1977.
"Director Series: Lee Grant: *Tell Me a Riddle*," interview with P. Mascuch, in *Films in Review* (New York), April 1981.
"Lee Grant: The Actress-Director Charts Her Climb from the Blacklist to the A-List," interview in *American Film* (Los Angeles), February 1990.

On GRANT: articles—

Current Biography 1974, New York, 1974.

Buckley, Michael, "Lee Grant," in *Films in Review* (New York), vol. 38, no. 8/9, 1987.

Gross, Ken, in *People Weekly* (New York), 23 October 1989.

* * *

Lee Grant is the only Hollywood actress of her generation successfully to move into the field of direction. After directing television and stage productions, she made her first film in 1976, an adaptation of Strindberg's *The Stronger*, on an American Film Institute grant. She followed that with *The Wilmar 8*, a documentary on a group of eight female bank employees on strike against job discrimination, and a touching feature about an aging Jewish couple, *Tell Me a Riddle*.

Beginning as a stage actress, she made her film debut in *Detective Story* (the same role she won a Tony for in the Broadway production). That role brought her an Oscar nomination and a prize at Cannes. Then, as quickly as she had become a Hollywood name, she was blacklisted. After delivering an anti-HUAC eulogy for blacklisted actor J. Edward Bromberg, she was called before the committee to testify against her husband Arnold Manoff, who had been blacklisted. Her refusal to do so made it nearly impossible for her to find work in television or film for the better part of 12 years.

When the political witch-hunts of the fifties were over, she began to work at a feverish pitch in both television and film, her first major achievement being an Emmy for her role as Stella Chernick on *Peyton Place*. In film she has traveled the route of the character actress, most notably as an obnoxious mother of some sort, perhaps best typified by Sophie Portnoy, the smothering mother in *Portnoy's Complaint*, and Norma Hubley, the harassed mother of the bride in *Plaza Suite*.

Her first major screen notices of the 1960s came as the unbelieving widow Leslie Colbert in *In the Heat of the Night*. Displaying her ability to move from comedy to drama she then played nasal and tough Fritzie Braddock, the acidic nagging wife to Telly Savalas in the underrated comedy *Buona Sera, Mrs. Campbell*, and Celia Pruett, the hand-wringing wife to trapped-in-orbit astronaut Richard Crenna in *Marooned*.

She then met Hal Ashby who ushered her to a second Oscar nomination as the squinting mad Mrs. Enders in *The Landlord*, and her first Oscar as Felicia, one of the rich women who enjoys the sexual favors of handsome George (Warren Beatty), in *Shampoo*. The latter role highlighted her ability to alternate between class and coarseness. Fresh from her Oscar win, she joined the star cargo of *Voyage of the Damned*, and as Lillian Rosen, the wife of a disbarred lawyer, was nominated for a fourth time.

Never one to miss an opportunity to play an unusual character, Grant has unfortunately found herself in a number of negligible films since 1976. Her career as a director, however, is now in full bloom: in 1986 she won an Oscar for her documentary feature *Down and Out in America*, then became the first female director to win the Directors Guild of America Award for her direction of *Nobody's Child*. Marlo Thomas starred in this fact-based television movie about a woman confined to a mental institution for 20 years. Thomas gave the performance of her career. This film is representative of Grant's intensity and ability to delve deep into, and dramatically bring out, what makes her characters tick.

—Doug Tomlinson, updated by Linda J. Stewart

GREENSTREET, Sydney

Nationality: American. **Born:** Sydney Hughes Greenstreet in Sandwich, Kent, England, 27 December 1879. **Education:** Attended Dane Hill Preparatory School, Margate, Kent. **Family:** Married Dorothy Marie Ogden, 1918, son: John Ogden. **Career:** 1899-1901—worked as tea planter in Ceylon; 1901-02—agency manager, Watneys Coombes and Reed's Brewery, Harrow, Middlesex; 1902—joined Ben Greet School of Acting: debut in *Sherlock Holmes* in Ramsgate, Kent; 1904—toured with the Ben Greet company in the United States, and stayed; then acted in Shakespeare for five years; subsequently acted for several groups, including the Harry Davis Stock Company, Pittsburgh, the Henry W. Savage company, the Margaret Anglin company; 1941—film debut in *The Maltese Falcon*. **Died:** 18 January 1954.

Films as Actor:

1941   *The Maltese Falcon* (Huston) (as Kasper Gutman); *They Died with Their Boots On* (Walsh) (as General Scott)

1942   *Across the Pacific* (Huston) (as Dr. H. F. C. Lorenz); ***Casablanca*** (Curtiz) (as Ferrari)

1943   *Background to Danger* (Walsh); *Conflict* (Bernhardt) (as Dr. Mark Hamilton)

1944   *Passage to Marseille* (Curtiz) (as Commandant Duval); *Between Two Worlds* (Blatt) (as Thompson); *The Mask of Dimitrios* (Negulesco) (as Mr. Peters); *The Conspirators* (Negulesco) (as Riccardo Quintanilla); *Hollywood Canteen* (Daves) (as guest)

1945   *Pillow to Post* (Sherman) (as Col. Otley); *Christmas in Connecticut* (*Indiscretion*) (Godfrey)

1946   *Three Strangers* (Negulesco) (as Jerome K. Arbutney); *Devotion* (Bernhardt) (as W. M. Thackeray); *The Verdict* (Siegel)

1947   *That Way with Women* (de Cordova) (as James P. Alden); *The Hucksters* (Conway)

1948   *Ruthless* (Ulmer); *The Woman in White* (Godfrey) (as Count Fosco); *The Velvet Touch* (Gage) (as Capt. Danbury)

1949   *Flamingo Road* (Curtiz) (as Titus Semple); *It's a Great Feeling* (Butler) (as guest); *Malaya* (*East of the Rising Sun*) (Thorpe)

Publications

On GREENSTREET: book—

Sennett, Ted, *Masters of Menace: Greenstreet and Lorre*, New York, 1979.

On GREENSTREET: article—

Pickard, Roy, "Sydney Greenstreet," in *Films in Review* (New York), August-September 1972.

* * *

Sydney Greenstreet's merrily monstrous screen persona sprang belatedly forth in the actor's 61st year with his first film role as Kasper Gutman in *The Maltese Falcon*. His decade as a screen villain (1941-49) stood in contrast to a 40-year stage career in England and America which nurtured his outlandish presence in Warner Brothers films.

His 285-pound bulk filled the frame, often in low angle shots (such as those in *The Maltese Falcon*) that magnified the impression he gave of looming menace. Clever as well as corrupt, charmingly dandi-

Sydney Greenstreet

fied when sybaritic, Greenstreet's typical villain mocked his victims with throaty laughter that seemed to detach him from the awful deeds he plotted to commit. He took obvious pleasure in playing cat-and-mouse, and satisfaction in his own greedy amorality. Concerned only with financial gain, he remained unflinchingly objective, able to appreciate his adversaries (Sam Spade in *The Maltese Falcon* and Rick in *Casablanca*, for example) and to acknowledge it when outfoxed in the end.

Such physical distortion in a film character reassures the viewer of his own comparative inadequacy, and may elicit revulsion or mirth. Greenstreet at his best elicited both responses simultaneously. But his villains never became buffoons, remaining sinister by contrast with the weasels played by Peter Lorre, Greenstreet's foil in eight Warners films, even as he exploited the comic possibilities of his dialogue with a knowing delivery. "As leader of all illegal activities in Casablanca, I am an influential and respected man," boasts his fly-swatting black marketeer Ferrari. Moments later, moved by the plight of Ilsa Lund and her freedom-fighter husband, Ferrari suggests a possible way for them to escape, and seems as surprised by his grand gesture as they are, since, he almost apologetically declares, "it cannot possibly profit" him.

Greenstreet vainly sought to display on film the acting range he had earlier demonstrated in the theater, where he performed a variety of classic and contemporary roles (including, triumphantly, numerous Shakespearean clowns), toured America with the Lunts for the Theatre Guild, and even played a feature part in Jerome Kern's Broadway musical *Roberta*. Among his few permitted forays into screen comedy, only *Christmas in Connecticut* (where he's cast as a circulation-crazy magazine publisher) reveals the Greenstreet talent for mischief. He played detectives (*The Verdict*, *The Velvet Touch*), the novelist Thackeray (*Devotion*), a celestial interrogator (*Between Two Worlds*), and General Winfield Scott in a Western (*They Died with Their Boots On*), but Greenstreet's fame rests on his gallery of desperate schemers which made him one of the great movie villains.

—Mark W. Estrin

GREENWOOD, Joan

Nationality: British. **Born:** Chelsea, London, 4 March 1921. **Education:** Attended St. Catherine's School, Bramley, Surrey; Royal Academy of Dramatic Art, London. **Family:** Married André Morell, 1960 (died 1978), one son. **Career:** 1938—stage debut in *Le Malade imaginaire* in London; 1940—film debut in *John Smith Wakes Up*; 1944—played Ophelia in *Hamlet*; later stage work includes roles in *The Confidential Clerk* in New York, 1957, *Hedda Gabler*, 1960 and 1964, *The Chalk Garden*, 1971, and *The Understanding*, 1982; 1983—in TV series *Girls on Top*. **Died:** In London, 28 February 1987.

Films as Actress:

1940 *John Smith Wakes Up* (Weiss—short) (as herself)
1941 *My Wife's Family* (Mycroft) (as Irma Bagshott); *He Found a Star* (Carstairs) (as Babe Cavour)
1943 *The Gentle Sex* (Howard) (as Betty)
1945 *They Knew Mr. Knight* (Walker) (as Ruth Blake); *Latin Quarter* (Sewell) (as Christine Minetti)
1946 *A Girl in a Million* (Searle) (as Gay)
1947 *The Man Within* (*The Smugglers*) (Knowles) (as Elizabeth); *The October Man* (Baker) (as Jennie Carden); *The White Unicorn* (*Bad Sister*) (Knowles) (as Lottie Smith)

1948 *Saraband for Dead Lovers* (*Saraband*) (Dearden) (as Sophie/Dorothea)
1949 *The Bad Lord Byron* (Macdonald) (as Lady Caroline Lamb); *Whisky Galore!* (*Tight Little Island*) (Mackendrick) (as Peggy Maccroon); **Kind Hearts and Coronets** (Hamer) (as Sibella)
1950 *Garou-Garou, le passe-muraille* (*Le Passe-Muraille*; *Mr. Peek-a-boo*) (Boyer)
1951 *Flesh and Blood* (Kimmins) (as Wilhelmina Cameron); *Young Wives' Tale* (Cass) (as Sabina Pennant); *The Man in the White Suit* (Mackendrick) (as Daphne Birnley); *The Importance of Being Earnest* (Asquith) (as Gwendolen Fairfax)
1954 *Knave of Hearts* (*Monsieur Ripois*; *Lovers, Happy Lovers*; *Lover Boy*) (Clément) (as Norah); *Father Brown* (*The Detective*) (Hamer) (as Lady Warren)
1955 *Moonfleet* (Lang)
1958 *Stage Struck* (Lumet)
1959 *Horse on Holiday* (English-language version of Danish film *Hest pá sommerferie*) (Henning-Jensen) (as voice)
1962 *Mysterious Island* (Endfield) (as Lady Mary Fairchild); *The Amorous Prawn* (*Playgirl and the War Minister*; *The Amorous Mr. Prawn*) (Kimmins) (as Lady Fitzadam)
1963 **Tom Jones** (Richardson) (as Lady Bellaston)
1964 *The Moon-Spinners* (Neilson) (as Frances Ferris)
1971 *Girl Stroke Boy* (Kellett)
1977 "London, 1912" ep. of *The Uncanny* (Héroux); *The Hound of the Baskervilles* (Morrissey)
1978 *The Water Babies* (Jeffries)
1983 *Country* (Eyre)
1984 *Ellis Island* (London—for TV)
1985 *Wagner* (Palmer)
1987 *Little Dorrit: Part I, Nobody's Fault* and *Little Dorrit: Part II, Little Dorrit's Story* (Edzard) (as Mrs. Clennam)
1988 *Melba* (Fisher)

Publications

On GREENWOOD: article—

"People of Talent: Joan Greenwood," in *Sight and Sound* (London), Spring 1956.

*   *   *

And how, Dennis Price inquires of Joan Greenwood on her return from abroad, did she enjoy her honeymoon? "Not at all." "Not at all?" "Not—at all." By means of the briefest possible pause, Greenwood invests the line with an infinite wealth of sexual innuendo.

Being at once sexy and witty was Greenwood's forte. Petite and graceful, she moved with a delicate feline sensuality; her breathily husky voice, accentuating unexpected vowels, hovered always on the verge of self-parody. She countered questionable situations with an exquisitely inquiring stare, poised somewhere between amusement and mock outrage. When she was given the chance—which happened nowhere near often enough—she brought to her roles a quality of playful eroticism all too rare in British cinema.

Kind Hearts and Coronets (in which the above dialogue occurs) provided one of her finest opportunities. As the hero's mistress, Sibella, her stylish playing was perfectly attuned to the ironic elegance of Hamer's wit. She was well used by Mackendrick, too, in *Whisky Galore!* and *The Man in the White Suit*—displaying in the latter a delectable subtlety of inflexion when attempting, half-reluctantly and half-willingly, to seduce Alec Guinness. Near-manda-

501

Joan Greenwood in *Kind Hearts and Coronets*

tory casting for Gwendolen in *The Importance of Being Earnest*, she almost rivaled Edith Evans for Wildean hauteur, and was equally well chosen as Lady Caroline Lamb in *The Bad Lord Byron*; unfortunately, the film was abysmal.

Hollywood seemed even less capable than Britain of knowing what to do with an actress of Greenwood's style and individuality. Perhaps the French might have given her the films she deserved. In *Monsieur Ripois* her performance as one of Gérard Philipe's victims revealed unexpected depths of pathos, though her only other French film, *Le Passe-Muraille*, proved disappointing. After the mid-1950s, perhaps discouraged, she devoted herself largely to the stage, and to married life, only occasionally turning up in small cameo roles to suggest what we had been missing.

—Philip Kemp

GRIFFITH, Melanie

Nationality: American. **Born:** New York City, 9 August 1957; daughter of the actress Tippi Hedren. **Education:** Attended Hollywood Profes-

sional School, California; studied acting with Stella Adler in 1975, 1981. **Family:** Married 1) the actor Don Johnson, 1976 (divorced 1977; re-married 1989, divorced 1995), daughter: Dakota Mayi; 2) the actor Steven Bauer (aka Steven Echevarria), 1982 (divorced), son: Alexander; 3) the actor Antonio Banderas. **Career:** 1970s—model; 1975—feature film acting debut; 1976—TV movie debut in mini-series, *Once an Eagle*; 1977—debut as TV series regular in *Carter Country* (1978-79); 1981—starred with mother, Tippi Hedren, in *Roar* (produced by stepfather, Noel Marshall); 1981—took a year's sabbatical to study acting with Stella Adler; 1984—returned to feature films as the female lead in Brian DePalma's *Body Double*; 1987—guest starred in an episode of TV's *Miami Vice*, directed by Don Johnson, her once-and-future husband; 1995—role as Dora in TV mini-series *Buffalo Girls*. **Awards:** Best Actress Golden Globe, for *Working Girl*, 1988.

Films as Actress:

1973   *The Harrad Experiment* (Ted Post) (as extra, uncredited)
1975   *Night Moves* (Arthur Penn) (as Delly Grastner); *The Drowning Pool* (Stuart Rosenberg) (as Schuyler Devereaux); *Smile* (Ritchie) (as Karen Love/"Miss Simi Valley")

1977   *Joyride* (Joseph Ruben) (as Susie); *One on One* (Lamont Johnson) (as hitchhiker)

1978   *Daddy, I Don't Like It Like This* (Adell Aldrich—for TV) (as girl in hotel room); *Steel Cowboy* (Laidman—for TV) (as Johnnie)

1980   *Underground Aces* (Robert Butler)

1981   *Roar* (Noel Marshall) (as Melanie); *The Star Maker* (Antonio—for TV) (as Dawn Bennett); *She's in the Army Now* (Averback) (as Sylvie Knoll); *Golden Gate* (Wendkos—for TV)

1984   *Body Double* (DePalma) (as Holly); *Fear City* (Abel Ferarra) (as Loretta)

1985   *Cherry 2000* (DeJarnatt) (as E. Johnson)

1986   *Something Wild* (Jonathan Demme) (as Audrey "Lulu" Hankel)

1988   *The Milagro Beanfield War* (Redford) (as Flossie Devine); *Stormy Monday* (Figgis) (as Kate); *Working Girl* (Mike Nichols) (as Tess McGill)

1990   *Pacific Heights* (Schlesinger) (as Patty Palmer); *The Bonfire of the Vanities* (DePalma) (as Maria Ruskin); *In the Spirit* (Seacat) (as Lureen); *Women and Men: Stories of Seduction* (Raphael, Richardson, and Russell—for TV) (as Hadley)

1991   *Paradise* (Donoghue) (as Lily Reed)

1992   *Shining Through* (Seltzer) (as Linda Voss); *A Stranger among Us* (Lumet) (as Emily Eden)

1993   *Born Yesterday* (Mandoki) (as Billie Dawn)

1994   *Milk Money* (Richard Benjamin) (as V); *Nobody's Fool* (Benton) (as Toby Roebuck)

1995   *Now and Then* (Glatter) (as Tina)

1996   *Mulholland Falls* (Tamahori); *Lolita* (Lyne) (as Mother); *Two Much* (Trueba) (as Betty Ferner)

Publications

By GRIFFITH: articles—

"Flirting with Success," interview with Craig Unger and Paul Jasmin, in *Interview* (New York), November 1988.

"Girl Talk: Melanie Griffith Opens Up," interview with Jill Feldman, in *Rolling Stone* (New York), 26 January 1989.

"Melanie Unplugged," interview with Eric Alterman, in *Vanity Fair* (New York), July 1994.

On GRIFFITH: book—

Salamon, Julie, *The Devil's Candy*, Boston, 1991.

On GRIFFITH: articles—

Infante, G. Cabrera, "Blonde on Blonde: A Love Letter to Melanie Griffith," in *American Film* (Washington, D.C.), March 1988.

Hinson, Hal, "The Rewards of a Working Girl," in *Washington Post*, 29 December 1988.

McGuigan, Cathleen, "Working Her Way to the Top: Melanie Griffith Used to Be Something Wild; Now She's Really Something," in *Newsweek* (New York), 2 January 1989.

Current Biography 1990, New York, 1990.

Bravin, Jess, "Working Whirl," in *Harper's Bazaar* (New York), November 1990.

Stanley, Allessandra, "The Mellowing of Melanie," in *Lear's* (New York), 1 April 1993.

Avins, Mimi, "Melanie Griffith Faces Adversity with Style," in *New Woman* (New York), 1 September 1994.

Biskind, Peter, "More Than He Bargained For," in *Premiere* (New York), 1 October 1994.

*   *   *

Melanie Griffith has been called the reincarnation of Jean Harlow, Judy Holliday, and Marilyn Monroe, but more than anything else, Melanie Griffith is a late twentieth-century Hollywood original. Mike Nichols, her director on her most successful performance, *Working Girl*, finally harnessed her considerable talents and made her a star. Her face, her eyes, are transparent; you can see right into her feelings, yet the audience never knows what her character is thinking. She is able to harness an intense power yet not seem to be acting, but just being herself. She is profane and virginal, street-smart and gossamer, completely spontaneous while totally in control. Yet she is probably more famous for her frequent appearances in gossip columns, the daughter of a 1960s star, the child companion of television star Don Johnson at age 14 (he was 22), a life filled with drugs, automobile accidents, and alcohol.

Melanie Griffith's career has been built on roles that call upon her to encompass these contradictions. Not quite a child actress, she made her feature film debut before she would have been graduated from high school, as the promiscuous neglected daughter of an actress in Arthur Penn's *Night Moves* (1975). That same year, she played Miss Simi Valley in Michael Ritchie's *Smile* before proceeding to specialize in playing precocious teens who were less innocent than they appeared. But then her personal problems overwhelmed her and she did not return to important roles until Brian DePalma's *Body Double* (1984). Impressed by her work, director Jonathan Demme cast Griffith as the adventurous lead of *Something Wild* (1986). The crest of this period of accomplishment came with *Working Girl*, which earned her not only stardom, but praise as an actress.

But immediate follow-up proved difficult. Through the early 1990s Melanie Griffith was surely busy, but none too successful in such films as *Paradise* and DePalma's ill-fated *Bonfire of the Vanities*. In 1992 Griffith, attempting to expand her screen image, endured two back-to-back failures with her performances as a legal secretary turned World War II spy in *Shining Through* and a tough New York City cop in love with a Hassidic Jewish man in Sidney Lumet's *A Stranger among Us*. Like other actresses and actors of the late twentieth century she has been more frequently on television than on the theatrical screen. Her television appearances include a score of television movies, both network and HBO, one modestly successful series, and more failed pilots than she surely would like to remember.

The remake of a classic screwball comedy *Born Yesterday* should have been her hit, but while her performance as ex-show girl Billie Dawn was highly praised, the public was lukewarm. *Born Yesterday* was the vehicle that made Judy Holliday a household name in 1950; Griffith redid Billie in her own fashion, sassy but hip, never as dumb as one might think. Indeed *Born Yesterday* seemed more a sequel to *Working Girl* than any faithful recreation of a role Judy Holliday made famous before Melanie Griffith was born. *Born Yesterday* has at the core of its comedy mocking the ways and woes of Washington, D.C. Perhaps in the age of cynicism of the final decade of the twentieth century, the remake of *Born Yesterday* represented too much a tale of optimism, a celebration of the people over corrupt powers of money and influence.

Yet Melanie Griffith did a wonderful send-up of Washington pretension. In a delightful scene Cynthia Schreiber (played by Nora Dunn), ace reporter for National Public Radio, interviews the guileless Billie as a representative of everything that is hick outside the beltway. But the joke turns out to be on Schreiber, when Billie has actually read *Democracy in America* while the National Public Radio host only knows it is important.

Melanie Griffith and Harrison Ford in *Working Girl*

It all worked in *Working Girl*. Griffith played a classic rags to riches climber with a feminist twist. Her Tess McGill from the wrong side of New York City, working class, gains access to a top job on Wall Street through smarts and some luck. With all the contradictions of Frank Capra and Jimmy Stewart two generations earlier, *Working Girl* taps into the myths of upward mobility in the United States, with a rare power. One can not help liking Tess McGill, even if one can see the cracks in the story logic. One sees those cracks only after the film is over and Tess is in her Manhattan high-rise, seeming to start her climb to the top of making money. This is a formula film, but Melanie Griffith proved a great actress in this genre movie.

—Douglas Gomery

GUINNESS, (Sir) Alec

Nationality: British. **Born:** London, England, 2 April 1914. **Education:** Attended Pembroke Lodge, Southbourne; Roborough, Eastbourne; studied acting at the Fay Compton Studio of Dramatic Art, London. **Military Service:** Royal Navy, 1941-46. **Family:** Married the actress Merula Salaman, 1938, son: Matthew. **Career:** Copywriter for Arks Publicity; 1934—stage debut in *Libel*, Hammersmith, London; film debut in *Evensong*; 1942—on leave from Royal Navy to appear in British play on Broadway, *Flare Path*; 1946—debut in featured role in film *Great Expectations*; 1948—directed the stage play *Twelfth Night*; 1948—roles in films *Oliver Twist* and *Kind Hearts and Coronets*, 1949, brought international popularity; followed by a series of Ealing comedies; continued to act and direct on stage: directed and acted in *The Cocktail Party*, London, 1968, and co-devised and acted in *Yahoo*, London, 1976; 1982—in TV mini-series *Tinker, Tailor, Soldier, Spy* and *Smiley's People*. **Awards:** Best Actor Academy Award, Best Actor, New York Film Critics, and Best British Actor, British Academy, for *The Bridge on the River Kwai*, 1957; Best Actor, Venice Festival, for *The Horse's Mouth*, 1958; Special Academy Award, "for advancing the art of screen acting through a host of memorable and distinguished performances," 1979; Fellow of the British Academy of Film and Television Arts, 1989, and of the British Film Institute, 1991; UK Film Critics' Circle Special Prize "for the brilliance of his career over more than forty years," 1989; Hon. D. Litt. (Oxon); Hon. Litt. D. (Cantab); Commander, Order of the British Empire, 1955; Knighted, 1959; made Companion of Honour, 1994. **Address:** c/o McReddie, 91 Regent Street, London W1R 7TB, England.

Films as Actor:

1934   *Evensong* (Saville) (as extra)
1946   *Great Expectations* (Lean) (as Herbert Pocket)

1948 *Oliver Twist* (Lean) (as Fagin)
1949 **Kind Hearts and Coronets** (Hamer) (as eight members of the d'Ascoyne family); *A Run for Your Money* (Frend) (as Whimple)
1950 *Last Holiday* (Cass) (as George Bird); *The Mudlark* (Negulesco) (as Disraeli)
1951 **The Lavender Hill Mob** (Charles Crichton) (as Henry Holland); *The Man in the White Suit* (Mackendrick) (as Sidney Stratton)
1952 *The Card* (*The Promoter*) (Neame) (as Edward Henry "Denry" Machin)
1953 *The Captain's Paradise* (*Paradise*) (Kimmins) (as Capt. Henry St. James); *Malta Story* (Hurst) (as Flight Lt. Peter Ross); *The Square Mile* (Pine—short) (as narrator)
1954 *Father Brown* (*The Detective*) (Hamer) (title role); *To Paris with Love* (Hamer) (as Col. Sir Edgar Fraser); *Stratford Adventure* (Parker—short) (as guest)
1955 *The Prisoner* (Glenville) (as the Cardinal); *The Ladykillers* (Mackendrick) (as Prof. Marcus); *Rowlandson's England* (Hawkesworth—short) (as narrator)
1956 *The Swan* (Charles Vidor) (as Prince Albert)
1957 *The Bridge on the River Kwai* (Lean) (as Col. Nicholson); *Barnacle Bill* (*All at Sea*) (Frend) (as William Horatio Ambrose)
1958 *The Horse's Mouth* (Neame) (as Gulley Jimson, + sc); *The Scapegoat* (Hamer) (as John Barratt/Jacques de Gue)
1959 *Our Man in Havana* (Reed) (as Jim Wormold)
1960 *Tunes of Glory* (Neame) (as Lt. Col. Jock Sinclair)
1961 *A Majority of One* (LeRoy) (as Koichi Asano)
1962 *H.M.S. Defiant* (*Damn the Defiant!*) (Lewis Gilbert) (as Capt. Crawford); **Lawrence of Arabia** (Lean) (as Prince Feisal)
1964 *The Fall of the Roman Empire* (Anthony Mann) (as Marcus Aurelius)
1965 *Situation Hopeless—But Not Serious* (Reinhardt) (as Herr Wilhelm Frick); *Doctor Zhivago* (Lean) (as Gen. Yevgraf Zhivago)
1966 *Hotel Paradiso* (Glenville) (as Boniface); *The Quiller Memorandum* (Anderson) (as Pol)
1967 *The Comedians* (Glenville) (as Major Jones); *The Comedians in Africa* (short on the making of *The Comedians*)
1970 *Cromwell* (Hughes) (as Charles I); *Scrooge* (Neame) (as Marley's Ghost)
1972 *Fratello Sole, Sorella Luna* (*Brother Sun, Sister Moon*) (Zeffirelli) (as Pope Innocent III)
1973 *Hitler: The Last Ten Days* (De Concini) (title role)
1976 *Murder by Death* (Moore) (as Jamessir Bensonmum, the butler)
1977 **Star Wars** (Lucas) (as Ben Obi-Wan Kenobi); *To See Such Fun* (Scofield—compilation)
1980 **The Empire Strikes Back** (Kershner) (as Ben Obi-Wan Kenobi); *Raise the Titanic* (Jameson) (as John Bigalow); *Little Lord Fauntleroy* (Gold—for TV) (as Earl de Dorincourt)
1983 *Lovesick* (Brickman) (as Freud); **Return of the Jedi** (Marquand) (as Ben Obi-Wan Kenobi)
1984 **A Passage to India** (Lean) (as Prof. Godbole); *Future Schlock* (Kiely and Peak) (as man in the white suit); *Edwin* (Rodney Bennett—for TV) (as Sir Fennimore Truscott)
1985 *Monsignor Quixote* (Rodney Bennett—for TV) (title role)
1987 *Little Dorrit* (Part I: *Nobody's Fault*, and Part II: *Little Dorrit's Story*) (Edzard) (as William Dorrit)
1988 *A Handful of Dust* (Sturridge) (as Mr. Todd)
1991 *Kafka* (Soderbergh) (as the Chief Clerk)
1992 *Tales from Hollywood* (Howard Davies—for TV) (as Heinrich Mann)
1993 *A Foreign Field* (Sturridge—for TV) (as Amos)
1995 *Mute Witness* (Waller) (as the Reaper)

Publications

By GUINNESS: book—

Blessings in Disguise, London, 1985.

By GUINNESS: articles—

"The Artist Views the Critics," in *Atlantic* (New York), March 1953.
"Man of Many Faces," interview with D. Hill, in *Films and Filming* (London), February 1955.
"Life with a Pinch of Salt," interview in *Films and Filming* (London), November 1965.
Interview with John Russell Taylor, in *American Film* (Los Angeles), April 1989.

On GUINNESS: books—

Tynan, Kenneth, *Alec Guinness*, New York, 1954.
Hunter, Allan, *Alec Guinness on Screen*, Glasgow, 1982.
Taylor, John Russell, *Alec Guinness: A Celebration*, London, 1984.
Missler, Andreas, *Alec Guinness: Sein Filme, Sein Leben*, Munich, 1987.
Von Gunden, Kenneth, *Alec Guinness: The Films*, Jefferson, North Carolina, 1987.
Harwood, Ronald, editor, *Dear Alec: Guinness at 75*, London, 1989.
Tanitch, Robert, *Guinness*, London, 1989.

On GUINNESS: articles—

McVay, Douglas, "Alec Guinness," in *Films and Filming* (London), May 1961.
Billings, P., "Sir Alec Guinness," in *Focus on Film* (London), Autumn 1972.
Current Biography 1981, New York, 1981.
Millar, Gavin, "Goonery and Guinness," in *Films and Filming* (London), January 1983.
Kennedy, Harlan, "Sir Alec," in *Film Comment* (New York), July/August 1983.
Thomson, David, "Gray Ghost," in *Film Comment* (New York), vol. 23, no. 2, 1987.

*   *   *

The consummate chameleon, Alec Guinness has successfully portrayed a timid but larcenous bank clerk, a brashly eccentric artist, a tortured Cardinal, the villainous Fagin, a fiery Scottish braggart, and a sad-eyed Arab prince of great cunning. According to Harlan Kennedy: "Almost alone among film actors, Guinness can assume the paraphernalia of makeup and funny voices and eccentric walks without losing a molecule of credibility. He never allows the weight of disguise to panic him into a matching hyperbole of voice and gesture." Guinness admits: "I try to get inside a character and project him—one of my own private rules of thumb is that I have not got a character unless I have mastered exactly how he walks . . . It's not sufficient to concentrate on his looks. You have got to know his mind—to find out what he thinks, how he feels, his background, his mannerisms."

Guinness rarely succumbs to excess. This probably has more to do with his naturally withdrawn and reflective character, his passion for anonymity. One cannot imagine Olivier stating, for example, that he became an actor to escape himself, which is precisely the reason Guinness has given. Guinness's artistic goals ("learning to pare down

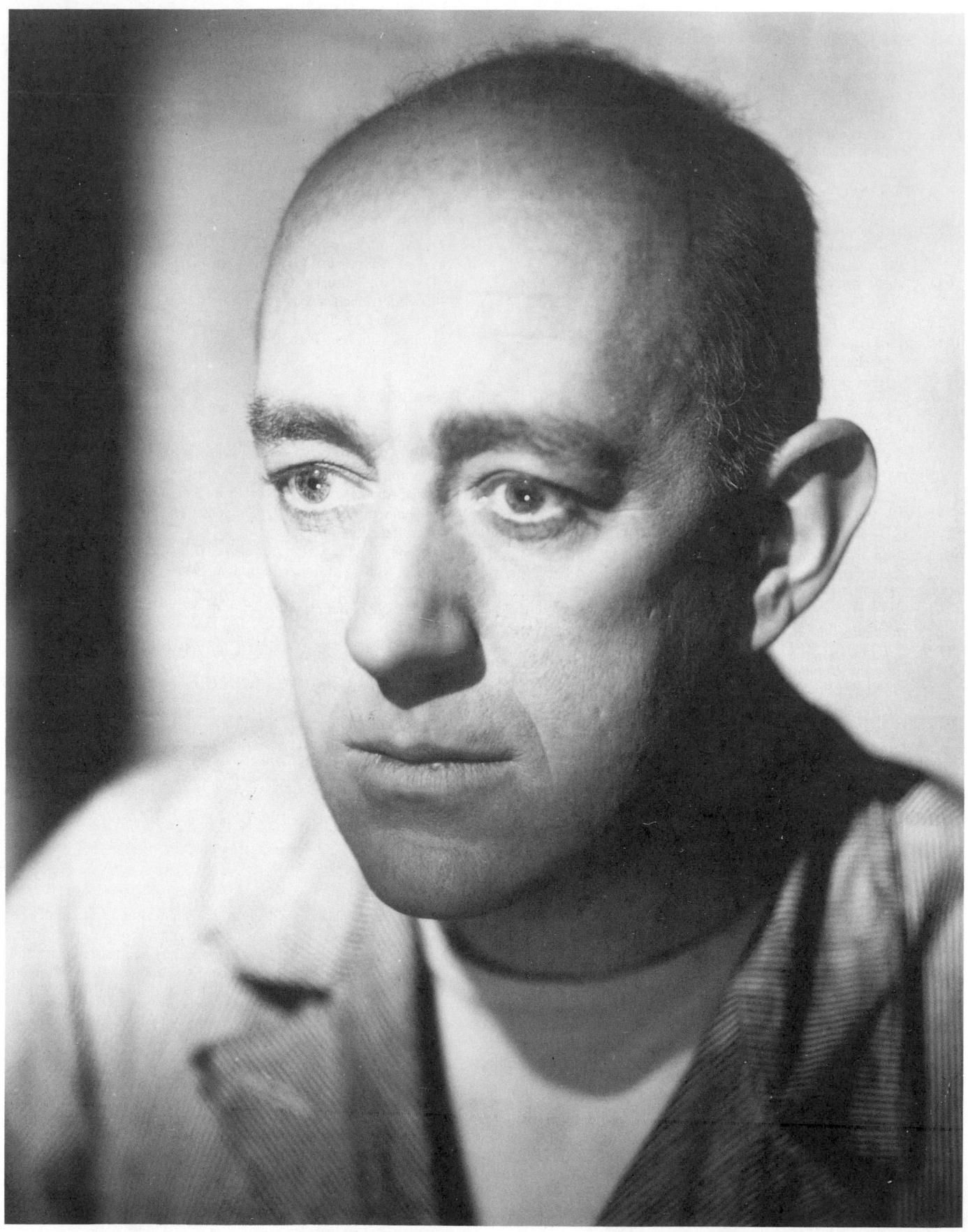

Alec Guinness in *The Prisoner*

one's performance: learning to cut the flourishes") reflect that personal reserve.

It is to another great British actor, John Gielgud, that Guinness owes his beginnings. Gielgud recommended him as a student to actress-teacher Martita Hunt (with whom Guinness would later co-star in *Great Expectations*) who, after several lessons, gave Guinness back his money: "I'm afraid you're wasting your time. You'll never be an actor." Luckily, Guinness persevered, winning a two-year scholarship to the Fay Compton Studio of Dramatic Art, where he was awarded (by Gielgud) the school's annual prize at graduation. Later, Gielgud offered him the part of Osric in his production of *Hamlet*. It was the turning point in Guinness's career. He worked for Gielgud and at the Old Vic until the outbreak of World War II, registering most strongly as a modern-day Hamlet at the Old Vic.

Guinness's film career began after he returned from the war, when he played Herbert Pocket in David Lean's *Great Expectations*, a role he had played in his own stage version of the Dickens novel. Guinness then pestered Lean into allowing him to play Fagin in *Oliver Twist*. Despite the elaborate makeup, he made the role completely credible—a full-blooded, pathetic Victorian monster. In the United States, critics deemed the performance anti-Semitic, and the film was heavily cut.

But it was his fourth film, *Kind Hearts and Coronets*, that made him a star. Beginning a long association with Ealing Studios, he appeared as eight characters, ranging from a doddering parson to a militant suffragette, whom the ninth in line to a duchy (Dennis Price) has to prune from the family tree. He received an Oscar nomination for *The Lavender Hill Mob* (as an obsequious bank clerk who succumbs to temptation). His reputation as a serious actor came with *The Prisoner*, a harrowing drama in which he played a persecuted cardinal behind the iron curtain.

Guinness's next important role was as the arrogant Colonel Nicholson, obsessed with his own code of rules and conventions in *The Bridge on the River Kwai*, a performance that garnered him several major awards. Ironically, it was a role director David Lean had to persuade him to take on because Guinness had a difficult time getting a grip on the character. Although memorable in *The Horse's Mouth* (his screenplay for the film was nominated for the Oscar), his next great role was in *Tunes of Glory*. Eschewing the more familiar role of a rigid martinet outsider (effectively portrayed by John Mills), he opted for the role of Jock Sinclair, an insensitive, hotheaded braggart whose outrageously clannish behavior brings about Mills's suicide and his own character's ultimate downfall.

His next leading role was the first one for which Guinness received unfavorable reviews. As the widowed Japanese diplomat Koichi Asano in *A Majority of One*, his only possible consolation was that Rosalind Russell, as the Yiddish widow Erma Jacoby, was as badly miscast as he. In the years that followed, Guinness played a number of supporting roles, the most significant of which were Prince Feisal in *Lawrence of Arabia*, Charles I in *Cromwell*, Ben Obi-Wan Kenobi in *Star Wars*, and Professor Godbole in *A Passage to India*, David Lean's comeback film after almost 16 years of directorial inactivity.

Over the years, Guinness has also turned in some outstanding performances on television—most notably in *Tinker, Tailor, Soldier, Spy* and *Smiley's People*, based on the espionage novels of John Le Carré; *Little Lord Fauntleroy*; and *Monsignor Quixote*, from the novel by Graham Greene. Guinness returned to the big screen, and to Dickens country, in the epic length *Little Dorrit* in 1987. He also had a small role in *Kafka*, released in 1991.

—Catherine Henry, updated by John McCarty

HACKMAN, Gene

Nationality: American. **Born:** Eugene Alden Hackman in San Bernardino, California, 30 January 1931. **Education:** Studied journalism, University of Illinois, Urbana, for six months; studied at a New York school for radio. **Military Service:** Served in the U.S. Marine Corps, 1947-52; disc jockey and newscaster for unit's radio station. **Family:** Married 1) Fay Maltese, 1956 (divorced 1985), children: Christopher, Elizabeth, Leslie; 2) Betsy Arakawa. **Career:** 1953—worked briefly for civilian radio and TV stations; then studied acting at Pasadena Playhouse; 1958—off-Broadway debut in *Chaparral*; 1959—television debut; 1961—film debut in *Mad Dog Coll*; 1963—Broadway debut in *Children from Their Games*; 1970—formed production company Chelly Ltd. **Awards:** Best Actor, Academy Award and Best Actor, New York Film Critics, for *The French Connection*, 1971; Best Actor, British Academy, for *The French Connection* and *The Poseidon Adventure*, 1972; Best Supporting Actor, Academy Award, for *Unforgiven*, 1992. **Address:** c/o Guttman, 118 South Beverly Drive #201, Beverly Hills, CA 90212, U.S.A.

Films as Actor:

1961   *Mad Dog Coll* (Balaban) (as cop)
1964   *Lilith* (Rossen) (as Norman)
1966   *Hawaii* (Hill) (as the Rev. John Whipple)
1967   *A Covenant with Death* (Johnson) (as Harmsworth); *First to Fight* (Nyby) (as Sgt. Tweed); **Bonnie and Clyde** (Arthur Penn) (as Buck Barrow); *Banning* (Winston) (as Tommy Del Gaddo)
1968   *Shadow on the Land* (Sarafian—for TV); *The Split* (Flemyng) (as Lt. Walter Brill); *Riot* (Kulik) (as Red Fletcher)
1969   *The Gypsy Moths* (Frankenheimer) (as Joe Browdy); *Downhill Racer* (Ritchie) (as coach); *Marooned* (John Sturges) (as Buzz Lloyd); *I Never Sang for My Father* (Cates) (as Gene Garrison)
1970   *Doctors' Wives* (Schaefer) (as Dr. Dave Randolph); *Confrontation* (Hiller—short)
1971   *The Hunting Party* (Medford); *The French Connection* (Friedkin) (as Jimmy "Popeye" Doyle)
1972   *Prime Cut* (Ritchie) (as "Mary Ann"); *Cisco Pike* (Norton) (as Holland); *The Poseidon Adventure* (Neame) (as the Rev. Frank Scott)
1973   *Scarecrow* (Schatzberg) (as Max)
1974   *The Conversation* (Coppola) (as Harry Caul); *Zandy's Bride* (Troell) (as Zandy); *Young Frankenstein* (Mel Brooks) (as guest)
1975   *Night Moves* (Arthur Penn) (as Harry Moseby); *Bite the Bullet* (Richard Brooks) (as Sam Clayton); *French Connection II* (Frankenheimer) (as Jimmy "Popeye" Doyle); *Lucky Lady* (Donen) (as Kibby)
1976   *The Domino Principle* (*The Domino Killings*) (Kramer) (as Roy Tucker)

1977   *A Bridge Too Far* (Attenborough) (as Maj. Gen. Sosabowski); *March or Die* (Richards) (as Maj. William Sherman Foster); *A Look at Liv* (*Liv Ullmann's Norway*) (Kaplan) (appearance)
1978   *Formula I, febbre della velocità* (*Speed Fever*) (Orefici and Morra) (as interviewee); *Superman* (Donner) (as Lex Luthor)
1980   *Superman II* (Lester) (as Lex Luthor); *The Making of Superman: The Movie* (Johnstone—doc) (appearance)
1981   *All Night Long* (Tramont) (as George Dupler); *Reds* (Beatty) (as Pete Van Wherry)
1983   *Under Fire* (Spottiswoode) (as Alex); *Superman III* (Lester) (as Lex Luthor); *Uncommon Valor* (Kotcheff) (as Col. Rhodes)
1984   *Misunderstood* (Schatzberg) (as Ned); *Eureka* (Roeg—produced in 1982) (as Jack McCann)
1985   *Twice in a Lifetime* (Yorkin) (as Harry Mackenzie); *Target* (Arthur Penn) (as Walter Lloyd)
1986   *Hoosiers* (*Best Shot*) (Anspaugh) (as Coach Norman Dale); *Power* (Lumet) (as Wilfred Buckley)
1987   *No Way Out* (Donaldson) (as David Brice, Secretary of Defense); *Superman IV: The Quest for Peace* (Furie) (as Lex Luthor)
1988   *Another Woman* (Woody Allen) (as Larry); *Bat 21* (Markle) (as Lt. Col. Iceal Hambleton); *Full Moon in Blue Water* (Masterson) (as Floyd); *Split Decisions* (*Kid Gloves*) (Drury) (as Dan McGuinn); *Mississippi Burning* (Parker) (as Anderson)
1989   *The Package* (Davis) (as Johnny Gallagher); *Loose Cannons* (Clarke) (as Mac)
1990   *Narrow Margin* (Hyams) (as Robert Caulfield); *Postcards from the Edge* (Nichols) (as Lowell); *Class Action* (Apted) (Jedediah Tucker Ward)
1991   *Company Business* (Meyer) (as Sam Boyd); *Class Action* (Apted) (as Jedediah Tucker Ward)
1992   **Unforgiven** (Eastwood) (as Sheriff "Little Bill" Daggett)
1993   *Geronimo: An American Legend* (Walter Hill) (as Brig.Gen. George Crook); *The Firm* (Pollack) (as Avery Tolar); *Earth and the American Dream* (Couturie—doc) (voice only)
1994   *Wyatt Earp* (Kasdan) (as Nicholas Earp)
1995   *Crimson Tide* (Scott) (as Frank Ramsey); *The Quick and the Dead* (Raimi) (as Herod); *Get Shorty* (Sonnenfeld) (as Harry Zimm)
1996   *The Birdcage* (Mike Nichols)

Publications

By HACKMAN: articles—

Interview with N. Mills, in *Stills* (London), April 1986.
Interview with B. Paskin, in *Films and Filming* (London), May 1986.
"Hackman: The Last Honest Man in America," interview with Beverly Walker, in *Film Comment* (New York), November/December 1988.

On HACKMAN: book—

Hunter, Allan, *Gene Hackman*, London, 1987.

On HACKMAN: articles—

Current Biography 1972, New York, 1972.
Hamill, P., "Hackman," in *Film Comment* (New York), September-October 1974.
Luft, H. G., "Gene Hackman: An American of Strength and Doubts," in *Films in Review* (New York), January 1975.
Ecran (Paris), October 1978.
Ward, Robert, "I'm Not a Movie Star: I'm an Actor!," in *American Film* (Washington, D.C.), March 1983.
Elia, M., "Gene Hackman. Monsieur Tout-le-monde," in *Séquences* (Montreal), November 1989.
Emerson, Jim, "Man of Iron," in *Premiere* (New York), February 1991.
Stars, September 1992.

*   *   *

Gene Hackman is one of that rare breed of actor whose star status has been built on talent alone. He may not be the handsomest or sexiest performer in the picture; his romantic roles have been infrequent, and mostly marginal to the plot. But you cannot stop watching him whenever he is on screen, even when the film in which he is appearing is run-of-the-mill. Hackman is an instinctive, intensely physical actor, as much at home playing loud-mouthed bullies and cunningly manipulative bad guys as stalwart or brooding heroes. He is especially adept at expressing himself by modulating his voice and subtly altering his expression, both of which communicate more to the audience than any dialogue. Few actors are more expert at giving ordinary people shadings of psychological complexity, and making larger-than-life characters seem more vulnerable and believable.

The first phase of Hackman's career commenced in the late 1960s. He had made his screen debut in a bit part as a cop in *Mad Dog Coll*, when he already had turned 30; six years were to pass before his appearance in *Bonnie and Clyde*, the first film in which he earned critical and audience attention. His performance as the genial but dimwitted older brother of Clyde Barrow won him an Oscar nomination, and instant stardom. He cemented his fame four years later with an Academy Award-winning star turn as "Popeye" Doyle, the bellicose, bigoted narcotics cop, in *The French Connection*. In between, he was splendid as the dutiful son unable to connect with his elderly parent in *I Never Sang for My Father*. Afterwards, he was equally fine as the obsessive surveillance expert in *The Conversation*; the itinerant bum lurching toward fellowship with another drifter in *Scarecrow*; and the dogged but emotionally torn-apart detective in *Night Moves*. His versatility may be exemplified by contrasting his performances in *The French Connection* and *Night Moves*. In each, he plays a good guy in search of bad guys, yet in *The French Connection* his performance befits his role in that it is outward and in-your-face; "Popeye" Doyle is a character whose actions affect others in the story. Conversely, in *Night Moves*, his outward toughness masks an inner vulnerability as he plays a character who not so much acts as is acted upon.

Hackman's career continued in a similar vein into the 1980s, at which point he offered equally fine performances as the television journalist who is intent upon becoming an anchorman in *Under Fire*; the tough, unorthodox basketball coach in *Hoosiers*; and the veteran FBI agent in *Mississippi Burning*. His way of getting inside a character is best summed up by critic Roger Ebert, writing about *Under Fire*: "Hackman never really convinced me that he could be an anchorman, but he did a better thing. He convinced me that he thought he could be one."

Not all of Hackman's films, however, have been of the highest caliber. His career has been littered with appearances in films ranging from the awful to the merely forgettable. This list begins with *The Split*, *Riot*, *Doctors' Wives*, *The Hunting Party*, *Prime Cut*, *Cisco Pike*, *Zandy's Bride*, *The Domino Principle*, and *March or Die*; and continues with *Bat 21*, *Full Moon in Blue Water*, *Split Decisions*, *The Package*, *Loose Cannons*, *Narrow Margin*, *Company Business*, and *The Quick and the Dead*. Mixed in were prestige roles in high-profile, big-budget Hollywood spectacles which required little more than his imposing presence. In *Superman* and its various sequels, he is the comically oily villain Lex Luthor. He is top-billed above an all-star cast in *The Poseidon Adventure*, one of the 1970s best disaster films, playing a heroic minister who cooly takes control after the capsizing of an ocean liner. Perhaps it was his coming to stardom at such a relatively advanced age—he was past 40 when he made *The French Connection*—that compelled him to be less selective in his choice of roles.

The second phase of Hackman's career started in the mid-1980s, when he began accepting juicy co-starring and supporting roles as corrupted authority figures. Some have been downright villainous: the scheming secretary of defense, who tries to cover up his murder of his mistress and in so doing makes an imposing foil for hero Kevin Costner, in *No Way Out*; and the ruthless outlaw-turned-sheriff, who hides his viciousness beneath a folksy demeanor, in *Unforgiven* (for which he earned a second Oscar). Other, similar characters have been more complexly twisted and deluded: the high-powered attorney who becomes mentor to hero Tom Cruise, and proves to be anguished and regretful, in *The Firm*; and the crusty, set-in-his-ways nuclear submarine commander, whose faulty judgment is challenged by hero Denzel Washington, in *Crimson Tide*.

But you can always expect a curve ball from Hackman. Once viewers became used to seeing him as foils for the hero, he offered an equally impressive performance in *Get Shorty* as a schlock movie producer who becomes comically involved with gangsters while attempting to finance his next project. In *Get Shorty*, actors other than Hackman—John Travolta, Delroy Lindo, Dennis Farina—get to play tough guy.

Despite his frequent lapses in judgment in selecting his film projects, Hackman has over the course of three decades appeared in an impressive list of exceptional films. In each, he has proved time and again to be a master of his craft.

—Fiona Valentine, updated by Rob Edelman

HANKS, Tom

Nationality: American. **Born:** Concord, California, 9 July 1956. **Education:** Attended California State University, Sacramento. **Family:** Married 1) Samantha Lewes, 1978 (divorced 1985), two children; 2) the actress Rita Wilson, 1988, sons: Chester, Truman Theodore. **Career:** Intern with the Great Lakes Shakespeare Festival, Cleveland, Ohio, and actor with the Riverside Shakespeare Company, New York City; 1980—film debut in *He Knows You're Alone*; TV work includes *Bosom Buddies*, 1980-82, *Happy Days*, 1982, and *Family Ties*, 1983-84. **Awards:** Best Actor Award, Los Angeles Film Critics, for *Big* and *Punchline*, 1988; Best Actor Academy Awards, for *Philadelphia*, 1993, and *Forrest Gump*, 1994. **Agent:** c/o Creative Artists Agency, 9830 Wilshire Blvd., Beverly Hills, CA 90212, U.S.A.

Films as Actor:

1980   *He Knows You're Alone* (Mastrioianni) (as Elliot)
1982   *Mazes and Monsters* (Stern—for TV)

Tom Hanks in *Forrest Gump*

1984   *Splash* (Ron Howard) (as Allan Bauer); *Bachelor Party* (Israel) (as Rick Gasko); *The Dollmaker* (Petrie—for TV)

1985   *The Man with One Red Shoe* (Dragoti) (as Richard); *Volunteers* (Meyer) (as Lawrence Bourne III)

1986   *The Money Pit* (Benjamin) (as Walter Fielding); *Nothing in Common* (Garry Marshall) (as David Basner); *Everytime We Say Goodbye* (Mizrahi) (as David)

1987   *Dragnet* (Mankiewicz) (as Pep Streebek)

1988   *Big* (Penny Marshall) (as Josh Baskin); *Punchline* (Seltzer) (as Steven Gold)

1989   *The 'Burbs* (Dante) (as Ray Peterson); *Turner and Hooch* (Spottiswoode) (as Scott Turner)

1990   *The Bonfire of the Vanities* (De Palma) (as Sherman McCoy); *Joe versus the Volcano* (Shanley) (as Joe Banks)

1992   *Radio Flyer* (Donner) (as narrator); *A League of Their Own* (Penny Marshall) (as Jimmy Dugan)

1993   *Sleepless in Seattle* (Ephron) (as Sam Baldwin); ***Philadelphia*** (Jonathan Demme) (as Andrew Beckett)

1994   ***Forrest Gump*** (Zemeckis) (title role)

1995   *Apollo 13* (Ron Howard) (as Jim Lovell); *Toy Story* (Lasseter) (as voice of Woody); *The Celluloid Closet* (Epstein and Friedman—doc) (as interviewee)

Film as Director:

1996   *That Thing You Do* (+ ro, sc)

Publications

By HANKS: articles—

Interview, in *Films* (London), July 1984.

Interview, in *Photoplay* (London), September 1984.

Interview, in *Time Out* (London), 26 October 1988.

Interview with Beverly Walker, in *Film Comment* (New York), March/April 1989.

"An Interview with Geena Davis," in *Interview* (New York), March 1992.

Interview with Brendan Lemon, in *Interview* (New York), December 1993.

"A Philadelphia Story," interview with Brad Gooch, in *Advocate*, 14 December 1993.

"Peaking Tom," interview with Brian D. Johnson, in *Maclean's* (Toronto), 11 July 1994.

On HANKS: books—

Trakin, Roy, *Tom Hanks: Journey to Stardom*, 1987; rev. ed.1995.

Salamon, Julie, *The Devil's Candy: "The Bonfire of the Vanities" Goes to Hollywood,* Boston, 1991.

Wallner, Rosemary, *Tom Hanks: Academy Award-Winning Actor*, Edina, Minnesota, 1994.

Pfeiffer, Lee, *The Films of Tom Hanks*, Secaucus, New Jersey, 1996.

On HANKS: articles—

Current Biography 1989, New York, 1989.
Troy, C., "It's a Cool Gig," in *American Film* (Hollywood), April 1990.
DeNicolo, David, "Right behind Mr. Nice Guy Lurks an Edgy Tom Hanks," in *New York Times*, 20 June 1993.
Conant, Jennet, "Tom Hanks Wipes That Grin off His Face," in *Esquire* (New York), December 1993.
Ebert, Roger, "Thanks, Hanks," in *Playboy* (Chicago), December 1994.

*   *   *

It is a cliché of press-agentry that comedians are always looking for a "stretch," seeking to redefine themselves as serious actors. Much rarer is the remarkable transformation of Tom Hanks from moderately successful television sitcom co-star to one of America's most beloved actors, matching only Spencer Tracy in winning two consecutive Oscars for Best Actor. Having firmly established his own comic persona, Hanks in certain recent roles seems to be deliberately playing against his type, or using it as a subtext, rather than simply abandoning it. Less a comedian with acting ability than an actor with a wry sensibility that lends itself to comic roles, Hanks has managed better than most comic actors of his generation to make a transition to dramatic leads. It is indicative of his post-Gump status as an all-American icon that his decent, solid performance as a decent, solid astronaut in *Apollo 13* was widely touted as deserving yet another Oscar.

Looking back on the 1984 *Splash*, which gave the young actor his first leading role and immediate stardom, one finds that he does not give an "apprentice" performance, one that affords mere glimpses of his future screen persona, but rather a full-blown Tom Hanks performance. Already in evidence is the distinctive combination of shyness and a cool knowingness. He already makes full use of his slightly pudgy boyish face with its crooked, perhaps impish smile; in particular he has mastered a great variety of facial reactions to others' bizarre or obnoxious behavior (a brother's outrageous schemes, a scientist's rudeness, a mermaid-lover eating a lobster, shell and all), as if he were engaged in an inner dialogue with himself. In the scene where the mermaid rejects the youth's marriage proposal, one sees a glimpse too of the petulant sarcastic anger that he will display more prominently in his dramatic roles in *Nothing in Common* and *Punchline*. He is often funniest when his character is unhappiest, as in the wedding scene, where the guests' queries about the youth's absent girlfriend (who has just rejected him) provoke increasingly exasperated reactions.

Splash also establishes a favorite situation for a Tom Hanks comedy: a relatively normal, reasonably sophisticated person reacting with surprisingly little hysteria to the most preposterous situations: a mermaid, a collapsing house, spooky neighbors, an insufferable dog, a human sacrifice to a volcano, or the vicissitudes of the Peace Corps. With the special exception of *Big*, the light comedies do not develop the Hanks persona so much as reprise it; indeed, they offer only a pale reflection of the original when the writing and direction are weak, as in *The 'Burbs*.

Hanks's boyish looks and, sometimes, air of mischief have suited him for roles in which an immature youth, not so much callow as heedless or self-centered, must grow up. In *Volunteers* the involuntary Peace Corps hero must (however perfunctorily) shape up; in *Nothing in Common* a self-characterized "childish, selfish" advertising executive has not yet become a "bona fide adult" because his estrangement from his parents has left him emotionally arrested; and in *Punchline*, a would-be comedian is (again) estranged from his father and capable only of an Oedipal crush upon an older woman. Even in *Sleepless in Seattle*, where the older Hanks is a widower with a small son and none of the impishness, the role calls for him to replay those anxious boyish days of having to learn the "rules" for dating all over again.

The maturity motif is treated most interestingly in *Big*, which critiques the perennial appeal of the American child-man to American women and to popular film audiences (while capitalizing upon that appeal at the same time). To portray a 13-year-old inside a man's body Hanks must eliminate the hip side of his persona altogether, but a surprising amount of the Hanks manner remains: the shyness, the wary alertness, the moments of exuberance and playfulness. Perhaps the really new dimension in this role is the occasional moment of naked vulnerability, notably in the moving scene of the man-child's first night in a sinister hotel.

Released the same year as *Big*, *Punchline* features one of Hanks's most complex dramatic performances. Here, besides successfully handling several virtuoso scenes, such as the on-stage emotional breakdown and the comic-pathetic "Singin' in the Rain" number, Hanks is able to make something consistent, scene by scene, of an extremely mercurial character, not to mention creating some sympathy for a frequently rude egotist. Of his performance as a gay lawyer with AIDS in the didactic *Philadelphia*, the cynical could argue that much of his physical decline is accomplished with makeup and much of the power of his "Maria Callas" monologue, virtually an aria in itself, comes from the diva's own voice and the director's near-expressionistic lighting and high camera angles. But certainly the actor must be credited for conveying the character's moments of overwhelming terror, determination to achieve justice, sardonic bitterness on occasion, and, with a touch of the Hanks boyish smile in the scene on the witness stand, an idealistic love for the law.

As for his incarnation of the "simpleton" Forrest Gump, it must suffice to say that behind the American-Gothic frown and near-monotone delivery, Hanks finds a remarkably subtle range of voice tones and glances to suggest an inner life for this fantasy character who is already "old" in suffering but never crushed by sorrow, an Ancient Mariner with a story to tell America but no guilt to expiate. The weight behind each reiteration of "That's all I have to say about that"; the merest hint of knowing disapproval in references to Richard Nixon; the rare outbursts of glee in reunions with Lieutenant Dan: these and countless other details add shadings to what could have been a stiffly allegorical figure.

Still occasionally choosing lighter roles he can breeze through, Hanks remains most memorable when he takes a risk in parts with curious mixes of comedy and drama, as with Gump or—a true character role—his drunken baseball coach in *A League of Their Own*. Only in *The Bonfire of the Vanities*, valiantly sporting an upper-crust accent but sabotaged by an ill-conceived script (and incidentally by his own nonpatrician looks), does Hanks fail to create a coherent character, although he at least gets to do a splendid display of outrage in the scene where he drives away the party guests.

—Joseph Milicia

HARA, Setsuko

Nationality: Japanese. **Born:** Masae Aida in Yokohama, 17 June 1920. **Career:** 1935—introduced to Nikkatsu studio by brother-in-law, the director Hisatora Kumagai; 1936—chosen by Dr. Arnold Franck for Japanese-German co-production *New Earth*; 1949—first of series of films with director Ozu, *Late Spring*; 1963—retired from films upon death of Ozu.

Setsuko Hara (center) with Chiyeko Higashijama (left) and Chishu Ryu in *Tokyo monogatari*

Films as Actress:

1937   *Atarashiki tsuchi* (*Die Tochter des Samurai*; *Die Liebe der Mitzu*; *The New Earth*) (Franck and Itami)

1938   *Denen Kokyogaku* (*Pastoral Symphony*) (Yamamoto)

1942   *Boro no kesshitai* (*Suicide Troops of the Watchtower*) (Imai)

1943   *Kessen no ozura e* (*Toward the Decisive Battle in the Sky*) (Watanabe); *Neppu* (*Hot Wind*) (Yamamoto)

1946   *Hikaritokage* (*Light and Shadow*); *Waga koiseshi otome* (*The Girl I Loved*) (Kinoshita); *Waga seishun ni kui nashi* (*No Regrets for My Youth*; *No Regrets for Our Youth*) (Kurosawa) (as Yukie); *Midorino furusato* (*Green Native Country*); *Reijin* (*A Beauty*)

1947   *Anjoke no butokai* (*A Ball at the Anjo House*; *The Ball of the Anjo Family*) (Yoshimura); *Onna dake no yuro* (*Ladies of the Night*)

1948   *Katug nogenkai*; *Yuwaku* (*Temptation*) (Yoshimura)

1949   **Banshun** (*Late Spring*) (Ozu) (as Noriko, the daughter); *Ojosan kampai* (*Here's to the Girls*) (Kinoshita); *Aoi sanmyaku* (*Blue Mountains*) (Imai)

1951   *Hakuchi* (*The Idiot*) (Kurosawa) (as Taeko Nasu); *Bakushu* (*Early Summer*) (Ozu) (as Noriko); *Meshi* (*Repast*) (Naruse) (as Michiyo Okamoto)

1953   ***Tokyo monogatari*** (*Tokyo Story*) (Ozu) (as Noriko); *Hakugy*

1954   *Yama no oto* (*Sounds from the Mountains*) (Naruse)

1956   *Shuu* (*Shower*) (Naruse)

1957   *Chieko-sho* (*The Chieko Story*) (Kumagai); *Tokyo boshoku* (*Tokyo Twilight*) (Ozu) (as Takako Numata); *Joshu to tomoni* (*Women in Prison*) (Hisamatsu)

1958   *Onnade arukoto* (*Women Unveiled*) (Kawashima); *Tokyo no kyujitsu* (*Holiday in Tokyo*) (Yamamoto)

1959   *Onna-gokoru* (*Woman's Heart*) (Maruyama); *Fujinkai no himitsu* (*A Woman's Secret*) (Yoshimura)

1960   *Robo no ishi* (*The Wayside Pebble*) (Hisamatsu) (as Oren Aikawa); *Kibo no aozora* (*Hope of Blue Sky*) (Kurata); *Musume tsuma haha* (*Daughters, Wives, and a Mother*) (Naruse); *Akibiyori* (*Late Autumn*) (Ozu) (as Akiko Miwa, the mother); *Fundoshi isha* (*The Country Doctor*; *Life of a Country Doctor*) (Inagaki) (as Iku, his wife)

1961   *Bojo no hito* (*Love and Fascination*) (Maruyama); *Kohayagawa-ke no aki* (*The End of Summer*; *Early Autumn*; *Last of Summer*) (Ozu) (as Akiko)

1962   *Chushingura* (*Loyal 47 Ronin*; *47 Samurai*) (Inagaki) (as Riku); *Musume to watashi* (*My Daughter and I*) (Horikawa) (as Mari's mother)

Publications

On HARA: books—

Richie, Donald, *Five Pictures of Yasujiro Ozu*, Tokyo, 1962.

Sato, Tadao, *Ozu Yasujiro no Geijutsu* [The Art of Yasujiro Ozu], Tokyo, 1971.

Ozu Yasujiro to Shigoto [Yasujiro Ozu—The Man and His Work], edited by Jun Satomi and others, Tokyo, 1972.

Richie, Donald, *Ozu*, Berkeley, California, 1974.

Richie, Donald, *Different People*, New York, 1987.

Bordwell, David, *Ozu and the Poetics of Cinema*, Princeton, New Jersey, 1988.

On HARA: articles—

Harvey, Stephen, "Setsuko Hara," in *Film Comment* (New York), November/December 1974.

Gillett, J., "Setsuko Hara," in *Film Dope* (London), September 1981.

Masson, A., "Setsuko Hara," in *Positif* (Paris), May 1982.

Wood, Robin, "The 'Noriko' Trilogy," in *cineAction* (Toronto), Winter 1992.

*   *   *

Although her career was prolific and her roles diverse, Setsuko Hara is known in the West primarily as a self-effacing character in six films of Yasujiro Ozu. Her range was far broader than the films made with Ozu would imply; her changes in behavior and appearance just within Kurosawa's *No Regrets for Our Youth*, for example, are astonishing. Nevertheless, Ozu captured the essence of her roles; feminine but strong, often traditional in dress but attracted to modern ways; part of a family unit but independent in spirit. For Ozu, Hara effectively embodies the complex position of modern Japan between its rich cultural heritage and its central role in the post-World War II global economy.

In *Currents in Japanese Cinema* Tadao Sato wrote, "Setsuko Hara had the image of a modern and intelligent woman, qualities that endeared her to Japanese audiences." (Comparisons to American stars such as Katharine Hepburn and Joan Crawford were common.) Perhaps her most representative role apart from her work with Ozu was as the persecuted widow in *No Regrets for Our Youth*, where, through her perseverance, she shows herself to be stalwart and indomitable. In many films she played characters who had careers or who were able to retain their own identities—and often to assert themselves—within the male-dominated society.

For Ozu, Setsuko Hara played a considerably more subtle version of the independent woman. In each of the six films she is without a husband, and her relationship with the family is predicated to a degree on their desire for her not to remain single. In *Late Spring* she is reluctant to marry and leave her widowed father; a decade later in *Late Autumn* Ozu cast her in the widowed role, as a mother whose daughter is similarly reluctant to leave home. In *The End of Summer*, Hara, again a widow, remains unmarried despite her family's concern. Choosing essentially to do what she wishes, she also advises her younger sister to marry for love rather than by arrangement. The independence never alienates her from her relatives. Indeed, Hara's characters are often the core of loving care within the family structure; in *Tokyo Story*, for example, Hara plays Noriko, a widowed daughter-in-law (again with no desire to remarry) whose affection for her husband's parents is greater than that of their own children. Hara's portrayal of Noriko (her role in three Ozu films, which critic Robin Wood has identified as a loose trilogy built around her) finally stands as one of the great portraits of human generosity and selflessness in world cinema.

Ozu captured Setsuko Hara in certain recurrent images. Most familiar is the enigmatic smile, often as she looks straight into the camera, in response to another character's solicitousness: in *Tokyo Story*, after a character asks her "Isn't life disappointing?," Hara's reply, "Yes, it is," is followed by just that smile, deepening the moment immeasurably. Ozu also contrasted her, particularly as she grew older, in formal, traditional kimono with another character wearing a dress (the younger sister in *The End of Summer*, the daughter in *Late Autumn*). That contrast is especially pointed during one scene in *The End of Summer* as the two sisters kneel by the water while discussing the differences in their lives. Although Ozu's films are commonly considered restrained, in the special moments when Hara's characters cry, after otherwise accepting all of life's misfortunes, the effect of emotional release for the audience can be devastating. For Ozu, Setsuko Hara must have been the perfect actress to play the genuinely loving daughter; it was only fitting that she chose to retire when he died, apparently also retiring her stage name to live in seclusion in Kamakura.

—Jerome Delamater, updated by Corey K. Creekmur

HARDY, Oliver. *See* **LAUREL, Stan, and Oliver HARDY.**

HARLOW, Jean

Nationality: American. **Born:** Harlean Carpenter in Kansas City, Missouri, 3 March 1911. **Education:** Attended Hollywood School for Girls. **Family:** Married 1) Charles Fremont McGrew 1927 (divorced 1929); 2) the producer Paul Bern 1932 (he committed suicide 1932); 3) Harold Rosson 1933 (divorced 1935). **Career:** Entered films as extra and bit player; 1930—contract with Howard Hughes, and played lead in *Hell's Angels*; 1932—contract with MGM; 1937—died during filming of *Saratoga*. **Died:** Of kidney failure, 7 June 1937.

Films as Actress:

1928   *Moran of the Marines* (Strayer); *Liberty* (McCarey—short)
1929   *Fugitives* (Beaudine); *Close Harmony* (Cromwell and Sutherland); *Double Whoopee* (Foster—short); *The Unkissed Man* (Roach—short); *Bacon Grabbers* (Foster—short); *This Thing Called Love* (Stein); *New York Nights* (Milestone); *The Saturday Night Kid* (Sutherland) (as Hazel)
1930   *Hell's Angels* (Hughes) (as Helen); *The Love Parade* (Lubitsch)
1931   *City Lights* (Chaplin) (as extra); **The Public Enemy** (*Enemy of the People*) (Wellman) (as Gwen Allen); *The Iron Man* (Browning) (as Rose); *The Secret Six* (Hill) (as Anne); *Goldie* (Stoloff) (title role); *Platinum Blonde* (Capra) (as Anne); *Three Wise Girls* (Beaudine) (as Cassie Barnes)
1932   *The Beast of the City* (Brabin) (as Daisy); *Red-Headed Woman* (Conway) (as Lil Andrews); *Red Dust* (Fleming) (as Vantine)
1933   *Hold Your Man* (Wood) (as Ruby Adams); *Dinner at Eight* (Cukor) (as Kitty); *What the Scotch Started* (short); *Bombshell* (*Blonde Bombshell*) (Fleming) (as Lola Burns)
1934   *The Girl from Missouri* (*100% Pure*) (Conway) (as Eadie)
1935   *Reckless* (Fleming) (as Mona Leslie); *China Seas* (Garnett) (as China Doll); *Riffraff* (Ruben) (as Hattie)
1936   *Wife vs. Secretary* (Brown) (as Whitey Wilson); *Suzy* (Fitzmaurice) (title role); *Libeled Lady* (Conway) (as Gladys Benton)
1937   *Personal Property* (Van Dyke)

Jean Harlow with Robert Williams in *Platinum Blonde*

Publications

On HARLOW: books—

Shulman, Irving, *Harlow: An Intimate Biography*, New York, 1964.
Conway, Michael, and Mark Ricci, *The Films of Jean Harlow*, New York, 1965.
Morella, Joe, and Edward Epstein, *Gable & Lombard & Powell & Harlow,* London, 1971.
Marx, Samuel, and Joyce Vanderveen, *Deadly Illusions: Jean Harlow and the Murder of Paul Bern*, New York, 1990.
Golden, Eve, *Platinum Girl: The Life and Legends of Jean Harlow*, New York, 1991.
Stenn, David, *Bombshell: The Life and Death of Jean Harlow*, New York, 1993.

On HARLOW: articles—

Almira, J., "Jean Harlow," in *Lumière du Cinéma* (Paris), March 1977.

Mank, G., "Jean Harlow 1911-1937," in *Films in Review* (New York), December 1978.
Schickel, Richard, "Jean Harlow" in *The Movie Star*, edited by Elisabeth Weis, New York, 1981.
Johnson, William, "Harlow's Time-Bomb," in *Film Comment* (New York), May/June 1992.
Hackett, Pat, "Jean Harlow, the Woman Who Made the World Believe Blonds Have More Fun," in *Interview*, September 1993.
James, Caryn, "A No-Apologies Woman for the 90's: Harlow," in *New York Times*, 1 October 1993.

On HARLOW: film—

Hollywood Remembers: Harlow: The Blonde Bombshell, television documentary, 1993.

*   *   *

Jean Harlow remains one of the more tragic instances of a talented star whose career was cut short by intense personal problems and ill health. Like Marilyn Monroe (in many respects both her psychological and artistic successor), Harlow died prematurely, in her case from kidney failure at the age of 26, after three failed marriages and a bittersweet affair with co-star William Powell.

The scandalous rumors surrounding both Harlow's death (could her Christian Scientist mother have intervened sooner to save her life?) and her second husband Paul Bern's suicide (did he kill himself to be free of his unhinged common-law wife Dorothy Milette?) resurface periodically in well-researched books such as *Platinum Girl* (1991). Although these regurgitated tragedies keep Harlow's name alive, they do little to shed light on her contradictory screen image of joyous sexuality.

Her entrance into films was an uncertain one, as an extra in such movies as *Love Parade* and Chaplin's *City Lights*, and in supporting roles in shorts appearing, for example, with Laurel and Hardy in *Double Whoopee*. After she secured a part in the 1929 feature film, *The Saturday Night Kid*, the maverick producer-director Howard Hughes put a nineteen-year-old Harlow under contract when he was converting his silent World War I aviation movie, *Hell's Angels*, into sound. Hughes, in effect, exploited her and her initial, more notorious image of the sluttish peroxided siren in loan-outs such as *Public Enemy*.

The next stage in Harlow's career came in 1932 when, parallel with her brief marriage to Paul Bern, MGM took over her contract, and permitted her to extend her image in the direction of satirical comedy. Harlow at last revealed herself to be a good actress with a subtle sense of humor, giving her public at once the glamorous image to which they were accustomed while developing a burlesque "send-up" of platinum blondes and their ways.

In Jack Conway's *Red-Headed Woman*, Harlow put her own irrepressible spin on the good-time girl image popularized by Clara Bow, the "It" Girl of the 1920s. This film, as well as Victor Fleming's *Red Dust*, with Harlow seductive and funny opposite Gable, and his saucy screwball farce *Blonde Bombshell* were made before the censorship code of the Hays office came into force. In the highly entertaining all-star comedy *Dinner at Eight*, Harlow outshone the veteran players.

In congenial vehicles (*Libeled Lady*, *Girl from Missouri*), lovable Harlow registers as a tomboy sidetracked by her own curves. Despite the persona of a boudoir goddess, Harlow seemed ill at ease as a maraboued mantrap in her early talkies. Allowed to reveal a bubbly sense of humor about her own voluptuousness, she hit her stride as a star. And even then, it is not oomph that lands her a dreamboat such as Clark Gable (*China Seas*) or Robert Taylor (*Personal Property*) or Spencer Tracy (*Riff-Raff*), but tenacity. Surprisingly touching in dramatic fare (ripping off Libby Holman's life in *Reckless* and playing seriocomic con games in *Hold Your Man*), Harlow displays a defensive vulnerability that illuminates all her memorable performances. The platinum hair, penciled eyebrows, and slinky wardrobe are just female drag Harlow donned as bait; what her co-stars and adoring fans discover is that she is sexiest when she reveals the soft allure under the Max Factor war paint. What gives the Harlow oeuvre a contemporary kick is her self-awareness, the sense that playing this role of shimmering vamp is a hoot for her and that she is forever trick-or-treating us in the costume of a seductress. Harlow was proud of her evident sex appeal, boasting that she never wore a bra even under her most revealing costumes. Her virtue as an actress lay in her innate sense of comedy, seeing through the artificial glamour by means of which she had originally gained her stardom, while at the same time fully appreciating its value.

—Roger Manvell, updated by Robert Pardi

HARRIS, Ed

Nationality: American. **Born:** Edward Allen Harris in Englewood, New Jersey, 28 November 1950. **Education:** Attended California Institute of the Arts, B.F.A., 1975; also attended Columbia University

and the University of Oklahoma. **Family:** Married the actress Amy Madigan, 1983, daughter: Lily Dolores. **Career:** 1981—stage appearance in *True West*, at South Coast Repertory, Costa Mesa, California; 1983—made off-Broadway debut in *Fool for Love*, Circle Repertory Theatre; 1985—appointed trustee, California Institute of the Arts; 1986—Broadway debut in *Precious Sons*, Longacre Theatre; 1994—in TV mini-series *The Stand*, and as one of the voices in *Baseball*. **Agent:** Contemporary Artists Agency, 9830 Wilshire Boulevard, Beverly Hills, CA 90212, U.S.A.

Films as Actor:

1977   *The Amazing Howard Hughes* (William A. Graham—for TV) (as Russ)
1978   *Coma* (Michael Crichton) (bit role)
1979   *The Seekers* (Hayers—for TV) (as Lt. William Clark)
1980   *Borderline* (Freedman) (as Hotchkiss); *The Aliens Are Coming* (Harvey Hart—for TV) (as Chuck Polchek)
1981   *Knightriders* (George Romero) (as Billy); *Dream On* (Harker)
1982   *Creepshow* (George Romero) (as Hank)
1983   *The Right Stuff* (Philip Kaufman) (as John Glenn); *Under Fire* (Spottiswoode) (as Oates)
1984   *Places in the Heart* (Benton) (as Wayne Lomax); *A Flash of Green* (Nuñez) (as Jimmy Wing); *Swing Shift* (Jonathan Demme) (as Jack Walsh)
1985   *Alamo Bay* (Malle) (as Shang); *Code Name: Emerald* (Sanger) (as Gus Lang); *Sweet Dreams* (Reisz) (as Charlie Dick)
1987   *Walker* (Alex Cox) (title role); *The Last Innocent Man* (Spottiswoode—for TV) (as Harry Nash)
1989   *To Kill a Priest* (Agnieszka Holland) (as Stefan); *Jacknife* (David Jones) (as Dave); *The Abyss* (James Cameron) (as Bud Brigman)
1990   *State of Grace* (Joanou) (as Frankie Flannery)
1991   *Paris Trout* (Gyllenhaal—for TV) (as Harry Seagraves)
1992   *Glengarry Glen Ross* (Foley) (as Dave Moss); *Running Mates (Dirty Tricks)* (Lindsay-Hogg—for TV) (as Hugh Hathaway)
1993   *Needful Things* (Fraser C. Heston) (as Sheriff Alan Pangborn); *The Firm* (Sydney Pollack) (as Wayne Tarrance)
1994   *China Moon* (John Bailey) (as Kyle Bodine); *Milk Money* (Richard Benjamin) (as Tom Wheeler)
1995   *Apollo 13* (Ron Howard) (as Gene Kranz); *Just Cause* (Glimcher) (as Blair Sullivan); *Nixon* (Oliver Stone) (as E. Howard Hunt)
1996   *Eye for an Eye* (Schlesinger) (as Mack McCann); *The Rock* (Bay)

Publications

By HARRIS: articles—

"Ed: The Private Faces of a Fierce Actor," interview with Amy Madigan, in *Interview* (New York), September 1992.
"Fredanded: Fred Ward and Ed Harris: Two Actors Who Give a Damn," interview with Brook Smith, in *Interview* (New York), March 1995.

On HARRIS: articles—

Griffin, Nancy, "Tough Enough," in *Premiere* (New York), November 1990.
Koehler, Robert, "Profile," in *Los Angeles Times*, 22 March 1992.
McNeil, Donald G. Jr., "George Wolfe and His Theater of Inclusion," in *New York Times*, 23 April 1995.
"Idol Chatter," in *Premiere* (New York), 1 August 1995.

*   *   *

Ed Harris in *The Right Stuff*

By the mid-1990s Ed Harris's acting career has fallen into three distinctive parts. He started on stage, beginning in 1975. After studying acting at the California Institute of the Arts, for a half dozen years his life became an almost nonstop whirl of theater activity in California (both Los Angeles and San Francisco), culminating in an acclaimed performance in Sam Shepard's *Fool for Love*. This staging was subsequently transferred to New York's Circle Repertory Company, signaling Harris's off-Broadway debut. In this intense period his stage appearances also include roles in *A Streetcar Named Desire*, *Sweet Bird of Youth*, *Julius Caesar*, *Hamlet*, *Camelot*, *The Time of Your Life*, and *The Grapes of Wrath*.

But then Hollywood called and Harris answered. His casting as astronaut John Glenn in *The Right Stuff* changed his whole life. He became a star. In a mid-1980s poll, Harris was named, with Jack Nicholson, as one of the sexiest balding men in America. Certainly this was just another silly testing of public opinion, but it meant praise bequeathed only on true movie stars, and by 1985 Harris was among them. On the screen, his powerful magnetism made him a lock for top roles in seemingly hot movies such as *Swing Shift*, *Places in the Heart*, and *Sweet Dreams*. Yet the work of this middle period with which Harris remains proudest of is in the virtually unseen *A Flash of Green*, a PBS "American Playhouse" project directed by Victor Nuñez which had a limited theatrical release.

But then something went wrong. In the late 1980s one after another of Harris's films bombed, or, if they made money, as with *The Abyss*, the take came in well below expectations. It was not as if Harris could not select moneymaking filmmakers with whom to work. James Cameron (*The Abyss*), Jonathan Demme (*Swing Shift*), and Louis Malle (*Alamo Bay*) were proven at the box-office and with the critics. Yet Harris's career as a movie star went south.

By nature a quietly intense man, Ed Harris worked best in Hollywood, with his compact, square-jawed face, in the role of a baffled Middle American working-stiff, trying to liberate himself from the chains of stoic masculinity. But by 1990 casting agents seemed uninterested, and Ed Harris began to rethink his career, setting aside a desire to become famous or make a lot of money, and seeking to doing projects he cared about. In the 1990s Ed Harris thus placed his film career on hold and returned to the theater. In 1992 he starred in Murray Mednick's play *Scar*, marking Harris's return to Los Angeles stages where he started.

Yet he continued to essay minor roles for Hollywood. He regularly appeared in television movies and as a top character actor in feature films. Dedicated to his craft, be it on stage or in front of the camera, he is nonetheless often wasted. For example in *Milk Money* he did a fine job in a small role as the proenvironmentalist, bashful widower. His work is tops, but minor in the blockbuster *The Firm*, in which Tom Cruise and Gene Hackman star while Harris did his usual first-rate job as an FBI investigator. His range as a supporting performer has rarely been surpassed and so Ed Harris seems forever stuck in this rut as a character actor. But when he shines, few surpass him. As abusive husband Charlie Dick in *Sweet Dreams*, the story of the life of country music legend Patsy Cline, Ed Harris is chilling, loving, and dangerous all at the same time. It is this type of work in minor roles that is underappreciated, but does make a lasting contribution to film history.

—Douglas Gomery

HARRIS, Richard

Nationality: Irish. **Born:** Limerick, 1 October 1933. **Education:** Studied at the London Academy of Music and Dramatic Art. **Family:** Married 1) Elizabeth Rees-Williams, 1957 (divorced 1969), four children, including the director Damian, and the actors Jared and Jamie; 2) Ann Turkel, 1975 (divorced 1982). **Career:** Mid-1950s—member of Joan Littlewood's Theatre Workshop Company; 1956—West End debut; 1958—film debut in *Alive and Kicking*; 1968—signed three-picture contract with Paramount; success as a recording artist; 1990—returned to London stage in *Henry IV*. **Awards:** Best Actor Award, Cannes Festival, for *This Sporting Life*, 1963.

Films as Actor:

1958 *Alive and Kicking* (Frankel) (as lover)
1959 *Shake Hands with the Devil* (Michael Anderson) (as Terence O'Brien); *The Wreck of the Mary Deare* (Michael Anderson) (as Higgins)
1960 *A Terrible Beauty* (*Night Fighters*) (Garnett) (as Sean Reilly)
1961 *The Long and the Short and the Tall* (*Jungle Fighters*) (Norman) (as Cpl. Johnstone); *The Guns of Navarone* (Thompson) (as Barnsby); *Mutiny on the Bounty* (Milestone) (as John Mills)
1963 *This Sporting Life* (Lindsay Anderson) (as Frank Machin); *Major Dundee* (Peckinpah) (as Capt. Benjamin Tyreen)
1964 *Il deserto rosso* (*The Red Desert*) (Antonioni) (as Corrado Zeller)
1965 *I tre volti* (Antonioni and Bolognini); *The Heroes of Telemark* (Anthony Mann) (as Knut Straud)
1966 *Hawaii* (George Roy Hill) (as Rafer Hoxworth); *The Bible . . . in the Beginning* (*The Bible*) (Huston) (as Cain)
1967 *Caprice* (Tashlin) (as Christapher White); *Camelot* (Logan) (as King Arthur)
1968 *The Molly Maguires* (Ritt) (as James McParlan/McKenna)
1970 *A Man Called Horse* (Silverstein) (title role); *Cromwell* (Hughes) (title role)
1971 *Man in the Wilderness* (Sarafian) (as Zachary Bass); *The Snow Goose* (for TV)
1973 *The Deadly Trackers* (Shear) (as Kilpatrick)
1974 *99 and 44/100 Per Cent Dead* (*Call Harry Crown*) (Frankenheimer) (as Harry Crown); *Juggernaut* (Lester) (as Fallon)
1976 *Echoes of a Summer* (Taylor) (as Eugene Striden, + exec pr, mus); *Robin and Marian* (Lester) (as King Richard); *The Return of a Man Called Horse* (Kershner) (title role)
1977 *Gulliver's Travels* (Hunt) (title role); *The Cassandra Crossing* (Cosmatos) (as Chamberlain); *Orca* (Michael Anderson) (as Capt. Nolan); *Golden Rendezvous* (Lazarus) (as John Carter)
1979 *The Wild Geese* (McLaglen) (as Rafer Janders); *The Ravagers* (Compton) (as Falk); *The Last Word* (Boulting) (as Danny Travis)
1980 *A Game for Vultures* (Fargo) (as David Swansey)
1981 *Your Ticket Is No Longer Valid* (Kaczender); *Tarzan, the Ape Man* (Derek) (as Parker)
1982 *Triumphs of a Man Called Horse* (Hough) (title role)

1984 *Highpoint* (Carter) (as Louis Kinney)
1985 *Martin's Day* (Gibson) (as Martin Steckert)
1988 *Maigret* (Paul Lynch—for TV)
1989 *Mack the Knife* (*The Threepenny Opera*) (Golan) (as Mr. Peachum); *King of the Wind* (Duffell) (as King George II)
1990 *The Field* (Sheridan) (as "Bull" McCabe)
1992 *Unforgiven* (Eastwood) (as English Bob); *Patriot Games* (Noyce) (as Paddy O'Neil); *Silent Tongue* (Shepard) (as Prescott Roe)
1993 *Wrestling Ernest Hemingway* (Haines) (as Frank)
1994 *Abraham* (Sargent—for TV) (title role); *This Is the Sea* (McGuckian)
1995 *Cry, the Beloved Country* (Roodt) (as James Jarvis); *Savage Hearts* (Ezra) (as Sir Roger Foxley; *The Great Kankinsky* (Winsor—for TV) (title role)

Film as Director:

1969 *Bloomfield* (+ ro as Eitan)

Other Film:

1970 *La Dame dans l'auto avec des lunettes et un fusil* (*The Lady in the Car with Glasses and a Gun*) (Litvak) (co-sc)

Publications

By HARRIS: book—

Honor Bound (novel), 1982.

By HARRIS: articles—

Interview, in *Films and Filming* (London), April 1965.
Interview, in *Photoplay* (London), June 1977.
Interview with T. Perlmutter, in *Cinema Canada* (Montreal), February 1986.
Interview with Lynn Barber, in the *Independent on Sunday* (London), 1 July 1990.

On HARRIS: books—

Smith, Gus, *Richard Harris: An Actor by Accident*, London, 1990.
Callan, Michael Feeney, *Richard Harris: A Sporting Life*, London, 1992.

On HARRIS: article—

Current Biography 1964, New York, 1964.
Collins, G., "Richard Harris: At Work in 'The Field,'" in *New York Times*, 16 December 1990.

*   *   *

Richard Harris's career is linked to a pair of his contemporaries: Peter O'Toole (who, like Harris, is an Irishman), and South Wales-born Richard Burton. All three were outstanding actors who burst onto the international film scene in a flash and were heralded for their ability to command movie screens. And similarly, all three dissipated themselves by carousing and dallying with spirits, in the process dulling their talents and losing their looks. But of the three, Harris's career has never quite equalled that of Burton or O'Toole.

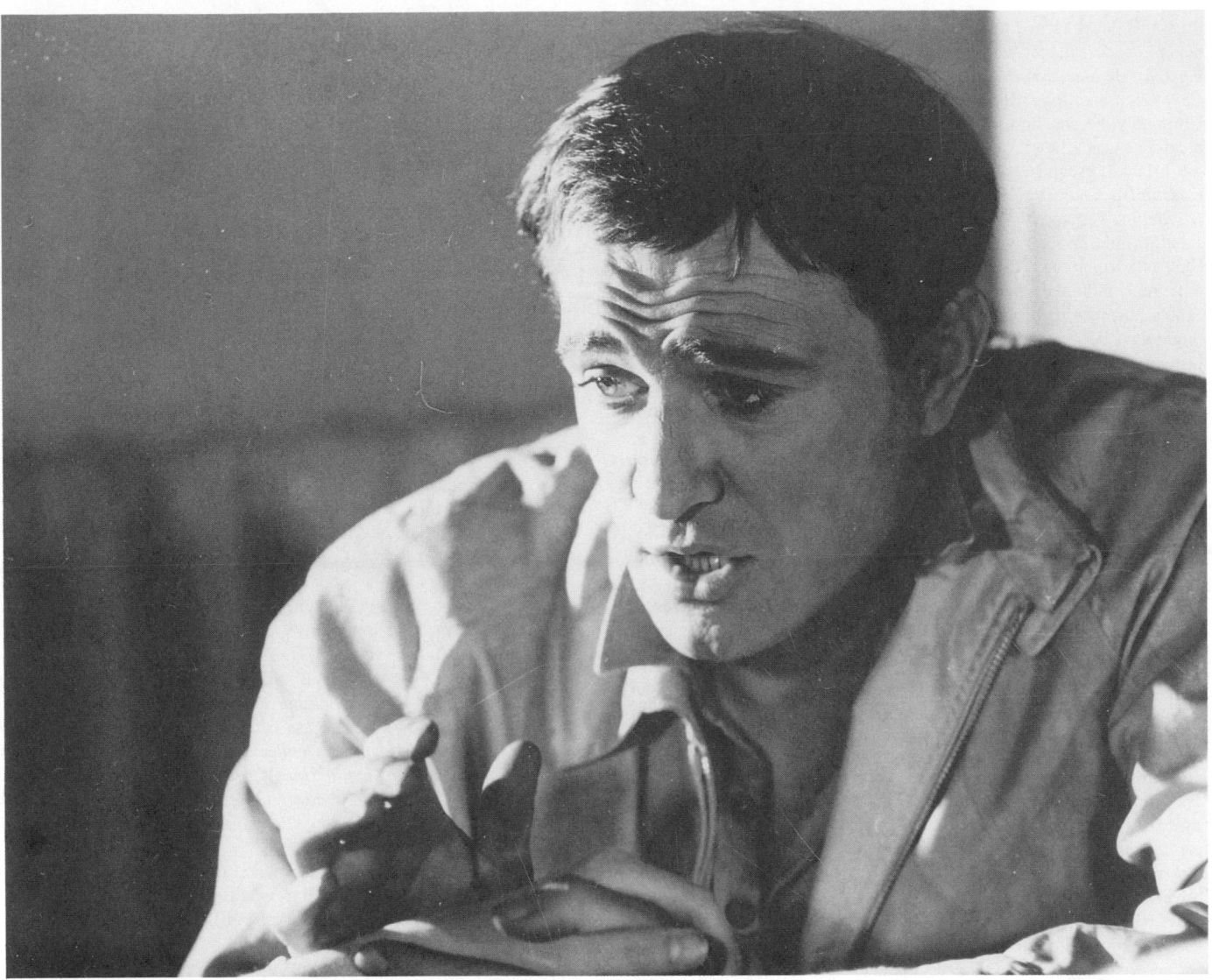

Richard Harris in *This Sporting Life* **courtesy of The Rank Organisation Plc**

After acting on stage during the 1950s as a member of Joan Littlewood's Theatre Workshop Company, Harris appeared in supporting roles in various, mostly British-made features. More often than not he is the macho Irishman, representing the lower ranks against effete officers and higher-billed movie stars in the likes of *Shake Hands with the Devil* and *A Terrible Beauty* (in which he serves in the Irish Republican Army), *The Guns of Navarone* and *The Long and the Short and the Tall* (in which he grunts through World War II), and *The Wreck of the Mary Deare* and *Mutiny on the Bounty* (in which he is a mutinous scoundrel). His key early career performance came in a starring role, as one of the classic angry young men of early 1960s British cinema. In Lindsay Anderson's *This Sporting Life*, Harris offers a soul-rattling performance as a rugged, discontented Yorkshire coal miner who becomes a fiercely brutal professional rugby player. The actor perfectly conveys his character's masochistic tendencies as he takes his physical and emotional knocks on and off the playing field.

As the years passed, however, Harris became known more for his headline-grabbing bouts of public drunkenness than for his work on screen. He had become established as a name actor, and he traded in on his fame to earn paychecks by appearing in a variety of international productions. Several were action and historical dramas, including *The Heroes of Telemark*, *The Bible*, and *Cromwell*; his performances became ever more hammy, as evidenced by his work in *Major Dundee* and *The Molly McGuires*. On rare occasion, he fully succeeded in a role: he had his best part since *This Sporting Life* in the violent back-to-nature cult hit *A Man Called Horse*, playing a nineteenth-century English aristocrat who is seized by the Sioux and suffers through torture to demonstrate his worth. But this success did not propel him upward. Rather, he repeated himself in two shabby sequels, *The Return of a Man Called Horse* and *Triumphs of a Man Called Horse*, and covered similar terrain in *Man in the Wilderness* and *The Deadly Trackers*. Unlike *Little Big Man* and *Dances with Wolves*, there is no attempt at liberal political correctness in any of these films; their chief ingredient is suffering, for the sake of suffering.

Harris did enjoy several offscreen successes. His song "MacArthur's Park" was a freak hit, and he played King Arthur on stage in the musical *Camelot* (earlier, he had appeared in the role in the ill-conceived screen version). But Harris mostly bounced around the movies. He co-wrote the screenplay of a dull thriller with a colorful title, *The Lady in the Car with Glasses and a Gun*. He executive produced and wrote a song for *Echoes of a Summer*, in which Jodie Foster has a fatal

519

illness. He even turned to direction with *Bloomfield*, a drama about a battered soccer player which harkens desperately back to *This Sporting Life*. He appeared in a pair of wry potboilers, *99 and 44/100 Per Cent Dead* and *Juggernaut* (in which he is reduced to self-parody). Ultimately, he was content to accept any old role in any old action picture he was offered, wearily plodding without commitment through the hijacks, escapes, shootouts, and travelogue locations in *The Cassandra Crossing*, *Golden Rendezvous*, *The Wild Geese*, and *Highpoint*. Perhaps his low points were appearances in a couple of standing-joke movies with Bo Derek, *Orca* (in which he snaps at Charlotte Rampling, "I resent it when a pretty and intelligent woman tells me I'm dumber than a fish") and *Tarzan, the Ape Man* (playing Jane's put-upon explorer father). Had his stature been greater, he might have been cast opposite Audrey Hepburn in *Robin and Marian*; instead, Sean Connery got the role, with Harris reduced to a cameo as Richard the Lion-Hearted. In the early 1980s, with his career languishing, he semiretired to Paradise Island in the Bahamas, where he rid himself of his drinking and embraced a more simple lifestyle.

In the 1990s, well into middle age, Harris has enjoyed a celluloid renaissance. This was sparked by his Academy Award-nominated performance in *The Field*, in which he has his best role in years: "Bull" McCabe, a charismatic Irish tenant farmer who has spent his life toiling his land. Conflict arises when the acreage is made available for auction, and it appears that the highest bidder will be a rich American planning to pave it and make it into an access road. Harris gives a resounding, commanding performance as the self-respecting farmer, a relic of a more uncomplicated era, who perceives that divinity and nature are one in the same.

He later made a brief but colorful appearance in *Unforgiven* as the insolent railroad gunman English Bob. Most recently, he has been paired in star turns with equally powerful actors whose characters outwardly have virtually nothing in common but who come to bond in the course of the story. In *Wrestling Ernest Hemingway*, he is an Irish ex-sea captain—a character he was born to play—whose need for camaraderie links him with Robert Duvall's Cuban barber. *Cry, the Beloved Country*, a remake of the 1951 film of Alan Paton's esteemed novel of South Africa, is the story of two fathers, one black and the other white, who know each other only by sight but become united in tragedy. Harris is quietly effective as a conservative South African farmer who becomes embittered upon the murder of his social reformer son, whose killer so happens to be the son of an elderly Zulu priest (James Earl Jones). Despite these recent successes, Harris's career will forever be characterized not by what was, but by what might have been.

—Kim Newman, updated by Rob Edelman

HARRISON, (Sir) Rex

Nationality: British. **Born:** Reginald Carey Harrison in Huyton, Lancashire, 5 March 1908. **Education:** Attended Birkdale Preparatory School; Liverpool College. **Military Service:** Royal Air Force, 1942-45: flight lieutenant. **Family:** Married 1) Marjorie Noel Collette Thomas, 1934 (divorced 1942), son: the actor Noel; 2) the actress Lilli Palmer, 1942 (divorced 1957), son: Carey; 3) the actress Kay Kendall, 1957 (died 1959); 4) the actress Rachel Roberts, 1962 (divorced 1971); 5) Elizabeth Harris, 1971 (divorced); 6) Mercia Mildred Tinker, 1978. **Career:** 1924-27—member of Liverpool Playhouse; 1927—toured in *Charley's Aunt*; 1931—West End debut in *Getting George Married*; 1931-35—alternated touring with London stage appearances; 1936—Broadway debut in *Sweet Aloes*; contract with Alexander Korda, began making films for Denham Studios; 1945—

seven-year contract with 20th Century-Fox; 1950s—worked principally in theater; 1956-58—in *My Fair Lady* on Broadway; continued stage work through 1980s. **Awards:** Best Actor Academy Award and Best Actor, New York Film Critics, for *My Fair Lady*, 1964; Order of Merit (Italy), for *The Agony and the Ecstasy*, 1965; knighted, June 1989. **Died:** Of pancreatic cancer, in New York City, 2 June 1990.

Films as Actor:

1930   *The School for Scandal* (Elvey) (bit role); *The Great Game* (Raymond) (as George)

1934   *Get Your Man* (George King) (as Tom Jakes); *Leave It to Blanche* (Harold Young) (as Ronnie)

1935   *All at Sea* (Kimmins) (as Aubrey Bellingham)

1936   *Men Are Not Gods* (Reisch) (as Tommy Stapleton)

1937   *Storm in a Teacup* (Saville and Dalrymple) (as Frank Burdon); *School for Husbands* (Marton) (as Leonard Drummond); *Over the Moon* (Freeland and William K. Howard) (as Dr. Freddie Jarvis)

1938   *St. Martin's Lane* (*Sidewalks of London*) (Whelan) (as Harley Prentiss); *The Citadel* (King Vidor) (as Dr. Lawford)

1939   *The Silent Battle* (*Continental Express*) (Herbert Mason) (as Jacques Sauvin); *Ten Days in Paris* (*Missing Ten Days*; *Spy in the Pantry*) (Whelan) (as Bob Stevens)

1940   *Night Train to Munich* (*Night Train*) (Reed) (as Gus Bennett)

1941   *Major Barbara* (Pascal) (as Adolphus Cusins)

1945   *Journey Together* (John Boulting) (bit role); *I Live in Grosvenor Square* (*A Yank in London*) (Wilcox) (as Major David Bruce); *Blithe Spirit* (Lean) (as Charles Condomine); *The Rake's Progress* (*Notorious Gentleman*) (Gilliat) (as Vivian Kenway)

1946   *Anna and the King of Siam* (Cromwell) (as King Mongkut)

1947   *The Ghost and Mrs. Muir* (Joseph L. Mankiewicz) (as the Ghost of Capt. Daniel Gregg); *The Foxes of Harrow* (Stahl) (as Steven Fox)

1948   *Escape* (Joseph L. Mankiewicz) (as Matt Denant); *Unfaithfully Yours* (Preston Sturges) (as Sir Alfred de Carter)

1951   *The Long Dark Hall* (Bushell and Beck) (as Arthur Groome)

1952   *The Four Poster* (Reis) (as John)

1953   *The Charm of Life* (Grémillon and Kast—short, English-language version of *Les Charmes de l'existence*) (as narrator); *Main Street to Broadway* (Garnett) (as guest)

1954   *King Richard and the Crusaders* (David Butler) (as Emir Ilderim/Saladin); *The Constant Husband* (Gilliat) (as Charles Hathaway)

1956   *This Is London* (Jago—short) (as narrator)

1958   *The Reluctant Debutante* (Minnelli) (as Jimmy Broadbent)

1960   *Midnight Lace* (David Miller) (as Tony Preston)

1962   *The Happy Thieves* (*Once a Thief*) (George Marshall) (as Jimmy Bourne)

1963   *Cleopatra* (Joseph L. Mankiewicz) (as Julius Caesar)

1964   *My Fair Lady* (Cukor) (as Professor Henry Higgins); "England" ep. of *The Yellow Rolls-Royce* (Asquith) (as Marquess of Frinton)

1965   *The Agony and the Ecstasy* (Reed) (as Pope Julius II); *Flashes Festivals* (Gérard—short)

1967   *The Honey Pot* (*It Comes Up Murder*) (Joseph L. Mankiewicz) (as Cecil Fox); *Dr. Doolittle* (Fleischer) (title role)

1968   *A Flea in Her Ear* (Charon) (as Victor Chandebisse/Poche)

1969   *Staircase* (Donen) (as Charlie Dyer)

1973   *The Adventures of Don Quixote* (Rakoff—for TV) (title role)

1975   *The Gentleman Tramp* (Patterson)

1977   *Behind the Iron Mask* (*The Fifth Musketeer*) (Annakin) (as Colbert)

1978   *Shalimar* (*Deadly Thief*) (Shah); *Crossed Swords* (*The Prince and the Pauper*) (Fleischer) (as Duke of Norfolk)

1979 *Ashanti* (Fleischer) (as Brian Walker)
1983 *The Kingfisher* (James Cellan Jones—for TV); *A Time to Die* (*Seven Graves for Rogan*) (Cimber) (as Von Osten)
1986 *Anastasia: The Mystery of Anna* (Chomsky—for TV) (as Grand Duke Cyril Romanov); *Heartbreak House* (Page—for TV)

Publications

By HARRISON: books—

Rex: An Autobiography, New York, 1975.
If Love Be Love (poetry anthology), editor, London, 1979.
A Damned Serious Business, London, 1990.

By HARRISON: article—

Interview in *Plays and Players*, March 1974.

On HARRISON: books—

Harrison, Elizabeth, *Love, Honour, and Dismay*, London, 1976.
Eyles, Allen, *Rex Harrison*, London, 1985.
Moseley, Roy, with Philip and Martin Masheter, *Rex Harrison: The First Biography*, London, 1987; as *Rex Harrison: A Biography*, New York, 1987.
Wapshott, Nicholas, *Rex Harrison: A Biography*, New York, 1992.
Walker, Alexander, *Fatal Charm: The Life of Rex Harrison*, New York, 1993.

On HARRISON: articles—

Behlmer, Rudy, "Rex Harrison," in *Films in Review* (New York), December 1965.
Bradshaw, J., "Oozing Charm from Every Pore," in *Esquire* (New York), July 1972.
Ecran (Paris), November 1979.
Current Biography 1986, New York, 1986.
Obituary in *Variety* (New York), 6 June 1990.
Ferguson, K., obituary in *Film Monthly* (Berkhamsted, England), August 1990.

*   *   *

Although Rex Harrison was such a commanding presence on screen, and seemed to have been a star for an incalculable number of years, in reality he did not make his mark until the 1940s. Given co-starring or featured roles in British films of the 1930s, Harrison always appeared to be overshadowed or out-acted by his colleagues, particularly Vivien Leigh in *Storm in a Teacup* and *St. Martin's Lane*, two films that should have helped the actor's career. As the King in *Anna and the King of Siam*, and as the jealous symphony conductor in *Unfaithfully Yours*, Harrison at last gained a substantial audience, but gossip concerning the suicide of Carole Landis, with whom he had had an affair, effectively ended his first Hollywood career.

This tragedy, rather than hurting Harrison, helped in the long run, for it allowed him to refine his acting on stage, and to recreate the image of the suave, urbane Englishman suggested by some of the actor's early films, such as *Blithe Spirit* and *The Rake's Progress*, but never fully developed. Harrison's portrayal of Professor Henry Higgins in *My Fair Lady*, of course, epitomized the new characterization, and it was further developed in *The Yellow Rolls-Royce*. Nevertheless, one should not categorize Harrison. *Cleopatra* gave him, out of everyone in the cast, an opportunity to dominate the scene as Caesar, and to rise above the banal script and production (and his first Oscar nomina-

tion). Yet again, in *The Agony and the Ecstasy*, as Pope Julius II, he was able to overcome the poor production, while *Staircase* presented him with a rare opportunity for "camp" comedy.

Following *Staircase* until his death in 1990, Harrison appearing only infrequently in films and only in supporting roles, including two swashbuckling failures, *Behind the Iron Mask* and *Crossed Swords*. He found more success on the stage in this period, however, including another go at Caesar in George Bernard Shaw's *Caesar and Cleopatra*, touring revivals of *My Fair Lady*, and up to a month before his death a lead role on Broadway in W. Somerset Maugham's *The Circle*. Over a 65-year career, Harrison had established himself as a top-notch performer of sophisticated roles on stage and on screen, and had secured a permanent place in the film pantheon as Professor Henry Higgins.

—Anthony Slide, updated by David E. Salamie

HART, William S.

Nationality: American. **Born:** William Surrey Hart in Newburgh, New York, 6 December 1865 (some sources give 1870). **Family:** Married Winifred Westover, 1921 (divorced 1927), son: William, Jr. **Career:** Lived for a time with a family in Dakota territory; 1888—worked at New York City post office, began studying acting with F. F. Markey; then actor with various troupes, established as supporting actor; 1899—created role of Messala in *Ben-Hur*; 1905—Broadway success as cowboy in *The Squaw Man*; 1907-08—performed lead in *The Virginian*; 1914—first film, 2-reeler *His Hour of Manhood* and first feature, *The Bargain*; first picture as director and star, *In the Sage Brush Country*; contract with Thomas Ince; 1915—joined Triangle Film Corp. formed by Ince, Harry Aitken, and D. Griffith; 1917—followed Ince to Famous Players-Lasky, given lucrative contract by Adolph Zukor; 1919—began association with director Lambert Hillyer; early 1920s—decline in production, negative publicity surrounding paternity suit (suit dismissed); 1925—made last film *Tumbleweeds* for United Artists; retired to ranch in Newhall, California. **Died:** 23 June 1946.

Films as Actor:

1914 *His Hour of Manhood* (Chatterton or Barker) (as Pete Larson); *Jim Cameron's Wife* (Chatterton or Barker) (as Andy Stiles); *The Bargain* (Barker) (as Jim Stokes)
1915 *On the Night Stage* (Barker—reissued 1918 as *The Bandit and the Preacher*) (as "Silent" Texas Smith)
1916 *The Captive God* (Swickard) (as Chippa)
1917 "War Relief" ep. of *All Star Production of Patriotic Episodes for the Second Liberty Loan* (Neilan) (as himself); *The Narrow Trail* (Hillyer) (as Ice Harding)
1919 *Wagon Tracks* (Hillyer) (as Buckskin Hamilton); *John Petticoats* (Hillyer) (as "Hardwood" John Haynes)
1920 *Sand* (Hillyer) (as Dan Kurrie); *The Toll Gate* (Hillyer) (as Black Deering, + co-sc); *The Cradle of Courage* (Hillyer) (as "Square" Kelly); *The Testing Block* (Hillyer) (as "Sierra" Bill, + story)
1921 *O'Malley of the Mounted* (Hillyer) (as Sergeant O'Malley, + story); *The Whistle* (Hillyer) (as Robert Evans); *White Oak* (Hillyer) (as Oak Miller, + story); *Three Word Brand* (Hillyer) (as Three Word Brand/Governor Paul Marsden/Ben Trego)
1922 *Travelin' On* (Hillyer) (as J. B., + story)

William S. Hart

1923 *Wild Bill Hickok* (Smith) (title role, + story); *Hollywood* (Cruze)
      (as guest)
1924 *Singer Jim McKee* (Smith) (title role, + story)
1925 *Tumbleweeds* (Baggot—reissued 1939 with spoken 8-minute
      prologue by Hart) (as Dan Carver)
1928 *Show People* (Vidor) (as guest)
1934 *The Hollywood Gad-About* (Lewyn—short) (appearance)

Films as Director and Actor:

1914 *The Passing of Two-Gun Hicks* (*Taming the Four-Flusher*)
      (title role); *In the Sage Brush Country* (*Mr. Nobody*) (as Jim
      Brandon)
1915 *The Scourge of the Desert* (*Reformed Outlaw*) (as Bill Evers);
      Mr. "Silent" Haskins (*The Marked Deck*; *Dealing for
      Daisy*; *His Royal Flush*; *Man against Man*) (as Lon
      Haskins); *The Sheriff's Streak of Yellow* (as Sheriff Hale);
      The Grudge (*The Haters*) (as Rio Ed); *The Roughneck*
      (*The Gentlemen from Blue Gulch*) (as Dave Page); *The
      Taking of Luke McVane* (*The Fugitive*) (title role); *The

Man from Nowhere (*The Silent Stranger*; *His Duty*) (as
Buck Varley); *"Bad Buck" of Santa Ynez* (*The Bad Man*;
Revolver Bill; *A Desperate Chance*) (as "Bad Buck" Pe-
ters); *The Darkening Trail* (*Hell Hound of Alaska*) (as
Yukon Ed); *The Conversion of Frosty Blake* (*The Con-
vert*; *Staking His Life*) (title role); *Tools of Providence*
(*Dakota Dan*; *Every Inch a Man*; *The Struggle in the
Steeple*) (as Dakota Dan); *Cash Parrish's Pal* (*Double
Crossed*) (title role); *The Ruse* (*Square Deal Man*; *A
Square Deal*) (as "Bat" Peters); *Pinto Ben* (*Horns and
Hoofs*) (as Boss Rider); *Keno Bates, Liar* (*The Last Card*)
(title role); *A Knight of the Trails* (*Prowlers of the Plains*)
(as Jim Treer); *The Disciple* (as Jim Houston)
1916 *Between Men* (as Bob White); *Hell's Hinges* (co-d: Swickard) (as
      Blaze Tracy); *The Aryan* (as Steve Denton); *The Primal Lure*
      (as Angus McConnell); *The Apostle of Vengeance* (as David
      Hudson); *The Dawn Maker* (as Joe Elk); *The Return of Draw
      Egan* (*The Fugitive*) (as "Draw" Egan/William Blake); *The
      Patriot* (as Bob Wiley); *The Devil's Double* (as "Bowie" Blake)
1917 *Truthful Tulliver* (title role); *The Gun Fighter* (as Cliff Hudspeth);
      The Square Deal Man (as Jack O'Diamonds); *The Desert

Man (as Jim Action); Wolf Lowry (as Tom "Wolf" Lowry); The Cold Deck (as Jefferson "On-the-Level" Leigh); The Silent Man (as "Silent" Budd Marr)

1918   Wolves of the Trail (as "Buck" Andrade); Blue Blazes Rawden (title role); The Tiger Man (as Hank Parsons); Selfish Yates (title role); Shark Monroe (title role); Riddle Gawne (as Jefferson "Riddle" Gawne); A Bullet for Berlin (as himself); The Border Wireless (as Steve Ransom); Branding Broadway (as Robert Sands)

1919   Breed of Men (as Careless Carmody); The Poppy Girl's Husband (as Hairpin Harry Dutton); The Money Corral (as Lem Beason); Square Deal Sanderson (co-d: Hillyer) (as Square Deal Sanderson/"Will Bransford")

Film as Consultant:

1930   Billy the Kid (Vidor)

Publications

By HART: books—

Pinto Ben and Other Stories, New York, 1919.
The Golden West Boys, Injun and Whitey, series, 3 vols., Boston and New York, 1919-22.
Told under a White Oak Tree, Boston, 1922.
William S. Hart in Wild Bill Hickok, Los Angeles, 1923.
A Lighter of Flames, New York, 1923.
The Order of Chanta Sutas, Los Angeles, 1925.
My Life East and West, Boston, 1929.
Hoofbeats, New York, 1933.
The Law on Horseback and Other Stories, Los Angeles, 1935.
And All Points West!, with Mary E. Hart, Binghamton, New York, 1940.

By HART: articles—

"Living Your Characters," in Motion Picture Magazine, December 1917.
"Cow-Punchers of the Antipodes," in Photoplay (New York), April 1919.
"And They Are All Beautiful," in Motion Picture Magazine, August 1919.
"My Pinto and Me," in Photoplay (New York), February 1920.
"The Compleat Cowboy," in Pictures and Picturegoer, September 1921.

On HART: books—

Fenin, George, and William K. Everson, The Western, From Silents to Cinerama, New York, 1962.
Horwitz, James, They Went Thataway, New York, 1976.
Koszanski, Diane, The Complete Films of William S. Hart: A Pictorial Record, New York, 1980.
Bell, Geoffrey, The Golden Gate and the Silver Screen, New York, 1984.
McDonald, Archie P., editor, Shooting Stars: Heroes and Heroines of the Western Film, Bloomington, Indiana, 1987.
MacCann, Richard Dyer, The First Filmmakers, Metuchen, New Jersey, 1989.

On HART: articles—

Codd, Elsie, "The Retirement of Bill Hart," in Pictures and Picturegoer, April 1921.
Daugherty, Frank, "Ol' Bill Hart Is Coming Back!," in Photoplay (New York), December 1930.
Mitchell, George, "William S. Hart," in Films in Review (New York), April 1955, and letter from Mitchell, May 1955.

Card, James, "The Films of William S. Hart," in Image (Rochester, New York), March 1956.
Mitchell, George, "The William S. Hart Museum," in Films in Review (New York), August-September 1962.
"The Stage Career of William S. Hart 1898-1912," in Silent Picture (London), Autumn 1972.

*   *   *

Writing of William S. Hart in 1918, the great French actor Charles Dullin commented: "He has the tenderness and simplicity of the hero who is always surprised at the evil intentions of men. He never doubts the word of others, since his own is sacred. He does not hate his enemy because of the harm he has done to him, but because of the contempt with which lies and treason inspire him." Even when playing a villain, as was so often the case at the beginnings of his films, Hart was an honorable man. He upheld honesty and integrity, particularly in his dealings with women. He never showed anything but respect for women (unless they happened to be the sort, usually played in his early films by Louise Glaum, who hung around in saloons). He was a storybook hero, worshipped by men and women, as popular in France as he was in the United States.

A veteran stage actor before he entered films, William S. Hart brought theatricality to his screen characterizations, but he also brought an image of the West which was far from realistic, but was an image in which most Americans wished to believe. Men were rugged individualists, while women were sweet and innocent. Hart's attitude towards women, both on and offscreen, is curious. Despite his obvious middle-age, he had no problem in having his characters fall in love with women who were usually little more than teenagers; in real life he easily fell in love with his leading ladies, proposing marriage to at least three of them. However his one marriage ended in early divorce and Hart remained for much of his life under the thumb of a domineering sister.

The plots of most Hart Westerns are similar in design. Typical is "Bad Buck" of Santa Ynez, in which Hart plays an outlaw, apparently totally evil but with one spark of goodness, a spark that is usually ignited by a good woman, but in this case by a child. The films were very much Hart's creations; by the mid-1910s he was almost always the director of his features and he would allow producer Thomas H. Ince no part in their creation. Hart obviously cherished the authorship of his films, eager to spread his image of the Old West and his version of Victorian morality. He did not glamorize the Old West, as did his closest rival Tom Mix; he used natural scenery (such as the Grand Canyon in The Bargain), his sets were primitive, and his clothing shabby and worn.

Although primarily a Western filmmaker, Hart did take his Western philosophy to other areas of the country: Shark Monroe is set in Alaska, The Poppy Girl's Husband and The Cradle of Courage in San Francisco. The Whistle is pro-labor. The Captive God has Hart cast as an Aztec leader.

William S. Hart continued to make films into the 1920s, but his characters and his morality belong more to the 1910s. By the mid-1920s, when his career ended, it was obvious that audiences were more interested in the easygoing antics of Tom Mix, Hoot Gibson, and Ken Maynard than in the antiquated moralizing Hart.

—Anthony Slide

HASEGAWA, Kazuo

Nationality: Japanese. **Born:** Kyoto, 27 February 1908. **Education:** Attended Fushimi No. 3 Elementary School to 1921. **Military Service:** Served three-months basic training for Japanese Army, and

523

spent the remainder of the war touring with theater groups, 1944-45. **Family:** Married 1) Tami Nakamura 1930 (divorced 1942); 2) Shige Iijima 1942, children: actor Narutoshi Hayashi and actresses Toshiko and Kiyo Hasegawa. **Career:** 1913—first role in his uncle's Kabuki theater; over the next few years used the stage names Kazuo Nakamura, Kazuo Arashi, and Chomaru Hayashi; underwent training as Kabuki actor; 1927—joined Shochiku Studio and made film debut (using name Chojiro Hayashi) in *Chigo no kempo*; made about 120 films in the next ten years for this studio; 1937—joined Toho Studio; his popularity was enhanced after being attacked by a thug, allegedly hired by rival studio; from this point began using his real name, Kazuo Hasegawa; 1942—established the Shin Engi-za theater group; 1946-47—engaged by Shin-Toho Studio; 1948-52—the Shin Engi-za company began producing films as well as plays; 1949-63—member of Daiei Studio and executive officer, 1957-63; 1964—first TV appearance; 1960s—concentrated on stage work. **Awards:** Japanese Government Shiju-hosho, 1965; Minister of Education Award, 1978. **Died:** From cerebral tumor, 6 April 1984.

Films as Actor:

(as Chojiro Hayashi)

1927 *Chigo no kenpo* (Inuzuka); *Ojo Kissa* (Kinugasa); *Rangun* (Inuzuka); *Doku azami* (Kinugasa); *Kinno jidai* (Kinugasa); *Itawari Asataro* (Inuzuka); *Jofusei* (Fuyushima); *Goyosen* (Kinugusa); *Yabure amigasa* (Inuzuka); *Akatsuki no yushi* (Kinugawa); *Korui* (Yamazaki); *Komori zoshi* (Yamazaki); *Gekka no kyoba* (Kingugasa); *Tempo hiken-roku* (Yamazaki)

1928 *Benten-kozo* (Kinugasa) (title role); *Kyoraku hicho* (Kinugasa); *Kaikoku-ki* (Kinugasa); *Fuunjo-shi* (Yamazaki) (as Shinpachi Aizawa); *Chokon yasha* (Kinugasa); *Hookibi* (Hoshi); *Shirai Gonpachi* (Yamazaki); *Ose Hangoro* (Hoshi); *Kaito Sayamaro* (Koishi); *Tsurugi no ketsuen* (Koishi); *Jinpinin* (Tomonari); *Edo sodachi* (Tomonari); *Kirare Yosa* (Kioshi); *Shigure-gasa* (Koishi); *Ningyo bushi* (Koishi); *Toribe-yama shinju* (Fuyushima)

1929 *Kurode-gumi Sukeroku* (Furuno); *Jigoku kaido* (Ishiyama); *Obo Kissa* (Fuyushima); *Fubuki-toge* (Fuyushima); *Omokage* (Hattori); *Yari no Gonzo* (Furuno); *Tsukigata Hanpeita* (Fuyushima) (title role); *Ise ondo* (Takeuchi); *Sanza shigure* (Hoshi); *Chi ni somuku mono* (Tomonari); *Kuruheru meikun* (Inoue)

1930 *Nogitsune Sanji* (Koishi); *Jisei wa utsuru* (Fuyushima); *Jikizamurai* (Inoue); *Fuyuki shinju* (Fuyushima); *Matsudaira Choshichiro* (Hoshi); *Seki no Yatappe* (Hoshi); *Naniwa hina* (Inoue); *Satsunan sodoin* (Fuyushima); *Chiyoda no ninjo* (Hoshi); *Shochiku biggu paredo* (Shimazu)

1931 *Fubuki ni sakebu ookami* (Fuyushima); *Bijobu Sakyo* (Hoshi); *Monzaburo no Hide* (Watanabe); *Reimei izen* (Kinugasa); *Jurokuya seishin* (Inuzuka); *Bato no zeni: Kesho-bosatsu no maki* (Inoue); *Kagoya Dainagon* (Futakawa); *Bata no zeni: Ogon oni ranbu no maki* (Inoue); *Jonan no Yoemon* (Inuzuka); *Nagebushi Yasuke: Michinoku no maki* (Futakawa); *Nagebushi Yasuke: Edo no maki* (Futakawa); *Hiren hikui-zuka* (Inuzuka)

1932 *Yaji Kita bijn sodo* (Futakawa); *Konjiki-yasha* (Nomura) (as Kanichi); *Tabigaeru kokyo no uta* (Inuzuka); *Nezumi-kozo Jirokichi* (Kinugasa) (as Jirokichi); *Matsuri-uta Mitokichi goroshi* (Inuzuka); *Rikigun daikoshin* (Shimizu); *Edo gonomi Ryogoku-zoshi* (Inoue); *Kamiyui Shinza* (Inuzuka); *Dogo no kishi* (Inoue); *Hototogisu* (Gosho); *Nezumi-kozo Kirokichi: Kaiketsu-hen* (Akiyama) (as Jirokichi); *Kikugoro*

goshi (Inuzuka); *Chushingura* (Kinugasa) (as Asano Takuminokami and Yoshida Sawaemon)

1933 *Adauchi kyodai kagami* (Futakawa); *Kikugoro goshi* (Fuyushima); *Ten-ichibo to Iganosuke* (Kinugasa); *Kyokaku harusame-gasa* (Fuyushima); *Irezumi hangan* (Fuyushima); *Futatsu dore* (Kinugasa); *Irezumi hangan: Hyaku-san kiki no maki* (Fuyushima); *Irezumi hangan: Kanketsu-hen* (Fuyushima); *Koina no Ginpei* (Kinugasa); *Uijin* (Fuyushima); *Yaji Kita* (Inoue)

1934 *Kutsukake Tokijiro* (Kinugasa) (as Tokijiro); *Yashu Honno-ji* (Fuyushima); *Ishii Tsuneemon* (Oosone); *Myoreki meikenshi* (Inoue); *Tsukigata Hanpeita* (Fuyushima) (title role); *Yakko Kagami-san* (Oosone); *Ippon-gatana dohyo-iri* (Kinugasa); *Rinzo shusse-tabi* (Futakawa); *Edo wa utsuru* (Fuyushima); *Genzaburo ihen: Hissatsuken oni no maki* (Kimura); *Genzaburo ihen: Shokuran renbo no maki* (Fuyushima); *Watashi no niisan* (Shimazu) (as Fumio); *Kyokaku Soga* (Inoue)

1935 *Hanayome no negoto* (Gosho) (as Yasuo); *Haha no ai* (Ikeda); *Kurayami no Ushimatsu* (Kinugasa); *Ronintabi sassho bosatsu* (Kondo); *Yokino-jo henge* Parts I and II (Kingugasa) (as Yokino-jo, Yamitaro, and Yukino-jo's mother); *Kagoya hangan* (Fuyushima) (as Ooka Echizen ni kami); *Tenpo Yasubei* (Inuzuka); *Megumi ni kenka* (Fuyushima)

1936 *Yokino-jo henge: Kaiketsu-hen* (Kinugasa) (as Yokino-jo, Yamitaro, and Yokino-jo's mother); *Onatsu Seijuro* (Inuzuka) (as Seijuro); *Arakawa no Sakichi* (Oosone); *Oduro Meikun* (Inoue); *Toribeyama shinju: Osome Hankuro* (Fuyushima) (as Hankuro); *Harusugata gonin-otoko* (Fuyushima)

1937 *Oosaka natsu-no-jin* (Kinugasa) (as Sakazaki Izumo no kami); *Tabi no kagero* (Inuzuka); *Tsuchiya Chikara: Rakka no make* (as Tsuchiya Chikara and Sugino Jubeita); *Sekkai no maki* (Fuyushima); *Suzukamori* (Inoue); *Moko raishu: Tekikoku Kofuku*; *Shishi-hen* (Akiyama); *Bancho sarayashiki* (Fuyushima)

(as Kazuo Hasegawa)

1938 *Tojuro no koi* (Yamamoto) (as Sakata Tojuro); *Mabuta no haha* (Kondo); *Tsuruhachi Tsurujiro* (Naruse) (as Tsurujiro); *Gekka no wakamusha* (Nakagawa)

1939 *Ronin fubuki* (Kondo); *Chushingura* Parts I and II (Takizawa and Yamamoto); *Kenka-tobi* Parts I and II (Ishida) (released as short 1951); *Echigo-jishi matsuri* (Watanabe); *Byakuran no uta* (Watanabe) (as Kokichi Matsumura); *Gozonji asumaotoko* (Takizawa)

1940 *Adauchi goyomi* (Kondo); *Hebihime-sama* (Kinugasa) (as Hinokiya Sentaro); *Shina no yoru* Parts I and II (Hase) (released as *Soshu yakyoku* 1952—short) (as Tetsuo Hase); *Zoku Hebihime-sama* (Kinugasa) (as Hinokiya Sentaro); *Moyuru daichi* (Abe) (as Lt. Ohashi); *Nessa no chikai* Parts I and II (Watanabe) (as Kenji Sugiyama)

1941 *Sakujitsu kieta otoko* (Makino) (as Bunkichi); *Hasegawa Roppa no Iemitsu to Hikosa* (Makino) (as Tokugawa Iemitsu and Kawamura Keibu); *Orizushichi nana-henge* Parts I and II (Ishida); *Awa no odoriko* (Makino) (released as *Kenun Naruto shibuki* 1960—short); *Kawanakajima gassen* (Kinugasa) (as Hyakuzo); *Otoko no hanamichi* (Makino) (as Utaemon III)

1942 *Matteita otoko* (Makino); *Fukei-zu* (Makino) (as Hayase Chikara); *Zoku Fukei-zu* (Makino) (as Hayase Chikara); *Omokage no machi* (Hagiwara)

1943 *Ina no Kantaro* (Takizawa) (released as *Ina-bushi jinji* 1953—short) (title role); *Ongaku dai-shingun* (Watanabe); *Meijin*

Kazuo Hasegawa (left) in *Yokino-jo henge*

Choji-bori (Hagiwara) (as Choji); *Susume dokuritsu-ki* (Kinugasa and Imai); *Himetaru kakugo* (Takizawa)

1944 *Idaten kaido* (Hagiwara); *Shibai-do* (Naruse); *Inochi no minato* (Watanabe)

1945 *Ato ni tsuzuku o shinzu* (Watanabe); *Sanju-san-gen-do toshi-ya monogatari* (Naruse)

1946 *Hinok butai* (Toyoda); *Aru yo no tonosama* (Kinugasa) (as Kiichiro Taira); *Kiri no yobanashi* (Hagiwara)

1947 *Toho Sen-ichi-ya* (Ichikawa); *Sakura-ondo: Kyo wa odotte* (Watanabe); *Oedo no oni* (Hagiwara); *Bonbon* (Saeki)

1948 *Yurei akatsuki ni shisu* (Makino); *Yukyo no mure* (Oosone); *Koban-zame: Dogo-hen* (Kinugasa)

1949 *Koban-zame: Aizo-hen* (Kinugasa); *Heiji happy-aku-ya-cho* (Saeki); *Ashi o arrata otoko* (Fuyushima); *Koga-yashiki* (Kinugasa); *Hebihime dochu* (Kimura); *Zoku Hebihime dochu* (Kimura); *Fukei-zu* (Makino) (short version of *Fukei-zu* and *Zoku Fukei-zu*, 1942)

1950 *Kizudarake no otoko* (Makino); *Otomi to Yosaburo* Parts I and II (Fuyushima) (as Yosaburo); *Jogashima no ame* (Tanaka); *Senryo-hada* (Fuyushima); *Hi no tori* (Tanaka); *Oni azami* (Fuyushima); *Beni-komori* (Kinugasa)

1951 *Ashura hangan* (Mori); *Tsuki no wataridori* (Kinugasa); *Zenigata Heiji* (Mori) (title role); *Meigetsu somato* (Kinugasa); *Orizuru-gasa* (Fuyushima); *Genji monogatari* (*Tale of Genji*) (Yoshimura) (as Hikari Genji); *Tsuki kara kita otoko* (Saeki); *Zenigata Heiji torimono-hikae: Koibumi*

dochu (Fuyushima) (title role); *Hebihime-sama* (Kinugasa) (short version of *Hebihime-sama* and *Zoku Hebihime-sama*, 1940)

1952 *Jirokichi goshi* (Ito) (as Jirokichi); *Shura-jo hibun: Soryu no maki* (as Momotaro and Shin-nosuke); *Hiun no maki* (Kinugasa); *Zenigata Heiji torimon-hikae: Jigoku no mon* (Mori) (title role); *Furisode kyojo* (Yasuda); *Kantaro tsukiyo-uta* (Tasaka) (as Kantaro); *Daibutsu kaigen* (Kinugasa) (as Kunihito); *Fuun senryo-bune* (Inagaki)

1953 *Zenigata Heiji torimono-hikae: Karakuri yashiki* (Mori) (title role); *Asama no mozu* (Kinugasa); *Hana no Kodo-kan* (Mori); *Shishi no za* (Ito) (as Hosho Yagoro); *Hana no kenka-jo* (Inuzuka); ***Jigokumon*** (*Gate of Hell*) (Kinugasa) (as Morito); *Omatsuri Hanjiro* (Inagaki) (as Hanjiro); *Zenigata Heiji torimon-hikae: Konjiki no ookami* (Mori) (title role)

1954 *Hanano sandogasa* (Inuzuka); *Okiku to Harima* (Ito) (as Aoyama Harima); *Yoidore nito-ryu* (Mori); *Hana no nagawakizashi* (Kinugasa); *Shirazu no Yataro* (Makita); *Tekka bugyo* (Kinugasa); *Zenigata Heiji torimono-hikae: Yurei daimyo* (Hirozu) (title role); *Chikamatsu monogatari* (*A Story from Chikamatsu; The Tale of the Crucified Lovers*) (as Mohei)

1955 *Itaro jishi* (Tasaka); *Nanatsu no kao no Ginji* (Misumi); *Jako yashiki* (Tasaka); *Bara wa ikutabika* (Kinugasa); *Tsubakuro-gasa* (Tasaka); *Tojuro no koi* (Mori) (as Sakata Tojuro);

Zenigata Heiji torimono-hikae: Doguro-kago (Tasaka) (title role); *Nagasaki no yuro* (Mori); *Ore was Tokichiro* (Mori)

1956   *Hana no wataridori* (Tasaka); *Yoshinaka o meguru san-nin no onna* (Kinugasa) (as Kiso Jiro Yoshinaka): *Zangiku monogatari* (Shima) (as Kikunosuke); *Zenigata Heiji torimono-hikae: Shibijin-buro* (Kado) (title role); *Nezumi-kozo shinobikomi-hikae* (Kado) (as Nazumi-kozo); *Zenigata Heiji torimono-hikae: Hitohada-gumo* (Mori) (title role); *Aizome-gasa* (Kato); *Tsukigata Hanpeita* (Kinugasa) (title role)

1957   *Zenigata Heiji torimono-hikae: Madara-hebi* (Kado) (title role); *Nezumi-kozo shinobikomi-hikae: Ne-no-koku sanjo* (Tasaka) (as Nezumi-kozo); *Genji monogatari: Ukifune* (Kinugasa) (as Kaeru no kimi); *Ninjo misui* (Kato); *Zenigata Heiji torimono-hikae: Megitsune yashiki* (Kato) (title role); *Naruto hicho* (Kinugasa); *Yuki no wataridori* (Kato)

1958   *Zenigata Heiji torimono-hikae: Hachi-nin no hanayome* (Makita) (title role); *Yukyo gonin otoko* (Kato); *Edokko matsuri* (Shima); *Chushingura* (Watanabe) (as Oishi Kuranosuke and Tamura); *Inochi o kakeru otoko* (Kato); *Kuchibue o fuku wataridori* (Tasaka); *Zenigata Heiji torimono-hikae: Onibi doro* (Kato) (title role); *Hana no yukyo-den* (Yasuda); *Nicherin to Moko daishurai* (Watanabe) (as Nichiren); *Igano minatsuki*; *Zenigata Heiji torimono-hikae: Yuki-onna no ashiato* (Kato) (title role)

1959   *Kagero-gasa* (Misumi); *Onna tokaizoku* (Ito); *Yamada Nagamasa Oja no tsurugi* (Kato) (title role); *Jirocho Fuji* (Mori) (as Jirocho); *Yotsuya kaidan* (Misumi); *Oyashiki-zame* (Kato); *Utamaro o meguru gonin no onna* (Kimura) (as Utamaro); *Furai monogatari: Ninkyo-hen* (Watanabe); *Seki no Yatappe* (Kato) (title role)

1960   *Futari no Musashi*; *Zenigata Heiji torimono-hikae: Bijin-gumo* (Misumi) (title role); *Oeyama Shuten-doji* (Tanaka); *Zoku jirocho Fuji* (Mori) (as Jirocho); *San-nin no kaoyaku* (Inoue); *Hi-sen-ryo* (Tanaka); *Furai monogatari: Abare Hisha*; *Ippon-gatana dohyo-iri* (Yasuda); *Kyokaku harusame-gasa* (Watanabe); *San-kyodai no ketto* (Tanaka)

1961   *Hare-kosode* (Yasuda); *Zenigata Heiji torimono-hikae: Yoru no emmacho* (Watanabe) (title role); *Sakurada-mon* (Nishiyama); *Mito Komon umi o wataru* (Watanabe); *Kuroi sando-gasa* (Nishiyama); *Zenigata Heiji torimono-hikae: Bijin-zame* (Misumi) (title role)

1962   *Sabakareru Echizen no kami* (Tanaka); *Nakayoshi ondo Nippon ichi dayo* (Inoue); *Aoba-jo no oni* (Misumi); *Shin no shi-kotei* (*The Great Wall*) (Tanaka)

1963   *Yokino-jo henge* (*An Actor's Revenge*) (Ichikawa) (as Yokino-jo and Yamitaro); *Edo mujo* (Nishiyama)

Publications

By HASEGAWA: books—

Watashi no niju-nen.
Butai ginmaku rokuju-nen.

On HASEGAWA: article—

Obituary, in *Revue du Cinéma* (Paris), July/August 1984.

*   *   *

Kazuo Hasegawa, a handsome Kabuki star known as Chojiro Hayashi until 1938, attracted an enormous following as soon as he joined the Shochiku Studio. His romantic features and soft movements, which he

learned from his training as an *onnagata* (female impersonator), thoroughly enchanted his fans. He studied with the director Teinosuke Kinugasa who had also been an *onnagata*. Kinugasa understood this actor's quality well, and continued to collaborate with him for several decades. Hasegawa also made countless swordplay films for the directors Fuyushima, Inuzuka, Inoue, Koishi, Hoshi, and Futakawa. Not content to rely on his Kabuki background, Hasegawa meticulously studied camera positions and lighting to understand how to present his attractive features most effectively in the film medium. For example, he consciously favored his left profile which was believed to be the better.

Among his 301 films, Hasegawa played period heroes such as samurais and lords, as well as detectives, actors, burglars, and gamblers. He most often played the familiar romantic type with high moral standards, struggling against injustice with the power of his sword. His acting style is elegant, with well-paced movement and delivery of dialogue. One of his most successful roles was in Kinugasa's *Yokino-jo-henge* in 1935-36, which Hasegawa remade for Kon Ichikawa in 1963. Drawn from the Kabuki theater are such elements as the complicated plot, the actor playing multiple roles (Hasegawa plays the vengeful Kabuki actor Yukino-jo, his mother, and the Robin Hood-like burglar who assists the actor in obtaining vengeance), as well as the concept of a play-within-a-play. The critical and popular success of this film led to the production of several sequels, all using Hasegawa.

Hasegawa's contemporary roles include romantic lovers in the Shochiku Studio's light-comic *shomingeki* (ordinary people's life) film genre and in the Toho Studio's wartime romances set in China, in which he played a Japanese man loved by a Chinese girl. His other successful roles include those of a doomed lover in Mizoguchi's *Chikamatsu monogatari*, which brought him international recognition, and his role as a brave warrior in Kinugasa's *Jigoku-mon*. These films were energetically exported under the auspices of the Daiei Studio, for which Hasegawa was the main star of the 1950s.

—Kyoko Hirano

HAWKINS, Jack

Nationality: British. **Born:** John Edward Hawkins in Wood Green, London, 14 September 1910. **Education:** Trinity County School, and Italia Conti School of Acting. **Military Service:** Served in Royal Welsh Fusiliers, 1940-45; later in charge of entertainment units in India and South East Asia Command: Colonel. **Family:** Married 1) the actress Jessica Tandy 1932 (divorced 1942), daughter: Susan; 2) the actress Doreen Lawrence, 1947; three children. **Career:** 1923—London stage debut as child actor in *Where the Rainbow Ends*; 1929—adult debut in *Young Woodley*; New York debut in *Journey's End*; 1930—film debut in *Birds of Prey*; 1951—last stage appearance; 1956—TV debut in *Caesar and Cleopatra*; 1958—formed Allied Film Makers distribution company with Bryan Forbes and others; 1963—co-founder, Tricastle Productions; 1966—after throat operation, unable to use his own voice in films (voice dubbed in subsequent performances); 1968—co-founder, Keep Films; 1974—in TV mini-series *QB VII*. **Awards:** Commander, Order of the British Empire, 1958. **Died:** Of throat cancer, 18 July 1973.

Films as Actor:

1930   *Birds of Prey* (*The Perfect Alibi*) (Dean) (as Alfred)
1932   *The Lodger* (*The Phantom Fiend*) (Elvey) (as Joe Martin)

Jack Hawkins in *Angels One Five*

1933 *The Good Companions* (Saville) (as Albert); *The Lost Chord* (Elvey) (as Dr. Jim Selby); *I Lived without You* (Elvey) (as Mort); *The Jewel* (Denham) (as Peter Roberts); *A Shot in the Dark* (Pearson) (as Normal Paul)

1934 *Autumn Crocus* (Dean) (as Alaric Craven); *Death at Broadcasting House* (Denham) (as Herbert Evans)

1935 *Peg of Old Drury* (Wilcox) (as Michael O'Taffe)

1937 *Beauty and the Barge* (Edwards) (as Lt. Seton Boyne); *The Frog* (Raymond) (as Capt. Gordon)

1938 *Who Goes Next?* (Elvey) (as Capt. Beck); *A Royal Divorce* (Raymond) (as Capt. Charles)

1939 *Murder Will Out* (Neill) (as Stamp); *Hamlet* (Boisen) (documentary on Kronborg production of play)

1940 *The Flying Squad* (Brenon) (as Mark McGill)

1942 *The Next of Kin* (Dickinson) (as Major)

1948 *The Fallen Idol* (Reed) (as Detective Ames); *Bonnie Prince Charlie* (Kimmins) (as Lord George Murray); *The Small Back Room* (Powell and Pressburger) (as Waring)

1950 *State Secret* (*The Great Manhunt*) (Gilliat) (as Col. Galcon); *The Black Rose* (Hathaway) (as Tristram Griffen); *The Elusive Pimpernel* (*The Fighting Pimpernel*) (Powell and Pressburger) (as Prince of Wales); *The Adventurers* (*The Great Adventure*) (MacDonald) (as Pieter Brandt)

1951 *No Highway* (*No Highway in the Sky*) (Koster) (as Denis Scott); *Angels One Five* (O'Ferrall) (as Tiger Small)

1952 *Home at Seven* (*Murder on Monday*) (Richardson) (as Dr. Sparling); *Mandy* (*Crash of Silence*) (Mackendrick) (as Richard Searle); *The Planter's Wife* (*Outpost in Malaya*) (Annakin) (as Jim Frazer); *The Cruel Sea* (Frend) (as Lt. Commander Ericson)

1953 *Twice upon a Time* (Pressburger) (as Dr. Matthews); *Malta Story* (Hurst) (as Air Officer Commanding); *The Intruder* (Hamilton) (as Wolf Merton); *Front Page Story* (Parry) (as John Grant); *Prince Philip* (Thomas—short) (as narrator)

1954 *The Seekers* (*Land of Fury*) (Annakin) (as Philip Wayne)

1955 *The Prisoner* (Glenville) (as Interrogator); *Land of the Pharaohs* (Hawks) (as Pharaoh); *Touch and Go* (*The Light Touch*) (Truman) (as Jim Fletcher)

1956 *The Long Arm* (*The Third Key*) (Frend) (as Supt. Tom Halliday); *The Man in the Sky* (*Decision against Time*) (Crichton) (as John Mitchell)

1957   *Fortune Is a Woman* (*She Played with Fire*) (Gilliat) (as Oliver Branwell); *The Bridge on the River Kwai* (Lean) (as Major Warden); *Battle for Britain* (Ashwood and Lloyd—short) (as narrator)

1958   *Gideon's Day* (*Gideon of Scotland Yard*) (Ford) (as Inspector George Gideon); *The Two-Headed Spy* (de Toth) (as General Alex Scottland)

1959   *Ben-Hur* (Wyler) (as Quintus Arrius); *The League of Gentlemen* (Dearden) (as Norman Hyde)

1961   *Two Loves* (*Spinster*) (Walters) (as W. W. J. Abercrombie); *La Fayette* (Dréville) (as General Cornwallis)

1962   *Five Finger Exercise* (Mann) (as Stanley Harrington); ***Lawrence of Arabia*** (Lean) (as General Allenby); *Rampage* (Karlson) (as Otto Abbot)

1963   *Zulu* (Enfield) (as the Rev. Otto Witt)

1964   *The Third Secret* (Crichton) (as Sir Frederick Belline); *Guns at Batasi* (Guillermin) (as Lt. Col. John Deal); *Masquerade* (Dearden) (as Col. Drexel); *Lord Jim* (Brooks) (as Marlow)

1965   *Victory at Yorktown* (Dréville—short; reedited version of *La Fayette* battle sequence, 1961) (as General Cornwallis); *Judith* (Mann) (as Major Lawton)

1966   *Danger Grows Wild* (*The Poppy Is Also a Flower*) (Young) (as General Behar); *The Party's Over* (Hamilton) (+ exec co-pr)

1967   *Great Catherine* (Flemyng) (as Sir George Gorse)

1968   *Shalako* (Dmytryk) (as Sir Charles Daggett)

1969   *Oh! What a Lovely War* (Attenborough) (as Emperor Franz Josef); *Monte Carlo or Bust!* (*Those Daring Young Men in Their Jaunty Jalopies*) (Annakin) (as Count Levinovitch); *Twinky* (*Lola*) (Donner) (as Judge Millington Draper)

1970   *The Adventures of Gerard* (Skolimowski) (as Millefleurs); *Waterloo* (Bondarchuk)

1971   *Jane Eyre* (Mann—for TV) (as Brocklehurst); *When Eight Bells Toll* (Périer); *Nicholas and Alexandra* (Schaffner); *Kidnapped* (Mann) (as Captain Hoseason); *The Beloved* (*The Sin*; *Restless*) (Cosmatos)

1972   *Young Winston* (Attenborough); *Habrichka el hashemersh* (*Niet!*; *Escape to the Sun*) (Golan)

1973   *The Last Lion* (de Witt); *Theatre of Blood* (Hickox); *Tales That Witness Madness* (Francis)

Publications

By HAWKINS: book—

Anything for a Quiet Life: The Autobiography of Jack Hawkins, London, 1973.

On HAWKINS: articles—

"Jack Hawkins," in *Films and Filming* (London), March 1955.

Hall, D. J., "Gentleman Jack," in *Films and Filming* (London), September 1970.

Lacourbe, R., "La Fin d'un gentleman," in *Ecran* (Paris), September-October 1973.

*   *   *

Jack Hawkin's rise to stardom in the late 1940s and early 1950s, after more than a decade in unimportant supporting roles, is explained largely by his ability to embody a cultural myth that, in postwar Britain, was fast becoming outmoded and could be presented only as the object of nostalgic longing. With his self-effacing restraint and yet obvious confidence, Hawkins easily suggested that public school pluck which British war documentaries and films had presented as the Empire's salvation during World War II.

By the 1950s, of course, that stiff upper-lipped and upper-class figure clearly belonged to the past. Hence Hawkins evoked him in films that celebrated national moments of triumph. As the long-suffering corvette captain in *The Cruel Sea*, Hawkins endures the dullness and horrors of war, and rises to its challenges with a determination to do the job right. In David Lean's *The Bridge on the River Kwai*, Hawkins's gentleman officer interrupts his scholarly career to do his bit in Burma, only momentarily losing his control when faced with the destructive paradoxes of war.

Since the character he created did belong to the past, it was perhaps inevitable that Hawkins remained uninvolved with the movement of British film toward "kitchen sink" realism in the late 1950s. Hawkins's policeman in *Gideon of Scotland Yard* is a romanticized image of the kindly bobby, a lower-middle-class figure who does his appointed job without complaint. Instead, Hawkins found work in those costume or historical epics produced in such great numbers during the 1960s on both sides of the Atlantic. He played character roles in films such as *Ben-Hur* (as a ramrod-stiff Roman admiral) and *Nicholas and Alexandra* as well as different incarnations of the upper-crust Englishman in *Waterloo*, *Jane Eyre*, and *Young Winston*, films whose mythic quality was certainly enhanced by his presence.

The most memorable of these always competent and sometimes distinguished performances is his role (once again for David Lean) as General Allenby in *Lawrence of Arabia*, a film that attacks the notion of English reserve. Here Hawkins provides ironic contrast for the spectacularly successful self-actualization of Lawrence's megalomania; Hawkins's Allenby is an empire builder who must resign himself, somewhat bitterly, to the anonymity of his role, to obeying rules both written and unwritten.

—R. Barton Palmer

HAWN, Goldie

Nationality: American. **Born:** Goldie Jeanne Hawn in Washington, D.C., 21 November 1945. **Education:** Attended Montgomery Blair High School, Silver Spring, Maryland; American University, Washington, D.C. **Family:** Married 1) the director Gus Trikonis, 1969 (divorced 1976); 2) the musician-comedian Bill Hudson in 1976 (divorced 1980), son: Oliver, daughter: Kate Garry; also son Wyatt with longtime partner the actor Kurt Russell. **Career:** 1965—toured as dancer in *Kiss Me Kate*; danced at The Desert Inn, Las Vegas; 1967—TV debut as dancer on Andy Griffith special; 1967-68—regular on TV show *Good Morning World*; 1968-70—regular on *Rowan and Martin's Laugh-In*; 1968—film debut in *The One and Only, Genuine, Original Family Band*; 1980—co-founder of Hawn-Mayers-Shyer-Miller Productions, subsequently active as producer. **Awards:** Best Supporting Actress, Academy Award for *Cactus Flower*, 1969.

Films as Actress:

1968   *The One and Only, Genuine, Original Family Band* (O'Herlihy) (as giggly girl)

1969   *Cactus Flower* (Saks) (as Toni Simmons)

1970   *There's a Girl in My Soup* (Boulting) (as Marion)

1971   *$* (*Dollars*; *The Heist*) (Richard Brooks) (as Dawn Divine)

1972   *Butterflies Are Free* (Katselas) (as Jill)

1974   *The Sugarland Express* (Spielberg) (as Lou Jean Poplin); *The Girl from Petrovka* (Miller) (as Oktyabrina)

1975   *Shampoo* (Ashby) (as Jill)

1976   *The Duchess and the Dirtwater Fox* (Frank) (as Amanda Quaid)

1978   *Foul Play* (Higgins) (as Gloria)
1979   *Viaggio con Anita* (*Travels with Anita*; *Lovers and Liars*) (Monicelli) (as Anita)
1980   *Private Benjamin* (Zieff) (title role, + exec pr); *Seems Like Old Times* (Jay Sandrich) (as Glenda)
1982   *Best Friends* (Jewison) (as Paula McCullen)
1984   *Swing Shift* (Jonathan Demme) (as Kay Walsh, + pr); *Protocol* (Ross) (as Sunny Davis, + exec pr)
1986   *Wildcats* (Ritchie) (as Molly McGrath)
1987   *Overboard* (Garry Marshall) (as Joanna Stayton/"Annie Proffitt")
1990   *Bird on a Wire* (Badham) (as Marianne Graves)
1991   *Deceived* (Harris) (as Adrienne Saunders); *Here's Looking at You, Warner Brothers* (Guenette—for TV) (as herself)
1992   *Housesitter* (Oz) (as Gwen); *Death Becomes Her* (Zemeckis) (as Helen Sharp); *Crisscross* (Menges) (as Tracy Cross)
1996   *The First Wives Club* (P. J. Hogan)

Films as Executive Producer:

1990   *My Blue Heaven* (Ross) (co-exec pr)
1995   *Something to Talk About* (Hallström)

Publications

By HAWN: articles—

Films and Filming (London), August 1978.
Photoplay (London), December 1981 and August 1982.

On HAWN: books—

Berman, Connie, *Solid Goldie: An Illustrated Biography of Goldie Hawn*, New York, 1981.
Haining, Peter, *Goldie*, London, 1985.

On HAWN: articles—

Current Biography 1971, New York, 1971.
Thomson, David, "Goldie Gets Serious," in *Film Comment* (New York), November/December 1982.
"Jonathan Demme: On the Line," in *American Film* (Washington, D.C.), January-February 1984.
McGillivray, D., "Goldie Hawn," in *Films and Filming* (London), July 1985.
Hadleigh, B., "Goldie Looks to the Future," in *Film Monthly*, October 1990.
Hirschberg, Lynn, "Solid Goldie," *Vanity Fair* (New York), March 1992.

*   *   *

It is the rare film fan who does not know that Goldie Hawn began her career playing the dumb, forgetful blond on television's *Laugh-In*. But few, save industry insiders, realize that during the 1980s Goldie Hawn had become one of the most powerful producers in Hollywood, occupying a rung of power below only the likes of a Steven Spielberg or a George Lucas. *Private Benjamin* proved her mettle; *Swing Shift* and *Protocol*, while fascinating films, failed at the box office.

The remarkable fact is that Hawn, with her image as the "dizzy blond," was able to acquire so much clout in the first place. In the 1960s few women were able to make their way from television fame to stardom on the silver screen. Goldie Hawn's Emmy-winning work on the hit *Laugh-In* changed that, launching her movie career, as well as introducing the world to the considerable talents of Lily Tomlin.

Goldie Hawn made her first major motion picture count. She won an Oscar, as best supporting actress, for *Cactus Flower* in 1969. By the early 1970s she was considered a rising young star. Her performance in Steven Spielberg's *The Sugarland Express* brought her notice among the rising young talents behind the camera; her fame spread because of the millions paid to see Hal Ashby's *Shampoo*. But Goldie Hawn aspired to gain control of her projects.

After a disappointment producing *The Girl from Petrovka*, her break came with *Private Benjamin* for which she served as executive producer and star. *Private Benjamin* is the tale of a bubbleheaded, spoiled Jewish American Princess who enlists in the army and changes into a strong, mature woman. This was tailor-made for Hawn by Hawn, made a lot of money, and was eventually turned into an short-lived television series in which she did not star.

But being a producer was fraught with peril. *Wildcats*, directed by Michael Ritchie, has Hawn as a divorced mother of two who asks to become the football coach and with grit takes on the job for an inner-city Chicago high school. Eventually she earns the team's respect and in the end coaches the team to a win in the big game (over the high school she worked at) and "proves" that women can coach football as well as men. Hawn the producer seems to be satisfied with obvious comic situations; it was hard to locate fresh "Goldie Hawn" vehicles.

Yet there were major exceptions. Her best work proved very, very good. For example, as the creative force behind *Swing Shift*, released in 1984 through Warner Brothers, producer Hawn and director Jonathan Demme crafted a complex tale of the female workers in a defense plant during World War II. The reaction of a Los Angeles, emerging into a mature city, and the sexual tension of the war—women doing traditionally men's roles—was contrast with the difficulties of maintaining relationships near and far away. This is a rare Hollywood film told from a woman's point of view. But therein comes the contradiction. *Swing Shift* was not what the public thought of a typical "Goldie Hawn" film and the movie quietly disappeared into the world of home video.

The contradiction can be fully appreciated by contrasting *Swing Shift* with a more typical Hawn-produced farce, *Protocol*. With a more conventional director, Herbert Ross, and a promising screenplay by Buck Henry, we have a scatterbrained "Goldie" (here named Sunny) who gets caught up in the world of politics in our nation's capitol. Critics called it, appropriately, "Goldie Goes to Washington." The pace was rapid fire, the jokes sometimes offensive (in particular to Arabs), but the laughs were genuine. In the end the critics found the film contrived. The film also made not as much money as expected and so the star of Goldie Hawn, the perpetual scatterbrained, blond smarter than she seemed at first glance, was giving way to a 45-year-old woman with few available roles.

The 1990s have not been good to Hawn, with little success associated with *Deceived*, *Crisscross*, or *Housesitter*. Her work as co-executive producer of *My Blue Heaven* also did not change the downward direction of her acting career. The 1990s were better on television with *An Evening with Bette, Cher, Goldie, Meryl, Olivia, Lily and Robin*, for ABC, and regular appearances on the annual Academy Awards shows. One wishes her luck as she begins to transform her career as a motion picture director.

—Douglas Gomery

HAYAKAWA, Sessue

Nationality: Japanese. **Born:** Kintaro Hayakawa in Nanaura township, Chiba, Japan, 10 June 1890. **Education:** Navy Preparatory School, Tokyo, graduated 1908; Naval Academy, Etajima, 1908; University of Chicago, graduated 1913. **Family:** Married the actress Tauru Aoki in 1914 (died 1961), son: Yukio, daughters: Yoshiko and Fujiko. **Career:** 1913—joined Japanese Theatre, Los Angeles, as actor and director, where his production of *Typhoon* led to his film debut with Thomas Ince; 1915—contract with Jesse Lasky Company; 1918—formed his own company, Haworth Pictures Corporation, and produced over 20 films in the next four years; 1922-39—made films in several countries, and also did stage work; 1923—toured US with stage play *Tiger Lily*; 1923—in London and on tour with *The Samurai*; 1927—founded Zen study hall in New York; 1931—acted in and directed *The Honorable Mr. Wong* in Tokyo; 1932—made lecture tour of Far East; 1934—appeared in production of *Hamlet* in Tokyo; 1939-45—lived in Paris during the war; 1949—produced his own play *The Life of the Buddha* in Tokyo; early 1950s—ordained as a Zen Buddhist priest. **Died:** 23 November 1973.

Films as Actor:

1914　*The Wrath of the Gods* (*The Destruction of Sakura-Jima*) (Barker) (as son of Samurai); *The Typhoon* (Barker) (as Dr. Tokoramo); *The Ambassador's Envoy* (as Kamura); *The Last of the Line* (*Pride of Race*) (Hunt) (as Gray Otter); *The Vigil* (Osborne) (as Kenjiro); *O Mimi san* (*The Courtship of O'Sann*) (Barker); *The Geisha* (Barker) (as Takura); *A Tragedy of the Orient* (Barker) (as Kato)

1915　*After Five* (Apfel) (as Valet); *The Clue* (Neill) (as secret agent); *The Secret Sin* (Reicher) (as Lin Foo); *The Cheat* (Cecil B. DeMille) (as Hishuru Tori); *The Famine* (Barker); *The Relic of Old Japan* (Barker); *The Chinatown Mystery* (Barker)

1916　*Temptation* (Cecil B. DeMille) (as opera admirer); *Alien Souls* (Reicher) (as Sakata); *The Honorable Friend* (Le Saint) (as Makino); *The Soul of Kura-san* (Le Saint) (as Toya)

1917　*The Victoria Cross* (*Honour Redeemed*) (Le Saint) (as Azimoolah); *Each to His Kind* (Le Saint) (as Rhandah); *The Bottle Imp* (Neilan) (as Lopoka); *The Jaguar's Claws* (Neilan) (as "El Jaguar"); *Forbidden Paths* (Thornby) (as Sato); *Hasimura Togo* (William C. DeMille) (title role); *The Call of the East* (Melford) (as Aria Takada); *The Secret Game* (William C. DeMille) (as Nara-Nara)

1918　*Hidden Pearls* (Melford) (as Maki); *The Honor of His House* (William C. DeMille) (as Count Ito Onato); *The City of Dim Faces* (Melford) (as Jang); *The Temple of Dusk* (Young) (as Akira); *The White Man's Law* (Young) (as John A. Ghengis); *The Bravest Way* (Melford) (as Tanura); *His Birth Right* (Worthington) (as Yukio)

1919　*Bonds of Honor* (Worthington) (as Yamashito and Sasamoto); *A Heart in Pawn* (Worthington) (as Toyama); *His Debt* (*The Debt*) (Worthington) (as Goro Moriyama); *The Courageous Coward* (Worthington) (as Tsuru Aoki); *The Man Beneath* (Worthington) (as Dr. Chindi Ashutor); *The Gray Horizon* (*A Dead Line*) (Worthington) (as Yano Masuto); *The Dragon Painter* (Worthington) (as Tatsu); *The Illustrious Prince* (Worthington) (as Prince Maiyo of Japan); *The Tong Man* (Worthington) (as Luk Chan)

1920　*The Beggar Prince* (Worthington) (as Prince of the Island of Desire and Niki); *The Brand of Lopez* (De Grasse) (as Vasco Lopez); *The Devil's Claim* (Swickard) (as Akbar Khan); *Li Ting Lang* (Swickard) (title role); *An Arabian Knight* (Swickard) (as Ahmed); *The Cradle of Courage* (Hillyer)

1921　*The First Born* (Campbell) (as Chan Wang); *Black Roses* (Campbell) (as Yoda); *Where Lights Are Low* (Campbell) (as Tsu Wong Shih); *The Swamp* (Campbell) (as Wang, + co-sc, exec pr)

1922　*Five Days to Live* (Dawn) (as Tai Leung); *The Vermilion Pencil* (Dawn) (as Tse Chan, Li Chan, and the Unknown)

1923　*La Bataille* (*The Danger Line*) (Violet) (as Marquis Yorisaka Sadao)

1924　*J'ai tué!* (Lion); *The Great Prince Shan* (Coleby) (title role); *Sen Yan's Devotion* (Coleby) (title role)

1929　*The Man Who Laughed Last*

1931　*Daughter of the Dragon* (as Ah Kee)

1935　*Tohjin Okichi* (Fuyishima) (as Townsend Harris)

1937　*Yoshiwara* (Ophüls) (as Ysamo); *Forfaiture* (L'Herbier) (as Li-Lang); *Die Tochter des Samurai* (*La Fille du samourai*; *Die Liebe der Mitzu*) (Fanck) (as the Star)

1938　*Tempête sur l'Asie* (Oswald) (as Prince Ling)

1939　*Macao, L'Enfer du jeu* (*Gambling Hell*) (Delannoy) (as Ying Tchai)

1941　*Patrouille Blanche* (Chamborant) (as the Star); *Le Soleil de minuit* (Roland) (as Matsui); *Malaria* (Gourguet) (as Saidi); *Tornavara* (Dreville)

1946　*Le Cabaret du grand large* (Javet) (as Wang)

1947　*Quartier Chinois* (Sti) (as Tong)

1949　*Tokyo Joe* (Heisler) (as Baron Kimura)

1950　*Three Came Home* (Negulesco) (as Col. Suga); *Les Misérables* Part I—"Daisuke Ito" and Part II—"Masahiro Makino" (as Iwakichi)

1953　*Higegi no shogun Yamashita Yasubumi* (*The Tragic General*; *Yamashita Yasubumi*) (Saeki) (as Yamashita)

1955　*House of Bamboo* (Fuller) (as Inspector Kita)

1957　*The Bridge on the River Kwai* (Lean) (as Col. Saito)

1958　*The Geisha Boy* (Tashlin) (as Mr. Sikita)

1959　*Green Mansions* (Ferrer) (as Runi)

1960　*Hell to Eternity* (Karlson) (as General Matsui); *Swiss Family Robinson* (Annakin) (as Kuala)

1962　*The Big Wave* (Danielewski) (as the Old Gentleman); *Daydreamer* (Bass) (as voice)

Publications

By HAYAKAWA: books—

The Bandit Prince (novel), New York, 1926.
Zen Showed Me the Way, Indianapolis, 1960.

On HAYAKAWA: articles—

Passek, J.-L., "Hommage: Sessue Hayakawa, Le Grand Ambassadeur japonais du cinéma muet," in *Cinéma* (Paris), January 1974.
Tessier, M., "Sessue Hayakawa: Le Péril jaune," in *Ecran* (Paris), January 1974.
Films in Review (New York), April 1976 and June-July 1983.

*　　*　　*

A man of many talents, Sessue Hayakawa published plays, novels, an autobiography, and exhibited his watercolors on silk during an acting career than spanned five decades. Both a graduate in political science from the University of Chicago and a Zen priest, he brought his rich cultural background and his keen intelligence to every screen role. Although he had no formal training in acting, he demonstrated complete control of movement and gesture—aided greatly by his mastery of judo, kendo, and ju jitsu. This control resulted in a noble bearing and a quiet but authoritative screen presence.

He was discovered by Thomas H. Ince while playing in a Japanese acting troupe in San Francisco, and hired at $500 a week to star in the 1914 *Typhoon*. The role that thrust him into the limelight, contribut-

Sessue Hayakawa with Fanny Ward in *The Cheat*

ing greatly to Hayakawa's exalted position in Hollywood, was that of Tori in Cecil B. DeMille's *The Cheat*. In it he portrays a rich, unscrupulous man who demands sexual favors from a woman in payment of a loan he had given her. When she tries to pay him back with money instead, he brands her on the shoulder, marking her as one of his possessions. This role made him the favorite arch villain of the silent era.

No Japanese actor has become as popular in the United States; in the 1920s he was earning $7,000 a week. He was highly regarded, being invited both to the White House by President Harding, and to give a command performance for George V and Queen Mary in the 1930s. He had a lifestyle that matched his popularity and proudly entertained at his 32-room Hollywood castle.

The roles he played were usually in turgid melodramas, such as *The City of Dim Faces* in which he loves a white woman, tries to sell her to his own people rather than lose her to a white man, and, in the end, freely gives his life in atonement. His exotic handsomeness and sensual bearing in well-tailored clothes made him also a favorite as a screen lover. He said in his autobiography that "public acceptance of me in romantic roles was a blow of sorts against racial intolerance, even though I lost the girl in the last reel."

He set up his own studio in the late 1910s, producing 23 films, then left Hollywood after an accident to work on stage and founded a Zen study group in New York in 1927. He also made films abroad, such as the tremendously successful *Danger Line* which played for two years straight in Paris. In France he made 17 films besides appearing in major stage productions. During the war he was forbidden to leave France and finally, after a 13-year absence, was allowed to return to the United States to star in *Tokyo Joe* opposite Humphrey Bogart.

His became a houshold name once again because of his remarkable performance as Colonel Saito in *The Bridge on the River Kwai* playing opposite Alec Guinness. Hayakawa's portrayal of this commander of a Japanese prisoner of war camp, who is obsessed by duty and military decorum, brought him a nomination for an Academy Award. Hayakawa said that in his entire career no character capitivated or challenged him more. In the later years of his career, Hayakawa directed an acting company in Japan and made many guest appearances in such American television shows as *Studio One*, *Wagon Train*, and *The Red Skelton Show*.

—Elaine Mancini

HAYDEN, Sterling

Nationality: American. **Born:** Sterling Relyea Walter in Montclair, New Jersey, 26 March 1916. **Education:** Attended Brown-Nichols School, Wassookeag School, and others before dropping out at age 17. **Military Service:** Joined the Marine Corps, and later with Office of Strategic Services serving in Greece and Yugoslavia, 1943-45; served under name John Hamilton. **Family:** Married 1) the actress Madeleine Carroll, 1942 (divorced 1945); 2) Betty Ann DeNoon, 1947 (divorced 1955), four children; 3) Catherine McConnell, 1960, two children. **Career:** 1930s—left school and became ordinary seaman on schooner *Puritan*, and served as first mate on *Yankee* on round-the-world voyage, 1935-36; then captain of brig *Florence C. Robinson*, 1938, and owner of schooner *Aldebaran*, 1939; 1940—contract with Paramount: film debut in *Virginia*, 1941; 1946—member of Communist Party for 6 months; 1950-51—after being blacklisted, voluntarily submitted to questioning by House Un-American Committee; 1959—voyage with his children aboard his schooner *The Wanderer* became subject of his autobiographical work *Wanderer*; 1973—stage appearance in *Are You Now or Have You Ever Been*; 1976—published the novel *Voyage*; 1982—in TV mini-series *The Blue and the Gray*. **Died:** In California, 23 May 1986.

Films as Actor:

1941 *Virginia* (Griffith); *Bahama Passage* (Griffith)
1947 *Blaze of Noon* (Farrow); *Variety Girl* (Marshall)
1949 *El Paso* (Foster); *Manhandled* (Foster)
1950 **The Asphalt Jungle** (Huston) (as Dix Handley)
1951 *Journey into Light* (Heisler); *Flaming Feather* (Enright); *Denver and Rio Grande* (Haskin)
1952 *The Golden Hawk* (Salkow); *Hellgate* (Warren); *Flat Top* (*Eagles of the Fleet*) (Selander); *The Star* (Heisler); *Kansas Pacific* (Nazarro)
1953 *Take Me to Town* (Sirk); *Fighter Attack* (Selander)
1954 *Crime Wave* (*The City Is Dark*) (De Toth); **Johnny Guitar** (Ray) (title role); *Prince Valiant* (Hathaway); *Arrow in the Dust* (Selander); *Naked Alibi* (Hopper); *Suddenly* (Allen); *So Big* (Wise); *Timberjack* (Kane); *Battle Taxi* (Strock)
1955 *The Eternal Sea* (Auer); *Shotgun* (Selander); *The Last Command* (Lloyd); *Top Gun* (Nazarro)
1956 *The Come-On* (Birdwell); *The Killing* (Kubrick); *Crime of Passion* (Oswald); *Five Steps to Danger* (Kesler)
1957 *The Iron Sheriff* (Salkow); *Valerie* (Oswald); *Gun Battle at Monterrey* (Hittleman and Franklin); *Zero Hour* (Bartlett)
1958 *Terror in a Texas Town* (Lewis); *Ten Days to Tulara* (Sherman)
1963 **Dr. Strangelove, or: How I Learned to Stop Worrying and Love the Bomb** (Kubrick) (as Gen. Jack D. Ripper)
1964 *A Carol for Another Christmas* (Mankiewicz—for TV)
1969 *Sweet Hunters* (Guerra); *Hard Contract* (Pogostin) (as Michael Carlson)
1970 *Loving* (Kershner) (as Lepridon)
1971 *Le Saut de l'ange* (Cobra) (Boisset); *Le Grand Départ* (Taysse)
1972 **The Godfather** (Coppola) (as McCluskey)
1973 *The Long Goodbye* (Altman); *The Final Program* (*The Last Days of Man on Earth*) (Fuest)
1974 *Deadly Strangers* (Hayers)
1975 *Cipola Colt* (*Cry Onion*) (Castellari); *Bertolucci secondo il cinema* (*Il cinema secondo Bertolucci*) (Giuseppe Bertolucci—doc)
1976 *1900* (*Novecento*) (Bernardo Bertolucci) (as Leo Dalco)
1978 *King of the Gypsies* (Pierson) (as King Zharko Stepanovicz)
1979 *Winter Kills* (Richert); *The Outsider* (Luraschi)

1980 *Nine to Five* (Higgins)
1981 *Venom* (Haggard); *Gas* (Rose); *Charlie Chan and the Curse of the Dragon Queen* (Donner)
1983 *La dolce cinema* (Masenza); *Leuchtturm des Chaos* (Buhler)

Publications

By HAYDEN: books—

Wanderer, New York, 1963.
Voyage (novel), New York, 1976.

By HAYDEN: articles—

Interview, in *Films Illustrated* (London), February 1981.
Interview with B. Berg, in *Cahiers du Cinéma* (Paris), June 1986.

On HAYDEN: articles—

Gow, G., "Vibes," in *Films and Filming* (London), December 1973.
Ciné Revue (Paris), 30 October 1980.
Obituary, in *Variety* (New York), 28 May 1986.

On HAYDEN: film—

Pharos of Chaos, directed by Wolf-Eckhart Bulher and Manfred Blank, West Germany, 1983.

*   *   *

Throughout his career, Sterling Hayden maintained that acting in film was only a means to an end, getting together enough money to buy a boat and go to sea. The claim has not been mere studio hype: from 1941 until the early 1980s Hayden worked only enough to finance his ocean voyages which he chronicled in his best-selling autobiography *Wanderer*, a book that says much about life and ships and little about movies.

Though he repeatedly denied his talent as an actor, he made several screen appearances that display his rare capacity for erasing the line between acting and being. Playing such roles as the hired gunman who dies trying to get back to his horses in Kentucky in *The Asphalt Jungle*, the hardboiled leader of a doomed gang of race track thieves in *The Killing*, and the mad General Ripper who destroys the world in *Dr. Strangelove*, Hayden has become fixed in the public mind as the doomed man of conviction, the man who lives and dies by a bizarre and somewhat perverted moral code.

His portrayals in those three films highlight a career that saw Hayden move from quiet, handsome leading man to weathered character actor. In his later films, most notably *The Long Goodbye*, *Loving*, and *Hard Contract*, he is a bearded, self-confident, and possibly mad Ahab who has forgotten that the meaning in his life came from searching for the whale.

Hayden, who in later years lived in a barge on the Seine, was always the uneasy hero in a series of Westerns and crime films, most at Republic. Hayden's early screen characters might hold a grudge or have a goal, but they just didn't want to talk about it. His more recent characters want to do nothing else but talk about their lost goals and dreams.

Perhaps it was his unconventional lifestyle that led directors to seek him out for the slightly neurotic heroes of films in the 1950s. *The Asphalt Jungle* and *The Killing* are good examples, but even more striking is his appearance in eccentric B pictures such as *Terror in a Texas Town* directed by Joseph Lewis. In this film Hayden plays a seaman who finds himself in a shootout with a gunman. The

Sterling Hayden in *Dr. Strangelove, or; How I Learned to Stop Worrying and Love the Bomb*

twist is that instead of a gun Hayden carries a harpoon. In *Valerie*, directed by Gerd Oswald, who directed Marlon Brando in *The Wild One*, Hayden played a Westerner who is viewed in radically different ways by the witnesses at a trial for murder. In this variation on *Rashomon*, Hayden's character proves to be as much of an enigma as the actor himself.

It is somewhat ironic that Hayden's most visible performance was in *The Godfather* as the corrupt policeman who is shot by Michael Corleone (Al Pacino). In the film Hayden's character is neither mad nor misunderstood. He is coolly and cruelly corrupt, a chilling facet of the Hayden persona that was seldom explored.

—Stuart Kaminsky

HAYWARD, Susan

Nationality: American. **Born:** Edythe Marrener in Brooklyn, New York, 30 June 1919. **Education:** Attended Girls' Commercial High School, Brooklyn. **Family:** Married the actor Jess Barker, 1944 (divorced 1954), twin sons Timothy and Gregory. **Career:** 1937—photographer's model in New York; option from David Selznick led to film debut, then a short Warner Brothers contract; 1939—contract with Paramount, and films by Paramount and other studios during the next few years; 1945—signed with independent producer Walter Wanger; 1949—contract with 20th Century-Fox; 1959—formed own production company, Carrollton, Inc.; 1969—stage role in *Mame*; 1970s—worked in TV. **Awards:** Best Actress, Cannes Film Festival, for *I'll Cry Tomorrow*, 1955; Best Actress, Academy Award and Best Actress, New York Film Critics, for *I Want to Live*, 1958. **Died:** Of a brain tumor, 14 March 1975.

Films as Actress:

1937   *Hollywood Hotel* (Berkeley) (as starlet at table)
1938   *The Amazing Dr. Clitterhouse* (Litvak); *The Sisters* (Litvak) (as telephone operator); *Comet over Broadway* (Berkeley) (as amateur actor); *Campus Cinderella* (Smith) (as coed); *Girls on Probation* (McGann) (as Gloria Adams)

1939 *Beau Geste* (Wellman) (as Isobel Rivers); *Our Leading Citizen* (Santell) (as Judith Schofield); *One Thousand Dollars a Touchdown* (Hogan) (as Betty McGlen)

1941 *Among the Living* (Heisler) (as Millie Pickens); *Sis Hopkins* (Santley) (as Carol Hopkins); *Adam Had Four Sons* (Ratoff) (as Hester Stoddard)

1942 *Reap the Wild Wind* (C. B. DeMille) (as Drusilla Alston); *The Forest Rangers* (Marshall) (as Tana Mason); *I Married a Witch* (Clair) (as Estelle Masterson); *A Letter from Bataan* (Pine—short); *Star Spangled Rhythm* (Marshall) (as Genevieve)

1943 *Hit Parade of 1943* (Rogell) (as Jill Wright); *Young and Willing* (E. Griffith) (as Kate Benson); *Jack London* (Santell) (as Charmain Kittredge)

1944 *Skirmish on the Home Front* (short); *And Now Tomorrow* (Pichel) (as Janice Blair); *The Fighting Seabees* (Ludwig) (as Constance Chesley); *The Hairy Ape* (Santell) (as Mildred Douglas)

1946 *Deadline at Dawn* (Clurman) (as June Goff); *Canyon Passage* (Tourneur) (as Lucy Overmire)

1947 *Smash-Up: The Story of a Woman* (Heisler) (as Angie Evans); *They Won't Believe Me* (Pichel) (as Verna Carlson); *The Lost Moment* (Gabel) (as Tina Bordereau)

1948 *Tap Roots* (Marshall) (as Morna Dabney); *The Saxon Charm* (Binyon) (as Janet Busch)

1949 *Tulsa* (Heisler) (as Cherokee Lansing); *House of Strangers* (Mankiewicz) (as Irene Bennett); *My Foolish Heart* (Robson) (as Eloise Winters)

1951 *I'd Climb the Highest Mountain* (King) (as Mary Elizabeth Eden Thompson); *Rawhide* (Hathaway) (as Vinnie Holt); *David and Bathsheba* (King) (as Bathsheba); *I Can Get It for You Wholesale* (Gordon) (as Harriet Boyd)

1952 *With a Song in My Heart* (Lang) (as Jane Froman); *The Snows of Kilimanjaro* (King) (as Helen); *The Lusty Men* (Ray) (as Louise Merritt)

1953 *The President's Lady* (Levin) (as Rachel Donalson Robards); *White Witch Doctor* (Hathaway) (as Ellen Burton)

1954 *Demetrius and the Gladiators* (Daves) (as Messalina); *Garden of Evil* (Hathaway) (as Leah Fuller)

1955 *Untamed* (King) (as Katie O'Neill); *Soldier of Fortune* (Dmytryk) (as Jane Hoyt); *I'll Cry Tomorrow* (Mann) (as Lillian Roth)

1956 *The Conqueror* (Powell) (as Borta)

1957 *Top Secret Affair* (Potter) (as Dottie Peale)

1958 *I Want to Live* (Wise) (as Barbara Graham)

1959 *Woman Obsessed* (Hathaway) (as Mary Sharron); *Thunder in the Sun* (Rouse) (as Gabrielle Dauphin)

1960 *The Marriage-Go-Round* (W. Lang) (as Content Delville)

1961 *Ada* (Mann) (title role); *Back Street* (Miller) (as Rae Smith)

1962 *I Thank a Fool* (Stevens) (as Christine Allison)

1963 *Stolen Hours* (Petrie) (as Laura Dember)

1964 *Where Love Has Gone* (Dmytryk) (as Valerie Hayden)

1967 *The Honey Pot* (Mankiewicz) (as Mrs. "Lone Star" Crockett Sheridan); *Think Twentieth* (Fleischer—short); *Valley of the Dolls* (Robson) (as Helen Lawson)

1972 *Heat of Anger* (D. Taylor—for TV) (as Jessie Fitzgerald); *The Revengers* (Daniel Mann) (as Elizabeth Reilly); *Say Goodbye, Maggie Cole* (J. Taylor—for TV) (title role)

Publications

On HAYWARD: books—

Anderson, Christopher, *A Star, Is a Star, Is a Star! The Lives and Loves of Susan Hayward*, New York, 1980.

Parish, James, and Don Stanke, *The Forties Gals*, Westport, Connecticut, 1980.

Linet, Beverly, *Susan Hayward: Portrait of a Survivor*, New York, 1980.

Moreno, Eduardo, *The Films of Susan Hayward*, Secaucus, New Jersey, 1981.

La Guardia, Robert, and Gene Arceri, *Red: The Tempestuous Life of Susan Hayward*, New York, 1985.

On HAYWARD: articles—

McClelland, D., "Susan Hayward," in *Films in Review* (New York), May 1962.

McClelland, D., "The Brooklyn Bernhardt," in *Films and Filming* (London), March 1965.

* * *

Susan Hayward's career was in certain respects quite curious. Few stars of her stature have appeared in so few interesting films or worked so seldom with distinguished directors (*Canyon Passage, The Lusty Men* . . . except from the viewpoint of Hayward's intrinsic interest there is really not much else to salvage). Considering the conditions within which female stars functioned in the classical period, the personality itself presents difficulties: abrasive, aggressive, intractable, it is not surprising that she took so long to become established, for years playing "other woman" roles (*Forest Rangers, I Married a Witch*) or being relegated to insipid or underdeveloped minor characters (*Reap the Wild Wind*); nor is it surprising that her major star roles tended to the solo tour de force rather than to the romantic love story (*I'll Cry Tomorrow, I Want to Live*).

Untamed is perhaps the ideal Hayward title: her personality at all points resists the "taming" represented by the traditional Hollywood happy ending, the subordination of female desire to male desire, the woman's surrender of her autonomy. Her two finest films make interesting and contrasted use of her intractability. The "happy ending" of *Canyon Passage* (one of the most underestimated of all Westerns) teams her with a "wanderer hero" (Dana Andrews) who equally refuses the confines of domesticity. Nicholas Ray's use of her in *The Lusty Men* is, on the contrary, fascinating in its perversity: her aggressiveness is allowed its full expression (including rage and physical violence) but exclusively in the interests of home and settling.

It is again not surprising that the "taming" of Hayward took, in her most celebrated roles, extreme and drastic forms. The punishments that characterize her career begin early: already in *The Forest Rangers* the "happy ending" (the union of Fred MacMurray and Paulette Goddard at Hayward's expense) requires that she be brutally assaulted with a fire hose. Most striking is the recurrent burden of alchoholism imposed on the Hayward characters (*Smash Up, My Foolish Heart, I'll Cry Tomorrow*); but she is also crippled in *With a Song in My Heart* and (most extremely) executed in the electric chair in *I Want to Live*.

—Robin Wood

HAYWORTH, Rita

Nationality: American. **Born:** Margarita Carmen Cansino in New York City, 17 October 1918. **Education:** Attended Hamilton High School, and Carthay School, Los Angeles. **Family:** Married 1) Edward C. Judson, 1936 (divorced 1942); 2) the director and actor Orson Welles, 1943 (divorced 1948), daughter: Rebecca; 3) Prince Ali Khan, 1949 (divorced 1953), daughter: Princess Yasmin; 4) the singer Dick

Haymes, 1953 (divorced 1955); 5) the producer James Hill, 1958 (divorced 1961). **Career:** 1926—film debut with her family group The Dancing Cansinos in *La Fiesta*; 1932—professional stage debut in Los Angeles; 1934-35—dancer with her father at Foreign Club, Tijuana, Mexico, and on California gambling boat; 1935—adult film debut in *Dante's Inferno*, then one-year contract with Fox; 1937—contract with Columbia; 1958—freelance acting career began with *Separate Tables*, and continued into 1970s. **Died:** In New York City, 14 May 1987.

Films as Actress:

(as Rita Cansino)

1926   *La Fiesta* (short) (as Anna Case)

1934   *Cruz diablo* (*The Devil's Cross*) (De Fuentes)

1935   *Under the Pampas Moon* (Tinling) (as Carmen); *Charlie Chan in Egypt* (King) (as Nayda); *Dante's Inferno* (Lachman) (as speciality dancer); *Paddy O'Day* (Seiler) (as Tamana Petrovich); *Piernas de seda* (*Silk Legs*) (Boland)

1936   *Human Cargo* (Dwan) (as Carmen Zorro); *Meet Nero Wolfe* (Biberman) (as Maria Maningula); *Rebellion* (*Lady from Frisco*) (Shores) (as Paula Castillo); *A Message to Garcia* (Marshall)

1937   *Trouble in Texas* (Bradbury) (as Carmen); *Old Louisianna* (*Treason*) (Willat) (as Angela Gonzales); *Hit the Saddle* (Wright) (as Rita)

(as Rita Hayworth)

1937   *Criminals of the Air* (Coleman) (as Rita); *Girls Can Play* (Hillyer) (as Sue Collins); *The Shadow* (*The Circus Shadow*) (Coleman) (as Mary Gillespie); *The Game That Kills* (Lederman) (as Betty Holland); *Paid to Dance* (Coleman) (as Betty Morom)

1938   *Who Killed Gail Preston?* (Barsha) (title role); *There's Always a Woman* (Hall) (as Mary); *Convicted* (Barsha) (as Jerry Wheelen); *Juvenile Court* (Lederman) (as Marcia Adams); *The Renegade Ranger* (Howard) (as Judith Alvarez); *Homicide Bureau* (Coleman) (as J. G. Bliss)

1939   *The Lone Wolf Spy Hunt* (*The Lone Wolf's Daughter*) (Godfrey) (as Karen); *Special Inspector* (*Across the Border*) (Barsha) (as Patricia Lane); *Only Angels Have Wings* (Hawks) (as Judy MacPherson); *Music in My Heart* (Santley) (as Patricia O'Malley)

1940   *Blondie on a Budget* (Strayer) (as Jean Forrester); *Susan and God* (*The Gay Mrs. Trexel*) (Cukor) (as Leonora Stubbs); *The Lady in Question* (C. Vidor) (as Natalie Rougin); *Angels over Broadway* (Hecht and Garmes) (as Nina Barona)

1941   *The Strawberry Blonde* (Walsh) (as Virginia Bush); *Affectionately Yours* (Bacon) (as Irene Malcolm); *Blood and Sand* (Mamoulian) (as Doña Sol); *You'll Never Get Rich* (Lanfield) (as Sheila Winthrop)

1942   *My Gal Sal* (Cummings) (as Sally Elliot); *Tales of Manhattan* (Duvivier) (as Ethel Halloway); *You Were Never Lovelier* (Seiter) (as Marina Aluna)

1943   *Show Business at War*

1944   *Cover Girl* (C. Vidor) (as Rusty Parka/Maribelle Hicks)

1945   *Tonight and Every Night* (Saville) (as Rosalind Bruce)

1946   *Gilda* (C. Vidor) (title role)

1947   *Down to Earth* (Hall) (as Terpsichore/Kitty Pendleton)

1948   *The Lady from Shanghai* (Welles) (as Elsa Barrister); *The Loves of Carmen* (C. Vidor) (title role)

1951   *Champagne Safari* (Leighter—documentary of Hayworth and Khan wedding trip)

1952   *Affair in Trinidad* (Sherman) (as Chris Emery)

1953   *Salome* (Dieterle) (title role); *Miss Sadie Thompson* (Bernhardt) (title role)

1957   *Fire Down Below* (Parrish) (as Irena); *Pal Joey* (Sidney) (as Vera Simpson)

1958   *Separate Tables* (Mann) (as Ann Shankland)

1959   *They Came to Cordura* (Rossen) (as Adelaide Gears)

1960   *The Story on Page One* (Odets) (as Jo Morris)

1962   *The Happy Thieves* (Marshall) (as Eve Lewis)

1964   *Circus World* (*The Magnificent Showman*) (Hathaway) (as Lila Alfredo)

1966   *The Money Trap* (Kennedy) (as Rosalie Kenny); *The Poppy Is Also a Flower* (*Danger Grows Wild*) (Young) (as Monique)

1967   *The Rover* (*L'Avventuriero*) (Young) (as Caterina)

1971   *Sons of Satan* (*I Bastardi, I gatti*; *The Cats*) (Tessari) (as Martha); *Road to Salina* (*La Route de Salina*) (Lautner) (as Mara); *The Naked Zoo* (*The Naked Lovers*; *The Hallucinators*) (Grefé)

1972   *The Wrath of God* (Nelson) (as Semona de la Plata)

1976   *Circle* (Seidelman)

Publications

On HAYWORTH: books—

Rosen, Marjorie, *Popcorn Venus*, New York, 1973.

Ringgold, Gene, *The Films of Rita Hayworth: The Legend and Career of a Love Goddess*, Secaucus, New Jersey, 1974.

Kobal, John, *Rita Hayworth: The Time, the Place, and the Woman*, New York, 1978.

Hill, James, *Rita Hayworth: A Memoir*, New York, 1983.

Morella, Joseph, and Edward Z. Epstein, *Rita: The Life of Rita Hayworth*, New York, 1983.

Dureau, Christian, *Rita Hayworth*, Paris, 1985.

Merrill, Gary, *Bette, Rita, and the Rest of My Life*, Augusta, Maine, 1988.

Leaming, Barbara, *If This Was Happiness: A Biography of Rita Hayworth*, New York, 1989.

On HAYWORTH: articles—

Kobal, John, "The Time, the Place and the Girl: Rita Hayworth," in *Focus on Film* (London), Summer 1972.

Stanke, Don, "Rita Hayworth," in *Films in Review* (New York), November 1972

Drew, Bernard, "Heartbreak Hollywood," in *American Film* (Washington, D.C.), June 1977.

Obituary, in *Variety* (New York), 20 May 1987.

Pulleine, Tim, obituary, in *Films and Filming* (London), July 1987.

Mille, A., "Rita Hayworth: Star en mouvement," in *Positif* (Paris), September 1987.

*   *   *

Rita Hayworth's life might serve as the prototype for that of the glamorous movie queen, the classic story of the beautiful young woman trapped in a profession that took over her life in ways she found difficult to understand, much less control. Born into a show-business family, Hayworth went to work early as a dancing partner for her father, Eduardo Cansino of The Dancing Cansinos. Her grace and beauty soon attracted Hollywood, and, after a lackluster beginning playing bit parts as a Latin type in B pictures, she was remade from an ethnic beauty into an all-American glamour girl through new makeup,

Rita Hayworth in *Gilda*

hair color, and an electrolysis treatment that lifted her hairline. The careful exploitation of her as the ultimate in Hollywood 1940s desirability brought her fame and wealth, but little happiness.

The Hayworth image was always sexy and alluring, but she didn't play in only one type of film. She was the dancing star of 1940s escapist musicals, and at the same time she played femmes fatales in a series of films noir. Her first real success as a leading lady came in 1941, and her films that year reflect these differences: Rouben Mamoulian's *Blood and Sand*, in which she was the temptress Doña Sol, and *You'll Never Get Rich*, in which she was Fred Astaire's dancing partner. She made another film with Astaire, *You Were Never Lovelier*, and many felt that Hayworth, a natural dancer with great stamina and rhythm, was Astaire's best on-screen partner. Although her singing had to be dubbed, she found great success in the musicals of the 1940s.

Two of the most financially successful and best remembered films of the war years starred Hayworth: the musical *Cover Girl*, in which she co-starred with Gene Kelly, and the sexually suggestive *Gilda*, opposite Glenn Ford. *Cover Girl* presented Hayworth in a Technicolor version of her own story. An ordinary dancer is transformed before the audience's eyes via clothing and makeup into a dazzling face on a magazine cover. She becomes a famous model as well as a successful musical comedy star, descending, as it seems, from the very heavens as she dances down a gigantic ramp in flowing chiffon. (Needless to say, none of it brings her happiness.) In *Gilda* she is used and abused by more than one man, and her apparent passivity allows her to be victimized and degraded, culminating in her famous striptease "Put the Blame on Mame, Boys." Hayworth's image as a destructive but pliable woman seemed to stick with her after *Gilda*. "Every man I've known has fallen in love with Gilda and wakened with me," she allegedly told a friend. One of her ex-husbands, Orson Welles, used Hayworth's image as a passive yet destructive temptress in his film *The Lady from Shanghai*.

Whether Hayworth played in musicals or dramas, she was always the ultimate in desirability. When in 1948 *Life* magazine dubbed her "The Love Goddess," she was officially marked with the tagline that would plague her the rest of her life. The issue coincided with the release of her film *Down to Earth*, in which she played the Greek goddess of dance, Terpsichore. Her image as a woman men could not resist was further enhanced by her five unhappy marriages, in particular her wedding to Prince Ali Khan in 1949. This publicity bonanza, fully exploited by the tabloids, made Hayworth into an international celebrity. She soon returned to Hollywood, however, and resumed her career, although she would never regain the fame she had in the 1940s.

Hayworth continued to perform during the 1960s and 1970s, occasionally trying her hand at television or a serious drama, such as her role in Rattigan's *Separate Tables*, for which she received good reviews. Hayworth's most famous and successful films, musical or dramatic, tend to deal with her as a woman whose image does not truthfully reflect her personality, and for whom success, riches, and beauty bring no real and lasting personal satisfaction. Sadly enough, it seemed to be the story of her own life.

—Jeanine Basinger

HENIE, Sonja

Nationality: American. **Born:** Oslo, Norway, 8 April 1912; became U.S. citizen, 1941. **Family:** Married 1) Daniel Reid Topping, 1940 (divorced 1946); 2) Winthrop Gardiner, Jr., 1949 (divorced); 3) Niels Onstadt. **Career:** 1923—became national skating champion of Norway; 1927—first of 10 world figure skating championships; 1928—first of three Olympic gold medals for figure skating;

1936—became professional skater, and for the next 15 years appeared in ice shops and exhibitions, sponsoring and producing her own shows after 1938; 1937—Hollywood film debut in 20th Century-Fox's *One in a Million*; 1945—toured American army hospitals as USO entertainer; 1950s—did TV ice shows; 1960s—interest in art lead to her founding Henie-Onstadt Stiftelser in Hovikodden, Norway. **Awards:** Knight of the Order of St. Olaf, 1937. **Died:** 11 October 1969.

Films as Actress:

1927 *Svy Dager for Elisabeth*
1937 *One in a Million* (Lanfield) (as Gretta Müller); *Thin Ice* (Lanfield) (as Lili Heiser)
1938 *Happy Landing* (Del Ruth) (as Trudi Erickson); *My Lucky Star* (Del Ruth)
1939 *Second Fiddle* (Lanfield) (as Trudi Horland); *Everything Happens at Night* (Cummings)
1940 *Sun Valley Serenade* (Humberstone)
1942 *Iceland* (Humberstone)
1945 *Wintertime* (Brahm); *It's a Pleasure* (Seiter)
1948 *The Countess of Monte Cristo* (de Cordova)
1958 *Hello London* (*London Calling*) (Smith)

Publications

By HENIE: books—

Mitt Livs Eventyr, Oslo, 1938.
Wings on My Feet, New York, 1940.

On HENIE: book—

Strait, Raymond, and Leif Henie, *Queen of Ice, Queen of Shadows: The Unsuspected Life of Sonja Henie*, New York, 1985.

*   *   *

During the late 1930s Sonja Henie was one of the most popular stars in Hollywood. The *Motion Picture Herald* ranked her in the top ten stars in 1937, 1938, and 1939. No one has ever argued that this ice skater-turned-actress was a great performer by traditional standards, but few familiar with the U.S. film industry of the 1930s can fail to acknowledge her box-office power during the years immediately prior to World War II. Twentieth Century-Fox certainly acknowledged it by paying her hundreds of thousands of dollars a year.

Henie was the greatest female ice skater of her age, winning three Olympic crowns before turning professional. As part of a U.S. tour during the spring of 1936, one of her performances was seen by Darryl F. Zanuck, who had recently taken charge of production at the newly merged Twentieth Century-Fox. He was in the process of developing new stars, and so cast Henie in *One in a Million* along with Fox contract players Adolphe Menjou, Don Ameche, and the Ritz Brothers. This film was such a success at the box office that its sequel, *Thin Ice*, vaulted Henie into the rankings of the top Hollywood stars. She was a shrewd business person, and pressed to have her contract renegotiated. It was, and her salary in 1939 topped $250,000.

By 1941, however, Henie's career as a movie star began to falter. In 1943, the studio did not renew her contract, and she moved to an independent company, International Pictures. The shift did not help, and so she voluntarily ended her movie career in 1948, and returned to her annual ice shows on a full-time basis. She retired from skating in

Sonja Henie

1952, a millionaire several times over. Like Esther Williams in the late 1940s, Henie was a unique athletic talent who was fully exploited by a then-powerful movie industry. No one can doubt she was a great ice show performer, but few have found any criteria for appreciating her ability as a motion picture actress.

—Douglas Gomery

HENREID, Paul

Nationality: American. **Born:** Paul George Julius von Hernreid in Trieste, Austria (now Italy), 10 January 1908; became U.S. citizen, 1946. **Education:** Attended Maria Theresianische Akademie, Vienna; Graphische Akademie, Vienna. **Family:** Married Elizabeth Camilla Julia Gluck, daughter: Monica. **Career:** 1929—joined book publishers A. G. Strobl, and attended the New Vienna Conservatory Dramatic Academy at night; 1932—film debut in *Baroud*; 1933—given contract by Max Reinhardt, and made stage debut in *Faust*; 1938—left Vienna after Nazi takeover of Austria; 1939—first British film, *Goodbye, Mr. Chips*; 1940—emigrated to America; played in *Victoria and Albert* in New York; 1941—joined the cast of radio serial *Joyce Jordan, Girl Interne*; contract with RKO; 1950s—much work as TV actor and director (he estimated he had directed 300 TV segments or

plays); 1962—directed the play *Everyman*; 1972—appeared in *Don Juan in Hell* on stage. **Died:** Of pneumonia, in Santa Monica, California, 29 March 1992.

Films as Actor:

1932   *Baroud* (*Love in Morocco*) (Ingram)
1934   *Hohe Schule* (*Das Geheimnis des Carlo Cavelli*) (Engels)
1935   *Eva* (Riemann); *. . . nur ein Komödiant* (Engel)
1937   *Victoria the Great* (Wilcox) (bit role)
1939   *Goodbye, Mr. Chips* (Wood) (as Max Staefel); *An Englishman's Home* (*Madmen of Europe*) (de Courville) (as Victor Brandt)
1940   *Night Train to Munich* (*Night Train*) (Reed) (as Karl Marsen); *Under Your Hat* (Elvey)
1942   *Joan of Paris* (Stevenson) (as Paul Lavallier); *Now, Voyager* (Rapper) (as Jerry Durrance); *Casablanca* (Curtiz) (as Victor Laszlo)
1944   *In Our Time* (Sherman) (as Count Stephen Orvid); *Between Two Worlds* (Blatt) (as Henry); *The Conspirators* (Negulesco) (as Vincent); *Hollywood Canteen* (Daves) (as guest)
1945   *The Spanish Main* (Borzage) (as Laurent Van Horn)
1946   *Devotion* (Bernhardt) (as Nichols); *Of Human Bondage* (Goulding) (as Philip Carey)
1947   *Deception* (Rapper) (as Karel Novak); *Song of Love* (Brown) (as Robert Schumann)
1948   *Hollow Triumph* (*The Scar*) (Sekely) (as John Muller/Dr. Bartok, + pr)
1949   *Rope of Sand* (Dieterle) (as Commandant Paul Vogel)
1950   *So Young, So Bad* (Vorhaus) (as Dr. Jason); *Last of the Buccaneers* (Landers) (as Jean Lafitte); *Dans la vie tout s'arrange* (Cravenne); *Pardon My French* (*The Lady from Boston*) (Vorhaus—English version of *Dans la vie tout s'arrange*) (as Paul Rencourt)
1952   *Thief of Damascus* (Jason) (as Abu Andar); *Stolen Face* (Fisher) (as Dr. Philip Ritter); *There Is No Escape* (Fisher)
1953   *Mantrap* (*Man in Hiding*; *Woman in Hiding*) (Fisher) (as Hugo Bishop); *Siren of Bagdad* (Quine) (as Kazah)
1954   *Kabarett* (*Dieses Leid bliebt bei dir*) (Forst); *Deep in My Heart* (Donen) (as Florenz Ziegfeld); *Pirates of Tripoli* (Feist) (as Edri-Al-Gadrian)
1956   *Meet Me in Las Vegas* (*Viva Las Vegas!*) (Rowland) (as Maria's manager)
1957   *Ten Thousand Bedrooms* (Thorpe) (as Anton)
1959   *Holiday for Lovers* (Levin) (as Eduardo Barroso); *Never So Few* (John Sturges) (as Nikko Regas)
1961   *The Four Horsemen of the Apocalypse* (Minnelli) (as Etienne Laurier)
1965   *Operation Crossbow* (Anderson) (as General Zeimann)
1966   *Peking Remembered* (Butler) (as narrator)
1969   *The Madwoman of Chaillot* (Forbes) (as the General)
1971   *The Failing of Raymond* (Sagal—for TV)
1975   *Death among Friends* (*Mrs. R.—Death among Friends*) (Wendkos—for TV)
1977   *Exorcist II: The Heretic* (Boorman) (as the Cardinal)
1987   *Hollow Triumph* (Sekely—for TV)

Films as Director:

1951   *For Men Only* (*The Tall Lie*) (+ pr, ro as Dr. Stephen Brice)
1956   *A Woman's Devotion* (*War Shock*; *Battleshock*) (+ ro as Capt. Henrique Monteros)

1958   *Girls on the Loose*; *Live Fast, Die Young*
1964   *Dead Ringer* (*Dead Image*); *Ballad in Blue* (*Blues for Lovers*)
            (+ co-story)

Publications

By HENREID: book—

Ladies Man: An Autobiography, with Julius Fast, New York, 1984.

On HENREID: articles—

Current Biography 1943, New York, 1943.
Classic Images (Indiana, Pennsylvania), March and April 1983.
Obituary, in *Variety* (New York), 6 April 1992.

                              *   *   *

Paul Henreid knew how to play the continental gentleman, a debonair character who could display bravery and patriotism with quiet grace. He played that type of role in two Hollywood classics which are so solidly etched in the minds of film enthusiasts that the remainder of this actor's full screen career dims against their bright lights. The first of these films, *Now, Voyager*, probably would have been remembered mainly as a tear-filled Bette Davis vehicle, in which the actress plays Charlotte Vance, a dowdy old maid headed for a nervous breakdown as the film begins. But Henreid, as Jerry Durrance, the unattainable love of Charlotte's life, created an indelible image when, in a recurring motif, he lit two cigarettes simultaneously and then handed one to Davis, one of the great romantic gestures in silver screen history.

A few months later *Casablanca* was released. In it he plays Victor Laszlo, archetypal freedom-fighting Resistance leader/political refugee whose brave efforts against Nazi tyranny, and the subsequent tortures he suffered during a year in a German concentration camp, have left him just a couple steps below sainthood. His finest moment, in a film made up of memorable moments, is the scene at Rick's Place in which he leads French citizens, demoralized under Nazi occupation, in a stirring rendition of the Marseillaise, drowning out the voices of German soldiers raised in a Nazi war song.

While Henreid's characters never flirted or gave a heavy come-on toward female co-stars, the actor exuded an air of romance which most women—on-screen and in the audience—could not resist. Even when he vied for the woman he loved with actors who had more zip and flash (Bogart in *Casablanca*, Claude Rains in *Deception*), his reserved elegance won out. As the powers at Warner Brothers came to recognize the appeal of their continental gentleman, they took a giant step in imaginative casting by starring him in the swashbuckler adventure *The Spanish Main*, in which he plays a bold pirate who rescues Maureen O'Hara from the villainous Walter Slezak. In the Technicolor entertainment *Last of the Buccaneers*, he plays dashing Jean Lafitte most effectively, and he went on to star in a string of swashbucklers in the 1950s.

Henreid's career dates to 1933, when he was discovered in Vienna by Otto Preminger. Shortly after that, he was given prominent stage roles in Max Reinhardt's Viennese theater. In addition to honing his acting craft, he learned enough about directing from Reinhardt and later from an array of Warner Brothers's filmmakers to begin directing in the 1950s. He pursued directing motion pictures, television shows (mainly for Alfred Hitchcock), and subsequently, television films until his death in 1992. Henreid's autobiography *Ladies Man* appeared in 1984. In it he discussed aspects of his life practically unknown to many, including his prestigious acting career in Europe, his own real-life flight from the Nazis, his liberal politics, and the infamous blacklisting period in Hollywood which he claimed had a detrimental effect on his movie career.

—James D. Wilson, updated by Audrey E. Kupferberg

HEPBURN, Audrey

Nationality: British. **Born:** Edda van Heemstra Hepburn-Ruston in Brussels, Belgium, 4 May 1929, to a British father and Dutch mother. **Education:** Studied ballet at Arnhem Conservatory of Music, Amsterdam, and in Marie Rambert's ballet school, London. **Family:** Married 1) the actor Mel Ferrer, 1954 (divorced 1968), son: Sean; 2) Andrea Dotti, 1969 (divorced), son Luca. **Career:** 1949—stage debut in chorus of *High Button Shoes*, London; studied acting with Felix Aylmer; 1951—film debut in Britain in small parts in several films; chosen by Colette to play title role in Broadway production of *Gigi*; 1953—American film debut in *Roman Holiday*; 1954—on Broadway stage in title role of *Ondine*; 1976—returned to films after long absence, in *Robin and Marian*; 1988—Special Ambassador for UNICEF. **Awards:** Best Actress Academy Award, Best Actress, New York Film Critics, and Best British Actress, British Academy, for *Roman Holiday*, 1953; Best British Actress, British Academy, for *The Nun's Story*, 1959; Best British Actress, British Academy, for *Charade*, 1964; Commander, Order of Arts and Letters, France, 1987; Jean Hersholt Humanitarian Award, 1993. **Died:** Of cancer, in Tolochenaz, Switzerland, 20 January 1993.

Films as Actress:

(as Edda Hepburn)

1948   *Nederland in 7 Lessen* (*Dutch at the Double*) (Linden and
            Josephson)

(as Audrey Hepburn)

1951   *One Wild Oat* (Saunders) (as extra); *Laughter in Paradise*
            (Zampi) (as cigarette girl); *Young Wives' Tale* (Cass) (as Eve
            Lester); ***The Lavender Hill Mob*** (Charles Crichton) (as
            Chiquita); *Nous irons à Monte Carlo* (Jean Boyer) (as Melissa Walter); *Monte Carlo Baby* (Jean Boyer and Fuller)
            (English version of *Nous irons à Monte Carlo*) (as Linda
            Farrel); *Secret People* (Dickinson) (as Nora Brent)
1953   *Introducing Audrey Hepburn* (Dickinson—short); *Roman
            Holiday* (Wyler) (as Princess Anne)
1954   *Sabrina* (*Sabrina Fair*) (Wilder) (title role)
1956   *War and Peace* (King Vidor) (as Natasha Rostov)
1957   *Funny Face* (Donen) (as Jo Stockton); *Love in the Afternoon*
            (Wilder) (as Ariane Chevasse); *Mayerling* (Anatole Litvak—
            for TV)
1959   *The Nun's Story* (Zinnemann) (as Sister Luke); *Green Mansions* (Ferrer) (as Rima); *The Unforgiven* (Huston) (as Rachel
            Zachary)
1961   ***Breakfast at Tiffany's*** (Edwards) (as Holly Golightly); *The
            Children's Hour* (*The Loudest Whisper*) (Wyler) (as Karen
            Wright)
1963   *Charade* (Donen) (as Reggie Lambert)
1964   *Paris When It Sizzles* (Quine) (as Gabrielle Simpson); *My Fair
            Lady* (Cukor) (as Eliza Doolittle)
1966   *How to Steal a Million* (Wyler) (as Nicole Bonnet); *Two for the
            Road* (Donen) (as Joanna Wallace)

1967 *Wait until Dark* (Terence Young) (as Susy Hendrix)
1976 *Robin and Marian* (Lester) (as Marian)
1979 *Bloodline* (*Sidney Sheldon's Bloodline*) (Terence Young) (as Elizabeth Roffe)
1981 *They All Laughed* (Bogdanovich) (as Angela Niotes)
1986 *Directed by William Wyler* (Slesin—doc) (as herself)
1987 *Love among Thieves* (Roger Young—for TV) (as Baroness Caroline DuLac)
1989 *Always* (Spielberg) (as Hap)
1990 *A Chance to Live* (Barnes—for TV) (as presenter)

Publications

By HEPBURN: article—

Interview in *Photoplay* (London), August 1982.

On HEPBURN: books—

Higham, Charles, *Audrey: A Biography of Audrey Hepburn*, London, 1984.
Latham, Caroline, *Audrey Hepburn*, London, 1984.
Woodward, Ian, *Audrey Hepburn*, London, 1984.
Stresau, Norbert, *Audrey Hepburn: ihre Filme, ihr Leben*, Munich 1985.
Maychick, Diana, *Audrey Hepburn: An Intimate Portrait*, Secaucus, New Jersey, 1993.
Harris, Warren G., *Audrey Hepburn: A Biography*, New York, 1994.
Hofstede, David, *Audrey Hepburn: A Bio-Bibliography*, Westport, Connecticut, 1994.
Karney, Robyn, *A Star Danced: The Life of Audrey Hepburn*, New York, 1995.
Vermilye, Jerry, *The Complete Films of Audrey Hepburn*, Secaucus, New Jersey, 1995.
Walker, Alexander, *Audrey: Her Real Story*, New York, 1995.
Paris, Barry, *Audrey Hepburn*, 1996.

On HEPBURN: articles—

Current Biography 1954, New York, 1954.
Viotti, S., "Britain's Hepburn," in *Films and Filming* (London), November 1954.
Simon, Brett, "Audrey Hepburn," in *Films and Filming* (London), March 1964.
Braun, E., "The Hepburn Quality Revisited," in *Films* (London), August 1981.
Thompson, F., "Audrey Hepburn," in *American Film* (Hollywood), May 1990.
Obituary in *New York Times*, 21 January 1993.
Wilson, Elizabeth, "Audrey Hepburn: Fashion, Film and the 50s," in *Screen* (London), March 1993.
Corliss, Richard, "Serene Majesty," obituary in *Film Comment* (New York), March/April 1993.
Collins, Amy Fine, "When Hubert Met Audrey," in *Vanity Fair* (New York), December 1995.

*   *   *

When Audrey Hepburn died in 1993 at the age of 63, the world mourned a film star who on-screen and off embodied grace, elegance, and strength. At the pinnacle of her screen career, Hepburn gave her audience the perfect postwar combination of tomboy and sophisticate. After her semiretirement from film in the late 1960s, Hepburn held an honorary place among the Hollywood royalty. In 1988 she began her second career as a tireless special ambassador for the United Nations Children's Fund (UNICEF).

Holly Golightly—whether dressed in a black Givenchy, enormous hat, and oval sunglasses hailing a taxi with a shrill whistle or in pigtails, sitting on the fire escape strumming "Moon River" on her guitar—epitomizes for many fans the essence of Audrey Hepburn's film career. Marked by the internal contradictions of big city sophistication and rural, childlike innocence, Holly appears fragile, yet by the end of *Breakfast at Tiffany's* the audience discovers her inner strength.

Like Holly Golightly, Hepburn's past contributed greatly to the complexity and richness of her public persona. Hepburn was born in Belgium in 1929 to a Dutch baroness and an English banker who left when Hepburn was six years old. Trapped in Nazi-occupied Holland with her mother throughout World War II, Hepburn was reduced to eating tulip bulbs. She survived the war, but suffered many problems associated with malnutrition. The waiflike fragility which so many have admired and emulated was one result of wartime hardship.

After the war, Hepburn moved to London where she studied ballet and worked as a dancer and model. Her film career began unnoticeably with several small parts in English movies. A chance meeting with the writer Colette landed Hepburn on Broadway in the title role of the hit show *Gigi*. She received critical acclaim, but was not chosen to recreate the role on-screen. (The role went to Leslie Caron who has similar physical attributes.) Two years later, in her first major U.S. film role as Princess Anne in William Wyler's *Roman Holiday*, Hepburn captured her audience's heart and won an Academy Award.

Part of Hollywood's royalty, Hepburn played opposite the realm's most handsome charming princes—Gregory Peck, Humphrey Bogart, Cary Grant, Gary Cooper, Burt Lancaster, Henry Fonda, and Fred Astaire. That most of her leading men were older than her added to her gamine elegance and mystique.

As Sabrina Fairchild, a chauffeur's daughter, Hepburn was torn between the smooth, handsome bachelor played by William Holden and his serious, businesslike older brother (Humphrey Bogart). Following her heart, Sabrina makes the right choice. Audrey Hepburn's characters would continue to make the heart's choice in all her best-loved movies. Her audiences loved and trusted her because she played characters whose hearts, if occasionally misguided, in the end were true and kind.

Sabrina also marked the beginning of Hepburn's lifelong intimate friendship with the French fashion designer Hubert de Givenchy. She considered Givenchy one of her best friends and he has referred to her as a sister. He designed most of her screen clothes and she wore his designs offscreen as well. The clothes he designed for her almost always accentuated her long neck and showed off her strong shoulders. The Hepburn/Givenchy look countered the torpedo-breasted voluptuousness of the 1950s ideal woman. Hepburn gave women the possibility of a dignified, comfortable look in which intelligence and wit matter as much as physical beauty.

Princess Anne, Sabrina, and Holly Golightly share qualities with all of Audrey Hepburn's roles: as the daughter of a private detective in *Love in the Afternoon*, an empathicist bookseller turned photographer's muse in *Funny Face*, a typist in *Paris When It Sizzles*, and the daughter of an eccentric art forger in *How to Steal a Million*, Hepburn charmed with her gamine elegance, her chic wardrobe, her indistinctly European accent, her intelligent, simple beauty, and her wide, expressive eyes. With *The Nun's Story*, *The Children's Hour*, and *Two for the Road*, she successfully attempted grittier roles. Her 1967 portrayal of Suzie Hendrix, a blind woman trapped by a killer in *Wait until Dark*, proved Hepburn capable of an edgy, tensile performance. During her semiretirement following *Wait until Dark*, Hepburn returned to the big screen a few times, most notably perhaps in her critically acclaimed role opposite Sean Connery in *Robin and Marion*.

Hepburn's two-decade reign as one of Hollywood's most extraordinary stars seems almost a fairy-tale interlude in a life ravaged by war and then spent serving others similarly ravaged. A former recipient of UNICEF relief aid, she considered her role as UNICEF special ambas-

Audrey Hepburn in *Charade*

sador one of the most important in her life. Her final film appearance as Hap, the romantic angel in Steven Spielberg's *Always*, left us with a screen image of what Hepburn always was—a serene, radiant presence with force of spirit whose effortless elegance and sovereignty inspires us all.

—Ilene S. Goldman

HEPBURN, Katharine

Nationality: American. **Born:** Katharine Houghton Hepburn in Hartford, Connecticut, 9 November 1907 (or 1909). **Education:** Attended West Middle School; Oxford School for Girls, Hartford; Bryn Mawr College, Pennsylvania, 1924-28. **Family:** Married Ludlow Ogden Smith, 1928 (divorced 1934). **Career:** 1928—professional stage debut with Edwin H. Knopf's stock company, Baltimore, in *The Czarina*; New York debut in September under name Katharine Burns in *Night Hostess*; appearance on Broadway in November under own name in *These Days*; 1932—appearance in *The Warrior's Husband* led to Hollywood offers; contract with RKO; film debut in George Cukor's *A Bill of Divorcement*; 1934—returned to Broadway to star in *The Lake*; 1936-37—toured in *Jane Eyre* for the Theatre Guild; 1938—bought out of RKO contract rather than star in *Mother Cary's Chickens*; 1938—on Broadway in *The Philadelphia Story* (written for her by Philip Barry); 1941—teamed with Spencer Tracy for first time in *Woman of the Year*; 1950—on Broadway as Rosalind in *As You Like It*; continued through 1950s to tour in Shakespeare productions; later stage roles through the early 1980s. **Awards:** Best Actress, Academy Award for *Morning Glory*, 1932-33; Best Actress, Venice Festival, for *Little Women*, 1934; Best Actress, New York Film Critics, for *The Philadelphia Story*, 1940; Best Acting (collectively awarded), Cannes Festival, for *Long Day's Journey into Night*, 1962; Best Actress, Academy Awards, for *Guess Who's Coming to Dinner?*, 1967, and *The Lion in Winter*, 1968; Best Actress, British Academy, for *Guess Who's Coming to Dinner?* and *The Lion in Winter*, 1968; Best Actress, Academy Award, for *On Golden Pond*, 1981.

Films as Actress:

1932   *A Bill of Divorcement* (Cukor) (as Sydney Fairfield)
1933   *Christopher Strong* (Arzner) (as Lady Cynthia Darrington); *Morning Glory* (Sherman) (as Ada Love/"Eva Lovelace"); *Little Women* (Cukor) (as Jo)
1934   *Spitfire* (Cromwell) (as Trigger Hicks); *The Little Minister* (Wallace) (as Lady Babbie)
1935   *Break of Hearts* (Moeller) (as Constance Dane); *Alice Adams* (Stevens) (title role)
1936   *Sylvia Scarlett* (Cukor) (title role); *Mary of Scotland* (Ford) (title role); *A Woman Rebels* (Sandrich) (as Pamela Thistlewaite)
1937   *Quality Street* (Stevens) (as Phoebe Throssel); *Stage Door* (La Cava) (as Terry Randall)
1938   *Bringing Up Baby* (Hawks) (as Susan Vance); *Holiday* (Cukor) (as Linda Seton)
1940   *The Philadelphia Story* (Cukor) (as Tracy Lord)
1942   *Woman of the Year* (Stevens) (as Tess Harding)
1943   *Keeper of the Flame* (Cukor) (as Christine Forrest); *Stage Door Canteen* (Borzage) (as herself)
1944   *Dragon Seed* (Bucquet) (as Jade)
1945   *Without Love* (Bucquet) (as Jamie Rowan)
1946   *Undercurrent* (Minnelli) (as Ann Hamilton)

1947   *The Sea of Grass* (Kazan) (as Lutie Cameron); *Song of Love* (Brown) (as Clara Schumann)
1948   *State of the Union* (Capra) (as Mary Matthews)
1949   *Adam's Rib* (Cukor) (as Amanda Bonner)
1951   *The African Queen* (Huston) (as Rose Sayer)
1952   *Pat and Mike* (Cukor) (as Pat Pemberton)
1955   *Summertime* (Lean) (as Jane Hudson)
1956   *The Rainmaker* (Anthony) (as Lizzie)
1957   *The Iron Petticoat* (Thomas) (as Vinka Kovelenko); *Desk Set* (Walter Lang) (as Bunny Watson)
1959   *Suddenly, Last Summer* (Mankiewicz) (as Mrs. Violet Venable)
1962   *Long Day's Journey into Night* (Lumet) (as Mary Tyrone)
1967   *Guess Who's Coming to Dinner?* (Kramer) (as Christina Drayton)
1968   *The Lion in Winter* (Anthony Harvey) (as Eleanor of Aquitaine)
1969   *The Madwoman of Chaillot* (Forbes) (as Countess Aurelia)
1971   *The Trojan Women* (Cacoyannis) (as Hecuba)
1973   *A Delicate Balance* (Richardson) (as Agnes); *The Glass Menagerie* (Anthony Harvey—for TV) (as Amanda Wingfield)
1975   *Rooster Cogburn* (Millar) (as Eula Goodnight); *Love among the Ruins* (Cukor—for TV) (as Jessica Medlicott)
1977   *Olly, Olly, Oxen Free* (*The Great Balloon Adventure*) (Colla) (as Miss Pudd)
1978   *The Corn Is Green* (Cukor—for TV) (as Lilly C. Moffat)
1981   *On Golden Pond* (Rydell) (as Ethel Thayer)
1983   *The Ultimate Solution of Grace Quigley* (*Grace Quigley*) (Anthony Harvey) (title role)
1984   *George Stevens: A Filmmaker's Journey* (Stevens, Jr.)
1986   *Mrs. Delafield Wants to Marry* (Schaefer—for TV) (title role); *Spencer Tracy Legacy: A Tribute by Katharine Hepburn* (Heeley—for TV)
1988   *Laura Lansing Slept Here* (Schaefer—for TV) (title role)
1993   *The Man Upstairs* (Schaefer—for TV) (as Victoria Brown)
1994   *Love Affair* (Caron) (as Ginny); *This Can't Be Love* (Anthony Harvey—for TV) (as Marion Bennett); *One Christmas* (Tony Bill—for TV) (as Cornelia Beaumont)

Publications

By HEPBURN: books—

The Making of The African Queen: Or How I Went to Africa with Bogart, Bacall, and Huston and Almost Lost My Mind, London 1987.
Me, New York, 1991.

By HEPBURN: articles—

Interview with I. McAsh, in *Films* (London), May 1982.
"Katharine Hepburn: 'It's My Last Day of Acting,'" interview with Army Archerd, in *TV Guide*, 17 December 1994.

On HEPBURN: books—

Newquist, Roy, *A Special Kind of Magic*, New York, 1967.
Dickens, Homer, *The Films of Katharine Hepburn*, New York, 1971.
Kanin, Garson, *Tracy and Hepburn*, New York, 1971.
Huston, John, *An Open Book*, New York, 1972.
Marill, Alvin H., *Katharine Hepburn*, New York, 1973.
Rosen, Marjorie, *Popcorn Venus*, New York, 1973.
Higham, Charles, *Kate: The Life of Katharine Hepburn*, New York, 1975.
Wallis, Hal, and Charles Higham, *Starmaker*, New York, 1980.

Katharine Hepburn in *Holiday*

Navarro, Marie-Louise, *Katharine Hepburn dans l'objectif*, Paris, 1981.

Britton, Andrew, *Katharine Hepburn: Star as Feminist*, Newcastle upon Tyne, 1983; rev. ed., 1995.

Carey, Gary, *Katharine Hepburn: A Biography*, London, 1983.

Freedland, Michael, *Katharine Hepburn*, London, 1984.

Morley, Sheridan, *Katharine Hepburn: A Celebration*, London, 1984; rev. ed., 1989.

Spada, James, *Hepburn: Her Life in Pictures*, London, 1984.

Edwards, Anne, *A Remarkable Woman: A Biography of Katharine Hepburn*, New York, 1985.

Anderson, Christopher, *Young Kate*, New York, 1988.

Bryson, John, *The Private World of Katharine Hepburn*, London, 1990.

Tarshis, Lauren, *Kate: The Katharine Hepburn Album*, New York, 1993.

Leaming, Barbara, *Katharine Hepburn*, New York, 1995.

On HEPBURN: articles—

Mason, G., "Katharine the Great," in *Films and Filming* (London), August 1956.

Tozzi, Romano, "Katharine Hepburn," in *Films in Review* (New York), December 1957.

Cowie, P., "Katharine Hepburn," in *Films and Filming* (London), June 1963.

Current Biography 1969, New York, 1969.

Bowers, R., "Hepburn since '57," in *Films in Review* (New York), August-September 1970.

Gilliatt, Penelope, "The Most Amicable Combatants," in *New Yorker*, 23 September 1972.

Phillips, Gene, "Cukor and Hepburn," in *American Classic Screen* (Shawnee Mission, Kansas), Fall 1979.

Crist, Judith, "Katharine Hepburn," in *The Movie Star*, edited by Elisabeth Weis, New York, 1981.

Watney, S., "Katharine Hepburn and the Cinema of Chastisement," in *Screen* (London), September/October 1985.

Cronyn, Hume, "Tracy, Hepburn, and Me," in *New York Times*, 15 September 1991.

McClurg, Jocelyn, "Kate on Kate," in *Saturday Evening Post*, January-February 1992.

*   *   *

Any account of Katharine Hepburn must necessarily be indebted to Andrew Britton's book on her, which (together with Richard Dyer's *Stars*) represents a significant breakthrough in attempts to deal with the star phenomenon that transcend the gossip column and career outline.

Hepburn has represented, on a number of levels, a problem that Hollywood never quite managed to solve, although it proposed a number of partial solutions. Aspects of the problem were how to publicize her; how to deal with her intransigent demands for better or different types of roles; which leading man, or *type* of male lead, to cast with or against her; and what sort of star vehicles to construct around her. Central to the problem is her famous rebelliousness. It is fitting that one of her 1930s films should be titled *A Woman Rebels*, since this characteristic was consistently expressed both by the characters she played and in her offscreen image. The rebelliousness could be used, up to a point, to construct her as an attractive identification-figure for the female viewer; but it threatened continuously to become too subversive, too radical, too incontainable. The problem Hollywood faced with Hepburn was, precisely, that of containment. This gives her career, of course, a very special interest in relation to feminism: both on and off screen, Hepburn repeatedly challenged a male-dominated social order and the male-dominated industry that is at once a part of that order and represents its structures to the general public.

Britton argues convincingly that, from a feminist viewpoint, Hepburn's most progressive work is located in the 1930s rather than in her more popular and famous later films such as *The Philadelphia Story* or the movies in which she was teamed with Spencer Tracy. Many of the films of this early period were explicitly concerned with a woman's rebellion against male determination; some (*Little Women, Stage Door*) add to this strong connotations of lesbianism, in the wider sense in which that term is now commonly used in feminist discourse: female bonding for mutual support and solidarity. This in turn merges with strong overtones of androgyny, developed most fully in *Sylvia Scarlett*, in which for much of the film she is disguised as a boy. Gender, in fact, becomes a central issue when considering the Hepburn persona during this period, as the films frequently deal with (and undermine) the socially constructed norms of masculinity and femininity. It is interesting that in her first film (*A Bill of Divorcement*) and at all periods of her career Hepburn worked with George Cukor, producing much of her best, most responsive and vivid work in collaboration with a gay (and woman-oriented) director. She also in this period found her ideal co-star, Cary Grant. Her 1930s work culminates in two masterpieces in which they were teamed, Cukor's *Holiday* and Hawks's *Bringing Up Baby*. The Grant and Hepburn personas lent themselves with special aptness and felicity to Hawks's comedy of sexual role reversal.

The Philadelphia Story marks a watershed: it contains some of Hepburn's most brilliant and radiant moments, but ascribes her rebelliousness to the egocentricity of a spoiled socialite, the film's project being essentially her chastisement and conversion into what patriarchal culture defines as a "real woman." The teaming with Tracy is a logical next step: the rebellion, the struggle for independence, are still thematically present (*Adam's Rib* is perhaps the most *explicitly* feminist of all Hepburn's movies), but the continued expression of those drives is made more acceptable by the presence of a male co-star who represents an entirely unambiguous and irreducible "masculinity."

Of Hepburn's transition into old age, one might say that she at least retained her dignity, without the descent into exploitation horror movies suffered by Bette Davis, Joan Crawford, and Tallulah Bankhead. The alternative has proved, however, to be a move into the sort of "class" productions deemed respectable in middle-of-the-road bourgeois culture, and one may question whether it is really any happier a fate to spend one's old age appearing in *The Lion in Winter* and *The Madwoman of Chaillot* than in *Straitjacket* or *Die, Die, My Darling*.

Hepburn's best work in this period has been, again, with George Cukor: the television movies *Love among the Ruins* and *The Corn Is Green*. *On Golden Pond*, a central movie of the Reagan era, finally subordinates her to the patriarchal order; yet her extraordinary vitality movingly survives.

In recent years, two biographical works have shed further light on Hepburn's background and motivation. One is an autobiography, called *Me*, in which she reveals her relationships with family and friends, and her need to be in control both personally and professionally. The second is Barbara Leaming's controversial tome, *Katharine Hepburn*, which serves to draw a very different and often unpleasant portrait of the Tracy-Hepburn relationship, and also her alleged romance with John Ford. In her late seventies and eighties, she continued acting in made-for-television movies (*Mrs. Delafield Wants to Marry, Laura Lansing Slept Here, The Man Upstairs, This Can't Be Love*) which are rare in story content in that each focuses on an elderly woman. But she did not altogether abandon the big screen, appearing as Warren Beatty's brittle but vigorous, wise aunt in *Love Affair*.

—Robin Wood, updated by Audrey E. Kupferberg

HERSHEY, Barbara

Nationality: American. **Born:** Barbara Herzstein in Hollywood, California, 5 February 1948. **Family:** Lived with the actor David Carradine, 1969-75, one son (Free, who changed his name to Tom at age nine); married Stephen Douglas, 1992 (divorced 1993). **Education:** Attended Hollywood High School. **Career:** 1966-67—regular on TV series *The Monroes*; 1968—made screen debut in *With Six You Get Eggroll*; 1973—changed name to Barbara Seagull, a name she kept for two years; 1979—in TV mini-series *A Man Called Intrepid* and *From Here to Eternity*; 1993—in TV mini-series *Return to Lonesome Dove*. **Awards:** Best Actress, Cannes Festival, for *Shy People*, 1987; Co-Best Actress, Cannes Festival, for *A World Apart*, 1988; Emmy Award, Best Dramatic Actress, for *A Killing in a Small Town*, 1990. **Agent:** Creative Artists Agency, 9830 Wilshire Boulevard, Beverly Hills, CA 90212, U.S.A.

Films as Actress:

(as Barbara Hershey)

1968   *With Six You Get Eggroll* (Morris) (as Stacey Iverson); *Yours, Mine and Ours* (Shavelson)
1969   *Heaven with a Gun* (Katzin) (as Leloopa); *Last Summer* (Perry) (as Sandy)
1970   *The Liberation of L. B. Jones* (Wyler) (as Nella Mundine); *The Baby Maker* (Bridges) (as Tish Gray)
1971   *The Pursuit of Happiness* (Mulligan) (as Jane Kauffman)
1972   *Dealing: Or the Berkeley-to-Boston Forty-Brick Lost-Bag Blues* (Williams) (as Susan); *Boxcar Bertha* (Scorsese) (title role)
1973   *Time to Run* (Adamson)

(as Barbara Seagull)

1974   *The Crazy World of Julius Vrooder* (*Vrooder's Hooch*) (Hiller) (as Zanni)
1975   *Love Comes Quietly* (*Angela*) (van der Heyde) (as Angela); *You and Me* (Carradine); *Diamonds* (Golan) (as Sally)

Barbara Hershey in *A World Apart*

(as Barbara Hershey)

1976 *Dirty Knight's Work* (*Trial by Combat*; *Choice of Weapons*) (Connor) (as Marion); *The Last Hard Men* (McLaglen) (as Susan Burgade); *Flood!* (Bellamy—for TV) (as Mary Cutler)

1977 *In the Glitter Palace* (Butler—for TV) (as Ellen Lange); *Just a Little Inconvenience* (Flicker—for TV) (as Nikki Klausing); *Sunshine Christmas* (Glenn Jordan—for TV) (as Cody)

1980 *The Stunt Man* (Rush) (as Nina Franklin); *Angel on My Shoulder* (Berry—for TV) (as Julie)

1981 *Take This Job and Shove It* (Trikonis) (as J. M. Halstead); *Americana* (Carradine—produced in 1973) (as Jess's daughter)

1983 *The Entity* (Furie) (as Carla Moran); *The Right Stuff* (Kaufman) (as Glennis Yeager)

1984 *The Natural* (Levinson) (as Harriet Bird)

1985 *My Wicked, Wicked Ways . . . The Legend of Errol Flynn* (Taylor—for TV) (as Lili Damita); *Passion Flower* (Sargent—for TV) (as Julia Maitland)

1986 *Hannah and Her Sisters* (Woody Allen) (as Lee); *Hoosiers* (*Best Shot*) (Anspaugh) (as Myra Fleener)

1987 *Tin Men* (Levinson) (as Nora); *Shy People* (Konchalovsky) (as Ruth Sullivan)

1988 *A World Apart* (Menges) (as Diana Roth); *The Last Temptation of Christ* (Scorsese) (as Mary Magdalene); *Beaches* (Garry Marshall) (as Hillary Whitney Essex)

1990 *Tune in Tomorrow* (*Aunt Julia and the Scriptwriter*) (Amiel) (as Aunt Julia); *A Killing in a Small Town* (*Evidence of Love*) (Gyllenhaal—for TV) (as Candy Morrison)

1991 *Paris Trout* (Gyllenhaal—for TV) (as Hanna Trout); *Defenseless* (Campbell) (as T. K. Katwuller); *Julia Has Two Lovers* (Shbib)

1992 *The Public Eye* (Franklin) (as Kay Levitz); *Stay the Night* (Winer—for TV) (as Jimmie Sue Finger)

1993 *Swing Kids* (Carter) (as Frau Muller); *Falling Down* (Schumacher) (as Beth); *Splitting Heirs* (Robert Young) (as Duchess Lucinda); *A Dangerous Woman* (Gyllenhaal) (as Aunt Frances)

1994 *Abraham* (Sargent—for TV) (as Sarah)

1995 *Last of the Dogmen* (Murphy) (as Lillian Sloan)

1996 *The Pallbearer* (Reeves); *Portrait of a Lady* (Campion)

Publications

By HERSHEY: articles—

Interview, in *Look Magazine* (New York), 3 November 1970.
"Barbara Hershey," interview with L. Geller, in *Interview* (New York), March 1986.

"The Fall and Rise of Barbara Hershey," interview with Ron Rosenbaum, in *American Film* (Washington, D.C.), May 1986.
Interview with Jeff Silverman, in *Chicago Tribune*, 22 March 1987.
Interview with Myra Forsberg, in *New York Times*, 29 March 1987.
"20 Questions: Barbara Hershey," interview with D. Rensin, in *Playboy* (Chicago), May 1987.
"Stretching Out," interview with M. Gray, in *Photoplay Movies & Video* (London), August 1987.
Interview with Mike Downey, in *GQ* (New York), November 1987.

On HERSHEY: articles—

"La vedette de la semaine," in *Ciné Revue* (Brussels), 25 June 1987.
Kearney, Jill, in *American Film* (New York), December 1987.
Gray, M., "Barbara Hershey," in *Photoplay Movies & Video* (London), March 1988.
Canby, Vincent, "Stardom Seen in Light of the 80's," in *New York Times*, 17 July 1988.
"Fanfair—Hershey Bliss," in *Vanity Fair* (New York), October 1988.
Current Biography 1989, New York, 1989.
Drucker, Elizabeth, "*Paris Trout*: Barbara Hershey Is Not Herself," in *American Film* (Washington, D.C.), April 1991.
Clements, Marcelle, "Decent Exposure," in *Premiere* (New York), October 1993.
Hemple, H. S., filmography in *Premiere* (New York), October 1993.

*   *   *

Barbara Hershey is a generally fine actress who, too often, has been wasted in films not worthy of her talents. Her critical reputation was resuscitated in the late 1980s when she accomplished the feat of winning back-to-back Best Actress prizes at the Cannes Film Festival.

Hershey was a gifted drama student at Hollywood High School when she obtained a talent agent through a teacher. The good-looking 17-year-old brunette quickly found regular work on the television series *The Monroes*, and later in other small-screen shows before making her big-screen debut as Brian Keith's possessive daughter in the Doris Day comedy *With Six You Get Eggroll*.

In 1969, Hershey played the first important lead of her career as Sandy in *Last Summer*, Frank Perry's artful and controversial study of four upper-class teenagers idling away a summer in a beach community. Here, Hershey was cast as a vivacious, willful beauty who manipulates her two male friends and taunts a plain-looking, less sexually experienced female. Observed the *Variety* critic, "Barbara Hershey has the sexual provocativeness and hoydenishness that is not calmed by any perceptive maturity."

Another significant early role for Hershey came in Martin Scorsese's first studio production, *Boxcar Bertha*. In this low-budget drama about the Great Depression, shot in 24 days in Arkansas, she appears in the title role, an orphaned vagrant who hops one freight train after another with her derelict lover, an embittered ex-labor agitator (David Carradine) and his band of train robbers. In retrospect, given the director with whom she was working, Hershey's presence becomes notable and even historic, but at the time of its release the movie was criticized as being excessively violent and was not a success.

In the 1970s, when Hershey was an attractive young actress who should have been peaking in popularity, her marketability was limited. This was partly because she had acquired a reputation as a hippie, which, in the eyes of many industry powers and moviegoers, meant she was flaky. Hershey was a flower-child, living out-of-wedlock with David Carradine and naming their baby boy "Free." She had changed her own name to Barbara Seagull sometime after the making of *Last Summer*, during which she accidentally was involved in the killing of a seagull. Furthermore, she put off audiences by taking roles considered outrageous. For instance, in *The Baby Maker*, Hershey played a

nonconformist hired to be impregnated by a man whose wife was sterile. And so, for the rest of the decade, she appeared mainly in minor and forgettable projects.

Then in 1980, director Richard Rush chose her for the outstanding black comedy *The Stunt Man*. This bit of casting took Hershey out of the second-rate ingenue roles to which she had been relegated, and placed her in her first womanly part. She played a quirky motion picture actress who appears to give her heart to a fugitive Vietnam veteran hiding on a set, when she actually is having an affair with the film's egomaniacal director (Peter O'Toole). *The Stunt Man* received critical accolades, and has become something of a cult film. Hershey's performance may have been passed over or panned by the reviewers, but it nonetheless pulled her out of a casting rut.

Two years later began a string of interesting roles in significant films by leading directors. In *The Right Stuff*, she is the wife of astronaut Chuck Yeager; in *The Natural*, she is the personification of evil, an erotic mystery woman who comes on to baseball phenom Roy Hobbs, then shoots him and commits suicide. Her dark sexual appeal was exploited further in *Hannah and Her Sisters*, in which she plays the pivotal part of Lee, the girlfriend of a moody artist, who becomes the love object of her brother-in-law; and again in the black comedy *Tin Men*, where she appears as the wife of an aluminum siding salesman who is seduced by her husband's arch enemy. During the making of *Boxcar Bertha*, Hershey gave Martin Scorsese the idea of filming Nikos Kazantzakis's controversial novel *The Last Temptation of Christ*. When he made the film 16 years later, the filmmaker handed her the coveted role of Mary Magdalene. But for many fans of three-handkerchief weepies, Hershey's most dynamic role came playing opposite Bette Midler in the quintessential woman's film *Beaches*.

The apex of three decades of filmic output came for Hershey when she was awarded the Best Actress Prize at Cannes two consecutive years. In 1987 she earned the award for *Shy People*, playing the head of a backwoods bayou clan. The following year, she was recognized for a riveting performance as a political zealot dedicated to the abolishment of apartheid in South Africa in *A World Apart*.

Hershey's more notable recent roles have been as characters who are secondary to the film's primary focus: Michael Douglas's estranged wife in *Falling Down*; a mystery woman opposite Joe Pesci in *The Public Eye*; and Debra Winger's sister in *A Dangerous Woman*.

—Audrey E. Kupferberg

HESTON, Charlton

Nationality: American. **Born:** Charlton Carter in Evanston, Illinois, 4 October 1924 (some sources say 1923); adopted name of stepfather as a child. **Education:** Attended school in St. Helens, Minnesota; New Trier High School, Winnetka, Illinois; Northwestern University, Evanston, Illinois. **Military Service:** Served in Eleventh Air Force, 1944-47. **Family:** Married Lydia Clarke, 1944, son: the director Fraser Heston, daughter: Holly Ann. **Career:** 1947-48—co-director and actor, Thomas Wolfe Memorial Theatre, Asheville, North Carolina; 1947—Broadway debut in Katharine Cornell's production of *Antony and Cleopatra*; 1948—TV actor on *Studio One* series; 1950—professional film debut in *Dark City*; 1953—narrator for radio series *Kaleidoscope*; 1965—founded first production company for *The War Lord*; 1973—directed film *Antony and Cleopatra*; performed in *The Crucible* on stage; 1975—in stage version of *Macbeth*; 1983—in TV mini-series *Chiefs*; 1985-87—in TV series *The Colbys*. **Awards:** Best Actor, Academy Award, for *Ben-Hur*, 1959; Academy Jean Hersholt Humanitarian Award, 1977. **Address:** c/o Michael Levine, Levine Communications, 433 North Camden, Suite 400, Beverly Hills, CA 90210, U.S.A.

Films as Actor:

1945   *Peer Gynt* (Bradley) (title role)

1950   *Julius Caesar* (Bradley) (as Marc Antony); *Dark City* (Dieterle) (as Danny Hale)

1952   *The Greatest Show on Earth* (Cecil B. DeMille) (as Brad); *The Savage* (*War Bonnet*) (George Marshall) (as Jim Ahern); *Ruby Gentry* (King Vidor) (as Boake Tackman); *Pony Express* (Jerry Hopper) (as Buffalo Bill)

1953   *The President's Lady* (Levin) (as Andrew Jackson); *Arrowhead* (C. Warren) (as Ed Bannon); *Bad for Each Other* (Rapper) (as Dr. Tom Owen); *The Naked Jungle* (Haskin) (as Christopher Leiningen); *Three Lives* (Dmytryk)

1954   *Secret of the Incas* (Hopper) (as Harvey Steele); *The Far Horizons* (Maté) (as William Clark); *Lucy Gallant* (Parrish) (as Casey Cole); trailer for North Carolina Safe Driving Campaign

1955   *The Private War of Major Benson* (Jerry Hopper) (title role)

1956   *The Ten Commandments* (Cecil B. DeMille) (as Moses); *Three Violent People* (Maté) (as Colt Saunders); *Many Voices* (short) (as narrator)

1958   *Touch of Evil* (Welles) (as Ramon Vargas); *The Big Country* (Wyler) (as Steve Leech); *The Buccaneer* (Quinn) (as Andrew Jackson)

1959   *The Wreck of the Mary Deare* (Anderson) (as John Sands); *Ben-Hur* (Wyler) (title role)

1961   *El Cid* (Anthony Mann) (title role); trailer for Mental Health Campaign (Pemberton)

1962   *The Pigeon That Took Rome* (Shavelson) (as Captain Paul MacDougall); *Diamond Head* (Green) (as Richard "King" Howland); *55 Days at Peking* (Nicholas Ray) (as Major Matt Lewis)

1963   *The Five Cities of June* (Herschensohn—short) (as narrator)

1965   *Major Dundee* (Peckinpah) (title role); *The Greatest Story Ever Told* (Stevens) (as John the Baptist); *The Agony and the Ecstasy* (Reed) (as Michelangelo); *The War Lord* (Schaffner) (as Chrysagon); *Peer Gynt* (Bradley—revised version of 1945 film with added soundtrack) (title role); *The Egyptologists* (short) (as narrator)

1966   *Khartoum* (Dearden) (as General Gordon); *While I Run This Race* (Levy) (as narrator)

1967   *Planet of the Apes* (Schaffner) (as George Taylor); *Will Penny* (Gries) (title role); *Counterpoint* (Nelson) (as Lionel Evans); *The American Film* (George Stevens, Jr.) (as narrator); *All about People* (for United Jewish Welfare Fund) (appearance); *Think Twentieth* (Fleischer) (appearance)

1968   *The Movie Experience: A Matter of Choice* (Ward—short) (as narrator); trailer about the dangers of air pollution

1969   *Number One* (*The Pro*) (Gries) (as Ron Catlan); *Beneath the Planet of the Apes* (Post) (as George Taylor); *The Festival Game* (Klinger and Lytton); *Rowan and Martin at the Movies* (for US Treasury Bonds); *The Heart of Variety* (short—for Variety Clubs International); *Rod Laver's Wimbledon* (Seligman) (as narrator)

1970   *King: A Filmed Record ... Montgomery to Memphis* (Lumet and Mankiewicz) (as narrator); *Julius Caesar* (Burge) (title role); *The Hawaiians* (*Master of the Islands*) (Gries) (as Whip Hoxworth)

1971   *The Omega Man* (Segal) (as Robert Neville); *Vietnam! Vietnam!* (Beck) (as narrator); *Skyjacked* (Guillermin) (as Captain Hank O'Hara)

1972   *The Call of the Wild* (Annakin) (as John Thornton); *Our Active Earth* (Hennessy—short) (as narrator)

1973   *Soylent Green* (Fleischer) (as Detective Thorn); *The Three Musketeers* (*The Queen's Diamonds*) (Lester) (as Cardinal Richelieu); *Lincoln's Gettysburg Address* (Kurtz and Johnson—short) (as narrator)

1974   *Airport 1975* (Smight) (as Murdock); *Earthquake* (Robson) (as Stuart Graff); *The Four Musketeers* (*The Revenge of Milady*) (Lester) (as Cardinal Richelieu)

1975   *The Fun of Your Life* (Hennessy—short) (as narrator)

1976   *The Last Hard Men* (McLaglen) (as Sam Burgade); *Midway* (*Battle of Midway*) (Smight) (as Captain Matt Garth); *America at the Movies* (George Stevens, Jr.) (as narrator); *Two-Minute Warning* (Peerce) (as Captain Peter Holly)

1977   *The Prince and the Pauper* (*Crossed Swords*) (Fleischer) (as Henry VIII)

1978   *Gray Lady Down* (Greene) (as Capt. Paul Blanchard)

1980   *The Awakening* (Newell) (as Corbeck); *The Mountain Men* (Richard Lang) (as Bill Tyler); *The Nairobi Affair* (Chomsky—for TV) (as Lee Cahill)

1985   *The Colbys* (Courtland—for TV) (as Jason Colby)

1986   *Directed by William Wyler* (Slesin—doc) (as himself)

1987   *Proud Men* (Graham—for TV)

1989   *Original Sin* (Satlof—for TV) (as Louis Mancini)

1990   *Treasure Island* (Fraser C. Heston) (as Long John Silver); *Solar Crisis* (Sarafian) (as Skeet Kelso); *The Little Kidnappers* (Shebib—for TV) (as James MacKenzie); *Almost An Angel* (Cornell) (as God)

1991   *Crucifer of Blood* (Fraser C. Heston—for TV) (as Sherlock Holmes)

1992   *Crash Landing: The Rescue of Flight 232* (*A Thousand Heroes*) (Lamont Johnson—for TV) (as Capt. Al Haynes)

1993   *Wayne's World 2* (Surjik) (as good actor); *Tombstone* (Cosmatos) (as Henry Hooker)

1994   *True Lies* (Cameron) (as Spencer Trilby)

1995   *In the Mouth of Madness* (Carpenter) (as Jackson Harglow); *Avenging Angel* (Baxley—for TV) (as Brigham Young)

1996   *Alaska* (Archainbaud); *Hamlet* (Branagh) (as Player King)

Films as Director:

1973   *Antony and Cleopatra* (+ ro as Antony, sc)

1983   *Mother Lode* (co-d, + roles as Silas McGee/Ian McGee)

1988   *A Man for All Seasons* (for TV) (+ ro as Sir Thomas More)

Publications

By HESTON: books—

The Actor's Life: Journals, 1956-1976, edited by Hollis Alpert, New York, 1978.
Beijing Diary, New York, 1990.
In the Arena: An Autobiography, New York, 1995.

By HESTON: articles—

"It's All a Matter of Size," interview with D. Austen, in *Films and Filming* (London), April 1968.
"Actor's Country," interview with Gordon Gow, in *Films and Filming* (London), May 1972.
"Heston on Welles," interview with J. Delson, in *Take One* (Montreal), October 1972.
"I Like to Think of Myself as a Professional," interview with F. A. Macklin, in *Film Heritage* (Dayton, Ohio), Fall 1974.
Interview with O. Eyquem and M. Henry, in *Positif* (Paris), March 1977.
"Point of View: The Face at the Cutting Room Door," in *American Film* (Washington, D.C.), September 1984.
"The Heston Commandments: Charlton Heston's Career Is Reaching Biblical Length," interview with George Wayne, in *Vanity Fair* (New York), September 1994.

Charlton Heston in *The Agony and the Ecstasy*

On HESTON: books—

Williams, John, *The Films of Charlton Heston*, Farncombe, Surrey, 1977; rev. ed., 1982.
Crowther, Bruce, *Charlton Heston: The Epic Presence*, London, 1986.
Munn, Michael, *Charlton Heston: A Biography*, London, 1986.
Reinhardt, Hans, and Andrea Rennschmidt, *Charlton Heston: Seine Filmischen Werke*, Landshut, Germany, 1993.

On HESTON: articles—

Higham, C., "Charlton Heston," in *Sight and Sound* (London), Autumn 1966.
Morris, George, "Charlton Heston," in *The Movie Star*, edited by Elisabeth Weis, New York, 1981.
McGilligan, Patrick, "Star Wars," in *Films and Filming* (London), May 1982.
Buskin, R., "Charlton Heston at the NFT," in *Films and Filming* (London), June 1985.
Current Biography 1986, New York, 1986.
Fuller, Graham, "Shots in the Dark," in *Interview* (New York), September 1993.

*   *   *

Before Charlton Heston evolved into the archetypal bigger-than-life man of action and towering presence of historical films, his screen career was devoted almost exclusively to playing tormented young men caught between some overpowering desire and a rigid sense of responsibility. *Dark City*, Cecil B. De Mille's *The Greatest Show on Earth*, and *Bad for Each Other* feature this earlier image. As the Heston persona evolved, the vulnerability of the character became more evident. For example, although his character is ultimately redeemed in *The Naked Jungle*, *Secret of the Incas*, and *The Big Country*, the Heston character is essentially a brooding villain in each.

The major irony of Heston's film career is that he is singly identified with historical epics. His strapping frame and timeless, regal looks made him ideal for the genre, one that he has enjoyed because of the broad canvas it allowed him to paint his various characters. He was 32 when he played the white bearded Moses in *The Ten Commandments* for Cecil B. De Mille—the role that brought him to prominence, but in which he feels he gave a less-than-stellar performance, believing it was really Yul Brynner's Ramses who stole the show. De Mille cast him a third time in *The Buccaneer*, playing Andrew Jackson (a part Heston had played previously in *The President's Lady* and for which he was a dead ringer). De Mille's then son-in-law Anthony Quinn directed the picture, which starred Heston's scene-stealing adversary from *The Ten Commandments*, Yul Brynner, in the title role. As *Ben-Hur*, Heston won the Best Actor Oscar for 1959. For producer Samuel Bronston, he made a series of epics in Europe, *El Cid* (which underwent a major restoration and theatrical rerelease in 1994), and *55 Days to Peking*. And for British director Basil Dearden and producer Julian Blaustein, Heston delivered one of his best (and most underrated) performances as a historical figure in *Khartoum*, where he played the doomed visionary general, Charles "Chinese" Gordon.

In spite of this public and critical perception of Heston as "King of Epics," the actor, in truth, has been one of the most adventuresome major stars in modern film history. Beginning with his portrayal of the Mexican border detective Vargas in Orson Welles's *Touch of Evil*, Heston has been enthusiastically willing to risk supporting the work of a director or writer who appears to be commercially off-limits. In each case, Heston has chosen to play characters who question the rigid ideals of heroism, the very ideals with which he is most often associated. Such roles include the Ahab-like title character of *Major Dundee* for Sam Peckinpah (for which Heston gave up his salary to support Peckinpah's vision of the film when Columbia threatened to shut the production down because of cost overruns); the loner cowpoke in Tom Gries's *Will Penny*; and, more recently, his decidedly antiheroic role in *The Mountain Man* and his Scottish miner, almost a horror film character, in *Mother Lode*, both of which were written by Heston's son, Fraser.

As John Williams has written in his excellent monograph, *The Films of Charlton Heston:* "Charlton Heston cares, not just for his own personal future, but for the future of the film-making industry. A decision to make a possibly uncommercial film, or to back a director in a major confrontation with a studio, is no small risk in days when stardom does not necessarily relate to box-office success." This conviction echoes throughout *In the Arena*, Heston's own autobiography, published in 1995.

Because of his association with screen epics, and indeed his willingness to appear in them, Heston's versatility has often been overlooked. For example, in *Soylent Green* Heston plays a policeman of an overpopulated and environmentally polluted New York of the future. The sense of his being a part of that world is made clear by the actor's movement. In one scene Heston must carry on a conversation while descending a stairway crowded with lounging, homeless people. He tiptoes, winding his way down without missing a beat, not pausing to pay obvious attention to his surroundings. He is a man accustomed to this nightmare world, a man whose sense of the limitation of space is always evident, an attitude that may be contrasted, for example, with Heston's *Will Penny* who moves about rather sluggishly in the less familiar, civilized indoors he shares with widow Joan Hackett than in the rather unrestricted outdoors where he allows his arms to move freely, and takes swift, confident steps.

Heston, in short, has mastered the ability to create a character who inhabits the fictive world the film is attempting to make real for us. The boiling hot metal cup grasped without hesitation by the mad miner in *Mother Lode*, the familiar handling of a paintbrush in the epic *The Agony and the Ecstasy,* and the hand automatically gripping the football across the seams in *Number One* all demonstrate the actor's attention and devotion to detail.

While Heston's ideal may be a tormented Shakespearean hero like Mark Antony (a role he has played twice on film), his strengths serve him well in popular genres, and have likely contributed to his longevity as a major star long after so many of his contemporaries have retired from the scene. He put in a cameo appearance in the gonzo comedy *Wayne's World 2* and was back as a historical figure in *Tombstone*. And he convincingly made action star extraordinaire Arnold Schwarzenegger back down in *True Lies*, something no younger actor has yet done on-screen.

—Stuart M. Kaminsky, updated by John McCarty

HOFFMAN, Dustin

Nationality: American. **Born:** Los Angeles, California, 8 August 1937. **Education:** Attended Los Angeles High School; Santa Monica City College for one year; acting classes at Pasadena Playhouse, 1956-

58; also studied music at the Los Angeles Conservatory of Music. **Family:** Married 1) Anne Byrne, 1969 (divorced), two daughters; 2) Lisa Gottsegen, 1980, two sons, two daughters. **Career:** 1958—in New York as aspiring actor; 1961—Broadway debut in *A Cook for Mr. General*; 1967—film debut in *The Tiger Makes Out*; 1976—member of First Artists Productions; 1982—producer of his film *Tootsie*; 1984—starring role in New York stage version of *Death of a Salesman*; 1989—as Shylock in *The Merchant of Venice*, London. **Awards:** Most Promising Newcomer, British Academy, for *The Graduate*, 1968; Best Actor, British Academy, for *Midnight Cowboy* and *John and Mary*, 1969; Best Actor Academy Award, and Best Actor, New York Film Critics, for *Kramer vs. Kramer*, 1979; National Society of Film Critics Award, for *Tootsie*, 1983; Best Actor Academy Award, and Golden Bear, Berlin Festival, for *Rain Man*, 1988. **Address:** c/o Punch Productions, 711 Fifth Avenue, New York, NY 10022, U.S.A.

Films as Actor:

1967   *The Tiger Makes Out* (Hiller) (as Hap); **The Graduate** (Mike Nichols) (as Benjamin Braddock)

1969   **Midnight Cowboy** (Schlesinger) (as Ratso Rizzo); *John and Mary* (Yates) (as John)

1970   *Un dollaro per 7 vigliacchi* (*El millón de Madigan; Madigan's Millions*) (Ash, Gentili, and Praeger—produced in 1967) (as Jason Fisher); *Little Big Man* (Arthur Penn) (as Jack Crabb); *Arthur Penn Films "Little Big Man"* (Erwitt—doc); *Arthur Penn 1922—: Themes and Variants* (Hughes—doc)

1971   *Who Is Harry Kellerman and Why Is He Saying Those Terrible Things about Me?* (Grosbard) (as George Sacourey); *Straw Dogs* (Peckinpah) (as David Sumner)

1972   *Alfredo Alfredo* (Germi) (title role)

1973   *Papillon* (Schaffner) (as Louis Dega); *Sunday Father* (Leaf—short)

1974   *Lenny* (Fosse) (as Lenny Bruce)

1975   *Lost in the Garden of the World* (Williams) (as interviewee)

1976   *All the President's Men* (Pakula) (as Carl Bernstein); *Marathon Man* (Schlesinger) (as Babe Levy)

1978   *Straight Time* (Grosbard) (as Max Dembo, + initial d)

1979   *Agatha* (Apted) (as Wally Stanton); *Kramer vs. Kramer* (Benton) (as Ted Kramer)

1982   *Tootsie* (Pollack) (as Michael Dorsey/Dorothy Michaels, + co-pr)

1983   *The Best of Everything* (Johnson)

1985   *Death of a Salesman* (Schlöndorff—for TV) (as Willie Loman); *Private Conversations* (Blackwood—doc)

1987   *Ishtar* (Elaine May) (as Chuck Clarke)

1988   *Rain Man* (Levinson) (as Raymond Babbitt)

1989   *Family Business* (Lumet) (as Vito McMullen); *Common Threads* (Epstein and Friedman—doc) (as narrator)

1990   *Dick Tracy* (Beatty) (as Mumbles)

1991   *Billy Bathgate* (Benton) (as Dutch Schultz); *Hook* (Spielberg) (as Captain Hook)

1993   *Earth and the American Dream* (Couturie—doc) (as voice)

1992   *Hero* (*Accidental Hero*) (Frears) (as Bernie LaPlante)

1995   *Outbreak* (Petersen) (as Colonel Sam Daniels M.D.)

1996   *American Buffalo* (Corrente) (as Teach); *Sleepers* (Levinson)

Publications

By HOFFMAN: articles—

Interview, in *Interview* (New York), June 1976.
Interview with P. Maraval, in *Cinématographe* (Paris), December 1978.

Dustin Hoffman in *Midnight Cowboy*

"Dialogue on Film: Dustin Hoffman," in *American Film* (Washington, D.C.), April 1983.

Interview with Mark Rowland, in *American Film* (Los Angeles), December 1988.

"Tales of Hoffman," interview with Peter Biskind, in *Premiere* (New York), February 1989.

On HOFFMAN: books—

Cornelsen, Peter, *Dustin Hoffman*, Bergisch Gladbach, 1980.

Dagneau, Gilles, *Dustin Hoffman*, Paris, 1981; rev. ed., 1985.

Sandre, Didier, *Dustin Hoffman*, Paris, 1981.

Brode, Douglas, *The Films of Dustin Hoffman*, Secaucus, New Jersey, 1983.

Lenburg, Jeff, *Dustin Hoffman: Hollywood's Anti-Hero*, New York, 1983.

Johnstone, Ian, *Dustin Hoffman*, Tunbridge Wells, Kent, 1984.

Agan, Patrick, *Hoffman vs. Hoffman: The Actor and the Man*, London, 1986.

Freedland, Michael, *Dustin: A Biography of Dustin Hoffman*, London, 1989.

Jelot-Blanc, Jean Jacques, *Dustin Hoffman*, Paris, 1990.

Bergan, Ronald, *Dustin Hoffman*, London, 1991.

On HOFFMAN: articles—

Current Biography 1969, New York, 1969.

Amata, C., "Dustin Hoffman," in *Focus on Film* (London), April 1980.

Boyum, Joy Gould, "Dustin Hoffman," in *The Movie Star Book*, edited by Elisabeth Weis, New York, 1981.

Smith, Gary, in *Rolling Stone* (New York), 3 February 1983.

Clark, John, filmography in *Premiere* (New York), February 1989.

Alfven, I., "I Love You Dustin," in *Chaplin*, vol. 34, no. 5, 1992.

Weinraub, Bernard, "Ratso Rizzo Redux? Not If He Can Help It," in *New York Times*, 27 September 1992.

*   *   *

Dustin Hoffman was the first American movie star to bring the intensity of Method acting to the kind of nebbishy, sex-struck characters Robert Morse played in commercial comedies and Woody Allen played in his stand-up/slapstick comedies. Hoffman's best scenes as

Benjamin in *The Graduate*, the movie that made him a star, are the comic seductions with Anne Bancroft. Benjamin's adenoidal dimness is a great joke on innocence. We like him because he seems unworthy of this sophisticated catch. The basic deliberateness of Hoffman's craft is clearer in his next picture, *Midnight Cowboy*, in which he gets into the crawly skin of Ratso Rizzo, a seedy New York drifter who befriends Jon Voight's Joe Buck, a newcomer trying to make it as a hustler. Hoffman as Ratso practically plots the coordinates of corruption and unworldliness on graph paper—but expertly. Usually, catching the actor acting lessens the viewer's enjoyment; Hoffman makes it work for him. This is not to say that his most intently acted performances lack depth. His finest performance is as Max Dembo in Ulu Grosbard's too little seen *Straight Time*, a study of criminal psychology. The picture does not team him up with a co-star but shows him in relation to a whole slate of superb supporting players, and every interaction reveals more of Dembo's locked-in mentality. Here Hoffman merges his focus as an actor with Dembo's bone-dry focus on burglary. The scene in which Dembo stays too long while robbing a jewelry store, and a consequent one in which he punishes the junkie getaway driver who panicked, are the most frighteningly inaccessible scenes Hoffman has ever dared as an actor.

In *Tootsie*, Sydney Pollack's deserved-smash comedy, Hoffman parodied his own reputation as a "difficult" actor. His Michael Dorsey cannot even get hired in commercials because he argued with a director about the motivation of the vegetable he was dressed up as. He can only get a job on a soap opera by reading for it in drag, as Dorothy Michaels. Hoffman's vanity lies mainly in his reputation as an actor rather than as a star, so he does not hesitate to make Dorothy womanly in an appropriately ungainly way. The combination of self-satire and the very scrupulousness being satirized enable him to give the most entertaining as well as the most thoroughly thought-out male drag performance in movie history. Watching him try to reach the challenging blond beauty he co-stars with on the soap while he is dressed up as the woman she has come to confide in like a mother, gives the wild transvestite comedy the added dimension of an unusually textured romantic comedy.

You get much more from Hoffman in drag in *Tootsie* than from his showy performance as Raymond, an autistic savant in *Rain Man*, a very wet, commercial picture about redemption through sacrifice. You *have* to watch Hoffman because Raymond's affliction means he cannot integrate himself into the scenes—you cannot take him for granted. With the incentive of getting to show up his much younger, "hot" co-star, Hoffman's performance is meticulously limited and yet totally shameless. Better is his naturalistic performance in 1989's *Family Business*, as Vito, a hard-working merchant caught between Sean Connery as his elementally attractive criminal father and Matthew Broderick as Vito's self-righteous son who is infatuated with Connery. Perhaps Hoffman's performance did not get the attention it deserved for the very reason that it is uncharacteristically unassuming. Hoffman shows how Vito's rage and frustration are inextricable from his love for his son. We believe that he would do anything for him, and feel affronted by the son's contempt.

Hoffman has remained a star for 30 years because the audience can see and appreciate his effort. Actors who are so apparently striving are rarely so expert. He even uses this as the basis of his dogged performance in *Agatha* as a newspaperman rising to the challenge of Vanessa Redgrave's emotionally overwrought Agatha Christie. He is less memorable in his big action hits, *Papillon*, *Marathon Man*, and *Outbreak*. Furthermore, when he is too openly ingratiating, as in *Kramer vs. Kramer*, his effort can all be waste, though we are willing to watch him go through ancient shtick—such as a single father who cannot cook a meal—that we would not at this date watch anyone else in. And he does not have the kind of expansive personality that can overcome fundamental miscasting; in *Lenny* he is not at all believable as a foul-mouthed junkie who shines like the white underbelly of show

biz. But he has never been just plain boring. He always gets to the theater ahead of you, and he is always working.

—Alan Dale

HOLDEN, William

Nationality: American. **Born:** William Franklin Beedle Jr. in O'Fallon, Illinois, 17 April 1918. **Education:** Attended South Pasadena High School and Pasadena Junior College, California. **Family:** Married the actress Brenda Marshall, 1941 (divorced 1971), sons: Peter and Scott. **Career:** 1938—stage debut in *Manya* at Pasadena Playhouse workshop theater; short Paramount contract and film debut in *Prison Farm*; 1942-45—served in U.S. Army: lieutenant; 1945—reentered films with Columbia; 1950s—TV actor and narrator in documentaries. **Awards:** Best Actor Academy Award, for *Stalag 17*, 1953; co-recipient, Special Jury Prize for Ensemble Acting, Venice Festival, for *Executive Suite*, 1954. **Died:** In Santa Monica, California, 12 November 1981.

Films as Actor:

1938   *Prison Farm* (Louis King) (as an inmate)

1939   *Million Dollar Legs* (Dmytryk) (as a graduate); *Golden Boy* (Mamoulian) (as Joe Bonaparte)

1940   *Each Dawn I Die* (Keighley) (bit role); *Invisible Stripes* (Lloyd Bacon) (as Tim Taylor); *Our Town* (Sam Wood) (as George Gibbs); *Those Were the Days* (J. T. Reed) (as P. J. "Petey" Simmons); *Arizona* (Ruggles) (as Peter Muncie)

1941   *I Wanted Wings* (Leisen) (as Jeff Young); *Texas* (George Marshall) (as Dan Thomas)

1942   *The Remarkable Andrew* (Heisler) (as Andrew Long); *The Fleet's In* (Schertzinger) (as Casey Kirby); *Meet the Stewarts* (Alfred E. Green) (as Michael Stewart)

1943   *Young and Willing* (E. H. Griffith) (as Norman Reese)

1947   *Blaze of Noon* (Farrow) (as Colin McDonald); *Dear Ruth* (William Russell) (as Lt. William Seacroft); *Variety Girl* (George Marshall) (appearance)

1948   *Rachel and the Stranger* (Norman Foster) (as Big Davey); *Apartment for Peggy* (Seaton) (as Jason); *The Man from Colorado* (Levin) (as Captain Del Stewart)

1949   *The Dark Past* (Maté) (as Al Walker); *Streets of Laredo* (Fenton) (as Jim Dawkins); *Miss Grant Takes Richmond* (Lloyd Bacon) (as Dick Richmond); *Dear Wife* (Haydn) (as Bill Seacroft)

1950   *Father Is a Bachelor* (Norman Foster and Berlin) (as Johnny Rutledge); **Sunset Boulevard** (Wilder) (as Joe Gillis); *Union Station* (Maté) (as Lt. William Calhoun); *Born Yesterday* (Cukor) (as Paul Verall)

1951   *Force of Arms* (Curtiz) (as Peterson); *Submarine Command* (Farrow) (as Commander White)

1952   *Boots Malone* (Dieterle) (title role); *The Turning Point* (Dieterle) (as Jerry McKibbon)

1953   *Stalag 17* (Wilder) (as Sefton); *The Moon Is Blue* (Preminger) (as Donald Gresham); *Forever Female* (Rapper) (as Stanley Krown); *Escape from Fort Bravo* (John Sturges) (as Capt. Roper)

1954   *Executive Suite* (Wise) (as McDonald Walling); *Sabrina* (Wilder) (as David Larrabee); *The Country Girl* (Seaton) (as Bernie Dodd); *Miyamoto Musashi* (*Samurai*) (Inagaki) (as narrator)

William Holden (right) with Cliff Robertson in *Picnic*

1955 *The Bridges at Toko-Ri* (Robson) (as Lt. Harry Brubaker);
      Love Is a Many Splendored Thing (Henry King) (as Mark
      Elliott); *Picnic* (Logan) (as Hal Carter)
1956 *The Proud and the Profane* (Seaton) (as Lt. Col. Colin Black);
      Toward the Unknown (LeRoy) (as Maj. Lincoln Bond)
1957 *The Bridge on the River Kwai* (Lean) (as Shears)
1958 *The Key* (Reed) (as David Ross)
1959 *The Horse Soldiers* (Ford) (as Maj. Henry Kendall)
1960 *The World of Suzie Wong* (Quine) (as Robert Lomax)
1962 *Satan Never Sleeps* (McCarey) (as Father O'Banion); *The
      Counterfeit Traitor* (Seaton) (as Eric Erickson); *The Lion*
      (Cardiff) (as Robert Hayward)
1964 *Paris When It Sizzles* (Quine) (as Richard Benson); *The Sev-
      enth Dawn* (Lewis Gilbert) (as Ferris)
1966 *Alvarez Kelly* (Dmytryk) (title role)
1967 *Casino Royale* (Huston and others) (as Ransome)
1968 *The Devil's Brigade* (McLaglen) (as Lt. Col. Robert T.
      Frederick)
1969 ***The Wild Bunch*** (Peckinpah) (as Pike Bishop); *The Christmas
      Tree* (Terence Young) (as Laurent)
1971 *Wild Rovers* (Edwards) (as Ross Bodine)
1972 *The Revengers* (Daniel Mann) (as John Benedict)
1973 *The Blue Knight* (Robert Butler—for TV) (as Bumper Mor-
      gan); *Breezy* (Eastwood) (as Frank Harmon)

1974 *Open Season* (Collinson) (as Wolkowski); *The Towering In-
      ferno* (Irwin Allen and Guillermin) (as Jim Duncan)
1976 *Network* (Lumet) (as Max Schumacher); *21 Hours at Munich*
      (William A. Graham—for TV) (as Manfred Schreiber)
1978 *Damien—Omen II* (Taylor) (as Richard Thorn); *Fedora*
      (Wilder) (as Barry Detweiler)
1979 *Ashanti* (Fleischer) (as Jim Sandell)
1980 *The Earthling* (Collinson) (as Patrick Foley); *When Time Ran
      Out* (Goldstone) (as Shelby Gilmore)
1981 *S.O.B.* (Edwards) (as Tim Culley)

Publications

By HOLDEN: article—

"I'm Old-Fashioned—and This Is Why," in *Films and Filming* (London), January 1961.

On HOLDEN: books—

Parish, James, and Don Stanke, *The All Americans*, New Rochelle, New
      York, 1977.
Thomas, Bob, *Golden Boy: The Untold Story of William Holden*, New
      York, 1983.

Quirk, Lawrence J., *The Complete Films of William Holden*, Secaucus, New Jersey, 1986.

On HOLDEN: articles—

Current Biography 1954, New York, 1954.
Drew, B., "Where Has Everybody Gone?," in *American Film* (Washington, D.C.), February 1977.
Obituary, in *New York Times*, 17 November 1981.
Obituary, in *Maclean's* (Toronto), 28 December 1981.
The Annual Obituary 1981, New York, 1982.
Marill, Alvin H., "William Holden," in *Films in Review* (New York), February 1982.
Cieutat, M., "William Holden ou le syndrome du vilain américain," in *Positif* (Paris), July/August 1982.

* * *

In the truest sense of a misused phrase, it was impossible to dislike William Holden. Enshrining the philosophy of "Never apologize, never explain," his screen character epitomized the engagingly unreliable drinking pal or feckless nephew to whom one lends money, confident the loan will be neither repaid nor—more importantly—resented. A Holden character seldom descended to self-pity, or flinched from the worst results of rapacity, superficiality, or cowardice. Paradoxically, audiences were convinced by this cordial venality that under the chromium shell hid a good man awaiting rescue, a hero who only needed the right stimulus to make his mother proud.

In 1939, when he slipped into *Golden Boy* by the back door, after Warner Brothers's refusal to lend Columbia the play's original star, John Garfield, Hollywood had few roles for the uncultured and weak-willed wise guys Holden was later to play with such ease. A flop as Odets's Italian working-class hero, torn between boxing and the violin, Holden marked time in unmemorable Westerns and comedies until Montgomery Clift's last-minute defection from Billy Wilder's *Sunset Boulevard* gave Holden the sleazy screenwriter role.

His Joe Gillis, an amalgam of Pat Hobby and Sammy Glick, is the faultlessly realized portrait of a Hollywood loser whose ambitions have shrunk to a second-hand Oldsmobile and half a feature credit. But even shot dead and floating in Gloria Swanson's pool, he can still, in a sardonic commentary, view his fate with unconceited irony.

Since writing a part with Holden in mind must have been a scenarist's nightmare, many of his best roles came, like that in *Sunset Boulevard*, on the rebound. Wilder wanted Charlton Heston for the prison camp profiteer Sefton in *Stalag 17*, and favored someone younger for *Sabrina* until Cary Grant's replacement by Humphrey Bogart dictated an older man for his playboy brother. Yet for both roles he seems the natural choice. Our belief in Holden's unflinching opportunism convinces us that Sefton should be more able than his fellow prisoners to spot the spy in their midst, and as David Larrabee, a thoroughbred stallion permanently at stud among the organdied daughters of Long Island, Holden catches the exact balance of tarnished golden boy and calculating seducer.

Holden was seldom convincing as a man who gave orders. No army would follow an officer so patently protective of his own skin. Nevertheless, he often played such roles: a cavalry captain in *Escape from Fort Bravo*, a jet pilot in *The Bridges at Toko-Ri*, an infantry officer in *The Devil's Brigade* and *The Bridge on the River Kwai*, and a cop who coped efficiently, if skeptically, with his duty in *The Blue Knight*. Only John Ford saw more in this character and made him, in *The Horse Soldiers*, a pacifist military doctor grappling with John Wayne's hard-nosed Civil War raider, a minor milestone in Holden's career.

One of the handsomest men ever to grace a movie screen, the Adonis-like Holden seemed ill-at-ease with his physical perfection, as if it were an impediment to being taken seriously as an actor. As with Robert Taylor and Montgomery Clift, two other stars whose personas were linked to their exquisiteness, Holden seemed less persuasive with the passage of time. With a few graceful exceptions, Holden's work as a character-star from the sixties onward seems curiously uncommitted and unfocused. As a leading man, Holden's key role as Hal, the aging charm boy of *Picnic*, in which Holden is unforgettable as a self-conscious drifter unable to recapture his college athletics halcyon days. After this overheated Americana in which Holden's sensuous body language underscored by "Moonglow" ignited the libidos of an entire Kansas town, and after that soggy valentine to miscegenation, *Love Is a Many Splendored Thing*, this star's charisma flickered on the back burner until he reemerged as a noticeably aged, somewhat burned-out leading man.

Still billed above the title, Holden stopped coasting long enough to unleash some staggering achievements in his twilight years. Amidst the raging violence of *The Wild Bunch*, and the hyperbolic fever of *Network*, Holden functions as a voice of reason and grounds both of these classic exercises in hysteria in a discernible reality. Ineffably sad-looking, Holden reaches out to the audience in *Fedora*, *The Blue Knight*, and *Wild Rovers* with intimations of his own mortality. In his final film, Blake Edwards's nihilistic black comedy *S.O.B.*, he could play a one-bottle and two-women-a-day man with complete credibility, but by now the residue of his cocky swagger from *Stalag 17* could be viewed as a defense mechanism against loneliness. We could see more clearly that his trademark cynicism was always a pose. In his late career knock-outs, Holden seems to be saying that he was a man who had everything but for whom *everything* was somehow not enough. Whatever psychological emptiness Holden carried around inside himself, neither a distinguished movie career nor alcoholic marathons could fill the void. On-screen, at least, this tarnished hero could redeem himself by fadeout. His legacy is an unusual one for a major star—an antiheroic presence embraced by filmgoers despite an angles-playing pragmatism that takes a circuitous route from the self-serving to the grudgingly altruistic.

—John Baxter, updated by Robert Pardi

HOLLIDAY, Judy

Nationality: American. **Born:** Judith Tuvim in Manhattan, New York, 21 June 1921. **Education:** Julia Richman High School, New York, graduated 1938. **Family:** Married David Oppenheim, 1948 (divorced 1957), son: Jonathan. **Career:** 1938—switchboard operator for Orson Welles's Mercury Theatre; 1939-44—formed sketch troupe The Revuers with Betty Comden, Adolph Green, John Frank, and Alvin Hammer; group appeared in New York clubs including Village Vanguard and on radio and television; about 1944—contract with Fox; 1945—New York stage debut in *Kiss Them for Me*; 1946—replaced ailing Jean Arthur in *Born Yesterday*: 3-year run of play established reputation; 1950—contract with Columbia; 1952—called to testify before Senate Internal Security Subcommittee because of activity in liberal organizations later labeled "communist"; 1954-55—TV appearances in 3 episodes of *Max Liebman Presents*; 1956—in stage play *Bells Are Ringing* in role written for her by Comden and Green, and in film version, 1960. **Awards:** Best Actress, Academy Award for *Born Yesterday*, 1950. **Died:** Of cancer, 7 June 1965.

Films as Actress:

1938   *Too Much Johnson* (Welles) (as extra)
1944   *Greenwich Village* (Walter Lang) (as one of The Revuers); *Something for the Boys* (Seiler) (as welder); *Winged Victory* (Cukor)

1949   *Adam's Rib* (Cukor) (as Doris Attinger)
1950   *Born Yesterday* (Cukor) (as Billie Dawn)
1952   *The Marrying Kind* (Cukor) (as Florence Keefer)
1954   *It Should Happen to You* (Cukor) (as Gladys Glover); *Phffft!* (Robson) (as Nina Tracy); *Extra Dollars* (Quine—short for U.S. Treasury Dept.)
1956   *The Solid Gold Cadillac* (Quine) (as Laura Partridge); *Full of Life* (Quine) (as Emily Rocco)
1960   *Bells Are Ringing* (Minnelli) (as Ella Peterson)

Other Film:

1965   *A Thousand Clowns* (Coe) (title song)

Publications

On HOLLIDAY: books—

Carey, Gary, *Judy Holliday: An Intimate Life Story*, New York, 1982.
Holtzman, Will, *Judy Holliday: Only Child*, New York, 1982.

On HOLLIDAY: articles—

Ciné Revue (Paris), 1 March 1979.
Shout, John D., "Judy Holliday," in *Films in Review* (New York), December 1980.

*   *   *

Judy Holliday did not star in many films—only seven. In her short career, however, she won an Academy Award for her first starring role in *Born Yesterday*. The first indication that Judy had a unique quality was evidenced in her part in *Adam's Rib*. She practically stole the show from Katharine Hepburn and Spencer Tracy. It was on Katharine Hepburn's insistence that Holliday got the part in *Adam's Rib* as a ploy to ensure that she got the part of Billie Dawn in *Born Yesterday*, a part she made famous on Broadway. *Born Yesterday* cast Holliday as a dumb blonde, but that is really an unfair description. Billie Dawn is not dumb, merely uneducated. As the film progresses we see through Holliday's fine acting a growth of character that an education can provide.

Holliday was a stunning success as Billie Dawn and a successful career seemed eminent. But it was short-lived. Her fame brought her to the attention of the U.S. Congressional Committee on Un-American Activities. In addition to Holliday's sympathy for certain left-wing or liberal causes, *Born Yesterday* was being criticized in certain right-wing circles as communist propaganda. A lot of background maneuvering relieved some of the pressure on Holliday's career, and she filmed *The Marrying Kind*, a comedy/drama that was a social commentary on the pressures of the working class. Once again Holliday gave a stunning performance in a part quite different from that in *Born Yesterday*. Holliday displayed a wide acting range and proved that she was able to handle drama as well as comedy. Judy's unofficial blacklisting ended with *It Should Happen to You*, her fourth film with the director George Cukor. Holliday was cast as Gladys Glover, a woman striving to become famous. Gladys wasn't a dumb blonde exactly: she was more of an oddball. Judy took a mediocre script and turned her character into a dazzling kook.

It is discouraging, however, that Hollywood was so shallow that an actress like Judy Holliday succeeds as one character and is forever cast in that mold. In *Adam's Rib*, *Born Yesterday*, and *The Marrying Kind*, Holliday demonstrated that she was an accomplished actress who could display a wide range of emotion and a naive, womanly innocence. It

was unfortunate that her death was so untimely. It would have been interesting to see Holliday in films that she chose for herself.

—Maryann Oshana

HOMOLKA, Oscar

Nationality: Austrian. **Born:** Vienna, Austria, 12 August 1898 (some sources give 1901 and 1903). **Education:** Attended the Royal Dramatic Academy, Vienna. **Military Service:** Served in the Austrian Army during World War I. **Family:** Married 1) the actress Grete Mosheim (divorced); 2) the actress Vally Hatvany, 1937 (died 1938); 3) Florence Meyer (divorced), sons: Vincent, Laurence; 4) the actress Joan Tetzel, 1949 (died 1977). **Career:** On stage in *Edward II* (also co-director with Brecht) in Munich, then member for ten years of Max Reinhardt's troupe in Berlin; 1926—film debut in *Die Abenteuer eines Zehnmarkscheines*; 1932—directed stage play *Pygmalion*; 1933—left Germany with rise of the Nazis, and worked in the United Kingdom; 1935—West End debut in *Close Quarters*; 1936-66—lived and worked in the United States; 1940—Broadway debut in *Grey Farm*; later acted on stage in *I Remember Mama*, 1944 and in film version, 1948, and *Rashomon*, 1959; lived in England after 1966. **Died:** In Sussex, England, 27 January 1978.

Films as Actor:

1926   *Die Abenteuer eines Zehnmarkscheines (K13 513)* (Viertel); *Brennende Grenze* (Waschneck); *Das Mädchen ohne Heimat (Vom Freudenhaus in die Ehe; Aftermath)* (David)
1927   *Dirnentragödie (Women without Men; The Tragedy of the Street)* (Rahn); *Fürst oder Clown* (Rasumny); *Die heilige Lüge* (Holger-Madsen); *Der Kampf des Donald Westhof* (Wendhausen); *Die Leibeigenen* (Eichberg); *Petronella* (Schwartz); *Regine, die Tragödie einer Frau* (Waschneck); *Schinderhannes (The Prince of Rogues)* (Bernhardt)
1928   *Die Rothausgasse* (Oswald)
1929   *Masken* (Meinert); *Revolte im Erziehungshaus* (Asagaroff)
1930   *Hokuspokus (Der Prozess der Kitty Kellermann; Hocuspocus)* (Ucicky); *Dreyfus (The Dreyfus Case)* (Oswald) (as Esterhazy)
1931   *1914, die letzten Tage vor dem Weltbrand* (Oswald); *Der Wege nach Rio* (Oswald); *Zwischen Nacht und Morgen (Dirnentragödie)* (Lamprecht); *Im Geheimdienst (In the Employ of the Secret Service)* (Ucicky); *Nachtkolonne* (Bauer); *Die Nächte von Port Said* (Mittler)
1932   *Spione am Werk (Spies at Work)* (Lamprecht)
1933   *Moral und Liebe* (Jacoby); *Unsichtbare Gegner* (Katscher)
1936   *Rhodes (Rhodes of Africa)* (Viertel) (as Paul Kruger); *Sabotage (The Woman Alone)* (Hitchcock) (as Carl Verloc); *Everything Is Thunder* (Rosmer)
1937   *Ebb Tide* (Hogan)
1940   *Seven Sinners* (Garnett); *Comrade X* (King Vidor)
1941   *The Invisible Woman* (Sutherland); *Rage in Heaven* (Van Dyke); *Ball of Fire* (Hawks) (as Prof. Gurkakoff)
1943   *Mission to Moscow* (Sutherland) (as Litvinoff); *Hostages* (Tuttle)
1946   *The Shop at Sly Corner (The Code of Scotland Yard)* (King)
1948   *I Remember Mama* (Stevens) (as Uncle Chris)
1949   *Anna Lucasta* (Rapper)
1950   *The White Tower* (Tetzlaff)
1951   *Der schweigende Mund* (Hartl)

Oscar Homolka in *Sabotage* **courtesy of The Rank Organisation Plc**

1952 *Top Secret* (*Mr. Potts Goes to Moscow*) (Zampi)
1953 *The House of the Arrow* (Anderson)
1954 *Prisoner of War* (Marton)
1955 *The Seven Year Itch* (Wilder)
1956 *War and Peace* (King Vidor) (as Gen. Kutuzov)
1957 *A Farewell to Arms* (Charles Vidor)
1958 *The Key* (Reed) (as Van Dam)
1959 *La tempestà* (*The Tempest*) (Lattuada) (as Savelic)
1961 *Mr. Sardonicus* (Castle) (as Krull)
1962 *Boys' Night Out* (Gordon) (as Dr. Prokosch); *The Wonderful World of the Brothers Grimm* (Levin) (as the Duke); *The Mooncussers* (Neilson—for TV)
1964 *The Long Ships* (Cardiff) (as Krok); *Ambassador at Large* (Schaffner—for TV)
1965 *Joy in the Morning* (Segal) (as Stan Pulaski)
1966 *Funeral in Berlin* (Hamilton) (as Col. Stok)
1967 *The Happening* (Silverstein) (as Sam); *Billion Dollar Brain* (Russell) (as Col. Stok)
1968 *The Strange Case of Dr. Jekyll and Mr. Hyde* (Jarrott—for TV)
1969 *Assignment to Kill* (Reynolds) (as Inspector Ruff); *The Madwoman of Chaillot* (Forbes) (as The Commissar)
1970 *Song of Norway* (Stone) (as Engstrand); *The Executioner* (Wanamaker) (as Racovsky)
1974 *The Tamarind Seed* (Edwards) (as Gen. Golitsyn)
1975 *One of Our Own* (Sarafian—for TV)

Publications

On HOMOLKA: article—

Profile, in *The New Yorker*, 2 December 1944.

* * *

Arriving in Germany from Vienna in 1918, Oscar Homolka soon achieved success on the stage, where for ten years he was a leading man in Max Reinhardt's famous theatrical troupe. In 1926 Homolka began his long film career, one that became international when, in 1933, Hitler assumed power. Homolka fled to Paris, then London where his career soon resumed on the stage and in film.

Soon thereafter he was invited to the United States where he spent most of the next 14 years as a character actor, generally playing a cruel or bumbling European whose thick accent and thicker eyebrows were the key defining attributes. Predictably, Hollywood loved him most as the blustering Uncle Chris in *I Remember Mama*.

In a 1944 *New Yorker* profile Homolka is quoted thus, "In Europe I played Othello, but in American pictures.... I am just the mean fellow who leers at the little heroine and dies hideously in the end." Howard Hawks, thankfully, showed us another side of Homolka when he cast him in *Ball of Fire* as the pipe-sucking Professor Gurkakoff, one of eight hermetic encyclopedia writers childishly lovestruck by Barbara Stanwyck's nightclub singer, Sugarpuss O'Shea.

Beginning in 1951, Homolka began working outside the United States. In the mid-1960s he settled in England where once again he specialized in playing the heavy foreign adversary. In both *Funeral in Berlin* and *Billion Dollar Brain* he played the Russian intelligence officer Stok, adversary to Michael Caine's Harry Palmer. In Blake Edwards's *The Tamarind Seed* he was the nasty Russian General Golitsyn. His most famous Russian characterization, however, was as Tolstoy's General Kutuzov in King Vidor's version of *War and Peace*. His gravel-voiced Russian commandant brought him excellent notices; in retrospect, the performance seems as gratuitous in its showiness as the film itself.

Such, however, cannot be said of his best screen role, that of Verloc in Alfred Hitchcock's *Sabotage*. Rather than cast him as a stereotypical German heavy, Hitchcock, while never excusing Verloc's guilt, perversely endowed this character with a sympathetic edge. Verloc is guilty of sabotage, but is also clearly a man trapped between loyalties. Homolka's tense and frightened performance heightens this complex conception. He literally seems to shrink with guilt over his role in the death of his young brother-in-law, Stevie. Verloc's death, visualized in Hitchcock's famous dinner-table montage, seems an act of mercy. In these last moments, Homolka effectively releases the tensions built up across the narrative and greets death with a peculiar calm.

—Doug Tomlinson

HOPE, Bob

Nationality: American. **Born:** Leslie Townes Hope in Eltham, London, 29 May 1903; emigrated with family to the United States, 1908, naturalized citizen 1920. **Education:** Attended Fairmont High School, Cleveland. **Family:** Married Dolores Reade 1933, four adopted children. **Career:** 1922—clerk for Chandler Motor Company; 1922—entered vaudeville as comedian and singer-dancer with Fatty Arbuckle's traveling show, then appeared (teamed with Lloyd Durbin and later George Byrne) on vaudeville circuit for next few years; 1927—Broadway debut in *The Sidewalks of New York*; 1928—emerged as solo monologist; in next few years was a headliner on RKO circuit, and appeared in plays on Broadway; 1934—film debut in short *Going Spanish*; 1935—radio debut, eventually leading to his own radio show *The Bob Hope Pepsodent Show*, 1939-48; 1940—teamed with Bing Crosby in first of the popular "Road" films, *Road to Singapore*; early 1940s—began series of overseas tours to entertain American troops; 1948—founded first of several film production companies; 1951-52—host, *Chesterfield Sound Off Time* TV series; 1952-53—host, *The Colgate Comedy Hour* TV series; 1963-67—host and occasional star of *Bob Hope Presents the Chrysler Theatre* TV series; appeared in numerous TV specials, through mid-1990s. **Awards:** Honorary Academy Awards, 1940, 1952, 1965; Jean Hersholt Humanitarian Award, 1959. **Address:** c/o 10000 Riverside Drive, Suite 3, North Hollywood, CA 91602, U.S.A.

Films as Actor:

1934 *Going Spanish* (Christie—short); *Paree, Paree* (Mack—short) (as Peter Forbes)
1935 *The Old Grey Manor* (French—short); *Watch the Birdie* (French—short); *Double Exposure* (French—short)
1936 *Calling All Tars* (French—short); *Shop Talk* (French—short)
1938 *The Big Broadcast of 1938* (Leisen) (as Buzz Fielding); *College Swing* (Walsh) (as Bub Brady); *Give Me a Sailor* (Nugent) (as Jim Brewster); *Thanks for the Memory* (Archainbaud) (as Steve Merrick); *Don't Hook Now* (Poleise) (as himself)
1939 *Never Say Die* (Nugent) (as Jim Kidley); *Some Like It Hot* (*Rhythm Romance*) (Archainbaud) (as Nicky Nelson); *The Cat and the Canary* (Nugent) (as Wally Hampton)
1940 *Road to Singapore* (Schertzinger) (as Ace Lannigan); *The Ghostbreakers* (Marshall) (as Harry Lawrence)
1941 *Road to Zanzibar* (Schertzinger) (as Fearless Hubert Frazier); *Caught in the Draft* (Butler) (as Don Bolton); *Nothing but the Truth* (Nugent) (as Steve Bennett); *Louisiana Purchase* (Cummings) (as Jim Taylor); *Star Spangled Rhythm* (Marshall) (as himself)

1942   *My Favorite Blonde* (Lanfield) (as Larry Haines); *Road to Morocco* (Butler) (as Turkey Jackson)

1943   *They Got Me Covered* (Butler) (as Robert Kittredge); *Let's Face It* (Lanfield) (as Jerry Walker); *Welcome to Britain* (Asquith) (as himself)

1944   *The Princess and the Pirate* (Butler) (as Sylvester the Great)

1945   *All Star Bond Rally* (Audley—short) (as himself); *Hollywood Victory Caravan* (Russell) (as himself)

1946   *Road to Utopia* (Walker) (as Chester Hooton); *Monsieur Beaucaire* (Marshall) (title role)

1947   *My Favorite Brunette* (Nugent) (as Ronnie Jackson); *Where There's Life* (Lanfield) (as Michael Valentine); *Variety Girl* (Marshall) (as himself)

1948   *Road to Rio* (McLeod) (as Hot Lips Barton); *The Paleface* (McLeod) (as Painless Peter Potter)

1949   *Sorrowful Jones* (Lanfield) (title role); *The Great Lover* (Hall) (as Freddie Hunter)

1950   *Fancy Pants* (Marshall) (as Humphrey)

1951   *The Lemon Drop Kid* (Lanfield) (title role); *My Favorite Spy* (McLeod) (as Peanuts White)

1952   *Son of Paleface* (Tashlin) (as Junior); *Road to Bali* (Walker) (as Harold Gridley); *The Greatest Show on Earth* (DeMille) (appearance)

1953   *Off Limits* (Marshall) (as Wally Hogan); *Here Come the Girls* (Binyon) (as Stanley Snodgrass); *Scared Stiff* (Marshall) (appearance)

1954   *Casanova's Big Night* (McLeod) (as Pippo Poppolino)

1955   *The Seven Little Foys* (Shavelson) (as Eddie Foy)

1956   *That Certain Feeling* (Panama) (as Francis X. Digman); *The Iron Petticoat* (Thomas) (as Chuck Lockwood)

1957   *Beau James* (Shavelson) (as Jimmy Walker)

1958   *Paris Holiday* (Oswald) (as Robert Leslie); *Showdown at Ulcer Gulch*

1959   *Alias Jesse James* (McLeod) (as Milford Farnsworth); *Five Pennies* (Shavelson) (as himself)

1960   *The Facts of Life* (Frank) (as Larry Gilbert)

1961   *Bachelor in Paradise* (Arnold) (as Adam J. Niles)

1962   *Road to Hong Kong* (Panama) (as Chester Babock)

1963   *Critic's Choice* (Weis) (as Parker Ballantine); *Call Me Bwana* (Douglas) (as Matt Merriwether)

1964   *A Global Affair* (Arnold) (as Frank Larrimore)

1965   *I'll Take Sweden* (De Cordova) (as Bob Holcomb)

1966   *Boy, Did I Get a Wrong Number* (Marshall) (as Tom Meade); *The Oscar* (Rouse) (as himself)

1967   *Eight on the Lam* (Marshall) (as Henry Dimsdale)

1968   *The Private Navy of Sgt. O'Farrell* (Tashlin) (title role)

1969   *How to Commit Marriage* (Panama) (as Frank Benson)

1972   *Cancel My Reservation* (Bogart) (as Dan Bartlett)

1979   *The Muppet Movie* (Frawley) (as Ice Cream Man)

1985   *Spies Like Us* (Landis) (as himself)

1986   *A Masterpiece of Murder* (Dubin—for TV)

Publications

By HOPE: books—

They Got Me Covered, Hollywood, 1941.
I Never Left Home, New York, 1944.
So This Is Peace, Hollywood, 1946.
Have Tux, Will Travel, as told to Pete Martin, New York, 1954.
I Owe Russia $1200, New York, 1963.
Five Women I Love: Bob Hope's Vietnam Story, New York, 1966.
The Last Christmas Show, as told to Pete Martin, New York, 1974.

The Road to Hollywood: My Forty Year Love Affair with the Movies, with Bob Thomas, New York, 1977.
Confessions of a Hooker: My Lifelong Love Affair with Golf, as told to Dwayne Netland, New York, 1985.
Don't Shoot, It's Only Me, with Melville Shavelson, New York, 1990.
We Could've Finished Last without You: An Irreverent Look at the Atlanta Braves, 1991.

By HOPE: articles—

"Unforgettable Lucille Ball," in *Reader's Digest* (Canadian), June 1990.
"Thanks for the Memory," interview with Bonnie Angelo and Jordan Bonfante, in *Time*, 11 June 1990.

On HOPE: books—

Thompson, Charles, *Bob Hope: Portrait of a Superstar*, New York, 1981.
Faith, William, *Bob Hope: A Life in Comedy*, New York, 1982.
Trescott, Pamela, *Bob Hope: A Comic Life*, London, 1987.
Carrick, Peter, *Thanks for the Memory: A Tribute to Bob Hope*, London, 1988.
Haining, Peter, *Bob Hope: Thanks for the Memory*, London, 1989.
Marx, Arthur, *The Secret Life of Bob Hope*, New York, 1993.

On HOPE: articles—

Kaplan, P. W., "On the Road with Bob Hope," in *Film Comment* (New York), January-February 1978.
Schickel, Richard, "Bob Hope," in *The Movie Star*, edited by Elisabeth Weis, New York, 1981.
Crnkovich, T., "On the Road with Bing, Bob, and Dorothy," in *Classic Images*, November 1992.
"Hollywood Recycles the Western Film," in *New York Times*, 3 May 1993.

*   *   *

Bob Hope was certainly a major movie star during the 1940s and 1950s, but his stay in Hollywood was only one short phase in an extraordinary show business career. Although Hope made feature films from the 1930s to the 1970s, it was his Paramount years from 1941 to 1953 that were his most successful. He became a star with the first Hope-Crosby "Road" film, *Road to Singapore* in 1940, and then quickly moved into the top ten ranking movie stars, usually occupying a slot several notches below Crosby.

The five "Road" films were all major box-office successes, but so were ten other films in which Hope starred without Crosby. These included *Paleface, Caught in the Draft, My Favorite Blond, Let's Face It, My Favorite Brunette, The Great Lover*, and *Fancy Pants*. All these films ranked among the top grossers for their respective years. This is an extraordinary list, and more importantly in the film business of the period they represented nearly half of all of Paramount's major hits of the 1940s. During the 1940s, Hope and Crosby powered Paramount past Loew's/MGM to number one in the film industry profit race.

Hope also achieved as much success in radio (a long-running top ten show) and television (a continuous contract with NBC since 1950 for specials). Concert dates and other appearances by this seemingly indefatigable performer have helped make him one of the highest paid show business personalities ever. Hope invested his earnings wisely and became one of the richest persons in the history of the American mass media.

All this wealth and fame has emerged from a character Hope first created in vaudeville in the 1920s, and successfully transferred—with the aid of a stable of writers personally under contract—to radio, then

Bob Hope

the movies, and finally to television. His character is boyishly auda-cious, a smart-aleck kid seeming to know it all. But at the first sign of trouble this character's eyes become enlarged, and he becomes a whim-pering coward who will do anything to save his skin. The character always surrounds himself with beautiful women, but rarely ever gets the girl. Using these traits, Hope can be the wisecracking stand-up comic, but offend no one. This well-manufactured image, with noth-ing left to chance, has appealed to middle-class Americans for some 40 years, and rightly or wrongly must take its place beside the Chaplin figure as the comic image of the mass media era that has attracted the greatest following.

Critical opinion of Hope's work spans the spectrum. Many find his character lacking elegance and charm because of its assembly-line patter. For this group, Hope has simply turned out a standardized product and nothing more. But there is a growing faction which has begun to honor Hope as the quintessential American comic, following in the Chaplin tradition. Thus, Hope ought to be praised for his speed of delivery, his adaption to new technological forms of entertainment, and even his obvious links to corporate America. Woody Allen, among others, has stepped forward to acknowledge his admiration for Hope's comedy. (Allen, for example, has claimed his *Love and Death* owes its origins to Hope's *Monsieur Beaucaire*.) However these arguments are resolved in the fu-ture, by the 1960s Bob Hope had moved beyond his status as a stand-up comic and into the realm of cultural icon.

—Douglas Gomery

HOPKINS, (Sir) Anthony

Nationality: British. **Born:** Port Talbot, South Wales, 31 December 1937. **Education:** Attended Cowbridge Grammar School, Glamorgan; Royal Academy of Dramatic Art, London, 1961-63; Cardiff College of Drama. **Family:** Married 1) Petronella Barker, 1967 (divorced 1972), daughter: Abigail; 2) Jennifer Lynton, 1973. **Career:** 1960—stage debut in *The Quare Fellow*, followed by repertory work; 1964—London stage debut in *Julius Caesar*; 1966-73—member of the Na-tional Theatre, London; 1967—film debut in *The White Bus*; 1974—appeared in *Equus* on Broadway, and directed the Los Angeles produc-tion, 1977; 1980s—theater work includes *Pravda*, *King Lear*, *Antony and Cleopatra*, and *M. Butterfly*; TV mini-series include *War and Peace*, 1973, *QB VII*, 1974, *Hollywood Wives*, 1985, *and Great Expectations*, 1989. **Awards:** Commander, Order of the British Empire, 1987; Best Actor, Academy Award, for *The Silence of the Lambs*, 1991; knighted, 1 January 1993. **Agent:** c/o CAA, 9830 Wilshire Boulevard, Beverly Hills, 90212, U.S.A.

Films as Actor:

1967 *The White Bus* (Anderson) (as Brechtian)
1968 *The Lion in Winter* (Harvey) (as Richard the Lion-Hearted)
1969 *Hamlet* (Richardson) (as Claudius); *The Looking Glass War* (Pierson) (as John Avery)
1971 *When Eight Bells Toll* (Périer) (as Philip Calvert)
1972 *Young Winston* (Attenborough) (as David Lloyd George)
1973 *A Doll's House* (Garland) (as Torvald Helmer)
1974 *The Girl from Petrovka* (Miller) (as Kostya); *Juggernaut* (Lester) (as Supt. John McCleod); *All Creatures Great and Small* (Whatham) (as Siegfried Farnon)
1976 *Dark Victory* (Butler—for TV) (as Michael); *Victory at Entebbe* (Chomsky—for TV) (as Yitzhak Rabin); *The Lindbergh Kid-napping Case* (Kulik—for TV) (as Bruno Hauptmann)

1977 *Audrey Rose* (Wise) (as Elliot Hoover); *A Bridge Too Far* (Attenborough) (as Lt. Col. John Frost)
1978 *Magic* (Attenborough) (as Corky/Fats); *International Velvet* (Forbes) (as Capt. Johnson); *Kean* (Jones—for TV) (title role)
1979 *Mayflower: The Pilgrim's Adventure* (Schaefer—for TV) (as Capt. Jones)
1980 *The Elephant Man* (Lynch) (as Frederick Treves); *A Change of Seasons* (Richard Lang) (as Adam Evans)
1981 *The Bunker* (Schaefer—for TV) (as Adolf Hitler); *Othello* (Miller—for TV) (title role); *Peter and Paul* (Day—for TV) (as St. Peter)
1983 *The Hunchback of Notre Dame* (Tuchner—for TV) (as Quasimodo)
1984 *The Bounty* (Donaldson) (as Captain Bligh); *Io e il duce* (*Mussolini and I*) (Negrin—for TV) (as Count Ciano); *A Married Man* (Davies and Jarrott—for TV) (as John Strickland)
1985 *Arch of Triumph* (Hussein—for TV) (as Dr. Ravic); *Guilty Conscience* (Greene—for TV) (as Arthur Jamison); *Heart-land* (Billington—for TV)
1986 *Blunt* (Glenister—for TV) (as Guy Burgess); *84 Charing Cross Road* (Jones) (as Frank Doel); *The Good Father* (Newell) (as Bill Hooper)
1988 *The Dawning* (Knights—released in U.S. 1993) (as Major Angus Barry/Cassius); *The Tenth Man* (Gold—for TV) (as Chavel); *Across the Lake* (Maylam—for TV) (as Donald Campbell)
1989 *A Chorus of Disapproval* (Winner) (as Dafydd Ap Llewellyn)
1990 *Desperate Hours* (Cimino) (as Tim Cornell); *One Man's War* (Toledo—for TV) (as Joel Filartiga)
1991 ***The Silence of the Lambs*** (Jonathan Demme) (as Dr. Hannibal "Cannibal" Lecter)
1992 ***Howards End*** (Ivory) (as Henry Wilcox); *Freejack* (Murphy) (as McCandless); *The Efficiency Expert* (*Spotswood*) (Joffe) (as Wallace); *Chaplin* (Attenborough) (as George Hayden); *Bram Stoker's Dracula* (Coppola) (as Prof. Abraham Van Helsing); *To Be the Best* (Wharmby—for TV) (as Jack Figg)
1993 *The Remains of the Day* (Ivory) (as Stevens); *The Trial* (David Jones) (as the priest); *Shadowlands* (Attenborough) (as Jack Lewis); *... und der Himmel steht still* (*The Innocent*) (Schlesinger) (as Bob Glass); *Selected Exits* (Tristram Powell—for TV) (as Gwyn Thomas); *Earth and the Ameri-can Dream* (Couturie—doc) (voice only)
1994 *The Road to Wellville* (Parker) (as Dr. John Harvey Kellogg); *Legends of the Fall* (Zwick) (as Colonel William Ludlow)
1995 *Nixon* (Stone) (title role)
1995 *Surviving Picasso* (Ivory)

Films as Director:

1990 *Dylan Thomas: Return Journey*
1995 *August* (+ ro)

Publications

By HOPKINS: book—

Anthony Hopkins' Snowdonia, with Graham Nobles, Grantown-on-Spey, 1993.

By HOPKINS: articles—

Interviews, in *Photoplay* (London), August 1978 and September 1984.
Interview with Rod Lurie, in *Empire* (London), June 1991.

Anthony Hopkins in *Howards End*

"I Like That," interview in *New Yorker*, 16 March 1992.

"Nicholson? Brando? (April Fool) It's . . . an Interview with Anthony Hopkins," interview with Lisa Liebman, in *Interview* (New York), April 1992.

"O.K., Says Anthony Hopkins, More Mr. Nice Guy," interview with Alex Witchel, in *New York Times*, 19 December 1993.

Interview with Lawrence Grobel, in *Playboy* (Chicago), March 1994.

On HOPKINS: books—

Falk, Quentin, *Anthony Hopkins: Too Good to Work: A Biography*, London, 1989; rev. ed., 1993.

Hare, David, *Writing Left-Handed*, London, 1991.

Callan, Michael Feeney, *Anthony Hopkins: In Darkness and Light*, London, 1993.

On HOPKINS: articles—

Ecran (Paris), May 1979.

Current Biography 1980, New York, 1980.

Films Illustrated (London), December 1980.

L'Ecran Fantastique (Paris), July-August 1984.

Wilson, P., "Anthony Hopkins," in *Film Monthly*, June 1991.

Kaye, Elizabeth, "Anthony Hopkins for Your Approval," in *Premiere* (New York), February 1994.

Kiener, Robert, "The Rebirth of Anthony Hopkins," in *Reader's Digest* (Canadian), July 1994.

*   *   *

Anthony Hopkins appeared in films for two decades without advancing to screen stardom. His performances, many of them in smaller-budget films, were lauded by critics, but audiences did not eagerly await his next movie appearance or place his name on lists of screen favorites. Perhaps his problem was that he lacked an identifiable persona and never developed into a Hollywood "type"; he seemed always to be hiding in period costumes or thick makeup. All the years of relative anonymity ended with his Oscar-winning performance in the most abhorrent role of his career, that of Hannibal "The Cannibal" Lecter in *The Silence of the Lambs*, one of the most popular and well-publicized pictures of 1991.

Now, in middle age, Hopkins's rugged looks and extraordinarily appealing voice (which often have led critics and fans to comparisons with fellow Welshman Richard Burton) are adding zest to an array of projects with which he has been associated, whether they be television movies, prestige art films, or extravagant Hollywood productions. His authoritative presence and incomparable acting ability are the elements which make him a standout performer, but it is his screen magnetism, displayed finally in choice star roles, which made him an international movie star.

Like his mentor Laurence Olivier, who often acted while camouflaged in thick makeup, Hopkins acquired a remarkable chameleon quality in his acting quite early in his career and kept with it for years. This has suited him particularly when taking on a series of biographical roles—Lloyd George, Adolf Hitler, Bruno Hauptmann, Donald Campbell, Captain Bligh, Yitzhak Rabin, Richard the Lion-Hearted, and even Richard Nixon—as well as with outrageous fictional grotesques such as Quasimodo, Lambert Le Roux, and Hannibal Lecter.

Besides the historical pieces in which he appeared, his pre-1990s performances do include a few unbalanced characters who may have laid a foundation for him to become celluloid's most credible cannibal killer. For instance, in *Magic* he played a demented ventriloquist, and in *Audrey Rose* he was a menacing stranger who claims a 12-year-old girl is his dead daughter reincarnated.

The international celebrity that he had sought since his humble, lower-middle-class boyhood in South Wales finally arrived with his chilling performance as a psychotic serial killer in *The Silence of the Lambs*. Hopkins's definitive interpretation of the warped, nightmarish criminal who not only murders but also dines on his prey flabbergasted audiences. His odd facial expressions, and the wiggling of his tongue in an eel-like manner, heavily contributed to the film's well-earned status as a classic of the horror genre.

Hopkins's two follow-up pictures were James Ivory's *Howards End* and *The Remains of the Day*. These two cinematic gems (both of which co-starred Emma Thompson) made him a darling of the art-house crowd. In the first film, which is based on a novel of Edwardian England by E. M. Forster, he plays a widower with a mahogany veneer that hides a chip-board heart. The subtle bearing of Hopkins's character underscores the snobbery among Britain's classes of that time, and the repression of emotion that was called for by the existing social conventions. In the second film, Hopkins plays a tradition-bound head butler who sacrifices his personal emotions and desires in the line of duty. Both of these characters are quiet beings who internalize their feelings. As such, their on-screen depictions could well have been stiff, blank signposts in the hands of a lesser actor, but Hopkins made both into three-dimensional and exciting individuals.

Shadowlands brought Hopkins the opportunity to play a full-fledged romantic gentleman in the character of real-life British writer C. S. Lewis. For this film, Hopkins began as a rather stiff, cloistered middle-aged Oxford educator who flowers as he becomes infused with love for a forthright American poet (Debra Winger). Hopkins's development from bookworm to enthusiastic lover showed audiences a most welcomed romantic quality. This role was, in a way, a graduated version or expansion of the character of the kindly bookstore salesman he played in *84 Charing Cross Road*.

Hopkins is an actor who can take on most any role. His presence can even make an otherwise mundane film mandatory viewing. Such is the case in *The Road to Wellville*, a disappointing adaptation of T. Coraghessan Boyle's comic novel, in which he transcends the poor script to give a delightfully animated, over-the-top performance—complete with silly, bucktoothed grin—as John H. Kellogg, the real-life inventor of corn flakes. In *Legends of the Fall*, the more sobering saga of early twentieth-century life in Montana, he is seen as the independent, feisty, and humanistic patriarch who has sired a trio of sons. In the latter part of this film, he is called upon to portray an elderly, partially paralyzed stroke victim who is left with marred speech. Under heavy makeup (again), he drags his disfigured body without ever losing his character's sense of eminence and dignity. It is the sort of specialty role Olivier himself would have fancied.

—Quentin Falk, updated by Audrey E. Kupferberg

HOPKINS, Miriam

Nationality: American. **Born:** Ellen Miriam Hopkins in Bainbridge, Georgia, 1902. **Education:** Attended Goddard Seminary, Vermont, and Syracuse University, New York. **Family:** Married 1) the actor Brandon Peters, 1926 (divorced 1931); 2) Austin Parker, 1931 (divorced 1932), one adopted son; 3) the director Anatole Litvak, 1937 (divorced 1939); 4) Raymond D. Brock, 1945 (divorced 1951). **Career:** 1921—stage debut as chorus girl in *The Music Box Revue*, followed by vaudeville tours and dramatic roles on Broadway; 1928—film debut in short *The Home Girl*; 1931—contract with Paramount; later contracts with Goldwyn, 1935, and Warner Brothers, 1938; 1940s—as leading parts declined, returned to stage, and appeared in summer

Miriam Hopkins in *These Three* **© 1936, Samuel Goldwyn**

stock and touring companies; 1949—TV debut; 1953—directed and starred in *Hay Fever*. **Died:** 9 October 1972.

Films as Actress:

1928 *The Home Girl* (Lawrence—short)
1930 *Fast and Loose* (Newmeyer) (as Marion Lenox)
1931 *The Smiling Lieutenant* (*Le Lieutenant souriant*) (Lubitsch) (as Princess Anna); *Twenty-Four Hours* (*The Hours Between*) (Gering) (as Rosie Duggan)
1932 ***Dr. Jekyll and Mr. Hyde*** (Mamoulian) (as Ivy Pearson); *Two Kinds of Women* (DeMille) (as Emma Krull); *Dancers in the Dark* (Burton) (as Gloria Bishop); *The World and the Flesh* (Cromwell) (as Maria Yaskaya); ***Trouble in Paradise*** (Lubitsch) (as Lily Vantier)
1933 *The Story of Temple Drake* (Roberts) (title role); *The Stranger's Return* (King Vidor) (as Louise Storr); *Design for Living* (Lubitsch) (as Gilda Farrell)
1934 *All of Me* (Flood) (as Lydia Darrow); *She Loves Me Not* (Nugent) (as Curly Flagg); *The Richest Girl in the World* (Seiter) (as Dorothy Hunter)

1935 *Becky Sharp* (Mamoulian) (title role); *Barbary Coast* (Hawks) (as Mary Rutledge "Swan"); *Splendor* (Nugent) (as Phyllis)
1936 *These Three* (Wyler) (as Martha Dobie); *Men Are Not Gods* (Reisch) (as Ann Williams)
1937 *The Woman I Love* (*The Woman Between*) (Litvak) (as Helene Maury); *Woman Chases Man* (Blystone) (as Virginia Travis); *Wise Girl* (Jason) (as Susan Fletcher)
1939 *The Old Maid* (Goulding) (as Delia Lovell)
1940 *Virginia City* (Curtiz) (as Julia Haynes); *The Lady with Red Hair* (Bernhardt) (as Mrs. Leslie Carter)
1942 *A Gentleman after Dark* (Marin) (as Flo Melton)
1943 *Old Acquaintance* (Sherman) (as Millie)
1944 *Skirmish on the Home Front* (short)
1949 *The Heiress* (Wyler) (as Lavinia Penniman)
1950 *The Mating Season* (Leisen) (as Fran Carleton)
1951 *Carrie* (Wyler) (as Julia Hartswood)
1952 *The Outcasts of Poker Flat* (Newman) (as Duchess)
1961 *The Children's Hour* (*The Loudest Whisper*) (Wyler) (as Mrs. Lily Mortar)
1964 *Fanny Hill* (*Fanny Hill: Memoirs of a Woman of Pleasure*) (Meyer) (as Maude Brown)

1965   *The Chase* (Penn) (as Mrs. Reeves)
1970   *Comeback* (*Hollywood Horror House*) (Wolfe)

Publications

On HOPKINS: article—

Checklist, in *Monthly Film Bulletin* (London), December 1978.

*   *   *

Petite Mariam Hopkins commanded attention on-screen. Her Hollywood vogue lasted less than a decade, but Southern breeding and accent gave her work a no-nonsense graciousness which (particularly in her early films) proved attractively diverting.

Hopkins's work in musical and, later, dramatic theater led to Paramount's signing her in 1931. After a slow start, she essayed a succession of well-received portrayals and earned a top star position. She was Maurice Chevalier's partner in *The Smiling Lieutenant*, the trollop in *Dr. Jekyll and Mr. Hyde*, a charming jewel thief in *Trouble in Paradise*: apparent versatility served to her advantage.

Actually, the same ladylike bitchiness characterized most of her screen work. By the mid-1930s, fewer scripts met with her approval, and she switched to Goldwyn Studios and later to Warners. She played *Becky Sharp*, patterned on Thackeray's *Vanity Fair*, competing with the novelty of the first three-color process Technicolor feature. But *These Three*—Lillian Hellman's *The Children's Hour* reconstructed as a conventional triangle drama—displayed Hopkins at her best: likably crisp and energetic, capable of connecting with the emotional demands of the part.

She rivaled Bette Davis off and twice on-screen (in *Old Acquaintance* and *The Old Maid*) but Davis won the audience sympathy and critical praise, since Hopkins tended to overdramatize. Increasingly, Hopkins abandoned Hollywood for the stage; she had picked up a reputation for feuding with co-stars.

Her own temperament and bad judgment of material, as much as the decreasing demand for her brand of histrionics, virtually ended her film career by the 1940s. She returned later in occasional character parts as shrewish, meddlesome relatives in *The Heiress*, *Carrie*, and, oddly, the remake of *The Children's Hour*.

—Richard Sater

HOPPER, Dennis

Nationality: American. **Born:** Dodge City, Kansas, 17 May 1936. **Education:** Attended high school in San Diego, California. **Family:** Married 1) Brooke Hayward, 1961 (divorced 1969), daughter: Marin; 2) Michelle Phillips, 1970 (divorced 1970); 3) Daria Halprin, 1972 (divorced 1976), daughter: Ruthana; 4) Katherine LaNasa, 1989 (divorced 1992), son: Henry Lee; 5) Victoria Duffy, 1996. **Career:** Mid-1950s—appeared in repertory at Pasadena Playhouse, and studied acting with Dorothy McGuire and John Swope at Old Globe Theatre, San Diego; 1955—film debut in *Rebel without a Cause*; contract with Warner Brothers; sculptor and still photographer—several one-man shows of photographs; 1969—directed first film *Easy Rider*. **Awards:** Best Supporting Actor, National Society of Film Critics, and LA Film Critics, for *Blue Velvet*, 1986. **Address:** Box 1889, Taos, NM 87571, U.S.A.

Films as Actor:

1954   *Johnny Guitar* (Nicholas Ray) (bit as posse member)
1955   ***Rebel without a Cause*** (Nicholas Ray) (as Groon); *I Died a Thousand Times* (Heisler)
1956   ***Giant*** (Stevens) (as Jordan Benedict III); *Gunfight at the O.K. Corral* (John Sturges) (as Billy Clanton)
1957   *No Man's Road* (Martinson—for TV); *A Question of Loyalty* (Doniger—for TV); *The Story of Mankind* (Irwin Allen) (as Napoleon); *Sayonara* (Logan) (as voice); *The Young Land* (Teztlaff) (as Hatfield Carnes)
1958   *From Hell to Texas* (*Manhunt*) (Hathaway) (as Tom Boyd); *Key Witness* (Karlson) (as "Cowboy")
1961   *Night Tide* (Harrington) (as Johnny Drake)
1963   *Tarzan and Jane Regained . . . Sort of* (Warhol)
1965   *The Sons of Katie Elder* (Hathaway) (as Dave Hastings)
1966   *Queen of Blood* (*Planet of Blood*) (Harrington) (as Paul)
1967   *Cool Hand Luke* (Roseberg) (as Babalugats); *The Trip* (Corman) (as Max); *The Glory Stompers* (Lanza) (as Chino); *Panic in the City* (Davis) (as Goff)
1968   *Hang 'em High* (Post) (as the Prophet); *Head* (Rafelson)
1969   *True Grit* (Hathaway) (as Moon); *The Festival Game* (Klinger and Lytton) (as interviewee)
1971   *Crush Proof* (Ménil)
1973   *Kid Blue* (Frawley) (as Bickford Waner)
1975   *James Dean, the First American Teenager* (Connolly—doc) (as interviewee)
1976   *Mad Dog Morgan* (*Mad Dog*) (Mora) (as Daniel Morgan); *Tracks* (Jaglom) (as Jack Falen)
1977   *Der Amerikanische Freund* (*The American Friend*) (Wenders) (as Tom Ripley); *Les Apprentis sorciers* (Cozarinsky)
1978   *Couleur chair* (Weyergans); *L'ordre et la sécurité du monde* (d'Anna)
1979   ***Apocalypse Now*** (Coppola) (as freelance photographer)
1980   *Wild Times* (Compton—for TV)
1981   *Renacida* (*Reborn*) (Luna); *King of the Mountain* (Nosseck) (as Cal)
1982   *Human Highway* (Shakey) (as Cracker); *The Osterman Weekend* (Peckinpah) (as Richard Tremayne)
1983   *Rumblefish* (Coppola) (as Father)
1984   *The Inside Man* (Clegg) (as Miller)
1985   *White Star* (Klick); *My Science Project* (Betuel) (as Bob Roberts); *Stark* (Holcomb—for TV); *O. C. and Stiggs* (Altman) (as Sponson)
1986   *Running Out of Luck* (Temple) (as video director); *The American Way* (*Riders of the Storm*) (Phillips) (as Captain); ***Blue Velvet*** (Lynch) (as Frank Booth); *Hoosiers* (*Best Shot*) (Anspaugh) (as Shooter); *The Texas Chainsaw Massacre Part II* (Hooper) (as Lt. "Lefty" Enright)
1987   *River's Edge* (Hunter) (as Feck); *Black Widow* (Rafelson) (as Ben Dumers); *Straight to Hell* (Cox) (as I. G. Farben); *The Pick-Up Artist* (Toback) (as Flash Jensen)
1988   *Blood Red* (Masterson) (as William Bradford Berrigan)
1989   *Chattahoochee* (Jackson) (as Walker Benson); *Flashback* (Amurri)
1990   *Superstar: The Life and Times of Andy Warhol* (Workman—doc); *Black Leather Jacket* (Mead) (as narrator); *Motion and Emotion* (as himself); *Hollywood Mavericks* (as himself)
1991   *Paris Trout* (Gyllenhaal—for TV) (title role); *Indian Runner* (Sean Penn) (as Caesar); *A Hero of Our Time*; *Eye of the Storm* (Zeltser) (as Marvin Gladstone); *Doublecrossed* (Young—for TV) (as Barry Seal)
1992   *Sunset Heat* (for TV); *Nails* (Flynn—for TV) (as Harry "Nails" Niles)

Dennis Hopper in *The Last Movie*

1993   *Boiling Point* (Harris) (as Red Diamond); *Red Rock West*
        (Dahl) (as Lyle); *Super Mario Bros.* (Morton and Jankel)
        (as King Koopa); *True Romance* (Scott) (as Clifford
        Worley); *The Heart of Justice* (Baretto—for TV) (as Aus-
        tin Blair)
1994   *Speed* (de Bont) (as Howard Payne); *Witch Hunt* (Schrader—for
        TV) (as H. Phillip Lovecraft)
1995   *Search and Destroy* (Salle) (as Dr. Luther Waxling); *Waterworld*
        (Kevin Reynolds) (as Deacon); *Basquiat* (*Build a Fort, Set
        It on Fire*) (Schnabel)
1996   *James Dean: A Portrait* (Legon—doc) (as himself); *Carried
        Away* (Barreto) (as Joseph)

Films as Director:

1969   ***Easy Rider*** (+ co-sc, ro as Billy)
1971   *The Last Movie* (+ co-sc, ro)
1980   *Out of the Blue* (+ ro as Don)
1988   *Colors*
1989   *Backtrack* (*Catchfire*) (d as "Allen Smithee," + ro as Milo)
1990   *The Hot Spot*
1994   *Chasers* (+ ro as Doggie)

Publications

By HOPPER: book—

Dennis Hopper: Out of the Sixties, Pasadena, California, 1986.

By HOPPER: articles—

"Dennis Hopper, Riding High," in *Playboy* (Chicago), December 1969.
Interview with G. O'Brien and M. Netter, in *Inter/View* (New York),
    February 1972.
Interview, in *Cahiers du Cinéma* (Paris), July-August 1980.
"How Far to the Last Movie?," in *Monthly Film Bulletin* (London),
    October 1982.
"Citizen Hopper," interview with C. Hodenfield, in *Film Comment* (New
    York), November/December 1986.
Interview with B. Kelley, in *American Film* (Los Angeles), March
    1988.
Interview with David Denicolo, in *Interview* (New York), February 1990.
Interview with C. Bierinckx, in *Film en Televisie + Video*, February 1991.
"Sean Penn," interview with Julian Schnabel and Dennis Hopper, in
    Interview (New York), September 1991.
"Gary Oldman," in *Interview* (New York), January 1992.

"Question and Answer Game with Dennis Hopper," interview in *Blimp*, Summer 1992.

"Rebel-ution," interview with Sean Penn, in *Interview* (New York), October 1994.

On HOPPER: book—

Rodriguez, Elean, *Dennis Hopper: A Madness to His Method*, New York, 1988.

On HOPPER: articles—

Macklin, F. A., "*Easy Rider*: The Initiation of Dennis Hopper," in *Film Heritage* (Dayton, Ohio), Fall 1969.

Burke, Tom, "Dennis Hopper Saves the Movies," in *Esquire* (New York), December 1970.

Burns, Dan E., "Dennis Hopper's *The Last Movie*: Beginning of the End," in *Literature/Film Quarterly*, 1979.

Algar, N., "Hopper at Birmingham," in *Sight and Sound* (London), Summer 1982.

Herring, H. D., "Out of the Dream and into the Nightmare: Dennis Hopper's Apocalyptic Vision of America," in *Journal of Popular Film* (Washington, D.C.), Winter 1983.

Scharres, B., "From Out of the Blue: The Return of Dennis Hopper," in *Journal of the University Film and Video Association* (Carbondale, Illinois), Spring 1983.

Current Biography 1987, New York, 1987.

Martin, A., "Dennis Hopper: Out of the Blue and into the Black," in *Cinema Papers* (Melbourne), July 1987.

Weber, Bruce, "A Wild Man Is Mellowing, Albeit Not on Screen, in *New York Times*, 8 September 1994.

*   *   *

Perhaps no other persona better signifies the lost idealism of the 1960s than that of Dennis Hopper. From his beginnings in *Rebel without a Cause, Giant*, and *Gunfight at the O.K. Corral*, to such surrealist epics as *Apocalypse Now* and *Blue Velvet*, the sight of Hopper's face alone now conjures up a menacing, violent, drug-ridden character.

As with many actors with such potent personas, Hopper's has stemmed in large part from his offscreen behavior. His violent nature, as well as a long ordeal of substance abuse (both alcohol and cocaine), has led to a typecasting that generally results in Hopper playing a psychotic villain. A significant turning point came with Hopper's 1969 directorial debut *Easy Rider*, in which he played a cynical biker in contrast to Peter Fonda's idealistic biker. The film left an indelible impression on American popular culture, as an indictment of American conformity and a celebration of the drug counterculture permeating the nation at the time. Another standout performance came with Coppola's *Apocalypse Now*, in which Hopper played a mad photographer—again, apparently his on-screen performance here (boisterous, drug-starved, and generally crazy) is very similar to that of his offscreen behavior during the shoot.

Another landmark and perhaps Hopper's greatest "comeback" came with David Lynch's *Blue Velvet*, in which he played a sadistic kidnapper who, among other things, inhales an unspecified gas and screams "Mommy" at Isabella Rossellini during bizarre sex scenes. A star was reborn, and Hopper's performance became as much a conversation piece as the film itself. This lead to similarly offbeat performances in *River's Edge, Paris Trout*, and *Search and Destroy*.

In the action thriller *Speed*, Hopper seemed to perfect the psychotic villain, and sharpened his black-humor edge. The film was a massive box-office success, and thus ensured further typecasting, this time in the most expensive movie ever made, *Waterworld*. Hopper managed to be surprisingly fresh in his role as a postapocalyptic psychotic villain, and proved the only decent element in an otherwise mediocre film. Not to be overlooked are the less widely seen but nonetheless fine performances delivered in *The American Friend* and *Out of the Blue*, among others. Ever since *Easy Rider*, virtually all of Hopper's films suggest an overwhelming loss, the loss of faith, hope, and idealism so closely identified culturally with the 1960s.

—Matthew Hays

HORTON, Edward Everett

Nationality: American. **Born:** Brooklyn, New York, 18 March 1886. **Education:** Attended Boys' High School, Brooklyn, Polytechnic of Brooklyn; Oberlin College, Ohio; Columbia University, New York. **Career:** 1906—chorus boy on Broadway; 1907—joined Dempsey Light Opera Company, Staten Island; 1908—joined Louis Mann's company, and had small roles on Broadway; 1912—joined Orpheum Players in Philadelphia; 1919—joined Los Angeles Stock Company; 1922—film debut (as Edward Horton) in *Too Much Business*; 1923—starred in his own company's production of *Clarence*, and in other plays in Los Angeles in the next few years; 1932—starred in *Springtime for Henry*, a role he played many times in the next 25 years on tour; and in New York in 1951; 1950—in the TV series *Holiday Hotel*; 1960—on tour with *Once upon a Mattress*; 1960s—in TV series *The Bullwinkle Show*, 1961-62, *The Cara Williams Show*, 1965-66, and *F Troop*, 1965-67. **Died:** 29 September 1970.

Films as Actor:

(as Edward Horton)

1922 *Too Much Business* (Robbins) (as John Henry Jackson); *The Ladder Jinx* (Robbins) (as Arthur Barnes); *A Front Page Story* (Robbins) (as Rodney Marvin)

1923 *Ruggles of Red Gap* (Cruze) (title role); *To the Ladies* (Cruze) (as Leonard Beebe)

1924 *Try and Get It* (Tate) (as Glenn Collins); *Flapper Wives* (Murfin and McCloskey) (as Vincent Platt); *The Man Who Fights Alone* (Worsely) (as Bob Alten)

(as Edward Everett Horton)

1924 *Helen's Babies* (Seiter) (as Uncle Harry)

1925 *Marry Me* (Cruze) (as John Smith); *Beggar on Horseback* (Cruze) (as Neil McRae); *The Business of Love* (Reis and Robbins)

1926 *La Boheme* (King Vidor) (as Colline); *The Nut-Cracker* (Ingraham) (as Horatio Slipaway); *Poker Faces* (Pollard) (as Jimmy Whitmore); *The Whole Town's Talking* (Laemmle) (as Chester Binney)

1927 *No Publicity* (short); *Dad's Choice* (short); *Find the King* (short); *Behind the Counter* (short); *Taxi! Taxi!* (Brown) (as Peter Whitby)

1928 *The Terror* (Del Ruth) (as Ferdinand Fane)

1929 *The Right Bed* (short); *Trusting Wives* (short); *Prince Babby* (short); *Good Medicine* (short); *Sonny Boy* (Mayo) (as Crandall Thorpe); *The Hottentot* (Del Ruth) (as Sam Harrington); *The Sap* (Mayo) (as Big Small); *The Aviator* (Del Ruth) (as Robert Street)

1930 *Take the Heir* (Ingraham) (as Smithers); *Wide Open* (Mayo) (as Simon Haldane); *Holiday* (E. H. Griffith) (as Nick Potter); *Once a Gentleman* (Cruze) (as Oliver)

1931   *Kiss Me Again* (*Toast of the Legion*) (Seiter) (as Réne); *Reaching for the Moon* (Goulding) (as Rogers); *Lonely Wives* (Mack); *The Front Page* (Milestone); *Six Cylinder Love* (Freeman); *Smart Woman* (La Cava); *The Age of Love* (Lloyd); *The Poor Rich* (Sedgwick)

1932   *But the Flesh Is Weak* (Conway); *Roar of the Dragon* (Ruggles); **Trouble in Paradise** (Lubitsch) (as François)

1933   *It's a Boy* (Whelan); *A Bedtime Story* (Taurog) (as Victor); *The Way to Love* (Taurog) (as Professor Gaston Bibi); *Design for Living* (Lubitsch); *Alice in Wonderland* (McLeod)

1934   *Soldiers of the King* (Elvey) (as Sebastian Marvello); *Easy to Love* (Keighley); *Sing and Like It* (Seiter) (as Adam Frink); *Smarty* (Florey); *Success at Any Price* (Roben); *Uncertain Lady* (Freund); *Kiss and Make Up* (Thompson); *The Merry Widow* (Lubitsch) (as Ambassador Popoff); *Ladies Should Listen* (Tuttle); *The Gay Divorcee* (Sandrich) (as Egbert Fitzgerald); *His Night Out* (Nigh)

1935   *The Private Secretary* (Edwards); *Biography of a Bachelor Girl* (Griffith); *All the King's Horses* (Tuttle) (as Peppi); *The Night Is Young* (Murphy) (as Szereny); **The Devil Is a Woman** (von Sternberg) (as Don Paquito); *In Caliente* (Bacon) (as Harold Brandon); *Ten Dollar Raise* (Marshall); *Going Highbrow* (Florey) (as Augie); *Little Big Shot* (Curtiz); **Top Hat** (Sandrich) (as Horace Hardwick)

1936   *Your Uncle Dudley* (E. Ford); *The Singing Kid* (Keighley) (as Davenport Rogers); *His Master's Voice*; *Hearts Divided* (Borzage) (as John Hataway); *Nobody's Fool* (Greville); *The Man in the Mirror* (Elvey) (as Jeremy Dike)

1937   *The King and the Chorus Girl* (Le Roy) (as Count Humbert); *Let's Make a Million* (R. McCarey); *Lost Horizon* (Capra) (as Alexander P. Lovett); *Shall We Dance* (Sandrich) (as Jeffrey Baird); *Oh, Doctor!* (McCarey); *Wild Money* (King); *Angel* (Lubitsch); *The Perfect Specimen* (Curtiz); *Danger—Love at Work* (Preminger); *The Great Garrick* (Whale); *Hitting a New High* (Walsh) (as Blynn)

1938   *Bluebeard's Eighth Wife* (Lubitsch); *College Swing* (Walsh) (as Hubert Dash); *Holiday* (Cukor); *Little Tough Guys in Society* (Kenton)

1939   *Paris Honeymoon* (Tuttle) (as Ernest Figg); *That's Right—You're Wrong* (Butler) (as Tom Village); *The Gang's All Here* (*The Amazing Mr. Forrest*) (Freeland) (as Treadwell)

1941   *You're the One* (Murphy) (as Death Valley Joe Frink); *Ziegfeld Girl* (Leonard) (as Noble Sage); *Sunny* (Wilcox) (as Henry Bates); *Bachelor Daddy* (Young); *Here Comes Mr. Jordan* (Hall) (as Messenger 7013); *Week-End for Three* (Reis); *Sandy Steps Out*

1942   *The Body Disappears* (Lederman); *I Married An Angel* (Van Dyke) (as Peter); *The Magnificent Dope* (Walter Lang); *Springtime in the Rockies* (Cummings) (as McTavish)

1943   *Forever and a Day* (Clair); *Thank Your Lucky Stars* (Butler) (as Farnsworth); *The Gang's All Here* (Berkeley) (as Peyton Potter)

1944   *Summer Storm* (Sirk); *Her Primitive Man* (Lamont); *San Diego, I Love You* (Le Borg); *Arsenic and Old Lace* (Capra); *Brazil* (Santley) (as Everett St. John Everett); *The Town Went Wild* (Murphy)

1945   *Steppin' in Society* (Esway); *Lady on a Train* (David) (as Haskell)

1946   *Cinderella Jones* (Berkeley) (as Keating); *Faithfully in My Fashion* (Salkow); *Earl Carroll's Sketch Book* (Rogell) (as Dr. Milo Edwards)

1947   *The Ghost Goes Wild* (Blair); *Down to Earth* (Hall) (as Messenger 7013); *Her Husband's Affair* (Simon)

1957   *The Story of Mankind* (Allen)

1961   *Pocketful of Miracles* (Capra) (as Butler)

1963   *It's a Mad, Mad, Mad, Mad World* (Kramer) (as Dinckler)

1964   *Sex and the Single Girl* (Quine) (as the Chief)

1967   *The Perils of Pauline* (Leonard) (as Casper Coleman)

1969   *Two Thousand Years Later* (Tenzer) (as Evermore)

1971   *Cold Turkey* (Lear)

Publications

On HORTON: book—

Parish, James Robert, and William T. Leonard, *The Funsters*, New Rochelle, New York, 1979.

On HORTON: article—

"Edward Everett Horton" in *Current Biography 1946*, New York, 1946.

*   *   *

Edward Everett Horton was one of the most frequently seen character actors on the screen. He appeared in more than 120 films, most of them being produced in the 1930s and 1940s. Horton rarely played the lead, but he frequently stole the show in his supporting roles. He specialized in comedy, often playing an individual who fretted and worried over every little problem, real or imagined. Horton's flustered manner of speech and anxious glances suggested a man on the brink of hysteria, but his comic approach kept this from becoming a matter for concern.

Many of the films in which this character appeared are screwball comedies of the 1930s. Horton was often the good friend and confidant of the romantic lead in these films. He worked with many well-known comedy directors of this period, such as George Cukor (*Holiday*), Ernst Lubitsch (*Design for Living, Trouble in Paradise*), and Frank Capra (*Lost Horizon*). Horton also appeared in three Fred Astaire-Ginger Rogers musicals (*The Gay Divorcee, Top Hat,* and *Shall We Dance?*). In 1941 Horton's bumbling and confused persona was perfectly employed in *Here Comes Mr. Jordan*, as the overzealous Messenger 7013 who collects the soul of Joe Pendleton just a little bit prematurely.

Although the frequency of Edward Everett Horton's screen appearances diminished with time, he never did officially retire. In the 1960s he made occasional guest appearances on TV's *F Troop* as the Indian medicine man Roaring Chicken. His voice became very familiar to children (and adults) as the narrator of "Fractured Fairy Tales" on the cartoon program *Rocky and His Friends* and its successor *The Bullwinkle Show*. He continued to work steadily up until only a few weeks before his death in 1970 at the age of 84.

—Linda J. Obalil

HOSKINS, Bob

Nationality: British. **Born:** Bury St. Edmunds, Suffolk, 26 October 1942. **Education:** Attended Stroud Green School, Finsbury Park, London. **Family:** Married 1) Jane Livesey (divorced), two children; 2) Linda, two children. **Career:** Worked in a variety of jobs, then became actor with the Unity Theatre, London; later theater work for the Royal Court Theatre, the Royal Shakespeare Company, 1976, and the National Theatre, including *Guys and Dolls*, 1982; 1972—film debut in *Up the Front*; 1974—in TV mini-series *Shoulder to Shoulder*, *Pennies from Heaven*, 1978, *Flickers*, 1981; 1987—directed first

Bob Hoskins (center) with Helen Mirren and Brian Hall in *The Long Good Friday* **© 1981 Paragon Entertainment Corporation/ Courtesy of HandMade Films**

film, *The Raggedy Rawney* (released 1990). **Awards:** Best Actor Awards from Cannes Festival, New York Film Critics and Los Angeles Film Critics, and British Academy of Film and Television Arts Award for Best Actor, for *Mona Lisa*, 1986. **Agent:** Hutton Management Ltd., 200 Fulham Road, London SW10 9PN, England.

Films as Actor:

1972   *Up the Front* (Kellet) (as recruiting sargeant)
1973   *The National Health* (Gold) (as Foster)
1975   *Inserts* (Byrum) (as Big Mac)
1976   *Royal Flash* (Lester)
1979   *Zulu Dawn* (Hickox) (as Sgt. Maj. Williams)
1980   *The Long Good Friday* (Mackenzie) (as Harold Shand)
1981   *Othello* (Jonathan Miller—for TV) (as Iago)
1982   *Pink Floyd—The Wall* (Alan Parker) (as rock 'n' roll manager)
1983   *The Honorary Consul* (*Beyond the Limit*) (Mackenzie) (as Colonel Perez)
1984   *The Cotton Club* (Francis Ford Coppola) (as Owney Madden); *Lassiter* (Roger Young) (as Becker)
1985   *Brazil* (Gilliam) (as Spoor); *The Dunera Boys* (Lewin); *Io e il duce* (*Mussolini and I*) (Negrin—for TV) (as Mussolini)
1986   *Mona Lisa* (Neil Jordan) (as George); *Sweet Liberty* (Alda) (as Stanley Gould)

1987   *The Lonely Passion of Judith Hearne* (Clayton) (as James Madden); *A Prayer for the Dying* (Hodges) (as Father Da Costa)
1988   *Who Framed Roger Rabbit?* (Zemeckis) (as Eddie Valiant)
1990   *Heart Condition* (Parriott) (as Jack Mooney); *Mermaids* (Benjamin) (as Lou Landsky)
1991   *Shattered* (Petersen) (as Gus Klein); *The Favor, the Watch, and the Very Big Fish* (Lewin) (as Louis Aubinard); *Hook* (Spielberg) (as Smee); *The Inner Circle* (Konchalovsky) (as Beria)
1992   *Passed Away* (Peters) (as Johnny Scanlan); *Blue Ice* (Mulcahy) (as Sam García)
1993   *Super Mario Bros.* (Morton and Jankel) (as Mario Mario)
1994   *World War II: When Lions Roared* (Sargent—for TV) (as Winston Churchill); *The Changeling* (Simon Curtis—for TV) (as De Flores)
1995   *Nixon* (Oliver Stone) (as J. Edgar Hoover); *Balto* (Wells—animation) (as voice of Boris); *Ding Dong* (Todd Hughes) (as himself)
1996   *The Secret Agent* (Hampton) (as Mr. Verloc, +co-pr)

Films as Director:

1990   *The Raggedy Rawney* (produced in 1987) (+ ro as Darky, co-sc)
1994   *The Rainbow* (+ ro)

Publications

By HOSKINS: articles—

Interviews in *Time Out* (London), 12 October 1985 and 23 November 1988.
Interview in *Film Directions* (Belfast), vol. 8, no. 32, 1986.
Interview with D. Hill, in *Stills* (London), March 1987.
Interview in *Première* (Paris), June 1988.
Interview in *Interview* (New York), February 1990.

On HOSKINS: book—

Moline, Karen, *Bob Hoskins: An Unlikely Hero*, London, 1988.

On HOSKINS: articles—

Hitchens, Christopher, "Tough Guys Do Dance," in *American Film* (Washington, D.C.), September 1987; see also January/February 1989.
Denby, David, "England's Little Big Man," in *Premiere* (New York), April 1989.
Current Biography 1990, New York, 1990.
Frutkin, Alan, "Bob Hoskins," in *Advocate* (Los Angeles), 23 January 1996.

*   *   *

Britain can boast precious few contemporary film stars with the screen presence to bring off that extraordinary, seemingly endless final shot in *The Long Good Friday* in which London gang boss Harold Shand is captured at the doors of the Savoy by the very IRA gang he believes he has just liquidated, and driven through the streets of the West End to an uncertain, but undoubtedly unpleasant, fate. If ever there was an illustration of Hoskins's remark that "the camera can see you think" then this is it. Indeed his whole incarnation of Shand in *The Long Good Friday* amply justifies director John Mackenzie's description of Hoskins as "the most exciting, explosive natural film acting talent that [Britain] has produced in years."

Hoskins's roles, and especially that of Shand, are often memorable for their Cagneyesque sense of barely suppressed violence, their sense of seething passions simmering just beneath the surface. But what is sometimes overlooked is his ability to incarnate ordinary, everyday people and, more to the point, to do so in a way that makes them compulsively interesting and watchable. This was one of the reasons which made the television mini-series *Flickers*, about the early days of British cinema, and *Pennies from Heaven* (infinitely preferable in every way to the feature film version) such memorable experiences and, doubtless, such milestones in Hoskins's acting career. As Kenith Trodd, the producer of the latter, put it, "because [Hoskins's character] Arthur Parker was an Everyman figure he had to be both very squalid and very identifiable. He had to be loved, despised and pitied, and Bob had the quality to get that over." The novelist and screenwriter William Boyd has also picked up on this quality in the actor; remarking on his "gritty ordinariness" and "potent banality" he notes that he has "an ability to play the ordinary man with a kind of tender veracity which is unrivalled."

It should also be pointed out that Hoskins has by no means confined himself to roles such as these—one has only to think of his Irish priest in *A Prayer for the Dying*, the neurotic Jewish screenwriter in *Sweet Liberty*, the fruity, power-mad J. Edgar Hoover in Stone's *Nixon,* and especially the vulnerable, suffering character playing opposite Maggie Smith in *The Lonely Passion of Judith Hearne* to realize just how versatile and adaptable an actor Hoskins actually is. And even if, in *The Cotton Club* and *Who Framed Roger Rabbit?*, Hollywood pre-

sented us with a rather different Hoskins to the inimitable Arthur Parker of *Pennies* or the lovable Cockney rogue of *Mona Lisa*, both films are a remarkable testimony to Hoskins's tremendous screen presence. Many other actors would have disappeared beneath the elaborate mise-en-scène, whereas Hoskins not only remains triumphantly visible, he shines.

The same is true of Hoskins's performance as the cartoonish pirate Smee, aide to Dustin Hoffman's insufferably mugging title character, in Spielberg's *Hook*. All but Hoskins seem swallowed up in this gargantuanly bloated—and remarkably tedious—variation on the J. M. Barrie fable *Peter Pan*. Even Hoskins's performance in *Super Mario Bros.*, a feature film based on—of all things—a video game, has much to recommend it, although why an actor of Hoskins's gifts would consent to appear in such drivel (apart from the obvious money factor, of course) is a mystery.

Only Hoskins's turn in the television docudrama *World War II: When Lions Roared* evidenced the possibility that occasionally a role may indeed be beyond his versatile grasp. His performance as Churchill, especially when contrasted with Michael Caine's remarkably well-realized Stalin, was more caricature of the man than realistic portrait.

—Julian Petley, updated by John McCarty

HOWARD, Leslie

Nationality: British. **Born:** Leslie Howard Stainer (some sources say Laszlo Horvath) in London, 3 April 1893. **Education:** Dulwich College, London. **Military Service:** Discharged from service in World War I suffering from shell shock. **Family:** Married Ruth Evelyn Martin, son: Ronald; daughter: Leslie Ruth. **Career:** After working in a bank, became stage actor; 1914—film debut in short *The Heroine of Mons*; 1917—stage debut in *Peg o' My Heart* on tour; 1919—co-founded Minerva Productions; 1920—American stage debut in *Just Suppose*; 1930—American film debut in version of his stage success *Outward Bound*, then a series of films in the United States for Warner Brothers, MGM, and Selznick; 1938—returned to England to direct, produce, and act in his own films; co-directorial debut with *Pygmalion*; 1940—began series of broadcast talks *Britain Speaks*. **Awards:** Best Actor, Venice Festival, for *Pygmalion*, 1938. **Died:** Plane shot down by Nazis, 1 June 1943.

Films as Actor:

1914   *The Heroine of Mons* (Noy—short)
1917   *The Happy Warrior* (Thornton) (as Rollo)
1919   *The Lackey and the Lady* (Bentley) (as Tony Dunciman)
1920   *Five Pound Reward* (Brunel—short) (as Tony Marchmont); *Bookworms* (Brunel—short) (as Richard)
1930   *Outward Bound* (Milton) (as Tom Prior)
1931   *Five and Ten* (*Daughter of Luxury*) (Leonard) (as Berry); *Never the Twain Shall Meet* (Van Dyke) (as Dan Pritchard); *Devotion* (Milton) (as David Trent); *A Free Soul* (Brown) (as Dwight Winthrop)
1932   *Service for the Ladies* (*Reserved for Ladies*) (Korda) (as Max Tracey); *Smilin' Through* (Franklin) (as John Carteret); *The Animal Kingdom* (*The Woman in His House*) (Griffith) (as Tom Collier)
1933   *Secrets* (Borzage) (as John Carlton); *Captured!* (Del Ruth) (as Captain Fred Allison); *Berkeley Square* (Lloyd) (as Peter Standish)

Leslie Howard in *The Scarlet Pimpernel* **courtesy of CTE (Carlton) Limited**

1934   *The Lady Is Willing* (Miller) (as Albert Latour); *Of Human Bondage* (Cromwell) (as Philip Carey); *British Agent* (Curtiz) (as Stephen Locke)
1935   *The Scarlet Pimpernel* (Young) (as Sir Percy Blakeney); *The Petrified Forest* (Mayo) (as Alan Squier)
1936   *Romeo and Juliet* (Cukor) (as Romeo); *Master Will Shakespeare* (Tourneur—short) (includes footage from *Romeo and Juliet*)
1937   *It's Love I'm After* (Mayo) (as Basil Underwood); *Stand-In* (Garnett) (as Atterbury Dodd)
1939   *Intermezzo: A Love Story* (*Escape to Happiness*) (Ratoff) (as Holger Brand); *Gone with the Wind* (Fleming) (as Ashley Wilkes)
1940   *Common Heritage* (Hanau—short) (as narrator)
1941   *From the Four Corners* (Havelock-Allen—short); *The White Eagle* (Cekalski—short) (as narrator); *49th Parallel* (*The Invaders*) (Powell) (as Philip Armstrong Scott)
1942   *In Which We Serve* (Coward and Lean) (as voice)
1943   *War in the Mediterranean* (Hanau—short) (as narrator)

Films as Producer:

1920   *The Bump* (Brunel—short); *Twice Two* (Brunel—short); *Too Many Cooks* (Brunel—short); *The Temporary Lady* (Brunel—short)
1943   *The Lamp Still Burns* (Elvey)

Films as Director:

1938   *Pygmalion* (co-d with Asquith, + ro as Professor Higgins)
1941   *Pimpernel Smith* (*Mister V*) (pr, + title role); publicity film for the Royal Institute for the Blind, title unknown
1942   *The First of the Few* (*Spitfire*) (pr, + ro as R. J. Mitchell)
1943   *The Gentle Sex* (narrator, + ro as silhouette)

Publications

By HOWARD: book—

Trivial Fond Records, edited by Ronald Howard, London, 1982.

By HOWARD: article—

"Where the Actor Ends," in *Saturday Evening Post* (Philadelphia), 28 June 1930.

On HOWARD: books—

Howard, Leslie Ruth, *A Quite Remarkable Father*, New York, 1959.
Memo from David O. Selznick, edited by Rudy Behlmer, New York, 1972.
Howard, Ronald, *In Search of My Father: A Portrait of Leslie Howard*, New York, 1982.
Richards, Jeffrey, *The Age of the Dream Palace: Cinema and Society 1930-39*, London, 1984.

On HOWARD: articles—

Dickens, Homer, "Leslie Howard," in *Films in Review* (New York), April 1959.
Shipman, David, in *The Great Movie Stars: The Golden Years*, New York, 1971.

Richards, Jeffrey, "Speaking for England," in *Listener* (London), 14 January 1982.
Braun, E., "Leslie Howard: Variations on an Enigma," in *Films* (London), July 1982.

*   *   *

In an article he wrote for the *Saturday Evening Post* in 1930, Leslie Howard asserted that "what the actor is in private life, he is to a large extent on the stage, because he cannot conceal himself and his true personality from his audience." Indeed in his films, as well as in plays, Leslie Howard was Leslie Howard—an idealistic, dreamy, upright Englishman. His "natural" approach to acting created a new style in the late 1920s when he became established on Broadway. Rather than adopt the modish and overwrought declamatory style of, say, a John Barrymore, he spoke conversationally, underplaying and relaxing into his roles.

His approach was tailor-made for the screen. He became very popular in the 1930s, a time when Hollywood was a haven for "aristocratic" English actors—Herbert Marshall, Sir Cedric Hardwicke, and Charles Laughton, to name a few. While American actors such as James Cagney and John Garfield slugged their way out of predicaments, the British actors demonstrated the supremacy of brains over brawn. As the Scarlet Pimpernel, for example, Howard fought the French with trickery and daring disguises rather than fisticuffs and swordplay. Whether or not his characters were brave, Howard usually played men of superior intellect—Henry Higgins in Shaw's *Pygmalion*, a writer in *The Petrified Forest*, a violinist in *Intermezzo*, a professor in *Pimpernel Smith*, a well-read humanist in *The 49th Parallel*, and an aeronautical engineer in *Spitfire*.

Unlike Marshall, Hardwicke, and Laughton, Howard was never a villain and frequently played characters who were unrelentingly noble. The effete Ashley Wilkes in *Gone with the Wind* notwithstanding, his nobility usually shone through acts of singular courage—sacrificing his life for Bette Davis in *The Petrified Forest*, risking his life to save others in *The Scarlet Pimpernel* and *Pimpernel Smith*, and fighting the Nazis (in a brains over brawn sort of way) in the aforementioned film and *The 49th Parallel*.

Although he was popular with women, the basis of his appeal was asexual. His characters were charming, witty, honorable, and intelligent; they liked and seemed to understand women. They did not pose the threat of a domineeringly masculine Rhett Butler. According to Molly Haskell, "women's preference for the English gentleman—witty, under-refined, unsexual or apparently misogynous, paternal—is rooted in an instinct for self-preservation.... A woman wants a hero who will look into her eyes and embrace her soul and demand nothing sexually," thereby allowing her to retain her strength and selfhood. Howard's characters liked and respected women (as Howard did in real life) and, with the exception of Professor Higgins, let them be.

Howard appeared in 25 films in 13 years, giving his most acclaimed performances in *Berkeley Square* (nominated for the 1933 Academy Award), *Of Human Bondage*, *The Scarlet Pimpernel*, and *Pygmalion* (nominated for the 1938 Academy Award). Yet he viewed acting principally as a financial means for engaging in other pursuits—writing plays, directing plays and films (*Pygmalion*, *Pimpernel Smith*, and *Spitfire*), and producing (*Intermezzo*, *Pimpernel Smith*). He intended, after the war, to give up acting and to produce and direct both plays and films. But on 1 June 1943, returning from a trip to Lisbon (to lecture on the theater and indirectly on the war), he was shot down by the Nazis, who believed Churchill was on board his commercial airliner. Britain had lost a fine actor and a great patriot. According to David Shipman, "it is no exaggeration to say that no figure in British show business was so deeply mourned, or missed, during this century."

—Catherine Henry

HOWARD, Trevor

Nationality: British. **Born:** Cliftonville, Kent, 29 September 1916. **Education:** Attended Clifton College, Bristol; Royal Academy of Dramatic Art, London. **Military Service:** Served in the Royal Artillery in Norway and Sicily, 1940-43; invalided out. **Family:** Married the actress Helen Cherry, 1944. **Career:** 1934—stage debut in *Revolt in a Reformatory*; then played in repertory; 1938—in West End production of *French without Tears*; 1944—film debut in *The Way Ahead*; 1960—began series of plays and movies for TV. **Awards:** Best British Actor, British Academy, for *The Key*, 1958. **Died:** In Bushey, Hertfordshire, 7 January 1988.

Films as Actor:

1944   *The Way Ahead* (Reed)
1945   *The Way to the Stars* (*Johnny in the Clouds*) (Asquith) (as S/L Carter); ***Brief Encounter*** (Lean) (as Dr. Alec Harvey)
1946   *I See a Dark Stranger* (*The Adventuress*) (Launder) (as Lt. David Bayne); *Green for Danger* (Gilliat) (as Dr. Barney Barnes)
1947   *They Made Me a Fugitive* (*I Became a Criminal*) (Cavalcanti) (as Clem Morgan); *So Well Remembered* (Dmytryk) (as Dr. Whiteside)
1949   *The Passionate Friends* (*One Woman's Story*) (Lean) (as Steve Stratton); ***The Third Man*** (Reed) (as Major Galloway); *Golden Salamander* (Neame) (as David Redfern)
1950   *Odette* (Wilcox) (as Captain Peter Churchill); *The Clouded Yellow* (Thomas) (as David Somers)
1951   *Lady Godiva Rides Again* (Launder) (as guest); *Outcast of the Island* (Reed) (as Peter Willems); *The Gift Horse* (*Glory At Sea*) (Bennett) (as Lt. Col. Hugh Fraser)
1953   *The Heart of the Matter* (O'Ferrall) (as Harry Scobie); *La Mano dello straniero* (*The Stranger's Hand*) (Soldati) (as Major Court)
1954   *April in Portugal* (as narrator)
1955   *Les Amants du Tage* (*The Lovers of Lisbon*) (Verneuil); *Cockleshell Heroes* (Ferrer) (as Captain Thompson)
1956   *Run for the Sun* (Boulting); *Around the World in Eighty Days* (Anderson); *Deception* (Bricken)
1957   *Interpol* (*Pickup Alley*) (Gilling) (as Frank McNally); *Manuela* (*Stowaway Girl*) (Hamilton) (as James Prothero)
1958   *The Key* (Reed) (as Chris Ford); *The Roots of Heaven* (Huston)
1960   *Moment of Danger* (*Malaga*) (Benedek) (as John Bain); *Sons and Lovers* (Cardiff) (as Walter Morel)
1962   *The Lion* (Cardiff) (as John Bullitt); *Mutiny on the Bounty* (Milestone) (as Captain Bligh)
1963   *Man in the Middle* (Hamilton) (as Major Kennsington)
1964   *Father Goose* (Nelson) (as Commander Frank Houghton)
1965   *Operation Crossbow* (Anderson) (as Professor Lindemann); *Von Ryan's Express* (Robson) (as Major Frank Finchman); *Morituri* (*The Saboteur Code Name "Morituri"*) (Wicki) (as Col. Statter); *The Liquidators* (Cardiff) (as Col. Mostyn)
1966   *Danger Grows Wild* (*The Poppy Is Also a Flower*) (Young—for TV) (as Lincoln); *Triple Cross* (Young) (as a civilian)
1967   *The Long Duel* (Annakin) (as Freddy Young); *Pretty Polly* (*A Matter of Innocence*) (Green) (as Robert Hook)
1968   *The Charge of the Light Brigade* (Richardson) (as Lord Cardigan)
1969   *Battle of Britain* (Hamilton) (as Air Vice Marshal Keith Park); *Twinky* (*Lola*) (Donner)
1970   *Ryan's Daughter* (Lean) (as Father Collins); *The Night Visitor* (Benedek)
1971   *Catch Me a Spy* (Clement); *Mary, Queen of Scots* (Jarrott); *Kidnapped* (Mann)
1972   *Pope Joan* (Anderson) (as Pope Leo); *The Offence* (Lumet); *Ludwig* (Visconti)
1973   *A Doll's House* (Losey); *Catholics* (Gold—for TV); *Craze* (Francis)
1974   *Eleven Harrowhouse* (Avakian); *Persecution* (*The Terror of Sheba*) (Chaffey); *The Count of Monte Cristo* (Greene); *Who?* (Gold); *Cause for Concern* (Benson) (as narrator)
1975   *Hennessy* (Sharp); *Conduct Unbecoming* (Anderson); *The Bawdy Adventures of Tom Jones* (Owen); *Der flüsternde Tod* (*Death in the Sun*; *Night of the Askari*; *Whispering Death*; *Blind Spot*) (Goslår)
1976   *Eliza Fraser* (*A Faithful Narrative of the Capture, Sufferings, and Miraculous Escape of Eliza Fraser*; *The Rollicking Adventures of Eliza Fraser*) (Burstall); *Aces High* (Gold)
1977   *Slavers* (Goslår); *The Last Remake of Beau Geste* (Feldman); *Babel Yemen* (Gane) (as narrator)
1978   *Superman* (Donner) (as First Elder); *Stevie* (Enders) (as The Man); *How to Score a Movie* (Enders) (as narrator); *One, Take Two* (*Die Rebellen*) (Megahy); *Vol de nuit* (*Night Flight*) (Davis—for TV)
1979   *Hurricane* (Troell) (as Father Malone); *Meteor* (Neame)
1980   *The Sea Wolves* (McLaglen) (as Jack Cartwright); *Sir Henry at Rawlinson End* (Roberts); *Staying on* (Narizzano—for TV)
1981   *Windwalker* (Merrill) (title role); *Light Years Away* (*Les Années lumières*) (Tanner)
1982   *Gandhi* (Attenborough) (as Judge Broomfield); *The Missionary* (Loncraine) (as Lord Ames); *The Deadly Game* (Shaefer—for TV)
1983   *Sword of the Valiant: The Legend of Gawain and the Green Knight* (Weeks)
1984   *George Washington* (Kulik—for TV)
1985   *Dust* (Hansel) (as the Father); *Time after Time* (Hays—for TV); *God Rot Tunbridge Wells* (Palmer—for TV)
1986   *Foreign Body* (Neame) (as Dr. Stirrup); *Christmas Eve* (Oper—for TV); *Peter the Great* (Chomsky—for TV); *Shaka Zulu* (Faure)
1987   *White Mischief* (Radford) (as Jack Soames)
1988   *The Unholy* (Vila) (as Father Silva); *The Dawning* (Knights)

Publications

On HOWARD: books—

Knight, Vivienne, *Trevor Howard: A Gentleman and a Player*, London, 1986.
Munn, Michael, *Trevor Howard: The Man and His Films*, London, 1989.

On HOWARD: articles—

Conrad, D., "Living Down a Classic," in *Films and Filming* (London), May 1958.
Whitehall, R., "Trevor Howard," in *Films and Filming* (London), February 1961.
Obituary, in *Variety* (New York), 13 January 1988.
Baxter, Brian, obituary, in *Films and Filming* (London), March 1988.

*   *   *

Trevor Howard has the clearly enunciated speech of the English gentleman, and in his youth possessed the modest good looks and unassuming manners that qualified him for stage training at the Royal

Trevor Howard with Earl Cameron in *The Heart of the Matter*

Academy of Dramatic Art. When World War II started he was still in his early twenties, and had had little time to make a mark. After service in the Royal Artillery, he was invalided out, and began to show his high qualities as an actor in repertory at the Arts Theatre in London, while at the same time appearing in uniform in such excellent war films as Carol Reed's *The Way Ahead* and Anthony Asquith's *The Way to the Stars*.

His lengthy roster of British film appearances (usually in starring or top supporting roles) began after his outstanding success as the quiet, sincere small-town doctor, a married man, who falls in love with Celia Johnson's guilt-stricken housewife and mother in Noël Coward's and David Lean's *Brief Encounter*, a film that attracted exceptional critical attention and made a lasting reputation for its authenticity in the wake of the key British war films of 1944-45 that had consolidated the realist style. It matched exactly the quieter, more unassuming characteristics of the middle-class English lifestyle, which could nonetheless be revealed through the intimacy of film to be fraught with hidden emotional disturbances. Moving beyond the efficient, somewhat withdrawn but selflessly loyal English army officer—seen, for example in *The Third Man*, *Odette*, and *Cockleshell Heroes*—Howard gradually enlarged his screen image to embrace the civilian, quietly romantic hero typical of the kind of man many Englishwomen (and others) hoped to meet and marry, the hero of such films as Lean's *The*

Passionate Friends and George More O'Ferrall's *The Heart of the Matter*.

To some audiences, this image of the sincere, good-looking, unassuming but often deeply emotional Englishman could appear to lack dash, even to be dull and unenterprising, except that Howard's intuitive control over the nuances of feeling made these performances dramatically powerful. At the same time, with gathering age and experience, he began even as early as Reed's *Outcast of the Islands* to enlarge his range still further and establish a reputation as a character actor. By the time of *Sons and Lovers* he was playing the miner Walter Morel, morose and difficult in his impoverished, working-class home, to such good effect that he was nominated for an Oscar. He also began to appear in American and Continental as well as British films.

By the 1960s and 1970s, his character range included such fine performances as the corseted, lecherous Lord Cardigan in *The Charge of the Light Brigade*, the toughly independent priest in Lean's *Ryan's Daughter*, Pope Leo in *Pope Joan*, Richard Wagner in the Italian production of *Ludwig*, and his effectively moving Dr. Rank in Joseph Losey's version of *A Doll's House*. He was ceaselessly employed in films for over 40 years, and remained a very favorite actor, especially in the eyes of the British public.

—Roger Manvell

HUDSON, Rock

Nationality: American. **Born:** Roy Harold Scherer, Jr. in Winnetka, Illinois, 17 November 1925. **Education:** Attended New Trier High School, Winnetka. **Military Service:** Served in U.S. Navy in Philippines, 1944-46. **Family:** Married Phyllis Gates 1955 (divorced 1958). **Career:** 1948—personal contract with Raoul Walsh, and film debut in *Fighter Squadron*; 1949—contract with Universal; studied acting with Sophie Rosenstein; 1956—founded first production company 7 Pictures; 1971—series pilot film *Once Upon a Dead Man* led to long-running TV series *McMillan and Wife*, 1971-76, and *McMillan*, 1976-77; 1973—stage debut in *I Do! I Do!*; 1976—toured with *John Brown's Body*; 1978—in TV mini-series *Wheels*, and *The Martian Chronicles*, in TV series *The Devlin Connection*, 1982, and *Dynasty*, 1984-85; 1985—announcement of his having AIDS focused national attention on the disease. **Died:** Of AIDS, in Beverly Hills, California, 2 October 1985.

Films as Actor:

1948 *Fighter Squadron* (Walsh) (as lieutenant)

1949 *Undertow* (Castle) (as detective)

1950 *I Was a Shoplifter* (Lamont) (as store detective); *One Way Street* (Fregonese) (as truck driver); *Winchester '73* (Anthony Mann) (as Young Bull); *Peggy* (de Cordova) (as Johnny Higgins); *The Desert Hawk* (de Cordova) (as Captain Ras)

1951 *Tomahawk* (Sherman) (as Burt Hanna); *Air Cadet* (Pevney) (as upper classman); *The Fat Man* (Castle) (as Roy Clark); *Iron Man* (Pevney) (as Speed O'Keefe); *Bright Victory* (Robson) (as Corporal John Flagg)

1952 *Here Come the Nelsons* (*Meet the Nelsons*) (de Cordova) (as Charles Jones); *Bend of the River* (Anthony Mann) (as Trey Wilson); *Scarlet Angel* (Salkow) (as Frank Truscott); *Has Anybody Seen My Gal?* (Sirk) (as Dan); *Horizons West* (Boetticher) (as Neal Hammond); *The Lawless Breed* (Walsh) (as John Wesley Hardin)

1953 *Seminole* (Boetticher) (as Lance Caldwell); *Sea Devils* (Walsh) (as Gilliat); *The Golden Blade* (Juran) (as Harun); *Back to God's Country* (Pevney) (as Peter Keith)

1954 *Taza, Son of Cochise* (Sirk) (title role); *Magnificent Obsession* (Sirk) (as Bob Merrick); *Bengal Brigade* (Benedek) (as Captain Jeffrey Claybourne)

1955 *Captain Lightfoot* (Sirk) (as Michael Martin); *One Desire* (Hopper) (as Clint Saunders); **All That Heaven Allows** (Sirk) (as Ron Kirby)

1956 *Never Say Goodbye* (Hopper) (as Dr. Michael Parker); **Written on the Wind** (Sirk) (as Mitch Wayne); **Giant** (Stevens) (as Bick Benedict); *Four Girls in Town* (Sher)

1957 *Battle Hymn* (Sirk) (as Col. Dean Hess); *Something of Value* (Richard Brooks) (as Peter McKenzie); *The Tarnished Angels* (Sirk) (as Burke Devlin); *A Farewell to Arms* (Charles Vidor) (as Lt. Frederick Henry)

1958 *Twilight for the Gods* (Pevney) (as David Bell)

1959 *This Earth Is Mine* (Henry King) (as John Rambeau); *Pillow Talk* (Gordon) (as Brad Allen)

1961 *The Last Sunset* (Aldrich) (as Dana Stribling); *Come September* (Mulligan) (as Robert Talbot); *Lover Come Back* (Delbert Mann) (as Jerry Webster)

1962 *The Spiral Road* (Mulligan) (as Dr. Anton Drager)

1963 *A Gathering of Eagles* (Delbert Mann) (as Jim Caldwell); *Marilyn* (Henry Koster—doc) (as narrator)

1964 *Man's Favorite Sport?* (Hawks) (as Roger Willoughby); *Send Me No Flowers* (Jewison) (as George Kimball); *Strange Bedfellows* (Frank) (as Carter Harrison)

1965 *A Very Special Favor* (Gordon) (as Paul Chadwick)

1966 *Blindfold* (Dunne) (as Dr. Bartholomew Snow); *Seconds* (Frankenheimer) (as Antiochus Wilson); *Tobruk* (Hiller) (as Major Donald Craig)

1968 *Ice Station Zebra* (John Sturges) (as Commander James Farraday)

1969 *Ruba al prossimo tuo* (*A Fine Pair*) (Maselli) (as Captain Mike Harmon); *The Undefeated* (McLaglen) (as Col. John Henry Thomas)

1970 *Darling Lili* (Edwards) (as Major William Larrabee); *Hornet's Nest* (Karlson) (as Captain Turner)

1971 *Pretty Maids All in a Row* (Vadim) (as Michael "Tiger" McDrew); *Once Upon a Dead Man* (Stern—for TV) (as Stewart McMillan)

1973 *Showdown* (Seaton) (as Chuck Jarvis)

1976 *Embryo* (*Created to Kill*) (Nelson) (as Dr. Paul Holliston)

1978 *Avalanche* (Corey Allen) (as David Shelby)

1980 *The Mirror Crack'd* (Hamilton) (as Jason Rudd)

1981 *The Star Maker* (Antonio—for TV)

1982 *World War III* (Greene—for TV)

1984 *The Ambassador* (J. Lee Thompson) (as Frank Stevenson); *The Vegas Strip War* (Englund—for TV) (as Neil Chaine)

Publications

By HUDSON: book—

Rock Hudson: His Story, with Sara Davidson, London, 1986.

By HUDSON: articles—

Interview, in *Films Illustrated* (London), August 1980.
Interviews, in *Ciné Revue* (Paris), 23 August and 11 October 1984.
Interview with John Kobal, in *Films and Filming* (London), October 1985.
"Scared Straight," interview with Boze Hadleigh, in *American Film* (Washington, D.C.), January/February 1987.

On HUDSON: books—

Parish, James, and Don Stanke, *The All Americans*, New Rochelle, New York, 1977.
Friedman, Jeannette, *Rock Hudson: The Story of a Giant*, Cresskill, New Jersey, 1985.
Althen, Michael, *Rock Hudson: Seine Filme, sein Leben*, Munich, 1986.
Bego, Mark, *Rock Hudson: Public and Private: An Unauthorized Biography*, New York, 1986.
Oppenheimer, Jerry, and Jack Vitek, *Idol, Rock Hudson: The True Story of an American Film Hero*, New York, 1986.
Gates, Phyllis, with Bob Thomas, *My Husband Rock Hudson*, New York, 1987.
Clark, Tom, with Dick Kleiner, *Rock Hudson: Friend of Mine*, New York, 1989.
Parker, John, *Five for Hollywood*, Secaucus, New Jersey, 1990.
Parker, John, *The Trial of Rock Hudson*, London, 1990.
Royce, Brenda Scott, *Rock Hudson: A Bio-Bibliography*, Westport, Connecticut, 1995.

On HUDSON: articles—

Current Biography, 1961, New York, 1961.
Hicks, J., "Rock Hudson: The Film Actor as Romantic Hero," in *Films in Review* (New York), May 1975.
Obituary, in *Variety* (New York), 9 October 1985.

Rock Hudson

Lippe, Richard, "Rock Hudson: His Story," in *CineAction!* (Toronto), no. 10, 1987.

Davidson, Casey, "AIDS Claims Its First Star: A Sad and Startled Nation Said Goodby to Rock Hudson 10 Years Ago," in *Entertainment Weekly*, 29 September 1995.

On HUDSON: film—

Rock Hudson, television movie, directed by John Nicolella.

* * *

Rock Hudson was an actor who never quite found his niche in Hollywood. Basically a competent performer, and quite a fine one when directed well, Hudson appeared in more than his share of bad movies. He began his film career with almost no training when he appeared in Raoul Walsh's *Fighter Squadron*. Legend has it that 38 takes were required for him to deliver his one line adequately. Hudson literally learned his craft on the job, a luxury not afforded to actors since the demise of the studio system. Although he started at Warner Brothers he moved to Paramount for his next film, William Castle's *Undertow*. Then he appeared in Anthony Mann's *Winchester '73*, Frederick de Cordova's *The Desert Hawk*, Joseph Pevney's *Air Cadet*, and Mark Robson's *Bright Victory*.

Hudson's parts grew longer in a series of adventure films made during Hollywood's last great production splurge: Mann's *Bend of the River*, Sidney Salkow's *Scarlet Angel*, Douglas Sirk's *Has Anybody Seen My Gal?*, Budd Boetticher's *Horizons West* and *Seminole*, and Walsh's *Sea Devils* and *Gun Fury*. In the mid-1950s Sirk, the most influential director in Hudson's career, used him perceptively in a number of better-than-average films: *Taza, Son of Chochise, Captain Lightfoot, Magnificent Obsession*, and *All That Heaven Allows*. The last two movies established him as a leading actor in "women's" films. After a fine performance in George Stevens's *Giant*, he made three additional films for Sirk, two of which, *Written on the Wind* and *The Tarnished Angels*, revealed a depth of character not previously evident in his films.

Hudson's third shift in career came when he was cast in a series of light comedies, several opposite Doris Day. Although the films vary greatly in quality, they afforded Hudson an opportunity to explore his comedic talents. Michael Gordon's *Pillow Talk*, Robert Mulligan's *Come September*, Delbert Mann's *Lover Come Back*, Norman Jewison's *Send Me No Flowers*, Melvin Frank's *Strange Bedfellows*, and Gordon's *A Very Special Favor* culminated with Hudson's comic tour de force in Howard Hawks's slapstick farce, *Man's Favorite Sport?*, in which Hudson gave a performance worthy of Cary Grant at his best.

From the mid-1960s Hudson appeared in a series of mediocre films including Roger Vadim's *Pretty Maids All in a Row*, in which he played an aging lothario who degenerates from a life of sex to violent crime among a bevy of nubile high school girls. He reunited with his *Giant* co-star Elizabeth Taylor for *The Mirror Crack'd*, a big-budget adaptation of an Agatha Christie Miss Marple novel (Angela Lansbury played Miss Marple), an engaging murder mystery that hinted at a career upswing. He also had a major role in the compelling, critically acclaimed 1982 telefilm *World War III*.

Hudson made his last screen appearance in the 1984 telefilm *The Las Vegas Strip Wars*. A year later, while on a trip to Paris seeking medical treatment for an "unstated" illness, Hudson collapsed and the story broke that the actor had been diagnosed with AIDS. And the secret was finally out: the longtime romantic idol of the silver screen was gay. Hudson, his managers, and the studios for which he worked had successfully skirted the rumors of Hudson's homosexuality for years. Hudson believed his career as a leading man would be finished if the truth ever got out. The revelation he had sought to avoid

for years made headlines everywhere after his diagnosis, but it resulted in an outpouring of sympathy and good wishes, rather than scorn, from his many fans in virtually every corner of the globe. His last public appearance at a benefit hosted by former leading lady Doris Day revealed the awful truth of AIDS to the world in vivid and uncompromising terms, Hudson's once strapping figure and handsome face now ravaged almost beyond recognition by the insidious virus. Five years after Hudson's death of AIDS, his secret life and public career became the subject of an inevitable television docudrama, with Thomas Ian Griffith starring as Hudson.

—Charles L. P. Silet, updated by John McCarty

HUNTER, Holly

Nationality: American. **Born:** Conyers, Georgia, 20 March (or 2 February) 1958. **Education:** Attended Carnegie-Mellon University, Pittsburgh, B.F.A., 1980. **Family:** Married the cinematographer Janusz Kaminski, 1995. **Career:** Moved to New York immediately after graduating, worked as waitress and temporary secretary to support herself while acting part-time; 1981—Harvey Weinstein gave her her first film role in *The Burning*; appeared in off-Broadway play *Battery*; 1982—auditioned for Beth Henley's *The Wake of Jamey Foster*, and the playwright was suitably impressed with Hunter's reading, which led to a lead role in *Crimes of the Heart*. **Awards:** Best Actress, New York and Los Angeles Film Critics, Berlin Film Festival, and best actress honors from National Board of Review, for *Broadcast News*, 1987; Best Actress in a made-for-TV movie Emmy Award, for *Roe vs. Wade*, 1989; Best Actress in a made-for-TV movie Emmy Award, for *The Positively True Adventures of the Alleged Texas Cheerleader-Murdering Mom*, 1993; Best Actress Academy Award, Best Actress Golden Globe Award, and Best Actress, Cannes Film Festival, for *The Piano*, 1993. **Agent:** Steven Dontanville, ICM, 8942 Wilshire Boulevard, Beverly Hills, CA 90211, U.S.A.

Films as Actress:

1981 *The Burning* (Maylam) (bit role as Sophie)

1983 *Svengali* (Harvey—for TV) (as Leslie); *An Uncommon Love* (Steven Hilliard Stern—for TV) (as Karen)

1984 *With Intent to Kill* (*Urge to Kill*) (Robe—for TV) (as Wynn Nolen); *Swing Shift* (Jonathan Demme) (as Jeannie Sherman)

1987 *Raising Arizona* (Coen) (as Edwina); *A Gathering of Old Men* (*Murder on the Bayou*) (Schlöndorff—for TV) (as Candy Marshall); *Broadcast News* (James L. Brooks) (as Jane Craig)

1988 *End of the Line* (Russell) (as Charlotte Haney)

1989 *Miss Firecracker* (Schlamme) (as Carnelle Scott); *Animal Behavior* (Jenny Bowen) (as Coral Grable); *Roe vs. Wade* (Hoblit—for TV) (as Ellen Russell/"Roe"); *Always* (Spielberg) (as Dorinda Durston)

1991 *Once Around* (Hallström) (as Renata Bella)

1992 *Crazy in Love* (Coolidge—for TV) (as Georgie Symonds)

1993 *The Positively True Adventures of the Alleged Texas Cheerleader-Murdering Mom* (Ritchie—for TV) (as Wanda Holloway); *The Firm* (Pollack) (as Tammy Hemphill); **The Piano** (Campion) (as Ada McGrath)

1995 *Copycat* (Amiel) (as Detective M. J. Monahan); *Home for the Holidays* (Jodie Foster) (as Claudia Larson)

1996 *Crash* (Cronenberg)

Holly Hunter in *Raising Arizona*

Publications

By HUNTER: articles—

Interview in *Time* (New York), 21 December 1987.
Interview in *Newsweek* (New York), 28 December 1987.
"Hunter Season," in *Advocate* (Los Angeles), no. 634, 1993.
Interview with Jodie Foster, in *Interview* (New York), November 1995.

On HUNTER: articles—

Pooley, Eric, "Hey, Man, It's Holly Hunter: The Relentless March of *Broadcast News*'s Star," in *New York*, 14 December 1987.
Handelman, David, "Three Men and a Lady," in *Rolling Stone* (New York), 28 January 1988.
Mathews, Jack, "No Southern Comfort," in *American Film* (Washington, D.C.), December 1989.
Weinraub, Bernard, "Miss Firecracker's Career Is Glowing Again, and It's Brighter Than Ever," in *New York Times*, 1 July 1993.
Baldinger, Scott, "Fringe Chick," in *Harper's Bazaar* (New York), October 1993.
Kroll, Jack, "The Return of Holly's Comet," in *Newsweek* (New York), 15 November 1993.
Current Biography 1994, New York, 1994.

*   *   *

Despite appearing in a mere 20-odd films (both made-for-television and features), Holly Hunter has proven herself as one of the most versatile actors working today. Her penchant for screwy characterizations, from the beauty queen wannabe in *The Miss Firecracker Contest* to an overly neurotic workaholic in *Broadcast News* to a mute pianist in *The Piano*, has allowed Hunter to leave an indelible mark on the cinema of the past two decades.

Hunter's acting began on the stage, where, after moving to New York City in 1980, she landed work with noted playwright Beth Henley in such plays as *Crimes of the Heart* and *The Miss Firecracker Contest*. Her break into film came when director Jonathan Demme saw her perform and cast her in *Swing Shift* in 1983. Sadly, the film suffered a bad edit job, but Hunter's turn as a war-widow was spirited, and rightly attracted critical attention.

Several appearances in feature and made-for-television movies later, Hunter starred in *Raising Arizona*, which remains one of her finest moments and one of the defining of her career. The film was made by the maverick filmmaking team of Joel and Ethan Coen, and their decidedly offbeat, obtuse style is a perfect match for the wildly eccentric characterizations Hunter does best. Hunter played a cop who marries a convict on parole (Nicolas Cage), a man she had booked many times for robbing convenience stores. What is intriguing about watching Hunter in *Arizona* is her keen ability to take this weird, rather grating character—one which most actors would play flat—and flesh her out to full dimension.

In 1986, Hunter was cast at the last minute as an overly neurotic news program producer in *Broadcast News*, James L. Brooks's acerbic take on television infotainment. If the character was not quite as eccentric as the one in *Raising Arizona*, it did not matter; Hunter brought such boundless energy to the role as to virtually steal the film from its considerable remaining cast, copping several awards as well as an Oscar nomination. Adding to what could be called an Eccentricity Portfolio was her surprise supporting role in *The Firm*, in which she played a rather tarty secretary, picking up another Oscar nomination.

But the biggest and most delightful surprise in Hunter's career came with the 1993 film *The Piano*, directed by New Zealand filmmaker Jane Campion. As with *Broadcast News*, Hunter was not initially seen as a logical choice for the film's lead (at first glance, *The Piano* would more easily be associated with the oeuvre of Meryl Streep). But Hunter exhibits a graceful, elegant power in the film. Playing a mute woman who expresses herself through her piano playing, Hunter was apparently drawn to the role in part because of the film's challenging gender dynamic. Contrary to typical cinematic female roles, Hunter's character is driven primarily by sexual interests, while the two men in the film (Harvey Keitel and Sam Neill) desperately want commitment. Hunter's strengths here are inarguable; she gives the lead in *The Piano* a captivating depth which perfectly matches the profoundly moving tone of the film.

While working on a wide range of feature film characterizations, also of note is Hunter's formal versatility. In addition to her considerable stage work, she has done several made-for-television movies. Hunter won an Emmy Award for *Roe vs. Wade* (1989), in which she played the woman best known as Jane Roe, who with the aid of feminist lawyers, challenged state law on abortion rights and won the landmark U.S. Supreme Court decision guaranteeing a woman's right to abortion. Echoing some of the career choices of Jane Fonda, Hunter cited her conviction in the role as married to her offscreen activist work (Hunter sits on the board of directors of the California Abortion Rights Action League). Another Emmy came with *The Positively True Adventures of the Alleged Texas Cheerleader-Murdering Mom* (1993), in which Hunter plays (with relish) a grotesque southern maternal figure, eager to help her cheerleader daughter claw her way to the top at any cost. Again, Hunter's instinct here appears perfect; the film itself, made for cable television, is a hilarious satire of the based-on-a-true-story made-for-television movie.

While Hunter has a penchant for the offbeat, her talents are not as well served by more conventional films. Her weakest performances have come in her efforts at more normal characterizations, in such films as *Always*, *Once Around*, and *Home for the Holidays*. In *Always*, Hunter seems constrained by the film's simplistic, romantic premise. In *Once Around* and *Home for the Holidays*, the audience's offscreen knowledge of Hunter, and the baggage she carries with her from previous films, makes her portrayal of a woman in dire need of a man ring false. Hunter is clearly best suited to highly unusual, quirky characters.

—Matthew Hays

HUPPERT, Isabelle

Nationality: French. **Born:** Isabelle Anne Huppert in Paris, 16 March 1955. **Education:** Attended Lycée de St. Cloud; Versailles Conservatory; studied Russian at Faculté de Clichy; studied with Antoine Vitz, Conservatoire National d'Art Dramatique. **Family:** Daughter: Lolita, and son: Lorenzo. **Career:** 1971—TV debut in *Proust*; film debut in *Faustine et le bel été*; 1973—stage debut in *Viendra-t-il un autre été?*; 1980—first American film, *Heaven's Gate*. **Awards:** Most Promising Newcomer, British Academy, for *La Dentellière*, 1977; Best Actress, Cannes Festival, and César Award, for *Violette Nozière*, 1978; Best Actress, Venice Film Festival, for *Une Affaire des femmes*, 1989; César Award, for *La Ceremonie*, 1995. **Agent:** Artmédia, 10 av George V, 75008 Paris, France.

Films as Actress:

1971   *Faustine et le bel été (Faustine and the Beautiful Summer; Growing Up)* (Companeez)
1972   *Le Bar de la Fourche* (Levent) (as Annie); *César et Rosalie (César and Rosalie)* (Sautet) (as Marite)

Isabelle Huppert in *Violette Noziere*

1973   *L'Ampélopède* (Weinberg)

1974   *Glissements progressifs du plaisir* (Robbe-Grillet); *Les Valseuses* (*Going Places*) (Blier) (as Jacqueline); *Sérieux comme le plaisir* (*As Serious as Pleasure*) (Benayoun); *Dupont Lajoie* (Boisset); *Le Grand Délire* (*The Big Delirium*) (Berry); *Aloise* (de Kermadec) (title role)

1975   *Rosebud* (*Rape of Innocence*) (Preminger) (as Hélène); *Docteur Françoise Gailland* (*No Time for Breakfast*) (Bertuccelli) (as Elisabeth Gailland); *Je suis Pierre Rivière* (*I Am Pierre Rivière*) (Lipinksa); *Le Petit Marcel* (*Little Marcel*) (Fansten) (as Yvette); *Flash Back* (Coggio)

1976   *Le Juge et l'assassin* (*The Judge and the Assassin*) (Tavernier) (as Rose)

1977   **La Dentellière** (*The Lacemaker*) (Goretta) (as Beatrice, "Pomme"); *Des Enfants gâtés* (Tavernier); *Les Indiens sont encore loin* (*The Indians Are Still Far Away*) (Moraz) (as Jenny Kern)

1978   *Violette Nozière* (*Violette*) (Chabrol) (title role); *Retour à la bien aimée* (*Return to the Beloved*) (Adam) (as Jeanne)

1979   *Les Soeurs Brontë* (*The Brontë Sisters*) (Téchiné) (as Anne)

1980   *Sauve qui peut (la vie)* (*Slow Motion*; *Every Man for Himself*) (Godard) (as Isabelle Rivière); *Orökseg* (*Les* *Héritières*; *The Heiresses*) (Mészáros); *Loulou* (Pialat) (as Nelly); **Heaven's Gate** (Cimino) (as Ella Watson); *La Dame aux Camélias* (*The True Story of Camille*; *La vera storia della signora delle camelie*; *Die Kameliendame*) (Bolognini and Festa Campanile) (as Alphonsine Plessis)

1981   *Coup de torchon* (*Clean Slate*) (Tavernier) (as Rose); *Les Ailes de la colombe* (*Wings of a Dove*) (Jacquot); *Eaux profondes* (*Deep Water*) (Deville) (as Melanie)

1982   *La Femme de mon pote* (*My Best Friend's Girl*) (Blier) (as Viviane Arthaud); *Passion* (*Passion, travail et amour*) (Godard) (as Isabelle); *La Truite* (*The Trout*) (Losey) (as Frédérique)

1983   *Coup de foudre* (*Entre Nous*; *At First Sight*) (Kurys) (as Lena); *Storia de Piera* (Ferreri) (as Piera)

1985   *Signé Charlotte* (*Signed Charlotte*; *Sincerely Charlotte*) (Caroline Huppert) (as Charlotte); *Sac de noeuds* (*All Mixed Up*) (Balasko) (as Rose Marie); *La Plus Grande Musée* (Lander—for TV)

1986   *Cactus* (Cox) (as Colo)

1987   *Les Possédés* (*The Possessed*) (Wajda) (as Maria Shatov); *The Bedroom Window* (Hanson) (as Sylvia Wentworth)

1989   *Une Affaire des femmes* (*Story of Women*) (Chabrol) (as Marie Latour); *La Guerre la plus glorieuse* (Petrovic); *Milan noir* (*Black Milan*) (Chammah) (as Sarah); *La Garce* (*The Bitch*) (Pascal) (as Aline Kaminker/Edith Weber)

1990   *La Vengeance d'une femme* (*A Woman's Revenge*) (Doillon) (as Cecile); *Malina* (Schroeter) (as the Woman)

1991   *Madame Bovary* (Chabrol) (title role); *Becoming Colette* (Danny Huston)

1992   *Apres l'Amour* (*Love after Love*) (Kurys) (as Lola); *Contre l'oubli* (*Against Oblivion*) (Akerman and others) (as herself)

1993   *L'Inondation* (*The Flood*) (Minaev) (as Sofia)

1994   *Amateur* (Hartley) (as Isabelle); *Le Separation* (*The Separation*) (Vincent) (as Anne)

1995   *La Ceremonie* (*A Judgment in Stone*) (Chabrol) (as Jeanne)

1996   *Le Affinita elettive* (*The Elective Affinities*) (Paolo and Vittorio Taviani) (as Carlotta)

Publications

By HUPPERT: articles—

"Claude Goretta and Isabelle Huppert," interview with Judith Kass, in *Movietone News* (Seattle), 14 August 1978.

"Huppert: A Parisian Country Girl," interview with John Simon, in *New York*, 6 October 1980.

Interview with Stephen Harvey, in *New York Times*, 16 November 1980.

Interview with Serge Daney and Serge Toubiana, in *Cahiers du Cinéma* (Paris), May 1981.

Interview with M. Amiel, in *Cinéma* (Paris), February 1982.

Interview with D. Parra, in *Revue du Cinéma* (Paris), April 1985.

Interview with Nick Roddick, in *Cinema Papers* (Melbourne), May 1986.

Interview with Tim Pulleine, in *Films and Filming* (London), January 1987.

Interview with Serge Toubiana, in *Cahiers du Cinéma* (Paris), September 1988.

Interview with M. Buruiana and M.-C. Abel, in *Séquences* (Montreal), March 1989.

Interview with A. Philippon and S. Toubiana, in *Cahiers du Cinéma* (Paris), January 1990.

Interview with D. Roth-Bettoni, in *Revue du Cinéma* (Paris), April 1991.

Interview in *Cahiers du Cinéma* (Paris), March 1994.

On HUPPERT: book—

Ruscart, Marc, *Isabelle vue par . . .*, Paris, 1989.

On HUPPERT: articles—

Yakir, Dan, in *After Dark*, October 1980.

Current Biography 1981, New York, 1981.

Stars (Mariembourg, Belgium), September 1990.

Strauss, F., "Scènes de la passion," in *Cahiers du Cinéma* (Paris), September 1990.

Roth-Bettoni, D., "Isabelle Huppert," in *Revue du Cinéma* (Paris), April 1991.

Schaefer, Stephen, "Femme Fatale," in *Connoisseur*, December 1991.

Allamand, C., "Isabelle Huppert est-elle bête?," in *Rectangle* (Geneva), Winter 1991/92.

Brantley, Ben, "Huppert Star," in *Vanity Fair* (New York), January 1992.

*   *   *

Isabelle Huppert's graduation from brief appearances to substantial roles came quickly. Within five years of making her debut she had achieved prominence as the rebellious middle-class teenager happily losing her virginity in *Les Valseuses* and had earned critical recognition for her exquisitely judged performance as the culturally alienated and sexually exploited "Pomme" of *La Dentellière*. As an unassuming hairdresser thrown into a pressurized student milieu by her immature lover, she copes bravely until, abandoned by him, she has a nervous breakdown. Huppert's understated rendering of internalized emotions, through minimal gestures imbued with tragic poignancy, was outstanding.

Further portrayals of the emotionally repressed or unfulfilled character, often at odds with her sexual or social situation, were to follow. In *Les Indiens sont encore loin* she conveyed the secret anguish of a reserved and emotionally confused schoolgirl choosing death; in *Les Soeurs Brontë* she was a convincing Anne, the most self-absorbed of the frustrated literary sisters; in *Loulou*, a bored middle-class wife falling for a plausible working-class rogue (Depardieu), and suffering the lacerating tensions of class differences; in *Eaux profondes*, a pathetic wife shackled to a perverse husband; in *La vera storia della signora delle camelie*, a demythologizing account of Marguerite Gauthier's life, she was the lonely, unloved heroine; and in *Cactus*, an unhappily married woman who builds a new life with a sightless partner, after losing an eye herself in an accident.

Huppert's performance as the enigmatic murderess in *Violette Nozière* was both an extension of previous roles and a platform for others. A complex figure seeming to dutifully comply with the stuffy constraints of her cramped family life, Violette not only spends her nights as a good-time girl working the hotels but also seeks the death of her parents. Huppert brilliantly projects this disturbing duality: the self-effacing homely girl of earlier films is now dovetailed with the sexual woman of others.

In subsequent roles the image of the sexual Huppert was developed. In *La Garce* and *The Bedroom Window* she was a ruthless femme fatale; in the romantic thriller *Milan noir* she held sway over three men; in *Coup de torchon* she provided temptation for the lubricious Philippe Noiret; as Frédérique in *The Trout* she ensnared men for her self-advancement; while in *Retour à la bien aimée* she is a murderous fetishist's obsession. *La Femme de mon pote* brought a comic variation as she desperately tried to seduce an uninterested disc-jockey played by Coluche. For Cimino she was the charismatic whorehouse madame in *Heaven's Gate*, while for Godard, in *Sauve qui peut*, her role as the jaded prostitute illustrated the vacuity of commercialized sex. In *Amateur*, a typically bizarre outing from the American Hal Hartley, Huppert plays a nymphomaniac yet still virginal nun who leaves the convent to write pornography, whereupon she encounters a sadistic amnesiac pornographer and his porn-queen wife.

Unattractive, morally dubious roles have often been Huppert's domain. Renewing her links with Chabrol she became his wartime backstreet abortionist of *Une Affaire des femmes*, and again in a performance of considerable depth and subtlety, she successfully conveyed the woman's unconscious rationalization of her actions. For Doillon in *La Vengeance d'une femme* she gave a brilliant performance as a cruel yet vulnerable wife sharing the news of her husband's death with his former mistress and making every barbed word count. The following year, however, Huppert suffered her first major failure in a roundly panned title portrayal of *Madame Bovary*—her third film for Chabrol; Huppert's Emma was too level-headed and icy to have so thoroughly ruined her life by the end of the story. She subsequently returned to form, such as in Christian Vincent's *La Separation* in which Huppert and co-star Daniel Auteuil make a fine duet as a couple whose relationship is slowly disintegrating.

Several of Huppert's roles have invited consideration of feminist issues and many of her films have been directed by women, though not necessarily from a feminist perspective. In *Coup de foudre*, Diane

Kurys has her abandon her oafish husband to start a new life with a similarly unfulfilled female friend; in *Orökseg*, Márta Mészáros tackles the issue of surrogate motherhood with Huppert as the child-bearer for a sterile friend and embroiled in subsequent jealousies and rivalries. In Josiane Balasko's challenging comedy *Sac de noeuds*, reminiscent of *Les Valseuses* in its forceful dialogue, she played a suburban platinum-blond having a good time with a virile criminal. For her own sister Caroline Huppert she was an amusing punk rock singer chancing her fortune in *Signé Charlotte*. Again for Kurys, Huppert portrayed a strong-willed novelist trapped between two lovers—one a cad, the other a weakling—in *Apres l'Amour*.

With more than 25 years of cinema behind her, Huppert can claim considerable achievements. As a comic performer she has been engaging; as a seductress she has projected a potent sensuality; as a sensitive exponent of the feelings of the inarticulate she has been peerless. She has enjoyed a rewarding association with female directors, and her roles have reflected her awareness of sexual and/or social conditioning. The quality of most of her recent performances suggest that a great deal is still to come from this talented actress.

—R. F. Cousins, updated by David E. Salamie

HURT, John

Nationality: British. **Born:** Chesterfield, Derbyshire, 22 January 1940. **Education:** Attended Lincoln School; St. Martin's School of Art, London; Royal Academy of Dramatic Art, London. **Family:** Married 1) the actress Annette Robertson (divorced 1964); 2) Marie-Lise Volpelière-Pierrot (died 1983); 3) Donna Peacock, 1984 (divorced 1990); 4) Jo Dalton, 1990, one son: Alexander John Vincent. **Career:** 1962—stage debut in *Infanticide in the House of Fred Ginger*; film debut in *The Wild and the Willing*; 1966-67—in repertory with the Royal Shakespeare Company; from 1970s—in TV plays, including *The Naked Civil Servant*, 1975, and *I, Claudius*, 1976; 1979—in TV mini-series *Crime and Punishment*, and *Red Fox*, 1991. **Awards:** Best Supporting Actor Award, British Academy, for *Midnight Express*, 1978; Best Actor Award, British Academy, for *The Elephant Man*, 1980.

Films as Actor:

1962   *The Wild and the Willing (Young and Willing)* (Thomas) (as Phil)

1963   *This Is My Street* (Hayers) (as Charlie)

1966   *A Man for All Seasons* (Zinnemann) (as Richard Rich)

1967   *The Sailor from Gibraltar* (Richardson) (as John)

1968   *Before Winter Comes* (J. Lee Thompson) (as Lt. Francis Pilkington)

1969   *Sinful Davey* (Huston) (as Davey Haggart)

1970   *In Search of Gregory* (Wood) (as Daniel)

1971   *10 Rillington Place* (Fleischer) (as Timothy John Evans); *Mr. Forbush and the Penguins (Cry of the Penguins)* (Viola) (title role); *The Pied Piper* (Demy) (as Franz, Baron's son)

1974   *Little Malcolm and His Struggle against the Eunuchs* (Cooper) (as Malcolm Scrawdyke)

1975   *Do Yourself Some Good* (Marquand—short) (as narrator); *The Ghoul* (Francis) (as Tom)

1976   *East of Elephant Rock* (Boyd); *La linea del fiume (Stream Line)* (Scavarda); *Shadows of Doubt* (Bolt); *The Island* (Fuest—for TV)

1977   *The Disappearance* (Cooper) (as Atkinson); *Spectre* (Clive Donner—for TV)

1978   *Watership Down* (Rosen—animation) (as voice of Hazel); **Midnight Express** (Alan Parker) (as Max); *The Shout* (Skolimowski) (as Anthony); *The Lord of the Rings* (Bakshi—animation) (as voice of Aragorn)

1979   *Alien* (Ridley Scott) (as Kane)

1980   *The Elephant Man* (Lynch) (as John Merrick); **Heaven's Gate** (Cimino) (as Billy Irvine)

1981   *History of the World, Part I* (Mel Brooks) (as Jesus)

1982   *Partners* (Burrows) (as Kerwin); *Night Crossing* (Delbert Mann) (as Peter Strelzyk); *The Plague Dogs* (Rosen—animation) (as voice of Snitter)

1983   *King Lear* (Elliott—for TV) (as the Fool); *The Osterman Weekend* (Peckinpah) (as Lawrence Fassett); *Champions* (Irvin) (as Bob Champion)

1984   *1984* (Radford) (as Winston Smith); *The Hit* (Frears) (as Braddock); *Success Is the Best Revenge* (Skolimowski) (as Dino Montecurva)

1985   *The Black Cauldron* (Berman and Rich—animation) (as voice of horned king); *After Darkness* (Othenin-Gerard) (as Peter Huninger); *Free at Last* (Lewis) (as narrator)

1986   *Jake Speed* (Lane) (as Sid); *Rocinunte* (Guedes) (as Bill)

1987   "Segment X" of *Aria* (Bryden) (as Garuso); *From the Hip* (Clark) (as Douglas Benoit); *Macheath* (Higgs); *Vincent—The Life and Death of Vincent van Gogh* (Vincent) (Cox—doc) (as voice of Vincent); *Spaceballs* (Mel Brooks) (as himself)

1988   *White Mischief* (Radford) (as Gilbert Colvile); *Nuit Bengali (Bengali Night)* (Klotz) (as Lucien Metz); *Deadline* (Stroud); *Little Sweetheart (Poison Candy)* (Simmons—for TV)

1989   *Scandal* (Caton-Jones) (as Stephen Ward); *Windprints* (Wicht) (as Charles Rutherford)

1990   *Romeo-Juliet* (Acosta); *Frankenstein Unbound* (Corman) (as Dr. Joseph Buchanan); *The Field* (Sheridan) (as "Bird" O'Donnell); *Who Bombed Birmingham? (The Investigation: Inside a Terrorist Bombing)* (Beckham—for TV) (as Chris Mullin)

1991   *King Ralph* (Ward) (as Lord Percival Graves); *I Dreamt I Woke Up* (Boorman) (as Boorman's Alter Ego); *Resident Alien* (Nossiter—doc)

1992   *L'Oeil qui ment (Dark at Noon, or Eyes and Lies)* (Raul Ruiz) (as Anthony/the Marquis); *Mémoire tranquee (Lapse of Memory)* (DeWolf) (as Conrad Farmer)

1993   *Monolith* (Eyres) (as Villano); *Great Moments in Aviation* (Kidron) (as Rex Goodyear)

1994   *Foerraederi (Betrayal)* (Von Krasenstjerna—doc) (as narrator); *Hans Christian Andersen's Thumbelina* (Bluth and Goldman—animation) (as voice of Mr. Mole); *Second Best* (Menges) (as Uncle Turpin); *Even Cowgirls Get the Blues* (Van Sant) (as the Countess)

1995   *Two Nudes Bathing* (Boorman) (as Marquis de Prey); *Rob Roy* (Caton-Jones) (as Marquis of Montrose); *Wild Bill* (Walter Hill) (as Charley Prince); *Saigon Baby* (Attwood—for TV) (as Jack Lee)

1996   *Dead Man* (Jarmusch) (as John Scholfield)

Publications

By HURT: articles—

Interview with D. Toyeux, in *Cahiers du Cinéma* (Paris), November 1984.

"The Outsider," interview with Gavin Smith, in *Film Comment* (New York), March/April 1989.

Interview with J. Smith, in *Skoop* (Amsterdam), July/August 1989.

On HURT: book—

Nathan, David, *John Hurt: An Actor's Progress*, London, 1986.

On HURT: articles—

Current Biography 1982, New York 1982.
Buckley, Michael, "John Hurt," in *Films in Review* (New York), May 1989.
Matousek, Mark, "English Accents," in *Harper's Bazaar* (New York), April 1990.
Winnert, D., "Great Outsider," in *Radio Times* (London), 13 October 1990.
Norman, Michael, "John Hurt: Always in Character," in *New York Times Magazine*, 2 December 1990.

*   *   *

The least macho of any serious (as opposed to comic) actor who has ever risen to a kind of stardom, however sporadic and precarious, the basis of John Hurt's image has always been weakness (physical, but most frequently also psychological) and unhealth (that thin, anxious, pasty face, and that frail body). It is not surprising that the cinema has consistently associated him with affliction. The first film in which he made a really strong impression (playing, typically, a very weak man) was *10 Rillington Place*. His unforgettable Timothy Evans—hapless, nervous, unstable, marginally retarded, eventually executed for a murder he did not commit and constitutionally unable effectively to defend himself—stole the movie from a distinguished cast that included Richard Attenborough as the actual guilty party, notorious British mass murderer John Reginald Christie. Interestingly, Hurt almost did not get the part. He was the last of dozens of British actors to be considered and got the role only when he arrived for his audition and the producers, who had previously dismissed him as a possibility, were stunned by his remarkable resemblance to the real Evans.

Since then, the array of afflictions from which Hurt has suffered on-screen has been formidable indeed, and the enormous weight of makeup under which he played the incomparably afflicted eponymous protagonist of the grim David Lynch film *The Elephant Man*—produced by, of all people, Mel Brooks!—might be taken as symbolic. Homosexuality (*The Naked Civil Servant, Partners*), alcoholism (*Heaven's Gate*), cancer (*Champions*), slimy space creatures erupting out of his chest (*Alien*), transvestism (*Even Cowgirls Get the Blues*), and protracted torture (*1984*) are among the many other crosses he has had to bear on film.

Through all these ordeals Hurt has maintained a remarkable dignity and integrity. If the image constructed by the totality of the roles has become something of a joke (what will they find for him to suffer from next?), the actor has never given a bad performance, and can hardly be blamed for the fact that, in the commercial cinema, if you do not look like Sylvester Stallone you do not get to play *Rambo* (one assumes in any case that Hurt would not wish to). His performances in gay roles, while the persona falls well within a certain cultural stereotyping, go some way in fact towards challenging the conventional view of homosexuality as an affliction; his much-maligned Billy Irvine in the much-maligned *Heaven's Gate*, the extravagantly excessive Cimino film which sank United Artists, actually constitutes a brilliantly realized component in that film's extraordinary total architecture.

Hurt's recent roles have offered him contrasting opportunities: a rare chance to play a conventional "leading man" (one might even say a "romantic" lead as he gets to sleep with Mary Shelley) as the time-traveling scientist in cult director Roger Corman's return to the megaphone after a twenty-year absence, *Frankenstein Unbound*, and a particularly colorful and excessive character-role in the Irish drama *The Field*. There is no question of Hurt's ability to "carry" a film as its star, but only when his character is anything but a conventional lead and has the advantage of eccentric makeup (*The Naked Civil Servant, The Elephant Man*). It is not his fault that he makes very little impression in *Frankenstein Unbound*, as the character (in a highly unconventional situation, but very conventionally conceived) could have been played by almost anyone, and the film, although apparently an instant "cult classic," is really quite bad.

The Field is another matter. Mistaken by some for a quasi-neorealist "slice of life," it is in fact an all-stops-out melodrama with many of the strengths of that genre: vividly realized characters built upon the solid foundation of strong and enduring stereotypes, a relishing of "excess" in performance and direction, and the dramatization of impossible tensions and contradictions within the society. In this context, Hurt's grotesque portrayal of a grotesque character, combining near-imbecility with a disturbingly malicious craftiness, is something of a tour de force, demonstrating once again his versatility and formidable technical control.

—Robin Wood, updated by John McCarty

HURT, William

Nationality: American. **Born:** Washington, D.C., 20 March 1950. **Education:** Attended Tufts University, Medford, Massachusetts; Juilliard School, New York. **Family:** Married 1) the actress Mary Beth Hurt, 1971 (divorced 1982); 2) Heidi Henderson, 1989 (divorced 1993), sons: Sam and William; son with the ballet dancer Sandra Jennings: Alex; daughter with the actress Sandrine Bonnaire: Jeanne. **Career:** 1976—actor with New York Civic Repertory Company; 1979—theatrical film debut in *Altered States*. **Awards:** Best Actor Academy Award, and Best Actor Award, Cannes Festival, for *Kiss of the Spider Woman*, 1985.

Films as Actor:

1978   *Verna—USO Girl* (Maxwell—for TV) (as Walter)
1979   *Altered States* (Ken Russell) (as Eddie Jessup)
1980   *Eyewitness (The Janitor)* (Yates) (as Daryll Deever)
1981   *Body Heat* (Kasdan) (as Ned Racine)
1983   *Gorky Park* (Apted) (as Arkady Renko); ***The Big Chill*** (Kasdan) (as Nick)
1985   *Kiss of the Spider Woman* (Babenco) (as Luis Molina)
1986   *Children of a Lesser God* (Haines) (as James Leeds)
1987   *Broadcast News* (James L. Brooks) (as Tom Grunick)
1988   *A Time of Destiny* (Nava) (as Martin Lawrence); *The Accidental Tourist* (Kasdan) (as Macon Leary)
1990   *I Love You to Death* (Kasdan) (as Harlan James); *Alice* (Woody Allen) (as Doug Tate)
1991   *Bis ans Ende der Welt (Until the End of the World)* (Wenders) (as Trevor McPhee/Sam Farber); *The Doctor* (Haines) (as Jack McKee)
1993   *The Plague (La Peste)* (Puenzo) (as Dr. Bernard Rieux); *Mr. Wonderful* (Minghella) (as Tom)
1994   *Trial by Jury* (Gould) (as Tommy Vesey); *Second Best* (Menges) (as Graham Holt)
1995   *Smoke* (Wang) (as Paul Benjamin); *Confidences a un inconnu (Secrets Shared with a Stranger)* (Bardawil)
1996   *Jane Eyre* (Zeffirelli) (as Edward Rochester); *Michael* (Nora Ephron) (as reporter); *Loved* (Dignam); *Un Divan a New York (A Couch in New York)* (Akerman) (as Henry Harriston)

William Hurt in *Kiss of the Spider Woman*

Publications

By HURT: articles—

Interview in *Films* (London), February 1982.
Interview with Dan Yakir, in *Film Comment* (New York), July/August 1985.
"Zen and the Art of Film Acting," interview with Susan Linfield, in *American Film* (Washington, D.C.), July/August 1986.

On HURT: book—

Goldstein, Toby, *William Hurt: The Man, the Actor*, New York, 1987.

On HURT: articles—

Rickey, Carrie, and Artie West, "The Return of the WASP Hero," in *American Film* (Washington, D.C.), November 1981.
"A New Breed of Actor," in *Newsweek* (New York), 7 December 1981.
Films and Filming (London), September 1984.
Current Biography 1986, New York, 1986.
Rothstein, M., "At Home Again, William Hurt Takes Stock," in *New York Times*, 15 October 1989.

* * *

After compiling a solid résumé of stage credits, blond-haired William Hurt found celluloid stardom in the early 1980s, at which point he was touted as his generation's Robert Redford. In fact, he was nominated by *Time* magazine as "the WASP movie idol of the 80s." But he also is a steadfastly dedicated actor committed to giving intelligent performances, as witnessed by his impressive work in three early films: *Altered States*, his screen debut, playing a scientist who uses himself as a guinea pig in his research experiments; *Eyewitness*, as a janitor enamored of an attractive television reporter; and *Body Heat*, as a lawyer manipulated by a devious femme fatale.

As he might be the first to acknowledge, Hurt has had no movie idol aspirations. He wanted to be an actor first, with versatility and a commitment to craft being his prominent concerns. His ability to thoroughly transform himself into his characters is best exemplified by his performances in two disparate roles. In *Broadcast News*, he plays Tom Grunick, the cardboard-handsome bubblehead whose looks alone allow him to become Washington correspondent of a major network news division, and who is being groomed to anchor the evening news; in *Kiss of the Spider Woman*, he is Luis Molina, the effeminate homosexual prisoner obsessed with the high camp of old Hollywood movies. Tom Grunick is all facade, a pretty boy who has mastered the art of looking good. An original thought has never entered his head, and he must be spoon-fed questions, words, and ideas. Conversely, Luis Molina is all feeling, all emotion. He is coquettish, flamboyant, amusing—and as extroverted as so many of Hurt's other characters are restrained. In both roles, the actor offers knowing performances, inhabiting each character and making him thoroughly believable within the framework of the story.

Quite a few of Hurt's other characters also have been cerebral: the enigmatic Edward Rochester, in *Jane Eyre*; Nick, the rootless, impotent drug-dealing Vietnam veteran who lives out of his beat-up sports car, in *The Big Chill*; James Leeds, the teacher of deaf pupils, in *Children of a Lesser God*; and Macon Leary in *The Accidental Tourist* and Paul Benjamin in *Smoke*, both of whom have been shattered by the premature demise of loved ones. Hurt's ability to project quietude might serve as a mask for his character's sensitivity (as in *The Accidental Tourist* and *Smoke*), or might be plain thickheadedness (as in *Broadcast News* and *Body Heat*). Indeed, as Kathleen Turner's bitch-goddess so properly observes in *Body Heat*, "You're not very bright, are you? I like that in a man."

In the early 1980s, Hurt was considered a hot actor and premier leading man; by the 1990s, he had been stricken from the Hollywood A-list. His inability to maintain a movie star profile resulted from his proclivity for selecting idiosyncratic screen roles. *The Plague* (in which he plays a doctor) is an ambitious but ultimately unwatchable adaptation of the Albert Camus novel, and never even earned a U.S. theatrical release. *Second Best*, in which he offers a sensitive performance as an aging Welsh bachelor who decides to adopt a troubled ten-year-old boy, is not the kind of film to have audiences lining up at movie theaters. In the 1990s, his highest profile roles have come in *Smoke* and *Jane Eyre*. In *Smoke*, he is part of an ensemble; in *Jane Eyre*, Rochester is subordinate to the title character.

Additionally, Hurt's career situation was exacerbated by his various legal scuffles and stormy romantic relationships (most notoriously, a 1989 palimony case brought on by his ex-lover, ballet dancer Sandra Jennings)—a predicament which resulted in his seeming to be more often mentioned in the headlines than the film reviews.

—Rob Edelman

HUSTON, Anjelica

Nationality: American. **Born:** Los Angeles, California, 8 July 1951; daughter of the director John Huston. **Education:** Attended schools in England; trained for the stage at the Loft Studio and with Peggy Furey, David Craig, and Martin Landau. **Family:** Married the sculptor Robert Graham, 1992. **Career:** 1967—film debut in *A Walk with Love and Death*; 1970s—worked as photographic model, New York City, then moved to California with partner Jack Nicholson and took acting lessons; in TV mini-series *Lonesome Dove*, 1989, *Family Pictures*, 1993, and *Buffalo Girls*, 1995. **Awards:** Best Supporting Actress, Academy Award, and Best Supporting Actress Awards, New York Film Critics and Los Angeles Film Critics, for *Prizzi's Honor*, 1985; Independent Spirit Award for Best Supporting Actress, for *The Dead*, 1987. **Agent:** c/o Toni Howard, William Morris Agency, 151 El Camino Drive, Beverly Hills, CA 90212, U.S.A.

Films as Actress:

1967 *A Walk with Love and Death* (John Huston) (as Lady Claudia)
1969 *Sinful Davey* (John Huston); *Hamlet* (Richardson) (as Court Lady)
1976 *The Last Tycoon* (Kazan) (as Edna); *Swashbuckler* (*The Scarlet Buccaneer*) (Goldstone) (as woman of dark visage)
1981 *The Postman Always Rings Twice* (Rafelson) (as Madge)
1982 *Frances* (Clifford)
1984 *This Is Spinal Tap* (Rob Reiner) (as Polly Deutsch); *The Ice Pirates* (Raffill) (as Maida); *The Cowboy and the Ballerina* (Jerry Jameson—for TV)
1985 *Prizzi's Honor* (John Huston) (as Maerose Prizzi)
1986 *Captain Eo* (Coppola—short); *Good to Go* (*Short Fuse*) (Novak)
1987 *Gardens of Stone* (Coppola) (as Samantha Davis); *The Dead* (John Huston) (as Gretta Conroy)
1988 *Mr. North* (Danny Huston) (as Persis Bosworth-Tennyson); *A Handful of Dust* (Sturridge) (as Mrs. Rattery)
1989 *Enemies, a Love Story* (Mazursky) (as Tamara); *Crimes and Misdemeanors* (Woody Allen) (as Dolores Paley)
1990 *The Grifters* (Frears) (as Lilly Dillon); *The Witches* (Roeg) (as Miss Ernst/Grand High Witch)
1991 *The Addams Family* (Sonnenfeld) (as Morticia Addams)
1992 *The Player* (Altman) (as herself)

Anjelica Huston in *The Addams Family*

1993   *Addams Family Values* (Sonnenfeld) (as Morticia Addams); *Man-
        hattan Murder Mystery* (Woody Allen) (as Marcia Fox); *And
        the Band Played On* (Spottiswoode—for TV) (as Dr. Betsy
        Reisz); *Family Pictures* (Saville—for TV) (as Lainey Eberlin)
1995   *The Perez Family* (Nair) (as Carmela Perez); *The Crossing
        Guard* (Sean Penn) (as Mary)

Publications

By HUSTON: articles—

Interviews, in *Inter/View* (New York), April 1974, September 1985,
    December 1987, July 1991, and December 1991.
Interview with Beverly Walker, in *Film Comment* (New York), Septem-
    ber/October 1987.
Interview with Joan Juliet Buck, in *Interview* (New York), December 1987.
Interview with Susan Morgan, in *Interview* (New York), December
    1991; see also July 1991.
Interview, in *Time Out* (London), 11 November 1987.
Interview with Sofia Coppola, in *Interview* (New York), October 1994.

On HUSTON: books—

Grobel, Lawrence, *The Hustons*, New York, 1989.
Harris, Martha, *Anjelica Huston: The Lady and the Legacy*, New York, 1989.

On HUSTON: articles—

Harmetz, Aljean, "Anjelica of the Hustons: Back in the Family Fold,"
    in *New York Times*, 27 June 1985.
Kaplan, James, "Anjelica Rising: Stardom for Another Huston," in *New
    York Times Magazine*, 12 February 1989.
Current Biography 1990, New York, 1990.
Thomson, D., "A Bit of a Coyote, A Hell of a Woman," in *American Film*
    (Hollywood), November 1990.
Hample, Henry S., "Anjelica Huston," in *Premiere* (New York), Novem-
    ber 1993.

*   *   *

In the movie world, nepotism has probably blighted as many careers
as it has advanced. In the case of Anjelica Huston it did both. Luckily
the damage came first, and early, giving her the chance to recover.
By the time opportunity presented itself again she was ready to succeed on her own evident merits.

The daughter of John Huston and his fourth wife, the late Ricky
Soma (to whom she bears a remarkable resemblance), Huston found
herself at age 16 pushed into the female lead in her father's medieval
romance, *A Walk with Love and Death*. Her co-star was the equally
unskilled Assaf (son of Moshe) Dayan. Unhappy about her inexperience and her own looks, she found the whole film "uncomfortable."
Like most of her father's films of this period, the movie was trashed by

the critics—although, again like most of his films of this period, its esteem has improved over the years. Nevertheless, the debacle effectively put her off acting for the next 15 years.

Further unsettled by the death of her mother in a car crash ("It drove me a little mad for five years") she took up fashion modeling, her oblique, elegant features attracting the attention of Richard Avedon and Helmut Newton. At a Hollywood party, an encounter with Jack Nicholson led to a relationship that was to last, on and off, for 17 years.

For most of the 1970s Huston was relegated to being her father's daughter and Nicholson's partner—a status that occasional small screen parts (*Swashbuckler*, *The Last Tycoon*) did little to change. But in 1981 a serious car accident inspired "the need not to waste my life." Ironically, during his own early years in Hollywood, her father had also been involved in a car crash, which claimed a life; the trauma prompted him to turn his life around. With Nicholson's encouragement she took up acting classes and started building a career. Her striking looks and imperious presence gained her strong-women roles in some worthwhile films (Rafelson's *The Postman Always Rings Twice*, as a lion tamer) and some cheerful rubbish (a pirate queen in *Ice Pirates*).

It was John Huston, making amends for her teenage debacle, who offered his daughter her breakthrough role. In his Mafioso black comedy, *Prizzi's Honor*, she played the vengeful Maerose Prizzi, a Brooklyn Lucrezia Borgia, in a lethally funny performance that stole the film from its stars, Nicholson and Kathleen Turner. She herself ascribed her success to the script ("a part so solid that it protected me—one could wear the part like a coat") and to her father's direction. She won a Best Supporting Oscar nomination. Her father was also nominated for his direction, mirroring the 1948 ceremonies when he and his own father, Walter Huston, were nominated (and won) in the same categories for *The Treasure of the Sierra Madre*. History failed to repeat itself, however, and this time, only one Huston, Anjelica, took home the prize.

Huston's elegiac side was superbly drawn out in her father's valedictory masterpiece, *The Dead*, adapted from the James Joyce short story by her brother, Tony. A film of flawless ensemble playing, it found its still center in the moment when Gretta Conroy, about to depart, halts on the stairway transfixed by the memory evoked by an old ballad. Huston played the scene with heart-stopping simplicity, her eyes and whole posture suggesting a grief held inside her for years, like an unborn child.

Huston rounded off the 1980s with four startlingly contrasted performances. Her concentration-camp survivor in Paul Mazursky's *Enemies: A Love Story* was wryly down-to-earth, recognizing with sardonic compassion that time and suffering have matured her far beyond her husband's inept reach. As chief of Roeg's *The Witches* she played the comic-strip villainy to the hilt, pulverizing recalcitrant underlings and changing small boys into mice with mocking relish. For Woody Allen's *Crimes and Misdemeanors* Huston turned her strength into neurotic tenacity, endowing Martin Landau's possessive mistress with an edge of desperation that was painful to watch. And she dominated Stephen Frears's bleak thriller, *The Grifters*, as Lilly Dillon, a predatory survivor driven by her own greed and terror into a downward spiral of destruction.

Huston's appearance is highly distinctive—poised, stylish, often beautiful, but never pretty. There is, underlying her tall, angular physique, a hint of fragility, of a capacity for hurt; naturally suited to tough roles, she can also appear touchingly warm and vulnerable. The one thing she cannot play is ordinary, which made her the ideal Morticia opposite Raul Julia's Gomez in *The Addams Family* (drawn from Charles Addams's macabre cartoons and the classic television sitcom), with her deadpan delivery of every deliciously perverse line. A cameo in Robert Altman's Hollywood broadside *The Player* and a small part among a very large and impressive cast in the made-for-cable AIDS drama, *And the Band Played On*, followed in rapid suc-

cession. Then it was back to comedy with Woody Allen for an ensemble part in *Manhattan Murder Mystery* and a reprise of her role as Morticia in the equally funny sequel, *Addams Family Values*. Her versatility has since shined in the comedy-drama, *The Perez Family*, where she was convincingly Hispanic, and on television as Calamity Jane in *Buffalo Girls*, based on Larry McMurtry's best-seller.

All these roles, in the space of a decade, showed, in case anyone doubted it, how far Anjelica Huston had come as an actress in a career of increasingly impressive potential.

—Philip Kemp, updated by John McCarty

HUSTON, John

Nationality: Irish/American. **Born:** John Marcellus Huston in Nevada, Missouri, 5 August 1906; son of the actor Walter Huston; became Irish citizen, 1964. **Family:** Married 1) Dorothy Jeanne Harvey, 1926 (divorced 1933); 2) Leslie Black, 1937 (divorced 1944); 3) Evelyn Keyes, 1946 (divorced 1950), one adopted son; 4) Ricki Soma, 1950 (died 1969), one son, two daughters including the actress Anjelica; 5) Celeste Shane, 1972 (divorced 1977); also son Daniel by Zoë Sallis. **Education:** Attended boarding school in Los Angeles and at Lincoln High School, Los Angeles, 1923-24. **Career:** 1916—taken to California for cure after doctors in St. Paul, Minnesota, diagnose enlarged heart and kidney disease; 1920s—boxer in California; 1924—actor in New York; 1927—competition horseman, Mexico; 1928-30—journalist in New York; 1930—scriptwriter and actor in Hollywood; 1932—worked for Gaumont-British, London; 1933—moved to Paris, intending to study painting; 1934—returned to New York, editor *Midweek Pictorial,* and stage actor; 1936—writer for Warner Brothers, Hollywood; 1941—directed first film, *The Maltese Falcon*; 1942-45—served in Signal Corps, Army Pictorial Service, discharged as major; 1947—with William Wyler and Philip Dunne, formed Committee for the 1st Amendment to counteract HUAC investigation; 1948—formed Horizon pictures with Sam Spiegel; 1952—formed John Huston Productions for unrealized project *Matador*; 1955—moved to Ireland; from mid-1960s—narrator for TV; 1972—moved to Mexico. **Awards:** Legion of Merit, U.S. Armed Services, 1944; Oscar for Best Direction, for *Treasure of the Sierra Madre*, 1947. **Died:** Of pneumonia, in Newport, Rhode Island, 28 August 1987.

Films as Actor:

1929   *The Shakedown* (William Wyler) (unbilled); *Two Americans* (short)
1930   *Hell's Heroes* (William Wyler) (unbilled); *The Storm* (William Wyler) (unbilled)
1963   *The Cardinal* (Preminger) (as Cardinal Glennon); *The Directors* (pr: Greenblatt) (appearance)
1968   *Candy* (Marquand) (as Dr. Dunlap); *The Rocky Road to Dublin* (Lennon—doc) (appearance)
1970   *Myra Breckenridge* (Sarne) (as Buck Loner); *The Other Side of the Wind* (Welles) (uncompleted)
1971   *The Bridge in the Jungle* (Kohner) (as Sleigh); *Man in the Wilderness* (Sarafian) (as Captain Filmore Henry); *The Deserter* (Kennedy) (as General Miles)
1973   *Battle for the Planet of the Apes* (J. Lee Thompson) (as Lawgiver)
1974   **Chinatown** (Polanski) (as Noah Cross)
1975   *Breakout* (Gries) (as Harris Wagner); *The Wind and the Lion* (Milius) (as John Hay)
1976   *Sherlock Holmes in New York* (Sagal—for TV) (as Professor James Moriarty)

John Huston

1977   *The Rhinemann Exchange* (Kennedy—for TV) (as Ambassador
        Henderson Granville); *Tentacles* (Hellman) (as Ned Turner); *Il
        Grande Attacco* (*The Biggest Battle*; *The Great Battle*; *Battle
        Force*; *The Battle of Mareth*) (Lenzi); *Angela* (Sagal) (as Hogan);
        Hollywood on Trial (Helpern Jr.—doc) (appearance)

1978   *The Word* (Richard Long—for TV) (as Nathan Randall); *El
        Triangulo diabolico de la Bermudas* (*The Bermuda Triangle*)
        (Cardona)

1979   *Jaguar Lives!* (Pintoff) (as Ralph Richards); *Winter Kills* (Richert)
        (as Pa Kegan)

1980   *Il Visitatore* (*The Visitor*) (Paradisi) (as Jersey Colsowitz); *Head
        On* (*Fatal Attraction*) (Grant) (as Clarke Hill); *Agee* (Spears—
        doc) (appearance); *John Huston's Dublin* (McGreevy—doc)
        (appearance)

1981   *To the Western World* (Kinmonth) (as narrator); *John Huston: A
        War Remembered* (Washburn—doc) (appearance)

1982   *Cannery Row* (Ward) (as narrator); *Lights! Camera! Annie!*
        (Kuehn—doc) (appearance)

1983   *Lovesick* (Brickman) (as Larry Geller, M.D.); *A Minor Miracle*
        (*Young Giants*) (Tannen)

1985   *The Black Cauldron* (Berman and Rich—animation) (as narrator); *George Stevens: A Filmmaker's Journey* (Stevens Jr.—doc) (appearance)

1986   *Directed by William Wyler* (Slesin—doc) (appearance)

Films as Director:

1941   **The Maltese Falcon** (+ sc)
1942   *In This Our Life* (+ co-sc, uncredited); *Across the Pacific* (co-d)
1943   *Report from the Aleutians* (doc) (+ ro as narrator, sc); *Tunisian Victory* (Capra and Boulting; directed some replacement scenes when footage lost, + co-commentary)
1944   *The Battle of San Pietro* (doc) (+ ro as narrator, sc)
1946   *Let There Be Light* (doc) (+ ro as narrator, co-sc, co-ph); *A Miracle Can Happen* (*On Our Merry Way*) (King Vidor and Fenton; directed some Henry Fonda/James Stewart sequences, uncredited)
1948   **The Treasure of the Sierra Madre** (+ ro as American tourist, sc); *Key Largo* (+ co-sc)
1949   *We Were Strangers* (+ bit role as bank clerk, co-sc)
1950   **The Asphalt Jungle** (+ pr, co-sc)
1951   *The Red Badge of Courage* (+ sc); **The African Queen** (+ co-sc)
1952   *Moulin Rouge* (+ pr, co-sc)
1953   *Beat the Devil* (+ co-pr, co-sc)
1956   *Moby Dick* (+ pr, co-sc)
1957   *Heaven Knows, Mr. Allison* (+ co-sc); *A Farewell to Arms* (Charles Vidor; direction begun by Huston)
1958   *The Barbarian and the Geisha*; *The Roots of Heaven*
1960   *The Unforgiven*
1961   *The Misfits*
1962   *Freud* (*Freud: The Secret Passion*) (+ ro as narrator)
1963   *The List of Adrian Messenger* (+ bit role as Lord Asthon)
1964   *The Night of the Iguana* (+ co-pr, co-sc)
1966   *La Bibbia* (*The Bible . . . in the Beginning*; *The Bible*) (+ ro as Noah/narrator)
1967   *Casino Royale* (co-d, + ro as McTarry); *Refelections in a Golden Eye* (+ voice heard at film's beginning)
1969   *Sinful Davey*; *A Walk with Love and Death* (+ ro as Robert the Elder); *De Sade* (Enfield; d uncredited) (+ ro as the Abbe)
1970   *The Kremlin Letter* (+ ro as Admiral, co-sc)
1971   *The Last Run* (Fleischer; d begun by Huston)
1972   *Fat City* (+ co-pr); *The Life and Times of Judge Roy Bean* (+ ro as Grizzly Adams)
1973   *The Mackintosh Man*
1975   *The Man Who Would Be King* (+ co-sc)
1976   *Independence* (short)
1979   *Wise Blood* (+ ro as Grandfather, billed as "Jhon" Huston)
1980   *Phobia*
1981   *Victory* (*Escape to Victory*)
1982   *Annie*
1984   *Under the Volcano*
1985   *Prizzi's Honor*
1987   *The Dead*

Other Films:

1931   *A House Divided* (William Wyler) (dialogue, sc); *Law and Order* (co-sc)
1932   *Murders in the Rue Morgue* (Florey) (dialogue, sc)
1935   *It Happened in Paris* (Robert Wyler and Carol Reed) (co-adapt, sc); *Death Drives Through* (Cahn) (co-sc)

1938   *Jezebel* (William Wyler) (co-sc); *The Amazing Dr. Clitterhouse* (Litvak) (co-sc)
1939   *Juarez* (Dieterle) (co-sc)
1940   *The Story of Dr. Ehrlich's Magic Bullet* (*Dr. Ehrlich's Magic Bullet*) (Dieterle) (co-sc)
1941   **High Sierra** (Walsh) (co-sc); *Sergeant York* (Hawks) (co-sc)
1946   **The Killers** (Siodmak) (sc, uncredited); *The Stranger* (Welles) (co-sc, uncredited); *Three Strangers* (Negulesco) (co-sc)
1988   *Mr. North* (Danny Huston) (co-sc, exec pr)

Publications

By HUSTON: books—

Frankie and Johnny, New York, 1968.
The Maltese Falcon, edited by Richard J. Anobile, New York, 1974.
High Sierra, edited by Douglas Gomery, Madison, Wisconsin, 1979.
The Treasure of the Sierra Madre, edited by James Naremore, Madison, Wisconsin, 1979.
The Asphalt Jungle, with Ben Maddow, Carbondale, Illinois, 1980.
An Open Book, New York, 1980.
Juarez, with Acncas Mackenzie and Wolfgang Reinhardt, edited by Paul J. Vanderwood, Madison, Wisconsin, 1983.

By HUSTON: articles—

Interview with Karel Reisz, in *Sight and Sound* (London), January/March 1952.
"How I Make Films," interview with Gideon Bachmann, in *Film Quarterly* (Berkeley), Fall 1965.
"Huston!," interview with C. Taylor and G. O'Brien, in *Inter/View* (New York), September 1972.
"Talk with John Huston," with D. Ford, in *Action* (Los Angeles), September/October 1972.
"The Innocent Bystander," interview with D. Robinson, in *Sight and Sound* (London), Winter 1972/73.
"Talking with John Huston," with Gene Phillips, in *Film Comment* (New York), May/June 1973.
Interview with D. Brandes, in *Filmmakers Newsletter* (Ward Hill, Massachusetts), July 1977.
Interview with P. S. Greenberg, in *Rolling Stone* (New York), June/July 1981.
"Dialogue on Film: John Huston," in *American Film* (Washington, D.C.), January/February 1984.
"Interview with John Huston," interview with S. Hachem, in *Millimeter* (New York), July 1985.
"Filmsa: een gesprek met John Huston," interview with G. Cillario, in *Skrien* (Amsterdam), February/March 1986.
Interview with Michel Ciment and D. Allison, in *Positif* (Paris), October 1987.
Studlar, Gaylyn, and David Desser, editors, *Reflections in a Male Eye: John Huston & the American Experience* (includes interview with and short stories by Huston), Washington, D.C., 1993.

On HUSTON: books—

Davay, Paul, *John Huston*, Paris, 1957.
Allais, Jean-Claude, *John Huston*, Paris, 1960.
Nolan, William, *John Huston, King Rebel*, Los Angeles, 1965.
Benayoun, Robert, *John Huston: La grande ombre da l'aventure*, Paris, 1966; rev. ed., 1985.
Cecchini, Riccardo, *John Huston*, 1969.
Tozzi, Romano, *John Huston, a Picture Treasure of His Films*, New York, 1971.

Pratley, Gerald, *The Cinema of John Huston*, South Brunswick, New Jersey, 1977.

Kaminsky, Stuart, *John Huston: Maker of Magic*, Boston, 1978.

Madsen, Axel, *John Huston*, Garden City, New York, 1978.

Giannetti, Louis D., *Masters of the American Cinema*, Englewood Cliffs, New Jersey, 1981.

Hammen, Scott, *John Huston*, New York, 1985.

Ciment, Gilles, editor, *John Huston*, Paris, 1987.

McCarty, John, *The Films of John Huston*, Secaucus, New Jersey, 1987.

Grobel, Lawrence, *The Hustons*, New York, 1989.

Hart, Clive, *Joyce, Huston & the Making of* The Dead, London, 1989.

The Making of The African Queen: Or How I Went to Africa with Bogart, Bacall, and Huston and Almost Lost My Mind, London 1987.

Viertel, Peter, *Guys and Pals, Dangerous Friends: At Large with Huston and Hemingway in the Fifties*, New York 1992.

Cooper, Stephen, *Perspectives on John Huston*, New York, 1994.

On HUSTON: articles—

"Huston" issues of *Positif* (Paris), August 1952 and January 1957.

Mage, David, "The Way John Huston Works," in *Films in Review* (New York), October 1952.

Laurot, Edouard, "An Encounter with John Huston," in *Film Culture* (New York), no. 8, 1956.

Archer, Eugene, "John Huston—The Hemingway Tradition in American Film," in *Film Culture* (New York), no. 19, 1959.

"John Huston, the Bible, and James Bond," in *Cahiers du Cinema in English* (New York), no. 5, 1966.

Konigsberger, Hans, "From Book to Film—via John Huston," in *Film Quarterly* (Berkeley), Spring 1969.

"Huston" issue of *Film Comment* (New York), May/June 1973.

Bachmann, Gideon, "Watching Huston," in *Film Comment* (New York), January/February 1976.

Jameson, R. T., "John Huston," in *Film Comment* (New York), May/June 1980.

Drew, B., "John Huston: At 74 No Formulas," in *American Film* (Washington, D.C.), September 1980.

Current Biography 1981, New York, 1981.

Millar, G., "John Huston," in *Sight and Sound* (London), Summer 1981.

"John Huston," in *Film Dope* (London), January 1983.

Hachem, S., "*Under the Volcano*," in *American Cinematographer* (Los Angeles), October 1984.

Marill, Alvin H., "The Films of John Huston," in *Films in Review* (New York), April 1985.

Canby, Vincent, "John Huston: A master at His Art," in *New York Times*, 23 June 1985.

Combs, Richard, "The Man Who Would Be Ahab: The Myths and Masks of John Huston," in *Monthly Film Bulletin* (London), December 1985.

"Huston" issue of *Positif* (Paris), January 1986.

Taylor, John Russell, "John Huston: The Filmmaker as Dandy," in *Films and Filming* (London), August 1986.

Negulesco, Jean, "John Huston: l'artiste que a du punch," in *Positif* (Paris), October 1986.

Obituary in *New York Times*, 29 August 1987.

Huston, Tony, "Family Ties," in *American Film* (New York), September 1987.

McCarthy, Todd, obituary in *Variety* (New York), 2 September 1987.

Ansen, David, "A Hollywood Iconoclast: A World-Class Director," in *Newsweek* (New York), 7 September 1987.

Schickel, Richard, "Wicked Gleams of the Good Life," in *Time* (New York), 7 September 1987.

Schulz-Keil, Weiland, and B. Walker, "Huston," in *Film Comment* (New York), September/October 1987.

Buckley, Michael, obituary in *Films in Review* (New York), November 1987.

Combs, Richard, "John Huston: An Account of One Man Dead," in *Monthly Film Bulletin* (London), December 1987.

Immergut, S., filmography and obituary in *Premiere* (New York), December 1987.

Schickel, Richard, "Huston's Serene Farewell," in *Time* (New York), 4 January 1988.

Carpenter, Gerald, "John Huston," in *Video Review* (New York), September 1988.

Literature/Film Quarterly (Salisbury, Maryland), vol. 17, nos. 2 and 4, 1989.

American Film (Washington, D.C.), June 1989.

On HUSTON: films—

On Location: "The Night of the Iguana," television documentary, directed by William Kronick, 1964.

The Life and Times of John Huston, Esquire, directed by Roger Graef, 1967.

Ride This Way Grey Horse, directed by Paul Joyce, 1970.

The Directors Guild Series: John Huston, documentary directed by Crain, 1982.

Observations under the Volcano, documentary directed by Christian Blackwood, 1984.

Huston: The Man, the Movies, the Maverick, television documentary, 1989.

The Making of The Dead, directed by Danny Huston, 1989.

* * *

Directors from John Cassavetes to Quentin Tarantino, Vittorio De Sica to Rainer Werner Fassbinder, have regularly worked in front of the camera. Even casual movie fans know that Alfred Hitchcock made celebrated cameo appearances in his films, and Orson Welles not only directed but starred in *Citizen Kane*.

But one of the most prolific of all actor-directors is John Huston. Certainly, performing was in Huston's genes. His father was the fine actor Walter Huston; his daughter is the equally fine actress Anjelica Huston. In fact, he is the only filmmaker ever to direct a father (for *The Treasure of the Sierra Madre*) and a daughter (for *Prizzi's Honor*) to Academy Awards.

Huston himself was graced with a deep, full, instantly recognizable voice. On occasion he narrated films; he is very much a faceless presence in his three World War II-era documentaries (*Report from the Aleutians*, *The Battle of San Pietro*, and *Let There Be Light*), which he directed while a member of the U.S. Army Signal Corps. His voice adds a certain stature to each film, as he describes the war's various military campaigns over some sobering, graphically realistic footage or illustrates the plight of deeply troubled returning veterans.

But Huston also had a photogenic face and a commanding screen presence, and he could work magic with a solid, juicy role. Had he not been such an outstanding director, he could have carved out a stellar career as a character actor, perhaps one to rival his illustrious father. He gave notable performances in Otto Preminger's *The Cardinal* (as the brusque but benevolent Boston Cardinal); William Richert's *Winter Kills* (as a patriarch whose son, a U.S. president, had been assassinated years earlier); and most especially Roman Polanski's *Chinatown* (as the insidiously evil powerbroker Noah Cross). He effectively directed himself in *The Life and Times of Judge Roy Bean* (as a properly grizzled Grizzly Adams) and *Wise Blood* (as a fire-and-brimstone preacher). While at his very best playing corrupted, hell-bent authority figures, Huston also could play farce, as he did in Marshall Brickman's romantic comedy *Lovesick*, cast as Dudley Moore's psychiatrist (who is predisposed to dropping off into slumberland during their sessions).

Nevertheless, Huston—like Orson Welles—far too often chose to slum on screen, accepting throwaway roles in schlocky films far beneath his stature. His filmography is littered with undistinguished parts in one-too-many potboilers, along with trashy Hollywood fare (most specifically, Christian Marquand's *Candy*, Cy Endfield's *De Sade*, and Mike Sarne's *Myra Breckenridge*). By accepting such work, Huston simply traded in on his name. He phoned in his performance in the minimum amount of time, and with the minimum effort. His reward: a paycheck, no more, no less. Had he been so inclined, Huston might have left us with just as many memorable film roles as films he directed.

—Rob Edelman

HUSTON, Walter

Nationality: American. **Born:** Walter Houghston in Toronto, Canada, 6 April 1884. **Education:** Attended Lansdowne School, Toronto; dramatic classes at Toronto College of Music. **Family:** Married 1) Rhea Gore, 1905 (divorced 1913), son: the director John Huston; 2) Bayonne Whipple, 1914; 3) Nanette Eugenia Sunderland, 1931. **Ca-**

reer: 1902-05—unsuccessful attempt at acting with road company and vaudeville; 1905-09—engineer in electric light and water plants in Montana, Texas, and Missouri; 1909—returned to vaudeville after forming a team with Bayonne Whipple, whom he later married; 1924—Broadway debut in *Mr. Pitt*; also appeared the same year in *Desire under the Elms*; 1929—film debut in short *The Carnival Man*; 1934—returned to Broadway for successful role in *Dodsworth*, later in film version; **Awards:** Best Actor, New York Film Critics, for *Dodsworth*, 1936; Best Supporting Actor Academy Award, for *Treasure of the Sierra Madre*, 1948. **Died:** 7 April 1950.

Films as Actor:

1929   *The Carnival Man* (Abbott—short); *The Bishop's Candlesticks* (Abbott—short); *Gentlemen of the Press* (Webb) (as Wickland Snell); *Two Americans* (Meehan or Santley); *The Lady Lies* (Henley) (as Robert Rossiter); *The Virginian* (Fleming) (as Trampas); *Abraham Lincoln* (Griffith) (title role); *The Bad Man* (Badger) (as Pancho López); *The Virtuous Sin* (*Cast Iron*) (Gasnier and Cukor) (as General Gregori Platoff); *The Criminal Code* (Hawks)

Walter Huston with Mary Astor in *Dodsworth* © 1936, Samuel Goldwyn

1931 *The Star Witness* (Wellman); *The Ruling Voice* (Lee)
1932 *A House Divided* (Wyler); *The Woman from Monte Carlo* (Curtiz); *Law and Order* (Cahn); *The Beast of the City* (Brabin); *American Madness* (Capra); *Night Court* (*Justice for Sale*) (Van Dyke); *The Wet Parade* (Fleming); *Rain* (Milestone); *Kongo* (Cowen)
1933 *Gabriel over the White House* (La Cava) (as President); *Hell Below* (Conway); *Storm at Daybreak* (Boleslawsky); *Ann Vickers* (Cromwell); *The Prizefighter and the Lady* (*Every Woman's Man*) (Van Dyke); *How I Play Golf No. 7: The Spoon* (Marshall—short)
1934 *Keep 'em Rolling* (Archainbaud)
1935 *The Tunnel* (*Transatlantic Tunnel*) (Elvey)
1936 *Rhodes of Africa* (*Rhodes*) (Viertel); *Dodsworth* (Wyler)
1938 *Of Human Hearts* (Brown)
1939 *The Light That Failed* (Wellman)
1941 *The Outlaw* (Hughes); *All That Money Can Buy* (*The Devil and Daniel Webster*; *Here Is a Man*; *Daniel and the Devil*) (Dieterle); *Safeguarding Military Information* (short) (as narrator); **The Maltese Falcon** (John Huston) (as Captain Jacoby); *Swamp Water* (*The Man Who Came Back*) (Renoir); *The Shanghai Gesture* (von Sternberg); *Our Russian Front* (Milestone and Ivens) (as narrator)
1942 *Always in My Heart* (Graham); *In This Our Life* (John Huston) (as barman); **Yankee Doodle Dandy** (Curtiz) (as Jerry Cohan); **Prelude to War** (Capra) (as narrator); *America Can Give It* (as narrator)
1943 *Edge of Darkness* (Milestone); *Mission to Moscow* (Curtiz); *The North Star* (Milestone); *The Battle of Britain* (Vieller) (as narrator); *December 7th* (Toland and Ford); *For God and Country* (Cahn—short) (as narrator); *Know Your Enemy: Japan* (Capra and Ivens) (as narrator)
1944 *Dragon Seed* (Conway and Bucquet) (as Ling Tau); *Pacific Northwest* (*Northwest U.S.A.*) (Van Dyke—short) (as narrator); *Suicide Battalion* (training film) (as narrator); *Knickerbocker Holiday* (Brown) (as Pieter Stuyvesant)
1945 *And Then There Were None* (*Ten Little Niggers*) (Clair); *The American People* (Litvak—short) (as narrator); *War Comes to America* (Litvak—short) (as narrator)
1946 *Let There Be Light* (John Huston) (as narrator); *Dragonwyck* (Mankiewicz); *Duel in the Sun* (Vidor) (as "The Sinkiller")
1947 *Summer Holiday* (Mamoulian)
1948 **The Treasure of the Sierra Madre** (John Huston) (as Howard)
1949 *The Great Sinner* (Siodmak)
1950 *The Furies* (Anthony Mann)

Publications

By HUSTON: articles—

"In and Out of the Bag: Othello Sits Up in Bed the Morning After and Takes Notice," in *Stage*, March 1937.
"There's No Place Like Broadway," in *Stage*, September 1983.

On HUSTON: books—

Huston, John, *An Open Book*, New York, 1980.
Grobel, Lawrence, *The Hustons*, New York, 1989.

On HUSTON: articles—

Grant, J., "Walter Huston Says, 'If I Were Roosevelt—,'" in *Movie Classic*, May 1933.
Vermilye, J., "Walter Huston," in *Films in Review* (New York), February 1960.
Ciné Revue (Paris), 16 October 1980.

* * *

For most of his screen career Walter Huston was typecast as the pillar of American respectability; he was a bank manager in *American Madness*, a successful businessman in *Dodsworth*, a prison warden in *The Criminal Code*, a fictitious American president in *Gabriel over the White House*. In historical roles, Huston was very much a patriarchal figure: President Lincoln in *Abraham Lincoln* and Pieter Stuyvesant in *Knickerbocker Holiday*. Even in *Yankee Doodle Dandy* he is typecast as the father of that ultimate figure of American patriotism, George M. Cohan.

Playing non-Americans Huston was cast in equally conservative roles. He was suitably imperial as Cecil Rhodes in *Rhodes of Africa*. He was kind yet commanding as the doctor/commune head of a Soviet village in that curiously middle-American study of rural Russian life under German attack, *The North Star*.

Huston's performance in *Dodsworth* is masterly and quietly understated, with his eyes and body movements indicating the hurt that he feels at his wife's leaving him. Yet, on the whole, it is thanks to his less typical roles that Huston can be considered as great a screen performer as stage actor. He is tyrannical as the circuit preacher in *Of Human Hearts* and magnificently hypocritical as the "Sin Killer" bent on saving Jennifer Jones's soul in *Duel in the Sun*. Above all he demonstrated a surprising impish quality as the devil in the guise of Mr. Scratch in *The Devil and Daniel Webster*, and as the old prospector (with that wickedly gleeful dance on discovering the gold) in his son John's *The Treasure of the Sierra Madre*.

—Anthony Slide

INFANTE, Pedro

Nationality: Mexican. **Born:** Pedro Infante Cruz in Mazatlán, November-December 1917. **Family:** Married María Luisa León (divorced—but divorce not recognized in Mexican courts); had two children with Lupita Torrentera; lived with Irma Dorantes. **Career:** Left school after fourth grade, and worked as errand boy and carpenter; 1939—singer of *rancheras* on Radio Station XEB in Mexico City; 1942—film debut as extra; 1947—role in *Nosotros los pobres* made him into a celebrity. **Awards:** Mexican Ariele Awards, 1955 and 1956; Best Actor, Berlin Festival, for *Tizoc*, 1957. **Died:** In plane crash in Mérida, 15 April 1956.

Films as Actor:

1942 *La feria de las flores* (Benavides); *Jesusita en Chihuahua* (Cardona) (as Valentin Terraza); *La razón de la culpa* (Ortega) (as Roberto)

1943 *Arriba las mujeres* (Orellana) (as Chuy); *Cuando habla el corazón* (Segura); *El Ametralladora* (Castillo) (as Salvador Pérez Gómez "El Ametralladora"); *Mexicanos al grito de guerra* (Gálvez Fuentes) (as Luis Sandoval); *Viva mi desgracia* (Rodríguez) (as Ramón Pineda)

1944 *Escándalo de estrellas* (Rodríguez) (as Ricardo del Valle y Rosales)

1945 *Cuandolloran los valientes* (Rodríguez) (as Agapito Treviño "Caballo Blanco")

1946 *Si me han de matar manaña* (Zacarías) (as Ramiro); *Los tres Garcia* and *Vuelen los Garcia* (Rodríguez) (as Luis Antonio Garcia)

1947 *La barca de oro* (Paradavé) (as Lorenzo); *Soy charro de Rancho Grande* (Paradavé) (as Paco Aldama); *Nosotros los pobres* (Rodríguez) (as Pepe "El Toro"); *Cartas marcadas* (Cardona) (as Manuel)

1948 *Los tres huastecos* (Rodríguez) (as Lorenzo, Victor, and Juan de Dios Andrade); *Angelitos negros* (Rodríguez) (as José Carlos); *Ustedes los ricos* (Rodríguez) (as Pepe "El Toro"); *Dicen que soy mujeriego* (Rodríguez) (as Pedro)

1949 *El seminarista* (Rodríguez) (as Miguel Morales); *La mujer que yo perdí* (Rodríguez) (as Pedro Montaño); *La oveja negra* and *No desearás la mujer de tu hijo* (Rodríguez) (as Silvano)

1950 *Sobre las olas* (Rodríguez) (as Juventino Rosas); *Tambíen de dolor se canta* (Cardona) (as Braulio Peláez); *Islas Marias* (Fernandez) (as Felipe); *El gavilán pollero* (González) (as José Inocencio Meléndez "El Gavilán"); *Las mujers de mi general* (Rodríguez) (as General Juan Zepeda)

1951 *Necesito dinero* (Zacarías) (as Manuel); *A toda máquina* and *¿Qué te ha dado esa mujer?* (Rodríguez) (as Pedro Chávez); *Ahi viene Martin Corona* and *El enamorado* (Zacarías) (as Martin Corona)

1952 *Un rincón cerca del cielo* and *Ahora soy rico* (González) (as Pedro González); *Por ellas aunque mal paguen* (Oro) (as himself); *Los hijos de Maria Morales* (de Fuentes) (as Pepe Morales); *Dos tipos de cuidado* (Rodríguez) (as Pedro Malo); *Ansiedad* (Zacarías) (as Rafael—father and son); *Pepe El Toro* (Rodríguez) (title role)

1953 *Reportaje* (Fernández) (as Damian); *Gitana tenias que ser* (Baledón) (as Pablo Mendoza)

1954 *Cuidado con el ser* (Baledón) (as Salvador Allende); *Cuidado con el amor* (Zacarías) (as Salvador Allende); *El mil amores* (González) (as Bibiano Villarreal); *Escuela de vagabundos* (González) (as Alberto Medina); *La vida no vale nada* (González) (as Pablo Galván); *Pueblo, canto, y esperanza* (González) (as Lencho Jiménez); *Los Gavilanes* (Oroná) (as Juan Menchaca)

1955 *Escuela de música* (Zacarías) (as Javier Prado); *La tercera palabra* (Soler) (as Pablo Saldaña); *El inocente* (González) (as Cutberto Gaudázar "Cruci"); *Pablo y Carolina* (de la Serna) (as Pablo Garza)

1956 *Tizoc* (Rodríguez) (title role); *Escuela de rateros* (González) (as Raúl Cuesta Hernández and Victor Valdés)

Publications

On INFANTE: books—

Riera, Emilio García, *Historia documental del cine mexicano*, vols. 2-6, Mexico, 1970-74.

Blanco, Jorge Ayala, *La aventura del cine mexicano*, Mexico, 1979.

Mora, Carl J., *Mexican Cinema: Reflections of a Society 1896-1980*, Berkeley, California, 1982.

Blanco, Jorge Ayala, *La búsqueda del cine mexicano*, Mexico City, 1986.

Blanco, Jorge Ayala, *La condición del cine mexicano*, Mexico City, 1986.

On INFANTE: article—

De la Colina, José, "La gran familia del cine mexicano: Pedro Infante," in *Dicine* (Mexico City), October 1987.

*   *   *

Some 30 years after his death, Pedro Infante, the unrivaled idol of Mexican film, remains alive in the culture of Latin America. More a personality than an actor, it could be said that Infante essentially played himself on the screen: an open, uncomplicated, and sincere representative of the people. His most memorable roles cast him as an urban worker or a rural charro, the Mexican cowboy. In contrast to the icy distance of similar male actors such as Jorge Negrete or Pedro Armendáriz, Infante recognized and reveled in the audience's presence, often looking directly into the camera, winking and laughing, while singing his *rancheras*. He charmed everyone but the bad guys as he sang and acted his way through screen vehicles usually constructed around him. Directors, co-stars, and scriptwriters were of secondary importance; everyone from Tierra del Fuego to the Rio Grande went to see Pedro.

Although he demonstrated his acting skills by playing multiple roles in several films, he was at his best in the male-bonding movies such as *Dos tipos de cuidado* ("Two wild and crazy guys") *A toda máquina* ("Full speed ahead"), and *¿Qué te ha dado esa mujer?* ("What did that woman give you?"). In *Dos tipos* Infante pointed to the primacy of the male-male relationship in machismo when he compared treachery by a woman and a man: "When a woman betrays us, well, we forgive her—because finally she's a woman. But, when we're betrayed by the man we think is our best friend—ay, Chihuahua—that really hurts." In *Dicen que soy mujeriego* ("They say I'm a womanizer"—a reference to Infante's off-screen exploits), Infante undercuts the expectation created by the film's title that a typically macho attitude towards women would be displayed. Instead he suggested that it is more virile to suffer than to cause suffering, dolefully complaining, "They say I'm a womanizer who plays around, but I feel lonely."

A folk hero who could be tender or sentimental without compromising his masculine image, Infante met his end in the flamboyant manner that gives meaning to such a character. He felt that although his first wife had made him an actor, God had made him a pilot. Other flyers demurred, describing him as "loco"—a judgment confirmed by several near-fatal crashes prior to the final one. His funeral was a tumultuous event, complete with thousands of mourners, the leading stars of Mexican cinema, and mariachi bands. He is still the idol of the popular classes: his films are shown weekly on Mexican television, his records sell widely, and some 10,000 people attended an event commemorating the 25th anniversary of his death. The vitality of Pedro Infante—his style, grace, and charm—has not lost its allure.

—John Mraz

IRONS, Jeremy

Nationality: British. **Born:** Jeremy John Irons in Cowes, the Isle of Wight, Hampshire, 19 September 1948. **Education:** Studied at Sherborne School and the Bristol Old Vic Theatre School. **Family:** Married 1) Julie Hallam; 2) the actress Sinead Cusack, 1978, sons: Samuel and Maximilian. **Career:** 1971—actor for Bristol Old Vic repertory company; subsequent stage work includes *Godspell*, 1972-73, *Wild Oats* for the Royal Shakespeare Company, 1976, *The Real Thing* on Broadway, 1983, and *The Rover*, *The Winter's Tale*, and *Richard II* for the RSC, late 1980s; 1974—in TV mini-series *Notorious Woman*; 1979—in TV mini-series *Love for Lydia*; 1980—film debut in *Nijinsky*; 1981—role as Charles Ryder in *Brideshead Revisited* mini-series for TV; 1985—directed video promo for Carly Simon; 1990—narrator for TV mini-series *The Civil War*. **Awards:** Best Actor, Award, New York Film Critics, for *Dead Ringers*, 1988; Best Actor Academy Award, and Best Actor Award, Los Angeles Film Critics, for *Reversal of Fortune*, 1990. **Address:** 194 Old Brompton Street, London SW5, England.

Films as Actor:

1980   *Nijinsky* (Ross) (as Mikhail Fokine)
1981   *The French Lieutenant's Woman* (Reisz) (as Charles Smithson/ Mike)
1982   *Moonlighting* (Skolimowski) (as Nowak)
1983   *Betrayal* (David Jones) (as Jerry); *The Wild Duck* (Safran) (as Harold Ackland)

1984   *Swann in Love* (*Un Amour de Swann*) (Schlöndorff) (as Charles Swann)
1986   *The Mission* (Joffé) (as Father Gabriel); *The Statue of Liberty* (Ken Burns—doc) (as voice)
1988   ***Dead Ringers*** (Cronenberg) (as Beverly and Elliot Mantle)
1989   *A Chorus of Disapproval* (Winner) (as Guy Jones); *Danny, the Champion of the World* (Millar—for TV) (as William Smith); *Australia* (Andrien) (as Edouard Pierson)
1990   *Reversal of Fortune* (Schroeder) (as Claus von Bulow)
1991   *Operation Zebracka* (*Zebracka Opera*) (Golan and Menzel) (as prisoner); *Kafka* (Soderbergh) (as Franz Kafka)
1992   *Waterland* (Gyllenhaal) (as Tom Crick); *Damage* (Malle) (as Dr. Stephen Fleming); *Tales from Hollywood* (Davies—for TV) (as Odon Von Horvath); *From Time to Time* (Blyth) (as H. G. Wells)
1993   *M. Butterfly* (Cronenberg) (as Rene Gallimard); *The House of the Spirits* (August) (as Esteban Trueba); *Earth and the American Dream* (Couturie—doc) (as voice)
1994   *The Lion King* (Minkoff—animation) (as voice of Scar)
1995   *Die Hard with a Vengeance* (McTiernan) (as Simon Peter Gruber)
1996   *Lolita* (Lyne) (as Humbert Humbert); *Stealing Beauty* (Bertolucci)

Publications

By IRONS: articles—

Interview, in *Films in Review* (New York), November 1981.
Interview with M. Bygrave, in *Film Comment* (New York), March/April 1983.
Interview with M. Smith, in *Cinema Papers* (Melbourne), July 1984.
Interview with M. Open, in *Film Directions* (Belfast), vol. 8, no. 32, 1986.
"Double Trouble," interview with Karen Jaehne, in *Film Comment* (New York), September/October 1988.
Interview with David DeNicolo, in *Interview* (New York), June 1990.
"A Question of Character," interview with Georgina Howell, in *Vogue* (New York), January 1993.

On IRONS: articles—

Current Biography 1984, New York, 1984.
Hibbin, S., "Jeremy Irons," in *Films and Filming* (London), July 1984.
Dossier on *The Mission*, in *Stills* (London), May/June 1986.
Kennedy, Harlan, "Metamorphosis Man," in *American Film* (Washington, D.C.), November/December 1991.
James, C., "Wrapping Himself inside Enigmas," in *New York Times*, 18 November 1992.
Johnson, Brian D., "Irons Mines a New Vein," in *Maclean's* (Toronto), 11 April 1994.

*   *   *

With his first major role in *The French Lieutenant's Woman* starring opposite Meryl Streep, Jeremy Irons's screen presence as an up-and-coming dramatic actor attracted an enormous amount of attention. Beginning his career on stage, Irons worked with the Bristol Old Vic repertory company and the Royal Shakespeare Company in the 1970s. Throughout his stardom, he has remained devoted to stage performances, with a major Broadway performance *The Real Thing* by Tom Stoppard, and a few productions with the Royal Shakespeare Company in the late 1980s. In that Irons is a relatively young actor,

Jeremy Irons with Geneviève Bujold in *Dead Ringers* courtesy of The Rank Organisation Plc

whose film career has spanned less than two decades, it is far too early to come to any conclusive view of his accomplishment.

Irons's striking matinee idol looks and melodious voice, his classical training and devotion to the theater, have resulted in gratuitous and premature comparisons to the young Laurence Olivier. Although potentially capable of Olivier's range, Irons gives the appearance of being a much more consciously restrained actor than Olivier, one less given to the bravura turn, more concerned with the *repressed* elements in the characters he plays than with their tempestuous external behavior. Even his most flamboyant roles—including his tours de force in *Reversal of Fortune* and *Dead Ringers*—convey the notion that Irons defers instinctively to the subtle nuance and unarticulated silence more readily associated with his parts in works such as Pinter's *Betrayal*, in which characters reveal as little as possible by speaking in ellipses. ("I'm very interested in what one conveys without words because I think it's one of the ways we communicate best in films or plays," he said in 1984. "I hate *acting* acting, seeing the wheels turn," he once told an interviewer. "I dislike the vulgarity of excessive effort.")

The dual roles Irons plays in *The French Lieutenant's Woman* (a screen adaptation of John Fowles's novel by Pinter), complemented by Streep's equally powerful performance, trace the shocking similarities between the Victorian era and its modern counterpart. As Damian Cannon puts it: "A classical tale of passion, betrayal and loss is related using a mixture of Victorian costume drama and contemporary fiction." In the film and the film within the film, Irons successfully portrays two men swamped by the mysterious power of love, or, more

accurately, that of obsession and descending into the spiral of ultimate despair. Marked by his looks of confused desires and an increasingly warped physique and psyche, the two characters, in different time zones, mesh into one perpetual image of loss. Irons's next major role came as the Jesuit priest in Roland Joffé's award-winning film, *The Mission*. Despite the highly problematic, revisionist treatment of eighteenth-century colonialism in South America, Irons and Robert De Niro (playing Father Mendoza, a former slaver) render convincing portrayals of two sides of religious faith. While De Niro relentlessly emits powerhouse forcefulness out of repentance and a hope for redemption, Irons quietly yet unblinkingly sustains an iron will for sainthood through martyrdom.

Irons's acting, however, did not get official recognition until another dual role performance in David Cronenberg's 1988 *Dead Ringers*. Hailed as the best actor of the year by the New York Film Critics, Irons plays Elliot and Beverly Mantle, twin doctors, both gynecologists, both sexually deviant, obsessed men. One is a dashing playboy, the other inhibited and private. One becomes addicted to drugs, the other, in attempting to cure him, becomes hooked as well. One woos women, the other impersonates him in order to sleep with the women his twin has wooed and won. Both die a mutually macabre death. The ingredients of a Cronenberg horror film are present, a fact excessively trumpeted in the film's inappropriate marketing, but the literary screenplay and Irons's dazzling, contrasting performance as the twins properly emphasized the film's true focus on filial obsession and descent into madness.

The most important role for Irons to date, however, came two years later as the mysterious Dutch socialite, Claus von Bulow, in Schroeder's *Reversal of Fortune* in 1990. In this Oscar-winning role, Irons plays a "cold, emotionless, and calculating" (Mark R. Leeper) European aristocrat who has been found guilty of the attempted murder of his wife (played brilliantly by Glenn Close). Hiring a trial lawyer and professor of law Alan Dershowitz to defend him, von Bulow enigmatizes his entire defense team by his immaculately articulate power of speech and cultured yet ominous demeanor demonstrating absolute self-control. With or without words, Irons's performance balances the detached charm and wit of the sophisticated rake of Restoration comedy (who never takes himself too seriously) with an antithetical air of menace calculated to invite speculation that von Bulow may indeed be a man capable of unspeakable acts. It is a difficult role that requires succinctly enunciated words and gesture, speech and the "unspeakable." It is also in a role like this that one sees most clearly Irons's ability to interlace the precision of stage acting and the minute yet significant details that filmic language is best at revealing.

For many, Irons's performances in both Louis Malle's 1992 *Damage* and Cronenberg's 1993 *M. Butterfly* came as a double disappointment. The mediocrity of both films, however, seems less a shock than the cardboard villain he plays in McTiernan's 1995 *Die Hard with a Vengeance*. Simon—brother of the terrorist, Hans, in the first *Die Hard*—is played with an embarrassing combination of Hopperish delirium and Travoltarian pretentious unwit. As the production of a remake of the classic *Lolita* is underway, one cannot help but hope Irons will once again render a heartfelt performance that utilizes his talent to the fullest.

—Mark W. Estrin, updated by Guo-Juin Hong

JACKSON, Glenda

Nationality: British. **Born:** Hoylake, Merseyside, 9 May 1936. **Education:** Attended West Kirby County Grammar School for Girls; Royal Academy of Dramatic Art, London. **Family:** Married Roy Hodges (divorced), son: Daniel. **Career:** 1957—London debut in *All Kinds of Men*; 1963—film debut in *This Sporting Life*; 1964—critically acclaimed role in *Marat/Sade* for Royal Shakespeare Company, London; also made Broadway debut in this role, and played it in film; 1971—in TV mini-series *Elizabeth R*; 1974—on stage as *Hedda Gabler*; from 1970s—continues to work in films and on stage; 1983—joined United British Artists production group; 1985—on stage in *Strange Interlude*; 1988—on stage in *Macbeth* as Lady Macbeth; 1990—selected as parliamentary candidate for the Labour Party, lost election; 1992—elected to House of Commons for the Labour Party, representing Hampstead and Highgate; announced her retirement from acting. **Awards:** Best Actress, Academy Award, National Society of Film Critics Award for Best Actress, Best Actress award, from the New York Film Critics, and D. W. Griffith Award from the National Board of Review, for *Women in Love*, 1970; two Emmy awards for performances in *Elizabeth R*, 1971; Etoile de Cristal, 1972; Best Actress, British Academy, and David Di Donatello award (Italy), for *Sunday, Bloody Sunday*, 1971; Best Actress, Academy Award, for *A Touch of Class*, 1973; Commander, Order of the British Empire, 1978; D. W. Griffith Award from National Board of Review for Best Actress, and Best Actress Award, New York Film Critics, for *Stevie*, 1981. **Agent:** Crouch Associates, 59 Frith Street, London W1, England.

Films as Actresses:

1963 *This Sporting Life* (Anderson) (bit role)
1965 *Benefit of the Doubt* (Whitehead) (documentary appearance in on-stage role)
1967 *Marat/Sade* (Brook) (as Charlotte Corday)
1968 *Tell Me Lies* (Brook); *Negatives* (Medak) (as Vivien)
1970 *Women in Love* (Russell) (as Gudrun Brangwen)
1971 *The Music Lovers* (Russell) (as Nina Milyukova); *Sunday, Bloody Sunday* (Schlesinger) (as Alex Greville); *Mary, Queen of Scots* (Jarrott) (as Elizabeth I); *The Boy Friend* (Russell) (as Rita)
1973 *Triple Echo* (Apted) (as Alice); *A Bequest to the Nation* (*The Nelson Affair*) (Jones) (as Emma Hamilton); *A Touch of Class* (Frank) (as Vicki Allessio); *Il soriso del grande tentatore* (*The Tempter*; *The Devil Is a Woman*) (Damiani) (as Sister Geraldine)
1974 *The Maids* (Miles) (as Solange)
1975 *The Romantic Englishwoman* (Losey) (as Elizabeth Fielding); *Hedda* (Nunn) (title role)
1976 *The Incredible Sarah* (Fleischer) (as Sarah Bernhardt); *Nasty Habits* (Lindsay-Hogg) (as Alexandra)
1978 *House Calls* (Zieff) (as Ann Atkinson); *Stevie* (Enders) (title role)
1979 *Lost and Found* (Frank) (as Tricia); *The Class of Miss MacMichael* (Narizzano) (as Conor MacMichael); *Build Me a World* (Gane—doc) (as narrator)
1980 *Hopscotch* (Neame) (as Isobel von Schmidt); *Health* (Altman)
1981 *Stop Polio* (Keefe—doc) (as narrator); *The Patricia Neal Story* (Page and Harvey—for TV) (title role)
1982 *The Return of the Soldier* (Bridges) (as Margaret); *Giro City* (Karl Francis—for TV) (as Sophie)
1984 *And Nothing but the Truth* (Francis); *Sakharov* (Gold—for TV) (as Elena Bonner)
1985 *Turtle Diary* (Irvin) (as Nearer)
1986 *Man-Made Famine* (Sauvageot)
1987 *Beyond Therapy* (Altman) (as Charlotte); *Business as Usual* (Barrett) (as Babs Flynn)
1988 *Salome's Last Dance* (Russell) (as Herodias/Lady Alice); *Strange Interlude* (Wise)
1989 *The Rainbow* (Russell) (as Anna Brangwen); *King of the Wind* (Duffell) (as Queen Caroline)
1990 *Doombeach* (Finbow) (as Miss); *Open Space: Death on Delivery* (TV doc)
1991 *The Castle* (Foreman); *A Murder of Quality* (Millar); *The House of Bernarda Alba* (for TV)

Publications

By JACKSON: articles—

"One-Take Jackson," interview with G. Gow, in *Films and Filming* (London), January 1977.
Interviews, in *Photoplay* (London), May 1981 and March 1983.
Interview, in *Time Out* (London), 29 October 1982.
Interview with Hal Rubenstein, in *Interview*, May 1988.

On JACKSON: books—

Nathan, David, *Glenda Jackson*, Tunbridge Wells, Kent, 1984.
Woodward, Ian, *Glenda Jackson: A Study in Fire and Ice*, London, 1985.

Glenda Jackson in *Stevie*

On JACKSON: articles—

Current Biography 1971, New York, 1971.
Spunner, S., and P. Longmore, "Glenda Jackson," in *Cinema Papers* (Melbourne), July-August 1975.
Ecran (Paris), March 1978.
Drew, Bernard, "Glenda Jackson," in *The Movie Star*, edited by Elisabeth Weis, New York, 1981.
Silvester, Christopher, "Labour Pains," in *Connoisseur*, July 1991.
Gam, Rita, "Enter Glenda, State Left," in *World Monitor: The Christian Science Monitor Monthly*, July 1992.

*   *   *

A stage-trained British actress, Glenda Jackson worked for the Royal Shakespeare Company and for Peter Brook before entering films. Her first important film performance was the re-creation of her stage role in Brook's filming of his own stage production of the Peter Weiss play *The Persecution and Assassination of Jean-Paul Marat as Performed by the Inmates of the Asylum of Charenton under the Direction of the Marquis de Sade* (*Marat/Sade*). Though not comprehensively distributed, the film excited critics in part because of Jackson's bold performance as the narcoleptic inmate. Critical acclaim and an Academy Award came to her in 1970 for her performance as Gudrun in Ken Russell's adaptation of D. H. Lawrence's *Women in Love*. In a cold and often repellent interpretation, Jackson created a Gudrun who is sexually driven, intelligent, lyrical, and aloof.

Jackson is noted for her full and expressive voice, her theatrical diction, and performances based less on naturalistic precepts than a declamatory theatrical tradition. Her face, though sometimes charged with eroticism, is by no means conventionally attractive, nor is her body, often bared in her films. Her dark, probing eyes are vaguely unsettling, and her mannerisms of touching her tongue to her teeth and curling her lips are both erotic and unpleasant. Her presence, which is considerable, demands attention and attracts the eye; her assured self-consciousness about her technique helps her to create a variety of characterizations. She followed her performance in *Women in Love* by starring in another Russell film, *The Music Lovers*, playing Tchaikovsky's nymphomaniac wife. It was a powerful, all-out performance in a film of such visual and sexual excess that many critics recoiled. Jackson subsequently made a small industry of playing Queen Elizabeth, first in *Elizabeth R*, a series for British television which was more responsible than anything else for gaining Jackson her American stardom, and then in the film *Mary, Queen of Scots*, opposite Vanessa Redgrave as Mary. The two women gave extraordinary and completely different kinds of performances: Jackson's stylized and mannered, Redgrave's more naturalistic and lyrical—a contrast that perfectly expressed the differences between the characters.

The remainder of Jackson's film roles are noteworthy for their variety: as a woman who begins an affair with a married man in an American screwball comedy, *A Touch of Class*, in which Jackson proved surprisingly adept at repartee and slapstick, and for which she won her second Academy Award; as Hedda Gabler in the virtually undistributed *Hedda*, for which Jackson adapted her controversial stage performance and was given an Academy Award nomination; as poet Stevie Smith in *Stevie*, also based on a stage role, which presented a wry and much warmer Jackson than had heretofore been seen; as the contemporary heroine of John Schelsinger's *Sunday, Bloody Sunday*, an examination of a love triangle with a bisexual apex, for which Jackson received another Academy Award nomination; as a conniving and conspiratorial nun patterned after Richard Nixon in the Watergate-inspired comedy, *Nasty Habits*; as Sarah Bernhardt in the underrated *The Incredible Sarah*, in which Jackson was also given the opportunity to portray Bernhardt acting in her most famous roles, including

Joan of Arc and Camille; as an Adlai-Stevenson-inspired, health faddist and possible transsexual, in Robert Altman's comedy *Health*; and as the repressed heroine in the odd, Harold Pinter-written love story, *Turtle Diary*.

Jackson's reputation as a film actress has declined somewhat in recent years, with the critical judgment that her screen persona remains unusually cold, whatever the role, and that her technique, from film to film, tends to be too unvarying. Unlike, say, Meryl Streep, who is the master of accents, Jackson has been unwilling, for example, to adjust her declamatory vocal technique—even in otherwise powerful, biographical performances in *The Patricia Neal Story* and *Sakharov* (both for television), playing well-known women (from Kentucky and Russia) who sound not even vaguely like Jackson. And yet it must be noted that Jackson has garnered extraordinary notice for her stage work in this period, including raves for the 1985 *Strange Interlude* (which has been preserved on video for television) and fascination for her controversial 1988 stage performance as Lady Macbeth. Perhaps the truth is that Jackson has a strong understanding of her own strengths and weaknesses and therefore sees no need to push beyond them; if she has lost some of her passion for acting, she has found her passion for politics and social commitment growing ever greater. Certainly, this political passion has been present as far back as her earliest, professional theatrical experiences (such as Peter Brook's anti-Vietnam play and film, *Tell Me Lies*). Clearly, *Sakharov* interested Jackson because playing Elena Bonner allowed her to make a statement about human rights; similarly, *Business as Usual* was a pro-labor, didactic drama that allowed Jackson to comment upon sexual harassment in Margaret Thatcher's England. Although Jackson made up with director Ken Russell, with whom she had had a falling out, to appear in *Salome's Last Dance* and, more notably, to appear in *The Rainbow* in the role of Anna Brangwen (the mother of Gudrun, the character she played in *Women in Love*), Jackson has virtually retired from acting, since her election to a seat in the British House of Commons, representing a working-class neighborhood for the Labour Party.

—Charles Derry

JACKSON, Samuel L.

Nationality: American. **Born:** Atlanta, Georgia, 21 December 1948. **Family:** Married the actress LaTanya Richardson, child: Zoe. **Education:** Attended Morehouse College, major in theater arts. **Career:** 1970s-1980s—worked in the theater; 1981—made screen debut in small role in *Ragtime*; late 1980s—originated roles of Willie Boy and Wolf on stage in August Wilson's *The Piano Lesson* and *Two Trains Running* at Yale Rep; co-founder of Just Us Theater Company, Atlanta, Georgia. **Awards:** Best Supporting Performance, Cannes Festival, and Best Supporting Actor, New York Film Critics Circle, for *Jungle Fever*, 1991. **Agent:** ICM, 8942 Wilshire Boulevard, Beverly Hills, CA 90211, U.S.A.

Films as Actor:

1981   *Ragtime* (Forman) (as gang member no. 2)
1987   *Eddie Murphy Raw* (Townsend—concert film)
1988   *Coming to America* (Landis) (as hold-up man); *School Daze* (Spike Lee) (as Leeds)
1989   *Sea of Love* (Becker) (as black guy); *Do the Right Thing* (Spike Lee) (as Senor Love Daddy); *Dead Man Out* (Pearce—for TV) (as Calvin Fredricks)

Samuel L. Jackson in *Pulp Fiction*

1990   *GoodFellas* (Scorsese) (as Stack Edwards); *Mo' Better Blues* (Spike Lee) (as Madlock); *Def by Temptation* (Bond III); *A Shock to the System* (Egleson) (as Ulysses); *Betsy's Wedding* (Alda) (as taxi dispatcher); *The Exorcist III* (*The Exorcist III: Legion*) (Blatty) (as Dream Blind Man); *The Return of Superfly* (Shore) (as Nate); *Common Ground* (Newell—for TV) (as the Reverend Bob McClain)

1991   *Jungle Fever* (Spike Lee) (as Gator Purify); *Strictly Business* (Hooks) (as Monroe); *Dead and Alive: The Race for Gus Farace* (Markle—for TV)

1992   *Patriot Games* (Noyce) (as Robby); *White Sands* (Donaldson) (as Greg Meeker); *Jumpin' at the Boneyard* (Stanzler) (as Mr. Simpson); *Juice* (Dickerson) (as Trip); *Johnny Suede* (DiCillo) (as B-Bop); *Fathers and Sons* (Paul Mones) (as Marshall)

1993   *Amos & Andrew* (Frye) (as Andrew Sterling); *National Lampoon's Loaded Weapon 1* (Quintano) (as Wes Luger); *Menace II Society* (Allen Hughes and Albert Hughes) (as Tat Lawson); *Jurassic Park* (Spielberg) (as Arnold); *True Romance* (Tony Scott) (as Big Don); *The Meteor Man* (Robert Townsend) (as Dre); *Simple Justice* (Helaine Head—for TV) (as the Steward)

1994   *Pulp Fiction* (Tarantino) (as Jules Winnfield); *The New Age* (Tolkin) (as Dale Deveaux); *Fresh* (Yakin) (as Sam); *Hail Caesar* (Anthony Michael Hall) (as mailman); *Assault at West Point: The Court-Martial of Johnson Whittaker* (Moses— for TV) (as Richard Greener); *Against the Wall* (Frankenheimer—for TV) (as Jamaal); *Quentin Tarantino: Hollywood's Boy Wonder* (Thompson—doc for TV) (appearance)

1995   *Losing Isaiah* (Gyllenhaal) (as Kadar Lewis); *Kiss of Death* (Schroeder) (as Calvin); *Die Hard with a Vengeance* (McTiernan) (as Zeus); *Fluke* (Carlei) (as voice of Rumbo); *Mob Justice* (Peter Markle)

1996   *The Great White Hype* (Hudlin) (as the Rev. Fred Sultan); *A Time to Kill* (Joel Schumacher) (as Carl Lee Hailey); *The Island of Dr. Moreau* (Frankenheimer)

Publications

By JACKSON: articles—

Interview with David Rensin, in *Playboy* (Chicago), April 1995.
"Sam I Am," interview with Claudia Dreifus, in *Premiere* (New York), June 1995.

On JACKSON: articles—

Williams, L., "Samuel L. Jackson: Out of Lee's *Jungle* into the Limelight," in *New York Times*, 9 June 1991.
Ickes, B., "Jackson Heights," in *New York*, 10 June 1991.

Chambers, Veronica Victoria, "Samuel L. Jackson," in *Premiere* (New
  York), May 1992.
Title, Stacey, "The Main Man," in *Harper's Bazaar* (New York), Feb-
  ruary 1993.
Angeli, Michael, "Samuel L. Jackson Climbs among the Glittering
  Stars," in *New York Times*, 7 February 1993.
Schoemer, Karen, "The 'L' Is for Lucky," in *Newsweek* (New York), 5
  June 1995.

*   *   *

The early career of Samuel L. Jackson closely parallels that of
another exemplary African-American character actor, Morgan Freeman. Both worked for years on stage and had unimportant movie
roles before cementing their reputations in searing, eye-opening, award-
caliber supporting performances.

In *Street Smart*, Freeman played a vicious pimp; in *Jungle Fever*,
Jackson is brilliant as the pitiful, crack-addicted brother of the film's
main character (Wesley Snipes). Jackson's Gator Purify constantly
hits on brother Flipper for money and favors, endlessly and patheti-
cally promising to clean up his life. He is a burden not only to Flipper
but to his righteous parents. Nevertheless, Gator is not just another
stereotypical African-American street hustler, a black villain in a
story whose heroes all are white. *Jungle Fever* is directed by an African American, Spike Lee; while the character serves to mirror a certain very real segment of the urban black population, in the context
of the story it is clear that he represents just one of many aspects of
that community. Jackson's riveting performance did not go unnoticed
by critics. The actor may have failed to earn a well-deserved Oscar
nomination, but he was cited with the first-ever Best Supporting Performance award at the Cannes Film Festival.

After establishing themselves in their breakthrough roles, the careers of Jackson and Morgan Freeman veer in different directions. On
more than one occasion, Freeman has played characters who are
sweetly sympathetic and gentle, while Jackson's roles—even when
cast as a hero or good guy—mostly remain hard-edged and frenetic. In
the 1990s, Jackson has become one of our most prolific movie actors,
consistently bringing a raw, kinetic energy to his work. He appears in
roles of varying lengths in megabudget epics whose scenarios are driven
not by character exploration but by special effects (*Jurassic Park*, *Die
Hard with a Vengence*); less splashier, more character-driven Hollywood fare (*Losing Isaiah*, *Kiss of Death*); made-for-television movies
(*Against the Wall*, *Assault at West Point: The Court-Martial of Johnson
Whittaker*); and high-profile releases of the New Wave of African-
American filmmakers (the Hughes brothers' *Menace II Society* and
Ernest Dickerson's *Juice*, in addition to *Jungle Fever*). Earlier, the
actor also had roles in Lee's *Do the Right Thing* and *Mo' Better Blues*.

Three Jackson performances—each in a very different role—serve
to mirror the actor's unfailing excellence and electrifying screen presence. In Quentin Tarantino's *Pulp Fiction*, he has the showy role of
Jules Winnfield, the bible-spouting hitman who is companion to John
Travolta's Vincent Vega. In Michael Tolkin's *The New Age*, he plays
Dale Deveaux, a "New Age" psychological motivator who shows up in
the film's final section to inspire the main character (Peter Weller).
In Stephen Gyllenhaal's *Losing Isaiah*, he is Kadar Lewis, an attorney
who encourages a former crack addict (Halle Berry) to reclaim her
young son, who has been adopted by a white family.

In each film, Jackson is surrounded by outstanding actors. Yet whenever he is spouting dialogue—whether confronting and confounding
"those who are about to die" in *Pulp Fiction*, or doing his high-
pressure sermonizing in *The New Age*, or declaring that black babies
belong with black mothers in *Losing Isaiah*—all other performers and
all other action around him cease to exist.

—Rob Edelman

JAFFE, Sam

Nationality: American. **Born:** New York City, 8 March 1891 (some
sources say 1893). **Education:** Attended Townsend Harris High School;
City College of New York, B.S. in engineering 1911, Columbia School
of Engineering. **Military Service:** Served in the U.S. Army, 1919.
Family: Married 1) Lillian Talz, 1924 (divorced 1941); 2) Bettye
Ackerman, 1956. **Career:** Taught math at Bronx Cultural Institute
to 1915; 1915—joined Washington Square Players, New York; 1921—
played on Broadway in *The Idle Inn*; 1934—film debut in *We Live
Again*; 1937—in Max Reinhardt's *The Eternal Road*; 1948—co-
founder, Equity Library Theatre, New York; 1961-65—played Dr.
Zorba in TV series *Ben Casey*, and appeared in TV mini-series *QB VII*,
1974. **Died:** 24 March 1984.

Films as Actor:

1934   *We Live Again* (Mamoulian); ***The Scarlet Empress*** (Von
          Sternberg) (as Grand Duke Peter)
1937   *Lost Horizon* (Capra) (as High Lama)
1939   *Gunga Din* (Stevens) (title role)
1943   *Stage Door Canteen* (Borzage)
1946   *13 Rue Madeleine* (Hathaway)
1947   *Gentleman's Agreement* (Kazan)
1948   *The Accused* (Dieterle)
1949   *Rope of Sand* (Dieterle)
1950   ***The Asphalt Jungle*** (Huston) (as Dr. Riedenschneider); *Under
          the Gun* (Tetzlaff)
1951   *I Can Get It for You Wholesale* (Gordon); *The Day the Earth
          Stood Still* (Wise)
1957   *All Mine to Give* (Reisner); *Les Espions* (Clouzot)
1958   *The Barbarian and the Geisha* (Huston)
1959   *Ben-Hur* (Wyler) (as Simonides)
1967   *A Guide for the Married Man* (Kelly)
1968   *Guns for San Sebastian* (Verneuil) (as Father Joseph)
1969   *The Great Bank Robbery* (Averback) (as Brother Lilac); *Night
          Gallery* (Shear)
1970   *The Kremlin Letter* (Huston); *Quarantined* (Penn—for TV);
          The Old Man Who Cried Wolf (Grauman—for TV); *The
          Dunwich Horror* (Haller) (as Old Whateley)
1971   *Bedknobs and Broomsticks* (Stevenson); *Sam Hill: Who
          Killed the Mysterious Mr. Foster?* (Cook—for TV)
1980   *Battle beyond the Stars* (Murakami); *Nothing Lasts Forever*
          (Schiller)

Publications

On JAFFE: books—

Huston, John, *An Open Book*, New York, 1972.
Young, Jordan R., *Reel Characters: Great Movie Character Actors*,
  Beverly Hills, California, 1986.

On JAFFE: article—

Obituary, in *Revue du Cinéma* (Paris), July/August 1984.

*   *   *

Sam Jaffe acted for over a decade on the New York stage before he
went to Hollywood in 1933. He was a "commuter" from then on, shut-
tling back and forth between the two coasts and his two professions.

Considered one of the great character actors, Jaffe always specialized in eccentric personalities: the mad Grand Duke Peter in *The Scarlet Empress*, the outrageous ex-convict Dr. Riedenschneider in *The Asphalt Jungle*, and the humble and suicidally loyal Gunga Din. His best-known and most beloved role was that of the 250-year-old High Lama in Frank Capra's classic *Lost Horizon*. Although he appeared in only one brief scene, his performance was the highlight of the film, etching itself permanently into one's memory. The ability consistently to turn the smallest of roles into a virtuoso moment was the key factor of Jaffe's career. This talent continued into the 1960s as evidenced by his portrayal of Dr. Zorba on the television series *Ben Casey*.

Giving an overview of his more than 50-year career in three media, he avowed a preference for the stage. "The movies take the cream off the top, and television is movies in a pressure cooker. The theatre gives you a better chance to develop character." Over 90 years old, Jaffe continued to work, playing the villainous head of a space station in *Battle beyond the Stars* and later appearing in *Nothing Lasts Forever*. During one of his last interviews, Jaffe announced that he was still looking for more roles. "When you stop working, you're dead."

—Constance Clark

JANNINGS, Emil

Nationality: Austrian. **Born:** Theodor Friedrich Emil Janenz in Rohrschach, Switzerland, 23 July 1884, of American father and German mother; naturalized Austrian citizen, 1947. **Family:** Married 1) Hanna Ralph; 2) Lucie Höflich; 3) the actress Gussy Holl. **Career:** After a short stint as a cook on a cargo boat, joined Gardelegen theater company at age 18; 1906—joined Max Reinhardt's Berlin theater as established actor; 1914—film debut in *Im Schützengraben*; 1927-29—made several films in Hollywood; early 1930s—formed the Deutsches Theater in Berlin; 1934—supervisor of State Theater; 1938—chairman of Tobis Film Company, which produced his films; 1941—became Artist of the State; 1944—last film *Wo ist Herr Belling?* not completed; blacklisted after the war, and made no more films though he was officially "de-Nazified." **Awards:** Best Actor Academy Award for *The Last Command* and *The Way of All Flesh*, 1927-28; Best Actor, Venice Festival, for *Der Herrscher*, 1937. **Died:** In Stroblhof, Austria, 2 January 1950.

Films as Actor:

1914   *Im Schützengraben* (Schmidthässler)
1916   *Frau Eva* (Wiene); *Im Angesicht des Toten*; *Aus Mangel an Beweisen* (Edel); *Passionels Tagebuch* (Ralph); *Stein unter Steinen* (Basch); *Nächte des Grauens* (Robison); *Der Zehnte Pavillon der Zitadelle* (Kaden); *Die Bettlerin von St. Marien* (Halm); *Unheilbar* (Hanus)
1917   *Die Ehe der Luise Rohrbach* (Biebrach); *Das Geschäft* (Reicher); *Lulu* (von Antalffy); *Wenn vier dasselbe tun* (Lubitsch); *Das Fidele Gefängnis* (Lubitsch); *Der Ring der Giuditta Foscari* (Halm)
1918   *Nach zwanzig Jahren* (Zeyn); *Die Augen der Mumie Ma* (*The Eyes of the Mummy*) (Lubitsch) (as Radu)
1918-19   *Keimendes Leben* (2 parts) (Jacoby)
1919   *Der Mann der Tat* (Janson); *Vendetta* (Jacoby); *Die Tochter des Mehemed* (Halm); *Madame DuBarry* (*Passion*) (Lubitsch) (as Louis XV)

1920   *Kohlhiesels Töchter* (Lubitsch) (as Peer Xavero); *Die Brüder Karamasoff* (*The Brothers Karamazov*) (Froelich) (as Mitya); *Das grosse Licht* (Henning); *Algol* (Werckmeister); *Colombine* (Hartwig); *Der Schädel der Pharaonentochter* (Tollen); *Anna Boleyn* (Lubitsch) (as Henry VIII)
1921   *Der Stier von Olivera* (Schönfelder); *Der Schwur des Peter Hergatz* (Halm); *Danton* (Buchowetzki) (title role); *Die Ratten* (Kobe); *Das Weib des Pharao* (*Loves of Pharaoh*) (Lubitsch) (as Amenes)
1922   *Othello* (Buchowetzki) (title role); *Peter der Grosse* (Buchowetzki) (title role)
1923   *Tragödie der Liebe* (May) (as Ombrade); *Alles für Geld* (*Fortune's Fool*) (Schünzel); *Das Wachsfigurenkabinett* (*Waxworks*) (Leni) (as Haroun-al-Rachid); *Quo Vadis* (Jacoby and d'Annunzio) (as Nero)
1924   *Nju* (*Husbands or Lovers*) (Czinner); ***Der letzte Mann*** (*The Last Laugh*) (Murnau) (as Doorman)
1925   *Liebe macht blind* (Mendes); ***Variété*** (Dupont) (as Boss); *Tartuff* (*Herr Tartuff*) (Murnau) (title role)
1926   *Faust: Eine deutsche Volkssage* (Murnau) (as Mephisto)
1927   *The Way of All Flesh* (Fleming) (as August Schillings)
1928   *The Last Command* (von Sternberg); *The Street of Sin* (*King of Soho*) (Stiller); *The Patriot* (Lubitsch) (as Paul I); *Sins of the Father* (Berger)
1929   *Betrayal* (Milestone)
1930   ***Der blaue Engel*** (*The Blue Angel*) (von Sternberg) (as Prof. Unrath); *Liebling der Götter* (*Darling of the Gods*) (Schwartz)
1931   *Stürme der Leidenschaft* (*Storms of Passion*) (Siodmak)
1933   *Die Abenteur des Königs Pausole* (*König Pausole*; *The Merry Monarch*) (Granowsky) (title role)
1934   *Der schwarze Walfisch* (Wendhausen) (as César)
1935   *Der alte und der junge König* (Steinhoff)
1936   *Traumulus* (Froelich)
1937   *Der Herrscher* (Harlan); *Der zerbrochene Krug* (Ucicky)
1939   *Robert Koch* (Steinhoff) (title role)
1941   *Ohm Krüger* (Steinhoff) (as Krüger)
1942   *Die Entlassung* (Liebeneiner) (as Bismarck, + pr)
1943   *Altes Herz wird wieder jung* (Engel)
1944   *Wo ist Herr Belling?* (Engel—unfinished)

Publications

By JANNINGS: books—

Wie ich zum Film kam, edited by Kurt Mühsam and Egon Jacobsohn, Berlin, 1926.
Das Filmgesicht, edited by Wolfgang Martini and Margarete Lange-Kosak, Munich, 1928.
Wir über uns selbst, edited by Hermann Treuner, Berlin, 1928.
Theater und Film, edited by C. C. Bergius, Berchtesgaden, 1951, as *Theater, Film, Das Leben, und Ich*, edited by C. C. Bergius, Berchtesgaden, 1961.

On JANNINGS: books—

Mitry, Jean, *Emil Jannings*, Paris, 1927.
Bie, Richard, *Emil Jannings*, Berlin, 1936.
Ihering, Herbert, *Emil Jannings*, Heidelberg, 1941.
Kurtz, Rudolf, *Emil Jannings*, Berlin, 1942.

On JANNINGS: articles—

Johnson, Julian, "A Visit with Emil Jannings," in *Photoplay* (New York), February 1926.

Emil Jannings with Pola Negri in *Madame DuBarry*

Smith, Frederick, "The Big Boy from Berlin Is Here," in *Photoplay* (New York), December 1926.

Tully, Jim, "Emil Jannings," in *Vanity Fair* (New York), November 1927.

Collier, Lionel, "Something in the Herr," in *Pictures and Picturegoer*, January 1929; also September 1930.

Dreyer, Carl, "Sur un film de Jannings," and "Du jeu de l'acteur," in *Cahiers du Cinéma* (Paris), January 1962.

Ford, Charles, "Emil Jannings," in *Anthologie du Cinéma*, vol 5, Paris, 1969.

Truscott, Harold, "Emil Jannings—A Personal View," in *Silent Picture* (London), Autumn 1970.

"Emil Jannings," in *Film Dope* (London), July 1983.

*   *   *

One of the great pleasures of film-going in the mid-1920s was to see the latest film starring the well-known German actor Emil Jannings. Of all the theater people who lent their talents to the new medium, he was arguably the greatest. In the 1920s he created a gallery of historical characters as well as people of his own time. Just after World War I,

German films were not welcomed in the Allied countries, a fact advertised by numerous distribution companies. One of the first films to break this embargo was Ernst Lubitsch's *Madame DuBarry*. Made in 1919 by an industry remarkable for its technical skills and the high artistic quality of its product, it was not released in the United States and western Europe until years later. Jannings portrayed Louis XV of France, making an impact that was to continue through his career.

Born of an American father and a German mother, the young Theodor Friedrich Emil Janenz took his first job as an assistant cook on a small cargo boat bound for London. Returning home, he toured Central Europe for a number of years as a member of the Gardelegen troupe of stage players. Eventually he joined the company of theatrical genius Max Reinhardt where his colleagues included Conrad Veidt, Werner Kraus, Paul Wegener, Lucie Hoflich, and Ernst Lubitsch. In 1914 he worked in some minor films and the following year he played in *Nächte des Grauens*, a typical horror film of its time. He then appeared in his first starring role in *Frau Eva*. Next Jannings was directed in three films by his old friend Lubitsch, of which the most important was *Die Augen der Mumie Ma*, before appearing in Lubitsch's spectacular *Madame DuBarry*.

Jannings furthered his popularity and status by making a number of films with the actress Henny Porten and the director Dmitri Buchowetzki. By 1924 he had established a worldwide reputation as a great actor. He starred with Conrad Veidt and Elisabeth Bergner in Paul Czinner's *Nju* and as the jealous trapeze artist in E. A. Dupont's *Variété*. His association with F. W. Murnau lead to the three masterpieces which will be his monument: *Der letzte Mann*, *Tartuffe*, and *Faust*. In *Der letzte Mann* he gave what most consider his greatest performance as an old hotel porter too weak for his job, who is reduced to working in the basement lavatories. His smug Tartuffe was full of subtle nuance, while his Mephistopheles was played with a slightly humorous cynicism that still suggested the blazing anarchy underneath. Even with an ego as great as his talent, Jannings subordinated himself to the disciplines of his art.

Jannings now sought a larger field for his activities and accepted an invitation from Paramount to play in the United States. Many of his old colleagues had already travelled west. He moved to Hollywood where he lived like a prince with his wife, Gussy. His first two films for Paramount, *The Way of All Flesh* and *The Last Command*, exploited his amazing capacity for the portrayal of suffering, and secured for Jannings the first Academy Award for best actor of 1927-28.

With the emergence of sound, Jannings returned to Germany, beginning a new career with the film best known to the present generation—*Der blaue Engel*. Jannings portrayed an old professor dragged to his destruction by an amoral cabaret singer played by Marlene Dietrich. Throughout the 1930s he continued to play large roles in film adaptations of Pierre Louys and Marcel Pagnol as well as more Germanic subjects such as Hauptmann's *Vor Sonnenuntergang* (*Der Herrscher*) and von Kleist's *Der zerbrochene Krug*.

With Hitler's rise to power, Jannings took full advantage of the opportunities the regime offered, playing in films that expressed the new morality and gave him good parts. His last film, *Wo ist Herr Belling?*, was never completed due to his suffering from intense neurasthenia. At the end of the war he retired to his estate on the Saltzkammergut in Austria. Much derogatory criticism has been written about Jannings's role within the Nazi regime. One writer would even remark, "Jannings was a miserable human being . . . uncultured and semi-illiterate." This seems to be little more than name calling, yet his participation in Nazism needs to be addressed.

No finer tribute could be paid him than that from his old director, Josef von Sternberg: "Jannings had every right to the universal praise that was his for many years, and his position in the history of the motion picture is secure, not only as a superlative performer but also as a source of inspiration for the writers and directors of his time. This in my opinion is the highest compliment within the scope of an actor to earn."

—Liam O'Leary

JOHNSON, Celia

Nationality: British. **Born:** Richmond, Surrey, 18 December 1908. **Education:** St. Paul's Girls' School, London; Royal Academy of Dramatic Art, London. **Family:** Married the writer Peter Fleming, 1935 (died 1971), one son and two daughters. **Career:** 1928—stage debut in *Major Barbara*, Huddersfield; 1934—film debut in *Dirty Work*; 1945—role in *Brief Encounter* gave her an international reputation; 1964-65—played in *The Master Builder* and *Hay Fever* in National Theatre season; 1971—played Gertrude in *Hamlet*, London. **Awards:** Best Actress, New York Film Critics, for *Brief Encounter*, 1946; Best Supporting Actress, British Academy, for *The Prime of Miss Jean*

Brodie, 1969. Commander, Order of the British Empire, 1958; Dame Commander, 1981. **Died:** 25 April 1982.

Films as Actress:

1934   *Dirty Work* (Walls)
1941   *We Serve* (short); *A Letter from Home* (short)
1942   *In Which We Serve* (Coward) (as Alix Kinross)
1943   *Dear Octopus* (*The Randolph Family*) (French) (as Cynthia)
1944   *This Happy Breed* (Lean) (as Ethel Gibbons)
1945   *Brief Encounter* (Lean) (as Laura Jesson)
1950   *The Astonished Heart* (Darnborough and Fisher) (as Barbara Faber)
1952   *I Believe in You* (Dearden) (as Matty); *The Holly and the Ivy* (O'Ferrall) (as Jenny Gregory)
1953   *The Captain's Paradise* (Kimmins) (as Maud St. James)
1955   *A Kid for Two Farthings* (Reed) (as Joanna)
1957   *The Good Companions* (Lee Thompson) (as Miss Trant)
1969   *The Prime of Miss Jean Brodie* (Neame) (as Miss Mackay)
1978   *Les Misérables* (Glenn Jordan—for TV)
1980   *The Hostage Tower* (Guzman—for TV); *Staying On* (Narizzano—for TV)

Publications

On JOHNSON: book—

Fleming, Kate, *Celia Johnson: A Biography*, London, 1991.

On JOHNSON: articles—

Obituary, in *Films and Filming* (London), June 1982.
Annual Obituary 1982, New York, 1983.

*   *   *

Night. A suburban English railway station. As a train approaches at speed, a neatly dressed woman, bleak despair in her eyes, steps to the edge of the platform—and, at the last second, hesitates. Rachmaninov thunders on the soundtrack; the lights of the rushing train slap across the woman's face as she stands horrified by the nearness of death.

The dramatic climax of *Brief Encounter* also proved to be the climax of Celia Johnson's screen career. No matter what other roles she played, the near-adulterous, near-suicidal, suburban wife of David Lean's film was the part she was remembered for. Not without reason: the film's classic status rests on the intelligence, subtlety, and emotional honesty of her performance.

Not that Johnson made many films—less than a dozen features in all, and few of them particularly distinguished. The best were probably the three she made for Lean, all scripted by Noël Coward. *In Which We Serve* offered her little more than a cameo role, though beautifully executed; and she was clearly less than comfortable with a working-class part in *This Happy Breed*. Her range was a narrow one; within it she could be superb, but outside it her subtlety looked merely overcautious.

She also possessed a notable talent for sophisticated comedy, often displayed on stage but all too rarely on screen. As one of Alec Guinness's bigamous wives in *The Captain's Paradise*, she made the material seem better than it deserved; but her finest comic performance on film was in *The Prime of Miss Jean Brodie*, where her delicately acidulous Scots headmistress nearly stole the picture from Maggie Smith—no small achievement.

Celia Johnson in *Brief Encounter* courtesy of The Rank Organisation Plc

That was her last film, though *Staying On*, made for TV, reunited her with her co-star of *Brief Encounter*, Trevor Howard, and demonstrated that in the intervening years her playing had lost nothing of its warmth and quiet skill.

—Philip Kemp

JOLSON, Al

Nationality: American. **Born:** Asa Yoelson in Srednike, Russia, 26 May 1886; emigrated with family to the United States, 1890; settled in Washington, D.C., 1894. **Family:** Married: 1) Henrietta Keller, 1906 (divorced 1919); 2) Alma Osborne, 1922 (divorced 1926); 3) the dancer Ruby Keeler, 1928 (divorced 1939), adopted son; 4) Earle Galbraith, 1945, adopted son. **Career:** Several abortive ventures to become singer or actor as a boy; 1899—debut on legitimate stage in *Children of the Ghetto*; then with various vaudeville and minstrel troupes, including the Lew Dockstader's Minstrels; 1909—big success singing in blackface with the minstrel troupe; for the next 15 years appeared in many productions (loosely termed the Winter Garden Shows); 1921—played in *Bombo* in a theater named after him; 1927—feature film debut in *The Jazz Singer*, billed as the first talking picture; 1931—on Broadway in *Wonderbar*, his last stage role; 1932—radio debut with his own program; entertained American troops overseas during World War II; 1946-49—provided the offscreen voice in two films based on his life, *The Jolson Story* and *Jolson Sings Again*. **Died:** Of heart attack, in San Francisco, 23 October 1950.

Films as Actor:

1926 *April Showers* (short)
1927 *The Jazz Singer* (Crosland) (as Jackie Rabinowitz/Jack Robin)
1928 *The Singing Fool* (Bacon) (as Al Stone)
1929 *Say It with Songs* (Bacon) (as Joe Lane); *New York Nights* (Milestone) (as guest); *Lucky Boy* (Taurog and Wilson) (as singer)
1930 *Mammy* (Curtiz) (as Al Fuller); *Big Boy* (Crosland) (as Gus); *Showgirl in Hollywood* (LeRoy) (as guest)
1933 *Hallelujah, I'm a Bum* (*Hallelujah I'm a Tramp*; *Lazy Bones*) (Milestone)
1934 *Wonder Bar* (Bacon) (as Al Wonder)
1935 *Go into Your Dance* (*Casino de Paree*) (Mayo) (as Al Howland)
1936 *The Singing Kid* (Keighley) (as Al Jackson)
1939 *Rose of Washington Square* (Ratoff) (as Ted Cotten); *Hollywood Cavalcade* (Cummings) (as guest); *Swanee River* (Lanfield) (as Edwin Dalmen)
1940 *The Cavalcade of Academy Awards* (Genet) (as guest)
1945 *Rhapsody in Blue* (Rapper) (as guest)
1946 *The Jolson Story* (Green) (voice)
1949 *Jolson Sings Again* (Levin) (voice)

Publications

On JOLSON: books—

Jolson, Harry, *Mistah Jolson*, as told to Alban Emley, Hollywood, 1951.
Sieben, Pearl, *The Immortal Jolson: His Life and Times*, New York, 1962.

Freedland, Michael, *Al Jolson*, New York, 1972.
Anderton, Barrie, *Sonny Boy! The World of Al Jolson*, London, 1975.
Geduld, Harry M., *Birth of the Talkies: From Edison to Jolson*, Bloomington, Indiana, 1975.
Oberfirst, Robert, *Al Jolson: You Ain't Heard Nothin' Yet*, San Diego, 1980.
McLelland, Doug, *Blackface to Blacklist: Al Jolson, Larry Parks and The Jolson Story*, Metuchen, New Jersey, 1987.
Goldman, Herbert G., *Jolson: The Legend Comes to Life*, New York, 1988.
Kiner, Larry F., *Al Jolson: A Bio-Discography*, Metuchen, New Jersey, 1992.
Fisher, James, *Al Jolson: A Bio-Bibliography*, Westport, Connecticut, 1994.

On JOLSON: articles—

Kobal, John, "Al Jolson and *Wonder Bar*," in *Film* (London), Summer 1970.
National Film Theatre Booklet (London), September-November 1972.
Sarris, Andrew, "The Cultural Guilt of Musical Movies: The Jazz Singer, 50 Years After," in *Film Comment* (New York), September-October 1977.
Ciné Revue (Paris), 10 September 1981.

* * *

Al Jolson was more than a film star; he was one of the truly legendary figures in American show business. Delivering songs, he was overpowering. He simply seized whatever limelight was available, and then strutted his special vocal magic. He established himself as a show business legend by 1910, outshining all who dared appear on stage with him. His Broadway shows contained little in the way of plot, but his audiences seemed not to care. All they wanted were a few hit songs, and more often than not, Jolson delivered.

In 1923, fabled director D. W. Griffith decided he would try to capture Jolson's electrifying persona on film, and the two started *Mammy's Boy*. This film was never finished, and only resulted in several nasty lawsuits. Success in the movies came for Jolson with the coming of sound. He recorded several of the earliest Vitaphone shorts for Warner Brothers. In 1927, he was instrumental in popularizing talkies with *The Jazz Singer*. That film simply interpolated several Jolson numbers into an otherwise lackluster silent film. But it was *The Singing Fool* which signaled Jolson as a major film star by establishing a box-office record which would last for nearly a decade.

The coming of sound helped Jolson bring his act to countless millions of new fans, but movie audiences seemed to tire quickly of that act. Jolson's 1930s releases of *Mammy* and *Big Boy* were not all that popular. Indeed, after 1930 he appeared in only five more films, and severely cut back his stage appearances. It was only through radio that Jolson reached audiences during the 1930s. He thus made a "comeback" of sorts during World War II, touring and singing for the troops. This exposure to another generation of fans helped result in two film biographies: *The Jolson Story* and *Jolson Sings Again*. Jolson himself provided the vocals; Larry Parks played the entertainer. The latter film was the highest grosser of 1949, and represented the top box-office attraction for the Columbia Pictures studio up to that time. As a result of the films, Jolson had come full circle, and was back on top again as a live entertainer during the last few years of his life.

—Douglas Gomery

603

Al Jolson

JONES, James Earl

Nationality: American. **Born:** Arkabutla, Mississippi, 17 January 1931; son of the actor Robert Earl Jones. **Education:** Attended Norman Dickson High School, Brethren, Michigan; University of Michigan, Ann Arbor, B.A. in drama 1953. **Military Service:** U.S. Army, 1953-55: lieutenant. **Family:** Married 1) Julienne Marie, 1967; 2) Cecilia Hart, 1982. **Career:** 1955-57—studied acting at American Theatre Wing, and with Lee Strasberg and Tad Danielewski, New York; 1955-59—performed in summer stock at Manistee Summer Theatre, Michigan; 1957—New York role in *Wedding in Japan*; 1961—breakthrough role in *The Blacks*, New York; 1964—title role in *Othello*, New York; also made film debut in *Dr. Strangelove*; 1965—continuing role in TV series *As the World Turns*; 1968—role in Broadway hit *The Great White Hope*, repeated in film version, 1970; in TV mini-series *Jesus of Nazareth*, 1977, *Roots: The Next Generation*, 1979, and *Signs and Wonders*, 1996; in TV series *Paris*, 1979-80, *Me and Mom*, 1985, *Gabriel's Fire*, 1990-92, and *Under One Roof*, 1995. **Awards:** Emmy Awards, for *Gabriel's Fire*, and *Heat Wave*, 1990; National Medal of Arts, 1992. **Agent:** Bauman/Hiller, 5750 Wilshire Boulevard, Suite 512, Los Angeles, CA 90036, U.S.A.

Films as Actor:

1964 *Dr. Strangelove: Or, How I Learned to Stop Worrying and Love the Bomb* (Kubrick) (as Lt. Lothar Zagg)
1967 *The Comedians* (Glenville) (as Dr. Magiot)
1970 *King: A Filmed Record . . . Montgomery to Memphis* (Lumet and Joseph L. Mankiewicz—doc); *End of the Road* (Avakian) (as Dr. D); *The Great White Hope* (Ritt) (as Jack Jefferson)
1972 *Malcolm X* (Worth and Perc—doc) (as narrator); *The Man* (Sargent—for TV but released theatrically) (as President Douglass Dilman)
1974 *Claudine* (Berry) (as Roop)
1975 *The UFO Incident* (Colla—for TV)
1976 *Deadly Hero* (Nagy) (as Rabbit); *The River Niger* (Shah) (as Johnny Williams); *The Bingo Long Traveling All-Stars and Motor Kings* (Badham) (as Leon); *Swashbuckler (The Scarlet Buccaneer)* (Goldstone) (as Nick Debrett)
1977 *Star Wars* (Lucas) (as voice of Darth Vader); *The Greatest* (Gries) (as Malcolm X); *Exorcist II: The Heretic* (Boorman) (as older Kokumo); *The Last Remake of Beau Geste* (Feldman) (as Sheikh Abdul); *A Piece of the Action* (Poitier) (as Joshua Burke); *The Greatest Thing that Almost Happened* (Moses—for TV)
1978 *The Bushido Blade* (Kotani) (as Harpooner); *Paul Robeson* (Lloyd Richards—for TV)
1980 *The Empire Strikes Back* (Kershner) (as voice of Darth Vader); *The Golden Moment: An Olympic Love Story* (Sarafian); *Guyana Tragedy: The Story of Jim Jones* (William A. Graham—for TV) (as Father Div)
1981 *Amy and the Angel* (Rosenblum—for TV) (as the Angel Gabriel)
1982 *Blood Tide* (Jeffries) (as Frye); *Conan the Barbarian* (Milius) (as Thulsa Doom)
1983 *Return of the Jedi* (Marquand) (as voice of Darth Vader)
1984 *The Vegas Strip War* (Englund—for TV) (as Jack Madrid); *Aladdin and His Wonderful Lamp* (Burton—for TV)
1985 *1877: The Grand Army of Starvation* (Briers); *The Atlanta Child Murders* (Erman—for TV); *City Limits* (Lipstadt) (as Albert)
1986 *My Little Girl* (Kaiserman) (as Ike Bailey); *Soul Man* (Miner) (as Prof. Banks)

1987 *Allan Quatermain and the Lost City of Gold* (Gary Nelson and Newt Arnold) (as Umslopogaas); *Gardens of Stone* (Francis Ford Coppola) (as Sgt.-Major "Goody" Nelson); *Matewan* (Sayles) (as "Few Clothes" Johnson); *Pinocchio and the Emperor of the Night* (Hal Sutherland—animation) (as voice of Emperor of the Night)
1988 *Coming to America* (Landis) (as King Jaffe Joffer)
1989 *Three Fugitives* (Veber) (as Detective Dugan); *Field of Dreams* (Robinson) (as Terence Mann); *Best of the Best* (Radler) (as Coach Couzo)
1990 *The Hunt for Red October* (McTiernan) (as Adm. James Greer); *Grim Prairie Tales* (Coe) (as Morrison); *Last Flight Out* (Elikann—for TV) (as Al Topping); *The Ambulance* (Cohen) (as Lt. Spencer); *Heat Wave* (Hooks—for TV) (as Junius Johnson); *Ivory Hunters (The Last Elephant)* (Sargent—for TV) (as Inspector Nkuru); *By Dawn's Early Light* (Sholder—for TV) (as Alice)
1991 *Terrorgram* (Kienzle) (as Voice of Retribution); *True Identity* (Lane) (as himself); *Convicts* (Masterson) (as Ben Johnson)
1992 *Scorchers* (Beaird) (as Bear); *Sneakers* (Robinson) (as Mr. Bernard Abbott); *Patriot Games* (Noyce) (as Adm. James Greer); *Lincoln* (Kunhardt—doc for TV) (as narrator)
1993 *Excessive Force* (Hess) (as Jake, the bar owner); *Percy and Thunder* (Dixon—for TV) (as Percy Banks); *Hallelujah* (Lane—for TV) (as Old Man Taylor); *The Meteor Man* (Townsend) (as Mr. Moses); *The Sandlot* (Evans) (as Mr. Mertle); *Sommersby* (Amiel) (as Judge Isaacs); *Dreamrider* (Bill Brown)
1994 *The Lion King* (Minkoff—animation) (as voice of Mufasa); *Clean Slate* (Mick Jackson) (as Dolby); *Clear and Present Danger* (Noyce) (as Adm. James Greer); *Naked Gun 33 1/3: The Final Insult* (Segal) (as himself, uncredited); *Twilight Zone: Rod Serling's Lost Classics* (Markowitz—for TV) (as host); *Africa: The Serengeti* (doc) (as narrator); *Confessions: Two Faces of Evil* (Cates—for TV) (as Charlie Lloyd); *The Vernon Johns Story* (Fink—for TV) (title role)
1995 *Jefferson in Paris* (Ivory) (as Madison Hemings); *Cry, the Beloved Country* (Roodt) (as the Rev. Stephen Kumalo)
1996 *A Family Thing* (Richard Pearce) (as Ray Murdock); *Looking for Richard* (Pacino)

Publications

By JONES: book—

James Earl Jones: Voices and Silences, with Penelope Niven, New York, 1993.

By JONES: articles—

Interview in *Jet* (Chicago), 4 July 1994.
Interview in *Jet* (Chicago), 16 January 1995.

On JONES: book—

Null, Gary, *Black Hollywood: The Negro in Motion Pictures*, Secaucus, New Jersey, 1975.

On JONES: articles—

Hellman, P., "The Great Black Hope," in *New York*, 21 October 1968.
Clark, John, filmography in *Premiere* (New York), June 1992.
Current Biography 1994, New York, 1994.

Culhane, John, "How James Earl Jones Found His Voice," in *Reader's Digest*, July 1994.

Mesic, Penelope, "Real Heat," in *Chicago*, February 1996.

*   *   *

When James Earl Jones was a young actor, it would have been impossible for him to have attained celluloid stardom. From the early 1950s through the late 1960s/early 1970s, only one African-American performer was allowed to achieve eminence on screen: Sidney Poitier. Such was the manner in which the racial politics of the era affected the movies. In the 1990s, Denzel Washington, Morgan Freeman, Wesley Snipes, Laurence Fishburne, and others have become movie stars—and Jones, too old to play romantic leads or action heroes, has aged into a venerable celluloid elder statesman and character actor.

Jones began pursuing an acting career in the 1950s, at which point he cut his teeth on the New York stage, often appearing with Joseph Papp's New York Shakespeare Festival. He was past 30 when he debuted on-screen in *Dr. Strangelove*, and he was barely noticeable in a minor role. His first important movie work came in 1970, when he was approaching the age of 40. In *The Great White Hope*, he offers a mesmerizing performance as Jack Jefferson, a character based on Jack Johnson, the first black-American heavyweight boxing champion. It was a part he had originated on Broadway two years earlier. Jones did go on to play some starring parts—most intriguingly, the first black U.S. president in *The Man*, and most memorably, the Josh Gibson-like Negro League home-run hitter opposite Billy Dee Williams's Satchel Paige-like hurler in *The Bingo Long Traveling All-Stars and Motor Kings*. Over the years, Jones frequently returned to the stage, and began appearing in television movies and mini-series (with one of his more distinguished roles being Alex Haley in *Roots: The Next Generation*).

But in most of his better films, including *Matewan*, *Field of Dreams*, *The Sandlot*, and the trilogy *The Hunt for Red October*, *Patriot Games*, and *Clear and Present Danger*, Jones has had supporting roles. As he began surfacing on screen with more frequency, many of his films—from *Swashbuckler* in 1976 through *Excessive Force* and *The Meteor Man* in 1993—have been unimpressive. Still, Jones is such an imposing presence that his impact is felt even when only his voice is employed on screen. Such is the case in the animated feature *The Lion King*, where he speaks the character of Mufasa, and most especially in the *Star Wars* trilogy, where he is the voice of Darth Vader.

In the mid-1990s, Jones has had two interesting starring roles: a back-country South African priest in *Cry, the Beloved Country* and a Chicago cop in *A Family Thing*. In these films, he is paired with a white actor (Richard Harris in the former, Robert Duvall in the latter). Both scenarios begin with the characters living in separate worlds; through the course of the story, they come to understand one another, realizing that they have much in common as human beings. In *Cry, the Beloved Country*, they are fathers whose sons suffer cruel fates; in *A Family Thing*, they are, in fact, half-brothers. The manner in which they learn to coexist serves to present a humanistic antidote to the racial polarization that pervades contemporary society.

While publicizing *A Family Thing*, Jones noted, "We are who we are for much more interesting reasons than our color": a deeply humane observation, which reflects upon his own life and career as much as it does the theme of the movie he was promoting.

—Rob Edelman

JONES, Jennifer

Nationality: American. **Born:** Phylis Isley in Tulsa, Oklahoma, 2 March 1919. **Education:** Attended Monte Cassino Junior College,

Tulsa; Northwestern University, Evanston, Illinois, one year; American Academy of Dramatic Arts, New York, 1938. **Family:** Married 1) the actor Robert Walker, 1939 (divorced 1945), sons: Robert and Michael; 2) the producer David Selznick, 1949 (died 1965), daughter: Mary (deceased); 3) Norton Simon, 1971. **Career:** Acted in some of her parents' touring productions; some roles in New York with Cherry Lane Troupe; 1938—radio actress, Tulsa, followed by a couple of bit parts in films; 1941—contract with David Selznick was followed by stage work in John Houseman's *Hello Out There*, and by study at Group Theatre with Sanford Meisner; 1943—starring role in Selznick's *The Song of Bernadette*; 1966—played title role in *The Country Girl* on stage. **Awards:** Best Actress, Academy Award, for *The Song of Bernadette*, 1943. **Address:** P.O. Box 367, Malibu, CA 90265, U.S.A.

Films as Actress:

1939   *New Frontier* (*Frontier Horizon*) (Sherman) (as Celia Braddock, billed as Phylis Isley); *Dick Tracy's G-Men* (Witney and English) (as Gwen Andrews)

1943   *The Song of Bernadette* (Henry King) (title role)

1944   *Since You Went Away* (Cromwell) (as Jane Hilton)

1945   *Love Letters* (Dieterle) (as Singleton/Victoria Remington)

1946   *The American Creed* (Robert Stevenson—short); *Cluny Brown* (Lubitsch) (title role); *Duel in the Sun* (King Vidor) (as Pearl Chavez)

1948   *Portrait of Jennie* (*Jennie*) (Dieterle) (title role)

1949   *We Were Strangers* (Huston) (as China Valdez); *Madame Bovary* (Minnelli) (title role)

1950   *Gone to Earth* (Powell) (as Hazel Woodus); *The Wild Heart* (Powell and Pressburger—revised version of *Gone to Earth*, shortened)

1952   *Carrie* (Wyler) (title role); *Ruby Gentry* (King Vidor) (title role)

1953   *Beat the Devil* (Huston) (as Gwendolyn Chelm); *Stazione termini* (*Indiscretion of an American Wife*; *Terminal Station*; *Indiscretion*) (de Sica) (as Mary Forbes)

1955   *Love Is a Many-Splendored Thing* (Henry King) (as Han Suyin); *Good Morning, Miss Dove* (Koster) (title role)

1956   *The Man in the Gray Flannel Suit* (Johnson) (as Betsy Rath)

1957   *The Barretts of Wimpole Street* (Charles Vidor) (as Elizabeth Barrett); *A Farewell to Arms* (Charles Vidor) (as Catherine Barkley)

1961   *Tender Is the Night* (Henry King) (as Nicole Diver)

1966   *The Idol* (Petrie) (as Carol)

1969   *Angel, Angel, Down We Go* (*Cult of the Damned*) (Thom) (as Astrid)

1974   *The Towering Inferno* (Guillerman) (as Lisolette Mueller)

1977   *She Came to the Valley* (Band) (as Srita)

Publications

On JONES: books—

Huston, John, *An Open Book*, New York, 1972.

Memo from David O. Selznick, edited by Rudy Behlmer, New York, 1972.

Bowers, Ronald, *The Selznick Players*, New York, 1976.

Linet, Beverly, *Star-Crossed: The Story of Robert Walker and Jennifer Jones*, New York, 1986.

Carrier, Jeffrey L., *Jennifer Jones: A Bio-Bibliography*, Westport, Connecticut, 1990.

Epstein, Edward Z., *Portrait of Jennifer: A Biography of Jennifer Jones*, New York, 1995.

Jennifer Jones

On JONES: articles—

Current Biography 1944, New York, 1944.
Hume, R., "She Saw the Vision and Became the Star," in *Films and Filming* (London), June 1956.
Doyle, N., "Jennifer Jones," in *Films in Review* (New York), August-September 1962.
Ciné Revue (Paris), 28 April 1983.
Hamel, Raymond, "Portrait of Jennifer," in *Classic Images* (Muscatine, Iowa), February 1993.

* * *

Jennifer Jones remains one of the more controversial actresses in the Hollywood cinema. In general, her professional and personal involvement with David O. Selznick has been given a prominence that has colored assessments of Jones's distinctive contribution to 1940s cinema. Interestingly, the central issue is not that Jones lacked talent or screen presence. The longstanding criticism is that Selznick, because of his commitment to Jones, had no critical distance and, with King Vidor's *Duel in the Sun*, tried to fashion an erotic identity for her, making Jones into a ridiculous creation. Previously, Jones's screen persona was as an innocent child/woman, an image established by her first starring role in Henry King's *The Song of Bernadette*. She had also given an intense and emotionally charged performance as a girl making the transition from youth to maturity in John Cromwell's *Since You Went Away*.

As the sensual half-breed Pearl in *Duel in the Sun*, Jones succeeds in giving an audaciously conceived performance employing a degree of physical gesture having more in common with silent-screen acting technique than with the naturalistic behavioral mannerisms associated with the sound cinema. In addition, while Jones's physical presence is intended to be provocative, she does not allow her physicality to undermine the complex psychological dimensions of the character. *Duel in the Sun* is thus a remarkable achievement but, like Jones's performance, it has often been misinterpreted as degrading to female sexuality. Though conceived on a lesser scale, Vidor's *Ruby Gentry* is equally successful in dealing with the same themes, and again Jones's sensuality is central to the expression of those concerns.

From the beginning, Jones's screen persona was imbued with a degree of hysteria, and in Vincente Minnelli's underrated *Madame Bovary* this characteristic erupts with particular impact. Minnelli, a director very sensitive to the various aspects of Jones's sensibility, including her romantic indulgence, encourages her to give a subtle performance without relinquishing the extravagant conception the character has of her identity. These same elements might have been as fully articulated in the Michael Powell/Emeric Pressburger version of *The Wild Heart*, but unfortunately Selznick's reworking of their footage does not present a rounded characterization.

Whether Jones would have ascended to the Hollywood Pantheon without her Svengali is less intriguing than revelations in the recent book *Portrait of Jennifer*, that she regretted the pact she made with David O. Selznick, recast in this biography as a lumbering Lucifer. No matter what coloration one paints the envied Selznick-Jones collaboration with, her status as melodramatic princess of the forties is indisputable. If adjectives such as "ethereal" and "luminous" became excess baggage with the passage of time, these qualities were responsible for Jones's realizing the evocative fantasy of *Portrait of Jennie*, the fortunes fools romance of *Love Letters*, and the valentine to homefront frustration, *Since You Went Away*, projects in which this actress's breathtaking vulnerability aroused the audience's protectiveness. If Selznick overproduced *Portrait of Jennie*, he stayed out of William Wyler's way long enough for Jones to hold her own against Olivier with her superb characterization of an unwittingly destructive demimonde in the underappreciated *Carrie*.

Ultimately, Selznick's make-or-break desire to out-Thalberg Thalberg with his very own Norma Shearer plaything named Jennifer proved fatal to both their careers. Surviving the Hollywood-in-flux fifties due to the unexpected box-office bonanza of a two different-worlds weepie, *Love Is a Many Splendored Thing*, Jones invested *Good Morning, Miss Dove* with appropriate starchy decorum and erased memories of kindred spirit Shearer in a four-hanky revisit with *The Barretts of Wimpole Street*. It was Selznick's overblown, unnecessary revamp of *A Farewell to Arms* that proved a farewell to his moguldom and Jones's major stardom. Deftly imbricating the complexities in Jones's persona with F. Scott Fitzgerald's themes, the flawed *Tender Is the Night* is the last film to resurrect Jones's patented fragility to good effect. Afterwards, the neurotic mannerisms consume her performances in the unworthy *The Idol* and the downright cheesy *Angel, Angel Down We Go*. Having purchased the rights to the novel, *Terms of Endearment*, Jones was cheated out of the plum role of Aurora by the director she had handpicked to helm her comeback. Perhaps, such ignominious treatment proved that cutthroat Hollywood had not changed much since her heyday. Offscreen, she has found philanthropist Norton Simon to protect her, but her radiance has been sorely missed on the big screen for many years.

—Richard Lippe, updated by Robert Pardi

JONES, Tommy Lee

Nationality: American. **Born:** San Saba, Texas, 15 September 1946. **Education:** Attended Saint Mark's School, Dallas; Harvard University, B.A. in English Literature, 1969. **Family:** Married 1) Kate Lardner (divorced); 2) Kimberlea Cloughley, 1981, children: Austin and Victoria. **Career:** 1969—Broadway stage debut in *A Patriot for Me*; 1970—film debut in *Love Story*; 1971-75—appeared in TV soap *One Life to Live*; mid-1970s—began appearing in numerous TV movies and theatrical films; earlier TV and film work is highlighted by performances in *Coal Miner's Daughter*, 1980, and as Gary Gilmore in *The Executioner's Song* (TV), 1982; 1989—appearance in the highly acclaimed miniseries *Lonesome Dove* helps revitalize career. **Awards**: Emmy Award, for *The Executioner's Song*, 1983; Academy Award, Golden Globe Award, and Los Angeles Critics Award, Best Supporting Actor, for *The Fugitive*, 1993. **Agent:** Michael Black, c/o International Creative Management, 8942 Wilshire Boulevard, Beverly Hills, CA 90212, U.S.A.

Films as Actor:

1970   *Love Story* (Hiller) (as Hank); *Eliza's Horiscope* (Sheppard) (as Tommy)
1973   *Life Study* (Nebbia) (as Gus)
1976   *Smash-Up on Interstate 5* (Moxey—for TV); *Jackson County Jail* (Miller) (as Coley Blake); *Charlie's Angels* (Moxey—for TV)
1977   *Rolling Thunder* (Flynn) (as Johnny Vohden); *The Amazing Howard Hughes* (William A. Graham—for TV) (title role)
1978   *Eyes of Laura Mars* (Kershner) (as John Neville); *The Betsy* (Petrie) (as Angelo Perino)
1980   *Coal Miner's Daughter* (Apted) (as Doolittle "Mooney" Lynn); *The Barn Burning* (Werner—for TV)
1981   *Back Roads* (Ritt) (as Elmore Pratt)
1982   *The Executioner's Song* (Schiller—for TV) (as Gary Gilmore); *The Rainmaker* (for TV)
1983   *Nate and Hayes* (Fairfax) (as Captain Bully Hayes)

Tommy Lee Jones in *The Fugitive*

1984 *The River Rat* (Rickman) (as Billy)
1985 *The Park Is Mine* (Steven Hilliard Stern—for TV) (as Mitch);
       Cat on a Hot Tin Roof (Hofsiss—for TV) (as Brick)
1986 *Yuri Nosenko, KGB* (Jackson—for TV); *Black Moon Rising*
       (Cokliss) (as Quint)
1987 *Broken Vows* (Taylor—for TV); *The Big Town* (Bolt) (as George
       Cole)
1988 *Stranger on My Land* (Elikann—for TV); *Stormy Monday*
       (Figgis) (as Cosmo); *Gotham* (Fonvielle—for TV) (as
       Eddie Mallard); *April Morning* (Delbert Mann) (as Moses
       Cooper)
1989 *The Package* (Andrew Davis) (as Thomas Boyette)
1990 *Fire Birds* (David Green) (as Brad Little)
1991 *JFK* (Oliver Stone) (as Clay Shaw)
1992 *Under Siege* (Andrew Davis) (as William Strannix)
1993 *House of Cards* (Lessac) (as Jake Beerlander); *Heaven and
       Earth* (Oliver Stone) (as Steve Butler); *The Fugitive* (An-
       drew Davis) (as U.S. Marshal Samuel Gerard)
1994 *Cobb* (Shelton) (title role); *Natural Born Killers* (Oliver
       Stone) (as Dwight McCloskey); *Blue Sky* (Richardson—
       produced in 1990) (as Hank Marshall); *Blown Away*
       (Hopkins) (as Ryan Gaerity); *The Client* (Schumacher)
       (as Roy Foltrigg)
1995 *Batman Forever* (Schumacher) (as D.A. Harvey "Two-Face"
       Dent)
1996 *Men in Black* (Sonnenfeld)

Film as Director:

1995 *The Good Old Boys* (for TV) (+ ro as Huey Calloway, co-
       sc)

Publications

On JONES: book—

Marill, Alvin H., *The Films of Tommy Lee Jones*, Secaucus, New Jersey, 1996.

By JONES: articles—

Interview with Carole Zucker, in *Figures of Light: Actors and Direc-
  tors Illuminate the Art of Film Acting*, New York, 1994.
Interview with Gavin Smith, in *Film Comment* (New York), January/
  February 1994.
"Onward and Upward with the Arts: Keeping up with Mr. Jones," inter-
  view with Lillian Ross, in *New Yorker*, 4 April 1994.

On JONES: articles—

Swartz, Mimi, "The Fugitive: Tommy Lee Jones," in *Texas Monthly*,
  October 1993.

Hample, Henry S., "Tommy Lee Jones," in *Premiere* (New York), January 1994.
Current Biography 1995, New York, 1995.

*   *   *

Tommy Lee Jones is capable of ferociously intense performances that verge on the extreme. Because of this, it is often easy to overlook his extraordinary range as an actor. Jones has shifted easily among film, television, and theater in a career that spans more than 25 years and often alternates between flamboyant and more understated roles. Recently associated with larger than life (some might say cartoonish) roles such as Ty Cobb in *Cobb*, "Two-Face" in *Batman Returns*, and Dwight McCloskey in *Natural Born Killers*, Jones appeared in nearly 15 films from 1989 through 1995 making him easily one of the busiest actors in Hollywood.

Always an actor of intelligence with a powerful screen presence, Jones's career in the mid to late 1970s yielded some interesting work from such exploitation fare as *Jackson County Jail* to the more ambitious *Rolling Thunder* and *Eyes of Laura Mars*. It does seem that the first phase of his career had more than its share of country-boy parts, killers, and "heavies."

An early turning point was his appearance in Michael Apted's *Coal Miner's Daughter*. Although Sissy Spacek garnered most of the critical attention and an Academy Award, Jones's understated portrayal of Doolittle "Mooney" Lynn gave the film a realistic center it otherwise lacked. His next key performance was his intense turn as Gary Gilmore in the television adaptation of Norman Mailer's *The Executioner's Song*, a film whose direction was not up to the imaginative performance of its leading man.

The 1980s seem to have been something of an unfocused time for the actor. He made his share of ordinary films and his career seemed as if it would not fulfill its early promise. He alternated between serious fare such as *Cat on a Hot Tin Roof* (television), playing Brick to Jessica Lange's Maggie and Rip Torn's Big Daddy, and action films such as *Black Moon Rising*, and familiar psycho roles such as *The Park Is Mine* (television). Jones's career seemed to be floundering. The turning point came with his beautifully understated performance in the highly acclaimed mini-series *Lonesome Dove*. His exquisitely detailed performance as the withdrawn Woodrow Call plays against Robert Duvall's more extroverted Gus with great subtlety. The performance reminded audiences that Jones was an actor of considerable range whose talents had been wasted in too many unremarkable films.

This range is clearly displayed in his astonishing performance as the elegant, refined Clay Shaw in Oliver Stone's controversial *JFK*, a role that would garner Jones an Academy Award nomination for Best Supporting Actor. This performance illustrates how physical his work as an actor is and how he uses props and makeup (in this case cigarette and white wig) to good effect. Jones thoroughly inhabits the masochistic Shaw with especially good use of speech rhythms that are both Louisiana-bound and pure Tommy Lee Jones. The actor strings together long sentences without seeming to come up for air, and occasionally shifts to a higher vocal pitch in a performance that rivets the audience's attention.

Jones's appearance as the deranged rocker/terrorist William Strannix in *Under Siege* confirmed that the actor was now commercially bankable. His rich, focused performance (along with Andrew Davis's skillful direction) elevated the film several notches above the usually monotonous, Steven Seagal action picture. Jones was reunited with Davis (for a third time) in the hugely successful, Harrison Ford vehicle *The Fugitive*, playing the determined Samuel Gerard. The film won Jones the most critical acclaim of his career, and he received an Oscar as Best Supporting Actor for his efforts. This last performance spurred

Gavin Smith to ask "Is it only the character or also Tommy Lee Jones up there, funnier, faster and smarter than everybody else."

At this point Jones's career entered overdrive and he risked serious overexposure. He worked twice more with Oliver Stone in the 1990s. He gave an underrated performance in the critical and commercial flop *Heaven and Earth*, and appeared in the controversial *Natural Born Killers* in a role that seems excessive but is in keeping with every other aspect of the film. He appeared in several high-profile, big-budget films with director Joel Schumacher, *The Client* and *Batman Forever*; gave an extravagantly flamboyant performance as Ty Cobb in *Cobb*, and once more essayed the action genre in *Blown Away*. Tony Richardson's understated *Blue Sky* was also released in this period (three years after it was made) to remind audiences that Jones could still play realistic characters with honest emotions. Finally, Jones appeared in, and made his directorial debut, in the earnest but unremarkable *The Good Old Boys*, a television film he also co-wrote.

Luckily, throughout this period of intense activity Jones's inventiveness and range are always on view. Tommy Lee Jones may not be the prettiest actor working in Hollywood with his rough-hewn face and slightly threatening presence, but he is unquestionably one of the best. The fact that he is only at mid-career gives us much to anticipate.

—Mario Falsetto

JOSEPHSON, Erland

Nationality: Swedish. **Born:** Stockholm, 15 June 1923. **Career:** Actor with the Municipal Theatre, Helsingborg, Sweden, 1945-49; Gothenburg Theatre, 1949-56; and Royal Dramatic Theatre, Stockholm, from 1956; 1958—film debut in *Ansiktet*; director, Royal Dramatic Theatre, Stockholm, 1966-75; 1977—in TV version of *Scenes from a Marriage*; co-director of first film, *En och En*, 1978; also writer and producer. **Awards:** Swedish Gold Bug Award for Best Actor, for *The Sacrifice* and *Amorosa*, 1986. **Address:** c/o Royal Dramatic Theatre, Nybroplan, Box 5037, 102 41 Stockholm, Sweden.

Films as Actor:

1958   *Ansiktet (The Magician; The Face)* (Bergman) (as Egerman); *Nära livet (Brink of Life; So Close to Life)* (Bergman) (as Anders)

1968   *Vargtimmen (Hour of the Wolf)* (Bergman) (as Baron Von Merkens); *Flickorna (The Girls)* (Zetterling and Hughes)

1969   *En Passion (A Passion of Anna; The Passion)* (Bergman) (as Elis Vergerus)

1972   *Viskningar och rop (Cries and Whispers)* (Bergman) (as doctor)

1973   *Scenes from a Marriage* (Bergman) (as Johan)

1975   *Monismanien 1995 (Monismania 1995)* (Fant) (as teacher)

1976   *Ansikte mot Ansikte (Face to Face)* (Bergman) (as Dr. Tomas Jacobi)

1977   *Den Allvarsamma Leken (Games of Love and Loneliness; The Serious Game)* (as Editor-in-Chief Doncker); *Oltre il bene e il male (Beyond Good and Evil; Au-dela du bien et du male)* (Cavani) (as Friedrich "Fritz" Nietzsche)

1978   *Herbstsonate (Autumn Sonata; Hostsonaten)* (Bergman) (as Josef)

1979 *Die erste Polka* (*The First Polka*) (Emmerich) (as Leo Maria);
      Dimenticare Venezia (*To Forget Venice*) (as Nicky); *A Look
      at Liv* (*Norway's Liv Ullmann*; *Liv Ullman's Norway*)
      (Kaplan—doc)
1980 *Karlekan* (*Love*) (as Erland)
1981 *Montenegro* (*Montenegro—Or Pigs and Pearls*) (Makavejev)
      (as Martin Jordan)
1982 *Bella Donna* (Keglevic) (as Max); **Fanny och Alexander**
      (*Fanny and Alexander*) (Bergman) (as Isak Jacobi); *Variola
      vera* (Markovic)
1983 *La casa del tappetto giallo* (*The House of the Yellow Carpet*)
      (as stranger); *Nostalghia* (*Nostalgia*) (Tarkovsky) (as
      Domenico)
1984 *Un caso di incoscienza* (*A Case of Irresponsibility*) (as Erik
      Sander); *Dirty Story* (as Gabriel Berggren); *Efter Repetitioner*
      (*After the Rehearsal*) (Bergman) (as Henrik Vogler); *Angelas
      Krig* (*Angela's War*) (as Goldberg); *Bakom Jalusin* (*Behind
      the Shutters*)
1985 *The Flying Devils* (*De Flyngande Djavlarna*) (Refn) (as Oscar
      Seidenbaum)
1986 *Amorosa* (Zetterling) (as David Sprengel); *L'ultima Mazurka*
      (Bettettini) (as Serra); *Le Mal d'aimer* (*The Malady of Love*;
      The Devil's Tail) (Trcves) (as Robert's father); **Offret** (*The
      Sacrifice*) (Tarkovsky) (as Alexander); *Saving Grace* (Rob-
      ert M. Young) (as Monsignor Francesco Ghezzi); *Garibaldi—
      The General* (as Cavour)
1987 *Il giorno prima* (*The Day Before*) (Montaldo); *Testament d'un
      poete Juif assassine* (*Testament of a Murdered Jewish Poet*)
      (as Zupanev); *Control* (Montaldo—for TV)
1988 *The Unbearable Lightness of Being* (Kaufman) (as the Ambas-
      sador); *La donna spezzata* (*A Woman Destroyed*) (as
      Maurizio)
1989 *La Guerre la plus glorieuse* (*Migrations*) (Petrovic); *Hanussen*
      (Szabó) (as Dr. Bettelheim); *Directed by Andrei Tarkovsky*
      (Leszczylowski—doc) (as narrator)
1990 *God afton, Herr Wallenberg* (*Good Evening, Mr. Wallenberg*)
      (Grede) (as Stockholm rabbi); *Il Sole buio* (*The Dark
      Sun*)
1991 *The Ox* (*Oxen*) (Nykvist) (as Silver); *Cattiva* (Eggleston and
      Lizzani) (as Prof. Brokner); *Meeting Venus* (Szabó) (as Jorge
      Picabia); *Prospero's Books* (Greenaway) (as Gonzalo)
1992 *Sofie* (Ullmann) (as Semmy); *Den ofrivillige golfaren* (*The
      Accidental Golfer*) (Aaberg) (as the critic)
1993 *The Dancer*; *The Last Witness* (Sundvall) (as Samuel Rosenbaum)
1994 *Dromspel* (*Dreamplay*) (Straume) (as blind man)
1995 *To Vlemma tou Odyssea* (*Ulysses' Gaze*; *The Gaze of Odysseus*;
      Le Regarde d'Ulysse) (Angelopoulos) (as preserver); *Ven-
      detta* (Haafström) (as OM); *The Forbidden Fruit* (as land-
      lord); *Kristin Lavransdatter* (Ullmann) (as Brother Edvin);
      Pakten (*The Sunset Boys*) (Risan)

Films as Actor and Co-Director:

1978 *En och En* (*One and One*) (with Nykvist and Thulin) (as
      Uncle Dan, + co-pr, sc)
1980 *Marmeladupproret* (*The Marmalade Revolution*; *La Revolte
      des confitures*) (with Nykvist) (as Karl Henrik Eller, + pr,
      sc)

Other Film:

1964 *För att inte tala om alla dessa kvinnor* (*All These Women*; *Now
      about All These Women*) (Bergman) (co-sc)

Publications

By JOSEPHSON: books—

Cirkel, 1946.
Spegeln och en portvakt, 1946.
Spel med bedrovade artister, 1947.
Ensam och fri, 1948.
Lyssnarpost, 1949.
De vuxna barnen, 1952.
Utflykt, 1954.
Sallskapslek, 1955.
En berattlelse om herr Silberstein, 1957; published as *A Story about Mr.
   Silberstein*, Evanston, Illinois, 1995.
Kungen ur leken, 1959.
Doktor Meyers sista dagar, 1964.
Kandidat Nilssons forsta natt, 1964.
Lejon i Overgangsaldern (*pjas Dromaten*), 1981.
Loppans kvallsvard: roman, Stockholm, 1986.
Sanningslekar, Stockholm, 1990.
Föreställningar, Stockholm, 1991.
Sjalvportratt: en egocentrisk dialog, Stockholm, 1993.

By JOSEPHSON: articles—

Interview with F. Grosoli, in *Cineforum* (Bergamo), June/July 1984.
Interview with A. Philippon, in *Cahiers du Cinéma* (Paris), March
   1985.
Interview with C. Blanchet, in *Cinéma* (Paris), 15 January 1986.
"Bergmans vaccinationsmetod eller Har Gud ont i magen?," in *Chaplin*
   (Stockholm), vol. 30, nos. 2-3, 1988.
Interview with Hubert Niogret, in *Positif* (Paris), February 1988.
"Den exotiska galenskapen," in *Chaplin* (Stockholm), vol. 33, no. 1,
   1991.
"Mastaren och erland," in *Chaplin* (Stockholm), vol. 33, no. 2, 1991.
"Ich war neugierig auf diese Heraus forderung," in *Film und Fersehen*
   (Potsdam, Germany), vol. 21, no. 3, 1993.

*   *   *

In *Prospero's Books*, Erland Josephson plays Gonzalo to Gielgud's
eponymous hero, and has most of his lines spoken for him. He is not
seen till near the end of the picture. When he finally appears, his
grizzled physiognomy and guttural tones, that earthiness he brings to
his screen roles are ill-matched against Greenaway's graphics and against
the full armory of Japanese video technology. Steeped in Ibsen and
Strindberg, a distinguished Swedish actor, here, Josephson discovers,
his accomplishments count for nothing. Not that Josephson is unused
to indignity. In *The Unbearable Lightness of Being*, he plays the role
of a former ambassador reduced to barroom status by 1968 and all
that. Nevertheless, he makes a natural Lear or Prospero himself,
albeit rather less mellifluous than Gielgud, and Ingmar Bergman and
Andrei Tarkovsky in particular have used him to depict teetering
monarchs of one sort or another.

As Alexander in Tarkovsky's *The Sacrifice*, Josephson surveys death
and destruction, imagines a holocaust. There is something saturnine,
verging on the leaden, in his playing: his features, suffused with gloom
and mapped with wrinkles, easily lend themselves to the grim melancholy of close-ups. On a more intimate level, as the "husband" to Liv
Ullmann's wife in Bergman's *Scenes from a Marriage*, Josephson
offers an effective rendering of that old archetype, the middle-class,
middle-aged and largely sedentary man driven to menopausal despair.
Here, he starts off as a bearded bourgeois gentleman, chewing on his
pipe, but, as his marriage frays at the edges, and as he and Ullmann
engage in a fit of anguished psychodrama, stripping each others' char-

acters and pretensions bare, he emerges as a confused, baffled outcast, estranged from his family, background, and profession. This is television territory. The marital conflict is mainly confined to the home: to bedroom, sitting room, kitchen. As Ullmann gains in strength, Josephson seems to dwindle. By the end of the film, he has reconciled himself to disappointment (and has forsaken the family Volvo in favor of a tiny, cramped Citroen).

Unlike his contemporaries in Bergman Rep, most notably Max Von Sydow and Ullmann, Josephson has not been lured to America to caricature his gloomy Scandinavian persona in Woody Allen comedies or to take parts as assassins in political thrillers. He has been too busy in Sweden. He has published poetry, novels, short stories, stage plays, plays for radio and plays for television, and he has written several film scripts. He is active in Swedish Equity. He finds time to teach drama. Still, outside his native country, he remains in Bergman's shadow.

When Tarkovsky, having recently left Russia, wanted an actor to convey his poignant longing for his homeland, his "nostalgia," he chose Josephson. It is Josephson's face which makes him so effective on film, that bearlike aspect, his ability to look lost and forlorn, to convey a sense of suffering and bewilderment, in spite of his bluff exterior. Were one to repeat Kuleshov's famous experiment of the 1920s and to intercut the same shot of Josephson with images of joy, of sadness, of anger, of hunger, the audience would find the Swedish actor, even though he had not moved a muscle, wondrously expressive, capable of embodying every emotion just through "being there," in front of the cameras. Nevertheless, he has the rare ability to combine a capacity for rage—for the grand gesture on the blasted heath—with a more subtle skill for understatement and comedy.

—G. C. Macnab

JOURDAN, Louis

Nationality: French. **Born:** Louis Gendre in Marseilles, 19 June 1919 (some sources say 1920). **Family:** Married Berthe Frédérique (second marriage), 1946, son: Louis. **Education:** Studied drama with René Simon in Paris. **Career:** Worked as assistant director to Marc Allégret; 1939—film debut in *Le Corsaire*; 1947—signed contract with David O. Selznick; contract taken over by 20th Century-Fox; 1954—in *The Immoralist* on New York stage; 1979—in TV mini-series *The French Atlantic Affair*, and *The First Olympics: Athens 1896*, 1984; 1984—on tour in stage play *Gigi*.

Films as Actor:

1939 *Le Corsaire* (Marc Allégret—not completed)
1940 *La Comédie du bonheur* (L'Herbier)
1941 *Premier rendez-vous* (*Her First Affair*) (Decoin) (as Pierre Mortemard); *Parade en sept nuits* (Marc Allégret)
1942 *L'Arlesienne* (Marc Allégret); *Félicie Nanteuil* (*Histoire comique*) (Marc Allégret); *La Vie de Bohême* (L'Herbier); *La Belle Aventure* (*Twilight*) (Marc Allégret)
1943 *Les Petites du Quai aux Fleurs* (Marc Allégret); *Untel Pere et Fils* (*The Heart of a Nation*) (Duvivier)
1947 *The Paradine Case* (Hitchcock) (as André Latour)
1948 *No Minor Voices* (Milestone) (as Ottavio Quaglini); ***Letter from an Unknown Woman*** (Max Ophüls) (as Stefan Brand)
1949 *Madame Bovary* (Minnelli) (as Rodolphe Boulanger)
1951 *Anne of the Indies* (Jacques Tourneur) (as Capt. Pierre François La Rochelle); *Bird of Paradise* (Daves) (as André Laurence)
1952 *The Happy Time* (Fleischer) (as Uncle Desmonde)

1953 *Rue de l'Estrapade* (Jacques Becker); *Decameron Nights* (Fregonese) (as Boccaccio/Paganino/Giulio/Bertrando)
1954 *Three Coins in the Fountain* (Negulesco) (as Prince Di Cessi)
1956 *La Mariée est trop belle* (*The Bride Is Much Too Beautiful*) (Gaspard-Huit) (as Michel); *The Swan* (Charles Vidor) (as Dr. Nicholas Agi); *Julie* (Andrew L. Stone) (as Lyle Benton)
1957 *Escapade* (Habib)
1958 *Dangerous Exile* (Hurst) (as Duc de Beauvais); *Gigi* (Minnelli) (as Gaston Lachaille)
1959 *The Best of Everything* (Negulesco) (as David Savage)
1960 *Can-Can* (Walter Lang) (as Philippe Forstier); *Leviathan* (Keigel) (as Paul)
1961 *Le vergine di Roma* (*Amazons of Rome*) (Bragaglia and Cottafavi) (as Drusco); *Le Comte de Monte Cristo* (*The Count of Monte Cristo*; *The Story of the Count of Monte Cristo*) (Autant-Lara) (as Edmond Dantès)
1962 *Il disordine* (*Le desorde*; *Disorder*) (Brusati) (as Tom); *Mathias Sandorf* (Lampin) (title role)
1963 *The V.I.P.s* (Asquith) (as Marc Champselle)
1965 *Les Sultans* (Delannoy)
1966 *Made in Paris* (Sagal) (as Marc Fontaine)
1967 *Peau d'espion* (*To Commit a Murder*) (Molinaro) (as Charles Beaulieu)
1968 *Le Avventure e gli amori di Miguel Cervantes* (*The Young Rebel*; *Cervantes*; *Les Aventures extraordinaires de Cervantes*) (Sherman) (as Cardinal Acquaviva); *A Flea in Her Ear* (Charon) (as Henri)
1969 *Run a Crooked Mile* (Levitt—for TV); *Fear No Evil* (Wendkos—for TV)
1970 *Ritual of Evil* (Day—for TV)
1973 *The Great American Beauty Contest* (Day—for TV) (as Ralph Dupree)
1974 *The Count of Monte Cristo* (David Greene) (as De Villefort)
1977 *The Man in the Iron Mask* (Newell—for TV) (as D'Artagnan)
1978 *Silver Bears* (Passer) (as Prince di Siracusa)
1982 *Swamp Thing* (Craven) (as Arcane)
1983 *Octopussy* (Glen) (as Kamal)
1984 *Double Deal* (Kavanagh) (as Peter Sterling); *Cover Up* (Crane)
1986 *Beverly Hills Madam* (Hart—for TV) (as Douglas Corbin)
1988 *Grand Larceny* (Swarz—for TV) (as Charles Grand); *Counterforce* (*Escuadron*) (Loma—for TV) (as Kassar)
1989 *The Return of Swamp Thing* (Wynorski) (as Dr. Anton Arcane)
1992 *Year of the Comet* (Yates) (as Philippe)
1994 *That's Entertainment! III* (Friedgen and Sheridan—compilation)

Publications

By JOURDAN: articles—

Interiew with S. Flett, in *Ciné Revue* (Paris), 25 August 1977.
Interview in *Screen International* (London), 11 June 1983.

On JOURDAN: book—

Bowers, Ronald, *The Selznick Players*, New York, 1976

On JOURDAN: articles—

Current Biography 1967, New York, 1967.
Films in Review (New York), June-July 1969.
Cottom, J. v., "Les immortels du cinéma," in *Ciné Revue* (Paris), 23 January 1975.

"La vedette de la Semaine: Louis Jourdan," in *Ciné Revue* (Paris), 13 January 1977.

Bulnes, J., "Les immortels du cinéma," in *Ciné Revue* (Paris), 2 January 1986.

* * *

The career of Louis Jourdan—among the most wasted stars of the Hollywood cinema—must be seen in the context of Hollywood's shifting but consistently uneasy flirtation with the specific forms of "otherness" represented by continental Europe. There have been many attempts to import European performers and build them into major stars. Most have been unsuccessful, their Hollywood careers short-lived, though women (Garbo, Dietrich, Bergman, Lamarr, and to an extent Alida Valli) have enjoyed more success than men (in the sound period, really only Charles Boyer).

With the important exception of the so-called woman's film (generally the domestic or romantic melodrama), Hollywood movies imply a male spectator. Laura Mulvey suggests in her seminal article "Visual Pleasure and Narrative Cinema" (*Screen*, Autumn 1975), that the male protagonist carries the action forward; the woman, as "object of the gaze," actually impedes it, functioning as a necessary spectacle, the "to-be-looked-at." Woman, then, is intrinsically constructed as "other," and her otherness (woman-as-mystery, the "eternal feminine") is underlined, made even more exotic, by foreignness. The male protagonist is the main identification-figure, with whom we look at the woman. Herein lies the problematic otherness of male European stars: their exotic appeal is postulated on notions of sophistication, allure, beauty (rather than a ruggedly masculine handsomeness), and threatening overtones of decadence. They are to-be-looked-at, constructing the spectator as feminine and evoking, for the male, all the dangers of repressed homosexual desire. After World War II, Hollywood's restoration of women to their "rightful" place was inevitably accompanied by a new insistence on masculinity. Boyer became increasingly sinister (*Gaslight*), and was subsequently relegated to character roles. There was really no place for a Louis Jourdan.

Jourdan's definitive (though rarely recognized) performance is in one of the finest, and most atypical, films ever produced in Hollywood: Ophüls's *Letter from an Unknown Woman*. Joan Fontaine's inexhaustibly complex and moving assumption of the title role has been widely celebrated, but Jourdan's contribution is scarcely less remarkable. Without his sensitivity and vulnerability the entire project would become much simpler: a foolish woman infatuated with a callous, incorrigibly promiscuous concert pianist for whom she sacrifices all. Jourdan's intensity gives to the role a sense of enormous (if dissipated) potential which confers dignity and substance not only on Stefan but on Lisa's love for him.

Jourdan worked in only two other distinguished films in the 1940s, both quite central to their respective directors' work, and both underrated by most critics: Minnelli's *Madame Bovary* and Hitchcock's *The Paradine Case*. The former inflects Jourdan's persona in the direction of aristocratic decadence, while retaining the sense of vulnerability. The latter, far more remarkably (especially in the 1950s), eliminates the decadence altogether yet defines the character, at least by implication, as gay. We are informed that Jourdan as the valet has no interest in women, has totally resisted the advances of Mrs. Paradine (Alida Valli, no less), and has been completely dedicated to his master, Colonel Paradine. The valet's dedication is the moral center of this remarkable film, and is combined very disturbingly with Valli's erotic dedication to Jourdan—although Hitchcock later felt Jourdan's character should have been rougher and more "manly" to account for the frustrated Valli's fixation upon him.

Throughout the fifties, Jourdan languished in big-budget CinemaScope soap operas and musicals. Only one deserves notice: Minnelli's *Gigi*, in which Jourdan functions splendidly in a role that,

like Stefan in *Letter*, could easily have been merely unpleasant. His meatiest recent role was the title one in a BBC television version of *Dracula*, the most faithful adaptation of Stoker's novel yet made, therefore the only one that does full justice to the novel's conception of Dracula as the embodiment of a dangerous sexuality that escapes the norms of the patriarchal order.

Appearances in the occasional major studio film such as *Octopussy* (as the less-than-agile villain opposite Roger Moore's equally long-in-the-tooth James Bond) and, more frequently, in exploitation pictures such as *Swamp Thing* and its lame sequel, *The Return of Swamp Thing*, have kept Jourdan's aging continental looks before the cameras, but have added little luster to his long career.

—Robin Wood, updated by John McCarty

JOUVET, Louis

Nationality: French. **Born:** Jules Eugène Louis Jouvet in Crozon, Finistère, Brittany, 24 December 1887. **Education:** Attended schools at Toulouse, Vorey-sur-Arzon, Le Puy-en-Velay, and elsewhere; studied pharmacy, 1905-07. **Military Service:** Performed military service, 1914-17. **Family:** Married; three children. **Career:** 1908—co-founder and administrator of Théâtre d'Action et d'Art; 1910—stage debut as member of Léon Noël troupe; 1911—joined Théâtre des Arts company; 1913—joined Jacques Copeau's Théâtre du Vieux-Colombier as actor and stage manager; 1917—assisted in preparation for Copeau season on Broadway; 1919-21—actor-designer with Vieux-Colombier following reopening; 1923-34 actor-manager of Comédie-Théâtre in Champs-Elysées; formed group "théâtre de cartel" with aim of reviving traditions of French theater; 1928—began association with playwright Jean Giraudoux: produced Giraudoux's subsequent plays; 1932—film debut in *Topaze*; 1934—began managing Athénée Théâtre and collaboration with designer Christian Bérard; appointed to faculty of Paris Conservatoire; 1936—worked on Comédie Française productions; 1940-45—self-imposed exile from German-occupied France; 1945—returned to Paris with production of Giraudoux's *La Folle de Chaillot*. **Died:** 16 August 1951.

Films as Actor:

1932 *Topaze* (Gasnier) (title role)
1935 ***La Kermesse héroïque*** (Feyder) (as the Chaplain)
1936 *Mister Flow* (Siodmak) (title role); *Les Bas-Fonds* (Renoir) (as the baron)
1937 *Mademoiselle Docteu (Salonique, nid d'espions)* (Pabst) (as Simonis); *Un Carnet de bal* (Duvivier) (as the lawyer); *Drôle de drame* (Carné) (as the bishop); *Forfaiture* (L'Herbier) (as Wolfar); *Alibi* (Chenal) (as the commissioner); *La Marseillaise* (Renoir) (as Roederer)
1938 *Ramuntcho* (Barberis) (as the leader of the smugglers); *La Maison du Maltais* (Chenal) (as Rossignol); *Entrée des artistes* (Allégret) (as Lambertin); *Education de prince* (Rim) (as Cercleux); *Le Drame de Shanghaî* (Pabst) (as Ivan); *Hôtel du Nord* (Carné) (as M. Edmond)
1939 *La Fin du jour* (Duvivier) (as Saint-Clair); *La Charrette fantôme* (Duvivier) (as Le Charretier de la Mort); *Volpone* (Tourneur) (as le parasite cynique)
1940 *Untel Père et fils* (Duvivier) (as the colonial); *Sérénade* (Boyer) (as the Viennese chief of police)

Louis Jouvet

1946 *Un Revenant* (Christian-Jaque) (as Jean-Pierre); *Copie conforme (Monsieur Alibi)* (Dréville) (as Gabriel Dupont and Isamora)
1947 *Quai des Orfèvres* (Clouzot) (as Inspector Antoine)
1948 *Les Amoureux sont seuls au monde* (Decoin) (as Favier); *Entre onze heures et minuit* (Decoin) (as Inspecteur Carrel); "Le Retour de Jean" ep. of *Retour à la vie* (Clouzot) (as Gérard)
1949 *Miquette et sa mère* (Clouzot) (as Monchablon); *Lady Paname* (Jeanson) (as Bagnolet)
1950 *Knock ou Le Triomphe de la médecine* (Lefranc) (as Dr. Knock, + artistic direction); *Une Histoire d'amour* (Lefranc) (as inspector); *Comédiens ambulants* (Canolle—short)

Publications

By JOUVET: books—

Prestiges et perspectives du théâtre français, Paris, 1945.
Quatre ans de tournée en Amérique Latine, 1941-45, Paris, 1945.
Ecoute, mon ami, Paris, 1952.
Le Comédien désincarné, Paris, 1954.
Reflexions du comédien, Paris, 1978.

By JOUVET: articles—

"Le cinéma? Que voulez-vous que j'en sache! Je débute . . . j'apprends," interview with Nino Frank in *Pour Vous* (Paris), 9 June 1932.
"L'Acteur à l'écran," in *Festival International* (Cannes), May 1965.

On JOUVET: books—

Canaille, Caro, *Etoiles en pantoufles*, Paris, 1954.
Knapp, Bettina, *Louis Jouvet: Man of the Theatre*, New York, 1957.
Kerien, Wanda, *Louis Jouvet, notre patron*, Paris, 1963.
Capara, Leo, *Dix ans avec Jouvet*, Paris, 1975.
Loubier, Jean-Marc, *Louis Jouvet: Biographie*, Paris, 1986.
Ozeray, Madeleine, *A Toujours Monsieur Jouvet*, Paris, 1987.
Mignon, Paul Louis, *Louis Jouvet: Qui êtes-vous?*, Paris, 1988.
Cathala, Josée, *Louis Jouvet*, Paris, 1989.

On JOUVET: articles—

Cournot, Christine, "Vie d'un grand comédien: Louis Jouvet," in *Cinémonde* (Paris), 24 September 1946.
Lemoine, A., "Jouvet le magnifique," in *Ciné-Digest* (Paris), October 1949.
Lefranc, Guy, "Louis Jouvet n'aimait pas le cinéma: une légende," and "La Prodigieuse Carriére de Louis Jouvet," by Bob Bergut in *L'Ecran Français* (Paris), 29 August 1951.
Aguettand, Lucien, "La Grande Probité de Louis Jouvet," in *Technicien du Film* (Paris), 15 September 1956.
Sadoul, Georges, "Jouvet et le cinéma," and "Notre revanche de cinéastes: lui donner la survie," by Julien Duvivier in *Les Lettres Françaises* (Paris), 25 August 1961.
Peyraud, Marcel, "Les Immortels du cinéma français," in *Ciné Revue* (Paris), 26 October 1967.
Régent, Roger, "Louis Jouvet, 1887-1951," in *Anthologie du Cinéma* vol. 5, Paris, 1969.
"Louis Jouvet," in *Film Dope* (London), December 1983.
Virmaux, A., and O. Virmaux, "Max Ophüls, Madeleine Ozeray, Louis Jouvet: Le Toboggan," in *Cinématographe* (Paris), April 1986.

Philippe, C.-J., and others, "Le comédien exemplaire," in *Cinématographe* (Paris), January 1987.
Chirat, R., "Télé-Jouvet," in *Cinéma* (Paris), 28 October 1987.

* * *

Louis Jouvet was already established as a giant of the French theater before he made his first film at the age of 46. Theater always remained his priority; he sometimes claimed, provocatively, that he acted in movies only for the money. True or not, there was nothing casual about his screen performances. Memorable even in mediocre films, he brought to good material a subtlety and complexity of characterisation that set him among the finest of cinema actors.

Lean, saturnine, faintly reptilian in appearance, Jouvet regarded the world sardonically through narrowed eyes, evidently expecting the worst of humankind. In *La Kermesse héroïque*, his Spanish chaplain, lecherous and mercenary, openly revels in his own hypocrisy, certain of finding it echoed in all those he meets. He was richly sanctimonious as another clergyman, the Anglican bishop of Carné's *Drôle de drame*, set in a wildly improbable Edwardian London; at one point, wishing to avoid the conspicuousness of clerical garb, he appears deliriously camouflaged in kilt and dark glasses.

Under weak direction, Jouvet could edge towards self-plagiarism, as he himself recognized: "If I'm being too Jouvet, stop me," he warned the director of his last film. His disenchanted air suited him to the failures and parasites of society: Arletty's unsavoury pimp in *Hôtel du Nord*, the shifty lawyer of Duvivier's *Carnet de bal*, or, in a more sympathetic vein, the proud, ruined count in Renoir's masterly treatment of Gorky, *Les Bas-Fonds*.

Almost all Jouvet's finest screen roles came during the five years from 1935 to 1940. His postwar films were unremarkable, with one exception: Clouzot's misanthropic *policier*, *Quai des Orfèvres*. Jouvet was the police detective, shabby and stubborn, retaining through his weary disillusionment a cold thin edge of compassion for the denizens of his seedy underworld. The hard-won humanity of his portrayal redeemed the film from facile cynicism.

—Philip Kemp

JULIA, Raul

Nationality: American. **Born:** Raul Rafael Carlos Julia y Arcelay in San Juan, Puerto Rico, 9 March 1940. **Family:** Divorced from first wife; married the dancer-actress Merel Poloway, 1976, two sons. **Education:** Attended University of Puerto Rico, B.A., liberal arts; studied theater with Wynn Handman, founder and artistic director of the American Place Theater. **Career:** 1964—came to the United States, settling in New York; 1964—made New York stage debut in Spanish-language play, *La vida es sueno*; 1964—member of Phoebe Brand's Theater in the Street, performing in Spanish and English; 1966—first began appearing with Joseph Papp's New York Shakespeare Festival; 1968—made Broadway debut in Jack Gelber's *The Cuban Thing*; 1971—made screen debut in small roles in *The Organization* and *The Panic in Needle Park*; 1971—had breakthrough stage role as Proteus in *Two Gentlemen of Verona*; briefly appeared on soap opera *Love of Life*, and was Rafael the Fixit Man on *Sesame Street*; served on Board of Directors of the New York Shakespeare Festival; 1988—in TV mini-series *The Richest Man in the World: The Story of Aristotle Onassis*. **Awards:** Emmy Award, Best Actor, for *The Burning Season*, 1994. **Died:** Of complications from a stroke, 24 October 1994.

Raul Julia in *Kiss of the Spider Woman*

Films as Actor:

1969   *Stiletto* (Kowalski)

1970   *McCloud: Who Killed Miss U.S.A.?* (Colla—for TV) (as Father Nieves)

1971   *Panic in Needle Park* (Schatzberg) (as Marco); *The Organization* (Medford) (as Juan Mendoza); *Been Down So Long It Looks Like Up to Me* (Young) (as Juan)

1975   *Death Scream* (*The Woman Who Cried Murder*) (Heffron—for TV) (as Detective Nick Rodriguez)

1976   *The Gumball Rally* (Bail) (as Franco)

1978   *Eyes of Laura Mars* (Kershner) (as Michael Reisler)

1979   *Strong Medicine* (Foreman)

1982   *The Escape Artist* (Deschanel) (as Stu Quinones); *Tempest* (Mazursky) (as Kalibanos); *One from the Heart* (Coppola) (as Ray)

1985   *Kiss of the Spider Woman* (Babenco) (as Valentin Arregui); *Compromising Positions* (Perry) (as David Suarez); *Overdrawn at the Memory Bank* (Kennedy—for TV) (Douglas Williams—for TV) (as Aram Fingal)

1986   *The Morning After* (Lumet) (as Joaquin Manero); *Florida Straights* (Hodges—for TV) (as Carlos Jayne)

1987   *Trading Hearts* (Leifer) (as Vinnie); *La Gran Fiesta* (Zurinaga) (as The Poet); *The Alamo: Thirteen Days to Glory* (Kennedy—for TV) (as Gen. Lopez de Santa Ana)

1988   *Tequila Sunrise* (Towne) (as Commandante Escalante); *Moon over Parador* (Mazursky) (as Roberto Strausmann); *Tango Bar* (Zurinaga) (as Ricardo); *The Penitent* (Osmond) (as Ramon Guerola)

1989   *Romero* (Duigan) (as Archbishop Oscar Romero); *Mack the Knife* (Golan) (as Macheath)

1990   *Presumed Innocent* (Pakula) (as Alejandro "Sandy" Stern); *Frankenstein Unbound* (Corman) (as Dr. Frankenstein); *The Rookie* (Eastwood) (as Strom); *Havana* (Pollack) (as Arturo Duran—uncredited)

1991   *The Addams Family* (Sonnenfeld) (as Gomez Addams)

1992   *La Peste* (*The Plague*) (Puenzo) (as Cottard); *A Life of Sin* (Neris) (as Paulo)

1993   *Addams Family Values* (Sonnenfeld) (as Gomez Addams)

1994   *The Burning Season* (Frankenheimer—for TV) (as Chico Mendez); *Street Fighter* (de Souza) (as General Bison)

1995   *Down Came a Blackbird* (Sanger—for TV) (as Tomas Ramirez)

Publications

By JULIA: articles—

Interview with Guy Flatley, in *New York Times*, 26 December 1971.
Interview with Brock Brower, in *New York Times*, 6 August 1978.
"Hooray for Julia," interview with M. Gray, in *Photoplay Movies & Video* (London), January 1986.

On JULIA: articles—

Current Biography 1982, New York, 1982.
Van Gelder, L., "At the Movies," in *New York Times*, 27 January 1989.
Hoban, Phoebe, "Meeting Raul," in *New York*, 25 November 1991.
Obituary, in *New York Times*, 25 October 1994.
Natale, Richard, obituary in *Variety* (New York), 31 October 1994.

*   *   *

Despite several fine roles in distinguished (not to mention popular) motion pictures, the legacy of Raul Julia primarily is as a stage actor. In 1966, he began a 16-year association with Joseph Papp's New York Shakespeare Festival; he also appeared on and off Broadway, and on stages throughout the country. Julia was equally adept in musicals and dramas, playing leading men and character roles in productions whose settings ranged from the classic to the contemporary.

A survey of Julia's many important stage credits serves to exemplify his breadth and scope as an actor. He first came to notice in 1971 playing Proteus in the musical *Two Gentlemen of Verona*. Other key Julia performances are as Charley Wykeham in a revival of the Loesser-Abbott musical *Where's Charley?*; Mack the Knife in Brecht-Weill's *The Threepenny Opera*; Lopakhin in Chekhov's *The Cherry Orchard*; Count Dracula in *Dracula*; Jerry in Pinter's *The Betrayal*; and Guido Contini in *Nine*, a musical adaptation of Fellini's *8½*. Add to the list various straight Shakespearean roles, including Orlando in *As You Like It*, Petruchio in *The Taming of the Shrew*, and the title role in *Othello*.

Unfortunately, with few exceptions, Julia was not allowed to transfer his acting brilliance to the screen. Despite his swarthy good looks, he rarely was a leading man in movies. In order to explain this slight, one only can point to the fact that he was Puerto Rican by birth. During Hollywood's Golden Age, traditional leading men most often were named Gable or Cooper or Taylor; by the 1970s, their surnames could be De Niro or Pacino. Had Julia come of age in the 1990s, he might have joined Spanish-born Antonio Banderas as a sexy leading man. But at the time of his premature death in 1994, when he was just in his early fifties, Julia already was beginning to play character villains. Witness his presence in *Street Fighter*, released after his death, in which he is cast (and overacts outrageously) as a crazed warlord who is determined to rule the world, and who battles action movie star Jean-Claude Van Damme.

By far Julia's best screen role came in *Kiss of the Spider Woman*, playing a political activist who shares a jail cell with an apolitical, flamboyantly gay man (William Hurt). Julia's performance was every bit as fine as that of Hurt. But Hurt's role, by its nature, was the showier of the two, and so he was the one who went on to win the Academy Award. The other key Julia movie character is the one that belatedly brought him widespread popularity: Gomez Addams in *The Addams Family* (released in 1991) and its sequel *Addams Family Values* (which came to movie screens two years later), both based on the popular 1960s television sitcom. Julia offers a delightfully broad comedy performance, further displaying his range as an actor.

If there is a thread that remains present through Julia's screen career, it is that he more than occasionally accepted roles in humanist-oriented films that related directly to Latino political concerns. Two of his better roles were as controversial real-life public figures. He offers a subtly forceful performance as martyred El Salvador Archbishop Oscar Romero in *Romero*; almost a year after his death, he was awarded an Emmy for his compelling performance as Brazilian political activist Chico Mendes in the made-for-cable feature *The Burning Season*. Furthermore, he accepted roles in two features directed by Marcos Zurinaga, both of which mix politics with Puerto Rican and Argentinian history and culture: *La Gran Fiesta*, a drama set on the evening before Puerto Rico's takeover by the American military in 1942; and *Tango Bar*, about the reunion of a pair of Argentinian tango dancers who were separated by a military coup.

—Rob Edelman

KAGAWA, Kyoko

Nationality: Japanese. **Born:** Kyoko Ikebe in Ibaragi prefecture, 5 December 1931. **Education:** Attended Municipal 10th Women's High School, Tokyo, graduated 1949. **Family:** Married the writer Takuji Makino, 1963, one son and one daughter. **Career:** 1949—joined Shin-Toho Studio: film debut in *Damoi*; stage debut; 1952—freelance actress; 1957—television debut; 1965-68—lived with her husband in New York. **Address:** 2-6-6 Aoba-dai, Meguro-ku, Tokyo 153, Japan.

Films as Actress:

1949   *Damoi* (Sato); *Kage o matoite*
1950   *Mado kara tobidase* (Shima); *Seishun dekameron*; *Sasameyuki* (Abe); *Kimi to yuku amerika-kogo* (Shima); *Ohtone no yogiri*; *Wakasama zamurai torimonocho: Nazo no noh-men yashiki* (Nakagawa)
1951   *Kujaku no sono* (Shima); *Ginza gesho* (Naruse); *Wakasama zamurai torimonocho: Noroi no ningyo-shi* (Nakagawa); *Kogen no eki yo sayounara* (Nakagawa); *Onna-gokoro dare ga shiru* (*Who Knows a Woman's Heart?*) (Yamamoto); *Karate Sanshiro*; *Asa no namon* (Gosho)
1952   *Oozora no chikai*; *Arashi no naka no haha*; *Shanhai gaeri no Riru* (Shima); *Chakkari fujin to ukkari fujin* (Watanabe); *Reimei hachigatsu jugo-nichi*; *Kin no tamago*; *Okasan* (*Mother*) (Naruse) (as Toshiko Fukuhara, the daughter); *Daigaku no kotengu*; *Kantaro tsukiyo-uta* (Tasaka); *Inazuma* (*Lightning*) (Naruse); *Montenruba no yo wa hukete*
1953   *Himeyuri no to* (*The Tower of Lilies*) (Imai); *Idaten kisha*; *Himegimi to ronin*; *Aiyoku no sabaki*; *Sono imoto*; *Asu wa docchi da*; *Yugato* (Yamamoto); ***Tokyo monogatari*** (*Tokyo Story*) (Ozu) (as Kyoko); *Koibumi* (Tanaka)
1954   *Hanran* (Abe); *Utsukushii hito*; ***Sansho dayu*** (*Sansho: The Bailiff*; *The Bailiff*) (Mizoguchi) (as Anju); *Kunsho* (Shibuya); *Onna no koyomi* (Hisamatsu); *Tomoshibi* (Ieki); *Tekka Bugyo*; *Haha no hatsukoi*; *Jihishincho* (Matsubayashi); *Chikamatsu monogatari* (*A Story from Chikamatsu*; *The Tale of the Crucified Lovers*) (Mizoguchi) (as Osan)
1955   *Aisureba koso*; *Nanatsu no kao no Ginji*; *Akatsuki, no Gassho*; *Nonki saiban*; *Gokumoncho*; *Shiinomi Gakuen* (Shimizu); *Aogashima no kodomotachi: Onnakyoshi no kiroku* (Nakagawa); *Oosho ichidai*; *Seido no Kirisuto* (Shibuya); *Irrashaimase* (Inizuho)
1956   *Abare andon* (Watanabe); *Shuu* (Watanabe); *Kuroobi sangokushi*; *Naze kanojo wa sonatta ka*; *Okusama wa daigaku-sei* (Sugie); *Ruten*; *Nezumi-kozo shinobikomi-hikae* (Kaido); *Morishaige yo doko e iku* (Mizuho); *Neko to Shozo to futaru no onna* (*The Cat, Shozo, and the Two Women*) (Toyoda); *Shin-Heike monogatari: Shizuka to Yoshitsune*; *Tenjodaifu*
1957   *Joshu to tomoni* (*Women in Prison*) (Hisamatsu); *Arashi no naka no otoko* (*The Man in the Storm*) (Taniguchi) (as

Akiko); *Osaka monogatari* (Yoshimura); *Yagyu bugei-cho* (*The Yangyu*; *Secret Scrolls*) (Inagaki) (as Oki); *Hikage no musume*; *Donzoko* (*The Lower Depths*) (Kurosawa) (as Okayo, her sister); *Onna Goroshi abura jigoku* (*The Prodigal Son*) (Horikawa) (as Sister); *Chijo* (Yoshimura)

1958   *Kanpai!*; *Miai-kekkon*; *Onna de arukoto* (Kawashima); *Tokyo no kyujitsu*; *Anzukko* (Naruse); *Zenigata Heiji torimono-hikae: Onibi-doro* (Kato); *Tsuzurikata kyodai* (Hisamatsu); *Akai jinbaori* (Yamamoto); *Boku wa san-nin mae*; *Mori to mizuumi no matsuri* (Uchida); *Zenigata Heiji torimono-hikae: Yukionna no ashiato*; *Soryu hiken* (*Ninjutsu*; *Secret Scrolls, Part II*) (Inagaki) (as Oki)
1959   *Kagero-gasa* (Misumi); *Aijo fudo*; *Ai no kane*; *Ningen no kabe* (Yamamoto); *Nippon tanjo* (Inagaki); *Fuunji: Oda Nobunaga*
1960   *Oedo no kyoji*; *Arakure daimyo*; *Yurei hanjo-ki*; *Hi-sen-ryo* (Tanaka); *Warui yatsu hodo yoku nemuru* (*The Bad Sleep Well*; *The Rose in the Mud*; *The Worse You Are, the Better You Sleep*) (Kurosawa) (as Keiko)
1961   *Osaka-jo monogatari* (*Daredevil in the Castle*; *Devil in the Castle*) (Inagaki) (as Ai); *Kuroi Gashu: Aru sogu*; *Aru sonan* (*Death on the Mountain*) (Sugie); *Mosura* (*Mothra*; *Godzilla vs. the Thing*; *Mothra tai Godzilla*) (Honda) (as showman); *Onna bakari no yoru*
1962   *Kiri no minato no akai hana*; *Asu aru kagiri* (*Till Tomorrow Comes*; *Ashita aru kagiri*) (Toyoda); *Saotome-ke no musumetachi* (Hisamatsu)
1963   *Tengoku to-jigoku* (*High and Low*; *Heaven and Hell*; *The Ransom*) (Kurosawa) (as Reiko, Gondo's wife); *Dokuritsu bijin-tai*; *Shichi-nin no keiji: Onn o sagase*
1965   *Akahige* (*Red Beard*) (Kurosawa) (as mental patient)
1974   *Kareinaru Ichizoku* (*The Family*) (Yamamoto)
1978   *Tsubasa wa kokoro ni tsukete* (Horikawa)
1979   *Otoko wa tsuraiyo: Torajiro Haru no yume* (*Tora's Spring Dream*) (Yamada)
1986   *Harukoma no Uta*
1990   *Shikibu monogatari* (Kumai) (as Isa Otomo)
1993   *Madadayo* (*Not Yet*) (Kurosawa) (as professor's wife)
1995   *Deep River*

Publications

On KAGAWA: article—

Anderson, Joseph L., and Donald Richie, in *The Japanese Film: Art and Industry*, Princeton, New Jersey, 1982.

*   *   *

Early in her career, Kyoko Kagawa worked in various film genres, specializing in the roles of innocent and sincere girls. She established her expertise at portraying this type of character in such roles as the

Kyoko Kagawa in *Tokyo monogatari*

kindhearted daughter in Mikio Naruse's *Okasan*, as the youngest and most sensitive daughter in Ozu's *Tokyo monogatari*, and as the student who tragically dies defending her native Okinawa in Tadashi Imai's *Himeyuri no to*. Throughout her early performances, Kagawa demonstrated an acting style that was very natural, pragmatic, and realistic.

Kenji Mizoguchi expanded her capacity for believable suffering by giving her lead roles as the enslaved daughter who sacrifices her life for her brother in *Sansho dayu* and as a wife who elopes with her husband's employer in the Kabuki-inspired *Chikamatsu monogatari*. In the latter role especially, Kagawa showed the tenacity required to survive the physical conflicts of human emotions. Her depiction of the dramatic changes a woman undergoes from a protected, wealthy wife to an independent, passionate lover was without compromise. Her next portrayal, of a helplessly shrewish wife in Toyoda's *Neko to Shozo to futaru no onna*, was a surprising departure; with a stylized cynicism replacing the naturalistic innocence that was her trademark. Kagawa's success in this unusual role, contradicting the actress's image, widened her scope and reputation.

After appearing once more as an ingenue in Kurosawa's *Warui yatsu hodo yoku nemuru*, she starred in another peculiar and stylized role as the apprehensive wife of a kidnapped president in Kurosawa's *Tengoku to jigoku*. In *Akahige*, Kurosawa incorporated both facets of Kagawa's image by casting her as an innocent girl who turns into a nymphomaniac at night. The performance, which was alternately naively idyllic and knowingly horrifying, was the highpoint of Kagawa's career.

—Kyoko Hirano

KARINA, Anna

Nationality: Danish. **Born:** Hanne Karin Blarke Bayer in Copenhagen, 22 September 1940. **Education:** Studied painting in Copenhagen. **Family:** Married 1) the director Jean-Luc Godard, 1961 (divorced 1967); 2) Pierre-Antoine Fabre, 1968 (divorced); 3) Daniel-Georges Duval, 1978. **Career:** Worked in France as photographer's model; 1959—actress in short film *Pigen og skoene*; 1960—first of a series of films directed by Godard, *Le Petit Soldat*; 1965—TV debut; 1972—set up production company Raska for her film *Vivre ensemble*, of which she also wrote a novelization. **Awards:** Best Actress, Berlin Film Festival, for *Une Femme est une femme*, 1961. **Agent:** 78 Boulevard Malesherbes, 75008 Paris, France.

Films as Actress:

1959 *Pigen og skoene* (*The Girl and the Shoes*) (Schmedes—short)
1960 *Le Petit Soldat* (*The Little Soldier*) (Godard—banned until 1963) (as Veronica Dreyer)
1961 *Ce soir ou jamais* (Deville); *Présentation ou Charlotte et son steak* (Rohmer—short) (shot in 1953 with dubbed voice); *Une Femme est une femme* (*A Woman Is a Woman*) (Godard) (as Angela); *Maid for Murder* (*She'll Have to Go*) (Asher) (as Toni); *Le Soleil dans l'oeil* (Bourdon); *Les Fiancés du Pont Macdonald* (Varda—short burlesque film from *Cléo de cinq à sept* shown in advance of the feature)
1962 *Cléo de cinq à sept* (*Cleo from 5 to 7*) (Varda); *Vivre sa vie* (*My Life to Live*; *It's My Life*) (Godard) (as Nana Kleinfrankenheim); *Shéhérazade* (*La Schiava di Bagdad*) (Gaspard-Huit) (title role); *Le Joli Mai* (Marker); "Le Corbeau et renard" ("The Fox and the Crow") ep. of *Les Quatre Vérités* (*Three Fables of Love*) (Bromberger)
1963 *Dragées au poivre* (*Sweet and Sour*) (Baratier) (as Giselle); *Un Mari à prix fixe* (de Givray)
1964 *Petit jour* (Pierre—short); *Band à part* (*Band of Outsiders*; *The Outsiders*) (Godard) (as Odile); *Le Voleur du Tibidabo* (*La vida es magnifica*) (Ronet); *De l'amour* (Aurel) (as Hélène)
1965 *La Ronde* (*Circle of Love*) (Vadim) (as the chambermaid); *Le Soldatess* (Zurlini); *Alphaville* (*Une étrange aventure de Lemmy Caution*; *Alphaville: A Strange Adventure of Lemmy Caution*; *Tarzan versus I.B.M.*) (Godard) (as Natasha von Braun); *Pierrot le fou* (*Peter the Crazy*) (Godard) (as Marianne Renoir); *La Religieuse* (*The Nun*) (Rivette) (as Suzanne Simonin); *Anna* (Koralnik—for TV)
1966 *Zärliche Haie* (*Tendres requins*) (Deville); *Made in U.S.A.* (Godard) (as Paula Nelson)
1967 *Lo straniero* (*The Stranger*; *L'Etranger*) (Visconti) (as Maria Cardona); "Anticipation" ep. of *Le Plus Vieux Métier du monde* (*The Oldest Profession*) (Godard) (as Natasha, Miss Conversation); *Lamiel* (Aurel)
1968 *The Magus* (*The God Game*) (Guy Green) (as Anne)
1969 *Michael Kohlhaas—Der Rebell* (Schlöndorff) (as Elisabeth); *Laughter in the Dark* (Richardson); *Justine* (Cukor) (as Melissa); *Le temps de mourir* (Farwagi); *Before Winter Comes* (J. Lee Thompson) (as Maria Holz)
1970 *L'alliance* (de Chalonge); *Cran d' Arret* (Boisset)
1971 *Rendez-vous à Bray* (Delvaux); *Carlos* (Geissendörfer)
1972 *The Salzburg Connection* (Katzin) (as Anna Bryant)
1973 *Pane e cioccolata* (*Bread and Chocolate*) (Brusati) (as Elena)
1974 *L'invenzione di Morel* (Greco)
1975 *L'Assassin musicien* (Jacquot); *Les Oeufs brouillés* (Santoni)
1976 *Chinesisches Roulette* (*Chinese Roulette*) (Fassbinder) (as Irene); *Also es war so . . .* (*Willi eine Zauberposse*) (Thome)
1978 *Chaussette surprise* (*Surprise Sock*) (Davy) (as Nathalie)
1979 *Just Like at Home* (Mészáros) (as Anna); *Historien om en moder* (*The Story of a Mother*) (Weeke)
1980 *Ausgerechnet Bananen* (Lommel); *Also es war so* (Thome—for TV)
1981 *L'Ami de Vincent* (*A Friend of Vincent*) (Granier-Deferre)
1984 *Ave Maria* (Richard) (as Berthe Granjeux)
1986 *Dame des Dunes* (Joyce Buñuel—for TV); *Dernière chanson* (*Last Song*) (Berry) (+ co-sc); *Anna* (Koralnik)
1987 *Dernier été à Tanger* (*Last Summer at Tangiers*) (Arcady) (as Myrrha); *Cayenne-Palace* (Maline) (as Lola)
1988 *L'Oeuvre au noir* (*The Abyss*) (Delvaux) (as Catherine)
1990 *Manden, der ville vaere Skyldig* (*The Man Who Wanted to Be Guilty*) (Roos) (as Edith)
1991 *Treasure Island* (as Mother)
1995 *Haut bas fragile* (Rivette) (as Sarah)

Film as Actress and Director:

1974 *Vivre Ensemble*

Publications

By KARINA: books—

Vivre ensemble, Paris 1973.
Golden City, Paris, 1983.
On n'achete pas le soleil, Paris, 1988.

By KARINA: articles—

"Anna Karina: *Vivre ensemble*," interview with L. Vigo, in *Jeune Cinéma* (Paris), September/October 1973.
"Elle est actrice, elle est femme, et pourtant . . . elle tourne; elle s'appelle Anna Karina," interview with G. Charest and A. Leroux, in *Cinéma Québec* (Montreal), November/December 1973.
Interview with A. Warhol, in *Interview* (New York), March 1974.
Ciné Revue (Paris), 28 December 1978 and 1 December 1983.

On KARINA: book—

Godard, Jean-Luc, *Godard par Godard: Les années Karina (1960 à 1967)*, Paris, 1985.

On KARINA: articles—

Ecran (Paris), December 1978; additions in issue for September 1979.
Ciné Revue (Paris), 24 November 1983.
Jousse, T., "Entretien avec Anna Karina," in *Cahiers du Cinéma* (Paris), November 1990.

* * *

Anna Karina is best known for her work with her director/husband Jean-Luc Godard. Their relationship was a classic example of the male auteur constructing his personal film universe, as well as constructing his wife's persona to fit or perform within that universe. Godard's work with Karina is the best of his repertoire, and Karina's work with most other directors is merely ordinary.

Originally from Denmark, Karina arrived in Paris in 1958 with limited facility in the French language, and having only modeling experience and one short film in her country to her credit. She turned down the part in *A bout de souffle* played by Jean Seberg, and instead performed in 1960's *Le Petit Soldat*, Godard's second feature, which earned her international recognition. The following year she appeared in Godard's *Une Femme est une femme*, the same year the two were married.

Godard was able to use Karina's occasional awkwardness as an asset by emphasizing the vulnerability that was the most distinguishing trait of her youthful performances. Despite his almost palpable adoration for her expressed in such films as *Une Femme est une femme* and *Vivre sa vie*, both of which have been described as documentaries on Karina herself, her characters were never mere victims or innocents. In *Vivre sa vie*, Karina's character and her lover read Edgar Allan Poe's *The Oval Portrait*, a foreshadowing of the ultimate dilemma Godard would face when the artist allows his cherished love to perish as he refines her portrait. As the series of collaborations progressed and, perhaps

Anna Karina in *Une Femme est une femme*

coincidentally, their marriage dissolved, Karina became definitively an active agent, an initiator of the action, even a betrayer. As an actress she had become an axiom of the Godardian cinema, a relative constant in his most highly animated period, representing herself as much as any fictional creation.

Apart from Godard's films, Karina's rather melancholy fragility has rarely been employed to full advantage. Jacques Rivette's densely developed portrait of *La Religieuse* and, much later, Fassbinder's *Chinese Roulette* emerge as the plainest exceptions. Her foray into the English-speaking cinema was, for the most part, disastrous, and her roles in such universally unpopular, expensive fiascos as *The Magus* and *Justine* were inconsequential at best. Although international stardom may have been unattainable, and while the French cinema is no longer the vanguard institution it was at the time, Anna Karina was clearly a contributing member of a group that set about actively to rethink the aims and the means of filmmaking.

—Richard Wilson, updated by Kelly Otter

KARLOFF, Boris

Nationality: British. **Born:** William Henry Pratt in London, England, 23 November 1887. **Education:** Attended Merchant Taylors' School, London, Uppingham School, 1903-06; King's College, London, 1906-09. **Family:** Married 1) the dancer Helene Vivian Soule, 1924 (divorced 1928); 2) Dorothy Stine, 1930 (divorced 1945), one daughter; 3) Evelyn Helmore, 1946. **Career:** 1909—emigrated to Canada, and joined the Ray Brandon Players in western Canada; during the next ten years played with other touring companies, including the Henry St. Clair Players and Billie Bennett's road company; 1919—billed film debut in *His Majesty, the American*; 1930—in stage version of *The Criminal Code*, and in film version the following year; 1931—acclaim for his role as the monster in *Frankenstein*; Universal contract; 1941—stage success in *Arsenic and Old Lace*, and later in *The Shop at Sly Corner*, 1949, as Captain Hook in *Peter Pan*, 1950, and in *The Lark*, 1955; 1949—host and star in TV series *Starring Boris Karloff*; 1954-55 panelist on TV series *Down You Go*; 1960-62—host and occasional star of TV series *Thriller*. **Died:** 2 February 1969.

Films as Actor:

1916   *The Dumb Girl of Portici* (Ratinoff) (as extra)
1919   *The Masked Raider* (Kennedy); *The Lightning Raider* (Seitz); *His Majesty, the American* (Henabery) (bit role); *The Prince and Betty* (Thornby) (bit role); *The Deadlier Sex* (Thornby) (as Jules Borney); *The Courage of Marge O'Doone* (Smith) (as Tavish)
1920   *The Last of the Mohicans* (Tourneur) (as Huron Indian)
1921   *Without Benefit of Clergy* (Young) (as Ahmed Khan); *The Hope Diamond Mystery* (*The Romance of the Hope Diamond*) (Payton) (as Priest of Kama-Sita/Dakar); *Cheated Hearts* (Henley) (as Nei Hamid); *The Cave Girl* (Franz) (as Baptiste)
1922   *The Man from Downing Street* (*The Jade Elephants*) (José) (as Dell Monckton/Maharajah Jehan Dharwar); *The Infidel* (Young) (as Nabob); *The Altar Stairs* (Hillyer) (as Hugo); *Omar the Tentmaker* (Young) (as Holy Imam Mowaffak); *The Woman Conquers* (Forman) (as Raoul Maris)
1923   *The Gentleman from America* (Sedgwick); *The Prisoner* (Conway) (as Prince Kapolski)
1924   *Riders of the Plains* (Jaccard); *The Hellion* (Bruce Marshall) (as outlaw); *Dynamite Dan* (Bruce Marshall) (as Tony Garcia)

1925   *Perils of the Wind* (Francis Ford); *Parisian Nights* (Santell) (as Pierre); *Forbidden Cargo* (*Dangerous Cargo*) (Buckingham) (as Pietro Castillano); *The Prairie Wife* (Ballin) (as Diego); *Lady Robin Hood* (Ince) (as Cabraza); *Never the Twain Shall Meet* (Tourneur) (as South Sea villain)
1926   *The Greater Glory* (Rehfeld) (as scissors grinder); *Her Honor, the Governor* (*The Second Mrs. Fenway*) (Withey) (as Snipe Collins); *The Bells* (Young) (as mesmerist); *The Eagle of the Sea* (Lloyd) (as pirate); *Old Ironsides* (*Sons of the Sea*) (Cruze) (as Saracen pirate); *Flames* (Moomaw) (as Blackie Blanchette); *The Golden Web* (Lang) (as Dave Sinclair); *Flaming Fury* (Hogan) (as Gaspard); *The Man in the Saddle* (Clifford Smith) (bit role); *The Nickel Hopper* (Yates) (as lecher); *Valencia* (*The Love Song*) (Buchowetzki) (bit role)
1927   *Tarzan and the Golden Lion* (McGowan) (as Owaza); *Let It Rain* (Cline) (as crook); *The Middlin' Stranger* (Thorpe) (as Al Meggs); *The Princess from Hoboken* (Dale) (as Pavel); *The Phantom Buster* (Bertram) (as Mexican smuggler); *Soft Cushions* (Cline) (as Chief Conspirator); *Two Arabian Knights* (Milestone) (as Purser); *The Love Mart* (Fitzmaurice) (as Fleming)
1928   *Vanishing Rider* (Taylor); *Vultures of the Sea* (Thorpe); *The Little Wild Girl* (Mattison) (as Maurice Kent)
1929   *Burning the Wind* (MacRae and Blache) (as Pug Doran); *The Fatal Warning* (Thorpe) (as Mullins); *The Devil's Chaplain* (Worne) (as Boris); *The Phantom of the North* (Webb) (as Jules Gregg); *Anne against the World* (Worne); *Two Sisters* (Cummings) (as Cecil); *Behind That Curtain* (Cummings) (as Soudanese servant); *The Unholy Night* (*The Green Ghost*) (Barrymore) (as Abdoul)
1930   *The Bad One* (Fitzmaurice) (as prison guard); *The Sea Bat* (Ruggles) (as Corsican); *The Utah Kid* (Thorpe) (as Baxter); *Mother's Cry* (Henley) (as murder victim)
1931   *King of the Wild* (Thorpe) (as Mustapha); *The Criminal Code* (Hawks) (as Ned Galloway); *Cracked Nuts* (Cline) (as revolutionary); *Young Donovan's Kid* (*Donovan's Kid*) (Niblo) (as Cokey Joe); *The Public Defender* (Ruben) (as Professor); *Smart Money* (Green) (as Sport Williams); *I Like Your Nerve* (McGann) (as Luigi); *Pardon Us* (Parrott) (as convict); *Five Star Final* (LeRoy) (as T. Vernon Isopod); *The Mad Genius* (Curtiz) (as father); *Dirigible* (Capra) (bit role); *The Last Parade* (Kenton) (bit role); *The Guilty Generation* (Lee) (as Ton Ricca); *Graft* (Cabanne) (as Joe Terry); *The Yellow Ticket* (*The Yellow Passport*) (Walsh) (as drunken Czarist aide); *Tonight or Never* (LeRoy) (as waiter); *Frankenstein* (Whale) (as the Monster); *Business and Pleasure* (Butler) (as Sheik)
1932   *Behind the Mask* (Dillon) (as Jim Henderson); *Alias the Doctor* (Curtiz) (as Autopsy Surgeon); *Scarface* (Hawks) (as Gaffney); *The Cohens and Kellys in Hollywood* (Dillon) (as himself); *The Miracle Man* (McLeod) (as Nikko); *Night World* (Henley) (as Happy MacDonald); *The Old Dark House* (Whale) (as Morgan); *The Mummy* (Freund) (as Im-Ho-Tep/Ardath Bey); *The Mask of Fu Manchu* (Brabin) (title role)
1933   *The Ghoul* (Hunter) (as Professor Morlant)
1934   *The Lost Patrol* (John Ford) (as Sanders); *The House of Rothschild* (Werker) (as Count Ledrantz); *Screen Snapshots, Number Eleven* (as himself); *The Black Cat* (*The House of Doom*; *The Vanishing Body*) (Ulmer) (as Hjalmar Poelzig); *Gift of Gab* (Freund) (as himself)
1935   *Bride of Frankenstein* (Whale) (as the Monster); *The Raven* (Friedlander) (as Edmond Bateman); *The Black Room* (Neill) (as Baron Gregor de Berghman/Anton de Berghman)

623

1936 *The Invisible Ray* (Hillyer) (as Dr. Janos Rukh); *The Walking Dead* (Curtiz) (as John Ellman); *The Man Who Lived Again* (*The Man Who Changed His Mind*; *Dr. Maniac*; *The Brainsnatcher*) (Stevenson) (as Dr. Laurience); *Juggernaut* (*The Demon Doctor*) (Henry Edwards) (as Dr. Sartorius); *Charlie Chan at the Opera* (Humberstone) (as Gravell)

1937 *Night Key* (Corrigan) (as Dave Mallory); *West of Shanghai* (*The War Lord*) (Farrow) (as General Wu Yen Fang)

1938 *The Invisible Menace* (*Without Warning*) (Farrow) (as Jevries); *Mr. Wong, Detective* (Nigh) (title role)

1939 *Son of Frankenstein* (Lee) (as the Monster); *The Mystery of Mr. Wong* (Nigh) (title role); *Mr. Wong in Chinatown* (Nigh) (title role); *The Man They Could Not Hang* (Grinde) (as Dr. Henryk Savaard); *Tower of London* (Rowland V. Lee) (as Mord)

1940 *Devil's Island* (Clemens) (as Dr. Charles Gaudet); *The Fatal Hour* (*Mr. Wong at Headquarters*) (Nigh) (as Mr. Wong); *British Intelligence* (*Enemy Agent*) (Morse) (as Franz Strendler); *Black Friday* (Lubin) (as Dr. Ernest Sovac); *The Man with Nine Lives* (*Behind the Door*) (Grinde) (as Dr. Leon Kravaal); *Doomed to Die* (*The Mystery of Wentworth Castle*) (Nigh) (as James Lee Wong); *Before I Hang* (Grinde) (as Dr. John Garth); *The Ape* (Nigh) (as Dr. Bernard Adrian); *You'll Find Out* (Butler) (as Judge Mainwaring)

1941 *The Devil Commands* (Dmytryk) (as Dr. Julian Blair); *Information Please Number Eight* (as guest panelist); *Information Please Number Twelve* (as guest panelist)

1942 *The Boogie Man Will Get You* (Landers) (as Professor Nathaniel Billings)

1944 *The Climax* (Waggner) (as Dr. Hohner); *House of Frankenstein* (Kenton) (as Dr. Gustav Niemann)

1945 *The Body Snatcher* (Wise) (as John Gray); *Isle of the Dead* (Robson) (as General Nikolas Pherides)

1946 *Bedlam* (Robson) (as Master George Sims)

1947 *Lured* (*Personal Column*) (Sirk) (as Charles Van Druten); *The Secret Life of Walter Mitty* (McLeod) (as Dr. Hollingshead); *Dick Tracy Meets Gruesome* (*Dick Tracy's Amazing Adventure*) (Rawlins) (as Gruesome); *Unconquered* (Cecil B. DeMille) (as Seneca Chief Guyasura)

1948 *Tap Roots* (George Marshall) (as Tishomingo)

1949 *Abbott and Costello Meet the Killer, Boris Karloff* (Barton) (as Swami Tapur)

1951 *The Strange Door* (Pevney) (as Voltan); *The Emperor's Nightingale* (*Cisaruv Slavik*) (Makovec) (as narrator)

1952 *The Black Castle* (Juran) (as Dr. Meissen)

1953 *Colonel March Investigates* (*Colonel March of Scotland Yard*) (Endfield) (title role); *The Hindu* (*Sabaka*) (Ferrin) (as General Pollegar); *Abbott and Costello Meet Dr. Jekyll and Mr. Hyde* (Lamont) (as Dr. Henry Jekyll); *The Monster of the Island* (*Il mostro dell'isola*) (Montero and Vecchietti) (as smuggler)

1957 *The Juggler of Our Lady* (Kousel) (as narrator); *Silent Death* (*Voodoo Island*) (Le Borg) (as Phillip Knight)

1958 *Frankenstein* (Koch) (as Baron Victor von Frankenstein); *The Haunted Strangler* (*Grip of the Strangler*) (Day) (as James Rankin/Dr. Tenant)

1963 *Corridors of Blood* (*The Doctor of Seven Dials*) (Day) (as Dr. Thomas Bolton); *The Raven* (Corman) (as Dr. Scarabus)

1964 *The Comedy of Terrors* (Jacques Tourneur) (as Amos Hinchley); *Black Sabbath* (*I tre volti della paura*) (Bava) (as Gorca); *Bikini Beach* (Asher) (as art dealer)

1965 *Die, Monster, Die!* (*Monster of Terror*; *The House at the End of the World*) (Haller) (as Nahum Whitley)

1966 *The Ghost in the Invisible Bikini* (Weis) (as Hiram Stokeley); *The Daydreamer* (Bass) (as voice)

1967 *Blind Man's Bluff* (*Cauldron of Blood*; *The Shrinking Corpse*) (Edward Mann) (as Charles Badulescu); *The Venetian Affair* (Jerry Thorpe) (as Dr. Pierre Vaugiroud); *Mondo balordo* (Montero) (as narrator); *Mad Monster Party* (Bass) (as Karloff puppet); *The Sorcerers* (Reeves) (as Professor Monserrat)

1968 *Targets* (Bogdanovich) (as Baron Orlok)

1970 *The Crimson Cult* (*Curse of the Crimson Affair*) (Sewell) (as Professor Marshe); *Isle of the Snake People* (Ibañez and Hill) (as Dr. Carl Van Boulder)

1971 *The Incredible Invasion* (*Sinister Invasion*) (Ibañez and Hill) (as scientist); *The Fear Chamber* (Ibañez and Hill) (as scientist)

1972 *House of Evil* (Ibañez and Hill) (as menace)

Publications

By KARLOFF: articles—

"My Life as a Monster," in *Films and Filming* (London), November 1957.
"Memories of a Monster," in *Saturday Evening Post* (New York), 3 November 1962.

On KARLOFF: books—

Clarens, Carlos, *An Illustrated History of the Horror Film*, New York, 1968.
Butler, Ivan, *Horror in the Cinema*, rev. ed., New York, 1970.
Aylesworth, Thomas, *Monsters from the Movies*, Philadelphia, 1972.
Underwood, Peter, *Karloff: The Life of Boris Karloff*, New York, 1972.
Gifford, Denis, *Karloff: The Man, The Monster, The Movies*, New York, 1973.
Glut, Donald, *The Frankenstein Legend: A Tribute to Mary Shelley and Boris Karloff*, Metuchen, New Jersey, 1973.
Bojarski, Richard, and Kenneth Beale, *The Films of Boris Karloff*, Secaucus, New Jersey, 1974.
Everson, William, *Classics of the Horror Film*, Secaucus, New Jersey, 1974.
Frank, Alan, *Horror Movies*, London, 1974.
Jensen, Paul, *Boris Karloff and His Films*, New York, 1974.
Lindsay, Cynthia, *Dear Boris: The Life of William Henry Pratt a.k.a. Boris Karloff*, New York, 1978.
Mank, Gregory William, *Karloff and Lugosi: The Story of a Haunting Collaboration*, Jefferson, North Carolina, 1990.
Nollen, Scott Allen, *Boris Karloff: A Critical Account of His Screen, Stage, Radio, Television, and Recording Work*, Jefferson, North Carolina, 1991.
Buehrer, Beverley Bare, *Boris Karloff: A Bio-Bibliography*, Westport, Connecticut, 1993.
McCarty, John, *Movie Psychos and Madmen*, New York, 1993.
McCarty, John, *The Fearmakers*, New York, 1994.

On KARLOFF: articles—

Gordon, A , "Boris Karloff," in *Cinema* (Beverly Hills), no. 1, 1969.
Roman, Robert C., "Boris Karloff," in *Films in Review* (New York), August-September 1969.
Gerard, Lillian, "Boris Karloff: The Man behind the Myth," in *Film Comment* (New York), Spring 1970.
Ecran (Paris), May 1978.
Starburst, no. 57, 1983.

Boris Karloff

American Classic Screen (Shawnee Mission, Kansas), March-April 1983.

Prédal, René, "L'Usine aux maléfices," in *Avant-Scène du Cinéma* (Paris), March 1985.

*   *   *

In one sense, Boris Karloff could be judged a failure. A lifetime of roles intended to create horror and loathing only succeeded in making him one of the most loved of actors. Audiences who shuddered pleasurably at his ghouls saw straight through them, to the gentle, dignified man beneath. Karloff ended up a white-haired, grandfatherly figure telling spooky tales to delight the children, any suggestion of menace belied by the kindliness in his eyes. That same sympathy animated the monsters he created—grave, vulnerable beings, victims of the "normal" world around them.

Unlike Lorre or Lugosi, serious actors who chafed at the narrow range into which Hollywood forced them, Karloff never strongly objected to being typecast in horror movies. In part, his reaction was practical: the relief of a 45-year-old actor, with ten years of ramshackle stock companies and ten more of movie bit-parts behind him, suddenly finding fame and security in his 65th film, the 1931 James Whale version of *Frankenstein*. But he was also doing what he could do best. To the end of his days, he called the Frankenstein Monster the best friend any actor could have had.

Tall, gaunt, lantern-jawed, Karloff moved with a somnolent slowness that aptly evoked the inexorable, slow-motion menace of a bad dream. Deep-set eyes, overhanging brows, and a voice that seemed to echo from cobwebby vaults enhanced the intensity of his presence. Karloff never needed to gesticulate or rave; the quietly understated malevolence of his acting gained the more by contrast with the B movie hamming that often surrounded him.

Karloff began acting in silent films, most notably *The Bells*, where he played an evil mesmerist opposite hero Lionel Barrymore. But it was *Frankenstein* that made him a star—though a couple of good roles just before, in Hawks's *The Criminal Code* and LeRoy's *Five Star Final* (as the ineffably named phony clergyman, T. Vernon Isopod), helped bring him to James Whale's attention when the original star of *Frankenstein*, Bela Lugosi, opted out of the role of the monster because he did not want to disguise his features under pounds of makeup and his distinctive voice with inarticulate grunts. Thus, Karloff got his most famous role by default. Nevertheless, the inarticulate pathos of Karloff's portrayal of the monster, innocent and bewildered, staggering beneath the burden of emotions it can neither express nor control, lent the film dignity and depth, creating a lasting classic. Universal billed him in the credits only as "Karloff"; for future films, his first name was reinstated, but for filmgoers everywhere, young and old, generation after generation, no other name but "Karloff" was ever needed.

Karloff played the monster in two sequels for Universal (and once on television, in an episode of the hit television series *Route 66*). Without his presence, further sequels collapsed into routine programmers. (Ironically, Bela Lugosi finally did overcome his antipathy for the role of the monster and played it himself—long after Karloff had discarded it to go on to bigger things—in Universal's *Frankenstein Meets the Wolfman*, the fourth entry in the studio's long-running series.) Both *Frankenstein* sequels in which Karloff reprised his role, *Bride of Frankenstein* and *Son of Frankenstein*, were made during the 1930s, the period of Universal's great horror cycle, and Karloff's best decade. As *The Mummy*, a virtual remake of Universal's smash hit *Dracula*, set in Egypt, he slowed his movements yet further into an ancient, hieratic solemnity, eyes burning fiercely in a face of weathered sandstone. Death-in-life roles suited his cadaverous deliberation: in Edgar G. Ulmer's broodingly atmospheric *The Black Cat*, pacing gravely through galleries of women's corpses preserved behind glass; a

resurrected convict in Curtiz's *The Walking Dead*; and, chuckling darkly, the clubfooted executioner Mord, henchman to Rathbone's Richard III in *Tower of London*.

Within the narrow range of his work, Karloff varied each role through subtle individual touches. Often, he undercut them with ironic humor: lumbering and grunting as the drunkenly lecherous butler of *The Old Dark House*; silkily urbane in *The Mask of Fu Manchu* (a rendition later reworked for virtue in the Mr. Wong series); ultimately over the top as a religious fanatic driven to mania by the sunbaked desert as a member of *The Lost Patrol*. Val Lewton provided Karloff with three quality assignments in the 1940s: *The Body Snatcher*, *Isle of the Dead*, and the elegantly Hogarthian *Bedlam*. Lewton's belief that horror can best be elicited through understatement and suggestion matched Karloff's talents perfectly, and he responded with some of his most stylishly controlled playing, especially in *The Body Snatcher*, as murderous cabman and protege of Burke and Hare, John Gray, arguably his greatest performance outside the original Frankenstein. The role is easily one of the subtlest, and scariest, dual-personality villains in the history of screen horror.

He was also adept at comedy, originating the role of the murderous Karloff lookalike Jonathan Brewster in the classic stage comedy *Arsenic and Old Lace*, where he sent up his own image as the ultimate bogeyman; Raymond Massey took the role in the Frank Capra film version because Karloff was still playing it on tour at the time.

Karloff again enjoyed sending up his image in Roger Corman's Edgar Allan Poe spoof, *The Raven*, and *The Comedy of Terrors*, where he appeared with fellow screen bad guys Peter Lorre, Basil Rathbone, and Vincent Price. One of Karloff's best roles came almost at the last, more or less playing himself in Bogdanovich's directorial debut, *Targets*. As an avowed "antique, an anachronism" in an age of impersonal slaughter, Karloff manifested a touching dignity, and the film provided an affectionate farewell tribute—although, crippled by arthritis to the point of virtual immobility, he tread the boards through five more shockers the same year, one in England, the others in Mexico. Like one of the undead characters he often played, he arose from the grave four years after his death in his last released film, *Blind Man's Bluff*, a feature he shot in Spain in 1967.

—Philip Kemp, updated by John McCarty

KAYE, Danny

Nationality: American. **Born:** David Daniel Kominski (some sources say Kaminski) in Brooklyn, New York, 18 January 1913. **Education:** Attended Thomas Jefferson High School, Brooklyn. **Military Service: Family:** Married Sylvia Fine, 1940, one daughter. **Career:** Singer and comic after leaving school: worked on radio station WBBC, Brooklyn, and on the Borscht Circuit in the Catskill Mountains, New York; 1933-39—toured with dancing act of Dave Harvey and Kathleen Young, and later as a single act, with material often written by Sylvia Fine; 1939—Broadway debut in *The Straw Hat Revue*; 1940—nightclub act at La Martinique, New York; 1940-41—parts in *Lady in the Dark* and *Let's Face It* on Broadway; performed for war bond rallies, and in camps and hospitals overseas during World War II; 1944—feature film debut in *Up in Arms* for Samuel Goldwyn; 1945—inaugurated popular radio show; 1948—began regular seasons at London Palladium; 1953—co-founder, with Sylvia Fine, Dena Productions; 1954—started his work for the United Nations Children's Fund; 1960—formed Belmont Television Company, and appeared on *The Danny Kaye Show*, 1963-67. **Awards:** Special Academy Award, 1954; Jean Hersholt Humanitarian Award, 1982; Member of French Legion of Honor, 1986. **Died:** Of a heart attack, in Los Angeles, 3 March 1987.

Danny Kaye with Vera Ellen in *Wonder Man* © 1945, Beverly Productions, Inc.

Films as Actor:

1937 *Dime a Dance* (Christie—short)

1938 *Getting an Eyeful* (Christie—short); *Cupid Takes a Holiday* (Watson—short); *Money on Your Life* (Watson—short)

1942 *Night Shift* (Kanin—short)

1944 *Up in Arms* (Nugent) (as Danny Weems); *The Birth of a Star* (*The Danny Kaye Story*) (Pollard—compilation of Kaye's shorts)

1945 *Wonder Man* (Humberstone) (as Buzzy Bellew/Edwin Dingle)

1946 *The Kid from Brooklyn* (McLeod) (as Burleigh Sullivan)

1947 *The Secret Life of Walter Mitty* (McLeod) (title role); *A Song Is Born* (Hawks) (as Professor Hobart Frisbee); *Bob Hope Reports to the Nation* (USO short) (appearance)

1949 *It's a Great Feeling* (Butler) (as guest); *The Inspector General* (Koster) (as Georgi)

1951 *Bernard Shaw's Village* (Frieze—short); *On the Riviera* (Walter Lang) (as Henri Duran/Jack Martin)

1952 *Hans Christian Andersen* (Charles Vidor) (title role)

1954 *Knock on Wood* (Panama and Frank) (as Jerry); *Hula from Hollywood* (Staub—short); *White Christmas* (Curtiz) (as Phil Davis); *Assignment Children* (short for UNICEF)

1955 *The Court Jester* (Panama and Frank) (as Hawkins)

1958 *Merry Andrew* (Kidd) (as Andrew Larabee); *Me and the Colonel* (Glenville) (as S. I. Jacobowsky)

1959 *The Five Pennies* (Shavelson) (as Red Nichols)

1961 *On the Double* (Shavelson) (as Pfc. Ernest Williams/Gen. Sir Lawrence Mackenzie-Smith)

1963 *The Man from the Diners' Club* (Tashlin) (as Ernie Klenk)

1969 *The Madwoman of Chaillot* (Forbes) (as Ragpicker)

1972 *Pied Piper* (short for UNICEF)

1981 *Skokie* (Wise—for TV) (as Max Feldman)

Publications

On KAYE: books—

Freedland, Michael, *The Secret Life of Danny Kaye*, London, 1985.
Gottfried, Martin, *Nobody's Fool: The Lives of Danny Kaye*, New York, 1994.

On KAYE: articles—

Current Biography 1952, New York, 1952.
Baker, P., "Kaye Dreams Are Hard to Capture on Film," in *Films and Filming* (London), December 1955.
Buckley, M., "Danny Kaye," in *Films in Review* (New York), May 1973.
Ecran (Paris), April 1979.
Obituary, in *Variety* (New York), 4 March 1987.
Obituary, in *Films and Filming* (London), April 1987.

*   *   *

The films of Danny Kaye comprise only one aspect of his overall career as a comedian. Kaye's initial rise to fame came on the stage, in various revues and on Broadway. He also was extremely successful on the New York nightclub circuit. Reportedly, it was in one of these nightclubs that Sam Goldwyn caught Kaye's act and offered him a film contract. This was not his first contact with the motion picture business. In the late 1930s he appeared in a few two-reelers for Educational Pictures which were not particularly entertaining or successful. In 1941 he turned down an MGM contract, choosing instead to continue working before live audiences. By the time Kaye decided to accept Sam Goldwyn's offer, he already had established himself as one of the hottest young comedians in New York, and he came to Hollywood as a star before he made his first feature.

Because of Kaye's success on the stage, Goldwyn spared no expense in launching his film career. His early films were lavish in their settings and featured extravagant musical numbers. Kaye's own routines were tailor-written for him by his wife and creative partner, Sylvia Fine. With their complicated patter and witty lyrics, her songs complemented his style of comedy. Kaye had become famous for his verbal acrobatics and foreign double-talk. He had specialized in such tongue twisters and rhymes as "The pellet with the poison's in the vessel with the pestle, the chalice from the palace has the brew that is true," from *The Court Jester*. Other examples include "The Lobby Number" in Kay's feature debut, *Up in Arms*, in which he sings to a crowd in a theater lobby; and *Wonder Man*, in which he uses an opera to sing out the clues of a murder.

In many of his films Kaye was cast in dual roles, sometimes playing twins or lookalikes (as in *Wonder Man* and *On the Double*). Other times he played characters with multiple personalities (as in *The Secret Life of Walter Mitty*). Generally speaking, one side of Kaye's character would be weak and helpless while the other would be strong and resourceful. During the course of the film, Kaye would learn to blend the two personalities in order to become a better individual.

In 1953 Kaye and his wife formed their own production company, Dena Productions. Together with the writers Norman Panama and Melvin Frank, they produced three pictures. One of these, *The Court Jester*, is not only Kaye's finest film but one of the all-time-classic screen comedies. Its $4-million budget made it the most expensive comedy up to that time. Kaye also was capable of playing the graceful romantic, as he so capably did in *White Christmas*. Here, his soft singing voice was never utilized so effectively. It is a shame that he was not allowed to play such roles more often.

Kaye also proved to be an equally fine dramatic actor. In the television movie *Skokie*, he offered a powerful performance as a concentration camp survivor who has settled in Middle America, and who sets out to thwart an attempt by neo-Nazis to hold a street demonstration. Earlier, in *The Five Pennies*, he was effective in the role of jazz musician Red Nichols.

Kaye also was noted for his many offstage and offscreen charitable endeavors, most specifically his varied activities on behalf of UNICEF.

—Linda Obalil, updated by Audrey E. Kupferberg

KEATON, Buster

Nationality: American. **Born:** Joseph Francis Keaton in Piqua, Kansas, 4 October 1895. **Family:** Married 1) Natalie Talmadge, 1921 (divorced 1933), sons: Joseph and Robert; 2) Mae Scribbens, 1933 (divorced 1936); 3) Eleanor Norris, 1940. **Career:** 1898-1917—beginning at the age of four, appeared with his parents, Joe and Myra Keaton, in vaudeville act billed as The Three Keatons; 1917—moved to California; 1917-20—appeared in 15 two-reelers for Comique Film Corporation, with Roscoe "Fatty" Arbuckle as director-actor-scriptwriter, starting with first film *The Butcher Boy*, 1917; 1918—as member of U.S. Army, entertained troops in France; 1919—offered own production company with Metro Pictures by Joseph Schenk; 1920-23—produced 19 two-reelers; 1923-28—directed ten features for Metro, starting with *The Three Ages*; 1929-31—plagued with marital problems and alcoholism, career faded during the transition from silent to sound films; 1934-39—starred in 16 comedies for Educational Pictures; 1935—became uncredited gag writer for the Marx Brothers and in the 1940s for Red Skelton's features; 1939-41—appeared in ten two-reelers for Columbia; from 1949—moved to TV to execute innovative commercials and become frequent guest in both comic and dramatic TV series; 1949—in TV series *The Buster Keaton Comedy Show*; 1950-51—in TV series *The Buster Keaton Show*; 1951—appearance with Chaplin in Chaplin's *Limelight* revived Keaton's career. **Awards:** "George Award," at first annual George Eastman Festival of Film Arts in Rochester, New York, 1956; special Academy Award, "for his unique talents which brought immortal comedies to the screen," 1959; honored at the screening of *Film*, written by Samuel Beckett, at the Venice Film Festival, 1965. **Died:** Of lung cancer in Woodland Hills, California, 1 February 1966.

Films as Actor:

(two-reelers with Roscue "Fatty" Arbuckle as director-actor-scriptwriter)

1917   *The Butcher Boy* (as village pest); *A Reckless Romeo* (as a rival); *The Rough House* (as grocer's boy and cop); *His Wedding Night* (as delivery boy); *Oh, Doctor!* (as doctor's son); *Coney Island* (*Fatty at Coney Island*) (as lifeguard); *A Country Hero* (as the dancer)
1918   *Out West* (as Bill Bullhum); *The Bell Boy* (as Arbuckle's assistant); *Moonshine* (as assistant revenue agent); *Good Night, Nurse!* (as the doctor/a visitor); *The Cook* (as the waiter and general helper)
1919   *A Desert Hero* (as badman); *Back Stage* (as stagehand); *The Hayseed* (as store clerk)
1920   *The Garage* (*Fire Chief*) (as garage mechanic)

(silent features with Keaton as leading actor)

1920   *The Saphead* (Blaché) (as Bertie "The Lamb" Van Alstyne)
1927   *College* (Horne) (as Ronald)
1928   *Steamboat Bill, Jr.* (Reisner) (as Willie Canfield); *The Cameraman* (Sedgwick) (as Luke Shannon, + pr)
1929   *Spite Marriage* (Sedgwick) (as Elmer Edgemont)

(1930s sound features with Keaton in minor and some major roles)

1929   *The Hollywood Revue of 1929* (Reisner) (as an oriental dancer)
1930   *Free and Easy* (*Easy Go*) (Sedgwick) (as Elmer Butts); *Doughboys* (*The Big Shot; Forward March!*) (Sedgwick) (as Elmer Stuyvesant, + pr)

1931 *Parlor, Bedroom, and Bath* (Sedgwick) (as Reginald Irving, + pr); *The March of Time* (Reichner—not completed); *Side-walks of New York* (Jules White and Zion Myers) (as Homer Van Tine Harmon, + pr)

1932 *The Passionate Plumber* (Sedgwick) (as Elmer Tuttle); *Speak Easily* (Sedgwick) (as Professor Timoleon Zanders Post); *What! No Beer?* (Sedgwick) (as Elmer J. Butts); *The Little King* (not completed)

1934 *Le Roi des Champs Elysées* (*Champ of the Champs Elysées*) (Nosseck) (as Buster Garnier/Jim Le Balafre)

1936 *The Invader* (*The Intruder*; *An Old Spanish Custom*) (Brunel) (as Leander Proudfoot)

(sound two-reelers for Educational Pictures starring Keaton; role as Elmer unless otherwise noted)

1934 *The Gold Ghost* (Lamont) (as Wally); *Allez Oop* (Lamont)

1935 *Palooka from Paducah* (Lamont) (as Jim); *One-Run Elmer* (Lamont); *Hayseed Romance* (Lamont); *Tars and Stripes* (Lamont); *The E-Flat Man* (Lamont); *The Timid Young Man* (Sennett) (as Milton)

1936 *Three on a Limb* (Lamont) (as Elmer Brown); *Grand Slam Opera* (Lamont) (as Elmer Butts); *Blue Blazes* (Raymond Kane); *The Chemist* (Al Christie) (as Elmer Triple); *Mixed Magic* (Raymond Kane)

1937 *Jail Bait* (Lamont); *Ditto* (Lamont); *Love Nest on Wheels* (Lamont)

(two-reeler Columbia shorts starring Keaton)

1939 *Pest from the West* (Del Lord) (as American yachtsman); *Mooch-ing through Georgia* (Jules White) (as Homer Cobb)

1940 *Nothing but Pleasure* (Jules White) (as Clarence Plunkett); *Pardon My Berth Marks* (Jules White) (as Elmer Pin-feather); *The Taming of the Snood* (*Four Thirds Off*) (Jules White) (as a hat shop owner); *The Spook Speaks* (Jules White) (as magician's housekeeper); *His Ex Marks the Spot* (*Buster's Last Stand*) (Jules White) (as the hus-band)

1941 *So You Won't Squawk* (Del Lord) (as Eddie); *General Nuisance* (*The Private General*) (Jules White) (as Peter Hedley Lamar Jr.); *She's Oil Mine* (Jules White) (as Buster Waters)

(feature films with Keaton in minor role, from 1939)

1939 *Hollywood Cavalcade* (Cummings) (as himself)

1940 *The Villain Still Pursued Her* (Edward F. Cline) (as William); *Li'l Abner* (Rogell) (as Lonesome Polecat); *New Moon* (Rob-ert Z. Leonard) (as Prisoner "LuLu")

1943 *Forever and a Day* (in sequence directed by Hardwicke) (as Dabb's assistant)

1944 *San Diego, I Love You* (LeBorg) (as bus driver); *Two Girls and a Sailor* (Thorpe) (as Durante's son)

1945 *That's the Spirit* (Lamont) (as L. M.); *That Night with You* (Seiter) (as Sam, the short-order cook); *She Went to the Races* (Goldbeck) (as bellboy)

1946 *God's Country* (Tansey); *El Moderno Barba Azul* (*Boom in the Moon*; *A Modern Bluebeard*) (Jamie Salvador) (as pris-oner of Mexicans who is sent to the moon)

1949 *The Lovable Cheat* (Oswald) (as Curt Bois); *In the Good Old Summertime* (Robert Z. Leonard) (as Hickey); *You're My Everything* (Walter Lang) (as waiter)

1950 *Sunset Boulevard* (Wilder) (as himself)

1951 *The Misadventures of Buster Keaton* (compilation of three episodes of *The Buster Keaton Show* TV series)

1952 *Limelight* (Chaplin) (as piano accompanist); *L'incantevole nemica* (*Captivating Enemy*) (Gora) (bit role)

1956 *Around the World in Eighty Days* (Michael Anderson) (as train conductor)

1960 *The Adventures of Huckleberry Finn* (*Huckleberry Finn*) (Curtiz) (as lion tamer)

1962 *Ten Girls Ago* (Harold Daniels—not completed)

1963 *It's a Mad, Mad, Mad, Mad World* (Stanley Kramer) (as Jimmy the Crook)

1964 *Pajama Party* (*The Maid and the Martian*) (Wies) (as Chief Rotten Eagle)

1965 *Beach Blanket Bingo* (Asher) (as himself); *How to Stuff a Wild Bikini* (Asher) (as Bwana); *Sergeant Deadhead* (*Sergeant Deadhead the Astronaut*) (Taurog) (as Pvt. Blinken); *The Man Who Bought Paradise* (*Hotel Paradise*) (Ralph Nelson—for TV) (as Mr. Blore)

1966 *A Funny Thing Happened on the Way to the Forum* (Richard Lester) (as Erronius)

1967 *Due Marines e un Generale* (*War, Italian Style*) (Scattini) (as Gen. Von Kassler)

(miscellaneous shorts)

1929 *The Voice of Hollywood, Number 10* (Lewyn)

1931 *The Stolen Jools* (*The Slippery Pearls*) (McGann) (as a Key-stone Kop)

1933 *Hollywood on Parade* (Lewyn)

1935 *La Fiesta de Santa Barbara* (Lewyn)

1936 *Sunkist Stars at Palm Springs*

1950 *Un Duel à Mort* (as a comic duelist, + co-sc)

1965 *Film* (Alan Schneider); *The Railrodder* (Potterton)

(industrial films)

1952 *Paradise for Buster* (Del Lord)

1960 *The Devil to Pay* (Skoble) (as Diablos)

1963 *The Triumph of Lester Snapwell* (James Calhoun) (title role)

1965 *The Fall Guy* (Bateman) (as Mr. Goodfarmer/Mr. Badfarmer)

1966 *The Scribe* (Sebert) (as newspaper reporter)

Films as Actor and Director:

(two-reelers with Keaton in the leading role, co-directed and co-scripted by Keaton with Eddie Cline, unless otherwise noted)

1920 *One Week* (as the husband); *Convict 13* (as the golfer/the vic-tim); *The Scarecrow* (as roommate); *Neighbors* (as the boy)

1921 *The Haunted House* (as bank clerk); *Hard Luck* (as the melan-choly boy); *The High Sign* (as the boy); *The Goat* (co-d and co-sc with Mal St. Clair) (as the boy); *The Boat* (as the captain of the DAMFINO)

1922 *The Paleface* (as Little Chief Paleface); *The Playhouse* (as the stage hand); *Cops* (as the unsuspecting victim); *My Wife's Relation* (as the husband); *The Blacksmith* (co-d and co-sc with Mal St. Clair) (as the blacksmith's assistant); *The Fro-zen North* (as the adventurer); *The Electric House* (as an electrical engineer); *Daydreams* (as the boy)

1923 *The Balloonatic* (as the boy); *The Love Nest* (as sailor)

(silent features directed by Keaton, with Keaton as leading actor)

1923 *The Three Ages* (co-d with Cline) (as the boy); *Our Hospitality* (co-d with Blystone) (as Willie McKay)

1924 *Sherlock, Jr.* (as the theater projectionist/title role); *The Navi-gator* (co-d with Crisp) (as Rollo Treadway)

1925   *Seven Chances* (as Jimmie Shannon); *Go West* (as Friendless, +
         story)
1926   *Battling Butler* (Alfred Butler); ***The General*** (as Johnnie Gray)

(one-reelers directed by Keaton; sound)

1938   *Life in Sometown, U.S.A.*; *Hollywood Handicap*; *Streamlined
         Swing*

Other Films:

1939   *The Jones Family in Hollywood* (Mal St. Clair) (co-sc); *The
         Jones Family in Quick Millions* (Mal St. Clair) (co-sc)

Publications

By KEATON: book—

My Wonderful World of Slapstick, with Charles Samuels, New York,
   1960; rev. ed., 1982.

By KEATON: articles—

"What Are the Six Ages of Comedy," in *The Truth about the Movies*,
   Hollywood, 1924.
"Why I Never Smile," in *Ladies Home Journal* (New York), June
   1926.
Interview with Christopher Bishop, in *Film Quarterly* (Berkeley), Fall
   1958.
"Keaton: Still Making the Scene," interview with Rex Reed, in *New York
   Times*, 17 October 1965.
"Keaton at Venice," interview with John Gillett and James Blue, in *Sight
   and Sound* (London), Winter 1965.
Interview with Arthur Friedman, in *Film Quarterly* (Berkeley), Summer
   1966.

On KEATON: books—

Turconi, Davide, and Francesco Savio, *Buster Keaton*, Venice, 1963.
Blesh, Rudi, *Keaton*, New York, 1967.
Lebel, Jean-Pierre, *Buster Keaton*, translated by P. D. Stovin, New York,
   1967.
Brownlow, Kevin, *The Parade's Gone By*, New York, 1968.
McCaffrey, Donald W. , *Four Great Comedians: Chaplin, Lloyd, Keaton,
   Langdon*, New York, 1968.
Robinson, David, *Buster Keaton*, London, 1968.
Kerr, Walter, *The Silent Clowns*, New York, 1975.
Anobile, Richard J., *The Best of Buster: The Classic Comedy Scenes
   Direct from the Films of Buster Keaton*, New York, 1976.
Wead, George, *Buster Keaton and the Dynamics of Visual Wit*, New York,
   1976.
Dardis, Tom, *Keaton: The Man Who Wouldn't Lie Down*, New York,
   1979.
Benayoun, Robert, *The Look of Buster Keaton*, Paris, 1982; London,
   1984.
Kline, Jim, *The Complete Films of Buster Keaton*, New York, 1993.
Edwards, Larry, *Buster: A Legend in Laughter*, Bradenton, Florida,
   1995.
Meade, Marion, *Buster Keaton: Cut to the Chase*, New York, 1995.
Rapf, Joanna E., and Gary L. Green, *Buster Keaton: A Bio-Bibliogra-
   phy*, New York, 1995.
Oldham, Gabriella, *Keaton's Silent Shorts: Beyond the Laughter*,
   Carbondale, Illinois, 1996.

On KEATON: articles—

Keaton, Joe, "The Cyclone Baby," in *Photoplay* (New York), May
   1927.
Review of *The General*, in *Motion Picture Magazine*, May 1927.
Agee, James, "Comedy's Greatest Era," in *Life* (New York), 5 Septem-
   ber 1949.
"Gloomy Buster Is Back Again," in *Life* (New York), 13 March 1950.
Dyer, Peter, "Cops, Custard—and Keaton," in *Films and Filming* (Lon-
   don), August 1958.
"Keaton" issue of *Cahiers du Cinéma* (Paris), August 1958.
Bishop, Christopher, "The Great Stone Face," in *Film Quarterly* (Ber-
   keley), Fall 1958.
Baxter, Brian, "Buster Keaton," in *Film* (London), November/Decem-
   ber 1958.
Robinson, David, "Rediscovery: Buster," in *Sight and Sound* (London),
   Winter 1959.
"Buster Keaton in Beckett's First Film," in *New York Times*, 21 July 1964.
Garcia Lorca, Federico, "Buster Keaton Takes a Walk," in *Sight and
   Sound* (London), Winter 1965.
Obituary in *New York Times*, 2 February 1966.
Crowther, Bosley, "Keaton and the Past," in *New York Times*, 6 Febru-
   ary 1966.
McCaffrey, Donald, "The Mutual Approval of Keaton and Lloyd," in
   Cinema Journal (Evanston, Illinois), no. 6, 1967.
Houston, Penelope, "The Great Blank Page," in *Sight and Sound*
   (London), Spring 1968.
Maltin, Leonard, "Buster Keaton," in *The Great Movie Shorts*, New
   York, 1972.
Mast, Gerald, "Buster Keaton," in *The Comic Mind*, New York, 1973.
Rubinstein, E., "Observations on Keaton's *Steamboat Bill, Jr.*," in *Sight
   and Sound* (London), Autumn 1975.
Everson, William, "Rediscovery: *Le Roi des Champs Elysées*," in *Films
   in Review* (New York), December 1976.
Houston, Penelope, "Buster Keaton," in *The National Society of Film
   Critics on Movie Comedy*, New York, 1977.
Wade, G., "The Great Locomotive Chase," in *American Film* (Wash-
   ington, D.C.), July/August 1977.
Denby, David, "Buster the Great," in *Premiere* (New York), March
   1991.
Sanders, Judith, and David Lieberfeld, "Dreaming in Pictures: The
   Childhood Origins of Buster Keaton's Creativity," in *Film Quarterly*
   (Berkeley), Summer 1994.
Gunning, Tom, "Buster Keaton: Or the Work of Comedy in the Age of
   Mechanical Reproduction," in *Cineaste* (New York), vol. 21, no. 3,
   1995.
Telotte, J. P., "Keaton Is Missing," in *Literature/Film* (Salisbury, Mary-
   land), Spring 1995.
Hogue, Peter, "Eye of the Storm: Buster Keaton," in *Film Comment*
   (New York), September/October 1995.
Lane, Anthony, "The Fall Guy: Buster Keaton's Genius Turned Slapstick
   and Catastrophe into Comic Gold," in *New Yorker*, 23 October 1995.

On KEATON: films—

The Buster Keaton Story, directed by Sidney Sheldon, 1957.
Sad Clowns (also known as *Silents, Please*), The History of Motion
   Pictures film series, 1961.
Buster Keaton Rides Again, documentary directed by John Spotten,
   1965.
Episode 8 ("Comedy: A Series Business") of *Hollywood: A Celebration
   of the American Silent Film*, television documentary, 1980.
Buster Keaton: A Hard Act to Follow, television documentary, 1987.

*   *   *

Buster Keaton

When motion picture critics began to reevaluate the comedy of Buster Keaton, he was the best-known silent screen comedian of the fifties and early sixties. This came about because he, more than any of his peers of the silent period, had made frequent appearances in television commercials, variety shows, and such series programs as *Eddie Cantor Comedy Theatre*, *The Martha Raye Show*, *Playhouse 90*, and *Route 66*. In some of the variety shows and commercials, Buster would execute some of his dangerous pratfalls that distinguished the knockabout comedy of his first film *The Butcher Boy* in 1917. These balletlike tumbles led early viewers to marvel at the physical comedy he had perfected in his vaudeville act with his father and mother. This sometimes resulted in an evaluation of his acting as merely physical, deadpan, and mechanical. In fact, as early as 1924, an unidentified evaluator noted in a review of *Sherlock, Jr.* in *Exceptional Photoplays* that Keaton was the "Humpty Dumpty of the screen. . . . always falling from the wall and always getting up again."

As critics attributed the essence of Keaton's comedy to a type of mechanistic theory similar to that advanced by French philosopher Henri Bergson, the views on his comic acting became oversimplified. Coupled with this was an admiration of the lack of the sentimental that appealed to the intellectuals who viewed his twenties features. These facets of his comedy also appealed to those who revisited Keaton's work after seeing him on television in the 1950s. Nearly 40 years after an evaluation of the comedian's comedy was formulated into a reductionistic mold, Tom Gunniny repeated the same concept in a 1995 *Cineaste* article entitled "Buster Keaton: Or the Work of Comedy in the Age of Mechanical Reproduction." In 1958 Christopher Bishop in *Film Quarterly* set the error of reduction in stone with the statement that Keaton "seems detached from his surroundings, uninvolved to the point of lunacy, an extraordinarily neutral figure, driven by compulsion beyond his comprehension, his behavior without source in any conscious motivation."

Such evaluations of Keaton's character and acting are quite common, and they are intended as penetrating views on the quintessence of the comedian's uniqueness in creating laughter. They fail to take into account many of the character traits that the actor uses in the development of the drama which would give dimension to the comedian's acting. In *Sherlock, Jr.*, for example, there are many of the obsessed, young boy characteristics that are quite fundamental to the plot and not "abstract" or lacking in "conscious motivation." Granted, Keaton utilized anesthesia of his emotion, somewhat in the manner exhibited by Harry Langdon and Stan Laurel, to create comedy of understatement. Underneath a placid exterior, burning desires existed in his character. The young, small-town movie projectionist dreams of a life as a famous detective. In the opening shot of *Sherlock, Jr.*, his childish enthusiasm becomes obvious as he reads with dogged intensity a book entitled *How to Become a Detective*.

In this scene Buster is caught reading on the job by the theater manager. With his eyes, the turn of the head, and protests of explanation by mouth movements, the comedian shows his motivation to get out of this predicament. Within ten minutes of the first reel of *Sherlock, Jr.* Keaton displays a variety of emotions. With hesitating arm and hand movements he shyly attempts to hold the hand of his girlfriend and present her with an engagement ring. Keaton does not smile but his eyes show his love for the young woman. When the small-town youth he portrays becomes an amateur detective, his full body comes into play as he pursues the villain of the drama. As if bent forward against a strong wind, he tails the suspect with great determination.

It is valid to compare the features of Buster Keaton's films with those of Harold Lloyd. Most of the plots and the characterizations are tied to the tradition of the genteel comedy, often involving a pursuit of some magnitude. In *Sherlock, Jr.* it is the goal of solving a crime; in *The General* it is a struggle to recover a stolen locomotive; in *The Cameraman* it becomes the desire to shoot a significant movie newsreel event. Each of these plots follows the Horatio Alger Jr. success story, developed along comic lines. Keaton, like Lloyd and Charles Chaplin, utilized the struggle of the little man pitted against a hostile world.

In his 12 silent film features Buster Keaton was able to provide variety in the skillful acting of broad, comic scenes or sequences and restrained, subtle, humorous character-building scenes. His acting skills in the broader portions of his features proved to be equal to the skills of Chaplin and Lloyd by handling such material. Again, using *Sherlock, Jr.* as an example, his dangerous race on a motorcycle to rescue his girlfriend seemed to be on the level of Harold Lloyd's "thrill comedy" that Lloyd executed climbing a skyscraper. Keaton also executed pratfalls with an agility and grace that surpassed the deftness of Chaplin and Lloyd.

An example of Keaton's ability to handle subtle, character-developing humor evolves from his departure from the portrait of a poor, young man to that of a rich, young man in the 1924 *The Navigator*. Since he is spoiled through pampering and money that usually will buy anything, everything has become routine. As if he were going to buy a new suit, he tells his valet that he is going to get married; he marches formally up to a young woman who is a friend of the family and asks unemotionally: "Will you marry me?" She instantly and vehemently replies, "Certainly not!" He looks blankly away from her, turns on his heels, takes his cane and hat from a servant, and leaves without another word being spoken.

The four kings of comedy of the 1920s—Chaplin, Lloyd, Keaton, and Harry Langdon—created comic characters that were distinctive. Chaplin was the lost soul, the little tramp, on the edge of society; Lloyd portrayed the eager young man struggling for success, mostly on a social plain; Langdon enacted a child-man baffled by a big world. Buster Keaton seemed to be a combination of Lloyd and Langdon. His character, like Lloyd's, struggled mightily to reach a goal. But, like Langdon, he found his environment perplexing. In a gesture used in many of his films Keaton executed an Indian-style survey of the horizon as he climbed a hill, a locomotive, or even an animal such as a cow or horse. This pose proved to be symbolic of a poor fellow lost in a broad, unknown, hostile world.

Those critics who try to apply Henry Bergson's comic theory of mechanism to his character are only looking at the facet that appeals to them. True, Keaton achieves some of his comedy by a fine-tuned, smooth working of his body, but the exclusion of other traits of his portrayal (especially his link with the genteel comedy character of the popular fiction of the day) seems to be a grievous simplification of Keaton's comedy. Furthermore, the so-called frozen face does reflect a tradition of the sad clown of the circus (Emmett Kelly, for example) handed down through the ages by the commedia dell' arte, the moonstruck Pierrot, who never smiled, creating understated, deviant emotions that audiences found so entertaining.

—Donald W. McCaffrey

KEATON, Diane

Nationality: American. **Born:** Diane Hall in Los Angeles, California, 5 January 1946. **Education:** Attended Santa Ana High School, California; Santa Ana College and Orange Coast College; studied acting with Sanford Meisner at the Neighborhood Playhouse, New York. **Family:** Adopted daughter, Dexter. **Career:** 1967—acted in Woodstock summer theater, New York; 1968—Broadway debut in *Hair*; later stage roles in *Play It Again, Sam* with Woody Allen, 1969, and *The Primary English Class*, 1976; 1970—film debut in *Lovers and Other Strangers*; also a singer: engagements at Reno Sweeney, New York, and other clubs and theaters; 1980—book of photographs published; 1987—directed first feature, *Heaven*; 1990—directed music video for Belinda Carlisle; directed episode of *Twin Peaks* for TV; directed TV After School Special, "The Girl with the Crazy Brother." **Awards:** Oscar for Best Actress, Best Actress, British Academy, and Best Actress, New York Film Critics, for *Annie Hall*, 1977. **Agent:** Stan Kamen, William Morris Agency, 151 El Camino Drive, Beverly Hills, CA 90212, U.S.A.

Films as Actress:

1970	*Lovers and Other Strangers* (Cy Howard) (as Joan Vecchio)
1972	*The Godfather* (Coppola) (as Kay Adams); *Play It Again, Sam* (*Aspirins for Three*) (Ross) (as Linda Christie)
1973	*Sleeper* (Woody Allen) (as Luna Schlosser)
1974	*The Godfather Part II* (Coppola) (as Kay Adams)
1975	*Love and Death* (Woody Allen) (as Sonja)
1976	*I Will I Will . . . for Now* (Panama) (as Katie Bingham); *Harry and Walter Go to New York* (Rydell) (as Lissa Chestnut)
1977	*Looking for Mr. Goodbar* (Richard Brooks) (as Theresa Dunn); *Annie Hall* (Woody Allen) (title role)
1978	*Interiors* (Woody Allen) (as Renata)
1979	*Manhattan* (Woody Allen) (as Mary Wilke)
1981	*Reds* (Beatty) (as Louise Bryant)
1982	*Shoot the Moon* (Parker) (as Faith Dunlap)
1984	*The Little Drummer Girl* (Hill) (as Charlie); *Mrs. Soffel* (*Dear Hearts*) (Armstrong) (title role)
1986	*Crimes of the Heart* (Beresford) (as Lenny)
1987	*Radio Days* (Woody Allen) (as New Year's singer); *Baby Boom* (Shyer) (as J. C. Wiatt)
1988	*The Good Mother* (Nimoy) (as Anna Dunlap)
1990	*The Lemon Sisters* (Chopra) (as Eloise Hamer, + co-pr); *The Godfather, Part III* (Coppola) (as Kay Adams)
1991	*Success* (Hunter); *Father of the Bride* (Shyer) (as Nina Banks)
1992	*Running Mates* (*Dirty Tricks* (Lindsay-Hogg—for TV) (as Aggie Snow)
1993	*Look Who's Talking Now* (Ropelewski) (as voice of Daphne); *Manhattan Murder Mystery* (Woody Allen) (as Carol Lipton)
1994	*Amelia Earhart: The Final Flight* (Simoneau—for TV) (title role)
1995	*Father of the Bride, Part II* (Shyer) (as Nina Banks)
1996	*The First Wives Club* (P. J. Hogan); *Marvin's Room* (Zaks)

Films as Director:

1982	*What Does Dorrie Want?* (doc)
1987	*Heaven* (doc) (+ sc)
1991	*Secret Society* (+ ro); *Wildflower* (for TV)
1995	*Unstrung Heroes*

Publications

By KEATON: books—

Reservations, New York, 1980.
Still Life, edited with Marvin Heiferman, New York, 1983.
Mr. Salesman: A Book (editor), Santa Fe, New Mexico, 1993.

By KEATON: articles—

"Heaven," interview with M. Glicksman, in *Film Comment* (New York), March/April 1987.

"Plane Speaking," interview with Benjamin Svetkey, in *Entertainment Weekly*, 10 June 1994.
"Annie Hall Doesn't Live Here Anymore," interview with Nancy Collins, in *Vanity Fair* (New York), November 1995.

On KEATON: book—

Moor, Jonathan, *Diane Keaton: The Story of the Real Annie Hall*, New York, 1989.

On KEATON: articles—

Monaco, James, "Looking for Diane Keaton," in *Take One* (Montreal), November 1977.
Current Biography 1978, New York, 1978.
Cowie, Peter, "Diane Keaton and *Looking for Mr. Goodbar*," in *Focus on Film* (London), no. 29, 1978.
Reed, Rex, "Diane Keaton," in *The Movie Star*, edited by Elisabeth Weis, New York, 1981.
Revue de Cinéma/Image et Son (Paris), January 1983.
Hibbin, S., "Diane Keaton," in *Films and Filming* (London), May 1985.
Ferguson, K., "Woody, Mia and Diane," in *Film Monthly*, July 1990.
Dowd, M., "Diane and Woody, Still a Fun Couple," in *New York Times*, 15 August 1993.
Greenberg, James, "Not at All Unstrung, and Calling the Shots," in *New York Times*, 3 September 1995.

* * *

Diane Keaton gained attention in Woody Allen's early comedies in which her sidekick's awkwardness serves as character. She is not a professional ingenue but does not seem amateurish; in *Play It Again, Sam*, *Sleeper*, and *Love and Death* she wins us with her game responsiveness to Allen's leads. With *Annie Hall* her freshness became an original style. She gets laughs from the play of half-thoughts and second-thoughts that do not quite keep Annie from developing the confidence to act on her impulses. Keaton's career after *Annie Hall* has been an exploration of experience by women who either have not had the chance to develop their instincts (*Mrs. Soffel*, *Crimes of the Heart*, *The Good Mother*), or have not shaped an attitude toward life that can handle what life sends them (*Interiors*, *Manhattan*, *Reds*, *Shoot the Moon*, *The Little Drummer Girl*). Keaton's gift is to discover her characters on camera; in the comedies there is dew in the air of her performance, and in the dramas the real pain of confusion, and sometimes both in the same movie.

Allen finally freed Keaton from her dependence on him by casting her as a Bergmanesque poet repelled by human involvement in *Interiors*. Playing Renata with the same hesitations and emotional elusiveness as her comic roles, she became a star with as identifiable a manner as Bette Davis or Katharine Hepburn. Unfortunately, she broke through when character acting achieved critical ascendancy. Thus while Meryl Streep garnered praise for much more deliberately and narrowly conceived performances, Keaton breathtakingly explored her star persona. Streep is famous for working by externals. Keaton, making her debut in 1970, helped reinvent movie naturalism in a freer, more explicit era; there is a feeling of transition, both internal and external, in her best performances.

Of course, even her fans see that in underwritten roles, such as Louise Bryant in *Reds* and Amelia Earhart in a 1994 television movie (a debunking of the aviatrix as her husband-promoter's media creation), Keaton's distinctive manner is too much up front. If we do not know what makes her character disconcerted and edgy she can grate. And in as thinly conceived a comedy as *The Lemon Sisters* Keaton

Diane Keaton with Woody Allen in *Annie Hall*

courts and weds preciousness (her failing as a director, both in the documentary *Heaven* and the comic family drama *Unstrung Heroes*). This is the downside of being one of the least ingratiating of stars. The upside is that when she is likable, she is likable in character, and she is fearless about being many things besides likable. As Faith in Alan Parkers's *Shoot the Moon*, opposite Albert Finney as the writer-husband she throws out when she discover he is having an affair, Keaton is a bitter, adamant antagonist to the helpless George, even though battling weighs her down. No actress has outdone Keaton at the comedy-drama of divided feelings. On a date, Peter Weller asks if he can kiss her, and she fumbles, "No . . . I mean, yes." Keaton, one of the first actresses of the counterculture generation to become a star, plays out the confusions of women trained in vanishing conventions. Faith, a mother of four with a living husband, "should not" be dating, but she *should* know whether she wants to be kissed. Annie Hall's charming diffidence becomes Faith's desolation, both pervasive and remote, while at the same time Keaton displays new comic gusto in the restaurant scene when Faith and George's fight spills over to another table. As Faith, caught between lives, Keaton gave the greatest performance by an American actress since Hepburn in *Long Day's Journey into Night* combined unreachable pain with eccentric comic outbursts.

Since 1982 only Gillian Armstrong's period piece *Mrs. Soffel*, about a prison warden's wife who helps convict brothers escape,

has been truly worthy of her. Keaton may be anachronistic, but she daringly probes the antisocial realms of female dissatisfaction with marriage and motherhood. Her other 1980s pictures are not major but she chose them intelligently for the roles they offered her. In *The Little Drummer Girl* she is an actress drafted into an antiterrorist plot. Charlie is an exaggeration of Keaton's traits as an actress, pushed to the edge by a supervolatile situation. When Charlie realized the enormity of seducing and betraying a terrorist leader, she gropes for a division between acting and life; Keaton makes us feel the agony of dangling. In *The Good Mother* she suffers melodramatic punishment for a late awakening with a lover whose uninhibitedness around her daughter leads to a custody battle. Anna's discovery of carnality, without coyness or prurience, is amazingly vivid. When Anna loses her daughter Keaton despairingly weighs the merits of sexuality and motherhood in face of a culture that polarizes them.

Keaton brings her remarkable physicality to comedy as well, especially *Baby Boom*. J. C., a corporate shark, has the personality for big business but her nerve endings lack the competitive training that men's receive. She cannot keep her legs from shaking as she closes deals; the excitement is overwhelming—and infectious. Forced to care for an infant, J. C. moves to New England where she does not even have business into which she can channel her energy; in crises she is liable to fritz out completely and keel over. Keaton's pratfalls are no less funny for the fact that she keeps J. C.'s motivation clear. Slapstick performances by female leads are rare; this is among the best.

Keaton's subsequent career includes a return as Kay in the third *Godfather*, which never gives her material that engages her advanced skill; a funny reteaming with Woody Allen in *Manhattan Murder Mystery*; and supporting roles in the *Father of the Bride* pictures, in which, practically reduced to pantomime, her reactions give these family comedies their only distinction. Keaton's recent work is not as triumphant as her 1980s movies, but she is adaptable, evergreen. She is always a good enough reason to see a movie.

—Alan Dale

KEATON, Michael

Nationality: American. **Born:** Michael Douglas in Coraopolis, Pennsylvania, 9 September 1951. **Family:** Married the actress Caroline MacWilliams, son: Sean. **Education:** Attended Kent State University for two years, majored in speech. **Career:** Early 1970s—began performing in Pittsburgh coffeehouses; 1972—worked as technical crew member of WQED, Pittsburgh's public TV station; 1975—moved to Los Angeles; 1977-82—did stand-up comedy at the Comedy Store and other comedy clubs, performed improvisational theater with the Los Angeles offshoot of Chicago's Second City troupe, began writing comedy material and making appearances on television shows, and was cast in the TV sitcoms *All's Fair* (1977), *Working Stiffs* (1979), and *Report to Murphy* (1982), and the comedy-variety shows *Mary* (1978) and *The Mary Tyler Moore Hour* (1979); 1982—made screen debut in *Night Shift*; 1985—cast as male lead in Woody Allen's *The Purple Rose of Cairo*, but was replaced by Jeff Daniels after a week of shooting. **Awards:** Best Actor, National Society of Film Critics, for *Beetlejuice* and *Clean and Sober*, 1988. **Agent:** Creative Artists Agency, 9830 Wilshire Boulevard, Beverly Hills, CA 90212, U.S.A.

Films as Actor:

1982 *Night Shift* (Ron Howard) (as Bill Blazejowski)
1983 *Mr. Mom* (Dragoti) (as Jack)
1984 *Johnny Dangerously* (Heckerling) (title role)
1986 *Gung Ho* (*Working Class Man*) (Ron Howard) (as Hunt Stevenson); *Touch and Go* (Mandel) (as Bobby Barbato)
1987 *The Squeeze* (Roger Young) (as Harry Berg)
1988 *Beetlejuice* (Burton) (as Betelgeuse); *Clean and Sober* (Caron) (as Daryl Poynter); *She's Having a Baby* (John Hughes) (uncredited cameo)
1989 *The Dream Team* (Zieff) (as Billy Caulfield); *Batman* (Burton) (as Bruce Wayne/Batman)
1990 *Pacific Heights* (Schlesinger) (as Carter Hayes)
1991 *One Good Cop* (Gould) (as Artie Lewis)
1992 *Batman Returns* (Burton) (as Bruce Wayne/Batman)
1993 *Much Ado about Nothing* (Branagh) (as Dogberry); *My Life* (Rubin) (as Bob Jones); *Earth and the American Dream* (Couturie—doc) (voice only)
1994 *The Paper* (Ron Howard) (as Henry Hackett); *Speechless* (Underwood) (as Kevin)
1996 *Multiplicity*

Publications

By KEATON: articles—

Interview with Tom Zito, in *Washington Post*, 30 October 1982.
"Michael Keaton Reaches to His Dark Side," interview with Adam Belanoff, in *Video Review* (New York), November 1988.
Interview with Bill Zehme, in *Rolling Stone* (New York), 29 June 1989.
"Batman and the New World Order," interview with Carol Caldwell, in *Esquire* (New York), June 1991.
Interview with L. Linderman, in *Playboy* (Chicago), July 1992.

On KEATON: articles—

Roman, S., in *Esquire* (New York), September 1983.
Lee, Luaine, in *Chicago Tribune*, 9 March 1986.
Edelstein, David, "Mixing *Beetlejuice*," in *Rolling Stone* (New York), 2 June 1988.
McGuigan, Cathleen, "Keaton Plays It Straight," in *Newsweek* (New York), 29 August 1988.
Roman, S., "First You Die," in *Video* (New York), November 1988.
Rodman, Ronald, "They Shoot Comic Books, Don't They?," in *American Film* (New York), May 1989.
Clark, John, filmography in *Premiere* (New York), July 1989.
Current Biography 1992, New York, 1992.
Schneller, Johanna, "Hanging Upside Down with Michael Keaton," in *GQ* (New York), June 1992.
Schreurs, Fred, "Bat Mitzvah," in *Premiere* (New York), July 1992.

* * *

There is a bit of larceny lurking in Michael Keaton's eyes, and he has made that mischievous expression work well for him in comedies and dramas, playing men disturbed by the business of business and the business of life. On occasion, he turns that look into pure wickedness to play berserk and otherworldly characters.

Keaton burst onto the film scene with his attention-grabbing performance in *Night Shift*, playing manic morgue worker Bill Blazejowski, who brings in extra earnings by moonlighting as a pimp. His follow-up, *Mr. Mom*, in which he plays a breadwinner who loses his job and consequently switches roles with his homemaker wife, may not have offered the most original comic script, but it was a box-office hit and solidified Keaton's stardom. He scored again in the 1920s-gangster spoof *Johnny Dangerously*. If the film was a bit too sketchy to sustain its running time, Keaton offers an attractive performance as the title hoodlum. His Johnny Dangerously is a deft burlesque on Cagney, with his lines delivered in flawless deadpan. After several lackluster efforts—*Gung Ho*, *Touch and Go*, *The Squeeze*—Keaton got back on track in two diverse films which, when contrasted, serve to show off his range.

In *Beetlejuice*, he donned heavy, homely makeup to play a comically macabre no-goodnik named Betelgeuse, a vulgar maverick ghost who markets himself as a "bio-exorcist" to frighten the living. Keaton is outrageous, taking a sometimes vulgar and often broadly theatrical approach to the hilarious, mangy character who is so suitable to the bizarre mood of Tim Burton's horror film. In *Clean and Sober*, Keaton once again is an unlikable, antisocial character. This time, his style is tense and energy-packed, but also more subdued, because the film is a drama of realism. It is the story of a lowlife hustler who checks into a private drug rehabilitation clinic to hide out after a young woman he has picked up at a bar overdoses from cocaine while in his bed. More than any of his previous roles, his Daryl Poynter goes through stages of character development as he is forced to look at the sad fact that he really is a cocaine addict whose life is spinning out of control as a result of his addiction.

Michael Keaton in *Clean and Sober*

Perhaps Keaton's most famous performance to date is the title character in the megahit *Batman* and its sequel, *Batman Returns*. If the showcase performance in the former is Jack Nicholson's (as The Joker) and
the latter is Michelle Pfeiffer's (playing Catwoman), Keaton more than
holds his own as a sturdy superhero. He was a surprise casting choice for
the dual role of Batman, the Caped Crusader, and his alter-ego, neurotic
millionaire Bruce Wayne. But given the moody and repressed sides of
Wayne's personality, Keaton surely was the right actor for the job (especially after being given an extra layer of muscle by the kindly costume
designer!). After a dispute over salary, he was replaced by Val Kilmer in
the third Batman feature, *Batman Forever*.

Keaton took aspects of his Betelgeuse character and built them into
the vulgar comedy part of Dogberry in Kenneth Branagh's production
of Shakespeare's *Much Ado about Nothing*. This time the effect was
less than spectacular, and there are moments when one wonders if he
really is part of the same movie as the actors who share screen time
with him. His follow-ups, however, were two powerful dramatic roles.
In *My Life*, a four-handkerchief weeper, he is a successful career man
whose body is being eaten away by cancer just as he is about to become
a father. In *The Paper*, a fast-paced yarn about New York City journalists, he appears as an overworked but dedicated tabloid metro editor
whose pregnant wife (Marisa Tomei) is pressuring him to find a higher
paying job. Though the former role gives Keaton the better opportunity to thoughtfully build a three-dimensional character, both roles
allowed the actor to present credible characters in well-conceived
melodramas.

Keaton has the look of a playground scrapper, and maybe that is
why he is at his best as an energetic fighter. He may be battling for
truth and justice, or for absurdly comical and ridiculous reasons. In any
case, when Keaton lets loose, one cannot be bored.

—Audrey E. Kupferberg

KEELER, Ruby

Nationality: American. **Born:** Ethel Keeler in Halifax, Nova Scotia,
Canada, 25 August 1910; emigrated with her family to New York City,
1913. **Education:** Attended St. Catherine of Siena grammar school;
Professional Children's School. **Family:** Married 1) the singer Al
Jolson, 1928 (divorced 1939), one adopted son; 2) John Homer Lowe,
1941 (died 1969), three children. **Career:** 1923—as a 13-year-old,
appeared as a chorus girl in *The Rise of Rosie O'Reilly*, followed by
nightclub work and roles in *Bye Bye Bonnie*, 1927, *The Sidewalks of
New York*, 1927, and *Whoopee!*, 1928; 1928—made short film *Ruby
Keeler*, but made feature film debut in 1933 with *42nd Street*; made TV
appearances after 1950, and returned to the stage in *Bell, Book, and
Candle*, 1968; 1971—in successful Broadway revival of *No, No
Nanette*. **Died:** Of cancer, in Rancho Mirage, California, 28 February
1993.

Films as Actress:

1928   *Ruby Keeler* (short)

1933   ***42nd Street*** (Lloyd Bacon) (as Peggy Sawyer); *Gold Diggers of 1933* (LeRoy) (as Polly Parker); *Footlight Parade* (Lloyd Bacon) (as Bea Thorn)

1934   *Dames* (Enright) (as Barbara Hemingway); *Flirtation Walk* (Borzage) (as Kit Fitts)

1935   *Go into Your Dance* (Mayo) (as Dorothy Wayne); *Shipmates Forever* (Borzage) (as June Blackburn)

1936   *Colleen* (Alfred E. Green) (title role)

1937   *Ready, Willing and Able* (Enright) (as Jane Clarke)

1938   *Mother Carey's Chickens* (Rowland V. Lee) (as Kitty Carey)

1941   *Sweetheart of the Campus* (*Broadway Ahead*) (Dmytryk) (as Betty Blake)

1970   *The Phynx* (Katzin) (cameo role)

1989   *Beverly Hills Brats* (Sotos)

Publications

On KEELER: book—

Thomas, Tony, *That's Dancing!*, New York, 1985.

On KEELER: articles—

Gorton, D., "Busby and Ruby," in *Newsweek* (New York), 3 August 1970.
Current Biography 1971, New York, 1971.
"Hooray for Busby Berkeley," in *Films in Review,* New York, October 1973.
Obituary, in *New York Times*, 1 March 1993.
Natale, Richard, obituary in *Variety* (New York), 8 March 1993.

*   *   *

Ruby Keeler's title as the mother of film tap dancing remains secure in American popular culture. She serves as both a legitimate and a nostalgic (if not camp) icon of the Busby Berkeley musicals of the 1930s. Between 1933 and 1937 she made nine films for Warner Brothers, a concentrated stardom which yielded a bright but short-lived career.

Keeler established the route typical of many Hollywood dancers: starting as a specialty act in nightclubs, joining a Broadway chorus, graduating to lead roles in revues, and finally testing for the screen. Her 1928 short, *Ruby Keeler*, was her screen test, but a screen test with a difference. Fox Studio wanted to hear how well their new sound system, Movietone, could record tap dancing. Keeler's success on Broadway in *Whoopee!* made her an obvious choice to test this system. *Variety* exclaimed that in the two-minute short "Ruby Keeler, revue dancer, snapped through a short but nifty tap dance. The [sound] machine gets every tap and reveals Miss Keeler as an exceptional female hoofer." If true, why did Keeler not make her first film until five years later, and for another studio? Movietone most likely recorded every tap, but Keeler could never be considered an "exceptional" dancer. In fact, her dancing demonstrates such an uncomfortable stiffness and clumsiness, one wonders how she became so popular. As David Shipman notes, "She danced ... a spirited but unexpressive tap, a suitable counterpoint to her cracked nasal soprano." Keeler herself acknowledges her limitations: "I was all personality and no talent. I couldn't act, I had that terrible singing voice, and now I can see I wasn't the greatest tap dancer in the world either."

On what then does her stardom rest if she "lacked" basic musical talent? Her marriage to Al Jolson, the top entertainer of the 1930s, interested the public very much. Warner Brothers exploited this curi-

osity to a very profitable degree when they co-starred Keeler and Jolson in *Go into Your Dance*. Tap dancing, emerging from a variety of folk traditions, began to enjoy a vogue as a form of mass entertainment. Keeler appeared as the first female solo tap dancer a Hollywood studio nurtured in this area. Depression audiences enjoyed her naive, ingenuous, and incessantly optimistic characters. In each film her character blindly pushes forward and eventually wins romantic fulfillment and economic security. This attribute of the Keeler persona became established (and immortalized) in her first film, *42nd Street*. When she must replace the star on opening night, her director tells her, "You're going out a youngster, but you've got to come back a star!" Depression audiences also enjoyed her participation in the escapist fantasies of Busby Berkeley. Berkeley choreographed Keeler's first four films, and since his style of choreography depended on kaleidoscopic group formations, her weakness as a dancer was often hidden. In "Shadow Waltz" from *Gold Diggers of 1933*, "Honeymoon Hotel" from *Footlight Parade*, and "I Only Have Eyes for You" from *Dames*, Keeler performs by simply walking through elaborate sets. And perhaps most significantly, her narrow abilities reinforced one of the most enduring myths about stardom: anyone can become a star. Clive Hirschhorn explains the process very succinctly: "The fact that Ruby Keeler ... couldn't sing, and wasn't a particularly good dancer, somehow didn't matter. On the contrary, if she was able to become a star, so could every other kid like her in America."

Keeler set the stage for the solo female tap dancer in Hollywood musicals. As her brief career ended, she passed the torch to Eleanor Powell who carried it to the top based on accomplished skill and talent.

—Greg S. Faller

KEITEL, Harvey

Nationality: American. **Born:** Brooklyn, New York, 13 May 1939. **Education:** Attended Actor's Studio under Frank Corsaro, Lee Strasberg, and Stella Adler. **Military Service:** U.S. Marine Corps. **Family:** Married the actress Lorraine Bracco (divorced 1993), daughter: Stella. **Career:** 1965—off-Broadway debut in Edward Albee's *The American Dream*; 1965—on stage in *Up to Thursday*; 1968—film debut in *Who's that Knocking at My Door?*, first of several appearances in Martin Scorsese's early films; 1975—on stage played Happy Loman in *Death of a Salesman*, with George C. Scott; 1983-84—on stage in David Rabe's *Hurly Burly*, directed by Mike Nichols; 1986—on stage in *A Lie of the Mind*; 1992—co-produced *Reservoir Dogs*. **Agent:** William Morris, 151 El Camino Drive, Beverly Hills, CA 90212, U.S.A.

Films as Actor:

1968   *Who's that Knocking at My Door?* (*I Call First*) (Scorsese) (as J. R.)

1970   *Street Scenes* (Scorsese—doc)

1973   ***Mean Streets*** (Scorsese) (as Charlie)

1974   *The Virginia Hill Story* (Schumacher—for TV) (as Bugsy Siegel)

1975   *Alice Doesn't Live Here Anymore* (Scorsese) (as Ben Everhart); *That's the Way of the World* (*Shining Star*) (Shore) (as Coleman Buckmaster)

1976   ***Taxi Driver*** (Scorsese) (as Sport); *Mother, Jugs & Speed* (Yates) (as Speed); *Buffalo Bill and the Indians, or Sitting Bull's History Lesson* (Altman) (as Ed Goodman); *Welcome to L.A.* (Rudolph) (as Ken Hood)

1977   *The Duellists* (Ridley Scott) (as Gabriel Ferand)

1978   *Fingers* (Toback) (as Jimmy Angelelli); *Blue Collar* (Schrader) (as Jerry Bartkowski)

1979   *Health* (Altman); *Eagle's Wing* (Harvey) (as Henry); *La Mort en Direct* (*Deathwatch*) (Tavernier) (as Roddy)

1980   *Bad Timing: . . . A Sensual Obsession* (Roeg) (as Inspector Netusil); *Saturn 3* (Donen) (as Benson)

1981   *La Nuit de Varennes* (*That Night in Varennes*; *The New World*) (Scola) (as Thomas Paine)

1982   *The Border* (Richardson) (as Cat)

1983   *Exposed* (Toback) (as Rivas); *Une pierre dans la bouche* (*A Stone in the Mouth*) (Leconte) (as the Fugitive); *Corrupt* (*Order of Death*; *Cop Killer*) (Faenza) (as Lt. Fred O'Connor)

1984   *Falling in Love* (Grosbard) (as Ed Lasky); *Dream One* (*Nemo*) (Selignac) (as Mr. Legend)

1985   *El Caballero del Dragon* (*The Knight of the Dragon*; *Star Knight*) (Colomo)

1986   *Camorra* (*Vicoli e delitti*; *Un complicato intrigo di donne, vicoli e delitti*; *The Naples Connection*) (Wertmüller) (as Frankie Acquasanta); *La Sposa Americana* (*The American Wife*) (Soldati); *Wise Guys* (De Palma) (as Bobby Dilea); *Off Beat* (Dinner) (as Mickey); *The Men's Club* (Medak) (as Solly Berliner)

1987   *Corsa in Discesa*; *L'inchiesta* (*The Inquiry*; *The Investigation*) (Damiani) (as Pontius Pilate); *The Pick-Up Artist* (Toback) (as Alonzo); *Dear America: Letters Home from Vietnam* (Couturie—doc) (as narrator); *Blindside* (Lynch) (as Penfield Gruber)

1988   *The Last Temptation of Christ* (Scorsese) (as Judas Iscariot); *Caro Gorbaciov* (*Dear Gorbachev*; *Cordial Gorbatschev*) (Lizzani); *Down Where the Buffalo Go* (Knox—for TV)

1989   *The January Man* (O'Connor) (as Frank Starkey); *La bataille des trois rois* (*The Battle of Three Kings*; *Tambores de fuego*; *Drums of Fire*) (Barka); *Imagining America* (for TV)

1990   *The Two Jakes* (Nicholson) (as Jake Berman); *Due occhi diabolici* (*Two Evil Eyes*) (Romero and Argento) (as Rod Usher); *Grandi Cacciatori* (*The Great Hunter*) (Camino); *Martin Scorsese Directs* (doc for TV)

1991   *Mortal Thoughts* (Rudolph) (as Det. John Woods); **Thelma & Louise** (Ridley Scott) (as Hal Slocumb); *Bugsy* (Levinson) (as Mickey Cohen); *Miracle on 44th Street: A Portrait of the Actor's Studio* (doc for TV)

1992   *Sister Act* (Ardolino) (as Vince LaRocca); **Reservoir Dogs** (Tarantino) (as Mr. White, + co-pr); *Bad Lieutenant* (Ferrara) (title role); *The Specialist* (Badham)

1993   *Dangerous Game* (*Snake Eyes*) (Ferrara) (as Eddie Israel); *Point of No Return* (*The Assassin*) (Badham) (as Victor the Cleaner); *The Young Americans* (Cannon) (as John Harris); *Rising Sun* (Kaufman) (as Tom Graham); **The Piano** (Campion) (as George Baines)

1994   **Pulp Fiction** (Tarantino) (as Winston Wolf); *Monkey Trouble* (*Pet*) (Amurri) (as Shorty); *Imaginary Crimes* (Drazan) (as Ray Weiler); *Somebody to Love* (Rockwell) (as Harry Harrelson)

1995   *Smoke* (Wang) (as Auggie Wren); *Clockers* (Spike Lee) (as Rocco Klein); *Blue in the Face* (Wang and Auster) (as Auggie Wren, + assoc pr); *Get Shorty* (Sonnenfeld) (cameo); *To Vlemma tou Odyssea* (*Ulysses' Gaze*; *The Gaze of Odysseus*; *Le Regarde d'Ulysse*) (Angelopoulos) (as A.); *American Cinema* (doc for TV)

1996   *From Dusk Till Dawn* (Rodríguez) (as Jacob Fuller); *Head above Water* (Jim Wilson) (as George); *City of Industry* (John Irvin)

Publications

By KEITEL: articles—

"Jake Jake: Jack Nicholson and Harvey Keitel," interview with Julian Schnabel, in *Interview* (New York), August 1990.
"Harvey Keitel, Zoe Lund, and Abel Ferrara: The Unholy Trinity that Makes *Bad Lieutenant* a Religious Experience," interview with Julian Schnabel, in *Interview* (New York), December 1992.
"The Gospel According to Harvey," interview with Georgina Howell, in *Vogue* (New York), December 1993.
Interview with Lawrence Grobel, in *Playboy* (Chicago), November 1995.

On KEITEL: articles—

Clark, John, filmography in *Premiere* (New York), September 1990.
Lyons, Donald, "Scumbags," in *Film Comment* (New York), November/December 1992.
Thompson, David, "Harvey Keitel: Staying Power," in *Sight and Sound* (London), January 1993.
Tosches, Nick, "Heaven, Hell, Harvey Keitel," in *Esquire* (New York), September 1993.
Schoemer, Karen, "Harvey Keitel Tries a Little Tenderness," in *New York Times*, 7 November 1993.
Current Biography 1994, New York, 1994.
Roberts, Chris, "It's the Way Keitel 'em," in *Melody Maker* (London), 8 January 1994.

*   *   *

Praised since his first screen appearances for his versatility and intensity, Harvey Keitel has steadily constructed one of the cinema's most prolific and adventurous acting careers. He first emerged, a fully formed talent out of the legendary Actors Studio, as the central and most compassionate figure in Martin Scorsese's semiautobiographical early films. In spite of Keitel's later, frequent divergence from those early roles, his performances for Scorsese—especially as the anguished Charlie in *Mean Streets*, torn between the Catholic Church and the Mob—have continued to shadow his ongoing identification with gritty, streetwise urban characters whose greatest conflicts are nevertheless internal or even metaphysical. (It thus seems impossible to imagine Scorsese casting any other actor as Judas in his controversial *Last Temptation of Christ*.) Although Keitel can be explosive on screen, his skills as an actor are most powerfully conveyed through small expressive gestures, often the result of his early training in improvisational techniques—reportedly his character's quiet, intimate dance with Jodie Foster in *Taxi Driver* was Keitel's idea, and it is the single scene in the film that clarifies the young prostitute's devotion to her pimp.

In the two decades following his indelible early performances, Keitel worked constantly in interesting but often little-seen films, increasingly in Europe (especially Italy, perhaps since his association with Scorsese perpetuated the illusion that Keitel, a Jew of Polish-Romanian descent, was himself Italian American). Along with a number of impressive performances—with his French officer in *The Duellists* and auto worker in *Blue Collar* standouts—a retrospective glance at Keitel's credits demonstrates his prescient knack for attaching himself to first-time directors who would soon thereafter become prominent filmmakers: after Scorsese, Keitel appears in the debut feature films of Ridley Scott (*The Duellists*), Alan Rudolph (*Welcome to L.A.*), Paul Schrader (*Blue Collar*), and Quentin Tarantino (*Reservoir Dogs*, which Keitel co-produced); he has also worked with such independently minded figures as Robert Altman (twice), Ettore Scola, Bertrand Tavernier, James Toback (in three films), Nicolas Roeg, Tony Richardson, Dario Argento, Lina Wertmüller, Abel Ferrara (twice), Jane Campion, Spike Lee, and Wayne Wang (in a pair of films shot

Harvey Keitel in *Reservoir Dogs*

simultaneously from Paul Auster scripts). In his diverse work for such a range of distinctive filmmakers, Keitel seemed to risk the pursuit of a career that was more personally rewarding than aimed at pleasing a large audience.

After working steady in rarely successful films, the early 1990s signaled a renaissance for Keitel, who continued to appear in diverse roles but finally again in popular and widely discussed films; he plays the sympathetic cops in *Mortal Thoughts*, *Thelma & Louise*, and *Clockers* (a delicate performance in Spike Lee's most focused narrative), and their nightmarish double as the (frequently naked, even crucified) *Bad Lieutenant*; that the same actor could appear almost simultaneously in the light comedy *Sister Act*, the ultraviolent neo-noir *Reservoir Dogs*, and the art-house hit *The Piano* (as an uneducated man who has gone half Maori), demonstrated the astonishing range of his skills to a wider audience. Although Keitel's willingness, in his early fifties, to appear nude in both *Bad Lieutenant* and *The Piano* was taken as evidence of his risk-taking as an actor, his real risks in those complex roles are far more than just dropping his pants.

Keitel's introductory line in Tarantino's *Pulp Fiction*—"I'm Winston Wolf, I solve problems"—may be a subtle comment on the actor's own assurance at this point in his career: his presence, in both commercial entertainments and more challenging works, now virtually guarantees at least one riveting and thoroughly committed performance in those films.

—Corey K. Creekmur

KELLY, Gene

Nationality: American. **Born:** Eugene Curran Kelly in Pittsburgh, Pennsylvania, 23 August 1912. **Education:** Attended Sacred Heart School and Peabody High School; Pennsylvania State University; University of Pittsburgh, A.B., 1933. **Military Service:** Served in U.S. Navy, 1944-47. **Family:** Married 1) the actress Betsy Blair, 1941 (divorced 1957), child: Kerry; 2) Jeanne Coyne, 1960 (died 1973), son: Timothy, daughter: Bridget; 3) Patricia Ward, 1990. **Career:** While still in college, had song-and-dance act with his brother Fred; assisted his mother in her dance school, and opened the Gene Kelly School of Dance, 1934; 1938—small parts in Broadway shows *Leave It to Me* and *One for the Money*; 1939—dance director for Billy Rose's Diamond Horseshoe club; 1940—lead role in stage musical *Pal Joey*; 1942—film debut in *For Me and My Gal* for Selznick; then contract with MGM; 1950—directed first film (with Stanley Donen), *On the Town*; later directed pure dance film, *Invitation to the Dance*, 1956; 1957—left MGM, and became freelance actor and director; 1958—directed *Flower Drum Song* on Broadway; 1960—choreographed ballet *Pas de dieux* for Paris Opera; 1962-63—in TV series *Going My Way*; also host or narrator of several TV works, and in the series *The Funny Side*, 1971, and the mini-series *North and South*, 1985. **Awards:** Honorary Oscar, "in appreciation of his versatility as an actor, singer, director and dancer, and specifically for his brilliant achievements in the art of choreography on film," 1951; Cecil B. DeMille Career Prize, 1980. **Died:** In Beverly Hills, California, 2 February 1996.

Films as Actor:

1942   *For Me and My Gal* (Berkeley) (as Harry Palmer)
1943   *Pilot Number Five* (Sidney) (as Alessandro); *DuBarry Was a Lady* (Del Ruth) (as Alec Howe/Black Arrow); *Thousands Cheer* (Sidney) (as Eddy Marsh); *The Cross of Lorraine* (Garnett) (as Victor)

1944   *Cover Girl* (Charles Vidor) (as Danny McGuire); *Christmas Holiday* (Siodmak) (as Robert Manette)
1945   *Anchors Aweigh* (Sidney) (as Joseph Brady)
1946   *Ziegfeld Follies* (Minnelli)
1947   *Living in a Big Way* (La Cava) (as Leo Gogarty)
1948   *The Pirate* (Minnelli) (as Sarafin); *The Three Musketeers* (Sidney) (as Dartagnan); *Words and Music* (Taurog)
1949   *Take Me Out to the Ball Game* (Berkeley) (as Eddie O'Brien)
1950   *The Black Hand* (Thorpe) (as Johnny Columbo); *Summer Stock* (Walters) (as Joe Ross)
1951   ***An American in Paris*** (Minnelli) (as Jerry Mulligan)
1952   *It's a Big Country* (Thorpe and others) (as Icarus Xenophon); *The Devil Makes Three* (Marton) (as Capt. Jeff Eliot)
1954   *Crest of the Wave* (*Seagulls over Sorrento*) (John and Roy Boulting) (as Lt. Bradville); *Brigadoon* (Minnelli) (as Tommy Albright)
1955   *Deep in My Heart* (Donen) (cameo role)
1957   *Les Girls* (Cukor) (as Barry Nicols)
1958   *Marjorie Morningstar* (Rapper) (as Noel Airman)
1960   *Inherit the Wind* (Kramer) (as E. K. Hornbeck); *Let's Make Love* (Cukor) (as guest)
1964   *What a Way to Go!* (Thompson) (as Jerry Benson)
1968   *The Young Girls of Rochefort* (Demy) (as Andy Miller)
1973   *Forty Carats* (Katselas) (as Billy Boyland)
1974   *That's Entertainment!* (Haley, Jr.) (as host)
1977   *Viva Knievel!* (Douglas)
1980   *Xanadu* (Greenwald) (as Danny McGuire)
1981   *Reporters* (Depardon)
1985   *That's Dancing!* (Haley Jr.)
1986   *Sins* (Hickox)
1994   *That's Entertainment! III* (Friedgen and Sheridan)

Films as Director:

1950   ***On the Town*** (co-d with Donen, + ro as Gaby)
1952   ***Singin' in the Rain*** (co-d with Donen, + ro as Don Lockwood)
1956   *Invitation to the Dance* (+ ro)
1957   *It's Always Fair Weather* (co-d with Donen, + ro as Ted Riley)
1958   *The Tunnel of Love*
1962   *Gigot*
1967   *A Guide for the Married Man*
1969   *Hello, Dolly!*
1970   *The Cheyenne Social Club*
1976   *That's Entertainment, Part Two* (co-d with Astaire, + ro as host)

Publications

By KELLY: articles—

Interview by C. L. Hanson, in *Cinema* (Beverly Hills), December 1966.
Interviews, in *American Film* (Washington, D.C.), February 1979.
Interview with R. Haver, in *Film Comment* (New York), November/December 1984.
Interview with J. Basinger, R. Haver, and Saul Chaplin, in *American Film* (Washington, D.C.), March 1985.
"And Now, the Real Kicker...," interview by Graham Fuller, *Interview*, May 1994.
"Toeing the Lion: Gene Kelly of *That's Entertainment! III*, interview in *Entertainment Weekly*, 13 May 1994.

Gene Kelly with Rita Hayworth in *Cover Girl*

On KELLY: books—

Griffith, Richard, *The Cinema of Gene Kelly*, New York, 1962.
Springer, John, *All Talking, All Singing, All Dancing*, New York, 1966.
Kobal, John, *Gotta Sing, Gotta Dance*, New York, 1970.
Burrows, Michael, *Gene Kelly*, Cornwall, England, 1971.
Thomas, Lawrence B., *The MGM Years*, New Rochelle, New York, 1972.
Knox, Donald, *The Magic Factory*, New York, 1973.
Hirschhorn, Clive, *Gene Kelly: A Biography*, London, 1974; rev. ed., 1984.
Thomas, Tony, *The Films of Gene Kelly, Song and Dance Man*, Secaucus, New Jersey, 1974; rev. ed., 1991.
Delameter, Jerome, *Dance in the Hollywood Musical*, Ann Arbor, Michigan, 1981.
Thomas, Tony, *That's Dancing*, New York, 1985.
Altman, Rick, *The American Film Musical*, Bloomington, Indiana, 1989.

On KELLY: articles—

Isaacs, H. R., "Gene Kelly," in *Theatre Arts* (New York), March 1946.
Behlmer, Rudy, "Gene Kelly," in *Films in Review* (New York), January 1964.
Cutts, John, "Kelly, Dancer, Actor, Director," in *Films and Filming* (London), August and September 1964.
Corliss, Richard, "Gene Kelly" in *The Movie Star*, edited by Elisabeth Weis, New York, 1981.
Film Criticism (Edinboro, Pennsylvania), Spring 1984.
Basinger, Jeanine, "Gene Kelly: Who Could Ask for Anything More?," in *American Film* (Washington, D.C.), March 1985.
McCullough, John, "Imagining Mr. Average," in *CineAction!* (Toronto), no. 17, 1989.
Ringgenberg, P., "Gene Kelly—The Dancing Cavalier," in *Hollywood: Then and Now*, vol. 24, no. 8, 1991.
Parkinson, D., "Dancing in the Streets," in *Sight & Sound*, January 1993.
Updike, John, "Gotta Dance," in *New Yorker*, 21 March 1994.
Obituary, in *New York Times*, 3 February 1996.

*   *   *

Gene Kelly established his reputation as an actor and dancer, but his contribution to the Hollywood musical embraces choreography and direction. His experiments with dance and with ways of filming it include combining dance and animation (*Anchors Aweigh* and *Invitation to the Dance*), and special effects (The "Alter Ego" number in *Cover Girl* and the split-screen dance of *It's Always Fair Weather*). His first attempts at film choreography relied on the established formulas of the film musical, but subsequently, particularly in the three films he co-directed with Stanley Donen, he developed a flexible system of choreography for the camera that took into account camera setups and movement, and editing.

Kelly consciously integrated dance and filmic elements with his on-screen characterizations, thereby developing a persona (and also a recognizable popular culture figure) that is manifested in the films' plots, songs, and especially dances. Like his dance style, this complex persona draws on a variety of sources. The song-and-dance man of *For Me and My Gal* is a vaudeville hoofer, and his principal dances are tap routines. The introspective Pierrot of *Invitation to the Dance*, and the Pierrot-sailor of the "A Day in New York" sequence from *On the Town*, are derived from commedia dell'arte, and their dances are more balletic. The swashbuckler of the dream dances in *Anchors Aweigh* and *The Pirate* is an athletic performer, combining the tours de force of ballet with acrobatic stunts.

Without disparaging his towering achievements as triple threat, it is clear that Kelly's happy-go-lucky Yankee Doodle dancin' boy image seems less resonant in today's pop culture vacuum. Despite superb supporting turns in *What a Way to Go* and *Forty Carats*, it is obvious that Kelly's grinning goodwill ambassador fell out of step with the sixties antiestablishment antiheroes. But Kelly's image does not need a rehabilitation so much as a reshifting "perception-wise," to paraphrase a tune from *It's Always Fair Weather*. Mesmerized by Gene's athleticized self-approval and tireless *cherchez la femme*-ing, critics and audiences have overlooked the contradictions in his cocky all-American huckster persona. Debuting as a draft dodger in *For Me and My Gal*, Kelly used his charisma's sinister edge to limn a mother-fixated killer in *Christmas Holiday*, camouflaged his rendition of a gigolo in *An American in Paris*, deftly enacted a womanizing summer schlocker in *Marjorie Morningstar*, and capped off his musical comedy career as a small-time fight promoter toying with a fix in *It's Always Fair Weather*.

Even in lighter fare (*On the Town*, *Summer Stock*), he often portrayed fellas bent on impressing people to get what they wanted. Reconsidering the Kelly persona from a distance of several decades, one can enjoy his eventual triumphs over shortcomings (including his own robust ego) in *Singin' in the Rain*, etc. It is a tribute to his unflappable charisma that unsavory character flaws all registered as temporary slippage, indiscretions cured by true love and transformed by joyfully aggressive dance. In his most seductive choreography (*The Pirate*, *Cover Girl*), he seemed to be dancing his demons away, and it is time to credit him for a more complex image than previously assumed.

If his solo work reveals a pretentiousness that never darkened Astaire's sunny horizons, no male dancer was ever as sexually potent in tandem on-screen; he can make a soft shoe with Debbie Reynolds an adventure in eros. Betrayed by overreaching with the ill-fated *Invitation to the Dance*, Kelly minimized his true gifts as entertainer and misjudged his audience's appetite for his brand of high culture. It was barbarous of MGM not to lend him for *Guys and Dolls* and *Pal Joey* and to saddle him with the airless *Brigadoon* and heavy-handed *Les Girls*. If the last four decades were dotted by the dashing of tantalizing projects and by Kelly's inability to stamp his post-Donen directorial assignments with his own personality, Kelly could take comfort in his singular contribution to the all-but-extinct musical form; time will reveal an icon more complex than the quixotic puddle jumper of *Singin' in the Rain*. In film after film, this superb actor choked back darker impulses to earn his goodness; he is the all-American operator who plays all the angles, but ultimately seeks the light in a song-and-dance spotlight.

—Jerome Delameter, updated by Robert Pardi

KELLY, Grace

Pseudonym: Princess Grace of Monaco. **Nationality:** American/Monégasque. **Born:** Grace Patricia Kelly in Philadelphia, Pennsylvania, 12 November 1929; became citizen of Monaco, 1956. **Education:** Attended Ravenhill Academy of the Assumption, Philadelphia; Stevens School, Chestnut Hill, Pennsylvania, graduated 1947; American Academy of Dramatic Art, New York, 1947-49. **Family:** Married Prince Rainier III of Monaco, 1956, children: Caroline, Albert, and Stephanie. **Career:** 1947-49—supported acting studies by modeling and appearing in TV commercials; 1949—stage debut in *The Torch Bearers*, written by uncle George Kelly, at Bucks County Playhouse; Broadway debut in Strindberg's *The Father*; 1951—film debut in *Fourteen Hours*; 1952—studied with Sanford Meisner at Neighborhood

Grace Kelly

Playhouse; seven-year contract with MGM; 1954—borrowed from MGM by Hitchcock for *Dial M for Murder*, first of three films with Hitchcock; 1965—founded Princess Grace Foundation; 1976—joined board of 20th Century-Fox. **Awards:** Oscar for Best Actress, for *The Country Girl*, 1954; Best Actress, New York Film Critics, for *The Country Girl, Rear Window*, and *Dial M for Murder*, 1954. **Died:** Following automobile accident in Monte Carlo, 14 September 1982.

Films as Actress:

1951   *Fourteen Hours* (Hathaway) (as Mrs. Fuller)
1952   **High Noon** (Zinnemann) (as Amy Kane)
1953   *Mogambo* (John Ford) (as Linda Nordley)
1954   *Dial M for Murder* (Hitchcock) (as Margot Wendice); **Rear Window** (Hitchcock) (as Lisa Fremont); *The Country Girl* (Seaton) (as Georgie Elgin); *The Bridges at Toko-Ri* (Robson) (as Nancy Brubaker); *Green Fire* (Marton) (as Catherine Knowland)
1955   *To Catch a Thief* (Hitchcock) (as Frances Stevens)
1956   *The Swan* (Charles Vidor) (as Princess Alexandra); *High Society* (Walters) (as Tracy Lord); *The Wedding in Monaco* (documentary short)
1964   *Mediterranean Holiday* (Leitner and Nussgruber—doc)
1977   *The Children of Theatre Street* (Dornhelm and Mack) (as narrator)
1979   *Rearranged* (Dornhelm) (as herself)

Publications

By KELLY: book—

My Book of Flowers, with Gwen Robyns, New York, 1980.

On KELLY: books—

Gaither, Gant, *Princess of Monaco: The Story of Grace Kelly*, New York, 1957.
Robyns, Gwen, *Princess Grace: A Biography*, 1976.
Parish, James, and Don Stanke, *The Hollywood Beauties*, New Rochelle, New York, 1978.
Hall, Trevor, *Her Serene Highness, Princess Grace of Monaco*, 1982.
Hart-Davis, Phyllidia, *Grace: The Story of a Princess*, New York, 1982.
Bradford, Sarah, *Princess Grace*, London, 1984.
England, Steven, *Princess Grace*, London, 1984.
Spada, James, *Grace: The Secret Lives of a Princess*, London, 1987.
Cohen, George, *Grace Kelly*, Paris, 1989.
Quine, Judith Balaban, *The Bridesmaids: Grace Kelly, Princess of Monaco, and Six Intimate Friends*, London, 1989.
Robinson, Jeffrey, *Rainier and Grace*, New York, 1989.
Wayne, Jane Ellen, *Grace Kelly's Men*, New York, 1991.
Conant, Howell, *Grace*, New York, 1992.
Edwards, Anne, *The Grimaldis of Monaco*, New York, 1992.
Surcouf, Elizabeth Gillen, *Grace Kelly, American Princess*, Minneapolis, 1992.
Sakol, Jeannie, *About Grace: An Intimate Notebook*, Chicago, 1993.
Lacey, Robert, *Grace*, New York, 1994.

On KELLY: articles—

Current Biography 1977, New York, 1977.
Bowers, Ron, "Grace Kelly," in *Films in Review* (New York), November 1978.
Cook, P., "The Sound Track," in *Films in Review* (New York), November 1982.

Obituary, in *Films and Filming* (London), November 1982.
Jomy, A., obituary, in *Cinéma* (Paris), November 1982.
Corliss, Richard, "Green Fire: Grace Kelly," in *Film Comment* (New York), November/December 1982.
The Annual Obituary 1982, New York, 1983.
Ciné Revue (Paris), 19 July 1984.
"Remembering Grace," in *Good Housekeeping*, September 1992.

On KELLY: film—

Grace Kelly, television movie, directed by Anthony Page, 1983.

*   *   *

Grace Kelly's career as a film actress was brief (1951-56), her rise meteoric, her end abrupt. At the height of her career, she married Prince Rainier of Monaco and never again acted in a film—although Alfred Hitchcock attempted to draw her out of retirement and make a comeback as the star of his film *Marnie*. Some sources say the former actress-turned-royalty was tempted, but that her prince scotched the idea. Tippi Hedren got the role.

Despite the brief five-year span of her career, and only 11 films, she captured the imagination of the moviegoing audience with her beauty, intelligence, and what Alfred Hitchcock referred to as her "sexual elegance." She is still capturing it, years after her death, as one of the most-biographied stars Hollywood has ever produced.

After a small role as the wife of a man (Richard Basehart) who threatens to commit suicide by jumping from a skyscraper in Henry Hathaway's taut *Fourteen Hours*, Kelly leaped into the big leagues opposite Gary Cooper in *High Noon*. Here, and thereafter, her roles often centered on the emergence of concealed passion after a thawing of her icy or principled front. Before she became a princess in real life, she exuded in her films an aloof and aristocratic if not royal manner that, within the films' cliché-ridden plots, broke down into a touching and warm sexual feeling for a man socially beneath her, and a search for self-respect. This change, as manifested in *Mogambo, Rear Window, The Country Girl, To Catch a Thief, The Swan*, and *High Society*, seemed a response to the public being fascinated with elegant upper-class manners, dress, and speech, while desiring a classless equality underneath it all.

Her screen metamorphosis often resulted in a moving love scene containing a surprisingly torrid kiss that, in its dramatic and sensual flavor, gave vent to the undercurrents her performance to that point had implied. A supreme example is *Mogambo*, her third film; in it she plays a naive, recently married English woman who falls for the charms of worldly safari guide Clark Gable. Her long-repressed surrender to his embrace and kiss generates a tremendous, almost explosive sexual heat. In *The Swan*, her last film before becoming a princess—in which she ironically prepared for her soon-to-be-real-life-role by playing a princess—the *Variety* reviewer found a similar scene "that must be figured as belonging to the ranks of the best love scenes ever filmed." In *To Catch a Thief*, when she kisses Gary Grant, the screen literally erupts with fireworks in the Riviera sky. This thawing kiss, releases her passion which, though resulting sometimes in just a dalliance, reveals the phoniness of her airs and the honesty of her feelings.

Hitchcock cast Kelly in his films as his quintessential heroine—a beautiful blond victim subject to brutal violence, or the threat of violence, or as the partner of a man in dangerous pursuit of something. It was the perfect pairing of director and actress. Delmore Schwartz, reviewing *To Catch a Thief*, suggested that Hitchcock and Kelly in their three films together succeeded in supplying the public's need for "vividness and vitality of personality, genuineness of experience, a renewal of the excitement of curiosity and wonder." In *Rear Window*, perhaps Kelly's best film with Hitchcock, a basic Hitchcockian situation—a callous male protagonist discovers love for his girlfriend when she is in danger and he is nearly helpless to protect her—is made all the more compelling by the presence of Kelly's wit, charm, and attractiveness.

Kelly's most accomplished performance was in the film version of Clifford Odets's *The Country Girl* as she became more than a director's tool or a vessel for audience excitement. In this role she was cast against type as the cynical, old-before-her-time, combative wife of a washed-up actor (Bing Crosby) who gets a last chance when a director (William Holden) puts faith in him. Her appearance contrasts with the clotheshorse elegance of her previous role in *Rear Window*. Here she dresses dowdily, in cardigan, glasses, and skirt, slouches, looks worn and haggard, and has a glazed look to her eyes. But she is a fighter, first for her husband, later for herself. The childlike happiness and gaiety present in previous roles only appears in a flashback which serves to point out all the more forcefully her frustrated condition. The range she covered in this role showed her potential for giving complex performances in roles not of her normal type. Unfortunately her studio, MGM, subsequently gave her no comparable role; they suspended her for turning down two of their choices. But Kelly got the last laugh and went on to become the most famous princess in the world until Di came on the scene.

—Alan Gevinson, updated by John McCarty

KENDALL, Kay

Nationality: British. **Born:** Justine Kendall McCarthy in Yorkshire, England, 21 May 1927. **Education:** Attended convent school. **Family:** Married the actor Rex Harrison, 1957. **Career:** 1939—stage debut, then with sister Kim Kendall, in a touring variety act; 1944—film debut in *Fiddlers Three*; 1946-49—on stage in plays and revues; 1957—American film debut in *Les Girls*. **Died:** Of leukemia, 6 September 1959.

Films as Actress:

1944   *Champagne Charlie* (Cavalcanti); *Fiddlers Three* (Watt); *Dreaming* (Baxter)

1945   *Waltz Time* (Stein) (as Lady-in-waiting)

1946   *Caesar and Cleopatra* (Pascal); *London Town* (Ruggles) (as Patsy); *Spring Song* (Tully)

1950   *Night and the City* (Dassin); *Dance Hall* (Crichton) (as Doreen)

1951   *Lady Godiva Rides Again* (Launder) (as Sylvie)

1952   *Wings of Danger* (*Dead on Course*) (Fisher) (as Alexia); *Curtain Up* (Smart) (as Sandra); *It Started in Paradise* (Bennett) (as Lady Caroline)

Kay Kendall in *Genevieve* courtesy of The Rank Organisation Plc

1953 *Mantrap* (Fisher) (as Vera); *Street of Shadows* (Vernon) (as Barbara); *Genevieve* (Cornelius) (as Rosalind); *The Square Ring* (Dearden) (as Eve Lewis); *Meet Mr. Lucifer* (Pelissier) (as Lonely Hearts Singer)

1954 *Fast and Loose* (Parry) (as Carol); *Doctor in the House* (Thomas) (as Isobel)

1955 *The Constant Husband* (Gilliat) (as Monica); *Simon and Laura* (Box) (as Laura); *The Adventures of Quentin Durward* (Thorpe) (as Isabelle)

1956 *Abdulla the Great* (*Abdullah's Harem*) (Ratoff) (as Ronnie)

1957 *Les Girls* (Cukor) (as Lady Wren)

1958 *The Reluctant Debutante* (Minnelli) (as Sheila Broadbent)

1959 *Once More, With Feeling* (Donen) (as Dolly Fabian)

Publications

On KENDALL: articles—

Shipman, David, in *The Great Movie Stars: The International Years*, London, 1972.

Lloyd, A., "Funny Girls and Funny Ladies: Kay Kendall," in *Films and Filming* (London), November 1983.

*   *   *

When Kay Kendall died at the age of 32, she had made a couple of dozen films, nearly all of them mediocre or worse, and none using more than a fraction of her talents. That she can still, 30 years later, be remembered with affection and regret, shows how far she was capable of transcending her material.

Startlingly tall (at 12, she qualified for the chorus line at the London Palladium), beautiful, and never more graceful than when she was acting helplessly drunk, Kendall brought to comedy a sharp intelligence and a sense of spirited self-mockery. Her ability to be at once sexy and funny—and all the sexier *because* she was funny—led several critics to compare her to Carole Lombard. But it also puzzled the studios, who never knew quite what to do with her. By the time they found out, it was too late.

Early in her career, she got what looked like her big break. At 19, with only a few negligible bit parts to her credit, she landed the female lead in one of the then most expensive British pictures ever made. This, unfortunately, was *London Town*, a direly inept musical with which Rank misguidedly hoped to storm the American market. That it flopped was no fault of Kendall's, but her career was blighted: no films for four years, and then back to the bit parts—mostly socialites and gangsters' molls.

Not until *Genevieve*, which she and Kenneth More stole from the nominal leads, John Gregson and Dinah Sheridan, were Kendall's idiosyncratic talents revealed. Her performance as More's fashion-model girlfriend, progressing through hauteur, disbelief and fury to final resignation in the face of rampant male lunacy, was witty and appealingly bemused, culminating in the tour de force of her drunken trumpet solo. Here, for all the evident lack of experience, was one of the great screen comediennes in the making.

Rank, disconcerted, pushed her into some unsuitable dross. She fought back with spirit, holding out for better roles, and matters improved slightly: *Simon and Laura*, with Peter Finch, and *The Constant Husband*, with Rex Harrison (whom she married), at least verged on sophistication, though hardly stretched her in either case. Kendall made no secret of her dissatisfaction with the material on offer. "If you're a film actress in Britain," she told the press, "you spend your life smuggling your physical equipment through the Customs."

By now, Hollywood had taken notice. *Quentin Durward* required little of her except to look elegant in period costume, but there fol-

lowed her two best films since *Genevieve*. Not that either of them was that good. *Les Girls* found its promising team of George Cukor, Cole Porter, and Gene Kelly all a long way below their best. Kendall, as the scattiest of a trio of hoofers, walked off with the picture, and did the same for *The Reluctant Debutante*, a routine West End comedy, with another off-form director (Minnelli this time). Her vitality and sparkle made both films seem far better than they actually were.

She had contracted leukemia, and made one last movie. *Once More, With Feeling*, a feeble comedy with Yul Brynner, was released after her death by way of inadequate memorial. But the sense of waste—at her early death, at her misuse by imperceptive producers—cannot finally overshadow the memory of her lithe, volatile presence, all too briefly illuminating the screen.

—Philip Kemp

KENNEDY, Arthur

Nationality: American. **Born:** John Arthur Kennedy in Worcester, Massachusetts, 17 February 1914. **Education:** Attended Worcester Academy; studied acting at Carnegie Technical Institute, Pittsburgh. **Military Service:** Served in U.S. Air Force, 1943-45; made training films. **Family:** Married actress Mary Cheffey, 1938, children: Terence and Laurie. **Career:** 1936—toured with Globe Theater; 1937—Broadway debut in *Richard III* with Maurice Evans's company; 1939—appeared with Evans company in *Henry IV, Part I*; in Federal Theater production *Life and Death of an American*; 1940—film debut in *City for Conquest* opposite James Cagney: contract with Warners; 1947—appeared as Chris Keller in Miller's *All My Sons* on Broadway (also originated roles of Biff in *Death of a Salesman*, 1947, John Proctor in *The Crucible*, 1954, and the doctor brother in *The Price*, 1968); 1954—first TV appearance; 1961—replaced Laurence Olivier in title role of *Becket* on Broadway; 1974—in TV series *Nakia*. **Awards:** Best Actor, New York Film Critics, for *Bright Victory*, 1951. **Died:** From a brain tumor, in Branford, Connecticut, 5 January 1990.

Films as Actor:

1940 *City for Conquest* (Litvak); *Santa Fe Trail* (Curtiz)

1941 **High Sierra** (Walsh) (as Red); *Knockout* (Clemens); *Strange Alibi* (Lederman); *Highway West* (McCann); *Bad Men of Missouri* (Enright) (as Jim Younger); *They Died with Their Boots On* (Walsh)

1942 *Desperate Journey* (Walsh)

1943 *Air Force* (Hawks)

1946 *Devotion* (Bernhardt—produced 1943) (as Branwell Brontë)

1947 *Cheyenne* (Walsh) (as The Sundance Kid); *Boomerang!* (Kazan)

1949 *Champion* (Robson); *The Window* (Tetzlaff); *Too Late for Tears* (Haskin); *Chicago Deadline* (Allen); *The Walking Hills* (Sturges)

1950 *The Glass Menagerie* (Rapper) (as Tom Wingfield)

1951 *Red Mountain* (Dieterle); *Bright Victory* (*Lights Out*) (Robson)

1952 *Bend of the River* (*Where the River Bends*) (Anthony Mann); *Rancho Notorious* (Lang); *The Girl in White* (*So Bright the Flame*) (Sturges); *The Lusty Men* (Ray)

1954 *Impulse* (de Lautour)

1955 *Crashout* (Foster); *The Naked Dawn* (Ulmer); *The Man from Laramie* (Anthony Mann); *Trial* (Robson); *The Desperate Hours* (Wyler)

1956 *The Rawhide Years* (Maté)

1957 *Peyton Place* (Robson) (as Lucas Cross)

1958 *Twilight for the Gods* (Pevney); *Some Came Running* (Minnelli)

1959 *Home Is the Hero* (Cook); *A Summer Place* (Daves)

1960 *Elmer Gantry* (Brooks)

1961 *Murder She Said* (Pollock); *Claudelle Inglish* (*Young and Eager*) (Douglas)

1962 *Adventures of a Young Man* (Ritt) (as Doc Adams); *Barabbas* (Fleischer) (as Pontius Pilate); *Lawrence of Arabia* (Lean)

1964 *Cheyenne Autumn* (Ford) (as Doc Holliday); *Italiani brava gente* (*Attack and Retreat*) (De Santis); *Joaquin Murieta* (*Vendetta*) (Sherman); *Joy in the Morning* (Segal)

1966 *Il chica del Lunes* (*Monday's Child*) (Torre-Nilsson); *Nevada Smith* (Hathaway); *Fantastic Voyage* (Fleischer); *The Brave Rifles* (as narrator)

1968 *Day of the Evil Gun* (Thorpe); *Lo sbarco di Anzio* (*Anzio*; *The Battle for Anzio*) (Dmytryk); *Un minuto per pregare, un instante per morire* (*Escondido*; *A Minute to Pray, a Second to Die*; *Dead or Alive*) (Giraldi)

1969 *Hail Hero* (Miller)

1970 *Shark!* (Fuller—produced 1967); *The Movie Murderer* (Sagal— for TV)

1971 *My Old Man's Place* (*Glory Boy*) (Sherin); *A Death of Innocence* (Wendkos—for TV); *The President's Plane Is Missing* (Duke—for TV); *Crawlspace* (Newland—for TV)

1973 *Bacciamo le mani* (*Ferrente*; *Kiss My Hand*; *Mafia War*) (Schiraldi); *Ricco* (De Micheli)

1974 *Nakia* (Horn—for TV); *Fin de semana para los muertos* (*The Living Dead at the Manchester Morgue*; *Don't Open the Window*) (Grau); *L'anticristo* (*The Antichrist*; *The Tempter*) (De Martino) (as the Bishop); *La polizia ha le mani legate* (*The Police Can't Move*; *Killer Cop*) (Ercoli)

1976 *Roma a mano armato* (*Rome Armed to the Teeth*; *Brutal Justice*) (Lenzi); *La spiaggia del desiderio* (*Emmanuelle on Taboo Island*) (D'Ambrosio); *Nove ospiti per un delitto* (*Nine Guests for a Crime*) (Baldi); *The Sentinel* (Winner)

1977 *Ab Morgen sind wir reich und ehrlich* (*Rich and Respectable*) (Antel); *Gli ultimi angeli* (*L'avventurosa fuga*; *Last Angels*) (Doria); *Ciclon* (*Cyclone*) (Cardona)

1978 *Sono stato un'agente CIA* (*Covert Action*) (Guerrieri); *Bermuda: la fossa maledetta* (*La cueva de los tiburones*; *Cave of Sharks*; *The Sharks' Cave*) (Richmond); *Porco mondo* (*Porno*) (Bergonzelli)

1979 *L'unanoide* (*The Humanoid*) (Lewis)

1980 *Movies Murderer* (Sagal—for TV)

1989 *Signs of Life* (for TV)

Publications

On KENNEDY: articles—

Marill, Alvin H., "Arthur Kennedy," in *Films in Review* (New York), March 1974.

Buckley, Michael, "Arthur Kennedy," in *Films in Review* (New York), December 1988 and January 1989; see also issues for August/September 1989 and January/February 1990.

Obituary, in *Variety* (New York), 10 January 1990.

Cieutat, Michel, "Arthur Kennedy (1925-1990): Le desperado de l'ombre," in *Postif* (Paris), April 1990.

*   *   *

Arthur Kennedy's acting career represents one of solid, mainstream performance. In the 1940s he moved from minor roles in Warner Brothers staples (*High Sierra, Air Force*) to starring in "social problem" films such as *Champion*. The 1950s and 1960s saw Kennedy reach the peak of his movie career with appearances in a number of highly regarded Westerns (*The Man from Laramie, Bend of the River*) plus several money-making spectacles (*Elmer Gantry, Lawrence of Arabia*).

Kennedy, like many character actors of Hollywood's Golden Age, aspired to the stage. He received classical acting training at Carnegie Institute of Technology and in the mid-1930s moved to New York to "make it" on Broadway. At this point in his career he never did. There were occasional triumphs, including, for example, a Broadway debut in *Richard III* with Maurice Evans's company. But with his "discovery" by a Warner Brothers' talent scout, Kennedy, like many before him, moved to Hollywood. Success on Broadway (in *Death of a Salesman*) came only after he became a name in the movies.

Kennedy's best film work came in a series of Westerns in the 1950s. In one brief span at the beginning of that decade he worked with Nicholas Ray, Fritz Lang, and Anthony Mann in three of the best Westerns ever made: *The Lusty Men, Rancho Notorious*, and *Bend of the River*. Later in the 1950s came yet another solid performance in Anthony Mann's *The Man from Laramie*.

For a time in the mid-1950s it seemed Kennedy might even become a movie star. He received Academy Award nominations for best supporting actor in 1955, 1957, and 1958, the last for the box office smash *Peyton Place*. But it was not to be. Rather than leading to major roles this succession of nominations (with no win) only permanently established him as an ever-reliable character actor.

Kennedy's career after 1960 produced few artistic triumphs. In part this is because he rarely worked for top-flight directors. Exceptions include John Ford (*Cheyenne Autumn*) and Sam Fuller (*Shark*). Like many a character actor of his generation, Kennedy turned more and more to television work. Although his lone attempt at a weekly series (*Nakia*) lasted for only 15 episodes, he achieved a degree of fame as a guest star in such anthology programs as General Electric Theater and Playhouse 90, and later in a number of movies made for television.

—Douglas Gomery

KERR, Deborah

Nationality: British. **Born:** Deborah Jane Kerr-Trimmer in Helensburgh, Scotland, 30 September 1921. **Education:** Attended Northumberland House Boarding School, Bristol, until 1936; Hicks-Smale Drama School (run by aunt Phyllis Smale), Bristol, 1936; studied ballet at Sadler's Wells, 1937. **Family:** Married 1) Anthony Charles Bartley, 1945 (divorced 1959), daughters: Melanie and Francesca; 2) the writer Peter Viertel, 1960. **Career:** 1936—radio work in Bristol, reading children's stories for BBC; 1937—first London stage appearance with Sadler's Wells Ballet; 1941—film debut in *Major Barbara*; one-year contract with Gabriel Pascal; 1945—toured France, Belgium, and Holland in *Gaslight* for Allied forces; 1946—MGM contract: U.S. film debut in *The Hucksters*, 1947; 1952—role in Columbia's *From Here to Eternity*; 1953—released from contract; in *Tea and Sympathy* on Broadway; 1972-73—on stage in *The Day after the Fair*; 1975—on Broadway in Edward Albee's *Seascape*; 1977—in London in Shaw's *Candida*; later in *The Corn Is Green*, 1985; TV work includes mini-series *A Woman of Substance*, 1984, and *Hold the Dream*, 1986; also subject of documentary, *Deborah Kerr: Not Just an English Rose*, for BBC TV, 1986. **Awards:** Best Actress, New York Film Critics, for *Black Narcissus* and *The Adventuress*, 1947; Best Actress, New York Film Critics, for *Heaven Knows, Mr. Allison*, 1957; Best Actress, New York Film Critics, for *The Sundowners*, 1960; honorary Academy Award, 1994.

Films as Actress:

1941 *Major Barbara* (Pascal) (as Jenny Hill); *Love on the Dole* (Baxter) (as Sally Hardcastle)

1942 *Penn of Pennsylvania* (*The Courageous Mr. Penn*) (Comfort) (as Gulielma Springett); *Hatter's Castle* (Comfort) (as Mary Brodie); *The Day Will Dawn* (*The Avengers*) (French) (as Kari)

1943 ***The Life and Death of Colonel Blimp*** (Powell and Pressburger) (as Edith Hunter)

1945 *Perfect Strangers* (*Vacation from Marriage*) (Korda) (as Catherine Wilson)

1946 *I See a Dark Stranger* (*The Adventuress*) (Launder) (as Bridie Quilty)

1947 ***Black Narcissus*** (Powell and Pressburger) (as Sister Clodagh); *The Hucksters* (Conway) (as Kay Dorrance)

1948 *If Winter Comes* (Saville) (as Nona Tybar)

1949 *Edward, My Son* (Cukor) (as Evelyn Boult)

1950 *Please Believe Me* (Taurog) (as English heiress); *King Solomon's Mines* (Bennett and Marton) (as Elizabeth Curtis)

1951 *Quo Vadis?* (LeRoy) (as Lygia)

1952 *The Prisoner of Zenda* (Thorpe) (as Princess Flavia)

1953 *Thunder in the East* (Vidor) (as Joan Willoughby); *Dream Wife* (Sheldon) (as Priscilla Effington); *Young Bess* (Franklin) (as Catherine Parr); ***From Here to Eternity*** (Zinnemann) (as Karen Holmes); *Julius Caesar* (Mankiewicz) (as Portia)

1955 *The End of the Affair* (Dmytryk) (as Sarah Miles)

1956 *Tea and Sympathy* (Minnelli) (as Laura Reynolds); *The Proud and Profane* (Seaton) (as Nurse Lee Ashley); *The King and I* (Lang) (as Mrs. Anna Leonowens)

1957 *Heaven Knows, Mr. Allison* (Huston) (as Sister Angela); *An Affair to Remember* (McCarey) (as Nickie)

1958 *Bonjour Tristesse* (Preminger) (as Anne); *Separate Tables* (Mann) (as Sybil Railton-Bell)

1959 *The Journey* (Litvak) (as Lady Diana Ashmore); *Count Your Blessings* (Negulesco) (as Grace Allingham); *Beloved Infidel* (King) (as Sheilah Graham)

1960 *The Sundowners* (Zinnemann) (as Ida Carmody); *The Grass Is Greener* (Donen) (as Hilary Rhyall)

1961 *The Naked Edge* (Anderson) (as Martha Radcliffe); *The Innocents* (Clayton) (as Miss Giddens)

1964 *The Chalk Garden* (Neame) (as Miss Madrigal); *The Night of the Iguana* (Huston) (as Hannah Jelkes)

1965 *Marriage on the Rocks* (Donohue) (as Valerie Edwards)

1967 *Eye of the Devil* (Thompson—produced 1966) (as Catherine de Montfaucon); *Casino Royale* (Huston and others) (as Agent Mimi ["Lady Fiona McTarry"])

1968 *Prudence and the Pill* (Cook and Neame) (as Prudence Hardcastle)

1969 *The Gypsy Moths* (Frankenheimer) (as Elizabeth Brandon); *The Arrangement* (Kazan) (as Florence Anderson)

1982 *Witness for the Prosecution* (Gibson—for TV)

1985 *Reunion at Fairborough* (Wise—for TV); *The Assam Garden* (McMurray) (as Helen)

Publications

By KERR: articles—

Interview with Bruno Villien, in *Cinématographe* (Paris), December 1983.

Interview with Brian Baxter, in *Films and Filming* (London), December 1984.

On KERR: book—

Braun, Eric, *Deborah Kerr*, London, 1977.

On KERR: articles—

Current Biography 1947, New York, 1947.

Braun, Eric, "From Here to Esteem," in *Films and Filming* (London), May 1970.

Doeckel, K., "Deborah Kerr," in *Films in Review* (New York), January 1978.

Lloyd, A., "Deborah Kerr," in *Films and Filming* (London), September 1984.

Denby, David, "Fire and Ice," in *Premiere*, January 1994.

*   *   *

The preeminent English gentlewoman, Deborah Kerr performed with a ladylike spiritedness and wholesome sincerity that proved equally popular in Great Britain and America.

A stage actress in her late teens, Kerr graduated from a small role in *Major Barbara* that led to three skillfully varied roles in *The Life and Death of Colonel Blimp* and an authoritative nun in *Black Narcissus*; afterward, MGM brought her to Hollywood to play opposite Clark Gable in *The Hucksters*.

A decorative period—*King Solomon's Mines* and others—did not take advantage of her surprising intensity, but her self-possession and well-bred personality worked to advantage in these popular films. Cast against type in *From Here to Eternity* as Burt Lancaster's adulterous lover, Kerr broadened her emotional range in the minds of cinemagoers with a memorably sensual roll in the surf.

Extraordinarily versatile, the six-time Oscar nominee stood her ground in hoopskirts opposite Yul Brynner in *The King and I*, sparred charmingly with Cary Grant and David Niven several times, and smoldered opposite Robert Mitchum, most notably as a housewife made transcendent by sacrifice in *The Sundowners*.

When Kerr did not have a handle on a role (e.g., *Beloved Infidel*) her neurotic tremulousness (used tellingly to portray a neglected closet drinker in *Edward, My Son*) wound up parodying her cashmere-sweatered earth mother role in *Tea and Sympathy*. At her sharpest, however, Kerr memorably agonized to find a balance between submerged desire and a self-imposed code of honor, whether as a wallflower doomed to *Separate Tables* or a nun taxed by her chastity habit in *Heaven Knows, Mr. Allison*.

Kerr's abandonment of Hollywood after the failures of *The Arrangement* and *Gypsy Moths* was especially disheartening since the decade started so promisingly with her repressed governess in *The Innocents*, a spellbinding spin through Capote's Freudinizing of *Turn of the Screw*, a splendidly evasive Miss Madrigal in the civilized *Chalk Garden*, and a definitive study in the denial of the flesh in a *Night of the Iguana* vulgarized by director John Huston but redeemed by its stars.

Adept at teary melodrama and light comedy, Kerr recently entranced a new generation of fans through the *Affair to Remember* clips that filled (and that were the sole reason to tolerate) *Sleepless in Seattle*. A superb theatrical performer, Kerr toured in made-to-order warhorses, enjoyed a Broadway return in Albee's *Seascape*, and demonstrated that time had not withered her variety in such television showcases as the BBC's *Ann and Debbie* and the opulent mini-series *A Woman of Substance*. Through a kaleidoscopic career, Kerr never lost the cool beauty and inborn gentility that initially established her stardom.

—Richard Sater, updated by Robert Pardi

Deborah Kerr in *Black Narcissus* **courtesy of The Rank Organisation Plc**

KINGSLEY, Ben

Nationality: British. **Born:** Krishna Banji in Scarborough, England, 31 December 1943. **Education:** Attended Manchester Grammar School; Salford University, M.A. (hon.); assoc. artist, Royal Shakespeare Co., 1968. **Family:** Married 1) the actress Angela Morant; 2) Alison Sutcliffe, 1978; children: Edmund William Macaulay, Ferdinand James Macaulay, Thomas Alexis, Jasmin Anna. **Career:** Appeared in plays including *Hamlet*, 1975-76, *Edmund Kean*, 1981-83, *Othello*, 1985-86; 1973—film debut in *Fear Is the Key*; 1984—in TV mini-series documentary *Playing Shakespeare*; 1987—in TV mini-series *The Secret of the Sahara*. Awards: Best Actor and Best Newcomer, British Academy of Film and Television Arts, 1982, Best Actor, Standard Film Awards London, 1983, and Best Actor Academy Award, 1983, for *Gandhi*; Distinguished Service Award, for *Murderers among Us: The Simon Wiesenthal Story*, 1989; Best Actor, Golden Camera Berlin award, and Evening Standard Film award, for *Schindler's List*, 1995. **Address:** c/o Zakiya & Associates, 110 St. Martin's Lane, London WC2N 4AD, England.

Films as Actor:

1973 *Fear Is the Key* (Tuchner) (as Roche)
1982 *Gandhi* (Attenborough) (title role); *The Merry Wives of Windsor* (David Jones—for TV) (as Frank Ford)
1983 *Betrayal* (David Jones) (as Robert)
1984 *Sleeps Six* (James Cellan Jones)
1985 *Harem* (Joffe) (as Selim); *Turtle Diary* (Irvin) (as William Snow); *Silas Marner: The Weaver of Raveloe* (Giles Foster—for TV) (title role); *Camille* (Desmond Davis—for TV) (as Duval)
1987 *Testimony* (Tony Palmer) (as Dmitri Shostakovich); *Maurice* (Ivory) (as Lasker-Jones)
1988 *Pascali's Island* (Dearden) (as Basil Pascali); *Without a Clue* (*Sherlock and Me*) (Eberhardt) (as Dr. Watson)
1989 *Slipstream* (Lisberger) (as Avatar); *Murderers among Us: The Simon Wiesenthal Story* (Brian Gibson—for TV) (title role)
1990 *The Children* (Tony Palmer) (as Martin Boyne); *Una Vita Scellerata* (*A Violent Life*) (Battiato); *The Fifth Monkey* (Rochat) (as Cunda); *Romeo-Juliet* (Acosta) (voice only)
1991 *L'Amour necessario* (*Necessary Love*) (Fabio Capri) (as Ernesto); *Bugsy* (Levinson) (as Meyer Lansky); *The War That Never Ends* (Jack Gold—for TV) (as Pericles)
1992 *Sneakers* (Robinson) (as Cosmo); *Freddie as F.R.O.7* (*Freddy the Frog*) (Acevski—animation) (as voice of Freddie)
1993 *Dave* (Reitman) (as Vice President Nance); **Schindler's List** (Spielberg) (as Itzhak Stern); *Searching for Bobby Fisher* (*Innocent Moves*) (Zaillian) (as Bruce Pandolfini)
1994 *Death and the Maiden* (Polanski) (as Dr. Roberto Miranda); *Liberation* (Schwartzmann—doc) (as narrator)
1995 *Joseph* (Roger Young—for TV) (as Potiphar); *Species* (Donaldson) (as Xavier Fitch)
1996 *Twelfth Night* (Trevor Nunn)

Publications

On KINGSLEY: articles—

Current Biography 1983, New York, 1983.
Golightly, Bill, "Ben Kingsley," *Horizon* (New York), March-April 1989.
Morrison, Mark, Arion Berger, Kathy Bishop, and Steve Pond, "Double Impact," in *Harper's Bazaar* (New York), December 1991.
Connelly, Christopher, "The Young and the Restless," in *Premiere* (New York), October 1992.
Heilpern, John, "Empire of the Stage," in *Vanity Fair* (New York), November 1995.

*   *   *

Ben Kingsley rose to fame as the star of Richard Attenborough's biopic *Gandhi* (1981), his second screen appearance following a supporting role in the Alistair MacLean thriller *Fear Is the Key* released almost a decade earlier. Actor Attenborough had sought to film the life of the martyred Indian leader since the 1960s after turning producer-director. His friend and mentor, David Lean, had been fascinated with the subject for a long time as well, but had been unable to secure financing or approvals from the various powers that be in and out of the government of India necessary to shoot the film on location. Attenborough persevered, using a substantial amount of his own money to develop the project, which eventually found a backer in Goldcrest Entertainment. After considerable give and take (mostly give), the director received permission to film his considerably watered down, politically correct look at the life and times of Gandhi in India. His boldest stroke was casting the unknown Kingsley, whose father was Indian and mother British, in the title role. On screen for most of the epic's rather ponderous 188 minutes, Kingsley carried the weight of the film almost entirely on his own shoulders and did so magnificently, delivering a performance of such restrained fire and spiritual strength that he earned a Best Actor Oscar. His selection of roles and films the remainder of the decade were very much a mixed bag, however.

The pretentious *Betrayal* (1983), from a play by Harold Pinter, found Kingsley in a love triangle with Jeremy Irons and Patricia Hodge, the central gimmick of which is that the events of the story unfold in reverse, beginning with their resolution. He played an Arab sheik who kidnaps Nastassja Kinski for his desert nights in the sex and sand epic *Harem* (1985), a French-made extravaganza marked by all the subtlety of a Harlequin Romance novel. In the gentle drama *Turtle Diary* (1985), scripted by Pinter, he and Glenda Jackson play a pair of shy people who form a romantic relationship based on their mutual need to save some giant turtles in a zoo. And as Dr. Watson in *Without a Clue*, he hires a bumbling actor played by Michael Caine to bring his fictional character of Sherlock Holmes to life. Alternately too stiff and too strained in his efforts to hit his comic marks, Kingsley demonstrated here that comedy, particularly farce-comedy, is not his forte, and has avoided it since.

Although he had played the composer Dmitri Shostakovich in the Tony Palmer-directed biopic *Testimony* (1987), the film was barely released. Only when the 1980s began to wind down would Kingsley find another role equal in challenge and visibility to the one that brought him fame as the decade began. In the title role of the Abby Mann-scripted made-for-television biopic *Murderers among Us: The Simon Wiesenthal Story*, Kingsley was, in the words of critic Leonard Maltin, "mesmerizing ... as the Holocaust survivor who dedicated the rest of his life to hunting down the war's Nazi bigwigs."

The 1990s have provided a range of roles for Kingsley, many of them in the kind of big-budget, commercial Hollywood product he had seemed studiously intent on avoiding after *Gandhi*. He brought a disturbing, smiler-with-a-knife sincerity to the part of gangster Meyer Lansky in *Bugsy* (1991). In *Searching for Bobby Fischer* (1993), based on a true story, he movingly revealed the inner turmoil of a chessmaster guiding a child prodigy whose genius for the game he too had exhibited in childhood but failed to fulfill. As the vice president in the political comedy *Dave*, he all but disappeared into the background, but that is the nature of the position itself, as the film suggests.

Ben Kingsley

As the Jewish business manager, Itzhak Stern, of the German profiteer Oskar Schindler (Liam Neeson) who saves the lives of more than a thousand Holocaust victims in *Schindler's List*, Kingsley perfectly conveyed the conflicting emotions of a man who keeps expecting his benefactor to turn against him and his people while coming to trust and admire the man for daring to stand against the exterminating Nazi tide. The performance earned Kingsley a Best Supporting Actor Academy Award nomination, although the role is actually a co-starring one.

Kingsley fared best among the largely miscast three-character drama *Death and the Maiden*, Roman Polanski's adaptation of Ariel Dorfman's play about a Chilean woman (Sigourney Weaver) who seizes the opportunity to get back at the man (Kingsley) who she believes raped and tortured her while she was a political prisoner, when he unwittingly stops by with her husband (Stuart Wilson) for a drink. As Weaver applies the screws, Kingsley almost convinces the viewer *he's* the victim in this dark and twisted tale of revenge and role reversal. The following year, however, found Kingsley slumming for the first time in his career in *Species*, a sexy ripoff of *Alien*, wherein, as the head scientist in pursuit of the extraterrestrial "whatsit," he appears on the verge of breaking into tears at any moment—perhaps from signing onto the project without having read the script.

—John McCarty

KINSKI, Klaus

Born: Nikolaus Günther Nakszynski in Sopot (Zoppot), Free State of Danzig (later Germany; now Gdansk, Poland), 8 October 1926; grew up in Berlin. **Military Service:** German Army, 1944; captured by the British on second day of combat, spending rest of war as POW. **Family:** Married first wife in 1950s, daughter: the actress Pola; 2) Ruth Brigitte Tocki, daughter: the actress Nastassja; 3) Minhoi Wiggers, son: Nanhoi. **Career:** After World War II, acted in theater companies in Tübingen and Baden-Baden; 1948—film debut in *Morituri*; 1950s and 1960s—appeared in dozens of films, gaining European stardom; 1973—appeared in *Aguirre, the Wrath of God*, first of several collaborations with the director Werner Herzog; 1989—directorial debut with *Paganini*. **Awards:** Deutscher filmpreis for Acting, for *Nosferatu—Phantom der Nacht*, 1979. **Died:** In Lagunitas, California, 23 November 1991.

Films as Actor:

1948 *Morituri* (York)
1951 *Decision before Dawn* (Litvak) (as whining soldier)
1954 *Ludwig II* (*Lanz und Elend eines Königs*) (Käutner); *Kinder, Mütter, und ein General* (*Hauen Sie ab mit Heldentum*) (Benedek)
1955 *Sarajewo* (*Um Thron und Liebe*) (Kortner); *Hanussen* (Fischer and Marischka)
1956 *Waldwinter* (Liebeneiner) (as Otto Hartwig); *Geliebte Corinna* (von Borsody)
1958 *A Time to Love and a Time to Die* (Sirk) (as Gestapo lieutenant)
1960 *Der Rächer* (*The Avenger*) (Anton) (as Lorenz Voss)
1961 *Die toten Augen von London* (*Geheimnis von London*; *The Dead Eyes of London*; *Dark Eyes of London*) (Vohrer) (as Edgar Strauss); *Das Geheimnis der gelben Narzissen* (*The Devil's Daffodil*; *Daffodil Killer*) (von Rathony) (as Peter Keene); *Bankraub in der Rue Latour* (Jürgens); *Die seltsame*

Gräfin (*The Strange Countess*) (von Baky) (as Stuart Bresset); *Das Rätsel der roten Orchidee* (*The Puzzle of the Red Orchid*; *Gangster in London*) (Ashley) (as Steve); *Die Kurve* (Zadek—for TV)
1962 *Der rote Rausch* (Schleif); *Dir Tür mit den sieben Schlössern* (*Das Gasthaus an der Themse*; *The House with Seven Locks*) (Vohrer) (as Gregor Gubanow); *The Counterfeit Traitor* (Seaton) (as Kindler)
1963 *Der schwarze Abt* (*The Black Abbot*) (Gottlieb); *Der Zinker* (*The Squeaker*) (Vohrer); *Die schwarze Kobra* (Zehetgruber); *Das indische Tuch* (Vohrer); *Scotland Yard jagt Doktor Mabuse* (*Die scharlachrote Dschunke*; *Scotland Yard Hunts Dr. Mabuse*) (Paul May); *Das Geheimnis der schwarzen Witwe* (*Secret of the Black Widow*) (Gottlieb); *Piccadilly null Uhr swölf* (Zehetgruber); *Kali-Yug, la dea della vendetta* (*Die Göttin der Rache*) (Camerini); *Il mistero del tempio indiano* (*Aufruhr in Indien*; *Das Geheimnis des indischen Tempels*) (Camerini—this film and the previous edited into one version titled *Kali-Yug, Goddess of Vengeance*)
1964 *Die Gruft mit dem Räselschloss* (Gottlieb); *Wartezimmer zum Jenseits* (Vohrer); *Der letzte Ritt nach Santa Cruz* (*Last Stage to Santa Cruz*) (Olsen); *Winnetou: II Teil* (*Giorni di fuoco*; *Le Tresor des montagnes bleues*; *Last of the Renegades*) (Reinl) (as Luke); *Das Geheimnis der chinesischen Nelke* (*Secret of the Chinese Carnation*) (Zehetgruber)
1965 *Das Verratertor* (*Traitor's Gate*) (Francis); *The Pleasure Girls* (*Die Goldpuppen*) (O'Hara) (as Nikko); *Neues vom Hexer* (Vohrer); *La Guerre secrète* (*The Dirty Game*) (Terence Young); *Estambul 65* (*Operación Istanbul*; *L'homme d'Istanbul*; *That Man in Istanbul*) (Isasi-Isasmendi) (as Schenck); *Doctor Zhivago* (Lean) (as Kostoyed)
1966 *Per qualche dollaro in più* (*For a Few Dollars More*) (Leone) (as hunchback); *Our Man in Marrakesh* (*Bang! Bang! You're Dead*) (Sharp) (as Jonquil); *Das Geheimnis der gelben Mönche* (*Wie tötet man eine Dame*; *Target for Killing*) (Köhler); *Spie contro il mondo* (*Gern hab' ich die Frau'n gekillt*; *Spy against the World*; *Killers Carnival*; *Carnival of Killers*) (Cardiff)
1967 *Quien sabe?* (*A Bullet for the General*) (Damiani) (as El Santo); *Circus of Fear* (*Psycho-Circus*) (Moxey) (as Manfred); *Die blaue Hand* (*Creature with the Blue Hand*) (Vohrer); *Carmen, Baby* (Metzger); *Su-muru* (*The Million Eyes of Su-muru*) (Shonteff) (as President Boong); *Five Golden Dragons* (Summers) (as Gert); *L'uomo, l'orgoglio, la vendetta* (*Man, Pride, and Vengeance*; *Mit Django kam der Tod*) (Bazzoni); *Coplan sauve sa peau* (*Les Jardins du diable*; *Requiem for a Snake*; *Devil's Garden*) (Boisset); *Mister Zehn Prozent—Miezen und Moneten* (*Sigpress contro Scotland Yard*) (Zurli)
1968 *Ad ogni costo* (*Grand Slam*; *Top Job*) (Montaldo) (as Erich Weiss); *Ognuno per se* (*Das Gold von Sam Cooper*; *The Ruthless Four*; *Sam Cooper's Gold*) (Holloway, i.e. Capitani) (as blond); *Sartana* (*Se incontri Sartana, prega per la tua morte*) (Kramer, i.e. Parolini); *A qualsiasi prezzo* (*Vatican Story*) (Miraglia); *Due volte Giuda* (Cicero); *Cinque per l'inferno* (*Five into Hell*) (Kramer, i.e. Parolini); *Il grande silenzio* (*La grand Silence*) (Corbucci); *Marquis de Sade: Justine* (*Justine and Juliet*; *Justine*) (Franco)
1969 *I bastardi* (*I gatti*; *Sons of Satan*; *The Cats*) (Tessari) (as Adam); *Il dito nell piaga* (*Salt in the Wound*; *The Dirty Two*) (Ricci); *La legge dei gangsters* (*Quintero*) (Marcellini); *Double Face* (*Das Gesicht im Dunkeln*; *A doppia faccia*; *Puzzle of horrors*) (Hampton, i.e. Freda); *Sono Sartana, il vostro bechino* (*I'll Dig Your Grave*) (Ascott, i.e. Carnimeo); *Paroxismus* (*Black Angel*; *Venus in Furs*) (Biliam and Franco) (as Ahmed); *La Peau de Torpédo* (*Children of Mata Hari*; *Pill of Death*)

Klaus Kinski in *Fitzcarraldo*

(Delannoy); *E Dio disse a Caino . . .* (*And God Said to Cain*) (Dawson, i.e. Margheriti)

1970 *Wie dommt ein so reizendes Mädchen zu diesem Gewerbe?* (*Mir hat es immer Spass gemacht; How Did a Nice Girl Like You Get into This Business?*) (Tremper); *Per una bara piena di dollari* (*Nevada Kid; A Barrel Full of Dollars; Adios companeros*) (Deem, i.e. Fidani); *La belva* (Costa); *Prega il morte e ammazza il vivo* (Warren, i.e. Vari); *Giù le mani . . . carogna* (Fidani); *Appuntamento col disonore* (*Rendezvous with Dishonor; The Night of the Assassins*) (Bolzoni); *I leopardi di Churchill* (*Commando Attack*) (Pradeaux)

1971 *El Conde Dracula* (*Count Dracula*) (Franco); *Nella stretta morsa del ragno* (*Dracula im Schloss des Schreckens; Web of the Spider; And Comes the Dawn . . . but Colored Red*) (Dawson, i.e. Margheriti) (as Edgar Allan Poe); *La bestia uccide a sangue freddo* (*Der Triebmörder; The Cold-blooded Beast; Slaughter Hotel; Asylum Erotica*) (Di Leo); *Lo chiamavano King . . .* (Reynolds, i.e. Romitelli); *Black Killer* (Moore, i.e. Oroccolo); *L'occhio del ragno* (*Eye of the Spider*) (Bianchi-Montero); *La vendetta e un piatto che si serve freddo* (*Vengeance Trail*) (William Redford, i.e. Squitier); *La mano nascosta di Dio* (Palli)

1972 *Il venditore di morte* (*The Price of Death*) (Thomas, i.e. Alberto); *Doppia taglia per Monnesota Stinky* (Deem, i.e. Fidani); *Il ritorno di Clint il solitario* (*Ti attende una corda . . . Ringo*) (Bagram, i.e. Balcazar)

1973 ***Aguirre, der Zorn Göttes*** (*Aguirre, the Wrath of God*) (Herzog) (title role); *Il mio nome è Shanghai Joe* (*Mezzogiorno di fuoco par Lin-Hao; Cinque pistole di violenca; To Kill or to Die*) (Caiano); *La mano spietat della legge* (*The Bloody Hands of the Law*) (Gariazzo); *La morte sorride all'assassino* (*Sette strani cadaveri*) (Massacesi); *Imperativo categorio: control il crimine con rabbia* (Gariazzo); *La mano che nutre la morte* (Garrone)

1974 *Le orme* (*Footprints*) (Bazzoni); *Le amanti del mostro* (Garrone); *Who Stole the Shah's Jewels?* (Leoni)

1975 *L'important c'est d'aimer* (*The Most Important Thing Is Love; The Main Thing Is to Love*) (Zulawski) (as Karl); *Lifespan* (Whitelaw) (as Industrialist); *Un genio, due compari, un pollo* (*The Genius*) (Damiani) (as Doc Foster); *Das Netz* (*The Web*) (Purzer)

1976 *Jack the Ripper* (*Der Dirnenmörder von London*) (Franco); *Madame Claude* (Jaeckin)

1977 *Nuit d'or* (Maoti); *Entebbe: Operation Thunderbolt* (Golan); *Mort d'un pourri* (Lautner)

653

1978   *La Chanson de Roland* (Cassenti); *Zoo zéro* (Fleischer)
1979   *Nosferatu—Phantom der Nacht* (*Nosferatu—The Vampire*)
(Herzog) (as Count Dracula); *Woyzeck* (Herzog) (title role);
Haine (*Traquenard*) (Goult)
1980   *Schizoid* (*Murder by Mail*) (Paulsen) (as Dr. Pieter Fales)
1981   *Buddy Buddy* (Wilder) (as Dr. Zuckerbrot)
1982   *Fitzcarraldo* (Herzog) (as Brian Sweeney Fitzgerald/title role);
The Soldier (*Codename: The Soldier*) (Glickenhaus) (as
Dracha); *Venom* (Haggard) (as Jacmel); *Love and Money*
(Toback) (as Frederick Stockheinz); *La Femme enfant*
(Billetdoux) (as Marcel); *Fruits of Passion* (Terayama) (as
Sir Stephen); *Burden of Dreams* (Blank—doc on making of
Fitzcarraldo); *Android* (Lipstadt) (as Dr. Daniel)
1983   *Beauty and the Beast* (Vadim—for TV)
1984   *The Little Drummer Girl* (George Roy Hill) (as Kurtz); *The
Secret Diary of Sigmund Freud* (Danford B. Greene) (as Dr.
Max Bauer); *Titan Find* (*Creature*) (Malone) (as Hans Rudy
Hofner); *Hitchhiker* (Hodges and Zetterling); *Codename
Wildgeese* (*Geheimecode Wildganse*) (Dawson, i.e.
Margheriti) (as Charlton)
1985   *Kommando Leopard* (*Commando Leopard*) (Dawson) (as
Silveira); *Creature* (Malone) (as Hofner); *El Caballero del
dragon* (*The Knight of the Dragon*; *Star Knight*) (Colomo)
(as Boetius); *Revenge of the Stolen Stars* (Lommel) (as
Duncan McBride)
1986   *Crawlspace* (Schmoeller) (as Dr. Karl Gunther)
1987   *Timestalkers* (Schultz—for TV) (as Dr. Joseph Cole); *Cobra
Verde* (Herzog); *Rough Justice* (Costa)
1988   *Nosferatu a Venezia: Il ritorno di Nosferatu* (Caminito)

Film as Actor, Director, and Scriptwriter:

1989   *Paganini* (title role)

Publications

By KINSKI: books—

Ich bin so wild nach deinem Erdbeermund, Munich, 1975.
All I Need Is Love: A Memoir, New York, 1988 (withdrawn for legal reasons).
Kinski Uncut: The Autobiography of Klaus Kinski, New York, 1996.

By KINSKI: article—

Interview in *Image et Son* (Paris), July 1976.

On KINSKI: books—

Sabatier, J. M., *Klaus Kinski*, Paris, 1979.
Setbon, Philippe, *Klaus Kinski*, Paris, 1979.
Rège, Philippe, *Klaus Kinski*, Paris, 1987.

On KINSKI: articles—

Thomson, David, "The Many Faces of Klaus Kinski," in *American Film*
(Washington, D.C.), May 1980.
Goodwin, Michael, "Herzog: The God of Wrath," in *American Film*
(Washington, D.C.), June 1982.
"Klaus Kinski," in *Film Dope* (London), September 1984.
Obituary in *New York Times*, 26 November 1991.
Obituary in *Variety* (New York), 2 December 1991.

*   *   *

Klaus Kinski's screen career began 25 years before his performance in Werner Herzog's remarkable *Aguirre, the Wrath of God*. Yet, of the numerous directors with whom Kinski worked, only Herzog captured the full range and originality of the actor's talents. In their films together, Kinski's passion and power became the brush with which Herzog painted his vivid portraits; it was an inspired wedding of an actor's style and a director's vision.

The Polish-born Kinski was a renowned and often controversial stage actor in Germany as a young man, but his work in films consisted almost entirely of well-paid roles in second-rate European features. There were a few memorable exceptions to this pattern—he appears briefly in *Doctor Zhivago* as a passenger on the long train ride, and as a villain in Leone's *For a Few Dollars More*—but not until 1973 and *Aguirre* did a film role reveal the true measure of Kinski's menacing power and maniacal fervor.

As a Spanish conquistador going slowly mad in the jungles of South America, Kinski is the personification of Herzog's theme of the destructiveness of absolute power. Yet Kinski is also a strangely heroic figure, a man obsessed with his fantasies and, in his own mind, the instrument of an angry God. There is a romantic bravura to Kinski's performance that is the antithesis of the naturalistic style of acting so prevalent in recent years, and its tone is exactly right for Herzog's epic tale.

In *Nosferatu—Phantom der Nacht*, Herzog's eerie, philosophical retelling of the classic vampire story, Kinski is again an obsessive, terrifying character. The richly atmospheric film pays homage to the great tradition of the German silent era, and Kinski is made up to resemble Max Schreck in Murnau's 1922 *Nosferatu*. Despite ashen face, sunken eyes, and razor-sharp fangs, Kinski's performance conveys the powerful eroticism inherent in the vampire legends, and it is this blend of oppressive horror and sexuality that sets the tone for Herzog's film.

In *Woyzeck* Herzog again makes use of Kinski's compelling intensity this time channeling it through a powerless character driven to an act of terrible violence. As the soldier whose sanity snaps under the crushing circumstances of his life—in a role that was perhaps frighteningly close to the actor's own experience as a prisoner of war during World War II—Kinski reveals a vulnerability as raw and dangerous as an exposed nerve. His final explosion is an agonizing release from the pain and helplessness that has marked the character's life.

Fitzcarraldo returns to the South American settings of *Aguirre*, and once more Kinski was cast (in place of the originally slated Jason Robards) as a man who becomes heroic through his willingness to sacrifice everything to achieve his dream. Yet the dream here is a benign and curiously joyful one, not the expression of a lust for power, but a desire to bring opera to a remote jungle town. Kinski's portrayal of the man in pursuit of this mad fantasy has the now familiar gleam of obsessive zeal, but the threatening quality has gone, leaving in its place a character who is driven but also possessed of a childlike innocence. The vital role that dreams and impossible quests play in our lives has been a pervasive theme in Herzog's work, and never has it been more eloquently articulated than by Kinski's performance in *Fitzcarraldo*.

Kinski's work with Herzog won him international recognition, as well as roles in films by other well-known directors, most notably James Toback's *Love and Money* and George Roy Hill's *The Little Drummer Girl*, in which he gives a memorable performance as Kurtz, the complex, charismatic Israeli spymaster. Kinski appeared in one final Herzog film, *Cobra Verde*, in 1987. He then made his directorial debut two years later with *Paganini*, which he also wrote and played the title role in. Critic David Thomson called the sexually explicit and intense screen biography of the violinist and composer "close to unwatchable." It ironically became Kinski's final film credit after he died two years later, ending a 43-year movie career.

Kinski will certainly be best remembered, however, for his roles in Herzog films; it was in these few films that Kinski enjoyed his finest moments on screen. In bringing Herzog's very personal visions to life, Kinski achieved the highest expression of his own unique abilities.

—Janet E. Lorenz, updated by David E. Salamie

KINSKI, Nastassja

Pseudonym: At one time, spelled first name "Nastassia." **Nationality:** German. **Born:** Nastassja Nakszynski in Berlin, 24 January 1961; daughter of the actor Klaus Kinski. **Education:** Attended schools in Rome, Munich, Caracas, and New York; studied acting with Lee Strasberg at the Actors Studio. **Family:** Married Ibrahim Moussa, 1984 (separated), children: Aljosha, Sonja Leila; daughter with Quincy Jones, Kenya Niambi Jones. **Career:** 1974—film debut in *Falsche Bewegung*; 1976—first English-language film, *To the Devil a Daughter*; 1980—international fame with *Tess*; 1980s—established Leila production and distribution company. **Awards:** Deutscher Filmpreis for Acting, for *Spring Symphony*, 1983. **Agent:** c/o William Morris, 151 El Camino Drive, Beverly Hills, CA, 90212, U.S.A.

Films as Actress:

1974 *Falsche Bewegung (The Wrong Move)* (Wenders) (as Mignon)
1976 *To the Devil a Daughter* (Sykes) (as Catherine Beddows); *Reifezeugnis (For Your Love Only)* (Petersen) (as Sina Wolf)
1978 *Cosi come sei (Stay as You Are)* (Lattuada) (as Francesca); *The Passion Flower Hotel (Leidenschaftliche Bluemchen; Boarding School)* (Farwagi) (as Deborah Collins)
1980 *Tess* (Polanski) (as Tess Durbeyfield)
1982 *One from the Heart* (Coppola) (as Leila); *Cat People* (Schrader) (as Irena Gallier)
1983 *Exposed* (Toback) (as Elizabeth Carlson); *La Lune dans le caniveau (The Moon in the Gutter)* (Beineix) (as Loretta Channing)
1984 *Unfaithfully Yours* (Zieff) (as Daniella Eastman); *The Hotel New Hampshire* (Richardson) (as Susie the Bear); *Paris, Texas* (Wenders) (as Jane); *Maria's Lovers* (Konchalovsky) (as Maria Bosic)
1985 *Harem* (Joffe) (as Diane); *Revolution* (Hudson) (as Daisy McConnahay); *Fruhlingssinfonie (Spring Symphony; Symphony of Love)* (Schamoni) (as Clara Wieck)
1987 *Maladie d'amour (Malady of Love)* (Deray) (as Juliette); *Intervista* (Fellini)
1988 *Magdalene (Stille nacht; Silent Night)* (Teuber) (as Magdalene)
1989 *Acque di primavera(Torrents of Spring)* (Skolimowski) (as Maria Nikolaevna Polozov)
1990 *Il sole anche di notte (Night Sun)* (Tavianis) (as Cristina); *Il Segreto (The Secret)* (Pachard)
1991 *L'Envers du decors: Portrait de Pierre Guffroy (Behind the Scenes: A Portrait of Pierre Guffroy)* (Salis—doc) (as herself); *The Insulted and the Injured*; *Dawn* (Maselli)
1992 *In Camera Mia* (Martino); *La Bionda (The Blonde)* (Rubini) (as Christine)
1993 *Faraway, So Close (In Weiter Ferne, So Nah!)* (Wenders) (as Raphaela)
1994 *Crackerjack* (Mazzo—for TV) (as K. C.); *Terminal Velocity* (Sarafian) (as Chris/Krista Morrow)
1996 *The Foolish Heart*

Publications

By KINSKI: articles—

Interview, in *Cinema* (West Germany), November 1979.
Interview with Andy Warhol, in *Inter/View* (New York), August 1980.
Interview with Jodie Foster, in *Film Comment* (New York), September/October 1982.
Interview, in *Photoplay* (London), September 1983.
Interviews, in *Première* (Paris), November 1985 and June 1987.
"And Now for ... Nastassja Kinski," interview with Sheila Benson, in *Interview* (New York), December 1993.

On KINSKI: book—

Sinclair, Marianne, *Hollywood Lolita: The Nymphet Syndrome in the Movies*, London, 1988.

On KINSKI: articles—

Biskind, P., "Will Overexposure Spoil Nastassia Kinski?," in *American Film* (Washington, D.C.), April 1982.
Current Biography 1984, New York, 1984.
Hibbin, S., "Nastassia Kinski," in *Films and Filming* (London), June 1984.
Film Français (Paris), 11 March 1988.
Lovece, Frank, "The Kinski Report," in *Entertainment Weekly*, 7 October 1994.

*   *   *

After very auspicious beginnings—having been discovered by Wim Wenders and elevated to stardom by Roman Polanski—Nastassja Kinski has so far had a less distinguished film career than a great many critics and early fans had predicted. Questions of talent aside, one likely reason why Kinski did not quickly become the next Ingrid Bergman or Audrey Hepburn (among the classic stars to whom she was compared) was her choice of projects after *Tess*, her breakthrough film. Her choices were admirably adventuresome and varied, and often for important directors, but most of the resulting films were considered highly flawed or at least controversial, though Kinski's performances were often cited as saving graces rather than part of the problem.

Following her debut as the deaf-mute Mignon figure in Wenders's update of *Wilhelm Meister*, and various European films that established her as a charming, sexually provocative teenager, *Tess* introduced Kinski to a much wider audience. These viewers saw a face with remarkably large eyes and lips (the wide mouth more prominent in later films), and heard a unique voice, with slurred, almost warbled sounds, especially the vowels preceding "r"s (not to be explained simply by her adoption of a Dorset accent). Much of the film called for her to be silent, eyes downcast, suggesting an inwardness, a soul perplexed and suffering. (Almost nothing is shown of the passionate side of Hardy's Tess, as if a subtext of Polanski's affair with the teenaged Kinski were allowed to suffice. Significantly, one never even overhears Tess's quarrel with Alec before she murders him, as reported in the novel.)

Kinski's first American role, a supporting one as the tightrope-walking vamp in *One from the Heart*, called for her to be little more than odd and exotic. A much more challenging role was the lead in Paul Schrader's *Cat People*, calling for a more intense version of the persona from *Tess*: sweetly innocent, miserably victimized, yet latently erotic and violent. As a woman who finds that she turns into a black panther when she has sex, Kinski has the appropriate haunted look, and of course the unusual facial features and voice that sounds American yet with some untraceable accent. She is convincingly shy and terror-stricken, less convincingly demonic in the weakly motivated

Nastassja Kinski in *Tess*

swimming-pool scene. Today *Cat People* may seem repellently voyeuristic, without a trace of the ironic distance one finds in, say, Hitchcock, and tiresome in its "take" on the myth of the virgin woman becoming a deadly animal when sexually aroused, but it made Kinski more of a star.

Her next roles, in *Exposed* and *The Moon in the Gutter*, allowed her to play less passive women, though hardly more in control of their destinies; but both films received notoriously negative reviews for directorial pretentiousness. By comparison, her portrayal of Clara Wieck in *Spring Symphony* was notably conservative and innocuous, like the film itself. *Unfaithfully Yours* at least demonstrated that Kinski could handle light comedy in charming fashion (here with an Italian accent).

But in 1984 Kinski achieved two major performances. *Maria's Lovers*, a curious fantasia on motifs from *Tess*, features her as the virginal bride of a young World War II veteran who proves to be impotent (only with the woman he loves) and deserts her; later she is seduced and made pregnant by a traveling musician, but consequently reunited with her husband. Kinski, her hair pulled back to reveal a less glamorized version of her striking features, is allowed more vivacity and intense emotional expression by director Andrei Konchalovsky than Polanski had permitted Tess: most notable are a tender scene with the father-in-law (Robert Mitchum) and an outburst at her unfaithful though tormented husband (John Savage).

In *Paris, Texas*, 90 minutes go by before Kinski, as the object of the protagonist's quest, is glimpsed on the screen, except in a home movie,

and another ten minutes before she looks directly at the screen (through a peepshow window, the viewpoint of her estranged husband [Harry Dean Stanton]) and begins to speak, in a Texas accent that is not flawless but still acceptable, almost touching. Asked in *Film Quarterly* about Kinski's public image as a "nymphet," Wim Wenders, who conceived the part for her, said that she fitted into the film's "subtext . . . which is a man insisting on a certain image of a woman. . . . I've followed Nastassia's career . . . and some of [her films] were painful to me because I felt there was someone who was trapped. There's a really great actress, and she's totally exploited because of her image. . . . I felt she was waiting to show the other side of that image. And she did." Wenders eventually takes the audience to the other side of the peepshow frame, to the woman's point of view. Kinski is tremendously affecting in an exposed role that essentially consists of two scenes with Stanton, in the second of which she mostly just reacts to his long monologue, then delivers a four-minute monologue of her own.

Following these performances, Kinski appears to have focused primarily upon her private life, including children; her roles have been less frequent, and seldom remarkable. As the "other woman" in the Turgenev costume drama *Torrents of Spring* she is rather flat, like the rest of the cast. As the angel Raphaela in *Faraway, So Close,* Wenders's sequel to *Wings of Desire*, she is, at least, quite perfect for the supporting role: hauntingly lovely of face and voice, ineffably sad. Playing conventional heroines in recent thrillers, she has little to do but look charming in the low-budget *Crackerjack*, while in *Terminal Velocity*, in the meatier role of an ex-KGB agent who becomes the sidekick of an

American flyboy (Charlie Sheen), she is a sexier sort of Nancy Drew as she snoops along dark corridors. One can only wonder if this featured role in a standard Hollywood action film signifies a new phase in a unique, seemingly unfulfilled career.

—Joseph Milicia

KLINE, Kevin

Nationality: American. **Born:** St. Louis, Missouri, 24 October 1947. **Education:** Attended Indiana University (major in music), 1972; studied at Juilliard. **Family:** Married the actress Phoebe Cates, 1989, two children: Joseph and Greta. **Career:** 1972-76—founding member of the Acting Company, New York City; 1977—played role of Woody Reed in TV soap opera, *Search for Tomorrow*; 1982—film debut in *Sophie's Choice*; 1987-88—artistic associate, Acting Company; 1990—acted and directed in production of *Hamlet*, later produced for television; 1993—artistic associate, New York Shakespeare Festival. **Awards:** Tony Award, for *On the Twentieth Century*, 1978; Tony Award, for *The Pirates of Penzance*, 1980; Academy Award for Best Supporting Actor, for *A Fish Called Wanda*, 1988.

Films as Actor:

1982   *Sophie's Choice* (Pakula) (as Nathan)
1983   *The Pirates of Penzance* (Leach) (as Pirate King); *The Big Chill* (Kasdan) (as Harold)
1985   *Silverado* (Kasdan) (as Paden)
1986   *Violets Are Blue* (Fisk) (as Henry Squires)
1987   *Cry Freedom* (Attenborough) (as Donald Woods)
1988   *A Fish Called Wanda* (Charles Crichton) (as Otto West)
1989   *The January Man* (O'Connor) (as Nick Starkey)
1990   *I Love You to Death* (Kasdan) (as Joey)
1991   *Soapdish* (Hoffman) (as Jeffrey Anderson); *Grand Canyon* (Kasdan) (as Mack)
1992   *Chaplin* (Attenborough) (as Douglas Fairbanks); *Consenting Adults* (Pakula) (as Richard Parker)
1993   *George Balanchine's The Nutcracker* (Ardolino) (as narrator); *Dave* (Reitman) (as Dave Kovic/Bill Mitchell)
1994   *Princess Caraboo* (Austin) (as Frixos)
1995   *French Kiss* (*Paris Match*) (Kasdan) (as Luc Teyssier)
1996   *Fierce Creatures* (Cleese and Robert M. Young) (as Rod McKane/Vince McKane); *The Hunchback of Notre Dame* (Trousdale and Kirk Wise—animation) (as voice of Phoebus)

Film as Director:

1990   *Hamlet* (for TV) (+ title role)

Publications

By KLINE: article—

"'You've Heard of Watergate—This Is Surrogate,'" telephone conversation with Sigourney Weaver, in *Interview* (New York), May 1993.

On KLINE: articles—

Current Biography 1986, New York, 1986.
Clark, John, "Kevin Kline," in *Premiere* (New York), May 1990.
Hoffman, Jan, "A Pair of Aces," in *Premiere* (New York), May 1990.
Morgenstern, Joe, "Kevin's Choice," in *Connoisseur*, July 1991.
Wetzseon, Ross, "Kevin Can Wait," in *New York*, 10 May 1993.
Gates, Anita, "Other Methods, Other Madness, and Always Slings and Arrows," in *New York Times*, 2 July 1995.

*   *   *

His first words on film were in an assumed Southern accent, announcing the technical virtuosity that would be the hallmark of his best work. Contravening the conventional wisdom that in screen acting less is more, Kline, trained in both classical and popular theater, is most arresting when allowed to import the large gestures favored, when not actually required by the stage. His screen persona thus tends to be that of a man who gets carried away with his enthusiasms, his ideas, most often himself. Roles requiring him to exhibit restraint or signal inner reflection can deaden his reflexes; Kline never seems so intelligent an actor as when he is playing stupid—witness his hilariously, self-enraptured, testosterone-driven dolt in *A Fish Called Wanda*. So exuberant is his performance that it literally takes a steamroller to halt the flow of his comic invention.

When no overt technical demand is made on the expressiveness of his voice or his body, Kline can be subdued, even dispirited. His debut in *Sophie's Choice* was an exception, a film in which Kline's uncanny impersonations, impulsive humor, and physical glamour were unpredictably fused in his portrayal of an irresistible and charismatic madness. His subsequent dramatic parts, however, have been less successful in exploiting his physical and emotional volatility to unexpected or fresh use. The irrepressible narcissism of his comic persona is not so much expunged as sublimated into a much more subtle, sometimes more objectional form of good guyism in such films as the environmentally and emotionally correct *Violets Are Blue*. Nor has Kline fared well in genres, such as the Western, that call upon him to simplify his emotions into archetypal attitudes. As Paden, the quiet and aimless cowboy out to change his luck in *Silverado*, Kline is meant to evoke the taciturn and secretly troubled masculinity of the classic Western hero (especially in the *High Noon*ish final shoot-out), but at best manages to suggest a muted rather than heroically restrained psyche.

His most frequent and somewhat uneven work has been with Lawrence Kasdan, for whom Kline epitomizes the white liberal male afflicted with all the pieties and perplexities such a species is heir to. Kline is Kasdan's model for the aging radical whose midlife anomie manifests itself in the form of earnest soul-searching rather than sexual lunacy. In *The Big Chill* he is such a genial host to the friends of his radical youth that he even agrees to father a child for a woman whose biological clock is about to ring its final alarm. Eleven years later, he plays virtually the same decent white liberal befuddled rather than appalled by the state of the world in *Grand Canyon*, only in this film Kasdan offers a less admiring view of Kline's sensitive husband, generous friend, and preternaturally patient "good father." He gives Kline a superman dream of flight that hints at the moral giddiness underlying his quiet decencies.

The trouble with a morally unimpeachable Kline is that he is no match for his impeachable comic double who invariably proves not only to be more entertaining, but finally, a better ethical monitor. In the confession scene that opens *I Love You to Death*, Kline gives a hilarious rendering of a happy sinner's uncontrite, but dutiful effort to recall the time, frequency, and number of his adulterous encounters with all the precision due to a ritual confession. In *Soapdish* he does a rollicking turn as a former soap star (as he once was) condemned to do dinner theater in Florida until his deceased character is recalled to life, only to find himself at the center of an equally absurdist Oedipal drama offstage.

But it is *Dave* that represents the quintessential Kline performance since in this film he gets to impersonate himself. Two halves of his screen persona confront each other in this dizzy tale of a presidential

Kevin Kline in *Dave*

double taking on the role, then the power, and finally the wife of a comatose president: the white liberal who has lost the values that once defined and sustained him (for the first time Kline plays the philandering husband without a trace of exculpatory male sentimentalism) and the comic ego, reincarnated in the gentle form of a populist who appreciates the simple joys of life. It helps to have Sigourney Weaver assisting in the comic transfer of power and affection. Kline is less fortunate in *French Kiss*, in which Meg Ryan's unrelievedly mannered performance almost overwhelms the subtle allure of Kline's larcenous charmer. Imitating not only a French accent but the mumble that gives movie Frenchmen their cachet, Kline reconciles the Gallic shrug and American double-take to register a surprising array of emotions—from a bemused laissez-faire sexuality to a conniving thievery to the unanticipated dawn of love. In such performances, Kline reminds us how comic theatricality can not only entertain, but also reveal as much about personal and national character as the most studied naturalism.

—Maria DiBattista

KORTNER, Fritz

Born: Fritz Nathan Kohn in Vienna, Austria, 12 May 1892. **Education:** Studied at the Academy of Music and Dramatic Arts, Vienna.

Family: Married the actress Johanna Hofer, son: Peter Kortner. **Career:** Actor in Mannheim and Hamburg; 1911—joined Max Reinhardt's theater, Berlin; achieved star status with his performance in *Die Wandlund*, 1919, and became a leading actor-director in German-language theater; 1915—film debut in *Manya, Die Türkin*; 1918—film directing debut with *Gregor Marold*; 1933—left Germany with rise of Nazis, and found refuge in New York after stays in Vienna, Prague, and London; wrote two Broadway plays, and worked as actor and screenwriter in Hollywood; returned to Germany after the war, and regained his stage reputation. **Awards:** Deutscher Filmpreis for career, 1966. **Died:** Of leukemia in Munich, 25 July 1970.

Films as Actor:

1915   *Die grosse Gafahr* (Sauer); *Im Banne der Vergangenheit* (Piel); *Manya, die Türkin* (Piel); *Police Nr. 1111* (Piel)

1916   *Das zweite Leben*

1917   *Der Brief einer Toten* (Friesler)

1918   *Die andere Ich* (Friesler) (as Professor); *Frauenehre* (Kundert) (as Jagdehilfe); *Sonnwendhof* (Leyde); *Der Stärkere* (Wiene)

1919   *Satanas* (Murnau); *Das Auge des Buddha* (Mondet) (as Indian servant); *Ohne Zeugen* (Baron and Kundert)

1920   *Die Brüder Karamasoff* (*The Brothers Karamazov*) (Buchowetzki and Froelich); *Katherina die Grosse* (*Catherine the Great*) (Schünzel) (as Potemkin); *Weltbrand*

(Gad); *Danton* (*All for a Woman*) (Buchowetzki); *Das Haus zum Mond* (Martin); *Der Schädel der Pharoanentochter* (Tollen); *Die Lieblingsfrau des Maharadscha* (Mack); *Die Nacht der Königin Isabeau* (Wiene); *Gerechtigkeit* (Lux)

1921 *Hintertreppe* (*Backstairs*) (Jessner); *Am roten Kliff* (Henning); *Aus dem Schwarzbuch eines Polizeikommissars* (Hanus); *Der Eisenbahnkönig* (Illès); *Die Verschwörung zu Genua* (Leni); *Landstrasse und Gross-stadt* (Wilhelm)

1922 *Peter der Grosse* (*Peter the Great*) (Buchowetzki); *Am Rande der Gross-stadt* (Kobe); *Der Graf von Essex* (Felner); *Der Ruf des Schicksals* (Guter); *Die Finsternis und ihr Eigentum* (Hartwig); *Luise Millerin* (Froelich); *Sterbende Völker* (Reinert)

1923 **Schatten** (*Warning Shadows*) (Robison); *Arme Sünderin* (Gariazzo); *Nora* (Viertel)

1924 *Armes kleines Mädchen* (Kayser); *Dr. Wislizenus* (Kobe); *Moderne Ehen* (Otto)

1925 *Orlacs Hände* (*The Hands of Orlac*) (Wiene) (as Nera)

1926 *Dürfen wir schweigen* (Oswald)

1927 *Beethoven* (*The Life of Beethoven*) (Löwenstein) (title role); *Maria Stuart* (Feher) (as Bothwell); *Mata Hari* (*Mata Hari, the Red Dancer*) (Feher); *Primanerliebe* (Land); *Alpentragödie* (Land); *Die Ausgestossenen* (Gerger); *Die Geliebte des Gouverneurs* (Feher) (+ co-sc); *Mein Leben für das Deine* (Morat); *Revolutions-hochzeit* (*The Last Night*) (Sandberg); *Die Frau auf der Folter* (*A Scandal in Paris*); **Die Büchse der Pandora** (*Pandora's Box*) (Pabst) (as Dr. Schön); *Frau Sorge* (Land)

1929 *Die Frau, nach der Mann sich sehnt* (*Three Loves*) (Bernhardt); *Atlantik* (Dupont); *Giftgas* (Dubson); *Die Nacht des Schreckens* (Righelle); *Das Schiff der verlorenen Menschen* (Tourneur); *Die Frau im Talar* (Trotz); *Somnambul* (Trotz)

1930 *Dreyfus* (*The Dreyfus Case*) (Oswald) (title role); *Menschen in Käfig* (*Love Storm*) (Dupont); *Der Andere* (Wiene) (dual role); *Die grosse Sehnsucht* (Szekely)

1931 *Der Mörder Dmitri Karamasoff* (*The Murderer Dimitri Karamazov*) (Ozep) (title role)

1932 *Danton* (Behrendt) (title role)

1934 *Chu Chin Chow* (Forde) (as Abu Hassan); *Evensong* (Saville) (as Kober)

1935 *Abdul the Damned* (Grune) (title role); *The Crouching Beast* (Hanbury) (as Ahmed Bey)

1936 *Midnight Menace* (*Bombs over London*) (Hill) (as Peters)

1943 *The Strange Death of Adolf Hitler* (Hagan) (as Marbach, + sc)

1944 *The Hitler Gang* (Farrow) (as Otto Strasser)

1946 *The Wife of Monte Cristo* (Ulmer); *Somewhere in the Night* (Mankiewicz); *The Razor's Edge* (Goulding) (as Kosti)

1947 *The Brasher Doubloon* (Brahm)

1948 *Berlin Express* (Tourneur); *The Vicious Circle* (*The Woman in Brown*) (Wilder)

1949 *Der Ruf* (*The Last Illusion*) (von Maky) (+ sc)

1950 *Epilog* (Käutner)

1952 *Blaubart* (Christian-Jacque) (as Haushofmeister); *Die Stimme des Anderen* (Engel) (+ co-sc)

Films as Director:

1918 *Gregor Marold*

1919 *Else von Erlenhof*

1931 *Der brave Sünder* (*The Upright Sinner*) (+ co-sc)

1932 *So ein Mädel vergisst man nicht* (+ co-sc)

1955 *Die Stadt ist voller Geheimnisse* (*City of Secrets*; *Secrets of the City*) (+ co-sc); *Sarajevo*

1960 *Die Sendung der Lysistrata* (for TV)

Publications

By KORTNER: book—

Alle Tage Abend, 1960.

On KORTNER: books—

Fritz Kortner, Berlin, 1970.

Brand, Matthias, *Fritz Kortner in der Weimarer Republik: Annäherungsversuche an die Entwicklung eines jüdischen Schauspielers in Deutschland*, Rheinfelden, 1981.

Völker, Klaus, *Fritz Kortner: Schauspieler und Regisseur*, Berlin, 1987.

* * *

Fritz Kortner, like his contemporary Conrad Veidt and the slightly older Emil Jannings, was associated with Max Reinhardt's Berlin theater in the years before and after World War I, and like them he became an important stage actor, combining a stage and a film career. His long life allowed him to continue after World War II as a leading, if often controversial, figure on the German-language stage.

His acting had a wider range than that of Werner Krauss, though like Krauss he was often cast in important parts in the expressionist films of the 1920s. He could be flamboyant (as in *Warning Shadows*), or more contained, as Lotte Eisner's description of him in *Backstairs* indicates: "Everything is motivated: the slow reactions of a poor indecisive man scared of love, the hesitations of an outcast of fortune who, having won his happiness by dint of guile, stops wanting to believe in it. . . . This instinctively Expressionistic actor blends into the setting." But he was also able to play such characters as Dr. Schön in *Pandora's Box*, Beethoven, Dmitri Karamazov, Bothwell, and Dreyfus.

England failed to recognize his ability when he went into exile after Hitler's taking power in Germany, and he acted in such minor films as *Chu Chin Chow* and *Abdul the Damned*; he had slightly better luck in the United States. After World War II he made a few films in Germany, but concentrated on stage work.

—George Walsh

KRAUSS, Werner

Nationality: Austrian. **Born:** Gestunghausen, Germany, 23 July 1884, became citizen of Austria. **Family:** Married Marie Bard (died 1944). **Career:** Stage actor, first in German provinces; 1914—film debut in *Die Pagode*; 1916—on Berlin stage under Max Reinhardt; 1933—appeared on London stage; in Nazi propaganda films, and named Actor of the State; continued acting on stage, and in a few films, after World War II; 1955—directed stage play *The Caine Mutiny Court Martial*. **Died:** In Vienna, 20 October 1959.

Films as Actor:

1914 *Die Pagode* (Fekete) (as Mr. Wu)

1915 *Die vertauschte Braut*

1916 *Hoffmanns Erzählungen* (*Tales of Hoffman*) (Oswald) (as Dapertutto); *Nacht des Grauens* (Robison); *Zirkusblut* (Oswald)

1917 *Der Friedensreiter*; *Der Fremde*; *Die Rache der Toten* (Oswald); *Die Seeschlacht* (Oswald); *Wenn Frauen lieben und hassen* (Speyer)

Werner Krauss in *Das Kabinett des Dr. Caligari*

1918   *Es werde Licht* (Part III) (Oswald); *Das Tagebuch einer Verloren* (Oswald); *Opium* (Reinert); *Stürme des lebens*

1919   *Die Frau mit den Orchideen* (Rippert); *Rose Bernd* (Halm); *Die Prostitution* (Rippert); *Totentanz* (Rippert); *Christus*; *Fräulein Pfiffikus*; *Das Mädchen und die Männer*

1920   ***Das Kabinett des Dr. Caligari*** (*The Cabinet of Dr. Caligari*) (Wiene) (title role); *Die Brüder Karamasoff* (*The Brothers Karamazov*) (Buchowetzki and Froelich) (as Dmitri); *Der Bucklige und die Tänzerin* (Maurnau); *Johannes Goth* (Gerhardt); *Das lachende Grauen* (Pick); *Danton* (*All for a Woman*) (Buchowetzki) (as Robespierre); *Die Beichte einer Toten*; *Der Mann ohne Namen* (*The Man without a Name*) (Jacoby)

1921   *Christian Wahnschaffe* (Gad); *Die Frau ohne Seele* (Lasko); *Grausige Nächte* (Pick); *Das Medium* (Rosenfeld); *Der Roman der Christine von Herre* (Berger); *Scherben* (*Shattered*) (Pick); *Sappho* (Buchowetzki); *Zirkus des Lebens* (Guter); *Die Beute der Erinnyen* (Rippert); *Der Tanz um Liebe und Glück* (Zeyn)

1922   *Der brennende Acker* (*Burning Soil*) (Murnau); *Josef und seine Brüder* (Froelich); *Lady Hamilton* (Oswald); *Luise Millerin* (Froelich); *Die Nacht der Medici* (Grune); *Nathan der Weise* (Noa); *Othello* (Buchowetzki) (as Iago); *Tragikomödie* (Wiene); *Der Graf von Essex* (Felner); *Die Marquise von Pompadour* (Halm)

1923   *Der Puppenmacher von Kiang-Ning* (Wiene); *I.N.R.I.* (*Crown of Thorns*) (Wiene); *Zwischen Abend und Morgen* (Robison); *Das alte Gesetz* (*This Ancient Law*) (Dupont); *Fridericus Rex* (von Cserepy); *Der Schatz* (*The Treasure*) (Pabst); *Das unbekannte Morgen* (Korda); *Adam und Eva* (Porges); *Alt-Heidelberg* (*Student Prince*) (Behrendt); *Fräulein Raffke* (Eichberg); *Der Kaufmann von Venedig* (Felner); *Der Menschenfeind* (Walther-Fein)

1924   *Dekameron-Nächte* (*Decameron Nights*) (Wilcox) (as Sultan); *Ein Sommernachtstraum* (*A Midsummer Night's Dream*) (Neumann) (as Bottom); *Das Wachsfigurenkabinett* (*Waxworks*) (Leni) (as Jack the Ripper)

1925   *Eifersucht* (*Jealousy*) (Grune); *Das Haus der Lüge* (*Die Wildente*) (Pick); *Die freudlose Gasse* (*Streets of Sorrow*; *Joyless Streets*) (Pabst) (as butcher); *Die Dame aus Berlin* (von Kabdebo); *Die Moral der Gasse* (Speyer); *Reveille, das grosse Wecken* (Kaufmann); *Der Trödler von Amsterdam* (Janson)

1926   *Tartüff* (*Tartuffe*) (Murnau) (as Orgon); *Geheimnisse einer Seele* (*Secrets of a Soul*) (Pabst); *Man spielt nicht mit der Liebe* (*Don't Play with Love*) (Pabst); *Nana* (Renoir) (as Muffat); *Der Student von Prag* (*The Student of Prague*; *The Man Who Cheated Life*) (Galeen) (as Devil); *Kreuzzug des Weibes* (*Unwelcome Children*) (M. Berger); *Uberflussige Menschen* (Rasumny)

1927   *Funkzauber* (Oswald); *Die Hose* (*A Royal Scandal*; *The Trousers*) (Behrendt); *Laster der Menschheit* (Meinert); *Die Hölle der Jungfrauen* (Dinesen); *Da hält die Welt dem Atem an* (Basch); *Der fidele Bauer* (Seitz); *Unter Ausschluss der Offentlichkeit* (Conrad Wiene)

1928   *Looping the Loop* (Robison)

1929   *Napoleon auf St. Helena* (Pick)

1931   *Yorck* (Ucicky) (title role)

1932   *Mensch ohne Namen* (*The Man without a Name*) (Ucicky)

1935   *Hundert Tage* (Wenzler—German version of *Campo di maggio*)

1936   *Burgtheater* (*Vienna Burgtheater*) (Forst)

1939   *Robert Koch* (Steinhoff) (as Dr. Rudolf Virchow)

1940   *Jud Süss* (Harlan) (several roles)

1941   *Annelie* (*Die Geschichte eines Lebens*) (von Baky)

1942   *Die Entlassung* (Liebeneiner); *Zwischen Himmel und Erde* (Braun)

1943   *Paracelsus* (Pabst)

1950   *Prämien auf den Tod* (Jurgens); *Der fallende Stern* (Braun)

1955   *Sohn ohne Heimat* (Deppe)

Publications

By KRAUSS: book—

Schauspiel meines Lebens (autobiography), edited by H. Weigel, 1957.

On KRAUSS: book—

Kracauer, Siegfried, *From Caligari to Hitler: A Psychological History of the German Film*, Princeton, New Jersey, 1947.

On KRAUSS: article—

Retro, March-April 1981 and January-February 1982.

*   *   *

Perhaps the greatest actor of the German Expressionist era, Werner Krauss is best known today for his work as Dr. Caligari in Robert Wiene's *The Cabinet of Dr. Caligari*, as the obsessed Count Muffat in Jean Renoir's version of Emile Zola's *Nana*, and for his part in Veit Harlan's antisemitic rendering of *Jud Süss*.

In *The Cabinet of Dr. Caligari* Krauss epitomizes the German Expressionist performance aesthetic which would dominate the next decade: an obvious external expression of interiority. Throughout the central part of the film, Krauss hobbles through nightmare sets, his crippled walk an expression of a crippled mind, his dark and menacing facial and body makeup of the rot within, his sparse and erratic white hair of his overall decrepitude. His posture, rounded inward to symbolize mystery and enclosure, refuses the spectator any sympathetic identification. At the film's end, when Caligari is shown to be the head of an asylum and the film the rantings of an inmate, Krauss expressionistically softens all aspects of posture and characterization to appear the epitome of benevolence.

In the wake of *Caligari*, Krauss continued to play evil or obsessed characters. Notable roles include Iago in Buchowetzki's *Othello* and Jack the Ripper in Leni's *Waxworks*.

By 1926, Krauss was the leading German film actor of his time, having worked with F. W. Murnau, G. W. Pabst, Lupu Pick, E. A. Dupont, Carl Froelich, Richard Oswald, and Paul Leni. But as he admitted to Jean Renoir, his general physical character had become a cliché. He had invested every character with the bowed head, drooping shoulders, and studied walk of an individual burdened with the cares of

the world. That posture had become his prop, and Renoir, then attracted to Expressionism, utilized it. In *Nana* Count Muffat falls prey to the demands of the exploitative Nana. Totally submissive to her demands, he ultimately disgraces himself by barking, sitting, rolling over, and playing dead like a dog. His utterly degraded character is reflected in his lumpish posture. That same year he appeared to much acclaim as the devil in Henrik Galeen's version of *The Student of Prague*.

Unlike many of the major talents of his time, Krauss did not flee Germany upon the rise of Nazism. Instead, he starred in many of their cinematic vehicles. The most notorious was *Jud Süss*, a film demanded by the Nazi Minister of Propaganda, Joseph Goebbels. In the years following the war, all associated with this film were plagued with recriminations for their participation. After the fall of Hitler, Krauss appeared in only three more films before his death in 1959.

—Doug Tomlinson

KUMAR, Dilip

Nationality: Indian. **Born:** Yusuf Khan, in Peshawar (now Pakistan), 1922. **Family:** Married the actress Saira Banu. **Career:** 1940—worked in a British army canteen, Bombay; 1944—film debut in *Jwar Bhata*; also producer until *Ganga Jumna*, 1961; appointed Sheriff of Bombay, 1980.

Films as Actor:

1944   *Jwar Bhata* (Amiya Chakravarty) (as Jagdish)

1945   *Pratima*

1946   *Milan* (*Nauka Dubi*) (Nitin Bose)

1947   *Jugnu*; *Neel Kamal* (Kidar Nath Sharma)

1948   *Anokha Pyar*; *Ghar Ki Izzat* (Daryani) (as Chanda); *Mela*; *Nadiya Ke Paar*; *Shaheed*

1949   *Andaz* (*A Matter of Style*; *Beau Monde*) (Mehboob Khan) (as Dilip); *Shabnam* (B. Mitra) (as Manoj)

1950   *Arzoo*; *Babul* (Sunny) (as Ashok); *Jogan* (Kidar Nath Sharma) (as Vijay)

1951   *Deedar* (*Vision*) (Nitin Bose) (as Shamu); *Hulchul*; *Tarana*

1952   *Aan* (*Savage Princess*; *Pride*) (Mehboob Khan) (as Jai Tilak); *Daag* (Amiya Chakravarty) (as Shankar); *Sangdil*

1953   *Footpath* (Sarhadi) (as Noshu); *Shikast*

1954   *Amar* (*Eternal*) (Mehboob Khan) (title role)

1955   *Azad* (*Free*) (Naidu) (as Khan Saheb/title role); *Devdas* (Bimal Roy) (title role); *Insaniyat* (*Humanity*) (Vasan) (as Mangal); *Udan Khatola* (Sunny) (as Kashi)

1957   *Naya Daur* (B. R. Chopra) (as Shankar); *Musafir* (*Traveller*) (Mukherjee)

1958   *Madhumati* (Bimal Roy) (as Devendra); *Yahudi* (Bimal Roy) (as the Roman Prince Marcus)

1959   *Paigham* (Vasan) (as Ratanal)

1960   *Kohinoor*; *Mughal-e-Azam* (K. Asif) (as Prince Salim)

1961   *Ganga Jumna* (Nitin Bose) (as Ganga)

1964   *Leader*

1966   *Dil Diya Dard Liya* (A. R. Kardar) (as Shankar); *Pari*

1967   *Ram Aur Shyam* (Tapi Chanakya)

1968   *Admi*; *Sangharsh* (H. S. Rawail); *Sadhu Aur Shaitan*

1970   *Sagina Mahato* (Tapan Sinha—in Bengali); *Gopi*

1972   *Anokha Milan*; *Dastaan*

1974   *Sagina*; *Phir Kabb Milogi*

1976   *Bairaag*

1980   *Chanayaka Chandragupta* (B. R. Chopra) (as Chanayaka)
1981   *Kranti*
1982   *Shakti* (*Power*) (Ramesh Sippy) (as Ashwini Kumar); *Vidhata*
1983   *Mazdoor*
1984   *Duniya*; *Mashaal*
1986   *Karma* (Subhash Ghai) (as Rana Vishnu Pratap Singh); *Dharam Adhikari*
1989   *Kanoon Apna Apna*
1990   *Izzatdar*
1991   *Saudagar* (Subhash Ghai) (as Bir Singh "Biru")

Publications

By KUMAR: articles—

Interviews in *Film World* (India), no. 6, 1970, November 1972, November 1976, and January 1980.
Interview with K. Mohamed, in *Cinema in India* (Bombay), vol. 3, no. 1, 1992.

On KUMAR: books—

Barnouw, Erik, and S. Krishnaswamy, *Indian Film*, New York, 1965; rev. ed., 1980.
Willemen, Paul, and Behroze Ghandy, *Indian Cinema*, London, 1982.
Ramachandran, T. M., *70 Years of Indian Cinema (1913-1983)*, Bombay, 1985.

On KUMAR: articles—

Film World (India), January 1975, January 1979, and June 1980.
Thomas, R., "Indian Cinema: Pleasures and Popularity," in *Screen* (London), May/August 1985.
Khalid, "Golden Era Begins," in *Cinema in India* (Bombay), vol. 4, no. 6, 1990.
Sathe, V. P., "The Three Aces," in *Cinema in India* (Bombay), vol. 4, no. 4, 1993.
Rajadhyaksha, Ashish, and Paul Willemen, in *Encyclopaedia of Indian Cinema*, New Dehli, 1994.

*   *   *

There is a persistent notion of a division in the Hindu tradition between the renouncer and the man of the world. Writers have noticed such features in modern Indian models of masculinity and heroism, in fields ranging from the world of cricket to that of commercial film narratives. Devdas, a character who is forbidden his beloved for social reasons, and drinks his life away, is one of the key renouncer figures in modern Indian literature and cinema. When a second film version was made in 1955, it was inevitable that, of the contemporary crop of film stars, it would be Dilip Kumar who played the lead role. The *Devdas* of 1955 is *the* Devdas for generations of Indian audiences. The tragic hero and the failed love became such staples of folklore that even today any variation on the said theme evokes a comparison with Dilip Kumar.

The renouncer failed in romance and withdrew from social life not because he was inadequate, but because of social prejudice. He could also simply be ill-fated. Kumar played a number of roles that essentially came from this character-type, though there were often quite complicated variations. He did of course play more positive heros, such as in the swashbuckling stunt films *Aan* (*Pride*) and *Azad* (*Free*), perhaps in a conscious move to diversify his screen presence. Even in such generic shifts, the legacy of his conventional "loser" image is discernible; in the costume action film *Insaniyat* (*Humanity*) his be-

loved marries another, and Kumar dies saving her child; and his outlaw peasant hero in *Ganga Jumna* first loses his wife and is then killed by his policeman brother for taking the law into his own hands.

There was evidently something glamorous in the renouncer hero's obsession with an impossible romance. But the highlighting of social prejudice as a factor in the narrative of romantic failure could make the conception quite powerful, exposing the injustice of the social order, and the inhuman ways in which intimate marital and familial ties were cynically arranged for material gain. Examples of this are Kumar's *Deedar* (*Vision*), and *Pyaasa* (*The Thirsty One*) for which it is said Guru Dutt initially wanted Kumar before casting himself in the lead role.

There are other, darker variations of the renouncer narrative. In the fascinatingly contrived *Andaz* (*A Matter of Style*) Dilip (Kumar) falls in love with Nina (Nargis) who, unknown to him, is already betrothed to Rajen (Raj Kapoor), absent while their friendship is developing. Nina is unaware that her friendly behavior has been misinterpreted by Kumar, and is shocked to hear his confession of love the day after she has married Rajen. Later, after a violent encounter with Rajen, Kumar becomes deranged and tries to force himself on Nina, who is compelled to kill him. The bulk of the story is seen from Nina's viewpoint, and there are definite indications that her feelings towards Kumar are ambiguous; given this, and the imperative that the popular film reassert a traditional morality, the glamorous romantic failure cannot remain glamorous; he has to become repulsive so that Nina can destroy him and so quell any residual ambiguity regarding her feelings.

Perhaps most intriguing is *Amar* (*Eternal*). Kumar is a debonair lawyer, practicing in the countryside, is engaged to the sophisticated Madhubala, daughter of a local estate owner. His urbane poise is undone when he meets a lively young peasant woman, played by Nimmi. He displays vicious, uncontrollable feelings towards her which culminate in his shocking rape of the girl. He finally renounces his betrothal to Madhubala, and marries Nimmi. This renunciation destabilizes genres and star discourses. The story of urban sophistication and comedy is deconstructed by combining it with the tale of rural simplicity and innocence: the hero of the first genre becomes the villain of the second. Further, Kumar is paired with Nimmi, a secondary female star who, in earlier work, was always shown to desire the hero without his reciprocating her love (*Deedar, Aan*)

These kinds of sophisticated variations on Kumar's star personality and his relationship to the renouncer archetype tended to give way before the altogether different type of genre that emerged in Hindi movies in the 1960s. *Leader*, for example, is a fascinatingly vulgar exercise in performance; its narrative, about the way Gandhian political values are threatened by corruption and violence, is merely a topical excuse to string together a series of boisterous romantic and comic routines. The aging Kumar was engaged in holding onto a youthful image by presenting himself as irresponsible and carefree and as leader of a group of teenage boys. Throughout his career and growth, Kumar is noted for his consummate skill in taking any role and bringing it to life, becoming an icon figure in the process. Contrived or otherwise, Kumar had an opportunity that many of the image-bound stars of Bombay never had. He always insisted and got a wide variety of roles, diverse plot structures, and complex climaxes that gave vent to his acting talents.

In the 1970s Kumar's appeal waned, but he has recently reemerged in a series of powerfully recessive performances. As an older character in *Shakti* (*Power*), for instance, he displays a relentless authoritarian face quite remote from the images of romantic loss and longing that defined his early career. In *Saudagar*, he takes on the legendary hero Raj Kumar, as they both get embroiled in the fights of two legendary friends who become archenemies. From the Bombay Talkies' *Jwar Bhata* in 1944, Kumar has traversed many ups and downs to reach *Izzatdar* in 1990, an aging actor with a younger heartthrob Govinda starring in the lead role. Now Kumar holds his position as the veteran of Bollywood. All the young actors may not aspire to achieve his success but certainly do wish to acquire at least a portion of the thespian's legendary talent.

In the 1990s, the 72-year-old actor has other interests that take up most of his time. Kumar has said, "as an actor who can get people to respect me, I must do more than act. I must take actions." With that as his guiding line, he has been taking active part in mitigating social distresses. He threw open the gates of his huge house, which he had used to seclude himself from society, to house the riot victims of the Bombay religious strife in 1993. He traveled all over the United States to raise money for the Bosnian Muslims. The thespian now has the role of his lifetime, and like all the other complex characterizations he took on, he is doing full justice to this one too.

—Ravi Vasudevan, updated by Usha Venkatachallam

KYO, Machiko

Nationality: Japanese. **Born:** Motoko Yamo in Osaka, 25 March 1924. **Education:** Attended Azuma Elementary School. **Career:** 1936—joined the Osaka Shochiku Girls Opera as dancer: stage debut, 1936; 1944—film debut in *Tengu-daoshi*; 1949—joined the Daiei Studio and first groomed as a "glamour girl" under the producer Masaichi Nagata; 1964—television debut in *Aburaderi*, and in film version, *Amai shiru*, 1964. **Awards:** Mainichi Eiga Concourse Awards for Best Actress, 1950 and 1964; Kinema Jumpo Award for Best Actress, for *Sweet Sweat*, 1964; also Special Citation, D. W. Griffith Awards, "for the modernization of traditional Japanese acting," 1954. **Address:** Olimpia Copu-35, 6-35 Jingumae, Shibuya-ku, Tokyo 151, Japan.

Films as Actress:

1944   *Tengu-daoshi* (Inoue); *Danjuro sandai* (*Three Generations of Danjuro*) (Mizoguchi)

1949   *Saigo ni warau otoko* (Yasuda) (as dancer); *Hanakurabe tanuki-goten* (Kimura); *Chika-gai no dankon*; *Mitsu no shinju*; *Chijin no ai* (Kimura) (as Naomi); *Hebi-hime dochu* (Kimura and Marune)

1950   *Zoku Hebi-hime dochu* (Kimura and Marune); *Harukanari haha no kuni* (Ito); *Asakusa no hada* (Kimura); *Bibo no umi* (Hisamatsu); *Fukkatsu*; **Rashomon** (*In the Woods*) (Kurosawa) (as Masago); *Hi no tori* (Tanaka); *Itsuwareru seiso* (Yoshimura) (as Kimicho)

Machiko Kyo in *Rashomon*

1951   *Koi no Oranda-zaka* (Suzuki); *Jiyu-gakko* (Yoshimura) (as
       Yuri); *Joen no hatoba*; *Mesuinu* (Kimura); *Genji monogatari*
       (Tale of Genji) (Yoshimura) (as Awaji no kami); *Bakuto*
       ichidai (Kimura)

1952   *Asakusa kurenai-dan*; *Nagasaki no uta wa wasureji*; *Taki-no*
       Shiraito (Nobuchi) (title role); *Bijo to tozoku* (Kimura); *Daibutsu*
       kaigen (Kinugasa) (as Maya-no-uri); *Bijo no tokudane*

1953   **Ugetsu monogatari** (*Ugetsu; Tales of a Pale and Mysterious Moon*
       after the Rain) (Mizoguchi) (as Lady Wakasa); *Kurohyo*; *Ani*
       imoto (*Older Brother, Younger Sister*) (Kimura) (as Mon);
       Jigokumon (*The Gate of Hell*) (Kinugasa) (as Kesa)

1954   *Aru onna* (Toyoda) (as Yoko); *Aizen katsura* (Kimura) (as
       Katsue Takaishi); *Shunkin monogatari* (Ito) (as Okoto);
       Asakusa no yoru (Shima); *Sen-hime* (Kimura); *Bazoku gei-*
       sha (Shima); *Haru no uzumaki*

1955   *Bara ikutabika* (Kinugasa); *Yokihi* (*Princess Yang Kwei-fei*)
       (Mizoguchi) (title role); *Tojuro no koi* (Mori); *Shin josei*
       mondo (Shima)

1956   *Shin Heike monogatari: Yoshinaka o meguru san-nin no onna*
       (Kinugasa) (as Tomoc); *Niji ikutabi*; **Akasen chitai** (*Street of*
       Shame) (Mizoguchi) (as Mickie); *Tsukigata Hanbeita*
       (Kinugasa) (as Hagino); *The Teahouse of the August Moon*
       (Daniel Mann) (as Lotus Blossom)

1957   *Itohan monogatari* (Ito) (as Itohan); *Stajio wa tenya wanya*;
       Odoriko; *Onna no hada*; *Jigoku-bana*; *Yoru no cho*
       (Yoshimura); *Ana* (*The Pit*; *The Hole*) (Ichikawa)

1958   *Yurakucho de aimasho* (Shima); *Kanashimi wa onna dakeni*
       (Shindo) (as the niece); *Haha*; *Chushingura* (Watanabe) (as
       Rui); *Osaka no onna* (Kinugasa) (as Osen); *Akasen no hi wa*
       kiezu; *Yoru no sugao*; *Musume no boken* (Shima)

1959   *Anata to watashi no ai-kotoba: Sayonara, konnichiwa* (*Goodbye,*
       Hello) (Ichikawa); *Sasameyuki* (Shima); *Onna to kaizoku* (Ito);
       Yoru no togyo; *Jirocho Fuji* (Mori); *Kagi* (*Odd Obsession*)
       (Ichikawa) (as Ikuko Kenmochi); *Ukigusa* (*Floating Weeds*;
       The Duckweed Story; *Drifting Weeds*) (Ozu) (as Sumiko)

1960   *Jokei* (Yoshimura); *Ruten no oohi*; *Bonchi* (Ichikawa); *San-*
       nin no kaoyaku (Inoue); *Ashi ni sawatta onna* (Masumura);
       Kao; *Oden jigoku* (Kimura)

1961   *Konki* (Yoshimura); *Nuregame Botan*; *Onna no kunsho*
       (Yoshimura); *Kodachi o tsukau onna* (*Samurai Daughter*)
       (Ikehiro); *Shaka* (*Buddha*) (Misumi) (as Yashas Nandabala)

1962   *Kurotokage* (*Black Lizard*) (Inoue); *Nakayoshi-ondo: Nippon*
       ichi dayo; *Shin no shikotei* (*The Great Wall*) (Tanaka); *Onna*
       no issho (Masumura) (as Kei Nunobiki)

1963   *Jokei kazoku*; *Dendai inchiki monogatari: Dotanuki*

1964   *Amai shiru* (*Sweet Sweat*) (Toyoda)

1966   *Tanin no kao* (*The Face of Another*) (Teshigahara) (as the
       wife); *Jinchoge* (*The Daphne*) (Chiba) (as first daughter);
       Chiisai tobosha (Yinugasa) (as Yayoi Yamamura)

1969   *Senba-zuru* (*Thousand Cranes*) (Manumura) (as Chikako
       Kurimoto)

1970   *Yabure kabure*

1974   *Kareinaru ichizoku* (*The Family*) (Yamamoto)

1975   *Kinkan-shoku* (Yamamoto) (as Mrs. Prime Minister)

1976   *Yoba* (Imai) (title role); *Otoko wa tsuraiyo: Torajiro junjo-*
       shishu (*Tora's Pure Love*) (Yamada)

1985   *Kesho* (*Make Up*) (Ikehiro)

Publications

On KYU: articles—

Trumball, Robert, "Rising Star of Japan," in *New York Times Magazine*,
   24 April 1955.

"Industry: Beauty from Osaka," in *Newsweek* (New York), 10 October
   1955.

Richie, Donald, "The Face of '63—Japan," in *Films and Filming* (London), July 1963.

Gillett, J., "Machiko Kyo," in *Film Dope* (London), March 1985.

*   *   *

Machikyo Kyo was perhaps the first Japanese actress to be
"groomed" as a star through the more typically Western attention
to glamour. Drawing upon her background as a dancer, her sex
appeal was emphasized by Daiei and her early director Masaichi
Nagata, and she quickly became a successful actress for the studio.
Her style was unique on the Japanese screen in its sensuality and
unbounded eroticism. The most representative of her early roles is
as a devilish girl trifling with her lover in *Chijin no ai*, based on the
novel by Tanizaki. She seemed at her best at portraying the sensual
women in his novels, as she later demonstrated in Ichikawa's mod-
ernistic adaptation of *Kagi*, incorporating a comic flair into her
role as the young and stimulating wife.

Typecast because of her alluring appearance, she successfully
extended her range in Kurosawa's *Rashomon*, which brought her
and the Japanese cinema international attention. Her explosive
performance in the role of a temperamental woman who is both
shockingly assertive and audaciously seductive startled the public
and critics. Her next great success came in Yoshimura's *Itsuwareru*
seiso, a remake of Mizoguchi's prewar masterpiece *Gion no shimai*.
Kyo played with enthusiasm a geisha attempting to vanquish men
who exploit women. Her reputation at the studio was gradually
established through her work in a series of fine films for Yoshimura
and Kimura.

For Mizoguchi, Kyo played the role of the ghost princess who
bewitches a potter in *Ugetsu monogatari*. Employing the type of
movement used in Noh drama, she successfully conveyed the chilling
atmosphere typical of the ghost genre within the Noh repertoire,
combining a horrifying effect with a mysterious eroticism. She also
collaborated with Mizoguchi in the title role of *Yokihi*, and as a West-
ernized prostitute in his final film *Akasen chitai*; at one moment while
simultaneously eating, smoking, chewing gum, and talking, she outrageously summarizes both her character's tactile eroticism as well as
her own considerable comic skills.

Kyo established an international reputation with these performances, as well as in Kinugasa's *Jigokumon*, to which she contributed
a visually stunning portrayal as a tragic aristocratic wife. Her first
American film, *The Teahouse of the August Moon*, was also her first
comedy, but her success in it inexplicably led to no other American
films, and even for a short while seemed to reduce her popularity in
Japan.

Her performances in Ozu's *Ukigusa* and in Toyoda's *Amai shiru*
show her mature acting style, which combines her passion with a new
contemplative quality. Her role in the latter film (which earned her
many awards) is particularly sublime, a depiction of a woman at the
bottom of society, managing to survive despite her suffering and vic-
timization. She further expanded her range by undertaking complicated new roles. These include the wife in Teshigahara's *Tanin no kao*,
whose husband secretly undergoes plastic surgery to alter his appearance. She nevertheless recognizes him, and allows him to seduce her.
Opposed to such characters is her portrayal of an extremely ambitious
woman in Satsuo Yamamoto's political entertainment film, *Kareinaru*
ichizoku. Through her unforgettable work with many of Japan's greatest directors, and since many of her films were distributed internationally, Kyo remains one of the most diverse and recognizable talents in
the Japanese cinema.

—Kyoko Hirano, updated by Corey K. Creekmur

LADD, Alan

Nationality: American. **Born:** Alan Walbridge Ladd in Hot Springs, Arkansas, 3 September 1913. **Education:** Hollywood High School. **Family:** Married 1) Marjorie Jane Harrold, 1936 (divorced 1941), son: the film executive Alan Ladd, Jr., 2) Sue Carol, 1942, daughter: the actress Alana, son: David. **Career:** During the early 1930s, "discovered" several times, but given only small parts, beginning in 1932 with *Once in a Lifetime*; worked as studio grip, attended Bard Dramatic School for one term, and eventually worked as a one-man variety show on radio station KFWB; 1942—Paramount contract; 1943-44—served in U.S. Army (medical discharge); 1948—formed his own radio production company; 1954-59—contract with Warner Brothers; 1954—formed Jaguar Productions; 1959—began TV production. **Died:** 29 January 1969.

Films as Actor:

1932   *Once in a Lifetime* (Mack)
1933   *Saturday's Millions* (Sedgwick)
1936   *Pigskin Parade (The Harmony Parade)* (Butler)
1937   *The Last Train from Madrid* (Hogan); *All over Town* (Horne); *Hold 'em Navy (That Navy Spirit)* (Neumann)
1938   *The Goldwyn Follies* (Marshall); *Come on Leathernecks* (Cruze); *Freshman Year* (McDonald)
1939   *Rulers of the Sea* (Lloyd); *The Green Hornet* (Beebe and Taylor—serial); *Hitler, Beast of Berlin (Beasts of Berlin; Hell's Devils; Goose Step)* (Scott)
1940   *Brother Rat and a Baby (Baby Be Good)* (Enright); *In Old Missouri* (McDonald); *The Light of Western Stars* (Selander); *Gangs of Chicago* (Lubin); *Those Were the Days (Good Old School Days)* (Laird); *Cross Country Romance* (Woodruff); *Wildcat Bus* (Woodruff); *Captain Caution* (Wallace); *The Howards of Virginia (The Tree of Liberty)* (Lloyd); *Meet the Missus* (St. Clair); *Her First Romance* (Dmytryk); *Blame It on Love* (doc); *Meat and Romance* (doc)
1941   *Petticoat Politics* (Kenton); *The Reluctant Dragon* (Werker); *I Look at You* (short); *The Black Cat* (Rogell); ***Citizen Kane*** (Welles) (as reporter); *Paper Bullets (Gangs Inc.)* (Rosen); *Great Guns* (Banks); *Cadet Girl* (McCarey); *Unfinished Rainbows* (doc)
1942   *Joan of Paris* (Stevenson); *This Gun for Hire* (Tuttle) (as Raven); *The Glass Key* (Heisler) (as Ed Beaumont); *Star Spangled Rhythm* (Marshall) (as guest)
1943   *Lucky Jordan* (Tuttle) (title role); *China* (Farrow) (as Mr. Jones); *Letters from a Friend* (Shourds—doc)
1944   *And Now Tomorrow* (Pichel) (as Dr. Merek Vance); *Skirmish on the Home Front* (doc)
1945   *Salty O'Rourke* (Walsh) (title role); *Hollywood Victory Caravan* (Russell—doc); *Duffy's Tavern* (Walker) (as guest)
1946   *The Blue Dahlia* (Marshall) (as Johnny Morrison); *O.S.S.* (Pichel) (as John Martin); *Two Years before the Mast* (Farrow) (as Charles Stewart)

1947   *My Favorite Brunette* (Nugent) (as guest); *Calcutta* (Farrow) (as Neale Gordon); *Variety Girl* (Marshall) (as guest); *Wild Harvest* (Garnett) (as Joe Madigan)
1948   *Saigon* (Fenton) (as Maj. Larry Briggs); *Beyond Glory* (Farrow) (as Rocky Gilman); *Whispering Smith* (Fenton) (as Luke Smith)
1949   *The Great Gatsby* (Nugent) (as Jay Gatsby); *Chicago Deadline* (Allen) (as Ed Adams); *American Portrait* (doc); *Eyes of Hollywood* (doc)
1950   *Captain Carey U.S.A. (After Midnight)* (Leisen) (as Webster Carey)
1951   *Appointment with Danger* (Allen) (as Al Goddard); *Branded* (Maté) (as Choya); *The Road to Hope* (doc)
1952   *Red Mountain* (Dieterle) (as Brett); *The Iron Mistress* (Douglas) (as Jim Bowie); *The Sporting Oasis* (short)
1953   *Thunder in the East* (Charles Vidor) (as Steve Gibbs); ***Shane*** (Stevens) (title role); *The Desert Legion* (Pevney) (as Paul Lartal); *Botany Bay* (Farrow) (as Hugh Tallant); *Paratrooper (The Red Beret)* (Young) (as Canada)
1954   *Saskatchewan (O'Rourke of the Royal Mounted)* (Walsh) (as O'Rourke); *Hell below Zero* (Robson) (as Duncan Craig); *The Black Knight* (Garnett) (as John); *Drum Beat* (Daves) (as Johnny MacKay)
1955   *The McConnell Story (Tiger in the Sky)* (Douglas) (as Mac McConnell)
1956   *Hell on Frisco Bay* (Tuttle) (as Steve Rollins); *Santiago (The Gun Runner)* (Douglas) (as Cash Adams); *A Cry in the Night* (Tuttle) (as narrator)
1957   *The Big Land (Stampeded)* (Douglas) (as Chad Morgan); *Boy on a Dolphin* (Negulesco) (as James Clader)
1958   *The Deep Six* (Maté) (as Alec Austen); *The Proud Rebel* (Curtiz) (as John Chandler); *The Badlanders* (Daves) (as Peter Van Hook)
1959   *The Man in the Net* (Curtiz) (as John Hamilton)
1960   *Guns of the Timberland* (Webb) (as Jim Hadley); *All the Young Men* (Bartlett) (as Kincaid); *One Foot in Hell* (Clark) (as Mitch Barrett)
1961   *Orazi e Curiazi (Duel of Champions)* (Baldi and Young) (as Horatio)
1962   *Thirteen West Street* (Leacock) (as Walt Sherill)
1963   *The Carpetbaggers* (Dmytryk) (as Nevada Smith)

Publications

On LADD: books—

Linet, Beverly, *Ladd: The Life, The Legend: The Legacy of Alan Ladd: A Biography*, New York, 1979.
Henry, Marilyn, and Ron DeSourdis, *The Films of Alan Ladd*, Secaucus, New Jersey, 1981.

On LADD: articles—

Roman, Robert C., "Alan Ladd," in *Films in Review* (New York), April 1964.

Alan Ladd

Fox, J., "The Good Bad Ladd: A Profile of the Gentle Gunman" and "Spirit of the West," in *Films and Filming* (London), June and July 1972.
Ciné Revue (Paris), 14 July 1983.

* * *

In the opening moments of *This Gun for Hire*, Alan Ladd checks his gun, feeds a kitten, slaps the maid, tosses a ball to a cute little girl, and cold-bloodedly shoots down two people whom he has been hired to rub out. With Veronica Lake's guidance, he eventually does the Right Thing, but it was his clear-eyed amorality that audiences responded to; *This Gun for Hire* made Ladd a star overnight.

He was already, by that time, a veteran of a decade in films, but had never made much of an impact: he was a college student in *Pigskin Parade*, a sailor in *Hold 'em Navy*, one of the reporters at the end of *Citizen Kane*, a cheerful animator explaining a storyboard to Robert Benchley in *The Reluctant Dragon*. After *This Gun for Hire* Ladd became more prolific and quite popular, but his range never extended appreciably. Stalwart and manly, he could also be dour; he seldom smiled without irony. Never a personable figure on the screen, Ladd's appeal was that of an icon: serene face, athletic body, piercing eyes, and an overall tough-guy demeanor that was precisely appropriate for the dark side of the 1940s.

His enigmatic, slightly mocking persona was used to diverse effect by his more perceptive directors—John Farrow, Tay Garnett, Raoul Walsh—and his frequent teamings with insolent twin-soul Veronica Lake provided his stolid imperturbability with a dash and resonance that did not always surface without her. Ladd and Lake were an inspired team; they were so alike in both countenance and manner that they often seem incestuous siblings rather than the conventional lovers that the script means for them to be. Ladd's sullen calm could also take on a veneer of Old World charm which made him a natural and courtly swashbuckler in colorful, exciting entertainments: *Desert Legion*; *The Iron Mistress* (in which he played Jim Bowie), *The Red Beret*, *Santiago*, *Saskatchewan*.

Shane was Ladd's last great part; his character looks back on a life of gunfire and bloodshed with a complex mixture of nostalgia and regret. Shane's past was, in short, like Ladd's filmic history. When the gunfighter rides away, we feel the loss of this cool and violent man who so wanted to be a hero, but who just didn't have it in him.

—Frank Thompson

LAKE, Veronica

Nationality: American. **Born:** Constance Ockelman, in Brooklyn, New York, 14 November 1919. **Family:** Married 1) John Detlie, 1940 (divorced 1943); 2) the director Andre de Toth, 1944 (divorced 1952); 3) Joseph A. McCarthy, 1955 (divorced 1959). **Education:** Attended Bliss Hayden School of Acting. **Career:** 1939—got small parts in films, beginning with *Sorority House*; several successful films before being teamed with Alan Ladd in *This Gun for Hire* made her a star. **Died:** Of hepatitis, in Burlington, Vermont, 7 July 1973.

Films as Actress:

(as Constance Keane)

1939   *The Wrong Room* (Brock—short); *Sorority House* (*That Girl from College*) (Farrow); *All Women Have Secrets* (Neumann)

1940   *Young as You Feel* (St. Clair); *Forty Little Mothers* (Berkeley)

(as Veronica Lake)

1941   *I Wanted Wings* (Leisen) (as Sally Vaughn); *Hold Back the Dawn* (Leisen); ***Sullivan's Travels*** (Preston Sturges) (as The Girl)
1942   *This Gun for Hire* (Tuttle) (as Ellen Graham); *The Glass Key* (Heisler) (as Janet Henry); *I Married a Witch* (Clair) (as Jennifer)
1943   *Star Spangled Rhythm* (Marshall); *So Proudly We Hail* (Sandrich) (as Lt. Olivia D'Arcy)
1944   *The Hour before the Dawn* (Tuttle) (as Dora Bruckmann)
1945   *Bring on the Girls* (Lanfield) (as Teddy Collins); *Out of This World* (Walker) (as Dorothy Dudge); *Duffy's Tavern* (Walker) (as guest); *Hold That Blonde!* (Marshall) (as Sally Martin)
1946   *Miss Susie Slagle's* (Berry) (as Nan Rogers); *The Blue Dahlia* (Marshall) (as Joyce Harwood); *Ramrod* (De Toth) (as Connie Dickason)
1947   *Variety Girl* (Marshall) (as guest)
1948   *Saigon* (Fenton) (as Letty Stanton); *Isn't It Romantic?* (McLeod) (as Candy); *The Sainted Sisters* (Russell) (as Letty Stanton)
1949   *Slattery's Hurricane* (De Toth) (as Dolores)
1952   *Stronghold* (Sekeley) (as Mary Stevens)
1966   *Footsteps in the Snow* (Green)
1973   *Flesh Feast* (*Time for Terror*) (Grinter) (as Dr. Elaine Frederick, + co-pr)

Publications

By LAKE: book—

Veronica: The Autobiography of Veronica Lake, with Donald Bain, London, 1969.

On LAKE: book—

Lenburg, Jeff, *Peekaboo: The Story of Veronica Lake*, New York, 1983.

On LAKE: article—

Braun, Eric, "Veronica Lake: Hollywood Comet," in *Films and Filming* (London), May 1974.

* * *

Veronica Lake, the girl with the "peek-a-boo hairstyle," is a consummate product of the Hollywood star machine. In the golden years of the studio system, stars were created overnight by media hype and studio-released "hot tips." It was this system that transformed aspiring actress Constance Ockelman into glamour sensation Veronica Lake. Her image "sold" so well that, in the early years of the war, Lake herself was asked to appeal to women factory workers to clip their copycat tresses to avoid industrial accidents.

Veronica Lake emerged in 1938 when, following an unsuccessful screen test at MGM, her film clip reached the desk of a producer at Paramount. Paramount was then suffering a drought and the producers were looking for a new face. In 1941 they cast Lake in the war film *I Wanted Wings*. An eight-year contract with Paramount followed. Later that year, Preston Sturges noticed Lake and cast her opposite Joel McCrea in the classic social comedy *Sullivan's Travels*. Her sultry, dry-humored vamp was the perfect complement to actors of McCrea's type. It was this success that motivated the studio to pair Lake with

Veronica Lake

Alan Ladd in what became billed as one of the romantic duos of the decade.

Many feel that Ladd and Lake created a model for the "toughs and vamps" breed of acting that was later to be perfected by Bogart and Bacall. Four major films highlight this most successful period of Lake's career: *This Gun for Hire*, followed by *The Glass Key*, *The Hour before Dawn*, and *Saigon*. In 1948, when her contract expired, Lake left Hollywood. Interviews suggested that she felt she had outgrown her stereotypic vamp image. Yet, in spite of her frustration at being typecast, she did not escape the image in her one notable role of her post-Hollywood period, in an action picture called *Stronghold*, independently produced in Mexico, partly with her own money.

—Rob Winning

LAMARR, Hedy

Nationality: American. **Born:** Hedwig Eva Maria Kiesler in Vienna, Austria, 9 November 1913; became U.S. citizen, 1953. **Education:** Attended Max Reinhardt's drama school, Berlin, and an acting school in Vienna before 1930. **Family:** Married 1) Friedrich Alexander Mandl, 1933; 2) the writer Gene Markey, 1939 (divorced), one adopted son; 3) the actor John Loder, 1943 (divorced 1947), one daughter and one son; 4) Ted Stauffer, 1951 (divorced 1952); 5) W. Howard Lee, 1953 (divorced 1960); 6) Lewis Boies, 1963 (divorced 1965). **Career:** 1930—film debut in *Geld auf der Strasse* (also script girl on the film) as Hedy Kiesler; some stage roles in Vienna; 1933—role in *Extase* brought international publicity; 1937—left her husband and soon arrived in Hollywood; 1938—contract with MGM, and renamed Hedy Lamarr; first American film, *Algiers*; for the next decade worked steadily in Hollywood and on radio; 1945—formed own production company; 1957—worked in TV; 1965—arrest on shoplifting charge made headlines; later exonerated; 1966—autobiography published aiming to revive her notoriety; later she sued her ghostwriters claiming that portions misrepresented her; 1984—wrote songs that were performed in a cabaret in Greenwich Village; 1992—charged again with shoplifting. **Address:** 568 Orange Drive, #47, Attamonte Springs, FL 32701, U.S.A.

Films as Actress:

(as Hedy Kiesler or Hedwig Kiesler)

1930   *Geld auf der Strasse* (*Money on the Street*) (Jacoby) (as young girl at nightclub table)
1931   *Die Blumenfrau von Lindenau* (*Sturm in Wasserglas*; *Flower Woman of Lindenau*; *Storm in a Water Glass*) (Jacoby) (as Burdach's secretary); *Man braucht kein Geld* (*Wir brauchen kein Geld*; *His Majesty, King Ballyhoo*; *We Need No Money*) (Boese) (as Käthe Brandt); *Die Koffer des Herrn O.F.* (*The Trunks of Mr. O.F.*; *The Thirteen Trunks of Mr. O.F.*) (Granowsky) (as Helene)
1933   *Symphonie der Liebe* (*Extase*; *Symphony of Love*; *Ecstasy*) (Machaty) (as Eva)

(as Hedy Lamarr)

1938   *Algiers* (Cromwell) (as Gaby)
1939   *Lady of the Tropics* (Conway) (as Manon de Vargnes)

1940   *I Take This Woman* (Van Dyke) (as Georgi Gragore); *Boom Town* (Conway) (as Karen Vanmeer); *Comrade X* (King Vidor) (as Theodora); *The Miracle of Sound* (Shearer—doc, short) (as herself)
1941   *Come Live with Me* (Clarence Brown) (as Johnny Jones); *Ziegfeld Girl* (Leonard) (as Sandra Kolter); *H. M. Pulham, Esq.* (King Vidor) (as Marvin Myles)
1942   *Tortilla Flat* (Fleming) (as Dolores "Sweets" Ramirez); *Crossroads* (*The Man Who Lost His Way*) (Conway) (as Lucienne Talbot); *White Cargo* (Thorpe) (as Tondelayo)
1943   *The Heavenly Body* (Hall) (as Vicky Whitley); *Show Business at War* (De Rochemont—doc, short) (as herself)
1944   *The Conspirators* (Negulesco) (as Irene); *Experiment Perilous* (Jacques Tourneur) (as Allida Bedereaux)
1945   *Her Highness and the Bellboy* (Thorpe) (as Princess Veronica)
1946   *The Strange Woman* (Ulmer) (as Jenny Hager)
1947   *Dishonored Lady* (Stevenson) (as Madeleine Damien)
1948   *Let's Live a Little* (Wallace) (as Dr. J. O. Loring)
1949   *Samson and Delilah* (Cecil B. DeMille) (as Delilah)
1950   *A Lady without Passport* (Joseph H. Lewis) (as Marianne Lorress); *Copper Canyon* (Farrow) (as Lisa Roselle)
1951   *My Favorite Spy* (McLeod) (as Lily Dalbray)
1954   *Eterna femmina* (*L'amante di Paride*; *Loves of Three Queens*; *The Face that Launched a Thousand Ships*; *Eternal Woman*) (Marc Allégret and Ulmer) (as Hedy Windsor/Helen of Troy/ Empress Josephine/Genevieve de Brabant)
1957   *The Story of Mankind* (Irwin Allen) (as Joan of Arc)
1958   *The Female Animal* (Keller) (as Vanessa Windsor)
1988   *Entertaining the Troops*; *Going Hollywood: The War Years*
1991   *Instant Karma* (Roderick Taylor) (as Movie Goddess)
1994   *That's Entertainment! III* (Friedgen and Sheridan—compilation)

Publications

By LAMARR: book—

Ecstasy and Me: My Life as a Woman, New York, 1966.

By LAMARR: articles—

Interview with S. Birmingham, in *New York Times*, 23 August 1970.
Interview with B. Edison, in *Films in Review* (New York), June/July 1974.

On LAMARR: book—

Young, Christopher, *The Films of Hedy Lamarr*, Secaucus, New Jersey, 1978.

On LAMARR: articles—

Ciné Revue (Paris), 7 October 1982.
Cinema Magazine (Paris), February 1983.
Bourgeois, T. R., "Dorothy Lamour and Hedy Lamarr," in *Hollywood Studio Magazine* (Studio City), vol. 23, no. 5, 1990.
Meeks, Fleming, "I Guess They Just Take and Forget about a Person," in *Forbes* (New York), 14 May 1990.
Steinem, Gloria, "Women in the Dark: Of Sex Goddesses, Abuse, and Dreams," in *Ms. Magazine* (New York), January/February 1991.
Briggs, C., "Classic Continental Beauties," in *Hollywood: Then and Now* (Studio City), vol. 25, no. 4, 1992.

*   *   *

Hedy Lamarr in *Extase*

Was Hedy Lamarr's only contribution to the cinema the fact that she was the first woman to walk naked across the screen in a commercially distributed film? Some would argue that this was the case, while others would maintain that, despite her lack of natural talent, she brought to the screen a unique presence that transcended the poor scripts she was often given. *Symphonie der Liebe*, which was retitled *Extase* following its favorable reception in France, is the film by which the Austrian-born actress will always be remembered not only for Lamarr's nudity but also for her simulation of the first on-screen female orgasm which she later revealed the director literally prodded out of her by repeated insertions of a large pin into her bare buttocks.

The film proved to be a popular box-office attraction in Europe, but was heavily cut when it was eventually released in America. Lamarr's role in the film certainly raised more than an eyebrow or two and won her the accolade of "the most beautiful woman in Europe."

Her early film career is closely linked with the emergent German and Austrian cinema of the 1930s, where she worked under the direction of Georg Jacoby, Karl Boese, and Alexis Granowsky. Lamarr successfully applied the skills she had learned on the stage in Weimar Berlin to the handful of films she made in Europe. But it was for her brunette beauty that she won her contract with MGM, not her acting ability.

670

In Hollywood she was renamed by Louis B. Mayer after the beautiful silent screen actress Barbara La Marr in the hope that some of the magic associated with the name would rub off. Lamarr was never quite as successful, artistically or commercially, as her fellow émigrés Greta Garbo, Greer Garson, and Marlene Dietrich. She was typecast as a provocative temptress, and her development as an actress was severely restricted by the reputation she held for her appearance in *Extase*. Paradoxically, her sheer beauty was a drawback to her ever being considered for more demanding roles, although her physical appearance on the screen influenced fashions during the late 1930s and early 1940s, with actresses and female cinemagoers dyeing their hair brunette and parting it in the center. MGM cast her in a variety of films—costume dramas, comedies, musicals—but the parts tended to be too similar and she never became a top box-office star, despite some critically acclaimed performances in two early 1940s King Vidor films: *Comrade X*, opposite Clark Gable, in the Garbo role of a sort of spinoff of the superior *Ninotchka*; and *H. M. Pulham, Esq.*, opposite Robert Young, as a career woman who briefly provides a spark to the proper Young's otherwise dull life—Lamarr later called this movie the favorite of her career.

Lamarr was an unusually independent actress for her time—very choosy about the roles she would take—and she turned down the parts in *Casablanca* and *Gaslight* played by Ingrid Bergman. Soon after, Lamarr's MGM contract expired and her career began to fade, but not before her dynamic female lead in *Samson and Delilah*. The role of the biblical seductress seemed tailor-made for her and represented what was, in the end, the peak of her cinematic achievement.

After her retirement from the screen in the late 1950s (save the rare cameo of 1991's *Instant Karma*), Lamarr subsequently became the object of some ridicule for her *Extase*-induced notoriety, obscuring the life of a woman whose intelligence helped invent an antijamming radio (for which she never earned a penny) and whose patriotism to her adopted country led her to donate the invention to the U.S. government for the World War II effort and to raise enormous sums selling war bonds (ironically enough, Bob Hope was one to later joke at her expense). Because Lamarr's true story deserves a wider audience, one hopes that she follows up on something she told *Forbes* in 1990: "I should probably sell my life story to Ted Turner, because it's unbelievable."

—Curtis Hutchinson, updated by David E. Salamie

LAMOUR, Dorothy

Nationality: American. **Born:** Mary Leta Dorothy Slaton in New Orleans, Louisiana, 10 December 1914. **Education:** Attended Spencer Business College. **Family:** Married 1) the bandleader Herbie Kay, 1935 (divorced 1939); 2) William Ross Howard III, 1943 (died 1977), two sons and one stepson. **Career:** 1930—appeared professionally in a Fanchon and Marco vaudeville revue; 1931—female vocalist for Herbie Kay band, in Chicago and on tour, and later appeared with Rudy Vallee and Eddie Duchin; 1934—radio singer on *The Dreamer of Songs* program: later radio programs include *The Chase and Sanborn Show*, 1937, and *The Sealtest Variety Theatre*, 1947; 1936—film debut in short *The Stars Can't Be Wrong* and the feature *The Jungle Princess*, in which she wore her famous sarong for the first time; 1939—first of the "Road" movies with Bob Hope and Bing Crosby, *Road to Singapore*; 1951—stage debut in *Roger the Sixth*; 1958—Broadway debut in *Oh! Captain*, and later toured with *DuBarry Was a Lady*, 1963, and *Hello, Dolly!*, 1967; 1961—toured with her own nightclub act.

Films as Actress:

1936 *The Jungle Princess* (Thiele) (as Ulah)
1937 *Swing High, Swing Low* (Leisen) (as Anita Alvarez); *High, Wide, and Handsome* (Mamoulian) (as Molly Fuller); *The Last Train from Madrid* (Hogan) (as Carmelita Castillo); *Thrill of a Lifetime* (Archainbaud) (as speciality act); *The Hurricane* (Ford) (as Marama)
1938 *The Big Broadcast of 1938* (Leisen) (as Dorothy Wyndham); *Her Jungle Love* (Archainbaud) (as Tura); *Tropic Holiday* (Reed) (as Manuela); *Spawn of the North* (Hathaway) (as Nicky Duval); *St. Louis Blues* (Walsh) (as Norma Malone)
1939 *Man about Town* (Sandrich) (as Diana Wilson); *Disputed Passage* (Borzage) (as Audrey Hilton); *Road to Singapore* (Schertzinger) (as Mima)
1940 *Johnny Apollo* (Hathaway) (as "Lucky" Dubarry); *Moon over Burma* (Louis King) (as Arla Dean); *Chad Hanna* (Henry King) (as Albany Yates); *Road to Zanzibar* (Schertzinger) (as Donna Latour)
1941 *Caught in the Draft* (Butler) (as Toni Fairbanks); *Aloma of the South Seas* (Santell) (as Aloma); *Beyond the Blue Horizon* (Santell) (as Tama); *The Fleet's In* (Schertzinger) (as the Countess)
1942 *Road to Morocco* (Butler) (as Princess Shalimar); *They Got Me Covered* (Butler) (as Christina Hill); *Star Spangled Rhythm* (Marshall) (as herself)
1943 *Dixie* (Sutherland) (as Millie Cook); *Riding High* (Marshall) (as Ann Castle); *And the Angels Sing* (Marshall) (as Nancy Angel); *Rainbow Island* (Murphy) (as Lona)
1944 *Road to Utopia* (Walker) (as Sal Van Hoyden); *A Medal for Benny* (Pichel) (as Lolita Sierra)
1945 *Masquerade in Mexico* (Leisen) (as Angel O'Reilly); *Duffy's Tavern* (Walker) (as herself)
1946 *My Favorite Brunette* (Nugent) (as Carlotta Montay); *Wild Harvest* (Garnett) (as Fay Rankin)
1947 *Variety Girl* (Nugent) (as herself); *Road to Rio* (McLeod) (as Lucia Maria De Andrade); *On Our Merry Way* (King Vidor) (as Gloria Manners); *Lulu Belle* (Fenton) (title role)
1948 *Slightly French* (Sirk) (as Mary O'Leary); *The Girl from Manhattan* (Green) (as Carol Maynard); *The Lucky Stiff* (Foster) (as Anna Marie St. Claire); *Manhandled* (Foster) (as Meri Kramer)
1951 *Here Comes the Groom* (Capra) (as herself)
1952 *The Greatest Show on Earth* (DeMille) (as Phyllis); *Road to Bali* (Walker) (as Lalah)
1961 *Road to Hong Kong* (Panama) (as herself)
1962 *Donovan's Reef* (Ford) (as Fleur)
1964 *Pajama Party* (Weiss) (as head saleslady)
1976 *Death at Love House* (*The Shrine of Lorna Love*) (Swackhamer—for TV)
1987 *Creepshow II* (Gornick) (as Martha Spruce)
1988 *Entertaining the Troops* (Mugge—for TV)

Publications

By LAMOUR: book—

My Side of the Road, as told to Dick McInnes, Englewood Cliffs, New Jersey, 1980.

By LAMOUR: articles—

Interview with C. Van Wyck, in *Photoplay* (New York), December 1938.
Interview with F. Dudley, in *Photoplay* (New York), July 1941.
"This Was My Favorite Role," *Movie Digest*, March 1972.

On LAMOUR: article—

"Mrs. Wm. Howard Always Carries a Sarong," in *Photoplay* (New York), March 1972.

*   *   *

Dorothy Lamour was an important fixture at Paramount Pictures during the 1940s, appearing in eight films that ranked among the top money earners for their respective years. Yet surprisingly she never was able to achieve major stardom. In film after film she served as a foil for bigger stars, in particular Bob Hope and Bing Crosby. The five 1940s "Road" films she made with Hope and Crosby (to Singapore, Zanzibar, Morocco, Utopia, and Rio), contributed millions to Paramount's coffers but never moved Lamour beyond her initial image of a beautiful woman wrapped in a sarong essaying a supporting role.

Like many of Paramount's stars of the 1940s, Dorothy Lamour started her show business career in another medium. Before she signed with the studio in 1936 she sang in nightclubs and on the radio. Her first few years under contract at Paramount were not too successful. Directors at other studios used her with far more skill: John Ford in *The Hurricane* (made for United Artists), and Henry Hathaway in *Johnny Apollo* (for Twentieth Century-Fox). *Road to Singapore* established her at Paramount, but after World War II, the studio system began to change, and in 1947 Paramount dropped her.

In 1949, pregnant with her son Richard, she and her husband William Ross Howard III moved to Howard's hometown of Baltimore and she settled in as a rich housewife. She made a brief comeback in 1952 with two films, the highly successful Cecil B. DeMille extravaganza, *The Greatest Show on Earth*, and yet another "Road" film, this time to Bali. During the 1950s, Lamour turned to television, making guest appearances on the *Colgate Comedy Hour*, *Damon Runyon Theatre*, and *Arthur Murray Party*. And there were two more nostalgic romps when she appeared in the final "Road" film (in a small part), and in John Ford's underrated *Donovan's Reef*. At the end of her career, during the 1960s and 1970s, she made innumerable tours on the dinner circuit, and surfaced briefly on the national scene as a replacement in the title role of *Hello Dolly!*

—Douglas Gomery

LANCASTER, Burt

Nationality: American. **Born:** Burton Stephen Lancaster in New York City, 2 November 1913. **Education:** Attended DeWitt Clinton High School; New York University, 1930-32. **Family:** Married 1) circus performer June Ernst, 1935 (divorced 1936); 2) Norma Anderson, 1946 (divorced 1969), children: William, James, Susan, Joanna, Sighle; 3) Susie Martin, 1990. **Career:** 1932-39—toured vaudeville and played in circuses in acrobatic act with Nick Cravat, Lang and Cravat; 1939-42—after injury, worked as salesman in Marshall Field's, fireman, and in meatpacking plant, all in Chicago; 1942-45—served in entertainment section of the U.S. Army; 1945—role in play *A Sound of Hunting* on Broadway; then contract with Hal Wallis; 1946—critical success in film debut *The Killers*; 1948—co-founder, with Harold Hecht, Hecht-Norma production company (later Hecht-Lancaster, then Hecht-Hill-Lancaster); 1955—directed the film *The Kentuckian*; 1971—on stage in *Knickerbocker Holiday*, and *The Boys of Autumn*, 1981, both in San Francisco; 1977—narrator of TV series *The Unknown War*, and in mini-series *Marco-Polo*, 1982, *On Wings of Eagles*, 1986; also council member and past president, American Civil Liber-

ties Union. **Awards:** Best Actor, New York Film Critics, for *From Here to Eternity*, 1953; Best Actor, Berlin Festival, for *Trapeze*, 1956; Best Actor, Academy Award, for *Elmer Gantry*, 1960; Best Foreign Actor, British Academy, for *Birdman of Alcatraz*, 1962; Best Actor Award, New York Film Critics, Los Angeles Film Critics, and British Academy, for *Atlantic City*, 1981. **Died:** In Century City, California, 20 October 1994.

Films as Actor:

1946 **The Killers** (Siodmak) (as the Swede)
1947 *Desert Fury* (Lewis Allen) (as Tom Hanson); *Brute Force* (Dassin) (as Joe Collins); *Variety Girl* (George Marshall) (as guest)
1948 *I Walk Alone* (Haskins) (as Frankie Madison); *All My Sons* (Reis) (as Chris Keller); *Sorry, Wrong Number* (Litvak) (as Henry Stevenson); *Kiss the Blood off My Hands* (*Blood on My Hands*) (Foster) (as Bill Saunders); *Criss Cross* (Siodmak) (as Steve Thompson)
1949 *Rope of Sand* (Dieterle) (as Mike Davis)
1950 *The Flame and the Arrow* (Jacques Tourneur) (as Dardo); *Mister 880* (Goulding) (as Steve Buchanan)
1951 *Jim Thorpe: All American* (*Man of Bronze*) (Curtiz) (title role); *Vengeance Valley* (Thorpe) (as Owen Daybright); *Ten Tall Men* (Goldbeck) (as Sgt. Mike Kincaid)
1952 *The Crimson Pirate* (Siodmak) (as Capt. Vallo)
1953 *Come Back, Little Sheba* (Daniel Mann) (as Doc); *The Key* (Parker—doc); *South Sea Woman* (Lubin) (as Sgt. O'Hearn); **From Here to Eternity** (Zinnemann) (as Sgt. Warden); *Three Sailors and a Girl* (Del Ruth) (as guest)
1954 *His Majesty O'Keefe* (Haskins) (title role); *Apache* (Aldrich) (as Massai); *Vera Cruz* (Aldrich) (as Joe Erin)
1955 *The Rose Tattoo* (Daniel Mann) (as Alvaro Mangiacavallo)
1956 *Trapeze* (Reed) (as Mike Ribble); *The Rainmaker* (Anthony) (as Starbuck); *Playtime in Hollywood* (short)
1957 *Gunfight at the O.K. Corral* (John Sturges) (as Wyatt Earp); **The Sweet Smell of Success** (Mackendrick) (as J. J. Hunsecker); *The Heart of Show Business* (Staub—doc) (as narrator)
1958 *Run Silent, Run Deep* (Wise) (as Lt. Jim Bledsoe); *Separate Tables* (Delbert Mann) (as John Malcolm)
1959 *The Devil's Disciple* (Hamilton) (as Anthony Anderson)
1960 *The Unforgiven* (Huston) (as Ben Zachary); *Elmer Gantry* (Richard Brooks) (title role)
1961 *The Young Savages* (Frankenheimer) (as Hank Bell); *Judgment at Nuremberg* (Kramer) (as Ernst Janning)
1962 *Birdman of Alcatraz* (Frankenheimer) (as Robert Stroud)
1963 *A Child Is Waiting* (Cassavetes) (as Dr. Matthew Clark); *The List of Adrian Messenger* (Huston) (as guest); *Il gattopardo* (*The Leopard*) (Visconti) (as Prince Don Fabrizio Salinas)
1964 *Seven Days in May* (Frankenheimer) (as Gen. James M. Scott)
1965 *The Train* (Frankenheimer) (as Labiche); *The Hallelujah Trail* (John Sturges) (as Col. Thadeus Gearhart); *Handle With Care* (doc) (as narrator); *Operation Head Start* (doc) (as narrator)
1966 *The Professionals* (Richard Brooks) (as Bill Dolworth)
1967 *All about People* (doc)
1968 *The Scalphunters* (Pollack) (as Joe Bass); *The Swimmer* (Perry) (as Ned Merrill)
1969 *Castle Keep* (Pollack) (as Maj. Falconer); *Jenny Is a Good Thing* (Horvath—doc) (as narrator); *The Gypsy Moths* (Frankenheimer) (as Mike Rettig); *In Name Only* (Swackhamer—for TV)

Burt Lancaster

1970 *Airport* (Seaton) (as Mel Bakersfield); *King: A Filmed Record ... Montgomery to Memphis* (Mankiewicz and Lumet—doc) (as co-narrator)

1971 *Lawman* (Winner) (as Jerred Maddox); *Valdez Is Coming* (Sherin) (as Bob Valdez); *H + 2* (Coombs—doc) (as narrator)

1972 *Ulzana's Raid* (Aldrich) (as McIntosh); *Mose* (*Moses*) (De Bosio—for TV) (title role)

1973 *Scorpio* (Winner) (as Cross); *Graduation* (Stanfield—doc) (as narrator); *Executive Action* (Miller) (as Farrington)

1974 *Gruppo di famiglia in un interno* (*Conversation Piece*) (Visconti) (as the Professor); *James Wong Howe* (Quo—doc) (as narrator)

1975 *A Life in Your Hands* (doc) (as narrator)

1976 *Buffalo Bill and the Indians* (Altman) (as Ned Buntline); *1900* (*Novecento*) (Bertolucci) (as Alfredo Berlinghieri); *Victory at Entebbe* (Chomsky—for TV) (as Defense Minister Peres)

1977 *The Cassandra Crossing* (Cosmatos) (as MacKenzie); *The Island of Dr. Moreau* (Taylor) (title role); *On the Edge of Reality* (doc); *Twilight's Last Gleaming* (Aldrich) (as Lawrence Dell)

1978 *Go Tell the Spartans* (Post) (as Major Asa Barker)

1979 *Zulu Dawn* (Hickox) (as Col. Durnford); *Arthur Miller on Home Ground* (Rasky—doc); *Cattle Annie and Little Britches* (Johnson) (as Bill Doolin)

1981 *La Pelle* (*The Skin*) (Cavani) (as Gen. Mark Cork); *Atlantic City* (Malle) (as Lou)

1983 *The Osterman Weekend* (Peckinpah) (as Maxwell Darnforth); *Local Hero* (Forsyth) (as Happer); *The Making of a "Local Hero"* (*With a Little Help from His Friends*) (Turner—doc)

1985 *Scandal Sheet* (Rich—for TV) (as Harold Fallen); *Little Treasure* (Sharp) (as Teschemacher)

1986 *Tough Guys* (Kanew) (as Harry Doyle)

1987 *Il giorno prima* (Montaldo); *Jeweller's Shop* (Anderson); *The Legacy of the Hollywood Blacklist* (Chailin—for TV) (as narrator); *Control* (Montaldo—for TV) (as Herbert Monroe)

1988 *Rocket Gibraltar* (Petrie) (as Levi Rockwell)

1989 *Field of Dreams* (Robinson) (as Dr. "Moonlight" Graham)

1990 *Voyage of Terror: The Achille Lauro Affair* (Negrin—for TV) (as Leon Klinghoffer); *Phantom of the Opera* (Richardson—for TV) (as Gerard Carrier)

1991 *Separate but Equal* (Stevens, Jr.—for TV) (as John W. Davis)

Films as Director:

1955 *The Kentuckian* (+ ro as Big Eli)
1974 *The Midnight Man* (co-d, + co-pr, co-sc, ro as Jim Slade)

Publications

By LANCASTER: article—

"Hollywood Drove Me to a Double Life," in *Films and Filming* (London), January 1962.

On LANCASTER: books—

Vermilye, J., *Burt Lancaster: A Pictorial Treasury of His Films*, New York, 1970.
Thomas, Tony, *Burt Lancaster*, New York, 1975.
Richards, Jeffrey, *Swordsmen of the Screen: From Douglas Fairbanks to Michael York*, London, 1977.

Clinch, Minty, *Burt Lancaster*, London, 1984.
Hunter, Allan, *Burt Lancaster: The Man and His Movies*, London, 1984.
Windeler, Robert, *Burt Lancaster*, London, 1984.
Lacourbe, Roland, *Burt Lancaster*, Paris, 1987.
Fury, David, *The Cinema History of Burt Lancaster*, Minneapolis, Minnesota, 1989.
Crowther, Bruce, *Burt Lancaster: A Life in Films*, London, 1991.
Fishgall, Gary, *Against Type: The Biography of Burt Lancaster*, New York, 1995.

On LANCASTER: articles—

Morgan, J., "Hecht-Lancaster Productions," in *Sight and Sound* (London), Summer 1955.
Schuster, Mel, "Burt Lancaster," in *Films in Review* (New York), August-September 1969.
Drew, Bernard, "Burt Lancaster," in *The Movie Star*, edited by Elisabeth Weis, New York, 1981.
Hunter, Allan, "A Perfectly Mysterious Man," in *Films and Filming* (London), October 1983.
Current Biography 1986, New York, 1986.
Lantos, J., "The Last Waltz," in *American Film* (New York), October 1986.
"Burt Lancaster," in *Shooting Stars: Heroes and Heroines of the Western Film*, edited by Archie P. McDonald, Bloomington, Indiana, 1987.
Buford, Kate, "Lancaster: Dance with the Leopard," in *Film Comment* (New York), January/February 1993.
Obituary, in *New York Times*, 22 October 1994.
Obituary, in *Variety* (New York), 24 October 1994.
Goodman, Mark, "The Daredevil," in *People Weekly*, 7 November 1994.
Lane, Anthony, in *New Yorker*, 14 November 1994.
Obituary, in *Current Biography 1995*, New York, 1995.

*   *   *

Burt Lancaster started his life by running off to the circus, leaving New York University where he had been a basketball star, and becoming an acrobat with partner Nick Cravat, who would later appear alongside Lancaster in many films, such as *Trapeze*, the actor's sober tribute to the daredevil life of the aerial artist he once had been. Lancaster's circus experience supplied him with certain qualities that were advantageous to a movie actor: a powerful physique and complete physical control. Nature supplied him with other features that contributed to his star quality: rugged good looks and, especially, the keyboard smile that would become his trademark.

His first screen roles, obtained for him by agent Harold Hecht, usually cast Lancaster as a brooding ex-convict, a taciturn villain, or a tense goon—most notably in Ernest Hemingway's *The Killers*, Lancaster's screen debut, where he played a crooked prizefighter nicknamed the Swede who is marked for death. It was only a few years after this that Lancaster followed the groundbreaking lead of actor James Stewart and went freelance, starting his own film production company in partnership with Hecht and James Hill. Hecht, Hill, and Lancaster's first picture was the well-received *Apache*, directed by Robert Aldrich. Lancaster starred as Massai, a warrior who refuses to surrender to the white man's ways after the capture of Geronimo, and is marked for extinction. Over Lancaster and Aldrich's objections, the film's grim conclusion was compromised in favor of a happier one for box-office reasons. The same star-director team followed *Apache* later that year with the acerbic Western adventure, *Vera Cruz*, a smash hit. Several decades later, Aldrich and Lancaster teamed again for *Ulzana's Raid*, a potent saga of the Indian Wars that also mirrored the then-current Vietnam conflict; it concluded on the bleak, more realistic note denied them earlier on *Apache*.

Lancaster has projected earnestness as the truth-seeking son of Edward G. Robinson in *All My Sons*, lovability as the truck driver opposite Anna Magnani in *The Rose Tattoo*, and perseverance as the Native American athlete Jim Thorpe in *Jim Thorpe: All-American*. For all of his brawn, he was also quite good at communicating vulnerability, gentleness, and self-doubt. All these elements were combined in his Oscar-nominated performance as Sergeant Warden in *From Here to Eternity* and as convicted killer Robert Stroud in *Birdman of Alcatraz*, a pet project.

Early in his career, Lancaster also developed another quite different character: the grinning mischief-maker. This character first appeared in *The Flame and the Arrow*, which was followed by the delightful adventure comedy *The Crimson Pirate*, a hilarious parody of—and homage to—the films of Douglas Fairbanks, Sr. that Lancaster had enjoyed as a youth. Lancaster seized every opportunity to take his shirt off, swing on ropes from ship to ship, and smile from ear to ear. He brought the same qualities to his role as *The Rainmaker*, one of the most ingratiating conmen in the history of the movies—and then combined them with his unique brand of bravado, energy, and physicality to create his Oscar-winning role as *Elmer Gantry* in which he was the embodiment of Sinclair Lewis's famous charlatan evangelist, orator, businessman, hustler, and lover.

A former president of the American Civil Liberties Union, Lancaster espoused liberal causes most of his life. Perhaps to understand them himself—and illuminate them for others—he liked playing characters diametrically opposed to his own political beliefs. Examples include John Frankenheimer's *Seven Days in May*, as the chairman of the Joint Chiefs who tries to orchestrate a military coup d'etat, and Robert Aldrich's potent political thriller *Twilight's Last Gleaming*, where he played the messianic General Dell, who commandeers a nuclear silo and threatens to launch a strike if the Pentagon refuses to own up to the real motives behind the Vietnam War. The latter role and film remained among his favorites.

In another favorite role, he was again the embodiment of a character taken from a famous novel, although of a totally different nature from Elmer Gantry. Guiseppe Di Lampedusa's physical description of the Sicilian prince in his novel *The Leopard* fits Lancaster to a tee, and director Luchino Visconti saw to it that Lancaster got the part in the Italian-made film version of the novel. Though not of the Method school, Lancaster always carefully prepared for and immersed himself in his roles. In fact, he reportedly knew more about Sicilian aristocracy, customs, traditions, and history than anyone else connected with the film except Visconti and Di Lampedusa. His authoritative demeanor, melancholic expression, and meditative mien contribute to one of the most believable historical figures in modern cinema. He starred again for Visconti as a retired, reclusive professor besieged by modernity in *Conversation Piece*. Also noteworthy is one of Lancaster's last screen appearances in *Atlantic City* where he plays an aging two-bit crook still hoping for his big chance, a performance that earned him another Oscar nomination.

Lancaster's career remains unmatched for his persistent refusal to allow Hollywood to typecast him strictly as a he-man. Because of his deep concern for the content of his films and eagerness to work with directors he considered important, he was willing to undertake virtually any kind of part.

—Elaine Mancini, updated by John McCarty

LANCHESTER, Elsa

Nationality: American. **Born:** Elsa Sullivan Lanchester (or Elizabeth Sullivan) in Lewisham, London, 28 October 1902; became U.S. citizen, 1950. **Education:** Attended Isadora Duncan's Bellevue School, Paris, 1912, and assistant on lecture tours; Margaret Morris's school, Chelsea, London. **Family:** Married the actor Charles Laughton, 1929 (died 1962). **Career:** 1918—taught dancing at Margaret Morris's school on the Isle of Wight; 1920—stage debut in a music hall act; founded children's theater, Soho; 1922—West End debut in *Thirty Minutes in a Street*; 1924—opened the London nightclub The Cave of Harmony; film debut in the amateur film *The Scarlet Woman*; other stage and film work in the 1920s, often with Laughton; 1930—in stage play *Payment Deferred* in London, and in 1931 in New York; 1932—short contract with MGM; 1933-34—acted at the Old Vic with Laughton; 1939—settled permanently in the United States; active in revue sketches from 1941, touring nightclubs with Ray Henderson, and in her own one-woman show *Elsa Lanchester—Herself*, 1951-61; in TV series *The John Forsythe Show*, 1965-66, and *Nanny and the Professor*, 1971. **Died:** In Woodland Hills, California, 26 December 1986.

Films as Actress:

1927   *One of the Best* (Hunter) (as Kitty)

1928   *The Constant Nymph* (Brunel) (as lady); *Bluebottles* (Montague—short); *The Tonic* (Montague—short); *Daydreams* (Montague—short)

1929   *Mr. Smith Wakes Up* (Hill—short)

1930   *Comets* (Geneen) (as herself)

1931   *The Love Habit* (Lachman); *The Stronger Sex* (Gundrey); *Potiphar's Wife* (Elvey) (as Mathilde); *The Officer's Mess* (Haynes) (as Cora Melville)

1933   *The Private Life of Henry VIII* (Korda) (as Anne of Cleves)

1934   *David Copperfield* (Cukor) (as Clickett)

1935   *Naughty Marietta* (Van Dyke); *The Bride of Frankenstein* (Whale) (as Mary Shelley/The Bride)

1936   *The Ghost Goes West* (Clair) (as dinner guest); *Rembrandt* (Korda) (as Hendrickie Stoffels); *Miss Bracebirdle Does Her Duty* (Garmes—short)

1938   *Vessel of Wrath* (*The Beachcomber*) (Pommer) (as Martha Jones)

1941   *Ladies in Retirement* (Charles Vidor) (as Emily Creed)

1942   *Son of Fury* (Cromwell) (as prostitute); *Tales of Manhattan* (Duvivier)

1943   *Forever and a Day* (Clair and others) (as waitress); *Thumbs Up* (Santley) (as Emmy Finch); *Lassie Come Home* (Wilcox)

1944   *Passport to Destiny* (McCarey) (as charwoman)

1946   *The Spiral Staircase* (Siodmak) (as Mrs. Oakes); *The Razor's Edge* (Goulding) (as secretary)

1947   *Northwest Outpost* (Dwan) (as chaperone); *The Bishop's Wife* (Koster) (as maid)

1948   *The Big Clock* (Farrow) (as artist)

1949   *The Secret Garden* (Wilcox) (as maid); *Come to the Stable* (Koster) (as artist); *The Inspector General* (Koster) (as mayor's wife)

1950   *Buccaneer's Girl* (De Cordova) (as madam); *Mystery Street* (Sturges) (as landlady); *The Pretty Girl* (Levin) (as spinster); *Frenchie* (King) (as Duenna)

1952   *Dreamboat* (Binyon) (as school president); *Les Misérables* (Milestone) (as Madame Magloire); *Androcles and the Lion* (Erskine) (as Megaera)

1953   *Girls of Pleasure Island* (Herbert, Gunzer) (as housekeeper)

1954   *Hell's Half Acre* (Auer) (as Lida O'Reilly); *Three Ring Circus* (Pevney) (as bearded lady)

1955   *The Glass Slipper* (Walters) (as wicked stepmother)

1957   *Witness for the Prosecution* (Wilder) (as nurse)

1958   *Bell, Book, and Candle* (Quine) (as matchmaker witch)

1964   *Honeymoon Hotel* (Levin) (as chambermaid); *Mary Poppins*
         (Stevenson) (as nanny); *Pajama Party* (Weis) (as house-
         keeper)
1965   *That Darn Cat* (Stevenson) (as nosy neighbor)
1967   *Easy Come, Easy Go* (Rich) (as yoga teacher)
1968   *Blackbeard's Ghost* (Stevenson)
1969   *Rascal* (Tokar) (as housekeeper); *Me Natalie* (Coe) (as land-
         lady)
1971   *Willard* (Mann)
1973   *Terror in the Wax Museum* (Fenady)
1974   *Arnold* (Fenady)
1976   *Murder by Death* (Moore) (as Dame Jessie Marbles)
1980   *Die Laughing* (Werner) (as Sophie)

Publications

By LANCHESTER: books—

Charles Laughton and I, New York, 1968.
Elsa Lanchester Herself, New York, 1983.

By LANCHESTER: article—

Interview, in *Radio Times* (London), 9 July 1983.

On LANCHESTER: articles—

Roberts, Florain, "Elsa Lanchester," in *Films in Review* (New York),
    August-September 1976.
Shipman, David, in *The Great Movie Stars: The Golden Years*, revised
    edition, London, 1979.

                    *   *   *

Elsa Lanchester, the daughter of two prominent socialists, had
always been a free spirit, studying with Isadora Duncan at the age of
11, teaching dance and directing a children's theater while still in her
teens, then starting a London theatrical club called The Cave of Harmony. By the time she met Charles Laughton, her future husband, in
1927, she had tired of her bohemian life and was attracted to his
"middle-class respectability." She and Laughton appeared together in
several plays (to favorable reviews), but as Laughton's film career
took off, her career began to suffer.

There were probably two reasons for this. First, she was not beautiful; though perkily attractive, she was small, with frizzy red hair and
an oddly blunted nose. Not considering her leading-lady material,
Hollywood might have forgotten her altogether had it not been for
her husband, who in turn represented her second problem. According
to Lanchester, producers resented the implied pressure of "if Charles
works, Elsa must be used, too," and she began to lose ground professionally. Her bits as maids, prudes, and assorted eccentrics seemed a far
cry from her London theatrical successes, including her role as the last
Peter Pan to be personally approved by James Barrie. Sometimes
producers would even fabricate Lanchester vehicles to lure the
Laughtons, "changing" their plans once the two were hooked. If she
did get into a Laughton picture, she felt she was "acting with a pistol
at my head" and that she *had* to be good.

Luckily, she almost always was, whether or not she appeared with
Laughton. Given the prejudice against her looks, it is ironic that she is
probably best known in this country for her role as the Bride of
Frankenstein (in the film of the same name). Wrapped in yards of
bandage, a wire cage with hair pieces on her head and three to four
hours' worth of makeup on her face, she hissed in imitation of swans
she had heard as a child in London (some of her hisses and screams

were run backward on the soundtrack). Yet she was pleased to be in the
film because, as the sweet-as-sugar Mary Shelley, she was allowed to
show the range of her acting.

She was able to demonstrate that range under less grueling circumstances, registering most effectively in *The Beachcomber* (she and
Laughton played the leads in this film produced by his Mayflower
production company), *The Private Life of Henry VIII* (as Anne of
Cleves, she gave the best performance of Laughton's wives), and
Witness for the Prosecution (both she and Laughton winning Oscar
nominations). She also contributed delightful cameos in a number of
other pictures, notably *Bell, Book, and Candle* (as an addled witch),
The Big Clock (as an eccentric artist), *Honeymoon Hotel* (as yet
another maid), and *The Razor's Edge* (as a social secretary).

To supplement these rather meager and intermittent opportunities,
Lanchester ultimately returned to the cabaret of her youth. In the
1940s she joined the Turnabout Theatre, performing cabaret songs,
and in the 1960s, she took an elaborate, one-woman show (*Elsa
Lanchester—Herself*) on the road, to rave reviews. The free spirit of
Elsa Lanchester appealed to live audiences denied the opportunity to
experience it in films by Hollywood's commercial cowardice.

                                                    —Catherine Henry

LANDAU, Martin

Nationality: American. **Born:** Brooklyn, New York, 20 June 1928
(some sources say 1931). **Family:** Married the actress Barbara Bain
(divorced), children: Susan Meredith, Juliet Rose. **Education:** Attended Pratt Institute and the Art Students League; studied for three
years at the Actors Studio. **Career:** 1950s—worked as a cartoonist
and staff artist for the New York *Daily News*; mid-1950s through mid-
1960s—appeared on TV series episodes; 1966-69—starred as Rollin
Hand on the hit TV series *Mission: Impossible*; 1975-77—starred as
Commander John Koenig on the syndicated TV series *Space: 1999*;
member of the Board of Directors, Actors Studio, and executive director, Actors Studio West. **Awards:** Golden Globe Award, for *Mission:
Impossible*, 1966-69; Golden Globe Award, for *Crimes and Misdemeanors*, 1989; Golden Globe Award, Los Angeles Critics Award, New
York Critics Circle Award, National Society of Film Critics Award,
Screen Actors Guild Award, and Best Supporting Actor Academy Award,
for *Ed Wood*, 1994. **Address:** 7455 Palo Vista Drive, Los Angeles,
CA 90046, U.S.A.

Films as Actor:

1959   *Pork Chop Hill* (Milestone) (as Marshall); **North by Northwest**
         (Hitchcock) (as Leonard); *The Gazebo* (George Marshall)
         (as the Duke)
1962   *Stagecoach to Dancer's Rock* (Bellamy) (as Dade Coleman)
1963   *Cleopatra* (Joseph L. Mankiewicz) (as Rufius)
1965   *The Greatest Story Ever Told* (Stevens) (as Caiaphas); *The
         Hallelujah Trail* (John Sturges) (as Chief Walks-Stooped-
         Over)
1966   *Nevada Smith* (Hathaway) (as Jesse Coe)
1970   *They Call Me Mr. Tibbs!* (Douglas) (as the Rev. Logan Sharpe);
         Operation Snafu (*Situation Normal All Fouled Up*) (Loy)
1971   *A Town Called Hell* (*A Town Called Bastard*) (Parrish) (as the
         Colonel)
1972   *Black Gunn* (Hartford-Davis) (as Capelli); *Welcome Home,
         Johnny Bristol* (McCowan—for TV) (as Captain Johnny
         Bristol)

Martin Landau (left) with Johnny Depp in *Ed Wood*

1973   *Savage* (Spielberg—for TV) (as Paul Savage); *Destination Moonbase Alpha* (Tom Clegg) (as Commander John Koenig)

1976   *Tony Saitta* (*Tough Tony*; *Strange Shadows in an Empty Room*; *Blazing Magnums*) (Herbert) (as Dr. George Tracer)

1979   *Meteor* (Neame) (as General Barry Adlon); *The Death of Ocean View Park* (Swackhamer—for TV) (as Tom Flood)

1980   *The Last Word* (Boulting) (as Captain Garrity); *Without Warning* (*It Came without Warning*) (Greydon Clark) (as Fred Dobbs); *The Return* (*The Alien's Return*) (Greydon Clark) (as Marshal)

1981   *The Harlem Globetrotters on Gilligan's Island* (Baldwin—for TV) (as J. J. Pierson)

1982   *Alone in the Dark* (Sholder) (as Byron "Preacher" Sutcliff); *The Fall of the House of Usher* (Conway—for TV) (as Roderick Usher)

1983   *The Being* (*Easter Sunday*) (Kong) (as Garson Jones)

1984   *Access Code* (Sobel)

1986   *Kung Fu: The Movie* (Richard Lang—for TV) (as John Martin Perkins III)

1987   *Cyclone* (Fred Olen Ray) (as Bosarian); *Sweet Revenge* (Sobel) (as Cicero); *Empire State* (Peck) (as Chuck); *Run If You Can* (Virginia Lively Stone); *Delta Fever* (William Webb) (as Bud); *Death Blow* (Nussbaum); *The Return of the Six-Million-Dollar Man and the Bionic Woman* (Ray Austin—for TV) (as Lyle Stenning)

1988   *Tucker: The Man and His Dream* (Francis Ford Coppola) (as Abe Karatz)

1989   *Trust Me* (Houston); *Crimes and Misdemeanors* (Woody Allen) (as Judah Rosenthal); *Paint It Black* (Hunter) (as Daniel Lambert)

1990   *Real Bullets* (Lindsay); *Firehead* (Yuval) (as Admiral Pendleton); *By Dawn's Early Light* (Sholder—for TV) (as the President); *Max and Helen* (Saville—for TV) (as Simon Wiesenthal)

1992   *Tipperary*; *The Color of Evening*; *Mistress* (Primus) (as Jack Roth); *Legacy of Lies* (May—for TV); *Something to Live For: The Alison Gertz Story* (*Fatal Love*) (McLoughlin—for TV) (as Jerry Gertz)

1993   *Eye of the Stranger* (Heavener) (as Mayor Howard Baines); *Sliver* (Noyce) (as Alex Parsons); *No Place to Hide* (Danus) (as Frank McCay); *12:01* (Sholder—for TV) (as Dr. Thadius Moxley)

1994   *Intersection* (Rydell) (as Neal); *Ed Wood* (Burton) (as Bela Lugosi); *Time Is Money* (Paolo Barzman) (as Mac)

1995   *Joseph* (Roger Young—for TV) (as Jacob)

1996   *City Hall* (Harold Becker) (as Judge Walter Stern); *The Adventures of Pinocchio* (as Gepetto)

Publications

By LANDAU: articles—

"Alfred Hitchcock ne ma jamais donne qu'un ordre celui d'aimes ce metier," interview with M. Deriez, in *Ciné Revue* (Brussels), 24 April 1986.

"A Mercurial Man Plays Aging, Cranky, and Elegant," interview with Steve Oney, in *New York Times*, 2 October 1994.

On LANDAU: articles—

Lindsay, R., "Martin Landau Rolls Up in a New Vehicle," in *New York Times*, 7 August 1988.
McGuigan, Cathleen, "From Heavy to Everyman," in *Newsweek* (New York), 16 October 1989.
"A Survivor of B-Movie Hell," in *New Yorker*, 3 April 1995.

*   *   *

After appearances in several prestige features—most notably Alfred Hitchcock's *North by Northwest* and Joseph L. Mankiewicz's *Cleopatra*—Martin Landau became a star as Rollin Hand in the hit television series *Mission: Impossible*. But the actor and his then-wife, Barbara Bain, who co-starred with him on the show, left after two seasons in a contract dispute. Neither of their careers were to recover. For almost two decades, Landau was just another working actor, appearing in seemingly endless low-budget throwaways and such made-for-television fare as *The Harlem Globetrotters on Gilligan's Island*.

His renaissance from the industry scrap heap came when he was cast in Francis Coppola's *Tucker: The Man and His Dream*, which netted Landau critical kudos and an Oscar nomination. He offers an eye-opening performance as Abe Karatz, a New York financier who helps Preston Tucker (Jeff Bridges) start up an automobile manufacturing company. Finally, Landau had a movie role worthy of his gift for fleshing out character. His performance is at once entertaining and quite moving; the character of Karatz is at the core of the story, and Landau adds some genuine heart to what is an otherwise slickly made film. Those who had forgotten Landau existed, or had considered him a has-been (or worse, a never-was), had no choice but to acknowledge his talent.

The actor earned further acclaim, and a second Oscar nomination, in Woody Allen's *Crimes and Misdemeanors*, a high drama of ethics and morality in contemporary American society. Landau plays Judah Rosenthal, a pillar of his community whose neurotic, possessive mistress (Anjelica Huston) threatens to expose his extramarital activities. Judah feels he has no choice but to initiate her murder. He at first is horrified by his decision, but soon comes to rationalize the action as being necessary to his survival. And in Tim Burton's *Ed Wood*, Landau was never better as the aging horror film star Bela Lugosi. He walked off with virtually every critics' prize, along with the Best Supporting Actor Oscar, for his beautifully rendered performance.

But perhaps his most revealing late-career role is in *Mistress*, in which Landau plays a character one senses he knows all too well: Jack Roth, an aging film producer who has come upon an old screenplay written by a movie purist/failed writer (Robert Wuhl). Roth feels that the script is a "knockout," and wants to get it made. But there is a catch: The producer notes that the script "does get heavy in places." It is, after all, about a painter who commits suicide. In order to secure funding for the project, Roth declares that perhaps the suicide part can be deleted—even though the act is the entire point of the story.

Roth is an intriguing character. He takes his meetings not at Le Dome or another A-list eatery but at a glorified diner. He "used to be a big shot at Universal," but he blew his career after standing up to his boss in a show of integrity. If the project in question had been a success, Roth might have gotten away with his indiscretion. But it bombed, and for 15 years he has had to "crawl around on my hands and knees to get a couple of bucks for something." Landau's departure from *Mission: Impossible* might be contrasted to Jack Roth's indiscre-

tion. Thankfully for Landau, however, he eventually was able to reestablish himself on the A-list of Hollywood actors—albeit after too many years, and too many bad movie roles.

—Rob Edelman

LANGDON, Harry

Nationality: American. **Born:** Council Bluffs, Iowa, 15 June 1884. **Family:** Married 1) the actress Rose Francis, 1903 (divorced 1928); 2) Helen Walton, 1929 (divorced 1931); 3) Mabel Georgena Sheldon, 1934, son: Harry Jr. **Career:** 1896—appeared on stage as child in Omaha amateur show; 1897—joined Dr. Belcher's Kickapoo Indian Medicine Show; then worked in circuses, tent show, and stock companies; 1903—formed "Johnny's New Car" act with Rose Francis, toured Orpheum Circuit until early 1920s; 1923—contract with Principal Pictures (Sol Lesser), then with Mack Sennett: film debut in short *Picking Peaches*, 1924; 1925—formed Harry Langdon Corporation, with Frank Capra as writer; 1926—first feature film, *Tramp, Tramp, Tramp*; 1927—directed the film *Three's a Crowd*; from 1929, worked for Hal Roach, Educational Films, Columbia, and Producers Releasing Corporation; worked as gag-man on Laurel and Hardy films, 1938-40. **Died:** Of a cerebral hemorrhage, 22 December 1944.

Films as Actor:

(in two-reel shorts)

1924   *Picking Peaches* (Kenton); *Smile Please* (Del Ruth); *Shanghaied Lovers* (Del Ruth); *The Cat's Meow* (Del Ruth); *His New Mama* (Del Ruth); *The First Hundred Years* (F. Richard Jones); *The Luck of the Foolish* (Harry Edwards); *The Hansom Cabman* (Edwards); *All Night Long* (Edwards); *Feet of Mud* (Edwards)
1925   *The Sea Squawk* (Edwards); *Boobs in the Wood* (Edwards); *His Marriage Wow* (Edwards); *Plain Clothes* (Edwards); *Remember When?* (Edwards); *Horace Greeley, Jr.* (Edwards); *The White Wing's Bride* (Goulding); *Lucky Stars* (Edwards); *There He Goes* (Edwards)
1926   *Saturday Afternoon* (Edwards and Capra)

(in features)

1926   *Tramp, Tramp, Tramp* (Edwards); *Ella Cinders* (Alfred E. Green) (cameo); *The Strong Man* (Capra) (as Harry Selby, the boy)
1927   *Long Pants* (Capra) (as Harry Selby); *His First Flame* (Edwards); *Fiddlesticks* (Edwards—short); *Soldier Man* (Edwards—short)

(in two-reel sound shorts)

1929   *Hotter than Hot* (Lewis R. Foster); *Sky Boy* (Rogers); *Skirt Shy* (Cruze)
1930   *A Soldier's Plaything* (*A Soldier's Pay*) (Curtiz—feature) (as Tim); *See America Thirst* (Craft—feature) (as Wally); *The Shrimp* (Rogers); *The Head Guy* (Guiol); *The Fighting Parson* (Guiol); *The Big Kick* (Doane); *The King* (Horne)
1932   *The Big Flash* (Gillstrom)
1933   *Hallelujah, I'm a Bum* (*Hallelujah, I'm a Tramp*; *New York*) (Milestone—feature) (as Egghead); *My Weakness* (David Butler—feature) (as Cupid); *Tired Feet* (Gillstrom); *The Hitch Hiker* (Gillstrom); *Knight Duty* (Gillstrom); *Tied for Life* (Gillstrom); *Hooks and Jabs* (Gillstrom); *Marriage Humor*

(Edwards); *The Stage Hand* (Edwards); *Leave It to Dad* (Edwards); *On Ice* (Gillstrom); *Pop's Pal* (Edwards); *A Roaming Romeo* (Gillstrom)

1934 *Trimmed in Furs* (Lamont); *Circus Hoodoo* (Gillstrom); *No Sleep on the Deep* (Lamont); *Petting Preferred* (Gillstrom); *Counsel on De Fence* (Ripley); *Shivers* (Ripley)

1935 *His Bridal Sweet* (Goulding); *The Leather Necker* (Ripley); *His Marriage Mixup* (Black); *I Don't Remember* (Black); *Atlantic Adventure* (Rogell—feature) (as Snapper)

1938 *He Loved an Actress* (*Mad about Money*) (Melville Brown—feature) (as Otto); *There Goes My Heart* (McLeod—feature) (as minister); *A Doggone Mixup* (Lamont); *Sue My Lawyer* (White)

1939 *Zenobia* (*Elephants Never Forget*) (Gordon Douglas) (as Prof. McCrackle)

1940 *Misbehaving Husbands* (Beaudine—feature) (as Henry Butler); *Cold Turkey* (Lord)

1941 *All-American Co-ed* (Prinz—feature) (as Hap Holden); *Double Trouble* (West—feature)

1942 *House of Errors* (Bernard B. Ray—feature); *What Makes Lizzy Dizzy?* (White); *Tire Man, Spare My Tires* (White); *Carry Harry* (Edwards); *Piano Mooner* (Edwards)

1943 *A Blitz on the Fritz* (White); *Blonde and Groom* (Edwards); *Here Comes Mr. Zerk* (White); *Spotlight Scandals* (Beaudine—feature)

1944 *Hot Rhythm* (Beaudine—feature) (as Whiffie); *Block Busters* (Fox—feature) (as Higgins); *To Heir Is Human* (Godsoe); *Defective Detectives* (Edwards); *Mopey Dope* (Lord)

1945 *Swingin' on a Rainbow* (Beaudine—feature) (as Chester Willoby); *Snooper Service* (Edwards); *Pistol Packin' Nitwits* (Edwards)

1960 *When Comedy Was King* (pr: Youngson)

Films as Director:

1927 *Three's a Crowd* (+ ro)
1928 *The Chaser* (+ ro); *Heart Trouble* (+ ro)
1937 *Wise Guys*

Films as Co-Scriptwriter:

1938 *Block-Heads* (Blystone)

Harry Langdon in *Tramp, Tramp, Tramp*

1939   *The Flying Deuces* (A. Edward Sutherland)
1940   *A Chump at Oxford* (Alfred Goulding); *Saps at Sea* (Gordon Douglas)
1941   *Road Show* (Roach)
1944   *Bride by Mistake* (Wallace)

Publications

By LANGDON: article—

"The Serious Side of Comedy Making," in *Theatre* (New York), December 1927.

On LANGDON: books—

Sennett, Mack, and Cameron Shipp, *King of Comedy*, New York, 1954.
Brownlow, Kevin, *The Parade's Gone By*, London, 1968.
McCaffrey, Donald, *Four Great Comedians*, New York, 1969.
Mast, Gerald, *The Comic Mind: Comedy and the Movies*, Chicago, 1974; rev. ed., 1979.
Slide, Anthony, *The Idols of Silence*, New York, 1976.
Parish, James Robert, and William T. Leonard, *The Funsters*, New York, 1979.
Schelly, William, *Harry Langdon*, Metuchen, New Jersey, 1982.
Rheuban, Joyce, *Harry Langdon: The Comedian as Metteur-en-Scène*, Rutherford, New Jersey, 1983.

On LANGDON: articles—

North, Jean, "It's No Joke to Be Funny," in *Photoplay* (New York), June 1925.
Hall, Leonard, "Hey! Hey! Harry's Coming Back," in *Photoplay* (New York), June 1929.
Albert, Katherine, "What's Happened to Harry Langdon?," in *Photoplay* (New York), February 1932.
Obituary in *New York Times*, 23 December 1944.
Agee, James, "Baby," in *Life* (New York), 5 September 1949.
Schonert, V. L., "Harry Langdon," in *Films in Review* (New York), October 1967; see also issues for November and December 1967.
Vitoux, Frédéric, "Harry Langdon et Frank Capra," in *Positif* (Paris), December 1971.
Orsini, M., "Le candide follie di Harry Langdon," in *Filmcritica* (Rome), April/May 1972.
Truscott, Harold, "Harry Langdon," in *Silent Picture* (London), Summer 1972.
Leary, R., "Capra and Langdon," in *Film Comment* (New York), November/December 1972.
Gilliatt, Penelope, in *Unholy Fools*, London, 1973.
Simsolo, N., "L'Athlète incomplet," and "V.I.P. B.I.S.," by G. Allombert, in *Image et Son* (Paris), no. 296, 1973.
Kral, P., "Harry, ailleurs ou on comique autre," in *Positif* (Paris), July/August and September 1978.
Eyquem, O., "Les Films de Harry Langdon," in *Positif* (Paris), September 1978.
Weinberg, Herman, "Harry Langdon," in *Films in Review* (New York), August/September 1981.
Everson, William K., "Souls of Wit: The Short Films of the Other Clowns," in *Video Movies* (Skokie, Illinois), June 1984.

*   *   *

His character had the moon face and the tight smile of an idiot child. Comedian Harry Langdon gave his clown a pathetic loneliness combined with a feline curiosity. With a rare gift for subtle, smooth pantomime, Langdon rose from a mediocre position as a vaudeville comedian to rival and nearly equal the great clowns who had already achieved success in the motion pictures by the mid-1920s.

Under the supervision of Harry Edwards and Frank Capra, Langdon captured the hearts of the critics and the general public with three excellent comedies, *Tramp, Tramp, Tramp*; *The Strong Man*; and *Long Pants*. The critic James Agee in his famous 1949 *Life* essay "Comedy's Greatest Era," rated the comedian higher than most commentators did. Agee described Langdon as a "virtuoso of hesitation and of delicately indecisive motions" with "a subtle emotional and mental process" similar to Charlie Chaplin's.

The one obvious difference between Langdon's and Chaplin's characters, however, is the mentality of the portraits. Langdon falls into the class of "dumb" clowns—somewhat like Stan Laurel's creative efforts. Most of the humor of the character springs from a childlike man who is lost in a sophisticated world. Unlike Chaplin's character, this little fellow is a simpleton who seldom takes action; he is a sexless baby who concentrates on his bag of popcorn when a prostitute makes eyes at him. Without a will of any consequence, this frail creature evokes laughter and sympathy when he is pitted against physical and mental superiors. This passive attitude is quite different from the comic creations of both Chaplin and Harold Lloyd whose characters had an aggressiveness which involved them in sharp, strong struggles. They had moments of violent action—kicking and biting their opposition—generally a bully twice their size. Their works, therefore, were sprinkled with the spice of invective comedy which provided variety and fast-paced conflict. Even Capra, noted for his excellent fast-paced films, realized he had to let Langdon work a scene slowly to use the detailed pantomimed routines which were the comedian's forte.

This whimsy of Langdon's comic portrait did not seem to click when he dismissed Frank Capra, who had directed *The Strong Man* and *Long Pants*. Langdon tried to direct three of his own features in the late 1920s, and the works were neither critical nor popular successes. It is possible that Langdon leaned too heavily on what some evaluators of the day thought was "Chaplinesque pathos" in such features as *Three's a Crowd*, an approach Harry Edwards and Capra had avoided. Langdon never fully recovered from his failure in the late 1920s. Many of his later two-reel shorts show some brilliant refurbishing of his silent screen routines, but he more often appeared providing some comedy in low-budget musical features.

The strength of Langdon's best films lies in his acting. Like Chaplin in his approach to his little tramp, Langdon brought a captivating intensity to his portrayal of the little-boy-lost. Langdon seemed to live the role he was acting. He became a skilled creator of an unusual comic character and deserves to be placed among the kings of silent screen comedy, Chaplin, Lloyd, and Buster Keaton.

—Donald McCaffrey

LANGE, Jessica

Nationality: American. **Born:** Cloquet, Minnesota, 20 April 1949. **Education:** Attended Cloquet High School, Minnesota; University of Minnesota, St. Paul. **Family:** Married the photographer Paco Grande, 1970 (divorced 1982); one daughter with the dancer Mikhail Baryshinikov: Alexandra; two children with the actor/writer Sam Shepard: Hannah Jane and Samuel Walker. **Career:** 1971-73—lived in Paris, where she studied mime with Etienne DeCroux, and danced at the Opera Comique; then worked as a model for the Wilhelmina agency in New York; 1976—film debut in *King Kong*, and given contract with the producer Dino De Laurentiis (broken, 1979); 1980—professional stage debut in *Angel on My Shoulder*; 1982—nominated for Academy Award as both Best Actress (in *Frances*) and Best Supporting Actress (in *Tootsie*) in same year; founder, Far West productions. **Awards:** Best Supporting Actress Academy Award, and Best Supporting Actress, New York Film Critics, for *Tootsie*, 1982; Best Actress Academy Award, for *Blue Sky*, 1994; Golden Globe Award, for *A Streetcar Named Desire*, 1995. **Agent:** Creative Artists Agency, 9830 Wilshire Boulevard, Beverly Hills, CA 90212, U.S.A.

Films as Actress:

1976   *King Kong* (Guillermin) (as Dwan)
1979   *All That Jazz* (Fosse) (as Angelique)
1980   *How to Beat the High Co$t of Living* (Scheerer) (as Louise)
1981   *The Postman Always Rings Twice* (Rafelson) (as Cora Papadakis); *The Best Little Girl in the World* (O'Steen—for TV)
1982   *Tootsie* (Pollack) (as Julie); *Frances* (Clifford) (as Frances Farmer)
1984   *Country* (Pearce) (as Jewel Ivy, + co-pr); *Cat on a Hot Tin Roof* (Hofsiss—for TV) (as Maggie)
1985   *Sweet Dreams* (Reisz) (as Patsy Cline)
1986   *Crimes of the Heart* (Beresford) (as Meg Magrath)
1988   *Everybody's All-American* (*When I Fall in Love*) (Hackford) (as Babs Rogers Grey); *Far North* (Shepard) (as Kate)
1989   *Music Box* (Costa-Gavras) (as Ann Talbot)
1990   *Men Don't Leave* (Brickman) (as Beth Macauley)
1991   *Cape Fear* (Scorsese) (as Leigh Bowden)
1992   *Night and the City* (Irwin Winkler) (as Helen Nasseros); *O Pioneers!* (Glenn Jordan—for TV) (as Alexandra Bergson)
1994   *Blue Sky* (Richardson—produced in 1990) (as Carly Marshall)
1995   *Rob Roy* (Caton-Jones) (as Mary); *Losing Isaiah* (Gyllenhaal) (as Margaret Lewin); *A Streetcar Named Desire* (Glenn Jordan—for TV) (as Blanche Dubois)

Publications

By LANGE: articles—

"Jessica Lange: From Kong to Cain," interview with Dan Yakir, in *Film Comment* (New York), March-April 1981.
Interview with B. Frank and B. Krohn, in *Cahiers du Cinéma* (Paris), June 1982.
"Dialogue on Film: Jessica Lange," in *American Film* (New York), June 1987 and August 1990.
"American Independent," interview with Linda Bird Francke and Brigitte LaCombe, in *Interview* (New York), December 1989.

On LANGE: book—

Jeffries, J. T., *Jessica Lange: A Biography*, New York, 1986.

On LANGE: articles—

Drew, Bernard, "Gorilla Power," in *American Film* (Washington, D.C.), December 1976-January 1977.
Drew, Bernard, "Life as a Long Rehearsal," in *American Film* (Washington, D.C.), November 1979.
Thompson, David, "Raising Cain," in *Film Comment* (New York), March-April 1981.
McGilligan, Patrick, "The Postman Rings Again," in *American Film* (Washington, D.C.), April 1981.
Current Biography 1983, New York, 1983.

Cameron, Julia, "Jessica Lange," in *American Film* (Washington, D.C.), January-February 1983.
Russo, Vito, "Jessica Lange: The Girl Who Went Away in a Limousine and Never Came Back," in *Moviegoer*, February 1983.
Patterson, Richard, "Cinematography for *Frances*," in *American Cinematographer* (Hollywood), March 1983.
Stivers, Cyndi, "Jessica Lange: From Frog to Movie Princess," in *Life* (New York), March 1983.
Rosenthal, David, "Jessica Lange," in *Rolling Stone* (New York), 17 March 1983.
Hibbin, S., "Jessica Lange," in *Films and Filming* (London), February 1985.
Schruers, Fred, "Lange-froid," in *Premiere* (New York), January 1990.
Elia, M., "Jessica Lange ou l'ironie des choix," in *Séquences* (Montreal), June 1990.
Monroe, Valerie, "Jessica," in *Harper's Bazaar* (New York), January 1991.
Sessums, Kevin, "Lange on Life," in *Vanity Fair* (New York), March 1995.

*   *   *

While talented contemporaries such as Spacek and Keaton deal with flickering sex appeal, Jessica Lange exudes a European quality, call it passion perfumed by mystery, that has not dampened Lange's leading lady allure. What the sensual Lange brings to all her roles is an intense conviction that bowls over audiences and sometimes sends her directors screaming into the night. Locking horns, for example, with Paul Brickman over his own conception, *Men Don't Leave*, she remolds his sunnier personality-driven seriocomedy into a melodrama worthy of Stanwyck or Dunne. The light touch necessary for a star-vehicle comedy may forever elude her, but as a dramatic actress she burns through directors' shortcuts and limitations in material to the heart of the matter.

In her dramas, when Lange approaches a man, it is almost a challenge to put up or shut up (Nicholson in *The Postman Always Rings Twice*, Powers Boothe in *Blue Sky*, Ed Harris in *Sweet Dreams*); she is just as direct in other circumstances. The only occasions when the resilient Lange crumbles are when her antagonists are dishonest (*Music Box*, *Losing Isaiah*, *Frances*)—a lying heart is an affront to the driven women she plays.

That solar-powered honesty was there from the beginning. Isn't it time to reevaluate that notorious remake of *King Kong*—to stop disparaging it for failing to top the thrills of the original classic and to view it as a lyrical romance between a cover girl and the world's tallest leading man. An incredibly sexy fairy tale, the excoriated *King Kong*, which critics used as a wedge to drive Lange's career into bimbo oblivion, actually contains the first evidence of that pulverizing sincerity audiences now accept. You could tell she really felt sorry for that big ape, a compassion which she more selectively meted out to future co-stars.

Recovering from a critical drubbing that would have sent lesser souls to a permanent room at the Betty Ford Clinic, Lange slowly proved she was more than just the plaything of a gigantic rubber monkey. Anger over her mistreatment seems to fester in subsequent performances which carry the subtext of I-Told-You-Jerks-I-Could Act. Shouting out what Lana Turner could only whisper in the remake of *The Postman Always Rings Twice*, a movie whose obviousness was no match for the original's film noir glamour, Lange wipes everyone else off the screen. Although she won a consolation prize Oscar for her supporting work in *Tootsie*, she should have beaten the Queen of Accents, Meryl Streep, to the best actress prize for *Frances*. As Dunaway accomplished with her *Mommie Dearest*, *Frances* is a tribute from one kindred-spirit actress to another, in this case a celebration of a misfit actress who religiously fought the studio system. This tour de force as Frances Farmer is a brave, audience-distancing perfor-

Jessica Lange in *Frances*

mance in which Lange remains true to Farmer's neurotic distaste for dissembling; as she journeys into this lost soul's emotional inferno, one feels one is witnessing acting attuned to the dark vision of Ingmar Bergman which has somehow been misplaced in a conventional Hollywood biopic.

Despite a predilection for folksy reverence that makes *Country*, *Far North*, and *O, Pioneers*, tediously noble, Lange purred tantalizingly in *Cat on a Hot Tin Roof*, soulfully embodied country-and-western legend Patsy Cline in *Sweet Dreams*, and saved *Everybody's All-American* from meretriciousness with another scalding portrayal, this time as a beauty queen whose will of iron lets her rise above being taken for granted. Going mad once more in *Blue Sky*, Lange won a best actress Oscar for this bittersweet fable abandoned by Orion Pictures after bankruptcy proceedings, but her second Tennessee Williams outing rang hollow as she barely scratched the surface of Blanche Dubois's tormented psyche, although she was light-years better than her co-star Alec Baldwin and his cartoonish Stanley Kowalski. All of Lange's work, even in the disappointing *A Streetcar Named Desire*, is creditable, and she can illuminate social problem dramas such as *Music Box* or *Losing Isaiah* even if they are really television movies masquerading as big-screen events. In fact, Lange is even good in Scorcese's bloated spook-show vulgarization of *Cape Fear*. Heeding the call of

commercial cinema, she has matured into a more womanly beauty in *Rob Roy*, less the Lorelei than the Life-mate, but she cannot be strait-jacketed into the confinement of just being some male star's leading lady. Capable of Sturm und Drang like the film Duses of yesteryear, Lange is the movie star as drama-queen, and she deserves to have flashy roles built to suit her core of anger and tempestuousness.

—Robert Pardi

LANSBURY, Angela

Nationality: American. **Born:** Angela Brigid Lansbury in London, England, 16 October 1925; granddaughter of the politician George Lansbury; became U.S. citizen, 1951. **Education:** Attended Webber-Douglas School of Singing and Dramatic Art, London; Feagin School of Drama and Radio, New York. **Family:** Married 1) Richard Cromwell, 1945 (divorced 1946); 2) Peter Pullen Shaw, 1949, one son and one daughter. **Career:** 1942—in nightclub act in Montreal; 1943—given seven-year contract with MGM, and made debut in *Gaslight* the following year; 1957—Broadway debut in *Hotel Paradiso*: later stage roles in *A Taste of Honey*, 1960, *Mame*, 1966, *Dear World*, 1969, and *Sweeney Todd*, 1979; from 1984—in TV series *Murder, She Wrote*; also in 1984, in TV mini-series *Lace*, and *The First Olympics: Athens 1896*; 1986—in TV mini-series *Rage of Angels: The Story Continues*. **Awards:** 4 Tony Awards for Best Actress in a Musical. **Agent:** William Morris Agency, 1350 Avenue of the Americas, New York, NY 10019, U.S.A.

Films as Actress:

1944   *Gaslight* (Cukor) (as Nancy Oliver); *National Velvet* (Brown) (as Edwina Brown)

1945   **The Picture of Dorian Gray** (Lewin) (as Sibyl Vane)

1946   *The Harvey Girls* (Sidney) (as Em); *The Hoodlum Saint* (Taurog) (as Dusty Willard); *Till the Clouds Roll By* (Whorf) (as guest star)

1947   *The Private Affairs of Bel Ami* (Lewin) (as Clotilde de Marelle); *If Winter Comes* (Saville) (as Mabel Sabre)

1948   *Tenth Avenue Angel* (Rowland) (as Susan Bratten); *State of the Union* (Capra) (as Kay Thorndyke); *The Three Musketeers* (Sidney) (as Queen Anne)

1949   *The Red Danube* (Sidney) (as Audrey Quail); *Samson and Delilah* (Cecil B. DeMille) (as Semadar)

1951   *Kind Lady* (John Sturges) (as Mrs. Edwards)

1952   *Mutiny* (Dmytryk) (as Leslie)

1953   *Remains to Be Seen* (Weis) (as Valeska Chauvea)

1954   *Key Man* (*A Life at Stake*) (Guilfoyle) (as Doris Hillman)

1955   *A Lawless Street* (Joseph H. Lewis) (as Tally Dickinson); *The Purple Mask* (Humberstone) (as Madame Valentine)

1956   *The Court Jester* (Panama and Frank) (as Princess Gwendolyn); *Please Murder Me* (Godfrey) (as Myra Leeds)

1958   *The Long Hot Summer* (Ritt) (as Minnie Littlejohn); *The Reluctant Debutante* (Minnelli) (as Mabel Claremont)

1959   *Season of Passion* (*Summer of the 17th Doll*) (Norman) (as Pearl)

1960   *The Dark at the Top of the Stairs* (Delbert Mann) (as Mavis Pruitt); *A Breath of Scandal* (Curtiz) (as Countess Lina)

1961   *Blue Hawaii* (Taurog) (as Sarah Lee Gates)

1962   *The Four Horsemen of the Apocalypse* (Minnelli) (as voice of Marguerite Laurier); *All Fall Down* (Frankenheimer) (as Annabel Willart); *The Manchurian Candidate* (Frankenheimer) (as Raymond's mother)

1963   *In the Cool of the Day* (Robert Stevens) (as Sibyl Logan)

1964   *The World of Henry Orient* (George Roy Hill) (as Isabel Boyd); *Dear Heart* (Delbert Mann) (as Phyllis)

1965   *The Greatest Story Ever Told* (George Stevens) (as Claudia); *The Amorous Adventures of Moll Flanders* (Terence Young) (as Lady Blystone); *Harlow* (Douglas) (as Mama Jean Bello)

1966   *Mister Buddwing* (*Woman without a Face*) (Delbert Mann) (as Gloria)

1970   *Something for Everyone* (Prince) (as Countess Herthe von Orstein)

1971   *Bedknobs and Broomsticks* (Stevenson) (as Eglantine Price)

1975   *The Story of the First Christmas Snow* (Bass and Rankin—animation for TV) (as voice of Sister Theresa)

1978   *Death on the Nile* (Guillermin) (as Mrs. Salome Otterbourne)

1979   *The Lady Vanishes* (Page) (as Miss Froy)

1980   *The Mirror Crack'd* (Hamilton) (as Miss Marple)

1982   *The Last Unicorn* (Rankin Jr. and Bass—animation) (as voice of Mommy Fortuna); *Little Gloria . . . Happy at Last* (Hussein—for TV) (as Gertrude Vanderbilt Whitney); *Sweeney Todd* (Hughes and Prince) (as Nellie Lovett)

1983   *The Pirates of Penzance* (Leach) (as Ruth); *The Gift of Love: A Christmas Story* (Delbert Mann—for TV)

1984   *Ingrid* (Feldman—for TV)

1985   *The Company of Wolves* (Neil Jordan) (as Granny); *The Murder of Sherlock Holmes* (Corey Allen—for TV)

1986   *A Talent for Murder* (Rakoff—for TV)

1988   *Shootdown* (Pressman—for TV)

1989   *The Shell Seekers* (Hussein—for TV) (as Penelope Keeling)

1990   *The Love She Sought* (Sargent—for TV) (as Agatha McGee)

1991   **Beauty and the Beast** (Wise and Trousdale—animation) (as voice of Mrs. Potts)

1992   *Mrs. 'Arris Goes to Paris* (Shaw—for TV) (title role)

Publications

By LANSBURY: book—

Angela Lansbury's Positive Moves (physical fitness), with Mimi Avins, New York, 1990.

By LANSBURY: articles—

"Safety Zone," interview with T. Gilling, in *Sight and Sound* (London), Summer 1972.

Interview, in *Radio Times*, 17 December 1983.

"Auntie Angela," interview with Kevin Allman, in *Advocate* (Los Angeles), 22 September 1992.

"That's All She Wrote," interview with Robert Massello, in *TV Guide* (Radnor, Pennsylvania), 4 November 1995.

On LANSBURY: books—

Parish, James, *Good Dames*, New York, 1974.

Bonanno, Margaret Wander, *Angela Lansbury: A Biography*, New York, 1987.

Edelman, Rob, *Angela Lansbury*, New York, 1996.

On LANSBURY: articles—

Hallowell, John, "A Smashing New Dame to Play Mame," in *Life* (New York), 17 June 1966.

Current Biography 1967, New York, 1967.

"Angela Lansbury, Sondheim, Prince and *Sweeney Todd*," in *Horizon*, April 1979.

Pacheco, Patrick, "Angela Lansbury: A Bloomin' Wonder," in *After Dark*, January 1980.

Bodeen, DeWitt, "Angela Lansbury," in *Films in Review* (New York), February 1980.

Films Illustrated (London), October 1980.

Olmsted, Dan, "Why Angela Lansbury Is Everyone's Cup of Tea," in *USA Weekend* (Arlington, Virginia), 29 November-1 December 1991.

Murphy, Mary, "Angela Gets Tough," in *TV Guide* (Arlington, Virginia), 26 December 1992.

*   *   *

Although recent years have seen the enormously talented Angela Lansbury become the definitive leading lady of Broadway musicals, she has never enjoyed a similar stardom on the screen despite the many film roles and awards she has to her credit. While she possesses unarguable acting ability and star quality, under the scrutiny of the camera her less than glamorous looks have made leading-lady, star-vehicle roles difficult for her to obtain from the very beginning.

Born in London, Lansbury began dramatic training as a child, continuing in the United States after being evacuated during the German blitz. After signing with MGM, she was nominated for an Oscar for

Best Supporting Actress in her first film, *Gaslight*. Although still in her teens at the time, this role started her on a path of character parts in which she was often younger than the unsympathetic character.

A second Academy Award nomination followed for *The Picture of Dorian Gray*, an adaptation of the Oscar Wilde novel. Lansbury subsequently appeared in a series of fine supporting performances, notably in Capra's *State of the Union*, Martin Ritt's *The Long Hot Summer*, and Delbert Mann's version of *The Dark at the Top of the Stairs*. Perhaps the best example of Lansbury's ability to play characters much older than herself is her unforgettably chilling portrayal of Laurence Harvey's devious mother in *The Manchurian Candidate*. In reality, she was only three years Harvey's senior.

Watching Lansbury the television hostess pop up on awards shows like a latter-day Toastmaster General seems a thorough waste of this versatile actress's time. These great lady stints could also be viewed, however, as a measure of the respectful affection audiences feel for her reassuring Jessica Fletcher, a television detective character with a record number of relatives to clear of murder charges. Since resoundingly garnering the megastardom denied her during her MGM contract period, Lansbury has evidenced a regrettable taste for bland, but high-rated, star vehicles such as *The Shell Seekers* and *Mrs. 'Arris Goes to Paris*. Lansbury acolytes who have experienced her glamorous *Mame*, indefatigable Mama Rose in *Gypsy*, and homicidally enterprising Mrs. Lovett in *Sweeney Todd*, know that Jessica Fletcher and subsequent television appearances only tap a smidgen of this powerhouse's talent. On-screen, Lansbury remains an unparalleled character star who can look back with pride on her psychologically crippling mother in *All Fall Down*, her divine poseur in *Death on the Nile*, her foolish adulteress in *The World of Henry Orient*, and her stylishly decadent countess in *Something for Everyone*.

After being shortsightedly passed over for the movie of *Mame* in favor of human foghorn Lucille Ball, Lansbury did get to kick up her heels in *Bedknobs and Broomsticks*, an affable treat but no *Mary Poppins*. Mothballing her musical comedy ambitions and once again donning old lady drag in *The Mirror Crack'd* and *The Lady Vanishes*, is it any wonder Lansbury embraced the nonfrumpy vistas of *Murder, She Wrote* in which she could play her own age and display the personal warmth not required by most of her celebrated acting outings? After her long-running series is history, Lansbury will continue to delight and astonish her fans, but one hopes her hard-won and long-overdue stardom will not tempt her to orphan her unscrupulous schemers and larger-than-life eccentrics in favor of variations on reliable, gracious, down-to-earth buttinski, J. B. Fletcher.

—Bill Wine, updated by Robert Pardi

LAUGHTON, Charles

Nationality: American. **Born:** Scarborough, Yorkshire, 1 July 1899; became U.S. citizen, 1950. **Education:** Attended Stonyhurst School until 16 years old; studied at Royal Academy of Dramatic Art, London, 1925-26. **Military Service:** Served in the British Army, 1917-18; gassed in final German advance of war. **Family:** Married the actress Elsa Lanchester, 1929. **Career:** 1916—sent to London to learn hotel business; 1918-25—worked in family hotel, took part in amateur theatricals; 1926—professional acting debut in *The Government Inspector*; 1928—appeared in bit roles in short filmed plays written by H. G. Wells for Elsa Lanchester; 1929—feature film debut in Dupont's *Piccadilly*; 1931—played with Lanchester in *Payment Deferred*, in London and New York; contract with Paramount; 1933-34—acted with Old Vic, London; 1937—taken into partnership, along with John Maxwell, in Erich Pommer's Mayflower Pictures; 1939—

moved permanently to United States; mid-1940s—collaborated with Bertolt Brecht on *Galileo* (premiered 1947 in Los Angeles); late 1940s—toured in programs of readings from great literature; as member of The First Drama Quartet (with Agnes Moorehead, Charles Boyer, and Cedric Hardwicke), toured in *Don Juan in Hell*; 1952—co-produced and directed Broadway production of *The Caine Mutiny Court Martial*; 1955—directed the film *The Night of the Hunter*. **Awards:** Best Actor, Academy Award for *The Private Life of Henry VIII*, 1932-33; Best Actor, New York Film Critics, for *Mutiny on the Bounty* and *Ruggles of Red Gap*, 1935. **Died:** Of cancer 15 December 1962.

Films as Actor:

1928   *Daydreams* (Montague—short) (as Rajah); *Bluebottles* (Montague—short) (as policeman); *Frankie and Johnnie* (Montague—short)
1929   *Piccadilly* (Dupont) (bit role)
1930   *Wolves* (*Wanted Men*) (De Courville)
1931   *Down River* (Godfrey)
1932   *The Old Dark House* (Whale) (as a Lancashire knight); *The Devil and the Deep* (Gering) (as submarine captain); *Payment Deferred* (Mendes); *The Sign of the Cross* (DeMille) (as Nero); in Lubitsch-directed ep. of *If I Had a Million* (anthology film)
1933   *Island of Lost Souls* (Kenton); ***The Private Life of Henry VIII*** (Korda) (title role); *White Woman* (Walker) (as Horace Prin)
1934   *The Barretts of Wimpole Street* (Franklin) (as Mr. Barrett)
1935   *Ruggles of Red Gap* (McCarey) (title role); *Les Misérables* (Boleslawsky) (as Javert); *Mutiny on the Bounty* (Lloyd) (as Captain Bligh)
1936   *Rembrandt* (Korda) (title role); *I, Claudius* (von Sternberg—not completed) (title role)
1937   *Vessel of Wrath* (*The Beachcomber*) (Pommer)
1939   *St. Martin's Lane* (*The Sidewalks of London*) (Whelan); *Jamaica Inn* (Hitchcock); *The Hunchback of Notre Dame* (Dieterle) (as Quasimodo)
1940   *They Knew What They Wanted* (Kanin) (as Tony Patucci)
1941   *It Started with Eve* (Koster)
1942   *The Tuttles of Tahiti* (Charles Vidor); *Tales of Manhattan* (Duvivier); *Stand by for Action* (Leonard)
1943   *Forever and a Day* (Clair and others); *This Land Is Mine* (Renoir); *The Man from Down Under* (Leonard)
1944   *The Canterville Ghost* (Dassin) (title role); *The Suspect* (Siodmak)
1945   *Captain Kidd* (Lee) (title role)
1946   *Because of Him* (Wallace)
1948   *The Paradine Case* (Hitchcock); *On Our Merry Way* (*A Miracle Can Happen*) (King Vidor) (as guest); *The Big Clock* (Farrow); *Arch of Triumph* (Milestone); *The Girl from Manhattan* (Green)
1949   *The Bribe* (Leonard); *The Man on the Eiffel Tower* (Meredith) (as Inspector Maigret)
1951   *The Blue Veil* (Bernhardt); *The Strange Door* (Pevney); "The Cop and the Anthem" ep. of *O. Henry's Full House* (Koster); *Abbott and Costello Meet Captain Kidd* (Lamont) (as Captain Kidd)
1953   *Salome* (Dieterle) (as King Herod); *Young Bess* (Sidney) (as Henry VIII)
1954   *Hobson's Choice* (Lean) (title role)
1957   *Witness for the Prosecution* (Wilder)
1960   *Sotto dieci bandiere* (*Under Ten Flags*) (Coletti) (as British Admiral); *Spartacus* (Kubrick) (as Gracchus)
1962   *Advise and Consent* (Preminger) (as Senator Seab Cooley)

Charles Laughton in *The Private Life of Henry VIII* **courtesy of CTE (Carlton) Limited**

Film as Director:

1955   *The Night of the Hunter* (+ co-sc)

Publications

On LAUGHTON: books—

Singer, Kurt, *The Laughton Story*, Philadelphia, 1954.
Lanchester, Elsa, *Charles Laughton and I*, New York, 1968.
Burrows, Michael, *Charles Laughton and Frederic March*, New York, 1970.
Brown, William, *Charles Laughton: A Pictorial Treasury of His Films*, New York, 1970.
Higham, Charles, *Charles Laughton: An Intimate Biography*, New York, 1976.
Lanchester, Elsa, *Elsa Lanchester Herself*, New York, 1983.
Callow, Simon, *Charles Laughton: A Difficult Actor*, London, 1987.
Missler, Andreas, *Charles Laughton: Seine Filme, sein Leben*, Munich, 1990.

On LAUGHTON: articles—

Gordon, Ruth, "Legitimate Laughton," in *Theatre Arts* (New York), November, 1950.
McVay, D., "The Intolerant Giant," in *Films and Filming* (London), March 1963.
Vermilye, Jerry, "Charles Laughton," in *Films in Review* (New York), May 1963.
Lorcey, J., "La Pesanteur et la grâce: Charles Laughton acteur," in *Avant-Scène du Cinéma* (Paris), 15 February 1978.
Turner, G. E., "Creating *The Night of the Hunter*," in *American Cinematographer* (Hollywood), December 1982.
Taylor, John Russell, "Tales of the Hollywood Raj," in *Films and Filming* (London), June 1983.
Mills, M. C., "Charles Laughton's Adaptation of *The Night of the Hunter*," in *Literature/Film Quarterly* (Salisbury, Maryland), January 1988.

*   *   *

Charles Laughton, one of the most distinguished actors of the century, was successful alike on stage and in film, yet, full of artistic self-doubts throughout his career, he was fraught by worries, largely of his own making, including problems arising from his homosexuality. Like Michel Simon in France, he was haunted by concern about his appearance; both men found themselves repellently ugly yet both had features which, though homely and far from conventionally handsome, possessed wonderful mobility of expression. In their particular cases, their appearance in fact became a great dramatic asset. Intended by his father, a hotelier in Scarborough, to follow the same occupation, Laughton broke away to train at the Royal Academy of Dramatic Art where he became a gold medalist in 1925. Once on the stage, he found his lifelong supporter and fellow-artist in the young character actress Elsa Lanchester, with whom in 1928 he appeared in two notable experimental two-reel film comedies *Bluebottles* and *Day Dreams*. His feature film debut was in a silent production, E. A. Dupont's *Piccadilly*, followed by appearances in other British features. Meanwhile, his stage career took him to America in 1931 as the murderer in the play *Payment Deferred*, which was subsequently filmed.

Laughton's outstanding success in films came, in both Britain and America, in the early 1930s in a long succession of star character parts—parallel to his commanding position in the theater, where he starred notably in Shakespeare at the Old Vic and, much later, at Stratford upon Avon. He played an effetely sadistic Nero in DeMille's *The Sign of the Cross* and an amusing bit part in the composite film *If I Had a Million*, developing a genius alike for comedy and drama. His brilliance in Korda's *The Private Life of Henry VIII* won him an Academy Award; he followed this with a veritable gallery of impressive character portraits—as Elizabeth Barrett Browning's father in the Sidney Franklin version of *The Barretts of Wimpole Street*, as the dignified English butler in Leo McCarey's *Ruggles of Red Gap*, as Javert in Richard Boleslawski's version of *Les Misérables*, and as Captain Bligh in Frank Lloyd's *Mutiny on the Bounty*. He was the artist in Korda's *Rembrandt*, the beachcomber in Erich Pommer's *Vessel of Wrath* (*The Beachcomber*), the street entertainer in Tim Whelan's *St. Martin's Lane* (*Sidewalks of London*), and Quasimodo in William Dieterle's version of *The Hunchback of Notre Dame*.

By the 1940s, with the Laughtons settled in Hollywood, films became his principal source of income, enabling him to own a handsome home and establish a collection of paintings. His roles alternated between the excellent and the mediocre, the excellent including those in Garson Kanin's *They Knew What They Wanted* (with Carole Lombard) and Henry Koster's *It Started with Eve*, his cowardly ghost in Jules Dassin's *The Canterville Ghost*, the Crippen-like murderer in Robert Siodmak's *The Suspect*, and the magazine tycoon in *The Paradine Case*. He starred in John Farrow's thriller, *The Big Clock* and was Inspector Maigret in the French-American production *The Man on the Eiffel Tower*. Many films of this period, however, were indifferent vehicles for Laughton's great talent, and it was good that in his final years he was given certain characters in which he could shine—as Hobson, the north of England bootmaker in David Lean's version of Stanley Houghton's play *Hobson's Choice*, as the elderly barrister in Billy Wilder's version of Agatha Christie's *Witness for the Prosecution*, and finally as the wily, crusty senator in Otto Preminger's *Advise and Consent*. This part he just managed to get through before his death.

Laughton had also in his later career established a new departure, giving dramatic readings, notably from the Bible and from Bernard Shaw's *Man and Superman*. He also directed one film with evident skill, *The Night of the Hunter*, a sinister thriller of great atmospheric power, containing a fine performance by Robert Mitchum.

—Roger Manvell

LAUREL, Stan, and Oliver HARDY

LAUREL. Nationality: British/American. **Born:** Arthur Stanley Jefferson in Ulverston, England, 16 June 1890. **Education:** Attended King James Grammar School, Bishop Auckland, Co. Durham. **Family:** Married 1) Mae Dahlberg (common-law marriage), 1919-25; 2) Lois Nelson, 1926 (divorced 1935), daughter: Lois Jr.; 3) Ruth Rogers, 1935 (divorced 1936); 4) Illeana Shuvalona, 1938 (divorced 1939); 5) remarried Ruth Rogers, 1941 (divorced 1946); 6) Ida Kitaeva Raphael, 1946. **Career:** 1906—stage debut in Glasgow; joined Levy and Cardwell Pantomime Company as stage manager, then as actor and featured comedian; 1910—joined the Fred Karno Company, worked as Charlie Chaplin's understudy on two U.S. tours, 1910 and 1912; from 1912—stayed in the U.S. and worked in vaudeville, first with Alice and Baldwin Cooke, then as a single act; 1917—film debut in *Nuts in May* (some scholars suggest an earlier appearance); 1917-26—more than 70 films for Universal, Vitagraph, Hal Roach, Pathe, and Metro as writer, performer, and occasionally director. **Awards:** Special Oscar, "for his creative pioneering in the field of cinema comedy," 1960. **Died:** In Santa Monica, California, 23 February 1965.

HARDY. Nationality: American. **Born:** Norvell Hardy Jr. in Harlem, Georgia, 1892. **Education:** Attended Georgia Military College; Atlanta Conservatory of Music; studied law briefly at the University of Georgia, Atlanta. **Family:** Married 1) Madelyn Saloshin, 1913 (divorced); 2) Myrtle Lee, 1921 (divorced 1937); 3) Virginia Lucille Jones, 1940. **Career:** 1900—debut as singer with the Coburn Minstrel Show, then toured with his own singing act; 1910-13—operated a movie theater in Milledgeville, Georgia; 1913—joined the Lubin film company in Jacksonville, Florida, and made film debut in *Outwitting Dad*, 1914; 1914-26—made films for Vim, Edison, and other companies in New York and Florida (and after 1918 in California). **Died:** In North Hollywood, California, 7 August 1957.

1926—Laurel and Hardy brought together as a team by Hal Roach (though they had both appeared in *A Lucky Dog*, 1917); worked together as team for the next 30 years, making both shorts and features for Hal Roach until 1940, then for other studios; toured Britain with a music hall revue, 1947 and 1954; Laurel stopped acting upon Hardy's death, but continued to write.

Films as Actor: Hardy—

(as Oliver "Babe" Hardy or Babe Hardy in early films)

1914   *Outwitting Dad*; *Back to the Farm* (Louis); *Pins Are Lucky*; *The Soubrette and the Simp* (Hotaling?); *The Smuggler's Daughter* (Hevener); *The Female Cop* (Hevener); *Those Love Pangs* (*The Rival Mashers*; *Busted Hearts*) (Chaplin); *The Rise of the Johnsons*

1915   *What He Forgot* (Hevener); *Cupid's Target* (Hevener); *Spaghetti and Lottery* (Louis); *Gus and the Anarchists* (Murphy); *Shoddy the Tailor* (Louis); *The Paperhanger's Helper*; *Spaghetti a la Mode*; *Charley's Aunt*; *Artists and Models*; *The Tramps*; *The Prize Baby* (Hevener); *An Expensive Visit* (Louis); *Cleaning Time* (Louis); *Mixed Flats* (Louis); *Safety Worst*; *Twin Sisters* (Hotaling); *Baby* (Myers); *Who Stole the Doggies?*; *A Lucky Strike* (Hotaling); *The New Butler* (Hotaling); *Matilda's Legacy* (Hotaling); *Her Choice* (Price); *Cannibal King*; *What a Cinch* (Louis); *Clothes Make the Man* (Louis); *The Dead Letter* (Louis); *Avenging Bill* (Hotaling); *The Haunted Hat* (Louis); *The Simp and the Sophomores* (Louis); *Babe's School Days* (Louis); *Ethel's*

Romeos (Middleton); *The New Adventures of J. Rufus Wallingford* (Wharton—serial); *Something in Her Eye*; *A Janitor's Joyful Job*; *Fatty's Fatal Fun*; *Ups and Downs* (Stull and Burns); *This Way Out* (Stull and Burns)

1916 *Chickens* (Stull and Burns); *Frenzied Finance* (Stull and Burns); *Busted Hearts* (Stull and Burns); *A Sticky Affair* (Stull and Burns); *Bungles' Rainy Day* (Stull and Burns); *The Tryout* (Stull and Burns); *Bungles Enforces the Law* (Stull and Burns); *Bungles' Elopement* (Stull and Burns); *Bungles Lands a Job* (Stull and Burns); *One Too Many*; *The Serenade*; *Nerve and Gasoline*; *Their Vacation*; *Mamma's Boy's*; *A Battle Royal*; *All for a Girl*; *Hired and Fired*; *What's Sauce for the Goose*; *The Brave Ones*; *The Water Cure*; *Thirty Days*; *Baby Doll*; *The Schemers*; *Sea Dogs*; *Hungry Hearts*; *Edison Bugg's Invention* (Hevener); *Never Again*; *Better Halves*; *A Day at School*; *A Terrible Tragedy* (Hevener); *Spaghetti*; *Aunt Bill*; *The Heroes*; *It Happened in Pikersville* (Hevener); *Human Hounds*; *Dreamy Knights*; *Life Savers*; *Their Honeymoon*; *An Aeriel Joyride* (Walter or Charles Reed); *Sidetracked*; *Stranded* (Burstein); *Love and Duty*; *Artistic Atmosphere*; *The Reformers*; *Royal Blood*; *The Candy Trail*; *The Precious Parcel* (*The Precious Packet*); *A Maid to Order*; *Twin Flats*; *A Warm Reception*; *Pipe Dreams*; *Mother's Child*; *Prize Winners*; *Ambitious Ethel*; *The Guilty Ones*

1917 *He Winked and Won*; *Fat and Fickle*; *The Boycotted Baby*; *Wanted—A Bad Man*; *The Other Girl*; *The Love Bugs*; *Back Stage* (Gillstrom); *The Hero* (Gillstrom); *Dough-Nuts* (Gillstrom); *Cupid's Rival* (Gillstrom); *The Villain* (Gillstrom); *A Millionaire* (Gillstrom); *A Mixup in Hearts* (Gillstrom); *The Goat* (Gillstrom); *The Genius* (Gillstrom); *The Stranger* (Gillstrom); *The Fly Cop* (Gillstrom); *The Modiste* (Gillstrom); *The Star Boarder* (Gillstrom); *The Chief Cook* (Gillstrom); *The Candy Kid* (Gillstrom); *The Station Master* (Gillstrom); *The Hobo* (Gillstrom); *The Pest* (Gillstrom); *The Prospector* (Gillstrom); *The Band Master* (Gillstrom); *The Slave* (Gillstrom)

1918 *The Artist* (Gillstrom); *The Barber* (Gillstrom); *King Solomon* (Gillstrom); *His Day Out* (Gillstrom); *The Orderly* (Gillstrom); *The Rogue* (Gillstrom); *The Scholar* (Gillstrom); *The Messenger* (Gillstrom); *The Handy Man* (Parrott); *Bright and Early* (Parrott); *The Straight and Narrow* (Parrott); *Playmates* (Parrott)

1919 *Freckled Fish* (Le Brandt); *Hop the Bell-Hop* (Parrott); *Lions and Ladies* (Griffin); *Mules and Mortgages* (Howe); *Tootsie and Tamales* (Noel Smith) (+ co-sc); *Healthy and Happy* (Noel Smith); *Flips and Flops* (Pratt); *Yaps and Yokels* (Noel Smith); *Mates and Models* (Noel Smith); *Squabs and Squabbles* (Noel Smith); *Bungs and Bunglers* (Noel Smith); *Switches and Sweeties* (Noel Smith)

1920 *Dames and Dentists* (Noel Smith); *Maids and Muslin* (Noel Smith); *Squeaks and Squawks* (Noel Smith); *Fists and Fodder* (Robbins); *Pals and Pugs* (Robbins); *He Laughs Last* (Robbins); *Springtime* (Robbins); *The Decorator* (Robbins); *His Jonah Day* (Robbins); *The Back Yard* (Robbins)

1921 *The Nuisance* (Robbins); *The Blizzard* (Robbins); *The Tourist* (Robbins); *Straight from the Shoulder* (Van Dyke); *The Fall Guy* (Semon); *The Sawmill* (Semon); *The Fly Cop* (Peebles, Semon, and Taurog)

1922 *Golf* (Semon); *The Counter Jumper* (Semon); *Fortune's Mask* (Ensminger); *The Little Wildcat* (Divad); *One Stolen Night* (Ensminger)

1923 *The Three Ages* (Keaton and Cline); *Rex, King of the Wild Horses* (Jones); *Be Your Age* (McCarey)

1924 *The Girl in the Limousine* (Semon); *Her Boy Friend* (Semon); *Kid Speed* (Semon); *The Wizard of Oz* (Semon) (as the tin woodsman); *The Perfect Clown* (Newmeyer)

1925 *Is Marriage the Bunk?* (McCarey); *Isn't Life Terrible?* (McCarey); *Enough to Do* (Laurel); *Wandering Papas* (Laurel); *Yes, Yes, Nanette* (Laurel and Hennecke); *Navy Gravy* (Parrott); *Stick Around*; *Hop to It*; *Should Sailors Marry?*

1926 *Stop, Look, and Listen* (Semon); *Madame Mystery* (Laurel and Wallace); *Long Live the King* (McCarey); *Thundering Fleas* (McGowan); *Along Came Auntie* (Guiol); *Crazy Like a Fox* (McCarey); *Be Your Age* (McCarey); *Should Men Walk Home?* (McCarey); *The Nickel Hopper* (Jones); *The Gentle Cyclone* (Van Dyke); *A Bankrupt Honeymoon* (Seiler); *A Sea Dog's Tale* (Lord); *Crazy to Act*; *Say It with Babies*

1927 *No Man's Law* (Jackman); *Fluttering Hearts* (Parrott); *The Lighter that Failed* (Parrott); *Love 'em and Feed 'em* (Bruckman); *Assistant Wives* (Parrott); *Galloping Ghosts* (Parrott); *Barnum and Ringling Inc.* (McGowan); *Why Girls Say No* (McCarey); *The Honorable Mr. Buggs* (Jackman)

1939 *Zenobia* (*Elephants Never Forget*) (Gordon Douglas) (as Dr. Tibbitt)

1949 *The Fighting Kentuckian* (*A Strange Caravan*) (Waggner) (as Willie Paine)

1950 *Riding High* (Capra) (as horse player)

Films as Actor: Laurel—

1917 *Nuts in May* (Williamson); *The Evolution of Fashion*

1918 *Hickory Hiram* (Frazee); *Phoney Photos* (Frazee); *Whose Zoo* (Hutchinson); *It's Great to Be Crazy*; *Huns and Hyphens* (Semon); *Bears and Bad Men* (Semon); *Frauds and Frenzies* (Semon) (as second prisoner)

1919 *No Place Like Jail* (Roach and Terry); *Just Rambling Along* (Roach and Terry); *Do You Love Your Wife?* (Roach and Terry); *Hustling for Health* (Roach and Terry); *Hoot Mon* (Roach and Terry); *Scars and Stripes* (Semon); *Mixed Nuts* (Parrott)

1920 *Oranges and Lemons* (Jeske); *The Spilers*

1921 *The Rent Collector* (Semon and Taurog)

1922 *The Carpenter*; *The Bootlegger*; *The Gardener*; *The Miner*; *The Egg* (Pratt); *Weak-End Party* (Pratt); *When Knights Were Cold* (Rouse); *Mud and Sand* (Pratt); *White Wings* (Jeske); *The Pest*

1923 *The Handy Man* (Kerr); *The Noon Whistle* (Jeske); *Under Two Jags* (Jeske); *Pick and Shovel* (Jeske); *Collars and Cuffs* (Jeske); *Kill or Cure* (Pembroke); *Gas and Air* (Jeske); *Wild Bill Hiccup* (Jeske); *Short Orders* (Roach); *A Man about Town* (Jeske); *Roughest Africa* (Cedar); *Frozen Hearts* (Howe); *The Whole Truth*; *Save the Ship* (Roach); *The Soilers* (Cedar); *Scorching Sands* (Roach); *Mother's Joy* (Cedar); *A Dark House*; *Cowboys Cry for It* (Bruckman)

1924 *Smithy* (Jeske); *Postage Due* (Jeske); *Zeb vs. Paprika* (Cedar); *Brothers under the Chin* (Cedar); *Near Dublin* (Cedar); *Rupert of Cole-Slaw* (*Rupert of Hee-Haw*) (Pembroke); *Wide Open Spaces* (Jeske); *Short Kilts* (Jeske); *Mandarin Mix-Up* (Rock and Pembroke); *Detained* (Rock and Pembroke); *Monsieur Don't-Care* (Rock and Pembroke); *West of Hot Dog* (Rock and Pembroke)

1925 *Somewhere in Wrong* (Rock and Pembroke); *Twins* (Rock and Pembroke); *Pie-Eyed* (Rock and Pembroke); *The Snow Hawk* (Rock and Pembroke); *Navy Blue Days* (Rock and Pembroke); *The Sleuth* (Semon and Taurog); *Dr. Pickle and Mr. Pryde* (Rock and Pembroke); *Half a Man* (Rock and Pembroke)

1926   *Atta Boy* (Goulding); *Now I'll Tell One* (Parrott); *Should Tall Men Marry?* (Bruckman); *Eve's Love Letters* (McCarey); *Get 'em Young* (Guiol); *On the Front Page*

1927   *Seeing the World* (McGowan)

Films Directed by Laurel:

1925   *Yes, Yes, Nanette* (co-d with Hennecke); *Unfriendly Enemies* (co-d with Finlayson); *Moonlight and Noses*; *Wandering Papas*; *Enough to Do*

1926   *On the Front Page* (+ ro); *Madame Mystery* (co-d with Wallace); *Never Too Old* (co-d with Wallace); *The Merry Widower*; *Wise Guys Prefer Brunettes*; *Raggedy Rose* (co-d with Wallace)

Film Co-Produced by Laurel:

1939   *Knight of the Plains* (Newfield)

Films as Actors: Laurel and Hardy—

(shorts)

1917   *A Lucky Dog* (Robbins)

1926   *45 Minutes from Hollywood* (Guiol)

1927   *Duck Soup* (Guiol); *Slipping Wives* (Guiol) (Laurel as handyman; Hardy as butler); *Love 'em and Weep* (Guiol) (Laurel as business associate; Hardy as party guest); *Why Girls Love Sailors* (Guiol) (Laurel as Willie Smelt; Hardy as Second Mate); *The Second Hundred Years* (Guiol) (as convicts); *Call of the Cuckoos* (Bruckman) (as asylum inmates); *Sailors Beware!* (Yates) (Laurel as cab driver; Hardy as purser); *With Love and Hisses* (Guiol) (as recruits); *Sugar Daddies* (Guiol) (Laurel as lawyer; Hardy as butler); *Hats Off* (Yates); *Do Detectives Think?* (Guiol) (as detectives); *Putting Pants on Philip* (Bruckman) (Laurel as Philip; Hardy as J. Piedmont Mumblethunder); *The Battle of the Century* (Bruckman) (Laurel as prize fighter; Hardy as manager); *Should Tall Men Marry?* (Bruckman)

1928   *Leave 'em Laughing* (Bruckman); *Flying Elephants* (Butler); *The Finishing Touch* (Bruckman); *From Soup to Nuts* (Kennedy); *You're Darn Tootin'* (*The Music Blasters*) (Kennedy); *Their Purple Moment* (Parrott); *Should Married Men Go Home?* (Parrott); *Two Tars* (Parrott); *Habeus Corpus* (Parrott); *We Faw Down* (*We Slip Up*) (McCarey); *Early to Bed* (Flynn)

1929   *Liberty* (*Criminals at Large*) (McCarey); *Wrong Again* (McCarey); *That's My Wife* (French); *Big Business* (Horne); *Unaccustomed as We Are* (Foster); *Double Whoopee* (Foster); *Berth Marks* (Foster); *Men of War* (Foster); *Perfect Day* (Parrott); *They Go Boom* (Parrott); *Bacon Grabbers* (Foster) (as process servers); *The Hoose-Gow* (Parrott); *Angora Love* (Foster)

1930   *Night Owls* (Parrott); *Blotto* (Parrott); *Brats* (Parrott) (Laurel as Stanley/Stanley's son; Hardy as Oliver/Oliver's son); *Below Zero* (Parrott); *Hog Wild* (*Aerial Antics*; *Hay Wire*) (Parrott); *The Laurel and Hardy Murder Case* (Parrott); *Another Fine Mess* (Parrott);

1931   *Be Big* (Parrott); *Chickens Come Home* (Horne); *The Stolen Jools* (*The Slippery Pearls*) (McGann) (Laurel as policeman; Hardy as police driver); *Laughing Gravy* (Horne); *Our Wife* (Horne); *Come Clean* (Horne); *One Good Turn* (Horne); *Beau Hunks* (*Beau Chumps*) (Horne); *On the Loose* (Roach)

1932   *Helpmates* (Parrott); *Any Old Port* (Parrott); **The Music Box** (Parrott); *The Chimp* (Parrott); *County Hospital* (Parrott); *Scram!* (McCarey); *Their First Mistake* (George Marshall); *Towed in a Hole* (George Marshall); *Wild Poses* (McGowan)

1933   *Twice Two* (Parrott) (Laurel as Stanley/Mrs. Hardy, + sc; Hardy as Oliver/Mrs. Laurel); *Me and My Pal* (Rogers and French) (+ sc by Laurel); *The Midnight Patrol* (French); *Busy Bodies* (French) (+ sc by Laurel); *Dirty Work* (French)

1934   *Oliver the Eighth* (*The Private Life of Oliver the Eighth*) (French); *Going Bye-Bye!* (Rogers); *Them Thar Hills!* (Rogers) (+ co-sc by Laurel); *The Live Ghost* (Rogers)

1935   *Tit for Tat* (Rogers) (+ sc by Laurel); *The Fixer-Uppers* (Rogers); *Thicker than Water* (Horne) (+ story by Laurel)

1936   *On the Wrong Trek* (Parrott and Law) (as hitchhikers)

1943   *The Tree in a Test Tube* (doc)

(features)

1929   *Hollywood Revue of 1929* (Riesner)

1930   *The Rogue Song* (Lionel Barrymore and Roach) (Laurel as Ali-Bek; Hardy as Murza-Bek)

1931   *Pardon Us* (*Jailbirds*; *Gaol Birds*) (Parrott)

1932   *Pack Up Your Troubles* (George Marshall and McCarey)

1933   *Fra Diavolo* (*The Devil's Brother*; *The Virtuous Tramps*) (Roach and Rogers) (Laurel as Stanlio; Hardy as Olio); *Sons of the Desert* (*Sons of the Legion*; *Fraternally Yours*) (Seiter)

1934   *Hollywood Party* (Boleslawski and Dwan); *Babes in Toyland* (*March of the Wooden Soldiers*; *Laurel and Hardy in Toyland*; *Revenge Is Sweet*; *Wooden Soldiers*) (Meins and Rogers) (Laurel as Stanley Dum; Hardy as Oliver Dee)

1935   *Bonnie Scotland* (Horne) (Laurel as Stanley McLaurel, + co-sc; Hardy as Ollie)

1936   *The Bohemian Girl* (Horne and Rogers); *Our Relations* (Lachman) (Laurel as himself/Alfie Laurel, + pr; Hardy as himself/Bert Hardyl)

1937   *Way Out West* (Horne) (+ pr by Laurel); *Pick a Star* (Sedgwick)

1938   *Swiss Miss* (Blystone); *Block-Heads* (Blystone)

1939   *The Flying Deuces* (A. Edward Sutherland)

1940   *A Chump at Oxford* (Alfred Goulding); *Saps at Sea* (Gordon Douglas)

1941   *Great Guns* (Banks)

1942   *A-Haunting We Will Go* (Werker)

1943   *Air Raid Wardens* (Sedgwick); *Jitterbugs* (St. Clair); *The Dancing Masters* (St. Clair)

1944   *The Big Noise* (St. Clair)

1945   *Nothing but Trouble* (Sam Taylor); *The Bullfighters* (St. Clair)

1951   *Atoll K* (*Robinson Crusoeland*; *Utopia*; *Escapade*) (Joannon)

Selected Compilation Films Featuring Laurel and Hardy:

1957   *The Golden Age of Comedy* (pr: Youngson and Sennett)

1960   *When Comedy Was King* (pr: Youngson)

1963   *Days of Thrills and Laughter* (pr: Youngson); *30 Years of Fun* (pr: Youngson)

1965   *Laurel and Hardy's Laughing Twenties* (pr: Youngson)

1966   *The Crazy World of Laurel and Hardy* (Garry Moore)

1967   *The Further Perils of Laurel and Hardy* (pr: Youngson)

1970   *Four Clowns* (pr: Youngson)

Publications

By LAUREL: articles—

"Laurel without Hardy," interview with Boyd Verb, in *Films in Review* (New York), March 1959.

"An Interview with Stan Laurel," with Larry Goldstein, reprinted in *Pratfall*, vol. 2, no. 2, 1977.

On LAUREL and HARDY: books—

McCabe, John, *Mr. Laurel and Mr. Hardy*, New York, 1961; new ed., 1966.
Borde, Raymonde, and Charles Perrin, *Laurel et Hardy*, Lyon, France, 1965.
Coursodon, Jean-Pierre, *Laurel et Hardy*, Paris, 1965.
Barr, Charles, *Laurel and Hardy*, London, 1967.
Everson, William K., *The Films of Laurel and Hardy*, Secaucus, New Jersey, 1967.
Maltin, Leonard, and others, *The Laurel and Hardy Book*, New York, 1973.
McCabe, John, *The Comedy World of Stan Laurel*, New York, 1974.
Anobile, Richard J., *A Fine Mess* (photographs), New York, 1975.
Lacourbe, Roland, *Laurel et Hardy: au l'enfance de l'art*, Paris, 1975.
McCabe, John, Al Kilgore, and Richard W. Bann, *Laurel and Hardy*, New York, 1975.
Scagnetti, Jack, *The Laurel and Hardy Scrapbook*, Middle Village, New York, 1976.

Giusti, Marco, *Laurel and Hardy*, Venice, 1978.
Gehring, Wes D., *Leo McCarey and the Comic Anti-Hero in American Film*, New York, 1980.
Guiles, Fred, *Stan: The Life of Stan Laurel*, New York, 1980.
Owen-Pawson, Jenny, and Bill Mouland, *Laurel before Hardy*, Kendal, Cumbria, 1984.
Governi, Giancarlo, *Laurel and Hardy: due teste senza cervello*, Turin, 1985.
Jones, Lori S., ed., *Laurel and Hardywood* (special quadruple ed. of *Pratfall* magazine), Universal City, California, 1985.
Pantieri, José, *I magnifica Laurel e Hardy*, Forli, 1986.
Crowther, Bruce, *Laurel and Hardy: Crown Princes of Comedy*, London, 1987.
Skretvedt, Randy, *Laurel and Hardy: The Magic behind the Movies*, Beverly Hills, California, 1987.
Leeflang, Thomas, *The World of Laurel and Hardy*, Leicester, England, 1988.
Smith, Leon, *Following the Comedy Trail: A Guide to Laurel and Hardy and Our Gang Locations*, Los Angeles, 1988.
McCabe, John, *Babe: The Life of Oliver Hardy*, London, 1989.
Nollen, Scott Allen, *The Boys: The Cinematic World of Laurel and Hardy*, Jefferson, North Carolina, 1989.

Stan Laurel and Oliver Hardy

Gehring, Wes D., *Laurel and Hardy: A Bio-Bibliography*, New York, 1990.

Oust, Ken, *Laurel and Hardy in Hull*, Beverley, England, 1990.

Blees, Christian, *Laurel and Hardy: ihr Leben, ihre Filme*, Berlin, 1993.

On LAUREL and HARDY: articles—

Robinson, David, "The Lighter People," in *Sight and Sound* (London), July/September 1954.

Obituary on Hardy, in *New York Times*, 8 August 1957.

Barnes, Peter, "Cuckoo," in *Films and Filming* (London), August 1960.

Roach, Hal, "Living with Laughter," in *Films and Filming* (London), October 1964.

Obituary on Laurel, in *New York Times*, 24 February 1965.

"L. & H. Cult," in *Time* (New York), 14 July 1967.

Pope, Dennis, "Stan Laurel and Oliver Hardy," in *Film* (London), Autumn 1967.

Everson, William K., "The Crazy World of Laurel and Hardy," in *Take One* (Montreal), no. 9, 1968.

Maltin, Leonard, "Laurel and Hardy," in *Movie Comedy Teams*, New York, 1970.

Braucourt, Guy, "Non, Lorèléardi n'est pas mort! (Ah! Ce cher vieil Ollie . . .)," in *Ecran* (Paris), April and May 1972.

Le Gueay, Philippe, "Laurel et Hardy: une allégorie de la catastrophe," in *Positif* (Paris), July/August 1978.

Gehring, Wes, on Leo McCarey and Laurel and Hardy, in *Films in Review* (New York), November 1979; see also issues for February and April 1980.

Classic Images (Indiana, Pennsylvania), July 1981; see also issues for September 1981, July 1982, and April 1984.

Robinson, Jeffrey, "Laurel and Hardy," in *Teamwork: The Cinema's Great Comedy Teams*, New York, 1982.

Anderson, Janice, "Laurel and Hardy," in *History of Movie Comedy*, New York, 1985.

Torgov, S., "Hardy Har Har!," in *American Film* (New York), October 1986.

Kimmel, D., "Life Imprisonment," in *Film Comment* (New York), July/August 1987.

Christon, Lawrence, "The Discreet Charm of Laurel and Hardy," in *Los Angeles Times* (Calendar section), 10 January 1988.

Berglund, B., "Did Stan Laurel Make His Film Debut as Early as 1915?," in *Griffithiana* (Gemona, Italy), September 1988.

*   *   *

Of all the truly great screen clowns of the silent and early sound periods, Laurel and Hardy took longest to gain serious critical recognition, perhaps because, unlike Chaplin and Keaton, they were never their own directors. Nevertheless, Charles Barr's book—one of the most delicate and sensitive works of film criticism so far published, to which this present note is, inevitably, heavily indebted—amply makes amends.

It was their peculiar distinction to be the great comic poets of the mainstream bourgeoisie. Chaplin was always "the tramp;" Lloyd was too genteel to be representative. Fields's character deliberately withdrew into alcoholism and misanthropy; Keaton was by nature—if quite unconsciously and reluctantly—alienated from *everything*. But Stan and Ollie, even when they played convicts or down-and-outs, were incorrigibly addicted to the bourgeois norm. Not that they represented conformity to those norms—not in the least. On the contrary, they dramatize the contradictions of bourgeois life carried to their most extreme. Everything they do is based on contradiction. Totally committed to each other, they are also totally and continuously at odds. Similarly, their apparent total commitment to the norms, mores, manners, conventions, and rituals of bourgeois culture is accompanied by an equally absolute resistance to them. Even when they are not knowingly transgressing (because they can never resist tempta-

tion), they are expressing their discontent, their instinctive refusal to be safely contained, by an extraordinary and virtually continuous barrage of accidents, destruction, misunderstandings and Freudian slips. In this they surely speak, more eloquently than any other comedians, most hilariously and touchingly, for the great mass of human individuals trapped within bourgeois norms (because, like Stan and Ollie, they do not know there are or could be any other), continually trying to adjust, continually, in their behavior, betraying their frustrations and resentment. Laurel and Hardy represent the bourgeois condition simply taken to its logical absurdity.

The main body of their great work lies clearly in the shorts, and it can hardly be accidental that their work during their finest, most consistently brilliant period was under the supervision of Leo McCarey. It is not clear how much McCarey actually contributed, but what *is* clear, is the perfect compatibility: the same contradictions, the same tensions between conformity and anarchy, structure many of McCarey's finest feature films (*Make Way for Tomorrow*, *The Bells of St. Mary's*, *Rally 'round the Flag, Boys!*).

There are extraordinary shorts in which they play tramps, servants, and convicts, in which much of the humor derives from the contradiction between their situation and their inveterate commitment to bourgeois gentility; but perhaps the most fully characteristic are those in which they act out the contradictions directly, in representations of bourgeois marriage, courtship, family, or (as in *Big Business*) capitalist competition. There are "doubling" films: *Brats*, in which they play themselves and their own children, a film about the horrors of "socialization;" and *Twice Two*, in which they play themselves and each other's wives, a film about the horrors of bourgeois marriage. Or there are those in which they try to circumvent the constraint of domesticity: *Helpmates* and, arguably their finest feature-length film, *Sons of the Desert*. As Charles Barr argues, the essence of their subversiveness lies in their connotations of the childish or childlike: they are children arrested somewhere in the middle of the process of socialization, still committed to the pleasure principle but extremely uneasy about it, vaguely grasping the reality principle but instinctively resistant to its domination, more polymorphously perverse than homosexual (for all their scenes in bed together), preferring each other's company to anyone else's (including, and especially, their wives') because, although continually at loggerheads, they know they are two of a kind (however different in physique and temperament), in their reluctant, unwitting, but absolute incorrigible refusal to be definitively integrated within the culture they also represent.

—Robin Wood

LÉAUD, Jean-Pierre

Nationality: French. **Born:** Paris, 5 May 1944; son of the scriptwriter Pierre Léaud and the actress Jacqueline Pierreux. **Career:** Child actor: film debut in *Les Quatre Cents Coups* by Truffaut, 1959; subsequently made several other films with Truffaut, and worked as assistant to Truffaut and Godard; 1967—stage debut at Avignon Festival; 1986—received suspended prison sentence for assaulting 80-year old neighbor with flowerpot. **Awards:** Best Actor, Berlin Festival, for *Masculin-féminin*, 1966.

Films as Actor:

1959   *Les Quatre Cents Coups* (*The 400 Blows*) (Truffaut) (as Antoine Doinel); *Le Testament d'Orphée* (*The Testament of Orpheus*) (Cocteau) (as schoolboy)

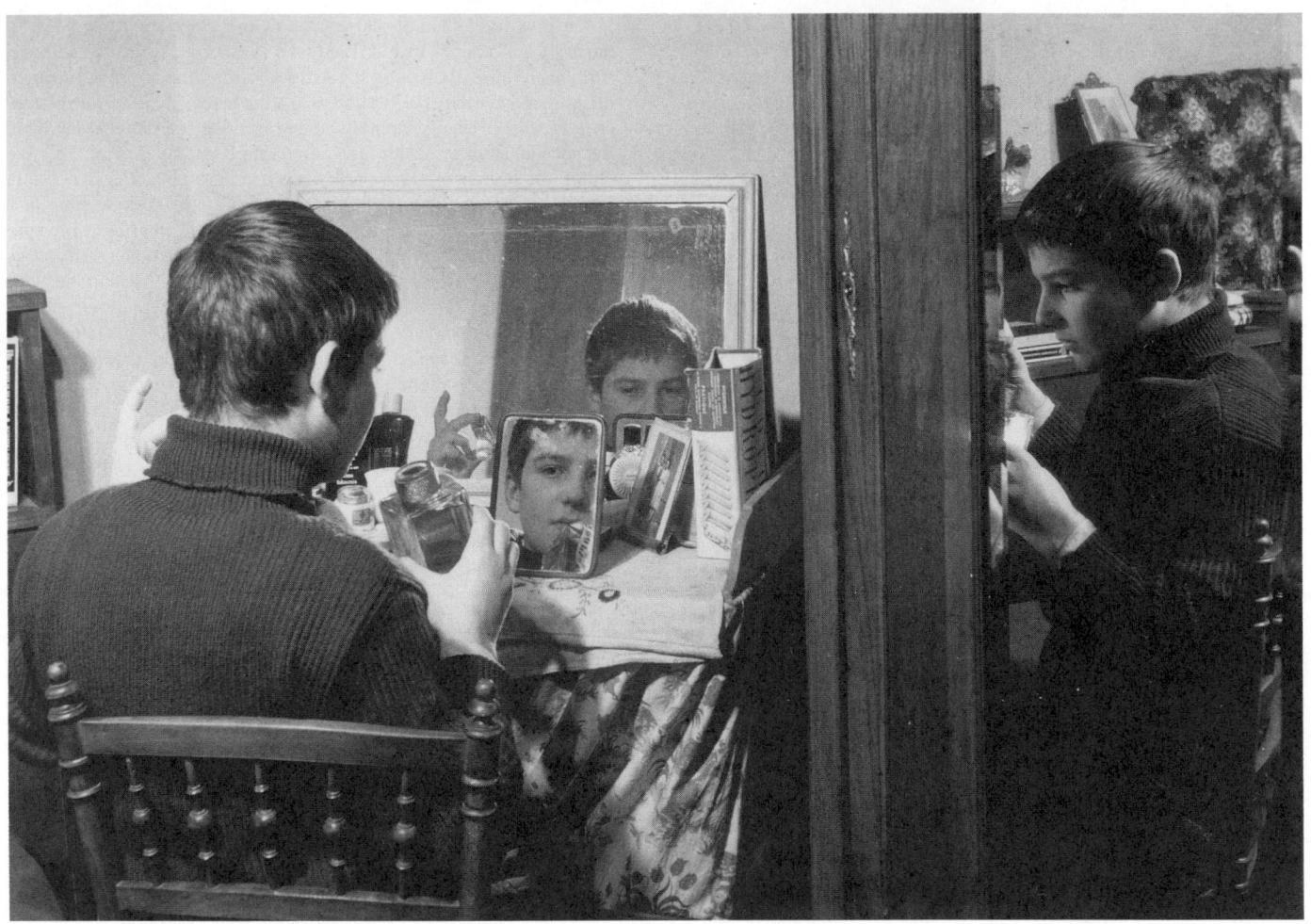

Jean-Pierre Léaud in *Les Quatre Cents Coups*

1962 "France" ep. of *L'Amour à vingt ans* (*Love at Twenty*) (Truffaut) (as Antoine Doinel)

1965 *Pierrot le Fou* (*Peter the Crazy*) (Godard) (as young man in cinema); *Mata-Hari Agent H.21* (Richard)

1966 *Masculin-féminin* (*Masculine-Feminine*) (Godard) (as Paul); *Le Départ* (Skolimowski) (as Marc); *Made in U.S.A.* (Godard) (as Donald Siegel)

1967 *La Chinoise* (Godard) (as Guillaume Meister); "Anticipation" ep. of *Les Plus Vieux Métier du monde* (*The Oldest Profession*) (Godard) (as bellboy); "Le Pere Noël a les yeux bleus" ("Santa Claus Has Blue Eyes") ep. of *Les Mauvaises Fréquentations* (*Bad Company*) (Eustache) (as Daniel); **Le Week-end** (Godard) (as Saint-Just/man in phone booth)

1968 *Le Gai Savoir* (*The Joy of Learning*) (Godard—for TV) (as Emile Rousseau); *Baisers volés* (*Stolen Kisses*) (Truffaut) (as Antoine Doinel); *Dialog* (*Dialogue*) (Skolimowski)

1969 *Porcile* (*Pigsty*; *Pigpen*) (Pasolini); *Los herederos* (*The Heirs*) (Diegues)

1970 *Der leone have sept cabecas* (*The Lion Has Seven Heads*) (Rocha); *Domicile conjugal* (*Bed and Board*) (Truffaut) (as Antoine Doinel)

1971 *Les Deux Anglaises et le continent* (*Two English Girls*; *Anne and Muriel*) (Truffaut) (as Claude Roc)

1972 **Last Tango in Paris** (*Ultimo tango a Parigi*) (Bertolucci) (as Tom)

1973 *Une Aventure de Billy le Kid* (Moullet); *Le Maman et la putain* (*The Mother and the Whore*) (Eustache) (as Alexandre); *La*

Nuit américaine (*Day for Night*) (Truffaut) (as Alphonse); *Spectre* (*Out One—Out Two*) (Rivette)

1976 *Les Lolas de Lola* (Dubois); *Umarmungen und andere Sachen* (Richter)

1979 *L'Amour en fuite* (*Love on the Run*) (Truffaut) (as Antoine Doinel)

1982 *Pour Bonnie* (Muret)

1983 *Rebelote* (Richard)

1984 *Rue Fontaine* (Garrel); *Paris vu par . . . 20 ans après* (Akerman)

1985 *Détective* (Godard) (as Inspector Neveu); *L'Education sentimentale* (Cravenne); *Csak egy mozi* (Sandor) (as Peter); *Herbe rouge* (Kast—for TV)

1986 *Corps et biens* (Jacquot) (as Marcel); *Grandeur et Decadence d'un petit commerce du cinéma* (Godard—for TV)

1987 *Boran—Zeit zum zielen* (Zuta); *Keufs* (Balasko); *Osseg Oder die Warheit uber Hansel und Gretel* (Klahn) (as Georg Osseg)

1988 *Jane B. par Agnès V.* (*A. V. sur J. B.*) (Varda); *36 Fillette* (Breillat) (as Boris Golovine)

1989 *Bunker Palace Hotel* (Bilal) (as Solal); *Femme de papier* (Schiffman) (as Marc)

1990 *I Hired a Contract Killer* (Aki Kaurismaki) (as Henri Boulanger)

1991 *Treasure Island* (as Midas/narrator); *Paris s'eveille* (*Paris Awakens*; *Paris at Dawn*) (as Clement); *J'Embrasse Pas* (Téchiné); *C'est la vie* (Cohn-Bendit and Steinbach)

1992 *Missä on Musette?* (*Where Is Musette?*) (Nieminen and Vesteri) (as himself)

1993   *La Vie de Boheme* (*Bohemian Life*) (Aki Kaurismaki) (as
        Blancheron); *La Naissance de l'amour* (*The Birth of Love*)
        (Garrel) (as Marcus); *De force avec d'autres* (Simon Reggiani)
1994   *Personne ne m'aime* (*Nobody Loves Me*) (Vernoux) (as Lucien)
1995   *Les Cent et une Nuits* (*A Hundred and One Nights*) (Varda) (as
        Furtive and Friendly Appearance)
1996   *Mon homme* (Blier) (as Claude); *Irma Vep* (Assayas)

Films as Assistant Director:

1964   *La Peau douce* (*The Soft Skin*) (Truffaut); *Une Femme mariée*
        (*The Married Woman*) (Godard)
1965   *Alphaville* (*Une étrange aventure de Lemmy Caution*;
        Alphaville: A Strange Adventure of Lemmy Caution; *Tarzan
        versus I.B.M.*) (Godard)

Publications

By LÉAUD: articles—

"Getting beyond the Looking Glass," interview with Jan Dawson, in
    Sight and Sound (London), Winter 1973-74.
Interview with Nan Robertson, in *New York Times*, 22 March 1985.
Interview with F. Revault d'Allonnes, in *Cinéma* (Paris), 23 May
    1986.

On LÉAUD: articles—

The Velvet Light Trap (Madison, Wisconsin), Winter 1972/73.
Cahiers du Cinéma (Paris), September 1983.
Romney, Jonathan, in *Guardian* (London), 14 February 1991.

*   *   *

Jean-Pierre Léaud is best known for his work with the director
François Truffaut, who chose him, at the age of 14, to portray the
young Antoine Doinel in *Les Quatre Cents Coups*. Léaud went on to
play Doinel in four more films over the next 20 years, creating an
unprecedented cinematic portrait of a character's development from
adolescence to adulthood. Léaud has also worked extensively with
Jean-Luc Godard, appearing in several of the director's most acclaimed
films. His association with both filmmakers made Léaud one of the
key actors of the influential French New Wave, as well as a familiar
figure in international cinema.

Léaud's long collaboration with Truffaut has had an immeasurable
impact on his career, and it is as Antoine Doinel that the actor has
given his most memorable performances. The character of Antoine
represents Truffaut's public—and highly personal—examination of
his own life, and Léaud has become, in effect, the director's alter ego.
In *Les Quatre Cents Coups* Truffaut presents a scathing record of his
own unhappy childhood, and Léaud captures perfectly the humor and
pain of misunderstood adolescence. This is childhood's dark side, and
Truffaut's famous freeze-frame of the runaway Léaud's haunting young
face at the film's conclusion is one of the classic images of modern
cinema. The later films adopt a much lighter tone as Antoine encounters love, marriage, fatherhood, and, finally, divorce, and Léaud's
performances provide an engaging combination of humor, intensity,
and hopeless romanticism. In *Baisers volés* and *Domicile conjugal*
Antoine pursues and weds the bemused Claude Jade, yet there is an
underlying strain of self-absorption in the character that will eventually end the relationship in *L'Amour en fuite*. Léaud manages to retain
Antoine's boyish appeal even as he reveals himself to be ill-equipped
to deal with the responsibilities of adult life.

The qualities Léaud displays in the Doinel films are also present in
much of his other work. In Truffaut's Academy Award-winning *La
Nuit américaine*, the young love-struck actor who asks "Are women
magic?" might easily be Antoine, while the hero of *Les Deux Anglaises
et le continent* shares Doinel's single-minded romantic obsessions.
Léaud is an actor of decidedly limited range, and he is most effective
within the framework of a particular character type. It is impossible
to think of him in the wide spectrum of roles open to a De Niro or a
Depardieu; he is, rather, a performer capable of bringing to life specific qualities in the characters he plays. The casting of Léaud as
Doinel was a fortuitous one, both for Truffaut, who found in the actor
the ideal personification of his autobiographical creation, and for
Léaud, who was presented with a part tailor-made for his talents.

Léaud's work for other directors, among them Godard, Bertolucci,
and Pasolini, also relies on his familiar mannerisms and style. There is
something inherently (and intentionally) amusing in Léaud's intensity, and he brings a wry edge of humor to such socio-political com-
mentaries as Godard's *Masculin-Féminin*, *La Chinoise*, and *Le Weekend*. In Bertolucci's *Last Tango in Paris* he appears as Maria Schneider's
boyfriend, performing a clever send-up of a self-important young
filmmaker as he follows her endlessly with his camera. All of these
roles bear the characteristic stamp of Léaud's passionate, ingenuous
personality.

—Janet E. Lorenz

LEE, Bruce

Nationality: American. **Born:** Lee Yuen Kam in San Francisco, California, 27 November 1940, of Chinese parents. **Education:** Attended
the University of Washington, Seattle. **Family:** Married Linda (Lee),
son the actor Brandon Lee (deceased). **Career:** Lived in Hong Kong
as a child, and made a number of films as a child actor; appeared as
Kato in the *Green Hornet* TV series, 1966-67, and also in *Batman*,
Ironside, *Blondie*, and *Longstreet* series, usually as a karate practitioner or teacher; from 1971, associated with series of kung-fu films
made in Hong Kong; he directed one himself (released posthumously).
Died: In Hong Kong, 20 July 1973.

Films as Actor:

(as Lee Siu Lung)

1946   *The Birth of Mankind*
1948   *My Son A-Chen*
1949   *Kid Cheung*
1951   *Infancy*
1953   *A Mother's Tears*; *Blame It on Father*; *Countless Families* (*A
        Myriad Homes*)
1954   *In the Face of Demolition*
1955   *An Orphan's Tragedy*; *We Owe It to Our Children*; *Orphan's
        Song*
1956   *Those Wise Guys Who Fool Around*; *Too Late for Divorce*
1957   *Thunderstorm*
1958   *The Orphan* (*The Orphan Ah-Sam*)
1961   *A Goose Alone in the World*

(as Bruce Lee)

1969   *Marlowe* (Bogart) (as Winslow Wong)
1971   *Fists of Fury* (*The Big Boss*) (Lo Wei) (as Chen)

1972 *The Chinese Connection* (*Fist of Fury*) (Lo Wei) (as Chen Chen)
1973 *Enter the Dragon* (*The Deadly Three*) (Clouse) (as Lee); *The Unicorn Fist*
1974 *Kato and the Green Hornet* (compilation of three *Green Hornet* episodes) (as Kato)
1979 *Game of Death* (*Bruce Lee's Game of Death*) (Clouse) (as Billy Lo)
1990 *The Best of the Martial Arts Films* (Weintraub—compilation)

Film as Actor, Director, and Scriptwriter:

1973 *Return of the Dragon* (*The Way of the Dragon*) (as Tang Lung)

Other Films:

1969 *The Wrecking Crew* (Karlson) (karate adviser)
1979 *Circle of Iron* (*The Silent Flute*) (co-story)

Publications

By LEE: books—

Chinese Gung Fu: The Philosophical Art of Self Defense, Oakland, California, 1965.
Tao of Jeet Kune Do, Burbank, California, 1975.
Bruce Lee's Fighting Method: Advanced Techniques, with M. Uyehara, Burbank, California, 1977.
Bruce Lee's Fighting Method: Basic Training, with M. Uyehara, Burbank, California, 1977.

By LEE: articles—

"Bruce Lee: The Final Screen Test," interview with C. Golden, in *Interview* (New York), November 1974.
Interview with Liu Chia-Liang, in *Cahiers du Cinéma* (Paris), September 1984.

On LEE: books—

Block, Alex Ben, *The Legend of Bruce Lee*, New York, 1974.
Bruce Lee, King of Kung Fu, edited by Lynne Waites, London, 1974.
Dennis, Felix, *Bruce Lee, King of Kung Fu*, London, 1974.
Lee, Linda, *Bruce Lee: The Only Man I Knew*, New York, 1975.
Château, René, *Bruce Lee: La Légende du petit dragon*, Paris, 1976.
Clouse, Robert, *Bruce Lee: The Biography*, Burbank, California, 1988.
Uyehara, M., *Bruce Lee: The Incomparable Fighter*, Burbank, California, 1988.
Lee, Linda, and Tom Bleecker, *The Bruce Lee Story*, Burbank, California, 1989.
Thomas, Bruce, *Bruce Lee*, New York, 1993.
Chunovic, Louis, *Bruce Lee: The Tao of the Dragon Warrior*, New York, 1996.

On LEE: articles—

Flanigan, B. P., "Kung Fu Krazy, or The Invasion of the 'Chop Suey Easterns'," in *Cineaste* (New York), vol. 6, no. 3, 1974.
Kaminsky, S. M., "Kung Fu Film as Ghetto Myth," in *Journal of Popular Film* (Bowling Green, Ohio), Spring 1974.
Ochs, P., "Requiem for a Dragon Departed," in *Take One* (Montreal), May 1974.
Moore, J., "I Was Bruce Lee's Voice," in *Take One* (Montreal), March 1975.
Braucourt, G., "Bruce Lee, superstar posthume," in *Ecran* (Paris), April 1975.

Gauthier, C., "Quand Superman se fit Chinois," and "Bruce Lee: repères biographiques et filmographiques," by D. Sauvaget, in *Image et Son* (Paris), March 1976.
Chiao, Hsiung-Ping, "Bruce Lee: His Influence on the Evolution of the Kung Fu Genre," in *Journal of Popular Film and Television* (Washington, D.C.), Spring 1981.
Appelo, Tim, "Tears of the Dragon," in *Entertainment Weekly* (New York), 14 May 1993.

On LEE: films—

Bruce Lee: The Legend, documentary, 1984.
Bruce Lee: The Man/The Myth, film biography, 1984.
Bruce Lee: Curse of the Dragon, documentary, 1993.
Dragon: The Bruce Lee Story, directed by Rob Cohen, 1993.

*   *   *

Bruce Lee was a phenomenon—a martial artist who, as an actor, became the hero and teacher of millions. As a child, Lee appeared in at least 20 Hong Kong film productions. Pursuing a career there and in the United States as a martial artist, Lee became well known and frequently taught actors, developing his own style of martial arts known as Jeet Kune Do. Due to his reputation, he was offered the role of Kato in the television series *The Green Hornet*.

After a few small parts in American films, Lee's breakthrough came when he returned to Hong Kong with his family in 1970. Due to the popularity of *The Green Hornet*, Lee found himself greeted by Hong Kong citizens as a local hero. Raymond Chow, the founder of Golden Harvest Productions, saw in Lee the great potential of a superstar and signed him for a two-film contract. With the immense box-office success of both *Fists of Fury* and *The Chinese Connection*, Lee went on to make his first English-language production, *Enter the Dragon*. Three months after the completion of the film and one month before its premiere, Lee's sudden death at the moment of his emerging international stardom shocked and saddened the world.

Another explanation for Lee's status as a cult figure may have something to do with his screen image. Because he was physically a small man, with the persona of a shy incompetent or a bumbling boy-next-door, it was hard to imagine that he could destroy any number of armed opponents singlehandedly. To many, Lee was the avenger of the underprivileged and oppressed, the "little man" rising up to battle the corruption surrounding him. He was a member of an oppressed minority who reflected the frustrations of minorities everywhere; he was the underdog who came out on top.

The 1990s have seen not only Jet Li's remake of *Fists of Fury* but also Jackie Chan's breakthrough in the United States with *Rumble in the Bronx*; like Lee, in the late 1970s Chan was discovered by Raymond Chow, who groomed him as a new Bruce Lee. People still remember Lee. A new generation of kung-fu movie stars, though employing different styles and incorporating more modern techniques, still have to prove that they can match up with—in terms of physical agility and fighting ability—the legendary Bruce Lee.

—Maryann Oshana, updated by Guo-Juin Hong

LEE, Christopher

Nationality: British. **Born:** Christopher Frank Carandini Lee in London, 27 May 1922. **Education:** Attended Summerfield Preparatory School; Wellington College. **Military Service:** Served in the Royal Air Force and in British Intelligence during World War II; mentioned in dispatches, 1944; **Family:** Married Birgit Kroencke, 1961, daughter: Christina. **Career:** 1947-51—contract with J. Arthur Rank: film debut in *Corridor of Mirrors*, 1948; early 1950s—appeared regularly in the TV series *Douglas Fairbanks Presents*; 1957—first horror film role, that of the Creature in *The Curse of Frankenstein*; many later horror films, often for Hammer Productions; 1972—founder, Charlemagne Productions, Ltd.; 1991—in TV mini-series *Sherlock Holmes and the Incident at Victoria Falls*. **Awards:** Officier, Ordre des Arts et Lettres, France, 1973. **Agent:** c/o James Sharkey and Associates Ltd., 21 Golden Square, London W1R 3PA, England.

Films as Actor:

1948   *Corridor of Mirrors* (Terence Young) (as Charles); *Scott of the Antarctic* (Frend) (as Bernard Day); *Hamlet* (Olivier); *One Night with You* (Terence Young); *Penny and the Pownall Case* (Hand) (as Jonathan Blair); *A Song for Tomorrow* (Fisher) (as Auguste); *Saraband for Dead Lovers* (*Saraband*) (Dearden); *My Brother's Keeper* (Roome)

1949   *Trottie True* (*The Gay Lady*) (Hurst)

1950   *Prelude to Fame* (McDonnell) (as newsman); *They Were Not Divided* (Terence Young) (as Lewis)

1951   *Captain Horatio Hornblower* (Walsh) (as Spanish Captain); *Valley of the Eagles* (Terence Young) (as detective)

1952   *Paul Temple Returns* (Rogers) (as Sir Felix Reybourne); *The Crimson Pirate* (Siodmak); *Top Secret* (Zampi)

1953   *Innocents in Paris* (Parry); *Babes in Baghdad* (Ulmer); *Moulin Rouge* (Huston)

1955   *That Lady* (Terence Young) (as Captain); *Man in Demand* (McDonald); *Crossroads* (Fitchen—short) (as the ghost); *The Dark Avengers* (*The Warriors*) (Levin) (as Captain of the Guard); *Storm over the Nile* (*None but the Brave*) (Korda and Young) (as Karaga Pasha); *The Cockleshell Heroes* (Ferrer); *Private's Progress* (Boulting) (as German officer)

1956   *Port Afrique* (Maté) (as Franz Vermes); *Beyond Mombasa* (George Marshall) (as Gil Rossi); *The Battle of the River Plate* (*Pursuit of the Graf Spee*) (Powell and Pressburger) (as Manola); *Moby Dick* (Huston); *Alias John Preston* (MacDonald) (title role)

1957   *The Curse of Frankenstein* (Fisher) (as the Creature); *The Traitors* (*The Accursed*) (McCarthy); *Fortune Is a Woman* (*She Played with Fire*) (Gilliatt) (as Charles Highbury); *Bitter Victory* (Ray) (as Sgt. Barney); *Ill Met by Moonlight* (*Night Ambush*) (Powell and Pressburger)

1958   *A Tale of Two Cities* (Thomas) (as Marquis de St. Evremonde); *The Battle of the V 1* (*Unseen Heroes*) (Scwell) (as Brunner); *The Truth about Women* (Box) (as François); *Dracula* (*Horror of Dracula*) (Fisher) (title role); *Corridors of Blood* (Day) (as Resurrection Joe)

1959   *The Hound of the Baskervilles* (Fisher) (as Sir Henry Baskerville); *The Man Who Could Cheat Death* (Fisher) (as Dr. Pierre Gerard); *Tempi duri per vampiri* (*Uncle Was a Vampire*; *Hard Times for Vampires*) (Steno); *The Mummy*

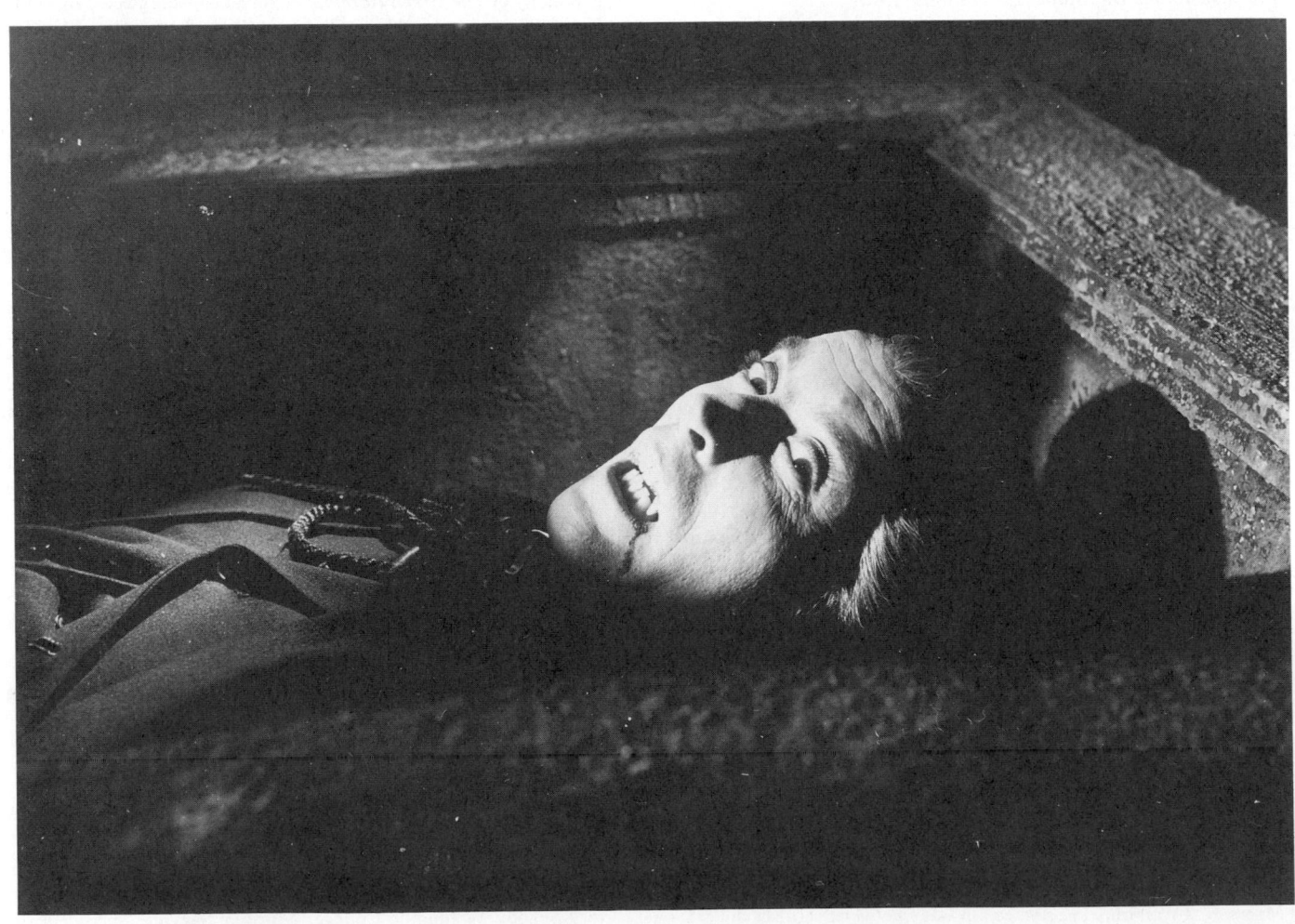

Christopher Lee in *Dracula* (1958)

(Fisher) (as Kharis); *Treasure of San Teresa* (*Hot Money Girls*) (Rakoff) (as Jaeger)

1960 *The City of the Dead* (*Horror Motel*) (Moxey) (as Professor Driscoll); *Too Hot to Handle* (Terence Young) (as Novak); *Beat Girl* (*Wild for Kicks*) (Greville) (as Kenny); *The Two Faces of Doctor Jekyll* (*House of Fright*) (Fisher) (as Paul Allen); *The Hands of Orlac* (*Les Mains d'Orlac*) (Gréville) (as Nero)

1961 *Taste of Fear* (*Scream of Fear*) (Holt) (as Dr. Gerrard); *The Terror of the Tongs* (Bushell) (as Chung King); *The Devil's Agent* (Carstairs) (as Baron von Staub); *Das Rätsel der röten Orchidee* (*The Puzzle of the Red Orchid*) (Ashley); *Ercole al centro della terra* (*Hercules at the Center of the Earth*; *Haunted World*) (Bava) (as Lichas)

1962 *Devil's Daffodil* (*Das Geheimnis der gelben Narzissen*) (Rathony) (as Ling Chu; *The Pirates of Blood River* (Gilling) (as La Roche); *Sherlock Holmes und das Halsband des Todes* (*Sherlock Holmes and the Deadly Necklace*) (Fisher and Witherstein) (title role)

1963 *La cripta de l'incubo* (*Terror in the Crypt*) (Mastrocinque) (as Count Karnstein); *La frusta e il corpo* (*Night Is the Phantom, What!*) (Bava) (as Kurt Menliff)

1964 *The Devil-Ship Pirates* (Sharp) (as Captain Robeles); *La vergine de Norimberga* (*Horror Castle*; *Castle of Terror*) (Dawson) (as Erich); *The Gorgon* (Fisher) (as Professor Carl Meister); *Dr. Terror's House of Horrors* (Francis) (as Franklyn Marsh); *Il castello dei morti viva* (*Castle of the Living Dead*) (Ricci and Wise) (as Count Drago)

1965 *She* (Day) (as Billali); *The Face of Fu Manchu* (Sharp) (title role); *The Skull* (Francis) (as Sir Matthew Phillips)

1966 *Dracula—Prince of Darkness* (Fisher) (title role); *Rasputin the Mad Monk* (Sharp) (title role); *The Brides of Fu Manchu* (Sharp) (title role)

1967 *Circus of Fear* (*Psycho-Circus*) (Moxey) (as Gregor); *Theatre of Death* (*Blood Fiend*) (Gallu) (as Phillipe Darvas); *Five Golden Dragons* (Summers) (as Dragon); *The Vengeance of Fu Manchu* (Summers) (title role); *Die Schlangengrube und das Pendel* (*The Blood Demon*) (Reinl) (as Count Regula); *Victims of Terror* (*Victims of Vesuvius*) (Bain—short); *Night of the Big Heat* (*Island of the Burning Damned*) (Fisher) (as Hanson)

1968 *The Devil Rides Out* (*The Devil's Bride*) (Fisher) (as Duc de Richleau); *The Face of Eve* (*Eve*) (Summers) (as Colonel Stuart); *Curse of the Crimson Altar* (*The Crimson Cult*) (Sewell) (as J. D. Morley); *The Blood of Fu Manchu* (*Kiss and Kill*) (Franco) (title role); *Dracula Has Risen from the Grave* (Francis) (title role)

1969 *The Oblong Box* (Hessler) (as Dr. Neuhartt); *The Magic Christian* (McGrath) (as Dracula); *Vampir* (Portobella)

1970 *Scream and Scream Again* (Hessler) (as Fremont); *The Castle of Fu Manchu* (Franco) (title role); *Julius Caesar* (Burge) (as Artemidorus); *Taste the Blood of Dracula* (Sasdy) (title role); *The Private Life of Sherlock Holmes* (Wilder) (as Mycroft Holmes); *The Scars of Dracula* (Baker) (title role); *The House That Dripped Blood* (Duffell) (as John Reid); *I, Monster* (Weeks) (as Marlowe); *Eugenie—The Story of Her Journey into Perversion* (*Philosophy of the Boudoir*) (Franco) (as Dolmance); *El processo de las brujas* (*Throne of Fire*; *The Bloody Judge*; *Night of the Blood Monster*) (Franco) (as Lord Chief Justice); *El umbracle* (Portobella); *One More Time* (Lewis) (bit role)

1971 *Hannie Caulder* (Kennedy) (as Bailey); *El Conde Dracula* (*Count Dracula*) (Franco) (title role); *In Search of Dracula* (Floyd—doc) (title role/narrator)

1972 *The Creeping Flesh* (Francis) (as James Hildern); *Dracula A.D. 1972* (Gibson) (title role); *Death Line* (*Raw Meat*) (Sherman) (as Stratton-Villiers); *Nothing but the Night* (Sasdy) (as Colonel Bingham)

1973 *The Satanic Rites of Dracula* (*Count Dracula and His Vampire Brides*) (Gibson) (title role); *The Three Musketeers* (*The Queen's Jewels*) (Lester) (as Rochefort); *The Wicker Man* (Hardy) (as Lord Summerisle); *Evlalie quitte les champs* (*Le Boucher, la star, et l'orpheline*; *The Star, The Orphan, and the Butcher*) (Savary) (as Van Krig); *Poor Devil* (Sheerer—for TV) (title role)

1974 *Horror Express* (Martin) (as Professor Alex Saxton); *The Four Musketeers* (*Revenge of Milady*) (Lester) (as Rochefort); *The Man with the Golden Gun* (Hamilton) (as Scaramanga); *Dark Places* (Sharp) (as Dr. Ian Mandeville)

1975 *Diagnosis: Murder* (*Diagnosis for Murder*) (Hayers—for TV); *To the Devil a Daughter* (Sykes) (as Father Michael Rayner); *Killer Force* (*The Diamond Mercenaries*) (Guest) (as Major Chilton); *Whispering Death* (Goslar) (as Albino); *Revenge of the Dead* (Evan Lee) (as narrator); *Dracula's Son* (*Dracula, père et fils*) (Molinaro) (as Dracula)

1976 *Alien Encounter* (*Starship Invasions*) (Hunt—for TV) (as Capt. Ramses)

1977 *Airport '77* (Jameson) (as Martin Wallace); *Meatcleaver Massacre* (Evan Lee)

1978 *End of the World* (Hayes) (as Father Pergado); *Caravans* (Fargo) (as Sardar Khan); *The Passage* (Thompson) (as gypsy); *Return to Witch Mountain* (Hough) (as Dr. Victor Gamon); *The Silent Flute* (*Circle of Iron*) (Moore) (as Zetan); *Jaguar Lives!* (Pintoff) (as Adam Cain); *Bear Island* (Sharp) (as Professor Lechinski); *The Pirate* (Annakin—for TV) (as Samir)

1979 *1941* (Spielberg) (as Captain von Kleinschmidt); *Nutcracker Fantasy* (Takeo Nakamura—animation) (as voice); *An Arabian Adventure* (Connor) (as Caliph Alquazar)

1980 *The Salamander* (Zinner—for TV); *Once upon a Spy* (Nagy—for TV) (as Marcus Valorium); *Rally* (*Safari 3000*; *Two in the Bush*) (Hurwitz) (as Lorenzo Borgia); *Serial* (Persky) (as Luckman Skull)

1981 *A Desperate Case*; *An Eye for an Eye* (Carver) (as Morgan Canfield); *Dance—Steigler & Steigler*

1982 *Charles and Diana: A Royal Love Story* (Goldstone—for TV) (as Prince Philip); *The Last Unicorn* (Rankin and Bass) (as voice of King Haggard); *Massarati and the Brain* (Hart)

1983 *House of the Long Shadows* (Walker) (as Corrigan); *The Keeper* (Drake); *The Return of Captain Invincible* (Mora) (as Mr. Midnight)

1984 *The Far Pavilions* (Duffell—for TV) (as Kaka-ji Rao); *Rosebud Beach Hotel* (Hurwitz) (as King)

1985 *The Howling II: Your Sister Is a Werewolf* (Mara) (as Stefan Crosscoe)

1986 *The Disputation* (Sax); *Shaka Zulu* (Faure); *Desperate Moves* (Hellman) (as Dr. Boxer)

1987 *The Girl* (Mattson) (as Peter Storm); *Jocks* (Carver) (as President White); *Mio, moy Mio* (*Mio in the Land of Faraway*) (Grammatikov) (as Kato)

1989 *The Return of the Musketeers* (Lester) (as Rochefort); *Murder Story* (Arno); *Treasure Island* (Fraser C. Heston) (as Blind Pew)

1990 *Gremlins II: The New Batch* (Dante) (as Dr. Catheter); *The Rainbow Thief* (Jodorowsky) (as Uncle Rudolf); *Honeymoon Academy* (Quintano); *L'avaro* (*The Miser*) (Cervi); *Il monastero* (*The Monastery*) (de Simone); *Shogun Mayeda* (Hessler); *Sherlock Holmes and the Leading Lady* (Sasdy) (as Sherlock Holmes)

1991   *Curse III: Blood Sacrifice* (Barton) (as Dr. Pearson)
1992   *Double Vision* (Knights) (as Mr. Bernard); *Journey of Honor* (Hessler) (as King Philip); *Jackpot* (as Cedric)
1993   *Alistair MacLean's Death Train* (Jackson—for TV) (as General Konstantin Benin); *Cybereden* (Orfini) (as Cedric)
1994   *Bandit: Bandit Goes Country* (for TV); *The No-Tell Hotel*; *Police Academy 7: Mission to Moscow* (Metter) (as Commandent Rakov); *Funny Man* (Sprackling) (as Callum Chance)
1995   *A Feast at Midnight* (Justin Hardy) (as Major Longfellow/ Raptor)
1996   *Im Brunnen der Traeume* (Lamberto Bava—for TV)

Publications

By LEE: books—

Christopher Lee's Treasury of Terror, London, 1966.
Christopher Lee's New Chamber of Horrors, London, 1974.
Christopher Lee's Archives of Horror, London, volume 1, 1975, and volume 2, 1976.
Tall, Dark and Gruesome (autobiography), London, 1977.
Lurking Shadows: An Anthology, edited with Michael Parry, 1979.
The Great Villains, London, 1979.

By LEE: articles—

Interview, in *L'Ecran Fantastique* (Paris), July/August 1984.
Interview with D. Parra and P. Ross, in *Revue du Cinéma* (Paris), May 1989.
"Interview with the Ex-Vampire," interview with R. Valley, in *Scarlet Street*, Fall 1991 and Winter 1992.
"Horror after Hammer," interview with D. Fischer, in *Midnight Marquee*, Summer 1993.
"Christopher and His Kind," interview with Glenn Kenny, in *TV Guide*, 24 September 1994.

On LEE: books—

Pirie, David, *Heritage of Horror: The English Gothic Cinema 1946-1972*, London, 1973.
Eyles, Allen, Robert Adkinson, and Nicholas Fry, *The House of Horror: The Story of Hammer Films*, London, 1973; rev. ed., 1973.
Pohle, Robert Jr., and Douglas C. Hart, *The Films of Christopher Lee*, Metuchen, New Jersey, 1983.
McCarty, John, *Splatter Movies: Breaking the Last Taboo of the Screen*, New York, 1984.
McCarty, John, *The Modern Horror Film*, New York, 1990.
McCarty, John, *The Fearmakers*, New York, 1994.
Miller, Mark A., *Christopher Lee and Peter Cushing and Horror Cinema*, Jefferson, North Carolina, 1995.

On LEE: articles—

Current Biography 1975, New York, 1975.
Ecran (Paris), December 1978.
Del Valle, D., "Tall, Dark and Gruesome," in *Films and Filming* (London), September 1985.

*   *   *

Since the mid-1950s Christopher Lee's name has been synonymous with horror, and Hammer horror in particular. It is a pity, although perhaps inevitable, that his association with one of the most critically despised and derided of all film genres has tended to obscure the quality of his performances within numerous horror productions and his activities elsewhere.

Christopher Lee's entrance into the acting profession was hardly an auspicious one. With only minimal acting experience and through the assistance of family contacts, he managed in 1947 to secure for himself a place at what came to be known as the Rank Charm School, an institution devised by British film tycoon J. Arthur Rank to foster and groom new acting talent. There followed nearly ten years of undistinguished small roles in films, television, and the theater, with Lee quickly establishing himself as an actor who did not fit readily into any of the accepted categories for British film actors: too tall (6' 4") to be a matinee idol, with looks altogether too striking to be a character performer.

But with Hammer's 1956 production of *The Curse of Frankenstein*, British cinema finally found a place for Lee's talents. Cast as the Creature, Lee managed through skillful mime to convey a real sense of physical pain and suffering. While not a performance to rival Karloff's classic Monster from the 1930s (Hammer's filmmakers would subsequently be much more interested in Baron Frankenstein himself rather than his inhuman progeny), it did earn Lee a place in the Hammer team and ensured that he would be a key player in that company's enormously successful construction of a recognizably British horror cinema.

The two most distinctive features of Lee's acting style as revealed in the Hammer films are his ability to project a sense of physicality through stance and gesture and his deep, sonorous voice. These two elements were combined to perfection in Hammer's version of *Dracula*, the film that finally made Lee a star. In what was one of his most meticulous performances, Lee endowed the vampire count with an overwhelmingly sexual presence that was light years away from Bela Lugosi's more melodramatic posturings in the part.

Lee continued to work in the horror genre throughout the 1960s and 1970s, playing a variety of authority figures, both good and evil, in some of the most noteworthy horror films of the period—*The Gorgon*, *The Devil Rides Out*, *The Creeping Flesh*, and *The Wicker Man*, to name but a few. He also brought a much-needed dignity to other, less distinguished products of the genre, including, sadly, Hammer's own Dracula cycle which by the late 1960s was increasingly reliant on Lee's charismatic presence to carry some rather uninspired scripts. At the same time, Lee was handing in characteristically assured and precise performances in a variety of nonhorror parts, with perhaps the best of these being the role of Mycroft Holmes in Billy Wilder's *The Private Life of Sherlock Holmes*. (Lee is probably the only actor who in the course of his career has played both Sherlock and Mycroft Holmes as well as Henry Baskerville.)

It is fair to say that despite his undoubted versatility Lee is at his best in fantastic or stylized settings—whether this be Castle Dracula or Scaramanga's exotic island retreat in the James Bond film *The Man with the Golden Gun*. In more realistically depicted worlds, he appears slightly uncomfortable and out of place. Whatever the reasons are for this (and the main one is probably his height, which handicapped his career for so long) it does seem that Christopher Lee is in every sense a larger-than-life actor who was fortunate enough to have found a space in the horror genre within which he could develop his formidable talent.

—Peter Hutchings, updated by John McCarty

LEE, Spike

Nationality: American. **Born:** Shelton Jackson Lee in Atlanta, Georgia, 1957. **Education:** Attended Morehouse College, B.A., 1979; New York University's Institute of Film and Television/Tisch School of the Arts, M.A. in Film, 1982. **Family:** Married Tonya Lewis, 1993, daughter: Satchel. **Career:** 1986—first feature film, *She's Gotta Have It*, which Lee directed, wrote, edited, and produced through his company 40 Acres and a Mule Filmworks, as well as co-starred in; 1989—*Do the Right Thing*, his third feature, is enormously controversial on issues of racial tension and violence; 1992—much-publicized struggle with Warner Brothers to get *Malcolm X* produced according to Lee's vision. **Awards:** Academy Award, for Best Student Film, for *Joe's Bed-Stuy Barbershop: We Cut Heads*, 1983; Prix de Jeunesse, Cannes Film Festival, for *She's Gotta Have It*, 1986. **Address:** 40 Acres and a Mule Filmworks, 124 De Kalb Avenue, Brooklyn, NY 11217, U.S.A.

Films as Actor, Director, Writer, and Producer:

1986	*She's Gotta Have It* (as Mars Blackmon, + ed)	
1988	*School Daze* (as Darryl "Half-Pint," co-sc)	
1989	*Do the Right Thing* (as Mookie, co-sc)	
1990	*Mo' Better Blues* (as Giant)	
1991	*Jungle Fever* (as Cyrus)	
1992	**Malcolm X** (as Shorty, co-sc, co-pr)	
1994	*Crooklyn* (as Snuffy, co-sc)	
1995	*Clockers* (as Chucky, co-sc, co-pr)	
1996	*Girl No. 6* (as Jimmy, + d, pr only)	

Films as Actor Only:

1991 *Lonely in America* (Barry Alexander Brown) (as himself)
1993 *The Last Party* (Marc Benjamin and Marc Levin—doc) (as himself)
1994 *The Drop Squad* (D. Johnson) (cameo as himself, + co-pr); **Hoop Dreams** (Steve James—doc) (as himself)

Other Films:

1983 *Joe's Bed-Stuy Barbershop: We Cut Heads* (d, sc, pr)
1995 *New Jersey Drive* (exec pr)

Publications

By LEE: books:

Spike Lee's Gotta Have It: Inside Guerilla Filmmaking, New York, 1987.
Uplift the Race: The Construction of School Daze, with Lisa Jones, New York, 1988.
Do the Right Thing: A Spike Lee Joint, with Lisa Jones, New York, 1989.
Mo' Better Blues, with Lisa Jones, New York, 1990.
Five for Five: The Films of Spike Lee (screenplays, with essays by Terry McMillan and others), New York, 1991.
By Any Means Necessary: The Trials and Tribulations of the Making of Malcolm X, with Ralph Wiley, New York, 1992.

By LEE: articles—

Interview, in *Village Voice* (New York), 12 August 1986.
Interview with M. Glicksman, in *Film Comment* (New York), July/August 1989.
"Spike Lee: The Do-the-Right-Thing Revolution," interview with Henry Louis Gates Jr., in *Interview* (New York), October 1994.
"Spike," interview with Anna Deavere Smith, in *Premiere* (New York), October 1995.

"Spike Speaks," interview with Alan Frutkin, in *Advocate* (Los Angeles), 31 October 1995.

On LEE: books—

Patterson, Alex, *Spike Lee*, New York, 1992.
Guerrero, Ed, *Framing Blackness: The African American Image in Film*, Philadelphia, 1993.
Bogle, Donald, *Toms, Coons, Mulattoes, Mammies, and Bucks: An Interpretive History of Blacks in American Films*, 3rd ed., New York, 1995.

On LEE: articles—

Tate, G., "Spike Lee," in *American Film* (Washington, D.C.), September 1986.
Current Biography 1989, New York, 1989.
Sharkey, B., and T. Davis, "Knocking on Hollywood's Door," in *American Film* (Washington, D.C.), July-August 1989.
Norment, Lynn, "A Revealing Look at Spike Lee's Changing Life," *Ebony* (Chicago), May 1994.

* * *

In a 1994 *Ebony* interview Spike Lee remarked that he does not like to perform in his own movies, "because I feel we're detracting from the movie, so I just do enough to not get in the way. . . . I don't have the skills to be an actor"; he has written roles for himself only because it is "better for the box office if I'm in the movies." This is a modest claim for someone whose performances in *She's Gotta Have It* and *Do the Right Thing* are major contributions to those films' overall success, artistically and financially. Yet it is also an honest assessment of someone whose acting skills may be considerably less than the power of his screen image. Lee seems well aware that his greatest asset as an actor is his iconic presence on the screen: the small, intense face and wiry body (familiar from television ads and cantankerous interviews as well as his movie roles) energizing his every scene.

If Lee as actor does not simply outshine his male colleagues in *She's Gotta Have It*, he is at the very least their perfect complement. Of the three rivals for the exclusive sexual attention of the central female character, Lee's Mars Blackmon—a comedian all too pleased with his own sense of humor, and a conspicuously diminutive figure next to Tracy Camilla Johns's strapping Nola—stands out against Tommy Hicks's alternately gently romantic and meanly possessive Jamie and John Terrell's humorless, preeningly narcissistic Greer. Early in the film Lee the writer-director designs a brilliantly edited introduction to Lee the actor, who swoops toward the camera on his bike and crashes. Lee makes the most of props such as gold accessories and oversized black-rimmed glasses, and has a perfect handle on the character's strutting and wheedling, as in Mars's oft-quoted signature line, "Please, baby, please, baby, please, baby, baby, baby, please!"

For his second film, *School Daze*, Lee created a much less central but quite disturbing character for himself. Darryl, better known as Half-Pint, the pathetic cousin of the film's hero, is a brainwashed initiate of a college campus's fascistic Gamma fraternity, a nerdy virgin who is ordered to have sex with the frat leader's girlfriend by the leader himself (supposedly to "test" her ability to go against orders). Playing him with puppy-dog eyes (behind thin wire-rims this time), Lee makes him less of a comical type, more a hopelessly conformist youth too dense to notice the woman's humiliation.

Lee's most notable achievement as an actor to date is surely his performance as Mookie, the pizza delivery boy in *Do the Right Thing*. In an otherwise ensemble film Mookie is a central character, along with Danny Aiello's Sal, the pizza parlor owner: the two of them utterly contrasted in bulk and outlooks, but having a fleeting, grudging

Spike Lee in *Do the Right Thing*

respect for one another that is the film's only flicker of hope for racial harmony in the last scene. Amid a large cast of acting veterans and at least one stunning newcomer (Rosie Pérez), Lee holds his own in all of Mookie's scenes, from his inimitable stride down the block in a memorable tracking shot, through his confrontations with the racist Pino (John Turturro), friendlier encounters with several others, outrage over the killing of Radio Raheem and stunned gaping at the riot he initiates, to his final stubborn and wary dialogue with Sal.

His next three roles in his own films were all as sidekicks to the leading man, each role decreasingly central to the plot. In *Mo' Better Blues* he is the mockingly named Giant, best friend and manager of jazz trumpeter Bleek (Denzel Washington), and an addictive gambler

who is indirectly responsible for ruining his friend's career. Lee's performance—abetted by an astonishing series of hats and jackets—is a little more jittery, the character more irritable, with a couple of speeches seeming to mimic the jazz riffs that are almost constantly on the soundtrack. In *Jungle Fever* he is again an instigator of trouble for his friend, the buppie architect Flipper (Wesley Snipes), this time by spreading the word of the latter's affair with a white woman. Here Lee gives himself some good lines, but delivers an appropriately low-key performance. Low key too are his line readings as Shorty, Malcolm Little's companion in crime who cannot appreciate his friend's transformation into Malcolm X (Washington again). Shorty is the first character to be seen in the film, in an especially striking tracking shot of the zoot-suited figure striding under some el tracks with jitterbug music on the soundtrack; yet if Lee at first seems to be hogging screen time, we come to realize that his character embodies a world Malcolm will utterly reject later in the film. Indeed, Shorty simply drops out of the narrative about halfway through.

Lee's roles in his next two films are little more than cameos, though not quite Hitchcockian walkthroughs. In *Crooklyn* he is a glue-sniffing neighborhood type observed by the ten-year-old heroine; in *Clockers*, he is a bystander at crime scenes early and late in the film, grimly looking on, as if a surrogate for the director in his angry examination of wasted lives. A more substantial role in *Girl No. 6* may bring Lee the actor back to relative prominence, though still as servant to Lee the auteur.

—Joseph Milicia

LEIGH, Janet

Nationality: American. **Born:** Jeanette Helen Morrison in Mercedes, California, 26 July 1927. **Education:** Studied music and psychology, College of the Pacific. **Family:** Married 1) John Carlyle, 1942 (marriage annulled 1942); 2) Stanley Reames, 1945 (divorced 1948); 3) the actor Tony Curtis, 1951 (divorced 1962), children Kelly Lee, and the actress Jamie Lee Curtis; 4) Robert Brandt, 1964. **Career:** 1946—seven-year contract with MGM; 1947—film debut in *The Romance of Rosy Ridge*; 1949—borrowed by Howard Hughes for three RKO films, beginning with *Holiday Affair*; 1950s—worked with Columbia and Universal; 1957—began TV work on *Schlitz Playhouse of Stars*; 1962—toured South America to promote Peace Corps; 1975—in Broadway play *Murder among Friends*; 1980—appeared with daughter Jamie Lee Curtis in *The Fog*. **Address:** 1625 Summit Ridge Drive, Beverly Hills, CA 90210, U.S.A.

Films as Actress:

1947 *The Romance of Rosy Ridge* (Rowland) (as Lissy Anne MacBean); *If Winter Comes* (Saville) (as Effie Bright)
1948 *Hills of Home* (*Master of Lassie*) (Wilcox) (as Margit Mitchell); *Words and Music* (Taurog) (as Dorothy Feiner Rodgers)
1949 *Act of Violence* (Zinnemann) (as Edith Enley); *Little Women* (LeRoy) (as Meg); *That Forsyte Woman* (*The Forsyte Saga*) (Bennett) (as June Forsyte); *The Doctor and the Girl* (Bernhardt) (as Evelyn Heldon); *The Red Danube* (Sidney) (as Maria Buhlen); *Holiday Affair* (Hartman) (as Connie)
1951 *Strictly Dishonorable* (Panama and Frank) (as Isabelle Dempsey); *Angels in the Outfield* (*Angels and the Pirates*) (Brown) (as Jennifer Paige); *Two Tickets to Broadway* (Kern) (as Nancy Peterson); *It's a Big Country* (Charles Vidor and others) (as Rose Szabo)
1952 *Just This Once* (Weis) (as Lucy Duncan); *Scaramouche* (Sidney) (as Aline de Guarillac de Bourbon); *Fearless Fagan* (Donen) (as Abby Ames)
1953 *Confidentially Connie* (Buzzell) (as Connie Bedloe); *The Naked Spur* (Anthony Mann) (as Linda Patch); *Houdini* (George Marshall) (as Bess); *Walking My Baby Back Home* (Lloyd Bacon) (as Chris Hall)
1954 *Prince Valiant* (Hathaway) (as Aleta); *Living It Up* (Taurog) (as Wally Cook); *The Black Shield of Falworth* (Mate) (as Lady Ann); *Rogue Cop* (Rowland) (as Karen)
1955 *Pete Kelly's Blues* (Webb) (as Ivy Conrad); *My Sister Eileen* (Quine) (as Eileen Sherwood)
1956 *Safari* (Terence Young) (as Linda Latham)

1957 *Jet Pilot* (von Sternberg—produced in 1950) (as Anna)
1958 *Touch of Evil* (Welles) (as Susan Vargas); *The Vikings* (Fleischer) (as Morgana); *The Perfect Furlough* (Edwards) (as Lieutenant Vicki Loren)
1960 *Who Was That Lady?* (Sidney) (as Ann Wilson); *Psycho* (Hitchcock) (as Marion Crane); *Pepe* (Sidney) (as guest)
1962 *The Manchurian Candidate* (Frankenheimer) (as Rosie)
1963 *Bye Bye Birdie* (Sidney) (as Rosie DeLeon); *Wives and Lovers* (Rich) (as Bertie Austin)
1966 *Kid Rodelo* (Carlson) (as Nora); *Three on a Couch* (Jerry Lewis) (as Dr. Elizabeth Acord); *Harper* (*The Moving Target*) (Smight) (as Susan Harper); *An American Dream* (*See You in Hell, Darling*) (Gist) (as Cherry McMahon); *The Spy in the Green Hat* (*One Spy Too Many*) (Sargent—edited from eps. of *The Man from U.N.C.L.E.* TV series) (as Miss Diketon)
1968 *Ad Ogni Costo* (*Grand Slam*; *Top Job*) (Montaldo) (as Mary Ann)
1969 *Hello Down There* (*Sub-A-Dub-Dub*) (Arnold) (as Vivian Miller); *The Monk* (McCowan—for TV); *Honeymoon with a Stranger* (Peyser—for TV)
1970 *The House on Green Apple Road* (Day—for TV)
1971 *Deadly Dreams* (Kjellin—for TV)
1972 *One Is a Lonely Number* (Stuart) (as Gert Meredith); *Night of the Lepus* (Claxton) (as Gerry Bennett)
1973 *Murdoch's Gang* (Dubin—for TV)
1977 *Murder at the World Series* (McLaglen—for TV); *Telethon* (Rich—for TV) (as Elaine)
1978 *The Sea Gypsies* (Raffill) (as Aline de Gravillac)
1979 *Boardwalk* (Verona) (as Florence)
1980 *The Fog* (Carpenter) (as Kathy Williams); *Mirror, Mirror* (Lee—for TV) (as Millie Gorman)
1985 *On Our Way* (Pressman—for TV); *Hitchcock: il brividio del geno* (*The Thrill of Genius*) (Bortolini and Masenza)

Publications

By LEIGH: books—

There Really Was a Hollywood, New York, 1984.
House of Destiny (novel), Ontario, Canada, 1995.
Psycho: Behind the Scenes of the Classic Thriller, New York, 1995.

By LEIGH: articles—

"*Psycho*, Rosie and a Touch of Orson: Janet Leigh Talks," interview with Rui Nogueria, in *Sight and Sound* (London), Spring 1970.
"Janet Leigh and Anthony Perkins: Don't Go Near the Shower," interview with Rod Lurie, in *Los Angeles Magazine*, July 1990.

On LEIGH: books—

Farber, Stephen, and Marc Green, *Hollywood Dynasties*, New York, 1984.
Rebello, Stephen, *Alfred Hitchcock and the Making of* Psycho, New York, 1990.

On LEIGH: articles—

Films in Review (New York), January 1979; April 1980.
Sanz, Cynthia, and E. X. Feeney, "Coming Clean: Janet Leigh, Still Shower-Shy, Tells All about *Psycho*," in *People Weekly* (New York), 7 August 1995.

*   *   *

For the first decade of her career (and to a great extent subsequently as well), Janet Leigh's screen persona was restricted almost exclusively to Hollywood's most conventional image of the "nice girl." Before *Psycho*, she appeared in a few distinguished films (the swashbuckler *Scaramouche*; *The Naked Spur*, one of Anthony Mann's most intense Westerns; the charming if minor *My Sister Eileen*; and of course *Touch of Evil*), but none of them gave her the opportunity to construct a star identity that transcended the persona's conventionality, nor, unfortunately, have any of her films since *Psycho*.

Her roles in *Touch of Evil* and *Psycho* are so strikingly (if superficially and coincidentally) similar that it is instructive to compare the use made of her by Welles and Hitchcock. In both, she is trapped in an otherwise deserted and isolated motel and cruelly terrorized. It is in *Touch of Evil* that the animus against women—and, especially, female sexuality—that disfigures all of Welles's films except *The Magnificent Ambersons* is most blatantly exposed. He gives Leigh's Suzie the film's tritest dialogue (occasionally sprinkled with automatic smart-ass racism), establishing a brash superficiality that, while at odds with Leigh's conventional "nice girl" persona, can scarcely be said to extend it profitably. She is encouraged to be both spunky and sexual, but any possible positive connotations those qualities might suggest are neutralized by the character's shrillness and insensitivity (as far as men are concerned, she is a real nuisance). She can then be punished in the film's protracted terrorization and rape sequences, shot and edited with unmistakable relish, the character reduced to an object on which any horror can be inflicted.

The objectification of Leigh in *Touch of Evil* has its answer in *Psycho*, where, throughout the film's first part, she is the central identification-figure for audience and director, the movement of her consciousness conveyed with almost unprecedented intimacy and inwardness. Hitchcock's point-of-view methodology produces a performance whose effectiveness might seem dependent upon editing (Marion Crane's car journey contains few shots lasting more than a few seconds, and, after one brief establishing two-shot, the entire Marion/Norman dialogue on which the film hinges is built on cross-cutting). Yet the more one sees the film the more one is convinced that the inexhaustible fascination of its first half owes a great deal to Leigh's presence: the precise communication of Marion's shifting perceptions and states of mind is the fruit of one of the cinema's great performer/director collaborations, dwarfing everything else in Leigh's career.

Although Leigh has not officially retired from acting, she has devoted most of her time in recent years to appearing on the lecture circuit discussing her work with Hitchcock in *Psycho*, Welles in *Touch of Evil*, and John Frankenheimer in *The Manchurian Candidate*, the best film of her post-*Psycho* period even though she had a relatively thankless role in it as Frank Sinatra's love interest.

She has also turned to writing, producing an autobiography in 1984 and a chatty memoir about the making of *Psycho* in 1995. The book is entertaining and readable but relatively lightweight in the research department compared with Stephen Rebello's definitive *Alfred Hitchcock and the Making of "Psycho"* published five years earlier.

Like a number of Hollywood stars in the twilight of their careers, a list that includes Kirk Douglas and Leigh's former husband Tony Curtis, she has also tried her hand at fiction—using Hollywood as a backdrop for her first novel, *House of Destiny*, the story of an aging star not unlike Leigh herself.

—Robin Wood, updated by John McCarty

LEIGH, Jennifer Jason

Nationality: American. **Born:** Jennifer Jason Leigh Morrow in Los Angeles, California, 5 February 1962; daughter of the actor Vic Morrow and the writer Barbara Turner. **Education:** Trained at the Lee Strasberg Institute. **Career:** 1978—began appearing as guest actress on such TV series as *Family*, *The Waltons*, and *Trapper John, M.D.*; 1979—made stage debut in Los Angeles Valley College production of *The Shadow Box*; 1981—made screen debut in *Eyes of a Stranger*; 1982—earned first important notices in *Fast Times at Ridgemont High*. **Awards:** Best Supporting Actress, New York Film Critics Circle and Boston Society of Film Critics, for *Miami Blues* and *Last Exit to Brooklyn*, 1990; honored with a tribute at the Telluride Festival, 1994; Independent Spirit Film Award, Best Actress, National Society of Film Critics and Chicago Film Critics, for *Mrs. Parker and the Vicious Circle*, 1994; Best Actress, Montreal Festival, for *Georgia*, 1995. **Agent:** ICM, 8942 Wilshire Boulevard, Beverly Hills, CA 90211, U.S.A.

Films as Actress:

1980   *Angel City* (Leacock—for TV) (as Kristy Teeter)
1981   *Eyes of a Stranger* (Wiederhorn) (as Tracy); *The Killing of Randy Webster* (Wanamaker—for TV) (as Amy Wheeler); *The Best Little Girl in the World* (O'Steen—for TV) (as Cascy Powell)
1982   *Fast Times at Ridgemont High* (Heckerling) (as Stacy Hamilton); *Wrong Is Right* (*The Man with the Deadly Lens*) (Richard Brooks) (as young girl); *The First Time* (Nosseck—for TV) (as Bonny Dillon)
1983   *Easy Money* (Signorelli) (as Allison Capoletti); *Girls of the White Orchid* (*Death Ride to Osaka*) (Kaplan—for TV) (as Carol Heath)
1984   *Grandview, U.S.A.* (Kleiser) (as Candy Webster)
1985   *Flesh + Blood* (*The Rose and the Sword*) (Verhoeven) (as Agnes)
1986   *The Hitcher* (Harmon) (as Nash); *The Men's Club* (Medak) (as Teensy)
1987   *Under Cover* (Stockwell) (as Tanille La Rue); *Sister, Sister* (Condon) (as Lucy Bonnard)
1988   *Heart of Midnight* (Chapman) (as Carol Rivers); *God Bless the Child* (Elikann—for TV)
1989   *Last Exit to Brooklyn* (Edel) (as Tralala); *The Big Picture* (Guest) (as Lydia Johnson)
1990   *Miami Blues* (Armitage) (as Susie "Pepper" Waggoner); *Buried Alive* (*Till Death Do Us Part*) (Darabont—for TV) (as Joanna Goodman)
1991   *Rush* (Zanuck) (as Kristen); *Backdraft* (Ron Howard) (as Jennifer Vaitkus); *Crooked Hearts* (Bortman) (as Marriet)
1992   *Single White Female* (Schroeder) (as Hedra Carlson); *The Prom* (Shainberg) (as Lana)
1993   *Short Cuts* (Altman) (as Lois Kaiser)
1994   *The Hudsucker Proxy* (Coen) (as Amy Archer); *Mrs. Parker and the Vicious Circle* (Rudolph) (as Dorothy Parker)
1995   *Dolores Claiborne* (Hackford) (as Selena St. George); *Georgia* (Grosbard) (as Sadie, + co-pr)
1996   *Kansas City* (Altman)

Publications

By LEIGH: articles—

"Actors, Agents, Atmosphere," interview, in *Interview* (New York), September 1985.
"Ice Cold Spain," interview by K. Ferguson, in *Photoplay Movies & Video* (London), January 1986.
"Midnight Heart," interview with Gavin Smith, in *Film Comment* (New York), March-April 1990.

Jennifer Jason Leigh in *The Hudsucker Proxy*

Interview with Lance Loud, in *Interview* (New York), May 1990.
Interview with Jeff Yarbrough, in *Interview* (New York), April 1991.
Interview with D. Rensen, in *Playboy* (Chicago), February 1992.
"Jennifer Jason Leigh Feels Your Pain," interview with Lynn Darling, in *Esquire* (New York), December 1994.
Interview with Jancee Dunn, in *Rolling Stone* (New York), 30 November 1995.
Interview with John Turturro, in *Interview* (New York), January 1996.

On LEIGH: articles—

Seidenberg, R., "Jennifer Jason Leigh," in *Premiere* (New York), March 1989.
Blue, Carol, "Leighway," in *Interview* (New York), October 1989.
Collins, G., "A Galaxy of Fallen Women Conjured Up by a Rising Star," in *New York Times*, 9 May 1990.
Weiss, Philip, "Jennifer Jason Leigh Flirts with Stardom," in *Rolling Stone* (New York), 17 May 1990.
Wolcott, James, "Gold Rush," in *Vanity Fair* (New York), February 1991.
Current Biography 1992, New York, 1992.
Hooper, J., "The Devil and Miss Leigh," in *Esquire* (New York), January 1992.
Rebello, S., "Quick Change Artist," in *Movieline* (Los Angeles), September 1992.
Sessums, Kevin, "Single White Phenomenon," in *Vanity Fair* (New York), July 1993.

Gaitskill, Mary, "Actress Seen in Strip Joint," in *Harper's Bazaar* (New York), September 1993.
Johnson, Brian D., "Acting on the Edge: Jennifer Jason Leigh Likes to Play the Extremes," in *Maclean's* (Toronto), 15 January 1996.

*   *   *

Jennifer Jason Leigh's most typical roles have been young women who are deeply vulnerable, and whose lives have taken disastrous, potentially tragic turns. Her characters often are quite sexually active, using their bodies and their sexuality to temporarily—but never permanently—ward off their demons.

Her performances are consistently memorable. Her first substantial screen role came in *Fast Times at Ridgemont High*, released in 1982, when Leigh was 20 years old. Her character is a forerunner of many of her later roles: Stacy Hamilton, a virginal high school student who is so curious about sex that she soon is "doing it" with everyone in sight, much to her eventual disillusionment and degradation. *Fast Times at Ridgemont High* featured a large cast of up-and-comers, including Sean Penn, Judge Reinhold, Phoebe Cates, and Forest Whitaker (and, in smaller roles, Eric Stoltz, Anthony Edwards, and Nicolas Cage). Yet Leigh was singled out as a star-to-be. "Don't they know they have a star on their hands?" raved critic Roger Ebert. "I didn't even know who Leigh was when I walked into [the film], and yet I was completely won over by her. She contained so much life and light that she was a joy to behold."

Through the 1980s, Leigh found herself in a series of mostly unmemorable movies. Her next eye-catching performances came in

Miami Blues, playing an ingenuous young woman whose boyfriend is a killer, and *Last Exit to Brooklyn*, cast as a troubled prostitute struggling to survive in a chaotic world. Two impressive follow-ups were *Rush* (as a narcotics cop who becomes addicted to both drugs and her troubled partner) and *Single White Female* (playing a psycho roommate—and an all-out villainess). Leigh's most representative performances were in *Miami Blues* and *Rush*; both are related to *Fast Times at Ridgemont High* in that her characters start out as well-scrubbed or well-meaning innocents but end up exploited and mistreated.

Leigh has not always played the bleary-eyed, substance-abusing victim. In *The Big Picture*, she displays a flair for comedy as a zany performance artist. In *Short Cuts*, she is a matter-of-fact working-class housewife employed as a phone-sex worker, who diapers her baby as she purrs erotic nothings into the ears of faceless strangers at the other end of the line. And in *The Hudsucker Proxy*, Leigh is Amy Archer, Pulitzer Prize-winning reporter who sets out to destroy paper-tiger corporate president Norville Barnes (Tim Robbins). The actress plays the role with more than a touch of Katharine Hepburn in her voice and mannerisms. Archer might be a variation of the character Hepburn played opposite Spencer Tracy decades earlier in *Woman of the Year*: a tough and respected journalist who is feminized in the course of the story.

A truly outstanding—and controversial—starring role came in *Mrs. Parker and the Vicious Circle*, Alan Rudolph's take on the famed Algonquin Round Table of the 1920s. At the film's core is the character of the writer-humorist Dorothy Parker (played by Leigh). She renders Parker as a brittle, sensitive lost soul, a woman who attained a certain level of professional success but who was not destined to find personal contentment. Some felt Leigh's acting to be Oscar-worthy; others were convinced she was grossly miscast, and garbled her way through her performance. In any case, she did not have the central role in her follow-up to *Mrs. Parker*. In *Dolores Claiborne*, Leigh is Selena St. George, a psychologically scarred journalist who is long estranged from the title character, her mother (Kathy Bates). Bates's performance is the commanding one here; Leigh's role is the less sensational. But the two actresses play off one another quite effectively.

In her next film, *Georgia*, scripted by her mother, Barbara Turner—her father is the late actor Vic Morrow—Leigh finally secured what may prove to be the role of a lifetime. *Georgia*, to be sure, is not a great film. But it does offer what was to be one of the most outstanding performances of 1995. As in *Dolores Claiborne*, Leigh plays a character with a complex bond to a female relative. She commands the screen as Sadie, a young woman whose older sister, Georgia, is a famous and beloved folk-rock singer who is as well-adjusted as she is beautiful. Sadie is something else altogether. She is a self-destructive wannabe singer who toils as a motel housekeeper and plays with bands in dreary bars and bowling alleys, while her sister fills concert halls. Sadie drinks "whatever's cheap or free," and often does so first thing in the morning. She at once admires and loves her sister, and is jealous of her success. This only partially explains the underlying tension between the two, which plays itself out as the story unfolds. The film's major flaw is that Sadie is depicted as having little talent, which simply is not true. Sadie might be a clone of Janis Joplin; in the person of Leigh, she offers moving renditions of various songs, especially Van Morrison's "Take Me Back." The result is a case of an actress transcending her character's limitations.

—Rob Edelman

LEIGH, Vivien

Nationality: British. **Born:** Vivian Mary Hartley in Darjeeling, India, 5 November 1913. **Education:** Attended Convent of the Sacred Heart, Roehampton; schools in Europe; Royal Academy of Dramatic

Art, London. **Family:** Married 1) Leigh Holman, 1932 (divorced 1940), daughter: Suzanne; 2) the actor Laurence Oliver, 1940 (divorced 1960). **Career:** 1934—film debut in *Things Are Looking Up*; 1935—stage debut in *The Green Sash*; 1935—contract with Alexander Korda, and, in 1938, contract with David O. Selznick; 1940—Broadway debut with Olivier in *Romeo and Juliet*: later stage roles in *Caesar and Cleopatra* and *Antony and Cleopatra* (with Olivier), *The Skin of Our Teeth*, *A Streetcar Named Desire* (in London, and in film version), *Look after Lulu*, and *Tovarich*; also a season with Olivier at Stratford upon Avon. **Awards:** Academy Award, for Best Actress, and Best Actress, New York Film Critics, for *Gone with the Wind*, 1939; Academy Award, for Best Actress, Best Actress, New York Film Critics, Best Actress, Venice Festival, and Best British Actress, British Academy, for *A Streetcar Named Desire*, 1951. **Died:** In London, England, 8 July 1967.

Films as Actress:

1934   *Things Are Looking Up* (de Courville) (as schoolgirl)
1935   *The Village Squire* (Denham) (as Rose Venables); *Gentleman's Agreement* (Pearson) (as Phil Stanley); *Look Up and Laugh* (Dean) (as Marjorie Belfer)
1936   *Fire over England* (William K. Howard) (as Cynthia)
1937   *Dark Journey* (Saville) (as Madeleine Godard); *Storm in a Teacup* (Saville and Dalrymple) (as Victoria Grow); *21 Days* (*Twenty-One Days Together*; *The First and the Last*) (Dean) (as Wanda)
1938   *A Yank at Oxford* (Conway) (as Elsa Craddock); *St. Martin's Lane* (*Sidewalks of London*) (Whelan) (as Libby)
1939   *Gone with the Wind* (Fleming—additional scenes directed by Cukor, Wood, Menzies, and David O. Selznick) (as Scarlett O'Hara)
1940   *Waterloo Bridge* (LeRoy) (as Myra Lester)
1941   *That Hamilton Woman* (*Lady Hamilton*) (Korda) (title role)
1946   *Caesar and Cleopatra* (Pascal) (as Cleopatra)
1948   *Anna Karenina* (Duvivier) (title role)
1951   *A Streetcar Named Desire* (Kazan) (as Blanche Dubois)
1954   *Elephant Walk* (Dieterle) (as Ruth Wiley in Ceylon long shots)
1955   *The Deep Blue Sea* (Litvak) (as Hester Collyer)
1961   *The Roman Spring of Mrs. Stone* (Quintero) (title role)
1965   *Ship of Fools* (Kramer) (as Mary Treadwell)

Publications

On LEIGH: books—

Barker, Felix, *The Oliviers*, Philadelphia, 1953.
Dent, Alan, *Vivien Leigh: A Bouquet*, London, 1969.
Robyns, Gwen, *Light of a Star: The Career of Vivien Leigh*, New York, 1971.
Memo from: David O. Selznick, edited by Rudy Behlmer, New York, 1972.
Edwards, Anne, *Vivien Leigh: A Biography*, New York, 1977.
Lasky, Jesse Jr., with Pat Silver, *Love Scene: The Story of Laurence Olivier and Vivien Leigh*, New York, 1978.
O'Connor, Garry, *Darlings of the Gods: One Year in the Lives of Laurence Olivier and Vivien Leigh*, London, 1984.
Taylor, John Russell, *Vivien Leigh*, London, 1984.
Walker, Alexander, *Vivien: The Life of Vivien Leigh*, London, 1987.
Vickers, Hugo, *Vivien Leigh*, London, 1988.
McBean, Angus, *Vivien Leigh: A Love Affair in Camera*, Oxford, 1989.
Guandalini, Gina, *Vivien Leigh*, Rome, 1990.
Molt, Cynthia Marylee, *Vivien Leigh: A Bio-Bibliography*, Westport, Connecticut, 1992.

Vivien Leigh in *That Hamilton Woman* **courtesy of CTE (Carlton) Limited**

On LEIGH: articles—

Current Biography 1946, New York, 1946.

Raper, M., "They Called Her a Dresden Shepherdess," in *Films and Filming* (London), August 1955.

Bowers, Ronald, "Vivien Leigh," in *Films in Review* (New York), August-September 1965.

Obituary, in *New York Times*, 9 July 1967.

Ciné Revue (Paris), 5 July 1984.

*   *   *

Vivien Leigh was a complex personality though she appeared at first to be just a petite, distinctly upper-class young girl with an unusual, refined kind of beauty that seemed to approach perfection. She was determined to go on the stage in spite of a privileged upbringing, a convent education, and an early marriage which brought her a house in Mayfair. By 1935 she had appeared on the London stage and in her first film.

It was her romantic supporting role in *Fire over England* in 1936, opposite Laurence Olivier as a dashing young man in the court of Elizabeth I, that led to one of the cinema's most celebrated acting partnerships, as famous a love-match in its time as that between Burton and Taylor in the 1960s. Olivier's Hollywood engagement to play Heathcliff in *Wuthering Heights* drew Leigh to California in his wake, and her arrival coincided with the prolonged search for a suitable actress to appear as the seductive, self-willed Scarlett O'Hara in *Gone with the Wind*. In the face of the fiercest competition, Myron Selznick persuaded his brother David to give her the part, and her success in a role that seemed made to her measure led to world fame and an Academy Award. Nevertheless, her special qualities—elfin stature, a grace of movement and gesture, and a porcelain-like facial beauty always enhanced by subtle black-and-white cinematography—had already been revealed in the romantic British film *St. Martin's Lane*, opposite Charles Laughton as a street entertainer entranced by her vagrant, waiflike girl.

The outbreak of World War II brought Olivier back to London, and Leigh (who was free to marry him only in 1940 due to the complications of their respective divorces) temporarily halted her promising Hollywood career in order to be with him during his period of war service in the Fleet Air Arm. Nevertheless, she appeared with Robert Taylor in the American film *Waterloo Bridge*, made in Britain, and with Olivier in Alexander Korda's *That Hamilton Woman*, in which she was again able to play the siren in a romanticized version of the notorious, obsessive relationship between Lord Nelson and Emma Hamilton.

From this point on, Leigh was to maintain an active stage career, together with infrequent film appearances. She worked closely with Olivier in many stage productions, notably Shakespearean seasons in Britain and America. She was effective in Gabriel Pascal's ponderous screen adaptation of Shaw's *Caesar and Cleopatra* and as the ill-fated heroine in Julien Duvivier's filming of *Anna Karenina*. Having played Blanche Dubois in Olivier's London stage production of *A Streetcar Named Desire*, she was invited by Elia Kazan to recreate the role in his 1951 screen version of the Tennessee Williams play.

One wishes Leigh had not treated the movies disdainfully in favor of living up to the demands of being Lady Olivier on stage. Despite health problems stemming from tuberculosis and spells of nervous exhaustion, she managed to enchant audiences on both sides of the Atlantic, even winning a Tony Award for her musical comedy brio in *Tovarich*. It is one of the cinema's great ironies that a genteel Englishwoman's most notable screen roles were both quintessentially American Southern belles. In inhabiting the fierce soul of Dixie in *Gone with the Wind* and then illuminating the decline visited upon Southern hospitality in *Streetcar Named Desire*, Leigh rose to the occasion of giving definitive interpretations to two great roles in one lifetime. If one examines Joanne Whaley-Kilmer chafing under her starched petticoats in television's *Scarlett* or Ann-Margret and Jessica Lange riding their respective *Streetcars*, one is confronted with understudies barely scratching the surface of indelible creations Leigh clawed to singular life. If Tennessee Williams's *The Roman Spring of Mrs. Stone* fails to camouflage its homosexual undercurrents, Leigh brings great dignity to a crudely directed film about the symbolic link between death and the decay of desirability. After this hothouse chronicle of the unloved (which can be viewed as a menopausal horror film), she turned up her pert nose at another gambol through the magnolias, the scary *Hush ... Hush, Sweet Charlotte*, and instead graced the stage once more. Booked aboard the metaphoric claptrap of *Ship of Fools*, Stanley Kramer's floating *Judgment at Nuremberg*, Leigh sails above her material with a luminous portrait of a coquette unwilling to sell herself short despite the ravages of time. Magically when Leigh does her Charleston, the years melt away; Leigh always acted with her entire being, and one can sense her feeding the role of Mrs. Treadwell with her own despair about time running out. Whatever physical or psychological demons she wrestled with, she was never an actress for half-measures and she danced out of her film career on a high note on the high dramatic seas of *Ship of Fools*. She died in 1967 while rehearsing with Michael Redgrave for a stage production of Albee's *Delicate Balance*.

—Roger Manvell, updated by Robert Pardi

LEMMON, Jack

Nationality: American. **Born:** John Uhler Lemmon in Boston, 8 February 1925. **Education:** Attended Rivers Country Day School, Chestnut Hill, Massachusetts; Phillips Academy, Andover, Massachusetts, graduated 1943; Harvard University, Cambridge, Massachusetts, B.A. and B.S., 1947. **Military Service:** Served as communications officer in Naval Reserve, 1945. **Family:** Married 1) the actress Cynthia Stone, 1950 (divorced 1956), son: Christopher; 2) the actress Felicia Farr, 1962. **Career:** After graduating from Harvard, worked as piano player at Old Nick saloon in New York; 1948—actor in radio soap opera; producer and actor in several TV series: *That Wonderful Guy*, 1949-50, *The Couple Next Door*, 1950, *The Ad-Libbers*, 1951, and *Heaven for Betsy*, 1952, all with Cynthia Stone; 1953—Broadway debut in *Room Service*; contract with Columbia; 1954—film debut in *It Should Happen to You*; 1957-58—regular on TV series *Alcoa Theatre*; 1958—on Broadway in *Face of a Hero*; 1971—directed the film *Kotch*; 1993—narrator of *The Wild West* TV mini-series. **Awards:** Best Supporting Actor, Academy Award, for *Mister Roberts*, 1955; Best Foreign Actor, British Academy, for *Some Like It Hot*, 1959, and for *The Apartment*, 1960; Best Actor, Academy Award, for *Save the Tiger*, 1973; Best Actor, British Academy, and Best Actor, Cannes Festival, for *The China Syndrome*, 1979; Best Actor, Berlin Festival, for *Tribute*, 1981; Best Actor, Cannes Festival for *Missing*, 1982; Life Achievement Award, American Film Institute, 1988. **Agent:** Jalem Productions, 141 El Camino, Suite 201, Beverly Hills, CA 90212, U.S.A.

Films as Actor:

1954   *It Should Happen to You* (Cukor) (as Pete Sheppard); *Phffft!* (Robson) (as Robert Tracy)
1955   *Three for the Show* (Potter) (as Marty Stewart); *Mister Roberts* (Ford and LeRoy) (as Ensign Pulver); *My Sister Eileen* (Quine) (as Bob Baker)

1956 *You Can't Run Away from It* (Powell) (as Peter Warne)
1957 *Fire Down Below* (Parrish) (as Tony); *Operation Mad Ball* (Quine) (as Pvt. Hogan)
1958 *Cowboy* (Daves) (as Frank Harris); *Bell, Book and Candle* (Quine) (as Nicky Holroyd)
1959 **Some Like It Hot** (Wilder) (as Jerry/Daphne); *It Happened to Jane* (Quine) (as George Denham)
1960 **The Apartment** (Wilder) (as Baxter); *Pepe* (Sidney) (as himself)
1961 *The Wackiest Ship in the Army* (Murphy) (as Lt. Rip Crandall)
1962 *Stowaway in the Sky* (Lamorisse) (as narrator); *The Notorious Landlady* (Quine) (as William Gridley); *Days of Wine and Roses* (Edwards) (as Joe)
1963 *Irma la Douce* (Wilder) (as Nestor); *Under the Yum-Yum Tree* (Swift) (as Hogan)
1964 *Good Neighbor Sam* (Swift) (as Sam Bissel)
1965 *How to Murder Your Wife* (Quine) (as Stanley Ford); *The Great Race* (as Prof. Fate) (Edwards)
1966 *The Fortune Cookie* (Wilder) (as Harry Hinkle)
1967 *Luv* (Donner) (as Harry Berlin)
1968 *The Odd Couple* (Saks) (as Felix Ungar)
1969 *The April Fools* (Rosenberg) (as Howard Brubaker)

1970 *The Out-of-Towners* (Hiller) (as George Kellerman)
1972 *The War between Men and Women* (Shavelson) (as Peter Wilson); *Avanti!* (Wilder) (as Wendell Armbruster)
1973 *Save the Tiger* (Avildsen) (as Harry Stoner)
1974 *Wednesday* (Kupfer); *The Front Page* (Wilder) (as Hildy Johnson)
1975 *The Prisoner of Second Avenue* (Frank) (as Mel)
1976 *The Entertainer* (Wrye—for TV) (as Archie Rice); *Alex and the Gypsy* (Korty) (as Alexander Main)
1977 *Airport '77* (Jameson) (as Don Gallagher)
1979 *The China Syndrome* (Bridges) (as Jack Godell)
1980 *Tribute* (Clark) (as Scottie Templeton)
1981 *Buddy Buddy* (Wilder) (as Victor Clooney)
1982 *Missing* (Costa-Gavras) (as Ed Horman)
1985 *Mass Appeal* (Glenn Jordan) (as Father Tim Farley); *Macaroni* (Scola) (as Robert)
1986 *That's Life* (Edwards) (as Harvey Fairchild)
1987 *Long Day's Journey into Night* (Miller—for TV)
1988 *The Murder of Mary Phagan* (Hale—for TV) (as Gov. John Staton)
1989 *Dad* (Goldberg) (as Jake Tremont)
1991 *JFK* (Stone) (as Jack Martin)

Jack Lemmon in *The China Syndrome*

1992   *Glengarry Glen Ross* (Foley) (as Shelley Levine); ***The Player*** (Altman) (as himself); *For Richer, for Poorer* (Sandrich—for TV) (as Aram Katourian)

1993   *A Life in the Theater* (Mosher—for TV) (as Robert); ***Short Cuts*** (Altman) (as Paul Finnigan); *Grumpy Old Men* (Petrie) (as John Gustafson); *Earth and the American Dream* (Couturie—doc) (voice only)

1995   *The Grass Harp* (Charles Matthau); *Grumpier Old Men* (Deutch) (as John Gustafson); *Getting Away with Murder* (Harvey Miller)

1996   *Hamlet* (Branagh) (as Marcellus)

Film as Director:

1971   *Kotch* (+ ro as stranger on bus)

Publications

By LEMMON: articles—

"Such Fun to Be Funny," in *Films and Filming* (London), November 1960.

"Interview: Jack Lemmon," in *Playboy* (Chicago), May 1964.

"I Never Had a Better Experience in My Professional Life," interview with B. Thomas, in *Action* (Los Angeles), January-February 1972.

Interview with S. Greenberg, in *Film Comment* (New York), May-June 1973.

"Dialogue on Film: Jack Lemmon," interview in *American Film* (Washington, D.C.), September 1982.

Interview, in *Films and Filming* (London), December 1984 and January 1985.

Interview with Gary Crowdus and Dan Georgakas, in *Cineaste* (New York), vol. 14, no. 3, 1986.

"Jack of All Trades," interview with Burt Prelutsky, in *American Film* (New York), March 1988.

Interview in *Talking Films: The Best of the Guardian Film Lectures*, edited by Andrew Britton, London, 1991.

On LEMMON: books—

Widenen, Don, *Lemmon: A Biography*, New York, 1975.

Baltake, Joe, *The Films of Jack Lemmon*, Secaucus, New Jersey, 1977; rev. ed., 1986.

Freedland, Michael, *Jack Lemmon*, London, 1985.

On LEMMON: articles—

Baltake, Joe, "Jack Lemmon," in *Films in Review* (New York), January 1970.

Eyles, A., "Jack Lemmon," in *Focus on Film* (London), Spring 1972.

Crist, Judith, "Jack Lemmon," in *The Movie Star*, edited by Elisabeth Weis, New York, 1981.

Wood, Michael, "In Search of *Missing*," in *American Film* (Washington, D.C.), March 1982.

Cieutat, Michel, "Jack Lemmon, un Arlequin d'Amérique," in *Positif* (Paris), September 1983.

Buckley, Michael, "Jack Lemmon," in *Films in Review* (New York), December 1984, January and February 1985.

Current Biography 1988, New York, 1988.

Junod, Tom, and Michael O'Neill, "Laughing on the Outside," in *Life*, October 1992.

Mitchell, Sean, "A Slice of Lemmon," in *Premiere* (New York), November 1992.

Wilmington, Michael, "Saint Jack," in *Film Comment* (New York), March/April 1993.

*   *   *

In Jack Lemmon's special brand of comedy, he spotlights the futility of the well-brought-up and well-intentioned male who flounders in a society rife with corruption and hypocrisy. His characters can triumph only when they develop a stronger sense of self, and take stands against those who abuse them. The flip side of this marvelous actor is that he is equally adept at playing dramatic roles. He is at his best when cast as characters who either are sadly and tragically deluded, or are complacent, average Americans who become radicalized by events that shatter their value systems.

As a younger movie star, Lemmon's best roles were as characters who moved from states of innocence to states of awareness through painful, if often humorous, experience. This type of character development highlighted Lemmon's nuances of gesture and facial expressions to their best advantage, as the characters endured bafflement and disorientation in their brave attempts to understand their world. In *Mr. Roberts*, Lemmon's Ensign Pulver starts out a comical wheeler-dealer, a jester-schemer who is far more adept at talking than functioning. But upon hearing of the death of the title character, who had been in conflict with his ship's martinet captain, Pulver's face and entire form are energized as he defiantly throws the captain's sacred palm tree overboard. Through most of *The Apartment* (in which Lemmon, as he often was throughout his career, is directed by Billy Wilder), his character, C. C. Baxter, is caught in a web of petty corporate corruption. In order to curry favor with his superiors, Baxter lends them his apartment for their overnight trysts, resulting in habitual inconvenience and many a sleepless night. Finally, having fallen in love with his boss's mistress, Baxter regains his dignity and quits his job. Lemmon plays this spineless organization man to perfection, making his transformation all the more impressive. Few viewers can resist the moment when Baxter thrusts out his formerly weak chin and tells his boss what he can do with the job and his key to the executive washroom.

Lemmon's other great early career comic performance came in a classic concoction meant strictly for laughs, *Some Like It Hot*, in which he and Tony Curtis dress in drag and join an all-girl band after accidentally witnessing the St. Valentine's Day Massacre. In 1966, still barely over a quarter-way through his career, Lemmon was paired with Walter Matthau in *The Fortune Cookie*, an inspired teaming which has continued through various other films into the 1990s. Lemmon and Matthau are at their best when playing polar opposites who find themselves united by happenstance. They have never been funnier than in *The Odd Couple*, in which both actors' comic abilities are exploited to the extreme with Lemmon as the neurotically obsessive neatnik Felix Ungar and Matthau as the glorious slob Oscar Madison.

In Lemmon's initial noteworthy roles, he was called upon to be a comic actor. But as his career progressed, he displayed his flip side as a superb dramatic actor-tragedian. His first great dramatic role is Joe, the pathetic alcoholic, in *Days of Wine and Roses*. In *Save the Tiger*, he brilliantly plays another miserable creature, Harry Stoner, a dress manufacturer who (like so many of his comic characters) has lost his innocence. But in so doing, he has become a weaker rather than stronger man as he shrugs his shoulders and submits to the daily acts of degradation he feels are necessary to his survival in the business world. Lemmon plays a variation on this character in *Glengarry Glen Ross*, David Mamet's emotionally gripping adaptation of his stage play, in which Lemmon gives what is perhaps his most riveting late-career performance as real estate salesman Shelley "The Machine" Levine. As with Willy Loman in *Death of a Salesman*—and Harry Stoner in *Save the Tiger*—Levine is an aging, desperate man. He will say anything and do anything to get the good leads that will allow him an audience for his tired sales pitches. Levine is all sweat and angst beneath his superficially friendly handshake, and Lemmon plays him with a master touch.

The actor has also played more sympathetic dramatic characters. He commands the screen in two overtly political dramas in which his characters undergo catharses similar to the ones experienced by his more comic alter-egos. In *The China Syndrome*, Lemmon plays nuclear power plant worker Jack Godell, a loyal company man who is transformed upon realizing that the authorities have failed to deal with the causes of an accidental meltdown at his plant. In *Missing*, he is conservative American businessman Ed Horman, who becomes radicalized upon the disappearance of his son in a Latin American country, and by his realization of America's squalid complicity in the country's repressive policies.

As Lemmon's career entered its fifth decade, the actor made a brief but memorable appearance in *The Grass Harp*, directed by Charles (son of Walter) Matthau, in which Lemmon plays just the type of character who might have been his nemesis in *The Apartment*: a slick, scheming entrepreneur-shyster who entices and then cons a narrow-minded, naive small-town businesswoman. He is especially fine in his poignant vignette in *Short Cuts*, playing a character who has forgotten how to feel: a father, estranged for many years from his son, who reenters the latter's life from out of nowhere—and who does not even know his own grandson's name. Another excellent late-career starring role came in *A Life in the Theater*, a television movie which, like *Glengarry Glen Ross*, is based on a David Mamet play. Lemmon plays Robert, an older actor who has devoted his life to the stage; in fact, to him, life *is* the theater. He and a younger actor are seen rehearsing, performing, and forever discussing and arguing about the craft of acting during a season of repertory plays. Primarily, *A Life in the Theater* serves as a showcase for Lemmon, who offers a canny, knowing performance as Robert—yet one more in a seemingly unending line of colorful, memorable characterizations.

—Rodney Farnsworth, updated by Rob Edelman

LEWIS, Jerry

Nationality: American. **Born:** Joseph Levitch in Newark, New Jersey, 16 March 1926. **Education:** Attended Irvington High School, Irvington, New Jersey. **Family:** Married 1) the singer Patti Palmer, 1944 (divorced), six children: Gary, Ron, Scott, Chris, Anthony, Joseph; 2) the actress/dancer Sandra Pitnick, 1983, one daughter. **Career:** 1931—made stage debut; 1942—developed comic routines, attracting Irving Kaye as manager; 1946—formed comedy team with Dean Martin; 1948—with Martin, signed by Hal Wallis for Paramount; 1949—feature film debut in *My Friend Irma*; 1952—became chairman of Muscular Dystrophy Association of America, raising funds from annual telethons; 1956—started solo career; formed Jerry Lewis Productions, Inc.; 1957—film debut as single, *The Delicate Delinquent*; 1959—signed seven-year contract with Paramount-York; 1963—lead in variety TV series *The Jerry Lewis Show*; 1967-69—lead in comedy-variety TV series *The Jerry Lewis Show*; 1972—after abandonment of *The Day the Clown Cried*, left films for eight years; 1988-89—in TV series *Wiseguy*; 1995—Broadway debut playing the devil in *Damn Yankees*. **Awards:** Commander of the Order of Arts and Letters, and Commander of the Legion of Honor, France, 1984; DHL (hon.), Mercy College, 1987; Prof. cinema, University of Southern California. **Agent:** William Morris Agency, Inc., 151 El Camino Drive, Beverly Hills, CA 90212, U.S.A.

Films as Actor:

1949 *My Friend Irma* (George Marshall) (as Seymour)
1950 *At War with the Army* (Walker) (as Pfc. Alvin Korwin); *My Friend Irma Goes West* (Walker) (as Seymour); *The Milkman* (Barton) (as milkman)
1951 *That's My Boy* (Walker) (as Junior Jackson); *Sailor Beware* (Walker) (as Melvin Jones)
1952 *Road to Bali* (Walker) (cameo); *Jumping Jacks* (Taurog) (as Hap Smith)
1953 *The Stooge* (Taurog—produced in 1951) (title role); *The Caddy* (Taurog) (title role); *Money from Home* (George Marshall) (as Virgil Yokum); *Scared Stiff* (George Marshall) (as Myron Myron Mertz)
1954 *Living It Up* (Taurog) (as Homer Flagg); *Three Ring Circus* (*Jerrico, the Wonder Clown*) (Pevney) (as Jerry Hotchkiss)
1955 *You're Never Too Young* (Taurog) (as Wilbur Hoolick); *Artists and Models* (Tashlin) (as Eugene Fullstack)
1956 *Pardners* (Taurog) (as Wade Kingsley Jr./Wade Kingsley Sr.); *Hollywood or Bust* (Tashlin) (as Malcolm Smith)
1957 *The Delicate Delinquent* (McGuire) (as Sidney Pythias, + pr); *The Sad Sack* (George Marshall) (as Bixby)
1958 *Rock-a-Bye-Baby* (Tashlin) (as Clayton Poole, + pr); *The Geisha Boy* (Tashlin) (title role, + pr)
1959 *L'il Abner* (Frank) (cameo); *Don't Give Up the Ship* (Taurog) (as John Paul Steckler)
1960 *Visit to a Small Planet* (Taurog) (as Kreton); *Cinderfella* (Tashlin) (title role, + pr)
1962 *It'$ Only Money* (Tashlin) (as Lester March)
1963 *It's a Mad, Mad, Mad, Mad World* (Kramer) (cameo as mad driver); *Who's Minding the Store?* (Tashlin) (as Raymond Phiffier)
1964 *The Disorderly Orderly* (Tashlin) (title role)
1965 *Boeing, Boeing* (Rich) (as Robert Reed)
1966 *Way . . . Way Out* (Gordon Douglas) (as Peter Mattemore)
1968 *Don't Raise the Bridge, Lower the River* (Paris) (as George Lester)
1969 *Hook, Line and Sinker* (George Marshall) (as Peter Ingersoll, + pr)
1983 **The King of Comedy** (Scorsese) (as Jerry Langford)
1984 *Slapstick of Another Kind* (Steven Paul); *Par out'es Rentre? On t'a pas vue sortir* (Philippe Clair); *Retenez moi . . . ou je Fais un Malheur!* (*To Catch a Cop*) (Michel Gerard) (as Jerry Logan); *Jerry Lewis Live* (Forrest)
1987 *Fight for Life* (Silverstein—for TV)
1989 *Cookie* (Susan Seidelman) (as Arnold Ross)
1992 *Mr. Saturday Night* (Crystal) (as himself)
1993 *Arizona Dream* (Kusturica) (as Leo Sweetie)
1995 *Funny Bones* (Chelsom) (as George Fawkes)

Films as Director and Actor:

1960 *The Bellboy* (title role, + pr, sc)
1961 *The Ladies' Man* (as Herbert Herbert Heebert/Heebert's mother, + pr, co-sc); *The Errand Boy* (title role, + co-sc)
1963 *The Nutty Professor* (as Professor Julius Kelp/Buddy Love, + co-pr, co-sc)
1964 *The Patsy* (as Stanley Belt, + co-sc)
1965 *The Family Jewels* (as Willard Woodward/the Peyton Brothers, + pr, co-sc)
1966 *Three on a Couch* (as Christopher Pride/Warren/Ringo/Rutherford/Heather, + pr)
1967 *The Big Mouth* (title role, + pr, co-sc)
1970 *Which Way to the Front?* (as Brendan Byers III, + pr); *One More Time* (d only)

Jerry Lewis

1972 *The Day the Clown Cried* (not completed) (title role, + sc)
1981 *Hardly Working* (as Bo Hooper, + co-sc)
1983 *Cracking Up* (*Smorgasbord*) (as Warren Nefron/Dr. Perks, + co-sc)

Publications

By LEWIS: books—

The Total Filmmaker, New York, 1971.
Jerry Lewis, in Person, New York, 1982.

By LEWIS: articles—

"Mr. Lewis Is a Pussycat," interview with Peter Bodganovich, in *Esquire* (New York), November 1962.
"America's Uncle," interview with Axel Madsen, in *Cahiers du Cinéma in English* (New York), no. 4, 1966.
"Five Happy Moments," in *Esquire* (New York), December 1970.
"Dialogue on Film: Jerry Lewis," in *American Film* (Washington, D.C.), September 1977.
Interview with D. Rabourdin, in *Cinéma* (Paris), April 1980.
Interview with Serge Daney, in *Cahiers du Cinéma* (Paris), May 1983.
"Thank You Jerry Much," interview with Graham Fuller, in *Interview* (New York), April 1995.

On LEWIS: books—

Gehman, Richard, *That Kid: The Story of Jerry Lewis*, New York, 1964.
Maltin, Leonard, *Movie Comedy Teams*, New York, 1970.
Marx, Arthur, *Everybody Loves Somebody Sometime (Especially Himself): The Story of Dean Martin and Jerry Lewis*, New York, 1974.
Etaix, Pierre, *Croquis: Jerry Lewis*, Paris, 1983.
Marchesini, Mauro, *Jerry Lewis: Un comico a perdere*, Verona, Italy, 1983.
Benayoun, Robert, *Bonjour Monsieur Lewis: Journal ouvert, 1957-1980*, Paris, 1989.
Lewis, Patti, and Sarah Anne Coleman, *I Laffed Till I Cried: Thirty-Six Years of Marriage to Jerry Lewis*, Waco, Texas, 1993.
Neibaur, James L., and Ted Okuda, *The Jerry Lewis Films: An Analytical Filmography of the Innovative Comic*, Jefferson, North Carolina, 1994.
Levy, Shawn, *The King of Comedy: The Life and Art of Jerry Lewis*, New York, 1996.

On LEWIS: articles—

Farson, Daniel, "Funny Men: Dean Martin and Jerry Lewis," in *Sight and Sound* (London), July/September 1952.
Kass, Robert, "Jerry Lewis Analyzed," in *Films in Review* (New York), March 1953.
Hume, Rod, "Martin and Lewis: Are Their Critics Wrong?," in *Films and Filming* (London), March 1956.
Current Biography 1962, New York, 1962.
Taylor, John, "Jerry Lewis," in *Sight and Sound* (London), Spring 1965.
Sarris, Andrew, "Editor's Eyrie," in *Cahiers du Cinéma in English* (New York), no. 4, 1966.
Schickel, Richard, "Jerry Lewis Retrieves a Lost Ideal," in *Life* (New York), 15 July 1966.
Vialle, G., and others, "Jerry Lewis," in *Image et Son* (Paris), no. 278, 1973.
Coursodon, J.-P., "Jerry Lewis's Films: No Laughing Matter?," in *Film Comment* (New York), July/August 1975.
LeBour, F., and R. DeLaroche, "Which Way to Jerry Lewis?," in *Ecran* (Paris), July 1976.

Shearer, H., "Telethon," in *Film Comment* (New York), May/June 1979.
McGilligan, P., "Recycling Jerry Lewis," in *American Film* (Washington, D.C.), September 1979.
Jerry Lewis Section of *Casablanca* (Madrid), June 1983.
Polan, Dana, "Being and Nuttiness: Jerry Lewis and the French," in *Journal of Popular Film and Television* (Washington, D.C.), Spring 1984.
Liebman, R. L., "Rabbis or Rakes, Schlemiels or Supermen? Jewish Identity in Charles Chaplin, Jerry Lewis, and Woody Allen," in *Literature Film Quarterly* (Salisbury, Maryland), vol. 12, no. 3, July 1984.
"Jerry Lewis," in *Film Dope* (London), September 1986.
Beynaud, B., "Qui a peur de Jerry Lewis? Pas nous, pas nous," in *Cahiers du Cinéma* (Paris), February 1989.
Angeli, Michael, "God's Biggest Goof," in *Esquire* (New York), February 1991.
Hoberman, J., "Before There Was Scarface, There Was Rubberface," in *Interview* (New York), February 1993.
Rapf, Joanna E., "Comic Theory from Feminist Perspective: A Look at Jerry Lewis," in *Journal of Popular Culture* (Bowling Green, Ohio), Summer 1993.
Krutnik, Frank, "Jerry Lewis: The Deformation of the Comic," in *Film Quarterly* (Berkeley, California), Fall 1994.
Krutnik, Frank, "The Handsome Man and His Monkey: The Comic Bondage of Dean Martin and Jerry Lewis, in *Journal of Popular Film and Television* (Bowling Green, Ohio), Spring 1995.

*   *   *

Lionized by the French critics as a comic auteur equal to Chaplin and Keaton, Jerry Lewis has seldom found much favor with critics in his own country. While other comedians such as Abbott & Costello (even The Three Stooges) who were similarly dismissed by contemporary reviewers but have since achieved a degree of artistic respectability—in some quarters, more than that—with the passage of time, Lewis has yet to experience such reappraisal. He remains more honored in Europe—especially France, although Germany and Spain have showered him with honors, too—than at home despite a career as prolific in its output as those of his more esteemed comic colleagues.

The reason for this may be that Lewis's style of comedy—which, in its post-Dean Martin period, focused almost exclusively on Lewis himself, almost never the characters or events surrounding him—strikes people as self-indulgent, self-centered, even egotistical; this is a major turnoff, particularly to critics. Also, the screen character he created and lavished so much attention on—the child who never grew up, a mugging simpleton Lewis dubbed "the Kid"—is very much an acquired taste. Children, especially young tots, find the character amusingly simpatico. But many older viewers, from age 20 on, find it forced, grating, shallow, stupid, and excruciatingly witless.

Lewis began his career as a borscht belt comedian and impersonator of well-known singers of the day whose voices and mannerisms he mimicked to the accompaniment of recordings. His career was going nowhere until a chance meeting with a crooner named Dean Martin, whose career was likewise stalled, led to their teaming up. Their mostly improvised act involved Lewis's manic attempts to destroy Martin's numbers by breaking him up on-stage. It was audiences who broke up; within months, Martin & Lewis was the hottest comedy team in show business. Word spread, Hollywood called, and Martin & Lewis made their screen debut low down in the cast list of *My Friend Irma*, a comedy based on a hit radio show of time. The team essentially reprised its stage act in the film. Audiences felt they stole the picture, a hit, which was followed by a sequel, *My Friend Irma Goes West*, in which the duo was top-billed with stars John Lund and Marie Wilson. Signed to a long-term contract by Paramount, Martin & Lewis starred in more than a dozen wildly popular comedies for the studio until their celebrated split in 1956 following the appropriately titled *Hollywood or Bust*. Many believed their Hollywood careers would go bust without each other, but Martin & Lewis proved them wrong. Martin went on to achieve a successful solo career as a singer, actor, and television star. After *The Delicate Delinquent*, his first film without Martin (in which Darren McGavin stepped into the Martin straight man role), Lewis decided he no longer needed a straight man for his antics, and went solo himself.

Lewis's disenchantment with the nature of the team's screen persona was among the stated reasons for the break-up. Critic David Thomson has described the persona as that of ". . . two men at odds: Lewis seems hurt by Martin's callousness, just as Martin seems offended by the proximity of a slob." As the team's films progressed, Martin's suave and sophisticated character seemed to become increasingly scornful and unscrupulously manipulative of Lewis's nitwit character, whose antics escalated into an insufferably annoying plague on both their houses. But some critics have voiced another possible reason for the split: Lewis's ambivalent desire to be *like* Martin and simultaneously hostility toward him. These critics have pointed to Lewis's *The Nutty Professor* (1963) as a not-so-subtle expression of this inner war. In the film—a comic take on Stevenson's *Dr. Jekyll and Mr. Hyde* that Lewis starred in, co-wrote and directed—he plays a nerdy, lovesick chemistry professor in the "Kid" mold and the alter-ego he unleashes with his magic formula: suave singer and lounge lizard Buddy Love, a character viewed as a vicious takeoff on Martin. Later, in *Boeing, Boeing*, a romantic farce co-starring Tony Curtis, Lewis ironically played the more subdued, straight man role, a role Dean Martin could easily have stepped in himself, so there may be some validity to the critics' assessment.

Lewis's most important collaboration after the break-up with Martin was with Frank Tashlin, a former Warner Brothers cartoon director turned feature filmmaker, whose satiric style and eye for the cartoonlike, belly-laugh sight gag strongly influenced Lewis's subsequent career and own directorial approach. Lewis made two films for Tashlin with Martin (*Artists and Models, Hollywood or Bust*) and six without, arguably the best of which is *Rock-a-Bye-Baby* (1958), a remake of the Preston Sturges classic *The Miracle of Morgan's Creek* (1944).

Lewis turned to directing with *The Bellboy* (1960), hailed by French critics as Lewis's breakthrough film and funniest movie to date. It was quickly followed by *The Ladies' Man* and *The Errand Boy* (both 1961), then *The Nutty Professor*, which the French named the best picture of the year and Lewis's masterpiece—his intervening films with Tashlin notwithstanding. By 1965, Lewis was being deified by the French as the greatest comic artist since Buster Keaton, an inapt comparison on a number of levels. For one thing, Lewis's increasing penchant for inserting pathos and the occasional "message" into his work was less like Keaton than Chaplin, whose career Lewis seemed bent most in emulating. Unlike Chaplin, however, Lewis's scenes of pathos tend to be more mawkish than tear-jerkingly sentimental.

Lewis's *The Day the Clown Cried* (1972), a seriocomic look at the Holocaust from the perspective of a Jewish comic imprisoned in a Nazi death camp, remains his most ambitious attempt to emulate Chaplin. Whether he succeeded or not we still do not know as the film has yet to be released due to legal entanglements with its backers. The debacle apparently crushed Lewis's spirits for a time; he did not make another film until 1979's aptly titled *Hardly Working*, a critically scorned (in America) but commercial hit.

Since then, Lewis has chosen to remain in the public mind primarily as host of the Labor Day Muscular Dystrophy Telethon, an annual charitable rite with which he has been associated for years. His film performances have mostly been for other directors, the most notable being Martin Scorsese, in whose 1983 *The King of Comedy* Lewis undertook his first dramatic role as a late night television talk show entertainer in the vein of Johnny Carson stalked by an ambitious fan.

Lewis's performance garnered well-deserved accolades not just in France, but, at last, in the United States as well. In 1995 he made his Broadway debut as the devil in a revival of the musical comedy *Damn Yankees* and was similarly acclaimed. Perhaps these two atypical roles, and the impressive kudos he received for his performances in them, auger better things to come for the indominatable "Kid" in his native land.

—John McCarty

LEWIS, Juliette

Nationality: American. **Born:** Los Angeles, California, 21 June 1973; daughter of the actor Geoffrey Lewis. **Education:** Received high school equivalency diploma. **Career:** 1985—acting debut in the cable TV mini-series *Home Fires*; mid to late 1980s, appeared in several TV situation comedies, including *I Married Dora*, 1987-88, and a recurring role on *Wonder Years*, 1989-90; 1988—theatrical movie debut in *My Stepmother Is an Alien*; 1990—first leading role in the TV movie *Too Young to Die?*; 1990s—continued work in films, as well as in television commercials and music videos. **Agent:** William Morris Agency, 151 El Camino Drive, Beverly Hills, CA 90212, U.S.A.

Films as Actress:

1988   *My Stepmother Is an Alien* (Benjamin)
1989   *Meet the Hollowheads* (*Life on the Edge*) (Burman) (as Cindy Hollowhead); *National Lampoon's Christmas Vacation* (Chechik) (as Audrey Griswold); *The Runnin' Kind* (Tash)
1990   *Too Young to Die?* (Markowitz—for TV) (as Amanda Sue Bradley)
1991   *Crooked Hearts* (Bortman) (as Cassie Warren); *Cape Fear* (Scorsese) (as Danielle Bowden)
1992   *Husbands and Wives* (Woody Allen) (as Rain)
1993   *That Night* (*One Hot Summer*) (Bolotin (as Sheryl O'Connor); *Kalifornia* (Sena) (as Adele Corners); *What's Eating Gilbert Grape* (Hallström) (as Becky)
1994   *Romeo Is Bleeding* (Medak) (as Sheri); *Natural Born Killers* (Oliver Stone) (as Mallory Knox); *Mixed Nuts* (*Lifesavers*) (Nora Ephron) (as Gracie Barzini)
1995   *The Basketball Diaries* (Kalvert) (as Diane Moody); *Strange Days* (Bigelow) (as Faith Justin)
1996   *From Dusk Till Dawn* (Rodríguez) (as Kate Fuller); *The Audition* (Lightfield Lewis) (+ pr); *The Evening Star* (as granddaughter)

Publications

By LEWIS: articles—

"Hot Actress," interview with J. Colapinto, in *Rolling Stone* (New York), 14 May 1992.
"Big Girl Now," interview with David Handleman, in *Vogue* (New York), February 1993.
"Juliette and Her Friends," interview with Wolf Schneider, in *Interview* (New York), July 1993.

On LEWIS: articles—

Rimer, S., "The Lonely Lolita of *Cape Fear*," in *New York Times*, 24 November 1991.

Juliette Lewis in *Kalifornia*

Smith, C. S., "Fair Juliette," in *New York*, 25 November 1991.
Park, J., "She's Got a Foot in the Door," in *People Weekly* (New York), 9 December 1991.
Mithers, C. L., "Screen Angel," in *Mademoiselle*, September 1993.
Greene, Ray, "Caught in the Act," in *Boxoffice*, December 1993.
Diamond, Jamie, "The Quirky Allure of Juliette Lewis," in *Cosmopolitan* (New York), January 1995.
Current Biography 1996, New York, 1996.

*   *   *

In her relatively short film career, Juliette Lewis has amassed an impressive array of screen credits. Inspired by her well-known character actor father, Geoffrey Lewis, she has been acting in films and television since the age of 13. Although she has no formal acting training, Lewis has consistently demonstrated her astonishing ability to craft well-studied and fascinating performances. Accordingly, she has been sought out by a number of major directors and actors, and despite her youth, she has chosen roles that have given her the opportunity to exercise her wide-ranging acting skills—regardless of the commercial or star-making potential of the films.

Lewis earned her first significant critical praise with her appearance in the television movie *Too Young to Die?*, in which she played a bereft young teenager who is manipulated into murdering a former lover by Brad Pitt's smarmy hustler. Then, her breakthrough theatrical film performance was in Scorsese's *Cape Fear*, for which she received Golden Globe and Academy Award nominations, and which confirmed her reputation as a major young Hollywood talent. Her riveting performance is both confident and complex: she plays a shy, confused teenager in the awkward throes of her sexual awakening who gets caught in the web of a psychotic rapist. In the film's extraordinarily memorable and chilling seduction scene, Lewis perfectly conveys her young character's sense of attraction and repulsion for Robert De Niro's oddly compelling stranger.

More of a gamine than a conventionally pretty actress, Lewis is able to accommodate a variety of "looks"—from the perfect embodiment of threatened innocence, as in *Too Young to Die?* and *Cape Fear*, to the sexy, scantily clad, and aggressive femme fatale/rock star of *Strange Days*. In both her leading roles and her ensemble film work, Lewis typically has played naive, dispossessed, working-class characters, who are either strangely menacing or even coldly violent, as in *Kalifornia* and *Natural Born Killers*. Indeed, her role as the sexually abused and disaffected serial killer in the latter further confirmed her unusual willingness to risk playing mostly unsympathetic characters. An example of this occurs in the eccentric, over-the-top film *Romeo Is Bleeding*, in which she plays the underage mistress of Gary Oldman's crooked cop. But, she also delivered an inspired and convincing performance in *Husbands and Wives* as an upper-middle class, east-coast collegian who is the sexually knowing object of desire for Woody Allen's middle-aged character. Likewise, her performance in *What's Eating Gilbert Grape*—as a smart, sensitive, and worldly young woman traveling with her grandmother through the Midwest in a trailer, who captivates and enlightens Johnny Depp's Gilbert—displays her uncanny ability to produce quiet and subtly nuanced characterizations.

In her rare press and television interviews, Lewis repeatedly has expressed her desire to elude Hollywood's conventional star system, in order to continue taking chances and hone her already admirable talents as a performer. Still in her early twenties, Lewis fortunately has ample time in which to pursue and to demonstrate her creative and artistic priorities.

—Cynthia Felando

LINDER, Max

Nationality: French. **Born:** Gabriel-Maximilien Leuvielle in Caverne, near Saint-Loubes, 16 December 1882 (some sources say 1883). **Education:** Studied diction with Adrien Caillard at the Bordeaux Conservatory for two years. **Military Service:** Served in French Army, 1914; wounded; made propaganda tour in Italy and Switzerland, 1915, then served in air force, 1916; **Family:** Married Hélène Peters, 1923, daughter: Maud Max Linder. **Career:** Small parts (as Lacerda) at Théâtre des Arts, Bordeaux; 1904—acted at Théâtre de l'Ambigu, Paris; 1905—film debut (as Max Linder) in *La Vie de Polichinelle*; 1907-14—comedy film series for Pathe as "Gentleman of Paris"; directed most of his own films after 1910; 1910—personal appearance in Berlin, and in Spain, 1912, and Russia, 1913; 1917—made several films in the United States for Essanay; opened Cine Max Linder, Paris; 1919—in feature comedy, *Le Petit Café*; 1921-22—formed production company in Hollywood: made a non-Max film, *The Three Must-Get-Theres*; 1925—made his last film, in Vienna. **Died:** Double suicide with wife, 31 October 1925.

Films as Actor:

1905   *La Vie de Polichinelle*; *La Première Sortie d'un collégien* (Gasnier); *Une Représentation au cinéma*

1906   *Le Première Cigare d'un collégien* (Gasnier); *Le Pendu* (Gasnier); *Le Poison* (Gasnier); *Les Contrebandiers* (Nonguet)

1907   *Un Mariage d'amour*; *Indée d'apache* (Nonguet); *Une Mauvaise Vie* (Nonguet); *La Mort d'un toréador* (Gasnier); *Sagnarelle* (Capellani); *La Légende de Polichinelle* (Capellani)

1908   *Les Débuts d'un patineur* (Gasnier); *Le Duel de Monsieur Myope* (Gasnier); *La Rencontre imprévue* (Monca); *La Très Moutarde* (Monca); *Une Conquête* (Monca)

1909   *Le Petit Jeune Homme* (Gasnier); *Mariage à l'américaine* (Gasnier); *En bombe* (*En bombe après l'obtention de son bachot*) (Gasnier); *La Petite Rosse* (Gasnier); *Une Séance de cinématographe* (Gasnier); *Une Jeune Fille romanesque* (*A Romantic Young Lady*) (Gasnier); *La Timidité vaincue* (*A Cure for Timidity*) (Gasnier); *Trop aimée* (Gasnier); *Le Mariage forcé* (Gasnier); *Je voudrais un enfant* (Gasnier); *Je bridge au plafond* (Gasnier); *Mes voisins me font danser* (Gasnier); *Kyrelor, bandit par amour* (Gasnier); *L'Ingénieux Attendat* (Gasnier); *Une Poursuite mouvementée* (Gasnier); *Une Campagne electorale* (Gasnier); *Un Mariage au puzzle* (Gasnier); *Les Débuts d'un yachtman* (Gasnier); *Un Cross-Country original* (Gasnier); *N'embrassez pas votre bonne* (Monca); *Un Chien qui rapporte* (*Mon Chien rapporte*) (Monca); *Le Râtelier de la belle-mère* (Monca); *Le Soulier trop petit* (*Max's Feet Are Pinched*) (Monca); *Le Chapeau-Claqué* (Monca); *Le Baromètre de la fidélité* (Monca)

(as scriptwriter and actor, directed by Nonguet unless otherwise noted)

1910   *Max aéronaute* (*Max aviateur*); *Max se trompe d'etage*; *Max prend un bain*; *Max fait de la photo*; *Max joue le drame*; *Les Débuts de Max au cinéma* (*Débuts au cinématographe*); *Max et l'Edelweiss*; *Max fait au ski* (*Max Goes Skiing*); *Max fait du patinage à roulette*; *Max champion de boxe* (*Max Has the Boxing Fever*); *Max et la belle négresse*; *Max célibataire*; *Max et l'inauguration de la statue*; *Max et son rival* (*Tout est bien qui finit bien*); *Max et Clancy tombe d'accord*; *Max et le téléphone*; *Max et ses trois mariages*; *Le Cauchemar de Max*; *Max a le feu sacré*; *Max maîtresse de piano*; *L'Idiot qui se croit Max*; *Max hypnotisé*; *Une Bonne pour monsieur, un domestique pour madame*; *Max cherche une fiancée*; *Max manque un riche mariage* (*Max Is Almost Married*); *Max ne se mariera pas*; *Max a trouvé une fiancée*; *Max se marie* (*Le Mariage de Max*); *Max et sa belle-mère*; *La Flûte merveilleuse* (d: unknown)

1919   *Le Petit Café* (Bernard) (+ co sc)

1920   *Le Feu sacré* (Diamant-Berger)

1923   *Au secours!* (Gance)

Films as Director and Actor:

1911   *Max dans sa famille* (+ sc); *Max en convalescence* (+ sc); *Max est charitable*; *Max est distrait* (*Max Is Absent-Minded*); *Max et son âne* (*L'Ane jaloux*); *Voisin . . . voisin* (*Max et son voisin*) (+ sc); *Max a un duel*; *Max victime du Quinquina*; *Max veut faire du théâtre* (+ sc); *Max et Jane font des crêpes* (*Max cuisinier par amour*) (+ sc); *Max et Jane en voyage de noces* (+ sc); *Max lance la mode* (+ sc); *Max reprend sa liberté* (+ sc); *Max et son chien Dick* (+ sc); *Max amoureux de la teinturière* (+ sc)

1912   *Max Linder contre Nick Winter*; *Max bandit par amour*; *Que peut-il avoir? Max escamoteur* (*Le Succès de la prestidigitation*) (+ sc); *Une Nuit agitée* (+ sc); *La Malle au mariage* (+ sc); *Max cocher de fiacre* (+ sc); *Match de boxe entre patineurs à roulettes* (+ sc); *Max professeur de tango* (*Max Tango Teacher*; *Too Much Mustard*) (+ sc); *Max et les femmes* (*Oh les femmes!*) (+ sc); *Une Idylle à la ferme* (+ sc); *Un Par original* (+ sc); *Max peintre par amour* (+ sc); *La Fuite de gaz*; *Max boxeur par amour*; *Le Mal de mer* (+ sc); *La Vengeance du domestique* (+ sc); *Max collectionneur de chaussures*; *Max jockey par amour*; *Voyage de noces en Espagne* (*Le Voyage de noces*) (+ sc); *Max toréador*; *Max emule de Tartarin*; *Amour tenace*; *Max et l'Entente Cordiale* (+ sc); *Max veut grandir* (+ sc); *Un Mariage au téléphone* (+ sc); *Le Roman de Max* (+ sc); *Max pratique tous les sports* (+ co-sc)

1913   *Comment Max fait le tour du monde* (*How Max Went around the World*) (+ sc); *Max fait des conquêtes* (+ sc); *Max n'aime pas les chats* (+ sc); *Max et le billet doux* (+ sc); *Max part en vacances* (*Les Vacances de Max*) (+ sc); *Max à Monaco* (+ sc); *Max a peur de l'eau* (*La Peur de l'eau*) (+ sc); *Un Enlèvement en hydroplane* (+ sc); *Max asthmatique* (+ sc); *Le Rendezvous de Max* (+ sc); *La Rivalité de Max* (*Rivalité*) (+ sc); *Le Duel de Max*; *Un Mariage imprévu* (+ sc); *Le Hasard et l'amour* (+ sc); *Qui a tué Max?* (*Max assassinés, quel est l'assassin?*; *Who Killed Max?*); *Max au convent*; *Les Escarpins de Max* (+ sc); *La Ruse de Max* (+ sc); *Le Chapeau de Max* (+ sc); *Max virtuose* (+ sc)

1914   *Max sauveteur* (*Max décoré*; *La Médaille de sauvetage*); *Max et le commissaire*; *Max pédicure* (+ sc); *Max illusioniste* (+ sc); *N'embrassez pas votre bonne*; *Max et le bâton de rouge*;

Max Linder

L'Anglais tel que Max le parle (+ sc); *Max et le mari jaloux* (*Max jaloux*) (+ sc); *Max et la doctoresse* (+ sc); *Max maître d'hôtel* (+ sc); *Max médicin malgré lui* (+ sc); *Max dans les airs* (*Les Débuts d'un aviateur*) (+ sc); *Le 2 Août 1914*

1915 *Max devrait porter des bretelles* (+ sc); *Max et le sac* (+ sc); *Max et l'espion* (+ sc)

1916 *Max et la main qui etreint* (*Max victime de la main qui etreint*) (+ sc); *Max entre deux feux* (*Max entre deux femmes*) (+ sc)

1917 *Max Comes Across* (*Max in America*; *Max part en Amérique*) (+ sc); *Max Wants a Divorce* (*Max's Divorce Case*; *Max veut divorcer*) (+ sc); *Max in a Taxi* (*Max et son taxi*) (+ sc)

1921 *Be My Wife* (*Who Pays My Wife's Bill?*; *Soyez ma femme*) (+ sc); *Seven Years' Bad Luck* (*Sept ans de malheur*) (+ sc)

1922 *The Three Must-Get-Theres* (*L'Etroit mousquetaire*) (+ sc)

1924 *Der Zirkuskönig* (*Le Roi du cirque*; *King of the Circus*; *The Circus King*) (co-d: E.-E. Violet, + sc)

Publications

On LINDER: books—

Ford, Charles, *Max Linder*, Paris, 1966.
Lindner, Maud, *Max Linder etait mon pere*, Paris, 1992.

On LINDER: articles—

"Colloque autour de Max Linder," in *Cinéma* (Paris), January 1964.
Spears, J., "Max Linder," in *Films in Review* (New York), May 1965.
Mitry, Jean, "Max Linder," in *Anthologie du cinéma* (Paris), vol. 2, 1966.
Ciné Revue (Paris), 23 July 1981.
Classic Images (Indiana, Pennsylvania), September 1982.
Benson, S., "Max Linder Returns," in *Film Comment* (New York), September/October 1984.
Beylie, Claude, "Le Charme discret de Max Linder," in *Avant-Scène du Cinéma* (Paris), November 1984.
Kral, P., "Linder le prétendant 1883-1925," in *Positif* (Paris), January 1986.

* * *

In 1925, depressed by the sagging box-office receipts of his films, Max Linder entered into a suicide pact with his wife; they killed themselves in a Paris hotel room. Only a decade earlier Linder had been universally acclaimed as one of the cinema's most popular comedians. He had a profound influence on an entire generation of silent clowns; for years he treasured a portrait inscribed, "To the one and only Max, 'the Professor,' from his disciple, Charles Chaplin."

Chaplin's oft-acknowledged debt to Linder has kept the French comic's name alive in the intervening years, but the general unavailability of his work has kept his reputation shadowy otherwise. Happily, since the 1960s a great many of Linder's films have been found (though not all; he made over 500 features and shorts during his 20-year career) and a reevaluation may yet firmly establish his place in the pantheon. Like Raymond Griffith and Charley Chase, models of subtle urbanity, Linder built his comedy on character: suave, dapper, handsome, his perpetual befuddlement keenly offset by immaculate evening dress, top hat, opera cape, cane. Though he could be brilliantly physical, Max was characteristically the earnest and bemused eye of calm in the midst of a violent comic hurricane. In his unhurried style, imperturbability is the source of humor. Linder's comedy was at dead odds with the broad, fast, and vulgar Mack Sennett School, anticipating instead the slow, measured lunacy of the films of Hal Roach.

Linder was the total *auteur*. He wrote, produced, and directed nearly all of his hundreds of comedies. As a director, he exhibited what one is tempted to label a peculiarly "French" fascination with camera tricks and special effects. In *Max Is Jealous* (*Max and His Dog*) he splits the screen into three panels to show a phone conversation between Max and the dog. In *The Three Must-Get-Theres*, a Fairbanks parody, Linder utilizes slow-motion techniques and extreme camera angles, notably two overhead shots. In *Seven Years' Bad Luck* his precision and invention are demonstrated in a scene in which Max's servant breaks a full-length mirror and, in order to disguise the accident, must act as Max's reflection. That the idea is rich in comic promise can be proven by the number of succeeding comics who have borrowed the gag with excellent results: the Marx Brothers, Lucille Ball, Bob Hope, and others.

After World War I Linder's popularity faltered in a Chaplin-mad world, and his later films have been unjustly neglected. *Be My Wife*, *Seven Years' Bad Luck*, and *The Three Must-Get-Theres* are delightful features filled with inventive gags, imaginative camera work, and confident, resourceful direction. *Au secours*, a short directed in France by Abel Gance, is a startling and original haunted-house comedy that reflects both Gance's bold, innovative style and Linder's lifelong love of cinema trickery. *Au secours* was never released theatrically, perhaps because no one could decide how to market such a strange, and in some ways unsettling, film.

Linder was to make but one more film after *Au secours*, and his final works attest to the fact that he was still approaching the peak of his powers. However, all the facts are not yet in and many of Linder's films remain lost. Thus it may be a while before we can evaluate his importance in relation to those whom he inspired and (in some cases) anticipated.

—Frank Thompson

LLOYD, Harold

Nationality: American. **Born:** Burchard, Nebraska, 20 April 1893. **Education:** Studied acting at School of Dramatic Art, San Diego. **Family:** Married the actress Mildred Davis, 1923 (died 1969), daughters: Mildred Gloria and Marjorie Elizabeth (nickname "Peggy," adopted), son: Harold Jr. **Career:** 1906—acted with the Burwood Stock Company, Omaha; 1913—joined a stock company playing in Los Angeles; worked as extra at Edison and Universal studios; 1914—made several "Willie Work" comedies for Hal Roach, now lost; 1915—featured actor in *Just Nuts*; 1915-17—made series of comedies, "Lonesome Luke," often with Bebe Daniels and Snub Pollard; 1917-19—made series of comedies featuring "young man with horn-rimmed glasses," often with Mildred Davis; 1922—began making feature films exclusively; 1923—formed Harold Lloyd Corporation; 1929—first sound film, *Welcome Danger*; 1949-50—served as Supreme Imperial Potentate of Shriners; 1960s—produced two compilation films of his films. **Awards:** Honorary Oscar, for being "master comedian and good citizen," 1952; George Eastman Awards, 1955 and 1957. **Died:** Of cancer, in Hollywood, 8 March 1971.

Films as Actor:

1913 *The Old Monk's Tale* (Dawley—995 feet) (as extra)

1914 *Samson* (Macdonald) (as extra); *The Patchwork Girl of Oz* (*The Ragged Girl of Oz*) (Macdonald) (as Hottentot)

1915 *Love, Loot and Crash* (Cogley—one-reeler); *Their Social Splash* (Gillstrom—553 feet) (as the Minister); *Miss Fatty's Seaside Lovers* (Arbuckle—one-reeler) (as masher); *From Italy's Shores* (Otis Turner—two-reeler) (as gangster); *Courthouse Crooks* (Parrott—two-reeler) (as Tom, youth out of work)

(in one-reel comedies directed by Hal Roach)

1915 *Just Nuts* (as Willie Work); *Lonesome Luke; Once Every Ten Minutes; Spit-Ball Sadie; Soaking the Clothes; Pressing His Suit; Terribly Stuck Up; A Mixup for Mazie; Some Baby; Fresh from the Farm; Giving Them Fits; Bughouse Bellhops; Tinkering with Trouble; Great While It Lasted; Ragtime Snap Shots; A Fozzle at a Tee Party; Ruses, Rhymes and Roughnecks; Peculiar Patients' Pranks; Lonesome Luke, Social Gangster*

1916 *Luke Leans to the Literary; Luke Lugs Luggage; Lonesome Luke Lolls in Luxury; Luke the Candy Cut-Up; Luke Foils the Villain; Luke and the Rural Roughnecks; Luke Pipes the Pippins; Lonesome Luke, Circus King; Luke's Double; Them Was the Happy Days!; Luke and the Bomb Throwers; Luke's Late Lunches; Luke Laughs Last; Luke's Fatal Flivver; Luke's Society Mix-Up; Luke's Washful Waiting; Luke Rides Roughshod; Luke—Crystal Gazer; Luke's Lost Lamb; Luke Does the Midway; Luke Joins the Navy; Luke and the Mermaids; Luke's Speedy Club Life; Luke and the Bang-Tails; Luke, the Chauffeur; Luke's Preparedness Preparations; Luke, the Gladiator; Luke, Patient Provider; Luke's Newsie Knockout; Luke's Movie Muddle (Luke's Model Movie; Director of the Cinema); Luke's Fireworks Fizzle; Luke Locates the Loot; Luke's Shattered Sleep*

(alternately directed by Hal Roach and Alf Goulding, with several directed by Lloyd)

1917 *Luke's Lost Liberty; Luke's Busy Days; Luke's Trolley Trouble; Lonesome Luke, Lawyer; Luke Wins Ye Ladye Faire*

(two-reelers)

1917 *Lonesome Luke's Lively Life; Lonesome Luke on Tin Can Alley; Lonesome Luke's Honeymoon; Lonesome Luke, Plumber; Stop! Luke! Listen!; Lonesome Luke, Messenger; Lonesome Luke, Mechanic; Lonesome Luke's Wild Women; Lonesome Luke Loses Patients; Birds of a Feather; Lonesome Luke from London to Laramie; Love, Laughs, and Lather; Clubs Are Trump; We Never Sleep*

(one-reelers as young man with horn-rimmed glasses)

1917 *Over the Fence* (as Ginger, + co-d with Macdonald); *Pinched; By the Sad Sea Waves; Bliss; Rainbow Island; The Flirt; All Aboard* (as the boy); *Move On; Bashful; Step Lively*

1918 *The Tip; The Big Idea; The Lamb; Hit Him Again; Beat It; A Gasoline Wedding; Look Pleasant, Please; Here Come the Girls; Let's Go; On the Jump; Follow the Crowd; Pipe the Whiskers; It's a Wild Life* (Pratt); *Hey There!; Kicked Out; The Non-Stop Kid* (as the boy); *Two-Gun Gussie* (as Harold); *Fireman, Save My Child; The City Slicker* (as Harold); *Sic 'em Towser; Somewhere in Turkey; Are Crooks Dishonest?* (as Jitney Jim); *An Ozark Romance; Kicking the Germ out of Germany; That's Him; Bride and Gloom; Two Scrambled; Bees in His Bonnet; Swing Your Partners; Why Pick on Me?* (as the boy); *Nothing but Trouble; Hear 'em Rave; Take a Chance; She Loves Me Not*

1919 *Wanted—$5000; Going! Going! Gone!; Ask Father* (as the boy); *On the Fire (The Chef)* (Roach) (as Winkle); *I'm on My Way* (as the boy); *Look Out Below; The Dutiful Dub; Next Aisle Over; A Sammy in Siberia; Just Dropped In; Crack Your Heels; Ring Up the Curtain* (as the boy); *Young Mr. Jazz; Si, Senor; Before Breakfast; The Marathon; Back to*

the Woods; *Pistols for Breakfast; Swat the Crook; Off the Trolley; Spring Fever* (as Billy); *Billy Blazes, Esq; Just Neighbors* (as the boy); *At the Old Stage Door; Never Touched Me* (as the boy); *A Jazzed Honeymoon; Count Your Change (Step Lively)* (as the boy); *Chop Suey and Co.* (as Officer Harold); *Heap Big Chief; Don't Shove* (as the boy); *Be My Wife; The Rajah; He Leads, Others Follow; Soft Money; Count the Votes; Pay Your Dues* (as the boy); *His Only Father*

(two-reelers, unless otherwise noted)

1919 *Bumping into Broadway* (as the boy); *Captain Kidd's Kids* (Roach) (as the boy); *From Hand to Mouth* (Goulding) (as the boy)

1920 *His Royal Slyness* (Roach) (as the American boy); *Haunted Spooks* (Roach and Goulding) (as the boy); *An Eastern Westerner* (Roach) (as the boy); *High and Dizzy* (Roach) (as Harold Hal); *Get Out and Get Under* (Roach); *Number, Please* (Roach and Newmeyer) (as the boy)

1921 *Now or Never* (Roach and Newmeyer—three-reeler); *Among Those Present* (Newmeyer) (as O'Reilly, the boy); *I Do* (as the boy); *Never Weaken* (Newmeyer—three-reeler) (as the boy)

(feature-length films)

1921 *Sailor-Made Man* (Newmeyer) (as the boy)

1922 *Grandma's Boy* (Newmeyer) (as the boy, Sonny/Granddaddy in flashback); *Dr. Jack* (Newmeyer) (title role)

1923 *Safety Last* (Newmeyer and Sam Taylor) (as the boy); *Dogs of War* (Roach—two-reeler) (as himself); *Why Worry?* (Newmeyer and Sam Taylor) (as Harold Van Pelham)

1924 *Girl Shy* (Newmeyer and Sam Taylor) (as the poor boy, Harold Meadows, + pr); *Hot Water* (Sam Taylor and Newmeyer) (as Hubby, + pr)

1925 *The Freshman* (Sam Taylor and Newmeyer) (as Harold "Speedy" Lamb, + pr)

1926 *For Heaven's Sake* (Sam Taylor) (as "The Uptown Boy," J. Harold Manners, + pr)

1927 *The Kid Brother* (Milestone, Howe, Neal, and Wilde) (as Harold Hickory, + pr)

1928 *Speedy* (Wilde) (as Harold "Speedy" Swift, + pr)

1929 *Welcome Danger* (Mal St. Clair and Bruckman) (as Harold Bledsoe, + pr)

1930 *Feet First* (Bruckman) (as Harold Horne, + pr)

1932 *Movie Crazy* (Bruckman) (as Harold Hall, + pr)

1934 *The Cat's Paw* (Sam Taylor) (as Ezekiel Cobb, + pr)

1936 *The Milky Way* (McCarey) (as Burleigh "Tiger" Sullivan, + pr)

1938 *Professor Beware* (Nugent) (as Prof. Dean Lambert, + pr)

1947 *Mad Wednesday (The Sin of Harold Diddlebock)* (Preston Sturges) (as Harold Diddlebock)

1962 *Harold Lloyd's World of Comedy* (compilation) (+ pr)

1966 *Harold Lloyd's Funny Side of Life* (compilation) (+ pr)

Films as Producer:

1941 *A Girl, a Guy, and a Gob (The Navy Steps Out)* (Wallace)

1942 *My Favorite Spy* (Garnett)

Publications

By LLOYD: book—

An American Comedy: An Autobiography, with Wesley W. Stout, New York, 1928.

Harold Lloyd

By LLOYD: articles—

"My Ideal Girl," in *Motion Picture Magazine* (New York), July 1918.

"For the People, by the People," in *Filmplay Journal*, April 1922.

"We Interview the Boy," interview with Gladys Hall and Adele Fletcher, in *Motion Picture Magazine* (New York), July 1922.

"Comedy Development," in *The Truth about the Movies by the Stars*, Hollywood, 1924.

"The Autobiography of Harold Lloyd," in *Photoplay* (New York), May/June 1924.

"What Is Love," in *Photoplay* (New York), February 1925.

"Harold Lloyd Tells the Most Dramatic Moments of His Life," in *Motion Picture*, December 1925.

"Hardships of Fun-Making," in *Ladies Home Journal*, May 1926.

"When They Gave Me the Air," in *Ladies Home Journal*, February 1928.

"Looking at the World through Horn-Rimmed Specs," in *Motion Picture Magazine* (New York), September 1933.

"Meeting with Harold Lloyd," interview with M. Calman, in *Sight and Sound* (London), Winter 1958/59.

"Interview with Harold Lloyd," interview with Arthur Friedman, in *Film Quarterly* (Berkeley), Summer 1962.

"The Funny Side of Life," in *Films and Filming* (London), January 1964.

"The Serious Business of Being Funny," interview with Hubert I. Cohen, in *Film Comment* (New York), Fall 1969.

"Harold Lloyd Talks to Anthony Slide about His Early Career," in *Silent Picture* (London), Summer/Autumn 1971.

Memoirs in *Ciné-Magazine*, 1930, reprinted in *Avant-Scène du Cinéma* (Paris), 15 October 1980.

On LLOYD: books—

Cahn, William, *Harold Lloyd's World of Comedy*, New York, 1964.

Borde, Raymonde, *Harold Lloyd*, Lyon, 1968.

McCaffrey, Donald W., *Four Great Comedians: Chaplin, Lloyd, Keaton, Langdon*, New York, 1968.

Lacourbe, Roland, *Harold Lloyd*, Paris, 1970.

Bowser, Eileen, *Harold Lloyd's Short Comedies*, New York, 1974.

Schickel, Richard, *Harold Lloyd: The Shape of Laughter*, Greenwich, Connecticut, 1974.

McCaffrey, Donald W., *Three Classic Silent Screen Comedies Starring Harold Lloyd*, Cranbury, New Jersey, 1976.

Reilly, Adam, *Harold Lloyd: The King of Daredevil Comedy*, New York, 1977.

Kerr, Walter, *The Silent Clowns*, New York, 1979.

Mast, Gerald, *The Comic Mind: Comedy and the Movies*, Chicago, rev. ed., 1979.

Tichy, Wolfram, *Harold Lloyd*, Frankfurt, 1979.

Dardis, Tom, *Harold Lloyd: The Man on the Clock*, New York, 1983.

D'Agostino, Annette M., *Harold Lloyd: A Bio-Bibliography*, Westport, Connecticut, 1994.

On LLOYD: articles—

Leigh, Anabel, "Specs without Glass," in *Photoplay* (New York), January 1920.

St. Johns, Adela Rogers, "What about Harold Lloyd," in *Photoplay* (New York), August 1922.

St. Johns, Adela Rogers, "How Lloyd Made *Safety Last*," in *Photoplay* (New York), July 1923.

Taylor, Sam, "Directing Harold Lloyd," in *Motion Picture Director*, November 1925.

Sherwood, Robert E., "The Perennial Freshman," in *New Yorker*, 30 January 1926.

Current Biography 1949, New York, 1949.

Agee, James, "Boy," in *Life* (New York), 5 September 1949.

Garringer, Nelson E., "Harold Lloyd Made a Fortune by Combining Comedy and Thrills," in *Films in Review* (New York), August/September 1962.

Borde, Raymonde, "L'Insolence de Harold Lloyd," in *Positif* (Paris) Summer 1966.

McCaffrey, Donald W., "The Mutual Approval of Keaton and Lloyd," in *Cinema Journal* (Evanston, Ill.), no. 6, 1966-67.

Obituary in *New York Times*, 9 March 1971.

Sarris, Andrew, "Harold Lloyd 1893-1971," in *New York Times*, 21 March 1971.

Slide, Anthony, obituary in *Silent Picture* (London), Summer/Autumn 1971.

Kaminsky, Stuart, "Harold Lloyd: A Reassessment of His Film Comedy," in *Silent Picture* (London), Autumn 1972.

Sarris, Andrew, "Harold Lloyd: A Rediscovery," in *American Film* (Washington, D.C.), September 1977.

Lacourbe, Roland, "Harold Lloyd, 1893-1971," in *Avant-Scène du Cinéma* (Paris), 1 May 1979.

Kral, P., "Harold l'insouciant ou portrait du poète en jeune entrepreneur," in *Positif* (Paris), December 1979.

Fernett, Gene, "A Retrospective: Harold Lloyd," in *Classic Images* (Muscatine, Iowa), March 1983.

deCroix, Rick, "Fighting for Reappraisal," in *Classic Images* (Muscatine, Iowa), November and December 1988, and January and February 1989.

"Gripping Stuff," in the *Listener* (London), 15 February 1990.

Brownlow, Kevin, "Harold Lloyd: A Renaissance Palace for One of the Silent Era's Great Comic Pioneers," in *Architectural Digest*, April 1990.

Santilli, Ernie, "Harold Lloyd: The Overlooked Overachiever," in *Filmfax* (Evanston, Illinois), April/May 1992.

Champlin, Charles, "Silent Film's Third Genius," in *Los Angeles Times*, 31 March 1993.

Brownlow, Kevin, "Preserved in Amber," in *Film Comment* (New York), March/April 1993.

Rivers, Scott, "Harold Lloyd: The Third Genius," in *Classic Images* (Muscatine, Iowa), September 1993.

Siegel, Scott, and Barbara Siegel, "Harold Lloyd," in *American Film Comedy*, New York, 1994.

Bassan, R., "Harold Lloyd, ou le comique ascenionnel," in *Le Mensuel du Cinéma* (Paris), January 1994.

D'Agostino, Annette, "Harold Lloyd: A Comic Genius Learns Comedy," in *Classical Images* (Muscatine, Iowa), April 1995.

On LLOYD: film—

Harold Lloyd: The Third Genius, television documentary directed by Kevin Brownlow and David Gill, 1989.

*   *   *

The sophistication and maturation of the silent screen comedy feature emerged in only a few years in the early 1920s—a phenomenon that came from the innovative efforts of Charlie Chaplin, Harold Lloyd, and Buster Keaton. As these three comedians graduated from one- and two-reel films, the scope of the five- and six-reel works dictated a need for a wider range of story material and a variety in acting levels and styles. An article entitled "Comedy Development," by Lloyd in the 1924 *Truth about the Movies by the Stars* indicated the actor saw the necessity of avoiding the same theme and type of film: "It is our intention to mix up the type of offering we will present. That has been our policy in the past, and it has worked out highly satisfactorily. . . . For no matter how great the appeal of a player, he cannot go on forever giving his public the same kind of picture, release after release."

As a very popular comedian in his one- and two-reelers, the actor first employed a character with limited dimension. From 1915 to 1918 Lloyd used an oddball tramp, Lonesome Luke, closely related to the circus clown and relied on wacky comic material that became the staple of a Mack Sennett slapstick short. When he switched to a character closer to that developed by the light comedians of the time—the young man next door—his acting style changed and his characterization became more appealing. A more realistic mode of acting became evident in his 1919 one-reel, *Just Neighbors*. The comedian developed incidents of frustration in the beginning of the film as he played a young man from the suburbs trying to catch a commuter train to his job in the city. The struggle of this character, called simply "The Boy," exhibited subtle facial expressions of annoyance, avoiding the broad body gestures of the earlier Lonesome Luke tramp character. Nevertheless, when Lloyd's young man gets into an altercation with his neighbor, a broad, slapstick fistfight shows a return to the comedy acting style of Lloyd's early films.

When Lloyd adopted the story material of the genteel comedians of the twenties—Charles Ray, Wallace Reid, and Douglas MacLean—he surpassed them in acting skills and the quality and quantity of laughable movies. In the development of a comic character in his first feature, *Grandma's Boy* (1922), the comedian could create a lighter, character-based humor of humiliation set against a stronger, broader, and ludicrous situation when his shy, withdrawn character metamorphosizes into an aggressive young man battling a villain. From hangdog expressions and wilted bodily movements the comedian showed a transition to a bold, erect stature of a man with a jutting aggressive jaw.

The key to understanding the comic character created by Lloyd lies in the leading figure's zeal. The enthusiasm of this character gives it distinction. Leading comedians of the time—Chaplin, Keaton, and Langdon—seldom used this trait in their comic characters. Lloyd, on the other hand, used this trait as the basic facet of his portrait. Some of the best comic moments of his films occur when Harold's zeal leads him into situations that backfire. His eagerness to be successful socially or financially leads him into the path of a rival who is a villain or into a scheme with many pitfalls. The comedian's acting ability comes into play as he attempts to cover his distress with a twisted smile. Attempts to impress a college clique in the 1925 *The Freshman* show the comedian exhibiting overeagerness to the point that he becomes the subject of the group's ridicule. As the character is humiliated, Lloyd provides a variety of humorous, pained expressions. But eventually the character's enthusiasms turns the tide in his favor. The fault that gains laughter is also the virtue that wins the victory. And victory quite often is achieved with the assistance of luck.

One of the misconceptions that has distorted the evaluation of Harold Lloyd's comic abilities is the view of some critics that he merely used a string of clever gags in his features—that he was in the same league as the lightweight, genteel comedians such as Ray, Reid, and MacLean who were popular actors in the silent features of the twenties. In the essay "Harold Lloyd: Comedy through Characterization" in *Harold Lloyd: The King of Daredevil Comedy*, Leonard Maltin refutes this concept. Maltin considers the comedian's acting talent to be an integral part of the characterization in the pictures he created: "For in order for that character to succeed as he did, there had to be a basic credibility . . . in his disarmingly natural performances. Like so many great performers who make their work look easy, Lloyd suffered the natural consequence of having certain critics believe that he wasn't really contributing much to his own films—that he was simply a likable fellow surrounded by funny incidents, and therefore a success by circumstance. This does a great injustice to a major comedy talent."

There is little doubt that Harold Lloyd has the credentials to be ranked as one of the kings of comedy of the silent period. A showing today of his *Grandma's Boy*, *Safety Last*, *The Freshman*, and *The Kid*

Brother brings high praise from sophisticated audiences. Not well known are his sound films. Lloyd made the transition to sound pictures more easily than the other three kings of comedy: Chaplin, Keaton, and Langdon. Like the eager, adventurous character he portrayed, Lloyd plunged into sound films with *Welcome Danger* in 1929. Under his own supervision he did five more feature in the thirties: *Feet First*, *Movie Crazy*, *The Cat's Paw*, *The Milky Way*, and *Professor Beware*. His last feature in 1947 under the direction of Preston Sturges, *The Sin of Harold Diddlebock* (renamed *Mad Wednesday*), did not meet with Lloyd's high standards. Nevertheless, this forties film and his sound films of the thirties were a match for if not superior to other comedies created in these two decades.

—Donald McCaffrey

LOCKWOOD, Margaret

Nationality: British. **Born:** Karachi, India (now Pakistan), 15 September 1916. **Education:** Attended Sydenham High School; studied dance at the Italia Conti school; Royal Academy of Dramatic Arts, 1933. **Family:** Married Rupert Leon, 1937 (divorced 1950), daughter: Margaret Julia. **Career:** 1931—stage debut in *A Midsummer Night's Dream* at the Holborn Empire; 1935—film debut in *Lorna Doone*; 1939—brief visit to Hollywood; 1948—TV debut in *Pygmalion* as Eliza Doolittle, also played role on stage, 1951; later stage work included *An Ideal Husband*, 1965, and *Lady Frederick*, 1970; 1952—contract with Herbert Wilcox; 1965—in TV series *The Flying Swan* with daughter Julia; later work included *Justice*, 1972-73. **Awards:** Commander, Order of the British Empire, 1980. **Died:** In London, 15 July 1990.

Films as Actress:

1935   *Lorna Doone* (Dean) (as Annie Ridd); *The Case of Gabriel Perry* (*Wild Justice*) (de Courville) (as Mildred Perry); *Some Day* (Powell) (as Emily); *Honours Easy* (Mycroft) (as Ann); *Man of the Moment* (Banks) (as Vera); *Midshipman Easy* (*Men of the Sea*) (Reed) (as Donna Agnes)

1936   *Jury's Evidence* (Ince) (as Betty Stanton); *The Amateur Gentleman* (Freeland) (as Georgina Hunstanton); *The Beloved Vagabond* (Bernhardt) (as Blanquette); *Irish for Luck* (Woods) (as Ellen O'Hare)

1937   *Street Singer* (de Marguenat) (as Jenny Green); *Who's Your Lady Friend?* (Reed) (as Mimi); *Dr. Syn* (Neill) (as Imogene); *Melody and Romance* (Elvey) (as Margaret Williams)

1938   *Owd Bob* (*To the Victor*) (Stevenson) (as Jeannie McAdam); *Bank Holiday* (*Three on a Weekend*) (Reed) (as Catherine Lawrence); **The Lady Vanishes** (Hitchcock) (as Iris Henderson)

1939   *Rulers of the Sea* (Lloyd) (as Mary Shaw); *Susannah of the Mounties* (Seiter) (as Vicky Standing); *A Girl Must Live* (Reed) (as Leslie James); *The Stars Look Down* (Reed) (as Jenny Sunley)

1940   *Night Train to Munich* (*Night Train*; *Gestapo*) (Reed) (as Anna Bomasch); *The Girl in the News* (Reed) (as Anne Graham)

1941   *Quiet Wedding* (Asquith) (as Janet Royd)

1942   *Alibi* (Hurst) (as Helene Ardouin)

1943   *The Man in Grey* (Arliss) (as Hesther Shaw); *Dear Octopus* (*The Randolph Family*) (French) (as Penny Randolph)

1944   *Give Us the Moon* (Guest) (as Nina); *Love Story* (*A Lady Surrenders*) (Arliss) (as Lissa Campbell)

Margaret Lockwood with James Mason in *The Wicked Lady*

1945   *A Place of One's Own* (Knowles) (as Annette); *I'll Be Your Sweetheart* (Guest) (as Edie Story); *The Wicked Lady* (Arliss) (as Barbara Worth/Lady Skelton)

1946   *Bedelia* (Comfort) (as Bedelia Carrington)

1947   *Hungry Hill* (Hurst) (as Fanny Ross); *Jassy* (Box) (as Jassy Woodroffe); *The White Unicorn* (*Bad Sister*) (Knowles) (as Lucy)

1948   *Look before You Love* (Huth) (as Ann Markham)

1949   *Cardboard Cavalier* (Forde) (as Nell Gwynne); *Madness of the Heart* (Bennett) (as Lydia Garth)

1950   *Highly Dangerous* (Baker) (as Frances Gray)

1952   *Trent's Last Case* (Wilcox) (as Margaret Manderson)

1953   *Laughing Anne* (Wilcox) (as Anne)

1954   *Trouble in the Glen* (Wilcox) (as Marissa Mengues)

1955   *Cast a Dark Shadow* (Gilbert) (as Freda Jeffries)

1976   *The Slipper and the Rose* (Forbes) (as Stepmother)

Publications

By LOCKWOOD: books—

My Life and Films, London, 1948.
Lucky Star: The Autobiography of Margaret Lockwood, London, 1955.

By LOCKWOOD: articles—

Interview, in *Film Weekly* (London), 2 September 1939.
Interview, in *Picturegoer* (London), 9 December 1944.
Interview, in *TV Times* (London), 20 November 1975.
Interview, in *Films Illustrated* (London), December 1975.

On LOCKWOOD: books—

Aspinall, Sue, and Robert Murphy, editors, *Gainsborough Melodrama*, London, 1983.
Tims, Hilton, *Once a Wicked Lady: A Biography of Margaret Lockwood*, London, 1989.

On LOCKWOOD: articles—

Picturegoer (London), 29 July 1939, 22 February 1941, 4 April 1942, 2 September 1944, 3 August 1946, 6 November 1948, 23 March-22 April 1950, and 31 January 1953.
Films and Filming (London), July 1963 and September 1973.
"Margaret Lockwood—the Gainsborough Lady," in *National Film Theatre Booklet* (London), September/October 1986.
"Margaret Lockwood," in *Film Dope* (London), February 1987.

Adair, Gilbert, Phyllis Calvert, and Michael Winner, obituaries in the *Independent* (London), 17 July 1990.
Obituary, in *Variety* (New York), 18 July 1990.

*   *   *

Although Margaret Lockwood had made 31 films in the preceding years, *The Wicked Lady* (1945) is the one film for which she is most remembered. For Margaret Lockwood the role and the title were destined to become synonymous with her. In a career of more than 40 films and numerous television appearances, Margaret Lockwood was "wicked" in only three of them. But it was her ability to play this type of character that remains the key point of identity for her star image in popular memory.

The "quota quickie" era of the 1930s had allowed Lockwood to make a large number of cheap films that familiarized her with studio techniques and enabled her to develop an acting style for camera. In 1935 alone she made six films—more than any other year of her career. This intense apprenticeship in film acting established Margaret Lockwood as a *film* actress at a time when most of British stars came from a strong theater or music hall tradition. Her biographer sees this point as a significant aspect of her later appeal: "The British cinema hadn't so far discovered and groomed a star it could call its own. Margaret, unmannered and possessing a technique which hadn't been schooled in the theater, was a natural for the camera and the microphone. The first favoured her pretty, well-defined features, the second a pleasant, musical voice free of the curlicues and exaggerations which most young actresses of that time assumed."

By the end of the 1930s, Margaret Lockwood was emerging as a star with a career modeled through a Hollywood-style British studio system. In 1937, Margaret Lockwood was offered a three-year contract with Gainsborough Studios as the company's first move to implement the plan to create Britain's first custom-made film star. The success of films such as *The Lady Vanishes* and *The Stars Look Down* established her star status and enabled her to go on to become the most popular and successful British screen actress of the 1940s.

The significance of *The Wicked Lady* then is not so much in terms of establishing Margaret Lockwood's star image as in changing it. When she had played a cheap, scheming hussy who trapped the hero into marriage in *The Stars Look Down* the critics acclaimed her performance, but fans all over the country wrote indignant letters to the star and the producer. The prospect of a similar reaction caused a certain amount of anxiety when she was cast as a wicked murderess in her first costume melodrama for Gainsborough, *The Man in Grey*. However, the result was a huge increase in fan mail for Lockwood. The wickedness of this character proved thrilling in a way that the mere bitchiness of the character in *The Stars Look Down* was not.

The Stars Look Down had certainly been a departure for Margaret Lockwood. While the performance might have confused her star image of the 1930s, *The Man in Grey* was the first step in transforming it in the mid-1940s. Most of her films prior to this had contributed to the establishment of an unremarkable star image—the genteel, demure and very English middle-class woman. But with this established track record it was all the more shocking to see the display of ruthless independence, sexual desire and wickedness that the *The Man in Grey* unleashed. The advent of *The Wicked Lady* in 1945 offered the prospect of taking the image to its limits with a part designed to be the most ruthless, amoral character any British film had ever dared to present. From being the "nice girl," she suddenly became exciting, daring, glamorous and independent—a transformation that was greeted with astounding adulation by her audiences.

If the potency of the wicked lady image lay in the shock of seeing a dramatic change in Margaret Lockwood's star image, it also touched a chord in the "new woman" emerging from the disciplines of a long war. As Hilton Tims notes, this wicked lady was "a woman of independence, flouting hidebound convention, flaunting her superiority over men and contempt for them with courage, singlemindedness and feminine wiles."

Such characteristics were enormously appealing and exciting for those British women who had tasted independence during the war years and were striving against attempts to return them to submissive domesticity. Appearing as she did in the popular women's genre of melodrama, Margaret Lockwood provided her female audience with a fantasy role model for the immediate postwar years. The intensity of this portrayal and the strength of the chord that was struck ensured that Margaret Lockwood would carry this image into the history of British cinema.

—Margaret O'Connor

LOLLOBRIGIDA, Gina

Nationality: Italian. **Born:** Subiaco, 4 July 1928 (some sources give 1927). **Education:** Studied sculpture and painting at the Academy of Fine Arts, Rome, 1944-47. **Family:** Married Drago Milko Skofic, 1950 (divorced), one son. **Career:** Singer and model for photographed comic strips (as Diana Loris) in mid-1940s; 1946—film debut in *Aquila Nera*; 1949—contract with Howard Hughes, who did not use her services for the next ten years; 1970s—devoted herself to photography and work for a fashion and cosmetics firm; 1975—directed the documentary film *Portrait of Fidel Castro*; 1984—appeared in TV series *Falcon Crest*; on Broadway in *The Rose Tattoo*. **Awards:** Silver Ribbon, Italy, for *Pane, amore, e fantasia*, 1953. **Address:** Via Appia Antica 223, 11078 Rome, Italy.

Films as Actress:

1946 *Aquila Nera* (*The Black Eagle*) (Freda); *Lucia di Lammermoor* (Ballerini)

1947 *Il segreto di Don Giovanni* (Mastrocinque); *Il delitto di Giovanni Episcopo* (Lattuada); *Vendetta nel sole* (*A Man about the House*) (Arliss and Amato); *L'elisir d'amore* (Costa)

1948 *Follie per l'opera* (Costa) (as Dora); *I pagliacci* (Costa) (as Nedda)

1949 *Campane a martello* (*Children of Chance*) (Zampa) (as Agostina Bortolizzi); *La sposa non può attender* (Franciolini) (as Donata)

1950 *Miss Italy* (Coletti) (as Lisetta Minneci); *Cuori senza fontiere* (*The White Line*) (Zampa) (as Donata Sebastian); *Vita da cani* (Steno and Monicelli) (as Margherita); *Aline* (Pastina) (title role)

1951 *Passaporto per l'Oriente* (*A Tale of Five Cities*; *A Tale of Five Women*) (Tully and others) (as Maria Severini); *La città si difende* (*Four Ways Out*) (Germi) (as Daniela); *Enrico Caruso, leggenda di una voce* (Gentilomo) (as Stella); *Achtung! Bandit!* (Lizzani) (as Anna); *Fanfan la Tulipe* (*Fanfan the Tulip*; *Soldier in Love*) (Christian-Jaque) (as Adeline); *Amor non ho . . . pero . . . pero* (Bianchi) (as Gina)

1952 "The Trial of Frine" ep. of *Altri tempi* (*Times Gone By*) (Blasetti) (as Frine); *Les Belles de nuit* (*La belle della notte*; *Beauties of the Night*) (Clair) (as Leila); *Moglie per una notte* (Camerini) (as Ottavia)

1953 *Le infedeli* (*The Unfaithfuls*) (Steno and Monicelli) (as Lulla Possenti); *La provinciale* (Soldati) (as Gemma Foresi); *Il maestro di Don Giovanni* (*Crossed Swords*) (Krims) (as

Francesca); *Pane, amore, e fantasia* (*Bread, Love and Dreams*) (Comencini) (as the girl, "Frisky"); *Beat the Devil* (Huston) (as Maria Dannreuther)

1954 *Le Grand Jeu* (*Flesh and the Woman*; *Il grande giuoco*; *The Big Game*) (Siodmak) (as Elena/Silvia); *La romana* (*Woman of Rome*) (Zampa) (as Adriana); *Pane, amore, e gelosia* (Comencini) (as Carotenuto)

1955 *La donna più bella del mundo* (Leonard) (as Lina Cavalieri); *Frisky* (Comencini) (title role)

1956 *Trapeze* (Reed) (as Lola); *Notre Dame de Paris* (*The Hunchback of Notre Dame*) (Delannoy) (as Esmeralda)

1958 *Anna di Brooklyn* (*Anna of Brooklyn*; *Fast and Sexy*) (Lastricati and Denham) (as Anna)

1959 *La Loi* (*Where the Hot Wind Blows*; *Le legge*; *The Law*) (Dassin) (as Marietta); *Never So Few* (John Sturges) (as Carla Vesari); *Solomon and Sheba* (King Vidor) (as Sheba)

1961 *Go Naked in the World* (MacDougall) (as Giulietta Cameron); *Come September* (Mulligan) (as Lisa Fellini)

1962 *Venere imperiale* (*Imperial Venus*; *Vénus impériale*) (Delannoy) (as Paolina Borghese)

1963 *Mare matto* (Castellani) (as Margherita)

1964 *Woman of Straw* (Dearden) (as Maria Marcello); "Monsignor Cupido" ep. of *Le bambole* (*Four Kinds of Love*; *The Dolls*) (Bolognini) (as Beatrice)

1965 *Strange Bedfellows* (Frank) (as Toni Vincente)

1966 *Io, io, io . . . e gli altri* (Blasetti) (as Titta); *Les Sultans* (*L'amante italiana*) (Delannoy) (as Lisa); *Hotel Paradiso* (Glenville) (as Marcelle Cot); *Le piacevoli notti* (Crispino and Lucignani) (as Domicilla)

1967 *La morte la fatto, l'uovo* (*Plucked*; *A Curious Way to Love*) (Questi) (as Anna)

1968 *The Private Navy of Sgt. O'Farrell* (Tashlin) (as Maria); *Un bellissimo novembre* (*That Splendid November*) (Bolognini) (as Cettina); *Le Avventure e gli amori di Miguel Cervantes* (*The Young Rebel*; *Cervantes*; *Les Aventures extraordinaires de Cervantes*) (Sherman) (as Giulia Toffolo)

1969 *Buona Sera, Mrs. Campbell* (Frank) (as Carla Campbell); *Stuntman* (Baldi) (as Evelyn Lake)

1970 *. . . e eontinuavano a fregarsi il milione di dollari* (Martin) (as Alicia)

1971 *Le avventure di Pinocchio* (Comencini) (as la fata turchina)

1972 *Herzbube* (*King, Queen, Knave*) (Skolimowski) (as Martha Dreyer); *Peccato mortale* (Rovira-Beleta) (as Netty); *Bad Man's River* (*Matalo*) (Gene Martin) (as Alicia)

1975 *Roses rouges et piments verts* (*The Lonely Woman*) (Rovira-Beleta)

1977 *Nido de viudas* (*Widow's Nest*) (Navarro)

1983 *Stella emigranti* (Masenza) (as herself)

Gina Lollobrigida in *Pane, amore, e gelosia*

1985   *Deceptions* (Shavelson and Chenault—for TV) (as Princess
        Alexandra)

1986   *The Love Boat: The Christmas Cruise* (for TV) (as Carla Lucci)

1995   *Les Cent et une Nuits* (*A Hundred and One Nights*) (Varda) (as
        Actor for a Day)

Film as Director:

1975   *Portrait of Fidel Castro* (doc)

Publications

By LOLLOBRIGIDA: books—

Italia mia (photographs), Florence, 1972.
Manila (photographs), 1972.
The Philippines (photographs), Liechtenstein, 1976.
Il segreto della rose, Milan, 1984.
Magica innocenza (photographs), Sao Paulo, 1993; as *The Wonder of
Innocence*, New York, 1994.

By LOLLOBRIGIDA: article—

Interview in *Ciné Revue* (Paris), 6 May 1982.

On LOLLOBRIGIDA: books—

Ponzi, Mauricio, *Gina Lollobrigida*, Rome, 1982; as *The Films of Gina
Lollobrigida*, Secaucus, New Jersey, 1982.
Canales, Luis, *Imperial Gina: The Strictly Unauthorized Biography of
Gina Lollobrigida*, Boston, 1990.

On LOLLOBRIGIDA: articles—

Current Biography 1960, New York, 1960.
Ecran (Paris), July 1978.
Stars (Mariembourg, Belgium), December 1990 and March 1992.
Canales, L., "Letters: Bread, Love and Dreams of Gina," in *Movieline*
(Escondido, California), September 1993.

*   *   *

Gina Lollobrigida will always be remembered as the first sex symbol
to emerge from the rubble of postwar Europe. Her rise in Italy coincided with the decline of the neorealist movement. Italian filmmakers
had been concentrating on making films that showed the depressing
reality of Italy after the war, and although these films were critically
acclaimed in other countries, they were unpopular in their home market, where audiences wanted escapist Hollywood-style glamour rather
than confrontation with the day-to-day reality of their drab lives.
Lollobrigida became the embodiment of their escapist fantasies
after Italian producers realized her potential and cast her in films
providing Italian cinemagoers with "rosy realism." As a result she
played a role in boosting Italy to a major position on the world's
film market.

From the outset of her career, she was typecast as a seductress,
whether in costume dramas, romantic comedies, or thrillers; her acting ability was clearly limited, and her range varied little from film to
film. Nonetheless, she received numerous awards for her acting, including the Italian equivalent of the Oscar, the Silver Ribbon, for her
performance in *Pane, amore, e fantasia*. The Italian film critics awarded
her the Grolla d'Oro for her performance in *La provinciale*, the French
public and film industry voted her Best Foreign Actress for three

successive years, and the International Cinema Club awarded her a
prestigious David trophy. All these awards demonstrate that, within
the confines in which she worked, Lollobrigida was unbeatable.

It was only natural that this buxom beauty should come to the
attention of Hollywood. Howard Hughes gave her a contract but was
not forthcoming in giving her a film, so after waiting around in Hollywood for three months she decided to pack her bags and return to
Italy. The legal battles that followed kept her out of Hollywood for
several years, possibly doing irreparable damage to her career. She did,
however, appear in a number of successful American productions shot
in Europe, including *Trapeze*, *Solomon and Sheba*, and *Come September*, which helped to maintain her popularity in America. As
Europe's most sought-after actress, Lollobrigida was fortunate to work
under the direction of Vittorio De Sica, René Clair, and John Huston,
and opposite actors as diverse as Jean-Paul Belmondo, Burt Lancaster,
Frank Sinatra, Alec Guinness, and Errol Flynn.

—Curtis Hutchinson

LOM, Herbert

Nationality: Czech. **Born:** Herbert Charles Angelo Kuchacevich ze
Schluderpacheru in Prague, Austria-Hungary (now Czech Republic),
11 September 1917. **Education:** Attended University of Prague; studied acting at the Prague School of Acting; scholarships to the London
Embassy School, the Sadlers Wells School, and the Westminster School.
Family: Married Dina Scheu, 1948, two sons. **Career:** 1937—film
debut; 1939—moved to England, studied acting, also one of the "voices
of freedom" for the BBC European service; late 1950s—began working in Hollywood; 1978—published novel *Enter a Spy*; 1984—in TV
mini-series *Lace*; also a painter and composer.

Films as Actor:

1937   *Žena pod křižem* (*Woman under the Cross*)

1940   *Mein Kampf My Crimes* (Norman Lee)

1942   *The Young Mr. Pitt* (Reed) (as Napoleon); *Secret Mission*
        (French) (as medical officer); *Tomorrow We Live* (*At Dawn
        We Die*) (King)

1943   *The Dark Tower* (Harlow) (as Torg)

1944   *Hotel Reserve* (Hanbury, Comfort, and Greene) (as Monsieur
        Andre Roux)

1945   *The Seventh Veil* (Bennett) (as Dr. Larson); *Night Boat to
        Dublin* (Huntington) (as Keitel)

1946   *Appointment with Crime* (Harlow) (as Gregory Lang)

1947   *Dual Alibi* (Travers) (as Jules and George de Lisle); *Snow-
        bound* (Macdonald) (as Keramikos)

1948   *Good Time Girl* (Macdonald) (as Max); *Portrait from Life* (*The
        Girl in the Painting*) (Fisher) (as Hendleman); *The Brass
        Monkey* (*Lucky Mascot*) (Freeland) (as Peter Hobart)

1949   *The Lost People* (Knowles); *Golden Salamander* (Neame) (as
        Ranki)

1950   *Night and the City* (Dassin) (as Kristo); *State Secret* (*The Great
        Manhunt*) (Gilliat) (as Karl Theodor); *The Black Rose*
        (Hathaway) (as Anthemus); *Cage of Gold* (Dearden) (as
        Rahman)

1951   *Hell Is Sold Out* (Anderson) (as Dominic Danges); *Two on the
        Tiles* (*School for Brides*) (Guillermin) (as Ford); *Mr. Den-
        ning Drives North* (Kimmins) (as Mados); *Whispering Smith
        Hits London* (*Whispering Smith versus Scotland Yard*)
        (Searle) (as Ford)

1952 *The Ringer* (Hamilton) (as Maurice Meister); *The Net* (*Project M7*) (Asquith) (as Alex Leon); *The Man Who Watched Trains Go By* (*Paris Express*) (French) (as Julius de Koster Jr.)

1953 *Rough Shoot* (*Shoot First*) (Parrish) (as Peter Sandorski); *The Love Lottery* (Crichton) (as Amico); *Star of India* (Lubin) (as Narbonne)

1954 *Beautiful Stranger* (*Twist of Fate*) (Miller) (as Emil Landosh)

1955 *The Ladykillers* (Mackendrick) (as Louis)

1956 *War and Peace* (King Vidor) (as Napoleon)

1957 *Fire Down Below* (Parrish) (as harbor master); *Hell Drivers* (Endfield) (as Gino); *Action of the Tiger* (Young) (as Trifon); *I Accuse!* (Ferrer) (as Major DuPaty de Clam)

1958 *Chase a Crooked Shadow* (Anderson) (as Vargas); *The Roots of Heaven* (Huston) (as Orsini); *Intent to Kill* (Cardiff) (as Juan Menda)

1959 *No Trees in the Street* (Thompson) (as Wilkie); *The Big Fisherman* (Borzage) (as Herod Antipas); *Passport to Shame* (*Room 43*) (Rakoff) (as Nick); *Flame over India* (*Northwest Frontier*) (Thompson) (as Van Leyden); *Third Man on the Mountain* (*Banner in the Sky*) (Annakin) (as Emil Saxon)

1960 *I Aim at the Stars* (Thompson) (as Anton Reger); *Spartacus* (Kubrick) (as Tigranes)

1961 *Mr. Topaze* (*I Like Money*) (Sellers) (as Castel Benac); *El Cid* (Anthony Mann) (as Ben Yussuf); *Mysterious Island* (Endfield) (as Captain Nemo); *The Frightened City* (Lemont) (as Waldo Zhernikov)

1962 *The Phantom of the Opera* (Fisher) (title role); *The Treasure of Silver Lake* (Reinl) (as Brinkley); *Tiara Tahiti* (Kotcheff) (as Chong Sing)

1963 *The Horse without a Head* (Chaffey)

1964 *A Shot in the Dark* (Edwards) (as Chief Inspector Charles Dreyfus)

1965 *Return from the Ashes* (Thompson) (as Dr. Charles Bovard)

1966 *Our Man in Marrakesh* (*Bang! Bang! You're Dead*) (Sharp) (as Mr. Casimir); *Gambit* (Neame) (as Shabhandar); *Die Nibelungen* (*Whom the Gods Wish to Destroy*) (Reinl) (as Koenig Etzel)

1967 *Die Nibelungen II* (Reinl) (as Koenig Etzel); *Assignment to Kill* (*The Assignments*) (Reynolds) (as Matt Wilson); *The Karate Killers* (Shear) (as Randolph)

1968 *The Face of Eve* (*Eve*) (Summers) (as Diego); *Villa Rides!* (Kulik) (as General Huerta); *99 Women* (*Island of Despair*) (Franco) (as the governor); *Uncle Tom's Cabin* (as Simon Legree)

1969 *Doppelganger* (*Journey to the Far Side of the Sun*) (Parrish) (as Dr Hassler); *Mister Jericho* (Hayers—for TV)

1970 *Count Dracula* (Franco) (as Van Helsing); *Dorian Gray* (*The Secret of Dorian Gray*) (Dallamano) (as Lord Henry Wotten); *Mark of the Devil* (*Burn Witch Burn*; *Hexen bis aufs Blutgeqvält*) (Armstrong) (as Count Cumberland)

1971 *Murders in the Rue Morgue* (Hessler) (as Marot)

1972 *Asylum* (*House of Crazies*) (Baker) (as Byron)

1973 *Dark Places* (Sharp) (as Prescott); *And Now the Screaming Starts* (Baker) (as Henry Fengriffen)

1974 *The Return of the Pink Panther* (Edwards) (as Dreyfus); *And Then There Were None* (*Ten Little Indians*) (Collinson) (as Dr. Armstrong)

1976 *The Pink Panther Strikes Again* (Edwards) (as Dreyfus)

1977 *Charleston* (Fondato) (as Inspector Watkins)

1978 *Revenge of the Pink Panther* (Edwards) (as Dreyfus)

1979 *The Lady Vanishes* (Page) (as Dr. Hartz); *The Man with Bogart's Face* (*Sam Marlow, Private Eye*) (Day) (as Mr. Zebra)

1980 *Hopscotch* (Neame) (as Mikhail Yaskov)

1982 *The Trail of the Pink Panther* (Edwards) (as Dreyfus)

1983 *Memed, My Hawk* (*The Lion and the Hawk*) (Ustinov) (as Ali Safa Bey); *The Dead Zone* (Cronenberg) (as Dr. Sam Weizak); *Curse of the Pink Panther* (Edwards) (as Dreyfus)

1985 *King Solomon's Mines* (Thompson) (as Col. Bockner)

1987 *Whoops Apocalypse* (Bussmann) (as Gen. Mosquera); *Scoop* (Gavin Miller—for TV) (as Mr. Baldwin)

1988 *Dragonard* (*Master of Dragonard Hill*) (Kikoine); *Skeleton Coast* (*Coast of Skeletons*) (Cardos) (as Elia); *Going Bananas* (*My African Adventure*) (Davidson) (as Mackintosh); *The Crystal Eye* (Tornatore)

1989 *River of Death* (Carver) (as Col. Ricardo Diaz); *Ten Little Indians* (*Death on Safari*) (Birkinshaw) (as Gen. Romensky); *Masque of the Red Death* (Birkinshaw) (as Ludwig)

1991 *The Pope Must Die* (*The Pope Must Diet*) (Richardson) (as Vittorio Corelli); *La Setta* (*The Devil's Daughter*; *The Sect*) (Soavi) (as Gran Vecchio)

1993 *Son of the Pink Panther* (Edwards) (as Inspector Dreyfus)

Publications

By LOM: books—

Enter a Spy (novel), 1978.
Dr. Guillotine: The Eccentric Exploits of an Early Scientist (novel), 1993.

By LOM: articles—

Interview, in *Films and Filming* (London), March 1979.
Interview, in *Films* (London), April 1983.
Letter, in *Screen International* (London), 13 December 1986.

On LOM: articles—

Picturegoer (London), 28 September 1946, 26 July 1947, 1 May 1948, and 3 June 1950.
Ciné Revue (Paris), 18 September 1980.
Screen International (London), 4 May 1984.

* * *

Although he has tackled such exotic roles as Napoleon (twice; in *The Young Mr. Pitt* and *War and Peace*), Captain Nemo (in *The Mysterious Island*), Herod Antipas (in *The Big Fisherman*), the Phantom of the Opera, Simon Legree, and Oscar Wilde's Lord Henry Wotten, Herbert Lom is liable to be best remembered for his continuing role as Chief Inspector Dreyfus, the French police commissioner driven to murderous madness by his blithely inept junior, Inspector Clouseau (Peter Sellers) in the Blake Edwards Pink Panther series, introduced in *A Shot in the Dark* and reaching a climax of insanity in *The Pink Panther Strikes Again*. After so many screen roles as villains, Lom obviously relished the chance to unbend—as he had done earlier, also alongside Sellers, in *The Ladykillers*. Lom's presence in the Pink Panther series became as indispensable to their comic value as that of Sellers himself—and all that lifts the three Panther sequels produced after Sellers's death from the comic doldrums. The last, to date, was *Son of the Pink Panther*, starring Italian comic Roberto Begnini as the bumbling scion of Drefyus's nemesis.

Making a strong impression, after some minor roles, as the concerned and suave psychoanalyst in *The Seventh Veil*—a role he later reprised in the television series *The Human Jungle*—Lom established a screen image as an intelligent, foreign, ambiguous character whose suave purring could mask either benevolence or larceny. Between services in historical epics such as *War and Peace*, *The Black Robe*, *El*

Herbert Lom

Cid, and *Spartacus*, Lom became a fixture of British crime movies—equally well cast as a Pole, an Italian, a Greek, a Maltese, a Frenchman, a German, or a Hungarian—and provided interesting villainy to a run of fine-to-outstanding movies (*Appointment with Crime, Good Time Girl, Intent to Kill, Passport to Shame*) set in a rainy, jazz-driven, smoky-club-clotted Soho that constitutes London's answer to Chandler country.

As Kristo, the suave Greek who runs all the wrestling in London, he is a sinister but tender presence in Jules Dassin's *Night and the City*, mourning his father by ordering Richard Widmark's murder, and bringing far more to the screen than is actually in the role, while he had fun in a rare lead in *The Frightened City*, as a corrupt accountant named Waldo Zhernikov who tries to enforce a protection racket on the clubs with the aid of Alfred Marks and Sean Connery as London hardmen. His overdone Italian martyr in the otherwise perfectly cast *Hell Drivers*, a gritty tale of British truckers not to be confused with the 1932 Wallace Beery movie of the same name, was a rare slip (the film was directed by Cy Endfield after fleeing the Hollywood blacklist and also featured Sean Connery). Ironically, it was a comedy, *The Ladykillers*, that was the culmination of this run of criminal/gangster roles, proving that Lom, who turns up in a white tie/black shirt combo with a violin case under his arm as if it were a machine gun, could play sly comedy as well as suave menace.

In the 1960s and 1970s, Lom's roles made excursions into spying (*Our Man in Marrakesh, The Karate Killers, Assignment to Kill, Hopscotch, The Man with Bogart's Face*), mini-epic (*Flame over India, Whom the Gods Wish to Destroy*—the low-rent remake of Fritz Lang's *Nibelungen, Peter and Paul*), science fiction (a future spy with a camera eyeball in *Journey to the Far Side of the Sun*), Nazi villainy (*The Lady Vanishes*) and Euro-Western (*Villa Rides!*) dotted in among cosmopolitan assignments such as *Gambit*, opposite Shirley MacLaine and Michael Caine, a clever gimmick movie in which Lom plays two versions of the richest man in the world.

When Cary Grant turned down the role, Hammer Films selected Lom for its classy remake of the classic *The Phantom of the Opera*, directed by Terence Fisher. Though the film has gained in esteem over the years, it was neither a critical nor commercial success when it came out, and Lom made no more films for Hammer, drifting instead into horror movies for other studios and directors. He made a stolid Dr. Van Helsing in Jesus Franco's feeble attempt to finally film Bram Stoker's *Count Dracula* "as written," a grim witchfinder in the notorious *Mark of the Devil*, which was rated "V for Violence" and for which "vomits bags" were issued at the box office. Occasional class acts did ensue, however, notably *And Now the Screaming Starts*, where he was the cause of a family curse, *Asylum* (as a mad psychic sending his consciousness out to kill as wax mannequins), and a survivor of the holocaust, now a psychiatrist, who gets a firsthand demonstration of Christopher Walken's sixth sense in Cronenberg's *The Dead Zone*.

—Kim Newman, updated by John McCarty

LOMBARD, Carole

Nationality: American. **Born:** Jane Alice Peters, in Fort Wayne, Indiana, 6 October 1908 (some sources say 1909). **Education:** Attended dancing and acting schools as a child; Fairfax High School, California. **Family:** Married 1) the actor William Powell, 1931 (divorced 1933); 2) the actor Clark Gable, 1939. **Career:** 1921—film debut as a 13-year-old in *A Perfect Crime*; 1925—contract with Fox, and appeared in *Marriage in Transit*; 1927-29—made a series of Mack Sennett shorts; 1930-37—under contract to Paramount, made a series of successful comedies; later films made for David O. Selznick and RKO. **Died:** In plane crash, 16 January 1942.

Films as Actress:

1921   *A Perfect Crime* (Dwan)
1925   *Dick Turpin* (Blystone); *Gold and the Girl* (Mortimer); *Marriage in Transit* (Neill) (as Celia Hathaway); *Hearts and Spurs* (Van Dyke) (as Sybil Estabrook); *Durand of the Badlands* (Reynolds) (as Ellen Boyd)
1926   *The Road to Glory* (Hawks)
1927   *The Fighting Eagle* (Crisp); *Smith's Pony* (short); *The Girl from Everywhere* (Cline—short)
1928   *Half a Bride* (La Cava); *The Divine Sinner* (Pembroke) (as Millie Claudert); *Me, Gangster* (Walsh) (as Blonde Rosie); *Show Folks* (Stein) (as Cleo); *Power* (Higgin); *Run, Girl, Run* (Goulding—short); *The Beach Club* (Edwards—short); *The Best Man* (Edwards—short); *The Swim Princess* (Goulding—short); *The Bicycle Flirt* (Edwards—short); *The Girl from Nowhere* (Edwards—short); *His Unlucky Night* (Edwards—short); *The Campus Carmen* (Edwards—short)
1929   *Matchmaking Mamas* (Edwards—short); *Ned McCobb's Daughter* (Cowen) (as Jennie); *High Voltage* (Higgin) (as Billie Davis); *Big News* (La Cava) (as Marg); *The Racketeer* (Higgin) (as Rhoda); *Dynamite* (DeMille)
1930   *The Arizona Kid* (Santell) (as Virginia Hoyt); *Safety in Numbers* (Schertzinger) (as Pauline); *Fast and Loose* (Newmeyer) (as Alice O'Neil)
1931   *It Pays to Advertise* (Tuttle) (as Mary Grayson); *Man of the World* (Wallace) (as Mary Kendall); *Ladies' Man* (Mendes) (as Rachel Fendley); *Up Pops the Devil* (Sutherland) (as Anne Merrick); *I Take This Woman* (Gering and Vorkapich) (as Kay Dowling)
1932   *No One Man* (Corrigan) (as Penelope Newbold); *Sinners in the Sun* (Hall) (as Doris Blake); *Virtue* (Buzzell) (as Mae); *No More Orchids* (Walter Lang) (as Anne Holt); *No Man Of Her Own* (Ruggles) (as Connie Randall)
1933   *From Hell to Heaven* (Kenton) (as Colly Tanner); *Supernatural* (Halperin) (as Roma Courtney); *Brief Moment* (Burton) (as Abby Fane); *The Eagle and the Hawk* (Walker) (as the beautiful lady); *White Woman* (Walker) (as Judith Denning)
1934   *Bolero* (Ruggles) (as Helen Hathaway); *We're Not Dressing* (Taurog) (as Doris Worthington); *Twentieth Century* (Hawks) (as Lily Garland); *Now and Forever* (Hathaway) (as Toni Carstairs); *Lady by Choice* (Burton) (as Alabam' Lee)

1935   *The Gay Bride* (Conway) (as Mary); *Rumba* (Gering) (as Diana Harrison); *Hands across the Table* (Leisen) (as Regi Allen)
1936   *Love before Breakfast* (Walter Lang) (as Kay Colby); *My Man Godfrey* (La Cava) (as Irene Bullock); *The Princess Comes Across* (Howard) (as Princess Olga)
1937   *Swing High, Swing Low* (Leisen) (as Maggie King); *Nothing Sacred* (Wellman) (as Hazel Flagg); *True Confession* (Ruggles) (as Helen Bartlett)
1938   *Fools for Scandal* (LeRoy) (as Kay Winters)
1939   *Made for Each Other* (Cromwell) (as Jane Mason); *In Name Only* (Cromwell) (as Julie Eden)
1940   *Vigil in the Night* (Stevens) (as Anne Lee); *They Knew What They Wanted* (Kanin) (as Amy Peters)
1941   *Mr. and Mrs. Smith* (Hitchcock) (as Ann Smith)
1942   *To Be or Not to Be* (Lubitsch) (as Maria Tura)

Publications

On LOMBARD: books—

Memo from: David O. Selznick, edited by Rudy Behlmer, New York, 1972.
Ott, Frederick W., *The Films of Carole Lombard*, Secaucus, New Jersey, 1972.
Swindell, Harry Win, *Screwball: The Life of Carole Lombard*, New York, 1975.
Maltin, Leonard, *Carole Lombard*, New York, 1976.
Morella, Joe, and Edward Epstein, *Gable & Lombard & Powell & Harlow*, London, 1976.
Matzen, Robert D., *Carole Lombard: A Bio-Bibliography*, Westport, Connecticut, 1988.

On LOMBARD: articles—

Photoplay (New York), June and September 1931, October 1933, March and May 1938, May 1939, and October 1940.
Busch, N. F., "A Loud Cheer for the Screwball Girl," in *Life* (New York), 17 October 1938.
Dickens, Homer, "Carole Lombard," in *Films in Review* (New York), February 1961.
Kanin, Garson, in *Hollywood* (New York), 1975.
McVay, D., "Eternal Images: Carole Lombard," in *Films and Filming* (London), June 1977.
Chaplin, Charlie, "Carole Lombard" in *The Movie Star*, edited by Elisabeth Weis (New York), 1981.
Lloyd, A., "Carole Lombard," in *Films and Filming* (London), October 1983.
Sarris, Andrew, "Carole Lombard," in *American Film* (New York), March 1989.

*   *   *

Legend has it that Carole Lombard was cast for her first screen role, as a 13-year old tomboy in Allan Dwan's *A Perfect Crime*, after the director spotted her playing baseball in the street. Whatever the truth to the story, that role was the beginning of a prolific and often hectic career in which she made more than 40 talking films before her tragic death in a plane crash. Except for a brief interlude to allow her to graduate from junior high school, the actress, appearing first as Carol, and after 1930 Carole, Lombard, made movie after movie—creating some of Hollywood's most memorable comedic roles.

Signed by Fox in 1925, she had small parts in *Marriage in Transit* with R. William Neill and *Hearts and Spurs* with W. S. Van Dyke before a car accident resulted in the cancellation of her contract. By

Carole Lombard

1927 she was working for Mack Sennett, for whom she made more than a dozen two-reel comedy shorts with such Sennett stars as Billy Bevan, Mack Swain, Chester Conklin, and Billy Gilbert. Some bit parts in other feature films, such as Raoul Walsh's *Me, Gangster*, finally led to a Pathé contract resulting in her first all-talking picture, *High Voltage*, directed by Howard Higgin. In 1930, she signed a seven-year contract with Paramount where she was allowed to develop her comic talents in such films as *Fast and Loose*, *It Pays to Advertise*, and *Man of the World*, in between being used as a decorative blonde in routine roles.

During these years she also appeared in Wesley Ruggles's *No Man of Her Own*, opposite Clark Gable; Stuart Walker's *White Woman*, with Charles Laughton; and Ruggles's *Bolero*, starring George Raft. In 1934 she emerged as a truly first-rate comedienne when she appeared opposite John Barrymore in *Twentieth Century*, directed by Howard Hawks. This turned out to be the first of four remarkable roles that characterized the best of her performances in the "Screwball" comedies of the 1930s.

From the mid-1930s until her death in 1942, Carole Lombard bounced from studio to studio out on loan from Paramount, appearing in a wide variety of films. At the end of the decade she made two serious films which suggest the potential depth of her talent, George Stevens's *Vigil in the Night* and Garson Kanin's *They Knew What They Wanted*. One critic has remarked that it could only have been the need for a dark-haired heroine that kept her from getting the Scarlett O'Hara role in *Gone with the Wind*.

Her last two films, Alfred Hitchcock's *Mr. and Mrs. Smith* and Ernst Lubitsch's *To Be or Not to Be*, further broadened her talents and provided a brief glimpse of how those talents could have been used. Her cool reserve might have made her one of Hitchcock's blonde heroines, and Lombard's wit and glamour seem exactly right for Lubitsch's stylish comedies.

Her death, while on a bond-selling tour to aid the war effort, stunned the American people. Clark Gable, her second husband, remained emotionally crushed for years. The telegram of condolence sent to Gable by President Roosevelt seemed to sum up the feelings of the time: "She brought great joy to all who knew her and to millions who knew her only as a great artist.... She is and always will be a star, one we shall never forget nor cease to be grateful to."

—Charles L. P. Silet

ŁOMNICKI, Tadeusz

Nationality: Polish. **Born:** Podhajce, 18 July 1927. **Career:** Stage and film actor; 1945—stage debut in Kraków; 1947—film debut in *Stalowe serca*; played leading roles in Polish films of the 1950s and 1960s; 1971—rector of the State Academy of the Performing Arts; 1975—director of the Teatr na Woli, Warsaw. **Died:** 1992.

Films as Actor:

1947   *Stalowe serca* (*Hearts of Steel*) (Urbanowicz)
1948   *Dwie brygady* (Cękalski)
1952   *Załoga* (*The Crew*) (Fethke)
1953   *Żołnierz zwycięstwa* (*A Soldier of Victory*) (Jakubowska)
1954   *Piątka z ulicy Barskiej* (*Five Boys of Barska Street*) (Aleksander Ford)
1955   *Pokolenie* (*A Generation*) (Wajda)
1957   *Trzy koniety* (*Three Women*) (Różewicz)
1958   "Ostinato Lugubre" ep. of **Eroica** (Munk) (as Zawistowski); *Ósmy dzień tygodnia* (*The Eighth Day of the Week*) (Aleksander Ford) (as Gregor)

1959   *Zamach* (*Partisan Mission/Answer to Violence*) (Passendorfer); *Baza ludzi umarłlych* (Petelski); *Kamienne niebo* (Petelski)
1960   *Niewinni czarodzieje* (*Innocent Sorcerers*) (Wajda) (as Bazyli)
1961   *Czas przeszły* (*Time Past*) (Buczkowski)
1963   *Zerwany most* (*The Lost Bridge*) (Passendorfer); *Mansarda* (*The Mansard*) (Nalecki)
1964   *Wiano* (*The Dowry*) (J. Łomnicki); *Pierwszy dzień wolności* (*The First Day of Freedom*) (Aleksander Ford)
1965   *Życie raz jeszcze* (*Life Begins Again*) (Morgenstern)
1966   *Potem nastąpi cisza* (*The Rest Is Silence*) (Morgenstern); *Bariera* (*Barrier*) (Skolimowski) (as doctor); *Angeklagt nach Paragraph 218* (*The Doctor Says*) (Aleksander Ford) (as Dr. Maurer)
1967   *Kontrybucja* (*The Contribution*) (J. Łomnicki); *Rece de gory* (*Hands Up!*) (Skolimowski)
1969   *Pan Wołodyjowski* (*Colonel Wolodyjowski*) (Hoffman) (title role)
1971   *Pan Dodek* (*Mr. Dodek*) (J. Łomnicki)
1972   *Poślizg* (J. Łomnicki)
1974   *Nagrody i odznaczenia* (J. Łomnicki); *Potop* (*The Deluge*) (Hoffman) (as Wolodyjowski)
1976   *Kommunisti* (Ozierov)
1977   *Granica* (Rybkowski)
1978   **Człowiek z marmaru** (*Man of Marble*) (Wajda) (as Jerzy Burski); *... gdziekolwiek jesteś, Panie Prezydencie* (Trzos-Rastawiecki) (as Stefan Starzyński)
1980   *Wizja lokalna 1901* (*Inspection of the Crime Scene 1901*) (Bajon)
1981   *Kontrakt* (*The Contract*) (Zanussi) (as Adam)
1982   *Daimler-Benz Limuzyna* (*The Consul*) (Bajon); *Przygody Pana Michala* (Komorowski); *Przypadek* (*Blind Chance*) (Kieślowski) (as Werner)
1984   *Dom Wariatow* (Koterski)
1986   *Kronika wypadkow milosnych* (*Chronicle of a Love Affair*) (Wajda) (as the Rev. Baum)
1988   **Dekalog 8** (Kieślowski) (as tailor)
1989   *Lawa* (Konwicki) (as priest)
1990   *Pension sonnenschein* (Bajon) (as Gustaw)
1991   *All of Me* (Bettina Wilhelm)

Publications

On ŁOMNICKI: book—

Filler, Witold, *Tadeusz Łomnicki*, Warsaw, 1976.

On ŁOMNICKI: articles—

Ecran (Paris), July 1978.
Filmowy Serwis Prasowy (Warsaw), May 1981 and August 1981.
Obituary, in *Filmowy Serwis Prasowy*, vol. 38, no. 4, 1992.
Poros, G., obituary in *Filmvilag*, vol. 35, no. 5, 1992.
Joris, L., "A Dieu," obituary in *Film en Televisie + Video*, July 1993.

*   *   *

The career of Tadeusz Łomnicki parallels the development of Polish cultural life since World War II. During the Occupation he had studied drama secretly, and finished his studies in Kraków after the war. His film debut in 1947 was in *Stalowe serca*, and he appeared in *Dwie brygady*, *Załoga*, and *Żołnierz zwycięstwa*, but his small roles, and the mediocrity of these films, did not permit him to display the range of his ability. In spite of this, he did manage to create interesting and thoughtful characters.

He soon had the chance to show the many sides of his talent in films by more eminent directors. Beginning in the mid-1950s, he played the roles of young fighters in Aleksander Ford's *Five Boys of Barska Street* and in Andrzej Wajda's *A Generation*. The most successful years of his film acting career were the 1960s, when he appeared in a series of films by such individualistic directors as Wajda, Janusz Morgenstern, and Jerzy Skolimowski. The spectrum of his roles includes convincing performances as intellectual, villager, soldier, hero, traitor, and coward—both extroverts expressing themselves through extravagant behavior, and introverted, thoughtful men. These characters are exemplified in his roles as Bazyli in *Innocent Sorcerers*, and as the title character in the historical film *Pan Wołodyjowski* whom he portrayed with all the outward bravura of a military hero, and simultaneously with an understanding of inner motivation.

In the 1970s Łomnicki was less prominent because of his theatrical and pedagogic activities. In 1971 he became rector of the state academy for performing arts, and in 1975 he became the director of the Teatr na Woli in Warsaw, where he also performed. His face, made more expressive by age, has not been lost to film audiences, however, since he appeared in several films that are highlights of recent Polish cinema—*Poślizg*, *The Deluge*, *Man of Marble*, and *Granica*. The most important of these, in terms of his performance, is . . . *gdziekolwiek jesteś, Panie Prezydencie*, in which he plays Stefan Starzyński, the Mayor of Warsaw forced to face the consequences of Poland's defeat at the beginning of World War II.

Łomnicki brought his career as a public figure to an end at the beginning of the 1980s after the dramatic events caused by the revolutionary appearance of the Solidarity movement which found its tragic culmination in the declaration of martial law. He gave up both his post as director of the Warsaw Theater and as rector of the Academy of Dramatic Arts, devoting himself to his original profession—acting. There was no lack of parts, since he was sought after by older directors—his contemporaries—as well as members of the younger generation. Together with a change in the climate of Polish society and cultural life, the character of both films and film figures changed; naturally this was true of the characters played by Łomnicki. Typical examples of these changes are found in *The Contract* with the part of an influential head doctor in a Warsaw hospital, who after becoming well-off loses his moral compass, and in *Blind Chance* with the part of an old communist, who is incapable of critically examining the false ideas he has believed in all his life (the latter film was directed by Krzysztof Kieślowski, banned on its release, and not shown until seven years later).

Łomnicki was not fully satisfied by acting in films. He was obsessed with the wish to play Shakespeare's King Lear. He succeeded at last, but died during one of the rehearsals, shortly before opening night.

—Blažena Urgošiková

LOREN, Sophia

Nationality: Italian. **Born:** Sofia Villani Scicolone in Rome, 20 September 1934. **Family:** Married the producer Carlo Ponti, 1957, sons: Carlo Jr. and Eduardo. **Career:** Began her film career as an extra in *Quo Vadis?* (produced in 1949), also a model for photographed cartoon strips and appeared in beauty contests; "discovered" by Carlo Ponti; 1957—first American film, *The Pride and the Passion*; 1988—in TV mini-series *Mario Puzo's The Fortunate Pilgrim*. **Awards:** Best Actress, Venice Festival, for *The Black Orchid*, 1959; Best Actress Academy Award, Best Actress, Cannes Festival, and Best Foreign Actress, British Academy, for *Two Women*, 1961; Honorary Oscar, for being "one of the genuine treasures of world cinema who, in a career

rich with memorable performances, has added permanent luster to our art form," 1990; created Knight, French Légion d'honneur, 1991; Cecil B. DeMille Lifetime Achievement Award, Hollywood Foreign Press Association, 1994; also eight David Di Donatello Awards. **Address:** c/o La Concordia Ranch, 1151 Hidden Valley Road, Thousand Oaks, CA 91361, U.S.A.

Films as Actress:

(as Sofia Scicolone-Lazzaro)

1950 *Cuori su mare* (*Hearts upon the Sea*) (Bianchi); *Il voto* (*The Vote*) (Bonnard); *Le sei mogli di Barbablu'* (*Bluebeard's Six Wives*) (Ludovico); *Io sono il capatz* (Simonelli); *Luci del varietà* (*Variety Lights*) (Fellini)

1951 *Quo Vadis?* (LeRoy—produced in 1949); *Era lui, sì! sì!* (*It's Him, Yes! Yes!*) (Metz); *Milano miliardaria* (*Milana the Millionairess*) (Metz); *Anna* (Lattuada); *The Magician in Spite of Himself* (Metz); *Il sogno di Zorro* (*The Dream of Zorro*) (Soldati); *E' arrivato l'accordatore* (*The Piano Tuner Has Arrived*) (Coletti); *Lebbra bianca* (Trapani)

1952 *La favorita* (*The Favorite*) (Barlacchi)

(as Sophia Loren)

1952 *White Slave Trade* (Comencini)

1953 *Aida* (Fracassi) (title role); *La domenica della buona gente* (*Good People's Sunday*) (Majano); *Il paese dei campanelli* (*The Country of Bells*) (Boyer); *Pellegrini d'amore* (*Pilgrim of Love*) (Forzano); *Carosella napolitano* (*Neapolitan Carousel*) (Giannini) (as Sisina); *Ci troviamo in Galleria* (*We'll Meet in the Gallery*) (Bolognini); *Tempi nostri* (*Anatomy of Love*) (Blasetti); *Due notti con Cleopatra* (*Two Nights with Cleopatra*) (Mattóli) (as Nisca/title role)

1954 *Attila flagello di dio* (*Attila*; *Attila the Hun*) (Francisci) (as Honoria); *Un giorno in pretura* (*A Day in Court*) (Steno) (as Anna); "Pizza on Credit" ep. of *L'oro di Napoli* (*The Gold of Naples*; *Every Day's a Holiday*) (de Sica) (as the wife); *La donna del fiume* (*Woman of the River*) (Soldati) (as Nives Mongolini); *Miseria e nobiltà* (*Poverty and Nobility*) (Mattóli); *Peccato che sia una canaglia* (*Too Bad She's Bad*) (Blasetti) (as Lina)

1955 *Il segno di Venere* (*The Sign of Venus*) (Risi) (as Agnese); *La bella mugnaia* (*The Miller's Wife*) (Camerini) (as Carmela); *Pane, amore, e . . .* (*Scandal in Sorrento*) (Risi) (as Donna Sofia); *La fortuna di essere donna* (*Lucky to Be a Woman*) (Blasetti) (as Antoinette)

1957 *The Pride and the Passion* (Kramer) (as Juana); *Boy on a Dolphin* (Negulesco) (as Phaedra); *Legend of the Lost* (*Timbuktu*) (Hathaway) (as Dita)

1958 *Desire under the Elms* (Delbert Mann) (as Ana Cabot); *Houseboat* (Shavelson) (as Cinzia Zaccardi); *The Key* (Reed) (as Stella)

1959 *The Black Orchid* (Ritt) (as Rose Bianco); *That Kind of Woman* (Lumet) (as Kay)

1960 *Heller in Pink Tights* (Cukor) (as Angela Rossini); *It Started in Naples* (*La baia di Napoli*) (Shavelson) (as Lucia Curcio); *A Breath of Scandal* (*Olympia*) (Curtiz) (as Princess Olympia); *The Millionairess* (Asquith) (as Epifania Parerga)

1961 *Lo ciociara* (*Two Women*) (de Sica) (as Cesira); *El Cid* (Anthony Mann) (as Chimene); "La Riffa" ep. of *Boccaccio '70* (de Sica) (as Zoe); *Madame Sans-Gêne* (*Madame*) (Christian-Jaque) (as Catherine Huebscher/Madame)

Sophia Loren

1962	*Le Couteau dans la plaie* (*Five Miles to Midnight*) (Litvak) (as Lisa Macklin); *I sequestrati di Altona* (*The Condemned of Altona*) (de Sica) (as Johanna)
1963	*Ieri, oggi, e domani* (*Yesterday, Today, and Tomorrow*) (de Sica) (as Adelina/Anna/Mara)
1964	*The Fall of the Roman Empire* (Anthony Mann) (as Lucilla); *Matrimonio all 'italiana* (*Marriage Italian Style*) (de Sica) (as Filomena Marturano)
1965	*Judith* (Daniel Mann) (title role); *Operation Crossbow* (*The Great Spy Mission*; *Operazione Crossbow*) (Anderson) (as Nora); *Lady L* (Ustinov) (title role)
1966	*Arabesque* (Donen) (as Yasmin Azir); *A Countess from Hong Kong* (Chaplin) (as Natasha)
1967	*C'era una volta* (*More than a Miracle*; *Cinderella, Italian Style*; *Happily Ever After*) (Rosi) (as Isabella); *Questi fantasmi* (*Ghosts, Italian Style*; *Three Ghosts*) (Castellani) (as Maria)
1969	*I girasoli* (*Sunflower*; *Les Fleurs du soleil*) (de Sica) (as Giovanna)
1971	*La moglie del prete* (*The Priest's Wife*) (Risi) (as Valeria Billi); *Bianco, rosso e . . .* (*The White Sister*; *The Sin*) (Lattuada) (as Sister Germana)
1972	*La mortadella* (*Lady Liberty*) (Monicelli) (as Maddalena Ciarrapico); *Man of La Mancha* (Hiller) (as Dulcinea/Aldonza)
1973	*Il viaggio* (*The Voyage*; *The Journey*) (de Sica) (as Adriana De Mauro)
1974	*Le testament* (*Jury of One*; *The Verdict*) (Cayatte) (as Teresa Leoni); *Brief Encounter* (Bridges—for TV); *Poopsie* (*Gun Moll*) (Capitani) (title role)
1977	*Una giornata speciale* (*A Special Day*) (Scola) (as Antonietta); *The Cassandra Crossing* (Cosmatos) (as Jennifer); *Angela* (Sagal) (title role)
1978	*Brass Target* (Hough) (as Mara)
1979	*Firepower* (Winner) (as Adele Tosca); *Revenge* (*Blood Feud*) (Wertmüller) (as Titina Paterno); *Shimmy Lugano e tarantelle e vino* (Wertmüller)
1980	*Oopsie Poopsie* (Capitani) (as Poopsie); *Sophia Loren: Her Own Story* (Stuart—for TV) (as herself)
1981	*Tieta d'agreste*
1985	*Qualcosa di biondo* (*Aurora*) (Ponzi) (as Aurora)
1986	*Courage* (Kagan—for TV) (as Marianna Miraldo)
1988	*The Fortunate Pilgrim* (Cooper—for TV) (as Lucia)

1990   *Sobato, Domenica e Lunedi (Saturday, Sunday and Monday)* (Wertmüller) (as Rosa Priore)
1994   *Ready to Wear (Prêt-a-Porter)* (Altman) (as Isabella de la Fontaine)
1995   *Grumpier Old Men* (Deutch) (as Maria Rigetti)
1996   *Messages*

Publications

By LOREN: books—

Eat with Me, London, 1972.
In the Kitchen with Love, Garden City, New York, 1972.

By LOREN: articles—

"This Is Your Life: Sophia Loren," interview with Alberto Moravia, in *Show* (Hollywood), September 1962.
Ciné Revue (Paris), 16 August 1984.
Photoplay (London), January 1985.
"Sofia Scicolone," interview with Graham Fuller, in *Interview* (New York), October 1993.

On LOREN: books—

Crawley, Tony, *The Films of Sophia Loren*, London, 1974.
Zec, Donald, *Sophia*, New York, 1975.
Hotchner, A. E., *Sophia: Living and Loving: Her Own Story*, New York, 1979.
Shaw, Sam, *Sophia Loren in the Camera Eye*, New York, 1980.
Degioanni, Bernard, *Sophia Loren*, Paris, 1984.
Levy, Alan, *Forever, Sophia: An Intimate Portrait*, New York, 1986.
Moscati, Italo, *Sophia Loren: tutto comincio quando al madre di un ragazza di Pozzuoli sogno di diventare Greta Garbo*, Venice, 1994.

On LOREN: articles—

Lane, J. F., "Neapolitan Gold," in *Films and Filming* (London), April 1957.
Current Biography 1959, New York, 1959.
Silke, J. R., "Sophia Loren: Earth Mother," in *Cinema* (Beverly Hills), February-March 1964.
Noble, Peter, in *Screen International* (London), 20 September 1980.
Canby, Vincent, "Sophia Loren and Marcello Mastroianni," in *The Movie Star*, edited by Elisabeth Weis, New York, 1981.
Ciné Revue (Paris), 26 April 1984.
Collins, Nancy, "Sophia," in *Vanity Fair* (New York), January 1991.
James, C., "Sophia Loren Recalls a Beloved Paisan," in *New York Times*, 4 October 1991.

*   *   *

Screen goddesses are rare enough, but celluloid divinities who can act are a breed apart. Although her impoverished beginnings as beauty pageant hopeful held little promise for success, the former Neapolitan dessert became one of the screen's glittering superstars. Enjoying a recent comeback in the stuck-on-itself *Ready to Wear* and the enjoyable but sitcomish *Grumpier Old Men*, incandescent Loren demonstrates how devalued cinema stars have become in an era rife with computer-programmed box-office lures (Demi Moore, Meg Ryan) and vapid starlets who would have been bit players in the forties (Sandra Bullock, Sarah Jessica Parker). When Loren sashays across the screen, the years slip by and a property's shortcomings can be overlooked because moviegoers feel they are getting more than their

money's worth. With few exceptions (e.g., Susan Sarandon), the current crop of actresses are fast-food vamps who leave one hungry for something more. That tasty something more is called star quality, and Loren had it from her earliest days as amply endowed sex symbol.

In her de Sica comedies, Sophia seemed amused by her own lusciousness, as if she could not believe the foolishness of men trailing after her oregano-scented splendor. Like all transplants to Tinseltown, Loren was vulgarized for American consumption into an all-purpose earth mother. Unlike the other pneumatic wonders of her day (Bardot, Ekberg, Lollobrigida), Loren could do more than stick out her chest. Although her Hollywood output has been denigrated by critics, such a blanket dismissal overlooks tangy romantic comedy pairings with Cary Grant (*Houseboat*) and Gable (*It Started in Naples*) in which she holds her own as shining star, not as imported decoration; a competent soap opera, *The Black Orchid*, illuminated by Loren's dramatic skill; and George Cukor's celebration of frontier spirit and outdoor ham, *Heller in Pink Tights*, which fuses Sophia's sharp comic timing and technicolored awesomeness.

When Magnani refused to play her mother in *Two Women*, Loren assumed that role and amazed even her enthusiasts. The first actress ever to win an Oscar for a foreign-language film, Loren deserved that accolade against stiff competition because she embodied the devastation of every displaced soul brought down by war. Deglamorized but still radiant, she was perfectly attuned to de Sica's humanism and was unforgettable in quiet scenes with her traumatized daughter as well as in her shattering aria of denunciation about her child's rape—shouted at passing soldiers who turn a deaf ear.

After that acting triumph, Loren returned to Hollywood as a Star Eminence. As one of the last traditional movie queens, she gracefully enlivened the superior epic, *El Cid*, stunningly clotheshorsed her way through the spyjinks of *Arabesque*, and brought enchantment to bear on a beggarman's version of *Man of La Mancha*, one of the musical genre's last gasps. An inestimable star in English, she is perhaps a finer actress in her native tongue. Having danced a comic-dramatic two-step with Mastroianni in such smash hits as *Yesterday, Today, and Tomorrow*, and *Marriage Italian Style*, she also paired beautifully with him in Scola's *A Special Day*, as a love-starved fascist-brainwashed housewife enjoying a respite from unhappiness.

Although many of her American projects were drivel, and although her later Italian films are drivel on a smaller budget, nothing can bank those Loren fires. Television has not been fruitful (she did not even play herself persuasively in her own biopic), and in retrospect, one is relieved she did not become a television diva on *Dynasty* since Joan Collins was their second choice and better suited to the crassness. With so few opportunities encircling her brand of endangered species stardom (consider the twilight years of Kim Novak and Elizabeth Taylor), one hopes the resurgence of interest in Loren will bring worthy vehicles. What the world needs now, more than love, is a return to bona fide movie stars who take us beyond ourselves and dare us to dream. Since they do not make them like they used to, Loren is too precious a resource for the contemporary cinema to waste.

—Robert Pardi

LORRE, Peter

Born: Laszlo Loewenstein in Rosenberg, Hungary, 26 June 1904. **Education:** Studied acting in Vienna. **Family:** Married 1) Cecilia Lovovsky, 1934; 2) Kaaren Verne, 1951 (divorced); 3) Anna Marie Brenning. **Career:** Stage debut in Zurich, and also acted in Breslau and other German-language cities: in Galsworthy's *Society* in Zurich, and in *Die Pionere von Ingolstadt* at the Volksbühne, Berlin, 1928; 1931—

played a child murderer in his film debut, *M*; 1933—left Germany with rise of Nazis, and made English-language film debut *The Man Who Knew Too Much* 1934; over the next ten years made films in Hollywood for Columbia, 20th Century-Fox (including the Mr. Moto series beginning 1937), and Warner Brothers; free-lance after 1947, often in horror films; 1951—directed and acted in *Der Verlorene* in Germany. **Died:** 24 March 1964.

Films as Actor:

1931   *M* (Fritz Lang) (as Hans Beckert); *Die Bomben auf Monte Carlo* (*The Bombardment of Monte Carlo*; *Monte Carlo Madness*) (Schwarz) (as Pawlitschenk); *Die Koffer des Herrn O.F.* (*The Thirteen Trunks of Mr. O.F.*) (Granowsky) (as Stix)

1932   *Fünf von der Jazzband* (*Five of the Jazzband*) (Engel); *Der weisse Dämon* (*The White Demon*) (Gerron) (as hunchback); *F.P. 1 antwortet nicht* (*F.P. 1 Doesn't Answer*) (Siodmak) (as Johnny); *Schuss im Morgengrauen* (*A Shot at Dawn*) (Zeisler) (as Klotz)

1933   *Was Frauen träumen* (*What Women Dream*) (von Bolvary) (as Füssli); *Unsichtbare Gegner* (*Invisible Opponent*) (Katscher) (as Henry Pless); *De haut à bas* (Pabst) (as beggar); *The Man Who Knew Too Much* (Hitchcock) (as Abbott)

1935   *Mad Love* (Freund) (as Dr. Gogol); *Crime and Punishment* (von Sternberg) (as Raskolnikov)

1936   *The Secret Agent* (Hitchcock) (as General)

1937   *Crack-Up* (St. Clair) (as Col. Gimpy); *Nancy Steele Is Missing* (Marshall) (as Prof. Sturm); *Think Fast, Mr. Moto* (Foster) (as Mr. Moto); *Lancer Spy* (Ratoff) (as Maj. Sigfried Gruning); *Thank You, Mr. Moto* (Foster) (as Mr. Moto)

1938   *Mr. Moto's Gamble* (Tinling) (as Mr. Moto); *Mr. Moto Takes a Chance* (Foster) (as Mr. Moto); *I'll Give a Million* (Walter Lang) (as Louie); *Mysterious Mr. Moto* (Foster) (as Mr. Moto)

1939   *Danger Island* (Leeds) (as Mr. Moto); *Mr. Moto's Last Warning* (Foster) (as Mr. Moto); *Mr. Moto Takes a Vacation* (Foster) (as Mr. Moto)

1940   *Strange Cargo* (Borzage) (as Cochon/M'sieu Pig); *I Was an Adventuress* (Ratoff) (as Polo); *Island of Doomed Men* (Barton) (as Stephen Danel); *Stranger on the Third Floor* (Ingster) (as Stranger); *You'll Find Out* (Butler) (as Fenninger)

1941   *The Face behind the Mask* (Florey) (as James Szabo); *Mr. District Attorney* (Morgan) (as Mr. Hyde); *They Met in Bombay* (Brown) (as Capt. Chang); *The Maltese Falcon* (Huston) (as Joel Cairo)

1942   *All through the Night* (Sherman) (as Pepi); *Invisible Agent* (Marin) (as Baron Ikito); *The Boogie Man Will Get You* (Landers) (as Dr. Lorentz); *Casablanca* (Curtiz) (as Ugarte)

1943   *Background to Danger* (Walsh) (as Zalenkoff); *The Constant Nymph* (Goulding) (as Fritz Bercovy); *The Cross of Lorraine* (Garnett) (as Sgt. Berger)

1944   *Passage to Marseille* (Curtiz) (as Marius); *The Mask of Dimitrios* (Negulesco) (as Cornelius Leyden); *Arsenic and Old Lace* (Capra) (as Dr. Einstein); *The Conspirators* (Negulesco) (as Jan Bernazsky); *Hollywood Canteen* (Daves) (as guest)

1945   *Hotel Berlin* (Godfrey) (as Johannas Koenig); *Confidential Agent* (Shumlin) (as Contreras)

1946   *Three Strangers* (Negulesco) (as West); *Black Angel* (Neill) (as Marko); *The Chase* (Ripley) (as Gino); *The Verdict* (Siegel) (as Victor Emmric); *The Beast with Five Fingers* (Florey) (as Hilary Cummins)

1947   *My Favorite Brunette* (Nugent) (as Kismet)

1948   *Casbah* (Berry) (as Slimane)

1949   *Rope of Sand* (Dieterle) (as Toady)

1950   *Quicksand* (Pichel) (as Nick)

1953   *Double Confession* (Annakin)

1954   *Beat the Devil* (Huston) (as O'Hara); *Twenty Thousand Leagues under the Sea* (Fleischer) (as Conseil)

1956   *Congo Crossing* (Pevney) (as Col. Arragas); *Around the World in Eighty Days* (Anderson) (as Japanese Steward); *Meet Me in Las Vegas* (Rowland) (as guest)

1957   *The Buster Keaton Story* (Sheldon) (as Kurt Bergner); *Silk Stockings* (Mamoulian) (as Brankov); *The Story of Mankind* (Allen) (as Nero); *The Sad Sack* (Marshall) (as Abdul); *Hell Ship Mutiny* (Sholem and Williams) (as Lamouet)

1959   *The Big Circus* (Newman) (as Skeeter)

1960   *Scent of Mystery* (Cardiff) (as Smiley)

1961   *Voyage to the Bottom of the Sea* (Allen) (as Emery)

1962   "The Black Cat" ep. of *Tales of Terror* (Corman) (as Montresor); *Five Weeks in a Balloon* (Allen) (as Ahmed)

1963   *The Raven* (Corman) (as Dr. Bedlo)

1964   *The Comedy of Terrors* (Tourneur) (as Felix Gillie); *Muscle Beach Party* (Asher) (as Mr. Strangdour); *The Patsy* (Lewis) (as Morgan Heywood)

Film as Director:

1951   *Der Verlorene* (*The Lost One*) (+ co-sc, ro as Dr. Karl Rothe)

Publications

On LORRE: books—

Sennett, Ted, *Masters of Menace: Greenstreet and Lorre*, New York, 1979.
Youngkin, Stephen D., James Bigwood, and Raymond G. Cabana, Jr., *The Films of Peter Lorre*, Secaucus, New Jersey, 1982.

On LORRE: articles—

Luft, Herbert, "Peter Lorre," in *Films in Review* (New York), May 1960.
Dyer, P. J., "Fugitive from Murder," in *Sight and Sound* (London), Summer 1964.
Classic Images (Indiana, Pennsylvania), November 1980.
Cinema (W. Germ), March 1984.
Film und Fernsehen (Berlin), no. 1, 1985.

*   *   *

"I want to escape ... to escape from myself! . . . But it's impossible. I can't. I can't escape ... Who knows what it feels like to be me? How I'm forced to act.... " Cringing, pathetic, grotesque, a giveaway M (for murderer) still chalked on his back, the cornered child-killer makes his agonized plea to a grim-faced jury of criminals. Peter Lorre's first film performance (barring an unconfirmed bit part or two), it was also one of his finest, and made him internationally famous. Yet at the same time it trapped him. Hollywood, having seen Lang's film, waited for Lorre to arrive, slapped an indelible M (for melodrama) on his back, and set him to 30 years of playing sad-eyed psychopaths. Throughout his subsequent career, the lines from *M* echo in ironic commentary.

But Lorre was also trapped by his own utterly distinctive physique. Squat, stocky, round-faced, at once pitiable and terrifying, he seemed a textbook illustration of schizophrenia: the eyes, liquid and soulful, that could abruptly bulge with murderous rage or ungovernable terror; the voice, a gentle middle-European whisper, pitching without warning into a shrill fury of frustration and hate; the cigarette drooping

Peter Lorre in *M*

from a twitching mouth; the caged, prowling walk, driven by some intolerable restlessness of spirit. Otis Ferguson described him as "childlike, beautiful, unfathomably wicked, always hinting at things it would not be good to know." Small wonder if he found himself cast as madmen and murderers.

His first appearance on a Hollywood screen, as Dr. Gogol in *Mad Love*, gave fair warning of what was to come. Leaning forward from the darkness of a theater box, moon-round face totally bald above a fur collar and neatly bisected by shadow, Lorre gazed with depraved desire at the spectacle of Frances Drake being tortured on a wheel. Although one of his better films, as it turned out, it pushed him over the edge of self-parody, using (as the *New York Times* remarked of a later movie) "his tricks but not his talent."

Lorre himself, longing to extend his range, always claimed that his true bent lay in comedy, and his most enjoyable roles were certainly those in which comic and sinister were finely balanced. As Joel Cairo in *The Maltese Falcon*, querulous and frizzy-haired, with his spats and gardenia-scented calling cards, he made one of a memorable gang of villains (along with Greenstreet, Mary Astor, and Elisha Cook), just occasionally allowing the killer to glare through the fop. His two roles for Hitchcock drew on a similar vein of quirky ambiguity: the kindly, soft-spoken nihilist in *The Man Who Knew Too Much*, so good with children; and the flamboyantly overdressed "Hairless Mexican" in *Secret Agent*, vain and temperamental, given to sudden outbursts of irrational fury. Lorre could effect the switch, from genial to chilling, with utmost subtlety—a twitch of the scalp, a spasm briefly contorting the mouth, and his shy, vulnerable face would smooth into an inhuman mask.

After *The Maltese Falcon* Warners teamed him eight more times with Greenstreet. They acted well together, effectively playing off Greenstreet's vast urbanity against Lorre's scuttering nervousness, even (perhaps especially) when, as in *The Mask of Dimitrios* or *The Verdict*, Lorre played hero to the other's villain. The *Mr. Moto* series also allowed him a rare escape from evil—routine Fox program-fodder, redeemed by Lorre's resilient wit. Otherwise it was mostly psychopaths, spies, and sadists, though Lorre could bring individuality to the most hackneyed parts, transforming them (in David Thomson's words) "into portraits of delicate, deranged kindness, pushed to the point of frantic malice."

Privately, Lorre was known as a charming man, gentle and intelligent. In later life, troubled by ill-health and overweight, and hurt by the undeserved failure of his sole attempt at directing, *Der Verlorene*, he wandered with resigned sadness through some disastrously bad movies. He was, Peter John Dyer wrote, "a victim of his own precocious fame ... too intractably unique in accent, form and expression for producers to reorient their attitude towards him. He was too obviously nearly mad. He was too dangerously sane."

—Philip Kemp

LOY, Myrna

Nationality: American. **Born:** Myrna Williams in Raidersburg (or Helena), Montana, 2 August 1905. **Education:** Attended Westlake School, Los Angeles, 1918-20; Venice High School, graduated 1923. **Family:** Married 1) the producer Arthur Hornblow Jr., 1936 (divorced 1942); 2) John Hertz, Jr. (divorced); 3) Gene Markey, 1946 (divorced 1950); 4) Howland Sargeant, 1951 (divorced 1960). **Career:** 1920—taught in private dance academy while in high school; 1923—chorus girl at Grauman's Chinese Theatre; also worked in Warners cutting department; 1925—film debut in *Pretty Ladies*; 1926—5-year contract with Warners; 1931—contract with MGM; 1942—

devoted time to Red Cross Work; 1945—attended United Nations sessions in San Francisco, subsequently U.S. representative to UNESCO for over 3 years; 1950s and 1960s—active in electoral campaigns of liberal Democrats including Adlai Stevenson and Eugene McCarthy; 1985—Motion Picture Academy sponsored tribute to Loy at Carnegie Hall, New York. **Awards:** Honorary Oscar, 1991. **Died:** In New York City, 14 December 1993.

Films as Actress:

1923   *The Ten Commandments* (Cecil B. DeMille) (uncredited)
1925   *Pretty Ladies* (Bell) (bit role)
1926   *Ben-Hur* (Niblo) (bit role); *Cave Man* (Milestone) (as chorus girl); *Across the Pacific* (Del Ruth); *Why Girls Go Back Home* (Flood); *The Gilded Highway* (Blackton); *Don Juan* (Crosland); *The Exquisite Sinner* (von Sternberg and Rosen); *So This Is Paris* (Lubitsch); *Finger Prints* (Bacon)
1927   *Ham and Eggs at the Front* (*Ham and Eggs*) (Del Ruth); *Bitter Apples* (Hoyt); *Heart of Maryland* (Bacon) (bit role); *The Jazz Singer* (Crosland) (as chorus girl); *If I Were Single* (Del Ruth); *The Girl from Chicago* (Enright); *The Climbers* (Stein); *Simple Sis* (Raymaker); *A Sailor's Sweetheart* (Bacon)
1928   *What Price Beauty* (Buckingham); *Beware of Married Men* (Mayo); *Turn Back the Hours* (Bretherton); *Crimson City* (Mayo); *Pay as You Enter* (Bacon); *State Street Sadie* (*The Girl from State Street*) (Mayo) (as "Slinky"); *Midnight Taxi* (Adolfi) (as Mrs. Joe Brant); *Noah's Ark* (Curtiz) (as dancer/slave girl)
1929   *Fancy Baggage* (Adolfi) (as Myrna); *The Desert Song* (Del Ruth) (as Azuri); *Black Watch* (*King of the Khyber Rifles*) (Ford) (as Yasmini); *The Squall* (Korda) (as Nubi); *Hardboiled Rose* (Weight) (as Rose Duhamel); *Evidence* (Adolfi) (as native girl); *Show of Shows* (Adolfi)
1930   *The Great Divide* (Barker) (as Manuella); *Cameo Kirby* (Cummings) (as Lea); *Isle of Escape* (Bretherton) (as Moira); *Under a Texas Moon* (Curtiz) (as Lolita Romero); *Cock o' the Walk* (Lane and Neill) (as Narita); *Bride of the Regiment* (Dillon) (as Sophie); *Last of the Duanes* (Werker) (as Lola); *The Truth about Youth* (Seiter) (as Kara the Firefly); *Renegades* (Fleming) (as Eleanore); *Rogue of the Rio Grande* (Bennet) (as Carmita); *The Devil to Pay* (Fitzmaurice) (as Mary Carlyle); *Jazz Cinderella* (*Love Is Like That*) (Pembroke) (as Mildred Vane)
1931   *Naught Flirt* (Cline) (as Linda Gregory); *Body and Soul* (Santell) (as Alice Lester); *A Connecticut Yankee* (*The Yankee at King Arthur's Court*) (Butler) (as Morgan Le Fay); *Hush Money* (Lanfield) (as Flo Curtis); *Transatlantic* (William K. Howard) (as Kay Graham); *Rebound* (Edward H. Griffith) (as Evie Lawrence); *Skyline* (Taylor) (as Paula Lambert); *Consolation Marriage* (Sloane) (as Elaine); *Arrowsmith* (Ford) (as Joyce Lanyon)
1932   *Emma* (Brown); *The Wet Parade* (Fleming); *Vanity Fair* (Franklin) (as Becky Sharp); *The Woman in Room Thirteen* (Henry King) (as Sari Loder); *New Morals for Old* (Brabin) (as Myra); *Love Me Tonight* (Mamoulian) (as Countess Valentine); *Thirteen Women* (Archainbaud) (as Ursula Georgi); *The Mask of Fu Manchu* (Brabin) (as Fah Lo See); *The Animal Kingdom* (*The Woman in His House*) (Edward H. Griffith) (as Cecilia Henry)
1933   *Topaze* (D'Arrast) (as Coco); *The Barbarian* (*A Night in Cairo*) (Wood) (as Diana); *The Prizefighter and the Lady* (Van Dyke) (as Belle Morgan); *When Ladies Meet* (Beaumont) (as Mary Howard); *Penthouse* (*Crooks in Clover*) (Van Dyke) (as Gertie Waxted); *Night Flight* (Brown) (as Brazilian pilot's wife); *Scarlet River* (Selznick) (as herself)

1934   *Men in White* (Boleslawsky) (as Laura); *Manhattan Melo-
        drama* (Van Dyke) (as Eleanor); **The Thin Man** (Van
        Dyke) (as Nora Charles); *Stamboul Quest* (Wood) (as
        "Fraulein Doktor"); *Evelyn Prentice* (William K. Howard)
        (title role); *Broadway Bill* (*Strictly Confidential*) (Capra)
        (as Alice)
1935   *Wings in the Dark* (Flood) (as Sheila Mason); *Whipsaw* (Wood)
        (as Vivian Palmer)
1936   *Wife versus Secretary* (Brown) (as Linda Stanhope); *Petti-
        coat Fever* (Fitzmaurice) (as Irene Campion); *The Great
        Ziegfeld* (Leonard) (as Billie Burke); *To Mary—with Love*
        (Cromwell) (as Mary Wallace); *Libeled Lady* (Conway)
        (as Connie Allenbury); *After the Thin Man* (Van Dyke) (as
        Nora Charles)
1937   *Parnell* (Stahl) (as Katie O'Shea); *Double Wedding* (Thorpe)
        (as Margit Agnew)
1938   *Man-Proof* (Thorpe) (as Mimi Swift); *Test Pilot* (Fleming) (as
        Ann Barton); *Too Hot to Handle* (Conway) (as Alma
        Harding)
1939   *Lucky Night* (Taurog) (as Cora Jordan); *The Rains Came*
        (Brown) (as Lady Edwina Esketh); *Another Thin Man* (Van
        Dyke) (as Nora Charles)
1940   *I Love You Again* (Van Dyke) (as Kay Wilson); *Third Finger,
        Left Hand* (Leonard) (as Margot Sherwood)
1941   *Love Crazy* (Conway) (as Susan Ireland); *Shadow of the Thin
        Man* (Van Dyke) (as Nora Charles)
1943   *Show Business at War* (short)
1944   *The Thin Man Goes Home* (Thorpe) (as Nora Charles)
1946   *So Goes My Love* (*A Genius in the Family*) (Ryan) (as Jane);
        The Best Years of Our Lives (Wyler) (as Milly)
1947   *The Bachelor and the Bobby Soxer* (*Bachelor Knight*) (Reis)
        (as Margaret); *Song of the Thin Man* (Buzzell) (as Nora
        Charles); *The Senator Was Indiscreet* (*Mr. Ashton Was Indis-
        creet*) (Kaufman) (bit role as Mrs. Ashton)
1948   *Mr. Blandings Builds His Dream House* (Potter) (as Muriel
        Blandings)
1949   *The Red Pony* (Milestone) (as Alice Tiflin)
1950   *Cheaper by the Dozen* (Walter Lang) (as Mrs. Lillian Gilbreth);
        That Dangerous Age (*If This Be Sin*) (Ratoff) (as Lady
        Cathy Brooke)
1952   *Belles on Their Toes* (Levin) (as Mrs. Gilbreth)
1956   *The Ambassador's Daughter* (Krasna) (as Mrs. Cartwright)
1958   *Lonelyhearts* (Donahue) (as Florence Shrike)
1960   *From the Terrace* (Robson) (as Martha Eaton); *Midnight Lace*
        (Miller) (as Aunt Bea)
1969   *The April Fools* (Rosenberg)
1971   *Death Takes a Holiday* (Butler—for TV); *Do Not Fold, Spindle
        or Mutilate* (Post—for TV)
1972   *The Couple Takes a Wife* (Paris—for TV)
1974   *Indict and Convict* (Sagal—for TV); *Airport 1975* (Smight)
        (as Mrs. Devaney)
1975   *The Elevator* (Jameson—for TV)
1977   *It Happened at Lakewood Manor* (*Panic at Lakewood Manor*;
        Ants!) (Sheerer—for TV) (as Ethel Adams)
1978   *The End* (Burt Reynolds) (as Maureen Lawson)
1980   *Just Tell Me What You Want* (Lumet) (as Stella Liberti)
1983   *Summer Solstice* (Rosenblum—for TV)

Publications

By LOY: book—

Myrna Loy: Being and Becoming, with James Kotsilibas-Davis, London, 1987.

By LOY: articles—

"Myrna Loy on Comedy," interview with Eric Braun in *Films and
   Filming* (London), March 1968.
"Nora on Nick," interview with J. Hurley, in *Films in Review* (New York),
   October 1982.
Interview with James Kotsilibas-Davis, in *American Film* (New York),
   vol. 13, no. 2, 1987.

On LOY: books—

Kay, Karyn, *Myrna Loy*, New York, 1977.
Quirk, Lawrence J., *The Films of Myrna Loy*, Secaucus, New Jersey,
   1980.
Baxt, George, *The William Powell and Myrna Loy Murder Case* (fiction),
   New York, 1996.

On LOY: articles—

Current Biography 1950, New York, 1950.
Ringgold, Gene, "Myrna Loy," in *Films in Review* (New York), Febru-
   ary 1963.
Bowers, Ron, "Legendary Ladies of the Movies," in *Films in Review*
   (New York), June-July 1973.
Braun, Eric, "The Dream Machine," in *Films and Filming* (London),
   March 1975.
Classic Images (Indiana, Pennsylvania), April 1982.
Films in Review (New York), October 1982.
Buckley, Michael, "A Tribute to Myrna Loy," in *Films in Review* (New
   York), May 1985.
Denby, David, "The Aristocrat Next Door," in *Premiere* (New York),
   November 1993.
Obituary, in *New York Times*, 15 December 1993.
Natale, Richard, obituary in *Variety* (New York), 27 December 1993.

*   *   *

Perhaps no other actress of her refinement has been so encumbered
by the star epithets meant to promote her than Myrna Loy. Touted as
the perfect wife and crowned Queen to Clark Gable's virile King, she
managed to retain her popular appeal while transcending the stereotypes affixed, but never adhering to her ebullient personality. A laugh
always seems fermenting deep within her, the happy product of some
distillation of good and high spirits.

Loy began her career as a dancer and bit player (one early "part"
cast her as the leg of a human chandelier!) but soon found her singular
beauty appropriated to play dark-skinned sirens and Oriental wan-
tons. She exhibited a fiendish glee in such lurid roles as the vindictive
half-caste with hypnotic powers out to revenge herself against her
white sorority sisters in *Thirteen Women* and the "sadistic nymphomaniac" (as Loy described her) in *The Mask of Fu Manchu*. A supporting role in *Love Me Tonight* released the levity in her nature. Her
drowsy Valentine, whose narcolepsy results not from lack of sleep, but
want of men, immediately revives whenever an eligible male wanders
in her vicinity. When asked whether she could go for a doctor, this
sleeping beauty responds with an enthusiastic, grateful "Yes!" Loy had
a way of reading of her lines, even the monosyllabic ones, that uncovered unexpected reserves of energy and irony ready for use.

Loy's Valentine, enchanting as she was, could have lived at any
time since the sixteenth century—providing she was lodged in a chateau. It was her early films with Woody Van Dyke, such as *Penthouse*
and *Manhattan Melodrama* which teamed her with William Powell
and Clark Gable, that naturalized Loy as a sophisticated woman very
much of her own times. Powell won out over the rough, but generous
Gable in the latter film, forming an enduring screen partnership that

Myrna Loy in *The Best Years of Our Lives* © 1946, Samuel Goldwyn

would have fun making fun of the modern sex relation. In 1934's *The Thin Man* Loy literally hurled the modern wife at the feet of an unsuspecting public by executing a three-point landing on a barroom floor. She rose, dignity intact, to assume her place in the popular imagination as the perfect wife who was in every way an equal to her mate—drink for drink, repartee for repartee, but mostly wink for wink. Though never canonized as the perfect husband, Powell knew how to cherish Loy as the most companionable of modern women—witty, unaffectedly but unmistakably intelligent, and remarkably good-natured.

Her rapport with Powell, while unique, nevertheless revealed her untroubled instinct for what her screen mates needed and saw in her. She is not as droll with Gable, who liked his women sassy but not ironic. Her staunch but giving heart so impresses him that he is ready to compromise his macho code and become gentler than he generally feels he can afford to be, a transformation she works on him in the *Test Pilot* and *Too Hot to Handle*. Opposite Cary Grant in *The Bachelor and the Bobby Soxer* and *Mr. Blandings Builds His Dream House* she maintains an imperturbable calm in the face of his frenzied attempts to create order out of chaos, calmly proceeding with her business whatever he thinks his—or hers—might be.

Loy persisted in the national psyche as the womanly ideal after the war. In Wyler's *The Best Years of Our Lives* she suggested how the generosity that in her comic roles manifested itself in good-spirited camaraderie also subsisted in the forbearing wife patiently assisting her husband's readjustment to civilian life. But Loy was no stranger to the dark side of the happy marriages she continued humanizing in films such as *Cheaper by the Dozen* and *Belles on Their Toes*. Her wrenching portrait as the alcoholic mother in *From the Terrace* and the sardonic wife in *Lonelyhearts* offer a bleak counterface to the festive mien she generally presented to the camera. Her last roles played on the knowledge that the qualities she embodied were fast becoming legendary, so that there is to her performances in *April Fools* and *Just Tell Me What You Want* the melancholy suggestion that her wit, womanly tact, and ironic intelligence had indeed transported her to some unreachable, yet still visible realm of perfection.

—Maria DiBattista

LUGOSI, Bela

Born: Bela Ferenc Denzso Blasko in Lugos, Hungary (now Romania), 20 October 1882. **Education:** Attended State Superior Gymnasium, Lugos, and Academy of Performing Arts, Budapest. **Family:** Married 1) Ilona Szmik, 1917 (divorced 1920); 2) the actress Ilona von Montagh, 1921 (divorced 1924); 3) Beatrice Woodruff Weeks, 1929 (divorced 1929); 4) Lillian Arch, 1933 (divorced 1953), son: Bela, Jr.; 5) Hope Linniger, 1955. **Career:** 1902—first stage appearance in *Ocskay Brigaderos*, Deva, Hungary (under name Bela Lugossy); later acted with Franz Joseph Repertory Theatre, Szeged Repertory Theatre, Hungarian Theatre, 1911-13, and National Theatre, 1913-19; 1917—Hungarian film debut in *A Leopard*; 1919—left Hungary when leftists were defeated, and appeared in several German films in 1920-21; formed a Hungarian Repertory Theatre in New York, and made his U.S. stage debut in *The Red Poppy* in 1922; 1923—U.S. film debut in *The Silent Command*; 1927—successful Broadway performance in title role of *Dracula*, repeated in film version in 1931, and in later tours with the play; mid-1940s—host and star of radio program *Mystery House*; 1955—voluntarily received treatment for drug addiction. **Died:** Of heart attack in Los Angeles, 16 August 1956.

Films as Actor:

(as Arisztid Olt)

1917   *A Leopard* (*The Leopard*) (Deesy); *Az azredes* (*The Colonel*) (Kertesz, i.e. Curtiz)

1918   *Alarcosbal* (*The Masked Ball*) (Deesy); *Naszdal* (*Song of Marriage*) (Deesy); *Küzdelem a letert* (*A Struggle for Life*) (Deesy); *99* (Kertesz, i.e. Curtiz); *Tacaszi vihar* (*The Wild Wind of Spring*) (Deesy); *Az elet kiralya* (*The King of Life*) (Deesy); *Lili* (Hintner)

(as Bela Lugosi)

1920   *Der Fluch der Menschheit* (Eichberg); *Der Januskopf* (*Janus-Faced*; *Dr. Jekyll and Mr. Hyde*) (Murnau) (as butler); *Die Frau im Delphin, oder 30 Tage auf dem Meeresgrund* (Kiekebusch-Brenken); *Die Teufelsanbeter*; *Lederstrumpf* (*The Deerslayer*) (Welling) (as Uncas)

1921   *Der Tanz auf dem Vulkan* (*Daughter of the Night*) (Eichberg) (as Andrew Fleurot); *Nat Pinkerton*; *Johann Hopkins der Dritte*

1923   *The Silent Command* (Edwards) (as Hisston)

1924   *The Rejected Woman* (Parker) (as Jean Gagnon)

1925   *The Midnight Girl* (Noy) (as Nicholas Harmon); *Daughters Who Pay* (Terwilliger) (as Serge Oumansky)

1928   *How to Handle Women* (Craft); *The Veiled Woman* (Flynn)

1929   *Prisoners* (Seiter) (as Brottos); *The Thirteenth Chair* (Browning) (as Insp. Delzante)

1930   *Such Men Are Dangerous* (Hawks) (as Dr. Goodman); *Wild Company* (McCarey) (as Felix Brown); *Viennese Nights* (Crosland) (as Hungarian Ambassador); *Renegades* (Fleming) (as thc Marabout)

1931   *Oh, For a Man* (MacFadden); ***Dracula*** (Browning) (as Count Dracula); *Fifty Million Frenchmen* (Bacon); *Women of All Nations* (Walsh) (as Prince Hassan); *The Black Camel* (MacFadden) (as Tarneverro); *Broad Minded* (Le Roy) (as Pancho); *Murders in the Rue Morgue* (Florey) (as Dr. Mirakle)

1932   *White Zombie* (Halperin) (as "Murder" Legendre); *Chandu, The Magician* (Varnel and Menzies) (as Roxor)

1933   *Island of Lost Souls* (Kenton) (as Leader of the Apemen); *The Death Kiss* (Marin) (as Joseph Steiner); *International House* (Sutherland) (as Gen. Nicholas Petronovich); *Night of Terror* (Stoloff) (as Degar); *The Whispering Shadow* (Hermand and Clark—serial) (as Prof. Strang); *The Devil's in Love* (Dieterle) (as prosecutor)

1934   *The Black Cat* (Ulmer) (as Dr. Vitus Werdegast); *Gift of Gab* (Freund) (as man in closet); *The Return of Chandu* (Taylor—serial—features *The Return of Chandu* and *Chandu on the Magic Island* released 1935) (as Chandu)

1935   *The Best Man Wins* (Kenton) (as Doc Boehm); *Mysterious Mr. Wong* (Nigh) (as Mr. Wong); *Mark of the Vampire* (Browning) (as Count Mora); *The Raven* (Landers) (as Dr. Richard Vollin); *Murder by Television* (Sanforth) (as Arthur Perry); *The Phantom Ship* (*The Mystery of the Marie Celeste*) (Clift) (as Anton Lorenzen)

1936   *The Invisible Ray* (Hillyer) (as Dr. Benet); *Postal Inspector* (Brower) (as Benez); *Shadow of Chinatown* (Hill—serial) (as Victor Poten)

1937   *S.O.S. Coastguard* (Witney and James—serial) (as Boroff)

1939   *Son of Frankenstein* (Lee) (as Ygor); *The Gorilla* (Dwan) (as Peters); *The Phantom Creeps* (Beebe and Goodkind—serial) (as Dr. Alex Zorka); ***Ninotchka*** (Lubitsch) (as Razinin); *The Human Monster* (*Dark Eyes of London*) (Summers) (as Dr. Orloff)

Bela Lugosi

1940   *The Saint's Double Trouble* (Hively) (as Partner); *Black Friday* (Lubin) (as Eric Marnay); *You'll Find Out* (Butler) (as Prince Saliano)

1941   *The Devil Bat* (Yarborough) (as Dr. Paul Carruthers); *The Black Cat* (Rogell) (as Eduardo); *The Invisible Ghost* (Lewis) (as Mr. Kessler); *Spooks Run Wild* (Rosen) (as Nardo the monster); *The Wolf Man* (Waggner) (as Bela)

1942   *Ghost of Frankenstein* (Kenton) (as Ygor); *Black Dragons* (Nigh) (as Dr. Melcher/Colomb); *The Corpse Vanishes* (Fox) (as Dr. Lorenz); *Bowery at Midnight* (Fox) (as Prof. Brenner/Karl Wagner); *Night Monster* (Beebe) (as Rolf)

1943   *Frankenstein Meets the Wolf Man* (Neill) (as monster); *The Ape Man* (Beaudine) (as Dr. Brewster); *Ghosts on the Loose* (Beaudine) (as Emil)

1944   *The Return of the Vampire* (Landers) (as Armand Tesla); *Voodoo Man* (Beaudine) (as Dr. Marlowe); *Return of the Ape Man* (Rosen) (as Prof. Dexter); *One Body Too Many* (McDonald) (as Larchmont)

1945   *The Body Snatcher* (Wise) (as Joseph); *Zombies on Broadway* (Douglas) (as Prof. Renault)

1946   *Genius at Work* (Goodwins) (as Stone)

1947   *Scared to Death* (Cabanne) (as Leonide)

1948   *Abbott and Costello Meet Frankenstein* (Barton) (as Count Dracula)

1952   *Old Mother Riley Meets the Vampire* (*Vampire over London*; *My Son, The Vampire*) (Gilling) (as Von Housen); *Glen or Glenda?* (*I Changed My Sex*) (Wood); *Bela Lugosi Meets a Brooklyn Gorilla* (*The Boys from Brooklyn*; *The Monster Meets the Gorilla*) (Beaudine) (as Dr. Zabor)

1955   *Bride of the Monster* (Wood) (as Dr. Eric Vornoff)

1956   *The Black Sleep* (Le Borg) (as Casimir)

1959   *Plan Nine from Outer Space* (*Grave Robbers from Outer Space*) (Wood) (as ghoul man)

Publications

On LUGOSI: books—

Lenning, Arthur, *The Count—The Life and Films of Bela "Dracula" Lugosi*, New York, 1974.

Everson, William K., *Classics of the Horror Film*, Secaucus, New Jersey, 1974.

Lander, Edgar, *Bela Lugosi: Biografia di una metamorfosi*, Milan, 1984.

Mank, Gregory William, *Karloff and Lugosi: A Haunting Collaboration*, Jefferson, North Carolina, 1990.

On LUGOSI: articles—

Lennig, A., "Bela Lugosi: The Raven," in *Film Journal* (Virginia), January-March 1973.

Classic Images (Indiana, Pennsylvania), September 1982.

Beylie, Claude, "Lugosi, bel ange noir," in *Avant-Scène du Cinéma* (Paris), March 1985.

*   *   *

Though his talents were limited, Bela Lugosi was a screen original. His Count Dracula has become part of movie folklore; one cannot imagine the vampire without a black cape and aristocratic manner, intoning dramatically ironic or romantic lines such as "I don't drink—wine" or "To die, to be really dead—that must be glorious!" in a mellifluous or sinister Hungarian accent. Lugosi had been a matinee idol in the Hungarian theater and, to some extent, in the American:

on Broadway, he played a Valentino-like sheik in *Arabesque*. His continental charm carried over to his Dracula—Valentino, the Sheik, through a glass darkly. Both are lady-killers, one figurative, one actual.

Lugosi rarely had the opportunity on screen to exhibit his persona's fatal charm. After he achieved movie stardom in *Dracula*, neither he nor Hollywood knew how to exploit his success or capitalize properly on his image. His one cinematic reprise of the Count was true to the original's spirit, but its context, *Abbott and Costello Meet Frankenstein*, precluded the possibility for any of the original's dark passion and sexual suggestion, as did his two Dracula imitations in *Return of the Vampire* and *Mark of the Vampire* (a stupid "elaborate hoax" movie, wherein Lugosi is a mute, snarling monster, revealed to be an actor impersonating a vampire; all references to the supposed vampire's incest were deleted).

Lugosi made one bad career choice after another. He rejected the part of Frankenstein's monster, but more damaging were the parts he too often accepted: supporting roles or red-herring parts in murder mysteries (when he should have been playing the actual menace), leads in "B" and "C" pictures, often serials. His poor judgment hurt him; each time a horror cycle ended, he was unable, unlike Boris Karloff, to find employment. (His only appearance in an "A" picture after 1933 was a one-scene cameo in *Ninotchka*.)

In only a handful of films did Lugosi exhibit the passion and obsession that were the mark of his most successful characters. Karloff's "mad" scientists were usually kindly, misguided, fatherly types whose attempts to aid humanity went awry. Lugosi's were monomaniacal, driven men who often labored all for love of (or lust for) a woman (for example, in *The Raven*, *The Corpse Vanishes*, and *Voodoo Man*). *White Zombie* and *Murders in the Rue Morgue* concern Lugosi's power over women; the loss of his wife and daughter spur Lugosi's revenge in *The Black Cat* and, for a change, a woman exerts hypnotic power over him in *Invisible Ghost*.

The equally obsessed Ygor—broken-necked, self-serving companion to Frankenstein's monster—was his other memorable creation, which displayed Lugosi's versatility but didn't help his career. He was more and more frequently cast as servants—either imperious (like his Dracula) or uncouth (like Ygor)—in somebody else's horror film, usually to lend menace to the production or another recognizable name to the cast.

By the time he played his last butler in *The Black Sleep*, he was associated with the inept Ed Wood, Jr., who, whatever his shortcomings as a filmmaker, treated Lugosi like a star. Wood cast him as the sage counselor in his very personal *Glen or Glenda?*, allowed him one last mad-scientist role in *Bride of the Monster*, and planned to star him as a vampire in the film that eventually became the infamous *Plan 9 from Outer Space*—built around the few minutes of Lugosi footage shot before his death. Wood's dim awareness of Lugosi's power and presence bestowed on the actor's last works a certain ignominious nobility.

—Anthony Ambrogio

LUKAS, Paul

Born: Pal Lukasz in Budapest, Hungary, 26 May 1895. **Education:** Attended College of Budapest; National Theatre Actors School. **Military Service:** Served in the Hungarian army, 1913-15: invalided out. **Family:** Married 1) Daisy Benes, 1927 (died 1962); 2) Annette Dreisens. **Career:** 1916—stage debut with National Theatre; 1917—Hungarian film debut in *Sphinx*; 1918-27—member of the Comedy Theatre, Budapest; also appeared in Max Reinhardt productions in

Vienna and Berlin; 1922—German film debut in *Samson und Delilah*; 1927—invited to Hollywood by Zukor, but U.S. film debut delayed while he learned English: debut in *Two Lovers*, 1928; also appeared on U.S. stage, most notably in *Watch on the Rhine*, 1941 (also in film version); also appeared on television, in series *The F.B.I.* and *Hotel Paradis*. **Awards:** Best Actor Academy Award, and Best Actor, New York Film Critics, for *Watch on the Rhine*, 1943. **Died:** 15 August 1971.

Films as Actor:

1915   *Man of the Earth*

1917   *Spynx* (*Sphinx*) (Balogh); *Udvari levego* (*Song of the Heart*) (Balogh)

1920   *Sarga Arnyèk* (Garas); *Little Fox* (Garas); *Castle without a Name*; *Masamod* (*The Milliner*) (Markus); *Szinèszno* (*The Actress*) (Forgacs); *Nevtelen vàr* (Garas); *Olavi* (Lajthay)

1921   *New York exprez kabel* (*Telegram from New York*) (Garas); *Hetszàzeves szerelem* (Garas); *Love of the Eighteenth Century*

1922   *The Lady in Grey*; *A szurkerahàs hölgy* (Deesy); *Samson und Delilah* (*Samson and Delilah*) (Curtiz); *Lady Violette* (Geroffy); *Eine Versunkene Welt*

1923   *The Glorious Life*; *Diadalmas elet* (Gaël); *Egy fiunak a fele* (von Bolvary); *A Girl's Way*; *Das unbekannte Morgen* (Korda)

1928   *Two Lovers* (Niblo) (as Ramón de Linea); *Three Sinners* (Lee) (as Count Dietrich Wallentin); *Loves of an Actress* (Lee) (as Dr. Durande); *Hot News* (Badger) (as James Clayton); *The Night Watch* (Korda) (as Captain Corlais); *The Woman from Moscow* (Berger) (as Vladimir); *Manhattan Cocktail* (Arzner) (as Renov)

1929   *The World of Wall Street* (Lee) (as David Tyler); *The Shopworn Angel* (Wallace) (as Bailey); *Illusion* (Mendes) (as Count Fortuny); *Half-Way to Heaven* (Abbott) (as Nick)

1930   *Slightly Scarlet* (Gasnier and Knopf) (as Malatroff); *Behind the Make-Up* (Milton) (as Boris); *Young Eagles* (Wellman) (as Von Baden); *Grumpy* (Cukor and Gardner) (as Berci); *The Benson Murder Case* (Tuttle) (as Adolph Mohler); *The Devil's Holiday* (Goulding) (as Dr. Reynolds); *Anybody's Woman* (Arzner) (as Gustav Saxon); *The Right to Love* (Wallace) (as Eric Helge)

1931   *City Street* (Mamoulian); *Unfaithful* (Cromwell); *The Vice Squad* (Cromwell); *Women Love Once* (Goodman); *Strictly Dishonorable* (Stahl); *The Beloved Bachelor* (Corrigan); *Working Girls* (Arzner)

1932   *No One Man* (Corrigan) (as Dr. Karl Bemis); *Tomorrow and Tomorrow* (Wallace); *Thunder Below* (Wallace); *A Passport to Hell* (Lloyd); *Rockabye* (Cukor); *Downstairs* (Bell)

1933   *Grand Slam* (Dieterle); *The Kiss before the Mirror* (Whale); *Sing Sinner Sing* (Christy); *Captured!* (Del Ruth); *Secret of the Blue Room* (Neumann); *Little Women* (Cukor) (as Professor Bhaer)

1934   *By Candlelight* (Whale); *Glamour* (Wyler); *The Countess of Monte Cristo* (Freund); *Affairs of a Gentleman* (Marin); *I Give My Love* (Freund); *The Fountain* (Cromwell); *Gift of Gab* (Freund)

1935   *The Casino Murder Case* (Fenton); *Father Brown—Detective* (Sedgwick) (title role); *Age of Indiscretion* (Ludwig); *I Found Stella Parish* (LeRoy); *The Three Musketeers* (Lee)

1936   *Dodsworth* (Wyler); *Ladies in Love* (Griffith)

1937   *Espionage* (Neumann); *Dinner at the Ritz* (Schuster); *Brief Ecstasy* (Gréville)

1938   *The Mutiny on the Elsinore* (Lockwood); **The Lady Vanishes** (Hitchcock) (as Dr. Hartz); *Dangerous Secrets* (Gréville)

1939   *Confessions of a Nazi Spy* (Litvak) (as Dr. Kassel); *Lady in Distress* (Mason); *Captain Fury* (Roach)

1940   *The Ghost Breakers* (Marshall); *Strange Cargo* (Borzage) (as Hessler)

1941   *The Monster and the Girl* (Heisler); *They Dare Not Love* (Whale); *The Chinese Bungalow* (*Chinese Den*) (G. King) (as Yuan Sing)

1943   *Watch on the Rhine* (Sherman and Shumlin) (as Kurt Mueller); *Hostages* (Tuttle)

1944   *Uncertain Glory* (Walsh); *Address Unknown* (Menzies); *Experiment Perilous* (Tourneur)

1946   *Deadline at Dawn* (Chapman); *Temptation* (Pichel)

1947   *Whispering City* (Ozep)

1948   *Berlin Express* (Tourneur)

1950   *Kim* (Saville)

1954   *20,000 Leagues under the Sea* (Fleischer) (as Professor Aronnax)

1958   *The Roots of Heaven* (Huston)

1960   *Scent of Mystery* (*Holiday in Spain*) (Todd and Cardiff); *Tender Is the Night* (King) (as Dr. Dohmler)

1962   *The Four Horsemen of the Apocalypse* (Minnelli) (as Karl von Hartrott)

1963   *Fifty-Five Days at Peking* (Ray) (as Dr. Steinfeldt); *Fun in Acapulco* (Thorpe) (as Maximillian)

1965   *Lord Jim* (Brooks) (as Stein)

1968   *Sol Madrid* (Hutton) (as Capo Riccione)

1970   *The Challenge* (Smithee)

Publications

On LUKAS: book—

Parish, James Robert, and William T. Leonard, *Hollywood Players: The Thirties*, New Rochelle, New York, 1976.

On LUKAS: articles—

Photoplay (New York), December 1930, June 1931, January 1932, June 1933, November 1934, and September 1940.
Time (New York), 14 April 1941.
New Yorker, 10 May 1941.
Ciné Revue (Paris), 30 April 1984.

*　　*　　*

In his more than 40 years in Hollywood, Hungarian-born Paul Lukas enjoyed an active career playing a combination of the suave, continental leading man to some of the screen's most glamorous actresses—Ruth Chatterton in *Anybody's Woman*, Sylvia Sidney in *City Streets*, Constance Bennett in *Rockabye*, and Loretta Young in *Grand Slam*—to the suave, continental villain in numerous Nazi-based war films. Rarely were his roles substantial enough for him to draw upon his extensive theatrical training. However, he did achieve top-ranking star status with his portrayal of Kurt Mueller in *Watch on the Rhine* in 1943.

Few of his films of the 1930s stand out, but he was particularly memorable as Professor Bhaer in *Little Women*. He played detective Philo Vance in *The Casino Murder Case*, Athos in *The Three Musketeers*, and Arnold Iselin in William Wyler's excellent *Dodsworth*. He was appropriately mysterious as the charming Dr. Hartz in Alfred Hitchcock's *The Lady Vanishes*, but probably his best 1930s role was as Dr. Kassel, the propaganda chief, in *Confessions of a Nazi Spy*. This was patriotic wartime melodrama brilliantly acted by Edward G. Robinson, Francis Lederer, and Lukas with swiftly paced direction by Anatole Litvak.

It was the Nazism of World War II that also set the scene for Lukas's greatest film success, *Watch on the Rhine*. He had starred in the 1941 New York stage version of this, Lillian Hellman's most subtly written play. His portrayal of Kurt Mueller, the German émigré with an American wife, was universally lauded by critics. Brooks Atkinson wrote in the *New York Time,* "As the enemy of fascism. Mr. Lukas' haggard, loving, resourceful determination becomes heroic by virtue of his sincerity and his superior abilities as an actor." When Warner Brothers produced the film version, they hired five members of the original Broadway cast, including Lukas, and the director, Herman Schumlin. They enlisted Hellman's friend Dashiell Hammett to write the screenplay and cast Bette Davis as Mueller's wife to ensure box-office success. However, it was Lukas's film, and he received the Academy Award and the New York Film Critics Award for his moving performance.

Despite the success of *Watch on the Rhine*, Lukas's career remained one of fairly cardboard leading roles opposite beautiful actresses (for example Hedy Lamarr in *Experiment Perilous*), and eventually evolved into mature character roles: he was Professor Aronnax in *20,000 Leagues under the Sea* and Stein in *Lord Jim.*

—Ronald Bowers

LUPINO, Ida

Nationality: American. **Born:** London, England, 4 February 1918, daughter of the actor Stanley Lupino and the actress Connie Emerald; became U.S. citizen in 1948. **Education:** Attended Clarence House School, Hove, Sussex; Royal Academy of Dramatic Art, London. **Family:** Married 1) the actor Louis Hayward, 1938 (divorced 1945); 2) the writer Collier Young, 1948 (divorced 1951); 3) the actor Howard Duff, 1951 (divorced 1972), daughter: Bridget. **Career:** Stage debut at Tom Thumb Theatre, London, at age 12; late 1920s—extra in films for British International Studios; 1932—first lead role in *Her First Affaire*; 1933-37—contract with Paramount; 1939—success in *The Light that Failed*: contract with Warner Brothers; 1949—co-founder, with Anson Bond, Emerald Productions: producer, co-director, and co-scriptwriter of *Not Wanted*; 1950—director of the film *Never Fear*, 1950-80—co-owner, with Collier Young, Film-makers Company; 1952—co-founder, with Dick Powell, Charles Boyer, and David Niven, Four Star Productions for television; 1956—director for TV series *On Trial*; 1957-58—in TV series *Mr. Adams and Eve*; 1957-66—worked exclusively in television. **Awards:** Best Actress, New York Film Critics, for *The Hard Way*, 1943. **Died:** Of cancer, in Burbank, California, 3 August 1995.

Films as Actress:

1932   *Her First Affaire* (Dwan) (as Anne)
1933   *Money for Speed* (Vorhaus) (as Jane); *High Finance* (George King) (as Jill); *The Ghost Camera* (Vorhaus) (as Mary Elton); *I Lived with You* (Elvey) (as Ada Wallis); *Prince of Arcadia* (Schwartz) (as Princess)
1934   *Search for Beauty* (Kenton) (as Barbara Hilton); *Come on, Marines!* (Hathaway) (as Esther Cabot); *Ready for Love* (Gering) (as Marigold Tate)
1935   *Paris in Spring* (Milestone) (as Mignon De Charelle); *Smart Girl* (Scotto) (as Pat Reynolds); *Peter Ibbetson* (Hathaway) (as Agnes)

1936   *Anything Goes* (*Tops Is the Limit*) (Milestone) (as Hope Harcourt); *One Rainy Afternoon* (*Matinee Scandal*) (Rowland V. Lee) (as Monique Pelerin); *Yours for the Asking* (Hall) (as Gert Malloy); *The Gay Desperado* (Mamoulian) (as Jane)
1937   *Sea Devils* (Stoloff) (as Doris Malone); *Let's Get Married* (Alfred E. Green) (as Paula Quinn); *Artists and Models* (Walsh) (as Paula Sewell); *Fight for Your Lady* (Stoloff) (as Marietta)
1939   *The Lone Wolf Spy Hunt* (Godfrey) (as Val Carson); *The Lady and the Mob* (Stoloff) (as Lila Thorne); *The Adventures of Sherlock Holmes* (Werker) (as Ann Brandon); *The Light that Failed* (Wellman) (as Bessie Broke)
1940   *They Drive by Night* (Walsh) (as Lana Carlsen)
1941   **High Sierra** (Walsh) (as Marie Garson); *The Sea Wolf* (Curtiz) (as Ruth Webster); *Out of the Fog* (Litvak) (as Stella Goodwin); *Ladies in Retirement* (Charles Vidor) (as Ellen Creed)
1942   *Moontide* (Mayo) (as Ada); *The Hard Way* (Sherman) (as Helen Chernen); *Life Begins at 8:30* (*The Light of Heart*) (Pichel) (as Kathi Thomas)
1943   *Forever and a Day* (Clair and others) (as Jenny); *Thank Your Lucky Stars* (David Butler) (appearance)
1944   *In Our Time* (Sherman) (as Jennifer Whittredge); *Hollywood Canteen* (Daves) (appearance)
1945   *Pillow to Post* (Sherman) (as Jean Howard)
1946   *Devotion* (Bernhardt) (as Emily Brontë); *The Man I Love* (Walsh) (as Petey Brown)
1947   *Deep Valley* (Negulesco) (as Libby); *Escape Me Never* (Godfrey) (as Gemma Smith)
1948   *Road House* (Negulesco) (as Lily Stevens)
1949   *Lust for Gold* (Simon) (as Julia Thomas); *Woman in Hiding* (Gordon) (as Deborah Chandler Clark)
1951   *On Dangerous Ground* (Nicholas Ray) (as Mary Malden)
1952   *Beware, My Lovely* (Horner) (as Mrs. Helen Gordon)
1953   *Jennifer* (Newton) (as Agnes)
1954   *Private Hell 36* (Siegel) (as Lilli Marlowe, + co-sc)
1955   *Women's Prison* (Seiler) (as Amelia Van Zant); *The Big Knife* (Aldrich) (as Marion Castle)
1956   *While the City Sleeps* (Fritz Lang) (as Mildred); *Strange Intruder* (Rapper) (as Alice)
1969   *Backtrack* (Bellamy) (as Mama Delores)
1972   *Junior Bonner* (Peckinpah) (as Elvira Bonner); *Deadhead Miles* (Zimmerman) (as herself); *Women in Chains* (Kowalski—for TV) (as Tyson); *The Strangers in 7A* (Wendkos—for TV) (as Iris Sawyer)
1973   *Female Artillery* (Chomsky—for TV) (as Martha Lindstrom); *I Love a Mystery* (Leslie Stevens—for TV) (as Randolph Cheyne); "Dear Karen" ep. of *The Letters* (Krasny—for TV) (as Mrs. Forrester)
1975   *The Devil's Rain* (Fuest) (as Mrs. Preston)
1976   *Food of the Gods* (Bert I. Gordon) (as Mrs. Skinner)
1978   *My Boys Are Good Boys* (Buckalew)

Films as Director:

1949   *Not Wanted* (co-d with Clifton, + co-pr, co-sc)
1950   *Never Fear* (*The Young Lovers*) (+ pr, co-sc); *Outrage* (+ co-pr, co-sc)
1951   *Hard, Fast, and Beautiful* (+ co-pr)
1953   *The Hitch-Hiker* (+ co-pr, co-sc); *The Bigamist* (+ co-pr, ro as Phyllis Martin)
1966   *The Trouble with Angels* (+ co-pr)

Ida Lupino in *Her First Affair*

Publications

By LUPINO: articles—

"The Trouble with Men Is Women," in *Silver Screen*, April 1947.
"Who Says Men Are People?," in *Silver Screen*, October 1948.
"I Cannot Be Good," in *Silver Screen*, June 1949.
"Me, Mother Directress," in *Action* (Los Angeles), May/June 1967.
"This Was My Favorite Role," in *Movie Digest*, November 1972.
Interview with Graham Fuller, in *Interview* (New York), October 1990.

On LUPINO: books—

Vermilye, Jerry, *Ida Lupino*, New York, 1977.
Stewart, Lucy, and Ann Liggett, *Ida Lupino as Film Director, 1949-1953: An Auteur Approach*, Ann Arbor, Michigan, 1979.
Kowalski, Rosemary, *A Vision of One's Own: Four Women Film Directors*, Ann Arbor, Michigan, 1980.
Parish, James, and Don Stanke, *The Forties Gals*, Westport, Connecticut, 1980.
Heck-Rabi, Louise, *Women Filmmakers: A Critical Reception*, Metuchen, New Jersey, 1984.
Kuhn, Annette, editor, *Queen of the 'B's: Ida Lupino behind the Camera*, Westport, Connecticut, 1995.
Donati, William, *Ida Lupino: A Biography*, Lexington, Kentucky, 1996.

On LUPINO: articles—

Current Biography 1943, New York, 1943.
"Director Only?," in *Films and Filming* (London), January 1955.
Vermilye, Jerry, "Ida Lupino," in *Films in Review* (New York), May 1959.
Parker, F., "Discovering Ida Lupino," in *Action* (Los Angeles), July/August 1973.
Siclier, J., and O. Eyquem, "Le Cinéma feminin d'Ida Lupino," in *Cahiers de la Cinémathèque* (Perpignan, France), no. 28, 1979.
Scheib, R., "Ida Lupino: Auteuress," in *Film Comment* (New York), January/February 1980.
"Newsreel: Lost Lupino," in *American Film* (Washington, D.C.), June 1981.
Films in Review (New York), October 1982.
Interim, L., "Une Femme dangereuse," in *Cahiers du Cinéma* (Paris), May 1983.
Nacache, J., "Sur six films d'Ida Lupino," in *Cinéma* (Paris), October 1983.
Ida Lupino section of *Positif* (Paris), March 1986.
Ciacchiari, F., "Ida Lupino," in *Cineforum* (Bergamo, Italy), May 1991.
Hallensleben, S., "Ida Lupino," in *EPD Film* (Frankfurt), April 1993.
Mallory, M., "Ida Lupino," in *Scarlet Street*, Winter 1994.
Flint, Peter B., obituary, in *New York Times*, 5 August 1995.
Obituary in *Variety* (New York), 14 August 1995.
Scorsese, Martin, "Behind the Camera, a Feminist," in *New York Times Magazine*, 31 December 1995.

*   *   *

A heart-shaped face, bowed lips, and large clear eyes gave her a Bo-Peepish quality, but Ida Lupino's strongest screen characterizations would make any self-respecting nursery-rhyme shepherdess blush! Lupino excelled in playing vixens and society's cast-offs. After spending six teenaged years appearing in mediocre parts, she attained stardom in the role of the selfish Cockney prostitute who is driven to madness after posing as a model for an obsessive artist (Ronald Colman) in *The Light that Failed*. She followed that role with an equally strong interpretation of a brazen lowlife in *They Drive by Night*. In that film, she dazzled critics as a bitch who kills her husband, goes after a man who spurns her, and then goes mad when things do not go her way.

Lupino once allegedly called herself "a poor man's Bette Davis." This is a cheapening remark, because Lupino had a screen presence unlike Davis or any other Hollywood leading lady. Like Davis, she was able to show backbone and ingenuity, especially when her character was up against the wall. What made her unique, however, was her ability to utilize soft, refined good looks and delicate mannerisms to play tough, unsympathetic women. In *High Sierra*, Lupino is at her best as a young thing who latches onto mobster Humphrey Bogart. What might have been no more than a one-dimensional helpless female role becomes a vivid characterization. She is like a stray cat, a rootless little-girl-lost who begs Bogart not to make her go back to the seedy "nightspot" where she used to work. At the same time she is determined and womanly, a warm beacon of sorts for a mobster who craves to retire to home and hearth.

In the films that are among the high points of her career, Lupino worked for William Wellman and several times for Raoul Walsh—two directors noted for creating pictures with rough, sometimes gritty brush strokes. When Lupino formed her own production company in 1949, she chose to produce motion pictures dealing with social themes, films reflecting the toughness of Wellman and Walsh. But these films presented social dramas with a new frankness. Lupino may have been influenced by the postwar Italian neorealist films, or perhaps she simply saw the power the genre of social drama could have when it renounced Hollywood glitz. In any case, *Not Wanted*, *Outrage*, and *The Bigamist* deal with, respectively, unwed mothers, rape, and bigamy. These are topics that were considered taboo by the major studios. At a time when no other woman was directing Hollywood feature films, Lupino was directing—and her films were not feminine powder-puff drivel. She paid detailed attention to the miseries women-as-victims were encountering as underdogs in society. Her success in directing these low-budget but effective and durable films is linked to her prior experience of acting troubled female characters. By then, she knew what worked, and what did not.

As a feminist film theory developed, it was ironic that Lupino actually was scoffed at for presenting women as victims rather than aggressors. Then, the tide turned and she was properly lauded as a significant pioneer among women directors.

From the mid-1950s on, Lupino practically disappeared from the screen. Of her scant celluloid roles during her last years, by far the best is Elvira Bonner, the estranged wife of Ace Bonner (Robert Preston), in *Junior Bonner*. Here she is acting with an intensity reminiscent of her strongest Hollywood roles. Age, however, had added a craggy naturalism to her looks and moves. Once again, critics hailed her acting achievement. Rather than catapult her into another round of first-rate parts, it turned out to be her last important role.

—Audrey E. Kupferberg

MacDONALD, Jeanette

Nationality: American. **Born:** Philadelphia, Pennsylvania, 18 June 1901. **Family:** Married Gene Raymond, 1937. **Career:** 1920—New York stage debut in chorus of *The Demi-Tasse Revue*; worked as model; 1923—second lead in singing role in *The Magic Ring*, contract with Henry Savage; 1925-29—starring roles in stage musicals for Savage and Shubert organization; 1929—film debut in *The Love Parade*; contract with Paramount; recording debut for RCA Victor; 1931—concert tour in Europe; 1933-42—contract with MGM; 1935—co-starred for first time with Nelson Eddy in *Naughty Marietta*; 1937—first solo starring feature, *The Firefly*; 1943—operatic debut in Montreal, in *Romeo and Juliet* with Ezio Pinza; American debut in *Faust* at Chicago Civic Opera; 1951—on Broadway with Gene Raymond in revival of *The Guardsman*; 1950s—television appearances with Raymond; 1957—in Las Vegas nightclub act. **Died:** 14 January 1965.

Films as Actress:

1929 *The Love Parade* (Lubitsch) (as Queen Louise of Sylvania)
1930 *The Vagabond King* (Berger) (as Katherine); *Monte Carlo* (Lubitsch); *Let's Go Native* (McCarey); *The Lottery Bride* (Stein); *Oh, For a Man* (MacFadden)
1931 *Don't Bet on Women* (Howard); *Annabelle's Affairs* (Werker)
1932 *One Hour with You* (Cukor and Lubitsch); *Love Me Tonight* (Mamoulian) (as Princess Jeannette)
1934 *The Cat and the Fiddle* (Howard); *The Merry Widow* (Lubitsch) (as Sonia)
1935 *Naughty Marietta* (Van Dyke) (as Princess Marie)
1936 *Rose Marie* (Van Dyke) (title role); *San Francisco* (Van Dyke)
1937 *Maytime* (Leonard); *The Firefly* (Leonard)
1938 *The Girl of the Golden West* (Leonard); *Sweethearts* (Van Dyke)
1939 *Broadway Serenade* (Leonard)
1940 *New Moon* (Leonard); *Bitter Sweet* (Van Dyke)
1941 *Smilin' Through* (Borzage)
1942 *I Married an Angel* (Van Dyke)
1943 *Cairo* (Van Dyke)
1944 *Follow the Boys* (Sutherland)
1948 *Three Daring Daughters* (Wilcox)
1949 *The Sun Comes Up* (Thorpe)

Publications

On MacDONALD: books—

Parish, James Robert, *The Jeanette MacDonald Story*, New York, 1976.
Goodrich, D., and S. Rich, *Farewell to Dreams*, Los Angeles, 1979.
Castanza, Philip, *The Films of Jeanette MacDonald and Nelson Eddy*, Secaucus, New Jersey, 1981.

On MacDONALD: articles—

Bodeen, DeWitt, "Jeanette MacDonald," in *Films in Review* (New York), March 1965.
Robb, Florence, in *Classic Images* (Indiana, Pennsylvania), November 1982 and April 1984.

* * *

Although typed by a "legitimate" soprano voice suited to operetta, Jeanette MacDonald had a career with two distinct phases. Under the direction of Ernst Lubitsch, in *The Love Parade* and subsequent films, she reveals an irony, a sense of the ridiculous, an ability to comment, with great subtlety, upon the conventions of operetta that Lubitsch himself so lovingly satirizes. In a sexual war of nerves with her co-star, Maurice Chevalier, MacDonald raises an eyebrow and defines

Jeanette MacDonald with Nelson Eddy

"the Lubitsch touch." After a brief flurry of success, MacDonald went into an equally brief decline and reemerged, a second choice (Grace Moore was unavailable) for *The Merry Widow*, again with Chevalier and again directed by Lubitsch. This was the last, precious expression of the bittersweet sentiment and trenchant humor that so suited director and star.

The second phase of MacDonald's career marks her peak of greatest popularity and contains the eight films in which her co-star was Nelson Eddy. MGM's most lavish productions and the strenuous vocalizing of the soprano and the baritone proved powerful at the box office. In these films MacDonald plays her operetta straight, the sentiment unadulterated. The beginning of World War II coincided with the waning and death of the series and the genre. Clark Gable, not Nelson Eddy, is the hero of her best-remembered film, *San Francisco*. In the celebrated title song, performed just before the spectacular earthquake sequence, MacDonald's energy and spirit prove just as infectious to audiences in movie theaters today as they did to the audience we see responding within the film.

—Charles Affron

MacLAINE, Shirley

Nationality: American. **Born:** Shirley MacLean Beaty in Richmond, Virginia, 24 April 1934; sister of the actor Warren Beatty. **Education:** Attended Washington School of Ballet; Washington and Lee High School, Arlington, Virginia, graduated 1952. **Family:** Married Steve Parker, 1954 (divorced 1977), daughter: Stephanie (known as the actress Sachi Parker). **Career:** In dancing chorus of *Oklahoma*, 1950, *Me and Juliet*, 1952, and understudy to Carol Haney in *The Pajama Game*, 1954; 1954-61—contract with Hal Wallis; 1955—film debut in *The Trouble with Harry*; 1971-72—in TV series *Shirley's World*; 1974—co-directed film *The Other Half of the Sky*; 1974—formed nightclub act for Las Vegas, and in 1976 toured with the act in Europe and Latin America. **Awards:** Best Actress, Berlin Festival, and Best Foreign Actress, British Academy, for *Ask Any Girl*, 1959; Best Actress, Venice Festival, and Best Foreign Actress, British Academy, for *The Apartment*, 1960; Best Actress, Berlin Festival, for *Desperate Characters*, 1971; Best Actress, Academy Award, and Best Actress, New York and Los Angeles Film Critics, for *Terms of Endearment*, 1983. **Agent:** c/o MacLaine Enterprises, 25200 Old Malibu Road, Malibu, CA 90262, U.S.A.

Films as Actress:

1955   *The Trouble with Harry* (Hitchcock) (as Jennifer Rogers); *Artists and Models* (Tashlin) (as Bessie Sparrowbush)
1956   *Around the World in Eighty Days* (Anderson) (as Princess Aouda)
1958   *Hot Spell* (Daniel Mann) (as Virginia Duval); *The Sheepman* (George Marshall) (as Dell Payton); *The Matchmaker* (Anthony) (as Irene Molloy); *Some Came Running* (Minnelli) (as Ginny Moorehead)
1959   *Ask Any Girl* (Walters) (as Meg Wheeler); *Career* (Anthony) (as Sharon Kensington)
1960   *Can-Can* (Walter Lang) (as Simone Pistache); *The Apartment* (Wilder) (as Fran Kubelik); *Ocean's Eleven* (Milestone) (as tipsy girl)
1961   *All in a Night's Work* (Anthony) (as Katie Robbins); *Two Loves* (Walters) (as Anna Vorontosov); *The Children's Hour* (Wyler) (as Martha Dobie)

1962   *My Geisha* (Cardiff) (as Lucy Dell/Yoko Mori); *Two for the Seesaw* (Wise) (as Gittel Mosca)
1963   *Irma La Douce* (Wilder) (title role)
1964   *What a Way to Go!* (Thompson) (as Louisa); *John Goldfarb, Please Come Home* (Thompson) (as Jenny Ericson)
1965   *The Yellow Rolls-Royce* (Asquith) (as Mae Jenkins)
1966   *Gambit* (Neame) (as Nicole Chang)
1967   *Woman Times Seven* (De Sica) (as Paulette)
1968   *The Bliss of Mrs. Blossom* (McGrath) (title role)
1969   *Sweet Charity* (Fosse) (as Charity Hope Valentine)
1970   *Two Mules for Sister Sara* (Siegel) (title role)
1971   *Desperate Characters* (Gilroy) (as Sophie Brentwood)
1972   *The Possession of Joel Delaney* (Hussein) (as Norah Benson)
1977   *The Turning Point* (Ross) (as Deedee Rogers)
1979   *Being There* (Ashby) (as Eve Rand)
1980   *A Change of Seasons* (Richard Lang) (as Karen Evans); *Loving Couples* (Smight) (as Evelyn)
1983   *Terms of Endearment* (James L. Brooks) (as Aurora Greenway)
1984   *Cannonball Run II* (Needham) (as Veronica)
1987   *Out on a Limb* (Butler—for TV) (as herself)
1988   *Madame Sousatzka* (Schlesinger) (title role)
1989   *Steel Magnolias* (Ross) (as Ouiser Boudreaux)
1990   *Waiting for the Light* (Monger) (as Zena); *Postcards from the Edge* (Nichols) (as Doris Mann)
1991   *Defending Your Life* (Albert Brooks) (as woman at past lives pavillion)
1993   *Used People* (Kidron) (as Pearl); *Wrestling Ernest Hemingway* (Haines) (as Helen)
1994   *Guarding Tess* (Wilson) (title role)
1995   *West Side Waltz* (for TV); *The Celluloid Closet* (Eptsein and Friedman—doc) (as interviewee)
1996   *The Evening Star* (as Aurora Greenway); *Mrs. Winterbourne*

Film as Director:

1974   *The Other Half of the Sky: A China Memoir* (doc) (co-d, + pr, sc)

Publications

By MacLAINE: books—

Don't Fall Off the Mountain, New York, 1970.
You Can Get There from Here, New York, 1975.
Out on a Limb, New York, 1983.
Dancing in the Light, New York, 1986.
It's All in the Playing, New York, 1987.
Going Within, New York, 1989.
Dance While You Can, New York, 1991.
My Lucky Stars: A Hollywood Memoir, New York, 1995.

By MacLAINE: articles—

"The Two Faces of Shirley," interview with R. Bean, in *Films and Filming* (London), February 1962
Photoplay (London), April 1984.
Interview with L. Farrah, in *Films and Filming* (London), May 1988.
"Shirley MacLaine Lives," interview with Pat Dowell, in *Washingtonian*, October 1988.
Interview with Janet Fitch, in *American Film* (New York), November 1989.

Shirley MacLaine in *Irma La Douce*

On MacLAINE: books—

Erens, Patricia, *The Films of Shirley MacLaine*, South Brunswick, New Jersey, 1978.
Denis, Christopher, *The Films of Shirley MacLaine*, Secaucus, New Jersey, 1980.
Pickard, Roy, *Shirley MacLaine*, London, 1985.
Spada, James, *Shirley and Warren*, London, 1985.
Freedland, Michael, *Shirley MacLaine*, London, 1986.
Hanck, Frauke, *Shirley MacLaine: Ihre Filme, ihr Leben*, Munich, 1986.

On MacLAINE: articles—

Current Biography 1978, New York, 1978.
Dowell, Pat, "Collector's Choice: Woman of the Year: Coming to Terms with the Career of Shirley MacLaine," in *American Film* (Washington, D.C.), April 1984.
Séquences (Montreal), July 1984.
Haskell, Molly, "Shirley MacLaine: Still Here," in *Film Comment* (New York), May-June 1995.

*   *   *

Shirley MacLaine's career has continued to thrive since she won her Academy Award in 1983. *Terms of Endearment* brought MacLaine full recognition as a performer and it also gave the actress an image for the latter stages of her career. The films that follow *Terms of Endearment* tend to present her as a combative person who, like Aurora Greenway in Brooks's film, struggles to set and maintain the "terms of endearment" of her personal relationships. In such films as *Madame Sousatzka* and *Postcards from the Edge* MacLaine is demanding, irascible, and generally exasperating; yet, by the film's resolution, she acknowledges that the relationship in question is at base essential and loving. The films illustrate the actress's willingness to play a difficult person who is in danger of alienating both the film's other characters and the viewer. MacLaine seems to delight in testing how far she can go before she pulls back and lets the viewer see that her character is in fact sensitive and capable of tenderness.

MacLaine has been highly successful in combining her status as a major star with that of a character actress; and the films are a testament to MacLaine's ability to sustain a career at an age when most of her contemporaries are no longer professionally active. Of the more recent films, *Madame Sousatzka* is perhaps the most outstanding and it provides MacLaine with an acting challenge she fully meets—Madame Sousatzka, a formidable piano teacher, is, in addition to being intelligent and creative, in equal measure bombastic and contemplative, willful and pliable. And John Schlesinger, who surrounds the actress with a group of strong performers, handles the material with insight and assurance. Similarly, *Postcards from the Edge*, another fine film, allows MacLaine to inject a degree of delicacy into her conception of an overbearing but insecure aging actress. Mike Nichols's film takes a gentle approach to satirizing Hollywood and tempers the mother-daughter conflict between MacLaine and Meryl Streep with low-key humor and a strong sense of compassion for both of these resilient but highly fragile characters. In these two films MacLaine is given the opportunity to bring depth and dimension to her characterizations; on the other hand, she also appears in *Steel Magnolias* and *Used People*, both shrill and crude films, and the bland *Guarding Tess*.

Besides working regularly as an actor, MacLaine continues to pursue her career as a writer. Her dual identity as actor/author came together most spectacularly with a telefilm dramatization of her book *Out on a Limb* in which she deals with transcendentalism. *Out on a Limb* is, aesthetically, undistinguished. The narrative is soap operaish,

the performances are merely adequate and the direction is flat. MacLaine, like the film itself, is highly self-conscious and strains to convince that the material is engrossing and deserving of the time and money spent on the project. *Out on a Limb*'s primary significance is that it forcefully acknowledges MacLaine's ongoing desire to control her star image. The film is essentially concerned with verifying that MacLaine is a serious thinker, has a social conscience, and aspires to personal growth.

In the film version of *Out on a Limb*, MacLaine wonders if the public is going to take her beliefs seriously or think that she is making a fool of herself; by the time of *Postcards from the Edge*, she manages to make on film a joking reference to her transcendent experiences. Yet, *Out on a Limb* stands as an extraordinary attempt by an actor to fashion her image and MacLaine's ambitious effort deserves credit. And, arguably, the project is influenced by a feminist impulse—MacLaine appears to be indicating that she takes sole responsibility for her actions and identity.

There is recent evidence that suggests MacLaine's screen image is undergoing a modification. Although she is currently shooting a sequel to *Terms of Endearment*, two recent works, *Guarding Tess* and *West Side Waltz*, feature a MacLaine that is stately but without sacrificing her humor and prickly nature. The image she projects evokes the latter day Katharine Hepburn for whom, incidentally, *West Side Waltz* was a star vehicle on Broadway.

Like *Terms of Endearment*, the MacLaine films that have followed are "women's films." In these films, the actress invariably plays an imperfect person. MacLaine does not offer idealized images of women but, instead, she attempts to show that women are complex and very human beings. And, like her filmic creations, MacLaine herself, is a survivor.

—Richard Lippe

MacMURRAY, Fred

Nationality: American. **Born:** Frederick Martin MacMurray in Kankakee, Illinois, 30 August 1908. **Education:** Attended Shattuck Boys Academy; Beaver Dam High School, Wisconsin; Carroll College, Waukesha, Wisconsin. **Family:** Married 1) Lillian Lamont, 1936 (died 1953), daughter: Susan, son: Robert; 2) the actress June Haver, 1954, adopted daughters: Katie and Laurie. **Career:** 1928—singer and saxophone player in The Royal Purples band, Chicago; 1929—film debut as extra in *Girls Gone Wild*; also joined The California Collegians band, and made Broadway debut with the band in *Three's a Crowd*, 1930; 1934—contract with Paramount; 1935—first leading role in *Grand Old Girl*; 1945—contract with 20th Century-Fox; 1946—produced the film *Pardon My Past*; 1959—first of many Disney films, *The Shaggy Dog*; 1960-72—in popular TV series *My Three Sons*. **Died:** 5 November 1991.

Films as Actor:

1929 *Girls Gone Wild* (Seiler) (as extra); *Tiger Rose* (Fitzmaurice) (as rancher)
1935 *Grand Old Girl* (Robertson) (as Sandy); *The Gilded Lily* (Ruggles) (as Peter Dawes); *Car Ninety-Nine* (Barton) (as Ross Martin); *Men without Names* (Murphy) (as Richard Hood/Richard "Dick" Grant); *Alice Adams* (Stevens) (as Arthur Russell); *Hands across the Table* (Leisen) (as Theodore Drew III); *The Bride Comes Home* (Ruggles) (as Cyrus Anderson)

Fred MacMurray in *The Caine Mutiny*

1936 *The Trail of the Lonesome Pine* (Hathaway) (as Jack Hale); *Thirteen Hours by Air* (Leisen) (as Jack Gordon); *The Princess Comes Across* (Howard) (as King Mantell); *The Texas Rangers* (King Vidor) (as Jim Hawkins)

1937 *Maid of Salem* (Lloyd) (as Roger Coverman); *Champagne Waltz* (Sutherland) (as Buzzy Bellew); *Swing High, Swing Low* (Leisen) (as Skid Johnson); *Exclusive* (Hall) (as Ralph Houston); *True Confession* (Ruggles) (as Kenneth Bartlett)

1938 *Coconut Grove* (Santell) (as Johnny Prentice); *Sing You Sinners* (Ruggles) (as Joe Beebe); *Men with Wings* (Wellman) (as Pat Falconer)

1939 *Cafe Society* (Griffith) (as Chick O'Bannon); *Invitation to Happiness* (Ruggles) (as Albert "King" Cole); *Honeymoon in Bali* (Griffith) (as Bill Burnett)

1940 *Remember the Night* (Leisen) (as John Sargent); *Little Old New York* (Henry King) (as Charles Browne); *Too Many Husbands* (Ruggles) (as Bill Cardew); *Rangers of Fortune* (Wood) (as Gil Farra)

1941 *Virginia* (Griffith) (as Stonewall Elliott); *One Night in Lisbon* (Griffith) (as Dwight Houston); *New York Town* (Charles Vidor) (as Victor Ballard); *Dive Bomber* (Curtiz) (as Commander Joe Blake)

1942 *The Lady Is Willing* (Leisen) (as Dr. Corey McBain); *Take a Letter, Darling* (Leisen) (as Tom Verney); *The Forest Rangers* (Marshall) (as Don Stuart); *Star Spangled Rhythm* (Marshall)

1943 *Flight for Freedom* (Mendes) (as Randy Britton); *Above Suspicion* (Thorpe) (as Richard Myles)

1944 *Standing Room Only* (Lanfield) (as Lee Stevens); *And the Angels Sing* (Binyon) (as Happy Morgan); ***Double Indemnity*** (Wilder) (as Walter Neff); *Practically Yours* (Leisen) (as Lt. Daniel Bellamy)

1945 *Murder, He Says* (Marshall) (as Pete Marshall); *Where Do We Go from Here?* (Ratoff) (as Bill); *Captain Eddie* (Bacon) (as Edward Rickenbacker)

1946 *Pardon My Past* (Fenton) (as Eddie York/Francis Pemberton); *Smoky* (Louis King) (as Clint Barkley)

1947 *Suddenly It's Spring* (Leisen) (as Peter Morely); *The Egg and I* (Erskine) (as Bob MacDonald); *Singapore* (Brahm) (as Matt Gordon)

1948 *On Our Merry Way* (*A Miracle Can Happen*) (King Vidor and Fenton) (as Al); *The Miracle of the Bells* (Pichel) (as Bill Dunnigan); *Don't Trust Your Husband* (*An Innocent Affair*) (Bacon) (as Vincent Doane); *Family Honeymoon* (Binyon) (as Grant Jordan)

1949 *Father Was a Fullback* (Stahl) (as George Cooper)

1950 *Borderline* (Seiter) (as Johnny Macklin); *Never a Dull Moment* (Marshall) (as Chris); *A Millionaire for Christy* (Marshall) (as Peter Lockwood)

1951 *Callaway Went Thataway* (Panama and Frank) (as Mike Frye)

1953 *Fair Wind to Java* (Kane) (as Captain Boll); *The Moonlighter* (Rowland) (as Wes Anderson)

1954 *The Caine Mutiny* (Dmytryk) (as Lt. Tom Keefer); *Pushover* (Quine) (as Paul Sheridan); *Woman's World* (Negulesco) (as Sid)

1955 *The Far Horizons* (Mate) (as Meriwether Lewis); *The Rains of Ranchipur* (Negulesco) (as Tom Ransome); *At Gunpoint* (Werker) (as Wright)

1956 *There's Always Tomorrow* (Sirk) (as Clifford Groves)

1957 *Gun for a Coward* (Biberman) (as Will Keough); *Quantez* (Keller) (as Gentry/John Coventry)

1958 *Day of the Bad Man* (Keller) (as Jim Scott); *Good Day for a Hanging* (Juran) (as Ben Cutler)

1959 *The Shaggy Dog* (Barton) (as Wilson Daniels); *Face of a Fugitive* (Wendkos) (as Jim Larsen/Kincaid); *The Oregon Trail* (Fowler) (as Neal Harris)

1960 ***The Apartment*** (Wilder) (as J. D. Sheldrake)

1961 *The Absent-Minded Professor* (Stevenson) (as Prof. Ned Brainard)

1962 *Bon Voyage* (Neilson) (as Harry Willard)

1963 *Son of Flubber* (Stevenson) (as Prof. Ned Brainard)

1964 *Kisses for My President* (Bernhardt) (as Thad McCloud)

1966 *Follow Me, Boys!* (Tokar) (as Lemual Siddons)

1967 *The Happiest Millionaire* (Tokar) (as Anthony J. Drexel Biddle)

1973 *Charley and the Angel* (McEveety) (as Charley Appleby)

1974 *The Chadwick Family* (Rich—for TV) (as Ned Chadwick)

1975 *Beyond the Bermuda Triangle* (Graham—for TV) (as Harry Ballinger)

1978 *The Swarm* (Allen) (as Clarence)

Publications

By MacMURRAY: article—

"I've Been Lucky," as told to P. Martin, in *The Saturday Evening Post* (Philadelphia), 24 February 1962.

On MacMURRAY: book—

Parish, James, and Don Stanke, *The All-Americans*, New Rochelle, New York, 1977.

On MacMURRAY: articles—

Obituary, in the *Times* (London), 6 November 1991.
Pulleine, Tim, in the *Guardian* (London), 7 November 1991.

* * *

Fred MacMurray enjoyed one of the longest careers in American filmmaking because of his all-purpose (and enduring) good looks and versatility. On the strength of some song and dance experience on Broadway, he was signed to a long-term contract by Paramount at the beginning of the sound era. One of his first films at the studio, *The Gilded Lily*, marked the beginning of his working relationship with Mitchell Leisen who, during the 1930s and 1940s, was perhaps Hollywood's most expert director of light farce and comedy. MacMurray did his best comedic work for Leisen in three 1940s films: *The Lady Is Willing, No Time for Love*, and *Take a Letter, Darling*. For Leisen he developed the lovable schlemiel persona that served him so well (the character's apotheosis comes much later in Disney's *The Absent-Minded Professor*). At the same time MacMurray did competent work in a number of other genres—notably as a supporting actor in action films such as *The Trail of the Lonesome Pine* and *The Texans*.

In dramatic roles, however, he often projected a weakness which undercut the narrative. In *Above Suspicion*, for example, he quite unsuccessfully impersonates an Oxford don called to work for British Intelligence; in a series of contretemps with blustering Nazis he simply cannot respond with the appropriate American toughness. The weakness of his persona—always, of course, an exploitable resource in farce and comedy—was occasionally well used in dramatic films, notably by Billy Wilder. As Walter Neff in *Double Indemnity*, MacMurray quite plausibly falls victim to Barbara Stanwyck's aggressive sexuality. Here his indecisiveness becomes an appropriate response to film noir's inhospitable and uncertain world. In *The Apartment* MacMurray plays a calculating executive who cold-heartedly exploits a series of female employees. As played by MacMurray, however, the character becomes an easily toppled predator, henpecked by an overbearing wife and undone by a jealous secretary, and this reversal admirably suits the film's debunking of social hierarchies.

Giving his finest screen performance, MacMurray plays a similar character in *The Caine Mutiny*. His Lieutenant Keefer is a supercilious intellectual, a man who is able to complain about his captain's inadequacies but who nevertheless lacks moral conviction. MacMurray's spinelessness perfectly expresses the film's underlying McCarthyite politics.

—R. Barton Palmer

MADSEN, Harald, and Carl SCHENSTRØM

MADSEN. Nationality: Danish. **Born:** Silkeborg, Denmark, 20 November 1890. **Career:** Joined the Zircus Miehe at age 14, and remained with it for 11 years; he formed a trio of clowns called "Die drei Miehes" and toured Scandinavia and Germany with the group; 1917—film debut in *Alexander den store* (Alexander the Great). **Died:** 13 July 1949.

SCHENSTRØM. Nationality: Danish. **Born:** Copenhagen, 13 November 1881. **Career:** Emigrated with his family to Chicago in the 1890s, but the family returned to Denmark after his father was hit by a streetcar; trained as a bookbinder, but went on the stage in 1903, and joined Nordisk Film Company in 1909; 1918—appeared in the Asta Nielsen film *Mod Lyset*. **Died:** 1942.

In 1921—the two comics were brought together by the director Lau Lauritzen, and made over 40 films until 1940; after Schenstrøm's death in 1942, Madsen made one final film, *Hjältar mot sin vilja*.

Films as Actors:

1917   *Alexander den store* (*Alexander the Great*) (Madsen only)
1918   *Mod Lyset* (Holger-Madsen) (Schenstrøm only)
1919   *Vaeddeløberen* (Lauritzen) (Schenstrøm only);   *Et sommereventyr* (*De keder sig pålandet*) (Lauritzen) (Schenstrøm only)
1921   *Tyvepak*; *Film, flirt og forlovelse* (Lauritzen)
1922   *Sol, sommer og studiner* (Lauritzen); *Landligger-idyl vandgang* (Lauritzen); *Han, Hun og Hamlet* (Lauritzen); *Mellem muntre musikanter* (Lauritzen); *Blandt byens børn* (Lauritzen)
1923   *Kan kaerlighed kureres?* (Lauritzen); *Dårskab, dyd og driverter* (Lauritzen); *Vore venners vinter* (Lauritzen)
1924   *Professor Petersens plejebørn* (Lauritzen); *Lille Lise Letpåtå* (Lauritzen); *Raske Riviera rejsende* (Lauritzen); *Ole Opfinders offer* (Lauritzen)
1925   *Takt, tone og tosser* (Lauritzen); *Zwei vagabunden in Prater* (Lowenstein); *Polis Paulus' Påskasmäll* (*Spritsmuglerne*) (Molander); *Grønkøbings glade gavtyve* (Lauritzen)
1926   *Dødsbokseren* (Lauritzen); *Ulvejaegerne* (Lauritzen); *Ebberöds Bank* (*Ebberød Bank*) (Wallén); *Don Quixote* (Lauritzen); *Die Swiegersöhne* (*Svigersønnerne*) (Steinhoff); *Lykkehjulet* (Gad)
1927   *Kongen af Pelikanien* (Andersen); *Vestervovvov* (Lauritzen); *Cocktails* (*For fuld Fart*) (Banks); *Tordenstenene* (Lauritzen)
1928   *Kraft og Skønhed* (Lauritzen); *Filmens Helte* (Lauritzen)
1929   *Kys, Klap og Kommers* (Lauritzen); *Hallo, Afrika forude* (Lauritzen); *Højt på en Kvist* (Lauritzen); *Hr. Tell og Søn* (Lauritzen); *The Rocket Bus* (*Raketbussen*; *Alf's Carpet*) (Kellino)

1930   *Tausend Worte Deutsch* (*Taler De tysk?*) (Jacoby); *Pas på Pigerne* (Lauritzen); *Fy og Bi Prøvefilm* (Lauritzen)
1931   *Krudt med Knald* (Lauritzen); *Fy og Bi i Kantonnement* (Lauritzen)
1932   *Han, Hun og Hamlet* (Lauritzen); *Lumpenkavaliere* (*Glade Gøglere*) (Boese)
1933   *Med fuld musik* (Lauritzen) (Schenstrøm only)
1935   *Knox und die lustigen Vagabunden* (*Zirkus Saran*) (Emo)
1936   *Mädchenräuber* (*Kvinderøverne*) (Sauer); *Blinde Passagiere* (*Blinde Passagerer*) (Sauer)
1937   *Bleka Greven* (*Raske Detektiver*) (Rodin); *Eine Insel wird entdeckt* (*Pat und Patachon im Paradies*; *Fy og Bi i Paradis*) (Lamác)
1938   *Midt i byens hjerte*
1940   *I de gode gamle Dage* (Jacobsen)
1947   *Hjältar mot sin vilja* (Husberg) (Madsen only)

Publications

On MADSEN and SCHENSTRØM: books—

Lange-Fuchs, Hauge, *Pat und Patachon*, Berlin, 1979.
Engberg, Marguerite, *Fy & Bi*, Copenhagen, 1980.

On MADSEN and SCHENSTRØM: articles—

Retro, November-December 1981 and January-February 1982.
Sauvaget, D., "Les Z'héros du cinéma—Doublepatte et Patachon," in *Revue du Cinéma* (Paris), June 1986.

*   *   *

Harald Madsen and Carl Schenstrøm were established as a comic team in Danish films in 1921 and through 1940 they made 46 films, 13 of them outside Denmark, in Sweden, Germany, Austria, and England. In Denmark they were known as Fyrtaarnet & Bivognen (literally the Light Tower and the Trailer), abridged to Fy & Bi. They were not the first film comedy team, but they were the earliest to gain international recognition, and in the 1920s they were immensely popular all over Europe. In France they were called Doublepatte and Patachon, in England Long & Short, and in the United States, where only a few of their films were distributed and where they never succeeded in attracting an audience, they were called Ole & Axel. Internationally they were best known by their German names Pat and Patachon.

Schenstrøm was a tall, lean man with a melancholy face and a drooping moustache. Madsen was a short and fat little fellow with a sly or sheepish smile on his childlike moon face. There was a strikingly classic contrast in their visual appearance, which immediately appealed to the cinema-going public, and they were an instant success.

Schenstrøm was the clever and inventive fellow, a kind of father figure to the short and naive Madsen. This simple relationship, once established, never led to more stimulating characterizations of their types. They were likable simpletons and their innocent humor was enjoyed by an audience which found the American slapstick comedies of the period too fast and too violent.

Schenstrøm and Madsen were both born and raised in petit bourgeois families. Schenstrøm was trained as a bookbinder before he went to the stage in 1903 and he had a solid theatrical background before he entered films in 1914. Madsen started in circus as a boy and was a partner in a clown trio before his film career began. Madsen and Schenstrøm were brought together by the director Lau Lauritzen, who had worked for six years at Nordisk Films, making two-reel comedies, before he became the artistic manager and leading director at Palladium, founded in 1921. In 1919 Lauritzen made the short comedy *Vaeddeløberen*, in which he used Schenstrøm and a short actor. This couple made another two-reeler, but in 1921 Lauritzen saw Madsen in a circus, and Fyrtaarnet & Bivognen were born. Lauritzen directed 30 of the comedies made in Denmark, and he also wrote many of the films.

The stories were simplistic tales, often about a young man and a young girl in love, but separated because of social barriers. Fy & Bi, the eternal outsiders, were often marginal characters in the story, but they played an important part as the instruments of love's fulfilment. The films ridiculed the nouveau riches of the time, and were mildly satirical of the upper middle-class establishment. Lauritzen preferred shooting outdoors (the Danish landscape is nicely used as a background), and he also garnished the films with pretty young girls. But as a director Lauritzen was pedestrian and uninventive, the films being loosely structured and slow. The infrequent gags depended on the simple presentation of the two amiable figures. The films represented an idyllic alternative to the highly professional products of the major film-producing countries, and they mirrored the innocent provinciality of a small country. In the 1930s Fy & Bi's popularity faded in most countries, but they still had a large and loyal audience in Denmark, Sweden, Germany, and Austria.

—Ib Monty

MAGNANI, Anna

Nationality: Italian. **Born:** Rome, 7 March 1908. **Education:** Attended a French convent school in Rome; Academy of Dramatic Art, Rome. **Family:** Married the director Goffredo Alessandrini, 1935 (separated), son: Luca. **Career:** Joined a touring repertory company, and made stage debut in 1926; also sang in night clubs; 1934—film debut in *La cieca di Sorrento*; continued theater work; 1954—first American film, *The Rose Tattoo*; later stage successes were *La Lupa*, 1965, and *Medea*, 1966. **Awards:** Best Actress, Venice Festival, for

Anna Magnani

L'onorevole Angelina, 1947; Best Actress Academy Award and Best Actress, New York Film Critics, for *The Rose Tattoo*; 1955; Best Actress, Berlin Festival for *Wild Is the Wind*, 1958; also received Italian Nastri d'argento Awards for Best Actress, 1945-46, 1947-48, 1948-49, 1951-52, and 1956; Italian Grolle d'oro Award, 1958-59. **Died:** Of cancer in Rome, 26 September 1973.

Films as Actress:

1934	*La cieca di Sorrento* (Malasomma); *Tempo massimo* (Mattoli)
1936	*Cavalleria* (Alessandrini); *Trenta secondi d'amore* (*Trente secondes d'amour*) (Bonnard)
1938	*Tarakanowa* (Ozep)
1940	*Una lampada alla finestra* (Talamo)
1941	*Teresa Venerdi* (De Sica); *Finalmente soli* (Gentilomo); *La fuggitiva* (Ballerini)
1943	*La fortuna viene dal cielo* (Rathonyi); *L'avventura di Annabella* (Menardi); *La vita è bella* (Bragaglia); *Campo dei fiori* (Bonnard); *L'ultima carrozzella* (Mattoli); *Il fiore sotto gli occhi* (Brignone)
1944	*Quartetto pazzo* (Salvani)
1945	**Roma città aperta** (*Rome, Open City*; *Open City*) (Rossellini) (as Pina); *Abbasso la miseria* (Righelli)
1946	*Devanti a lui tremava tutta Roma* (*Before Him All Rome Trembled*; *Tosca*) (Gallone); *Abbasso la richezza* (Righetti); *Un uomo ritorna* (Neufeld); *Il bandito* (Lattuada)
1947	*La sconosciuto di San Marino* (Cottafavi); *L'onorevole Angelina* (*Angelina*) (Zampa); *Assunta spina* (Mattoli); *Molti sogni per le strade* (Camerini); *L'Amore* (*Woman*; *Ways of Love*) (Rossellini)
1949	*Vulcano* (Dieterle)
1951	*Bellissima* (Visconti)
1952	*Camicie rosse* (Alessandrini)
1953	**Le Carrosse d'or** (*The Golden Coach*) (Renoir) (as Camilla/Colombine); "We, the Women" ep. of *Siamo donne* (Visconti)
1955	*The Rose Tattoo* (Daniel Mann)
1956	*Suor letizia* (Camerini)
1957	*Wild Is the Wind* (Cukor)
1958	*Nella città l'inferno* (*And the Wild, Wild Women*) (Castellani)
1960	*The Fugitive Kind* (Lumet); *Risate di Gioia* (*The Passionate Thief*) (Monicelli)
1962	*Mamma Roma* (Pasolini)
1963	*Le Magot de Joséfa* (Autant-Lara)
1965	*Made in Italy* (Loy)
1969	*The Secret of Santa Vittoria* (Kramer); *Nell' anno del signore* (Magni)
1972	*Roma* (*Fellini Roma*) (Fellini)

Publications

On MAGNANI: books—

Wallis, Hal, and Charles Higham, *Starmaker*, New York, 1980.
Governi, Giancarlo, *Nannarella: La vita di Anna Magnani*, Milan, 1981.
Hochkofler, Matilde, *Anna Magnani*, Rome, 1984.
Carrano, Patrizia, *La Magnani*, Milan, 1986.
Pistagnesi, Patrizia, editor, *Anna Magnani*, Milan, 1989.
Di Giammatteo, Fernaldo, *Roberto Rossellini*, Florence, 1990.

On MAGNANI: articles—

Kobler, J., "Tempest on the Tiber," in *Life* (New York), 13 February 1950.

Whitehall, Richard, "Gallery of Great Artists: Anna Magnani," in *Films and Filming* (London), July 1961.

Bianciotti, H., "Hommage: La Magnani, l'intensité de la passion," in *Cinéma* (Paris), December 1973.

Mitchell, T., "The Construction and Reception of Anna Magnani in Italy and the English-Speaking World," in *Film Criticism* (Meadville, Pennsylvania), Fall 1989.

*   *   *

Anna Magnani's persona was, above all, that of "great actress"; yet, in relation to her career, that description has to be understood in a very particular way. Conventionally, "actor" and "star" have been defined in an opposing manner: the latter is defined in terms of "presence," of an authentic and immediately recognizable personality, often glamorous and permitting identification on the level of fantasy-fulfillment; the former is defined in terms of the ability to transform the self, to "be" different characters. Magnani was always, irreducibly, Magnani, yet she lacked the most obvious attributes of the female star: though she had a remarkably expressive face, she was by no means conventionally beautiful; neither did she have a body that could be conventionally fetishized; her roles were never of the kind to encourage fantasy-identification. For American audiences, she represented exactly what Hollywood had consistently failed to produce: "reality," the nonglamorous human being. Hence, she could never be successfully promoted in Hollywood beyond a certain point (soon reached); for audiences conditioned by Hollywood expectations, "reality" is exotic, a striking novelty that swiftly palls.

Magnani's persona as a great actress is built, not on transformation, but on emotional authenticity (or, more precisely, on the *signification* of authenticity): she doesn't portray characters but expresses "genuine" emotions, the guarantee of genuineness being the rejection of glamour. There is clearly a problem here, exemplified but never resolved throughout Magnani's career. As an "unknown" in *Rome, Open City*, she was a "real" person, expressing real emotions; yet, overnight, she became a famous actress celebrated for her *acting* of "real" emotions. One might say that she spent the rest of her career acting authenticity. The problem is readily apparent in the films made with Rossellini. In *Rome, Open City* she is one of a team of largely nonprofessional players; her performance is extraordinary, but it is fully integrated in the ensemble. In *The Miracle* she is also extraordinary but in a far more dubious way: the film is so obviously a vehicle for her, and her acting of authenticity is so strenuous that we are impressed not so much by the sense of genuine emotions but by the sheer effort of their expression.

Perhaps her greatest performance is in Renoir's *The Golden Coach*, and there are very particular reasons for this (apart from, though not unconnected with, Renoir's fascination with and sympathy for actors): the entire film plays upon notions of theater and reality, the interaction between them, the relation between roles on stage and roles in real life. Opening and closing with the rise and fall of a theater curtain, it announces itself as "theater" and gives us the *commedia dell'arte* performances of Magnani's troupe as theater-within-the-ater. Every character, except Magnani the actress, is trapped in a social role or stereotype, and each man wants to impose an identity on Magnani who, in the film's final paradox, retreats back into the theater as the only place where, by consciously acting roles, she can be herself. It is a film that calls into question the very concept of authenticity and asks whether we do not, everywhere and always, act. While the film is centered unequivocally on Magnani, her performance is fully integrated in it, and we never have the sense that the material has been conceived merely as a showcase for her talents.

It is sad but predictable that Hollywood could find nothing more appropriate for her than the spurious pretensions of Tennessee Williams at his worst (*The Rose Tattoo*, *The Fugitive Kind*); and finally wasted her in a thoroughly conventional role in *The Secret of Santa Vittoria*. (What an amazing Cleopatra she might have made to Charlton Heston's Antony.) Her most distinguished work in Hollywood was acheived (again, predictably) under the sympathetic guidance of George Cukor, the American cinema's greatest director of actresses, whose distinction lies more in his ability to draw out the individual essence of a player than in encouraging the externalities of "great acting." *Wild Is the Wind*, a project Cukor took over at a very late stage of its development, awkwardly scripted, repeatedly sounding like a stage play, transcends such limitations through Magnani's sensitive and inward performance.

—Robin Wood

MALDEN, Karl

Nationality: American. **Born:** Mladen Sekulovich in Chicago, Illinois, 22 March 1914. **Education:** Attended Emerson High School, Gary, Indiana; the Art Institute of Chicago, 1933-36; Goodman Theatre Dramatic School, Chicago. **Military Service:** U.S. Army Air Force, 1943-45. **Family:** Married the actress Mona Graham, 1938, daughters: Mila and Carla. **Career:** 1937—Broadway debut in *Golden Boy*; 1940—film debut in *They Knew What They Wanted*; 1945—resumed Broadway career following military service; 1947—in Broadway production of *A Streetcar Named Desire*, and in film version, 1951; 1957—directed the film *Time Limit*; 1966-69—director, Screen Actors Guild; 1972-77—starring role in TV series *The Streets of San Francisco*; 1980—in TV series *Skag*; 1989-93—president of the Academy of Motion Picture Arts and Sciences. **Awards:** Best Supporting Actor Academy Award, for *A Streetcar Named Desire*, 1951. **Address:** 1845 Mandeville Canyon Road, Los Angeles, CA 90049, U.S.A.

Films as Actor:

1940	*They Knew What They Wanted* (Kanin) (as Red)
1944	*Winged Victory* (Cukor) (as Adams)
1946	*13 Rue Madeleine* (Hathaway) (as flight sergeant)
1947	*Boomerang* (Kazan) (as Lt. White); *Kiss of Death* (Hathaway) (as Sgt. William Cullen)
1950	*Where the Sidewalk Ends* (Preminger) (as Lt. Thomas); *The Gunfighter* (Henry King) (as Mac); *Halls of Montezuma* (Milestone) (as Doc)
1951	*The Sellout* (Mayer) (as Buck Maxwell); ***A Streetcar Named Desire*** (Kazan) (as Mitch); *Decision before Dawn* (Litvak)
1952	*Diplomatic Courier* (Hathaway) (as Ernie); *Ruby Gentry* (King Vidor) (as Jim Gentry); *Operation Secret* (Seiler) (as Maj. Latrec)
1953	*Take the High Ground* (Richard Brooks) (as Sgt. Laverne Holt); *I Confess* (Hitchcock) (as Larrue)
1954	*Phantom of the Rue Morgue* (Del Ruth) (as Dr. Marais); ***On the Waterfront*** (Kazan) (as Father Barry)
1956	*Baby Doll* (Kazan) (as Archie Lee)
1957	*Fear Strikes Out* (Mulligan) (as John Piersall); *Bombers B-52* (*No Sleep till Dawn*) (Gordon Douglas) (as Sgt. Chuck Brennan)
1959	*The Hanging Tree* (Daves) (as Frenchy Plante)
1960	*Pollyanna* (Swift) (as Rev. Paul Ford); *The Great Imposter* (Mulligan) (as Father Devlin)
1961	*One-Eyed Jacks* (Brando) (as Dad Longworth); *Parrish* (Daves) (as Judd Raike)

Karl Malden (right) with Marlon Brando in *On the Waterfront*

1962   *All Fall Down* (Frankenheimer) (as Ralph Willart); *Birdman of Alcatraz* (Frankenheimer) (as Harvey Shoemaker); *Gypsy* (LeRoy) (as Herbie Sommers)

1963   "The Rivers" ep. of *How the West Was Won* (Hathaway) (as Zebulon Prescott); *Come Fly with Me* (Levin) (as Walter Lucas)

1964   *Dead Ringer* (*Dead Image*) (Henreid) (as Sgt. Jim Hobbson); *Cheyenne Autumn* (Ford) (as Capt. Wessels)

1965   *The Cincinnati Kid* (Jewison) (as Shooter)

1966   *Nevada Smith* (Hathaway) (as Tom Fitch); *Murderers' Row* (Levin) (as Julian Wall)

1967   *The Adventures of Bullwhip Griffin* (Neilson) (as Judge Higgins); *Hotel* (Quine) (as Keycase); *Billion Dollar Brain* (Ken Russell) (as Leo Newbegin)

1968   *Blue* (Narizzano) (as Doc Morton); *Hot Millions* (Till) (as Carlton J. Klemper)

1969   *Il gatto a nove code* (*Cat o' Nine Tails*) (Argento) (as Franco Arno)

1970   *Patton* (*Patton: Lust for Glory*) (Schaffner) (as Gen. Omar Bradley)

1971   *Wild Rovers* (Edwards) (as Walter Buckman)

1972   *The Streets of San Francisco* (Grauman—for TV) (as Det. Lt. Mike Stone)

1973   *Summertime Killer* (Isasi) (as John Kiley)

1977   *Captains Courageous* (Hart—for TV)

1979   *Meteor* (Neame) (as Harry Sherwood); *Beyond the Poseidon Adventure* (Irwin Allen) (as Wilbur Hubbard)

1980   *The Wildcatters* (for TV); *Skag* (Perry—for TV)

1981   *Miracle on Ice* (Steven Hilliard Stern—for TV); *Word of Honor* (Damski—for TV)

1983   *The Sting II* (Kagan) (as Macalinski); *Twilight Time* (Paskaljevic) (as Marko)

1984   *Fatal Vision* (David Greene—for TV) (as Freddy Kassab); *With Intent to Kill* (Robe—for TV) (as Thomas E. Nolan)

1985   *Alice in Wonderland* (Harry Harris—for TV) (as Walrus)

1986   *Billy Galvin* (John Gray) (as Jack Galvin)

1987   *Nuts* (Ritt) (as Arthur Kirk)

1988   *My Father, My Son* (Bleckner—for TV) (as Adm. Elmo Zumwalt Jr.)

1989   *The Hijacking of the Achille Lauro* (Collins—for TV) (as Klinghoffer)

1990   *Call Me Anna* (Cates—for TV) (as Dr. Harold Arlen)

1991   *Absolute Strangers* (Cates—for TV) (as Fred Zusselman)

1992   *Back to the Streets of San Francisco* (Damski—for TV) (as Mike Stone)

1993   *Earth and the American Dream* (Couturie—doc) (as voice); *They've Taken Our Children: The Chowchilla Kidnapping* (Gillum—for TV) (as Ed Ray)

Film as Director:

1957 *Time Limit*

Publications

By MALDEN: article—

"What the Hell, I'm a Frank Guy," interview in *Cinema* (Beverly Hills), February/March 1964.

On MALDEN: articles—

Current Biography 1957, New York, 1957.
Marill, Alvin H., in *Films in Review* (New York), April 1977.

* * *

Karl Malden was already an established young Broadway character actor when he came to Hollywood to do several minor roles in such films as *13 Rue Madeleine* and *Kiss of Death*. Elia Kazan did not (as is often reported) introduce Malden to films, but he did give the actor's career a new direction by making available to him roles in which Malden's dramatic intensity and Method-influenced acting style could be displayed. Malden had returned to Broadway to play Mitch in *A Streetcar Named Desire* for Kazan, and afterward followed the director to Hollywood to appear in his *Boomerang*. A few years later he repeated his role in Kazan's screen version of *Streetcar*, and won an Oscar as Best Supporting Actor.

His performance in that film revealed an underlying and uneasily repressed well of emotion that was effectively exploited by Kazan. In *On the Waterfront*, Malden plays the parish priest as a man who cannot refrain from either righteous anger or direct involvement in waterfront politics. His intensity suits Kazan's social message and contrasts nicely with Brando's subtle characterization of the ex-prizefighter who turns crusader. More often, however, Malden's energy was channeled into portrayals of an evil bordering on obsession or neurosis. As a crooked sheriff who cannot control his temper, he is once again effectively contrasted with the coolness and self-possession of Brando's outlaw in *One-Eyed Jacks*. Or if not outright evil, his characters were misguided and obsessive. This especially was so when he played weak-willed parents. As the neurotic father who is determined that his son achieve his own frustrated dream of athletic stardom in *Fear Strikes Out*, Malden is effectively contrasted to the twitchy insecurity of Anthony Perkins's Jimmy Piersall. As the superficially friendly, semi-alcoholic father of Warren Beatty and Brandon de Wilde in *All Fall Down*, he is just as equally contrasted to Angela Lansbury's exasperating, clinging mother.

Malden has repeated these characterizations with only minor variations in a number of films, most notably *Birdman of Alcatraz*, *Cheyenne Autumn*, and *Nevada Smith*, where he played off the cooler styles of Burt Lancaster, Richard Widmark, and Steve McQueen respectively. The self-effacing subordination of Mitch in *Streetcar* also has been employed successfully in other roles. As Omar Bradley in *Patton*, for example, he is almost insistently ordinary in a way that contrasts to George C. Scott's obsessive and self-concerned hero.

But Malden's best work on screen came in the 1950s, under the guidance of Elia Kazan, a director who has been able to channel and emphasize the subtler qualities of his acting style. His most memorable role is that of Archie Lee in *Baby Doll*, where his acting meshes beautifully with the ensemble work of Carroll Baker and Eli Wallach. Malden lends the character a sense of repressed sexuality which perfectly suits the erotic subtext of Williams's story.

In later years, Malden has starred on television in a popular weekly crime drama, *The Streets of San Francisco* (not to mention a series of credit card commercials). He has appeared in higher-quality made-for-television movies, often playing fathers who have complex relationships with their sons (such as *My Father, My Son* and *Billy Galvin*) or leaders of younger men (e.g., Coach Herb Brooks in *Miracle on Ice*).

—R. Barton Palmer, updated by Rob Edelman

MALKOVICH, John

Nationality: American. **Born:** Christopher, Illinois, 9 December 1953. **Education:** Attended Eastern Illinois State University; Illinois State University. **Family:** Married the actress Glenne Headly, 1982 (divorced 1990); one daughter, Armandine, and one son, Loewy, with Nicoletta Peyran. **Career:** 1976—co-founder of Chicago's Steppenwolf Theatre Group; 1982—New York theatrical debut in *True West*; 1984—theatrical film debut in *Places in the Heart*; 1994—director and producer of *Libra*, Steppenwolf Theatre, Chicago. **Awards:** Best Actor, Obie Award, for *True West*, 1983; Best Supporting Actor, National Society of Film Critics and National Board of Review, for *Places in the Heart*, 1984; Emmy for Outstanding Supporting Actor, for *Death of a Salesman*, 1986. **Agent:** Tracy Jacobs, International Creative Management, 8942 Wilshire Boulevard, Beverly Hills, CA 90211, U.S.A. **Address:** 346 South Lucerne Boulevard, Los Angeles, CA 90020, U.S.A.

Films as Actor:

1981 *American Dream* (Damski—for TV) (as Gary); *Word of Honor* (Damski—for TV)
1982 *True West* (Sinise and Goldstein—for TV) (as Lee)
1984 *Places in the Heart* (Benton) (as Mr. Will); *The Killing Fields* (Joffé) (as Al Rockoff)
1985 *Eleni* (Yates) (as Nicholas Gage)
1986 *Death of a Salesman* (Schlöndorff—for TV) (as Biff); *Rocket to the Moon* (John Jacobs—for TV) (as Ben Stark)
1987 *Making Mr. Right* (Susan Seidelman) (as Dr. Jeff Peters/Ulysses); *The Glass Menagerie* (Paul Newman) (as Tom); *Empire of the Sun* (Spielberg) (as Basie)
1988 *Miles from Home* (*Farm of the Year*) (Sinise) (as Barry Maxwell); *Dangerous Liaisons* (Frears) (as Vicomte de Valmont)
1990 *Old Times* (Simon Curtis—for TV); *The Sheltering Sky* (Bertolucci) (as Port Moresby)
1991 *Queens Logic* (Rash) (as Eliot); *The Object of Beauty* (Lindsay-Hogg) (as Jake)
1992 *Shadows and Fog* (Woody Allen) (as a clown); *Jennifer 8* (Robinson) (as St. Anne); *Of Mice and Men* (Sinise) (as Lennie)
1993 *In the Line of Fire* (Petersen) (as Mitch Leary); *Alive* (Frank Marshall) (as narrator, uncredited); *We're Back! A Dinosaur's Story* (Zondag and others—animation) (as voice)
1994 *Heart of Darkness* (Roeg—for TV) (as Kurtz)
1995 *Par dela les nuages* (*Al di la delle nuvole*; *Beyond the Clouds*) (Antonioni and Wenders) (as director); *O Convento* (*The Convent*; *Le Couvent*) (de Oliveira) (as Michael)
1996 *Mary Reilly* (Frears) (as Dr. Jekyll/Mr. Hyde); *Mulholland Falls* (Tamahori) (as Gen. Thomas Timms); *Der Unhold* (*The Ogre*; *Le Rois des aulnes*) (Schlöndorff); *Portrait of a Lady* (Campion)

Other Film:

1988   *The Accidental Tourist* (Kasdan) (co-exec pr)

Publications

By MALKOVICH: articles—

"The Malkovich Magnetism," interview with Dena Kleiman, in *New York Times Magazine*, 15 September 1985.
"Between the Lines," interview with Hal Hinson, in *Vogue* (New York), October 1985.
"Acting's Burning Talent," interview in *Harper's Bazaar* (New York), November 1987.
"Honest John," interview with Clifford Terry, in *Plays and Players* (Croydon, Surrey), April 1992.
"Malkovich and Moor," interview with Hamish Bowles, in *Vogue* (New York), September 1993.
"Character/Actor," interview in *Psychology Today* (New York), July/ August 1994.

On MALKOVICH: article—

Gritten, David, "What Is John Malkovich?," in *Cosmopolitan* (New York), November 1992.

*   *   *

Before he first appeared on movie screens in Robert Benton's *Places in the Heart*, John Malkovich had already earned a formidable reputation as a stage actor, a director and as a co-founder of the Steppenwolf Theatre Ensemble in Chicago. In many ways Malkovich is still more identified with the theater than with Hollywood, not only for his considerable successes on the stage, but also for his often disparaging remarks about the film business. (He told *Psychology Today* he never acts in films for artistic expression, that he does it only "for the money.") Yet with just a few exceptions, his film work seems passionate, daring, and finely crafted. He works in Hollywood films with nary a trace of movie star vanity, disclosing dark and truly unpleasant aspects of his characters in a way that is almost unknown with other "leading men." At the same time Malkovich is able to transcend his rebarbative demeanor and make his flawed, angry characters the emotional center of many of the films he appears in. Despite maintaining this precarious balance in his acting for almost a decade, Malkovich's self-deprecatingly theatrical tendencies have recently shifted him to the place where he has nearly lost his star status to the rank of "character actor" and "heavy"; his recent dual role as Dr. Jekyll and Mr. Hyde in *Mary Reilly* only exemplifies the conundrum in his acting persona.

John Malkovich's first two theatrical film appearances—in *Places in the Heart* and *The Killing Fields*—arrived almost back-to-back in the fall of 1984 and he was singled out for praise with both. Malkovich won multiple awards and nominations for *Places in the Heart*, yet even in Benton's innocent, rural film—as a gentle, blinded World War I veteran critics noticed something both excit-

John Malkovich in *Eleni*

ing and troubling in the actor's work. (Pauline Kael in the *New Yorker* referred to his "great acting" and almost immediately followed the accolade with the comment "he's so touching he's creepy.") The next year Malkovich had a large film role in Peter Yates's *Eleni*, but was generally considered miscast in a poorly realized production. In that same year, however, he won recognition doing a radically new interpretation of Arthur Miller's Biff opposite Dustin Hoffman in *Death of a Salesman* on Broadway. Malkovich's haunted, soft-spoken performance would be recreated for a television version in 1986 and his reputation as a major American actor was secured.

Not surprisingly, Malkovich would distinguish himself most in the coming years in cinematic adaptations of theatrical productions: first, in 1987, as Tennessee Williams's autobiographical Tom in Paul Newman's version of *The Glass Menagerie* and in 1988 in Stephen Frears's adaptation of Christopher Hampton's play *Les Liaisons Dangereuses*. In the former Malkovich suggests—not for the first time or the last—a subtle but nearly hypnotic homosexual component to the role. In the latter, as Valmont, the actor triumphs over his seeming miscasting as a sexual games-player who finally falls in love with one of the women he has toyed with. Holding his own against Glenn Close, Michelle Pfeiffer, and Uma Thurman, Malkovich made *Dangerous Liaisons* his greatest (and almost only real) "star turn" in the cinema.

Subsequently Malkovich has had slightly less good fortune in film. His Port Moresby in Bernardo Bertolucci's problematic *The Sheltering Sky* was arrestingly smug, self-destructive, and mesmerizing; the film never recovered from the character's death two-thirds of the way through. In *The Object of Beauty* Malkovich astonished again, this time with his ability to play a (merely) likable would-be sophisticate. The film was much more suitable to his talents than the earlier comedy, *Making Mr. Right*, and it raised hopes that the actor might become a postmodern Cary Grant, but few people saw the picture. Malkovich's role in Woody Allen's *Shadows and Fog* in 1992 was nearly a cameo and after all the intelligence and self-loathing he had been showing on-screen up to that point, his Lennie in *Of Mice and Men*, directed by his *Steppenwolf* colleague Gary Sinise, rang a bit false.

To date, Malkovich's one great film performance in the 1990s was in Wolfgang Petersen's *In the Line of Fire*. Playing opposite an iconic Clint Eastwood, Malkovich took the clichéd part of a brilliant assassin and created something so frightening and horrifyingly human, that he single-handedly raised the film out of its genre conventions. From there, though, Malkovich was very nearly over the top as Kurtz in Nicolas Roeg's *Heart of Darkness*. Oddly, he seemed strangely uninvolved playing Dr. Jekyll and Mr. Hyde, working with Frears and Hampton again, in *Mary Reilly*.

—Daniel Humphrey

MALONE, Dorothy

Nationality: American. **Born:** Dorothy Eloise Maloney in Chicago, Illinois, 30 January 1925. **Education:** Student at Ursuline Convent; Highland Park High School, Hockaday Junior College, and Southern Methodist University, all in Dallas; studied dancing and diction in Hollywood. **Family:** Married 1) the actor Jacques Bergerac, 1959 (divorced 1964), two daughters; 2) Robert Tomarkin, 1969 (marriage annulled 1969); 3) Charles H. Bell, 1971. **Career:** 1943—contract with RKO, and film debut in *The Falcon and the Co-Eds*; 1964-68—played Constance in TV series *Peyton Place*; 1976—in TV mini-series *Rich Man, Poor Man*. **Awards:** Best Supporting Actress, Academy

Award for *Written on the Wind*, 1956. **Agent:** Ann Waugh Talent Agency, 4731 Laurel Canyon Boulevard, Suite 5, North Hollywood, CA 91607, U.S.A.

Films as Actress:

1943   *The Falcon and the Co-Eds* (Clemens)
1944   *One Mysterious Night* (Boetticher); *Show Business* (Marin)
1945   *Too Young to Know* (de Cordova);*Hollywood Canteen* (Daves)
1946   *Janie Gets Married* (Sherman); **The Big Sleep** (Hawks) (as bookshop clerk); *Night and Day* (Curtiz)
1948   *To the Victor* (Daves); *Two Guys from Texas* (Butler); *One Sunday Afternoon* (Walsh)
1949   *South of St. Louis* (Enright); *Colorado Territory* (Walsh)
1950   *The Nevadan* (Douglas); *Convicted* (Levin); *The Killer That Stalked New York* (McEvory); *Law and Order* (Juran)
1953   *Scared Stiff* (Marshall); *Jack Slade* (Schuster)
1954   *Loophole* (Schuster); *Pushover* (Quine); *Young at Heart* (Douglas); *Private Hell 36* (Siegel)
1955   *Five Guns West* (Corman);*Battle Cry* (Walsh);*Artists and Models* (Tashlin); *At Gunpoint* (Werker)
1956   *Pillars of the Sky* (Marshall); *Tension at Table Rock* (Warren); **Written on the Wind** (Sirk) (as Marylee Hadley)
1957   *Quantez* (Keller); *Man of a Thousand Faces* (Pevney); *Tip on a Dead Jockey* (Thorpe)
1958   *The Tarnished Angels* (Sirk); *Too Much, Too Soon* (Napoleon) (as Diana Barrymore)
1959   *Warlock* (Dmytryk)
1960   *The Last Voyage* (Stone)
1961   *The Last Sunset* (Aldrich) (as Belle Breckenridge)
1963   *Beach Party* (Asher) (as Marianne)
1964   *Fate Is the Hunter* (Nelson) (as Lisa Bond)
1969   *Gli insaziabili* (de Martino); *The Pigeon* (Bellamy—for TV)
1975   *The Man Who Would Not Die* (*Target in the Sun*) (Chessbro and Taylor—for TV); *Abduction* (Zito)
1976   *The November Plan* (Medford)
1977   *Little Ladies of the Night* (Chomsky—for TV); *Murder in Peyton Place* (Kessler—for TV); *Golden Rendezvous* (Lazarus)
1978   *Katie: Portrait of a Centerfold* (Greenwald—for TV)
1979   *Winter Kills* (Richert) (as Emma Kegan); *Good Luck, Miss Wyckoff* (Chomsky) (as Mildred)
1980   *The Day Time Ended* (Cardos) (as Ana); *Condominium* (Hyers)
1982   *The Being* (Kong) (as Marge Smith)
1984   *He's Not Your Son* (Taylor—for TV) (as Dr. Sullivan)
1985   *Peyton Place—The Next Generation* (Elikann—for TV) (as Constance MacKenzie Carson)
1986   *Descanse en piezas* (*Rest in Pieces*) (Braunstein)
1992   *Basic Instinct* (Verhoeven) (as Hazel Dobkins)

Publications

On MALONE: article—

"Dorothy Malone," in *Stars*, September 1992.

*   *   *

In the Hollywood of the 1950s and 1960s, with its system of casting by type, Dorothy Malone came to be identified by her luxurious coif of platinum blonde hair and her provocative, sidling walk. Her appearance defined her screen persona of the ignominious woman, which determined the direction of her career.

She began in pictures in minor roles, but soon was getting larger parts in everything from Westerns to musicals to films noir. In one memorable early role, Malone plays the reserved yet sensuous bookshop clerk in *The Big Sleep* who lets her hair down for private eye Marlowe (Humphrey Bogart). During these years she generally got parts that capitalized on her looks, but did not give her much opportunity for real acting.

If there was a peak in her career it was in the mid-1950s, when, under contract to Universal, she made two films with director Douglas Sirk, whose work set a standard for the genre of American melodrama. Appearing opposite Robert Stack and matinee idol Rock Hudson in *Written on the Wind* and *The Tarnished Angels*, she was afforded the chance to explore the full range of her sultry persona. It explodes with full force in the character of Marylee, the rich girl who cannot get enough stimulation in *Written on the Wind*. She despises her alcoholic brother (Stack) and lustfully pursues their childhood companion (Hudson), who is in love with Stack's wife (Lauren Bacall). Malone's exaggerated appearance provides an effective dramatic contrast to Bacall's reserved, demure beauty.

As a devoted wife and mother in *Tarnished Angels*, her appearance changes only by degrees, as she is ignored by her husband (Stack), a carnival stunt flier, and must continually fend off the naive advances of the newspaper man played by Hudson. One interesting exception to the pattern of Malone's 1950s roles is her portrayal of Diana Barrymore in *Too Much, Too Soon*, a seldomly seen film made in the wake of the success of *Written on the Wind*.

Despite winning the best supporting actress Oscar for her work in *Written on the Wind*, Malone found relatively few good parts coming her way—perhaps it was that her physical beauty lent itself most readily to more decorative roles in the studio executives' eyes. Eventually she shifted to television, where she found success in the mid-1960s in the long-running melodrama *Peyton Place*. In recent years she has acted in films only occasionally.

—Rob Winning, updated by Frank Uhle

MANGANO, Silvana

Nationality: Italian. **Born:** Rome, 21 April 1930. **Education:** Studied as a dancer. **Family:** Married the producer Dino De Laurentiis, 1949, daughters: Veronica Raffaella and Francesca, son: Federico. **Career:** Worked as a model; 1946—won Miss Rome beauty contest; 1947—film debut in *L'elisir d'amore*; 1949—international attention with film *Bitter Rice*; a number of leading roles followed; 1960s-70s—roles in series of films by both Pasolini and Visconti. **Awards:** Italian Nastro d'argento Awards for Best Actress, 1954-55 and 1963, and for Best Supporting Actress, 1971-72; Italian Grolle d'oro Awards for Best Actress, 1962-63 and 1966-67. **Died:** In Madrid, 16 December 1989.

Films as Actress:

1947   *L'elisir d'amore* (Costa); *Il delitto di Giovanni Episcopo* (*Flesh Will Surrender*) (Lattuada)
1948   *Gli uomini sono nemici* (*Carrefour de passion*) (Giannini); *Riso amaro* (*Bitter Rice*) (De Santis)
1949   *Cagliostro* (*Black Magic*) (Ratoff)
1950   *Il lupo della Sila* (*The Lure of the Sila*) (Coletti); *Brigante Musolino* (*Fugitive in 6B*) (Camerini)
1952   *Anna* (Lattuada)

1954   *Mambo* (Rossen); *Ulisse* (*Ulysses*) (Camerini) (as Penelope and Circe)
1955   "Teresa" ep. of *L'oro di Napoli* (*The Gold of Naples*; *Every Day's a Holiday*) (De Sica)
1957   *Uomini e lupi* (De Santis)
1958   *La Diga sul Pacifico* (*The Sea Wall*; *Angry Age*) (Clément)
1959   *La tempesta* (*Tempest*) (Lattuada) (as Nasha); *La grande guerra* (*The Great War*) (Monicelli) (as Constantina)
1960   *Jovanda e le altre* (*Five Branded Women*) (Ritt); *Crimen* (. . . *And Suddenly It's Murder!*; *Killing in Monte Carlo*) (Camerini) (as Marina Strucchi)
1961   *Il guidizio universale* (*The Last Judgment*) (De Sica); *Barabba* (*Barabbas*) (Fleischer) (as Rachel); *Una vita difficile* (Risi)
1963   *Il processo a Verona* (*The Verona Trial*) (Lizzani)
1964   *La mia signora* (two eps.) (Bolognini and Comencini)
1965   *Il Disco Volante* (*The Flying Saucer*) (Brass)
1966   *Io, io, io . . . e gli altri* (*I, I, I . . . and the Others*) (Blasetti)
1967   *Scusi, lei e favorevole o contrario* (*Excuse Me . . .*) (Sordi); *Edipo Re* (*Oedipus Rex*) (Pasolini) (as Jocasta); *La streghe* (*The Witches*) (Visconti, Bolognini, Pasolini, Rossi, and De Sica) (different roles in each ep.)
1968   "La Bambinala" ep. of *Capriccio all'italiana* (Monicelli); *Viaggio de lavoro* (Zac); *Teorema* (*Theorum*) (Pasolini) (as the mother)
1969   *Medea* (Pasolini)
1971   **Morte a Venezia** (*Death in Venice*) (Visconti) (as Tadzio's mother); *Scipione detto anche l'Africano* (Magni); *Il Decamerone* (*The Decameron*) (Pasolini); *Ludwig* (Visconti)
1972   *Lo scopone scientifico* (Comencini); *D'amore si muore* (Carunchio)
1975   *Gruppo di famiglia in un interno* (*Conversation Piece*) (Visconti)
1984   *Dune* (Lynch)
1987   *Oci ciorinia* (*Dark Eyes*) (Mikhalkov) (as Elisa)

Publications

On MANGANO: articles—

Apon, A., "Silvana Mangano," in *Skrien* (Amsterdam), January 1972.
Ciné Revue (Paris), 7 February 1985.
Obituary, in *Cinéma* (Paris), January 1990.
Obituary, in *Positif* (Paris), March 1990.

*   *   *

Silvana Mangano was trained as a dancer and worked as a model before winning the Miss Rome beauty contest in 1946 which brought her into the movies. In her first starring role, as a migrant farm worker in *Bitter Rice*, caught between social awareness and jealousy born of a passionate love affair, she was instantly thrust into the international limelight. American critics called her the Italian Rita Hayworth, with an extra 20 pounds; she was the first of the postwar stars to represent the full-figured, fiery Italian beauty.

Her fame brought her offers from Hollywood and Alexander Korda but she turned them down in favor of marriage to Dino De Laurentiis who produced most of her films. Unlike several of her counterparts, Mangano quickly moved beyond the stereotype of an earthy sex symbol, and developed her skills as a dramatic actress. Her role in *The Gold of Naples* as the prostitute trapped in a marriage of honor to a rich uncaring man was critically acclaimed. Another role as a prostitute, in *The Great War*, revealed an ability at satirical comedy, while *Crimean* displayed her as a sophisticate.

Silvana Mangano in *Edipo Re*

She accepted few film offers and chose her roles carefully, usually preferring to collaborate with directors whose work she admired. Pasolini used her as Jocasta in *Oedipus Rex*, in *The Decameron*, and as an upper-middle-class mother whose life is profoundly changed by the visit of a young man to her home in *Theorem*. Pasolini said that she was practically contemptuous of her great beauty and that she worked hard at constantly improving her dramatic capabilities. She often worked with Luchino Visconti, and in fact played in four of his last six films. She reportedly accepted the role of Tadzio's mother in *Death in Venice* for no salary; her portrayal of the impeccably groomed aristocratic woman relied entirely on mime for its effect. At the opposite extreme was her role as a vulgar and pushy nouveau-riche mother in *Conversation Piece*. She played both the grand sophisticate of the past and the reptilian modern mother with equal conviction.

—Elaine Mancini

MANSFIELD, Jayne

Nationality: American. **Born:** Vera Jayne Palmer in Bryn Mawr, Pennsylvania 19 April 1933. **Education:** Studied acting with Baruch Lumet, 1952. **Family:** Married 1) Paul Mansfield, 1950 (divorced

1956), daughter: Jayne Maria; 2) the actor Mickey Hargitay, 1958 (divorced 1964), three children including the actress Mariska Hargitay; 3) Matt Cimber, 1964, son: Anthony Richard. **Career:** 1951—stage debut in *Ten Nights in a Barroom* in Austin, Texas; 1953—appeared in several productions for Dallas Institute for the Performing Arts; joined Blue Book Model Agency, Hollywood; 1954—television debut on *Lux Video Theatre*; 1955—short contract with Warner Brothers, and film debut in *Pete Kelly's Blues*; Broadway stage debut in *Will Success Spoil Rock Hunter?*; 1956—regular panelist on TV show *Down You Go*; 1956—contract with 20th Century-Fox, not renewed; 1965—TV comedy pilot *The Jayne Mansfield Show* never developed into series. **Died:** In car accident, 29 June 1967.

Films as Actress:

1955   *Pete Kelly's Blues* (Webb); *Illegal* (Allen); *Hell on Frisco Bay* (*The Darkest Hour*) (Tuttle)

1956   *The Girl Can't Help It* (Tashlin); *Female Jungle* (*Hangover*) (Ve Sota—produced 1954); *The Wayward Bus* (Vicas)

1957   *Will Success Spoil Rock Hunter?* (Tashlin); *The Burglar* (Wendkos—produced 1955); *Kiss Them for Me* (Donen)

1958   *The Sheriff of Fractured Jaw* (Walsh)

1960   *Too Hot to Handle* (*Playgirl after Dark*) (Young); *Gli amori di Ercole* (*The Loves of Hercules*) (Bragaglia)

Jayne Mansfield

1961   *The George Raft Story* (*Spin of a Coin*) (Newman); *It Takes a Thief* (*The Challenge*) (Gilling)
1962   *It Happened in Athens* (Marton)
1963   *Promises! Promises!* (Donovan)
1964   *Heimlich nach St. Pauli* (Jacobs); *Panic Button* (Sherman); *Einer frisst den anderern* (*When Strangers Meet*; *Dog Eat Dog*) (Nazarro); *L'amore primitivo* (*Primitive Love*) (Scattini)
1966   *The Fat Spy* (Cates); *Las Vegas Hillbillies* (*Country Music U.S.A.*) (Pierce)
1967   *A Guide for the Married Man* (Kelly); *Spree* (*Here's Las Vegas*) (Leisen and Green—produced 1963); *Single Room Furnished* (Cimber)

Publications

On MANSFIELD: books—

Saxton, Martha, *Jayne Mansfield and the American Fifties*, Boston, 1975.
Jackson, Jean-Pierre and Françoise, *Jayne Mansfield*, Paris, 1984.
Luijters, Guus, and Gerald Timmer, *Sexbomb: The Life and Death of Jayne Mansfield*, Secaucus, New Jersey, 1988.
Callan, Michael Feeney, *Jayne Mansfield: ihre Filme, ihr Leben*, Munich, 1989.
Betrock, Alan, compiler, *Jayne Mansfield vs. Mamie Van Doren: Battle of the Blondes: A Pictorial History*, Brooklyn, New York, 1993.
Faris, Jocelyn, *Jayne Mansfield: A Bio-Bibliography*, Westport, Connecticut, 1994.

On MANSFIELD: articles—

McClure, M., "Defense of Jayne Mansfield," in *Film Culture* (New York), no. 32, 1964.
Calendo, J., "Saint Jayne Mansfield," in *Inter/View* (New York), June 1975.
Haspiel, James Robert, and Charles Herschberg, "Jayne Mansfield's Starlet Days," in *Films in Review* (New York), June 1976, see also issue for November 1977.
Ciné Revue (Paris), 10 April 1984.

On MANSFIELD: films—

The Wild, Wild World of Jayne Mansfield, documentary, 1958.
The Jayne Mansfield Story, directed by Dick Lowry for television, 1980.

*   *   *

Lacking Monroe's overrated vulnerability, Mansfield survives as a fifties icon more for what she represents than for her bodacious body of work. To feminist authors such as Martha Saxton (*Jayne Mansfield and the American Fifties*), Mansfield's a shapely club to beat over the head of sexist pigs; to gay men, Jayne's an outrageous cartoon of heterosexuality; to wolf-whistlers, she is the ultimate love machine, a depersonalized bosom to rest one's weary head on. Yet, Mansfield's potent image has outlasted all the other Monroe derivatives for a special reason; you can sense Mansfield savoring her Hollywood stardom and inviting the audience to share in her improbable good fortune.

A master of publicity, Mansfield was far more popular as an outrageous public figure than as a film star, and this attention-getting resourcefulness became her prime asset when her movie career peaked in less than three years. It is not surprising that Jayne Mansfield was inescapably typed in films as the caricature of a dumb blonde, for she

tirelessly promoted the same image off the screen as well. She exploited her attributes at a time when the media were obsessed with such matters. But her most artistically successful films were also those that took the most thorough advantage of her physical presence: her work with director Frank Tashlin in *The Girl Can't Help It* and the film version of *Will Success Spoil Rock Hunter?* In both, Tashlin was able simultaneously to elevate her to a representation of exaggerated sexuality and humanize her as a sympathetic character. But such opportunities were unique for Mansfield, who by 1960 had been dropped by Twentieth Century-Fox and had retreated to minor international films and nightclub appearances.

If her truest talent was for self-promotion, one can only speculate about felicitous turns her career might have taken. Consideration for the Lee Remick role in *Anatomy of a Murder* seems less screwy if you have seen Mansfield's uncluttered dramatic work on an episode of *Alfred Hitchcock Presents*. Perhaps if she had signed for the role of Ginger created for her on *Gilligan's Island*, she would not have been killed while driving to reach her next nightclub engagement.

But television, in Mansfield's philosophy, was a step down. Reduced to gyrating in a Hercules flick or undulating in such lower depth cinema as *Las Vegas Hillbillies*, Jayne still radiated the excitement of a little girl who had just landed the lead in the school play. Shrewdly manufacturing herself as a goddess of excess, Mansfield skyrocketed to stardom but did not know how to manage her career once she arrived. Before her American success story soured, fans had a good time at the party Mansfield always seemed to be throwing herself. That trademark squeal of delight was genuine.

—Richard Wilson, updated by Robert Pardi

MARAIS, Jean

Nationality: French. **Born:** Jean Alfred Villain-Marais in Cherbourg, 11 December 1913. **Education:** Attended Collège de Saint-Germain-en-Laye; Lycées Condorcet and Janson-de-Sailly; Saint Nicolas, Buzenal. **Military Service:** French Army, beginning in 1939; joined Leclerc division of the American Third Army, 1943. **Family:** One son. **Career:** 1930—apprenticed to a photographer in Le Vésinet, but soon was painting and studying acting with Charles Dullin; 1933—film debut in *L'epervier* (also assistant director); also appeared in walk-on roles in Dullin's productions; 1937—in chorus of Cocteau's *Oedipe* on stage in Paris; beginning of a personal and professional relationship with Cocteau; appeared in several plays written for him by Cocteau, and in films written or directed by Cocteau; stage work included roles at the Comédie Française, and acting in and directing Cocteau's *Les Parents terribles* in 1977. **Awards:** Croix de Guerre. **Address:** c/o Les Films 13, 15 Ave. Hoche, 75008 Paris, France.

Films as Actor:

1933   *L'epervier* (*Bird of Prey*) (L'Herbier) (+ asst d)
1934   *Le Bonheur* (L'Herbier); *Le Scandale* (L'Herbier)
1941   *Le Pavillon brûle* (de Baroncelli)
1942   *Le Lit à Colonne* (Tual)
1943   *L'Eternal Retour* (*The Eternal Return*) (Delannoy) (as Tristan); *Voyage sans espoir* (Christian-Jaque); *Carmen* (Christian-Jaque) (as Don Jose)
1946   ***La Belle et la bête*** (*Beauty and the Beast*) (Cocteau and Clément) (as the Beast/the Prince)

1947   *Les Chouans* (Colef); *L'Aigle à deux têtes* (*The Eagle with Two Heads*) (Cocteau) (as Stanislas)

1948   *Ruy Blas* (Billon) (title role/Don Cesari); *Les Parents terribles* (*The Storm Within*; *Intimate Relations*) (Cocteau) (as Michel)

1949   *Aux yeux du souvenir* (*Souvenir*) (Delannoy); *Le Secret de Mayerling* (*The Secret of Mayerling*) (Delannoy) (as Crown Prince Rudolph)

1950   *Orphée* (*Orpheus*) (Cocteau) (title role); *Le Château de verre* (Clément)

1951   *Les miracles n'ont lieu qu'une fois* (Yves Allégret)

1952   *La voce del silenzio* (Pabst); *Nez de cuir* (Yves Allégret)

1953   *Julietta* (Marc Allégret) (as André Landecourt); *Le Comte de Monte-Cristo* (*Count of Monte Cristo*) (Vernay) (as Edmond Dantes); *Dortoir des grandes* (*Inside a Girls' Dormitory*) (Decoin); *Si Versailles m'était conte* (*Affairs in Versailles*; *Royal Affairs in Versailles*) (Guitry) (as Louis XV)

1954   *Le Guérisseur* (Ciampi); *Napoléon* (Guitry) (as Count de Montholon)

1955   *Futures vedettes* (Marc Allégret); *Si Paris nous était conté* (*If Paris Were Told to Us*) (Guitry) (as François I)

1956   *Élena et les hommes* (*Paris Does Strange Things*; *Elena and Her Men*) (Renoir) (as Gen. François Rollan); *S.O.S. Noronha* (Rouquier); *Typhon sur Nagasaki* (*Typhoon over Nagasaki*) (Ciampi)

1957   *Le notti bianche* (*White Nights*) (Visconti) (as Lodger); *Un Amour de poche* (*Nude in His Pocket*; *Girl in His Pocket*) (Kast) (as Professor Jérôme)

1959   *Le Testament d'Orphée* (*The Testament of Orpheus*) (Cocteau) (as Oedipus)

1960   *Le Capitan* (Hunebelle); *Austerlitz* (*The Battle of Austerlitz*) (Gance and Richebé) (as Carnot)

1961   *La Princesse de Clèves* (Delannoy); *Le Capitain Fracasse* (Gaspard-Huit)

1962   *Ponzio Pilato* (*Pontius Pilate*) (Rapper) (title role); *Le Masque de fer* (Decoin) (as D'Artagnan)

1964   *Patate* (*Friend of the Family*) (Thomas) (as Noel Carradine); *Fantômas* (Hunebelle) (title role/Fandor)

1965   *Fantômas se déchaine* (*Fantômas Strikes Back*) (Hunebelle) (title role); *Le Gentleman de Cocody* (*Man from Cocody*) (Christian-Jaque) (as Jean-Luc Hervé de la Tommeraye)

1966   *Le Saint prend l'affût* (Christian-Jaque) (title role)

1967   *Fantômas contre Scotland Yard* (Hunebelle) (title role)

1968   *Le paria* (Carliez)

1970   *La Provocation* (Charpak); *Le Jouet Criminel* (Thomas); *Peau d'âne* (*The Magic Donkey*; *Donkey Skin*) (Demy) (as Blue King)

1980   *Les Parents Terribles* (Hubert—for TV)

1982   *Ombre et secrets* (Delabre)

1985   *Parking* (Demy) (as the Devil)

1986   *Le lien de Parenté* (*Parental Claim*; *Next of Kin*) (Rameau) (as Victor Blaise)

1988   *Johanna D'Arc of Mongolia* (Ottinger)

1992   *Les Enfants du Naufrageur* (*Shipwrecked Children*) (Foulon) (as old man with a limp)

1995   *Les Misérables* (Lelouch) (as Monsieur Myriel)

1996   *Stealing Beauty* (Bertolucci)

Publications

By MARAIS: books—

Mes quatres verités, Paris, 1957.

Histoire de ma vie, Paris, 1975.
Contes, Paris, 1978.
L'inconcevable Jean Cocteau: suivi de, Cocteau-Marais, Monaco, 1993.

By MARAIS: articles—

Interview in *L'Ecran Fantastique* (Paris), no. 21, 1981.
Ciné Revue (Paris), 18 February 1982 and 2 August 1984.

On MARAIS: books—

Cocteau, Jean, *Jean Marais*, Paris, 1951.
Jelot-Blanc, Jean-Jacques, *Jean Marais: biographie*, Paris, 1994.

On MARAIS: articles—

Current Biography 1962, New York, 1962.
Stars (Mariembourg, Belgium), Spring 1993.

*   *   *

Few actors have been so lucky as to have their roles tailor-made for them by a writer and director of Jean Cocteau's stature. As screenwriter, director, and often author of the original stage play on which the film was based, Cocteau developed the characters, the milieu, and even the camera techniques around the personality, physical features, and acting capabilities of his intimate friend Jean Marais. But Cocteau was for his part also very fortunate to find in Marais the perfect embodiment of his archetypal heroes.

It is in those films of Cocteau having a clear mythic basis that the collaboration between director and actor reached its height. In *L'Eternal Retour*, scripted by Cocteau, Marais acts the part of the desperately enamored Tristan in a modernized telling of the medieval legend of love and death. *L'Aigle à deux têtes* is a legendary view of a stormily romantic 19th-century world, in which Marais plays an anarchistic student who almost becomes a prince consort; here, too, the ending is a Wagnerian one of love in death. That Marais seems a bit old for the part fits perfectly the Hamletesque overtones of the film; the student is a youth old in spirit. Marais's chiseled features are perfect for this film, for they are strong enough to be those of the peasant's son he seems to be and noble enough for the prince he should or even might be. In *La Belle et la bête* Marais's attractive monster changes into an almost too charming prince.

The actor's sublime (if certainly not beautiful) facial features are perfect for portraying a mythological Greek figure such as Orpheus; and no less valuable in this and similar roles is Marais's severe acting style, the result of his classical training as an actor with the Comédie Française. *Orphée*, second of the director's three films on the subject, is the culmination of the collaboration between Cocteau and Marais. The actor conveys perfectly the brooding poet-visionary, seeking to escape the unwanted adulation and the criticism of the hostile and cliquish world of modern Paris. Cocteau adapted the role from that of the chatty Orpheus of a stage play, written long before the two met, into a figure of monumental reticence classically embodied by Marais. A similar effect is achieved in an appearance by the actor, this time as Oedipus in Cocteau's *Testament d'Orphée*. The role is brief and non-speaking; the effect is eternal.

The actor's other films are disappointing; the closer Marais's roles came to a Cocteauesque poesis—for example, in Visconti's *Le notti bianche*—the better they are. As an actor, Marais has been no more and no less than the lyre of an Orpheus.

—Rodney Farnsworth

Jean Marais in *Orphée*

MARCH, Fredric

Nationality: American. **Born:** Frederick Ernest McIntyre Bickel in Racine, Wisconsin, 31 August 1897. **Education:** Racine High School, University of Wisconsin, Madison, B.A. in economics. **Military Service:** Served as artillery lieutenant during World War I. **Family:** Married the actress Florence Eldridge, 1927, two adopted children. **Career:** 1920—apprentice at National City Bank, New York, but decided to become an actor: bit part in stage play *Deburau* in Philadelphia; film debut as extra in *Paying the Piper*; 1926—lead in Broadway play *The Devil in the Cheese*; later toured with Theatre Guild Repertory Company; 1928—contract with Paramount to make talking films; 1933—Paramount contract ended, and most later work done on short 2-film contracts or as freelance; 1943—on Broadway stage in *The Skin of Our Teeth*; 1956—on stage in world premiere of O'Neill's *Long Day's Journey into Night*, New York and Paris. **Awards:** Best Actor Academy Award for *Dr. Jekyll and Mr. Hyde*, 1931-32; Best Actor Academy Award for *The Best Years of Our Lives*, 1946; Best Actor, Venice Festival, for *Death of a Salesman*, 1952; Best Actor, Berlin Festival, for *Inherit the Wind*, 1960. **Died:** 14 April 1975.

Films as Actor:

1928   *The Dummy* (Milton) (as Trumbull Meredith); *The Studio Murder Mystery* (Tuttle) (as Richard Hardell)

1929   *Paris Bound* (Griffith) (as Jim Hutton); *Jealousy* (De Limur) (as Pierre); *Footlights and Fools* (Seiter) (as Gregory Pyne); *The Marriage Playground* (Mendes) (as Martin Boyne); *Sarah and Son* (Arzner) (as Howard Vanning); *The Wild Party* (Arzner)

1930   *Ladies Love Brutes* (Lee) (as Dwight Howell); *Paramount on Parade* (as doughboy); *Manslaughter* (Abbott) (as Dan O'Bannon); *Laughter* (D'Arrast) (as Paul Lockridge); *The Royal Family of Broadway* (Cukor) (as Tony Cavendish); *True to the Navy* (Tuttle); *Honor among Lovers* (Arzner) (as Jerry Stafford); *The Night Angel* (Goulding) (as Rudek Berkem); *My Sin* (Abbott) (as Dick Grady)

1932   ***Dr. Jekyll and Mr. Hyde*** (Mamoulian) (title role); *Strangers in Love* (Mendes) (as Buddy Drake/Arthur Drake); *Merrily We Go to Hell* (Arzner) (as Jerry Corbett); *Make Me a Star* (as himself); *Smilin' Through* (Franklin) (as Jeremy Wayne/Kenneth Wayne); *The Sign of the Cross* (DeMille) (as Marcus Superbus)

1933   *Tonight Is Ours* (Walker) (as Sabien Pastal); *The Eagle and the Hawk* (Walker) (as Jerry Young); *Design for Living* (Lubitsch) (as Tom Chambers)

1934   *All of Me* (Flood) (as Don Ellis); *The Affairs of Cellini* (La Cava) (as Benvenuto Cellini); *The Barretts of Wimpole Street* (Franklin) (as Robert Browning); *Death Takes a Holiday* (Leisen) (as Death); *Good Dame* (Gering); *We Live Again* (Mamoulian)

1935   *Anna Karenina* (Brown) (as Vronsky); *The Dark Angel* (Franklin) (as Alan Trent); *Les Misérables* (Boleslawski)

1936   *Mary of Scotland* (Ford) (as Earl of Bothwell); *Anthony Adverse* (LeRoy) (title role); *The Road to Glory* (Hawks)

1937   *A Star Is Born* (Wellman) (as Norman Maine); *Nothing Sacred* (Wellman) (as Wally Cook)

1938   *The Buccaneer* (DeMille) (as Jean Lafitte); *There Goes My Heart* (McLeod) (as Bill Spencer); *Trade Winds* (Garnett) (as Sam Wye)

1939   *China's 400,000,000* (doc); *Lights Out in Europe* (doc)

1940   *So Ends Our Night* (Cromwell) (as Josef Steiner); *Susan and God* (Cukor)

1941   *One Foot in Heaven* (Rapper) (as William Spence); *Bedtime Story* (Hall) (as Lucius Drake); *Victory* (Cromwell)

1942   *I Married a Witch* (Lubitsch) (as Wallace Wooley); *Black Sea Fighters* (doc)

1944   *The Adventures of Mark Twain* (Rapper) (title role); *Tomorrow the World* (Fenton) (as Mike Frame)

1946   ***The Best Years of Our Lives*** (Wyler) (as Dr. Stephenson)

1948   *Another Part of the Forest* (Gordon) (as Marcus Hubbard); *Live Today for Tomorrow* (Gordon) (as Judge Calvin Cooke); *An Act of Murder* (Gordon)

1949   *Christopher Columbus* (McDonald) (title role); *The Titan-Michaelangelo* (doc)

1951   *Death of a Salesman* (Benedek) (as Willy Loman)

1952   *It's a Big Country* (Wellman and others) (as Papa Esposito)

1953   *Man on a Tightrope* (Kazan) (as Karel Cernik)

1954   *Executive Suite* (Wise) (as Lorne Phineas Snow); *The Bridges at Toko-Ri* (Robson) (as Adm. George Tarrant)

1955   *The Desperate Hours* (Wyler) (as Don Hilward); *Alexander the Great* (Rossen) (as Philip of Macedonia); *Albert Schweitzer* (doc)

1956   *The Man in the Gray Flannel Suit* (Johnson) (as Hopkins)

1959   *Middle of the Night* (Delbert Mann) (as Jerry Kingsley)

1960   *Inherit the Wind* (Kramer) (as Matthew Harrison Brady)

1961   *The Young Doctors* (Karlson) (as Dr. Joseph Pearson)

1963   *The Condemned of Altona* (De Sica) (as Gerlach); *Seven Days in May* (Frankenheimer) (as President Jordan Lyman)

1966   *Hombre* (Ritt) (as Alexander Favor)

1969   *. . . Tick . . . Tick . . . Tick . . .* (Nelson) (as Mayor Parks)

Publications

On MARCH: books—

Blum, Daniel, *Great Stars of the American Stage: A Pictorial Record*, New York, 1952.

Burrows, Michael, *Charles Laughton and Fredric March*, Cornwall, England, 1970.

Quirk, Lawrence J., *The Films of Fredric March*, New York, 1971.

On MARCH: articles—

Lee, Sonia, "Fredric March Gambled with Death—and Won," in *Motion Picture Magazine* (New York), December 1933.

Manners, Dorothy, "Fredric March Defends Hollywood's Morals," in *Motion Picture Magazine* (New York), November 1934.

Vandour, Cyril, "Freddie Marches On," in *Motion Picture Magazine* (New York), December 1937.

Paxton, John, "This Militant March," in *Stage*, 15 May 1939.

Isaacs, Hermine Rich, "Two Girls and Fredric March," in *Theatre Arts* (New York), April 1944.

Tozzi, Romano, "Fredric March," in *Films in Review* (New York), December 1958.

Moret, H., "Fredric March," in *Ecran* (Paris), June-July 1975.

Braun, Eric, "The Seven Ages of March," in *Films and Filming* (London), November and December 1975.

*   *   *

Fredric March was one of the most durable Hollywood performers, playing, as a young man, a wide variety of leading roles in different genres, and creating, in middle age, a number of notable characterizations. The longevity of his career and range of his successes are somewhat surprising since he disdained an internal Method approach to acting as well as the building of a distinctive screen persona. Instead

March preferred, in Richard Gehman's interesting formulation, to put on a role "much as a man fits himself into a Grafton street suit." For both stage and screen performances March would study the role intensely, memorizing the dialogue early, and let the character take shape as a comfortable mask. Thus his screen performances are remarkable for their subtlety, and so are all the more cinematic, while being dependent for their effectiveness on directorial support. In the wrong part March would tend to become stolid and weak; this is especially true of his 1930s work as a romantic lead, where he was often outplayed by the actresses with whom he appeared.

Unlike that of most screen actors, March's career in films developed simultaneously with his stage career. In the early 1920s he worked as an extra in several films shot in New York and appeared in a number of minor theatrical roles, finally landing a leading part in a light comedy, *The Devil in the Cheese*. His subsequent impersonation of John Barrymore in *The Royal Family* brought him to the notice of Hollywood. He was signed to a five-year contract by Paramount, a studio whose glossy and sophisticated romantic comedies suited March's good looks and slightly cynical demeanor. Most notably, he repeated the role of John Barrymore in *The Royal Family of Broadway*, where he strikes just the right note of humorous dissolute talent. Even in his light comedy roles, however, March always suggests a repressed anger or dissatisfaction, a quality exploited especially in the Barrymore part. This may explain his somewhat surprising choice for the title role in Rouben Mamoulian's *Dr. Jekyll and Mr. Hyde*. Unlike Spencer Tracy's later version, March's performance is a tour de force of impersonation (aided by makeup and directorial touches) rather than characterization. March was awarded the Oscar for his performance.

In the years immediately following, however, he was not afforded another opportunity to play such a complex character. Instead he became involved, now as a freelancer, in a number of costume epics and historical films, casting decisions influenced by the fact that he looked good in period clothes and had a resonant delivery. He was competent, if not convincing, as Browning in *The Barretts of Wimpole Street*, rather dashing as the picaresque hero of *Anthony Adverse*, and a powerful Bothwell in *Mary of Scotland*. He did impressive work, always in an essentially supporting capacity, in a number of films with contemporary settings, most notably Howard Hawks's *The Road to Glory* and William Wellman's *A Star Is Born*, where once again, he strikes just the right note of dissolute talent.

In these two roles suggestions of a darker, repressed, and perhaps self-destructive energy emerges, a side of March's persona only previously exploited in his double role as Jekyll and Hyde. He returned to Broadway during the later stages of World War II to appear in an acclaimed production of *A Bell for Adano*, in which he was a very optimistic (and perhaps one-dimensional) Major Joppolo. In *The Best Years of Our Lives*, however, William Wyler was able to make better use of March's persona. The original treatments of the script had made Al Stephenson a returning veteran who cannot fit back into a comfortable civilian niche, and rejects his job at the bank. In the final version, however, Stephenson is a more complex character—a man whose dissatisfactions are revealed in occasional tippling but who represses his anger for the sake of social appearances and convention. March's embodiment of the role is near perfect, a triumph of casting and effective direction (particularly Wyler's feel for slowly developed drama). March received the Oscar for his role, which is in a sense a study for his James Tyrone in the stage version of *Long Day's Journey into Night*.

In the 1950s March's career deteriorated, in spite of competent performances as Willy Loman in Benedek's *Death of a Salesman* and as a besieged homeowner in Wyler's *The Desperate Hours*. Even late in his career, however, March was able to turn in a finely conceived characterization as a villainous Indian agent in *Hombre*.

—R. Barton Palmer

MARETSKAYA, Vera

Nationality: Russian. **Born:** Vera Petrovna Maretskaya in Moscow, 31 July 1906. **Education:** Attended the Bakhtangova Theatre Actors Studio, Moscow, graduated 1924. **Career:** 1924-30—stage actress in Moscow, then actress in Rostov-on-Don, 1936-40, and after 1940 at Mossovet Theatre, Moscow; 1925—film debut in *The Tailor from Torzhok*. **Awards:** State Prize of the USSR, 1942, 1946, 1948, 1951; People's Artist of the USSR, 1949; Heroine of Socialist Labor, 1976. **Died:** In Moscow, 17 August 1978.

Films as Actress:

1925 *Zakroishchik iz Torzhka* (*The Tailor from Torzhok*) (Protazanov)
1926 *Zelenyi Zmii* (*The Green Serpent*) (Kabalov)
1928 *Dom na Trubnoi* (*The House on Trubnaya Street*) (Barnet); *Prostye serdtsa* (*Simple Hearts*) (Khudoleev)
1929 *2-Buldi-2* (Kuleshov); *Zhivoi trup* (*The Living Corpse*) (Otsep); *Sto dvadtsat tysyach v god* (*One Hundred Twenty Thousand a Year*) (Chernyak)
1930 *Stydno skazat* (*It's a Shame to Say It*) (Armand)
1933 *Chernyi barak* (*The Black Hut*) (Yashin and Gorchakov)
1934 *Chetyre vizity Samuelya Vulfa* (*The Four Visits of Samuel Wolf*) (Stolper)
1935 *Lyubov i nenavist* (*Love and Hate*) (Gendelshtein) (as Vera)
1936 *Pokolenie pobeditelei* (*A Generation of Conquerors*) (Stroeva) (as Varya Postnikova); *Zori Parizha* (*Paris Commune*) (Roshal)
1939 *Chlen pravitelstva* (*A Member of the Government*) (Zarkhi and Heifitz) (as Aleksandra Sokolova)
1941 *Delo Artamonovykh* (*The Artamonov Affair*) (Roshal)
1942 *Kotovsky* (Faintsimmer)
1943 *Ona zashchishchaet Rodinu* (*She Defends Her Country*; *No Greater Love*) (Ermler) (as Praskovya Lukyanova)
1944 *Svadba* (*The Wedding*; *Marriage*) (Annensky)
1947 *Selskaya uchitelnitsa* (*A Village School-Teacher*) (Donskoi) (as Varvara Vasilevna)
1955 *Mat* (*Mother*) (Donskoi)
1956 *Polyushko-pole* (*My Little Field*) (Stroeva)
1962 *Sredi dobrykh lyudei* (*Mother and Daughter*) (Bryunchugin and Buchovsky) (as Mikhailina)
1964 *Legkaya zhizn* (*An Easy Life*) (Dorman)

Publications

By MARETSKAYA: books—

30 let sovetskoi kinematografi, with others, Moscow, 1950.
Vasily Vasilyevich Vanin, with others, Moscow, 1955.

On MARETSKAYA: books—

Dunina, S., *Narodnaia artistka SSSR Vera Petrovna Maretskaya*, Moscow, 1953.
Boiadzhiev, G., *Maretskaya*, Moscow, 1954.
Zak, M., *Aktery sovetskogo kino*, Moscow, 1964.

On MARETSKAYA: articles—

Iskusstvo Kino (Moscow), September 1976, January and December 1979.

*   *   *

Vera Maretskaya in *Selskaya uchitelnitsa*

Vera Maretskaya's first film role was as the maidservant in Yakov Protazanov's silent comedy *Zakroishchik iz Torzhka*. Her talent for comedy and vivacious temperament drew the attention of Boris Barnet, and he offered her the role of a peasant girl who comes to town looking for a job and has a series of humorous adventures in *Dom na Trubnoi*. Beginning with this film, the social characteristics and background of her roles were carefully worked out and made clear in her performances. In the silent era she appeared in several more films, and created the persona of an honest, pure-hearted, and somewhat naive girl who knew how to maintain her social and moral dignity.

In the mid-1930s she acted in two films, *Lyubov i nenavist* and *Pokolenie pobeditelei*, in which her characters took an active part in the October Revolution and the Civil War. The young mine worker Vera in the first film, and Varya Postnikova in the second, were not only ardent believers in revolutionary ideals but were also willing to fight for them. At the same time they were sensitive and feminine, with a lively sense of humor, which was the basic quality of Maretskaya's memorable cinematic presence.

Zarkhi and Heifitz's *Chlen pravitelstva* presented her character, Aleksandra Sokolova, as a symbol of the social achievements and possibilities of emancipated Soviet women. An ordinary villager, she becomes the organizer of a big *kolkhoz* and then a member of the government. Maretskaya created a full-blooded character who, despite the restrictions imposed by the Soviet cinema of the time, experienced suffering and disappointment as well as joy.

Her success in this role was followed by several films in which she played contemporary women: roles as doctor, mother, worker, and so on. All of them were actively involved in constructing a new Soviet society. Her ability to bring such characters to life made Maretskaya one of the most famous Soviet actresses prior to the war. Her role as Praskovya Lukyanova ("Comrade P") in *Ona zashchishchaet Rodinu* is of this type. The actress created the character of a woman who, having suffered the cruelties of war, becomes the leader of a group of partisans fighting the fascist occupying army. Her heroic life and death personified the heroism of millions of Soviet women who fought the fascists as bravely as their men did.

The role that best demonstrates the range of her ability is that of Varvara Vasilevna in Mark Donskoi's *Selskaya uchitelnitsa*. As the village teacher of the title she ages from youth to middle age. Again, this character is not an extraordinary person; building a type, the actress lived the life of a real woman, whose days were devoted to the emotional and spiritual education of her students. In 1955 she played the mother in Donskoi's version of Gorki's *Mat*. Though this film did not make the powerful impression of Pudovkin's 1926 masterpiece, Maretskaya once again showed the deep understanding and love for the women of her country expressed through the unforgettable characters she created on the screen.

—Christina Stoyanova

MARSH, Mae

Nationality: American. **Born:** Mary Warne Marsh in Madrid, New Mexico, 9 November 1895. **Education:** Convent of the Immaculate Heart, Hollywood. **Family:** Married Louis Lee Arms, 1918, children: Mary, Brewster, and Marguerite. **Career:** 1906—family moved to Los Angeles; 1911—telephone operator; 1912—first screen appearance in Mary Pickford film *The Lesser Evil*; given name "Mae" by Griffith to distinguish her from Pickford; first leading role in *Man's Genesis*: teamed with Bobby Harron for first time; 1915-16—with Bobby Harron in series in films for Triangle; 1916-19—contract with Goldwyn; 1920—contract with Robertson-Cole Company; stage debut in comedy *Brittie*; 1922—first British film, *Flames of Passion*; last Griffith film, *The White Rose*; 1931—resumed film acting in character parts; 1955—named one of five outstanding screen actresses of silent era at George Eastman House Festival of Fine Arts. **Died:** In Hermosa Beach, California, 13 February 1968.

Films as Actress:

1912 *The Lesser Evil* (Griffith) (as extra); *The Old Actor* (Griffith) (as extra); *Man's Genesis* (Griffith) (as Lily White); *Sands of Dee* (Griffith); *The New York Hat* (Griffith); *Brute Force* (Griffith) (as Lily White)

1913 *The Telephone Girl and the Lady* (O'Sullivan); *Love in an Apartment Hotel*; *A Girl's Strategem*; *Fate* (Griffith)

1914 *The Battle of Elderbush Gulch* (Griffith); *Judith of Bethulia* (Griffith) (as Naomi); *The Escape* (Griffith); *Home Sweet Home* (Griffith) (as Apple-Pie Mary); *The Avenging Conscience* (Griffith); (in films supervised by Griffith: *The Outcast*; *The Victim*; *The Great Leap*; *Paid with Interest*)

1915 ***The Birth of a Nation*** (Griffith) (as Flora Cameron)

1916 *Intolerance* (Griffith) (as The Little Dear One); *Hoodoo Ann* (Ingraham) (title role); *The Marriage of Molly O*; *The Wild Girl of the Sierras* (Powell); *A Child of the Paris Streets* (Ingraham); *The Little Liar* (Ingraham); *The Wharf Rat* (Withey)

1917 *Polly of the Circus* (Horan and Hollywood); *Sunshine Alley* (Noble); *The Cinderella Man* (Tucker)

1918 *Fields of Honour* (Ince); *Beloved Traitor* (Worthington); *The Face in the Dark* (Henley); *The Glorious Adventure* (Henley); *All Women* (Henley); *Money Mad* (Henley); *Hidden Fires* (Irving); *The Racing Strain* (Flynn)

1919 *The Bondage of Barbara* (Flynn); *Spotlight Sadie* (Trimble); *The Mother and the Law* (Griffith—"modern" sequence from *Intolerance* with added footage) (as The Little Dear One)

1920 *The Little 'fraid Lady* (Adolfi)

1921 *Nobody's Kid* (Hickman)

1922 *Till We Meet Again* (Cabanne); *Flames of Passion* (Wilcox)

1923 *Paddy the Next Best Thing* (Cutts); *The White Rose* (Griffith) (as Teazie)

1924 *Daddies* (Seiter); *Arabella* (Guine); *A Woman's Secret* (Wilcox)

1925 *Tides of Passion* (Blackton); *The Rat* (Cutts)

1931 *Over the Hill* (Henry King) (as Ma Shelby)

1932 *Rebecca of Sunnybrook Farm* (Santell); *That's My Boy* (Neill)

1933 *Alice in Wonderland* (McLeod)

1934 *Little Man, What Now?* (Borzage); *Bachelor of Arts* (Louis King)

1935 *Black Fury* (Curtiz)

1936 *Hollywood Boulevard* (Florey)

1940 *Young People* (Dwan); ***The Grapes of Wrath*** (Ford); *The Man Who Wouldn't Talk* (Burton)

1941 *Great Guns* (Banks); *Blue, White, and Perfect* (Leeds)

1942 *Tales of Manhattan* (Duvivier)

1943 *Dixie Dugan* (Brower)

1944 *Jane Eyre* (Stevenson)

1945 *A Tree Grows in Brooklyn* (Kazan)

1946 *The Late George Apley* (Mankiewicz) (as Agnes's dresser); ***My Darling Clementine*** (Ford)

1948 *Deep Waters* (Henry King); *The Snake Pit* (Litvak)

1949 *Three Godfathers* (Ford); *Impact* (Lubin); *A Letter to Three Wives* (Mankiewicz) (as maid); *The Fighting Kentuckian* (Waggner)

1950 *The Gunfighter* (Henry King); *When Willie Comes Marching Home* (Ford)

1951 *That's My Boy* (Walker)

1952 *Night without Sleep* (Baker)

1953 *A Blueprint for Murder* (Stone); *The Sun Shines Bright* (Ford)

1954 ***A Star Is Born*** (Cukor) (as party guest)

1955 *Prince of Players* (Dunne); *The Tall Men* (Walsh)

1956 *While the City Sleeps* (Fritz Lang); *Julie* (Stone); *Girls in Prison* (Cahn); ***The Searchers*** (Ford)

1957 *Wings of Eagles* (Ford)

1958 *Cry Terror* (Stone)

1960 *Sergeant Rutledge* (Ford)

1961 *Two Rode Together* (Ford)

1963 *Donovan's Reef* (Ford)

1964 *Cheyenne Autumn* (Ford)

1967 *Arabella* (Bolognini)

Publications

By MARSH: book—

Screen Acting, Los Angeles, 1921.

By MARSH: article—

"What I Want to Do in My New Pictures," in *Movie Weekly*, 23 December 1922.

On MARSH: book—

Lahue, Kalton C., *Ladies in Distress*, South Brunswick, New Jersey, 1971.

On MARSH: articles—

Bruce, Robert, "The Girl on the Cover," in *Photoplay* (New York), July 1915.

Simpson, Hazel, "Too Many Marys Make a Mae," in *Motion Picture Classic* (Brooklyn), June 1918.

Smith, Frederick, "Mae, Mary, and Matrimony," in *Motion Picture Classic* (Brooklyn), March 1920.

Evans, Delight, "Will Mae Marsh Come Back?" in *Photoplay* (New York), March 1923.

Dunham, H., "Mae Marsh," in *Films in Review* (New York), June-July 1958, see also issues for October 1968 and March 1969.

"Farewell Little Sister!," in *Classic Film Collector* (Indiana, Pennsylvania), Spring 1968.

Dunham, H., "Mae Marsh, Robert Harron, and D. W. Griffith," in *Silent Picture* (London), Autumn 1969.

Böhler, W.-E., "Mae Marsh," in *Filmkritik* (Munich), January 1972.

Kael, Pauline, "Lillian Gish and Mae Marsh," in *The Movie Star*, edited by Elisabeth Weis, New York, 1981.

* * *

Mae Marsh

Contemporary audiences probably know Mae Marsh through the scores of minor character roles she played during the sound era. At that point in her lengthy career, she was often at the periphery of the screen's action, registering in bit parts such as Rochester's wife in *Jane Eyre* or a fear-crazed woman in John Ford's *Two Rode Together*. Much earlier, however, she gave two of the silent screen's finest performances, in D. W. Griffith's *The Birth of a Nation* and *Intolerance*.

Marsh's first films were made in 1912, where she acted in one-reelers directed by Griffith for the Biograph Company. Her combination of fair-haired vulnerability and plucky resolve made her an early favorite with her director, her colleagues, and her audience. Pauline Kael has contrasted her with Griffith's other great actress, Lillian Gish, finding Gish "pure and fluid and lilylike . . . idealized femininity," and Marsh "less ethereal, somehow less actressy, more solid and 'normal,' and yet, in her own way, as exquisite and intuitive."

Griffith broke from Biograph in 1913 and Marsh had a featured role in three of his first four independent productions, most notably as "Apple Pie Mary" opposite Robert Harron's sophisticated easterner in *Home Sweet Home*. Harron and Marsh became one of Griffith's favorite teams, as adept at light comedy as in the more dramatic Biographs in which they were paired (*Man's Genesis*, *The Sands of Dee*). Flora Cameron, the "Little Sister" in Griffith's Civil War epic *The Birth of a Nation*, was the first role to show her true dramatic range, progressing from the irrepressible energy of a child to the barely contained joy and melancholy of a young woman greeting her brother home from a lost war. Critics compared Marsh to Eleanora Duse after her portrayal of "The Little Dear One" in the Modern Story of Griffith's mammoth four-part *Intolerance*. Again teamed with Harron, her performance traces a similar path from innocence to maturity. She is impassioned yet naturalistic, emphasizing subtlety over histrionics. Marsh was adored in England, where she went to make several films. A final collaboration with Griffith, *The White Rose*, was a largely successful attempt to recapture the quality of her best work. Feeling stereotyped, she retired in the mid-1920s, but Fox coaxed her back to work for *Over the Hill*, beginning the series of cameos that kept her on the screen until 1967. She worked often during this period for Andrew Stone and John Ford, but it was Griffith to whom she owed the development of her character and the refinement of her art.

—Lee Tsiantis

MARSHALL, Herbert

Nationality: British. **Born:** Herbert Brough Falcon Marshall in London, England, 23 May 1890. **Education:** Attended St. Mary's College, Harlow, Essex. **Military Service:** Served in the British forces during World War I: lost a leg. **Family:** Married 1) Mollie Maitland, 1915; 2) the actress Edna Best, 1928 (divorced 1940), one daughter; 3) Elizabeth Russell, 1940, one daughter; 4) Patricia Mallory (died 1958); 5) Dee Anne Kahmann, 1960. **Career:** Apprenticed at a chartered accountant, then business manager for an impresario; 1911—stage debut in Buxton; 1913—London stage debut; 1918—joined the Lyric Opera House, Hammersmith, London, and subsequently became leading man on London and New York stage during the 1920s; 1927—film debut in *Mumsie*; concentrated on films after 1932, and settled in Hollywood; 1944-52—in radio series *The Man Called X*. **Died:** Of heart attack, 22 January 1966.

Films as Actor:

1927 *Mumsie* (Wilcox) (as Colonel Armytage)
1928 *Dawn* (Wilcox)

1929 *The Letter* (De Limur) (as Geoffrey Hammond)
1930 *Murder* (Hitchcock) (as Sir John Menier)
1931 *The Calendar (Bachelor's Folly)* (Hunter) (as Garry Anson); *Michael and Mary* (Saville) (as Michael Rowe); *Secrets of a Secretary* (Abbott)
1932 *The Faithful Heart (Faithful Hearts)* (Saville) (as Waverly Ango); *Blonde Venus* (von Sternberg) (as Edward Faraday); **Trouble in Paradise** (Lubitsch); *Evenings for Sale* (Walker)
1933 *Clear All Wires* (Hill); *The Solitaire Man* (Conway); *I Was a Spy* (Saville)
1934 *Four Frightened People* (DeMille); *Riptide* (Goulding); *Outcast Lasy* (Leonard); *The Painted Veil* (Boleslawsky)
1935 *The Good Fairy* (Wyler); *The Flame Within* (Goulding); *Accent on Youth* (Ruggles); *The Dark Angel* (Franklin); *If You Could Only Cook* (Seiter)
1936 *The Lady Consents* (Roberts); *Till We Meet Again* (Goulding); *Forgotten Faces* (Dupont); *Girls' Dormitory* (Cummings); *A Woman Rebels* (Sandrich); *Make Way for a Lady* (Burton)
1937 *Angel* (Lubitsch) (as Sir Frederick Barker); *Breakfast for Two* (Santell)
1938 *Mad about Music* (Taurog); *Always Goodbye* (Lanfield); *Women against Women* (Sinclair)
1939 *Zaza* (Cukor)
1940 *A Bill of Divorcement* (Farrow); *Foreign Correspondent* (Hitchcock); *The Letter* (Wyler) (as Robert Crosbie)
1941 *Adventures in Washington* (Green); **The Little Foxes** (Wyler) (as Horace Giddons); *When Ladies Meet* (Leonard); *Kathleen* (Bucquet)
1943 *The Moon and Sixpence* (Lewin) (as Somerset Maugham); *Forever and a Day* (Goulding and others); *Flight for Freedom* (Mendes); *Young Ideas* (Dassin)
1944 *Andy Hardy's Blonde Trouble* (Seitz)
1945 *The Enchanted Cottage* (Cromwell); *The Unseen* (Allen)
1946 *Crack-Up* (Reis); *The Razor's Edge* (Goulding) (as Somerset Maugham)
1947 *Duel in the Sun* (Vidor) (as Scott Chavez); *Ivy* (Wood)
1948 *The High Wall* (Bernhardt)
1949 *The Secret Garden* (Wilcox)
1950 *The Underworld Story* (Endfield); *Black Jack* (Duvivier)
1951 *Anne of the Indies* (Tourneur)
1952 *Something to Live For* (Preminger)
1953 *Angel Face* (Preminger)
1954 *Riders to the Stars* (Carlson); *The Black Shield of Falworth* (Maté); *Gog* (Strock); *Wicked as They Come* (Hughes)
1955 *The Virgin Queen* (Koster)
1957 *The Weapon* (Chester)
1958 *Stage Struck* (Lumet); *The Fly* (Neumann)
1960 *College Confidential* (Zugsmith); *Midnight Lace* (Miller)
1961 *A Fever in the Blood* (Sherman) (as Governor Thornwall)
1962 *Five Weeks in a Balloon* (Allen) (as the Prime Minister)
1963 *The List of Adrian Messenger* (Huston) (as Sir Wilfred Lucas); *The Caretakers* (Bartlett) (as Dr. Jubal Harrington)
1965 *The Third Day* (Smight) (as Austin Parsons)

Publications

On MARSHALL: article—

Ciné Revue (Paris), 28 July 1977.

* * *

Essentially the urbane, upper-class English gentleman with perfect diction and gracious manners, Herbert Marshall remained a somewhat old-world, romantic figure who became a much beloved character actor and skillful comedian of stage and screen with an expert sense of timing in the kind of social comedy associated with Somerset Maugham or Noël Coward, reaching its height of perfection in Lubitsch's exquisite *Trouble in Paradise*. He appeared on the stage including the West End London theater in the years immediately preceding his service in World War I, in which he lost a leg. He successfully overcame the effects of his disability, managing to disguise it perfectly in performance.

His principal career in the 1920s was in the theater of both London and New York, working notably with Edna Best (whom he married in 1928) as a husband-and-wife team. At the same time he began to work in films, his debonair English manner making him an inevitable draw once sound was introduced to the cinema. His first notable film appearance was, typically enough, in a Somerset Maugham adaptation, *The Letter*, co-starring with Jeanne Eagels. This was also his first Hollywood film. (He was to reappear in the same subject a decade later in 1940, playing opposite Bette Davis and directed by William Wyler.) After appearing in several early British talkies, he returned to America to make what should surely stand as his most perfect film performance in the 1932 *Trouble in Paradise*. As a gentleman crook, he was suave, unruffled, never at a loss in handling women, in this most sophisticated of high, romantic comedies. Never was skilful dialogue so beautifully timed, never was comic action so adroit as in this masterpiece, which remains perfect, timeless entertainment after half a century. With this success behind him, he abandoned the stage for the screen, and made Hollywood his base, appearing in virtually no more British films after 1933.

Marshall was to work with many notable women stars of the time, such as Marlene Dietrich (*Blonde Venus*), Claudette Colbert (*Four Frightened People*), Greta Garbo (*The Painted Veil*), Merle Oberon (*The Dark Angel*), Katharine Hepburn (*A Woman Rebels*), Bette Davis (*The Little Foxes*), Joan Crawford and Greer Garson (*When Ladies Meet*), Gene Tierncy (*The Razor's Edge*), and Jean Simmons (*Angel Face*). As his particular British-style image ceased to find an outlet in later films, he became increasingly a character actor, working solidly from the 1940s until his death in his mid-seventies in 1966. His later films are unfortunately indifferent, but with over half a century of professional work behind him he was one of the most notable actors of his generation.

—Roger Manvell

MARTIN, Dean

Nationality: American. **Born:** Dino Paul Crocetti in Steubenville, Ohio, 17 June 1917. **Education:** Left school in 10th grade. **Family:** Married 1) Elizabeth Ann McDonald, 1940 (divorced 1949), four children; 2) Jeanne Rieggers, 1949 (divorced 1973), three children; 3) Catherine Mae Hawn, 1973 (divorced 1976), adopted daughter: Sasha. **Career:** Amateur boxer as "Kid Crocket," then worked in steel mill and as clerk and croupier; singer, as Dino Martino, with Ernie McKay's Band; then singer and dealer in gambling houses; 1946—booked in Rio Bamba, New York; teamed with Jerry Lewis in double act, and worked in clubs, radio, and television; 1949—film debut in *My Friend Irma*; 1950-55—host, with Lewis, *The Colgate Comedy Hour* on television; 1956—broke with Lewis, and became solo performer as singer and actor; 1965-74—star of *The Dean Martin Show*, on television. **Died:** Of acute respiratory failure, in Beverly Hills, California, 25 December 1995.

Films as Actor:

1949 *My Friend Irma* (George Marshall) (as Steve Baird)

1950 *My Friend Irma Goes West* (Walker) (as Steve Baird); *At War with the Army* (Walker) (as Sgt. Puccinelli)
1951 *That's My Boy* (Walker) (as Bill Baker); *Sailor Beware* (Walker) (as Al Crowthers)
1952 *Jumping Jacks* (Taurog) (as Chick Allen); *Road to Bali* (Walker) (as himself)
1953 *The Stooge* (Taurog) (as Bill Miller); *Scared Stiff* (George Marshall) (as Larry Todd); *The Caddy* (Taurog) (as Joe Anthony); *Money from Home* (George Marshall) (as Honey Talk Nelson)
1954 *Living It Up* (Taurog) (as Steve); *Three-Ring Circus* (Pevney) (as Pete Nelson)
1955 *You're Never Too Young* (Taurog) (as Bob Miles); *Artists and Models* (Tashlin) (as Rick Todd)
1956 *Pardners* (Taurog) (as Slim Mosely, Jr.); *Hollywood or Bust* (Tashlin) (as Steve Wiley)
1957 *Ten Thousand Bedrooms* (Thorpe) (as Ray Hunter)
1958 *The Young Lions* (Dmytryk) (as Michael Whiteacre); *Some Came Running* (Minnelli) (as Bama Dillert)
1959 *Rio Bravo* (Hawks) (as Dude); *Career* (Anthony) (as Maury Novak)
1960 *Who Was That Lady?* (Sidney) (as Michael Haney); *Bells Are Ringing* (Minnelli) (as Jeffrey Moss); *Ocean's Eleven* (Milestone) (as Sam Harmon); *Pepe* (Sidney) (as himself)
1961 *All in a Night's Work* (Anthony) (as Tony Ryder); *Ada* (Daniel Mann) (as Bo Gillis)
1962 *Sergeants 3* (John Sturges) (as Sgt. Chip Deal); *The Road to Hong Kong* (Panama) (as himself); *Who's Got the Action* (Daniel Mann) (as Steve Flood)
1963 *Come Blow Your Horn* (Yorkin) (as the Bum); *Toys in the Attic* (Hill) (as Julian Berniers); *Who's Been Sleeping in My Bed?* (Daniel Mann) (as Jason Steel); *Four for Texas* (Aldrich) (as Joe Jarrett)
1964 *What a Way to Go!* (Thompson) (as Leonard Crawley); *Robin and the Seven Hoods* (Douglas) (as Little John); *Kiss Me, Stupid* (Wilder) (as Dino)
1965 *The Sons of Katie Elder* (Hathaway) (as Tom Elder); *Marriage on the Rocks* (Donohue) (as Ernie Brewer)
1966 *The Silencers* (Karlson) (as Matt Helm); *Texas across the River* (Gordon) (as Sam Hollis); *Murderer's Row* (Levin) (as Matt Helm)
1967 *Rough Night in Jericho* (Laven) (as Alex Flood); *The Ambushers* (Levin) (as Matt Helm)
1968 *Bandolero!* (McLagen) (as Dee Bishop); *How to Save a Marriage—and Ruin Your Life* (Cook) (as David Sloane); *Five Card Stud* (Hathaway) (as Van Morgan); *The Wrecking Crew* (Karlson) (as Matt Helm)
1970 *Airport* (Seaton) (as Vernon Demerest)
1971 *Something Big* (McLagen) (as Joe Baker)
1973 *Showdown* (Seaton) (as Billy Massey)
1975 *Mr. Ricco* (Bogart) (as Joe Ricco)
1980 *Cannonball Run* (Needham) (as Jamie Blake)
1982 *Bonjour, Monsieur Lewis* (Benayoun—doc)
1984 *Cannonball Run II* (Needham) (as Jamie Blake)
1985 *Half-Nelson* (Bilson—for TV)

Publications

On MARTIN: books—

Parish, James Robert, and William T. Leonard, *The Funsters*, New Rochelle, New York, 1979.
Wallis, Hal, and Charles Higham, *Starmaker*, New York, 1980.
Freedland, Michael, *Dino: The Dean Martin Story*, London, 1984.

Tosches, Nick, *Dino: Living High in the Dirty Business of Dreams*, New York, 1992.

On MARTIN: articles—

Ciné Revue (Paris), 12 March 1981.
Barth, J., "Kino Dino," in *Premiere*, February 1992.
Murphy, Mary, "The Days and Nights of Dean Martin," in *TV Guide*, 16 July 1994.
Obituary, in *New York Times*, 26 December 1995.

* * *

Like no other act of the late 1940s, Dean Martin and Jerry Lewis burst onto and dominated the American show business scene. An immediate hit in nightclubs, the duo was signed by producer Hal Wallis for Paramount Pictures. With their third film, *At War with the Army*, released in 1951, Martin and Lewis began a six-year run as major movie stars. In 1952, they moved into first place in the annual *Motion Picture Herald* listing of top ten ranking stars. Only *Artists and Models* and *Hollywood or Bust* (both directed by Frank Tashlin), however, are remembered today except by hardcore Martin and Lewis fans.

In 1956 Martin and Lewis split. Lewis continued in the movies, going on to produce and direct his own pictures, and for a time Martin's career seemed to flounder. Ironically, in retrospect, it was during this period of the late 1950s in which Martin produced his most significant work as a motion picture actor. He was good in *The Young Lions*, but superb in Howard Hawks's *Rio Bravo*, in which his reforming drunk demonstrated that in the right part Martin could be a great actor.

Also during this period, Martin shifted away from movies toward other media, principally popular music. In 1958, he produced a pair of million-selling singles in "Return to Me," and "Volare." At that time he also linked up with Frank Sinatra and became a charter member of the so-called "Rat Pack." Sinatra-led films followed: *Ocean's Eleven*, *Sergeants 3*, and *Robin and the Seven Hoods*. This work led Martin to a revitalized film career in the mid-1960s and so he reemerged back onto the ranking of top stars because of a dismal but popular spoof of James Bond in *The Silencers*. Martin again played Matt Helm in the sequel, *Murderer's Row*, but at that point moved to television complete with a popular NBC variety show. This led to gigs in Las Vegas and later Atlantic City so that alone *Rio Bravo*, sadly, will remain the lone monument to an acting talent wasted.

—Douglas Gomery

MARTIN, Steve

Nationality: American. **Born:** Waco, Texas, 14 August 1945. **Education:** Attended Long Beach State College and the University of California, Los Angeles. **Family:** Married the actress Victoria Tennant, 1986 (separated). **Career:** As a child performer, worked with Wally Boag at Disneyland, then at Birdcage Theatre, Knott's Berry Farm; 1967—while at University, accepted contract to write for *The Smothers Brothers Comedy Hour* for CBS TV; from 1970—writer and stand-up comic, working on TV through the 1970s, including *Saturday Night Live*, on tour, and on best-selling records; 1979—feature film debut as writer/performer in *The Jerk*, 1979; partner in Aspen Film Society (an independent production company) and 40 Share Productions (a television production company). **Awards:** Best Actor Awards, U.S. National Society of Film Critics, and New York Film Critics, for

All of Me, 1984; Best Actor Awards, U.S. National Society of Film Critics, and Los Angeles Film Critics, for *Roxanne*, 1987. **Address:** P.O. Box 929, Beverly Hills, CA 90213, U.S.A.

Films as Actor:

1977 *The Absent-Minded Waiter* (Gottlieb—short) (+ co-sc)
1978 *Sergeant Pepper's Lonely Hearts Club Band* (Schultz) (as Maxwell Edison); *The Kids Are Alright* (Stein)
1979 *The Muppet Movie* (Frawley); *The Jerk* (Carl Reiner) (as Navin, + co-sc)
1981 *Pennies from Heaven* (Ross) (as Arthur)
1982 *Dead Men Don't Wear Plaid* (Carl Reiner) (as Rigby Reardon, + co-sc)
1983 *The Man with Two Brains* (Carl Reiner) (as Dr. Michael Hfuhruhurr, + co-sc)
1984 *The Lonely Guy* (Miller) (title role); *All of Me* (Carl Reiner) (as Roger Cobb, + co-sc)
1985 *Movers and Shakers* (Asher) (as Fabio Longio)
1986 *Little Shop of Horrors* (Oz) (as Orin Scrivello, D.D.S.); *Three Amigos* (Landis) (as Lucky Day, + co-sc, exec pr)
1987 *Planes, Trains and Automobiles* (Hughes) (as Neal Page); *Roxanne* (Schepisi) (as Charlie "C. D." Bales, + sc)
1988 *Dirty Rotten Scoundrels* (Oz) (as Freddy Benson)
1989 *Parenthood* (Howard) (as Gil Buckman)
1990 *My Blue Heaven* (Ross) (as Vinnie Antonelli)
1991 *L.A. Story* (Mick Jackson) (as Harris K. Telemacher, + sc, exec pr); *Father of the Bride* (Shyer) (as George Banks); *Grand Canyon* (Kasdan) (as Davis)
1992 *Housesitter* (Oz) (as Newton Davis); *Leap of Faith* (Pearce) (as Jonas Nightengale)
1993 *And the Band Played On* (Spottiswoode—for TV) (as Brother)
1994 *A Simple Twist of Fate* (MacKinnon) (as Michael McMann, + sc, exec pr); *Mixed Nuts* (Ephron) (as Philip)
1995 *Father of the Bride, Part II* (Shyer) (as George Banks)
1996 *Sgt. Bilko* (Lynn) (title role)

Publications

By MARTIN: books—

Cruel Shoes, New York, 1977.
Picasso at the Lapin Agile (play), 1993.

By MARTIN: articles—

Interview with B. Fong-Torres, in *American Film* (New York), June 1982.
Interview with Jack Barth, in *Film Comment* (New York), September/October 1984.
Interview, in *Photoplay* (London), March 1985.
Interview, in *Time Out* (London), 21 October 1987.
"I'm Just a White Guy from Orange County," interview with Elvis Mitchell, in *American Film* (New York), November 1988.
Interview with D. Sheff, in *Playboy*, January 1993.
"A Not So Wild and Crazy Writer," interview with Alex Witchel, in *New York Times*, 22 October 1995.

On MARTIN: book—

Lenburg, Greg, Randy Skretvedt, and Jeff Lenburg, *Steve Martin: The Unauthorized Biography*, New York, 1980.

On MARTIN: articles—

Current Biography 1978, New York, 1978.
Allen, Steve, in *Funny People*, New York, 1981.
McGillivray, David, "Steve Martin," in *Films and Filming* (London), December 1985.
Worrell, Denise, in *Icons: Intimate Portraits*, New York, 1989.
Fiddy, Dick, "Steve Martin: Wild and Crazy Guy," in *National Film Theatre Booklet* (London), December 1989.
Friedman, Bruce Jay, "Steve Martin, National Treasure," in *Playboy*, April 1991.
Van Biema, David, and Joe McNally, "Steve Martin Gets Serious," in *Life*, March 1992.
de Jonge, Peter, "Cool Jerk," in *New York Times*, 31 May 1992.
Gopnik, Adam, "Steve Martin: The Late Period," in *New Yorker*, 29 November 1993.

*   *   *

With each passing year, Steve Martin's achievement in the American cinema seems stronger and more secure. He is now clearly the most versatile comic actor in American film today, as well as one of its most sensitive writers and cautious risk takers. Martin began as a writer for other comics and television variety shows, but soon developed for himself an incredibly successful career as a stand-up comedian. His routines tended toward the zany, his persona that of the jerky, egocentric comic. There was always a clear, almost philosophical, intelligence at work in his routines, even when he performed with an arrow through his head. His comic bit of using a single flashcube to take a photo of his large audience worked as a sly comment on misguided photographers among his typical amphitheater crowds. His use of catchphrases (such as "*Excuuuuuuse* me," and "I'm a wild and crazy guy") entered popular parlance, although they were as much reflexive ruminations on the concept of the catchphrase, as they were catchphrases. Indeed, his egocentric persona was so self-consciously a put-on that on their second level, his routines became structural treatises on the stand-up form: "New Comedy" which was funny because it was sly *parody* of comedy, rather than comedy. His famous "happy feet" bit, whereby Martin's feet involuntarily start to dance, introduced the theme that would become a primary hallmark of the comedian's work: the split between the mind and the body.

In his first feature, *The Jerk*, a picaresque tale that marked the first of many collaborations with director Carl Reiner, Martin played a black sharecropper's adopted son who discovers only as an adult that he is white. *The Jerk* draws heavily on Martin's stand-up traditions, particularly a sequence in which Martin—in cliched Mexican *bandido* drag—engages in dastardly cat juggling. *The Man with Two Brains*, co-written by Martin, continued to draw upon his traditions: the white suit; the tendency to wear bunny ears; the persona of the self-deluded, yet vulnerable jerk; and the verbal silliness ("Into the mud, scum queen!").

A clear, artistic departure took place with the 1981 *Pennies from Heaven*, directed by Herbert Ross. A very downbeat musical, Martin and co-star Bernadette Peters danced and lip-synced to authentic contemporary performances from the Great Depression era. If generally considered a noble failure, *Pennies from Heaven* distinguished Martin as one of the few American comic actors of his time (along with Woody Allen) willing to take chances on risky material. Risky, too, was his 1982 film *Dead Men Don't Wear Plaid* (again with director Reiner), in which Martin—through the magic of special effects and the most sophisticated Kuleshovian editing—performs opposite stars such as Ingrid Bergman, Humphrey Bogart, and Barbara Stanwyck in scenes borrowed from their greatest period vehicles.

With the exception of occasional films that appear designed to appeal to a juvenile audience (for instance, *Three Amigos*, a disappointing collaboration with John Landis and alumni of the *Saturday Night Live* television show or the slapstick *Planes, Trains and Automobiles*, directed by John Hughes), Martin's films have continued to show laudable ambitiousness and fascinating inspiration. Several films in which Martin worked only as performer particularly stand out: In the musical *Little Shop of Horrors*, directed by Muppet alumnus Frank Oz, Martin turned in an overwhelmingly energetic supporting turn as a sadistic dentist. In *All of Me*, co-starring Lily Tomlin, Martin's physical mastery was so impressive that he won a number of film critics' awards for performance. In *Parenthood*, directed by Ron Howard, Martin played a more reflective leading man in a decidedly ensemble piece, although his stand-up tradition is nicely exploited in a scene as "Cowboy Gil," maker of balloon animals. And in *Father of the Bride* and its sequel, Martin showed definitively that he could follow in Spencer Tracy's footsteps as a totally credible actor, easily capable of exuding warmth and human feeling.

Many of Martin's recent acting projects alternate, too, it would seem, between safer works of mass appeal which entertain and ambitious works of more limited appeal which intellectually engage. *Housesitter*, for instance, with Goldie Hawn, is an absolutely charming comedy in the tradition of the Hollywood screwball, with Martin and Hawn exhibiting considerable chemistry in a well-written formula, while Lawrence Kasdan's *Grand Canyon* (a key film of the nineties) challenges spectators to question their life choices, with Martin willing to take on a relatively serious role and to potentially undermine his star status by appearing in an ensemble context. Ambitious and disturbing, too, is *Leap of Faith*, in which Martin puts his kinetic energy to use as the prancing, dancing, strutting preacher Jonas Nightingale. The insincerity which had always been an integral part of Martin's stand-up persona is transferred wholesale to the business of the faith healer, and this satirical portrait of the shamans of Christian fundamentalism is surprisingly hard-hitting and unsentimental.

In general, Martin's film work is marked by an incredible physical gracefulness which recalls Keaton and Chaplin; a sweetness and vulnerability which recalls Stan Laurel, but which is often (particularly early in his career) projected through a surface persona of egoism and jerkiness, which recalls Jerry Lewis; and an almost schizophrenic split between the performer's mind and his body. Indeed, Martin is invariably most memorable in scenes that display the actor-writer's incredible physical gracefulness in conflict with his mental state: one thinks of *All of Me*, with the crazy scene of physical conflict as a transmogrified female soul takes control of one side of Martin's body; or of *Roxanne*, with Martin's balletic fight using his tennis racket as a weapon and his later hilarious attempt to drink a glass of wine without his huge nose interfering. On a less conflicted note, one thinks of Martin's triumphant dance with Lily Tomlin in *All of Me* and his moving dance of joy after his son catches a baseball in a Little League game in *Parenthood*.

Especially impressive about Martin's development as a comedian is his increased activity as the screenwriter of his own projects. In *Roxanne*, directed by Australian Fred Schepisi in 1987 from a screenplay by Martin, Martin plays C. D. Bales, a fire chief with a huge nose. A witty and moving updating of the Rostand play *Cyrano de Bergerac* to a mountain resort community, *Roxanne* seems Martin's masterpiece so far. More than merely clever, Martin showed the relevance of *Cyrano* to contemporary culture, in the process providing himself a dazzling opportunity for his verbal wit and acrobatic grace. Particularly impressive is Martin's revision of Cyrano's monologue on nose-insults, which offers some continuity with the actor's stand-up tradition. Martin the writer even provides some beautiful, romantic, wistful love scenes which Martin the actor interprets with subtlety and expressiveness. *L.A. Story*, directed by Mick Jackson in 1991, also written by Martin, looks increasingly like a major satirical statement about life in Hollywood: not so bitter as Altman's *The Player*, but certainly as insightful, if more whimsical, and definitely possessing a

Steve Martin in *Leap of Faith*

moral vision—which seems a hallmark of Martin as writer. Although *A Simple Twist of Fate*, directed by Gillies MacKinnon in 1994, was—like *Roxanne*—written by Martin as a contemporary, updating of a literary classic (in this case, George Eliot's *Silas Marner*), it was not particularly successful with audiences or critics. As a dramatist, Martin fills his story with feeling (one thinks of Martin dancing with his baby girl while doing a deft Harry Belafonte impression or of father and daughter mugging to music as they look into each other's eyes), but never to that sentimental point where he forgets the truth—that in the real world, money, unfortunately, always matters. Martin also reveals himself to be a writer strongly focused on structure—with the spinning discs the recurring symbols of the twists of fate that underlie our lives.

In his professional life, Martin has also demonstrated the not inconsiderable ability to collaborate respectfully with a variety of other skillful artists, a canny eye for quality material, an intelligence which emerges in all his performances, and a generosity as actor to his co-stars. Many of these qualities are in marked contrast to so many of his contemporary, such as Chevy Chase or Eddie Murphy, whose work has so consistently been rather artless, hypocritical, or opportunistic. Martin's latest project has resulted in at least a temporary departure from film: his original play, *Picasso at the Lapin Agile*, played successfully in Chicago and Los Angeles in 1995, with other Martin plays currently in process. If there remains any major disappointment from

Martin, it is that he has not evidently aspired to direct, for one would certainly welcome films even more fully dictated by Martin's own creative impulses.

—Charles Derry

MARVIN, Lee

Nationality: American. **Born:** New York City, 19 February 1924. **Education:** Attended a number of schools, including Public School 165, New York, Lakewood High School, Florida, and St. Leo's Preparatory School, Dade City, Florida. **Family:** Married 1) Betty Edeling, 1952 (divorced 1965), four children; 2) Pamela Freely, 1970. **Career:** Quit school to join the U.S. Marine Corps; wounded, 1944, and hospitalized for 13 months; worked at odd jobs, then became a plumber's apprentice, Woodstock; 1947—stage debut in *Roadside* at Maverick Theatre, Woodstock; then studied at the American Theatre Wing, New York; 1950—film debut in *You're in the Navy Now*; 1951—stage role in Broadway success *Billy Budd*; 1957-60—in TV series *M-Squad*; 1979—involved in landmark legal case concerning "palimony." **Awards:** Best Actor Academy Award and Best Actor, Berlin Festival,

Lee Marvin in *Cat Ballou*

for *Cat Ballou*, 1965; Best Foreign Actor, British Academy, for *The Killers* and *Cat Ballou*, 1965. **Died:** Of a heart attack in Tucson, Arizona, 29 August 1987.

Films as Actor:

1951   *You're in the Navy Now* (Hathaway); *Down among the Sheltering Palms* (Goulding) (as Snively); *Diplomatic Courier* (Hathaway) (as an M.P.); *The Duel at Silver Creek* (Siegel) (as Tinhorn Burgess)

1952   *We're Not Married* (Goulding) (as Pinky); *Hangman's Knot* (Huggins) (as Ralph Bainter); *Seminole* (Boetticher) (as Sergeant Magruder); *The Glory Brigade* (Webb) (as Corporal Bowman); *Eight Iron Men* (Dmytryk) (as Mooney)

1953   *Gun Fury* (Walsh) (as Blinky); *The Stranger Wore a Gun* (De Toth) (as Dan Kurth); *The Wild One* (Benedek) (as Chino); *The Big Heat* (Fritz Lang) (as Vince Stone); *The Caine Mutiny* (Dmytryk) (as Meatball); *Gorilla at Large* (Jones)

1954   *The Raid* (Fregonese) (as Lt. Keating); *A Life in the Balance* (Horner) (as the killer); *Bad Day at Black Rock* (Sturges) (as Hector David); *Not as a Stranger* (Kramer) (as Brundage)

1955   *Violent Saturday* (Fleischer) (as Dill); *I Died a Thousand Times* (Heisler) (as Babe Kossuk); *Pete Kelly's Blues* (Webb) (as Al Gannaway); *Shack Out on 101* (Dein); *Pillars of the Sky* (Marshall) (as Sgt. Lloyd Carractart); *Seven Men from Now* (Boetticher) (as Big Masters); *The Rack* (Laven) (as Captain John Miller)

1956   *Attack!* (Aldrich) (as Colonel Bartlett); *Raintree County* (Dmytryk) (as Orville "Flash" Perkins)

1957   *The Missouri Traveler* (Hopper) (as Tobias Brown)

1961   *The Comancheros* (Curtiz) (as Tully Crow); **The Man Who Shot Liberty Valance** (Ford) (as Liberty Valance)

1962   *Donovan's Reef* (Ford) (as Boots Gilhooley)

1963   *Sergeant Ryker* (Kulik—for TV) (title role); *The Killers* (Siegel) (as Charlie)

1964   *Ship of Fools* (Kramer) (as Bill Tenny)

1965   *The Professionals* (Brooks) (as Fardan); *Cat Ballou* (Silverstein) (as Tim Strawn/Kid Shelleen)

1966   *The Dirty Dozen* (Aldrich) (as Major Reisman)

1967   *Point Blank* (Boorman) (as Walker)

1968   *Hell in the Pacific* (Boorman) (as the American); *Tonight Let's All Make Love in London* (Whitehead) (as himself); *Paint Your Wagon* (Logan) (as Ben Rumson)

1969   *Monte Walsh* (Fraker) (title role)

1971   *Pocket Money* (Rosenberg) (as Leonard); *Prime Cut* (Ritchie) (as Nick Devlin)

1972   *The Emperor of the North Pole* (*Emperor of the North*) (Aldrich) (as A Number 1)

1973	*The Iceman Cometh* (Frankenheimer) (as Hickey); *The Spikes Gang* (Fleischer) (as Harry Spikes)
1974	*The Klansman* (Young) (as the sheriff)
1975	*Shout at the Devil* (Hunt) (as Flynn O'Flynn)
1976	*The Great Scout and Cathouse Thursday* (*Big Sam*) (Taylor) (as Sam Longwood)
1978	*Avalanche Express* (Robson) (as Colonel Harry Wargrave); *The Big Red One* (Fuller) (as Sgt. Possum)
1980	*Death Hunt* (Hunt) (as Sgt. Edgar Millen)
1982	*Gorky Park* (Apted) (as Jack Osborne)
1983	*Canicule* (*Dog Day*) (Boisset) (as Jimmy Cobb)
1985	*The Dirty Dozen—The Next Mission* (McLaglen—for TV)
1986	*The Delta Force* (Golan) (as Col. Nick Alexander)

Publications

By MARVIN: articles—

Interview, in *Playboy* (Chicago), January 1969.
Interview with Bruno Villien and J. S. Sabria, in *Cinématographe* (Paris), January 1984.
Interview with Allan Hunter, in *Films and Filming* (London), April 1984.

On MARVIN: book—

Zec, Donald, *Marvin: The Story of Lee Marvin*, London, 1979.

On MARVIN: articles—

Ciné Revue (Paris), 5 February 1981 and 15 September 1983.
Obituary, in *Variety* (New York), 2 September 1987.
Obituary, in *Films and Filming* (London), November 1987.

*   *   *

Lee Marvin was one of the greatest practitioners of minimalist American screen acting. He made a memorable appearance in Fritz Lang's *The Big Heat*, playing a sadistic gangster who scorches Gloria Grahame's face with a pot of hot coffee, making Jimmy Cagney's grapefruit assault on Mae Clarke look like a mere chilly caress. This early, shocking role displayed a vicious side to Marvin's screen personality which continued to simmer just under the surface, and occasionally to erupt, throughout his career.

Marvin is primarily known for his aggressive action roles, many directed by such stalwarts of the American cinema as John Ford, Don Siegel, Robert Aldrich, and Sam Fuller. His screen persona can be described as cold, but with the capacity for sudden, brutal heat. His pale hair, icy blue-gray eyes, and stony face, in later films craggy but no less cruel, added force to his screen image. Like other minimalist actors (Bronson, Eastwood, Norris), Marvin's characters are most frequently verbally terse and emotionally recondite. His roles are often the embodiment of an exaggerated "macho" ideal: tough men seemingly devoid of feelings or vulnerability, figures often impenetrable and remote to movie audiences.

He has played villains, as well as heroes, in war films (*Hell in the Pacific*, *The Big Red One*), in Westerns (*The Man Who Shot Liberty Valance*, *The Professionals*), and in gangster films (*The Killers*, *Prime Cut*). Often in these genre films, Marvin is less a full-bodied character than a one-dimensional force projecting the director's attitude towards violence, revenge, authority, or heroism. In *Point Blank* he gives a shuddering performance as a man betrayed by his gangster cohorts. As the frozen center of this jumpy, cold, modernist film,

Marvin portrays a character so emotionally dead that not even murderous revenge can bring him back to life.

Most critics agree that Marvin's other great performances are in *The Dirty Dozen*, as a hard-nosed major unable to conceal his basic decency and fairness, and *Cat Ballou*, a comic tour de force for which he won his only Academy Award. He received excellent notices for his performance as Hickey in the film of Eugene O'Neill's *The Iceman Cometh*; critic Stanley Kaufmann thought it better than Jason Robard's stage version. More recently, a small but effective performance in *Gorky Park* (where he gently closes a woman's eyes before he blows her away) showed he had lost none of his chilly power.

Marvin's screen and television career prospered in the 1950s. His TV series *M-Squad* was a big hit from 1957-60. The success of *M-Squad* boosted his stock with film producers, and in the 1960s Marvin's career hit its stride. He did his best work and achieved his greatest popularity during this period. His career faltered in the 1970s when a younger generation of actors emerged; moviegoers went to see "the new Eastwood film" as they had gone to see his movies a decade earlier. Aside from the powerful screen presence he brought to the movies, Lee Marvin's career can also be seen as a bridge, the cinematic link between the tough guys of the 1930s and 1940s (Cagney, Bogart) and the minimalist heroes of the 1970s and 1980s.

—Joanne Abrams

THE MARX BROTHERS

Nationality: American. **Chico. Born:** Leonard Marx in New York City, 22 March 1891 (some sources say earlier). **Family:** Married Betty Harp, 1912; one daughter. **Harpo. Born:** Adolph (later used the name Arthur) Marx in New York City, 23 November 1893 (some sources say earlier). **Family:** Married Susan Fleming, 1936, four adopted children. **Groucho. Born:** Julius Marx in New York City, 2 October 1890 (some sources say 1895). **Family:** Married 1) Ruth Johnson, 1920 (divorced 1942), one daughter and one son; 2) Kay Marvis Gorcey, 1945 (divorced 1951), one daughter; 3) Eden Hartford, 1954 (divorced 1969). **Zeppo. Born:** Herbert Marx in New York City, 25 February 1901. **Family:** Married 1) Marion Benda, 1927 (divorced), one son; 2) Barbara Blakely, 1959 (divorced 1973). A fifth brother, **Gummo**, born Milton Marx, was involved in some of the early show business career.
Career: Chico, Harpo and Groucho all entered vaudeville as singers; Groucho toured with a "girls" singing group; 1910s—their mother formed the vaudeville act The Three Nightingales, later The Four Nightingales, incorporating the brothers; they left vaudeville for the music stage, 1920s; 1925—first big success with Broadway show *The Cocoanuts* (film version in 1929); 1933—Zeppo left the group to become a theatrical agent and a manufacturer of aircraft parts; 1934—Chico and Groucho appeared in radio show *Flywheel, Shyster and Flywheel*; 1940s—both Chico and Harpo appeared with their own bands; 1943-44—Groucho in radio show *The Pabst Blue Ribbon Show*; 1947-58—Groucho hosted radio quiz *You Bet Your Life*, also TV version, 1950-58; 1948—Groucho's play, *Time for Elizabeth*, written with Norman Krasna, produced on Broadway; 1950-51—Chico in TV series *The College Bowl*; 1962—Groucho in TV series *Tell It to Groucho* and toured in one-man show *An Evening with Groucho*, 1972. **Awards:** (Groucho): Cannes Festival Special Award, 1972; Honorary Oscar, "in recognition of his brilliant creativity and for the unequalled achievements of the Marx Brothers in the art of motion picture comedy," 1973. **Died:** Chico—11 October 1961; Harpo—28 September 1964; Groucho—19 August 1977; Zeppo—13 December 1979.

Films as Actors:

1925   *Too Many Kisses* (Sloane) (Harpo only)
1929   *The Cocoanuts* (Florey and Santley) (Groucho as Mr. Hammer, Harpo as Harpo, Chico as Chico, and Zeppo as Jamison)
1930   *Animal Crackers* (Heerman) (Groucho as Capt. Jeffrey T. Spaulding, Harpo as the Professor, Chico as Signor Emanuel Ravelli, and Zeppo as Horatio Jamison)
1931   *Monkey Business* (McLeod) (as stowaways)
1932   *Horse Feathers* (McLeod) (Groucho as Prof. Quincey Adams Wagstaff, Harpo as Pinky, Chico as Barovelli, and Zeppo as Frank Wagstaff)
1933   *Duck Soup* (McCarey) (Groucho as Rufus T. Firefly, Harpo as Pinkie, Chico as Chicolini, and Zeppo as Bob Rolland)
1935   *A Night at the Opera* (Wood) (Groucho as Otis B. Driftwood, Harpo as Tomasso, and Chico as Fiorello)
1937   *A Day at the Races* (Wood) (Groucho as Dr. Hugo Z. Hackenbush, Harpo as Stuffy, and Chico as Toni)
1938   *Room Service* (Weiter) (Groucho as Gordon Miller, Harpo as Faker Englund, and Chico as Harry Binelli)
1939   *At the Circus* (Buzzell) (Groucho as J. Cheever Loophole, Harpo as Punchy, and Chico as Antonio Pirelli)
1940   *Go West* (Buzzell) (Groucho as S. Quentin Quale, Harpo as Rusty Panello, and Chico as Joseph Panello)
1941   *The Big Store* (Reisner) (Groucho as Wolf J. Flywheel, Harpo as Wacky, and Chico as Ravelli)
1946   *A Night in Casablanca* (Mayo) (Groucho as Ronald Kornblow, Harpo as Rusty, and Chico as Corbaccio)
1947   *Copacabana* (Green) (Groucho as Lionel L. Devereaux)
1949   *Love Happy* (Miller) (Groucho as Sam Grunion, Harpo as Harpo, and Chico as Faustino the Great)
1950   *Mr. Music* (Haydn) (Groucho as himself)
1951   *Double Dynamite* (Cummings) (Groucho as Emil J. Kech)
1952   *A Girl in Every Port* (Erskine) (Groucho as Benny Linn)
1957   *Will Success Spoil Rock Hunter?* (*Oh! For a Man!*) (Tashlin) (Groucho as surprise guest); *The Story of Mankind* (Irwin Allen) (Groucho as Peter Minuit, Harpo as Isaac Newton, and Chico as Monk)
1968   *Skidoo* (Preminger) (Groucho as "God")

Publications

By MARX BROTHERS: books—

Beds by Groucho Marx, New York, 1930.
Many Happy Returns by Groucho Marx, New York, 1942.
Groucho and Me by Groucho Marx, New York, 1959.
Harpo Speaks!, with Rowland Barber, New York, 1961.
Memoirs of a Mangy Lover by Groucho Marx, New York, 1963.
The Groucho Letters: Letters from and To by Groucho Marx, New York, 1967.
The Groucho Marx Scrapbook, with Richard J. Anobile, New York, 1973.
The Groucho File: An Illustrated Life, Indianapolis, 1976.

By MARX BROTHERS: articles—

"Groucho Writes," in *Take One* (Montreal), no. 11, 1968.
Interview with Groucho Marx, in *Take One* (Montreal), January 1970.
"Alias Julius Henry Marx," interview with Groucho by J. Adamson in *Take One* (Montreal), December 1975.

On MARX BROTHERS: books—

Crichton, Kyle, *The Marx Brothers*, New York, 1951.

Marx, Arthur, *Life with Groucho*, New York, 1954.
Zimmerman, Paul, and Burt Goldblatt, *The Marx Brothers and the Movies*, New York, 1968.
Eyles, Allen, *The Marx Brothers: Their World of Comedy*, New York, 1969.
Anobile, Richard, *Why a Duck?: Visual and Verbal Gems from the Marx Brothers Movies*, New York, 1971.
Marx, Arthur, *Son of Groucho*, New York, 1972.
Adamson, Joseph, *Groucho, Harpo, Chico, and Sometimes Zeppo: A History of the Marx Brothers and a Satire on the Rest of the World*, New York, 1973.
Chesler, Judd, *Toward a Surrealistic Film Aesthetic, with an Investigation into the Elements of Surrealism in the Marx Brothers and Jean Vigo*, Ann Arbor, Michigan, 1977.
Chandler, Charlotte, *Hello, I Must Be Going: Groucho and His Friends*, New York, 1978.
Mast, Gerald, *The Comic Mind: Comedy and the Movies*, Chicago, revised edition, 1979.
Arce, Hector, *Groucho*, New York, 1979.
Marx, Maxine, *Growing Up with Chico*, Englewood Cliffs, New Jersey, 1980.
Alion, Yves, *Les Marx Brothers*, Paris, 1985.
Marx, Arthur, *My Life with Groucho: A Son's Eye View*, New York, 1988.

On MARX BROTHERS: articles—

"Horse Feathers," in *Time* (New York), 15 August 1932.
Rowland, R., "American Classic," in *Hollywood Quarterly*, April 1947 (reprinted in *Penguin Film Review* (London), September 1948).
Perelman, S. J., "The Winsome Foursome," in *Show* (Hollywood), November 1961.
Gili, J.-A., and others, "Sur les Marx Brothers," in *Ecran* (Paris), January 1972.
Stone, E., "Groucho and Adolf; or, The Summer of 1941," in *Journal of Popular Film* (Bowling Green, Ohio), Summer 1973.
Ghezzi, E., "I fratelli Marx nelle strutture del sogno," in *Filmcritica* (Rome), October-December 1973.
Schippers, K., "'We Were Brothers Long before Warner!' Groucho Marx," in *Skoop* (Amsterdam), September 1977.
Passek, J.-L., "Groucho Marx," in *Cinéma* (Paris), November 1977.
Thomson, D., "Groucho Marx: A Retrospective," in *Take One* (Montreal), November 1977.
Calman, M., "Perelman in Cloudsville," in *Sight and Sound* (London), Autumn 1978.
"Marx Brothers Issue" of *Avant-Scène du Cinéma* (Paris), April 1983.
Winokur, Mark, "'Smile, Stranger': Aspects of Immigrant Humor in the Marx Brothers' Humor," in *Literature/Film Quarterly* (Salisbury, Maryland), July 1985.
Mossis, C.D., "The Ithyphallus as Lacanian Signifier in the Marx Brothers Comedies," in *Film Criticism* (Meadville, Pennsylvania), Fall 1987.

On MARX BROTHERS: musical—

Minnie's Boys by Arthur Marx and Robert Fisher, produced on Broadway, 1970.

*   *   *

The Marx Brothers' irreverent brand of humor has been described as surrealistic, absurdist, and anarchic. Consistently anti-authoritarian, their films mock serious institutions and professions, figures of authority, and "high art," with special abuse reserved for anyone deemed pompous, rich, or respectable. For example, *Horse Feathers* ridicules

American colleges, *Duck Soup* takes jabs at governmental officials and international relations, and *A Night at the Opera* lambastes opera and its rich patrons. At their best, the Brothers not only run circles around figures of authority, but also undermine Hollywood film conventions and the authority of language, from official institutional language with its specialized jargon to everyday language ordinarily taken for granted. They have influenced countless filmmakers, comedians, authors, and playwrights.

The Brothers' individual comic personae were established early in their careers and remained consistent: Groucho's sardonic punster, Chico's immigrant with a phony Italian accent who never comprehends social conventions but creates his own logical alternatives, and Harpo's devious mischief-maker who never speaks but communicates brilliantly with facial expressions and props. Two other brothers, Zeppo and Gummo, participated in their vaudeville acts, with Zeppo continuing as a straight man in their first five films before quitting to become a Hollywood agent. Margaret Dumont joined their vaudeville act and remained a regular cast member during their film careers, always playing the role of a rich dowager.

Vaudeville provided the Brothers with the opportunity to develop their personae and their unique way of relating to one another. First as solo performers and then together as a team, the Brothers perfected their vaudeville skits by improvising in response to the exigencies of each audience. Their first two films were actually vaudeville routines adapted for the screen. Even after relinquishing the vaudeville circuit for film careers, the Brothers continued to improvise around their scripts. For *A Night at the Opera* and *A Day at the Races*, they refined their film scenarios by testing them before live audiences. Vaudeville exerted the strongest influence on the Brothers' comedic styles; its quick pace and reliance on visual combined with verbal gags were integral to their development. Other important influences were silent films (especially Chaplin) and the scriptwriters who worked with them over the years.

Working in the film industry gradually altered the Marx Brothers' comedy, a process that some commentators have interpreted as one of restraining the more confrontational aspects of their humor. Their earlier films are generally considered to be their best. In *Monkey Business*, for example, the Brothers are stowaways on an ocean liner, which they terrorize with their pranks before trying to get through Customs with Maurice Chevalier imitations. *Duck Soup* is considered by many to be their finest, most irreverent film, but it also led to a split from Paramount, their first producer, due to the film's poor box-office performance and to changes in Paramount's administration. Set in the fictional country of Freedonia, *Duck Soup* casts Groucho as

The Marx Brothers: Groucho, Harpo and Chico

the country's intransigent president, Rufus T. Firefly, who insults everyone, whether friend or foe, and capriciously launches a war that he declines to end because "I've paid a month's rent on the battlefield."

After their switch to MGM, the Brothers' films began to soften their barbed wit. *A Night at the Opera* and *A Day at the Races*, their first two MGM releases, were their most financially successful films and displayed some memorable zaniness. In *A Night at the Opera* Harpo and Chico get the orchestra to play "Take Me Out to the Ballgame" during the overture to *Il trovatore*, Groucho sells popcorn in the aisles, Harpo and Chico join the action on stage while Groucho yells "boogie boogie," and they raise and lower inappropriate backdrops behind the confused singers. Nevertheless, under the guidance of Irving J. Thalberg, the Brothers were restrained by more rigid plots and by serious romantic subplots involving young lovers faced with obstacles to their happiness. Placed within the confines of having to help the romantic couples, who were spared from mockery, the Brothers' humor lost some of its all-inclusiveness. Musical interludes became standard elements as well, and while Groucho's singing, Chico's piano playing, and Harpo's harp playing exhibited talented horseplay, other musical performers tended to plod.

Their films following Thalberg's death in 1936 became increasingly formulaic while still displaying some outstanding comic moments. Hollywood of the 1930s, with its Production Code and Wall Street bosses, was not conductive to unleashed anti-authoritarian humor. Following *Love Happy*, their last film, the Brothers went their separate ways, but all three continued to perform: Groucho as host of a quiz show, *You Bet Your Life*, on radio and television, and Chico and Harpo as guests on televised variety shows.

A few elements in the Marx Brothers films are disturbing, such as the ethnic stereotypes and the limited roles for women characters who exist solely as the objects of the Brothers' jokes and lechery. Ultimately, the Marx Brothers' humor can be characterized as good satirical fun. Rather than construct a vision of a better society, the Brothers ridicule an immutable society before becoming integrated into the world of success by the happy endings. Their genius lies in casting fresh light on social mores by undermining conventional manifestations of seriousness.

—Claudia Springer

MASINA, Giulietta

Nationality: Italian. **Born:** Giulia Anna Masina in San Giorgio di Piano, 22 February 1920 (other sources say 1921 or 25 October 1920). **Education:** Attended the University of Rome. **Family:** Married the director Federico Fellini, 1943 (died 1993). **Career:** 1939—professional stage debut in Wilder's *Felice Viaggio*, Rome; worked as radio actress; acted with the University of Rome dramatic group: in the university's production of *Angelica*, with Marcello Mastroianni, 1948; 1946—film debut in *Paisà*; 1952—appeared in minor role in her first film directed by Fellini, *Lo sceicco bianco*; this led to critically acclaimed performances in *La strada*, 1954, *Nights of Cabiria*, 1956, and *Juliet of the Spirits*, 1965, all for Fellini; late 1960s through mid-1980s—in semi-retirement, appearing in infrequent Italian TV productions, and host of Italian radio show *Open Letters to Giulietta Masina*, 1966-69; 1985—movie comeback; 1986—swansong with *Ginger and Fred*. **Awards:** Best Actress, Cannes Festival, for *Nights of Cabiria*, 1957; also Italian Nastro d'argento Awards for Best Actress, 1957 and 1985-6, and for Best Supporting Actress, 1948-49 and 1950-51; Italian Grolle d'oro Award for Best Actress, 1957-58. **Died:** Of cancer, in Rome, 23 March 1994.

Films as Actress:

1946   *Paisà* (*Paisan*) (Rossellini) (bit role)
1948   *Senza pietà* (*Without Pity*) (Lattuada) (as Marcella)
1951   *Luci del varietà* (*Variety Lights*; *Lights of Variety*) (Lattuada and Fellini) (as Melinda Amour); *Persiane chiuse* (*Behind Closed Shutters*) (Comencini) (as Pippo); *Europa '51* (*The Greatest Love*) (Rossellini) (as Passerotto); *Cameriera bella presenza offres* (Pastina)
1952   *Lo sceicco bianco* (*The White Sheik*) (Fellini) (as Cabiria)
1953   *Donne proibite* (*Angels of Darkness*; *Forbidden Women*) (Amato); *Cento anni d'amore* (De Felice); *Ai Margini della Metropoli*
1954   *La strada* (*The Road*) (Fellini) (as Gelsomina); *Via Padova 46* (*Lo Scocciatore*) (Bianchi)
1955   *Il bidone* (*The Swindle*; *The Swindlers*) (Fellini) (as Iris); *Buonanotte . . . avvocato!* (Bianchi) (as Carla Santi)
1956   *Le notti di Cabiria* (*Nights of Cabiria*; *Cabiria*) (Fellini) (as Cabiria)
1958   *Fortunella* (de Filippo); *Nella città l'inferno* (*And the Wild, Wild Women*; *Hell in the City*) (Castellani) (as Lina)
1959   *Jons und Erdme* (Käutner)
1960   *La Grande Vie* (*Das kunstseidene Mädchen*; *La gran vita*) (Duvivier)
1965   *Giulietta degli spiriti* (*Juliet of the Spirits*) (Fellini) (title role)
1967   *Non stuzzicate la zanzara* (*Don't Tease the Mosquito*) (Wertmuller)
1969   *The Madwoman of Chaillot* (Forbes) (as Gabrielle, the Madwoman of Sulpice)
1985   *Frau Holle* (Jakubisco) (title role); *Perinbaba* (Jakubisco) (as Perinbaba/Mrs. Winter)
1986   *Ginger e Fred* (*Ginger and Fred*) (Fellini) (as Ginger/Amelia Bonetti)
1991   *Aujourd'Hui Peut-Etre . . .* (*A Day to Remember*)

Publications

By MASINA: books—

Il diario degli altri, Torino, 1975.
Giulietta Masina (interviews with Tullio Kezich), Bologna, 1991.

By MASINA: article—

Interview with O. Volta, in *Positif* (Paris), September 1985.

On MASINA: book—

Kezich, Tullio, *Giulietta Masina (la Chaplin mujer)*, Valencia, 1985.

On MASINA: articles—

Current Biography 1958, New York, 1958.
Wolf, W., "Italy's Movie Greats," in *Cue*, 6 November 1965.
Kast, P., "Giulietta and Federico," in *Cahiers du Cinéma in English*, no. 5, 1966.
Neubourg, M., and O. Dazat, "Ginger and Fred," in *Cinématographe* (Paris), January 1986.
Barabas, K., and others, "Fellinirol," in *Filmkultura* (Budapest), vol. 25, no. 6, 1989.
Harrysson, K., "Ett livsode ristat I ansiktet," in *Chaplin* (Stockholm), vol. 34, no. 2, 1992.
Obituary in *New York Times*, 24 March 1994.

*   *   *

Giulietta Masina in *La strada*

Although she attained a virtually mythic status during the 1950s and 1960s, as the symbolic center of such films as *La strada* and *Juliet of the Spirits*, Giulietta Masina's performances are seldom discussed apart from the considerable directorial achievements of her noted husband, Federico Fellini.

Before she became the focus of his autobiographical outpourings, she was a highly regarded actress. She made her debut in Roberto Rossellini's *Paisà* in 1946 and, two years later, won the Italian film critics' award for best supporting actress in *Senza pietà*. Collaborating with Fellini in films of the early 1950s such as *Luci del varietà* and *Lo sceicco bianco*, she shaped a gamine screen persona often compared to Chaplin's little tramp. Some reviewers have criticized her for simply conveying the superficial feelings and sentimentality on which Fellini's slick and mechanical stories were based, but one need only view her performance in *La strada* to see a sensitivity and subtlety of expression that are anything but mechanical. Again, in *Nights of Cabiria*, she delivered a restrained but heartrending interpretation of a naive prostitute.

During the 1960s her husband elevated her to the status of resident muse in the Fellini household, and her filmic presence in those years cannot be accounted for by her performance alone. Fellini's films of that decade, particularly the masterpiece *Juliet of the Spirits*, obsessively examine the relationship of Masina to her husband's midlife artistic crises and achievements. Unfortunately, because these films so thoroughly established her as the feminine side of Fellini's psyche, other directors did not offer her the variety of roles deserved by her talent.

As a result, Masina effectively went into semiretirement following 1969's *The Madwoman of Chaillot*, appearing only on Italian radio and television for the next decade and a half. She returned to the screen in 1985, but her swansong occurred the following year in Fellini's nostalgic *Ginger and Fred*, which paired her with Fellini's favorite actor, Marcello Mastroianni, in a highly praised performance. Masina and Fellini became more reclusive after the release of *Ginger and Fred*, both falling into ill health. Fellini died in October 1993, the day after the couple celebrated their 50th wedding anniversary; an increasingly despondent Masina succumbed to cancer less than five months later.

—Stephen L. Hanson, updated by David E. Salamie

MASON, James

Nationality: British. **Born:** James Neville Mason in Huddersfield, Yorkshire, 15 May 1909. **Education:** Marlborough College; Cambridge University, degree in architecture. **Family:** Married 1) Pamela Kellino, 1941 (divorced 1964), daughter: Portland, son: Morgan; 2) Clarissa Kaye, 1971. **Career:** Acted with Hull and Croydon repertory companies after leaving university; 1933—West End stage debut in *Gallows Glorious*; 1935—film debut in *Late Extra*; contract with Fox-British; 1938—formed own production company Gamma Productions;

James Mason in *Odd Man Out* **courtesy of The Rank Organisation Plc**

1946—Broadway debut in *Bathsheba*; 1949—U.S. film debut in *Caught*; 1954-55—host of the TV series *Lux Video Theatre*, and in mini-series *Jesus of Nazareth*, 1977, and *A.D.*, 1985. 1978—on Broadway in *The Faith Healer*. **Awards:** London Evening Standard Special Award, 1977; Acting Award, UK Critics, for *The Shooting Party*, 1985. **Died:** Of heart attack in Lausanne, Switzerland, 27 July 1984.

Films as Actor:

1935 *Late Extra* (Parker) (as Jim Martin)
1936 *Twice Branded* (Rogers) (as Henry Hamilton); *Troubled Waters* (Parker) (as John Merriman); *Prison Breaker* (Brunel) (as Bunny Barnes); *Blind Man's Bluff* (Parker) (as Stephen Neville); *The Secret of Stambov* (*The Spy in White*) (Marton) (as Larry); *Fire over England* (Howard) (as Ambassador)
1937 *The Mill on the Floss* (Whelan) (as Tom Tulliver); *Catch as Catch Can* (*Atlantic Episode*) (Kellino) (as Robert Leyland); *The Return of the Scarlet Pimpernel* (Schwartz) (as Jean Tallion)
1939 *I Met a Murderer* (Kellino) (as Mark Warrow)
1941 *This Man Is Dangerous* (*The Patient Vanishes*) (Huntington) (as Mick Cardby); *Hatter's Castle* (Comfort) (as Dr. Renwick); *The Night Has Eyes* (*Terror House*) (Arliss) (as Stephen)
1942 *Alibi* (Hurst) (as André Laurent); *Secret Mission* (French) (as Raoul de Carnot); *Thunder Rock* (Boulting) (as Streeter)
1943 *The Bells Go Down* (Dearden) (as Ted Robbins); *The Man in Grey* (Arliss) (as Marquis de Rohan); *They Met in the Dark* (Lamec) (as Commander Heritage); *Candlelight in Algeria* (George King) (as Alan Thurston)
1944 *Fanny by Gaslight* (*Man of Evil*) (Asquith) (as Lord Manderstoke); *Hotel Reserve* (Hanbury, Comfort, and Greene) (as Peter Vadassy)
1945 *A Place of One's Own* (Knowles) (as Mr. Smedhurst); *They Were Sisters* (Crabtree) (as Geoffrey); *The Seventh Veil* (Bennett) (as Nicholas); *The Wicked Lady* (Arliss) (as Capt. Jackson)
1947 **Odd Man Out** (Reed) (as Johnny McQueen); *The Upturned Glass* (Huntington) (as Michael Joyce)
1949 *Caught* (Ophüls) (as Larry Quinada); *Madame Bovary* (Minnelli) (as Gustave Flaubert); *The Reckless Moment* (Ophüls) (as Marlon Donnelly); *East Side, West Side* (LeRoy) (as Brandon Bourne)
1950 *One Way Street* (Fregonese) (as Doc Matson)
1951 *Pandora and the Flying Dutchman* (Lewin) (as Hendrick van der Zee); *The Desert Fox* (Hathaway) (as Rommel)
1952 *Five Fingers* (Mankiewicz) (as Cicero); *Lady Possessed* (Spier and Kellino) (as Del Palma); *The Prisoner of Zenda* (Thorpe) (as Rupert); "Secret Sharer" ep. of *Face to Face* (Brahm) (as Captain)
1953 *Charade* (Kellino—for TV) (as The Murderer, Major Linden, and Jonah Watson, + co-sc); *The Man Between* (Reed) (as Ivo Kern); *The Story of Three Loves* (Reinhart) (as Charles Coutray); *The Desert Rats* (Wise) (as Rommel); *Botany Bay* (Farrow) (as Capt. Paul Gilbert); *Julius Caesar* (Mankiewicz) (as Brutus)
1954 *Prince Valiant* (Hathaway) (as Sir Brack); **A Star Is Born** (Cukor) (as Norman Maine); *20,000 Leagues under the Sea* (Fleischer) (as Capt. Nemo)
1956 *Forever Darling* (Hall) (as Guardian Angel); *Bigger than Life* (Ray) (as Ed Avery); *Island in the Sun* (Rossen) (as Maxwell Fleury)
1958 *Cry Terror* (Stone) (as Jim Molner); *The Decks Ran Red* (Stone) (as Capt. Edwin Rummill)

1959 **North by Northwest** (Hitchcock) (as Phillip Vandamm); *Journey to the Center of the Earth* (Levin) (as Prof. Oliver Lindenbrook); *A Touch of Larceny* (Hamilton) (as Comm. Max Easton)
1960 *The Trials of Oscar Wilde* (*The Man with the Green Carnation*) (Hughes) (as Sir Edward Carson)
1961 *The Marriage-Go-Round* (Lang) (as Paul Delville); *Escape from Zahrain* (Neame) (as Johnson)
1962 **Lolita** (Kubrick) (as Humbert Humbert); *Hero's Island* (Stevens) (as Jacob Webber, + pr); *Tiara Tahiti* (Kotcheff) (as Capt. Brett Aimsley)
1964 *Finchè dura la tempesta* (*Torpedo Bay*) (Frend) (as Blayne); *The Fall of the Roman Empire* (Anthony Mann) (as Timonedes); *The Pumpkin Eater* (Clayton) (as Bob Conway)
1965 *Lord Jim* (Brooks) (as Gentleman Brown); *Genghis Khan* (Levin) (as Kam Ling); *Les Pianos mécaniques* (*The Uninhibited*) (Bardem) (as Regnier)
1966 *The Blue Max* (Guillermin) (as Count von Klugermann); *Georgy Girl* (Narizzano) (as James Leamington); *The Deadly Affair* (Lumet) (as Charles Dobbs)
1967 *Stranger in the House* (Rouve) (as John Lawyer); *The London Nobody Knows* (Cohen) (as narrator)
1968 *Duffy* (Parrish) (as Charles Calvert); *Mayerling* (Young) (as Emperor Franz Josef)
1969 *Age of Consent* (Powell) (as Bradley Monahan); *The Sea Gull* (Lumet) (as Trigorin)
1970 *Spring and Port Wine* (Hammond) (as Rafe Crompton)
1971 *L'uomo dalle due ombre* (*Cold Sweat*) (Young) (as Ross)
1972 *Bad Man's River* (Martin) (as Montero)
1973 *Child's Play* (Lumet) (as Malley); *The Last of Sheila* (Ross) (as Philip); *The Mackintosh Man* (Huston) (as Wheeler)
1974 *Frankenstein: The True Story* (Smight—for TV) (as Dr. Polidari); *11 Harrow House* (Avarian) (as Watts); *The Marseille Contract* (Parrish) (as Brizard)
1975 *Great Expectations* (Hardy) (as Magwich); *Mandingo* (Fleischer) (as Maxwell)
1978 *Heaven Can Wait* (Beatty and Henry) (as Mr. Jordan); *The Boys from Brazil* (Schaffner) (as Eduard Seibert)
1979 *Murder by Decree* (Clark) (as Dr. Watson); *Salem's Lot* (Hooper—for TV); *The Passage* (Thompson) (as Professor Bergson)
1980 *Ffolkes* (*North Sea Hijack*; *Assault Force*) (McLagen) (as Admiral Brinsden)
1982 *The Verdict* (Lumet) (as Ed Concannon); *Evil under the Sun* (Hamilton) (as Odell Gardener); *Ivanhoe* (Camfield—for TV)
1983 *Yellowbeard* (Damski)
1984 *The Assisi Underground* (Ramati)
1985 *Dr. Fischer of Geneva* (Lindsay-Hogg—for TV) (title role); *The Shooting Party* (Bridges) (as Sir Randolph Nettleby)

Film as Director:

1954 *The Child*

Publications

By MASON: books—

The Cats in Our Lives, with Pamela Kellino, 1949.
Before I Forget, London, 1981.

By MASON: articles—

Interview with I. McAsh, in *Films* (London), November 1981.

Interview, in *Time Out* (London), 4 March 1983.
Interview with P. Carcassonne, in *Cinématographe* (Paris), May 1983.
Interview with D. Rabourdin, in *Cinéma* (Paris), September 1984.

On MASON: books—

Hirschorn, Clive, *The Films of James Mason*, London, 1975.
De Rosso, Diana, *James Mason: A Personal Biography*, Oxford, 1989.
Haver, Ronald, *A Star Is Born: The Making of the 1954 Movie and Its 1983 Restoration*, London, 1989.
Morley, Sheridan, *James Mason: Odd Man Out*, London, 1989.

On MASON: articles—

Canby, Vincent, "The Performer vs the Role: Catherine Deneuve and James Mason," in *The Movie Star*, edited by Elisabeth Weis, New York, 1981.
Buckley, Michael, "James Mason," in *Films in Review* (New York), May 1982; see also issues for June/July and November 1982.
Obituary, in *Variety* (New York), 1 August 1984.
Buckley, Michael, "A Final Tribute: James Mason 1904-1984," in *Films in Review* (New York), October 1984.
Cieutat, Michel, "James Mason, Bigger than Stars," in *Positif* (Paris), November 1984.

* * *

James Mason spent a few years on the stage before turning in the late 1930s to the screen. He appeared in a series of quota films in which his dark, somewhat sinister good looks qualified him as a type of ruthless but romantic villain. He was seen in such bravura romances as *The Man in Grey*, *The Seventh Veil*, and *The Wicked Lady*, successful at the box office and distinguished chiefly for his star quality. Apart from a supporting role in *Thunder Rock*, his first important film was Carol Reed's *Odd Man Out*. As Johnny, the Irish-partisan being hunted through the streets of Belfast by both the police and by those seeking to aid him, he achieved the feat of playing a leading character who is mute through much of the action, an odyssey of fear and terror spanning some 24 hours.

It was on the strength of this performance that Mason went to Hollywood, embarking on what proved a busy if somewhat directionless career in which his considerable talent and unusual screen personality were too often wasted in indifferent films. Mason's screen image was of the highly educated English gentleman, with a soft touch of Irish in his speech, and the capacity to reveal a cruel streak, especially in his relations with women. Always an impressive presence, he twice appeared effectively as Field-Marshal Rommel, in *The Desert Fox* and *The Desert Rats*, and was a thoughtful but unexciting Brutus in Joseph Mankiewicz's filming of *Julius Caesar*. In the early 1950s he also returned to the romantic costume genre in which he had originally made his name, playing Rupert of Hentzau in *The Prisoner of Zenda* and bringing sinister authority to the part of Captain Nemo in *20,000 Leagues under the Sea*.

Mason gave one of his best performances in George Cukor's 1954 version of *A Star Is Born*, as husband of the star, Judy Garland. He returned to England to make *The Man Between* and a three-part television film, *Charade*, which he co-scripted. Mason's other notable roles include the charmingly well-bred villain in Hitchcock's *North by Northwest*, his appearance in Ken Hughes's *The Trials of Oscar Wilde*, and Humbert Humbert in Kubrick's *Lolita*, in which Mason is for once the victim. Unfortunately, the censorship of the day required that the eroticism of the relationship between middle-aged man and nymphette be somewhat muted.

—Roger Manvell

MASSEY, Raymond

Nationality: American. **Born:** Raymond Hart Massey in Toronto, Ontario, Canada, 30 August 1896; became U.S. citizen, 1944. **Education:** Attended Appleby School, Oakville, Ontario; Canadian Officers' Training Corps, University of Toronto, 1915; Balliol College, Oxford. **Military Service:** Canadian Field Artillery, 1915-19; wounded at Ypres, 1916; Canadian Army, 1942: major. **Family:** Married 1) the stage designer Peggy Fremantle (divorced), son: Geoffrey; 2) the actress Adrianne Allen, 1929 (divorced 1939), children: Daniel and Anna; 3) Dorothy Ludington Whitney, 1939. **Career:** About 1920—worked in family business, Massey-Harris Agricultural Implement Company, Toronto; 1922—moved to London to pursue stage career: debut in Eugene O'Neill's *In the Zone*; 1926—with Allan Wade and George Carr, began managing Everyman Theatre, Hampstead; 1931—New York debut in title role of Norman Bel Geddes's production of *Hamlet*; talking film debut as Sherlock Holmes in *The Speckled Band* (may have appeared in English silents as early as 1923); 1934—returned to New York in his own production of *The Shining Hour*; continued alternating between London and New York theaters; worked in both British and American films; 1939—created title role in Robert Sherwood's play *Abe Lincoln in Illinois*, and in film version, 1942; long-term contract with Warners; 1952—his play *The Hanging Judge* presented in London; 1961-66—played Dr. Gillespie in TV series *Dr. Kildare*. **Died:** In Los Angeles, 29 July 1983.

Films as Actor:

1931   *The Speckled Band* (Raymond) (as Sherlock Holmes)
1932   *The Old Dark House* (Whale) (as Philip Waverton); *The Face at the Window* (Hiscott) (as Paul le Gros)
1935   *The Scarlet Pimpernel* (Korda) (as Chauvelin)
1936   ***Things to Come*** (Menzies) (as John and Oswald Cabal); *Fire over England* (William K. Howard) (as Philip of Spain)
1937   *Under the Red Robe* (Seastrom) (as Cardinal Richelieu); *Dreaming Lips* (Czinner) (as Miguel del Vayo); *The Prisoner of Zenda* (Cromwell) (as Black Michael); *The Hurricane* (Ford) (as Gov. Eugene De Laage)
1938   *The Drum* (*Drums*) (Zoltan Korda) (as Prince Ghul)
1939   *Black Limelight* (Stein) (as Peter Charrington)
1940   *Abe Lincoln in Illinois* (*Spirit of the People*) (Cromwell) (title role); *Santa Fe Trail* (Curtiz) (as John Brown)
1941   *Dangerously They Live* (Florey) (as Dr. Ingersoll); *49th Parallel* (*The Invaders*) (Powell) (as Andy Brock)
1942   *Desperate Journey* (Walsh) (as Maj. Otto Baumeister); *Reap the Wild Wind* (Cecil B. DeMille) (as King Cutler)
1943   *Action in the North Atlantic* (Lloyd Bacon) (as Capt. Steve Jarvis)
1944   *Arsenic and Old Lace* (Capra) (as Jonathan Brewster); *The Woman in the Window* (Fritz Lang) (as Frank Lalor)
1945   *God Is My Co-Pilot* (Florey) (as General Chennault); *Hotel Berlin* (Godfrey) (as Arnim Von Dahnwitz)
1946   ***A Matter of Life and Death*** (*Stairway to Heaven*) (Powell and Pressburger) (as Abraham Farlan)
1947   *Mourning Becomes Electra* (Dudley Nichols) (as Brig. Gen. Ezra Mannon); *Possessed* (Bernhardt)
1949   *The Fountainhead* (King Vidor) (as Gail Wynand); *Roseanna McCoy* (Reis) (as Old Randall McCoy)
1950   *Barricade* (Godfrey) (as Boss Kruger); *Challenge—Science against Cancer* (Parker—doc) (as narrator); *Dallas* (Heisler); *Chain Lightning* (Heisler) (as Leland Willis)
1951   *Sugarfoot* (Marin) (as Jacob Stint); *Come Fill the Cup* (Gordon Douglas) (as John Ives); *David and Bathsheba* (Henry King) (as Nathan the Prophet)

1952	*Carson City* (De Toth) (as "Big Jack" Davis)
1953	*The Desert Song* (Humberstone) (as Yousseff)
1955	*Battle Cry* (Walsh) (as Gen. Snipes); *Seven Angry Men* (Warren) (as John Brown); *Prince of Players* (Dunne) (as Junius Brutus Booth); ***East of Eden*** (Kazan) (as Adam Trask)
1956	*The True Story of the Civil War* (Stoumen) (as narrator)
1957	*Omar Khayyam* (*The Life, Loves and Adventures of Omar Khayyam*) (Freeman) (as the Shah); *The Naked Eye* (Stoumen) (as narrator); rerelease of 1927 *Uncle Tom's Cabin* (as narrator); *Mayerling* (Litvak—for TV) (as prime minister)
1958	*The Naked and the Dead* (Walsh) (as General Cummings)
1960	*The Great Imposter* (Mulligan) (as Abbott Donner) (as Abbott Donner)
1961	*The Fiercest Heart* (Sherman) (as Willem); *The Queen's Guards* (Powell) (as Capt. Fellowes)
1962	*Jacqueline Kennedy's Asian Journey* (Seltzer) (as narrator)
1963	*How the West Was Won* (Ford) (as Abraham Lincoln); *Report on China* (as narrator)
1969	*Mackenna's Gold* (J. Lee Thompson) (as the Preacher)
1971	*The President's Plane Is Missing* (Duke—for TV)
1972	*All My Darling Daughters* (Rich—for TV) (as Matthew Cunningham)
1973	*My Darling Daughters' Anniversary* (Pevney—for TV) (as Matthew Cunningham)

Publications

By MASSEY: books—

When I Was Young, Boston, 1976.
A Hundred Different Lives: An Autobiography, London, 1979.

On MASSEY: book—

Richards, Jeffrey, *Swordsmen of the Screen: From Douglas Fairbanks to Michael York*, London, 1977.

On MASSEY: articles—

Current Biography 1946, New York, 1946.
Stein, Jeanne, "Raymond Massey," in *Films in Review* (New York), August/September 1963.
Obituary in *New York Times*, 31 July 1983.
Obituary in *Variety* (New York), 3 August 1983.
O'Toole, Lawrence, "A Gentleman of Character," obituary in *Maclean's* (Toronto), 8 August 1983.

* * *

The thunder and the lightning became Raymond Massey more than any other screen actor of his day. His booming, authoritative voice, grand manner, and tall, broad-shouldered body were made for command, and Massey exploited them with skill and intelligence.

Prophets and driven men were his meat. He hunted the Scarlet Pimpernel with the full messianic fury of the Terror, and as Black Michael intrigued so ruthlessly for the throne of Zenda that his hatchet man Rupert of Hentzau said admirably, "There are times in the presence of your majesty when I feel myself an amateur." His monocled arrogance as Black Michael made him a natural to play villainous Nazi generals during World War II, which he did, most memorably, in Raoul Walsh's *Desperate Journey*. His capacity for personal menace was also used by Frank Capra in *Arsenic and Old Lace*, a lumbering Massey replacing Boris Karloff, who created the role on stage of the murderous Brewster brother who is constantly mistaken for Karloff himself.

Massey's definitive Abraham Lincoln, and his preaching abolitionist John Brown capture the charismatic personalities of men who know they are born to change history. He played both roles twice on film, Lincoln in *Abe Lincoln in Illinois* and *How the West Was Won* and Brown in *Santa Fe Trail* and *Seven Angry Men*. He was no less convincing in *Things to Come* as John and Oswald Cabal, members of a dynasty committed to a new order of scientific government. The last shot in the Korda fantasy, with Massey intoning a technocratic prayer over scenes of the first moon voyage—"All the universe or nothingness. . . . Which shall it be?"—makes him seem a kind of god.

Michael Powell liked Massey's radical Canadian belligerence, and used the actor three times: as the hero of the War of Independence who prosecutes David Niven in the heavenly court of *A Matter of Life and Death*; more briefly, but to good effect, as a Canadian soldier in *49th Parallel*, stuck in a railroad truck with fleeing Nazi Eric Portman, whom he gleefully demolishes; and last in *The Queen's Guards*, Powell's ill-fated attempt at a comeback following the critical disaster of *Peeping Tom,* which almost wrecked the director's career.

Massey rose to the demands of even the fruitiest melodrama. His newspaper magnate in *The Fountainhead*, as pathologically pigheaded as the Gary Cooper with whom he competes for Patricia Neal; the patriarch of the acting Booth clan in *Prince of Players*, and the father of James Dean in *East of Eden*; even his roles as routine heavy in a dozen 1950s Westerns and period films never lost the sense that, as he spoke, thunder rumbled somewhere beyond the horizon. That thunder was relatively muted, however, in his final screen appearances in the sitcomlike made-for-television movies *All My Darling Daughters* and *My Darling Daughters' Anniversary*, where he played second fiddle to star Robert Young's harried judge whose four vivacious daughters get married, and subsequently celebrate their first wedding anniversaries, on the same day.

—John Baxter, updated by John McCarty

MASTROIANNI, Marcello

Nationality: Italian. **Born:** Fontana Liri, 28 September 1924. **Family:** Married the actress Flora Carabella, 1950, daughter: Barbara; one daughter by the actress Cathérine Deneuve. **Career:** Worked in his father's carpentry shop; put to work by the Germans drawing maps during World War II, and imprisoned in a forced-labor camp, 1943-44; 1944—cashier for Eagle Lion Films, Rome; also acted with the University of Rome dramatic group: in the university's production of *Angelica*, with Giulietta Masina, 1948; 1948—hired by Visconti for his theatrical troupe; also acted in radio plays; 1949—first substantial film role in *Una domenica d'agosto*; 1966—formed independent film production company, Master Films; 1984—on stage in *Tchin Tchin*, Paris. **Awards:** Best Foreign Actor, British Academy, for *Divorce, Italian Style*, 1963; and for *Yesterday, Today, and Tomorrow*, 1964; Best Actor, Cannes Festival, for *Drama della gelosia*, 1970, and for *Oci ciornie*, 1986; also Italian Nastro d'argento Awards for Best Actor, 1954-55, 1957, 1960, 1961, 1985-86, and 1987-88; Italian Grolle d'oro Awards for Best Actor, 1954-55, 1975-76, and 1977-78; Lifetime Achievement Award, European Film Awards, 1988. **Address:** c/o Giovanna Cau, Via Maria Adelaide 8, Rome 1-00196, Italy.

Films as Actor:

1938	*Marionette* (Gallone)
1940	*La colonna di ferro* (Blasetti)
1942	*Una storie d'amore* (Camerini); *I bambini ci guardano* (De Sica)

1947   *I miserabili* (Freda)
1950   *A Tale of Five Cities* (Marcellini); *Una domenica d'agosto* (Emmer); *Vita da cani* (*A Dog's Life*) (Steno and Monicelli); *Cuori sul mare* (Bianchi); *Contro la legge* (Calzavara)
1951   *Parigi e sempre Parigi* (Emmer); *Atto di accusa* (Gentilomo)
1952   *Sensualità* (*Barefoot Savage*) (Fracassi) (as Carlo); *La ragazze di Piazza di Spagna* (*Three Girls from Rome*) (Emmer); *Tragico ritorno* (Faraldo); *Penne nere* (Biancoli); *Gli eroi della domenica* (Camerini); *Il viale della speranza* (Risi); *Febbre di vivere* (Gora)
1953   *Non e mai troppe tardi* (Ratti); *Lulu* (Cerchio)
1954   *Cronache di poveri amanti* (Lizzani); *Giorni d'amore* (De Santis); *Casa Ricordi* (*House of Ricordi*) (Gallone) (as Donizetti); *La muta di Portici* (Ansoldi); *La principessa delle Canarie* (Moffa and Serrano de Osma)
1955   *Peccato che sia una canaglia* (*Too Bad She's Bad*) (Blasetti) (as Paolo); *La belle mugnaia* (*The Miller's Beautiful Wife*) (Camerini) (as Luca); *Tam-Tam Mayumbe* (Napolitano)
1956   *Il bigamo* (*The Bigamist*) (Emmer); *La fortuna di essere donna* (*Lucky to Be a Woman*) (Blasetti) (as Corrado)
1957   *Pari e figli* (*A Tailor's Maid*) (Monicelli); *Il momento più bello* (*The Most Wonderful Moment*) (Emmer); *Le notti bianche* (*White Nights*) (Visconti) (as Mario); *La ragazza della Salina* (Cap); *Il medico e lo stregone* (Monicelli)
1958   *I soliti ignoti* (*Big Deal on Madonna Street*) (Monicelli) (as Tiberio); *Racconti d'estate* (*Love on the Riviera*; *Summer Tales*) (Francolini) (as police inspector); *Un ettaro di cielo* (Casadio); *Amore e guai* (Dorigo)
1959   *Il legge* (*La Loi*; *Where the Hot Wind Blows*) (Dassin) (as engineer); *Il nemico di mia moglie* (*My Wife's Enemy*) (Puccini) (as Marco); *Tutti innamorati* (Orlandini); *Ferdinando I, re di Napoli* (Franciolini)
1960   ***La dolce vita*** (Fellini) (as Marcello Rubino); *Il bell'Antonio* (Bolognini) (as Antonio Magnano); *Adua e la compagne* (*Love à la Carte*) (Pietrangeli) (as Piero)
1961   *La notte* (*The Night*) (Antonioni) (as Giovanni Pontano); *Fantasmi a Roma* (*Ghosts of Rome*) (Pietrangeli); *L'assassino* (*The Lady Killer of Rome*) (Petri) (as Nello Poletti); *Divorzio all'italiana* (*Divorce, Italian Style*) (Germi) (as Ferdinando Cefalù)
1962   *La Vie privée* (*A Very Private Affair*) (Malle) (as Fabio); *Cronaca familiare* (*Family Diary*) (Zurlini) (as Enrico)
1963   ***Otto e mezzo*** (*8 1/2*) (Fellini) (as Guido Anselmi); *I compagni* (*The Organizer*) (Monicelli) (as Prof. Sinigaglia); *Il giorno più corto* (*The Shortest Day*) (Corbucci) (as himself); *Ieri, oggi, domani* (*Yesterday, Today, and Tomorrow*) (De Sica) (as Carmine/Renzo/Augusto Rusconi)
1964   *Matrimonio all'italiana* (*Marriage Italian Style*) (De Sica) (as Domenico Soriano)
1965   *Casanova '70* (Monicelli) (as Maj. Andrea Rossi-Colombetti); *La decima vittima* (*The Tenth Victim*) (Petri) (as Marcello Polletti); *Oggi, domani, dopodomani* (Ferreri, De Filippo, and Salce—eps. released as *Kill the Other Sheik* and *The Man with the Balloons*); *L'uomo dai cinque palloni* (Ferreri—revised version of ep. in previous film)
1966   *The Poppy Is Also a Flower* (Young) (as Insp. Mosca); *Spara forte, piu forte ... non capisco* (*Shoot Loud, Louder ... I Don't Understand*) (De Filippo) (as Alberto Saporito); *Io, io, io ... e gli altri* (*I, I, I ... and the Others*) (Blasetti)
1967   *Questi fantasmi* (*Ghosts—Italian Style*) (Castellani); *La straniero* (*The Stranger*) (Visconti) (as Arthur Meursault)
1968   *Diamonds for Breakfast* (Morahan); *Gli amanti* (*A Place for Lovers*) (De Sica) (as Valerio)
1969   *I girasoli* (*Sunflower*) (De Sica) (as Antonio); *Block-Notes di un regista* (*A Director's Notebook*) (Fellini—for TV)

1970   *Leo the Last* (Boorman) (as Leo); *Drama della gelosia* (*The Pizza Triangle*) (Scola) (as Oreste); *Giochi particolari* (Indovina)
1971   *La moglie del prete* (*The Priest's Wife*) (Risi); *Permette? Rocco Papaleo* (*Rocco Papaleo*) (Scola); *Ca n'arrive qu'aux autres* (*It Only Happens to Others*) (Trintignant); *Scipione detto anche l'africano* (Magni); *Fellini Roma* (Fellini)
1972   *La cagna* (*Liza*) (Ferreri); *Che?* (*What?*; *Diary of Forbidden Dreams*) (Polanski); *Mordi e fuggi* (Risi)
1973   *Rappresaglia* (*Massacre in Rome*) (Cosmatos); *Salut l'artiste* (Robert); ***La Grande Bouffe*** (*Blow-Out*) (Ferreri); *L'Evènement le plus important que l'homme a marché sur la lune* (*A Slightly Pregnant Man*) (Demy)
1974   *Touchez pas le femme blanche* (Ferreri); *Poopsie* (Capitani) (as Charlie the Collar); *Allonsanfan* (P. and V. Taviani) (as Fulvio Imbriani)
1975   *Per le antiche scale* (*Down the Ancient Stairs*) (Bolognini); *C'eravamo tanto amati* (*We All Loved Each Other So Much*) (Scola); *La pupa del gangster* (Capitani)
1976   *La donna della domenica* (*The Sunday Woman*) (Comencini); *La divina creatura* (*The Divine Nymph*) (Griffi) (as Michele Barra); *Todo modo* (Petri); *Culastrice nobile veneziano* (Mogherini); *Signore e signori buonanotte* (Comencini and others)
1977   *Una giornata speciale* (*A Special Day*) (Scola); *Mogliamante* (*Wifemistress*) (Vicario) (as Luigi DeAngelis)
1978   *Doppio delitto* (Steno); *Bye Bye Monkey* (Ferreri); *Cosi come sei* (*Stay as You Are*) (Lattuada) (as Giulio); *Ciao maschio* (Ferreri); *Le mani sporche* (Petri—for TV); *Fatto di sangue fra due uomini per causa di una vedova* (*Blood Feud*; *Revenge*) (Wertmüller) (as Lawyer Spallone)
1979   *L'ingorgo* (*Bottleneck*; *Traffic Jam*) (Comencini); *La città delle donne* (*City of Women*) (Fellini) (as Snaporaz); *Shimmy Lugano e tarantelle e vino* (Wertmüller); *Giallo napoletano* (Corbucci); *La terrazza* (Scola) (as Luigi)
1980   *Fantasma d'amore* (*Ghost of Love*) (Risi) (as Nino); *Oopsie Poopsie* (Capitani) (as Charlie the Collar)
1981   *La pelle* (*The Skin*) (Cavani) (as Curzio Malaparte); *La Nuit de Varennes* (*That Night in Varennes*) (Scola) (as Casanova)
1982   *Oltre la porta* (*Beyond the Door*) (Cavani); *La Storia di Piera* (*The Story of Piera*) (Ferreri) (as Lorenzo, Piera's father); *Le Général de l'armée morte* (Tovoli)
1983   *Gabriela* (Barreto) (as Nacib Saad)
1984   *Enrico IV* (*Henry IV*) (Bellochio) (title role)
1985   *Maccheroni* (*Macaroni*) (Scola) (as Antonio Jasiello); *La due vita di Mattia Pascal* (*The Two Lives of Mattia Pascal*) (Monicelli) (as Mattia); *I soliti ignoti vent' anni dopo* (*Big Deal on Madonna Street ... Twenty Years Later*) (Todini) (as Tiberio)
1986   *Ginger e Fred* (*Ginger and Fred*) (Fellini) (as Fred); *O Melissokomos* (*The Beekeeper*) (Angelopoulos) (as Spyros); *Melissokomos Patheni—O Alles Mythos* (*A Beekeeper Dies—The Other Tale*) (Papilou)
1987   *Intervista* (*The Interview*) (Fellini) (as himself); *Oci ciornie* (*Dark Eyes*) (Mikhalkov) (as Romano); *Globalny Pressing* (Boronin)
1988   *Miss Arizona* (Sandor) (as Rozsnyai); *Vacanza* (Guillot); *O Samba* (Constantini); *Il mitico Gianluca* (Lazotti)
1989   *Splendor* (*The Last Movie*) (Scola) (as Jordan)
1990   *Che ora e?* (*What Time Is It?*) (Scola) (as Father); *Stanno tutti bene* (*Everybody's Fine*) (Tornatore) (as Matteo Scuro); *Verso sera* (Archibugi) (as Prof. Bruschi)
1991   *To Meteoro Vima tou Pelargou* (*Le Pas Suspendu de la Cigogne*; *Suspended Step of the Stork*) (Angelopoulos) (as the vanished politician); *La Voleur d'enfants* (*The Children Thief*) (as Bigua/the Colonel)

Marcello Mastroianni

1992   *Used People* (Kidron) (as Joe); *A Fine Romance* (*Tchin-Tchin*)
        (Saks) (as Cesareo Gramaldi)
1993   *Do Eso No Se Habla* (*I Don't Want to Talk about It*) (Bemberg)
        (as Ludovico D'Andrea); *1, 2, 3, Soleil* (*1, 2, 3, Sun*) (Blier)
        (as Constantin); *El Ladron de Ninos* (De Chalonge)
1994   *Ready to Wear* (*Prêt-a-Porter*) (Altman) (as Sergei); *La Vera
        Vita di Antonio H.* (*The True Life of Antonio H.*) (Monteleone)
        (as himself)
1995   *Les Cent et une Nuits* (*A Hundred and One Nights*) (Varda) (as
        the Italian friend); *Par dela les nuages* (*Aldila della nuvole*;
        Beyond the Clouds) (Antonioni and Wenders) (as Maestro)
1996   *Trois Vies et une Seule Mort* (Raul Ruiz); *Sostiene Pereira*
        (*Afirma Pereira*; *Pereira Declares*) (Roberto Faenza)

Publications

By MASTROIANNI: articles—

"Interview: Marcello Mastroianni," in *Playboy* (Chicago), July 1965.
Interview with A. Lacombe, in *Ecran* (Paris), July-August 1975.
Interview with M. Chion, in *Cahiers du Cinéma* (Paris), February 1986;
    see also April 1987.
Interview with Gregory Speck, in *Interview* (New York), November
    1987.
Interview with Allan Hunter and Alan Stanbrook, in *Films and Film-
    ing* (London), August 1988.
"Marcello? Marcello? Mar-cell-ooo!," interview with Marcelle
    Clements, in *Premiere* (New York), June 1991.

On MASTROIANNI: books—

Fava, Claudio, and Matilde Hochkofler, *Marcello Mastroianni*, Rome,
    1980.
Labrid, Herve, *Marcello Mastroianni*, Paris, 1980.
Hochkofler, Matilde, *Marcello Mastroianni: il gioco del cinema*, Rome,
    1992.
Dewey, Donald, *Marcello Mastroianni: His Life and Art*, Secaucus, New
    Jersey, 1993.

On MASTROIANNI: articles—

Current Biography 1963, New York, 1963.
Canby, Vincent, "Sophia Loren and Marcello Mastroianni," in *The
    Movie Star*, edited by Elisabeth Weis, New York, 1981.
Neubourg, M., and O. Dazat, "Ginger and Fred," in *Cinématographe*
    (Paris), January 1986.
Howell, Georgina, "The 35-Second Seduction; Movie Legend Marcello
    Mastroianni Shows Just How It's Done," *M Inc.*, April 1991.
Bachmann, Gideon, "Marcello Mastroianni and the Game of Truth,"
    Film Quarterly, Winter 1992.

*   *   *

Since the 1950s, Marcello Mastroianni has been Italy's favorite
leading man, as well as one of his country's finest actors. Until the
emergence of Gérard Depardieu on the international film scene,
Mastroianni also was the most famous European actor in America.
This renown is symbolized by his earning the astonishing total of
three Academy Award nominations (for *Divorce, Italian Style*, *A Special Day*, and *Dark Eyes*), quite an accomplishment for an actor working in non-English-language films.

After World War II, Mastroianni joined Luchino Visconti's repertory company, which was bringing to Italy a new kind of theater and
novel ideas of staging. The young actor played Mitch in *A Streetcar

Named Desire, Happy in *Death of a Salesman*, Stanley Kowalski in
Visconti's second staging of *Streetcar*, and roles in Chekhov's *Three
Sisters* and *Uncle Vanya*. At this time, he also was appearing on-
screen, with his roles gradually increasing in importance. Mastroianni
permanently sealed his stardom in Italy in 1957, playing a timid clerk
whose love is not reciprocated, in Visconti's *White Nights*. Three years
later, he graduated to international superstardom with his role as the
jaded, world-weary journalist in Fellini's *La dolce vita*, a film that
changed the look and direction of Italian cinema. Since then, he has
remained a major box-office draw around the world.

From the 1960s on, Mastroianni regularly worked with the top
Italian and French filmmakers (including Antonioni, Malle, and De
Sica, in addition to Fellini and Visconti), in some of the highest profile
foreign-language releases (beginning with *Il bell'Antonio* in 1960 and
The Night in 1961). While he was to become known for playing Latin
lover roles, his characters often were far more complexly drawn.
They were not one-dimensional pretty boys; rather, beneath their
handsome exteriors they were lazy, world-weary, and doubt-ridden.
But Mastroianni also was adept at spoofing the image of the Casanova,
as he did so memorably in *Divorce, Italian Style*. With waxed moustache and glossy, matted-down hair, he plays a married man who
schemes to rid himself of his witless and unattractive wife so that he
may marry his sexy young cousin. He further played against his image
in *A Special Day*, cast as a lonely homosexual. Earlier on, he had
displayed a light touch for comedy in *Big Deal on Madonna Street*,
playing the exasperated member of an inept group of burglars. His
seemingly detached air was perfectly suited to satire as well, as he
demonstrated in films as diverse as *The Tenth Victim*, *Allonsanfan*, and
City of Women. Yet he remained perfectly capable of playing highly
dramatic roles, as he did so well in *The Organizer*, cast as a highborn
but now indigent professor who becomes involved in union organizing
activities in turn-of-the-twentieth-century Italy.

Mastroianni was the logical choice to star as Fellini's film director/
alter-ego in *8½*; one cannot imagine any other actor in this role. But
he is perhaps best remembered for his pairings with Sophia Loren,
with whom he was cast in the deliciously funny three-part sex farce
Yesterday, Today, and Tomorrow and the equally amusing sex comedy
Marriage Italian Style. In both these films, Mastroianni's masculinity
blends perfectly with Loren's exuberant earthy personality. After these
successes, the two appeared together in the less-successful drama *Sunflower*, playing a couple separated by war, and *A Special Day*, in which
Mastroianni's homosexual and Loren's oppressed wife come together
on the day in 1938 when Hitler was cheered on the streets of Rome
during his visit to Mussolini.

In the latter stages of his career, Mastroianni has continued to take
serious dramatic roles. For instance, in *The Suspended Step of the
Stork*, he is quietly poignant as an obscure man who may have once
been an important Greek politician who had disappeared years earlier.
The actor has been especially effective in roles as aging romantics. In
Used People, one of his few English-language films, he plays a man
who begins courting the woman he has admired from afar for two
decades. Sometimes he is romantically entangled with women young
enough to be his daughter (or even granddaughter). In *I Don't Want to
Talk about It*, he is a suave bachelor who becomes involved with two
women, a young dwarf and her physically attractive but obnoxiously
manipulative mother. In both of these films, Mastroianni is never
anything less than charming.

He has also played the senior citizen who simply looks back on his
past. In *Everybody's Fine*, he is an elderly man who is absorbed in his
memories, and who travels through Italy to call on his five adult
children. In *Dark Eyes*, he gives a tour-de-force performance as a once
young and idealistic aspiring architect, who married a banker's daughter, fell into a lifestyle of afternoon snoozes and philandering, and
proved incapable of holding onto what was important to him. His on-
screen presence has also been directly linked to his earlier screen

characterizations. In *Ready to Wear*, he is reunited with Sophia Loren, and at one point in the scenario, she recreates her famous steamy striptease sequence from *Yesterday, Today, and Tomorrow*. Loren is as beguiling as she had been 30 years earlier but Mastroianni is no longer the attentive young lover, so Sophia's seductive moves only put him to sleep. Mastroianni's appearance in two of Fellini's final features is especially sentimental. *Ginger and Fred* is sweetly nostalgic for its union of Mastroianni and Giulietta Masina, two of the maestro's then-aging but still vibrant stars of the past. In *Intervista*, he appears as himself with Anita Ekberg, with whom he had starred decades before in *La dolce vita*. Mastroianni's entrance is especially magical; the sequence in which he and Ekberg (who, he remarks, he has not seen since making *La dolce vita*) observe their younger selves in some famous clips from that film is wonderfully nostalgic.

In his long and prolific career, Mastroianni almost singlehandedly defined the contemporary type of Latin lover, then proceeded to redefine it a dozen times and finally parodied it and played it against type. He remains unsurpassed as one of the most universally popular and beloved of all motion picture personalities.

—Elaine Mancini, updated by Rob Edelman

MATTHAU, Walter

Nationality: American. **Born:** Walter Matthau (some sources say Matthow or Matuschanskayasky) in New York City, 1 October 1920. **Education:** Attended the New School for Social Research Dramatic Workshop under Irwin Piscator. **Military Service:** U.S. Air Force as a radioman-gunner, 1942-45. **Family:** Married 1) Grace Johnson, 1948 (divorced 1958), one son and daughter; 2) Carol Marcus Saroyan, 1959, one son: the director Charles Matthau. **Career:** Child actor in New York Yiddish theater; 1946—professional adult stage debut; then worked in summer stock and on Broadway, 1948; later stage work include roles in *Once More, with Feeling*, 1958, *A Shot in the Dark*, 1962, and *The Odd Couple*, 1965, and film version, 1968; 1955—film debut in *The Kentuckian*; 1959—in TV series *Tallahassee 7000*. **Awards:** Best Supporting Actor, Academy Award, for *The Fortune Cookie*, 1966; Best Actor, British Academy, for *Pete 'n' Tillie* and *Charley Varrick*, 1973. **Address:** c/o The Matthau Company, 10100 Santa Monica Boulevard, Suite 2200, Los Angeles, CA 90067, U.S.A.

Films as Actor:

1955 *The Kentuckian* (Lancaster) (as Sam Bodine); *The Indian Fighter* (De Toth) (as Wes Todd)
1956 *Bigger Than Life* (Nicholas Ray) (as Wally Gibbs)
1957 *A Face in the Crowd* (Kazan) (as Mel Miller); *Slaughter on Tenth Avenue* (Laven) (as Al Dahlke)
1958 *King Creole* (Curtiz) (as Maxie Fields); *Voice in the Mirror* (Keller) (as Dr. Leon Karnes); *Onionhead* (Taurog) (as Red Wildoe); *Ride a Crooked Trail* (Hibbs) (as Judge Kyle)
1960 *Strangers When We Meet* (Quine) (as Felix Andrews)
1962 *Lonely Are the Brave* (Miller) (as Sheriff Johnson); *Who's Got the Action?* (Daniel Mann) (as Tony Gagoots)
1963 *Island of Love* (De Costa) (as Tony Dallas); *Charade* (Donen) (as Hamilton Bartholomew/Carson Dyle)
1964 *Ensign Pulver* (Logan) (as Doc); *Fail-Safe* (Lumet) (as Groeteschele); *Goodbye Charlie* (Minnelli) (as Sir Leopold Sartori)
1965 *Mirage* (Dmytryk) (as Ted Caselle)
1966 *The Fortune Cookie* (Wilder) (as Willie Gingrich)

1967 *A Guide for the Married Man* (Kelly) (as Paul Manning)
1968 *The Odd Couple* (Saks) (as Oscar Madison); *The Secret Life of an American Wife* (Axelrod) (as Movie Star "Charlie"); *Candy* (Marquand) (as Gen. Smight)
1969 *Hello, Dolly!* (Kelly) (as Horace Vandergelder); *Cactus Flower* (Saks) (as Julian Winston)
1971 *A New Leaf* (May) (as Henry Graham); *Plaza Suite* (Hiller) (as Sam Noah/Jesse Kiplinger/Roy Hubley); *Kotch* (Lemmon) (title role)
1972 *Pete 'n' Tillie* (Ritt) (as Pete)
1973 *Charlie Varrick* (Siegel) (title role); *The Laughing Policeman* (*An Investigation of Murder*) (Rosenberg) (as Jake Martin)
1974 *The Taking of Pelham One Two Three* (Sargent) (as Garber); *Earthquake* (Robson) (as token drunk); *The Front Page* (Wilder) (as Walter Burns)
1975 *The Sunshine Boys* (Ross) (as Willy Clark); *The Gentleman Tramp* (Patterson—doc) (as narrator)
1976 *The Bad News Bears* (Ritchie) (as Morris Buttermaker)
1978 *House Calls* (Zieff) (as Dr. Charley Nichols); *Casey's Shadow* (Ritt) (as Lloyd Bourdell); *California Suite* (Ross) (as Marvin Michaels)
1979 *Sunburn* (Serafian)
1980 *Little Miss Marker* (Berstein) (as Sorrowful Jones); *Hopscotch* (Neame) (as Miles Kendig); *Portrait of a 60% Perfect Man* (Trescot—doc) (as himself)
1981 *First Monday in October* (Neame) (as Dan Snow); *Buddy Buddy* (Wilder) (as Trabucco)
1982 *I Ought to Be in Pictures* (Ross) (as Herbert Tucker)
1983 *The Survivors* (Ritchie) (as Sonny Paluso)
1985 *Movers and Shakers* (Asher) (as Joe Mulholland)
1986 *Pirates* (Polanski) (as Capt. Thomas Bartholomew Red)
1988 *The Couch Trip* (Ritchie) (as Donald Becker); *Il piccolo diavolo* (*The Little Devil*) (Benigni) (as Maurice)
1990 *The Incident* (Sargent—for TV) (as Harmon Cobb)
1991 *Visitor* (Newman); *JFK* (Stone) (as Sen. Russell Long); *Mrs. Lambert Remembers Love* (Charles Matthau—for TV) (as Clifford)
1992 *Against Her Will: An Incident in Baltimore* (Delbert Mann—for TV) (as Harmon Cobb)
1993 *Dennis the Menace* (Castle) (as Mr. Wilson); *Grumpy Old Men* (Petrie) (as Max Goldman)
1994 *Incident in a Small Town* (Delbert Mann—for TV) (as Harmon Cobb); *I.Q.* (Schepisi) (as Albert Einstein)
1995 *The Grass Harp* (Charles Matthau) (as Judge Cool); *Grumpier Old Men* (Deutch) (as Max Goldman)

Film as Director:

1960 *Gangster Story* (+ ro as Jack Martin)

Publications

By MATTHAU: articles—

"Rumpled Royalty" (excerpt from "The Player - III," *New Yorker*, 4 November 1961), interview with Lillian Ross, in *New Yorker*, 31 May 1993.
"Genius," interview with Karen Duffy, in *Interview* (New York), December 1994.

On MATTHAU: book—

Hunter, Allan, *Walter Matthau*, New York, 1984.

Walter Matthau with Goldie Hawn in *Cactus Flower*

On MATTHAU: articles—

Current Biography 1966, New York, 1966.
Eyles, Allen, "Walter Matthau," in *Focus on Film* (London), Spring 1972.
Photoplay (London), January 1981 and April 1982.
Rubinstein, Leslie, "One Fortunate Cookie," in *American Film* (Washington, D.C.), July-August 1983.

*   *   *

Walter Matthau is one of the motion picture industry's solid, respected character actors. He has more than 40 films to his credit, commencing—after years of acting on the stage, where he honed his craft—with *The Kentuckian* and *The Indian Fighter* in 1955. He is at his beloved best playing comically persnickety characters, generally opposite Jack Lemmon, his longtime co-star.

Early in his career, Matthau displayed his versatility in roles as dissimilar as Mel Miller, the astutely perceptive writer who sees through the sham of cynically manipulative television personality Lonesome Rhodes, in *A Face in the Crowd*; Maxie Fields, the crime boss who menaces Elvis Presley, in *King Creole*; and Sheriff Johnson, the Western lawman who doggedly pursues Kirk Douglas, in *Lonely Are the Brave*. At this stage of his career, Matthau did some extraordinary work in otherwise slight, forgettable films. In the Audie Murphy Western *Ride a Crooked Trail*, he offers a spirited performance as a flamboyant, dipsomaniacal judge.

Matthau did not transcend his status as all-purpose character actor until, in an inspired bit of casting, he and Jack Lemmon played opposite each other in *The Fortune Cookie*. Matthau won an Oscar for his role as a crooked lawyer who fast-talks television cameraman Lemmon into an insurance fraud. In their best pairings, Lemmon and Matthau are cast as opposite character types who are contrasted to comic effect. Perhaps their best film is *The Odd Couple*, with its humor deriving from the contrasting characters of slob-supreme Oscar Madison (a role which Matthau originated on Broadway), and fastidious neatnik Felix Ungar (Lemmon). Over the course of three decades, Matthau and Lemmon have become as famous a team as Tracy and Hepburn and Hope and Crosby. A Matthau-Lemmon-like relationship is the basis of the comedy in *The Sunshine Boys*, in which Matthau and George Burns play two cantankerous former vaudevillains induced into reuniting for a television show.

Matthau has been at his funniest playing the gloriously ornery slob whom you might find sitting across a card table, with cigar in one hand

and beer can in the other as he hangs with his cronies. The comedy is derived from his characters' becoming involved in unlikely situations. In *The Odd Couple*, Matthau's Oscar Madison becomes the roomate of Felix Ungar. In *The Bad News Bears*, Matthau's Morris Buttermaker, another slob-supreme, is coerced into coaching a team of Little League misfits. In these films, he combines a sort of grouchy shiftiness with soul, wit, cunning, nonjudgmental forbearance, and obstinate persistence. Later on in his career, he caricatured this persnickety persona in *Dennis the Menace*, playing the forever-flustered Mr. Wilson.

He also is expert at playing drawing room comedy, cast in roles that in an earlier era would have been tailor-made for Spencer Tracy. In these films, Matthau effectively plays on the tensions between social coexistence and masculine awkwardness. Indeed, in *First Monday in October*, he and co-star Jill Clayburgh, playing Supreme Court justices with contrasting political philosophies, closely replicate a Tracy-Hepburn relationship. In *Plaza Suite*, he offers a tour de force playing three disparate roles, teamed with three different actresses: the jaded, adulterous husband of Maureen Stapleton; a Hollywood producer attempting to seduce ex-girlfriend Barbara Harris; and a father of the bride, married to Lee Grant. He has also played the older man who becomes a romantic object. In *Hello, Dolly!*, he is a brusque self-made man matrimonially targeted by Barbra Streisand. In *Cactus Flower*, he is a defensively overworked dentist targeted by Ingrid Bergman. In *House Calls*, he is a widowed doctor targeted by Glenda Jackson.

In the early 1970s, Matthau had become a top ten box-office star, quite an accomplishment for a craggy-faced actor with an unpolished gait and drooping posture, not to mention his trademark New York snarl. Lemmon, feeling that no film had really tapped Matthau's depths, directed him in *Kotch*, a humanistic comedy in which he plays an irascible grandfather put to pasture by his family. He also appeared in several straight dramatic roles, as cops (*The Laughing Policeman*, *The Taking of Pelham One Two Three*), a stunt pilot-turned-luckless bank robber (*Charley Varick*), and an ex-CIA agent defying official embargoes on his memoirs (*Hopscotch*).

Matthau's better late-career parts have included roles as sage senior citizens. In *I.Q.*, he brings warmth to his role as Albert Einstein, who plays matchmaker for his niece and a garage mechanic. In *The Grass Harp*, directed by his son Charles—who looks like a younger, leaner, less craggier version of his dad—he plays a wizened, widowed retired judge who idles away his hours sitting in his small town's barbershop and drugstore. As the scenario progresses, he comes to share a deeply moving relationship with a gentle-souled maiden aunt. Here, Matthau displays his ability to play tender as well as persnickety, as his character talks of his late wife, and the meaning of love and how difficult and elusive it is to find. These sequences seem to be gifts that a devoted director-son would aspire to present to a beloved actor-father.

—Raymond Durgnat, updated by Rob Edelman

MATURE, Victor

Nationality: American. **Born:** Victor John Mature in Louisville, Kentucky, 29 January 1915. **Education:** Attended George H. Tingley Public School and St. Paul's and St. Xavier's parochial schools, Louisville; St. Joseph's Academy, Bardstown, Kentucky; Kentucky Military Institute, Linden; Spenserian Business School. **Military Service:** U.S. Coast Guard, 1942-45. **Family:** Married 1) the actress Frances Evans, 1938 (divorced 1941); 2) Martha Stephenson, 1941 (divorced 1943); 3) Dorothy Stanford Berry, 1948 (divorced), daughter: Victoria; two other marriages. **Career:** Worked briefly as scissor grinder, in wholesale candy house, and in restaurant business; 1935—attended the Pasadena Community Playhouse drama school; 1936—stage debut in *Paths*

of Glory, and leading role in *Autumn Crocus*, 1937; 1939—film debut in *The Housekeeper's Daughter*; 1940—contract with Hal Roach-MGM; leading role in *One Million B.C.*; 1941—Broadway stage debut in *Lady in the Dark*; 1942—contract with 20th Century-Fox; 1949—successful role as Samson in *Samson and Delilah*; then series of leading roles into the mid-1950s. **Address:** P.O. Box 706, Rancho Santa Fe, CA 92067, U.S.A.

Films as Actor:

1939   *The Housekeeper's Daughter* (Roach) (as Lefty)
1940   *One Million B.C. (Man and His Mate)* (Roach) (as Tumak); *Captain Caution* (Wallace) (as Dan Marvin); *No No Nanette* (Wilcox) (as William)
1941   *Hot Spot (I Wake Up Screaming)* (Humberstone) (as Frankie Christopher/Botticelli); *The Shanghai Gesture* (von Sternberg) (as Dr. Omar)
1942   *Song of the Islands* (Walter Lang) (as Jefferson Harper); *My Gal Sal* (Cummings) (as Paul Dreiser); *Footlight Serenade* (Ratoff) (as Tommy Lundy); *Seven Days' Leave* (Whelan) (as Johnny Grey)
1943   *Show Business at War* (De Rochemont—doc) (as himself)
1946   **My Darling Clementine** (Ford) (as Doc John Holliday)
1947   *Moss Rose* (Ratoff) (as Sir Alexander Sterling); *Kiss of Death* (Hathaway) (as Nick Bianco)
1948   *Fury at Furnace Creek* (Humberstone) (as Cash); *Cry of the City* (Siodmak) (as Lt. Candella)
1949   *Easy Living* (Jacques Tourneur) (as Pete Wilson); *Red, Hot, and Blue* (Farrow) (as Denny James); *Samson and Delilah* (Cecil B. DeMille) (as Samson)
1950   *Wabash Avenue* (Koster) (as Andy Clark); *I'll Get By* (Sale) (cameo role); *Stella* (Binyon) (as Jeff De Marco); *Gambling House* (Tetzlaff) (as Marc Fury)
1952   *The Las Vegas Story* (Stevenson) (as Dave Andrews); *Something for the Birds* (Wise) (as Steve Bennett); *Million Dollar Mermaid (The One-Piece Bathing Suit)* (LeRoy) (as James Sullivan); *Androcles and the Lion* (Erskine) (as Captain)
1953   *Affair with a Stranger* (Rowland) (as Bill Blakely); *The Glory Brigade* (Webb) (as Lt. Sam Prior); *The Robe* (Koster) (as Demetrius); *The Veils of Bagdad* (Sherman) (as Antar)
1954   *Dangerous Mission* (Louis King); *Demetrius and the Gladiators* (Daves) (as Demetrius); *The Egyptian* (Curtiz) (as Horemheb); *Betrayed* (Reinhardt) (as the Scarf)
1955   *Chief Crazy Horse (Valley of Fury)* (Sherman) (title role); *Violent Saturday* (Fleischer) (as Shelley Martin); *The Last Frontier* (Anthony Mann) (as Jed)
1956   *Safari* (Terence Young) (as Ken Duffield); *The Sharkfighters* (Jerry Hopper) (as Lt. Cmdr. Ben Staves); *Zarak* (Terence Young) (title role)
1957   *Interpol (Pickup Alley)* (Gilling) (as Charles Sturgis); *The Long Haul* (Hughes) (as Harry Miller)
1958   *China Doll* (Borzage) (as Cliff Brandon); *No Time to Die (Tank Force)* (Terence Young) (as Sgt. David Thatcher)
1959   *Escort West* (Lyon) (as Ben Lassiter); *The Bandit of Zhobe* (Gilling) (as Kasin Khan); *The Big Circus* (Joseph M. Newman) (as Hank Whirling); *Timbuktu* (Jacques Tourneur) (as Mike Conway)
1960   *Annibale (Hannibal)* (Ulmer and Bragaglia) (title role)
1961   *I tartari (The Tartars)* (Thorpe) (as Oleg)
1966   *Caccia alla volpe (After the Fox)* (de Sica) (as Tony Powell)
1968   *Head* (Rafelson) (as The Big Victor)
1972   *Every Little Crook and Nanny* (Cy Howard) (as Carmine Ganucci)

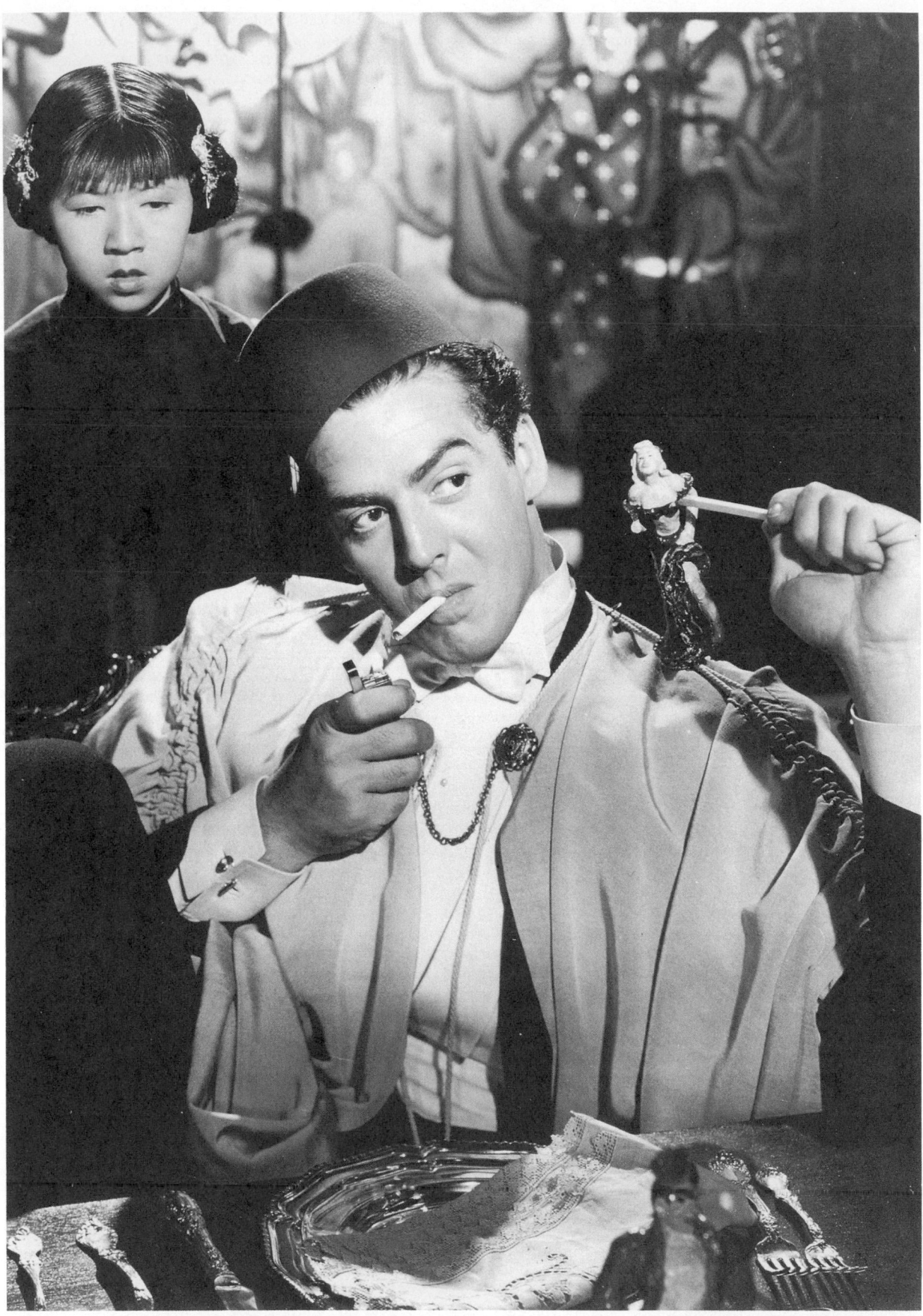

Victor Mature in *The Shanghai Gesture*

1976 *Won Ton Ton, the Dog Who Saved Hollywood* (Winner) (as Nick)
1979 *Firepower* (Winner) (as Harold Everett)
1984 *Samson and Delilah* (Philips—for TV) (as Manoah)

Publications

By MATURE: articles—

Interview with J. Marks, in *Interview* (New York), May 1972.
"Schauspieler I: Victor lernt beten," interview with Delmer Daves, in *Filmkritik* (Munich), January 1975.
Interview in *Ciné Revue* (Paris), 16 June 1983.

On MATURE: book—

Parish, James Robert, and Don E. Stanke, *The Swashbucklers*, New Rochelle, New York, 1976.

On MATURE: articles—

Current Biography 1951, New York, 1951.
TV Times (London), 11-17 February 1982.

*   *   *

Victor Mature had one of the most underrated and misunderstood careers in Hollywood history. Nicknamed "the gorgeous hunk" and ridiculed by the Harvard *Lampoon* (their annual award for worst actor is named for him), Mature nevertheless has earned a permanent place in film history through a series of roles in distinguished movies by major directors. Mature's noteworthy roles include "Doc" Holliday in John Ford's *My Darling Clementine*, the savage hero of Anthony Mann's *The Last Frontier*, the seducer of Joseph von Sternberg's *The Shanghai Gesture*, and the strongman of DeMille's *Samson and Delilah*. (Thirty-five years later, he took the role of Manoah, Samson's father, in a made-for-television remake.) He also brings the appropriate physical characteristics and a relaxed, low-key acting style to excellent, lesser-known films such as Jacques Tourneur's *Easy Living*, Frank Borzage's *China Doll*, and two films noir of the 1940s, Henry Hathaway's *Kiss of Death* and Robert Siodmak's *Cry of the City*. Mature has, in truth, appeared in more films that are revived and respected today than many of his contemporaries whose work was more celebrated at the time.

When Mature came to Hollywood (from a successful Broadway role as, appropriately, a movie star in *Lady in the Dark*), his sexy good looks, open personality, and impressive physique made him an overnight success as a leading man. He was typecast as a persuasive man—a con artist, really—who was crooked, but not really evil, and who had a keen eye for the ladies. His film roles may be separated into three separate genres, all of which utilize this basic persona: (1) escapist musicals and comedies, which emphasize his sense of humor, sex appeal, and flamboyant style (he played leading man to the pinup queens of the 1940s, Betty Grable in *Song of the Islands*, *Footlight Serenade*, and *Wabash Avenue*, and Rita Hayworth in *My Gal Sal*); (2) costume dramas or epics, including Westerns, which emphasized his remarkable physique and florid exaggerated style, suggesting a hero of mythic proportions; and (3) films noir, which implied that his broad smile and obviously Mediterranean good looks hid a violent and passionate nature.

Though Mature was a major name in the 1940s and 1950s he had virtually retired by the early 1960s. His occasional return to the screen found him gracefully lampooning his own image in such films as *After the Fox* and *Head*, the latter a pseudo-hip Bob Rafelson-Jack Nicholson concoction featuring The Monkees, Annette Funicello,

Timothy Carey, Sonny Liston, Frank Zappa, Carol Doda, Ray Nitschke, and Teri Garr. Here, Mature can be found playing the aptly named "Big Victor." In so doing, he proved it was he who best understood the nature of his appeal.

—Jeanine Basinger, updated by Rob Edelman

MAURA, Carmen

Nationality: Spanish. **Born:** Madrid, 1945; greatniece of the politician Antonio Maura. **Education:** Attended University of Madrid. **Family:** Married, 1965 (marriage annulled), two children. **Career:** From mid-1960s—actress in Madrid and on tour, becoming leading actress of the Maria Guerrero Theatre; presenter of TV show *Esta noche*, 1980s. **Awards:** National Prize of Cinematography, Spanish Ministry of Culture, 1988; Goya Award for Best Actress, and European Felix Award for Best Actress, for *Women on the Verge of a Nervous Breakdown*, 1988; European Felix Award for Best Actress, for *¡Ay, Carmela!*, 1990.

Films as Actress:

1977 *Tigres de Papel* (*Paper Tigers*) (Colomo) (as Carmen)
1980 *Pepi, Luci, Bom y otras chicas del montón* (*Pepi, Luci, Bom, and Other Girls on the Heap*) (Almodóvar) (as Pepi); *Aquella Casa en las Afueras* (*That House in the Outskirts*) (Martin)
1983 *Entre Tinieblas* (*Into the Dark*; *The Sisters of Darkness*) (Almodóvar) (as Sister); *Sal Gordo* (*Garbage*) (Colomo); *Chi Trova, un Amico, Trova un Tesoro* (*Who Finds a Friend Finds Treasure*) (Corbucci)
1984 *¿Qué he hecho yo para merecer esto?* (*What Have I Done to Deserve This?*) (Almodóvar) (as Gloria)
1985 *Extramuros* (Picazo); *Se infiel y no mires con quien* (Trueba)
1986 *Matador* (Almodóvar) (as Julia); *Tata Mia* (*Nanny Dear*) (Borau) (as Elvira)
1987 *La Ley del Deseo* (*Law of Desire*) (Almodóvar) (as Tina Quintero)
1988 ***Mujeres al borde de un ataque de nervios*** (*Women on the Verge of a Nervous Breakdown*) (Almodóvar) (as Pepa Marcos); *Baton Rouge* (Moleon) (as Isabel Harris)
1990 *¡Ay, Carmela!* (Saura) (title role)
1991 *Como ser Mujer y no morir en el intento* (*How to Be a Woman and Not Die Trying*) (Belen) (as Carmen); *Chatarra* (as Zabu); *Extramuros* (*The Outskirts*) (Picazo) (as Sister Ana)
1992 *La Reina Anonima* (*The Anonymous Queen*) (Suarez) (as Ana Luz)
1993 *Entre el cielo y la tierra* (*In Heaven as on Earth*; *Sur la terre comme au ciel*) (Hansel) (as María García); *Louis, L'enfant du roi* (*Louis, the Child King*) (Planchon) (as Queen Anne of Austria); *Sombras en una Batalla* (*Shadows in a Conflict*) (Mario Camus) (as Ana)
1994 *Como Ser Infeliz y Disfrutarlo* (*How to Be Miserable and Enjoy It*) (Urbizu) (as Carmen)
1995 *King of the River* (as Carmen Costa); *Una Pareja de Tres* (Verdaguer) (as Ana); *El Paloma Cojo* (De Arminan)
1996 *Tres Desejos* (Luis Galvao Teles)

Publications

By MAURA: articles—

Interview with Elliot Stein, in *Village Voice* (New York), 15 November 1988.

Interview, in *Films and Filming* (London), June 1989.
Interview with Dominic Wells, in *Time Out* (London), 8 May 1991.
"'Taisez-vous les canaris!' Entretien avec Carmen Maura," interview with P. Piazzo, in *Jeune Cinéma*, September/October 1991.

On MAURA: articles—

Lida, David, "Comic Chaos," in *Connoisseur*, March 1991.
Current Biography 1992, New York, 1992.

*   *   *

Simply put, Carmen Maura is Spain's most popular screen actress, and one of her country's most famous and acclaimed international movie stars. But her career remains inexorably linked to that of the director who cast her in some of her best roles, Pedro Almodóvar. If, cinematically speaking, Almodóvar is the prince of *La Movida* (The Movement), a term referring to Spain's burgeoning pop culture in the post-Franco era, then Maura is its undisputed queen.

Maura began her screen career a decade before she first was directed by Almodóvar. She had roles in various films that barely were seen outside Spain, made by such directors as Javier Aguirre, Pilar Muro, Miguel Angel Diaz, and Jaime Bayarri, who are familiar only to the most ardent aficionado of Spanish cinema. She also appeared on Spanish television, for a year even hosting a weekly talk show, *Esta Noche*.

Maura's career was to be inexorably altered upon meeting Almodóvar, then an aspiring director, around the time that both were cast in a stage production of Sartre's *Dirty Hands*. Because of her age—Maura was close to 30 at Franco's demise, and 35 when she first worked with Almodóvar in *Pepi, Luci, Bom, and Other Girls on the Heap*—the director could not cast her as young, self-assured women reaching their prime in a censorship-free society. Her most typical characters came to maturity in a prefeminist, Franco-influenced era, a time in which passion—especially for women—was considered antisocial. The claws of fascism and chauvinism have entrapped them, causing them to be "on the verge of nervous breakdowns." But it now is the time of *La Movida*. Franco is dead. It is the destiny of women to break free from bondage, to defiantly thrust off their shackles, to learn to live for themselves and become their own persons.

While the Maura/Almodóvar heroines struggle with liberation, to the point where they are driven to commit murder or change their sexual preference (or even their sex), they also are deliciously sexy and charmingly off-kilter. And Maura is a perfect presence in Almodóvar's best black comedies, most especially *Women on the Verge of a Nervous Breakdown*, in which she plays a desperate actress who responds in a most outrageous manner upon learning, by a message on her telephone answering machine, that she has been abandoned by her lover; and *What Have I Done to Deserve This?*, cast as an off-the-wall housewife who undergoes various trials and crises in a contemporary Madrid that is depicted as a repressive hell of pavement, bricks and stones, and prisonlike apartment buildings.

Sexuality, and a woman's reaction to the sexual brutality of men at a time of sexual and political liberation, is at the core of most Maura/

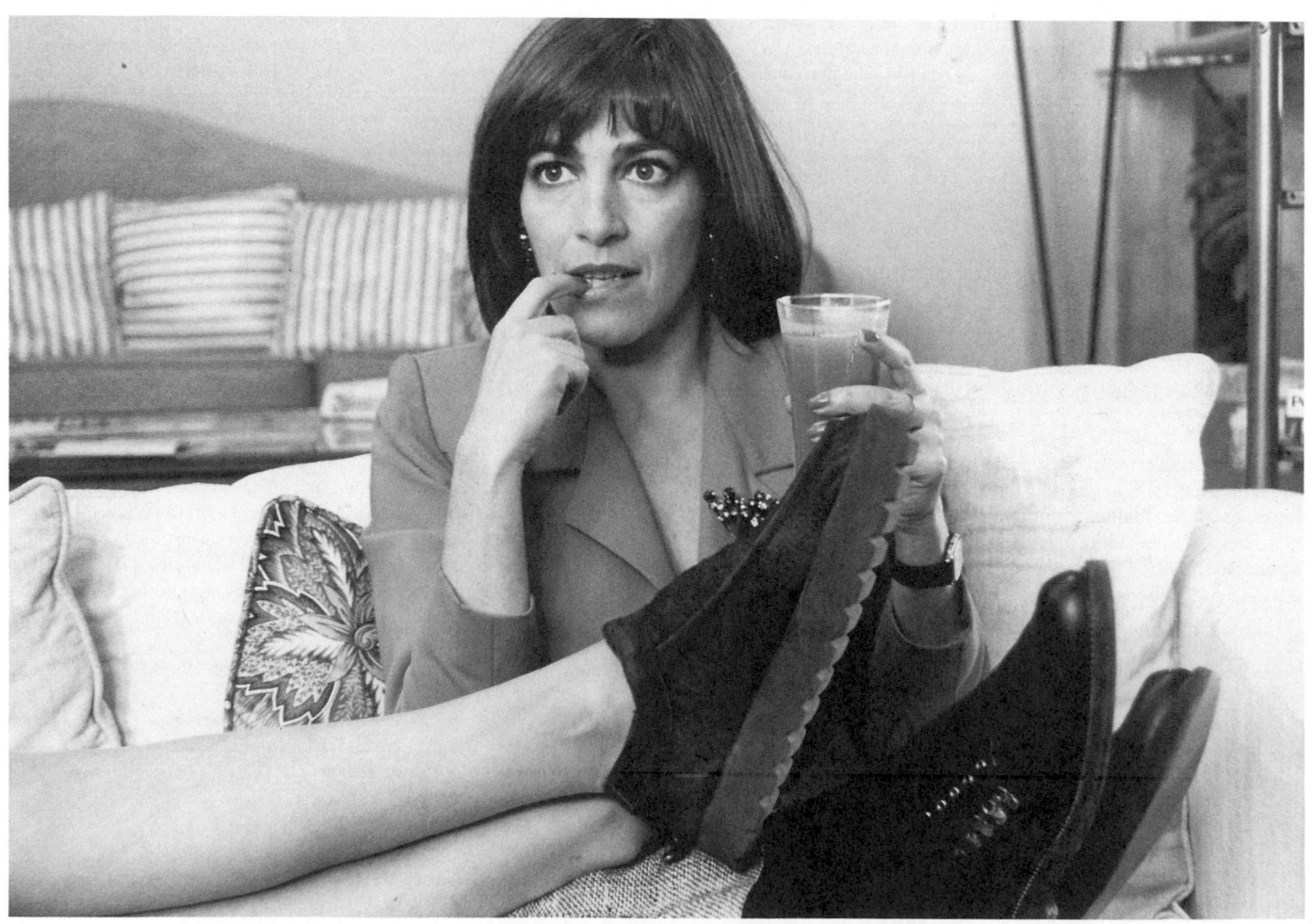

Carmen Maura in *Mujeres al borde de un ataque de nervios*

Almodóvar characters. In *What Have I Done to Deserve This?*, the frustrated heroine's ultimate response to her boorish husband is a murderous whack with the handiest nearby object. In *Pepi, Luci, Bom, and Other Girls on the Heap*, her character becomes a lesbian after her husband rapes their neighbor. Finally, in *Law of Desire*, Maura offers a bravura performance as a free-spirited, man-hating transsexual, formerly named Tino but now called Tina.

None of these characters are staunchly political, nor are they dictated by doctrine. They simply respond to their life situations; their ideology manifests itself in their actions. These women have come to feel passion, the only emotion that can give meaning to their existence. And for them, passion quickly transforms itself into anger at the manner in which they have been treated by society, and by men. That anger eventually transforms itself into revenge, as they evolve from repressed, passive victims into autonomous individuals who think and act freely—and, often, outrageously.

While shooting *Women on the Verge of a Nervous Breakdown*, Maura and Almodóvar had a falling out and did not speak for two years. His most recent film, the well-received *The Flower of My Secret*, features Almodóvar regulars Marisa Paredes, Rossy de Palma, and Chus Lampreave—but not Maura.

But this did not slow down Maura's career, as she has been a star presence playing a wide spectrum of roles in her non-Almodóvar-directed films. They include *Baton Rouge*, in which she plays a wealthy, married middle-aged woman who has an affair with a duplicitous younger man; *Extramuros*, chronicling the secret endeavors of two nuns, who also are lovers, at the time of the Spanish Inquisition; *Louis, L'enfant du roi*, as Anne of Austria; *Shadows in a Conflict*, as a rural woman who becomes lovers with an ex-con; *In Heaven as on Earth*, playing a globe-trotting television journalist who becomes pregnant and whose unborn child speaks to her, informing her that all fetuses have decided not to be born; and especially *¡Ay, Carmela!*, cast as a tempestuous, highly principled—and, ultimately, heroic—vaudevillian who gets lost behind enemy lines while entertaining the partisans during the Spanish Civil War.

—Rob Edelman

McCREA, Joel

Nationality: American. **Born:** Joel Albert McCrea in South Pasadena, California, 5 November 1905. **Education:** Attended Hollywood High School; Pomona College, graduated 1928. **Family:** Married the actress Frances Dee, 1933, sons: Jody, David, Peter. **Career:** Extra in several films in mid-1920s; 1928—stock contract with MGM, followed by 1929 contract with RKO; 1930—first featured film role in *The Silver Horde*; followed by a succession of starring roles; later worked with Paramount and Samuel Goldwyn; after 1946—played only in Western films; 1959-60—in TV series *Wichita Town*. **Awards:** Life Achievement Award, Los Angeles Film Critics, 1987. **Died:** In Woodland Hills, California, 20 October 1990.

Films as Actor:

1927   *The Fair Co-Ed* (Wood); *The Enemy* (Niblo)
1929   *The Jazz Age* (Shores) (as Tod Sayles); *Single Standard* (Robertson); *Dynamite* (DeMille) (as Marco); *So This Is College* (Wood)
1930   *The Silver Horde* (Archainbaud) (as Boyd Enerson); *Lightnin'* (King) (as John Marvin)

1931   *Once a Sinner* (McClintic) (as Tommy Mason); *Kept Husbands* (Bacon) (as Dick Brunton); *Born to Love* (Stein) (as Barry Craig); *The Common Law* (Stein) (as John Neville, Jr.); *Girls about Town* (Cukor) (as Jim Baker)
1932   *Business and Pleasure* (Butler) (as Lawrence Ogle); *The Last Squadron* (Archainbaud) (as Red); *Bird of Paradise* (Vidor) (as Johnny Baker); *The Most Dangerous Game* (Pichel and Schoedsack) (as Bob Whitney); *Rockabye* (Cukor) (as Jacob Van Riker Pell); *The Sport Parade* (Murphy) (as Sandy Baker)
1933   *The Silver Chord* (Cromwell) (as David Phelps); *Scarlet River* (Brower) (as himself); *Bed of Roses* (La Cava) (as Dan Walters); *One Man's Journey* (Robertson) (as Jimmy Watt); *Chance at Heaven* (Seiter) (as Blacky Gorman)
1934   *Gambling Lady* (Mayo) (as Garry Madison); *Half a Sinner* (*Alias the Deacon*) (Neumann) (as John Adams); *The Richest Girl in the World* (Seiter) (as Tony Travers)
1935   *Private Worlds* (La Cava) (as Dr. Alex MacGregor); *Our Little Girl* (Robertson) (as Dr. Donald Middleton); *Woman Wanted* (*Manhattan Madness*) (Seitz) (as Tony Baxter); *Barbary Coast* (Hawks) (as James Carmichael); *Splendor* (Nugent) (as Brighton Lorrimore)
1936   *These Three* (*The Loudest Whisper*) (Wyler) (as Dr. Joseph Cardin); *Two in a Crowd* (Green) (as Larry Stevens); *Adventure in Manhattan* (Ludwig) (as George Melville); *Come and Get It* (Wyler and Hawks) (as Richard Glasgow); *Banjo on My Knee* (Cromwell) (as Ernie Holley)
1937   *Interns Can't Take Money* (Santell) (as Dr. Jimmie Kildare); *Woman Chases Man* (*The Woman's Touch*) (Blystone) (as Kenneth Nolan); *Dead End* (Wyler) (as Dave Connell); *Wells Fargo* (Lloyd) (as Ramsay MacKay)
1938   *Three Blind Mice* (Seiter) (as Van Smith); *Youth Takes a Fling* (Mayo) (as Joe Meadows)
1939   *Union Pacific* (DeMille) (as Jeff Butler); *They Shall Have Music* (*Melody of Youth*) (Mayo) (as Peter McCarthy); *Espionage Agent* (Bacon) (as Barry Corvall)
1940   *He Married His Wife* (Del Ruth) (as "Randy" Randall); *The Primrose Path* (La Cava) (as Ed Wallace); *Foreign Correspondent* (Hitchcock) (as Johnny Jones)
1941   *Reaching for the Sun* (Wellman) (as Russ Elliot); **Sullivan's Travels** (Sturges) (as John Sullivan)
1942   *The Great Man's Lady* (Wellman) (as Ethan Hoyt); *The Palm Beach Story* (Sturges) (as Tom Jeffers)
1943   *The More the Merrier* (Stevens) (as Joe Carter)
1944   *Buffalo Bill* (Wellman) (title role); *The Great Moment* (Sturges) (as W. T. G. Morton)
1945   *The Unseen* (Allen) (as David Fielding)
1946   *The Virginian* (Gilmore) (title role)
1947   *Ramrod* (De Toth) (as Dave Nash)
1948   *Four Faces West* (Green) (as Ross McEwan)
1949   *South of St. Louis* (Enright) (as Kip Davis); *Colorado Territory* (Walsh) (as Wes McQueen)
1950   *Stars in My Crown* (Tourneur) (as Josiah Doziah Grey); *The Outriders* (Rowland) (as Will Owens); *Saddle Tramp* (Fregonese) (as Chuck Conner); *Frenchie* (King) (as Tom Banning)
1951   *Hollywood Story* (Castle) (as himself); *Cattle Drive* (Neumann) (as Dan Matthews)
1952   *The San Francisco Story* (Parrish) (as Rick Nelson)
1953   *Lone Hand* (Sherman) (as Zachary Hallock); *Shoot First* (*Rough Shoot*) (as Lt. Colonel Robert Tanie)
1954   *Border River* (Sherman) (as Clete Mattson); *Black Horse Canyon* (Hibbs) (as Dee Rockwell)
1955   *Stranger on Horseback* (Tourneur) (as Rick Thorne); *Witchita* (Tourneur) (as Wyatt Earp)

1956   *The First Texan* (Haskins) (as Sam Houston)
1957   *The Oklahoman* (Lyon) (as Dr. John Brighton); *Trooper Hook* (Warren) (as Sgt. Hook); *Gunsight Ridge* (Lyon) (as Mike Ryan); *The Tall Stranger* (Carr) (as Ned Bannon)
1958   *Cattle Empire* (Warren) (as John Cord); *Fort Massacre* (Newman) (as Vinson)
1959   *The Gunfight at Dodge City* (Newman) (as Bat Masterson)
1962   ***Ride the High Country*** (*Guns in the Afternoon*) (Peckinpah) (as Steve Judd)
1970   *Cry Blood, Apache* (Starrett) (as Pitcairn)
1974   *The Great American Cowboy* (doc—for TV) (as narrator)
1977   *Mustang Country* (Champion) (as Dan)
1980   *The Oklahoma* (Lyon)
1990   *Preston Sturges: The Rise and Fall of an American Dreamer* (Bowser—TV doc)

Publications

By McCREA: article—

Interview with P. McGilligan and Allen Eyles, in *Focus on Film* (London), no. 30, 1978.

On McCREA: articles—

Eyles, Allen, "Joel McCrea," in *Focus on Film* (London), Winter 1976.
Bodeen, DeWitt, "Joel McCrea and Frances Dee," in *Films in Review* (New York), December 1978.
Obituary, in *Variety* (New York), 21 October 1990.

*   *   *

Of the great American male film stars, Joel McCrea is arguably the most underrated. In a career that lasted over 30 years, his characters ranged from tuxedoed escorts for the likes of Kay Francis and Constance Bennett in *Girls about Town* and *Bed of Roses* to adventurers in *The Most Dangerous Game* and *Bird of Paradise*, from Western "heroes" in *Colorado Territory* and *Ramrod* to comic leading men in *The Palm Beach Story* and *The More the Merrier*. But in spite of his extraordinary filmography, it is unlikely that McCrea will ever become a screen icon of the order of a John Wayne or a Gary Cooper, since, among film heroes, he is one of the least prone to self-mythologizing—with the possible exception of his role in Peckinpah's *Ride the High Country*; and perhaps not coincidentally, he virtually retired after its completion. His search for adventure is seldom more than that and largely free of any sort of neurotic drives. It is this fundamental sanity of McCrea's that probably appealed to Gregory La Cava and Preston Sturges, and which forms the emotional center in the extraordinary series of films that McCrea collaborated on with these two directors. The dramatic tone of the La Cava and Sturges films could range from melodrama (*Private Worlds*) to comedy (*The Palm Beach Story*), or an audacious mixture of the two (*Primrose Path, Sullivan's Travels*), but in most of them McCrea remains an essentially passive male figure surrounded by chaos and insanity. The narratives tend to be controlled by either the female or the subsidiary male characters, and even when they are not, McCrea's attempts at control (as in *Sullivan's Travels*) generally result in total disorder.

While McCrea projects an obvious heterosexuality, it is so relaxed that, in fleeting moments, a film will eroticize him. He becomes the object of an aging widow's affections in *Sullivan's Travels* and she hopefully peers down at him from a second-story window as he chops wood for her, shirtless and sweating. His highly photogenic torso is also featured prominently in *The More the Merrier* as he takes a shower while beating his arms against his chest and barking like a seal,

a primeval mating call that is answered in the film by a sexually unfulfilled Jean Arthur. And *Bird of Paradise* is one of the most erotic of the pre-Production Code films, in which McCrea and Dolores Del Rio set up an idyllic romance, largely unhampered by dress codes.

McCrea appeared in a few films after *Ride the High Country* but they are less than memorable and he seems to have done them more as a lark than anything else. Ultimately, these late films emerge as nothing more than postscripts in his career rather than presenting any sort of revisionist portraits of him. For those who traffic in puncturing the "myths" of popular culture, Joel McCrea was given precious little with which to work.

—Joe McElhaney

McDANIEL, Hattie

Nationality: American. **Born:** Wichita, Kansas, 10 June 1895. **Family:** Married twice. **Career:** 1910s—band vocalist; 1932—film debut in *The Golden West*; 1930s-40s—performer on radio series *Amos 'n' Andy*, *Eddie Cantor Show*, and others; 1947-51—played title role in radio series *Beulah*, and in TV version, 1951. **Awards:** Best Supporting Actress Academy Award for *Gone with the Wind*, 1939. **Died:** 2 October 1952.

Films as Actress:

1932   *The Golden West* (Howard); *Blonde Venus* (von Sternberg); *Hypnotized* (Sennett); *Washington Masquerade* (Brabin)
1933   *I'm No Angel* (Ruggles); *The Story of Temple Drake* (Roberts)
1934   *Operator Thirteen* (Boleslawsky); *Little Men* (Rosen); *Judge Priest* (Ford); *Lost in the Stratosphere* (M. Brown); *Babbitt* (Keighley); *Imitation of Life* (Stahl)
1935   *Music Is Magic* (Stone); *Another Face* (Cabanne); *China Seas* (Garnett); *Alice Adams* (Stevens); *The Little Colonel* (Butler); *The Traveling Saleslady* (Enright)
1936   *Gentle Julia* (Blystone); *High Tension* (Dwan); *Star for a Night* (Seiler); *Can This Be Dixie?* (Marshall); *Postal Inspector* (Brower); *Hearts Divided* (Borzage); *Libeled Lady* (Conway); *The First Baby* (Seiler); *Reunion* (Taurog); *The Bride Walks Out* (Jason); *Big Time Vaudeville Reels* (shorts); *Valiant Is the Word for Carrie* (Ruggles); *Next Time We Love* (Griffith); *The Singing Kid* (Keighley)
1937   *Don't Tell the Wife* (Cabanne); *Racing Lady* (Fox); *Over the Goal* (Smith); *The Wildcatter* (Collins); *The Crime Nobody Saw* (Barton); *True Confession* (Ruggles); *Saratoga* (Conway); *Forty-Five Fathers* (Tinling); *Nothing Sacred* (Wellman)
1938   *Battle of Broadway* (Marshall); *The Shining Hour* (Borzage); *The Mad Miss Manton* (Jason); *Shopworn Angel* (Potter)
1939   ***Gone with the Wind*** (Fleming) (as Mammy); *Everybody's Baby* (St. Clair); *Zenobia* (Douglas)
1940   *Maryland* (Henry King)
1941   *Affectionately Yours* (Bacon); *The Great Lie* (Goulding); *They Died with Their Boots On* (Walsh)
1942   *The Male Animal* (Nugent); *In This Our Life* (Huston); *George Washington Slept Here* (Keighley); *Reap the Wild Wind* (DeMille)
1943   *Thank Your Lucky Stars* (Butler); *Johnny Come Lately* (Howard)
1944   *Since You Went Away* (Cromwell); *Janie* (Curtiz); *Three Is a Family* (Ludwig); *Hi, Beautiful* (Goodwins)

Hattie McDaniel

1946 *Margie* (Henry King); *Never Say Goodbye* (Kern); *Janie Gets Married* (Sherman)
1947 *Song of the South* (Foster)
1948 *The Flame* (Auer); *Mr. Blandings Builds His Dream House* (Potter); *Mickey* (Murphy); *Family Honeymoon* (Binyon)
1949 *The Big Wheel* (Ludwig)

Publications

On McDANIEL: books—

Leab, Daniel J., *From Sambo to Superspade: The Black Experience in Motion Pictures*, Boston, 1975.
Black Films and Filmmakers, edited by Lindsay Patterson, New York, 1975.
Null, Gary, *Black Hollywood: The Negro in Motion Pictures*, Secaucus, New Jersey, 1975.
Sampson, Henry B., *Blacks in Black and White: A Source Book on Black Films*, Metuchen, New Jersey, 1977.
Jackson, Carlton, *Hattie: The Life of Hattie McDaniel*, Lanham, Massachusetts, 1990.

On McDANIEL: article—

Bourne, S., "Star Equality," in *Films and Filming* (London), December 1983.

*   *   *

Hattie McDaniel once said that it was better to play a maid in the movies for $7,000 a week than to work as a real maid for $7. As a black actress, McDaniel was undeniably stifled by Hollywood's racism, which confined her to domestic roles for her entire career.

However, her personal acting ability and comic delivery enabled her to transcend racial stereotypes, and to obtain official recognition as the first black to win an Oscar (for Best Supporting Actress in *Gone with the Wind*). At the height of her career, McDaniel's roles suggested a personal if not social equality with her white co-stars, and even an intellectual superiority. Big, bossy, and never hesitating to speak her mind, McDaniel was at her best in this period, displaying her remarkable comic talent unrestrainedly.

This was not always the case. Early in her career, McDaniel played a one-dimensional, loyal black servant. The role of the "mammy" fitted her like a glove, and she became the helpmate of some of the screen's biggest stars. Before long, though, her rebellious spirit began to emerge and her characters gained greater depth. Her tough, no-nonsense attitude first became apparent in *Judge Priest*, but the best example from this period is probably the Katharine Hepburn film *Alice Adams*. Encouraged by the director George Stevens, McDaniel broke free from the subservient mold. Instead of being merely a walk-on character in uniform, she became a scene-stealer, expressing her contempt for her white employers' pretentious attempts at upperclass chic. Having once obtained success with this new characterization, McDaniel continued to refuse the standard acting opportunities given black actresses at the time.

Rising to new heights of comic rebellion in *The Mad Miss Manton*, McDaniel's characterization became downright sassy. She mouths off to her society boss, Barbara Stanwyck, and refuses to take any guff from either her or her friends. In total control, delivering her lines with comic aplomb, McDaniel's character, despite her subservient status, approaches her employer on an equal social footing. It was not surprising that, given a role expanded to suit her broadening talents, McDaniel would win the Oscar a year later.

The Oscar-winning McDaniel role was that of Mammy in *Gone with the Wind*, a culmination of her roles in earlier films. McDaniel was still the feisty maid, but the possibilities of her role were extended to the fullest, making her a prominent character in the story. The role featured emotions and attributes not usually associated with an auxiliary character—Mammy demonstrates love, warmth, and understanding for her white family. In fact, she becomes an integral part of it; she is the mother figure holding the family together through the worst hardships of the Civil War, when no one else is capable.

Sadly, after *Gone with the Wind* McDaniel's roles reverted to the submissive stereotype she had worked so hard to escape, particularly in films such as *Since You Went Away*. Bringing the servant characterization full circle, McDaniel took on the radio character *Beulah* in 1948, which she continued playing until she died.

—Maryann Oshana

McDOWALL, Roddy

Born: Roderick Andrew McDowall in London, England, 17 September 1928. **Education:** Attended St. Joseph's School, London; 20th Century-Fox school for child actors. **Career:** 1938—film debut as child actor in *Murder in the Family*; 1941—U.S. film debut in *Man Hunt*; 1946—stage debut in *Young Woodley* in Westport, Connecticut; 1955—in *Julius Caesar* and *The Tempest* at Stratford, Connecticut, Shakespeare Festival; other stage work in roles in *No Time for Sergeants*, 1952, *Compulsion*, 1957, *Look After Lulu*, 1959, and *Camelot*, 1960; 1970s—in several TV mini-series, and the series *The Planet of the Apes*, 1974, and *Fantastic Journey*, 1977; 1971—directed the film *Tam Lin*; 1980s and 1990s—in TV mini-series *Around the World in 80 Days*, 1989, *An Inconvenient Woman*, 1991, *The Sands of Time*, 1992. **Agent:** Philip Gersch Agency, 222 North Cannon Drive, Beverly Hills, CA 90210, U.S.A.

Films as Actor:

1938 *Murder in the Family* (Banks) (as Peter Osborne); *Scruffy* (Faye); *Hey! Hey! USA!* (Varnel); *I See Ice* (Kimmins); *Convict Ninety-Nine* (Varnel); *Yellow Sands* (Brenon); *John Halifax, Gentleman* (George King); *Sarah Siddons*
1939 *Just William* (Cutts) (as Ginger); *Dirt*; *Dead Men's Shoes* (Bentley); *Poison Pen* (Stein); *Brother's Keeper*; *Murder Will Out* (Neill)
1940 *The Outsider* (Stein); *Saloon Bar* (Forde)
1941 *You Will Remember* (Raymond) (as young Bob Slater); *This England* (MacDonald); *Man Hunt* (Fritz Lang) (as Vaner, the cabin boy); *How Green Was My Valley* (Ford) (as Huw Morgan); *Confirm or Deny* (Mayo) (as Albert Perkins)
1942 *Son of Fury* (Cromwell) (as Benjamin as a boy); *The Pied Piper* (Pichel) (as Ronny Cavanaugh); *On the Sunny Side* (Schuster) (as Hugh Aylesworth)
1943 *My Friend Flicka* (Schuster) (as Ken McLaughlin); *Lassie Come Home* (Wilcox) (as Joe Carraclough)
1944 *The Keys of the Kingdom* (Stahl) (as Francis as a boy); *The White Cliffs of Dover* (Brown) (as John Ashwood II as a boy)
1945 *Thunderhead—Son of Flicka* (Louis King) (as Ken McLaughlin); *Molly and Me* (Seiler) (as Jimmy Graham); *Hangover Square* (Brahm) (as voice)
1946 *Holiday in Mexico* (Sidney) (as Stanley Owen)
1948 *Green Grass of Wyoming* (Louis King); *Rocky* (Barry); *Macbeth* (Welles) (as Malcolm); *Kidnapped* (Beaudine) (as David Balfour, + assoc pr)

1949   *Tuna Clipper* (Beaudine) (as Alec, + assoc pr); *Black Midnight* (Boetticher) (as Scott Jordan)

1950   *Everybody's Dancing* (Berke); *Killer Shark* (Boetticher) (as Ted); *Big Timber* (*Tall Timber*) (Yarbrough) (as Jimmy)

1951   *The Steel Fist* (Barry) (as Erik)

1960   *Midnight Lace* (Miller) (as Malcolm); *The Subterraneans* (MacDougall) (as Yuri Gligoric)

1962   *The Longest Day* (Annakin and others) (as Pvt. Morris)

1963   *Cleopatra* (Joseph L. Mankiewicz) (as Octavian)

1964   *Shock Treatment* (Sanders) (as Martin Ashly)

1965   *The Greatest Story Ever Told* (Stevens) (as Matthew); *The Loved One* (Richardson) (as D. J., Jr.); *That Darn Cat!* (Stevenson) (as Gregory Benson); *The Third Day* (Smight) (as Oliver Parsons); *Inside Daisy Clover* (Mulligan) (as Walter Baines)

1966   *Lord Love a Duck* (Axelrod) (as Alan "Mollymauk" Musgrave); *The Defector* (*L'Espion*; *Lautlose Waffen*) (Levy) (as CIA Agent Adam); *Paris brûle-t-il?* (*Is Paris Burning?*) (Clément)

1967   *The Adventures of Bullwhip Griffin* (Neilson) (title role); *It!* (*Return of the Golem*) (Leder) (as Arthur Pimm); *The Cool Ones* (Nelson) (as Tony)

1968   *Planet of the Apes* (Schaffner) (as Cornelius); *Five Card Stud* (Hathaway) (as Nick Evers)

1969   *Hello Down There* (Arnold) (as Nate Ashbury); *The Midas Run* (*A Run on Gold*) (Kjellin) (as Wister); *Angel, Angel, Down We Go* (*Cult of the Damned*) (Thom) (as Santoro); *Night Gallery* (Sagal—for TV)

1971   *Pretty Maids All in a Row* (Vadim) (as Mr. Proffer); *Escape from the Planet of the Apes* (Taylor) (as Cornelius); *Bedknobs and Broomsticks* (Stevenson) (as Mr. Jelk); *Terror in the Sky* (Kowalski—for TV); *A Taste of Evil* (Moxey—for TV); *Corky* (*Lookin' Good*) (Horn)

1972   *The Poseidon Adventure* (Neame) (as Acres); *Conquest of the Planet of the Apes* (Thompson) (as Caesar); *The Life and Times of Judge Roy Bean* (Huston) (as Frank Gass); *What's a Nice Girl Like You . . .?* (Paris—for TV)

1973   *Battle for the Planet of the Apes* (Thompson) (as Caesar); *The Legend of Hell House* (Hough) (as Ben Fischer); *Arnold* (Fenady) (as Robert)

1974   *The Elevator* (Jameson—for TV); *Miracle on 34th Street* (Cook—for TV); *Dirty Mary, Crazy Larry* (Hough) (as Stanton)

1975   *Funny Lady* (Ross) (as Bobby)

1976   *Mean Johnny Barrows* (Williamson) (as Tony DaVinci); *Embryo* (Nelson) (as Riley); *Flood* (Bellamy—for TV)

1977   *Sixth and Main* (Cain) (as Skateboard)

1978   *Laserblast* (Rae) (as Dr. Mellon); *The Cat from Outer Space* (Tokar) (as Stallwood); *Rabbit Test* (Rivers) (as Gypsy Grandmother/Dr. Fishbind)

1979   *The Thief of Baghdad* (Conner—for TV); *Hart to Hart* (T. Mankiewicz—for TV); *Nutcracker Fantasy* (Nakamura—animation) (as voice of Franz Fritz); *Scavenger Hunt* (Michael Schultz) (as Jenkins); *Circle of Iron* (*The Silent Flute*) (Moore) (as White Robe); *The Martian Chronicles* (Anderson—for TV)

1980   *The Memory of Eva Ryker* (Grauman—for TV)

1981   *Charlie Chan and the Curse of the Dragon Queen* (Clive Donner) (as Gillespie)

1982   *Evil under the Sun* (Hamilton) (as Rex Brewster); *Mae West* (Phillips—for TV)

1983   *Class of 1984* (Lester) (as Terry Corrigan); *This Girl for Hire* (Jameson—for TV)

1984   *Zany Adventures of Robin Hood* (Austin—for TV)

1985   *Fright Night* (Holland) (as Peter Vincent); *Deceptions* (Chaenault—for TV)

1986   *GoBots: Battle of the Rock Lords* (Patterson—animation) (as voice of Nuggit)

1987   *Dead of Winter* (Arthur Penn) (as Mr. Murray); *Overboard* (Garry Marshall) (as Andrew, the butler, + exec pr)

1988   *Doin' Time on Planet Earth* (Charles Matthau) (as Minister)

1989   *Fright Night Part 2* (Wallace) (as Peter Vincent); *The Big Picture* (Guest) (as the Judge); *Cutting Class* (Pallenberg) (as Dr. Dante)

1990   *Shakma* (Parks) (as Sorenson); *The Color of Evening* (Stafford); *Carmilla* (Beaumont)

1991   *Going Under* (Travis) (as secretary of defense/Mr. Neighbor); *Earth Angel* (Napolitano—for TV) (as Mr. Tatum); *Deadly Game* (Wright—for TV) (as Dr. Aaron/Osiris); *Los Gusanos no Llevan Bufanda* (*The Naked Target*) (Elorrieta) (as Ernest Peabody)

1992   *The Magical World of Chuck Jones* (Daugherty—doc) (as himself); *Double Trouble* (Paragon) (as Chamberlain)

1994   *Hart to Hart: Home Is Where the Hart Is* (Peter R. Hunt—for TV) (as Jeremy Sennet); *Mirror Mirror 2: Raven Dance* (Lifton); *Heads* (Shapiro—for TV) (as Fibris Drake); *Angel 4: Undercover* (Axmith) (as Geoffrey Kagen)

1995   *The Alien Within* (for TV) (as Dr. Henry Lazarus); *Last Summer in the Hamptons* (Jaglom) (as Thomas)

1996   *It's My Party* (Kleiser) (as Damian Knowles)

Film as Director:

1971   *Tam Lin* (*The Devil's Widow*)

Publications

By McDOWALL: books—

Double Exposure (photographs), New York, 1966.
Double Exposure Take Two (photographs), New York, 1989.
Double Exposure, Take Three (photographs), New York, 1993.
Double Exposure, Take Four (photographs), New York, 1993.

By McDOWALL: articles—

"A Life in Pictures," interview with Gavin Lambert, in *Interview* (New York), September 1989.
"Dark Star," interview of Louise Brooks by Roddy McDowall, in *Interview* (New York), October 1989.
"Tim Burton and Vincent Price," interview by Graham Fuller and Roddy McDowall, in *Interview* (New York), December 1990.
"The Redgrave Sisters," interview by Roddy McDowall, in *Interview* (New York), February 1991.
"Sitting Pretty: After a Twenty-Year Absence, Actress Maureen O'Hara Returns to the Silver Screen," interview by Roddy McDowall, in *Premiere* (New York), July 1991.

On McDOWALL: articles—

Current Biography 1961, New York, 1961.
Buckley, Michael, "Roddy McDowall," in *Films in Review* (New York), August/September and October 1988.

*   *   *

Although Roddy McDowall has appeared in more than 100 motion pictures playing a variety of roles and characters (and has an equal number of television credits) he seems to have been plagued by type-casting during much of his career. He began acting in films at the age of nine in Great Britain. His family emigrated to America in 1940 when he was signed to a movie contract by Darryl F. Zanuck at Twentieth Century-Fox. His first major role in an American film was in John Ford's *How Green Was My Valley*. Soon afterwards followed *My Friend Flicka* and *Lassie Come Home*. These films helped to establish McDowall as a major child star, generally playing the role of sensitive, winsome youngsters. He kept extremely busy making two or three films each year throughout the 1940s. Although McDowall was growing into an adult during this period, producers and audiences continued to think of him as a "child" star. His youthful appearance allowed him to play characters much younger than his actual years (the most outlandish situation coming in 1965 with *Lord Love a Duck* in which the 35-year-old McDowall played a high school teenager), but it limited the kinds of film roles he was being offered. His initial stardom in America had typecast him into one specific kind of role that he had now outgrown.

Many child stars fade away after this period in their careers, but McDowall was able to continue with his acting by moving to the New York stage. Live television was another medium that enabled McDowall to expand his acting talents with a variety of roles. While he has not been honored by the Academy of Motion Picture Arts and Sciences, McDowall has won both Emmy and Tony awards for his work in these other mediums.

In the early 1960s he cautiously ventured back into motion pictures as an "adult" actor, taking mainly character roles. In 1967 his career took a different turn with *Planet of the Apes*. McDowall, in Oscar-winning ape makeup, played Cornelius, a chimpanzee scientist sympathetic to human time traveler Charlton Heston in a future world where humans are subservient to apes. The film was extremely popular at the box office, and there were four sequels, plus a short-lived television series. Although he continued to take other film roles during this period, McDowall's name became synonymous with the ape series. And while it is true that McDowall has appeared in several science-fiction films (such as *The Legend of Hell House, Arnold, Embryo, Laserblast,* and *The Martian Chronicles*), he also continues to play many varying roles in other films. A quick glance at his screen credits shows an amazing diversity of films, and McDowall should perhaps be considered more of a character actor than one who has been typecast in any one specific role.

—Linda J. Obalil, updated by Frank Uhle

McDOWELL, Malcolm

Nationality: British. **Born:** Leeds, 15 June 1943. **Education:** Attended Cannock College, Kent. **Family:** Married 1) Margot Bennett Dullea, 1975 (divorced 1980); 2) the actress Mary Steenburgen, 1980 (divorced 1990), two children: Lilly and Charlie; 3) Kelley Kuhr. **Career:** Early 1960s—worked in coffee factory, then as coffee salesman in Yorkshire; actor in regional repertory companies in Shanklin, Isle of Wight, and Torquay; mid-1960s—with Royal Shakespeare Company for 18 months; 1967—film debut in *Poor Cow*; 1975—on stage in *Entertaining Mr. Sloane*, London, and in *Look Back in Anger*, New York, 1980. **Agent:** Cauden Inc., 822 South Robertson Boulevard, Suite 200, Los Angeles, CA 90035, U.S.A.

Films as Actor:

1967   *Poor Cow* (Loach) (as Billy, scene was deleted from released film)

1968   *If . . .* (Lindsay Anderson) (as Mick Travis)
1970   *Figures in a Landscape* (Losey) (as Ansell)
1971   *The Raging Moon* (*Long Ago Tomorrow*) (Forbes) (as Bruce Pritchard); *A Clockwork Orange* (Kubrick) (as Alex)
1973   *O Lucky Man!* (Lindsay Anderson) (as Mick Travis)
1975   *Royal Flash* (Lester) (as Capt. Harry Flashman)
1976   *Voyage of the Damned* (Rosenberg) (as Max Gunter)
1977   *Aces High* (Gold) (as Gresham)
1978   *She Fell among Thieves* (Clive Donner—for TV); *The Cat from Outer Space* (Tokar) (as Mr. Stallwood)
1979   *The Passage* (J. Lee Thompson) (as Capt. Von Berkow); *Time after Time* (Meyer) (as H. G. Wells)
1980   *Caligula* (Brass—produced in 1977) (title role); *Look Back in Anger* (David Jones)
1981   *Britannia Hospital* (Lindsay Anderson) (as Mick Travis)
1982   *The Compleat Beatles* (Montgomery—doc) (as narrator); *Cat People* (Schrader) (as Paul Gallier); *Hardcore* (James Kenelm Clark)
1983   *Get Crazy* (*Flip Out*) (Arkush) (as Reggie Wanker); *Blue Thunder* (Badham) (as Col. Cochrane); *Cross Creek* (Ritt) (as Maxwell Perkins)
1985   *Arthur the King* (*Merlin and the Sword*) (Clive Donner—for TV, produced in 1983) (as Arthur); *Gulag* (Roger Young—for TV) (as the Englishman)
1986   *Monte Carlo* (Page—for TV) (as Christopher Quinn)
1988   *Buy & Cell* (Boris) (as Warden Tennant); *Sunset* (Edwards) (as Alfie Alperin)
1989   *The Caller* (Arthur Allan Seidelman—produced in 1987) (title role); *Il Maestro* (Hansel) (as Walter Goldberg); *The Hateful Dead* (*Mortacci*) (Citti)
1990   *Disturbed* (Charles Winkler) (as Dr. Derek Russell); *Moon 44* (*Intruder*) (Emmerich) (as Major Lee); *Class of 1999* (Mark Lester) (as Dr. Miles Langford); *Jezebel's Kiss* (Keith) (as Ben Faberson); *Snake Eyes* (Reid); *Happily Ever After* (Howley—animation, for TV) (as voice of Lord Maliss)
1991   *Tsareubiitsa* (*Assassin of the Tsar*) (Shakhnazarov) (as Timofeef/Yurovsky); *The Light in the Jungle* (Schweitzer) (Hofmyer) (as Dr. Albert Schweitzer)
1992   *The Player* (Altman) (as himself)
1993   *Chain of Desire* (Lopez) (as Hubert Bailey); *Bopha!* (Freeman) (as De Villiers); *Night Train to Venice* (Quinterio) (as stranger); *Vend d'est* (*East Wind*) (Enrico) (as Gen. Smyslowosky); *The Second Greatest Story Ever Told* (as Gabriel)
1994   *Milk Money* (Benjamin) (as Waltzer); *Star Trek Generations* (David Carson) (as Dr. Tollan Soran); *Seasons of the Heart* (Lee Grant—for TV) (as Alfred McGinnis); *Fatal Pursuit* (Louzil)
1995   *Dangerous Indiscretion* (as Roger Everett); *Tank Girl* (Talalay) (as Kesslee); *Exquisite Tenderness* (Schenkel) (as Dr. Roger Stein); *The Man Who Wouldn't Die* (for TV) (as Bernard Drake); *Kids of the Round Table* (Tinnell) (as Merlin); *Fist of the North Star* (Randel)
1996   *The Little Riders* (Connor) (as Capt. Kessel)

Publications

By McDOWELL: articles—

"Malcolm McDowell: The Liberals, They Hate *Clockwork*," interview with Tom Burke, in *New York Times*, 30 January 1972.
"Malcolm McDowell: A Very Low Tea with Jude Jade," interview in *Interview* (New York), July 1973.
"O Lucky Man!," interview in *Take One* (Montreal), September 1973.

Malcolm McDowell in *A Clockwork Orange*

"Something More," interview with G. Gow, in *Films and Filming* (London), October 1975.

Interview in *Photoplay* (London), February 1980.

L'Ecran fantastique (Paris), July/August 1983.

Interview with D. Parra, in *Revue du Cinéma* (Paris), June 1989.

Interview with Kitty Bowe Hearty, in *Premiere* (New York), April 1995.

On McDOWELL: articles—

Photoplay (London), December 1981.

Ciné Revue (Paris), 19 January 1984.

Bernstein, R., "Malcolm McDowell Post-*Clockwork*," in *New York Times*, 14 March 1993.

*   *   *

Malcolm McDowell began his film career in the late 1960s and early 1970s in highly regarded and frequently daring British films. Later following in the tradition of the "working actor," McDowell moved often and without apology from highly praised work to less artistically justifiable appearances in mediocre productions. His major collaborative relationship has been with the late director Lindsay Anderson, who discovered him and gave him the role of Mick Travis in *If . . .*: a metaphorical examination of conformity and rebellion among young gentlemen in boarding school. McDowell went on to work with Anderson (playing a completely dissimilar Mick Travis) in the satire *O Lucky Man!*, the script of which was based in part on the actor's own experiences as a coffee salesman. Subsequently McDowell made his New York stage debut in Anderson's off-Broadway revival of *Look Back in Anger*. The two collaborated a final time in 1981 with *Britannia Hospital*, where—again as a "Mick Travis"—McDowell had

one of the most spectacularly violent and funny death scenes in cinema.

The role McDowell has been most associated with, however, is the raping, murderous gang-leader Alex in Stanley Kubrick's *A Clockwork Orange*. Now considered a key performance of seventies cinema, McDowell's Alex is a character both winsome and appalling, pathetic and high-spirited. Despite the fact that this performance was followed by one as a suddenly sweet Mick in *O Lucky Man!*, McDowell would never completely avoid the typecasting set in place by his bloodthirsty characters in *If . . .* and *A Clockwork Orange*. This reputation for villainy would be cemented by McDowell's turn as the eponymous Roman Emperor in the ballyhooed *Caligula*, a pornographic cult film financed by Penthouse magazine.

Although he maintains a reputation for on-screen carnage and sexually explicit material, McDowell has played other types of characters with alacrity. McDowell starred in *Long Ago Tomorrow* as a gentle paraplegic and had other notable roles during the 1970s in *Royal Flash*, *Voyage of the Damned*, and *Aces High*, in which the actor essayed the role of a disillusioned World War I officer in the Royal Flying Corps.

During the 1980s and 1990s McDowell worked on both sides of the Atlantic, but to sporadic and fading accolades. His last memorable roles were once more at polar extremes. He played H. G. Wells opposite his future wife Mary Steenburgen in the fantasy *Time after Time*. Here again, McDowell was a master of conflicting qualities; his Wells was both innocent and shrewdly brilliant as he attempted to capture Jack the Ripper in modern day San Francisco. Also arresting was his role as Nastassja Kinski's disturbed brother in Paul Schrader's *Cat People*, where incest was a key motivation behind his character. Unfortunately, McDowell's luck seemed to run out in the mid-eighties. *Blue Thunder* was a financial success but gave McDowell only a conventional villain's role. His other parts in that period were usually as supporting characters or in uninteresting films, many made for television.

McDowell seemed the perfect choice to "kill off" Captain James T. Kirk in *Star Trek Generations*, but his Soran in that film was a stock character with only McDowell's piercing eyes to distinguish him in an overcrowded cast. Virtually all of McDowell's roles since *Cat People* hint at what he could contribute to the cinema if given an opportunity. His Mick Jagger parody in *Get Crazy* would have seemed hilarious if given better lines, while the awful *Night Train to Venice* suggests how good he might have been as Hannibal Lecter in *The Silence of the Lambs*.

—Daniel Humphrey

McLAGLEN, Victor

Born: Tunbridge Wells, Kent, England, 10 December 1886. **Military Service:** Boy soldier during the Boer War; served as Captain in Irish Fusiliers during World War I; Provost Marshal of Bagdad. **Family:** Married 1) Mary Lamont, 1919, son: the director Andrew McLagen, daughter: Sheila; 2) Suzanna Maria Brueggemann, 1943. **Career:** Prizefighter in Canada, and vaudeville and circus performer; 1920—film debut in *The Call of the Road*; 1924—U.S. film debut in *The Beloved Brute*; 1925—appeared in the first of many films of the director John Ford, *The Fighting Heart*. **Awards:** Best Actor Academy Award for *The Informer*, 1935. **Died:** 7 November 1959.

Films as Actor:

1920   *The Call of the Road* (Coleby)
1921   *The Sport of Kings* (Rooke); *Carnival* (Knoles) (as Baron); *Corinthian Jack* (Rowden)
1922   *The Glorious Adventure* (Blackton) (as Bulfinch); *A Romance of Old Bagdad* (Foss)
1923   *In the Blood* (West) (as Tony Crabtree); *The Romany* (Thornton); *M'Lord of the White Road* (Rooke)
1924   *The Beloved Brute* (Blackton) (as Charles Hinges)
1925   *The Unholy Three* (Browning) (as Hercules); *The Gay Corinthian* (Rooke); *Winds of Chance* (Lloyd) (as Poleon Doret); *The Fighting Heart* (Ford) (as Soapy Williams)
1926   *The Isle of Retribution* (Hogan) (as Doomsdorf); *Men of Steel* (Archainbaud) (as Pete Masarick); *Beau Geste* (Brenon) (as Hank); *What Price Glory* (Walsh) (as Capt. Flagg)
1927   *Loves of Carmen* (Walsh) (as Escamillo)
1928   *A Girl in Every Port* (Hanks) (as Spike Madden); *Mother Machree* (Ford) (as Terrence O'Dowd); *Hangman's House* (Ford) (as Citizen Hogan); *The River Pirate* (Howard) (as Sailor Fritz)
1929   *Captain Lash* (Blystone) (title role); *Strong Boy* (Ford) (title role); *The Black Watch* (Ford) (as Capt. Donald Gordon King); *The Cock-Eyed World* (Walsh) (as Sgt. Flagg); *Hot for Paris* (Walsh) (as John Patrick Duke)
1930   *On the Level* (Cummings) (as Biff Williams); *A Devil with Women* (Cummings) (as Jerry Maxton); *Three Rogues*
1931   *Dishonored* (von Sternberg); *Women of All Nations* (Walsh); *Annabelle's Affairs* (Werker); *Wicked* (Dwan)
1932   *The Gay Caballero* (Werker); *While Paris Sleeps* (Dwan); *Devil's Lottery* (Taylor); *Guilty as Charged* (Kenton); *Rackety Rax* (Werker)
1933   *Hot Pepper* (Blystone); *Laughing at Life* (Beebe); *Dick Turpin* (Stafford and Hanbury) (title role)

1934   *No More Women* (Rogell); *The Lost Patrol* (Ford); *The Wharf Angel* (Menzies and Somnes); *Murder at the Vanities* (Leisen); *The Captain Hates the Sea* (Milestone)
1935   *Under Pressure* (Walsh); *The Great Hotel Murder* (Forde); **The Informer** (Ford) (as Gypo Nolan)
1936   *Professional Soldier* (Garnett); *Klondike Annie* (Walsh); *Under Two Flags* (Lloyd); *The Magnificent Brute* (Blystone)
1937   *Nancy Steele Is Missing* (Marshall); *Sea Devils* (Stoloff); *This Is My Affair* (Seiter); *Wee Willie Winkie* (Ford); *Battle of Broadway* (Marshall)
1938   *The Devil's Party* (McCarey); *We're Going to Be Rich* (Banks)
1939   *Pacific Liner* (Landers); *Gunga Din* (Stevens); *Let Freedom Ring* (Conway); *Ex-Champ* (Rosen); *Captain Fury* (Roach); *Full Confession* (Farrow); *Rio* (Brahm); *The Big Guy* (Lubin)
1940   *South of Pago-Pago* (Green); *Diamond Frontier* (Schuster)
1941   *Broadway Limited* (Douglas)
1942   *Call Out the Marines* (Ryan and Hamilton); *Powder Town* (Lee)
1943   *China Girl* (Hathaway)
1944   *Tampico* (Mendes); *Roger Touhy—Gangster* (Florey); *The Princess and the Pirate* (Butler)
1945   *Rough, Tough, and Ready* (Lloyd)
1946   *Whistle Stop* (Moguy)
1947   *The Foxes of Harrow* (Stahl); *Calendar Girl* (Dwan)
1948   *Fort Apache* (Ford)
1949   **She Wore a Yellow Ribbon** (Ford) (as Sgt. Quincannon)
1950   *Rio Grande* (Ford)
1952   **The Quiet Man** (Ford) (as "Red" Will Danaher)
1953   *Fair Wind to Java* (Kane)
1954   *Prince Valiant* (Hathaway); *Trouble in the Glen* (Wilcox) (as Parlan)
1955   *Many Rivers to Cross* (Rowland); *City of Shadows* (Witney); *Lady Godiva* (Lubin); *Bengazi* (Brahm)
1956   *Around the World in Eighty Days* (Anderson) (as Helmsman)
1957   *The Abductors* (Andrew McLagen)
1958   *Sea Fury* (Endfield) (as Capt. Bellew)

Publications

By McLAGLEN: book—

Express to Hollywood, London, 1934.

On McLAGLEN: articles—

Johnston, A., "Victor McLaglen, Master of the Light Horse," in *Women's Home Companion*, November 1936.
Obituary, in *New York Times*, 8 November 1959.
Classic Images (Indiana, Pennsylvania), October 1983.
Leibfred, Philip, "Victor McLaglen," in *Films in Review* (New York), April 1990.

*   *   *

There is something essentially mindless in the expressionistic style of acting; in it actors are just short of being automatons who *express* puppet-like the artistic vision of the auteur. In this respect, Victor McLaglen is the perfect lead for the two American filmic masterpieces in this style—John Ford's *The Lost Patrol* and *The Informer*. The frenetic vision of a group of soldiers lost in a patrol in the Mesopotamian desert finds central focus in the sergeant played by McLaglen. His exaggerated gestures seem appropriate when viewed against the otherworldly backdrop of sand dunes and tortuous palms. This realm of heat-induced hallucinations and even insanity provides

Victor McLaglen

an excuse for an actor whose body and voice function best at their extremes. One of the reasons that *The Informer* has fallen out of the high critical esteem in which it was once held is that its pervasive expressionism, above all in McLaglen's Academy-Award-winning performance, has been overborne by the movement to film outside the studio and the corresponding turn to a self-conscious, indeed intellectual approach inherent in the Stanislavsky method which, since the 1940s and 1950s has come to dominate English-language films.

Given this change in style and given his acting strengths, McLaglen could only continue to flourish as the comic character actor—his oscillation between farce and sentimentality in the role of sergeant in John Ford's cavalry films such as *Fort Apache*, *She Wore a Yellow Ribbon*, and *Rio Grande*. This role was a continuation of that of the sergeant in *Wee Willie Winkie* in the 1930s—which was in many ways a parody of his role in *The Lost Patrol*. It may be a fulsome but not inappropriate analogy to compare McLaglen's sergeant in the cavalry films and his role of the overbearing squire in *The Quiet Man* to some of Shakespeare's clowns, if in no other way than their common exuberance and almost excessive sense of life.

Outside of John Ford's realm—when McLaglen is playing neither the *acharné* role of the 1930s nor the ingratiating buffoon of the later films—he is nothing beyond mere histrionic grimaces and gestures. This fact is a tribute to Ford's choice of actor for his ensemble pieces—McLaglen's absence from the director's vision would be like a Franz Hals low-life canvas without its drunken, wide-mouthed clown.

—Rodney Farnsworth

McQUEEN, Steve

Nationality: American. **Born:** Terence Steven McQueen in Slater, Missouri (or Indianapolis, Indiana), 24 March 1930. **Military Service:** Marine Corps, 1947-50. **Family:** Married 1) the actress Neile Adams, 1956 (divorced), children: Terry Leslie and Chadwick Steven; 2) the actress Ali McGraw, 1973 (divorced). **Career:** Abandoned by father while an infant; spent part of childhood at Boys' Republic, Chino, California, a reform school; 1950—worked at various jobs, lumberjack, sailor, oil field worker; 1952—began studying at Uta Hagen-Herbert Berghof School of Acting, New York; stage debut in walk-on role in a Second Avenue Yiddish theater; early 1950s—appeared in summer stock and on TV; 1956—film debut in bit role in *Somebody Up There Likes Me*; replaced Ben Gazzara on Broadway in *A Hatful of Rain*; 1957—first featured film role in *Never Love a Stranger*; 1958-61—in TV series *Wanted: Dead or Alive*; early 1960s—formed production company Socar; 1969—co-founder, First Artists Production Company. **Died:** Of cancer at clinic Santa Rosa in Juarez, Mexico, 7 November 1980.

Films as Actor:

1956 *Somebody Up There Likes Me* (Wise) (as Fidel)
1957 *Never Love a Stranger* (Stevens) (as Martin Cabell)
1958 *The Blob* (Yeaworth) (as Steve); *The Great St. Louis Bank Robbery* (Guggenheim and Stix) (as George Fowler)
1959 *Never So Few* (John Sturges) (as Bill Ringa)
1960 *The Magnificent Seven* (John Sturges) (as Vin)
1961 *The Honeymoon Machine* (Thorpe) (as Lieutenant Fergie Howard)

1962 *Hell Is for Heroes* (Siegel) (as Reese); *The War Lover* (Leacock) (as Buzz Rickson)
1963 *The Great Escape* (John Sturges) (as Hilts); *Love with the Proper Stranger* (Mulligan) (as Rocky Papasano); *Soldier in the Rain* (Nelson) (as Sergeant Eustis Clay)
1964 *Baby the Rain Must Fall* (Mulligan) (as Henry Thomas)
1965 *The Cincinnati Kid* (Jewison) (title role)
1966 *Nevada Smith* (Hathaway) (as Max Sand/Nevada Smith); *The Sand Pebbles* (Wise) (as Holman)
1968 *The Thomas Crown Affair* (Jewison) (title role); *Bullitt* (Yates) (as Frank Bullitt)
1969 *The Reivers* (Rydell) (as Boon Hogganbeck)
1971 *Le Mans* (Katzin) (as Michael Delaney); *On Any Sunday* (Bruce Brown—doc)
1972 *Junior Bonner* (Peckinpah) (title role); *The Getaway* (Peckinpah) (as Doc McCoy)
1973 *Papillon* (Schaffner) (title role)
1974 *The Towering Inferno* (Guillermin and Irwin Allen) (as Michael O'Hallorhan)
1978 *An Enemy of the People* (Schaefer—never released theatrically) (as Dr. Thomas Stockmann)
1980 *Tom Horn* (Wiard) (title role, + exec pr); *The Hunter* (Kulik) (as Ralph "Papa" Thorson)

Publications

On McQUEEN: books—

Campbell, Joan, *The Films of Steve McQueen*, Farncombe, Surrey, 1977.
Ferrari, Philippe, *Steve McQueen*, Paris, 1981.
Satchell, Tim, *Steve McQueen*, London, 1981.
Ragsdale, Grady, *Steve McQueen, the Final Chapter*, Ventura, California, 1983.
Durant, Philippe, *Steve McQueen*, Paris, 1984.
Nolan, William F., *McQueen*, New York, 1984.
St. Charnez, Casey, *The Films of Steve McQueen*, Secaucus, New Jersey, 1984.
Kirberg, Robert J., *Steve McQueen: seine Filme, sein Leben*, Munich, 1985.
Spiegel, Penina, *McQueen: The Untold Story of a Bad Boy in Hollywood*, Garden City, New York, 1986.
Toffel, Neile McQueen, *My Husband, My Friend*, New York, 1986.
Guerif, Françoise, *Steve McQueen*, Paris, 1988.
McGraw, Ali, *Moving Pictures: An Autobiography*, London, 1991.
Terrill, Marshall, *Steve McQueen: Portrait of an American Rebel*, New York, 1994.

On McQUEEN: articles—

Current Biography 1960, New York, 1960.
Harper's Bazaar (New York), February 1965.
Obituary in *New York Times*, 8 November 1980.
Obituary in *Newsweek*, 29 December 1980.
The Annual Obituary 1980, New York, 1981.
Eyman, S., and D. Elley, "The Under-Achiever: The Outsider," in *Focus on Film* (London), March 1981.
Cieutat, Michel, "Steve McQueen, ou les limites de la nouvelle frontière," in *Positif* (Paris), June 1981.
Beaver, J., "Steve McQueen," in *Films in Review* (New York), August/September 1981.
On TV work in *Films in Review* (New York), February 1982.
Sragow, Michael, "The Films of Steve McQueen," in *Video Movies* (Skokie, Illinois), May 1984.

Steve McQueen with Lee Remick in *Baby the Rain Must Fall*

Norman, Barry, in *The Film Greats*, London, 1985.

Cohen, Meg, "McQueen of Hearts," in *Harper's Bazaar* (New York), February 1993.

*   *   *

Stories of Steve McQueen's troubled childhood and roustabout adolescence never squared with the fastidiousness of his screen persona, the aristocracy of his best roles. McQueen did not need to act snobbery and elitism; his whole being vibrated with a sense of natural superiority. Only once, in *The Thomas Crown Affair*, did he play the wealthy and powerful man he was in real life, and then the role fitted him as perfectly as his tailoring.

Even as early as his 1958 role in a cheap sci-fi feature, *The Blob*, it was possible to see something different about Steve McQueen. This actor could play people who instigated events rather than simply responded to them. Undeterred by civic disbelief and police disapproval, he almost single-handedly rouses the town to the menace from outer space, even emptying the local cinema one step ahead of the flood of red jelly.

His Vin in *The Magnificent Seven* is one of the great roles of Western cinema, an intricate portrait of youthful professionalism which may draw on McQueen's early days as a student actor in New York. It is not the callow Horst Buchholz but McQueen who is the real tyro of the group. A Hemingway hero, his experience of life has not caught up with his expertise, and for much of the film he is concerned to define himself by the standards of the job he has been given. The other gunmen either sympathize with the Mexicans or are antagonistic; only McQueen is indifferent to them. But he is enough of a romantic to wonder at the absence of women, and when a cache of them is discovered, hidden by anxious relatives, his response is a touching solicitude. As Buchholz unceremoniously heaves Rosenda Monteros over his saddle McQueen murmurs, "Gently, boy . . . gently."

Repressed loners in search of standards were McQueen's speciality. His wintry blue eyes, neat movements, and clipped unemotional voice told you everything you needed to know about life on the road, in the trenches, in prison, or on the trail. He did not mind being unsympathetic; audiences knew he was a cut above those around him, and identified with his locked-tongue loneliness, his private obsession—something Peckinpah explored (and exploited) to great effect in *The Getaway*.

The best McQueens are in the 1960s. His ambitious young professional gambler in *The Cincinnati Kid*, psychopathic World War II G.I. in *Hell Is for Heroes*, World War II pilot in *The War Lover*, itinerant jazz musician in *Love with the Proper Stranger*, and rootless wanderer in *Baby the Rain Must Fall* all flirt with villainy, particularly in their callous attitude toward the women who love these driven men. His Frank Bullitt in *Bullitt* is no better, but when, in the final enigmatic scene, he returns to his apartment after the bloody airport shootout, sees his mistress sleeping, and impassively washes his hands before joining her, the line between hero and clod is decisively drawn.

Yearning for critical respectability as a versatile actor, not just a film star, McQueen grew a beard and took on the change-of-pace role of the whistleblowing title character who earns the enmity of the society he is trying to protect in an ambitious film version of Ibsen's *The Enemy of the People*, financed by his own company. No one but McQueen, it seemed, believed the arty film had a chance of finding an audience, and it was never released to theaters; it languished on the shelf for several years before being shuttled to television.

McQueen bounced back in a pair of films more in harmony with his traditional image, the Western *Tom Horn* (ironically a sort of cowboy variation on *The Enemy of the People*) and the action film *The Hunter*, in which he played a real-life tracker of crooks who jump bail. *Horn* was a flop but *The Hunter* proved the commercial shot in the arm the actor needed to maintain his star status. Unfortunately, he had earlier

been diagnosed with cancer and spent the last months of his life seeking miracle cures in Mexico and elsewhere before succumbing to the disease at the young age of 50.

—John Baxter, updated by John McCarty

MENJOU, Adolphe

Nationality: American. **Born:** Adolphe Jean Menjou in Pittsburgh, Pennsylvania, 18 February 1890. **Education:** Attended St. Joseph's Seminary, Rockwell Public School, and East High School, all in Cleveland; Culver Military Academy, Indiana, 1906-07; Stiles University Preparatory School, Ithaca, New York; Cornell University, Ithaca, 1908-11. **Military Service:** Served in the Ambulance Corps, 1917-19; Captain. **Family:** Married 1) Katherine Tinsley (divorced); 2) Kathryn Carver (divorced); 3) the actress Verree Teasdale, 1934, adopted son: Peter. **Career:** Managed one of his father's restaurants in Cleveland, 1911-12; then a variety of jobs in New York; 1914—film debut in *The Man behind the Door*; 1919—production manager for Van Buren film company in New York; 1923—first starring role, in Chaplin's *A Woman of Paris*; 1929-30—worked in Paris on several French-language films; 1930—MGM contract: starred with Cooper and Dietrich in *Morocco*; 1944—co-founder, Motion Picture Alliance for the Preservation of American Ideals; 1947—"friendly" witness before the HUAC; 1952-54—host on TV series *Favorite Story*. **Died:** 29 October 1963.

Films as Actor:

1914   *The Man behind the Door* (Van) (as ringmaster)
1916   *A Parisian Romance* (Thompson) (as Juliani); *Nearly a King* (Thompson); *The Habit of Happiness* (Dwan); *The Price of Happiness* (Lawrence); *The Crucial Test* (John Ince) (as Russian colonel); *Romeo and Juliet* (Noble) (as a Capulet); *The Scarlet Runner* (Van—serial); *Manhattan Madness* (Dwan); *The Devil at His Elbow* (B. King); *The Kiss* (Henderson); *The Reward of Patience* (Vignola); *The Blue Envelope Mystery* (North)
1917   *The Valentine Girl* (Dawley) (as Joe Winder); *An Even Break* (Hillyer); *The Amazons* (Kaufman) (as Count de Grivel); *The Moth* (Jose) (as husband)
1920   *What Happened to Rosa?* (Schertzinger) (as reporter)
1921   *The Faith Healer* (Melford) (as Dr. Littlefield); *Courage* (Franklin) (as Bruce Ferguson); *Through the Back Door* (Green and J. Pickford) (as James Brewster); *The Three Musketeers* (Niblo) (as Louis XIII); *Queenie* (Mitchell) (as Count Michael); *The Sheik* (Melford) (as Raoul de Saint Hubert)
1922   *Head over Heels* (Schertzinger) (as Sterling); *Is Matrimony a Failure?* (Cruze) (as Dudley King); *The Eternal Flame* (Lloyd) (as Duc de Langeais); *The Fast Mail* (Durning) (as Cal Baldwin); *Clarence* (DeMille) (as Hubert Stem); *Pink Gods* (Stanlaws) (as Louis Barney); *Singed Wings* (Stanlaws) (as Bliss Gordon)
1923   *The World's Applause* (W. DeMille) (as Robert Townsend); *Bella Donna* (Fitzmaurice) (as Mr. Chepstow); *Rupert of Hentzau* (Heerman) (as Count Rischenheim); *A Woman of Paris* (Chaplin) (as Pierre Revel); *The Spanish Dancer* (Brenon) (as Don Salluste)
1924   *The Marriage Circle* (Lubitsch) (as Prof. Josef Stock); *Shadows of Paris* (Brenon) (as Georges de Croy); *The Marriage*

Adolphe Menjou

Cheat (Wray) (as Bob Canfield); *For Sale* (Archainbaud) (as Joseph Hudley); *Broadway after Dark* (Bell) (as Ralph Norton); *Broken Barriers* (Barker) (as Tommie Kemp); *Sinners in Silk* (Henley) (as Arthur Merrill); *Open All Night* (Bern) (as Edmond Duverne); *The Fast Set* (W. DeMille) (as Ernest Steel); *Forbidden Paradise* (Lubitsch) (as Chancellor)

1925 *The Swan* (Buchowetski) (as Albert of Kersten-Rodenfels); *A Kiss in the Dark* (Tuttle) (as Walter Grenham); *Are Parents People?* (St. Clair) (as Mr. Hazlitt); *Lost—A Wife* (W. DeMille) (as Tony Hamilton); *The King on Main Street* (Bell) (as Serge IV, King of Molvania)

1926 *The Grand Duchess and the Waiter* (St. Clair) (as Albert Durant); *A Social Celebrity* (St. Clair) (as Max Haber); *Fascinating Youth* (Wood) (as himself); *The Ace of Cads* (Reed) (as Chappel Maturin); *The Sorrows of Satan* (Griffith) (as Prince Lucio de Rimanez)

1927 *Blonde or Brunette* (Rosson) (as Henri Martel); *Evening Clothes* (Reed) (as Lucien D'Artois); *Service for Ladies* (D'Arrast) (as Albert Leroux); *A Gentleman of Paris* (D'Arrast) (as Marquis de Marignan); *Serenade* (D'Arrast) (as Franz Rossi)

1928 *A Night of Mystery* (Mendes) (as Capt. Ferreol); *His Tiger Wife* (Henley) (as Henri); *His Private Life* (Tuttle) (as Georges St. Germain)

1929 *Marquis Preferred* (Tuttle) (as Marquis d'Argenville); *Fashions in Love* (Schertzinger) (as Paul de Remy)

1930 *Mon gosse de père* (de Limur; also in English-language version, *The Parisian*) (as Gerome); *L'Enigmatique Monsieur Parkes* (Gasnier—French-language version of *Slightly Scarlet*; also in Spanish-language version, *Amore audaz*) (as M. Parkes); *Morocco* (von Sternberg) (as La Bessier); *New Moon* (Conway) (as Gov. Boris Brusiloff)

1931 *Wir um schalten auf Hollywood* (Reicher—German-language version of *The March of Time*); *Soyons gai* (Robinson—French-language version of *Let Us Be Gay*); *The Easiest Way* (Conway) (as Willard Brockton); *The Front Page* (Milestone) (as Walter Burns); *Men Call It Love* (Selwyn) (as Tony Minot); *The Great Lover* (Beaumont) (as Paurel); *Friends and Lovers* (Schertzinger) (as Capt. Roberts)

1932 *Forbidden* (Capra) (as Bob Grover); *Prestige* (Garnett) (as Capt. Remy Baudoin); *Bachelor's Affairs* (Werker) (as Andrew Hoyt); *Night Club Lady* (Cummings) (as Thatcher Colt); *Two White Arms* (*Wives Beware*) (Niblo) (as Maj. Carey Liston); *Blame the Woman* (*Diamond Cut Diamond*) (Niblo) (as Dan McQueen); *A Farewell to Arms* (Borzage) (as Maj. Rinaldi)

1933 *The Circus Queen Murder* (Neill) (as Thatcher Colt); *Morning Glory* (Sherman) (as Louis Easton); *The Worst Woman in Paris?* (Bell) (as Adolphe Ballou); *Convention City* (Mayo) (as T. R. Kent)

1934 *Easy to Love* (Keighley) (as John Townsend); *The Trumpet Blows* (Roberts) (as Pancho Gomez); *Journal of a Crime* (Keighley) (as Paul Molet); *Little Miss Marker* (Hall) (as Sorrowful Jones); *The Great Flirtation* (Murphy) (as Stephen Karpath); *The Human Side* (Buzzell) (as Gregory Sheldon); *The Mighty Barnum* (Walter Lang) (as B. Walsh)

1935 *Gold Diggers of 1935* (Berkeley) (as Nicoleff); *Broadway Gondolier* (Bacon) (as Prof. de Vinci)

1936 *The Milky Way* (McCarey) (as Gabby Sloan); *Sing, Baby, Sing* (Lanfield) (as Bruce Farraday); *Wives Never Know* (Nugent) (as J. Hugh Ramsey)

1937 *One in a Million* (Lanfield) (as Ted Spencer); *A Star Is Born* (Wellman) (as Oliver Niles); *Cafe Metropole* (E. Griffith) (as Monsieur Victor); *100 Men and a Girl* (Koster) (as John Cardwell); *Stage Door* (La Cava) (as Anthony Powell)

1938 *The Golden Follies* (Marshall) (as Oliver Merlin); *Letter of Introduction* (Stahl) (as John Mannering); *Thanks for Everything* (Seiter) (as J. B. Harcourt)

1939 *King of the Turf* (Green) (as Jim Mason); *Golden Boy* (Mamoulian) (as Tom Moody); *That's Right—You're Wrong* (Butler) (as Stavey Delmere); *The Housekeeper's Daughter* (Roach) (as Deakon Maxwell)

1940 *A Bill of Divorcement* (Farrow) (as Hilary Fairfield); *Turnabout* (Roach) (as Phil Manning)

1941 *Road Show* (Roach and Douglas) (as Col. Carleton Carraway); *Father Takes a Wife* (Hively) (as Frederic Osborne)

1942 *Roxie Hart* (Wellman) (as Billy Flynn); *Syncopation* (Dieterle) (as George Latimer); *You Were Never Lovelier* (Seiter) (as Edwardo)

1943 *Hi Diddle Diddle* (Stone) (as Col. Hector Phyffe); *Sweet Rosie O'Grady* (Cummings) (as Thomas Moran)

1944 *Step Lively* (Whelan) (as Wagner)

1945 *Man Alive* (Enright) (as Kismet)

1946 *Heartbeat* (Wood) (as ambassador); *The Bachelor's Daughter* (Stone) (as Mr. Moody)

1947 *I'll Be Yours* (Seiter) (as Weschsberg); *District Attorney* (Sinclair) (as Craig Warren); *The Hucksters* (Conway) (as Mr. Kimberly)

1948 *State of the Union* (Capra) (as Jim Conover)

1949 *My Dream Is Yours* (Curtiz) (as Thomas Hutchins); *Dancing in the Dark* (Reis) (as Crossman)

1950 *To Please a Lady* (Brown) (as Gregs)

1951 *The Tall Target* (Anthony Mann) (as Caleb Jeffers); *Across the Wide Missouri* (Wellman) (as Pierre)

1952 *The Sniper* (Kramer) (as Lt. Kafka)

1953 *Man on a Tightrope* (Kazan) (as Fesker)

1955 *Timberjack* (Kane) (as Swiftwater Tilton)

1956 *The Ambassador's Daughter* (Krasna) (as Senator Cartwright); *The Fuzzy Pink Nightgown* (Taurog) (as Arthur Martin)

1957 **Paths of Glory** (Kubrick) (as Gen. Broulard)

1958 *I Married a Woman* (Kanter) (as Frederick W. Sutton)

1960 *Pollyanna* (Swift) (as Mr. Prendergast)

Publications

By MENJOU: book—

It Took Nine Tailors, 1948.

By MENJOU: article—

"Man of Two Worlds—and 250 Movies," in *Films and Filming* (London), August 1961.

On MENJOU: articles—

Current Biography 1948, New York, 1948.

Obituary, in *New York Times*, 30 October 1963.

Buñuel, Luis, "Variations sur la moustache de Menjou," in *Cinématographe* (Paris), September-October 1983.

Holland, Larry Lee, in *Films in Review* (New York), October 1983, see also issues for November 1983 and January and April 1984.

*   *   *

One of the most amazing things about that most sophisticated of boulevard-actors, Adolphe Menjou, is that his mother was a Gaelic-speaking peasant girl from Connemara, Nora Joyce. True, his father was a French hotelier in Pittsburgh where Adolphe was born. It does not appear that he imbibed the principles of the French Revolution from his father nor did the conservative Catholicism of his mother produce in him an active social consciousness. It is not surprising then that he proved the most cooperative witness before the Committee on Un-American activities in later years.

Educated in Cleveland and at the Culver Military Academy in Indiana and the Engineering school at Cornell University, but smitten with acting fever, he arrived in New York at the age of 23. At that time New York and New Jersey were the centers of the American film industry. After assorted jobs Menjou drifted into films, working with Vitagraph and independent companies. In a Fox film, *A Parisian Romance*, Menjou moved out of the ranks of extras. He continued in films, appearing in *The Scarlet Runner* serial, a version of *Romeo and Juliet* with Francis X. Bushman, and gained experience in bit parts. Eventually he joined an ambulance unit from Cornell and spent two years military service in Europe. After the war he moved to Hollywood, the new home of the film industry. He was helped by his old acquaintance Fatty Arbuckle, and played in Mabel Normand and Mary Pickford films until he landed the juicy part of Louis XIII in Fairbanks's *The Three Musketeers*. His reputation was now made. He had already established his stock-in-trade—the well-dressed figure and the cultivated moustache. He was in *The Sheik* with Valentino, *The Eternal Flame* (as the Duc de Langeais) with Norma Talmadge, in *Bella Donna* with Pola Negri, and even in a Western with Buck Jones, *The Fast Mail*. But it was in Chaplin's *A Woman of Paris* that the Menjou style was once and for all perfected. Apart from the unusual fact that this was a serious Chaplin film in which the great comedian did not appear (except in a walk-on part) but was a highly imaginative piece of filmmaking, it was bound to attract attention. Menjou as the elegantly cynical man-about-town created a memorable figure. Under Chaplin's meticulous direction—the film took eight months in production and as many as 200 takes were sometimes made for one scene—Menjou created a style which was to become his trademark on the screen, particularly in the films of Mal St. Clair and Harry D'Arrast. In 1924 he had big roles in Lubitsch's *Forbidden Paradise* and *The Marriage Circle*, both masterpieces of sophistication. The three D'Arrast films he worked on were *A Gentleman of Paris*, *Serenade*, and *Service for Ladies*, all of 1927. He appeared with Lillian Gish in Molnar's *The Swan*, directed by Dmitri Buchowetzski. Another of his successes was St. Clair's *The Grand Duchess and the Waiter* which made him a highly paid star, and accepted as one of Hollywood's elite.

With the coming of talking pictures Menjou actually went to France and played in Jean de Limur's *Mon gosse de père*. He spoke many languages including Gaelic. He appeared in French versions of other films in Hollywood including *L'Enigmatique Monsieur Parkes* with Claudette Colbert. And then came two big breaks. He played in von Sternberg's *Morocco* with Dietrich and Gary Cooper, again playing the debonair man-of-the-world who loses in the game of love. In Lewis Milestone's *The Front Page* he played a tough newspaper editor in a script by Hecht and MacArthur. It was an exacting role, and Menjou rose to the occasion most successfully. From then on his career was well and truly established. He played for most of the important directors and in films such as *A Farewell to Arms* with Helen Hayes and Gary Cooper, *Morning Glory* with Katharine Hepburn, *The Milky Way* with Harold Lloyd, *100 Men and a Girl* with Deanna Durbin, and even partnered Shirley Temple in *Little Miss Marker*. He was in William Wellman's version of *A Star Is Born* in 1937. His professionalism never flagged and his reliability as an actor kept him in constant demand.

To the end of his career he continued to shine, and few will forget his superb performance as the defense counsel in *Roxie Hart* where he is coaching Ginger Rogers who is on trial for her life. In Stanley Kubrick's *Paths of Glory* in 1957 Menjou gives a fine performance as the cynical General Broulard. Cynicism being one of his stocks in trade it was fitting that it should be he who played Satan in the D. W. Griffith silent film *The Sorrows of Satan* in 1926, not one of Griffith's best.

—Liam O'Leary

MERCOURI, Melina

Nationality: Greek. **Born:** Maria Amalia Mercouris in Athens, 18 October 1925. **Education:** Studied acting at the Academy of the National Theatre, Athens, 1943-46. **Family:** Married 1) Panayiotis Harakopos, 1942; 2) the director Jules Dassin, 1966. **Career:** 1946—stage debut in modern play by Alexis Solomos followed by a series of modern plays on the Greek stage; 1955—film debut in *Stella*; 1960—international attention in role in *Never on Sunday*; then appeared in several international productions; 1967—debut on Broadway, in *Ilya, Darling*; 1977—earlier political activity against the regime of the "colonels" led to being elected to Parliament; 1981—named Minister of Culture and Sciences; 1985—became Minister of Culture, Youth and Sports; 1989—lost post when her party was voted out of office; regained post in 1993 when her party was returned to power. **Awards:** Best Actress, Cannes Festival, for *Never on Sunday*, 1960. **Died:** Of lung cancer, in New York City, 6 March 1994.

Films as Actress:

1955   *Stella* (Cacoyannis) (title role)
1957   *Celui qui doit mourir* (*He Who Must Die*) (Dassin) (as Mary Magdalene)
1958   *The Gypsy and the Gentleman* (Losey) (as Belle)
1959   *La Loi* (*Where the Hot Wind Blows*; *Le legge*; *The Law*) (Dassin) (as Donna Lucrezia)
1960   *Pote tin kryiaki* (*Never on Sunday*) (Dassin) (as Ilya)
1961   *Vive Henri IV, Vive l'amour* (Autant-Lara); *Il giudizio universale* (*The Last Judgment*) (de Sica)
1962   *Phaedra* (Dassin) (title role)
1963   *The Victors* (Foreman) (as Magda)
1964   *Topkapi* (Dassin) (as Elizabeth Lipp)
1965   *Les Pianos mécaniques* (*The Uninhibited*) (Bardem) (as Jenny)
1966   *A Man Could Get Killed* (Neame and Owen) (as Aurora-Celeste da Costa); *10:30 P.M. Summer* (Dassin) (as Maria)
1969   *Gaily, Gaily* (*Chicago, Chicago*) (Jewison) (as Queen Lil)
1970   *La Promesse de l'aube* (*Promise at Dawn*) (Dassin) (as Nina Kacew)
1975   *Once Is Not Enough* (Guy Green) (as Karla)
1976   *Nasty Habits* (*The Abbess*) (Lindsay-Hogg) (as Sister Gertrude)
1978   *A Dream of Passion* (Dassin) (as Maya/Medea)
1980   *Diving for Roman Plunder: The Cousteau Odyssey* (doc) (as commentator)
1984   *Keine zufällige Geschichte* (*Not by Coincidence*) (Kerr)

Publications

By MERCOURI: book—

I Was Born Greek, London, 1971.

By MERCOURI: article—

"The Time Has Come for American Travelers to Return to Europe," in *USA Today Magazine* (Arlington, Virginia), May 1987.

On MERCOURI: book—

Arnold, Frank, and Michael Esser, editors, *Hommage für Melina Mercouri und Jules Dassin*, Berlin, 1984.

On MERCOURI: articles—

Reed, Rex, in *Do You Sleep in the Nude?*, New York, 1968.

Melina Mercouri

Eyles, A., "Melina Mercouri," in *Focus on Film* (London), March-April 1970.

Ciné Revue (Paris), 28 January 1982.

Sight and Sound (London), Summer 1982.

Current Biography 1988, New York, 1988.

Orth, Maureen, "'La Pasionaria' of the Acropolis," in *Vanity Fair* (New York), February 1991.

Stars (Mariembourg, Belgium), March 1992.

Obituary in *New York Times*, 7 March 1994.

Obituary in *Variety* (New York), 14 March 1994.

*   *   *

"To be born Greek," Melina Mercouri once wrote, "is to be magnificently cursed." The statement is wholly in character; like her acting, it is unashamedly larger than life, and its bearing on literal truth is beside the point. As an actress, Mercouri was a phenomenon, and objecting that she overacted is like pointing out that the Parthenon would make an uncomfortable living room.

With *Never on Sunday* Mercouri burst upon an undefended world. It was her third film with the expatriate American director Jules Dassin, though their first Greek film together. They had previously teamed for *Where the Hot Wind Blows*, a neorealist love triangle drama set in Italy co-starring Yves Montand and Gina Lollobrigida, and the Christ story parable *He Who Must Die*, based on the novel by her fellow countryman Nikos Kazantzakis. Suggestions that she lured Dassin into pretension may be unjustified, since *He Who Must Die* was well into preparation before she was cast as the Magdalene figure. There was nothing pretentious about *Never on Sunday*, though—it was glorious hokum, frank and unabashed, and Mercouri as the tart with a heart was loud, brash, and irresistible. Dassin himself took the part of the sailor who falls for her. Made for $150,000 (and looking it), it raked in $15 million worldwide.

Tawny-haired, green-eyed, with a husky voice extending well down the baritone range, Mercouri could handle melodrama or broad comedy, but hardly high tragedy, as *Phaedra*, another of her films with Dassin, proved conclusively. *Topkapi* worked better for both of them. In it, Dassin recycled elements from his earlier classic about a not-so-perfect crime, *Rififi*, into a comedy about an even more intricate heist of a diamond in an Istanbul museum. The film was a crowd pleaser and critical hit. Mercouri acted up a storm, though Peter Ustinov stole the film and won a Best Supporting Actor Oscar as the bumbling member of the gang.

Mercouri and Dassin's final collaborations were *10:30 P.M. Summer*; *Promise at Dawn*, from writer Romain Gary's memoir about his mother; and *A Dream of Passion*, a modern-day version of the classic

Greek tragedy *Medea*. None fared well with either audiences or critics. Mercouri remained in demand as an international star, however, appearing in a string of high-profile American and European films that did little to satisfy her artistic appetite. She played a roaring twenties Chicago prostitute in Jewison's *Gaily, Gaily*—and was mercifully lost among the slumming ensemble cast of *Once Is Not Enough,* a jet-set soap opera from the pen of Jacqueline Susann.

Politics were in Mercouri's blood. Her grandfather had been mayor of Athens, her father minister of the interior, and Dassin, whom she married, was a victim of the Hollywood blacklist—as was director Joseph Losey, with whom she also made a film, *The Gypsy and the Gentleman.* When the Colonels seized power she quit Greece and, despite threats to her life, campaigned tirelessly against them all over the world. The regime revoked her citizenship, incurring her resplendent scorn: "I was born Greek and I shall die Greek. They were born fascists and they will die fascists."

After returning to Greece she made only three more films; increasingly, politics took over. Appointed minister of culture in the Socialist government, she temporarily renounced acting, turning her energies to revitalizing the rickety Greek film industry. Mercouri once numbered among her ambitions "to win an Oscar, and become President of Greece." She died in 1994, both goals having eluded her.

—Philip Kemp, updated by John McCarty

MEREDITH, Burgess

Nationality: American. **Born:** Cleveland, Ohio, 16 November 1908. **Education:** Attended Cathedral Choir School, Cleveland; Hoosac Falls Preparatory School, New York; Amherst College, Massachusetts. **Military Service:** Air Force, 1942-45; then transferred to the Office of War Information and involved in making films for G.I.s. **Family:** Married 1) Helen Berrian Derby, 1932 (divorced 1935); 2) Margaret Perry, 1936 (divorced 1938); 3) the actress Paulette Goddard, 1944 (divorced 1948); 4) Kaja Sundsten, 1952 (separated 1976), two children. **Career:** 1930-33—member of Eva Le Gallienne's Civic Repertory Theatre, debut in *Romeo and Juliet*; 1933—in Broadway production of *The Threepenny Opera*; 1934—radio debut in the program *Red Davis*; 1935—successful role in *Winterset*, written by Maxwell Anderson with Meredith in mind; made film debut in the film version the following year; 1939—in stage production of Orson Welles's *Five Kings*, based on Shakespeare's history plays; host for radio program *Pursuit of Happiness*; 1949—directed the film *The Man on the Eiffel Tower*; 1950—directed and acted in *Happy as Larry* on television; 1963—on London stage in title role of *Hughie*; 1964-65—in TV series *Mr. Novak*, as The Penguin in *Batman*, 1966-68, *Search*, 1972-73, host of *Those Amazing Animals* series, 1980-81, and *Gloria*, 1982-83. **Awards:** Emmy, for *Tail Gunner Joe*, 1977.

Films as Actor:

1936   *Winterset* (Santell) (as Mio)
1937   *There Goes the Groom* (Santley) (as Dick Mathews)
1938   *Spring Madness* (Simon) (as the Lippencott)
1939   *Idiot's Delight* (Brown) (as Quillery); *Of Mice and Men* (Milestone) (as George Milton)
1940   *Castle on the Hudson* (*Years without Days*) (Litvak) (as Steven Rockford); *Second Chorus* (Potter) (as Hank Taylor)
1941   *San Francisco Docks* (Lubin) (as Johnny Barnes); *The Forgotten Village* (Kline) (as narrator); *That Uncertain Feeling* (Lubitsch) (as Sebastian); *Tom, Dick, and Harry* (Kanin) (as Harry)

1942   *Street of Chance* (Hively) (as Frank Thompson)
1944   *Tunisian Victory* (doc) (as narrator)
1945   *The Story of G.I. Joe* (*G.I. Joe*; *War Correspondent*) (Wellman) (as Ernie Pyle)
1946   *Diary of a Chambermaid* (*Le Journal d'une femme de chambre*) (Renoir) (as Capt. Mauger, + co-pr, sc); *Magnificent Doll* (Borzage) (as James Madison); *Hymn of Nations* (doc) (as narrator)
1948   *On Our Merry Way* (*A Miracle Can Happen*) (King Vidor and Fenton) (as Oliver Pease, + co-pr); *Mine Own Executioner* (Kimmins) (as Felix Milne)
1949   *Jigsaw* (Markle) (as bartender)
1953   *Golden Arrow* (*The Gay Adventure*; *Three Men and a Girl*) (Parry) (as Dick)
1957   *Albert Schweitzer* (Hill) (as narrator); *Joe Butterfly* (Hibbs) (title role)
1958   *Sorcerer's Village* (doc) (as narrator)
1961   *Universe* (doc) (as narrator)
1962   *Advise and Consent* (Preminger) (as Herbert Gelman)
1963   *The Cardinal* (Preminger) (as Father Ned Halley)
1964   *The Kidnappers* (*Man on the Run*) (Romero) (as Louis Halliburton)
1965   *In Harm's Way* (Preminger) (as Cmdr. Egan Powell)
1966   *Crazy Quilt* (Korty) (as narrator); *A Big Hand for the Little Lady* (Cook) (as Doc Scully); *Madame X* (Rich) (as Dan Sullivan); *Batman* (Martinson) (as The Penguin)
1967   *Discover America* (doc) (as narrator); *Hurry Sundown* (Preminger) (as Judge Purcell); *Torture Garden* (Francis) (as Dr. Diablo)
1968   *Stay Away, Joe* (Peter Tewksbury) (as Charlie Lightcloud); *Skidoo* (Preminger) (as the warden)
1969   *MacKenna's Gold* (J. Lee Thompson) (as storekeeper); *The Reivers* (Rydell) (as narrator); *Hard Contract* (Pogostin) (as Ramsey Williams)
1970   *There Was a Crooked Man* (Joseph L. Mankiewicz) (as the Missouri Kid)
1971   *Such Good Friends* (Preminger) (as Bernard Kalman); *Clay Pigeon* (Tom Stern and Slate) (as the sculptor); *Lock, Stock, and Barrel* (Thorpe—for TV); *The Strange Monster of Strawberry Cove* (Shea—for TV)
1972   *The Man* (Sargent—for TV but released theatrically) (as Sen. Watson); *Probe* (*Search*) (Mayberry—for TV); *A Fan's Notes* (Till) (as Mr. Blue); *Getting Away from It All* (Philips—for TV)
1973   *Hay que matar a B.* (*B. Must Die*) (Borau)
1974   *Golden Needles* (Clouse) (as Winters)
1975   *The Day of the Locust* (Schlesinger) (as Harry); *Ninety-Two in the Shade* (McGuane) (as Goldsboro); *The Hindenburg* (Wise) (as Emilio Pajetta)
1976   *Rocky* (Avildsen) (as Mickey); *Burnt Offerings* (Dan Curtis) (as Brother)
1977   *The Last Hurrah* (Sherman—for TV); *Johnny, We Hardly Knew Ye* (Cates—for TV); *Golden Rendezvous* (Lazarus) (as Van Heurden); *The Great Georgia Bank Hoax* (*The Great Bank Hoax*; *Shenanigans*) (Jacoby) (as Jack Stutz); *SST—Death Flight* (*SST—Disaster in the Sky*; *Death Flight*) (Rich—for TV); *The Manitou* (Girdler) (as Dr. Ernest Snow); *Tail Gunner Joe* (Jud Taylor—for TV) (as Joseph N. Walsh); *The Sentinel* (Winner) (as Charles Chazen)
1978   *Foul Play* (Higgins) (as Hennessey); *Magic* (Attenborough) (as Ben Greene); *Kate Bliss and the Ticker Tape Kid* (Kennedy—for TV); *The Amazing Captain Nemo* (March) (as Prof. Waldo Cunningham)
1979   *Rocky II* (Stallone) (as Mickey)
1980   *When Time Ran Out* (*Earth's Final Fury*) (Goldstone) (as Rene Valdez); *Final Assignment* (Almond) (as Zak)

1981   *True Confessions* (Grosbard) (as Seamus Fargo); *The Last Chase*
        (Burke) (as Capt. J. G. Williams); *Clash of the Titans*
        (Desmond Davis) (as Ammon)
1982   *Rocky III* (Stallone) (as Mickey)
1983   *Twilight Zone—The Movie* (Landis, Spielberg, and Dante) (as
        narrator)
1984   *Wet Gold* (Lowry—for TV) (as Sampson)
1985   *Santa Claus: The Movie* (Szwarc) (as Ancient Elf)
1986   *Outrage!* (Grauman—for TV) (as Judge Aaron Klein); *Elephant
        Games* (Blumberg—for TV)
1987   *King Lear* (Godard) (as Don Learo); *Mr. Corbett's Ghost* (Danny
        Huston)
1988   *Full Moon in Blue Water* (Masterson) (as the General); *Hot to
        Trot* (Dinner) (as voice of Don's dad, uncredited)
1990   *Rocky V* (Avildsen) (as Mickey); *State of Grace* (Joanou) (as
        Finn)
1991   *Oddball Hall* (Hunsicker) (as Ingersol); *Night of the Hunter*
        (David Greene—for TV) (as Birdy); *Preminger: Anatomy
        of a Filmmaker* (Robins—doc) (as narrator)
1992   *Mastergate* (for TV) (as Wylie Slaughter); *Lincoln* (Kunhardt—
        doc for TV) (as Winfield Scott)
1993   *Grumpy Old Men* (Petrie) (as Grandpa Gustafson); *Jean Renoir*
        (David Thompson—doc)
1994   *Camp Nowhere* (Prince) (as Fein); *Across the Moon* (Gottlieb)
        (as Barney)
1995   *Grumpier Old Men* (Deutch) (as Grandpa Gustafson)

Films as Director:

1944   *Salute to France* (co-d); *Welcome to Britain* (co-d); *Rear Gunner*
1947   *A Yank Came Back* (co-d, + ro as narrator)
1949   *The Man on the Eiffel Tower* (+ ro as Huertin)
1969   *The Third Eye* (*The Ying and the Yang*) (+ ro)

Publications

By MEREDITH: book—

So Far, So Good: A Memoir, Boston, 1994.

By MEREDITH: articles—

"Talking with . . . Burgess Meredith: The Old Men and the Sea," in
    People Weekly (New York), 13 June 1994.
Interview with Henry Cabot Beck, in *Interview* (New York), January
    1996.

On MEREDITH: book—

Parish, James Robert, and William T. Leonard, *Hollywood Players: The
    Thirties*, New Rochelle, New York, 1976.

On MEREDITH: articles—

Current Biography 1940, New York, 1940.
Ciné Revue (Paris), 2 July 1981 and 12 January 1984.
Henderson, J. A., "Burgess Meredith," in *Film Dope* (Nottingham,
    England), October 1989.

*   *   *

Burgess Meredith has, for the most part, always played the eccentric on screen; his roles have included everything from Tweedledee in

Alice in Wonderland to "The Penguin" in *Batman* to a ninetysomething
whippersnapper in the *Grumpy Old Men* films. Nevertheless, his screen
career has been an off-and-on affair. He once remarked, ever-so-
aptly, "I disappear from the public eye and get rediscovered quite
often."

Meredith made his film debut as the idealistic, revenge-seeking Mio
in the highly stylized screen version of Maxwell Anderson's verse-
play *Winterset*, a role he created on Broadway. Some of his best roles
came early in his career: George, the migrant worker and protector of
the simple-minded, oversized Lennie, in *Of Mice and Men*; the nonconformist suitor in *Tom, Dick, and Harry*; the malcontent pianist in
That Uncertain Feeling; and the loony neighbor in Renoir's *Diary of
a Chambermaid*. For Hollywood's purposes, Meredith's small frame
made him more appropriately cast as the war correspondent, rather
than the warrior; he was the personal choice of Ernie Pyle to star as
the fabled war reporter in *The Story of G.I. Joe*.

Still, Meredith never did make a full commitment to film. Between
the 1930s and mid-1960s, he often could be found on the stage,
appearing in the likes of *High Tor*, *The Threepenny Opera*, *Liliom*,
and *Candida*, and writing and directing *Ulysses in Nighttown* and *A
Thurber Carnival*.

His most famous screen role—the pugnacious fight manager in
Rocky—came exactly four decades after his screen debut. Meredith
then became a major Hollywood personality, and was very much in
demand. He gave a masterful performance as attorney Joseph N.
Walsh on television in *Tail Gunner Joe*, although his other screen and
television appearances, ranging from hosting *Those Amazing Animals*
to playing a vet on *Gloria*, a short-lived spin-off of *All in the Family*,
have been less than impressive.

Back in 1937, critic Wolcott Gibbs hailed Meredith, in *The New
Yorker*, as "brilliant, impressive, heartbreaking, vibrant and eloquent."
Gibbs was, of course, talking of Meredith the stage performer. Sadly,
there are only a handful of film roles that live up to that estimation.

—Anthony Slide, updated by Audrey E. Kupferberg

MIDLER, Bette

Nationality: American. **Born:** Honolulu, Hawaii (some sources say
Paterson, New Jersey), 1 December 1945. **Education:** Attended the
University of Hawaii; studied acting at the Berghof Studio. **Family:**
Married Martin von Haselberg, 1984, daughter: Sophie. **Career:**
1966—film debut in bit part in *Hawaii*, then returned to Hollywood
with unit; moved to New York, worked off-Broadway (including *Salvation*, 1969) and in Broadway production of *Fiddler on the Roof*;
1970—singer/entertainer (with Barry Manilow) at The Continental
Bathhouse, Manhattan; 1971—recording contract; 1979—film debut
in starring role in *The Rose*; 1985—signed three-picture contract with
Touchstone Pictures (extended 1987); also co-founder, All Girls Productions. **Address:** c/o Rick Nicita, Creative Artists Agency, 9830
Wilshire Boulevard, Beverly Hills, CA 90212, U.S.A.

Films as Actress:

1966   *Hawaii* (George Roy Hill) (as passenger)
1969   *Goodbye, Columbus* (Peerce) (bit part)
1974   *The Divine Mr. J* (Alexander—filmed record of 1969 off-
        Broadway musical *Salvation*) (as the Virgin Mary)
1979   *The Rose* (Rydell) (as Rose)
1980   *Divine Madness!* (Ritchie—filmed record of a concert)
1982   *Jinxed!* (Siegel) (as Bonita Friml)

Bette Midler in *The Rose*

1986   *Down and Out in Beverly Hills* (Mazursky) (as Barbara Whiteman); *Ruthless People* (Abrahams) (as Barbara Stone)
1987   *Outrageous Fortune* (Hiller) (as Sandy Brozinsky)
1988   *Big Business* (Abrahams) (as Sadie Ratliff/Sadie Shelton); *Oliver & Company* (Scribner—animation) (as voice of Georgette); *Beaches* (Garry Marshall) (as C. C. Bloom, + co-mus, co-pr)
1990   *Stella* (Erman) (as Stella Claire)
1991   *For the Boys* (Rydell) (as Dixie Leonard, + co-pr); *Scenes from a Mall* (Mazursky) (as Deborah Fifer)
1993   *Hocus Pocus* (Ortega) (as Winifred Sanderson); *Gypsy* (Ardolino—for TV) (as Rose Hovick); *Earth and the American Dream* (Couturie—doc) (voice only)
1995   *Get Shorty* (Sonnenfeld) (as Doris)
1996   *The First Wives Club* (Hogan)

Publications

By MIDLER: books—

A View from a Broad, New York, 1980.
The Saga of Baby Divine, New York, 1983.

By MIDLER: articles—

Interview in *Interview* (New York), no. 11, 1974.

Interview in *American Film* (Washington, D.C), September 1978.
Interview in *Films Illustrated* (London), March 1981.
Interview in *Photoplay* (London), February 1982.
Interview in *Hollywood Reporter*, 50th Anniversary Issue, 1986.

On MIDLER: books—

Spada, James, *The Divine Bette Midler*, New York, 1984.
Bego, Mark, *Bette Midler, Outrageously Divine: An Unauthorized Biography*, New York, 1987.
Collins, Ace, *Bette Midler*, New York, 1989.
Mair, George, *Bette: An Intimate Biography of Bette Midler*, Secaucus, New Jersey, 1995.

On MIDLER: articles—

Current Biography 1973, New York, 1973.
Films and Filming (London), February 1980.
Time Out (London), 9 September 1987.
Worrell, Denise, in *Icons: Intimate Portraits*, New York, 1989.
Revue du Cinéma (Paris), February 1989.
"Bette Midler," in *Film Dope* (London), January 1990.
Holden, Stephen, "The Two Sides of Bette Midler, Mushy and Divine," in *New York Times*, 16 July 1995.

*   *   *

Bette Midler represents one of the best examples of a movie star during the sharply focused business mentality of the "New Hollywood" of the 1980s. Developing a persona based on eight previous years of hit records and sold-out concerts, Midler became one of the major film stars of the late 1980s (in 1986 and 1988 she ranked as the top female box-office attraction).

Before entering the film industry, Midler established a devout following focused on her singing and an outrageous personality modeled after Mae West, Sophie Tucker, and Rosalind Russell. Known as "The Divine Miss M," she projected an image of brassy vulgarity, aggressive humor, and bawdy sexuality. Not surprisingly, her film debut as *The Rose* (constructed as a "fictionalized biography" of Janis Joplin) emphasized these traits. Besides showcasing her well-known talents as a singer/comedienne, the film also demonstrated she could act; she received an Academy Award nomination for Best Actress. After the ironically titled *Jinxed!* nearly ended her film career, Midler signed an exclusive contract with Disney (Touchstone Pictures) in 1985. While working for Disney, Midler achieved her greatest success, mostly because she also began to modify her image. Her first six Touchstone films tamed and contained her earlier over-the-top persona to fit the Disney mold and appeal to a wider audience. Midler's characters begin as vulgar, abrasive, and egocentric, but end, after contact with characters exhibiting opposing qualities, as genteel, ingratiating, and cooperative. In *Down and Out in Beverly Hills* she plays a crass, nouveau riche housewife struggling with sexual frigidity. Once "cured" by a homeless man, she softens and contributes to the fight against social inequality. In *Ruthless People* she starts as an unattractive, ostentatious, spoiled, and loudmouthed heiress whose contact with working-class kidnappers reveals generosity, beauty, and self-assured independence. In *Outrageous Fortune*, her vulgarity and overt sexuality become refined and romantic after a series of adventures with an upper-class actress. This interplay between opposites receives its fullest expression in *Big Business*. Midler plays identical twins separated at birth: one a demure daydreamer and the other a ruthless business executive. Each adopts qualities of the other to produce two well-balanced individuals.

Big Business also signaled Midler's move away from comedy and into melodrama. Both *Beaches* and *Stella* functioned as "Women's Films," using a strong, well-known star to address notions of friendship, romance, children, work, self-sacrifice, and death. The synthesis of contradictory personality traits remains however. In *Beaches*, an independent, extroverted celebrityhood turns into a mature sense of private responsibility when her best friend dies and she adopts the orphaned daughter. The film also featured Midler's No. 1 Grammy award winning song ("The Wind beneath My Wings") reinforcing her legacy as a singer. In *Stella* (the third film adaptation of Olive Higgins Prouty's *Stella Dallas*), Midler arranges for her daughter's upward social mobility by sacrificing their relationship. These two films, with their emphasis on romance, work, and children, occurred soon after the birth of her daughter. To make the point even clearer, Midler also played "Mother Earth" on an Earth Day 1990 television special.

This maternal inflection of her star image manifests itself in her most recent films. In *Hocus Pocus*, she parodies herself as a witch who must sacrifice children for her own immortality. In *Gypsy* (a remake of the Rosalind Russell film), she plays the ultimate stage mother whose obsessive nature nearly alienates her daughter; the songs are also tailor-made for Midler's typical performance style. *For the Boys* is perhaps the most revealing of her recent films. Produced by her own company (All Girls Productions), the film combines ribald humor, song and dance, and maternal melodrama. Tracing 50 years in the life of a very popular entertainer and her relationship to her husband, son, and partner, the film highlights and synthesizes every facet of Midler's stardom (and resulted in her second Oscar nomination for Best Actress).

Midler continues to record music, tour, write, and star in films and television specials (her farewell song to Johnny Carson, "Dear Mr. Carson," was the highlight of Carson's televised retirement and won her an Emmy). This ability to successfully perform in a number of interrelated media should secure her stardom in the even more business-oriented Hollywood of the 1990s.

—Greg S. Faller

MIFUNE, Toshiro

Nationality: Japanese. **Born:** Tsingtao, China, of Japanese parents, 1 April 1920. **Education:** Attended Schools in China, and was graduated from Port Arthur High School; studied aerial photography. **Military Service:** Japanese Army, 1939-45. **Family:** Married Takeshi Shiro, 1950, two sons, one daughter. **Career:** 1946—joined Toho Film Company, and made debut in *These Foolish Times*; also studied acting in the Toho drama school; 1948—first of several films for the director Kurosawa, *Drunken Angel*; 1963—formed Mifune Productions; also directed the first film of the company, *The Legacy of the 500,000*; 1966—appeared in first English-language film, *Grand Prix*; 1981—in TV mini-series *Shogun*. **Awards:** Best Actor, Venice Festival, for *Yojimbo*, 1961; Best Actor, Venice Festival, for *Red Beard*, 1965; also Kinema Jumpo Awards for Best Actor, 1961 and 1968. **Address:** Mifune Production Company, 9-30-7 Seijyo, Setagayaku, Tokyo, Japan.

Films as Actor:

1946 *Shin baka jidai (The New Age of Fools; These Foolish Times)* (Yamamoto) (as Genzaburo Ohno)
1947 *Ginrei no hate (Snow Trail)* (Taniguchi) (as Ejima)
1948 *Yoidore tenshi (Drunken Angel)* (Kurosawa) (as Matsunaga)
1949 *Jaokman to Tetsu (Jackoman and Tetsu)* (Taniguchi) (as Tetsu); *Shizukanaru ketto (The Quiet Duel; A Silent Duel)* (Kurosawa) (as Dr. Kyoki Fujisaki); *Norainu (Stray Dog)* (Kurosawa) (as Det. Murakami)
1950 *Datsugoku (Escape from Prison)* (Yamamoto) (as Shinkichi); *Shubun (Scandal)* (Kurosawa) (as Ichiro Aoe); *Konyaku yubiwa (Engagement Ring)* (Kinoshita) (as Takeshi Ema); *Kaizoki-sen (Pirates)* (Inagaki) (as Tora); *Ishinaka-sensei gyojoki datsugoko (Conduct Report on Professor Ishinaka)* (Naruse) (as Nagasawa); *Rashomon (In the Woods)* (Kurosawa) (as Tajomaru)
1951 *Ai to nikushimi no kaneta e (Beyond Love and Hate)* (Taniguchi) (as Goru Sakata); *Hakuchi (The Idiot)* (Kurosawa) (as Denkichi Akama); *Bakuro ich-dai (Life of a Horse-Trader)* (Kimura) (as Yonetaro Katayama); *Kanketsu Sasaki Kojiro (Kojiro Sasaki)* (Inagaki) (as Musashi Miyamoto); *Onna-gokoro dare ga shiru (Who Knows a Woman's Heart?)* (Yamamoto) (as Mizuno); *Ereji (Elegy)* (Yamamoto); *Sengo-ha obake taikai (The Meeting of the Ghost of Après Guerre)* (Saeki)
1952 *Tokyo no koibito (Jewels in Our Hearts; Tokyo Sweetheart)* (Chiba) (as Kurokawa); *Sengoku-burai (Sword for Hire)* (Inagaki) (as Hayatenosuke Sasa); *Saikaku ichidai onna (Life of Oharu; Diary of Oharu)* (Mizoguchi) (as Katsunosuke); *Ketto kagiya no tsuji (Vendetta of Samurai)* (Mori) (as Mataemon Araki); *Muteki (Foghorn)* (Taniguchi) (as Chiyokichi); *Gekiryu (A Swift Current)* (Taniguchi) (as Shunsuke Kosugi); *Minato e kita otoko (The Man Who Came to the Port)* (Honda) (as Goro Shinnuma)

1953 *Himawari-musume* (*Love in a Teacup*; *Sunflower Girl*) (Chiba) (as Ippei Hitachi); *Taiheiyo no washi* (*Eagle of the Pacific*) (Honda) (as Lt. Tomonage); *Fukeyo harukaze* (*My Wonderful Yellow Car*; *Blow! The Spring Breeze*) (Taniguchi) (as Matsumura); *Hoyo* (*The Last Embrace*) (Makino) (as Shinkichi and Hayakawa)

1954 **Shichi-nin no samurai** (*Seven Samurai*) (Kurosawa) (as Kikuchiyo); *Mitsuyu-sen* (*The Black Fury*) (Sugie) (as Eiichi Tsuda); *Miyamoto Musashi* (*Samurai*) (Inagaki) (as Shinmen Musashi); *Shiosai* (*The Surf*) (Taniguchi)

1955 *Zoko Miyamoto Musashi* (*Duel at Ichijoji Temple*) (Inagaki) (as Musashi Miyamoto); *Dansei No. 1* (*A Man among Men*) (Yamamoto); *Ikimoto no kiroki* (*I Live in Fear*; *Record of a Living Being*; *What the Birds Knew*) (Kurosawa) (as Kiichi Nakajima); *Tenka taihai* (*All Is Well*) (Sugie) (as Daikichi Risshun); *Ichijoji no ketto* (*Samurai, Part II*) (Inagaki) (as Miyamoto Musashi); *Otoko arite* (*No Time for Tears*) (Maruyama) (as Mitsuo Yano)

1956 *Ketto ganryu-jima* (*Musashi and Kojiro*; *Samurai, Part III*) (Inagaki) (as Miyamoto Musashi); *Kuroobi sangokushi* (*Rainy Night Duel*) (Taniguchi) (as Masahiko Koseki); *Ankoku-gai* (*The Underworld*) (Kamamoto) (as Det. Kumada); *Aijo no kessan* (*Settlement of Love*; *Accounts of Affection*) (Saburi) (as Shuntaro Ohira); *Tsuma no kokoro* (*A Wife's Heart*) (Naruse) (as Kenkichi Takemura); *Narazumono* (*Scoundrel*; *A Rascal*) (Aoyagi) (as Kanji); *Shujin-sen* (*Rebels of the High Sea*) (Inagaki) (as Tokuzo Matsuo)

1957 *Kumonosu-jo* (*Throne of Blood*; *Cobweb Castle*; *The Castle of the Spider's Web*; *Macbeth*) (Kurosawa) (as Taketoki Washizu); *Shitamachi* (*Downtown*) (Chiba) (as Yoshio Tsuruishi); *Donzoko* (*The Lower Depths*) (Kurosawa) (as Sutebichi); *Arashi no naka no otoko* (*The Man in the Storm*) (Taniguchi) (as Saburo Wataki); *Yagyu bugei-cho* (*The Yangyu*; *Secret Scrolls*) (Inagaki) (as Tasaburo); *Kono futari ni sachi are* (*Be Happy These Two Lovers*) (Honda) (as Toshio Maruyama); *Kiken no eiyu* (*Dangerous Hero*) (Suzuki) as Kawata)

1958 *Muhomatsu no issho* (*The Rickshaw Man*) (Inagaki) (as Matsugoro Tomishima); *Soryu hiken* (*Ninjutsu*; *Secret Scrolls, Part II*) (Inagaki) (as Tasaburo); *Tokyo no kyujitsu* (*Holiday in Tokyo*) (Yamamoto) (as Jiro); *Jinsei gekijo seishun-hen* (*Theatre of Life*) (Sugie) (as Hishakaku); *Kakushi toride no san akunin* (*The Hidden Fortress*; *Three Bad Men in a Hidden Fortress*) (Kurosawa) (as Rokurota Makabe)

1959 *Ankokugai no kaoyaku* (*The Big Boss*) (Okamoto) (as Daisuke Kashimura); *Aru kengo no shogai* (*Samurai Saga*) (Inagaki) (as Heihachiro Komaki); *Sengoku gunto-sen* (*Saga of the Vagabonds*) (Sugie) (as Rokuro); *Nippon tanjo* (*The Three Treasures*) (Inagaki) (as Prince Yamato Takeru); *Dokuritsu gurenta* (*Desperado Outpost*) (Okamoto) (as Capt. Kodama)

1960 *Ankoku-gai no taiketsu* (*The Last Gunfight*) (Okamoto) (as Saburo Fujioka); *Kunisada Chuji* (*The Gambling Samurai*) (Taniguchi) (title role); *Otoko tai otoko* (*Man against Man*) (Taniguchi) (as Kaji); *Taiheiyo no arashi* (*I Bombed Pearl Harbor*) (Matsubayashi) (as Adm. Yamaguchi); *Warui yatsu hodo yoku nemuru* (*The Bad Sleep Well*; *The Rose in the Mud*; *The Worse You Are, the Better You Sleep*) (Kurosawa) (as Koichi Nishi)

1961 *Animas Trujano* (*The Important Man*) (Rodríguez) (title role); **Yojimbo** (*The Bodyguard*) (Kurosawa) (as Sanjuro Kuwabatake); *Osaka-jo monogatari* (*Daredevil in the Castle*) (Inagaki) (as Mohei); *Gen to Fudo-myoh* (*The Youth and His Amulet*) (Inagaki) (as Fudo-myoh)

1962 *Tsubaki Sanjuro* (*Sanjuro*) (Kurosawa) (title role); *Toburoku no Tatsu* (*Tatsu*) (Inagaki) (as Tatsu); *Chushingura* (*Loyal 47 Ronin*; *47 Samurai*) (Inagaki) (as Genban Tawaraboshi)

1963 *Taiheiyo no tsubasa* (*Attack Squadron*) (Matsubayashi) (as Commander Senda); *Tengoku to-jigoku* (*High and Low*; *Heaven and Hell*; *The Ransom*) (Kurosawa) (as Kingo Gondo)

1964 *Daitozuku* (*Samurai Pirate*; *The Lost World of Sinbad*) (Taniguchi) (as Sukazaemon/Luzon); *Dai-tatsumaki* (*Whirlwind*) (Inagaki) (as Morishige Niiro)

1965 *Samurai* (*Samurai Assassin*) (Okamoto) (as Tsuruchiyo Niino); *Akahige* (*Red Beard*) (Kurosawa) (as Dr. Niide); *Sugata sanshiro* (*Judo Saga*) (Uchikawa) (as Shogoro Yano); *Taiheyo kiseki no sakusen Kiska* (*The Retreat from Kiska*) (Maruyama) (as Adm. Kawashima); *Chi to suna* (*Fort Graveyard*) (Okamoto) (as Sgt. Kosugi)

1966 *Abare Goemon* (*Rise against the Sword*) (Inagaki) (title role); *Daibosatsu toge* (*The Sword of Doom*) (Okamoto) (as Toranosuke Shimada); *Kiganjo no boken* (*Adventures of Takla Makan*) (Taniguchi) (as Oosumi); *Doto ichi man kairi* (*The Mad Atlantic*) (Fukuda) (as Heihachiro Murakami); *Grand Prix* (Frankenheimer) (as Izo Yamura)

1967 *Joi-uchi* (*Rebellion*) (Kobayashi) (as Isaburo Sasahara); *Nippon no ichiban nagai hi* (*The Emperor and a General*) (Maruyama) (as War Minister Anami)

1968 *Yamamoto Isoruku* (*Admiral Yamamoto*) (Maruyama) (title role); *Gion matsuri* (*The Day the Sun Rose*) (Yamanuchi) (as Kuma); *Korube no taiyo* (*Tunnel to the Sun*) (Kumai) (as Kitagawa)

1969 *Hell in the Pacific* (*The Enemy*) (Boorman) (as Japanese soldier); *Furin kaza* (*Samurai Banners*; *Under the Banner of Samurai*) (Inagaki) (as Kansuke Yamamoto); *Nippon-kai dai-kaisen* (*Battle of the Japan Sea*) (Maruyama) (as Adm. Togo); *Akage* (*Red Lion*) (Okamoto) (as Gonzo, + co-pr); *Shinsen-gumi* (*Band of Assassins*) (Sawashima) (as Isami Kondo); *Eiko eno 5000 kiro* (*Safari 5000*) (Kurahara) (as Tuichiro Takase)

1970 *Bakumatsu* (*The Ambitious*) (Itoh) (as Shojiro Goto); *Machibuse* (*The Incident at Blood Pass*; *The Ambush*) (Inagaki) (as Tosaburo Hanawa); *Gunbatsu* (*The Militarists*) (Horikawa) (as Isoruku Yamamoto); *Zatoichi to Yojimbo* (*Zatoichi Meets Yojimbo*) (Okamoto) (as Yojimbo)

1971 *Soleil rouge* (*Red Sun*) (Terence Young) (as Kuroda)

1974 *Paper Tiger* (Annakin) (as Ambassador Kagoyama)

1976 *Midway* (*Battle of Midway*) (Smight) (as Adm. Isoroku Yamamoto)

1977 *Ningen no shomei* (*Proof of the Man*) (Sato)

1978 *The Bushido Blade* (Kotani) (as Shogun's commander)

1979 *Winter Kills* (Richert) (as Keith); *1941* (Spielberg) (as Commander Mitamura); *Oginsawa* (*Love and Death of Ogin*) (Kumai)

1981 *Inchon* (Terence Young) (as Saito-San)

1982 *The Challenge* (*Sword of the Ninja*) (Frankenheimer) (as Toru Yoshida)

1984 *Sanga Moyu*

1985 *No More God, No More Love* (Murakawa) (as Kozo Kanzaki)

1987 *Taketori monogatari* (*Princess from the Moon*) (Ichikawa) (as Taketore-no-Miyatsuko); *Otoko wa tsuraiyo: Shiretoko bojo* (*Tora-San Goes North*) (Yamada) (as Junkichi Ueno)

1989 *Sen no Rikyu* (*The Death of a Tea Master*) (Kumai)

1991 *Shogun Mayeda* (*Journey of Honor*) (Hessler) (as Lord Takugawa Ieyasu); *Strawberry Road*

1993 **Map of the Human Heart** (*Le Carte du Tendre*) (Vincent Ward); *Shadow of the Wolf* (*Agakuk*) (Dorfman) (as Ramoof)

1994 *Picture Bride* (Hatta) (as the Benshi)

1995 *Deep River*

Toshiro Mifune with Machiko Kyo in *Rashomon*

Film as Actor and Director:

1963   *Goju man-nin no isan* (*The Legacy of the 500,000*) (as Takeichi Matsuo)

Publications

By MIFUNE: articles—

Interview with J. Gambol, in *Cinema* (Beverly Hills), Winter 1967.
Interview with R. Guy, in *Cinema* (Beverly Hills), no. 1, 1969.
"New York Salutes Japan's John Wayne," interview with C. Haberman, in *New York Times*, 4 March 1984.
Interview with Y. Alion and Y. Oshima, in *Revue du Cinéma* (Paris), February 1990.
Interview with H. Niogret, in *Postif* (Paris), June 1990.

On MIFUNE: articles—

LaBadie, D. W., "Toshiro Mifune: Japan's Top Sword," in *Show* (Hollywood), May 1963.
Milius, John, "Toshiro Mifune: An Appreciation," in *Cinema* (Beverly Hills), Winter 1967.
Checklist in *Monthly Film Bulletin* (London), August 1971.
Current Biography 1981, New York, 1981.
Niogret, H., "Toshiro Mifune," in *Positif* (Paris), May 1982.
Belie, D. de, "Toshiro Mifune," in *Ciné Revue* (Paris), 21 July 1983.
Grilli, Peter, "Civil Samurai," in *Film Comment* (New York), July/August 1984.
"His Studio and Indie Less Active, Mifune to Hike Acting Chores," in *Variety* (New York), 23 September 1987.
Gillett, J., "Toshiro Mifune," in *Film Dope* (Nottingham, England), January 1990.

*　　*　　*

Akira Kurosawa said this of Toshiro Mifune's acting: "Many contemporary actors unfortunately do not bother too much with creative process. They acquired several acting procedures and they then use them whether it is suitable or not. I often remember Mifune. When we worked together on the film *Shichi-nin no samurai* [*Seven Samurai*] we shot the scene in which he explains to the samurais the disgrace of the peasants, and he cries. 'My hero is a peasant, and therefore he must cry like a peasant,' Mifune said to me. I was totally fascinated when he performed for me in front of the camera. In his acting performances there was always such remarkable sincerity and truth."

Kurosawa and Mifune met for the first time in 1947 during the shooting of the film *Yoidore tenshi* [*Drunken Angel*]. It was a tragic story of a doctor in a postwar city, and Mifune splendidly played the character of a gangster ill with tuberculosis. It was his first great chance, after a short career of photography and two unimportant films. From that time on he only rarely missed playing in Kurosawa's films. The pairing is among the most famous in cinema, like that of John Ford and John Wayne and Martin Scorsese and Robert De Niro. Under Kurosawa's direction, Mifune gradually became Japan's premier film actor. His fame, and Kurosawa's, spread abroad with *Rashomon*, a masterly treatment of a samurai story of love and revenge narrated in five different forms.

Mifune managed economically to interpret the characteristics of his heroes, their motivations, efforts, and ideas. He was boyishly direct and sensitive in *Seven Samurai*; magnificent and cruel in *Throne of Blood*, Kurosawa's reworking of Shakespeare's *Macbeth* in a Japanese setting; heroic and courageous in a series of Samurai dramas (*Yojimbo*, *Sanjuro*); and self-complacent but at the same time mor-

ally upright and courageous in Kurosawa's absorbing crime film *High and Low*, based on a novel by the American writer Ed McBain. The collaboration was more than that of actor and director. Mifune and Kurosawa understood one another and complemented each other perfectly. Mifune contributed ideas to the realization of particular scenes—for example, the filming of the duels in *Sanjuro*. He also contributed to entire films; for example, Kurosawa's *Ran*, a version of *King Lear*, is virtually Mifune's conception, even though he did not act in the film itself.

An international star since 1966 when he appeared for director John Frankeheimer in the epic racing film *Grand Prix*, Mifune has acted in numerous films outside his native Japan. They include John Boorman's World War II epic *Hell in the Pacific*, opposite Lee Marvin; the Euro-Western *Red Sun* opposite Charles Bronson; the Kennedy conspiracy thriller *Winter Kills*; and the epic television mini-series *Shogun*. More recently he appeared as an Eskimo in the Canadian-French adventure film *Shadow of the Wolf*. His most recent Japanese film, for director Kayo Hatta, was *Picture Bride*, a period tale set in the early years of this century, where he had a cameo as a narrator for silent films. Mifune and Kurosawa teamed for the last time as actor and director on *Red Beard* in 1965, a medical drama not unlike *Drunken Angel*, the film that brought the two together.

—Vacláv Merhaut, updated by John McCarty

MILLAND, Ray

Born: Reginald Truscott-Jones in Neath, Glamorganshire, Wales, 3 January 1907; as a child took the name of his stepfather, Mullane, and was known in early career as Jack Mullane, then Raymond Milland. **Education:** Attended King's College, Cardiff. **Military Service:** Served in the Household Cavalry, 1925-28. **Family:** Married Muriel Weber, 1932, son: Daniel David, daughter: Victoria Francesca. **Career:** Actor in several provincial repertory companies; 1929—film debut; 1934-53—contract with Paramount; 1944—entertained the troops in the South Pacific; 1953-54—in TV series *Meet Mr. McNutley*, later renamed *The Ray Milland Show*, 1954-55; 1954—contract with Republic as actor-director; then independent producer and sometime director; 1958—host of TV series *Trails West*; 1959-60—in TV series *Markham*, and in the mini-series *Rich Man, Poor Man*, 1976, and *Seventh Avenue*, 1977. **Awards:** Best Actor Academy Award, Best Actor, New York Film Critics, and Best Actor, Cannes Festival, for *The Lost Weekend*, 1945. **Died:** In Torrance, California, 10 March 1986.

Films as Actor:

(as Raymond Milland)

1929   *The Plaything* (Knight) (as Ian); *The Informer* (Robinson); *The Flying Scotsman* (Knight) (as Jim Edwards); *The Lady from the Sea* (Knight) (as Tom Roberts)
1930   *Way for a Sailor* (Wood) (as ship's officer); *Passion Flower* (William DeMille) (bit role)
1931   *The Bachelor Father* (Leonard); *Just a Gigolo* (Conway) (as Freddie); *Bought* (Mayo) (as Charles Carter); *Ambassador Bill* (Taylor) (as Lothar); *Blonde Crazy* (Del Ruth) (as Joe Reynolds)
1932   *The Man Who Played God* (Adolfi) (as Eddie); *Polly of the Circus* (Santell) (as a rich young man); *Payment Deferred* (Mendes) (as James Medland)

1933   *Orders Is Orders* (Forde) (as Dashwood); *This Is the Life* (de Courville) (as Bob Travers)

1934   *Bolero* (Ruggles) (as Lord Coray); *We're Not Dressing* (Taurog) (as Prince Michael Stofani); *Many Happy Returns* (McLeod) (as Ted Mabert); *Charlie Chan in London* (Forde) (as Neil Howard); *Menace* (Murphy) (as Freddie Bastion)

1935   *One Hour Late* (Murphy) (as Tony St. John); *The Gilded Lily* (Ruggles) (as Charles Gray/Granville)

(as Ray Milland)

1935   *Four Hours to Kill* (Leisen) (as Carl); *The Glass Key* (Tuttle) (as Taylor Henry); *Alias Mary Dow* (Neumann) (as Peter Marshall)

1936   *Next Time We Love* (Edward Griffith) (as Tommy Abbott); *The Return of Sophie Lang* (Archainbaud) (as Jimmy Lawson); *The Big Broadcast of 1937* (Leisen) (as Bob Miller); *The Jungle Princess* (Thiele) (as Christopher Powell); *Three Smart Girls* (Koster) (as Lord Michael Stuart)

1937   *Bulldog Drummond Escapes* (Hogan) (title role); *Wings over Honolulu* (Potter) (as Lt. Stony Gilchrist); *Easy Living* (Leisen) (as John Ball, Jr.); *Ebb Tide* (Hogan) (as Robert Herrick); *Wise Girl* (Jason) (as John O'Halloran)

1938   *Her Jungle Love* (Archainbaud) (as Bob Mitchell); *Tropic Holiday* (Reed) (as Ken Warren); *Men with Wings* (Wellman) (as Scott Barnes); *Say It in French* (Stone) (as Richard Carrington, Jr.)

1939   *French without Tears* (Asquith) (as Alan Howard); *Hotel Imperial* (Florey) (as Lt. Nemassy); *Beau Geste* (Wellman) (as John Geste); *Everything Happens at Night* (Cummings) (as Geoff Thompson)

1940   *Irene* (Wilcox) (as Don Marshall); *The Doctor Takes a Wife* (Hall) (as Dr. Timothy Sterling); *Untamed* (Archainbaud) (as William Crawford); *Arise, My Love* (Leisen) (as Tom Martin)

1941   *I Wanted Wings* (Leisen) (as Jeff Young); *Skylark* (Sandrich) (as Tony Kenyon)

1942   *The Lady Has Plans* (Lanfield) (as Kenneth Harper); *Reap the Wild Wind* (Cecil DeMille) (as Stephen Tolliver); *Are Husbands Necessary?* (Taurog) (as George Cugat); *The Major and the Minor* (Wilder) (as Major Kirby); *Star Spangled Rhythm* (Marshall) (as himself)

1943   *The Crystal Ball* (Nugent) (as Brad Cavanaugh); *Forever and a Day* (Goulding and others) (as Bill Trimble)

1944   *The Uninvited* (Allen) (as Roderick Fitzgerald); *Lady in the Dark* (Leisen) (as Charley Johnson); *Till We Meet Again* (Borzage) (as John); *Ministry of Fear* (Fritz Lang) (as Stephen Neale)

1945   **The Lost Weekend** (Wilder) (as Don Birnam)

1946   *Kitty* (Leisen) (as Sir Hugh Marcy); *The Well-Groomed Bride* (Lanfield) (as Lt. Briggs)

1947   *California* (Farrow) (as Jonathan Trumbo); *The Imperfect Lady* (Allen) (as Clive Loring); *The Trouble with Women* (Lanfield) (as Professor Gilbert Sedley); *Variety Girl* (Marshall) (as himself); *Golden Earrings* (Leisen) (as Colonel Ralph Denistour)

1948   *The Big Clock* (Farrow) (as George Stroud); *So Evil My Love* (Allen) (as Mark Bellis); *Miss Tatlock's Millions* (Haydn) (as himself); *Sealed Verdict* (Allen) (as Major Robert Lawson)

1949   *Alias Nick Beale* (Farrow) (title role); *It Happens Every Spring* (Bacon) (as Vernon Simpson)

1950   *A Woman of Distinction* (Buzzell) (as Alec Stevenson); *A Life of Her Own* (Cukor) (as Steve Harleigh); *Copper Canyon* (Farrow) (as Johnny Carter)

1951   *Circle of Danger* (Tourneur) (as Clay Douglas, + co-pr); *Night into Morning* (Markle) (as Phillip Ainley); *Close to My Heart* (Keighley) (as Brad Sheridan)

1952   *Bugles in the Afternoon* (Rowland) (as Kern Shafter); *Something to Live For* (Stevens) (as Alan Miller); *The Thief* (Rouse) (as Allan Fields)

1953   *Jamaica Rum* (Foster) (as Patrick Fairlie); *Let's Do It Again* (Hall) (as Gary Stuart)

1954   *Dial M for Murder* (Hitchcock) (as Tom Wendice)

1955   *The Girl in the Red Velvet Swing* (Fleischer) (as Stanford White)

1956   *Three Brave Men* (Dunne) (as Joe di Marco); *The River's Edge* (Dwan) (as Nardo Denning); *High Flight* (Gilling) (as Commander David Rudge)

1962   *Premature Burial* (Corman) (as Guy Carrell)

1963   *The Man with the X-Ray Eyes* (Corman) (title role)

1964   *The Confession* (*Quick, Let's Get Married. Seven Different Ways*) (Dieterle) (as Mario Farni)

1968   *Rose rosse per il Fuhrer* (*Red Roses for the Führer*) (Di Leo)

1970   *Daughter of the Mind* (Grauman—for TV) (as Professor Constable); *Company of Killers* (Thorpe) (as George DeSalles); *Love Story* (Hiller) (as Oliver Barrett III)

1971   *River of Gold* (Friedkin—for TV) (as Evelyn Rose); *Black Noon* (Kowalski—for TV)

1972   *The Big Game* (Day); *Frogs* (McCowan) (as Jason Crockett); *The Thing with Two Heads* (Frost) (as Dr. Maxwell Kirshner); *Embassy* (Hessler) (as the Ambassador)

1973   *The House in Nightmare Park* (*Crazy House*) (Sykes) (as Stewart Henderson); *Terror in the Wax Museum* (Fenaday) (as Henry Flexner)

1974   *Gold* (Hunt) (as Hurry Hirschfield)

1975   *The Dead Don't Die* (Harrington—for TV) (as Jim Moss); *Escape to Witch Mountain* (Hough) (as Aristotle Bolt); *Ellery Queen* (*Too Many Suspects*) (Greene—for TV)

1976   *Aces High* (Gold); *Look What's Happened to Rosemary's Baby* (*Rosemary's Baby II*) (O'Steen—for TV); *The Last Tycoon* (Kazan); *Mayday at 40,000 Feet* (Butler—for TV)

1977   *Slavers* (Goslar); *Blackout* (Matalon) (as Mr. Stafford); *Survival Run* (Spiegel); *The Swiss Conspiracy* (Arnold); *The Uncanny* (Heroux) (as Frank Richards)

1978   *La ragazza in Pigiamo Giallo* (*The Girl in the Yellow Pajamas*) (Mogherini); *Cruise into Terror* (Kessler—for TV); *Oliver's Story* (Korty) (as Oliver Barrett III); *Battlestar Galactica* (Colla)

1979   *The Darker Side of Terror* (Trikonis—for TV); *Cave In!* (Fenaday); *Game for Vultures* (Fargo)

1980   *The Attic* (Edwards)

1982   *The Royal Romance of Charles and Diana* (Levin—for TV)

Films as Director:

1955   *A Man Alone* (+ ro as Wes Steele)

1956   *Lisbon* (+ pr, ro as Captain Robert John Evans)

1958   *The Safecracker* (+ ro as Colley Dawson)

1962   *Panic in Year Zero* (+ ro as Harry Baldwin)

1967   *Hostile Witness* (+ ro as Simon Crawford)

Publications

By MILLAND: book—

Wide-Eyed in Babylon (autobiography), London, 1974.

By MILLAND: article—

"Glamour and Catastrophe: Ray Milland, Irwin Allen Interviewed," by Gordon Gow in *Films and Filming* (London), September 1975.

On MILLAND: book—

Parish, James Robert, and Don E. Stanke, *The Debonairs*, New Rochelle, New York, 1975.

On MILLAND: articles—

Current Biography 1946, New York, 1946.
Obituary, in *New York Times*, 11 March 1986.
Obituary, in *Variety* (New York), 12 March 1986.
Decaux, E., "Ray Milland," in *Cinématographe* (Paris), April 1986.

* * *

Ray Milland had made over 60 feature films by the time he won an Oscar for his role as an alcoholic in Billy Wilder's *The Lost Weekend*. The surprise shown by the critical establishment at Milland's proficiency in the role suggests that nothing much had ever been expected of him. It is now clear, however, that *The Lost Weekend* simply reveals a more obvious aspect of Milland's style; he had already built an impressive body of work and was to go on to deliver performances of increasing depth, vitality, variety, and originality.

Milland first appeared in films in 1929 and his easy charm and smooth good looks proved appropriate to many sorts of roles. He regularly turned in competent, sometimes excellent performances in comedies (*Easy Living*), musicals (*Three Smart Girls*), adventures (*Beau Geste*), and exotic romances (*The Jungle Princess* and its Technicolor remake *Her Jungle Love*, both with Dorothy Lamour). Milland signed a contract with Paramount in 1934 and the studio kept him continually busy; the actor averaged five features per year throughout the 1930s. He worked with most of Paramount's top directors—Taurog, Ruggles, Tuttle, Wellman, Florey, Sandrich, Borzage—but the two who would make the films most representative of Milland's styles were Mitchell Leisen and John Farrow.

Not only did Milland work often with the two directors (six features with Leisen, four with Farrow), his stylistic development can be seen clearest when his roles for them are compared. The quintessential Milland performances of the "leading man" variety are contained in Leisen's delightful *Easy Living* and *Kitty*. The darker, more sinister side of his personality first came to the fore in Farrow's *Alias Nick Beal*, a film in which Milland plays the Devil himself. It was, undoubtedly, *The Lost Weekend* that first suggested the less savory aspects of Milland's character, but it was Farrow who developed and nurtured the duality of a suave, handsome gentleman who contains within himself the suggestion of blackest evil. In Farrow's Westerns *California* and *Copper Canyon*, Milland portrays an ostensible hero, but with the suggestion of a cruel and violent past; in *The Big Clock*, he essays the role of an "innocent" man in the intriguing position of trying to track himself down in a murder investigation.

There had been, throughout his career, a certain element of smugness behind the Milland smile, though earlier it was generally used for comedic effect. As Milland grew older and his value as a romantic lead began to wane, the more sinister aspects of this self-assuredness became more evident. Once this rich vein had been tapped by Farrow, Wilder, and Lang (in the excellent *Ministry of Fear*), other directors turned to Milland for parts that demanded this sort of coloring: Hitchcock's *Dial M for Murder*, Rouse's *The Thief*, and Fleischer's *The Girl in the Red Velvet Swing* each exploited the murderous glint in Milland's eloquent eyes.

In 1955 Milland directed his first film, *A Man Alone* (in which he also starred) and proved that his increasingly original and iconoclastic style was a personal creation, not simply the result of eccentric interpretations of routine scripts. The five films he signed as director show the influence of personalities as diverse as Farrow, Russell Rouse and (particularly in his handling of *Panic in Year Zero*) Roger Corman, but all five are ultimately highly personal, subversive expressions of his unique vision. *Panic in Year Zero* and *The Safecracker* are marvelously tense, moody and imaginative; *Hostile Witness* and *Lisbon* are not as accomplished but are similarly intriguing.

Between directing stints Milland continued to take whatever acting jobs came his way. Two Corman quickies—*The Premature Burial* and *The Man with the X-Ray Eyes*—are fascinating, the latter providing Milland with the wittiest, most energetic role of his later career, but he appeared in a cavalcade of terrible films. One of the worst, the inexplicably popular *Love Story*, temporarily found a wide audience for Milland. One of the best of a bad lot is the surprisingly entertaining *Frogs*.

Hollywood never quite knew what it had in Ray Milland, but he continuously showed himself to be an adventurous artist, always interested in exposing his established image to radical and surprising lights.

—Frank Thompson

MILLER, Ann

Nationality: American. **Born:** Johnny Lucille Collier in Houston, Texas, 12 April 1923. **Family:** Married 1) Reese Miller (divorced); 2) William Moss, 1958 (divorced); 3) Arthur Cameron, 1961 (marriage annulled). **Career:** Dancer as child: entered show business playing clubs; 1937—contract with RKO; 1939—Broadway debut in *George White's Scandals*; 1942—contract with Columbia; 1948—contract with MGM after success in *Easter Parade*; late 1950s—mainly in television and nightclub appearances; 1960s—toured in musicals *Can-Can*, *Dolly*, and others; 1969—in Broadway run of *Mame*; 1972—appeared in *Anything Goes* in St. Louis, and later on tour; 1979-82—on Broadway in *Sugar Babies* with Mickey Rooney, and toured with it, 1982-85. **Agent:** c/o Artists Group, 10100 Santa Monica Blvd #305, Los Angeles, CA 90067, U.S.A.

Films as Actress:

1936   *The Devil on Horseback* (Wilbur)
1937   *New Faces of 1937* (Jason); *Stage Door* (La Cava) (as Annie); *The Life of the Party* (Seiter) (as Betty)
1938   *Radio City Revels* (Stoloff) (as Billie Shaw); *Having Wonderful Time* (Santell) (as Vivian); *You Can't Take It with You* (Capra) (as Essie Carmichael); *Room Service* (Seiter) (as Hilda Manney); *Tarnished Angel* (Goodwins) (as Violet McMaster)
1940   *Too Many Girls* (Abbott) (as Pepe); *Hit Parade of 1941* (Auer) (as Annabelle Potter)
1941   *Melody Ranch* (Santley) (as Julie Shelton); *Time Out for Rhythm* (Salkow) (as Kitty Brown); *Go West, Young Lady* (Strayer) (as Lola); *True to the Army* (Rogell) (as Vicki Marlow)
1942   *Priorities on Parade* (Rogell) (as Donna D'Arcy)
1943   *Reveille with Beverly* (Barton) (title role); *What's Buzzin' Cousin?* (Barton) (as Ann Crawford)
1944   *Jam Session* (Barton) (as Terry Baxter); *Hey Rookie* (Barton) (as Winnie Clark); *Carolina Blues* (Jason) (as Julie Carver)
1945   *Eve Knew Her Apples* (Jason) (as Eve Porter); *Eadie Was a Lady* (Dreifuss) (title role)
1946   *The Thrill of Brazil* (Simon) (as Linda Lorens)
1948   *The Kissing Bandit* (Benedek) (as fiesta dancer); *Easter Parade* (Walters) (as Nadine Gale)
1949   **On the Town** (Kelly and Donen) (as Claire Huddesen)
1950   *Watch the Birdie* (Donohue) (as Miss Lucky Vista)

Ann Miller

1951   *Two Tickets to Broadway* (Kern) (as Joyce Campbell); *Texas Carnival* (Walters) (as Sunshine Jackson)
1952   *Lovely to Look At* (LeRoy) (as Bubbles Cassidy)
1953   *Small Town Girl* (Kardos) (as Lisa Bellmount); *Kiss Me Kate* (Sidney) (as Bianca)
1954   *Deep in My Heart* (Donen)
1955   *Hit the Deck* (Rowland) (as Ginger)
1956   *The Opposite Sex* (David Miller) (as Gloria Dell); *The Great American Pastime* (Hoffman) (as Mrs. Doris Patterson)
1976   *Won Ton Ton, the Dog Who Saved Hollywood* (Winner) (cameo)
1994   *That's Entertainment! III* (Friedgen and Sheridan) (as host)

Publications

By MILLER: books—

Miller's High Life, with N. L. Browning, New York, 1972.
Tapping into the Force, with Dr. Maxine Astor, Norfolk, Virginia, 1990.

By MILLER: article—

Interview, in *After Dark* (New York), November 1979.

On MILLER: books—

Condor, Jim, *Ann Miller: Tops in Tap*, New York, 1981.
Thomas, Tony, *That's Dancing!*, New York, 1985.

On MILLER: articles—

Shipman, David, in *The Great Movie Stars*, rev. ed., London, 1979.
Current Biography 1980, New York, 1980.
Ciné Revue (Paris), 20 August 1981.

*   *   *

Ann Miller's reputation as Hollywood's virtuoso female tap dancer is challenged only by Eleanor Powell, whose career was ending as Miller's was beginning. It is a tribute to Miller's ability—and her long, shapely legs, and spirited personality—that she is as well known as she is, given that her roles were often second leads in minor musicals. Indeed, in only four of her films (*Easter Parade, On the Town, Lovely to Look At,* and *Kiss Me Kate*) did she work with other significant performers of the genre. Nevertheless, she managed to achieve a long and respectable career within the Hollywood studio system and subsequently on stage.

Although Miller's dancing was limited to tap (she had to learn basic ballet steps to play Essie Carmichael in *You Can't Take It with You*), within that form she incorporated almost limitless variations. Since speed was her particular skill, she was able to include extra heel and toe in standard tap steps. Moreover, the dynamic quality of her dancing was often heightened by the spectacular nature of the routines. Many of her roles, particularly those at Columbia, were as a singer-dancer in nightclubs or vaudeville, and a climactic musical number highlighted Miller's tapping. "Thumbs Up and V for Victory" in *Reveille with Beverly* and "No Name Jive" in *Jam Session* are examples; in each, she is backed by a chorus that, through arrangement of the sets and choreography, makes her dancing the center of attention.

When she worked with major figures of the genre (Fred Astaire and Gene Kelly, for example), Miller's acting and singing as well as dancing became part of the MGM ensemble approach. Although she shares the screen in *On the Town*, for instance, she contributes to the whole film; there is at least one number that presents each character through song and dance. In hers, "Prehistoric Man," she captures the libidinous nature of Claire Huddesen precisely because she *dances* that character. Without diminishing the air of glamour that Miller had cultivated throughout her career, her roles at MGM also allowed her to contribute to the musical genre while displaying her always stunning tap dancing ability.

Miller's screen career, for all intents and purposes, ended with the death of the studio system and the decline of the Hollywood musical. This is a shame, because the persona she had established, which mainly won her the parts of comic (albeit attractive) ladies and bitches, might have sustained her well into middle age.

In recent years, she (along with her old MGM cohort, Mickey Rooney) has been touring in the musical revue *Sugar Babies*, demonstrating that after all these years her natural charm and dancing talents have not failed her.

—Jerome Delamater, updated by Audrey E. Kupferberg

MILLS, (Sir) John

Nationality: British. **Born:** Felixstowe, Suffolk, England, 22 February 1908. **Military Service:** Royal Engineers, 1940, began making propaganda films; medical discharge for duodenal ulcer, 1941. **Family:** Married 1) the actress Aileen Raymond, 1931 (divorced 1940); 2) the actress Mary Hayley Bell, 1941, daughters: the actresses Juliet and Hayley, son: Jonathan. **Career:** At 16, clerk with Ipswich corn merchant; 1927—London stage debut in chorus of *The Five O'Clock Revue*; joined repertory company The Quaints, tour of Far East; 1931—in stage version of Noël Coward's *Cavalcade*; 1932—film debut opposite Jessie Matthews in *The Midshipmaid*; 1938—invited by Tyrone Guthrie to join Old Vic company; 1949-50—produced and appeared in two films, *The History of Mr. Polly* and *The Rocking-Horse Winner*; 1961—on Broadway in Terence Rattigan's *Ross*; 1967—in TV series *Dundee and the Culhane*; 1977—on stage in *Separate Tables*, *Goodbye, Mr. Chips*, 1982, *Little Lies*, 1983, and *Pygmalion*, 1987; 1989—in TV mini-series *Around the World in 80 Days*, *Night of the Fox*, 1990, and *The Sands of Time*, 1992. **Awards:** Best Actor, Venice Festival, for *Tunes of Glory*, 1960; Best Supporting Actor Academy Award, for *Ryan's Daughter*, 1970; knighted, 1977; London Evening Standard Special Award, 1979. **Agent:** ICM, 388 Oxford Street, London W1, England.

Films as Actor:

1932 *The Midshipmaid* (*Midshipmaid Gob*) (de Courville) (as Golightly)

1933 *Britannia of Billingsgate* (Hill) (as Fred); *The Ghost Camera* (Vorhaus) (as Ernes Elton)

1934 *A Political Party* (Norman Lee) (as Tony Smithers); *The River Wolves* (Pearson) (as Peter Farrell); *The Lash* (Henry Edwards) (as Arthur Haughton); *Doctor's Orders* (Norman Lee) (as Ronnie Blake); *Those Were the Days* (Bentley) (as Bobby); *Blind Justice* (Vorhaus) (as Ralph Summers)

1935 *Brown on Resolution* (*Forever England*; *Born for Glory*; *Torpedo Raider*) (Forde) (as Able Seaman Albert Brown); *Car of Dreams* (Melford and Cutts) (as Robert Miller); *Royal Cavalcade* (*Regal Cavalcade*) (Bentley and others) (as boy); *Charing Cross Road* (de Courville) (as Tony)

1936 *First Offence* (*Bad Blood*) (Mason) (as Johnnie Penrose); *Tudor Rose* (*Nine Days a Queen*; *Lady Jane Grey*) (Stevenson) (as Lord Guildford Dudley)

1937 *O.H.M.S.* (*You're in the Army Now*) (Walsh) (as Cpl. Bert Dawson); *The Green Cockatoo* (*Four Dark Hours*; *Race Gang*) (Menzies and William K. Howard) (as Jim Connor)

1939 *Goodbye Mr. Chips* (Wood) (as Peter Colley as a young man)

1940 *Old Bill and Son* (Dalrymple) (as young Bill Busby); *All Hands* (Carstairs—short); *Dangerous Comment* (short); *Now You're Talking* (short)

1941 *Cottage to Let* (*Bombsight Stolen*) (Asquith) (as Lt. George Perrey); *The Black Sheep of Whitehall* (Hay and Dearden) (as Bobby)

1942 *The Young Mr. Pitt* (Reed) (as William Wilberforce); *In Which We Serve* (Coward and Lean) (as Shorty Blake); *The Big Blockade* (Frend) (as Tom)

1943 *We Dive at Dawn* (Asquith) (as Lt. Freddie Taylor)

1944 *Victory Wedding* (Matthews—short); *This Happy Breed* (Lean) (as Billy Mitchell); *Waterloo Road* (Gilliat) (as Jim Colter)

1945 *Total War in Britain* (Rotha—doc) (as narrator); *The Way to the Stars* (*Johnny in the Clouds*) (Asquith) (as Peter Penrose)

1946 ***Great Expectations*** (Lean) (as Pip Pirrip); *Land of Promise* (Rotha—doc) (as voice)

1947 *So Well Remembered* (Dmytryk) (as George Boswell); *The October Man* (Baker) (as Jim Ackland)

1948 *Scott of the Antarctic* (Frend) (as Capt. Robert Falcon Scott)

1949 *The History of Mr. Polly* (Pelissier) (as Alfred Polly, + pr); *Friend of the Family* (Hill—doc) (as narrator); *The Flying Skyscraper* (short) (as narrator)

1950 *The Rocking-Horse Winner* (Pelissier) (as Bassett, + pr); *Morning Departure* (*Operation Disaster*) (Baker) (as Lieut. Comdr. Armstrong)

1951 *Mr. Denning Drives North* (Kimmins) (as Tom Denning)

1952 *The Gentle Gunman* (Relph and Dearden) (as Terence Sullivan)

1953 *The Long Memory* (Hamer) (as Davidson)

1954 *Hobson's Choice* (Lean) (as Willie Mossop)

1955 *The Colditz Story* (Hamilton) (as Pat Reid); *The End of the Affair* (Dmytryk) (as Albert Parkis); *Above Us the Waves* (Thomas) (as Commander Frazer); *Escapade* (Leacock) (as John Hampden)

1956 *War and Peace* (King Vidor) (as Platon Karatayev); *It's Great to Be Young* (Frankel) (as Mr. Dingle); *The Baby and the Battleship* (Jay Lewis) (as "Puncher" Roberts); *Around the World in Eighty Days* (Anderson) (as London cabbie)

1957 *Town on Trial* (Guillermin) (as Supt. Mike Halloran); *The Circle* (*The Vicious Circle*) (Thomas) (as Dr. Howard Latimer)

1958 *Dunkirk* (Norman) (as Corporal Tubby Binns); *Ice Cold in Alex* (*Desert Attack*) (J. Lee Thompson) (as Capt. Anson); *I Was Monty's Double* (*Hell, Heaven or Hoboken*) (Guillermin) (as Major Harvey)

1959 *Tiger Bay* (J. Lee Thompson) (as Superintendent Graham); *Season of Passion* (*Summer of the 17th Doll*) (Norman) (as Barney)

1960 *Swiss Family Robinson* (Annakin) (as Mr. Robinson); *Tunes of Glory* (Neame) (as Lt. Col. Basil Barrow)

1961 *The Singer Not the Song* (Baker) (as Father Keogh)

1962 *Flame in the Streets* (Baker) (as "Jacko" Palmer); *The Valiant* (Baker) (as Captain Morgan); *Tiara Tahiti* (Kotcheff) (as Lt. Col. Clifford Southey)

1964 *The Chalk Garden* (Neame) (as Maitland)

1965 *The Truth about Spring* (Thorpe) (as Tommy Tyler); *King Rat* (Forbes) (as Smedley-Taylor); *Operation Crossbow* (*The Great Spy Mission*) (Anderson) (as General Boyd)

1966 *The Wrong Box* (Forbes) (as Masterman Finsbury)

1967 *The Family Way* (Boulting) (as Ezra Fitton); *Chuka* (Gordon Douglas) (as Colonel Stuart Valois); *Africa—Texas Style!* (Marton) (as Wing Commander Howard Hayes)

1969 *Run Wild, Run Free* (Sarafian) (as Moorman); *Oh! What a Lovely War* (Attenborough) (as Field Marshal Sir Douglas Haig); *Lady Hamilton* (*Emma Hamilton*; *The Making of a Lady*) (Christian-Jaque) (as Sir William Hamilton); *La morte non ha sesso* (*A Black Veil for Lisa*) (Dallamano) (as Insp, Franz Bulov)

1970 *Adam's Woman* (*Return of the Boomerang*) (Leacock) (as Sir Philip); *Ryan's Daughter* (Lean) (as Michael)

1971 *Dulcima* (Nesbitt) (as Mr. Parker)

1972 *Lady Caroline Lamb* (Bolt) (as Canning); *Young Winston* (Attenborough) (as General Kitchener)

1973   *Oklahoma Crude* (Kramer) (as Cleon Doyle)
1975   *The Human Factor* (Dmytryk) (as Mike McCallister)
1976   *Dirty Knight's Work* (*Trial by Combat*; *Choice of Weapons*)
       (Connor) (as Bertie Cook)
1977   *The Devil's Advocate* (Green) (as Blaise Meredith)
1978   *The Big Sleep* (Winner) (as Inspector Jim Carson); *The Thirty-*
       Nine Steps (Sharp) (as Colonel Scudder); *Dr. Strange* (De
       Guere—for TV)
1979   *Zulu Dawn* (Hickox) (as Sir Henry Bartle Frere); *Quatermass*
       Conclusion (Haggard) (as Prof. Bernard Quatermass)
1982   *Gandhi* (Attenborough) (as Lord Chelmsford)
1983   *Sahara* (McLaglen) (as Cambridge); *A Woman of Substance*
       (Sharp—for TV) (as Henry Rossiter)
1984   *Masks of Death* (Baker)
1985   *Murder with Mirrors* (Lowry—for TV) (as Lewis Serrocold);
       Edge of the Wind (Ives—for TV)
1986   *When the Wind Blows* (Murukami—animation) (as voice of
       Jim Bloggs); *Hold the Dream* (Sharp—for TV) (as Henry
       Rossiter); *Witnesses*
1987   *Who's That Girl?* (Foley) (as Montgomery Bell)
1989   *The Lady and the Highwayman* (Hough) (as Sir Lawrence
       Dobson); *A Tale of Two Cities* (Monnier)
1990   *Ending Up* (Sasdy—for TV) (as Bernard)
1991   *The Last Straw*
1992   *Galaxies Are Colliding*
1993   *Harnessing Peacocks* (James Cellan Jones—for TV) (as Ber-
       nard); *Frankenstein* (Wickes—for TV) (as DeLacey)
1994   *Deadly Advice* (Fletcher) (as Jack the Ripper)
1996   *Hamlet* (Branagh) (as Old Norway)

Film as Director and Producer:

1966   *Sky West and Crooked* (*Gypsy Girl*)

Publications

By MILLS: book—

Up in the Clouds, Gentlemen Please, New Haven, 1981.

By MILLS: article—

Interview in *Photoplay* (London), July 1980.

On MILLS: book—

Tanitch, Robert, *John Mills*, London 1993.

On MILLS: articles—

Johnson, Ian, "Mills," in *Films and Filming* (London), June 1962.
Current Biography 1963, New York, 1963.
Williams, J., "Oscar, Oscar," in *Films Illustrated* (London), July 1971.
Marill, Alvin, "John Mills," in *Films in Review* (New York), August/
   September 1971.
Dacre, R., "John Mills," in *Film Dope* (Nottingham, England), Janu-
   ary 1990.
Stars (Mariembourg, Belgium), September 1991.
Roberts, J., "John Mills," in *Classic Images* (Muscatine, Iowa), August
   1992.

*   *   *

Whether stuck in the middle of the desert (*Ice Cold in Alex*) or stuck in the frozen climes of the South Pole (*Scott of the Antarctic*) or stuck at sea (*In Which We Serve*) or stuck in a prisoner-of-war camp (*The Colditz Story*), John Mills is so unfailingly cheerful, brave, and decent one gets the sense that were he to be cast against type, perhaps to play Adolf Hitler or Genghis Khan, we would warm to his performance and have him home to tea nonetheless.

It is surely significant that Mills first came to prominence in the war years, a period of consensus in British politics when decency—as embodied in 1946 by the Attlee government—was briefly fashionable, and where class, privilege, and good looks were not the sole criteria on which the British movie star was judged. As Jeffrey Richards has observed, Mills's great achievement has been "to show the qualities of English decency operating at every level of society." In 1947, Mills toppled Gainsborough Studios' aristocratic "cad and rotter," James Mason, from his perch at the top of the popularity polls. It is quite inconceivable that Mills would ever have bludgeoned Margaret Lockwood with an iron poker (as Mason did in *The Man in Grey*). Nor, in later life, would Mills have been happy corrupting nymphets (as Mason did in *Lolita*). Whether as character actor or leading man, Mills maintained morals, principles, and basic humanity. Given the opportunity to follow Granger and Mason to Hollywood, he plumped for Britain.

Sometimes, Mills could exude an irritating sanctimony and smugness. As Pip in David Lean's *Great Expectations*, he is dull and bland beside the gallery of Dickensian grotesques (Finlay Currie as the shaven-headed convict, Mr. Jaggers, Miss Havisham, and company); it seems very unlikely that Jean Simmons would ever have fallen for such a lackluster hero. And in Lean's *This Happy Breed*, Mills's decency and loyalty to Nöel Coward's quaint ideal of the family—Mills's portrayal of the boy-next-door—as in *In Which We Serve*, is faintly grating.

In the 1950s, as prosperity set in, and as Churchill and then Macmillan attempted to gnaw away at the "consensual decency" of the previous decade, Mills stood as a totem of the old values. Generally, British 1950s war films are seen as symptomatic of imperial anxiety, of Albion attempting to cope with its loss of significance in the world, with the growing pains of Suez and the disappearing empire. As British world influence dwindles, British filmmakers try to reinvoke martial myths of the recent past. Seen in such a light, Mills, forever dressed in khaki, seems a reactionary figure in such films as *Tunes of Glory*, which was, of course, that film's point about his character.

It comes as something of a surprise to discover that Mills, like Cagney (to whom, although gentler with grapefruits, he is in some sense a British parallel), started off his career in musical comedy. Somehow, one does not think of him singing and dancing. In later years, Mills tried to break away from his Mr. Decent type; he played a deformed deaf-mute in Lean's *Ryan's Daughter*, a performance that won a him a Best Supporting Actor Oscar, although it borders on the freakish. He marvelously played the stiff-necked dad of newlyweds Hywell Bennett and daughter Hayley in *The Family Way*. And he has even attempted to play the villain from time to time—as in the serial killer omnibus *Deadly Advice*, where he played Jack the Ripper. As General Haig, the butcher of the Somme who sent hundreds of thousands of British soldiers to their death, in the earlier *Oh! What a Lovely War*, he laced his villainy with sympathy to create a realistic human portrait. In all these films, he demonstrated that he is a far more versatile actor than his war-hero persona often allowed. Nonetheless, he will always be remembered as brave Shorty Blake with the stiff upper lip or as Courageous Captain Scott—as the chivalric and conscientious protagonist of a dozen British war movies.

—G. C. Macnab, updated by John McCarty

John Mills in *Great Expectations* courtesy of The Rank Organisation Plc

MINEO, Sal

Nationality: American. **Born:** Salvatore Mineo, Jr. in the Bronx, New York, 10 January 1939. **Education:** Attended Christopher Columbus High School, New York. **Career:** Child actor on Broadway in *The Rose Tattoo*; 1952—appeared in *The King and I* on Broadway; 1955—film debut in *Six Bridges to Cross*; also appeared on television; 1969—director of stage play *Fortune and Men's Eyes* in New York. **Died:** Stabbed by robber, 12 February 1976.

Films as Actor:

1955   *Six Bridges to Cross* (Pevney); ***Rebel without a Cause*** (Ray) (as Plato); *The Private War of Major Benson* (Hopper)
1956   *Crime in the Street* (Siegel); *Rock Pretty Baby* (Bartlett); *Somebody up There Likes Me* (Wise); *Giant* (Stevens)
1957   *Dino* (Carr); *The Young Don't Cry* (Werker)
1958   *Tonka* (Foster)
1959   *A Private Affair* (Walsh); *The Gene Krupa Story* (Weis) (title role)
1960   *Exodus* (Preminger) (as Dov Landau)
1962   *Escape from Zahrain* (Neame) (as Tahar); *The Longest Day* (Annakin and others) (as Private Martini)
1964   *Cheyenne Autumn* (Kellogg) (as Red Shirt)
1965   *The Greatest Story Ever Told* (Stevens) (as Uriah); *Who Killed Teddy Bear?* (Cates) (as Lawrence)
1966   *The Dangerous Years of Kiowa Jones* (March—for TV)
1967   *Stranger on the Run* (Siegel—for TV)
1969   *Eighty Steps to Jonah* (Oswald) (as Jerry Taggart); *Krakatoa, East of Java* (Kowalski) (as Leoncavallo Borghese)
1970   *The Challengers* (Martinson—for TV)
1971   *Escape from the Planet of the Apes* (Taylor); *In Search of America* (Bogart—for TV); *How to Steal an Airplane* (Martinson—for TV)
1972   *The Family Rico* (Wendkos—for TV)

Publications

On MINEO: book—

Braudy, Susan, *Who Killed Sal Mineo?* (novel), New York, 1982.

On MINEO: articles—

Cook, G., "Three Days to Grow Up," in *Photoplay*, July 1961.
Ciné Revue (Paris), 24 June 1982.
Smith, Laura C., "Untimely End for a 'Rebel,'" in *Entertainment Weekly*, 10 February 1995.

*   *   *

Sal Mineo's career was dominated by a single role that swiftly achieved the status of icon or myth: his Plato in Nicholas Ray's *Rebel without a Cause*. Ray's film, its intense and powerful dramatic inspiration intermittently transcending its "textbook sociology" basis, is a striking example of a great opportunity almost seized and then fumbled: it opens up the possibility of constructing an alternative, nonrepressive and nonauthoritarian sexual/familial structure then opts for restoring "normality" at the end. Significantly, the vital move for completing this operation is the elimination of Plato, the character who, far more than Jim (James Dean) and Judy (Natalie Wood), resists assimilation into the norms of bourgeois culture.

Rebel is the only film in which Mineo's character is clearly coded as gay. Typically, as with the film's other teenage characters, his "problem" is "explained" in terms of an unsatisfactory family background; nevertheless, during the central sequences in the abandoned mansion, Plato's gayness achieves a resonance that escapes the film's glib sociologizing. The three characters move towards becoming an alternative family, mutually caring and protective, Jim as father, Judy as mother, Plato as child. Yet this is disturbed and complicated by the continual threat (produced as much by the sexual ambiguity of the Dean persona as by the presence of Mineo) of a sexual dimension to the men's relationship: the implications of connecting the familial and the sexual in this way could scarcely be more radical. The strategy by which the film repudiates (rather than resolves) those implications is interesting: Jim becomes preoccupied with Judy at Plato's expense, subsequently rendering him impotent by removing the bullets from his gun, hence unintentionally abetting in his death at the hands of patriarchal authority (in the form of the police). Thereafter, in the film's famous last line, the heterosexual couple can be definitively reestablished and reintegrated into bourgeois normality.

Mineo's persona has two aspects, vulnerability and aggressiveness. If *Rebel* offers the most complete realization of the former, the latter perhaps received fullest expression in *Cheyenne Autumn*, where Mineo played a transgressive and intractable Indian brave. It was Preminger who made possible the ideal fusion of the two sides: the young Irgun initiate of *Exodus* is surely Mineo's finest performance, though achieved through the explicit repudiation of the persona's gay connotations. ("They used me as you would use a woman.") The extraordinary intensity of the interrogation scene is due as much to Mineo's vulnerable/aggressive dualism as to Preminger's iron control over editing and mise-en-scène.

—Robin Wood

MINNELLI, Liza

Nationality: American. **Born:** Liza May Minnelli in Los Angeles, California, 12 March 1946; daughter of the director Vincente Minnelli and the actress Judy Garland; sister of the actress Lorna Luft. **Education:** Attended public and private schools. **Family:** Married 1) Peter Allen, 1967 (divorced); 2) Jack Haley Jr., 1974 (divorced 1979); 3) Mark Gero, 1979 (divorced 1992). **Career:** Appeared as a small child in her mother's film *In the Good Old Summertime*, 1949, and on stage with her mother at the Palace Theatre, New York, 1953; 1960—toured with her school production of *The Diary of Anne Frank*; 1963—in Broadway production of *Best Foot Forward*; 1964—made first recording, and appeared as singer with her mother at London Palladium; 1965—cabaret debut; 1968—dramatic role in film *Charlie Bubbles*; 1972—successful television special *Liza with a Z*; 1978-80—with the Martha Graham Dance Co., New York. **Awards:** Best Actress, Academy Award and Best Actress, British Academy, for *Cabaret*, 1972. **Agent:** c/o PMK Public Relations, 1776 Broadway, New York, NY 10019, U.S.A.

Films as Actress:

1949   *In the Good Old Summertime* (Leonard) (as herself)
1968   *Charlie Bubbles* (Finney) (as Eliza)
1969   *The Sterile Cuckoo* (*Pookie*) (Pakula) (as "Pookie" Adams); *Tell Me That You Love Me, Junie Moon* (Preminger) (title role)
1972   *Cabaret* (Fosse) (as Sally Bowles)

Liza Minnelli

1974   *That's Entertainment!* (Haley Jr.—compilation) (as host); *Journey Back to Oz* (Sutherland—animation, produced in 1964) (as voice of Dorothy)
1975   *Lucky Lady* (Donen) (as Claire)
1976   *A Matter of Time* (Vincente Minnelli) (as Nina); *Silent Movie* (Mel Brooks) (as herself)
1977   *New York, New York* (Scorsese) (as Francine Evans)
1981   *Arthur* (Gordon) (as Linda Marolla)
1983   *The King of Comedy* (Scorsese) (as herself)
1984   *A Great Wind Cometh* (Golan); *The Muppets Take Manhattan* (Oz) (cameo)
1985   *That's Dancing!* (Haley Jr.—compilation) (as host); *A Time to Live* (Wallace—for TV) (as Mary-Lou Weisman)
1987   *Pinocchio and the Emperor of the Night* (Sutherland—animation) (voice only); *Minnelli on Minnelli: Liza Remembers Vincente* (Schickel—doc for TV)
1988   *Rent-a-Cop* (London) (as Della Roberts); *Arthur 2: On the Rocks* (Yorkin) (as Linda Marolla Bach)
1991   *Stepping Out* (Lewis Gilbert) (as Mavis Turner)
1994   *Parallel Lives* (Yellen—for TV) (as Stevie Merrill); *Unzipped* (as herself)
1995   *West Side Waltz* (for TV)

Publications

By MINNELLI: articles—

"At the Deli with Liza Minnelli," interview with M. Peterson, in *Inter/View* (New York), May 1972.
"Brève rencontre . . . avec Liza Minnelli et Vincente Minnelli," interview with G. Braucourt, in *Ecran* (Paris), December 1975.
Interview, in *Photoplay* (London), September 1981.
"Liza Minnelli," interview with K. D. Lang, in *Interview* (New York), March 1991.

On MINNELLI: books—

D'Arcy, Susan, *The Films of Liza Minnelli*, London, 1973; 2nd ed., Bembridge, England, 1977.
Parish, James Robert, and Jack Ano, *Liza: Her Cinderella Nightmare*, New York, 1975.
Petrucelli, Alan W., *Liza! Liza!: An Unauthorized Biography of Liza Minnelli*, London, 1983.
Spada, James, with Karen Swenson, *Judy and Liza*, New York, 1983.
Freedland, Michael, *Liza with a 'Z': A Biography of Liza Minnelli*, London, 1988.
Carrick, Peter, *Liza Minnelli*, London, 1993.
Leigh, Wendy, and Stephen Karten, *Liza: Born a Star*, New York, 1993.
Mair, George, *Under the Rainbow: The Real Liza Minnelli*, Secaucus, New Jersey, 1995.

On MINNELLI: articles—

Vallance T., "Liza Minnelli," in *Focus on Film* (London), Summer 1972.
Ecran (Paris), January 1978.
Current Biography 1988, New York, 1988.
"Liza!," in *Harper's Bazaar* (New York), August 1988.
Servin, James, "Liza," in *Harper's Bazaar* (New York), August 1990.
Clark, John, filmography in *Premiere* (New York), May 1991.
Scott, Jay, "Liza's Buffalo Shuffle," in *Premiere* (New York), May 1991.

*   *   *

Liza Minnelli has not had much of a film career since *New York, New York* and her output, including the telefilms, is slight. Nevertheless, she has appeared in works that have been important in illustrating that she remains a major talent who continues to evolve. Most striking in this regard is *A Time to Live*, Minnelli's first telefilm, in which she plays the role of a middle-class suburban woman whose son has muscular dystrophy. Playing a wife/mother who, in addition to fulfilling the caretaker role, struggles to accept the fact that her son will die young, Minnelli's role represents a radical departure. While she brings her familiar emotional intensity to the characterization, Minnelli tempers the character's emotionalism by emphasizing her innate intelligence, determination, and discipline. Minnelli's performance is deeply felt, she is given strong support by her co-stars and the script has an integrity which lifts it above the inherent melodramatics of the subject matter.

In contrast to the unrelenting dramatics of *A Time to Live*, *Stepping Out* is a musical that makes wonderful use of Minnelli's identity as a dancer, singer, and theatrical personality: an ideal Minnelli project allowing her to integrate her musical talents into a comedy/drama narrative. Unlike her previous musicals, the film has a contemporary setting and gives her a character who interacts with other women. It should have revived Minnelli's film career but both the critics and the public were indifferent. Perhaps the film lacked sufficient star power and Minnelli, while surrounded by a strong supporting cast, did not have a name co-star; in any case, *Stepping Out* is Minnelli's sole theatrical feature of quality and substance since *New York, New York*. The low point of the more recent projects is *Rent-a-Cop*, a film which clumsily tries to combine the genres of the action film and the romantic comedy. Minnelli's flamboyant performance as a brassy prostitute is a disaster and in great part because the film's writers and director give her no help whatsoever in integrating the character into what is clearly a Burt Reynolds vehicle.

Aside from their being strong projects and the opportunities they afford Minnelli as an actor, *A Time to Live* and *Stepping Out* are of interest in that both films present Minnelli as a person who accepts responsibility and makes a commitment to those who need help. Clearly, Minnelli's screen persona has grown considerably from the early 1970s. The image of a mature and caring person is present as early as *Tell Me That You Love Me, Junie Moon* but it was obscured by the unstable characters she played in *The Sterile Cuckoo* and *Cabaret*. *New York, New York* presents Minnelli as the responsible person in a relationship and in *Stepping Out*, Minnelli, playing a dance teacher, makes a professional and personal commitment to her students.

Minnelli's on-screen image as a more mature person is reinforced by her offscreen identity. From early on in her career, Minnelli publicly acknowledged her parents, their talent and creativity. *Minnelli on Minnelli: Liza Remembers Vincente* is an intelligent and affectionate documentary on her father's films; and Minnelli in concert and print has repeatedly honored her mother as a singer and actor. From another perspective, Minnelli has shown herself to be a caring person giving of her time and energy to the raising of money for AIDS victims. She has also been a high profile supporter of gay and lesbian rights.

There is no obvious explanation as to why Minnelli's film career has not fully succeeded. Possibly, she chose to make live performance work her priority and channeled her efforts to that end; or, it may be that her persona is a bit at odds with a popular image of the contemporary woman. Minnelli tends to display a highly emotional sensibility which counters the notion that today's women are in control of their feelings. Also, Minnelli has cultivated, through the ties to her parents, an identity that connects her image to the classical Hollywood cinema. The reference to Hollywood's past may cause some confusion in the publics' mind as to what era Minnelli's presence personifies.

Minnelli keeps active doing live performances. She maintains an enthusiasm and energy and has managed not to be locked into playing the diva. In her most recent film project, the telefilm *West Side Waltz*,

she undertakes a character part enacting the role of a naive and insecure middle-aged woman who discovers that she is capable of taking
on responsibilities and, in doing so, begins to value herself. While
Minnelli provides a charming and distinctive characterization in *West
Side Waltz*, she should not be relegated to older women character parts.
Minnelli is a vibrant and attractive woman and what she deserves is
the opportunity to fully utilize her talents on-screen and grow as a
person and artist.

—Richard Lippe

MIRANDA, Carmen

Nationality: Brazilian. **Born:** Maria do Carmo Miranda da Cunha in
Libson, Portugal, 9 February 1909; grew up in Rio de Janeiro. **Career:** Radio singer and recording star in Brazil from late 1920s; 1939—
debut on Broadway in *The Streets of Paris*; also appeared at the Waldorf-
Astoria; 1940—U.S. film debut in *Down Argentine Way* as featured
act; also appeared on television. **Died:** Of heart attack, in Beverly
Hills, California, 5 August 1955.

Films as Actress:

1933   *A voz do carnaval* (Gonzaga and Mauro)
1935   *Alô, alô, Brasil!* (Downey, de Barro, and Ribeiro); *Estudantes*
        (Downey)
1936   *Alô, alô carnaval!* (Gonzaga)
1939   *Banana da terra* (de Barro)
1940   *Down Argentine Way* (Cummings) (as herself)
1941   *That Night in Rio* (Cummings) (as Carmen); *Weekend in Ha-
        vana* (Walter Lang) (as Rosita Rivas)
1942   *Springtime in the Rockies* (Cummings) (as Rosita Murphy)
1943   *The Gang's All Here* (*The Girls He Left Behind*) (Berkeley) (as
        Dorita)
1944   *Four Jills in a Jeep* (Seiter) (as herself); *Greenwich Village*
        (Walter Lang) (as Princess Querida); *Something for the Boys*
        (Seiler) (as Chiquita Hart)
1946   *Doll Face* (*Come Back to Me*) (Seiler) (as Chita); *If I'm Lucky*
        (Seiler) (as Michele O'Toole)
1947   *Copacabana* (Alfred E. Green) (as Carmen Novarro)
1948   *A Date with Judy* (Thorpe) (as Rosita Cochellas)
1950   *Nancy Goes to Rio* (Leonard) (as Marina Rodriguez)
1953   *Scared Stiff* (George Marshall) (as Carmelita Castinha)

Publications

On MIRANDA: books—

Parish, James Robert, *The Fox Girls*, New York, 1971.
Cardoso, Abel Jr., *Carmen Miranda, a cantora do Brasil*, Sao Paulo,
    1978.
Saia, Luiz Henrique, *Carmen Miranda*, Sao Paolo, 1984.
Barsante, Cassio Emmanuel, *Carmen Miranda*, Rio de Janeiro, 1985.
Gil-Montero, Martha, *Brazilian Bombshell: The Biography of Carmen
    Miranda*, New York, 1989.

On MIRANDA: articles—

Current Biography 1941, New York, 1941.
Obituary, in *New York Times*, 6 August 1955.
Konder, Rodolfo, "The Carmen Miranda Museum: Brazilian Bombshell
    Still Box Office in Rio," in *Americas*, September 1982.
Terrell, Nena, "Helena Soldberg Unmasks a Brazilian Idol," in *Ameri-
    cas*, January-February 1996.

On MIRANDA: film—

Carmen Miranda: Bananas Is My Business, documentary, directed by
    Helena Soldberg, 1994.

*   *   *

Carmen Miranda's phenomenal but limited success in Hollywood
seems closely linked to the United States's Good Neighbor Policy
during World War II and Twentieth Century-Fox's skill at showcasing musical talent. The Good Neighbor Policy encouraged economic, cultural, and military alliance between the United States
and Central and South America. Within this political climate,
Miranda would fulfill the role of musical "ambassador" between
Latin America and the United States, giving American audiences a
taste of Brazilian culture. This "taste" however, as nurtured by
Fox, proved narrow, highly stereotyped, and offensive to Brazilian
audiences.

The most popular singer in Brazil during the 1930s, Miranda recorded more than 100 records, appeared in five films, and conducted
nine sold-out South American tours. These credentials brought her to
New York City in 1939 to appear in *The Streets of Paris*. Her stereotyping as a Brazilian "bimbo" began with her first American interview.
Hoping to impress with her sparse English she exclaimed, "I say
money, money, money and I say hot dog! I say yes, no, and I say
money, money, money...." When asked why she learned to say
money, Miranda answered, through an interpreter, that everyone
who comes to the United States must learn to say money. Financially insightful, but probably not the best first impression to make.
Nevertheless, after her six-minute performance garnered unani-
mous rave reviews, she became the toast of the town. Her costumes
set a fashion trend and the samba dominated New York City dance
floors.

Her return to Brazil after the show closed proved significantly
less triumphant. Held responsible for "Americanizing" and betraying Brazilian culture, Miranda's popularity plummeted. A cruel response from her own people to her Boradway success, but one that
became prophetic. When she signed an exclusive contract with
Twentieth Century-Fox, she remained essentially a "novelty act"
perpetuating her star image as the "Brazilian Bombshell" in film
after film.

From *Down Argentine Way* to *Scared Stiff*, Miranda was carefully
placed as a well-known and tempestuous Latin performer who spoke
broken English (her first three films were set in Argentina, Brazil, and
Cuba to legitimize her accent) and sang in Portuguese. Her frenetic
and incessant gesturing, whether performing or not, suggested a human whirligig. Her clothing copied her Broadway costumes which she
brought from South America: Brazilian native dress modeled on the
"bahiana," the African vendors of Bahia, Brazil. Their clothing features many layers of brightly colored and differently textured fabric topped with glittering jewelry and flower/fruit hats. Twentieth
Century-Fox modified and exaggerated this folk dress until her
exotic millinery became her trademark. Busby Berkeley created
the ultimate image of Miranda when he made her "The Lady in the
Tutti-Frutti Hat," in *The Gang's All Here*. Standing under a forced-
perspective set painting that suggested an impossibly gigantic banana hat, Miranda became the stereotyped embodiment of Brazil
her people feared.

Even when top-billed, Miranda was never cast as the romantic lead,
her non-American mannerisms and sexuality being "unsuitable" for

Carmen Miranda

the hero. Miranda's volatile nature juxtaposed the introverted demeanor (hence cultural "acceptability") of the romantic female leads with whom she was often paired: Alice Faye and Vivian Blaine. The only time she was cast as the romantic lead, in *Copacabana*, she played a dual role that demonstrated her typical position, fluctuating between her usual "Brazilian" performing style and a refined French chanteuse.

Remarkably, given the near caricature of her persona, Miranda became a major musical star and the highest-paid female performer in the United States during World War II. Even though she made only 14 Hollywood films, Miranda's star image is still readily recognized in the United States today. She has been parodied by everyone including Mickey Rooney in *Babes on Broadway*, Bugs Bunny, Milton Berle, and a number of Gary Larson cartoons. That she should be best remembered for her hats undercuts her talent. Her Brazilian legacy as one of that country's most popular performers provides a more fitting epithet.

—Greg S. Faller

MIRREN, Helen

Nationality: British. **Born:** Ilynea Lydia Mironoff in London, England, 26 July 1945. **Education:** Attended St. Bernard's Convent, Westcliff-on-Sea, Essex; also attended teacher training college in North London. **Family:** Has lived for many years with the producer-director Taylor Hackford. **Career:** 1963-64—member National Youth Theatre; 1967—member Manchester Repertory Theatre; 1967-71, 1974-75, 1977-78, 1982—member Royal Shakespeare Company; 1967—film debut in *Herostratus*; 1972—attended Peter Brook's International Centre of Theatre Research in Paris; in TV mini-series *Cousin Bette*; 1972-73—toured Africa and the United States with Peter Brook's company; 1991-96—starring role in "Prime Suspect" series of TV productions, including the mini-series *Prime Suspect*, 1991, *Prime Suspect 2*, 1992, and *Prime Suspect 3*, 1994, the TV movies *Prime Suspect: The Lost Child*, 1995, and *Prime Suspect: Inner Circles*, 1996; 1992—Los Angeles stage debut in *Woman in Mind*; 1995—Broadway debut in *A Month in the Country*. **Awards:** Best Actress Award, Cannes Film Festival, and Best Actress, British Academy of Film and Television Arts, for *Cal*, 1984; Best Actress Awards, British Academy of Film and Television Arts, for *Prime Suspect*, 1991, 1992, 1993; Best Actress Award, Cannes Film Festival, for *The Madness of King George*, 1995. **Agent:** Ken McReddie Ltd., 91 Regent Street, London W1R 7TB, England. **Address:** c/o ICM, 8942 Wilshire Boulevard, Beverly Hills, CA 90211, U.S.A.

Films as Actress:

1967   *Herostratus* (Don Levy)
1968   *A Midsummer Night's Dream* (Peter Hall) (as Hermia)
1969   *Age of Consent* (Michael Powell) (as Cora Ryan)
1972   *Savage Messiah* (Ken Russell) (as Gosh Smith-Boyle); *Miss Julie* (Phillips and Glenister) (title role)
1973   *O Lucky Man!* (Lindsay Anderson) (as Patricia)
1976   *Hamlet* (Coronado)
1978   *As You Like It* (Basil Coleman—for TV) (as Rosalind); *The Collection* (for TV)
1979   *S.O.S. Titanic* (William Hale—for TV) (as Stewardess May Sloan); *Blue Remembered Hills* (Brian Gibson—for TV)
1980   *Caligula* (Brass—produced in 1977) (as Cesonia); *Hussy* (Chapman) (as Beaty Simons); *The Fiendish Plot of Dr. Fu Manchu* (Haggard) (as Alice Rage); *The Long Good Friday* (Mackenzie) (as Victoria)
1981   *Excalibur* (Boorman) (as Morgana); *Priest of Love* (Christopher Miles); *A Midsummer Night's Dream* (Moshinsky—for TV) (as Titania)
1982   *Cymbeline* (Moshinsky—for TV) (as Imogen)
1984   *Cal* (O'Connor) (as Marcella Morton); *2010* (Hyams) (as Tanya Kirbuk); *The Little Mermaid* (Iscove—for TV)
1985   *White Nights* (Hackford) (as Galina Ivanova); *The Gospel According to Vic* (*Heavenly Pursuits*) (Gormley) (as Ruth Chancellor); *Coming Through* (Barber-Fleming—for TV) (as Frieda von Richtofer Weekly)
1986   *The Mosquito Coast* (Weir) (as Mother)
1987   *Invocation: Maya Deren* (doc) (as narrator); *Cause Celebre* (Gorrie—for TV) (as Alma Rattenbury)
1988   *Pascali's Island* (Dearden) (as Lydia Neuman)
1989   *When the Whales Came* (Rees) (as Clemmie Jenkins); ***The Cook, the Thief, His Wife & Her Lover*** (Greenaway) (as Georgina Spica, the Wife); *Red Knight, White Knight* (Geoff Murphy—for TV) (as Anna)
1990   *Bethune: The Making of a Hero* (*Dr. Bethune*) (Borsos—released in U.S. in 1993) (as Frances Penny Bethune)

1991	*The Comfort of Strangers* (Schrader) (as Caroline); *Where Angels Fear to Tread* (Sturridge) (as Lilia Herriton); *People of the Forest: The Chimps of Gombe* (TV doc) (as narrator)
1993	*The Hawk* (Hayman) (as Annie Marsh)
1994	*Prince of Jutland* (Axel) (as Queen Geruth); *The Madness of King George* (Hytner) (as Queen Charlotte)
1995	*Prime Suspect: The Lost Child* (John Madden—for TV) (as Supt. Jane Tennison)
1996	*Prime Suspect: Inner Circles* (Sarah Pia Anderson—for TV) (as Supt. Jane Tennison); *Losing Chase* (Kevin Bacon)

Publications

By MIRREN: articles—

Interview with James Saynor, in *Interview* (New York), January 1993.
Interview with Amy Rennert, in *New Orleans Magazine*, April 1994.

On MIRREN: book—

Rennert, Amy, ed., *Helen Mirren: Prime Suspect: A Celebration*, San Francisco, 1995.

On MIRREN: articles—

Hauptfuhrer, Fred, "She Played Caligula's Wife and Fu Manchu's Girlfriend, but Helen Mirren Is Fiercest of All in the Flesh," in *People* (New York), 3 November 1980.
Edwardes, Jane, "Mirren Image," in *Time Out* (London), 11 January 1989.
Sanderson, Mark, "Two-Way Mirren," in *Time Out* (London), 12 June 1991.
Taubin, Amy, "Misogyny, She Wrote," in *Village Voice* (New York), 28 January 1992.
Wolcott, James, "Columbo in Furs," in *New Yorker*, 25 January 1993.
"Mirren Image," in *Harper's Bazaar* (New York), February 1993.
Grimes, William, "Detective Tennison Returns to PBS, Still in Charge but Now in Command," in *New York Times*, 2 February 1993.
Fallon, James, "Helen's Prime Time," in *W* (New York), May 1994.
Hitchens, Christopher, "Mirren and *Middlemarch*," in *Vanity Fair* (New York), May 1994.
Ansen, David, "The Prime of Helen Mirren," in *Newsweek* (New York), 16 May 1994.
Current Biography 1995, New York, 1995.

Helen Mirren in *The Cook, the Thief, his Wife and her Lover*

Weinraub, Bernard, "Uninhibited, Opinionated, It Must Be Helen Mirren," in *New York Times*, 23 April 1995.

Wolcott, James, "Helen Mirren," in *New Yorker*, 24 April 1995.

*   *   *

Helen Mirren's career has been a remarkable blend of prestige and trashy roles, befitting an actress who has enjoyed long-term membership in the Royal Shakespeare Company and highly publicized exposés of her Bohemian lifestyle and romantic involvements with, most notably, Liam Neeson and Taylor Hackford (with whom Mirren has lived in Los Angeles since the mid-1980s). In the 1970s, she was know as "the Sex Bomb of the RSC," once quoted as proudly proclaiming, "I like sex; I'm extremely sensual." In her first major screen role, in Michael Powell's Australian feature, *Age of Consent*, she snorkeled nude along the Great Barrier Reef. She was provocatively naked in Ken Russell's *Savage Messiah*, and on stage in the 1971 Royal Shakespeare Company production of Jean Genet's *The Balcony*. Mirren was at ease, and superb, in Shakespearian roles, including Hermia and Titania in 1968 (film) and 1982 (stage) productions of *A Midsummer Night's Dream*, Lady Macbeth on stage in 1974, and Rosalind in the BBC's *As Your Like It*. At the same time, she enjoyed shocking the critics and her fans by performing in Gore Vidal's *Caligula*, but not, as she points out, "in the naughty bits."

Splendid as she was as Queen Charlotte, opposite Nigel Hawthorne, in the film adaptation of Alan Bennett's play, *The Madness of George III*, it is in the medium of television in recent years that Helen Mirren has garnered most praise and an international following. She first attracted the attention of American audiences in 1987 in Anglia Television's adaptation of Terence Rattigan's *Cause Celebre*, playing the real-life Alma Rattenbury, who, in 1935, took her 18-year-old chauffeur as her lover and encouraged him to murder her husband. From that performance as a lonely and confused middle-aged woman, Mirren moved on to an entirely different role, that of Detective Chief Inspector Jane Tennison in Lynda La Plante's *Prime Suspect*. Here, Mirren is cast as the highest ranking policewoman in the United Kingdom, fighting both sexism and the intrusion of her private life. Mirren's characterization is of a strong woman, plagued by self doubts and one whose place in the system forces her to display an unpleasant edge. Thanks to Alma Rattenbury and Jane Tennison, Mirren has become, in the words of James Wolcott in the *New Yorker,* "the heiress to Glenda Jackson as the queen of the quality mini-series."

From a major British stage performer of the 1970s, Helen Mirren graduated to secondary film roles in the 1980s and starring television performances in the late 1980s and 1990s. In middle age, the actress gives little indication as to what the future holds. The prurient will note that her body, as well displayed as it was in *The Cook, the Thief, His Wife & Her Lover*, shows no signs of aging, while her facial features have developed from a somewhat vacuous expression to those of a woman who has obviously enjoyed a very interesting life and whose few lines are suggestive of an intellectual interior rather than the aging process.

—Anthony Slide

MITCHUM, Robert

Nationality: American. **Born:** Robert Charles Duran Mitchum in Bridgeport, Connecticut, 6 August 1917. **Education:** Attended Haaren High School, New York, left at age 14. **Military Service:** U.S. Army, 1945. **Family:** Married Dorothy Spence, 1940, three children, including the actor Christopher. **Career:** Worked at a variety of jobs during the 1930s, including heavyweight boxing; joined Long Beach Civic Theatre as stage hand and actor in late 1930s, and worked for Lockheed Aircraft in early 1940s; 1943—film debut in *Hoppy Serves a Writ*; 1944—contract with RKO, later shared with David O. Selznick, then bought by Howard Hughes; 1945—starring role in *G.I. Joe*; 1948—well-publicized arrest for possession of marijuana; 1954— formed own production company, DRM Productions, later changed to Talbot Productions; 1980—in TV mini-series *The Winds of War*, *North and South*, 1985, and *War and Remembrance*, 1988; 1990— in TV series *A Family for Joe*. **Address:** P.O. Box 5216, Montecito, CA 93108, U.S.A.

Films as Actor:

(as Bob Mitchum)

1943   *Hoppy Serves a Writ* (Archainbaud) (as Rigney); *The Leather Burners* (Henabery) (as Randall); *Border Patrol* (Selander) (as a henchman); *Follow the Band* (Yarbrough) (as Tate Winters); *Aerial Gunner* (Pine) (as Sergeant); *Colt Comrades* (Selander) (as Bart); *Cry Havoc!* (Thorpe) (as groaning man); *The Human Comedy* (Brown) (as Horse); *Minesweeper* (Berke) (as Chuck); *We've Never Been Licked* (*Texas to Tokyo*) (Rawlins) (as Panhandle Mitchell); *Beyond the Last Frontier* (Bretherton) (as Trigger Dolan); *Bar Twenty* (Selander) (as Richard Adams); *Doughboys in Ireland* (Landers) (as Earnie Jones)

(as Robert Mitchum)

1943   *Corvette K-225* (Rossen) (as Shephard); *The Lone Star Trail* (Taylor) (as Ben Slocum); *False Colors* (Archainbaud) (as Rip Austin); *Dancing Masters* (St. Clair) (as Mickey); *Riders of the Deadline* (Selander) (as Drago); *Gung Ho!* (Enright) (as Pigiron Matthews)

1944   *Johnny Doesn't Live Here Anymore* (*And So They Were Married*) (Joe May) (as Jeff Daniels); *Mr. Winkle Goes to War* (*Arms and the Woman*) (Alfred E. Green) (as corporal); *When Strangers Marry* (*Betrayed*) (Castle) (as Fred); *Girl Rush* (Gordon Douglas) (as Jimmy Smith); *Thirty Seconds over Tokyo* (LeRoy) (as Bob Gray); *Nevada* (Killy) (as Jim "Nevada" Lacy)

1945   *West of the Pecos* (Killy) (as Pecos Smith); *The Story of G.I. Joe* (*G.I. Joe*; *War Correspondent*) (Wellman) (as Lt. Walker)

1946   *Till the End of Time* (Dmytryk) (as William Tabeshaw); *Undercurrent* (Minnelli) (as Michael Garraway); *The Locket* (Brahm) (as Norman Clyde)

1947   *Pursued* (Walsh) (as Jeb Rand); **Crossfire** (Dmytryk) (as Sgt. Peter Keeley); *Desire Me* (Cukor and LeRoy, both uncredited) (as Paul Albert); **Out of the Past** (*Build My Gallows High*) (Jacques Tourneur) (as Jeff Bailey)

1948   *Rachel and the Stranger* (Norman Foster) (as Jim Fairways); *Blood on the Moon* (Wise) (as Jimmy Garry)

1949   *The Red Pony* (Milestone) (as Billy Buck); *The Big Steal* (Siegel) (as Lt. Duke Halliday); *Holiday Affair* (Hartman) (as Steve Mason)

1950   *Where Danger Lives* (Farrow) (as Jeff Cameron)

1951   *My Forbidden Past* (Stevenson) (as Dr. Mark Lucas); *His Kind of Woman* (Farrow) (as Dan Miller); *The Racket* (Cromwell) (as Captain Thomas McQuigg)

1952   *Macao* (von Sternberg) (as Nick Cochran); *One Minute to Zero* (Garnett) (as Colonel Steve Janowski); *The Lusty Men* (Nicholas Ray) (as Jeff McLoud); *Angel Face* (Preminger) (as Frank Jessup)

Robert Mitchum

1953   *White Witch Doctor* (Hathaway) (as Lonnie Douglas); *Second Chance* (Maté) (as Russ Lambert)

1954   *She Couldn't Say No* (*Beautiful but Dangerous*) (Lloyd Bacon) (as Doc); *River of No Return* (Preminger) (as Matt Calder); *Track of the Cat* (Wellman) (as Curt Bridges)

1955   *Not as a Stranger* (Kramer) (as Lucas Marsh); **The Night of the Hunter** (Laughton) (as Preacher Harry Powell); *Man with the Gun* (*The Trouble Shooter*) (Wilson) (as Clint Tollinger)

1956   *Foreign Intrigue* (Sheldon Reynolds) (as Dave Bishop); *Bandido* (Fleischer) (as Richard Wilson)

1957   *Heaven Knows, Mr. Allison* (Huston) (title role); *Fire Down Below* (Parrish) (as Felix); *The Enemy Below* (Powell) (as Captain Murrell)

1958   *Thunder Road* (Ripley) (as Lucas Doolin, + pr, co-sc); *The Hunters* (Powell) (as Maj. Cleve Seville)

1959   *The Angry Hills* (Aldrich) (as Mike Morrison); *The Wonderful Country* (Parrish) (as Martin Brady)

1960   *Home from the Hill* (Minnelli) (as Captain Wade Hunnicut); *The Night Fighters* (*A Terrible Beauty*) (Garnett) (as Dermot O'Neill); *The Grass Is Greener* (Donen) (as Charles Delacro); *The Sundowners* (Zinnemann) (as Paddy Carmony)

1961   *The Last Time I Saw Archie* (Webb) (as Archie Hall)

1962   *Cape Fear* (J. Lee Thompson) (as Max Cady); *The Longest Day* (Annakin, Marton, Wicki, and Oswald) (as Brig. Gen. Norman Cota); *Two for the Seesaw* (Wise) (as Jerry Ryan)

1963   *The List of Adrian Messenger* (Huston) (as Jim Slattery); *Rampage* (Karlson) (as Harry Stanton)

1964   *Man in the Middle* (Hamilton) (as Lt. Colonel Barney Adams); *What a Way to Go!* (J. Lee Thompson) (as Rod Anderson)

1965   *Mr. Moses* (Neame) (title role)

1967   *The Way West* (McLaglen) (as Dick Summers); *El Dorado* (Hawks) (as J. D. Harrah)

1968   *Lo sbarco di Anzio* (*Anzio*; *The Battle for Anzio*) (Dmytryk) (as Dick Ennis); *Villa Rides* (Kulick) (as Lee Arnold); *Five Card Stud* (Hathaway) (as Jonathan Rudd)

1969   *Secret Ceremony* (Losey) (as Albert); *Young Billy Young* (Kennedy) (as Ben Kane); *The Good Guys and the Bad Guys* (Kennedy) (as James Flagg)

1970   *Ryan's Daughter* (Lean) (as Charles Shaughnessy)

1971   *Going Home* (Leonard) (as Harry K. Graham)

1972   *The Wrath of God* (Nelson) (as Van Horne)

1973   *The Friends of Eddie Coyle* (Yates) (as Eddie Coyle)

1975   *The Yakuza* (Pollack) (as Harry Kilmer); *Farewell, My Lovely* (Richards) (as Philip Marlowe)

1976   *Midway* (*Battle of Midway*) (Smight) (as Admiral William Halsey); *The Last Tycoon* (Kazan) (as Pat Brady)

1977   *The Amsterdam Kill* (Clouse) (as Quinlin)

1978   *Matilda* (Daniel Mann) (as Duke Parkhurst); *The Big Sleep* (Winner) (as Philip Marlowe)

1979   *Breakthrough* (*Sargent Steiner*) (McLaglen) (as Col. Rogers)

1980   *Night Kill* (Post—for TV) (as Donner)

1981   *Agency* (Kaczender) (as Ted)

1982   *That Championship Season* (Miller) (as Coach Delaney); *One Shoe Makes It Murder* (Hole—for TV) (as Harold Shillman)

1983   *A Killer in the Family* (Heffron—for TV) (as Gary Tison)

1984   *The Ambassador* (J. Lee Thompson) (as Peter Hacker)

1985   *Maria's Lovers* (Konchalovsky) (as Ivan's father); *The Hearst and Davies Affair* (Rich—for TV) (as William Randolph Hearst); *Reunion at Fairborough* (Wise—for TV); *Promises to Keep* (Black)

1986   *Thompson's Last Run* (Freedman—for TV)

1988   *Mr. North* (Danny Huston) (as James McHenry Bosworth); *John Huston: The Man, the Movies, the Maverick* (Martin—doc) (as narrator); *Scrooged* (Richard Donner) (as Preston Rhinelander); *Jake Spanner, Private Eye* (Katzin—for TV)

1989   *Brotherhood of the Rose* (Chomsky—for TV) (as John Eliot)

1990   *Presumé dangereux* (*Believed Violent*) (Lautner) (as Prof. Forrester); *A Family for Joe* (Melman—for TV) (as Joe)

1991   *Bis ans Ende der Welt* (*Until the End of the World*) (Wenders); *Cape Fear* (Scorsese) (as Lt. Elgart)

1993   *Tombstone* (Cosmatos) (as narrator); *Midnight Ride* (Bralver); *Woman of Desire* (Ginty) (as Walter J. Hill)

1995   *Backfire* (A. Dean Bell) (as Marshal Marc Marshall)

1996   *Dead Man* (Jarmusch) (as John Dickinson); *Pakten* (*The Sunset Boys*) (Risan)

Publications

By MITCHUM: articles—

Interview with B. Rehfield, in *Esquire* (New York), February 1983.

Interviews in *Photoplay* (London), November 1983 and February 1985.

Interview in *Films* (London), November 1984.

Interview in *Talking Films: The Best of the Guardian Film Lectures*, edited by Andrew Britton, London, 1991.

Interview with Graham Fuller, in *Interview* (New York), December 1991.

"Mitchum Russell," interview with Harlan Kennedy and Gerald Peary, in *Film Comment* (New York), July/August 1992.

"Rule 7: Remember the Advice of a Survivor," interview with David Freeman, in *Los Angeles Magazine*, October 1995.

On MITCHUM: books—

Tomkies, Mike, *The Robert Mitchum Story*, Chicago, 1972.

Belton, John, *Robert Mitchum*, New York, 1976.

Marill, Alvin H., *Robert Mitchum on the Screen*, South Brunswick, New Jersey, 1978.

Eells, George, *Robert Mitchum*, New York, 1984.

Malcolm, Derek, *Robert Mitchum*, Tunbridge Wells, Kent, 1984.

Downing, David, *Robert Mitchum*, London, 1985.

Mitchum, John, *Them Ornery Mitchum Boys: The Adventures of John and Robert Mitchum*, Pacifica, California, 1989.

Crowther, Bruce, *The Film Career of Robert Mitchum*, London, 1991.

Roberts, Jerry Wayne, *Robert Mitchum: A Bio-Bibliography*, Westport, Connecticut, 1992.

Marill, Alvin H., *The Films of Robert Mitchum*, Secaucus, New Jersey, 1995.

On MITCHUM: articles—

Ringgold, Gene, "Robert Mitchum," in *Films in Review* (New York), May 1964.

Current Biography 1970, New York, 1970.

Chevalier, J., "Une Fleur pour Bob Mitchum, le rebelle d'Hollywood," in *Ecran* (Paris), December 1975.

Ebert, Roger, "Robert Mitchum," in *The Movie Star*, edited by Elisabeth Weis, New York, 1981.

Ward, R., "Mr. Bad Taste and Trouble Himself: Robert Mitchum," in *Rolling Stone* (New York), 3 March 1983.

Thompson, Frank, "Robert Mitchum: The Original Mr. Attitude Can Act as Well as He Wants," in *American Film* (New York), May 1991.

Filmography in *Premiere* (New York), November 1991.

"Hot Icon: Robert Mitchum," in *Rolling Stone* (New York), 14 May 1992.

*   *   *

Whether due to natural modesty or shrewdness, Robert Mitchum has cultivated an image as Hollywood's I Don't Care Boy. A self-proclaimed graduate of the I-Just-Show-Up-and-Read-My-Lines School of Acting, Mitchum presents the media and his devotees with a portrait of himself as a no-nonsense underachiever who lucked into his career. For a man whose first minor break come when he volunteered to ride a horse that had just killed another bit player, the truth about his casual attitude might be complex enough for the kind of treatment Kurosawa gave *Rashomon*.

Brimming with the sort of he-man sexuality that swept away women's better judgment, Mitchum might have been stuck playing muscle-bound rascals if he had come to prominence sooner, but his ascendancy coincided with the postwar turmoil encapsulated in film noir. A man of few words, all of them packed with dynamite, the terse Mitchum was a minimalist actor; since he did not call attention to himself with Oscar-grabbing flourishes, his economical methods make his cleanly delivered performances seem all the more modern today. Winning his first and only Oscar nomination for *The Story of G.I. Joe*, Mitchum always had the luxury of alternating hero and villain roles as he effortlessly changed his wardrobe from leather chaps to soldier fatigue to P.I. trench coat, with an innate fashion sense of what the well-dressed antihero wore. How many of his fellow players from his B Westerns are even still working actors? Never letting up with his official line about not taking his career seriously, Mitchum outlasted his more highly regarded contemporaries until he was the last Golden Age male superstar still billed above the title.

At the time when he was RKO's resident screwed-over everyman, his notorious drug bust actually enhanced his reputation by jazzing up his social outlaw image. Ingrid Bergman, Tom Neal, Rory Calhoun and many others were not so fortunate in an era when *Confidential* magazine began invading stars' homes to look for skeletons in their closets.

Perpetuating his persona as a frontiersman with a past (*Rachel and the Stranger*, *Blood on the Moon*), Mitchum brought an equally haunted quality to bear on RKO's other genre staple, the fatalistic urban thriller in which Mitchum hinted that resignation to corruption was often an antihero's only recourse. If *Out of the Past* engraves the tough, soul-sick Mitchum image in stone, his other RKO standouts hint at something more sinister than entrapment in a cycle of crime. What is endlessly fascinating about movies such as *Angel Face*, *The Locket*, *Where Danger Lives*, and *My Foolish Past* is that the solidly built male star at the center of these whirlpools is primarily a fall guy for women. In the provocative *Angel Face*, Mitchum is the heterosexual's worst nightmare, a man of action turned impotent by a controlling beauty. Less perilously paired with Jane Russell in a series of robust adventures, Mitchum's lighter side received a workout, but he continued adding to his star luster with straightforward leading-man roles opposite Deborah Kerr, Marilyn Monroe, and others, in exciting romantic films that explored his good-natured skepticism while exercising his broad appeal to men and women.

In the course of easing into his own played-down legend, Mitchum broadened his range with subtle turns in sophisticated misfires such as *Secret Ceremony*, singlehandedly salvaged the epic *Ryan's Daughter* with his quiet authority, and brought heartbreaking purity to bear on his portrayal of an Australian sheep farmer cursed with wanderlust but blessed with Deborah Kerr in *The Sundowners*.

Knocking the socks off even his admirers, Mitchum also made chilled-to-the-marrow moviegoers shudder with his interpretations of rotten villains in *Cape Fear* and *The Night of the Hunter*. The former is a taut psycho-thriller about a sadist conversant with legal technicalities; Mitchum fashions a stalker monster clearly ahead of his time—an achievement all the more impressive since critics-darling Robert De Niro failed to outdo Mitchum in the dreadful Scorcese remake. Even finer is Mitchum's venal bible-thumper in *The Night of the Hunter*, Charles Laughton's expressionist fairy tale now regarded as a horror classic. If these two performances do not clinch the argument that Mitchum is a great screen actor then the definition of great screen acting needs to be modified.

Late in his career, Mitchum's seen-it-all wariness and offhanded gallantry redefined forties detective iconography for contemporary times with *Farewell, My Lovely*. In a fitting career capstone, the mini-series *The Winds of War* and *War and Remembrance* consolidated Mitchum's position as one of Hollywood's durable icons. It is fortunate that Mitchum has endured to receive accolades for a body of work that he has consistently undervalued. Somewhere behind those heavy-lidded eyes and are-you-kidding exterior, Mitchum must feel secretly vindicated. Although filmgoers have enjoyed this late bloomer's laconic presence for years, the critical and popular consensus has finally caught up with Mitchum's greatness as a screen star.

—Robert Pardi

MIX, Tom

Nationality: American. **Born:** Thomas Erwin Mix in Mix Run, Pennsylvania, 6 January 1880. **Military Service:** U.S. Army Artillery, 1898-1901; sergeant. **Family:** Married 1) Grace I. Allin, 1902 (marriage annullcd); 2) Kitty Jewel Perrine, 1905 (divorced); 3) Olive Stokes, 1907 (divorced 1917), daughter: Ruth; 4) Victoria Forde, 1918 (divorced 1930), daughter: Thomasina; 5) Mabel Hubbard Ward, 1932. **Career:** c.1903—drum major with Oklahoma Cavalry Band: played the St. Louis World's Fair; 1904—bartender, then deputy sheriff and night Marshal of Dewey, Oklahoma; 1906-09—with Miller Brothers 101 Real Wild West Ranch, home base of their Wild West Show; 1909—joined Widerman Wild West Show, Amarillo, Texas; played with Alaska-Yukon-Pacific Exposition, Seattle, in a show formed with his wife, Olive Stokes; joined Will A. Dickey's Circle D Ranch Wild West Show and Indian Congress, with contract to supply Selig Company with cowboys and Indians for films; off-screen wrangler; 1910—film debut in *Ranch Life in the Great Southwest*; personal contract with Selig; then made many films for Selig, often writing and directing them himself; 1917-28—contract with Fox; 1930-31—toured with Sells Floto Circus; 1936-38—toured with Tom Mix Circus. **Died:** In auto accident near Florence, Arizona, 12 October 1940.

Films as Actor:

1910 *Ranch Life in the Great Southwest* (Boggs); *Briton and Boer*; *On the Little Big Horn* (*Custer's Last Stand*) (Boggs); *The Range Rider* (Reynolds); *An Indian Wife's Devotion*; *The Long Trail* (Boggs); *The Millionaire Cowboy*; *Taming Wild Animals* (Boggs); *The Trimming of Paradise Gulch* (Boggs); *Up San Juan Hill*; *Pride of the Range* (Boggs)

1911 *Captain Kate* (Boggs); *Lost in the Jungle* (Boggs); *The Totem Mark* (Boggs); *The Wheels of Justice* (Boggs); *Back to the Primitive* (Boggs); *Lost in the Arctic* (Boggs); *Rescued by Her Lions* (Boggs); *Kit Carson's Wooing* (Boggs); *In the Days of Gold* (Boggs); *In Old California When the Gringos Came* (Boggs); *A Romance of the Rio Grande* (Campbell); *The Schoolmaster of Mariposa* (Boggs); *Western Hearts*; *The Telltale Knife* (Duncan); *Outlaw Reward*

1912 *A Reconstructed Rebel* (Campbell)

1913 *How It Happened* (Duncan); *The Range Law* (Duncan); *Juggling with Fate*; *The Sheriff of Yawapai County* (Duncan); *The Life Timer* (Duncan); *Pauline Cushman, the Federal Spy*; *A Prisoner of Cabanas* (Campbell); *The Shotgun Man and the Stage Driver* (Duncan); *His Father's Deputy* (Duncan); *The Noisy Six* (Campbell); *Religion and Gun Practice* (Duncan); *The Wordless Message* (Campbell); *The Law*

Tom Mix

and the Outlaw (Duncan) (+ co-sc); *The Marshal's Capture* (Duncan); *Songs of Truce* (Campbell); *Sallie's Sure Short* (Duncan); *Budd Doble Comes Back* (Campbell); *Made a Coward* (Duncan); *The Taming of Texas Pete* (Duncan); *An Apache's Gratitude* (Duncan); *The Stolen Moccasins* (Duncan); *The Good Indian* (Duncan); *Tobias Wants Out* (Eagle); *Saved by the Pony Express*; *The Sheriff and the Rustler* (Duncan) (+ sc); *A Muddle in Horse Thieves*; *The Escape of Jim Dolan* (Campbell) (+ sc)

1914 *The Little Sister*; *Shotgun Jones* (Campbell); *Me an' Bill* (Campbell); *The Leopard's Foundling* (Grandon); *In Defiance of the Law*; *His Fight* (Campbell); *Wiggs Takes the Rest Cure* (Grandon); *The Wilderness Mail* (Campbell); *When the Cook Fell Ill* (Campbell); *Etienne of the Glad Heart* (Campbell); *The Reveler* (Campbell); *The White Mouse* (Campbell); *Chip of the Flying U* (Campbell); *To Be Called For* (Grandon); *The Fifth Man* (Grandon); *Jim* (Grandon); *The Lonesome Trail* (Campbell); *The Livid Flame* (Grandon); *Four Minutes Late* (Grandon); *Hearts and Masks* (Campbell); *The Going of the White Swan* (Campbell); *Garrison's Finish* (Grandon); *The Losing Fight* (Campbell); *If I Were Young Again* (Grandon); *Out of Petticoat Lane* (Grandon); *Your*

Girl and Mine (Grandon); *In the Days of the Thundering Herd* (Campbell); *The Soul Mate* (Grandon); *Wade Brent Pays* (Grandon); *Buffalo Hunting* (Grandon); *The Lure of the Windigo* (Grandon); *The Flower of Faith* (Grandon)

1915 *Heart's Desire* (Grandon); *Hearts of the Jungle* (Grandon); *The Puny Soul of Peter Rand* (Grandon); *Jack's Pals* (Grandon); *The Face at the Window* (Grandon); *The Parson Who Fled West* (B. King)

1916 *When Cupid Slipped*

1917 *The Heart of Texas Ryan* (Martin); *Durand of the Bad Lands* (Stanton)

1918 *Cupid's Roundup* (Le Saint); *Six Shooter Andy* (C. Franklin and S. Franklin); *Western Blood* (Reynolds) (+ co-sc); *Ace High* (Reynolds); *Mr. Logan, U.S.A.* (Reynolds); *Fame and Fortune* (Reynolds)

1919 *Treat 'em Rough* (Reynolds); *Hell-Roarin' Reform* (Le Saint); *Fighting for Gold* (Le Saint); *The Coming of the Law* (Rosson); *The Wilderness Trail* (Le Saint); *Rough-Riding Romance* (Rosson); *The Speed Maniac* (Le Saint); *The Feud* (Le Saint)

1920 *The Cyclone* (Smith); *Desert Love* (Jaccard) (+ co-sc); *The Terror* (Jaccard) (+ co-sc); *Three Gold Coins* (Smith); *The Untamed* (Flynn); *The Texan* (Reynolds); *Prairie Trails* (Marshall)

1921 *The Road Demon* (Reynolds); *Hands Off* (Marshall); *A Ridin' Romeo* (Marshall) (+ co-sc); *Big Town Round-up* (Reynolds); *After Your Own Heart* (Marshall) (+ co-sc); *The Night Horsemen* (Reynolds); *The Rough Diamond* (Sedgwick) (+ co-sc); *Trailin'* (Reynolds)

1922 *Sky High* (Reynolds); *Chasing the Moon* (Sedgwick) (+ co-sc); *Up and Going* (Reynolds) (+ co-sc); *The Fighting Streak* (Rosson); *For Big Stakes* (Reynolds); *Just Tony* (Reynolds); *Do and Dare* (Sedgwick); *Tom Mix in Arabia* (Reynolds) (+ co-sc); *Catch My Smoke* (Beaudine)

1923 *Romance Land* (Sedgwick); *Three Jumps Ahead* (Ford); *Stepping Fast* (Franz); *Soft-Boiled* (Blystone); *The Lone Star Ranger* (Hillyer); *Mile-a-Minute Romeo* (Hillyer); *North of Hudson Bay* (Ford); *Eyes of the Forest* (Hillyer)

1924 *Ladies to Board* (Blystone); *The Trouble Shooter* (Conway); *The Heart Buster* (Conway); *The Last of the Duanes* (Reynolds); *Oh, You Tony!* (Blystone); *Teeth* (Blystone); *The Deadwood Coach* (Reynolds)

1925 *Dick Turpin* (Blystone); *Riders of the Purple Sage* (Reynolds); *The Rainbow Trail* (Reynolds); *The Lucky Horseshoe* (Blystone); *The Everlasting Whisper* (Blystone); *The Best Bad Man* (Blystone)

1926 *The Yankee Senor* (Flynn); *My Own Pal* (Blystone); *Tony Runs Wild* (Buckingham); *Hard-Boiled* (Blystone); *No Man's Gold* (Seiler); *The Great K & A Train Robbery* (Seiler); *The Canyon of Light* (Stoloff)

1927 *The Last Trail* (Seiler); *The Broncho Twister* (Dull); *Outlaws of Red River* (Seiler); *The Circus Ace* (Stoloff); *Tumbling River* (Seiler); *Silver Valley* (Stoloff); *The Arizona Wildcat* (Neill); *Life in Hollywood Number Four*

1928 *Daredevil's Reward* (Forde); *A Horseman of the Plains* (Stoloff); *Hello Cheyenne* (Forde); *Painted Post* (Forde); *Hollywood Today Number Four*; *Son of the Golden West* (Forde); *King Cowboy* (DeLacey)

1929 *Outlawed* (Forde); *The Drifter* (DeLacey); *The Big Diamond* (Forde)

1930 *Voice of Hollywood Nos. 1-2*

1932 *The Rider of Death Valley* (Rogell) (as Tom Rigby); *Texas Bad Man* (E. Laemmle); *Destry Rides Again* (Stoloff) (as Thomas J. Destry Jr.); *My Pal, the King* (Neumann) (as Tom Reed); *The Fourth Horseman* (MacFadden); *Flaming Guns* (Rosson); *Hollywood on Parade Nos. 3-4*

1933 *Hidden Gold* (Rosson); *Terror Trail* (Schaefer) (as Tom Munroe); *Rustler's Roundup* (MacRae); *The Miracle Rider* (Eason and Schaefer—serial)

Films as Director and Actor:

1913 *Local Color* (+ sc)

1914 *The Real Thing in Cowboys*; *The Moving Picture Cowboy* (+ sc); *The Way of the Redman* (+ sc); *The Mexican* (+ sc); *Jimmy Hayes and Muriel*; *Why the Sheriff Is a Bachelor* (+ sc); *The Ranger's Romance* (+ sc); *The Telltale Knife* (+ sc); *The Sheriff's Reward* (+ sc); *The Scapegoat* (+ sc); *The Rival Stage Lines*; *Saved by a Watch* (+ sc); *The Man from the East* (+ sc); *Cactus Jack Heartbreaker*; *A Militant School Ma'am*

1915 *Harold's Bad Man*; *Cactus Jim's Shopgirl*; *The Grizzly Gulch Chariot Race*; *Forked Trails*; *Roping a Bride*; *Bill Haywood, Producer*; *Slim Higgins* (+ sc); *The Man from Texas*; *Child of the Prairie* (+ sc); *The Stagecoach Driver and the Girl* (+ sc); *Sagebrush Tom* (+ sc); *The Outlaw's Bride*; *The Legal Light*; *Ma's Girls* (+ sc); *Getting a Start in Life*; *Mrs. Murphy's Cooks* (+ sc); *The Conversion of Smiling Tom*; *An Arizona Wooing*; *A Matrimonial Boomerang*; *Pals in Blue* (+ sc);

Saved by Her Horse; *The Heart of the Sheriff* (+ sc); *With the Aid of the Law* (+ pr); *The Foreman of Bar Z Ranch*; *The Child, the Dog, and the Villain*; *The Taking of Mustang Pete*; *The Gold Dust and the Squaw*; *A Lucky Deal* (+ pr, sc); *Never Again* (+ pr, sc); *How Weary Went Wooing* (+ pr); *The Auction Sale of Run-Down Ranch*; *The Range Girl and the Cowboy* (+ sc); *Her Slight Mistake*; *The Girl and the Mail Bag*; *The Brave Deserve the Fair* (+ sc); *The Stagecoach Guard* (+ sc); *The Race for a Gold Mine*; *The Foreman's Choice* (+ pr); *Athletic Ambitions*; *The Tenderfoot's Triumph*; *The Chef at Circle G* (+ pr); *The Impersonation of Tom* (+ pr); *Bad Man Bobbs* (+ pr); *On the Eagle Trail* (+ pr)

1916 *The Desert Calls Its Own* (+ pr); *A Mix-Up in Movies* (+ pr, sc); *The Passing of Pete* (+ pr, sc); *Trilby's Love Disaster* (+ pr, sc); *A Five Thousand Elopement* (+ pr); *Along the Border* (+ pr, sc); *Too Many Chefs* (+ pr, sc); *The Man Within*; *The Sheriff's Duty* (+ pr, sc); *Cooked Trails* (+ pr, sc); *Going West to Make Good* (+ pr, sc); *The Cowpuncher's Peril* (+ pr, sc); *Taking a Chance* (+ pr, sc); *The Girl of Gold Gulch* (+ pr); *Some Duel* (+ pr, sc); *Legal Advice* (+ pr, sc); *Shooting Up the Movies* (+ pr, sc); *Local Color* (+ pr, sc); *An Angelic Attitude* (+ pr, sc); *A Western Masquerade* (+ pr, sc); *A Bear of a Story* (+ pr, sc); *Roping a Sweetheart* (+ pr, sc); *Tom's Strategy* (+ pr, sc); *The Taming of Grouchy Bill* (+ pr, sc); *The Pony Express Rider* (+ pr, sc); *A Corner in Water* (+ pr, sc); *The Raiders* (+ pr, sc); *The Canby Hill Outlaws* (+ pr, sc); *A Mistake in Rustlers* (+ pr, sc); *An Eventful Evening* (+ pr); *The Way of the Rem Redman* (+ sc); *A Close Call* (+ pr, sc); *Tom's Sacrifice* (+ pr, sc); *The Sheriff's Blunder* (+ pr, sc); *Mistakes Will Happen* (+ pr, sc); *Twisted Trails* (+ pr); *The Golden Thought* (+ pr); *Starring in Western Stuff* (+ pr, sc); *In the Days of Daring* (+ pr)

1917 *The Saddle Girth* (+ pr, sc); *The Luck That Jealousy Brought* (+ pr); *Hearts and Saddles* (co-d, + sc); *A Roman Cowboy* (+ sc); *Six Cylinder Love* (+ sc); *A Soft Tenderfoot* (+ sc); *Tom and Jerry Mix* (+ sc)

1918 *Who's Your Father?*

1920 *The Daredevil* (+ sc)

Publications

By MIX: articles—

"Hunting with Roosevelt," in *Photo-Play World*, May 1919.

"My Life Story," in *Photoplay* (New York), February-April 1925, reprinted in *Classic Images* (Indiana, Pennsylvania), July 1981-June 1984.

"Sure You Can Make Money in California," in *Photoplay* (New York), September 1926.

"Romance and a Hard-Boiled Shirt," in *Photoplay* (New York), January 1927.

"Wound Stripes of Hollywood," in *Photoplay* (New York), April 1927.

"Advice to Husbands and Wives," in *Photoplay* (New York), June 1927.

"The Vacation Complex," in *Photoplay* (New York), September 1927.

"Wanted Dead or Alive—Edmund Hoyle," in *Photoplay* (New York), December 1927.

"Making a Million," in *Photoplay* (New York), January-May 1928.

"The Loves of Tom Mix," in *Photoplay* (New York), March 1929.

"Shaking Hands with Death," in *Pictures and Picturegoer*, 26 November 1932.

On MIX: books—

Mix, Olive Stokes, and Eric Heath, *The Fabulous Tom Mix*, Englewood, New Jersey, 1957.

Fenin, George, and William K. Everson, *The Western, from Silents to Cinerama*, New York, 1962.

Harmon, Jim, and Donald Glut, *The Great Movie Serials: Their Sound and Fury*, Garden City, New York, 1972.

Nicholas, John, *Tom Mix: Riding Up to Glory*, Oklahoma City, 1980.

Irving, Clifford, *Tom Mix and Pancho Villa*, New York, 1982.

Norris, M. G., *The Tom Mix Book*, Waynesville, North Carolina, 1989.

Mix, Paul E., *Tom Mix: A Heavily Illustrated Biography*, Jefferson, North Carolina, 1990.

Mix, Paul E., *Tom Mix, the Formative Years*, Austin, Texas, 1990.

Seiverling, Richard F., *Tom Mix, Portrait of a Superstar*, Hershey, Pennsylvania, 1991.

On MIX: articles—

Remont, Fritzi, "Mixing in at Mixville," in *Motion Picture Classic* (Brooklyn), October 1919.

Tilley, Frank, "On Location with Tom Mix," in *Pictures and Picturegoer*, September 1923.

Kenrick, J. N., "Tom Mix Comes Back," in *Pictures and Picturegoer*, 30 April 1932.

Phillips, Malcolm, "Last of the Cowboy Kings," in *Pictures and Picturegoer*, 2 November 1940.

Mitchell, G., and William K. Everson, "Tom Mix," in *Films in Review* (New York), October 1957.

Five-part biography in *Classic Images* (Indiana, Pennsylvania), September 1980-May 1981.

Oakes, Philip, "Tom Mix—America's Champion Cowboy," in *Listener* (London), 8 March 1984.

Birchard, R. S., "Earliest Days of the Tom Mix Legend," in *American Cinematographer* (Hollywood), June 1987.

Singer, Tom, "Keepers of the Flame," in *New Yorker*, 3 June 1991.

*   *   *

In a sense, Tom Mix was the victim of a Hollywood legend. Stills published in books on the Western show him in big, 20-gallon cowboy hats, exaggerated dude ranch garb, and with a less-than-intelligent grin on a face that can only be called homely. To those who have not seen Mix's films, he was the epitome of the good guy Western hero from his oversized white hat to his incredibly intelligent horse Tony. But the legend is wrong.

The image of the Western hero was already a cliché by the time Mix, a former rodeo rider, hit the screen in 1910, and was based on dime novels, popular theater, and early film. Mix's films, in fact, are primarily comedies and Mix was primarily a comic performer from his early two-reelers for Selig in Chicago through his features in the 1920s for Fox. This is not simply a perverse interpretation. It is a fact which was quite evident to the children and adults who delighted in seeing Mix drunkenly trying to impress a city girl in *The Heart of Texas Ryan* or desperately attempting to hide Tony behind a narrow drapery in *The Great K & A Train Robbery*. Mix, who was indeed an accomplished rider who did his own stunts (many of them quite dangerous, as in the aforementioned film where he leaps from his horse aboard a speeding train among other derring-do) was an equally accomplished comic actor who seldom took himself seriously. In an outright comedy such as *Soft-Boiled*, which is set in the present day with no Western trappings at all, he reveals himself to be the pratfalling equal of Harold Lloyd. The horn-rimmed glasses he wears in the film even make him look a little like Lloyd.

Among the few Mix films that are readily available to contemporary viewers is *Dick Turpin*, based on the legend of the British highwayman of the same name, one of Mix's few attempts at serious presentation. The stunts are there but this film, also a non-Western,

distorts the image and talent of the man whose studio biography, with almost no truth in it, says he duplicated the characters he played. Mix, according to the biography, was part-Indian; a hero of the Spanish-American War, the Boer War, the Boxer Rebellion, and the Mexican Intervention; an accomplished knife-thrower, a graduate of Virginia Military Academy; and a former Texas Ranger. He was none of these. But he was a showman.

A reexamination of Mix's actual work rather than hearsay reveals not a forerunner of star-spangled Western stars like Roy Rogers, Gene Autry, and Hopalong Cassidy, but a precursor of John Wayne—an actor well aware of the nuance of close-up, the potential weakness of the naive Western hero, and the importance of the small gesture. Mix was not himself a cliché, an anachronism, or an absurdity. He was a talented actor who suggested the possibility of an absurd and comic hero which questioned the tradition of the rugged American and foreshadowed Western film "heroes" from Lee Marvin's Kid Shelleen in *Cat Ballou* to Clint Eastwood's *Broncho Billy* to Bruce Willis as Mix himself in *Sunset*.

—Stuart M. Kaminsky, updated by John McCarty

MODOT, Gaston

Nationality: French. **Born:** Paris, 31 December 1887. **Education:** Studied architecture and painting. **Military Service:** Military service, 1909. **Career:** Painter; began acting in films in 1909; then joined troupe of "Pouics" of Jean Durant, and began acting for Gaumont; made Westerns in the Camargue region of France; associated with Louis Delluc in the late 1920s; 1928—directed the film *La Torture par l'espérance*; 1941—wrote script for *Nous les gosses*, and *Leçon de conduite*, 1945. **Died:** 20 February 1970.

Films as Actor:

1909-14   [various roles and frequent screenwriter for the Onésime series (Durand)]

1909   *Les Papas de Francine; Sur le Sentier de la guerre; Coeur de Tzigane; Fauves et Bandits; Cent Dollars mort ou vif; Le Collier vivant*

1910   *Les Poilus de la Neuvieme*

1911   *Nemrod et Compagnie*

1912   *Sous la Griffe* (Durand); *Ame de Pierre*

1914   *Le Comte de Monte-Cristo*

1916   *La Danseuse voilée*

1917   *Mater Dolorosa* (Gance); *La Zone de la mort* (Gance)

1918   *Elle*

1919   *Un Ours* (Burguet) (+ co-sc); *La Fête espagnole* (Dulac); *La Sultane de l'amour* (Le Somptier and Burguet)

1920   *Le Chevalier de Gaby* (Burguet) (+ co-sc)

1921   *Mathias Sandorf* (Fescourt); *Fièvre* (Delluc) (as barkeeper)

1922   *Les Mille et une nuits* (Tourjansky); *La Terre du Diable* (Luitz-Morat); *Le Sang d'Allah* (Luitz-Morat); *Les Mystères de Paris; Au-dèla de la Mort; Au deuil du Harem* (Luitz-Morat); *La Boquetière des Innocents*

1923   *Petit Hotel à louer; La Mediante de Saint-Sulpice* (Burguet); *Le Cousin Pons* (Robert)

1924   *Nene; Le Miracle des loups* (*The Miracle of the Wolves*) (Bernard); *A L'Horizon du Sud* (de Gastyne)

1925   *Les Elus de la mer* (Roudès, Dumont)

1926   *Veille d'Armes* (de Baroncelli); *La Châtelaine du Liban* (de Gastyne); *Carmen* (Feyder)

1928   *Naples au baiser de feu* (Nadedjine); *La Villa des mille joies; La Merveilleuse Vie de Jeanne d'Arc; Shéhérazade* (*Sous le Ceil d'Orient; Secrets of the Orient*) (Volkov) (as Prince Hussen)

1929   *Monte Cristo* (Fescourt); *Liberté enchaînée; Le Fantôme de bonheur; Le Monocle vert; Das Schiff der verlorene Menschen* (*The Ship of Lost Souls*) (Tourneur)

1930   *Sous les toits de Paris* (*Under the Roofs of Paris*) (Clair) (as Fred); **L'Age d'or** (Buñuel) (as The Man)

1931   *L'Opéra de Quat'sous* (Pabst—French-language version of **Die Dreigroschenoper**) (as Peachum); *Fantômas* (Féjos) (as Firmin); *Autour d'une enquête* (Siodmak—French-language version of *Voruntersuchung*)

1932   *Coups de feu à l'Aube; La Mille et Deuxième Nuits* (Volkov)

1933   *Crainquebille* (*Coster Bill of Paris*) (de Baroncelli); *Le Quatorze Juillet* (*July 14th*) (Clair); *Quequ'un a tue* (Forrester); *Colomba* (Séverac)

1934   *L'Auberge du Petit-Dragon* (de Limur); *Le Mystère Imberger* (Séverac)

1935   *Passage Interdit* (Bernan); *Lucrèce Borgia* (Gance); *La Bandera* (*Escape from Yesterday*) (Duvivier) (as Muller); *Le Clown bux* (Natanson)

1936   *La Vie est à nous* (Renoir); **Pépé le Moko** (Duvivier); *Les Réprouvés* (Séverac)

Gaston Modot in *L'Age d'or*

1937   *La Grande Illusion* (*Grand Illusion*) (Renoir) (as a surveyor);
        Mademoiselle Docteur (Pabst)
1938   *Le Joueur d'echecs* (*The Devil Is an Empress*) (Dréville) (as
        Major Nicolaieff); *La Marseillaise* (Renoir); *La Fin du jour*
        (*The End of a Day*) (Duvivier) (as the innkeeper)
1939   *La Règle du jeu* (*The Rules of the Game*) (Renoir) (as
        Schumacher); *Plein aux As* (Houssin)
1941   *Nous le Gosses* (*Portrait of Innocence*) (Daquin) (+ co-sc)
1942   *Dernier Atout* (Becker)
1943   *L'Homme de Londres* (Decoin)
1944   *Le Bossu* (Delannoy)
1945   *Les Enfants du paradis* (*The Children of Paradise*) (Carné) (as
        the blind beggar)
1946   *Antoine et Antoinette* (Becker) (as a civil servant)
1947   *Dernier Refuge* (Maurette); *Le Silence est d'or* (*Man-about-
        Town*) (Clair); *Eternel Conflit* (Lampin)
1948   *Le Mystère de la chambre jaune* (Aisner); *L'Amoire volante*
        (Rim); *Le Point du jour* (Daquin); *L'Ecole buissonnière*
        (*Passion for Life*) (Le Chanois) (as an examiner)
1949   *La Beauté du Diable* (*Beauty and the Devil*) (Clair) (as a
        gypsy); *Rendez-vous de Juillet* (Becker); *Le Parfum de la
        dame en noir* (Daquin)
1951   *Ce Coquin d'Anatole* (Couzinet); **Casque d'or** (*Golden Marie*;
        The Golden Helmet) (Becker) (as Danard)
1952   *La Môme vert-de-gris* (Borderie)
1954   *French Cancan* (*Only the French Can*) (Renoir)
1955   *Cela s'appelle l'aurore* (Buñuel)
1956   *Les Truands* (Rim)
1957   *Eléna et les hommes* (*Paris Does Strange Things*) (Renoir)
1958   *Les Amants* (*The Lovers*) (Malle) (as a servant)
1959   *Le Testament du Docteur Cordelier* (Renoir)
1961   *Les Menteurs* (*The Liars*; *Twisted Lives*) (Gréville) (as Carloti)
1962   *Le Diable et les dix commandments* (*The Devil and the Six
        Commandments*) (Duvivier) (as grandfather)

Film as Director and Screenwriter:

1928   *La Torture par l'espérance* (+ ro)

Publications

On MODOT: articles—

Lacasson, François, and Raymond Bellour, in *Cinéma* (Paris), Novem-
    ber/December 1961.
Télérama (Paris), 15 October 1983.

*   *   *

For more than 50 years, Gaston Modot was one of the most conspicuous and respected character actors in the French cinema. Whether
playing rogue or thug, beggar or barkeeper, soldier or surveyor, Modot
would turn the smallest role into a sound, and often striking, performance, making him a special favorite of French filmmakers. Inevitably, Modot's talents led to his being cast so frequently that today his
angularly handsome face is discernible in nearly 100 films.

The story of Modot's career in film reads like an abbreviated history of the French cinema, for his career began in 1909, not quite 15
years after the Lumière brothers had first publicly projected their
celluloid snippets of the world's doings, and ended in 1962, amidst the
potent innovations of the French New Wave. Between 1909 and
1962, Modot appeared in an array of films whose historical importance is, at the least, twofold. First, retrospectively, Modot's films

represent a near-gamut of established cinematic movements, genres,
and types, embracing such varieties as the avant garde and the film
noir. And second, his films include numerous examples of both classics
(for example, Julien Duvivier's *Pépé le Moko*) and masterpieces (Jean
Renoir's *La Grande Illusion*; Marcel Carné and Jacques Prévert's *Les
Enfants du paradis*) of the French cinema.

Modot first performed in film among the actors and acrobats of
Jean Durand's successful and prolific collection of comic shorts, the
Onésime series. The remainder of Modot's years in silent film, which
comprises a mixture of mysteries, historical subjects, *drames passionels*,
and adventure tales laced with the exotic, is distinguished by leading
roles in Abel Gance's dark melodrama *Mater Dolorosa* and in two
early examples of the symbolist branch of avant-garde cinematic
impressionism: Germaine Dulac's violent *La Fête espagnole* and Louis
Delluc's *Fièvre*, whose somber atmosphere and action prefigured the
film noir. During the silent years, Modot also completed his only
effort at scripting and directing a film, the well-received *La Torture
par l'espérance*.

Modot's personal interest in the European avant-garde movement,
which may have been influenced by his early training as a painter and
his friendships with Modigliani and Picasso, culminated in his participation in the surrealist branch of the avant-garde cinema as the
"leading man" in Luis Buñuel's *L'Age d'or*. Paradoxically, the performance for which Modot is best known is also the least well-known of
his performances. Fed by the destructive reactions of the Camelots du
Roi and the Jeunesses Politiques, and the malicious entreaties of *Le
Figaro*, which journalistically reduced what has since been called the
greatest surrealist film to "a collection of the most obscene, repellent,
and witless episodes," the "scandal of *L'Age d'or*" closed Paris 28,
where *L'Age d'or* had just opened, and expelled the film from public
theaters for 50 years. Those still powerful images of Modot's frustrated efforts, as both victim (of mankind's institutionalized authority figures) and victimizer (of animals and cripples), to satisfy the free
play of his desire for Lya Lys's heroine remained unavailable to
filmgoers, outside rare showings in cinémathéques and occasional private screenings, until *L'Age d'or* reopened in 1980 in New York City.

During the 1930s, Modot made his first appearances in films directed
by René Clair, Julien Duvivier, and Jean Renoir, three directors for whom
he would work repeatedly. For Clair, Modot played, among other roles,
both rogue, in Clair's musical comedy *Sous les toits de Paris*, one of the
first all-talking French films, and gypsy, in Clair's controversial version
of *Faust*, *La Beauté du Diable*. Modot performed in several of Duvivier's
romantically pessimistic gangster films, playing a supporting role to Jean
Gabin's lead in *Pépé le Moko*. Under Duvivier's direction, Modot also
acted in the film with which he ended his career, a collection of seven
vignettes entitled *Les Diable et les dix commandments*.

Modot worked with Jean Renoir more often than with any other
director, their association lasting through the end of the 1950s. And it
is in Renoir's greatest films, *La Grande Illusion* and *La Règle du jeu*,
that Modot gave two of his most notable performances. As the un-
named "engineer for the ordnance survey" and a prisoner of war in *La
Grande Illusion*, Modot shares a scene with the mechanic Maréchal,
played by Gabin, that is one of the film's many sensitive and multilay-
ered exchanges between pairs of human beings. In *La Règle du jeu*
Modot plays the gamekeeper Schumacher, the only character in the
film whose genuine but brutal attempts to observe the rules of the
"game" end in death and defeat.

Throughout his long career, Gaston Modot imparted both to and
through the characters he portrayed a great sense of natural artistry,
without ever losing sight of the essentially collaborative nature of
filmmaking. His performances remain hallmarks of the professional
character actor, forever informing and enriching the final textures of
each film, however plain or exquisite, in which he appeared.

—Nancy Jane Richards

MONROE, Marilyn

Nationality: American. **Born:** Norma Jean Mortenson (or Baker) in Los Angeles, California, 1 June 1926. **Education:** Studied acting at Actors Lab in Los Angeles and Actors Studio in New York. **Family:** Married 1) James Dougherty, 1942 (divorced 1948); 2) the baseball player Joe DiMaggio, 1954 (divorced 1954); 3) the writer Arthur Miller, 1956 (divorced 1961). **Career:** During World War II worked in aircraft factory, then began modeling; 1946—short contract with 20th Century-Fox; 1948—film debut in *Scudda Hoo! Scudda Hay!*; 1950—success in films *The Asphalt Jungle* and *All about Eve* led to long-term contract with Fox. **Died:** Probable suicide, 5 August 1962.

Films as Actress:

1948 *Scudda Hoo! Scudda Hay! (Summer Lightning)* (Herbert) (as extra); *Dangerous Years* (Pierson) (as Evie); *Ladies of the Chorus* (Karlson) (as Peggy Martin)
1949 *Love Happy* (Miller) (as extra)
1950 *A Ticket to Tomahawk* (Sale) (as Clara); ***The Asphalt Jungle*** (Huston) (as Angela Phinlay); ***All about Eve*** (Joseph L. Mankiewicz) (as Miss Caswell); *The Fireball (The Challenge)* (Garnett) (as Polly); *Right Cross* (John Sturges) (as girl at nightclub)
1951 *Home Town Story* (Pierson) (as Miss Martin); *As Young as You Feel* (Harmon Jones) (as Harriet); *Love Nest* (Joseph M. Newman) (as Roberta Stevens); *Let's Make It Legal* (Sale) (as Joyce)
1952 *Clash by Night* (Fritz Lang) (as Peggy); *We're Not Married* (Goulding) (as Annabel Norris); *Don't Bother to Knock* (Roy Ward Baker) (as Nell); *Monkey Business* (Hawks) (as Lois Laurel); "The Cop and the Anthem" ep. of *O. Henry's Full House (Full House)* (Koster) (as streetwalker)
1953 *Niagara* (Hathaway) (as Rose Loomis); *Gentlemen Prefer Blondes* (Hawks) (as Lorelei Lee); *How to Marry a Millionaire* (Negulesco) (as Pola Debevoise)
1954 *River of No Return* (Preminger) (as Kay Weston); *There's No Business Like Show Business* (Walter Lang) (as Vicky)
1955 *The Seven Year Itch* (Wilder) (as the Girl)
1956 *Bus Stop* (Logan) (as Cherie)
1957 *The Prince and the Showgirl* (Olivier) (as Elsie Marina)
1959 ***Some Like It Hot*** (Wilder) (as Sugar Kane)
1960 *Let's Make Love* (Cukor) (as Amanda Dell)
1961 ***The Misfits*** (Huston) (as Roslyn Tabor)

Publications

By MONROE: books—

My Story, New York, 1974.
Marilyn in Her Own Words, New York, 1983; as *Marilyn on Marilyn*, London, 1983.
A Never-Ending Dream, edited by Guus Luijters, New York, 1986.

On MONROE: books—

Martin, Pete, *Will Acting Spoil Marilyn Monroe?*, New York, 1956.
Zolotow, Maurice, *Marilyn Monroe*, New York, 1960; rev. ed., 1990.
Carpozi, George Jr., *Marilyn Monroe: "Her Own Story,"* New York, 1961.
Violations of the Child: Marilyn Monroe, by "Her Psychiatrist Friend," New York, 1962.

The Films of Marilyn Monroe, edited by Michael Conway and Mark Ricci, New York, 1964.
Hoyt, Edwin, *Marilyn: The Tragic Years*, New York, 1965.
Guiles, Fred, *Norma Jean: The Life of Marilyn Monroe*, New York, 1969.
Wagenknecht, Edward, *Marilyn Monroe: A Composite View*, Philadelphia, 1969.
Huston, John, *An Open Book*, New York, 1972.
Mailer, Norman, *Marilyn*, New York, 1973.
Mellen, Joan, *Marilyn Monroe*, New York, 1973.
Rosen, Marjorie, *Popcorn Venus*, New York, 1973.
Kobal, John, *Marilyn Monroe: A Life on Film*, New York, 1974.
Murray, Eunice, with Rose Shade, *Marilyn: The Last Months*, New York, 1975.
Sciacca, Tony, *Who Killed Marilyn?*, New York, 1976.
Weatherby, W. J., *Conversations with Marilyn*, New York, 1976.
Pepitone, Lena, and William Stadiem, *Marilyn Monroe Confidential: An Intimate Personal Account*, New York, 1979.
Dyer, Richard, editor, *Marilyn Monroe*, London, 1980.
Mailer, Norman, *Of Women and Their Elegance*, New York, 1981.
Anderson, Janice, *Marilyn Monroe*, New York, 1983.
Summers, Anthony, *Goddess: The Secret Lives of Marilyn Monroe*, London, 1985.
Kahn, Roger, *Joe and Marilyn: A Memory of Love*, New York, 1986.
Rollyson, Carl E., *Marilyn Monroe: A Life of the Actress*, Ann Arbor, Michigan, 1986.
Steinem, Gloria, and George Barris, *Marilyn*, New York, 1986.
Arnold, Eve, *Marilyn Monroe: An Appreciation*, London, 1987.
Crown, Lawrence, *Marilyn at Twentieth Century-Fox*, New York, 1987.
Dyer, Richard, *Heavenly Bodies: Film Stars and Society*, London, 1987.
Miller, Arthur, *Timebends*, New York, 1987.
Shevey, Sandra, *The Marilyn Scandal: Her True Life Revealed by Those Who Knew Her*, London, 1987.
McCann, Graham, *Marilyn Monroe*, Cambridge, 1988.
Mills, Bart, *Marilyn on Location*, London, 1989.
Schirmer, Lothar, *Marilyn Monroe and the Camera*, London, 1989.
Marriott, John, *Marilyn Monroe*, Philadelphia, 1990.
Haspiel, James, *Marilyn: The Ultimate Look at the Legend*, London, 1991.
Brown, Peter H., *Marilyn: The Last Take*, New York, 1992.
Strasberg, Susan, *Marilyn and Me: Sisters, Rivals, Friends*, New York, 1992.
Wayne, Jane Ellen, *Marilyn's Men: The Private Life of Marilyn*, New York, 1992.
Gregory, Adela, *Crypt 33: The Saga of Marilyn Monroe—The Final Word*, Secaucus, New Jersey, 1993.
Guiles, Fred Lawrence, *Norma Jean: The Life of Marilyn Monroe*, New York, 1993.
Spoto, Donald, *Marilyn Monroe: The Biography*, New York, 1993.
Miracle, Berniece Baker, and Mona Rae Miracle, *My Sister Marilyn: A Memoir of Marilyn Monroe*, Chapel Hill, North Carolina, 1994.
Baty, S. Paige, *American Monroe: The Making of a Body Politic*, Berkeley, 1995.
Lefkowitz, Frances, *Marilyn Monroe*, New York, 1995.

On MONROE: articles—

Baker, P., "The Monroe Doctrine," in *Films and Filming* (London), September 1956.
Current Biography 1959, New York, 1959.
Obituary in *New York Times*, 6 August 1962.
Odets, Clifford, "To Whom It May Concern: Marilyn Monroe," in *Show* (Hollywood), October 1962.
Roman, Robert, "Marilyn Monroe," in *Films in Review* (New York), October 1962.

Marilyn Monroe

Fenin, G., "M.M.," in *Films and Filming* (London), January 1963.

Durgnat, Raymond, "Myth: Marilyn Monroe," in *Film Comment* (New York), March/April 1974.

"Marilyn Monroe Issue" of *Cinéma d'aujourd'hui* (Paris), March/April 1975.

Haspiel, J. R., "Marilyn Monroe: The Starlet Days," in *Films in Review* (New York), June/July 1975.

Stuart, A., "Reflection of Marilyn Monroe in the Last Fifties Picture Show," in *Films and Filming* (London), July 1975.

Haspiel, J. R., "That Marilyn Monroe Dress," in *Films in Review* (New York), June/July 1980.

Gilliatt, Penelope, "Marilyn Monroe," in *The Movie Star*, edited by Elisabeth Weis, New York, 1981.

Stenn, D., "Marilyn Inc.," and David Thomson, "Baby Go Boom!," in *Film Comment* (New York), September/October 1982.

Belmont, Georges, "Souvenirs d'Hollywood," in *Cahiers du Cinéma* (Paris), July/August 1987.

Minifie, D., "Marilyn Monroe," in *Films and Filming* (London), August 1987.

Haun, H., "Marilyn Monroe," in *Films in Review* (New York), November 1987.

On MONROE: films—

Marilyn, documentary, narrated by Rock Hudson, 1963.

Marilyn Monroe, Life Story of America's Mystery Mistress, documentary, 1963.

Marilyn: The Untold Story, directed for television by John Flynn, Jack Arnold, and Lawrence Schiller, 1980.

Marilyn and the Kennedys, documentary for television, 1985.

Marilyn Monroe: Beyond the Legend, documentary, 1985.

Marilyn: Say Goodbye to the President, documentary, 1985.

Marilyn Monroe, documentary, 1990.

Marilyn Monroe: The Last Word, documentary, 1990.

Marilyn Monroe: The Woman behind the Myth, documentary, 1990.

Marilyn and Me, directed for television by John Patterson, 1991.

Marilyn Monroe: The Marilyn Files, documentary, 1991.

Norma Jean & Marilyn, television movie, 1996.

*   *   *

More pages have been written about Marilyn Monroe than any other movie star. She has inspired all sorts of fellow artists, from novelists to painters to rock songwriters. In 1996, 34 years after Monroe's death (at age 36), HBO brought Oscar winner Mira Sorvino to the small screen in yet another retelling of Monroe's life. Representations of femininity, sexuality, and American ambition created by and around Monroe continue to fascinate, indicating that tensions among these factors continue to exist.

To some she was a gifted comedienne, to others a sexual joke, but there is no doubt that Marilyn Monroe staked a claim for herself in film history as the quintessential "dumb" blond, the biggest of the blond bombshells. She had, according to Billy Wilder, "flesh impact." And her face was her fortune as much as her voluptuous figure (Wilder again): "The luminosity of that face! There has never been a woman with such voltage on the screen, with the exception of Garbo."

Monroe's appeal lay in more than her physical attributes. Another director, Joshua Logan, described her as "naive about herself and touching, rather like a little frightened animal." Lee Strasberg saw "a combination of wistfulness, radiance, yearning [that] set her apart and [made] everyone wish to . . . share in the childish naivete which was at once so shy and yet so vibrant." Or, in the words given to Cary Grant and Ginger Rogers in Monroe's film *Monkey Business*, she was "half child, but not the half that shows."

Monroe's triumphs in projecting the woman-as-child arose in part from the traumas of her personal life. Orphaned as a child by her father's desertion and mother's insanity, brought up in an orphanage and foster homes, and married at 16 to a boy of 20, she developed, according to critic Molly Haskell, a "painful, naked, and embarrassing need for love." Moreover, her mother's insanity, and the fact that both her mother's parents had also been committed to institutions, may have deepened fears of abandonment instilled by her childhood experiences. Certainly her genetic heritage did nothing to encourage her to envision a future as a responsible adult.

Yet she was adult enough to work throughout her life to develop her control over her psycho-physical actor's instrument. Most of all, Monroe engaged with Constantin Stanislavski's ideas—that an actor's job is to make every physical move meaningful, to embrace and embody the world as it is for her, not for convention—variations of which she studied in the early 1950s with Michael Chekhov and, more famously, in the mid-1950s with Lee and Paula Strasberg. To further clarify for herself ways to physicalize her characters' inner states, Monroe kept with her Mabel Elsworth Todd's book *The Thinking Body*. Once Monroe had the "handle" for a role or scene, she was, according to Montgomery Clift, "an incredible person to act with. . . . Playing a scene with her . . . was like an escalator. You'd do something, and she'd catch it and would go like that, just right up."

Her first films relegated her display of such talents to modeling jobs and acting classes. Under contract at Twentieth Century-Fox in 1946-47, she had bit parts in two forgettable films (*Scudda Hoo! Scudda Hay!* and *Dangerous Years*). In 1948 Columbia gave her a six-month contract and an introduction to the studio's head acting teacher Natasha Lytess, a former member of Max Reinhardt's company. Until the mid-1950s, Lytess would be Monroe's personal drama coach and a fixture on her sets. Monroe's official debut was a leading role in a B picture, *Ladies of the Chorus*. Though she showed promise, it wasn't until her first film for MGM, *The Asphalt Jungle*, that she made a real impact with both the public and the critics. Small parts in *All about Eve* and in several B pictures led to more substantial roles in *We're Not Married* and *Monkey Business*.

For her biggest role yet, in *Don't Bother to Knock*, Monroe received mixed reviews playing a psychotic babysitter obsessed with her dead lover. As Carl Rollyson notes, Monroe in this film builds perhaps too obviously upon what her second acting instructor, Stanislavski's associate Michael Chekhov, called "the psychological gesture." Such a keystone gesture—here Monroe's twisting together of her fingers—not only encapsulates a character's mental state but allows changes in it to be revealed over time. Throughout her career, as pinup girl, onstage USO diva in Korea, and movie star, Monroe can be seen carefully framing her own body—using her hands, arms and hips especially—for maximum emotional resonance. Her appeal as a screen actress and archetypal image rests upon this self-composition more than is commonly acknowledged.

Monroe's first starring role was in *Niagara*, which elevated her to the ranks of 1953's top-grossing stars. As a faithless wife, she delivered a credible performance while projecting a great deal of sex appeal. Her undulations across some cobblestones represented the longest walk in cinema history—116 feet of film.

Niagara was followed by other rich roles. As Lorelei in *Gentlemen Prefer Blondes*, she showed she could sing and anchored the first of many delightful production numbers. (These redeemed such lesser films as *River of No Return* and *Let's Make Love*.) *How to Marry a Millionaire* further proved her comic talents. As the innocent myopic Pola Debevoise, a gold digger reluctant to wear glasses, she walked into walls and read books upside down with comic aplomb.

Monroe's next big film was *The Seven Year Itch*, in which she played a lightly parodic media sex goddess with subtle sensitivity. But by then she was disillusioned with her success and bored with her "dumb blond" image. Wanting to continue her artistic growth as a working actress, she left Hollywood for New York and the Actors Studio. Public reaction was unkind. *Life* magazine called the move "irrational," and *Time* found her all wet: "her acting talents, if any, run a needless second" to her truest virtues—"her moist 'come-on' look . . . moist, half-closed eyes and moist, half-opened mouth."

But Monroe spent a year with Lee Strasberg, director of the Actors Studio, learning to tap her own experience to work into her characters. At the Strasbergs' prompting, she entered psychoanalysis to negotiate her new self-knowledge. By the end of the year she had more sophisticated tools for exploring her characters—but she was gradually disintegrating as a person. The ego she had so carefully assembled in her early twenties came unglued in her increasing, drug-fueled fears of something lacking in herself.

Still, *Bus Stop*, her first film upon returning to Hollywood, was a revelation to the critics: "get set for a surprise. Marilyn Monroe has finally proved herself an actress" (Bosley Crowther, *New York Times*). Working for the first time with a southern accent, Monroe caught the delicate balance the script sets between her character's self-image and her limitations, especially in her songs. Critics disagreed over whether Monroe's modulated, realistic portrayal was due to the Strasbergs' influence or to the fact that it was her first role of any depth.

Her next film was made by her own company, which she had set up with Milton Greene. Although she and Laurence Olivier, her co-star and director, delivered good performances in *The Prince and the Showgirl*, problems between them on the set exacerbated Monroe's growing insecurity and addictions and did little to offset her distress over a troubled third marriage, to playwright Arthur Miller.

Monroe's sex appeal and comic timing were happily arrayed again in *Some Like It Hot*. But her next film, *Let's Make Love*, was a critical failure that brought her into an unhappy romance with her co-star, Yves Montand. By the time she did *The Misfits* (written for her by Miller), although she delivered a multifaceted, poignant performance, her chronic lateness and addiction to alcohol and pills were out of control. These afflictions caused her removal from a subsequent film, *Something's Got to Give*, and she died two months later of a drug overdose.

Her death was a tragic conclusion to a promising career. According to director John Huston, something disturbing happened to Monroe between *The Asphalt Jungle* and *The Misfits*, but it deepened her responses; now her acting came from inside. As a child, Monroe "used to playact all the time. For one thing, it meant I could live in a more interesting world than the one around me." But the magnificent life she brought to the screen finally eluded her in reality.

—Catherine Henry, updated by Susan Knobloch

MONTAND, Yves

Nationality: French. **Born:** Ivo Livi in Monsummano Alto, Tuscany, Italy, 13 October 1921; raised in Marseilles, France, from age two. **Family:** Married the actress Simone Signoret, 1951 (died 1985), stepdaughter (adopted following Signoret's death): the actress Catherine Allégret; son with Carole Amiel: Valentin. **Career:** Left school at age 11, and worked at a variety of jobs before becoming a singer in Marseilles and Paris; 1945—performed at Moulin Rouge; Edith Piaf helped him in his career; 1946—feature film debut in *Étoile sans lumière* with Piaf; 1950-51—six-month musical tour of Europe and North Africa; 1953—breakthrough role in *Le Salaire de la peur*; 1954—appeared with Signoret in stage play *The Crucible*, and in film version, 1957; 1958—highly publicized and criticized tour of Soviet Union and Eastern-bloc countries, with Signoret; 1959—one-man show on Broadway; 1965—co-starred with Signoret in *Compartiment tueurs*, first of several films by Costa-Gavras; 1968—acclaimed one-man show in Paris; late 1970s—released enormously popular album of songs,

Montand d'hier à aujourd'hui (*Montand, from Yesterday to Today*); 1982—became first popular singer to perform solo at New York's Metropolitan Opera House, followed by U.S. caberet tour, then tour of Brazil and Japan; 1986—acclaimed performance in pair of international hits, *Jean de Florette* and *Manon des sources*; produced and starred in one-man TV special, *Montand à la une*; 1987—named president, Cannes Film Festival; 1988—long politically active, received serious mention as a possible French presidential candidate, but he declined to pursue; 1991—at time of death, was preparing a singing tour. **Awards:** Best Actor awards, French Étoile de cristal and New York Film Critics Circle, for *La Guerre est finie*, 1966; special tribute, Film Society of Lincoln Center, 1988. **Died:** Of a heart attack, in Senlis, France, 9 November 1991.

Films as Actor:

1945 *Silence . . . antenne* (Lucot—short) (as singer)
1946 *Étoile sans lumière* (*Star without Light*) (Blistène) (as Pierre); *Les Portes de la nuit* (*Gates of the Night*) (Carné—released in U.S. in 1950) (as Jean Diego)
1948 *L'Idole* (*The Idol*) (Esway) (as Luc Fenton)
1950 *Souvenirs perdus* (Christian-Jaque) (as singer); *Paris chante toujours* (Montazel) (as singer); *Parigi e sempre Parigi* (Emmer) (as singer)
1953 ***Le Salaire de la peur*** (*The Wages of Fear*) (Clouzot) (as Mario); "Mara" ep. of *Tempi nostri* (*Our Time*; *The Anatomy of Love*) (Blasetti)
1954 *Napoléon* (Guitry) (as Marshal Lefebvre)
1955 *Les Heros sont fatigués* (*Heroes and Sinners*) (Ciampi) (as Michel Rivière)
1956 *Marguerite de la nuit* (Autant-Lara) (as Mephistopheles); *Uomini e lupi* (De Santis) (as Ricuccio)
1957 *Les Sorcières de Salem* (*The Witches of Salem*; *The Crucible*) (Rouleau) (as John Proctor); *Poet Iv Montan* (*Yves Montand chante en U.S.S.R.*) (Sloutky and Yutkevitch)
1958 *La lunga strada azzura* (*La Grande Strada Azzura*; *The Wide Blue Road*) (Pontecorvo) (as Squarcio)
1959 *Le Père et l'enfant* (*Premier Mai*) (Saslavsky) (as Jean); *La Loi* (*Where the Hot Wind Blows*; *Le legge*; *The Law*) (Dassin) (as Matteo Brigante)
1960 *Let's Make Love* (*The Billionaire*; *The Millionaire*) (Cukor) (as Jean-Marc Clément); *Yves Montand Chante* (filmed concert/doc)
1961 *Sanctuary* (Richardson) (as Candy Man); *Aimez-vous Brahms?* (*Goodbye Again*) (Litvak) (as Roger Desmarest)
1962 *My Geisha* (Cardiff) (as Paul Robaix)
1963 *Le Joli Mai* (Marker—doc) (as narrator)
1965 *Compartiment tueurs* (*The Sleeping Car Murder*) (Costa-Gavras) (as Insp. Grazzi)
1966 *La Guerre est finie* (*The War Is Over*) (Resnais) (as Diego); *Paris-brûle-t-il?* (*Is Paris Burning?*) (Clément) (as Marcel Bizien); *Grand Prix* (Frankenheimer) (as Jean-Pierre Sarti)
1967 *Vivre pour vivre* (*Live for Life*) (Lelouch) (as Robert Colomb)
1968 *Un soir, un train* (*One Night, a Train*) (Delvaux) (as Mathias); *Le Diable par la queue* (*The Devil by the Tail*) (de Broca) (as Cesar Maricorne)
1969 *Mister Freedom* (Klein) (cameo as Capt. Formidable); *Z* (Costa-Gavras) (as Deputy Z); *Le Deuxième Procès d'Artur London* (Marker—doc); *Jour de tournage* (Marker and Depouey—doc)
1970 *L'Aveu* (*The Confession*) (Costa-Gavras) (as Gerard); *On a Clear Day You Can See Forever* (Minnelli) (as Dr. Marc Chabot); *Le Cercle rouge* (*The Red Circle*) (Melville) (as Jansen)

1971   *La Folie des grandeurs* (*Delusions of Grandeur*) (Oury) (as Blaze)
1972   *César et Rosalie* (*César and Rosalie*) (Sautet) (as César); *Le Fils* (Granier-Deferre) (as Ange Orahona)
1973   **Tout va bien** (*Just Great*) (Godard and Gorin) (as He); *Etat de siège* (*State of Siege*) (Costa-Gavras) (as Philip Michael Santore)
1974   *Le Hasard et la violence* (Labro) (as Laurent Berman); *Vincent, Francois, Paul, et les autres* (*Vincent, Francois, Paul and the Others*) (Sautet) (as Vincent); *La Solitude du chanteur de fond* (*The Loneliness of the Long-Distance Singer*) (Marker—doc) (as himself); *T'es fou, Marcel* (Rochefort—doc)
1975   *Le Sauvage* (*The Savage*; *Lovers Like Us*) (Rappeneau) (as Martin Coutances); *Section spéciale* (*Special Section*) (Costa-Gavras) (cameo)
1976   *Police Python 357* (Corneau) (as Marc Ferrot); *La Grand Escogriffe* (Pinoteau) (as Emile Morland)
1977   *Le Menace* (*The Threat*) (Corneau) (as Henri Savin)
1978   *Les Routes du sud* (*The Roads to the South*) (Losey)
1979   *Clair de femme* (*Womanlight*) (Costa-Gavras) (as Michel); *I comme Icarus* (*I as in Icarus*) (Verneuil)
1980   *The Case against Ferro* (Corneau) (title role)
1981   *Le Choix des armes* (*Choice of Arms*) (Corneau) (as Noel Durieux)
1982   *Tout feu tout flamme* (*All Fired Up*) (Rappeneau) (as Victor Valance)
1983   *Garçon!* (*Waiter!*) (Sautet) (as Alex)
1986   **Jean de Florette** (Berri) (as César "Le Papet" Soubeyran); **Manon des sources** (*Jean de Florette 2*; *Manon of the Spring*) (Berri) (as César "Le Papet" Soubeyran)
1988   *Trois places pour le 26* (*Three Seats for the 26th*) (Jacques Demy) (as himself)
1990   *Netchaïev est de retour* (*Netchaïev Is Back*) (Deray) (as Pierre Marroux)
1992   *IP5: L'île aux Pachydermes* (*IP5: The Island of Pachyderms*) (Beineix) (as Leon Marcel)

Publications

By MONTAND: books—

Du soleil plein la tête, with Jean Denys, Paris, 1955.
Tu vois, je n'ai pas oublie, with Herve Hamon and Patrick Rotman, France, 1990; published as *You See, I Haven't Forgotten*, New York, 1992.

By MONTAND: articles—

Interview with R. Predal, in *Cinéma* (Paris), March 1974.
Cinéma (Paris), July/August 1980.
Interview with Harlan Jacobson, in *Film Comment* (New York), vol. 23, no. 5, 1987.
Interview in *Film und Fernsehen* (Potsdam), no. 5, 1990.
Interview in *Talking Films: The Best of the Guardian Lectures*, edited by Andrew Britton, London, 1991.
Interview with Y. Poncelet, in *Grand Angle* (Mariembourg, Belgium), February 1991.

On MONTAND: books—

Megret, Christian, *Yves Montand*, Paris, 1953.
Remond, Alain, *Yves Montand*, Paris, 1977.
Rouchy, Marie-Elisabeth, *Yves Montand*, Paris, 1980.

Cannavo, Richard, and Henri Quiquere, *Yves Montand: Le Chant d'un homme*, Paris, 1981.
Laneque, M., and R. Gallot, *Montand: De Chansons et images*, Paris, 1981.
Remond, Alain, *Montand*, Paris, 1981.
Monserrat, Joëlle, *Yves Montand*, Paris, 1983.
Semprun, Joseph, *Montand: La vie continué*, Paris, 1983.
Desneux, Richard, *Yves Montand: L'artiste engagé*, Lausanne, 1989.
Pascuito, Bernard, *Montand: le livre du souvenir*, Paris, 1992.
Ginies, Michel, *Yves Montand*, Paris, 1995.

On MONTAND: articles—

Hamill, Pete, "Yves Montand," in *New York*, 6 September 1982.
Andriotakis, Pamela, "Paris Isn't Burning, Just Marking Time as Yves Montand Tours America," in *People Weekly* (New York), 20 September 1982.
Schupp, P., "Yves Montand: Le Rebelle au grand coeur," in *Séquences* (Montreal), August 1987.
Current Biography 1988, New York 1988.
Darrach, Brad, "Yves Montand: Amid Memories of Old Wars and Lost Loves, the Most Seductive of Frenchmen Looks Ahead to New Conquests," in *People Weekly* (New York), 16 May 1988.
"Yves Montand," in *Film Dope* (Nottingham, England), March 1990.
"Yves Montand," in *Stars* (Mariembourgh, Belgium), December 1990.
Obituary in *New York Times*, 10 November 1991.
Obituary in *Times* (London), 11 November 1991.
Obituary in *Variety* (New York), 18 November 1991.
Taboulay, C., obituary in *Cahiers du Cinéma* (Paris), December 1991.
Sineux, M., "Yves Montand: Eloge de l'intercesseur," in *Positif* (Paris), January 1992.

On MONTAND: film—

Montand, documentary directed by Jean Labib, 1994.

*   *   *

After a brilliant beginning as a cabaret singer, helped along the way by Edith Piaf, Yves Montand made a number of films that were disappointing. In fact, just at the time when he was about to abandon his film career, he accepted a role in Clouzot's *Le Salaire de la peur* that made him famous as a film star. The film, full of dramatic tension, depicts the desperately courageous trip of four drivers with a dangerous load on a treacherous road, and is now reckoned to be—because of its subject, its technical qualities, and its performances—one of the finest films of its time. Yet for the next decade Montand's films were not successful. Only in the late 1960s did he manage to move in a natural way before the camera, and from the time of his making *Compartiment tueurs* onwards, his acting took on an authority it lacked before. *La Guerre est finie*, *Vivre pour vivre*, and *Un soir, un train* show this, especially the last, about the complicated relations of a couple seemingly on the boundary of dream and reality.

With his association with the director Costa-Gavras, which began in 1965 with *Compartiment tueurs*, his acting reached a mid-career peak. His participation in Costa-Gavras's politically oriented works reflected his own political convictions, about which he was never silent. *Z* and *Etat de siège* deal with the restriction of civil rights in Greece and Chile, respectively. In *L'Aveu*, based on a book by Arthur London, one of the accused in Slansky's trial in Czechoslovakia, he created with a shocking persuasiveness the character of a man who suffers the monstrous power of a state determined to make good its charges of conspiracy, betrayal, and class and racial hatred.

Montand also made comedies and love stories as well as crime stories. In *Le Fils* he created the character of a mafioso who returns to

Corsica from America and is involved in a vendetta, and in *La Choix des armes* he played a man in whose house two escaped convicts take shelter. He acted with Cathérine Deneuve in *Le Sauvage*, with Romy Schneider in *César et Rosalie* and *Clair de femme*, and with Isabelle Adjani in *Tout feu, tout flamme*.

Although he had a notable late-career comedic role in 1983's highly praised light comedy *Garçon!* playing the waiter, Montand's film career had hit a valley in the late 1970s and early 1980s. A final climax would come in 1986, however, with his scheming village elder in the wonderful two-part multicontinent smash hit *Jean de Florette* and *Manon des sources*. Based on novels by Maurice Pagnol, the films were made back-to-back by director Claude Berri in the costliest production in France up to that time. For his part, Montand drew on his rural Italian roots in perfectly capturing a proud old peasant whose greed leads ultimately to an ending reminiscent of Greek tragedy. In one of his best performances ever, Montand held the central role through both films, even next to Gérard Depardieu's strong portrayal of Montand's nemesis in *Jean de Florette*—a fitting culmination to the career of an actor beloved by his fellow French and unusually popular outside France as well.

—Karel Tabery, updated by David E. Salamie

MONTGOMERY, Robert

Nationality: American. **Born:** Henry Montgomery, Jr. in Beacon, New York, 21 May 1904. **Education:** Attended Pawling School for Boys, New York. **Military Service:** Served in the U.S. Naval Reserve, 1941-45; Commander. **Family:** Married 1) Elizabeth Bryan-Allen, 1928 (divorced 1950), daughter: the actress Elizabeth, son: Robert Jr.; 2) Elizabeth Grant Harkness, 1950. **Career:** Worked as mechanic for New York New Haven and Hartford Railroad, and as an oiler on a Standard Oil tanker; 1924—stage debut in *The Mask and the Face*, New York; actor for Rochester repertory company; Broadway debut in *Dawn*; 1926—film debut in *College Days*; 1929—contract with MGM, and sound film debut in *So This Is College*; 1930s—influential in establishing Screen Actors Guild; 1942—founder with Elliott Nugent, Neptune Productions; 1945—helped with direction of film *They Were Expendable*, and solo director of film *Lady in the Lake*, 1946; 1948—contract with CBS radio for series of mystery dramas; 1949—on radio series *Robert Montgomery Speaking*, later called *A Citizen Views the News*; 1950-57—host, director, producer, and sometime actor, *Robert Montgomery Presents* TV series; 1952-60—media consultant to President Eisenhower. **Died:** In New York City, 27 September 1981.

Films as Actor:

1926 *College Days* (Thorpe)
1929 *So This Is College* (Wood) (as Biff); *Untamed* (Conway) (as Andy McAllister); *Their Own Desire* (Hopper) (as Jack Marlett); *Three Live Ghosts* (Freeland) (as William Foster)
1930 *Free and Easy* (Sedgwick) (as Larry); *The Divorcee* (Leonard) (as Don); *The Big House* (Hill) (as Kent Marlowe); *Sins of the Children* (Wood) (as Nick Higginson); *Our Blushing Brides* (Beaumont) (as Tony); *Love in the Rough* (Reisner) (as Kelly); *War Nurse* (Selwyn) (as Wally)
1931 *Inspiration* (Brown) (as Andre Martel); *The Easiest Way* (Conway) (as Johnny Madison); *Strangers May Kiss* (Fitzmaurice) (as Steve); *Shipmates* (Pollard) (as Jonesy); *The Man in Possession* (Wood) (as Raymond Dabney); *Private Lives* (Franklin) (as Elyot Chase)

1932 *Lovers Courageous* (Leonard) (as Willie Smith); *But the Flesh Is Weak* (Conway) (as Max Clement); *Letty Lynton* (Brown) (as Hale Darrow); *Blondie of the Follies* (Goulding) (as Larry Belmont); *Faithless* (Beaumont) (as William Wade)
1933 *Hell Below* (Conway) (as Lt. Thomas Knowlton); *When Ladies Meet* (Beaumont) (as Jimmy Lee); *Made on Broadway* (*The Girl I Made*) (Beaumont) (as Jeff Bidwell); *Another Language* (Edward Griffith) (as Victor Hallam); *Night Flight* (Brown) (as Auguste Pellerin); *Fugitive Lovers* (Boleslawsky) (as Paul Porter)
1934 *The Mystery of Mr. X* (Selwyn) (as Nicholas Revel); *Riptide* (Goulding) (as Tommy Trent); *Hide-Out* (Van Dyke) (as Lucky Wilson); *Forsaking All Others* (Van Dyke) (as Dill Todd)
1935 *Biography of a Bachelor Girl* (Griffith) (as Kurt); *Vanessa: Her Love Story* (Howard) (as Benjie); *No More Ladies* (Griffith) (as Sherry Warren)
1936 *Petticoat Fever* (Fitzmaurice) (as Dascom Dinsmore); *Trouble for Two* (Rubin) (as Prince Florizel); *Piccadilly Jim* (Leonard) (as Jim Crocker)
1937 *The Last of Mrs. Cheyney* (Boleslawsky) (as Lord Arthur Dilling); *Night Must Fall* (Thorpe) (as Danny); *Ever Since Eve* (Bacon) (as Freddy Matthews); *Live, Love, and Learn* (Fitzmaurice) (as Bob Graham)
1938 *The First 100 Years* (Thorpe) (as David Conway); *Yellow Jack* (Seitz) (as John O'Hara); *Three Loves Has Nancy* (Thorpe) (as Malcolm Niles)
1939 *Fast and Loose* (Marin) (as Joel Sloane)
1940 *The Earl of Chicago* (Thorpe) (as Silky Kilmount); *Haunted Honeymoon* (Woods) (as Lord Peter Wimsey)
1941 *Mr. and Mrs. Smith* (Hitchcock) (as David Smith); *Rage in Heaven* (Van Dyke) (as Phillip Monrell); *Here Comes Mr. Jordan* (Hall) (as Joe Pendleton); *Unfinished Business* (La Cava) (as Tommy Duncan)
1948 *The Saxon Charm* (Binyon) (as Matt Saxon); *The Secret Land* (doc) (as narrator); *June Bride* (Windust) (as Carey Jackson)

Films as Director:

1945 *They Were Expendable* (co-d with Ford, + ro as Lt. John Brickley)
1946 *Lady in the Lake* (+ ro as Philip Marlowe)
1947 *Ride the Pink Horse* (+ ro as Blackie Gagin)
1949 *Once More, My Darling* (+ ro as Collier Laing)
1950 *Your Witness* (*Eye Witness*) (+ ro as Adam Heywood)
1960 *The Gallant Hours* (+ pr, narrator)

Publications

By MONTGOMERY: book—

Open Letter from a Television Viewer, New York, 1968.

On MONTGOMERY: articles—

Reynolds, Quentin, "Man with a Union Card," in *Collier's* (New York), 1 April 1939.
Current Biography 1948, New York, 1948.
Bodeen, DeWitt, "Robert Montgomery," in *Films in Review* (New York), February 1981.
Obituary, in *New York Times*, 28 September 1981.
The Annual Obituary 1981, New York, 1982.

Mangravite, Andrew, "Republican Noir," in *Film Comment* (New York), January/February 1994.

* * *

Robert Montgomery's career is unique. He achieved success as actor and director in film, television, theater, and radio, and also gained considerable recognition in politics. In addition, he started what might be seen as a media dynasty by fathering a bona fide second generation star, his daughter, Elizabeth.

The arrival of sound to motion pictures brought many young men like Montgomery to Hollywood—men of good looks, polish, and enough stage experience to deliver dialogue well. After being placed under contract to MGM, Montgomery became a "tennis, anyone?" leading man for that studio's stable of beautiful actresses. His apprentice years found him supporting Norma Shearer (*The Divorcee, Riptide*), Joan Crawford (*Our Blushing Brides, Letty Lynton*), Marion Davies (*Blondie of the Follies*), and Greta Garbo (*Inspiration*), among others. Montgomery, however, was too intelligent and too versatile to be typecast with the limited range such roles afforded him. He undertook such parts as the frightened prison squealer in the key genre film, *The Big House*, as well as that of a homicidal maniac with a civilized veneer in *Night Must Fall*, a role which earned him an Oscar nomination. As a result of his own initiative, there were many Robert Montgomerys on screen—the arch comedian, the dapper cad, the crazy killer, the hard-boiled detective, the noble war hero. He was not one persona, but many.

Montgomery with also not content to be an idle screen actor in his private life. Always rebellious, he is said to have told Louis B. Mayer, when refused a deserved salary increase, "If you were a younger man, Mr. Mayer, I'd give you a beating." In 1933 he helped organize the Screen Actors Guild, and served four terms as its president. He proved an effective negotiator for better working conditions, higher pay, and steadier work for bit players. During World War II he saw action in PT boat service, an experience he used in John Ford's *They Were Expendable*, part of which he actually directed himself. He earned a Bronze Star for his destroyer service on D-Day.

After the war Montgomery turned to directing as well as acting. His most famous film is *Lady in the Lake*, in which he experimented with "first-person camera," allowing the camera to serve as the actual eyes of the leading character, Raymond Chandler's private-eye Philip Marlowe (played by Montgomery himself). This film, an experiment in the subjective point of view, stands as a landmark. Montgomery became executive producer-director-advisor to NBC, and created one of television's first anthology series, *Robert Montgomery Presents*. On stage, he directed *The Desperate Hours*, earning a Tony Award. Having been active in politics since his early days with SAG, he undertook the prestigious job as media adviser to President Eisenhower, a man he greatly admired. His book, *Open Letter from a Television Viewer*, denounced the networks as insisting on "fairy tales for grown-up children," and was ahead of its time in defining the media wasteland.

Montgomery was not only successful in four media, a capable director, an innovative producer, and a versatile actor, he was ahead of his own time in being an actor who understood that politicians would have to become masters of the media to win. He was in many ways a visionary and an experimentalist, but in all ways a man of intelligence.

—Jeanine Basinger

MOORE, Demi

Nationality: American. **Born:** Demetria Guynes in Roswell, New Mexico, 11 November 1962. **Education:** Left school at age 16. **Fam-** ily: Married 1) Freddy Moore, 1980 (divorced 1984); 2) the actor Bruce Willis, 1987, daughters: Rumer Glenn, Scout Larue, and Tallulah Belle. **Career:** 1981—film debut in *Choices*; 1982-83—played Jackie Templeton in TV daytime drama *General Hospital*; 1984—in TV series *The Master*; 1987—stage role in *The Early Girl*; 1991—co-produced *Mortal Thoughts*; on cover of August issue of *Vanity Fair*, nude and pregnant, again on cover of August 1992 issue, nude and painted; 1995—co-produced *Now and Then*. **Agent:** Ron Meyer, Creative Artists Agency, 9830 Wilshire Boulevard, Beverly Hills, CA 90212, U.S.A.

Films as Actress:

1981   *Choices* (Narizzano)
1982   *Young Doctors in Love* (Garry Marshall) (cameo); *Parasite* (Band) (as Patricia Welles)
1984   *No Small Affair* (Schatzberg) (as Laura Victor); *Blame It on Rio* (Donen) (as Nicole Hollis)
1985   *St. Elmo's Fire* (Schumacher) (as Jules)
1986   *Wisdom* (Estevez) (as Karen Simmons); *One Crazy Summer* (Savage Steve Holland) (as Cassandra); *About Last Night . . .* (Zwick) (as Debbie)
1988   *The Seventh Sign* (Schultz) (as Abby Quinn)
1989   *We're No Angels* (Neil Jordan) (as Molly)
1990   *Ghost* (Jerry Zucker) (as Molly Jensen)
1991   *Nothing but Trouble* (Aykroyd) (as Diane Lightston); *Mortal Thoughts* (Rudolph) (as Cynthia Kellogg, + co-pr); *The Butcher's Wife* (Terry Hughes) (as Marina)
1992   *A Few Good Men* (Rob Reiner) (as Lt. Cmdr. JoAnne Galloway)
1993   *Indecent Proposal* (Lyne) (as Diana Murphy)
1994   *Disclosure* (Levinson) (as Meredith Johnson)
1995   *The Scarlet Letter* (Brian Gibson) (as Hester Prynne); *Now and Then* (Glatter) (as Samantha, + co-pr)
1996   *The Juror* (Brian Gibson) (as Annie Laird); *Striptease* (Andrew Bergman) (as Erin Grant); *The Hunchback of Notre Dame* (Truesdale and Kirk Wise—animation) (as voice of Esmeralda); *Undisclosed* (*G. I. Jane*) (Ridley Scott); *If These Walls Could Talk* (Cher—for TV) (+ exec pr)

Publications

By MOORE: articles—

"Demi's Big Moment," interview with Nancy Collins, in *Vanity Fair* (New York), August 1991.
"Demi's Body Language," interview with Jennet Conant, in *Vanity Fair* (New York), August 1992.
"The Last Pinup," interview with Michael Angeli, in *Esquire* (New York), May 1993.
"Table Talk," panel discussion with Sally Field, Jodie Foster, and Nancy Griffin, in *Premiere* (New York), Winter 1993 (Special Issue: Women in Hollywood).
Interview with Mim Udovitch, in *Rolling Stone* (New York), 9 February 1995.
"Demi-Tough," interview with Tad Friend, in *Vogue* (New York), October 1995.

On MOORE: articles—

"Demi Moore: The Cool Beauty on ABC-TV's Sizzling Soap, *General Hospital*," in *Harper's Bazaar* (New York), June 1982.
Kaye, Elizabeth, "Ordinary People," in *Rolling Stone* (New York), 26 September 1985.

Demi Moore in *Indecent Proposal*

Skow, John, "Greetings to the Class of '86," in *Time* (New York), 26 May 1986.

Park, Jeannie, "They Heard It through the Grapevine," in *People Weekly* (New York), 12 November 1990.

Clark, John, filmography in *Premiere* (New York), January 1991.

Abramowitz, Rachel, "Reason to Believe," in *Premiere* (New York), April 1991.

Current Biography 1993, New York, 1993.

Gelman-Waxner, Libby, "A Decent Proposal," in *Premiere* (New York), July 1993.

Bennetts, Leslie, "Demi's State of Grace," in *Vanity Fair* (New York), December 1993.

Gelman-Waxner, Libby, "Brunets Have More Fun," in *Premiere* (New York), February 1995.

Cerio, Gregory, "Demi Moore," in *People Weekly* (New York), 8 May 1995.

Millea, Holly, "Anywhere but Here," in *Premiere* (New York), September 1995.

Walls, Jeannette, "Get Me Retrial!," in *Esquire* (New York), November 1995.

Schaefer, Karl-Heinz, in *Cinema* (Germany), no. 4, 1996.

*   *   *

Demi Moore's steady rise to superstar status by the early 1990s may appear surprising when the number of unsuccessful films she had made is compared to the hits, but her great popularity and increased power in Hollywood are undeniable. By 1996's *Striptease*, she could command a woman's-salary-record of $12.5 million, a figure which might look risky after the box-office disappointments of *The Juror* and *The Scarlet Letter*. Nevertheless, even Moore's potential to deliver hit films still makes her one of the few female stars in contemporary Hollywood to have films custom-tailored to her desires.

After an unremarkable film debut, Moore was noticed on the popular television soap opera *General Hospital* (which led to her cameo in the parody *Young Doctors in Love*), and then identified as one of Hollywood's 1980s "brat pack" of young actors, most notably through her role in the *Big Chill*-imitation *St. Elmo's Fire*. She finally achieved widespread recognition in *Ghost*, a huge hit in which her ability to generate audience sympathy while retaining her independence and strength established her popular image; while her co-stars worked with the special effects, Moore provided realistic emotional grounding for the story at the heart of the film's supernatural nonsense. Taking advantage of her new on-screen prominence, she began to take greater control of her career behind the scenes, co-producing *Mortal Thoughts*, in which she co-starred with husband Bruce Willis. *A Few Good Men* elevated Moore into the company of two male superstars, Jack Nicholson and Tom Cruise, but could not find much to do with her character.

Alongside her early television and film career, Moore's early marriage and divorce, drug problems, and brief engagement to Emilio Estevez (her co-star and director of the dreadful *Wisdom*) kept her frequently in the gossip columns. Her marriage to fellow superstar Bruce Willis in 1987, their public appearances at the openings of Planet Hollywood restaurants (of which they are co-owners), and especially her nude portraits on the cover of *Vanity Fair*—first in the eighth month of pregnancy, later with her figure regained and clothing only painted on—generated even more continual offscreen attention. Such activities have allowed Moore to successfully negotiate a range of otherwise contradictory identities: she appears as "the last pinup," an unapologetically sexy woman in a "postfeminist" age, as well as an ideal mother, supportive spouse, and shrewd businesswoman, whose advice and personal experiences are regularly featured in popular women's magazines. *Indecent Proposal* perhaps exploited the fantasies underlying these tensions most explicitly, with Moore playing a loyal wife who might nevertheless be purchased by millionaire Robert Redford for at least one night of sexual play. Her role in *Disclosure* as an aggressive businesswoman who sexually exploits male colleague Michael Douglas dealt with similar contradictions, but with a more distastefully reactionary twist.

The Scarlet Letter was a much-derided mistake, with Moore justifying the absurd changes in Hawthorne's classic plot by insisting that most people had not read the book, and *Now and Then* (her second co-production), while more successful, misled fans somewhat, since Moore and her adult co-stars appear only briefly in a film devoted to flashbacks of their characters as children. Advance publicity for *Striptease* suggests that Moore's erotic dancing will be the film's principal draw, with display of her body once again possibly diverting attention from whatever acting skills her role may demonstrate (yet another nude portrait for the film's poster created yet another minor controversy). Only her distinctive, husky voice, however, will be featured in the Disney animated adaptation of *The Hunchback of Notre Dame*.

In an industry that has always rewarded male stars with higher salaries and greater career control, Moore is in an unusual position to decide her future direction as a performer. Her determination to succeed seems unshakable, but the wisdom of her choices remains to be seen; there is no question that the rise, fall, or steady continuation of her career will be fully documented by an attentive media.

—Corey K. Creekmur

MOORE, Dudley

Nationality: British. **Born:** Dudley Stuart John Moore in Dagenham, Essex, 19 April 1935. **Education:** Attended Dagenham County High School; Guildhall School of Music, London; Magdalen College, Oxford, B.A., 1957, B.Mus., 1958. **Family:** Married 1) the actress Suzy Kendall, 1966 (divorced 1968); 2) the actress Tuesday Weld, 1975 (divorced 1976), son: Patrick; 3) the actress Brogan Lane, 1988 (divorced 1992); 4) Nicole Rothschild, 1994, son: Nicholas. **Career:** Jazz pianist, with John Dankworth and the Vic Lewis Band; 1960—stage debut in *Beyond the Fringe*, Edinburgh, later in long runs in London and New York; 1964—collaborated with the comedian Peter Cook in concerts, and TV series *Not Only . . . but Also*, repeated in 1966 and 1970; 1966—feature film debut in *The Wrong Box*; 1968—wrote first film score, for *Inadmissible Evidence*; 1969—in London stage version of *Play It Again, Sam*; 1981—pianist with the Los Angeles Philharmonic Orchestra; 1991—co-presenter, with Georg Solti, of TV series *Orchestra*; 1993—in TV series *Dudley* and *Daddy's Girls*, 1994; also narrator for National Geographic series *Really Wild Animals*. **Agent:** Lou Pitt, ICM, 8942 Wilshire Boulevard, Beverly Hills, CA 90210, U.S.A.; or Dennis Selinger, ICM, Oxford House, 76 Oxford Street, London, W1R 1RB, England.

Films as Actor:

1964   *The Hat* (as narrator)

1966   *The Wrong Box* (Forbes) (as John Finsbury)

1967   *Bedazzled* (Donen) (as Stanley Moon, + co-sc, mus)

1968   *30 Is a Dangerous Age, Cynthia* (McGrath) (as Rupert Street, + co-sc, mus)

1969   *Monte Carlo or Bust (Those Daring Young Men in Their Jaunty Jalopies)* (Annakin) (as Lt. Kit Barrington); *The Bed Sitting Room* (Lester) (as Police Sergeant)

1972   *Alice's Adventures in Wonderland* (Sterling) (as Dormouse)

1977　*The Hound of the Baskervilles* (Morrissey) (as Dr. Watson/Mrs. Ada Holmes/Mr. Spiggott, + co-sc, mus)

1978　*Foul Play* (Higgins) (as Stanley Tibbets, + mus); *Derek and Clive Get the Horn* (+ exec pr, co-sc, mus)

1979　*10* (Edwards) (as George Webber); *To Russia with Elton* (as narrator)

1980　*Wholly Moses!* (Weis) (as Harvey/Herschel)

1981　*Arthur* (Gordon) (title role)

1982　*Six Weeks* (Bill) (as Patrick Dalton, + mus)

1983　*Romantic Comedy* (Hiller) (as Jason Carmichael); *Lovesick* (Brickman) (as Saul Benjamin)

1984　*Best Defense* (Huyck) (as Wylie Cooper); *Micki and Maude* (Edwards) (as Rob Salinger); *Unfaithfully Yours* (Zieff) (as Claude Eastman)

1985　*Santa Claus: The Movie* (Szwarc) (as Patch)

1986　*W. C. Fields: Straight Up* (Adamson—doc) (as narrator)

1987　*Like Father, Like Son* (Daniel) (as Dr. Jack Hammond)

1988　*Arthur 2: On the Rocks* (Yorkin) (as Arthur Bach, + exec pr)

1989　*The Adventures of Milo and Otis* (*Koneko Monogatari*) (Hata) (as narrator)

1990　*Crazy People* (Bill) (as Emory Leeson)

1991　*Blame It on the Bellboy* (Herman) (as Melvyn Orton)

1993　*The Pickle* (Mazursky)

1994　*Parallel Lives* (Yellen—for TV) (as Una's imaginary friend/President Andrews)

1996　*The Mirror Has Two Faces*

Other Films:

1968　*Inadmissible Evidence* (Page) (mus)

1969　*Staircase* (Donen) (mus)

Publications

By MOORE: books—

Musical Bumps, London, 1986.
Off Beat: A Musical Companion, New York, 1993.

By MOORE: articles—

Interviews in *Photoplay* (London), December 1981 and May and June 1983.
Interview in *Films* (London), February 1982.
Interview with Roger Ebert, in *Chicago Sun-Times*, 25 November 1984.
Interview with B. Paskin, in *Films and Filming* (London), February 1988.

On MOORE: books—

Cook, Peter, *Dud & Pete: The Dagenham Dialogues*, London, 1971.
Lenburg, Jeff, *Dudley Moore: An Informal Biography*, New York, 1982.
Donovan, Paul, *Dudley*, London, 1988.
Bergan, Ronald, *Beyond the Fringe . . . and Beyond: A Critical Biography of Alan Bennett, Peter Cook, Jonathan Miller and Dudley Moore*, London, 1989.

On MOORE: articles—

Current Biography 1982, New York, 1982.
McGillivray, David, "Dudley Moore," in *Films and Filming* (London), May 1982.
Clarke, Gerald, "Cuddly Dudley, the Wee Wonder," in *Time* (New York), 21 February 1983.

Schreiberg, Stu, "Dudley Moore," in *Life* (New York), June 1988.
Blake, J. C., "Dudley Moore," in *Film Dope* (London), September 1990.
Siegel, Scott, and Barbara Siegel, "Dudley Moore," in *American Film Comedy: From Abbott and Costello to Jerry Zucker*, New York, 1994.
Hitchens, Christopher, "Kings of Comedy," in *Vanity Fair* (New York), December 1995.

*　　*　　*

When Dudley Moore and Peter Cook acted as a comic duo in the sixties and seventies, Moore created some of his most humorous characters. The partners' movie debut in *The Wrong Box* (1966) illustrated the contrasting characters that made their films so laughable.

In their first movie they play cousins who are hiding a body they think is their uncle killed in a train wreck. Cook as Cousin Morris orders Cousin John (Moore) to dig faster. When John complains, "Why do I always have to do the dirty work?" Morris shoots back, "Because you are remarkably stupid." John reflects for a second and meekly replies, "Yes. I forgot that. Sorry."

This type of exchange became typical in two movies that would follow. In some ways Moore seemed to be playing a dense Laurel to Cook's dominating Hardy. *Bedazzled* (1967) and *The Hound of Baskervilles* (1977 in Britain and 1980 in the United States) displayed Dudley Moore's ability to create a funny, meek bungler who is easily tyrannized by Cook's character who has a haughty disposition and an assumed superior position. As the subservient character, Moore replies to the browbeating he receives with a befuddled voice and well-timed phrasing.

Bedazzled proves to be a film that shows the range and variety of Dudley Moore's acting more than any single film in his career. From the occupation of a lowly short-order cook, Stanley Moon, the basic character Moore plays, the actor portrays many variations. This comes about when the fry cook sells his soul to the devil, a role played by Peter Cook, who is a supercilious, mod Mephistopheles named George Spiggot. In order to impress a woman he yearns for but who hardly notices him, the devil, George, gives Stanley the character of an intellectual who pursues the arts. As this sophisticated gentleman Moore changes his voice inflections and accent to that of a posh Englishman—a portrait of a pretender to culture. In another wish there is a transformation to a fly because he wants to spy undetected on the object of his desire, Margaret. Dudley mimics an insect by an odd slurring of consonants (like buzzing) and a falsetto. Realizing all his transformations were to obtain a lustful goal or a nefarious advantage, Stanley wishes for a pure love.

The devil Spiggot turns Moon into a cloistered nun where he meets Margaret who is also a nun. Moore enacts the part of a female with only a lighter, less deep voice in a subtle way which avoids the often overdone interpretation of a woman by a man. The humor, therefore, avoids heavy-handed burlesque.

In another work with Peter Cook, Moore executes three comic characters in *The Hound of Baskervilles*. Besides the role of Dr. Watson as the partner to Cook as Sherlock Holmes, he plays the characters of Mrs. Ada Holmes, Sherlock's mother, and Mr. Spiggot a one-legged messenger applicant. Moore handles these minor roles in a way that distinguishes them completely from the major role of Dr. Watson. His in-drag role of the mother is comic yet, again, not overdone. Spiggot hops about enthusiastically wishing to be given the job of a "runner" of confidential messages from Sherlock Holmes. Spiggot is not given the job. Engaged as a writer for the lampoon on the famous fictional detective, the actor is shown as Dr. Watson playing solo for long stretches, indicating a move away from his partnership with Peter Cook.

Moore took a new direction in his career in the late seventies as he became a lead actor without a male co-star to bounce off with comic replies of frustration. With this move—into what became known as

Dudley Moore in *Arthur*

romantic comedy and through which Moore gained the nickname "Cuddly Dudley"—he actually began a slow slide to less funny films, except for *10* (1979) and *Arthur* (1981).

When Moore's acting partner became a woman the laughter began to fade. There were no writers, directors, or actors to provide a resurgence of the sophisticated or romantic comedy of the thirties and early forties. Liza Minnelli in *Arthur* plays the common working-class woman who gets entangled with the society of the wealthy, almost in the way Jean Arthur does in the 1937 *Easy Living*. While Minnelli is no comedienne with the skills of such actresses as Arthur and Carole Lombard, she is better than most of the women who were teamed with Moore in his eighties comedies. Also, credit should go to writer-director Steve Gordon who provided some shades of the witty comedy of decades ago. In *10* Moore benefited from the directing of Blake Edwards for Moore's second movie in the United States. But, the woman in the movie, Bo Derek, proved to be merely a prop—the object of the comedian's unfulfilled desire.

Ironically, another actor who might provide a continuing partner and counterpoint as Peter Cook did in the earlier, more laughable movies appeared: John Gielgud in *Arthur* and *Arthur 2: On the Rocks* (1988). Winning a best supporting actor Oscar for his role, the butler Mr. Hobson, in the first *Arthur*, Gielgud interacted effectively with Dudley and provided the witty put-downs that gave a similar tone to the comedy of actor Moore's reaction humor—much like his earlier movies, *The Wrong Box*, *Bedazzled*, and *The Hound of Baskervilles*.

—Donald W. McCaffrey

MOOREHEAD, Agnes

Nationality: American. **Born:** Agnes Robertson Moorehead in Clinton, Massachusetts, 6 December 1906. **Education:** Attended school in Reedsburg, Wisconsin; Muskingum College, Ohio; University of Wisconsin, Madison, M.A. in English and public speaking. **Family:** Married 1) John Griffith Lee, 1930 (divorced 1951), son: Sean; 2) Robert Gist, 1953 (divorced 1958). **Career:** Taught public speaking at Soldiers Grove High School, Wisconsin; radio singer in St. Louis (stations KSO and KMOX), and appeared as dancer and singer with Municipal Opera, St. Louis, for three seasons; taught dramatics at Dalton School, and studied at American Academy of Dramatic Arts, both in New York; also appeared on Broadway in *Marco Millions*, 1928, and other plays; 1930s—radio actress; 1937—joined Orson Welles's Mercury Theater; 1941—film debut in *Citizen Kane*; contracts with Warner Brothers and MGM during next few years; 1948—on stage with Orson Welles in *Macbeth*; 1954—toured with one-woman show *An Evening with Agnes Moorehead*; 1964-71—in TV series *Bewitched*; 1973—on Broadway in *Gigi*. **Awards:** Best Actress, New York Film Critics, for *The Magnificent Ambersons*, 1942. **Died:** 30 April 1974.

Films as Actress:

1941   *Citizen Kane* (Welles) (as Mary Kane)

Agnes Moorehead in *The Magnificent Ambersons*

1942 *The Magnificent Ambersons* (Welles) (as Fanny Minafer); *The Big Street* (Reis) (as Violette); *Journey into Fear* (Norman Foster) (as Mrs. Mathews)

1943 *The Youngest Profession* (Buzzell) (as Miss Featherstone); *Government Girl* (Dudley Nichols) (as Mrs. Wright)

1944 *Jane Eyre* (Stevenson) (as Mrs. Reed); *Since You Went Away* (Cromwell) (as Emily Hawkins); *Dragon Seed* (Conway) (as cousin's wife); *The Seventh Cross* (Zinnemann) (as Mme. Marelli); *Mrs. Parkington* (Garnett) (as Aspasia Conti); *Tomorrow the World* (Fenton) (as Jessie)

1945 *Keep Your Powder Dry* (Buzzell) (as Lt. Colonel Spottiswoode); *Our Vines Have Tender Grapes* (Rowland) (as Ma Jacobson); *Her Highness and the Bellboy* (Thorpe) (as Countess Zoe)

1947 *Dark Passage* (Daves) (as Madge Rapf); *The Lost Moment* (Gabel) (as Juliana)

1948 *Summer Holiday* (Mamoulian) (as Cousin Lillie); *The Woman in White* (Godfrey) (as Countess Fosco); *Station West* (Lanfield) (as Mrs. Caslon); *Johnny Belinda* (Negulesco) (as Aggie McDonald)

1949 *The Stratton Story* (Sam Wood) (as Ma Stratton); *The Great Sinner* (Siodmak) (as Emma Getzel)

1950 *Without Honor* (Pichel) (as Katherine Williams); *Caged* (Cromwell) (as Ruth Benton)

1951 *Fourteen Hours* (Hathaway) (as Mrs. Cosick); *Show Boat* (Sidney) (as Parthy Hawks); *The Blue Veil* (Bernhardt) (as Mrs. Palfrey); *The Adventures of Captain Fabian* (William Marshall) (as Aunt Jezebel); *Captain Blackjack* (Duvivier) (as Mrs. Birk)

1952 *The Blazing Forest* (Ludwig) (as Jessie Crane)

1953 "The Jealous Lover" ep. of *The Story of Three Loves* (Reinhardt) (as Aunt Lydia); *Scandal at Scourie* (Negulesco) (as Sister Josephine); *Those Redheads from Seattle* (Lewis R. Foster) (as Mrs. Edmonds); *Main Street to Broadway* (Garnett) (as Mildred Waterbury)

1954 *Magnificent Obsession* (Sirk) (as Nancy Ashford)

1955 *Untamed* (Henry King) (as Aggie); *The Left Hand of God* (Dmytryk) (as Beryl Sigman); *All that Heaven Allows* (Sirk) (as Sara Warren)

1956 *Meet Me in Las Vegas* (*Viva Las Vegas*) (Rowland) (as Miss Hattie); *The Conqueror* (Powell) (as Hunlun); *The Revolt of Mamie Stover* (Walsh) (as Bertha Parchman); *The Swan* (Charles Vidor) (as Queen Maria Dominika); *Pardners* (Taurog) (as Matilda Kingsley); *The Opposite Sex* (Miller) (as the Countess)

1957 *The True Story of Jesse James* (Nicholas Ray) (as Mrs. Samuel); *Jeanne Eagels* (Sidney) (as Mme. Nielson); *Raintree County* (Dmytryk) (as Ellen Shawnessy); *The Story of Mankind* (Irwin Allen) (as Queen Elizabeth)

1958 *La tempesta* (*Tempest*) (Lattuada) (as Vassilissa)

1959 *Night of the Quarter Moon* (Haas) (as Cornelia Nelson); *The Bat* (Wilbur) (as Cornelia Van Gorder)

1960 *Pollyanna* (Swift) (as Mrs. Snow)

1961 *Twenty Plus Two* (Joseph M. Newman) (as Mrs. Delaney); *Bachelor in Paradise* (Arnold) (as Judge Peterson)

1962 *Jessica* (Negulesco) (as Maria Lombardo)

1963 *How the West Was Won* (Ford, Marshall, and Hathaway) (as Rebecca Prescott); *Who's Minding the Store?* (Tashlin) (as Mrs. Phoebe Tuttle)

1964 *Hush ... Hush, Sweet Charlotte* (Aldrich) (as Velma Cruther)

1966 *The Singing Nun* (Koster) (as Sister Cluny); *Alice through the Looking Glass* (Handley—for TV) (as the Red Queen)

1969 *The Ballad of Andy Crocker* (McCowan—for TV)

1971 *What's the Matter with Helen?* (Harrington) (as Sister Alma); *Marriage: Year One* (Graham—for TV); *Suddenly Single* (Taylor—for TV); *The Strange Monster of Strawberry Cove* (Shea—for TV)

1972 *Rolling Man* (Hyams—for TV); *Night of Terror* (Szwarc—for TV); *Dear, Dead Delilah* (Farris) (title role)

1973 *Frankenstein—The True Story* (Smight—for TV) (as Mrs. Blair); *Charlotte's Web* (Charles A. Nichols and Takamoto—animation) (as voice of the Goose)

Publications

By MOOREHEAD: articles—

Interview, in *Hollywood Speaks*, edited by Mike Steen, New York, 1974.
Interview with N. Bernheim and others, in *Image et Son* (Paris), April 1974.

On MOOREHEAD: books—

Parish, James Robert, *Good Dames*, New York, 1974.
Sherk, Warren, *Agnes Moorehead: A Very Private Person*, Philadelphia, 1976.
Kear, Lynn, *Agnes Moorehead: A Bio-Bibliography*, Westport, Connecticut, 1992.

On MOOREHEAD: articles—

Current Biography 1952, New York, 1952.
Sight and Sound (London), Autumn 1955.
Bowers, Ronald, "Agnes Moorehead," in *Films in Review* (New York), May 1966.
Obituary, in *New York Times*, 1 May 1974.

*   *   *

One might define hysteria as the response to the continual and irreversible frustration of the desire for power, authority, or (at least) personal dignity, which is why, within patriarchal culture, it is an ailment predominantly associated with women. Agnes Moorehead was one of Hollywood's most impressive spokespersons for female hysteria (whether overtly expressed or precariously and agonizingly controlled), linked in many of her most fully characteristic roles to an explicitly sexual frustration, the ignominious condition of the "spinster."

In the definitive role of her career in *The Magnificent Ambersons*, her Aunt Fanny—sexually repressed, tormented by physicality in all its forms, disappointed in love, her formidable energies permitted no other outlet in a world where power is by definition *male*—is the cinema's most eloquent realization of the term "spinster" and of its logical accompaniment of hysteria. Deviation from this prototype into heroine's friend roles (*All that Heaven Allows*) and even into motherhood (*The Stratton Story*), Agnes had her share of ignominious parts but intermittently displayed strength and intelligence in roles that position her outside direct male determination (*Caged, The Revolt of Mamie Stover*). An exemplary character actress, Moorehead received four Academy Award nominations, soldiered on histrionically when those she "supported" succumbed to flimsy material, and remained impossible to ignore even when going stratospherically over the top in big-budget flops such as the pseudo-Oriental turkey *The Conqueror*.

Before her Hollywood employment, the resonant Moorehead voice made her one of radio's most durable interpreters and the creator of the warhorse, *Sorry, Wrong Number*. Later as an antidote to the limitations of her contractual characterdom, she toured to great advantage onstage, particularly in Shaw's *Man and Superman*, with Boyer, Laughton, and Hardwicke. A Queen of all media, Moorehead tackled a diversity of parts on-screen from her debut as *Citizen Kane*'s pragmatic mother. Unfettered by a set image, her range extended from a tightly coiled murderess taking a classic tumble out the window in *Dark Passage* to a comic gadfly in *Pollyanna* in which her heart is melted by an orphan. Although intensity was the keynote of her acting, she could be salt of the earth as in *Johnny Belinda* or airily upper crust as in *Mrs. Parkington*, a countess role which prefigured her glamorous resurgence on television's *Bewitched*. Fondly remembered for another television role on a *Twilight Zone* episode as an outer space giantess peevishly crushing U.S. astronauts, she completely conquered television with her stylishly supernatural Endora on *Bewitched*; her interpretation of the ultimate mother-in-law joke armed with magical powers of reprisal won her the deserved celebrity that eluded her as a premiere character star in the movies. Prior to *Bewitched*, she tackled one of her unlikeliest assignments as the white trash Velma in the Grand Guignol picnic, *Hush ... Hush, Sweet Charlotte*; it was an outrageous send-up of a fugitive from *Tobacco Road*, the thickest ham Moorehead ever sliced, and it should have won her the Academy Award. Always a bridesmaid in the Oscar race, Moorehead possessed a flinty versatility which even such drive-in trash as *Dear, Dead Delilah* could not demean. Her place in film history is guaranteed by her sterling work in her first two films, and it is for these (especially *Ambersons*) that she will be most vividly remembered.

—Robin Wood, updated by Robert Pardi

MOREAU, Jeanne

Nationality: French. **Born:** Paris, 23 January 1928. **Education:** Attended the Lycée Edgar Quinet, Paris; Conservatoire National d'Art Dramatique, Paris. **Family:** Married 1) the actor Jean-Louis Richard, 1949 (divorced), son: Jérôme; 2) the director William Friedkin, 1977 (divorced 1980). **Career:** 1948-52—member of the Comédie Française: debut in *A Month in the Country*; 1948—film debut in *Dernier amour*; 1952—joined Théâtre National Populaire; 1975—president, Cannes Film Festival; 1976—directed the film *Lumière*; 1982—co-founder, with Klaus Hellwig, Moreau Productions; 1994—in TV mini-series *Catherine the Great*; also recorded several albums of songs. **Awards:** Best Actress, Cannes Festival, for *Moderato Cantabile*, 1960; Best Foreign Actress, British Academy, for *Viva Maria*, 1966; Chevalier, Légion d'honneur; Ordre Nationale du Merite et des Arts et Lettres. **Agent:** Artmédia, 10 av Georges V, 75008 Paris, France.

Films as Actress:

1948 *Dernier amour* (Stelli)
1950 *Meurtes* (*Three Sinners*) (Pottier); *Pigalle Sainte-Germain-des-Pres* (Berthomieu)
1951 *L'Homme de ma vie* (Lefranc)
1952 *Il est minuit, Docteur Schweitzer* (Haguet)
1953 *Touchez pas au grisbi* (*Grisbi; Don't Touch the Loot*) (Jacques Becker) (as Josy); *Dortoir des grandes* (*Inside a Girls' Dormitory*) (Decoin); *Julietta* (Marc Allégret) (as Rosie Facibey); *Les Intriguantes* (Decoin); *La Reine Margot* (Dréville)
1954 *Secrets d'alcôve* (*The Bed; Il Letto*) (Decoin, Delannoy, Habib, and Franciolini) (as Mother)
1955 *Les Hommes en blanc* (*The Doctors*) (Habib) (as Marianne); *Gas-Oil* (Grangier); *M'sieur la caille* (Pergament)
1956 *La Salaire du péché* (de la Patellière); *Jusqu-au dernier* (Billon)

1957 *Les Louves* (*Demoniaque; The She Wolves*) (Saslavsky) (as Agnes); *L'Etrange Mr. Steve* (Vailly); *Trois jours à vivre* (Grangier); *Echec au porteur* (Grangier)
1958 *Ascenseur pour l'échafaud* (*Elevator to the Gallows; Frantic*) (Malle) (as Florence Carala); *Le Dos au mur* (*Back to the Wall*) (Molinaro); *Les Amants* (*The Lovers*) (Malle) (as Jeanne Tournier)
1959 *Les Liaisons dangereuses* (*Dangerous Love Affairs; Relazioni Pericolose*) (Vadim) (as Juliette de Merteuil); *Le Dialogue des Carmélites* (Bruckberger); *Five Branded Women* (Ritt) (as Ljuba); **Les Quatre Cents Coups** (*The 400 Blows*) (Truffaut) (as woman with dog)
1960 *Moderato Cantabile* (*Seven Days . . . Seven Nights*) (Brook) (as Ann Desbaredes); **La notte** (*The Night*) (Antonioni) (as Lidia)
1961 *Une Femme est une femme* (*A Woman Is a Woman*) (Godard) (as woman in bar)
1962 **Jules et Jim** (*Jules and Jim*) (Truffaut) (as Catherine); *Eva* (Losey) (as Eva Olivier); *La Baie des anges* (*Bay of Angels*) (Demy) (as Jackie Demaistre); *Le Feu follet* (*The Fire Within*) (Malle) (as Jeanne)
1963 *The Victors* (Foreman) (as Frenchwoman); **Le Procès** (*The Trial*) (Welles) (as Miss Burstner)
1964 *Peau de banane* (*Banana Peel*) (Marcel Ophüls) (as Cathy); *Le Journal d'une femme de chambre* (*Diary of a Chambermaid*) (Buñuel) (as Celestine); *Le Train* (*The Train*) (Frankenheimer) (as Christine); *The Yellow Rolls-Royce* (Asquith) (as Marchioness Eloise of Frinton)
1965 *Viva Maria* (Malle) (as Maria I); *Mata Hari—Agent H-21* (Richard) (title role)
1966 *Mademoiselle* (*Summer Fires*) (Richardson) (title role); **Campanadas a Medianoche** (*Chimes at Midnight; Falstaff*) (Welles) (as Doll Tearsheet)
1967 *The Sailor from Gibraltar* (Richardson) (as Anna); "Mademoiselle Mimi" ep. of *Le Plus Vieux Métier du monde* (*The Oldest Profession*) (de Broca) (as Mimi)
1968 *La Mariée etait en noir* (*The Bride Wore Black*) (Truffaut) (as Julie Kohler); *Great Catherine* (Flemyng) (title role); *Une Histoire immortelle* (*The Immortal Story*) (Welles—for TV) (as Virginie Ducrot)
1969 "When Love Dies" ep. of *Le Petit théâtre de Jean Renoir* (*The Little Theater of Jean Renoir*) (Renoir—for TV) (as the singer); *Le Corps de Diane* (*Diane's Body*) (Richard) (title role)
1970 *Monte Walsh* (Fraker) (as Martine Bernard); *Alex in Wonderland* (Mazursky) (as herself); *Comptes à rebours* (Pigaut)
1971 *L'Humeur vagabonde* (Luntz)
1972 *Chère Louise* (de Broca); *Nathalie Granger* (Duras) (as other woman)
1973 *Joanna Francesca* (Diegues) (title role); *Je t'aime* (*I Love You*) (Duceppe) (as Elisa Boussac); *Les Valseuses* (*Going Places*) (Blier) (as Jeanne Pirolle)
1974 *La Race des seigneurs* (Granier-Deferre); *Hu Man* (Laperrousaz); *Le Jardin qui bascule* (Gilles)
1975 *Souvenirs d'en France* (*French Provincial*) (Téchiné)
1976 *Mr. Klein* (Losey) (as Florence); *The Last Tycoon* (Kazan) (as Didi)
1980 *Your Ticket Is No Longer Valid* (Kaczender); *Plein sud* (*Heat of Desire*) (Beraud) (as Helene)
1981 *Lucien chez les barbares* (Bernardi); *Mille milliards de dollars* (Berneuil)
1982 *La Truite* (*The Trout*) (Losey) (as Lou); *Querelle* (Fassbinder) (as Lysiane); *Autour de l'arbre* (Dillon)
1983 *Der Bauer von Babylon* (*The Wizard of Babylon*) (Schidor—doc)
1984 *Jean-Louis Barrault—Man of the Theatre* (Balash—doc)

Jeanne Moreau in *Les Amants*

1985   *Le Plus Grande Musée* (Lander—for TV); *Vicious Circle* (Ives—
for TV)

1986   *Le Paltoquet* (Deville) (as the Proprietress); *Sauve-toi Lola*
(Drach) (as Marie-Aude); *Le Tiroir secret* (Molinaro—for
TV); *François Simon—La présence* (Simon—doc); *Last Se-
ance* (Wyndham-Davies—for TV)

1987   *Le Miraculé* (Mocky) (as Sabine); *Renoir, les portraits de la
beauté* (Shigenobu—doc); *Hotel Terminus* (Ophüls)

1988   *Calling the Shots* (Cole and Dale—doc); *La Nuit de l'ocean*
(Perset)

1989   *La Femme fardée* (Pinheiro) (as La Doria)

1990   *La femme Nikita* (Besson) (as Amande); *Alberto Express* (Joffé)
       (as the Baroness)
1991   *Suspended Step of the Stork* (*To Meteoro Vima tou Pelargou*)
       (Angelopoulos) (as the wife); *Anna Karamazoff*; *The Archi-
       tecture of Doom* (as narrator); *Bis ans Ende der Welt* (*Until
       the End of the World*) (Wenders) (as Edith Farber)
1992   *The Lover* (*L'Amant*) (Annaud) (as voice of Marguerite Duras); *A
       Demain* (as Tete); *La Vielle qui marchait dans le mer* (*The Old
       Lady Who Walked in the Sea*) (Heynemann) (as Lady M)
1993   *The Absence* (Handke) (as wife of the old man); **Map of the
       Human Heart** (*La carte du tendre*) (Ward) (as Sister
       Banville); *Je M'Appelle Victor* (*My Name Is Victor*) (Jacques)
       (as Rose); *The Summer House* (Hussein) (as Lili); *A Foreign
       Field* (Sturridge—for TV) (as Angelique)
1995   *Les Cent et Une Nuits* (*A Hundred and One Nights*) (Varda) (as
       Actor for a Day); *Par dela les nuages* (Antonioni and
       Wenders)

Films as Director:

1976   *Lumière* (*Light*) (+ sc, ro as Sarah Dedieu)
1979   *L'adolescente* (+ co-sc)
1984   *Lillian Gish* (co-d, + pr)

Publications

By MOREAU: book—

*L'adolescente: d'apres un scenario de Henriette Jelinek et Jeanne
Moreau, sur une idée originale de Jeanne Moreau*, Paris, 1979.

By MOREAU: articles—

Interview with M. Lindsay, in *Cinema* (Beverly Hills), no. 3, 1969.
Interview with E. Decaux and Bruno Villien, in *Cinématographe* (Paris),
October 1982.
Interview with Michael Buckley, in *Films in Review* (New York), De-
cember 1983.
"Dialogue on Film: Jeanne Moreau," in *American Film* (New York),
July/August 1984.
Interview with M. Chevrie and Serge Toubiana, in *Cahiers du Cinéma*
(Paris), February 1987.
Interview with M. Buruiana, in *Séquences* (Montreal), January 1989.
Interview with Molly Haskell and Andrea R. Vaucher, in *Film Comment*
(New York), March/April 1990.

On MOREAU: books—

Erdelyi, Z. Agnes, *Jeanne Moreau*, Budapest, 1977.
Ruscart, Marc, editor, with Chantel Le Sauzel, *Jeanne Moreau, une
femme, une actrice*, Paris, 1986.
Moireau, Jean-Claude, *Jeanne Moreau*, Paris, 1988.
Lauermann, Gabriele, *Jeanne Moreau: ihre Filme, ihr Leben*, Munich,
1989.
Delmar, Michael, *Jeanne Moreau: portrait d'une femme*, Paris, 1994.
Gray, Marianne, *La Moreau: A Biography of Jeanne Moreau*, London, 1996.

On MOREAU: articles—

Stanbrook, Alan, "The Star They Couldn't Photograph," in *Films and
Filming* (London), February 1963.
Duras, Marguerite, "The Affairs of Jeanne Moreau," in *Show* (Holly-
wood), March 1963.

Current Biography 1966, New York, 1966.
Gilliatt, Penelope, "Jeanne Moreau," in *The Movie Star*, edited by
Elisabeth Weis, New York, 1981.
Allen, D., "Moreau in London," in *Sight and Sound* (London), Sum-
mer 1982.
Ferguson, S., "Jeanne Moreau," in *Ecran* (Paris), vol. 16, no. 4/5, 1991.
"Hot Number: Jeanne Moreau," in *Economist* (London), 11 February
1995.

*   *   *

Jeanne Moreau's canonization coincided with the assault of the
French New Wave on stale professional craftsmanship and conventional movie stardom. Toiling in the theater and forgettable movies
for more than a decade, Moreau was no spring chicken when Louis
Malle helped mold her image as the femme d'un certain age. At a
chronological age when American leading ladies were put out to the
pasture of television sitcoms and summer stock, Moreau flourished
not because she was refreshingly foreign but because, judged particularly against the backdrop of the rotting American studio system, she
was unique. Not cast as disposable used goods like Piper Laurie in *The
Hustler* or as a perennial spinster like Geraldine Page in *Summer and
Smoke*, the no-longer fresh-faced Moreau of *Jules and Jim* and *Frantic* was a vitally sexy woman far from ready for consignment to a
sexist junk heap. Defying bourgeois standards of propriety in *Les
Amants* or deliberately bastardizing social intercourse in *Les Liaisons
dangereuses* for her own pleasure, Moreau excited film buffs because
she played by her own rules which were subject to change dictated by
her will.

The charting of one's destiny was a luxury denied most of the
actresses working in Hollywood films of this same period. Adopted as
a patron saint by Truffaut, Malle, and Godard, and embraced by the
intelligentsia as a love goddess who did not insult their IQs, Moreau
followed the same course in her career as her characters did in her
movies: wherever your heart leads you, never compromise once you
reach the destination. By insisting on placing herself in the hands of
the top filmmakers of the era, her career span exceeded those who
thought they were being clever just by alternating a commercial hit
with an Oscar-nominated drama. Not constrained by an image, she
became a tabula rasa for innovators. If she was the embodiment of
soul-sickness for Antonioni in his unsparing dissection of a marriage
in *La notte*, she could also be perceived as the saucy spirit of plaisir for
Demy's *Bay of Angels* or the brutally frank spokesperson for the
superiority of the serving class in Buñuel's *Diary of a Chambermaid*.
If her American vehicles reveal her at half-mast, that may have been
the consequence of not aligning herself with major Yankee filmmakers (save for Welles, who was by this point an expatriate far out of the
Hollywood mainstream). In Europe, however, even intriguing misfires by Britishers Richardson and Brook, only enhanced her legend as
a femme fatale with the soul of a poet. All the diverse aspects of
Moreau's personality mesh seamlessly in Truffaut's masterpiece, *Jules
and Jim*, which could be called Moreau's *Camille*. Still exhilarating
today, this gloriously untidy film presents Moreau's maddeningly
modern Catherine as part unfettered child, part calculating vixen.
Bewitching the viewers just as she captivates her lovers, Moreau crystallizes the movie's romantic tragedy for us by creating a mystery
woman who never surrenders to either man the complete abandonment they desire.

Sometimes languidly sensual, sometimes raging with volcanic force,
the Empress of Art Cinema capped off the first phase of her stardom
with an enchanting rendition of a bittersweet song in *Le Petit théâtre
de Jean Renoir*, a valedictory to him and a tribute to her loveliness
which time seemed powerless to dim. As a character actress she continued to spark excitement, notably passing on the New Wave baton
from Truffaut to Blier in *Going Places* and instructing a declassé

850

assassin in social graces in *La femme Nikita*. Although space defeats anyone trying to summarize all of Moreau's acting benedictions, one can point out that as of 1993, her histrionic passion could still attain rapturous heights on the evidence of *The Summer House*. Fittingly for an actress who hitched her star to so many auteurs, she made a graceful transition to directing. Beginning with a contemplation of acting and friendship in the luminous *Lumière*, progressing through a lovely coming-of-age tale, *L'adolescente*, and culminating in an inspired documentary about Lillian Gish, Moreau proves that she is still the searching artist no matter where she positions herself on a movie set. The restless drive for self-expression which fueled some of her favorite moviemakers' greatest works now lives on in her own highly personal and adventurous efforts.

—Robert Pardi

MORGAN, Michèle

Nationality: French. **Born:** Neuilly-sur-Seine, 29 February 1920. **Education:** Studied acting under René Simon. **Family:** Married 1) William Marshall, 1942 (divorced 1949), one son; 2) Henri Vidal, 1950 (died 1959). **Career:** 1936—film debut in bit part in *Mademoiselle Mozart*; also worked on stage; 1937—contract with the director Marc Allégret; 1942-46—made several films in the United States under contract to RKO; 1966—exhibition of her paintings at Galerie Dina Vierny; 1978-80—on stage in *Le Tout pour le tout*, and in *Chéri*, 1982-83. **Awards:** Best Actress, Cannes Festival, for *La Symphonie pastorale*, 1946. Chevalier, Legion of Honor, 1969. **Address:** 5 rue Jacques Dulud, 92200 Neuilly-sur-Seine, France.

Films as Actress:

1936 *Mademoiselle Mozart* (Noé) (bit role); *La Vie parisienne* (Siodmak) (bit role); *Mes tantes et moi* (Noé) (as Michèle); *Le Mioche* (*Forty Little Mothers*) (Moguy) (as student); *Une Fille à papa* (Guissart) (bit role)

1937 *Gigolette* (Noé) (bit role); *Gribouille* (*Heart of Paris*) (Marc Allégret) (as Natalie Roguin); *Orage* (Marc Allégret) (as Pascaud)

1938 **Quai des brumes** (*Port of Shadows*) (Carné) (as Nelly); *Le Récif de corail* (Gleize) (as Lilian White)

1940 *L'Entraîneuse* (Valentin) (as Suzy); *Les Musiciens du ciel* (Lacombe) (as Lte. Saulnier)

1941 *Remorques* (*Stormy Waters*) (Grémillon) (as Catherine)

1942 *La Loi du nord* (Feyder) (as Jacqueline Bert); *Joan of Paris* (Stevenson) (title role)

1943 *Untel Père et Fils* (*The Heart of a Nation*) (Duvivier—produced in 1939) (as Marie Froment-Léonard); *Two Tickets to London* (Marin) (as Jeanne); *Higher and Higher* (Whelan) (as Millie)

1944 *Passage to Marseilles* (Curtiz) (as Paula)

1946 *La Symphonie pastorale* (Delannoy) (as Gertrude); *The Chase* (Ripley) (as Lorna Roman)

1948 *The Fallen Idol* (*The Lost Illusion*) (Reed) (as Julie); *Fabiola* (Blasetti) (title role); *Aux yeux du souvenir* (*Souvenir*) (Delannoy) (as Claire Magny)

1950 *Maria Chapdelaine* (*The Naked Heart*) (Marc Allégret—released in U.S. in 1955) (title role); *La Belle que voilà* (Le Chanois) (as Jeanne Morel); *Le Château de verre* (Clément) (as Evelyne Bertal)

1951 *L'Etrange Madame X* (Grémillon) (as Irène)

1952 "L'Orgueil" ("Pride") ep. of *Les Sept Péchés Capitaux* (*The Seven Deadly Sins*) (Autant-Lara) (as Anne-Marie de Pallières); *La Minute de vérité* (*The Moment of Truth*) (Delannoy) (as Madeleine Richard)

1953 *Les Orgueilleux* (*The Proud and the Beautiful*) (Yves Allégret) (as Nellie)

1954 "Jeanne" ep. of *Destinées* (*Daughters of Destiny*; *Love, Soldiers and Women*; *Lysistrata*) (Yves Allégret) (as Jeanne d'Arc); *Obsession* (Delannoy) (as Helene Giovanni)

1955 *Napoléon* (Guitry) (as Joséphine); *Oasis* (Yves Allégret) (as Francoise Lignières); *Les Grandes Manoeuvres* (*The Grand Maneuver*; *Summer Manoeuvres*) (Clair) (as Marie-Louise Rivière); *Si Paris nous était conté* (*If Paris Were Told to Us*) (Guitry) (as Gabrielle d'Estrées)

1956 *Marguerite de la nuit* (Autant-Lara) (as Marguerite); *Marie-Antoinette* (Delannoy) (title role)

1957 *The Vintage* (Hayden) (as Léonne Morel); *Retour de Manivelle* (*There's Always a Price Tag*) (de la Patellière) (as Hélène Freminger)

1958 *Le Miroir à deux faces* (*The Mirror Has Two Faces*) (Cayatte) (as Marie-José); *Maxime* (Verneuil) (as Jacqueline Monneron); *Racconti d'estate* (*Love on the Riviera*; *Summer Tales*; *Femmes d'un été*) (Francolini) (as Micheline)

1959 *Pourquoi viens-tu si tard?* (Decoin) (as Catherine Ferrer); *Vacanze d'inverno* (Mastrocinque) (as Steffa Tardier)

1960 *Menschen im Hotel* (*Grand Hotel*) (Reinhardt) (as La Grusinskaya); *Les Scélérats* (Hossein) (as Thelma Roland); *Fortunat* (Joffé) (as Juliette Valecourt)

1961 *Le Puits aux trois vérités* (*Three Faces of Sin*) (Villiers) (as Renée Plèges); *Les Lions sont lachés* (Verneuil) (as Cecile)

1962 *Un Coeur gros comme ça* (Reichenbach) (as herself); *Rencontres* (Agostini) (as Bella Krasner); "The Hugues Case" ep. of *Le Crime ne paie pas* (*Crime Does Not Pay*; *The Gentle Art of Murder*) (Oury) (as Jeanne Hugues 2)

1963 *Landru* (*Bluebeard*) (Chabrol) (as Célestine Buisson); *Méfiez-vous mesdames* (Hunebelle) (as Gisèle Duparc)

1964 *Il fornaretto di Venezia* (Tessari) (as Comtesse Sofia Zeno); *Constance aux enfers* (*Web of Fear*) (Villiers) (as Constance Brunel); *Les Pas perdus* (Robin) (as Yolande Simonnet); *Les Yeux cernés* (Hossein) (as Florence Vollmer)

1965 *Dis-moi qui tuer* (Périer) (as Geneviève Monthannet)

1966 *Lost Command* (*Not for Honor and Glory*) (Robson) (as Comtesse Nathalie de Clairefons)

1967 *La Bien-aimée* (Doniol-Valcroze—for TV) (as Fanny)

1968 *Benjamin ou Les mémoires d'un puceau* (*Benjamin*; *The Diary of an Innocent Boy*) (Deville) (as Comtesse Gabrielle de Valandry)

1975 *Le Chat et la souris* (*Cat and Mouse*) (Lelouch) (as Mme. Richard)

1978 *Robert et Robert* (Lelouch) (as herself)

1984 *Chéri* (Hubert—for TV)

1986 *Un Homme et une femme: vingt ans déjà* (*A Man and a Woman: 20 Years Later*) (Lelouch); *Le Tiroir secret* (Molinaro—for TV)

1990 *Stanno tutti bene* (*Everybody's Fine*) (Tornatore) (as woman on train)

Publications

By MORGAN: books—

Avec ces yeux, with Marcelle Routier, Paris, 1977, as *With Those Eyes*, London, 1978.
Le fil bleu: le roman de ma famille, Paris, 1993.

Michèle Morgan in *Quai des Brumes*

On MORGAN: book—

Bouniq-Mercier, Claude, *Michèle Morgan*, Paris, 1983.

On MORGAN: articles—

Ecran (Paris), February 1979.
Ciné Revue (Paris), 7 January 1982.
Stars (Mariembourg, Belgium), December 1989, June 1990, December
    1990, and June 1992.
Baker, B., "Michèle Morgan," in *Film Dope* (Nottingham, England),
    September 1990.

*   *   *

After a successful debut in the 1930s as an affecting, ill-fated heroine, Michèle Morgan survived a disappointing wartime period in Hollywood to become France's most acclaimed actress of the 1950s.
With her honest expression, serene open face, and fine features, she
possessed an almost unworldly beauty which seemed the outward manifestation of untainted virtue and intrinsic moral strength. In the bleak
mood of pre-war Europe she came to represent the contemporary
romantic heroine doomed through implacable adversity to unhappiness.

Morgan's first triumph came in *Gribouille* as the fetchingly innocent Natalie, unjustly accused of murdering her lover. Pathetic, self-
sacrificing roles followed. In *Orage* an impossible affair leads to suicide; in *L'Entraîneuse*, revelation of her dubious past destroys her
happiness, while in *La Loi du nord* and *Les Musiciens du ciel* a martyr's
death is her reward for loyalty and devotion. It was with Jean Gabin as
a romantic partner, however, that she achieved distinction. If in *La
Récif de corail* misfortune is conquered, in *Quai des brumes* and
Remorques their chance encounter secures only fleeting happiness.
As the hapless heroine, Morgan gave outstanding performances, particularly for Carné as Nelly, the precociously mature young woman
trapped in a corrupt society and experiencing love with the fugitive
Gabin. Her assorted and indifferent Hollywood performances included
that of a servant masquerading as a debutante in Whelan's comedy-
musical *Higher and Higher*, a romanticized Resistance heroine in
Joan of Paris, and in *Two Tickets to London* a widow romantically
involved with a serviceman.

Critical acclaim marked Morgan's return to French cinema in a
sensitive and restrained performance as the blind girl Gertrude in *La
Symphonie pastorale*. Reestablishing herself as the romantic heroine,
she now assumed professional roles as an air hostess dogged by memories in *Aux yeux du souvenir* and as a terminally ill ballerina in *La Belle
que voilà*. The postwar era brought co-productions and historical
roles, notably as a haughty aristocrat in *Fabiola*, a spirited Joan of

Arc in *Destinées*, as Joséphine de Beauharnais in *Napoléon*, the beautiful leading lady in *Marie-Antoinette*, and in *Si Paris nous était conté* as mistress to Henri IV. European directors cast her successively as the tearful mistress of *The Fallen Idol*, the fading, suicidal ballerina of *Menschen im Hotel*, and as a seductive thief in *Racconti d'estate*.

Invariably elegant and wealthy, in her 1950s roles she remained the victim, now bored and frustrated in her stifling ease. Escape is sought in adultery, as in *Le Château de verre*, *L'Etrange Madame X*, with a proletarian lover, and with an artist in *La Minute de vérité*. An alternative solution to personal unhappiness is found in alcohol in *Les Scélérats*, *Oasis*, and, most powerfully, as the unhappily married hard-drinking lawyer of *Pourquoi viens-tu si tard?* Distinguishing this era were roles as Gérard Philipe's courageous medical helper in *Les Orgueilleux* and, particularly, as the sincere, sophisticated, and suffering divorcée he seeks to seduce in *Les Grandes Manoeuvres*.

Rarely convincing as a wicked woman, Morgan was nevertheless cast as a defrauding vamp in *Retour de Manivelle*, a murderess in *Les Yeux cernés*, and in *Le Puits aux trois vérités* as a negligent, jealous mother. Lighter roles saw her as a witty partner to Bourvil in *Fortunat*, a would-be murderess in *Méfiez-vous mesdames*, an adventuress in *Dis-moi qui tuer*, and a murder suspect in *Le Chat et la souris*.

As a traditional star closely identified with established directors such as Yves Allégret and Delannoy, Michèle Morgan was all but ignored by the New Wave iconoclasts. Extending over five decades, her largely distinguished, if uneven, film career survived indifferent roles in nonindigenous productions. Eight years after her last screen appearance, as herself in *Robert et Robert*, she made a triumphant return to the stage in Colette's *Chéri*. More recently, she has enjoyed a popular following in the television serial *Le Tiroir secret* as a psychologist delving into her dead husband's past. She will be remembered for her exceptional beauty, her discreet, composed acting as the desirable young heroine, and her intelligent, sensitive performances as the sophisticated lady of later years.

—R. F. Cousins

MORI, Masayuki

Nationality: Japanese. **Born:** Yukimitsu Arishima in Sapporo City, Hakkaido, 13 January 1911; son of the writer Takeo Arishima. **Education:** Attended Imperial University, Kyoto, to 1932. **Family:** Married Toshie Yoshida, 1946; sons: Takeo and Junkichi. **Career:** 1929-31—member of the Tsukiji Sho-gekijo theater group, and later worked with Teruko Nagaoko's Teatoro Comedia, 1932-36, the Bungaku-za theater group, 1937-44, and the Tokyo Geijutsu Gekijo theater group Mingei, 1945; then freelance stage actor; 1942—film debut in *Haha no chizu*; 1950—international recognition for role in *Rashomon*. **Awards:** Japanese Kinema Jumpo Award for Best Actor, for *Floating Clouds*, 1955; also Mainichi Eiga Concourse Awards, 1947 and 1960. **Died:** Of cancer in Tokyo, 7 October 1973.

Films as Actor:

1942 *Haha no chizu* (Shimazu)
1943 *Susume dokuritsu-ki* (Kinugasa and Imai)
1944 *Dengeki Shutsudo*
1945 *Zoku Sugata Sanshiro* (*Sanshiro Sugata*; *Judo Saga, Part II*) (Kurosawa) (as Yoshima Dan); *Toro-no-o o fumu otokotachi* (*Men Who Tread on the Tiger's Tail*) (Kurosawa) (as Kamei)
1946 *Asu o tsukuru hitobito* (*Those Who Make Tomorrow*) (Kurosawa, Tamamoto, and Sekigawa)

1947 *Anjo-ke no buto-kai* (Yoshimura) (as eldest son)
1948 *Kofuku no isu*; *Ware nakinurete*; *Jutai* (Shibuya); *Hakai* (*Apostasy*) (Kinoshita)
1949 *Waga shogai no kagayakeru hi* (Yoshimura) (as ex-officer); *Kyo ware ren-ai su*; *Guddobai* (Shima); *Dai-tokai no ushimitsu-doki*; *Chijin no ai* (Kimura); *Yabure-daiko* (Kinoshita)
1950 *Ma no ogon*; *Kazan-myaku*; **Rashomon** (Kurosawa) (as Takehiro); *Senka no hate*; *Tokyo no hiroin*; *Re-mizeraburu* (two parts); *Okusama ni goyojin*
1951 *Kyujo hiroba* (Hisamatsu); *Zemma* (Kinoshita); *Hakuchi* (*The Idiot*) (Kurosawa) (as Myshkin); *Nusumareta koi*; *Junpaku no yoru*; *Musashinofujin* (*Lady Musashino*) (Mizoguchi) (as Tadao Akiyama); *Tokyo hika*
1952 *Joobachi*; *Taki no Shiraito*; *Bijo to tozoku* (Kimura); *Anote konote*
1953 *Senba-zuru* (Yoshimura); *Yosei wa hana no nioi ga suru* (Hisamatsu); **Ugetsu monogatari** (*Ugetsu*) (Mizoguchi) (as Genjuro); *Saikai*; *Ani imoto* (Naruse) (as older brother); *Kani-ko sen* (Yamamura); *Asakusa monogatari*; *Koibumi* (Tanaka)
1954 *Moeru Shanhai*; *Aru onna* (Toyoda) (as ship's captain); *Ai Midori no nakama*; *Aku no tanoshisa*
1955 *Ukigumo* (*Floating Clouds*) (Naruse); *Yokihi* (*The Princess Yang Kwei-fei*) (Mizoguchi) (as Emperor); *Kokoru* (Ichikawa) (as teacher); *Yushima no shiraume* (Kinugasa) (as Shuzo Sakai); *Nyubo yo, eien nare* (Tanaka)
1956 *Fusen*; *Iro-zange*; *Ai wa furu hoshi no kanata ni*; *Ningen gyorai shutsugeki su*
1957 *Arakure* (Naruse); *Kyo no inochi*; *Banka* (Gosho) (as Setsuo Katsuragi)
1958 *Onna de arukoto* (Kawashima); *Shiroi akuma*; *Yoru no tsuzumi* (Imai) (as drummer)
1959 *Suzukake no sampomichi* (Horikawa); *Dai-san no shikaku*; *Fubuki to tomo ni keiyukinu*; *Onna-gokoro*; *Kotan no kuchibue* (Naruse); *Aru rakujitsu*; *Kizoku no kaidan*; *Yogiri no ketto*
1960 *Onna ga kaidan o noboru toku* (*When a Woman Ascends the Stairs*) (Naruse) (as Nobuhiko); *Mususme tsuma haha* (Naruse); *Gametsui yatsu* (*This Greedy Old Skin*) (Chiba); *Otouto* (*Her Brother*) (Tchikawa) (as father); *Warui yatsu hodo yoku nemuru* (*The Bad Sleep Well*) (Kurosawa) (as Iwabuchi)
1961 *Onna wa yoru kesho-suru* (Inoue); *Tsuma to shite onnato shite* (Naruse); *Ai to honoo to* (*Challenge to Live*) (Sugawa); *Onna no kunsho* (Yoshimura); *Nyobo gakko*; *Shamisen to otobai* (Shinoda)
1963 *Bushido zankoku monogatari* (*Bushido*) (Imai) (as Lord Hori); *Taiheiyo hitoribotchi* (*Alone on the Pacific*; *My Enemy the Sea*) (Ichikawa) (as father); *Hikaru umi* (Nakahira)
1964 *Otoko-girai*; *Kikyo*
1966 *Haru ramman* (Chiba); *Kamo to negi*
1967 *Midaregumo* (*Scattered Clouds*) (Naruse)
1968 *Yamamoto Isoroku* (*Admiral Yamamoto*) (Maruyama); *Sogeki* (*Sun Above, Death Below*) (Horikawa) (as Katakura)
1969 *Hi mo tsuki* (*Through Days and Months*) (Nakamura) (as father); *Aa, kaigun* (*Gateway to Glory*) (Murayama)
1970 *Zatoichi: Abare Himatsuri* (Misumi)
1972 *Ken to hana*

*   *   *

The Shingeki (modern theater) actor Masayuki Mori first impressed the Japanese film audience with his performance as the nihilistic son of an aristocratic family in Yoshimura's 1947 film, *Anjo-ke no buto-*

kai. His intellectual and sophisticated characterization attracted critical attention, as well as establishing his career as a successful film star. His collaboration with Yoshimura continued through the 1950s: another of their masterpieces is *Waga shogai no kagayakeru hi*, in which Mori played an ex-officer with whom the heroine falls in love without knowing he has assassinated her father. The film vividly conveyed the confusing and disillusioned mood of postwar Japan, emphasized by Mori's skillful and explosively powerful performance.

He began to work with Kurosawa during the war, and Mori's international fame came when he played the husband in *Rashomon*. Despite the rather static acting style demanded by Mori's role (contrasting with the stormy performances of Mifune and Kyo), he projected an intensity at least equaling that of the more dramatic characters. As Myshkin in Kurosawa's adaptation of *The Idiot*, Mori created a character of sublime purity, enriched by his strong theater background. Especially skillful with his sense of timing and subtle expressions which made this almost nonhuman abstract character so convincing.

Of his several roles in Naruse's films, the most representative is that of the middle-aged man in *Ukigumo*. Mori played a disillusioned intellectual constantly betraying the heroine, who cannot leave him. This fatalistic character became incredibly rich and even sympathetic despite his negative aspects, as Mori created a sort of sincerity of the weak man in him. His achievement elicited an enthusiastic response from the critics and audience. For Mizoguchi, Mori portrayed the potter enchanted by the ghost princess in *Ugetsu monogatari* and the loving Emperor in *Yokihi*. The former role portrayed the extreme form of the doomed lover, contrasting with the calm style of the pure lover in the latter film. In both cases, Mori gave solid, well-rounded performances despite the director's harsh pursuit of realism.

In addition to the role of disillusioned intellectual, Mori was also admired as a romantic lover (Gosho's *Banka*), a simple but humanistic laborer (Naruse's *Ani imoto*), a poor *Ainu* man victimized by discrimination (Naruse's *Kotan no kuchibue*), and others in a wide range of melodrama, social drama, and comedy.

—Kyoko Hirano

MOZHUKIN, Ivan

Nationality: Russian. **Born:** Ivan Ilyitch Mozhukin in Penza, 26 September 1887 (some sources give 1889); adopted the spelling Mosjoukine in France. **Education:** Studied law at the University of Moscow, two years. **Family:** Married 1) the actress Nathalie Lissenko; 2) Agnes Peterson; illegitimate son: the writer Romain Gary. **Career:** 1910—actor with stage company in Kiev, also toured in the provinces; 1911—moved to Moscow: became famous for his roles in Dumas's *Kean* and Rostand's *L'Aiglon*; film debut in *The Kreutzer Sonata*; then made films for the Khanyonkov studios and for the director Evgeni Bauer; 1915—began long association with the director Yakov Protazanov; formed production company with Protazanov and the producer Joseph Ermoliev; 1917-19—during the revolution, Ermoliev relocated the company in Yalta, then in Istanbul and Paris; company re-formed as Société des Films Ermoliev; 1921—directed the film *L'Enfant du carneval*. **Died:** In Neuilly, France, 17 January 1939.

Films as Actor:

1911   *Kreitzerova sonata* (*The Kreutzer Sonata*) (Chardynin); *Zhizn na Tzarya* (*A Life for the Czar*) (Goncharov); *Oborono Sevastopolya* (*The Defense of Sebastopol*) (Goncharov) (as Napoleon III)

1912   *Kubok zhizhni i smerti* (*The Cup of Life and Death*) (Hansen); *Mirele Efros* (Gai); *Bratya razbotchniki* (*Brother Brigands*) (Goncharov); *Strasnia pokoynik* (*The Redoubtable Deceased*) (Yuriev); *Snotchak* (*The Daughter-in-Law*) (Gai); *Chelovek, drama nachidnya* (*Man: A Modern Drama*) (Chardynin); *Bratya* (*Brothers*) (Chardynin); *Krestyanskaya dolia* (*A Peasant's Fate*) (Goncharov); *Rabotchaia slobodka* (*Workers' Quarters*) (Goncharov); *Voina i mir* (*War and Peace*) (Chardynin); *Givoi troup* (*The Living Corpse*) (Chardynin); *Dourman* (*Vertigo*) (Chardynin); *Falchivi koupon* (*The False Note*) (Chardynin)

1913   *Tchaz Boulat* (Goncharov); *Gorre Sarri* (*The Sorrows of Sarah*) (Arkatov); *Pianstvo i yevo pozledstvia* (*Drunkenness and Its Consequences*) (Dvoretsky); *Obryv* (*The Precipice*) (Chardynin); *Domik v Kolomna* (*The Little House in Kolomn*) (Chardynin); *Vot mchitza troika potchtovaia* (*The Troika*) (Bauer); *Diadiouskina kvartira* (*In the Maiden's Room*) (Bauer); *Straschnaia miest* (*Terrible Vengeance*) (Starevitch); *Notch pered Rozdestvom* (*Christmas Eve*) (Starevitch) (as the Devil)

1914   *Revnost* (*Jealousy*) (Chardynin); *V roukatch bespotchadnogo roka* (*In the Hands of a Pitiless Destiny*) (as Chardynin); *Zhemtshina zavtrastchevo dnia* (*Woman of Tomorrow*) (Chardynin); *Ditya bolchogo goroda* (*Children of the City*) (Bauer); *Krisantemi* (*Chrysanthemums*) (Chardynin); *Tainstvennie nekto* (*The Beggar*) (Chardynin); *Sorvanetch* (*The Ballad*) (Chardynin); *Ty pomnis li?* (*Do You Remember?*) (Chardynin); *Shazka o spiatchek* (*Sleeping Beauty*) (Bauer); *V polnotch na kladbische* (*At Midnight in the Tomb*) (Bauer); *Rozdennie polzat utat ne mozet* (*The Silent Witnesses*) (Bauer); *Zlatcha notch* (*The Terrible Night*) (Bauer); *Zhizn na smerti* (*Life in Death*) (Bauer); *Slava nam, smert vragam!* (*Glory to Me, Death to the Enemy!*) (Bauer); *Taina Germanskovo posolstva* (*The Secrets of the German Ambassador*) (Bauer); *Ei gerochsky podvig* (*His Heroic Action; Honor of the Nation*) (Bauer)

1915   *Ruslan i Ludmila* (*Ruslan and Ludmila*) (Starevitch); *Natasha Rostova* (Chardynin); *Vlast tmy* (*The Powers of Darkness*) (Chardynin); *Vozrozhdennia* (*Resurrection*) (Chardynin); *Potop* (*The Deluge*) (Chardynin); *Klub nravstvennosti* (*The Suicide Club*) (Bauer); *Petersburgskiya trushchobi* (*Petersburg Slums*) (Protazanov and Gardin); *Komedia smerti* (*The Comedy of Death*) (Chardynin); *Nikolai Stavrogin* (Protazanov); *Taina niegorodskoi yamarki* (*The Mysteries of the Novgorod Fair*) (Protazanov); *Vot vspynulo utro* (*The Other Love*) (Sabinsky); *Vsyou zhizn pod maskoi* (*Life behind a Mask*) (Sabinsky); *Deti Vanyousina* (*The Girl of Vaniousine*) (Protazanov); *Para gnedych* (*Diary of a Madman*) (Protazanov); *Kaitchka* (*The Seagull*) (Protazanov); *Smerti doma* (*The House of Death*) (Protazanov); *The Silent Bell-Ringer* (Protazanov); *Vo vlasti gretcha* (*Under the Yoke of Sin*) (Protazanov and Asagarov)

1916   *Lyubov silna na strastyou potseluya* (*The Strange Passion of a Kiss*) (Sabinsky); *V boynoi slepote strastei* (*Blind Passion*) (Sabinsky); *Zhizn mig iskusstvo vetchno* (*Life Is Short but Art Is Eternal*) (Sabinsky); *A shchastiya bylo tak vozmotzno* (*And Happiness Will Be Possible*) (Asagarov); *Uchveli uzh davno krisantemi v sadu* (*When the Chrysanthemums Fade*) (Arkatov); *Pikovaya dama* (*The Queen of Spades*) (Protazanov); *Zhenshchina s kinzhalom* (*Woman with a Dagger*) (Protazanov); *Shkval* (*The Squall*) (Protazanov); *Le Parlementaire* (Volkov); *Na viershina slavy* (*The Height of Glory*) (Volkov); *Kulissi ekrana* (*Behind the Screen*) (Volkov) (+ sc); *Tanyets smerti* (*Danse Macabre*) (Protazanov) (+ sc); *Ugolok* (*The Right Sort*) (Sabinsky)

1916-17 *Grekh* (*Sin*) (Protazanov and Asagarov—serial) (+ co-sc)

1917 *Prokuror* (*Public Prosecutor*) (Protazanov) (+ sc); *Otets i syn* (*Father and Son*) (Perestiani); *Torguvi dom Karski* (*Karsky and Company*) (Sabinsky); *Dots Izrila* (*The Idol*; *The Daughter of Israel*) (Tourjansky); *Andrei Kozhukhov* (Protazanov); *Ni nado kruvi* (*Blood Need Not Be Spilled*) (Volkov); *Prokliatiye millioni* (*Cursed Millions*) (Protazanov); *Satana likuyushchii* (*Satan Triumphant*) (Protazanov) (+ co-sc); *Otets Sergii* (*Father Sergius*) (Protazanov)

1918 *Taina korolevy* (*The Queen's Secret*) (Protazanov)

1919 *Justice d'abord* (*The Public Prosecutor*) (Protazanov) (+ sc); *La Nuit du 11 Septembre* (Protazanov); *L'Angoissante Aventure* (*The Agonizing Adventure*) (Protazanov)

1921 *Tempêtes* (Boudrioz)

1922 *La Maison du mystère* (Volkov—serial)

1924 *Kean* (*Edmund Kean—Prince among Lovers*) (Volkov); *Les Ombres qui passent* (Nadejdine and Asagarov); *Le Lion des Mogols* (Epstein) (+ sc)

1925 **Feu Mathias Pascal** (*The Late Mathias Pascal*; *The Living Dead Man*) (L'Herbier)

1926 *Michel Strogoff* (*Michael Strogoff*) (Tourjansky)

1927 *Casanova* (Volkov); *The Surrender* (Sloman)

1928 *Der Präsident* (*The President*) (Righelli); *Der geheime Kurier* (*Le Rouge et le noir*) (Righelli)

1929 *Adjudant des Zaren* (*Au service du Tsar*) (Striljevsky); *Manolescu* (*Manolesco, roi des voleurs*) (Tourjansky)

1930 *Der weisse Teufel* (*The White Devil*) (Volkov)

1931 *Le Sergent X* (Striljevsky)

1932 *La Mille et Deuxième Nuits* (Volkov)

1933 *Les Amours de Casanova* (Barberis)

1934 *L'Enfant du carnaval* (Volkov) (+ sc)

1936 *Nitchevo* (de Baroncelli)

Films as Director:

1921 *L'Enfant du carnaval* (+ sc, ro)

1923 *Le Brasier ardent* (co-d, + sc, ro)

Publications

By MOZHUKIN: book—

Quand j'etais Michel Strogoff, with Jean Arroy, Paris, n.d.

Ivan Mozhukin in *Otets Sergii*

On MOZHUKIN: books—

Arroy, Jean, *Ivan Mosjoukine*, Paris, 1927.
Gary, Romain, *Promesse à l'aube*, Paris, 1959, translated as *Promise at Dawn*, New York, 1962.
Tsivian, Yuri, and others, *Silent Witnesses: Russian Films 1908-1919*, London and Pordenone, 1989.

On MOZHUKIN: articles—

Mitry, Jean, "Ivan Mosjoukine," in *Anthologie du cinéma*, vol. 2, Paris, 1968
O'Leary, Liam, "Ivan Mosjoukine," in *Silent Picture* (London), Summer and Winter 1969.
Flickers, January 1980.
Classic Images (Indiana, Pennsylvania), November 1982.

*   *   *

Ivan Mozhukin was always more than an actor. He was a man of the cinema, a very remarkable actor, scriptwriter, and director. Of his two careers one was as leading star of the Czarist cinema, matinee idol, and focal point of an early Russian film culture. The early Russian cinema was perfervid, highly emotional, and melodramatic. It also drew on classic Russian writers. Its standards were high, and it produced directors of the caliber of Volkov, Protazanov, Bauer, and Tourjansky. Many of its actors were later to enrich the cinema of Western Europe. When the Ermoliev company emigrated in 1919 with their actors, designers, and cameramen, Mozhukin came with them, adopting the name "Mosjoukine," by which he is best known.

Mozhukin was born in Penza in 1887 and was intended for a law career. Drawn to the stage, he gained experience in provincial and Moscow theaters and soon drifted into films. In many of these his leading lady was his wife, the talented Nathalie Lissenko. His first film, in 1911, was *The Kreutzer Sonata*. In 1913 he had the good luck to be directed by Evgeni Bauer, who influenced his acting style, giving it subtlety and depth. In 1915 he joined the Ermoliev company with whose destiny he was to be closely linked. Outstanding films of 1916 were Arkatov's *When the Chrysanthemums Fade*, Protazanov's *The Queen of Spades*, and Volkov's *Behind the Screen*, with a script by Mozhukin. 1917 was a critical year for Russia but Mozhukin registered some of his greatest successes, *Public Prosecutor*, *Satan Triumphant*, and *Father Sergius*. In the last film, based on Tolstoy and directed by Protazanov, Mozhukin gave a virtuoso performance as the young officer who becomes a monk and resists in his old age the temptations of the flesh. His last Russian film was an adaptation of Elinor Glynn's novel *Three Weeks*, retitled *The Queen's Secret*. The Ermoliev company, having relocated in Yalta, fled from there to France via Istanbul. The film *L'Angoissante Aventure* was made en route and finished in Paris. Mozhukin, Lissenko, and Nicolai Koline were its leading players, and it was directed by Protazanov. It is about a lighthearted young man-about-town who has a run of bad luck and experiences misery and dejection. It gave Mozhukin an opportunity for a versatile performance. The Russians settled in the old studios of Montreuil near Paris and Protazanov directed a remake of *Public Prosecutor* under the title *Justice d'abord*. In Volkov's serial *La Maison du mystère* he established his French reputation and himself directed *L'Enfant du carnaval*. His most striking work as a director, was however, in the avant-garde *Le Brasier ardent*, a delightful comedy, dreamlike in its fantasy, in which he played a whole range of characters.

Alexander Kamenka continued the work of Ermoliev with his Albatros company for which many brilliant young French directors worked. In *Kean*, based on the life of the great English tragedian, Mozhukin had a wonderful opportunity to bring the story of the actor to life and interpret Hamlet and Romeo, even if in silent mime. Jean

Epstein directed him in *Le Lion des Moguls* with designs by Bilinsky. L'Herbier's *Le Feu Mathias Pascal* gave him a Pirandello role which he played with memorable skill. *Michel Strogoff* by Tourjansky introduced him to the world's screens in a spectacular film widely distributed by Universal. Volkov's *Casanova*, also handled by Universal gave him similar exposure but a visit to Hollywood was not a success, and Edward Sloman's *The Surrender* did not enhance his reputation. He now played in several German films, *Manolescu*, directed by Tourjansky, and *Le Rouge et le noir* by Righelli, featuring Agnes Peterson whom he married, deserting his old partner Nathalie Lissenko. It is interesting to note that he was first choice for Gance's *Napoléon* but chose instead to take the role of *Michel Strogoff*.

He appeared in Volkov's sound film *Der weisse Teufel* (based on Tolstoy's *Hadshi Murad*) with some success, but from now on his star was in decline. Inferior remakes of past successes and minor roles in French films followed, and the once proud Russian star drifted into poverty and obscurity. He died destitute in the public ward of a Neuilly hospital and is buried with the brother Alexander in the lovely Russian Orthodox graveyard of Ste. Geneviève du Bois just south of Paris. He was a giant among silent screen actors, refined in his playing and dynamic and haunting in his personality. The second title of his great film *Kean* was *Désordre et genie* and that, alas, was true of him. He lived life to the fullest. Everyone I had asked who had known him always said "Mosjoukine, il etait fou."

—Liam O'Leary

MUELLER-STAHL, Armin

Nationality: German. **Born:** Tilsit, East Prussia (now Sovetsk, Russia), 17 December 1930. **Education:** Studied violin at Berlin Conservatory; attended drama school, starting in 1952. **Family:** Married Gabriele Scholz, 1973, son: Christian. **Career:** Concert violinist, then became actor; 1954—began long association with the Volksbühne, Berlin; 1956—film debut in *Heimliche Ehen*; 1960—in TV series *Fluchte aus der Hölle*; 1965—in TV mini-series, *Wolf unter Wölfen*, *Wege übers Land*, 1968, *and Die sieben Affären der Dona Juanita*, 1973; 1976—blacklisted from East German show business because of political activities; 1980—having been encouraged to leave the country, emigrated with family to West Germany; 1981—West German film debut in Fassbinder's *Lola*; in TV mini-series *Collin*, *Wohin und zurück*, 1984, *Jokehnen oder Wie lange fährtman von Ostpreussen nach Deutschland?*, 1987, and *Amerika (Topeka, Kansas . . . USSR)*, also 1987; 1989—American film debut in Costa-Gavras's *Music Box*, continued to work in Hollywood thereafter. **Awards:** Deutscher Filmpreis for Acting, for *Lola*, 1982; Silver Bear, Berlin Film Festival, for *Utz*, 1993. **Address:** Gartnweg 31, 2430 Sirksdorf, Germany. **Agent:** Paul Kohner, Inc., 9169 Sunset Boulevard, Los Angeles, CA 90069, U.S.A.

Films as Actor:

1956 *Heimliche Ehen* (*The Secret Marriage*) (Wagenheim)
1960 *Fünf Patronenhülsen* (Beyer) (as the Frenchman)
1962 *Königskinder* (Beyer); *. . . und deine Liebe auch* (Vogel)
1963 *Nackt unter Wölfen* (*Naked among the Wolves*) (Beyer) (as Höfel); *Christine* (Dudow)
1964 *Alaskafüchse* (Wallroth); *Preludio 11* (Maetzig)
1967 *Ein Lord am Alexander-Platz* (Reisch)
1970 *Tödlicher Irrtum* (Petzold)
1972 *Der Dritte* (*The Third*; *The Blind Man*) (Günter) (as the blind man); *Januskopf* (Maetzig)

1973 *Die Hosen des Ritters von Bredow* (Petzold)
1974 *Kit & Co.—Lockruf des Goldes* (Petzold)
1975 *Jakob der Lügner* (*Jacob the Liar*) (Beyer) (as Roman Schtamm)
1976 *Nelken in Aspik* (Reisch)
1977 *Die Flucht* (*The Flight*) (Gräf) (as Dr. Volkmar Schmith)
1978 *Geschlossene Gesellschaft* (Beyer—for TV) (as Robert)
1980 *Die längste Sekunda* (Kühn—for TV)
1981 **Lola** (Fassbinder) (as Von Bohm); *An uns glaubt Gott nicht mehr* (for TV); *Der Wessten leuchtet* (*Lite Trap*) (Schilling) (as Harald Liebe); *Ja und Nein* (Tölle—for TV)
1982 *Die Sehnsucht der Veronika Voss* (*Veronika Voss*) (Fassbinder) (as Max Rehbein); *Viadukt* (*Matushka*) (Sandor) (as Tetzlaff); *Un Dimanche de flics* (*A Cop's Sunday*) (Vicines) (as the lawyer); *Ich werde warten* (Barabas—for TV); *Die Gartenlaube* (Ballmann—for TV); *Die Flügel der Nacht* (*Wings of Night*) (Noever) (as Gödel); *Flucht aus Pommern* (*Flight from Pomerania*) (Schubert—for TV) (as Lyssek); *Der Fall Sylvester matuska* (Simo—for TV); *Ausgestossen* (Corti—for TV); *An uns glaubt Gott nicht mehr* (Corti—for TV)
1983 *Glut* (*Glut im Herzen*; *Embers*) (Koerfer) (as François Korb/ Andres Korb); *Eine Liebe im Deutschland* (*A Love in Germany*; *Un Amour en Allemagne*) (Wajda) (as SS-Untersturmfuhrer Mayer); *L'Homme blesse* (Chereau) (as Father); *Trauma* (Kubach) (as Sam); *Ruhe sanft, Bruno* (Gies—for TV)
1984 *Die Mitläufer* (*Following the Fuhrer*) (Leiser) (as Kurz); *Tausend Augen* (*Thousand Eyes*) (Blumenberg) (as Arnold); *Tatort—Freiwild* (Staudte—for TV) (as Dr. Konrad Ansbach); *Rita Ritter* (Achternbusch)
1985 *Der Angriff der Gegenwart aud die Ubrige Zeit* (*The Blind Director*) (Kluge) (as Blind Movie Director); *Zabudnite na Mozarta* (*Vergesst Mozart*; *Forget Mozart!*) (Luther) (as Count Pergen); *Redl Ezredes* (*Oberst Redl*; *Colonel Redl*) (Szabó) (as Crown Prince Franz-Josef); *An uns glaubt Gott nicht mehr* (*God Doesn't Believe in Us Anymore*) (Corti) (as Gandhi)
1986 *Bittere Ernte* (*Angry Harvest*) (Agnieszka Holland) (as Leon); *Hautnah* (Schulze-Rohr—for TV); *Unser Mann im Dschungel* (*The Jungle Mission*) (Steiner and Stripp—for TV) (as Mr. Kehlmann); *Momo* (Schaaf) (as Chief Grey Man); *Der Fall Franza* (*Franza*) (Schwarzenberger—for TV) (as Dr. Jordan/Dr. Korener); *Gauner im Paradies* (Fantl—for TV); *Auf den Tag genau* (Laehn)
1987 *Der Joker* (*Lethal Obsession*) (Patzak) (as Axel Baumgartner)
1988 *Das Spinnennets* (*Spider's Web*) (Wicki) (as Baron von Rastschuk); *Der Gorilla* (Rusnale); *Tagebuch für einen Mörder* (Gottlieb—for TV) (as Max Telligan)
1989 *Music Box* (Costa-Gavras) (as Michael Laszlo); *Midnight Cop* (*Killing Blue*) (Patzak) (as Inspector Alex Glas); *Schweinegold* (Kückelmann); *Ein Märchen der Gebruder Nimm Schweinegold* (*C.A.S.H.: A Political Fairy Tale*) (as Maxwell); *A Hecc* (*Just for Kicks*) (as Marno)
1990 *Avalon* (Levinson) (as Sam Krichinsky)
1991 *Kafka* (Soderbergh) (as Inspector Grubach); "New York" ep. of *Night on Earth* (Jarmusch) (as Helmut Grokenberger); *Bronsteins Kinder* (*Bronstein's Children*) (Kawalerowicz) (as Arno Bronstein)
1992 *The Power of One* (Avildsen) (as Doc); *Far from Berlin* (McNally) (as Otto Linder)
1993 *Utz* (Sluizer) (as Baron Kaspar Joachim von Utz); *Der Kinoerzaehler* (*The Movie Teller*) (Sinkel) (as the movie teller); *The House of the Spirits* (August) (as Severo)
1994 *Holy Matrimony* (Nimoy) (as Uncle Wilhelm); *The Last Good Time* (Balaban) (as Joseph Kopple)

1995 *A Pyromaniac's Love Story* (Brand) (as Mr. Linzer); *T. Rex* (*Theodore Rex*) (Betuel)
1996 *Taxandria* (Servais)

Publications

By MUELLER-STAHL: books—

Verordneter Sonntag (novel; title means "Lost Sunday"), Berlin, 1981.
Drehtage: Music Box *und* Avalon, Frankfurt, 1991.

On MUELLER-STAHL: book—

Hölzl, Gebhard, and Thomas Lassonczyk, *Armin Mueller-Stahl: seine Filme, sein Leben*, Munich, 1992.

On MUELLER-STAHL: articles—

Walsh, Michael, "A Star Is Reborn," in *Premiere* (New York), November 1990.
Farrell, Mary H. J., and Franz Spelman, "Emerging from behind the Iron Curtain, Armin Mueller-Stahl Finds Freedom—and Stardom in *Avalon*," in *People Weekly* (New York), 12 November 1990.
Rother, H.-J., "Drehtage *Music Box* und *Avalon*," in *EPD Film* (Frankfurt, Germany), July 1991.

*   *   *

Armin Mueller-Stahl's acting career began in East Germany with theatrical roles in a romantic vein: Romeo in *Romeo and Juliet*, the Prince in Lessing's *Emilia Galotti*, and Andrei in the stage version of *War and Peace*. In 1956 he made his cinema debut, and has subsequently had the opportunity to display his rare talent for projecting highly dramatic characters who unite the tragic and the everyday, the romantic and the down-to-earth.

He first attracted notice in the role of the Frenchman in *Fünf Patronenhülsen* by Frank Beyer (Mueller-Stahl was to appear in many of Beyer's later films). In the story of a group of soldiers forced to try and make their way out of an ambush during the Spanish Civil War, Mueller-Stahl was praised for the realism of his performance and for the fluidity and at the same time restraint of his dramatic talent. His part in the 1960 television series *Flucht aus der Hölle* brought him tremendous acclaim. His success was confirmed in the film version of Bruno Apiz's novel *Nackt unter Wölfen* in which he once again worked with Beyer as well as Erwin Geschonek. Hefel (Mueller-Stahl) sacrifices himself with dignity in order to save the Jewish child whom the prisoners have hidden in the beech woods.

After having been blacklisted in East Germany for his political activities, Mueller-Stahl was encouraged to emigrate, whereupon he took his family to West Germany. Although virtually unknown in the West, he soon worked with Fassbinder in *Lola* and *Die Sehnsucht der Veronika Voss*—films that formed a part of the director's great fresco in which he attempted to depict the social and spiritual development of Germany from the war years to the present. In *Lola* Mueller-Stahl laconically traces, almost as if from a distance, the downfall of a city administrator who becomes prey to the seductions of Lola (an obvious allusion to Josef von Sternberg's *The Blue Angel*) and the temptations of money and corruption.

In 1983 Mueller-Stahl reached a high point in his dramatic career with the film *Glut*, which deals with one of the central themes of the Swiss cinema: the wound left behind in the national consciousness by Swiss neutrality during World War II. Mueller-Stahl has a double role as a father, an arms producer actively involved with the Fascists in Germany, and his son, who bears the spiritual "wound" of his child-

857

hood. The family seem prosperous and content, but they are not spared the tragedy of war: the grandfather, a colonel in the Swiss Reserves, dies while trying to save a Polish prisoner of war, and the arms factory is shelled by the Allies. The son is made painfully aware of his "wound" when he meets a girl who was taken into a comfortable Swiss home during the war years—a little Polish girl, saved from annihilation in the ghetto and now grown into a beautiful, independent woman (Krystyna Janda). The collapse of a human life is shown here by Mueller-Stahl with great realism, and at the same time with that distancing irony that characterizes his best screen roles.

In the late 1980s, Hollywood discovered Mueller-Stahl, who soon played two astonishingly different characters in two of his first American films, Costa-Gavras's *Music Box* and Barry Levinson's *Avalon*. In the former he had to learn English and take on a Hungarian accent as a Nazi war criminal who has spent decades as a patriotic immigrant in the United States before his past crimes come to light. In the latter Mueller-Stahl spiced his English with some Yiddish to touchingly capture the patriarch of an extended family of Jewish immigrants to America who is unable to hold the family together against the strong currents of suburbanization and American culture. After a supporting role as an inspector in Steven Soderbergh's somewhat disappointing *Kafka*, Mueller-Stahl had an endearing comic role as the just-off-the-boat immigrant taxi driver who can barely drive or speak English but finds a friendly face in a streetwise Brooklynite fare in the "New York" episode of Jim Jarmusch's wildly uneven *Night on Earth*. Of special of note is Mueller-Stahl's deft touch at capturing his character's amazement at the sights he sees on the way to Brooklyn—it is little wonder that so many of his characters for Hollywood have been immigrants. His best later career role to date, however, is not in any of his Hollywood films, but in the international co-production *Utz*, directed by George Sluizer and based on the novel by Bruce Chatwin. Here Mueller-Stahl brings to vivid life a very eccentric Czechoslovak baron whose life obsession is collecting porcelain figurines. (The actor's son Christian also appears, portraying the baron at age 18.)

—Maria Racheva, updated by David E. Salamie

MUNI, Paul

Nationality: American. **Born:** Muni Weisenfreund in Lemberg, Austria (now Lvov, Ukraine), 22 September 1895; emigrated with his family to the United States, 1902. **Family:** Married Bela Finkel, 1921. **Career:** 1908—first stage appearance in *Two Corpses at Breakfast*, Cleveland; beginning 1910—toured with Samuel Grossman's theater troupe; 1914-17—worked with burlesque company, Philadelphia; 1917-18—worked with Molly Picon's company, Boston; 1918—joined Yiddish Art Theatre in New York; became star of Yiddish theater in 1920s; 1926—Broadway debut in *We Americans*; 1929—first film appearance in *The Valiant*; 1932—contract with Warner Brothers; 1939—on Broadway in *Key Largo*; 1955—stage success in *Inherit the Wind*. **Awards:** Best Actor, Academy Award, and Best Actor, Venice Festival, for *The Story of Louis Pasteur*, 1936; Best Actor, New York Film Critics, for *The Life of Emile Zola*, 1937. **Died:** In Santa Barbara, California, 25 August 1967.

Films as Actor:

1929   *The Valiant* (Howard) (as Dyke); *Seven Faces* (Viertel) (as Papa Chibou)
1932   *Scarface* (Hawks) (as Tony Camonte); *I Am a Fugitive from a Chain Gang* (LeRoy) (as James Allen)

1933   *The World Changes* (LeRoy) (as Nordholm)
1934   *Hi, Nellie!* (LeRoy)
1935   *Bordertown* (Mayo) (as Johnny Rodriguez); *Black Fury* (Curtiz) (as Joe Radek); *Dr. Socrates* (Dieterle) (title role); *The Story of Louis Pasteur* (Dieterle) (title role)
1937   *The Good Earth* (Franklin) (as Wang Lung); *The Woman I Love* (Litvak) (as Lieutenant Claude Maury); *The Life of Emile Zola* (Dieterle) (title role)
1939   *Juarez* (Dieterle) (as Benito Pablo Juarez); *We Are Not Alone* (Goulding) (as Dr. David Newcome)
1940   *Hudson's Bay* (Pichel) (as Pierre Radisson)
1942   *The Commandos Strike at Dawn* (Farrow) (as Eric Torensen)
1943   *Stage Door Canteen* (Borzage) (as himself)
1944   *A Song to Remember* (Charles Vidor) (as Joseph Elsner)
1945   *Counter-Attack* (Zoltan Korda) (as Alexei Kulkov)
1946   *Angel on My Shoulder* (Mayo) (as Eddie Kagle)
1952   *Imbarco a mezzanotte* (*Embarkation at Midnight*; *Stranger on the Prowl*; *Encounter*) (Losey) (as The Man)
1959   *The Last Angry Man* (Daniel Mann) (as Dr. Sam)

Publications

By MUNI: articles—

"Paul Muni Interviews Himself," in *Motion Picture Magazine* (New York), December 1933.
"Hollywood Is the World's Melting Pot," as told to Gladys Hall, in *Movie Classic*, November 1936.

On MUNI: books—

Lawrence, Jerome, *Actor: The Life and Times of Paul Muni*, New York, 1974.
Druxman, Michael B., *Paul Muni—His Life and Films*, New York, 1974
Parish, James Robert, *The Tough Guys*, New Rochelle, New York, 1976.
Wallis, Hal, and Charles Higham, *Starmaker*, New York, 1980.

On MUNI: articles—

Cooley, Donald G., "They Tried to Make a Chaney Out of Muni," in *Movie Classic*, April 1935.
Best, Katherine, "Danger: Man at Work," in *Stage*, 1 April 1939.
Eustis, Morton, "Paul Muni," in *Theatre Arts* (New York), March 1940.
Current Biography 1944, New York, 1944.
Jacobs, Jack, "Paul Muni," in *Films in Review* (New York), November 1961.
Obituary, in *New York Times*, 26 August 1967.
Kazan, Elia, in *Positif* (Paris), October 1989.

On Muni: film—

Actor: The Paul Muni Story, 1978.

*   *   *

During the 1930s Paul Muni was one of the most respected names in acting. He was a perfectionist and extremely selective in the scripts he would choose to do. (Muni's contracts at both Fox and Warner Brothers gave him script approval.)

Once a script was agreed upon, Muni required months to research his character and prepare for his performance. If the character was a historical figure, he would read every available book on the subject. If the character required a certain dialect, he would rehearse into a recorder until he was satisfied with his accent. Once filming began he

Paul Muni

would remain in character between takes and even when he was off the studio lot. Muni would literally become the person in the script, which helped to build his reputation as one of the finest character actors of his time.

Muni began his acting career on the Yiddish stage in New York City. As a teenager he developed an affinity for makeup and often played characters much older than his real years. In 1926 he appeared on Broadway in *We Americans* which brought him to the attention of Hollywood. He started at Fox, and his first film, *The Valiant*, brought him his first of four Academy nominations. Unfortunately, the film bombed at the box office. His second film, *Seven Faces*, was also a financial failure. During the production of *Scarface* the project received a lot of criticism from the censors. Their main objection was the glorification of the gangster, so the studio added a subtitle to the film—"the shame of the nation." When the film was finally released, it was a huge box-office success, and Muni decided to remain in Hollywood to make more films. (His new contract with Warner Brothers also allowed him to act on the stage between pictures.)

Muni's next film was *I Am a Fugitive from a Chain Gang*, based on the autobiography of Robert E. Burns. The film not only was a critical and financial success (both the film and Muni received Academy nominations), but also helped bring about public awareness of prison conditions in the south. Needless to say, the southern portion of the country did not take well to the film.

Muni's next milestone picture was *The Story of Louis Pasteur*. It took some good arguing on the part of Muni, the producer Henry Blanke, and the director William Dieterle to persuade Warner Brothers to back the film. The studio finally agreed, although they consented with a minimum budget and shooting schedule. The film was the sleeper of the year, and Muni won an Oscar for his role. After this film Muni appeared in several other historical films, such as *The Life of Emile Zola* and *Juarez*.

Although Muni did not make many pictures during his career (23 in all), he did appear in several significant films. *Scarface* was the first (and often considered to be the best) of the major gangster films of the 1930s. Other films, such as *I Am a Fugitive from a Chain Gang* and *Black Fury* dealt with social injustice, while historical films (although often containing more fiction than fact) were promoted as "important" and prestigious pictures. All of these films are based on strong leading characters, and Muni's ability to give substance to these parts helped to create several memorable roles for the screen.

—Linda J. Obalil

MURPHY, Eddie

Nationality: American. **Born:** Edward Regan Murphy in Brooklyn, New York, 3 April 1961. **Education:** Attended Roosevelt High School. **Family:** Married Nicole Mitchell, 1993, children: Bria, Miles Mitchell, Shayne Audra. **Career:** 1976—first public performance at a youth center on Long Island; 1980-84—regular on *Saturday Night Live* for NBC TV; 1982—film debut in *48 HRS.*; 1985—signed multifilm deal with Paramount; formed own film production company; 1986—formed Eddie Murphy Television Enterprises; 1989—directed first film, *Harlem Nights.* **Address:** c/o Eddie Murphy Productions, Inc., 152 West 57th Street, 47th Floor, New York, NY 10019, U.S.A.

Films as Actor:

1982 *48 HRS.* (Walter Hill) (as Reggie Hammond)
1983 *Trading Places* (Landis) (as Billy Ray Valentine)

1984 *Best Defense* (Huyck) (as Landry); *Beverly Hills Cop* (Brest) (as Axel Foley)
1986 *The Golden Child* (Ritchie) (as Chandler Jarrell)
1987 *Beverly Hills Cop II* (Tony Scott) (as Axel Foley, + story); *Eddie Murphy Raw* (concert performance)
1988 *Coming to America* (Landis) (as Prince Akeem/Clarence/Saul/ Randy Watson, + story)
1990 *Another 48 HRS.* (Walter Hill) (as Reggie Hammond)
1992 *The Distinguished Gentleman* (Lynn) (as Thomas Jefferson Johnson); *Boomerang* (Hudlin) (as Marcus Graham, + story)
1994 *Beverly Hills Cop III* (Landis) (as Axel Foley)
1995 *Vampire in Brooklyn* (Craven) (as Maximillian/Preacher Pauley/Guido, + pr)
1996 *The Nutty Professor*; *The Metro* (+ pr)

Film as Actor and Director:

1989 *Harlem Nights* (as Quick, + exec pr, sc)

Other Film:

1990 *The Kid Who Loved Christmas* (exec pr)

Publications

By MURPHY: articles—

Interviews in *Time Out* (London), 1 December 1983 and 6 July 1988.
Interview in *Jet* (Chicago), 18 March 1985.
Interview in *Photoplay* (London), May 1985.
Interview in *Interview* (New York), September 1987.
Interview with Bill Zehme, in *Rolling Stone* (New York), 24 August 1989.
Interview with David Rensin, in *Playboy* (Chicago), February 1990.
Interview with Walter Leavy, in *Ebony* (Chicago), June 1994.

On MURPHY: books—

Ruuth, Marianne, *Eddie: Eddie Murphy from A to Z*, Los Angeles, 1985.
Gross, Edward, *The Films of Eddie Murphy*, Las Vegas, Nevada, 1990.
Wilburn, Deborah A., *Eddie Murphy*, New York, 1993.

On MURPHY: articles—

Current Biography 1983, New York, 1983.
Corliss, Richard, "The Good Little Bad Little Boy," in *Time* (New York), 11 July 1983.
Connelly, Christopher, "Eddie Murphy Leaves Home," in *Rolling Stone* (New York), 12 April 1984.
Hibbin, S., "Eddie Murphy," in *Films and Filming* (London), December 1984.
"Inside Moves," in *Esquire* (New York), January 1985.
Berkoff, Steven, in *Time Out* (London), 1 February 1985.
Grenier, Richard, "Eddie Murphy, American," in *Commentary* (New York), March 1985.
Townsend, Robert, "Eddie, the Black Pack and Me," in *American Film* (Washington, D.C.), December 1987.
Ehrenstein, David, "The Color of Laughter," in *American Film* (New York), September 1988.
"Three Generations of Black Comedy," in *Ebony* (Chicago), January 1990.

Eddie Murphy in *Trading Places*

Schickel, Richard, "In Search of Eddie Murphy: The Gifts that Made Him a Star Have Disappeared into Self-Parody," in *Time* (New York), 25 June 1990.

Richardson, John H., "Murphy's Law," in *Premiere* (New York), January 1992.

Richmond, Peter, "Trading Places," in *GQ* (New York), July 1992.

Stivers, Cyndi, "Murphy's Law," in *Premiere* (New York), August 1992.

Brennan, J., "Murphy's Cool about Being Top Cat," in *Variety* (New York), 15 March 1993.

*   *   *

Young and ambitious, black comedian Eddie Murphy rose from the ranks of stand-up comedy and television to become one of the top box-office film stars of the 1980s only to see his career and popularity take a precipitous nosedive in the 1990s.

While still a teenager, Murphy began haunting the comedy clubs in New York City, honing his craft at night while attending school during the day. After high school, he was selected to join the cast of *Saturday Night Live*, the late-night television series that had launched the careers of celebrated comic actors John Belushi, Bill Murray, and Dan Aykroyd. The show offered a forum for Murphy to showcase his talent for mimicry as well as to develop a series of memorable characters, including Gumby, Buckwheat, and Mr. Robinson, which were biting takeoffs on television favorites from the past. A starring role opposite Nick Nolte in the action film *48 HRS.* helped to construct

his distinctive film persona—that of the sassy, self-confident, often abrasive con artist who is fast on his feet.

From *48 HRS.* to *Harlem Nights*, each of Murphy's roles has made use of this image, even the character of Officer Axel Foley in *Beverly Hills Cop* (a role originally slated for Sylvester Stallone) and its lackluster sequels, *Beverly Hills Cop II* and *III*. Like the fast-talking con-man characters in all of Murphy's films, Axel easily assumes other identities in order to get past some obstacle. Murphy's adeptness at mimicry—whether it is a recognizable character such as Buckwheat or a stereotype such as a fastidious government inspector—is his trademark. His roles emphasize this talent, which places most of his films in the category of star vehicles.

Other aspects of Murphy's comic persona, particularly as displayed in his stand-up routines earlier in his career, include a proclivity toward provocative, masculine humor. His speech is peppered with expletives and street slang, while his self-assured demeanor is assertive. Yet his comedy and his image do not threaten his white audiences. The best of Murphy's humor and the best of his film roles create a tension between the dangerously provocative and the brashly humorous: he makes a potentially volatile joke but tempers the delivery with a wide grin and a unique belly laugh.

Comparisons to Richard Pryor, the biggest black star of the last generation, are inevitable. Though Murphy claims Pryor as a major influence, profound differences mark their comedy styles and personas. Pryor's stand-up routines derive from growing up on society's margins. The characters in his routines—winos, junkies, prostitutes—are not easily adapted into mainstream television and films. Murphy grew up in a lower-middle-class neighborhood on Long Island; the primary source for many of his routines and comic impersonations is television. No matter how many four-letter words he uses, Murphy has an immediate bond with mainstream audiences who grew up with the tube.

Toward the end of the 1980s, Murphy experienced a backlash in the media. As occurs to many popular figures who suddenly become superstars, he began to be criticized by a press that had previously been friendly. Reviewers attacked such films as *Beverly Hills Cop II* and *Another 48 HRS.* for being uninspired vehicles chosen to cash in on his fame and the success of their forerunners, while stories about his numerous bodyguards, enormous wealth, and frequent womanizing added to the media-based perception that success had altered his personality. This criticism culminated in the beating he took for his vanity production *Harlem Nights,* an action comedy he wrote, co-produced, directed, and starred in. The film was poorly executed, but reviewers unfairly dismissed Murphy's interest in working behind the camera as the actions of an ego-driven superstar, conveniently forgetting that he had expressed a desire to produce and direct as far back as 1983. Suddenly, Murphy's self-confidence was deemed arrogance; his mainstream appeal was termed "a slick, Hollywood package."

All this negative press had repercussions at the box office. Murphy rebounded slightly with *The Distinguished Gentleman* in which he took his con-artist persona to Washington, D.C., to cash in on the gravy train as a freewheeling, wheeler-dealer member of the House of Representatives. The film was warmly received by reviewers for its satiric edge and was a moneymaker at the box office, albeit not in the blockbuster class of earlier Murphy films. *Boomerang*—a prefeminist

if somewhat crass comedy which traded on Murphy's image as a womanizer who, in the film, sees the error of his ways when he runs up against maneater Robin Givens—inspired neither good reviews nor good box office. A third installment in the popular *Beverly Hills Cop* series, which seemed like a sure bet, was an unexpected flop with audiences. As was *Vampire in Brooklyn,* a Wes Craven horror comedy in which Murphy played several roles, including the bloodsucker of the title. It remains to be seen if his latest effort at regaining his crown as a king of comedy, a planned remake of the Jerry Lewis vehicle *The Nutty Professor,* will do the trick.

Still relatively young, the talented comedian has come to a crossroad in his career. The critical backlash against him could result in a conscious attempt to alter his image, or, like so many other comic actors, including *Saturday Night Live* alumnus Chevy Chase, he could continue to choose roles tailored to his persona. Neither path is a guarantee for continued success.

—Susan M. Doll, updated by John McCarty

MURRAY, Bill

Nationality: American. **Born:** Evanston, Illinois, 21 September 1950. **Family:** Married Mickey Kelly, 1981, sons: Homer and Luke. **Education:** Attended Loyola Academy in Wilmette, Illinois, and Regis Col-

Bill Murray in *Scrooged*

lege, Denver, as a premed student. **Career:** Acted in plays in high school and worked summers as caddy; after droppping out of college joined his brother Brian Doyle-Murray in the Chicago improv troupe Second City, winning a scholarship to its workshop, and then traveling with its road company; appeared on radio in *The National Lampoon Radio Hour*; 1975—in off-Broadway revue *The National Lampoon Show*; 1976—on *Saturday Night Live with Howard Cosell*; 1977—gained fame on *Saturday Night Live* in its second season. **Agent:** Jay Moloney, Creative Artists Agency, 9830 Wilshire Boulevard, Beverly Hills, CA 90212, U.S.A.

Films as Actor:

1975 *Shame of the Jungle* (Picha and Szulzinger) (as voice)
1977 *Things We Did Last Summer* (Weis)
1978 *All You Need Is Cash* (*The Rutles*) (Idle and Weis—for TV) (as Bill Murray the K)
1979 *Meatballs* (Reitman) (as Tripper); *Mr. Mike's Mondo Video* (O'Donoghue); *The Main Event* (Zieff) (as Mantilla's cornerman)
1980 *Where the Buffalo Roam* (Linson) (as Dr. Hunter S. Thompson); *Caddyshack* (Ramis) (as Carl Spackler); *Loose Shoes* (Ira Miller) (as Lefty Schwartz)
1981 *Stripes* (Reitman) (as John Winger)
1982 *Tootsie* (Pollack) (as Jeff Slater, unbilled)
1984 *Nothing Lasts Forever* (Schiller) (as Lunar Cruise Director Ted Breughel); *Ghostbusters* (Reitman) (as Dr. Peter Venkman); *The Razor's Edge* (Byrum) (as Larry Darrell, + co-sc)
1986 *Little Shop of Horrors* (Oz) (as Arthur Denton)
1988 *Scrooged* (Richard Donner) (as Frank Cross); *She's Having a Baby* (John Hughes) (cameo, uncredited)
1989 *Ghostbusters II* (Reitman) (as Dr. Peter Venkman)
1991 *What about Bob?* (Oz) (as Bob Wiley)
1993 *Groundhog Day* (Ramis) (as Phil Connors); *Mad Dog and Glory* (McNaughton) (as Frank Milo)
1994 *Ed Wood* (Tim Burton) (as Bunny Breckinridge)
1996 *Kingpin*; *Space Jam* (Kahn, Pytka, and Bruce Smith); *Larger than Life*

Film as Director:

1990 *Quick Change* (co-d with Howard Franklin) (+ ro as Grimm, co-pr)

Publications

By MURRAY: articles—

Interview with Timothy Crouse, in *Rolling Stone* (New York), 16 August 1984.
Interview with Elisa Leonelli, in *Venice Magazine*, 16 March 1993.

On MURRAY: articles—

Grossberger, Lewis, "Bill Murray Making It Up as He Goes," in *Rolling Stone* (New York), 20 August 1981.
Blount, Roy Jr., "Have You Heard the One about Bill Murray and the Himalayan Women?," in *GQ* (New York), November 1984.
Chase, Chris, "Bill Murray: More than Just a Funnyman," in *Cosmopolitan*, December 1984.
Current Biography 1985, New York, 1985.

White, Timothy, "The Rumpled Anarchy of Bill Murray," in *New York Times Magazine*, 20 November 1988.
Connelly, Christopher, "The Man You Are Looking for Is Not There," in *Premiere* (New York), August 1990.
Corliss, Richard, "Bill Murray in the Driver's Seat," in *Time* (New York), 8 March 1993.
Solman, Gregory, "The Passion of Bill Murray," in *Film Comment* (New York), November/December 1993.

* * *

Like the original cast members of *Saturday Night Live*, whom he joined in 1977, Bill Murray developed his routines in response to the irradiating phoniness of post-World War II suburban culture. The Not Ready for Prime Time Players were expert at parodying the voice of both sententious and commercial fraudulence—the gelatinous precepts learned in home, school, and church (and in the homes, schools, and churches on television and in the movies), the nearly hysterical pitches of television advertising, the oiliness of show biz "intimacy." John Belushi flared out fast, while Dan Aykroyd was too manic a parodist for the big screen, and Chevy Chase quickly became another self-satisfied purveyor of low-grade product. Only Murray was able to broaden his counterculture cabaret attitude enough to be a popular movie comedian without becoming smug or another example of what he professed to despise. In the service comedy *Stripes* he took nothing seriously and still galvanized that scrappy production. In *Stripes* and the much more expensive *Ghostbusters* he used the concepts of the movies to goof on the movies themselves, without killing joy. He did his duty by *Ghostbusters* without getting implicated in the jumbo Hollywood machinations that engineered it.

He served the same function in *Tootsie* as Dustin Hoffman's roommate, in which his hilarious deadpan (and reportedly improvised) comments on Hoffman's scam turned the audience's disbelief to the movie's advantage. At the time he seemed oddly cast as an incorruptible, experimental playwright, but this does in fact tie in to Murray's deeper concerns, which for a while he had trouble bringing to the screen. The head-on approach produced *The Razor's Edge*, which Murray tried to enliven and make personal by anachronistic wisecracking in the role of the man shaken to his spiritual foundations. Murray's 1970s shtick was out of place, and he did not know how to animate Larry Darrell otherwise. But the main problem was that he seemed intellectually susceptible to a middle-brow epic like Maugham's novel in the first place; wanting to be profound he just got portentous.

Murray did come across in a slapstick turn in character (that is, a character other than his own put-on persona) in the nifty musical *Little Shop of Horrors*, but it was not until his breakthrough performance as Frank Cross in *Scrooged* that he found a way to play a fuller character in the kind of comedy that audiences wanted to see him in. He deepened his screen persona not by going around it but by going through it. Murray used this updated *Christmas Carol* to stage his career redemption—he learned how to play the emotional scenes straight without betraying his 1970s rejection of show biz fakery. He went even further as the burnt-out weatherman Phil Connors in *Groundhog Day*, allegorically doomed to replay his least favorite day of the year forever. Frank Cross is a hyperbolic monster; Phil's disgust with himself seems more life-sized, and it makes personal sense for Murray to play a man who has been drained of life in front of rather than behind the camera. *Groundhog Day* is, if anything, too enjoyable for the good of its reputation. Murray is not just good as the jaded television-caster, he is phenomenal. He knows in his bones how to show us what it is like to be encased in a media image, how remote your own and other people's responses become. Murray uses the disruption of Phil's routine to flip his own professional lid and to show us the emotional springs of his comedy, exactly what he always protected with comic cynicism. His performance in *Mad Dog and Glory* as the ruthless loan shark who wants to be a stand-up comic combines the scary and funny elements of Phil's remoteness. Murray convincingly integrates the stand-up comic's aggression as part of the gangster's hovering threat, but the script never comes together, and once again De Niro kills a teaming by his own kind of remoteness as an actor. But by drilling down to *genuine* sources of comic redemption in *Scrooged*, *Ghostbuster II*, *Quick Change*, and *Groundhog Day*, Murray has fulfilled a promise we never expected him to make.

—Alan Dale

NAZIMOVA, Alla

Nationality: American. **Born:** Yalta, Russia (now Ukraine), 4 June 1879; became U.S. citizen, 1927. **Education:** Attended private Catholic school, Montreux, Switzerland; studied music at Philharmonic Music Academy, Yalta; Academy of Acting, Moscow. **Family:** Married Paul Orleneff, 1904; lived with the actor Charles Bryant. **Career:** Apprenticeship at Stanislavsky's Moscow Art Theatre; then acted in repertory companies in Kostroma, Kerson, and Vilna; 1903—leading actress at Nemetti Theatre, St. Petersburg; 1904-05—toured Berlin and London with the play *The Chosen People*, banned in Russia; 1905—presented *The Chosen People* in Russian in New York, followed by other successful plays in Russian; 1906—studied English with the mother of Richard Barthelmess; debut in first English-speaking role in *Hedda Gabler*; her fame in New York became so great that a theater was named for her (later renamed the 39th Street Playhouse); 1912—presented *Bella Donna* in New York and on a year-long tour; 1916—film debut in *War Brides*; contract with Metro Company, and made several films written by June Mathis; 1922—made the film *A Doll's House* with her own money for release by United Artists; 1928—joined Eva Le Gallienne's Civic Repertory Company, New York, and later the Theatre Guild, 1929. **Died:** In Los Angeles 13 July 1945.

Films as Actress:

1916   *War Brides* (Brenon) (as Joan)
1918   *Revelation* (Baker) (as Joline); *Toys of Fate* (Baker) (as Hagar and Azah); *An Eye for an Eye* (Capellani) (as Hassouna)
1919   *Out of the Fog* (Capellani) (as Faith and Eve); *The Red Lantern* (Capellani) (as Mahlee and Blanche Sackville); *The Brat* (Blaché)
1920   *Stronger Than Death* (Blaché) (as Sigrid Fersen); *The Heart of a Child* (Smallwood) (as Sally Snape); *Madame Peacock* (Smallwood) (as mother and daughter) (+ sc); *Billions* (Smallwood) (as Princess Tirloff)
1921   *Camille* (Smallwood) (as Marguerite Gauthier, + pr)
1922   *A Doll's House* (Bryant) (as Nora, + pr, sc)
1923   *Salome* (Bryant) (title role, + pr, sc)
1924   *Madonna of the Streets* (Carewe)
1925   *The Redeeming Sin* (Blackton); *My Son* (Carewe) (as Ana Silva)
1940   *Escape* (LeRoy) (as Emmy Ritter)
1941   *Blood and Sand* (Mamoulian)
1944   *The Bridge of San Luis Rey* (Lee) (as Marquesa de Montmayor); *In Our Time* (Sherman) (as Zofya Orvid); *Since You Went Away* (Cromwell) (as Koslowska)

Film as Consultant and Research Adviser:

1939   *Zaza* (Cukor)

Publications

By NAZIMOVA: articles—

Hall, Gladys, and Adele Fletcher, "We Interview Camille," in *Motion Picture Magazine*, January 1922.
"I Come Full Circle," in *Theatre* (New York), April 1929.

On NAZIMOVA: book—

Blum, Daniel, *Great Stars of the American Stage: A Pictorial Record*, New York, 1952.

On NAZIMOVA: articles—

Dale, Alan, "Nazimova and Some Others," in *Cosmopolitan* (New York), April 1907.
Montanye, Lillian, "A Half Hour with Nazimova," in *Motion Picture Classic* (Brooklyn), July 1917.
Fredericks, Edwin, "The Real Nazimova," in *Photoplay* (New York), February 1920.
Howe, Herbert, "Nazimova Speaks," in *Picture Play*, September 1920.
Mullett, Mary, "How a Dull, Fat Little Girl Became a Great Actress," in *American Magazine*, April 1922.
Service, Faith, "Memoirs of Madame," in *Motion Picture Classic* (Brooklyn), November 1922.
Brush, Katherine, "Nazimova—Player of Roles," in *National Magazine* (New York), July 1923.
Thompson, E. R., "The Art of Alla Nazimova," in *Pictures and Picturegoer*, January 1925.
St. Johns, Adela Rogers, "Temperament? Certainly Says Nazimova," in *Photoplay* (New York), October 1926.
Barnes, Djuna, "Alla Nazimova, One of the Greatest of Living Actresses, Talks of Her Art," in *Theatre Guild Magazine*, June 1930.
Eustis, Morton, "The Actor Attacks His Part: Nazimova," in *Theatre Arts* (New York), December 1936.
Kirkland, Alexander, "The Woman from Yalta," in *Theatre Arts* (New York), December 1949.
Ashby, Clifford, "Alla Nazimova and the Advent of the New Acting in America," in *Quarterly Journal of Speech*, April 1954.
Bodeen, DeWitt, "Nazimova," in *Films in Review* (New York), December 1972.
"Alla Nazimova," in *Rebellin in Hollywood: 13 Porträts des Eigensinns*, Frankfurt, 1986.

*   *   *

Alla Nazimova, one of the most exotic actresses of the late 1910s and 1920s, had an exotic Russian background to begin with. Born of Jewish parents in Yalta, and educated in a Swiss Catholic convent, she took up the violin and in her school orchestra played under Tchaikovsky and Rimsky-Korsakov. Her acting aspirations led her to Moscow and an apprenticeship with Stanislavsky's Art Theatre. She found leading roles in the provinces and settled in St. Petersburg where

Alla Nazimova in *War Brides*

she married her theater partner Paul Orleneff. Eventually the pair took the Zionist play *The Chosen People* on a European tour, and to America in 1905.

She decided to remain in the United States while her husband and the company returned home. Success on the New York stage, after she had learned English, led to a film version of her stage triumph *War Brides* under the direction of Herbert Brenon. (In the film she introduced Richard Barthelmess, the son of her English coach.) Diminutive, but with a dynamic personality, she struck a new note in American films. The Irish actor Michael MacLiammóir described her quality as "agonized ecstasy."

Her next film, *Revelation*, confirmed her talent, and she soared to stardom. Charles Bryant, her lover and leading man in many of her films, helped her to set up a palatial establishment in Hollywood known as the Garden of Allah. She was now known simply as Nazimova, in the way one would speak of Bernhardt or Duse. Three films directed by the talented Paul Capellani, *An Eye for an Eye*, *Out of the Fog*, and *The Red Lantern*, featured some of her finest work, the last being outstanding.

From this point on, her work takes on an eclectic virtuosity. An association with the designer Natacha Rambova led to highly stylized productions of *Camille* (with Valentino) and *Salome* with designs based on Beardsley. *Salome* was made with no concessions whatever to popular taste, and was poorly received, though it is actually a courageous experiment aesthetically, and remains remarkable for Nazimova's catlike grace.

In the mid-1920s she returned to her first love, the theater, and had a most distinguished career in classic Russian plays at the New York Civic Repertory Company. She played in a few sound films, always in small character parts though they were impeccably done. Her last years were restless and not particularly happy, though she lived to see her nephew Val Lewton make his name in films. Those who remember her stage performance speak of her with respect and love.

—Liam O'Leary

NEAGLE, (Dame) Anna

Nationality: British. **Born:** Marjorie Robertson in Forest Gate, London, 20 October 1904. **Education:** Studied dancing as a child. **Family:** Married the director Herbert Wilcox, 1943 (died 1977). **Career:** Worked as a dance instructor, then as chorus girl; 1925—stage debut in *Charlot's Revue of 1925*; 1929—Broadway debut in *Wake Up and Dream*; 1931—lead role in *Stand Up and Sing*; film debut in *Should a Doctor Tell?*; first film by director Wilcox, *Goodnight, Vienna*; late 1950s—formed her own film production company; 1960—on stage in *The More the Merrier*; later stage work includes *Charlie Girl*, 1965-71, *No, No, Nanette*, 1973, *My Fair Lady* in London and Toronto, 1978-79, and *Cinderella*, 1982. **Awards:** Dame Commander, Order of the British Empire, 1969. **Died:** In Surrey, England, 3 June 1986.

Films as Actress:

(as Marjorie Robertson)

1931   *Should a Doctor Tell?* (Haynes)

(as Anna Neagle)

1931   *The Chinese Bungalow* (Williams) (as Charlotte)
1932   *Goodnight, Vienna* (Wilcox) (as Vicki)

1933   *The Flag Lieutenant* (Henry Edwards) (as Hermione Wynne); *The Little Damozel* (Wilcox) (title role); *Bitter Sweet* (Wilcox) (as Sara Linden)
1934   *The Queen's Affair* (Wilcox) (as Queen Nadina)
1935   *Nell Gwyn* (Wilcox) (title role)
1936   *Peg of Old Drury* (Wilcox) (title role); *Limelight* (Wilcox)
1937   *The Three Maxims* (Wilcox); *London Melody* (Wilcox); *Victoria the Great* (Wilcox) (title role)
1938   *Sixty Glorious Years* (Wilcox) (as Queen Victoria)
1939   *Nurse Edith Cavell* (Wilcox) (title role)
1940   *Irene* (Wilcox) (title role)
1941   *No, No, Nanette* (Wilcox) (title role); *Sunny* (Wilcox)
1942   *They Flew Alone* (Wilcox) (as Amy Johnson)
1943   *Forever and a Day* (episode) (Wilcox and others); *The Yellow Canary* (Wilcox)
1945   *I Live in Grosvenor Square* (Wilcox)
1946   *Piccadilly Incident* (Wilcox)
1947   *The Courtneys of Curzon Street* (Wilcox); *Royal Wedding* (doc) (as commentator)
1948   *Spring in Park Lane* (Wilcox) (as Judy Howard)
1949   *Elizabeth of Ladymead* (Wilcox) (as four wives); *Maytime in Mayfair* (Wilcox)
1950   *Odette* (Wilcox) (title role)
1951   *The Lady with a Lamp* (Wilcox) (as Florence Nightingale)
1952   *Derby Day* (Wilcox)
1955   *Lilacs in the Spring* (*The Glorious Days*) (Wilcox)
1956   *King's Rhapsody* (Wilcox) (as Marta Karillos); *My Teenage Daughter* (Wilcox) (as Valerie Carr)
1957   *No Time for Tears* (Frankel)
1958   *The Man Who Wouldn't Talk* (Wilcox) (as Mary Randall, Q.C.)
1959   *The Lady Is a Square* (Wilcox) (as Frances Baring)

Films as Producer:

1957   *These Dangerous Years* (Wilcox)
1958   *Wonderful Things* (Wilcox)
1959   *Heart of a Man* (Wilcox)

Publications

By NEAGLE: book—

Anna Neagle Says "There's Always Tomorrow": An Autobiography, London, 1974.

By NEAGLE: article—

Interview with T. Williams, in *Films and Filming* (London), May 1983.

On NEAGLE: articles—

Coulson, A. A., "Anna Neagle," in *Films in Review* (New York), March 1967.
Lewis, K., "Dame Anna Neagle: Eighty Glorious Years," in *Films in Review* (New York), October 1985.
Obituary in *Variety* (New York), 11 June 1986.
Obituary in *Films and Filming* (London), July 1986.

*   *   *

"She is as much a part of Britain as Dover's white cliffs," wrote one critic of Anna Neagle, an actress who for more than 40 years personified the attitudes and ideals of the British upper-middle class. She was

Anna Neagle

never a great actress, but in the eyes of her husband and director Herbert Wilcox she was incomparable, and he saw to it that she portrayed every type of role from prostitute to queen, from showgirl to spy. Neagle took each of these roles in her stride and, thanks in no small part to her professionalism and her outright "niceness," she pulled most of them off.

Although Neagle will best be remembered for her 1930s performances as Queen Victoria in *Victoria the Great* and *Sixty Glorious Years*, she is at her best in the title role of *Nell Gwyn*, a part that offered humor and pathos and allowed the actress to display a gamine quality almost totally lacking in her later work. In Hollywood she appeared chiefly in remakes of earlier stage and screen musicals which seem somewhat lifeless, and are not helped by Neagle's limited skills as a singer. Returning to Britain she became that country's top box-office star of the 1940s in a series of films named after London's better-known thoroughfares, in which she and Michael Wilding offered a welcome middle-class escape from the drab reality of a country suffering rationing and shortages in the postwar period.

Neagle was definitely out of style in the 1950s; she tried to come to grips with the new "beat generation" and failed. Happily she returned to the stage and never ceased working in that medium. Her charm and winning personality continued to delight audiences for whom the motion picture had become a medium strictly for the young.

—Anthony Slide

NEAL, Patricia

Nationality: American. **Born:** Patsy Louise Neal in Packard, Kentucky, 20 January 1926. **Education:** Attended Knoxville High School, Tennessee; Northwestern University, Evanston, Illinois, 1944-45. **Family:** Married the writer Roald Dahl, 1953 (divorced 1983), five children (one deceased). **Career:** Coached in acting as a child, and made stage debut at age 15 at Barter Theatre, Virginia; 1944—understudy on tour in *The Voice of the Turtle*, and in short Broadway run; 1946—Tony-Award winning performance in Broadway production of *Another Part of the Forest*; 1947—joined Strasberg's Actors Studio, New York; 1949—film debut in *John Loves Mary*; contract with Warner Brothers; 1952—on stage in *The Children's Hour*; 1958—in *Suddenly Last Summer* in London; 1964-68—series of strokes and long rehabilitation period; 1968—returned to films in *The Subject Was Roses*; 1978—in TV mini-series *The Bastard*. **Awards:** Best Actress Academy Award, Best Actress, New York Film Critics, and Best Foreign Actress, British Academy, for *Hud*, 1963; Best Foreign Actress, British Academy, for *In Harm's Way*, 1965. **Address:** P.O. Box 1043, Edgartown, MA 02539, U.S.A.

Films as Actress:

1949 *John Loves Mary* (David Butler) (as Mary McKinley); *The Fountainhead* (King Vidor) (as Dominique Francon); *It's a Great Feeling* (David Butler) (as herself)
1950 *The Hasty Heart* (Sherman) (as Sister Margaret Parker); *Bright Leaf* (Curtiz) (as Margaret Jane Singleton); *Three Secrets* (Wise) (as Phyllis Horn); *The Breaking Point* (Curtiz) (as Leona Charles)
1951 *Operation Pacific* (Waggner) (as Mary Stuart); *Raton Pass* (*Canyon Pass*) (Marin) (as Ann); *The Day the Earth Stood Still* (Wise) (as Helen Benson); *Weekend with Father* (Sirk) (as Jean Bowen)

1952 *Diplomatic Courier* (Hathaway) (as Joan Ross); *Something for the Birds* (Wise) (as Anne Richards); *Washington Story* (*Target for Scandal*) (Pirosh) (as Alice Kingsly)
1954 *La tua donna* (Paolucci); *The Stranger from Venus* (*Immediate Disaster*) (Burt Balaban) (as Susan North)
1957 *A Face in the Crowd* (Kazan) (as Marcia Jeffries)
1961 *Breakfast at Tiffany's* (Edwards) (as "2E")
1963 *Hud* (Ritt) (as Alma Brown)
1964 *Psyche '59* (Singer) (as Allison)
1965 *In Harm's Way* (Preminger) (as Lt. Maggie Haynes)
1968 *The Subject Was Roses* (Grosbard) (as Nettie Cleary)
1971 *The Road Builder* (*The Night Digger*) (Reid) (as Maura Prince); *The Homecoming: A Christmas Story* (Cook—for TV) (as Olivia Walton)
1973 *Baxter* (Jeffries) (as Dr. Clemm); *Hay que matar a B.* (*B. Must Die*) (Borau) (as Julia); *Happy Mother's Day—Love George* (*Run, Stranger, Run*) (McGavin) (as Cara)
1974 *Things in Their Season* (Goldstone—for TV)
1975 *Eric* (Goldstone—for TV) (as Lois Swenson)
1977 *Widow's Nest* (*Nido de viudas*) (Navarro) (as Lupe); *Tail Gunner Joe* (Jud Taylor—for TV)
1978 *A Love Affair: The Eleanor and Lou Gehrig Story* (Cook—for TV) (as Mrs. Gehrig)
1979 *The Passage* (J. Lee Thompson) (as Ariel Bergson); *All Quiet on the Western Front* (Delbert Mann—for TV) (as Paul's mother)
1981 *Ghost Story* (Irvin) (as Stella Hawthorne)
1984 *Glitter* (Beaumont—for TV); *Love Leads the Way* (Delbert Mann—for TV); *Shattered Vows* (Bender—for TV) (as Sister Carmelita)
1989 *An Unremarkable Life* (Chaudri) (as Frances McEllany)
1990 *Caroline?* (Sargent—for TV) (as the headmistress)
1992 *A Mother's Right: The Elizabeth Morgan Story* (Otto—for TV) (as Antonia Morgan)
1993 *Heidi* (Rhodes—for TV) (as Grandmother)

Publications

By NEAL: book—

As I Am: An Autobiography, with Richard DeNeut, New York, 1988.

On NEAL: books—

Farrell, Barry, *Pat and Roald*, New York, 1969.
Burrows, Michael, *Patricia Neal and Margaret Sullavan*, Cornwall, England, 1971.

On NEAL: articles—

Current Biography 1964, New York, 1964.
Buckley, Michael, "Patricia Neal," in *Films in Review* (New York), April 1983; see also letter in August/September issue.

On NEAL: film—

The Patricia Neal Story, directed by Anthony Harvey and Anthony Page for television, 1981.

* * *

As modern teachers of naturalistic acting would ask of her, Patricia Neal personifies true openness: to her characters' impulses both intellectual and sexual, to her fellow players, to all acting media, to the pursuit of work even after deep personal affliction and loss. Never a major star, she rose to prominence when Hollywood's "classical" period—characterized by the interlocking systems of studio/star/genre—was ending. She is in fact one of the earliest members of an ongoing post-1950s sorority of "working" actresses. These women's mastery of contemporary acting techniques clearly works in their every on-screen moment, but, unless they turn to television, they remain fairly anonymous working actors—nonstars—their film roles usually small or lost in low-quality productions.

The reasons femininity and Hollywood movie stardom became comparatively estranged between the studio era and the recent age of the blockbuster are complex: at the root is a perceived shift in movie viewership by the 1970s to young men, connected to the Hollywood commonplace that only male actors can turn films into megahits by virtue of their mere presence. But surely also a factor is some resistance to women, like Neal, able to combine practical control and a post-Production Code, expandingly erotic heat: one of her own favorite examples comes in *Hud* when her character swats a fly—which Neal fortuitously noticed on the set—in response to Paul Newman's kiss.

Neal was well-received on Broadway in the mid-1940s, having worked in local theaters and summer stock through high school and college. She was invited to be a founding member of the Actors Studio, the New York collective which would become the most famous workshop devoted to expanding the ideas of Constantin Stanislavski in the United States—although she writes that she was expelled temporarily when she went to Hollywood. There she met more critical than commercial success between 1949 and 1952, her two most memorable roles coming in *The Fountainhead* and *The Day the Earth Stood Still*. She studied screen acting with George Shdanoff and later Shdanoff's teacher Michael Chekhov, Stanislavski's associate.

Neal returned to Broadway in 1952 and spent the mid-1950s dividing her time between New York and England, occupied with a new marriage, children, renewed work at the Actors Studio, and jobs onstage and in television. Her best run of film work began in 1957 with *A Face in the Crowd*, as she moved into innocuous, reliable, supportive (and supporting) women's roles, including *Breakfast at Tiffany's*, *In Harm's Way*, and *Hud*, for which she won an Oscar.

Her career was drastically interrupted in the mid-1960s by a series of strokes. Her courageous attempts to reestablish herself across the 1970s and 1980s often found her characters also dealing with illness. Unsurprisingly, given developing industry patterns, her best recent roles have come on television. She brings a motherly, astute depth especially to 1990's *Caroline?*, with television star Stephanie Zimbalist and working actress Pamela Reed. Patricia Neal soldiers on, an actress of intelligence and fire never fully exploited by Hollywood film.

—Robin Wood, updated by Susan Knobloch

NEESON, Liam

Nationality: Irish. **Born:** Ballymena, Northern Ireland, 7 June 1952. **Family:** Married the actress Natasha Richardson, 1994, son: Micheal Richard Antonio. **Career:** 1981—film debut in *Excalibur*; 1983—in TV mini-series *A Woman of Substance*; 1984—in TV mini-series *Ellis Island*; 1986—in TV mini-series *If Tomorrow Comes*; theatrical appearances include *Anna Christie* (Broadway), 1993 ; **Agent:** Creative Artists Agency, 9830 Wilshire Boulevard, Beverly Hills, CA 90212, U.S.A.

Films as Actor:

1981   *Excalibur* (Boorman) (as Sir Gawain)
1983   *Krull* (Yates) (as Kegan)

1984   *The Bounty* (Donaldson) (as Churchill); *The Innocent* (Mackenzie) (as John Carns)
1985   *Arthur the King* (*Merlin and the Sword*) (Cliver Donner—for TV, produced in 1983) (as Grak); *Lamb* (Gregg) (as Brother Sebastian)
1986   *The Mission* (Joffe) (as Fielding); *Hold the Dream* (Don Sharp—for TV) (as Blackie O'Neill); *Duet for One* (Konchalovsky) (as Totter)
1987   *Suspect* (Yates) (as Carl Wayne Anderson); *A Prayer for the Dying* (Hodges) (as Liam Docherty); *Sweet as You Are* (Angela Pope—for TV) (as Martin Perry); *Sworn to Silence* (Peter Levin—for TV) (as Vincent Cauley)
1988   *Satisfaction* (*Girls of Summer*) (Freeman) (as Martin Falcon); *The Dead Pool* (Van Horn) (as Peter Swan); *The Good Mother* (Nimoy) (as Leo Cutter); *High Spirits* (Neil Jordan) (as Martin Brogan)
1989   *Next of Kin* (Irvin) (as Briar Gates)
1990   *Darkman* (Raimi) (Peyton Westlake/title role)
1991   *The Big Man* (*Crossing the Line*) (Leland) (as Danny Scoular)
1992   *Under Suspicion* (Simon Moore) (as Tony Aaron); *Shining Through* (Seltzer) (as Franz-Otto Dietrich); *Leap of Faith* (Pearce) (as Will); *Husbands and Wives* (Woody Allen) (as Michael); *Deception* (*Ruby Cairo*; *The Missing Link: Ruby Cairo*) (Clifford) (as Fergus Lamb)
1993   *Ethan Frome* (Madden) (title role); **Schindler's List** (Spielberg) (as Oskar Schindler)
1994   *Nell* (Apted) (as Jerome Lovell); *Out of Ireland* (Paul Wagner—doc) (voice only)
1995   *Rob Roy* (Caton-Jones) (title role)
1996   *Michael Collins* (Neil Jordan) (title role); *Before and After* (Schroeder) (as Ben Ryan)

Publications

By NEESON: articles—

"*Darkman*'s Liam Neeson Unmasked," interview with Marc Shapiro, in *Video Review* (New York), March 1991.
"Stranger in Paradise," interview with Joe Morgenstern, in *Harper's Bazaar* (New York), December 1992.
"Hold the Hunk Stuff, the Man's an Actor First," interview with Francis X. Clines, in *New York Times*, 10 January 1993.

On NEESON: book—

Millar, Ingrid, *Liam Neeson: The First Biography*, New York, 1996.

On NEESON: articles—

Greenberg, James, "Close-Up: Liam Neeson," in *American Film*, October 1988.
King, Patricia, "A Wee Bit of Hollywood Power," in *Newsweek* (New York), 7 November 1988.
Frankel, Martha, "Man of the Year: Mercurial Liam Neeson Can Play a Masked Avenger, a Desperate Boxer, a Lover and a Mute. But What Is He Really Like?," in *American Film* (Los Angeles), December 1990.
Kantrowitz, Barbara, "A Touch of the Poet," in *Newsweek* (New York), 8 February 1993.
Mansfield, Stephanie, "Liam Neeson Puts on the Kettle," in *GQ* (New York), December 1993.
Current Biography 1994, New York, 1994.
Howell, Georgina, "Liam's Leap," in *Vogue* (New York), January 1994.

Liam Neeson in *Schindler's List*

Smith, Dinitia, "It's . . . ! Liam Neeson," in *New York Times Magazine*, 4 December 1994.

* * *

Irish-born Liam Neeson has the features and presence of a film star of the 1930s or 1940s—a Paul Muni, perhaps, or Robert Mitchum. A laborer before becoming an actor, he cuts a strapping figure which makes him ideal for over-the-top hero roles in the grand tradition of Hollywood's Golden Age. But there is a vulnerability about him that makes him equally suitable for today's sensitive hero types, as well.

He brought both of these characteristics to his star-making, and Oscar-nominated, performance in Spielberg's *Schindler's List*, a film that accentuated Neeson's old-style Hollywood looks by being shot in noirish black and white. Neeson's Schindler, who saves the lives of more than a thousand Jews from the exterminating hands of the Nazis, is shady but honest, pragmatic but altruistic—the quintessential noir hero, a man walking a tightrope down some very dark, very mean streets. He is also a man with a desperate need to feel accepted—the prototypical Spielberg hero.

The real Oskar Schindler was an enigma. History still cannot put a finger on the actual motives that prompted him to save the lives of so many of his Jewish employees. Was he a humanist who saw a terrible wrong and did his best to right it? A charismatic scoundrel? Or a savvy exploiteer who saw no profit in sending productive workers to the gas chambers just because they were Jewish? (Does it even matter? What counts is that he saved lives when others in his position did not.)

For most of the film, Neeson plays Schindler as such an enigma, a genuine man in the middle—until Spielberg blows the character's fascinating ambiguity at the conclusion by having him break down in front of the Jews he has saved and be consoled in his despair over not having saved more. This behavior is simply not consistent with the character Neeson has created; it strikes such a false note of strained sentimentality (and trademark Spielbergian pathos) that one can almost feel the actor gritting his teeth to get through the scene. Tellingly, it is his only unconvincing moment in the three-hours-plus of the film.

Neeson made his screen debut as one of the knights of the Round Table among an ensemble cast of (then) largely unknown British and Irish players in *Boorman's Excalibur,* an exquisite recounting of the Arthurian legend; the role required little of him except a hardy build and a sense of physical and moral strength—his trademarks to this day. He is virtually unidentifiable behind beard and armor; one can see the film even now and not realize he is in it, though his role is not insubstantial.

A year later, he was back in Camelot, and identifiable this time, among the ensemble cast of Clive Donner's television epic *Arthur the King*, a decided come-down from the Boorman film and which mixed medieval derring-do with Lewis Carroll and sat on the shelf for nearly three years until the network aired it.

This seemed to form the pattern of much of Neeson's first decade of film work—substantial if not noticeable roles in high-profile action/period pieces (*The Bounty*, *The Mission*) and noticeable, high-profile roles in action-filled duds (*Next of Kin*, *A Prayer for the Dying*).

Sam Raimi's cartoonish *Darkman* changed Neeson's fortunes. As the gentle giant scientist turned avenging phantom of the title, Neeson revealed that he could not only handle action scenes but also register the kind of sensitivity audiences seemed to want in movie heroes of the 1990s. He started getting major parts in major films that stressed this side of his persona exclusively—the understanding lover who awakens Diane Keaton's sensuality in *The Good Mother*; the nice guy local who woos traveling huckster Debra Winger in *Leap of Faith*; the wily but vulnerable German soldier romanced and (improbably) manipulated by spy Melanie Griffith in *Shining Through*.

As the compassionate small town doctor who nurtures—and is nurtured by—a backwoods wild child in *Nell*, Neeson ably supported star Jodie Foster's bid for yet another Oscar-nominated performance. But as the legendary Scottish folk hero *Rob Roy*, he got his best role since *Schindler's List.*

Though the title character is by no means as multifaceted as Schindler, *Rob Roy* enabled Neeson to combine both aspects of his talents, support no one, and fully take the lead in the same manner as the Spielberg film. Here he is a man of action and pillar of integrity, as well as kind and loving husband and father. He even got to duel it out with villain Tim Roth in one of the best screen sword fights since the halcyon days of Flynn and Rathbone.

—John McCarty

NEGRI, Pola

Nationality: American. **Born:** Barbara Apollonia Chalupiec in Janowa, Poland, 31 December 1894 (or 1899). **Education:** Attended the boarding school of Countess Platen, Warsaw; studied at the Imperial Ballet School, St. Petersburg; Philharmonia drama school, Warsaw. **Family:** Married 1) Count Popper (died); 2) Count Eugene Domski, 1919 (divorced 1921); 3) Prince Serge Mdivani, 1927 (divorced 1931). **Career:** 1913—stage debut in Hauptmann's *Hannele* in Warsaw; 1914—film debut in *Niewolnica Zmyslow*; 1917—went to Berlin at urging of Max Reinhardt: acted in *Sumurun* in Berlin; 1918-20—series of German films, including several by Lubitsch; 1923—first U.S. film, *Bella Donna*; late 1920s—career faltered with advent of sound: made films in Germany, Austria, and England; returned to the United States at outbreak of World War II. **Awards:** Deutscher Filmpreis, 1964. **Died:** In San Antonio, Texas, 1 August 1987.

Films as Actress:

1914   *Niewolnica Zmyslow* (Pawlowski)
1915   *Pokoj no. 13* (Hertz); *Bestia* (Hertz); *Czarna Ksiazka* (Hertz)
1916   *Jego Ostatni Czyn* (Hertz); *Zona* (Hertz); *Studenci* (Hertz); *Arabella* (Hertz)
1917   *Küsse, die man in Dunkeln stiehlt* (Matull?); *Nicht lange täuschte mich das Glück* (Matull?); *Rosen, die der Sturm entblättert* (Matull?); *Zügelloses Blut* (*Gypsy Blood*); *Die toten Augen* (Matull?)
1918   *Der gelbe Schein* (*The Yellow Ticket*) (Janson); *Wenn das Herz in Hass erglüht* (Matull?); *Mania* (*Mad Love*) (Illes); *Die Augen der Mumie Ma* (*The Eyes of the Mummy*) (Lubitsch); *Carmen* (Lubitsch) (title role)
1919   *Das Karussell des Lebens* (Jacoby); *Kreuziget sie!* (Jacoby); *Madame DuBarry* (*Passion*) (Lubitsch) (title role); *Camille* (*The Red Peacock*); *Comptesse Doddy* (Jacoby)
1920   *Geschlossene Kette* (Stein); *Medea* (Lubitsch); *Das Martyrium* (Stein); *Die Marchesa d'Arminiani* (Halm); *Sumurun* (*One Arabian Night*) (Lubitsch); *Vendetta* (Jacoby)

1921   *Die Bergkatze* (Lubitsch); *Sappho* (Buchowetski); *Die Damme in Glashaus* (Janson); *Arme Violetta* (Stein)
1922   *Die Flamme* (*Montmartre*) (Lubitsch)
1923   *Bella Donna* (Fitzmaurice) (title role); *The Cheat* (Fitzmaurice) (as Carmelita De Córdoba); *Hollywood* (Cruze) (as guest); *The Spanish Dancer* (Brenon) (as Maritana)
1924   *Shadows of Paris* (Brenon) (as Clair); *Men* (Buchowetski) (as Cleo); *Lily of the Dust* (Buchowetski) (as Lily Czepanek); *Forbidden Paradise* (Lubitsch) (as Catherine the Great)
1925   *East of Suez* (Walsh) (as Daisy Forbes); *The Charmer* (Olcott) (as Mariposa); *Flower of Night* (Bern) (as Carlota y Villalon); *A Woman of the World* (St. Clair) (as Countess Elnora)
1926   *The Crown of Lies* (Buchowetski) (as Olga Kriga); *Good and Naughty* (St. Clair) (as Germaine Morris)
1927   *Hotel Imperial* (Stiller) (as Anna Sedlak); *Barbed Wire* (Lee) (as Mona); *The Woman on Trial* (Stiller) (as Julie)
1928   *Three Sinners* (Lee) (as Baroness Gerda Wallentin); *The Secret Hour* (Lee) (as Amy); *Loves of an Actress* (Lee) (as Rachel); *The Woman from Moscow* (Berger) (as Princess Fedora); *Are Women to Blame?*
1929   *Street of Abandoned Children*
1930   *The Woman He Scorned* (Czinner)
1932   *A Woman Commands* (Czinner)
1934   *Fanatisme* (Ravel and LeKain)
1935   *Mazurka* (Forst)
1936   *Moskau-Shanghai* (Wegener)
1937   *Madame Bovary* (Lamprecht) (title role)
1938   *Rudolph Valentino* (short); *Die Nacht der Entscheidung* (Malasomma); *Tango notturno* (Kirchhoff); *Die fromme Lüge* (Malasomma)
1943   *Hi Diddle Diddle* (Stone)
1964   *The Moon-Spinners* (Neilson)

Publications

By NEGRI: books—

Memoirs of a Star, New York, 1970.
La Vie et la rêve au cinéma, Paris, n.d.

By NEGRI: articles—

"The Autobiography of Pola Negri," in *Photoplay* (New York), January-April 1924.
"Robert W. Frazer," in *Photoplay* (New York), June 1924.
"What Is Love?" in *Photoplay* (New York), November 1924.
"I Become Converted to the Happy Ending," in *Motion Picture Director*, March 1926.
"My Ideal Screen Lover," in *Pictures and Picturegoer*, March 1931.

On NEGRI: books—

Rosen, Marjorie, *Popcorn Venus*, New York, 1973.
Von Cossart, Axel, *Pola Negri: Leben eines stars*, 1988.
Czapinska, Wieslawa, *Polita*, Warsaw, 1989.

On NEGRI: articles—

Haskins, Harrison, "Who Is Pola Negri?" in *Motion Picture Classic* (Brooklyn), February 1921.
Howe, Herbert, "The Real Pola Negri," in *Photoplay* (New York), November 1922.

Pola Negri

Howe, Herbert, "The Loves of Pola Negri," in *Photoplay* (New York), November 1923.

Frazer, Robert, "Pola Negri," in *Photoplay* (New York), July 1924.

Lyon, Ben, "Vampires I Have Known," in *Photoplay* (New York), February 1925.

St. Johns, Ivan, "How Pola Was Tamed," in *Photoplay* (New York), January 1926.

Hall, Leonard, "The Passing of Pola," in *Photoplay* (New York), December 1928.

Beinhorn, C. Wyche, "Pola Negri: Tempestuous Temptress," in *Take One* (Montreal), September 1978.

Article in *Film* (Poland), 9 September 1984.

Obituary in *Films and Filming* (London), September 1987.

*   *   *

Pola Negri—the very name summons up the exoticism that was her stock-in-trade. This image sometimes got in the way of the undeniable fact that she was one of the silent screen's more gifted actresses. But drama moved offscreen for Pola Negri, and as her film career in the United States faded, her life kept her in the public eye. As a personality, she was one of those characters that may justifiably be called "the self-enchanted." This is the part of her reputation that endures today, obscuring the fact that her film career was a long and notable one.

She began performing in Poland as an ingenue with the Rozmaitoczi Theatre, scoring early successes as Hedwig in Ibsen's *Wild Duck*, and in the title role of Hauptmann's *Hannele*. Her stage work brought her to the attention of Alexandr Hertz, the pioneer Polish film producer, who made several of her earliest films. She was also the star of Max Reinhardt's pantomime *Sumurun*, first in Poland and then in Berlin. While there, she met a member of Reinhardt's coterie, the fledgling movie director Ernst Lubitsch. After a series of wonderful comic short films (the best of which is *Die Bergkatze*), she was featured in one of the early historical spectacles, *Passion (Madame DuBarry)*. Her vital and uninhibited portrayal of the French courtesan won her the admiration of Europe, and also impressed the Hollywood studios. She was soon on her way to America, under contract to Paramount. Unfortunately, the caliber of her work in the United States was nowhere near that of her German pictures.

Negri was an excellent performer when guided by a forceful director such as Lubitsch, but was given to excess when unharnessed. The Americans who directed her 1920s silents were not able to contain her rebellious energy. She gained a reputation for being temperamental, and her pictures never rivaled the success of *Passion*. There were a few high points though: she was teamed with Lubitsch once more, and produced a brilliant comic character in *Forbidden Paradise*. Her dramatic performance as a hotel maid in Mauritz Stiller's *Hotel Imperial* was a pinnacle of silent-screen dramatics. These occasional triumphs did little to enhance her career, and she retired from the screen in 1928 (ostensibly because of her marriage to Prince Mdivani).

An English picture, *Street of Abandoned Children*, was made in 1929, and she returned to the United States for her first talkie, *A Woman Commands*, in which her good performance was wasted on a poor film. No other offers were forthcoming, so she made one film in France, *Fanatisme*. Her career was given a second life by a long-term contract with ufa in 1935. She was starred in a series of strong films: as the cafe singer in Willi Forst's musical *Mazurka*, as a cocaine addict in *Tango notturno*, and in the title role of Gerhardt Lamprecht's *Madame Bovary*. More comfortable with the German language, she proved herself to be a restrained and tasteful performer, as well as a distinctive cabaret singer. World War II interrupted her career there, and she returned to the United States, working only twice thereafter, in *Hi Diddle Diddle* and *The Moon-Spinners*.

—Joseph Arkins

NEILL, Sam

Nationality: Irish/New Zealander. **Born:** Nigel John Dermot Neill in Northern Ireland, 14 September 1947; raised in New Zealand from age seven. **Education:** Attended University of Canterbury, New Zealand. **Family:** Married 1) Lisa Harrow (divorced), son: Tim; 2) the makeup artist Noriko Watanabe, 1989, daughter: Elena. **Career:** 1970s—member of New Zealand's National Film Unit as documentary filmmaker; 1977—feature film debut as actor in *Sleeping Dogs*; 1983—enhanced leading man status with PBS series *Reilly, Ace of Spies*; 1985—in TV mini-series *Kane and Abel*; 1987—in TV mini-series *Amerika*; 1996—returned to documentary roots with his film *Cinema of Unease*. **Awards:** Order of the British Empire, 1992. **Agent:** Ed Limato, ICM, 8942 Wilshire Boulevard, Beverly Hills, CA 90211, U.S.A.

Films as Actor:

1975   *Landfall* (Maunder); *Ashes* (Barclay) (as priest)

1977   *Sleeping Dogs* (Roger Donaldson) (as Smith)

1979   ***My Brilliant Career*** (Gillian Armstrong) (as Harry Beecham); *Just Out of Reach* (Blagg) (as Mike); *The Journalist* (Thornhill) (as Rex)

1980   *Lucinda Brayford* (Gauci—for TV) (as Tony Duff)

1981   *Attack Force Z* (Burstall) (as Sgt. Danny J. Costello); *The Final Conflict* (*Omen III: The Final Conflict*) (Graham Baker) (as Damien Thorn); *Z dalekiego kraju* (*From a Far Country: Pope John Paul II*) (Zanussi—for TV) (as Marian); *Possession* (Zulawski) (as Marc)

1982   *Enigma* (Szwarc) (as Dimitri Vasilkov); *Ivanhoe* (Camfield—for TV) (as Brian de Bois-Guilbert)

1983   *The Country Girls* (Desmond Davis—for TV) (as Mr. Gentleman)

1984   *Robbery under Arms* (Crombie and Hannam—for TV) (as Captain Starlight); *Le Sang des autres* (*The Blood of Others*) (Chabrol—for TV) (as Dieter Bergman)

1985   *Plenty* (Schepisi) (as Lazar); *For Love Alone* (Stephen Wallace) (as James Quick)

1986   *The Good Wife* (*The Umbrella Woman*) (Ken Cameron) (as Neville Gifford); *Strong Medicine* (Guy Green—for TV) (as Vince Lord)

1988   *A Cry in the Dark* (*Evil Angels*) (Schepisi) (as Michael Chamberlain); *Leap of Faith* (*Question of Faith*) (Gyllenhaal—for TV) (as Oscar Ogg)

1989   *Dead Calm* (Noyce) (as John Ingram); *La Révolution Française* (*The French Revolution*) (Enrico and Heffron) (as Lafayette)

1990   *The Hunt for Red October* (McTiernan) (as Capt. Vasily Borodin)

1991   *Death in Brunswick* (*Nothing to Lose*) (Ruane) (as Carl Fitzgerald); *Bis ans Ende der Welt* (*Until the End of the World*) (Wenders) (as Eugene Fitzgerald); *Fever* (Elikann—for TV) (as Elliott Mandel); *One against the Wind* (Elikann—for TV) (as Capt. James Leggatt); *Shadow of China* (Yanagimachi) (as TV reporter, credited as John Dermot)

1992   *Hostage* (Robert Young) (as John Rennie); *Memoirs of an Invisible Man* (Carpenter) (as David Jenkins)

1993   *Jurassic Park* (Spielberg) (as Dr. Alan Grant); ***The Piano*** (Campion) (as Stewart); *Family Pictures* (Saville—for TV) (as David Eberlin)

1994   *Sirens* (Duigan) (as Norman Lindsay); *Rainbow Warrior* (*The Sinking of the Rainbow Warrior*) (Tuchner) (as Allan Galbraith); *The Jungle Book* (Sommers) (as Col. Brydon)

Sam Neill in *Dead Calm*

1995   *In the Mouth of Madness* (Carpenter) (as John Trent); *Victory* (Peploe) (as Mr. Jones);
1996   *Restoration* (Michael Hoffman) (as King Charles II)

Films as Director:

1974   *Telephone Etiquette* (doc) (+ sc, ed)
1975   *Four Shorts on Architecture* (doc) (+ sc, ed)
1977   *On the Road with Red Mole* (doc); *Architect Athfield* (doc)
1996   *Cinema of Unease* (*A Personal Journey by Sam Neill*) (doc) (+ ro as presenter, co-sc)

Publications

By NEILL: articles—

Interview, in *Films Illustrated* (London), October 1981.
"Sam Neill's Megalosaurus Talent," interview with Graham Fuller, in *Interview* (New York), June 1993.

On NEILL: articles—

Castell, D., "Will Sam Play It Again?," in *Films Illustrated* (London), February 1980.
"Sam Neill," in *Film a Doba* (Czech Republic), January 1984.
Gillivray, D., "Sam Neill," in *Films and Filming* (London), February 1984.
Murray, Scott, *Australian Film 1978-1992*, Melbourne, 1993.
Natale, Richard, "Jurassic Spark," in *Harper's Bazaar* (New York), June 1993.
Clark, John, "Sam Neill," in *Premiere* (New York), July 1993.
Thompson, Anne, "Who the Heck Is Sam Neill?," in *Entertainment Weekly* (New York), 23 July 1993.
"Sam Neill," in *Film Review* (London), August 1995.

*   *   *

Self-effacing thinking woman's sex symbol, Sam Neill is the closest commodity resembling James Mason that we have in contemporary cinema. That is high praise indeed. As a vis-à-vis for magnetic actresses round the world, Neill is in the business of making Meryl Streep, Holly Hunter, and Judy Davis look good; it could be argued that these unshrinking violets have given their finest performances opposite him. Only a few quietly authoritative film actors (such as Neill, Arliss Howard, and David Straithairn) can support female powerhouses without being burned up by their reflecting glory. Whether Neill packs the kind of attention-getting virility that will make him a household name is in doubt; he certainly did not stand out as the heroic centerpiece of the biggest moneymaker of all time, *Jurassic Park*, in which he is dwarfed by state-of-the-art special effects and juvenile thrills befitting a theme park methodology. He does, however, exhibit a charisma that sneaks up on you unlike the bravado of such superstars as Bruce Willis and Mel Gibson; he is sort of the boy next door whom you wish would move back in as a man.

Beginning his cinematic career in the fledgling New Zealand film industry as a documentary filmmaker (a pursuit he has reactivated with 1996's *Cinema of Unease*), the boyishly appealing Neill stood out immediately but garnered international attention as the liberal-minded plum that feminist author Judy Davis lets slip through her fingers in *My Brilliant Career*. In his own neck of the woods, Neill's unaggressive masculinity was equally at home in the trenches of *Attack Force Z* and the glorious outback of *Robbery under Arms* as well as in the boudoirs of *For Love Alone* and *The Good Wife*. What is remark-

able about these down-under vehicles is that the Australian industry allowed Neill to tackle some robust hero roles, whereas Hollywood second bananas him in its macho free-for-alls such as *The Hunt for Red October* and *The Jungle Book*.

If television has typecast him as a generic sensitive type in a slew of mini-series and movies, he can point with peacock pride to the PBS series *Reilly, Ace of Spies*, which contains his sexiest performance as he fills out evening clothes better than anyone since Cary Grant. Reunited memorably with Judy Davis in the haunting *One against the Wind*, he subtly underplays the high-voltage Anjelica Huston right off the television screen in the bitter breast-beating of *Family Pictures*, as a family man scrambling like Houdini to free himself of domestic chains. Varying his range previously with a villain role in *Ivanhoe* failed for the simple reason that Neill cannot camouflage his innate decency. Even when his characters disappoint or betray, Neill's likable persona blunts the impact of the transgression.

On the big screen, Neill always distinguishes himself except in roles requiring over-the-top flamboyance; on the evidence of *The Final Conflict*, *Possession*, and *In the Mouth of Madness* he would be wise to check out of horror venues forever. Because Neill has never disgraced himself with a bad performance, he often gets overlooked in the distribution of kudos in favor of more obvious performers. Not only is he the only actor keeping the audience from snoozing during the tenton, asleep-in-the-deep thriller, *The Hunt for Red October*, he also is so irresistibly bewildered in the pretentious *The Piano* that one loses all patience with Holly Hunter's intransigent mute. In Fred Schepisi's tricky media attack, *A Cry in the Dark*, Neill brilliantly complements Streep with a heartrending display of stoicism. This portrait of a grieving father vilified by the press and public is his finest performance to date. Lest the misconception persist that Neill is only a stalwart support system for bigger egoed film stars of both sexes, consider his exemplary work in the flawed *Death in Brunswick*, a searing delineation of an irresponsible man imbibing to drown out a surfeit of self-doubt (an acting turn even more noteworthy because it exists in a vacuum of a black comedy film). In a 360-degree reversal, Neill charmed audiences with his freethinking artist who admires female flesh as religiously as he loathes hypocrisy in the colorful fable, *Sirens*. In that movie's hothouse atmosphere, Neill's sex appeal has its most expansive workout since his womanizer role in *The Good Wife*.

Neither extinct dino-monsters nor formidable female stars can cow this pliable performer who rarely gets his proper due. Neill is one of the rare male stars able to unapologetically make emotional expressiveness not seem like a challenge that real he-men must meet and rise above. In all of his performances, psychological openness and virility go hand in hand. The contemporary cinema is richer for having nurtured a male star who confronts crises with intelligence before resorting to violence and who unabashedly admires women even when he cannot fathom their mysteries.

—Robert Pardi

NELLIGAN, Kate

Nationality: Canadian. **Born:** Patricia Colleen Nelligan in London, Ontario, Canada, 16 March 1951. **Education:** Attended York University, Ontario; Central School of Speech and Drama, London, England. **Family:** Married the pianist-songwriter Robert Reale, 1989. **Career:** 1974—London, England, stage debut in *Knuckle*; 1974—film debut in *The Count of Monte Cristo*; 1983—Broadway debut in *Plenty*; 1980—in TV mini-series *Therese Raquin*; 1980s—nominated for four Tony Awards; 1994—in TV mini-series *Million Dollar Babies*. Lives in New York. **Awards:** London Critics Award, Most Prom-

Kate Nelligan (center) with Andrea Laskaris (left) and Claudia Gough in *Eleni*

ising Actress, for *Knuckle*, 1974; Evening Standard Award, Best Actress, for *Plenty*; British Academy of Film and Television Arts and National Board of Review, Best Supporting Actress, for *Frankie and Johnny*, 1991. **Agent:** Joe Funicello, ICM, 8942 Wilshire Boulevard, Beverly Hills, CA 90211, U.S.A.

Films as Actress:

1974   *The Count of Monte Cristo* (David Greene) (as Mercedes); *The Arcata Promise* (Cunliffe—for TV) (as Laura)

1975   *The Romantic Englishwoman* (Losey) (as Isabel)

1977   *Licking Hitler* (Hare) (as Anna Seaton)

1978   *Measure for Measure* (Desmond Davis—for TV) (as Isabella)

1979   *Dracula* (Badham) (as Lucy Seward)

1980   *Mr. Patman* (Guillerman) (as Peabody)

1981   *Eye of the Needle* (Marquand) (as Lucy)

1982   *Victims* (Friedman—for TV) (as Ruth Hession)

1983   *Without a Trace* (Stanley R. Jaffe) (as Susan Selky)

1985   *Mystery of Henry Moore* (Rasky); *Eleni* (Yates) (title role)

1987   *Control* (Montaldo—for TV) (as Sarah Howell); *Kojak: The Price of Justice* (Metzger—for TV) (as Kitty Keeler)

1990   *The White Room* (Rozema) (as Jane); *Bethune: The Making of a Hero* (*Dr. Bethune*) (Borsos—released in U.S. in 1993); *Love and Hate: The Story of Colin and JoAnn Thatcher* (*Love and Hate: A Marriage Made in Hell*) (Francis Mankiewicz—for TV) (as JoAnn Thatcher)

1991   *The Prince of Tides* (Streisand) (as Lila Wingo Newbury); *Frankie and Johnny* (Garry Marshall) (as Cora)

1992   *Shadows and Fog* (Woody Allen) (as Eve); *The Diamond Fleece* (Waxman—for TV) (as Holly Plum); *Terror Stalks the Class Reunion* (*For Better and for Worse*) (Clive Donner—for TV) (as Kay)

1993   *Fatal Instinct* (Carl Reiner) (as Lana Ravine); *Liar, Liar* (Montessi—for TV) (as Susan Miori); *Shattered Trust: The Shari Karney Story* (Corcoran—for TV) (as Stephanie Chadford); *Old Times* (for TV) (as Kate)

1994   *Wolf* (Mike Nichols) (as Charlotte Randall); *Spoils of War* (David Greene—for TV) (as Elise); *Into the Deep* (Howard Hall—doc) (as narrator)

1995   *How to Make an American Quilt* (Moorhouse) (as Constance Saunders); *Margaret's Museum* (Ransen) (as Catherine MacNeil); *A Mother's Prayer* (Elikann—for TV) (as Sheila Walker)

1996   *Up Close and Personal* (Avnet) (as Joanna Kennelly); *Captive Heart: The James Mink Story* (Bruce Pittman—for TV) (as Elizabeth Mink)

Publications

On NELLIGAN: articles—

Wolcott, J., "Kate the Great," in *New York*, 25 October 1982.

Clarke, G., "Show Business: The Grail Came Parcel Post," in *Time* (New York), 10 January 1983.

Freedman, S. G., "For Kate Nelligan, Ghosts Haunt the Stage," in *New York Times Magazine*, 15 April 1984.

Kroll, J., "Kate Nelligan at Full Blast," in *Newsweek* (New York), 16 April 1984.

Darnton, N., "Eleni Enshrines a Mother's Legacy of Love," in *New York Times*, 27 October 1985.

Garel, A., "Kate Nelligan," in *Revue du Cinéma* (Paris), March 1989.

Witchel, A., "Brightness of a Star in Non-Stellar Roles," in *New York Times*, 14 November 1991.

Kaplan, Michael, "The Elegant Kate Nelligan," in *Cosmopolitan* (New York), April 1994.

*   *   *

Those privileged to catch Kate Nelligan's expressively raw emoting in the PBS mini-series, *Therese Raquin*, were thunderstruck by her intensity as the Zola heroine. Tearing off her clothes as if in a fever, sensualist Nelligan seemed poised for major stardom. More than two decades later, Nelligan is still handsomer than Hollywood's current flavors of the month and acts rings around better-known contemporaries. Hers is a case of one major stumble (*Eleni*) sabotaging an entire film career. Thrilling theater audiences, she remains an above-the-title attraction; in the movies, she is primarily a treasured supporting player.

From the time Nelligan completed her theatrical apprenticeship in London, she has been lavishly praised for her expansive range and risk-taking, notably a tour de force in *Moon for the Misbegotten*, in which she wrestled with an O'Neill role for which she was physically unsuited and triumphed in it. What was so striking about her early decorative appearances in *Dracula* and *The Count of Monte Cristo* was that such a young woman could be blessed with both surpassing beauty and a flawless command of acting technique. In 1981 her grace under fire in the spy thriller *Eye of the Needle* revealed an old-fashioned movie star presence. The Nelligan persona fell into place: an intelligent romantic waging a battle against her carnal instincts. Without her defining passion, the film would be warmed-over espionage claptrap, and she was within hailing distance of the Fonda-Dunaway-Glenda Jackson acting pantheon.

As for Nelligan's next outings, one, *Without a Trace*, was a hybrid of soap opera and tabloid sensationalism that reduced her to one-note suffering; the other, *Eleni*, snuffed out the promise of superstardom. One of the sloppiest prestige productions ever clumsily adapted from a beloved best seller, *Eleni* did a disservice to its poignant subject matter about a son searching for closure with his mother's World War II martyrdom in Greece. Examining the wobbly structure of the screenplay which favored the crusading son (drably limned by John Malkovich) over the noble mother should have tipped Nelligan off that this was not the dream role it appeared to be. Too young and too refined for a role ideal for Irene Pappas or Katina Paxinou, Nelligan visibly tries to bend the windbag role to her will but she is left twisting in the wind by flowery dialogue more suited to a Sarah Bernhardt comeback tour than to a simple peasant woman's dreams for her children's safety.

Since the critical excoriation heaped on *Eleni*, Nelligan has continued to astonish her theatrical following (*Virginia*, *Spoils of War*) and rebounded with magnificent starring roles on television in *Kojak: The Price of Justice*, as a manipulative child murderess modeled after Alice Crimmins; *Love and Hate*, as a battered wife whispering in a voice of protest; and *Spoils of War*, as an aging sixties radical selfishly clutching her son as a link to her ex-husband. Deftly scaling down her theatrical effects in television specials based on acclaimed plays (*Old Times*, *Three Hotels*), she can also scenery chew with the hungriest of hams as she proved with her savage caricature of a sob-story columnist fanning the Dionne Quints craze. What possessed her to trash her talent in *Terror Stalks the Class Reunion* seems less earth-shattering when fans can continue enjoying vindicating returns to cinema such as her silken performances as a brutally funny hash slinger in *Frankie and Johnny* and as a domineering mother suppressing a scandal with damaging aftershocks for her children in *The Prince of Tides*. And if such big-budget flicks as *Wolf* foolishly push her to the sidelines, at least television offers such juicy opportunities as *Spoils of War* in which Nelligan dazzles with her youthful allure intact as a flamboyant lost soul waxing nostalgic for the man that got away and for her limelight days as star protester on campus. As with her other major acting turns, Nelligan etches women defined by a sexual core which they allow to sweep better judgment aside (*Eye of the Needle, Therese Raquin, Frankie and Johnny*) or which they deliberately warp as a power tool against men (*Kojak: The Price of Justice, The Prince of Tides*).

Time has made Nelligan's beauty less remote and her talent more versatile. If movie megastardom is unlikely now, a slew of acting triumphs in all media seems guaranteed for this smashing artist who might have been miscast in the role of traditional movie star. Whereas stars fade, great actresses such as Nelligan go on working with their power undiminished.

—Robert Pardi

NEWMAN, Paul

Nationality: American. **Born:** Cleveland, Ohio, 26 January 1925. **Education:** Attended Shaker Heights High School; Kenyon College, Gambier, Ohio, degree in economics and dramatics, 1949; Yale Drama School, New Haven, Connecticut, 1951-52. **Military Service:** U.S. Navy on torpedo planes as radioman, 1943-46; **Family:** Married 1) Jackie Witte, 1949, three children (one deceased); 2) the actress Joanne Woodward, 1958, three daughters. **Career:** 1949—acted in repertory company in Williams Bay, Wisconsin, and with Woodstock Players, Illinois; 1950-51—ran the family sporting-goods business in Cleveland after the death of his father; 1952—worked in television in New York; 1953—Broadway debut in *Picnic*; 1954—contract with Warner Brothers, and film debut in *The Silver Chalice*; on New York stage in *The Desperate Hours*; 1959—on Broadway in *Sweet Bird of Youth*; 1968—directed first feature film, *Rachel, Rachel*, starring Joanne Woodward; 1969—founder, with Barbra Streisand and Sidney Poitier, First Artists Production Company; also professional race car driver and owner of food manufacturing company, Newman's Own Inc.; 1995—part owner of *The Nation*. **Awards:** Best Actor, Cannes Festival, for *The Long Hot Summer*, 1958; Best Foreign Actor, British Academy, for *The Hustler*, 1961; Best Direction, New York Film Critics, for *Rachel, Rachel*, 1968; Honorary Oscar, "in recognition of his many memorable and compelling screen performances and for his personal integrity and dedication to his craft," 1985; Best Actor, Academy Award, for *The Color of Money*, 1986; Doctor of Humane Letters, Yale University, 1988. **Address:** 1120 5th Avenue #1C, New York, NY 10128, U.S.A.

Films as Actor:

1954   *The Silver Chalice* (Saville) (as Basil the Defender)
1956   *The Rack* (Laven) (as Capt. Edward Hall Jr.); *Somebody Up There Likes Me* (Wise) (as Rocky Graziano)
1957   *The Helen Morgan Story* (*Both Ends of the Candle*) (Curtiz) (as Larry); *Until They Sail* (Wise) (as Capt. Jack Harding)
1958   *The Long Hot Summer* (Ritt) (as Ben Quick); *The Left-Handed Gun* (Arthur Penn) (as Billy Bonney); *Cat on a Hot Tin Roof* (Richard Brooks) (as Brick); *Rally 'round the Flag, Boys!* (McCarey) (as Harry Bannerman)
1959   *The Young Philadelphians* (*The City Jungle*) (Sherman) (as Tony Lawrence)
1960   *From the Terrace* (Robson) (as Alfred Eaton); *Exodus* (Preminger) (as Ari Ben Canaan)
1961   *Paris Blues* (Ritt) (as Ram Bowen); ***The Hustler*** (Rossen) (as "Fast Eddie" Felson)
1962   *Hemingway's Adventures of a Young Man* (*Adventures of a Young Man*) (Ritt) (as Ad Francis); *Sweet Bird of Youth* (Richard Brooks) (as Chance Wayne)

1963   *Hud* (Ritt) (as Hud Bannon); *A New Kind of Love* (Shavelson) (as Steve Sherman); *The Prize* (Robson) (as Andrew Craig)
1964   *What a Way to Go!* (Thompson) (as Larry Flint); *The Outrage* (Ritt) (as Juan Carrasco)
1965   *Lady L* (Ustinov) (as Armand)
1966   *Harper* (*The Moving Target*) (Smight) (as Lew Harper); *Torn Curtain* (Hitchcock) (as Professor Michael Armstrong)
1967   *Hombre* (Ritt) (as John Russell); *Cool Hand Luke* (Rosenberg) (as Luke Jackson)
1968   *The Secret War of Harry Frigg* (Smight) (title role)
1969   *Winning* (Goldstone) (as Frank Capua); *Butch Cassidy and the Sundance Kid* (Hill) (as Butch Cassidy)
1970   *WUSA* (Rosenberg) (as Rheinhardt)
1972   *Pocket Money* (Rosenberg) (as Jim Kane); *The Life and Times of Judge Roy Bean* (Huston) (title role)
1973   *The Mackintosh Man* (Huston) (as Rearden); *The Sting* (Hill) (as Henry Gondorff)
1974   *The Towering Inferno* (Guillermin and Irwin Allen) (as Doug Roberts)
1975   *The Drowning Pool* (Rosenberg) (as Lew Harper)
1976   *Buffalo Bill and the Indians, or Sitting Bull's History Lesson* (Altman) (as Buffalo Bill); *Silent Movie* (Mel Brooks) (cameo)
1977   *Slapshot* (Hill) (as Reggie Dunlop)
1979   *Quintet* (Altman) (as Essex)
1981   *Absence of Malice* (Pollack) (as Gallagher); *Fort Apache, the Bronx* (Petrie) (as Murphy); *When Time Ran Out* (*Earth's Final Fury*) (Goldstone) (as Hank Anderson)
1982   *The Verdict* (Lumet) (as Frank Galvin)
1986   *The Color of Money* (Scorsese) (as Eddie Felson)
1987   *Hello Actors Studio* (Tresgot—doc)
1989   *Fat Man and Little Boy* (*Shadow Makers*) (Joffé) (as Gen. Leslie R. Groves); *Blaze* (Shelton) (as Earl K. Long)
1990   *Mr. and Mrs. Bridge* (Ivory) (as Walter Bridge)
1991   *Why Havel?* (as himself)
1994   *The Hudsucker Proxy* (Coen) (as Sidney J. Mussburger); *Nobody's Fool* (Benton) (as Donald "Sully" Sullivan)

Films as Director:

1959   *On the Harmfulness of Tobacco*
1968   *Rachel, Rachel* (+ pr)
1971   *Sometimes a Great Notion* (*Never Give an Inch*) (+ ro as Hank Stamper)
1972   *The Effect of Gamma Rays on Man-in-the-Moon Marigolds* (+ pr)
1980   *The Shadow Box* (for TV)
1984   *Harry and Son* (+ ro as Harry, co-pr, co-sc)
1987   *The Glass Menagerie*

Publications

By NEWMAN: articles—

"Success Begins at Forty," in *Films and Filming* (London), January 1966.
"Interview: Paul Newman," in *Playboy* (Chicago), July 1968.
"The Anti-Hero as Director," interview with D. Diehl, in *Action* (Los Angeles), May-June 1969.
Interview with R. Sklar and A. Horton, in *Cineaste* (New York), vol. 12, no. 1, 1982.
"Newman on Nukes," interview with J. Goodman, in *American Film* (Washington, D.C.), October 1982.

Paul Newman (left) with Jackie Gleason in *The Hustler*

Interview with Brian Baxter, in *Films and Filming* (London), March 1987.

Interview with Michel Cieutat, in *Positif* (Paris), March 1987.

On NEWMAN: books—

Hamblett, Charles, *Paul Newman*, London, 1975.

Godfrey, Lionel, *Paul Newman, Superstar: A Critical Biography*, New York, 1978.

Quick, Lawrence J., *The Films of Paul Newman*, Secaucus, New Jersey, 1981.

Barbier, Philippe, and Jacques Moreau, *Album Photos: Paul Newman*, Paris, 1983.

Landry, J. C., *Paul Newman*, London, 1983.

Guerif, François, *Paul Newman*, Paris, 1987.

Kerbel, Michael, *Paul Newman: Seine Filme, sein Leben*, Munich, 1987.

Morella, Joe, and Edward Z. Epstein, *Paul and Joanne: A Biography of Paul Newman and Joanne Woodward*, New York, 1988.

Netter, Susan, *Paul Newman and Joanne Woodward*, London, 1989.

Oumano, Elena, *Paul Newman*, New York, 1989.

Stern, Stewart, *No Tricks in My Pocket: Paul Newman Directs*, New York, 1989.

Lax, Eric, *Paul Newman: A Biography*, Atlanta, 1996.

On NEWMAN: articles—

Eyles, Allen, "The Other Brando," in *Films and Filming* (London), January 1965.

Westerbeck, C. L., Jr., "Good Company," in *Sight and Sound* (London), Autumn 1973.

Gow, Gordon, "Closer to Life," in *Films and Filming* (London), April 1975.

Farber, Stephen, "Paul Newman," in *The Movie Star*, edited by Elisabeth Weis, New York, 1981.

Baxter, Brian, "Paul Newman," in *Films and Filming* (London), August 1984.

Current Biography 1985, New York, 1985.

Eisenberg, Lee, "Paul Newman: Him with His Foot to the Floor," in *Esquire* (New York), June 1988.

Worrell, Denise, in *Icons: Intimate Portraits*, New York, 1989.

Scheer, Robert, "The Further Adventures of Paul Newman," in *Esquire* (New York), October 1989.

Dowd, Maureen, "Paul Newman and Joanne Woodward: A Lifetime of Shared Passions," in *McCall's*, January 1991.

Carter, Betsy, "Paul Newman Acts His Age," in *Harper's Bazaar*, April 1994.

Hirschberg, Lynn, "Has Paul Newman Finally Grown Up?," in *New York*, 12 December 1994.

Ansen, David, "American's Own," in *Newsweek*, 19 December 1994.

* * *

Of his movie debut in *The Silver Chalice*, Paul Newman has been quoted as saying, "to have the honor of being in the worst picture of the fifties and surviving is no mean feat." Whether it really is the worst film of the 1950s is a matter for some debate; the fact of Newman's quite remarkable survival is not.

For in spite of a clutch of poor reviews for his role as "Basil the Defender" in that ignoble epic, Newman—fresh from the Actors Studio and some success in a Broadway production of *Picnic*—was to become one of the most accomplished of film actors. Reversing the customary relation between the sublime and the ridiculous, he went straight from *The Silver Chalice* to the role of Rocky Graziano in *Somebody Up There Likes Me*, and from that film until *Hud* in 1963 Newman did nothing but learn and improve. In his best performances of these years (*The Left-Handed Gun*, *The Hustler*, and *Hud* rather than the more theatrical material such as *Cat on a Hot Tin Roof* or *Sweet Bird of Youth*) he rose to the challenge of movie acting with apparently effortless skill.

Take *The Left-Handed Gun*. Arthur Penn's neurotically intense Freudian Western presents a young man constantly on the very edge of insanity, a Billy the Kid with all the traditional accoutrements but none of the heroics. Newman, typically, built his performance on detailed physical impressions, his every movement convoluted, his gestures conveying impossible tensions. He really is like a spring ready to snap. This Billy is clearly of the Actors Studio, of a piece with the work of Brando, Steiger, Wallach, and Clift. Expression of character comes from within, "absorbing other people's personalities and adding some of your own," as Newman once put it. The difficulty with this approach, the so-called Method, is that it was designed primarily for the stage and therefore all too easily led its exponents into overstatement on screen. It was essential to tone down Method techniques to meet the singular requirements of movie acting.

For Newman, unlike Rod Steiger and to some extent Marlon Brando, that proved no great problem, and by 1961 and *The Hustler* he had found the perfect balance. Newman's performance as Fast Eddie Felson, the consummately ambitious pool hustler who ultimately finds self-respect, harnesses the sheer physicality of Method technique to the understatement required of actors playing on the big screen. In *The Hustler* Newman uses many of the little contrivances on which he was to come to rely: suddenly looking away and turning back with a quizzical expression; restraining that luminous smile then switching it on like a spotlight; furrowing his brow in a way that breathes seriousness into the most trivial exchange. In this film, however, there is much more to his performance than skillful deployment of these techniques.

Partly, of course, that is a product of quality and depth in *The Hustler*'s writing and direction. Looks and smiles convey much more when writer, director, and cinematographer are as skilled as the actor, and it is likely that Fast Eddie would have been fascinating whoever played the role. But there is also a strong sense of involvement from Newman, an engagement with character which has not been found in many of his performances since. In *The Hustler* Newman the actor is subjugated to Eddie the character: all his considerable skills are placed in the service of the film. In his later big successes (*Butch Cassidy and the Sundance Kid*, *The Sting*, and even the rather better *Cool Hand Luke*) everything is built upon an already established Newman persona. These films are vehicles. Not in the sense that they are made solely to display him, but that they are movies in which his written character is sufficient of a tabula rasa to allow him to play it by resorting to the now familiar array of Newman techniques and mannerisms. These are roles molded by the requirements of the star system and played by reflex.

This is not to suggest that Newman has not given audiences and filmmakers excellent value. He has probably provided more consistent service than any other actor of the Method generation. It is only when you view his work of the 1970s and 1980s in the light of his best performances that you realize how much was lost when he was transformed from actor into star. Fortunately, it is no longer necessary to return to *The Hustler* to make that comparison. Since he turned 60 he seems to have found new commitment and energy, gracing several films with impeccable performances. One such is his hugely enjoyable portrait of the extrovert and eccentric Earl K. Long in *Blaze*. Another, perhaps the biggest delight to long-term admirers, is his recreation of Eddie Felson 25 years on in *The Color of Money*, for which he finally received the Academy Award that he merited for its prequel, *The Hustler*. Scorsese's film may not have the classical narrative qualities of Robert Rossen's original but it does have Newman giving an object lesson in refined movie acting. And the early 1990s have produced a little run of quality performances in *Mr. and Mrs. Bridge*, *The Hudsucker Proxy*, and, best of all, as Sully in *Nobody's Fool*, for which he received yet another Oscar nomination. Forty years since *The Silver Chalice,y* and Newman is still effortlessly proving that surviving that disaster was no accident.

—Andrew Tudor

NICHOLSON, Jack

Nationality: American. **Born:** Neptune, New Jersey, 22 April 1937. **Education:** Attended Manasquan High School in Neptune; studied acting in Los Angeles with Jeff Corey, 1957. **Family:** Married Sandra Knight, 1961 (divorced 1966), child: Jennifer; two children with actress Rebecca Broussard. **Career:** 1957—office boy in MGM cartoon department; some television appearances; 1957-58—stage work with Players Ring Theater; 1958—film debut in *The Cry Baby Killer*; 1963—first screenwriting credit for *Thunder Island*; 1971—directed first film, *Drive, He Said*. **Awards:** Best Supporting Actor, New York Film Critics, for *Easy Rider*, 1969; Best Actor, British Academy, for *Chinatown* and *The Last Detail*, 1974; Best Actor, Cannes Festival, for *The Last Detail*, 1974; Best Actor, New York Film Critics, for *Chinatown* and *The Last Detail*, 1974; Best Actor, Academy Award, Best Actor, New York Film Critics, and Best Actor, British Academy, for *One Flew over the Cuckoo's Nest*, 1976; Best Supporting Actor, Academy Award, for *Terms of Endearment*, 1983; Best Actor Awards, New York Film Critics and Los Angeles Film Critics, 1987; American Film Institute Life Achievement Award, 1994. **Agent:** Sandy Bressler and Associates, 15760 Ventura Boulevard, Suite 1730, Encino, CA 91436, U.S.A.

Films as Actor:

1958   *The Cry Baby Killer* (Addis) (as Jimmy)
1959   *Too Soon to Love* (Rush) (as Buddy)
1960   *The Wild Ride* (Corman) (as Johnny Varron); *Studs Lonigan* (Lerner) (as Weary Reilly); *Little Shop of Horrors* (Corman) (as Wilbur Force)

1961 *The Broken Land* (Bushelman) (as Will Broicous)
1962 *The Raven* (Corman) (as Roxford Bedlo)
1963 *The Terror* (Corman) (as Andre Duvalier)
1964 *Ensign Pulver* (Logan) (as crew member); *Back Door to Hell* (Hellman) (as Burnett)
1966 *The Shooting* (Hellman) (as Billy Spear, + co-pr)
1967 *Hell's Angels on Wheels* (Rush) (as Poet)
1968 *Psych-Out* (Rush) (as Stoney)
1969 ***Easy Rider*** (Dennis Hopper) (as George Hanson)
1970 *On a Clear Day You Can See Forever* (Minnelli) (as Tad Pringle); ***Five Easy Pieces*** (Rafelson) (as Robert Eroica Dupea)
1971 *Carnal Knowledge* (Nichols) (as Jonathan); *A Safe Place* (Jaglom) (as Mitch)
1972 *The King of Marvin Gardens* (Rafelson) (as David Staebler)
1973 *The Last Detail* (Ashby) (as Billy Buddusky)
1974 ***Chinatown*** (Polanski) (as J. J. Gittes); *The Fortune* (Nichols) (as Oscar Sullivan)
1975 ***Professione: Reporter*** (*The Passenger*) (Antonioni) (as David Locke); *Tommy* (Russell) (as Doctor); ***One Flew over the Cuckoo's Nest*** (Forman) (as Randall P. McMurphy)
1976 *The Missouri Breaks* (Arthur Penn) (as Tom Logan); *The Last Tycoon* (Kazan) (as Brimmer)
1980 *The Shining* (Kubrick) (as Jack Torrance)

1981 *The Border* (Richardson) (as Charlie Smith); *The Postman Always Rings Twice* (Rafelson) (as Frank Chambers); *Reds* (Beatty) (as Eugene O'Neill)
1983 *Terms of Endearment* (James L. Brooks) (as Garrett Breedlove)
1985 *Prizzi's Honor* (Huston) (as Charlie Fontana)
1986 *Heartburn* (Nichols) (as Mark)
1987 *Broadcast News* (James L. Brooks) (as Bill Rorich); *Ironweed* (Babenco) (as Francis Phelan); *The Witches of Eastwick* (Miller) (as Daryl Van Horne)
1989 *Batman* (Burton) (as the Joker/Jack Napier)
1992 *Hoffa* (DeVito) (title role); *Man Trouble* (Rafelson) (as Harry Bliss); *A Few Good Men* (Rob Reiner) (as Col. Nathan R. Jessep)
1994 *Wolf* (Nichols) (as Will Randall)
1995 *The Crossing Guard* (Sean Penn) (as Freddy Gale)
1996 *The Evening Star* (as Garrett Breedlove); *Mars Attacks!* (Tim Burton) (as President James Dale)

Films as Scriptwriter:

1963 *Thunder Island* (Leewood)
1966 *Ride the Whirlwind* (Hellman) (+ pr, ro as Wes); *Flight to Fury* (Hellman) (+ ro as Jay Wickham)

Jack Nicholson in *One Flew Over the Cuckoo's Nest*

1967 *The Trip* (Corman)
1968 *Head* (Rafelson) (co-sc, + co-pr, ro as himself)

Films as Director:

1970 *Drive, He Said* (+ co-pr, co-sc)
1978 *Goin' South* (+ ro as Henry Moon)
1990 *The Two Jakes* (+ ro as J. J. Gittes)

Publications

By NICHOLSON: articles—

"Jack Nicholson on the New York Film Festival," interview with V. Wade, in *Inter/View* (New York), December 1972.
"Jack Nicholson and Angelica Huston," interview with R. Kent, in *Inter/View* (New York), April 1974.
"Profession: Actor," interview with J. R. Taylor, in *Sight and Sound* (London), Summer 1974.
Interview with B. Walker, in *Film Comment* (New York), May/June 1985.
Interview with D. Caulfield and P. H. Broeske, in *Stills* (London), October 1985.
"Jake Jake: Jack Nicholson and Harvey Keitel," interview with Julian Schnabel, in *Interview* (New York), August 1990.
"Wolf, Man, Jack," interview with Nancy Collins, in *Vanity Fair* (New York), April 1994.

On NICHOLSON: books—

Crane, Robert David, and Christopher Fryer, *Jack Nicholson—Face to Face*, New York, 1975.
Dickens, Norman, *Jack Nicholson: The Search for a Superstar*, New York, 1975.
Braithwaite, Bruce, *The Films of Jack Nicholson*, Farncombe, Surrey, 1977.
Sandre, Didier, *Jack Nicholson*, Paris, 1981.
Downing, David, *Jack Nicholson: A Biography*, London, 1983.
Cagin, Seth, and Philip Dray, *Hollywood Films of the Seventies: Sex, Drugs, Rock 'n' Roll and Politics*, New York, 1984.
McGee, Mark Thomas, *Fast and Furious: The Story of American International Pictures*, Jefferson, North Carolina, 1984.
Brode, Douglas, *The Films of Jack Nicholson*, London, 1987; rev. ed., 1994.
Parker, John, *The Joker's Wild: The Biography of Jack Nicholson*, London, 1991.
Shepherd, Donald, *Jack Nicholson: An Unauthorized Biography*, New York, 1991.
Bingham, Dennis, *Acting Male: Masculinities in the Films of James Stewart, Jack Nicholson, and Clint Eastwood*, New Brunswick, New Jersey, 1994.
McGilligan, Patrick, *Jack's Life: A Biography of Jack Nicholson*, New York, 1994.

On NICHOLSON: articles—

Cieutat, Michel, "Jack Nicholson, ou la vocation de l'abandon," in *Positif* (Paris), May 1973.
Eyles, Allen, "Jack Nicholson," in *Focus on Film* (London), Summer 1974.
Haskell, Molly, "Gould vs. Redford vs. Nicholson: The Absurdist as Box Office Draw," in *The Movie Star*, edited by Elisabeth Weis, New York, 1981.

Wolf, Jamie, "It's All Right, Jack," in *American Film* (Washington, D.C.), January-February 1984.
Grimes, T., "BBS: Auspicious Beginnings, Open Endings," in *Movie* (London), Winter 1986.
Greenberg, J., "Forget It Jack, It's *The Two Jakes*," in *American Film* (New York), February 1990.
Schruers, Fred, "The Two Jacks," in *Premiere* (New York), September 1990.
Current Biography 1995, New York, 1995.

*   *   *

One is surprised that an actor of such obvious charisma as Jack Nicholson remained mired for so long in low-budget films made about and for the fringes of American society. During his early years, he appeared in a steady stream of quickies for Roger Corman and others. His masochistic dental patient in Corman's classic two-day wonder *Little Shop of Horrors* remains a high point, although it did little to advance Nicholson's career at the time. Only when the counterculture became a less peripheral force toward the end of the 1960s did Nicholson begin to exert widespread appeal.

Nicholson's background (a broken home) and intense personality suited him for roles as an alienated, rebellious biker and as a horror film hero always on the thin edge of psychosis. Significantly, his break came in *Easy Rider,* where he plays an alcoholic lawyer only too ready to hit the road and leave behind a meaningless settled life. Nicholson's *tour-de-forcey* performance in the role, which he took over at the last minute when the already cast Rip Torn himself hit the road, earned a supporting Oscar nomination. Like Richard Rush's *Hell's Angelsy* on Wheels, in which he appeared two years before, *Easy Rider* presented bikers as the image of nonconformity. The difference was that the ideas of freedom from responsibility and a dedication to self-enjoyment now found a wider audience which Nicholson was at last able to tap.

In subsequent films, Nicholson has made his drifter character more resonant. In *Five Easy Pieces* his Bobby Dupea is a man caught between the claims of different cultures. At the end, he sets out like Huck Finn for the frontier. But the character will undoubtedly find only another dead end in Alaska, only another correlative of his own incapacities. For demythologizing the character he had so vividly etched the year before in *Easy Rider*, Nicholson earned his first Oscar nomination as best actor. He has since taken his screen persona in the direction of continuing popular appeal, determined not to find himself for the second time on the outside of mainstream cinema.

In Mike Nichols's *Carnal Knowledge* he played a successful, Ivy League-educated lawyer whose youthful joy in sex, poisoned by male chauvinism, becomes a pitiful impotence. For Hal Ashby's *The Last Detail* he portrayed a dim-witted military policeman who instinctively grasps the injustices of his world but is only able to stage an ineffective (if heartwarming) protest against them. In Polanski's *Chinatown* Nicholson is a jaded detective whose "matrimonial work" is nevertheless an attempt to preserve innocence and indict the guilty (he fails at both). As McMurphy in Forman's *One Flew over the Cuckoo's Nest* he offers a variation on his character of the unrepressed outsider, who doubles as a healer of psychic wounds (a performance that won him an Oscar). In both *The Missouri Breaks* (opposite Brando) and *Reds* (as Eugene O'Neill, receiving another Oscar nomination), he is again an outsider battling or protesting against an unjust system—the flip side of his later role in Rob Reiner's military courtroom drama, *A Few Good Men*, wherein he personified the injustices of the system itself. In Kubrick's *The Shining*, he returned to a character much like those he had played for Corman—the potential psychopath who goes over the brink into madness—but pulled out all the stops in a creatively daring performance.

His role in *Terms of Endearment* further softened the rebel character he had created for the turbulent 1960s and 1970s. As a womanizing, alcoholic former astronaut, he is a comic and not a tragic figure, a man who does his own thing, hurts no one, and can be melodramatically transformed into a sensitive human being. The part won him another supporting actor Oscar.

Now conceiving himself more as a character actor, Nicholson has introduced a Cormanesque flair for the absurdly horrific as the devil in *The Witches of Eastwick*, as the Joker in *Batman,* and as the loser book editor turned lycanthropic winner in *Wolf.* The antihero of his earlier career, it seems, can now only be recreated—as the nostalgic performances in *The Two Jakes* (a sequel to *Chinatown*), *Ironweed,* and *Hoffa* make clear.

—R. Barton Palmer, updated by John McCarty

NIELSEN, Asta

Nationality: Danish. **Born:** Copenhagen, 11 September 1881. **Education:** Attended the children's school of the Royal Theatre, Copenhagen. **Family:** Married 1) the director Urban Gad, 1910 (divorced); four later marriages. **Career:** Actress in chorus of the Kongelige Theatre; stage debut at the Dagmar Theatre, then leading lady at the New Theatre; 1910—film debut in *Afgrunden*, directed by Gad; 1911-36—worked in Germany first with the producer Paul Davidson: directed by Lubitsch, Gerlach, Wiene, Pabst, and others; 1932—only sound film, *Unmögliche Liebe*; 1936—returned to Denmark. **Awards:** Deutscher filmpress, 1963. **Died:** In Copenhagen, 24 May 1972.

Films as Actress:

1910   *Afgrunden* (Gad); *Den sorte Drom* (Gad); *Balletdanserinden* (Blom); *Nachtfalter* (Gad); *Heissen Blut* (Gad); *Im grossen Augenblick* (Gad); *Zigeunerblut* (Gad); *Der fremde Vogel* (Gad)

1912   *Die Arme Jenny* (Gad); *Die Match des Goldes* (Gad); *Zum Tode gehetzt* (Gad); *Der Totentanz* (Gad); *Die Kinder des Generals* (Gad); *Wenn die Maske fällt* (Gad); *Das Mädchen ohne Vaterland* (Gad); *Jugend und Tollheit* (Gad); *Komodiaten* (Gad); *Die Sunden der Väter* (Gad)

1913   *Der Tod in Sevilla* (Gad); *Die Suffrageten* (Gad); *S.1.* (Gad); *Die Filmprimadonna* (Gad); *Engelein* (Gad)

1914   *Das Kind ruft* (Gad); *Zapatas Bande* (Gad); *Das Feuer* (Gad); *Die Tochter der Landstrasse* (Gad); *Vordertreppe-Hintertreppe* (Gad); *Engeleins Hochzeit* (Gad); *Die ewige Nacht* (Gad); *Aschenbrödel* (Gad); *Weisse Rosen* (Gad)

1916   *Dora Brandes* (Stifter); *Das liebes A.B.C.* (Stifter)

1917   *Das Waisenhauskind* (Schmidthassler); *Die Rose der Wildnes* (Schmidthassler); *Das Eskimo-Baby* (Schmidthassler); *Die Börsenkönigin* (Edekl)

1918   *Mod Lyset* (Holger-Madsen)

1919   *Nach dem Gesetz* (Grunwald); *Graf Sylvains Rache* (Grunwald); *Das Ende von Liede* (Grunwald); *Rausch* (Lubitsch)

1920   *Hamlet* (Gade); *Steuerman Holk* (Wolff); *Der Reigen* (Oswald); *Kurfurstendamm* (Oswald); *Brigaten Rache* (Bruck)

1921   *Sklaven der Sinne (Irrende Seelen)* (Froelich); *Die Spionin (Mata Hari)* (Wolff); *Die geliebte Roswolskys* (Basch and Galeen); *Fräulein Julie* (Jessner)

1922   *Vanina (Vanina Vanini)* (von Gerlach); *Der Absturz* (Wolff); *Die Tänzerin Navarro* (Wolff)

1923   *Erdgeist* (Jessner); *INRI* (Wiene)

1924   *Das am Meer* (Kaufmann); *Liebende Buddhas* (Wegener); *Die Frau im Feuer* (Bose); *Die Schmetterlingsschlacht* (Eckstein); *Hedda Gabler* (Eckstein) (title role); *Die Gesunkenen* (Walther-Fein)

1925   *Athleten* (Zelnik); *Die freudlose Gasse* (Pabst)

1927   *Laster den Menschheit* (Meinert); *Dirnentragödie* (Rahn); *Gehetzte Frauen* (Oswald); *Kleinstadtsunder* (Rahn); *Das gefahrliche Alter* (Illés)

1932   *Unmögliche Liebe (Vera Holgk und ihre Töchter)* (Waschneck)

Publications

By NIELSEN: book—

Die Tiende Muse, Copenhagen, 1945.

On NIELSEN: books—

Langsted, Adolph, *Asta Nielsen*, Copenhagen, 1918.

Diaz, Pablo, *Asta Nielsen: Eine Biographie unsere popularen Kunstlerin*, Berlin, 1920.

Urazov, Ismait, *Asta Nielsen*, Moscow, 1926.

Mungenast, Ernst, *Asta Nielsen*, Stuttgart, 1928.

Balázs, Béla, *Theory of the Film: Character and Growth of a New Art*, London, 1952.

Engenberg, Marguerite, *Asta Nielsen*, Copenhagen, 1966.

Drouzy, Maurice, *Le Cinéma Danois*, Paris, 1979.

Image: On the Art and Evolution of Film, edited by Marshall Deutelbaum, New York, 1979.

Asta Nielsen—ihr Leben in Fotodokumenten: Selbstzeugnissen und zeitgenössischen Bertrachtungen, edited by Renate Seydel and Allan Hagedorff, Munich, 1981.

Fonesca, M. S., *Panorama do Cinema Dinamarquês*, Lisbon, 1983.

On NIELSEN: articles—

Blakestone, Oswell, "Lusts of Mankind," in *Close-Up* (London), November 1928.

Winge, J. H., "Asta Nielsen," in *Sight and Sound* (London), April 1950.

Eisner, Lotte, "Asta Nielsen," in *Cahiers du Cinéma* (Paris), December 1953.

"The Screen's First Tragedienne: Asta Nielsen," in *Image* (Rochester, New York), March 1955.

Luft, H. G., "Asta Neilsen," in *Films in Review* (New York), January 1956.

Castello, Guilio, "Asta Nielsen," in *Bianco e nero* (Rome), October-November 1958.

Lindberg, I., "Ojeblikke med Asta," in *Kosmorama* (Copenhagen), September 1972.

Gress, E., "Die Asta: A Personal Impression," and "Asta Nielsen: The Silent Muse," by R. C. Allen in *Sight and Sound* (London), Autumn 1973.

Gramann, K., and H. Schlupmann, "Asta Nielsen: Pioniere van de filmtaal," in *Skrien* (Amsterdam), September 1983.

Monty, Ib, "Deres hengivne," *Kosmorama* (Copenhagen), Autumn 1986.

*   *   *

Asta Nielsen, muse of silence, began her career with *Afgrunden*, and from 1910 to 1916 (her formative period), carried fully the style of the cultivated Dane in cinema. Contrary to the practice of actors of the time toward excessive and emphatic gestures, Nielsen launched a style more suited to the cinematographic medium, characterized by her strife, by the play of various expressions which she completed with a distant gaze, holding generally to one point of view and then cut away, in contrast to the montage editing of America.

Asta Nielsen

With *Afgrunden* Asta Nielsen naturally introduced one of the fundamental components of her representational style. Here emerges a sense of dance, and her eroticism, touched with an aura of spirituality, commands a metaphysical fatalism—the marked Nordic presence—which made Nielsen so disturbing. When she created the vamp (preceding Musidora and Theda Bara) she came to be a sorceress and one of the forces of cinema, conveying innermost feelings in her melodramas. Her admirable use (similar to what Lillian Gish began to create much later) of her face and her gaze—a tremor of the eyelids or her immense eyes spoke concisely—made audiences feel a dialogue was transmitted despite the silence of the film.

Her relationship with Urban Gad symbolized a model of identification between actress and director which film history continually reproduces (for example, Stiller-Garbo, Sternberg-Dietrich, and Godard-Karina). Between the acting power of Nielsen and the mastery of mise-en-scène of Gad, a style completely appropriate and self-sustaining emerged. For example, *Vordertreppe-Hintertreppe*, in particular through the technique of lighting and stylized decor, shows the contribution of their relationship to the development of a type of worldly drama which foreshadowed what would be seen much later as "Lubitsch's touch."

Berlin did not delay in summoning her. With the support of the producer Paul Davidson, Nielsen became established as one of the key figures of the German cinema. Especially in the second stage of her career, after cutting away from Gad, Nielsen brought to the German screen the burden of tragic and mystic Scandinavian culture, and one can hear the echo of both Ibsen (not only by chance in the film *Hedda Gabler*) and Strindberg (by filming *Fräulein Julie* with Jessner).

This period gave her, consequently, the chance to make her major contributions to the art of cinematic representation. In one case we see her utilizing the slightest expressions of her visage (her "painted face" in front of the mirror in *Der Absturz*) as she is to receive her lover after ten years in prison. Her deceptively passive attitude toward the scene, in *Die freudlose Gasse*, of the jeweler making experimental jewels, while Nielsen fails to notice what is really seen, is a sovereign example of multiexpressive mimicry. And she is working not only with her face but also with her hands, which resignedly tumble down on long arms from her body, and which she uses to accent her voluntary mechanized portrayal. These are the same hands which "spoke" in *Vanina*, in a most typical product of "caligari-ism," as she waits to escape with her lover.

As others have said about Nielsen, she reminds one of a female Hamlet, a woman who worked with men who had a sense of dynasty, a fragile woman with melancholy ambiguity, reminding us of Mary Magdalene in Wiene's *INRI*, with a piousness of dynastic volume, or the Lulu of Jessner's *Erdgeist*. In her work with Jessner, Reinhardt's great rival in the development of German theater, she began her second phase. Nielsen worked with a variety of directors who chose theatrical texts of undeniable quality, from Ibsen and Strindberg to Wedekind and Schnitzler.

In the 1920s Nielsen also developed a persona in characteristic decline, changing from her old passion to the figure of an old dignified prostitute, quoting from *Der Absturz* in two noted "street films," *Die freudlose Gasse* of Pabst and *Dirnentragödie* of Bruno Rahn. Extracting life from the world of myth, Nielsen now herself seems mythic.

—M. S. Fonseca

NIVEN, David

Nationality: British. **Born:** James David Graham Niven in Kirriemuir, Scotland (some sources say London, England), 1 March 1910. **Educa-** **tion:** Attended Stowe House boarding school, near Buckingham, 1923-26; Royal Military College, Sandhurst, 1927-29: commissioned lieutenant in Highland Light Infantry: served in Malta and England to 1932. **Military Service:** Rifle Brigade, 1939-45: lieutenant colonel. **Family:** Married 1) Primula Rollo, 1940 (died 1946), sons: the producer-director David Jr. and James Graham; 2) Hjordia Tersmeden, 1948, adopted daughters: Kristina and Fiona. **Career:** After resigning commission, roamed Canada and United States; 1932—first role as extra in *There Goes the Bride*; 1935—contract with Samuel Goldwyn, first speaking role in film *Without Regret*; 1939—leading role in *Wuthering Heights*; 1946—returned to Hollywood after the war ended; 1951—on Broadway in *Nina*; 1952—on stage in *The Moon Is Blue* in Hollywood, and in film version, 1953; 1952—formed Four Star Playhouse, with Charles Boyer, Ida Lupino, and Dick Powell, and appeared in the TV series *Four Star Playhouse*, 1952-56, and *Alcoa Theatre*, 1957-58; 1959—host of TV series *The David Niven Show*; 1960—moved to Chateau-d'Oex, Switzerland; 1964-65—in TV series *The Rogues*; 1979—in TV mini-series *A Man Called Intrepid*, 1979. **Awards:** Best Actor Academy Award, and Best Actor, New York Film Critics, for *Separate Tables*, 1958; London Evening Standard Special Award, 1980. **Died:** Of ALS (Lou Gehrig's disease), in Chateau-d'Oex, Switzerland, 29 July 1983.

Films as Actor:

1932   *There Goes the Bride* (De Courville) (as extra)
1934   *All the Winners* (Malins) (as extra)
1935   *Mutiny on the Bounty* (Lloyd) (as extra); *Without Regret* (Harold Young) (as Bill Gage); *A Feather in Her Hat* (Santell) (as Leo Cartwright); *Barbary Coast* (Hawks) (as sailor); *Splendor* (Nugent) (as Clancey Lorrimore)
1936   *Rose Marie* (Van Dyke) (as Teddy); *Palm Springs* (*Palm Springs Affair*) (Scotto) (as George Brittel); *Dodsworth* (Wyler) (as Maj. Clyde Lockert); *Thank You, Jeeves* (*Thank You, Mr. Jeeves*) (Arthur Greville Collins) (as Bertie Wooster); *The Charge of the Light Brigade* (Curtiz) (as Capt. James Randall); *Beloved Enemy* (Potter) (as Gerald Preston)
1937   *We Have Our Moments* (Werker) (as Joe Gilling); *The Prisoner of Zenda* (Cromwell and Van Dyke) (as Capt. Fritz von Tarlenheim); *Dinner at the Ritz* (Schuster) (as Paul de Brack)
1938   *Bluebeard's Eighth Wife* (Lubitsch) (as Albert de Regnier); *Four Men and a Prayer* (Ford) (as Christopher Leigh); *Three Blind Mice* (Seiter) (as Steve Harrington); *The Dawn Patrol* (Goulding) (as Lt. Scott)
1939   *Wuthering Heights* (Wyler) (as Edgar Linton); *Bachelor Mother* (Kanin) (as David Merlin); *The Real Glory* (Hathaway) (as Lt. McCool); *Eternally Yours* (Garnett) (as Tony); *Raffles* (Wood and Wyler) (title role)
1942   *The First of the Few* (*Spitfire*) (Leslie Howard) (as Geoffrey Crisp)
1944   *The Way Ahead* (*The Immortal Battalion*) (Reed) (as Lt. Jim Perry)
1946   *A Matter of Life and Death* (*Stairway to Heaven*) (Powell and Pressburger) (as Squadron Leader Peter D. Carter); *Magnificent Doll* (Borzage) (as Aaron Burr); *The Perfect Marriage* (Lewis Allen) (as Dale Williams)
1947   *The Other Love* (de Toth) (as Dr. Anthony Stanton); *The Bishop's Wife* (Koster) (as Henry Brougham)
1948   *Bonnie Prince Charlie* (Kimmins) (title role); *Enchantment* (Reis) (as Gen. Sir Roland "Rolle" Dane)
1949   *A Kiss in the Dark* (Daves) (as Eric Phillips); *A Kiss for Corliss* (*Almost a Bride*) (Wallace) (as Kenneth Marquis)
1950   *The Elusive Pimpernel* (*The Fighting Pimpernel*) (Powell and Pressburger) (as Sir Percy Blakeney); *The Toast of New Orleans* (Taurog) (as Jacques Riboudeaux)

David Niven

1951	*Happy Go Lovely* (Humberstone) (as B. G. Bruno); *Soldiers Three* (Garnett) (as Capt. Pindenny); *The Lady Says No!* (Ross) (as Bill Shelby); *Appointment with Venus* (*Island Rescue*) (Thomas) (as Maj. Valentine Moreland)
1953	*The Moon Is Blue* (Preminger) (as David Slater); *The Love Lottery* (Charles Crichton) (as Rex Allerton)
1954	*Happy Ever After* (*Tonight's the Night*) (Zampi) (as Jasper O'Leary); *Carrington, V.C.* (*Court Martial*) (Asquith) (title role)
1955	*The King's Thief* (Leonard) (as Duke of Brampton)
1956	*The Birds and the Bees* (Taurog) (as Col. Harris); *Around the World in Eighty Days* (Anderson) (as Phileas Fogg); *The Little Hut* (Herbert and Robson) (as Henry Brittingham-Brett)
1957	*Oh Men! Oh Women!* (Nunnally Johnson) (as Dr. Alan Coles); *My Man Godfrey* (Koster) (title role); *The Silken Affair* (Kellino) (as Roger Tweakham, new accountant)
1958	*Bonjour Tristesse* (Preminger) (as Raymond); *Separate Tables* (Delbert Mann) (as Maj. Pollock); *Glamorous Hollywood* (Staub—short) (as himself)
1959	*Ask Any Girl* (Walters) (as Miles Doughton); *Happy Anniversary* (David Miller) (as Chris Walters)
1960	*Please Don't Eat the Daisies* (Walters) (as Laurence Mackay)
1961	*The Guns of Navarone* (J. Lee Thompson) (as Corporal Miller); *I due nemici* (*The Best of Enemies*) (Hamilton) (as Major Richardson)
1962	*La citta prigioniera* (*The Captive City*; *The Conquered City*) (Anthony) (as Maj. Peter Whitfield); *The Road to Hong Kong* (Panama) (cameo as Tibetan monk); *Guns of Darkness* (Asquith) (as Tom Jordan)
1963	*55 Days at Peking* (Nicholas Ray) (as Sir Arthur Robertson); *Il giorno più corto* (*The Shortest Day*) (Corbucci) (as himself)
1964	*The Pink Panther* (Edwards) (as Sir Charles Litton); *Bedtime Story* (Levy) (as Lawrence Jamieson)
1965	*Lady L* (Ustinov) (as Lord Lendale [Dicky]); *Where the Spies Are* (Guest) (as Dr. Jason Love)
1967	*Eye of the Devil* (J. Lee Thompson—produced in 1966) (as Philippe de Montfaucon); *Casino Royale* (Huston and others) (as Sir James Bond)
1968	*The Extraordinary Seaman* (Frankenheimer) (as Lt. Cmdr. Finchhaven, R.N.); *Prudence and the Pill* (Cook and Neame) (as Gerald Hardcastle); *The Impossible Years* (Michael Gordon) (as Jonathan Kingsley)
1969	*Before Winter Comes* (J. Lee Thompson) (as Maj. Giles Burnside); *Le Cerveau* (*The Brain*) (Oury) (as Col. Matthews ["The Brain"])
1970	*The Statue* (Amateau) (as Alex Bolt)
1972	*King, Queen, Knave* (*Herzbube*) (Skolimowski) (as Charles Dreyer)
1974	*Vampira* (*Old Dracula*) (Clive Donner) (as Count Dracula); *Paper Tiger* (Annakin) (as Walter Bradbury)
1976	*No Deposit, No Return* (Tokar) (as J. W. Osborne); *Murder by Death* (Robert Moore) (as Dick Charleston)
1978	*Candleshoe* (Tokar) (as Priory); *Death on the Nile* (Guillerman) (as Colonel Race)
1979	*Escape to Athena* (Cosmatos) (as Professor Blake); *A Nightingale Sang in Berkeley Square* (*The Biggest Bank Robbery*; *The Big Scam*; *The Mayfair Bank Caper*) (Thomas) (as Ivan/Gen. Bernard Drew)
1980	*Rough Cut* (Siegel) (as Chief Inspector Cyril Willis)
1981	*The Sea Wolves* (McLaglen) (as Col. W. H. Grice)
1982	*Better Late than Never* (*Ménage à Trois*; *Whose Little Girl Are You?*) (Forbes) (as Nicholas "Nick" Cartland); *Trail of the Pink Panther* (Edwards) (as Sir Charles Litton)
1983	*Curse of the Pink Panther* (Edwards) (as Sir Charles Litton)

Publications

By NIVEN: books—

Round the Rugged Rocks (novel), London, 1951; as *Once over Lightly*, New York, 1951.
The Moon's a Balloon: Reminiscences, London, 1971.
Bring on the Empty Horses, London, 1975.
Go Slowly, Come Back Quickly (novel), New York, 1981.

By NIVEN: articles—

Interview with J. Reid, in *Motion Picture*, July 1937.
"This Is Myself," in *Movieland Magazine*, June 1947.
"Turning the Tables on Todd," in *Hollywood Reporter*, 18 November 1957.
"I'm Always Surprising Myself," in *Saturday Evening Post*, July 1958.
Interview in *Newsweek* (New York), 22 December 1958.
"A Way with Words," interview in *Films and Filming* (London), November 1978.
"Odds against Success," in *Films* (London), December 1980.

On NIVEN: books—

Garrett, Gerard, *The Films of David Niven*, London, 1975.
Haining, Peter, *The Last Gentleman: A Tribute to David Niven*, 1984.
Hutchinson, Tom, *Niven's Hollywood*, London, 1984.
Morley, Sheridan, *The Other Side of the Moon: The Life of David Niven*, London, 1985.
Francisco, Charles, *David Niven: Endearing Rascal*, New York, 1986.
Fowler, Karin J., *David Niven: A Bio-Bibliography*, Westport, Connecticut, 1995.

On NIVEN: articles—

Hamilton, S., "Life Story," in *Photoplay* (New York), September 1939.
Current Biography 1957, New York, 1957.
Thomas, A., "David Niven," in *Films in Review* (New York), February 1962.
"The Screen Answers Back," in *Films and Filming* (London), May 1962.
Obituary in *Variety* (New York), 3 August 1983.
Obituary in *Films and Filming* (London), September 1983.
Gallagher, John A., "A Final Tribute: David Niven 1910-1983," in *Films in Review* (New York), October 1983.
Norman, Barry, in *The Film Greats*, London, 1985.
Niven, James G., "Life with Father," in *Vanity Fair* (New York), July 1988.
Hale, C., in *Film Dope* (Nottingham, England), July 1992.
Stars (Mariembourg, Belgium), Spring 1993.

*   *   *

Graceful and urbane David Niven excelled at light comedy and playing the gentleman rogue. He possessed considerable charm, not unlike Cary Grant or Errol Flynn, but his sexuality was presented in a more subtle style. Niven could be sexy by just clinking his champagne glass lightly against the tip of his partner's glass, or by tentatively clearing his throat and then half-smiling with a bright, searching gaze toward his leading lady.

Niven came from a long line of military men, but, after tough years at Sandhurst military academy and a stint in the British army, he chose a life of drifting and adventuring which eventually led him to find work as a $2.50-per-day Hollywood extra in 1934. These early years, as well as his later career, are chronicled in two eloquent, best-selling memoirs.

Niven quickly ingratiated himself with the influential British colony in Hollywood, and it was not long before his social contacts paid off. Samuel Goldwyn put him under contract at $100 per week, and he began working regularly. From an inexperienced and rather stiff bit player, he rose to minor dramatic roles in a variety of films, including quality pictures such as *Dodsworth*, *The Charge of the Light Brigade*, and *The Prisoner of Zenda*. Rapidly, his acting improved, and in *The Dawn Patrol* Niven played his first truly memorable part as Errol Flynn's flying buddy. A flair for drawing-room comedy surfaced in *Dinner at the Ritz*, and peaked in *Bachelor Mother*, in which his high-toned British dignity was a perfect foil to Ginger Rogers's working-class American brassiness.

At the onset of World War II, Niven was one of the first film stars to join (or, in his case, reenlist in) the military. Recruited twice for dramatic propaganda films, *First of the Few* and *The Way Ahead*, he was otherwise inactive in pictures for almost six years. Discharged as a colonel, he returned to Goldwyn and appeared in a number of forgettable films, with the exception being the silly but heartwarming comedy *The Bishop's Wife*, which has become a Christmas classic. His growing dissatisfaction with the studio resulted in a contractual release. Now middle-aged, Niven began his freelancing period without much luck; poor choices of scripts damaged his box-office drawing power.

Two films during the late 1950s reestablished his critical reputation and popularity. As the precise and unflappable Phileas Fogg, the character most closely associated with him, Niven held together the all-star extravaganza *Around the World in Eighty Days*. His pathetic bogus major in *Separate Tables* epitomized grace under pressure and proved that Niven could sustain a dramatic role. For the film, he was awarded a Best Actor Oscar.

At the beginning of the 1960s, he appeared in two very different but memorable motion pictures. In *Please Don't Eat the Daisies*, he gave a florid, funny performance as a drama critic with family ties. The part of the dry-witted corporal with an expertise in explosives in *The Guns of Navarone* catered to Niven's screen personality while allowing him an opportunity to play in a big-budget, macho story of brave saboteurs on an all-but-impossible endeavor. Unfortunately, however, his last years are littered with too many appearances in second-rate fare.

David Niven's career stands as credit to his persistence and versatility. He made transitions from decade to decade gracefully, bridging the old Hollywood and the new. He meshed well with any co-star; his effortlessly urbane style and distinctive sense of timing were unforgettable in his good films, and served him well in those that were less than memorable.

—Richard Sater, updated by Audrey E. Kupferberg

NOIRET, Philippe

Nationality: French. **Born:** Lille, 1 October 1930. **Education:** Attended Lycée Janson-de-Sailly, Paris; and Coll. Des oratoriens, Juilly; studied theater under Roger Blin, and at the Dramatic Centre of the West, and the Théâtre National Populaire. **Family:** Married the actress Monique Chaumette, 1962, daughter: Frédérique. **Career:** Worked in cabaret with the comedian Jean-Pierre Darras; 1948—film debut in *Gigi*; 1951—stage debut; then member of the Théâtre National Populaire; announcer on TV show *Discorama*. **Awards:** Best Actor, Venice Festival, for *Thérèse Desqueyroux*, 1962; Étoile de cristal for Best Actor, for *L'Horloger de Saint-Paul*, 1974; Césars for Best Actor, for *Le Vieux Fusil*, 1975, and *La Vie et rien d'autre*, 1989; European Film Award for Best Actor, 1989. **Address:** 104 rue des Sablons, Mareil-Marly 78750, France. **Agent:** Artmédia, 10 av George V, 75008 Paris, France.

Films as Actor:

1948   *Gigi* (Audry) (bit role)

1950   *Olivia* (Audry) (bit role)

1951   *Agence matrimoniale* (Le Chanois)

1955   *La Pointe courte* (Varda)

1960   *Zazie dans le métro* (Zazie; *Zazie in the Underground*) (Malle) (as Uncle Gabriel); *Ravissante* (Lamoureux) (as Maurice)

1961   *Le Capitaine Fracasse* (Gaspard-Huit) (as Hérode); "Lauzun" ep. of *Les Amours célèbres* (Boisrond) (as Louis XIV); *Le Rendez-vous* (Delannoy) (as Inspector Maillard); *Tout l'or du monde* (*All the Gold in the World*) (Clair) (as Victor Hardy)

1962   *Comme un poisson dans l'eau* (Michel) (as Lucien Barlemont); "L'affaire Hugues" ("The Hugues Case") ep. of *Le Crime ne paie pas* (*Crime Does Not Pay*; *The Gentle Art of Murder*) (Oury) (as Clovis Hugues); ***Thérèse Desqueyroux*** (*Thérèse*) (Franju) (as Bernard Desqueyroux); *Le Massaggiatrici* (Fulci) (as Bellini)

1963   *Ballade pour un voyou* (Bonnardot) (as Inspector Mathieu); *Clémentine Chérie* (Chevalier) (as Director General); *La Porteuse de pain* (Cloche) (as Jacques Garaud/Paul Harmant)

1964   *Cyrano et d'Artagnan* (Gance) (as Louis XIII); *Mort, où est ta victoire?* (*Death, Where Is Thy Victory?*) (Bromberger) (as Brassy); *Les Copains* (Robert) (as Bénin); *Monsieur* (Le Chanois) (as Edmond Bernadac)

1965   *Lady L* (Ustinov) (as Ambroise Gérôme)

1966   *La Vie de château* (*A Matter of Resistance*) (Rappeneau) (as Jérôme); *Qui êtes-vous, Polly Magoo?* (Klein) (as Jean-Jacques Georges); *Les Sultans* (Delannoy) (as gynecologist); *Tendre Voyou* (*Tender Scoundrel*) (Jean Becker) (as Bibi Dumonceux); *Le Voyage du père* (de la Patellière) (as traveler)

1967   *The Night of the Generals* (*La Nuit de generaux*) (Litvak) (as Inspector Morand); *L'Un et l'autre* (*The Other One*) (Allio) (as André); "Snow" ep. of *Woman Times Seven* (*Sette volta donna*; *Sept fois femme*) (De Sica) (as Victor)

1968   *Alexandre le bienheureux* (*Very Happy Alexander*; *Happy Alexander*) (Robert) (title role); *Adolphe, ou l'âge tendre* (Toublanc-Michel) (as de Pourtalain)

1969   *The Assassination Bureau* (Dearden) (as Lucoville); *Mister Freedom* (Klein) (as Moujik Man); *Justine* (Strick and Cukor) (as Pombal); *Clérambard* (Robert) (title role); *Topaz* (Hitchcock) (as Henri Jarré)

1970   *Les Caprices de Marie* (*Give Her the Moon*) (de Broca) (as Gabriel)

1971   *Time for Loving* (*Paris Was Made for Lovers*) (Miles) (as Marcel); *Les Aveux les plus doux* (Molinaro) (as Inspector Muller); *Murphy's War* (Yates) (as Louis Brézan)

1972   *La Vieille Fille* (Blanc) (as Gabriel Marcassus); *La Mandarine* (Molinaro) (as Georges); *Le Trèfle à cinq feuilles* (*Five-Leaf Clover*) (Freess) (as Alfred); *L'Attentat* (*Plot*; *The French Conspiracy*) (Boisset) (as Garcin); *Siamo tutti im libertà provvisoria* (Scarpelli) (as Judge Jannacone)

1973   *Poil de carotte* (Graziani) (as M. Lepic); *Le Serpent* (*The Serpent*; *Night Flight from Moscow*) (Verneuil) (as Berthon); *La Grande Bouffe* (*The Big Feast*; *Blow-Out*) (Ferreri) (as Phillippe); *Touche pas à la femme blanche* (*Don't Touch White Women*) (Ferreri) (as Gen. Terry)

1974   *L'Horloger de Saint-Paul* (*The Clockmaker*; *The Watchmaker of Lyon*) (Tavernier) (as Michel Descombe); *Un Nuage entre les dents* (Pico) (as Malisard); *Les Gaspards* (Tchernia) (as Gaspard de Montfermeil); *Le Secret* (*The Secret*) (Enrico) (as Thomas Berthelot)

1975   *Le Jeu avec le feu* (Robbe-Grillet) (as Georges de Saxe); "Les Nobles" ep. of *Que la fête commence!* (*Let Joy Reign Supreme*) (Tavernier) (as Philippe d'Orléans); *Le Vieux Fusil* (*The Old Gun*) (Enrico) (as Julien Dandieu)

1976 *Amici miei* (*My Friends*) (Monicelli) (as Giorgio Perozzi);
      Monsieur Albert (Renard) (title role); *Le Juge et l'assassin*
      (*The Judge and the Assassin*) (Tavernier) (as Judge Emile
      Rousseau); *Il commune senso del pudore* (*A Common Sense
      of Modesty*) (Sordi) (as Constanzo); *Une Femme à sa fenêtre*
      (*A Woman at Her Window*) (Granier-Deferre) (as Raoul
      Malfosse); *Coup de foudre* (Enrico) (as Ladislas)

1977 *Le désert des Tartares* (*Il deserto dei tartari*; *The Desert of the
      Tartars*) (Zurlini) (as "The General"); *Un Taxi mauve* (*The
      Purple Taxi*) (Boisset) (as Philippe Marchal)

1978 *La Barricade du point du jour* (Richon) (as Eugène Pottier);
      Tendre poulet (*Dear Detective*; *Dear Inspector*) (de Broca)
      (as Antoine Lemercier); *Le Témoin* (*The Witness*; *Il
      Testimone*) (Mocky) (as Robert Maurisson); *Due pezzi di
      pane* (Citti); *Who Is Killing the Great Chefs of Europe?* (*Too
      Many Chefs*) (Kotcheff) (as Jean-Claude Moulineau)

1979 *Salto nel vuoto* (*A Leap into the Void*) (Bellocchio); *La Mort
      en direct* (*Deathwatch*) (Tavernier)

1980 *On a volé la cuisse de Jupiter* (*Jupiter's Thigh*) (de Broca) (as
      Antoine Lemercier); *Une Semaine de vacances* (*A Week's
      Vacation*) (Tavernier) (as Michel Descombe); *Pile ou face*
      (*Heads or Tails*) (Enrico) (as Baroni)

1981 *Tre fratelli* (*Three Brothers*) (Rosi) (as Raffaele Giuranna); *Il faut
      tuer Birgitt Haas* (*Birgitt Haas Must Be Killed*) (Heynemann);
      Coup de torchon (*Clean Slate*) (Tavernier) (as Lucien Cordier)

1982 *L'Étoile du nord* (*The North Star*) (Granier-Deferre) (as Edouard
      Binet); *Amici miei, atto due* (Monicelli) (as Giorgio Perozzi)

1983 *L'Africain* (*The African*) (de Broca) (as Victor); *Un Ami de
      Vincent* (*A Friend of Vincent*) (Granier-Deferre); *La Grande
      Carnaval* (Arcady) (as Ètienne Labrouche)

1984 *Aurora* (Ponzi—for TV); *Fort Saganne* (Corneau) (as
      Dubreuilh); *Les Ripoux* (*My New Partner*; *Le Cop*) (Zidi) (as
      René); *Souvenirs, souvenirs* (Zeitoun)

1985 *Le Quatrième Pouvoir* (*The Fourth Power*) (Leroy) (as Yves
      Dorget); *Speriamo che sia femmina* (*Let's Hope It's a Girl*)
      (Monicelli) (as Count Leonardo); *L'Été prochain* (*Next Sum-
      mer*) (Trintignant) (as Edouard); *Qualcosa di biondo* (*Au-
      rora*) (Ponzi)

1986 *La Femme secrète* (*The Secret Wife*) (Grall) (as Pierre Franchin);
      Masques (Chabrol) (as Christian Legagneur); *Twist Again a
      Moscou* (*Twist Again in Moscow*) (Poure) (as Igor Tatiatev);
      Autour de minuit (*'Round Midnight*) (Tavernier) (as Redon)

1987 *Noyade interdite* (*Widow's Walk*) (Granier-Deferre) (as
      Molinat); *La famiglia* (*The Family*) (Scola) (as Jean-Luc);
      Gli occhiali d'oro (*The Gold Rimmed Glasses*; *Les Lunettes
      d'or*) (Montaldo) (as Dr. Fadigati)

1988 *Chouans!* (de Broca) (as Savinien de Kerfardec); *Il Frullo del
      passero* (Mingozzi); *Cinema Paradiso* (*Nuovo Cinema
      Paradiso*) (Tornatore) (as Alfredo)

1989 *La Vie et rien d'autre* (*Life and Nothing But*) (Tavernier) (as
      Maj. Dellaplanne); *The Return of the Musketeers* (Lester)
      (as Cardinal Mazarin)

1990 *Ripoux contre ripoux* (*My New Partner II*; *Le Cop 2*) (Zidi) (as
      René); *Faux et l'usage de Faux* (*Forgery and the Use of
      Forgeries*) (Heynemann) (as Anatole Hirsch)

1991 *Uranus* (Berri) (as Watrin); *Dimenticare Palermo* (*The
      Palermo Connection*) (Rosi) (as the hotel manager);
      J'embrasse pas (*I Don't Kiss*) (Téchiné) (as Romain); "The
      Blue Dog" ep. of *Specialmente la domenica* (*Especially on
      Sunday*) (Tornatore) (as Amleto); *Rossini, Rossini* (as
      Gioacchino Rossini)

1992 *Nous Deux* (*The Two of Us*) (Graziani) (as Toussaint); *Max et Jérémie*
      (*Max and Jeremy*) (Devers) (as Robert "Max" Maxendre); *Contre
      l'oubli* (*Against Oblivion*) (Akerman and others) (as himself);
      Zuppa Di Pesce (*Fish Soup*) (Infascelli) (as Alberto)

1993 *Tango* (Laconte) (as the elegant man)

1994 *Il Postino* (*The Postman*) (Radford) (as Pablo Neruda); *Veillees
      d'armes* (*The Troubles We've Seen: A History of Journalism
      in Wartime*) (Marcel Ophüls—doc) (as himself); *Grosse Fa-
      tigue* (*Dead Tired*) (Blanc) (as himself); *La Fille de
      D'Artagnan* (*D'Artagnan's Daughter*) (Tavernier) (as
      D'Artagnan); *Les Milles* (Graal) (as Le General)

1995 *Le Roi de Paris* (*The King of Paris*) (Maillet) (as Victor Derval);
      Facciamo paradiso (Monicello) (as Bertelli)

1996 *Les Grands ducs* (Leconte) (as Victor Vialat); *Fantôme avec
      chauffeur* (Oury) (as Philippe Bruneau-Tessier)

Publications

By NOIRET: articles—

Interview with I. F. McAsh, in *Films* (London), August 1982.
Interview with Joseph Hurley and Bertrand Tavernier, in *Films in
     Review* (New York), March and April 1983.
Interview with M. Amiel, in *Cinéma* (Paris), April 1983.
Interview with J. Zimmer and D. Parra, in *Revue du Cinéma* (Paris),
     April 1987.
Interview with M. Buruiana, in *Séquences* (Montreal), June 1989.
"La guerre n'est pas finie," interview with K. Jaehne, in *Cineaste* (New
     York), no 1, 1990.
Interview with G. Midding, in *Filmbulletin* (Winterthur, Switzerland),
     no. 4, 1991.
"Tango," interview with Y. Poncelet, in *Grand Angle* (Mariembourg,
     Belgium), February 1993.

On NOIRET: book—

Maillet, Dominique, *Philippe Noiret*, Paris, 1978; rev. ed., 1989.

On NOIRET: articles—

Ecran (Paris), March 1978.
Ciné Revue (Paris), 10 February 1983.
Schupp, P., "Philippe Noiret, la stabilité dans la diversité," in *Séquences*
     (Montreal), April 1984.
Stars (Mariembourg, Belgium), March 1990.
Dominicus, M., "Liegen met de blik van eel uilskuiken," in *Skrien*
     (Amsterdam, Netherlands), December 1990/January 1991.
"Philippe Noiret," in *Film Dope* (Nottingham, England), July 1992.

*   *   *

A tall, heavily built actor who only established himself in his thirties, Philippe Noiret has no youthful role to his credit and has usually
depicted middle-aged, and often middle-class, characters. Though initially cast in fairly predictable secondary roles such as the outsmarted
property developer in *Tout l'or du monde*, he gradually made his mark
both in comic creations and more serious roles. He excelled as the
complacent, sanctimonious husband of *Thérèse Desqueyroux* and as
the ruthless self-seeking businessman of *La Porteuse de pain*, while his
comic gifts were revealed as the diffident, city-fearing Jérôme of *La
Vie de château*, as the transvestite artiste of *Zazie dans le métro*, and
as the bogus priest giving sex sermons in *Les Copains*. With his endearing performance as the idle, misogynistic farmer of *Alexandre le
bienheureux*, Noiret confirmed his position as a leading comic actor.

His already varied career now became international. Noiret's first
English part was as a libertine politician in *Lady L*. He was a politi-
cian-cum-brothel keeper in *The Assassination Bureau*, a Nazi-hunter
in *The Night of the Generals*, and in *Woman Times Seven* an unhappily

married bourgeois. In America he was the sexually deficient diplomat of *Justine*, the NATO economist of *Topaz*, and the timid engineer of *Murphy's War*. Now a commercial star, Noiret generously appeared for emerging directors, but despite good performances the films were financial failures.

It was not until the 1970s that he worked regularly with Italian directors, often in co-productions and initially in outrageous satirical roles. His performances for Ferreri in the *La Grande Bouffe* and *Touche pas à la femme blanche* were landmarks: in the former as a degenerate oedipal judge hosting a decadent party; in the latter as General Terry in a loose parody of Custer's last stand. Weightier roles came as the cynical reporter in Pico's *Un Nuage entre les dents*, as Judge Jannacone in Scarpelli's *Siamo tutti im libertà provvisoria*, or as the magistrate in Rosi's *Tre fratelli*. For Enrico he gave an intensely moving portrayal of the surgeon dedicated to avenging the murder of his family by the Nazis in *Le Vieux Fusil*. Further notable interpretations came as the homosexual professor driven to suicide in Montaldo's *Gli occhiali d'oro* and two roles for Giuseppe Tornatore: Alfredo the projectionist who affectionately shares his love of the cinema with a young enthusiast in *Cinema Paradiso*, and Amleto the barber and shoemaker who is shadowed by a mysterious dog with a blue spot on its head in "The Blue Dog" episode of *Specialmente la domenica*. His most acclaimed performance of the 1990s to date came in Michael Radford's *Il Postino* as the poet Pablo Neruda whom he portrayed with a passion—for poetry, love, and the sleepy Italian island where he lives in exile—that brings a very fictional story to life.

Over the last two decades and a half of French cinema Noiret has been closely associated with de Broca, Tavernier, Claude Zidi, and Granier-Deferre. It has been through Tavernier, however, that Noiret's depth of talent has been revealed. In *L'Horloger de Saint-Paul* he was outstanding as Michel Descombe, the quiet widower protecting his criminal son, yet finding friendship with the investigator; in *Que la fête commence!* he brilliantly conveyed the human complexity of the Regent as a public and private person; in *Le Juge et l'assassin* he was the domineering and chillingly cruel investigating magistrate; and in *Coup de torchon* he was masterful as a cunning, authoritarian, and lubricious colonial policeman. There were only minor roles in *Une Semaine de vacances* (again as Michel Descombe) and as Redon in *Autour de minuit*, but in *La Vie et rien d'autre* Noiret again triumphed as the dedicated Major Dellaplanne intent on identifying the war-dead, despite official opposition. Noiret's latest Tavernier role came in 1994 with his portrayal of D'Artagnan in *La Fille de D'Artagnan*.

Memorable roles, both major and minor, have come with other directors: as the nasty, petty crook of *Monsieur Albert* (Renard); as the child murderer of *Le Témoin* (Mocky); as the principled journalist in *Le Quatrième Pouvoir* (Leroy); and as the corrupt television presenter of Chabrol's *Masques*. In *La Vieille Fille* (Blanc), Noiret gave one of his finest performances as the shy Gabriel Marcassus tentatively building a relationship with a withdrawn spinster. Among minor, but masterfully executed, roles he has appeared as the architect in *La famiglia*; an actor in *L'Un et l'autre*; the headmaster of *Souvenirs, souvenirs*; and, untypically, a morbid artist in *La Femme secrète*. Another noteworthy role came in the early 1990s among an ensemble French all-star cast in Claude Berri's *Uranus*, with Noiret portraying a sincere but deluded and naive schoolteacher in postwar 1945 France living amidst the rubble of a village bombed by the Allies, in a country obsessed with the search for wartime collaborators.

In a career of more than 125 disparate roles, Philippe Noiret has, in turn, appalled as the vicious, depraved, or despicable; reassured as a solid authority figure; disturbed and amused in comedy, satire, and farce; and yet subtly revealed the emotional complexities of human relationships. His contribution to French cinema has been significant, by encouraging talented newcomers and by setting high standards of performance.

—R. F. Cousins, updated by David E. Salamie

NOLTE, Nick

Nationality: American. **Born:** Omaha, Nebraska, 8 February 1941. **Education:** Attended Pasadena City College and Phoenix City College. **Family:** Married 1) Sheila Page (divorced); 2) Sharon Haddad, 1978; 3) Rebecca Linger, 1984, child: Brawley King. **Career:** Worked on stage in Phoenix, Denver, Minneapolis, and Chicago; 1974—TV film debut in *Winter Kill*; 1975—feature film debut in *Return to Macon County*; 1976—in TV mini-series *Rich Man, Poor Man*. **Address:** c/o Kingsgate Films Inc., 29555 Rainsford Place, Malibu, CA 90265, U.S.A.

Films as Actor:

1974	*Winter Kill* (Taylor—for TV); *The California Kid* (Heffron—for TV); *Death Sentence* (Swackhamer—for TV)
1975	*Return to Macon County* (Compton) (as Bo Hollinger); *The Runaway Barge* (Sagal—for TV)
1977	*The Deep* (Yates) (as David Sanders)
1978	*Who'll Stop the Rain* (Reisz) (as Ray Hicks); *North Dallas Forty* (Kotcheff) (as Phillip Elliott)
1980	*Heart Beat* (Byrum) (as Neal Cassady)
1982	*48 Hrs.* (Walter Hill) (as Jack Cates); *Cannery Row* (Ward) (as Doc)
1983	*Under Fire* (Spottiswoode) (as Russell Price)
1984	*The Ultimate Solution of Grace Quigley* (*Grace Quigley*) (Harvey) (as Seymour Flint); *Teachers* (Hiller) (as Alex)
1986	*Down and Out in Beverly Hills* (Mazursky) (as Jerry Baskin)
1987	*Extreme Prejudice* (Walter Hill) (as Jack Benteen, Texas Ranger); *Weeds* (Hancock) (as Lee Umstetter)
1989	*Three Fugitives* (Veber) (as Daniel Lucas); "Life Lessons" ep. of *New York Stories* (Scorsese) (as Lionel Dobie); *Farewell to the King* (Milius) (as Learoyd)
1990	*Everybody Wins* (Reisz) (as Tom O'Toole); *Q & A* (Lumet) (as Lieut. Mike Brennan); *Another 48 Hrs.* (Walter Hill) (as Jack Cates)
1991	*Prince of Tides* (Streisand) (as Tom Wingo); *Cape Fear* (Scorsese) (as Sam Bowden)
1992	*The Player* (Altman); *Lorenzo's Oil* (George Miller) (as Augusto Odone)
1993	*Gettysburg* (Maxwell)
1994	*I Love Trouble* (Shyer) (as Peter Brackett); *Blue Chips* (Friedkin) (as Pete Bell); *I'll Do Anything* (James L. Brooks) (as Matt Hobbs)
1995	*Jefferson in Paris* (Ivory) (title role)
1996	*Mulholland Falls* (Tamahori)

Publications

By NOLTE: articles—

Interview, in *Prevue*, December 1982-January 1983.
"Nick Nolte: 'I'm Action in Hollywood's Book,'" interview with B. Hadleigh, in *Film Monthly* (Berkhamsted, England), July 1991.

On NOLTE: articles—

Current Biography 1980, New York, 1980.
American Film (Washington, D.C.), September 1977.
Ciné Revue (Paris), 8 December 1983.
Photoplay (London), July 1984.
Films and Filming (London), November 1984.

McGuigan, Cathleen, "The Prime of Nick Nolte," in *Newsweek* (New York), 27 February 1989.

Oney, Steve, "The Nolte Nobody Knows," in *Premiere* (New York), March 1989.

Bordy, Meredith, "Prince of Hollywood," in *Connoisseur*, September 1991.

Mansfield, Stephanie, "Nick Nolte: Up from the Gutter," in *GQ* (New York), October 1991.

De Jonge, Peter, "Off-Balance Heroes," in *New York Times Magazine*, 27 October 1991.

Schwarzbaum, Lisa, "Nick's Time," in *Entertainment Weekly* (New York), 24 January 1992.

Cieutat, M., "Nick Nolte," in *Positif* (Paris), April 1993.

*   *   *

Nick Nolte resurfaced after *The Deep* with an amazing performance in *Who'll Stop the Rain* as Ray Hicks, a Marine in Vietnam caught up in a dope scam by Michael Moriarty as a disillusioned intellectual friend. Moriarty's trafficking is a *gesture* of disgust; he creates a mess he cannot clean up. Nolte, harking back to a pre-counterculture style of self-reliant heroic alienation, takes responsibility regardless of fault. He is sick of being pushed around, and thus in taking on crooked federal agents hits a nerve in the audience. Hicks is not above corruption—we see him take petty revenge on a party of swingers—but we are drawn to him in action hero terms which are deepened by the movie's morally complex view of the seventies drug culture.

Nolte followed this with *North Dallas Forty* in which Phillip Elliott, a pro football receiver, has the best hands in the game but cannot play the more important game of kissing the asses of corporate owners and managers. It is the same kind of sports melodrama as 1940s boxing pictures (he even sneaks around with the girls with one of the hostile managers), but Nolte has such a relaxed, expansive presence he makes a melodramatic bind seem like a naturalistic essay. In *Who'll Stop the Rain* Nolte starts out reading Nietzsche in Vietnam and ends up dead; in *North Dallas Forty* he starts out sleepless with pain and ends up unemployed but unencumbered, in love. Nolte has a sleepy-lion-headed magnificence that can plausibly go either way.

His finest performances have surprisingly been as artists. In Roger Spottiswoode's *Under Fire*, about photojournalists in Nicaragua during the Sandinista revolution, Nolte plays a photographer who agrees to aid the leftists by faking a photo. He does not *mime* the character's dilemma; he is too thoroughgoing a performer to put on masks. We see him heading toward his decision in his relations with Joanna Cassidy and Gene Hackman as colleagues and in his relations to guerrillas and mercenaries swirling in the conflict. In Martin Scorsese's *Life Lessons* he plays Lionel Dobie, an abstract-expressionist painter who is trying to keep his assistant from quitting but cannot give her the assurance she needs—that she has got talent and is profiting artistically from their association. Nolte nervily makes Dobie lumberingly foolish, repellently obsessive, yet palpably inspired as a painter.

Nolte is extraordinarily versatile for a big-guy star. He is believable as the bearlike bum who liberates Richard Dreyfuss and Bette Midler's Beverly Hills household in Paul Mazursky's *Down and Out in Beverly Hills* and again as the stolid small-town sheriff in Walter Hill's *Extreme Prejudice*. He can play sensitive without playing educated, as in *Weeds*, and without his sensitivity blocking the route to effective action. He can also play men who are outmaneuvered, as he is by Debra Winger's Angela Crispini in *Everybody Wins*, without losing his force. And in a big-budget romance such as *Prince of Tides*, he is a bit of everything—an overgrown adolescent baiting his wife; a sleek, solid romantic lead at Barbra Streisand's swank dinner party; even a collapsed analysand, crying in Streisand's arms.

He gets in trouble playing weak men in pictures that do not offer him compensation for what is lost. *Cape Fear* strings him up to satisfy Scorsese's meretricious insistence on turning a cheap revenge thriller into a redemp-

tion story, and Nolte seems beset less by De Niro's psycho than by the script that keeps coming at him with compromises and failures. Likewise, James L. Brooks's *I'll Do Anything* makes Nolte too small as an out-of-work actor hoping to star in a remake of *Mr. Deeds Goes to Town*, while in *Jefferson in Paris* the revisionist script has Frenchmen point out to Nolte's Jefferson the contradiction of being a slave owner and a freedom fighter and leaves the foundering father gaping without a rejoinder. If Nolte wants a befuddled role worthy of his talents he should play Bellow's *Henderson the Rain King*.

But Nolte, more than any other current star, leaves his bad roles behind him. He appears unusually often for a star nowadays, and the fact that he does not seem overexposed is a tribute to the fundamental honesty of his acting. You may have to seek him out a bit behind that squint, but once you do he does not put up barriers—he is as generous as nature made him.

—Alan Dale

NORMAND, Mabel

Nationality: American. **Born:** Staten Island, New York, 9 November 1892. **Family:** Married the actor Lew Cody, 1926. **Career:** Worked for Butterick dress-pattern company, then artists' model; 1910—extra in Vitagraph films: debut in *Over the Garden Wall*; then worked for Biograph, often for Mack Sennett, with whom she had a personal as well as professional relationship; 1912—left with Sennett to go to Keystone company; series of successful short films with Fatty Arbuckle; 1914—appeared in some of Chaplin's shorts, and in the feature-length *Tillie's Punctured Romance*; 1916—Sennett helped form the Mabel Normand Feature Company, but first feature, *Mickey*, made in 1916, was not released until 1918; 1918—contract with Samuel Goldwyn; 1922-23—the deaths of the director William Desmond Taylor, 1922, and Courtland Dines, 1923, both involved Normand peripherally, and her career suffered; 1925—in stage play *The Little Mouse*, which closed in its pre-Broadway tryouts; 1926-27—made a few shorts for Hal Roach. **Died:** Of tuberculosis in Monrovia, California, 23 February 1930.

Films as Actress:

1910   *Over the Garden Wall*
1911   *Picciola*; *Betty Becomes a Maid*; *The Maid's Night Out*; *The Troublesome Secretaries*; *The Subduing of Mrs. Nag* (Baker); *The Squaw's Love* (D. W. Griffith); *A Dash through the Clouds*; *The Diving Girl* (Sennett); *Her Awakening* (D. W. Griffith); *Saved from Himself* (D. W. Griffith); *The Unveiling* (D. W. Griffith); *The Eternal Mother* (D. W. Griffith)
1912   *The Water Nymph* (Sennett); *Pedro's Dilemma* (Sennett); *The Ambitious Butler* (Sennett); *Tomboy Bessie* (Sennett); *The Tourists* (Sennett); *A Spanish Dilemma* (Sennett); *The Brave Hunter* (Sennett); *The Mender of Nets* (D. W. Griffith); *The Fatal Chocolates*; *Oh Those Eyes!*; *Mabel's Adventures* (Sennett); *Mabel's Stratagem* (Nicholls); *Mabel's Lovers* (Sennett); *The Grocery Clerk's Romance* (Sennett); *The Deacon's Trouble* (Sennett); *A Temperamental Husband* (Sennett); *A Desperate Lover* (Sennett); *The New Neighbor* (Sennett); *The Flirting Husband* (Sennett); *Stolen Glory* (Sennett); *Cohen at Coney Island* (*Cohen Collects a Debt*) (Sennett); *At It Again* (Sennett); *The Rivals* (Sennett); *Mr. Fix-It* (Sennett); *Brown's Seance* (Sennett); *A Midnight Elopement* (Sennett); *The Duel* (Sennett)

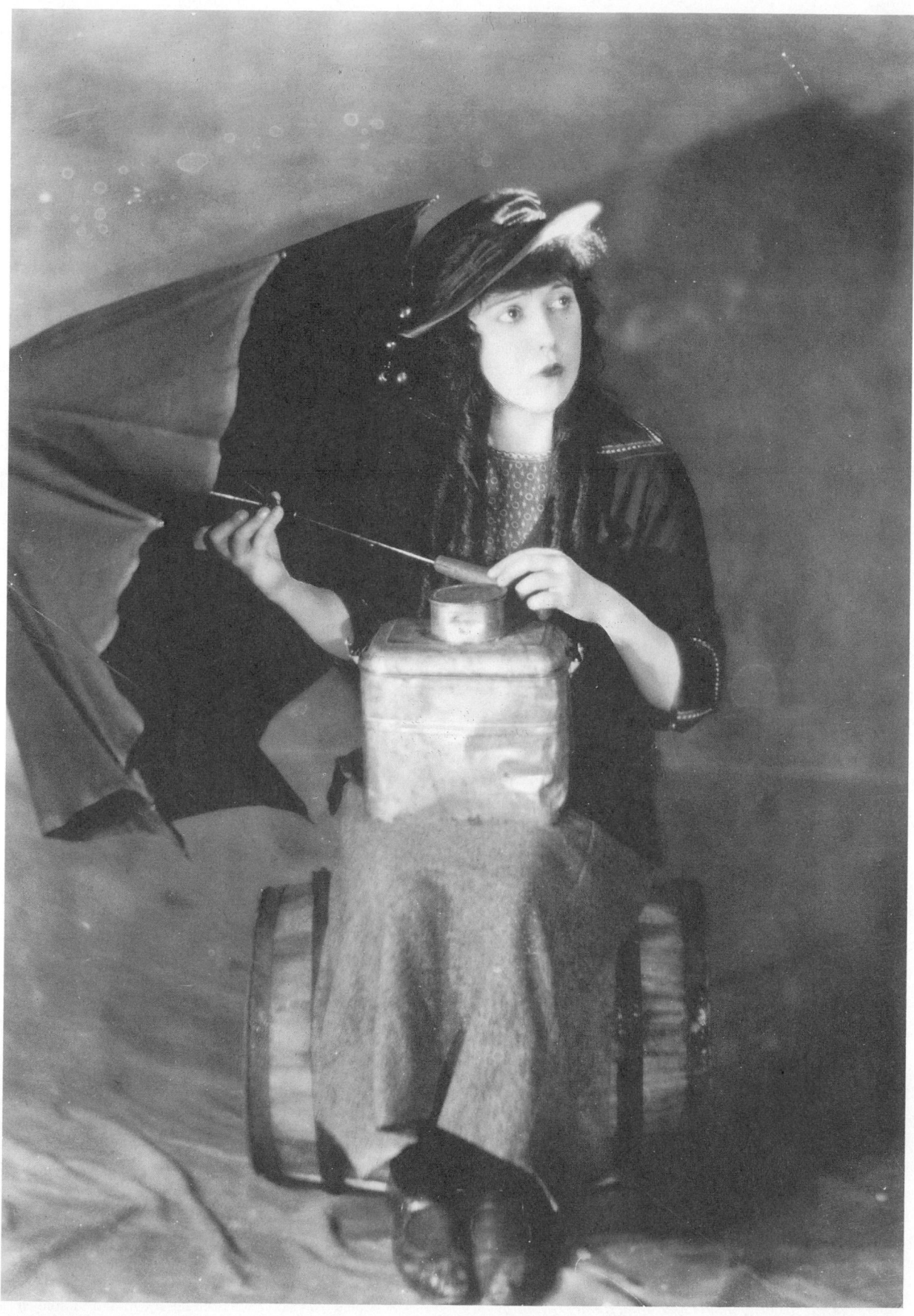

Mabel Normand in *Molly O'*

1913 *Betty in the Lions' Den* (Thomson); *Barney Oldfield's Race for a Life* (Sennett); *The Fatal Taxicab* (Sennett); *For the Love of Mabel* (Sennett); *A Strong Revenge* (Sennett); *Fatty's Flirtation* (Sennett); *Speed Kings* (Sennett); *Love Sickness at Sea* (Sennett); *Cohen Saves the Flag* (Sennett); *Zuzu the Band Leader* (Sennett); *The Cure That Failed* (Sennett); *For Lizzie's Sake* (Sennett); *The Battle of Who Ran* (Sennett); *Mabel's Awful Mistake* (*Her Deceitful Lover*) (Sennett); *Mabel's New Hero* (Sennett); *Mabel's Dramatic Career* (*Her Dramatic Debut*) (Sennett and Nicholls); *A Tangled Affair* (Sennett); *A Doctored Affair* (Sennett); *Saving Mabel's Dad* (Sennett); *The Champion* (Lehrman); *The Mistaken Masher* (Sennett); *Just Brown's Luck* (Sennett); *Heinze's Resurrection* (Sennett); *The Professor's Daughter* (Sennett); *A Red Hot Romance* (Sennett); *The Sleuths at the Floral Parade* (Sennett); *The Rube and the Baron* (Sennett); *The Chief's Predicament* (Sennett); *Those Good Old Days*; *Father's Choice* (Sennett); *A Little Hero* (Sennett); *Hubby's Job* (Sennett); *The Speed Queen* (Sennett); *A Noise from the Deep* (Sennett); *Professor Bean's Removal* (Sennett); *The Gypsy Queen* (Sennett); *Baby Day* (Sennett); *The Bowling Match* (Sennett); *Mabel's Heroes* (Nicholls); *The Gusher* (Sennett)

1914 *His Trysting Place* (*Family Home*) (Chaplin); *Tillie's Punctured Romance* (Sennett); *Getting Acquainted* (*A Fair Exchange*; *Hullo Everybody*) (Chaplin); *Mabel's Strange Predicament* (*Hotel Mixup*) (Lehrman and Sennett); *A Misplaced Foot* (Sennett); *Mabel's Stormy Love Affair* (Nicholls); *Mabel's Bear Escape* (Nicholls); *Mabel's Nerve* (Nicholls); *Mabel's New Job* (Nicholls); *Mabel's Blunder*; *Mabel's Latest Prank* (*Tour Rheumatism*) (Sennett); *Those Country Kids* (Dillon and Arbuckle); *Hello, Mabel!*; *Lovers Post Office* (Dillon and Arbuckle); *How Nerves Are Made* (Parrott); *Fatty's Wine Party* (Arbuckle and Dillon); *A Glimpse of Los Angeles* (Lucas—doc); *Won in a Closet* (Nicholls); *Mack at It Again* (Sennett); *The Alarm* (Arbuckle and Dillon); *Gentlemen of Nerve* (*Some Nerve, Charlie at the Races*) (Chaplin); *Fatty's Jonah Day* (Arbuckle and Dillon); *The Sea Nymphs* (*His Diving Beauty*) (Sennett); *In the Clutches of the Gang*

1915 *Fatty and Mabel at the San Diego Exposition* (Dillon); *That Little Band of Gold* (*For Better or Worse*); *Stolen Magic* (Sennett); *Wished on Mabel*; *My Valet* (Sennett); *The Little Teacher* (*A Small Town Bully*) (Sennett)

1916 *Fatty and Mabel Adrift* (Arbuckle); *The Bright Lights* (*The Lure of Broadway*) (Arbuckle); *He Did and He Didn't* (*Love and Lobsters*) (Arbuckle)

1918 *Dodging a Million* (Selwyn); *The Floor Below* (Badger); *Joan of Plattsburg* (Tucker); *The Venus Model* (Badger); *Back to the Woods* (Irving); *Mickey* (Sennett); *Peck's Bad Girl* (Giblyn); *A Perfect Thirty-Six* (Giblyn); *Stake Uncle Sam to Play Your Hand*

1919 *Sis Hopkins* (Badger); *The Pest* (Cabanne); *When Doctors Disagree* (Schertzinger); *Upstairs* (Schertzinger); *The Jinx* (Schertzinger)

1920 *Pinto* (Schertzinger); *The Slim Princess* (Schertzinger)

1921 *What Happened to Rosa?* (Schertzinger) (as Mayme Ladd); *Molly O'* (Jones) (title role)

1922 *Head over Heels* (Schertzinger) (as Tina); *Oh, Mabel Behave* (Sennett and Sterling) (as innkeeper's daughter); *Suzanna* (Jones) (title role)

1923 *The Extra Girl* (F. Richard Jones) (as Sue Graham)

1926 *Raggedy Rose* (Laurel and Wallace—short); *The Nickel Hopper* (Jones—short); *One Hour Married* (short)

1927 *Anything Once* (short); *Should Men Walk Home?* (McCarey—short)

Films as Actress and Director:

1914 *Mabel at the Wheel* (*His Daredevil Queen*; *Hot Finish*) (co-d with Sennett); *Caught in a Cabaret* (*Jazz Waiter*; *Faking with Society*) (co-d with Chaplin); *Mabel's Busy Day* (*Charlie and the Sausage*; *Love and Lunch*; *Hot Dogs*) (co-d with Chaplin); *Her Friend the Bandit* (*Mabel's Flirtation*; *The Thief Catcher*) (co-d with Chaplin); *The Fatal Mallet* (*The Pile Driver*; *The Rival Suitors*; *Hit Him Again*) (co-d with Chaplin); *Mabel's Married Life* (*When You're Married*; *The Squarehead*) (co-d with Chaplin)

1915 *Mabel and Fatty's Married Life* (*Fatty and Mabel's Married Life*) (co-d with Dillon); *Mabel and Fatty's Wash Day* (*Fatty and Mabel's Simple Life*) (co-d with Dillon); *Mabel and Fatty's Simple Life* (co-d with Dillon); *Mabel, Fatty, and the Law* (*Fatty's Spooning Day*) (co-d with Dillon); *Mabel Lost and Won*; *Mabel's Wilful Way* (co-d with Arbuckle); *Mabel and Fatty Viewing the World's Fair at San Francisco, California* (co-d with Arbuckle)

1949 *Down Memory Lane* (Karlson—compilation)

Publications

On NORMAND: books—

Fussell, Betty Harper, *Mabel*, New Haven, Connecticut, 1982.
Kirkpatrick, Sidney, *A Cast of Killers*, London, 1986.
Sinclair, Marianne, *Hollywood Lolita: The Nymphet Syndrome in the Movies*, London, 1988.
Sherman, William Thomas, *Mabel Normand: A Source Book to Her Life and Films*, Seattle, 1994.

On NORMAND: articles—

"Mabel Normand," in *Moving Picture World*, 11 July 1914.
Quirk, James, "The Girl on the Cover," in *Photoplay* (New York), August 1915.
St. Johns, Adela Rogers, "Hello Mabel!," in *Photoplay* (New York), August 1921.
Howe, Herbert, "The Diaries of Mabel Normand," in *Pantomime*, 12 October 1921.
Obituary in *New York Times*, 24 February 1930.
Quirk, James, "Mabel Normand Says Goodbye," in *Photoplay* (New York), May 1930.
Slide, Anthony, "Forgotten Early Women Directors," in *Films in Review* (New York), March 1974.
Normand, S., "Mabel Normand: Her Grandnephew's Memoir," in *Films in Review* (New York), August/September 1974.
Durfee, Minta, in *Classic Film/Video Images* (Indiana, Pennsylvania) July 1980.
Fussell, Betty, "The Films of Mabel Normand," in *Film History* (Bristol, Pennsylvania), vol. 2, no. 4, 1988.
Sherman, William Thomas, "Love and Courage: A Look at the Films and Career of Mabel Normand," in *Classic Images* (Muscatine, Iowa), November 1990, December 1990, January 1991, and February 1991.
Hale, C., "Mabel Normand," in *Film Dope* (Nottingham, England), July 1992.
Sherman, W. T., "Filmography Update: The Films of Mabel Normand," in *Classic Images* (Muscatine, Iowa), July 1992 and August 1992.

* * *

Schooled by Mack Sennett in the rough-and-tumble world of slapstick, the pixieish Mabel Normand was known as a deft thrower (and recipient) of the custard pie. In many of her films Normand was paired with Charlie Chaplin and Roscoe "Fatty" Arbuckle. In *Tillie's Punctured Romance*, usually considered America's first feature-length film comedy, she was Chaplin's accomplice in villainy as he bilks Marie Dressler of her fortune by marrying her. Though the film was adapted by Sennett from Dressler's successful stage comedy, it has all the characteristics of Normand's one-reelers for Biograph and Keystone. Discovering her husband's infidelity, the indignant Dressler pursues Chaplin and Normand in an elaborate chase sequence.

Normand had acted in more than 100 short films for Sennett by 1916, when he developed a genteel comedy vehicle for her titled *Mickey*. The film was so atypical of the entrepreneur's slapstick approach that he hesitated to release it until 1918, when more genteel comedies had begun to appear. The story, about a mischievous orphan mistreated by the people of a small town, resembled the typical plot of a Mary Pickford film, and when the film became a hit, Normand began to rival Pickford. Though the film cannot now be considered first-rate, Normand's performance has sparkle, warmth, and sincerity.

Unhappy with Sennett's lack of support on *Mickey*, and their deteriorating personal relationship, Normand signed a contract with Samuel Goldwyn to make similar features. She proved the depth of her talent with such films as *Molly O'* and *The Extra Girl* in the early 1920s, but her career was cut short by a scandal involving her in the still-unsolved murder of director William Desmond Taylor. Because of her alleged romantic involvement with Taylor, and the fact that she was one of the last people to see him alive, she had difficulty in convincing the public of her innocence. Despite this and subsequent personal problems, her films remind us of her gaiety. On screen she was the sunshine girl, the greatest comedienne of the silent era.

—Donald McCaffrey

NOVAK, Kim

Nationality: American. **Born:** Marilyn Pauline Novak in Chicago, Illinois, 13 February 1933. **Education:** Attended Farragut High School, Chicago; Wright Junior College, Chicago; Los Angeles City College. **Family:** Married 1) the actor Richard Johnson, 1965 (divorced 1966); 2) Dr. Robert Malloy, 1977. **Career:** Model in Chicago, then with the Caroline Leonetti Modeling Agency in Hollywood; 1954—film debut in *The French Line*; Columbia contract led to publicity build-up as a sex symbol; 1961—formation of production company Kimco; 1970—acted and sang her own composition in the TV documentary *This Land Is Mine*; 1986-87—in TV series *Falcon Crest*. **Address:** c/o William Morris Agency, 151 El Camino Drive, Beverly Hills, CA 90212, U.S.A.

Films as Actress:

1954 *The French Line* (Lloyd Bacon) (as Paris model); *Pushover* (Quine) (as Lona McLane); *Phffft!* (Robson) (as Janis)

1955 *Picnic* (Logan) (as Madge Owens); *Five against the House* (Karlson) (as Kay Greylek); *Son of Sinbad* (*Nights in a Harem*) (Tetzlaff) (as daughter of the 40 thieves); *The Man with the Golden Arm* (Preminger) (as Molly)

1956 *The Eddy Duchin Story* (Sidney) (as Marjorie Oelrichs)

1957 *Jeanne Eagels* (Sidney) (title role); *Pal Joey* (Sidney) (as Linda English)

1958 *Vertigo* (Hitchcock) (as Madeleine Elster/Judy Barton); *Bell, Book and Candle* (Quine) (as Gillian Holroyd)

1959 *Middle of the Night* (Delbert Mann) (as Betty Preisser)

1960 *Strangers When We Meet* (Quine) (as Maggie Gault); *Pepe* (Sidney) (as herself)

1962 *Boys' Night Out* (Michael Gordon) (as Cathy); *The Notorious Landlady* (Quine) (as Carlye Hardwicke)

1964 *Of Human Bondage* (Hathaway, Forbes, and Hughes) (as Mildred Rogers); *Kiss Me, Stupid* (Wilder) (as Polly the Pistol)

1965 *The Amorous Adventures of Moll Flanders* (Terence Young) (title role)

1968 *The Legend of Lylah Clare* (Aldrich) (as Elsa Brinkmann/title role)

1969 *The Great Bank Robbery* (Averback) (as Lyda Kabanov)

1973 "Luau" ep. of *Tales that Witness Madness* (Francis) (as Auriol Pagaent); *The Third Girl from the Left* (Medak—for TV)

1974 *The Celebrity Art Portfolio* (D'Anjolell—short)

1975 *Satan's Triangle* (Roley—for TV) (as Eva)

1977 *The White Buffalo* (*Hunt to Kill*) (J. Lee Thompson) (as Poker Jenny Schermerhorn)

1979 *Just a Gigolo* (Hemmings) (as Helga)

1980 *The Mirror Crack'd* (Hamilton) (as Lola Brewster)

1983 *Malibu* (Swackhamer—for TV)

1987 *Es Hat Mich Sehr Gefreut* (as "Musikerinnen")

1990 *The Children* (Tony Palmer) (as Rose Sellars)

1991 *Liebestraum* (Figgis) (as Mrs. Anderssen)

Publications

By NOVAK: articles—

"The Legend of Kim Novak," interview with J. Calendo, in *Interview* (New York), June 1972.
"Fiction and Feelings," interview with Bruno Villien, in *Films* (London), May 1981.
Interview in *Vanity Fair* (New York), October 1995.

On NOVAK: books—

Kleno, Larry, *Kim Novak on Camera*, San Diego, 1980.
Brown, Peter Harry, *Kim Novak: The Reluctant Goddess*, New York, 1986.

On NOVAK: articles—

Current Biography 1957, New York, 1957.
Haspiel, J. R., "Kim Novak, Yesterday's Superstar," in *Films in Review* (New York), February 1978.
Ciné Revue (Paris), 7 February 1980 and 23 April 1981.
Lippe, Richard, "Kim Novak: A Resistance to Definition," in *cineAction* (Toronto), no. 7, December 1986.
Lurie, Rod, "The Last Temptation of Kim Novak," in *Los Angeles Magazine*, September 1990.
"Kim Novak," in *Film Dope* (London), July 1992.
"Kim Novak," in *Stars* (Mariembourg, Belguim), Spring 1993.

*   *   *

Kim Novak has often been disparaged as the last star manufactured by the studio system. In 1953, when Harry Cohn realized that Columbia's reigning sex goddess, Rita Hayworth, was becoming too rebellious, he supposedly decided to "create" a replacement. He selected Novak and, having her groomed and promoted through a huge publicity campaign, cast her in several films meant to display her sex appeal. Cohn's investment actually offered Novak an opportunity: she achieved stardom by developing an individualistic screen persona, and through her own accomplishments as an actress.

Kim Novak with James Stewart in *Vertigo*

Whatever Cohn's intentions may have been, Novak did not conform to the sex goddess concept. This is apparent in her first starring role, in Richard Quine's *Pushover*. Cast as a femme fatale, she undermines the implications of the character's destructive sexual appeal by projecting an extreme vulnerability. In Mark Robson's *Phffft!* her unease at playing a Marilyn Monroe-like dumb blond is very apparent. In *Picnic* and *The Man with the Golden Arm* she sensitively portrays characters who resist being treated merely as sex objects, and *Jeanne Eagels* remains interesting, despite George Sidney's crude direction and a clichéd script, because of Novak's ability to project the subjective identity of the character.

Although her performance as Madeleine/Judy in Hitchcock's *Vertigo* was considered perfunctory, it is, in hindsight, a remarkable contribution to what is, arguably, the director's finest achievement. Novak's reflective and essentially introverted personality, and undeniable screen presence, are ideally suited to the many nonverbal scenes involving the Madeleine character. Given the film's conception, Madeleine must convey both aloofness and intimacy to be effective, and Novak manages to sustain the resulting tension. The vulnerability implied by Madeleine's intimacy is given full expression in the Judy character, lending substance to a characterization crucial for the film's emotionally devastating climax. Her performance in *Vertigo* deserves as much acclaim as Jimmy Stewart's.

Richard Quine's *Bell, Book and Candle* and *Strangers When We Meet* also gave Novak splendid opportunities. To some extent, her work in the former, where she gives a muted performance in counterpoint to the film's comic aspects, is a variation on her *Vertigo* role. Again there is a contrast between her appearance and identity, and the question of her ability to deceive the hero into falling in love with an image. In *Strangers When We Meet* Quine uses Novak's sensitivity to give dimension to a character seeking fulfillment of emotional needs.

Novak's comic timing is outstanding in Wilder's *Kiss Me, Stupid*. To a typical 1950s Marilyn Monroe role Novak adds a self-awareness that makes the character more touching and stronger than Monroe could have managed. This trait is again evident in Novak's portrayal of an aging chorus girl in the made-for-television movie *The Third Girl from the Left*.

Novak's career faltered in the 1960s and by the end of the decade she had decided to be professionally less active. Nevertheless, Novak has not ceased to be serious about her identity as an actor. Several of the projects she has undertaken, including *Tales that Witness Madness*, *Satan's Triangle*, and *The White Buffalo*, turned out to be inferior works which, aside from giving her exposure, were unworthy of her effort. That Novak undertook these projects suggests that she was having difficulty finding quality material; but, it also may have been that she was uncertain as to what image she wanted to project. In both *Tales that Witness Madness* and *The White Buffalo*, Novak's participation is dependent on her status as a star but the films allow her to play character parts.

Novak's early 1980s films, *The Mirror Crack'd* and *Just a Gigolo*, also reflect this indecision as to what direction her career was taking. In the former, she is part of an ensemble cast; Elizabeth Taylor and Rock Hudson have bigger parts but Novak and Tony Curtis give better performances. Novak is cast as a vulgar and bitchy 1950s Hollywood star who sees herself as Taylor's rival. She plays the role to the hilt and is extremely convincing as a totally unlikable person. While her characterization functions to enliven an otherwise bland film and Novak demonstrates an ability to play broad comedy, the role offers her no scope. *Just a Gigolo* is another film with an intriguing star cast. Novak, in a supporting role, again plays an unsympathetic woman—a predatory widow who seduces David Bowie. As in *The Mirror Crack'd*, Novak here is sending up the sex goddess image that she had been identified with in the earlier stages of her career. (*Just a Gigolo* was drastically cut after its initial screening in an attempt to make the film more commercial.)

More recently, *The Children* and *Liebestraum* provided Novak with strong parts and the two films contain some of her finest work; in fact, her tour-de-force performance in the remarkable *Liebestraum* should have garnered her an Academy Award nomination. Unfortunately, neither film has received much exposure: *Liebestraum* because of its highly demanding nature. On the other hand, *The Children*, which never received a North American release, was heavily cut and reedited in its video version as the distributor had no faith in the film. In *The Children*, Novak portrays a cultured, reserved widow who has been courted by a man promising love and a commitment; instead, his attention is diverted and she is abandoned. Although *The Children* is centered on the Ben Kingsley character, Novak's role, which utilizes her skill in projecting vulnerability, is equally relevant to the film's theme of disillusionment and loss. In *Liebestraum*, Novak plays a bedridden woman dying of cancer who, when reunited with her now adult son, confronts the past in which she killed her husband. In contrast to the demands of *The Children*, *Liebestraum* gives her a much more demonstrative character who is physically and emotionally in anguish. Novak, in a series of short, intense scenes, constructs a forceful and compelling characterization. The performance is extremely disciplined; without sentimentalizing the character and her situation, Novak conveys the underlying sadness of this woman's identity.

Kim Novak has not made a film since *Liebestraum*. As her work has long shown, she is an intelligent, creative actor who has an extraordinary screen presence. Ideally, Novak will be back on-screen.

—Richard Lippe

NOVARRO, Ramon

Born: Durango, Mexico, 6 February 1899. **Career:** Emigrated to the United States, and worked as singing waiter and dancer with the Marion Morgan Dancers on Orpheum Circuit; 1916—extra in film *Joan the Woman* and many others; 1922—helped by Rex Ingram, and given part in *The Prisoner of Zenda*; 1930—directed Spanish and French versions of his film *Call of the Flesh*, and the original film *Contra la corrienta*, 1936; 1935—on stage in the operetta *A Royal Exchange* in London; continued to act in small parts after World War II. **Died:** Killed by intruders, 31 October 1968.

Films as Actor:

1917   *The Hostage*; *The Little American*; *Joan the Woman*; *The Jaguar's Claws*
1918   *The Goat* (Crisp)
1921   *Small Town Idol* (Kenton); ***The Four Horsemen of the Apocalypse*** (Ingram)
1922   *Mr. Barnes of New York* (Schertzinger) (as Antonio); *Trifling Women* (Ingram) (as Henri/Ivan de Maupin); *The Prisoner of Zenda* (Ingram) (as Rupert of Hentzau)
1923   *Where the Pavement Ends* (Ingram) (as Motauri); *Scaramouche* (Ingram) (as André-Louis Moreau)
1924   *The Arab* (Ingram) (as Jamil Abdullah Azam); *Thy Name Is Woman* (Niblo) (as Juan Ricardo); *The Red Lily* (Niblo) (as Jean Leonnec)
1925   *The Midshipman* (Cabanne) (as James Randall); *A Lover's Oath* (Earle) (as Ben Ali)
1926   *Ben-Hur* (Niblo) (title role)
1927   *Lovers?* (Stahl) (as José/Ernesto); *The Road to Romance* (Robertson) (as José Armando); *The Student Prince in Old Heidelberg* (Lubitsch) (as Prince Karl Heinrich)
1928   *Across to Singapore* (Nigh) (as Joel Shore); *A Certain Young Man* (Henley) (as Lord Gerald Brinsley); *Forbidden Hours* (Beaumont) (as Michael IV)
1929   *The Flying Fleet* (Hill) (as Tommy); *The Pagan* (Van Dyke) (as Henry Shoesmith Jr.)
1930   *Devil-May-Care* (Franklin) (as Armand); *In Gay Madrid* (Leonard) (as Ricardo); *Call of the Flesh* (Brabin) (as Juan)
1931   *Daybreak* (Feyder); *Son of India* (Feyder); *Mata Hari* (Fitzmaurice)
1932   *Huddle* (Wood); *Son-Daughter* (Brown)
1933   *The Barbarian* (Wood)
1934   *The Cat and the Fiddle* (Howard); *Laughing Boy* (Van Dyke); *The Night Is Young* (Murphy)
1937   *The Sheik Steps Out* (Pichel)
1938   *A Desperate Adventure* (Auer)
1940   *La Comédie du bonheur* (L'Herbier)
1942   *La Virgen que forjó una Patria* (Bracha)
1949   *We Were Strangers* (Huston); *The Big Steal* (Siegel)
1950   *The Outriders* (Rowland); *Crisis* (Brooks)
1960   *Heller in Pink Tights* (Cukor)

Films as Director:

1930   *La sevillana* and *Le Chanteur de Seville* (Spanish and French
          versions of *Call of the Flesh*)
1936   *Contra la corrienta* (+ sc)

Publications

By NOVARRO: articles—

"Alice Terry," in *Photoplay* (New York), July 1924.
"My Eleven Years of Stardom," in *Pictures and Picturegoer*, 1 July 1933.

On NOVARRO: articles—

Terry, Alice, "Ramon Novarro," in *Photoplay* (New York), July 1924.
Biery, Ruth, "Why Ramon Novarro Decided to Remain in the Movies,"
    in *Photoplay* (New York), October 1928.
Bodeen, DeWitt, "Ramon Novarro," in *Films in Review* (New York),
    November 1967.
Obituary in *New York Times*, 15 November 1968.
Bodeen, DeWitt, "Ramon Novarro," in *Silent Picture* (London), Summer 1969.

*   *   *

Ramon Novarro came to fame as a rival to Rudolph Valentino: he was the biggest name in a group of Latin Lovers that also included Antonio Moreno and Ricardo Cortez. He was less pretentious than Valentino and there was a natural style to his acting which to some extent removed Novarro from the "just a pretty face" class of performer. Despite the ease and charm of his performances, however, one is very much aware that he was a decidedly feminine actor, almost too beautiful to be taken seriously. He was a former male model, and his homosexuality was a fairly open secret in Hollywood. Presumably, his sexual preference did have some influence on his acting style, did persuade him to use a little too much facial makeup, and (most unfortunate of all) did encourage him to indulge in a considerable amount of seminude posing on-screen at a time when he was developing what looked suspiciously like a paunch.

Rex Ingram, who discovered and directed Rudolph Valentino in *The Four Horsemen of the Apocalypse*, also discovered Novarro and worked hard to make him a screen idol the equal of Valentino. From the villainous Rupert of Hentzau in *The Prisoner of Zenda*, Ingram transformed Novarro into the tragic lover of *Trifling Women*, and co-starred him in a series of romantic pictures with his wife, Alice Terry. With the title role in *Ben-Hur*, Novarro reached the pinnacle of his career, although he gave a better performance the following year in Ernst Lubitsch's *The Student Prince in Old Heidelberg*. Age began to take its toll, and despite Novarro's trying desperately to look youthful

Ramon Novarro with Alice Terry in *Scaramouche*

in his early talkies, it was pathetic to see the aging matinee idol playing a parody of himself in such films as *The Sheik Steps Out*.

—Anthony Slide

NOVELLO, Ivor

Nationality: British. **Born:** David Ivor Davies in Cardiff, Wales, 15 January 1893. **Education:** Attended Magdalen College Choir School, Oxford, and chorister of Magdalen College, 1905-11; studied composition with Dr. Brewer, Gloucester. **Career:** Published his first song at age 17; his World War I song "Keep the Home Fires Burning" made him famous; wrote songs for revues; 1920—film debut in *L'Appel du sang*; 1921—stage debut as actor; 1923—wrote successful play *The Rat* with Constance Collier; made U.S. film *The White Rose* for D. W. Griffith, but international career did not materialize; 1924—actor-manager, sometimes in collaboration; 1930-31—contract screenwriter for MGM; 1935—beginning of a series of stage musicals written, composed, and acted by Novello. **Died:** 6 March 1951.

Films as Actor:

1920 *L'Appel du sang* (*The Call of the Blood*) (Mercanton) (as Maurice Delarey); *Miarka, fille l'ours* (*Miarka, Daughter of the Bear*) (Mercanton) (as Ivor)
1921 *Carnival* (Knoles) (as Count Andrea Scipione)
1922 *The Bohemian Girl* (Knoles) (as Thaddeus)
1923 *The White Rose* (Griffith) (as Joseph Beaugarde); *Bonnie Prince Charlie* (Calvert) (title role)
1925 *The Rat* (Cutts) (as Pierre Boucheron)
1926 *The Triumph of the Rat* (Cutts) (as Pierre Boucheron); *The Lodger* (*The Case of Jonathan Drew*) (Hitchcock) (as Jonathan Drew)
1927 *Downhill* (*When Boys Leave Home*) (Hitchcock) (as Roddy Berwick); *The Vortex* (Brunel) (as Nicky Lancaster)
1928 *The Constant Nymph* (Brunel) (as Lewis Dodd); *A South Sea Bubble* (Hunter) (as Vernon Wilson); *The Gallant Hussar* (von Bolvary) (as Lt. Alrik); *The Return of the Rat* (Cutts) (as Pierre Boucheron)
1930 *Symphony in Two Flats* (Gundry) (as David Kennard)
1931 *Once a Lady* (McLintic) (as Bennett Cloud)
1932 *The Lodger* (*The Phantom Fiend*) (Elvey) (as Angeloff, + co-sc)
1933 *Sleeping Car* (Litvak) (as Gaston)
1934 *Autumn Crocus* (Dean) (as Andreas Steiner)

Film as Producer:

1923 *The Man without Desire* (*The Man without a Soul*) (Brunel) (+ ro as Vittorio Dandolo)

Film as Scriptwriter:

1933 *I Lived with You* (Elvey) (+ ro as Prince Felix Lenieff)

Publications

By NOVELLO: books (plays)—

The Truth Game, London, 1929.
I Lived with You, Party, Symphony in Two Flats, London, 1932.

Proscenium, London, 1934.
Fresh Fields, New York, 1936.
Careless Rapture, London, 1936.
Full House, London, 1936.
Comedienne, London, 1938.
Glamorous Night, London, 1939.
We Proudly Present, London, 1947.
The Dancing Years, London, 1953.
Perchance to Dream, London, 1953.
King's Rhapsody, London, 1955.

On NOVELLO: books—

Noble, Peter, *Ivor Novello, Man of the Theatre*, London, 1951.
Macqueen-Pope, W. J., *Ivor, The Story of an Achievement*, London, 1951, rev. ed., 1954.
Rose, Richard, *Perchance to Dream: The World of Ivor Novello*, London, 1974.
Wilson, Sandy, *Ivor*, London, 1975.
Harding, James, *Ivor Novello*, London, 1987.

On NOVELLO: articles—

National Film Theatre Booklet (London), August 1982.
Braun, Eric, "Ivor Novello: The Spirit of Romanticism," in *Films* (London), December 1982.
Classic Images (Indiana, Pennsylvania), July 1984.
"Noël Coward and Ivor Who?," in *Economist* (London), 27 November 1993.

* * *

Comparisons between Ivor Novello and Noël Coward are inevitable. Both were virtual one-man shows, equally adept at writing, composing, acting, and directing. Indeed, the story is told of Coward's asking for complimentary tickets at a suburban theater box office, explaining that he had written, composed, and directed the production currently playing there, and the woman in the box office responding with "A regular little Ivor Novello, aren't we." Of the two, Coward was unquestionably the better composer and writer; his dialogue could be brittle and witty while Novello's was basically sentimental. Novello was the more handsome, but he was a little too beautiful and fey, almost too handsome to be taken seriously as an actor. The major difference is in the two men's film careers. While Coward made an easy transition to films as actor, writer, and director, Novello was only a leading man on screen, immensely popular in Britain, but only moderately so in the United States.

Novello's attitude towards all aspects of show business was very straightforward and unadventurous. In 1949 he commented, "I'm no highbrow. The theater is a place of entertainment, and I'm an entertainer. I don't believe in using the theater for moralizing lectures on social behavior." After appearances in a few minor British and French features, Novello made his first major screen appearance under the direction of D. W. Griffith in *The White Rose*. He was well cast as the weak clergyman who impregnates and then betrays the heroine, Mae Marsh. Perhaps without intending, Novello plays the role with a total lack of spirit, and thus makes the part believable. Aside from his performance in *The White Rose*, Novello is best remembered as a screen actor for his title role in Alfred Hitchcock's *The Lodger*. He gives an extraordinarily languid performance but is not helped by what appears to be an overuse of heavy white makeup. Novello fares worse in the remake, with dialogue making the characterization ludicrous.

In Britain, Novello became a popular matinee idol with a series of films built around a French apache, the Rat, who steals from the rich. His love is a homely working-class girl who protects him from harm

Ivor Novello in *The White Rose*

and is even willing to die for him when he is accused of murder. Novello provided the script for the first film, *The Rat*, which is notable for Graham Cutts's direction and Hal Young's fluid camerawork. In later "Rat" films Novello was paired with Mabel Poulton and Ruth Chatterton, but none of his leading ladies looked as beautiful as the hero.

Novello tried once again for Hollywood stardom in 1931 with *Once a Lady*, but his part opposite Ruth Chatterton was small and made no impact. He starred in a half-dozen more British features, but decided he was better off in the theater where his fans were unable to come too close to their effete idol.

—Anthony Slide

NOWICKI, Jan

Nationality: Polish. **Born:** Kawal, 5 November 1939. **Family:** Married the director Marta Mészáros. **Education:** Attended the School of Theatre and Film, Kraków. **Career:** 1965—film debut in *Ashes*; in TV series *Dyrektorzy*.

Films as Actor:

1965 *Popioły (Ashes)* (Wajda)
1966 *Bariera (Barrier)* (Skolimowski) (as He)
1967 *Password: Korn* (Podgórski)
1968 *Pan Wołodyjowski (Colonel Wolodyjowski)* (Hoffman) (as Ketling)
1969 *Dziura w ziemi (A Hole in the Ground)* (Kondratiuk)
1970 *Doktor Eva* (Żuławski—for TV)
1971 *Życie rodzinne (Family Life)* (Zanussi); *The Third Part of the Night* (Zulawski)
1972 *Anatomy of Love* (Zaluski); *Skorpion, panna, i lucznik (Scorpio, Virgo, and Sagittarius)* (Kondratiuk); *Sanatorium pod klepsydra (The Hour-Glass Sanatorium)* (Has); *A Wasted Night* (Majewski—for TV)
1973 *Story in Scarlet* (Kluba)
1974 *Hour after Hour* (Zaluski)
1976 *Kilenc hónap (Nine Months)* (Mészáros); *Red Thorns* (Dziedzina)
1977 *Ok ketten (The Two of Them; Two Women)* (Mészáros)
1978 *Olyan, mint otthon (Just Like at Home)* (Mészáros) (as Andras Novak); *Spirála (The Spiral)* (Zanussi); *Moloch* (Szulkin)
1979 *Útközben (On the Move)* (Mészáros) (+ co-sc)
1980 *Orökseg (The Heiresses)* (Mészáros); *W. Bialy dzie in(In Broad Daylight)* (Zebrowski); *Golem* (Szulkin)
1981 *Anya és leánya (Mother and Daughter)* (Mészáros); *Spokojne lata* (Kotkowski)
1982 *Napló gyermekeimnek (Diary for My Children)* (Mészáros) (as Janos/Juli's father); *Kettevalt Mennyezet* (Pal Gabor)
1983 *Wielki Szu (The Great Szu)* (Chęciński); *Délibábok országa (The Land of Mirages)* (Mészáros)
1984 *Spassenieto* (Paunchev)
1985 *O-bi, O-bi—Koniec cywilizacji (O-bi, O-bi—The End of Civilization; Ga, Ga—chwala bohaterom)* (Szulkin); *Hulyeseg nem Akadaly* (Xantus) (as Dr. Korosi)
1986 *Biala Wizytowka* (Bajon); *Zygfryd (Siegfried)* (Domalik) (as Waldo, circus owner)
1987 *Magnat (The Magnate)* (Bajon) (as Ksiaze Hans von Teuss); *Napló szerelmeimnek (Diary for My Loves)* (Mészáros) (as Janos)
1988 *Schodami w Gore, Schodami w Dol (Upstairs, Downstairs)* (Domalik); *Piroska és a farkas (Bye-Bye Red Riding Hood)* (Mészáros) (as ornithologist)
1989 *Notater om Korlighedon* (Leth); *Lawa*
1990 *Napló apamanak, anyammnak (Diary for My Father and Mother)* (Mészáros) (as Janos); *Potyautasok* (as prison boss)
1991 *Konyortelen Idol* (Sara)
1993 *The Great Post Office Robbery* (as Bogdan, the cop); *A Magzat (Fetus)* (Mészáros)

Publications

On NOWICKI: articles—

Film a Doba (Prague), January 1982.
Mazierska, B., "Superwizja," in *Filmowy Serwis Prasowy*, vol. 39, no. 8/9, 1993.

*   *   *

Jan Nowicki first won wide critical acclaim for his portrayal of a member of the "lost generation" in Jerzy Skolimowski's *Bariera*. He was labeled the "Polish James Dean" and considered heir to the legacy of Zbigniew Cybulski. In subsequent roles, however, Nowicki demonstrated a range of characterizations that denied this early attempt at classification and cut against the grain of the young Polish film heroes of the time. In *Dziura w ziemi* he played a well-adjusted, energetic young man who charms people with his love of life. In *Życie rodzinne* he portrayed a cynical and introspective man plagued by a series of profound doubts. In *Spirála* his portrait of a man hopelessly awaiting an unheroic and undignified death was accomplished with an economy of gesture and an immobile face in which only the eyes showed animation. After this part, which was difficult for the audience, demanding almost the limit of what a spectator can bear, a number of others followed. It seems there is no character that Nowicki could not play. In *Wielki Szu* he acts with restraint the part of a confidence trickster whose dubious fame is nearing its bitter end. In three of Piotr Szulkin's films he adjusted to a future fantasy world. Finally, the figure of a powerful count of a Polish-German house in Filip Bajon's *Magnat* represents the culmination of his acting career. Here Nowicki portrays a man who over the course of dozens of years bears witness both to the gradual disappearance of old values and to growing fascism in Europe and in his own family.

A special chapter in Nowicki's career has been his involvement in several Hungarian films directed by Marta Mészáros, his wife. In *Útközben* he portrays an actor whose obsession is his profession. The role is frequently seen as a personal statement because of the similarity between Nowicki and the character and the fact that Nowicki collaborated on the screenplay.

Nowicki's list of film credits is rich and without interruption. He creates his characters either with mimicry or a deadpan face, and according to the character he applies irony, cynicism, metaphor, or a grotesque exaggeration. In spite of all this, in all of the characters he portrays he remains himself. Nowicki has also gained official recognition and popularity for his work in television and, more notably, in the theater.

—Blažena Urgošíková

OATES, Warren

Nationality: American. **Born:** Depoy, Kentucky, 5 July 1928. **Education:** Attended high school in Louisville, Kentucky; University of Louisville, 1950-53. **Family:** Married Vickery (Oates) (second marriage), two children. **Career:** 1948-50—served in the U.S. Marine Corps; studied drama in New York, worked as hat-check at 21 Club and tested gags on *Beat the Clock* TV show; worked on New York stage: roles in *Who's Happy Now?* and *The Wisteria Trees*; 1958—film debut in *Up Periscope!*; 1962-63—regular appearances in TV series *Stoney Burke*; 1978—in TV mini-series *Black Beauty*, and *East of Eden*, 1981. **Died:** Of heart attack, in Los Angeles, 3 April 1982.

Films as Actor:

1958   *Up Periscope!* (Douglas)
1959   *Yellowstone Kelly* (Douglas) (as Cavalry corporal); *The Rise and Fall of Legs Diamond* (Boetticher) (as Eddie Diamond); *Private Property* (Stevens) (as Boots)
1961   *Hero's Island* (*The Land We Love*) (Stevens) (as Wayte); **Ride the High Country** (*Guns in the Afternoon*) (Peckinpah) (as Henry Hammond)
1963   *Mail Order Bride* (Kennedy) (as Jace)
1964   *The Rounders* (Kennedy); *Major Dundee* (Peckinpah) (as O. W. Hadley)
1966   *Return of the Seven* (Kennedy) (as Colbee); *The Shooting* (Hellman) (as Willet Gashade); *Welcome to Hard Times* (*Killer on a Horse*) (Kennedy) (as Jenks)
1967   *In the Heat of the Night* (Jewison) (as Sam Wood)
1968   *The Split* (Flemying) (as Marty Gough); *Something for a Lonely Man* (Taylor—for TV) (as Angus Duren)
1969   **The Wild Bunch** (Peckinpah) (as Lyle Gorch); *Smith!* (O'Herlihy) (as Walter Charlie); *Crooks and Coronets* (*Sophie's Place*) (O'Connolly) (as Marty Miller)
1970   *Barquero* (Douglas) (as Jake Remy); *There Was a Crooked Man* (Mankiewicz) (as Floyd Moon); *The Movie Murderer* (Sagal—for TV) (as Alfred Fisher)
1971   *Two-Lane Blacktop* (Hellman) (as "G.T.O."); *The Hired Hand* (Fonda) (as Harris); *Chandler* (Magwood) (title role); *The Reluctant Heroes* (Day—for TV) (as Corporal Leroy Sprague)
1973   *The Thief Who Came to Dinner* (Yorkin) (as Dave Reilly); *Tom Sawyer* (Taylor) (as Muff Potter); *Kid Blue* (Frawley) (as Reese Ford); *Dillinger* (Milius) (title role); *Badlands* (Malick) (as Holly's father)
1974   *The White Dawn* (Kaufman) (as Billy); *Bring Me the Head of Alfredo Garcia* (Peckinpah) (as Bennie); *Cockfighter* (Hellman) (as Frank Mansfield)
1975   *Race with the Devil* (Starrett) (as Frank); *Ninety-Two in the Shade* (McGuane) (as Nichol Dance)
1976   *Dixie Dynamite* (Frost) (as Mack); *Drum* (Carver) (as Hammond Maxwell)
1977   *Sleeping Dogs* (Donaldson) (as Willoughby); *Prime Time* (*American Raspberry*) (Swirnoff) (as Celebrity Sportsman); *The African Queen* (Sarafian—for TV) (as Charlie Allnot)
1978   *Amore, piombo, e furore* (*China 9, Liberty 37*) (Hellman) (as Matthew Hellman); *The Brink's Job* (Friedkin) (as "Specs" O'Keefe); *True Grit* (Heffron—for TV) (as Rooster Cogburn)
1979   *1941* (Spielberg) (as Maddox); *And Baby Makes Six* (Hussein—for TV); *My Old Man* (Erman—for TV)
1981   *Stripes* (Reitman) (as Sergeant Hulka)
1982   *The Border* (Richardson) (as Red)
1983   *Blue Thunder* (Badham) (as Braddock); *Tough Enough* (Fleischer) (as James)

Publications

By OATES: articles—

Interview with A. Garel, in *Image et Son* (Paris), April 1974.
Interview with David Thomson, and others in *Film Comment* (New York), January-February 1981.

On OATES: articles—

Eyles, Allen, "Warren Oates," in *Focus on Film* (London), Spring 1973.
Checklist in *Monthly Film Bulletin* (London), June 1982.
Obituary in *Films and Filming* (London), June 1982.
The Annual Obituary 1982, New York, 1983.
McGillivray, David, "Warren Oates," in *Films and Filming* (London), September 1984.
Hoberman, J., "Home on the Range," in *Premiere*, February 1993.

On OATES: film—

Warren Oates: Across the Border, documentary, directed by Tom Thurman, 1993.

*   *   *

The character actor Warren Oates has been described by the critic David Thomson as ". . . on first sight grubby, balding, and unshaven. You can smell whisky and sweat on him, along with that mixture of bad beds and fallen women. He's toothy, he's small . . . and he has a face like prison bread, with eyes that have known too much solitary confinement. But the eyes bulge and shrink in a sweet game of fear and courage. And for some of us Oates is the only human being in pictures." The essential believability of Oates's characters is one of the most notable aspects of his film career. Rather than a simple projection of a man-on-the-street identity, however, his believability rests on a more sophisticated use of nuance and unpredictability, which, in combination with his unpolished physical appearance, gives his screen roles a substance that succeeds in suspending the audience's disbelief.

Whatever his role, Oates always manages to convey a certain degree of familiarity on the screen, as opposed to portraying an impos-

Warren Oates in *Dillinger*

sibly perfect hero. A case in point is his performance in the title role of *Dillinger*. At a time when roaring twenties desperadoes were being glamorized on film (for example, Warren Beatty's Clyde Barrow in *Bonnie and Clyde*), Oates's conception of "Public Enemy Number One" is neither glamorous nor romanticized. Instead, his swagger is offset by his insecurity, making his eruptions of violence seem the inevitable result of human frustration and frailty.

In an interview, Oates once expressed his feelings of insecurity about playing major figures, particularly in Westerns. In his opinion, John Wayne had become the model for that sort of mythic figure, and he himself possessed none of the requisite visual attributes. This "inadequacy" may be responsible for Oates's career as a supporting player, but all of Oates's characters are nonetheless memorable, because each has its idiosyncracies and quirks. The ability to project such qualities is indispensable for a supporting actor, as his roles are often fragmented and do not evolve over the duration of the film.

A particularly good example is Terrence Malick's *Badlands*, in which Oates plays Sissy Spacek's domineering father, who is brutally murdered by Spacek's boyfriend, played by Martin Sheen. Oates's appearance in the film is brief, and his characterization must therefore be drawn quickly. Rather than playing a more standard supporting role, Oates's character instead actually extends the film's plot. Just when Oates seems to be the most predictable, he explodes in a fashion which foreshadows the violence of Sheen's character. Oates's performance gives the film a cutting edge suggesting that Spacek's relationship with Sheen is not in fact escape, but a continuation of her relationship with her father.

To film enthusiasts, Oates's signature performances were undoubtedly those in his three films for director Sam Peckinpah. In *Ride the High Country*, *The Wild Bunch*, and *Bring Me the Head of Alfredo Garcia*, Oates got perhaps his widest exposure. These were certainly the only instances in which it could be said that Oates was in big-budget films. In fact, the final shoot-out in *The Wild Bunch* had a longer shooting schedule (about 25 days) than most of the rest of the films he appeared in. In *Alfredo Garcia* Oates played what may be his only major role. His character is central to the action and is sustained for the film's duration. Oates himself cited this as his favorite role for that very reason. *Alfredo Garcia* typifies Oates's role as the "bad guy," yet even his bad guys are charming, and not without a level of humor and humanity. Human, then, is the word for Warren Oates on screen. Not "real," necessarily, but believable and charming, because his characters possess a range of qualities the viewer can identify as his or her own.

—Rob Winning

OBERON, Merle

Born: Estelle Merle O'Brien Thompson in Bombay, India, 19 February 1911 (birthplace, date, and name vary in different sources). **Education:** Attended La Martinère College, Calcutta. **Family:** Married 1) the director Alexander Korda, 1939 (divorced 1945); 2) the camera-man Lucien Ballard (divorced); 3) Bruno Pagliai, 1957 (divorced), two adopted children: Bruno, Jr. and Francesca; 4) Robert Wolders, 1978. **Career:** Dance hostess at Cafe de Paris in London; 1930—film debut in *Alf's Button*; 1932—contract with London Film Productions; 1933—lead in film *The Private Life of Henry VIII*; followed by films for United Artists produced by Samuel Goldwyn, notably *Wuthering Heights*, 1939; 1957—host for TV series *Assignment Foreign Legion*; 1973—producer and co-editor of film *Interval*. **Died:** Of stroke in Los Angeles, 23 November 1979.

Films as Actress:

(as Estelle Thompson)

1930 *Alf's Button* (Kellino)
1931 *Never Trouble Trouble* (Lane); *Fascination* (Mander)
1932 *Service for Ladies* (*Reserved for Ladies*) (Korda); *For the Love of Mike* (Banks); *Ebb Tide* (Rosson); *Aren't We All* (Lachman); *Wedding Rehearsal* (Korda) (as Miss Hutchinson); *Men of Tomorrow* (Sagan) (as Ysobel d'Aunay)

(as Merle Oberon)

1933 *The Private Life of Henry VIII* (Korda) (as Anne Boleyn)
1934 *The Battle* (*Hara-Kiri*; *Thunder in the East*) (Farkas) (as Marquise Yorisaka); *The Broken Melody* (*Vagabond Violinist*) (Vorhaus) (as Germaine); *The Private Life of Don Juan* (Korda) (as Antonia)
1935 *The Scarlet Pimpernel* (Young) (as Marguerite Blakeney); *Beloved Enemy* (Potter) (as Helen Drummond); *Folies Bergeres* (Del Ruth) (as Baroness Genevieve Cassini); *The Dark Angel* (Franklin) (as Kitty Vane)
1936 *These Three* (Wyler) (as Karen Wright)
1937 *Over the Moon* (Freeland, Howard) (as June Benson)
1938 *The Divorce of Lady X* (Whelan) (as Leslie Steel); *The Cowboy and the Lady* (Potter) (as Mary Smith)
1939 *Wuthering Heights* (Wyler) (as Cathy Linton); *The Lion Has Wings* (Powell and Hurst) (as Mrs. Richardson)
1940 *'Til We Meet Again* (Goulding) (as Joan Ames)
1941 *That Uncertain Feeling* (Lubitsch) (as Jill Baker); *Affectionately Yours* (Bacon) (as Sue Mayberry); *Lydia* (Duvivier) (title role)
1943 *Forever and a Day* (Goulding and others) (as Marjorie); *Stage Door Canteen* (Borzage) (as herself); *First Comes Courage* (Arzner) (as Nicole Larsen)
1944 *The Lodger* (Brahm) (as Kitty); *Dark Waters* (de Toth) (as Leslie Calvin)
1945 *A Song to Remember* (Charles Vidor) (as George Sand); *This Love of Ours* (Dieterle) (as Karin)
1946 *A Night in Paradise* (Lubin) (as Delerai); *Temptation* (Pichel) (as Ruby)
1947 *Night Song* (Cromwell) (as Cathy)
1948 *Berlin Express* (Tourneur) (as Lucienne)
1951 *Pardon My French* (Vorhaus) (as Elizabeth Rockwell)
1952 *Twenty-Four Hours in a Woman's Life* (*Affair in Monte Carlo*) (Saville) (as Linda Venning)
1954 *Todo es posible en Granada* (de Heredia) (as Margaret Fobson); *Desirée* (Koster) (as Empress Josephine); *Deep in My Heart* (Donen) (as Dorothy Donnelly)
1956 *The Price of Fear* (Biberman) (as Jessica Warren)
1963 *Of Love and Desire* (Rush) (as Katherine Beckman)
1966 *The Oscar* (Rouse) (as herself)
1967 *Hotel* (Quine) (as The Duchess)

Film as Producer:

1973 *Interval* (Daniel Mann) (+ ro as Serena Moore)

Publications

By OBERON: articles—

"Merle Oberon Is Not a Hindu," interview with J. Calendo in *Inter/View* (New York), July 1973.

Merle Oberon in *The Scarlet Pimpernel* courtesy of CTE (Carlton) Limited

Interview (made in 1977) in *Films in Review* (New York), February 1982, see also the issue for June-July 1982.

On OBERON: books—

Parish, James Robert, and Don E. Stanke, *The Glamour Girls*, New Rochelle, New York, 1975.
Higham, Charles, and Roy Moseley, *Princess Merle: The Romantic Life of Merle Oberon*, New York, 1983.

On OBERON: articles—

Current Biography 1941, New York, 1941.
Obituary in *New York Times*, 24 November 1979.

On OBERON: film—

Queenie, television mini-series directed by Larry Peerce, 1987.

*   *   *

Merle Oberon represents a classical case of the woman whose sheer beauty secured her the kind of attention that eventually brought her into films. Raised in India, she did not come to London until she was 17; she then progressed from cafe hostess (name Queenie O'Brien) to film extra. This in turn led to minor roles in undistinguished British films during 1930-32 (name Estelle Thompson), until she finally caught the eye of the Hungarian-British producer, Alexander Korda.

Korda gave her the opportunity, personal patronage, and training which was to establish her as a beautiful star (name Merle Oberon) and acceptable actress. She was later to become his wife. Her first role of importance was as Anne Boleyn in Korda's film, *The Private Life of Henry VIII*, where her dark beauty and svelte grooming made a marked, if short-lived, impression among the King's succession of wives. Her appearance and panache won her many star roles in both London and Hollywood productions, including those in Korda's *The Private Life of Don Juan*, *The Scarlet Pimpernel*, and *The Dark Angel*.

Her career seemed threatened when she was in a severe car accident during the shooting of *I, Claudius*, in which she was to have played Messalina opposite Charles Laughton. (Korda made her accident his reason for closing down this troubled production.) After successful facial surgery, however, she was able to return to the screen, and starred from 1938 through to the 1960s in a range of films, largely American. The more notable, perhaps, are *The Divorce of Lady X*, *Wuthering Heights* (with Laurence Olivier), Ernst Lubitsch's *That Uncertain Feeling*, René Clair's *Forever and a Day*, and as George Sand in the Chopin biographical film *A Song to Remember*. Daniel Mann directed her last film, *Interval*, which she produced herself and co-edited, about an older woman who finds happiness with a younger man, played by Robert Wolders. He went on to become her husband in real life.

—Roger Manvell

O'BRIEN, Edmond

Nationality: American. **Born:** New York City, 10 September 1915. **Education:** Attended Fordham University, New York; studied acting at Neighborhood Playhouse School of the Theatre. **Family:** Married 1) the actress Nancy Kelly, 1941 (divorced 1942); 2) the actress Olga San Juan, 1948 (divorced 1967), three children, including the actress Maria O'Brien. **Career:** Worked as bank clerk while studying acting

and trying to get roles; 1937—joined Orson Welles's Mercury Theater, and acted on radio and stage; 1938—film debut in *Prison Break*; 1954—director, with Howard Koch, of feature film *Shield for Murder*; 1962-63—in TV series *Sam Benedict*, and series *The Long Hot Summer*, 1965-66: also directed some of the episodes. **Awards:** Best Supporting Actor Academy Award, for *The Barefoot Contessa*, 1954. **Died:** Of Alzheimer's disease, 8 May 1985.

Films as Actor:

1938   *Prison Break* (Lubin) (as prisoner)
1939   *The Hunchback of Notre Dame* (Dieterle) (as Pierre Gringoire)
1941   *Obliging Young Lady* (Wallace) (as Red Reddy); *A Girl, a Guy, and a Gob* (*The Navy Steps Out*) (Wallace) (as Stephen Herrick); *Parachute Battalion* (Goodwins) (as Bill Burke)
1942   *Powder Town* (Rowland V. Lee) (as Pennant)
1943   *The Amazing Mrs. Holliday* (Manning) (as Tom)
1944   *Winged Victory* (Cukor) (as Irving Miller)
1946   *The Killers* (Siodmak) (as Jim Riordan)
1947   *The Web* (Gordon) (as Bob Regan); *A Double Life* (Cukor) (as Bill Friend)
1948   *Another Part of the Forest* (Gordon) (as Ben Hubbard); *For the Love of Mary* (De Cordova) (as Lt. Tom Farrington); *Fighter Squadron* (Walsh) (as Maj. Ed Hardin); *An Act of Murder* (*Live Today for Tomorrow*) (Gordon) (as David Douglas)
1949   *White Heat* (Walsh) (as Hank Fallon/Vic Pardo)
1950   *The Redhead and the Cowboy* (Fenton) (as Dunn Jeffers); *Backfire* (Sherman) (as Steve Connolly); *D.O.A.* (Maté) (as Frank Bigelow); *711 Ocean Drive* (Joseph M. Newman) (as Mal Granger); *The Admiral Was a Lady* (Salkow) (as Jimmie Stevens); *Between Midnight and Dawn* (Gordon Douglas) (as Dan Purvis)
1951   *Two of a Kind* (Levin) (as Lefty Farrell); *Warpath* (Haskin) (as John Vickers); *Silver City* (*High Vermilion*) (Haskin) (as Larkin Moffatt)
1952   *Denver and the Rio Grande* (Haskin) (as Jim Vesser); *The Turning Point* (Dieterle) (as John Conroy); *The Greatest Show on Earth* (Cecil B. DeMille) (as midway barker)
1953   *Man in the Dark* (Comfort) (as Steve Rawley/James Blake); *Cow Country* (Selander) (as Ben Anthony); *The Hitch-Hiker* (Lupino) (as Roy Collins); *Julius Caesar* (Joseph L. Mankiewicz) (as Casca); *The Bigamist* (Lupino) (as Harry Graham); *China Venture* (Siegel) (as Capt. Matt Reardon)
1954   *The Shanghai Story* (Lloyd) (as Dr. Dan Maynard); *The Barefoot Contessa* (Joseph L. Mankiewicz) (as Oscar Muldoon)
1955   *Pete Kelly's Blues* (Webb) (as Fran McCarg)
1956   *1984* (Anderson) (as Winston Smith); *D-Day, the Sixth of June* (Koster) (as Col. Timmer); *A City in the Night* (Tuttle) (as Taggart); *The Rack* (Laven) (as Lt. Col. Frank Wasnick); *The Girl Can't Help It* (Tashlin) (as Marty Murdock)
1957   *The Big Land* (*Stampeded*) (Gordon Douglas) (as Jagger); *Stopover Tokyo* (Breen) (as George Underwood)
1958   *The World Was His Jury* (Sears) (as David Carson); *Sing Boy Sing* (Henry Ephron) (as Joseph Sharkey)
1959   *Up Periscope* (Gordon Douglas) (as Stevenson); *L'Ambitieuse* (*The Climbers*) (Yves Allégret)
1960   *The Last Voyage* (Andrew L. Stone) (as 2nd Engineer Walsh); *The Third Voice* (Cornfield) (as the Voice); *The Great Imposter* (Mulligan) (as Capt. Glover)
1962   *Moon Pilot* (Neilson) (as McClosky); *The Man Who Shot Liberty Valance* (Ford) (as Dutton Peabody); *Birdman of Alcatraz* (Frankenheimer) (as Tom Gaddis); *The Longest Day* (Annakin, Marton, Wicki, and Oswald) (as Gen. Raymond O. Barton)

1964   *Seven Days in May* (Frankenheimer) (as Sen. Raymond Clark); *Rio Conchos* (Gordon Douglas) (as Col. Theron Pardee)

1965   *Sylvia* (Gordon Douglas) (as Oscar Stewart); *The Hanged Man* (Siegel—for TV) (as Arnie Seeger); *Synanon (Get Off My Back)* (Quine) (as Chuck Dederich)

1966   *Fantastic Voyage* (Fleischer) (as Gen. Carter); *The Doomsday Flight* (Graham—for TV)

1967   *Le Vicomte règle ses comptes (The Viscount)* (Cloche) (as Ricco Barone); *Peau d'espion (To Commit a Murder)* (Molinaro) (as Sphax); *The Outsider* (Graham—for TV)

1969   *The Wild Bunch* (Peckinpah) (as Sykes); *The Love God?* (Hiken) (as Osborn Tremain); *River of Mystery* (Stanley—for TV)

1970   *The Intruders* (Graham—for TV) (as Col. William Bodeen)

1971   *What's a Nice Girl Like You . . . ?* (Paris—for TV)

1972   *They Only Kill Their Masters* (Goldstone) (as George); *Jigsaw (Man on the Move)* (Graham—for TV)

1973   *Isn't It Shocking?* (Badham—for TV) (as Justin Oates); *A proposito Lucky Luciano (Re: Lucky Luciano; Lucky Luciano)* (Rosi) (as Harry J. Anslinger)

1974   *99 and 44/100 Per Cent Dead (Call Harry Crown)* (Frankenheimer) (as Uncle Frank Kelly)

Films as Director:

1954   *Shield for Murder* (co-d with Koch, + ro as Barney Nolan)

1960   *Mantrap* (+ pr)

Publications

On O'BRIEN: articles—

Eyles, Allen, "Edmond O'Brien," in *Focus on Film* (London), Autumn 1974.

Obituary in *New York Times*, 10 May 1985.

Obituary in *Time* (New York), 20 May 1985.

*   *   *

To watch Edmond O'Brien unwrap a cigar or roll down a limousine window was to recognize a man comfortable with the realities of power. John Houseman, his old Mercury Theater radio producer, cast him in *Julius Caesar* as Casca, but O'Brien's conspirator lacked the credibility he might have brought to the title role (played with road-company broadness by Louis Calhern).

An emphasis on his ranting snarl of a voice and his inspired capacity for perspiration often obscured O'Brien's effortless flair for menace. His film debut as the babbling playwright Gringoire in *The Hunchback of Notre Dame* was his last chance as a potential leading man. In 1950 Rudolph Maté's paranoid thriller *D.O.A.* cast him as a doomed poison victim sweating out his last hours avenging his own murder. Thereafter, his snarl and beaded brow won him entrée to the ranks of classic unreliables.

By 1956 his persona as a heavy had become indelible, and Frank Tashlin in *The Girl Can't Help It* mocked the metamorphosis, having O'Brien's Marty "Fats" Murdock recall nostalgically his days as jukebox czar Marty "Slim" Murdock.

Nobody has better captured the humid flush and numbered belligerence of the serious drunk. O'Brien's only Oscar, for *The Barefoot Contessa*, was won with another perspiring performance as a boozy press agent, and he captured a further nomination for Frankenheimer's *Seven Days in May*, as the dipsomaniac Southern senator shakily assisting President Fredric March to unravel a military conspiracy. O'Brien was set to play the Lowell Thomas journalist who makes a household name of T. E. Lawrence in David Lean's epic *Lawrence of Arabia*, but he became ill at the last minute and was replaced by Arthur Kennedy. O'Brien had his last great film role in Sam Peckinpah's landmark Western *The Wild Bunch* as a grizzled gunslinger who has outlived his time and views life as a circle of disaster that must not be taken seriously. He is almost unrecognizable in the part, which he and Peckinpah intended as a nod to Walter Huston's character in *The Treasure of the Sierra Madre*.

As the television lawyer *Sam Benedict* in the early 1960s, O'Brien offered a down-market version of the then-popular *Defenders* formula, and in the series based on *The Long Hot Summer* he took over Burl Ives's duties as the bullying Southern patriarch. Neither these nor his efforts as director showed the skill he brought to roles that exploited his ability to roll a cigar between his pudgy finger, look a man in the eye, and convince the audience this is not a man one should even consider buying a used car from.

—John Baxter, updated by John McCarty

O'BRIEN, Margaret

Nationality: American. **Born:** Angela Maxine O'Brien in San Diego, California, 15 January 1937. **Education:** Attended University High School, Los Angeles. **Family:** Married 1) Harold R. Allen Jr., 1959 (divorced 1968); 2) Roy T. Thorsen, 1974, daughter: Mary. **Career:** Child model at age three; 1941—film debut at age four in *Babes on Broadway*; made some films after 1951, but has worked since mainly on stage and television, including the mini-series *Testimony of Two Men*, 1977; 1979—civilian aide to Secretary of the Army Clifford Alexander. **Awards:** Special Academy Award, as "outstanding child actress of 1944," 1944. **Address:** 1250 La Preresa Drive, Thousand Oaks, CA 91362, U.S.A.

Films as Actress:

1941   *Babes on Broadway* (Berkeley)

1942   *Journey for Margaret* (Van Dyke) (title role)

1943   *Dr. Gillespie's Criminal Case* (Goldbeck) (as Margaret); *Thousands Cheer* (Sidney); *Madame Curie* (LeRoy) (as Irene at age 5)

1944   *Lost Angel* (Rowland) (as Alpha); *Jane Eyre* (Stevenson) (as Adele); *The Canterville Ghost* (Dassin) (as Lady Jessica de Canterville); *Meet Me in St. Louis* (Minnelli) (as Tootie Smith); *Music for Millions* (Koster) (as Mike)

1945   *Our Vines Have Tender Grapes* (Rowland) (as Selma Jacobson)

1946   *Bad Bascomb* (Simon) (as Emmy); *Three Wise Fools* (Buzzell) (as Sheila O'Monohan)

1947   *The Unfinished Dance* (Koster)

1948   *Tenth Avenue Angel* (Rowland) (as Flavia Mills); *Big City* (Taurog) (as Midge)

1949   *Little Women* (LeRoy) (as Beth March); *The Secret Garden* (Wilcox) (as Mary Lennox)

1951   *Her First Romance* (Friedman) (as Betty Foster)

1956   *Glory* (David Butler) (as Clarabel Tilbee)

1960   *Heller in Pink Tights* (Cukor) (as Della Southby)

1968   *Split Second to an Epitaph* (Horn—for TV)

1971   *Diabolical Wedding*

1972   *Annabelle Lee*

1981   *Amy* (McEveety) (as Hazel Johnson)

Margaret O'Brien

Publications

On O'BRIEN: articles—

Ciné Revue (Paris), 21 August 1980.
Baker, B., "Margaret O'Brien," in *Film Dope* (London), July 1992.

* * *

Margaret O'Brien received a special Oscar in 1944 for being an "outstanding child actress," a distinction she shared with Shirley Temple, Jackie Cooper, and others. Unlike most of her contemporaries and subsequent child actors, however, O'Brien was not particularly "cute." Her success lay in her ability to stir the emotions of her audience in dramatic scenes rather than with childish charm or musical talent. Beginning with her first hit, and only her second film, *Journey for Margaret*, which was made at her home studio, MGM, O'Brien relied on scowls and cynicism as much as her dimples. She invariably wore a pointed cap and usually was deadly serious as she seemed to carry the weight of the world on her little shoulders.

Her two best films, both made in 1944, were *The Canterville Ghost* and *Meet Me in St. Louis*. In the former, O'Brien captured the audience, playing the pivotal role of a young duchess whose courage inspires both a 400-years-dead ghost played by Charles Laughton and a brash American G.I. played by Robert Young. In *Meet Me in St. Louis* O'Brien had a relatively minor role in comparison with star Judy Garland and many well-known members of the MGM stock company, but her big scene in which she hysterically destroys the snowmen on the front lawn on Christmas Eve has become famous, and led to her Oscar.

O'Brien appeared in a number of productions after the war, including *Little Women*, but her career declined dramatically, like so many other child stars, as she reached puberty. While she was in her prime, O'Brien was considered one of the best child actors on the screen, although in retrospect most of her films show her in a whiny, unattractive light. She has continued to act sporadically over the years, but has never risen above minor featured parts. Her most widely seen role as a adult was that of an overweight housewife in Robert Young's television series, *Marcus Welby, M.D.*

—Patricia King Hanson

O'CONNOR, Donald

Nationality: American. **Born:** Donald David Dixon Ronald O'Connor in Chicago, Illinois, 28 August 1925. **Family:** Married 1) Gwendolyn Carter, 1944 (divorced 1954), daughter: Donna; 2) Gloria Noble, 1956, three children. **Career:** Member of "The O'Connor Family" circus and vaudeville act as a child; 1937—film debut in *Melody for Two*; 1938-39—made films under contract with Paramount; then resumed family act; 1941—contract with Universal; 1944-46—served in entertainment division of the U.S. Army; 1949—starred in the film *Francis*, followed by five more in the series; 1951-54—star of the TV series *The Colgate Comedy Hour*, and *The Donald O'Connor Show: Here Comes Donald*, 1954-55; performed in nightclubs and cabarets;1956—his first symphony performed by the Los Angeles Philharmonic Orchestra; 1981—Broadway debut in musical *Bring Back Birdie*; 1982—in *Show Boat*, Houston and New York. **Address:** P.O. Box 4524, Valley Village Station, North Hollywood, CA 91607, U.S.A.

Films as Actor:

1937 *Melody for Two* (Louis King)

1938 *Sing You Sinners* (Ruggles) (as Mike Beebe); *Sons of the Legion* (Hogan) (as Butch Baker); *Men with Wings* (Wellman) (as Pat Falconer at age 10); *Tom Sawyer—Detective* (Louis King) (as Huck Finn)

1939 *Unmarried* (Neumann) (as Ted Streaver at age 12); *Night Work* (Archainbaud) (as Butch Smiley); *Boy Trouble* (Archainbaud) (as Butch); *Million Dollar Legs* (Grinde) (as Sticky Boone); *Beau Geste* (Wellman) (as Beau as a child); *Death of a Champion* (Florey) (as Small Fry); *On Your Toes* (Enright) (as Phil as a boy)

1942 *What's Cookin'?* (Cline) (as Tommy); *Private Buckaroo* (Cline) (as Donny); *Give Out Sisters* (Cline) (as Don); *Get Hep to Love* (Lamont) (as Jimmy Arnold)

1943 *When Johnny Comes Marching Home* (Lamont) (as Frankie); *It Comes Up Love* (Lamont) (as Ricky); *Strictly in the Groove* (Keays); *Mister Big* (Lamont) (as Donald); *Top Man* (Lamont) (as Don Warren)

1944 *Chip Off the Old Block* (Lamont) (as Donald Corrigan); *Follow the Boys* (Thorpe); *This Is the Life* (Feist) (as Jimmy Plum); *Bowery to Broadway* (Lamont); *The Merry Monahans* (Lamont) (as Jimmy Monahan)

1945 *Patrick the Great* (Ryan) (as Pat Donague Jr.)

1947 *Something in the Wind* (Pichel) (as Charlie Read)

1948 *Are You with It?* (Hively) (as Milton Haskins); *Feudin', Fussin', and A-Fightin'* (Sherman) (as Wilbur McMurty)

1949 *Yes Sir, that's My Baby* (Sherman) (as William Waldo Winfield); *Francis* (*Francis the Talking Mule*) (Lubin) (as Peter Stirling)

1950 *Curtain Call at Cactus Creek* (Lamont) (as Edward Timmons); *The Milkman* (Barton) (as Roger Bradley)

1951 *Double Crossbones* (Barton) (as Dave Crandall); *Francis Goes to the Races* (Lubin) (as Peter Stirling)

1952 **Singin' in the Rain** (Kelly and Donen) (as Cosmo Brown); *Francis Goes to West Point* (Lubin) (as Peter Stirling)

1953 *Call Me Madam* (Walter Lang) (as Kenneth); *I Love Melvin* (Weis) (as Melvin Hoover); *Francis Covers the Big Town* (Lubin) (as Peter Stirling); *Walkin' My Baby Back Home* (Lloyd Bacon) (as Jigger Millard)

1954 *Francis Joins the Wacs* (Lubin) (as Peter Stirling); *There's No Business Like Show Business* (Walter Lang) (as Tim Donahue)

1955 *Francis in the Navy* (Lubin) (as Peter Stirling/Slicker Donovan)

1956 *Anything Goes* (Robert Lewis) (as Ted Adams)

1957 *The Buster Keaton Story* (Sheldon) (title role)

1961 *Cry for Happy* (George Marshall) (as Murray Prince); *Le meraviglie di Aladino* (*Les Mille et une nuits*; *The Wonders of Aladdin*) (Levin) (as Aladdin)

1965 *That Funny Feeling* (Thorpe) (as Harvey Granson)

1974 *That's Entertainment!* (Haley Jr.—compilation) (as host)

1981 *Ragtime* (Forman) (as Evelyn's dance teacher)

1982 *Pandemonium* (*Thursday the 12th*) (Sole)

1985 *The Last Great Vaudeville Show* (Iscove—for TV); *Alice in Wonderland* (Harry Harris—for TV) (as Lory Bird)

1986 *Irving Berlin's America* (Dubose—for TV)

1987 *A Mouse, a Mystery and Me* (Nichols—for TV)

1990 *A Time to Remember* (Travers) (as Father Walsh)

1992 *Toys* (Levinson) (as Kenneth Zevo)

1994 *That's Entertainment! III* (Friedgen and Sheridan—compilation); *Bandit: Bandit's Silver Angel* (Needham—for TV) (as Uncle Cyrus)

Publications

By O'CONNOR: article—

Interview, in *Photoplay* (London), November 1982.

On O'CONNOR: book—

Thomas, Tony, *That's Dancing!*, New York, 1985.

On O'CONNOR: articles—

Current Biography 1955, New York, 1955.
Reed, J. D., "Can You Tap This," in *People Weekly* (New York), 21 December 1992.

* * *

Donald O'Connor's vaudeville background has been in evidence throughout his film career. Bing Crosby allegedly asked, "Isn't there anything he can't do?" Singer, dancer, and comedian, O'Connor played in many low-budget musicals and established his reputation by proving that, indeed, he could do just about everything. Perhaps his most popular role was as the straight man to a talking mule in six films of the *Francis* series. He was never stereotyped by that role, however, and throughout the several years of production of those films, he appeared in a number of important musicals and continued his vaudeville exploits in two successful television shows. It was fitting that, in one of his later films, he played Buster Keaton, whose multiple physical talents and vaudeville background were similar to O'Connor's.

During the early 1940s, under contract to Universal, O'Connor was cast in a number of musicals, often directed by Charles Lamont, that exploited his vaudeville talents and teenage charm. In *Top Man*, *Chip Off the Old Block*, and *The Merry Monahans*, for example, he was teamed with Peggy Ryan in films that seemed Universal's answer to MGM's Garland-Rooney films. Often called on to assume adult responsibilities, O'Connor's characters won their way in the world (and the girl's heart) by show-business expertise. Later, in more mature roles in *Singin' in the Rain*, *I Love Melvin*, and *Call Me Madam*, he retained some of that youthful quality and spirit of delight in performing.

"Make 'em Laugh" from *Singin' in the Rain* displays all of O'Connor's inventive vaudeville-based skills. As he sings the song, itself a paean to the virtues of popular entertainment, O'Connor performs a series of body maneuvers and slapstick gags: he gets hit by a plank, walks into a wall, gets his feet entangled and falls, and, finally, runs up a wall and backflips off it. Each of these displays him as the limber-legged and rubber-faced vaudeville comedian. Other numbers show his tapping ability, as well. In *I Love Melvin* he is required to tap on roller skates and, a frequent O'Connor trademark, to assume a variety of identities with quick costume changes.

Although he brought his trademark panache to the *Francis* series, O'Connor is more happily remembered partnering peppy Debbie Reynolds than a quadruped. It is regrettable that MGM could not have given O'Connor a permanent home after *Singin' in the Rain*: what other dancer stole scenes from Gene Kelly? Of O'Connor's five major shots at big studio musical comedy immortality, only one (*Singin' in the Rain*) is an undisputed masterwork. Whereas *I Love Melvin* is mere breezy escapism (a sort of upscale version of his Universal Studio romps), *Anything Goes* is a regrettably garish shortchanging of Cole Porter; yet O'Connor bucks and wings his way through both until their limitations evaporate. Blessed with a partner of equal merit in Vera-Ellen, O'Connor helps Ethel Merman turn *Call Me Madam* into one of the sunniest transfers of a Broadway hit to the screen. And if nothing in *There's No Business Like Show Business* matches his silken dancing to "It's a Lovely Day Today" in *Call Me Madam*, *Show Business* does provide him with ample opportunities to dazzle aficionados. Despite contending with squeaky-clean Johnny Ray and resistibly upbeat Mitzi Gaynor, not to mention the daunting prospect of coming face to face with Monroe's bosom, O'Connor energetically steals the film by dancing with the exuberance of someone born in a trunk, who could dance before he could walk. If it had been filmed earlier, he would have been the definitive leprechaun in *Finian's Rainbow*, but such major roles were sadly not his lot; lending class to vulgarly conceived production numbers was his forte.

Not faring well after the demise of the Hollywood musical, O'Connor failed to storm Broadway in a foolish sequel called *Bring Back Birdie*. Nevertheless, he continued to wow his fans in summer stock, embarked on a second career as a composer, and made a graceful all-too-brief comeback as a dance instructor in *Ragtime*. Watching his clowning around on a standout episode of *Frasier*'s 1995-96 season and struck by his galvanizing routines showcased in *That's Entertainment! III*, one can only regret the waste of his talents for the past 30 years. Despite the extinction of the film musical, O'Connor, one of the last movie stars to have trained in vaudeville, has achieved a special place as an indispensable link among various types of popular American entertainment.

—Jerome Delamater, updated by Robert Pardi

O'HARA, Maureen

Nationality: American. **Born:** Maureen Fitzsimmons in Milltown, Ireland, 17 August 1921; became U.S. citizen, 1946. **Education:** Attended Burke's School of Elocution; Abbey Theatre School, Dublin; Guildhall School of Music, London; London College of Music. **Family:** Married 1) the director George Hanley Brown, 1939 (divorced 1941); 2) the director Will Price, 1941 (divorced 1952), one daughter: Bronwyn; 3) Charles F. Blair 1968 (died 1978). **Career:** Radio performer from age 12; 1938—film debut in *Kicking the Moon Around*; 1939—leading role in *Jamaica Inn*; Hollywood contract with 20th Century-Fox/RKO; 1951—Co-Founder, Price Merman Productions; 1953—contract with Columbia; television work from 1960.

Films as Actress:

1938   *Kicking the Moon Around* (*The Playboy*; *Millionaire Merry-Go-Round*) (Forde) (as secretary)
1939   *My Irish Molly* (Bryce) (as Eileen O'Shea); *Jamaica Inn* (Hitchcock) (as Mary); *The Hunchback of Notre Dame* (Dieterle) (as Esmeralda)
1940   *A Bill of Divorcement* (Farrow) (as Sydney Fairfield); ***Dance, Girl, Dance*** (Arzner) (as Judy)
1941   *They Met in Argentina* (Goodwins and Hively) (as Lolita); *How Green Was My Valley* (Ford) (as Angharad Morgan)
1942   *To the Shores of Tripoli* (Humberstone) (as Mary Carter); *Ten Gentlemen from West Point* (Hathaway) (as Carolyn Bainbridge); *The Black Swan* (King) (as Margaret Denby)
1943   *The Immortal Sergeant* (Stahl) (as Valentine); *This Land Is Mine* (Renoir) (as Louise Martin); *The Fallen Sparrow* (Wallace) (as Toni Donne)
1944   *Buffalo Bill* (Wellman) (as Louis Cody)
1945   *The Spanish Main* (Borzage) (as Francisca)
1946   *Sentimental Journey* (Walter Lang) (as Julie); *Do You Love Me?* (Ratoff) (as Katherine Hilliard)
1947   *Sinbad the Sailor* (Wallace) (as Shireen); *The Homestretch* (Humberstone) (as Leslie Hale); *Miracle on 34th Street* (Seaton) (as Doris Walker); *The Foxes of Harrow* (Stahl) (as Odalie)
1948   *Sitting Pretty* (Walter Lang) (as Tracey)
1949   *The Forbidden Street* (*Britannia Mews*) (Negulesco) (as Adelaide Culver); *A Woman's Secret* (Ray) (as Marian Washburn); *Father Was a Fullback* (Stahl) (as Elizabeth Cooper); *Bagdad* (Lamont) (as Princess Marjan)

Maureen O'Hara

1950　*Comanche Territory* (Sherman) (as Katie); *Tripoli* (Price) (as Countess D'Arneau); *Rio Grande* (Ford) (as Kathleen Yorke)

1951　*Flame of Araby* (Lamont) (as Princess Tanya)

1952　*At Sword's Point* (Allen) (as Claire); *Kangaroo* (Milestone) (as Dell McGuire); **The Quiet Man** (Ford) (as Mary Kate Danaher); *Against All Flags* (Sherman) (as Spitfire Stevens)

1953　*The Redhead from Wyoming* (Sholem) (as Kate Maxwell)

1954　*War Arrow* (Sherman) (as Elaine Corwin); *Malaga* (*Fire over Africa*) (Benedek) (as Joanna Dane)

1955　*The Long Gray Line* (Ford) (as Mary O'Donnell); *The Magnificent Matador* (Boetticher) (as Karen Harrison); *Lady Godiva* (Lubin) (title role)

1956　*Lisbon* (Milland) (as Sylvia Merrill); *Everything but the Truth* (Hopper) (as Joan Madison)

1957　*The Wings of Eagles* (Ford) (as Minnie Wead)

1959　*Our Man in Havana* (Reed) (as Beatrice Severn)

1961　*The Parent Trap* (Swift) (as Maggie McKendrick); *The Deadly Companions* (*Trigger Happy*) (Peckinpah) (as Kit Tilden)

1962　*Mr. Hobbs Takes a Vacation* (Koster) (as Peggy Hobbs)

1963　*Spencer's Mountain* (Daves) (as Olivia Spencer); *McLintock!* (McLaglen) (as Katherine McLintock)

1965　*The Battle of the Villa Fiorita* (Daves) (as Moira)

1966　*The Rare Breed* (McLaglen) (as Martha Price)

1970　*How Do I Love Thee?* (Gordon) (as Elsie Waltz)

1971　*Big Jake* (Sherman) (as Martha McCandles)

1973　*The Red Pony* (Totten—for TV) (as Ruth Tiflin)

1991　*Only the Lonely* (Columbus) (as Rose Muldoon)

1995　*The Christmas Box* (for TV)

Publications

By O'HARA: article—

"Sitting Pretty: After a Twenty-Year Absence, Actress Maureen O'Hara Returns to the Silver Screen," interview by Roddy McDowall, in *Premiere*, July 1991.

On O'HARA: book—

Parish, James Robert, *The RKO Gals*, London, 1974.

On O'HARA: articles—

Current Biography 1953, New York, 1953.

Fox, J., "Maureen O'Hara: The Fighting Lady," in *Films and Filming* (London), December 1972.

Pickard, Roy, in *Radio Times* (London), 21-27 January 1984.

Lewis, K., "Maureen O'Hara," in *Films in Review* (New York), April and May 1990.

Ferguson, K., "The Screen Return of Maureen O'Hara," in *Film Monthly*, September 1991.

Brock, P., "These I Have Known: Maureen O'Hara," in *Classic Images*, December 1992.

*　　*　　*

The essential screen persona of Maureen O'Hara found its famous, if truncated, embodiment in the films of John Ford. Her persona usually follows the same pattern: she is an explosive Irish lass who rebels against an essentially patriarchally structured society, yet in the end is tamed into a type of submission by the John Wayne character.

But those critics who say there is nothing behind this strong, if only temporarily so, facade are wrong. In *Rio Grande*, for example, her acting during those scenes where she resists Wayne contain far more effective acting than those where she finally capitulates. In *The Quiet Man* she again plays the volatile woman who puts up a good fight, but, in the finale, is brought to heel—but it is her intransigence over her dowry that sticks in one's mind. Only in *The Wings of Eagles*, with Wayne, and in *The Long Gray Line*, without him, does Ford allow the Maureen O'Hara personality a certain dignity in something like an adult relationship—perhaps because in both films Ford was bound by the biographical bases of the narratives.

Is it heresy to suggest the most compelling reason to watch a John Ford movie today is the chance to glory in Maureen O'Hara? Much heralded by a hierarchy of male critics, Ford's cinema boasts undisputed masterpieces such as *The Searchers*, along with sentimental blarney and wearying sexism that would be unbearable without O'Hara.

Long dismissed as the Queen of Technicolor, O'Hara has been undervalued by critics who cannot see the forest for the Titian tresses. A bewitching Esmeralda in *Hunchback of Notre Dame*, O'Hara displayed a haunted duality as the tragically pragmatic Angharad in *How Green Was My Valley*, and gave a delicate performance as an artistically inclined ballerina in *Dance, Girl, Dance*. In O'Hara's canon of work, however, such showcase dramas took a backseat to rip-roaring escapism.

However much one laments the curve-hugging aesthetic straitjacket O'Hara was forced to model in male-dominated film after film, it is her vitality that outshines all studio era constraints. Whereas other Hollywood wenches were simply mannequins with cleavage, O'Hara heaved her bosom and hitched up her skirts in order to swashbuckle with the best of them (Power, Fairbanks Jr., Cornell Wilde). Nowhere in the action genre arena was she more suitably cast than as D'Artagnan's daughter in *At Sword's Point*, because she got to dress up like a man and raise hell. The essential O'Hara is a free spirit who refuses to behave like a lady. A force of nature born in a shamrock patch, she is a joy to behold even in escapist claptrap; what prevents exotic adventures such as *Sinbad the Sailor* and *Flame of Araby* from aging painfully is the tongue-in-cheek relish with which O'Hara attacked these roles.

Maturing gracefully, she played mothers who did not sacrifice their sexuality at the birthing stool in such films as *Parent Trap* and *Battle of the Villa Florita*. And then, after years of retirement, O'Hara delivered a deliciously unsympathetic turn in *Only the Lonely* which should have netted her critics' prizes and an Oscar. Perhaps it is her fate to be underrated for acting that is naturally graceful and aligned with an ageless beauty. As the controlling matriarch manipulating the apron strings wound around her adult son in *Only the Lonely*, O'Hara gets a cinematic revenge for all the occasions when male co-stars underestimated her and filmmakers misused her gifts.

—Rodney Farnsworth, updated by Robert Pardi

OKADA, Eiji

Nationality: Japanese. **Born:** Chiba Prefecture, 13 June 1920. **Education:** Attended Keio University, degree in economics. **Military Service:** Japanese Army, World War II. **Family:** Married Aiko Wasa. **Career:** 1946-54—member of Tomoyoshi Murayama's Shinkyo Gekidan (the second) theater group; later involved with the Gekidan Seinen Haiyu Club, Gendaijin Gekijo, and Gekidan Geki-kukan Kakuteru theater groups; also founded theater company with his wife; 1949—film debut in *Hana no sugao*; 1959—gained international attention with role in *Hiroshima, mon amour*. **Died:** In Tokyo, 14 September 1995.

Eiji Okada with Emmanuelle Riva in *Hiroshima, mon amour* **Argos Films for Hiroshima mon amour**

Films as Actor:

1949   *Hana no sugao* (Shibuya)
1950   *Mata au hi made* (*Until We Meet Again*; *Until the Day We Meet Again*) (Imai) (as Saburo)
1951   *Fusetsu ni ju-nen* (Saburi) (as Namikiri)
1952   *Yamabiko gakko* (*School of Echoes*) (Imai); *Okasan* (*Mother*) (Naruse) (as Shinjiro, the baker); *Shinku chitai* (*Vacuum Zone*) (Yamamoto) (as Okamoto)
1953   *Himeyuri ro to* (*The Tower of Lilies*; *Himeyuri Lily Tower*) (Imai)
1954   *Horoki* (Hisamatsu); *Okuman-choja* (*A Billionaire*) (Ichikawa)
1955   *Koko ni izuni ari* (*Here Is a Fountain*) (Imai); *Kao no nai otoko*
1956-7 *Shonen tanteidan* (Kobayashi) (parts I-IV) (as Kogoro Akechi)
1959   **Hiroshima, mon amour** (Resnais) (as Lui, the architect)
1963   *The Ugly American* (Englund) (as Deong); *Kanojo to kare* (*She and He*) (Hani) (as Eiichi); ***Suna no onna*** (*Woman in the Dunes*) (Teshigawara) (as Niki Jumpei)
1964   *Ansatsu* (*The Assassin*) (Shinoda)
1965   *Sugata Sanshiro* (*Judo Saga*) (Ichikawa) (as the Higaki brothers); *Sandai kaiju chikyu saidai no kessen* (*Ghidrah, the Three-Headed Monster*) (Honda); *Goben no tsubaki* (*The Scarlet Camellia*) (Nomura) (as General Maruu)
1966   *Tanin no kao* (*The Face of Another*) (Teshigahara)

1967   *Chieko-sho* (*Portrait of Chieko*) (Nakamura) (as Tsubaki); *Girara* (*The X from Outer Space*) (Nihonmatsu)
1968   *Showa no inochi* (*Stormy Era*) (Masuda); *Kurobe no taiyo* (*Tunnel to the Sun*) (Kumai)
1969   *Jotai* (*Vixen*) (Manumura) (as Nobuyuki Ishido); *Dankon* (*Bullet Wound*) (Moritani)
1971   *Yomigaeru daichi* (Nakamura); *This Transient Life* (Jissoji) (as sculptor)
1973   *Zatoichi's Conspiracy* (Yasuda) (as Shinbei)
1975   *The Yakuza* (*Brotherhood of the Yakuza*) (Pollack) (as Tono Toshiro)
1976   *Daichi no komoriuta* (Masumura); *Paamenento bruu: Manatsu no koi* (Yamane)
1982   *Ogin Sama* (*Love and Faith of Ogin*) (Kumai) (as Ankokuji); *Ningyo Girai* (Hikada)
1983   *Nankyoku monogatari* (*Antarctica*) (Kurahara) (as the captain); *Yogoreta Eiyu* (Kadokawa)
1986   *Haru No Kane*
1989   *Sen no Rikyu* (Kumai) (as Honkakubo)
1991   *Jutai* (*Traffic Jam*) (Kurotsuchi) (as son); *Hikarigoke* (as Nishikawa)
1994   *Bo no Kanashimi* (*Like a Rolling Stone*) (Kumashiro) (as Tanaka)
1995   *Love without a Person*; *Harukana Jidai No Daidan O* (as White Man)

Publications

On OKADA: article—

Obituary in *New York Times*, 5 October 1995.

*   *   *

As an experienced Shingeki (modern theater) actor, Eiji Okada always met the unique demands of complex and abstract roles. His quiet and philosophically oriented public image and modern, rather western physical features—rare for a Japanese actor—were well suited for the existentialist films that brought him international fame.

He established his image as an earnest, intellectual youth with the role of a wartime student in Tadashi Imai's romantic antiwar film, *Mata au hi made*. Okada's caring attitudes authenticated his image in the minds of the immediate postwar Japanese audiences. Through subsequent roles in the works of the leftist independent film production movement (by such directors as Yamamoto, Saburi, and Imai), he began to be recognized as an extremely reliable actor in socially oriented films. Starting at this time and continuing until his death in 1995, Okada also appeared in various genres, including melodrama, comedy, and detective films.

The two roles that brought Okada worldwide fame were as the Japanese architect in love with a French woman in Alain Resnais's *Hiroshima, mon amour*, and as the entomologist trapped in a frustrating and enigmatic situation in Hiroshi Teshigawara's emotionally draining *Woman in the Dunes*. In both performances his intelligent and convincing characterizations challenged and matched the rigid stylization of each film. His role in the former brought him to the attention of Marlon Brando who secured for Okada his only Hollywood credit in the disappointing *The Ugly American* playing a communist rebel leader in a southeast Asian country reminiscent of Vietnam. None of his latter career films were particularly noteworthy; he in fact devoted most of his energy to the theater during this period.

—Kyoko Hirano, updated by David E. Salamie

OLBRYCHSKI, Daniel

Nationality: Polish. **Born:** Lowicz, 27 February 1945. **Education:** Attended the School of Drama, Warsaw, graduated 1971. **Family:** Married, one son: Rafał. **Career:** 1964—film debut in *Ranny v lesie*; 1970—in title role of stage production of *Hamlet*; 1978—appeared in the Peter Handke play *Die Unvernünftigen sterben aus* in Nanterre, France; 1987—in TV mini-series *The Secret of the Sahara*. **Awards:** Bronze Lion of Gdansk, for *The Deluge*, 1974; Chevalier de l'Order des Arts et des Lettres, France.

Films as Actor:

1964   *Ranny v lesie* (*The Wounded in the Forest*) (Nasfeter) (as Lieutenant)
1965   *Popioły* (*Ashes*) (Wajda) (as Rafal)
1966   *Potem nastąpi cisza* (*The Silence Will Reign*) (Morgenstern); *Bokser* (*The Boxer*) (Dziedzina) (title role)
1967   *Jowita* (*Jovita*) (Morgenstern) (as Marc Arens); *Małżeństwo z rozsądki* (Bareja)
1968   *Hrabina Cosel* (Antczak)

1969   *Pan Wołodyjowski* (*Colonel Wolodyjowski*) (Hoffman) (as Azja); *Polowanie na muchy* (*Hunting Flies*) (Wajda); *Skok* (*Bank Robbery*) (Kutz); *Wszystko na sprzedaż* (*Everything for Sale*) (Wajda) (as Daniel); *Struktura kryształu* (Zanussi); *Różaniec z granatow* (Rutliewicz)
1970   *Brzezina* (*The Birch-wood*) (Wajda); *Egy Barany* (*Angel of Death*) (Jancso); *Krajobraz po bitwie* (*Landscape after the Battle*) (Wajda) (as Tadeusz); *La Pacifista* (Jancso); *Sól ziemi czarnej* (*The Salt of This Black Earth*) (Kutz)
1971   *Życie rodzinne* (*Family Life*) (Zanussi) (as Wit); *Liberation* (Ozierow); "Poslednii chturm" ep. of *Osvobojdienie* (Ozierow)
1973   *Wesele* (*The Wedding*) (Wajda) (as bridegroom); *Roma rivuole Cesare* (*Rome Wants Another Cacsar*) (Jancso) (as Claudius)
1974   *Potop* (*The Deluge*) (Hoffman)
1975   *Pilatus und andere—ein Film für Karfreitag* (*Pilate and Others*) (Wajda—for TV) (as Matthew the Levite); *Ziema obiecana* (*The Promised Land*) (Wajda) (as Karol Borowiecki)
1976   *Dagny* (Sandoy) (as Przybyszewski); *Zdjęcia próbne* (Holland, Kędzierski, and Domaraddzki)
1978   *Panny z Wilka* (*The Young Ladies from Wilko*) (Wajda) (as Wiktor Ruben); ***Die Blechtrommel*** (*The Tin Drum*) (Schlöndorff) (as Jan Bronski)
1980   *Kung-Fu* (Kijowski); *Wizja lokalna 1901* (*Inspection of the Crime Scene 1901*) (Bajon)
1981   *Les Uns et les autres* (*Bolero*) (Lelouch) (as Karl); *La Derelitta* (Igoux)
1982   *Roza* (Christofis); *Przgody pana Michala* (Komorowski)
1983   *Si j'avais mille ans* (Enkell); *La Truite* (*The Trout*) (Losey) (as Saint-Genis)
1984   *La Diagonale du fou* (*Dangerous Moves*) (Dembo) (as TacTac); *Casablanca, Casablanca* (Nuti); *Elakoon Itsemurhaaja* (Jasny); *Lieber Karl* (Knilli) (as teacher)
1985   *Der Bulle und das Mädchen* (*The Cop and the Girl*) (Keglevic) (as Fritz); *O-bi, O-bi—Koniec cywilizacji* (*O-bi, O-bi—The End of Civilization*; *Ga, Ga—chwala bohaterom*) (Szulkin); *Mariage blanc* (Kassovitz); *Le Monde desert* (Beuchot); *Music Hall* (Bluwal); *Pad Italje* (*The Fall of Italy*) (Zafranovic); *Eine Liebe in Deutschland* (*A Love in Germany*) (Wajda) (as Wiktorczyk)
1986   *Objection* (Trzos-Rastawiecki) (as Grzegorz); *Rosa Luxemburg* (von Trotta) (as Leo Jogiches); *Siekierezada* (*Axiliad*) (Leszczynski) (as Katny)
1987   *Mosca addio* (Bolognini) (as Yuli); *Teleftaio Stichima* (Zirnis)
1988   *The Unbearable Lightness of Being* (Kaufman) (as Interior Ministry Official); *Notturno* (Lehner); ***Dekalog 3*** (Kieślowski—for TV)
1989   *L'Orchestre rouge* (Rouffio) (as Giering); *Bugiarda* (Giraldi); *La Boutique de l'orfever* (as Adam)
1990   *Le Silence d'ailleurs* (Mouyal)
1992   *Das Lange Gespräch mit dem Vogel* (Zanussi—for TV) (as Angelo)
1993   *Ivan and Abraham* (as Stepan); *Kolejnosc uczuc* (*Sequence of Feelings*) (Piwowarski) (as Rafal Nawrot); *Jobb Szepnek es Gazdagnak Lenni* (*Better to Be Pretty and Rich*) (Bajon)
1995   *Transatlantis* (as Neuffer); *Bastard* (as Geza); *Pestka* (Janda) (as Borys)

Publications

By OLBRYCHSKI: articles—

"Rozmowa z Danielem Olbrzychskim," interview with A. Markowski, in *Kino* (Warsaw), October 1974.

Interview with J. Frenais, in *Cinéma* (Paris), April 1978.

"Daniel Olbrychski," interview with M. Martin, in *Ecran* (Paris), November 1979.

Interview with J. Bruller, in *Cahiers du Cinéma* (Paris), March 1980.

Interview, in *Filmfaust* (Frankfurt), October/November 1982.

On OLBRYCHSKI: articles—

Erdmann, L., "Daniel Olbrychski," in *Filmwissenschaftliche Beitrage* (Berlin), vol. 17, no. 2, 1976.

Filmowy Serwis Prasowy (Warsaw), 1-15 June 1981.

"Daniel Olbrychski in Profile," in *Polish Film* (Warsaw), no. 2, 1988.

Tabecki, J., "Daniel Olbrychski. Czlowiek sukcesu," in *Iluzjon* (Warsaw), January/June 1990.

*   *   *

The acting career of Daniel Olbrychski took shape under the influence of the great legend of Polish cinematography—the actor Zbigniew Cybulski. In 1967, Cybulski died in a tragic accident and thus their lives crossed only briefly: once they were acting partners in the same film (*Jowita*). In spite of this, Olbrychski's artistic career will be long compared and measured by the value of his older colleague, and rightly so. In spite of all that separates them, they have much in common: above all tremendous popularity, evoked by common aspirations, ideas, opinions, and moods of their generations.

Olbrychski debuted while still a student at the Theatrical University in *The Wounded in the Forest*, directed by Janusz Nasfeter. Foreshadowing future great performances, he played the role of a young lieutenant, captivating the audience with his appearance—slim, fair-haired, cherubic, and radiating youth, intellect, and emotionality. The destiny of a new acting personality of the Polish film was confirmed and in the next year he replaced Cybulski in the film *Ashes*. During his studies, Olbrychski acted in some other films while polishing his acting technique. Since then he has contributed a whole series of film characters to the Polish cinema.

Olbrychski does not represent an invariable type; he can convincingly play both contemporary and period roles. His heroes are energetic men of action, rejecting stability and security for a life full of reversals, dynamics, and surprises (there exist, naturally, exceptions). Olbrychski plays them with discipline, without effects, in a concentrated and sometimes even reserved manner. This is one of the most noticeable features of his acting method. His relation to the character played suggests a certain aloofness, reserve, inner inaccessibility, and insubordination. The Polish film critic and historian Kryzysztof Teodor Toeplitz expressed this aptly: "When Olbrychski plays a boxer, the suspicion arises in us that he is not a real boxer and that what he really is will remain a secret for us." This approach presents itself in its purest form in Wajda's *Everything for Sale* (dedicated to the memory of Cybulski), in which Olbrychski in a complicated way resolves the legend of his predecessor and finds his own way.

In other works this quality is less apparent but still present. In Wajda's *The Wedding* he plays the role of a bridegroom which at a glance differs from all his previous roles. The bridegroom in his interpretation is unusually merry and happy; but gradually the actor lets the spectator peer beneath the surface of this happiness. From the merriment, disquiet and alienation emerge, linking him with the heroes from earlier films. Olbrychski's temperament explodes in *The Deluge* whose hero is endowed with such vitality that the film was accepted as an excellent study of Polish national character, with all its positive and negative aspects.

In the 1970s a new feature appeared in Olbrychski's acting that is connected with his artistic and human ripening and with acquiring new experiences. We find it for the first time in Wajda's *The Promised Land* where this dynamic, explosive actor metamorphosizes before

our eyes into a sober, matter-of-fact man who, after a youth full of inspiration and enthusiasm, accepts in cold blood the cruel rules of play of his milieu. The roles in his subsequent films continue to be marked by this skepticism.

Since the beginning of the 1970s Olbrychski has acted in the films of both well-known and beginning European directors. The number of parts and different characters he has played is impressive: in the historical fresco *Die Blechtrommel*, based on Günther Grass's novel, he plays the part of a potential father of an undersized hero, Jan Bronski; in *Pad Italje* he portrays a partisan commander who because of his love for a girl from a rich family loses the trust of his comrades-in-arms; in Von Trotta's biographical *Rosa Luxemburg* he tackles the role of the co-founder of Polish Social Democracy. Even though Olbrychski has tasted success abroad, when offered a part in a Polish film, he never turns his countrymen down. In so doing, he takes on a range of contemporary, historical, dramatic, and even comedic roles.

In his advancing years, he is no longer a youngster with a cherub's face, nor is he a romantic hero. In his actor's biography this change is sharply documented by his part in Radosław Piwowarski's *Chronology of Sentiments*. Olbrychski plays with great charm an aging lady-killer, who in spite of his age charms and sweeps a young girl off her feet. Olbrychski continues to act on the stage and he has received a number of theater and film awards, including the Chevalier de l'Order des Arts et des Lettres from France. His son Rafał follows in his steps, appearing with him in *Pan Twardowski*.

—Blažena Urgošíková

OLDMAN, Gary

Nationality: British. **Born:** London, England, 21 March 1958. **Education:** Attended Rose Buford College of Speech and Drama, London. **Family:** Married 1) Lesley Manville (divorced), one son: Alfred; 2) the actress Uma Thurman, 1990 (divorced 1992); 3) the actress Isabella Rossellini, 1994. **Career:** 1980—stage debut in *Massacre at Paris*; 1980-86 theatrical appearances include *Chincilla*, *A Waste of Time*, *Summit Conference*, *The Pope's Wedding*, *Desert Air*, *Women Beware Women*, *Real Dreams*, and *Smart Money*; 1982—film debut in *Remembrance*; 1993—in "Dead End for Delia" ep. of *Fallen Angels* TV series. **Awards:** Fringe Best Newcomer Award, 1985-86; *Drama Magazine* Award, for Best Actor of the Year, 1985; Cable Ace Award, Best Actor in a Dramatic Series, for "Dead End for Delia" ep. of *Fallen Angels*, 1994. **Agent:** c/o Duncan Heath, 162-170 Wardour Street, London W1V 3AT, England.

Films as Actor:

1982   *Remembrance* (Gregg) (as Daniel)
1984   *Meantime* (Leigh—for TV) (as Coxy)
1985   *Honest, Decent and True* (Les Blair—for TV)
1986   *Sid and Nancy* (Cox) (as Sid Vicious)
1987   *Prick Up Your Ears* (Frears) (as Joe Orton)
1988   *We Think the World of You* (Gregg) (as Johnny Burney); *Track 29* (Roeg) (as Martin); *The Firm* (Alan Clarke—for TV) (as Bex Bissek)
1989   *Paris by Night*; *Criminal Law* (Campbell) (as Ben Chase)
1990   *Heading Home* (Hare) (as Ian Tyson); *State of Grace* (Joanou) (as Jack Flannery); *Chattahoochee* (Mick Jackson) (as Emmett Foley); *Rosencrantz and Guildenstern Are Dead* (Stoppard) (as Rosencrantz)
1991   *JFK* (Oliver Stone) (as Lee Harvey Oswald)

Gary Oldman

1992 *Bram Stoker's Dracula* (Francis Ford Coppola) (title role)
1993 *True Romance* (Tony Scott) (as Drexl Spivey); *Romeo Is Bleeding* (Medak) (as Jack Grimaldi); *Who Was Lee Harvey Oswald?* (doc for TV) (as voice of Oswald)
1994 *Leon* (*The Cleaner*; *The Professional*) (Besson) (as Stansfield); *Immortal Beloved* (Rose) (as Beethoven)
1995 *Murder in the First* (Rocco) (as Associate Warden Glenn); *The Scarlet Letter* (Joffe) (as the Reverend Arthur Dimmesdale); *Basquiat* (*Build a Fort, Set It on Fire*) (Schnabel) (as Albert Milo)

Publications

By OLDMAN: articles—

"Gary Oldman: Wildman of the Brit Pack," interview with Fred Schruers, in *Rolling Stone* (New York), 18 October 1990.
Interview with Dennis Hopper, in *Interview* (New York), January 1992.
"Dracula Speaks: Gary Oldman and His Role as the Count," interview in *Film Review* (London), February 1993.

On OLDMAN: articles—

Steinberg, Robert, "Gary Oldman Turns up the Heat in Hell's Kitchen," in *American Film* (Los Angeles), October 1990.
Abramowitz, Rachel, "Neck Romance," in *Premiere* (New York), December 1992.
Ascher-Walsh, Rebecca, "Immortal Bedeviled," in *Entertainment Weekly* (New York), 10 February 1995.
Current Biography 1996, New York, 1996.

*   *   *

Gary Oldman is one of those rare actors who inhabits his roles with an almost chameleon-like quality. From part to part—and a widely varying lot they are—he is utterly convincing; as often as not, he is also unrecognizable. Usually, this spells doom to an actor's potential for stardom. Audiences cannot follow an actor they cannot find. But Oldman has mysteriously avoided this trap; perhaps *because* of his versatility and range—both of which not even his closest competitor, fellow Brit Daniel Day Lewis, has matched—he has somehow managed to achieve that stardom. Unlike Day Lewis, however, he has yet to win an Oscar, but this cannot be for long.

After making his screen debut in *Remembrance* and then appearing among the cast of Mike Leigh's "kitchen sink" TV drama *Meantime*, Oldman shot into the public mind with his lacerating, in-your-face performance as the self-destructive punk rocker Sid Vicious in Alex Cox's *Sid and Nancy*, the first of several, disparate biopic roles he would undertake in the years to come.

Vicious's rebelliousness against society aside, there would seem to be little in the character or Oldman's uncanny incarnation of it to have made anyone think "That's just the guy to play avante-garde, gay British playwright Joe Orton!" But that is exactly what director Stephen Frears did think and Oldman was cast in *Prick Up Your Ears*, the film version of John Lahr's Orton biography which traced the short life of the working-class writer whose meteoric career was cut short when his lover Kenneth Halliwell (Alfred Molina) murdered him in 1967. Oldman's personification of Orton was so persuasive that even hard-to-please British director/film historian Ken Russell was given to note: "Gary Oldman as the gay genius turned in a remarkable performance, managing the transition from ingenuous provincial lad to glam metropolitan sophisticate with an invisible technique."

Sporting a variety of convincing regional accents and dialects, Oldman has played an array of thoroughly American characters no

less vividly, from lowlife drug running scum (*True Romance*, *The Professional*) to noir heroes fixated on the wrong woman (*Romeo Is Bleeding*). As the Boston defense lawyer who gets psycho Kevin Bacon acquitted then fights to get him behind bars when Bacon kills again, Oldman brought sorely needed dignity to the utterly exploitative *Criminal Law*, his American film debut. *State of Grace*, an Irish-American *Mean Streets* about the Hell's Kitchen gang known as the Westies, found Oldman on the opposite side of the law (not for the first time or the last) as a none-too-bright gangster killed by his own brother (Ed Harris) as a payoff to the Mob. In *Chattahoochee*, Oldman himself was behind bars as a Korean war vet suffering post-traumatic stress syndrome who is wrongfully incarcerated in a mental institution that makes Bedlam look like Sunnybrook Farm, and brings some welcome reform to it. In *Murder in the First*, he squared off once more against Kevin Bacon, a prisoner who goes mad due to the brutal treatment of Oldman's Alcatraz warden. The latter two films were based on true stories.

JFK on the other hand was based on theory and supposition. Marshaling mountains of information uncovered by Warren Report critics over the years, director Oliver Stone's provocative docudrama concluded that the Mob served as functionaries in a much broader, government-managed scheme to assassinate Kennedy, a scheme in which Lee Harvey Oswald was just what he said he was, a "patsy." While the veracity of the film's conspiracy theories were vigorously challenged by critics, Oldman's dead-on portrait of Oswald was roundly applauded as eerily accurate in voice and manner. Oldman even *looked* the part, without the use of much makeup—another trademark of the actor's amazing, and seemingless effortless, virtuosity in biopic roles. Two years later, he supplied the voice of Oswald, reading from Oswald's own diaries, in a PBS *Frontline* documentary rebutting much of the Stone epic's conspiracy evidence. Again, the effect was positively eerie.

Since then, Oldman has played everything from the screen's most passionate Dracula to Beethoven (bearing yet another uncanny physical resemblance to the character) to Nathaniel Hawthorne's guilt-ridden puritan adulterer who gets Demi Moore's anachronistically feminist Hester Prynne saddled with *The Scarlet Letter*. And yet his career is still in its prime. Typically, leading men add longevity to their working lives by aging gracefully, and almost imperceptibly, into character roles. Oldman has a strong leg up. He is a charismatic leading man and bravura character actor already.

—John McCarty

OLIN, Lena

Nationality: Swedish. **Born:** Stockholm, 22 March 1955; daughter of the actor/director Stig Olin and the actress Britta Olin. **Education:** Attended Royal Dramatic Theater School of Sweden. **Family:** Son with the actor Orjan Ramberg: August. Career: Began dramatic school at 20, and three years later was employed at the Royal Dramatic Theater; 1976— film debut in Ingmar Bergman's *Face to Face*; 1984—in Bergman's final directorial project, *After the Rehearsal*; 1988—established her alliance with passionate characters whose portrayals will pervade her later repertoire with *The Unbearable Lightness of Being*. **Awards:** New York Film Critics Circle Award for Best Supporting Actress, for *Enemies, a Love Story*, 1989. **Agent:** Martha Luttrell, International Creative Management, 8899 Beverly Boulevard, Los Angeles, CA 90048, U.S.A.

Films as Actress:

1976 *Ansikte mot Ansikte* (*Face to Face*) (Bergman—for TV, originally broadcast in serial form) (as shop assistant)

1978   *Picassos aeventyr* (*The Adventures of Picasso*) (Danielsson) (as Dolores)

1980   *Karleken* (*Love*)

1982   **Fanny och Alexander** (*Fanny and Alexander*) (Bergman) (as Rosa)

1984   *Efter Repetitionen* (*After the Rehearsal*) (Bergman) (as Anna Egerman)

1985   *Wallenberg: A Hero's Story* (Lamont Johnson—for TV)

1986   *Flucht in den Norden* (*Escape to the North*) (Engström); *Pa Liv Och Dod* (*A Matter of Life and Death*)

1988   *The Unbearable Lightness of Being* (Kaufman) (as Sabina)

1989   *S/Y Glaedjen* (*S/Y Joy*) (Du Rees); *Enemies, a Love Story* (Mazursky) (as Masha)

1990   *Havana* (Pollack) (as Bobby Duran)

1993   *Romeo Is Bleeding* (Medak) (as Mona Demarkov); *Mr. Jones* (Figgis) (as Dr. Libbie Bowen)

1994   *The Night and the Moment* (*La Nuit et le Moment*) (Tato) (as The Marquise)

1996   *Night Falls on Manhattan* (Lumet) (as Peggy Lindstrom); *The Golden Hour* (Hallström)

Publications

By OLIN: articles—

Interview with Margy Rochlin, in *Interview* (New York), January 1991.
Interview with David Rensin, in *Playboy* (Chicago), February 1991.

On OLIN: articles—

Harper's, January 1986.
American Film, November 1989.
Linfield, Susan, "How Swede She Is," in *Rolling Stone* (New York), 8 March 1990.
"Hot in Havana," in *Fame*, November 1990.
MacPherson, Malcolm, "The Thinking Man's Beauty," in *Premiere* (New York), January 1991.
"Swede Success," in *Vanity Fair* (New York), January 1991.
New York Times, 20 September 1991.
Hedges, Peter, "Driving Miss Olin," in *Harper's Bazaar* (New York), March 1993.

Lena Olin in *Havana*

"What's Wrong with This Picture?" in *Los Angeles Times*, 24 October 1993. Hooper, Joseph, "Love to Kill You," in *Esquire* (New York), December 1993.

* * *

Born to actor parents, Lena Olin, one of Sweden's leading actresses and a member of Ingmar Bergman's famed company, began her career on stage at the Royal Dramatic Theater where she acted in the classical repertoire, including Shakespeare, August Strindberg, and Anton Chekhov. On stage and in film, Olin has taken on classical and modern roles, but usually plays complicated, ambiguous women, such as the heroines of Strindberg and Lars Noren, a contemporary writer, who, like Strindberg, writes about perplexing Swedish women.

Her acting education in Sweden emphasized the minutiae of physical expression, unlike the education of many American actors who are indoctrinated into Method acting and its preoccupation with emotional states. "In school what was important was not how you felt inside, it was how you showed your feelings with your body and the sound of your voice. It was very practical work," she remarked. She admits this work was at times boring and tedious, but it has given her an unusually broad and precise physical vocabulary and the capacity for displaying contradictory feelings at the same time.

According to Jean Baudrillard, seduction is the process of letting oneself die in reality and become reconstituted in illusion, an idea that lends itself perfectly to Olin's screen persona. Her true nature is shy, and she claims to be embarrassed to walk down the street as herself rather than in a character. Yet she plays nude scenes unabashedly because she feels it is someone else who is bare, not her; she holds that "nudity is just another costume." Her seductiveness is the physical manifestation of fantasy, for herself as well as her audience. Sexuality is made visual and the illusion is unmistakably real. But her characters are more complicated than just being sexual, as they also live in worlds plagued by political upheavals such as Prague Spring, the Holocaust, and the Cuban Revolution. Her seductiveness is the product of courage and remarkable skill.

Following her 1976 film debut in a bit role in Bergman's *Face to Face*, she appeared in two more Bergman films, *Fanny and Alexander*, where she has only a minor role as a maid, and the ultracomplex *After the Rehearsal*, in which she portrays the chastising actress daughter of a womanizing director's (Erland Josephson) old lover. She was later playing Cordelia in a production of *King Lear*, directed by Bergman, when the executive producer of *The Unbearable Lightness of Being* spotted her. The resultant striking role of the hedonistic Sabina was her American film debut and earned her numerous other film offers. None interested her, however, until *Enemies, a Love Story*, where she plays Masha, the Russian concentration camp survivor, who uses physical passion to escape horrible memories and the future that awaits her. The portrayal also earned Olin her first Oscar nomination, as Best Supporting Actress.

To date, Olin has yet to match her successes of the late 1980s. Committed to art rather than celebrity, Olin's opportunities in Hollywood have certainly been limited, evidenced by the consecutive failures of *Havana*, *Romeo Is Bleeding*, and *Mr. Jones*. Her outrageous performance as a sexy Mafia hit woman in the second of these three, however, showed that she will simply need to seek out the right roles (and films) to recapture her earlier success.

—Kelly Otter

OLIVIER, (Lord) Laurence

Nationality: British. **Born:** Laurence Kerr Olivier in Dorking, Surrey, 22 May 1907. **Education:** Attended Church of All Saints Choir School, London; St. Edward's School, Oxford, 1921-24; Central School of Speech Training and Dramatic Art, London. **Family:** Married 1) the actress Jill Esmond, 1930 (divorced 1940), son: Tarquin; 2) the actress Vivien Leigh, 1940 (divorced 1960); 3) the actress Joan Plowright, 1961, son: Richard, daughters: Tamsin and Julie. **Career:** 1925—assistant stage manager and understudy, St. Christopher Theatre, Letchworth; stage debut in *Macbeth*; 1926-28—member of Birmingham Repertory Company; 1930—film debut in *Too Many Crooks*; 1941-44—served in the Fleet Air Arm, mainly in entertainment capacity; 1944-49—director of the Old Vic company; 1945—directed first film, *Henry V*; 1951—co-starred with Vivien Leigh in Shaw's *Caesar and Cleopatra* and Shakespeare's *Antony and Cleopatra* on alternate nights, in London and New York; 1961—in TV mini-series *The Power and the Glory*; 1962-65—director of Chichester Festival Theatre; 1965-73—director of the emerging National Theatre (one of the auditoria in the new building is named the Olivier Theatre); 1976—produced a series of plays for Granada Television; in TV mini-series *Jesus of Nazareth*, 1977, *Brideshead Revisited*, 1981, *The Last Days of Pompeii*, 1984, *Peter the Great*, 1986. **Awards:** Special Academy Award, and Best Actor, New York Film Critics, for *Henry V*, 1946; Best Actor Academy Award, and Best Actor, New York Film Critics, for *Hamlet*, 1948; Best British Actor, British Academy, for *Richard III*, 1955; Best Supporting Actor, British Academy, for *Oh! What a Lovely War*, 1969; Best Actor, New York Film Critics, for *Sleuth*, 1972; Special Academy Award, "for the full body of his work, for the unique achievements of his entire career and his lifetime contribution to the art of film," 1978. Knighted, 1947; made Baron Olivier of Brighton (the first actor to be given this distinction), 1970; Honorary Doctorates from Universities of Oxford, 1957, Edinburgh, 1964, London, 1968, Manchester, 1969, and Sussex, 1978. **Died:** In Steyning, Sussex, England, 11 July 1989.

Films as Actor:

1930   *Too Many Crooks* (G. King) (as the Man); *The Temporary Widow* (*Murder for Sale*) (Ucicky) (as Peter Billie)

1931   *Friends and Lovers* (Schertzinger) (as Lt. Nichols); *Potiphar's Wife* (*Her Strange Desire*) (Elvey) (as Straker); *The Yellow Ticket* (*The Yellow Passport*) (Walsh) (as Julian Rolphe)

1932   *Westward Passage* (Milton) (as Nick Allen)

1933   *No Funny Business* (Stafford) (as Clive Dering); *Perfect Understanding* (Gardner) (as Nicholas Randall)

1935   *Moscow Nights* (*I Stand Condemned*) (Asquith) (as Captain Ignatoff)

1936   *As You Like It* (Czinner) (as Orlando); *Conquest of the Air* (Korda) (as Vincent Lunardi); *Fire over England* (William K. Howard) (as Michael Ingolby)

1937   *21 Days* (*Twenty-One Days Together*; *The First and the Last*) (Dean) (as Larry Durant)

1938   *The Divorce of Lady X* (Whelan) (as Logan)

1939   *Wuthering Heights* (Wyler) (as Heathcliff); *Q Planes* (*Clouds over Europe*) (Wheelan) (as Tony McVane)

1940   *Pride and Prejudice* (Leonard) (as Mr. Darcy); *Rebecca* (Hitchcock) (as Maxim de Winter)

1941   *That Hamilton Woman* (*Lady Hamilton*) (Korda) (as Admiral Lord Nelson); *49th Parallel* (*The Invaders*) (Powell) (as Johnnie); *Words for Battle* (Jennings) (as commentator)

1943   *The Demi-Paradise* (*Adventure for Two*) (Asquith) (as Ivan Kouznetsoff)

1944   *The Volunteer* (Powell and Pressburger—doc)

1951   *The Magic Box* (Boulting) (as PC 94 B); *Carrie* (Wyler) (as George Hurstwood)

1959   *The Devil's Disciple* (Hamilton) (as General "Gentleman Johnnie" Burgoyne)

1960 *Spartacus* (Kubrick) (as Crassus); *The Entertainer* (Richardson) (as Archie Rice)

1962 *Term of Trial* (Glenville) (as Graham Weir)

1965 *Bunny Lake Is Missing* (Preminger) (as Supt. Newhouse)

1966 *Othello* (Burge) (title role); *Khartoum* (Dearden) (as the Mahdi)

1968 *The Shoes of the Fisherman* (Anderson) (as Premier Kamenev); *Romeo and Juliet* (Zeffirelli) (as speaker of the Prologue and the Epilogue)

1969 *The Dance of Death* (Giles) (as army captain); *Battle of Britain* (Hamilton) (as Sir Hugh Dowding); *Oh! What a Lovely War* (Attenborough) (as Sir John French)

1970 *David Copperfield* (Delbert Mann—for TV) (as Mr. Creakle)

1971 *Nicholas and Alexandra* (Schaffner) (as Prime Minister Witte)

1972 *Sleuth* (Mankiewicz) (as Andrew Wyke)

1973 *Lady Caroline Lamb* (Bolt) (as Duke of Wellington); *Long Day's Journey into Night* (Blakemore and Wood—for TV) (as James Tyrone); *The Merchant of Venice* (Miller and Sichel—for TV) (as Shylock)

1975 *Love among the Ruins* (Cukor—for TV) (as Sir Arthur Granville-Jones)

1976 *Marathon Man* (Schlesinger) (as Szell); *The Seven-Per-Cent Solution* (Ross) (as Professor Moriarty); *Cat on a Hot Tin Roof* (Moore—for TV) (as Big Daddy)

1977 *Come Back, Little Sheba* (Narizzano—for TV) (as Doc); *A Bridge Too Far* (Attenborough) (as Dr. Spaander)

1978 *The Betsy* (Petrie) (as Loren Hardeman Sr.); *The Boys from Brazil* (Schaffner) (as Ezra Lieberman)

1979 *A Little Romance* (Hill) (as Julius); *Dracula* (Badham) (as Van Helsing)

1980 *The Jazz Singer* (Fleischer) (as Cantor Rabinovitch)

1981 *Inchon* (Terence Young) (as Gen. MacArthur); *Clash of the Titans* (Desmond Davis) (as Zeus)

1982 *A Voyage Round My Father* (Rakoff—for TV) (as Father)

1983 *Wagner* (Palmer—for TV) (as Pfeufer); *A Talent for Murder* (Rakoff—for TV); *Mister Halpren and Mister Johnson* (Rakoff—for TV) (as Mr. Halpren); *King Lear* (Elliott—for TV) (title role)

1984 *The Jigsaw Man* (Terence Young) (as Adm. Sir Gerald Scaith); *The Bounty* (Donaldson) (as Adm. Hood); *Ebony Tower* (Knights—for TV)

1985 *Wild Geese II* (Hunt) (as Rudolf Hess)

1986 *Lost Empires* (Grine—for TV); *Directed by William Wyler* (Slesin—doc) (as himself)

1989 *War Requiem* (Jarman) (as Old Soldier)

Films as Actor and Director:

1945 *Henry V* (title role, + pr)

1948 *Hamlet* (title role, + pr)

1953 *The Beggar's Opera* (as MacHeath, pr only)

1955 *Richard III* (title role, + pr)

1957 *The Prince and the Showgirl* (as Grand Duke Charles, + pr)

1970 *The Three Sisters* (released in U.S. in 1974) (as Dr. Chebutikin)

Publications

By OLIVIER: books—

Five Seasons of the Old Vic Theatre Company, with Michel Saint-Denis, London, 1950.
Confessions of an Actor, London, 1982.
On Acting, London, 1986.

By OLIVIER: article—

"The Entertainer," in *American Film* (New York), November 1986.

On OLIVIER: books—

Barker, Felix, *The Oliviers*, Philadelphia, 1953.
Lunari, Gigi, *Laurence Olivier*, Bologna, 1959.
Whitehead, Peter, and Robin Bean, *Olivier—Shakespeare*, London, 1966.
Darlington, W. A., *Laurence Olivier*, London, 1968.
Fairweather, Virginia, *Cry God for Larry*, London, 1969.
Memo from: David O. Selznick, edited by Rudy Behlmer, New York, 1972.
Laurence Olivier, edited by Logan Gourlay, London, 1973.
Cottrell, John, *Laurence Olivier*, Englewood Cliffs, New Jersey, 1975.
Lasky, Jesse Jr., with Pat Silver, *Love Scene: The Story of Laurence Olivier and Vivien Leigh*, New York, 1978.
Olivier: The Films and Faces of Laurence Olivier, edited by Margaret Morley, Godalming, 1978.
Hirsch, Foster, *Laurence Olivier*, Boston, 1979; as *Laurence Olivier on Screen*, New York, 1984.
Daniels, Robert, *Laurence Olivier: Theatre and Cinema*, London, 1980.
Kiernan, Thomas, *Sir Larry: The Life of Laurence Olivier*, New York, 1981.
Lefevre, Raymond, *Laurence Olivier*, Paris, 1981.
Barker, Felix, *Laurence Olivier: A Critical Study*, Tunbridge Wells, Kent, 1984.
Bragg, Melvyn, *Laurence Olivier*, London, 1984; rev. ed., 1989.
O'Connor, Garry, *Darlings of the Gods: One Year in the Lives of Laurence Olivier and Vivien Leigh*, London, 1984.
Silviria, Dale, *Laurence Olivier and the Art of Filmmaking*, Rutherford, New Jersey, 1985.
Tanitch, Robert, *Olivier: The Complete Career*, London, 1985.
Holden, Anthony, *Olivier*, London, 1988.
Spoto, Donald, *Laurence Olivier: A Biography*, New York, 1991.
Olivier, Tarquin, *My Father Laurence Olivier*, London, 1992.
Vermilye, Jerry, *The Complete Films of Laurence Oliver*, 1992.

On OLIVIER: articles—

McVay, Douglas, "Hamlet to Clown," in *Films and Filming* (London), April 1962.
Brown, Constance, "Olivier's *Richard III*: A Reevaluation," in *Film Quarterly* (Berkeley), Summer 1967.
Hart, Henry, "Laurence Olivier," in *Films in Review* (New York), December 1967.
Coleman, Terry, "Olivier Now," in *Show* (Hollywood), June 1970.
Eyles, Allen, "Sir Laurence Olivier," in *Focus on Film* (London), Spring 1973.
Keleher, L., "Laurence Olivier: Getting on with It," in *Take One* (Montreal), July 1978.
Current Biography 1979, New York, 1979.
Bodeen, DeWitt, "Laurence Olivier: The Man and His Times," in *Films in Review* (New York), December 1979.
McDonald, N., "The Relationship Between Shakespeare's Stagecraft and Modern Film Technique (with Special Reference to the Films of Laurence Olivier)," in *Australian Journal of Screen Theory* (Kensington, New South Wales), no. 7, 1980.
Drew, Bernard, "Laurence Olivier," in *The Movie Star*, edited by Elisabeth Weis, New York, 1981.
Thomson, David, "Our Lord of Danger," in *Film Comment* (New York), March/April 1983.
Taylor, John Russell, "Olivier at Eighty," in *Films and Filming* (London), May 1987.

Laurence Olivier with Merle Oberon in *Wuthering Heights* **© MCMXXXIX by Samuel Goldwyn**

Donaldson, P., "Olivier, Hamlet and Freud," in *Cinema Journal* (Champaign, Illinois), Summer 1987.

Obituary in *Variety* (New York), 12 July 1989.

Schickel, Richard, obituary in *Film Comment* (New York), September/October 1989.

*   *   *

"I had the voice" said John Gielgud morosely, "but Larry had the legs." And Olivier knew it. The most starstruck and showy of the theatrical knights, he always flirted with the movies both as performer and director. Olivier the actor/producer who relished creating wild leaps and intricate fights for his plays, and took a Lon Chaney delight in mime, accent, and character makeup, was made for films. But the more thoughtful performer, such as his James Tyrone in *Long Day's Journey into Night*, saw the threat of popular success. He admits in his autobiography that, unlike stage work, "films and television do not usually tax one's energies beyond their normal capacities," yet it is evident that Olivier gave to most of them the benefit of a meticulous technique.

Hollywood offered him stardom in his days as a *jeune premier*, Goldwyn casting him as a lumpen Heathcliff in *Wuthering Heights* and MGM planning an appearance opposite Garbo in *Queen Christina*. This might have tipped Olivier inescapably toward a movie career, but Garbo rejected him in favor of old lover and slipping star John Gilbert, and thereafter, perhaps pettishly, he elected for character roles. His languid Darcy in *Pride and Prejudice*, Maxim de Winter in *Rebecca*,

Nelson in Korda's American-made *That Hamilton Woman* and Hurstwood, the hotel manager ruined by love in *Carrie* are performances by an actor, not the appearances of a star.

That Olivier took film playing less seriously after his Hollywood days is evident in two wartime propagandist roles, a Russian in *The Demi-Paradise* and a French-Canadian trapper in *49th Parallel*. Both embarrassingly dated now, they show a boyish glee in accent and disguise at the expense of character.

Touring with Vivien Leigh as an actor/manager in the 1930s and 1940s encouraged Olivier to embark on his first films as director/star. *Henry V* (made at government request to bolster morale), *Hamlet*, and *Richard III* are inspired popularizations, using only half the text but conveying the essence of Shakespeare with a combination of film production values and visual flair.

Olivier's adaptation of *Henry V* is highly praised by Andre Bazin. He describes its success in solving the dialectic between cinematic realism and theatrical convention: "The beginning traveling shot is to plunge us into the theater, to the courtyard of an Elizabethan inn.... [It] is not with the play *Henry V* that the film is immediately and directly concerned, but with the performance of *Henry V*."

As an accomplished stage actor, his endeavor in film can thus be seen as one that pertains to a language specific to cinema as well as the immediacy of theatricality.

Richard III is Olivier's triumph as director/star, a performance straight out of Lon Chaney's *The Penalty*, dignified by language and stagecraft. Olivier had discovered in his famous stage *Coriolanus* that sexual magnetism could make even evil glamorous, and his Richard explored that insight in rich detail. The realization seemed to alarm him. It was years before he dared play another outright monster.

His films of the 1950s and 1960s mostly recreated his stage hits *The Entertainer*, *Othello*, *The Three Sisters*, and *The Dance of Death*, thought he did direct and star opposite Marilyn Monroe in the unsuccessful *The Prince and the Showgirl*, and appeared in some cameos chosen from the range of international film and television productions that could always use an imposing figure with a commanding voice. His Mahdi in *Khartoum* used the makeup and mime from *Othello*, and while the generals, air vice marshals, Russian counts, and epicene Roman commanders he played in everything from *Spartacus* to *The Battle of Britain* occasionally seemed taken off the peg at some theatrical supplier, they are never less than memorable.

He returned to more abrasive material as declining health accentuated his hawkish profile and raised his voice to a grating rasp. A querulous Moriarty in *The Seven-Per-Cent Solution*, Nazi hunter Ezra Lieberman in *The Boys from Brazil*, and the monster of *Marathon Man* are all effective creations by a man who had little interest in the cinema, but who used it, like the piano learned in childhood, to pick out a few tunes when the mood took him. The craftsmanship, professionalism, practical intelligence and the highest seriousness that Richard Schickel profoundly admires and fondly remembers can be best summed up by the advice Olivier offered Dustin Hoffman during the making of *Marathon Man*:

"Hoffman kept himself awake for two days so that he could look— and above all, feel—properly haggard for one of his scenes with Olivier. 'You should learn to act, my dear boy,' his Lordship murmured. 'Then you wouldn't have to put yourself through this sort of thing.'"

—John Baxter, updated by Guo-Juin Hong

OLMOS, Edward James

Nationality: American. **Born:** East Los Angeles, California, 24 February 1947. **Family:** Married 1) Kaija Keel (divorced), sons: Mico and Bodie; 2) the actress Lorraine Bracco, 1994. **Education:** Attended East Los Angeles City College and California State University, Los Angeles; studied drama at the Lee Strasberg Institute. **Career:** 1960s—formed rock band, Eddie James and the Pacific Ocean, to help pay his college tuition; 1970s—began acting in small stage productions in Los Angeles and appearing in bit roles on such TV series as *Kojak* and *Hawaii Five-O*; 1978—starred as El Pachuco in *Zoot Suit* on the Los Angeles stage; in TV mini-series *Evening in Byzantium*; 1979— played El Pachuco in New York; 1982—had first important screen role in *The Ballad of Gregorio Cortez*; 1984-89—played Lt. Martin Castillo on TV series *Miami Vice*; 1988—in TV mini-series *Mario Puzo's The Fortunate Pilgrim*; 1992—formed YOY Productions with director Robert M. Young. **Awards:** Best Actor, Los Angeles Drama Critics Circle, for *Zoot Suit*, 1978; Emmy Award, Best Supporting Actor in a Drama Series, for *Miami Vice*, 1985. **Agent:** Artists Agency, 10000 Santa Monica Boulevard, Suite 305, Los Angeles, CA 90067, U.S.A.

Films as Actor:

1975   *aloha, bobby and rose* (Mutrux) (small role)
1977   *Alambrista!* (Robert M. Young) (as drunk)
1980   *Fukkatsu no hi* (*Virus*) (Fukasaku) (as Captain López)
1981   *Three Hundred Miles for Stephanie* (Ware—for TV) (as Art Vela); *Zoot Suit* (Valdez) (as El Pachuco); *Wolfen* (Wadleigh) (as Eddie Holt)
1982   *The Ballad of Gregorio Cortez* (Robert M. Young) (title role, + co-pr, co-mus); ***Blade Runner*** (Ridley Scott) (as Gaff); *Sequin* (Jesús Salvador Treviño—for TV)
1986   *Saving Grace* (Robert M. Young) (as Ciolino)
1988   *Stand and Deliver* (Menendez) (as Jaime Escalante)
1989   *Triumph of the Spirit* (Robert M. Young) (as Gypsy)
1990   *Maria's Story* (Wali and Cohen—doc) (as narrator)
1991   *Talent for the Game* (Robert M. Young) (as Virgil Sweet)
1993   *Roosters* (Robert M. Young) (as Gallo); *A Million to Juan* (*A Million to One*) (Paul Rodríguez) (as the Angel); *Menendez: A Killing in Beverly Hills* (Elikann—for TV) (as José Menendez)
1994   *The Burning Season* (Frankenheimer—for TV) (as Wilson Pinheiro)
1995   *Mirage* (Williams) (as Matteo Juárez); *My Family* (*Mi Familia*) (Nava) (as Paco, the narrator)
1996   *Caught* (Robert M. Young)

Film as Director:

1992   *American Me* (+ ro as Santana Montoya, co-pr)

Publications

By OLMOS: articles—

"Burning with Passion," interview with Guy D. Garcia and Elaine Dutka, in *Time* (New York), 11 July 1988.
Interview with M. Seligson, in *Playboy* (Chicago), June 1989.
"Ball Park Figures," interview with Lorraine Bracco, in *Interview* (New York), April 1991.
Interview with David Mills, in *Washington Post*, 21 March 1992.
"One Year Later—A Talk with Edward James Olmos," interview with Laura Meyers in *Los Angeles Magazine*, April 1993.

On OLMOS: articles—

Aufderheide, Pat, "Reel Life," in *Mother Jones* (San Francisco), April 1988.
Current Biography 1992, New York, 1992.
Leo, John, "The Melting Pot Is Cooking," in *U.S. News and World Report* (Washington, D.C.), 5 July 1993.

*   *   *

Edward James Olmos is a savvy, street-smart performer who is one of the rare Hispanic Americans to have found major stardom on stage, screen, and television. After years of knocking around Los Angeles playing theater and television roles, his breakthrough came when he was cast in the Los Angeles stage production of *Zoot Suit*, a stylized musical drama blending fact with fiction. *Zoot Suit* details the plight of the leader of a gang of Mexican Americans who are about to do time in San Quentin for their part in the zoot suit riots in 1942 Los Angeles. Olmos's role was the pivotal one in the scenario: El Pachuco, a mythical character who is the embodiment of the dashing, self-respecting and virile Latino who so disrupted the complacency of Caucasian Californians back in the 1940s. Olmos offered a dynamic, star-making performance as El Pachuco, playing the role for a year-and-a-half on the Los Angeles and New York stages, and again in the less-than-successful screen adaptation.

Olmos soon was to gain his foothold as a screen actor in a film with which he remains most proud: *The Ballad of Gregorio Cortez*, a turn-of-the-twentieth-century drama about a now-legendary Mexican

American, unjustly accused of murder, who manages to elude a 600-man Texas posse. The film was directed by veteran independent filmmaker Robert M. Young, who has become the actor's close friend and colleague. Over the years, they have worked on several projects (from 1977's *Alambrista!*, in which Olmos had a small role, to 1996's *Caught*).

But Olmos's best screen role to date has been in *Stand and Deliver*, a based-on-fact story featuring a most unusual movie hero: Jaime Escalante, a Bolivian-born computer scientist who relinquished a high-paying job to teach math in an East Los Angeles barrio high school. The bespeckled Escalante's slight paunch and nondescript appearance in no way obscure his intense dedication to his job. Escalante inspires his young Hispanic charges to pass an Advanced Placement calculus test. Olmos transformed his physical appearance to become Escalante; he gained 40 pounds, and each day endured an excruciating makeup process in order to camouflage his own abundant head of hair. For his efforts, he earned a well-deserved Best Actor Academy Award nomination.

You will never, ever find Olmos playing stereotypical Hispanics, or for that matter throwaway roles in mindlessly entertaining Hollywood fare. "I've been offered roles in many films," he told this writer before the release of *Stand and Deliver*, "including *Scarface*, *Streets of Fire*, *Firestarter* and *Band of the Hand*. If I'd accepted them, I feel I would be compromising myself. Of course, my family suffered for this, because we had to compromise our living standard. But this was balanced by my being able to keep hold of my integrity." He added, "I'm only interested in making films that I can be proud to take into my community." Indeed, Olmos reported that he at first had declined an offer to portray an American Indian in *Wolfen*. He only accepted the part when no appropriate actor could be found.

In fact, many of his roles have been infused with a political consciousness. This certainly is the case with El Pachuco, Gregorio Cortez, and Jaime Escalante. It is true in *My Family*, a warmhearted multigenerational chronicle of a Mexican-American family from the 1920s through 1980s. Given Olmos's status as an elder statesman of Latino stars, it is appropriate that his role is that of the narrator, the chronicler of the Sánchez family saga. And it also is true of the film in which Olmos made his directorial debut: *American Me*, a searing indictment of the violence and chaos which are becoming rampant in American society. The scenario is set over a 30-year time span, with Olmos starring as Santana, described as "a child of the Pachuco riots of the 1940s"; in this regard, the film is linked to the time and place depicted in *Zoot Suit*. Santana forms his own gang at age 16, and eventually ends up doing an 18-year prison stretch. Olmos's purpose for making *American Me* was to depict the hard, brutal reality of the criminal life. Indeed, the *Variety* reviewer was on target when he called Santana "one of the least romanticized film gangsters since Paul Muni's *Scarface*."

Finally, and most impressively, Edward James Olmos is unlike the many actors and sports stars from modest backgrounds who upon attaining celebrityhood have slammed the door on their roots. Not only is he deeply concerned about the way in which Hispanics are depicted on movie screens, but he remains active in a hands-on manner in the East Los Angeles community in which he came of age.

—Rob Edelman

Edward James Olmos (left) with Jaime Escalante on the set of *Stand and Deliver*

O'SULLIVAN, Maureen

Born: Roscommon, Ireland, 17 May 1911. **Education:** Attended Roehampton School, London. **Family:** Married 1) the director John Farrow, 1936 (died 1963), seven children: Michael, Patrick, the actress Mia Farrow, John, Prudence, Tisa, Stephanie; 2) James E. Cushing, 1983. **Career:** 1929—film debut in *Song o' My Heart*; contract with Fox, followed by short contracts with other studios; 1932-42—contract with MGM; first of six Tarzan films, *Tarzan, the Ape Man*; 1942-48—off the screen; 1963—on stage in *Roomful of Roses*, followed by other plays, including *It's Never Too Late* and *Morning's at Seven*, 1980. **Agent:** Milton Goldman, International Creative Management, 40 West 57th Street, New York, NY 10019, U.S.A.

Films as Actress:

1930 *Song o' My Heart* (Borzage) (as Eileen O'Brien); *So This Is London* (Blystone) (as Elinor Worthing); *Just Imagine* (David Butler) (as LN-18); *The Princess and the Plumber* (Korda) (as Princess Louise)

1931 *A Connecticut Yankee* (David Butler) (as Alisande); *Skyline* (Taylor) (as Kathleen Kearny); *The Silver Lining* (*Thirty Days*) (Crosland) (as Joyce Moore); *The Big Shot* (*The Optimist*) (Murphy) (as Doris)

1932 *Tarzan, the Ape Man* (Van Dyke) (as Jane Parker); *Fast Companions* (*The Information Kid*) (Neumann) (as Sally); *Skyscraper Souls* (Selwyn) (as Lynn Harding); *Strange Interlude* (Leonard) (as Madeline); *Okay America* (*Penalty of Fame*) (Garnett) (as Miss Barton); *Payment Deferred* (Mendes) (as Winnie Marble)

1933 *Robber's Roost* (Louis King) (as Helen); *The Cohens and the Kellys in Trouble* (Stevens) (as Mollie Kelly); *Tugboat Annie* (LeRoy) (as Pat Severn); *Stage Mother* (Brabin) (as Shirley Lorraine)

1934 *Tarzan and His Mate* (Gibbons and Conway) (as Jane Parker); ***The Thin Man*** (Van Dyke) (as Dorothy Wynant); *Hide-Out* (Van Dyke) (as Pauline); *The Barretts of Wimpole Street* (Franklin) (as Henrietta)

1935 *David Copperfield* (Cukor) (as Dora); *West Point of the Air* (Rosson) (as Skip Carter); *Cardinal Richelieu* (Rowland V. Lee) (as Lenore); *The Flame Within* (Goulding) (as Lillian Belton); *Anna Karenina* (Brown) (as Kitty); *Woman Wanted* (Seitz) (as Ann); *The Bishop Misbehaves* (Dupont) (as Hester Grantham)

1936 *The Voice of Bugle Ann* (Thorpe) (as Camden Terry); *Tarzan Escapes* (Thorpe) (as Jane Parker); *The Devil Doll* (Browning) (as Lorraine Lavond)

1937 *A Day at the Races* (Wood) (as Judy); *The Emperor's Candlesticks* (Fitzmaurice) (as Maria); *Between Two Women* (*Surrounded by Women*) (Seitz) (as Claira Donahue); *My Dear Miss Aldrich* (Seitz) (as Martha Aldrich)

1938 *A Yank at Oxford* (Conway) (as Molly Beaumont); *Hold That Kiss* (Marin) (as June Evans); *Port of Seven Seas* (Whale) (as Madelon); *The Crowd Roars* (Thorpe) (as Sheila Carson); *Spring Madness* (Simon) (as Alexandra Benson)

1939 *Let Us Live* (Brahm) (as Mary Roberts); *Tarzan Finds a Son* (Thorpe) (as Jane)

1940 *Sporting Blood* (*Sterling Metal*) (Simon) (as Linda Lockwood); *Pride and Prejudice* (Leonard) (as Jane Bennet)

1941 *Maisie Was a Lady* (Marin) (as Abigail Rawlston); *Tarzan's Secret Treasure* (Thorpe) (as Jane)

1942 *Tarzan's New York Adventure* (Thorpe) (as Jane)

1948 *The Big Clock* (Farrow) (as Georgette Stroud)

1950 *Where Danger Lives* (Farrow) (as Julie)

1952 *Bonzo Goes to College* (de Cordova) (as Marion Drew); *No Resting Place* (Rotha) (as Nan Kyle)

1953 *All I Desire* (Sirk) (as Sara Harper); *Mission over Korea* (Sears) (as Nancy Slocum)

1954 *Duffy of San Quentin* (*Men behind Bars*) (Doniger) (as Gladys Duffy); *The Steel Cage* (Doniger) (as Gladys Duffy)

1957 *The Tall T* (Boetticher) (as Doretta Mims)

1958 *Wild Heritage* (Haas) (as Emma Breslin)

1965 *Never Too Late* (Yorkin) (as Edith Lambert)

1970 *The Phynx* (Katzin) (as herself)

1972 *The Crooked Hearts* (Sandrich—for TV)

1976 *The Great Houdinis* (Shavelson—for TV) (as Lady Doyle)

1985 *Too Scared to Scream* (Lo Bianco) (as Mother)

1986 *Hannah and Her Sisters* (Woody Allen) (as Norma, Hannah's mother); *Peggy Sue Got Married* (Francis Ford Coppola) (as Elizabeth Alvorg)

1987 *Stranded* (Fuller) (as Grace Clark)

1988 *Good Old Boy* (for TV) (as Aunt Sue)

1992 *The Habitation of Dragons* (Lindsay-Hogg—for TV) (as Miss Helen Taylor); *With Murder in Mind* (*With Savage Intent*) (Tuchner—for TV) (as Aunt Mildred)

1994 *Hart to Hart: Home Is Where the Hart Is* (Peter R. Hunt—for TV) (as Eleanor Biddlecomb)

Publications

By O'SULLIVAN: article—

"Maureen O'Sullivan," interview with Kingsley Canham, in *Focus on Film* (London), Summer 1974.

On O'SULLIVAN: book—

Billips, Connie J., *Maureen O'Sullivan: A Bio-Bibliography*, New York, 1990.

On O'SULLIVAN: articles—

Bodeen, DeWitt, "Maureen O'Sullivan," in *Films in Review* (New York), January 1984.

Hutchings, David, "Maureen O'Sullivan Finds Her Star Reborn Playing Mother to Her Daughter in *Hannah and Her Sisters*," in *People Weekly* (New York), 14 April 1986.

*   *   *

Maureen O'Sullivan's place in film history unfortunately has been relegated to that of an animal-skin-clad girl making a home for the king of the jungle. Although not her first film, *Tarzan, the Ape Man* was her first important role and her recitation of the words "Tarzan" and "Jane" (not "You Tarzan, me Jane" as so often misquoted) made her instantly famous to audiences worldwide. She appeared in several other Tarzan films with Johnny Weissmuller, but her contract at MGM also placed her in a large number of roles, usually playing the star's sister, best friend, or other secondary leads. She had a lovely speaking voice and a delicate beauty which suggested "well-bred young English lady" roles, such as the flighty Dora in *David Copperfield*, Henrietta in *The Barretts of Wimpole Street*, and the oldest sister, Jane, in *Pride and Prejudice*.

In the 1940s, when O'Sullivan was still in her prime and very active in films, she semiretired from acting to be a mother to her large family and a wife to the writer-director John Farrow, with whom she worked in the 1948 thriller *The Big Clock*. The marriage lasted until Farrow's

Maureen O'Sullivan

death in 1963 and produced, among its seven children, the actress Mia Farrow. During the 1950s O'Sullivan made a few films and did some television work, but she did not have any important roles until after John Farrow's death when she went to Broadway and starred in the successful comedy *Never Too Late*. After the long run of the play, it was turned into a film in which O'Sullivan again played opposite her Broadway co-star, Paul Ford. In the film, a gentle comedy, Ford and O'Sullivan, the middle-aged parents of a married daughter, discover that they are going to have another baby. Although she was well into her fifties, O'Sullivan was still very attractive and displayed a fine sensibility for light comedy, something which she seldom, if ever, was able to do as an ingenue.

In the 1980s, O'Sullivan's screen career was briefly jump-started in Woody Allen's *Hannah and Her Sisters*, cast as the mother of the character played by daughter Mia. Later on, she became a vocal supporter of her daughter (and denouncer of Allen) in the wake of the notorious Soon-Yi affair.

—Patricia King Hanson, updated by Rob Edelman

O'TOOLE, Peter

Nationality: Irish. **Born:** Peter Seamus O'Toole in Connemara, Ireland, 2 August 1932; grew up in Leeds, Yorkshire. **Education:** Attended St. Anne's convent school, Leeds. **Military Service:** British Submarine Service, 1950-52: signalman and decoder. **Family:** Married 1) the actress Sian Phillips, 1959 (divorced 1979), daughters: Kate and Pat; 2) Karen Brown, 1983 (divorced), child: Lorcan. **Career:** Worked as journalist for *Yorkshire Evening News*; 1952-54—attended Royal Academy of Dramatic Art, London; 1954-58—member of the Bristol Old Vic company: debut in *The Matchmaker*, 1955; 1959—on West End stage in *The Long and the Short and the Tall*; 1960—film debut in *Kidnapped*; in repertory at Stratford-upon-Avon Royal Shakespeare Theatre; later stage work includes roles in *Macbeth*, London, 1980, and *Man and Superman*, London, 1982; appeared in TV mini-series *Masada*, 1981, and *John Jakes' Heaven and Hell: North and South, Part III*, 1994. **Awards:** Best British Actor, British Academy, for *Lawrence of Arabia*, 1962; Best Actor, U.S. National Society of Film Critics, for *The Stunt Man*, 1980; also several Italian awards. **Address:** 98 Heath Street, London NW3, England.

Films as Actor:

1960   *Kidnapped* (Stevenson) (as Robin MacGregor); *The Savage Innocents* (*Ombre Bianche*) (Nicholas Ray) (as 1st Trooper); *The Day They Robbed the Bank of England* (Guillermin) (as Captain Fitch)

1962   *Lawrence of Arabia* (Lean) (title role)

1964   *Becket* (Glenville) (as King Henry II)

1965   *What's New Pussycat?* (Clive Donner) (as Michael James); *Lord Jim* (Richard Brooks) (title role); *The Sandpiper* (Minnelli) (as voice)

1966   *The Bible . . . in the Beginning* (*The Bible*; *La Bibbia*) (Huston) (as the Three Angels); *How to Steal a Million* (Wyler) (as Simon Dermott)

1967   *Night of the Generals* (Litvak) (as General Tanz); *Casino Royale* (Huston and others) (as Piper)

1968   *Great Catherine* (Flemyng) (as Captain Charles Edstaston); *The Lion in Winter* (Harvey) (as Henry II)

1969   *Goodbye, Mr. Chips* (Wood) (as Arthur Chipping); *Country Dance* (*Brotherly Love*) (J. Lee Thompson) (as Sir Charles Henry Arbuthnot Pinkerton Ferguson)

1971   *Murphy's War* (Yates) (as Murphy)

1972   *The Ruling Class* (Medak) (as Jack, 14th Earl of Gurney); *Man of La Mancha* (Hiller) (as Cervantes/Don Quixote)

1973   *Under Milk Wood* (Sinclair) (as Captain Cat)

1975   *Man Friday* (Gold) (as Robinson Crusoe); *Rosebud* (Preminger) (as Larry Martin); *Foxtrot* (*The Other Side of Paradise*) (Ripstein); *Rogue Male* (Clive Donner—for TV) (as The Earl)

1978   *Power Play* (Burke) (as Col. Zeller)

1979   *Zulu Dawn* (Hickox) (as Lord Chelmsford)

1980   *The Stunt Man* (Rush) (as Eli Cross); *Caligula* (Brass—produced in 1977) (as Tiberius)

1982   *My Favorite Year* (Benjamin) (as Alan Swann); *The Antagonists* (Sagal—for TV)

1983   *Svengali* (Harvey—for TV); *Pygmalion* (Cooke—for TV) (as Henry Higgins)

1984   *Supergirl* (Szwarc) (as Zaltar); *Sherlock Holmes and the Baskerville Curse* (Graham) (as voice); *Kim* (Davies—for TV)

1985   *Creator* (Passer) (as Harry)

1986   *Club Paradise* (Ramis) (as Gov. Anthony Croyden Hayes)

1987   ***The Last Emperor*** (Bertolucci) (as Reginald Johnston)

1988   *High Spirits* (Neil Jordan) (as Peter Plunkett)

1989   *In una notta di chiaro di luna* (*On a Moonlit Night*) (Wertmüller); *Dark Angel* (Hammond—for TV)

1990   *Wings of Fame* (Votoček) (as Cesar Valentin); *The Rainbow Thief* (Jodorowsky) (as Prince Meleagre); *Isabelle Eberhardt* (Pringle) (as Major Lyautey); *The Nutcracker Prince* (Schibli) (as voice of Pantaloon); *The Pied Piper* (*Crossing to Freedom*) (Norman Stone—for TV) (as John Sidney Howard)

1991   *King Ralph* (Ward) (as Willingham)

1992   *Rebecca's Daughters* (Francis) (as Lord Sarn); *The Seventh Coin* (Soref) (as Emil Saber)

1996   *Gulliver's Travels* (Sturridge—for TV) (as Emperor of Lilliput)

Publications

By O'TOOLE: book—

Loitering with Intent: The Child, London, 1992.

By O'TOOLE: articles—

"Interview: Peter O'Toole," in *Playboy* (Chicago), September 1965.
Interview with J. Buck, in *Inter/View* (New York), October 1972.
"O'Toole Ascending," interview with J. McBride, in *Film Comment* (New York), March-April 1981.

On O'TOOLE: books—

Freedland, Michael, *Peter O'Toole: A Biography*, New York, 1982.
Wapshott, Nicholas, *Peter O'Toole: A Biography*, Sevenoaks, Kent, 1983.

On O'TOOLE: articles—

Current Biography 1968, New York, 1968.
McGillivray, David, "Peter O'Toole," in *Focus on Film* (London), Summer 1972.
Houghton, M., "Slow Motion O'Toole," in *Films in Review* (New York), March 1985.

*   *   *

Peter O'Toole in *Lawrence of Arabia*

Losing themselves in the hollows of Peter O'Toole's craggy face in piddling television escapism such as *Gulliver's Travels*, his fans can flash backward to the more salubrious time when he was a blond god capable of standing astride a David Lean epic. Reduced to appearing in stentorian show-and-tell cameos, O'Toole has become a sort of John Barrymore for the nineties.

A promising light on London's West End and a potential matinee idol in minor films, O'Toole beat out Brando and Albert Finney for the coveted role of Lawrence of Arabia and breathed magnetic life-force into that enigmatic figure. Burnished by the sun and bundled up smashingly in a burnoose, a star was born. Like a lover with a fixation on piercing blue eyes, the camera could not get enough of him, but the ravishing-looking O'Toole was never interested in stripped-to-the-waist love god superstardom.

Despite forays into the fading Hollywood studio system, O'Toole never seemed comfortable twinkling at leading ladies in *What's New Pussycat?* or *How to Steal a Million*. Only when he brought passion to a role did he seem like a star. A shockingly changeable Henry II in *Becket* was resoundingly more forceful than any of the Anouilh's stage play interpreters such as Olivier and Anthony Quinn; O'Toole followed this regal triumph with a robust revisit to the same king in *The Lion in Winter*, even if that stage comedy was misinterpreted on film as a melodrama. Oddly touching in two deteriorative musicals made bearable by his genius (*Goodbye, Mr. Chips* and *Man of La Mancha*), he compensated for commonplace flops in the seventies by balancing them with exemplary turns such as his perfectly nuanced hit man who just misses assassinating Der Fuhrer in *Rogue Male*, and as the nutty

Earl of Gurney, who believes he is Christ but whose psychological cure transforms him into Jack the Ripper. Consummately hilarious and unsettling, this rabid satire is the movie *Clockwork Orange* pretends to be. A self-proclaimed vocational drinker as well as actor, O'Toole never set much store by his movie star visage and did not look back when character roles started rolling in. He superbly incarnated the concept of the film director as mini-God in the masterpiece, *The Stunt Man*, and was a comedic cyclone as the dipsomaniac has-been Alan Swann, pulling himself together for his biggest fan in the charming *My Favorite Year*.

Since that peak, the life seems to have been boiled out of him. As his physical decline became more and more pronounced, O'Toole retreated to self-parody which may be copacetic with *Supergirl* but certainly does not sit too well with Henry Higgins in *Pygmalion*. One still hopes inspiration will fire him up for more than showy displays of mellifluousness. Unapologetic about the way he has lived his life, the hell-raising Irishman may rebound with performances that do not rely on vocal tricks and mannerisms; after all, he is a man brave enough to have continued performing *Macbeth* after being savaged by the London critics. Even his ruined grandeur is spectacular and belongs to another risk-taking age when larger-than-life personalities ruled the stage and screen. Unfortunately, the nagging doubt persists that this flamboyant star's passion for acting may be as ravaged as his once-considerable physical beauty.

—Robert Pardi

PACINO, Al

Nationality: American. **Born:** Alfredo James Pacino in New York City, 25 April 1940. **Education:** Attended High School of the Performing Arts, New York; Herbert Berghof Studio under Charles Laughton; Actors Studio, New York, from 1966. **Career:** Worked as mail boy, in the offices of *Commentary* magazine, a movie usher, and building superintendent; then actor off-off-Broadway; 1969—Broadway debut in *Does the Tiger Wear a Necktie?*; film debut in *Me, Natalie*; 1970—member of the Lincoln Center repertory theater; director of stage play *Rats* in Boston; 1977—in stage play *The Basic Training of Pavlo Hummel* in Boston, and New York; 1982-84—co-artistic director, Actors Studio; 1984—London stage debut in *American Buffalo*. **Awards:** Best Actor, British Academy, for *The Godfather, Part II* and *Dog Day Afternoon*, 1975; Best Actor, Academy Award, for *Scent of a Woman*, 1992; Chevalier dans l'Orde des Arts et de Lettres, 1995. **Agent:** c/o CAA, 9830 Wilshire Boulevard, Beverly Hills, CA 90212, U.S.A.

Films as Actor:

1969   *Me, Natalie* (Coe) (as Tony)
1971   *Panic in Needle Park* (Schatzberg) (as Bobby)
1972   **The Godfather** (Coppola) (as Michael Corleone)
1973   *Scarecrow* (Schatzberg) (as Lion); *Serpico* (Lumet) (title role)
1974   **The Godfather, Part II** (Coppola) (as Michael Corleone)
1975   *Dog Day Afternoon* (Lumet) (as Sonny)
1977   *Bobby Deerfield* (Pollack) (title role)
1979   *. . . And Justice for All* (Jewison) (as Arthur Kirkland)
1980   *Cruising* (Friedkin) (as Steve Burns)
1982   *Author! Author!* (Hiller) (as Travalian)
1983   *Scarface* (De Palma) (as Tony Montana)
1985   *Revolution* (Hudson) (as Tom Dobb)
1989   *Sea of Love* (Becker) (as Frank Keller)
1990   *Dick Tracy* (Beatty) (as Big Boy Caprice); *The Godfather, Part III* (Coppola) (as Michael Corleone)
1991   *Frankie and Johnny* (Garry Marshall) (as Johnny)
1992   *Scent of a Woman* (Brest) (as Lt. Col. Frank Slade); *Glengarry Glen Ross* (Foley) (as Ricky Roma)
1993   *Carlito's Way* (De Palma) (as Carlito Brigante); *Jonas in the Desert* (as himself)
1995   *Two Bits* (*A Day to Remember*) (James Foley) (as Gitano Sabatoni); *Heat* (Michael Mann) (as Vincent Hanna)
1996   *City Hall* (Becker) (as Mayor John Pappas); *Donna Brasco* (Newell)

Film as Director:

1996   *Looking for Richard*

Publications

By PACINO: articles—

Interview, in *Time Out* (London), 6 September 1984.
Interview, in *Ciné Revue* (Paris), 30 January 1986.
Interview with J. Schnabel, in *Interview* (New York), February 1991.
Interview with Teresa Carpenter, in *Guardian* (London), 3 December 1991.

On PACINO: books—

Zuckerman, Ira, *The Godfather Journal*, New York, 1972.
Puzo, Mario, *The Making of* The Godfather, Greenwich, Connecticut, 1973.
Yule, Andrew, *Life on the Wire: The Life and Art of Al Pacino*, New York, 1991.
Schoell, William, *The Films of Al Pacino*, Secaucus, New Jersey, 1995.

On PACINO: articles—

Current Biography 1974, New York, 1974.
Thomson, D., "Two Gentlemen of Corleone," in *Take One* (Montreal), May 1978.
Strasberg, Lee, in *Photoplay* (New York), April 1980.
Williamson, Bruce, "Al Pacino," in *The Movie Star*, edited by Elisabeth Weis, New York, 1981.
Image et Son (Paris), January 1982.
Chute, David, "Scarface," in *Film Comment* (New York), February 1984.
Stivers, Cyndi, "Sunny-Side Up," in *Premiere* (New York), October 1991.
Richards, David, "Sunday View: Pacino's Star Turn Reflects the Glories of Rep," in *New York Times*, 5 July 1992.
Minsky, Terri, "Descent of a Man," in *Premiere* (New York), February 1993.
Dullea, Georgia, "Al Pacino Confronts a Gala, Kudos, Fame and His Own Shyness," in *New York Times*, 22 February 1993.
Weinraub, Bernard, "De Niro! Pacino! Together Again for First Time," in *New York Times*, 27 July 1995.

*   *   *

Al Pacino's career is connected to that of his Italian-American contemporary, Robert De Niro. Both New York City-born, they each became movie stars in the early 1970s, and have more often than not played vividly realized characters who exist (on both sides of the law) within contemporary urban milieus. Pacino's first major role is Michael Corleone in *The Godfather*; De Niro played Michael's father in the sequel, *The Godfather, Part II*. Two decades later, they were masterly paired in *Heat*, with Pacino the cop who obsessively tracks De Niro's hood. Finally, and most importantly, their acting styles clearly derive from the Method school, with Pacino remaining an important force in the continuation and development of New York's famed Actors Studio.

Al Pacino

Woman, playing a blind, cantankerous, ultimately suicidal ex-Army colonel. But he is even better in *Glengarry Glen Ross*, adapted by David Mamet from his stage play about the pressures on, and frustrations of, a group of real estate salesmen. Pacino plays Ricky Roma, a character who is tough, hard, and slick. Roma is a hotshot who lays a psychological-metaphysical line on his clients like a master manipulator. Those who have come to Roma to inquire about purchasing property are not so much his clients as his victims. As Roma, Pacino offers an acting tour de force. To watch him here, spouting Mamet's bristling dialogue—at once vivid and knowing, with brush strokes both subtle and broad—is to see a master actor at the top of his form.

—Robin Wood, updated by Rob Edelman

PAGE, Geraldine

Nationality: American. **Born:** Kirksville, Missouri, 22 November 1924. **Education:** Attended the Goodman Theatre Dramatic School, Chicago; also studied acting with Uta Hagen. **Family:** Married 1) Alexander Schneider, 1956 (divorced); 2) the actor Rip Torn; daughter: Angelica; twin sons: Anthony and Jonathan. **Career:** Actress in Lake Zurich, Illinois, summer theater, four summers; also with Woodstock, Illinois, repertory company for two years; worked in New York for International Thread Company while acting off-Broadway; 1947—film debut in *Out of the Night*; 1951—leading role in *Summer and Smoke* in New York, repeated in film version in 1961; film contract with Charles K. Feldman; 1953—Broadway debut in *Mid-Summer*; first featured film role in *Hondo*; later stage work includes roles in *Sweet Bird of Youth*, 1959, *Strange Interlude*, 1963, *Three Sisters*, 1964, *Clothes for a Summer Hotel*, 1980 and *Agnes of God*, 1982. **Awards:** Best Supporting Actress, British Academy, for *Interiors*, 1978; Oscar for Best Actress, for *The Trip to Bountiful*, 1985. **Died:** Of a heart attack, in New York City, 13 June 1987.

Films as Actress:

1947 *Out of the Night*
1953 *Hondo* (Farrow) (as Angie Lowe); *Taxi* (Ratoff) (as Florence Albert)
1961 *Summer and Smoke* (Glenville) (as Alma Winemiller)
1962 *Sweet Bird of Youth* (Brooks) (as Alexandra Del Lago)
1963 *Toys in the Attic* (Hill) (as Carrie Berniers)
1964 *Dear Heart* (Delbert Mann) (as Elvie Johnson)
1966 *Monday's Child* (Nilsson); *You're a Big Boy Now* (Coppola) (as Margery Chanticleer)
1967 *The Happiest Millionaire* (Tokar) (as Mrs. Duke)
1968 *What Ever Happened to Aunt Alice?* (Katzin) (as Mrs. Clair Marrable)
1969 "A Christmas Memory" ep. of *Trilogy* (Perry—for TV) (as the Woman)
1971 *The Beguiled* (Siegel) (as Martha); *J. W. Coop* (Robertson) (as Mama)
1972 *Pete 'n' Tillie* (Ritt) (as Gertrude)
1973 *Happy as the Grass Was Green* (*Hazel's People*) (Davis) (as Anna Witmer)
1974 *Live Again, Die Again* (Colla—for TV)
1975 *Day of the Locust* (Schlesinger) (as Big Sister)
1976 *Nasty Habits* (Hogg) (as Walburga)
1977 *The Rescuers* (Reitherman, Lounsbery, and Stevens—animation) (as voice of Mme. Medusa); *Something for Joey* (Antonio—for TV); *The Three Sisters* (Bogart) (as Olga)

Pacino's acting roots are apparent in his earliest performances, which emphasize spontaneity, improvisation and a flamboyance of manner and expression to a point where acting threatens to become the films' raison d'être. This is precisely the case in his roles as the young junkie in *Panic in Needle Park*, the drifter who has abandoned his family in *Scarecrow*, the honest New York cop singlehandedly fighting a corrupt police department in *Serpico*, and the would-be bankrobber who desires to finance his lover's sex change operation in *Dog Day Afternoon*. It is his appearances in these films (as well as *The Godfather* and *The Godfather, Part II*) which established Pacino as one of the 1970s' most important stars. His performances in the first four are tours de force of an almost crazed nervous energy combined with a deep intensity and vulnerability. This energy appears at once a positive trait, infectious and irresistible, and a mask, a defense against the constant threat posed by the other characters or forces at work in the story.

But it was his work in the two *Godfather* films which required Pacino to create a far more complexly psychological characterization. Here, his acting style changes drastically, as he becomes more restrained and understated. His Michael Corleone starts out a young, all-American war hero, a man with decent instincts and the type of guy one would expect to marry, raise a family, and become a pillar of his community. As time passes and Michael finds himself becoming more deeply and inexorably involved in his family's "business," Pacino gradually and ever-so-subtly develops his character into a powerful but nonetheless tragic figure: a man who has allowed himself to be seduced and ultimately corrupted, to the point where he is capable of instigating the most vicious and horribly evil actions (such as ordering the murder of Fredo, his own brother). Unlike his psychotic other brother Sonny, who is primarily ruled by his temper and emotions, Michael is an intelligent man who should know better. So his soul becomes tainted, and he becomes at once emotionally repressed and tragically incapable of altering his fate. He is consumed by a cloak of weariness which haunts him, overriding and defining his character more than any amount of power he has achieved. This aspect of his evolving character plays itself out dramatically in the third *Godfather* film, made a decade and a half after *The Godfather, Part II*, in which Michael Corleone suffers through the death of his beloved daughter.

Pacino's career has not been without its share of miscalculations. Chief among them are *Cruising*, a distasteful, embarrassing thriller in which his character, a New York City cop, goes undercover and enters a gay netherworld in order to seek out a killer; *Bobby Deerfield*, an awful soaper in which he plays a race car driver romancing a beautiful but seriously ill woman; *Revolution*, a preposterous Revolutionary War drama in which he is cast as a trapper; and *Scarface*, by far his worst screen performance, in which he overacts outrageously as a Cuban drug dealer. But Pacino's stardom remained intact, and he has endured into the 1990s as a major movie personality whose casting in a film makes that film an event. He ended the 1980s with a solid star turn as another New York cop in *Sea of Love*, generating sufficient heat in his love scenes with Ellen Barkin and exhibiting the abundant array of emotions experienced by his character. The same is the case in the aforementioned *Heat* as well as *Carlito's Way*, in which he plays a weary, streetwise Puerto Rican criminal attempting to go straight. He was never more ingratiating as an ex-con who falls for a reluctant waitress in *Frankie and Johnny*; he effectively reprised Michael Corleone in the otherwise disappointing *The Godfather, Part III*; he was fun to watch as the vividly menacing Big Boy Caprice in *Dick Tracy*; and he graduated to senior citizen roles, nicely playing a wise old Italian immigrant grandfather in *Two Bits*, a Depression-era nostalgia piece.

In two of Pacino's most important 1990s films, he plays flamboyant characters who are, in their manner, aging extensions of his roles in *The Panic in Needle Park*, *Scarecrow*, *Dog Day Afternoon*, and *Serpico*. He earned a long-overdue Academy Award for *Scent of a*

1978 *Interiors* (Allen) (as Eve)
1981 *Honky Tonk Freeway* (Schlesinger) (as Sister Mary Clarise);
      Harry's War (Merrill) (as Beverley)
1982 *I'm Dancing as Fast as I Can* (Hofsiss) (as Jean Martin)
1984 *The Pope of Greenwich Village* (Rosenberg) (as Mrs. Ritter); *The
      Parade* (*Hit Parade*) (Hunt); *The Dollmaker* (Petrie—for TV)
1985 *White Nights* (Hackford) (as Anne Wyatt); *The Trip to Bounti-
      ful* (Masterson) (as Mrs. Carrie Watts); *The Bride* (Roddam)
      (as Mrs. Baumann); *Flanagan* (Goldstein) (as Mama)
1986 *My Little Girl* (Kaiserman) (as Grandmother Molly); *Nazi
      Hunter: The Beate Klarsfield Story* (*Nazi Hunter: The Search
      for Klaus Barbie*) (Lindsay-Hogg); *Native Son* (Freedman)
      (as Peggy)

Publications

By PAGE: article—

Interview in *Actors in Acting: Performing in Theatre and Film Today*,
   by Joanmarie Kalter, New York, 1979.

On PAGE: articles—

Current Biography 1953, New York, 1953.
Eyles, Allen, "Geraldine Page," in *Focus on Film* (London), Spring 1973.
Obituary in *New York Times*, 15 June 1987.
Obituary in *Variety* (New York), 17 June 1987.

*   *   *

An exponent of the Method style of acting, Geraldine Page was best
known as a stage performer, particularly for her work in the plays of
Tennessee Williams. Her performances in the film versions of *Summer and Smoke*, as a shy spinster hopelessly in love with her neighbor, and *Sweet Bird of Youth*, as an aging movie star suffering from a
nervous breakdown, established her as a successful and important actress and indicated the wide range of her acting abilities.

In 1953, Page was brought to Hollywood to play opposite John
Wayne in *Hondo* as Angie Lowe, a homesteader with child, abandoned
by her husband. Warner Brothers executives were unimpressed with
her despite an Oscar nomination; she was not offered another Hollywood film until the 1960s. After the two Tennessee Williams roles,
she became somewhat typecast as a spinster or neurotic, as evidenced
by her characters in *Toys in the Attic*, *Dear Heart*, and *You're a Big
Boy Now*. Her eccentric image was pushed to its sinister extreme,
epitomizing evil behind a sweet facade, in such films as *The Beguiled*
and *Whatever Happened to Aunt Alice?*, while her comic abilities were
showcased in *Pete 'n' Tillie* (notably her frustration when police demand to know her real age).

Woody Allen used the accumulated resonance of her desperately
vulnerable character roles when he cast her as the self-pitying wife and
overbearing mother of *Interiors*, a woman whose well-ordered existence is shattered by her husband's desire for a divorce. Life becomes a
strain: a spilled drop of wine at her birthday celebration provides an
exquisite moment for Page to eloquently communicate long suffering.

Her stage career continued to be her prime focus, working both on
and off Broadway, and accepting only occasional television parts and
movie roles. In 1984, Page was awarded a seventh Oscar nomination
for *The Pope of Greenwich Village*, the record for actresses who had
yet to win.

The following year, the losing streak was ended with her glorious
performance in *The Trip to Bountiful* as Mrs. Carrie Watts, an aging
widow now living in a two-room Houston apartment with her son and
overbearing daughter-in-law. Aware her time is near, Mrs. Watts is
anxious to make one last trip to Bountiful, the place of her youth. As
a woman coping with the sorrows and frustrations of old age depen-
dency, Page brilliantly communicates Mrs. Watts' tendency for self-
dramatization: she will make it to Bountiful if she has to walk the last
12 miles from Harrison. The emotional journey Mrs. Watts takes on
this trip allows Page to use effectively the sense memory skills of her
Method background: upon her arrival at the homestead, her simple
statement "I'm home" is accompanied by a facial expression that
magnificently encompasses both the joy of arrival and a sadness over
those not present.

—Doug Tomlinson

PALANCE, Jack

Nationality: American. **Born:** Walter Jack Palahnuik (or Vladimir
Palanuik) in Lattimer, Pennsylvania, 18 February 1920 (some sources
give 1919). **Education:** Attended the University of North Carolina,
Chapel Hill; Stanford University, California. **Family:** Married 1) Virginia Baker, 1949 (divorced), two daughters and one son; 2) Elaine
Rogers, 1987. **Career:** Worked as coal miner, cook, radio repairman,
and boxer; then served in World War II as bomber pilot: shot down and
needed plastic surgery; after the war studied at Stanford; 1947—debut
on Broadway; 1950—film debut in *Panic in the Streets*; 1956—acclaimed role in TV play *Requiem for a Heavyweight*; appeared in TV
series *The Greatest Show on Earth*, 1963-64, and *Bronk*, 1975-76, and
in mini-series *Buck Rogers*, 1980, *The Chisholms*, 1980, and *Buffalo
Girls*, 1995. **Awards:** Best Supporting Actor Award for *City Slickers*,
1991. **Agent:** c/o Susan Smith & Associates, 121 North San Vicente
Boulevard, Beverly Hills, CA, 90211, U.S.A.

Films as Actor:

(as Walter Jack Palance)

1950 *Panic in the Streets* (Kazan) (as Blackie)

(as Jack Palance)

1950 *Halls of Montezuma* (Milestone) (as Pigeon Lane)
1952 *Sudden Fear* (Miller) (as Lester Blaine)
1953 *Shane* (Stevens) (as Stark Wilson); *Second Chance* (Maté) (as
      Cappy Gordon); *Arrowhead* (Warren) (as Toriano); *Flight
      to Tangier* (Warren) (as Gil Walker); *Man in the Attic*
      (Fregonese) (as Slade)
1954 *The Silver Chalice* (Saville) (as Simon Magus); *Sign of the
      Pagan* (Sirk) (as Attila the Hun)
1955 *Kiss of Fire* (Joseph M. Newman) (as El Tigre); *The Big Knife*
      (Aldrich) (as Charles Castle); *I Died a Thousand Times*
      (Heisler) (as Roy Earle)
1956 *Attack!* (Aldrich) (as Lt. Costa)
1957 *The Lonely Man* (Levin) (as Jacob Wade); *House of Numbers*
      (Rouse) (as twin brothers, Bill and Arne Judlow); *Flor de
      mayo* (*Beyond All Limits*) (Gavaldón) (as Gatsby)
1958 *The Man Inside* (Gilling) (as Milo March)
1959 *Ten Seconds to Hell* (Aldrich) (as Eric Koertner)
1960 *Austerlitz* (*The Battle of Austerlitz*) (Gance) (as Weirother)
1961 *I mongoli* (*The Mongols*) (De Toth, Savona, and Freda) (as
      Ogotai); *Rosemunda e Alboino* (*Sword of the Conqueror*)
      (Campogalliani) (as Alboino); *Il guidizio universale* (*The
      Last Judgment*) (De Sica)

1962 *Barabba* (*Barabbas*) (Fleischer) (as Torvald); *La guerra continua* (*Warriors Five*) (Savona) (as Jack)

1963 *Le Mépris* (*Contempt*) (Godard) (as Jeremy Prokosch)

1965 *Les Tueurs de San Francisco* (*Once a Thief*) (Nelson) (as Walter Pedak)

1966 *The Professionals* (Richard Brooks) (as Captain Jesús Raza); *The Spy in the Green Hat* (Sargent) (as Louis Strago)

1967 *Torture Garden* (Francis) (as Ronald Wyatt); *Kill a Dragon* (Moore) (as Rick)

1968 *Las Vegas 500 millones* (*They Came to Rob Las Vegas*) (Isasmendi) (as Douglas); *Marquis de Sade: Justine* (*Justine and Juliet*) (Franco)

1969 *Il mercenario* (*The Mercenary*; *A Professional Gun*) (Corbucci) (as Ricciolo); *The Desperados* (Levin) (as Parson Josiah Galt); *Che!* (Fleischer) (as Fidel Castro)

1970 *The McMasters* (Kjellin) (as Kolby); *Monte Walsh* (Fraker) (as Chet Rollins); *Vamos a matar, compañeros!* (*Compañeros*) (Corbucci) (as Xantos)

1971 *The Horsemen* (Frankenheimer) (as Tursen); *Si puo fare ... amigo* (*The Big and the Bad*) (Lucidi) (as gunman)

1972 *Chato's Land* (Winner) (as Quincey Whitmore); *Dr. Jekyll and Mr. Hyde* (Jarrott—for TV)

1973 *Oklahoma Crude* (Kramer) (as Hellman); *Te deum* (*The Con Men*) (Castallani)

1974 *Dracula* (Curtis—for TV) (title role); *Craze* (Francis) (as Neal Mottram); *The Godchild* (Badham—for TV)

1975 *The Hatfields and the McCoys* (Ware—for TV); *The Four Deuces* (Bushnell); *Africa Express* (Lupo); *The Diamond Mercenaries* (*Killer Force*) (Guest)

1976 *The Great Adventure* (Baldanello)

1977 *Welcome to Blood City* (Sasdy) (as Sheriff Frendlander); *I padroni della città* (*Mr. Scarface*; *Rulers of the City*) (di Leo); *Portrait of a Hit Man* (Buckhantz) (as Jim Buck)

1978 *One Man Jury* (Martin) (as Wade); *God's Gun* (Kramer)

1979 *Dead on Arrival* (Martin); *Seven from Heaven* (Clark); *The Shape of Things to Come* (McCowen) (as Omus); *Cocaine Cowboys* (Lommel) (as Raf); *Buck Rogers in the 25th Century* (Haller—for TV); *Angels Brigade* (Clark); *The Last Ride of the Dalton Gang* (Curtis—for TV)

1980 *The Ivory Ape* (Kotani—for TV); *Ladyfingers*; *Without Warning* (*It Came . . . without Warning*) (Clark); *Hawk the Slayer* (Marcell) (as Voltan)

1982 *Alone in the Dark* (Sholder) (as Frank Hawkes)

1987 *Bagdad Cafe* (*Out of Rosenheim*) (Adlon) (as Rudy Cox)

1988 *Gor* (Kiersch) (as Xenos); *Young Guns* (Cain) (as L. G. Murphy)

1989 *Batman* (Burton) (as Carl Grissom); *Outlaw of Gor* (Cardos) (as Xenos); *Tango and Cash* (Konchalovsky) (as Yves Perret)

1991 *City Slickers* (Underwood) (as Curly)

1992 *Solar Crisis* (Sarafian) (as Travis); *Keep the Change* (Tennant—for TV) (as Overstreet); *Salmonberries* (Adlon)

1993 *Cyborg II: Glass Shadows* (Schroeder) (as Mercy)

1994 *The Swan Princess* (Rich) (as voice of Rothbart); *Twilight Zone: Rod Serling's Lost Classics* (for TV) (as Jeremy Wheaton); *Cops & Robbersons* (Ritchie) (as Jack Stone); *City Slickers II: The Legend of Curly's Gold* (Weiland) (as Duke Washburn)

Publications

By PALANCE: article—

Interview with J.-L. Sablon, in *Revue du Cinéma* (Paris), October 1989.

On PALANCE: articles—

Ecran (Paris), December 1978.

Brock, Alan, in *Classic Images* (Indiana, Pennsylvania), July 1982.

Martin, D., "Jack Palance, Living the Western," in *New York Times*, 21 July 1991.

Current Biography 1992, New York, 1992.

Reilly, Anthony, "Off Palance," in *Premiere* (New York), July 1994.

*   *   *

As much as any other actor, the career of Jack Palance has been determined by his physical appearance. His taut-skinned and somewhat Asian features and the legacy of his Slavic background were rendered even more distinctive by the severe burns and resulting plastic surgery he endured after the crash of a bomber he was piloting during World War II. His resulting look never would allow him to be cast as a romantic hero. In short, Palance seemed destined to be typecast as a sadistic heavy.

After some Broadway experience (notably with Elia Kazan), the actor moved on to Hollywood like so many others associated with the Actors Studio. He started out in movies playing creepy villains in prestige films. In Kazan's *Panic in the Streets*, he is striking if somewhat hysterical as a trigger-happy, plague-stricken hood. In *Shane*, he is especially menacing as a gunslinger who is the very image of grim death. In *Sudden Fear*, his character is more outwardly respectable: Lester Blaine, an actor who woos and wins heiress-turned-playwright Joan Crawford. Only what she does not know is that he just may be a fortune hunter and killer. This should not be surprising, as Palance simply is not the romantic type. Given his developing screen image, Palance was in character as Blaine is transformed from attentive suitor to outright heavy. The actor's career was off to a fast start, as evidenced by his two Best Supporting Actor Oscar nominations (for *Sudden Fear* and *Shane*).

During this period, Palance also appeared as a villain in a number of costume epics, playing a very satanic Simon Magus in *The Silver Chalice* and an energetic Attila the Hun in *Sign of the Pagan*. But his best screen work was to come in several films directed by Robert Aldrich, who perceptively realized that Palance's daunting appearance could be made to suggest an inner vulnerability. In *The Big Knife*, he plays a movie star mired in a corrupt Hollywood that serves as a microcosm of American society. In this role, Palance powerfully conveys a moral decay to which he contributes but which eventually traps him as well. In *Attack!* and *Ten Seconds to Hell* he plays similar characters, soldiers who are inevitably (and sadly) doomed by their involvement in the deadly business of war.

From the 1960s on, Palance's career became run of the mill. He appeared in a seemingly endless number of foreign and domestic costume epics, throwaway melodramas and actioners, and uninspired television movies. Occasionally an interesting credit was thrown into the mix: Godard's *Contempt*, the Westerns *The Professionals* and *Monte Walsh*, and Percy Adlon's *Bagdad Cafe*. But Palance for the most part was earning his mortgage money by appearing in the likes of *Kill a Dragon*, *Africa Express*, *The Diamond Mercenaries*, *Dead on Arrival*, *The Last Ride of the Dalton Gang*, *Gor*, *Outlaw of Gor*, and so on.

In 1991, Palance was fortunate enough to be cast as Curly, the weather-beaten trail boss who interacts with Billy Crystal, in the popular baby boomer comedy *City Slickers*. His performance won him the Best Supporting Actor Oscar; that, along with his Oscarcast display of physical dexterity, earned him the kind of notoriety and publicity other faded veteran actors only dream of. Curly is a larger-than-life character if there ever was one, and Palance plays him broadly and with a partial wink at the viewer. He appears to be enjoying himself immensely as he offers a deft parody of all of his macho villain characters.

Still, one wishes that the career of Jack Palance had developed differently and that, over the decades, he had been able to maintain the high level of his earliest screen work.

—R. Barton Palmer, updated by Rob Edelman

PAPAS, Irene

Nationality: Greek. **Born:** Irene Lelekou in Chiliomodion, 9 March 1926. **Education:** Attended the Royal Drama School, Athens. **Family:** Married 1) Alkis Papas, 1947 (marriage dissolved 1951); 2) José Kohn, 1957 (marriage annulled). **Career:** Singer and dancer from her teens in variety shows; 1950—film debut in *Nekri Politeia*; contract with Lux films (Italy) in early 1950s; made several U.S. films in the mid-1950s, and international productions subsequently; 1967—on Broadway with Jon Voight in *That Summer—That Fall*. **Address:** c/o United Film Distribution, 115 Middle Neck Road, Great Neck, NY 11021, U.S.A.

Films as Actress:

1951 *Nekri Politeia (Dead City)* (Iliades)
1953 *Le infideli (The Unfaithfuls)* (Steno and Monicelli) (as Mrs. Luisa Azzali); *Dramma della Casbah* (Anton); *Vortice* (Matarazzo); *The Man from Cairo* (Enright) (as Yvonne)
1954 *Teodora, Imperatrice di Bisanzio (Theodora, Slave and Empress)* (Freda); *Attila flagello di dio (Attila; Attila the Hun)* (Francisci) (as Grune)
1956 *Tribute to a Bad Man* (Wise) (as Jocasta Constantine); *The Power and the Prize* (Koster)
1960 *Antigone (Rights for the Dead)* (Tzavellas) (title role)
1961 *The Guns of Navarone* (J. Lee Thompson) (as Maria Pappadimos)
1962 *Electra* (Cacoyannis) (title role)
1964 *The Moon-Spinners* (Neilson) (as Sophia); ***Zorba the Greek*** (Cacoyannis) (as the widow)
1965 *Die Zeugin aus der Hölle (Witness Out of Hell; Gorge Trave; Bitter Grass)* (Mitrovic) (as Lea Weiss)
1966 *Roger la Honte* (Freda)
1967 *Más allá de las montañas (Beyond the Mountains; The Desperate Ones)* (Ramati) (as Ajmi); *A ciascuno il sou (We Still Kill the Old Way)* (Petri) (as Luisa Roscio)
1968 *The Brotherhood* (Ritt) (as Ida Ginetta); *Ecce Homo* (Gaburro); *L'Odissea* (Rossi—for TV)
1969 *Z* (Costa-Gavras) (as Hélène); *A Dream of Kings* (Delbert Mann) (as Caliope); *Anne of the Thousand Days* (Jarrott) (as Queen Catherine of Aragon)
1971 *The Trojan Women* (Cacoyannis) (as Helen of Troy); *Roma Bene* (Lizzani); *N.P. (N.P.—The Secret)* (Agosti) (as housewife); *Un posto ideale per uccidere* (Lenzi)
1972 *Non si servizia un paperino (Don't Torture the Duckling)* (Fulci); *Piazza Pulita (1931: Once upon a Time in New York; Pete, Pearl and the Pole)* (Vanzi); *Sutjeska (The Fifth Offensive)* (Vanzi)
1974 *Le farò da padre (Bambina)* (Lattuada)
1975 *Mose (Moses; The Lawgiver)* (De Bosio—for TV) (as Zipporah)
1976 *The Message (Mohammad, Messenger of God; Al-Risalah)* (Akkad) (as Hind); *Bodas de sangre* (Barka)
1977 *L'uomo di Corleone* (Coletti); *Un ombra nell' ombra* (Carpi); *Iphigenia* (Cacoyannis) (as Clytemnestra)

1979 *Bloodline* (Terence Young) (as Simonetta Palazza); ***Cristo si e fermato a Eboli*** (*Christ Stopped at Eboli*) (Rosi) (as Giulia)
1981 *Lion of the Desert (Omar Mukhtar)* (Akkad—produced in 1979) (as Mabrouka)
1982 *Erendira* (Guerra) (as grandmother); *La Ballade de Mamlouk* (Bouassida)
1983 *Il disertore (The Deserter)* (Berlinquer) (as Mariangela); *Afghanistan porquoi* (Masbahi)
1984 *Steps* (Hirschfield); *The Assisi Underground* (Ramati) (as Mother Giuseppina)
1985 *Into the Night* (Landis) (as Shaheen Parvizi)
1987 *Sweet Country* (Cacoyannis) (as Mrs. Araya); *High Season* (Peploe) (as Penelope)
1988 *Cronaca di una morte annunciata (Chronicle of a Death Foretold)* (Rosi) (as Angela's Mother)
1989 *Island* (Cox) (as Marquise); *Ociano* (Deodato—for TV)
1990 *La Batalla de los Tres Reyes* (as Lalla Sahaba)
1991 *Drums of Fire*; *Banquet*
1992 *Lettera da Parigi (The Latest from Paris)* (Giordani) (as Gina); *Zoe*
1993 *Pano Kato Ke Plagios (Up, Down and Sideways)* (Cacoyannis) (as Maria)
1994 *Jacob* (Peter Hall—for TV) (as Rebekah); *Homecoming*

Publications

By PAPAS: article—

"Irene Papas a Toronto," interview with E. Castiel, in *Séquences* (Montreal), November/December 1993.

On PAPAS: articles—

Ecran (Paris), July 1978.
Ciné Revue (Paris), 16 August 1979.
García Márquez, Gabriel, "Behind the Scenes: Chronicle of a Film Foretold," in *American Film* (Washington, D.C.), September 1984.
McDonald, M., "Interviews with Michael Cacoyannis and Irene Papas," in *Bucknell Review*, vol. 35, no. 1, 1991.

*   *   *

Some actors and roles seem predestined for each other. From the opening shot of Michael Cacoyannis's *Electra*, as the proud, implacable face emerges from encroaching shadows, it becomes impossible to imagine anyone else as Euripides's heroine. Erect, immutably dignified, dark eyes burning fiercely beneath heavy black brows, Irene Papas visibly embodies the sublimity of classical Greece, tragic yet serene. "I had never thought," Dilys Powell wrote, "to see the face of the great Apollo from the Olympia pediment live and move. Now I have seen it."

Cacoyannis continued to provide some of her finest roles: as the caged Helen, eyes flashing, defying the execrations of *The Trojan Women*; and in *Iphigenia*, the third in his Euripidean trilogy, as Clytemnestra, terrible in her grief, even more terrible in the cold, vengeful tenacity that succeeds it. He also cast her, memorably, as the widow in *Zorba the Greek*: cool marble to Lila Kedrova's raddled plush, yet still conveying a powerful sensuality beneath the impassive surface which rendered wholly credible the final appalling explosion into violence.

So awe-inspiring a presence has often worked to Papas's detriment, tending to limit her roles—especially in Hollywood, where she has

Irene Papas in *Cristo si e fermato a Eboli*

generally been assigned Mother Earth parts, requiring little more than stoical suffering or elemental fury. Yet her range is certainly wider—she started out, after all, in Athenian musical reviews. Italy, her second home during the Colonels' regime (which she contemptuously termed "the fourth Reich"), has sometimes offered more imaginative scope. Her housekeeper in Rosi's *Cristo si e fermato a Eboli*, bathing Gian Maria Volonté in a tin tub and commenting with sly appreciation on his physique, suggests a talent for subtle comedy hitherto unsuspected by international audiences—and which it would be good to see developed.

—Philip Kemp

PATIL, Smita

Nationality: Indian. **Born:** 1954. **Education:** Attended Bombay University. **Career:** Involved with a theater group in Poona; 1972—newscaster on a Bombay television station; 1975—film debut in Shyam Benegal's *Nishant.* **Awards:** Indian National Film Awards for Best Actress, for *Bhumika,* 1977, and *Chakra,* 1980. **Died:** 13 December 1986.

Films as Actress:

1975 *Nishant* (Benegal)
1977 *Manthan* (*Churning*) (Benegal); *Bhumika* (*The Role*) (Benegal)
1978 *Gaman* (Ali); *Anugraham* (*The Boon*) (Benegal)
1980 *Akrosh*; *Naxalitees*; *Chakra* (*Vicious Circle*) (Dharmaraj)
1981 *Albert Pinto ko gussa kyon aati hai* (*Why Albert Pinto Is Angry*) (Mirza); *Sadgati* (*Deliverance*) (Ray—for TV); *Bhavni bhavai* (*A Folk Tale*) (Mehta) (as Ujjan); *Aswa medher ghora* (*Sacrificial Horse*) (Bhattarcharya)
1982 *Namak halal*; *Shakti*; *Bazaar*; *Dil e Nadaan*
1983 *Mandi* (Benegal); *Subah* (*Umbartha*; *Morning*; *Threshold*) (Patel) (as Sulabha); *Arth*; *Ardh Satya*; *Chatpatee*; *Ghungroo*; *Dard ka rishta*; *Qayamat*; *Haadsaa*
1984 *Situm*; *Anand nur Anand*; *Raawan*; *Pet Pyar nur Paap*; *Tarang* (Shahani)
1985 *Chidambaram* (Aravindan) (as Sivakami)
1986 *Debshishu* (Chakraborty); *Mirch Masala* (*Spices*) (Mehta) (as Sonbai)
1987 *Nazrana* (Tandon); *Sutradhar* (Joshi)
1988 *Akarshan*; *Hum Farishte Nahin*; *Waris*
1989 *Oonch Neech Beech*; *Galiyon Ka Badshah*

Publications

By PATIL: article—

Interview with C. Tesson, in *Cahiers du Cinéma* (Paris), February 1981.

On PATIL: articles—

Obituary in *Variety* (New York), 24 December 1986.
Obituary in *Cahiers du Cinéma* (Paris), January 1987.
Smita Patil 1953-1986: A Film Tribute, Greenwich Festival Booklet,
    London, 1987.
Rajadhyaksha, Ashish, and Paul Willemen, *Encyclopaedia of Indian
    Cinema*, London and New Delhi, 1994.

* * *

In India during the 1970s, the New Cinema movement arose as a challenge to mainstream popular cinema. Although it also hoped to alter mainstream cinema, the New Cinema's main thrust was a greater verisimilitude centered around contemporary social issues. Foremost among its concerns was the representation of an ideal modern woman. Smita Patil was the New Cinema actress most strongly identified with establishing the role model for this new woman.

Smita Patil was discovered by director Shyam Benegal while working as a newscaster for Bombay television. Her face soon appeared on every national magazine cover and she became a star overnight. Wearing little or no makeup and dressed in traditional saris, her "natural looking" image was somewhat antithetical to that of the usual Indian film star. She was increasingly cast in roles that used this image to blur any distinction between her personal and professional life. Originally described as the rural milkmaid "with fire in her eyes and a deep intensity in her soul," her screen persona was made concrete after appearing in Benegal's *Bhumika*, the story of a famous Marathi stage and screen actress (the Joan Crawford of India) whose life was fraught with drink and painful love affairs during her search for personal freedom in an orthodox society.

Although the art cinema world tended to champion her as a serious actress, Patil began an uneasy crossover towards more commercial films. A recipient of national awards within India, Smita Patil's talents also attracted attention outside her native land; Costa-Gavras organized a retrospective of her films in France.

—Behroze Gandhy

PECK, Gregory

Nationality: American. **Born:** Eldred Gregory Peck in La Jolla, California, 5 April 1916. **Education:** Attended high school in San Diego; St. John's Military Academy, Los Angeles; San Diego State University; University of California, Berkeley, graduated 1939; Neighborhood Playhouse theater school, New York, under Sanford Meisner, two years. **Family:** Married: 1) Greta Konen, 1942 (divorced 1955), three children, one deceased; 2) Veronique Passani, 1955, son: the actor Tony Peck, daughter: the actress Cecilia Peck. **Career:** Worked as talker at World's Fair, New York, and guide at Radio City; 1940—acted at Barter Theatre, Abingdon, Virginia, and later at theaters in New York; 1943—film debut in *Days of Glory*; contract with David O. Selznick, and several other film companies; 1948—co-founder, La Jolla Playhouse; 1958—co-producer of film *The Big Country*; 1965—charter member of National Arts Council; 1967-69—chairman of the Board of Trustees, American Film Institute; 1982—in TV mini-series

The Blue and the Gray, and as voice in *Baseball*, 1994; 1995—toured in one-man show *A Conversation with Gregory Peck*. **Awards:** Best Actor, New York Film Critics, for *Twelve O'Clock High*, 1949; Best Actor Academy Award, for *To Kill a Mockingbird*, 1962; Jean Hersholt Humanitarian Award, 1967; Life Achievement Award, American Film Institute, 1989. **Agent:** Mike Simpson, William Morris Agency, 151 El Camino Drive, Beverly Hills, CA 90212, U.S.A.

Films as Actor:

1943   *Days of Glory* (Jacques Tourneur) (as Vladimir)
1944   *Keys of the Kingdom* (Stahl) (as Father Francis Chisholm)
1945   *Spellbound* (Hitchcock) (as John "J. B." Ballantine); *The Valley of Decision* (Garnett) (as Paul Scott)
1946   *The Yearling* (Brown) (as Pa Baxter); *Duel in the Sun* (King Vidor) (as Lewt McCanles)
1947   *The Macomber Affair* (Korda) (as Robert Wilson); *Gentleman's Agreement* (Kazan) (as Phil Green); *The Paradine Case* (Hitchcock) (as Anthony Keane)
1948   *Yellow Sky* (Wellman) (as Stretch)
1949   *The Great Sinner* (Siodmak) (as Fedja); *Twelve O'Clock High* (Henry King) (as Gen. Frank Savage)
1950   *The Gunfighter* (Henry King) (as Johnny Ringo)
1951   *Captain Horatio Hornblower* (Walsh) (title role); *Only the Valiant* (Gordon Douglas) (as Capt. Richard Lance)
1952   *David and Bathsheba* (Henry King) (as David); *The World in His Arms* (Walsh) (as Jonathan Clark); *The Snows of Kilimanjaro* (Henry King) (as Harry Street); *Pictura* (as narrator)
1953   *Roman Holiday* (Wyler) (as Joe Bradley); *Night People* (Johnson) (as Col. Steve Van Dyke)
1955   *The Purple Plain* (Parrish) (as Forrester); *The Million Pound Note* (*Man with a Million*) (Neame) (as Jerry Adams)
1956   *The Man in the Gray Flannel Suit* (Johnson) (as Tom Rath); *Moby Dick* (Huston) (as Capt. Ahab)
1957   *Designing Woman* (Minnelli) (as Mike Hagen)
1958   *The Bravados* (Henry King) (as Jim Douglass)
1959   *Pork Chop Hill* (Milestone) (as Lt. Joe Clemons); *Beloved Infidel* (Henry King) (as F. Scott Fitzgerald); *On the Beach* (Kramer) (as Dwight Towers)
1961   *The Guns of Navarone* (J. Lee Thompson) (as Capt. Mallory)
1962   *Cape Fear* (J. Lee Thompson) (as Sam Bowden); *To Kill a Mockingbird* (Mulligan) (as Atticus Finch)
1963   "The Plains" ep. of *How the West Was Won* (Hathaway) (as Cleve Van Valen); *Captain Newman, M.D.* (Miller) (title role)
1964   *Behold a Pale Horse* (Zinnemann) (as Manuel Artiguez)
1965   *Mirage* (Dmytryk) (as David Stillwell)
1966   *Arabesque* (Donen) (as David Pollock); *John F. Kennedy: Years of Lightning, Day of Drums* (Herschensohn) (as narrator)
1968   *The Stalking Moon* (Mulligan) (as Sam Varner)
1969   *MacKenna's Gold* (J. Lee Thompson) (as MacKenna); *The Most Dangerous Man in the World* (*The Chairman*) (J. Lee Thompson) (as Dr. John Hathaway); *Marooned* (John Sturges) (as Charles Keith)
1970   *I Walk the Line* (Frankenheimer) (as Sheriff Henry Tawes)
1971   *Shootout* (Hathaway) (as Clay Lomax)
1973   *Billy Two Hats* (Kotcheff) (as Deans)
1978   *The Boys from Brazil* (Schaffner) (as Dr. Josef Mengele)
1981   *The Sea Wolves* (McLaglen) (as Col. Lewis Pugh)
1983   *The Scarlet and the Black* (London—for TV) (as Monsignor Hugh O'Flaherty)
1986   *Directed by William Wyler* (Slesin—doc) (as himself)

Gregory Peck in *Gentleman's Agreement*

1987	*Amazing Grace and Chuck* (*Silent Voice*) (Newell) (as President)
1989	*Old Gringo* (Puenzo) (as Ambrose Bierce)
1991	*Other People's Money* (Jewison) (as Andrew Jorgenson); *Cape Fear* (Scorsese) (as Lee Heller)
1993	*The Portrait* (Arthur Penn—for TV) (as Gardner Church, + exec pr)
1995	*Sinatra: 80 Years My Way* (doc) (as himself)

Films as Producer:

1958	*The Big Country* (Wyler) (+ ro as James McKay)
1972	*The Trial of the Catonsville Nine* (Davidson)
1974	*The Dove* (Jarrott)
1976	*The Omen* (Richard Donner) (+ ro as Robert Thorn)
1977	*MacArthur* (Sargent) (+ title role)

Publications

By PECK: book—

An Actor's Life, 1978.

By PECK: articles—

"Le Plus Beau Jour de notre vie," interview with Guy Braucourt, in *Ecran* (Paris), July-August 1972.

"Gregory Peck on *The Trial of the Catonsville Nine*," interview with G. Woodside, in *Take One* (Montreal), December 1972.

"Gregory Peck: He's the Man," interview with Ron Haver, in *American Film* (New York), March 1989.

On PECK: books—

Thomas, Tony, *Gregory Peck*, New York, 1977.
Freedland, Michael, *Gregory Peck: A Biography*, New York, 1980.
Griggs, John, *The Films of Gregory Peck*, Secaucus, New Jersey, 1984.
Molyneaux, Gerard, *Gregory Peck: A Bio-Bibliography*, Westport, Connecticut, 1995.

On PECK: articles—

Stein, J., "Gregory Peck," in *Films in Review* (New York), March 1967.
Films Illustrated (London), October 1980.

Haskell, Molly, "Gregory Peck," in *The Movie Star*, edited by Elisabeth Weis, New York, 1981.

Buckley, Michael, "Gregory Peck," in *Films in Review* (New York), April and May 1984.

Clark, John, filmography in *Premiere* (New York), October 1989.

Current Biography 1992, New York, 1992.

Murphy, Kathleen, "The World Is in His Arms," in *Film Comment* (New York), March-April 1992.

Denerstein, Robert, "A Class Act," in *Rocky Mountain News* (Denver), 18 September 1995.

*   *   *

When Gregory Peck was designated an enemy of the conservative Nixon establishment, it was as much a recognition of his role within the social symbolism of Hollywood films, as a reaction to his personal involvement with liberal causes. If James Stewart, in his work for Frank Capra, nostalgically embodies the populist image of the small-town good citizen, Peck creates the figure of the decent and fair-minded reformer or the fundamentally good man who rises to the moral demands of the occasion. Only rarely have other qualities of Peck's persona been explored, particularly the resentment and anger which his intensity suggests. It is in these uncharacteristic roles that he has done some of his most interesting as well as some of his worst acting.

After some experience with New York City's Neighborhood Playhouse, Peck moved to Hollywood where, classified as 4-F, he worked steadily during the war. In his first role, as an Eastern front guerilla in Jacques Tourneur's *Days of Glory*, he demonstrated the requisite qualities of the versatile leading man. By the end of the 1940s Peck had established himself as both a commercial and critical success. He received Oscar nominations for *Gentleman's Agreement*—a perfect show-case for his intensity and aroused righteousness, *The Yearling*, and *The Keys of the Kingdom*. The acclaim however, was more for the likable persona Peck had created than for any demonstration of acting virtuosity.

In the 1950s and 1960s he played many similar roles, the apotheosis of his reformer character coming in *To Kill a Mockingbird*, a film in which Peck's humble and antiracist small-town lawyer is a successful mix of populist goodwill and political commitment. Less impressive versions of the same conscience-stricken character are to be found in *Twelve O'Clock High*, *Captain Horatio Hornblower*, and *Pork Chop Hill*.

Those roles that explore the dark side of his personality indicate both his virtues and limitations as an actor. In the Freudian Western *Duel in the Sun* he demonstrated early in his career that he could successfully evoke both sexual obsession and sociopathy. Performances in *The Gunfighter*, *The Man in the Gray Flannel Suit*, *The Paradine Case*, and *The Snows of Kilimanjaro* exhibited a very human frailty that was only glimpsed in his more optimistic roles. Peck's failure to portray adequately the complexities of a compulsive figure in such films as *Moby Dick*, *MacArthur*, and *The Boys from Brazil* indicates the limitations of his skill as an actor.

Peck, like many of the characters he played, has a social conscience. He has been involved in charitable, political, and film industry causes. In 1965, he became a member of the National Council on the Arts, then he was elected chairman of the American Cancer Society the following year. From 1967 to 1969, he was on the Board of Trustees of the American Film Institute. He served as president of the Academy of Motion Picture Arts & Sciences. Peck also received the Medal of Freedom and the Academy's Jean Hersholt Humanitarian Award.

—R. Barton Palmer, updated by Linda J. Stewart

PENN, Sean

Nationality: American. **Born:** Burbank, California, 17 August 1960; son of the actor and television director Leo Penn and the actress Eileen Ryan; brother of the actor Christopher Penn. **Family:** Married 1) the singer-actress Madonna, 1985 (divorced 1989); 2) the actress Robin Wright, 1996, two children: Dylan and Hopper. **Education:** Attended Santa Monica High School. **Career:** In high school directed and acted in Super-8 movies; two years as backstage technician and assistant to actor/director Pat Hingle with the Los Angeles Group Repertory theater; directed play *Terrible Jim Fitch*, acted in *Earthworms* and *The Girl on the Via Flaminia*; studied acting with Peggy Feury; 1979—guest appearances on TV series *Barnaby Jones*; made Broadway debut in *Heartland*, which had a brief run but led to his movie debut in *Taps*; returned to Broadway in *Slab Boys*; 1982—breakthrough performance in *Fast Times at Ridgemont High*. **Agent:** c/o Brian Gersh, William Morris Agency, 151 El Camino Drive, Beverly Hills, CA 90212, U.S.A.

Films as Actor:

1979   *The Concrete Cowboys* (Burt Kennedy—for TV)
1981   *Hellinger's Law* (Leo Penn—for TV); *The Killing of Randy Webster* (Wanamaker—for TV); *Taps* (Harold Becker) (as Alex Dwyer)
1982   *Fast Times at Ridgemont High* (Heckerling) (as Jeff Spicoli)
1983   *Bad Boys* (Rosenthal) (as Mick O'Brien); *Summerspell* (Shanklin) (as Buddy)
1984   *Crackers* (Malle) (as Dillard); *Racing with the Moon* (Richard Benjamin) (as Henry "Hopper" Nash)
1985   *The Falcon and the Snowman* (Schlesinger) (as Andrew Daulton Lee)
1986   *At Close Range* (Foley) (as Bradford Whitewood Jr.); *Shanghai Surprise* (Goddard) (as Glendon Wasey)
1987   *Dear America: Letters Home from Vietnam* (Couturie—doc) (as voice only)
1988   *Colors* (Dennis Hopper) (as Danny McGavin); *Judgment in Berlin* (Leo Penn) (as Gunther X); *Cool Blue* (Mullin and Shepard) (as Phil the plumber, uncredited)
1989   *Casualties of War* (De Palma) (as Sergeant Meserve); *We're No Angels* (Neil Jordan) (as Jimmy)
1990   *State of Grace* (Joanou) (as Terry Noonan)
1991   *Schneeweissrosenrot* (*SnowwhiteRosered*) (Langhans and Ritter)
1993   *Carlito's Way* (De Palma) (as David Kleinfeld); *The Last Party* (Mark Benjamin and Marc Levin—doc) (as himself)
1995   *Dead Man Walking* (Tim Robbins) (as Matthew Poncelet)

Films as Writer and Director:

1991   *The Indian Runner*
1995   *The Crossing Guard*

Publications

By PENN: articles—

"... But Not Too Close," interview with Martha Frankel, in *American Film* (Los Angeles), August 1991.

Interview with Julian Schnabel and Dennis Hopper, in *Interview* (New York), September 1991.

Sean Penn in *At Close Range*

"Sean Penn at Close Range," interview with Gavin Smith, in *Film Comment* (New York), September 1991.

"Sean Penn," interview with Graham Fuller, in *Interview* (New York), October 1995.

On PENN: articles—

Haller, Scot, "Who Is Sean Penn—and Why Doesn't He Want Anyone to Find Out?," in *People* (New York), 11 February 1985.
Wolcott, James, "Tough Act," in *Vanity Fair* (New York), March 1986.
Carter, Graydon, "Sean Penn Pulls No Punches," in *Vogue*, May 1988.
Connelly, Christopher, "Sean Penn Bites Back," in *Premiere* (New York), October 1991.
Current Biography 1993, New York, 1993.
Weinraub, Bernard, "Ex-Bad Boy as Sensitive Director," in *New York Times*, 12 November 1995.

*   *   *

Sean Penn stood out in his first screen appearance as the calm eye of the melodramatic *Taps*. But his unself-conscious ease at centering his characters turned out to be only one of his distinctive modes. As appealingly unforced as he was in *Taps, Bad Boys,* and *Racing with the Moon,* his second performance (the one that made him popular), as the stoned surfer Spicoli in the teen comedy *Fast Times at Ridgemont High,* showed he also had the wit and nerve to play a character in a highly stylized manner. At the time it was odd to read that he took this performance so seriously that he insisted on staying in character off the set, because one of the great pleasures of watching him as Spicoli is how he uses his considerable technical skill in a comic vein. But whatever you thought of his pronouncements on his art, Penn, both as naturalist and cartoonist, was clearly a prodigy.

Penn's self-conscious style got the better of him in his grotesquely mannered performance as Daulton Lee in *The Falcon and the Snowman*. His debts to Dustin Hoffman (*Midnight Cowboy*) and Robert De Niro (*The King of Comedy*) stick out because the character has no center; all that registers is Penn's effort as an actor. This turn showed that Penn could think his way into a performance that reveals no experience and gives no pleasure. But after his interlude as Madonna's consort, brawling in the glare of tabloid flashbulbs, Penn gave a towering performance in Brian De Palma's *Casualties of War* as Sergeant Meserve, the American soldier in Vietnam who avenges the death of a buddy on a forlorn Vietnamese girl he and his patrol kidnap from her village. Meserve's outlines are as bold as Daulton Lee's in *Falcon*, but Penn fills them in with more saturated tones of confusion and rage. Penn's Meserve is much more than a melodramatic foil to Michael J. Fox's naturalistic Eriksson. Penn is the elemental man-at-war, with only the turn of circumstances separating courage from sadism. Penn is able to frighten you by bringing into his body, face, and voice the full potential range of organized male aggression, both the aggression that protects and the aggression that violates. Penn was the first of the actors of his generation to show the influence of De Niro, making him in effect Brando's oldest grandson. As Meserve he shot way past De Niro in his current black hole phase and seemed truly worthy of Brando's corona.

Penn now claims that he does not like acting and accepts roles only to pay bills or in order to work with certain directors on exceptional scripts. For instance, he was tempted back to work with Brian De Palma and Al Pacino on *Carlito's Way* in which he gives an ingenious performance as a sleazy lawyer. His Kleinfeld is not as great a character as Meserve, but it allows him to bring a rancid smack to his comic style. Kleinfeld is so amoral that he is funny. This is how Scorsese used Joe Pesci, but in a more heavy-handed way, both in terms of script and acting. Kleinfeld is untrustworthy the way a teenager is; he snickers at his fibs and stunts as if unaware that the mayhem he is setting in

motion could kill him. Again Penn uses the caricatural style he used for Daulton Lee, but that style is given variety and lift by De Palma's super-sophisticated sense of the comedy of disaster. If Penn keeps his word and gives up acting it will be an enormous loss to American moviegoers, who watch him with something like gratitude for the lean confidence of his talent as he slides into a difficult, confused character such as the weaselly condemned killer Matthew Poncelet in *Dead Man Walking*. The two pictures he has directed, *The Indian Runner* and *The Crossing Guard*, both steeped in lugubrious visuals and emotionally thin-textured despite a lot of acting-workshop searching for effect, are scanty compensation for the performances he has not given. But it is hard to believe that any actor as inventive as Penn, equally good when serious and funny, will abandon what he does so well.

—Alan Dale

PERKINS, Anthony

Nationality: American. **Born:** New York City, 4 April 1932. **Education:** Attended Browne and Nichols School, Cambridge, Massachusetts; Rollins College, Winter Park, Florida; Columbia University, New York. **Family:** Married Berinthia (Berry) Berenson, 1973, children: Osgood, Elvis. **Career:** 1946—professional stage debut in Brattleboro theater, Vermont; other summer stock and television work; 1953—film debut in *The Actress*; 1954—Broadway debut in *Tea and Sympathy*; later stage roles include *Look Homeward, Angel*, 1957, the musical *Green-Willow*, 1960, *Equus*, 1977, and *Romantic Comedy*, 1979; 1983—in TV mini-series *For the Term of His Natural Life*; 1987—in TV mini-series *Napoleon and Josephine: A Love Story*. **Awards:** Best Actor, Cannes Festival, for *Goodbye Again*, 1961. **Died:** 12 September 1992.

Films as Actor:

1953   *The Actress* (Cukor) (as Fred Whitmarsh)
1956   *Friendly Persuasion* (Wyler) (as Josh Birdwell)
1957   *Fear Strikes Out* (Mulligan) (as Jimmy Piersall); *The Lonely Man* (Levin) (as Riley Wade); *The Tin Star* (Anthony Mann) (as Sheriff Ben Owens)
1958   *Desire under the Elms* (Delbert Mann) (as Eben Cabot); *Barrage contre le Pacifique* (*This Angry Age; The Sea Wall*) (Clément) (as Joseph Dufresne); *The Matchmaker* (Anthony) (as Cornelius)
1959   *Green Mansions* (Ferrer) (as Abel); *On the Beach* (Kramer) (as Peter Holmes)
1960   *Tall Story* (Logan) (as Ray Blent); *Psycho* (Hitchcock) (as Norman Bates)
1961   *Goodbye Again* (*Aimez-vous Brahms?*) (Litvak) (as Philip Van Der Besh); *Phaedra* (Dassin) (as Alexis)
1962   *Le Procès* (*The Trial*) (Welles) (as Josef K.); *Five Miles to Midnight* (Litvak) (as Robert Macklin)
1963   *La Glaive et la balance* (*Two Are Guilty*) (Cayatte) (as Johnny)
1964   *Une Ravissante Idiote* (*A Ravishing Idiot*) (Molinaro) (as Harry Compton/Nicholas Maukouline)
1965   *The Fool Killer* (González) (as Milo Bogardus)
1966   *Paris brûle-t-il?* (*Is Paris Burning?*) (Clément) (as Sgt. Warren)
1967   *Le Scandale* (*The Champagne Murders*) (Chabrol) (as Christopher Balling)
1968   *Pretty Poison* (Black) (as Dennis Pitt)

Anthony Perkins

1970   *How Awful about Allan* (Harrington—for TV); *WUSA* (Rosenburg) (as Rainey); *Catch-22* (Mike Nichols) (as Chaplain Tappman)

1971   *Quelqu'un derrière la porte* (*Someone behind the Door*; *Two Minds for Murder*) (Gessner) (as Laurence Jeffries)

1972   *The Life and Times of Judge Roy Bean* (Huston); *Play It as It Lays* (Perry) (as B. Z.); *La Décade prodigieuse* (*Ten Days' Wonder*) (Chabrol) (as Charles Van Horn)

1974   *Lovin' Molly* (Lumet) (as Gid); *Murder on the Orient Express* (Lumet) (as Hector McQueen)

1975   *Mahogany* (Gordy) (as Sean)

1978   *First, You Cry* (Schaefer—for TV); *Remember My Name* (Rudolph) (as Neil Curry); *Les Misérables* (Glenn Jordan—for TV) (as Inspector Javert)

1979   *Winter Kills* (Richert); *The Black Hole* (Gary Nelson) (as Dr. Alex Durant); *The Horror Show* (Schickel)

1980   *Double Negative* (Bloomfield) (as Lawrence Miles); *Twee frouwen* (*Twice a Woman*) (Sluizer) (as Alfred); *ffolkes* (*North Sea Hijack*; *Assault Force*) (McLaglen) (as Kramer)

1983   *Psycho II* (Franklin) (as Norman Bates); *Sins of Dorian Gray* (Maylam—for TV)

1984   *Crimes of Passion* (*China Blue*) (Russell) (as the Rev. Peter Shayne); *Glory Boys* (Ferguson—for TV) (as Jimmy)

1988   *Destroyer* (Kirk) (as Robert Edwards)

1989   *Edge of Sanity* (*Dr. Jekyll and Mr. Hyde*) (Kikoine) (as Dr. Henry Jekyll/Jack Hyde)

1990   *Psycho IV: The Beginning* (Garris—for TV) (as Norman Bates); *I'm Dangerous Tonight* (Tobe Hooper—for TV) (as Buchanan); *Daughter of Darkness* (Stuart Gordon—for TV)

1991   *Los Gusanos no Llevan Bufanda* (*The Naked Target*) (Elorrieta) (as mechanical man); *Der Mann nebenan* (*A Demon in My View*) (Haffter) (as Arthur Johnson)

1992   *In the Deep Woods* (Correll—for TV) (as Paul)

Other Films:

1973   *The Last of Sheila* (Ross) (co-sc)
1986   *Psycho III* (d, ro as Norman Bates)
1988   *Lucky Stiff* (d)

Publications

By PERKINS: articles—

"Anthony Perkins," interview in *Cinema* (Beverly Hills), March-April 1965.

"Pinning Down the Quicksilver," interview with Robin Bean, in *Films and Filming* (London), July 1965.

"What's Tony Perkins Really Really Like?," interview with B. Berenson, in *Inter/View* (New York), November 1972.

"Berry and Tony: A Love Story," in *Interview* (New York), January 1974.

Interview in *L'Ecran Fantastique*, July-August 1983.

Interview with François Guerif, in *Revue du Cinéma* (Paris), May 1989.

"Live Bates," interview with Mim Udovitch, in *Interview* (New York), November 1990.

On PERKINS: books—

Palmer, Laura Kay, *Osgood and Anthony Perkins*, Jefferson, North Carolina, 1991.

Winekoff, Charles, *Split Image*, New York, 1996.

On PERKINS: articles—

Current Biography 1960, New York, 1960.

Gow, Gordon, "Closer to Life," in *Films and Filming* (London), April 1975.

Tanner, L., "Anthony Perkins," in *Films in Review* (New York), August/September 1986.

Obituary in *Variety* (New York), 21 September 1992.

Thomson, David, obituary in *Film Comment* (New York), November/December 1992.

Rose, Frank, "The Prodigal Son," in *Premiere* (New York), October 1993.

*   *   *

Looking back from *Crimes of Passion* through *Psycho* to Anthony Perkins's early career, it comes as something of a shock to realize that Hollywood initially fashioned his persona to signify healthy boy-next-door normality. His first two roles immediately established the opposing comic and serious sides of his image. He portrayed, on the one hand, an enthusiastic but callow and unimaginative suitor in *The Actress*, and, on the other hand, an earnest and sensitive Quaker boy reluctantly learning what it means to kill in *Friendly Persuasion*. Perkins was instantly perceived as immensely attractive, and the nature of the attractiveness posed a problem for a cinema dedicated overall to the preservation and reinforcement of clear-cut gender identity. Perkins's charm was centered on an abundance of qualities traditionally associated with femininity—sensitivity, vulnerability, diffidence, and a physical and emotional delicacy and frailty—a combination that might tend to arouse sexual feelings not only in women, but disturbingly and dangerously, in men.

Given a potential new star then, Hollywood was somewhat at a loss as to what he might star *in*. During the next few years several solutions were attempted: eccentric roles in eccentric comedy (*The Matchmaker*, *Tall Story*); a boy learning to become a man under the guidance of an older role model (*The Tin Star*); and roles in which vulnerability could be justified by an unbearable situation (*On the Beach*). But the pre-*Psycho* film that most closely suggests the solution that was finally adopted was *Fear Strikes Out*. Perkins's feminine characteristics could be at once contained and explained if they were associated with neurotic disorder. The Norman Bates of *Psycho*, clearly Perkins's greatest performance, is also the definitive one in which the solution is perfected, and Perkins was never able to live it down. Norman gives all those attractive Perkins qualities their most complete embodiment and expression and is then revealed as hopelessly insane. There have been many attempts to define the fascination of Hitchcock's extraordinary film, but most of them miss its core, the very basis of its power to disturb: the extremely complex play with gender and the transgression of traditional gender boundaries.

After *Psycho*, Perkins's career became problematic, although he never gave a phoned-in performance and he reaffirmed his acting credentials by replacing Anthony Hopkins in Broadway's *Equus*. After his misguided flight to Europe to find opportunities for "serious" acting he felt Hollywood had denied him, there were halfhearted attempts to reestablish him as a romantic lead. Instead Perkins eventually came to terms with the stigma of being everybody's favorite mama's boy although it is a bit disheartening to witness the deterioration of his youthful persona into a breeding ground for psychoses from *Psycho* onward. Within the limits imposed by typecasting, Perkins triumphed especially in *Pretty Poison*, as a garden variety mental case outclassed by a diabolically twisted high school honor student acted by Tuesday Weld in a parody of her Thalia Meninger role from television's *Dobie Gillis*. As the mask of fresh-faced good looks faded, Perkins seemed positively ferretlike, his eyes burning with secrets he had been hiding from movie audiences. If he is disproportionately jittery in the all-star company of *Murder on the Orient Express*, and so transparently dysfunctional in *Mahogany* and *Play It as It Lays* as to seem certifiable, he is haunting as the target of revenge in *Remember My Name* and eerily vindictive as unyielding Inspector Javert in a splendid television adaptation of *Les Misérables*.

After meshing with the blackly comic ironies of *Winter Kills* and lampooning his image as all-purpose nutcase in Ken Russell's florid *Crimes of Passion*, Perkins made peace with the person responsible for his stifled stardom: Norman Bates. Resurrecting that character's tragic flaws for campy effect in *Psycho II*, Perkins gives a moving performance as if finally reconciled with the cinema's most popular transvestite slasher. Directing himself in *Psycho III* brought the reward of teaming with another idiosyncratic presence, Diana Scarwid, but *Psycho IV* explained the unexplainable in overly explicit Freudian terms. The horror flicks that followed were cheapie exercises that incorporated Perkins shouting *boo!* as if his mere presence were so scary, decent scripts were unnecessary. An extremely gifted actor who inadvertently created his own Frankenstein monster, Perkins could point with pride to his singularly brilliant creation, even if an argument could be advanced that the saddest casualty of Norman Bates's murder spree was Perkins's career.

—Robin Wood, updated by Robert Pardi

PESCI, Joe

Nationality: American. **Born:** Newark, New Jersey, 9 February 1943. **Family:** Married and divorced three times; one daughter, Tiffany, from first marriage. **Career:** 1953—Began performing on stage as a child and became a regular on the TV variety show *Startime Kids*; 1961—made screen debut as a back-up guitarist with Joey Dee and The Starlighters in *Hey, Let's Twist*; 1960s—worked as lounge singer and stand-up comedian under the names "Jonathan Marcus," "Joey Prima," and "Joey Cannon," and recorded record album under the name "Joe Ritchie"; early 1970s—teamed with Frank Vincent in a nightclub act; had initial screen acting role in *Death Collector*, 1975; 1980—earned acclaim for first important role in *Raging Bull*; 1985—starred in short-lived TV sitcom, *Half Nelson*; 1988—appeared as "Mr. Big" in the Michael Jackson music video *Moonwalker*. **Awards:** British Academy Award, Best Newcomer to Film, New York Film Critics Circle Award, Best Supporting Actor, American Society of Film Critics Award, Best Supporting Actor, for *Raging Bull*, 1980; Academy Award, Best Supporting Actor, for *GoodFellas*, 1990. **Agent:** Contemporary Artists Agency, 9830 Wilshire Boulevard, Beverly Hills, CA 90212-1825, U.S.A.

Films as Actor:

1961   *Hey, Let's Twist* (Garrison) (extra)
1975   *Death Collector* (*Family Enforcer*) (De Vito) (billed as Joseph Pesci)
1980   *Raging Bull* (Scorsese) (as Joey LaMotta); *Don't Go in the House* (Ellison) (billed as Joey Pesci)
1982   *I'm Dancing as Fast as I Can* (Hofsiss) (as Roger); *Dear Mr. Wonderful* (*Ruby's Dream*) (Lilienthal) (as Ruby Dennis)
1983   *Easy Money* (Signorelli) (as Nicky); *Eureka* (Roeg) (as Mayakofsky)
1984   *Once upon a Time in America* (Leone) (as Frankie Monaldi); *Tutti dentro* (*Put 'Em All in Jail*; *Everybody in Jail*) (Sordi) (as Corrado Emilio Parisi)
1987   *Man on Fire* (Chouraqui) (as David)

1989   *Lethal Weapon 2* (Richard Donner) (as Leo Getz); *Backtrack* (*Catchfire*) (Dennis Hopper—released in U.S. in 1991) (as Leo Carelli)
1990   *GoodFellas* (Scorsese) (as Tommy De Vito); *Betsy's Wedding* (Alda) (as Oscar Henner); *Home Alone* (Columbus) (as Harry)
1991   *The Super* (Daniel) (as Louie Kritski); *JFK* (Oliver Stone) (as David Ferrie)
1992   *My Cousin Vinny* (Lynn) (as Vincent La Guardia Gambino); *The Public Eye* (Franklin) (as Leonard "The Great Bernzini" Bernstein); *Home Alone 2: Lost in New York* (Columbus) (as Harry); *Lethal Weapon 3* (Richard Donner) (as Leo Getz)
1993   *A Bronx Tale* (De Niro) (as Carmine)
1994   *With Honors* (Keshishian) (as Simon Wilder); *Jimmy Hollywood* (Levinson) (as Jimmy Alto)
1995   *Casino* (Scorsese) (as Nicky Santoro)

Publications

By PESCI: articles—

"20 Questions," interview with J. Bain, in *Playboy* (Chicago), December 1991.
"Whap! It's Joltin' Joe Pesci," interview with Dennis Hopper, in *Interview* (New York), November 1992.

On PESCI: articles—

Stern, Ellen, in *New York Times*, 5 December 1980.
"Interview *Dear Mr. Wonderful*: Peter Lilienthal on the Star of His Picture, Joe Pesci," in *Kino* (Berlin), no. 4, 1982.
McDonough, J., "Joe Pesci," in *Film Comment* (New York), November/December 1989.
Hoban, Phoebe, "Raging Joe Pesci," in *New York*, 4 March 1991.
Siedenberg, Robert, "Splashy Movies, Unsung Stars," in *American Film* (Los Angeles), June 1991.
Harrison, N., "Joe Pesci? That Guy Is Some Kind of Character," in *New York Times*, 8 March 1992.
Clark, John, filmography in *Premiere* (New York), October 1992.
Current Biography 1994, New York, 1994.

*   *   *

To date, two roles have defined Joe Pesci's screen career. Both came in films directed by Martin Scorsese, and in each he plays variations of the same character: a pint-sized New Yorker who is hilariously foul-mouthed and invariably in-your-face.

The first is *Raging Bull*, in which he earned celluloid stardom and a Best Supporting Actor Oscar nomination. For years, Pesci had been struggling to establish himself in the entertainment industry as an actor, stand-up comic and singer. Prior to *Raging Bull*, his sole previous screen acting had been in *Death Collector*, a low-budget crime melodrama in which he is billed as "Joseph" Pesci. When Scorsese cast him, he had retired from show business and was managing a restaurant in the Bronx. Pesci plays Joey, the ill-bred brother-manager of boxer Jake LaMotta (Robert De Niro). The latter is an inarticulate, irrationally jealous man, who throughout the course of the story self-destructively alienates himself from his loved ones, including his brother. Pesci proved himself more than up to the task of playing an important role in a high-powered movie which became an instant classic among biopics and boxing dramas. If Scorsese and De Niro won the lion's share of credit for the success of *Raging Bull*, Pesci (along with Cathy Moriarty, cast as LaMotta's wife) earned an entree into the celluloid main arena.

Joe Pesci (right) with Marisa Tomei and Fred Gwynne in *My Cousin Vinny*

Nevertheless, in the decade between *Raging Bull* and *GoodFellas*, his second film with Scorsese, Pesci's screen career floundered. None of his roles during this period was memorable; his best was in the little-seen *Dear Mr. Wonderful*, playing a character not unlike the pre-*Raging Bull* Joe Pesci: Ruby Dennis, a man who has show business aspirations but finds himself operating a bowling alley-nightclub in New Jersey.

Pesci had failed to fulfill the potential he exhibited in *Raging Bull*. But he was back in full force in *GoodFellas*—again with De Niro—and his work here not only thrust him into starring roles but earned him the Best Supporting Actor Oscar. *GoodFellas* is a tough, knowing, based-on-fact gangster epic, depicting the evolution of life in the New York Mafia for a quarter-century beginning in the mid-1950s. The primary character is Ray Liotta's Henry Hill, a young guy "from the neighborhood" who yearns to be a wiseguy, with De Niro playing James Conway, Hill's mentor. Pesci's role is strictly a supporting one, on hand to inject the film with a vivid dose of local color. He offers a graphic, scene-stealing performance as Tommy De Vito, a quick-tempered hoodlum. Tommy is no by-the-numbers mob executioner. He is a psychopath who savors being a gangster, and is obsessed with his machismo; he sticks a switchblade in the gut of a rival with the same emotion he would invest in sticking a carving knife in a Thanksgiving turkey. *GoodFellas* differs from *Raging Bull* in that Pesci is not overshadowed by De Niro, perhaps because the latter's role is neither the showiest nor the most important in the film.

Pesci was to prove equally adept at playing urban types who are comical rather than sinister. This certainly is the case in the *Home Alone* films, in which he is cast as Harry, one of a pair of street slime who tangle in cartoon-violent fashion with a young, resourceful boy (Macauley Culkin); and in *Lethal Weapon 2* and *Lethal Weapon 3*, in which he plays fast-talking money launderer Leo Getz. Here, according to a *Variety* critic, Pesci is allowed to showcase "his unique ability to go absolutely ballistic in rat-a-tat fashion." The actor gave what was perhaps his best post-*GoodFellas* performance in *My Cousin Vinny*, cast in a role he was born to play: Brooklyn "lawyer" Vincent La Guardia Gambino, who heads way out of his element—to the Deep South—to defend his cousin and a friend who have been falsely accused of murder. If you grew up in an Italian-American neighborhood in Brooklyn you knew guys like Gambino, a hopelessly uncouth but nonetheless persistent and thoroughly likable character who wears his accent on his sleeve.

Pesci also brought a creepy presence to *JFK*, cast as alleged Kennedy assassination conspirator David Ferrie, and had one of his most sympathetic roles in *The Public Eye*, playing a Weegee-like 1940s tabloid newspaper photographer. In *Casino*, his third film with Scorsese, he virtually repeats his *GoodFellas* characterization, playing Nicky Santoro, another ballsy mobster who is as short-fused as he is short in stature. Nicky's turf is Las Vegas, rather than New York. He is sent there by the "bosses" back east, to be the muscle behind Robert De Niro's casino manager, and he eventually builds himself into the town's most powerful enforcer. Nicky relishes being a gangster. No matter how big a guy is, Nicky will fearlessly take him on and beat him up.

Pesci's acting is letter-perfect, but one cannot escape the fact that Nicky Santoro is a virtual clone of Tommy De Vito.

Playing Tommy De Vito may have earned Pesci star stature, but more often than not his starring films—*The Super* (playing a New York City slumlord), *With Honors* (a homeless man), and *Jimmy Hollywood* (a Tinseltown wannabe)—have been undistinguished. Will he ever find a third (or fourth, or fifth) great role to rival the ones he played in *Raging Bull* and *GoodFellas*?

—Rob Edelman

PFEIFFER, Michelle

Nationality: American. **Born:** Santa Ana, California, 29 April 1957 (some sources say 1959); sister of the actress Dedee Pfeiffer. **Education:** Attended Fountain Valley High School. **Family:** Married 1) the actor Peter Horton, 1982 (divorced 1987); adopted daughter, Claudia Rose, 1993); 2) David E. Kelley, 1993, one child. **Career:** Worked as supermarket cashier; 1977—won Miss Orange County Beauty Pageant; 1979—TV debut in *Delta House* series; 1980—in TV series *B.A.D. Cats*; film debut in *The Hollywood Knights*; 1989—stage debut in *Twelfth Night*. **Awards:** Best Actress Awards, Los Angeles Film Critics, and New York Film Critics, for *The Fabulous Baker Boys*, 1989. **Agent:** Ed Limato, William Morris Agency, 151 El Camino Drive, Beverly Hills, CA 90212, U.S.A.

Films as Actress:

1979 *The Solitary Man* (Moxey—for TV)
1980 *The Hollywood Knights* (Mutrux) (as Suzi Q); *Falling in Love Again* (Paul) (as Sue Wellington)
1981 *Charlie Chan and the Curse of the Dragon Queen* (Clive Donner) (as Cordelia Farrington); *Splendor in the Grass* (Sarafian—for TV); *The Children Nobody Wanted* (Richard Michaels—for TV); *Callie & Son* (Hussein—for TV)
1982 *Grease II* (Birch) (as Stephanie Zinone)
1983 *Scarface* (De Palma) (as Elvira)
1985 *Into the Night* (Landis) (as Diana); *Ladyhawke* (Richard Donner) (as Isabeau)
1986 *Sweet Liberty* (Alda) (as Faith Healy)
1987 *Amazon Women on the Moon* (Dante) (as Brenda); *The Witches of Eastwick* (Miller) (as Sukie Ridgemont)
1988 *Married to the Mob* (Jonathan Demme) (as Angela De Marco); *Tequila Sunrise* (Towne) (as Jo Ann Vallenari); *Dangerous Liaisons* (Frears) (as Madame de Tourvel)
1989 *The Fabulous Baker Boys* (Kloves) (as Susie Diamond)
1990 *The Russia House* (Schepisi) (as Katya)
1991 *Frankie and Johnny* (Garry Marshall) (as Frankie)
1992 *Love Field* (Kaplan) (as Lurene Hallett); *Batman Returns* (Burton) (as Catwoman/Selina Kyle)
1993 *The Age of Innocence* (Scorsese) (as Countess Ellen Olenska)
1994 *Wolf* (Nichols) (as Laura Alden)
1995 *Dangerous Minds* (John N. Smith) (as LouAnne Johnson)
1996 *Up Close and Personal* (Avnet); *To Gillian on Her 37th Birthday*

Publications

By PFEIFFER: articles—

Interview, in *Cinéma* (Paris), September 1982.
Interview, in *Photoplay* (London), July 1985.

Interviews, in *Inter/View* (New York), March 1986, August 1988, and February 1989.
Interview, in *Vanity Fair* (New York), February 1989.
"Michelle Pfeiffer as Work in Progress," interview with Hal Hinson, in *Esquire* (New York), December 1990 .
Interview with Graham Fuller, in *Interview* (New York), July 1994.
"Michelle Pfeiffer, Sensuous to Sensible," interview with Tim Egan, in *New York Times*, 6 August 1995 .

On PFEIFFER: books—

Thompson, Douglas, *Pfeiffer: Beyond the Age of Innocence*, London, 1993.
Crowther, Bruce, *Michelle Pfeiffer: A Biography*, London, 1994.

On PFEIFFER: articles—

Thomson, D., "Class of 1985," in *Film Comment* (New York), March/April 1985.
McGillivray, David, "Michelle Pfeiffer," in *Films and Filming* (London), November 1985.
Current Biography 1990, New York, 1990.
Premiere (New York), March 1990.
Winnert, Derek, "The Fabulous Pfeiffer Girl," in *Radio Times* (London), 28 July 1990.
Seidenberg, Robert, "The Fabulous Pfeiffer Girl," in *American Film* (Washington, D.C.), January 1991.
Hirshey, Gerri, "The Bat's Meow: Catwoman Michelle Pfeiffer," in *Rolling Stone* (New York), 3 September 1992.
Kaplan, James, and Ty Burr, "Blond Ambivalence," in *Entertainment Weekly*, 29 January 1993.

*   *   *

Michelle Pfeiffer first entered moviegoers' awareness as a perfect *objet*—Al Pacino's affectless moll in *Scarface*, and the cursed damsel in *Ladyhawke*. Then, in her supporting roles in Alan Alda's *Sweet Liberty* as an actress who flickers startlingly in and out of character, and as an earth-mother journalist in *The Witches of Eastwick*, holding her own with those seasoned stars Cher, Susan Sarandon, and Jack Nicholson, it became clear that if Pfeiffer lacks theatrical skills she has such a fluid sense of character that it serves as technique.

In 1988 she began playing leads, in Jonathan Demme's crime burlesque *Married to the Mob* in which she is the liquid center of a nutty confection, and in *Tequila Sunrise* in which Mel Gibson and Kurt Russell, as pals on opposite sides of the law, vie for her simultaneously practical and romantic restaurateur. Those movies might also have worked with more conventional actresses, but Pfeiffer gives them something extra—unaffected warmth and surprising texture. She can use her big, clear eyes to express open longing for connection without going soft, because she is only half unearthly vision. The other half is a chick who says she can take care of herself (even if that means living with disappointment).

As Madame de Tourvel, the victim whose feverish destruction transforms and destroys her seducer in Stephen Frears's *Dangerous Liaisons*, Pfeiffer gained critical acceptance. She just *becomes* a proper but susceptible ancien régime wife, in the same unforced manner that makes the movie so strikingly timeless a period piece. She and Glenn Close—a thespian, by God—work in contrasting modes, but Pfeiffer does not suffer by comparison. In *Frankie and Johnny*, an engaging, nearly epic, sitcom about waitresses and a short-order cook, Pfeiffer and Kate Nelligan, the intuitive screen actress and the bravura stage star, *complement* each other's styles, like Garbo and Ina Claire in *Ninotchka*, but in a crummy setting. As a formerly battered woman afraid of involvement, Pfeiffer acts hopeless without killing the

Michelle Pfeiffer in *Dangerous Liaisons*

movie's last-resort romanticism. She is leery of Pacino's overriding optimism, but burns under the surface; her defensiveness glows.

Pfeiffer finally became a star in *The Fabulous Baker Boys* playing a singer added to two brothers' struggling lounge act. As the toughened, badly used singer, Pfeiffer flirts with Jeff Bridges's piano player—and the audience falls. Their affair, carried out not only offstage but on, all over the piano in fact, has a glamorous heat that most people thought was extinguished by the 1950s. But Pfeiffer never lets her beauty (or her singing talent) carry her. She always develops character in her own way; she is as uncorrupt as any big screen beauty ever.

Even her double performance as Selina Kyle and Catwoman in *Batman Returns* has authenticity. She is perfectly befuddled as the secretary who cringes at how servile she sounds but cannot help herself; as Catwoman she takes fantastic, porny compensation for Selina's subservience. Pfeiffer's seemingly effortless acting enables her to flow easily between comedy and drama; as Catwoman she springs to the wild extremes of bad girl comedy but always maintains a sense of the frumpy, intimidated secretary's conflicts.

Recently Pfeiffer has played the kind of blandly virtuous roles that win Oscar nominations. To her credit, she plays them as honestly as possible. In *Love Field* she at least sees the comedy in her Jackie Kennedy-obsessed housewife's racial awkwardness, but the basic story is about her reeducation. And in *Dangerous Minds*, Pfeiffer shows the performance sweat of a high school teacher reaching out to time-serving ghetto kids, so that you do not entirely object to the focus on *her* feelings, *her* triumph. Though disguised by "street" attitudes, in-

ner-city tragedies, and rap music, it is a very princessy movie which ends with the kids begging the lovely blond lady not to leave. Pfeiffer's real triumph is that you do not think of her as a princess, but as a resourceful teacher.

Yes, Pfeiffer is too careful in Scorsese's *Age of Innocence*, and she should know better than to sign up for something as dopey as *Wolf*, but she has never given a lazy performance. As an intuitive actress, her means are so simple that she has the double talent of seeming always in character and always herself, without the concept of "herself" calling up any mannerisms. She is inaccessibly beautiful but not actressy (she chews gum very well). She would be equally probable as a goddess or just some adventurous girl you went to high school with.

—Alan Dale

PHILIPE, Gérard

Nationality: French. **Born:** Cannes, 4 December 1922. **Education:** Attended Collège Stanislas; Institution Montaigne, Vence; School of Law, Nice; studied acting with Jean Wall. **Career:** Stage debut in *Une Grande Fille toute simple*, Nice; 1944—film debut in *La Boîte aux rêves*; 1945—in Camus's play *Caligula* in Paris; followed by a series of successful stage roles in *Le Cid*, 1951, *Lorenzaccio*, 1952, *Richard II*,

1953, and *On ne badine pas avec l'amour*, 1959; 1956—co-director of the film *Les Aventures de Till L'Espiègle*. **Awards:** French Etoile de Cristal for Best Actor, for *Monsieur Ripois*, 1955. **Died:** 25 November 1959.

Films as Actor:

1944	*La Boîte aux rêves* (Yves Allégret); *Les Petites du Quai aux Fleurs* (Marc Allégret)
1945	*Schéma d'une identification* (Resnais—short)
1946	*Le Pays sans étoiles* (Lacombe) (as Simon Frédéric); *L'Idiot* (Lampin) (as Prince Mychkin)
1947	*Le Diable au corps* (*Devil in the Flesh*) (Autant-Lara) (as François Jaubert)
1948	*La Chartreuse de Parme* (Christian-Jaque) (as Fabrice Del Dongo)
1949	*Une si jolie petite plage* (Yves Allégret) (as Pierre); *Tous les chemins mènent à Rome* (Boyer) (as M. Pégase)
1950	*La Beauté du Diable* (Clair) (as Henri, Faust, and Mephisto); *La Ronde* (Ophüls) (as Count); *Souvenirs perdus* (Christian-Jaque); *Saint-Louis ou l'ange de la paix* (Darène—short) (as narrator); *Avec André Gide* (Marc Allégret—doc) (as narrator); *Forêt sacrée* (Gaisseau—doc) (as narrator)
1951	*Juliette ou la clef des songes* (Carné) (as Michel); *Avignon, bastion de la provence* (Guenet—short)
1952	*Fanfan-la-tulipe* (Christian-Jaque) (title role); *Les Sept Péchés capitaux* (Lancombe); *Les Belles de nuit* (Clair) (as Claude)
1953	*Les Orgueilleux* (Yves Allégret) (as Georges)
1954	*Si Versailles m'était conté* (Guitry) (as D'Artagnan); *Monsieur Ripois* (Clément) (title role); *Les Amants de la Villa Borghese* (Franciolini); *Le Rouge et le noir* (Autant-Lara) (as Julien Sorel)
1955	*Les Grandes Manoeuvres* (Clair) (as Armand); *Si Paris m'était conté* (Guitry); *La Meilleure part* (Yves Allégret) (as Perrin)
1956	*Le Théâtre national populaire* (Franju—short)
1957	*Montparnasse 19* (Becker) (as Amedeo Modigliani); *Pot-Bouille* (Duvivier) (as Octave Mouret)
1958	*La Vie à deux* (Duhour) (as Désiré); *Le Joueur* (Autant-Lara) (as Alexei de Dostoievsky)
1959	*Les Liaisons dangereuses 1960* (Vadim) (as Valmont)
1960	*La Fièvre monte à El Pao* (Buñuel)

Film as Co-Director:

1956	*Les Aventures de Till L'Espiègle* (+ title role)

Publications

By PHILIPE: articles—

Interviews in *L'Ecran Français* (Paris), 16 December 1947, 12 April 1949, 16 May 1951, and 27 June 1951.
"In the Margin," in *Sequence* (London), Spring 1949.
Les Lettres Françaises (Paris), December 1953, 29 March 1956, and 1 November 1956.
Les Nouvelles Littéraires (Paris), 30 May 1957.

On PHILIPE: books—

Le Bolzer, Guy, and Michel Mardore, *Gérard Philipe*, Lyons, 1960.
Giannoli, Paul, *La Vie inspirée de Gérard Philipe*, Paris, 1960.
Gérard Philipe: souvenirs et témoignages, edited by Anne Philipe and Claude Roy, Paris, 1960, rev. ed. 1977.
Chapelle, Monique, *Gérard Philipe, notre éternelle jeunesse*, Paris, 1965.
Sadoul, Georges, *Gérard Philipe*, Paris, 1967; rev. ed., 1979.
Urbain, Jacques, *Il y a dix ans, Gérard Philipe*, Yverdon, 1969.
Périsset, Maurice, *Gérard Philipe*, Paris, 1975.
Périsset, Maurice, *Gérard Philipe, ou la jeunesse du monde*, Nice, 1979.
Durant, Philippe, *Gérard Philipe*, Paris, 1983.
Cadars, Pierre, *Gérard Philipe*, Paris, 1984.
Nores, Dominique, *Gérard: Qui êtes-vous?*, Lyons, 1988.
Bonal, Gérard, *Gérard Philipe: Biographie*, Paris, 1994.

On PHILIPE: articles—

Billard, Ginette, "Gérard Philipe, the Actor, May End His Career," in *Films and Filming* (London), October 1955.
"Philipe Issue," of *Les Lettres Françaises* (Paris), 3 December 1959.
Leprohon, Pierre, "Gérard Philipe," in *Anthologie du cinéma*, vol.6, Paris, 1971.
Ecran (Paris), December 1978.
Ciné Revue (Paris), 20 November 1980.
Cousins, R. F., "Recasting Zola: Gérard Philipe's Influence on Duvivier's Adaptation of Pot-Bouille," in *Literature/Film Quarterly* (Salisbury, Maryland), July 1989.

* * *

In a brilliant but sadly brief career, Gérard Philipe was celebrated as the most talented and most loved screen and stage actor of his generation. An enormously gifted, intelligent, and committed professional, he possessed a fine voice, a handsome, youthful appearance, and a charming freshness which suggested both residual innocence and emotional intensity. Encouraged by Marc Allégret, he trained under Jean Huret and later Jean Wall before making a promising stage debut at Cannes.

Philipe's film career was launched by Marc and Yves Allégret in their romantic comedies *La Boîte aux rêves* and *Les Petites du Quai aux Fleurs*, but his first leading role came in *Le Pays sans étoiles* as a dreaming clerk uncannily acting out a crime of passion. A more demanding part, executed with discerning subtlety, followed as the reforming, idealistic, and deranged Prince Myshkin in *L'Idiot*. However, in *Le Diable au corps*, as the adolescent passionately and perhaps irresponsibly involved with a nurse who, although engaged to a soldier, bears his child, he triumphed with a public deeply conscious of the personal moral dilemmas posed by wartime separations. The successful partnership with Micheline Presle led to a laborious romantic farce, *Tous les chemins mènent à Rome* and a later lesser variation on the adulterous couple relationship in *Les Amants de la Villa Borghese*.

Though Hollywood beckoned, Philipe preferred to remain within the European film tradition, working in France or Italy, and in co-productions. He resisted typecasting but invariably, though with considerable versatility, he played the romantic hero. He could epitomize the tragic hero as in *Une si jolie petite plage*, sensitively depicting the corrosive self-absorption of the spurned, suicidal adolescent, or in the later *Montparnasse 19* powerfully rendering the suffering and despair of the doomed alcoholic artist Modigliani. But he could also be the ebullient, swashbuckling romantic hero of *Fanfan-la-Tulipe* or in *Les Aventures de Till L'Espiègle* (co-directed with Joris Ivens) the sharp-witted, high-spirited Flemish folk hero.

The postwar tendency to film literary classics brought Philipe roles in adaptations of Stendhal and Zola, where his star presence determined the focus of the screen version. As Fabrice Del Dongo in *La Chartreuse de Parme* and Julien Sorel in *Le Rouge et le noir* he gave perceptive performances as the insecure, self-absorbed, yet immensely appealing and energetic Stendhalian heroes, while in Duvivier's reworking of Zola's *Pot-Bouille* he effortlessly portrayed the seducer

Gérard Philipe in *Le Diable au corps*

Octave Mouret. Sacha Guitry exploited his image in period dramas as D'Artagnan in *Si Versailles m'était conté* and in *Si Paris m'était conté* as a troubadour linking the historical tableaux. Films by René Clair in this period reveal his typical range. In *La Beauté du Diable* he was the pleasure-seeking young Faust; in *Les Belles de nuit* a dreamer privileged with amorous partners across the centuries; and in *Les Grandes Manoeuvres* with Michèle Morgan, he excelled as the cavalry officer frivolously bent on conquering a sophisticated divorcée, but falling deeply in love. He was again the unrequited, dreaming lover in Carné's *Juliette ou la clef des songes*, the rejected suitor turning to gambling in *Le Joueur*, but in *La Vie à deux* his love triumphs over social disparity.

Although predominantly the disarming screen lover, Philipe also appeared as less attractive characters: as a foolish, cynical count in *La Ronde*; a callous, calculating Valmont in *Les Liaisons dangereuses*, 1960; the master of ceremonies and eventual participant in *Les Sept Péchés capitaux*; the homicidal maniac in *Souvenirs perdus*; and in *Monsieur Ripois* as an impressively ruthless Don Juan of London society tragically blind to genuinely felt emotion. More serious dramatic roles for Yves Allégret revealed him as a disillusioned hard-drinking doctor rediscovering his purpose in *Les Orgueilleux*, and as the dedicated engineer heroically rescuing trapped workers in *La Meilleure Part*, while for Buñuel in *La Fièvre monte à El Pao* he was a reforming prison governor opposed to the fascist dictatorship.

In a remarkable career, Gérard Philipe worked with the leading directors and actresses of his day and was never less than accomplished. With his handsome looks, seductive voice, and engaging personality he endeared himself to audiences as the noble but often humble romantic hero. Through his dedicated craftsmanship, he won the respect of his fellow professionals to become one of the legendary figures of French cinema.

—R. F. Cousins

PICCOLI, Michel

Nationality: French. **Born:** Jacques Daniel Michel Piccoli in Paris of Italian parents, 27 December 1925. **Family:** Married 1) Eleno Eleonore Hirt (divorced), daughter: Anne-Cordélia; 2) the actress and singer Juliette Greco, 1966 (divorced 1977); 3) Ludivine Clerc, 1978. **Career:** 1944—film debut in *Sortilèges*; also worked on French stage and television. **Awards:** French Étoile de Cristal Award for Best Actor, for *La Curée*, 1966; Best Actor, Cannes Festival, for *Salto nel vuoto*, 1979.

Films as Actor:

1944 *Sortilèges* (Christian-Jaque)
1949 *Le Point du jour* (Daquin); *Le Parfum de la dame en noir* (Daquin)
1950 *Sans laisser d'adresse* (Chanois)
1951 *Terreur en Oklahoma* (Paviot—short)
1952 *Chicago Digest* (Paviot—short); *Torticola contre Frankensberg* (Paviot—short); *Saint-Tropez, devoir de vacances* (Paviot—short); "Jeanne d'Arc" ep. of *Destinées* (Delannoy)
1953 *Interdit de séjour* (de Canonge)
1954 *Tout chante autour de moi* (Gout)
1955 *French Cancan* (*Only the French Can*) (Renoir) (as Valorguil); *Les Mauvaises Rencontres* (Astruc); *Ernst Thälman Führer seiner Klasse* (Maetzig)

1956 *La Mort en ce jardin* (*Death in the Garden*; *Evil Eden*; *Gina*) (Buñuel) (as Father Lizzardi); *Les Sorcières de Salem* (*Witches of Salem*; *The Crucible*) (Rouleau); *Marie-Antoinette* (Delannoy); *Les Copains du dimanche* (Aisner)
1957 *Nathalie* (*The Foxiest Girl in Paris*) (Christian-Jaque) (as Frank Marchal, policeman); *Tabarin* (Pottier)
1958 *Rafles sur la ville* (*Sinners of Paris*) (Chenal)
1959 *La Bête à l'affût* (Chenal); *La Dragée haute* (Kerchner)
1960 *Le bal des espions* (Clément)
1961 *Le vergini di Roma* (*Amazons of Rome*) (Bragaglia and Cottafavi); *Le Rendez-vous* (Delannoy); *La Chevelure* (Kyrou—short); *Le Rendez-vous de Nöel* (Michel—short)
1962 *Climats* (Lorenzi); *Fumée, histoire et fantaisie* (Villiers and Berne—short)
1963 *Le Doulos* (*The Fingerman*; *Doulos—The Fingerman*) (Melville) (as Nuttheccio); *Le Jour et l'heure* (*The Day and the Hour*) (Clément) (as Antoine); *Le Mépris* (*Contempt*) (Godard) (as Paul Javal)
1964 *Le Journal d'une femme de chambre* (*Diary of a Chambermaid*) (Buñuel) (as Monsieur Monteil); *La Chance et l'amour* (Bitsch); *Marie-Soleil* (Bourseiller); *Pararazzi* (Rozier—short); *De l'amour* (Aurel) (as Raoul)
1965 *Masquerade* (Dearden) (as Sarrassin); *Lady L* (Ustinov) (as Lecoeur); *Le Coup de grâce* (Gayrol); *Compartiment tueurs* (*The Sleeping Car Murder*) (Costa-Gavras) (as Cabourg); *Les Ruses du Diable* (Vecchiali); *Café tabac* (Guillemot—short)
1966 *Paris brûle-t-il?* (*Is Paris Burning?*) (Clément) (as Edgar Pisani); *La Curée* (*The Game Is Over*) (Vadim) (as Alexandre Saccard); *La Guerre est finie* (*The War Is Over*; *Krigetar Slut*) (Resnais) (as customs inspector); *Les Créatures* (*Varelserna*) (Varda) (as Edgar); *La Voleuse* (Chapot)
1967 *Un Homme de trop* (*Shock Troops*) (Costa-Gavras) (as Extra Man); *Les Demoiselles de Rochefort* (*The Young Girls of Rochefort*) (Demy) (as Simon Dame); **Belle de jour** (Buñuel) (as Henri Husson); *Mon amour, mon amour* (Trintignant)
1968 *Benjamin ou Les mémoires d'un puceau* (*Benjamin*; *The Diary of an Innocent Boy*) (Deville) (as Count Philippe de Saint-Germain); *Danger: Diabolik* (*Diabolik*) (Bava) (as Inspector Ginco); *La Chamade* (Cavalier) (as Charles); *La Prisonnière* (*The Female Prisoner*; *La Prigioniera*) (Clouzot); *Dillinger è morto* (*Dillinger Is Dead*) (Ferreri) (as Glauco)
1969 *La Voie lactée* (*The Milky Way*; *La Via lattea*) (Buñuel) (as the Marquis); *Topaz* (Hitchcock) (as Jacques Granville); *L'invitata* (de Seta)
1970 *Les Choses de la vie* (*The Things of Life*) (Sautet) (as Pierre); *L'Invasion* (Yves Allégret); *Max et les ferrailleurs* (Sautet) (title role)
1971 *La Poudre d'escampette* (*Touch and Go*; *French Leave*) (de Broca) (as Valentin)
1972 *La Décade prodigieuse* (*Ten Days' Wonder*) (Chabrol) (as Paul Regis); **Le Charme discret de la bourgeoisie** (*The Discreet Charm of the Bourgeoisie*) (Buñuel) (as Home Secretary); *L'udienza* (*The Audience*; *The Papal Audience*) (Ferreri); *La cagna* (*Liza*) (Ferreri); *La Femme en bleu* (Deville); *César et Rosalie* (*Cesar and Rosalie*) (Sautet) (as narrator); *L'Attentat* (*The Plot*; *The French Conspiracy*) (Boisset) (as Colonel Kassar)
1973 *Themroc* (Faraldo) (title role, + co-pr); *Les Noces rouges* (*Wedding in Blood*; *Red Wedding*) (Chabrol); **La Grande Bouffe** (*Blow-Out*) (Ferreri) (as Michel, the TV producer); *Le Far-West* (Brel); *Grandeur nature* (*Life Size*; *Love Doll*) (Berlanga); *Touche pas à la femme blanche* (*Don't Touch White Women*) (Ferreri) (as Buffalo Bill)

1974   *Le Trio infernal* (Girod); *Le Fantôme de la liberté* (*The Phantom of Liberty*; *The Specter of Freedom*) (Buñuel) (as 2nd prefect); *La Faille* (Fleischmann); *Léonor* (Juan Buñuel) (as Richard)

1975   *Vincent, François, Paul, et les autres* (*Vincent, Paul, and the Others*) (Sautet); *Sept morts sur ordonnance* (Rouffio) (as Dr. Losseray)

1976   *Mado* (Sautet) (as Simon Leotard); *F comme Fairbanks* (Dugowson); *Todo modo* (Petri); *L'ultimata donna* (*The Last Woman*; *La Derniere femme*) (Ferreri)

1977   *L'Imprécateur* (Bertucelli); *René la Canne* (Girod); *Des Enfants gâtés* (*Spoiled Children*) (Tavernier) (as Bernardi); *La Part du feu* (Périer)

1978   *L'Etat sauvage* (*The Savage State*) (Girod) (as Orlaville); *Strauberg ist Da* (Gallé); *La Petite Fille en velours bleu* (Bridges); *Le Sucre* (Rouffio)

1979   *Giallo napoletano* (*Neapolitan Thriller*) (Corbucci); *Der Preiss für Überleben* (*Le Prix de la survie*) (Noever); *Le Mors aux dents* (Heynemann); *Le Divorcement* (Barouh); *Salto nel vuoto* (*A Leap in the Dark*; *Leap into the Void*) (Bellocchio) (as Judge Ponticelli)

1980   *La Fille prodigue* (Doillon)

1981   *Atlantic City* (Malle) (as Joseph); *Une Etrange Affaire* (Granier-Deferre) (as Bertrand Maler); *Espion, lève toi* (Boisset); *La Passante du Sans-Souci* (*La Passante*) (Rouffio and Kirsner) (as Max Baumstein); *La Nuit de Varennes* (*That Night in Varennes*; *The New World*) (Scola) (as King Louis XVI)

1982   *Passion* (Godard); *Une Chambre en ville* (*A Room in Town*) (Demy) (as Edmond Leroyer); *Le Prix du danger* (Boisset); *Oltre la porta* (*Beyond the Door*) (Cavani); *Que les gros salaires lèvent le doigt!!!* (Granier-Deferre) (as José Viss); *Le Général de l'armée morte* (*Il generale dell'armata morta*) (Tovoli) (+ co-sc); *Gli occhi, la bocca* (*The Eyes, the Mouth*) (Bellocchio) (as Uncle Nigi)

1983   *Viva la vie* (Lelouch)

1984   *La Diagonale du fou* (*Dangerous Moves*) (Dembo) (as Akiva Liebskind); *Adieu Bonaparte* (*Weda'an Bonapart*) (Chahine) (as Louis Caffarelli du Flaga); *Péril en la demeure* (*Peril*; *Death in a French Garden*) (Deville) (as Graham Tombsthay); *Le Matelot 512* (Allio); *Success Is the Best Revenge* (Skolimowski) (as French official)

1985   *Partir, revenir* (*Going and Coming Back*) (Lelouch) (as Simon Lerner)

1986   *Mauvais Sang* (*Bad Blood*; *The Night Is Young*) (Carax) (as Marc); *Mon beau-frère a tué ma soeur* (Rouffio) (as Ètienne); *Le Paltoquet* (Deville) (as The Nonentity); *La Puritaine* (Doillon) (as Pierre)

1987   *Maladie d'amour* (Deray) (as Raoul Bergeron); *La Terre étrangère* (Bondy); *L'Homme voilé* (*The Veiled Man*) (Bagdadi) (as Kassar); *La Rumba* (Hanin) (as Malleville)

1988   *Blanc de chine* (Granier-Deferre); *Y'a Bon les blancs* (Ferreri)

1989   *Actor* (Angelucci)

1990   *Milou en mai* (*May Fools*) (Malle) (as Milou); *Martha und Ich* (*Martha and I*) (Jiri Weiss) (as Uncle Ernst); *La Belle Noiseuse* (*The Beautiful Troublemaker*; *Divertimento*) (Rivette) (as Edouard Frenhofer)

1991   *L'Equilibriste* (*Walking a Tightrope*) (Papatakis) (as Marcel Spadice); *Das Schicksal des Freiherrn von Leisenbohg* (Molinaro); *El Ladron del Ninos* (*The Children Thief*; *Le Voleur d'enfants*) (De Chalonge) (as M. Armand); *Contre l'oubli* (*Against Oblivion*; *Ecrire contre l'oubli*) (Akerman and others)

1992   *Archipelago* (Granier-Deferre) (as Leonard Wilde); *Le Bal des casse-pieds* (Yves Robert) (as Desire); *From Time to Time* (Blyth) (as Jules Verne); *Le Souper* (*The Supper*) (Molinaro) (as voice of Chateaubriand); *La Vie crevee* (*Punctured Life*) (Nicloux) (as Raymond)

1993   *La Cavale des Fous* (*Loonies at Large*) (Pico) (as Henri Toussaint); *Ruptures* (Citti) (as Paul)

1994   *Bête de scène*; *L'Ange noir* (*The Black Angel*) (Brisseau) (as Georges Feuvrier); *Al Mohager* (*The Emigrant*) (Chahine) (as Adam)

1995   *Les Cent et une nuits* (*A Hundred and One Nights*) (Varda) (as Simon Cinema)

1996   *Tykho Moon* (Bilal); *Compagna di viaggio* (Del Monte); *Beaumarchais, l'insolent* (Molinaro) (as le Prince Conti)

Film as Actor and Director:

1994   *Train de nuit* (+ co-sc)

Publications

By PICCOLI: book—

Dialogues égoïstes, with Alain Lacombe, Paris, 1976.

By PICCOLI: articles—

Interviews in *Cinématographe* (Paris), September/October 1983 and November 1986.
Interviews with Serge Toubiana, in *Cahiers du Cinéma* (Paris), October 1984 and December 1986.
Interview with T. Jousse and N. Saada, in *Cahiers du Cinéma* (Paris), November 1990.
"Un moment étoile de l'humanite," interview with J. A. Gili and others, in *Positif* (Paris), January 1992.

On PICCOLI: book—

Chazal, Robert, *Michel Piccoli: Le provocateur*, Paris, 1989.

On PICCOLI: articles—

Ciné Revue (Paris), 8 May 1980 and 8 March 1984.
Film Français (Paris), 1 March 1985.
Merigeau, P., and J. Zimmer, "Toujours jouer le metteur en scène," in *Revue du Cinéma*, (Paris), September 1991.
Sartor, F., "Rivette, Piccoli & Béart," in *Film en Televisie + Video* (Brussels), November 1991.
Deville, M., "Le film de ma vie," in *Positif* (Paris), June 1994.

*   *   *

In a career spanning six decades and encompassing more than 130 films by major European directors, Michel Piccoli deservedly enjoys an international reputation as an accomplished, versatile actor. His repertoire extends from anodyne comic roles to those stamped by ferocious black humor, from the gentle and compassionate to the cynical and sadistic, from the respectable to the deliberately outrageous.

A powerful screen presence, he has constantly served his character creations. His dark, gaunt appearance in his mid-thirties lent conviction to tough, sinister roles in crime thrillers, particularly as Nuttheccio, the successful gangster of *Le Doulos*. Later physically imposing roles include that of Max the vice-squad detective in *Max et les ferrailleurs* and the ruthless Colonel Kassar in *L'Attentat*. The sexual charge in Piccoli's acting was regularly exploited by Luis Buñuel. After *La Mort en ce jardin* where he played a priest compromised by a prostitute, he became the eager womanizer Husson of *Belle de jour*, the frustrated Monteil pursuing his servants in *Le Journal d'une femme de chambre*, and the perverse sensualist de Sade in *La Voie lactée*.

Further perspectives on Piccoli's range are found in parts requiring a more reflective, detached, and experienced view of the world. He was the phlegmatic philosophy teacher undisturbed by horrendous events in *La Décade prodigieuse*; the knowledgeable music-shop manager in *Les Demoiselles de Rochefort*; the elegant opera-loving croupier Joseph of *Atlantic City* and in *Paris brûle-t-il?* the Gaullist politician Edgar Pisani. A more disturbing moral detachment is witnessed as the cynical businessman of *La Curée*, as the calculating and unfeeling manipulator of *Benjamin*, or as the callous, corrupt, and lustful lawyer of *Le Trio infernal*. Yet he has also played sensitive or insecure males: in *Le Mépris* he excelled as the self-doubting writer Paul Javal, in *Les Choses de la vie* he portrayed an architect torn between his mistress and family life, and in *Compartiment tueurs* he played the neurotic victim Cabourg.

In roles reflecting the sardonic, self-critical mood of the 1960s and 1970s Piccoli risked his established image by appearing in fiercely satirical and often scandalous films exposing the materialism, authoritarianism, gluttony, sexual depravity, and cupidity of contemporary society. His humanistic concerns are further reflected in later films by Buñuel, Godard, Tavernier, and Tovoli.

For emerging directors he extended his canon of tough characters, while in parodies of the genre he was the surly barman in Deville's *Le Paltoquet* indulging in murder fantasies about his clients, and in Rouffio's *Mon beau-frère a tué ma soeur* he was successfully teamed with Michel Serrault as an unworldly academic. Unusually cast as the victim, he was murdered by his duplicitous wife in Deville's compelling *Péril en la demeure*.

In studies of the jealous male losing a mistress he was impressive in Demy's *Une Chambre en ville* and in Deray's *Maladie d'amour*. Among Piccoli's most successful depictions of human complexity must rank his role in Bellochio's *Salto nel vuoto* as the apparently balanced, humane judge who in private is withdrawn, depressive, and despotic.

With age he has increasingly come to play the role of the father, particularly in explorations of the father/daughter relationship. In Cavani's *Oltre la porta* he convinced as the distraught parent of a prostitute daughter, but his most notable performances came for Doillon: as the tragic father nearing death in *La Fille prodigue*, and, in the emotionally intense performance of *La Puritaine*, as a stage director working out in dramatic terms his feelings for his wayward daughter.

Whether as gangster, glutton, sardonic observer, lustful womanizer, reflective intellectual, cynical manipulator, or the mature compassionate male, Michel Piccoli carries conviction in his accomplished variations on his powerful screen personality.

—R. F. Cousins

PICKFORD, Mary

Born: Gladys Mary Smith in Toronto, Ontario, Canada, 8 April 1893. **Family:** Married 1) the actor Owen Moore, 1911 (divorced 1920); 2) the actor Douglas Fairbanks, 1920 (divorced 1936); 3) the actor Buddy Rogers, 1937, two adopted children. **Career:** 1898—debut as child actress in stage play *Bootle's Baby*; played other roles in Valentine Stock Company, and toured with other companies; 1907—Broadway debut in *The Warrens of Virginia*; 1909—film debut as extra in *Her First Biscuits*; leading role in D. W. Griffith's *The Violin Maker of Cremona*; became known as "The Biograph Girl with the Curls"; 1913-18—contract with Zukor; 1918—independent producer; 1919—co-founder, with Douglas Fairbanks, Charlie Chaplin, and D. W. Griffith, of United Artists; 1923-24—roles in *Rosita* and *Dorothy Vernon of Haddon Hall* attempted to break her "little girl" image; 1929—first sound film, *Coquette*; 1937—formed Mary Pickford Cosmetic Company; 1956—sold the last of her United Artists stock. **Awards:** Best Actress Academy Award for *Coquette*, 1928/29. **Died:** In Santa Monica, California, 29 May 1979.

Films as Actress:

(all films directed by Griffith unless noted)

1909 *Her First Biscuits*; *The Violin Maker of Cremona*; *The Lonely Villa*; *The Son's Return*; *The Faded Lilies*; *The Peach Basket Hat*; *The Way of Man*; *The Necklace*; *The Mexican Sweethearts*; *The Country Doctor*; *The Cardinal's Conspiracy*; *The Renunciation*; *The Seventh Day*; *A Strange Meeting*; *Sweet and Twenty*; *The Slave*; *They Would Elope*; *The Indian Runner's Romance*; *His Wife's Visitor*; *Oh Uncle*; *The Sealed Room*; *1776, or The Hessian Renegades*; *The Little Darling*; *In Old Kentucky*; *Getting Even*; *The Broken Locket*; *What's Your Hurry*; *The Awakening*; *The Little Teacher*; *The Gibson Goddess*; *In the Watches of the Night*; *His Lost Love*; *The Restoration*; *The Light That Came*; *A Midnight Adventure*; *The Mountaineer's Honor*; *The Trick That Failed*; *The Test*; *To Save Her Soul*

1910 *All on Account of the Milk* (Powell); *The Woman from Mellon's*; *The Englishman and the Girl*; *The Newlyweds*; *The Thread of Destiny*; *The Twisted Trail*; *The Smoker*; *As It Is in Life*; *A Rich Revenge*; *A Romance of the Western Hills*; *May and December*; *Never Again!*; *The Unchanging Sea*; *Love among the Roses*; *The Two Brothers*; *Romona*; *In the Season of Buds*; *A Victim of Jealousy*; *A Child's Impulse*; *Muggsy's First Sweetheart*; *What the Daisy Said*; *The Call to Arms*; *An Arcadian Maid*; *Muggsy Becomes a Hero*; *The Sorrows of the Unfaithful*; *When We Were in Our Teens*; *Wilful Peggy*; *Examination Day at School*; *A Gold Necklace*; *A Lucky Toothache*; *Waiter No. 5*; *Simple Charity*; *The Masher*; *The Song of the Wildwood Flute*; *A Plain Song*

1911 *White Roses*; *When a Man Loves*; *The Italian Barber*; *Three Sisters*; *A Decree of Destiny*; *The First Misunderstanding* (Ince and Tucker); *The Dream* (Ince and Tucker) (+ sc); *Maid or Man* (Ince); *At the Duke's Command*; *The Mirror*; *While the Cat's Away*; *Her Darkest Hour* (Ince); *Artful Kate* (Ince); *A Manly Man* (Ince); *The Message in the Bottle* (Ince); *The Fisher-maid* (Ince); *In Old Madrid* (Ince); *Sweet Memories of Yesterday* (Ince); *The Stampede*; *Second Sight*; *The Fair Dentist*; *For Her Brother's Sake* (Ince and Tucker); *Back to the Soil*; *In the Sultan's Garden* (Ince); *The Master and the Man*; *The Lighthouse Keeper*; *For the Queen's Honor*; *A Gasoline Engagement*; *At a Quarter to Two*; *Science*; *The Skating Bug*; *The Call of the Song*; *A Toss of the Coin*; *The Sentinel Asleep*; *The Better Way*; *His Dress Shirt*; *'Tween Two Loves (The Stronger Love)*; *The Rose's Story*; *From the Bottom of the Sea*; *The Courting of Mary* (Tucker); *Love Heeds Not the Showers* (Moore); *Little Red Riding Hood* (Moore); *The Caddy's Dream* (Moore)

1912 *Honor Thy Father* (Moore); *The Mender of Nets*; *Iola's Promise*; *Fate's Inception*; *The Female of the Species*; *Just Like a Woman*; *Won by a Fish* (Sennett); *The Old Actor*; *A Lodging for the Night; A Beast at Bay; Home Folks; Lena and the Geese* (+ sc); *The School Teacher and the Waif; An Indian Summer; A Pueblo Legend; The Narrow Road; The Inner Circle; With the Enemy's Help; Friends; So Near, Yet So Far; A Feud in the Kentucky Hills; The One She Loved; My Baby; The Informer; The Unwelcome Guest; The New York Hat*

1913   *In the Bishop's Carriage* (Porter); *Caprice* (Dawley)

1914   *A Good Little Devil* (Porter); *Hearts Adrift* (Porter); *Tess of the Storm Country* (Porter); *The Eagle's Mate* (Kirkwood); *Such a Little Queen* (Hugh Ford); *Behind the Scenes* (Kirkwood); *Cinderella* (Kirkwood)

1915   *Mistress Nell* (Kirkwood); *Fanchon, the Cricket* (Kirkwood); *The Dawn of Tomorrow* (Kirkwood); *Little Pal* (Kirkwood); *Rags* (Kirkwood); *Esmerelda* (Kirkwood); *A Girl of Yesterday* (Dwan); *Madame Butterfly* (Olcott)

1916   *The Foundling* (O'Brien); *Poor Little Peppina* (Olcott); *The Eternal Grind* (O'Brien); *Hulda from Holland* (O'Brien); *Less Than Dust* (Emerson)

1917   *The Pride of the Clan* (Tourneur); *The Poor Little Rich Girl* (Tourneur); *A Romance of the Redwoods* (De Mille); *Rebecca of Sunnybrook Farm* (Neilan) (title role); *A Little Princess* (Neilan)

1918   *Stella Maris* (Neilan) (title role/Unity Blake); *Amarilly of Clothes-Line Alley* (Neilan); *M'Liss* (Neilan); *How Could You, Jean?* (Taylor); *Johanna Enlists* (Taylor); *One Hundred Percent American* (Rossen)

1919   *Captain Kidd, Jr.* (Taylor)

1927   *The Madonna in the Gaucho* (Jones)

Films as Producer:

1919   *Daddy Long-Legs* (+ ro); *The Hoodlum* (+ ro); *The Heart o' the Hills* (+ ro)

1920   *Pollyanna* (+ title role); *Suds* (+ ro)

1921   *The Love Light* (Marion) (+ ro as Angela); *Through the Back Door* (Green and Jack Pickford) (+ ro as Jeanne Budamere); *Little Lord Fauntleroy* (Green and Jack Pickford) (+ title role)

1922   *Tess of the Storm Country* (Robertson) (+ title role)

1923   *Rosita* (Lubitsch) (+ title role); *Garrison's Finish* (Rosson) (co-sc titles only)

1924   *Dorothy Vernon of Haddon Hall* (Neilan) (+ title role)

1925   *Little Annie Rooney* (Beaudine) (+ title role)

1926   *Sparrows* (Beaudine) (+ ro as Mama Mollie)

1927   *My Best Girl* (Sam Taylor) (+ ro as Maggie Johnson)

1929   *Coquette* (Sam Taylor) (+ ro as Norma Besant); *The Taming of the Shrew* (Sam Taylor) (+ ro as Katherine)

1931   *Kiki* (Sam Taylor) (+ title role)

1933   *Secrets* (Borzage) (+ roles as Mary Marlow/Mary Carlton)

Publications

By PICKFORD: books—

Pickfordisms for Success, Los Angeles, 1922.

Why Not Try God?, New York, 1934, as *Why Not Look Beyond?*, London, 1936.

Little Liar (novel), New York, 1934.

The Demi-Widow (novel), Indianapolis, 1935.

My Rendezvous with Life, New York, 1935.

Sunshine and Shadow, New York, 1955.

By PICKFORD: articles—

"What It Means to Be a Movie Actress," in *Ladies' Home Journal*, January 1915.

"The Body in the Bosphorus," in *Theatre*, April 1919.

"Greatest Business in the World," in *Chaplin* (Stockholm), 10 June 1922.

"Mary Is Looking for Pictures," in *Photoplay* (New York), June 1925.

"Mary Pickford Awards," in *Photoplay* (New York), October 1925.

On PICKFORD: books—

Niver, Kemp, *Mary Pickford: Comedienne*, Los Angeles, 1970.

Cushman, Robert, *Tribute to Mary Pickford*, Washington, D.C., 1970.

Lee, Raymond, *The Films of Mary Pickford*, South Brunswick, New Jersey, 1970.

Wagenknecht, Edward, *Movies in the Age of Innocence*, New York, 1971.

Windelen, Robert, *Sweetheart: The Story of Mary Pickford*, London, 1973 + biblio.

Rosen, Marjorie, *Popcorn Venus*, New York, 1973.

Carey, Gary, *Doug and Mary: A Biography of Douglas Fairbanks and Mary Pickford*, New York, 1977.

Herndon, B., *Mary Pickford and Douglas Fairbanks: The Most Popular Couple the World Has Ever Known*, New York, 1977.

Eyman, Scott, *Mary Pickford: America's Sweetheart*, New York, 1990.

On PICKFORD: articles—

Johnson, Julian, "Mary Pickford, Herself and Her Career," in *Photoplay* (New York), November 1915-February 1916.

Belasco, David, "When Mary Pickford Came to Me," in *Photoplay* (New York), December 1915.

Cheatham, Maude, "On Location with Mary Pickford," in *Motion Picture Magazine*, June 1919.

Russell, M. Lewis, "Mary Pickford—Director," in *Photoplay* (New York), March 1920.

St. Johns, Adela Rogers, "Why Does the World Love Mary?" in *Photoplay* (New York), December 1921.

Birdwell, Russell, "When I Am Old, as Told by Mary Pickford," in *Photoplay* (New York), February 1925.

St. Johns, Adela Rogers, "The Story of the Married Life of Doug and Mary," in *Photoplay* (New York), February 1927.

Whitaker, Alma, "Mrs. Douglas Fairbanks Analyzes Mary Pickford," in *Photoplay* (New York), March 1928.

St. Johns, Adela Rogers, "Why Mary Pickford Bobbed Her Hair," in *Photoplay* (New York), September 1928.

Harriman, M. C., "Mary Pickford," in *New Yorker*, 7 April 1934.

Current Biography 1945, New York, 1945.

Card, J., "The Films of Mary Pickford," in *Image* (Rochester, N.Y.), December 1959.

Spears, J., "Mary Pickford's Directors," in *Films in Review* (New York), February 1966.

"Lettre de Paris sur Mary Pickford," in *Cahiers du Cinéma* (Paris), September 1966.

Scaramazza, Paul, "Rediscovering Mary Pickford," in *Film Fan Monthly*, December 1970.

Harmetz, Aljean, "America's Sweetheart Lives," in *New York Times*, 28 March 1971.

Gow, Gordon, "Mary," in *Films and Filming* (London), December 1973.

"Album di Mary Pickford," in *Cinema Nuovo* (Turin), August 1979.

Mitry, J., "Le Roman de Mary Pickford," in *Avant-Scène du Cinéma* (Paris), 1 November 1980.

Arnold, Gary, "Mary Pickford," in *The Movie Star*, edited by Elisabeth Weis, New York, 1981.

Classic Images (Indiana, Pennsylvania), July 1984.

*   *   *

Mary Pickford

It is hard to imagine the impact and popularity of Mary Pickford during the height of her career since she retired from the screen in 1933 and refused to let her films be rereleased or shown on television. She sensed that the image she established of innocence, diligence, and uncomplicatedness was historically specific. Her embodiment of idealized, rural American values was essentially meaningless past the demise of the silent film era. She belonged in short to a different world, a world of rapidly expanding technology, star idolatry, and fantastic power. Fortunately, she donated most of her films to the American Film Institute, establishing the Mary Pickford Collection, and her third husband, Buddy Rogers, organized a small theater in her honor at the Library of Congress. These are the only two places where one can see the majority of her works.

Judging from her first one-reelers at Biograph, Pickford possessed a natural screen presence and mastery of mime technique that far exceeded her fellow performers. By the time she left Biograph, she had effectively redefined film acting. She later claimed, "I refused to exaggerate in my performance. . . . Nobody ever directed me, not even Mr. Griffith." She demonstrated intelligence, wit, grace, and ambition in quickly learning every detail of the film industry. She was fully aware of her popularity as "Little Mary" and "America's Sweetheart," and pressed the studios to pay her accordingly. By 1916 Pickford was earning $10,000 a week and choosing her scripts, cameraman, and director.

Her place in the pantheon of stars was secured by her performance in the title role of *Tess of the Storm Country*. This was followed by a string of brilliant roles that repeated the winning formula of innocence and pathos in such films as *Poor Little Rich Girl*, *Rebecca of Sunnybrook Farm*, *Pollyanna*, *Little Lord Fauntleroy*, and one of cinema's first split-screen double roles in *Stella Maris*. The public adored her long golden curls and her embodiment of the eternal child/woman: lovable, spirited, whimsical, and pure. Behind the scenes she was an accomplished businesswoman. Pickford, along with Charles Chaplin, D. W. Griffith, and her second husband, Douglas Fairbanks, founded United Artists to control the production and distribution of their films.

In the 1920s Pickford's career did not diminish. She graduated from "America's Sweetheart" to "World's Sweetheart"; hundreds of thousands lined the streets of Moscow to see her when she and Fairbanks visited the Soviet Union in 1926. She could play any role, as her performances in *Sparrows*, *Stella Maris*, *The Hoodlum*, and *The Taming of the Shrew* demonstrate. But the public wanted "Little Mary" and Pickford enjoyed the wealth and fame too much to attempt more than a few departures from her established image. Pickford explained, "My career was planned, there was never anything accidental about it. It was planned, it was painful, it was purposeful."

Unable completely to escape her stereotype, she was forced to quit filmmaking as its popularity waned. One of the figures who shaped the Hollywood aesthetic, she lived as a virtual recluse in her mansion, Pickfair, until her death. She said of her filmgoing audience, "Make them laugh, make them cry, and back to laughter. What do people go to the theater for? An emotional exercise. . . . I am a servant of the people. I have never forgotten that." Mary Pickford, although unseen for many years, cannot be forgotten.

—Elaine Mancini

PIDGEON, Walter

Nationality: American. **Born:** Walter Davis Pidgeon in East St. John, New Brunswick, Canada, 23 September 1897; became a U.S. citizen in 1943. **Education:** Attended Alexander School, East St. John; University of New Brunswick, Fredericton, 1914-15; studied singing at New England Conservatory of Music, Boston, 1924. **Military Service:** Canadian Field Artillery, during World War I: lieutenant; medical discharge, 1918. **Family:** Married: 1) Edna Pickles, 1922 (died 1924); daughter: Edna Verne; 2) Ruth Walker, 1930. **Career:** 1919—began work as messenger for Shawmut Bank, Boston; 1921-22—with the E. E. Clive repertory group; toured with Elsie Janis in musical; 1925—Broadway appearance in the musical *Puzzles of 1925*; 1926—film debut in *Mannequin*; then back on the stage; 1931-37—contract with First National, mainly for musical films; 1937-57—contract with MGM; 1942-43—on Lux Radio Theatre; 1956—host of TV series *MGM Parade*; later stage roles include *The Happiest Millionaire*, 1957, *Take Me Along*, 1959, *Take Her, She's Mine*, 1964, and *Dinner at Eight*, 1966. **Awards:** Co-recipient, Special Jury Prize for Ensemble Acting, Venice Festival, for *Executive Suite*, 1954. **Died:** In Santa Monica, California, 25 September 1984.

Films as Actor:

1926   *Mannequin* (Cruze) (as reporter); *The Outsider* (Rowland V. Lee); *Miss Nobody* (Hillyer) (as writer); *Old Loves and New* (Maurice Tourneur); *Marriage License* (Borzage); *Heart of Salome* (Schertzinger)

1927   *The Girl from Rio* (Terris); *The Gorilla* (Santell); *The Thirteenth Juror* (Laemmle)

1928   *The Gateway of the Moon* (Wray); *Woman Wise* (Wray); *Turn Back the Hours* (Bretherton); *Clothes Make the Woman* (Terriss); *Melody of Love* (Heath) (as Jack Clark)

1929   *Her Private Life* (Korda) (as Ned Thayer); *A Most Immoral Lady* (Wray) (as Tony Williams)

1930   *Bride of the Regiment* (*Lady of the Rose*) (Dillon) (as Col. Vultow); *Viennese Nights* (Crosland) (as Franz); *Sweet Kitty Bellairs* (Alfred E. Green) (as Lord Varney); *Show Girl in Hollywood* (LeRoy) (as himself)

1931   *Kiss Me Again* (Seiter) (as Paul de St. Cyr); *Going Wild* (Seiter) (as "Ace" Benton); *The Gorilla* (Foy) (as Arthur Marsden); *Hot Heiress* (Badger) (as Clay)

1932   *Rockabye* (Cukor) (as Commissioner Al Howard)

1933   *The Kiss before the Mirror* (Whale) (as Bachelor)

1934   *Journal of a Crime* (Keighley) (as Florestan, baritone)

1936   *Big Brown Eyes* (Walsh) (as Richard Morey); *Fatal Lady* (Ludwig) (as David Roberts); *Girl Overboard* (Salkow) (as Paul Stacey)

1937   *She's Dangerous* (*Blonde Dynamite*) (Carruth) (as Dr. Scott Logan); *As Good as Married* (Buzzell) (as Fraser James); *A Girl with Ideas* (Simon) (as Micky McGuire); *Saratoga* (Conway) (as Hartley Madison); *My Dear Miss Aldrich* (Seitz) (as Ken Morley)

1938   *Man-Proof* (Thorpe) (as Alan Wythe); *The Girl of the Golden West* (Leonard) (as Jack Rance); *The Shopworn Angel* (Potter) (as Sam Bailey); *Listen, Darling* (Marin) (as Richard Thurlow); *Too Hot to Handle* (Conway) (as Bill Dennis)

1939   *Society Lawyer* (Marin) (as Christopher Durant); *Six Thousand Enemies* (Seitz) (as Steve Donegan); *Stronger than Desire* (Fenton) (as Tyler Flagg); *Nick Carter, Master Detective* (Jacques Tourneur) (title role/Robert Chalmers)

1940   *It's a Date* (Seiter) (as John Arlen); *Dark Command* (Walsh) (as William Cantrell); *The House across the Bay* (Mayo) (as Tim Nolan); *Phantom Raiders* (Jacques Tourneur) (as Nick Carter); *Sky Murder* (Seitz) (as Nick Carter); *Flight Command* (Borzage) (as Squadron Cmdr. Bill Gary)

1941   *Man Hunt* (Fritz Lang) (as Briton Thorndyke); *How Green Was My Valley* (Ford) (as Mr. Gruffydd); *Blossoms in the Dust* (LeRoy) (as Sam Gladney); *Design for Scandal* (Taurog) (as Jeff Sherman)

1942   *Mrs. Miniver* (Wyler) (as Clem Miniver); *White Cargo* (Thorpe) (as Harry Witzel)
1943   *Madame Curie* (LeRoy) (as Pierre Curie); *The Youngest Profession* (Buzzell) (as himself)
1944   *Mrs. Parkington* (Garnett) (as Maj. Augustus Parkington)
1945   *Weekend at the Waldorf* (Leonard) (as Chip Collyer)
1946   *Holiday in Mexico* (Sidney) (as Jeffrey Evans); *The Secret Heart* (Leonard) (as Chris Matthews)
1947   *Cass Timberlane* (Sidney) (as man at cocktail party); *If Winter Comes* (Saville) (as Mark Sabre)
1948   *Julia Misbehaves* (Conway) (as William Sylvester Packett); *Command Decision* (Wood) (as Maj. Gen. Roland G. Kane)
1949   *The Red Danube* (Sidney) (as Col. Michael "Jokey" Nicobar); *That Forsyte Woman* (*The Forsyte Saga*) (Bennett) (as Jolyon Forsyte)
1950   *The Miniver Story* (Potter) (as Clem Miniver)
1951   *Soldiers Three* (Garnett) (as Col. Brunswick); *Calling Bulldog Drummond* (Saville) (title role); *The Unknown Man* (Thorpe) (as Dwight Bradley Mason); *Quo Vadis* (LeRoy) (as narrator); *The Sellout* (Mayer) (as Haven D. Allridge)
1952   *Million Dollar Mermaid* (*The One-Piece Bathing Suit*) (LeRoy) (as Professor Kellerman); *The Hoaxters* (doc) (as narrator); *The Bad and the Beautiful* (Minnelli) (as Harry Pebbel)
1953   *Scandal at Scourie* (Negulesco) (as Patrick J. McChesney); *Dream Wife* (Sheldon) (as Walter McBride)
1954   *Executive Suite* (Wise) (as Frederick Y. Alderson); *Men of the Fighting Lady* (Marton) (as Cmdr. Kent Dowling); *The Last Time I Saw Paris* (Richard Brooks) (as James Ellswirth); *Deep in My Heart* (Donen) (as J. J. Shubert)
1955   *The Glass Slipper* (Walters) (as narrator); *Hit the Deck* (Rowland) (as Rear Adm. Daniel Xavier Smith)
1956   *Forbidden Planet* (Wilcox) (as Dr. Morbius); *These Wilder Years* (Rowland) (as James Rayburn); *The Rack* (Laven) (as Col. Edward W. Hall Sr.)
1961   *Voyage to the Bottom of the Sea* (Irwin Allen) (as Admiral Nelson)
1962   *Big Red* (Tokar) (as James Haggin); *Advise and Consent* (Preminger) (as Sen. Bob Munson); *I due colonelli* (*The Two Colonels*) (Vanzina) (as Col. Timothy Henderson)
1963   *Il giorno più corto* (*The Shortest Day*) (Corbucci) (as himself); *Anniversary* (doc) (as narrator)
1967   *How I Spent My Summer Vacation* (*Deadly Roulette*) (Hale—for TV); *Cosa Nostra, an Arch Enemy of the F.B.I.* (Medford); *Warning Shot* (Kulik) (as Orville Ames)
1968   *Funny Girl* (Wyler) (as Florenz Ziegfeld); *A qualsiasi prezzo* (*The Vatican Affair*) (Miraglia)
1969   *Rascal* (Tokar) (as voice of Sterling North); *The Mask of Sheba* (Rich—for TV) (as Dr. Condon)
1970   *The House on Greenapple Road* (*The Red Kitchen Murder*) (Day—for TV)
1972   *Skyjacked* (*Sky Terror*) (Guillermin) (as Sen. Arne Lindner); *The Screaming Lady* (*The Screaming Woman*) (Smight—for TV) (as Dr. Larkin)
1973   *The Neptune Factor* (*An Underwater Odyssey*) (Petrie) (as Dr. Samuel Andrews); *Harry in Your Pocket* (*Harry Never Holds*) (Geller) (as Casey)
1974   *The Girl on the Late, Late Show* (Gary Nelson—for TV); *The Yellow Headed Summer*; *Live Again, Die Again* (Colla—for TV)
1975   *You Lie So Deep, My Love* (Rich—for TV)
1976   *Won Ton Ton, the Dog Who Saved Hollywood* (Winner) (as Grayson's butler); *Murder on Flight 502* (McCowan—for TV); *Two-Minute Warning* (Peerce) (as pickpocket); *The Lindbergh Kidnapping Case* (Kulik—for TV) (as Judge Trenchard)
1978   *Sextette* (Ken Hughes and Rapper) (as the Chairman)

Publications

On PIDGEON: articles—

Current Biography 1942, New York, 1942.
Marill, Alvin H., "Walter Pidgeon," in *Films in Review* (New York), November 1969.
Classic Images (Indiana, Pennsylvania), December 1983.
Obituary in *New York Times*, 26 September 1984.
Obituary in *Variety* (New York), 3 October 1984.
Buckley, Michael, "A Final Tribute: Walter Pidgeon 1897-1984," in *Films in Review* (New York), December 1984.

*   *   *

Tall, blandly handsome and dapper with a mellifluous even syrupy voice, Walter Pidgeon seemed to be the very archetype of a romantic leading man. In reality he was somewhat the Rodney Dangerfield of his day; he rarely got respect. One reviewer dubbed him "a handsome piece of stage furniture" and he was characterized as "looking and acting like a monument" and having "the temperament of a turtle."

Yet in his prime at MGM in the 1940s Pidgeon was a sought-after leading man and half of a romantic teaming with then very popular Greer Garson. He had reached this pinnacle slowly, said to have been initially encouraged by no less a personage than Fred Astaire in the mid-1920s. Possessed of a fine baritone singing voice he eventually landed in Broadway musicals and was supposedly the first to record the standards "What'll I Do?" and "All Alone."

Considering his voice had hitherto been his fortune, it is little wonder that Walter Pidgeon's 15 or so silent movies were an undistinguished lot in which he played villains or at least the "other man." It was happily back to the theater until talkies came.

With the craze for musicals at the dawn of sound Pidgeon was a natural and he was tapped for Universal's first all-talkie *Melody of Love* in 1928. He played a songwriter and thus could burst into song convincingly. For a couple of years thereafter he was First National's resident, if somewhat wooden, baritone warbling in frothy concoctions such as *Bride of the Regiment*, *Sweet Kitty Bellairs*, and *Viennese Nights*.

Walter Pidgeon hit several low points and this proved to be one of them. The audience's desire for movies that sang (and sang and sang) waned. His career lingered on, barely, and he managed to carve a small albeit unexciting niche for himself in dramatic roles in the early 1930s. When these, too, proved to be a dead end he returned to the stage for the hit play *Night of January 16* in which he played a gangster.

This was the entree to further movie offers and eventually a contract with MGM. Pidgeon seemed to be on his true path at last but even after his first top-billed role in *Society Lawyer* he was relegated to second leads and "decent fellow" parts. The three-film series in which he played the detective Nick Carter also took him nowhere.

Walter Pidgeon's best films came on loan-outs in 1941 in *Man Hunt* and *How Green Was My Valley* for Twentieth Century-Fox. The former picture revealed an appealingly rugged side to his persona that was rarely tapped. The latter, in which he convincingly played the Reverend Gruffydd, won the Best Picture Oscar for 1941.

Pidgeon and the flame-haired Garson first appeared together in *Blossoms in the Dust*. This led to *Mrs. Miniver*, the great schmaltzy patriotic film of World War II. It too won a Best Picture Academy Award and Pidgeon was nominated for the Oscar for Best Actor. A couple of years later their *Madame Curie* also proved popular and led to his second Oscar nomination.

Pidge, as he was known, starred with Garson in seven more films but he usually played second fiddle to her. It also was noticed by reviewers, if not by the studio, that Pidgeon did not exhibit much charisma on the screen and that he usually supported strong female stars.

The duo's films began bringing diminishing returns and yet another career low yawned before Walter Pidgeon. Once again, with 1948's *Command Decision*, he bounced back. It was only a temporary boost, however. He inevitably slipped into character parts and was dropped by MGM in the mid-1950s.

Always eager to work, Pidgeon remained active into the 1960s and even beyond, and there were a few notable films in which he gave worthy performances. Certainly the cult sci-fi classic *Forbidden Planet* was among them as was *Advise and Consent, Funny Girl, The Bad and the Beautiful*, and *Voyage to the Bottom of the Sea*. He also tried Broadway again, being seen on the boards as late as 1966.

Perhaps it is damning Pidgeon with faint praise to call him a dependable leading man who made his co-stars look good. In private life he was possessed of a very outgoing, even boisterous personality but on celluloid he was rarely allowed to rise above a limited range of emotions. This is not to say he *could* not do so.

Unfortunately most of Pidgeon's roles bring to mind the fatal words "gentlemanly," "decent," "solid," and, truth to tell, "*stolid*" as well. He has to be characterized as one of Hollywood's dullest major leading men and there is unlikely to be a festival of his films any time soon.

—Roy Liebman

PITT, Brad

Nationality: American. **Born**: William Bradley Pitt in Shawnee, Oklahoma, 18 December 1963. **Education**: Attended public school in Springfield, Missouri; majored in journalism with a focus on advertising at the University of Missouri but left in 1986 very shortly before graduating; studied acting with Roy London. **Career**: 1987—film debut, *Less than Zero*; TV debut in as guest on series *Dallas*; 1987-89, worked extensively on TV: guest starred in *Another World, Dallas, Growing Pains, Head of the Class, 21 Jump Street, thirtysomething, Tales from the Crypt* ("King of the Road," 1989); 1990—starred in the TV series *Glory Days* (as Walker Lovejoy); has done advertisements for Levi's jeans and Mountain Dew soda; 1991—breakthrough film role in *Thelma & Louise*; 1992—starred in the Oscar-nominated short, *Contact*; 1994—read for the audio-book of Cormac McCarthy's novel, *All The Pretty Horses*. **Awards**: Golden Globe for Best Supporting Actor, for *12 Monkeys*, 1995. **Agent**: Creative Artists Agency, 9830 Wilshire Boulevard, Beverly Hills, CA 90212, U.S.A.

Films as Actor:

1987   *Less than Zero* (Kanievska) (extra)
1988   *A Stoning in Fulham County* (Elikann—for TV)
1989   *Cutting Class* (Pallenberg) (as Dwight Ingalls); *Happy Together* (Damski) (as Brian); *The Image* (Werner—for TV)
1990   *Too Young to Die?* (Markowitz—for TV) (as Billy Canton)
1991   *Across the Tracks* (Tung) (as Joe Maloney); **Thelma & Louise** (Ridley Scott) (as J. D.)
1992   *Contact* (short); *Cool World* (Bakshi) (as Frank Harris); *Johnny Suede* (DiCillo) (title role); *A River Runs through It* (Redford) (as Paul Maclean)
1993   *Kalifornia* (Sena) (as Early Grayce); *True Romance* (Tony Scott) (as Floyd)
1994   *The Favor* (Petrie—produced in 1991) (as Elliott); *Interview with the Vampire* (Neil Jordan) (as Louis); *Legends of the Fall* (Zwick) (as Tristan Ludlow)
1995   *Seven* (Fincher) (as David Mills); *12 Monkeys* (Gilliam) (as Jeffrey Goines)

1996   *Devil's Own* (Pakula); *Seven Years in Tibet* (Annaud); *Sleepers* (Levinson); *David*

Publications

By PITT: articles—

Interview with Alison Powell, in *Interview* (New York), February 1992.
"Hot Actor," interview with Jay Martel, in *Rolling Stone* (New York), 14 May 1992.
"Slippin' Around on the Road with Brad Pitt," interview with Chris Mundy, in *Rolling Stone* (New York), 1 December 1994.
"Brad Attitude," interview with Johanna Schneller, in *Vanity Fair* (New York), February 1995.

On PITT: books—

Catalano, Grace, *Brad Pitt: Hot and Sexy*, New York, 1995.
Nickson, Chris, *Brad Pitt*, New York, 1995.

On PITT: articles—

McKenna, Kristine, "The Bad Boy Makes Good," in *New York Times*, 7 July 1991.
Snowden, Lynn, "Brad Pitt Is Afraid of Sharks," in *Premiere* (New York), October 1994.
Mooney, Josh, "Brad Pitt: Thief of Hearts," in *Cosmopolitan*, November 1995.
Current Biography 1996, New York, 1996.

*   *   *

With seven leading feature film roles, four of them in blockbusters, over the four years 1992-95, Brad Pitt has proved himself a movie star for the "alternative" generation. That is, like the "alternative" rock bands who achieved mainstream success in the 1990s by revisiting rock traditions with a vaguely troubled nonchalance—rather than either a knowing distance or a fully immersed sincerity—Pitt walks in the footsteps of James Dean and all the screen's subsequent good-looking rebel males, but with a certain low-key looseness to his torment, an extravagance to his toughness, a calculation to both his blankness and his brains. If Dean and Marlon Brando are filled with angst, Steve McQueen and Paul Newman's personas seem emptier, both more entrenched in their out-of-step positions and more lost in them. Robert Redford's image appears emptier still, but preoccupied with a lack of concern about it, personifying anomie or perhaps protesting it by embracing its extreme. Pitt's characters typically accept a core of emptiness as a given, too, but they do not let it get in the way of their good times. Often they or those they care most about wind up dead or otherwise destroyed, but their movies are all about the queasy fun they have on the way.

Across a prolific string of guest appearances on television soap operas, sitcoms, drama series, and movies of the week, Pitt found his type—confused but charming all-American boy—and worked two sides of it as the size of his roles quickly increased. In four key pre-stardom performances he divided his time equally between playing good boys trying to get up in the world (the short-lived television series *Glory Days*, the low-budget feature *Across the Tracks*), and bad boys trying to get back at it (the episode of the anthology horror series *Tales from the Crypt* called "King of the Road," the television film *Too Young to Die?*).

It was a character from the latter category—J. D., an outlaw who steals the bankroll in Ridley Scott's *Thelma & Louise*—which opened

Brad Pitt with Juliette Lewis in *Kalifornia*

the doors to stardom for Pitt. But the pattern of his career as a leading man suggests that, in the 1990s, the lines separating conventionally striving young man, rebel, psychopath, and victim are hardly clear-cut. Not only does Pitt play all four types in separate instances, he usually combines elements of all four at once. J. D. himself gets a free ride with the film's heroines by pretending to be an earnest colle-gian—and by feigning nonaggression, giving up his plea for their help as soon as one expresses disapproval. Later, the freewheeling vigor of the exploitative sexuality and criminality J. D. unleashes for (and against) Geena Davis's Thelma is situated by the film as just a cover for his weakness and guilt, when the cop played by Harvey Keitel takes out his anger at the women's impossible situation by blaming and humiliating J. D.

In each of the four big-budget (and big box-office) vehicles that Pitt has carried after *Thelma*—*A River Runs through It, Interview with the Vampire, Legends of the Fall,* and *Seven*—his character similarly rides a crosscurrent of mutually canceling traits: iconoclastic but family-centered, wounded but destructive, unstable but brave. Pitt's choice of projects has shaped his overall persona along similar lines: for every ambivalent leading character there is both a tame supporting role (a too-comfortable boyfriend in *The Favor*) and a wild one (a drug-dazed roommate in *True Romance*). The supporting character whose por-trayal earned Pitt his first Academy Award nomination, Jeffrey Goines in *12 Monkeys*, is another perfect encapsulation of the incongruity gathered around Pitt as his generation's angry young man. Jeffrey seems insane at the beginning of the film, in his obsessive, evidently terroristic rebellion against his father—but by the end, Jeffrey's good reasons and intentions are revealed, albeit along with his powerless-ness.

Pitt has demonstrated his interest in art as well as commerce with several offbeat leading roles, all of which ask him to delve even more deeply than his mainstream hits into the essences of strongly desiring but perversely flawed men. He plays a never-will-be rock star/crimi-nal/worthy lover in the low-budget *Johnny Suede*; a detective stranded across lines of being from his true love as the only human in the cartoon *Cool World*; and a committed lover and friend but casual killer in *Kalifornia*. The last film saw a lot of weight and facial hair added to the form which won him *People* magazine's acclamation as the "sexi-est man alive" in January 1995. Clearly Brad Pitt has become some-thing of a flashpoint for his social moment's ideas about, and conflicts over, masculinity. The impressively wide-ranging devotion to his craft he has shown thus far should keep him at the on-screen epicenter of such conflicts for a long time to come.

—Susan Knobloch

PLEASENCE, Donald

Nationality: British. **Born:** Worksop, Nottinghamshire, 5 October 1919. **Education:** Attended grammar school in Ecclesfield, York-shire. **Military Service:** Royal Air Force during World War II: in prison camp for a year: discharged 1946 as flight lieutenant. **Family:** Married 1) Miriam Raymond, 1941 (divorced 1958), daughters: An-gela and Jean; 2) Josephine Martin Crombie, 1959, daughters: Lucy and Polly Jo; 3) Meira Shore, 1971, daughter: Alexis. **Career:** Worked for the railways, becoming manager of a station at Swinton, York-shire; 1939—assistant stage manager, then manager, of a theater in Jersey: stage debut in *Wuthering Heights*; 1942—London debut in *Twelfth Night*; 1946—on stage in London in *Vicious Circle*, then at Birmingham Repertory Theatre, 1948-50, and Bristol Old Vic Com-pany, 1950-51; 1951—New York stage debut in *Caesar and Cleopatra*; 1954—film debut in *The Beachcomber*; 1960—stage role in *The Care-*

taker, repeated in film version, 1963; 1977—in TV mini-series *Jesus of Nazareth*, in *The Bastard*, 1978, *Centennial*, 1978, and *Sighs and Wonders*, 1995; in TV series *The Barchester Chronicles*, 1982; co-founder, with Harold Pinter and Robert Shaw, Glasshouse Productions. **Died:** In St.-Paul-de-Vence, France, 2 February 1995.

Films as Actor:

1954   *The Beachcomber* (Box) (as Tromp); *Orders Are Orders* (Paltenghi) (as Corporal Martin)

1955   *Value for Money* (Annakin) (as Limpy)

1956   *1984* (Anderson) (as Parsons); *The Black Tent* (Hurst) (as Ali)

1957   *The Man in the Sky* (*Deception against Time*) (Crichton) (as Crabtree); *Manuela* (*Stowaway Girl*) (Hamilton) (as Evans); *Barnacle Bill* (Frend) (as bankteller)

1958   *A Tale of Two Cities* (Thomas) (as Barsad); *Heart of a Child* (Clive Donner) (as Speil); *The Wind Cannot Read* (Thomas) (as doctor); *The Man Inside* (Gilling) (as organ grinder); *The Two Headed Spy* (de Toth) (as General Hardt)

1959   **Look Back in Anger** (Richardson) (as Hurst); *Killers of Kilimanjaro* (Thorpe) (as Captain); *The Battle of the Sexes* (Crichton) (as Irwin Hoffman)

1960   *The Shakedown* (Lemont) (as Jessel); *The Flesh and the Fiends* (*Mania*) (Gilling) (as William Hare); *Hell Is a City* (Guest) (as Gus Hawkins); *Circus of Horrors* (Hayers) (as Vanet); *Sons and Lovers* (Cardiff) (as Pappleworth); *The Big Day* (Scott) (as Victor Partridge); *Suspect* (*The Risk*) (Boulting) (as Brown); *The Hands of Orlac* (*Les Mains d'Orlac*) (Gréville) (as Coates); *A Story of David* (McNaught) (as Nabal)

1961   *No Love for Johnnie* (Thomas) (as Roger Renfrew); *The Wind of Change* (Sewell) (as Pop); *Spare the Rod* (Norman) (as Jenkins); *The Horsemasters* (Fairchild) (as Major Pinksy); *What a Carve Up!* (Jackson) (as Everett Sloane); *The In-spector* (*Lisa*) (Dunne) (as Sergeant Walters)

1962   *Dr. Crippen* (Lynn) (title role)

1963   *The Caretaker* (*The Guest*) (Clive Donner) (as Davis); *The Great Escape* (John Sturges) (as Blythe)

1965   *The Greatest Story Ever Told* (Stevens) (as the Dark Hermit); *The Hallelujah Trail* (John Sturges) (as Oracle Jones)

1966   *Cul-de-Sac* (Polanski) (as George); *Matchless* (Lattuada) (as Andreanu); *Eye of the Devil* (Thompson) (as Pere Dominic); *The Night of the Generals* (Litvak) (as General Kahlenberge); *Fantastic Voyage* (Fleischer) (as Dr. Michaels)

1967   *Will Penny* (Gries) (as Preacher Quint); *You Only Live Twice* (Gilbert) (as Blofeld)

1969   *The Madwoman of Chaillot* (Forbes) (as prospector); *Arthur Arthur* (Gallu) (cameo role)

1970   *THX 1138* (Lucas) (as SEN 5241); *Soldier Blue* (Nelson) (as Isaac Cumber); *Mister Freedom* (Klein) (as Dr. Freedom)

1971   *The Pied Piper* (Demy) (as Baron)

1972   *Kidnapped* (Delbert Mann) (as Ebenezer Balfour); *Innocent Bystanders* (Collinson) (as Loomis); *Henry VIII and His Six Wives* (Hussein) (as Thomas Cromwell); *The Jerusalem File* (Flynn) (as Maj. Samuels); *Death Live* (*Raw Meat*) (Sherman) (as Inspector Colquhoun)

1973   *Wedding in White* (Fruet) (as Jim); *From beyond the Grave* (Connor) (as peddler); *Tales That Witness Madness* (Francis) (as Tremayne)

1974   *The Black Windmill* (Siegel) (as Cedric Harper); *The Mutations* (Cardiff) (as Nolter); *Barry Mackenzie Holds His Own* (Beresford) (as Erich, Count Plasma); *Journey into Fear* (Daniel Mann) (as Kuvetli)

1975   *The Count of Monte Cristo* (Greene—for TV) (as Danglars); *Heart of the West* (*Hollywood Cowboy*) (Zieff) (as A. J. Nietz); *I Don't Want to Be Born* (*The Devil within Her*) (Sasdy) (as Dr. Finch); *Escape to Witch Mountain* (Hough) (as Deranian)

1976   *The Devil's Men* (*Land of the Minotaur*) (Carayiannis) (as Father Roche); *The Last Tycoon* (Kazan) (as Boxley); *The Passover Plot* (Campus) (as Pontius Pilate); *Dirty Knights' Work* (*Trial by Combat*; *A Choice of Weapons*) (Connor) (as Sir Giles Marley)

1977   *The Eagle Has Landed* (John Sturges) (as Heinrich Himmler); *Telefon* (Siegel) (as Nicolai Dalchimsky); *The Uncanny* (Heroux) (as Valentine De'Ath); *Oh, God!* (Carl Reiner) (as Dr. Harmon); *Night Creature* (Madden); *Goldenrod* (Hart—for TV)

1978   *Sergeant Pepper's Lonely Hearts Club Band* (Schultz) (as B. D. Brockhearst); *Halloween* (Carpenter) (as Loomis); *Power Play* (Burke) (as Blair); *The Dark Secret of Harvest Home* (Leo Penn—for TV) (as narrator); *L'Ordre et la securité du monde* (d'Anna); *The Defection of Simas Kurdirka* (Rich—for TV)

1979   *Gold of the Amazon Women* (Lester—for TV); *Tomorrow Never Comes* (Collinson) (as Dr. Todd); *All Quiet on the Western Front* (Delbert Mann—for TV) (as Kantoreck); *Les Liens du sang* (*Blood Relatives*) (Chabrol) (as Doniac); *Dracula* (Badham) (as Seward); *Better Late Than Never* (Crenna—for TV); *Good Luck, Miss Wyckoff* (Chomsky) (as Steiner); *Jaguar Lives* (Pintoff) (as General Villinova); *L'Homme en colère* (*The Angry Man*; *Jigsaw*) (Pinoteau) (as France)

1980   *Halloween II* (Rosenthal) (as Loomis)

1981   *Escape from New York* (Carpenter) (as President of the U.S.); *The Monster Club* (Baker) (as Pickering); *The Thing* (Carpenter)

1982   *Alone in the Dark* (Sholder); *Witness for the Prosecution* (Gibson—for TV); *Race for the Yankee Zephyr* (*Treasure of the Yankee Zephyr*) (Hemmings); *To Kill a Stranger* (Moctezuma) (as Col. Kostik)

1983   *The Devonsville Terror* (Lommel)

1984   *Warrior of the Lost Word* (Worth); *A Breed Apart* (Mora); *Where Is Parsifal?* (Helman); *The Ambassador* (*Peacemaker*) (Thompson) (as Minister Eretz)

1985   *The Corsican Brothers* (Sharp—for TV); *Terror in the Aisles* (Kuehn—compilation film) (as narrator); *Arch of Triumph* (Hussein—for TV) (as Haake); *Frankenstein's Great Aunt Tillie* (Gold); *Phenomena* (*Creepers*) (Argento) (as John McGregor); *Sotto il vestito niente* (*Nothing Underneath*) (Vanzina) (as Inspector); *Treasure of the Amazon* (Cardona) (as Klaus)

1986   *Cobra Mission* (*The Rainbow Professional*) (Ludman)

1987   *Scoop* (Millar—for TV); *Spettri* (*Specters*) (Avallone) (as Prof. Lasky, Archaeologist); *Warrior Queen* (*Pompeii*) (Vincent) (as Claudius); *Il grande ritorno di Django* (*Django Strikes Again*) (Ted Archer); *Prince of Darkness* (Carpenter) (as Priest); *Ground Zero* (Pattinson and Myles) (as Prosper Gaffney)

1988   *Commander* (Dawson); *The Great Escape II: The Untold Story* (Taylor—for TV); *Halloween IV: The Return of Michael Myers* (Little) (as Dr. Loomis); *Hanna's War* (Golan) (as Rosza); *Paganini Horror* (Coates); *Phantom of Death* (Deodato); *The House of Usher* (Birkinshaw) (as Clive Usher)

1989   *The Room* (Altman); *Halloween V: The Revenge of Michael Myers* (Othenin-Girard) (as Dr. Loomis); *Ten Little Indians* (Birkinshaw) (as Justice Wargrave); *River of Death* (Carver) (as Heinrich Spaatz)

1990   *I, Charles de Gaulle* (Granier-Deferre); *Miliardi* (*Billions*) (Vanzina) (as Ripa); *Buried Alive* (Kikoine) (as Dr. Schaeffer)

1991   *Dien Bien phu* (Schoendoerffer) (as Howard Simpson); *American Rickshaw* (Martino) (as the Reverend Morton)

1992   *Shadows and Fog* (Woody Allen) (as Doctor)

1994   *Hour of the Pig* (Megahey) (as Pincheon); *Femme Fatale* (Prasad) (as Victor Harty)

1995   *Merlin* (for TV); *Halloween VI: The Curse of Michael Myers* (Chapelle) (as Dr. Loomis)

Publications

By PLEASENCE: articles—

"Taking the Pick," in *Films and Filming* (London), August 1962.
Interview with L. Hart, in *Cinema Canada* (Montreal), June-July 1973.
Interview with Tim Pulleine, in *Films and Filming* (London), April 1985.

On PLEASENCE: articles—

Current Biography 1969, New York, 1969.
Obituary, in *New York Times*, 3 February 1995.

*   *   *

His distinctive bald pate, a slightly otherworldly glint in his pale blue eyes, and an unnerving fixated manner combined to make Donald Pleasence an arresting character actor. Most often cast as a Milquetoast or unctuous schemer in his early career, he absorbed the same traits into the predominantly villainous roles that became the trademark of his later screen career.

Pleasence made his film debut in Muriel Box's *The Beachcomber*, a remake of the 1938 Charles Laughton vehicle, opposite Robert Newton as the title character. Turns as the real-life murderer and body snatcher William Hare in John Gilling's *The Flesh and the Fiends* and the henpecked title character (his only starring role) in *Dr. Crippen*, a vivid recounting of the legendary case of the British wife murderer of that name, anticipated numerous horror roles to come.

Pleasence drew critical raves for his central role in the dark, absurdist comedy *The Guest*, based on Harold Pinter's play *The Caretaker*. The performance attracted the attention of Roman Polanski, who cast Pleasence in his own dark, absurdist comedy *Cul-de-Sac*, the Polish director's second English-language film. Pleasence played George, the quintessential Polanski protagonist, a man whose life comes undone when his insular world is intruded upon by outsiders, in this case a pair of fleeing gangsters.

The Great Escape, in which Pleasence appeared among a large international cast, opened the door to Hollywood, where he enjoyed a busy career on the big and small screens (appearing in such hit television series as *The Twilight Zone* and *The Outer Limits*). He made the transition to horror film staple for an entire generation when John Carpenter cast him as the obsessed doctor on the trail of the "ultimate evil," a mass-murdering former patient named Michael Myers, in *Halloween*. Pleasence's character was named Sam Loomis after the part played by John Gavin in Hitchcock's classic *Psycho*. Pleasence reappeared as Loomis in five *Halloween* sequels, the last of which, *Halloween VI: The Curse of Michael Myers*, was released after Pleasence's death in 1995.

—Bill Wine, updated by John McCarty

961

POITIER, Sidney

Nationality: American. **Born:** Miami, Florida, 20 February 1924 (some sources say 1927), grew up in the Bahamas. **Education:** Attended Western Senior High School and Governor's High School, both in Nassau. **Family:** Married 1) Juanita Hardy, 1950, daughters: Beverly, Pamela, Sherry, Gina; 2) the actress Joanna Shimkus, 1976, two children. **Career:** 1942-45—served in the U.S. Army as a physiotherapist; member of the American Negro Theater: in *Days of Our Youth* and other plays; 1946—Broadway debut in *Lysistrata* in all-black production; 1948—toured with play *Anna Lucasta*; 1949—film debut in Signal Corps documentary *From Whom Cometh My Help*; 1950—fiction film debut in *No Way Out*; 1959—in stage play *A Raisin in the Sun*, and in film version, 1961; 1968—directed Broadway play *Carry Me Back to Morningside Heights*; 1969—co-founder, with Paul Newman and Barbra Streisand, First Artists Productions; 1972—first directed film, *Buck and the Preacher*. **Awards:** Best Actor, Berlin Festival, and Best Foreign Actor, British Academy, for *The Defiant Ones*, 1958; Best Actor Academy Award, and Best Actor, Berlin Festival, for *Lilies of the Field*, 1963; Life Achievement Award, American Film Institute, 1992. **Address:** c/o Verdon Productions, 9350 Wilshire Boulevard, Beverly Hills, CA 90212, U.S.A.

Films as Actor:

1949	*From Whom Cometh My Help* (Signal Corps doc)
1950	*No Way Out* (Mankiewicz) (as Dr. Luther Brooks)
1952	*Cry, the Beloved Country* (Korda) (as Reverend Msimangu); *Red Ball Express* (Boetticher) (as Corporal Andrew Robertson)
1954	*Go, Man, Go!* (Howe) (as Inman Jackson)
1955	*Blackboard Jungle* (Richard Brooks) (as Gregory Miller)
1956	*Goodbye, My Lady* (Wellman) (as Gates)
1957	*Edge of the City* (Ritt) (as Tommy Tyler); *Something of Value* (Richard Brooks) (as Kimani); *Band of Angels* (Walsh) (as Rau-ru)
1958	*Mark of the Hawk* (Audley) (as Obam); *The Defiant Ones* (Kramer) (as Noah Cullen); *The Virgin Island* (Jackson) (as Marcus)
1959	*Porgy and Bess* (Preminger) (as Porgy)
1960	*All the Young Men* (Bartlett) (as Towler)
1961	*A Raisin in the Sun* (Petrie) (as Walter Lee Younger); *Paris Blue* (Ritt) (as Eddie Cook)
1962	*Pressure Point* (Cornfield) (as Doctor)
1963	*Lilies of the Field* (Nelson) (as Homer Smith)
1964	*The Long Ships* (Cardiff) (as Ali Mansuh)
1965	*The Greatest Story Ever Told* (Stevens) (as Simon of Cyrene); *The Bedford Incident* (Harris) (as Ben Munceford); *A Patch of Blue* (Green) (as Gordon Ralfe)
1966	*The Slender Thread* (Pollack) (as Alan Newell); *Duel at Diablo* (Nelson) (as Toller)
1967	*To Sir with Love* (Clavell) (as Mark Thackeray); *In the Heat of the Night* (Jewison) (as Virgil Tibbs); *Guess Who's Coming to Dinner* (Kramer) (as John Prentice)
1968	*For Love of Ivy* (Daniel Mann) (as Jack Parks)
1969	*The Lost Man* (Arthur) (as Jason Higgs)
1970	*They Call Me Mister Tibbs!* (Douglas) (title role)
1971	*The Organization* (Medford) (as Virgil Tibbs); *Brother John* (Goldstone) (as John Kane)
1975	*The Wilby Conspiracy* (Nelson) (as Shack Twala)
1988	*Shoot to Kill* (*Deadly Pursuit*) (Spottiswoode) (as Warren Stantin); *Little Nikita* (*The Sleeper*) (Benjamin) (as Roy Parmenter)
1991	*Separate but Equal* (Stevens Jr.—for TV) (as Thurgood Marshall)
1991	*Children of the Dust* (David Greene—for TV) (as Gypsy Smith)
1992	*Sneakers* (Robinson) (as Donald Crease)

Films as Director:

1972	*Buck and the Preacher* (+ ro as Buck)
1973	*A Warm December* (+ ro as Matt Younger)
1974	*Uptown Saturday Night* (+ ro as Steve Jackson)
1975	*Let's Do It Again* (+ ro as Clyde Williams)
1977	*A Piece of the Action* (+ ro as Manny Durrell)
1980	*Stir Crazy*
1982	*Hanky Panky*
1984	*Shootout*
1985	*Fast Forward*
1990	*Ghost Dad*

Publications

By POITIER: book—

This Life, New York, 1980.

By POITIER: articles—

"They Call Me a Do-It-Yourself Man," in *Films and Filming* (London), September 1959.

"Talking of Corruption," in *Films and Filming* (London), August 1961.

"Entertainment, Politics, and the Movie Business," interview with G. Noble, in *Cineaste* (New York), Winter 1977-78.

"Walking the Hollywood Color Line," in *American Film* (Washington, D.C.), April 1980.

Interview with Frank Spotnitz, in *American Film* (Washington, D.C.), September/October 1991.

On POITIER: books—

Newquist, Roy, *A Special Kind of Magic*, New York, 1967.
Hoffman, William, *Sidney*, New York, 1971.
Null, Gary, *Black Hollywood: The Negro in Motion Pictures*, Secaucus, New Jersey, 1975.
Marill, Alvin H., *The Films of Sidney Poitier*, Secaucus, New Jersey, 1978.
Keyser, Lester, and Andre Ruszkowski, *The Cinema of Sidney Poitier: The Black Man's Changing Role on the American Screen*, San Diego, 1980.
Kelley, Samuel L., *The Evolution of Character Portrayals in the Films of Sidney Poitier, 1950-78*, Jefferson, North Carolina, 1983.

On POITIER: articles—

Current Biography 1959, New York, 1959.
Cripps, Thomas, "Death of Rastus: Negro in American Films since 1945," in *Phylon*, Fall 1967.
Mason, Clifford, "Why Does White America Love Sidney Poitier So?," in the *New York Times*, 10 September 1967.
Sanders, Charles L., "Sidney Poitier: Man behind the Superman," in *Ebony* (Chicago), April 1968.
Hall, D. J., "Pride without Prejudice," in *Films and Filming* (London), December 1971 and January 1972.
Kael, Pauline, "Sidney Poitier," in *The Movie Star*, edited by Elisabeth Weis, New York, 1981.

Sidney Poitier in *Edge of the City*

Kelley, Samuel, "Sidney Poitier: héros intégrationiste," in *CinémAction* (Paris), January 1988.

*   *   *

As the Hollywood film industry ended the twentieth century, Eddie Murphy, Danny Glover, and Denzel Washington could be counted as major movie stars. But they owe a major part of their success to Sidney Poitier's pioneering efforts three decades earlier. In the late 1950s and through the 1960s Poitier singlehandedly transformed the Hollywood movie's image of the black man from the racist "coon" to the positive hero.

During the 1960s Poitier was *the* symbol of the liberal Hollywood, a black actor with dignity. But this had not been achieved "overnight," without struggle. During the early 1950s he took what parts he could land, from Joseph Mankiewicz's *No Way Out*, where he played an educated, bright, and dedicated doctor caught in a heated racial situation, to James Wong Howe's sole credit as a director, the creaky portrait of the Harlem Globetrotters' basketball enterprise, *Go, Man, Go!*

Richard Brooks's somewhat sanitized portrait of inner-city America, *Blackboard Jungle*, made Poitier a star. Thereafter his presence became a symbol to the rising consciousness about racial segregation in the United States. Noted producers cast him in roles designed for his new image. Most self-conscious was Stanley Kramer's *The Defiant Ones*, with black and white chained together trying to escape from a brutal Southern prison camp. Otto Preminger's *Porgy and Bess* was the director's homage to black life in the South, while in *Lilies of the Field* Poitier assisted a group of nuns, a "feel good" classic.

During this period he was much honored, winning many awards, from prizes from the Venice and Berlin Film Festivals to a New York Film Critics Award for best actor to the William J. German Human Relations Award from the American Jewish Congress. He won a much-deserved Oscar for *Lilies of the Field*, and so became a top box-office draw for *A Patch of Blue*, *To Sir, with Love*, *In the Heat of the Night*, and *Guess Who's Coming to Dinner?* In 1967 Poitier was rated number seven on a list of top moneymaking stars; the following year he ranked first.

By 1969 he had done so well he was able, with Paul Newman, Barbra Streisand, Steve McQueen, and Dustin Hoffman to create the First Artists Film Production Company. He had decided then to work within the Hollywood system and become a director, but *Buck and the Preacher*, *A Warm December*, and *Uptown Saturday Night* made precious little money. He returned to acting, with little success. *Little Nikita* ended his career as a leading man.

Poitier had become a member of the establishment, penning a celebrated autobiography in 1980. His black detective from the North made so famous with *In the Heat of the Night* was considered radical in the late 1960s. Two decades later no one commented on his roles as an FBI agent. In 1989 he was elected to the Board of Trustees for the American Museum of the Moving Image. In 1992 he was honored with the American Film Institute Life Achievement Award, in 1994 he earned the National Board of Review Career Achievement Award, and in 1995 he was honored with the Kennedy Center Honors Lifetime Achievement Award.

—Douglas Gomery

POWELL, Dick

Nationality: American. **Born:** Richard Ewing Powell in Mountain View, Arkansas, 14 November 1904. **Education:** Attended high school in Little Rock, Arkansas, Little Rock College, one year. **Family:** Married 1) M. Maund; 2) the actress Joan Blondell, 1936 (divorced 1945), daughter: Ellen, adopted son: Norman; 3) the actress June Allyson, 1945, adopted daughter. **Career:** Singer with his own band from age 17; also played baritone horn; toured with the Royal Peacock Band, then with Charlie Davis's orchestra, Indianapolis; 1930—singer, comedian, and master of ceremonies at Stanley Theatre, Pittsburgh; also sang on radio; 1932—film debut in *Blessed Event*; contract with Warner Brothers; also sang on radio series *Hollywood Hotel*; 1940s—changeover to dramatic roles in films; contracts with Paramount and RKO; on radio series *The Band Wagon*, *Rogue's Gallery*, 1945-46, and *The Front Page*, 1948; 1952—co-founder, with Charles Boyer, Ida Lupino, and David Niven, Four Star Productions for television, and regular actor in series *Four Star Playhouse*, 1952-56; host, *Dick Powell's Zane Grey Theatre*, 1956-61, and *The Dick Powell Show*, 1961-63; 1953—first directed film, *Split Second*. **Died:** 2 January 1963.

Films as Actor:

1932　*Blessed Event* (Del Ruth) (as night club owner); *Too Busy to Work* (*Jubilo*) (Blystone)

1933　*The King's Vacation* (Adolphi); ***42nd Street*** (Bacon) (as Billy Lawler); *The Gold Diggers of 1933* (LeRoy) (as Robert Treat Bradford/Brad Roberts); *Footlight Parade* (Bacon); *College Coach* (Wellman); *Convention City* (Mayo)

1934　*Dames* (Berkeley); *Wonder Bar* (Bacon); *Twenty Million Sweethearts* (Enright); *Happiness Ahead* (LeRoy); *Flirtation Walk* (Borzage)

1935　*The Gold Diggers of 1935* (Berkeley); *Page Miss Glory* (LeRoy); *Broadway Gondolier* (Bacon); *A Midsummer Night's Dream* (Reinhardt and Dieterle) (as Lysander); *Shipmates Forever* (Borzage); *Thanks a Million* (Del Ruth)

1936　*Colleen* (Green); *Hearts Divided* (Borzage) (as Jerome Bonaparte); *Stage Struck* (Berkeley); *The Gold Diggers of 1937* (Berkeley)

1937　*On the Avenue* (Del Ruth); *The Singing Marine* (Enright); *Varsity Show* (Berkeley); *Hollywood Hotel* (Berkeley)

1938　*Cowboy from Brooklyn* (Bacon); *Hard to Get* (Enright); *Going Places* (Enright)

1939　*Naughty but Nice* (Enright)

1940　*Christmas in July* (Preston Sturges); *I Want a Divorce* (Murphy)

1941　*Model Wife* (Jason); *In the Navy* (Lubin)

1942　*Star Spangled Rhythm* (Marshall) (as himself); *Happy Go Lucky* (Bernhardt)

1943　*True to Life* (Marshall); *Riding High* (Marshall)

1944　*It Happened Tomorrow* (Clair); *Meet the People* (Reisner); *Murder, My Sweet* (Dmytryk) (as Philip Marlowe)

1945　*Cornered* (Dmytryk)

1947　*Johnny O'Clock* (Rossen)

1948　*To the Ends of the Earth* (Stephenson); *The Pitfalls* (de Toth); *Station West* (Lanfield); *Rogue's Regiment* (Florey)

1949　*Mrs. Mike* (King)

1950　*The Reformer and the Redhead* (Panama); *Right Cross* (John Sturges)

1951　*Cry Danger* (Parrish); *The Tall Target* (Anthony Mann); *You Never Can Tell* (Breslow)

1952　*The Bad and the Beautiful* (Minnelli)

1954　*Susan Slept Here* (Tashlin)

Films as Director:

1953　*Split Second*

1956　*The Conqueror* (+ pr)

1957　*You Can't Run Away from It* (+ pr); *The Enemy Below* (+ pr)

1958　*The Hunters* (+ pr)

Publications

On POWELL: articles—

Current Biography 1948, New York, 1948.

Thomas, Anthony, "Dick Powell," in *Films in Review* (New York), May 1961.

Obituary in *New York Times*, 4 January 1963.

Corneau, E., "The Crooner Who Turned Tough Guy," in *Classic Film Collector*, Fall 1972.

*　　*　　*

Dick Powell was a rare performer in the motion picture business. While other, more talented performers came and went, Dick Powell managed to hang on as a star for more than two decades, evolving from boy crooner in the 1930s to tough guy in the 1940s. By the 1950s he was able to move directly into television and became a top producer. Powell understood his own limitations: "I started out with two assets: a voice that didn't drive audiences into the streets, and a determination to make money."

During the 1930s, beginning with *42nd Street*, Powell functioned as the leading man in innumerable Warner Brothers musicals. Cherubically smiling, he chased Ruby Keeler through such films as *The Gold Diggers of 1933*, *Dames*, and *Footlight Parade*. Powell's performances were workmanlike, and helped boost him into the Motion Picture Herald's list of top stars in 1935 (seventh place) and 1936 (sixth place).

From 1939 on, Dick Powell strove to break his image of adolescent singer. He moved to Paramount and took on different roles, including comedies for Preston Sturges (*Christmas in July*) and René Clair (*It Happened Tomorrow*). But only another move to RKO gave Powell the chance to develop an altogether new screen image. In *Murder, My Sweet* he became an active participant in the film noir cycle of the 1940s. Other films of this genre that starred Dick Powell include

Dick Powell

Cornered, *Johnny O'Clock*, and *Pitfall*. For the 1940s there was a "new, rough tough Dick Powell," popular but never reaching the fame of the boy crooner of the 1930s.

In the 1950s, Powell began to direct and produce television. He formed Four Star Television with David Niven, Ida Lupino, and Charles Boyer, but it was Powell who ran the corporation, producing such hits as *The Rifleman*, *Wanted—Dead or Alive*, and *The Detectives*.

—Douglas Gomery

POWELL, Eleanor

Nationality: American. **Born:** Springfield, Massachusetts, 21 November 1912. **Family:** Married the actor Glenn Ford, 1943 (divorced 1959), son: Peter. **Career:** Began studying ballet at age 6; appeared in Atlantic City clubs as a child; 1928—dance debut with Co-Optimists troupe in New York; then learned tap dancing; 1929—Broadway debut in *Follow Through*; 1935—film debut in *George White's Scandals*; 1936—lead role in film *Broadway Melody of 1936*; contract with

Eleanor Powell

MGM, and made series of successful musicals until 1940; 1953-56—created and acted in TV series *Faith of Our Children*; 1960-64—in musical revues in Las Vegas and New York. **Awards:** Five Emmys for *Faith of Our Children* TV series. **Died:** In Beverly Hills, California, 11 February 1982.

Films as Actress:

1935 *George White's Scandals* (*George White's 1935 Scandals*) (White) (as Marilyn Collins); *Broadway Melody of 1936* (Del Ruth) (as Irene Foster/Mlle. Arlette)
1936 *Born to Dance* (Del Ruth) (as Nora Paige)
1937 *Broadway Melody of 1938* (Del Ruth) (as Sally Lee); *Rosalie* (Van Dyke) (title role)
1939 *Honolulu* (Buzzell) (as Dorothy March)
1940 *Broadway Melody of 1940* (Taurog) (as Clare Bennett)
1941 *Lady Be Good* (McLeod) (as Marilyn Marsh)
1942 *Ship Ahoy* (Buzzell) (as Tallulah Winters)
1943 *I Dood It* (*By Hook or by Crook*) (Minnelli) (as Constance Shaw); *Thousands Cheer* (Sidney) (as featured performer)
1945 *Sensations of 1945* (*Sensations*) (Andrew L. Stone) (as Ginny Walker)
1950 *Duchess of Idaho* (Leonard) (as featured performer)

Publications

By POWELL: articles—

"Eleanor Powell Talking to John Kobal," in *Focus on Film* (London), Autumn 1974 and Spring 1975.
Interview with John Kobal, in *People Will Talk*, New York, 1985.

On POWELL: books—

Thomas, Tony, *That's Dancing!*, New York, 1985.
Schultz, Margie, *Eleanor Powell: A Bio-Bibliography*, Westport, Connecticut, 1994.

On POWELL: articles—

Pérez, M., "Un Fusée pointée vers les planches: Eleanor Powell, des Scandales à la Broadway Melody de 1940," in *Positif* (Paris), February 1977.
Classic Images (Indiana, Pennsylvania), April 1982.
The Annual Obituary 1982, New York, 1983.
Films in Review (New York), April 1984.

*   *   *

Eleanor Powell assumed the mantle of Hollywood's top female tap dancer from Ruby Keeler. But where one might question Keeler's dancing ability, Powell's films provide clear evidence that she danced without peer. This view seems confirmed by the Dance Masters of America who awarded her the title of world's greatest tap dancer and by MGM's willingness to showcase an unknown in her second film. MGM banked on America's tap-dancing craze during the 1930s to catapult Powell to immediate stardom; a gamble which paid off handsomely. Her weak acting and singing (she was usually dubbed by Marjorie Lane) failed to detract and she became a box-office smash. In 11 films from *Broadway Melody of 1936* to *Sensations of 1945* Powell remained the premier female tap dancer. Arturo Toscanini once said that the three things he would remember most about his trip to the West Coast were the sunset, the Grand Canyon, and

Eleanor Powell's dancing. As she retired, Ann Miller literally followed in her footsteps to dominate tap during the late 1940s and early 1950s.

Powell incorporated acrobatics and ballet (which she studied first) into tap, creating a unique dance style that emphasized high kicks, rapid "grands pirouettes," "chain turns," and gymnastics. She also employed steps, positions, and movements usually reserved for men. Her aggressive and powerful technique ultimately classified her as a solo performer. As Fred Astaire said in *Steps in Time*, "She 'put 'em down' like a man, no ricky-ticky-sissy stuff with Ellie. She really knocked out a tap dance in a class by herself." The consistency of her dancing also offers sufficient evidence that she worked as her own choreographer.

All Powell's films, except *Broadway Melody of 1940*, move to opulent finales which she dances without a partner; she does however dance with a chorus. In *Broadway Melody of 1936* she performs in a glittering tuxedo surrounded by 30 male dancers in top hat and tails. In *Born to Dance*, Powell commands a battleship (set), its "crew," two military bands, and a battalion of women. In *Rosalie*, she dances with 34 West Point cadets and 500 extras. This solo emphasis created an obvious problem for MGM when casting romantic musical comedies. In fact, MGM could not find her a suitable dancing partner. No male dancer with whom she teamed could match her tap virtuosity; only Fred Astaire in *Broadway Melody of 1940* proved an equal partner. (Their "Begin the Beguine" routine remains one of the most sublime performances in Hollywood musical history.) Consequently, MGM usually paired her with nondancing male stars such as Jimmy Stewart, Robert Taylor, and Nelson Eddie. Powell eventually courted seven leading men in nine films over an eight-year span, and even danced with Buttons the Dog in *Lady Be Good* and a horse in *Sensations of 1945*.

Powell always portrayed a self-assured, intelligent, and independent woman, with strong and supportive female friends, interested in romance but not as an exclusive goal. Her idealized placement was reinforced by her comparison to other women in the films who ranged from gold-diggers to the freakish to the vain. This characterization reflected her dance routines which, as already mentioned, also upset the romantic comedy formula of female to male capitulation. During the late 1930s and early 1940s, such a persona undoubtedly added to her popularity.

—Greg S. Faller

POWELL, William

Nationality: American. **Born:** William Horatio Powell in Pittsburgh, Pennsylvania, 29 July 1892. **Education:** Attended high school in Kansas City; University of Kansas, Lawrence, briefly; American Academy of Dramatic Arts, New York, 1911-12. **Family:** Married 1) the actress Eileen Wilson (divorced 1931), son: William David; 2) the actress Carole Lombard, 1931 (divorced 1933); 3) the actress Diana Lewis, 1940. **Career:** 1912—Broadway debut in *The Ne'er-Do-Well*; 1913-15—in road company of the melodrama *Within the Law*; then acted in the Harry Davis company, Pittsburgh, the Baker company, Portland, Oregon, the Jessie Bonsteele company, Buffalo, and others; 1918-19—with Castle Square Stock Company, Boston; 1922—film debut in *Spanish Love*; 1925-31—contract with Paramount, followed by contract with Warner Brothers, 1931-34, and MGM, 1934. **Awards:** Best Actor, New York Film Critics, for *Life with Father*, and *The Senator Was Indiscreet*, 1947. **Died:** 5 March 1984.

Films as Actor:

1922 *Spanish Love*; *Sherlock Holmes* (Parker) (as Forman Wells); *When Knighthood Was in Flower* (Vignola) (as Francis I); *Outcast* (Withey) (as DeValle)

1923 *The Bright Shawl* (Robertson)

1924 *Under the Red Robe* (Crosland) (as Duke of Orleans); *Romola* (King) (as Tito Melema); *Dangerous Money* (Tuttle)

1925 *Too Many Kisses* (Sloane); *Faint Perfume* (Gasnier); *My Lady's Lips* (Hogan); *The Beautiful City* (Webb)

1926 *White Mice* (Edward Griffith); *Sea Horses* (Dwan); *Desert Gold* (Seitz); *The Runaway* (William DeMille); *Aloma of the South Seas* (Tourneur); *Beau Geste* (Brenon) (as Boldoni); *Tin Gods* (Dwan); *The Great Gatsby* (Brenon) (as George Wilson)

1927 *New York* (Reed); *Love's Greatest Mistake* (Sutherland); *Special Delivery* (Goodrich); *Senorita* (Badger); *Paid to Love* (Hawks); *Time for Love* (Tuttle); *Nevada* (Waters); *She's a Sheik* (Badger); *Feel My Pulse* (La Cava)

1928 *Beau Sabreur* (Waters); *Partners in Crime* (Strayer); *The Last Command* (von Sternberg); *The Dragnet* (von Sternberg); *The Vanishing Pioneer* (Waters); *Forgotten Faces* (Schertzinger)

1929 *Interference* (Mendez); *The Canary Murder Case* (St. Clair) (as Philo Vance); *The Green Murder Case* (Tuttle) (as Philo Vance); *Charming Sinners* (Milton); *Four Feathers* (Schoedsack and Mendez); *Pointed Heels* (Sutherland)

1930 *The Benson Murder Case* (Tuttle) (as Philo Vance); *Paramount on Parade* (as himself/Philo Vance); *Shadow of the Law* (Gasnier); *Behind the Makeup* (Milton); *Street of Chance* (Cromwell); *For the Defense* (Cromwell)

1931 *Man of the World* (Wallace); *Ladies Man* (Mendez); *The Road to Singapore* (Green)

1932 *High Pressure* (Le Roy); *Jewel Robbery* (Dieterle); *One Way Passage* (Garnett); *Lawyer Man* (Dieterle)

1933 *Double Harness* (Cromwell); *Private Detective 62* (Curtiz); *The Kennel Murder Case* (Curtiz) (as Philo Vance)

1934 *Fashions of 1934* (Dieterle); *The Key* (Curtiz); *Manhattan Melodrama* (Van Dyke); **The Thin Man** (Van Dyke) (as Nick Charles); *Evelyn Prentice* (Howard)

1935 *Reckless* (Fleming); *Star of Midnight* (Roberts); *Escapade* (Leonard); *Rendezvous* (Howard)

1936 *The Great Ziegfeld* (Leonard) (title role); *The Ex-Mrs. Bradford* (Roberts); *Libeled Lady* (Conway); *My Man Godfrey* (La Cava) (title role); *After the Thin Man* (Van Dyke) (as Nick Charles)

1937 *The Last of Mrs. Cheyney* (Boleslawsky); *The Emperor's Candlesticks* (Fitzmaurice); *Double Wedding* (Thorpe)

1938 *The Baroness and the Butler* (Walter Lang)

1939 *Another Thin Man* (Van Dyke) (as Nick Charles)

1940 *I Love You Again* (Van Dyke)

1941 *Love Crazy* (Conway); *Shadow of the Thin Man* (Van Dyke) (as Nick Charles)

1942 *Crossroads* (Conway)

1943 *The Youngest Profession* (Buzzell) (as himself)

1944 *The Heavenly Body* (Hall); *The Thin Man Goes Home* (Thorpe) (as Nick Charles)

1946 *Ziegfeld Follies* (Minnelli) (as Florenz Ziegfeld); *The Hoodlum Saint* (Taurog)

1947 *Song of the Thin Man* (Buzzell) (as Nick Charles); *Life with Father* (Curtiz) (as Clarence Day); *The Senator Was Indiscreet* (Kaufman)

1948 *Mr. Peabody and the Mermaid* (Pichel) (as Mr. Peabody)

1949 *Take One False Step* (Erskine); *Dancing in the Dark* (Reis)

1951 *The Treasure of the Lost Canyon* (Tetzlaff); *It's a Big Country* (Wellman and others)

1953 *The Girl Who Had Everything* (Thorpe); *How to Marry a Millionaire* (Negulesco)

1955 *Mister Roberts* (Ford and LeRoy) (as Doc)

Publications

On POWELL: books—

Morella, Joe, and Edward Epstein, *Gable & Lombard & Powell & Harlow*, London, 1971.

Francisco, Charles, *Gentleman: The William Powell Story*, New York, 1985.

Quirk, Lawrence J., *The Complete Films of William Powell*, Secaucus, New Jersey, 1986.

On POWELL: articles—

Current Biography 1947, New York, 1947.

Jacobs, Jack, "William Powell," in *Films in Review* (New York), November 1958.

Hurley, J., "Nora on Nick: Myrna Loy Talks about Her Co-Star," and "Remembering William Powell," by S. Rabin, in *Films in Review* (New York), October 1982.

Obituary in *New York Times*, 6 March 1984.

Obituary in *Variety* (New York), 14 March 1984.

Buckley, Michael, "A Final Tribute: William Powell," in *Films in Review* (New York), May 1984.

Rickey, C., "Bittersweet William," in *Film Comment* (New York), May/June 1984.

Winokur, Mark, "Improbable Ethnic Hero: William Powell and the Transformation of Ethnic Hollywood," in *Cinema Journal* (Champaign, Illinois), Fall 1987.

Drabelle, Dennis, "The Art of William Powell," in *Film Comment* (New York), May/June 1993.

* * * .

William Powell specialized in urbane cynicism, signifying unflappable, upper-class charm with the smallest gesture. A dependable actor at the MGM stable in the late 1930s and the 1940s, Powell, whether romantic, comic, or sinister, kept his edge of witty sophistication invariably intact.

Brief stage training in the early 1920s led to film work. His features—trim moustache, expressive eyes, close haircut—were ideal for silent picture villainy. He remained a busy supporting actor during that decade. Powell easily bridged the transition to sound, which utilized his talents fully. With the addition of his persuasive, carnival-barker voice, Powell was roguishly slick rather than suspicious, suitable for lawyer and detective parts as well as smooth criminals. One of his earliest talkie assignments, as the private eye Philo Vance in *The Canary Murder Case*, served as a preliminary for the role most closely associated with him: Nick Charles to Myrna Loy's Nora in the screen adaptation of Dashiell Hammett's *The Thin Man*. Powell and Loy generated a rare, extraordinary chemistry on-screen, pioneering a concept that would become a staple in screwball comedy—marriage could be fun, a partnership. The stars paired in 13 films altogether, including five additional *Thin Man* outings.

His subsequent screen roles were variations on the Charles theme, igniting a succession of classic comedies—*Libeled Lady*, *My Man Godfrey*, *Double Wedding*. Health problems led to relative inaction in the 1940s and after, but by choosing his roles with care and accuracy, he eased into genial character parts. In *Life with Father*, as the irascible Clarence Day, Powell reached another career peak. He chose to retire after his warmly received portrait of Doc in *Mister Roberts*.

Talent and fortunate material contributed to Powell's success. He ranks among the best sophisticated comedy stars, and his work remains eminently entertaining.

—Richard Sater

POWER, Tyrone

Nationality: American. **Born:** Tyrone Edmund Power in Cincinnati, Ohio, 5 May 1913; son of the actor Tyrone Power Sr. **Education:** Attended Sisters of Mercy Academy and St. Xavier Academy, both in Cincinnati; Preparatory School of the University of Dayton, 1928-29; Purcell High School, 1929-31. **Family:** Married 1) the actress Annabella, 1939 (divorced 1948); 2) the actress Linda Christian, 1949 (divorced 1955), daughters: the actresses: Romina and Taryn; 3) Deborah Ann Minardos, 1958, son: Tyrone Jr. **Career:** 1931—short season in minor roles with Shakespearean repertory company in Chicago; then worked at Santa Barbara Community Theatre for two years, at the Circuit Theatre in Chicago, and in summer stock in West Falmouth, Massachusetts; 1932—film debut in *Tom Brown of Culver*; 1936—contract with 20th Century-Fox; 1942-46—served in the U.S. Marine Corps as pilot: discharged as First Lieutenant; 1953—toured with Charles Laughton's group in *John Brown's Body*; later toured the United Kingdom in the stage play *The Devil's Disciple*. **Died:** 15 November 1958.

Films as Actor:

1932   *Tom Brown of Culver* (Wyler) (as John)

1934   *Flirtation Walk* (Borzage) (as cadet)

1936   *Girl's Dormitory* (Cummings) (as Count Vallais); *Ladies in Love* (Edward Griffith) (as Karl Lanyi); *Lloyd's of London* (King) (as Jonathan Blake)

1937   *Love Is News* (Garnett) (as Steve Layton); *Café Metropole* (Edward Griffith) (as Alexis Penayev/Alexander Brown); *Thin Ice* (Lanfield) (as Prince Rudolph); *Second Honeymoon* (Walter Lang) (as Raoul)

1938   *In Old Chicago* (King) (as Dion O'Leary); *Alexander's Ragtime Band* (King) (as Alexander/Rofer Grant); *Marie Antoinette* (Van Dyke) (as Count Axel de Fersen); *Suez* (Dwan) (as Ferdinand de Lesseps)

1939   *Jesse James* (King) (title role); *Rose of Washington Square* (Ratoff) (as Bart Clinton); *Second Fiddle* (Lanfield) (as Jimmy Sutton); *The Rains Came* (Brown) (as Major Rama Safti); *Daytime Wife* (Ratoff) (as Ken Norton)

1940   *Johnny Apollo* (Hathaway) (as Bob Cain); *Brigham Young—Frontiersman* (Hathaway) (as Jonathan Kent); *The Mark of Zorro* (Mamoulian) (as Don Diego Vega/Zorro)

1941   *Blood and Sand* (Mamoulian) (as Juan Gallardo); *A Yank in the R.A.F.* (King) (as Tim Baker)

1942   *Son of Fury* (Cromwell) (as Benjamin Blake); *This above All* (Litvak) (as Clive Briggs); *The Black Swan* (King) (as Jamie Waring)

1943   *Crash Dive* (Mayo) (as Lt. Ward Stewart)

1946   *The Razor's Edge* (Goulding) (as Larry Darrell)

1947   *Nightmare Alley* (Goulding) (as Stan Carlisle); *Captain from Castile* (King) (as Pedro de Vargas)

1948   *The Luck of the Irish* (Koster) (as Stephen Fitzgerald); *That Wonderful Urge* (Sinclair) (as Thomas Jefferson Tyler)

1949   *Prince of Foxes* (King) (as Andrea Orsini)

1950   *The Black Rose* (Hathaway) (as Walter of Gurnie); *American Guerilla in the Philippines* (*Guerillas*) (Fritz Lang) (as Ensign Chuck Palmer)

1951   *Rawhide* (Hathaway) (as Tom Owens); *I'll Never Forget You* (Baker) (as Peter Standish)

1952   *Diplomatic Encounter* (Hathaway) (as Mike Kells); *Pony Soldier* (Newman) (as Duncan MacDonald)

1953   *The Mississippi Gambler* (Maté) (as Mark Fallon)

1955   *The Long Gray Line* (Ford) (as Marty Mahar); *Untamed* (King) (as Paul Van Riebeck)

1956   *The Eddie Duchin Story* (Sidney) (title role)

1957   *Abandon Ship* (Sale) (as Alec Holmes); *The Sun Also Rises* (King) (as Jake Barnes)

1958   *Witness for the Prosecution* (Wilder) (as Leonard Vole)

Publications

On POWER: books—

Cameron, Ian, *Adventure in the Cinema*, London, 1973.
Thomas, Tony, *Cads and Cavaliers*, New York, 1973.
Richards, Jeffrey, *Swordsmen of the Screen: From Douglas Fairbanks to Michael York*, London, 1977.
Arce, Hector, *The Secret Life of Tyrone Power*, New York, 1979.
Guiles, Fred, *Tyrone Power: The Last Idol*, New York, 1979.
Belafonte, Dennis, and Alvin Marill, *The Films of Tyrone Power*, Secaucus, New Jersey, 1981.

On POWER: articles—

Current Biography 1950, New York, 1950.
Connor, Edward, "The Genealogy of Zorro," in *Films in Review* (New York), August-September 1957.
Obituary in *New York Times*, 16 November 1958.
Roman, R., "Tyrone Power," in *Films in Review* (New York), January 1959, also see letters in March 1959 issue.
Behlmer, Rudy, "Swordplay on the Screen," in *Films in Review* (New York), June-July 1965.

*   *   *

Descended from a long line of actors, and the namesake of a distinguished stage father, Tyrone Power learned his craft on Broadway. Blessed with sweet-faced good looks and an insouciant manner, he was signed by Twentieth Century-Fox as an answer to MGM's Robert Taylor. Along with his close friend and frequent co-star Don Ameche, he became the mainstay of Darryl Zanuck's star roster.

Most often cast as the romantic lead in period pictures such as *Lloyds of London*, *Marie Antoinette*, *Suez*, and *In Old Chicago*, Power also proved adept at light comedy, especially in the much underrated farce *Love Is News*. Frequently directed by Henry King or Henry Hathaway, and usually appearing opposite Loretta Young or Alice Faye, he became one of Hollywood's reigning heartthrobs.

Power enjoyed his best parts during the period from 1939 to 1941. He enlisted in the Marines during World War II and emerged from combat a harder, tougher man, his baby-face countenance gone forever. Even though he succeeded in highly dramatic roles such as *The Razor's Edge* and *Nightmare Alley*, Zanuck insisted on bringing back the Tyrone Power audiences loved before the war. He appeared in a number of comedies, including a remake of *Love Is News* entitled *That Wonderful Urge*, and a series of lavish costume epics: *Captain from Castile*, *The Black Rose*, *King of the Khyber Rifles*, and *Rawhide*. Unlike many stars, he continued to get good

Tyrone Power

parts as he grew older. Tyrone Power died an untimely death at the age of 45 while filming King Vidor's *Solomon and Sheba* in Madrid.

—John A. Gallagher

PRESLE, Micheline

Nationality: French. **Born:** Micheline Chassagne in Paris, 22 August 1922; known in the United States as Micheline Prelle. **Education:** Attended a convent school. **Family:** Married the actor William Marshall. **Career:** 1938—film debut in *Je chante*; successful leading roles followed; 1946—international success with Gérard Philipe in *Le Diable au corps*; 1950-51—made several American films; also acted on stage and television. **Address:** 6 rue Antoine-Dubois, Paris 75006, France.

Films as Actress:

(as Micheline Michel)
1938   *Je chante* (Stengel); *Petite peste* (de Limur); *Sais seule que j'aime* (Fescourt)

(as Micheline Presle)
1939   *Jeunes filles en détresse* (Pabst) (as Jacqueline Presle)
1940   *Le Paradis perdu* (*Four Flights to Love*) (Gance) (as mother and daughter); *Fausse alerte* (*The French Way*) (de Baroncelli) (as Claire Ancelot); *Elles étaient 12 femmes* (Lacombe) (as Lucie); *Parade en 7 nuits* (Marc Allégret)
1941   *Historie de rire* (*Foolish Husbands*) (L'Herbier) (as Adélaîde Barbier); *Le Soleil a toujours raison* (Billon) (as Micheline)
1942   *La Comédie du bonheur* (L'Herbier) (as Lydia); *La Nuit fantastique* (*Fantastic Night*) (L'Herbier) (as Irène); *Félicie Nanteuil* (*Histoire comique*) (Marc Allégret) (title role); *La Belle Aventure* (*Twilight*) (Marc Allégret) (as Françoise Pinbrache)
1943   *Un Seul Amour* (Blanchar) (as Clara Biondi)
1944   *Falbalas* (*Paris Frills*) (Becker) (as Micheline Lafaurie)
1945   *Boule de suif* (*Angel and Sinner*) (Christian-Jaque) (as Elisabeth Rousset)
1946   **Le Diable au corps** (*Devil in the Flesh*) (Autant-Lara) (as Marthe Graingier)
1947   *Les Jeux sont faits* (*The Chips Are Down*) (Delannoy) (as Eve Charlier)
1948   *Les Derniers Jours de Pompéi* (*Sins of Pompeii*) (L'Herbier) (as Hélène); *Tous les chemins mènent à Rome* (Boyer) (as Laura)
1950   *Under My Skin* (*La Belle de Paris*) (Negulesco) (as Paule Manet); *American Guerilla in the Philippines* (*I Shall Return*; *Guerillas*) (Fritz Lang) (as Jeanne Martinez)
1951   *The Adventures of Captain Fabian* (*New Orleans Adventure*) (William Marshall) (as Léa Mariotte)
1952   *La Dame aux camélias* (Bernard) (as Marguerite Gautier)
1953   *L'Amour d'une femme* (Grémillon) (as Marie Prieur); *Si Versailles m'était conté* (*Affairs in Versailles*; *Royal Affairs in Versailles*) (Guitry) (as Madame de Pompadour); *Villa Borghese* (*Les Amants de villa Borghese*; *It Happened in the Park*) (Franciolini)
1954   *Casa Ricordi* (*House of Ricordi*; *La Maison du souvenir*) (Gallone) (as Virginia Marchi); *Les Impures* (Chevalier) (as Michèle); *Napoléon* (Guitry) (as Hortense de Beauharnais)
1955   *Treize à table* (Hunebelle) (as Madeleine Villardier)

1956   *Beatrice Cenci* (*Le Château des amants maudits*) (Freda) (as Lucrezia Cenci); *La Mariée est trop belle* (*The Bride Is Much Too Beautiful*) (Gaspard-Huit) (as Judith)
1957   *Les Louves* (*Demoniaque*; *The She Wolves*) (Saslavsky) (as Hélène); *Les Femmes sont marrantes* (Hunebelle) (as Nicole)
1958   *Christine* (Gaspard-Huit) (as Lena Eggersdorf); *Bobosse* (Périer) (as Régine) (Surin)
1959   *Blind Date* (*Chance Meeting*; *L'Enquête de l'inspecteur Morgan*) (Losey) (as Jacqueline Cousteau); *Une Fille pour l'été* (*A Mistress for the Summer*) (Molinaro) (as Paule); *Le Baron de l'Ecluse* (Delannoy) (as Perle); *Herrin der Welt* (*Mistress of the World*) (Dieterle) (as Mme. Latour)
1960   *L'Amant de cinq jours* (*The Five Day Lover*; *Infidelity*) (de Broca) (as Madeleine)
1961   *Les Grandes Personnes* (*Time Out for Love*) (Valère) (as Michèle); *L'Assassino* (*The Lady Killer of Rome*; *The Assassin*) (Petri) (as Adalgisa de Matteis); *I briganti italiani* (*Les Guerrilleros*) (Camerini) (as La Marquise)
1962   "La Luxure" ("Lust") ep. of *Les Sept Péchés capitaux* (*The Seven Capital Sins*) (Demy) (as Mother); *La Loi des hommes* (Gérard) (as Sophie Olivier); *If a Man Answers* (*Un Mari en laisse*) (Levin) (as Germaine Stacey); *Le Diable et les dix commandements* (*The Devil and the Ten Commandments*) (Duvivier) (as Micheline); *Venere imperiale* (*Vénus impériale*; *Imperial Venus*) (Delannoy) (as Josephine de Beauharnais)
1963   *Coup de bambou* (Boyer) (as Angèle Brissac); *The Prize* (Robson) (as Denise Marceau)
1964   *Dark Purpose* (*L'Intrigue*) (George Marshall) (as Monique); *La Chasse à l'homme* (*The Gentle Art of Seduction*; *Male Hunt*) (Molinaro) (as Isabelle Heurtin); *Les Pieds nickelés* (Chambon) (as Lady Van der Mèche)
1965   *Je vous salue, mafia* (*Hail, Mafia*) (Lévy) (as Daisy); *La Religieuse* (*The Nun*) (Rivette) (as Mme. de Moni)
1966   *Le Roi de coeur* (*King of Hearts*) (de Broca) (as Mme. Eglantine)
1969   *La Bal du Comte d'Orgel* (Marc Allégret) (as Mme. de Séryeuse); *Le Clair de terre* (Gilles) (as L'Antiquare)
1970   *Peau d'âne* (*The Magic Donkey*; *Donkey Skin*) (Demy) (as La Deuxième Reine [Red Queen])
1971   *Les Pétroleuses* (*The Legend of Frenchie King*) (Christian-Jaque) (as Tante Amélie); *Il Diavolo nel Cervello* (Sollima) (as La comtesse Claudia)
1973   *L'Oiseau rare* (Brialy); *L'Evénement le plus important depuis que l'homme a marché sur la lune* (*A Slightly Pregnant Man*) (Demy) (as Dr. Delavigne); *Le Boucher, la star, et l'orpheline* (Savary) (as Belladonna); *La Gueule de l'emploi* (Rouland) (as herself)
1974   *Deux grandes filles dans un pyjama* (Girault) (as Laurence); *La preda* (Paolella) (as Bessie Lester); *Trompe-l'oeil* (D'Anna) (as Laure Deschanel)
1975   *Mords pas, on t'aime* (*La Fête des pères*) (Yves Allégret)
1976   *Nea* (*Nea: A New Woman*) (Kaplan) (as Helen Ashby); *Le Diable dans la boîte* (Lary) (as Mme. Aubert); *Certaines nouvelles* (Davila) (as Hélène)
1977   *Va voir maman, papa travaille* (*Your Turn, My Turn*) (Leterrier) (as Vava)
1978   *On efface tout* (Vidal) (as Mme. Coeurdevey); *Démons de midi* (*La couleur de temps*) (Paureilhe) (as Rose); *S'il vous plaît . . . la mer?* (Lancelot) (as mother); *Je te tiens, tu me tiens par la barbichette* (Yanne) (as La femme d'argent)
1979   *Rien ne va plus* (Ribes) (as Carmen); *Tout dépend des filles* (Fabre) (as Betty)
1981   *Remueménage* (Davila) (as mother)

Micheline Presle with Gérard Philipe in *Le diable au corps*

1983   *Archipel des amours* (Treilhou); *En haut des marches* (Vecchiali); *Lili Lamont* (Logereau); *Thieves After Dark* (*Voleurs de la nuit*) (Fuller) (as Genevieve); *Le Sang des autres* (*The Blood of Others*) (Chabrol) (as Denise)

1984   *Le Chien* (Gallotte); *Les Fausses confidences* (Marivaux) (as Mme. Argante)

1986   *Beau temps, mais orageux en fin de journée* (Frot-Coutaz) (as Jacqueline)

1988   *Alouette, je te plumerai* (Zucca) (as lady with jewels)

1989   *Je veux rentrer à la maison* (*I Want to Go Home*) (Resnais) (as Isabelle Gauthier); *La Fête des pères* (Fleury) (as Mireille)

1990   *Après après-demain* (Frot-Coutaz) (as the neighbor)

1991   *Der Andere Blick* (*The Other Eye*) (Heer and Schmiedel)

1993   *Je m'appelle Victor* (*My Name Is Victor*) (Jacques) (as Luce); *Fanfan* (*Fanfan & Alexandre*) (Jardin) (as Maude)

1994   *Pas tres Catholique* (*Something Fishy*) (Tonie Marshall) (as Mme. Loussine); *Casque Bleu* (*Blue Helmet*) (Jugnot) (as Gisele)

1995   *Le Journal du Seducteur* (*Seducer's Diary*) (Du Broux) (as Diane); *Les Misérables* (Lelouche) (as Mother Superior)

Publications

By PRESLE: book—

L'Arriere Mémoire, 1994.

By PRESLE: articles—

Interview in *Cinématographe* (Paris), May 1982.
Interview in *Film Français* (Paris), 31 August 1984.
Interview with Raymond Chirat, in *La IVe République et ses films*, Paris 1985.
Interview with F. Audé and G. Grandmaire, in *Positif* (Paris), April 1989.
"Le rire de Pabst," in *Cahiers du Cinéma* (Paris), supplement, May 1991.

On PRESLE: articles—

Taboulay, C., "Son rire était formidable," in *Cahiers du Cinéma* (Paris), April 1992.
Stars (Mariembourg, Belgium), June 1992 and September 1992.
Ciné Revue (Paris), 21 April 1983.

*   *   *

After training for the stage under Raymond Rouleau, Micheline Presle made her screen debut with Charles Trenet in *Je chante*. An international career of more than a hundred films has followed with a variety of directors including Marc Allégret, Autant-Lara, Demy, Gance, L'Herbier, Losey, and her husband William Marshall. Her early appearances were in character as a mischievous adolescent, but she quickly graduated to more demanding roles and achieved critical recognition as Jacqueline in *Jeunes filles en détresse* and for her dual role as mother and daughter in *Le Paradis perdu*.

During the Occupation she appeared as the desirable young female in lighthearted romantic comedies directed by L'Herbier: *La Comédie du bonheur, Histoire de rire, La Nuit fantastique*. In the last two she played opposite Fernand Gravey whom she was later to partner in the acclaimed situation comedy *Treize à table*. Films with Marc Allégret consolidated her reputation; she played Françoise Pinbrache in the comic success *La Belle Aventure* and starred as the ambitious young actress of *Félicie Nanteuil*. In the immediate postwar years came more weighty parts, now as the mature, and often sophisticated, woman of the world. *Falbalas*, in which she was joined by her early mentor Raymond Rouleau, intitiated this transition: here brilliantly rendering the unpredictable Micheline Lafaurie, the inspiration behind a celebrated couturier. Three consecutive tragic roles in literary adaptations followed: she played the exploited and shunned prostitute of Maupassant's *Boule de suif*, was Eve Charlier in Sartre's *Les Jeux sont faits*, and in Radiguet's *Le Diable au corps* she played Marthe, the unfaithful wife of a serving soldier, in a memorable partnership with Gérard Philipe.

Popular success took Presle to Hollywood where she was teamed with established American stars: with John Garfield in *Under My Skin* she was a cabaret singer; with Tyrone Power in *American Guerilla in the Philippines* the seductive Jeanne Martinez; and with Errol Flynn in *New Orleans Adventure*, directed by her husband William Marshall and filmed in France, she was the irresistible Léa Mariotte. None of these parts extended her acting skills.

As Marguerite Gautier in Dumas's *La Dame aux camélias*, however, she reaffirmed her French roots, and for Sacha Guitry she appeared in lavish historical costume dramas. If these parts simply confirmed her versatility, more challenging roles as a professional woman came in the 1950s and 1960s, reflecting social changes of the period. After her engaging portrayal of a dedicated young doctor facing the sexual prejudices of a small community in *L'Amour d'une femme*, she was, in lighter vein, the director of a woman's magazine in *La Mariée est trop belle*, a successful businesswoman in *Les Grandes Personnes*, a busy reporter in *La Loi des hommes*, and a psychologist in *Mords pas, on t'aime*. Her comic gifts have also seen her cast as the socially outrageous or endearingly scatterbrained character. More sinister roles have included the sleazy cabaret singer in *Les Impures*, the atrocious Hélène of *Les Louves*, the alcoholic Bessie Lester of *La Préda*, and for Losey the deceptively genteel Jacqueline Cousteau of *Blind Date*.

With age Presle has been increasingly cast as the mother, good or bad, rather than the wife, faithful or unfaithful. There have been memorable performances as Laure Deschanel, the possessive mother of *Trompe-l'oeil*, or as Helen Ashby, the lesbian mother of *Néa*, or as the clinically depressive mother of *Beau temps, mais orageux en fin de journée*, while in Resnais's *I Want to Go Home* she gave a delightfully measured performance as the cultured Mme. Gauthier.

Presle's links with the theater have remained strong and she has often excelled in screen versions of plays, as, for example, in the role of Mme. Argante in Marivaux's *Les Fausses confidences*. In more than one film she has played the performer, either as cabaret singer or as actress. Her work for television has also met with acclaim, particularly as the star of the long-running series *Les Saintes Chéries*.

As an actress who enjoys her work immensely, Presle has responded readily to a variety of roles for the stage, the cinema, and television. Her range is impressive, extending from early comic and romantic parts through roles in thrillers, costume pieces, and social dramas, into darker, more tragic character studies. Her talents have been in demand by French, English, American, and Italian directors alike, and in her long career she has worked with the most famous names of the cinema and those who have quickly faded. Vitality, versatilty, and an enduring commitment to her profession have ensured Presle a permanent place in the annals of the cinema.

—R. F. Cousins

PRESLEY, Elvis

Nationality: American. **Born:** Elvis Aron Presley in Tupelo, Mississippi, 8 January 1935. **Education:** Attended L. C. Humes High School, Memphis, Tennessee, graduated 1953. **Family:** Married Priscilla Beaulieu, 1967 (divorced 1973), daughter: Lisa Marie. **Career:** Worked as truck driver; 1954—first recording: by 1956, the center of tremendous publicity based on his records and appearances on television and stage; 1956—contract with Hal Wallis: film debut in *Love Me Tender*, followed by a series of successful films until 1969; 1958-60—served in the U.S. Army in West Germany; returned to singing and moviemaking; occasional cabaret engagements. **Died:** In Memphis, 16 August 1977.

Films as Actor:

1956	*Love Me Tender* (Webb)
1957	*Loving You* (Kanter); *Jailhouse Rock* (Thorpe)
1958	*King Creole* (Curtiz)
1960	*G.I. Blues* (Taurog); *Flaming Star* (Siegel)
1961	*Wild in the Country* (Dunne); *Blue Hawaii* (Taurog)
1962	*Follow That Dream* (Douglas); *Kid Galahad* (Karlson); *Girls! Girls! Girls!* (Taurog)
1963	*It Happened at the World's Fair* (Taurog); *Fun in Acapulco* (Thorpe)
1964	*Kissin' Cousins* (Nelson); *Viva Las Vegas* (Sidney); *Roustabout* (Rich)
1965	*Girl Happy* (Sagal); *Tickle Me* (Taurog); *Harum Scarum* (Nelson)
1966	*Frankie and Johnny* (de Cordova); *Paradise, Hawaiian Style* (Moore); *Spinout* (Taurog)
1967	*Easy Come, Easy Go* (Rich); *Double Trouble* (Taurog); *Clambake* (Nadel)
1968	*Stay Away Joe* (Tewksbury); *Speedway* (Taurog); *Live a Little, Love a Little* (Taurog)
1969	*Charro!* (Warren); *The Trouble with Girls* (Tewksbury); *Change of Habit* (Moore)
1970	*Elvis—That's the Way It Is* (Sanders—doc)
1972	*Elvis on Tour* (Adidge and Abel—doc)

Publications

On PRESLEY: books—

Wallis, Hal, and Charles Higham, *Starmaker*, New York, 1980.

Crumbaker, Marge, and Gabe Tucker, *Up and Down with Elvis Presley*, New York, 1981.

Hawkins, Martin, and Colin Escott, *Elvis: The Illustrated Discography*, London, 1981.

Hopkins, Jerry, *Elvis: The Final Years*, London, 1981.

Rogale, Jean-Yves, *Le Roi Elvis*, Paris, 1981.

Whisler, John, *Elvis Presley—a Reference Guide and Discography*, Metuchen, New Jersey, 1981.

Sauers, Wendy, *Elvis Presley: A Complete Reference*, Jefferson, North Carolina, 1984.

McLafferty, Gerry, *Elvis in Hollywood: Celluloid Sell Out*, New York, 1989.

Schuster, Hal, *The Films of Elvis Presley*, Las Vegas, Nevada, 1989.

Bartel, Pauline C., *Reel Elvis: The Ultimate Trivia Guide to the King's Movies*, Dallas, 1994.

Esposito, Joe, *Good Rockin' Tonight: Twenty Years on the Road and on the Town with Elvis*, New York, 1994.

Hazen, Cindy, *The Best of Elvis: Recollections of a Great Humanitarian*, New York, 1994.

Elvis Presley

Stanley, David, *The Elvis Encyclopedia*, Los Angeles, 1994.
Nash, Bruce M., *Amazing but True Elvis Facts*, Kansas City, Missouri, 1995.

On PRESLEY: articles—

Meltzer, R., "The Films of Elvis Presley," in *Take One* (Montreal), March 1974.
Marill, Alvin H., in *Films in Review* (New York), December 1977.
Braun, Eric, "Elvis: In Search of Satisfaction," in *Films* (London), September 1982.
Hampton, Howard, "Elvis Dorado: The True Romance of *Viva Las Vegas*, in *Film Comment* (New York), July/August 1994.

*   *   *

No major star suffered through more bad movies than Elvis Presley. Of the 31 he made in his decade-and-a-half as a movie star, arguably only Don Siegel's *Flaming Star*, in which he played Pacer, a half-breed torn between loyalty to his Kiowa mother and his white father and stepbrother—a nonsinging role for Presley—has any redeeming value beyond the star's appearance. That he continued to make films for 13 years is testament to the durability of his star quality.

In 1956 Presley rose from obscurity to become a national figure as rock and roll's first superstar. Within months of his first national recording success Presley began making films; *Love Me Tender*, released before the year's end, recouped its $1 million cost in the first three days of release.

Presley's next three films featured some of his best work as both singer and actor. In *Loving You*, he played Deke Rivers, a sensitive, small town teenager who makes a rapid rise to national prominence as a rock 'n' roll singer. Among the many great performance pieces is the finale, "Got a Lot of Living to Do," which features Elvis in a thigh-slapping, hip-shaking performance. In his next film, *Jailhouse Rock*, Elvis was shown at his singular rockin' best: as inmate Vince Everett, he leads his fellow prisoners through a volcanic, snarling rendition of the title song. This film, like Elvis's other early movies, allowed him to create a more well-rounded character than in his later efforts. The final scene where he faces the possibility of losing his voice and realizes the importance of his friends is touching.

As with *Loving You* and *Jailhouse Rock*, Elvis's next film, *King Creole*, was a narrative about the complications of a rapid rise to stardom. Set in New Orleans, Presley played high school student Danny Fisher, an insolent punk who is "discovered" and becomes the toast of Bourbon Street. Similar to *Loving You*, *King Creole* contained autobiographical overtones: like Elvis, Danny Fisher's music was based in black culture—in the film's opening, Elvis and several black street vendors sing "Crawfish," while at the King Creole, Danny rocks in a Dixieland style with a call/response format. In *Loving You*, Presley had paid homage to his other major musical influence—country music—with his performance of "Lonesome Cowboy."

Considering his substantial following, it is curious that he was continually saddled with mediocre scripts and second-rate directors, particularly after his 1960 return from Army service. It was as if Hollywood knew he would bring in the customers despite the narratives. Loyal fans continued to see his films and eventually contributed in excess of $180 million to the Hollywood coffers. In addition they gave gold status to nine soundtrack albums.

While the early films featured Presley as a rock star, many of his 1960s vehicles had him in any number of improbable guises from which he broke into improbable song: as the rebellious Glen Tyler in *Wild in the Country*, he develops a relationship with a psychiatric counselor (Hope Lange) who encourages his flair for writing and arranges for him to receive a scholarship to college; as race car driver Lucky Jackson in *Viva Las Vegas* he uses his singing talents to woo a swimming instructor played by Ann-Margret; as American movie star Johnny Tyrone in *Harum Scarum*, he is kidnapped in the Middle East, escapes, and falls in love with Princess Shalimar (played by Miss America, Mary Ann Mobley). Of the 1960s films, *Roustabout* is arguably the most interesting. Here Elvis plays Charlie Rogers, an insolent, parentless entertainer who finds a new home with a carnival show operated by Barbara Stanwyck. His performances light up the midway and save the carnival from bankruptcy. The experience of working with the pop idol was a positive one for the screen veteran; as Stanwyck stated, "The idea of working with Mr. Presley intrigued me . . . . Mr. Wallis said he was a wonderful person to work with . . . and he is. His manners are impeccable, he is on time, he knows his lines, he asks for nothing outside of what any other actor or actress wants."

Throughout the 1960s Presley avoided the concert and public appearance route, opting for visibility through films. By the end of the decade this strategy had begun to fail, neither movies nor records selling at previous high levels. With the failure of *Change of Habit*—with Mary Tyler Moore as a nun—Elvis stopped making films. No one seemed interested in Presley, who at the height of his film career was earning $1 million per movie plus a substantial percentage of the gross.

Presley was able to break out of the confines of his now-dated image by leaving the silver screen for the small screen. In a 1968 television special that combined the hokey musical numbers familiar from his movies with leather-clad, bare-bones rocking and rolling (in front of a live audience), Elvis reintroduced himself to the public. His career was reinvigorated, with a return to concert tours and rootsier, bluesier recordings (his records of the 1960s generally having consisted of substandard movie soundtrack songs, which bore little resemblance to his seminal 1950s rockabilly style). To capitalize on Presley's change of direction, a movie was again considered, but this time it was to be a documentary of an Elvis concert tour. *Elvis, That's the Way It Is* brought forth Presley's charisma and musical talent far better than the mundane, studio-concocted fluff he had been forced to wade through for the previous decade. In typical Presley fashion, however, once was not enough. Two years later *Elvis on Tour* gave us another look at "the King" on- and off-stage, but the magic was wearing thin for both Elvis and his audiences. It was to be Elvis's last movie.

Presley's importance to film history is less for his continued popularity than for the trend he set within the musical genre. With the success of his vehicles, other recording stars were signed to movie roles and throughout the 1960s there continued a never-ending stream of jukebox musicals: minimal narratives with lots of hit tunes.

In the first scene of his movie debut, Elvis was seen deep in the frame laboriously dragging a plow. In retrospect we can only marvel at how prophetic that shot was considering the material he was made to drag through movie theaters for the next 14 years.

—Doug Tomlinson, updated by Frank Uhle

PRESTON, Robert

Nationality: American. **Born:** Robert Preston Meservey in Newton Highlands, Massachusetts, 8 June 1918. **Education:** Attended Lincoln High School, Hollywood. **Family:** Married Catherine Feltus Craig, 1941. **Career:** 1934—joined Shakespearian group managed by Mrs. Tyrone Power Sr.; then worked at Pasadena Community Theatre for two years; 1938—film debut in *King of Alcatraz*; contract with Paramount; also acted on stage in 18 Actors company; 1942-46—served in U.S. Army Air Force; 1951—in TV series *Man against Crime*, *Anywhere, U.S.A.* series, 1952-54, and mini-series *The Chisholms*,

1980; 1951—on stage in *Twentieth Century*; later stage roles include *The Male Animal*, *The Tender Trap*, 1954, *His and Hers*, 1954, *The Music Man*, 1957 (and film version, 1962), *I Do! I Do!*, 1968, and *Mack and Mabel*, 1974. **Awards:** Tony Awards, for *I Do! I Do!*, 1967, and *The Music Man*, 1958; Best Supporting Actor Award, U.S. National Film Critics, for *S.O.B.*, 1981. **Died:** Of lung cancer, in Santa Barbara, California, 21 March 1987.

Films as Actor:

1938   *King of Alcatraz* (Florey) (as Robert MacArthur); *Illegal Traffic* (Louis King) (as Bent Martin)

1939   *Disbarred* (Florey) (as Bradley Kent); *Union Pacific* (Cecil B. DeMille) (as Dick Allen); *Beau Geste* (Wellman) (as Digby Geste)

1940   *Typhoon* (Louis King) (as Johnny Porter); *Moon over Burma* (Louis King) (as Chuck Lane); *Northwest Mounted Police* (Cecil B. DeMille) (as Constable Ronnie Logan)

1941   *New York Town* (Charles Vidor) (as Paul Bryson Jr.); *Lady from Cheyenne* (Lloyd) (as Steve); *Night of January 16th* (Clemens) (as Steve Van Ruyle); *Parachute Battalion* (Goodwins) (as Donald Morse)

1942   *Pacific Blackout* (*Midnight Angel*) (Murphy) (as Robert Draper); *Reap the Wild Wind* (Cecil B. DeMille) (as Dan Cutler); *This Gun for Hire* (Tuttle) (as Michael Crane); *Wake Island* (Farrow) (as Joe Doyle); *Star Spangled Rhythm* (George Marshall) (cameo role)

1943   *Night Plane from Chung-King* (Murphy) (as Capt. Nick Stanton)

1947   *Wild Harvest* (Garnett) (as Jim Davis); *The Macomber Affair* (Zoltan Korda) (as Francis Macomber); *Variety Girl* (George Marshall) (cameo role)

1948   *Whispering Smith* (Fenton) (as Murray Sinclaire); *Blood on the Moon* (Wise) (as Tate Biling)

1949   *The Big City* (Taurog) (as the Reverend Phillip A. Andrews); *The Lady Gambles* (Gordon) (as David Boothe); *Tulsa* (Heisler) (as Brad Brady)

1950   *The Sundowners* (Templeton) (as Wichita Kid)

1951   *My Outlaw Brother* (Nugent) (as Joe Warnder); *When I Grow Up* (Kanin) (as Father Reed); *The Best of the Badmen* (Russell) (as Matthew Fowler)

1952   *Face to Face* (Windust) (as Sheriff); *Cloudburst* (Searle) (as John)

1955   *The Last Frontier* (Anthony Mann) (as Col. Frank Marston)

1960   *The Dark at the Top of the Stairs* (Delbert Mann) (as Rubin)

1962   *The Music Man* (Da Costa) (as Professor Howard Hill)

1963   *How the West Was Won* (Hathaway) (as Roger Morgan); *Island of Love* (Da Costa) (as Steve Blair); *All the Way Home* (Segal) (as Jay)

1972   *Junior Bonner* (Peckinpah) (as Ace Bonner); *Child's Play* (Lumet) (as Joseph Dobbs)

1974   *Mame* (Saks) (as Beauregard)

1975   *My Father's House* (Segal—for TV)

1977   *Semi-Tough* (Ritchie) (as Big Ed Bookman)

1980   *The Man That Corrupted Hadleyburg* (Rosenblum—for TV) (as Mr. Stranger)

1981   *S.O.B.* (Edwards) (as Dr. Irving Finegarten)

1982   *Victor/Victoria* (Edwards) (as Toddy); *Rehearsal for Murder* (Greene—for TV)

1984   *The Last Starfighter* (Castle) (as Centauri); *The September Gun* (Taylor—for TV)

1985   *Finnegan, Begin Again* (Joan Micklin Silver—for TV) (as Mike Finnegan)

1986   *Outrage!* (Grauman—for TV) (as Dennis Riordan)

Publications

By PRESTON: article—

Interview in *American Classic Screen* (Shawnee Mission, Kansas), September-October 1982.

On PRESTON: articles—

Preston, Catherine Craig, "The Movies and I," as told to John Springer, in *Films in Review* (New York), August-September 1957.
Current Biography 1958, New York, 1958.
Peper, W., "Robert Preston," in *Films in Review* (New York), March 1968.
Hurley, Joseph, in *Films in Review* (New York), August-September 1982.
Obituary in *Variety* (New York), 25 March 1987.
Obituary in *Films and Filming* (London), May 1987.

*   *   *

Robert Preston is best known for his stage and screen performances as "Professor" Harold Hill in *The Music Man*. His portrayal of the disarming confidence man underscores the paradox that informs his work: here and elsewhere, Preston's feather-light grace and sense of comedic timing belie his rugged and sturdy visage.

Preston was signed by Paramount in 1938, and first gained wide approval in *Union Pacific*. After serving in World War II, he was a success in *The Macomber Affair*. Tired of playing leads in only smaller pictures, Preston accepted an offer in 1951 to appear on Broadway, and he soon became known as a stage actor. In 1957, Preston arrived as "the music man," and won his first of two Tony Awards. Preston's success on Broadway renewed Hollywood's interest in him; he became known as one of the ablest character actors in Hollywood, and continued work on both coasts. In the 1980s, work with Blake Edwards brought Preston renewed acclaim. His performance as Toddy in *Victor/Victoria* brought Preston an Academy Award nomination.

There is always a touch of fraud about Preston's characters. They gain sympathy in direct proportion to the degree they acknowledge their own facade. Preston frequently emphasizes the function of acting in his roles, adding to his fraudulent image an element that colors and shades each performance. Preston's paradoxical image has been used in a variety of ways. Though often serving a humorous purpose, his double-sided quality can generate a deep tragic resonance: he dies playing a practical joke in *Beau Geste*, his whimsical attitude foreshadows his death in *All the Way Home*, and his delusions about aging impair his relationship with his wife and son in *Junior Bonner*.

Preston's persona has proved to be uncommonly malleable: witty and dashing in *Beau Geste*, devil-may-care in *Northwest Mounted Police*, romantic and rough-hewn in *Reap the Wild Wind*, heroic in *Wake Island*, stiff-backed and humorless in *The Last Frontier*, and explosively charming in *The Music Man*. The quality of his work ennobles even his contractual obligations and gives a sense of history to his career. When he gives a "Viking's Funeral" to Richard Mulligan in *S.O.B.* it reminds one of the funeral Preston gave Gary Cooper in *Beau Geste*. The difference between the two deny simple repetition; they represent significant variations of Preston's image and his incessant vitality.

—Frank Thompson, updated by Cynthia Baron

PRICE, Vincent

Nationality: American. **Born:** St. Louis, Missouri, 27 May 1911. **Education:** Attended Community School and Country Day School, both in St. Louis; Yale University, New Haven, Connecticut, B.A., 1933; University of London, 1934-35. **Family:** Married 1) the actress Edith Barrett, 1938 (divorced 1948), son: Vincent; 2) Mary Grant, 1949 (divorced 1973), daughter: Victoria; 3) the actress Coral Browne, 1974 (died 1991). **Career:** Apprentice teacher, Riverdale Country Day School; 1935—stage debut in *Chicago* in London; then in *Victoria Regina* in London and New York; 1938—in Orson Welles's Mercury Theatre production of *The Shoemaker's Holiday*, New York; film debut in *Service de Luxe*; 1947—contract with Universal-International, then contract with RKO, 1951; 1950-52—panelist on TV program *Pantomime Quiz*; 1953—in stage production of *Richard III*, and later in *Billy Budd*, 1955, and *Ardele*, 1975; Art Consultant for Sears Roebuck; 1960—host, TV series *The Chevy Mystery Show*; 1979—actor in TV series *Time Express*; 1980-88—host, TV series *Mystery*. **Died:** In Los Angeles, 25 October 1993.

Films as Actor:

1938 *Service de Luxe* (Rowland V. Lee) (as Robert Wade)

1939 *The Private Lives of Elizabeth and Essex* (Curtiz) (as Sir Walter Raleigh); *Tower of London* (Rowland V. Lee) (as the Duke of Clarence)

1940 *Green Hell* (Whale) (as David Richardson); *The Invisible Man Returns* (May) (title role); *House of Seven Gables* (May) (as Clifford Pyncheon); *Brigham Young—Frontiersman* (Hathaway) (as Joseph Smith)

1941 *Hudson's Bay* (Pichel) (as King Charles II)

1943 *The Song of Bernadette* (Henry King) (as Dutour)

1944 *Wilson* (Henry King) (as William McAdoo); *Laura* (Preminger) (as Shelby Carpenter); *The Keys of the Kingdom* (Stahl) (as the Reverend Angus Mealy); *The Eve of St. Mark* (Stahl) (as Pvt. Francis Marion)

1945 *A Royal Scandal* (*Czarina*) (Preminger) (as Marquis de Fleury); *Leave Her to Heaven* (Stahl) (as Russell Quinton)

1946 *Shock* (Werker) (as Dr. Cross); *Dragonwyck* (Mankiewicz) (as Nicholas Van Ryn)

1947 *Moss Rose* (Ratoff) (as Inspector Clinner); *The Long Night* (Litvak) (as Maximilian); *The Web* (Gordon) (as Andrew Colby)

1948 *Up in Central Park* (Seiter) (as Boss Tweed); *Rogue's Regiment* (Florey) (as Mark Van Ratten); *Abbott and Costello Meet Frankenstein* (Barton) (as voice of The Invisible Man); *The Three Musketeers* (Sidney) (as Cardinal Richelieu)

1949 *The Bribe* (Leonard) (as Carwood); *Bagdad* (Lamont) (as Pasha Al Nadim)

1950 *Champagne for Caesar* (Whorf) (as Burnbridge Waters); *The Baron of Arizona* (Fuller) (as James Addison Reavis); *Curtain Call at Cactus Creek* (Lamont) (as Tracy Holland)

1951 *Adventures of Captain Fabian* (William Marshall) (as George Brissac); *His Kind of Woman* (Farrow) (as Mark Cardigan)

1952 *Las Vegas Story* (Stevenson) (as Lloyd Rollins)

1953 *House of Wax* (de Toth) (as Prof. Henry Jarrod); *Pictura* (as narrator)

1954 *Dangerous Mission* (Louis King) (as Paul Adams); *The Mad Magician* (Brahm) (as Gallico); *Casanova's Big Night* (McLeod) (title role)

1955 *The Story of Colonel Drake* (Pierson—short) (title role); *Son of Sinbad* (*Nights in a Harem*) (Tetzlaff) (as Omar Khayyam)

1956 *Serenade* (Anthony Mann) (as Charles Winthrop); *While the City Sleeps* (Fritz Lang) (as Walter Kyne); *The Ten Commandments* (Cecil B. DeMille) (as Baka); *The Vagabond King* (Curtiz) (as narrator)

1957 *The Story of Mankind* (Irwin Allen) (as the Devil)

1958 *The Fly* (Neumann) (as Francois)

1959 *The House on Haunted Hill* (Castle) (as Frederick Loren); *The Big Circus* (Joseph M. Newman) (as Hans Hagenfeld); *The Bat* (Wilbur) (as Dr. Malcolm Wells); *The Return of the Fly* (Bernds) (as Francois Delambre)

1960 *The Tingler* (Castle) (as Dr. Richard Chapin); *The House of Usher* (*The Fall of the House of Usher*) (Corman) (as Roderick Usher)

1961 *Master of the World* (Witney) (as Robur); *The Pit and the Pendulum* (Corman) (as Nicholas Medina); *Nefertite—Regina del Nilo* (*Queen of the Nile*) (Cerchio); *Gordon, il Pirato Nero* (*Rage of the Buccaneer*; *The Black Buccaneer*) (Costa) (as Romero); *Naked Terror* (Brenner—doc) (as narrator)

1962 *Confessions of an Opium Eater* (Zugsmith) (as DeQuincey); *Convicts Four* (Kaufman) (as Carl Carmer); *Tower of London* (Corman) (as Richard of Gloucester); *Tales of Terror* (Corman) (as Locke/Fortunato/Valdemar)

1963 *The Raven* (Corman) (as Dr. Erasmus Craven); *Chagall* (Venturi—short) (as narrator); *Twice-Told Tales* (Salkow); *Diary of a Madman* (Le Borg) (as Simon Cordier); *Comedy of Terrors* (*The Graveside Story*) (Jacques Tourneur); *Beach Party* (Asher)

1964 *The Haunted Palace* (Corman) (as Charles Dexter Ward/Joseph Curwen); ***The Masque of the Red Death*** (Corman) (as Prince Prospero); *L'ultimo uomo della terra* (*The Last Man on Earth*) (Salkow)

1965 *The Tomb of Ligeia* (Corman); *City under the Sea* (*War Gods of the Deep*) (Jacques Tourneur); *I tabù* (*Taboos of the World*) (Marcellini—doc) (as narrator); *Dr. Goldfoot and the Bikini Machine* (Taurog) (as Dr. Goldfoot)

1966 *Dr. Goldfoot and the Girl Bombs* (Bava) (as Dr. Goldfoot)

1967 *Das Haus der tausend Freuden* (*House of a Thousand Dolls*) (Summers) (as Felix Manderville); *The Jackals* (Webb)

1968 ***Witchfinder General*** (*The Conqueror Worm*; *Matthew Hopkins—Witchfinder General*) (Reeves) (as Matthew Hopkins); *More Dead Than Alive* (Sparr) (as Dan Ruffalo); *Histoires extraordinaires* (*Spirits of the Dead*) (Fellini and others) (English-language version only) (as narrator)

1969 *The Trouble with Girls* (Tewksbury) (as Mr. Morality); *The Oblong Box* (Hessler) (as Julian Markham)

1970 *Cry of the Banshee* (Hessler); *Scream and Scream Again* (Hessler) (as Lord Edward Whitman)

1971 *The Abominable Dr. Phibes* (Fuest) (title role); *What's a Girl Like You . . . ?* (Paris—for TV)

1972 *Dr. Phibes Rises Again* (Fuest) (title role)

1973 *Theatre of Blood* (Hickox) (as Edward Lionheart)

1974 *Madhouse* (Clark) (as Paul Toombes); *The Devil's Triangle* (TV doc); *Percy's Progress* (*It's Not the Size That Counts*) (Thomas) (as Stavos Mammonian); *Journey into Fear* (Daniel Mann) (as Dervos)

1976 *The Butterfly Ball* (Klinger) (as narrator)

1978 *Days of Fury* (as narrator)

1980 *The Monster Club* (Baker) (as Erasmus); *Romance in the Jugular Vein*

1981 *The Thief and the Cobbler* (Williams) (as voice)

1983 *House of the Long Shadows* (Walker) (as Lionel); *Bloodbath at the House of Death* (Cameron); *Vincent* (Burton) (as voice)

1984 *Michael Jackson's Thriller* (Landis—short) (as narrator)

1986 *The Great Mouse Detective* (*Basil the Great Mouse Detective*) (Mattinson) (as voice of Professor Ratigan)

1986 *From a Whisper to a Scream* (*The Offspring*) (Burr) (as Julian White)

1987 *The Whales of August* (Anderson) (as Mr. Nikolai Maranov); *The Little Troll Prince* (Paterson) (as voice); *Escapes* (Steenland) (as Mailman)

Vincent Price in *The House of Usher*

1988 *Dead Heat* (Goldblatt) (as Arthur P. Loudermilk)
1989 *Backtrack* (*Catchfire*) (Smithee [Dennis Hopper]) (as Lino Avoca)
1990 *Edward Scissorhands* (Burton) (as the Inventor); *Once . . .* (Williams) (as voice)
1993 *The Heart of Justice* (Barreto—for TV) (cameo)

Publications

By PRICE: books—

I Like What I Know, New York, 1959.
The Book of Joe, New York, 1961.
A Treasury of Great Recipes, New York, 1965.
A National Treasury of Cooking, New York, 1967.
The Come into the Kitchen Cook Book, New York, 1969.
The Vincent Price Treasury of American Art, Waukesha, Wisconsin, 1972.
Monsters, with V. B. Price, New York, 1981.

By PRICE: articles—

"Mean, Moody, and Magnificent," interview in *Films and Filming* (London), March 1965.

"Black Cats and Cobwebs," in *Films and Filming* (London), August 1969.
Cahiers du Cinéma (Paris), January 1982.
"Tim Burton and Vincent Price," interview with Roddy McDowall, in *Interview* (New York), December 1990.

On PRICE: books—

Beck, Calvin Thomas, *Heroes of the Horrors*, New York, 1975.
McAsh, Iain F., *The Films of Vincent Price*, London, 1977.
McAsh, Iain F., *Vincent Price: A Biography*, Farncombe, Surrey, 1982.
McCarty, John, *The Modern Horror Film*, Secaucus, New Jersey, 1990.
McCarty, John, *The Fearmakers*, New York, 1994.
Williams, Lucy Chase, *The Complete Films of Vincent Price*, Secaucus, New Jersey, 1995.

On PRICE: articles—

Current Biography 1956, New York, 1956.
Marill, Alvin H., "Vincent Price," in *Films in Review* (New York), May 1969.
L'Ecran Fantastique (Paris), no. 17 and no. 18, 1981.
Buckley, Michael, "Vincent Price," in *Films in Review* (New York), May and June/July 1988; also letter in issue for November 1988.

"Vincent Price Issue" of *Cinefantastique* (Oak Park, Illinois), vol 19, nos 1-2, 1989.

Obituary in *Variety* (New York), 15 November 1993.

Obituary in *New York Times*, 26 October 1993 and 27 October 1993.

Obituary in *Current Biography 1994*, New York, 1994.

*   *   *

Like Boris Karloff, his predecessor as the American cinema's best-loved horror star, Vincent Price never disdained the genre slot into which he had been typecast. In fact, he relished it, a relish that came through clearly on screen, and turned his back on the genre only when the FX masters took over and bloodletting rather than barnstorming became the order of the day.

Throughout his career, Price's calling card had been the raised eyebrow and the sardonic smile, either sinister or ironic, and frequently both at the same time. Before *House of Wax* introduced him to his horror metier, he had been used in a variety of secondary leads, taking feckless noir roles that would have been done for George Sanders if they had been any meatier (*The Long Night*, *The Bribe*), and playing a variety of historical personages (Walter Raleigh, Joseph Smith, the Duke of Clarence, Charles II, Cardinal Richelieu, Casanova, Omar Khayyam). After a few smiling hero roles, notably *The House of Seven Gables* opposite George Sanders's villain, he snared the occasional bizarre lead that presaged his destiny: the title character in *The Invisible Man Returns* (reprising the role voice-only for a gag in the later *Abbott and Costello Meet Frankenstein*), as the drug-addicted patron in *Dragonwyck*, as an early (for him) mad scientist in the cheap *Shock*, or as the megalomanic schemer trying to steal a large portion of the United States in *The Baron of Arizona*. In other roles (*Curtain Call at Cactus Creek*, *Champagne for Caesar*, *His Kind of Woman*), he demonstrated a facility for crazed, hammy comedy that would feature prominently in his horror roles. A spell as a Twentieth Century-Fox contract player in the 1940s had dropped him a few plums—the gutless playboy in *Laura*—but mainly stranded him amid the glossy, stifling "quality" of *Brigham Young*, *The Song of Bernadette*, *The Keys of the Kingdom*, and *The Eve of St. Mark*, so he entered the 1950s with an interesting, but somewhat spotty, curriculum vitae.

Price's casting as the kindly sculptor concealing his hideous scars behind a mask in *House of Wax*, a 3-D remake of *Mystery of the Wax Museum*, changed all that. He followed it up with a stereoscopic variation, *The Mad Magician*, and was stuck with the role of the Devil in the unbelievable *Story of Mankind* before landing in three horror films whose seminal popularity did much to bring the waning horror genre back, and Price with it. *The Fly*, widescreen sci-fi, plays more like a Universal picture of the 1930s with its hooded mutant, the victim of a mistimed experiment in teleportation. Price did not take the lead, but the concerned, Lionel Atwill-type secondary figure (a situation that was rectified in the sequel, *The Return of the Fly*). *The House on Haunted Hill* and *The Tingler*, both directed by gimmick master William Castle, virtually created a modern American horror tradition with contemporary settings, cynical murder-twist storylines (courtesy of Clouzot's *Les Diaboliques*), jokey revivals of old horror clichés, and dead-straight grue. They set the pace for Price for years to come.

The House of Usher brought Price together with Roger Corman, Edgar Allan Poe, and American-International Pictures. Corman and AIP were looking to move away from the grade-B, black-and-white shockers that made them a small fortune toward something with a touch of class in the vein of the Gothic horrors being turned out by their British counterparts at Hammer Films. In Poe they found a bankable, homegrown source of Gothic material, and in Price they found an American actor on a par with Hammer stalwarts Peter Cushing and Christopher Lee. Price's neurasthenic Roderick Usher in the team's first effort is as colorful and decaying as his house, and he relishes his over-the-top dialogue and puffy-sleeved outfits, cringing perfectly when the whole edifice collapses on his head in the finale.

The Price-Corman-Poe-AIP combo would continue for most of the 1960s (*The Pit and the Pendulum*, *The Raven*, *Tales of Terror*, *Masque of the Red Death*, *Tomb of Ligeia*, and others) and make Price a top-of-the-line horror star, allowing him to branch out in such imitation efforts as the Hawthorne-derived *Twice-Told Tales*, the de Maupassant-derived *Diary of a Madman*, the Verne-derived *Master of the World*, such international oddities as *The Last Man on Earth* (unclassically adapted from Richard Matheson's classic vampire novel *I Am Legend*) and *The House of a Thousand Dolls*, and self-parodying vehicles like *Dr. Goldfoot and the Bikini Machine*.

Price eventually left the Poe series to appear in Michael Reeves's *Matthew Hopkins—Witchfinder General*, retitled *The Conqueror Worm* in the United States to make it appear Poe-like. Reeves demanded that Price play it thoroughly straight for a change, and he added a chilling touch of mercy to the pitiless monster at the center of the icy period piece. In the Dr. Phibes pictures, director Robert Fuest demanded that he play the ultimate incarnation of a comic-horror tradition, a mad vaudeville organist who favors unwieldly slapstick death-traps to dispose of his victims, and again Price rose to the challenge. Dr. Phibes was a dry run for Price's bravura comic-horror performance in *Theatre of Blood*, where he is a crazed Shakespearean who slaughters his unsympathetic critics using disgusting methods of murder derived from the Bard's plays.

Price curbed his frenzied film schedule from 1977 through 1982 to go on the road for a 200-city tour of his one-man show *Diversions and Delights* (written by John Gay) in which he played the dying Oscar Wilde. He returned to the screen with several feeble monster rallies (*The Monster Club*, *From a Whisper to a Scream*, *Dead Heat*) and one gem, *House of the Long Shadows*, in which he joined forces, memorably, with fellow horror icons Peter Cushing, Christopher Lee, and John Carradine. His lone "serious" credits before his death were Lindsay Anderson's octogenarian mood piece *The Whales of August* (appearing opposite Lillian Gish and Bette Davis) and the superior made-for-cable drama *The Heart of Justice*, where he provided a noteworthy cameo in the film's opening scene.

Price's unbilled bit as "Big Daddy" in AIP's *Beach Party* confirmed another aspect of his persona—his status as an honorary kid, a mod parent figure, either benevolent or malevolent, whose interests are aligned with the juveniles in the pictures and the audiences. This led to his becoming a minor hero to the younger generation, even appearing on the *Batman* show as Egghead, with Elvis Presley in *The Trouble with Girls*, and with Michael Jackson *on his Thriller* album. The culmination of this eventually came in an oddly touching association with Tim Burton, first in the short cartoon *Vincent*, about a boy who wants to be Vincent Price when he grows up, and then, in an extremely moving flashback, as the inventor in *Edward Scissorhands*, teaching his creation etiquette, poetry, and love of art (Price's great passion in real life).

—Kim Newman, updated by John McCarty

PRYOR, Richard

Nationality: American. **Born:** Peoria, Illinois, 1 December 1940. **Military Service:** U.S. Army, in Germany, 1958-60; discharged for attacking fellow soldier with a switchblade. **Family:** Married 1) Patricia Price (divorced), son: Richard Jr.; 2) Shelley Bonus (divorced), daughter: Rain; daughter, with Maxine Silverman: Elizabeth Anne; 3) Deboragh McGuire, 1977 (divorced 1978); 4) Jennifer Lee, 1981 (divorced); 5) Flynn BeLaine, 1986 (divorced 1987; remarried 1990, divorced), sons: Steven and Kelsey; also daughter: Renee and son: Franklin. **Career:** Professional debut as drummer at age of seven; 1961—began to develop comedy act in small clubs in Peoria, Cleveland, Chicago, and Buffalo, and from 1963, at the Café Wha? in New York; 1966—national exposure on several TV shows; then engagements in Las Vegas, and successful recordings; 1967—film debut in *The Busy Body*; later films include versions of his live performances; television scriptwriter for Flip Wilson, Lily Tomlin, and the series *Sanford and Son*; 1975—set up Richard Pryor Enterprises, Inc., Los Angeles; later founded Indigo Productions; 1977—in TV series *The Richard Pryor Show*; 1984-85—in TV series *Pryor's Place*; 1986—debut as feature director with *Jo Jo Dancer*; 1990s—stricken with multiple sclerosis, wrote autobiography, and continued to write comedy material. **Address:** c/o Edward Astrin, 16633 Ventura Boulevard, Suite 1450, Encino, CA 91436, U.S.A.

Films as Actor:

1967   *The Busy Body* (Castle) (as Whittaker)
1968   *Wild in the Streets* (Shear) (as Stanley X); *The Green Berets* (Wayne)
1969   *The Young Lawyers* (Hart—for TV)
1970   *Carter's Army* (McCowan—for TV) (as Jonathan Crunk); *The Phynx* (Katzin) (as himself)
1971   *You've Got to Walk It Like You Talk It or You'll Lose That Beat* (Locke) (as wino); *Dynamite Chicken* (Pintoff) (as himself)
1972   *Lady Sings the Blues* (Furie) (as Piano Man)
1973   *Some Call It Loving* (James B. Harris) (as Jeff); *Wattstax* (Stuart); *The Mack* (*The Mack and His Pack*) (Campus) (as Slim); *Hit!* (Furie) (as Mike Willmer)
1974   *Uptown Saturday Night* (Poitier) (as Sharp Eye Washington)
1975   *Adios Amigo* (Williamson) (as Sam)
1976   *Silver Streak* (Hiller) (as Grover Muldoon); *The Bingo Long Traveling All-Stars and Motor Kings* (Badham) (as Charlie Snow); *Car Wash* (Schultz) (as Daddy Rich)
1977   *Which Way Is Up?* (Schultz) (as Leroy Jones/Rufus Jones/the Rev. Thomas); *Greased Lightning* (Schultz) (as Wendell Scott)
1978   *Richard Pryor Live in Concert* (Jeff Margolis—filmed concert); *California Suite* (Ross) (as Dr. Chauncy Gump); *Blue Collar* (Schrader) (as Zeke Brown); *The Wiz* (Lumet) (title role)
1979   *Richard Pryor Is Back Live in Concert* (Jeff Margolis—filmed concert); *The Muppet Movie* (Frawley) (as balloon vendor)
1980   *Stir Crazy* (Poitier) (as Harry Monroe); *Wholly Moses* (Weis) (as Pharaoh); *In God We Trust* (Feldman) (as God)
1981   *Bustin' Loose* (Oz Scott) (as Joe Braxton, + co-pr, co-story); *Richard Pryor, Live and Smokin'* (Blum—filmed concert, produced in 1971)
1982   *The Toy* (Richard Donner) (as Jack Brown); *Richard Pryor Live on the Sunset Strip* (Layton—filmed concert) (+ co-pr); *Some Kind of Hero* (Pressman) (as Eddie Keller)
1983   *Superman III* (Lester) (as Gus Gorman)
1985   *Brewster's Millions* (Walter Hill) (as Montgomery Brewster)
1986   *Funny* (Wynn)
1987   *Critical Condition* (Apted) (as Eddie/Kevin)
1988   *Moving* (Metter) (as Arlo Pear)
1989   *See No Evil, Hear No Evil* (Hiller) (as Wally Karew); *Harlem Nights* (Murphy) (as Sugar Ray)
1990   *Look Who's Talking Too* (Heckerling) (as voice)
1991   *Another You* (Phillips) (as Eddie Dash)
1996   *Lost Highway* (Lynch)

Films as Director:

1983   *Richard Pryor Here and Now* (filmed concert)
1986   *Jo Jo Dancer, Your Life Is Calling* (+ ro as alter ego/title role, pr, co-sc)

Other Film:

1974   *Blazing Saddles* (Mel Brooks) (co-sc)

Publications

By PRYOR: book—

Pryor Convictions, and Other Life Sentences, with Todd Gold, New York, 1995.

By PRYOR: article—

"Richard Pryor in His Own Words," interview with David Schumacher, in *Entertainment Weekly* (New York), 30 April 1993.

On PRYOR: books—

Haver, Ronald, *Richard Pryor: The Legend of a Survivor*, New York, 1981.
Robbins, Fred, and David Ragan, *Richard Pryor: This Cat's Got 9 Lives*, New York, 1982.
Rovin, Jeff, *Richard Pryor: Black and Blue*, New York, 1983.
Haskins, Jim, *Richard Pryor: A Man and His Madness*, New York, 1984.
Lee, Jennifer, *Tarnished Angel: Surviving in the Dark Curve of Drugs, Violence, Sex, and Fame: A Memoir*, New York, 1991.
Williams, John A., and Dennis A. Williams, *If I Stop I'll Die: The Comedy and Tragedy of Richard Pryor*, New York, 1991.

On PRYOR: articles—

Current Biography 1976, New York, 1976.
Kael, Pauline, "Richard Pryor," in *The Movie Star*, edited by Elisabeth Weis, New York, 1981.
Rosenbaum, Jonathan, "The Man in the Great Flammable Suit," in *Film Comment* (New York), July/August 1982.
Geist, Kenneth L., "The Charlie Parker Story," in *Films in Review* (New York), May 1989.
Handelman, David, "The Last Time We Saw Richard," in *Premiere* (New York), January 1992.
Burr, Ty, "Pryor Engagements," in *Entertainment Weekly* (New York), 30 April 1993.
Schumacher, David, "Richard Pryor's Biggest Fight," in *Ebony* (Chicago), September 1993.
Plummer, William, and F. X. Feeney, "Nowhere to Hide," in *People Weekly* (New York), 29 May 1995.
Cover story in *Jet* (Chicago), 5 June 1995.

*   *   *

Black comedian Godfrey Cambridge once remarked on the vulnerability of African-American performers to Hollywood fads. Had he worked in the 1930s, he said, he would have mostly hung on plantation gates in ragged overalls, yelling "Massa Jim come home from de war," while in the 1940s he would have taken hormone injections and appeared as a bass in prison pictures singing "Nobody Knows the Trouble I Seen."

Malign providence has seemingly sentenced Richard Pryor, one of the cleverest of black comic writers and stand-up comedians, to be perpetually out of phase with movie fashion. He was too young to play the stern young professionals that made Sidney Poitier's name, too comic for the subsequent black thrillers dominated by Richard Roundtree, then too old for the sassy black stud cycle that made stars of Pryor acolytes such as Eddie Murphy. He tried comedy/drama just a little too soon and had to watch the infinitely less talented Bill Cosby turn black middle-class rectitude into a gold mine.

After small roles in films as improbable as John Wayne's *The Green Berets*, Pryor found a niche in the mid-1970s as a supporting and cameo player. His stock-in-trade was a gagging, capering, eye-rolling modern parody of the Stepin Fetchit/Rochester cliché black of the 1930s, its cornerstone a startled sidewise glance as some new horror bears down on him. He has the most memorable moment of *Car Wash* as a fake evangelist in a stretch limo, with the Pointer Sisters as his retinue, and in *Silver Streak* he hilariously coaches Gene Wilder in passing for black, turning him into a capering, jiving cliché in blackface. Pryor and Wilder continued this partnership in *Stir Crazy* as bumbling escaped convicts, then in the dismal *See No Evil, Hear No Evil* where they played fugitives with complementary physical disabilities, Wilder deaf and Pryor blind.

Wilder and Poitier have wisely used Pryor in almost every comedy they directed, usually as the startled innocent put upon by more cunning colleagues. It is a tribute to Pryor's comic invention (and that of director Richard Lester) that he even adapted this performance to *Superman III* and won laughs as a self-taught computer genius.

Pryor achieved starring roles in the mid-1980s, but his projects were unwisely selected. *Some Kind of Hero* and *Jo Jo Dancer, Your Life Is Calling*, which he also directed and co-wrote, were moralistic comedy/dramas, at odds with his farcical image. His straight comedy performances were no better. *The Toy*, in which he is purchased by millionaire Jackie Gleason as a plaything for his son, is bizarrely old-fashioned, a story more typical of late silent comics such as Harry Langdon than the streetwise Pryor. Two years after Eddie Murphy's *Trading Places*, Pryor, once more out of phase with fashion, was cast in the copycat *Brewster's Millions*, yet another version of George Barr McCutcheon's post-World War I farce about a millionaire's heir forced to waste millions in order to inherit even more. Heavily mired in plot, it was resistant to Pryor's comic skill, even with the talented John Candy in support.

The actor's ill-fortune at this time extended into a private life that became more and more notorious but ultimately merely sad. A long-time cocaine addict, Pryor nearly died from a 1977 heart attack, then in 1980 sustained severe burns in what was initially described as an accident suffered while Pryor was freebasing cocaine, but has since been revealed by Pryor to be a suicide attempt—he doused himself with cognac and ignited it with a lighter—brought on by the coke and his despondency over the death of his beloved grandmother, the only anchor he had had in a very rough childhood. His numerous wives, lovers, and children and revelations about his abuse of the women in this life—most notably revealed in ex-wife Jennifer Lee's memoir—only added to his notoriety.

That his next setback—he was diagnosed with multiple sclerosis in 1986—was not of his own doing, finally provided him with some public sympathy (incredibly enough, this was followed by quadruple-bypass heart surgery in 1991). Pryor is no doubt talented, thoughtful, and inventive, and is a more important performer than his ill-starred career suggests, but one wonders if, given his weakened physical condition, he will ever be given a chance to make the comeback that would provide the Hollywood ending to a most Hollywood-like life and career.

—John Baxter, updated by David E. Salamie

PURVIANCE, Edna

Nationality: American. **Born:** Lovelock, Nevada, 1894. **Career:** Secretary in San Francisco; 1915—joined the Essanay Company, and made film debut in *His Night Out*, directed by Chaplin; almost all her subsequent films were under Chaplin's direction, playing opposite him. **Died:** In Hollywood, 11 January 1958.

Films as Actress:

(films directed by Chaplin unless noted)

1915   *His Night Out* (short); *The Champion* (short); *In the Park* (short); *The Jitney Elopement* (short); *The Tramp* (short); *By the Sea* (short); *The Perfect Lady* (short); *Work* (short); *A Woman* (short); *The Bank* (short); *Shanghaied* (short); *Police* (short); *Burlesque on Carmen* (as Carmen); *A Night in the Show* (short)

1916   *The Floorwalker* (short); *The Fireman* (short); *The Vagabond* (short); *The Count* (short) (as Miss Moneybags); *The Pawnshop* (short); *Behind the Screen* (short); *The Rink* (short)

1917   *Easy Street* (short); *The Cure* (short); *The Immigrant* (short); *The Adventurer* (short)

1918   *Triple Trouble* (compilation); *A Dog's Life*; *Shoulder Arms*; *The Bond* (short)

1919   *Sunnyside*; *A Day's Pleasure*

1921   *The Kid*; *The Idle Class*

1922   *Pay Day*

1923   *The Pilgrim*; *A Woman of Paris* (as Marie St. Clair)

1926   *L'Education de prince* (Daimant-Berger); *A Woman of the Sea* (*The Seagull*) (von Sternberg)

1947   *Monsieur Verdoux* (as extra)

1952   *Limelight* (as extra)

Publications

On PURVIANCE: articles—

Interview with H. S. Naylor, in *Motion Picture Magazine*, April 1918.
Interviews with M. Cheatham, in *Motion Picture Classic*, November 1919 and August 1922.
Interview with C. Stuart, in *Motion Picture Magazine*, February 1922.
Obituary in *New York Times*, 16 January 1958.
Fieschi, J., "La Fin d'une liaison," in *Cinématographe* (Paris), January 1981.
See entry on Charlie Chaplin in *International Dictionary of Films and Filmmakers, Volume 2: Directors*.

*   *   *

Shortly after Charlie Chaplin accepted a contract with the Essanay Studio in 1915, he invited Edna Purviance, a young stenographer, to join him as his exclusive leading lady. For the next seven years, Purviance portrayed the love interest in more than 20 of the short features that Chaplin wrote, directed, and starred in before 1923, faithfully accompanying him in his travels from Essanay to Mutual (in 1916) and from Mutual to First National (in 1918). Consequently, Purviance appeared with Chaplin and, among others, Ben Turpin, Eric Campbell, and Mack Swain, in many of the most popular and now-classic films of the silent American cinema, including *The Tramp*, *Easy Street*, *The Immigrant*, and *The Kid*.

Edna Purviance

Purviance proved to be the perfect choice for Chaplin's films of 1915-22, whose themes and content reflected his growing social conscience. Unlike Mabel Normand, who had often played opposite Chaplin during his year with Keystone, Purviance richly and consistently embodied the contemporary ideal of woman as sympathetic and gentle creature. Unfailingly calm before the storm of the little tramp's vigorous horseplay and displays of affection, Purviance served Chaplin's character as a splendidly harmonious and appreciative foil. Yet she contributed more to Chaplin's productions than a placid presence and a beautiful face. Under Chaplin's direction, she developed into a sensitive and expressive silent actress, demonstrating her ability to rise above the level of appealing decoration, a position that Chaplin initially thought she would occupy in his films. Within the confines of essentially a single role, she portrayed an array of characters—a farmer's daughter, an organist for an urban mission, a woman of wealth and high fashion—as elegant, intelligent, and good-humored women.

Irony blighted the final years of Purviance's film career, which ostensibly ended in 1926. In an effort to reward Purviance for her personal and professional loyalty and to make her a star, Chaplin passed over *The Trojan Women* and Napoleon's Josephine to cast her as Marie St. Clair in *A Woman of Paris*, an original story tinged with the biographical. Although *A Woman of Paris* failed commercially, it introduced filmmaking to the sophisticated and psychologically suggestive, and made a star, not of Purviance, but of one of her leading men, Adolphe Menjou. Still on Chaplin's payroll, where she would remain until her death, Purviance acted in Henri Daimant-Berger's unsuccessful *L'Education de prince* before working with Chaplin on the film known alternately as *A Woman of the Sea* and *The Seagull*. Chaplin, who produced the film but asked Josef von Sternberg to direct it, was so displeased with the final print that he refused its release. Neither *The Seagull* nor *A Woman of Paris* became available, at least to Western audiences, until after Chaplin's death in 1977, nearly 20 years after Purviance's own death. Purviance made her final appearances on film in Chaplin's *Monsieur Verdoux* and *Limelight*. Despite returning to the studio in the era of sound, Purviance remained silent, for in both films, she played an extra.

—Nancy Jane Richards

983

QUAID, Dennis

Nationality: American **Born:** Houston, Texas, 9 April 1954; younger brother of the actor Randy Quaid. **Education:** Attended public school in Houston; and the University of Houston, which he left before graduating. **Family:** Married 1) the actress P. J. Soles (divorced); 2) the actress Meg Ryan, 1991, son: Jack Henry. **Career:** 1975—film debut in *Crazy Mama*; 1983—stage debut, off-Broadway, *The Last of the Knucklemen*, followed by stage work in both New York and Los Angeles (including *True West*, 1984); has also written songs; played piano and guitar, and sung with his band, the Eclectics; 1989—formed Summers/Quaid Productions with Cathleen Summers. **Agent:** International Creative Management, 8942 Wilshire Boulevard, Beverly Hills, CA 90212, U.S.A.

Films as Actor:

1975   *Crazy Mama* (Jonathan Demme) (as extra)
1977   *I Never Promised You a Rose Garden* (Page); *9/30/55 (September 30, 1955; 24 Hours of the Rebel)* (Bridges) (as Frank)
1978   *Are You in the House Alone?* (Grauman—for TV); *The Seniors* (Amateau) (as Alan); *Our Winning Season* (Ruben) (as Paul Morelli)
1979   *Amateur Night at the Dixie Bar and Grill* (Schumacher—for TV); *Breaking Away* (Yates) (as Mike)
1980   *Gorp* (Ruben) (as Mad Grossman); *The Long Riders* (Walter Hill) (as Ed Miller)
1981   *All Night Long* (Tramont) (as Freddie Dupler); *Caveman* (Gottlieb) (as Lar); *The Night the Lights Went Out in Georgia* (Maxwell) (as Travis Child); *Bill* (Page—for TV) (as Barry Morrow)
1982   *Johnny Belinda* (Harvey—for TV) (as Kyle)
1983   *Bill: On His Own* (Page—for TV) (as Barry Morrow); *Jaws 3-D (Jaws III)* (Alves) (as Mike Brody); *The Right Stuff* (Kaufman) (as Gordon "Gordo" Cooper); *Tough Enough* (Fleischer) (as Art Long)
1984   *Dreamscape* (Ruben) (as Alex Gardner)
1985   *Enemy Mine* (Petersen) (as Davidge)
1987   *The Big Easy* (McBride) (as Remy McSwain); *Innerspace* (Dante) (as Lt. Tuck Pendleton); *Suspect* (Yates) (as Eddie Sanger)
1988   *D.O.A.* (Morton and Jankel) (as Dexter Cornell); *Everybody's All-American* (Hackford) (as Gavin Grey)
1989   *Great Balls of Fire!* (McBride) (as Jerry Lee Lewis)
1990   *Come See the Paradise* (Alan Parker) (as Jack McGurn); *Postcards from the Edge* (Mike Nichols) (as Jack Falkner)
1993   *Flesh and Bone* (Kloves) (as Arlis Sweeney); *Undercover Blues* (Ross) (as Jeff Blue); *Wilder Napalm* (Caron) (as Wallace Foudroyant)
1994   *Wyatt Earp* (Kasdan) (as Doc Holliday)
1995   *Something to Talk About* (Hallström) (as Eddie Bichon)
1996   *Dragonheart* (Cohen) (as Bowen)

Publications

By QUAID: articles—

"When Dennis Met Meg," interview with George Kalogerakis, in *Vogue* (New York), November 1993.
"The (Almost) Born-Again Dennis Quaid," interview with Nancy Mills, in *Cosmopolitan*, June 1994.

On QUAID: book—

Birnbaum, Gail, *Dennis Quaid*, New York, 1988.

On QUAID: articles—

Taylor, Clarke, "Dennis Quaid: A Quandary at a Career Crossroads," in *Los Angeles Times*, 2 January 1984.
Seeley, David, "Dennis, Anyone?," in *Playboy* (Chicago), December 1987.
Haskell, Molly, "Sympathy for the Devilish: Hollywood's New Man—Not Afraid of Women," in *Vogue* (New York), March 1988.
Hoban, Phoebe, "The Quintessential Dennis Quaid," in *Cosmopolitan*, March 1988.
Greene, Bob, "Getting Quaid," in *Esquire* (New York), April 1988.
Norman, Michael, "Dennis Quaid Can't Sit Still: A Young Actor Rocks on the Cusp of Stardom," in *New York Times Magazine*, 6 November 1988.
Tosches, Nick, "Playing the Killer," in *Vogue* (New York), July 1989.
Natale, Richard, "Lose 43 Pounds. Ride a Horse. Emote. Just Another Day at the OK Corral," in *Los Angeles Times*, 19 June 1994.

*   *   *

Dennis Quaid is consummately a genre actor. His career alternates comedies, musicals, and Westerns with sci-fi films, neo-films noir, and melodramas. He thus works in a frame of Hollywood tradition: twice over, in that his physical form—tall, well-muscled yet lithe, with a trademark grin—echoes not his immediate "New Hollywood" predecessors but much earlier Hollywood leading men. Connecting to an even older tradition, Quaid specializes in men on quests. But he brings a responsiveness and humor to his adventurers which marks them as products of his feminist-influenced times.

His acting style itself injects a contemporary note. He works avidly to make his characters' contours and capacities part of his body: he learned to fly to play an astronaut, pounded a piano hours a day to play a rock star, gained 40 pounds for one role, lost 40 for another. In this Quaid is a quintessential "post-Method" actor. Whatever his personal take on Lee Strasberg's Method (which the *New York Times Magazine* reports he "will mention" but not "intellectualize"), his devotion, first, to "living" his parts, and, second, to transforming conventions demonstrates his embrace of the Method's two central precepts—which have exceeded their roots in the teachings of Stanislavski and Strasberg and permeated Hollywood since the 1950s.

Dennis Quaid

The conjunction of new techniques in acting—and in filmmaking overall—with established story structures makes Dennis Quaid's movies entertaining. Unfortunately, in Hollywood at a time when stars are defined by their ability to carry blockbuster franchises, usually through many sequels, Quaid's versatility may have kept him from becoming the superstar he seemed primed to become in the late 1980s. Nonetheless he has worked quite steadily since the late 1970s. The first phase of Quaid's career found him moving from bit parts to large supporting roles in a string of youth sex comedies and melodramas; in 1979, he got his first real notice as the angriest young man in *Breaking Away*. Over the next four years he worked at a middle level in television films and features, in some well-received projects (*The Long Riders*, *Bill*) and some misses (*Caveman*, *Jaws 3-D*).

In 1983 he found the wellspring of the adventurer type he would come to embody, with the role of cocky, intense but relaxed space traveler "Gordo" Cooper in *The Right Stuff* (one of three biopics in Quaid's catalog). Between 1984 and 1990 Quaid became a full-fledged leading man, playing the searcher in cycles of sci-fi films (*Dreamscape*, *Enemy Mine*, *Innerspace*), and perverse crime stories (*The Big Easy*, *Suspect*, *D.O.A.*). *Easy* made him a heartthrob of the moment, as his corrupt but charming police detective set out on a quest across the landscape of uptight female sexuality in the person of Ellen Barkin. Quaid's next two films also grapple with harsh romance. The aging athlete of *Everybody's All-American* seems a later chapter in the coming-of-age sports melodramas Quaid had done in his early days. Playing Jerry Lee Lewis in *Great Balls of Fire!* similarly followed from Quaid's previous, lesser-known country-rock musicals (*Amateur Night at the Dixie Bar and Grill*, *The Night the Lights Went Out in Georgia*, *Tough Enough*), bringing on-screen his talents for singing and songwriting.

But neither *All-American* nor *Fire!* were huge hits, perhaps in part because they both concern pioneering heroes who fail as much as they succeed. *Come See the Paradise* resembled some of Quaid's previous work with its theme of cross-racial inclusivity (*Enemy Mine*)—but its questioning of U.S. wartime policies did not match the tenor of the Gulf War. After taking two years off to kick cocaine, get married, and have a son, Quaid returned with three leading roles in 1993, the most well-reviewed being the country noir *Flesh and Bone* which co-starred his wife, Meg Ryan. Quaid turned to supporting roles for two years (it was to play tubercular Doc Holliday in *Wyatt Earp* that he lost 40 pounds). *Dragonheart* put him back at center stage, literalizing Quaid's affinity for his cardinal genre, the knight's quest, as revved up with state-of-the-art special effects, in an attempt to reunite a fine actor with box-office success.

—Susan Knobloch

QUAYLE, (Sir) Anthony

Nationality: British. **Born:** John Anthony Quayle in Ainsdale, Lancashire, 7 September 1913. **Education:** Attended Rugby School, Royal Academy of Dramatic Arts, London, 1930-31. **Family:** Married 1) Hermione Hanne (divorced); 2) Dorothy Hyson, 1947, son: Christopher, daughters: the actress Jennifer Quayle and Rosanna. **Career:** 1931—straight man to music hall comic; London debut in *Robin Hood*; 1932—joined the Old Vic company, London; 1935—film debut in *Moscow Nights*; 1936—New York debut in *The Country Wife*; 1939-45—served in the Royal Artillery, part of the time writing and directing pantomimes and revues: Major; 1948-56—director of the Shakespeare Memorial Theatre (later the Royal Shakespeare Theatre), Stratford-upon-Avon: produced the entire cycle of Shakespeare plays, and acted in many of them; later stage work includes roles in *A View from the Bridge*, in London, 1956, *Titus Andronicus* in Paris, 1957, *Long Day's Journey into Night*, 1958, *Galileo* in New York, 1967, *Sleuth* in London and New York, 1970, *King Lear*, 1978, and *The Clandestine Marriage* (also director), 1984; 1968—in TV series *Strange Report* (on U.S. television, 1971); 1971—U.S. narrator for TV mini-series *The Six Wives of Henry VIII*, and in mini-series *QB VII*, 1974, *Masada* (*The Antagonists*), 1981, and *The Last Days of Pompeii*, 1984; also narrator for Conservative Party broadcasts, 1980s; 1983—founder, Compass Theatre. **Awards:** Commander of the British Empire, 1952. Knighted, 1985. **Died:** In London, 20 October 1989.

Films as Actor:

1935	*Moscow Nights* (*I Stand Condemned*) (Asquith)
1938	*Pygmalion* (Asquith and Howard)
1948	*Hamlet* (Olivier) (as Marcellus); *Saraband for Dead Lovers* (Dearden)
1955	*Oh Rosalinda* (*Fledermaus '55*) (Powell and Pressburger) (as Orlovsky)
1956	*The Battle of the River Plate* (*Pursuit of the Graf Spee*) (Powell and Pressburger); *The Wrong Man* (Hitchcock)
1957	*Woman in a Dressing Gown* (Lee Thompson); *No Time for Tears* (Frankel)
1958	*The Man Who Wouldn't Talk* (Wilcox); *Ice Cold in Alex* (*Desert Attack*) (Lee Thompson)
1959	*Tarzan's Greatest Adventure* (Guillermin)
1960	*The Challenge* (*It Takes a Thief*) (Gilling)
1961	*The Guns of Navarone* (Lee Thompson); *Drums for a Queen* (doc) (as narrator)
1962	*This Is Lloyd's* (doc) (as narrator); ***Lawrence of Arabia*** (Lean)
1963	*The Fall of the Roman Empire* (Mann)
1964	*East of Sudan* (Juran)
1965	*Operation Crossbow* (*The Great Spy Mission*) (Anderson); *A Study in Terror* (*Fog*) (James Hill) (as Dr. Murray)
1966	*The Poppy Is Also a Flower* (*Danger Grows Wild*) (Young)
1967	*Incompreso* (*Misunderstood*) (Comencini)
1968	*Mackenna's Gold* (Lee Thompson)
1969	*Destiny of a Spy* (Sagal—for TV); *Before Winter Comes* (Lee Thompson)
1970	*Anne of the Thousand Days* (Jarrott) (as Cardinal Wolsey)
1971	*Island Unknown* (Newmann—doc) (as narrator)
1972	*Everything You Always Wanted to Know about Sex but Were Afraid to Ask* (Allen)
1973	*A Bequest to the Nation* (Jones) (as Lord Minto); *Jarret* (Shear—for TV) (as Basset Cosgrave)
1974	*The Tamarind Seed* (Edwards) (as Jack Loder); *Great Expectations* (Hardy—for TV) (as Jaggers)
1975	*Moses* (*The Lawgiver*) (De Bosio—for TV) (as Aaron)
1976	*The Eagle Has Landed* (John Sturges); *Twenty-One Hours at Munich* (Graham—for TV)
1978	*The Chosen* (De Martino) (as Prof. Griffith)
1979	*Murder by Decree* (Clark) (as Sir Charles Warren)
1984	*Lace* (Hale—for TV); *The Testament of John* (Taylor—for TV)
1985	*The Key to Rebecca* (Hemmings—for TV)
1986	*The Theban Plays by Sophocles* (Talor—for TV)
1988	*Magdalene* (*Stille nacht*; *Silent Night*) (Teuber) (as Father Nossler); *La leggenda del santo bevitore* (*The Legend of the Holy Drinker*) (Olmi); *Miracle* (Ross—for TV); *The Bourne Identity* (Young—for TV); *Buster* (Green) (as Sir James McDowell)
1989	*King of the Wind* (Duffell) (as Lord Granville); *The Endless Game* (Forbes—for TV); *Confessional* (Flemyng)
1990	*Once . . .* (Williams) (as voice)

Publications

By QUAYLE: book—

A Time to Speak, London, 1990.

On QUAYLE: articles—

Lewis, E., "Virtuoso from England," in *Cue*, 4 February 1956.
Current Biography 1971, New York, 1971.
Obituary in *New York Times*, 21 October 1989.
Obituary in *Variety* (New York), 25 October 1989.

* * *

Perhaps more than that of any other actor, the film career of Anthony Quayle exemplifies the substantial differences between the requirements of stage performance and what movie audiences demand of larger than life screen figures. Classically trained and an immense success in demanding theatrical roles from Shakespeare to Arthur Miller, Anthony Quayle has never been more than an interesting supporting player in the cinema. The reason is simple: possessed of a fine voice and capable of interesting impersonations, Quayle lacked the good looks and charisma necessary for screen popularity. In addition, he was never able to fit himself into any of the leading man stereotypes that emerged during the early stages of his career. Unlike Jack Hawkins, for example, he was unable to establish himself as a personification of the self-sacrifice and dedication which led to victory in World War II. Nor, like Richard Burton, Michael Caine, or Albert Finney, was he able to find success impersonating intense and hungry working-class men. Instead, he was forced to continue a pattern he discovered early in show business: playing a foil or straight man to the attractiveness and vitality of a featured character.

In *Lawrence of Arabia* he plays a British liaison officer assigned to command an inexperienced Lieutenant Lawrence just posted to the Arab army. Everything he tells Lawrence is conventional wisdom, and all of it proves wrong as the seemingly predestined hero accomplishes the unlikely and the impossible. Quayle's anger at his subordinate's unauthorized success thus seems the jealousy of an ordinary man encountering the extraordinary. *The Fall of the Roman Empire* finds Quayle as a robust gladiator promoted by newly crowned emperor Christopher Plummer to an important position of command; here Quayle's intensity and forcefulness provide an important mirror for the emperor, whose slide into suicidal self-

Anthony Quayle in *Lawrence of Arabia*

destructiveness is eventually measured by a murderous attack on his trusted subordinate.

In *The Guns of Navarone* (directed by J. Lee Thompson, for whom Quayle has done much of his screen work), Quayle plays an overconscientious officer put in charge of a dangerous, vital mission (a Jack Hawkins type who takes his work too seriously). This position of authority and narrative focus, however, is momentary; wounded early in the operation, Quayle becomes suicidal, making room for unlikely hero Gregory Peck to claim the command. In the turgid melodrama *The Tamarind Seed* Quayle is an overeager security officer, the bane of the furtive and complex lives lived by the diplomatic corps he is supposed to oversee; the film uses him as little more than an errand boy for star-crossed lovers Omar Sharif and Julie Andrews, whose love affair softens his north-country cynicism. In fact, anger and unpopularity seem to be the hallmark of many of Quayle's more minor screen roles: as the priest Aaron, foil to the main character in *Moses*; as a stuffy aristocrat, accessory to the murder plot detected by Christopher Plummer's cagey Sherlock Holmes in *Murder by Decree*; as the insanely jealous king who discovers that the fool has given his wife an aphrodisiac in *Everything You Always Wanted to Know about Sex*; as a briefly seen Marcellus in Olivier's *Hamlet*.

Roles with more promise show what Quayle's film career might have been, had he the requisite qualities. He is suitably intense and dedicated as Manny's defense attorney in Hitchcock's *The Wrong Man*; but the narrative doesn't offer him much chance for heroics as Manny's innocence is established by a chance encounter in the police station. In any case, the film's noir documentariness deemphasizes the personal qualities of its characters (including Henry Fonda as the victim/hero), making Quayle's performance even less noticeable. *Ice Cold in Alex* (another Thompson film) affords Quayle an interesting opportunity to emerge into narrative prominence. Here he plays a South African soldier picked up by the British main party (led by John Mills) retreating from Tobruk. Twice on the journey his cunning saves the group, and he seems much more in control than either the commander or the top NCO (played by Harry Andrews). Quayle's character is eventually discovered to be a German spy, but, because of his service to the group, they lie to save him, affirming to the authorities that he was in German uniform when they first saw him.

Perhaps his finest performance, however, as an embattled Cardinal Wolsey in *Anne of the Thousand Days*, depends on Quayle's successful portrayal of a foil, here to the romantic struggle between monarch and queen. It is ironic that a stage actor who achieved international success in principal Shakespearean parts should have been most rewarded (an Academy Award nomination) by film professionals for such a different kind of performance and, by extension, career.

—R. Barton Palmer

QUINN, Anthony

Nationality: American. **Born:** Anthony Rudolph Oaxaca Quinn in Chihuahua, Mexico, 21 April 1915 (some sources give 1916); became U.S. citizen, 1947. **Education:** Attended public school in Los Angeles, California. **Family:** Married 1) Katherine DeMille, 1937 (divorced 1965), sons: Christopher (deceased), Duncan, daughters: Christina, Kathleen, Valentina; 2) Iolanda Addolori, 1965 (separated 1995), sons: Francesco, Daniele, Lorenzo; child with Kathy Benvin. **Career:** Worked as cement mixer, ditchdigger, boxer, fruit picker, taxi driver; also with Federal Theater Project; 1936—stage debut in *Clean Beds*; film debut in *Parole*; then contract with Paramount, 1936-40; 1947—Broadway debut in *The Gentleman from Athens*; 1958—directed the film *The Buccaneer*; 1962—on stage in *Tchin-Tchin*; 1971-

72—in TV series *The Man and the City*; 1977—in mini-series *Jesus of Nazareth*; 1983—in musical version of the film, *Zorba!* on Broadway; 1988—in TV mini-series *The Richest Man in the World: The Story of Aristotle Onassis*. **Awards:** Best Supporting Actor Academy Award, for *Viva Zapata!*, 1952; Best Supporting Actor Academy Award, for *Lust for Life*, 1956. **Agent:** Johnnie Planco, William Morris Agency, 1350 Avenue of the Americas, New York, NY 10019, U.S.A.

Films as Actor:

1936 *Parole* (Landers) (as Browning); *Sworn Enemy* (Marin) (as gangster); *Night Waitress* (Landers) (as hood); *The Plainsman* (Cecil B. DeMille) (as Cheyenne Indian); *The Milky Way* (McCarey) (as extra)

1937 *Swing High, Swing Low* (Leisen) (as the Don); *Waikiki Wedding* (Tuttle) (as Kimo); *The Last Train from Madrid* (Hogan) (as Capt. Ricardo Alvarez); *Partners in Crime* (Murphy) (as Nicholas Mazaney); *Daughter of Shanghai* (Florey) (as Harry Morgan)

1938 *The Buccaneer* (Cecil B. DeMille) (as Beluche); *Dangerous to Know* (Florey) (as Nicholas Keisnoff); *Tip-Off Girls* (Louis King) (as Marty); *Hunted Men* (Louis King) (as Legs); *Bulldog Drummond in Africa* (Louis King) (as Deane Fordline); *King of Alcatraz* (Florey) (as Lou Gadney)

1939 *King of Chinatown* (Grinde) (as Mike Gordon); *Union Pacific* (Cecil B. DeMille) (as Jack Cordray); *Island of Lost Men* (Neumann) (as Chang Tai); *Television Spy* (Dmytryk) (as Forbes)

1940 *Emergency Squad* (Dmytryk) (as Nick Buller); *Road to Singapore* (Schertzinger) (as Caesar); *Parole Fixer* (Florey) (as Francis Bradmore); *The Ghost Breakers* (George Marshall) (as Ramon); *City for Conquest* (Litvak) (as Murray Bruno); *Texas Rangers Ride Again* (Hogan) (as Joe Yuma)

1941 *Blood and Sand* (Mamoulian) (as Manolo de Palma); *Knockout* (Clemens) (as Trego); *Thieves Fall Out* (Wright) (as Chic Collins); *They Died with Their Boots On* (Walsh) (as Crazy Horse); *The Perfect Snob* (McCarey) (as Alex Morens); *Bullets for O'Hara* (William K. Howard) (as Tony Van Dyne)

1942 *Larceny, Inc.* (Lloyd Bacon) (as Leo Dexter); *Road to Morocco* (David Butler) (as Mullay Kasim); *The Black Swan* (Henry King) (as Wogan); *The Ox-Bow Incident* (Wellman) (as the Mexican)

1943 *Guadalcanal Diary* (Seiler)

1944 *Buffalo Bill* (Wellman) (as Yellow Hand); *Roger Touhy, Gangster* (*The Last Gangster*) (Florey) (as George Carroll); *Ladies of Washington* (Louis King) (as Michael Romanescue); *Irish Eyes Are Smiling* (Ratoff) (as Al Jackson)

1945 *Where Do We Go from Here?* (Ratoff) (as Indian Chief); *China Sky* (Enright) (as Chen Ta); *Back to Bataan* (Dmytryk) (as Capt. Andres Bonifacio)

1946 *California* (Farrow) (as Don Luis Rivera y Hernandez)

1947 *Sinbad the Sailor* (Wallace) (as Emir); *The Imperfect Lady* (Lewis Allen) (as Jose Martinez); *Black Gold* (Karlson) (as Charley Eagle); *Tycoon* (Wallace) (as Enrique Vargas)

1951 *The Brave Bulls* (Rossen) (as Raul Fuentes); *Mask of the Avenger* (Karlson) (as Giovanni Larocca); *High Treason* (Boulting)

1952 *Viva Zapata!* (Kazan) (title role); *The Brigand* (Karlson) (as Carlos Delargo); *The World in His Arms* (Walsh) (as Portugee); *Against All Flags* (Sherman) (as Roc Brasiliano)

1953 *City beneath the Sea* (Boetticher) (as Tony Bartlett); *Seminole* (Boetticher) (as Osceola); *Ride Vaquero!* (Farrow) (as José Esqueda); *East of Sumatra* (Boetticher) (as Kiang); *Blowing Wild* (Fregonese) (as Ward Conway); *Cavalleria Rusticana* (*Fatal Desire*) (Gallone) (as Alfio); *Donne Proibite* (*Angels of Darkness*; *Forbidden Women*) (Amato) (as Francesco Caserto)

1954   *Ulisse* (*Ulysses*) (Camerini) (as Antinous); ***La strada*** (Fellini) (as Zampano); *The Long Wait* (Saville) (as Johnny McBride); *Attila flagello di dio* (*Attila*; *Attila the Hun*) (Francisci) (title role)

1955   *The Magnificent Matador* (Boetticher) (as Luis Santos); *The Naked Street* (Shane) (as Phil Regal); *Seven Cities of Gold* (Webb) (as Capt. Gaspar de Portola)

1956   *Lust for Life* (Minnelli) (as Paul Gauguin); *Man from Del Rio* (Horner) (as Dave Robles); *The Wild Party* (Horner) (as Big Tom Kupfen); *Notre Dame de Paris* (*The Hunchback of Notre Dame*) (Delannoy) (as Quasimodo)

1957   *The River's Edge* (Dwan) (as Ben Cameron); *The Ride Back* (Miner) (as Bob Kallen); *Wild Is the Wind* (Cukor) (as Gino)

1958   *Hot Spell* (Daniel Mann) (as Jack Duval)

1959   *The Black Orchid* (Ritt) (as Frank Valentine); *Warlock* (Dmytryk) (as Tom Morgan); *Last Train from Gun Hill* (John Sturges) (as Craig Beldon)

1960   *Heller in Pink Tights* (Cukor) (as Tom Healy); *Portrait in Black* (Gordon) (as Dr. David Rivera); *The Savage Innocents* (*Ombre Bianche*) (Nicholas Ray) (as Inok)

1961   *The Guns of Navarone* (J. Lee Thompson) (as Col. Andrea Stavros)

1962   *Barabbas* (Fleischer) (title role); *Requiem for a Heavyweight* (Nelson) (as Mountain Rivera); ***Lawrence of Arabia*** (Lean) (as Auda Abu Tayi)

1964   *Behold a Pale Horse* (Zinnemann) (as Capt. Vinolas); *Der Besuch* (*The Visit*) (Wicki) (as Serge Miller); ***Zorba the Greek*** (Cacoyannis) (title role)

1965   *La Fabuleuse Aventure de Marco Polo* (*Marco the Magnificent*) (de la Patellière and Noel Howard) (as Kublai Khan); *A High Wind in Jamaica* (MacKendrick) (as Juan Chavez)

1966   *Lost Command* (*Not for Honor and Glory*) (Robson) (as Lt. Col. Pierre Raspeguy)

1967   *La 25e Heure* (*La Vingt-cinquième Heure*; *The 25th Hour*) (Verneuil) (as Johann Moritz); *The Happening* (Silverstein) (as Roc Delmonico); *The Rover* (*L'Avventuriero*) (Terence Young) (as Peyrol)

1968   *Guns for San Sebastian* (Verneuil) (as Leon Alastray); *The Shoes of the Fisherman* (Anderson) (as Kiril Lakota); *The Magus* (Guy Green) (as Maurice Conchis)

1969   *The Secret of Santa Vittoria* (Kramer) (as Stalo Bambolini); *A Dream of Kings* (Daniel Mann) (as Matsverkas)

1970   *A Walk in the Spring Rain* (Guy Green) (as Will Cade); *R.P.M.* (Kramer) (as Paco); *Flap* (*The Last Warrior*) (Reed) (as Flapping Eagle); *King: A Filmed Record . . . Montgomery to Memphis* (Lumet and Joseph L. Mankiewicz—doc)

1971   *The City* (Petrie—for TV) (as Thomas Jefferson Alcala); *Arroza* (Boetticher) (as narrator)

1972   *Across 110th Street* (Shear) (as Capt. Frank Mattelli, + exec pr); *The Voice of La Raza* (Greaves) (as narrator)

1973   *Deaf Smith and Johnny Ears* (Cavara) (as Erastus "Deaf" Smith); *The Don Is Dead* (Fleischer) (title role)

1974   *The Marseilles Contract* (*The Destructors*) (Parris) (as Steve Ventura)

1976   *L'eredità Ferramonti* (*The Inheritance*) (Bolognini) (as Gregorio Ferramonti); *Bluff* (*High Rollers*); *The Message* (*Mohammad, Messenger of God*) (Akkad) (as Hazma); *Tigers Don't Cry* (Collinson)

1978   *The Greek Tycoon* (J. Lee Thompson) (as Theo Tomasis); *Caravans* (Fargo) (as Zulfigar); *The Children of Sanchez* (Bartlett)

1979   *The Passage* (J. Lee Thompson) (as the Basque)

1981   *High Risk* (Raffill) (as Mariano); *Lion of the Desert* (*Omar Mukhtar*) (Akkad—produced in in 1979) (as Omar Mukhtar); *The Con Artists* (Corbucci) (as Bang); *The Salamander* (Zinner) (as Bruno Manzini)

1982   *Regina* (*Roma*) (Prate)

1983   *Valentina* (Betancor) (as Mosen Joaquin)

1984   *Ingrid* (Feldman); *The Last Days of Pompeii* (Hunt—for TV)

1986   *Isola del tesoro* (Dawson)

1989   *A Man of Passion* (*Pasion de hombre*) (Loma); *Actor* (Angelucci)

1990   *Ghosts Can't Do It* (Derek); *A Star for Two* (Kaufman); *Revenge* (Tony Scott) (as Tiburon Mendez); *The Old Man and the Sea* (Storke—for TV) (as Santiago)

1991   *Only the Lonely* (Columbus) (as Nick); *Jungle Fever* (Spike Lee) (as Lou Carbone); *Mobsters* (Karbeinidoff) (as Don Masseria)

1993   *Last Action Hero* (McTiernan) (as Tony Vivaldi)

1994   *Somebody to Love* (Rockwell) (as Emilio); *Hercules in the Underworld* (Bill L. Norton—for TV) (as Zeus); *Hercules in the Maze of the Minotaur* (Bender—for TV) (as Zeus); *Hercules and the Lost Kingdom* (Cokliss—for TV) (as Zeus); *Hercules and the Circle of Fire* (Doug Lefler—for TV) (as Zeus); *Hercules and the Amazon Women* (Bill L. Norton—for TV) (as Zeus); *This Can't Be Love* (Harvey—for TV) (as Michael Reyman)

1995   *A Walk in the Clouds* (Arrau) (as Don Pedro Aragon)

Film as Director:

1958   *The Buccaneer*

Publications

By QUINN: books—

The Original Sin, a Self-Portrait (autobiography), New York, 1972.
One Man Tango, with Daniel Paisner, New York, 1995.

By QUINN: articles—

"The Loving World of Anthony Quinn," interview with Mary Simons, in *Look* (New York), 1 April 1969.
"Competing with Myself," interview in *Films and Filming* (London), February 1970.
Interview by Veronica Webb, in *Interview* (New York), May 1991.
"The Number It Takes to Tango," interview with Alex Witchel, in *New York Times*, 6 July 1995.

On QUINN: books—

Marill, Alvin H., *The Films of Anthony Quinn*, Secaucus, New Jersey, 1975.
Ball, Gregor, *Anthony Quinn: seine Filme, sein Leben*, Munich, 1985.
Amdur, Melissa, *Anthony Quinn*, New York, 1993.

On QUINN: articles—

Current Biography 1957, New York, 1957.
Johnson, Ian, "Anthony Quinn," in *Films and Filming* (London), February 1962.
Marill, Alvin H., "Anthony Quinn," in *Films in Review* (New York), October 1968.
Denby, David, "High on Anthony Quinn," in *Premiere* (New York), September 1992.

*   *   *

Pounding on his beefy chest and rolling his exotic eyes, Anthony Quinn is easily disparaged as an all-purpose Ethnic, but his vibrant approach to acting can be riveting. In the 1990s, in smaller doses, as in the macho shenanigans of *Last Action Hero*, the formulaic but diverting comedy of *Only the Lonely*, and especially the swooning lyricism of *A Walk in the Clouds*, Quinn seems looser and less pointedly vociferous. Maybe time has purified him of some of that much talked-about Life Force, that so memorably defined the spirit of *Zorba the Greek*. That was before it degenerated into meaninglessness when applied across the board to all the international characterizations that nipped at Zorba's heels. In his post-1964 heyday, Quinn was as overexposed as the cast of television's *Friends* are today.

Born in poverty in Mexico, Anthony Quinn served a long contractual apprenticeship in the movies as lummox-in-loincloth or scourge-with-scimitar. If menace of a foreign extraction was required, casting agents made a beeline to Tony. But small monotonous parts were as galling to Quinn as being dismissed as Cecil B. DeMille's son-in-law. Graduating from leads in B movies, Quinn remained the same stone-faced heavy in A pictures; the performance in *Viva Zapata!* that won him his first Oscar hardly seemed more challenging than dozens of scenery-chewing turns that preceded it.

Instead of turning his frustration at being typecast inward, Quinn started thesping his heart out more and more; the Quinn style was born—earthy, hearty, and above all, voluble. You could outfight Quinn but never outshout him. Several savvy breaks from the Hollywood rut paid off by building (maybe overbuilding) Quinn's confidence. After donning the Brando T-shirt as a replacement Stanley Kowalski, he also shared glory with Olivier himself as they switched lead roles in *Becket*, and then his career rose phoenixlike out of a past-his-prime graveyard with Fellini's *La strada*. Taken seriously by Hollywood thanks to his art-house circuit success as the brutal strongman, Zampano, Quinn snagged a second supporting Oscar for *Lust for Life* and then began stamping all his roles with the same lust for overacting.

Whether certain directors could handle him with more authority or whether he simply responded to simpatico material, Quinn got delightfully high on his own ego-puffery in Cukor's colorful *Heller in Pink Tights*, presented a memorably noncondescending portrayal of an Eskimo in Ray's *The Savage Innocents*, then shadow-boxed beautifully with despair in *Requiem for a Heavyweight*, a much subtler and affecting portrait of brute force than his *La strada* stint. Throughout the 1950s and early 1960s, whether top-billed as he gave us *Barabbas* or cameoed in *Lawrence of Arabia*, Quinn broke no new ground until the soulmate role of *Zorba the Greek* liberated him. After 1964, however, Tony the Quinn became Zorba the Greek, and it is difficult to rebut the prevailing wisdom that dubbed him a one-man UN. He could play Italian, Native American, Greek, or Basque—just go round the globe; Quinn acted there. This was thesping by way of Berlitz. Still, if there were many occasions when you wished he had moved on from Esperanto-translated populism, there was no denying this peacock actor's energy. If every performer seeks to improve upon reality, then Quinn is the Great Embellisher. Refusing to play in sotto voce, the man is a one-tenor opera. The feverish, life-forced quality of his performances (good and bad) sing out with the overabundant grace notes of a man whose love of acting is boundless.

—Robert Pardi

R

RAFT, George

Nationality: American. **Born:** George Ranft in New York City, 26 September 1895. **Family:** Married Grayce Mulrooney, 1923 (separated 1923, died 1970). **Career:** From age 13, worked as boxer, pool player, dancer; 1919—dancer in vaudeville, in the next few years touring on the Orpheum and Keith Circuits; also dancer at Jimmy Durante's Club Durante and Texas Guinan's El Fey Club; 1925—Broadway debut in *The City Chap*; 1929—film debut in *Queen of the Nightclubs* with Texas Guinan; early 1930s—several roles as gangsters in films, with much publicity concerning his friendship with nonfictional gangsters: 1932—classical role in *Scarface*, contract with Paramount, then in 1939 contract with Warner Brothers, and freelance after 1942; organized sports show for entertaining the troops during World War II; 1953—in TV series *I'm the Law*; early 1960s—public relations director for Consumer Marts stores; 1966-67—host of Colony Club casino, London, but banned from England as persona non grata because of alleged gangster connections. **Died:** In Los Angeles, 24 November 1980.

Films as Actor:

1929   *Queen of the Nightclubs* (Foy) (as gigolo)
1931   *Quick Millions* (Brown) (as Jimmy Kirk)
1932   *Hush Money* (Lanfield) (as Maxie); *Palmy Days* (Sutherland) (as Joe the Frog); *Taxi!* (Del Ruth) (as Willie Kenny); *Scarface* (Hawks) (as Guido Rinaldi); *Night Court* (Van Dyke); *Night World* (Hensley) (as Ed Powell); *Love Is a Racket* (Wellman) (as Stinky); *Dancers in the Dark* (Burton) (as Louie Brooks); *Madame Racketeer* (Hall) (as Jack Houston); *Night after Night* (Mayo) (as Joe Anton); *If I Had a Million* (Lubitsch and others) (as Eddie Jackson)
1933   *Under-Cover Man* (Flood) (as Nick Darrow); *Pick-Up* (Gering) (as Harry Glynn); *The Midnight Club* (Hall) (as Nick Mason); *The Bowery* (Walsh) (as Steve Brodi); *All of Me* (Flood) (as Honey Rogers); *Bolero* (Ruggles) (as Raoul Debaere)
1935   *Rumba* (Gering) (as Joe Martin); *The Trumpet Blows* (Roberts) (as Manuel); *Limehouse Blues* (Hall) (as Henry Young); *Stolen Harmony* (Werker) (as Ray Angelo/Ray Ferraro); *The Glass Key* (Tuttle) (as Ed Beaumont); *Every Night at Eight* (Walsh) (as Tops Cardona); *She Couldn't Take It* (Garnett) (as Spot Ricardi)
1936   *It Had to Happen* (Del Ruth) (as Enrico Scaffa); *Yours for the Asking* (Hall) (as Johnny Lamb)
1937   *Souls at Sea* (Hathaway) (as Rowdah)
1938   *You and Me* (Lang) (as Joe Dennis); *Spawn of the North* (Hathaway) (as Tyler Dawson)
1939   *The Lady's from Kentucky* (Hall) (as Marty Black); *I Stole a Million* (Tuttle) (as Joe Laurik); *Invisible Stripes* (Bacon) (as Cliff Taylor); *Each Dawn I Die* (Keighley) (as Hood Stacey)
1940   *The House across the Bay* (Mayo) (as Steve Larwitt); *They Drive by Night* (Walsh) (as Joe Fabrini)

1941   *Manpower* (Walsh) (as Johnny Marshall)
1942   *Broadway* (Seiter) (as George)
1943   *Background to Danger* (Walsh) (as Joe Barton); *Stage Door Canteen* (Borzage) (as himself)
1944   *Follow the Boys* (Sutherland) (as Tony West)
1945   *Nob Hill* (Hathaway) (as Johnny Angelo); *Johnny Angelo* (Marin) (title role)
1946   *Whistle Stop* (Moguy) (as Kenny); *Mr. Ace* (Marin) (as Eddie Ace); *Nocturne* (Marin) (as Lt. Joe Warne)
1947   *Christmas Eve* (Marin) (as Mario Torio)
1948   *Intrigue* (Marin) (as Brad Dunham); *Race Street* (Marin) (as Dan Gannin)
1949   *Outpost in Morocco* (Florey) (as Capt. Paul Garard); *Johnny Allegro* (Tetzlaff) (title role); *Red Light* (Del Ruth) (as John Torno); *A Dangerous Profession* (Tetzlaff) (as Vince Kane); *Nous irons à Paris* (Boyer) (as guest)
1951   *Lucky Nick Cain* (Newman) (title role); *I'll Get You* (Freidman) (as Steve Rossi)
1952   *Loan Shark* (Freidman) (as Joe Gargen); *Adventure in Algiers* (*Secret of the Casbah*)
1953   *The Man from Cairo* (Enright) (as Mike Cannelli)
1954   *Black Widow* (Johnson) (as Det. Bruce); *Rogue Cop* (Rowland) (as Dan Beaumonte)
1955   *A Bullet for Joey* (Allen) (as Joe Victor)
1956   *Around the World in Eighty Days* (Anderson) (as bouncer)
1959   **Some Like It Hot** (Wilder) (as Spats Columbo); *Jet over the Atlantic* (Haskin) (as Stafford)
1960   *Ocean's Eleven* (Milestone) (cameo role)
1961   *The Ladies Man* (Lewis) (as himself); *Two Guys Abroad* (Sharp)
1964   *For Those Who Think Young* (Martinson) (as detective); *The Patsy* (Lewis) (as himself)
1965   *Du Rififi à Paname* (de la Patellière) (as Charles Binnaggio)
1966   *Casino Royale* (Huston and others) (as himself)
1968   *Five Golden Dragons* (Summers) (as Golden Dragon); *Skidoo!* (Preminger) (as Capt. Garbaldo)
1972   *Hammersmith Is Out* (Ustinov) (as Guido Scartucci); *Deadhead Miles* (Zimmermann) (cameo role)
1978   *Sextette* (Hughes) (as himself); *The Man with Bogart's Face* (Fenady) (as Petey Cane)

Publications

By RAFT: articles—

Interview with R. Donaldson, in *Movie Classic Magazine*, June 1932.
"You've Got to Be Tough in Hollywood," in *Films and Filming* (London), July 1962.

On RAFT: books—

Yablonsky, Lewis, *George Raft*, New York, 1974.
Parish, James Robert, and Steven Whitney, *The George Raft File: The Unauthorized Biography*, New York, 1974.

George Raft

Neibaur, James L., *Tough Guy: The American Movie Macho*, Jefferson, North Carolina, 1989.

On RAFT: articles—

Beaver, J., "George Raft," in *Films in Review* (New York), April 1978.
The Annual Obituary 1980, New York, 1981.

* * *

George Raft was instrumental in the development of the character of the hardboiled gangster, a character that became a standard of the American cinema for decades. In fact, he fit the type so well that his rather shady background became the object of endless speculation, and both the public and the studio refused to accept him in any but the most indistinguishable tough-guy parts. Perhaps he filled these parts even too well, for he never became as popular or sympathetic as James Cagney or Humphrey Bogart, and, in his apparent effort to overcome the image, he rejected several roles that turned Bogart into a major star: *The Maltese Falcon*, *Casablanca*, and *High Sierra*.

Raft began his career as a dancer in clubs and on the stage, and although his physical grace was evident in even the most undignified roles and the most violent situations, his musical talent was exploited in very few of his films. Once his part as Paul Muni's coin-tossing sidekick in Howard Hawks's *Scarface* had established his career and his image, Raft played variations on that role as a Paramount contract player throughout the 1930s and then in a series of increasingly minor melodramas for less prestigious studios. Finally, when advancing age and the changing demands of the audience ended his leading roles once and for all, he turned to self-caricature, often appearing as himself in miniscule cameo parts.

In Hollywood, a strong personal image is usually seen as a lack of versatility, and George Raft's career is illustrative of this tendency which has limited many actors even at the height of their popularity. While few of his films were successful in any way, either with audiences or with the critics, Raft's real failure was in his inability to outgrow the character that he helped to create.

—Richard Wilson

RAIMU

Nationality: French. **Born:** Jules Auguste César Muraire in Toulon, 17 December 1883. **Military Service:** French Army, 1914-15: discharged for health reasons. **Family:** Married in 1936, daughter, Paulette. **Career:** Began performing as singer and actor in café-concerts in Toulon; changed name to Raimu for engagement at Casino de Toulon, 1899-1900, and toured in southern France and North Africa for the next few years; 1905—worked as croupier in Aix-les-Bains; 1910—in Felix Mayol's performing group in Paris, and became successful performer at the Folies-Bergère and other clubs; 1915—first legitimate theater role in Feydeau's *Monsieur Chasse*, followed by roles in other stage plays; 1929—created the famous role of César in Pagnol's *Marius*, later recreated in film version; 1931—sound film debut in *Le Blanc et le noir*; 1944-45—member of the Comédie Française. **Died:** In Neuilly, France, 20 September 1946.

Films as Actor:

1912-14 *L'Homme nu* (Desfontaines); *L'Agence Cacahuete* (Lion)

1931 *Le Blanc et le noir* (Florey); *Mam'zelle Nitouche* (Marc Allégret) (as Célestin-Floridor); *Marius* (Korda) (as César Olivier)

1932 *La Petite Chocolatière* (Marc Allégret) (as Félicien Bédarrides); *Fanny* (Marc Allégret) (as César Olivier); *Les Gaîtés de l'escadron* (Tourneur) (as Capitaine Hurluret)

1933 *Theodore et Cie* (Colombier) (as Clodomir); *Charlemagne* (Colombier) (title role)

1934 *Ces Messieurs de la santé* (Colombier) (as Tafard); *Tartarin de Tarascon* (Bernard) (title role); *J'ai un idée* (Richebé) (as Aubrey)

1935 *Minuit, Place Pigalle* (Richebé); *Faisons un rêve* (Guitry); *L'École des cocottes* (Colombier) (as Labaume); *Gaspard de Besse* (Hugon)

1936 *Le Secret de Polichinelle* (Berthomieu); *Le Roi* (Colombier) (as Bourdier); *Les Jumeaux de Brighton* (Heymann) (three roles); *César* (Pagnol) (title role)

1937 *Vous n'avez rien a déclarer?* (*Confessions of a Newlywed*; *Have You Nothing to Declare?*) (Joannon) (as the Professor); *Les Perles de la couronne* (*The Pearls of the Crown*) (Guitry and Christian-Jaque) (cameo); *La Chaste Suzanne* (Berthomieu) (as M. des Aubrais); *Les Rois du sport* (Colombier); *Le Fauteuil 47* (Rivers); *Gribouille* (*Heart of Paris*) (Marc Allégret) (as Camille); *Un Carnet de bal* (*Life Dances On, Christine*) (Duvivier) (as François Patusset)

1938 *Le Héros de la Marne* (Hugon); *L'Étrange Monsieur Victor* (Grémillon) (as Victor Agardanne); *Les Nouveaux riches* (Berthomieu) (as Legendre); *La Femme du boulanger* (*The Baker's Wife*) (Pagnol) (as Aimable Castenet, the baker)

1939 *Monsieur Brotonneau* (Esway) (as Loulou); *Dernière jeunesse* (*Last Desire*) (Musso) (as Georges); *L'Homme qui cherche la verité* (*The Man Who Seeks the Truth*) (Esway) (as Vernet)

1941 *Le Duel* (Fresnay); *Parade en sept nuits* (Marc Allégret); *Les Petits Riens* (Leboursier) (as Charpillon); *Monsieur la Souris* (*Midnight in Paris*) (Lacombe); *Le Bienfaiteur* (Decoin) (as Moulinet)

1942 *L'Arlésienne* (Allégret) (as Marc)

1943 *Le Colonel Chabert* (Le Hénaff) (title role); *Untel Père et fils* (*The Heart of a Nation*) (Duvivier) (as Jules Froment)

1946 *La Fille du puisatier* (*The Well-Digger's Daughter*) (Pagnol—produced in 1940); *Les Gueux au paradis* (*Hoboes in Paradise*) (Le Hénaff); *L'Homme au chapeau rond* (*The Eternal Husband*) (Billon) (as Nicolas Pavlovitch)

1948 *La Vie de Raimu* (Toedoc)

1949 *Les Inconnus dans la maison* (*Strangers in the House*) (Decoin—produced in 1942) (as Hector Loursat)

1957 *Les Étoiles ne meurent jamais* (de Vaucorbeil—doc)

Publications

By RAIMU: articles—

"Raimu m'a parle," interview with Chantal, in *Cinémonde* (Paris), 6 November 1930.
"Pourquoi l'acteur et le metteur en scène doivent étroitement collaborer?," in *Pour vous* (Paris), 24 December 1931.
"Quelques minutes avec Raimu," by Henri Calef, in *Paris-Midi* (Paris), 22 September 1932.
"Les Souvenirs de Raimu," in *Pour vous* (Paris), no. 213-218, 15 December 1932/19 January 1933.
"J'aime toujours le théâtre, mais . . . ," in *Le Jour* (Paris), 3 October 1933.
"Quand j'étais Tartarin," in *Ciné-Miroir* almanac, 1935.
"Raimu écrit et se décrit," interview with Claude Christians, in *Ecran Français* (Paris), 23 October 1946.

Raimu in *César*

On RAIMU: books—

Fronval, George, *Raimu, sa vie, ses films*, Paris, 1939.
Olivier, Paul, *Raimu, ou La Vie de César*, Paris, 1947.
Régent, Roger, *Raimu*, Paris, 1951.
Perisset, Maurice, *Raimu*, Paris, 1976.
Oliver, Paul, *Raimu, ou L'Epopée de César*, Paris, 1977.
Brun, Paulette, *Raimu, mon pere*, Paris, 1980.
Brun-Raimu, Paulette, *Raimu: Une Biographie*, Paris, 1982.
Lacotte, Daniel, *Raimu*, Paris, 1988.

On RAIMU: articles—

Moustier, J., "Raimu, ou le 'bon garçon' du Midi," in *Cinémonde* (Paris), 15 September 1932.
"Raimu" issue of *Visages* (Paris), December 1938.
Jeanson, Henri, "Quand M. Raimu joue rétrospectivement les héros de la Marne," in *La Flèche* (Paris), 16 December 1938 (also see Raimu's response in *La Flèche*, 23 December 1938).
Cocteau, Jean, "L'Arrivée de Raimu au Théâtre-Français," in *Comoedia* (Paris), 25 September 1943.
Cocteau, Jean, "M. Raimu à la Comédie-Français," in *Comoedia* (Paris), 1 April 1944.
Obituary in *New York Times*, 21 September 1946.
Pagnol, Marcel, "Raimu, mon compagnon," in *Opéra* (Paris), 2 October 1946.
Fronval, George, "Témoignages sur un comédien, recueillis et présentés par . . . " (series of ten articles), in *Cinémonde* (Paris), 22 October 1946 to 7 January 1947.
Senez, Monique, "Les Grand Jules va ressusciter," in *Ecran Français* (Paris), 22 and 29 July 1947.
Jacobson, H. L., "Homage to Raimu," in *Hollywood Quarterly*, Winter 1947-48.
Régent, Roger, "Il y a deux ans mourait Raimu," in *Ecran Français* (Paris), 5 October 1948.
Rim, Carlo, "Raimu chez Molière, tragédie en un acte," in *Ecran Français* (Paris), 3 October 1951.
"Souvenirs sur Raimu," in *Le Figaro Littéraire* (Paris), 7 September 1963.
"Pagnol raconte Raimu," in *Télérama* (Paris), 26 December 1965.
Leprohon, Pierre, "Raimu," in *Anthologie du Cinéma*, vol. 2, Paris, 1967.
"L'adieu de Marcel Pagnol à Raimu," in *L'Avant-Scène du Cinéma* (Paris), July-September 1970.
Cornand, A., "Raimu aurait cent ans," in *Revue du Cinéma* (Paris), October 1983.
Vincendeau, G., "Daddy's Girls," in *IRIS* (Iowa City, Iowa), no. 8, 1988.

*   *   *

Between 1931 and 1936 the playwright Marcel Pagnol, turned screenwriter and then director, brought to the screen a trilogy, *Marius*, *Fanny*, and *César*, starring one of the best-loved French comedians, Raimu, who proved that a simple, natural comic style would work best in the contemporary French cinema. As César, the father of the wronged Fanny, he depicted the dignity of a poor man in a waterfront world trying to get along in a difficult situation. Raimu's attempt to preserve the honor and happiness of his abandoned, pregnant daughter ran the gamut of humor with a grace in acting seldom seen on the screen.

In the early 1940s director Pagnol would rework the same theme in *La Fille du puisatier* with an effective pairing of Raimu as the father and Fernandel as the suitor whose marriage to the daughter would solve the delicate situation of having an unwed mother. An earlier film, *The Baker's Wife*, created in the late 1930s by Pagnol, was prob-

ably Raimu's most humorous film. The touch of sympathy he elicited for the character prompted some critics to compare Raimu's technique with Chaplin's method of combining pathos and humor. Raimu played the baker whose wife had run away with a younger man, depicting a mild-mannered soul who gives up his trade because of his sorrow over his unfaithful wife.

These works with Raimu as the star represent some of the best comedy made during the golden period of French film in the 1930s and early 1940s. The writing and directing genius of Marcel Pagnol merged and complemented the acting genius of Raimu to produce these comic masterpieces.

—Donald McCaffrey

RAINER, Luise

Born: Vienna, Austria, 12 January 1910. **Family:** Married 1) the playwright Clifford Odets, 1937 (divorced 1940); 2) Robert Knittel, 1945 (died 1989), one daughter. **Career:** Actress from childhood in Vienna and Berlin; acted in Max Reinhardt's Vienna theater ensemble in plays by Pirandello, Shakespeare, and many others; 1930—film debut in *Ja, der Himmel über Wien*; 1935-38—contract with MGM; U.S. film debut in *Escapade*, followed by two successive Oscar-winning roles in *The Great Ziegfeld* and *The Good Earth*; 1943—"comeback" film *Hostages*; some later stage and television work; 1978—paintings exhibited at Seale Gallery, London; 1981 and 1983—toured the United States in *Enoch Arden*, music by Strauss. **Awards:** Best Actress Academy Award, and Best Actress, New York Film Critics, for *The Great Ziegfeld*, 1936; Best Actress Academy Award, for *The Good Earth*, 1937. **Address:** 54 Eaton Square, London SW1W 9BE, England.

Films as Actress:

1930 *Ja, der Himmel über Wien* (short)
1932 *Sehnsucht, 202* (Neufeld)
1933 *Heut' kommt's drauf an* (Gerron)
1935 *Escapade* (*Masquerade*) (Leonard) (as Leopoldine)
1936 *The Great Ziegfeld* (Leonard) (as Anna Held)
1937 *The Good Earth* (Franklin) (as O-Lan); *The Emperor's Candlesticks* (Fitzmaurice) (as Countess Olga Muranova); *Big City* (*Skyscraper Wilderness*) (Borzage) (as Anna Benton)
1938 *The Toy Wife* (Thorpe) (as Gilberta Brigard); *The Great Waltz* (*Toute la ville danse*) (Duvivier) (as Poldi Vogelhuber); *Dramatic School* (Sinclair) (as Louise)
1943 *Hostages* (Tuttle) (as Milada Pressinger)
1988 *A Dancer* (Chase—video for TV)

Publications

On RAINER: articles—

Norden, H. B., in *Vanity Fair* (New York), September 1935.
Bronner, Edwin, "Luise Rainer," in *Films in Review* (New York), October 1955.

*   *   *

Luise Rainer's career withered under the curse of the Oscar, of two Oscars in fact. Reminiscent of Elisabeth Bergner, an exponent of the

Luise Rainer

laughter and tears school of acting, Rainer made an immediate impact with her hyperemotional style. Showing her changing moods with an arsenal of vocal and facial expressions, eyes darting, hands fluttering, Rainer's nervous energy was distinctively European, but also dissimilar to the slower rhythms of Garbo and Dietrich, the reigning European actresses in Hollywood. Portraying Anna Held, a less-than-starring role in the musical extravaganza *The Great Ziegfeld*, Rainer so impressed audiences with one highly emotional scene that she was rewarded with an Oscar. Her Anna is speaking on the phone to her ex-husband, Flo Ziegfeld. Still in love with him, she gallantly congratulates him on his marriage to Billie Burke. The camera records her agitation; Ziegfeld hears a voice that hovers between false gaiety and despair; when she hangs up she dissolves into tears.

In her next film, *The Good Earth*, Rainer played a role meant to be diametrically opposed to the vivacious Anna Held. Here she portrayed a humble Chinese peasant, utterly subservient to her husband, perpetually huddled in submission, barely speaking a word of dialogue or raising her eyes to the camera. The contrast (and perhaps MGM's strength among Academy members) allowed her to win her second Oscar in successive years.

At this point, Hollywood turned its back on Luise Rainer just as abruptly as it had celebrated her. Having gained the reputation of being "difficult," she was cast in a few unimportant or disappointing films, her whole Hollywood career having lasted three years (with the exception of *Hostages*, produced during World War II). Adding to her decline was the poor career advice given her by then-husband Clifford Odets. Her record of two successive Oscars stood, however, until Katharine Hepburn equaled it in 1967 and 1968.

Rainer came back to Hollywood in the early 1980s, and even appeared on an episode of television's *The Love Boat*. And in 1988 she starred in *A Dancer*, a 28-minute-long dramatic piece directed by independent video artist Doris Chase. Her role was that of an ex-dancer who currently teaches, choreographs, and runs her own ballet school, and who is reunited with a former lover after a 30-year separation. Rainer's mature, carefully crafted performance offers evidence that, had her career been charted on a different course, she might have flourished as a screen star.

—Charles Affron, updated by Rob Edelman

RAINS, Claude

Nationality: American. **Born:** William Claude Rains in London, England, 10 November 1889; son of the actor and film director Frederick William Rains; became U.S. citizen, 1938. **Family:** Married 1) the actress Isabel Jeans, 1913 (divorced); 2) the actress Marie Hemingway, 1920 (divorced 1920); 3) Beatrix Thomson, 1924 (divorced 1935); 4) Francis Propper, 1935 (divorced 1956), daughter: Jennifer; 5) Agi Jambor, 1959 (divorced 1959); 6) Rosemary Clark, 1960. **Career:** 1900—stage debut as boy singer in *Sweet Nell of Old Drury*; then callboy, prompter, and assistant stage manager at His Majesty's Theatre, London; 1911—adult stage debut in *Gods of the Mountain*; 1912—U.S. stage debut in tour with Granville Barker's troupe in *Androcles and the Lion*; 1915-19—served with the London Scottish regiment: Captain; after the war, returned to the stage; also taught at the Royal Academy of Dramatic Art, London; 1920—film debut in *Build Thy House*; 1926—stayed in the United States after tour with *The Constant Nymph*; 1928-33—contract with Theatre Guild: in *Volpone*, *Marco Millions*, *The Apple Cart* and other plays; 1933—U.S. film debut in *The Invisible Man*; 1949—speaker with the Philadelphia Orchestra for Copland's *A Lincoln Portrait*; 1954—in T. S. Eliot's *The Confidential Clerk* on Broadway. **Died:** 30 May 1967.

Films as Actor:

1920 *Build Thy House* (Goodwins) (as Clarkis)
1933 *The Invisible Man* (Whale) (as Dr. Jack Griffin)
1934 *Crime without Passion* (Hecht and MacArthur) (as Lee Gentry)
1935 *The Man Who Reclaimed His Head* (Ludwig) (as Paul Verin); *The Clairvoyant* (Elvey) (as Maximus); *The Mystery of Edwin Drood* (Walker) (as John Jasper); *The Last Outpost* (Barton) (as John Stevenson)
1936 *Anthony Adverse* (LeRoy) (as Don Luis); *Hearts Divided* (Borzage) (as Napoleon Bonaparte); *Stolen Holiday* (Curtiz) (as Stefan Orloff)
1937 *The Prince and the Pauper* (Keighley) (as Earl of Hertford); *They Won't Forget* (LeRoy) (as District Attorney Griffin)
1938 *Gold Is Where You Find It* (Curtiz) (as Col. Ferris); ***The Adventures of Robin Hood*** (Curtiz and Keighley) (as Prince John); *White Banners* (Goulding) (as Paul Ward); *Four Daughters* (Curtiz) (as Adam Lemp)
1939 *They Made Me a Criminal* (Berkeley) (as Detective Phelan); *Juarez* (Dieterle) (as Napoleon III); *Sons of Liberty* (Curtiz) (as Haym Solomon); *Daughters Courageous* (Curtiz) (as Jim Masters); ***Mr. Smith Goes to Washington*** (Capra) (as Senator Joseph Harrison Payne); *Four Wives* (Curtiz) (as Adam Lemp)
1940 *Saturday's Children* (Sherman) (as Mr. Halevy); *The Sea Hawk* (Curtiz) (as Don Jose Alvarez de Cordoba); *The Lady with Red Hair* (Bernhardt) (as David Belasco)
1941 *Four Mothers* (Keighley) (as Adam Lemp); *Here Comes Mr. Jordan* (Hall) (title role); *The Wolf Man* (Waggner) (as Sir John Talbot); *Kings Row* (Wood) (as Dr. Alexander Tower)
1942 *Moontide* (Mayo) (as Nutsy); ***Now, Voyager*** (Rapper) (as Dr. Jasquith); ***Casablanca*** (Curtiz) (as Louis Renault)
1943 *The Phantom of the Opera* (Lubin) (title role); *Forever and a Day* (Wilcox) (as Ambrose Pomfret)
1944 *Passage to Marseilles* (Curtiz) (as Capt. Freycinet); *Mr. Skeffington* (Sherman) (title role)
1945 *This Love of Ours* (Dieterle) (as Targel); *Strange Holiday* (Oboler) (as John Stephenson)
1946 *Angel on My Shoulder* (Mayo) (as the Devil); *Caesar and Cleopatra* (Pascal) (title role); ***Notorious*** (Hitchcock) (as Alexander Sebastian); *Deception* (Rapper) (as Alexander Hollenius)
1947 *The Unsuspected* (Curtiz) (as Victor Grandison)
1948 *The Passionate Friends* (Lean) (as Howard Justin)
1949 *Rope of Sand* (Dieterle) (as Arthur Martingale); *Song of Surrender* (Leisen) (as Elisha Hunt)
1950 *The White Tower* (Tetzlaff) (as Paul Delambre); *Where Danger Lives* (Farrow) (as Frederic Lannington)
1951 *Sealed Cargo* (Werker) (as Capt. Skalder)
1953 *The Paris Express* (*The Man Who Watched Trains Go By*) (French) (as Kees Popinga)
1956 *Lisbon* (Milland) (as Aristedes Mavros)
1959 *This Earth Is Mine* (Henry King) (as Philippe Rambeau)
1960 *The Lost World* (Allen) (as Prof. George Edward Challenger); *Il planet degli uomini spenti* (*Battle of the Worlds*) (Dawson)
1961 *The Pied Piper of Hamelin* (Windust) (as Mayor of Hamelin)
1962 ***Lawrence of Arabia*** (Lean) (as Dryden)
1963 *Twilight of Honor* (*The Charge Is Murder*) (Sagal) (as Art Harner)
1965 *The Greatest Story Ever Told* (Stevens) (as King Herod)

Publications

By RAINS: article—

Interview by H. Hall, in *Motion Picture Magazine*, March 1935.

On RAINS: books—

De Marinis, Rick, *A Lovely Monster: The Adventures of Claude Rains and Dr. Tellenbeck* (novel), New York, 1975.
Wallis, Hal, and Charles Higham, *Starmaker*, New York, 1980.

On RAINS: articles—

Current Biography 1949, New York, 1949.
Stein, Jeanne, "Claude Rains," in *Films in Review* (New York), November 1963.
Obituary in *New York Times* 31 May 1967.
Richards, Jeffrey, "In Praise of Claude Rains," and "Claude Rains—a Career to Remember," in *Films and Filming* (London), February and March 1982.

*   *   *

One of the greatest advantages of the Hollywood studio system was the chance it afforded actors to develop their careers through steady employment and carefully developed roles over a long number of years. This was particularly true for those performers who excelled in character parts and supporting roles, as audiences came to recognize their faces and appreciate their work in a way that is no longer possible today. Of this group, Claude Rains enjoyed one of Hollywood's most successful careers, bringing his combination of sophistication, subtlety, and dry wit to a remarkably varied selection of roles. Rains also achieved a distinction rare among supporting players—sufficient individual popularity to allow him occasional starring roles as well. His ability to transcend the supporting category placed him in an unusual position among his contemporaries as one of the few character actors who was also a star.

Rains had reached middleage and established himself as an accomplished stage actor in London and New York before his distinguished speaking voice won him the leading role in *The Invisible Man*. Rain's face appears only briefly in the film, after the character's death renders him visible again, but the strength of his vocal performance alone launched the actor's career in Hollywood. His work in films over the next three decades would win him four Academy Award nominations and include performances in such classic features as *The Adventures of Robin Hood*, *Casablanca*, and *Notorious*.

Rains followed *The Invisible Man* with a starring role in *Crime without Passion*, in which he portrays a man driven to the brink of madness by an unhappy love affair. Rains would play similar characters in subsequent films, as his reserved, ironic manner proved an ideal mask for slowly crumbling sanity. Yet his range as an actor was extraordinary, and he portrayed villains and sympathetic heroes with equal ease, a facility which was put to frequent use during his years under contract to Warner Brothers. In 1938 he portrayed the dastardly King John in *The Adventures of Robin Hood* back to back with his warmhearted performance as the father of a family of girls in *Four Daughters*. The following year brought his first Oscar nomination, as best supporting actor, for his role as the corrupt senator who retains a spark of decency in Capra's *Mr. Smith Goes to Washington*.

His performance in the Capra film exemplifies Rains's ability to portray characters who remain charming—and sometimes sympathetic—in spite of their actions. As Louis Renault, the sardonic French police captain who collaborates with the Germans in *Casablanca*, Rains remains an engaging figure throughout the film, and his eventual

decision to join Humphrey Bogart in the Resistance comes as no great surprise. In Alfred Hitchcock's *Notorious,* Rains gives one of his finest performances as the Nazi sympathizer whose obsessive love for American agent Ingrid Bergman makes him a complex, pathetic figure and causes his final downfall.

Rains also appeared in several films opposite Bette Davis, then at the height of her Hollywood career. In *Now, Voyager*, one of the classic "women's films" of the 1940s, he portrays Davis's wise, understanding psychiatrist, while his performance as her adoring, long-suffering husband in *Mr. Skeffington* brought him another Oscar nomination. The pairing of Davis's electric screen presence with Rains's precise, assured style lends a particular chemistry to their films together.

Rains's work in later years included roles in *Lawrence of Arabia*, *Twilight of Honor*, and *The Greatest Story Ever Told*, and he remained, until the end of his career, an actor of consummate professionalism and skill.

—Janet E. Lorenz

RASP, Fritz

Nationality: German. **Born:** Heinrich Rasp in Bayreuth, 13 May 1891. **Career:** 1908—extra in films; 1909—stage debut in *Jugend* in Munich, then actor in provincial theaters, 1910-13; in Berlin at Deutsches Theater, 1914-16, 1918-19, Metropoltheater, 1919-20, Kleines Schauspielhaus, 1920-21, Deutsches Theater, 1921-24, Volksbühne, 1936-44, Hebbeltheater, 1945-47, and Deutches Theater, 1947-50, and at the Staatstheater in Munich after 1951; 1916—billed film debut in *Schuhpalast Pinkus*; series of films by Lang and Pabst in the 1920s made him a leading film actor. **Died:** In Gräfelfing, 30 November 1976.

Films as Actor:

1916   *Schuhpalast Pinkus* (Lubitsch)
1917   *Hans Trutz im Schlaraffenland* (Wegener)
1920   *Lachte man gerne*
1922   *Jugend* (Sauer)
1923   *Der Mensch am Wege* (Dieterle); ***Schatten*** (*Le Montreur d'ombre*) (Robison); *Time Is Money* (Sauer); *Zwischen Abend und Morgen* (Robison)
1924   *Komödianten* (Grune); *Arabella, der Roman eines Pferdes* (Grune)
1925   *Ein Sommernachtstraum* (Neumann); *Menschen am Meer* (Lasko); *Götz von Berlichigen* (Moest); *Die Puppe vom Lunapark* (Speyer); *Die Wildentes* (*Das Haus der Lüge*) (Lupu-Pick)
1926   ***Metropolis*** (Lang) (as Slim); *Qualen der Nacht* (Bernhardt); *Die Waise von Lowood* (Bernhardt); *Der Liebe Lust und Lied* (Gerron); *Uberflüssige Menschen* (Rasumny)
1927   *Der Letzte Walzer* (Robinson); *Kinderseelen klagen euch an* (Bernhardt); *Die Liebe der Jeanne Ney* (*Un Amour de Jeanne Ney*) (Pabst)
1928   *Der Geheimnisvolle Spiegel* (Hoffman and Teschner); *Spione* (*Les Espions*) (Lang); *Schinderhannes* (Bernhardt); *Die Carmen von St. Pauli* (Waschneck)
1929   *Die Frau im Mond* (*La Femme sur la lune*) (Lang); *Fruehlings Erwachen* (Oswald); *Der Hund von Baskerville* (Oswald); *Die Drei um Edith* (Waschneck); *Das Tagebuch einer Verlorenen* (*Trois Pages d'un journal*) (Pabst)

Fritz Rasp in *Die Dreigroschenoper*

1930   *Dreyfus* (Oswald); *Die Grosse Sehnsucht* (Szekely)
1931   *Tropennächte* (Mittler); *Der Zinker* (Lamac and Fric); *Die Pranke* (Steinhoff); *Die Vier vom Bob* (Guter); *Der Mörder Dimitri Karamasoff* (*Les Frères Karamazov*) (Ozep); ***Die Dreigroschenoper*** (*L'Opéra de quat' sous*; *The Threepenny Opera*) (Pabst) (as Peachum); *Emil und die Detektive* (*Emile et les détectives*) (Lamprecht)
1932   *Der Hexer* (Lamac); *Die Grausame Freundin* (Lamac); *Der Sündige Hof* (Osten); *Judas von Tirol* (Osten); *Der Schuss am Nebelhorn* (Beck-Gaden)
1934   *Charley's Tante* (Stemmle); *Klein Dorrit* (Lamac); *Lockvogel* (Steinhoff); *Grenzfeuer* (Beck-Gaden)
1935   *Lockspitzel Asew* (Jutzi)
1936   *Die Leuchter des Kaisers* (Hartl); *Der Hund von Baskerville* (Lamac); *Onkel Bräsig* (Waschneck)
1937   *Togger* (von Alten); *Einmal werd' ich Dir gefallende* (Riemann)
1938   *Nanu, sie kennen Korff noch nicht?* (Holl)
1939   *Frau im Strom* (Lamprecht); *Es war eine rauschende Ballnacht* (Froelich)
1940   *Leidenschaft* (Janssen)
1941   *Alarm* (Fredersdorf)
1943   *Paracelsus* (Pabst)
1946   *Irgendwo in Berlin* (Lamprecht)
1950   *Skandal in der Botschaft* (Ode)
1952   *Haus des Lebens* (Hartl); *Die Mühle im Schwarzwäldertal* (Kugelstadt); *Hokuspokus* (Hoffman)
1955   *Der Cornet* (Reich)
1956   *Magic Fire* (Dieterle)
1959   *Der Frosch mit der Maske* (Reinl)
1960   *Der Rote Kreis* (Roland); *Die Rande des Schreckens* (Reinl); *Das Schwartze Schaf* (Ashley)
1961   *Die Selfsame Gräfin* (Baky)
1962   *Das Ratsel der roten Orchidee* (Ashley)
1963   *Der Zinker* (Vohrer)
1965   *Dr. Med. Hiob Preaetorius* (Hoffman)
1976   *Lina Braake* (Sinkel)

Publications

On RASP: article—

"Fritz Rasp," in *Cinéma* (Paris), February 1977.

*   *   *

Fritz Rasp became one of the principal character actors of the German silent cinema, and appeared in films for a span of half a century, beginning in 1916. Originally, like so many of his distinguished contemporaries, he trained in the theater under Max Reinhardt. His first film undertaking was his appearance in the early Lubitsch silent farce *Schuhpalast Pinkus*. It was not until 1923, however, that he began to establish himself as a sinister character actor, in Arthur Robinson's *Schatten*, one of the more celebrated of the macabre German silent films. Here, Rasp plays the leering observer in the hallucinations, conjured up by a traveling shadow play showman, which play on the subconscious fears and desires of a jealous husband, his wife, and her lovers.

After appearing in a silent version of *A Midsummer Night's Dream*, Rasp specialized in obnoxious characters in some of the finest films of the German cinema—in Fritz Lang's *Metropolis*, and as the lascivious and lurking secret agent in Pabst's *Die Liebe der Jeanne Ney*. He went on from this to play a series of sly villains in other films directed by Lang and Pabst, notably *Die Frau im Mond*.

With the coming of sound in 1931, Rasp portrayed the treacherous Peachum in the Pabst-Brecht-Weill film production of *The Threepenny*

Opera, the year in which he also starred as the epileptic servant who, obsessed with greed, murders his master in Fëdor Ozep's *Der Mörder Dimitri Karamasoff*.

Rasp remained in Germany during the period of the Third Reich, appearing most significantly, perhaps, in Pabst's *Paracelsus*. After the war, he was seen in one of the better films that dealt with society in Germany under Allied occupation, *Irgendwo in Berlin*, directed by Gerhard Lamprecht, which focused on the problems of young boys and soldiers returning to civilian life after the collapse of the Nazi regime.

—Roger Manvell

RATHBONE, Basil

Born: Johannesburg, South Africa, of British parents, 13 June 1892. **Education:** Attended Repton School, England. **Family:** Married 1) Ethel Marian Forman (divorced), one son; 2) the writer Ouida Bergere, late 1920s, daughter: Cynthia. **Career:** 1911—worked briefly for Globe Insurance Company, Liverpool; joined stage company of his cousin, Frank Benson: stage debut in *The Taming of the Shrew* in Liverpool; 1912—U.S. stage debut on tour with Benson's Shakespearean company; 1914—London stage debut in *The Sin of David*; 1916-19—served in Liverpool Scottish Regiment: Military Cross; 1921—film debut in *Innocent*; 1925—U.S. film debut in *The Masked Bride*; 1933-34—played opposite Katharine Cornell in *The Barretts of Wimpole Street* and *Romeo and Juliet*; later stage roles include work in *The Heiress*, 1947, *Julius Caesar*, 1950, and *The Gioconda Smile*, 1950; 1939—played Sherlock Holmes in the first of a series of films, *The Hound of the Baskervilles*; also played Holmes on radio for seven years, and acted in the radio series *Scotland Yard*, 1947, and the serial *Tales of Fatima*, 1948; 1950—narrator with Philadelphia Orchestra in *The Nightingale and the Rose*; 1952—host for TV series *Your Lucky Clue*. **Died:** 21 July 1967.

Films as Actor:

1921   *Innocent* (Elvey) (as Amadis de Jocelyn); *The Fruitful Vine* (Elvey) (as Don Cesare Carelli)
1923   *The School for Scandal* (Phillips) (as Joseph Surface)
1924   *Trouping with Ellen* (Hunter) (as Tony Winterslip)
1925   *The Masked Bride* (Cabanne) (as Antoine)
1926   *The Great Deception* (Higgin) (as Rizzio)
1929   *The Last of Mrs. Cheyney* (Franklin) (as Lord Arthur Dilling)
1930   *The Bishop Murder Case* (Grinde and Burton) (as Philo Vance); *A Notorious Affair* (Bacon) (as Paul Gherardi); *The Lady of Scandal* (Franklin) (as Edward); *This Mad World* (W. DeMille) (as Paul); *The Flirting Widow* (Seiter) (as Col. Smith); *A Lady Surrenders* (Stahl) (as Carl Vaudry); *Sin Takes a Holiday* (Stein) (as Durant)
1932   *A Woman Commands* (Stein) (as Capt. Alex Pastisch)
1933   *One Precious Year* (Edwards) (as Derek Nagel); *Loyalties* (Dean) (as Ferdinand de Levis)
1935   *David Copperfield* (Cukor) (as Mr. Murdstone); *Anna Karenina* (Brown) (as Karenin); *The Last Days of Pompeii* (Schoedsack) (as Pontius); *A Feather in Her Hat* (Santell) (as Capt. Courtney); *A Tale of Two Cities* (Conway) (as Marquis St. Evremonde); *Captain Blood* (Curtiz) (as Capt. Levasseur); *Kind Lady* (Seitz) (as Henry Abbott)
1936   *Private Number* (Del Ruth) (as Wroxton); *Romeo and Juliet* (Cukor) (as Tybalt); *The Garden of Allah* (Boleslawsky) (as Count Anteoni)

1937   *Confession* (May) (as Michael Michailow); *Love from a Stranger* (Lee) (as Gerald Lovell); *Make a Wish* (Neumann) (as Selden); *Tovarich* (Litvak) (as Gorotchenko)

1938   *The Adventures of Marco Polo* (Mayo) (as Ahmed); ***The Adventures of Robin Hood*** (Curtiz and Keighley) (as Sir Guy de Gisbourne); *If I Were King* (Lloyd) (as Louis XI); *The Dawn Patrol* (Goulding) (as Maj. Brand)

1939   *Son of Frankenstein* (Lee) (as Baron Frankenstein); *The Hound of the Baskervilles* (Lanfield) (as Sherlock Holmes); *The Sun Never Sets* (Lee) (as Clive Randolph); *The Adventures of Sherlock Holmes* (Werker) (as Sherlock Holmes); *Rio* (Braum) (as Paul Reynard); *Tower of London* (Lee) (as Richard III)

1940   *Rhythm on the River* (Schertzinger) (as Oliver Courtney); *The Mark of Zorro* (Mamoulian) (as Capt. Esteban Pasquale)

1941   *The Mad Doctor* (Whelan) (as Dr. George Sebastian); *The Black Cat* (Rogell) (as Hartley); *International Lady* (Whelan) (as Reggie Oliver); *Paris Calling* (Marin) (as Benoit)

1942   *Fingers at the Window* (Lederer) (as Dr. Santelle); *Crossroads* (Conway) (as Henri Sarrou); *Sherlock Holmes and the Voice of Terror* (Rawlins) (as Sherlock Holmes); *Sherlock Holmes and the Secret Weapon* (Neill) (as Sherlock Holmes)

1943   *Sherlock Holmes in Washington* (Neill) (as Sherlock Holmes); *Above Suspicion* (Thorpe) (as Sig von Aschenhausen); *Sherlock Holmes Faces Death* (Neill) (as Sherlock Holmes); *Crazy House* (Cline) (as guest)

1944   *The Spider Woman* (Neill) (as Sherlock Holmes); *The Scarlet Claw* (Neill) (as Sherlock Holmes); *Bathing Beauty* (Sidney) (as George Adams); *The Pearl of Death* (Neill) (as Sherlock Holmes); *Frenchman's Creek* (Leisen) (as Lord Rockingham)

1945   *The House of Fear* (Neill) (as Sherlock Holmes); *The Woman in Green* (Neill) (as Sherlock Holmes); *Passage to Algiers* (Neill) (as Sherlock Holmes)

1946   *Terror by Night* (Neill) (as Sherlock Holmes); *Heartbeat* (Wood) (as Prof. Aristide); *Dressed to Kill* (Neill) (as Sherlock Holmes)

1949   *Ichabod and Mr. Toad* (Kinney, Geronimi, and Algar) (as voice of Mr. Toad)

1954   *Casanova's Bad Night* (McLeod) (as Lucio)

1955   *We're No Angels* (Curtiz) (as Andre Trochard)

1956   *The Court Jester* (Panama and Frank) (as Sir Ravenhurst); *The Black Sleep* (LeBorg) (as Sir Joel Cadman)

1958   *The Last Hurrah* (Ford) (as Norman Cass)

1962   *The Magic Sword* (Gordon) (as Lodac); "The Case of M. Valdemar" ep. of *Tales of Terror* (Corman) (as Carmichael); *Two before Zero* (Faralla—doc) (as narrator)

1963   *The Comedy of Terrors* (Tourneur) (as John F. Black)

1964   *Pontius Pilate* (Rapper) (as Caiaphas)

1966   *Queen of Blood* (Harrington) (as Dr. Farraday); *Ghost in the Invisible Bikini* (Weis) (as Reginald Ripper)

1967   *Voyage to a Prehistoric Planet* (Sebastian, i.e. Harrington) (as Prof. Hartman); *Autopsy of a Ghost* (Rodriquez) (as Canuto Perez); *Hillbillys in a Haunted House* (Yarbrough) (as Gregor)

Publications

By RATHBONE: articles—

Interview by L. Soule, in *Motion Picture Magazine*, July 1936.
Interview by F. Baird, in *Photoplay*, August 1936.

By RATHBONE: book—

In and Out of Character, New York, 1962.

On RATHBONE: books—

Thomas, Tony, *Cads and Cavaliers*, South Brunswick, New Jersey, 1973.
Druxman, Michael B., *Basil Rathbone: His Life and His Films*, South Brunswick, New Jersey, 1975.
Richards, Jeffrey, *Swordsmen of the Screen: From Dougas Fairbanks to Michael York*, London, 1977.

On RATHBONE: articles—

Current Biography 1951, New York, 1951.
Obituary in *New York Times*, 22 July 1967.
Maltin, Leonard, "Basil Rathbone," in *Film Fan Monthly*, September 1967.
Cutts, J., "Superswine!" in *Films and Filming* (London), March 1969.
Gires, Pierre, "Basil Rathbone," in *L'Ecran Fantastique* (Paris), December 1970.

*   *   *

Basil Rathbone's film career is a lengthy one, spanning 45 years. During this time he played a variety of roles, both on the screen and stage, and he prided himself on his versatility. Nevertheless, Rathbone often found himself at the mercy of producers who typecast him within a limited range of characters.

In the earliest part of his film career, Rathbone was generally cast as a romantic lead. He certainly fitted the traditional description of tall, dark, and handsome, but these roles did little to advance his career. Then in 1935 Rathbone's cold portrayal of Murdstone in *David Copperfield* caught the attention of producers, who subsequently cast him as the heavy in such films as *Anna Karenina*, *A Tale of Two Cities* and *Captain Blood*. Perhaps his most famous villainous role was Sir Guy de Gisbourne in *The Adventures of Robin Hood*. For this role (and similar ones) Rathbone studied fencing and became quite an excellent swordsman, which made his portrayals still more convincing.

Although being typecast as a villain brought Rathbone a great deal of work and success, he felt the need to break out of that mold. In 1939 Rathbone changed his image when he portrayed Sherlock Holmes in *The Hound of the Baskervilles*. In many ways Basil Rathbone was the definitive Sherlock Holmes—he not only fit Conan Doyle's description of the character, but also played the part with precision and sincerity. Rathbone portrayed Holmes in 14 films (he also played the part on radio and on the stage). Although the series was very successful, Rathbone soon discovered that his association with the Sherlock Holmes character was even more constricting than his earlier identity as a villain. Finding it increasingly difficult to get acceptable film roles, in 1946 Rathbone acted on the New York stage in an attempt to escape his typecasting problems. He returned to Hollywood eight years later, only to discover that he had not quite escaped being typecast, continuing to play villains in such films as *We're No Angels* and *The Last Hurrah*. One especially memorable film from this period was *The Court Jester* in which Rathbone combined all the best elements from his earlier dastardly roles to create the consummate adversary for Danny Kaye.

Rathbone's final few roles were in mainly low-budget horror films. While two of these, *Tales of Terror* and *The Comedy of Terrors*, have become cult favorites, others are best forgotten. It is a pity that Rathbone's career should end on such a note, for the actor was capable of so much more. His earlier films showed great versatility when he was allowed the opportunity to play varied and challenging roles. Nevertheless, it is a tribute to his acting ability that he is so strongly associated with two quite opposite roles, both the classical screen villain and the ultimate proponent of law and justice, Sherlock Holmes.

—Linda J. Obalil

REAGAN, Ronald

Nationality: American. **Born:** Ronald Wilson Reagan in Tampico, Illinois, 6 February 1911. **Education:** Attended Dixon High School, Illinois; Eureka College, Illinois, B.A. in economics and sociology, 1932. **Family:** Married 1) the actress Jane Wyman, 1940 (divorced 1948), daughter: Maureen, adopted son: Michael; 2) the actress Nancy Davis, 1952, daughter: Patti, son: Ron. **Career:** 1932-37—sports announcer for radio station WOC, Davenport, Iowa (later consolidated with WHO in Des Moines); 1937—film debut in *Love Is on the Air*; contract with Warner Brothers; 1941—first lead role in big-budget film, *Kings Row*; 1942-45—served in U.S. Army; worked on air force training films; 1947-52—president of the Screen Actors Guild; 1953-54—host of TV show *The Orchid Awards*, and later host of TV series *General Electric Theater*, 1954-62, and *Death Valley Days*, 1965-66; 1964—last film, *The Killers*; 1966-74—served as governor of California; 1980—elected president of the United States: reelected in 1984, serving until January 1989; 1994—revealed to have Alzheimer's disease.

Films as Actor:

1937	*Love Is on the Air* (Grinde) (as Andy McLeod); *Hollywood Hotel* (Berkeley)
1938	*Swing Your Lady* (Enright); *Sergeant Murphy* (Eason); *Accidents Will Happen* (Clemens); *Cowboy from Brooklyn* (*Romance and Rhythm*) (Bacon); *Boy Meets Girl* (Bacon); *Girls on Probation* (McGann); *Brother Rat* (Keighley)
1939	*Going Places* (Enright); *Secret Service of the Air* (Smith); *Dark Victory* (Goulding); *Code of the Secret Service* (Smith); *Naughty but Nice* (Enright); *Hell's Kitchen* (Seiler and Dupont); *Angels Wash Their Faces* (Enright); *Smashing the Money Ring* (Morse)
1940	*Brother Rat and a Baby* (*Baby Be Good*) (Enright); *An Angel from Texas* (Enright); *Murder in the Air* (Seiler); *Knute Rockne—All American* (Bacon); *Tugboat Annie Sails Again* (Seiler); *Santa Fe Trail* (Curtiz)
1941	*The Bad Man* (Thorpe); *Million Dollar Baby* (Bernhardt); *Nine Lives Are Not Enough* (Sutherland); *International Squadron* (Mendes); *Kings Row* (Wood) (as Drake McHugh)
1942	*Juke Girl* (Bernhardt); *Desperate Journey* (Walsh)
1943	*This Is the Army* (Curtiz)
1947	*Stallion Road* (Kern); *That Hagen Girl* (Godfrey); *The Voice of the Turtle* (Rapper)
1949	*John Loves Mary* (Butler); *Night unto Night* (Siegel); *The Girl from Jones Beach* (Godfrey); *It's a Great Feeling* (Butler)
1950	*The Hasty Heart* (Sherman); *Louisa* (Hall)
1951	*Storm Warning* (Heisler) (as Burt Rainey); *Bedtime for Bonzo* (De Cordova) (as Prof. Peter Boyd); *The Last Outpost* (Foster) (as Vance Britten); *Hong Kong* (Foster) (as Jeff Williams)
1952	*She's Working Her Way through College* (Humberstone) (as John Palmer); *The Winning Team* (Seiler) (as Grover Cleveland Alexander)
1953	*Tropic Zone* (Foster) (as Dan McCloud); *Law and Order* (Juran) (as Frame Johnson)
1954	*Prisoner of War* (Marton) (as Web Sloane); *Cattle Queen of Montana* (Dwan) (as Farrell)
1955	*Tennessee's Partner* (Dwan) (as cowpoke)
1957	*Hellcats of the Navy* (Juran) (as Cmdr. Casey Abbott)
1961	*The Young Doctors* (Karlson) (as narrator)
1964	*The Killers* (Siegel—made for TV, but released theatrically instead) (as Browning)
1992	*Wisecracks* (Singer) (archival footage as himself)

Publications

By REAGAN: books—

Where's the Rest of Me?, with Richard Hubler, New York, 1965.
The Reagan Wit, edited by Bill Adler, Thornwood, New York, 1981.
An American Life, New York, 1990.

On REAGAN: books—

Gardner, Gerald, *The Actor: A Photographic Interview with Ronald Reagan*, Harmondsworth, England, 1980.
Thomas, Tony, *The Films of Ronald Reagan*, Secaucus, New Jersey, 1980.
Boyansky, Bill, *Ronald Reagan, His Life and Rise to the Presidency*, New York, 1981.
Smith, Hedrick, and others, *Reagan—The Man, The President*, New York, 1981.
Van der Linden, Frank, *The Real Reagan*, New York, 1981.
Anderson, Janice, *Ronald Reagan*, New York, 1982.
Leamer, Lawrence, *Make-Believe: The Story of Nancy and Ronald Reagan*, New York, 1983.
McLelland, Doug, *Hollywood on Ronald Reagan: Friends and Enemies Discuss Our President, the Actor*, Winchester, Massachusetts, 1983.
McDonald, Archie P., editor, *Shooting Stars: Heroes and Heroines of Western Film*, Bloomington, Indiana, 1987.
Rogin, Michael Paul, *Ronald Reagan, the Movie and Other Episodes in Political Demonology*, Berkeley, 1987.
Denton, Robert E. Jr., *The Primetime Presidency of Ronald Reagan: The Era of the Television Presidency*, New York, 1988.
Edwards, Anne, *Early Reagan: The Rise of an American Hero*, London, 1988.
Feiffer, Jules, *Ronald Reagan in Movie America*, New York, 1988.
McClure, Arthur F., C. David Rice, and William T. Stewart, editors, *Ronald Reagan, His First Career: A Bibliography of the Movie Years*, Lewiston, New York, 1988.
Webster, Duncan, *Looka Yonder!: The Imaginary America of Populist Culture*, London, 1988.
Morreale, Joanne, *A New Beginning: A Textual Frame Analysis of the Political Campaign Film*, New York, 1991.
Davis, Patti, *The Way I See It*, New York, 1992.
Edel, Wilbur, *The Reagan Presidency: An Actor's Finest Performance*, New York, 1992.
Vaughn, Stephen, *Ronald Reagan in Hollywood: Movies and Politics*, Cambridge, England, 1994.

On REAGAN: articles—

Hunter, J. F., "Ronald Reagan," in *Films in Review* (New York), April 1967.
Tuchman, M., "Ladies and Gentlemen, the Next President of the United States," in *Film Comment* (New York), July-August 1980.
Vaughn, Stephen, "Spies, National Security, and the 'Inertia Project': The Secret Service Films of Ronald Reagan," in *American Quarterly* (Philadelphia, Pennsylvania), vol. 39, no. 3, 1987.
Schickel, Richard, "No Method to His Madness," in *Film Comment* (New York), May/June 1987.

On REAGAN: film—

The Life and Times of Ronald Reagan, documentary, 1993.

*   *   *

Ronald Reagan

Because of the unfashionableness of his conservative politics in critical circles, and because of his starring role in *Bedtime for Bonzo*, which has become a kind of cult film exemplifying Hollywood mediocrity, Ronald Reagan, 40th president of the United States, has been largely dismissed as an actor. Indeed, it seems difficult to assess with any accuracy or perceptiveness the value of Reagan's work, even though that work is finally starting to be reconsidered. In truth, *Bedtime for Bonzo* is a likable film, not atypical of Hollywood, and certainly no more unambitious than, say, *Christmas in Connecticut* with Barbara Stanwyck or *June Bride* with Robert Montgomery and Bette Davis. The fact that Reagan was almost cast in the Humphrey Bogart role of Rick in *Casablanca* is generally used as a weapon to demonstrate the shortsightedness of Hollywood moguls. And yet, had Reagan been cast, the role might very well have catapulted him from the second string to the ranks of the major luminaries. Reagan did have a fairly undistinguished film career, but no more so than that of half a dozen others: Jeff Chandler, George Montgomery, and Richard Egan, for example, all of whom did consistently respectable work, but were never fortunate enough to connect with the one director or film that would have transformed their careers.

Ronald Reagan was actually a very good actor, with a sincerity and boyish charm that were at the same time genuine and endearing. His affable screen persona approached a synthesis of John Wayne and Jimmy Stewart: macho Americanism tempered with humility and good humor. At least three performances stand out as worthy of consideration: his portrayal as the "Gipper" in *Knute Rockne—All American*, simple, unaffected, and touching; his surprising turn as a villain in the Don Siegel film *The Killers*, in which his villainy is contrasted favorably with that of Angie Dickinson's femme fatale, who is unable to face her death with the sincerity and grace that Reagan's Browning does; and his strong portrayal as Drake McHugh in the very strange and powerful *Kings Row*—in which Reagan's own inherent optimism and innocence is somewhat ridiculed and punished, as small-town America is itself held up for criticism and scandal. *Kings Row* is the key film in the Reagan oeuvre, indeed, even the Reagan life: Drake's heartrending cry, "Where's the rest of me?" when he wakes to discover his legs have been amputated (unnecessarily, as it turns out), was chosen by Reagan as the title of his 1965 biography.

Reagan's role as president of the Screen Actors Guild involved him in politics (part of a tradition that would later extend to the conservative politics of future guild president Charlton Heston, as well as to the liberal politics of the future guild president Ed Asner), and Reagan found himself involved in events and issues relating to that ignoble Hollywood era of blacklisting. Although most commentators hold Reagan up as a villainous and right-wing ally to the House Committee on Un-American Activities, a close reading of his initial testimony before the committee reveals semantically precise language and a position far more subtle than that associated with the various and more strident reactionaries in the Hollywood community such as Adolphe Menjou. A rather schizophrenic Reagan film during this era, *Storm Warning*, which strongly advocates naming names, but in the context of exposing Ku Klux Klan lynchings of blacks, is also worth reconsideration.

One could say, with only a trace of irony, that Reagan's single most notable performance was as president of the United States. His appearance in the Republican National Committee's election film, with its uplifting message—"It's Morning in America," was imbued with an incredible archetypal grandeur which only John Wayne at his peak could have matched. It can be argued that turning points in his two presidential elections were both due to Reagan performance moments: the first, the famous "I paid for this microphone" reprimand where he communicated righteous anger during a debate prior to the Republican convention with wonderful economy; the second, in his reelection campaign debate with Michael Dukakis, where his joke about his own age was delivered so perfectly that he totally deflected any discussion of his potential mental incapacity or infirmity. Reagan was the perfect movie president—half Dr. Gillespie, half an American grandfather: self-deprecating, casual, stubborn, understanding. In his speeches and appearances, he discussed fictional characters and situations from the cinema as if they were real, blurring the line between the fictional and the actual. As well, he provided the American media with eight years of photo opportunities of himself. Of course, while Reagan's presidency received boffo business at the box office of contemporaneous public opinion, the overall judgment of long-term historical review remains much less secure—the most likely sustaining criticisms of his presidency being the increased homelessness and drug use in America; the Iran-Contra scandal; his almost total ignoring of the AIDS epidemic; and the rampant mentality of consumerism and excess inherent in the enlarging gap between the poor and the rich. And yet, it is unmistakably clear that Reagan is the acknowledged father of the Reagan Revolution, that he reenergized the Republican party, and that he helped bring down the Soviet Union and Communist Eastern Europe with his unyielding John Wayne stance toward the "evil empire."

As a kind of footnote to Reagan's career must be acknowledged the rather public personal soap opera played out so prominently during and after his presidency and the variety of ambivalence and contradic-

tions underlying this family saga. A conservative proponent of family values, Reagan did not have a conventional personal life: with divorce from actress Jane Wyman, temporary estrangement from at least one adopted child, public speculation on the sexual orientation of a (eventually married) son, and an ongoing, public Sturm und Drang with daughter Patti Davis, who publicly repudiated her father's politics, her mother's values, and essayed the careers of Hollywood actress and centerfold model before settling on a career as a writer, producing a steamy *roman à clef* as well as an unusually candid account of her family's interpersonal problems. Contradictory, too, to Reagan's strong image, Nancy Reagan (like many other first ladies) was widely accused of controlling her husband; in one videotaped public performance, when her husband faltered, she even prompted his line sotto voce, "We're doing the best we can." Was Nancy merely a protective partner covering for her spouse's hearing loss? Was she the director (or at other times, a chief adviser) of this drama and Reagan the dutiful studio player? Or was this incident (and the whole Iran/Contra scandal) the first evidence precursing the poignant announcement by Reagan in a 1994 farewell letter that he was suffering from Alzheimer's disease? In California, now, for Reagan's deathwatch, the family seems at last to be coming together, still attracting media attention, playing out their roles for an avid, caring public.

—Charles Derry

REDFORD, Robert

Nationality: American. **Born:** Charles Robert Redford, Jr. in Santa Monica, California, 18 August 1937. **Education:** Attended Van Nuys High School, California; University of Colorado, Boulder; Pratt Institute, New York; American Academy of Dramatic Arts, New York. **Family:** Married Lola Jean Van Wagenen, 1958 (divorced), children: Shauna, David James, Amy Hart. **Career:** 1959—Broadway debut in *Tall Story*; 1962—film debut in *War Hunt*; 1963—on Broadway in *Barefoot in the Park*, and in film version, 1967; 1980—directed the film *Ordinary People*; 1980s—set up Sundance Institute for young filmmakers; also owner of Sundance ski resort in Provo, Utah; and dedicated conservationist. **Awards:** Best Actor, British Academy, for *Tell Them Willie Boy Is Here* and *Butch Cassidy and the Sundance Kid*, 1970; Best Director Academy Award for *Ordinary People*, 1980; Lifetime Achievement Award, Screen Actors Guild, 1996. **Address:** 1223 Wilshire Boulevard #412, Santa Monica CA, 90403, U.S.A.

Films as Actor:

1962   *War Hunt* (Sanders) (as Private Ray Loomis)
1965   *Situation Hopeless, but Not Serious* (Reinhardt) (as Hank); *Inside Daisy Clover* (Pakula) (as Wade Lewis)
1966   *The Chase* (Arthur Penn) (as Eubber Reeves); *This Property Is Condemned* (Pollack) (as Owen Legate)
1967   *Barefoot in the Park* (Saks) (as Paul Bratter)
1969   *Butch Cassidy and the Sundance Kid* (Hill) (as Sundance Kid); *Downhill Racer* (Ritchie) (as David Chappellet); *Tell Them Willie Boy Is Here* (Polonsky) (as Cooper)
1970   *Little Fauss and Big Halsy* (Furie) (as Big Halsy)
1972   *The Hot Rock* (Yates) (as Dortmunder); *The Candidate* (Ritchie) (as Bill McKay); *Jeremiah Johnson* (Pollack) (title role)
1973   *The Way We Were* (Pollack) (as Hubbel Gardiner); *The Sting* (Hill) (as Johnny Hooker)
1974   *The Great Gatsby* (Clayton) (title role)

1975   *The Great Waldo Pepper* (Hill) (title role); *Three Days of the Condor* (Pollack) (as Turner)
1976   *All the President's Men* (Pakula) (as Bob Woodward, + co-pr)
1977   *A Bridge Too Far* (Attenborough) (as Maj. Cook)
1979   *The Electric Horseman* (Pollack) (as Sonny)
1980   *Brubaker* (Rosenberg) (title role)
1984   *The Natural* (Levin) (as Roy Hobbs)
1985   *Out of Africa* (Pollack) (as Denys Finch-Hatton)
1986   *Legal Eagles* (Reitman) (as Tom Logan)
1987   *Do You Mean There Are Still Real Cowboys?* (Blair—for TV) (as narrator)
1989   *Yosemite: The Fate of Heaven* (doc) (as narrator); *To Protect Mother Earth* (doc) (as narrator)
1990   *Havana* (Pollack) (as Jack Weil)
1992   *Incident at Oglala* (Apted—doc) (as narrator, + exec pr); *Sneakers* (Robinson) (as Martin Bishop)
1993   *Indecent Proposal* (Lyne) (as John Gage)
1996   *Up Close and Personal* (Avnet)

Films as Director:

1980   *Ordinary People*
1988   *The Milagro Beanfield War* (+ co-pr)
1992   *A River Runs through It* (+ ro as narrator, co-pr)
1994   *Quiz Show* (+ pr)

Other Films:

1988   *Promised Land* (Hoffman) (co-exec pr)
1989   *Some Girls* (*Sisters*) (Hoffman) (exec pr)
1991   *The Dark Wind* (Morris) (co-exec pr)
1993   *King of the Hill* (Soderbergh) (exec pr)
1995   *The American President* (Rob Reiner) (co-pr)

Publications

By REDFORD: book—

The Outlaw Trail, New York, 1978.

By REDFORD: articles—

Interview with N. Arnoldi and M. Ciment, in *Positif* (Paris), October 1972.
"Sydney Pollack: The Way We Are," interview with P. Erens, in *Film Comment* (New York), September-October 1975.
Interview with M. Cosandaey, in *Cineaste* (New York), vol. 16, nos. 1-2, 1987-88.
Interview with Stephen Schaefer, in *Film Comment* (New York), January/February, 1988.
Interview with Jill Kearney, in *American Film* (New York), March, 1988.
Interview with Allan Hunter, in *Films and Filming* (London), July 1988.
"Redford Talks: Our Man in Havana Breaks His Silence," interview with Neil Gabler, in *New York*, 10 December 1990.
"Weird Wild and Woolly; Welcome to the Offbeat World of Robert Redford," interview with Nicole Burdette, in *Harper's Bazaar*, October 1992.
Interview with Hal Rubenstein, in *Interview* (New York), September 1994.
Interview with Anthony DeCurtis, in *Rolling Stone* (New York), 6 October 1994.

On REDFORD: books—

Spada, James, *The Films of Robert Redford*, Secaucus, New Jersey, 1977; updated ed., 1984.
Bardavid, Gerard, *Robert Redford*, Paris, 1980.
Downing, David, *Robert Redford*, New York, 1982.
Jeier, Thomas, *Robert Redford: Seine Filme, sein Leben*, Munich, 1984.
Crowther, Bruce, *Robert Redford*, Tunbridge Wells, Kent, 1985.
Durant, Philippe, *Robert Redford*, Paris, 1985.
McKnight, Stephanie, editor, *Robert Redford*, London, 1988.
Clinch, Minty, *Robert Redford*, Sevenoaks, Kent, 1989.

On REDFORD: articles—

Life (cover story) (New York), 6 February 1970.
Eyles, Allen, "Robert Redford," in *Focus on Film* (London), Winter 1972.
Cieutat, Michel, "Robert Redford, ou la nostalgie du passé simple," in *Positif* (Paris), May 1974.
Chevallier, J., "Portrait Robert Redford," in *Cinéma* (Paris), May 1980.
Haskell, Molly, "Gould vs. Redford vs. Nicholson," in *The Movie Star*, edited by Elisabeth Weis, New York, 1981.
Perry, G., "Sundance," in *American Film* (Washington, D.C.), October 1981.
Current Biography 1982, New York, 1982.
Hanson, Steve, Patricia King Hanson, and Pat H. Broeske, "Ruling Stars," in *Stills* (London), June/July 1985.
Hibbin, S., "Robert Redford," in *Films and Filming* (London), March 1986.
Thomson, David, "Ordinary Bob: Can Robert Redford Ever Explode?," in *Film Comment* (New York), January/February 1988.
Thompson, A., "Sundance," in *Sight and Sound* (London), Winter 1988-89.
Alion, Y., "Robert Redford," in *Revue du Cinéma* (Paris), September 1990.
Caputo, Philip, "Robert Redford: Alone on the Range," in *Esquire* (New York), September 1992.
Clark, John, "Robert Redford," in *Premiere* (New York), October 1992.
Weinraub, Bernard, "Robert Redford Speaks His Mind on Truth, Justice, and Hollywood," in *New York Times*, 4 May 1992.

*   *   *

The price of popularity with the moviegoing public often is diminished stature with the critics. Such is the case with Robert Redford, whose exquisite all-American handsomeness has decorated movie screens since the early 1960s. After several years working on stage and as a guest actor in television series episodes, he debuted in *War Hunt*, a little-seen, low-budget war film. He slowly built up his career throughout that decade, earning his first commercial success by recreating his Broadway role as the stuffy lawyer in the Neil Simon comedy *Barefoot in the Park*. At the end of the 1960s, he became one of the world's top movie stars and box-office attractions with his fame-solidifying appearance opposite Paul Newman in *Butch Cassidy and the Sundance Kid*.

Newman and Redford are similar in that both are among the beautiful people whose fortunes are in their faces. But Newman, unlike Redford, has chosen not just to play ornaments in glossy Hollywood star vehicles. From *Somebody Up There Likes Me* in 1956 through *Nobody's Fool* in 1994, Newman has played a wide range of interesting, challenging, deeply complicated characters. Meanwhile, Redford's characters have been confined to a fairly narrow spectrum. He rarely has played unsympathetic types, two exceptions being the arrogant opportunists in *Downhill Racer* and *Little Fauss and Big Halsy*. Instead, nearly all of his roles have been charming heroes, or handsome

Robert Redford

icons who rarely display emotional fireworks. Extremes of anger or romantic ardor remain uncommon in his work. Rather, his characters remain dispassionate as they become involved in the dynamics of the story. They are like athletes who look good on the playing field, and are admired by the fans as they play their games, but whose inner workings remain known only to their coaches or fellow players. Even when his character is flawed (the idealistic, naively deluded candidate who compromises his integrity in *The Candidate*) or victimized (the tragedy-tainted baseball phenom in *The Natural*), Redford's overriding image is that of a Golden Boy. For this reason, recognition as a truly great actor (as opposed to truly great movie star) always has eluded him. The quintessential Redford-as-handsome-icon performance is found in *The Way We Were*. Here, his character is not so much a person as an object, a larger-than-life divine blond being to be admired by Barbra Streisand. Streisand has the meaty role, that of the ethnic, committed political activist who undergoes the bulk of the character development. Redford is for all intents and purposes a male Bo Derek—a shallow Joe College who is called upon to do little more than be beautiful.

In all fairness to the actor, however, it must be noted that he came to stardom in an era in which more and more major male movie stars were essentially character actors whose charisma compensated for their lack of classic good looks. By maintaining his stardom, Redford almost singlehandedly kept alive the image of the movie star as a diamond-bright alloy of glamour, celebrity, and erotic allure. He was able to accomplish this by exercising firm control over his career. Since *Butch Cassidy and the Sundance Kid*, Redford has selected parts which he feels are compatible with his established screen persona, thus ensuring his popularity with movie audiences. He also has chosen to work with such directors as Michael Ritchie, George Roy Hill, and Sidney Pollack, who seem to best understand that persona, and know how to successfully convey it on-screen.

Perhaps Redford has been at his best playing opposite Newman, in *Butch Cassidy* and *The Sting*. Newman's presence seems to loosen up Redford, and their on-screen chemistry is the key ingredient which makes both films such satisfying entertainments. In these films, Redford adds a pleasingly wry wit to his characterizations. And in his better screen moments, he is effectively able to hint, via subtle nuance, at a more complex psychology hidden beneath his surface presence.

In recent years, Redford has transcended his identity as an actor. In the 1980s, he established the Sundance Institute for young filmmakers, with his Sundance Film Festival, a showcase for the year's newest independent films, evolving into one of the motion picture industry's higher-profile events. He also entered the directing arena in 1980, winning an Academy Award for his maiden effort, *Ordinary People*. It remains an impressive drama examining the brittle reality beneath the veneer of an outwardly typical upper-middle-class American family that has been torn apart by tragedy. Unfortunately, none of Redford's subsequent directorial efforts have matched *Ordinary People*. *The Milagro Beanfield War* is set in a picturesque New Mexico town, mostly populated by poor and powerless Hispanics, that is about to be swallowed up by "progress" in the form of a fat-cat land developer. The result is at best pleasant and entertaining, enhanced by lyrical, wryly humorous moments, and at worst unnecessarily melodramatic. *A River Runs through It* is a much-too-taciturn drama about the relationships and opposing forces within another American family, this one an outdoors Montana household. Despite its wide acclaim, *Quiz Show*, an allegorical drama about the television quiz show scandals of the late 1950s, is wrought with oversimplifications and misstatements of fact.

On one level, a sense of social responsibility exists within Redford's more recent cinematic involvements, from the subjects he has chosen for the films he has directed to his involvement with the Sundance Institute and his narrating and executive producing Michael Apted's *Incident at Oglala*. The latter is a potent documentary presenting evidence of the railroading of Leonard Peltier, the American Indian

Movement activist convicted of killing a pair of FBI agents in 1975 at South Dakota's Pine Ridge Reservation. A number of Redford's earlier films work as examinations or exposes of inequities within the American system. *The Candidate* and *All the President's Men* deal with the seamy side of American politics. *Brubaker* uncovers corruption within the penal system. *The Electric Horseman* is a tract against crass commercialism and the exploitation of nature.

Whether, as one school of thought maintains, Redford's looks have been his albatross, limiting the directions in which a sizable talent might otherwise have taken him, or whether, as others argue, he is merely a competent actor with exceptional physical appeal, is a puzzle which remains obstinately difficult to solve. But unlike hundreds (if not thousands) of other pretty boy actors, Redford was no flavor of the month, a hot item one day and a has-been (or never-was) the next. He has been able to maintain his stardom over several decades, which in and of itself is quite an accomplishment.

—Fiona Valentine, updated by Rob Edelman

REDGRAVE, (Sir) Michael

Nationality: British. **Born:** Michael Scudamore Redgrave in Bristol, 20 March 1908. **Education:** Attended Clifton College, Bristol; Magdalene College, Cambridge, B.A. in French, German and English 1930. **Family:** Married the actress Rachel Kempson, 1935, daughters: the actresses Vanessa Redgrave and Lynn Redgrave, son: the actor Corin Redgrave. **Career:** Modern language teacher, Cranleigh school; 1934-36—member of Liverpool Repertory Theatre: professional debut in *Counsellor-at-Law*; in the following years acted at the Old Vic, London, and with John Gielgud's company; 1938—film debut in *The Lady Vanishes*; 1941-42—served in the Royal Navy; 1945—directed and appeared in the stage play *Jacobowsky and the Colonel*; 1947—U.S. film debut in *Mourning Becomes Electra*; 1948—U.S. stage debut in *Macbeth*; 1957—formed his own production company; 1959—appeared in his own adaptation of *The Aspern Papers* on London stage; continued to act in films and on stage, and also on television. **Awards:** Best Actor, Cannes Festival, for *The Browning Version*, 1951. Commander, Order of the British Empire, 1952. Knighted, 1959. **Died:** 21 March 1985.

Films as Actor:

1938   *The Lady Vanishes* (Hitchcock) (as Gilbert)
1939   *Stolen Life* (Czinner) (as Alan Mackenzie); *Climbing High* (Reed) (as Nicholas Brooke)
1940   *The Stars Look Down* (Reed) (as David Fenwick); *A Window in London* (Mason) (as Peter)
1941   *Kipps* (Reed) (title role); *Atlantic Ferry* (Forde) (as Charles MacIver); *Jeannie* (French) (as Stanley Smith)
1942   *The Big Blockade* (Frend) (as the Russian)
1943   *Thunder Rock* (Boulting) (as Charleston)
1945   *The Way to the Stars* (Asquith) (as Flight Lt. Archdale); ***Dead of Night*** (ep. dir by Cavalcanti) (as Maxwell Frere); *A Diary for Timothy* (Jennings) (as narrator)
1946   *The Captive Heart* (Dearden) (as Karel Hasek); *The Years Between* (Bennett) (as Michael Wentworth)
1947   *The Man Within* (Bennett) (as Carlyon); *Mourning Becomes Electra* (Nichols) (as Orin Mannon)
1948   *Secret behind the Door* (Fritz Lang) (as Mark Lamphere)
1951   *The Browning Version* (Asquith) (as Andrew Crocker-Harris)

1952   *The Importance of Being Earnest* (Asquith) (as John Worthington)
1954   *The Green Scarf* (O'Ferrall) (as Maitre Deliot)
1955   *The Sea Shall Not Have Them* (Gilbert) (as Air Commodore Walty); *Oh, Rosalinda!* (Powell and Pressburger) (as Col. Eisenstein); *The Night My Number Came Up* (Norman) (as Air Marshal); *The Dam Busters* (Anderson) (as Barnes Wallis); *Confidential Report* (Welles) (as Trebitsch)
1956   *1984* (Anderson) (as O'Connor)
1957   *Time without Pity* (Losey) (as David Graham); *The Happy Road* (Kelly) (as Gen. Medworth)
1958   *Vanishing Cornwall* (Browning—doc) (as narrator); *The Quiet American* (Mankiewicz) (as Fowler); *Law and Disorder* (Crichton) (as Percy); *The Immortal Land* (Wright—doc) (as narrator); *Behind the Mask* (Hurst) (as Sir Anthony Benson Gray)
1959   *Shake Hands with the Devil* (Anderson) (as Michael Collins); *The Wreck of the Mary Deare* (Anderson) (as Mr. Nyland)
1961   *No, My Darling Daughter* (Box and Thomas) (as Sir Matthew Carr); *The Innocents* (Clayton) (as the Uncle)
1962   *The Loneliness of the Long-Distance Runner* (Richardson) (as Governor)
1965   *Young Cassidy* (Cardiff) (as W. B. Yeats); *The Heroes of Telemark* (Anthony Mann) (as Uncle); *The Hill* (Lumet) (as the M.O.)
1968   *Assignment K* (Gielgud) (as Harris); *Heidi* (Delbert Mann—for TV)
1969   *Oh! What a Lovely War* (Attenborough) (as Gen. Wilson); *Goodbye, Mr. Chips* (Ross) (as Headmaster)
1970   *David Copperfield* (Delbert Mann—for TV) (as Peggotty); *Goodbye Gemini* (Gibson) (as the MP)
1971   *Connecting Rooms* (Gollings) (as James Wallraven); *The Go-Between* (Losey) (as Leo as adult)
1972   *Nicholas and Alexandra* (Schaffner) (as Grand Duke); *The Last Target* (Spenton-Foster) (as Erik Fritsch)

Publications

By REDGRAVE: books—

The Actor's Ways and Means, London, 1953; rev. ed., London, 1995.
The Mountebank's Tale (novel), London, 1958.
Mask or Face: Reflections in an Actor's Mirror, London, 1958.
The Aspern Papers (play), London, 1959.
In My Mind's I: An Actor's Autobiography, London, 1983.

By REDGRAVE: article—

"I Am Not a Camera," in *Films and Filming* (London), January-March 1955.

On REDGRAVE: books—

Findlater, Richard, *Michael Redgrave, Actor*, New York, 1956.
Redgrave, Deirdre, with Danaë Brook, *To Be a Redgrave*, London, 1982.
Kempson, Rachel, *A Family and Its Fortunes*, London, 1986.
Redgrave, Corin, *Michael Redgrave: My Father*, 1995.

On REDGRAVE: articles—

Current Biography 1950, New York, 1950.
De La Roche, C., "Master of His Destiny," in *Films and Filming* (London), December 1955.

Obituary in *New York Times*, 22 March 1985.
Obituary in *Variety* (New York), 27 March 1985.

*   *   *

Although he often gave the impression that he was only appearing on the screen under sufferance and would far rather have been treading the boards of the Old Vic, perhaps playing King Lear for Tyrone Guthrie or consorting in the dressing rooms with Dame Edith Evans, Sir Michael Redgrave had a long and varied career as a film actor, proving himself a plausible, if reluctant, leading man in his debut, the Hitchcock caper, *The Lady Vanishes*; displaying a stiff upper lip in a succession of war films, notably Basil Dearden's *The Captive Heart* and Michael Anderson's *The Dam Busters*; and even showing a knack for comedy as Jack Worthington in *The Importance of Being Earnest*.

"Earnest" Redgrave most certainly was: he generally acted briskly, with a bookish, schoolmasterly air, and was expert at conveying a sense of pained idealism. He was rather too intense to be classified with the "chaps," the tweed jacketed, pipe smoking squires/stars of 1950s British cinema, such as Jack Hawkins and Kenneth More. With Redgrave in front of the cameras, there is always the sense of a ferocious nervous energy ready to rip through the outward reserve. In Cavalcanti's segment of *Dead of Night*, for example, he plays the ventriloquist who becomes possessed by his own Charlie McCarthy of a dummy. Watching this performance is like seeing Mr. Chips give way to Hannibal Lecter. There is his brooding cameo as the Uncle in *The Innocents*, Jack Clayton's reworking of *The Turn of the Screw*; there is his crusading reformer of the mines in *The Stars Look Down*, his cuckolded husband in *The Browning Version*, or his political zealot of *Fame Is the Spur*: these are all parts that confirm that a Redgrave fueled by a sense of moral righteousness is a terrifying thing.

Basil Wright and Humphrey Jennings, doyens of the culturally respectable Documentary Movement, were his contemporaries at Cambridge, where Redgrave edited a magazine, *Venture*, and was film critic for *Granta*. His academic/high culture background perhaps goes some way to explaining his disdain for the medium that brought him popular success: "I, who believed that in good acting there must be a continual stream of improvisation, began to think that this business of hitting chalk marks, adjusting one's gaze . . . and all the rest of the paraphernalia . . . was a very mechanical, second-best thing indeed."

As a dissenting British film actor, he is in good company. James Mason, Stewart Granger, and Dirk Bogarde have also used their autobiographies to denigrate the British pictures they "graced." Nevertheless, it is surprising that Redgrave, who worked with Fritz Lang and Orson Welles, Carol Reed and Anthony Asquith among others, should still contrive to scoff at the bastard celluloid muse. Yet the key to Redgrave's acting is his quite palpable sense of discomfort: he always seems ill at ease. He was never accepted by either the theater or the film "establishment." He did not scale the heights of the holy triumvirate, Olivier/Richardson/Gielgud, on the stage. Nor was he a fully fledged film star. A quintessential Redgrave screen performance is his depiction of Barnes Wallis, builder of the bouncing bomb, in *The Dam Busters*. Here, he plays a nervous, stooped inventor in a mackintosh, clearly uncomfortable in a world of hearty RAF officers and their Labradors. Just as Redgrave the actor never received his due, Barnes Wallis finds that his schemes run aground on the rocks of Home Office and Bomber Command indifference. He is the boffin as outsider, the serious Stanislavskian caught in a world of West End farce. In the end, his perverse and unshakable self-belief see him triumph against the odds.

It used to be commonplace to say that British film actors were "emotionally frozen" and/or "sexually repressed." Unlike their Methodist American counterparts, they did not "explode": it is hard to think of Redgrave or Trevor Howard sweating it out à la Brando in *A Streetcar Named Desire*. What these consummate British stars can do

Michael Redgrave (right) with Richard Todd in *The Dam Busters*

is to hint at the seething turmoil of social, sexual, and political anxiety behind the carapace. They are expert at "imploding." And few manage better to convey the anguish engendered by having strong feelings but being denied the outlet to express them than Redgrave senior. In his bristling, schoolmasterly awkwardness, he remains an infinitely more interesting actor than either his children or grandchildren.

—G. C. Macnab

REDGRAVE, Vanessa

Nationality: British. **Born:** London, 30 January 1937; daughter of the actor Michael Redgrave and the actress Rachel Kempson; sister of the actress Lynn Redgrave and the actor Corin Redgrave. **Education:** Attended Queensgate School, London; Central School of Speech and Drama, London, 1954-57. **Family:** Married the director Tony Richardson, 1962 (divorced 1966), daughters: the actresses Natasha and Joely Richardson; one son by the actor Franco Nero. **Career:** 1958—London debut in *A Touch of the Sun*; film debut in *Behind the*

Mask; 1959—season with Royal Shakespeare Theatre in Stratford upon Avon; 1966—in stage play *The Prime of Miss Jean Brodie*; later stage work includes roles in *Antony and Cleopatra*, 1973, *Macbeth*, 1975, *The Seagull*, 1985, and *Orpheus Descending*; 1988. 1977—producer of the film *The Palestinian*; 1983—successfully sued the Boston Symphony for canceling her concert series for political reasons; 1986—in TV mini-series *Peter the Great,* and *Young Catherine*, 1991. **Awards:** Best Actress, Cannes Festival, for *Morgan! A Suitable Case for Treatment*, 1966; Best Actress, Cannes Festival, for *Isadora*, 1969; Best Supporting Actress Academy Award, for *Julia*, 1977; Best Supporting Actress, New York Critics, for *Prick Up Your Ears*, 1987. **Address:** 1 Ravenscourt Road, London W6, England.

Films as Actress:

1958   *Behind the Mask* (Hurst) (as Pamela Gray)
1966   *Morgan! A Suitable Case for Treatment* (Reisz) (as Leonie Delt); *Blow-Up* (Antonioni) (as Jane)
1967   *Red and Blue* (Richardson) (as Jacky); *Camelot* (Logan) (as Guinevere); *A Man for All Seasons* (Zinnemann) (as Anne Boleyn); *The Sailor from Gibraltar* (Richardson) (as Sheila); *The Charge of the Light Brigade* (Richardson) (as Clarissa)

Vanessa Redgrave in *Morgan, A Suitable Case for Treatment*

1968   *Isadora* (Reisz) (as Isadora Duncan); *The Sea Gull* (Lumet) (as Nina); *Un tranquillo posto di campagna* (*A Quiet Place in the Country*) (Petri) (as Flavia); *Tonight Let's All Make Love in London* (Whitehead) (as guest)

1969   *Oh! What a Lovely War* (Attenborough) (as Sylvia Pankhurst); *La vacanza* (*The Vacation*; *Dropout*) (Brass) (as Immacolata)

1971   *The Trojan Women* (Cacoyannis) (as Andromache); **The Devils** (Russell) (as Sister Jeanne); *Mary, Queen of Scots* (Jarrott) (title role)

1974   *Murder on the Orient Express* (Lumet) (as Mary Debenham)

1975   *Out of Season* (Alan Bridges) (as Ann)

1976   *The Seven-Per-Cent Solution* (Ross) (as Lola Deveraux)

1977   *Julia* (Zinnemann) (title role); *Agatha* (Apted) (as Agatha Christie); *The Palestinian* (Battersby) (+ pr)

1979   *Yanks* (Schlesinger) (as Helen); *Bear Island* (Sharp) (as Hedi Lindquist)

1980   *Playing for Time* (Daniel Mann—for TV) (as Fania Fenelon)

1982   *My Body, My Child* (Chomsky—for TV) (as Leenie Cabrezi)

1983   *Wagner* (Palmer—for TV) (as Cosima)

1984   *The Bostonians* (Ivory) (as Olive Chancellor)

1985   *Wetherby* (Hare) (as Jean Travers); *Steaming* (Losey) (as Nancy); *Three Sovereigns for Sarah* (Leacock—for TV) (as Sarah Cloyce)

1986   *Second Serve* (Page—for TV) (as Renee Richards); *Comrades* (Douglas) (as Mrs. Carlyle)

1987   *Prick Up Your Ears* (Frears) (as Peggy Ramsay)

1988   *Consuming Passions* (Foster) (as Mrs. Garza); *A Man for All Seasons* (Charlton Heston—for TV) (as Alice More)

1990   *Diceria dell'untore* (*The Plague Sowers*) (Cino) (as Sister Crucifix); *Romeo-Juliet* (Acosta) (voice of Mother Capulet); *A Breath of Life* (Cino) (as Sister Crocifissa); *Orpheus Descending* (Hall—for TV) (as Lady Torrance)

1991   *Stalin's Funeral* (Yevtuschenko); *The Ballad of the Sad Café* (Callow) (as Miss Amelia Evans); *What Ever Happened to Baby Jane?* (Greene—for TV) (as Blanche Hudson); *Behind the Mask* (doc)

1992   **Howards End** (Ivory) (as Ruth Wilcox)

1993   *Storia di una Capinera* (*Sparrow*) (Zeffirelli) (as Sister Agata); *The House of the Spirits* (August) (as Nivea); *Crime and Punishment* (as Mrs. Raskolnikov); *Un Muro de Silencio* (*A Wall of Silence*) (Stantic) (as Kate Benson); *They* (*They Watch*) (Korty—for TV) (as Florence Latimer); *Great Moments in Aviation* (Kidron) (as Dr. Angela Bead)

1994   *Mother's Boys* (Simoneau) (as Lydia); *Little Odessa* (Gray) (as Irina Shapira)

1995   *A Month by the Lake* (Irvin) (as Miss Bentley); *Down Came a Blackbird* (Jonathan Sanger—for TV) (as Anna Lenke)

1996   *Mission Impossible* (DePalma)

Publications

By REDGRAVE: book—

Vanessa Redgrave: An Autobiography, London, 1991.

By REDGRAVE: articles—

Interview with B. Lewis, in *Films and Filming* (London), October 1986.
"A Woman of Conscience," interview with Nicholas Wroe, in *New Statesman & Society*, 4 October 1991.

On REDGRAVE: books—

Redgrave, Deirdre, with Danaë Brook, *To Be a Redgrave*, London, 1982.
Kempson, Rachel, *A Family and Its Fortunes*, London, 1986.
Hare, David, *Writing Left-Handed*, London, 1991.

On REDGRAVE: articles—

Current Biography 1966, New York, 1966.
Haustrate, G., and W. Chmait, "Cinéma et Palestine," and "Oscar et protestations," in *Cinéma* (Paris), May 1978.
Corliss, Richard, "Vanessa Redgrave," in *The Movie Star*, edited by Elisabeth Weis, New York, 1981.
Ivory, James, "The Trouble with Olive," in *Sight and Sound* (London), Spring 1985.
Henry, William A. III, "Vanessa Ascending: The Pre-eminent Actress of Her Time Returns to Broadway," in *Time*, 9 October 1989.
Raymond, Gerard, "Redgrave on Redgrave," in *Advocate*, 12 February 1991.
Schiff, Stephen, "Who's Afraid of Vanessa Redgrave," in *Vanity Fair* (New York), July 1991.

* * *

Disappointing is the first word that comes to mind about Vanessa Redgrave's film career. But that perhaps says more about our expectations than her achievements. Being part of one of Britain's great theatrical families may have been more of a burden than an asset, so it is a credit to her persistence and intelligence that she has not given up on acting entirely, or sunk to the depths of a Hayley or Juliet Mills. Yet in virtually all of her films there remains a lingering sense of something great, of a performer of truly passionate intensity going to waste.

In some cases, this can be squarely blamed on the directors concerned. During her marriage to Tony Richardson, enduring *The Sailor from Gibraltar* and *The Charge of the Light Brigade* can only have hastened the divorce proceedings. And how could any performer communicate through the chaotic gore of *The Devils*? Redgrave almost succeeds in giving a startling performance, but is constantly thwarted by director Ken Russell's selfish grandiosity. Even her Academy Award-winning role in *Julia*, impressive as it is, cannot help but drown in the pale timidity of its surroundings, that Hollywood brand of liberal politics known as Zinnemannism. She demonstrably acts Jane Fonda off the screen; in fact, it is an embarrassingly one-sided contest—elegant intelligence versus radical pouting. But the film remains too pretty, too patronizing, and, crucially, too evasive about the women's relationship.

Many of Redgrave's films are limited by respectability, as if she were determined to prove her classical credentials. Hence she is adequately striking in *The Sea Gull*, lovingly embalmed by Sidney Lumet, and does what she can in the international stew of *The Trojan Women*. In *Mary, Queen of Scots* she succumbs to the tedious early 1970s vogue

for Tudor costume drama, half-heartedly sparring with Glenda Jackson when they should be asking each other how they got into such a dull film in the first place.

In the 1960s Redgrave played female lead in two films central to the inflated ego of that decade—*Blow-Up* and *Morgan*. In both, she had to contend with a smothering male presence (Antonioni and David Warner respectively), but very nearly captures the hearts of the two films. Her Guinevere in *Camelot* is suitably beautiful but, not surprisingly, her intelligence rarely seems engaged by the text. *Isadora* at least put her in the epicenter of a film, giving Redgrave her best early career leading role as Isadora Duncan and offering her a substantial dramatic showcase.

It took considerable courage, given the hysterical misinterpretation of her political views in certain quarters of the United States, to take the lead role in the made-for-television drama *Playing for Time*, and her success in it is heartening. She is never less than moving in her role as concentration camp prisoner Fania Fenelon. But perhaps her finest film performance, though less celebrated than many, came in *Yanks*. It is one of the only straightforwardly romantic films she has appeared in, but it never equates romanticism with sloppiness. Redgrave's acting, free of the responsibilities of a crushing classical role or of the need to punch home political points, is the strong, subtle, emotional center of the text.

As she has aged, Redgrave has taken on an assortment of roles. She was a solid presence in two films in which her characters are at once dissimilar and alike: they may come from opposite classes, yet the fact that each is dying is a key element in the story. In *Howards End*, she is a highborn matriarch who wills her cherished estate to the character played by Emma Thompson; in *Little Odessa*, she is a nondescript Russian-Jewish woman whose husband has been unfaithful and whose oldest son has become a hitman.

Redgrave gave an attractive star performance in *A Month by the Lake* playing an amiable British woman who comes to Italy's Lake Como for a vacation and becomes intrigued by the idea of a romance with a stylish but impulsive, ultimately enigmatic middle-aged businessman. Her performances in *Yanks* and *A Month by the Lake* are clear proof that if Redgrave's political commitments ever put an end to her acting career, it will be a significant loss. Yet even her political views, liked by few people and understood by fewer, seem somehow linked to the tenacity and conviction she has displayed in her films.

—Andy Medhurst, updated by Rob Edelman

REED, Oliver

Nationality: British. **Born:** Robert Oliver Reed in Wimbledon, Surrey, 13 February 1938; the nephew of the director Carol Reed. **Family:** Married 1) Kate Byrne, two children; 2) Josephine Burge, 1985. **Career:** Worked as nightclub bouncer, boxer, and cab driver; military service in the Medical Corps; 1960—film debut in *The Angry Silence*; 1968-69—roles in *Oliver!* and *Women in Love* brought critical attention; 1993—in TV mini-series *Return to Lonesome Dove*. **Agent:** ICM, 8899 Beverly Boulevard, Los Angeles, CA 90048, U.S.A.

Films as Actor:

1960   *The Angry Silence* (Green) (as Mick); *The League of Gentlemen* (Dearden); *The Bulldog Breed* (Asher); *Beat Girl* (*Wild for Kicks*) (Greville) (as Plaid Shirt); *Sword of Sherwood Forest* (Fisher) (as Melton); *The Two Faces of Dr. Jekyll* (*House of Fright*) (Fisher)

1961   *His and Hers* (Hurst) (as Poet); *The Curse of the Werewolf* (Fisher) (as Leon); *The Rebel* (*Call Me Genius*) (Day); *No Love for Johnnie* (Thomas)

1962   *The Damned* (*These Are the Damned*) (Losey) (as King); *The Pirates of Blood River* (Gilling) (as Brocaire); *Captain Clegg* (*Night Creatures*) (Scott) (as Harry Crabtree)

1963   *Paranoiac* (Francis) (as Simon Ashby); *The Scarlet Blade* (Gilling) (as Capt. Sylvester); *The Party's Over* (Hamilton) (as Moise)

1964   *The System* (*The Girl Getters*) (Winner) (as Tinker)

1965   *The Brigand of Kandahar* (Gilling) (as Eli Khan)

1966   *The Trap* (Hayers) (as Jean La Bete); *The Jokers* (Winner)

1967   *The Shuttered Room* (Greene) (as Ethan); *Dante's Inferno: The Life of Dante Gabriel Rossetti* (Russell—for TV) (title role); *I'll Never Forget What's 'is Name* (Winner) (as Andrew Quint)

1968   *Oliver!* (Carol Reed) (as Bill Sykes)

1969   *The Assassination Bureau* (Dearden) (as Ivan Dragomiloff); *Hannibal Brooks* (Winner) (as Brooks); *Women in Love* (Russell) (as Geral Crich)

1970   *La Dame dans l'auto avec des lunettes et un fusil* (*The Lady in the Car with Glasses and a Gun*) (Litvak) (as Michael Caldwell); *Take a Girl Like You* (Miller) (Patrick)

1971   **The Devils** (Russell) (as Father Grandier); *The Hunting Party* (Medford) (as Frank Calder)

1972   *Z.P.G.* (Campus) (as Russ McNeil); *Sitting Target* (Hickox) (as Harry Lomart); *Mordi e fuggi* (*Dirty Weekend*; *Bite and Run*) (Risi) (as Fabrizio)

1973   *Blue Blood* (Sinclair); *Triple Echo* (Apted) (as Sergeant); *Il giorno del furore* (*Days of Fury*; *One Russian Summer*) (Calenda)

1974   *The Three Musketeers* (Lester) (as Athos)

1975   *The Four Musketeers* (Lester) (as Athos); *Tommy* (Russell) (as Frank Hobbs); *Ten Little Indians* (Collinson) (as Hugh Lombard); *Royal Flash* (Lester) (as Bismark)

1976   *The Great Scout and Cathouse Thursday* (Taylor) (as Joe Knox); *Burnt Offerings* (Curtis) (as Ben); *Blood in the Streets* (*The Revolver*) (Sollima) (as Vito Caprini); *The Sell Out* (Collinson) (as Gabriel Lee)

1978   *The Big Sleep* (Winner) (as Eddie Mars); *Crossed Swords* (*The Prince and the Pauper*) (Fleischer) (as Miles Henderson); *Tomorrow Never Comes* (Collinson) (as Wilson); *Maniac* (*Assault on Paradise*; *The Town That Cried Terror*) (Compton) (as Nick McCormick)

1979   *The Class of Miss MacMichael* (Narizzano) (as Terence Sutton); *The Brood* (Cronenberg) (as Dr. Hal Raglan)

1980   *Dr. Heckyl and Mr. Hype* (Griffith) (title role)

1981   *Condorman* (Jarrott) (as Krokov); *Lion of the Desert* (Akkad) (as Gen. Rodolfo Graziani)

1982   *Venom* (Haggard) (as Dave); *Death Bite* (*Spasms*) (Fruet) (as Jason Kincaid)

1983   *Two of a Kind* (Herzfeld) (as Beazley); *The Sting II* (Kagan) (as Lonnegan); *Fanny Hill* (O'Hara); *The Great Question* (*Al Mas à la Al Kubra*) (Jameel)

1986   *Captive* (Mayerberg) (as Gregory Le Vay); *Castaway* (Roeg) (as Gerald Kingsland)

1987   *Wheels of Terror* (Hessler) (as the General)

1988   *Dragonard* (*Master of Dragonard Hill*) (Kikoine); *Captive Rage* (Sundstrom) (as Gen. Belmondo); *Skeleton Coast* (Cardos) (as Capt. Simpson); *The House of Usher* (Birkinshaw) (as Roderick Usher)

1989   *The Adventures of Baron Münchausen* (Gilliam) (as Vulcan); *Rage to Kill* (Winters); *The Return of the Musketeers* (Lester) (as Athos); *A Ghost in Monte Carlo* (Hough—for TV); *Gor* (Kiersch) (as Sarm)

1990   *Treasure Island* (Fraser C. Heston—for TV) (as Captain Billy Bones); *Panama Sugar and the Dog Thief* (Avallone)

1991   *Army* (Santostefano); *The Pit and the Pendulum* (Gordon) (as Cardinal); *Prisoner of Honor* (Russell—for TV) (as Gen. Boisdeffre); *Hired to Kill* (Mastorakis) (as Michael Bartos)

1992   *Severed Ties* (Santostefano and Roberts) (as Dr. Hans Vaughan)

1995   *Funny Bones* (Chelsom) (as Dolly Hopkins)

Publications

By REED: book—

Read All about Me (autobiography), London, 1979.

By REED: article—

Interview in *Arena* (London), Spring 1992.

On REED: book—

D'Arcy, Susan, *The Films of Oliver Reed*, London, 1975.

On REED: article—

Ecran (Paris), December 1979.

*   *   *

Time and more than his fair share of bad films have tended to relegate Oliver Reed to the status of a washed-up middle-aged actor whose early promise has expired under a morass of inferior work. Certainly his appearances in the grisly, post-*Wild Bunch* splatter Western *The Hunting Party*, the snake-on-the-loose horror thriller *Venom*, and the comic book *Condorman* offered little opportunity for him to reveal either talent or screen presence. Yet there is nothing to be gained from merely pointing to Reed's long list of bad films and dismissing him on this basis. Nor would it be justified. From his first starring role in Terence Fisher's *The Curse of the Werewolf* to collaborations with Richard Lester and, especially, Ken Russell, with whom Reed's tempestuous nature formed an ideal match, Oliver Reed exhibits at his best a powerful screen persona which bad films have tarnished but not destroyed completely.

Cast early on as a thug or teddy boy in several British kitchen sink and juvenile delinquency dramas, Reed had his first major role as the title character in *Curse* for Hammer Films (he had had a small part as a bouncer in the same studio's *The Two Faces of Dr. Jekyll*, also directed by Terence Fisher, released the previous year). Parts in other of the studio's horror and action thrillers quickly followed, most notably the scenery-chewing psycho in *Paranoiac*. His career advanced considerably when he met Ken Russell, for whom he starred as the poet Dante Gabriel Rossetti in Russell's BBC biopic *Dante's Inferno*. Their association continued with Russell's breakthrough film, *Women in Love*, in which Reed co-starred, through several other Russell extravaganzas (*Mahler*, *Lisztomania*) in which the actor took cameos. Reed had his biggest success as the murderous Bill Sikes in *Oliver!*, the film adaptation of the hit musical based on Charles Dickens's *Oliver Twist*. The director, Carol Reed, was his uncle, who, detesting nepotism, declined considering his nephew for the part; the latter won it entirely on his own by auditioning. He has worked steadily since, but has never quite achieved the star status *Oliver!* so auspiciously hinted at.

A comparison of several of Reed's major roles apart from Sikes, but certainly not excluding it—Leon in *Curse*, Grandier in *The Devils*, and Athos in *The Three Musketeers/The Four Musketeers*—provides some insight into his success. In the case of the first, we have a man torn

Oliver Reed

between a desire for love and a destructive animal rage which eventually overcomes and destroys him. Romance in the form of Christina (Catherine Feller) can conquer his werewolf side but circumstances tear them apart. Grandier is a priest who sees no contradiction between his clerical vôws and the pursuit of physical pleasure. This "immoral" man becomes the most moral of all when he takes a lone and fatal stand against the government figures who wish to destroy the independence of the city of Loudon. Athos, who drinks and fights with no regard for public opinion or his own safety, is also a nobleman whose genuine love for a harlot, Milady (Faye Dunaway), lost him his honor. In all three cases Reed skillfully conveys the contradictions inherent in the characters—quiet introspection alternating with harsh violence.

It is true that Reed cannot on his own redeem a mediocre film, but then it is difficult to think of any actor who could have salvaged anything from *Z.P.G.*, *Tomorrow Never Comes*, or *Sting II* (where Reed took the part created by Robert Shaw). He often seems uncaring in his choice of roles. But he clearly knows a good project when it comes along (he told David Cronenberg that *The Brood* was the best script he had read since *The Devils*).

It is encouraging, however, that recent supporting roles such as Vulcan in Gilliam's *The Adventures of Baron Münchausen*, Billy Bones in Fraser Heston's version of *Treasure Island*, and the wry, drunken priest in Stuart Gordon's Russell homage, *The Pit and the Pendulum*, have brought him the praise he often deserves.

—Daniel O'Brien, updated by John McCarty

REEVES, Keanu

Nationality: Canadian/American. **Born:** Beirut, Lebanon, 2 September 1964, to a Chinese-Hawaiian father and British mother. **Education:** Attended High School for the Performing Arts, Toronto, was graduated in 1982; studied acting at Hedgerow Theatre, Moylan, Pennsylvania, and at Lea Posluns Community Theatre, Toronto. **Career:** 1984—first professional stage and TV roles, in Toronto; 1986—moved to Los Angeles; 1987—won serious critical attention for role in *River's Edge*; 1994—popular success as action hero in *Speed* followed by stage production of *Hamlet* in Winnipeg. **Agent:** ICM, 8942 Wilshire Boulevard, Beverly Hills, CA 90211, U.S.A. **Address:** Chateau Marmont, Los Angeles, CA.

Films as Actor:

1986   *Dream to Believe* (*Flying*) (Paul Lynch) (as Tommy); *Youngblood* (Markle) (as Hoover); *Act of Vengeance* (Mackenzie—for TV) (as Buddy Martin); *Under the Influence* (Thomas Carter—for TV) (as Eddie Talbot); *Babes in Toyland* (Clive Donner—for TV) (as Alex/Jack Be Nimble); *Brotherhood of Justice* (Braverman—for TV) (as Derek); *Young Again* (Steven Hilliard Stern—for TV) (as Michael Riley, age 17)

1987   *River's Edge* (Hunter) (as Matt)

1988   *The Night Before* (Eberhardt) (as Winston Connelly); *The Prince of Pennsylvania* (Nyswander) (as Rupert Marshetta); *Permanent Record* (Marisa Silver) (as Chris Townsend); *Dangerous Liaisons* (Frears) (as the Chevalier Danceny)

1989   *Parenthood* (Ron Howard) (as Tod); *Bill & Ted's Excellent Adventure* (Herek) (as Ted "Theodore" Logan)

1990   *Tune in Tomorrow . . .* (*Aunt Julia and the Scriptwriter*) (Amiel) (as Martin Loader); *I Love You to Death* (Kasdan) (as Marlon James)

1991   *Bill & Ted's Bogus Journey* (Hewitt) (as Ted "Theodore" Logan); *My Own Private Idaho* (Van Sant) (as Scott Favor); *Point Break* (Bigelow) (as Johnny Utah)

1992   *Bram Stoker's Dracula* (Francis Ford Coppola) (as Jonathan Harker)

1993   *Much Ado about Nothing* (Branagh) (as Don John); *Little Buddha* (Bertolucci) (as Siddhartha Gautama); *Freaked* (*Hideous Mutant Freekz*) (Winter and Tom Stern) (as Ortiz the Dog Boy, uncredited)

1994   *Even Cowgirls Get the Blues* (Van Sant) (as Julian Glitche); *Speed* (De Bont) (as Jack Traven)

1995   *Johnny Mnemonic* (Longo) (title character); *A Walk in the Clouds* (Arau) (as Paul Sutton); *Children Remember the Holocaust* (doc) (as host)

1996   *Feeling Minnesota* (Baigleman) (as Jjaks Clayton); *Chain Reaction* (Andrew Davis)

Publications

On REEVES: book—

Keanu Reeves: Tear Out Photo Book, London, 1994.

On REEVES: articles—

Snowden, Lynn, "Keanu Reeves," in *Rolling Stone* (New York), 9 March 1989.

Ansen, David, "Goodbye, Airhead," in *Newsweek* (New York), 13 June 1994.

Current Biography 1995, New York, 1995.

Slack, Lyle, "Keanu's Excellent Adventure," in *Maclean's* (Toronto), 23 January 1995.

"Hollywood to Hamlet," in *Plays and Players* (London), March 1995.

Shnayerson, Michael, "Young and Restless," in *Vanity Fair* (New York), August 1995.

"Keanù Reeves," in *Film Review* (London), March 1996.

*   *   *

For someone whose acting talents have been judged slight by a number of critics, Keanu Reeves has nonetheless attracted the interest of several distinguished film directors, from Bernardo Bertolucci to Stephen Frears and Gus Van Sant, who have offered him important roles. And for someone who might well be able to sustain a major career in nothing but light comedies and action-adventure films, Reeves has sought out roles that are far from standard Hollywood routine, from a bisexual street hustler who is also a modern-day Prince Hal to a very different prince, Siddhartha the Buddha.

Largely a Torontoan in upbringing and theatrical training, Reeves retained a youthful demeanor which allowed him to play troubled or airheaded teenagers well into his twenties. In one of his earliest starring roles, in *The Prince of Pennsylvania*, a film that veers uneasily between family melodrama and farce, Reeves typically has little vocal range—often he sounds as if he has a head cold—and for the most part looks rather blank. All the same, he seems perfectly cast as a disaffected youth of the Eighties, guarded and unrevealing of inner feelings, yet with occasional surprisingly playful or sarcastic moments. It is very far from a Method performance: the difference is especially clear in *My Own Private Idaho*, in which every flicker of River Phoenix's face registers some dream or torment, while Reeves, as the unforthcoming "Prince Hal," the supposed best friend of Phoenix's narcolept, remains masked. Is it Reeves or the character who is masked, we may ask, and in either case is there anything behind the facade? This may be either good acting or astute casting on the director's part for the role of a seemingly affectless modern youth.

Keanu Reeves in *Little Buddha*

In the case of *Little Buddha*, the question of acting ability seems almost irrelevant. Bertolucci too made an inspired choice in casting Reeves as Prince Siddhartha, if only for his sheer screen presence: he has the bearing of an Indian prince (or a movie star), with the handsomeness of an undefined nationality along with a seeming inwardness, to make the pageantlike historical segments of the film work brilliantly.

Playing livelier, more impetuous characters, Reeves makes more use of a boyish intensity, whether he is the hippie lover of *Parenthood* or a more aristocratic swain in *Dangerous Liaisons*. In the *Bill and Ted* films, Reeves shows far greater animation in his jovial goofiness than his truly blank co-star, Alex Winter. Yet in certain roles where he must be a stock leading man (*Bram Stoker's Dracula*) or where the director seems incapable of getting anything interesting out of the character (*Johnny Mnemonic*), Reeves is a virtual cipher. In *A Walk in the Clouds* his extremely reserved demeanor does work, despite that the role calls for an old-fashioned heart-on-sleeve romantic warmth: perhaps because his performance is a striking contrast to the heated ones of his Hispanic and Italian co-stars, perhaps because the camera registers him as a genuine movie star, "the true prince," as Falstaff recognizes Hal by "instinct."

In *Speed* Reeves gives perhaps his best performance to date, despite the formula role. Still exhibiting traces of his Valley Boy persona while playing a heroic cop, he brings a deliciously comic note to moments of suspense, as when Jack tries to calm a gunman who cannot recognize the larger peril of the booby-trapped bus: "I don't know you, man. I'm not here for you. Let's not *do* this. . . . I don't care about your crime. Whatever you did, I'm sure (*pause*) that you're sorry. So it's cool now." Most important, he also brings a combination of physical energy and enough animation of face and voice to suggest possibilities of true range in future film roles.

—Joseph Milicia

REGGIANI, Serge

Born: Sanna, Italy, 2 May 1922; lived in France from age six. **Education:** Attended the Paris Conservatory, 1940-43. **Family:** Married 1) Janine Darcey, 1945; 2) Annie Noël. **Career:** 1938—film debut in *Conflict*; also stage actor and singer from the 1960s; on Italian television since 1962. **Awards:** Chevalier de la Légion d'honneur, Officier des Arts et des Lettres. **Address:** c/o Charley Marouani, 37 rue Marbeuf, 75008 Paris, France.

Films as Actor:

1938   *Conflict* (Moguy)
1939   *Le Jour se lève* (*Daybreak*) (Carné); *Nuits de décembre* (Bernhardt)

1942 *Le Voyageur de la Toussaint* (Daquin)
1943 *Le Carrefour des enfants perdus* (*Children of Chaos*) (Joannon) (as Jorisse)
1945 *François Villon* (Swoboda) (title role); *Étoile sans lumière* (*Star without Light*) (Blistène) (as Gaston)
1946 *Les Portes de la nuit* (*Gates of the Night*) (Carné) (as Guy Senechal); *Coïncidences* (Debecque)
1947 *La Fleur de l'age* (Carné—not completed); *La dessous des cartes* (Cayatte); *Manon* (Clouzot) (as Léon Lescaut); *Le Mystère de la chambre jaune* (Aisner); *Au Royaume des cieux* (*Woman Hunt*) (Duvivier) (as Pierre)
1948 *Les Amants de Vérone* (*The Lovers of Verona*) (Cayatte) (as Angelo)
1949 *Le Parfum de la dame en noir* (Daquin)
1950 *Les Anciens de Saint Loup* (Lampin); *Une Fille à croquer* (André) (as Loup); *La Ronde* (*Circle of Love*) (Max Ophüls) (as Franz, the soldier)
1951 *Camicie rosse* (*Anita Garibaldi*; *Red Shirts*) (Alessandrini and Rosi) (as Lantini); *Secret People* (Dickinson) (as Louis)
1952 *Casque d'or* (*Golden Helmet*) (Jacques Becker) (as Manda); *La Bergère et le ramoneur* (Grimault) (as voice); *Il mondo le condanna* (Franciotini); *Bufere* (*La Fille dangereuse*) (Brignone)
1953 *Act of Love* (*Une Acte d'amour*) (Litvak) (as Claude)
1954 *Napoléon* (Guitry) (as Lucien Bonaparte)
1955 *Les Salauds vont en enfer* (*The Wicked Go to Hell*) (Hossein) (as Rudel)
1956 *Elisa* (Richebé)
1957 *La donna del giorno* (*The Doll that Took the Town*) (Maselli) (as Mario); *Les Misérables* (Le Chanois) (as Marius); *Echec au porteur* (Grangier); *Le Passager clandestin* (Habib)
1959 *Marie-Octobre* (Duvivier) (as Rogier)
1960 *Tutti a casa* (*Everybody Go Home!*) (Comencini) (as Pvt. Ceccarelli)
1961 *Paris Blues* (Ritt) (as Michel Duvigne)
1962 *La guerra continua* (*Warriors Five*; *La Dernière attaque*) (Savona) (as Libero)
1963 *Le Doulos* (*The Fingerman*; *Doulos—The Fingerman*) (Melville) (as Maurice Fangel); *Il gattopardo* (*The Leopard*) (Visconti) (as Count Ciccio Tumeo)
1964 *Bestiare d'amour* (*The Lair of Love*) (Calderón) (as narrator)
1965 *Compartiment tueurs* (*The Sleeping Car Murder*) (Costa-Gavras); *Marie-Chantal contre le docteur Kha* (*Marie Chantal against Dr. Kha*) (Chabrol) (as Ivanov); *Lord Jim* (Richard Brooks) (as French lieutenant)
1967 *Les Aventuriers* (*The Last Adventure*) (Enrico) (as the pilot); *I sette fratelli Cervi* (Puccini); *La 25e Heure* (*La Vingt-cinquième heure*; *The 25th Hour*) (Verneuil) (as Trajan Koruga)
1968 *Il giorno della civetta* (*The Day of the Owl*; *La Maffia fait la loi*; *Mafia*) (Damiani) (as Parrinieddu)
1969 *L'Armée des ombres* (*The Shadow Army*) (Melville) (as barber)
1971 *Comptes à rebours* (Pigaut) (as Nolan)
1972 *Les Caïds* (Enrico) (as Theor); *Trois milliards sans ascenseur* (Pigaut) (as Pierrot)
1974 *Touche pas à la femme blanche* (*Don't Touch White Women*) (Ferreri) (as Mad One)
1975 *Le Chat et la souris* (*Cat and Mouse*) (Lelouch) (as Insp. Lechat); *Vincent, François, Paul, et les autres* (*Vincent, François, Paul, and the Others*) (Sautet) (as Paul)
1976 *Le Bon et les méchants* (Lelouch) (as Resistance Chief)
1977 *Une Fille cousue de fil blanc* (Michel Lang) (as Jérome); *Violette et François* (Rouffio) (as Father)
1979 *La terrazza* (Scola) (as Sergio)

1980 *L'Empreinte des géants* (*The Imprint of Giants*) (Enrico); *Fantastica* (Carle) (as Euclide)
1985 *Echo* (Failevic)
1986 *O Melissokomos* (*The Bee Keeper*) (Angelopoulos) (as Sick Man); *Mauvais Sang* (*Bad Blood*; *The Night Is Young*) (Carax) (as Charlie, + mus)
1988 *Ne réveillez pas un flic qui dort* (Pinheiro) (as "le stephanois"); *Êternelle Jeunesse* (de Sisti)
1989 *Coupe franche* (Sauné)
1990 *Il y a des jours . . . et des lunes* (*There Were Days and Moons*) (Lelouch) (as Sophie's father); *Plein Fer* (Dayan) (as Emilio)
1991 *J'ai engagé un tueur* (*I Hired a Contract Killer*) (Aki Kaurismaki) (as Vic); *Emile des Roses* (Gabrea)
1993 *De force avec d'autres* (Simon Reggiani) (as Serge/Sergio); *Le Petit garçon*

Publications

By REGGIANI: books—

La Question se pose, with Blaise N'Djehoya and Simon Reggiani, Paris, 1990.
Dernier courrier avant la nuit, 1995.

By REGGIANI: article—

Interview with R. Grelier, in *Image et Son* (Paris), January 1972.

*   *   *

After training at the Paris Conservatory and appearing at the Noctombules theater, Serge Reggiani was an extra in *Conflict* and *Le Jour se lève* before obtaining a minor part in *Nuits de décembre*. A more substantial role followed in *Le Voyageur de la Toussaint* where, as a wayward youth, he confirmed his promise.

As a slender, handsome young man with strikingly deep-set dark eyes and strong expressive features, he was readily cast in romantic and often tragic roles as a social outsider. He was the male lead in *Le Carrefour des enfants perdus*, the poet and outcast *François Villon*, the young French patriot in *Act of Love*, and Louis, an exiled revolutionary activist fighting a fascist dictator, in *Secret People*. In his more darkly tragic roles he was the despairing suicide of Carné's bleak *Les Portes de la nuit*; the charming but doomed Romeo figure of *Les Amants de Vérone*; the blind organist misled and murdered by the prostitute he has grown to love in ignorance of her profession in *Elisa*, and in *Paris Blues* the unstable drug-addicted guitarist in a jazz band. More rewarding romantic parts came as the young student Marius in *Les Misérables* and as the decent worker who finds pure love in a degrading society in *Au Royaume des cieux*, while in *La Ronde* he demonstrated his acting range as the soldier turned seducer with ever ambitious tastes.

His most complete romantic performance, however, came in *Casque d'or* as Manda, the young carpenter, who because of his love is drawn into crime, forced to kill, and finally dies bravely by the guillotine. In his tender but unsentimental portrayal of the fated lover, all the more convincing for its intense, controlled understatement, Reggiani gave a performance of considerable strength and subtlety. But if he can be various incarnations of the romantic hero he can also assume the myriad forms of the villain. In *Manon* he was the despicable pleasure-seeking black marketeer; in *Bufere* he was a trapeze artist mixed up in murder and blackmail; in *Les Salauds vont en enfer* he was a treacherous, vicious criminal; and in *Comptes à rebours* an embittered convict bent on revenge. Not all of his criminal characters are entirely unworthy, and in these roles Reggiani conveys a moral complexity based in notions of trust, loyalty, and integrity. In *Le Doulos* he is the betrayed gangster Maurice Fangel; in *Les Aventuriers* a tough, sympathetic pilot embroiled in crime; and in *Les Caïds* a gang leader who remains loyal to his associates.

His tough features have lent themselves to Resistance dramas. He was the Romanian Trajan Koruga in Verneuil's *La 25e Heure*; the barber in Melville's *L'Armée des ombres*; and a Resistance chief in Lelouch's *Le Bon et les méchants*. Among his many other notable roles he was the Russian spy Ivanov in *Marie-Chantal contre le docteur Kha*, Inspector Lechat in *Le Chat et la souris*, and Paul in Sautet's family drama *Vincent, François, Paul, et les autres*. In rare aristocratic parts he played Lucien Bonaparte in *Napoléon* and Count Ciccio in *Il gattopardo*.

After a brief absence from films, though not from television work, Reggiani has appeared for both well-established and emerging directors in minor roles that are almost a synthesis of his varied screen career. He played a terminally-ill Frenchman with a political past in Angelopoulos's *O Melissokomos*; he lent his presence to Pinheiro's thriller about right-wing police corruption in *Ne réveillez pas un flic qui dort*; he was Charlie in Carax's manipulation of traditional noir elements in the gangster film *Mauvais Sang*; he appeared in Sauné's drama of family loyalties in *Coupe franche*; and in Lelouch's *Il y a des jours . . . et des lunes* he was the delightfully nostalgic old man.

A talented actor, Serge Reggiani has an impressive repertoire of character creations. He has, in turn, transformed himself into lover, gangster, detective, spy, worker, aristocrat, family man, hero, and villain. In a career spanning over half a century he has won the respect of audiences and directors alike in France, England, Italy, and Greece as a totally committed professional.

—R. F. Cousins

REMICK, Lee

Nationality: American. **Born:** Boston, Massachusetts, 14 December 1935. **Education:** Attended Miss Hewitt's Classes (now the Hewitt School), New York, graduated 1953; studied ballet with Mme. Ruth Swoboda and modern dance with Charles Weidman; attended Barnard College, New York, one semester, 1954. **Family:** Married 1) William A. Colleran, 1957 (divorced 1969), daughter: Katherine, son: Matthew; 2) William Rory Gowans, 1970, stepdaughters: Justine and Nicola. **Career:** 1952—member of the Music Circus Tent in summer stock in Hyannis, Massachusetts; 1953—Broadway debut in *Be Your Age*; TV debut on *Armstrong Circle Theater*; 1957—film debut in *A Face in the Crowd*; later stage work included roles in *Anyone Can Whistle*, 1964, and *Wait until Dark*, 1966, both on Broadway, and *Bus Stop* in London, 1976; 1970—moved to London, England; 1973–89—in several TV mini-series, including *The Blue Knight*, 1973; *QB VII*, 1974; *Arthur Hailey's Wheels*, 1978; *Ike*, 1979; *Mistral's Daughter*, 1984; *Nutcracker: Money, Madness, Murder*, 1987; *Around the World in Eighty Days*, 1989; 1974—portrayed title role in critically acclaimed seven-part TV mini-series *Jennie: Lady Randolph Churchill*; 1981—returned to the United States, settling in Los Angeles; 1982—signed for three-month Broadway run of *Agnes of God*, but was replaced by Elizabeth Ashley in dispute over creative differences; 1988—formed production company with James Garner and Peter Duchow; 1989—diagnosed with kidney and lung cancer. **Awards:** Best Actress, Golden Globe Award, for *Days of Wine and Roses*, 1962; Golden Globe Award, for *The Blue Knight*, 1973; Best Actress, British Academy of Film and Television Arts, and Golden Globe Award, for *Jennie: Lady Randolph Churchill*, 1974; Prix Genie Award (Canada), for *Tribute*, 1980. **Died:** Of cancer, 2 July 1991.

Films as Actress:

1957 *A Face in the Crowd* (Kazan) (as Betty Lou Fleckum)
1958 *The Long Hot Summer* (Ritt) (as Eula Varner)
1959 *These Thousand Hills* (Fleischer) (as Callie); ***Anatomy of a Murder*** (Preminger) (as Laura Manion)
1960 *Wild River* (Kazan) (as Carol Baldwin)
1961 *Sanctuary* (Richardson) (as Temple Drake)
1962 *Experiment in Terror* (*The Grip of Fear*) (Edwards) (as Kelly Sherwood); *Days of Wine and Roses* (Edwards) (as Kirsten Arnesen)
1963 *The Running Man* (Reed) (as Stella Black); *The Wheeler Dealers* (*Separate Beds*) (Hiller) (as Molly Thatcher)
1965 *Baby the Rain Must Fall* (Mulligan) (as Georgette Thomas); *The Hallelujah Trail* (John Sturges) (as Cora Templeton Massingale)
1968 *No Way to Treat a Lady* (Smight) (as Kate Palmer); *The Detective* (Gordon Douglas) (as Karen Leland);
1969 *Hard Contract* (Pogostin) (as Sheila)
1971 *A Severed Head* (Dick Clement) (as Antonia Lynch-Gibson); *Loot* (Narizzano) (as Fay); *Sometimes a Great Notion* (*Never Give an Inch*) (Paul Newman) (as Viv Stamper)
1973 *A Delicate Balance* (Richardson) (as Julia); *Touch Me Not* (*The Hunted*) (Fifthian); *And No One Could Save Her* (Billington—for TV) (as Fern O'Neil)
1975 *Hennessy* (Sharp) (as Kate Brook); *Hustling* (Sargent—for TV) (as Fran Morrison); *A Girl Named Sooner* (Delbert Mann—for TV) (as Elizabeth McHenry)
1976 *The Omen* (Richard Donner) (as Katherine Thorn)
1977 *Telefon* (Siegel) (as Barbara); *The Ambassadors* (James Cellan Jones—for TV) (as Maria Gostrey)
1978 *The Medusa Touch* (Gold) (as Dr. Zonfeld); *Breaking Up* (Delbert Mann—for TV) (as JoAnn Hammil)
1979 *The Europeans* (Ivory) (as Eugenia); *Torn between Two Lovers* (Delbert Mann—for TV) (as Diane Conti)
1980 *The Competition* (Oliansky) (as Greta Vandemann); *Tribute* (Bob Clark) (as Maggie Stratton); *The Women's Room* (Glenn Jordan—for TV) (as Mira Adams); *Haywire* (Tuchner—for TV) (as Margaret Sullavan)
1982 *The Letter* (Erman—for TV) (as Leslie Crosbie)
1983 *Montgomery Clift* (*The Rebels: Montgomery Clift*) (Masenza—doc) (as interviewee); *A Gift of Love: A Christmas Story* (Delbert Mann—for TV) (as Janet Broderick)
1984 *A Good Sport* (Antonio—for TV) (as Michelle Tenney); *Rearview Mirror* (Antonio—for TV) (as Terry Seton)
1985 *Toughlove* (Glenn Jordan—for TV) (as Jan Charters)
1986 *Of Pure Blood* (Sargent—for TV) (as Alicia Browning); *Emma's War* (Jessop) (as Anne Grange)
1988 *The Vision* (Norman Stone—for TV); *Jesse* (Glenn Jordan—for TV) (as Jesse Maloney)
1989 *Bridge to Silence* (Arthur—for TV) (as Marge); *Dark Holiday* (*Passport to Terror*) (Antonio—for TV) (as Gene LePere)

Publications

By REMICK: articles—

Interview with Robert Emmett Ginna, in *Horizon* (New York), September 1960.
Interview with Gordon Gow, in *Films and Filming* (London), February 1971.
Interview with Brigid Keenan, in *Times* (London), 7 July 1974.
Interview in *Films Illustrated* (London), December 1975.

Lee Remick

"Lee Remick: The Aura of Movie Star at Its Best," interview with David Galligan, in *Drama-Logue*, 28 February 1985.

Interview in *On Performing*, by David Craig, New York, 1987.

On REMICK: book—

Rivadue, Barry, *Lee Remick: A Bio-Bibliography*, Westport, Connecticut, 1995.

On REMICK: articles—

Levy, Emanuel, "A Girl with a Lilt in Her Eyes," in *Life* (New York), 6 June 1960.
LaBadie, Donald W., "What Makes Remick Walk?," in *Show* (Hollywood), February 1963.
Stang, Joanne, "The Lady Known as Lee," in *New York Times*, 20 June 1965.
Current Biography 1966, New York, 1966.
Marill, Alvin H., in *Films in Review* (New York), November 1978.
Ecran (Paris), 15 June 1979.
Buckley, Michael, "Lee Remick," in *Films in Review* (New York), November 1988.
Obituary in *Hollywood Reporter*, 3 July 1991.
Obituary in *New York Times*, 3 July 1991.
Obituary in *Variety* (New York), 10 July 1991.

* * *

Central to Lee Remick's complex and fascinating screen presence during the first phase of her career is a sense of erotic warmth, an irreducible sensuality, capable (when combined with her remarkable gifts as an actress) of the most diverse inflections, depending on the degree to which it is allowed or denied free expression. Consider two of her finest performances, in the two finest films in which she appeared, made within a year of each other: *Anatomy of a Murder* and *Wild River*. The former is built upon the character's sexual knowingness, seductiveness, promiscuity, the latter on the character's sexual deprivation and subsequent reawakening. Preminger uses Remick's sensuality as one aspect of his detailed, multifaceted exercise in sustained ambiguity: she plays a woman ready deliberately to exploit her attractiveness as a means of manipulation, yet the erotic charge she communicates is so strong that its genuineness is never in question. The character's uninhibited sensuality, which might have been presented as merely degenerate (the Hollywood stereotype of the "nymphomaniac"), becomes in Remick's performance engaging, oddly touching. *Wild River* seems easily Kazan's best film, the only one in which his self-conscious pretensions to social significance are completely assimilated into a fully realized dramatic texture, and Remick's performance as the young, uneducated, widowed mother is crucial to its success. In her earlier scenes, she movingly communicates a potential for life stifled by calamity and deprivation, above all by erotic starvation. She then beautifully realizes the gradual transition to rebirth, a rebirth at once sexual and spiritual, made possible by contact, not with an overt, macho sexuality, but with the sensitivity, diffidence, and gentleness rendered by Montgomery Clift with an inwardness that equals Remick's—creating one of Hollywood's finest love stories.

A similar opposition can be found in her two films for Blake Edwards. Her character in *Experiment in Terror* is relatively sketchy and conventional, but (as the object of terrorization by a psychopath) it is built upon the necessity for self-control. *Days of Wine and Roses* plays on the converse of this, and on the corollary of the overt, flamboyant sensuality of *Anatomy of a Murder*: the character's surrender to alcoholic dissolution as an escape from the tensions and constraints of contemporary urban life.

Beginning particularly around the time of Remick's 1970 move to London following her marriage to the British director William "Kip"

Gowans, Remick faced the bane of so many ingenues turned mature women—a dearth of lead roles in major motion pictures. Over the next 21 years until her premature death in 1991 from cancer, the second phase of her career took her down the now-familiar path into television films and mini-series. Two of Remick's best performances during this period were in mini-series that offered her challenging roles: 1974's *Jennie: Lady Randolph Churchill* and 1987's *Nutcracker: Money, Madness, Murder*. In the former, Remick fulfilled a long-time ambition by playing the title role, the American-born mother of Winston Churchill, and was triumphant in capturing the woman's flamboyancy and in portraying her from age 18 to 67. Remick (and the series) won universal critical praise, but especially in England where she earned an award from the British Academy. The based-on-fact *Nutcracker* provided Remick with another memorable role—Frances Schreuder, a narcissistic socialite who plots, with her eldest son, the murder of her father fearing he plans to cut her out of his multimillion dollar fortune. Remick perfectly embodies the cold-blooded Schreuder, never once showing her in a sympathetic light.

Remick certainly made the most of the dwindling opportunities presented to her in the 1970s and 1980s, almost always elevating the not-always top-notch material she was presented with, but her real-life portrayal of cancer patient was perhaps the most inspiring role of her career. Following her 1989 diagnosis, she not only faced the dread disease with courage but also spoke publicly and without hesitation about her illness, trying to impart hope to others similarly afflicted and earning a Cancervive Victory award in the process. Her death in July 1991 at age 55 cut short the career of one of classiest and most-respected actresses of her time.

—Robin Wood, updated by David E. Salamie

REY, Fernando

Nationality: Spanish. **Born:** Fernando Casado Arambillet Veiga in La Coruña, 20 September 1917. **Education:** Attended Donoso Cortés Academy, Madrid; University of Madrid School of Architecture. **Military Service:** Fought for the Republic, Spanish civil war, 1936-39. **Family:** Married the actress Mabel Karr, 1960, daughter: Mabel. **Career:** 1936—film debut as extra in *Nuestra Natacha*; worked at dubbing foreign films (famous for his voice of Laurence Olivier); worked on stage in *Las mocedades del Cid* at Teatro Español and in plays for Francisco Melgares's company: a few later stage roles since the 1940s (in Anouilh's *Becket*, 1968); 1961—first of series of films by Buñuel, *Viridiana*; 1971—role in *The French Connection* brought international popularity; 1977—in TV mini-series *Jesus of Nazareth*, *A.D.*, 1985, *I Bromessi Sposi (The Betrothed)*, 1988; also served as president of the Spanish Academy of Cinematographic Arts & Sciences. **Awards:** Best Actor (co-recipient), Cannes Festival, for *Viridiana*, 1961; Best Actor, Cannes Festival, for *Elisa, My Love*, 1977; Best Actor, Spanish Goya Awards, for *Diario de invierno*, 1988. **Died:** Of bladder cancer, in Madrid, 9 March 1994.

Films as Actor:

1936 *Nuestra Natacha* (Perojo) (as extra)
1940 *La gitanilla*; *Los cuatro Robinsones (The Four Robinsons)* (Maroto)
1944 *Eugenia de Montijo* (Rubio); *El rey que rabió*
1945 *Los últimos de Filipinas* (Román); *Misión blanca*; *Tiera sedienta* (Gil)
1946 *La Pródiga* (Gil) (as José)

1947 *Reina Santa* (Gil) (as Infante Alfonso); *La Princesa de los Ursinos*; *Don Quixote de la Mancha* (Gil) (as Sanson Carrasco); *Fuentovejuna* (Román); *Noche de Reyes* (Lucia)

1948 *Locura de amor* (*The Mad Queen*) (Orduña) (as Don Filipe el Hermoso); *Si te hubieses casado con migo* (Tourjansky)

1949 *Las aventuras de Juan Lucas* (Gil)

1950 *Augustina de Aragón* (Orduña); *Mare Nostrum* (Gil) (as Ulises)

1951 *Cielo negro* (Mur-Oti); *La Señora de Fátima* (Gil); *Esa pareja feliz* (*That Happy Pair*) (Bardem and García Berlanga)

1952 *¡Bienvenido, Mr. Marshall!* (*Welcome, Mr. Marshall!*) (Bardem and García Berlanga) (as narrator); *Cómicos* (*Comedians*) (Bardem); *La laguna negra* (Castillo)

1953 *Rebeldia* (Conde); *El Alcalde de Zalamea* (Maesso); *Aeropuerto* (Lucía); *Cabaret* (Manzanos)

1954 *Marcelino, pan y vino* (*The Miracle of Marcelino*) (Vajda); *Tangier Assignment* (Leversuch) (as inspector)

1955 *Un marido de ida y vuelta* (Lucia)

1956 *Faustina* (de Heredia); *El amor de Don Juan* (Berry) (title role); *Una aventura de Gil Blas* (Jolivet); *Marcelino* (Vajda) (as Brother Moderno); *Pantaloons* (Berry) (as Don Inigo)

1957 *La vanganza* (*Vengeance*) (Bardem) (as Forastero); *Les Bijoutiers au clair de lune* (*The Night Heaven Fell*; *Heaven Fell That Night*) (Vadim)

1958 *Culpables* (Castillo); *Les habitantes de la casa deshabitada* (Ramirez); *Parque de Madrid* (Salabery)

1959 *Sonatas* (*Las adventuras del Marques de Bradomin*) (Bardem) (as Capt. Casares); *Operación Relampage*; *Las dos y media y venuno* (Ozores); *Nacido para la música* (*Né pour la musique*) (Salvia)

1960 *Fabiola* (Blasetti); *Los ultimos dias de Pompeya* (*The Last Days of Pompeii*) (Bonnard) (as High Priest); *Don Lucio y el harmano pio* (Conde); *A las cinco de la tarde* (Bardem); *Teresa de Jesús* (Orduña); *La rivolta degli schiavi* (*The Revolt of the Slaves*; *Die Sklaven Roms*) (Malasomma) (as Valerio)

1961 ***Viridiana*** (Buñuel) (as Don Jaime); *Goliat contra los gigantes* (*Goliath against the Giants*) (Malatesta) (as Bokan)

1962 *Schéhérazade* (*La Schiava di Bagdad*) (Gaspard-Huit and Bourdon); *Rogelia* (Gil); *La cara del terror* (*Face of Terror*; *Face of Fear*) (Ferry) (as Dr. Charles Taylor); *Tierra brutal* (*The Savage Guns*) (Carreras) (as Don Hernán)

1963 *El espontánes* (Grau) (as Painter); *Dios eligió sus viajeros* (Ozores); *The Ceremony* (Harvey) (as Sanchez); *The Running Man* (Reed) (as police official); *El valle de las espadas* (*The Castilian*; *Valley of the Swords*) (Setó) (as Ramiro II)

1964 *Los palomas* (Gomes); *El señor de la salle* (Amadori); *La nueva cenicienta* (Sherman); *Echappement libre* (*Backfire*; *Scappamento aperto*) (Jean Becker)

1965 *España insolita*; *Misión Lisboa* (Demicheli); *Zampó y yo* (Lucia); *Cartas boca arriba* (*Cards on the Table*) (Franco); *The Amazing Dr. G* (Simonelli); *Totò de Arabia* (*Totò d'Arabia*) (de la Loma); *Due mafiosi contre Goldginger* (*Dos de la Mafia*) (Simonelli); *Cartes sur table* (*Attack of the Robots*) (Franco)

1966 *Don Quixote* (Rim); *Dulcinea del Toboso*; *Das Vermachtnis des Inka* (*El Ultimo Rey de los Incas*; *Viva Gringo*; *Zevetut na Inkata*) (Marischka) (as President Castillo); ***Campanadas a medianoche*** (*Chimes at Midnight*; *Falstaff*) (Welles) (as Worcester); *Los jueces de la Biblia* (Dolz and Baldi); *El hijo del Pistolero* (*Son of a Gunfighter*) (Landres) (as Don Fortuna); *Return of the Seven* (Kennedy) (as priest); *El Greco* (Salce) (as King Philip II)

1967 *Un dollaro a testa* (*Navajo Joe*) (Corbucci) (as Parson Rattigan); *Robo de diamantes* (*Run Like a Thief*) (Glasser) (as Col. Romero); *Le Vicomte règle ses comptes* (*The Vis-*

count) (Cloche) (as Marco Demoigne); *Más allá de las montañas* (*Beyond the Mountains*; *The Desperate Ones*) (Ramati) (as Ibram); *Amor en el aire* (Amadori) (as Saldiez)

1968 *Villa Rides* (Kulik) (as Col. Fuentes); *Le Avventure e gliamori di Miguel Cervantes* (*The Young Rebel*; *Cervantes*; *Les Aventures extraordinaires de Cervantes*) (Sherman) (as Philip II); *I Grande condottieri* (*Gideon and Sampson*) (Baldi) (as the stranger); *Une Histoire immortelle* (*The Immortal Story*) (Welles—for TV) (as merchant)

1969 *Candidato per un assassino* (*Un sudario a la medida*; *Candidate for a Killing*) (Elorrieta); *Guns of the Magnificent Seven* (Wendkos) (as Quintero); *Fellini Satyricon* (*Satyricon*) (Fellini); *Il Prezzo del potere* (*The Price of Power*) (Valerii) (as Pinkerton); *El libro del buen amor* (Marcos) (as voice)

1970 *Land Raiders* (*Day of the Landgrabbers*) (Juran) (as priest); *¡Vamos a matar, compañeros!* (*Compañeros*) (Corbucci) (as Prof. Xantos); *The Adventurers* (Lewis Gilbert) (as Jaime Xenos); *Tristana* (Buñuel) (as Don Lope); *Muerte de un presidente* (Valerii); *Los frios ojos miedo* (Castellari); *Histoia de una traición* (Conde); *Coartada en disco rojo* (*I due volti della paura*) (Demicheli)

1971 *La cólera del viente* (Camus and Colizzi) (as Don Antonio); *La Luz del fin del mundo* (*The Light at the Edge of the World*) (Billington) (as Capt. Moriz); *The French Connection* (Friedkin) (as Alain Charnier); *A Town Called Hell* (*A Town Called Bastard*) (Parrish) (as blind farmer); *Bianco, rosso e . . .* (*The White Sister*; *The Sin*) (Lattuada) (as chief physician)

1972 *La duba* (Gil); *Chicas de club* (Grau); ***Le Charme discret de la bourgeoisie*** (*The Discreet Charm of the Bourgeoisie*) (Buñuel) (as Ambassador Raphael Acosta); *Questa specie d'amore* (Bevilacqua)

1973 *Antony and Cleopatra* (Charlton Heston) (as Lapidus); *La Chute d'un corps* (Palac); *Senso unico* (*One Way*) (Mauceri); *Zanna bianca* (*White Fang*) (Fulci); *La polizia incrimina, la legge assolve* (*High Crime*) (Castellari); *Tarot* (Forqué); *Pena de muerte* (Grau); *El mejor alcalde, el Rey* (Gil)

1974 *Dites-le avec des fleurs* (Grimblat) (as Jacques); *La Femme aux bottes rouges* (*The Lady with the Red Boots*; *The Women with the Red Boots*) (Juan Buñuel) (as Perrot); *Fatti di gente perbene* (*La Grande Bourgeoise*; *The Murri Affair*; *Drama of the Rich*) (Bolognini) (as Augusto Murri); *Corruzione al palazzo di giustizia* (Aliprandi)

1975 *Cadaveri eccellenti* (*Illustrious Corpses*) (Rosi) (as Minister of Security); *French Connection II* (Frankenheimer) (as Alain Charnier); *Pasqualino Settebelleze* (*Seven Beauties*; *Pasqualino: Seven Beauties*) (Wertmüller) (as Pedro); *Il Contesto*; *¿Existio Otra Humanidad?* (Marcos—doc)

1976 *Le désert des Tartares* (*Il deserto dei Tartari*; *The Desert of the Tartars*) (Zurlini) (as Nathanson); *Strip-Tease* (Lorente); *A Matter of Time* (Minnelli) (as Charles van Maar); *Voyage of the Damned* (Rosenberg) (as Cuban president)

1977 *Elisa, Vida mia* (*Elisa, My Love*) (Saura) (as Elisa's father); *Cet obscur objet de désir* (*That Obscure Object of Desire*) (Buñuel) (as Mathieu)

1978 *Uppdragnet* (*The Assignment*) (Arehn) (as Roberto Bidara); *Dulce Piel de Mujer* (*Honey*) (Angelucci)

1979 *Quintet* (Altman) (as Grigor); *Le Dernier amant romantique* (*The Last Romantic Lover*) (Jaeckin) (as Max); *L'Ingorgo* (*Traffic Jam*; *Bottleneck*) (Comencini) (as Carlo); *Caboblanco* (J. Lee Thompson) (as Tereda)

1980 *El Crimen de Cuenca* (Miro)

1981 *Tragala, pervo* (Artero); *La vera storia della signora delle Camelie* (Bolognini); *Casta e pura* (Samperi)

Fernando Rey with Silvia Pinal in *Viridiana*

1982   *Cercasi Gesu* (Comencini) (as Don Filippo); *Estrangeira* (Grilo); *Monsignor* (Perry) (as Santoni); *Pablo Picasso Pintor* (Rossif) (as voice); *Bekenntnisse des Hochstaplers Felix Krull* (Sinkel—for TV)

1983   *Bearn o la Sala de Munecas* (Chavarri)

1984   *The Hit* (Frears) (as Chief Inspector); *Un Amour interdit* (Dougnac); *Elogia della pazzia di desiderio erasmo* (Aquerre)

1985   *Padre Nuestro* (*Our Father*) (Regueiro) (as Cardinal); *Rustler's Rhapsody* (Wilson) (as railroad colonel); *El Caballero del dragon* (Colomo) (as Fray Lupo); *Black Arrow* (John Hough—for TV)

1986   *Saving Grace* (Robert M. Young) (as Cardinal Stefano Biondi); *Tiempo de silencio* (Aranda); *Hotel du paradis* (Bokova) (as Joseph); *Mi General* (*My General*) (de Arminan) (as Adm. Comesana)

1987   *El Bosque encantado* (*The Enchanted Forest*) (Cuerda) (as Mr. d'Abondo)

1988   *Captain James Cook* (Clark—for TV); *Diario de invierno* (Requeiro) (as Father); *Moon over Parador* (Mazursky) (as Alejandro); *Pasodoble* (Sanchez) (as Don Nuno); *El Tunel* (*The Tunnel*) (Drove) (as Allende); *El aire de un crimen* (Isasi-Isasmendi); *Esmeralda Bay* (Franco) (as Ramos)

1989   *La bataille des trois rois* (*The Battle of Three Kings*; *Tambores de fuego*; *Drums of Fire*) (Barka) (as Papa)

1990   *Diceria dell'untore* (*The Plague Sowers*; *A Breath of Life*) (Cino) (as doctor); *Naked Tango* (Schrader) (as Judge Torres); *A Breath of Life* (Cino)

1991   *La Vida Lactea* (*The Milky Life*) (Esterlich)

1992   *1492: The Conquest of Paradise* (Ridley Scott) (as Friar Marchena); *La Marrana* (José Luis Cuerda)

1993   *Al Otro Lado del Túnel* (*At the Other End of the Tunnel*; *The Other Side of the Tunnel*) (de Arminan); *Madregilda* (Regueiro)

Publications

By REY: article—

"Fernando Rey y la generosidad de los actores," interview with F. Sánchez, in *Cine* (Mexico), March 1979.

On REY: book—

Cebollada, Pascual, *Biografía y películas de Fernando Rey*, Barcelona, 1992.

On REY: articles—

Current Biography 1979, New York, 1979.
Bulnes, J., "Les immortels du cinema: Fernando Rey," in *Revue du Cinéma* (Paris), 18 January 1990.
Obituary in *New York Times*, 10 March 1994.

*   *   *

The cinema has produced a number of distinguished collaborations in which one senses a very special relationship between director, actor, and character: one thinks of Fellini and Mastroianni in *La dolce vita* and *8½*, of Bergman and von Sydow in the period from *The Seventh Seal* to *Shame*, of Ozu and Chishu Ryu through a long sequence of films. Such a relationship clearly existed between Luis Buñuel and Fernando Rey, and it is for his work with Buñuel that Rey is justly celebrated.

The precise nature of the director/actor/character relationship needs to be defined with care and delicacy: it is clearly different from case to case, and seldom a simple matter of the actor "representing" the director within the narrative. That description is perhaps closest to the truth in the case of Fellini and Mastroianni, and furthest from it in that of Buñuel and Rey. Superficially, it might even appear that Buñuel used Rey to depict precisely the kind of character toward which he has always been antagonistic—the wealthy bourgeois-capitalist patriarch. Yet for all his attacks on the bourgeoisie, Buñuel always had the honesty to acknowledge his own membership in it, and as he entered old age (the precise point where Rey enters his work) the acerbity of his films became increasingly mellowed by compassion and generosity. Rey's characters are always presented critically, they are always "wrong"; but Buñuel's point about them is that they *cannot* be right, that their entrapment in social structures and social conditioning is irreversible. So, while they are treated ironically and without sentimentality, Buñuel's love for them, rooted in a fellow feeling that derives doubtless from their age, is beyond dispute.

Rey's conservative Don Jaime in *Viridiana*, complexly associated with sexual repression, classical music, and emotional depth, commits suicide, making way for his illegitimate son, "progressive," promiscuous, opportunistic, and shallow. Both *Tristana* and *Cet obscur objet de désir* develop, painfully and sympathetically, a theme established in *Viridiana*, the elderly man's erotic and masochistic obsession with a beautiful young woman. Paradoxically, *Le Charme discret de la bourgeoisie* gives him the most monstrous characteristics yet extends to him the most explicit forgiveness: he, of all the characters, at the end of the film is allowed to enjoy a meal undisturbed. The forgiveness entails three conditions: he eats because he is hungry, not to enact a reassuring bourgeois ritual; he sends his servant to bed and gets the food himself; he has just dreamed of the annihilation of his entire class (or at least of all the characters who represent it in the film). The last point, especially, suggests the basis for Buñuel's tenderness towards Rey's characters: their patriarchal position is invariably qualified by vulnerability and a profound unease.

In addition to his seminal work with Buñuel, Rey also had a number of fine performances for other noteworthy directors: Juan Antonio Bardem and Luis García Berlanga (*¡Bienvenido, Mr. Marshall!* and *Esa pareja feliz*), Orson Welles (*Chimes at Midnight*), Lina Wertmüller (*Seven Beauties*), and Carlos Saura (*Elisa, My Love*, for which Rey won a best actor award at Cannes). But the role for which he is best known in the United States was his smooth French drug kingpin, Alain Charnier, in William Friedkin's worldwide smash *The French Connection*. Un-

fortunately, aside from his reprisal of Charnier in John Frankenheimer's excellent sequel *French Connection II*, Hollywood rarely handed Rey such juicy roles in which he could showcase his talent. The last two decades of his career until his death in 1994 pushed his number of film appearances over 150 but did not generate much of note. Rey did, however, in 1992 have a very well received lead role as Don Quixote in a critically acclaimed Spanish television series.

—Robin Wood, updated by David E. Salamie

REYNOLDS, Burt

Nationality: American. **Born:** Waycross, Georgia, 11 February 1936. **Education:** Attended Florida State College; Palm Beach Junior College. **Family:** Married 1) the actress Judy Carne, 1963 (divorced 1965); 2) the actress Loni Anderson, 1988 (divorced 1994), one adopted son. **Career:** Football player with the Baltimore Colts; 1958—actor at Hyde Park Playhouse, New York; 1959-60—in TV series *Riverboat*; 1961—on Broadway in *Look, We've Come Through*; film debut in *Angel Baby*; 1962-65—in TV series *Gunsmoke*, and in *Hawk* series, 1966, and *Dan August* series, 1970-71; 1976—directed first film, *Gator*; 1990-94—in TV series *Evening Shade*.

Films as Actor:

1961 *Angel Baby* (Wendkos) (as Hoke Adams); *Armored Command* (Haskin) (as Skee)
1965 *Operation C.I.A.* (Nyby) (as Mark Andrews)
1967 *Un dollaro a testa* (*Navajo Joe*) (Corbucci) (as Joe)
1968 *Fade-In* (*Iron Cowboy*) (Taylor) (as Rob)
1969 *Impasse* (Benedict) (as Pat Morrison); *100 Rifles* (Gries) (as Yaqui Joe); *Sam Whiskey* (Laven) (title role)
1970 *Hunters Are for Killing* (Girard—for TV); *Run, Simon, Run* (McGowan—for TV) (title role); *Skullduggery* (Gordon Douglas) (as Douglas Temple); *Shark* (*Maneater*; *Un Arma de dos filos*) (Fuller) (as Caine)
1972 *Fuzz* (Colla) (as Det. Steve Carella); ***Deliverance*** (Boorman) (as Lewis); *Everything You Always Wanted to Know about Sex but Were Afraid to Ask* (Woody Allen) (as Switchboard)
1973 *Shamus* (Kulik) (as McCoy); *White Lightning* (Sargent) (as Gator McKlusky); *The Man Who Loved Cat Dancing* (Sarafian) (as Jay Grobart)
1974 *The Longest Yard* (Aldrich) (as Paul Crewe)
1975 *W. W. and the Dixie Dancekings* (Avildsen) (as W. W. Bright); *At Long Last Love* (Bogdanovich) (as Michael Oliver Pritchard III); *Hustle* (Aldrich) (as Lt. Phil Gaines); *Lucky Lady* (Donen) (as Walker)
1976 *Silent Movie* (Mel Brooks) (as himself); *Nickelodeon* (Bogdanovich) (as Buck Greenaway)
1977 *Smokey and the Bandit* (Needham) (as Bandit); *Semi-Tough* (Ritchie) (as Billy Clyde Puckett)
1978 *Hooper* (Needham) (as Sonny Hooper)
1979 *Starting Over* (Pakula) (as Phil Potter)
1980 *Rough Cut* (Siegel) (as Jack Rhodes); *Smokey and the Bandit II* (Needham) (as Bandit)
1981 *The Cannonball Run* (Needham) (as J. J. McClure); *Paternity* (Steinberg) (as Buddy Evans)
1982 *The Best Little Whorehouse in Texas* (Higgins) (as Sheriff); *Best Friends* (Jewison) (as Richard Babson)

1983   *The Man Who Loved Women* (Edwards) (as David); *Stroker Ace*
       (Needham) (title role); *Smokey and the Bandit III* (Lowry)
       (as the real Bandit)
1984   *Cannonball Run II* (Needham) (as J. J. McClure); *City Heat*
       (Richard Benjamin) (as Mike Murphy)
1986   *Uphill All the Way* (Dobbs) (as poker player)
1987   *Heat* (Richards) (as Nick "Mex" Escalante); *Malone* (Cokliss)
       (as Richard Malone)
1988   *Switching Channels* (Kotcheff) (as John L. Sullivan IV); *Rent-
       a-Cop* (London) (as Tony Church); *The Story of Hollywood*
       (Gosling—for TV) (as narrator)
1989   *Physical Evidence* (Michael Crichton) (as Joe Paris); *Break-
       ing In* (Forsyth) (as Ernie Mullins); *All Dogs Go to Heaven*
       (Bluth—animation) (as voice of Charlie)
1990   *Modern Love* (Benson) (as Col. Parker); *A Day in the Life of
       Wood Newton* (Thomason)
1992   **The Player** (Altman) (as himself)
1993   *Cop and a Half* (Henry Winkler) (as Nick McKenna)
1995   *The Maddening* (Danny Huston)
1996   *Precious*; *Striptease* (Andrew Bergman) (as Congressman
       Dilbeck); *Trigger Happy* (Bishop)

Films as Actor and Director:

1976   *Gator* (as Gator McKlusky)
1978   *The End* (as Sonny Lawson)
1982   *Sharky's Machine* (as Sharky)
1985   *Stick* (title role)
1993   *The Man from Left Field* (for TV) (as Jack)

Publications

By REYNOLDS: books—

My Life, New York, 1994.
Seminole Seasons: Florida State's Rise to the National Title, with Bruce
   Chadwick, Dallas, Texas, 1994.

By REYNOLDS: articles—

"The End Is Just the Beginning," interview with J. McBride and B.
   Brooks, in *Film Comment* (New York), May-June 1978.
"Sophisticated Touch," interview in *Films and Filming* (London), June
   1980.
"Burt Offerings," interview with Rebecca Ascher-Walsh, in *Entertain-
   ment Weekly* (New York), 7 October 1994.

On REYNOLDS: books—

Hurwood, Bernhardt J., *Burt Reynolds*, New York, 1979.
Whitley, Dianna, *Burt Reynolds: Portrait of a Superstar*, New York, 1979.
Streebeck, Nancy, *The Films of Burt Reynolds*, Secaucus, New Jersey,
   1982.
Resnick, Sylvia Safran, *Burt Reynolds: An Unauthorized Biography*, New
   York, 1983.
Hall, Elaine Blake, *Burt and Me: My Days and Nights with Burt
   Reynolds*, New York, 1994.
Smith, Lisa, *Burt Reynolds*, Palm Beach, Florida, 1994.

On REYNOLDS: articles—

McGillivray, David, "Burt Reynolds," in *Focus on Film* (London),
   Autumn 1972.

Current Biography 1973, New York, 1973.
Lee, G., "The Burt Reynolds Game Plan," in *American Film* (Washing-
   ton, D.C.), June 1978.
Smith, J., "The Wooing of Burt Reynolds," in *American Film* (Wash-
   ington, D.C.), July-August 1980.
Haskell, Molly, "Burt Reynolds," in *The Movie Star*, edited by Elisabeth
   Weis, New York, 1981.
Sarne, M., "Taking a New Direction," in *Films* (London), May 1982.
Hanson, Steve, Patricia King Hanson, and Pat H. Broeske, "Ruling
   Stars," in *Stills* (London), June/July 1985.

*   *   *

Quipster Burt Reynolds was a wise guy stud whose sexy insolence
snowballed into box-office magic. For a film star who springboarded
to fame via talk show appearances (independent of the merits of his
screen work), Reynolds was a true media sensation whose celebrity
now rests on off-guard sightings on tabloid-television programs.

Cocksure on the surface, but inwardly peeved about the failure of
several television series, the young Reynolds was a product of the
waning days of Hollywood studio training programs. What he mainly
learned as a contract actor was that on-the-job acting lessons were
good but that playing a half-breed on *Gunsmoke* was bad. His gridiron
days as football star, ending with a crippling knee injury, stood him in
good stead when he became the prime symbol of macho knockabout in
the American cinema of the 1970s. What set Reynolds apart (as he
must have sensed when he posed nude for *Cosmopolitan* magazine),
was a teasing sexuality that endeared him to ladies just as his quick-
tempered brawling made him a hit with men.

A long time in coming, stardom hit Reynolds when he was already
the darling of late night television shows. Concurrently sending critics
in search of superlatives, *Deliverance* brought him the best notices of
his career for his well-rounded exploration of destructive machismo,
but this was not the Burt the public hankered for. Consolidated by the
boffo business registered by an unheralded road picture, Reynolds's
stardom made him the first good ol' boy megastar. After *Smokey and
the Bandit*, Reynolds reigned as King of the Road in a parallel universe
of CB radios, monster trucks, and trailer lifestyles.

Admirably never downgrading his shit-kickin' fans, Reynolds tried
to broaden his range beyond the drive-in set but never courageously or
farsightedly enough. Escalating his antics as a loose cannon in slapped-
together enterprises such as *The Cannonball Run*, Reynolds rode the
crest of the box office but seemed trapped in a country-western ghetto.
His bad boy image never seemed mature enough to fit comfortably
with traditional private eye role models; his cynicism seemed like a
pose not an existential outcry. By the time he foisted *Heat*, *Malone*,
and *Physical Evidence* on an unwaiting world, the tough-as-nails detective demeanor seemed more soft than hard-boiled.

For some reason, the off-the-cuff wit and bedroom eyes-flirting
that delighted insomniacs during his talk show interviews did not translate to big-screen appeal in a series of lightweight but strained romantic comedies: *Paternity*, *Switching Channels*, and *Best Friends*. For a
time, the razor-sharp satire, *Semi-Tough*, and the slick caper flick,
Rough Cut, showed glimmers of Reynolds's bantering sexiness but his
Manly Folk Hero of the Movies and his Class Cut-Up on television
never comfortably coexisted. Perhaps he had a longer ride at the top
than his talent deserved. On television, career resuscitation arrived in
the form of the "gosh-darning" *Evening Shade*, but a series of on-set
tantrums rocked his world followed by news of ugly irreconcilable
differences stemming from his divorce from Velvetta Cheesecake,
Loni Anderson. Having given him his start, the vast television wasteland reclaimed him.

Unlike his studio contract buddy, Clint Eastwood, who aged gracefully and sexily into the love interest of *Bridges of Madison County*,
Reynolds has toupéed and plastic surgeried himself almost beyond

recognition. (Not since Robert Taylor dyed his hair jet black has a famous leading man failed so totally at stopping the clock.) No doubt, his touted comeback opposite Demi Moore in *Striptease* can only be considered a stopgap measure. Perhaps comedies may bring respite but Reynolds no longer has the self-possessed good looks to unseat Schwarzenegger, Stallone, and dozens of up-and-comers who have usurped his place in the overcrowded action-movie meat market. The truth is that Reynolds has always been a television star; that hillbilly hero film career now seems like an aberration.

—Robert Pardi

REYNOLDS, Debbie

Nationality: American. **Born:** Mary Frances Reynolds in El Paso, Texas, 1 April 1932. **Education:** Attended high school in Burbank, California. **Family:** Married 1) the singer Eddie Fisher, 1955 (divorced 1959), daughter: the actress Carrie Fisher, son: Todd Fisher; 2) Harry Karl, 1960 (divorced 1973); 3) Richard Hamlett, 1985. **Career:** 1948—film debut in *June Bride*; contract with Warner Brothers, 1948-50, and with MGM, 1950-59; nightclub work since 1961; 1969-70—actress in *The Debbie Reynolds Show*; 1973—star of *Irene* on Broadway; 1981—in TV series *Aloha Paradise*. **Address:** Raymax Productions, 6514 Lankershim Boulevard, North Hollywood, CA 91606, U.S.A.

Films as Actress:

1948 *June Bride* (Windust) (as Boo's girl friend)
1950 *The Daughter of Rosie O'Grady* (Butler) (as Maureen O'Grady); *Three Little Words* (Thorpe) (as Helen Kane); *Two Weeks with Love* (Rowland) (as Melba Robinson)
1951 *Mr. Imperium* (Hartman) (as Gwen)
1952 *Singin' in the Rain* (Donen and Kelly) (as Kathy Selden); *Skirts Ahoy!* (Lanfield) (as herself)
1953 *I Love Melvin* (Weis) (as Judy Leroy); *The Affairs of Dobie Gillis* (Weis) (as Pansy Hammer); *Give a Girl a Break* (Donen) (as Suzy Doolittle)
1954 *Susan Slept Here* (Tashlin) (as Susan); *Athena* (Thorpe) (as Minerva Mulvain)
1955 *Hit the Deck* (Rowland) (as Carol Pace); *The Tender Trap* (Walters) (as Julie Gillis)
1956 *The Catered Affair* (Richard Brooks) (as Jane Hurley); *Bundle of Joy* (Taurog) (as Polly Parrish); *Meet Me in Las Vegas* (*Viva Las Vegas*) (Rowland)
1957 *Tammy and the Bachelor* (Pevney) (as Tammy)
1958 *This Happy Feeling* (Edwards) (as Janet Blake)
1959 *The Mating Game* (George Marshall) (as Marietta Larkin); *Say One for Me* (Tashlin) (as Holly); *It Started with a Kiss* (George Marshall) (as Maggie); *The Gazebo* (George Marshall) (as Nell Nash)
1960 *The Rat Race* (Mulligan) (as Peggy Brown); *Pepe* (Sidney) (as guest)
1961 *The Pleasure of His Company* (Seaton) (as Jessica Poole); *The Second Time Around* (Sherman) (as Lucretia)
1963 *How the West Was Won* (Hathaway, Ford, and Marshall) (as Lilith Prescott); *My Six Loves* (Champion) (as Janice Courtney); *Mary, Mary* (LeRoy) (title role)
1964 *The Unsinkable Molly Brown* (Walters) (title role); *Goodbye Charlie* (Minnelli) (as George)
1966 *The Singing Nun* (Koster) (as Sister Ann)

1967 *Divorce American Style* (Yorkin) (as Barbara Harmon)
1968 *How Sweet It Is!* (Paris) (as Jenny)
1971 *What's the Matter with Helen?* (Harrington) (as Adelle Bruckner)
1972 *Charlotte's Web* (Nichols and Takamoto) (as voice of Charlotte)
1974 *That's Entertainment!* (Haley Jr.) (as narrator)
1987 *Sadie and Jon* (Moxey—for TV)
1989 *Perry Mason: The Case of the Musical Murder* (Nyby—for TV) (as Amanda Cody)
1992 *The Bodyguard* (Jackson) (as herself); *Battling for Baby* (Art Wolff—for TV)
1993 *Heaven and Earth* (Stone) (as Eugenia); *Jack L. Warner: The Last Mogul* (Gregory Orr—doc)
1994 *That's Entertainment! III* (Friedgen and Sheridan) (as host)
1996 *Mother* (Albert Brooks)

Publications

By REYNOLDS: books—

If I Knew Then, New York, 1963.
Debbie: My Life, with David Patrick Columbia, New York, 1988.

On REYNOLDS: books—

Rosen, Marjorie, *Popcorn Venus*, New York, 1973.
Farber, Stephen, and Marc Green, *Hollywood Dynasties*, New York, 1984.

On REYNOLDS: articles—

Current Biography 1964, New York, 1964.
Hample, Henry S., "Debbie Reynolds," in *Premiere* (New York), January 1994.

*   *   *

Debbie Reynolds may have been crowned Miss Burbank of 1948, but the qualities she brought to her movie debut that same year were more those of the cheerleader than the beauty queen. Her ebullient girlishness hit exactly the right note in the musicals and comedies which became her staple, and her popularity was so immediate that she was given starring roles while still a novice. Her early parts did not vary much, but her charm was so effortless that she could nudge a movie into the next higher notch of entertainment by the sheer force of enthusiasm. Her singing and dancing were no more than competent yet she was repeatedly cast in musicals, perhaps because her sprightly and buoyant character so readily lent itself to the musical's unreal milieu.

Her gifts as a mimic, mined more thoroughly in the nightclub acts of her later career, are already in evidence in the delightful *I Love Melvin*, as is her inherent sense of comedy timing. She shows precocious skills as a farceur in such films as *The Affairs of Dobie Gillis* and *Susan Slept Here*, when the script requires only that she be adorable.

Her zeal began to seem a bit forced in *The Tender Trap*, *The Catered Affair*, and *A Bundle of Joy*. A slurpy sentimentality crept into her vehicles, beginning with *Tammy and the Bachelor*. She could be theatrical and obvious in *The Gazebo*, *How the West Was Won*, and *Mary, Mary*. Still, her talents remain formidable. Witness her popular star turn as *The Unsinkable Molly Brown*, a role she played on screen and stage. And when she allows herself an offbeat role, as in the witty *What's the Matter with Helen?*, the results can be agreeably loopy.

Reynolds's career of late has not focused on feature filmmaking. Since the 1970s, she has led a crusade to restore and preserve the objects and real estate of Hollywood history, including buildings, costumes, posters, and props. She also has assembled an impressive collection of vintage movie memorabilia. These activities have made her one of the most respected citizens of Hollywood. Professionally, her career has been relegated almost exclusively to the stage and club dates, and to her appearances in two aerobic exercise videotapes. She also wrote an autobiography, *Debbie: My Life*.

Still, her beauty and exuberance merely await the right screen role. Having acquitted herself so admirably with Gene Kelly in *Singin' in the Rain* when she was no more than 19, what might she be capable of now?

—Frank Thompson, updated by Audrey E. Kupferberg

RICHARDSON, Miranda

Nationality: British. **Born:** Lancashire, England, 3 March 1958. **Education:** Studied acting at the Bristol Old Vic Drama School. **Career:** Late 1970s—began her career appearing with a small theater in Manchester, England; early 1980s—toured in repertory, then moved to London and began appearing in stage and TV productions; 1985—earned raves for debut screen role in *Dance with a Stranger*; 1986—appeared as Queen Elizabeth I on the popular BBC series *The Black Adder*. **Awards:** Royal Television Society, Best Actress Award, for *Sweet as You Are*, 1987; British Academy of Film and Television Arts Award, Best Supporting Actress, for *Damage*, 1992; Golden Globe Award, Best Actress in a Comedy, for *Enchanted April*, 1992; New York Film Critics Circle, Best Supporting Actress, for *Damage*, *Enchanted April*, and *The Crying Game*, 1992; National Board of Review Award, Best Actress, for *Tom & Viv*, 1994; Golden Globe Award, Best Supporting Actress, for *Fatherland*, 1994. **Agent:** Kerry Gardner, 15 Kensington High Street, London W8 5NP, England.

Films as Actress:

1983   *A Woman of Substance* (Don Sharp—for TV) (as Paula)
1985   *Dance with a Stranger* (Newell) (as Ruth Ellis); *The Innocent* (Mackenzie) (as Mary Turner); *Underworld* (*Transmutations*) (Pavlou) (as Oriel); *The Death of the Heart* (Hammond—for TV) (as Daphne Heccomb)
1987   *Empire of the Sun* (Spielberg) (as Mrs. Victor); *Eat the Rich* (Peter Richardson) (as DHSS Blond); *After Pilkington* (Morahan—for TV) (as Penny); *Sweet as You Are* (Angela Pope—for TV) (as Julia Perry)
1988   *Black Adder's Christmas Carol* (Boden—for TV) (as Queen Elizabeth/Asphyxia)
1989   *El Sueno del Mono Loco* (*The Mad Monkey*; *Twisted Obsession*) (Trueba) (as Marilyn); *Ball-Trap on the Cote Sauvage* (Jack Gold—for TV) (as Early Bird)
1991   *Mio Caro Dr. Graessler* (*The Bachelor*) (Faenza) (as Frederica/ The Widow)
1992   *Enchanted April* (Newell) (as Rose Arbuthnot); **The Crying Game** (Neil Jordan) (as Jude); *Damage* (Malle) (as Ingrid)
1993   *Century* (Poliakoff) (as Clara); *The Line, the Cross, and the Curve* (Kate Bush—short) (as mysterious woman); *Old Times* (for TV) (as Anna)
1994   *The Night and the Moment* (Tato) (as Julie); *Tom & Viv* (Gilbert) (as Vivienne Haigh-Wood); *Fatherland* (Menaul—for TV) (as Charlie Maguire)
1996   *Kansas City* (Altman); *Evening Star* (Harling) (as Patsy)

Publications

By RICHARDSON: article—

"New Face: Miranda Richardson: From Bristol Old Vic to Ruth Ellis on Film," interview with N. Robertson, in *New York Times*, 16 August 1985.

On RICHARDSON: articles—

McAsh, L. F., "Introducing Miranda Richardson," in *Photoplay Movies & Video* (London), May 1985.
Canby, Vincent, "Spectacular Debuts Create Worry about the Future," in *New York Times*, 18 August 1985.
Linfield, Susan, "Close-up: Miranda Richardson," in *American Film* (New York), December 1987.
Ver Meulen, M., "Miranda's Brave New World," in *Premiere* (New York), December 1987.
Wolf, M., "Miranda Richardson Is at Home with the Extreme," in *New York Times*, 7 April 1991.
Specter, M., "Miranda Richardson: Running from Typecasters," in *New York Times*, 27 December 1992.
Kroll, Jack, and others, "Inheriting the Crown," in *Newsweek* (New York), 4 January 1993.
Current Biography 1994, New York, 1994.
Biskind, Peter, "Viv a Little," in *Premiere* (New York), March 1995.

*   *   *

Nineteen ninety-two certainly was Miranda Richardson's year. She impressed movie audiences by giving eye-popping performances as three very different characters. Any actress would have been delighted to earn attention for any one of these roles. The fact that she scored a trifecta is especially impressive.

Richardson is blessed with the chameleon-like ability to completely transform her appearance from role to role; if you look at stills from her various films, you will find it hard to connect all of the characters depicted in each as being played by the same person. Richardson can play characters out of different eras, characters who are victims and victimizers, character who are soft or tough, all with equal aplomb. Her three 1992 releases are Neil Jordan's *The Crying Game*, in which she plays a cold-blooded Irish Republican Army terrorist; Mike Newell's *Enchanted April*, in which she is an emotionally repressed Englishwoman who is one of a quartet who rents a picturesque Italian villa for a month; and Louis Malle's *Damage*, in which she is the wife of a high-powered member of Parliament, who is betrayed when he enters into a liaison with their son's girlfriend. Richardson might have earned Oscar nominations for any one of these roles but she was cited for *Damage*, in the Best Supporting Actress category. In this later film, she has never been better as her character reacts upon realizing the full extent of her husband's infidelity.

Prior to 1992, Richardson was best-known to moviegoers for her star-making performance in Newell's *Dance with a Stranger*. This based-on-fact melodrama is set during the 1950s, with the actress playing Ruth Ellis, a divorcee and prostitute turned nightclub manager who was found guilty of murdering her lover and became the last woman ever to be hanged in England. And she has offered fine performances in films not nearly as hyped as her 1992 releases. In *The Bachelor*, a subtle, thoughtful story of repressed emotion, Richardson even plays two roles. The first is Frederica, the unmarried longtime companion of her staid, middle-aged doctor-brother (Keith Carradine). As the film opens, Frederica seems bored, even disturbed. It is no surprise, then, that she promptly commits suicide. Richardson reappears later in the story as the last of several women with whom the doctor comes in contact. She is The Widow, a tactless, gossipy woman

Miranda Richardson in *Enchanted April*

with the brattiest of daughters this side of *The Children's Hour*—and a character totally unlike Frederica.

Richardson was to further her reputation as an actress willing to play fiercely complicated characters, picking up another Oscar nomination, this one as Best Actress, for *Tom & Viv*. The film is an austere, up-close-and-personal drama detailing the relationship between two deeply intertwined personalities: writer-poet T. S. Eliot (Willem Dafoe) and his deeply troubled wife, Vivienne Haigh-Wood (Richardson). The pair meet in 1914, and court in what seems like record time. But none of Viv's relatives informs Tom that she suffers from what her concerned brother calls "women's troubles . . . a shameful family secret." She is a fragile, delicate soul who actually is afflicted with a hormonal imbalance. Tom & Viv may love each other passionately, but end up being akin to two trains speeding down two vastly different tracks.

All of Richardson's best roles have been united in that they are psychologically complex. She is at her strongest when playing individuals who, either because of their own inner demons or the manner in which they have been treated by others, are forced to deal with deep, unrelenting emotion.

—Rob Edelman

RICHARDSON, (Sir) Ralph

Nationality: British. **Born:** Ralph David Richardson in Cheltenham, 19 December 1902. **Education:** Attended Xaverian College, Brighton. **Family:** Married 1) Muriel Hewitt, 1924 (died 1942); 2) Meriel Forbes, 1944, son: Charles David. **Career:** 1921—stage debut in *Les Misérables*, Brighton; then toured England and Ireland with a Shakespearean repertory company; 1925—London stage debut in *Oedipus at Colonus*; 1933—film debut in *The Ghoul*; 1936—directed the play *Bees on the Boat Deck*; 1939-44—served with Fleet Air Arm: Lt. Commander; 1944-49—associated with resuscitating the Old Vic theater, London as actor and director: in New York with the Old Vic company; on stage in plays by Shakespeare, Sheridan, Pirandello; 1952—directed the film *Home at Seven*; 1977—in TV mini-series *Jesus of Nazareth*. **Awards:** Best Actor, New York Film Critics, and Best British Actor, British Academy, for *The Sound Barrier*, 1952; Best Acting (collectively awarded), Cannes Festival, for *Long Day's Journey into Night*, 1962; Best Supporting Actor, New York Film Critics, for *Greystoke: The Legend of Tarzan*, 1982. Knighted, 1947. **Died:** In London, 10 October 1983.

Films as Actor:

1933 *The Ghoul* (Hunter) (as Nigel Hartley); *Friday the Thirteenth* (Saville) (as schoolmaster); *Java Head* (Ruben) (as William Ammidon)

1934 *The Return of Bulldog Drummond* (Summers) (as Hugh Drummond); *The King of Paris* (Raymond) (as Paul)

1935 *Bulldog Jack* (Forde) (as Morell)

1936 **Things to Come** (Menzies) (as the Boss)

1937 *The Man Who Could Work Miracles* (Mendes) (as Col. Winstanley); *Thunder in the City* (Gering) (as Manningdale); *South Riding* (Saville) (as Robert Carne)

1938 *The Divorce of Lady X* (Whelan) (as Lord Mere); *The Citadel* (King Vidor) (as Denny)

1939 *Q Planes* (*Clouds over Europe*) (Whelan) (as Maj. Hammond); *Smith* (Browne); *The Four Feathers* (Korda) (as Capt. John Durrance); *The Lion Has Wings* (Powell, Hurst, and Brunel) (as Wing Commander)

1940 *Health for the Nation* (doc) (as narrator); *On the Night of the Fire* (Hurst) (as Will Kobling)

1942 *The Day Will Dawn* (*The Avengers*) (French) (as Lockwood)

1943 *The Silver Fleet* (Wellesley and Sewell) (as Jaap Van Leyden)

1944 *The Volunteer* (Powell and Pressburger—doc) (as himself)

1946 *School for Secrets* (Ustinov) (as Prof. Heatherville)

1948 *Anna Karenina* (Duvivier) (as Alexei Karenin); *The Fallen Idol* (Reed) (as Baines)

1949 *The Heiress* (Wyler) (as Dr. Austin Sloper)

1951 *Outcast of the Islands* (Reed) (as Capt. Lingard)

1952 *The Sound Barrier* (*Breaking the Sound Barrier*) (Lean) (as John Richfield); *The Holly and the Ivy* (O'Ferrall) (as the Rev. Martin Gregory)

1955 *Richard III* (Olivier) (as Duke of Buckingham)

1956 *Smiley* (Kimmins) (as Rev. Lambeth); *The Passionate Stranger* (Box) (as Roger Wynter/Sir Clement)

1960 *Our Man in Havana* (Lean) (as "C"); *Oscar Wilde* (Ratoff) (as Sir Edward Carson); *Exodus* (Preminger) (as Gen. Sutherland)

1961 *The 300 Spartans* (Maté) (as Themistocles)

1962 *Long Day's Journey into Night* (Lumet) (as James Tyrone)

1964 *Woman of Straw* (Dearden) (as Charles Richmond)

1965 *Dr. Zhivago* (Lean) (as Alexander Gromeko)

1966 *Khartoum* (Dearden) (as Gladstone); *The Wrong Box* (Forbes) (as Joseph Finsbury)

1967 **Chimes at Midnight** (*Campanadas a medianoche*; *Falstaff*) (Welles) (as narrator)

1969 *Midas Run* (*A Run on Gold*) (Kjellin) (as Henshaw); *The Bed Sitting Room* (Lester) (as Lord Fortnum of Alamein); *Oh! What a Lovely War* (Attenborough) (as Sir Edward Grey); *The Battle of Britain* (Hamilton) (as Minister); *The Looking Glass War* (Pierson) (as Leclerc)

1970 *Eagle in a Cage* (Cook) (as Sir Hudson Lowe); *David Copperfield* (Delbert Mann—for TV) (as Mr. Micawber)

1971 *Who Slew Auntie Roo?* (Harrington) (as Mr. Benton)

1972 *Tales from the Crypt* (Francis) (as Crypt Keeper); *Alice's Adventures in Wonderland* (Miller—for TV) (as Caterpillar); *Lady Caroline Lamb* (Bolt) (as George III)

1973 *Frankenstein—The True Story* (Smight—for TV) (as Lacey); *O Lucky Man!* (Anderson) (as Sir James Burgess/Monty); *A Doll's House* (Losey) (as Dr. Rank)

1975 *Rollerball* (Jewison) (as Senator)

1976 *The Man in the Iron Mask* (Newell—for TV) (as Cardinal Richelieu)

1978 *Watership Down* (Rosen—animation) (as voice); *No Man's Land* (Hall—for TV) (as Hirst)

1981 *Time Bandits* (Gilliam) (as The Supreme Being); *Early Days* (Page—for TV) (as Kitchen); *Dragonslayer* (Robbins) (as Ulrich); *Witness for the Prosecution* (Gibson—for TV)

1982 *Wagner* (Palmer—for TV) (as Pfi)

1984 *Greystoke: The Legend of Tarzan* (Hudson); *Give My Regards to Broad Street* (Webb)

1985 *Invitation to the Wedding* (Brooks) (as Uncle Willie)

Film as Director:

1952 *Home at Seven* (+ ro as David Preston)

Publications

On RICHARDSON: books—

Hobson, Harold, *Ralph Richardson*, London, 1958.
O'Connor, Garry, *Ralph Richardson: An Actor's Life*, London, 1982; rev. ed., 1986.

Ralph Richardson in *Long Day's Journey into Night*

Tanitch, Robert, editor, *Ralph Richardson: A Tribute*, London, 1982.

On RICHARDSON: articles—

Current Biography 1950, New York, 1950.
"Ralph Richardson," in *Films and Filming* (London), May 1961.
Coulson, A. A., "Ralph Richardson," in *Films in Review* (New York), October 1969.
Obituary in *New York Times*, 11 October 1983.
The Annual Obituary 1983, Chicago, 1984.

*   *   *

Of the triumvirate of great British twentieth-century actors—John Gielgud, Laurence Olivier, and Ralph Richardson—only Richardson has enjoyed a screen career as long and as prolific as any film personality. As actress Barbara Jefford has commented, "He was always a wonderfully flexible film performer—better in many ways than Gielgud or Olivier." Thanks to a long-term contract he became a familiar figure in British films—"my film career had always been in the hands of Korda," Richardson said after the producer's death. "Korda looked after me." Yet the majority of Richardson's films are instantly forgettable. He began his screen career in an atrocious Boris Karloff vehicle, *The Ghoul*, which did nothing to enhance either actor's reputation, and did not obtain a decent screen role until *Things to Come* some three years later.

Things to Come features Richardson as the Hitler-Mussolini style Boss of a futuristic world crippled by wars. It was followed by *The Man Who Could Work Miracles*, in which the actor played an eccentric judge, and *The Citadel*, in which Richardson again played an eccentric, this time drunken Dr. Denny. He was rapidly becoming a major young British character actor, and at the same time getting a reputation for eccentricity in which he delighted. In later years he would ride around London on a motorbike with a parrot on his shoulder, and keep a pet ferret which he washed each week in Lux soap suds.

With *South Riding*, Richardson graduated from character actor to leading man, a position enhanced by his performances in *The Four Feathers* and *Anna Karenina*. But he was aging fast, and by the time Richardson made his Hollywood debut in *The Heiress*, he was old enough to play Olivia de Havilland's father, Dr. Austin

Sloper, in this adaptation of the Henry James classic. Elegant and refined, Richardson destroys his daughter's one chance at love in a performance that is, unquestionably, the first of his two great American screen roles.

Because Richardson accepted so many film roles, the bulk of his work seems minor and unimpressive. One can only ponder why he took parts in such unimportant features as *The 300 Spartans*, *Woman of Straw*, *Midas Run*, *Tales from the Crypt*, or *Rollerball*. Perhaps Korda's death in 1959 robbed the actor of the guidance he needed in his screen work. Only one other Hollywood feature gives Richardson a role equal to his talent, that of James Tyrone in *Long Day's Journey into Night*, a part to which he brings a strength of character and a sorrow strangely lacking from Laurence Olivier's highly regarded stage performance.

From the late 1950s onwards, Richardson's film roles were small, and yet each production was enhanced by his appearance, described by Kenneth Tynan as a "unique physical presence, at once rakish and stately, as of a pirate turned prelate." Richardson's eccentricity spilled over into his screen work, notably in *The Time Bandits*, in which, as the Supreme Being, he wears a three-piece suit and looks as if he had just wandered on to the set directly from the street, mumbling his lines and appearing totally confused.

—Anthony Slide

RITTER, Thelma

Nationality: American. **Born:** Brooklyn, New York, 14 February 1905. **Education:** Attended Manual Training High School, New York; American Academy of Dramatic Arts, New York. **Family:** Married Joseph Moran, 1927, son: Joseph Anthony, daughter: Monica Ann. **Career:** Acted in vaudeville and stock companies, then at the Poli Theatre, Elizabeth, New Jersey; retired from show business in the 1930s; 1944—acted in radio series; 1947—film debut in *Miracle on 34th Street* followed by a series of character parts; 1949-55—contract with 20th Century-Fox; 1955—television debut in play written for her by Paddy Chayevsky, *The Catered Affair*; 1957—in Broadway musical *New Girl in Town*. **Died:** 5 February 1969.

Films as Actress:

1947   *Miracle on 34th Street* (Seaton) (as Peter's mother)
1948   *Call Northside 777* (Hathaway) (as woman); *A Letter to Three Wives* (Mankiewicz) (as Sadie)
1949   *City across the River* (Shane) (as Mrs. Cusack); *Father Was a Fullback* (Stahl) (as Geraldine)
1950   *Perfect Strangers* (Windust) (as Lena Fassler); **All about Eve** (Mankiewicz) (as Birdie); *I'll Get By* (Sale) (as Miss Murphy)
1951   *The Mating Season* (Leisen) (as Ellen McNulty); *As Young as You Feel* (Jones) (as Dell Hodges); *The Model and the Marriage Broker* (Cukor) (as Mae Swazey)
1952   *With a Song in My Heart* (Lang) (as Clancy)
1953   *Titanic* (Negulesco) (as Maude Young); *The Farmer Takes a Wife* (Levin) (as Lucy Cashdollar); *Pickup on South Street* (Fuller) (as Moe)
1954   **Rear Window** (Hitchcock) (as Stella)
1955   *Daddy Long Legs* (Negulesco) (as Miss Pritchard); *Lucy Gallant* (Parrish) (as Molly Basserman)

1956   *The Proud and Profane* (Seaton) (as Kate Connors)
1959   *A Hole in the Head* (Capra) (as Sophie Manetta); *Pillow Talk* (Gordon) (as Alma)
1961   *The Misfits* (Huston) (as Isabelle Steers); *The Second Time Around* (Sherman) (as Aggie)
1962   *Birdman of Alcatraz* (Frankenheimer) (as Elizabeth Stroud)
1963   *How the West Was Won* (Ford and others) (as Agatha Clegg); *For Love or Money* (Gordon) (as Chloe Brasher); *A New Kind of Love* (Shavelson) (as Lena O'Connor); *Move Over Darling* (Gordon) (as Grace Arden)
1965   *Boeing-Boeing* (Rich) (as Bertha)
1967   *The Incident* (Peerce) (as Bertha Beckerman)
1968   *What's So Bad about Feeling Good?* (Seaton) (as Mrs. Schwartz)

Publications

On RITTER: book—

Parish, James, *Good Dames*, New York, 1974.

On RITTER: articles—

Current Biography 1957, New York, 1957.
Obituary in *New York Times*, 5 February 1969.
Roman, R. C., "Thelma Ritter," in *Films in Review* (New York), November 1969.

*   *   *

Thelma Ritter had what is referred to as "street smarts," a kind of instinctive intelligence acquired through years of survival in an often hostile urban environment. For Ritter, that urban environment was usually New York City, and she captured the vernacular and the character of its people—their mixture of forthright bad manners, shrewdness, and bluff—probably more accurately than any other actor of her generation.

Always intolerant of any sort of false or pretentious behavior, she sabotages Ann Sothern's hopes for an elegant dinner party in *A Letter to Three Wives* by refusing to put on any special airs as a maid for the occasion ("Soup's on"). As the ex-vaudevillian Birdie Coonan in *All about Eve*, she is the first to see through Eve Harrington's manipulative posturings ("What a story. Everything but the bloodhounds snappin' at her rear end").

Her screen career did not begin until she was in her forties, and the women she portrayed were generally single, widowed, or divorced. In such films as *The Mating Season*, *The Model and the Marriage Broker*, and *Rear Window*, she advises and consoles young and glamorous couples, patching up their romances and prodding them into marriage. This advice, however, was often unsolicited and unwanted, and her wisecracking exterior masked a vulnerable and complex human being whose own problems could be as deepseated as those of the people she so freely advises. Often, she was so much a part of her environment that she had difficulty in understanding anything beyond its confines. Birdie Coonan sees everything, even Civil War history, in theatrical terms ("I never played Fort Sumter"). When Jeanne Crain speaks romantically of Sherwood Forest in *The Model and the Marriage Broker*, Ritter asks, "Where's that—Jersey?"

It is in *Pickup on South Street* that she gives her best performance as the street peddler and informer, Moe. "You'd be doin' me a favor," she tells Richard Kiley as he points a pistol at her head. And lying on her deathbed, a gramophone playing a scratched recording of "Mam'selle," Thelma Ritter—aging, frightened, and

Thelma Ritter

utterly alone—evokes the most heartbreaking aspect of the type of woman she so skillfully portrayed.

—Joe McElhaney

ROBARDS, Jason

Nationality: American. **Born:** Jason Nelson Robards Jr., in Chicago, Illinois, 26 July 1922; son of the actor Jason Robards Sr.; often billed as Jason Robards, Jr. in early years of his career. **Education:** Attended Hollywood High School; American Academy of Dramatic Arts, New York, 1946-47. **Military Service:** U.S. Naval Reserve, 1940-46: radioman first class. **Family:** Married 1) the actress Eleanor Pitman, 1948 (divorced 1958), sons: Jason and David, daughter: Sarah; 2) Rachel Taylor, 1959; 3) the actress Lauren Bacall, 1961 (divorced 1973), son: Sam Prideaux; 4) Lois O'Connor, one daughter and one son. **Career:** School teacher and cab driver between acting engagements in New York; 1953—in the play *American Gothic*; 1956—success in New York production of *The Iceman Cometh* (in revival of the play, 1985); the successful production of the play led to O'Neill's widow allowing the premiere of his unproduced play *Long Day's Journey into Night* later the same year; 1959—film debut in *The Journey*; 1961—in TV series *Acapulco*; also appeared in many other TV roles, including roles in the mini-series *Washington: Behind Closed Doors*, 1977, *F.D.R.: The Last Year*, 1980, and *An Inconvenient Woman*, 1991. **Awards:** Best Acting (collectively awarded), Cannes Festival, for *Long Day's Journey into Night*, 1962; Best Supporting Actor Academy Award, and Best Supporting Actor, New York Film Critics, for *All the President's Men*, 1976; Best Supporting Actor Academy Award, for *Julia*, 1977. **Agent:** Buchwald Associates, 10 East 44th Street, New York, NY 10017, U.S.A.

Films as Actor:

1959 *The Journey* (Litvak) (as Paul Kedes)
1961 *By Love Possessed* (John Sturges) (as Julius Penrose); *Tender Is the Night* (Henry King) (as Dick Diver)
1962 *Long Day's Journey into Night* (Lumet) (as James Tyrone)
1963 *Act One* (Schary) (as George S. Kaufman)
1965 *A Thousand Clowns* (Coe) (as Murray Burns)
1966 *A Big Hand for the Little Lady* (*Big Deal at Dodge City*) (Cook) (as Henry Drummond); *Any Wednesday* (Miller) (as John Cleves)
1967 *Divorce American Style* (Yorkin) (as Nelson Downes); *Hour of the Gun* (John Sturges) (as Doc Holliday); *The St. Valentine's Day Massacre* (Corman) (as Al Capone)
1968 *The Night They Raided Minsky's* (Friedkin) (as Raymond Paine); *Isadora* (*The Loves of Isadora*) (Reisz) (as Paris Singer); *C'era una volta il West* (*Once upon a Time in the West*) (Leone) (as Cheyenne)
1970 *Tora! Tora! Tora!* (Fleischer) (as Gen. Walter C. Short); *Julius Caesar* (Burge) (as Brutus); *Fools* (Gries) (as Matthew South); *The Ballad of Cable Hogue* (Peckinpah) (as Cable Hogue); *Operation Snafu* (*Situation Normal All Fouled Up*; *Rosolino paternò, soldato . . .*) (Loy)
1971 *Murders in the Rue Morgue* (Hessler) (as Cesar Charron); *Johnny Got His Gun* (Trumbo) (as Joe's father)
1972 *The War between Men and Women* (Shavelson) (as Stephen Kozlenko); *The Execution* (Badiyi); *The House without a Christmas Tree* (Bogart—for TV)

1973 *Pat Garrett and Billy the Kid* (Peckinpah) (as Lew Wallace)
1975 *Mr. Sycamore* (Kohner) (as John Gwilt); *A Boy and His Dog* (L. Q. Jones) (as Lew Craddock); *Die Hinrichtung* (Badiyi); *A Moon for the Misbegotten* (for TV)
1976 *All the President's Men* (Pakula) (as Ben Bradlee)
1977 *Julia* (Zinnemann) (as Dashiell Hammett)
1978 *Comes a Horseman* (Pakula) (as Ewing); *A Christmas to Remember* (Englund—for TV) (as Daniel Larson)
1979 *Hurricane* (Troell) (as Capt. Bruckner); *Caboblanco* (J. Lee Thompson) (as Gunther Berkdorff)
1980 *Raise the Titanic!* (Jameson) (as Adm. James Sandecker); *Melvin and Howard* (Jonathan Demme) (as Howard Hughes); *Haywire* (Tuchner—for TV) (as Leland Hayward)
1981 *The Legend of the Lone Ranger* (Fraker) (as President Grant)
1982 *Burden of Dreams* (Blank—doc)
1983 *Max Dugan Returns* (Ross) (title role); *Something Wicked This Way Comes* (Clayton) (as Charles Halloway); *The Day After* (Meyer—for TV) (as Dr. Russell Oakes)
1984 *Sakharov* (Gold—for TV) (title role); *America and Lewis Hine* (Rosenblum—doc)
1985 *The Long Hot Summer* (Cooper—for TV) (as Will Varner); *The Atlanta Child Murders* (Erman—for TV)
1986 *Johnny Bull* (Weill—for TV); *The Last Frontier* (Wincer—for TV) (as Ed Stenning)
1987 *Laguna Heat* (Langton) (as Wade Shephard); *Square Dance* (*Home Is Where the Heart Is*) (Petrie) (as Dillard)
1988 *The Good Mother* (Nimoy) (as Muth); *Bright Lights, Big City* (Bridges) (as Alex Hardy, uncredited); *L'Ami Retrouvé* (*Reunion*) (Schatzberg) (as Henry Strauss); *The Christmas Wife* (David Hugh Jones—for TV); *Breaking Home Ties* (Wilder—for TV); *Inherit the Wind* (David Greene—for TV) (as Henry Drummond)
1989 *Dream a Little Dream* (Rocco) (as Coleman Ettinger); *Parenthood* (Ron Howard) (as Frank Buckman); *Black Rainbow* (Hodges) (as Walter Travis)
1990 *Quick Change* (Franklin and Bill Murray) (as Chief Rotzinger)
1991 *The Perfect Tribute* (Bender—for TV) (as Abraham Lincoln); *Chernobyl: The Final Warning* (*Final Warning*) (Page—for TV) (as Dr. Armand Hammer); *Mark Twain and Me* (Petrie—for TV) (as Mark Twain)
1992 *Storyville* (Frost) (as Clifford Fowler)
1993 *The Trial* (David Hugh Jones) (as Dr. Huld); **Philadelphia** (Jonathan Demme) (as Charles Wheeler); *The Adventures of Huck Finn* (Sommers) (as the King); *Heidi* (Rhodes—for TV) (as Grandfather)
1994 *The Paper* (Ron Howard) (as Graham Keighley); *Little Big League* (Scheinman) (as Thomas Heywood); *The Enemy Within* (Darby—for TV) (as Gen. R. Pendleton Lloyd)
1995 *Journey* (for TV) (as Marcus); *My Antonia* (Sargent—for TV)

Publications

By ROBARDS: articles—

"Coming Alive," interview with J. Craven, in *Films and Filming* (London), September 1978.
"The Players," interview with Andrew Corsell and Amy Donohue, in *Philadelphia Magazine*, December 1993.

On ROBARDS: book—

Lauren Bacall by Myself, New York, 1978.

On ROBARDS: articles—

Current Biography 1959, New York, 1959.
Bryson, J., "Jason Robard's Long Journey Home," in *New York*, 24 December 1973.

*   *   *

Jason Robards's acting career began in the 1950s on the New York stage, where he was quickly hailed as the definitive interpreter of the playwright Eugene O'Neill. His triumphant success in a 1956 revival of O'Neill's *The Iceman Cometh* prompted the playwright's widow Oona to allow her husband's autobiographical *Long Day's Journey into Night*, which the author had refused to let be staged during his lifetime, to receive its Broadway premiere in 1959, with Robards as star.

To the general public, however, Robards is known more for his films roles—and for his highly publicized 1961 marriage to the actress Lauren Bacall following the death of her first husband, the legendary Humphrey Bogart. The two were divorced in 1973.

Anatole Litvak's *The Journey*, with Deborah Kerr and Yul Brynner, launched Robards's film career, which, unlike his stage career, has often brought him more criticism than acclaim. In films such as John Sturges's *Hour of the Gun*, as Doc Holliday, and Sergio Leone's *Once upon a Time in the West*, as a mercenary gunslinger, Roabards's character is treacherous, unattached, and inaccessible; his minimal dialogue subtly conceals his violent nature. Just as often, however, Robards has a tendency to invest his film performances with a too-broad theatricality. His wildly over-the-top Al Capone in *The St. Valentine's Day Massacre* is a good case in point. The role, for which the slim, WASPish Robards was also physically miscast, was originally slated for Orson Welles.

In interviews, Robards often refers to his role as the loner symbol of America's pioneer and entrepreneurial spirit in Sam Peckinpah's *The Ballad of Cable Hogue* as one of his favorites. The highly anticipated film, following on the heels of Peckinpah's groundbreaking *The Wild Bunch*, was not a commercial success, largely due to Robards's gruff and grating interpretation of the character, who keeps losing our sympathy when he is most trying to gain it. The actor gave a much more human, and sympathetic, performance for Peckinpah as the doomed protagonist of the writer-director's *Noon Wine*, a television adaptation of Katherine Anne Porter's haunting short story.

Robards is at his best on screen when either he, the director, or both keeps his scenery chewing in check. As evidence of this, he won Academy Awards for Best Supporting Actor in 1976 and again in 1977 for two of his most restrained screen performances—as *Washington Post* editor Ben Bradlee in Alan J. Pakula's *All the President's Men* and as the writer Dashiell Hammett in Fred Zinneman's *Julia*. Given the alcoholic Hammett's brooding, self-destructive nature, the latter role gave Robards plenty of opportunities to engage in extravagant histrionics, but the tight rein he held on himself resulted in a Hammett that is both warm and likable. Robards received his last Academy Award nomination (so far) for his whimsical portrayal of billionaire-recluse Howard Hughes in Jonathan Demme's *Melvin and Howard*.

Though now in his seventies, Robards maintains a busy schedule on stage, television, and in the movies—his most notable recent role that of the villain in Jonathan Demme's AIDS drama *Philadelphia*.

—Rob Winning, updated by John McCarty

ROBBINS, Tim

Nationality: American. **Born:** Timothy Francis Robbins in West Covina, California, 16 October 1958; son of the folksinger Gil

Robbins, of The Highwaymen. **Family:** Longtime companion of the actress Susan Sarandon, sons: Jack Henry, Miles Guthrie. **Education:** Attended State University of New York at Plattsburgh; University of California, Los Angeles, graduated 1981; studied French with the actor George Bigot of the Theatre du Soleil. **Career:** 1970—began acting with the Theatre for the New City, an avant-garde theater; 1981—co-founded The Actor's Gang, an avant-garde theater company, later becoming its artistic director; 1986—made short film for TV's *Saturday Night Live*, which was later to serve as the inspiration for *Bob Roberts*; 1988—with Adam Simon, wrote the play *Carnage*, performed at Actor's Gang, Tiffany Theater, California; established his own independent company, HAVOC Productions. **Awards:** Best Actor, Cannes Festival, for *The Player*, 1992. **Agent:** William Morris Agency, 151 El Camino Drive, Beverly Hills, CA 90212, U.S.A.

Films as Actor:

1983   *Quarterback Princess* (Black—for TV) (as Marvin)
1984   *Toy Soldiers* (Fisher) (as Boe); *No Small Affair* (Schatzberg) (as Nelson)
1985   *Fraternity Vacation* (Frawley) (as Larry "Mother" Tucker); *The Sure Thing* (Rob Reiner) (as Gary Cooper); *Malice in Wonderland* (*The Rumor Mill*) (Trikonis—for TV) (as Joseph Cotten)
1986   *Howard the Duck* (Huyck) (as Phil Blumburtt); *Top Gun* (Tony Scott) (as Sam Wills)
1988   *Five Corners* (Bill) (as Harry Fitzgerald); *Bull Durham* (Shelton) (as Ebby Calvin "Nuke" LaLoosh); *Twister* (Almereyda) (as Jeff)
1989   *Tapeheads* (Fishman) (as Josh Tager, + mus); *Erik the Viking* (Terry Jones) (title role); *Miss Firecracker* (Schlamme) (as Delmount Williams)
1990   *Cadillac Man* (Donaldson) (as Larry); *Jacob's Ladder* (*Dante's Inferno*) (Lyne) (as Jacob Singer)
1991   *Jungle Fever* (Spike Lee) (as Jerry)
1992   *The Player* (Altman) (as Griffin Mill)
1993   *Short Cuts* (Altman) (as Gene Shepard)
1994   *The Hudsucker Proxy* (Coen) (as Norville Barnes); *The Shawshank Redemption* (Darabont) (as Andy Dufresne); *Ready to Wear* (*Prêt-a-Porter*) (Altman) (as Joe Flynn); *I.Q.* (Schepisi) (as Ed Walters)

Films as Director:

1992   *Bob Roberts* (+ title role, sc, mus)
1995   *Dead Man Walking* (+ sc)

Publications

By ROBBINS: articles—

Robbins, Tim, "Leaving the Demons at the Office," in *Premiere* (New York), January 1991.
Interview with Claudia Dreifus, in *Progressive* (Madison, Wisconsin), June 1991.
"Tim Robbins," interview with J. Morgan, in *Interview* (New York), August 1992.
Interview with W. Kalbacker, in *Playboy* (Chicago), October 1992.
"Rendezvous with Tim and Julia," interview in *Interview* (New York), January 1995.
Interview in *Playboy* (Chicago), February 1995.

Tim Robbins (left) with Paul Newman in *The Hudsucker Proxy*

On ROBBINS: articles—

Silberg, J., "Close-up: Tim Robbins," in *American Film* (Los Angeles), November 1988.

Carnahan, M., "Tim Robbins," in *Premiere* (New York), March 1989.

Kroll, Jack, "Two Coast Man," in *Newsweek* (New York), 12 November 1990.

Kloman, H., "Tim Robbins Running Hard," in *New York Times*, 12 January 1992.

Maslin, Janet, "Critic's Notebook: At Cannes, Tim Robbins Proves a Double Threat," in *New York Times*, 13 May 1992.

Ansen, David, "The Man of the Moment," in *Newsweek* (New York), 25 May 1992.

Giavarini, L., "Tim Robbins," in *Cahiers du Cinéma* (Paris), June 1992.

Weber, B., "Stumping with the Movies' Favorite Son," in *New York Times*, 30 August 1992.

Kopkind, Andrew, "A Player Ups the Ante," in *Premiere* (New York), September 1992.

"The Stars and Snipes," in *Maclean's* (Toronto), 14 September 1992.

Frankel, M., "The Cutest Serious Person in Showbiz," in *Movieline* (Los Angeles), October 1992.

Zehme, Bill, "Tim Robbins: The Running Man," in *Rolling Stone* (New York), 29 October 1992.

Current Biography 1994, New York, 1994.

* * *

Tim Robbins took two giant steps forward in 1992. Not only did he have the primary role in one of the year's most talked-about films, Robert Altman's *The Player*—a film featuring a who's who of Hollywood royalty in cameo appearances—but he wrote, directed, and starred in *Bob Roberts*, a pungent political satire structured as a mock documentary.

At the time of the release of *The Player* and *Bob Roberts*, Robbins had been appearing on-screen for almost a decade. After playing small roles in several films and even surviving the debacle of *Howard the Duck*, he came to critical attention in *Five Corners*, playing the pacifistic, socially committed Harry Fitzgerald—a character who closely mirrors the actor's offscreen concerns—and *Bull Durham*, cast as Ebby Calvin "Nuke" LaLoosh, fireballing minor league hurler with "a million-dollar arm, but a five-cent head." Robbins effectively adds a devilish but ultimately mindless frat-boy air to *Bull Durham*. But for the most part, he has been adept at playing more mature—and smarmier—characters such as Bob Roberts, and Griffin Mill in *The Player*, a laced-in-acid lampoon of the motion picture industry. Robbins is nothing short of perfection as Mill, the amoral, hotshot head of production at a large movie studio upon whom real life intrudes when he accidentally kills a screenwriter. And in *Short Cuts*, also directed by Robert Altman, he is fine as an egocentric cop, a macho manipulator who brazenly cheats on his wife.

Robbins's most telling film to date has been *Bob Roberts*, if only because of his participation behind as well as in front of the camera. Robbins cast himself as the title character, a folk singer and self-made millionaire-turned right-wing icon who is running for a seat in the U.S. Senate. Candidate Roberts is the Bob Dylan of the New Right. His second record album is titled *The Times Are Changin' Back*. He will parade the American flag as he says the right things to press the right buttons of the electorate. His politics are the politics of self-interest. Forget what is fair. Forget the responsibilities of government leadership. Forget human rights, women's rights, or the homeless. Just think of yourself.

In his speeches, Roberts lambasts the 1960s as "a dark stain on America" not because of the political climate which led to Watergate but because of social protest. If you disagree with Roberts, he is sure to call you a commie or, even worse, unpatriotic. Above all, the film is a deft satire of the media. Television news departments are more interested in regurgitating zippy sound bites and "good shots" of Roberts than in examining his stand on issues. The scenario lampoons the forced, superficial chit-chat in which bubbleheaded anchorpersons indulge after mindlessly reading news from teleprompters. In *Bob Roberts*, both the print and television media report on the latest allegations about candidates, resulting in shifts in the polls. But no journalist dares to investigate these allegations. The only person doing a proper journalist's job is a black radical (Giancarlo Esposito), who has discovered that Broken Dove, Roberts's organization, has been connected with failed savings and loans, drug smuggling, and more. Indeed, one of the messages in *Bob Roberts*, telegraphed by Robbins, is simple and clear: Think before you vote. The film—which came to movie houses during a presidential election year—is a cautionary tale about the need for substance and candor in American politics, and political campaigns. It reflects the progressive political concerns of Robbins and his longtime companion, Susan Sarandon (who appears in the film in a cameo role).

Robbins is not incapable of playing sympathetic characters. He is especially good in *Jacob's Ladder*, acting the role of a psychologically scarred Vietnam veteran; *I.Q.*, as a garage mechanic who falls in love with the niece of Albert Einstein; and *The Shawshank Redemption*, cast as a soft-spoken banker-accountant locked up in jail for decades after being falsely convicted of murdering his wife and her lover. He also can play the wide-eyed innocent. In *The Hudsucker Proxy*, a wicked satire of corporate greed and bureaucracy, he is bright-eyed Norville Barnes—the name of a character right out of a Preston Sturges satire. Norville, fresh out of the Muncie College of Business Administration, comes to New York to work in the mailroom of a fabulously successful conglomerate and promptly becomes a pawn in a scheme concocted by the company founder-and-president's venal right-hand man.

Once Robbins's stature in the industry was such that he could hand-pick his roles, his most interesting parts have been in films with a social conscience at their core. These films either have depicted individuals wronged by a viciously unfair bureaucracy (*The Shawshank Redemption*), or individuals who will use and abuse power within political, social or economic systems that have gone sour (*The Player*, *Bob Roberts*, *The Hudsucker Proxy*).

—Rob Edelman

ROBERTS, Julia

Nationality: American. **Born:** Smyrna, Georgia, 28 October 1967; sister of the actor Eric Roberts. **Family:** Married Lyle Lovett, 1993 (divorced 1995). **Career:** 1985—moved to New York; 1988—film debut with brother Eric in *Blood Red*; 1990—voted Performer of the Year by American cinema owners. **Agent:** Elaine Goldsmith, ICM, 8942 Wilshire Boulevard, Beverly Hills, CA 90211, U.S.A.

Films as Actress:

1988   *Blood Red* (Masterson—produced in 1986) (as Maria Collogero); *Satisfaction* (*Girls of Summer*) (Freeman) (as Daryle Shane); *Baja Oklahoma* (Roth—for TV); *Mystic Pizza* (Petrie) (as Daisy Arujo)
1989   *Steel Magnolias* (Ross) (as Shelby Eatenton Latcherie)
1990   *Pretty Woman* (Garry Marshall) (as Vivian Ward); *Flatliners* (Schumacher) (as Rachel Mannus)
1991   *Dying Young* (Schumacher) (as Hillary O'Neil); *Hook* (Spielberg) (as Tinkerbell); *Sleeping with the Enemy* (Ruben) (as Sara Waters/Laura Burney)
1992   *The Player* (Altman) (cameo)
1993   *The Pelican Brief* (Pakula) (as Darby Shaw)
1994   *I Love Trouble* (Shyer) (as Sabrina Peterson); *Ready to Wear* (*Prêt-à-Porter*) (Altman) (as Anne Eisenhower)
1995   *Something to Talk About* (Hallstrom) (as Grace)
1996   *Mary Reilly* (Frears) (title role); *Michael Collins* (Neil Jordan)

Publications

By ROBERTS: articles—

Interview with Catherine Seipp, in *Harper's Bazaar* (New York), September 1989.
Interview with Robert Palmer, in *Time Out* (London), 10 April 1991.
Interview with Elaine Dutka, in *Empire* (London), October 1991.
Interview in *Playboy* (Chicago), November 1991.
"Julia Makes Trouble," interview with David Rensin, in *Rolling Stone* (New York), 14 July 1994.
"Rendezvous with Tim and Julia," interview in *Interview* (New York), January 1995.

On ROBERTS: articles—

Palmer, Robert, "Suddenly, Julia," in *American Film* (New York), July 1990.
Thomas, Philip, in *Empire* (London), December 1990.
Current Biography 1991, New York, 1991.
Tighe, Michael, "Travels with Julia," in *Premiere* (New York), June 1991.
Connelly, Christopher, "Nobody's Fool," in *Premiere* (New York), December 1993.
Harris, Mark, "Julia Roberts," in *Entertainment Weekly* (New York), 24 June 1994.
Gordinier, Jeff, "The Next Julia Roberts," in *Entertainment Weekly* (New York), 11 August 1995.
McInerney, Jay, cover story in *Harper's Bazaar* (New York), September 1995.

*   *   *

A meteoric rise to fame is the classic Hollywood dream and one to which many young and talented actors still aspire. Despite the fact that the American film industry no longer has the studio star system of Dream Factory days, the phenomenal success of a star such as Julia Roberts is testimony to the enduring importance of film stardom for audiences and as an organizing factor for the film industry economy. It is, however, an oversimplification to describe Roberts's stardom as an overnight sensation, and far too early for comparisons with major talents such as Meryl Streep, as her performances have been rather uneven, her fame peaking and tumbling like a bumpy roller-coaster ride.

Julia Roberts in *Flatliners*

Making her film debut with her brother Eric in *Blood Red*, Julia Roberts appeared in three more films before getting a substantial role among the all-star cast in *Steel Magnolias*. Not dimmed by the acting of film veterans such as Shirley MacLaine and Sally Field and no less striking in beauty than Daryl Hannah, Roberts delivers a powerful performance as a young and courageous Southern belle (Shelby) who strives for a wholesome life by becoming a mother despite her unfit physical conditions. With her fiery red hair and what has now become a signature broad smile, Shelby represents a vitality that shines its brightest in the face of life's most fatal odds.

It was undoubtedly with the role as a happy-go-lucky whore in *Pretty Woman* that Julia Roberts captured the hearts of critics and public alike and was suddenly exposed to public attention on a grand scale. The story is no more than a modern version of Cinderella combined with a banal, "triumph of love over materialism," message. Its phenomenal success, on another level, indicates a transition from the 80s to 90s. Beyond the crude violence and idiotic patriotism in the *First Blood* series, beyond the paranoia and panic in the stiflingly conservative Reagan era as seen in *The Fly* and *Terminator*, and beyond the childish American narcissism masked as a comic-strip hero in the *Indiana Jones* trilogy, *Pretty Woman* moves towards a reconciliation with late capitalist exploitation and a deteriorating economy by way of recycling old values in a flashy and soft-core disguise. Julia Roberts stands for that transition, whose offscreen image has been presented as "freshness" and "intoxicating innocence"—submissive and unchallenging values for the 90s.

One of her next films, *Sleeping with the Enemy*, though another commercial success, taking $70 million within its first six weeks, was greeted by only mediocre reviews by the critics. Another moral tale celebrating traditional values and highlighting Roberts's image of youthful and wholesome vitality combined with vulnerability and sexual allure, this film secured Roberts's position as one of the leading actresses of the 90s, a position which she will have to struggle to maintain.

With a rumored $10 million per movie in 1991, Roberts really seemed to look like the girl who had it all—looks, talent, success, and money. Such an early success, however, also seems to warrant the enormous pressure of coming to fame too quickly and too young. "As we begin talking, it's abundantly clear that Julia Roberts distrusts journalists," wrote Robert Palmer in 1990. This inherent tension with media would continue to worsen when her last-minute cancellation of the wedding to actor Kiefer Sutherland in 1991 was widely exploited by reporters all over the world. Her sudden marriage and subsequent divorce with singer Lyle Lovett proved to be equally sensational for the press. Very soon, the once "ideal woman of the 90s" would be described as a "nail-biting, chain-smoking," "edgy and tense," and "hell-to-work-with" Julia Roberts. And soon followed reports of a total collapse.

Roberts is certainly not the first Hollywood star to find the pressure of fame too much to cope with. Comparisons were quickly made with the likes of Monroe and Taylor—sometimes with sympathy and sometimes with an unkind relish. Roberts and the ideals she has stood for seemed, if only temporarily, to have gone off the rails, bringing the fantasy of womanhood as enduring and magical innocence back down to earth with a bang. A series of attempts to live up to her early fame proved to be mostly disappointing. The 1993 *The Pelican Brief* failed to create any chill in the spine that a dark political thriller was expected to. *I Love Trouble* in 1994 was disastrous largely because of the mismatch of Roberts with an aged and far too grouchy Nick Nolte. While *Something to Talk About* strikes no sparks between Roberts and Dennis Quaid in a failed romantic comedy, *Mary Reilly* appears to be too dark, John Malkovich too gripping and grim, and Roberts too pale and vulnerable to be appealing to the masses. It is perhaps unfair to keep looking for the same pretty woman film after film—possibly the same kind of trap that Shirley Temple was unable to escape from.

—Margaret O'Connor, updated by Guo-Juin Hong

ROBERTS, Rachel

Nationality: British. **Born:** Llanelli, Wales, 20 September 1927. **Education:** Attended the University of Wales, B.A.; Royal Academy of Dramatic Arts, London. **Family:** Married 1) the actor Alan Dobie, 1955 (divorced 1961); 2) the actor Rex Harrison, 1962 (divorced 1971). **Career:** On stage from 1951; 1952—film debut in *Valley of Song*; 1953—London stage debut in *The Buccaneer*; 1956-57—member of the Bristol Old Vic company; 1971—in stage play *Alpha Beta* in London, and in film version, 1976; 1976-78—in TV series *The Tony Randall Show*; and in mini-series *A Man Called Intrepid*, 1979. **Awards:** Best British Actress, British Academy, for *Saturday Night and Sunday Morning*, 1960; Best British Actress, British Academy, for *This Sporting Life*, 1963; Best Supporting Actress, British Academy, for *Yanks*, 1979. **Died:** Suicide in Los Angeles, 26 November 1980.

Films as Actress:

1952   *Valley of Song (Men Are Children Twice)* (Gunn) (as Bessie Lewis)
1953   *The Limping Man* (de la Tour and Endfield) (as barmaid)
1954   *The Weak and the Wicked* (Lee Thompson) (as Pat); *The Crowded Day* (Guillermin) (as Maggie)
1957   *The Good Companions* (Lee Thompson) (as Elsie/Effie Longstaffe)
1960   ***Saturday Night and Sunday Morning*** (Reisz) (as Brenda)
1962   *Girl on Approval* (Frend) (as Anne Howland)
1963   *This Sporting Life* (Anderson) (as Mrs. Hammond)
1968   *A Flea in Her Ear* (Charon) (as Suzanne)
1969   *Destiny of a Spy (The Gaunt Woman)* (Sagal—for TV)
1970   *The Reckoning* (Gold) (as Joyce Eglington)
1971   *Doctors' Wives* (Schaefer) (as Della Randolph); *The Wild Rovers* (Edwards) (as Maybell)
1973   *O Lucky Man!* (Anderson) (three roles); *Baffled!* (Leacock—for TV); *The Belstone Fox (Free Spirit)* (Hill) (as Cathie)
1974   *Murder on the Orient Express* (Lumet) (as Hildegarde Schmidt); *Great Expectations* (Hardy—for TV) (as Mrs. Gargery)
1976   *Picnic at Hanging Rock* (Weir) (as Mrs. Appleyard); *Alpha Beta* (Page) (as Nora Elliot)
1977   *A Circle of Children* (Taylor—for TV)

1978   *Foul Play* (Higgins) (as Gerda)
1979   *When a Stranger Calls* (Walton) (as Dr. Monk); *Yanks* (Schlesinger) (as Mrs. Moreton)
1980   *The Hostage Tower* (Guzman—for TV)
1981   *Charlie Chan and the Curse of the Dragon Queen* (Donner) (as Mrs. Dangers)
1982   *The Wall* (Markowitz—for TV)

Publications

By ROBERTS: book—

No Bells on Sundays: The Rachel Roberts Journals, edited by Alexander Walker, London, 1984.

On ROBERTS: articles—

Klemesrud, J., "How to Vex the Ex. Mrs. Rex," in *New York Times Biographical Edition*, December 1973.
The Annual Obituary 1980, New York, 1981.

*   *   *

Rachel Roberts was a shy asthmatic child who emerged from her repressive home in the Welsh Valleys, "where the stage was something good girls kept away from," to become one of Britain's most talented actresses during the 1960s. Her father was a Welsh Baptist minister and she had to fight her parents' disapproval to go to grammar school, university and then onto the Royal Academy of Dramatic Arts where she won one of the top student prizes. She was first a stage actress and when she was 25 made her first film, *Valley of Song*, before going on to make *The Good Companions* and then *Our Man in Havana* with Alec Guinness, Ralph Richardson, and Noël Coward. She had a warm and earthy talent and specialized in roles that had a doomed or tragic edge.

Her three most remarkable parts were in *This Sporting Life*, *Saturday Night and Sunday Morning*, and *O Lucky Man!*; she was well suited to films that were in the British tradition of gritty social realism. Her difficult marriage to Rex Harrison brought about a hiatus in her career though she did appear in *Murder on the Orient Express*, in Peter Weir's *Picnic at Hanging Rock*, and more successfully, in John Schlesinger's *Yanks* where she won a British Academy Award for Best Supporting Actress.

She once said, "Until I get another skin, I am distinctly unhappy with the one I was born with." This lack of ease with herself propelled into the world of acting and for many people her most significant and unforgettable role was as the repressed and self-punishing North Country widow Mrs. Hammond, Richard Harris's landlady who dies so movingly with blood on her lips and a spider on the wall in *This Sporting Life*. The depth and intensity she brought to her acting unfortunately found its way into her life with more disastrous and destructive consequences. After the failure of her marriage to Rex Harrison and her expulsion from the jet-set world of champagne and furs, her career took a downturn, compounded by her depression and an alchohol problem which made her an unpredictable guest on talk shows and prevented her from being offered the parts she should have had. It was a sad ending to her film career and one she found impossible to live with, and in 1980 she took an overdose and was found dead at her home in California—a long way from Llanelli, Wales, where she was born. It was a journey marked by both personal loss and great cinematic verve.

—Sylvia Paskin

Rachel Roberts in *Saturday Night and Sunday Morning*

ROBERTSON, Cliff

Nationality: American. **Born:** Clifford Parker Robertson in La Jolla, California, 9 September 1925. **Education:** Attended La Jolla High School, graduated 1941; Antioch College, Yellow Springs, Ohio, one year; studied acting at Actors Studio, New York. **Family:** Married 1) Cynthia Stone, 1957 (divorced 1959), daughter: Stephanie; 2) the actress Dina Merrill, 1966 (divorced 1989), daughter: Heather. **Career:** 1941—seaman on the tramp steamer *Admiral Cole*; worked in merchant marine during World War II; 1943—film debut in *We've Never Been Licked*; 1947—on tour with the play *Three Men on a Horse*; 1948-50—on national tour with the play *Mister Roberts*; 1953—New York debut in *Late Love*; 1954—regular actor on TV series *Robert Montgomery Presents*; 1955—contract with Columbia; 1972—directed the film *J. W. Coop*; many television roles, including the mini-series *Washington: Behind Closed Doors*, 1977; late 1970s—sued Columbia executive David Begelman for illegal checking practices; 1983-84—in TV series *Falcon Crest*; 1995—in TV mini-series *Dazzle*. **Awards:** Best Actor Academy Award, for *Charly*, 1968.

Films as Actor:

1943   *We've Never Been Licked* (*Fighting Command*) (Rawlins) (as Adams); *Corvette K-225* (Rosson)
1955   *Picnic* (Logan) (as Alan)
1956   *Autumn Leaves* (Aldrich) (as Burt Hanson)
1957   *The Girl Most Likely* (Leisen) (as Pete)
1958   *The Naked and the Dead* (Walsh) (as Hearn)
1959   *Gidget* (Wendkos) (as Kahoona); *Battle of the Coral Sea* (Wendkos) (as Lt. Cmdr. Jeff Conway)
1960   *As the Sea Rages* (Haechler) (as Clements)
1961   *All in a Night's Work* (Anthony) (as Warren Kingsley Jr.); **Underworld, U.S.A.** (Fuller) (as Tolly Devlin); *The Big Show* (Clark) (as Josef Everard)
1962   *The Interns* (Swift) (as Dr. John Paul Otis)
1963   *My Six Loves* (Champion) (as the Rev. Jim Larkin); *PT 109* (Martinson) (as John F. Kennedy); *Sunday in New York* (Tewksbury) (as Adam Tyler)
1964   *The Best Man* (Schaffner) (as Joe Cantwell); *633 Squadron* (Grauman) (as Wing Cmdr. Roy Grant)
1965   *Masquerade* (Dearden) (as David Frazer); *Up from the Beach* (Parrish) (as Sgt. Edward Baxter); *Love Has Many Faces* (Singer) (as Pete Jordan)
1967   *The Honey Pot* (Mankiewicz) (as William McFly)
1968   *The Devil's Brigade* (McLaglen) (as Maj. Alan Crown); *Charly* (Nelson) (title role); *The Sunshine Patriots* (Sargent—for TV)
1970   *Too Late the Hero* (Aldrich) (as Lt. Lawson)
1971   *The Great Northfield Minnesota Raid* (Kaufman) (as Cole Younger)
1973   *The Man without a Country* (Delbert Mann—for TV) (as Philip Nolan); *Ace Eli and Rodger of the Skies* (Sampson) (as Eli)
1974   *Man on a Swing* (Perry) (as Lee Tucker); *A Tree Grows in Brooklyn* (Hardy—for TV)
1975   *Out of Season* (Bridges) (as Joe); *Three Days of the Condor* (Pollack) (as Higgins); *My Father's House* (Segal—for TV)
1976   *Return to Earth* (Taylor—for TV) (as Buzz Aldrin); *Obsession* (De Palma) (as Michael Courtland); *Midway* (Smight) (as Cmdr. Carl Jessop); *Shoot* (Hart) (as Maj. Rex Jeanette)
1977   *Fraternity Row* (Tobin) (as narrator)
1978   *Overboard* (Newland—for TV); *Dominique* (Anderson) (as David Ballard)
1982   *Two of a Kind* (Roger Young—for TV) (as Frank Minor)

1983   *Class* (Carlino) (as Burroughs); *Brainstorm* (Trumbull) (as Alex Terson); *Star 80* (Fosse) (as Hugh Hefner)
1985   *Shaker Run* (Morrison); *The Key to Rebecca* (Hemmings—for TV)
1986   *Dreams of Gold: The Mel Fisher Story* (Goldstone—for TV)
1987   *Malone* (Cokliss) (as Charles Delaney); *Ford: The Man and the Machine* (Eastman—for TV) (title role)
1990   *Dead Reckoning* (Robert Lewis—for TV) (as Dr. Daniel Barnard)
1991   *Wild Hearts Can't Be Broken* (Miner) (as Dr. Carver)
1992   *Wind* (Ballard) (as Morgan Weld)
1994   *Renaissance Man* (Penny Marshall) (as Col. James)
1995   *Pakten* (Risan)
1996   *Escape from L.A.* (John Carpenter)

Films as Director:

1971   *J. W. Coop* (+ title role)
1979   *The Pilot* (+ co-sc, ro)

Publications

On ROBERTSON: book—

McClintick, David, *Indecent Exposure: A True Story of Hollywood and Wall Street*, New York, 1982.

On ROBERTSON: articles—

Current Biography 1969, New York, 1969.
Hart, Henry, "Cliff Robertson," in *Films in Review* (New York), March 1969.
"Cliff Robertson and Hollywoodgate," in *Films in Review* (New York), August-September 1978.
Green, Michelle, "Cliff Robertson: Hollywood's Mr. Clean Shot Down David Begelman; Now the Actor Has Pulled His Career Out of a Nosedive," in *People Weekly* (New York), 5 December 1983.

*   *   *

A sturdy, interesting leading man and moderately versatile character actor/villain, Cliff Robertson played his most dramatic scenes thus far offscreen when he blew the whistle on Columbia president David Begelman for embezzlement. Although this led to his three-year blacklisting by the movie studios, Robertson weathered that particular storm, and is currently embarked on what is virtually a second movie career.

Initially, Joshua Logan, who had directed Robertson in the stage version of his *Mister Roberts*, provided him with his feature movie debut role in the film version of William Inge's play, *Picnic*; Robertson plays the Kansan who loses Kim Novak to drifter William Holden. After appearing in a number of films of varying quality, Robertson attracted considerable attention when he was chosen by President John F. Kennedy to portray him in Leslie Martinson's straightforward *PT 109*.

The group of films that followed were mostly routine, although his ruthless presidential candidate in Gore Vidal's political melodrama, *The Best Man*, is both effective and memorable. Ralph Nelson's *Charly*, however, in which Robertson portrays a retarded man whom a scientific experiment transforms to a genius and back again, gained him the Academy Award as Best Actor. Robertson had played the role on television in 1961 and purchased the rights to the material (Daniel Keyes's novel *Flowers for Algernon*), ensuring his appearance in the film version. He also directed, scripted, produced and starred in the well-received 1972 film *J. W. Coop*, a character study of a dumb but cocky ex-convict rodeo cowboy. Despite this success, Robertson has only directed one other film, *The Pilot*, in which he also starred.

After a number of other films in the early 1970s, including supporting performances in two solid box-office hits, *Midway* and *Three Days of the Condor*, Robertson had few jobs for more than three years during his blacklisting. He resumed his career in the 1980s, however, with supporting roles in Douglas Trumbull's *Brainstorm* and Bob Fosse's *Star 80* (portraying *Playboy* founder Hugh Hefner), among other film and television assignments. Robertson now seems well on his way back toward starring roles which call for quiet determination, evident authority, and understated intensity.

—Bill Wine, updated by Frank Uhle

ROBESON, Paul

Nationality: American. **Born:** Paul Leroy Robeson in Princeton, New Jersey, 9 April 1898. **Education:** Attended Rutgers University, New Brunswick, New Jersey (All-American football player), B.A., 1919 (Phi Beta Kappa); Columbia University Law School, New York,

graduated 1923; admitted to the New York Bar, and joined New York law firm, 1923. **Family:** Married Eslanda Cardozo Goode, 1921 (died 1965), son: Paul. **Career:** Professional football player while attending law school; 1921—professional debut on Broadway in *Taboo*; 1922—English debut in the same play, retitled *Voodoo*, in Blackpool opposite Mrs. Patrick Campbell; 1924—on stage in New York in *The Emperor Jones* and *All God's Chillun Got Wings*; 1925—film debut in *Body and Soul*; first professional singing tour; 1930—in stage play *Othello*: later appeared in the play on Broadway and on tour, 1940; 1950-58—after appearing before the House Un-American Activities Committee, passport revoked; 1958—farewell concert, Carnegie Hall, New York; in poor health from 1959 until his death. **Awards:** Stalin Peace Prize, 1952 (received 1958); admitted to Black Filmmakers Hall of Fame, 1974; inducted into College Football Hall of Fame, 1995. **Died:** In Philadelphia, 23 January 1976.

Films as Actor:

1925 *Body and Soul* (Micheaux); *Borderline* (MacPherson)
1933 *The Emperor Jones* (Dudley Murphy) (as Brutus Jones)

Paul Robeson with Dilys Thomas in *The Proud Valley*

1935   *Sanders of the River* (*Bosambo*) (Z. Korda) (as Bosambo)
1936   *Song of Freedom* (Wills) (as John Zinga); *Show Boat* (Whale)
       (as Joe)
1937   *King Solomon's Mines* (Stevenson) (as Umbopa); *Jericho* (*Dark
       Sands*) (Freeland) (as Jericho Jackson); *Big Fella* (Wills) (as
       Joe)
1940   *The Proud Valley* (Tennyson) (as David Goliath)
1942   *Native Land* (Hurwitz and Strand—doc) (as narrator); *Tales of
       Manhattan* (Duvivier) (as Luke)
1954   *Das Lied der Ströme* (*Song of the Rivers*) (Ivens—doc) (sing-
       ing voice only)

Publications

By ROBESON: books—

Here I Stand, New York, 1958.
Paul Robeson, Tributes, Selected Writings, edited by Roberta Yancy
Dent, New York, 1976.
Paul Robeson Speaks: Writings, Speeches, Interviews, 1918-1974,
edited by Philip Fowler, Larchmont, New York, 1978.

By ROBESON: article—

"The Culture of the Negro," in *Spectator*, 15 June 1934.

On ROBESON: books—

Robeson, Eslanda Goode, *Paul Robeson, Negro*, New York, 1930.
Graham, Shirley, *Paul Robeson, Citizen of the World*, New York, 1946.
Robeson, Eslanda Goode, *Paul Robeson Goes to Washington*, Salford,
Lancashire, 1956.
Seton, Marie, *Paul Robeson*, London, 1958.
Salk, Erwin, *Paul Robeson: The Great Forerunner*, New York, 1965.
Hoyt, Edwin, *Paul Robeson: The American Othello*, Cleveland, 1967.
Brown, Lloyd, *Lift Every Voice for Paul Robeson*, New York, 1971.
Hamilton, Virginia, *Paul Robeson: The Life and Times of a Free Black
Man*, New York, 1974.
Wright, Charles, *Labor's Forgotten Champion*, Detroit, 1975.
Brown, Lloyd, *Paul Robeson Rediscovered*, New York, 1976.
Gilliam, Dorothy, *Paul Robeson, All-American*, Washington, D.C.,
1976.
Nazel, Joseph, *Paul Robeson: Biography of a Proud Man*, Los Ange-
les, 1980.
Robeson, Susan, *The Whole World in His Hands: A Pictorial Portrait of
Paul Robeson*, Secaucus, New Jersey, 1981.
Dyer, Richard, *Heavenly Bodies: Film Stars and Society*, London,
1987.
Duberman, Martin Bauml, *Paul Robeson*, New York, 1989.
Larsen, Rebecca, *Paul Robeson, Hero before His Time*, New York, 1989.
McKissack, Pat, *Paul Robeson: A Voice to Remember*, Hillside, New
Jersey, 1992.
Holmes, Burnham, *Paul Robeson: A Voice of Struggle*, Austin, Texas,
1995.

On ROBESON: articles—

Hutchens, John K., "Paul Robeson," in *Theatre Arts* (New York), Oc-
tober 1944.
DuBois, W. E. B., "Paul Robeson, Right," in *Negro Digest*, March 1950.
Miers, Earl Schenk, "Paul Robeson: Made by America," in *Negro
Digest*, October 1950.
Rowan, Carl T., "Has Paul Robeson Betrayed the Negro?," in *Ebony*
(Chicago), October 1957.

Pittman, John, "Mount Paul," in *New World Review*, February 1962.
Fishman, George, "Paul Robeson's Student Days and the Fight against
Racism at Rutgers," in *Freedomways*, Summer 1969.
Cripps, Thomas, "Paul Robeson and Black Identity in American Mov-
ies," in *Massachusetts Review*, Summer 1970.
Weaver, Harold D., "Paul Robeson: Beleaguered Leader," in *Black
Scholar*, December 1973-January 1974.
Current Biography 1976, New York, 1976.
Obituary in *New York Times*, 24 January 1976.
Stuckey, Sterling, "'I Want to Be African': Paul Robeson and the End
of Nationalist Theory and Practice," in *Massachusetts Review*, Spring
1976.
Ward, Geoffrey C., "Robeson's Choice," in *American Heritage*, April
1989.
Sorel, Nancy Caldwell, "Paul Robeson and Peggy Ashcroft," in *Atlan-
tic* (New York), May 1992.

*   *   *

Paul Robeson's life story, of which his film career was a small
and sadly underdeveloped component, is one of the great inspira-
tions and tragedies of modern American history. An actor and
singer of great presence and power, Robeson tried, often in vain, to
find dignified roles for a black man in both American and British
studios. With the exceptions of the African-American pioneer
director Oscar Micheaux's *Body and Soul*, the avant-garde *Borderline*, and the British *Big Fella* he was cast as either a subhuman or
a super-leader with whom no one could identify. Nevertheless,
Robeson was America's Twentieth-Century Renaissance man: All-
American athlete at Rutgers, Columbia law school graduate, political activist, bass-baritone, public intellectual, linguist, and actor.
Born in 1898, he became famous in the mid-1920s for his roles in
two Eugene O'Neill plays, *All God's Chillun Got Wings* and *The
Emperor Jones*. He repeated the latter role in the 1933 indepen-
dently produced film version, and the play itself anticipates
Robeson's film career in several ways.

Like Robeson himself, Brutus Jones embarks on a journey of
self-discovery. This southern black laborer becomes first a criminal
and then the despot of a Caribbean Island. The transformation
repeats itself through Robeson's film career: severing ties with one
world, he must adopt a new persona in another. Two years after
making *The Emperor Jones*, in the Korda-produced *Sanders of the
River*, Robeson played a petty thief who has left Liberia and, by
kowtowing to the British imperialists, becomes an African chief.
In *Song of Freedom* he portrays an English dockworker who, after
becoming a famous singer, retraces his ancestry in an African village. Another transformation occurs in *King Solomon's Mines*, in
which Robeson's Umbopa, after traveling with white fortune-hunt-
ers to his native land, reveals himself as the rightful chief. He plays
the mythical David Goliath in Pen Tennyson's *The Proud Valley*.
After arriving in a Welsh coal-mining town as a vagabond who has
jumped his American ship, David becomes the pride of the men's
chorus and a miner who martyrs himself to save the less noble
white miners. (Although Robeson's characters obviously represent
moral choices, more recent critics have also openly acknowledged
their frequent eroticism.)

The Emperor Jones contains gratuitous songs for Robeson which
were not in the stage productions, again setting a precedent. In *Show
Boat*, recreating his stage role as Joe, he sings "Ol' Man River" (which
he would later reinvent in concert as a protest song) in a stunning
expressionistic sequence, and later performs a comic duet with Hattie
McDaniel written especially for the film once Robeson was cast. His
songs in *Sanders of the River* ("On to Battle") and *King Solomon's
Mines* ("Song of the Mountains") contain embarrassingly childish
lyrics, and in both *Song of Freedom* and *The Proud Valley* Robeson's

obtrusive lyrics can be best described as anglicized Socialist Realism. Robeson's singing is perhaps best experienced through his many recordings of spirituals and international folk songs, which often suggest the legendary power of his live concerts.

Robeson's life was as superhuman as David Goliath's in *The Proud Valley*: the Spanish Civil War stopped for a day for his concert; his *Othello* was the longest-running Shakespearean play in American theatrical history; he was as outspokenly pro-African liberation as he was anti-imperialist. He championed communism even when government pressure destroyed his health and career. That he accomplished so much in so many public arenas is still awe-inspiring, while his life continues to inspire debate and discussion; that the American and British film industries, not to mention the U.S. government, so consistently devalued and hampered his talents remains a major shame.

—Howard Feinstein, updated by Corey K. Creekmur

ROBINSON, Bill ("Bojangles")

Nationality: American. **Born:** Luther Robinson in Richmond, Virginia, 26 May 1878. **Education:** Formal education ended at age six. **Family:** Married Fannie S. Clay. **Career:** Danced as a child in beer gardens, and worked in racing stables; appeared as a dancer in *The South before the War*, but then worked as a waiter for 10 years; 1906—beginning of successful stage and nightclub dancing career: on Broadway in *Blackbirds of 1927* and *Brown Buddies* in the 1920s; 1930—film debut in *Dixiana*; 1935—role in *The Little Colonel*, first of several films with Shirley Temple; 1939—on stage in *The Hot Mikado*. **Died:** November 1949.

Films as Actor:

1930   *Dixiana* (Reed)
1935   *The Little Colonel* (Butler); *Hooray for Love* (Walter Lang) (as Bill); *In Old Kentucky* (Marshall); *The Big Broadcast of 1936* (Taurog); *The Littlest Rebel* (Butler)
1937   *One Mile from Heaven* (Dwan) (as Officer Joe)
1938   *Rebecca of Sunnybrook Farm* (Dwan); *The Road Demon* (Brower); *Harlem in Heaven* (J. and D. Goldberg—short); *Just around the Corner* (Cummings); *Up the River* (Werker) (as Memphis Bill)
1943   *Stormy Weather* (Stone)

Film as Choreographer:

1936   *Dimples* (Seiter)

Bill "Bojangles" Robinson

Publications

On ROBINSON: books—

Leab, Daniel, *From Sambo to Superspade: The Black Experience in Motion Pictures*, Boston, 1975.
Sampson, Henry, *Blacks in Black and White: A Source Book on Black Films*, Metuchen, New Jersey, 1977.
Haskins, Jim, and N. R. Mitgang, *Mr. Bojangles: The Biography of Bill Robinson*, New York, 1988.

On ROBINSON: articles—

Current Biography 1941, New York, 1941.
Obituary in *New York Times*, 26 November 1949.

*   *   *

Although he was in his fifties when he appeared in his first film, Bill Robinson still managed to demonstrate the tapping ability that had previously made him the exemplar of the black hoofer and a legend on the stage. Particularly through the four films he did with Shirley Temple (*The Little Colonel, The Littlest Rebel, Just around the Corner*, and *Rebecca of Sunnybrook Farm*), he helped to create an audience for an important form of popular dance. A somewhat limited performer, Robinson nevertheless became the film representative of the many black dancers of the 1920s and 1930s who strongly influenced—and often helped create—contemporary vernacular dance.

Robinson coached Shirley Temple for their routines together, and in all the films dance becomes the vehicle to accomplish their goals (e.g., overcoming the Great Depression in *Just around the Corner*). His most famous number, the so-called Stair Dance, becomes a showpiece of *The Little Colonel* when he uses it to persuade Shirley to go upstairs to bed. In the process he teaches her the dance while singing and humming his own accompaniment. Robinson used his dance style to inform his characters, as an expression of their control of a situation. Never flamboyant, Robinson emphasized the legs and feet (with little upper-body movement) in several basic tap steps that he turned into intricate combinations. (The Stair Dance, for example, uses the stair and riser to provide the percussive sound of a toe tap followed by a heel tap, also using a soft-shoe shuffle.) His restricted range avoided "flash" acts—and even many standard steps—but, as Marshall and Jean Stearns wrote in *Jazz Dance*, "Robinson's career is proof that a tap dancer with technique and personality can make relatively simple tap dancing an exciting art."

Stormy Weather, Robinson's last film, was an all-black revue with a slight story line fictionally paralleling Robinson's own life. Someone in the film refers to him as having "educated feet," and, although he has only one big number (in which he beats out the rhythm while jumping on drums), he plays a character who cannot keep his feet from moving whenever he hears a musical cue. As in many of his films, the camerawork of *Stormy Weather* alternated between full-figured medium long shots, showing his controlled elegance, and close-ups accentuating the intricacy of his footwork. His age may have contributed to his limitations in *Stormy Weather*, but the film still shows a hoofer performing with style and joie de vivre.

Bill Robinson's movie roles seem to serve two functions. His popularity among white audiences made it possible for other black dancers to follow him in films at a time when racial restrictions were strong in Hollywood. In addition, although there were many other—and maybe superior—black hoofers in vaudeville and in black musicals, all of whom strongly affected the popular dance associated with movie musicals of the 1930s, Robinson alone be-

came the direct evidence of their influence. Whatever his abilities—and they were considerable—his films are a legacy of the development of tap dance in America.

—Jerome Delamater

ROBINSON, Edward G.

Nationality: American. **Born:** Emanuel Goldenberg in Bucharest, Romania, 12 December 1893; acquired U.S. citizenship papers on emigrating with his parents at age 10. **Education:** Attended Townsend Harris Hall High School, New York; Columbia University, New York; American Academy of Dramatic Arts, New York, 1912-13. **Family:** Married 1) Gladys Lloyd, 1927 (divorced 1956), son: Emanuel; 2) Jane Adler, 1958. **Career:** 1913—member of Binghamton Stock Company, New York; 1915—Broadway debut in *Under Fire*; served in the U.S. Navy during World War I; 1923—film debut in *The Bright Shawl*; 1927—leading role in stage play *The Racket* (also co-wrote it); 1931—contract with Warner Brothers; 1937-40—in radio series *Big Town* with Claire Trevor; 1946—formed Film Guild Corporation production company; 1956—on Broadway in *Middle of the Night*. **Awards:** Best Actor, Cannes Festival, for *House of Strangers*, 1949; Special Academy Award, 1972 (awarded posthumously). **Died:** 26 January 1973.

Films as Actor:

1923 *The Bright Shawl* (Robertson) (as Domingo Escobar)
1929 *The Hole in the Wall* (Flory) (as the Fox); *Night Ride* (Robertson) (as Tony Garotta)
1930 *A Lady to Love* (Seastrom) (as Tony); *Outside the Law* (Browning) (as Cobra Collins); *East Is West* (Bell) (as Charlie Young); *Thunder in the City* (Gering) (as Dan Armstrong); *The Widow from Chicago* (Cline) (as Dominio)
1931 *Little Caesar* (LeRoy) (as Rico Bandello); *Smart Money* (Green) (as Nick "The Barber" Venizelos); *Five Star Final* (LeRoy) (as Joseph Randall)
1932 *The Hatchet Man* (Wellman) (as Wong Low Get); *Two Seconds* (LeRoy) (as John Allen); *Tiger Shark* (Hawks) (as Mike Mascarena); *Silver Dollar* (Green) (as Yates Martin)
1933 *The Little Giant* (Del Ruth) (as James Francis Ahearn); *I Loved a Woman* (Green) (as John Hayden)
1934 *Dark Hazard* (Green) (as Jim "Buck" Turner); *The Man with Two Faces* (Mayo) (as Damon Wells)
1935 *The Whole Town's Talking* (Ford) (as Arthur Ferguson Jones); *Barbary Coast* (Hawks) (as Louis Chamacis)
1936 *Bullets or Ballots* (Keighley) (as Johnny Blake)
1937 *Kid Galahad* (Curtiz) (as Nick Donati); *The Last Gangster* (Ludwig) (as Joe Krozac)
1938 *A Slight Case of Murder* (Bacon) (as Remy Marco); *The Amazing Dr. Clitterhouse* (Litvac) (title role); *I Am the Law* (Hall) (as John Lindsay)
1939 *Confessions of a Nazi Spy* (Litvak) (as Ed Renard); *Blackmail* (Potter) (as John Ingram)
1940 *Dr. Ehrlich's Magic Bullet* (Dieterle) (title role); *Brother Orchid* (Bacon) (as Little John Sarto); *A Dispatch from Reuters* (Dieterle) (as Julius Reuter)
1941 *The Sea Wolf* (Curtiz) (as Wolf Carsen); *Unholy Partner* (LeRoy) (as Bruce Corey); *Manpower* (Walsh) (as Hawk McHenry)

1942   *Larceny, Inc.* (Lloyd Bacon) (as Pressure Maxwell); *Tales of Manhattan* (Duvivier) (as Browne)

1943   *Destroyer* (Seiter) (as Steve Boleslauski); *Flesh and Fantasy* (Duvivier) (as Marshall Tyler)

1944   *Tampico* (Mendes) (as Capt. Bart Manson); *Mr. Winkle Goes to War* (Green) (title role); **Double Indemnity** (Wilder) (as Barton Keyes)

1945   *The Woman in the Window* (Fritz Lang) (as Prof. Richard Whanley); *Our Vines Have Tender Grapes* (Rowland) (as Martinius Jacobson)

1946   *Scarlet Street* (Fritz Lang) (as Christopher Cross); *Journey Together* (Boulting) (as Dean McWilliams); *The Stranger* (Welles) (as Wilson)

1947   *The Red House* (Daves) (as Peter Morgan)

1948   *All My Sons* (Reis) (as Joe Keller); *Key Largo* (Huston) (as Johnny Rocco); *The Night Has a Thousand Eyes* (Farrow) (as John Triton)

1949   *It's a Great Feeling* (Butler) (as himself)

1950   *My Daughter Joy* (*Operation X*) (Ratoff) (as George Constantin)

1952   *Actors and Sin* (Hecht) (as Maurice Tillayou)

1953   *Vice Squad* (Caven) (as Captain Barnaby); *Big Leaguer* (Aldrich) (as John "Hans" Lobart); *The Glass Web* (Arnold) (as Henry Hayes)

1954   *Black Tuesday* (Fregonese) (as Vincent Cavelli)

1955   *The Violent Men* (Maté) (as Lew Wilkison); *Tight Spot* (Karlsen) (as Lloyd Hallett); *A Bullet for Joey* (Lewis Allen) (as Inspector Raoul Leduc)

1956   *Hell on Frisco Bay* (Tuttle) (as Victor Amato); *Nightmare* (Shane) (as Rene); *The Ten Commandments* (Cecil B. DeMille) (as Dathan)

1959   *A Hole in the Head* (Capra) (as Mario Manetta)

1960   *Seven Thieves* (Hathaway) (as Theo Wilkins); *Pepe* (Sidney) (as himself)

1961   *My Geisha* (Cardiff) (as Sam Lewis)

1962   *Two Weeks in Another Town* (Minnelli) (as Maurice Kruger)

1964   *The Prize* (Robson) (as Dr. Max Stratman); *Good Neighbor Sam* (Swift) (as Simon Nurdlinger); *Robin and the Seven Hoods* (Douglas) (as Big Jim); *The Outrage* (Ritt) (as Cow Man); *Cheyenne Autumn* (Ford) (as Carl Schurr)

1965   *A Boy Ten Feet Tall* (Mackendrick) (as Cocky Wainwright); *The Cincinnati Kid* (Jewison) (as Cancey Howard)

1968   *La Blonde de Pekin* (*The Blonde from Peking*) (Gassner) (as Douglas); *Ad ogni costo* (*Grand Slam*) (Montaldo) (as Prof. James Anders); *Uno scacco tutto matto* (*Mad Checkmate*) (Fiz) (as MacDowell); *Operation St. Peter's* (Fucci) (as Joe); *Never a Dull Moment* (Paris) (as Leo Joseph Smooth)

1969   *MacKenna's Gold* (Thompson) (as Old Adams); *U.M.C.* (*Operation Heartbeat*) (Sagal—for TV)

1970   *The Old Man Who Cried Wolf* (Grauman—for TV); *Song of Norway* (Stone) (as Krogstad)

1973   *Soylent Green* (Fleischer) (as Sol Roth); *Neither by Day nor Night* (Stern) (as Father)

1979   *Arthur Miller on Home Ground* (Rasky—doc)

Publications

By ROBINSON: book—

All My Yesterdays, with Leonard Spigelgass, New York, 1973.

On ROBINSON: books—

Lee, Raymond, and B. C. Van Hecke, *Gangster and Hoodlums: The Underworld in Cinema*, foreword by Edward G. Robinson, New York, 1971.

Parish, James Robert, and Alvin H. Marill, *The Cinema of Edward G. Robinson*, South Brunswick, New Jersey, 1972.

Wallis, Hal, and Charles Higham, *Starmaker*, New York, 1980.

Gansberg, Alan L., *Little Caesar: A Biography of Edward G. Robinson*, Sevenoaks, Kent, 1983.

Neibaur, James L., *Tough Guy: The American Movie Macho*, Jefferson, North Carolina, 1989.

Marill, Alvin H., *The Complete Films of Edward G. Robinson*, Secaucus, New Jersey, 1990.

McCarty, John, *Hollywood Gangland*, New York, 1995.

On ROBINSON: articles—

Current Biography 1950 New York, 1950.

Eyles, Allen, "Edward G. Robinson," in *Films and Filming* (London), January 1964.

Roman, Robert, "Edward G. Robinson," in *Films in Review* (New York), August-September 1966.

Beylie, Claude, "Ave, Little Caesar!" in *Ecran* (Paris), March 1973.

Overbey, D., "Edward G. Robinson," in *Take One* (Montreal), May 1978.

*   *   *

His craggy frog-face, squat, stocky figure, and whine/growl of a voice made Edward G. Robinson the permanent property of generations of impressionists and caricaturists. That his acting never descended into the masochistic self-parody of many another distinctive talent is due to Robinson's skill and humor. He became famous through his startling and vivid portrayal of Rico Bandello in *Little Caesar*. This and other roles of the same vintage and mood (*The Hole in the Wall* and *Outside the Law*, to name but two) swiftly typed Robinson as a conscienceless, snarling thug. He was never trapped by this menacing persona. Instead, he played with it, using it as a foundation and weaving skillful variations on the public's perception of his range. Like Cagney he transcended typecasting; rather, he used it to his own ends. No matter with what preconceptions one approaches a Robinson characterization, the actor is able to bring to his work a freshness, an element of the unexpected.

Robinson's roles were sometimes thinly scripted but they inevitably emerged as full-blooded and emotionally shaded on the screen. Even the toughest of his maniacal killers is capable of moments of whimsy or unguarded pleasure. This often points to an essential weakness in the character which leads to his inevitable downfall. This is the key to Robinson's screen gangsters and bad guys, and what separates them from those of his fellow kings of the celluloid underworld, Cagney and Bogart. Robinson's characters are killers, but they are not clever, homicidal crazies (like Cagney's) or desperate loners looking for a way out (like Bogart's). They are fools guided by stupidity—essentially comic figures. This may be why many of Robinson's best gangster films following *Little Caesar* were, in fact, outright comedies in which he not only poked fun at the distinctive tough guy character he had created but further defined that character in ways that some of his dramas failed to do. In these comic films, such as *The Little Giant, The Whole Town's Talking, A Slight Case of Murder, Brother Orchid*, and so on, his cruel face softened and relaxed until it resembled that of an amiable, if unfortunate, baby.

In Robinson's best performances, he was able to walk the line between reason and rage. *Flesh and Fantasy* and *The Night Has a Thousand Eyes* show his vulnerability and susceptibility to madness; he is a hard-edged thug with a soft spot in *The Last Gangster*, a cuckold in *Manpower*, noble and tenacious in *Dr. Ehrlich's Magic Bullet*, shrewd and bemused in *Double Indemnity*, benevolent and fatherly in *Our Vines Have Tender Grapes*.

Robinson worked with some of the best directors in Hollywood—Browning, LeRoy, Wellman, Ford, Hawks, Farrow, Curtiz, Huston—but the archetypical Robinson roles are contained in Fritz Lang's *Scarlet Street* and *The Woman in the Window*. In the former, he is an easily manipulated artist driven to madness and murder by his wife's infidelity. In the latter, he portrays a cultured and intelligent professor who becomes embroiled in the seamier side of life by his obsession with the beautiful subject of a portrait. In both films, Lang's themes seem tailor-made to display the disparate facets of Robinson's personality: paranoia, impending insanity, and violence versus taste, trust, and an innate, if fragile, amiability.

—Frank Thompson, updated by John McCarty

ROGERS, Ginger

Nationality: American. **Born:** Virginia Katherine McMath in Independence, Missouri, 16 July 1911; adopted name of stepfather, Rogers. **Education:** Attended Benton Boulevard Elementary School, Kansas City; Sixth Ward Elementary School and Central High School, both in Fort Worth, Texas. **Family:** Married 1) the dancer Jack Pepper (Edward Jackson Culpepper), 1929 (divorced 1931); 2) the actor Lew Ayres, 1934 (divorced 1940); 3) the actor Jack Briggs, 1943 (divorced 1949); 4) the actor Jacques Bergerac, 1953 (divorced 1957); 5) William Marshall, 1961 (divorced 1970). **Career:** 1925—stage debut in Eddie Foy's vaudeville troupe; then toured for next few years as dancer, first with Jack Pepper, later as a solo act; 1929—New York debut in musical comedy *Top Speed*; 1930—feature film debut in *Young Man of Manhattan*; 1933—first film with Fred Astaire, *Flying Down to Rio*, 1951—on Broadway in *Love and Let Love*: later stage work in *Hello, Dolly!* in New York and tour, 1965-67, *Mame* in London, 1969, *Coco* on tour, 1971, *Our Town* in Sherman, Texas, 1972; 1971—fashion consultant to J. C. Penney chain; 1976—formed a nightclub review; 1985—directed play *Babes in Arms*, performed in Tarrytown, New York. **Awards:** Best Actress Academy Award, for *Kitty Foyle*, 1940. **Died:** In Rancho Mirage, California, 25 April 1995.

Films as Actress:

1929   *A Night in a Dormitory* (Delmar—short); *A Day of a Man of Affairs* (Basil Smith—short)

1930   *Office Blues* (Blumenstock—short) (as secretary); *Campus Sweethearts* (Meehan—short); *Young Man of Manhattan* (Bell) (as Puff Randolph); *Queen High* (Newmeyer) (as Polly Rockwell); *The Sap from Syracuse* (*The Sap from Abroad*) (A. Edward Sutherland) (as Ellen Saunders); *Follow the Leader* (Taurog) (as Mary Brennan)

1931   *Honor among Lovers* (Arzner) (as Doris Blake); *The Tip-Off* (*Looking for Trouble*) (Rogell) (as Baby Face); *Suicide Fleet* (Rogell) (as Sally)

1932   *Screen Snapshots* (short); *Hollywood on Parade* (Oakie—short); *Carnival Boat* (Rogell) (as Honey); *The Tenderfoot* (Enright) (as Ruth); *The Thirteenth Guest* (*Lady Beware*) (Albert Ray) (as Marie Morgan/Lela); *Hat Check Girl* (Lanfield) (as Jessie King); *You Said a Mouthful* (Lloyd Bacon) (as Alice Brandon)

1933   *Hollywood on Parade, No. 9* (short); **42nd Street** (Lloyd Bacon) (as Ann Lowell, "Anytime Annie"); *Broadway Bad* (*Her Reputation*) (Lanfield) (as Flip Daly); *Gold Diggers of 1933* (LeRoy) (as Fay Fortune); *Professional Sweetheart* (*Imaginary Sweetheart*) (Seiter) (as Glory Eden); *A Shriek*

in the Night (Albert Ray) (as Patricia Morgan); *Don't Bet on Love* (Roth) (as Molly Gilbert); *Sitting Pretty* (Harry Joe Brown) (as Dorothy); *Flying Down to Rio* (Freeland) (as Honey Hale); *Chance at Heaven* (Seiter) (as Marje Harris)

1934   *Rafter Romance* (Seiter) (as Mary Carroll); *Finishing School* (Tuchock and Nicholls Jr.) (as Cecelia "Pony" Ferris); *Twenty Million Sweethearts* (Enright) (as Peggy Cornell); *Change of Heart* (Blystone) (as Madge Roundtree); *Upperworld* (Del Ruth) (as Lily Linder); *The Gay Divorcee* (Sandrich) (as Mimi Glossop); *Romance in Manhattan* (Roberts) (as Sylvia Dennis)

1935   *Roberta* (Seiter) (as Countess Scharwenka/Lizzie Gatz); *Star of Midnight* (Roberts) (as Donna Mantin); **Top Hat** (Sandrich) (as Dale Tremont); *In Person* (Seiter) (as Carol Corliss)

1936   *Follow the Fleet* (Sandrich) (as Sherry Martin); *Swing Time* (Stevens) (as Penelope "Penny" Carrol)

1937   *Shall We Dance* (Sandrich) (as Linda Keene); *Stage Door* (La Cava) (as Joan Maitland)

1938   *Having Wonderful Time* (Santell) (as Thelma "Teddy" Shaw); *Vivacious Lady* (Stevens) (as Frances "Francey" Brent); *Carefree* (Sandrich) (as Amanda Cooper)

1939   *The Story of Vernon and Irene Castle* (Potter) (as Irene Foote Castle); *Bachelor Mother* (Kanin) (as Polly Parrish); *Fifth Avenue Girl* (La Cava) (as Mary Grey)

1940   *Primrose Path* (La Cava) (as Ellie May Adams); *Lucky Partners* (Milestone) (as Jean Newton); *Kitty Foyle* (Wood) (title role)

1941   *Tom, Dick, and Harry* (Kanin) (as Janie)

1942   *Roxie Hart* (Wellman) (title role); *Tales of Manhattan* (Duvivier) (as Diane); *The Major and the Minor* (Wilder) (as Susan Applegate); *Once upon a Honeymoon* (McCarey) (as Katie O'Hara/Katharine Butte-Smith)

1943   *Show Business at War* (*March of Times* series) (short); *Tender Comrade* (Dmytryk) (as Jo Jones)

1944   *Lady in the Dark* (Leisen) (as Liza Elliott); *Safeguarding Military Information* (WWII training film); *Battle Stations* (as narrator); *I'll Be Seeing You* (Dieterle) (as Mary Marshall)

1945   *Weekend at the Waldorf* (Leonard) (as Irene Malvern)

1946   *Heartbeat* (Wood) (as Arlette Lafon); *Magnificent Doll* (Borzage) (as Dolley Paine Madison)

1947   *It Had to Be You* (Hartman and Mate) (as Victoria Stafford)

1949   *The Barkleys of Broadway* (Walters) (as Dinah Barkley)

1950   *Perfect Strangers* (*Too Dangerous to Love*) (Windust) (as Terry Scott)

1951   *Storm Warning* (Heisler) (as Marsha Mitchell); *The Groom Wore Spurs* (Whorf) (as Abigail J. Furnival)

1952   *We're Not Married* (Edmund Goulding) (as Ramona); *Monkey Business* (Hawks) (as Edwina Fulton); *Dreamboat* (Binyon) (as Gloria)

1954   *Forever Female* (Rapper) (as Beatrice Page); *Black Widow* (Nunnally Johnson) (as Lottie); *Twist of Fate* (*Beautiful Stranger*) (Miller) (as Johnny Victor)

1955   *Tight Spot* (Karlson) (as Sherry Conley)

1956   *The First Traveling Saleslady* (Lubin) (as Rose Gillray); *Teenage Rebel* (Edmund Goulding) (as Nancy Fallon); *Oh, Men! Oh, Women!* (Nunnally Johnson) (as Mildred Turner)

1964   *The Confession* (*Seven Different Ways*; *Quick, Let's Get Married*) (Dieterle) (as Mme. Rinaldi)

1965   *Harlow* (Segal) (as Mama Jean); *Cinderella* (Dubin—for TV) (as the Queen)

1984   *George Stevens: A Filmmaker's Journey* (Stevens Jr.—doc)

1994   *That's Entertainment! III* (Friedgen and Sheridan—compilation)

Ginger Rogers

Publications

By ROGERS: book—

Ginger: My Story, New York, 1991.

By ROGERS: articles—

"How I Got My First Job," in *Dance*, December 1931.

"Roger!," interview with M. Arnold, in *Photoplay* (New York), August 1949.

"Candid Comments by an Actress," interview with Richard L. Coe, in *New York Times*, 23 September 1951.

"Doctor Ginger Rogers," interview with R. C. Hay, in *Inter/View* (New York), October 1972.

"Ginger Rogers: Things Do Seem to Pan Out," interview with Christine Winter, in *Chicago Tribune*, 1 December 1974.

"Taps for Ginger Rogers," interview with J. Goldberg, in *Village Voice* (New York), 15 March 1976.

"Ginger," interview with Andy Warhol, in *Interview* (New York), April 1976.

"And What Is Ginger Up To?," interview with J. Klemesrud, in *Esquire* (New York), August 1976.

On ROGERS: books—

Richards, Dick, *Ginger: Salute to a Star*, Brighton, 1969.

Croce, Arlene, *The Fred Astaire and Ginger Rogers Book*, New York, 1972.

Smith, Milburn, editor, *Astaire and Rogers*, New York, 1972.

Parish, James Robert, *The RKO Girls*, New Rochelle, New York, 1974.

Dickens, Homer, *The Films of Ginger Rogers*, Secaucus, New Jersey, 1975.

McGilligan, Patrick, *Ginger Rogers*, New York, 1975.

Eells, George, *Ginger, Loretta, and Irene Who?*, New York, 1976.

Topper, Susanne, *Astaire and Rogers*, New York, 1976.

Delameter, Jerome, *A Critical and Historical Analysis of Dance as a Code of the Hollywood Musical*, Ann Arbor, Michigan, 1979.

Carrrick, Peter, *A Tribute to Fred Astaire*, London, 1984.

Faris, Jocelyn, *Ginger Rogers: A Bio-Bibliography*, Westport, Connecticut, 1994.

Morley, Sheridan, *Shall We Dance?: The Life of Ginger Rogers*, New York, 1995.

On ROGERS: articles—

Crisler, B. R., "Ginger Takes the Town," in *New York Times*, 16 February 1936.

"Fred Astaire and Ginger Rogers" issue of *Visages* (Paris), January 1939.

"Dancing Girl," in *Time* (New York), 10 April 1939.

Strauss, Theodore, "The Young Lady from Independence," in *New York Times*, 22 February 1942.

"She Adds New Chapter to Her Success Story," in *Life* (New York), 2 March 1942.

Sarris, Andrew, "Ginger Rogers/Fred Astaire Musicals," in *Village Voice* (New York), 7 May 1964.

Dickens, Homer, "Ginger Rogers," in *Films in Review* (New York), March 1966.

Current Biography 1967, New York, 1967.

Spiegel, Ellen, "Fred and Ginger Meet Van Nest Polglase," in *The Velvet Light Trap* (Madison, Wisconsin), Autumn 1973.

"Ginger Rogers Today," in *Photoplay* (New York), November 1976.

McAsh, I. F., "Just Ginger Rogers," in *Films Illustrated* (London), May 1978.

Wood, Robin, "Never Never Change, Always Gonna Dance," in *Film Comment* (New York), September/October 1979.

"Footlights Again for Ginger Rogers," in *New York Times*, 2 May 1980.

Rickey, C., "Ginger Rogers Is a Great Actress. Really," in *Village Voice* (New York), 26 May 1980.

Telotte, J. P. "Dancing the Depression: Narrative Strategy in the Astaire-Rogers Films," in *Journal of Popular Film and Television*, November 1980.

Lauwaert, D., "Fred Astaire and Ginger Rogers," in *Film en Televisie* (Brussels), October 1983.

"Dishonored Lady," in *New Yorker*, 11 January 1993.

Bergan, Ronald, "Shall We Dance?," in *Guardian*, 12 April 1995.

Obituary in *New York Times*, 26 April 1995.

Shales, Tom, "Ginger Rogers, Dancing Chic to Chic, in *Washington Post*, 26 April 1995.

Kendall, Elizabeth, "Film View: An Actress First and Then a Dancer," in *New York Times*, 7 May 1995.

Croce, Arlene, "Ginger Rogers," in *New Yorker*, 8 May 1995.

*   *   *

One of the longest successful Hollywood film careers belongs to Ginger Rogers, a fact frequently overlooked. When fans and historians list those women who survived as stars despite age and changing styles and times, the names usually cited include Joan Crawford, Bette Davis, Katharine Hepburn, and Myrna Loy, but Rogers is rarely mentioned. It is perhaps a tribute to her lasting youthfulness that, although there is no question that she is a major star with a lengthy career, she is not thought of as someone who survived or kept her career going after great setbacks. Instead, she is a star who never had to make a comeback because she never left the limelight.

The best-known aspect of the Rogers career is her membership in the most beloved and celebrated dance team in the history of the American musical cinema—the Fred Astaire/Ginger Rogers combination which was paired in ten dance musicals. Together, from 1933 to 1939, they made nine films for RKO, managing to keep the financially unstable studio afloat for several years. Because many film scholars consider the Astaire/Rogers films to be the greatest dance musicals produced by Hollywood, they have been the subject of extensive analysis. Most of the research concerns the revolutionary aesthetic contributions that have been attributed to Fred Astaire; the integration of musical numbers and choreography with plot and story line, sound recording methods, and the use of camera work to maintain the integrity of the dance numbers.

Historically, the other half of the team, Rogers, has been continually overlooked. As film scholar Robin Wood so aptly states, "One habitually thinks of Rogers as Astaire's partner, rather than the other way around." Some have argued that Astaire, in fact, needed Rogers more than she him.

After Astaire's sister broke up the Broadway dance team of Fred and Adele Astaire in 1932, Astaire found his career in musical comedy faltering and embarked on a career in the motion picture industry. It was a risky undertaking. Already 33 and thin, balding, and not-classically handsome, Astaire did not possess the qualities of the typical Hollywood leading man. Rogers, however, was already well-established in the American film industry. Before being matched with Astaire, she appeared in 19 feature films, including 2 of Warner's Busby Berkeley musicals, *42nd Street* and *Golddiggers of 1933*. During the years in which she and Astaire were a team, Rogers made several films, both dramatic and comedic, without him. According to Croce, "By the end of 1939, RKO considered Rogers its No. 1 star and began laying plans for a straight dramatic career, while Astaire ran out his contract."

In their filmed musical pairings, Astaire and Rogers seemed wrong for one another, gloriously mismatched physically, intellectually, and stylistically. Rogers was down-to-earth, athletic—very much the "all-American" type. In the exaggerated manner of film stars, she represented the ordinary. Astaire was the elegant, European in grace, and so exceptional that he has never been equaled. Yet together, they personified the idiosyncrasy of romance—two people that friends would never match up, but who have been brought together by an inexplicable attraction. This attraction was physicalized and eloquently expressed through their dances. The best explanation of the Astaire/Rogers chemistry is a quote attributed to Katharine Hepburn: "She gave him sex, and he gave her class."

Had Rogers not been so ambitious, she might have settled for lasting fame as Astaire's most popular dance partner. But she wanted more for herself, and knew from her years in films before Astaire that she could play comedy and drama well. She broke off the partnership, a courageous career move for which she is seldom given credit.

Her first major success as a dramatic actress was *Kitty Foyle*, for which she won the 1940 Oscar for Best Actress. Having thus established herself as a solo performer, Rogers continued to pursue an active career in comedy as well as drama, occasionally returning to the musical format. Her screen image became that of a wise, tough-minded, humorous, hard-working, real-life American woman, an image built to last as it accommodated her advancing age and afforded her the versatility to play in different film genres. In later years, Rogers made a successful transition from films to television, and found equal acclaim in big Broadway musicals such as *Mame* and *Hello, Dolly!*

Any discussion of the career of Ginger Rogers must give credit to her mother, Leila Rogers, who managed her daughter with determination and intelligence. Together, the two women made the most of all opportunities they had, beginning with young Ginger's first triumph in a Charleston contest. Rogers was not considered the most beautiful woman in Hollywood, nor the best actress, singer, comedienne, or even dancer. But she was an attractive woman who could be glamorous or wholesome, depending on what the role required. She could sing and dance well, and she was versatile, with excellent comedic timing, and ability to mimic, and real dramatic skill. Putting it all together gave her the edge she needed which, supplemented by the Rogers family business acumen, and her own professionalism, made her a top star and kept her there.

Ginger Rogers and her mother represent pioneer career women. Active in politics, shrewd in business, and maintaining control of their careers in the difficult, frequently male-dominated world of Hollywood, they may be thought of as feminists in deed if not by label or self-definition.

—Jeanine Basinger, updated by Frances Gateward

ROGERS, Roy

Nationality: American. **Born:** Leonard Franklin Slye in Cincinnati, Ohio, 5 November 1911; used the names Len Slye and, briefly, Dick Weston in early years of show business. **Family:** Married 1) Arlene Wilkins, 1936 (died 1946), two children and one adopted child; 2) the actress Dale Evans, 1947, one child (deceased) and five adopted children (two deceased). **Career:** Worked in shoe factory and moved to California with his family as fruit picker; singer on radio and with groups Rocky Mountaineers, International Cowboys, and Cactus Mac and His O-Bar-O Cowboys; 1933—joined Jack Lefevre and His Texas Outlaws on radio station KFWB; formed Pioneer Trio, then expanded the group as Sons of the Pioneers; 1935—film debut as one of the Sons of the Pioneers in *The Old Homestead*; 1937—contract as actor with Republic Pictures: film debut as actor in *Under Western Stars*, 1938; his films over the next dozen years, with his horse Trigger, his sidekick George "Gabby" Hayes, and, after 1944, Dale Evans, established him as the leading cowboy star; 1948-57—star of *The Roy Rogers Show* on radio, and on television, 1951-57; also star of *The Roy Rogers and Dale Evans Show*, 1962, and host of *Kraft Music Hall*, 1967-71; also toured, marketed clothing and games, recorded songs, and established a family restaurant chain and the Roy Rogers-Dale Evans Museum in Victorville, California.

Films as Actor:

1935   *The Old Homestead* (as singer); *Slightly Static* (as singer); *Tumbling Tumbleweeds* (Kane) (as singer); *Way Up Thar* (as singer); *Gallant Defender* (as singer)

1936   *The Mysterious Avenger* (as singer); *Rhythm on the Range* (as singer); *The Big Show* (Wright) (as singer); *The Old Corral* (Kane) (as singer)

1937   *The Old Wyoming Trail* (as singer); *Wild Horse Rodeo* (as singer)

1938   *The Old Barn Dance* (Kane) (as singer); *Under Western Stars* (Kane); *Billy the Kid Returns* (Kane) (as Billy the Kid); *Come On, Rangers* (Kane); *Shine On, Harvest Moon* (Kane)

1939   *Rough Riders' Roundup* (Kane); *Frontier Pony Express* (Kane); *Southward Ho* (Kane); *In Old Caliente* (Kane); *Wall Street Cowboy* (Kane); *The Arizona Kid* (Kane); *Jeepers Creepers* (McDonald); *Saga of Death Valley* (Kane); *Days of Jesse James* (Kane)

1940   *Young Buffalo Bill* (Kane); *The Dark Command* (R. Walsh); *The Carson City Kid* (Kane); *The Ranger and the Lady* (Kane); *Colorado* (Kane); *Young Bill Hickok* (Kane) (title role); *The Border Legion* (Kane)

1941   *Robin Hood of the Pecos* (Kane); *Arkansas Judge* (McDonald); *In Old Cheyenne* (Kane); *Sheriff of Tombstone* (Kane); *Nevada City* (Kane); *Bad Man of Deadwood* (Kane); *Jesse James at Bay* (Kane) (as Jesse James); *Red River Valley* (Kane)

1942   *Man from Cheyenne* (Kane); *South of Santa Fe* (Kane); *Sunset on the Desert* (Kane); *Romance on the Range* (Kane); *Sons of the Pioneers* (Kane); *Sunset Serenade* (Kane); *Heart of the Golden West* (Kane); *Ridin' Down the Canyon* (Kane)

1943   *Idaho* (Kane); *King of the Cowboys* (Kane); *Song of Texas* (Kane); *Silver Spurs* (Kane); *Man from Music Mountain* (Kane); *Hands across the Border* (Kane)

1944   *The Cowboy and the Senorita* (Kane); *The Yellow Rose of Texas* (Kane); *Song of Nevada* (Kane); *San Fernando Valley* (English); *Lights of Old Santa Fe* (McDonald); *Brazil* (Stars and Guitars) (Santley) (as guest); *Hollywood Canteen* (Daves) (as guest)

1945   *Utah* (English); *Bells of Rosarita* (McDonald) (as himself); *The Man from Oklahoma* (McDonald); *Sunset in El Dorado* (McDonald); *Don't Fence Me In* (English); *Along the Navajo Trail* (McDonald)

1946   *Song of Arizona* (McDonald); *Rainbow over Texas* (McDonald) (as himself); *My Pal Trigger* (McDonald); *Under Nevada Skies* (McDonald); *Roll on Texas Moon* (Witney); *Home in Oklahoma* (Witney); *Out California Way* (Selander) (as guest); *Heldorado* (Witney)

1947   *Apache Rose* (Witney); *Hit Parade of 1947* (McDonald) (as guest); *Bells of San Angelo* (Witney); *Springtime in the Sierras* (Witney); *On the Old Spanish Trail* (Witney)

1948   *The Gay Ranchero* (Witney); *Under California Skies* (Witney); *Eyes of Texas* (Witney); *Melody Time* (Disney) (as guest); *Night Time in Nevada* (Witney); *Grand Canyon Trial* (Witney); *The Far Frontier* (Witney)

1949   *Susanna Pass* (Witney); *Down Dakota Way* (Witney); *The Golden Stallion* (Witney)

1950   *Bells of Colorado* (Witney); *Twilight in the Sierras* (Witney); *Trigger, Jr.* (Witney); *Sunset in the West* (Witney); *North of the Great Divide* (Witney); *Trail of Robin Hood* (Witney)

1951   *Spoilers of the Plains* (Witney); *Heart of the Rockies* (Witney); *In Old Amarillo* (Witney); *South of Caliente* (Witney); *Pals of the Golden West* (Witney)

1952   *Son of Paleface* (Tashlin)

1959   *Alias Jesse James* (McLeod) (as guest)

1975   *Mackintosh and T. J.* (Chomsky) (as Mackintosh)

Publications

By ROGERS: books—

My Favorite Christmas Story, with Frank S. Mead, Westwood, New Jersey, 1960.

Happy Trails: The Story of Roy Rogers and Dale Evans, with Carlton Stowers, Waco, Texas, 1979.

Happy Trails: Our Life Story, with Jane and Michael Stern, New York, 1994.

Roy Rogers: King of the Cowboys, edited by Georgia Morris and Mark Pollard, San Francisco, 1994.

On ROGERS: books—

Davis, Elise Miller, *The Answer Is God: The Inspiring Personal Story of Dale Evans and Roy Rogers*, New York, 1955.

Fenin, George, and William K. Everson, *The Western: From Silents to Cinerama*, New York, 1962.

Rothel, David, *The Singing Cowboys*, South Brunswick, New Jersey, 1978.

Rogers, Roy Jr., with Karen Ann Wojahn, *Growing Up with Roy & Dale*, Ventura, California, 1986.

Rothel, David, *The Roy Rogers Book*, Madison, North Carolina, 1987.

Phillips, Robert W., *Roy Rogers: A Biography, Radio History, Television Career Chronicle, Discography, Filmography, Comicography, Merchandising and Advertising History, Collectibles Description, Bibliography, and Index*, Jefferson, North Carolina, 1995.

On ROGERS: articles—

Current Biography 1983, New York, 1983.

Hoberman, J., "Home on the Range," in *Premiere*, February 1993.

Stern, Jane, and Michael Stern, "Happy Trails," in *Atlantic*, November 1993.

On ROGERS: film—

Roy Rogers, King of the Cowboys, documentary directed by Thys Ockersen, 1993.

*   *   *

In 1942 Roy Rogers inherited Gene Autry's mantle as the number one B Western movie star when the latter entered the U.S. Army Air Force. Autry was never able to regain his crown. From 1943 to 1954, Rogers, "King of the Cowboys," reigned as the top moneymaking B Western movie star in the annual *Motion Picture Herald* poll. Rogers reached the acme of his star power near the end of World War II when for a time he was ranked among the top ten of all movie box-office attractions.

Rogers's first wife, Arlene, died in 1946, six days after the birth of their third child. One year later, Rogers remarried, this time to his then leading lady, Dale Evans. From then on, the two constantly worked together, forever linking their names. After their marriage, the duo seemed to be everywhere—in the movies, on the radio, and eventually on television.

Rogers came to star in Republic Westerns in 1938 because Gene Autry, then tops on the B Western circuit, walked off the lot in order to gain more money from the notoriously tightfisted studio boss, Herbert J. Yates. Republic substituted Rogers in an already-planned Autry vehicle. The studio spent more than the normal $50,000 on the 65-minute *Under Western Stars*. When box-office returns proved to be higher than normal, Republic rushed Rogers into a series that would differentiate his image from Autry's. The Rogers B programmers were set in the traditional era of the Old West, not the 1930s America of Autry's adventures. Rogers also stuck more closely to the elements typically associated with Westerns in terms of locale and costume, sang less often (two times verses Autry's five times per film), and frequently took on the character of a famous Western hero (Buffalo Bill, or Wild Bill Hickok) while Autry always played himself.

Once Autry returned after his short-lived walkout, the two B Western stars coexisted at Republic. When in 1942 Autry entered the U.S. Army Air Force, Republic began to heavily promote Rogers as the "King of the Cowboys." Rogers's films then became Autry clones, complete with modern settings and up-to-date automobiles, radios, and airplanes. When Dale Evans came aboard in 1944, their production numbers moved far past the simple efforts of Gene Autry. It was at this point that Rogers and Evans began a weekly radio show and reached the apex of their fame as movie stars. From there Rogers moved into early television work. The premiere of *The Roy Rogers Show* in December 1951 was a gala affair featuring a live remote with Rogers, Evans, and special guest star Bob Hope. The second half of the program consisted of the initial episode of the 30-minute Western series which would appear on NBC Sunday nights. The series continued until 1957 with a total of more than 100 black-and-white episodes produced.

Since then, Rogers has made regular appearances at fairs and on television variety shows, opened a museum, and in a deal that made him a millionaire many times over teamed with the Marriott Corporation to help promote a chain of fast-food restaurants. Additional Rogers activities include a line of Western wear, the acquisition of real estate, and the raising of thoroughbred horses. Roy Rogers has never gone away, despite the fact he has made no movies for more than two generations.

—Douglas Gomery

ROGERS, Will

Nationality: American. **Born:** William Penn Adair Rogers in Indian Territory (now Oklahoma), 4 November 1879. **Education:** Attended Drumgoole School; Harrell International Institute; Halsell College; Scarritt Collegiate Institute; Kemper Military Institute, Missouri. **Family:** Married Betty Blake, 1908, two sons and one daughter. **Career:** Worked at a variety of jobs; entered show business as a lasso artist and rough rider in Texas Jack's Wild West Circus in Ladysmith, Natal; 1905—vaudeville performer in New York; 1907—legitimate stage debut in musical *The Girl Rangers*; 1912—legitimate Broadway debut in the musical *The Wall Street Girl*; 1916—first of many appearances in the *Ziegfeld Follies*—from 1918 appearing in "Timely Topics" sketches commenting on current events and personalities; 1918-21—contract with Samuel Goldwyn; film debut in *Laughing Bill Hyde*; 1919—first of many books, *The Cowboy Philosopher on the Peace Conference*; 1922—beginning of his newspaper column, soon widely syndicated; also a correspondent for *The Saturday Evening Post*; 1923—first of many recordings; 1927-28—wrote and appeared in a series of short films of his travels; 1934—in stage play *Ah, Wilderness!* in San Francisco. **Died:** In airplane crash, 15 August 1935.

Films as Actor:

1918   *Laughing Bill Hyde* (Henley) (title role)
1919   *Almost a Husband* (Badger) (as Sam Lyman)
1920   *Jubilo* (Badger) (title role); *Water, Water Everywhere* (Badger) (as Billy Fortune); *Just Call Me Jim* (Badger) (title role); *The Strange Boarder* (Badger) (as Sam Gardner); *Honest Hutch* (Badger) (title role); *Cupid the Cowpuncher* (Badger) (as Alec Lloyd)
1921   *Guile of Women* (Badger) (as Hjalmar Maartens); *Boys Will Be Boys* (Badger) (as Peep O'Day); *Doubling for Romeo* (Badger) (as Sam Cody); *A Poor Relation* (Badger) (as Noah Vale)
1922   *One Glorious Day* (Cruze) (as Ezra Botts); *The Headless Horseman* (Venturini) (as Ichabod Crane); *The Ropin' Fool* (Badger—short) (as "Ropes" Reilly, + sc); *Fruits of the Faith* (Badger—short) (as Larry, + sc)
1923   *Hollywood* (Cruze) (as himself); *Jus' Passin' Through* (Parrott—short); *Hustlin' Hawk* (Pembroke—short); *Two Wagons, Both Covered* (Wagner—short) (as William Banion/Bill Jackson); *Uncensored Movies* (Clements—short)
1924   *The Cowboy Sheik* (Howe—short) (as "Two Straw" Bill); *The Cake Eater* (Howe—short); *Going to Congress* (Wagner—short) (as Alfalfa Doolittle); *Our Congressman* (Wagner—short) (as Alfalfa Doolittle); *Big Moments from Little Pictures* (Howe—short); *High Brow Stuff* (Wagner—short); *Don't Park There* (Guiol—short); *A Truthful Liar* (Del Ruth—short) (as Alfalfa Doolittle); *Jubilo, Jr.* (McGowan—short) (as Jubilo); *Gee Whiz, Genevieve* (Howe)
1927   *Tip Toes* (Wilcox) (as Uncle Hen Kaye); *A Texas Steer* (Wallace) (as Maverick Brander); *They Had to See Paris* (Borzage) (as Pike Peters) *With Will Rogers in Dublin* (Clancy—short) (one of a series of shorts written by Rogers and all directed by Clancy); *With Will Rogers in Paris*; *Hiking through Holland with Will Rogers*; *Roaming the Emerald Isle with Will Rogers*; *Through Switzerland and Bavaria with Will Rogers*; *Hunting for Germans in Berlin with Will Rogers*; *With Will Rogers in London*; *Prowling around France with Will Rogers*; *Winging 'round Europe with Will Rogers*; *Exploring England with Will Rogers*; *Reeling down the Rhine with Will Rogers*
1928   *Over the Bouncing Blue with Will Rogers*
1929   *Happy Days* (Stoloff) (as himself)
1930   *So This Is London?* (Blystone) (as Hiram Draper); *Lightnin'* (King) (title role)

Will Rogers

1931   *A Connecticut Yankee* (Butler) (as Hank Martin); *Young as You Feel* (Borzage) (as Lemuel Morehouse); *The Plutocrat* (Butler); *Ambassador Bill* (Taylor) (as Bill Harper)

1932   *Business and Pleasure* (Butler) (as Earl Tinker); *Down to Earth* (Butler) (as Pike Peters); *Too Busy to Work* (Blystone) (as Jubilo)

1933   *State Fair* (King) (as Abel Frake); *Doctor Bull* (Ford) (title role); *Mr. Skitch* (Cruze) (title role)

1934   *David Harum* (Cruze) (title role); *Handy Andy* (Butler) (as Andrew Yates); *Judge Priest* (Ford) (title role)

1935   *Life Begins at Forty* (Marshall) (as Kenesaw H. Clark); *Doubting Thomas* (Butler) (as Thomas Brown); *In Old Kentucky* (Marshall) (as Steve Tapley); *Steamboat round the Bend* (Ford) (as Dr. John Pearly)

Publications

By ROGERS: books—

The Cowboy Philosopher on the Peace Conference, New York, 1919.
The Cowboy Philosopher on Prohibition, New York, 1919.
The Illiterate Digest, New York, 1919.
Letters of a Self-Made Diplomat to His President, New York, 1926.
There's Not a Bathing Suit in Russia, New York, 1927.
Ether and Me, New York, 1929.
Wit and Philosophy from the Radio Talks of America's Humorist, Chicago, 1930.
Will Rogers' Wit and Wisdom, edited by Jack Lait, New York, 1936.
Autobiography, edited by Donald Day, Boston, 1949.
How We Elect Our President, edited by Donald Day, Boston, 1952.
Sanity Is Where You Find It, edited by Donald Day, Boston, 1955.
The Will Rogers Book, edited by Paula McSpadden Love, Indianapolis, 1961.
The Writings of Will Rogers, edited by Joseph A. Stout, Peter C. Rollings, and Stephen K. Gragert, Stillwater, Oklahoma, 1976—ongoing.
The Best of Will Rogers, edited by Bryan B. Sterling, New York, 1979.
Will Rogers Reports, edited by Bryan B. and Frances N. Sterling, New York, 1982.
The Papers of Will Rogers, edited by Arthur Frank Wertheim and Barbara Bair, Norman, Oklahoma, 1995—ongoing.
Will Rogers Speaks: Over 1,000 Timeless Quotations for Public Speakers, compiled by Bryan Sterling and Frances Sterling, New York, 1995.

On ROGERS: books—

Hitch, A. M., *Cadet Days of Will Rogers*, Boonville, Missouri, 1935.
Milam, Irene McSpadden, *Will Rogers as I Knew Him*, Claremore, Oklahoma, 1935.
Milsten, David, *An Appreciation of Will Rogers*, San Antonio, 1935.
O'Brien, Patrick J., *Will Rogers*, Philadelphia, 1935.
Folks Say of Will Rogers, edited by William H. Payne and Jake Lyons, New York, 1936.
Trent, Spi M., *My Cousin, Will Rogers*, New York, 1939.
Rogers, Betty (Mrs. Will), *Will Rogers*, Indianapolis, 1941.
Croy, Homer, *Our Will Rogers*, New York, 1953.
Day, Donald, *Will Rogers*, New York, 1962.
Brown, William R., *Imagemaker: Will Rogers and the American Dream*, Columbia, Missouri, 1970.
Axtell, Margaret Shellabarger, *Will Rogers Rode the Range*, Phoenix, 1972.
McKetchum, Richard, *Will Rogers: His Life and Times*, New York, 1973.
Alworth, Paul, *Will Rogers*, New York, 1974.
The Will Rogers Scrapbook, edited by Bryan B. Sterling, New York, 1976.

Will Rogers: A Centennial Tribute, edited by Arrell Morgan Gibson, Oklahoma City, 1979.
Rollins, Peter C., *Will Rogers: A Bio-Bibliography*, Westport, Connecticut, 1984.
Sterling, Bryan B., and Frances N., *Will Rogers in Hollywood*, New York, 1984.
Yagoda, Ben, *Will Rogers: A Biography*, San Francisco, 1994.
Malone, Mary, *Will Rogers: Cowboy Philosopher*, Springfield, New Jersey, 1996.
Robinson, Ray, *American Original: A Life of Will Rogers*, New York, 1996.

On ROGERS: articles—

Rollins, P. C., "Will Rogers: Symbolic Man and Film Image," in *Journal of Popular Film* (Bowling Green, Ohio), Fall 1973.
Rubin, M., "Mr. Ford and Mr. Rogers," in *Film Comment* (New York), January-February 1974.
Rollins, P. C., "Regional Literature and Will Rogers: Film Redeems a Literary Film," in *Literature/Film Quarterly* (Salisbury, Maryland), Winter 1975.
"Will Rogers: The Cowboy Philosopher Spoke for the Folks," in *Life*, Fall 1990.

On ROGERS: film—

The Story of Will Rogers, directed by Michael Curtiz, 1952.

*   *   *

Will Rogers was more than a movie star; he was one of the greatest American show business personalities of the first third of the twentieth century. He reigned as a star of the Ziegfeld Follies, penned an influential newspaper column, and in 1934 topped the annual poll as the most popular movie star in America. During the bleak years of the Great Depression, Rogers came to represent the noble savage, the casual humorist and raconteur, the man who clung to the folkways of a mythical nineteenth-century America. John Ford, the great American director, best understood Rogers's image, and fully exploited it in *Doctor Bull*, *Judge Priest*, and *Steamboat round the Bend*, Rogers's best and most popular motion pictures.

But his origins were far from Hollywood Boulevard. He began as a performer in Wild West shows at the turn of the century. From there Rogers moved to the vaudeville stage and later to the Ziegfeld Follies. Lariat tricks provided the core of his first act, but he soon began to spin out homespun tales of folk humor and wisdom between tricks. Rogers reached the peak of this first phase of his career near the end of the second decade of the twentieth century. It was at this point famed Hollywood producer Samuel Goldwyn signed him to play in silent films. Between 1918 and 1922 he essayed cowboy roles but his career went nowhere. For the remainder of the silent era Rogers returned to the stage—save for a few shorts made for the Hal Roach studios.

It was the coming of sound that boosted Will Rogers's movie stardom. The new medium of the talkies captured a wit and style perfected by 20 years on the stage. From 1929, with *They Had to See Paris*, until his death in an airplane crash at Point Barrow, Alaska, Will Rogers was Fox's most important movie star. Indeed two films, *In Old Kentucky* and *Steamboat round the Bend* were released after the actor's untimely death, and for a newly merged Twentieth Century-Fox Film. Certainly for the first part of the Hollywood studio era, he ranked among the more important stars of American sound movies.

—Douglas Gomery

ROONEY, Mickey

Nationality: American. **Born:** Joe Yule Jr., in Brooklyn, New York, 23 September 1920. **Education:** Attended Dayton Heights and Vine Street elementary schools and Fairfax High School, Hollywood; Pacific Military Academy, Culver City, California; also attended a studio school at MGM. **Military Service:** U.S. Army, 1944-46. **Family:** Married 1) the actress Ava Gardner, 1942 (divorced 1943); 2) Betty Jane Rase, 1944 (divorced 1949), sons: Mickey Jr. and Timothy; 3) the actress Martha Vickers, 1949 (divorced 1951), son: Teddy; 4) Elaine Mahnken, 1951 (divorced 1958); 5) Barbara Ann Thomasen, 1958 (divorced), sons: Kerry and Kyle, daughters: Kelly Ann and Kimmy Sue; 6) Margie Lang, 1966 (divorced 1967); 7) Carolyn Hocket (divorced), two children; 8) the singer Jan Chamberlain, 1978. **Career:** Stage debut in his parents' vaudeville act at age 15 months as a midget; 1926—film debut as a midget in *Not to Be Trusted*; 1927-34—in series of short films about Mickey McGuire; 1937—first of the Andy Hardy films, *A Family Affair*; 1951—directed the film *My True Story*; 1963—in summer stock in the play *The Tunnel of Love*; 1964-65—in TV series *Mickey*, and a regular in TV series *NBC Follies*, 1973; 1964—toured nightclub circuit with dancer Bobby Van; has since toured in other plays; 1979—in theatrical revue *Sugar Babies* with Ann Miller, first in Los Angeles, then in long Broadway run, and touring (until 1985); 1992-94—in TV series *The Black Stallion*. **Awards:** Special Academy Award (with Deanna Durbin), "for their significant contribution in bringing to the screen the spirit and personification of youth and as juvenile players setting a high standard of ability and achievement," 1938; Best Actor César Award (France), for *Baby Face Nelson*, 1957; Special Academy Award, "in recognition of his 60 years of versatility in a variety of memorable film performances," 1982. **Address:** 7500 Devista Drive, Los Angeles, CA 90046, U.S.A.

Films as Actor:

1926   *Not to Be Trusted* (Buckingham—short)
1927   *Orchids and Ermine* (Santell)
1932   *Emma* (Brown); *The Beast of the City* (Brabin) (as Mickey Fitzpatrick); *Sin's Pay Day* (Seitz) (as Mickey McGuire); *High Speed* (Lederman) (as Mickey McGuire); *Officer 13* (Melford); *Fast Companions* (*The Information Kid*) (Neumann) (as Midge); *My Pal, the King* (Neumann) (as King Charles V)
1933   *The Big Cage* (Neumann) (as Jimmy); *The Life of Jimmy Dolan* (*The Kid's Last Flight*) (Mayo) (as Freckles); *The Big Chance* (Herman); *Broadway to Hollywood* (*Ring Up the Curtain*) (Mack and Rapf) (as Ted III, as child); *The World Changes* (LeRoy); *The Chief* (Reisner) (as Willie)
1934   *Beloved* (Schertzinger); *I Like It that Way* (Lachman) (as messenger boy); *Love Birds* (Seiter) (as Gladwyn Tootle); *Half a Sinner* (Neumann) (as Willie); *The Lost Jungle* (Schaefer and David Howard) (as Mickey); *Manhattan Melodrama* (Van Dyke) (as Blackie as a boy); *Upperworld* (Del Ruth) (as Jerry); *The Hide-Out* (Van Dyke) (as Willie); *Chained* (Brown) (as boy swimmer); *Blind Date* (Neill) (as Freddy); *Death on the Diamond* (Sedgwick) (as Mickey)
1935   *The County Chairman* (Blystone) (as Freckles); *Reckless* (Fleming); *The Healer* (*Little Pal*) (Barker); *A Midsummer Night's Dream* (Dieterle) (as Puck); *Ah, Wilderness* (Brown) (as Tommy Miller); *Riffraff* (Ruben)
1936   *Little Lord Fauntleroy* (Cromwell) (as Dick); *The Devil Is a Sissy* (*The Devil Takes the Count*) (Van Dyke) (as "Gig" Stevens); *Down the Stretch* (Clemens) (as Snapper Sinclair)

1937   *Captains Courageous* (Fleming) (as Dan); *Slave Ship* (Garnell) (as Swifty); *A Family Affair* (Seitz) (as Andy Hardy); *Hoosier Schoolboy* (Nigh) (as Shockey); *Live, Love, and Learn* (Fitzmaurice) (as Jerry Crump); *Thoroughbreds Don't Cry* (Alred E. Green) (as Tim Donahue)
1938   *Out West with the Hardys* (Seitz) (as Andy Hardy); *You're Only Young Once* (Seitz) (as Andy Hardy); *Love Is a Headache* (Thorpe) (as Mike); *Judge Hardy's Children* (Seitz) (as Andy Hardy); *Hold That Kiss* (Marin) (as Chick Evans); *Lord Jeff* (*The Boy from Bernardos*) (Wood) (as Terry O'Mulvaney); *Love Finds Andy Hardy* (Seitz) (as Andy Hardy); *Boys Town* (Taurog) (as Whitey Marsh); *Stablemates* (Wood) (as Mickey)
1939   *The Adventures of Huckleberry Finn* (Thorpe) (title role); *The Hardys Ride High* (Seitz) (as Andy Hardy); *Andy Hardy Gets Spring Fever* (Van Dyke) (as Andy Hardy); *Judge Hardy and Son* (Seitz) (as Andy Hardy); *Babes in Arms* (Berkeley) (as Mickey Moran)
1940   *Young Tom Edison* (Taurog) (title role); *Andy Hardy Meets Debutante* (Seitz) (as Andy Hardy); *Strike Up the Band* (Berkeley) (as Jimmy Connors)
1941   *Andy Hardy's Private Secretary* (Seitz) (as Andy Hardy); *Men of Boys Town* (Taurog) (as Whitey Marsh); *Life Begins for Andy Hardy* (Seitz) (as Andy Hardy); *Babes on Broadway* (Berkeley) (as Tommy Williams)
1942   *The Courtship of Andy Hardy* (Seitz) (as Andy Hardy); *A Yank at Eton* (Taurog) (as Timothy Dennis); *Andy Hardy's Double Life* (*Andy Hardy Steps Out*) (Seitz) (as Andy Hardy)
1943   *The Human Comedy* (Brown) (as Homer Macauley); *Girl Crazy* (*When the Girls Meet the Boys*) (Taurog) (as Danny Churchill Jr.); *Thousands Cheer* (Taurog)
1944   *Andy Hardy's Blonde Trouble* (Seitz) (as Andy Hardy); *National Velvet* (Brown) (as Mi Taylor)
1946   *Ziegfeld Follies* (Minnelli); *Love Laughs at Andy Hardy* (Goldbeck) (as Andy Hardy)
1947   *Killer McCoy* (Rowland) (as Tommy McCoy)
1948   *Summer Holiday* (Mamoulian) (as Richard Miller); *Words and Music* (Taurog) (as Lorenz "Larry" Hart)
1949   *The Big Wheel* (Ludwig) (as Billy Coy)
1950   *Quicksand* (Pichel) (as Dan Brady, auto mechanic); *He's a Cockeyed Wonder* (Godfrey) (as Freddie Frisby); *The Fireball* (Garnett) (as Johnny Casar)
1951   *My Outlaw Brother* (*My Brother, the Outlaw*) (Nugent) (as Denny O'More); *The Strip* (Kardos) (as Stanley Maxton)
1952   *Sound Off* (Quine) (as Mike Donnelly)
1953   *All Ashore* (Quine) (as Francis "Moby" Dickerson); *Mickey Rooney, Then and Now* (Staub); *Off Limits* (*Military Policemen*) (George Marshall) (as Herbert Tuttle); *A Slight Case of Larceny* (Weis) (as Augustus "Geechy" Cheevers)
1954   *Drive a Crooked Road* (Quine) (as Eddie Shannon); *The Atomic Kid* (Martinson) (as Blix Waterberry); *The Bridges at Toko-Ri* (Robson) (as Mike Forney)
1955   *The Twinkle in God's Eye* (Blair) (as the Rev. Macklin)
1956   *The Bold and the Brave* (Lewis R. Foster) (as Dooley); *Francis in the Haunted House* (Lamont) (as David Prescott); *Magnificent Roughnecks* (Rose) (as Frank Sommers)
1957   *Operation Mad Ball* (Quine) (as M/Sgt. Yancy Skibo); *Baby Face Nelson* (Siegel) (title role)
1958   *Andy Hardy Comes Home* (Koch) (as Andy Hardy); *A Nice Little Bank that Should Be Robbed* (*How to Rob a Bank*) (Levin) (as Gus Harris)
1959   *The Last Mile* (Koch) (as "Killer" John Mears); *The Big Operator* (Haas) (as Little Joe Braun)
1960   *Platinum High School* (*Rich, Young, and Deadly*) (Haas) (as Steven Conway)

Mickey Rooney

1961   *Breakfast at Tiffany's* (Edwards) (as Mr. Yunioshi); *King of the Roaring Twenties* (*The Big Bankroll*) (Joseph M. Newman) (as Johnny Burke); *Everything's Ducky* (Taylor) (as Beetle McKay)

1962   *Requiem for a Heavyweight* (Nelson) (as Army)

1963   *It's a Mad, Mad, Mad, Mad World* (Kramer) (as Ding Bell)

1964   *Secret Invasion* (Corman) (as Terrence Scanlon)

1965   *Twenty-Four Hours to Kill* (Bezencenet) (as Norman Jones); *How to Stuff a Wild Bikini* (Asher) (as Peachy Keane)

1966   *Il diavolo innamorato* (*The Devil in Love*; *L'arcidiavolo*) (Scola); *Ambush Bay* (Winston) (as Sgt. Ernest Wartell)

1968   *The Extraordinary Seaman* (Frankenheimer) (as W.W.J. Oglethorpe); *Skidoo* (Preminger) (as "Blue Chips" Packard)

1969   *The Comic* (Carl Reiner) (as Cockeye); *Eighty Steps to Jonah* (Oswald) (as Wilfred Bashford)

1970   *The Cockeyed Cowboys of Calico County* (Leader) (as Indian Tom); *Hollywood Blue* (Osco)

1971   *B. J. Lang Presents* (Yablonsky)

1972   *Evil Roy Slade* (Parish—for TV); *Richard* (Yerby and Hurwitz) (as Guardian Angel); *Pulp* (Hodges)

1973   *The Godmothers* (Grefe) (+ co-sc)

1974   *Az de corazon* (*Ace of Hearts*) (Demicelli); *Thunder County* (*Cell Block Girls*; *Convict Women*; *Women's Prison Escape*; *It Snows in the Everglades*) (Robinson); *That's Entertainment!* (Haley Jr.—compilation) (as narrator); *Journey Back to Oz* (Hal Sutherland—animation) (as voice); *The Year without a Santa Claus* (Bass and Rankin Jr.—animation, for TV) (as voice of Santa Claus)

1975   *Bon baisers de Hong Kong* (Chiffre); *Rachel's Man* (Mizrahi)

1976   *Find the Lady* (*Kopek and Broom*; *Call the Cops!*) (Trent)

1977   *Pete's Dragon* (Chaffey) (as Lampie); *The Domino Principle* (*The Domino Killings*) (Kramer) (as Spiventa)

1978   *The Magic of Lassie* (Chaffey) (as Gus)

1979   *The Black Stallion* (Ballard) (as Henry Dailey); *Donovan's Kid* (McEveety—for TV) (as Bailey); *Arabian Adventure* (Connor) (as Daad El Shur)

1980   *My Kidnapper, My Love* (*Dark Side of Love*) (Wanamaker—for TV)

1981   *The Fox and the Hound* (Stevens—animation) (as voice of Tod); *Leave 'em Laughing* (Cooper—for TV); *L'Empereur de Perou* (*The Emperor of Peru*; *Odyssey of the Pacific*) (Arrabal) (as Emperor of Peru); *Bill* (Page—for TV) (as Bill Sackter); *Senior Trip* (Kenneth Johnson—for TV) (cameo)

1982   *The Black Stallion Returns* (Dalva) (as Henry Dailey); *O'Malley* (O'Herlihy); *One of the Boys* (Baldwin)

1983   *Bill: On His Own* (Page—for TV) (as Bill Sackter)

1984   *It Came upon the Midnight Clear* (Hunt—for TV)

1985   *The Care Bears Movie* (Arna Selznick—animation) (as voice of Mr. Cherrywood)

1986   *Lightning—The White Stallion* (Levey) (as Barney Ingram); *Little Spies* (Beeman—for TV); *The Return of Mickey Spillane's Mike Hammer* (Danton—for TV); *There Must Be a Pony* (Sargent—for TV) (cameo)

1987   *Bluegrass* (Wincer—for TV) (as John Paul Jones)

1989   *Erik the Viking* (Terry Jones) (as Erik's grandfather)

1990   *Home for Christmas* (McGubbin—for TV) (as Elmer)

1991   *My Heroes Have Always Been Cowboys* (Rosenberg) (as Junior); *Silent Night, Deadly Night 5: The Toy Maker* (Kitrosser) (as Joe Petto); *La Vida Lactea* (*The Milky Life*) (Esterlich) (as Barry Reilly); *The Gambler Returns: Luck of the Draw* (Lowry—for TV) (as the Director)

1992   *The Magic Voyage* (as narrator); *The Legend of Wolf Mountain* (Clyde) (as Jensen); *Maximum Force* (Merhi) (as chief of police); *Little Nemo: Adventures in Slumberland* (Hurtz and Hata—animation) (as voice of Flip)

1993   *Sweet Justice* (Plone)

1994   *That's Entertainment! III* (Friedgen and Sheridan—compilation) (as host); *The Revenge of the Red Baron* (*Plane Fear*) (Robert Gordon) (as Grandpa James); *Radio Star—Die AFN-Story* (Karnick and Richter—doc) (as himself)

1995   *The Legend of O. B. Taggart* (Hitzig) (+ sc)

(1927-34 series of "Mickey McGuire" shorts, directed by Herman, Montgomery, and Duffy; Rooney was billed first as Mickey Yule, then Mickey "Himself" McGuire, and Mickey Rooney):

1927   *Mickey's Circus* (includes *Pals, Battle, Eleven*)

1928   *Mickey's Parade* (includes *In School, Nine, Little Eva, Wild West, In Love, Triumph, Babies, Movies, Rivals, The Detective, Athletes, Big Game Hunt*)

1929   *Mickey's Great Idea* (includes *Explorers, Menagerie, Last Chance, Brown Derby, Northwest Mounted, Initiation, Midnight Follies, Surprise, Mixup, Big Moment*)

1930   *Mickey's Champs* (includes *Strategy, Mastermind, Luck, Whirlwind, Warriors, The Romeo, Merry Men, Winners, Musketeers, Bargain*)

1931   *Mickey's Stampede* (includes *Crusaders, Rebellion, Diplomacy, Wildcats, Thrill Hunters, Helping Hand, Sideline*)

1932   *Mickey's Travels* (includes *Holiday, Golden Rule, Busy Day, Charity, Big Business*)

1933   *Mickey's Ape Man* (includes *Race, Big Broadcast, Disguises, Touchdown, Tent Show, Covered Wagon*)

1934   *Mickey's Minstrels* (includes *Rescue, Medicine Man*)

Films as Director:

1951   *My True Story*

1961   *The Private Lives of Adam and Eve* (co-d with Zugsmith, + ro as Nick Lewis/Devil)

Publications

By ROONEY: books—

I.E. An Autobiography, New York, 1963.
Life Is Too Short, New York, 1991.
The Search for Sonny Skies (novel), Secaucus, New Jersey, 1994.

By ROONEY: article—

Interview with George Christy, in *Interview* (New York), May 1992.

On ROONEY: book—

Marx, Arthur, *The Nine Lives of Mickey Rooney*, New York, 1986.

On ROONEY: articles—

Current Biography 1965, New York, 1965.
Jordan, D., and E. Connor, "Judge Hardy and Family," in *Films in Review* (New York), January 1974.
Shindler, Merrill, "'How I Did It!': Three Recent Comebacks that Have Worked," in *Los Angeles Magazine*, March 1980.
Marill, Alvin H., "Mickey Rooney," in *Films in Review* (New York), June/July 1982; see also letter in August/September issue.
Witchel, Alex, "At 73, Still the Star, Still the Child," in *New York Times*, 7 July 1993.

*   *   *

Mickey Rooney has done everything there is to do in show business—vaudeville, radio, legitimate theater, television, and film—all with equal success and, it might be said, equal failure. His is a career that reached the heights and plunged to the depths, but through it all Rooney kept on working and growing, the mark of a professional. His recent successes include nominations for the Tony (*Sugar Babies*), the supporting actor Oscar (*Black Stallion*, the inspiration for a later television series in which he also appeared), and an Emmy (*Bill*). The "comeback" such recognition indicates represents one of the most spectacular returns to the limelight in Hollywood history.

Rooney was born into a show business family. At the age of two, he joined his parents in their vaudeville act, and by the age of five was appearing in a series of filmed shorts under the name of Mickey McGuire. Throughout the late 1920s and early 1930s, he made more than 40 appearances in films. By the mid-1930s he was called Mickey Rooney and was under contract to MGM as a successful child star. In 1937 he was featured in a minor film called *A Family Affair*, which introduced the family of Judge Hardy (played in that original movie by Lionel Barrymore). Rooney's appearance as the Judge's son, Andy Hardy, was to turn into a box-office bonanza as he became one of Hollywood's best-loved characters. Hardy became the idealized image of the all-American teenager, real enough to get himself into trouble, but strong enough to find his way out of it (though not without the wise counsel of his beloved father, played in the later Hardy films by Lewis Stone). In 1938 Rooney was awarded a special honorary Oscar for "bringing to the screen the spirit and personification of youth" and for "setting a high standard of ability and achievement" as Andy Hardy. In 1939, 1940, and 1941 Rooney was among the top box-office stars in the United States, a success attributable not only to the Hardy series, but also to his pairings with co-stars as diverse as Wallace Beery and Judy Garland. In these famous MGM films, Rooney sang, danced, clowned, played various musical instruments, emoted, and generally did everything with seeming ease and an abundance of raw talent. He was nominated for Oscars in 1939 and 1943. He was on top of the world at the age of 20, full of youth and energy, and with an apparently unlimited career ahead of him. By the end of the 1940s, however, and by his own admission, he was an unwanted commodity. "In 1938," he said, "I starred in eight pictures. In 1948 and 1949 together, I starred in only three."

During the 1950s, Rooney kept his career going by appearing in nightclubs and on television, and by forming an independent film production company to present himself as the star of a series of movies, none of which was really successful. He also tried his hand at dramatic roles, many of which were much against type. Rooney received another Oscar nomination for his intense performance as a doomed G.I. during the invasion of Italy in the iconoclastic war film *The Bold and the Brave*; drew excellent notices for his supporting role in *Requiem for a Heavyweight*, the film version of Rod Serling's celebrated television drama; and won a Best Actor César award (the French equivalent of the Oscar) for his Cagneyesque performance as the psychopathic title character of Don Siegel's much underrated gangster film *Baby Face Nelson*. Despite these accomplishments, his career faltered. Bankruptcy in 1962, various emotional problems, and seven divorces (which made him the subject of many jokes) all contributed to a difficult period in which Rooney was considered finished in show business. He developed himself further as a character actor, however, and began to find acclaim in television. He published an autobiography, pursued various business ventures, and taught acting, continuing to work professionally when and where he could. In the early 1980s he returned to Broadway in the long-running hit musical, *Sugar Babies*, and found himself once more back on top. When the Motion Picture Academy gave him a second honorary Oscar at its 1982 ceremony, his long career as the boy who could do anything and everything, but who had to grow up, was placed in perspective.

Rooney's abundant talent, like his film image, might seem like a metaphor for America: a seemingly endless supply of natural resources that could never dry up, but which, it turned out, could be ruined by excessive use and abuse, by arrogance or power, and which had to be carefully tended to be returned to full capacity. From child star to character actor, from movie shorts to television specials, and from films to Broadway, Rooney ultimately did prove he could do it all, do it well, and keep on doing it. His is a unique career, both for its versatility and its longevity.

—Jeanine Basinger, updated by John McCarty

ROSAY, Françoise

Nationality: French. **Born:** Françoise de Nalèche in Paris, 19 April 1891. **Education:** Attended school in Versailles; studied at the National Conservatory of Declamation, Paris. **Family:** Married the director Jacques Feyder, 1917 (died 1948). **Career:** 1908—stage debut in *Fantaisies Parisiennes* in Paris; 1913—film debut in *Falstaff*; made several films directed by Feyder and Clair in the 1920s; then worked in the United States, Germany, and the United Kingdom over the next few decades. **Died:** 28 March 1974.

Films as Actress:

1913   *Falstaff*
1922   *Crainquebille* (Feyder)
1925   *Gribiche* (Feyder)
1928   *Le Bateau de verre* (David and Milliet); *Les Deux Timides* (Clair); *Madame Récamier* (Ravel and Lakain)
1929   *The One Woman Idea* (Viertel); *Le Procès de Mary Dugan* (de Sano); *Buster se marie* (Autant-Lara)
1930   *Le Petit Café* (Berger); *Si l'empereur savait ca!* (Feyder); *Saysons gais* (Robison)
1931   *Echec au roi, o Le Roi s'ennui* (d'Usseau and de la Falaise); *Jenny Lind* (Robison); *Olympia* (Feyder); *Quand on est belle* (Robison); *Casanove wider willen* (Brophy); *Magnificent Lie* (Viertel); *La Chance* (Guisart); *La Femme en homme* (*L'ultimo Lord*) (Genina)
1932   *Papa sans le savoir* (Mirande); *Le Rosier de Madame Husson* (Deschamps)
1933   *La Pouponnière* (Boyer); *Tambour battant* (Robison); *L'Abbé Constantin* (Paulin); *Tour Pour rien* (Pujon); *He*
1934   *Le Grand Jeu* (Feyder); *Die Insel* (Steinhoff); *Vers l'abine* (Steinhoff)
1935   *Pension Mimosas* (Feyder); *Coralie et Cie* (Cavalcanti); *Renous* (Gréville); *Le Billet de mille* (Didier); *Gangster malgré lui* (Hugon); *Maternité* (Choux); **La Kermesse héroïque** (Feyder); *Marie des Angoisses* (Bernheim); *The Robber Symphony* (Feher); *Marchand d'amour* (Gréville)
1936   *Le Secret de Polichinelte* (Baethomieu); *Die letzen vier von St. Paul* (Klinger); *Jenny* (Carné)
1937   *Drôle de drame* (Carné); *Mein Sohn, der Herr Minister* (Harlan); *Un Carnet de bal* (Duvivier); *Le Fanteuil 47* (Rivers)
1938   *Paix sur le Rhin* (Choux); *Ramuntcho* (Barberis); *Le Joueur d'echecs* (Dréville); *Le Ruisseau* (Lehmann and Autant-Lara); *Les Gens du voyage* (Feyder); *Fahrendes Volk* (Feyder)
1939   *Serge Panine* (Méré and Schiller); *Die Hochzeitsreise* (Ritter)
1940   *Elles étaient douze femmes* (Lacombe and Mirande)
1941   *Une Femme disparait* (Feyder)
1944   *The Halfway House* (Dearden)

Françoise Rosay in *La Kermesse héroïque*

1945   *Johnny Frenchman* (Frend)
1946   *Macadam* (Blistène); *La Dame de Haut-le-Bois* (Daroy); *Portrait of a Woman* (Burstyn)
1948   *Saraband for Dead Lovers* (Dearden); "Alien Corn" ep. of *Quartet* (French); *Le Joueur* (Autant-Lara); *Backstreet of Paris*
1949   *Le Mystère* (Barton) (Spaak); *Les Vagabonds du rêve* (Tavano); *Donne senza nome* (Radvanyi)
1950   *On n'aime qu'une fois* (Stelli); *Marie Chapdelaine* (*The Naked Heart*) (Marc Allégret); *The September Affair* (Dieterle); *The Thirteenth Letter* (Preminger)
1951   *L'Auberge Rouge* (Autant-Lara); *I figli di nessuno* (Matarazzo)
1952   "L'Orgueil" ("Pride") ep. of *Les Sept Péchés capitaux* (Autant-Lara); *Le Banquet des fraudeurs* (Storck); *Wanda la peccatrice* (Coletti); *Sul Ponte dei Sospiri* (Leonviola); *Chi è senza peccato* (Matarazzo)
1954   *La Reine Margot* (Dreville)
1955   *That Lady* (Young); *Ragazze d'oggi* (Zampa)
1956   *Le Long des trottoirs* (Moguy)
1957   *The Seventh Sin* (Neame); *Interlude* (Sirk)
1958   *Me and the Colonel* (Glenville)
1959   *The Sound and the Fury* (Ritt); *Du Rififi chez les femmes* (*Riff Raff Girls*) (Joffé) (as Bertha); *Une Fleur au fusil* (Käutner)
1960   *Le Bois des amants* (Autant-Lara); *Sans Tambour ni trompette* (Blanc)

1961   *The Full Treatment* (*Stop Me before I Kill*) (Guest) (as Mme. Prade); *La "Cave" se rebiffe* (*The Counterfeiters of Paris*) (Grangier) (as Pauline); *Frau Cheney's Ende* (Wild)
1962   *The Longest Day* (Annakin and others); *Volles Herz und leere taschen*
1965   *Up from the Beach* (*The Day After*) (Parrish)
1966   *Cloportes* (Granier-Deferre) (as Gertrude)
1967   *La 25e Heure* (*The 25th Hour*) (Verneuil) (as Mme. Nagy)
1968   *Faut pas prendre les enfants du bon dieu pour des canards sauvages* (*Operation Leontine*) (Audiard)
1969   *Un Merveilleux Parfum d'oseille* (Bassi)
1974   *Der Fussgänger* (*The Pedestrian*) (Schell)

Publications

By ROSAY: books—

La Traversée d'une vie, Paris, 1974.
Le Cinéma notre metier, with Jacques Feyder, Geneva, 1944.

On ROSAY: articles—

Obituary in *Times* (London), 30 March 1974.
Braucourt, Guy, "Françoise Rosay," in *Ecran* (Paris), May 1974.
"L'Enfer des filmographies," in *Ecran* (Paris), June 1974.

*   *   *

Being the wife to a famous man can often be a handicap. Not so in the case of Françoise Rosay, who became the wife of Jacques Feyder, one of France's greatest film directors. Some of her finest performances were given under his direction. Indeed, the two worked so well together that she also assisted him on films in which she did not appear. As an actress, she had a long and varied career creating characters as diverse as Catherine of Russia and Madame Husson. She played in France, Germany, the United States, England, and Switzerland.

Though she had embarked on a career of theater and opera before she married Feyder in 1917, she more or less devoted herself to a lifelong collaboration with her talented husband. She appeared in a small role in his *Crainquebille*. Then, in *Gribiche* she had a more fulfilling role as the rich American lady who adopts a small working-class boy, beautifully played by Jean Forest. In René Clair's *Les Deux Timides* she played Pierre Batcheff's aunt. In 1928 she accompanied her husband to Hollywood, where the following year she played a small part in Berthold Viertel's *The One Woman Idea* and also appeared in Feyder's French versions of Hollywood talking films. One of these was Ferenc Molnar's *Olympia*, made also in a German version. She also played in *Le Petit Café* and *Jenny Lind*. In these films she was learning dramatic techniques which were to make her one of the greatest actresses of French cinema.

Back in France, she was delightful in *Le Rosier de Madame Husson* with Fernandel. Feyder then returned to France himself, and in three of his films she established herself as a major actress. In *Le Grand Jeu* she played second lead to Marie Bell in a film about the Foreign Legion. In *Pension Mimosas* she suffered the loss of a worthless adopted son, but in *La Kermesse héroïque* she magnificently created a great comedy role as the Burgomaster's wife who welcomes and flirts with the Spanish commander in the Flemish town of Boom in 1616, playing the role in both the French and German versions. All three of these films represented a happy collaboration between Feyder and his scriptwriter, Charles Spaak. The war found the Feyders in Switzerland where Rosay played four roles in Feyder's last important film, *Une Femme disparait*. After his death, Rosay continued to act in films with some stage appearances in London and Paris. In England she made *Saraband for Dead Lovers*, *Johnny Frenchman*, *Quartet*, and *The Naked Heart*, and she appeared in Maximilian Schell's *Der Fussgänger* and in a number of American films, including *The Longest Day*.

—Liam O'Leary

ROSSELLINI, Isabella

Nationality: Italian. **Born:** Rome, 18 June 1952; daughter of the director Roberto Rossellini and the actress Ingrid Bergman. **Family:** Married 1) the director Martin Scorsese, 1979 (divorced 1983); 2) Jonathan Wiedemann (divorced), daughter: Elettra Ingrid; also has adopted son: Roberto; 3) the actor Gary Oldman, 1994; had long-term relationship with the director David Lynch. **Education:** Was graduated from Rome's Academy of Fashion and Costume; attended Finch College and The New School for Social Research. **Career:** 1972—moved to New York at age 19; 1970s—worked as a translator for the Italian News Bureau and as a New York correspondent for Italian TV; 1976—made her screen debut opposite her mother, Ingrid Bergman, in *A Matter of Time*; 1979—returned to Italy to play first leading movie role, in *Il Prato*; 1980—began modeling career; 1982—enrolled in acting classes; 1993—in "The Frightening Frammis" episode of the TV series *Fallen Angels*. **Address:** Click Model Management, Inc., 881 Seventh Avenue, New York, NY 10019, U.S.A.

Films as Actress:

1976   *A Matter of Time* (Minnelli) (as Sister Pia)
1979   *Il Prato* (*The Meadow*) (Paolo Taviani and Vittorio Taviani) (as Eugenia)
1981   *Il Pap'occhio* (*In the Pope's Eye*) (Arbore) (as Isabella)
1985   *White Nights* (Hackford) (as Darya Greenwood)
1986   **Blue Velvet** (David Lynch) (as Dorothy Vallens)
1987   *Tough Guys Don't Dance* (Mailer) (as Madeline); *Siesta* (Lambert) (as Marie); *Red Riding Hood* (Adam Brooks)
1988   *Zelly and Me* (Rathborne) (as Joan, "Zelly")
1989   *Cousins* (Schumacher) (as Maria Hardy)
1990   *Wild at Heart* (David Lynch) (as Perdita Durango); *Ivory Hunters* (*The Lost Elephant*) (Sargent—for TV) (as Maria Di Conti)
1991   *Dames Galantes* (*Gallant Ladies*) (Tacchella) (as Victoire); *Lies of the Twins* (Hunter—for TV) (as Rachel Marks)
1992   *Death Becomes Her* (Zemeckis) (as Lisle Von Rhoman)
1993   *Fearless* (Weir) (as Laura Klein); *The Pickle* (Mazursky) (as Planet Cleveland Woman); *. . . und der Himmel steht still* (*The Innocent*) (Schlesinger) (as Maria)
1994   *Wyatt Earp* (Kasdan) (as Big Nosed Kate); *Immortal Beloved* (Rose) (as Anna Marie Erdody)
1996   *The Funeral* (Ferrara); *Big Night*

Publications

By ROSSELLINI: articles—

Interview with Joseph Gelmis, in *Newsday* (Melville, New York), 18 April 1982.
Interview with Elaine Dutka, in *Time* (New York), 2 May 1983.
"On Her Own," interview with Alice Steinback, in *Saturday Review* (New York), November/December 1985.
"Isabella Rossellini Accesses the Role that Haunted Her," interview with L. Winer, in *New York Times*, 23 November 1986.
"Isabella Interview," interview with P. Stone, in *Interview* (New York), April 1988.
"Bella, Bella Isabella," interview with C. McGuigan and others, in *Newsweek* (New York), 2 May 1988.
"Silent Star," interview with Joan Juliet Buck, in *Vogue*, January 1993.

On ROSSELLINI: book—

Young, Cathleen, *Isabella Rossellini: Quiet Renegade*, New York, 1989.

On ROSSELLINI: articles—

"The Women We Love," in *Esquire* (New York), June 1987.
Current Biography 1988, New York, 1988.
"The Talk of the Town: Mother and Daughter," in *New Yorker*, 23 October 1989.

*   *   *

Isabella Rossellini was born into celluloid royalty; she is the daughter of Ingrid Bergman and Roberto Rossellini. Her fame rests mostly in her bloodline, her uncanny resemblance to her mother, and her extraordinary success as a model. Rossellini began the latter career at age 28, and soon became one of the world's highest-paid and most in-demand models. She has graced more than 500 magazine covers, and earned $2-million a year from a contract with Lancome, the French cosmetics company. In 1982, she appeared on the cover of the U.S.

Isabella Rossellini with Kyle MacLachlan in *Blue Velvet*

edition of *Vogue*, which became the magazine's biggest seller in over a decade.

White Nights, released in 1985 (in which her role is secondary to those of stars Mikhail Baryshnikov and Gregory Hines), was trumpeted as Rossellini's movie debut. Her actual first screen appearance, however, came almost a decade earlier in *A Matter of Time*, which starred her mother. The role was a small one, as a nurse; it is of interest mostly for her character's name, Sister Pia—Rossellini's older half sister is, of course, Pia Lindstrom (by Bergman's first husband, Dr. Peter Lindstrom). Also before *White Nights*, Rossellini had a key role in *Il Prato*, directed by Italy's Paolo and Vittorio Taviani, playing a young clerk in a small Tuscan village who becomes romantically involved with two men.

Rossellini's roles often have been secondary ones. A prime example is *Wyatt Earp*, in which her character—Big Nosed Kate, sweetheart of Doc Holliday (Dennis Quaid)—seems to evaporate from sight soon after initially appearing on-screen. Even when she does well in a fully conceived role, she finds herself eclipsed by characters (and performers) who are far more charismatic. In *Fearless*, she is fine as the wife of a plane crash survivor (Jeff Bridges), but she ultimately is outflanked by Bridges and Rosie Pérez (playing another survivor). The latter two have the showcase roles, and give the showcase performances.

But Rossellini was charming and appealing in *Cousins*, an American remake of *Cousin, Cousine*, Jean-Charles Tachella's French-language romantic comedy. Her character is married to a womanizer, and has

become accustomed to his infidelities. She finds herself attracted to her cousin-by-marriage (Ted Danson), and the two become romantically involved. Had Rossellini been cast in more roles like this, she might have developed into a widely popular leading lady.

Easily Rossellini's best screen work to date may be found in *Blue Velvet*, directed by David Lynch, with whom she had a long-term relationship. *Blue Velvet* is a dark and unsettling thriller in which she plays a bored, deranged nightclub singer who is raped by a psychopath (Dennis Hopper). Her presence here was controversial in that she appeared frontally nude. Rossellini also had a role in Lynch's violent, erotic *Wild at Heart*, playing Perdita Durango, ex-girlfriend of macho but tenderhearted, on-the-lam Sailor Ripley (Nicolas Cage). But here, too, the foremost female roles are played by other actresses—Laura Dern and Diane Ladd.

—Rob Edelman

ROURKE, Mickey

Nationality: American. **Born:** Philip Andre Rourke Jr., in Schenectady, New York, 16 September 1956; at age seven, moved to Miami. **Education:** Studied acting with Sandra Seacat in New York. **Family:** Married the actress Debra Feuer, 1980 (divorced); may have married companion, the actress and model Carre Otis. **Career:** Late 1970s—stage debut in *A View from the Bridge*; 1979—moved to Los Angeles, film debut in *1941*; 1991—took up professional boxing.

Films as Actor:

1979   *1941* (Spielberg) (as Reese)
1980   *City in Fear* ("Allan Smithee," i.e. Jud Taylor—for TV); *Act of Love* (Jud Taylor—for TV) (as Joseph Cybulkowski); **Heaven's Gate** (Cimino) (as Nick Ray); *Fade to Black* (Zimmerman) (as Richie); *Rape and Marriage: The Rideout Case* (Levin—for TV)
1981   *Body Heat* (Kasdan) (as Teddy Lewis)
1982   *Diner* (Levinson) (as Boogie)
1983   *Rumble Fish* (Francis Ford Coppola) (as Motorcycle Boy)
1984   *The Pope of Greenwich Village* (Rosenberg) (as Charlie); *Eureka* (Roeg—produced in 1982) (as Aurelio D'Amato)
1985   *Year of the Dragon* (Cimino) (as Stanley White)
1986   *9½ Weeks* (Lyne) (as John)
1987   *Angel Heart* (Alan Parker) (as Harry Angel); *Barfly* (Schroeder) (as Henry Chinaski); *A Prayer for the Dying* (Hodges) (as Martin Fallon)
1989   *Johnny Handsome* (Walter Hill) (as John Sedley); *Homeboy* (Seresin) (as Johnny Walker, + story); *Francesco* (Cavani) (title role)
1990   *Wild Orchid* (Zalman King) (as James Wheeler); *Desperate Hours* (Cimino) (as Michael Bosworth)
1991   *Harley Davidson and the Marlboro Man* (Wincer) (as Harley Davidson)
1992   *White Sands* (Donaldson) (as Gorman Lennox)
1993   *The Last Outlaw* (Geoff Murphy—for TV) (as Graff)
1994   *The Last Ride* (*F. T. W.*) (as Frank T. Wells)
1995   *Fall Time* (Paul Warner) (as Florence)

Publications

By ROURKE: articles—

Interview in *Interview* (New York), no. 3, 1985.
Hutchinson, C., "Year of the Rourke," in *Films and Filming* (London), January 1986.
"Acting Out," interview with Margy Rochlin, in *American Film* (New York), November 1987.
"Mickey Mouth," interview with Gisela Martine Getty, in *Interview* (New York), January 1988.
Interview in *Films and Filming* (London), March 1990.

On ROURKE: book—

Mills, Bart, *Mickey Rourke: An Illustrated Biography*, London, 1988.

On ROURKE: articles—

Allen, Jennifer, "Bad Boy: Actor Mickey Rourke Is a Hard Case with a Heart," in *New York*, 14 November 1983.
McGillivray, David, "Mickey Rourke," in *Films and Filming* (London), July 1985.
Ostria, V., "S'il continue à pleuvoir," in *Cahiers du Cinéma* (Paris), November 1985.
McDonough, Tom, "Down and (Far) Out," in *American Film*, November 1987.
Smith, Gavin, "Actors Face the Truth," in *Film Comment* (New York), January/February 1989.

Crawley, T., "The Man behind the Mask," in *Film Monthly* (Berkhamsted, England), September 1990.
Stanley, Alessandra, "Can 50 Million Frenchmen Be Wrong? The Nouvellest Vague: Mickey Rourke," in *New York Times Magazine*, 21 October 1990.
Current Biography 1991, New York, 1991.
Stars (Mariembourg, Belgium), Winter 1993.
Kennedy, Dana, "Knock-Knock Knockin' on Hollywood's Door," in *Entertainment Weekly* (New York), 9 December 1994.
Baumgold, Julie, "Tough Guys Don't Wear Underwear," in *Esquire* (New York), February 1995.
Raab, Scott, "Mickey Rourke Doesn't Smell," in *GQ* (New York), July 1995.

*   *   *

Mickey Rourke's career is one of unfulfilled potential. He might have developed into his generation's John Garfield, Marlon Brando, Montgomery Clift, James Dean: a foremost on-screen interpreter of the sexually attractive but disillusioned and world-weary rebel hero/loner, and a modern-era practitioner of the Method. Unfortunately, he has been restricted by poor judgment in choosing his screen roles and, even more haplessly, an inability to coexist with his fellow actors and film makers. Indeed, stories of Rourke playing out the role of off-camera spoiled brat/bad boy are legion—and, after a while, they grow tiresome.

He began his career in promising fashion, with a starring role in the made-for-television movie *Rape and Marriage: The Rideout Case*, playing a husband who is accused by his wife of rape, and he impressed as the quiet, intense explosives expert in *Body Heat*. He had a nice showcase as a member of the ensemble cast of *Diner* (playing the womanizing Boogie), and emerged unscathed from Francis Coppola's disappointing *Rumble Fish* (in the role of the Motorcycle Boy).

Diner and *Rumble Fish* feature casts laden with up-and-coming talent. In *Diner*, Rourke appears with Steve Guttenberg, Daniel Stern, Kevin Bacon, Ellen Barkin, and Paul Reiser; in *Rumble Fish*, his fellow actors include Matt Dillon, Diane Lane, Nicolas Cage, Christopher Penn, and Laurence Fishburne. Some of these actors have gone on to enjoy thriving celluloid careers. In particular, Bacon, Barkin, Dillon, Lane, Cage, Penn, and Fishburne have done arresting work on screen; in the mid-1990s, several—especially Bacon, Cage, and Fishburne—are entering their prime as major movie stars. But, while Rourke is not without several commendable credits on his filmography, as he nears his 40th birthday the sense about him is that his future movies will more than likely be of the direct-to-video variety.

Easily Rourke's best screen role came in *Barfly*, based on the autobiographical musings of cult writer Charles Bukowski. Rourke plays Henry Chinaski, a self-destructive fall-down drunk, and his bravura performance predates that of Cage's award-winning work almost a decade later in *Leaving Las Vegas*. *Barfly*, however, was to be the exception to, rather than the rule of, Rourke's career. His casting in *Johnny Handsome*, *Desperate Hours*, and *Harley Davidson and the Marlboro Man* is obscured by the fact that he turned down the leads in *Beverly Hills Cop* and *Top Gun*. After taking sixth billing in Nicolas Roeg's *Eureka*, he may have declared, "I'd rather do a small part on a Roeg film than a big one in a Hollywood meatball movie." But his attempts at "serious" filmmaking have been seriously misguided. A prime example: *Year of the Dragon*, a sloppily directed (by Michael Cimino) genre exercise in which he plays a Vietnam veteran/New York City cop. The scenario may have serious pretensions—Rourke's character is named White; his main life-skill is killing; and he has brought the war home to the extent that he is involved in Chinatown hostilities. But in *Year of the Dragon*, the bottom line is that Rourke plays yet another boring, stereotypically violent Vietnam vet.

Mickey Rourke

Rourke has, at the same time, chosen to work abroad, but with little impact. In the British-made *A Prayer for the Dying*, he sports a laughable accent playing an IRA hit man. In the Italian-German *Francesco* he plays Francis of Assisi, but the result is practically unwatchable. If his early performances were calm and cerebral, in *Francesco* Rourke embodies the worst stereotype of Method acting as he mumbles his way through the film.

Rourke also has specialized in erotically-charged roles. The best of these came in the ambitious but ultimately unsuccessful *Angel Heart*, playing a private eye; his erotic love scene (with Lisa Bonet) had to be cut to avoid an X-rating. In *9½ Weeks*, he is cast as a bondage-hooked banker, and the result is a mess of a movie that earned headlines for Rourke's lack of rapport with his co-star, Kim Basinger. The actor may have married his *Wild Orchid* co-star, Carre Otis; the film won notoriety for an infamous, supposedly unsimulated sex scene between the two. But *Wild Orchid* is a typical concoction of its director, Zalman King: dramatically inept soft-core pornography. At least Rourke did not appear in the sequel, *Wild Orchid 2: Two Shades of Blue*.

In 1991, Rourke became a professional boxer. As a youngster growing up on the mean streets of New York and Miami, his aspiration was to become a boxer. Nevertheless, his decision to turn pro at an age—35—when most career fighters are way beyond their primes was ill-advised. It was as if playing a pugilist on screen (as he had in *Homeboy*) was insufficient proof of his machismo. He had to one-up John Garfield, Robert Ryan, Kirk Douglas, and Sylvester Stallone—actors who appeared in classic boxing movies—by becoming the real McCoy.

Every actor is entitled to an occasional turkey, but Rourke's career, once past its early, promising stages, is the equivalent of a Thanksgiving feast. "I've watched actors I've admired over the years sell out. That's the worst crime of all," he has said. While a noble thought, Rourke's proclivity for misguided decision making (not to mention his oversized ego) is the dominating factor of his career.

—Rob Edelman

ROWLANDS, Gena

Nationality: American. **Born:** Virginia Cathryn Rowlands in Cambria, Wisconsin, 19 June 1934 (some sources give 1936). **Education:** Attended Washington and Lee High School, Arlington, Virginia; University of Wisconsin, two years; American Academy of Dramatic Arts, New York. **Family:** Married the director John Cassavetes, 1954 (died 1989), children: the actor/director Nick Cassavetes, Alexandra, Zoe. **Career:** Wardrobe mistress and actress with Provincetown Playhouse, New York; appeared in New York in plays *All about Love* and *Dangerous Corner*, and on tour in *Time Out for Ginger* and *The Seven Year Itch*; 1956—successful role in *Middle of the Night*; 1957—MGM contract: film debut in *The High Cost of Loving*, 1958; 1961-62—in TV series *87th Precinct*, and later in *Peyton Place*, 1967. **Awards:** Best Actress, Berlin Festival, for *Opening Night*, 1978; Italian Silver Ribbon for Best Foreign Actress, for *Love Streams*, 1983-84. **Address:** 7917 Woodrow Wilson Drive, Los Angeles, CA 90046, U.S.A.

Films as Actress:

1958   *The High Cost of Loving* (Ferrer) (as Virginia Fry)
1962   *A Child Is Waiting* (John Cassavetes) (as Sophie Widdicombe); *Lonely Are the Brave* (Miller) (as Jerri Bondi); *The Spiral Road* (Mulligan) (as Els)
1967   *Tony Rome* (Douglas) (as Rita Kosterman)

1968   *A qualsiasi prezzo* (*The Vatican Affair*) (Miraglia); *Faces* (John Cassavetes) (as Jeanni Rapp); *Gli intocabili* (*Machine Gun McCain*) (Montaldo) (as Rosemary Scott)
1969   *The Happy Ending* (Richard Brooks)
1971   *Minnie and Moskowitz* (John Cassavetes) (title role)
1974   *A Woman under the Influence* (John Cassavetes) (as Mabel Longhetti)
1976   *Two-Minute Warning* (Peerce) (as Janet)
1978   *The Brink's Job* (Friedkin) (as Mary Pine); *A Question of Love* (Thorpe—for TV)
1979   *Opening Night* (John Cassavetes) (as Myrtle Gordon); *Strangers: The Story of a Mother and Daughter* (Katselas—for TV)
1980   *Gloria* (John Cassavetes) (title role)
1982   *Tempest* (Mazursky) (as Antonia)
1983   *Thursday's Child* (Rich—for TV) (as Victoria Alden)
1984   *Love Streams* (John Cassavetes) (as Sarah Lawson)
1985   *An Early Frost* (Erman—for TV) (as Katherine Pierson)
1987   *The Betty Ford Story* (Greene—for TV) (title role); *Light of Day* (Schrader) (as Jeannete Rasnick)
1988   *Another Woman* (Woody Allen) (as Marion Post)
1990   *Montana* (Graham—for TV) (as Bess Guthrie)
1991   *Once Around* (Hallström) (as Marilyn Bella); *Night on Earth* (Jarmusch) (as Victoria Snelling); *Face of a Stranger* (Weill—for TV) (as Pat Foster); *Ted & Venus* (Cort) (as Mrs. Turner)
1992   *Crazy in Love* (Coolidge—for TV) (as Honora)
1993   *Silent Cries* (Anthony Page—for TV) (as Dr. Peggy Sutherland)
1994   *Parallel Lives* (Yellen—for TV) (as Francie Pomerantz); *The Neon Bible* (Terence Davies) (as Aunt Mae)
1995   *Something to Talk About* (Hallström) (as Georgia King)
1996   *Unhook the Stars* (Nick Cassavetes)

Publications

By ROWLANDS: articles—

"Gena Rowlands Is Gloria," interview with Rob Edelman, in *Films in Review* (New York), October 1980.
Interview with T. Jousse, in *Cahiers du Cinéma* (Paris), June 1992.
Interview with Gary Indiana, in *Interview* (New York), December 1992.

On ROWLANDS: articles—

Current Biography 1975, New York, 1975.
Farren, J., "Gena Rowlands," in *Cinéma* (Paris), February 1977.
Walker, Beverly, "Woman of Influence: Gena," in *Film Comment* (New York), May/June 1989.

*   *   *

Although Gena Rowlands made her film debut in 1958, she seemed to burst fresh onto the cinema screens with the 1968 release of John Cassavetes's *Faces*. Under the direction of her husband, she gave a performance of startling intensity as Jeanni Rapp, a prostitute who spends an evening with an errant husband played by John Marley.

Over the next 20 years, Rowlands's career was inextricably linked with that of her husband. She starred in an additional five films he directed, including three in which he co-starred; in 1982, they played husband and wife in Paul Mazursky's *Tempest*.

Unlike any other director with whom Rowlands has worked, Cassavetes was able to successfully tap into the actress's ability to depict a wide variety of female experiences, particularly playing women at extreme points of stress. Three years after the release of *Faces*,

Rowlands appeared in *Minnie and Moskowitz* as Minnie, a lonely, former prom queen about to turn 40 who, after being dumped by her married boyfriend (Cassavetes), takes up with Moskowitz, an aging hippie who works as a parking lot attendant.

Then, as the tortured housewife Mabel Longhetti in *A Woman under the Influence*, Rowlands garnered her greatest critical reviews, her depiction of a lower-middle-class woman's struggle to maintain sanity striking a resonant chord with many viewers and critics. Sadly, Mabel lives her life through her husband and children; according to Rowlands, Mabel was "totally vulnerable and giving, she had no sense of her own worth, and was completely mirrored in the eyes of men." In an intensely physical performance, Rowlands convincingly depicted the erratic behavior of a woman who finds she cannot always express herself in words. Mabel struggles valiantly but ineffectually with her psychological condition; never does Cassavetes romanticize her martyrdom. Made at a time when challenging, fully-developed roles for actresses were becoming increasingly rare, *A Woman under the Influence* (along with *An Unmarried Woman*, starring Jill Clayburgh) stands as a beacon amid a vast wasteland of one-dimensional women's roles as mothers and whores.

The next Cassavetes-Rowlands collaboration—*Opening Night*—had Rowlands playing Myrtle Gordon, an unmarried actress on the verge of a nervous breakdown, who attempts to come to terms with her private life through her theatrical career. It just so happens that she is undergoing a crisis of confidence while playing a woman who is facing the same situation. Here Cassavetes also plays the dual role: Myrtle's former lover in real life, who also plays opposite her on stage.

Then, beginning with a statement that Rowlands made to her husband about her desire to work with a child, came the script of *Gloria*. As a hardened ex-showgirl and former girlfriend to a Mafia boss, Gloria is living on her own, with, as she claims, her own money and her own apartment. That is until her neighbor squeals on the mob and Gloria is left holding his son and the book of evidence his father had compiled. Gloria walks tough; Rowlands explained that much of the power of her performance was communicated in the way she carried herself as she moves about on the streets of New York. According to her, it was a walk that said, "They'd better watch out." Ultimately, Gloria is a trapped woman; she admits she hates kids, yet in following her code of what is right, she protects and eventually develops a certain motherly responsibility to this six-year-old Puerto Rican orphan. Lines of dialogue such as "I'm saving your life, stupid" encapsulate her confusion. Throughout, Rowlands never hedges in her meanness, despite the well-known acting school dictum that you must never be mean to kids or old people.

Their final project—*Love Streams*—is perhaps Cassavetes's most successful film. As brother and sister, Rowlands and Cassavetes depict characters going through individual crises, she of divorce and custody, he as a writer in the throes of researching a book on prostitution. Ultimately, Rowlands's Sarah loves too much, particularly those who are less fortunate than she; she herself has recently been incarcerated in a mental institution. She desperately tries to prove that she is happy, and can function on her own. Sarah and Robert meet up and through several tumultuous scenes, reawaken childhood affections.

It is unfortunate that Rowlands no longer has Cassavetes to direct her, for very few others have tapped into her unique capabilities. In 1988, just before Cassavetes's death, Woody Allen directed her in his Bergmanesque *Another Woman*, about a writer coming to terms with her life; the role was very much the kind Bergman wrote for Liv Ullmann. Unfortunately, the project lacked the piercing insights that mark Bergman's work, and Rowlands was never fully able to plumb the depths of the character.

Perhaps Rowlands's most incisive performance outside her work with Cassavetes was as the mother dealing with her son's AIDS in the television movie *An Early Frost*. Here, her character, at a point in her life of extreme stress, compassionately acknowledges her love for her son. And her best recent role has been in Terence Davies's *The Neon Bible*, cast as Aunt Mae, an aging Southern belle who comes to live with her young nephew and his family in a small town. Mae, like a character out of a Tennessee Williams play, fills her nephew's ear with colorful stories, but beneath her surface bravado is a melancholy soul; she is like the forlorn subject of one of the blues songs she sings, as she goes on to impart her feelings and vulnerabilities to her nephew.

—Doug Tomlinson, updated by Rob Edelman

RUSSELL, Jane

Nationality: American. **Born:** Ernestine Geraldine Russell in Bemidji, Minnesota, 21 June 1921; grew up in California. **Education:** Was graduated from Van Nuys High School. **Family:** Married 1) the athlete Bob Waterfield, 1943 (divorced 1968), three adopted children: Thomas, Tracy, Robert; 2) Roger Barrett, 1968 (died 1968); 3) John Calvin Peoples, 1974. **Career:** Receptionist, then model; studied acting at Max Reinhardt's Theatre Workshop and Maria Ouspenskaya's school; 1939-late 1950s—under contract to Howard Hughes; 1943—enormous publicity with release of her debut film *The Outlaw*; also worked on stage and in nightclubs; 1971—in the stage musical *Company*; spokeswoman for the Playtex Company; 1983-84 appeared in some episodes of TV series *Yellow Rose*. **Address:** c/o Webb, 7500 Devista Drive, Los Angeles, CA 90046, U.S.A.

Films as Actress:

1943   *The Outlaw* (Hughes) (as Rio)
1946   *Young Widow* (Marin) (as Joan Kenwood)
1948   *The Paleface* (McLeod) (as Calamity Jane)
1951   *His Kind of Woman* (Farrow) (as Lenore Brent); *Double Dynamite* (Cummings) (as Mildred Goodhug)
1952   *Macao* (von Sternberg) (as Julie Benson); *Road to Bali* (Walker) (as herself); *The Las Vegas Story* (Stevenson) (as Linda Rollins); *Son of Paleface* (Tashlin) (as Mike); *Montana Belle* (Dwan) (as Belle Starr)
1953   *Gentlemen Prefer Blondes* (Hawks) (as Dorothy)
1954   *The French Line* (Lloyd Bacon) (as Mary Carson); *Underwater!* (John Sturges) (as Theresa)
1955   *Foxfire* (Pevney) (as Amanda Lawrence); *Gentlemen Marry Brunettes* (Sale) (as Bonnie/Mimi Jones); *The Tall Men* (Walsh) (as Nella Turner)
1956   *Hot Blood* (Nicholas Ray) (as Annie Caldash); *The Revolt of Mamie Stover* (Walsh) (title role)
1957   *The Fuzzy Pink Nightgown* (Taurog) (as Laurel Stevens)
1964   *Fate Is the Hunter* (Ralph Nelson) (as herself)
1966   *Johnny Reno* (Springsteen) (as Nona Williams); *Waco* (Springsteen) (as Jill Stone)
1967   *The Born Losers* (Laughlin) (as Mrs. Shorn)
1970   *Darker than Amber* (Clouse) (as Alabama Tiger)

Publications

By RUSSELL: book—

Jane Russell: My Path & My Detours: An Autobiography, New York, 1985.

Jane Russell

By RUSSELL: articles—

Interview with John Kobal, in *Films and Filming* (London), July 1984.
"Russell," interview with G. Peary, in *Film Comment* (New York), July/
August 1992.

On RUSSELL: book—

Parish, James Robert, *The RKO Gals*, New Rochelle, New York, 1974.

On RUSSELL: articles—

Hagen, Ray, "Jane Russell," in *Films in Review* (New York), March 1963.
Dangaard, C., "Jane Russell l'autre destin d'un symbole sexuel," in *Cine-
Tele-Revue*, 23 July 1987.
Kendall, R., "Jane Russell Speaks Out," in *Hollywood Studio*, no. 10,
1988.
Rubenstein, Hal, "Jane Russell," in *Interview* (New York), August 1988.
Kuerten, J., "Busenwunder und Boesewicht, in *Medium*, no. 2, 1991.
Peary, G., "Russell," in *Film Comment* (New York) , July/August 1992.
Stars (Mariembourg, Belgium), Autumn 1993.

*   *   *

Most stars develop an image, but Jane Russell was an image before she was properly a movie star. Even today, she is likely best remembered as the busty, cleavaged sex symbol of *The Outlaw*'s huge publicity campaign than as, for example, Dorothy in *Gentlemen Prefer Blondes*. The image (together with the accompanying slogan, "Mean, moody, magnificent") was much parodied, but hardly required it: it was a parody already. Of what? Female sexual provocation, of course, in a culture that has not been reluctant to endorse the equation sexuality = woman = evil. But even worse: an active, aggressive, desiring female sexuality. "How would you like to tussle with Russell?" was always meant, presumably, to be a question that daunted viewers as much as aroused them. How—within a male-dominated culture that takes the phallus as its symbol of power, a culture in which male potency is thus continuously threatened and which is characterized accordingly by male sexual anxiety in its many forms—can active female sexuality be represented *except* as parody? (There are, in fact, two other options: it can be set up in order to be punished and subdued, or it can be quite straightforwardly vilified.) Jane Russell was always something of a joke because what the image stood for could not be seriously contemplated.

Russell's role in *The Outlaw* is in fact remarkably innocuous: the film is so obsessed with male homosexuality that it marginalizes her completely. Movie reviewers routinely dismissed her performance, but they did note the contribution her breasts made to the production. Indeed, director Howard Hughes conducted a nationwide "talent" search for the perfect actress to play Rio; and he selected Russell based almost solely upon her amply endowed physique. Accordingly, it was clearly not the role but the image that made her a kind of star. But *what* kind? What could be done with her? It seems inevitable that, after one or two false starts, she would be shifted into comedy; inevitable even, that she would find a special if temporary niche partnering Bob Hope, most of whose humor is rooted in sexual ineffectuality, so that the comic-parodic side of the Russell persona becomes even more pronounced.

One might also have predicted—given a certain auteurist hindsight—that if Russell were to have a moment of real glory it would be in collaboration with Howard Hawks; one wonders how different her career might have been had Hawks directed her in *The Outlaw* as was originally intended (he directed only a couple of scenes at the beginning of the film, before Russell was introduced). Hawks's delight in assertive women, and his insistence that the role of Dorothy be developed especially for her, enabled Russell, in *Gentlemen Prefer Blondes*, to play comedy in which female sexual attractiveness becomes the positive norm in a ridiculous world of male incompetence and inanity. Although Marilyn Monroe was unequivocally the star of *Gentlemen*, Russell rises to this considerable challenge to deliver a clever performance as her wisecracking, sexually experienced, and less materially motivated friend. And, in one of the film's most memorable numbers, "Ain't There Anyone Here for Love?," Russell is enchanting as a woman who is quite comfortable in the company of scores of barely clad athletic men. Little wonder that the film's final scene, the double wedding, ends with the camera moving in to frame Russell and Monroe as they smile at each other rather than at their husbands.

—Robin Wood, updated by Cynthia Felando

RUSSELL, Rosalind

Nationality: American. **Born:** Waterbury, Connecticut, 4 June 1908. **Education:** Attended Notre Dame Academy, Waterbury; Marymount School, Tarrytown on the Hudson, New York; American Academy of Dramatic Arts, New York. **Family:** Married Frederic Brisson, 1941, son: Carl Lance. **Career:** Toured in a tent show; 1929—joined the Copley players, Boston; appeared in *Garrick Gaieties* in New York, on tour with *Roar China*, and in *Talent* and *Second Man*; 1934—contract with MGM: film debut in *Evelyn Prentice*; 1953—on Broadway in *Wonderful Town*, and then in *Auntie Mame*, 1956, and in film version, 1958. **Awards:** Jean Hersholt Humanitarian Award, 1972. **Died:** 28 November 1976.

Films as Actress:

1934   *Evelyn Prentice* (Howard) (as Nancy Harrison); *The President Vanishes* (Wellman) (as Sally Voorman); *Forsaking All Others* (Van Dyke) (as Eleanor)
1935   *The Night Is Young* (Murphy) (as Countess Rafay); *West Point of the Air* (Rosson) (as Dare); *The Casino Murder Case* (Marin) (as Doris); *Reckless* (Fleming) (as Jo); *China Seas* (Garnett) (as Sybil Barclay); *Rendezvous* (Howard) (as Joel Carter)
1936   *It Had to Happen* (Del Ruth) (as Beatrice); *Under Two Flags* (Lloyd) (as Lady Venetia); *Trouble for Two* (Ruben) (as Miss Vandeleur/Princess Brenda); *Craig's Wife* (Arzner) (as Harriet Craig)
1937   *Night Must Fall* (Thorpe) (as Olivia); *Live, Love, and Learn* (Fitzmaurice) (as Julie Stoddard)
1938   *Man-Proof* (Thorpe) (as Elizabeth); *Four's a Crowd* (Curtiz) (as Jean Christy); *The Citadel* (King Vidor) (as Christine Manson)
1939   *Fast and Loose* (Marin) (as Garda Sloane); *The Women* (Cukor) (as Sylvia Fowler)
1940   *His Girl Friday* (Hawks) (as Hildy Johnson); *No Time for Comedy* (Keighley) (as Linda Easterbrook); *Hired Wife* (Seiter) (as Kendal Browning)
1941   *This Thing Called Love* (*Married but Single*) (Hall) (as Ann Winters); *They Met in Bombay* (Brown) (as Anya Von Duren); *Design for Scandal* (Taurog) (as Cornelia Porter)
1942   *Take a Letter, Darling* (Leisen) (as A. M. MacGregor); *My Sister Eileen* (Hall) (as Ruth Sherwood)
1943   *Flight for Freedom* (Mendes) (as Tonie Carter); *What a Woman!* (Cummings) (as Carol Kingsley)

1945   *Roughly Speaking* (Curtiz) (as Louise Randall); *She Wouldn't Say Yes* (Hall) (as Susan Lane)
1946   *Sister Kenny* (Nichols) (title role)
1947   *The Guilt of Janet Ames* (Levin) (title role); *Mourning Becomes Electra* (Nichols) (as Lavinia Mannon)
1948   *The Velvet Touch* (Gage) (as Valerie Stanton)
1949   *Tell It to the Judge* (Foster) (as Marsha Meredith)
1950   *A Woman of Distinction* (Buzzell) (as Susan Middlecott)
1952   *Never Wave at a WAC* (McLeod) (as Jo McBain)
1955   *The Girl Rush* (Pirosh) (as Kim Halliday)
1956   *Picnic* (Logan) (as Rosemary Sydney)
1958   *Auntie Mame* (Da Costa) (title role)
1961   *A Majority of One* (LeRoy) (as Mrs. Jacoby)
1962   *Five Finger Exercise* (Mann) (as Louise Harrington); *Gypsy* (LeRoy) (as Rose)
1966   *The Trouble with Angels* (Lupino) (as Mother Superior)
1967   *Oh, Dad, Poor Dad* (Mackendricks) (as Madame Rosepettle)
1968   *Rosie!* (Rich) (title role); *Where Angels Go—Trouble Follows!* (Neilson) (as Mother Simplicis)
1971   *Mrs. Pollifax—Spy* (Martinson) (title role)
1972   *The Crooked Hearts* (Sandrich—for TV) (as Laurita Dorsey)

Film as Writer:

1956   *The Unguarded Moment* (Keller) (co-sc)

Publications

By RUSSELL: book—

Life Is a Banquet, with Chris Chase, New York, 1977.

On RUSSELL: books—

Rosen, Marjorie, *Popcorn Venus*, New York, 1973.
Yanni, Nicholas, *Rosalind Russell*, New York, 1975.
Parish, James, and Don Stanke, *The Leading Ladies*, New York, 1977.

On RUSSELL: articles—

Current Biography 1943, New York, 1943.
Ringgold, Gene, "Rosalind Russell," in *Films in Review* (New York), December 1970.
"Rosalind Russel (sic)," in *Cinéma* (Paris), February 1977.
Bowers, Ron, "Hors d'oeuvre," in *Films in Review* (New York), April 1977.

*   *   *

In 1965 Rosalind Russell gave David Zeitlin of *Life* magazine her prescription for success in acting: "It's okay to have talent, but talent is the least of it. In a performance or a career, you've got to have vitality. I've worked with actors and actresses far better than I'll ever be—as far as talent goes. But what they have just doesn't register because they don't have a ... drive underneath a project. ... Sometimes what you have to do is almost claw your work onto film." That two-fisted approach worked well in such larger-than-life characters as Sylvia Fowler (*The Women*), Hildy Johnson (*His Girl Friday*), Ruth Sherwood (*My Sister Eileen*), Mame Dennis (*Auntie Mame*), and Rose (*Gypsy*), but badly in more subtle or multidimensional roles as Lavinia Mannon (*Mourning Becomes Electra*), Bertha Jacoby (*A Majority of One*), and Louise Harrington (*Five Finger Exercise*). Still, despite her excesses, Russell cornered the market on the intelligent, fast-talking, well-dressed career woman, and her superb comic timing was arguably the best in the business.

Russell's film career can be divided into roughly three periods. In the 1930s she played the "other woman" in major films and the resilient leading lady of minor ones, usually getting Joan Crawford's or Myrna Loy's discarded roles. Her first real break came in 1935 when Myrna Loy decided not to play opposite William Powell in *Rendezvous*, a spy comedy in the *Thin Man* tradition. Russell's first starring role came a year later when MGM lent her out to Columbia to do *Craig's Wife*. Though too young for the part, she received excellent notices as a fastidious, domineering housewife. Despite this critical acclaim (or perhaps because of it), she was still locked into a type—the young, well-dressed sophisticate.

The Women marked a transition in her career and made her a star. Russell played a malicious chatterbox in a flamboyantly exaggerated comic style. Producer Hunt Stromberg had intended to cast Ilka Chase (who originated the role on stage), declaring Russell "too beautiful" and "a fine dramatic actress, but not a comedienne." Russell kept pushing for the part and made five tests until she got it.

After *The Women* Russell was accepted enthusiastically as a full-fledged comedienne and in 1940 played the role for which (with the possible exception of Mame) she is most remembered—Hildy Johnson. With a breakneck, clenched-teeth delivery, she deflates the lesser mortals around her (all men), lighting her own cigarettes and disarming a murderer, while trying to decide between a career (newspaper reporting) and marriage. She gets them both in the end, but opts for conniving Cary Grant (one of the few leading men able to stand up to her on screen) over the mealy-mouthed Ralph Bellamy.

Throughout the 1940s Russell played a seemingly endless series of career women with (she claimed) essentially the same office set. Once again she had been typecast. Although the 1940s brought her three Oscar nominations for parts deviating from type (*My Sister Eileen*, *Sister Kenny*, and, inexplicably, *Mourning Becomes Electra*), only *My Sister Eileen* was commercially successful and her career went into a decline.

By the 1950s Russell was too old for her "type," so she returned to the stage, appearing in *Bell, Book and Candle*, *Wonderful Town* (a musical version of *My Sister Eileen*), and *Auntie Mame*. She appeared in a few films during that period, the best of which was *Picnic*, for which she undoubtedly would have been nominated as Best Supporting Actress had she agreed to be considered for that category. Russell's two-year stage role as Mame Dennis led to her best film in over a decade—*Auntie Mame*. Modeling the role on one of her sisters, she received a fourth Oscar nomination for her zany portrayal, but did not work again in film until three years later.

With the exception of *Gypsy*, which offered her a part large enough to encompass her pull-out-all-the-stops theory of acting, Russell's film roles in the last decade of her career were an embarrassment—either because she misunderstood the characters (e.g., Bertha Jacoby and Louise Harrington) or because the films themselves were bad (e.g., *Where Angels Go, Trouble Follows* and *Mrs. Pollifax—Spy*).

Discussing her career, she remarked: "There are only two ways to get ahead in Hollywood. You either have to get one great picture a year—these propel you forward—or your impact has to be made with a lot of pictures." Clearly she went the latter route, her vivacious intelligence and snappy delivery remaining in our memories in the leaner years of her career.

—Catherine Henry

RUTHERFORD, (Dame) Margaret

Nationality: British. **Born:** London, 11 May 1892. **Education:** Attended Wimbledon Hill School; Ravenscroft. **Family:** Married Stringer Davis, 1945. **Career:** Taught speech and piano; then studied

Margaret Rutherford with Michael Redgrave in *The Importance of Being Earnest* courtesy of The Rank Organisation Plc

acting at the Old Vic, London; 1925—stage debut; then in repertory in Oxford, Croydon, and London; 1936—film debut in *Dusty Ermine*; 1939—first appearance as Miss Prism in *The Importance of Being Earnest*, London; repeated the role in film version, 1952; 1940—stage role of Mme. Arcati in *Blithe Spirit*; repeated in film, 1945; 1948—stage role of Miss Whitchurch in *The Happiest Days of Your Life*; repeated in film, 1950. **Awards:** Best Supporting Actress Academy Award for *The V.I.P.s*, 1963. Dame Commander, Order of the British Empire, 1967. **Died:** 22 May 1972.

Films as Actress:

1936   *Dusty Ermine* (*Hideout in the Alps*) (Vorhaus) (as Miss Butterby); *Talk of the Devil* (Reed) (as housekeeper); *Troubled Waters* (Parker)

1937   *Beauty and the Barge* (Edwards) (as Mrs. Baldwin); *Big Fella* (Wills); *Catch as Catch Can* (*Atlantic Episode*) (Kellino) (as Maggie Carberry); *Missing, Believed Married* (Carstairs) (as Lady Parke)

1941   *Spring Meeting* (Mycroft) (as Aunt Bijou); *Quiet Wedding* (Asquith) (as Magistrate)

1943   *The Yellow Canary* (Wilcox) (as Mrs. Towcester); *The Demi-Paradise* (*Adventure for Two*) (Asquith) (as Rowena Ventnor)

1944   *English without Tears* (*Her Man Gilbey*) (French) (as Lady Christobel Beauclerk)

1945   *Blithe Spirit* (Lean) (as Mme. Arcati)

1947   *While the Sun Shines* (Asquith) (as Dr. Winifred Frye); *Meet Me at Dawn* (*The Gay Duellist*) (Freeland) (as Mme. Vernorel)

1948   *Miranda* (Annakin) (as Nurse Cary); *Passport to Pimlico* (Cornelius) (as Prof. Hatton-Jones)

1950   *The Happiest Days of Your Life* (Launder) (as Miss Whitchurch); *Her Favourite Husband* (*The Taming of Dorothy*) (Soldati) (as Mrs. Dotherington)

1951   *The Magic Box* (Boulting) (as Lady Pond)

1952   *Curtain Up* (Smart) (as Jeremy St. Clare); *The Importance of Being Earnest* (Asquith) (as Miss Prism); *Castle in the Air* (Cass) (as Miss Nicholson); *Miss Robin Hood* (Guillermin) (as Miss Honey)

1953   *Innocents in Paris* (Parry) (as Gwladwys Inglott); *Trouble in Store* (Carstairs) (as Miss Bacon)
1954   *The Runaway Bus* (Guest) (as Cynthia Beeston); *Aunt Clara* (Kimmins) (as Clara Hilton); *Mad about Men* (Thomas) (as Nurse Carey)
1955   *An Alligator Named Daisy* (Thompson) (as Prudence Croquet)
1957   *The Smallest Show on Earth* (Dearden) (as Mrs. Fazackerlee); *Just My Luck* (Carstairs) (as Mrs. Dooley)
1959   *I'm All Right Jack* (Boulting) (as Aunt Dolly)
1961   *Murder She Said* (Pollock) (as Jane Marple); *On the Double* (Shavelson)
1963   *The Mouse on the Moon* (Lester) (as Grand Duchess Gloriana); *Murder at the Gallop* (Pollock) (as Miss Marple); *The V.I.P.s* (Asquith) (as Duchess of Brighton)
1964   *Murder Most Foul* (Pollock) (as Miss Marple); *Murder Ahoy* (Pollock) (as Miss Marple)
1965   *The Alphabet Murders* (Pollock) (as Miss Marple)
1966   *A Countess from Hong Kong* (Chaplin) (as Mrs. Gaulswallow); **Chimes at Midnight** (*Campanadas a medianoche*; *Falstaff*) (Welles) (as Hostess Quickly)
1967   *The Wacky World of Mother Goose* (Bass) (as voice); *Arabella* (Bolognini) (as Princess Ilaria)

Publications

By RUTHERFORD: book—

Margaret Rutherford: An Autobiography, as told to Gwen Robyns, London, 1972.

On RUTHERFORD: books—

Keown, Eric, *Margaret Rutherford*, New York, 1955.
Simmons, Dawn Langley, *Margaret Rutherford: A Blithe Spirit*, London, 1983.

On RUTHERFORD: articles—

Current Biography 1964, New York, 1964.
Obituary in *New York Times*, 23 May 1972.
Vermilye, Jerry, "Margaret Rutherford," in *Films in Review* (New York), August/September 1990.

*   *   *

James Mason, asked to name his favorite leading lady, said that he tried rating them all by stars and that the only five-star lady was Margaret Rutherford. She was an exceptional and well-loved comedienne, who began her working life as a teacher of piano and elocution before a small legacy enabled her to attend the Old Vic school to study drama. She had various successful stage roles before making her first film in 1936, *Dusty Ermine*. She had a highly unorthodox appearance—the demeanor of a startled turkey-cock, the jaws of a bloodhound and a highly unwieldy frame. All of this marked her out to be a character actress, a term applied to women not considered attractive enough to be the love interest in films. Margaret Rutherford's screen career depended on her playing variations on the theme of delightfully dotty "spinster," either intense, gushing, and absentminded or tweedy and austere.

She played all her roles with aplomb and perspicacity and had a superb sense of timing. She was the irrepressible and flamboyant Madame Arcati in *Blithe Spirit*, the enthusiastic Medieval expert in Ealing Studio's *Passport to Pimlico*, and the unforgettably fluttering and forgetful Miss Prism in *The Importance of Being Earnest*. In *The*

Happiest Days of Your Life she starred with Alastair Sim, who played the headmaster of the school upon which Rutherford and her truculent "gels" are billeted with uproarious consequences (shades of St. Trinian's). He was her male counterpart in the realms of the British Eccentric—realms that they ruled with equal gusto and gladiatorial insouciance. Raymond Durgnat writing in *A Mirror for England* noted that "British qualms about the grinding effect of puritanical submission to the system are often expressed in two ways: their veneration for eccentrics and their much touted sense of humour . . . (they) are usually 'upperclass' in origin and either of independent means or firmly ensconced in authority . . . they are usually variations on old-fashioned father and aunt figures and the eccentricity is not eccentricity at all, but the old upperclass way of speaking out boldly and rudely."

Several other eccentric roles followed for Margaret Rutherford for she played Miss Marple in several MGM Agatha Christie films, where once again her unlikely and sexually "unappealing" exterior hid a true and marvelous ingenuity and a remarkable and scrupulous intelligence. Her elegant comic touch and her warmth were triumphant in every role she played—a glorious galleon in full sail firing salvos at all who crossed her bow.

—Sylvia Paskin

RYAN, Meg

Nationality: American. **Born:** Margaret Mary Hyra in Fairfield, Connecticut, 19 November 1961. **Education:** University of Connecticut, studied journalism at New York University. **Family**: Married the actor Dennis Quaid, 1991, one son: Jack Henry. **Career:** 1981—film debut in *Rich and Famous*; 1982-84—appeared in TV daytime drama *As the World Turns*; 1993—started production company, Prufrock Pictures. **Awards:** Golden Apple, Hollywood Woman's Press Club, 1989; Crystal Award, Women in Film, 1995. **Agent:** Steve Dontanville, International Creative Management, 8942 Wilshire Boulevard, Beverly Hills, CA 90211, U.S.A. **Address:** Prufrock Pictures, 10201 West Pico Boulevard, Building 78, Los Angeles, CA 90035, U.S.A.

Films as Actress:

1981   *Rich and Famous* (Cukor) (as Debby at 18); *Amy and the Angel* (Rosenblum—for TV) (as Denise)
1983   *Amityville 3-D* (*Amityville: The Demon*) (Fleischer) (as Lisa)
1986   *Armed and Dangerous* (Lester) (as Maggie Cavanaugh); *Top Gun* (Tony Scott) (as Carole Bradshaw)
1987   *Innerspace* (Dante) (as Lydia Maxwell)
1988   *Promised Land* (*Young Hearts*) (Hoffman) (as Bev); *D.O.A.* (Morton and Jankel) (as Sydney Fuller); *The Presidio* (Hyams) (as Donna Caldwell)
1989   *When Harry Met Sally . . .* (Rob Reiner) (as Sally Albright)
1990   *Joe versus the Volcano* (Shanley) (as DeDe/Angelica/Patricia)
1991   *The Doors* (Oliver Stone) (as Pamela Courson)
1992   *Prelude to a Kiss* (René) (as Rita Boyle)
1993   *Sleepless in Seattle* (Nora Ephron) (as Annie Reed); *Flesh and Bone* (Kloves) (as Kay Davies)
1994   *I.Q.* (Schepisi) (as Catherine Boyd); *When a Man Loves a Woman* (Mandoki) (as Alice Green)
1995   *French Kiss* (*Paris Match*) (Kasdan) (as Kate, + co-pr); *Restoration* (Hoffman) (as Katherine)
1996   *Courage under Fire* (Zwick) (as Capt. Karen Walden); *Two for the Road* (as Joanna, + pr)

Meg Ryan with Billy Crystal in *When Harry Met Sally. . .*

Publications

By RYAN: articles—

"Brilliant Disguise," interview with Fred Schruers, in *Rolling Stone* (New York), 11 February 1988.

"That's the Way Love Goes," interview with Nancy Riffin, in *Premiere* (New York), July 1993.

"Tough Love," interview with Charles Salzberg, in *Redbook* (New York), July 1993.

"The Crying Game," interview with John Mosby, in *Film Review* (London), November 1993.

"Faces of Meg," interview with Amy Fine Collins, in *Harper's Bazaar* (New York), June 1994.

"Megabucks Megastar Meg Ryan," interview with Richard Natale, in *Cosmopolitan* (New York), 1 December 1994.

"Maximum Meg," interview with Kevin Sessums, in *Vanity Fair* (New York), May 1995.

"The French Connection," interview with Marianne Gray, in *Film Review* (London), December 1995.

"Private Meg," interview with Rachel Abramowitz, in *Premiere* (New York), May 1996.

On RYAN: articles—

Landman, Beth, and others, "The Meg Ryan Mystique," in *Redbook* (New York), April 1995.

Corliss, Richard, "Star Lite, Star Bright," in *Time* (New York), 22 May 1995.

*   *   *

Before Meg Ryan achieved the top rank of stardom with *When Harry Met Sally . . .* in 1989, she had attracted notice in a number of memorable supporting roles on television and in film. Her big-screen debut was as Candice Bergen's daughter in *Rich and Famous* in 1981 and she acquired fans with her role in the soap opera *As the World Turns* from 1982-84, but it was in *Top Gun*, as Anthony Edwards's wife and then widow, that she made her first major impression. Her line to Edwards, "Take me to bed or lose me forever," became something of a catch phrase for teenage girls in the summer of 1986 and Ryan and Edwards stole much of the spotlight away from the film's leads, Tom Cruise and Kelly McGillis.

Ryan's raw-nerve, wild-girl image in *Top Gun* may have caused Michael Hoffman to cast her in *Promised Land*, two years later. While the film sank under a surfeit of unstructured adolescent angst, Ryan's performance as Kiefer Sutherland's violence prone, white-trash bride impresses and even shocks today's viewers who only know her from her later romantic comedies. Her Bev in that film suggests that Ryan has a range that has gone sadly unused, even in her recent dramatic roles in *Flesh and Bone* and *When a Man Loves a Woman*.

After *Promised Land*, however, Ryan sank comfortably back into "girlfriend-of-the-lead" parts in *D.O.A.* and *The Presidio*. It was in

Rob Reiner's *When Harry Met Sally . . .*, that Ryan emerged as a major star and solidified the comic persona that would dominate much of her career in the coming years. Ryan's faked orgasm scene in that film would be widely replayed and comparisons would be drawn between her and Carole Lombard. Ryan offered a winsome amalgamation of innocence and big city savoir faire; her inchoate romantic schemes seemed to evaporate across her face before being fully solidified but Ryan always managed to land her man in the final reel. If the Lombard comparison was a bit pat, one could compare Ryan to the remarkably similar Clara Bow in the 1927 film, *It*. As with Bow in that Hoover-era picture, Ryan offered the Reagan-Bush years a post-Jane Fonda, post-Sally Field image of the "strong" woman who gets what she wants through feminine ingenuity while maintaining a supple, girlish demeanor. This was hardly a persona feminists took to—even Camille Paglia would criticize Ryan's image in print—but it won the actress a coveted place in the hearts of many filmgoers who yearned for a return to preliberation sex roles and attitudes.

Ryan did stretch a bit in *Joe versus the Volcano* (where she played three distinct roles) and *Prelude to a Kiss* (where her character's body is possessed by an elderly, ill man who fortuitously gets a new lease on life). Neither film, however, had the enormous impact of 1993's *Sleepless in Seattle*. In that Nora Ephron film, as an engaged woman who leaves her fiancé to track down a dream man she has heard about on the radio, Ryan offered another canny alternative to the "strong" and perhaps subliminally threatening female stars of the period.

While *Sleepless in Seattle* grossed $188 million, Ryan may have played out that film's kind of character to the point where audiences have became a bit wary. *I.Q.* for Fred Schepisi in 1994 was a critical and box-office disappointment and 1995's *French Kiss*, co-produced by her new production company, did not recapture the success of her earlier blockbusters. The latter's only modest box-office success, despite a witty script, sharp direction, and some of Ryan's most skillful and precise comic work, points to the actress's need to explore other options in film roles. *When A Man Loves a Woman*, where Ryan plays an alcoholic mother, earned her a certain amount of respect as a dramatic actress, and Edward Zwick's *Courage under Fire*, where she plays a Persian Gulf War hero, seems calculated to help Ryan shift gears into a more complex mode of performance for the second half of the nineties.

—Daniel Humphrey

RYAN, Robert

Nationality: American. **Born:** Robert Bushnell Ryan in Chicago, Illinois, 11 November 1909. **Education:** Attended Loyola Academy, Chicago; Dartmouth College, Hanover, New Hampshire (boxing champion), B.A. in literature 1931. **Military Service:** U.S. Marine Corps, 1944-45: drill instructor, Camp Pendleton barracks, San Diego. **Family:** Married Jessica Cadwalader, 1939 (died 1972), sons: Timothy, Cheyney, daughter: Lisa. **Career:** 1936—member of Edward Boyle's stock company, Chicago; 1939—studied at Max Reinhardt's Actors' Workshop in Los Angeles; professional stage debut in *Too Many Husbands* in Los Angeles; 1940—contract with Paramount; first significant film role in *Golden Gloves*; 1941—on Broadway in *Clash by Night*; then contract with RKO; 1943—first big break with lead role, opposite Ginger Rogers, in *Tender Comrade*; 1947—following military service, appeared in first of several films noir, *The Woman on the Beach*; 1951—with wife, founded Oakwood Elementary School in North Hollywood, a cooperative dedicated to humanistic education; political activism continued throughout his life, notably serving as co-chairman of the Holly-

wood branch of the National Committee for a Sane Nuclear Policy, starting in 1959; 1954—in off-Broadway play *Coriolanus*; 1959—co-founder with John Houseman and Sidney Harmon, Theatre Group at UCLA; 1960—on stage in *Antony and Cleopatra* at Stratford, Connecticut, and *The Front Page* on Broadway, 1969; 1964-65—narrator of TV series *World War I*. **Awards:** Special Prize, U.S. National Society of Film Critics, for *The Iceman Cometh*, 1973. **Died:** Of cancer, in New York City, 11 July 1973.

Films as Actor:

1927   *The College Widow* (Mayo) (as extra)

1929   *Strong Boy* (Ford) (bit role as baggage man)

1940   *Golden Gloves* (Dmytryk) (as Pete Wells); *Queen of the Mob* (Hogan) (as Jim); *The Ghost Breakers* (George Marshall) (as intern); *Northwest Mounted Police* (Cecil B. DeMille) (as Constable Dumont)

1941   *Texas Rangers Ride Again* (Hogan) (as Eddie)

1943   *Bombardier* (Wallace) (as Joe Connors); *The Sky's the Limit* (Edward H. Griffith) (as Reg Fenton); *Behind the Rising Sun* (Dmytryk) (as Lefty); *Gangway for Tomorrow* (Auer) (as Joe Dunham); *The Iron Major* (Enright) (as Father Tim Donovan); *Tender Comrade* (Dmytryk) (as Chris)

1944   *Marine Raiders* (Schuster) (as Capt. Dan Craig)

1947   *Trail Street* (Enright) (as Allen Harper); *The Woman on the Beach* (Renoir) (as Scott); *Crossfire* (Dmytryk) (as Monty Montgomery)

1948   *Berlin Express* (Tourneur) (as Robert Lindley); *Return of the Badmen* (Enright) (as Sundance Kid); *Act of Violence* (Zinnemann) (as Joe Parkson); *The Boy with Green Hair* (Losey) (as Dr. Evans)

1949   *Caught* (Max Ophüls) (as Smith Ohlrig); *The Set-Up* (Wise) (as Stoker Thompson); *The Woman on Pier 13* (*I Married a Communist*) (Stevenson) (as Brad Collins)

1950   *The Secret Fury* (Ferrer) (as David); *Born to Be Bad* (Nicholas Ray) (as Nick Bradley)

1951   *Best of the Badmen* (William D. Russell) (as Jeff Clanton); *Flying Leathernecks* (Nicholas Ray) (as Griff); *The Racket* (Cromwell) (as Nick Scanlon); *On Dangerous Ground* (Nicholas Ray) (as Jim Wilson)

1952   *Clash by Night* (Fritz Lang) (as Earl Pfeiffer); *Beware My Lovely* (Horner) (as Howard Wilton); *Horizons West* (Boetticher) (as Dan Hammond)

1953   *City beneath the Sea* (Boetticher) (as Brad Carlton); *The Naked Spur* (Anthony Mann) (as Ben Vandergroat); *Inferno* (Roy Baker) (as David Carson)

1954   *Alaska Seas* (Jerry Hopper) (as Matt Kelly); *About Mrs. Leslie* (Daniel Mann) (as George Leslie); *Her Twelve Men* (Leonard) (as Joe Hargrave); *Bad Day at Black Rock* (John Sturges) (as Reno Smith)

1955   *Escape to Burma* (Dwan) (as Jim Brecan); *House of Bamboo* (Fuller) (as Sandy Dawson); *The Tall Men* (Walsh) (as Nathan Stark)

1956   *The Proud Ones* (Webb) (as Marshal Cass Silver); *Back from Eternity* (Farrow) (as Bill Larnigan)

1957   *Men in War* (Anthony Mann) (as Lt. Benson)

1958   *God's Little Acre* (Anthony Mann) (as Ty Ty Walden); *Lonelyhearts* (*Miss Lonelyhearts*) (Donehue) (as William Shrike)

1959   *Day of the Outlaw* (De Toth) (as Blaise Starrett); *Odds against Tomorrow* (Wise) (as Earle Slater)

1960   *Ice Palace* (Sherman) (as Thor Storm)

1961   *The Canadians* (Kennedy) (as Inspector William Gannon); *King of Kings* (Nicholas Ray) (as John the Baptist)

1962   *The Longest Day* (Annakin, Marton, Wicki, and Oswald) (as
        Brig. Gen. James M. Gavin); *Billy Budd* (Ustinov) (as Mas-
        ter-at-Arms John Claggart)
1964   *The Inheritance* (Mayer—doc) (as narrator)
1965   *Battle of the Bulge* (Annakin) (as Gen. Grey); *The Crooked
        Road* (Chaffey) (as Richard Ashley)
1966   *La Guerre secrète* (*La guerra segreta*; *Spione untersich*; *The
        Dirty Game*; *The Dirty Agents*) (Terence Young, Christian-
        Jaque, and Lizzani) (as Gen. Bruce); *The Professionals* (Ri-
        chard Brooks) (as Hans Ehrengard)
1967   *The Busy Body* (Castle) (as Charley Barker); *The Dirty Dozen*
        (Aldrich) (as Col. Everett Dasher-Breed); *Hour of the Gun*
        (*The Law and Tombstone*) (John Sturges) (as Ike Clanton)
1968   *Custer of the West* (*Good Day for Fighting*) (Siodmak) (as Sgt.
        Mulligan); *Escondido* (*Un Minuto per Pregare un Instante
        per Morire*; *A Minute to Pray, a Second to Die*; *Dead or
        Alive*) (Giraldi) (as Governor Lem Carter); *Lo Sbarco di
        Anzio* (*Anzio*; *The Battle for Anzio*) (Dmytryk) (as Gen.
        Carson)
1969   *The Wild Bunch* (Peckinpah) (as Deke Thornton)
1970   *Captain Nemo and the Underwater City* (James Hill) (title
        role)
1971   *Lawman* (Winner) (as Marshal Cotton Ryan); *The Love Ma-
        chine* (Haley Jr.) (as Gregory Austin)
1972   *Le Course, du lièvre a travers les champs* (*. . . And Hope to
        Die*) (Clément) (as Charley)
1973   *The Lolly-Madonna War* (*Lolly-Madonna XXX*) (Sarafian) (as
        Pap Gutshall); *Executive Action* (David Miller) (as Foster);
        The Outfit (*The Good Guys Always Win*) (Flynn) (as Mailer);
        The Iceman Cometh (Frankenheimer) (as Larry Slade); *The
        Man without a Country* (Delbert Mann—for TV) (as
        Vaughan)

Publications

On RYAN: books—

Parish, James, *The Tough Guys*, New Rochelle, New York, 1976.
Jarlett, Franklin, *Robert Ryan: A Biography and Critical Filmography*,
    Jefferson, North Carolina, 1990.

On RYAN: articles—

Sight and Sound (London), Summer 1955.
Current Biography 1963, New York, 1963.
Stein, J., "Robert Ryan," in *Films in Review* (New York), January 1968.
Obituary in *New York Times*, 12 July 1973.
Ecran (Paris), November 1979.
Génin, T., "Robert Ryan: un héros américain," in *Avant-Scène du
    Cinéma* (Paris), 1 March 1980.
Thomson, David, "Ryan and Shaw," in *Film Comment* (New York),
    January/February 1994.

*   *   *

Robert Ryan was unique among Hollywood stars for having been
both an Ivy League graduate (Dartmouth, class of 1931) and an undefeated intercollegiate boxing champion, heavyweight class. Thus he
brought to his acting career the unusual combination of a fine education and an authentic tough-guy reputation. In his early years out of
college, he found work in a depression environment wherever he
could, first spending two hot and dirty years as engine room janitor on
a freighter that steamed from New York to East Africa around the
Cape and back, then touring the country in one odd job after another—gold prospecting and cowpunching in northern Montana, department store modeling and working a desk job with the board of
education in Chicago.

When he ended up in California in 1939, he enrolled at the Max
Reinhardt Actors' Workshop, which led to his stage debut in *Too
Many Husbands* at Belasco Theatre in Los Angeles. A Paramount
Pictures talent scout was impressed enough by Ryan's opening night
performance to offer him a $75 a week contract, which he accepted
on the spot. With Paramount, he then made his feature film debut,
appropriately cast as a boxer in a B movie entitled *Golden Gloves*. He
found steady work in small parts, with his first big break coming in
1943 as co-star to Ginger Rogers in *Tender Comrade*. This film was
later cited—ludicrously so—as an example of how communists had
infiltrated the film industry. Both its director, Edward Dmytryk, and
its screenwriter, Dalton Trumbo, were among the original blacklisted
Hollywood ten. Ryan, however, was helped by his appearance in *Tender Comrade*, although his enlistment in the Marines in 1944 temporarily halted his promising career.

It was after the war that Ryan found real success as a movie star by
being featured in a colorful dramatic role as a bigoted villain in *Crossfire*.
His chilling performance not only earned him an Oscar nomination as
Best Supporting Actor, it also tended to type him for the majority of
the screen roles to follow. His film persona relied on that of the
smooth surface which covers a twisted interior. Ryan was a big man, 6'
3" tall, with dark hair and good looks. He might have become a
traditional "handsome hero" leading man, but instead he began playing articulate villains, the kind who could talk their way out of places
and build alibis for themselves in any kind of situation. In addition to
the obvious acting skill such roles require, Ryan had the sort of Irishness
viewers often associate with blarney. He added to it a suspicious smile
and overly confident manner which seemed to suggest hidden strength
and possible danger, an undercurrent of violence and cruelty. With
these characteristics, he created a gallery of some of the most interesting villains ever seen on film, and built a career out of crime films,
films noir, melodramas, and Westerns.

For the majority of the moviegoing public, he is most associated
with the last genre. (Ryan himself referred to his "long, seamy face"
as being perfect for Westerns.) His filmography reads as a chronology
of the development of the genre in the postwar period, from such
classics as Anthony Mann's *The Naked Spur* and John Sturges's *Bad
Day at Black Rock* through Raoul Walsh's *The Tall Men*, Budd
Boetticher's *Horizons West*, and Andre De Toth's *Day of the Outlaw* to
the iconoclastic film by Sam Peckinpah, *The Wild Bunch*. Recently,
much critical attention has been given to Ryan's seminal contributions to film noir, especially given his appearance in films by many of
that genre's most important directors, notably Jean Renoir (*The Woman
on the Beach*), Max Ophüls (*Caught*), Robert Wise (*The Set-Up*),
Nicholas Ray (*On Dangerous Ground*), and Fritz Lang (*Clash by
Night*).

Always an actor to seek challenge and a change, Ryan returned to
the New York stage in 1954, starring in *Coriolanus*. From that time
on, he moved back and forth from his film career to his stage career,
creating successes in theater both in Los Angeles and New York, and
particularly finding praise for his outstanding performance in an excellent revival of *The Front Page* shortly before his death. Unfortunately, over the last eight years of his life Ryan was largely relegated
to cameos in big pictures, such as *The Dirty Dozen*, *Custer of the West*,
and *Anzio* (although he made more money in this period than in the
first 25 years of his film career combined).

Ryan guided his entire career with intelligence and seriousness of
purpose. Since his desire was to be more than a movie star, he willingly
accepted roles that did not create a lovable persona. Because of this,
he did not attract as large a following as some other stars. Nevertheless, he always maintained a reputation for quality and reliability. Seen
in retrospect, this quality places him at the center of film history, as

he appeared in many films which, although not Oscar winners of their day, are now considered classics worthy of serious attention and study. In this way, history and time are making Robert Ryan into one of the most interesting stars of Hollywood films.

—Jeanine Basinger, updated by David E. Salamie

RYDER, Winona

Nationality: American. **Born:** Winona Laura Horowitz in Winona, Minnesota, 29 October 1971. **Education:** Studied drama at the American Conservatory Theater in San Francisco. **Career:** Early 1980s—acted on the stage in small theaters; 1984—discovered by a talent scout while studying at the American Conservatory Theater and given screen test; 1986—made screen debut in *Lucas*; 1989—cast as Michael Corleone's daughter in *The Godfather: Part III*, but dropped out because of overwork. **Awards:** Best Actress, Gijon Festival, for *Square Dance*, 1987; National Board of Review Award, Best Supporting Actress, for *The Age of Innocence*, 1993. **Agent:** Carol Bodie.

Films as Actress:

1986   *Lucas* (Seltzer) (as Rina)
1987   *Square Dance* (*Home Is Where the Heart Is*) (Petrie) (as Gemma)
1988   *Beetlejuice* (Burton) (as Lydia Deetz); *1969* (Ernest Thompson) (as Beth)
1989   *Great Balls of Fire!* (McBride) (as Myra Gail Lewis); *Heathers* (*Lethal Attraction*; *Westerberg High*) (Lehmann) (as Veronica Sawyer)
1990   *Welcome Home, Roxy Carmichael* (Abrahams) (as Dinky Bossetti); *Mermaids* (Richard Benjamin) (as Charlotte Flax); *Edward Scissorhands* (Burton) (as Kim Boggs)
1991   *Night on Earth* (Jarmusch) (as Corky)
1992   *Bram Stoker's Dracula* (Francis Ford Coppola) (as Mina Murray/Elisabeta)
1993   *The Age of Innocence* (Scorsese) (as May Welland)
1994   *The House of the Spirits* (August) (as Blanca); *Reality Bites* (Stiller) (as Lelaina Pierce); *Little Women* (Armstrong) (as Jo March)
1995   *How to Make an American Quilt* (Moorhouse) (as Finn Dodd)
1996   *The Crucible* (Hytner) (as Abigail); *Looking for Richard* (Pacino) (as Lady Anne); *Boys* (Cochran)
1997   *Alien Resurrection*

Publications

By RYDER: articles—

"Winning Winona," interview with L. Tobey, in *Interview* (New York), May 1989.
"A Meeting of the Minds," interview with Timothy Leary, in *Interview* (New York), November 1989.
"Winona Ryder," interview with J. Giles, in *Interview* (New York), December 1990.
"Winona Ryder Beats the Heat," interview with David Wild, in *Rolling Stone* (New York), 16 May 1991.

On RYDER: articles—

Handleman, David, "Hot Actress: After *Heathers* Will Stardom 'Devirginize' Newcomer Winona Ryder?," in *Rolling Stone* (New York), 18 May 1989.

Hoban, Phoebe, "Wise Child," in *Premiere* (New York), June 1989.
Ansen, D., and L. Buckley, "Movies: Whole Lotta Shakin' Goin' On," in *Newsweek* (New York), 10 July 1989.
Harmetz, Aljean, "On and Off Screen, Winona Ryder Comes of Age," in *New York Times*, 9 December 1990.
Ostria, V., "Winona Ryder," in *Cahiers du Cinéma* (Paris), July/August 1991.
Hirschorn, Michael W., "Winona among the Grown-ups," in *Esquire* (New York), November 1992.
Abramowitz, R., "Neck Romance," in *Premiere* (New York), December 1992.
Clark, John, filmography in *Premiere* (New York), December 1992.
Current Biography 1994, New York, 1994.
Giles, Jeff, "Winona," in *Rolling Stone* (New York), 10 March 1994.
Frost, Polly, "The Woman in Winona," in *Harper's Bazaar* (New York), December 1994.
Allen, Jenny, "Little Woman, Big Star," in *Life* (New York), December 1994.
Corliss, Richard, "Take a Bow, Winona," in *Time* (New York), 9 January 1995.

*   *   *

At an age when young people are in the throes of starting high school, Winona Ryder was making her screen debut in *Lucas*. When many teenagers are thinking senior prom, she was starring in *Beetlejuice*. And when young adults are finishing college and pondering their futures, Ryder already had appeared on-screen in *Heathers*, *Great Balls of Fire!*, *Welcome Home, Roxy Carmichael*, *Edward Scissorhands*, *Mermaids*, and *Bram Stoker's Dracula*. Despite all of these credits, Ryder's career had not yet peaked. She was one adolescent actress who effortlessly would segue into adult roles.

In her early films, Ryder more often than not was cast as an intelligent but essentially ingenuous and alienated young person. In *Lucas* and *Square Dance*, she effectively plays sensitive adolescents. Later on, she did well as the friendless smalltown eccentric in *Welcome Home, Roxy Carmichael*; the thoughtful, distressed daughter in *Mermaids*; and, in particular, the teen who hangs out, albeit uncomfortably, with her high school's princess-shrews and eventually opts for independence in *Heathers*. But the film in which she really caught on was Tim Burton's *Beetlejuice*, playing a self-described "strange and unusual" adolescent with a morbid fashion sense. Not all of Ryder's characters were unconventional; in *Edward Scissorhands*, she is the otherwise average teen who comes to love an android. Another important Ryder role came in Francis Coppola's *Bram Stoker's Dracula*, in which she plays both Elisabeta (who kills herself upon obtaining erroneous news that her beloved, the fifteenth-century Romanian king Vlad the Impaler, had died in battle) and Mina Murray (the fiancée of Jonathan Harker and the love-object of Dracula).

In the Los Angeles segment of Jim Jarmusch's *Night on Earth*, Ryder plays one of her more centered characters: Corky, a rough-around-the-collar type who—horror of horrors—would much rather be a mechanic than a movie star; she is contrasted to a chic casting agent who drips Beverly Hills and is wedded to her portable telephone. But Ryder's most compelling contemporary "adult" role has been in Ben Stiller's *Reality Bites*, one of the earliest in a mid-1990s cycle of Generation X coming-of-age movies. The conflicts experienced by her character, Lelaina Pierce, mirror the personal and professional frustrations of post-Baby Boomer twentysomethings who grew up in dysfunctional families and are products of American pop culture. Ultimately, it is difficult for her to "find [her] own identity without having any heroes or role models." She also has come to adulthood in a declining economy. So despite her college diploma, she may not have a white-collar future. In one telling sequence, Lelaina, who was valedictorian of her college graduation class, applies for employment

Winona Ryder in *Heathers*

in a fast-food restaurant: the type of job which, under different circumstances, she would have had part-time back in high school. Still, some of the issues with which Lelaina deals are, in their essence, age-old. With whom does she fall in love? Does she sustain a relationship with the yuppie who is flashy and successful but lacking in substance and values? Or does she become involved with the product of grunge culture, who will never buy her a tennis bracelet but at least is honest in his response to the world around him? Ryder offers an attractive performance as Lelaina, capturing all of the character's confusion and frustration.

In her two Oscar-nominated roles to date—certainly, they are the first of several she will earn in her career—Ryder donned period costumes in adaptations of classic American novels. In Martin Scorsese's sumptuously produced but only intermittently involving *The Age of Innocence*, based on the book by Edith Wharton, she is the proper young lady whom proper lawyer Daniel Day Lewis is expected to marry. And in Gillian Armstrong's *Little Women*, based on the Louisa May Alcott classic, she makes a vibrant Jo March, the story's central character. Her follow-up to *Little Women* was similar in that it too was directed by a woman, and tells the story of female characters who bond: Jocelyn Moorhouse's *How to Make an American Quilt*. As in *Reality Bites*, Ryder plays a perplexed contemporary twentysomething: Finn Dodd, who is about to be married and who spends a summer at the home of her grandmother and great aunt. There, she interacts with various family members and friends who are part of a quilting circle.

As Ryder has gotten older, her roles only have gotten better. She is in line for a lengthy and important screen career.

—Rob Edelman

RYU, Chishu

Nationality: Japanese. **Born:** Kyushu, 13 May 1906. **Career:** 1925—joined the Shockiku Kamata film studio acting school; 1929—first of many films for the director Yasujiro Ozu, *Wakaki hi*. **Awards:** Best Actor Awards, Mainichi Eiga Concourse, Japan, 1948, 1951, 1970; Tokyo Blue Ribbon Prize for Best Supporting Actor, 1951. **Died:** Of cancer, in Yokohama, Japan, 16 March 1993.

Films as Actor:

1929 *Wakaki hi (Days of Youth)* (Ozu) (as student)
1930 *Rakudai wa shitakeredo (I Flunked, But . . .)* (Ozu) (as passing student); *Sono yo no tsuma (That Night's Wife)* (Ozu) (as policeman)
1932 *Umarete wa mita keredo (I Was Born, But . . .)* (Ozu); *Seishun no yume ima izuko (Where Now Are the Dreams of Youth?)* (Ozu) (as Shimazaki)
1933 *Tokyo no onna (Women of Tokyo)* (Ozu) (as reporter); *Hijosen no onna (Dragnet Girl)* (Ozu) (as policeman); *Dekigokoro (Passing Fancy)* (Ozu) (as man on boat)
1934 *Haka o kowazuya (A Mother Should Be Loved)* (Ozu) (as Hattori)
1935 *Tokyo no yado (An Inn in Tokyo)* (Ozu)
1936 *Daigaku yoitoko (College Is a Nice Place)* (Ozu) (as Amano); *Hotori musuko (The Only Son)* (Ozu) (as Okubo)
1941 *Todake no kyodai (Brothers and Sisters of the Toda Family)* (Ozu) (as friend)
1942 *Chichi ariki (There Was a Father)* (Ozu) (as Shuhei Horikawa); *Minami ni kaze (South Wind)* (Yoshimura)

1947 *Nagaya Shinshiroku (Record of a Tenement Gentleman)* (Ozu) (as Tashiro)
1948 *Kaze no naka no mendori (A Hen in the Wind)* (Ozu) (as Kazuichiro Satake)
1949 **Banshun** *(Late Spring)* (Ozu) (as Shukicki Somiya, the father)
1950 *Munekata shimai (The Munekata Sisters)* (Ozu) (as Takachika Munekata)
1951 *Bakushu (Early Summer)* (Ozu) (as Koichi); *Karemen Kyoko ni kaeru (Carmen Comes Home)* (Kinoshita)
1952 *Ochazuke no aji (The Flavor of Green Tea over Rice; Tea and Rice)* (Ozu) (as Sadao Hirayama)
1953 **Tokyo monogatari** *(Tokyo Story)* (Ozu) (as Shukicki Hirayama)
1954 *Nijushi no Hitomi (Twenty-Four Eyes)* (Kinoshita)
1956 *Shoshun (Early Spring)* (Ozu) (as Kiichi Onodera)
1957 *Tokyo boshoku (Twilight in Tokyo)* (Ozu) (as Shukichi Sugiyama)
1958 **Higanbana** *(Equinox Flower)* (Ozu) (as Shukichi Mikami); *Muhomatsu no issho (The Rickshaw Man)* (Inagaki) (as Mr. Yuki)
1959 *Ohayo (Good Morning)* (Ozu) (as Keitaro Hayashi); *Ukigusa (Floating Weeds; The Duckweed Story; Drifting Weeds)* (Ozu) (as theater owner)
1960 *Akibiyori (Late Autumn)* (Ozu) (as Shukichi Miwa, the uncle); *Warui yatsu hodo yoku nemuru (The Bad Sleep Well; The Rose in the Mud; The Worse You Are, the Better You Sleep)* (Kurosawa) (as Nonaka)
1961 *Yato kaze no naka o hashiru (Bandits on the Wind)* (Inagaki) (as village priest); *Kohayagawa-ke no aki (The End of Summer; Early Autumn; Last of Summer)* (Ozu) (as a farmer); *Gen to fudo-myoh (The Youth and His Amulet)* (Inagaki); **Ningen no joken III** *(A Soldier's Prayer)* (Kobayashi) (as village elder)
1962 *Onna no za (The Wiser Age; Woman's Status)* (Naruse); **Samma no aji** *(Autumn Afternoon)* (Ozu) (as Shuhei Hirayama)
1964 *Daikon to ninjin (Twilight Path; Radishes and Carrots)* (Shibuya) (as Tokichi Tamaki)
1965 *Akahige (Red Beard)* (Kurosawa) (as Yasumoto's father)
1967 *Nippon no ichiban nagai hi (The Emperor and a General)* (Okamoto) (as Prime Minister)
1969 *Nihonkai daikaisen (Battle of the Japan Sea)* (Maruyama) (as Gen. Nogi); *Eiko eno kurohyo (Fight for the Glory)* (Ichimura) (as Yonoshin)
1980 *Nikudan (Okamoto)*
1983 *When We Are Old* (Iyoda)
1984 *Gubijinso* (Ohyama); *I Lived But* (Inone); *Ososhiki (The Funeral Rites; The Funeral; Death, Japanese Style)* (Itami) (as the priest)
1985 *Otoko wa Tsuraiyo (Torajiro Shinjitsu Ichiro; Tora-San's Forbidden Love)* (Yamada) (as Priest); *Tokyo-ga* (Wenders)
1986 *Sorekara* (Morita); *Kinema no tenchi (Final Take: The Golden Age of Movies)* (Yamada) (as Tomo, studio janitor)
1988 *Otoko wa Tsuraiyo: Torajiro Salada kinenbi* (Yamada); *Marusa no Onna II* (as retired monk)
1989 *Otoko wa Tsuraiyo: Toraijiro kokoro no tabiji (Tora-San Goes to Vienna)* (Yamada) (as Gozen-Sama, Priest)
1990 "Village of the Watermills" ep. of *Akira Kurosawa's Dreams (Dreams)* (Kurosawa) (as 103 year old man)
1991 *Bis ans Ende der Welt (Until the End of the World)* (Wenders) (as Mr. Mori)
1992 *Hikarigoke (Luminous Moss)* (Kumai) (as judge)

Publications

By RYU: articles—

"Yasujiro Ozu," in *Sight and Sound* (London), vol. 92, Spring 1964.
Interview with M. Tessier, in *Avant-Scène du Cinéma* (Paris), 15 March 1978.

Chishu Ryu (right) in *Banshun*

"Ozu et moi: reflexions sur mon mentor" (reprinted from *Kinema Jumpo*, June 1958), in *Positif* (Paris), January 1979.

On RYU: articles—

Obituary in *Variety* (New York), 22 March 1993.
Niogret, H., "Chishu Ryu," in *Positif* (Paris), June 1993.
Obituary in *Skrien* (Amsterdam), June-July 1993.
Obituary in *Film en Televisie + Video* (Brussels), July 1993.

* * *

Yasujiro Ozu's method of filmmaking demanded a style of acting and a kind of actor at the opposite extremes from the Method school so familiar in the West. Every sequence, every shot within it, and every detail (whether of decor or gesture) within every shot, was planned by the director, his screenwriter (most often Kogo Noda), and his cinematographer (usually Yuharu Atsuya) during the evolution of the film. The actors were never asked to improvise or psychologize; instead they were expected to subordinate themselves to the overall compositional design of the film and be able to communicate the most meticulous and subtle inflections of expression and gesture under Ozu's direction. According to Chishu Ryu, Ozu "fixed each actor into each

shot," and so one imagines that the ascetic discipline required of Ryu's early (and abandoned) training to follow his father as a Buddhist priest had some lasting value for his acting career.

Chishu Ryu was Ozu's lifelong friend and the most regular member of the stock company of actors he drew together. He is in Ozu's earliest surviving film (his eighth) *Wakaki hi* (1929), played his first major role in *Daigaku yoitoko* (1936), and is in all the last 17 (and the star of many) of the director's films. Just how consistent his contributions were in between is somewhat difficult to determine, as many of the films are lost or inaccessible. In the later works, Ryu's appearances take on the character of a directorial trademark: if there is no star role for him, he turns up in a brief cameo, perhaps with no more than a line or two of dialogue. (Ryu's consistent dependability was perhaps his defining quality as a professional: he was reportedly also on hand for all 45 of director Yoji Yamada's inexplicably popular *Tora-san* films.)

In many of the later films the director/actor relationship becomes clearly symbiotic, in an extremely complex and fruitful way. There is no question of Ryu "playing" Ozu or being a mouthpiece for the director's statements, yet one repeatedly senses a special sympathy between the director and the Ryu character, a sympathy which never precludes the possibility of critical distance. In *Banshun* and *Tokyo monogatari*, for example, we are made firmly aware of the character's limitations: the film's vision is far wider than *his* vision, which it contains and transcends. The limitations (and this is consistent with other late Ozu works, not necessarily starring Ryu, for example *Equinox Flower*) are defined in relation to the female characters (especially those played by Setsuko Hara): Ozu's subtle feminism has never been as acknowledged as Mizoguchi's or Naruse's, and Ryu's most frequent role in Ozu's universe as a gentle yet somewhat obtuse patriarch deserves reviewing in this light.

In his final film appearances, Ryu is an explicitly revered icon, for both his aging contemporaries (such as Kurosawa) and younger acolytes, such as Wim Wenders, whose pilgrimage to meet Ryu in *Tokyo-Ga* is a moving tribute to both Ozu and his favorite actor.

—Robin Wood, updated by Corey K. Creekmur

SAINT, Eva Marie

Nationality: American. **Born:** Newark, New Jersey, 4 July 1924. **Education:** Attended Delmar High School, New Jersey; Bowling Green State University, Ohio, B.A. 1946; Actors Studio, New York. **Family:** Married the director Jeffrey Hayden, 1951, son: Darrell, daughter: Laurette. **Career:** Acted on radio in New York, including the serial *One Man's Family*, and later in TV version, 1950-52; 1953—role in the Broadway play *The Trip to Bountiful*; 1954—film debut in *On the Waterfront*; later worked on stage and television, sometimes directed by Hayden; 1986—in TV mini-series *A Year in the Life*; 1987-88—appeared in TV series *Moonlighting*; 1990—in TV mini-series *Voyage of Terror: The Achille Lauro Affair* and *People Like Us*. **Awards:** Best Supporting Actress Academy Award, for *On the Waterfront*, 1954; Emmy Award, for *People Like Us*, 1990. **Agent:** Kohner Agency, 9300 Wilshire Boulevard, #555, Beverly Hills, CA 90212, U.S.A.

Films as Actress:

1954   ***On the Waterfront*** (Kazan) (as Edie Doyle)
1956   *That Certain Feeling* (Panama and Frank) (as Dunreath Henry)
1957   *A Hatful of Rain* (Zinnemann) (as Celia Pope); *Raintree Country* (Dmytryk) (as Nell Gaither)
1959   ***North by Northwest*** (Hitchcock) (as Eve Kendall)
1960   *Exodus* (Preminger) (as Kitty Fremont)
1962   *All Fall Down* (Frankenheimer) (as Echo O'Brien)
1964   *36 Hours* (Seaton) (as Anna Hedler); *A Carol for Another Christmas* (Mankiewicz—for TV) (as Wave)
1965   *The Sandpiper* (*The Flight of the Sandpiper*) (Minnelli) (as Claire Hewitt)
1966   *The Russians Are Coming, the Russians Are Coming* (Jewison) (as Elspeth Whittaker); *Grand Prix* (Frankenheimer) (as Louise Frederickson)
1969   *The Stalking Moon* (Mulligan) (as Sarah Carver)
1970   *Loving* (Kershner) (as Selma Wilson)
1972   *Cancel My Reservation* (Bogart) (as Sheila Bartlett)
1976   *The Macahans* (McEveety—for TV) (as Kate Macahan)
1978   *A Christmas to Remember* (Englund—for TV) (as Emma Larson)
1979   *When Hell Was in Session* (Krasny—for TV) (as Mrs. Jeremiah Denton)
1980   *The Curse of King Tut's Tomb* (Leacock—for TV) (as Sarah Morrissey)
1981   *The Best Little Girl in the World* (O'Steen—for TV) (as Joanne Powell); *Splendor in the Grass* (Sarafian—for TV)
1983   *Malibu* (Swackhamer—for TV) (as Mary Wharton); *Jane Doe* (Nagy—for TV) (as Dr. Addie Coleman)
1984   *Fatal Vision* (David Greene—for TV) (as Mildred Kassab); *Love Leads the Way* (Delbert Mann—for TV) (as Mrs. Eustes)
1986   *Nothing in Common* (Garry Marshall) (as Lorraine Basner); *The Last Days of Patton* (Delbert Mann—for TV)

1988   *Breaking Home Ties* (*Norman Rockwell's Breaking Home Ties*) (John Wilder—for TV); *I'll Be Home for Christmas* (Chomsky—for TV) (as Martha Bundy)
1991   *Palamino* (*Danielle Steel's Palomino*) (Michael Miller—for TV) (as Caroline Lord)
1993   *Kiss of a Killer* (Elikann—for TV) (as Mrs. Wilson)
1995   *Mariette in Ecstasy* (Bailey) (as Mother Saint-Raphael); *My Antonia* (Sargent—for TV) (as Grandmother Burden)

Publications

By SAINT: article—

Interview with Michael Buckley, in *Films in Review* (New York), May 1983.

On SAINT: article—

Current Biography 1955, New York, 1955.

*   *   *

In one sense, Eva Marie Saint is the perfect example of a talent that Hollywood never quite figured out how to use. Her career failed to develop in any confident direction after she won an Academy Award for her first film, *On the Waterfront*. To paraphrase Marlon Brando's famous line, "she should've been a contender."

In almost all her films, Saint has been presented as an outwardly vulnerable, fragile woman who possesses a surprising inner strength. This image has carried her through a series of roles as either a supportive wife (*A Hatful of Rain*; *All Fall Down*; *36 Hours*; *The Russians Are Coming, the Russians Are Coming*; and *Loving*) or a determined, resourceful mother (*The Stalking Moon*, *Loving*, *The Best Little Girl in the World*, and *The Macahans*). Only Alfred Hitchcock employed the reverse of this image, casting Saint against type as an outwardly strong woman with a hidden vulnerability in *North by Northwest*.

While never cast in a role of central importance, Saint has frequently highlighted the talents of the men with whom she has starred. Her ability to pay attention, show interest, and respond has made many actors look very good indeed. Don Murray's strongest scenes in *A Hatful of Rain* are those with Saint, actually interacting with her instead of simply reciting monologues for the camera. Warren Beatty's initial recognition as a serious actor occurred when he appeared opposite Saint in *All Fall Down*. Gregory Peck's role as a resourceful Westerner in *The Stalking Moon* was made particularly poignant by Saint's portrayal of a complex woman who merits his protection. Perhaps George Segal's best work was in *Loving* with Saint. Ironically, Bob Hope recognized and used Saint's ability to make an actor look good and charge a film with believability in *That Certain Feeling* and *Cancel My Reservation*.

Following the latter, Saint has had little opportunity to show her acting skill on the big screen. Mostly, she has valiantly risen above the largely inferior television productions that predominate her late-ca-

Eva Marie Saint with Marlon Brando in *On the Waterfront*

reer filmography, with only occasional forays back to the screen, such as the underdeveloped role as mother of Tom Hanks and wife of Jackie Gleason, whom she leaves after 36 years of marriage, in *Nothing in Common*. Her better television performances include her wife of a Vietnam prisoner-of-war in *When Hell Was in Session*, her convincing portrayal of Marilyn Klinghoffer in the mini-series *Voyage of Terror: The Achille Lauro Affair*, her Emmy-winning role in the mini-series *People Like Us*, and her grandmother (alongside Jason Robards's grandfather) of Jim Burden in the adaptation of Willa Cather's novel *My Antonia*. Saint also had a widely seen, although only occasional, role as Cybill Shepherd's mother in one season of the television series *Moonlighting*.

—Stuart M. Kaminsky, updated by David E. Salamie

SANDA, Dominique

Nationality: French. **Born:** Dominique Varaigne in Paris, 11 March 1948. **Family:** Married at 15 (divorced two years later); one child by Christian Marquand. **Career:** Model, then actress; 1969—film debut

in *Une Femme douce*; 1992—in TV mini-series *De Avontuur lijke reis van Lukas* (*By Way of the Stars*), and *Joseph*, 1995. **Awards:** Best Actress, Cannes Festival, for *L'eredità Ferramonti*, 1976. **Agent:** Georges Beaume, Agents Associés, 3 Quia Malquais, 75006 Paris, France.

Films as Actress:

1969   *Une Femme douce* (*A Gentle Creature*) (Bresson) (as She)
1970   *Erste Liebe* (*First Love*) (Schell) (as Sinaida); *Il conformista* (*The Conformist*) (Bertolucci) (as Anna Quadri); *Il giardino dei Finzi Contini* (*The Garden of the Finzi-Continis*) (De Sica) (as Micol)
1971   *Sans mobile apparent* (*Without Apparent Motive*) (Ladro) (as Sandra Forest)
1972   *La notte dei fiori* (*Night of the Flowers*) (Baldi)
1973   *The Mackintosh Man* (Huston) (as Mrs. Smith); *L'Impossible Objet* (*Impossible Object*; *Story of a Love Story*) (Frankenheimer) (as Nathalie)
1974   *Gruppo di famiglia in un interno* (*Conversation Piece*; *Violence et Passion*) (Visconti) (as Mother); *Steppenwolf* (Haines) (as Hermine)

1976 *Le Berceau de cristal* (Garrel); *1900* (*Novecento*) (Bertolucci) (as Ada); *L'eredità Ferramonti* (*The Inheritance*) (Bolognini) (as Irene)

1977 *Oltre il bene e il male* (*Beyond Good and Evil*; *Au-dela du bien et du mal*) (Cavani) (as Lou Andreas-Salome); *Damnation Alley* (Smight) (as Janice)

1978 *Utopia* (Azimi); *Le Navire Night* (Duras)

1979 *La Chanson de Roland* (Cassenti); *Caboblanco* (J. Lee Thompson) (as Marie Allesandri)

1980 *Le Voyage en douce* (Deville) (as Hélène)

1981 *Les Ailes de la Colombe* (Jacquot); *La Naissance du jour* (Demy—for TV)

1982 *Une Chambre en ville* (*A Room in Town*) (Demy) (as Edith Leroyer); *L'Indiscretion* (Lary) (as Beatrice)

1983 *Poussière d'Empire* (Lam-Lé)

1984 *Le Matelot 512* (Allio)

1985 *Une Femme ou deux* (*One Woman or Two*; *A Woman or Two*) (Vigne)

1986 *Corps et bien* (Jacquot) (as Helene)

1987 *Les Mendiants* (Jacquot) (as Hélène); *Le Train* (Damiani—for TV)

1989 *Il decimo clandestino* (Wertmüller—for TV) (as landlady); *In una notte di chiaro di Luna* (Wertmüller); *Guerriers et captives* (*Warriors and Captives*; *Warriors and Prisoners*) (Cozarinsky); *Voglia di vivere* (Gasparini—for TV); *Crystal or Ash, Fire or Wind, as Long as It's Love* (as Carola)

1990 *Yo, la peor de Todas* (*I, the Worst of Them All*) (Bemberg) (as Vice-Reine Maria Luisa); *Come un bambino* (Risi); *Voyage of Terror: The Achille Lauro Affair* (Negrin—for TV)

1991 *Tolgo il disturbo* (Risi)

1992 *El Viaje* (*The Journey*; *The Voyage*) (Solanas) (as Helen); *Albert Savarus*

1993 *Der Grüne Heinrich* (*Green Henry*) (Körfer) (as Mother); *Emile des Roses* (as Bertha); *Der Fall Lucona* (*The Lucona Affair*) (Jack Gold) (as Lili Wolff)

1994 *Nobody's Children* (Wheatley—for TV) (as Dr. Stephanie Vaugier)

1995 *Brennendes Herz* (*Burning Heart*) (Patzak)

Publications

By SANDA: articles—

Interview with C. Clouzot, in *Ecran* (Paris), April 1977.
Interview with D. Maillet, in *Cinématographe* (Paris), May 1977.
Interview with M. Amiel, in *Cinéma* (Paris), November 1982.
Interview with Serge Toubiana, in *Cahiers du Cinéma* (Paris), April 1986.
"Prorochestvia fei sbylis," interview with A. Braginskii, in *Iskusstvo Kino* (Moscow), no. 7, 1990.
"Autour de *Peter Ibbetson*," in *Cahiers du Cinéma* (Paris), supplement, May 1991.

* * *

Dominique Sanda's career seems to have dwindled to the point of invisibility, her attempts to establish herself in the American cinema having come to nothing. Yet in her early films she made an indelible impression. Certainly, nothing she has done since has either affected or significantly developed the image she established in her work for Bresson and Bertolucci, an image centered on the twin notions of female emancipation and sexual liberation. In their different ways, both *Une Femme douce* and *The Conformist* are extremely troubled, to the point of unresolved confusion, about these issues, and Sanda's

presence is in both cases central to their ambivalence. In Bresson's film, Catholicism confronts feminism, finds it very disturbing, and seeks to define it in terms of "lost souls" (the path of the "liberated woman" leads inevitably to suicide because, without the guidance of men and God, she does not know where to go). The project is complicated partly by Bresson's integrity (he is too intelligent a filmmaker to reduce the debate to a simple, preconceived resolution) and partly by Sanda's participation, which sets up a pronounced resistance to the director's habitual and perverse repression of his actors: if the "liberated woman" is damned, she is also the most alive and vivid presence in the film.

The current impasse of Bertolucci's career can be read as the logical result of his failure to resolve the confusions about sexuality and sexual politics that made *The Conformist* at once so vital and so frustrating. Again, the Sanda character (Anna) is at the heart of the confusion. The film asserts that (a) Fascism is linked to the *repression* of homosexuality (the protagonist Marcello), and (b) that it is linked to homosexuality itself (his friend and mentor Italo). The ambivalence is embodied most vividly in Anna, who is presented as a positive contrast to the repressed hero (as a liberated bisexual woman ready to allow free expression to her lesbian impulses), yet is also associated with decadence. The characterization (though without the lesbianism) is more or less repeated in *1900*, but it is surely for *The Conformist* that we think of Sanda, the character's beauty and energy inseparable from her androgyny, her ability to be at once "masculine" and "feminine."

—Robin Wood

SANDERS, George

Nationality: British. **Born:** St. Petersburg, Russia, of English parents, 3 July 1906. **Education:** Attended a Russian grade school; Dunhurst Preparatory School; Bedales School; Brighton College; Manchester Technical School. **Family:** Married 1) the actress Susan Larson, 1940 (divorced 1949); 2) the actress Zsa Zsa Gabor, 1949 (divorced 1957); 3) the actress Benita Hume, 1958 (died 1967); 4) the actress Magda Gabor, 1970 (divorced 1970). **Career:** Worked in a Birmingham textile mill, in the tobacco business, and as an advertising writer; then in show business as a chorus boy, in a cabaret act, on radio, and as understudy in London; 1936—film debut in *Find the Lady*; contract with 20th Century-Fox: U.S. film debut in *Lloyd's of London*; in the Saint and the Falcon series over the next few years; 1957—host of TV series *The George Sanders Mystery Theatre*. **Awards:** Best Supporting Actor Academy Award for *All about Eve*, 1950. **Died:** Suicide, 25 April 1972.

Films as Actor:

1936 *Find the Lady* (Gillett) (as Curly Randall); *Strange Cargo* (Huntington) (as Roddy Burch); *The Man Who Could Work Miracles* (Mendes) (as Indifference); *Dishonor Bright* (Walls) (as Lisle); *Lloyd's of London* (Henry King) (as Lord Everett Stacy); *Things to Come* (Menzies) (as Pilot)

1937 *Love Is News* (Garrett) (as Count Andre de Guyon); *Slave Ship* (Garrett) (as Lefty); *The Lady Escapes* (Forde) (as Rene Blanchiard); *Lancer Spy* (Ratoff) (as Lt. Michael Bruce)

1938 *International Settlement* (Forde) (as Del Forbes); *Four Men and a Prayer* (Forde) (as Wyatt)

George Sanders with Ingrid Bergman in *Viaggio in Italia*

1939 *Mr. Moto's Last Warning* (Foster) (as Eric Norvell); *So This Is London* (Freeland); *The Saint Strikes Back* (Farrow) (as Simon Templar); *Confessions of a Nazi Spy* (Litvak) (as Schlager); *The Saint in London* (Carstairs) (as Simon Templar); *Allegheny Uprising* (Seiter) (as Captain Swanson); *Nurse Edith Cavell* (Wilcox) (as Captain Heinrichs)

1940 *The Outsider* (Stein) (as Ragatzy); *Green Hell* (Whales) (as Forrester); *Rebecca* (Hitchcock) (as Jack Flavell); *The Saint's Double Trouble* (Hively) (as Simon Templar/The Boss); *The House of the Seven Gables* (May) (as Jaffrey Pynchon); *The Saint Takes Over* (Hively) (as Simon Templar); *Foreign Correspondent* (Hitchcock) (as Ffolliott); *Bitter Sweet* (Van Dyke) (as Baron von Tranisch); *The Son of Monte Cristo* (Lee) (as Gurko Lanen)

1941 *Rage in Heaven* (Van Dyke) (as Ward Andrews); *The Saint in Palm Springs* (Hively) (as Simon Templar); *Man Hunt* (Fritz Lang) (as Major Quive-Smith); *The Gay Falcon* (Reis) (title role); *A Date with the Falcon* (Reis) (title role); *Sundown* (Hathaway) (as Major Coombes)

1942 *Son of Fury* (Cromwell) (as Sir Arthur Blake); *The Falcon Takes Over* (Reis) (title role); *Her Cardboard Lover* (Cukor) (as Tony Barling); *Tales of Manhattan* (Duvivier) (as Williams); *The Moon and Sixpence* (Lewin) (as Charles Strickland); *The Falcon's Brother* (Logan) (as Gay Lawrence); *The Black Swan* (Henry King) (as Captain Billy Leech); *Quiet Please, Murder* (Larkin) (as Fleg)

1943 *This Land Is Mine* (Renoir) (as George Lambert); *They Came to Blow Up America* (Ludwig) (as Carl Stealman); *Appointment in Berlin* (Green) (as Keith Wilson); *Paris after Dark* (Moguy) (as Dr. André Marbel)

1944 *Action in Arabia* (Moguy) (as Gordon); *The Lodger* (Brahm) (as John Warwick); *Summer Storm* (Sirk) (as Fedor Michailovitch Petroff)

1945 ***The Picture of Dorian Gray*** (Lewin) (as Lord Henry Wotton); *Hangover Square* (Brahm) (as Dr. Allan Middleton); *Uncle Harry* (*The Strange Affair of Uncle Harry*) (Siodmak) (title role)

1946 *A Scandal in Paris* (Sirk) (as Vidocq); *The Strange Woman* (Ulmer) (as John Evered)

1947 *The Private Affairs of Bel Ami* (Lewin) (as George Duroy); *The Ghost and Mrs. Muir* (Mankiewicz) (as Miles Fairley); *Lured* (Sirk) (as Robert Fleming); *Forever Amber* (Preminger) (as Charles II)

1949 *The Fan* (*Lady Windermere's Fan*) (Preminger) (as Lord Darlington); *Samson and Delilah* (DeMille) (as The Saran of Gaza)

1950   *Captain Blackjack* (Duvivier) (as Mike Alexander); ***All about Eve*** (Mankiewicz) (as Addison De Witt)

1951   *I Can Get It for You Wholesale* (Gordon) (as Noble); *The Light Touch* (Brooks) (as Felix Guignol)

1952   *Ivanhoe* (Thorpe) (as De Bois-Guilbert); *Assignment—Paris* (Parrish) (as Nick Strang)

1953   ***Viaggio in Italia*** (*Journey to Italy*; *Voyage to Italy*) (Rossellini) (as Alexander Joyce); *Call Me Madam* (Walter Lang) (as Cosmo Constantine)

1954   *Witness to Murder* (Rowland) (as Albert Richter); *King Richard and the Crusaders* (Butler) (as Richard I); *Jupiter's Darling* (Sidney) (as Fabius Maximus)

1955   *Moonfleet* (Lang) (as Lord Ashwood); *The Scarlet Coat* (Sturges) (as Dr. Odell); *The King's Thief* (Leonard) (as Charles II); *Night Freight* (Yarborough) (as disc jockey)

1956   *Never Say Goodbye* (Hopper) (as Victor); *While the City Sleeps* (Fritz Lang) (as Mark Loving); *That Certain Feeling* (Panama and Frank) (as Larry Larkin); *Death of a Scoundrel* (Martin) (as Clementi Sabourin)

1957   *The Seventh Sin* (Neame and Minnelli) (as Tim Waddington)

1958   *The Whole Truth* (Guillermin) (as Carliss); *From Earth to the Moon* (Haskin) (as Stuyvesant Nicholl)

1959   *That Kind of Woman* (Lumet) (as the man); *Solomon and Sheba* (King Vidor) (as Adonijah)

1960   *A Touch of Larceny* (Hamilton) (as Sir Charles Holland); *The Last Voyage* (Stone) (as Captain Robert Adams); *Bluebeard's Ten Honeymoons* (Wilder) (as Landru); *Village of the Damned* (Rilla) (as Gordon Zellaby); *The Rebel* (*Call Me Genius*) (Day) (as Sir Charles Brouard)

1961   *Cone of Silence* (*Trouble in the Sky*) (Friend) (as Sir Arnold Hobbes); *Cinque ore in contanti* (*Five Golden Hours*) (Zampi) (as Mr. Bing); *Le Rendez-vous* (Delannoy) (as J. K.)

1962   *Operation Snatch* (Day) (as Major Hobson); *In Search of the Castaways* (Stevenson) (as Thomas Ayerton)

1963   *Cairo* (Rilla) (as Major Pickering); *The Cracksman* (Scott) (as the guv'nor); *Ecco* (*Mondo di notte*) (Proia—doc) (as narrator)

1964   *Dark Purpose* (Marshall) (as Raymond Fontaine); *A Shot in the Dark* (Edwards) (as Benjamin Ballon); *The Golden Head* (Thorpe) (as Basil Palmer)

1965   *The Amorous Adventures of Moll Flanders* (Young) (as the banker)

1966   *The Quiller Memorandum* (Anderson) (as Gibbs); *Trunk to Cairo* (Golan) (as Professor Schlieben)

1967   *Good Times* (Friedkin) (as Mr. Mordicus); *Warning Shot* (Kulik) (as Calvin York)

1968   *One Step to Hell* (Howard) (as Captain Phillips); *The Jungle Book* (Reitherman) (as voice of Shere Khan)

1969   *The Candy Man* (Leder) (as Sidney Carter); *The Best House in London* (Saville) (as Sir Francis Leybourne); *The Body Stealers* (*Thin Air*; *Invasion of the Body Stealers*) (Levy) (as General Armstrong)

1970   *The Kremlin Letter* (Huston) (as the warlock); *Rio '70* (*The Seven Secrets of Su-Muru*; *Future Women*) (Franco); *Appuntamento col disonore* (*Rendezvous with Dishonor*) (Bolzoni)

1971   *Endless Night* (Gilliatt)

1972   *Doomwatch* (Sasdy) (as the Admiral); *The Living Dead* (*Psychomania*; *The Frog*; *The Death Wheelers*) (Sharp) (as Shadwell)

Publications

By SANDERS: book—

Memoirs of a Professional Cad, New York, 1960.

On SANDERS: books—

Thomas, Tony, *Cads and Cavaliers*, South Brunswick, New Jersey, 1973.

Richards, Jeffrey, *Swordsmen of the Screen: From Douglas Fairbanks to Michael York*, London, 1977.

Aherne, Brian, *A Dreadful Man*, assisted by George Sanders and Benita Hume, New York, 1979.

Van Der Beets, Richard, *George Sanders: An Exhausted Life*, Lanham, Maryland, 1990.

On SANDERS: articles—

Current Biography 1943, New York, 1943.

Obituary in *New York Times*, 26 April 1972.

Beylie, C., "Trois hommes morts," in *Ecran* (Paris), June 1972.

"George Sanders," in *Films and Filming* (London), June 1972.

"George Sanders," letter from G. Shawcross in *Films in Review* (New York), October 1975.

Interim, L., "Homage à l'ironie," in *Cahiers du Cinéma* (Paris), March 1981.

*   *   *

George Sanders was the smoothest of villains; a cool, dangerous cad who could outsneer Basil Rathbone and outpurr Vincent Price. He deployed irresistible charm with an edge of menace, qualified by a disconcerting sense of languid indifference. Given the quality of many of his films, this feeling of ennui was often justified.

Despite frequently proclaimed laziness ("My own desire as a boy was to retire. That ambition has never changed") and contempt for the whole business of acting, Sanders made an impressive quantity of movies. From time to time he was cast as a good chap, or even a romantic lead, but the impersonation was rarely convincing. During the war years he inevitably played despicable Nazis, most notably in Lang's *Man Hunt*. But it was the morally ambiguous roles, the charmingly cynical bounders, that suited him best. "I was beastly but I was never coarse. I was a high-class sort of heel." Highly literate and multilingual, Sanders responded thankfully to intelligent scripts. Albert Lewin, master of overblown cultural decadence, served him well in three films, but his finest part came from another word-oriented director, Joseph Mankiewicz, in *All about Eve*. As the adder-tongued drama critic Addison De Witt, Sanders effortlessly walked off with the picture and a thoroughly deserved Oscar.

Such ideal roles were sadly rare. Sanders occasionally worked for major directors such as Renoir and Lang, but only in their lesser films. Towards the end of his career the overall quality of his material slipped from mediocre to abysmal, and he often looked as weary as he must have felt. One of his last assignments was Disney's *Jungle Book*, impeccably cast as the voice of Shere Khan, the soft-spoken, razor-clawed tiger. His suicide note was wholly in character: "Dear World, I am leaving because I am bored."

—Philip Kemp

SARANDON, Susan

Nationality: American. **Born:** Susan Tomalin in New York City, 4 October 1946; grew up in Edison, New Jersey. **Education:** Attended Catholic University of America, Washington, D.C., B.A., 1968. **Family:** Married the actor Chris Sarandon, 1967 (divorced 1979); daughter with the writer Franco Amurri; two sons with actor Tim Robbins. **Career:** 1970—film debut in *Joe*; member of improvisational group,

New York; 1981—stage debut in *A Couple White Chicks Sitting around Talking*. **Awards:** Best Actress Academy Award, and Screen Actors Guild Award for drama actor, for *Dead Man Walking*, 1995. **Agent:** William Morris Agency, 1350 Avenue of the Americas, New York, NY 10019, U.S.A.

Films as Actress:

1970   *Joe* (Avildsen) (as Melissa Compton)
1972   *Lady Liberty* (Monicelli) (as Sallyi)
1973   *The Haunting of Rosalind* (for TV) (as Dita)
1974   *The Satan Murders* (Swift—for TV) (as Kate); *The Front Page* (Wilder) (as Peggy Grant); *The Great Waldo Pepper* (Hill) (as Mary Beth); *Lovin' Molly* (Lumet) (as Sarah); *F. Scott Fitzgerald and the Last of the Belles* (Schaefer—for TV)
1975   **The Rocky Horror Picture Show** (Sharmon) (as Janet Weiss)
1976   *One Summer Love* (Dragonfly) (Cates—for TV) (as Chloe)
1977   *The Other Side of Midnight* (Jarrott) (as Catherine Douglas)
1978   *Pretty Baby* (Malle) (as Hattie); *King of the Gypsies* (Pierson) (as Rose); *Checkered Flag or Crash* (Gibson); *The Great Smokey Roadblock* (*The Last of the Cowboys*) (Leone) (as Ginny, + co-pr)
1979   *Something Short of Paradise* (Helpern) (as Madeleine Ross)
1980   *Loving Couples* (Smight) (as Stephanie)
1981   *Atlantic City* (Malle) (as Sally); *Owen Marshall, Counselor at Law* (*Pattern of Morality*) (Kulik—for TV)
1982   *The Tempest* (Mazursky) (as Aretha); *Who Am I This Time?* (Demme—for TV)
1984   *The Hunger* (Tony Scott) (as Sarah Roberts); *The Buddy System* (Glenn Jordan) (as Emily); *Talking Nicaragua* (Engel—doc)
1985   *Compromising Positions* (Perry) (as Judith Singer); *Io e il duce* (*Mussolini and I*) (Negrin—for TV)
1986   *Women of Valor* (Kulik—for TV)
1987   *The Witches of Eastwick* (Miller) (as Jane Spofford)
1988   *Bull Durham* (Shelton) (as Annie Savoy); *Sweet Heart's Dance* (Greenwald) (as Sandra Boon); *Da grande* (Amurri)
1989   *The January Man* (O'Connor) (as Christine Starkey); *A Dry White Season* (Palcy) (as Melanie Bruwer); *The Monkey People* (doc) (as narrator)
1990   *White Palace* (Mandoki) (as Nora Baker); *Through the Wire* (doc) (as narrator)
1991   *Thelma and Louise* (Ridley Scott) (as Louise Sawyer)
1992   *Bob Roberts* (Robbins) (as news anchor Tawna Titan); *Lorenzo's Oil* (Miller) (as Michaela Odone); **The Player** (Altman); *Light Sleeper* (Schrader) (as Ann)
1994   *The Client* (Schumacher) (as Reggie Love); *Little Women* (Armstrong) (as Marmee March); *Safe Passage* (as Mag Singer)
1995   *Dead Man Walking* (Robbins) (as Sister Helen Prejean)
1996   *James and the Giant Peach* (Selick) (as voice)

Publications

By SARANDON: articles—

Interview in *Inter/View* (New York), June 1983.
Interview in the *Guardian* (London), 24 May 1989.
Interview by Claudia Dreifus, in *Playboy*, May 1989.
Interview by Graham Fuller, in *Interview*, June 1991.
Interview by W. Schneider, in *American Premiere*, vol. 13, no. 1, 1993.
"Susan Sarandon: Uncompromising Positions," interview by Gavin Smith, in *Film Comment*, March-April 1993.

"Susan Sarandon: Lover, Lawyer, Marmee," interview by Bruce Newman, in *New York Times*, 17 July 1994.
"Susan Sarandon: The Bigger-Picture Revolution," interview by Graham Fuller, in *Interview*, October 1994.

On SARANDON: articles—

Kessler, Stephen, "Extremities," in *Film Comment* (New York), April 1985.
Farber, Stephen, "Who Is She This Time?," in *American Film* (Washington, D.C.), May 1983; see also June 1988.
Current Biography 1989, New York, 1989.
Queenan, Joe, "Miss Congeniality," in *Rolling Stone*, 9 February 1989.
Yagoda, Ben, "The Prime of Susan Sarandon," in *American Film*, May 1991.
Ruuth, M., "Susan Sarandon," in *Chaplin*, vol. 35, no. 2, 1993.
Cagle, Jess, "Laying down the Law," in *Entertainment Weekly*, 29 July 1994.

*   *   *

Flashing the most hypnotic movie star eyes since Bette Davis overworked her optic nerves, Susan Sarandon graduated from utility performer (*Joe, Other Side of Midnight*) to respected actress (*Atlantic City*, television's *Who Am I This Time?*) to one of the most durable stars of contemporary cinema. At an age when most actresses are scrambling for second leads and TV sitcoms, Sarandon became the rare kind of star you would go to see in anything. Unfortunately, at earlier periods in her career, she seemed to appear in just about anything (*The Great Smokey Roadblock*) and got by on cover girl looks alone (*The Great Waldo Pepper, The Front Page*) until Louis Malle recognized that her European sensuality was being miscast as Apple Pie Americana. Once Malle released her self-deprecating wit and unabashed sexuality, Sarandon seemed to relax on-screen.

Having shucked off the sorority sister wholesomeness (that netted her cult status as the square in *Rocky Horror Picture Show*), Sarandon plowed through the eighties in Hollywooden properties save for one bright spot: a sassy amateur detective in *Compromising Positions*, the first evidence an entire film could be fashioned around her star-presence.

In 1987 she was asked (via Cher's clout) to switch roles with that living legend in the unaccountably popular *Witches of Eastwick* and was then convinced to audition for *Bull Durham*. She landed the juicy part of Annie Savoy and has not looked back. Covering all of that rollicking romance's bases, her screen persona emerged: a sensualist who flaunts conventions because the rules make no sense to her. Obliterating the double standard that has always plagued popular entertainment, Sarandon did not accept the Madonna or Whore dichotomy, but instead created the figure of a sexual missionary who made no apology for her largesse. A lucky project for her, *Bull Durham* introduced her to co-star Tim Robbins, her now long-time companion with whom she has had two children.

Refining her blue collar earth mother image further by bedding a younger man in *White Palace*, Sarandon then struck a nerve in the feminist fantasia *Thelma and Louise*. Harmoniously teamed with Geena Davis, Sarandon's fiercely guarded vulnerability lit up this turnabout-is-fair-play escapism and made the film seem more novel than it was.

Heart-wrenchingly, she next threw herself into the challenge of interpreting an unsympathetic character, a grimly determined mother alienating anyone who rains on her anti-medical establishment parade in *Lorenzo's Oil* as she seeks a cure for her dying son. In this unwieldy movie, which is a terminal illness weepie so clinical it turns into a horror film, crusading Sarandon provides the bleak life-and-death struggles with a heartbeat.

Susan Sarandon in *The Hunger*

This unwavering, nurturing quality is an integral part of Sarandon's refurbished appeal. Known for her humanitarian efforts offscreen, Sarandon's compassion is imprinted on her roles as a mother surrogate outsmarting the Goodfellas in *The Client* (a creaky vehicle that solidified her box office power), as a Civil War matriarch role-modeling her brood in a perceptive remake of *Little Women* and as a nun grappling with capital punishment in *Dead Man Walking*. Even cast as a recreational drug dispenser in *Light Sleeper*, she zeroed in on this weary hedonist's speck of conscience.

Like all great stars, Sarandon rivets the attention whether she is merely marking time as a decorative blood bank in *The Hunger*, weathering the arty, forced exuberance of *The Tempest*, or purposefully lending her gravity to a liberal property such as *A Dry White Season*.

Unlike technically proficient above-the-title leading ladies such as Meryl Streep and Glenn Close, Sarandon is a welcome throwback to the studio era's personality-driven stars who did not submerge themselves in roles but stamped each individualized characterization with their own unique, unmistakable imprint. If any one scene crystallizes her image as fearless protector, it is the sequence in *A Safe Place*, in which she risks her life fending off a vicious dog threatening her son. Ferocity and passion characterize her every move as she invests the often-disparaged role of American mother with quiet heroism.

Whereas other stars condescend to mother roles to preserve the last vestiges of stardom, Sarandon has rediscovered herself in such

parts without mummifying herself as a sexless, aproned martyr. If female stars over forty finally start attaining big screen prominence instead of being exiled to television problem dramas, dinner theaters, or book deals, pioneering Sarandon will be largely responsible. More vividly beautiful with the passage of time, Sarandon unapologetically shows audiences that there is more to womanhood than Sharon Stone can reveal.

—Robert Pardi

SCACCHI, Greta

Nationality: British/Italian. **Born:** Milan, Italy, 18 February 1960. **Family:** One daughter, Leila, with the actor Vincent D'Onofrio. **Education:** Attended the University of Western Australia; studied theater in England at the Bristol Old Vic Theatre School. **Career:** Late 1970s—began acting on the stage in Perth, Australia; late 1970s-early 1980s—came to England, where she appeared on stage with the Bristol Old Vic and on British TV; 1983—earned initial international acclaim for performance in *Heat and Dust*. **Agent:** Smith-Freedman and Associates, 121 North San Vicente Boulevard, Beverly Hills, CA 90211, U.S.A.

Greta Scacchi in *Heat and Dust*

Films as Actress:

1982 *Das Zweite Gesicht* (*The Second Face*) (Graf)
1983 *Dr. Fischer of Geneva* (Lindsay-Hogg—for TV) (as Anna-Louisa); *Heat and Dust* (Ivory) (as Olivia Rivers)
1984 *The Ebony Tower* (Knights—for TV) (as Mouse); *Camille* (Desmond Davis—for TV) (as Marguerite Gautier)
1985 *The Coca-Cola Kid* (Makavejev) (as Terri); *Defence of the Realm* (Drury) (as Nina Beckman); *Burke & Wills* (Clifford) (as Julia Matthews)
1987 *Good Morning, Babilonia* (*Good Morning, Babylon*) (Paolo Taviani and Vittorio Taviani) (as Edna); *Un homme amoureux* (*A Man in Love*) (Kurys) (as Jane Steiner)
1988 *White Mischief* (Radford) (as Diana Broughton); *Paura e amore* (*Trois soeurs*; *Love and Fear*; *Three Sisters*) (von Trotta) (as Maria); *La donna della luna* (*Woman in the Moon*) (Zagarrio) (as Angele)
1990 *Presumed Innocent* (Pakula) (as Carolyn Polhemus)
1991 *Fires Within* (Gillian Armstrong) (as Isabel); *Shattered* (Petersen) (as Judith Merrick)
1992 *The Player* (Altman) (as June Gudmundsdottir); *Turtle Beach* (*The Killing Beach*) (Wallace) (as Judith); *Salt on Our Skin* (*Desire*) (Birkin) (as George)
1994 *The Browning Version* (Figgis) (as Laura Crocker-Harris); *Country Life* (Blakemore) (as Deborah Voysey)
1995 *Jefferson in Paris* (Ivory) (as Maria Cosway)
1996 *Rasputin* (for TV) (as Alexandra); *Bravo Ready* (D'Alatri); *Emma* (McGrath)

Publications

By SCACCHI: article—

Interview with M. Brennan, in *Films and Filming* (London), August 1985.

On SCACCHI: articles—

Gray, M., "Globetrotting Greta," in *Photoplay Movies & Video* (London), November 1987.
Schiff, Stephen, "Spotlight: Steamy Scacchi," in *Vanity Fair* (New York), May 1989.
Rochlin, Margy, "Foreign Intrigue," in *Harper's Bazaar* (New York), June 1991.
Clark, John, filmography in *Premiere* (New York), September 1991.
Schruers, Fred, "Greta," in *Premiere* (New York), September 1991.
Ferguson, K., "Classy Scacchi," in *Film Monthly* (Berkhamsted, England), November 1991.
Gritten, David, "The Transformation of Greta Scacchi," in *Cosmopolitan*, April 1994.

* * *

Had she been working in movies during an earlier era, Greta Scacchi would have made a great heroine/villainess in classic film noir mysteries. One can see her playing Brigid O'Shaughnessy, toying with Bogie's Sam Spade in *The Maltese Falcon*; Phyllis Dietrichson, trapped in a stifling marriage and making insurance salesman Walter Neff (Fred MacMurray) go through hoops in *Double Indemnity*; or Cora Smith, also stifled by her marriage to an unglamorous older man, who charms drifter Frank Chambers (John Garfield) in *The Postman Always Rings Twice*.

What audiences missed out on back in the 1940s was a captivating blond actress who instinctively blends a feeling of innocence and impish girlishness with a beguiling seductiveness. In her various screen roles, however, Scacchi often is found shedding her clothes—something she never could have done back in Hollywood's heyday. For this reason alone, she has become a popular cinema icon for more discerning male moviegoers.

Scacchi is also blessed with enchantingly expressive eyes, which frequently communicate more to the camera and viewer than her conversation. This description perfectly characterizes her performance in the film in which she first attracted attention: *Heat and Dust*, in which she is cast as Olivia, an attractive young Englishwoman, wed to a proper British civil servant stationed in India, whose passions are aroused upon becoming romantically involved with an Indian prince. She further established herself in *The Coca-Cola Kid*, a satire about the representative of an American soft drink company who is sent to Australia as a troubleshooter. She is a bright and attractive presence as a secretary with whom the Yank tussles, and then seduces.

Scacchi has played characters who are ruled by their feelings rather than their intellect. In *Love and Fear*, she is cast as Maria, the middle of three sisters, who has no career goals and lives an aimless existence. Her elder sibling (Fanny Ardant) is the sensitive intellectual, and her younger one (Valeria Golino) is the fervent idealist. The latter two are roles which one cannot imagine Scacchi playing. More often than not, her characters, as the one she played in *Heat and Dust*, are wed to unsuitable partners, and are involved in extramarital relations. In *The Browning Version*, an updating of the Terrence Rattigan play (which previously had been filmed in 1951), Scacchi plays a role not dissimilar to that of Phyllis Dietrichson or Cora Smith: a beautiful woman, lovelessly married to an older man (Albert Finney, cast as a scholarly but bureaucratic professor of languages at a stuffy British boys' school), who fools around with a younger man (the school's American-born science teacher, played by Matthew Modine).

Indeed, Scacchi is miscast in roles where intellect (or even, for that matter, romantic longing) takes precedence over sexual desire. Such is the case in *Jefferson in Paris*. She plays yet another unfulfilled married woman: Maria Cosway, whose husband is a fop, and who falls for Thomas Jefferson (Nick Nolte). Scacchi is most believable when she asks the object of her desire, "How far do you go in America?" You wait for Maria to seduce Jefferson, but this is not to be, given the man with whom she is dealing. When Jefferson does tell her he missed her after a long absence, she only can smile seductively—a reaction that is completely out of place for her character.

Scacchi is far better suited to playing film noirish vamps and mystery women. In *The Player*, she is June Gudmundsdottir, the amoral girlfriend of a screenwriter who is accidentally killed by Griffin Mill (Tim Robbins), hotshot head of production of a large movie studio. In *Presumed Innocent*, she plays Carolyn Polhemus, an ambitious, sexually adventurous assistant prosecutor who becomes a murder victim—and who was the object of the sexual fixation of the co-worker (Harrison Ford) who is accused of the crime. Perhaps her best—and most typically provocative—role to date has been in *White Mischief*, a based-on-fact story in which she also is cast as the wayward wife of a much older, less-than-sexually attentive man. Scacchi plays Diana Broughton, the elegant, decadent mate of a British diplomat (Joss Ackland) who is stationed in Kenya during the early years of World War II. The essence of the story revolves around the manner in which the husband responds when Diana commences an affair with an impoverished earl (Charles Dance) who is a notorious womanizer. Scacchi has never been more striking than in *White Mischief*—and never more coolly seductive.

—Rob Edelman

SCHEIDER, Roy

Nationality: American. **Born:** Roy Richard Scheider in Orange, New Jersey, 10 November 1935. **Education:** Attended Franklin and Marshall College, Lancaster, Pennsylvania, B.A. 1955. **Military Service:** U.S. Air Force. **Family:** Married 1) Cynthia Eddenfield Bebout, 1962, one daughter; 2) Brenda King, one son. **Career:** Member of the Lincoln Center Repertory Company; 1964—film debut in *Curse of the Living Corpse*; 1980—on Broadway in *Betrayal*; 1993-95—in TV series *seaQuest DSV*; 1993—in TV mini-series *Wild Justice*, and *Leopold & Loeb*, 1994.

Films as Actor:

1964   *Curse of the Living Corpse* (Tenney) (as Philip Sinclair)
1968   *Paper Lion* (March); *Star!* (Wise)
1969   *Stiletto* (Kowalski) (as Bennett)
1970   *Loving* (Kershner) (as Skip); *Puzzle of a Downfall Child* (Schatzberg) (as Mark)
1971   *The French Connection* (Friedkin) (as Buddy "Cloudy" Russo); *Klute* (Pakula) (as Frank Ligourin)
1972   *Assignment Munich* (Rich—for TV) (as Jake Webster)
1973   *The Seven-Ups* (D'Antoni) (as Buddy Manucci); *Un Homme est morte* (*The Outside Man*; *Funerale a Los Angeles*) (Deray) (as Lenny); *L'Attendat* (*The French Conspiracy*) (Boisset) (as Michael Howard)
1975   *Jaws* (Spielberg) (as Sheriff Martin Brody); *Sheila Levine Is Dead and Living in New York* (Furie) (as Sam Stoneham)
1976   *Marathon Man* (Schlesinger) (as Doc Levy)
1977   *Sorcerer* (Friedkin) (as Jackie Scanlon/ "Juan Dominiguez")
1978   *Jaws II* (Szwarc) (as Sheriff Brody)
1979   *Last Embrace* (Jonathan Demme) (as Harry Hannan); *All That Jazz* (Fosse) (as Joe Gideon)
1982   *Still of the Night* (Benton) (as Sam Rice)
1983   *Blue Thunder* (Badham) (as Frank Murphy); *Tiger Town* (Shapiro) (as Billy Young); *Jacobo Timerman: Prisoner without a Name, Cell without a Number* (Yellen—for TV) (title role)
1984   *2010* (Hyams) (as Heywood Floyd)
1985   *Mishima* (Schrader) (as narrator)
1986   *The Men's Club* (Medak) (as Cavanaugh); *52 Pick-Up* (Frankenheimer) (as Harry Mitchell)
1988   *Cohen and Tate* (Red) (as Cohen)
1989   *Night Game* (Masterson) (as Mike Seaver); *Listen to Me* (Stewart) (as Charlie Nichols)
1990   *The Fourth War* (Frankenheimer) (as Colonel Jack Clark); *The Russia House* (Schepisi) (as Russell); *Somebody Has to Shoot the Picture* (Pierson—for TV) (as Paul Marish)
1991   *Naked Lunch* (Cronenberg) (as Dr. Benway); *Contact: The Yahomani Indians of Brazil* (doc)
1993   *Romeo Is Bleeding* (Medak) (as Don Falcone)
1994   *Covert Assassin* (as Col. Peter Stride)
1996   *Myth of Fingerprints*

Publications

By SCHEIDER: articles—

Interview in *Films Illustrated* (London), January 1976.
Interview with James Cameron-Wilson, in *Film Review* (London), November 1980.
Interviews in *Ecran Fantastique*, July/August 1983 and April 1985.
Interview in *Time Out* (London), 14 March 1985.

On SCHEIDER: article—

Hamill, Pete, "Recognizing Roy Scheider," in *New York*, 23 May 1983.

*   *   *

Roy Scheider's career is marked by variety and diversity, but it has not been varied by degrees. Instead, Roy Scheider characters can always be seen at the extremes. He is at once the heroic, everyman, Sheriff Martin Brody in *Jaws* and *Jaws II* and Frank, the sadistic pimp in *Klute*. On both counts, at whatever end of the character spectrum he operates, he is always believable, and most importantly, accessible.

The best way to visualize the extremes in Scheider's long film career is to look at the year 1971. In that year he had roles in two Academy Award-winning motion pictures. In *Klute* he played Jane Fonda's pimp Frank, a necessarily small, seedy character from whose lips syrupy wooing and brutal epithets flow with equal credibility. Later that year, Scheider got what was to become perhaps his breakthrough role. As Buddy Russo, Gene "Popeye Doyle" Hackman's partner in *The French Connection*, he was the ideal, play-it-by-the-book offset to Hackman's obsessive Doyle.

Scheider's most memorable role, and subsequently his most marketable persona, is that of Sheriff Martin Brody in *Jaws*. Brody is the perfect commoner's hero: a former New York cop, who is afraid of the water, but lives and works on a small resort island. Brody himself wittily underscores this fact saying, "It's only an island if you're looking at it from out there [the water]." Brody, like so many later Scheider characters—the mild-mannered psychiatrist in *The Still of the Night* or the daring copter pilot in *Blue Thunder*—must rise above his personal limitations or hang-ups to overcome an adversary seemingly much better prepared. The task of these characters is made harder by the fact that they are also outsiders. But Scheider has worked his way up the ranks (i.e., "paid his dues" as an actor—anyone who has seen the low-budget *Curse of the Living Corpse* will agree), and been a tough guy in real life (Golden Gloves boxer in high school). These factors have helped bring a special kind of realism to his roles.

A less visible aspect of Scheider's career, but one that is just as significant, is the number of times he has played against his usual persona. In films such as William Friedkin's *Sorceror*, Scheider finds characters that seem to have no precedent in his prolific past. *All That Jazz* is the best example of how Scheider has willingly taken career chances. In the film, which Bob Fosse loosely based on his own self-destructive lifestyle, Scheider plays a famed choreographer/filmmaker named Joe Gideon. As such, he must dance, sing, and most importantly, develop a character that is credible within such a world. Scheider did an excellent job of making Gideon a three-dimensional character, managing to create a sympathetic side to a self-indulgent womanizer. His performance earned him an Academy Award nomination.

Among other things, Scheider has been fortunate enough to have worked with the major directorial talents of the last two decades: Steven Spielberg, William Friedkin, Robert Benton, Alan J. Pakula, and Bob Fosse. It is also, decidedly, a tribute to Roy Scheider's talents that the foremost names continue to want to work with him.

—Rob Winning, updated by Linda J. Stewart

SCHELL, Maria

Nationality: Swiss. **Born:** Maria Margarethe Anna Schell in Vienna, Austria, 5 January 1926; sister of the actor Maximilian Schell; became Swiss citizen. **Education:** Attended a convent school in Colmar, Germany; business school in Switzerland; School of the Theatrical Arts,

Zurich. **Family:** Married 1) the director Horst Hächler, 1957; 2) the stage director Veit Relin, 1966. **Career:** 1942—film debut in *Der Steinbruch*; then acted on Swiss stage; 1946—member of the State Theater of Bern; film contract with Alexander Korda; continued to act on stage: in *Faust* opposite Albert Bassermann on European tour; 1958—first U.S. film, *The Brothers Karamazov*; 1980—in TV miniseries *The Martian Chronicles*, *Inside the Third Reich*, 1982, and *Der Clan der Anna Voss*, 1995. **Awards:** Best Actress, Cannes Festival, for *Die letzte Brücke*, 1954; Best Actress, Venice Festival, for *Gervaise*, 1955; Deutscher Filmpreis Career Award, 1977.

Films as Actress:

1942 *Der Steinbruch* (Steiner)
1943 *Maturareise* (Steiner)
1948 *Der Engel mit der Posaune* (Hartl) (as Anna Linden); *Maresi* (Thimig)
1949 *Die letzte Nacht* (York)
1950 *Nach dem Sturm* (Ucicky); *Es kommt ein Tag* (*A Day Will Come*) (Jugert) (as Madeline)
1951 *The Magic Box* (John Boulting) (as Helena Friese-Greene); *The Angel with the Trumpet* (Bushell) (as Anna Linden); *Angelika* (*Affairs of Dr. Holl*; *Dr. Holl*) (Hansen) (title role)
1952 *So Little Time* (Bennett) (as Nicole de Malvines)
1953 *The Heart of the Matter* (O'Ferrall) (as Helen Rolt); *Bis wir uns Wiedersehen* (Ucicky) (as Pamela); *Tagebuch einer Verliebten* (*Diary of a Lover*) (von Baky) (as Barbara Holzmann); *Solange du da bist* (*As Long as You're Near Me*) (Braun); *Der traumende Mund* (*Dreaming Lips*) (von Baky) (as Liss)
1954 *Die letzte Brücke* (*The Last Bridge*) (Käutner) (as Helga Reinbeck); *Napoléon* (Guitry) (as Marie-Louise of Austria)
1955 *Die Ratten* (*The Rats*) (Siodmak) (as Pauline Karka); *Urgano sul Po*; *Herr über Leben und Tod* (*No Way Back*) (Vicas); *Gervaise* (Clément) (title role)
1956 *Liebe* (*Love*) (Hächler)
1957 *Rose Bernd* (*The Sins of Rose Bernd*) (Staudte) (title role); *Le notti bianche* (*White Nights*) (Visconti) (as Natalia); *Ungarn in Flammen* (as narrator)
1958 *The Brothers Karamazov* (Richard Brooks) (as Grushenka); *Une Vie* (*End of Desire*; *One Life*) (Astruc) (as Jeanne Dandieu); *Der Schinderhannes* (*Duel in the Forest*) (Käutner)
1959 *The Hanging Tree* (Daves) (as Elizabeth Mahler)
1960 *Hellas* (*As the Sea Rages*) (Hächler) (as Mana); *Cimarron* (Anthony Mann) (as Sabra Cravet)
1961 *Das Reisenrad* (von Radvanyi); *The Mark* (Guy Green) (as Ruth Leighton)
1962 *Ich bin auch nur eine Frau* (*Only a Woman*; *I, Too, Am Only a Woman*) (Weidenmann) (as Lilli Koenig)
1963 *L'Assassin connait la musique* (Weidermann); *Zwei Whisky und ein Sofa* (*Rendezvous in Trieste*) (Gräwert)
1965 *Who Has Seen the Wind?* (Sidney—for TV); *Nora oder Ein Puppenheim* (Moszkowicz—for TV)
1968 *99 mujeres* (*99 Women*; *Island of Despair*; *Isle of Lost Women*) (Franco) (as Leonie); *Le Diable par la queue* (*The Devil by the Tail*) (de Broca) (as Diane)
1969 *La Provocation* (Charpak)
1970 *El processo de las brujas* (*Throne of Fire*; *The Bloody Judge*; *Night of the Blood Monster*) (Franco)
1971 *Such a Pretty Cloud*; *Dans la poussière du soleil* (*Lust in the Sun*) (Balducci)
1972 *Chamsin* (Rilen); *Die Pfarrhauskomödie* (Rilen)
1973 *Immobilien* (Jägersberg)

1974 *The Odessa File* (Neame) (as Frau Miller); *Change* (Fischerauer); *Marie* (Geissendörfer); *Die Kurpfuscherin* (*The Quack*) (Cremer—for TV)
1975 *Das Konzert* (Haugk—for TV); *Die Heiratsvermittlerin* (Matiasek—for TV); *Die Abrechnung* (Wolfgang Becker—for TV)
1976 *Voyage of the Damned* (Rosenberg); *So oder so ist das Leben* (Rilen—for TV); *Folies bourgeoises* (*The Twist*) (Chabrol) (as Gretel)
1977 *Spiel der Verlierer* (Hohoff); *Teerosen* (Rolf Von Sydow—for TV)
1978 *Superman* (Richard Donner) (as Vond-Ah)
1979 *Die erste Polka* (Emmerich) (as Valeska); *Schöner Gigolo—armer Gigolo* (*Just a Gigolo*) (Hemmings) (as Mutti); *Christmas Lilies of the Field* (Ralph Nelson—for TV); *Der Wald* (Ten Haaf—for TV); *Moral* (Wilhelm—for TV)
1980 *Der Thronfolger* (Döpke—for TV); *Liebe bleibt nicht ohne Schmerzen* (Bohrer)
1981 *La Passante du Sans-Souci* (*La Passante*) (Ruoffio) (as Anna Helwig); *Frau Jenny Triebel* (Franz Josef Wild—for TV); *Inside the Third Reich* (Chomsky—for TV) (as Mrs. Speer)
1982 *Der Besuch der alten Dame* (Ammann—for TV) (as Claire Zachanassian)
1983 *Der Trauschein* (Kishon—for TV)
1984 *Samson and Delilah* (Philips—for TV); *Koenig Drosselbart* (*Kral drozdi brada*) (Beck and Luther)
1985 *1919* (Brody) (as Sophie Rubin)
1991 *Le Dernier mot* (Behat)

Publications

By SCHELL: book—

Die Kostbarkeit des Augerblicks, Gedanken Erinnerungen, Munich, 1985.

By SCHELL: article—

In *Seventeen Interviews*, by Edwin Miller, New York, 1970.

On SCHELL: book—

Spaich, Herbert, *Maria Schell: Ihre Filme—ihre Leben*, Munich, 1986.

On SCHELL: articles—

"The Golden Look" (cover story), in *Time* (New York), 30 December 1957.
Current Biography 1961, New York, 1961.
Spelman, F., "The Explosive Schell Family," in *Show* (Hollywood), January 1963.

*   *   *

Throughout the 1950s, Maria Schell dazzled rows of moviegoers in Europe and Great Britain with a series of extraordinarily moving performances. German audiences, who were especially enamored of her intense portrayals of unjustly suffering women, voted Schell their favorite actress in 1951, 1952, 1954, 1955, and 1956. Critical tongues likewise wagged approbation, frequently citing Schell's instinctual talent as an actress, the emotional range of her acting, and her goldstruck beauty. Recognizing that her presence in a film could help assure its commercial and often critical success, filmmakers throughout Europe cast Schell in nearly 25 films before 1960. Her role as a central character would also cancel the need for dubbing as Schell spoke five languages.

After her critical successes in *Die letzte Brücke* and *Gervaise*, MGM acknowledged Schell's abilities and the healthy box-office receipts of her films by inviting her to appear in *The Brothers Karamazov* as Grushenka, a coveted role for which Marilyn Monroe had originally been considered. Schell's arrival in Hollywood provoked both enthusiastic speculations on her becoming the newest international screen star, and favorable comparisons with Ingrid Bergman who had captured Hollywood in the 1940s. But, a brief series of miscastings, including her performance as Grushenka, revealed the potential weakness of box-office casting and soured Schell's three years in Hollywood. The miscastings only highlighted her shortcomings and misused her strengths. As Grushenka, Schell reduced the complexity of Dostoevsky's character to a frustrating ambiguity, replete with a nervous giggle. For MGM's remake of *Cimarron*, Schell undermined the role of Sabra Cavet through a number of inexplicable acts such as repeatedly flashing the famous Schell smile while in childbirth.

Critical response to Schell had so deteriorated by the early 1960s that, despite her strong performance in *Le notti bianche*, Bosley Crowther would write in a review of the film, "Miss Schell is enough to blunt one's perceptivity to the poetry and meaning of the [film's] theme." The additional waning of her popularity with the moviegoing public induced Schell in 1963 to leave film and work full-time in the theater, where she had begun her career as an actress. Schell returned to motion pictures in 1968, once again as an international performer, to play a diversity of roles, including a cameo appearance in *Superman*.

—Nancy Jane Richards

SCHELL, Maximilian

Nationality: Swiss. **Born:** Vienna, Austria, 8 December 1930; brother of the actress Maria Schell; became Swiss citizen. **Education:** Attended the universities of Zurich and Munich. **Military Service:** Swiss Army. **Family:** Married Natalya Andreichenko, 1985, one child. **Career:** Following military service, actor in London, Germany, and Switzerland; 1955—film debut in *Kinder, Mütter, und ein General*; 1958—English-language role in *The Young Lions* brought international attention; stage debut in New York in *Interlock*; 1959—in *Hamlet* on American television; followed by other film, stage, and television roles; 1968—produced the film *Das Schloss*; 1970—directed the film *Erste Liebe*; also stage director; 1977—directed the stage plays *Tales from the Vienna Woods*, London, and *The Undiscovered Country*, London, 1979; 1986—in TV mini-series *Peter the Great*; 1990—in TV series *Wiseguy*; 1991—in TV mini-series *Young Catherine*. **Awards:** Best Actor Academy Award, and Best Actor, New York Film Critics, for *Judgment at Nuremberg*, 1961; Best Supporting Actor, New York Film Critics, for *Julia*, 1977; Deutscher Filmpreis for Best Actor, 1984, and for Career, 1989-90. **Address:** Keplerstrasse 2, 8000 Munich 80, Germany.

Films as Actor:

1955 *Kinder, Mütter, und ein General* (Benedek); *Der 20 Juli* (Harnak); *Reifende Jugend* (Erfurth)
1956 *Ein Mädchen aus Flandern* (*The Girl from Flanders*) (Kautner); *Die Ehe des Dr. Med. Danwitz* (Rabenalt); *Ein Herz kehrt Heim* (York)

1957 *Die Letzten werden die Ersten sein* (Hansen); *Taxichauffeur Bänz* (Dueggelin) (as Toni Schellenberg)
1958 *Das Gluck auf der Alm* (*Ein wunderbaren Sommer*) (Tressler); *The Young Lions* (Dmytryk) (as Capt. Hardenberg)
1960 *Hamlet* (Wirth) (title role)
1961 *Judgment at Nuremberg* (Kramer) (as Hans Rolfe)
1962 *Five Finger Exercise* (Delbert Mann) (as Walter); *The Reluctant Saint* (Dmytryk) (as Giuseppe Desa); *I sequestri di Altona* (*The Condemned of Altona*) (De Sica) (as Franz)
1964 *Topkapi* (Dassin) (as William Walter)
1965 *Return from the Ashes* (J. Lee Thompson) (as Stanislaus Pilgrim)
1966 *John F. Kennedy: Years of Lightning, Day of Drums* (Herschensohn—doc) (as narrator)
1967 *The Deadly Affair* (Lumet) (as Dieter Foey); *Más allá de las montañas* (*Beyond the Mountains*; *The Desperate Ones*) (Ramati) (as Marek); *Counterpoint* (Nelson) (as Schiller)
1968 *Heidi* (Delbert Mann—for TV) (as Herr Sesseman)
1969 *Krakatoa, East of Java* (*Volcano*) (Kowalski) (as Captain Chris Hanson); *Simon Bolivar* (Blasetti); *L'assoluto naturale* (Bolognini)
1972 *Paulina 1880* (Bertucelli) (as Count); *Pope Joan* (*The Devil's Imposter*) (Anderson) (as Adrian)
1974 *The Odessa File* (Neame) (as Eduard Roschmann)
1975 *The Man in the Glass Booth* (Hiller) (as Arthur Goldman); *The Days that Shook the World* (*Atentat u Sarajevu*; *Assasination at Sarajevo*; *Assassination*) (Bulajic) (as Djuro Sarac)
1976 *St. Ives* (J. Lee Thompson) (as Dr. John Constable)
1977 *A Bridge Too Far* (Attenborough) (as Gen. Wilhelm Bittrich); *Cross of Iron* (Peckinpah) (as Stransky); *Julia* (Zinnemann) (as Johann)
1978 *Amo non Amo* (*Together*; *I Love You, I Love You Not*) (Balducci) (as John)
1979 *Avalanche Express* (Robson) (as Bunin); *The Black Hole* (Nelson) (as Dr. Hans Reinhardt); *Players* (Harvey) (as Marco)
1980 *The Diary of Anne Frank* (Sagal—for TV)
1982 *The Chosen* (Kagan) (as Professor David Malter)
1983 *Phantom of the Opera* (Markovic—for TV)
1984 *The Assisi Underground* (Ramati) (as Col. Mueller); *Morgen in Alabama* (*Man under Suspicion*) (Kuckelmann) (as lawyer Landau)
1989 *The Rose Garden* (Rademakers) (as Aaron Reichenbacher)
1990 *The Freshman* (Andrew Bergman) (as Larry London)
1992 *Labyrinth* (Jires) (as himself); *Miss Rose White* (Sargent—for TV) (as Mordechai); *Stalin* (Passer—for TV) (as Lenin)
1993 *A Far Off Place* (Salomon) (as Col. Mopani Theron); *Justiz* (*Justice*) (Geissendörfer) (as Isaak Kohler)
1994 *Little Odessa* (Gray) (as Arkady Shapira); *Abraham* (Sargent—for TV)

Films as Producer:

1968 *Das Schloss* (*The Castle*) (Noelte) (+ ro as "K")
1976 *Einsichten eines Clowns* (co-pr)

Films as Director:

1970 *Erste Liebe* (*First Love*) (+ co-pr, co-sc, ro as the father)
1974 *Der Fussgänger* (*The Pedestrian*) (+ co-pr, sc, ro as Andreas Giese)
1975 *Der Richter und sein Henker* (*Murder on the Bridge*; *End of the Game*; *Getting Away with Murder*) (+ co-pr, co-sc)

1981   *Geschichten aus dem Wienerwald* (*Tales from the Vienna Woods*)
       (+ pr, sc)
1984   *Marlene* (doc) (+ co-sc, ro as interviewer)
1993   *Candles in the Dark* (for TV) (+ ro as Colonel Arkush)

Film as Scriptwriter:

1971   *Trotta* (Schaaf)

Publications

By SCHELL: books—

Odon von Horvath, Geschichten aus dem Wienerwald, Frankfurt, 1979.
Anni und Josef Albers: eine Retrospektive, Munich, 1989.

By SCHELL: articles—

Interview with G. Flatley, in *New York Times*, 16 September 1977.
Interview with T. Buckley, in *New York Times*, 3 March 1978.
"Maximilian Schell akteur en kineast," interview with R. Pede, in *Film en Televisie* (Brussels), October 1980.
Interview with C. Chase, in *New York Times*, 31 December 1981.
Interview with B. Reisfeld, in *Photoplay* (London), January 1985.
"Europe at the fin de siecle," interview, by Schell, with Vaclav Havel, in *Society*, September/October 1995.

On SCHELL: articles—

Current Biography 1962, New York, 1962.
Spelman, F., "The Explosive Schell Family," in *Show* (Hollywood), January 1963.
Baxter, B., "Schell Schock," in *Films Illustrated* (London), January 1974.
"La vedette de la semaine: Maximilian Schell," in *Ciné Revue* (Paris), 9 October 1975.
"Maximilian Schell," in *Ecran* (Paris), 15 December 1979.
Dangaard, C., "Maximilian Schell," in *Ciné Revue* (Paris), 7 February 1980.
Bulnes, J., "Les immortals du cinéma: Maximilian Schell," in *Ciné Revue* (Paris), 28 July 1983.

*   *   *

The specter of Nazism seems to have haunted Schell throughout his acting career. Although born in Vienna and raised in Switzerland, he is best known for his work in films about World War II and its aftermath, wherein he has most often been cast as a Nazi officer. In fact, his first Hollywood part was that of the devout storm trooper who commanded Marlon Brando's morally troubled German captain in *The Young Lions*, based on the Irwin Shaw best-seller. He subsequently donned the uniform of the Third Reich in war films as varied as *Counterpoint*, *A Bridge Too Far*, and Sam Peckinpah's *Cross of Iron*, where he played a scheming German general determined to win the titular medal for valor even if he has to sacrifice his entire command.

In 1961, Schell won the Academy Award as best actor for his intense performance as the German attorney defending Nazis charged with war crimes in *Judgment at Nuremburg*—a role he had originated on television in the CBS series *Playhouse 90* where the Abby Mann drama first appeared. In 1975, more than a decade later, Schell was again nominated for the same award for his role in the American Film Theater's production of *The Man in the Glass Booth* in which he portrayed a war criminal, based on Adolf Eichmann, brought to justice

in an Israeli court after the end of the war. Later, in *The Odessa File*, he played a similar war criminal, who this time manages to escape justice and is bent on reviving the Third Reich. Still another instance of Schell's interpretation of the Nazi mentality may be found in Zinnemann's *Julia*.

Despite the undeniable quality of his acting, Schell's continued casting as a Nazi has tended to limit his career. For even in roles that do not deal with the World War II experience, he seems to be expected to portray figures with Nazi-like characteristics. For example, in *The Black Hole*, an artistically and commercially unsuccessful science fiction film released by Disney in 1979, Schell portrayed a mad scientist. Derived obviously from James Mason's treatment of Captain Nemo in *20,000 Leagues under the Sea*, the character created by Schell evinces the same sort of authoritarianism and cold dedication to cause at the expense of humane concerns which marks the stereotype of the Nazi in much film and literature. His performance as Lenin in the made-for-cable docudrama *Stalin* was cut from the same cloth.

Perhaps because his acting career has been somewhat restricted in breadth, Schell turned to other aspects of filmmaking. In 1968 he produced a treatment of Franz Kafka's *The Castle*, and in 1970 he directed his first film, *First Love*, based on a short novel by Ivan Turgenev. In 1974 *The Pedestrian*, which Schell co-produced, directed, wrote, and acted in, was nominated for an Academy Award as best foreign-language film. But his 1984 documentary *Marlene* on the life of the legendary film star Marlene Dietrich remains one of his most interesting achievements. Dietrich agreed to cooperate with Schell in the making of the film, but when the cameras started to roll, she turned the tables on him by refusing to appear on camera. His sleight-of-hand in suggesting her presence through the use of silhouettes and other techniques turned what might otherwise have been a standard "talking head" piece into a visually stunning tour de force.

Schell's acting career has not languished with his involvement in production, direction, and screenwriting. After all, two of his Academy Award nominations for acting occurred in the 1970s, after he had taken on other filmmaking responsibilities. Yet it is clear that his place in cinematic history will be more than that of an actor, for his achievements behind the camera will have to enter into the final account. Also, perhaps as the trauma of Nazism recedes more and more into the historical past, the casting of Schell as a Nazi may become less frequent, and he can just play Germans, even sympathetic ones, as he did quite memorably in the television remake of *The Diary of Anne Frank* as the title character's father.

—William M. Clements, updated by John McCarty

———

SCHENSTRØM, Carl. *See* **MADSEN, Harald, and Carl SCHENSTRØM.**

———

SCHNEIDER, Romy

Nationality: Austrian. **Born:** Rosemarie Magdalena Albach-Retty in Vienna, Austria, 23 September 1938. **Education:** Attended school in Berchtesgaden; Pensionnat Goldstein, Salzburg. **Family:** Married 1) Harry Meyen-Haubenstock, 1966 (divorced 1975), son: David Christophe; 2) Daniel Biassini, 1975 (separated), daughter: Sarah Magdalena. **Career:** 1952—left school to appear in her mother's film *Wenn der weisse Flieder wieder blüht*; 1959—moved to Paris; 1961—on stage in *'Tis Pity She's a Whore*; 1963-65—appeared in leading roles in Hollywood films; 1966—returned to Paris and starred in numerous international productions. **Awards:** Deutscher Filmpreis for Acting, 1977; French César Awards for Best Actress, 1975 and 1978. **Died:** In Paris, 29 May 1982.

Films as Actress:

1953 *Wenn der weisse Flieder wieder blüht* (Deppe)
1954 *Feuerwerk* (Hoffmann); *Mädchenjahre einer Königen* (*The Story of Vickie*) (Marischka) (as Queen Victoria)
1955 *Der letzte Mann* (Braun); *Die Deutschmeister* (*Mam'zelle Cricri*) (Marischka)
1956 *Sissi* (Marischka) (as Princess Elisabeth of Austria); *Kitty und die grosse Welt* (Wiedermann)
1957 *Sissi—die junge Kaiserin* (Marischka) (as Empress Elisabeth of Austria); *Robinson soll nicht sterben* (*The Girl and the Legend*) (von Baky) (as Maud); *Monpti* (Käutner)
1958 *Sissi—Schichsalsjahre einer Kaiserin* (Marischka—edited version of the three Sissi films released as *Forever My Love*, 1962) (as Empress Elisabeth of Austria); *Scampolo* (Wiedermann); *Mädchen in Uniform* (Radvanyi) (as Manuela von Mainhardis)
1959 *Die schöne Lügnerin* (von Ambesser); *Die Halbzart* (Thiele); *Christine* (Gaspard-Huit) (title role); *Ein Engel auf Erden* (*Angel on Earth*) (Radvanyi) (as air stewardess/guardian angel)
1960 *Katia* (*Magnificent Sinner*) (Siodmak) (title role); *Plein soleil* (*Purple Noon*; *Lust for Evil*) (Clément)
1961 *Le Combat dans l'île* (Cavalier); *Die Sendung der Lysistrata* (Kortner)
1962 *Le Procès* (*The Trial*) (Welles) (as Leni); "Il lavoro" ("The Job") ep. of *Boccaccio '70* (Visconti) (as Pupe)
1963 *The Victors* (Foreman) (as Regine); *The Cardinal* (Preminger) (as Annemarie)
1964 *Good Neighbor Sam* (Swift) (as Janet Lagerhof)
1965 *What's New Pussycat?* (Donner) (as Carole Werner)
1966 *La Voleuse* (*Schornstein No. 4*) (Chapot); *10.30 P.M. Summer* (Dassin) (as Claire); *Triple Cross* (Young) (as the Countess)
1968 *Otley* (Dick Clement) (as Imogen)
1969 *La Piscine* (*The Swimming Pool*) (Deray) (as Marianne)
1970 *My Lover, My Son* (Newland) (as Francesca Anderson); *Qui?* (*The Sensuous Assassin*) (Keigel); *Les Choses de la Vie* (*The Things of Life*) (Sautet) (as Hélène)
1971 *La califfa* (Bevilacqua); *Max et les ferrailleurs* (Sautet); *Bloomfield* (*The Hero*) (Harris)
1972 *César et Rosalie* (Sautet); *The Assassination of Trotsky* (Losey)
1973 *Ludwig* (*Ludwig: Twilight of the Gods*) (Visconti) (as Empress Elisabeth of Austria); *Le Train* (Granier-Deferre); *Le Trio infernal* (*The Infernal Trio*) (Girod) (as Philomene)
1974 *Un Amour de pluie* (*Loving in the Rain*) (Brialy); *Le Mouton enragé* (*Love at the Top*; *The French Way*) (Deville)
1975 *L'Important c'est d'aimer* (*The Most Important Thing Is Love*) (Zulawski); *Les Innocents aux mains sales* (*Dirty Hands*) (Chabrol); *Le Vieux Fusil* (*The Old Gun*) (Enrico)
1976 *Une Femme à sa fenêtre* (*A Woman at Her Window*) (Granier-Deferre) (as Margot)
1977 *Gruppenbild mit Dame* (*Group Picture with Lady*) (Petrović)
1978 *Mado* (Sautet) (as Helene); *Une Histoire simple* (*A Simple Story*) (Sautet) (as Marie)
1979 *Last Embrace* (Demme); *Bloodline* (Young); *Clair de femme* (Costa-Gavras) (as Lydia); *Lo sconosciuto*; *La Mort en direct* (*Deathwatch*) (Tavernier) (as Katherine Mortonhoe)

1980 *Garde à vue* (*Under Suspicion*) (Miller) (as Chantal Martinaud); *La Banquière* (Girod)
1981 *Fantasma d'amore* (*Ghost of Love*) (Risi) (as Anna); *La Passante du Sans-Souci* (*La Passante*) (Rouffio) (as Elsa Weiner/Lina Baumenstein)

Publications

By SCHNEIDER: book—

Ich, Romy, Munich, 1988.

On SCHNEIDER: books—

Benichou, Pierre, and Sylviane Pommier, *Romy Schneider*, Paris, 1976.
Knef, Hildegard, *Romy: Betrachtung eines Lebens*, Hamburg, 1983.
Arnould, Françoise, and Françoise Gerber, *Romy Schneider, Princesse de l'écran*, Paris, 1985.
Hermary-Vieille, Catherine, *Romy*, Paris, 1986.
Steenfatt, Margret, *Eine gemachte Frau: Die Lebengeschichte der Romy Schneider*, Hamburg, 1986.
Seydel, Renate, *Romy Schneider: Bilder ihres Lebens*, Munich, 1987.
Cohen, Georges, *Romy Schneider*, Paris, 1988.
Riess, Curt, *Romy Schneider*, Rastatt, 1990.

On SCHNEIDER: articles—

Haustrate, Gaston, "Romy Schneider," in *Cinéma* (Paris), July/August 1982.
Elley, Derek, "Romy Schneider," in *Films and Filming* (London), August 1982.
Tavernier, Bertrand, obituary, in *Positif* (Paris), February 1986.

* * *

Born into an old-established and famous theatrical family, Romy Schneider was almost predestined to become an actress. As an internationally known German film star, she is second in fame only to Marlene Dietrich. Like Dietrich, she had an ambiguous relationship to Germany and chose not to live there.

Schneider's screen debut, at the age of 14, was alongside her mother Magda Schneider, in *Wenn der weisse Flieder wieder blüht*. This led to further film offers and to playing the saccharine-sweet eponymous heroine in the trilogy *Sissi*, a kitsch bio-pic of Elisabeth, the Austrian Empress. As Sissi, Schneider had become the darling of the German speaking public. Ute Schneider suggests that the Sissi films provided a safety valve for Germans in their inability to mourn (i.e. the collective disavowal of the fascist past): "Hardly any other 1950s tearjerker film had been more effective in letting the audience sob their heart out. It is a pertinent example of the continuing repression of political reality that can be traced in [German] entertainment cinema. Sissi demonstrated yet again the victory of the heart over the 'evil' of politics, the dream of conquering people and countries with no more than a feminine smile and maternal care." The role of Sissi typecast Schneider for the early part of her career and she came to hate the image, but was haunted by it for the rest of her life.

Her engagement to Alain Delon seems to have given her enough determination to leave for France, escaping parental control and the smothering Sissi image (although initially she continued to be typecast). Nevertheless, Schneider's first serious role came from the German director Fritz Kortner, as Myrrhine in Kortner's adaptation of Aristophanes's *Die Sendung der Lysistrata*. Then in Paris Visconti offered Schneider her first theater engagement, in *'Tis Pity She's a Whore*. Despite having to act in French, she won audience and critical

Romy Schneider

acclaim. It also marked the beginning of her international career as a character actress. Subsequently, Schneider gained a major prize for her performance in Welles's *Le Procès* and Visconti cast her again in *Boccaccio '70*. Following a brief interlude in Hollywood, playing in Preminger's *The Cardinal*, and demonstrating her ability for comedy alongside Jack Lemmon in *Good Neighbor Sam*, and Peter Sellers and Peter O'Toole in *What's New, Pussycat?*, Schneider returned to France. Subsequently, while working with the director Claude Sautet and with Michel Piccoli as her film partner, Schneider embarked on the most fruitful period of her career. Sautet cast her in a range of roles, playing the modern sexually liberated woman. Having created a new persona, Schneider had the courage to accept again the role of Elisabeth in Visconti's *Ludwig*. She depicted the woman as cold and unyielding, thereby erasing any trace of the sweet Sissi character.

Over the years Schneider achieved success in her career by great discipline and ambition. She stated frankly that she used her classical beauty as a handmaiden in the service of her craft. Despite Schneider's professional emancipation and her rebellion against the values of her parents' generation, she cannot be considered a feminist, even in the widest sense. She mostly played women as perceived from a typical male position: the housewife, the mother, the mistress or the whore. She rarely depicted independent professional women, but rather came to represent those women who revolt, only to settle eventually for compromise.

Even while in France, however, she deliberately chose roles that critically engaged with Germany's fascist history, albeit from a French perspective. *La Passante du Sans-Souci*, a French-German co-production, is a striking case in point, since the film illustrates differing national perspectives on recent history. The German version has a happy end, whereas in the French the couple are killed by the neo-Nazis. Another pertinent example is the German film *Gruppenbild mit Dame* (based on Heinrich Böll's sociohistorical critique of Germany). Schneider could strongly identify with her role of Leni, a woman misunderstood in her own country. Though the film was dismissed by the critics (lacking the complexity of the novel), Schneider won an important German prize for her performance.

Towards the end, Romy Schneider knew both sadness and tragedy. After serious kidney surgery and her divorce from her second husband, her young son, David Christophe, was killed climbing over his own front gate. Although she threw herself into her work, the pressure and stress proved too much and Romy Schneider died of heart failure a year later.

—Ulrike Sieglohr

SCHWARZENEGGER, Arnold

Nationality: Austrian/American. **Born:** Graz, Austria, 30 July 1947; became U.S. citizen, 1983. **Education:** Studied at University of Wis-

Arnold Schwarzenegger in *Terminator 2: Judgment Day*

consin, Superior, B.A. in business and international economics. **Family:** Married Maria Schriver, 1986, three children: Katherine, Christina, Patrick. **Career:** From 1962—bodybuilder, in England, then in U.S. from late 1960s; 1976—retired from bodybuilding, film debut as Arnold Schwarzenegger, in *Stay Hungry;* 1980—appointed chairman of the President's Council on Physical Fitnesss and Sports (resigned 1993); 1991—reputedly paid $15 million for his role in *Terminator 2.* Part-owner of Planet Hollywood and Schatzi restaurants. **Awards:** 13 world champion bodybuilding titles, 1965-80; Golden Globe for Best Newcomer, for *Stay Hungry,* 1976. **Address:** 3110 Main Street, #330, Santa Monica, CA 90405, U.S.A.

Films as Actor:

(as Arnold Strong)

1970　*Hercules in New York* (*Hercules Goes to New York; Hercules: The Movie; Hercules Goes Bananas*) (Arthur Allan Seidelman) (title role)
1973　*The Long Goodbye* (Altman) (as a hood)

(as Arnold Schwarzenegger)

1976　*Stay Hungry* (Rafelson) (as Joe Santo)
1977　*Pumping Iron* (George Butler—doc) (as himself)
1979　*Scavenger Hunt* (Michael Schultz); *The Villain* (*Cactus Jack*) (Needham) (as handsome stranger)
1981　*The Jayne Mansfield Story* (*Jayne Mansfield: A Symbol of the 50's*) (Lowry—for TV) (as Mickey Hargitay)
1982　*Conan the Barbarian* (Milius) (title role)
1984　*Conan the Destroyer* (Fleischer) (title role); *The Terminator* (Cameron) (title role)
1985　*Red Sonja* (Fleischer) (as Kalidor); *Commando* (Lester) (as John Matrix)
1986　*Raw Deal* (Irvin) (as Kaminski)
1987　*The Running Man* (Glaser) (as Ben "Butcher of Bakersfield" Richards); *Predator* (McTiernan) (as Maj. Alan "Dutch" Schaefer)
1988　*Red Heat* (Walter Hill) (as Capt. Ivan Danko); *Twins* (Reitman) (as Julius Benedict)
1990　*Total Recall* (Paul Verhoeven) (as Douglas Quaid); *Kindergarten Cop* (Reitman) (as Detective John Kimble)
1991　*Terminator 2: Judgment Day* (Cameron) (as the Terminator)
1992　*Feed* (Rafferty and Ridgeway—doc) (as himself); *Lincoln* (Kunhardt—doc) (as voice of John G. Nicolay)
1993　*Last Action Hero* (McTiernan) (as Sergeant Jack Slater/himself, + exec pr); *Dave* (Reitman) (as himself)
1994　*True Lies* (Cameron) (as Harry Tasker); *Junior* (Reitman) (as Dr. Alexander Hesse); *Beretta's Island* (as himself)
1996　*Eraser* (Chuck Russell) (as John Kruger, the Eraser); *Crusade* (Verhoeven)

Film as Director:

1992　*Christmas in Connecticut* (for TV)

Publications

By SCHWARZENEGGER: books—

Arnold's Bodyshaping for Women, New York, 1979.
Arnold's Bodybuilding for Men, New York, 1981.

Arnold's Encyclopaedia of Modern Bodybuilding, New York, 1984.
Arnold: The Education of a Bodybuilder, with Douglas Kent Hall, New York, 1986.
Arnold's Fitness for Kids Ages Birth-5: A Guide to Health, Exercise, and Nutrition, with Charles Gaines, New York, 1993.
Arnold's Fitness for Kids Ages 6-10: A Guide to Health, Exercise, and Nutrition, with Charles Gaines, New York, 1993.
Arnold's Fitness for Kids Ages 11-14: A Guide to Health, Exercise, and Nutrition, with Charles Gaines, New York, 1993.

By SCHWARZENEGGER: articles—

Interview with K. Honeycutt, in *American Film* (Washington, D.C.), May 1982.
"Schwarzenegger on *Predator,*" interview with Dann Gire, in *Cinefantastique* (Oak Park, Illinois), vol. 18, no. 1, 1987.
Interview with Pat H. Broeske and Herb Ritts, in *Interview* (New York), July 1991.
Interview with Jenny Cooney, in *Empire* (London), September 1991.

On SCHWARZENEGGER: books—

Green, Tom, *Arnold!,* New York, 1987.
Butler, George, *Arnold Schwarzenegger: A Portrait,* New York, 1990.
Dorsey, Charles B., *Arnold Schwarzenegger,* Paris, 1990.
Leigh, Wendy, *Arnold: An Unauthorized Biography,* London, 1990.
Flynn, John L., *The Films of Arnold Schwarzenegger,* Secaucus, New Jersey, 1993; rev. ed., 1995.
Conklin, Thomas, *Meet Arnold Schwarzenegger,* New York, 1994.
McCabe, Bob, *Arnold Schwarzenegger,* London, 1994.
Wright, Adrian, *Arnold Schwarzenegger: A Life on Film,* London, 1994.

On SCHWARZENEGGER: articles—

McGillivray, David, in *Films and Filming* (London), June 1986.
Brauerhoch, A., "Glanz und Elend der Muskelmänner," in *Frauen und Film* (Frankfurt), August 1986.
Thompson, Anne, and Tom Soter, "*Total Recall,* Total Arnie," in *Empire* (London), August 1990.
Current Biography 1991, New York, 1991.
Desanglois, L., "Arnold Schwarzenegger," in *Revue du Cinéma* (Paris), October 1991.
Briggs, Joe Bob, "Whatever You Say, Arnold," in *Playboy* (Chicago), January 1992.
Svetkey, Benjamin, "What, Me Worry?," in *Entertainment Weekly* (New York), 11 June 1993.
James, C., "Film View: Arnold as Icon: From Hulk to Hero," in *New York Times,* 27 June 1993.

*　　*　　*

Considering he has made a mere 20-odd movies, Arnold Schwarzenegger's career has gone through numerous distinct and bizarre phases. His evolution, from a bodybuilder who appeared in such consciously silly entries as *Hercules in New York* and *Conan the Barbarian* to sci-fi death machine in the Terminator movies to comic actor in such films as *Twins* and *Junior,* has been strange, to say the least. His films have shown consistency, however, in that Schwarzenegger's performance style has always exhibited the basic hallmarks of postmodernity: pastiche and parody. First gaining notoriety as a professional bodybuilder, he recognized opportunities to appear in such outrageously over-the-top films as the Conan series, for example, which were little more than pumped-up B movies (with big budgets), films Schwarzenegger clearly (and quite rightly) did not take entirely seriously. His constant mugging to the camera in the documentary *Pumping Iron* did more than win him the Mr. Universe title: it proved his innate theatrical sensibility and his canny comic abilities.

But Schwarzenegger's first real breakthrough came with *The Terminator*, in which he cleverly turned down the offer to play the hero and opted instead for the role of evil robot. The film, a characteristically action-packed entry from director James Cameron, had an entertaining but intelligent Oedipal time-warp sci-fi concept, some excusably cheesy special effects, and a, well, perfectly robotic performance by Schwarzenegger. The subsequent huge box-office success of the film secured Schwarzenegger's place in the American cultural Zeitgeist.

Schwarzenegger's deadpan performance immediately drew comparisons to Clint Eastwood, an actor famous for his minimalist style. This performance style would carry on in other films, including *Commando*, *Raw Deal*, *The Running Man*, *Predator*, *Total Recall*, and *Terminator 2: Judgment Day*, among others. Schwarzenegger also appropriated Eastwood's stinging penchant for the one-liner (e.g., "Make my day"), many of which became popular catchphrases and Schwarzenegger trademarks ("I'll be back" in particular). Eastwood would acknowledge the debt Schwarzenegger owed him when he referred to the former bodybuilder as "my son" during the 1995 Academy Award ceremonies.

Schwarzenegger's career took a disastrous turn in 1993 with *The Last Action Hero*, an ultra-self-reflexive take on the action movie. The film has its entertaining moments, but fans appeared uncomfortable with the artifices of the action film being laid quite so bare—thus the film flopped despite one of the most expensive publicity campaigns in Hollywood history (including an ad posted on the space shuttle, the first of its kind). Schwarzenegger has also been far less successful when trying his hand at out-and-outright comedies (*Twins* and *Junior*), where he is simply uncontrolled as a performer. *Junior* was a brave and interesting gender-challenging role for Schwarzenegger; the film's premise had him the first man ever to become pregnant. Again, audiences seemed uncomfortable with this wall of muscles in a maternal position, and the film did mediocre box office.

Schwarzenegger's last major success was *True Lies*, a film which divided critics with its misogynist and racist overtones, resurrecting speculation that the actor had far-right leaning politics. Schwarzenegger has become something of an anti-Jane Fonda, notorious for his support of conservative causes and politicians, including Ronald Reagan and George Bush. Like Fonda, Schwarzenegger's persona is also not without contradictions (he is married to Maria Schriver, a member of America's most famous liberal clan the Kennedys, for example). Like his politics and personal life, Schwarzenegger's appearances on-screen can be read as perfect open texts: the audience can choose to see his machismo as role-model material to be emulated and adored, or as astute po-mo parody of the ludicrous masculine male ideal.

—Matthew Hays

SCHYGULLA, Hanna

Nationality: German. **Born:** Katowice, Poland (then German-occupied Kattowitz), 25 December 1943; brought up in Munich, Germany. **Education:** Attended Munich University; Fridi-Leophard Studio. **Career:** Stage actress, particularly with Fassbinder's troupe; 1968—film debut in *Der Bräutigan, die Komödiantin, und der Zuhalter*; 1969—first of several films by Fassbinder, *Liebe ist kalter als der Tod*; 1971—assistant director on Peer Raben's TV film *Die Ahnfrau*; 1972—in TV mini-series *Acht Stunden sind kein Tag*, and in *Die Dämonen*, 1977, *Die grosse Flatter*, 1978, and *Peter the Great*, 1986. **Awards:**

Deutscher Filmpreis for Acting, 1971 and 1979; Best Actress, Berlin Festival, for *The Marriage of Maria Braun*, 1979. **Agent:** ZBF Agentur, Leopoldstr 19, 8000 Munich 40, Germany.

Films as Actress:

1968   *Der Bräutigan, die Komödiantin, und der Zuhalter* (*The Bridegroom, the Comedienne, and the Pimp*) (Straub—short) (as the comedienne)

1969   *Liebe ist kalter als der Tod* (*Love Is Colder than Death*) (Fassbinder) (as Joanna); *Katzelmacher* (Fassbinder) (as Marie); *Gotter der Pest* (*Gods of the Plague*) (Fassbinder) (as Joanna); *Warum lauft Herr R amok?* (*Why Does Herr R Run Amok?*) (Fassbinder and Fengler) (as school friend); *Jagdszenen aus Niederbayarn* (*Hunting Scenes in Lower Bavaria*) (Fleischmann) (as Paula); *Baal* (Schlöndorff—for TV)

1970   *Rio das mortes* (Fassbinder—for TV) (as Hanna); *Das Kaffeehaus* (*The Coffee House*) (Fassbinder—for TV) (as Lisaura); *Whity* (Fassbinder) (as Hanna); *Die Niklashauser Fahrt* (*The Niklashausen Journey*) (Fassbinder—for TV) (as Johanna); *Warnung vor einer heiligen Nutte* (*Beware of a Holy Whore*) (Fassbinder) (as Hanna); *Pionere in Ingolstadt* (*Recruits in Ingolstadt*; *Pioneers in Ingolstadt*) (Fassbinder—for TV) (as Berta); *Kuckucksei im Gangsternest* (Spieker); *Matthias Kneissel* (Hauff—for TV); *Baal* (Schlöndorff—for TV)

1971   *Der Händler der vier Jahreszeiten* (*The Merchant of Four Seasons*) (Fassbinder) (as first sister); *Das Haus am Meer* (*The House by the Sea*) (Hauff—for TV); *Jakob von Günten* (Lilienthal—for TV)

1972   *Die bitteren Tranen der Petra von Kant* (*The Bitter Tears of Petra von Kant*) (Fassbinder) (as Karin Thimm); *Wildwechsel* (*Jail Bait*; *Wild Game*) (Fassbinder) (as gynecologist); *Bremer Freiheit* (*Bremen Freedom*) (Fassbinder and Lohmann—for TV) (as Luise Maurer)

1974   *Fontane: Effi Briest* (*Effi Briest*) (Fassbinder) (title role); *Falsche Bewegung* (*Wrong Move*) (Wenders) (as Therese)

1975   *Der Stumme* (Meili); *Ansichten eines Clowns* (*The Clown*) (Jasny) (as Marie)

1977   *Die Heimkehr des alten Herrn* (Jasny)

1978   *Aussagen nach einer Verhaftung* (Moorse—for TV); ***Die Ehe der Maria Braun*** (*The Marriage of Maria Braun*) (Fassbinder) (title role)

1979   *Die Dritte Generation* (*The Third Generation*) (Fassbinder) (as Susanne)

1980   *Lili Marleen* (Fassbinder) (as Wilkie Bunterberg); *Berlin Alexanderplatz* (Fassbinder) (as Eva)

1981   *Die Fälschung* (*Circle of Deceit*; *False Witness*) (Schlöndorff) (as Arianne Nassar); *La Nuit de Varennes* (*That Night in Varennes*; *The New World*) (Scola) (as Countess Sophie de la Borde)

1982   *Passion* (*Passion, travail et amour*) (Godard); *La Storia di Piera* (*The Story of Piera*) (Ferreri) (as Eugenia); *Antonieta* (*Maria Antonieta Rivas Mercado*) (Saura); *Heller Wahn* (*L'Amie*; *Sheer Madness*; *A Labor of Love*; *Friends and Husbands*) (von Trotta) (as Olga)

1983   *Eine Liebe im Deutschland* (*A Love in Germany*; *Un Amour en Allemagne*) (Wajda) (as Paulina Kropp)

1984   *Il futuro e donna* (*The Future Is Woman*) (Ferreri) (as Anna)

1986   *Barnum* (Philips—for TV) (as Jenny Lind); *Forever, Lulu* (*Crazy Streets*) (Kollek) (as Elaine Hines); *The Delta Force* (Golan) (as Ingrid)

1987   *Casanova* (Langton—for TV) (as Casanova's mother)

Hanna Schygulla in *Die Ehe der Maria Braun*

1988   *El verano de la Señorita Forbes* (*The Summer of Miss Forbes*)
        (Hermosillo) (title role); *Miss Arizona* (Sandor) (as Mitzi)
1990   *Abraham's Gold* (Graser) (as Bärbel); *Aventure de Catherine
        C.* (Beuchot)
1991   *Dead Again* (Branagh) (as Inga)
1992   *Golem, l'Esprit de l'Exil* (*Golem, the Spirit of the Exile*) (Gitai);
        Warszawa Year 5703 (*Warsaw—Year 5703*; *Tragarz puchu*)
        (Kijowski) (as Stephania)
1993   *Metamorphosis of a Melody*; *Petrified Garden* (as Woman);
        Mavi Surgun (*The Blue Exile*) (Kiral) (as the Actress); *Aux
        Petits Bonheurs* (*Life's Little Treasures*) (Deville) (as Lena);
        Ich Will Nicht Nur, Dass Ihr Mich Liebt (as herself); *Madame
        Bäurin* (Bogner)
1994   *Hey Stranger* (Woditsch) (as Tania)
1995   *Die Nacht der Regisseure* (*The Night of the Filmmakers*)
        (Reitz—doc) (as herself, uncredited); *Les Cent et une Nuits*
        (*A Hundred and One Nights*) (Varda) (as Actor for a Day)
1996   *Pakten* (*The Sunset Boys*) (Risan)

Publications

By SCHYGULLA: book—

Romy Schneider: Portraits 1954-1981, text by Schygulla, Munich,
1988.

By SCHYGULLA: articles—

Interview with Bruno Villien, in *Cinématographe* (Paris), June 1983.
"La Schygulla: Is There Life after Fassbinder?," interview with Gideon
    Bachmann, in *Vanity Fair* (New York), January 1984.
Interview with E. Colina, in *Cine Cubano* (Havana), no. 122, 1988.
"Nous, débutants," in *Cahiers du Cinéma* (Paris), March 1990.
"Ein Geschichtsbuch in Filmen," interview with H. Hurst, in *CICIM:
    Revue pour le Cinéma Francais* (Munich), June 1991.
"Ha!," interview with Gary Indiana and Michael Comte, in *Interview*
    (New York), September 1991.

On SCHYGULLA: books—

Hanna Schygulla: Bilder aus Filmen von Rainer Werner Fassbinder,
    text by Schygulla, Munich, 1981.
Birnbaum, Lillian, and Peter Stephan Jungk, *Vier Frauen: Porträts*,
    Heidelberg, [1993?]

On SCHYGULLA: articles—

Bensoussan, G., "Star ou pas?," in *Cahiers du Cinéma* (Paris), April
    1981.
Current Biography 1984, New York, 1984.
Penkert, S., "Hanna Schygulla im Portrait," in *Filmfaust* (Frankfurt),
    February/March 1985.
Sante, Luc, "Screen Gem," in *Interview* (New York), March 1989.
Emerson, Jim, "Regarding Hanna," in *Film Comment* (New York), July/
    August 1991.
Seesslen, G., "Heilige Huren, bleiche Mütter," in *EPD Film* (Frankfurt),
    August 1991.
Mazierska, E., "Tragarz puchu," in *Filmowy Serwis Prasowy* (Warsaw),
    no. 11, 1992.

*   *   *

Screen performances of German actress Hanna Schygulla are most
often associated with the work of the prolific German director Rainer

Werner Fassbinder, and, indeed, Schygulla acted in about half of the
almost 40 films written and directed by this talented filmmaker before
his death in 1982. Schygulla's outstanding performance in the title
role of *The Marriage of Maria Braun* helped this film to its critical
and—for the first time for a New German film—international commercial success.

The actress has, however, appeared in leading roles in many films
by other directors, in Germany and elsewhere, among them Volker
Schlöndorff, Reinhard Hauff, Vojtèch Jasny, Jean-Luc Godard,
Margarethe von Trotta, and Andrej Wajda. While the roles Schygulla
played seemed less than satisfactory in some of these films, her performances in most of them reveal her adaptability as well as her
brilliance as an actress of international stature.

She stands out among her fellow co-founders of the "antitheater"
in Munich in the late 1960s, who formed a tight ensemble around
Fassbinder and acted in most of his films in a largely intact group for
almost 15 years, with such talented performers as Margaret Carstens,
Ingrid Caven, Irm Hermann, and Kurt Raab working exclusively with
Fassbinder on stage and on the movie set. The unique role that Hanna
Schygulla played in this group is revealed in Fassbinder's intensely
self-reflective film about filmmaking, *Beware of a Holy Whore*. Most
of the members of the ensemble represent themselves and bear their
real names, but amidst various bizarre and sadomasochistic gestures by
the others. "Hanna" remains uniquely calm, understanding of the
others' conflicts, yet somehow aloof and clearly independent-minded.
It is she who counsels and reassures the others philosophically as they
lie strewn about in exhausted poses, despondent at the failure of their
project, at the film's end.

Schygulla's characters in many other appearances for Fassbinder in
the early period of her career (1969-72, during which time she acted
in almost two dozen films, television productions, and stage plays,
about half of which were directed by Fassbinder) are often called
"Johanna" or "Hanna"; she usually portrays the girlfriend, initially
supporting but often ultimately opposing the driven male lead. This
character emerges quite early in Schygulla's film roles. In *Katzelmacher*,
she plays the girlfriend of a rather narrow- and vicious-minded youth
in a shifting set of bored provincial couples. Her character, here called
Marie (with reference, some critics would have it, to the Virgin Mary),
alone in the group shows sympathy to the hated foreign worker,
enacted by Fassbinder.

After this first stage of her career, which Schygulla says happened
very easily and quickly, without much intention, Schygulla quit acting
to resume her university studies. "I broke these off not long before my
comprehensive examinations and acted in *Effi Briest*, then came a
long pause between me and work in film. I hitchhiked through America
and worked in children's theater in Germany. I can only explain my
leaving film work with this dissatisfaction I felt in myself." Schygulla
next acted in Wim Wenders's rather abstract stylized *Wrong Move*,
based on Goethe's *Wilhelm Meister*, and a more naturalistic role as
Marie in the adaptation by Czech filmmaker Vojtèch Jasny of Heinrich
Böll's *The Clown*. Her next work with Fassbinder was in the title role
of his original script *The Marriage of Maria Braun*, as a young bride
during World War II who survives the deprivations of the postwar
years and becomes a successful career woman in the 1950s during long
and repeated forced separation from her husband.

In this and succeeding roles, Schygulla's screen persona as an intelligent and independent, yet feeling, career woman emerged. She has
on occasion been likened to Marlene Dietrich: certainly a complex
but confident sexuality has been a component of many of Schygulla's
characters. Altogether during the second phase of her screen career
(1974-83), Schygulla played leading roles in major commercial films
and was billed as a star. Yet, Schygulla has had little sense of "stardom." She emanates a remarkable physical presence which does not
derive from any conventional standards of star beauty. Rather, what
some have called an essentially "pancake-faced" and somewhat dumpy

figure is so highly, though subtly, expressive that an elusive smile, a nuanced arching of the brows, or a slight hand gesture can transform her image into that of a vibrant beauty. To a large extent she retained the distanced acting style she developed early on—in avoiding displays of emotion but rather manifesting what has been deemed "exaggerated understatement." While this style occasionally seems unconvincing in a more realistic context, as in *Lili Marleen*, she usually carries it off. Certainly, few leading actresses of this period could utter, as she did, rather flatly in German, "I'm so happy, I'm so unhappy," in one breath and seem entirely believable.

In her career's third phase, from 1984 into the mid-1990s, Schygulla's career foundered, not coincidentally around the time she reached middle age. Particularly unfortunate, but not surprising, is that since 1986—when she made an amazingly inauspicious entrance into U.S. films with *Forever, Lulu* and *The Delta Force*—Hollywood has found little use for Schygulla's talent. Aside from a minor but stylish role as a housekeeper in Kenneth Branagh's overloaded film noir *Dead Again*, she probably missed her best chance (to date) at a Hollywood role worthy of her skills when she turned down the female lead (subsequently played by Isabella Rossellini) in David Lynch's *Blue Velvet* for the characteristically down-to-earth reason that she needed to take care of her ailing, aged mother. A glance at her 1990s filmography begs the question: is this a mid-career slump or a career permanently adrift without the anchor of an ongoing actor-director relationship?

—Ramona Curry, updated by David E. Salamie

SCOTT, George C.

Nationality: American. **Born:** George Campbell Scott in Wise, Virginia, 18 October 1927; grew up in Detroit. **Education:** Attended Redford High School, Detroit; University of Missouri School of Journalism, Columbia to 1953. **Military Service:** 1945-49—served in the U.S. Marine Corps. **Family:** Married 1) Carolyn Hughes (divorced); 2) the actress Patricia Reed (divorced); 3) the actress Colleen Dewhurst, 1960 (divorced 1965; remarried 1967, divorced 1972), sons: Alexander and the actor Campbell; also four other children; 4) the actress Trish Van Devere, 1972. **Career:** 1953-57—actor in stock in Toledo, Washington, D.C., and Ontario, while working as laborer and clerk; 1957—New York stage role in *Richard III* in Joseph Papp's Shakespeare Festival season brought critical recognition; later stage work includes roles in *Comes a Day* on Broadway, 1958, *The Andersonville Trial*, 1959, *The Merchant of Venice*, 1962, and *The Three Sisters* in London, 1965; 1959—film debut in *The Hanging Tree*; 1961—in TV mini-series *The Power and the Glory*; 1963-64—in TV series *East Side, West Side*; 1969—directed the play *Hello and Goodbye*; also appeared in *Plaza Suite* on Broadway with Maureen Stapleton; 1972—directed the film *Rage*; 1985—in TV mini-series *Mussolini—The Untold Story*; 1987-88—in TV series *Mr. President*; 1994—in TV series *Traps*. **Awards:** Best Actor Academy Award (award refused), and Best Actor, New York Film Critics, for *Patton*, 1970. **Address:** c/o Stern Agency, 11755 Wilshire Boulevard, Suite 2320, Los Angeles, CA 90025, U.S.A.

Films as Actor:

1959   *The Hanging Tree* (Daves) (as Dr. George Grubb); ***Anatomy of a Murder*** (Preminger) (as Claude Dancer)
1961   ***The Hustler*** (Rossen) (as Bert Gordon)

1963   *The List of Adrian Messenger* (Huston) (as Anthony Gethryn)
1964   ***Dr. Strangelove: Or, How I Learned to Stop Worrying and Love the Bomb*** (Kubrick) (as Gen. "Buck" Turgidson)
1965   *The Yellow Rolls Royce* (Asquith) (as Paolo Maltese)
1966   *La Bibbia* (*The Bible . . . in the Beginning*; *The Bible*) (Huston) (as Abraham); *Not with My Wife You Don't!* (Panama) (as Tank Martin); *This Savage Land* (*The Road West*) (McEveety—for TV, released theatrically in 1969) (as Jud Barker)
1967   *The Flim-Flam Man* (*One Born Every Minute*) (Kershner) (as Mordecai)
1968   *Petulia* (Lester) (as Archie Bollen)
1970   *Patton* (*Patton: Lust for Glory*) (Schaffner) (title role)
1971   *They Might Be Giants* (Harvey) (as Justin Playfair/Sherlock Holmes); *Jane Eyre* (Delbert Mann—for TV) (as Edward Rochester); *The Last Run* (Fleischer) (as Harry Garmes); *The Hospital* (Hiller) (as Dr. Herbert Bock)
1972   *The New Centurions* (Fleischer) (as Sgt. Kilvinski)
1973   *Oklahoma Crude* (Kramer) (as Noble Mason); *The Day of the Dolphin* (Mike Nichols) (as Dr. Jake Terrell)
1974   *Bank Shot* (Champion) (as Walter Upjohn Ballantine)
1975   *The Hindenberg* (Wise) (as Col. Ritter); *Fear on Trial* (Johnson—for TV) (as Louis Nizer)
1976   *Beauty and the Beast* (Cook—for TV)
1977   *Islands in the Stream* (Schaffner) (as Thomas Hudson)
1978   *Crossed Swords* (*The Prince and the Pauper*) (Fleischer) (as the Ruffler); *Movie Movie* (Donen) (as Gloves Malloy/Spats Baxter)
1979   *Hardcore* (*The Hardcore Life*) (Schrader) (as Jake Van Dorn); *Arthur Miller on Home Ground* (Rasky)
1980   *The Formula* (Avildsen) (as Barney Caine); *The Changeling* (Medak) (as John Russell)
1981   *Taps* (Harold Becker) (as Gen. Harlan Bache)
1982   *Oliver Twist* (Clive Donner—for TV) (as Fagin)
1983   *China Rose* (Day—for TV)
1984   *A Christmas Carol* (Clive Donner—for TV) (as Ebenezer Scrooge); *Firestarter* (Lester) (as John Rainbird)
1985   *The Indomitable Teddy Roosevelt* (Engle—doc) (as narrator)
1986   *Choices* (Rich—for TV); *The Last Days of Patton* (Delbert Mann—for TV) (title role); *The Murders in the Rue Morgue* (Szwarc—for TV) (as Auguste Dupin)
1987   *Pals* (Antonio—for TV) (as Jack Stobbs)
1989   *The Ryan White Story* (Herzfeld—for TV)
1990   *Descending Angel* (Kagan—for TV) (as Florian Stroia); *The Exorcist III* (*The Exorcist III: Legion*) (Blatty) (as Lt. Kinderman); *The Curse of the Starving Class* (Masterson); *The Rescuers Down Under* (Butoy—animation) (as voice of Percival McLeach)
1991   *Finding the Way Home* (Holcomb—for TV) (as Max Mittelmann)
1993   *Curacao* (Carl Schultz—for TV); *Malice* (Harold Becker) (as Dr. Kessler)
1994   *In the Heat of the Night: A Matter of Justice* (Badiyi—for TV) (as Judge Walker); *The Whipping Boy* (Macartney—for TV) (as Blind George)
1995   *Angus* (Patrick Read Johnson) (as Ivan); *Tyson* (Edel—for TV) (as Cus D'Amato)

Films as Director:

1970   *The Andersonville Trial* (for TV)
1972   *Rage* (+ ro as Dan Logan)
1974   *The Savage Is Loose* (+ pr, ro as John)

George C. Scott in *Hardcore*

Publications

By SCOTT: articles—

"Rage," interview in *Action* (Los Angeles), January-February 1973.
"What Directors Are Saying," in *Action* (Los Angeles), January-February 1974.
"George C. Scott/Trish Van Devere Seminar," in *Dialogue on Film* (Beverly Hills), January 1975 (also released in booklet form).
Interview in *Playboy* (Chicago), December 1980.

On SCOTT: book—

Harbinson, Allen, *George C. Scott: The Man, The Actor, The Legend*, New York, 1977.

On SCOTT: articles—

Current Biography 1971, New York, 1971.
Reed, Rex, "George C. Scott," in *The Movie Star*, edited by Elisabeth Weis, New York, 1981.

*   *   *

George C. Scott is one of the most powerful of American actors, and he often plays characters who are unique, individualistic, intense, and sometimes angry in films with such forceful titles as *Rage*, *Crossed Swords*, *Bank Shot*, *Not with My Wife You Don't!*, *They Might Be Giants*, *The Savage Is Loose*, *Firestarter*, and *Malice*. It is almost too easy to classify him as an "angry man," for some of his most memorable moments in films are where he exhibits extreme rage: slapping a soldier as Patton (*Patton*), glaring at a slum landlord as a Los Angeles policeman (*The New Centurions*), smashing up a pornographic headquarters as an angry father (*Hardcore*). But he can also show great tenderness on the screen, which can be clearly seen in many of the above-mentioned films and especially in *The Day of the Dolphin* and *Petulia*. He also has a great flair for comedy. Two of his most famous comic roles are General "Buck" Turgidson (*Dr. Strangelove*) and the flim-flam man (*The Flim-Flam Man*). Whether it is in a title role (*Patton*) or in a brief appearance (*Malice*), with his rasping voice, piercing eyes, and chiseled features, he creates characters who are believable, multidimensional, and exciting.

Scott began in the theater, but from the beginning and throughout his career, he divides his acting choices between stage, film, and television. One of his early roles in film that brought acclaim was as gambler/manager Bert Gordon opposite Paul Newman, Jackie Gleason, and Piper Laurie in *The Hustler* (1961), where he brought just the right blend of menace, cruelty, and charm to the morality tale of an eager pool player. His roles necessarily changed as he aged. He moved from playing a divorced father (Archie Bollen) with young children in *Petulia* (1968) to a father (Jake Van Dorn) with a runaway daughter in *Hardcore* (1979) to a grandfather (Ivan) with an adult daughter and grandson in *Angus* (1995). Even in the short-lived 1994 television series *Traps* he played Joseph Trapcheck, the grandfather of three generations of police detectives.

Although his roles have included several soldiers, doctors, and police detectives, including a character who thought he was Sherlock Holmes (*They Might Be Giants*), his work cannot be stereotyped. He is just as comfortable playing the rogue Fagin (*Oliver Twist* for television) or a music composer (*The Changeling*).

What may account for Scott's staying power as an actor for so many years is his three-dimensional qualities. He is often cast in very masculine, assertive roles, and to these and his other roles he brings a depth of feeling which can touch an audience deeply. For example, he played General George S. Patton (probably his most well-known characterization) in two films, *Patton* (1970), directed by Franklin Schaffner, and *The Last Days of Patton* (1986), directed for television by Delbert Mann. Scott had to play much of the latter film lying in bed, as Patton had broken his neck in an automobile accident. The camera is in close on him in many shots, and Scott runs through a range of emotions which convey to the viewer Patton's sadness, anger, sentimentality, and courage. It is a remarkable performance, considering that earlier in the film Scott showed his usual toughness in sparring with his superiors and his ability to do comedy by singing a silly song.

Though Scott has worked with some of the best Hollywood directors and actors, he has never fitted the typical Hollywood stereotype and has always had an independent spirit. For example, he turned down the Academy Award for best actor in *Patton*. He fought with the program practices department of CBS in order to obtain more realism for his television series *East Side, West Side*. He opposed the rating given the excellent film he produced, directed, and starred in, *The Savage Is Loose*. Being so outspoken, he has sometimes been called difficult, but he is always the professional. He has aged well, and has provided a series of original and memorable performances throughout his career.

—H. Wayne Schuth

SCOTT, Randolph

Nationality: American. **Born:** George Randolph Crane Scott in Orange, Virginia, 23 January 1903. **Education:** Attended private school; Georgia Institute of Technology, Atlanta; University of North Carolina, Chapel Hill, degree in engineering; studied acting at Pasadena Playhouse. **Family:** Married 1) Marianna du Pont Somerville, 1936 (divorced 1939); 2) Patricia Stillman, 1944, one son and one daughter. **Career:** 1928—film debut in *Sharp Shooters*; also worked as voice coach for Gary Cooper and stuntman; some stage work; contract with Paramount, then variety of roles; 1950-55—founding member of Scott-Brown Productions, with Harry Joe Brown; 1956-60—famous series of seven Westerns for Budd Boetticher; 1962—retired. **Died:** In Los Angeles, 2 March 1987.

Films as Actor:

1928   *Sharp Shooters* (Blystone)
1929   *Dynamite* (DeMille); *The Far Call* (Dwan) (as Helms); *The Virginian* (Fleming); *The Black Watch* (Ford)

1931   *The Women Men Marry* (Hutchinson) (as Steve Bradley)
1932   *Sky Bride* (Roberta); *Hot Saturday* (Seiter) (as Fadden); *A Successful Calamity* (Adolfi) (as Larry)
1933   *Island of Lost Souls* (Kenton); *Wild Horse Mesa* (Hathaway) (as Chane Weymer); *Hello Everybody!* (Seiter) (as Hunt Blake); *Heritage of the Desert* (Hathaway) (as Jack Hare); *Murders in the Zoo* (Sutherland) (as Dr. Woodford); *Supernatural* (Halperin) (as Grant Wilson); *Cocktail Hour* (Schertzinger) (as Randolph Morgan); *Man of the Forest* (Hathaway) (as Brett Dale); *To the Last Man* (Hathaway) (as Lynn Hayden); *Sunset Pass* (Hathaway); *Broken Dreams* (Vignola) (as Dr. Robert Morely); *Thundering Herd* (Hathaway)
1934   *The Last Round-Up* (Hathaway) (as Jime Cleve); *Wagon Wheels* (Barton) (as Clint Belmet)
1935   *The Rocky Mountain Mystery* (*The Fighting Westerner*) (Barton); *Roberta* (Seiter) (as John); *Home on the Range* (Jacobson) (as Tom Hartfield); *Village Tale* (Cromwell) (as Slaughter Somerville); *She* (Pichel and Holden) (as Leo Vincey); *So Red the Rose* (King Vidor) (as Duncan Bedford)
1936   *Follow the Fleet* (Sandrich) (as Bilge); *And Sudden Death* (Barton) (as Lt. James Knox); *The Last of the Mohicans* (Seitz) (as Hawkeye); *Go West, Young Man* (Hathaway) (as Bud)
1937   *High, Wide, and Handsome* (Mamoulian) (as Peter Cortlandt)
1938   *Rebecca of Sunnybrook Farm* (Dwan) (as Anthony Kent); *Road to Reno* (Simon) (as Steve Fortness); *The Texans* (as Kirk Jordan)
1939   *Jesse James* (Henry King) (as Will Wright); *Susannah of the Mounties* (Seiter) (as Monty Montague/Inspector Angus); *Coast Guard* (Ludwig) (as Speed Bradshaw); *Frontier Marshall* (Dwan) (as Wyatt Earp); *Twenty Thousand Men a Year* (Green) (as Brad Reynolds)
1940   *Virginia City* (Curtiz) (as Vance Irby); *My Favorite Wife* (Kanin) (as Burkett); *When the Daltons Rode* (Marshall) (as Tod Jackson)
1941   *Western Union* (Fritz Lang) (as Vance Shaw); *Belle Starr* (Cummings) (as Sam Starr); *Paris Calling* (Marlin) (as Nick)
1942   *To the Shores of Tripoli* (Humberstone) (as Sgt. Dixie Smith); *The Spoilers* (Enright) (as Alexander McNamara); *Pittsburgh* (Seiler) (as Cash Evans)
1943   *The Desperadoes* (Charles Vidor) (as Steve Upton); *Bombardier* (Wallace) (as Capt. Buck Oliver); *Corvette K-225* (Rosson) (as Lt. Commander MacClain); *Gung Ho!* (Enright) (as Col. Thorwald)
1944   *Belle of the Yukon* (Seiter) (as Honest John Calhoun)
1945   *China Sky* (Enright) (as Dr. Gray Thompson); *Captain Kidd* (Lee) (as Adam Mercy)
1946   *Abilene Town* (Marin) (as Dan Mitchell, + co-pr); *Badman's Territory* (Whelan) (as Mark Rowley); *Home Sweet Homicide* (Bacon) (as Bill Smith)
1947   *Trail Street* (Enright) (as "Bat" Masterson); *Gunfighters* (Waggner) (as Brazos Kane); *Christmas Eve* (*Sinner's Holiday*) (Marin) (as Jonathan)
1948   *Albuquerque* (Enright) (as Cole Armin); *Return of the Badmen* (Enright) (as Vance); *Coroner Creek* (Enright) (as Chris Denning)
1949   *Canadian Pacific* (Marin) (as Tom Andrews); *The Walking Hills* (Sturges) (as Jim Carey); *The Doolins of Oklahoma* (Douglas) (as Bill Doolin); *Fighting Man of the Plains* (Marin) (as Jim Dancer)
1950   *The Nevadan* (Douglas) (as Andrew Barclay); *Colt 45* (Marin) (as Steve Farrell); *The Cariboo Trail* (Marin) (as Jim Redfern)
1951   *Sugarfoot* (Marin) (as Jackson "Sugarfoot" Redan); *Starlift* (Del Ruth) (as himself); *Santa Fe* (Pichel) (as Britt Canfield); *Fort Worth* (Marin) (as Ned Britt); *Man in the Saddle* (De Toth) (as Owen Meritt)
1952   *Carson City* (De Toth) (as Jeff); *Hangman's Knot* (Huggins) (as Matt Stewart); *The Man Behind the Gun* (Feist) (as Major Callicut)

Randolph Scott in *Comanche Station*

1953   *The Stranger Wore a Gun* (De Toth) (as Jeff Travis); *Thunder
        over the Plains* (De Toth) (as Captain David Porter)
1954   *Riding Shotgun* (De Toth) (as Larry Delong); *The Bounty
        Hunter* (De Toth) (as Jim Kipp)
1955   *Rage at Dawn* (Whelan) (as James Barlow); *Ten Wanted Men*
        (Humberstone) (as John Stewart); *Tall Man Riding* (Selander)
        (as Larry Madden); *A Lawless Street* (Lewis) (as Calem Ware)
1956   *Seven Men from Now* (Boetticher) (as Ben Stride, + co-pr);
        Seventh Cavalry (Lewis) (as Captain Tom Benson)
1957   *The Tall T* (Boetticher) (as Pat Brennan, + co-pr); *Shoot-Out
        at Medicine Bend* (Bare) (as Cap Devlin); *Decision at Sun-
        down* (Boetticher) (as Bart Allison, + co-pr)
1958   *Buchanan Rides Alone* (Boetticher) (title role, + co-pr)
1959   *Westbound* (Boetticher) (as John Hayes, + co-pr); *Ride Lone-
        some* (Boetticher) (as Ben Brigade, + co-pr)
1960   *Comanche Station* (Boetticher) (as Jefferson Cody, + co-pr)
1962   **Ride the High Country** (*Guns in the Afternoon*) (Peckinpah)
        (as Gil Westrum)

Publications

On SCOTT: books—

Fenin, George, and William K. Everson, *The Western: From Silents to
    Cinerama*, New York, 1962.

Lahue, Kalton C., *Riders of the Range*, Cranbury, New Jersey, 1973.
Parish, James Robert, *Great Western Stars*, New York, 1976.
Crow, Jefferson Brim III, *Randolph Scott: The Gentleman from Vir-
    ginia*, Carrollton, Texas, 1987.
McDonald, Archie P., editor, *Shooting Stars: Heroes and Heroines of
    Western Film*, Bloomington, Indiana, 1987.
Crow, Jefferson Brim, *Randolph Scott: A Film Biography*, Madison,
    North Carolina, 1994.
Scott, C. H., *Whatever Happened to Randolph Scott?*, Madison, North
    Carolina, 1994.

On SCOTT: articles—

McCarthy, Todd, obituary in *Variety* (New York), 4 March 1987.
Boetticher, Budd, "Un gentleman," in *Cahiers du Cinéma* (Paris), April
    1987.
Obituary in *Revue du Cinéma* (Paris), May 1987.

*   *   *

Randolph Scott had a long career in the movies, beginning during
the coming of sound, and ending with his final performance in director
Sam Peckinpah's celebrated Western, *Ride the High Country*, in 1962.
Throughout this remarkable 35-year span Scott remained true to one
role—the character of the bashful but feared Western hero. But in real
life he was neither a Westerner nor a cowboy. Scott was born and bred

a Southerner; he attended Georgia Tech and was graduated from the University of North Carolina. He broke into Hollywood through a series of menial jobs, the most illustrious of which was being Gary Cooper's voice coach for a short time.

Scott's break came with the revival of the B Western in the 1930s. Quickly he became a minor star, graduating to making Westerns for Paramount. Through the 1930s and 1940s he appeared in an amazing 66 films and rarely worked with distinguished directors (and when he did, it was in mediocre films such as Fritz Lang's *Western Union* and Rouben Mamoulian's *High, Wide, and Handsome*). More often than not Scott was grinding them out under the guiding hand of a Ray Enright or a Henry Hathaway.

In the early 1950s (at almost 50 years of age) Scott "overnight" became a star. In the first four years of that decade he made his only appearances in the annual ten list of most popular actors. The Westerns seemed unchanged from the vehicles of the 1940s, save for the addition of color. But during the early 1950s the public embraced Randolph Scott's "new" screen persona as dished up in a series of three or four Westerns per year.

Based on this newfound popularity, Scott formed his own production company with producer Harry Joe Brown. This enterprise provided Scott with the freedom to create his own Westerns and at the same time become a very wealthy man. In what is now known as the "Ranown" cycle of films, Randolph Scott made his greatest contribution to film history by portraying an aging cowboy in seven films directed by Budd Boetticher, and produced by Scott and Brown. These seven films (from *Seven Men from Now* in 1956 to *Comanche Station* in 1960), established, according to noted critic Andrew Sarris, "a new style of the [Western] genre." Film theorist André Bazin called *Seven Men from Now* "the most intelligent Western I know of . . . and the most beautiful."

Scott's final film was *Ride the High Country*. Many critics consider this tribute to the Western to be director Sam Peckinpah's best film. Randolph Scott retired in 1962 as one of Hollywood's richest men. He made this fortune, estimated to be in the tens of millions of dollars, from the movies plus wise investments in oil wells and real estate. Unlike many of his generation Scott appeared on television only in his old films, not in movies made for television or as a guest star on a series.

—Douglas Gomery

SEBERG, Jean

Nationality: American. **Born:** Jean Dorothy Seberg in Marshalltown, Iowa, 13 November 1938. **Education:** Attended schools in Marshalltown; University of Iowa, Iowa City. **Family:** Married 1) Francois Moreuil, 1958 (divorced 1960); 2) the writer Romain Gary, 1963 (divorced); 3) Dennis Berry. **Career:** 1956—chosen amid great publicity as unknown to play the lead in Preminger's film *Saint Joan*; 1958—Preminger turned over her contract to Columbia after the failure of both *Saint Joan* and *Bonjour Tristesse*; 1959—role in Godard's *A bout de souffle* gave her international critical recognition; later French and international films; 1970s—career embittered by political harassment of her by the media; breakdown after the miscarriage of her child, and lawsuit concerning its paternity. **Died:** In Paris, 31 August 1979.

Films as Actress:

1957   *Saint Joan* (Preminger) (title role)
1958   *Bonjour Tristesse* (Preminger) (as Cecile)

1959   *The Mouse That Roared* (Arnold) (as Helen)
1960   *A bout de souffle* (*Breathless*) (Godard) (as Patricia Franchini); *Let No Man Write My Epitaph* (Leacock) (as Barbara Holloway); *La Recreation* (*Playtime*; *Love Play*) (Moreuil) (as Kate Hoover)
1961   *Les Grandes Personnes* (*Time Out for Love*) (Valere) (as Ann); *L'Amant de cinq jours* (*The Five-Day Lover*) (de Broca)
1962   *Congo Vivo* (Bennati)
1963   *In the French Style* (Parrish) (as Christina James); *Le Grand Escroc* (Godard—short)
1964   *Echappement libre* (*Backfire*) (Becker) (as Olga Celan); *Lilith* (Rossen) (title role)
1965   *Moment to Moment* (LeRoy) (as Kay Stanton); *Un Millard un billard* (*Diamonds Are Brittle*) (Gessner)
1966   *La Ligne de demarcation* (*Line of Demarcation*) (Chabrol); *A Fine Madness* (Kershner) (as Lydia West)
1967   *Estouffade à la Carabei* (*The Looters*; *Stew in the Caribbean*) (Besnard); *La Route de Corinthe* (*The Road to Corinth*; *Who's Got the Black Box?*) (Chabrol) (as Shanny)
1968   *Les Oiseaux vont mourir au Perou* (*Birds Come to Die in Peru*) (Gary) (as Adriana)
1969   *Pendulum* (Schaefer) (as Adele Matthews); *Paint Your Wagon* (Logan) (as Elizabeth)
1970   *Airport* (Seaton) (as Tanya Livingston); *Ondata di calore* (*Dead of Summer*) (Risi) (as Joyce Grasse); *Macho Callahan* (Kowalski) (as Alexandra Mountford)
1971   *Kill!* (*Kill! Kill! Kill!*) (Gary) (as Emily)
1972   *Quaeta specie d'amore* (*This Kind of Love*) (Bevilacqua); *L'Attentat* (*The French Conspiracy*) (Boisset) (as Edith Lemoine); *Camorra!* (Squitieri)
1973   *La corrupción de Chris Miller* (*The Corruption of Chris Miller*; *Behind the Shutters*) (Bardem) (as Ruth)
1974   *Mousey* (*Cat and Mouse*) (Petrie—for TV) (as Laura Anderson/Richardson); *Les hautes solitudes* (*The Outer Limit of Solitude*) (Garrel)
1975   *Bianchi cavalli d'Agosto* (*The White Horses of Summer*) (Del Balzo); *Le Grande Délire* (*The Great Frenzy*) (Berry)
1976   *Die Wildente* (*The Wild Duck*) (Geissendoerfer) (as Gina)

Film as Director:

1974   *Ballad for the Kid* (+ ro)

Publications

By SEBERG: articles—

"Lilith et moi," in *Cahiers du Cinéma* (Paris), April 1966, reprinted in English as "Lilith and I," in January 1967 issue.
"Re-birth," interview with G. Gow, in *Films and Filming* (London), June 1974.
Interview with Susan d'Arcy, in *Films Illustrated* (London), August 1974.

On SEBERG: books—

Frischauer, Willi, *Behind the Scenes of Otto Preminger*, New York, 1974.
Richards, David, *Played Out: The Jean Seberg Story*, New York, 1981.
Athill, Diana, *Make Believe: A True Story*, South Royalton, Vermont, 1993.

On SEBERG: articles—

LaBadie, D. W., "Everybody's Galatea," in *Show* (Hollywood), August 1963.

Jean Seberg in *Lilith*

Current Biography 1966, New York, 1966.

Obituary in *New York Times*, 9 September 1979.

Lewis, Kevin, "Jean Seberg of Iowa and Paris," in *Films in Review* (New York), April 1980, corrections in February 1981 issue.

Alpert, Hollis, "Jean Seberg: Falling Star," in *American Film* (Washington, D.C.), September 1981.

Kramer, M., and R. Shafrensky, in *Jump Cut* (Berkeley, California), April 1983.

* * *

In the 34 features and 2 shorts that Iowa-born Jean Seberg made, she frequently played the all-American woman abroad. Her first two films, *Saint Joan* (in which the 17-year-old Seberg won the title role in a highly publicized open casting call) and *Bonjour Tristesse*, failed to gain her a critical or popular audience in the United States. *Saint Joan* in particular was a notorious failure, and easily might have plunged her back into obscurity. In France, however, she became a star overnight after her performance in the film that launched the French New Wave, *A bout de souffle*. Here, Jean-Luc Godard developed what he saw as her essential image, a fetching ambiguity of incorruptible wholesomeness that cloaked a casual amorality. The French were immediately charmed by her short-cropped blond hair, midwestern-accented French, and relaxed naturalistic acting.

A bout de souffle also established Seberg as the archetypal American girl abroad, and prompted Robert Rossen to cast her in her finest American film, *Lilith*. She plays a beautiful young schizophrenic in a luxurious mental asylum who seduces an occupational therapist. A genuine departure for her, the role allowed Seberg to use her wholesomeness as a cover for Lilith's malevolence. In one hauntingly lovely scene, Seberg draws her skirt to her knees, wades into a misty lake, and bends over to kiss her own image, an act that illuminates not only Lilith's destructive narcissism but also Seberg's delicate grace. Following *Lilith*, she became quickly stereotyped as a sophisticated, occasionally disturbed, cheating wife through such films as *Moment to Moment*, *A Fine Madness*, and *Pendulum*. Yet she also developed into an actress capable of playing roles of determination and quiet strength in such films as *Line of Demarcation* and *Paint Your Wagon*.

During the last decade of her life, Seberg's mental health deteriorated, due in part to a miscarriage and harassment by the FBI for supporting the Black Panthers. Hoping to revitalize a faltering career, she worked with many promising directors in Europe. Her only demanding role was in the prize-winning *Ondata di calore*, in which she gave a tour-de-force performance in a familiar role as a schizophrenic American woman stranded in Morocco. Two of her films drew their material directly from her life: *Ballad for the Kid* and *Les hautes solitudes*. In the latter she portrays herself—an American actress and left-wing activist living in exile. Neither film was successful.

At her best an actress of uncommon intelligence and feeling, Seberg never completely lost her all-American wholesomeness on the screen, even in films that explicitly tried to undermine it: *La corrupción de Chris Miller* and *Les Oiseaux vont mourir au Perou*. As the critic Vincent Canby said, she was "one of the most appealing and enigmatic movie stars of the 1960s." But she also was one of the more notorious casualties of the times, on levels personal, professional, and political. In 1995, 16 years after her tragic and much-too-early death, independent filmmaker Mark Rappaport reconstructed her life in the celluloid essay *From the Journals of Jean Seberg*, in which he examined her on- and off-screen persona from a social and cultural perspective.

—Arthur Nolletti Jr., updated by Rob Edelman

SEGAL, George

Nationality: American. **Born:** Great Neck, New York, 13 February 1934. **Education:** Attended George School, Haverford, Pennsylvania; Haverford College; Columbia University, New York, B.A. 1955. **Military Service:** U.S. Army, 1956-57. **Family:** Married 1) Marion Sobel, 1956 (divorced 1983), daughters: Elizabeth and Patty; 2) Linda Rogoff, 1983. **Career:** Organized Bruno Lynch and His Imperial Jazz Band while a student; 1955—understudy and factotum for Circle in the Square Theatre, New York; 1956—professional stage debut in *Don Juan*; Broadway debut in *The Iceman Cometh*; original member of the improvisational group The Premise; 1961—film debut in *The Young Doctors*; 1967—recording *George Segal, the Yama Yama Man*; a later group, The Beverly Hills Unlisted Jazz Band, has played at Carnegie Hall; 1987—in TV series *Take Five*, and *Murphy's Law*, 1988-89, and syndicated TV series *High Tide*, 1994.

Films as Actor:

1961   *The Young Doctors* (Karlson) (as Dr. Howard)

1962   *The Longest Day* (Annakin, Marton, Wicki, and Oswald) (as first commando up cliff)

1963   *Act One* (Schary) (as Lester Sweyd)

1964   *The New Interns* (Rich) (as Dr. Tony Parelli); *Invitation to a Gunfighter* (Wilson) (as Matt Weaver)

1965   *King Rat* (Forbes) (as Corporal King); *Ship of Fools* (Kramer) (as David)

1966   *Who's Afraid of Virginia Woolf?* (Mike Nichols) (as Nick); *Lost Command* (*Not for Honor and Glory*) (Robson) (as Lt. Mahidi); *The Quiller Memorandum* (Anderson) (as Quiller)

1967   *The St. Valentine's Day Massacre* (Corman) (as Peter Gusenberg)

1968   *No Way to Treat a Lady* (Smight) (as Morris Brummel); *Bye Bye Braverman* (Lumet) (as Monroe Rieff); *Il suo modo di fare* (*Tenderly*; *The Girl Who Couldn't Say No*) (Brusati) (as Franco)

1969   *L'Etoile du Sud* (*The Southern Star*) (Hayers) (as Dan Rockland); *The Bridge at Remagen* (Guillermin) (as Lt. Phil Hartman)

1970   *Loving* (Kershner) (as Brooks Wilson); *The Owl and the Pussycat* (Ross) (as Felix); *Where's Poppa?* (Carl Reiner) (as Gordan Hocheiser); *The Lie* (Alan Bridges—for TV)

1971   *Born to Win* (Passer) (as Jay Jay)

1972   *The Hot Rock* (Yates) (as Kelp)

1973   *Blume in Love* (Mazursky) (title role); *A Touch of Class* (Frank) (as Steve Blackburn)

1974   *California Split* (Altman) (as Bill Denny); *The Terminal Man* (Hodges) (as Harry Benson)

1975   *Russian Roulette* (Lombardo) (as Timothy Shaver); *The Black Bird* (Giler) (as Sam Spade Jr.)

1976   *The Duchess and the Dirtwater Fox* (Frank) (as Charlie Malloy)

1977   *Rollercoaster* (Goldstone) (as Harry Calder); *Fun with Dick and Jane* (Kotcheff) (as Dick Harper)

1978   *Who Is Killing the Great Chefs of Europe?* (Kotcheff) (as Robby)

1979   *Lost and Found* (Frank) (as Adam)

1980   *The Last Married Couple in America* (Cates) (as Jeff Thompson)

1981   *Carbon Copy* (Schultz) (as Walter Whitney)

1983   *Trackdown: Finding the Goodbar Killer* (Persky—for TV) (as John Grafton); *The Man in 5A* (*Killing 'em Softly*) (Fisher)

1984   *Zany Adventures of Robin Hood* (Austin—for TV); *The Cold Room* (Dearden—for TV) (as Hugh Martin)

1985   *Not My Kid* (Tuchner—for TV); *Stick* (Burt Reynolds) (as Barry Brahn)

1986   *Many Happy Returns* (Steven Hilliard Stern—for TV)

1988   *All's Fair* (Lane)

1989   *Look Who's Talking* (Heckerling) (as Albert); *The Endless Game* (Forbes—for TV) (as Jock)

1991   *The Clearing* (Alenikov); *For the Boys* (Rydell) (as Art Silver)

1992   *Me, Myself & I* (Ferro) (as Buddy Arnett)

1993   *Taking the Heat* (Tom Mankiewicz—for TV) (as District Attorney Kepler); *Look Who's Talking Now* (Ropelewski) (as Albert)

1994   *Army of One* (Vic Armstrong) (as Severence); *Direct Hit* (Merhi) (as James Tronson); *The Feminine Touch* (Janis) (as Sen. "Beau" Ashton); *Following Her Heart* (Lee Grant—for TV) (as Harry Haussman); *Seasons of the Heart* (Lee Grant—for TV) (as Ezra Goldstine); *Deep Down* (Travers—direct to video) (as Gil)

1995   *To Die For* (Van Sant) (cameo); *The Babysitter* (Ferland—direct to video) (as Bill Holsten)

1996   *The Good Doctor: The Paul Fleiss Story* (for TV); *Flirting with Disaster* (David O. Russell) (as Mr. Copland); *It's My Party* (Kleiser) (as Paul Stark)

Publications

On SEGAL: articles—

Current Biography 1975, New York, 1975.

Drew, B., "The Ambivalent Star," in *American Film* (Washington, D.C.), May 1978.

Marx, Linda, "With a Touch of Brash, George Segal Finally Plays the Big Time," in *People Weekly* (New York), 29 June 1981.

*   *   *

Back in the 1960s, George Segal was considered an attractive and talented young actor with leading man potential. He had showy supporting roles in a number of films, two of which became major critical and commercial successes: *Ship of Fools*, playing David, the painter and lover of Julie (Elizabeth Ashley) and *Who's Afraid of Virginia Woolf?*, as Nick, cast opposite Elizabeth Taylor, Richard Burton, and Sandy Dennis. Around this time he graduated to starring roles, which kept him busy into the 1970s. He was well-cast in the role of hero: a cop, on the trail of Rod Steiger's killer of lonely middle-aged ladies, in *No Way to Treat a Lady* and an American secret agent, in the intelligent, Harold Pinter-scripted thriller *The Quiller Memorandum*. He skillfully played addicts (to gambling, in *California Split*, and heroin, in *Born to Win*), and he was attractively cast in romantic comedies (especially *A Touch of Class*, opposite Glenda Jackson, and *The Owl and the Pussycat*, paired with Barbra Streisand).

But Segal's best roles were as contemporary urban/suburban neurotics with serious woman trouble, whether with wives (*Loving* and *Blume in Love*) or mothers (*Where's Poppa?*). At the same time, while a viable star capable of carrying a film, he was not averse to taking a role in which he was part of a male ensemble (notably in *Bye Bye Braverman* and *The Hot Rock*).

Significantly, many of Segal's films (including *The Owl and the Pussycat*, *Where's Poppa?*, *Bye Bye Braverman*, *The Hot Rock*, and *Born to Win*) are set in New York City. In many of these scenarios, he exudes a Jewish boyishness; but his persona is that of a more handsome (but no less obsessive and neurotic) version of Woody Allen.

From the mid-1970s through early 1980s, Segal's failures (*The Black Bird*, *The Duchess and the Dirtwater Fox*, *The Last Married Couple in America*, and *Lost and Found*, the latter an inferior attempt to reprise the success of *A Touch of Class*) began outnumbering

his successes (*Fun with Dick and Jane*)—and even the latter did not approach the quality of his earlier work. By the 1980s, his career as a celluloid star had ended, so he segued into starring parts in made-for-television movies and, eventually, supporting roles on-screen (most memorably as the self-centered married lover of Kirstie Alley in *Look Who's Talking*, the head writer for entertainer James Caan in *For the Boys*, and the husband of compulsive-obsessive Mary Tyler Moore in *Flirting with Disaster*). In a film such as *Flirting with Disaster*, he is perfectly cast as an older (but no less wiser) extension of his characters in *Loving*, *Blume in Love*, and *Where's Poppa?*

Segal occasionally continued to win starring roles. In *Me, Myself & I*, he plays another New York neurotic, a writer who becomes involved with his schizophrenic neighbor (JoBeth Williams). But the film, low-budget and independently produced, lacks the stature (let alone quality) of his earlier work.

—Rob Edelman

SELLERS, Peter

Nationality: British. **Born:** Peter Richard Henry Sellers in Southsea, Hampshire, 8 September 1925. **Education:** Attended St. Aloysius College, London. **Family:** Married 1) the actress Anne Howe, 1951 (divorced 1964), son: Michael, daughter: Sarah; 2) the actress Britt Ekland, 1964 (divorced 1969), daughter: Victoria; 3) Miranda Quarry, 1970 (divorced 1974); 4) the actress Lynne Frederick, 1977. **Career:** Appeared as child actor in revue at age five, *Splash Me*; worked as a drummer in a dance band after leaving school; 1943-46—served in the Royal Air Force; toured with the Gang Show in the Middle East, discharged as corporal; 1946-47—entertainment director of holiday camp; then vaudeville comedian: at Windmill Theatre, London, 1948, and on vaudeville circuit until 1956; 1951—film debut in *Penny Points to Paradise*; 1952-59—on radio shows *Show Time*, *Ray's a Laugh*, and *The Goon Show*, the last becoming a popular cult favorite; 1958—stage debut in *Brouhaha* in London; 1959—role in *I'm All Right, Jack* brought wide popularity; later films in the Pink Panther series made him an international star. **Awards:** Best British Actor, British Academy, for *I'm All Right, Jack*, 1959; Commander, Order of the British Empire, 1966. **Died:** In London, 24 July 1980.

Films as Actor:

1951   *Penny Points to Paradise* (Young) (as the Major/Arnold Fringe); *London Entertains* (Faucey); *Let's Go Crazy* (Cullimore—short) (as Groucho/Guiseppe/Cedric/Izzy Gozzunk/Crystal Jollibottom)

1952   *Down among the Z Men* (Rogers) (as Major Bloodnok)

1953   *Super Secret Service* (Green)

1954   *Orders Are Orders* (Paltenghi) (as Private Goffin)

1955   *John and Julie* (Fairchild) (as P. C. Diamond); *The Ladykillers* (Mackendrick) (as Harry); *The Case of the Mukkinese Battlehorn* (Stirling—short) (as Inspector Quilt/Henry Crun/ Sid Crimp/Sir Jervis Fruit); *The Man Who Never Was* (Neame) (voice of Winston Churchill)

1957   *The Smallest Show on Earth* (Dearden) (as Percy Quill); *Death of a Salesman* (Arliss—short); *Cold Comfort* (Hill); *Insomnia Is Good for You* (as Hector Dimwiddle)

1958   *The Naked Truth* (*Your Past Is Showing*) (Zampi) (as Sonny MacGregor); *Up the Creek* (Guest) (as Chief Petty Officer Doherty); *Tom Thumb* (Pal) (as Tony); *Carlton-Browne of the F.O.* (*Man in a Cocked Hat*) (Boulting) (as Amphibulous)

1959 *The Mouse That Roared* (Arnold) (as Bascombe/Grand Duchess Gloriana/Count Mountjoy); *I'm All Right, Jack* (Boulting) (as Fred Kite)

1960 *Battle of the Sexes* (Crichton) (as Mr. Martin); *Two-Way Stretch* (Day) (as "Dodger" Lane)

1961 *Never Let Go* (Guillermin) (as Lionel Meadows); *The Millionairess* (Asquith) (as Dr. Ahmed el Kabir/Parerga); *The Road to Hong Kong* (short)

1962 *Only Two Can Play* (Gilliat) (as John Lewis); *Waltz of the Toreadors* (Guillermin) (as General Leo Fitzjohn); *Lolita* (Kubrick) (as Clare Quilty)

1963 *The Dock Brief* (Hill) (as Morgenhall); *Heavens Above* (Boulting) (as the Reverend John Aspinall); *The Wrong Arm of the Law* (Owen) (as Pearly Gates); *The Pink Panther* (Edwards) (as Inspector Clouseau)

1964 **Dr. Strangelove: Or, How I Learned to Stop Worrying and Love the Bomb** (Kubrick) (title role/Captain Mandrake/President Muffley); *The World of Henry Orient* (Hill) (title role); *A Shot in the Dark* (Edwards) (as Inspector Clouseau)

1965 *What's New, Pussycat?* (Clive Donner) (as Fritz Fassbender)

1966 *The Wrong Box* (Forbes) (as Dr. Pratt); *After the Fox* (De Sica) (as Aldo Vanucci)

1967 *Casino Royale* (Huston and others) (as Evelyn Tremble); *The Bobo* (Parrish) (as Juan Bautista); *Woman Times Seven* (De Sica) (as Jean)

1968 *The Party* (Edwards) (as Hrundi Vakshi); *I Love You, Alice B. Toklas* (Averback) (as Harold Fine)

1969 *The Magic Christian* (McGrath) (as Sir Guy Grand)

1970 *Hoffman* (Rakoff) (title role); *There's a Girl in My Soup* (Boulting) (as Robert Danvers); *A Day at the Beach* (Hesera); *Simon, Simon* (Stark—short)

1972 *Where Does It Hurt?* (Amateau); *Alice's Adventures in Wonderland* (Sterling) (as King of Hearts)

1973 *The Blockhouse* (Rees) (as Bouquet); *The Optimist* (*The Optimist of Nine Elms*) (Simmons) (as Sam); *Soft Beds and Hard Battles* (*Undercover Hero*) (Boulting) (as Gen. Latour/Major Robinson/Schroeder/Adolf Hitler/Prince Kyoto/French President)

1974 *Ghost in the Noonday Sun* (Medak); *The Great McGonagall* (McGrath) (as Queen Victoria); *The Return of the Pink Panther* (Edwards) (as Inspector Clouseau)

1976 *Murder by Death* (Moore) (as Sidney Wang); *The Pink Panther Strikes Again* (Edwards) (as Inspector Clouseau)

1978 *Revenge of the Pink Panther* (Edwards) (as Inspector Clouseau)

1979 *Being There* (Ashby) (as Chance); *The Prisoner of Zenda* (Quine) (as Prince Rudolph/Syd Frewin)

1980 *The Fiendish Plot of Dr. Fu Manchu* (Haggard) (title role/Nayland Smith)

1982 *Trail of the Pink Panther* (Edwards) (as Inspector Clouseau)

Film as Producer:

1960 *The Running, Jumping, and Standing Still Film* (Lester—short)

Film as Director:

1961 *Mister Topaze* (+ title role)

Publications

By SELLERS: books—

Seller's Market, with Joe Hyams, London, 1966.
The Book of the Goons, with Spike Milligan, London, 1974.

On SELLERS: books—

Evans, Peter, *Peter Sellers: The Mask Behind the Mask*, 1968, rev. ed., 1981.
Sellers, Michael, with Sarah and Victoria Sellers, *P.S. I Love You: Peter Sellers, 1951-80*, London, 1981.
Sylvester, Derek, *Peter Sellers: An Illustrated Biography*, London, 1981.
Walker, Alexander, *Peter Sellers: The Authorised Biography*, London, 1981.
Stark, Graham, *Remembering Peter Sellers*, London, 1990.
Starr, Michael, *Peter Sellers: A Film History*, Jefferson, North Carolina, 1991.
Lewis, Roger, *The Life and Death of Peter Sellers*, London, 1994.

On SELLERS: articles—

Current Biorgaphy 1960, New York, 1960.
McVay, D., "The Man Behind," in *Films and Filming* (London), May 1963.
McGillivray, D., "Peter Sellers," in *Focus on Film* (London), Spring 1974.
Thomson, D., "The Rest Is Sellers," in *Film Comment* (New York), September-October 1980.
The Annual Obituary 1980, New York, 1981.
Ansen, David, "Peter Sellers," in *The Movie Star*, edited by Elisabeth Weis, New York, 1981.
Sinoux, M., "Bye Bye Birdie—num-num," in *Positif* (Paris), February 1981.
Braun, Eric, "Authorized Sellers," in *Films* (London), August 1982.
Millar, M., "Goonery and Guinness," in *Films and Filming* (London), January 1983.
Peary, Gerald, "Peter Sellers," in *American Film* (New York), April 1990.

*   *   *

English comedy pre-1945 was usually modest, rueful, cheerful, uncritical; back from the war Sellers's generation brought more anarchic attitudes, and Sellers found fame, with Spike Milligan, Harry Secombe, and, initially, Michael Bentine, in *The Goon Show* radio comedy. Like some missing link between Edward Lear and Monty Python, the Goons combined anarcho-daffy parodies of Englishness with the Dada-logic of crazy cartoons, yet being sound-only, were crazier still. Sellers was the voices of, inter alia, Bluebottle, Major Dennis Bloodnok, and Henry Crum, later developing a quieter, more populist, humor on records. Goonery boggles visual live action; the early, very cheap, shorts get odd licks of it, though Richard Lester's 1960 *The Running, Jumping, and Standing Still Film* (which Sellers produced) is a gem.

Having risen to fame as a gaggle of lunatic voices, Sellers hesitated before plunging into film, as if uncertain what the rest of him could add; indeed, throughout certain roles, and periodically in all of them, his voice seems to float over a face which, however deadly its mimicry, also seems blank. His immense diversity of characters—mad-keen officer-class types, the "shabby genteel," polite misfits, demented liberals—all share a gleaming-eyed obstinacy with a Nelsonian blindness to some obvious and enormous truth.

His movie career developed slowly, through character acting, especially lower-class character parts: a Cockney crook in *The Ladykillers*, a Scottish clerk in *Battle of the Sexes*, an "Old Mate" cinema projectionist in *Smallest Show on Earth*, the caricature-suave criminal kingpin in *The Wrong Arm of the Law*, a misanthropic television star in *The Naked Truth*, and above all Fred Kite, the earnest Communist shop-

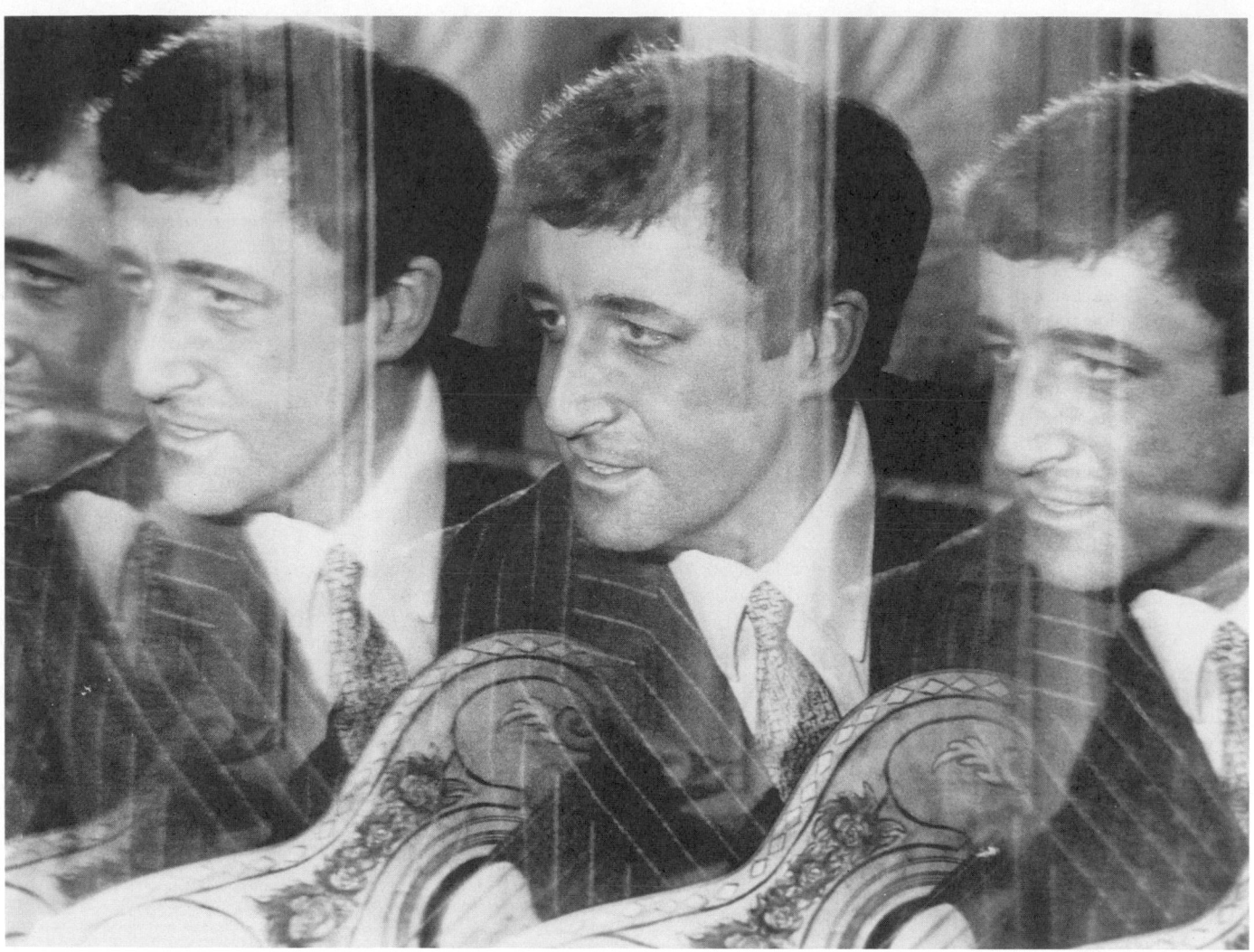

Peter Sellers

steward, in *I'm All Right, Jack*, the performance that earned Sellers a British Academy Award and brought him international attention. A cold energy, a deadly accurate detail, an association of deference with pathos, and an absence of team spirit set Sellers's lower-class characters nearer the "angry young men" of the time and the subsequent "satire boom" than the general 1950s ethos.

Wistful pathos keynoted his first star part in an international film, as the idealistic Indian doctor pursued by Sophia Loren's Shavian Superwoman in *The Millionairess*. But two stronger, atypical dramatic roles, as a ravingly irate crook in the gangster film *Never Let Go*, and as the worldly colonel in *Waltz of the Toreadors*, from Anouilh's play, strengthened the, perhaps unfair, critical opinion that, unlike Alec Guinness, he was more an impersonator of types than an actor. In three films about middle-class innocents finally learning the prevalent cynicism—*Mister Topaze* (self-directed), *Only Two Can Play* (from Kingsley Amis), and *The Dock Brief* (from John Mortimer)—his talent seemed stalled for lack of heart, or at least, modulations between his "home keys": icy rage and stiff bewilderment.

His gifts revived under a group of American directors. Pulling a Guinness, he played several roles in Jack Arnold's *The Mouse That Roared* (including a fruitily Edwardian Margaret Rutherford-type duchess). Sellers then repeated the feat in Kubrick's *Dr. Strangelove* (a liberal President being desperately reasonable during nuclear apoca-

lypse, his ex-Nazi scientific adviser, and a decent but dumb RAF colonel who almost saves the world from the brink of destruction; Sellers was set to play a fourth role in the film, as the Texas bombardier who rides a nuke to oblivion, but suffered an accident after several scenes were shot and was replaced by Slim Pickens). He had warmed up for this job with several identity-jugglings in Kubrick's earlier *Lolita*, as an enigmatic intellectual playacting a succession of characters to hound James Mason's nymphet-obsessed Humbert Humbert.

Hollywood snared Sellers for Blake Edwards's lighthearted Pink Panther films, a fusion of slapstick and "comedy of manners," about the (mis)adventures of Inspector Clouseau, an accident-prone detective braving social humiliations which would have finished a less insensitive and dimwitted man. The role was a supporting one in the first Panther film, but Sellers's tomfoolery stole the picture out from under David Niven and its other big-name stars, and Sellers's character was made the lead in the immediate follow-up, *A Shot in the Dark*, and all the remaining (and gradually deteriorating) Panther comedies from then on.

Disagreements during the shooting of Sellers's first film actually made in Hollywood, *Kiss Me, Stupid!*, generated much publicity, first from a reported clash of egos between Sellers and his director, Billy Wilder, then from the near-fatal heart attack that prompted Sellers's replacement by Ray Walston. Trimmer and healthier, he returned in

What's New, Pussycat?, scripted by Woody Allen, in which Sellers's swinging psychiatrist intriguingly mixed gaucheries à la Clouseau with a smidgeon of Strangelove. But many unsuccessful films ensued, in which he offered awkward variations on his swinging sixties specialities (parody, pathos, awkwardness, stiffly frozen fury). Nevertheless, the Clouseau sequels proved highly popular, and kept his name in the public eye long enough for him to achieve a fine swansong (and an Oscar nomination) as the simpleminded gardener taken for a guru in Hal Ashby's quiet, mournful, comedy, *Being There*. Sellers had pursued the role for years, bombarding the novel's author, Jerzy Kosinski, with marathon telegrams signed by its hero, Chauncey Gardiner. He imbued the film with a chilling superficiality of feeling, which a number of Sellers biographers suggest was a self-portrait. It is often said that in every clown is a Hamlet struggling to get out; Sellers was a chameleon struggling to contain a vacuum within, his biographers say. His characters' propensity to quietly fixed stares suggests not so much Stan Laurel, from whom Sellers learned them, but some furious frustration, some tantrumy dominance. If Goonish lunacy generally was exuberantly obsessive, and had soul, its essence was a manic triumph over some inner deadness.

Sellers was the type of actor-comedian whose basic character shades into a myriad of impersonations—like Peter Ustinov (for whom the role of Clouseau was first intended) or Danny Kaye (the original choice for the old Cockney busker of *The Optimist of Nine Elms*). He drew much inspiration from two more fully dramatic chameleons, Alec Guinness, renowned for stiff-upper-lip melancholy, and Laurence Olivier, especially in his cynically hollow roles (parodied by Sellers repeatedly, almost vengefully). On an abidingly popular comedy record, Sellers speaks Lennon and McCartney's *A Hard Day's Night* like Laurence Olivier doing Shakespeare; but the Sellers combines Henry V (noble resolution) and Richard III (dark treachery). So many incongruous identities, cultures, moralities, in one even vocal line, is Sellers's essence—and *ars celare artis*.

It is reputedly Sellers who endowed Fred Kite with soul, where the Boultings had envisaged only a schematically nasty "bolshie" militant. On *Strangelove*, Kubrick used three or more cameras to catch Sellers's unscripted, unpredictable, yet always in-character, improvisations. Clouseau is a classic comic figure, a silhouette as appropriate to mass affluence and its embarrassments as Tati's Hulot, but always exact and intimate, where Tati's films became remote and overblown. Sellers was surely an auteur, even if one can only dream about the Wilder film as it might have been, with Sellers and Monroe (as first envisaged), or Sellers in deeper Woody Allen films (Allen's *Zelig*, for example, another fable about "being there"). It is fittingly sardonic that Sellers's many happy collaborations with Edwards ended on a sour note, with litigation over Sellers's last "performance" as Clouseau, which was cobbled together, after his death, from the outtakes of earlier films, a life-size cutout, and other simulacra of an actor "being there."

—Raymond Durgnat, updated by John McCarty

SEYRIG, Delphine

Nationality: French. **Born:** Delphine Claire Beltiane Seyrig in Beirut, Lebanon, of French parents, 10 April 1932. **Family:** Married Jack Youn-German, 1950. **Career:** 1952-55—actress on French stage; then studied at the Actors Studio, New York; 1961—French film debut in *L'Année dernière à Marienbad* brought international fame; stage work included roles in *A Month in the Country*, 1964, *Rosencrantz and Guildenstern Are Dead*, 1967, and *The Beast in the Jungle*, 1981; 1970s—directed video shorts. **Awards:** Best Actress, Venice Festival, for *Muriel*, 1963. **Died:** Of a lung disease, in Paris, 15 October 1990.

Films as Actress:

1958 *Pull My Daisy* (Frank) (as Mrs. Larry Rivers)
1961 *L'Année dernière à Marienbad* (*Last Year at Marienbad*) (Resnais) (as the woman)
1963 *Muriel* (Resnais) (as Helene)
1965 *Qui êtes-vous, Polly Magoo?* (Klein)
1966 *La Musica* (Duras and Seban) (as She)
1967 *Accident* (Losey) (as Francesca)
1968 *Mr. Freedom* (Klein) (as Marie/Madeleine); *Baisers volés* (*Stolen Kisses*) (Truffaut) (as Fabienne Tabard); *La Voie lactée* (*The Milky Way*) (Buñuel) (as prostitute)
1970 *Peau d'âne* (*The Magic Donkey*; *Donkey Skin*) (Demy) (as Fairy Godmother)
1971 *Le Rouge aux lèvres* (*Daughters of Darkness*) (Kumel) (as Countess Elizabeth Bathory)
1972 *Le Charme discret de la bourgeoisie* (*The Discreet Charm of the Bourgeoisie*) (Buñuel) (as Mme. Thevenot); *Le Journal d'un suicide* (Stanojevic) (as interpreter)
1973 *Evlalie quitte les champs* (*The Star, The Orphan, and the Butcher*) (Savary); *A Doll's House* (Losey) (as Kristine Linde); *The Day of the Jackal* (Zinnemann) (as Colette)
1974 *The Black Windmill* (Siegel) (as Cecil Burrows); *Dites-le avec des fleurs* (Grimblat) (as Françoise); *Le Cri de coeur* (Lallemand) (as wife)
1975 *India Song* (Duras) (as Anne-Marie); *Le Jardin qui bascule* (Gilles) (as Kate); *Jeanne Dielman, 23 Quai du Commerce, 1080 Bruxelles* (Akerman) (title role); *Aloise* (de Kermadec) (title role); *Voyage en Amérique*; *Je t'aime, tu danses*
1976 *Caro Michele* (Monicelli) (as Adriana); *Son nom de Venise dans Calcutta désert* (Duras)
1977 *Repérages* (*Faces of Love*) (Soutter) (as Julie); *Der letzte Schrei* (van Ackeren); *Baxter—Véra Baxter* (Duras)
1980 *Le Chemin perdu* (Moraz); *Cher Inconnu* (*I Sent a Letter to My Love*) (Mizrahi) (as Yvette)
1981 *Freak Orlando* (Ottinger); *Man of Destiny* (Davis—for TV)
1983 *Le Grain de sable* (Meffre)
1984 *Dorian Gray im Spiegel der Boulevardpresse* (Ottinger)
1985 *Sarah et le cri de la langouste* (Bluwal)
1986 *Letters Home* (Akerman); *The Golden Eighties* (Akerman) (as Jeanne)
1987 *Seven Women, Seven Sins* (Sander)
1989 *Johanna d'Arc of Mongolia* (Ottinger)

Publications

By SEYRIG: articles—

"The Lily of the Valley," interview with Rui Nogueira in *Sight and Sound* (London), Autumn 1969.
Interview with A. Drewnowski in *Inter/View* (New York), June 1972.
"Delphine Seyrig," by G. Heathwood in *Cinema Papers* (Melbourne), January 1978.
Interview by E. Bonn and T. Deknut in *Ecran* (Paris), March 1978.
Interview in *Talking Films: The Best of the Guardian Film Lectures*, edited by Andrew Britton, London, 1991.

On SEYRIG: articles—

Amiel, M., "Alain Resnais raconté par ses acteurs," in *Cinéma* (Paris), July-August 1980.
Hervo, B., in *Filmfaust*, December-January 1981-82.
Obituary, in *Variety* (New York), 22 October 1990.

*   *   *

Delphine Seyrig with Vernon Dobtcheff and Claude Juan in *India Song*

The haunting screen image of Delphine Seyrig stands at the center of French avant-garde filmmaking since the 1960s. Her elevation to this stature is based on two films, *L'Année dernière à Marienbad* and *India Song*. Not only significant as films, these works are important for their connections with the *nouveau roman*, a style that seeks to achieve an image of the eternal present through a dynamic of frozen gesture and glances. Only the face, body, and intellect of Seyrig could lend the subtleties demanded of this form which emphasizes image and psychology over plot and dialogue. David Bordwell admirably summed up Seyrig's novelistic qualities by calling her a Proustian actress. She endows her characters with a historical complexity brought to life in the present through the simplest of gestures.

Alain Robbe-Grillet, who wrote *L'Année denière à Marienbad*, had hoped Kim Novak would play the female lead. He wanted an actress who was less cerebral and more carnal than Seyrig. Fortunately for the dramatic and visual complexity of the film, Seyrig won the role. The film is about brainwashing; a man attempts to create in a woman's mind a past that never was in order to gain control over her present. The dramatic energy of the film is based on the woman's psychic resistance to the man. At times, the woman posed like a model, moments when the fashion-plate beauty of Seyrig works to perfection. Other times, the woman rebels or at least recoils from this positioning and rebuffs the man with wit and sophistication. Here the persona of Seyrig comes into full play. Even when capitulating to the man, there is enough lingering resistance to make the spectator question the validity of the image and wonder if it is not part of the man's fantasy. Novak, who plays to perfection a woman conforming to all aspects of imagistic male fantasy, as in *Vertigo*, would not have been able to generate this sense of resistant intellect.

In *India Song* Seyrig perfectly embodies the upper-class *hauteur* of the femme fatale. She portrays a woman who, in the grand French manner of de Pompadour, de Staël, and George Sand, has emotional and intellectual power to enslave certain males even into her middle age. *India Song*, even more than *L'Année dernière à Marienbad*, gives the false impression of stasis. Treating mental actions and developments rather than physical ones, the film requires a commanding yet illusive presence that only Seyrig could provide. Any other actress would have made the character appear like a dressmaker's dummy in a shop window.

Between *L'Année dernière à Marienbad* and *India Song* lie other fine, if less historically significant, films: *Muriel, Accident*, and *Baisers volés*. Throughout her career, Delphine Seyrig embodied the intelligent and beautiful woman who approximates human perfection. She remains one of film history's most important actresses.

—Rodney Farnsworth

SHARIF, Omar

Nationality: Egyptian. **Born:** Michael Shalhoub in Alexandria, 10 April 1932; grew up in Cairo. **Education:** Attended English schools; British Victoria College, Cairo. **Family:** Married the actress Faten Hamama, 1955 (divorced), son: Tarek. **Career:** Worked in the family lumber business for three years; 1953—film debut in Egypt; formed own production company; 1962—western film debut in *Lawrence of Arabia*; 1966—member of the team the Bridge Circus; also a bridge columnist, and made tapes for the TV series *Grand Slam*; 1986—in TV mini-series *Peter the Great*; 1987—presenter of TV show *Play Bridge with Omar Sharif*; 1990s—in TV mini-series *Sidney Sheldon's Memories of Midnight*, 1991, *and Lie Down with Lions*, 1994. **Agent:** Ames Cushing, William Morris Agency, 31/32 Soho Square, London W1V 5DG, England.

Films as Actor:

1953   *Sera's fil Wadi (Struggle in the Valley)* (Shahin)

1954   *Ayamna el Hilwa (Our Happy Days)* (Halim); *Shaitan el Sahara (Devil of the Desert)* (Shahin)

1955   *Sera'a fil Mina (Struggle in the Pier)* (Shahin); *Ard el Salam (Land of Peace)* (El-Chiekh)

1956   *La Anam (No Sleep)* (Saif)

1957   *Shati el Asrar (Shore of Mystery)* (Salem); *Ghaltit Habibi (My Lover's Mistake)* (Bideir)

1958   *Goha* (Baratier); *Min Ajl Imraa (For the Sake of a Woman)* (El-Cheikh); *Mouid maa el Maghoul (A Date with an Unknown)* (Salem); *Fediha fil Zamalek (Scandal at Zamalek)* (Mustafa)

1959   *Ehne el Talamza (We Students)* (Salem); *Sera's fil Nil (Struggle in the Nile)* (Salem)

1960   *Eshaet Hub (Love Rumor)* (Abdel-Wahab); *Lowat el Hub (Agony of Love)* (Saif); *Nahr el Hub (River of Love)* (Zukfikar); *Hubbi el Wahid (My Only Love)* (El-Cheikh); *Gharam el Asyad (I Love My Boss)* (Naguib); *Bidaya wa Nihaya (Beginning and End)* (Saif)

1961   *Fi Baitina Rajul (A Man in Our House)* (Barakat)

1962   **Lawrence of Arabia** (Lean) (as Sherif Ali ibn el Kharish)

1964   *The Fall of the Roman Empire* (Anthony Mann) (as Sohamus); *Behold a Pale Horse* (Zinnemann) (as Father Francisco); *The Yellow Rolls-Royce* (Asquith) (as Davich)

1965   *La Fabuleuse Aventure de Marco Polo (Marco the Magnificent)* (de la Patellière and Noel Howard) (as Emir Alaou); *Genghis Khan* (Levin) (title role); *Doctor Zhivago* (Lean) (title role)

1966   *The Poppy Is Also a Flower* (Terence Young) (as Dr. Rad)

1967   *The Night of the Generals* (Litvak) (as Major Grau); *C'era una volta (More than a Miracle; Cinderella, Italian Style; Happily Ever After)* (Rosi) (as Prince Ramon)

1968   *Funny Girl* (Wyler) (as Nick Arnstein); *Mayerling* (Terence Young) (as Crown Prince Rudolf)

1969   *MacKenna's Gold* (J. Lee Thompson) (as Colorado); *The Appointment* (Lumet) (as Federico Fendi); *Che!* (Fleischer) (title role)

1970   *The Last Valley* (Clavell) (as Vogel); *The Horsemen* (Frankenheimer) (as Uraz)

1971   *Le Casse (The Burglars)* (Verneuil) (as Abel Zacharia)

1972   *Le Droit d'aimer (The Right to Love; Brainwashed)* (Le Hung)

1973   *L'isola misteriosa e il capitano Nemo (The Mysterious Island of Captain Nemo)* (Bardem) (as Captain Nemo)

1974   *The Tamarind Seed* (Edwards) (as Feodor Sverdlov); *Juggernaut* (Lester) (as Captain Brunel); *The Return of the Pink Panther* (Edwards)

1975   *Funny Lady* (Ross) (as Nick Arnstein); *Crime and Passion (Ace Up Your Sleeve)* (Passer) (as André Ferren)

1976   *The Pink Panther Strikes Again* (Edwards) (as Egyptian assassin)

1979   *Bloodline* (Terence Young) (as Ivo Palazzi); *Ashanti* (Fleischer) (as the Prince)

1980   *The Baltimore Bullet* (Miller) (as the Deacon); *Oh, Heavenly Dog!* (Camp) (as Malcolm Bart); *S*H*E* (Robert Lewis—for TV) (as Cesare Magnasco); *Pleasure Palace* (Grauman—for TV)

1981   *Green Ice* (Day) (as Meno Argenti)

1982   *Inchon* (Terence Young)

1984   *Top Secret!* (Zucker, Abrahams, and Zucker) (as Cedric); *Far Pavilions* (Duffell—for TV)

1985   *Edge of the Wind* (Ives—for TV); *Vicious Circle* (Ives—for TV)

1986   *Anastasia: The Mystery of Anna* (Chomsky—for TV) (as Czar Nicholas II); *Harem* (Hale—for TV) (as Sultan Hassan)

Omar Sharif in *Lawrence of Arabia*

1987   *Les Possédés* (*The Possessed*) (Wajda) (as Stephan Verkhovensky)
1988   *Grand Larceny* (Szwarc—for TV) (as Rashid Saud); *Les Pyramides bleue* (*Paradise Calling*) (Dombasle) (as Alex); *Keys to Freedom* (Feke)
1989   *Michelangelo and Me* (De Moro—for TV); *No Justice* (Tessari)
1990   *Mountains of the Moon* (Rafelson) (uncredited); *Quatro piccole donne* (Albano—for TV); *The Rainbow Thief* (Jodorowsky) (as Dima the Thief); *Lion in the Desert* (Tessari—for TV); *Viaggio d'Amore* (*Journey of Love*) (as Rico)
1991   *The Castle* (Foreman); *Al Moaten Al Myssri* (*War in the Land of Egypt*) (Salah Abou Serif); *Mayrig* (Verneuil) (as Hagop)
1992   *Tengoku No Taizai* (*Heavenly Sin*) (Masuda) (as Tsai Mang Hua); *Mrs. 'Arris Goes to Paris* (Shaw—for TV) (as Marquis DeChassange); *588 Rue Paradis* (Verneuil) (as Hagop); *Beyond Justice* (Tessari) (as Emir)
1996   *Gulliver's Travels* (Sturridge—for TV) (as the Sorcerer)

Publications

By SHARIF: books—

L'eternel Masculin, with Marie Guinchars, Paris, 1976; as *The Eternal Male*, Paris, 1976.
Omar Sharif's Life in Bridge, London, 1983.

On SHARIF: articles—

Current Biography 1970, New York, 1970.
Jabara, A., and others, "The Arab Image in American Film and Television," in *Cineaste* (New York), vol. 17, no. 1, 1989.

*   *   *

After almost ten years as a star of the Egyptian cinema, Omar Sharif received desired international critical and popular acclaim with his performance as Sherif Ali, Lawrence's fierce ally in David Lean's *Lawrence of Arabia*. The film won an Oscar as Best Picture and Sharif was nominated as Best Supporting Actor. Quickly he became a gossip-magazine staple as the hottest new screen sex symbol. In the years that immediately followed, he courageously took on further historical characters, including Sohamus, King of the Armenians in *The Fall of the Roman Empire*, and the title role of *Genghis Khan*.

David Lean, who brought him to international acclaim, then altered Sharif's established image as a fierce warrior, when he next cast him as Dr. Yuri Zhivago, the idealistic poet caught up in the Russian Revolution and an illicit love affair. Sharif's role in the epic *Doctor Zhivago* is still the part many moviegoers primarily identify him with. The film was produced on a mammoth scale, by a major director and co-starred Julie Christie (who also was extremely popular at the time). This all contributed to *Zhivago*'s current status as a cinematic classic and Sharif's association to the main character. Three years later he was cast as Nick Arnstein opposite Barbra Streisand's Fanny Brice in *Funny Girl*. (This was his ultimate role as a man wounded in love.) For the third time in less than ten years, he was in a top-grossing film and the focus of much media attention. His real life escapades as a bridge player fueled the fan magazines with parallels between Sharif and Arnstein.

The year 1969 saw the beginning of his fall from major stardom. Once again he took on the role of a historic figure: Che Guevara in *Che!*. This time the film was a disaster and Sharif did not weather the failure. He then began to work in Europe. In the mid-1970s he returned to English-speaking roles only to be involved in three all-star failures: as Soviet spy Sverdlov opposite Julie Andrews in Blake

Edwards's *The Tamarind Seed*, as Captain Brunel in Richard Lester's *Juggernaut*, and once again as Nick Arnstein opposite Streisand in Herbert Ross's *Funny Lady*. Despite an interesting performance as the opportunistic investment counselor André Ferren in Ivan Passer's underrated *Crime and Passion*, Sharif has since received only mediocre roles in mediocre or poor films. Most recently, he was uncharacteristically cast as a villain in the television movie *Gulliver's Travels*.

Sharif's offscreen life as an international playboy kept his name active in the gossip columns in the 1980s. His box-office power, however, has waned significantly from the promise of the 1960s.

—Doug Tomlinson, updated by Linda J. Stewart

SHAW, Robert

Nationality: British. **Born:** Westhoughton, Lancashire, 9 August 1927. **Education:** Attended Truro School, Cornwall; Royal Academy of Dramatic Arts, London. **Family:** Married 1) the actress Jennifer Bourke, 1952 (divorced), four daughters; 2) the actress Mary Ure, 1963 (died 1975), four children; 3) Virginia Hansen, 1976, two children. **Career:** 1948-49—member of the Shakespeare Memorial Theatre, Stratford upon Avon; 1951—West End debut in *Hamlet*; joined Old Vic troupe, and toured in Europe and South Africa; film debut in *The Lavender Hill Mob*; 1956—in TV series *The Scarlet Pimpernel*; 1956-57—in TV series *The Buccaneers*; 1959—first of several prize-winning novels, *The Hiding Place*; later dramatized by Shaw; 1961—Broadway debut in *The Caretaker*; 1968—his play *The Man in the Glass Booth*, based on his novel, produced in both London and New York, and in 1975 made into a movie; 1976—co-host of Academy Awards show. **Died:** In Tourmakeady, Ireland, 28 August 1978.

Films as Actor:

1951   *The Lavender Hill Mob* (Charles Crichton) (as police scientist)
1955   *The Dam Busters* (Anderson) (as Flight Sgt. Pulford)
1956   *Doublecross* (Squire); *A Hill in Korea* (*Hell in Korea*) (Amyes) (as Lance-Cpl. Hodge)
1959   *Sea Fury* (Enfield) (as Gorman); *Libel* (Asquith) (as first photographer)
1962   *The Valiant* (*L'affondamento della Valiant*) (Roy Ward Baker) (as Lt. Field)
1963   *Tomorrow at Ten* (Comfort) (as Marlow); *The Caretaker* (*The Guest*) (Clive Donner) (as Aston); *From Russia with Love* (Terence Young) (as Red Grant)
1964   *The Luck of Ginger Coffey* (Kershner) (title role); *Carol for Another Christmas* (Joseph L. Mankiewicz—for TV)
1965   *Battle of the Bulge* (Annakin) (as Col. Hessler)
1966   *A Man for All Seasons* (Zinnemann) (as King Henry VIII)
1968   *Custer of the West* (*Good Day for Fighting*) (Siodmak) (as Gen. George Custer); *The Birthday Party* (Friedkin) (as Stanley Weber)
1969   *Battle of Britain* (Hamilton) (as Squadron Leader Skipper); *The Royal Hunt of the Sun* (Lerner) (as Francisco Pizarro)
1970   *Figures in a Landscape* (Losey) (as MacConnachie, + sc)
1971   *A Town Called Hell* (*A Town Called Bastard*) (Parrish) (as town priest)
1972   *Young Winston* (Attenborough) (as Lord Randolph Churchill)
1973   *A Reflection of Fear* (*Labyrinth*; *Autumn Child*) (Fraker) (as Michael); *The Hireling* (Bridges) (as Steven Leadbetter); *The Sting* (George Roy Hill) (as Doyle Lonnegan)

1974 *The Taking of Pelham One Two Three* (Sargent) (as Blue)
1975 *Jaws* (Spielberg) (as Quint); *Der Richter und sein Henker* (*Murder on the Bridge*; *End of the Game*) (Schell) (as Richard Gastmann)
1976 *Robin and Marion* (Lester) (as Sheriff of Nottingham); *Swashbuckler* (*The Scarlet Buccaneer*) (Goldstone) (as Ned Lynch); *Diamonds* (Golan) (as Charles/Earl Hodgson)
1977 *Black Sunday* (Frankenheimer) (as Kabakov); *The Deep* (Yates) (as Romer Treece)
1978 *Force Ten from Navarone* (Hamilton) (as Mallory)
1979 *Avalanche Express* (Robson) (as Marenkov)

Publications

By SHAW: books—

The Hiding Place (novel), London, 1959.
The Sun Doctor (novel), London, 1961.
The Flag (novel), London, 1965.
The Man in the Glass Booth (play), London, 1967 (also novel version, 1967).
A Card from Morocco (novel), New York, 1969.
Cato Street (play), London, 1972.

By SHAW: articles—

"Running Figure in Landscape," interview with A. Guerin and H. Grossman, in *Show* (Hollywood), January 1970.
"Robert Shaw: No More Food for Fish," interview with B. Drew, in *American Film* (Washington, D.C.), November 1977.

On SHAW: books—

Carmean, Karen, and Georg Gaston, *Robert Shaw: More than a Life*, Lanham, Maryland, 1993.
French, John, *Robert Shaw: The Price of Success*, London, 1993.

On SHAW: articles—

Current Biography 1968, New York, 1968.
Obituary, in *Washington Post*, 29 August 1978.
Thomson, David, "Ryan and Shaw," in *Film Comment* (New York), January/February 1994.

*   *   *

At the time Robert Shaw died of a heart attack in 1978, his status as a bona fide movie star was still in its infancy. But this late recognition was preceded by a long and memorable career as a character actor and villain. His classical training at the Royal Academy of Dramatic Art interested him in writing as well as acting. Shaw was a playwright, scenarist, and award-winning novelist, bringing a literate and literary sensibility to his screen acting.

But it was the other side of Shaw's personality—that of an extremely competitive, quick-tempered, greedy man whose infidelities resulted in his first and second wives each giving birth to one of his children within a five-week span, and led his second wife, the actress Mary Ure, and mother of four of his ten children to suicide—that provided the raw material for his initial film image. Built on a foundation of harnessed anger, Shaw's image was cemented through numerous performances in character roles and as arch-villains. Most notable of these were his roles as Red Grant, stalking James Bond and sporting outrageously dyed blond hair, in *From Russia with Love*; Lord Randolph Churchill, the father of Winston Churchill, in Attenborough's *Young*

Winston; and perhaps the role that best-suited the dark side of Shaw's psyche, King Henry VIII in *A Man for All Seasons*, for which, appropriately enough, he was nominated for a Best Supporting Actor Academy Award.

The two films most responsible for altering Shaw's career were *The Sting* and *Jaws*. In co-starring roles he fixed himself indelibly in the public eye and secured his status as a leading man. This new position however, was unfortunately brief. The few films that followed granted him top-billing but little else in terms of popular or critical acceptance. Had he lived, he might have been able to create a leading man as colorful, memorable, or dynamic as his best villains. His failed attempts at heroic stardom seem to indicate that Shaw's particular brand of blustery ferocity was best utilized in support of, or in opposition to, the protagonist of a film.

—Bill Wine, updated by David E. Salamie

SHEARER, Norma

Nationality: American. **Born:** Edith Norma Shearer in Westmont, Montreal, Quebec, Canada, 10 August 1900; became U.S. citizen, 1932. **Education:** Attended Westmont High School; Canadian Royal Academy of Music. **Family:** Married 1) the producer Irving Thalberg, 1927 (died 1936), son: Irving, daughter: Katherine; 2) Martin Arrouge, 1942. **Career:** Model, movie hall pianist, and stage actress, New York; 1920—film debut as extra in *The Flapper*; 1923—MGM contract; then a series of minor parts in films; 1927—marriage with Thalberg, an MGM producer, then series of leading roles and international popularity; 1942—last film, *Her Cardboard Lover*. **Awards:** Best Actress Academy Award for *The Divorcee* (also nominated for *Their Own Desire*), 1929/30; Best Actress, Venice Festival, for *Marie Antoinette*, 1938. **Died:** In Woodland Hills, California, 12 June 1983.

Films as Actress:

1920 *The Flapper* (Crosland) (as extra); *The Restless Sex* (Leonard) (as extra); *Way Down East* (Griffith) (as extra); *The Stealers* (Cabanne) (as Julia Martin)
1921 *Torchy's Millions*
1922 *The Leather Pushers* (Pollard—serial); *The Man Who Paid* (Apfel) (as Jeanne); *The Bootleggers* (Sheldon) (as Helen Barnes); *Channing of the Northwest* (Ince) (as Jess Driscoll)
1923 *A Clouded Name* (Huhn) (as Marjorie Dare); *Man and Wife* (McCutheon) (as Dora Perkins); *The Devil's Partner* (Fleming) (as Jeanne); *Pleasure Mad* (Barker) (as Elinor Benton); *The Wanters* (Stahl) (as Marjorie); *Lucretia Lombard* (Conway) (as Mimi)
1924 *The Trail of the Law* (Apfel) (as Jerry Varden); *The Wolf Man* (Mortimer) (as Elizabeth Gordon); *Blue Water* (Hartford) (as Lilian Denton); *Broadway after Dark* (Bell) (as Rose Dulane); *Broken Barriers* (Barker) (as Grace Durland); *Married Flirts* (Vignola) (as herself); *Empty Hands* (Fleming) (as Claire Endicott); *The Snob* (Bell) (as Nancy Claxton); *He Who Gets Slapped* (Seastrom) (as Consuelo)
1925 *Lady of the Night* (Bell) (as Molly/Florence Banning); *Waking Up the Town* (Keyes) (as Mary Ellen Hope); *A Slave of Fashion* (Henley) (as Katherine Emerson); *Pretty Ladies* (Bell) (as Frances White); *The Tower of Lies* (Seastrom) (as Glory); *His Secretary* (Henley) (as Ruth Lawrence)
1926 *The Devil's Circus* (Christensen) (as Mary); *The Waning Sex* (Leonard) (as Nina Duane); *Upstage* (Bell) (as Dolly Haven)

Norma Shearer

1927 *The Demi-Bride* (Leonard) (as Criquette); *After Midnight* (Bell) (as Mary); *The Student Prince* (Lubitsch) (as Kathie)

1928 *Voices across the Sea* (short); *The Latest from Paris* (Wood) (as Ann Dolan); *The Actress* (Franklin) (as Rose Trelawney); *A Lady of Chance* (Henley) (as Dolly)

1929 *The Trial of Mary Dugan* (Veiller) (title role); *The Last of Mrs. Cheyney* (Franklin) (title role); *The Hollywood Revue* (Reisner) (as herself); *Their Own Desire* (Hopper) (as Lally)

1930 *The Divorcee* (Leonard) (as Jerry); *Let Us Be Gay* (Leonard) (as Kitty Brown)

1931 *The Stolen Jools* (McCann—short); *Jackie Cooper's Christmas Party* (short) (as herself); *Strangers May Kiss* (Fitzmaurice) (as Lisbeth); *A Free Soul* (Brown) (as Jan Ashe); *Private Lives* (Franklin) (as Amanda Prynne)

1932 *Smilin' Through* (Franklin) (as Moonyean Clare/Kathleen)

1934 *Riptide* (Goulding) (as Lady Mary Rexford); *The Barretts of Wimpole Street* (Franklin) (as Elizabeth Barrett)

1936 *Mister Will Shakespeare* (Tourneur-short); *Romeo and Juliet* (Cukor) (as Juliet)

1938 *Marie Antoinette* (Van Dyke) (title role)

1939 *Idiot's Delight* (Brown) (as Irene Fellara); *The Women* (Cukor) (as Mrs. Stephen Haines)

1940 *Escape* (LeRoy) (as Countess Von Treck)

1941 *We Were Dancing* (Leonard) (as Vicki Wilomirski)

1942 *Her Cardboard Lover* (Cukor) (as Consuelo Croydon)

Publications

By SHEARER: article—

"I'm Tame as a Lion," in *American Magazine*, July 1935.

On SHEARER: books—

Thomas, Bob, *Thalberg: Life and Legend*, New York, 1969.
Memo from: David O. Selznick, edited by Rudy Behlmer, New York, 1972.
Rosen, Marjorie, *Popcorn Venus*, New York, 1973.
Jacobs, Jack, and Myron Braun, *The Films of Norma Shearer*, South Brunswick, New Jersey, 1976.
Quirk, Lawrence J., *Norma: The Story of Norma Shearer*, New York, 1988.
Lambert, Gavin, *Norma Shearer: A Life*, London, 1990.

On SHEARER: articles—

Howe, Herbert, "What Is Norma Shearer's Charm for Men?" in *Photoplay* (New York), November 1925.
St. Johns, Adela Rogers, "I'm Not Going to Marry Says Norma Shearer," in *Photoplay* (New York), May 1927.
Fletcher, Adele, "Beauty, Brains, or Luck?" in *Photoplay* (New York), August 1930.
Lee, Basil, "The First Real Lady of Films," in *Photoplay* (New York), July 1934.
Tully, Jim, "Early Struggles of Norma Shearer," in *Pictures and Picturegoer*, 17 August 1935.
Manners, Dorothy, "How Norma Shearer Faces the Future," in *Photoplay* (New York), December 1936.
Baskette, Kirtley, "A Queen Comes Back," in *Photoplay* (New York), July 1938.
Willson, Dixie, "Norma Shearer's Handful of Memories," in *Photoplay* (New York), October 1938.
Jacobs, J., "Norma Shearer," in *Films in Review* (New York), August-September 1960.

McCarthy, Todd, obituary, in *Variety* (New York), 15 June 1983. Obituary in *Films and Filming* (London), July 1983.

*   *   *

During the Great Depression, Norma Shearer represented all the glamour and chic associated with MGM. Although her acclaimed talent as an actress rested on little more than fan magazine publicity, she was, undeniably, a major star. She consistently ranked among Hollywood's most popular performers during the 1930s, winning six Academy Award nominations for best actress between 1929 and 1938. Her marriage to Irving Thalberg was of great importance; his position made her a first lady of Hollywood while his power secured for Shearer some of her best roles. This is not to imply that Shearer's career depended upon her husband's connections. She had learned from working in silent films for such marginal outfits as Allied Producers, New Brunswick, and FBO Studios, how best to utilize her limited talents to create the ultimate image of a glamorous woman. After Thalberg's death, she completed her studio contract and then retired to a life of wealth and leisure, only rarely appearing in public. Of her films, only *The Student Prince*, *Romeo and Juliet*, and *The Women* seem to hold any interest for audiences today.

—Douglas Gomery

SHEEN, Martin

Nationality: American. **Born:** Ramon Estevez in Dayton, Ohio, 3 August 1940. **Education:** Attended Chaminade High School, Dayton. **Family:** Married Janet (Sheen), 1961, sons: the actors Charlie Sheen, Emilio Estevez, and Ramon Estevez, daughter: the actress Renée Estevez. **Career:** Late 1950s—joined Beck and Malina's off-off-Broadway Living Theatre, New York; 1961—important role in *The Connection*; 1964—Broadway debut in *Never Live over a Pretzel Factory*; also in *The Subject Was Roses*; 1967—film debut in *The Incident*; 1967-68—in TV soap opera *As the World Turns*; also in several made-for-TV movies; 1968—title role in Joseph Papp's "mod" production of *Hamlet*; in TV mini-series *The Missiles of October*, 1974, *Blind Ambition*, 1979, *Kennedy*, 1983, *Alex Haley's Queen*, and *A Matter of Justice*, 1993. **Agent:** Innovative Artists, 1999 Avenue of the Stars, #2850, Los Angeles, CA 90067, U.S.A.

Films as Actor:

1967 *The Incident* (Peerce) (as Artie Connors)

1968 *The Subject Was Roses* (Grosbard) (as Timmy Cleary)

1969 *Then Came Bronson* (William Graham—for TV)

1970 *Catch-22* (Mike Nichols) (as Lt. Dobbs); *The Andersonville Trial* (George C. Scott—for TV)

1971 *Goodbye, Raggedy Ann* (Cook—for TV); *Mongo's Back in Town* (Chomsky—for TV); *No Drums, No Bugles* (Ware) (as Ashby Gatrell)

1972 *Pickup on 101* (Florea) (as Les Cavanaugh); *Rage* (George C. Scott) (as Major Holliford); *Welcome Home, Johnny Bristol* (McCowan—for TV) (as Graytak); *That Certain Summer* (Lamont Johnson—for TV); *Pursuit* (Michael Crichton—for TV) (as Timothy Drew)

1973 *Crime Club* (Rich—for TV) (as Deputy Wilson); *Letters from Three Lovers* (Erman—for TV); *Catholics* (Gold—for TV) (as Father John Kinsella); *Message to My Daughter* (Robert Michael Lewis—for TV)

Martin Sheen in *Apocalypse Now*

1974   ***Badlands*** (Malick) (as Kit); *The Execution of Private Slovik* (Lamont Johnson—for TV) (title role); *The Story of Pretty Boy Floyd* (Ware—for TV); *The California Kid* (Heffron—for TV)

1975   *The Legend of Earl Durand* (John Patterson) (as Luther Sykes); *The Last Survivors* (Katzin—for TV); *Sweet Hostage* (Philips—for TV) (as Leonard Hatch)

1977   *The Cassandra Crossing* (Cosmatos) (as Robby Navarro); *The Little Girl Who Lives Down the Lane* (Gessner) (as Frank Hallett)

1978   *Eagle's Wing* (Harvey) (as Pike)

1979   ***Apocalypse Now*** (Francis Ford Coppola) (as Capt. Willard)

1980   *The Final Countdown* (Don Taylor) (as Warren Lasky); *Loophole* (*Break In*) (Quested) (as Stephen Booker)

1982   *Gandhi* (Attenborough) (as Walker); *That Championship Season* (Miller) (as Tom Daley); *In the Custody of Strangers* (Greenwald—for TV)

1983   *Enigma* (Szwarc) (as Alex Holbeck); *Man, Woman, and Child* (Richards) (as Bob Beckwith); *The Dead Zone* (Cronenberg) (as Sen. Greg Stillson); *No Place to Hide* (Johnson and Bird) (as narrator); *Choices of the Heart* (Sargent—for TV); *In the King of Prussia* (De Antonio—doc)

1984   *The Guardian* (David Greene—for TV) (as Charlie Hyatt); *Firestarter* (Lester) (as Capt. Hollister)

1985   *Out of the Darkness* (Jud Taylor—for TV) (as Ed Zigo); *Consenting Adult* (Gates—for TV) (as Ken Lynd); *In the Name of the People* (Christopher—doc) (as narrator); *Broken Rainbow* (Mudd—doc) (as narrator); *The Fourth Wise Man* (Michael Ray Rhodes—for TV); *From Blitzkrieg to the Bomb* (doc) (as narrator); *The Real Thing* (Schnall—doc) (as narrator); *Shattered Spirits* (Greenwald—for TV); *The Atlanta Child Murders* (Erman—for TV)

1986   *News at Eleven* (Robe—for TV) (as Frank Kenley); *Samaritan: The Mitch Snyder Story* (Heffron—for TV) (as Mitch Snyder); *State of Emergency* (Bennett) (as Dr. Alex Carmody)

1987   *Secrets of the Titanic* (Hurley—doc) (as narrator); *Siesta* (Lambert) (as Del, Claire's husband); *Wall Street* (Oliver Stone) (as Carl Fox); *Conspiracy: The Trial of the Chicago 8* (Kagan—for TV) (as James Marion Hunt); *The Believers* (Schlesinger) (as Dr. Cal Jamison)

1988   *Da* (Clark) (as Charlie); *Judgment in Berlin* (Leo Penn) (as Herbert J. Stern); *Walking after Midnight* (Kay—doc)

1989   *Beverly Hills Brats* (Sotirakis) (as Jeffrey Miller); *Beyond the Stars* (*Personal Choice*) (Saperstein) (as Paul Andrews); *Cold Front* (Goldstein) (as John Hyde); *Nightbreaker* (Markle—for TV) (as Dr. Alexander Brown)

1991   *The Maid* (Toynton) (as Anthony Wayne); *Paper Hearts* (McCall); *JFK* (Oliver Stone) (as narrator); *Guilty until Proven Innocent* (Wendkos—for TV) (as Harold Hohne)

1992   *My Home, My Prison* (Marcus and Muñoz—doc) (as narrator); *Original Intent* (Marcarelli) (as Joe); *Touch and Die* (Solinas) (as Frank); *The Water Engine* (Schachter—for TV) (as chain letter voice); *Blood on the Badge* (McCormick)

1993   *Hear No Evil* (Greenwald) (as Lt. Philip Brock); *Gettysburg* (Maxwell) (as Gen. Robert E. Lee); *The Killing Box* (*Ghost Brigade*) (Hickenlooper) (as Gen. Haworth); *The Last P.O.W.? The Bobby Garwood Story* (Georg Sanford Brown—for TV) (as Capt. Ike Eisenbraun); *Hot Shots!, Part Deux* (Abrahams)

1994   *Roswell* (Kagan—for TV) (as Townsend); *When the Bough Breaks* (Cohn) (as Police Capt. Swaggert); *Boca* (Avancini—for TV) (as Jesse James Montgomery); *The Floating Outfit: Trigger Fast* (*Guns of Honor*; *Trigger Fast*) (Lister) (as Jackson Baines Hardin); *Running Wild* (Humer—doc) (as Dan Walker); *Fortunes of War* (Notz) (as Francis Labeck); *Hits!* (Greenblatt) (as Kelly); *One of Her Own* (Armand Mastroianni—for TV) (as Asst. D.A. Pete Maresca)

1995   *Gospa* (Sedlar) (as Jozo Zovko); *The Break* (Katzin) (as Gil Robbins); *Les Cent et une Nuits* (*A Hundred and One Nights*) (Varda) (as Furtive and Friendly Appearance); *Dillinger and Capone* (Purdy) (as Dillinger); *Dead Presidents* (as judge); *The American President* (Rob Reiner) (as A. J. MacInerney)

1996   *Project ALF* (for TV); *The War at Home* (Estevez)

Other Films:

1986   *Babies Having Babies* (d—for TV)
1988   *No Means No* (Auerbach) (exec pr)
1989   *Cadence* (*Stockade*) (d, co-sc, + ro as Sgt. Otis V. McKinney)

Publications

By SHEEN: article—

Interview with Emile De Antonio, in *American Film* (Washington, D.C.), December 1982.

On SHEEN: books—

Riley, Lee, and David Schumacher, *The Sheens: Martin, Charlie and Emilio Estevez*, New York, 1989.
Press, Skip, *Charlie Sheen, Emilio Estevez & Martin Sheen*, Parsippany, New Jersey, 1996.

On SHEEN: articles—

Current Biography 1977, New York, 1977.
Vallely, J., "Martin Sheen: Heart of Darkness, Heart of Gold," in *Rolling Stone* (New York), 1 November 1979.
Hingley, Audrey T., "The Luster of Martin Sheen," in *Saturday Evening Post*, December 1983.
McGillivray, David, "Martin Sheen," in *Films and Filming* (London), December 1985.
Kellner, Elena, "All in the Family" (cover story), in *Hispanic* (Austin, Texas), May 1994.

*   *   *

Martin Sheen is a prolific, reliable actor whose versatility has been evident from the very beginning of his screen career. In his first two films, he offered fine performances as altogether different characters: a thug who terrorizes the passengers in a New York City subway car, in *The Incident*; and a young World War II veteran who becomes immersed in his parents' marital problems, in *The Subject Was Roses* (a role for which he had won acclaim on Broadway).

Early on, Sheen—along with a seemingly endless list of actors who, over the decades, have been able to strike nonconformist poses—was heralded as a "new James Dean." He gave his most Dean-like performance in Terrence Malick's cult classic, *Badlands*, playing an alienated and amoral young rebel-on-the-run who, joined by a female counterpart, goes on a killing binge. *Badlands* is a film that serves as a major link in a cinematic chain that includes *They Live by Night*, *Bonnie and Clyde*, *Thieves Like Us*, and *Natural Born Killers*. Unlike so many James Dean clones who quickly proved to be flavors-of-the-month, however, Sheen has had a substantial career. Yet his early, flashy roles never did propel him to major screen stardom. By far, the major body of his best work came in made-for-television movies and mini-series, including *That Certain Summer*, *Catholics*, *The Execution of Private Slovik*, *Sweet Hostage*, *Kennedy* (as John F. Kennedy), *The Missiles of October* (as Robert Kennedy), *News at Eleven*, *The Long Road Home*, and *Samaritan: The Mitch Snyder Story*.

Far and away the penultimate Sheen screen appearance—and most consequential credit of his career—is in Francis Coppola's much-publicized, much-analyzed Vietnam War epic, *Apocalypse Now*. Sheen has the pivotal role of the fatigued Captain Willard, who is dispatched to seek out and kill the renegade officer Colonel Kurtz (Marlon Brando). Sheen even suffered a heart attack during the film's endlessly exhausting shoot in the Philippines. Still, with regard to its actors, it was the controversial presence and performance of Brando that was the most discussed upon the film's release, and remains so to this day. This focus on Brando does not reflect on Sheen's talent, but it does symbolize his inability to break through as a major movie star.

As he has aged, Sheen has had nice supporting roles in films ranging from Oliver Stone's *Wall Street* (playing the father of real-life son Charlie Sheen) to Rob Reiner's *The American President*; has been one of the cast members of prestigious epics (*Gandhi* and *Gettysburg*, playing General Robert E. Lee in the latter); and has narrated an endless number of documentaries and features (including Stone's *JFK*). Also of note is his political activism. Sheen is a humanist and progressive who has never avoided being at the center of an organized protest; in April 1996, he was one of 20 people arrested during a Good Friday demonstration outside the Riverside Research Institute, a Manhattan-based nuclear research facility. Sheen has translated his politics to the screen via his involvement in such projects as Maria Florio's and Victoria Mudd's *Broken Rainbow*, an Oscar-winning documentary about the resettling of Navajo Indians, and Emile De Antonio's *In the King of Prussia*, about a trial of Roman Catholic activists in Pennsylvania.

Today, Sheen's identity is related as much to his being the father of Charlie Sheen and Emilio Estevez as to his own professional accomplishments. In this regard, he joins the likes of Henry Fonda, John Carradine, Lloyd Bridges, Kirk Douglas, and others as the senior member of a Hollywood acting family.

—Rob Edelman

SHEPARD, Sam

Nationality: American. **Born:** Samuel Shepard Rogers VII in Fort Sheridan, Illinois, 5 November 1943. **Education:** Attended Mount Antonio Junior College, Walnut, California, 1960-61. **Family:** Mar-

Sam Shepard in *Country*

ried 1) the actress O-Lan Johnson, 1969 (divorced), son: Jesse Mojo; children with the actress-producer Jessica Lange, daughter: Hannah Jane, and son: Samuel Walker. **Career:** 1962—joined a theatrical repertory group but left the next year; by 1966 several of his one-act plays had been produced off-Broadway; by the late 1960s began to write film scripts and continued to write plays which were performed nationwide; 1978—selected to play the lead in *Days of Heaven*, his first of several major acting roles; 1988—wrote and directed *Far North*, and *Silent Tongue*, 1993; 1995—in TV mini-series *Streets of Laredo*. **Awards:** Three Obie Awards, 1965-66; Brandeis University Creative Arts Medal, 1976; Pulitzer Prize, for play *Buried Child*, 1978. Agent: Toby Cole, 234 West 44th Street, New York, NY 10036, U.S.A.

Films as Actor:

1969   *Bronco Bullfrog* (Platts-Mill) (as Jo)
1970   *Brand X*
1978   ***Days of Heaven*** (Malick) (as the Farmer); *Renaldo and Clara* (Dylan) (+ co-sc)
1980   *Resurrection* (Daniel Petrie) (as Cal Carpenter)

1981   *Raggedy Man* (Fisk) (as Bailey)
1982   *Frances* (Clifford) (as Harry York)
1983   *The Right Stuff* (Kaufman) (as Chuck Yeager)
1984   *Country* (Pearce) (as Gil Ivy); ***Paris, Texas*** (Wenders) (+ sc)
1985   *Fool for Love* (Altman) (as Eddie, + sc)
1986   *Crimes of the Heart* (Beresford) (as Doc Porter)
1987   *Baby Boom* (Shyer) (as Dr. Jeff Cooper)
1989   *Steel Magnolias* (Ross) (as Spud Jones)
1991   *Defenseless* (Martin Campbell) (as George Beutel); *Voyager* (*Homo Faber*) (Schlöndorff) (as Walter Faber); *Bright Angel* (Fields) (as Jack Russell)
1992   *Thunderheart* (Apted) (as Frank Coutelle)
1993   *The Pelican Brief* (Pakula) (as Thomas Callahan)
1994   *Safe Passage* (Ackerman) (as Patrick Singer)
1996   *Lily Dale* (Masterson—for TV) (as Peter Davenport)

Films as Scriptwriter:

1968   *Me and My Brother* (Frank) (co-sc)
1970   *Zabriskie Point* (Antonioni) (co-sc)

1972 *Oh! Calcutta!* (Aucion) (co-sc)
1982 *True West* (Sinise and Goldstein—for TV) (+ pr)
1995 *Curse of the Starving Class* (McClary—for TV)

Films as Director and Scriptwriter:

1988 *Far North*
1993 *Silent Tongue*

Publications

By SHEPARD: plays—

Five Plays (includes *Chicago, Icarus's Mother, Fourteen Hundred Thousand, Red Cross, Melodrama Play*), Indianapolis, 1967.
La Turista, Indianapolis, 1968.
Operation Sidewinder, Indianapolis, 1970.
Mad Dog Blues and Other Plays (includes *Cowboy Mouth, Cowboys No. 2*), New York, 1971.
The Unseen Hand and Other Plays (includes *The Rock Garden, 4-H Club, Forensic and the Navigators, Cowboys No. 2, The Holy Ghostly, Shaved Splits, Back Bog Beast Bait*), Indianapolis, 1971.
The Tooth of Crime and Geography of a Horse Dreamer, New York, 1974.
Action and The Unseen Hand, London, 1975.
Angel City and Other Plays (includes *The Rock Garden, Cowboys No. 2, Cowboy Mouth, Mad Dog Blues, Action, Killer's Head, Curse of the Starving Class*), New York, 1976.
Buried Child and Other Plays (includes *Suicide in B : A Mysterious Overture, Seduced*), New York, 1979.
Buried Child and Seduced and Suicide in B : A Mysterious Overture, London, 1980.
Four Two-Act Plays (includes *La Turista, The Tooth of Crime, Geography of a Horse Dreamer, Operation Sidewinder*), New York, 1980.
Seven Plays (includes *Buried Child, Curse of the Starving Class, The Tooth of Crime, La Turista, True West, Tongues, Savage/Love*), New York, 1981.
True West, London, 1981.
Chicago and Other Plays, 1982.
Fool for Love and *The Sad Lament of Pecos Bill on the Eve of Killing His Wife,* San Francisco, 1983.
Fool for Love and Other Plays (includes *Angel City, Cowboy Mouth, Suicide in B : A Mysterious Overture, Seduced, Geography of a Horse Dreamer, Melodrama Play*), New York, 1984.
States of Shock, New York, 1991.
Simpatico, New York, 1995.

By SHEPARD: books—

Hawk Moon: A Book of Short Stories, Poems, and Monologues, Los Angeles, 1973.
Rolling Thunder Logbook, New York, 1977.
Motel Chronicles, with photographs by Johnny Dark, San Francisco, 1982.
Paris, Texas (screenplay), with Wim Wenders, edited by Chris Sievernich, New York, 1984.
Joseph Chaikin and Sam Shepard: Letters and Texts: 1972-1984, edited by Barry Daniels, New York, 1989.
Cruising Paradise, New York, 1996.

By SHEPARD: articles—

"Sam Shepard, Writer on the Way Up," interview with Mel Gussow, in *New York Times*, 12 November 1969.

"Metaphors, Mad Dogs, and Old Time Cowboys," interview with Kenneth Chubb, in *Theatre Quarterly*, August/October, 1974.
"Saga of Sam Shepard," interview with Robert Coe, in *New York Times Magazine*, 23 November 1980.
"The New American Hero," interview with Pete Hamill, in *New York*, 5 December 1983.
"Myths, Dreams, Realities—Sam Shepard's America," interview with Michiko Kakutani, in *New York Times*, 29 January 1984.
"The Natural," interview with Blanche McCrary Boyd, in *American Film*, October 1984.
"Who's That Tall, Dark Stranger?," interview with Jack Kroll, in *Newsweek* (New York), 11 November 1985.
"Strong Words," interview with Jonathan Cott, in *Vogue* (New York), September 1988.
"The Man on the High Horse," interview with Jennifer Allen, in *Esquire* (New York), November 1988.

On SHEPARD: books—

Auerbach, Doris, *Sam Shepard, Arthur Kopit, and the Off-Broadway Theatre*, Boston, 1982.
Shewey, Don, *Sam Shepard: The Life, the Loves behind the Legend of a True American*, New York, 1985.
Oumano, Ellen, *Sam Shepard: The Life and Work of an American Dreamer*, New York, 1986.
DeRose, David J., *Sam Shepard*, New York, 1992.
Tucker, Martin, *Sam Shepard*, New York, 1992.

On SHEPARD: articles—

Brantley, Ben, "Sam Shepard, Storyteller," in *New York Times*, 13 November 1994.
"Fool for Sam," in *Village Voice* (New York), in 20 February 1996.
Schiff, Stephen, "Shepard on Broadway," in *New Yorker*, 22 April 1996.
Marks, Peter, "Sam Shepard Is Happy to Be on Broadway, but It's Just a Visit," in *New York Times*, 28 May 1996.

*   *   *

Sam Shepard has spent almost his entire adult life as an artist. He has written numerous plays, has published short fiction and screenplays, and has acted, directed, and collaborated on a variety of film projects with artists ranging from Bob Dylan to Wim Wenders.

After a brief stint with a theatrical repertory group and writing several one-act plays that were produced off-Broadway, it was the "transformation" techniques of actor-director Joseph Chaikin in the mid-sixties that inspired Shepard to act. Many of his film characters are concealed and enigmatic, a reflection of his own publicity-shy nature.

Shepard made his feature motion picture debut when director Terrence Malick cast him as a wealthy and mysterious farmer in *Days of Heaven*. In 1980 he co-starred opposite Ellen Burstyn in *Resurrection*. He was featured in *Raggedy Man* with Sissy Spacek, and then co-starred with Jessica Lange in *Frances*, where the two met and established a long-term relationship. He followed his performance in *Frances* with one as test pilot Chuck Yeager in *The Right Stuff* for which he received an Oscar nomination for Best Actor. Again he teamed with Jessica Lange in *Country*, then played the starring role of "Eddie" in his own screen adaptation of his long-running play *Fool for Love*, directed by Robert Altman. He also appeared in *Crimes of the Heart* with Diane Keaton, Lange, and Spacek; followed by *Baby Boom* with Keaton; *Steel Magnolias*; and nonlead roles in *Thunderheart, The Pelican Brief*, and *Safe Passage*. He made his film directing debut with *Far North* in 1988.

—Kelly Otter

SHIMURA, Takashi

Nationality: Japanese. **Born:** Shoji Shimazaki in Hyogo prefecture, 12 March 1905. **Education:** Attended night courses in English at Kansai University, late 1920s. **Family:** Married Masako, 1937. **Career:** 1928—formed amateur theater group, Shichigatsu-za; then joined a commercial group, Kindai-za, 1930, and appeared on stage in Osaka and on tour; 1939—joined the Shinsen-za group; 1934—joined the Shinko Kinema studio, Kyoto: first important film role in *Chuji uridasu*, 1935; later worked for other studios, including Makino, Nikkatsu, Shochiku, and, from 1941, Toho; 1950-54—roles in *Rashomon* and *Seven Samurai* brought international attention; appeared on television from the mid-1960s. **Died:** Of emphysema in Tokyo, 11 February 1982.

Films as Actor:

1935 *Chuji uridasu* (Itami); *Tora-ko* (Sasukita)

1936 *Umon torimonocho: Harebare gojusan-tsugi*; **Naniwa ereji** (*Osaka Elegy*) (Mizoguchi) (as the detective); *Akanishi Kakita* (Itami) (as Tsunomata); *Shura yako: Edo no hana-osho*; *Hasshu kyokakujin*; *Maisen*; *Churetsu nikudan sanyushi*; *Hatsugaro-ondo*; *Irezumi chohan* (Kinugasa)

1937 *Seishun gonin otoko* (Part I, II); *Ryuko sokitai*; *Katana o nuite*; *Kisoji no tabigasa*

1938 *Jigoku no mushi* (Inagaki)

1939 *Myohoin Kanpachi* (Tsuji); *Shunju-ittoryu* (Marune); *Mumyo-yumyo* (Matsuda)

1940 *Genroku bushido*; *Adauchi kokyogaku* (Marune); *Zoko Shimizu-minato* (Makino); *Maboroshi-jo*; *Uemon torimono-cho: Uemon Edo-sugata* (as Abata no Keishiro)

1941 *Uchiiri zenya* (Marune); *Umi o wataru sairei* (Inagaki); *Edo saigo no hi* (Inagaki); *Miyamoto Musashi: Ichijo-ji no ketto* (Inagaki)

1942 *Torii Kyozaemon* (Uchida)

1943 *Sugata Sanshiro* (*Sanshiro Sugata*)) (Kurosawa) (as Hansuke Murai)

1944 *Ichiban utsukushiku* (*The Most Beautiful*) (Kurosawa) (as Goro Ishida)

1945 *Tota no o o fumu otokotachi* (*The Men Who Tread on the Tiger's Tail*) (Kurosawa) (as Kakaoka)

1946 *Waga seishun ni kui nashi* (*No Regrets for Our Youth*) (Kurosawa) (as Dokuazami)

1947 *Ginrei no hate* (*Snow Trail*) (Taniguchi)

1948 *Yoidore Tenshi* (*Drunken Angel*) (Kurosawa) (as Dr. Sanada)

1949 *Shizukanaru ketto* (*The Quiet Duel*) (Kurosawa) (as Kyonosuke Fujisaki); *Nora-inu* (*Stray Dog*) (Kurosawa) (as Chief Detective Sato)

1950 *Sukyandaru* (*Shubun*; *Scandal*) (Kurosawa) (as Hiruta); **Rashomon** (Kurosawa) (as the woodcutter)

1951 *Hakuchi* (*The Idiot*) (Kurosawa) (as Ono); *Mesu-inu* (Kimura); *Bakui ichidai* (Kimura)

1952 **Ikiru** (*To Live*; *Doomed*) (Kurosawa) (as Kanji Watanabe); *Ketto Kagiyanotsuji*; *Muteki*; *Bijo to yaju*

1954 *Saikaku ichidai-onna* (*The Life of Oharu*) (Mizoguchi); **Shichinin no samurai** (*The Seven Samurai*) (Kurosawa) (as Kambei); *Gojira* (*Godzilla, King of the Monsters*) (Honda) (as Dr. Yamane)

1955 *Otoko arite* (Maruyama); *Geisha Konatsu*; *Hitori neru yo no Konatsu* (Aoyagi); *Ikimono no kiroku* (*Record of a Living Being*; *I Live in Fear*; *What the Birds Knew*) (Kurosawa) (as Harada)

1956 *Ketto Ganryu-Jima* (*Musashi and Kojiro*; *Samurai Part III*) (Inagaki) (as official)

1957 *Kumonosujo* (*Throne of Blood*) (Kurosawa) (as Noriyasu Odaguru); *Ohtoro-jo no hanayome* (Matsuda); *Dotanba* (Uchida)

1958 *Chushingura* (Watanabe) (as Jubei Otake); *Ten to sen*; *Kakushi toride no san-akunin* (*Hidden Fortress*) (Kurosawa) (as General Izumi Nagakura)

1959 *Kotan no kuchibue* (Naruse); *Shobushi ro sono musume* (Shima); *Sengoki gunto-den* (*Saga of the Vagabonds*) (Sugie) (as Toki Saemon-no-jo)

1960 *Taiheiyo no arashi* (*I Bombed Pearl Harbor*) (Matsubayashi) (as Tosaku); *Warui yatsu hodo yoku nemuru* (*The Bad Sleep Well*) (Kurosawa) (as Moriyama); *Otoko tai otoko* (*Man against Man*) (Taniguchi) (as Taniguchi)

1961 *Yojimbo* (*The Bodyguard*) (Kurosawa) (as Tokuemon); *Osaka-jo monogatari* (*Daredevil in the Castle*) (Inagaki); *Ai to honoho to* (*Challenge to Live*) (Sugawa); *Mosura* (*Mothra*) (Honda)

1962 *Tsubaki Sanjuro* (*Sanjuro*) (Kurosawa) (as Kurofuji); *Chusingura* (Inagaki); *Futari no musuko* (*Different Sons*) (Chiba); *Yosei Gorath* (*Gorath*) (Honda)

1963 *Tengoku to jigoku* (*High and Low*) (Kurosawa) (as the director)

1964 **Kaidan** (*Kwaidan*) (Kobayashi) (as priest); *Samurai* (*Samurai Assassin*) (Okamoto); *Dai-tozoku* (*Samurai Pirate*) (Taniguchi)

1965 *Akahige* (*Red Beard*) (Kurosawa) (as Tokubei Izumiya); *Sandai kaiju chikyu saidai no kessen* (*Ghidrah*; *The Three Headed Monster*) (Honda)

1966 *Furankenshutain tai Baragon* (*Frankenstein Conquers the World*) (Honda); *Bankokku no yuro* (*Night in Bangkok*) (Chiba)

1967 *Nippon no ichiban nagai hi* (*The Emperor and a General*) (Okamoto) (as information clerk)

1968 *Kurobe no taiyo* (Kumai); *Zatoichi hatashi-jo* (Yasuda); *Gion matsuri* (*The Day the Sun Rose*) (Yamanuchi) (as Tsuneemon)

1969 *Furin-kazan* (*Samurai Banners*) (Inagaki); *Showa zankyo-den: Karajishi jingi*; *Zoku otoko wa tsuraiyo* (Yamada) (as the father)

1970 *Gunbatsu* (Horikawa)

1971 *Otokowa tsuraiyo: Torajiro koiuta* (Yamada)

1973 *Zatoichi's Conspiracy* (Yasuda) (as Sakuebi)

1974 *Ranru, no hata* (Yoshimura); *Shinkansen diabakuha* (Sato)

1976 *Zoku ningen kakumei* (Masuda); *Ninjutsu Sarutobi Sasuke*

1982 *Ogin Sama* (*Love and Faith of Ogin*) (Kamai) (as Sen Rikyu)

Publications

On SHIMURA: article—

The Annual Obituary 1982, New York, 1983.

* * *

Takashi Shimura began his career playing villains or fools in many prewar films. His first major performance in Akira Kurosawa's *Sugata Sanshiro* began his ascendancy as one of Japan's most skillful and distinctive actors. Although he worked in numerous genres throughout his career, he is most often associated with Kurosawa's films, becoming an indispensible partner with him for 30 years.

Shimura's first starring role was as the alcoholic ghetto doctor of *Drunken Angel*. He attempts to save the life of a reckless gangster, played by Toshiro Mifune, who suffers from tuberculosis. Their performances, showing strength beneath human frailty, depicted opposing attitudes towards the confusion of optimism and despair in post-war Japan. Shamiru continued to play characters with paternal relationships to the younger Mifune: in *The Quiet Duel* as a doctor who encourages his son to follow his profession; in *Stray Dog* as an older detective paired with a rookie; and in *Seven Samurai* as the leader of a group of samurai which includes Mifune.

Two of Shimura's most impressive roles were as a villainous lawyer who awakens to the meaning of justice in *Scandal* and as a middle-aged bureaucrat in *Ikiru*. Learning he has terminal cancer, Shimura's character wishes to redeem his egocentric life by building a children's park. The dramatic change of this ordinary businessman as he wavers between hope and disillusionment became Shimura's screen monument.

—Kyoko Hirano

SIDNEY, Sylvia

Nationality: American. **Born:** Sophie Koscow in the Bronx, New York, 8 August 1910 (some sources give August 10); adopted by her stepfather, and took the name Sidney. **Education:** Attended Washington Irving High School; studied acting at the Theatre Guild School, New York. **Family:** Married 1) the publisher Bennett Cerf, 1935 (divorced 1936); 2) the actor Luther Adler, 1938 (divorced 1946), son: Jacob; 3) Carlton Alsop, 1947 (divorced). **Career:** 1926—professional stage debut in *Challenges of Youth*, Washington, D.C.; 1927—Broadway debut in *The Squall*; 1929—film debut (credited) in *Thru Different Eyes*; 1931-35—contract with Paramount; then worked with Walter Wanger and other producers and studios; also continued to work on stage, and, from the 1950s, on television; toured with the National Repertory Company in the 1960s; later roles in *Enter Laughing*, 1963, *Barefoot in the Park*, 1964, and *Vieux Carré*, 1977; 1978—appeared as Mrs. Carlson in the pilot for TV series *WKRP in Cincinnati*; 1986—in TV series *Morningstar/Eveningstar*.

Films as Actress:

1927   *Broadway Nights* (Boyle) (uncredited)
1929   *Thru Different Eyes* (Blystone) (as witness)
1931   *City Streets* (Mamoulian) (as Nan Cooley); *Confessions of a Co-ed* (Burton and Murphy) (as Patricia); *An American Tragedy* (von Sternberg) (as Roberta Alden); *Street Scene* (King Vidor) (as Rose Maurrant)
1932   *Ladies of the Big House* (Gering) (as Kathleen Storm); *The Miracle Man* (McLeod) (as Helen Smith); *Merrily We Go to Hell* (Arzner) (as Joan Prentice); *Make Me a Star* (Beaudine) (as herself); *Madame Butterfly* (Gering) (title role)
1933   *Pick-Up* (Gering) (as Mary Richards); *Jennie Gerhardt* (Gering) (title role)
1934   *Good Dame* (Gering) (as Lillie Taylor); *Thirty Day Princess* (Gering) (as Nancy Lane/Princess Catterina Theodora Margerita Zizzi)
1935   *Behold My Wife* (Leisen) (as Tonita Stormcloud); *Accent on Youth* (Ruggles) (as Linda Brown); *Mary Burns, Fugitive* (William K. Howard) (title role)
1936   *Trail of the Lonesome Pine* (Hathaway) (as June Tolliver); *Fury* (Fritz Lang) (as Katherine Grant)
1937   *Sabotage* (*Hidden Power*; *A Woman Alone*) (Hitchcock) (as Sylvia Verloc); *You Only Live Once* (Fritz Lang) (as Joan Graham); *Dead End* (Wyler) (as Drina)

1938   *You and Me* (Fritz Lang) (as Helen Dennis)
1939   *. . . One Third of a Nation* (Murphy) (as Mary Rogers)
1941   *The Wagons Roll at Night* (Enright) (as Flo Lorraine)
1945   *Blood on the Sun* (Lloyd) (as Iris Hilliard)
1946   *The Searching Wind* (Dieterle) (as Cassie Bowman); *Mr. Ace* (Marin) (as Margaret Wyndham Chase)
1947   *Love from a Stranger* (Whorf) (as Cecily Harrington)
1952   *Les Misérables* (Milestone) (as Fantine)
1955   *Violent Saturday* (Fleischer) (as Elsie)
1956   *Behind the High Wall* (Biberman) (as Hilda Carmichael)
1971   *Do Not Fold, Spindle, or Mutilate* (Post—for TV)
1973   *Summer Wishes, Winter Dreams* (Cates) (as Mrs. Pritchett)
1975   *The Secret Night Caller* (Jameson—for TV) (as Kitty); *Winner Take All* (Bogart—for TV)
1976   *God Told Me To* (*Demon*) (Cohen) (as Elizabeth Mullin); *Raid on Entebbe* (Kershner—for TV) (as Dora Bloch); *Death at Love House* (*The Shrine of Lorna Love*) (Swackhamer—for TV)
1977   *I Never Promised You a Rose Garden* (Page) (as Miss Coral); *Snowbeast* (Wallerstein—for TV)
1978   *Siege* (Pearce—for TV); *Damien: Omen II* (Taylor) (as Aunt Marion)
1980   *FDR: The Last Year* (Page—for TV); *The Gossip Columnist* (Sheldon—for TV); *The Shadow Box* (Paul Newman—for TV)
1981   *Small Killing* (Stern—for TV)
1982   *Having It All* (Zwick—for TV) (as Marney)
1983   *Hammett* (Wenders) (as Donaldina Cameron); *Corrupt* (*Order of Death*) (Faenza) (as Margaret Smith)
1984   *Finnegan Begin Again* (Joan Micklin Silver—for TV) (as Margaret Finnegan)
1985   *An Early Frost* (Erman—for TV) (as Beatrice McKenna)
1986   *Morning Star/Evening Star* (Jameson—for TV)
1987   *Pals* (Antonio—for TV) (as Fern Stobbs)
1988   *Beetlejuice* (Burton) (as Juno)
1991   *Andre's Mother* (Reinisch)
1992   *Used People* (Kidron) (as Becky)
1996   *Mars Attacks!* (Tim Burton) (as heartland youth's grandma)

Publications

By SIDNEY: books—

Needlepoint Book, New York, 1968.
Question and Answer Book on Needlepoint, New York, 1974.

By SIDNEY: article—

"Screen Gem: The Bright Star of *Fury*, *City Streets*, *Blood on the Sun* Talks Frankly about Times Past," in *Interview* (New York), January 1990.

On SIDNEY: book—

Parish, James Robert, *The Paramount Pretties*, New Rochelle, New York, 1972.

On SIDNEY: articles—

Springer, John, "Sylvia Sidney," in *Films in Review* (New York), January 1966.
Bowers, Ron, "Legendary Ladies of the Movies," in *Films in Review* (New York), June-July 1973.
Tuchman, M., "Checklist 102: Sylvia Sidney," in *Monthly Film Bulletin* (London), November 1974.

Sylvia Sidney

Current Biography 1981, New York, 1981.

Shipman, David, in *The Great Movie Stars*, rev. ed., London, 1990.

*   *   *

Sylvia Sidney was one of Paramount's biggest stars during the 1930s. What made her unique during the heyday of the studio system was her physical type and her persistent emphasis of professionalism over stardom. In comparison with her contemporary female stars, Sidney was far from the recognized ideal of beauty. Her tiny figure, heart-shaped face, deep expressive eyes, and large mouth were in direct contrast to the tall, linear elegance embodied by Greta Garbo and Katharine Hepburn. Instead of enjoying a position of superiority because of classical beauty, Sidney was usually dominated, evoking an image of the vulnerable girl, the type an audience immediately responded to with loving protection. Her disregard for the trappings of celebrity rewarded her with unglamorous yet distinctive roles. She specialized in poor or criminal women characters. Unlike other actresses who occasionally played girls from the wrong side of the tracks, her heroines did not find economic comfort or acquire an elevated social status. Such socioeconomic criticism of the Great Depression era was singular in the American cinema, and Sidney was the only actress continually associated with this type of film.

Sidney worked with some of the period's best filmmakers, beginning with Josef von Sternberg, King Vidor, William Wyler, Alfred Hitchcock, and a lesser-known but equally fine director, Marion Gering. Rouben Mamoulian used her to establish the archetypical film gunmoll in *City Streets*. This stage of her career culminated in Fritz Lang's *Fury* and *You Only Live Once*. In these psychologically motivated roles, Sidney once again demonstrated her unmatched emotional range.

Ironically, Sidney claimed her critically praised roles were restricting her versatility. Her few ventures into comedy, *Thirty Day Princess* and *Accent on Youth*, did little to prevent her continued typecasting. After virtually retiring from Hollywood films in the mid-1940s, Sidney acted on stage and television. She made a triumphant comeback to feature films in *Summer Wishes, Winter Dreams*, winning her first and only Oscar nomination, and since then has enlivened several theatrical features and television films. Her best roles have been Robert Preston's elderly, delusional wife in *Finnegan Begin Again*; the grandmother of AIDS-afflicted Aidan Quinn in *An Early Frost*; and what must be her most unusual role, the tough "spiritual world" caseworker in *Beetlejuice*. Ironically, in her old age, Sidney has been able to achieve a versatility that eluded her earlier in her career.

—Věroslav Hába, updated by Audrey E. Kupferberg

SIGNORET, Simone

Nationality: French. **Born:** Simone-Herniette-Charlotte Kaminker in Wiesbaden, Germany, to French parents, 25 March 1921. **Education:** Attended schools in Paris; teaching degree. **Family:** Married 1) the director Yves Allégret, 1947 (divorced 1950), daughter: Catherine; 2) the actor Yves Montand, 1951. **Career:** Early 1940s—worked as teacher, then typist for *Le Nouveau Temps* newspaper; 1942—film debut in *Le Prince charmant*; 1946—leading role in *Macadam*; 1954—in stage version of French version of Miller's *The Crucible* in Paris with Montand, and in later film version, 1957; 1958—English-language role in *Room at the Top*; also appeared in *Macbeth* in London, and on television in the U.S. **Awards:** Best Foreign Actress, British Academy, for *Casque d'or*, 1952; Best Foreign Actress, British Academy, for *Witches of Salem*, 1957; Best Foreign Actress, British Academy, Best Actress Academy Award, and Best Actress, Cannes Festival,

for *Room at the Top*, 1959; French César for Best Actress, for *La Vie devant soi*, 1977. **Died:** 30 September 1985.

Films as Actress:

1942   *Le Prince charmant* (Boyer); *Les Visiteurs du soir* (*The Devil's Envoy*) (Carné); *Bolero* (Boyer)

1943   *La Bôite aux rêves* (Yves Allégret); *Adieu Léonard* (Prévert); *L'Ange de la nuit* (Berthomieu); *Beatrice devant le désir* (de Marguenat)

1945   *Les Démons de l'Aube* (Yves Allégret); *Le Couple idéal* (Roland)

1946   *Macadam* (*Back Streets of Paris*) (Blistène)

1947   *Fantômas* (Sacha)

1948   *Dédée d'Anvers* (Yves Allégret) (title role); *Against the Wind* (Crichton) (as Michele); *L'Impasse de deux anges* (Tourneur)

1949   *Manèges* (*The Cheat*) (Yves Allégret) (as Dora); *Four Days Leave* (*Swiss Tour*) (Lindtberg) (as Yvonne)

1950   *Le Traqué* (*Gunman in the Streets*) (Tuttle); *Ombre et lumière* (Calef) (as Isabell); *La Ronde* (*Circle of Love*) (Ophüls) (as the Whore)

1952   *Casque d'or* (*The Golden Helmet*) (Becker) (as Marie)

1953   *Thérèse Raquin* (*The Adultress*) (Carné) (title role)

1955   *Les Diaboliques* (*Diabolique*; *The Fiends*) (Clouzot) (as Nicole Horner)

1956   *La Mort en ce jardin* (*Death in the Garden*; *Evil Eden*; *Gina*) (Buñuel) (as Djin); *Die Wind Rose* (Bellon)

1957   *Les Sorcières de Salem* (*Witches of Salem*) (Rouleau) (as Elizabeth Proctor)

1958   *Room at the Top* (Clayton) (as Alice Aisgill)

1960   *Les Mauvais Coups* (*Naked Autumn*) (Leterrier) (as Roberte); *Adua e le compagne* (*Love à la Carte*) (Pietrangeli) (as Adua)

1961   "Jenny de Lacours" ep. of *Les Amours célébrés* (Girod) (title role)

1962   *Term of Trial* (Glenville) (as Anna Weir)

1963   *Le Jour et l'heure* (*The Day and the Hour*) (Clément) (as Thérèse Dutheil); *Dragées au poivre* (*Sweet and Sour*) (Baratier) (as Geneviève); *Le Joli Mai* (Marker—doc) (as narrator)

1965   *Ship of Fools* (Kramer) (as La Condesa); *Compartiment tueurs* (*The Sleeping Car Murders*) (Costa-Gavras) (as Elaine Darrès)

1966   *Paris, brûle-t-il?* (*Is Paris Burning?*) (Clément) (as cafe owner)

1967   *The Deadly Affair* (Lumet) (as Elsa Fennan); *Games* (Harrington) (as Lisa Schindler)

1968   *The Sea Gull* (Lumet) (as Arkadina)

1969   *L'Armée des ombres* (*The Shadow Army*) (Melville) (as Mathilde); *Mister Freedom* (Klein)

1970   *L'Aveu* (*The Confession*) (Costa-Gavras) (as Lise); *Comptes à rebours* (*Countdown*) (Pigaut); *L'Américain* (Bozzuffi) (as Leone)

1971   *Le Chat* (*The Cat*) (Granier-Deferre) (as Clemence); *La Veuve Couderc* (*The Widow Couderc*) (Granier-Deferre) (title role)

1973   *Rude journée pour la reine*(*Rough Day for the Queen*) (Allio) (as Jeanne); *Les Granges brulées* (*The Investigator*) (Chapot) (as Rose)

1974   *La Chair de l'orchidée* (*Flesh and the Orchid*; *Flesh of the Orchid*) (Chereau) (as Lady Vamos)

1976   *The Case against Ferro* (Corneau) (as Térèse Ganay)

1977   *Madame Rosa* (*La Vie devant soi*) (Mizrahi) (title role)

1978   *Judith Therpauve* (Chereau) (title role)

1981   *Cher Inconnu* (*I Sent a Letter to My Love*) (Mizrahi) (as Louise)

1982   *L'Adolescente* (*The Adolescent*) (Moreau) (as Mamie)

1983   *L'Etoile du nord* (Granier-Deferre) (as Madame Baron)

Simone Signoret with Laurence Harvey in *Room at the Top*

Publications

By SIGNORET: books—

La Nostalgie n'est plus ce qu'elle etait, Paris, 1976, as *Nostalgia Isn't What It Used to Be*, New York, 1976.
Le Lendemain, cela était souriante?, Paris, 1979.
Adieu, Volodia (novel), Paris, 1985.

On SIGNORET: books—

Sandre, Didier, *Simone Signoret*, Paris, 1981.
Monserrat, Joëlle, with Jacques Lorcey, *Simone Signoret*, Paris, 1983.
Durant, Philippe, *Simone Signoret: Une Vie*, Paris, 1988.
Périsset, Maurice, *Simone Signoret*, Paris, 1988.
David, Catherine, *Simone Signoret, ou la mémoire par partagée*, Paris, 1990.
Allégret, Catherine, *Les souvenirs—et les regrets aussi*, Paris, 1994.

On SIGNORET: articles—

Current Biography 1960, New York, 1960.
Schupp, P., "Simone Signoret: Le courage de la détermination," in *Séquences* (Montreal), July 1983.

Obituary in *Variety* (New York), 2 October 1985.
Toubiana, Serge, "Sacré monstre," in *Cahiers du Cinéma* (Paris), November 1985.
Granier-Deferre, P., obituary in *Positif* (Paris), February 1986.

*   *   *

Film stars—female ones, at any rate—are not supposed to grow old, and certainly not faster than the rest of us. At worst, they should age gradually and gracefully, retaining slimness and glamour well into their sixties, prompting envious mutters of "She doesn't look a day over...." Simone Signoret broke all these rules, which may be why she inspired so many ungallant comparisons. Writers likened her to an aging boxer, to Brando, Michel Simon, and Margaret Rutherford. Loss of glamour may be condoned, but deliberate rejection of it, Signoret's trademark in her later years, arouses resentment. With characteristic forthrightness she titled her 1976 autobiography *Nostalgia Isn't What It Used to Be*, as if to call attention to this deliberate rejection of her earlier, glamour days.

The young Signoret radiated beauty and a ripe sensuality which glowed tangibly from the screen. She moved with the indolent languor of a woman supremely confident in her own powers of attraction; the slow, sleepy smile and the heavy-lidded eyes irresistibly evoked thoughts of warm bedrooms and summer meadows. Inevitably, she was cast time and again as a prostitute, a profession amply represented in the post-war French cinema.

So it was as a streetwalker that she first came to international notice, opening and closing the sexual carousel in Ophüls's shimmering *La Ronde*, and touchingly bemused in her scene with Gérard Philipe's emotionally anesthetized count. A year later, another period piece raised her to the summit of her early years: as Serge Reggiani's lover in Becker's *Casque d'or*, she brought to the scenes of their brief, doomed idyll an erotic intensity which suffused the whole film with immediacy and warmth.

Signoret was never petite. The breadth of her shoulders and her squarely planted stance suggested a tenacious practicality, a vulnerable strength. As a murderess, she could be both credible and sympathetic: as one of Zola's pair of guilt-ridden lovers in *Thérèse Raquin*, or as the seemingly vulnerable yet scheming blond bombshell accomplice in the homicidal labyrinth of Clouzot's *Les Diaboliques*, the role that cemented her international renown and became an archetype thereafter in imitation upon ripoff of the Boileau-Narcejac thriller, including three remakes with Tuesday Weld, Kate Vernon, and, most recently, Sharon Stone filling Signoret's shoes.

According to rumor, no British actress could be found with the requisite blend of sophistication and sensuality to play the older woman driven to suicide by her social climbing lover (Laurence Harvey) in Jack Clayton's *Room at the Top*. True or not, Signoret indisputably lacked neither; feline and exotic amid the bleak Northern terraces of the British New Wave, she picked up an Oscar for her performance in this, her first English-language film, and a string of Hollywood offers, all refused. Politics and her marriage to singer-turned-actor Yves Montand (whose international renown was also cemented by an appearance in a Clouzot film, *The Wages of Fear*) increasingly took precedence in her life. Both of them were banned from French television, radio, and state-run theaters during the 1960s, and at one point were refused entry to the United States for their left-wing views.

Defiantly unconventional, Signoret made no attempt to conceal the growing heaviness of her face and figure, even emphasizing it with drably unglamorous roles. Often she played women oppressed by the past: a survivor of the concentration camps in Lumet's downbeat thriller *The Deadly Affair* based on a John Le Carré novel; an impressive Arkadina in the same director's *The Sea Gull*, co-starring Vanessa Redgrave, another actress known and ostracized for her political views; movingly dignified as the fated Resistance fighter in *L'Armée des ombres*; hiding frustrated love beneath outward bitterness in *Le Chat*; and vulnerability to her illicit love for doomed Oskar Werner in *Ship of Fools*. Such roles were never depressing, given the vitality of her presence.

Age could do nothing to lessen the beauty of her smile, which when it came still lit up her face with protective tenderness. Signoret had always said she would go on acting until she could play grandmothers, and now she could, superbly: a surrogate in *La Vie devant soi* and the real thing in Jeanne Moreau's nostalgically evocative *L'Adolescente*. From every man's dream mistress to every child's ideal grandmother—there are worse progressions.

—Philip Kemp, updated by John McCarty

SIMMONS, Jean

Nationality: British/American. **Born:** Jean Merilyn Simmons in London, England, 31 January 1929; became U.S. citizen, 1956. **Education:** Attended the Orange Hill School for Girls; Aida Foster School of Dancing. **Family:** Married 1) the actor Stewart Granger, 1950 (divorced 1960), daughter: Tracy; 2) the director Richard Brooks, 1960 (divorced 1977), daughter: Kate. **Career:** 1944—film debut in *Give Us the Moon*; 1945—contract with J. Arthur Rank; 1949—on English stage in *Power of Darkness*; 1951-52—contract with Howard Hughes (RKO); 1964—U.S. stage debut in *Big Fish, Little Fish*; also toured with the musical *A Little Night Music*; in TV mini-series *The Dain Curse*, 1978, *Beggarman, Thief*, 1979, *The Thorn Birds*, 1983, *North and South*, 1985, *North and South II*, 1986, *Great Expectations* (as Miss Havisham), 1989, and *Dark Shadows*, 1991; in TV series *Dark Shadows*, 1991, and *Angel Falls*, 1993. **Awards:** Best Actress, Venice Festival, for *Hamlet*, 1948. **Address:** c/o A. Morgan Maree, Jr. & Associates, 6363 Wilshire Boulevard, Los Angeles, CA 90048, U.S.A.

Films as Actress:

1944   *Give Us the Moon* (Guest) (as Heidi); *Mr. Emmanuel* (French); *Kiss the Bride Goodbye* (Stein) (as Molly Dodd); *Meet Sexton Blake* (Harlow) (as Eva Watkins)

1945   *Sports Day* (*The Colonel's Cup*) (Short); *The Way to the Stars* (*Johnny in the Clouds*) (Asquith) (as singer)

1946   *Caesar and Cleopatra* (Pascal) (as handmaiden/harpist); ***Great Expectations*** (Lean) (as young Estella)

1947   *Hungry Hill* (Hurst) (as Jane Brodrick); ***Black Narcissus*** (Powell and Pressburger) (as Kanchi); *Uncle Silas* (*The Inheritance*) (Frank) (as Caroline Ruthyn); *The Woman in the Hall* (Jack Lee) (as Jay Blake)

1948   *Hamlet* (Olivier) (as Ophelia)

1949   *Adam and Evalyn* (*Adam and Evelyne*) (French) (as Evalyn Wallace); *The Blue Lagoon* (Launder) (as Emmeline Foster)

1950   "Sanatorium" ep. of *Trio* (French) (as Eve Bishop); *Cage of Gold* (Dearden) (as Judith Moray); *So Long at the Fair* (Darnborough and Fisher) (as Vicky Barton); *The Clouded Yellow* (Thomas) (as Sophie Malraux)

1953   *Androcles and the Lion* (Erskine) (as Lavinia); *Angel Face* (Preminger); *Affair with a Stranger* (Rowland) (as Carolyn Parker); *The Actress* (Cukor) (as Ruth Gordon Jones); *The Robe* (Koster) (as Diana); *Young Bess* (Sidney) (title role)

1954   *She Couldn't Say No* (Lloyd Bacon) (as Corby Lane); *The Egyptian* (Curtiz) (as Merit); *Desiree* (Koster) (title role); *A Bullet Is Waiting* (Farrow) (as Cally Canham)

1955   *Guys and Dolls* (Mankiewicz) (as Sarah Browne); *Footsteps in the Fog* (Lubin) (as Lily Watkins)

1956   *Hilda Crane* (Dunne) (title role)

1957   *This Could Be the Night* (Wise) (as Anne Leeds); *Until They Sail* (Wise) (as Barbara Leslie Forbes)

1958   *Home before Dark* (LeRoy) (as Charlotte Bronn); *The Big Country* (Wyler) (as Julie Maragon)

1959   *This Earth Is Mine* (Henry King) (as Elizabeth Rambeau)

1960   *Spartacus* (Kubrick) (as Varinia); *Elmer Gantry* (Richard Brooks) (as Sister Sharon Falconer); *The Grass Is Greener* (Donen) (as Hattie Durant)

1963   *All the Way Home* (Segal) (as Mary Follet)

1965   *Life at the Top* (Kotcheff) (as Susan Lampton)

1966   *Mister Buddwing* (*Woman without a Face*) (Delbert Mann) (as the blond)

1967   *Divorce American Style* (Yorkin) (as Nancy Downes); *Rough Night in Jericho* (Laven) (as Molly Lang)

1968   *Heidi* (Delbert Mann—for TV) (as Fräulein Rottenmeier)

1969   *The Happy Ending* (Richard Brooks) (as Mary Wilson)

1971   *Say Hello to Yesterday* (Rakoff) (as Woman)

1975   *Mr. Sycamore* (Kohner) (as Estelle Benbow)

1978   *Dominique* (Anderson) (title role)

Jean Simmons

1981   *A Small Killing* (Steven Hilliard Stern—for TV); *Golden Gate* (Wendkos—for TV); *Valley of the Dolls* (Grauman—for TV) (as Helen Lawson)

1984   *December Flower* (Frears—for TV)

1985   *Midas Valley* (Trikonis—for TV)

1987   *Perry Mason: The Case of the Lost Love* (Satlof—for TV) (as Laura Kilgallen)

1988   *Going Undercover* (Clarke) (as Maxine De La Hunt); *The Dawning* (Knights—released in U.S. in 1993) (as Aunt Mary); *Inherit the Wind* (David Greene—for TV) (as Lucy Brady); *A Friendship in Vienna* (Arthur Allan Seidelman—for TV) (as narrator)

1990   *The Laker Girls* (Bruce Seth Green—for TV) (as Connie Harrison); *People Like Us* (Billy Hale—for TV) (as Peach); *Sensibility and Sense* (David Hugh Jones—for TV)

1992   *They Do It with Mirrors* (Norman Stone—for TV) (as Carrie-Louise Serrocold)

1994   *One More Mountain* (Lowry—for TV) (as Sarah Keyes)

1995   *Daisies in December* (Haber—for TV) (as Katherine Palmer); *How to Make an American Quilt* (Moorhouse) (as Em)

Publications

On SIMMONS: articles—

Current Biography 1952, New York, 1952.

Marrill, Alvin H., "Jean Simmons," in *Films in Review* (New York), February 1972.

*   *   *

In an early screen appearance—a cameo in *The Way to the Stars* in which she briefly sang "Let him go, let him tarry" at a troop show—Jean Simmons made an instant and indelible impression. The fascination of that appearance—a song of adult sexuality performed quite unselfconsciously by a very young girl—lay in the way it collapsed any such opposition. The ambiguity was brilliantly used by David Lean in Simmons's young Estella of *Great Expectations*: indeed, the film never quite recovers from the shock of Jean Simmons growing up to be Valerie Hobson.

Typically, the British cinema of the late 1940s, divided among plodding "good taste," elephantine comedy, and determinedly risqué and much be-cleaveged period melodrama, was quite incapable of developing this extraordinary talent, or even of understanding its nature. Powell and Pressburger grasped something of the persona's possibilities, but her role in *Black Narcissus* (Sabu's Indian seductress) was small and underdeveloped. Otherwise, predictably, the "innocent" side of the persona was played at the expense of the sexual; even so, her presence was registered as sufficiently provocative (especially in one so young and "sweet") for strenuous efforts to be necessary to chastise and subdue it in *The Clouded Yellow*. Yet the presence survived it all; it even survived *Hamlet*, in which her Ophelia, despite (or perhaps because of) her inexperience in Shakespeare, despite the encumbrance of an absurd blond wig, and Olivier's turgid direction, was one of the more bearable performances.

It was Preminger in *Angel Face* who first realized fully the complexity of her potential, much to the consternation of the British critics. Here the innocent/sexual tension is fully developed in a characterization that manages to be touching, vulnerable, sensitive, selfish, manipulative, pathological, and horrific all at the same time; the devastating effect of the ending derives as much from the accumulated energies and frustrations conveyed by Simmons's performance as from Preminger's casual and poker-faced abruptness. Perfectly complementing this was her work in *The Actress*, where the unerring instinct

and feminine sympathy of Cukor helped her to realize most captivatingly the persona's positive connotations, its eagerness, energy, and exuberance. These two films, with *Elmer Gantry*, mark the peak of Simmons's achievement.

Ultimately, Simmons's Hollywood career has proved scarcely more satisfying than her British one. The problem has lain partly in the persona itself and its resistance to age: its fascination, suggestiveness, and ambiguity are necessarily contingent upon youthfulness, and as the girl became a woman the persona had to be restructured. Her relationship (marital and professional) with Richard Brooks produced one more rounded and complex realization of Simmons's potentiality, her Sister Sharon in *Elmer Gantry*. Here the innocent/knowing ambiguity reaches a definitive formulation, the film playing on Sharon's genuineness/fraudulence, integrity/self-deception. The other Brooks collaboration, *The Happy Ending*, suffers from the director's heavy-handed approach to social significance: the film looks as if he had just read an introductory guide to feminism.

Mired in television dreck such as the soapy *Angel Falls* and the recycled *Dark Shadows*, Jean Simmons remains a gallant trouper who, unlike many contemporaries, gives fully realized performances even as a guest on *Murder, She Wrote*. For adoring fans, a big-screen return in the A-picture ensemble of *How to Make an American Quilt* was cause for celebration. Pinpointing what went wrong with her film career is a graver pastime. Rumors still abound that disgruntled eccentric Howard Hughes set out to wreck her American career when he ran RKO. Whether that charge can ever be proven does not explain why she so often settled for comfortable leading lady status (*Spartacus*, *The Big Country*, *The Robe*, *The Egyptian*) when she should have been toplining her own star vehicles. In 1958 she gave heart and soul to the quasi-feminist soap opera, *Home before Dark* by audaciously conveying a woman belittled into a breakdown for not measuring up to the 1950s ideals of physical beauty and womanliness. Unleashing a tour de force in this little-seen movie, Simmons lends her radiance also to more popular melodramas such as *This Earth Is Mine*, *Until They Sail*, and the now-campy *Hilda Crane*. Is there a more apropos symbol of fifties's domestic directives than Simmons's used-goods Hilda eyeing two gorgeous marital prospects while snuggled in a mink that has seen better days? Pausing to praise her comedic éclat in *Divorce American Style* and *The Grass Is Greener* and marveling at her grasp of heart-ravaged grief in *All the Way Home*, aficionados can only shake their heads at her descent into television's *Laker Girls*. Sort of *The Star* that Got Away, Simmons's iridescent work brings a tinge of regret about the wasted potential of an indisputably great actress and an unrealized movie superstar.

—Robin Wood, updated by Robert J. Pardi

SIMON, Michel

Nationality: Swiss. **Born:** François Simon in Geneva, 9 April 1895. **Education:** Attended the École Evangeliste de la rue Calvin; Collège du Genève. **Family:** Married; son: François. **Career:** Worked as photographer and boxer; debut in music hall as an acrobat-clown-dancer; 1920—legitimate stage debut in *Measure for Measure* in Paris; 1922-25—member of Pitoëff troupe, Paris; 1925—film debut in *La Puissance du travail*; 1929—first big stage success in *Jean de la Lune*, and in film version, 1931; later stage roles in *Hamlet*, *Siegfried*, and *Pygmalion*; also a singer. **Awards:** Best Actor, Berlin Festival, for *Le Vieil Homme et l'enfant*, 1967. **Died:** In Bry-sur-Marne, 30 May 1975.

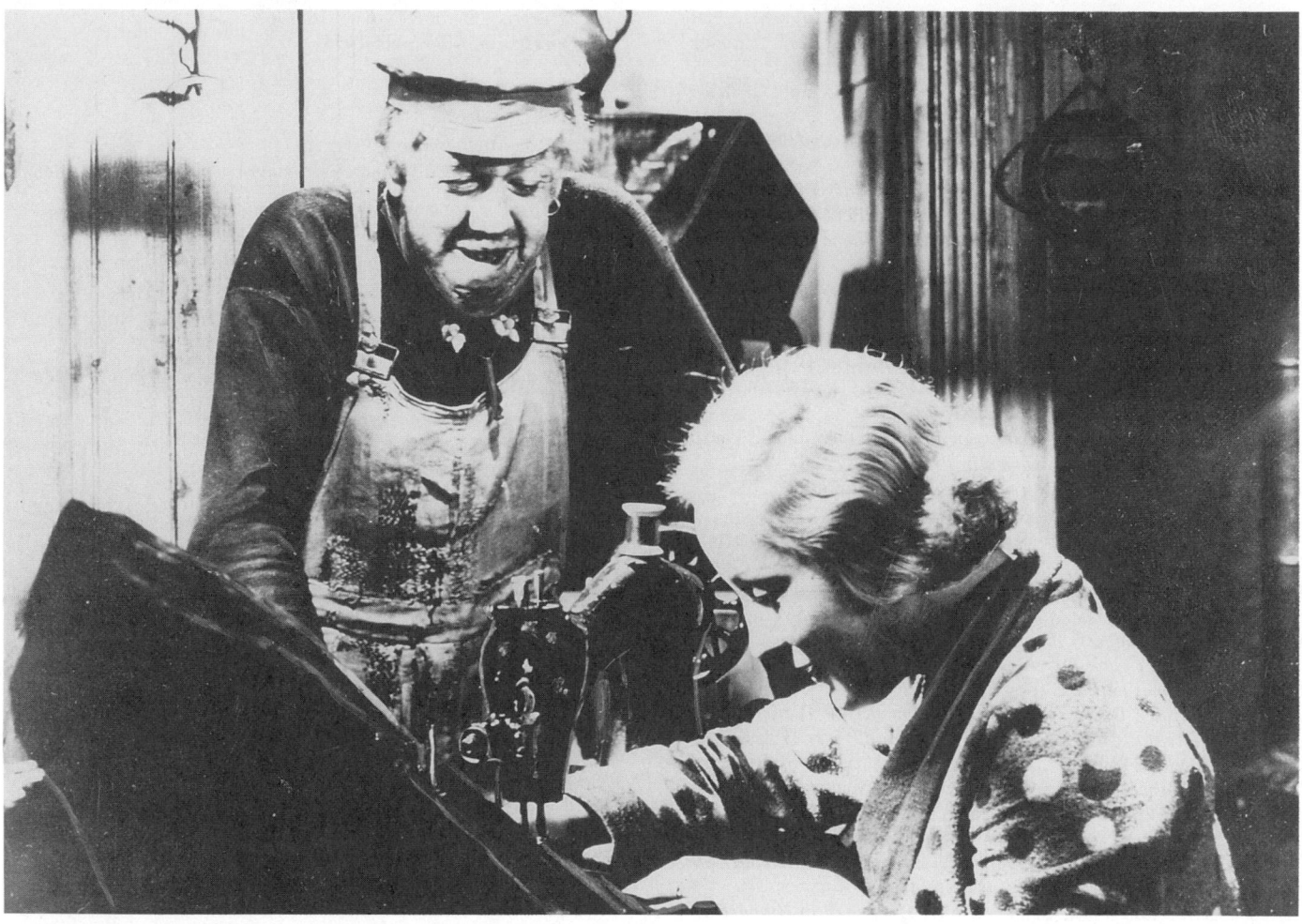

Michel Simon with Dita Parlo in *L'Atalante*

Films as Actor:

1925   *La Puissance du travail* (*La Vocation d'André Carrel*) (Choux) (as Marius Duret); **Feu Mathias Pascal** (*The Late Matthew Pascal*) (L'Herbier) (as Pomino)

1926   *L'Inconnue des six jours* (Sti) (as servant)

1927   *Casanova* (Volkoff)

1928   **La Passion de Jeanne d'Arc** (*The Passion of Joan of Arc*) (Dreyer) (as Judge Lemaitre); *Tire au flanc* (Renoir) (as Joseph)

1929   *Pivoine* (Sauvage) (title role); *L'Enfant de l'amour* (L'Herbier) (as Loredan)

1931   *Jean de la Lune* (Choux) (as Clotaire); *On purge Bébé* (Renoir) (as Chouilloux); *La Chienne* (Renoir) (as Maurice Legrand); *Baleydier* (Mamy) (title role)

1932   **Boudu sauvé des eaux** (*Boudu Saved from Drowning*) (Renoir) (title role)

1933   *Miquette et sa mère* (Maurice) (as Monchablon); *Du haut en bas* (Pabst) (as Bodoletz); *Leopold le bien-aimé* (Brun) (as Ponce)

1934   *L'Atalante* (Vigo) (as Le Père Jules); *Lac aux Dames* (Marc Allégret) (as Oscar Lissenhop); *Le Bonheur* (L'Herbier) (as Noël Malpias)

1935   *Quand la vie était belle* (*Le Bébé de l'Escadron*) (Sti) (as Perrot-Joly); *Ademat au Moyen-Age* (de Marguenat) (as Lord Pickwickdam); *Amants et voleurs* (Bernard) (as Doizeau)

1936   *Sous les yeux d'occident* (*Razumov*) (Marc Allégret) (as Lespera); *Moutonnet* (*Moutonnet à Paris*; *Une Aventure de Moutonnet*) (Sti) (as Frecheville); *Les Jumeaux de Brighton* (Heymann) (as La Brosse); *Le Mort en fuite* (Berthomieu) (as Achille Baluchet); *Jeunes filles de Paris* (Vermorel) (as Milord et Baron de Beaupoil); *Faisons un rêve* (Guitry) (as himself)

1937   *La Bataille silencieuse* (*Le Poisson Chinois*) (Billon) (as Captain Sauvin); *Naples au baiser de feu* (*The Kiss of Fire*) (Genina) (as Michel); *Boulot aviateur* (*Fripons, voleurs, et cie*) (de Canonge) (as Baron Bobeche); *Drôle de drame* (*Bizarre Bizarre*) (Carné) (as Félix Chapel/Irwin Molyneux); *Si tu m'aimes* (*Mirages*) (Ryder) (as Michel); *Le Choc en retour* (Monca and Keroul) (as Laverdac)

1938   *Les Disparus de Saint-Agil* (*Boys School*) (Christian-Jaque) (as Lemel); **Le Quai des brumes** (*Port of Shadows*) (Carné) (as Zabel); *Les Nouveaux Riches* (Berthomieu) (as Martinet); *La Chaleur du sein* (Boyer) (as Michel Quercy); *Le Ruisseau* (Autant-Lara) (as Comte Edouard de Bourgogne); *Belle étoile* (de Baroncelli) (as Leon)

1939   *Eusèbe Deputé* (Berthomieu) (as Eusèbe Bonbonneau); *Le Dernier Tournant* (Chenal) (as Nick Marino); *Noix de Coco* (Boyer) (as Josserand); *Le Fin de jour* (*The End of a Day*) (Duvivier) (as Cabrissade); *Cavalcade d'amour* (Bernard) (as Diogene); *Circonstances atténuantes* (*Extenuating Circumstances*) (Boyer) (as the lawyer); *Fric-Frac* (Autant-Lara) (as Jo-les-bras-coupés); *Derrière la façade* (*32 Rue*

Montmartre) (Lacombe) (as Picking); *Les Musiciens du ciel* (Lacombe) (as Captain Simon); *Paris New York* (Mirande and Heymann) (as Boucheron)

1940   *La Comédie du bonheur* (L'Herbier) (as Jourdain); *La Tosca* (*The Story of Tosca*) (Koch) (as Scarpia)

1942   *Il re sè diverte* (*The King's Jester*) (Bonnard) (as Triboulet); *La Dame de l'ouest* (Koch) (as Carras)

1943   *Au bonheur des Dames* (*Shop-Girls of Paris*) (Cayatte) (as Baudu); *Vautrin* (*Vautrin the Thief*) (Billon) (title role)

1945   *Un Ami viendra ce soir* (*A Friend Will Come Tonight*) (Bernard) (as Michel Lemaret)

1946   *Panique* (*Panic*) (Duvivier) (as Hire); *La Taverne de poisson couronne* (Chanas) (as Captain Palmer)

1947   *Non coupable* (*Not Guilty*) (Decoin) (as Dr. Ancelin); *Les Amants du Pont Saint-Jean* (Decoin) (as Garonne); *La Carcasse et le Tord-Cou* (Chanas) (as Le Tord-Cou)

1948   *Fabiola* (Blasetti) (as Fabian Sévère)

1949   *La Beauté du diable* (*Beauty and the Devil*) (Clair) (as Faust/Mephistopheles); *Women in Prison* (Radvanyi)

1950   *Les Deux Verités* (Leonviola) (as Maitre Simoni)

1951   *La Poison* (Guitry) (as Paul Braconier)

1952   *La Fille au fouet* (Dreville); *Brelan d'As* (Verneuil) (as Maigret); *Monsieur Taxi* (Hunebelle) (as Pierre Verger); *Le Rideau rouge* (Barsacq) (as Lucien Bertal); *Le Chemin de Damas* (Glass) (as Caiphe); *La Vie d'un honnête homme* (*The Virtuous Scoundrel*) (Guitry) (as Alain/Albert); *Il mercante de Venezia* (*The Merchant of Venice*) (Billon) (as Shylock); *Femmes de Paris* (Boyer) (as Buisson)

1953   *L'Etrange Désir de M. Bard* (Radvanyi) (as Bard); *Saadia* (Lewin) (as Bou Rezza); *Par ordre du Tsar* (Haguet) (as Général Witgenstein); *Quelques pas dans la vie* (Blasetti)

1955   *L'Impossible M. Pipelet* (Hunebelle) (as Maurice Martin); *Les Mémoires d'un flic* (Foucaud) (as Inspector Dominique)

1956   *La Joyeuse Prison* (Berthomieu) (as Benoit)

1957   *Les Trois font la paire* (Duhour) (as Commissar Bernard); *Un Certain M. Jo* (Jolivet) (title role)

1959   *Es geschah am hellichten Tag* (*It Happened in Broad Daylight*) (Vajda); *La Femme nue et Satan* (*The Head*) (Trivas) (as Professor Abel); *Austerlitz* (Gance)

1960   *Pierrot la tendresse* (Villiers) (title role); *Candide* (Carbonnaux) (as Colonel Nanar)

1961   *Le Bateau d'Emile* (*Le Homard flambé*) (de la Patellière) (as Charles-Edmond Larmentiel)

1962   *Le Diable et les dix commandments* (*The Devil and the Ten Commandments*) (Duvivier) (as Jerome Chambard); *Cyrano et D'Artagnan* (Gance) (as Mauvieres)

1963   *The Train* (Frankenheimer) (as Papa Boule); *Mondo di notte* (Ecco) (Proia—doc)

1965   *Deux heures à tuer* (Govar) (as Nénette)

1967   *Le Vieil Homme et l'enfant* (*The Two of Us*) (Berri) (as Pépé); *Ce sacre grand-père* (*The Marriage Came Tumbling Down*) (Poitrenaud) (as Jéricho)

1970   *Contestation Generale* (Zampa); *La Maison* (Brach) (as Jacques Compiegne)

1971   *Blanche* (Borowczyk) (as the lawyer)

1972   *La più bella serata della mia vita* (Scola) (as Zorn)

1973   *Evlalie quitte les champs* (*The Star, The Orphan, and the Butcher*) (Savary)

1975   *L'Ibis rouge* (Mocky) (as Zizi)

Publications

By SIMON: articles—

Interview in *Entr'acte* (Brussels), October 1960.
Télé Ciné (Paris), February-March 1962.

Plexus (Paris), October-November 1968.
Cinéma (Paris), November 1974.

On SIMON: books—

Guth, Paul, *Michel Simon*, Paris, 1951.
Buache, Freddy, *Michel Simon: Un Acteur et ses personnages*, Bienne, 1962.
Fernand Sequin rencontre Michel Simon, Ottowa, 1969.
Fansten, Jacques, *Michel Simon*, Paris, 1970.
Gauteur, Claude, and André Bernard, *Michel Simon*, Paris, 1975.
Carré, Jeanne, *728 jours avec Michel Simon*, Paris, 1978.
Plume, Christian, and Xavier Pasquini, *Michel Simon*, Nice, 1981.
Gauteur, Claude, *Michel Simon*, Paris, 1987.
Loubier, Jean-Marc, *Michel Simon, ou le roman d'un jouisseur*, Paris, 1989.

On SIMON: articles—

Beylie, C., "Michel Simon l'unique," in *Ecran* (Paris), July-August 1975.
"La Chienne," in *Avant-Scène du cinéma* (Paris), October 1975.
Doneux, M., "Hommage à Michel Simon," in *APEC—Revue belge du cinéma* (Brussels), v. 13, no. 1-2, 1975-76.
Beylie, C., "L'Enfer Simon," in *Ecran* (Paris), September 1978.
Gauteur, Claude, "Michel Simon" in *Anthologie du Cinéma*, vol. 10, Paris, 1979.
Gauteur, Claude, "Michel Simon (1895-1975)," in *Avant-Scène du Cinéma* (Paris), 15 October 1979.
Sellier, G., "L'inquiétante étrangeté de Michel Simon," in *Cinéma* (Paris), July/August 1983.
Ostria, V., "Le dernier des hommes," in *Cahiers du Cinéma* (Paris), September 1987.

*   *   *

Michel Simon shared with a very few other great stars, notably Charles Laughton, a kind of lifelong personal struggle with his physical appearance, an appearance which nevertheless was to be the essence of his very special appeal as an actor. Like Laughton, Simon's homeliness, even ugliness, was in itself a part of his deeply sympathetic personality on the screen. Before going on stage he had been a professional boxer and acrobatic clown, entering the theater in 1918 when in his early twenties. He was already in his thirties before he made any mark in films, though well-established in the theater. There are glimpses of him, however, in notable silent films, such as Marcel L'Herbier's Pirandellian *Feu Mathias Pascal* and Carl Dreyer's *La Passion de Jeanne d'Arc*, but he achieved film stardom in Jean Choux's *Jean de la lune*, a film version of the play by Marcel Achard in which he had achieved success on the stage. It was in sound films that he best fulfilled his unique capacity to interpret the more bizarre character roles that matched his massive bulk, his twisted-up facial expression, and his rough, corn-creaky, semiarticulate voice, with which he managed to project extraordinary comic effects. Jean Renoir, who himself had to cope with an ungainly body and a homely, if kindly, face, took to him, and together, with the coming of sound, they created two eccentric comedies, *On purge Bébé* (after Feydeau) and *Boudu sauvé des eaux*, and, in total contrast, the tragic *La Chienne*. Renoir describes with delight the eccentric character of Simon and his pleasure at working with him in his book *My Life and My Films*.

Simon's output of films was to continue for the next quarter century, led initially by his grotesquely comic performance in the star role of a good-natured mate of a barge plying the Seine in Jean Vigo's film, *L'Atalante*. His more notable prewar serious parts came in the films of Marcel Carné, *Drôle de drame* and the poetic *Quai des brumes*, in

Christian-Jaque's film of a boy's school, *Les Disparus de Saint-Agil*, and in Julien Duvivier's *La Fin de jour*. He also appeared with Arletty in a farcical film, *Fric-Frac*, which they had both played on the stage.

With the coming of war and the occupation, Simon, now in his fifties, remained in France, but appeared in fewer films, and those of a kind very different from the predominantly proletarian parts of the past. He worked in costume drama, playing, for example, Scarpia in the film *La Tosca* and Rigoletto in *Il re sè diverte*, both Italian films, a genre he was to continue after the war in the Italian *Fabiola*; he starred as Shylock in *Il mercante di Venezia* and as Faust/Mephistopheles in Réne Clair's *La Beauté du diable*. His other principal genre became crime films, including the title role of the thief in *Vautrin* and the criminal in Duvivier's *Panique*.

In his private life, apart from a single brief period of marriage, Simon remained virtually a recluse, and in 1957 he suffered near exclusion from his profession through a serious injury to the nervous system caused by a dye he had used for makeup; this brought on partial paralysis from which it took time for him to recover. Nevertheless, he achieved a magnificent performance in 1967 in *Le Vieil Homme et l'enfant* as a French peasant whose anti-Jewish prejudice is overcome through caring for a small Jewish boy during the period of the occupation. Simon continued to appear in French and Italian productions until 1975, the year of his death.

—Roger Manvell

SIMON, Simone

Nationality: French. **Born:** Bethune, 23 April 1910 (other sources give 1911 or 1914); grew up in Marseilles. **Career:** Worked briefly as fashion designer and model, Paris; 1931—stage debut in the operetta *Balthazar*, Paris; film debut in *Le Chanteur inconnu*; 1935-38—contract with 20th Century-Fox: U.S. film debut in *Girls' Dormitory*; 1938—in French film with Jean Gabin, *La Bête humaine*; on U.S. stage in *Three after Three*; 1941—in *Charlot's Revue* in Hollywood, and on vaudeville tour; 1966—on Paris stage in *La Courte Paille*. **Address:** 5 rue de Tilsitt, Paris 75008, France.

Films as Actress:

1931 *Le Chanteur inconnu* (Tourjansky); *Un Opère sans Douleur* (Tarride); *La petite chocolatiere* (Hervil); *Mam'zelle Nitouche* (Marc Allégret)

1932 *Un Fils d'Amerique* (Gallone); *Le Roi des palaces* (Gallone); *L'Étoile de valence* (de Poligny)

1933 *Tire au flanc* (Renoir)

1934 *Le Voleur* (Jacques Tourneur)

1935 *Les Yeux no irs* (*Dark Eyes*) (Tourjansky) (as Tania); *Les Beaux Jours* (Marc Allégret); *Prenez Garde à la Peinture* (Chomette); *Lac aux Dames* (Marc Allégret) (as Puck)

1936 *Girls' Dormitory* (Cummings) (as Marie Claudel); *Ladies in Love* (Edward H. Griffith) (as Marie Armand)

1937 *Seventh Heaven* (Henry King) (as Diane); *Love and Hisses* (Lanfield) (as Yvette Guerin)

1938 ***La Bête humaine*** (*Judas Was a Woman*) (Renoir) (as Séverine); *Josette* (Dwan) (as Renée Le Blanc)

1941 *All that Money Can Buy* (*The Devil and Daniel Webster*) (Dieterle) (as Belle)

1942 ***Cat People*** (Jacques Tourneur) (as Irena Dubrovna)

1943 *Tahiti Honey* (Auer) (as Suzie)

Simone Simon with Jean Gabin in *La Bête humaine*

1944 *The Curse of the Cat People* (Fritsch and Wise) (as Irena); *Mademoiselle Fifi* (Wise) (as Elizabeth Rousset); *Johnny Doesn't Live Here Anymore* (*And So They Were Married*) (Joe May) (as Kathie Aumont)

1946 *Pétrus* (Marc Allégret)

1947 *Temptation Harbour* (*Le Port de la tentation*) (Comfort) (as Camelia)

1950 *Olivia* (*Pit of Loneliness*) (Audry); ***La Ronde*** (*Circle of Love*) (Max Ophüls) (as Marie, the maid)

1951 *Donna senza nome* (*Women without Names*) (Radvanyi) (as Yvonne)

1952 "The Model" ep. of *Le Plaisir* (*House of Pleasure*) (Max Ophüls) (as Josephine)

1954 *I tre ladri* (De Felice); *Double Destin* (Vicas)

1956 *The Extra Day* (Fairchild) (as Michele Blanchard)

1973 *La Femme en bleu* (Deville)

Publications

On SIMON: article—

Brisset, S., "Les hommes qui aimaient les femmes ...," in *Cinéma 90*, November 1990.

On SIMON: book—

Parish, James Robert, and William T. Leonard, *Hollywood Players: The Thirties*, New Rochelle, New York, 1976.

*   *   *

Simone Simon was originally brought to the United States to repeat her French ingenue roles. Even though a talented actress, she never achieved any level of popularity with American audiences. Twentieth Century-Fox even attempted to promote her as a singing star in *Love and Hisses* and *Josette*, but her weak voice undid that strategy. Her Hollywood films are mostly forgotten except for the quartet she made at RKO.

In *All that Money Can Buy*, Simon plays the devil's emissary who steals a good man away from his wife. This role probably led to her selection as the lead in her best-known American film, *Cat People*, and its sequel *The Curse of the Cat People*. Playing a foreign wife who fears the consequences of sex, her accent adds to the films' strange atmospheric qualities. Finally she made *Mademoiselle Fifi*, an adaptation of two de Maupassant stories about a French laundress who defies the occupying German forces during the Franco-Prussian War. This patriotic indictment of collaboration was unpopular in the United States, and although it was the first American film to be shown in France after the Normandy invasion, it failed to find an audience. Thus, what some critics consider to be Simon's best Hollywood work went largely unseen, and she returned to Europe and her minor triumphs in Ophüls's *La Ronde* and *Le Plaisir*.

—Anthony Ambrogio

SINATRA, Frank

Nationality: American. **Born:** Francis Albert Sinatra in Hoboken, New Jersey, 12 December 1915. **Education:** Attended David E. Rue Junior High School and Demarest High School, Hoboken. **Family:** Married 1) Nancy Barbato, 1939 (divorced 1950), daughters: the singer Nancy and Christina, son: Frank Jr.; 2) the actress Ava Gardner, 1951 (divorced 1957); 3) the actress Mia Farrow, 1966 (divorced 1968); 4) Barbara Marx, 1976. **Career:** 1935—singer with Hoboken Four: winner of Major Bowes' Amateur Hour contest, and appeared in short film; solo singer at clubs; 1939—singer with Harry James Band; first recordings; 1940-42—singer with Tommy Dorsey Band; 1942—first appearance as solo singer in New York; 1943-44—on radio program *Your Hit Parade* (also appeared on the show, 1947-49); 1945-47—on radio program *Songs by Sinatra*; 1950-52—in the musical TV series *The Frank Sinatra Show*; 1953—serious film role in *From Here to Eternity*; 1956—produced the film *Johnny Concho*; 1957-58—in the music and drama TV series *The Frank Sinatra Show*; 1960—formed his own record company, Reprise Records; 1965—directed the film *None but the Brave*. **Awards:** Best Supporting Actor Academy Award, for *From Here to Eternity*, 1953; Jean Hersholt Humanitarian Award, 1970. **Agent:** Burson-Marsteller, 3333 Wilshire Boulevard, Los Angeles, CA 90010, U.S.A.

Films as Actor:

1935   *Major Bowes' Amateur Theatre of the Air* (Auer) (as singer)
1941   *Las Vegas Nights* (Murphy) (as band singer)
1942   *Ship Ahoy* (Buzzell) (as band singer)

1943   *Reveille with Beverly* (Barton) (as singer); *Higher and Higher* (Whelan) (as Frank); *Show Business at War* (*March of Time* series) (short)
1944   *The Road to Victory* (Prinz) (as himself); *Step Lively* (Whelan) (as Glen)
1945   *The All Star Bond Rally* (Audley) (as himself); *Anchors Aweigh* (Sidney) (as Clarence Doolittle); *The House I Live In* (LeRoy) (as himself)
1946   *Till the Clouds Roll By* (Whorf) (as himself)
1947   *It Happened in Brooklyn* (Whorf) (as Danny Miller)
1948   *The Miracle of the Bells* (Pichel) (as Father Paul); *The Kissing Bandit* (Benedek) (as Ricardo)
1949   *Take Me Out to the Ball Game* (Berkeley) (as Dennis Ryan); **On the Town** (Donen and Kelly) (as Chip); **Adam's Rib** (Cukor) (voice only)
1951   *Double Dynamite* (Cummings) (as Emile Keck); *Meet Danny Wilson* (Pevney) (title role)
1953   **From Here to Eternity** (Zinnemann) (as Angelo Maggio)
1954   *Suddenly* (Lewis Allen) (as John Baron)
1955   *Young at Heart* (Gordon Douglas) (as Barney Sloan); *Not as a Stranger* (Kramer) (as Alfred Boone); *The Tender Trap* (Walters) (as Charlie Reader); *Guys and Dolls* (Joseph L. Mankiewicz) (as Nathan Detroit); *The Man with the Golden Arm* (Preminger) (as Frankie Machine)
1956   *Meet Me in Las Vegas* (*Viva Las Vegas*) (Rowland) (as himself); *High Society* (Walters) (as Mike Connor); *Around the World in Eighty Days* (Anderson) (as piano player)
1957   *The Pride and the Passion* (Kramer) (as Miguel); *The Joker Is Wild* (Charles Vidor) (as Joe E. Lewis); *Pal Joey* (Sidney) (title role)
1958   *Kings Go Forth* (Daves) (as Lt. Sam Loggins); *Some Came Running* (Minnelli) (as Dave Hirsh)
1959   *Invitation to Monte Carlo* (Lloyd) (as himself); *A Hole in the Head* (Capra) (as Tony Manetta); *Never So Few* (John Sturges) (as Captain Tom Reynolds)
1960   *Can-Can* (Walter Lang) (as Francois Durnais); *Ocean's Eleven* (Milestone) (as Danny Ocean); *Pepe* (Sidney) (as himself)
1961   *The Devil at Four O'Clock* (LeRoy) (as Harvey)
1962   *Sinatra in Israel* (short) (as himself); *The Road to Hong Kong* (Panama) (as himself); *The Manchurian Candidate* (Frankenheimer) (as Bennett Marco)
1963   *Come Blow Your Horn* (Bud Yorkin) (as Alan Baker); *The List of Adrian Messenger* (Huston) (as Gypsy stableman); *Four for Texas* (Aldrich) (as Mack Thomas)
1964   *Paris When It Sizzles* (Quine) (as singing voice)
1965   *Von Ryan's Express* (Robson) (as Colonel Joseph Ryan); *Marriage on the Rocks* (Donohue) (as Dan Edwards)
1966   *Cast a Giant Shadow* (Shavelson) (as David "Mickey" Marcus); *The Oscar* (Rouse) (as himself); *Assault on a Queen* (Donohue) (as Mark Brittain)
1967   *The Naked Runner* (Furie) (as Sam Laker); *Tony Rome* (Gordon Douglas) (title role)
1968   *The Detective* (Gordon Douglas) (as Joe Leland); *Lady in Cement* (Gordon Douglas) (as Tony Rome)
1970   *Dirty Dingus Magee* (Kennedy) (title role)
1974   *That's Entertainment!* (Haley—compilation) (as narrator)
1977   *Contract on Cherry Street* (Graham—for TV) (as Detective Frank Horannes)
1984   *Cannonball Run II* (Needham) (as himself)
1988   *Who Framed Roger Rabbit?* (Zemeckis) (as voice of Singing Sword)
1989   *Entertaining the Troops* (doc)
1990   *Listen Up!: The Lives of Quincy Jones* (Weissbrod—doc)
1995   *Young at Heart* (for TV) (as himself)

Frank Sinatra in *Guys and Dolls* © MCMLV by Samuel Goldwyn Productions, Inc.

Films as Actor and Producer:

1956   *Johnny Concho* (McGuire) (title role)
1962   *Sergeants 3* (John Sturges) (as Sgt. Mike Merry)
1964   *Robin and the Seven Hoods* (Gordon Douglas) (as Robbo)
1980   *The First Deadly Sin* (Hutton) (as Edward Delaney, exec pr)

Film as Actor, Director, and Producer:

1965   *None but the Brave* (as Chief Pharmacist Mate Maloney)

Publications

By SINATRA: books—

Sinatra in His Own Words, compiled by Guy Yarwood, New York, 1982.
A Man and His Art, New York, 1991.

By SINATRA: article—

"Frank Sinatra: My Meeting with the Chairman of the Board," interview with Walter Thomas, in *Interview* (New York), July 1991.

On SINATRA: books—

Shaw, Arnold, *Sinatra*, New York, 1968.
Ringgold, Gene, and Clifford McCarty, *The Films of Frank Sinatra*, New York, 1971.
Barnes, Ken, *Sinatra and the Great Song Stylists*, London, 1972.
Romero, J., *Sinatra's Women*, New York, 1976.
Howlett, John, *Frank Sinatra*, New York, 1979.
Lonstein, Albert, and Vito Marino, *The Revised Compleat Sinatra: Discography, Filmography, Television Appearances, Motion Picture Appearances, Radio Appearances, Concert Appearances, Stage Appearances*, Ellenville, New York, 1979.
Frank, Alan, *Sinatra*, London, 1984.
Jewell, Derek, with George Perry, *Frank Sinatra: A Celebration*, Boston, 1985.
Sinatra, Nancy, *Frank Sinatra: My Father*, Garden City, New York, 1985.
Kelley, Kitty, *His Way: The Unauthorized Biography of Frank Sinatra*, New York, 1986.
Adler, Bill, *Sinatra, the Man and the Myth: An Unauthorized Biography*, New York, 1987.
De Stefano, Gildo, *Frank Sinatra*, Venice, 1991.
Doctor, Gary L., *The Sinatra Scrapbook*, Secaucus, New Jersey, 1991.
Pickard, Roy, *Frank Sinatra at the Movies*, London, 1994.
Britt, Stan, *Sinatra: A Celebration*, New York, 1995.
Coleman, Ray, *Sinatra: Portrait of the Artist*, Atlanta, 1995.
Friedwald, Will, *The Song Is You: A Singer's Art*, New York, 1995.
Petkov, Steven, and Leonard Mustazza, *The Frank Sinatra Reader*, New York, 1995.
Shirak, Ed Jr., *Our Way: Based on the Song a Time that Was*, Hoboken, New Jersey, 1995.
Sinatra, Nancy, *Frank Sinatra: An American Legend*, Los Angeles, 1995.
Vare, Ethlie Ann, editor, *Legend: Frank Sinatra and the American Dream*, New York, 1995.

On SINATRA: articles—

Current Biography 1960, New York, 1960.
Tercinet, A., "Frank Sinatra," in *Avant-Scène du Cinéma* (Paris), 15 June 1980.

Horton, R., "Ol' Blue Eyes," in *American Film* (New York), July/August 1988.
Plagens, Peter, "Stranger in the Night," in *Newsweek* (New York), 21 March 1994.
Ressner, Jeffrey, "And Again, One More for the Road," in *Time* (New York), 21 March 1994.
Schwartz, Jonathan, "And Now the End Is Near . . . Sinatra's Last Audition," in *Esquire* (New York), May 1995.
Holden, Stephen, "They Did It His Way," in *New York Times*, 10 December 1995.
Tosches, Nick, "The Death, and Life, of the Rat Pack," in *New York Times*, 7 January 1996.

On SINATRA: films—

Sinatra, mini-series directed by James Sadwith, 1992.
Sinatra: 80 Years My Way, documentary, 1995.

*   *   *

Frank Sinatra's acting has been notable for its variety of roles and versatility of styles. Appearing in many different types of films, he has made particular contributions to musicals, dramas, action/adventure films, and comedies. To a certain extent his film career has paralleled his singing career. As he grew older, he became more serious and introspective, sometimes more personal, as a singer. He sought new material and different arrangements in a conscious evolution of vocal style. Similarly, in films he turned from youthful, singing roles to serious, dramatic ones during the 1950s in an attempt to establish himself as an actor. His uncanny ability to choose just the right material to sing, however, has not always worked for him on the screen. Although he has had remarkable success in certain, very disparate films—*On the Town, From Here to Eternity, A Hole in the Head, The Manchurian Candidate*, and *The Detective*—he has also seemed frequently miscast or indifferent in others—*Guys and Dolls, Can Can*, and *The Pride and the Passion*. Nevertheless, he is probably as well known as a screen star as he is as a recording artist.

Sinatra's earliest roles exploited an image that had contributed to his popularity as a singer—the skinny kid who needs mothering. In several of the films, he played opposite a strong female character who had to teach him about love. In *Take Me Out to the Ball Game*, for example, Betty Garrett's Shirley chases Sinatra's Dennis Ryan, aggressively overcoming his reticence. At one point, she even picks him up and carries him off the baseball field. The two were paired in almost identical roles in *On the Town* as well. He was also cast in *Anchors Aweigh* as the younger partner who could not succeed in getting the leading lady to fall for him, but who realizes in time that a less sophisticated girl is the one he really loves.

Dissatisfied, however, with that image and the roles in those musicals, Sinatra left MGM. Although he appeared in subsequent musicals, it is primarily in dramatic roles that Sinatra has achieved success since he played Maggio in *From Here to Eternity* (the role that won him an Oscar for Best Supporting Actor). Pivotal to that change in emphasis for his career, Maggio was a role for which Sinatra campaigned, and it led to further roles of dramatic power and significance, usually as a character whose tough facade hides his vulnerability. Such contradictions often lead to the film's dramatic conflict as in *The Man with the Golden Arm, The Joker Is Wild, Some Came Running*, and *The Detective*.

Sinatra's versatility as a screen actor is especially represented by his roles in comedies and adventure films. In both genres he avoids the pretentiousness of some of his less successful serious roles while still displaying a personal style akin to some of his best work as a singer. As Alan Baker, the older brother teaching the younger about sex in *Come Blow Your Horn*, as Tony Manetta, the playboy father working to raise a son in *A Hole in the Head*, or as Colonel Joseph Ryan leading a group of soldiers in a dangerous act of sabotage during World War II in *Von Ryan's Express*, Sinatra plays characters who assert themselves in precarious, though often funny, situations. They frequently make big mistakes in the process, but manage ultimately to turn the mistakes into successes. Moreover, as a result, the character learns a great deal about himself and proves to be a more responsible, endearing individual than the self-centered cad he seemed at first.

In the 1950s and 1960s, Sinatra and other actors such as Shirley MacLaine, Dean Martin, and Sammy Davis Jr.—who appeared in several films together—became known as the "Rat Pack." (Sinatra has also been nicknamed "Chairman of the Board of Show Business," or just "Chairman of the Board.") His leadership of the Rat Pack and the stories of Sinatra's impatience with film production practices and lack of cooperation on the set are legendary. Certain films, particularly *The Pride and the Passion*, may have been compromised because of his intransigence. In addition, many other aspects of his offscreen life are often difficult to separate from his on-screen performances. Nevertheless, such a separation must be made because he created a significant number of diverse roles over a 40-year career.

—Jerome Delamater, updated by Linda J. Stewart

SLOANE, Everett

Nationality: American. **Born:** New York City, 1 October 1909. **Education:** Attended Public School No. 46; Townsend Harris High School, New York; University of Pennsylvania, Philadelphia. **Family:** Married Luba Herman, 1933, son: Ned, daughter: Erika. **Career:** 1927—joined Jasper Deeter's stock company, Moylan, Pennsylvania; 1928—New York stage debut; then worked for a Wall Street broker; 1929—radio actor: over the next few years appeared in *The Goldbergs*, *The Crime Doctor*, and, for eight years, *The Shadow*; 1935—Broadway debut in *Boy Meets Girl*; 1938—joined Orson Welles's Mercury Theatre, and appeared in many of its radio productions; 1941—film debut in Welles's *Citizen Kane*; 1944—on Broadway in *A Bell for Adano*; 1950s—in many television series and plays, notably Rod Sterling's *Patterns* and *Noon on Doomsday*; directed the stage plays *Twilight Bar* and *The Dancer*. **Died:** Suicide, 6 August 1965.

Films as Actor:

1941   *Citizen Kane* (Welles) (as Bernstein)
1942   *Journey into Fear* (Foster) (as Kopeikin)
1948   *The Lady from Shanghai* (Welles) (as Arthur Bannister)
1949   *Prince of Foxes* (King) (as Belli)
1950   *The Men* (Zinnemann) (as Dr. Brock)
1951   *The Enforcer* (Windust) (as Albert Mendoza); *Bird of Paradise* (Daves) (as beachcomber); *The Prince Who Was a Thief* (Maté) (as Yussef); *Sirocco* (Bernhardt) (as General LaSalle); *The Blue Veil* (Bernhardt) (as District Attorney); *The Desert Fox* (Hathaway) (as General Burgdoff)
1952   *The Sellout* (Mayer) (as Nelson Tarsson); *Way of a Gaucho* (Tourneur) (as Falcon)
1955   *The Big Knife* (Aldrich) (as Nat Danziger)
1956   *Patters* (Cook) (as Walter Ramsey); *Somebody Up There Likes Me* (Wise) (as Irving Cohen); *Lust for Life* (Minnelli) (as Dr. Gachet)
1958   *Marjorie Morningstar* (Rapper) (as Arnold Morgenstern); *The Gun Runners* (Siegel)
1960   *Home from the Hill* (Minnelli) (as Albert Halstead)

1961   *By Love Possessed* (Sturges) (as Reggie)
1962   *Brushfire* (Warner) (as Chevern McCase)
1963   *The Man from the Diner's Club* (Tashlin) (as Martindale)
1964   *The Patsy* (Lewis) (as Caryl Ferguson); *Ready for the People* (Kulik) (as Paul Boyer); *The Disorderly Orderly* (Tashlin) (as Mr. Tuffington)

Publications

By SLOANE: article—

Interview in *Film* (London), no. 37, 1965.

On SLOANE: articles—

"One of Radio's Best and Highest-Priced Actors," in *Newsweek*, 4 September 1944.
Current Biography 1957, New York, 1957.
Coulson, A., "Everett Sloane," in *Film* (London), Autumn 1963.
Obituary in *New York Times*, 7 August 1965.
Letter from Roy Pickard in *Films in Review* (New York), July 1972.

*   *   *

Everett Sloane ranks as one of Hollywood's great character actors. His subtle performance as Bernstein in *Citizen Kane* guarantees him a secure niche in any history of film. Indeed, when Everett Sloane's name is mentioned the image which comes to mind is "Bernstein," the thin, little man with huge piercing eyes, and the vitriolic voice. Sloane will also long be remembered for his work in *The Lady from Shanghai*, *The Men*, and *The Big Knife*.

But Sloane had another distinguished acting career before he ever made his way to Hollywood. A native New Yorker, he first gravitated to the stage at age seven and from then on vowed to become an actor. But try as he might, initially he could not "make it" on Broadway. So like many of his generation he gravitated to the then-fledgling world of radio drama.

During the 1930s Sloane was a fixture on America's airwaves. He acted in everything from *Buck Rogers* to *Crime Doctor* to *The Goldbergs*, and appeared for eight years in *The Shadow*. In this last show he met up with the then-radio wunderkind Orson Welles and joined the Mercury Theatre of the Air in 1938. Sloane went on to act in the most famous of the Mercury radio productions, including *War of the Worlds*.

Subsequently Welles took Sloane with him to Hollywood in 1940. Their first collaboration was *Citizen Kane*. Many critics have commented upon Sloane's crucial role in that classic film. Sloane's best scene comes when Bernstein (reflecting upon his career as Kane's business manager) remembers a girl with a white dress and parasol whom he only saw for a second "but I'll bet a month hasn't gone by since, that I haven't thought of that girl." Memory is at the core of *Citizen Kane*, and Welles provided Sloane with the film's most unforgettable line.

Sloane acted for Welles again in *Journey into Fear* and *The Lady from Shanghai*. This success in Hollywood led to what he always wanted—a triumph on Broadway, in this case in *Native Son*. But like that of his mentor, Orson Welles, Sloane's later career never matched its early triumphs. He slipped into the category of top-flight character actor in such vehicles as *Lust for Life* and *Marjorie Morningstar* and ended his movie career in two of Jerry Lewis's most acclaimed films, *The Patsy* and *The Disorderly Orderly*.

Yet film was never Sloane's first love. He continued (unsuccessfully) to try Broadway. To this end he supported himself with work on the radio, and later as an active participant in numerous early television anthology programs. His death by suicide in 1965 robbed the entertainment world of one of its most distinguished performers.

—Douglas Gomery

SMITH, (Dame) Maggie

Nationality: British. **Born:** Ilford, Essex, 28 December 1934. **Education:** Attended the Oxford School for Girls; studied at the Oxford Playhouse School. **Family:** Married 1) the actor Robert Stephens, 1967, (divorced 1975), sons: Christopher and Toby; 2) the writer Beverley Cross, 1975. **Career:** Played in revues in Oxford and London. 1956—New York stage debut in *New Faces of 1956*; 1958—film debut in *Nowhere to Go*; 1959-60—season at the Old Vic, London; 1963-68—member of the National Theatre, London; also acted at the Shakespeare Festival in Stratford, Ontario; later work includes *The Way of the World*, 1984, and *Lettice and Lovage*, 1987; 1987—in TV mini-series *Talking Heads*, the "Bed among the Lentils" episode. **Awards:** Best Actress Academy Award, and Best Actress, British Academy, for *The Prime of Miss Jean Brodie*, 1969; Best Supporting Actress Academy Award, for *California Suite*, 1978; Best Actress, British Academy, for *A Private Function*, 1985, *A Room with a View*, 1986, and *The Lonely Passion of Judith Hearne*, 1987. Dame Commander, Order of the British Empire, 1990. **Agent:** ICM, 388 Oxford Street, London W1N 9HE, England.

Films as Actress:

1958   *Nowhere to Go* (Holt) (as Bridget Howard)
1962   *Go to Blazes* (Truman) (as Chantal)
1963   *The V.I.P.s* (Asquith) (as Miss Mead)
1964   *The Pumpkin Eater* (Clayton) (as Philpot)
1965   *Young Cassidy* (Cardiff and Ford) (as Nora)
1966   *Othello* (Burge) (as Desdemona)
1967   *The Honey Pot* (Joseph L. Mankiewicz) (as Sarah Watkins)
1968   *Hot Millions* (Till) (as Patty Terwilliger)
1969   *The Prime of Miss Jean Brodie* (Neame) (title role); *Oh! What a Lovely War* (Attenborough) (as music hall star)
1972   *Travels with My Aunt* (Cukor) (as Aunt Augusta); *Love and Pain and the Whole Damn Thing* (Pakula) (as Lola Fisher)
1976   *Murder by Death* (Moore) (as Dora Charleston)
1978   *California Suite* (Ross) (as Diana Barrie); *Death on the Nile* (Guillermin) (as Miss Bowers)
1981   *Evil under the Sun* (Hamilton) (as Daphne Castle); *Clash of the Titans* (Desmond Davis) (as Thetis); *Quartet* (Ivory) (as Lois Heidler)
1982   *The Missionary* (Loncraine) (as Lady Ames); *Better Late than Never* (*Whose Little Girl Are You?*) (Forbes) (as Miss Anderson)
1985   *A Private Function* (Mowbray) (as Joyce Chilvers); *Lily in Love* (*Jatszani Kell*) (Makk) (title role)
1986   *A Room with a View* (Ivory) (as Charlotte Bartlett)
1987   *The Lonely Passion of Judith Hearne* (Clayton) (title role)
1990   *Romeo-Juliet* (Acosta) (as voice of Rozaline)
1991   *Hook* (Spielberg) (as Granny Wendy Darling)
1992   *Sister Act* (Ardolino) (as Mother Superior); *Memento Mori* (Clayton and Hubbard—for TV) (as Mrs. Mabel Pettigrew)
1993   *The Secret Garden* (Holland) (as Mrs. Medlock); *Sister Act 2: Back in the Habit* (Duke) (as Mother Superior); *Suddenly Last Summer* (Eyre—for TV) (as Violet Venable)
1996   *Richard III* (Loncraine) (as the Duchess of York); *The First Wives Club* (Hogan)

Publications

By SMITH: articles—

Interview with Clive Goodwin, in *Acting in the Sixties*, edited by Hal Burton, London, 1970.
Interview in *Show* (Hollywood), November 1972.
Interview with Mary Harron, in the *Observer* (London), 18 November 1982.
Interview with Sheridan Morley, in the *Times* (London), 14 July 1990.

On SMITH: book—

Coveney, Michael, *Maggie Smith: A Bright Particular Star*, London, 1992.

On SMITH: articles—

Current Biography 1970, New York, 1970.
Wolf, Matt, "There Is Nothing Like This Dame," in *New York Times Magazine*, 18 March 1990.

*   *   *

As a younger dramatic actress making a splash in *Othello*, Maggie Smith seemed as proficient as other English stage contemporaries but unremarkable on-screen. It was as a flustered comedienne, England's daffiest export since Kay Kendall, that Smith truly emerged as a star. What makes Smith so funny is that she is often the sole cast member diligently trying to remain the voice of reason; the loss of her dignity to chaos can be overwhelmingly hilarious, whether it is her Oscar-nominee in *California Suite*, who drowns her desire for her gay hubby in booze; her mousy nurse uncovering a rapscallion's murder scheme in *The Honey Pot*; or her Dora Charleston trying to keep her wits about her while the world's most famous detectives lose their cool in *Murder by Death*. Often cast as a low-level professional (e.g., the enterprising secretary in *Hot Millions*, the paid companion in *Death on the Nile*), who is sometimes a spinster, Smith specializes in playing underappreciated ugly ducklings who often save the day for their love objects as Patty Terwilliger does in *Hot Millions* by wisely investing her spouse's embezzled funds.

When Smith seamlessly combines the frustration of the unmarried woman with her trademark frazzled composure in melodramas, the comedy technique heightens her characters' predicaments. In her Oscar-winning performance as the disciplinarian molder of little girls in *The Prime of Miss Jean Brodie*, she is both pathetic and laughable as she misinterprets the range of her influence. What is so heartbreaking about Smith's roles that play tears off laughter is that her insular characters have no sense of their own ridiculousness; when the self-image is shattered by the perception of the outside world as in *Jean Brodie*, the effect on the spectator is devastating. In the transmuting tragicomedy *Love and Pain and the Whole Damn Thing*, the slapstick sequences brilliantly reverse audience expectations; Smith's dazzling physical comedy shtick becomes a slap in the audience's face once it is revealed that Smith's character is terminally ill. We are so conditioned to draw enjoyment from Smith's lively self-deprecation, that this knowledge of Lola Fisher's mortality is shocking. Daringly, both *A Room with a View* and *The Lonely Passion of Judith Hearne* employ ludicrous aspects of the characters' deportment to underscore their fragility. Not since Katharine Hepburn cornered the market on the unloved (*The African Queen*, *Summertime*, *Rainmaker*), has a star brought so much poignancy to bear on the plight of the spinster.

A comparison between these two great eccentrics is telling even if Hepburn was a great beauty who relied on mannerisms to emphasize her characters' uniqueness, whereas Smith is a plain woman who some-

Maggie Smith in *The Lonely Passion of Judith Hearne* © 1987 Paragon Entertainment Corporation/Courtesy of HandMade Films

times falls back on mannerisms to undercut her characters' despair. But when Smith colors her unloved women with humor not for sugar-coating but for ironic counterpoint, her artistry is profoundly moving, as with her moral watchdog chaperon in *Room with a View* and her tippling neurasthenic, *Judith Hearne*, one of cinema's incontrovertibly great performances. Foolishly pinning her old maid hope on an obvious con man, Hearne is driven round the bend by this final rejection as if it were a personal affront from a God she has come to question. Superb in British television productions such as *Memento Mori* and a remake of Hepburn's chilling *Suddenly Last Summer*, Smith is admittedly something of a one-woman band as an actress. If her performance gimmickry is not as well-suited to the all-star bitchery of *Evil under the Sun* as it is to the inspired satire of *A Private Function* or *The Missionary*, she can never be accused of tasteful dullness; her bag of tricks is unmistakably hers, not the generic posturing of female clowns such as Goldie Hawn and Meg Ryan.

Lately, somewhat toned-down in supporting roles as the stern Mrs. Medlock in the stylish children's film *The Secret Garden* or as the disgusted mother of a political monster in the revisionist *Richard III*, Smith is restrained but still impactful. In the tepid box-office-smash the *Sister Act* films, Smith provides a welcome soupçon of class, but she is much too distinctive a funnywoman to play straight lady to other comediennes. Her only dreadful performance in a brilliant career forms the centerpiece of *Travels with My Aunt*, a crippled project she inherited from Katharine Hepburn after a power play between that actress and MGM. Encouraged in an interpretation owing more to Auntie Mame than Graham Greene's beloved book, Smith offers a circus clown rendition of *The Madwoman of Chaillot*. For the only time in her career, those much written-about star mannerisms strangle her authority. One misstep in a body of work this bright and singular only throws the other magnificent achievements into sharper relief. Whereas other versatile stars manage to give superb comic and searing dramatic acting displays in different films, Smith magically combines comic and tragic masks inside the spirit of the same character. How she creates these breathtaking histrionic effects may be the province of sorcery.

—Robert Pardi

SNIPES, Wesley

Nationality: American. **Born:** Orlando, Florida, 31 July 1962; grew up in the South Bronx. **Family:** Divorced, son: Jelani Asar. **Education:** Was graduated from the State University of New York at Purchase, where he studied acting. **Career:** Early 1980s—moved back to New York to establish career as an actor; 1985—made Broadway debut in *The Boys of Winter*; 1987—had attention-getting role as a gang leader in the Michael Jackson music video *Bad*; 1989-90—made first important movie appearances in *Major League*, *King of New York*, and *Mo' Better Blues*; 1990—in TV series H.E.L.P. **Awards:** Cable Ace Award, Best Actor, for *Vietnam War Story 2*, 1989. **Agent:** Baker Winokur Ryder, 405 South Beverly Drive, 5th Floor, Beverly Hills, CA 90212, U.S.A.

Films as Actor:

1986 *Wildcats* (Ritchie) (as Trumaine); *Streets of Gold* (Roth) (as Roland Jenkins)
1987 *Critical Condition* (Apted) (as ambulance driver)
1988 *Vietnam War Story 2* (for TV)
1989 *Major League* (Ward) (as Willie Mays Hayes)

1990 *King of New York* (Ferrara) (as Thomas Flannigan); *Mo' Better Blues* (Spike Lee) (as Shadow Henderson)
1991 *New Jack City* (Van Peebles) (as Nino Brown); *Jungle Fever* (Spike Lee) (as Flipper Purify)
1992 *White Men Can't Jump* (Shelton) (as Sidney Deane); *The Waterdance* (Jimenez and Steinberg) (as Raymond Hill); *Passenger 57* (Hooks) (as John Cutter)
1993 *Boiling Point* (James B. Harris) (as Jimmy); *Rising Sun* (Kaufman) (as Web Smith); *Demolition Man* (Brambilla) (as Simon Phoenix); *Harlem* (*Sugar Hill*) (Ichaso) (as Roemello Skuggs)
1994 *Drop Zone* (Badham) (as Pete Nessip)
1995 *To Wong Foo, Thanks for Everything! Julie Newmar* (Kidron) (as Noxeema Jackson); *Money Train* (Ruben) (as John); *Waiting to Exhale* (Whitaker) (as James, uncredited)
1996 *The Fan* (Tony Scott)

Publications

By SNIPES: articles—

"New Face: Wesley Snipes: How an Actor Turned into a Jazzman," interview with Stephen Holden, in *New York Times*, 24 August 1990.
Interview with Paul D. Colford, in *Newsday* (Melville, New York), 23 October 1990.
"Hollywood's Hottest New Star Talks about His Divorce, His Days on the Streets and Why He Doesn't Have *Jungle Fever*," interview with Laura B. Randolph, in *Ebony* (Chicago), September 1991.
"Stars Recall Their Encounters with Racism," interview with Clarence Waldron, in *Jet* (Chicago), 7 December 1992.
Interview in *Playboy* (Chicago), October 1993.

On SNIPES: articles—

Rohter, L., "The Star of *New Jack City* Is Building on Its Success," in *New York Times*, 27 March 1991.
Washington, Elsie B., "That's My Baby," in *Essence* (New York), May 1991.
Seidenberg, Robert, "Splashy Movies, Unsung Stars," in *American Film* (Hollywood), June 1991.
Rugoff, R., "Wesley Fever," in *Premiere* (New York), July 1991.
"Wesley Snipes: Busiest Actor in Hollywood," in *Jet* (Chicago), 18 May 1992.
Current Biography 1993, New York, 1993.
Hirschberg, Lynn, "Living Large," in *Vanity Fair* (New York), September 1993.
Norment, Lynn, "Bachelors with Money and Clout," in *Ebony* (Chicago), October 1993.
Fink, Mitchell, "Could It Be the Title?," in *People Weekly* (New York), 6 March 1995.

*   *   *

Wesley Snipes is best-known to the moviegoing public as a durable star of action-adventure films. He has in fact become an action hero to rival Stallone and Schwarzenegger. The actor's success in the likes of *Passenger 57* (playing a specialist in antiterrorism who goes up against airline hijackers) and *Drop Zone* (cast as a U.S. marshal battling sky-diver villains) confirms that an African-American actor is not incapable of finding major stardom playing such roles. Snipes also has been cast as other standard characters in action epics. He has been the wizened veteran hero's youthful partner (in *Rising Sun*, paired with Sean Connery); and the deranged, ultradangerous villain (in *Demolition Man*, opposite Stallone). His cumulative success in all these

Wesley Snipes in *Demolition Man*

roles has allowed him to enter the upper echelon of the Hollywood acting hierarchy, as he reportedly now earns upwards of $5 million per movie.

But what truly marks Snipes as a motion picture personality is his versatility; his interest in playing not only in action-adventure fare but in character-driven films; and his willingness to experiment in roles that a Sylvester Stallone would never, ever accept. He initially attracted attention as the gang leader in the popular Michael Jackson music video *Bad*, a role that served as his calling card for feature film work. After impressive supporting turns in three films—*Major League* (as the speedy baseball player Willie Mays Hayes); *King of New York* (as a tough, honest cop); and *Mo' Better Blues* (as a jazz musician)—Snipes hit the mark in two 1991 releases. Not only did his performances in *New Jack City* and *Jungle Fever* establish him as a rising young star, but they effectively displayed his range as an actor. In *New Jack City*, he offered a chillingly sinister performance as Nino Brown, a Harlem drug lord; and in *Jungle Fever*, he gave a subtle performance as Flipper Purify, a guilt-ridden architect, married to a black woman, who enters into an affair with his white secretary.

Around the time he made *The Waterdance* and *White Men Can't Jump*, Snipes quickly was emerging as one of the decade's top stars. In *The Waterdance*, he is Raymond Hill, a streetwise black who has become a paraplegic and is confined to a rehabilitation center. In *White Men Can't Jump*, he plays another street-smart type: Sidney Deane, a Southern California basketball hustler. At first glance, both characters are contemporary African-American stereotypes. Raymond Hill is a self-described ladies' man who before becoming wheelchair-bound had lived a "wild life"; admittedly, he was not much of a husband to his wife or father to his little girl. And Sidney Deane seems the type who, if given the opportunity, would hustle you out of your last dime. Nevertheless, in both *The Waterdance* and *White Men Can't Jump*, Snipes adds unusual depth and poignancy to his characterizations. His performances allow you to see beyond the characters' surface hype, making both men at once deeply flawed and deeply human.

Snipes also is not apprehensive about playing against type—in the broadest possible sense. He lampooned his macho image in *To Wong Foo, Thanks for Everything! Julie Newmar*, in which he, along with Patrick Swayze and John Leguizamo, play drag queens. Snipes's Noxeema Jackson comes complete with blond wig and red high-heel shoes. He/she is co-winner of a drag queen beauty pageant, and he/she is not afraid of wiggling his/her hips. Arnold Schwarzenegger may be amenable to gently spoofing his screen image, playing the "twin" of Danny DeVito in *Twins* and a scientist who finds himself pregnant in *Junior*. But one cannot imagine Schwarzenegger playing a homosexual, let alone a drag queen. It is to Snipes's credit that he is willing to risk alienating his action-adventure audience by stretching himself in a role like Noxeema Jackson.

—Rob Edelman

SORDI, Alberto

Nationality: Italian. **Born:** Rome, 15 June 1920. **Career:** 1932—won contest for imitating Oliver Hardy; subsequent work in dubbing U.S. films into Italian (besides Hardy's voice, he dubbed Robert Mitchum); also in music hall in Ermete Zacconi's troupe; 1938—film debut in *La principessa Tarahanova*; 1966—directed the film *Fumo di Londra*; 1988—in TV mini-series *I Promessi sposi* (*The Betrothed*). **Awards:** Best Actor, Berlin Festival, for *Detenuto in attesa di giudizio*, 1971; Italy's Nastro Argento Award, 1953-54, 1955-56, 1959, 1976-77; also won David Di Donatello Award 9 times since 1959. **Address:** Via Pruso 45, Rome 00184, Italy.

Films as Actor:

1938   *La principessa Tarahanova* (*Princess Tarahanova*) (Ozep and Soldati)

1940   *La notte delle beffe* (*The Night of Tricks*) (Campogalliani); *Cuori nella tormenta* (*Tormented Hearts*) (Campogalliani)

1941   *Le signorine della villa accanto* (*The Women Next Door*) (Rosmino)

1942   *I tre aquilotti* (*The Three Pilots*) (Mattòli) (as Filippo); *La Signorina* (Kish); *Giarabub* (Alessandrini); *Casanova farebbe cosi* (*Casanova Would Do It That Way!*) (Bragaglia); *Santa Elena piccolo isola* (Simoni)

1944   *Tre ragazze cercano marito* (*Three Girls Looking for Husbands*) (Coletti) (as Giulio); *Circo equestre Za-Bum* (*The Za-Bum Circus*) (Mattòli)

1945   *Chi l'ha visto?* (*Who's Seen Him?*) (Allessandrini); *L'innocente Casimiro* (*The Innocent Casimiro*) (Campogalliani)

1946   *Le miserie del signor Travet* (*His Young Wife*) (Soldati) (as Barbarotti)

1947   *Il delitto di Giovanni Episcopo* (*Flesh Will Surrender*) (Lattuada) (as Doberti); *Il passatore* (*A Bullet for Stefano*; *The Ferryman*) (Coletti) (as the boyfriend)

1948   *Il vento mi ha cantato una canzone* (*The Wind Sang Me a Song*) (Mastrocinque); *Che Tempi!* (*What Times!*) (Bianchi) (as Mario Aguirre); *Sotto il sole di Roma* (*Under the Sun of Rome*) (Castellani)

1951   *Mamma mia, che impressione* (Savarese) (+ co-sc); *Cameriera bella presenza offresi* (Pastini)

1952   *Lo sceicco bianco* (*The White Sheik*) (Fellini) (title role); *Totò e i re di Roma* (Steno and Monicello); *E arrivato l'accordatore* (*The Tuner Has Arrived*) (Coletti); *Giovinezza* (Pastina)

1953   **I vitelloni** (*The Young and the Passionate*; *Vitelloni*) (Fellini) (as Alberto); *Ci troviamo in galleria* (Bolognini) (as Alberto); *L'incantevole nemica* (Gora); *Canzoni, canzoni, canzoni* (Paolella); *Due notti con Cleopatra* (*Two Nights with Cleopatra*) (Mattòli) (as Cesarino)

1954   *Il seduttore* (Rossi) (+ co-sc); *Amori di mezzo secolo* (Chiari); *Tempi nostri* (*Anatomy of Love*; *Our Time*) (Blasetti); *Gran varietà* (Paolella) (as Premoli); *Tripoli, bel suol d'amore* (Cerio) (as Alberto); *Via Padova 46* (*Lo Scocciatore*) (Bianchi); *Un giorno in pretura* (*A Day in Court*) (Steno) (as Meniconi, + co-sc); *Una parigina a Roma* (Kobler); *L'allegro squadrone* (Moffa); *Le Rouge et le noir* (Autant-Lara); *Accadde al commissariato* (Simonelli) (as Alberto Tadini); *Il matrimonio* (Petrucci); *Un americano a Roma* (Steno) (as Nando Moriconi, + co-sc)

1955   *L'arte di arrangiarsi* (Zampa); *Il segno di Venere* (*The Sign of Venus*) (Risi) (as Romolo Proietti); *La bella di Roma* (Comencini); *Bravissimo* (D'Amico); *Piccolo posta* (Steno) (as Rodolfo Vanzino); *Un eroe dei nostri tempi* (Monicelli); *Accadde al penitenziario* (Bianchi); *Buonanotte ... avvocato!* (Bianchi) (as Alberto Santi, + co-sc)

1956   *Lo scapolo* (Pietrangeli); *I pappagalli* (Paolinelli); *Mio figlio Nerone* (*Nero's Mistress*; *Nero's Weekend*) (Steno) (as Nero); *Da qui all 'eredità*; *Guardia, guardia scelta, brigadiere e maresciallo* (Bolognini); *Era du venerdi 17* (*The Virtuous Bigamist*) (Soldati) (as Mario); *Mi permette babbo!* (Bonnard)

1957   *Souvenir d'Italie* (*It Happened in Rome*) (Pietrangeli) (as Sergio); *Arrivano i dollari!* (Costa); *A Farewell to Arms* (Charles Vidor) (as Father Galli); *Il conte Max* (Bianchi)

1958   *Il medico e lo stregone* (Monicelli); *Il marito* (Loy and Puccini); *Fortunella* (De Filippo); *Ladro lui, ladra lei* (Zampa); *Domenica e sempre domenica* (Mastrocinque) (+

co-sc); *Le Septième Ciel* (Bernard); *Venezia, la luna, e tu* (Risi); *Nella città l'inferno* (*... and the Wild Wild Women*; *Hell in the City*) (Castellani) (as Adonis); *Racconti d'estate* (*Love on the Riviera*; *Summer Tables*; *Femmes d'un été*) (Franciolini) (as Aristarco Bertolini); *Oh! Que Mambo!* (Berry)

1959 *Il moralista* (*The Moralist*) (Bianchi) (as Agostino); *I magliari* (*The Swindlers*) (Rosi) (as Totonno); *La grande guerra* (*The Great War*) (Monicelli) (as Orseste Jacovacci); *Brevi amori a Palma di Majorca* (Bianchi); *Il vedovo* (Risi); *Il giovane leone*; *Vacanze d'inverno* (Mastrocinque); *Costa azzurra* (Sala); *Policarpo, ufficiale di scrittura* (Soldati)

1960 *Tutti a casa* (*Everybody Go Home!*) (Comencini) (as Alberto Innocenzi); *Gastone* (Bonnard); *Il vigile* (Zampa); *Crimen* (*. . . And Suddenly It's Murder!*; *Killing in Monte Carlo*) (Camerini) (as Alberto Franzetti)

1961 *I due nemici* (*The Best of Enemies*) (Hamilton) (as Captain Blasi); *Il giudizio universale* (*The Last Judgment*) (de Sica); *Una vita difficile* (Risi) (as Silvio Magnozzi)

1962 *Mafioso* (Lattuada) (as Antonio Badalamenti); *Il commissario* (Comencini) (as Dante Lombardozzi)

1963 *Il diavolo* (*To Bed or Not to Bed*; *The Devil*) (Polidoro) (as Amadeo Ferretti); *Il boom* (de Sica) (as Giovanni Alberti); *Il maestro di Vigevano* (Petri) (as Monbelli); *Tentazione proibite* (Civirani)

1964 *La mia signora* (Bolognini, Comencini, and Brass) (five roles)

1965 *Il disco volante* (*The Flying Saucer*) (Brass) (four roles); *Those Magnificent Men in Their Flying Machines* (Annakin) (as Count Emilio Ponticelli); *Made in Italy* (*A L'Italienne*) (Loy) (as errant husband); "Latin Lover" ep. of *I tre volti* (*Three Faces of a Woman*) (Indovina) (as Armando Tucci, + co-sc); "Guglirlmo il dentone" ep. of *I complessi* (D'Amico) (+ co-sc); *Thrilling* (Scola, Polidoro, and Lizzani)

1966 *I nostri mariti* (*Our Husbands*) (Risi, d'Amico, and Zampa); "Queen Marta" ("Giovanni") ep. of *Le fate* (*The Queens*; *Sex Quartet*) (Pietrangeli) (as Giovanni)

1967 "Senso civico" ("Civic Sense") ep. of *Le streghe* (*The Witches*) (Bolognini) (as truckdriver)

1968 *Il medico della mutua* (*The Family Doctor*) (Zampa) (as Dr. Guido Tersilli, + co-sc); *Riusciranno i nostri eroi a ritrovare l'amico misteriosamente scomparso in Africa?* (Scola) (as Fausto di Salvio)

1970 "La camera" (as Antonio) and "Il leone" (as Giacinto Colonna) eps. of *Le coppie* (*The Couples*) (+ d of first ep.; de Sica); *Contestazione generale* (Zampa) (as Don Giuseppe)

1971 *Detenuto in attesa di giudizio* (*Detained While Waiting for Justice, Why?*) (Loy) (as Giuseppi Di Noi)

1972 *La più bella serata della mia vita* (*The Most Wonderful Evening of My Life*) (Scola) (as Alfredo Rossi); *Lo scopone scientifico* (*The Scientific Cardplayer*) (Comencini) (as Peppino); *Roma* (*Fellini's Roma*) (Fellini)

1973 *Anastasia mio fratello* (Steno) (as Don Salvatore Anastasia, + co-sc)

1975 *To Love, Perhaps to Die*; *Tra moglie e Mario*

1977 *Un borghese piccolo piccolo* (*An Average Man*) (Monicelli) (as Giovanni Vivaldi); "L'ascensore" ep. of *Quelle strane occasioni* (Comencini) (as Monsignor); "First Aid," "Like a Queen," and "Funeral Elegy" eps. of *I nuovi mostri* (*Viva Italia!*; *The New Monsters*) (Monicelli, Risi, and Scola)

1978 *Le Temoin* (*The Witness*) (Mocky) (as Antonio)

1979 *L'Ingorgo* (*Traffic Jam*) (Comencini); *Il Malato Imaginario* (*The Imaginary Invalid*) (Tonino Cervi) (as Arganti, + co-sc)

1982 *Il Marchese del Grillo* (Monicelli) (as Onofrio Del Grillo/Gasperino, + co-sc)

1984 *Bertoldo, Bertoldino e Cacasenno* (Monicelli) (as Friar Cipolla)

1985 *Sono un fenomeno paranormale* (*I'm a Paranormal Phenomenon*) (Corbucci) (+ co-sc)

1986 *Troppo forte* (*Great!*) (Verdone) (as lawyer, + co-sc)

1989 *Una botta di vita* (*A Blast of Life*) (Oldoini) (as Battistini, + co-sc)

1990 *El Avaro* (*The Miser*) (Cervi) (+ sc); *In nome del popolo sovrano* (*In the Name of the Sovereign People*) (Magni) (as Marchese Arquati)

1992 *Vacanze di Natale '91* (*Christmas Vacation '91*) (Oldoini) (as Sabino, + co-sc)

Films as Director:

1966 *Fumo di Londra* (+ ro as Dante Fontane, co-sc); *Scusi, lei favorevole o contrario?*; *Un italiano in America* (+ ro as the father, sc)

1969 *Amore mio, aiutami* (+ ro as Giovanni Macchiavelli, co-sc)

1973 *Polvere di stelle* (*Stardust*) (+ ro as Mimmo Adami, sc)

1974 *Finche c'è guerra c'è speranza* (*While There's War, There's Hope*) (+ ro as Pietro Ciocca, co-sc)

1976 *Il commune senso del pudore* (*A Common Sense of Modesty*) (+ ro, co-sc)

1978 "Le Vacanze intelligenti" ep. of *Dove vai in vacanza?* (+ ro as Remo, co-sc)

1980 *Io e Caterina* (*Catherine and I*) (+ ro as Enrico)

1982 *Io so che tu sai che io so* (*I Know that You Know that I Know*) (as Fabio Bonetti); *In viaggio con papa* (*Journey with Papa*) (+ ro as Armando Ferretti, co-sc)

1983 *Un tassinaro* (*The Taxi Driver*) (+ ro as Pietro, co-sc)

1984 *Tutti dentro* (*Everybody in Jail*) (+ ro as Judge Annibale Salvemini)

1987 *Un tassinaro a New York* (*A Taxi Driver in New York*) (+ ro as Pietro, co-sc)

1992 *Assolto per aver commesso il Fatto* (*Acquitted for Having Committed the Deed*) (+ ro as Emilio Garrone, co-sc)

1994 *Nestore l'Ultima Corsa* (*Nestor's Last Trip*) (+ ro as Gaetano, co-sc)

Publications

By SORDI: articles—

Interview, in *Ecran* (Paris), November 1977.
"Alberto Sordi: 'Sur la scène, ce que je sais faire dans la vie,'" interview with A. Tournès, in *Jeune Cinéma* (Paris), April/May 1978.
Interview, in *Interview* (New York), July 1986.
"I mille volti di Alberto Sordi," interview with I. Jachini, in *Rivista del Cinematografo* (Rome), June 1993.

On SORDI: books—

Fava, Claudio G., *Alberto Sordi*, Rome, 1979.
Governi, Giancarlo, *Alberto Sordi: un italiano come noi*, Milan, 1979.
Porro, Maurizio, *Alberto Sordi*, Milan, 1979.

On SORDI: articles—

Mazzetti, L., "People of Talent: Alberto Sordi," in *Sight and Sound* (London), Summer 1956.
Cineforum (Bergano), May 1980.
CinemAction (Conde-sur-Noireau, France), March 1987.

"Un ricordo di Alberto Sordi per Zamap," in *Cinema Sud* (Avellino, Italy), December/January/February 1991/1992.

Grimes, W., "Comical Everyman of Italian Cinema," in *New York Times*, 11 March 1993.

*   *   *

Alberto Sordi is probably the most beloved personality of the Italian cinema. He commands a public so varied and a reputation so large that it is surprising he is little known outside his own country. His participation in international productions is also unfortunately rare.

Sordi entered films in 1938, but his comic sensibilities were not used to full advantage until Federico Fellini cast him as the false hero of photo-romances in *Lo sceicco bianco* and as a weak-willed provincialist in *I vitelloni*. From then on, Sordi was the king of satirical comedy, specializing in portrayals of inept, foolish, and pompous petite bourgeoisie frightened by progress and change. The films he starred in were far from exceptional, but Sordi's screen persona was powerful enough to transcend the limitations of his directors and production companies. These socially conscious comedies serve as an excellent barometer of the Italian cultural phenomena during the 1950s. His immense popularity generated the demand for at least six films a year. *Un americano a Roma* has become a repertory favorite while *Un eroe dei nostri tempi* serves as a final distillation of his image: cowardly, conformist, and very, very funny.

Sordi's screen image developed more and more tragic overtones during the 1960s and 1970s, culminating in his masterful performance in *Un borghese piccolo piccolo*. He plays a man so blindly dedicated to his common son's vain attempts at social climbing that he becomes a criminal maniac. Since the late 1960s, Sordi has directed and scripted as well as starred in many critically neglected films which have been relatively successful at the box office. One of Sordi's favorite subjects in his own films is the generation gap, a theme he handles with concern and intelligence.

—Elaine Mancini

SPACEK, Sissy

Nationality: American. **Born:** Mary Elizabeth Spacek in Quitman, Texas, 25 December 1949. **Education:** Attended Quitman High School; Lee Strasberg Theatrical Institute, New York. **Family:** Married the art director Jack Fisk, 1974, one child. **Career:** Late 1960s—in New York as a budding rock singer: some work in commercials and as background singer; 1970—film extra in Warhol's *Trash*; 1972—first film role in *Prime Cut*; 1974—worked with Jack Fisk as set decorator on *Phantom of the Paradise*; 1995—in TV mini-series *Streets of Laredo*, a sequel to *Lonesome Dove*. **Awards:** Best Supporting Actress, New York Film Critics, for *Three Women*, 1977; Best Actress Academy Award, and Best Actress, New York Film Critics, for *Coal Miner's Daughter*, 1980, and for *Crimes of the Heart*, 1986. **Agent:** c/o Creative Artists Agency, 9830 Wilshire Boulevard, Beverly Hills, CA 90212, U.S.A.

Films as Actress:

1970   *Trash* (Morrissey) (as extra)
1972   *Prime Cut* (Ritchie) (as Poppy)
1973   *Ginger in the Morning* (Wiles) (title role); *Badlands* (Malick) (as Holly Sargis); *The Girls of Huntingdon House* (Kjellin—for TV)

1974   *The Migrants* (Gries—for TV) (as Wanda Trimpin)
1975   *Katherine* (Kagan—for TV) (title role)
1976   *Carrie* (De Palma) (title role)
1977   *Three Women* (Altman) (as Pinky); *Welcome to L.A.* (Rudolph) (as the maid)
1978   *Verna—USO Girl* (Maxwell—for TV) (title role)
1980   *Coal Miner's Daughter* (Apted) (as Loretta Lynn); *Heart Beat* (Byrum) (as Carolyn Cassady)
1981   *Raggedy Man* (Fisk) (as Nita Longley)
1982   *Missing* (Costa-Gavras) (as Beth Horman)
1983   *The Man with Two Brains* (Carl Reiner) (as voice of Ann Uumellmahaye)
1984   *The River* (Rydell) (as Mae Garvey)
1985   *Marie* (Donaldson) (title role)
1986   *'night, Mother* (Moore) (as Jessie Cates); *Crimes of the Heart* (Beresford) (as Babe Magrath); *Violets Are Blue* (Fisk) (as Gussie Sawyer)
1990   *The Long Walk Home* (Pearce) (as Miriam Thompson)
1991   *JFK* (Stone) (as Liz Garrison)
1992   *A Private Matter* (Joan Micklin Silver—for TV); *Hard Promises* (Grant) (as Chris Coalter)
1994   *Trading Mom* (*Mommy Market*) (Brelis—produced in 1992) (as Mommy/Mama/Mom/Natasha); *A Place for Annie* (for TV) (as Susan Lansing)
1995   *The Good Old Boys* (Jones—for TV); *The Grass Harp* (Charles Matthau) (as Verena)

Film as Art Director:

1977   *Death Game* (*The Seducers*) (Traynor)

Publications

On SPACEK: book—

Emerson, Mark, and Eugene E. Pfaff, *Country Girl: The Life of Sissy Spacek*, New York, 1988.

On SPACEK: articles—

Current Biography 1978, New York, 1978.
Hibbin, S., "Sissy Spacek," in *Films and Filming* (London), April 1985.
Mills, N., "Big Sissy," in *Stills* (London), February 1986.
Houtchens, C. J., "The Country Girl," in *Harper's Bazaar*, January 1990.
Bandler, Michael J., "'I've Kinda Found My Rhythm'," in *McCall's*, February 1991.

*   *   *

The Texas accent, which she has retained throughout her career, has allowed Sissy Spacek to play a variety of characters with Southern-American roots. But beyond this geographic similarity, she has been able to submerge her personality in various screen roles, instilling in them a genuine sincerity and bringing to them much subtlety and intelligence and an impressive emotional range. In the initial phase of her career she played victims: troubled teens and eccentrics, and characters who suffered much even after finding success. In her middle period, she was at her best as heroines, strong-willed women attempting to transcend obstacles as they carved out their lives or battled hypocrisy and bureaucracy. In her career's third period, she graduated to character roles.

Spacek's two best early-career roles were as adolescent outcasts, one a bored, brainlessly misguided teen who links up with a James Dean-obsessed killer in the cult classic *Badlands*, the other a deeply disturbed and repressed teen who comes to realize that she possesses

Sissy Spacek in *Badlands*

telekinetic powers in *Carrie*. She was equally fine in *Three Women* playing Pinky, a strange, psychologically complex young woman who comes to work in a health care facility for senior citizens and forms a bond with a co-worker. In *Coal Miner's Daughter*, she won an Oscar playing the most solidly grounded of her early roles: Loretta Lynn, who emerged from a poverty-stricken life in the Kentucky coal fields to win fame as a country music legend. Still, Spacek's Loretta is a deeply vulnerable character. With her success comes feelings of self-doubt, which play themselves out in self-destructive behavior and an eventual on-stage breakdown.

Phase two of Spacek's career commences with *Raggedy Man*, in which she gives an energetic, naturalistic performance as a young divorcee attempting to establish a life for herself and her two children. She was equally effective in *Missing*, as a wife whose husband has mysteriously disappeared in a Latin American country; *The River*, as a Tennessee farm woman fighting to keep the family land out of the hands of bankers; and *Marie*, about a divorced mother who battles corruption in the Tennessee state government.

The next transformation of her career begins with *'night, Mother* (playing an unhappy, suicidal woman) and *Crimes of the Heart* (as the

weirdest of three flaky Southern sisters), roles which are older variations of her early-career characterizations. Around this time, she also played a rare, strictly romantic lead in *Violets Are Blue*. Another, albeit different, character part came in *The Long Walk Home*, playing a proper, upper-class representative of traditional Southern womanhood who slowly has her consciousness raised in the preintegration 1950s.

In the 1990s, Spacek began appearing more frequently in prestige television movies. And she played her first nonglamorous middle-aged screen character in *The Grass Harp*, cast as a haughty, close-minded businesswoman in a small pre-World War II Southern town who is most concerned with making money and owning people. Her character (who is closer in appearance to Edna May Oliver than any freckle-faced ingenue or determined heroine) is contrasted to her gentle-souled sister (Piper Laurie). Both Spacek and Laurie offer award-caliber performances (ironically, almost two decades earlier, Laurie had been cast in *Carrie* as Spacek's religious-fanatic mother). Her success in *The Grass Harp* at once mirrors Spacek's versatility and serves as proof that she will yet again successfully alter her career to fit her age.

—Rob Edelman

STALLONE, Sylvester

Nationality: American. **Born:** Michael Sylvester Stallone in New York City, 6 July 1946. **Education:** Attended Devereux High School, Berwyn, Pennsylvania; an American college in Leysin, Switzerland (also served as athletic coach); University of Miami, Coral Gables. **Family:** Married 1) Sasha Czack, 1974 (divorced 1985), sons: Sage Moonblood, Seth; 2) the actress Brigitte Nielsen, 1985 (divorced 1987). **Career:** Late 1960s—worked as pizza demonstrator, swept zoo cages, and usher in New York while trying to get acting parts; 1970—film debut in *Party at Kitty and Studs*; 1976—role in film based on his own script, *Rocky*; 1978—directed first film, *Paradise Alley*. **Awards:** Honorary César, 1992. **Agent:** c/o William Morris Agency, 151 El Camino Drive, Beverly Hills, CA 90212, U.S.A.

Films as Actor:

1970   *The Italian Stallion* (*Party at Kitty and Studs*) (Milton Lewis and Morton Lewis) (as Stud)

1971   *Bananas* (Woody Allen) (as mugger)

1974   *No Place to Hide* (Shaftel) (as Jerry); *The Prisoner of Second Avenue* (Frank) (as youth in park); *The Lords of Flatbush* (Verona and Davidson, + co-sc) (as Stanley)

1975   *Farewell My Lovely* (Richards) (as Kelly/Jonnie); *Capone* (Carver) (as Frank Nitti); *Death Race 2000* (Bartel) (as "Machine Gun" Joe Vitebo); *Rebel* (Schnitzer) (as Jerry Savage)

1976   *Rocky* (Avildsen) (as Rocky Balboa, + sc); *Cannonball* (*Carquake*) (Bartel) (cameo)

1978   *F.I.S.T.* (Jewison) (as Johnny Kovak, + co-sc)

1981   *Victory* (*Escape to Victory*) (Huston) (as Robert Hatch); *Nighthawks* (Malmuth) (as Deke DeSilva)

1982   *First Blood* (Kotcheff) (as John Rambo, + co-sc)

1984   *Rhinestone* (Clark) (as Nick, + co-sc)

1985   *Rambo: First Blood, Part II* (Cosmatos) (as John Rambo, + co-sc)

1986   *Cobra* (Cosmatos) (as Marion Cobretti, + co-sc); *Over the Top* (Golan) (as Lincoln Hawk, + co-sc)

1988   *Rambo III* (MacDonald) (title role, + co-sc)

1989   *Lock Up* (Flynn) (as Frank Leone); *Tango and Cash* (Konchalovsky) (as Ray Tango)

1990   *Rocky V* (Avildsen) (title role, + sc)

1991   *Oscar* (Landis) (as Angelo "Snaps" Provolone)

1992   *Stop! Or My Mom Will Shoot* (Spottiswoode) (as Sgt. Joe Bomowski)

1993   *Cliffhanger* (Harlin) (as Gabe Walker, + sc); *Demolition Man* (Brambilla) (as Sgt. John Spartan)

1994   *The Specialist* (Llosa) (as Ray Quick)

Sylvester Stallone as Rambo

1995 *Judge Dredd* (Cannon) (title role); *Assassins* (Richard Donner)
     (as Robert Rath)
1996 *Daylight* (Rob Cohen); *Firestorm* (Andrew Davis)

Films as Director and Scriptwriter:

1978 *Paradise Alley* (+ ro as Cosmo Carboni)
1979 *Rocky II* (+ title role)
1982 *Rocky III* (+ title role)
1983 *Staying Alive* (co-sc, + co-pr)
1985 *Rocky IV* (+ title role)

Publications

By STALLONE: books—

The Official Rocky Handbook, New York, 1977.
Paradise Alley (novel), New York, 1977.

By STALLONE: articles—

Interview with Pat H. Broeske, in *Stills* (London), December 1985/
     January 1986.
"Sly's Body Electric," interview with Zoe Heller, in *Vanity Fair* (New
     York), November 1993.
"The Underdog Triumphs!," interview with Graham Fuller, in *Interview*
     (New York), October 1994.
"Sly," interview with Joel Silver, in *Interview* (New York), July 1995.

On STALLONE: books—

Daly, Marsha, *Sylvester Stallone: An Illustrated Life*, New York, 1984.
L., Christophe, and Guy Braucourt, *Sylvester Stallone*, Paris, 1985.
Rovin, Jeff, *Stallone! A Hero's Story*, New York, 1985.
Neibaur, James L., *Tough Guy: The American Movie Macho*, Jefferson,
     North Carolina, 1989.

On STALLONE: articles—

Calhoun, J., "Sylvester Stallone," in *Films in Review* (New York),
     August/September 1982.
Hibbin, S., "Star Profile: Sylvester Stallone," in *Films and Filming*
     (London), March 1984.
Pally, M., "Red Faces," in *Film Comment* (New York), January/Febru-
     ary 1986.
Gauthier, G., "Western-Eastern," in *Revue du Cinéma* (Paris), April
     1986.
Brauerhoch, A., "Glanz und Elend der Muskelmänner," in *Frauen und
     Film* (Frankfurt), August 1986.
Stauth, Cameron, "Requiem for a Heavyweight," in *American Film*
     (New York), January 1990.
Brown, Ian, "Portrait of the Artist as a Movie Star," in *Premiere* (New
     York), February 1991.
Crawley, T., "The End of Stallone's Rocky Road," in *Film Monthly*
     (Berkhamsted, England), February 1991.
Weinraub, Bernard, "All Right, Already, No More Mr. Funny Guy," in
     New York Times, 9 June 1993.
Current Biography 1994, New York, 1994.

*   *   *

Regardless of how one may feel about Sylvester Stallone and what
he represents, he is still a bankable star of the first magnitude. With
Arnold Schwarzenegger, he is the preeminent action-movie star of his
era, an actor whose mere presence in films with such generic titles as
Cobra, Cliffhanger, The Specialist, Demolition Man, and *Judge Dredd*
signals to audiences a certain kind of contemporary movie: mindlessly
violent action films where character development is secondary to
special effects, gushing blood, and high body counts. Stallone's appeal
in such films is based on a combination of his brawn and the physical
heroics his character undergoes, rather than any acting ability. Often,
Stallone grunts his way through his films, having been given hardly
any dialog lasting beyond a few sentences at a time. But then, his
characters are meant to be men of action, rather than words.

This is not to say that Stallone has made flawless career choices. He
has involved himself in movies that have flopped. In *F.I.S.T.*, a box-
office failure (which is nonetheless one of his best films), he had one
of his more ambitious roles as a Jimmy Hoffa-like labor leader. Not all
of his action films have been successes, either. One example is *Judge
Dredd*, a film which on paper seemed a sure-fire hit but which disappointed at the box office. And for the most part, he has met disaster
whenever attempting a change of pace. *Rhinestone*, for example,
starred him with Dolly Parton as a New York cabdriver who becomes
a hillbilly singer. As with most Stallone films, it earned dreadful reviews, but in this case audiences stayed away en masse. Stallone's
failures when veering from tried-and-true formulas are what separates
him from Schwarzenegger, who has worked successfully in other film
genres, even to the point of self-parody (as in *Twins* and *Junior*).

Stallone's most popular and enduring characters remain boxer Rocky
Balboa and Vietnam-veteran John Rambo; he appeared in each role in
a separate, hugely successful film series. Indeed, it was a combination
of his performance as the lovable proletarian lug Rocky Balboa, compounded by the real-life, rags-to-riches story of how the film came to
movie screens, which earned Stallone his initial mass fame. Stallone
was just another struggling, unbankable actor, playing bit parts and
featured roles as hoods (in, respectively, *Bananas* and *The Lords of
Flatbush*), when he penned the *Rocky* screenplay. In a schrewd move,
he refused to sell the script unless he would be allowed to play the title
role. He won out, and in so doing became one of Hollywood's most
well-publicized success stories and an American myth come to life.

In the great American tradition, the characters of Rocky Balboa
and John Rambo reflect the idealized triumph of the individual, and
herein lies the essence of the characters' appeal. At the same time,
politics also plays no small part in the *Rocky-Rambo* films. Rocky
Balboa may have started out as an endearing pug, a heartfelt symbol of
the common man who lives out the fantasies of millions of other
common men in that he gets his one shot at fame by fighting for the
world championship. But as the story of Rocky continued through its
sequels, Rocky literally wraps himself in the American flag. John
Rambo, meanwhile, rises out of the ashes of the Vietnam folly. He is a
bigger-than-life, thoroughly indestructible superhero—the good guy
who can never, ever be defeated, and the good guy that America
wishes itself to be. As Rambo battles the yellow and red perils (in
Rambo: First Blood, Part II and *Rambo III*), American males are
meant to fantasize about filling his shoes, just as they fantasize about
filling the shoes of a Don Mattingly or Dan Marino.

The *Rambo* films in particular are throwbacks to the 1950s, a
simpler age. America was then the self-proclaimed leader of the free
world. Good and bad were clearly defined, and war movies were popular
because they reenacted battles in conflicts from which the United
States emerged victorious. So for the Rambo films to have been popular, they must portray a soldier as a winner in battle—even if the facts
tell you that the war is lost. *First Blood*, the initial Rambo film,
focuses on the character's status as a Vietnam veteran. Next, he returns to the Asian jungle to liberate MIAs and rewrite the Vietnam
history book. Then, he finds a new war. This one may be set in
Afghanistan, but it is against the usual enemy: ludicrous commie-
miscreant caricatures who claim that they "try to be civilized" as they

beat unconscious their red, white, and blue-blooded foes. But after being exposed to a strong dose of Rambo, they are destined to fall like cattle rustlers in a John Wayne Western. Indeed, in the 1980s, Stallone came to replace Wayne as the celluloid symbol of love-it-or-leave-it, hit-first-and-ask-questions-later conservatism.

In effect, in his subsequent big-budget action extravaganzas, Stallone has played thinly disguised Rambo variations. In the trailer for *The Specialist*, viewers are told all they need to know about Stallone's character when informed that "the government taught him to kill"—a description that also holds true for John Rambo. In *Nighthawks*, Stallone plays a stalwart New York City cop who learned his killing skills—where else?—on the battlefields of Southeast Asia.

To Stallone's credit, he cannot be faulted for attempting to extend his screen persona, and he does understand his liabilities as an actor. Even if Rambo and Rocky will not carry him into the next century, he has made his mark. His screen persona should not easily be dismissed, just as his pop-cultural success cannot be ignored.

—James M. Welsh, updated by Rob Edelman

STAMP, Terence

Nationality: British. **Born:** Terence Henry Stamp in Stepney, London, England, 22 July 1938. **Education:** Attended the Webber-Douglas Drama School, London. **Career:** Stage actor: role in *Why the Chicken*; 1962—film debut in title role in *Billy Budd*; later stage roles in *Dracula, The Lady from the Sea*, and *Alfie*; 1980s—published three volumes of autobiography. **Awards:** Best Actor, Cannes Festival, for *The Collector*, 1965. **Address:** c/o Markham and Froggatt, 4 Windmill St, London W1, England **Agent:** IFA Talent Agency, 8730 Sunset Boulevard, Suite 490, Los Angeles, CA 90069, U.S.A.

Films as Actor:

1962   *Billy Budd* (Ustinov) (title role); *Term of Trial* (Glenville) (as Mitchell)
1965   *The Collector* (Wyler) (as Freddie Clegg)
1966   *Modesty Blaise* (Losey) (as Willie Garvin)
1967   *Far from the Madding Crowd* (Schlesinger) (as Sgt. Troy); *Poor Cow* (Loach) (as Dave)
1968   "Toby Dammit" ep. of *Histoires extraordinaires* (*Spirits of the Dead*) (Fellini) (title role); *Blue* (Narizzano) (title role); *Teorema* (*Theorem*) (Pasolini) (as the visitor)
1970   *The Mind of Mr. Soames* (Cooke) (as John Soames)
1971   *Una stagione all' inferno* (Risi)
1974   *Hu Man* (Lapperrousaz)
1976   *Strip-Tease* (Lorente); *La divina creatura* (*The Divine Nymph*) (Griffi) (as Duke Daniele di Bagnasco)
1978   *The Thief of Bagdad* (Clive Donner—for TV) (as Wazir Jaudur); *Superman* (Richard Donner) (as Gen. Zod)
1979   *Amo non amo* (*I Love You, I Love You Not*) (Balducci); *Meetings with Remarkable Men* (Peter Brook) (as Prince Lubovedsky)
1980   *Misterio en la isla de los monstruos* (*Monster Island*; *Mystery of Monster Island*) (Piquer) (as Taskinar); *Superman II* (Lester) (as Gen. Zod)
1982   *Morte in Vaticano* (*Death in the Vatican*) (Aliprandi)
1983   *Bloody Chamber* (Lewin); *Chess Game* (Tucker—for TV)
1984   *The Hit* (Frears) (as Willie Parker); *The Company of Wolves* (Jordan)

1986   *Hud* (Lokkeberg) (as Edward, an artist); *Legal Eagles* (Reitman) (as Victor Taft); *Link* (Franklin) (as Dr. Steven Philip); *Directed by William Wyler* (Slesin—doc) (as himself)
1987   *The Sicilian* (Cimino) (as Prince Borsa); *Wall Street* (Stone) (as Sir Larry Wildman)
1988   *Alien Nation* (Baker) (as William Harcort); *Young Guns* (Cain) (as John Henry Tunstall)
1990   *Genuine Risk* (Voss) (as Paul Hellwart)
1991   *Beltenebros* (*Prince of Shadows*) (Pilar Miro) (as Darman)
1993   *The Real McCoy* (Mulcahy) (as Jack Schmidt); *The Adventures of Priscilla, Queen of the Desert* (Elliott) (as Bernadette)
1996   *Tire a part* (Bernard Rapp)

Film as Director:

1990   *Stranger in the House* (+ sc, ro)

Publications

By STAMP: books—

Stamp Album, London, 1987.
Coming Attractions, London, 1988.
Double Feature, London, 1989.
The Night, London, 1991.

By STAMP: articles—

Interviews with Robin Bean, in *Films and Filming* (London), December 1968 and January 1969.
Interview with Sheila Johnston, in *Stills* (London), October 1984.
Interview with F. Guérif and P. Mérigeau, in *Revue du Cinéma* (Paris), October 1985.
Interview with Allan Hunter, in *Films and Filming* (London), June 1988.
"Terence Stamp's Summer Camp," interview with Jonathan Bernstein, in *Interview* (New York), August 1994.
"He's Every Woman," interview with Charles Busch, in *Advocate*, 24 January 1995.

On STAMP: article—

Dowd, Maureen, "He's Got Legs," in *Premiere* (New York), August 1994.

*   *   *

After years in which he had pretty much been out of the consciousness of moviegoers, Terence Stamp served notice that he still is an actor of considerable range with his eye-opening star turn in *The Adventures of Priscilla, Queen of the Desert*. Stamp had not exactly been absent from movie screens, but he was commanding neither memorable featured parts nor the prestige starring roles he had won earlier in his career. For instance, when one thinks of *Wall Street*, in which he had a supporting role, one thinks of Oliver Stone, Michael Douglas, Charlie Sheen, and featured cast members Hal Holbrook, Martin Sheen, Daryl Hannah, and James Spader. When one thinks of *Young Guns*—in which Stamp has one of his better later-career roles as a British gentleman who becomes mentor to six youthful hooligans in the American West—one thinks of Charlie Sheen, Emilio Estevez, Lou Diamond Phillips, and the other actors cast in the title roles.

Back in the 1960s, his decade of stardom, Stamp established himself with his Oscar-nominated supporting performance as the ingenu-

Terence Stamp in *The Collector*

ous, ill-fated seaman in Melville's *Billy Budd*. This success led to his being cast with varying degrees of success in high-profile, prestige productions. Stamp's best roles were complex, enigmatic ones. In *Poor Cow*, he is impressive as the petty criminal whose tenderness towards Carol White is countered by his vicious beating of an elderly victim. He gave his best star performances in *The Collector*, playing a warped young amateur lepidopterist who kidnaps an art student, hoping that during her imprisonment she will come to love him; the Fellini-directed segment of the three-part *Spirits of the Dead*, a surreal adaptation of an Edgar Allan Poe story in which Stamp is cast as a cynical, alcoholic, ill-fated movie star; and *Teorema*, the story of a mysterious, ambiguous figure who disrupts and transforms the lives of a bourgeois Italian family. While the latter is very much the creation of its writer-director, Pier Paolo Pasolini, the film gains immeasurably from Stamp's imposing presence and otherworldly features. His lesser roles of the period came in *Far from the Madding Crowd*, in which he has little to do but look good in a cavalry uniform and wave his saber for the benefit of Julie Christie, and the comic-strip film *Modesty Blaise*, in which he is stranded as Monica Vitti's sidekick.

In the 1970s and 1980s, Stamp made the transition from leading man to supporting actor. Among his best roles were the hunted ex-con in *The Hit* and the thoroughly evil General Zod in *Superman II* (also seen briefly in *Superman*). The character of General Zod may have been one-dimensional, but Stamp is highly effective as he adopts a calm, detached attitude to his acts of destruction. But for the most part, his roles (as well as films) remained undistinguished until, in a brilliant bit of casting, he signed on to play his highest-profile character in years: Bernadette, the dignified yet vulnerable transsexual in *Priscilla*. The film is a funny, moving, sleeper hit comedy in which Stamp is one-third of a drag queen act touring the Australian provinces. Bernadette is a risky character for any actor, one which easily might have degenerated into a campy caricature. But the actor's striking features and sheer presence lent much to the role, which ends up a sensational star turn—and, perhaps, Stamp's most memorable screen characterization.

—Daniel O'Brien, updated by Rob Edelman

STANTON, Harry Dean

Nationality: American. **Born:** West Irvine, Kentucky, 14 July 1926. **Education:** Attended the University of Kentucky, Lexington. **Career:** Served in the U.S. Navy during World War II; 1950s—began acting in bit parts in films; 1962—first billed part in *Hero's Island*. **Agent:** Bresler Kelly Kipperman, 15760 Ventura Boulevard, Suite 1730, Encino, CA 91436, U.S.A.

Films as Actor:

1962 *Hero's Island* (Stevens) (as Dixey)
1963 *The Man from the Diner's Club* (Tashlin) (as Beatnik)
1966 *The Hostage* (Doughten) (as Eddie)
1967 *Cool Hand Luke* (Rosenberg) (as tramp); *A Time for Killing* (Karlson) (as Sgt. Dan Way)
1968 *Day of the Evil Gun* (Thorpe) (as Sgt. Parker); *The Mini-Skirt Mob* (Dexter) (as Spook)
1970 *Rebel Rousers* (Cohen); *Kelly's Heroes* (Hutton) (as Willard)
1971 *Two-Lane Blacktop* (Hellman) (as Oklahoma hitchhiker)
1972 *Cisco Pike* (Norton) (as Jesse)

1973 *Dillinger* (Milius) (as Homer Van Meter); *Pat Garrett and Billy the Kid* (Peckinpah) (as Luke)
1974 *Where the Lilies Bloom* (Graham) (as Kiser Pease); *Cockfighter* (Hellman) (as Jack); *The Godfather, Part II* (Coppola) (as FBI Agent)
1975 *Farewell, My Lovely* (Richards) (as Billy Rolfe); *Ninety-Two in the Shade* (McGuane) (as Carter); *Rafferty and the Gold Dust Twins* (Richards) (as Billy Winston); *Rancho Deluxe* (Perry) (as Curt)
1976 *The Missouri Breaks* (Penn) (as Calvin)
1978 *Renaldo and Clara* (Dylan) (as Lafkezio); *Straight Time* (Grosbard) (as Jerry Schue)
1979 *Flatbed Annie and Sweetiepie: Lady Truckers* (Greenwald—for TV); *Alien* (Scott) (as Brett); *The Rose* (Rydell) (as Billy Ray); *Wise Blood* (Huston) (as Asa Hawks)
1980 *The Black Marble* (Becker) (as Philo Skinner); *Private Benjamin* (Zieff) (as Sgt. Jim Ballard)
1981 *Escape from New York* (Carpenter) (as Brain)
1982 *One from the Heart* (Coppola) (as Moe); *Deathwatch* (Tavernier) (as Vincent Ferriman); *Young Doctors in Love* (Marshall) (as Dr. Oliver Ludwig)
1983 *Repo Man* (Cox) (as Bud); *I Want to Live* (Rich—for TV); *Christine* (Carpenter) (as Rudolph Junkins); **Paris, Texas** (Wenders) (as Travis Clay Henderson)
1984 *Red Dawn* (Milius) (as Mr. Eckert); *The Bear* (Sarafian) (as Coach Thomas)
1985 *One Magic Christmas* (Borso) (as Gideon); *Fool for Love* (Altman) (as Old Man); *The Care Bears Movie* (Selznick) (as voice of Brave Heart Lion); *Uforia* (Binder) (as Brother Bud)
1986 *Pretty in Pink* (Deutsch) (as Jack Walsh)
1987 *Slamdance* (Wang) (as Smiley)
1988 *Stars and Bars* (O'Connor) (as Loomis Gage); *Mr. North* (Danny Huston) (as Henry Simmons); *The Last Temptation of Christ* (Scorsese) (as Saul/Paul)
1989 *Dream a Little Dream* (Rocco) (as Ike Baker); *Twister* (Almereyda) (as Eugene Cleveland); *Monster Maker* (Foster—for TV)
1990 *The Fourth War* (Frankenheimer) (as General Roger Hackworth); *Wild at Heart* (Lynch) (as Johnnie Farragut); *Stranger in the House* (Stamp); *Motion and Emotion* (as himself)
1991 *The Payoff* (Cooper) (as Harry Hook)
1992 *Man Trouble* (Rafelson) (as Redmond Layls); *Twin Peaks: Fire Walk with Me* (Lynch) (as Carl Rodd)
1993 *Hostages* (Wheatley—for TV) (as Frank Reed); *Hotel Room* (Signorelli and Lynch—for TV)
1994 *Blue Tiger* (Barba—for TV) (as Smith); *Against the Wall* (Frankenheimer—for TV) (as Hal Smith)
1995 *Never Talk to Strangers* (P. Hall) (as Max Cheski); *A Hundred and One Nights* (as Furtive and Friendly Appearance)
1996 *Down Periscope* (David S. Ward) (as Howard)

Publications

By STANTON: articles—

Interview with Roger Ebert, in *Chicago Sun-Times*, 9 December 1984.
Interview in *The Face* (London), June 1985.
Interview with Madonna, in *Inter/View* (New York), December 1985.
Interview in *Premiere* (New York), December 1985.
Interview in *Time Out* (London), 6 August 1986.
Interview by Ingrid Sischy, in *Interview*, January 1991.
"The Freshest Car Fresheners," in *Interview*, June 1993.

Harry Dean Stanton in *Alien*

On STANTON: articles—

Yakir, Dan, "Harry Dean Stanton: The Outsider Is Now 'In'," in *USA Today*, 13 December 1984.

Oney, Steve, "A Character Actor Reaches Cult Status," in *New York Times*, 16 November 1986.

*   *   *

Harry Dean Stanton is a Kentucky-born character actor who has appeared in numerous films since the mid-1960s. His sullen, dour appearance has served him in a wide range of roles, particularly that of burnt-out misfits living on the fringe of society. His lean frame, coupled with a long, lonely face is well-suited for Westerns and Western characters. One of his most memorable was featured in *The Missouri Breaks* as the elderly, dignified Calvin, a traditional cowboy of the Old West who did not care for his gang leader's plans for starting a farm.

Since the late 1970s Stanton has demonstrated his versatility in a series of low-key roles. As an Army recruiter in *Private Benjamin*, he conned the vulnerable Goldie Hawn into joining the armed forces. In *The Rose* he was the legendary country singer who quietly admonished the trashy rock star to "not talk trash to my boy."

Stanton has etched memorable portraits of some of society's losers. He received critical acclaim for his performance in *Farewell, My Lovely* as the washed-up musician living with his wife and son in the shadows of a seedy apartment. In the futuristic *Escape from New York* he was Brain, whose domain was a burnt-out Manhattan Public Library. Stanton did a comic variation on these roles in *Young Doctors in Love* and *Repo Man*, in which his rumpled, liquor-soaked characters were openly defiant of polite society and whose very appearance was a mockery.

Stanton has been especially prized by directors of art house and independent films. Paul Cox, David Lynch, and Wim Wenders have all given him important roles. Wenders chose Stanton to star in *Paris, Texas*, in which Stanton movingly portrays a drifter who seeks to be reunited with his family. The film won top honors at the 1984 Cannes Film Festival, and Stanton's performance was critically praised.

In the tradition of great supporting players, he has also given on-screen support to some of film's finest actors, including Marlon Brando, Jack Nicholson, Robert Mitchum, and Dustin Hoffman. His is the memorable face with the unfamiliar name, whose film appearances have earned him something of a cult reputation.

—Donald Liebenson, updated by Frank Uhle

STANWYCK, Barbara

Nationality: American. **Born:** Ruby Stevens in Brooklyn, New York, 16 July 1907. **Education:** Attended elementary schools in Brooklyn. **Family:** Married 1) Frank Fay, 1928 (divorced 1935); 2) the actor Robert Taylor, 1939 (divorced 1951). **Career:** Working girl from early age; wrapper in a department store, telephone operator, pattern cutter, file clerk; then dancer in night clubs; 1923—first stage appearance in musical comedy; toured with *Ziegfeld Follies of 1923*; 1926— in dramatic role in stage play *The Noose*; 1927—film debut in *Broadway Nights*; 1931—contract with Warner Brothers; 1935—freelance actress; 1936—began radio acting with *Lux Radio Theatre*; 1956— formed Barwyk Corporation production company; 1960-61—host of TV series *The Barbara Stanwyck Show*, and in *The Big Valley* series, 1965-69; 1980s—in TV mini-series *The Thorn Birds*, 1983, and 1985-86 in series *The Colbys*. **Awards:** Co-recipient, Special Jury Prize for Ensemble Acting, Venice Festival, for *Executive Suite*, 1954; Special Academy Award, for "superlative creativity and unique contribution to the art of screen acting," 1981. **Died:** In Santa Monica, California, 20 January 1990.

Films as Actress:

1927   *Broadway Nights* (Boyle) (as dancer)

1929   *The Locked Door* (Fitzmaurice) (as Ann Carter); *Mexicali Rose* (Kenton) (title role)

1930   *Ladies of Leisure* (Capra) (as Kay Arnold)

1931   *Illicit* (Mayo) (as Anne Vincent); *Ten Cents a Dance* (Barrymore) (as Barbara O'Neil); *Night Nurse* (Wellman) (as Lora Hart); *The Miracle Woman* (Capra) (as Florence Fallon)

1932   *Forbidden* (Capra) (as Lulu Smith); *Shopworn* (Grinde) (as Kitty Lane); *So Big* (Wellman) (as Selina Peake Dejong); *The Purchase Price* (Wellman) (as Joan Gordon)

1933   *The Bitter Tea of General Yen* (Capra) (as Megan Davis); *Ladies They Talk About* (Bretherton) (as Nan Taylor); *Baby Face* (Green) (as Lily Powers); *Ever in My Heart* (Mayo) (as Mary Archer)

1934   *Gambling Lady* (Mayo) (as Lady Lee); *A Lost Lady* (Green) (as Marian Ormsby)

1935   *The Secret Bride* (Dieterle) (as Ruth Vincent); *The Woman in Red* (Florey) (as Shelby Barrett); *Red Salute* (Lanfield) (as Drue Van Allen); *Annie Oakley* (Stevens) (title role)

1936   *A Message to Garcia* (George Marshall) (as Raphaelita Maderos); *The Bride Walks Out* (Jason) (as Carolyn Martin); *His Brother's Wife* (Van Dyke) (as Rita Wilson); *Banjo on My Knee* (Cromwell) (as Pearl Holley); *The Plough and the Stars* (Ford) (as Nora Clitheroe)

1937   *Interns Can't Take Money* (Santell) (as Janet Haley); *This Is My Affair* (Seiter) (as Lil Duryea); *Stella Dallas* (King Vidor) (title role); *Breakfast for Two* (Santell) (as Valentine Ransom)

1938   *Always Goodbye* (Lanfield) (as Margot Weston); *The Mad Miss Manton* (Jason) (title role)

1939   *Union Pacific* (Cecil B. DeMille) (as Mollie Monahan); *Golden Boy* (Mamoulian) (as Lorna Moon)

1940   *Remember the Night* (Leisen) (as Lee Leander)

1941   **The Lady Eve** (Preston Sturges) (as Jean Harrington); *Meet John Doe* (Capra) (as Ann Mitchell); *You Belong to Me* (Ruggles) (as Helen Hunt); *Ball of Fire* (Hawks) (as Sugarpuss O'Shea)

1942   *The Great Man's Lady* (Wellman) (as Hannah Sempler); *The Gay Sisters* (Rapper) (as Fiona Gaylord)

1943   *Lady of Burlesque* (Wellman) (as Dixie Daisy); *Flesh and Fantasy* (Duvivier) (as Joan Stanley)

1944   **Double Indemnity** (Wilder) (as Phyllis Dietrichson); *Hollywood Canteen* (Daves) (as herself)

1945   *Christmas in Connecticut* (Godfrey) (as Elizabeth Lane)

1946   *My Reputation* (Bernhardt) (as Jessica Drummond); *The Bride Wore Boots* (Pichel) (as Sally Warren); *The Strange Love of Martha Ivers* (Milestone) (title role); *California* (Farrow) (as Lily Bishop)

1947   *The Two Mrs. Carrolls* (Godfrey) (as Sally Morton Carroll); *The Other Half* (de Toth) (as Karen Duncan); *Cry Wolf* (Godfrey) (as Sandra Marshall); *Variety Girl* (George Marshall) (as herself)

1948   *B. F.'s Daughter* (Leonard) (as Polly Fulton); *Sorry, Wrong Number* (Litvak) (as Leona Stevenson)

1949   *The Lady Gambles* (Gordon) (as Joan Boothe); *East Side, West Side* (LeRoy) (as Jessie Brown)

Barbara Stanwyck

1950   *The File on Thelma Jordan* (Siodmak) (title role); *No Man of Her Own* (Leisen) (as Helen Ferguson); *The Furies* (Anthony Mann) (as Vance Jeffords); *To Please a Lady* (Brown) (as Regina Forbes)
1951   *The Man with a Cloak* (Markle) (as Lorna Bounty)
1952   *Clash by Night* (Fritz Lang) (as Mae Doyle)
1953   *Jeopardy* (John Sturges) (as Helen Stilwin); *Titanic* (Negulesco) (as Julia Sturges); *All I Desire* (Sirk) (as Naomi Murdoch); *The Moonlighter* (Rowland) (as Rela); *Blowing Wild* (Fregonese) (as Marina)
1954   *Executive Suite* (Wise) (as Julie Tredway); *Witness to Murder* (Rowland) (as Cheryl Draper); *Cattle Queen of Montana* (Dwan) (as Sierra Nevada Jones)
1955   *The Violent Men* (Maté) (as Martha Wilkinson); *Escape to Burma* (Dwan) (as Gwen Moore)
1956   *There's Always Tomorrow* (Sirk) (as Norma Miller); *The Maverick Queen* (Kane) (as Kit Banion); *These Wilder Years* (Rowland) (as Ann Dempster)
1957   *Crime of Passion* (Oswald) (as Kathy); *Trooper Hook* (Warren) (as Cora); *Forty Guns* (Fuller) (as Jessica Drummond)
1962   *Walk on the Wild Side* (Dmytryk) (as Jo Courtney)
1964   *Roustabout* (Rich) (as Maggie Morgan)
1965   *The Night Walker* (Castle) (as Irene Trent)
1970   *The House That Wouldn't Die* (Llewellyn—for TV) (as Ruth Bennett)
1971   *A Taste of Evil* (Llewellyn—for TV) (as Miriam Jennings)
1973   *The Letters* (Nelson—for TV) (as Geraldine Parkington)

Publications

By STANWYCK: articles—

"Stanwyck Speaks," interview with B. Drew, in *Film Comment* (New York), March-April 1981.
Interview with Robert Blees, in *American Film* (Washington, D.C.), April 1987.

On STANWYCK: books—

Rosen, Marjorie, *Popcorn Venus*, New York, 1973.
Smith, Ella, *Starring Miss Barbara Stanwyck*, New York, 1974; rev. ed., 1985.
Vermilye, Jerry, *Barbara Stanwyck*, New York, 1975.
DiOrio, Al, *Barbara Stanwyck*, New York, 1983.
Dickens, Homer, *The Films of Barbara Stanwyck*, Secaucus, New Jersey, 1984.
Wayne, Jane Ellen, *Stanwyck*, New York, 1985.
Madsen, Axel, *Stanwyck*, New York, 1994.

On STANWYCK: articles—

Current Biography 1947, New York, 1947.
Ringgold, Gene, "Barbara Stanwyck," in *Films in Review* (New York), December 1963.
Lewis, Joseph H., "Barbara Stanwyck: A Fiery Devotion," in *Close-Ups: The Movie Star Book*, edited by Danny Peary, New York, 1978.
Corliss, Richard, "Barbara Stanwyck," in *The Movie Star*, edited by Elisabeth Weis, New York, 1981.
"Class," by J. McCourt, "Stella Stanwyck," by D. Thomson, "Stanwyck & Capra," by R. T. Jameson, and "The Strange Fate of Barbara Stanwyck," by S. Harvey, in *Film Comment* (New York), March-April 1981.
"Barbara Stanwyck," letter from M. Buckley, in *Films in Review* (New York), June-July 1981.

Lloyd, A., "Barbara Stanwyck," in *Films and Filming* (London), July 1984.
Viviani, C., and Yann Tobin, "Capra et Barbara Stanwyck: éclat et éclatement du mélo," in *Positif* (Paris), July/August 1987.
Peary., G., "Barbara Stanwyck," in *American Film* (New York), July/August 1989.
McBride, Joseph, obituary in *Variety* (New York), 24 January 1990.
Murphy, Kathleen, "Farewell My Lovelies," in *Film Comment* (New York), July/August 1990.

*   *   *

Of strong and resolute character, the Stanwyck woman seemed equal to whatever life might bring her, and the result was that there was little in the way of struggle, corruption, sacrifice, hysteria, or fun that Barbara Stanwyck did not experience and convey with startling honesty.

It was Frank Capra who first recognized and elicited Stanwyck's ability to render emotion before it has been rationalized or repressed. Under his direction, she gave her most sensual performance in *The Bitter Tea of General Yen* as a straight-laced, yet fervent missionary who comes to not only accept but love the cultivated warlord who abducts her. The expected changes of heart that Capra's populist comedies would dramatize were first and more subtly worked out in his films with the young, pliant Stanwyck. Capra brought out the moral passion lurking in Stanwyck's intensity, the counterpart to the talent for evil that her film noir roles would later explore.

Stanwyck's capacity for self-transfiguration, which Capra put to ironic use in his tale of a compromised female evangelist, *The Miracle Woman*, has been overlooked by even her most sympathetic critics, but the last shot of *Stella Dallas* proclaims and glorifies it. Even in less high-toned films about female self-betterment such as *Shopworn* and Capra's *Ladies of Leisure*, Stanwyck showed undisguised feeling for the dreams, often understandably shabby, dreamt by those with little hope and no faith except in themselves.

Her comic heroines never quite forget their relation to their hard-boiled, often manhandled cousins. Even when presented the assured blessings of comic existence, Stanwyck never trusts to luck alone; romantic kismet, in particular, is notoriously unreliable. In *The Lady Eve* she spends the first half of the film falling for her chosen dupe, the irresistibly naive Henry Fonda, the second half revenging herself on him for not seeing that good girls are not as good as they look and bad girls not as bad as he thinks. She is equally convincing in admitting the limits of her wisdom, as in her savvy, yet tenderhearted performance as the newspaperwoman who pleads for the populist idealism she once scoffed at in *Meet John Doe*.

In the late 1940s and through the 1950s, Stanwyck was called upon to exhibit and endure a battery of female neuroses—invalidism, masochism, helpless addiction, and baffled desire—taking on such parts as the hysteric in *Sorry, Wrong Number* and a gambler beaten within an inch of her life in *The Lady Gambles*. Even when possessed of power she would turn it against herself, nursing her impotent hatred for the tycoon who rejected her in *Executive Suite* or, more strikingly, concealing a murderous hatred and even more fatal love in *The Strange Love of Martha Ivers*. But she also struggled against quieter forms of desperation, nowhere with more dignity than in two of Douglas Sirk's less gaudy melodramas of life desiccated by convention, *All I Desire* and *There's Always Tomorrow*. These years touched more boldly, too, on a sexual ambiguity that could shadow her femme fatales and self-reliant frontier women. Her harsh blond in *Double Indemnity* intensifies rather than interrupts the relationship between Fred McMurray's Walter and Edward G. Robinson's Keyes, giving a peculiar suggestion to the desperation in Walter's passion for her. By the time of *Walk on the Wild Side* she unabashedly plays a lesbian madam.

Fearless in whatever psychic territory she was asked to explore, she braved the wilds of the first patently Freudian Western, *The Furies*, and in old age was mortified by sexual desire in *The Thorn Birds*. Whether playing a struggling working girl, burlesque queen, madcap heiress, sassy gunmoll, doting mother, lonely career woman, restless wife, murderous adulteress, or rugged frontier woman, Stanwyck could gaze into the heart of her character and never blink.

—Arthur Nolletti Jr., updated by Maria DiBattista

STEENBURGEN, Mary

Nationality: American. **Born:** Newport, Arkansas, 8 February 1953. **Family:** Married 1) the actor Malcolm McDowell, 1980 (divorced 1990), children: Lilly and Charlie; 2) the actor Ted Danson, 1995. **Education:** Attended Hendrix College where she studied drama; continued her studies in New York at the Neighborhood Playhouse, with Sanford Meisner. **Career:** Mid-1970s—acted on stage at the Neighborhood Playhouse, and with a comedy improvisational group; 1978—selected by Jack Nicholson to make her screen debut in *Goin' South*; 1985—in TV mini-series *Tender Is the Night*; 1992—politically involved with liberal causes, and actively campaigned for Bill Clinton. **Awards:** Best Supporting Actress Academy Award, and Golden Globe Award, for *Melvin and Howard*, 1980; honorary doctorate degrees from Hendrix College, Conway, Arkansas, and the University of Arkansas at Little Rock. **Agent:** William Morris Agency, 151 El Camino Drive, Beverly Hills, CA 90212, U.S.A.

Films as Actress:

1978   *Goin' South* (Nicholson) (as Julia Tate); *Rabbit Test* (Joan Rivers)
1979   *Time after Time* (Meyer) (as Amy Robbins)
1980   *Melvin and Howard* (Jonathan Demme) (as Lynda Dummar)
1981   *Ragtime* (Forman) (as Mother)
1982   *A Midsummer Night's Sex Comedy* (Woody Allen) (as Adrian)
1983   *Cross Creek* (Ritt) (as Marjorie Kinnan Rawlings); *Romantic Comedy* (Hiller) (as Phoebe)
1985   *One Magic Christmas* (Borsos) (as Ginny Grainger)
1987   *Dead of Winter* (Arthur Penn) (as Julie Rose/Katie McGovern/ Evelyn); *The Whales of August* (Lindsay Anderson) (as Young Sarah)
1988   *End of the Line* (Russell) (as Rose Pickett, + exec pr); *The Attic: The Hiding of Anne Frank* (Erman—for TV) (as Miep Gies)
1989   *Miss Firecracker* (Schlamme) (as Elain Rutledge); *Parenthood* (Ron Howard) (as Karen Buckman)
1990   *Back to the Future, Part III* (Zemeckis) (as Clara Clayton); *The Long Walk Home* (Pearce) (as narrator)
1991   *The Butcher's Wife* (Terry Hughes) (as Stella)
1993   *Philadelphia* (Jonathan Demme) (as Belinda Conine); *What's Eating Gilbert Grape* (Hallström) (as Betty Carver); *Earth and the American Dream* (Couturie—doc) (voice only)
1994   *Clifford* (Flaherty) (as Sarah Davis); *Pontiac Moon* (Medak) (as Katherine Bellamy); *It Runs in the Family* (*My Summer Story*) (Bob Clark) (as Mom)
1995   *My Family* (*Mi Familia*) (Nava) (as Gloria); *The Grass Harp* (Matthau) (as Sister Ida); *Powder* (Salva) (as Jessie Caldwell); *Nixon* (Oliver Stone) (as Hannah Nixon)
1996   *Gulliver's Travels* (Sturridge—for TV) (as Mary Gulliver)

Publications

By STEENBURGEN: articles—

Interview with A. Foley, in *Mademoiselle* (New York), November 1979.
"At the Movies," interview with Stephen Holden, in *New York Times*, 22 August 1986.

On STEENBURGEN: articles—

Gottlieb, A., "Mary Steenburgen: A Country Girl Finds Happiness in Hollywood," in *Mademoiselle* (New York), November 1980.
Eisenberg, L., "The Mary Steenburgen Story," in *Rolling Stone* (New York), 2 September 1982.
"Keep Your Eye on . . . a Star Named Steenburgen," in *Harper's Bazaar* (New York), October 1983.
Yakir, Dan, "A Special Way of Life," in *Horizon* (New York), October 1983.
Garel, A., "Mary Steenburgen Bio-Filmography," in *Revue du Cinéma* (Paris), May 1989.
Farrell, Mary, and Vicki Sheff, "After Years on the Mommy Track, Mary Steenburgen Knows the Full Route of Parenthood," in *People Weekly* (New York), 28 August 1989.
Cerio, Gregory, and Vicki Sheff-Cahan, "Merry Mary," in *People Weekly* (New York), 21 November 1994.

*   *   *

Mary Steenburgen is a bright screen presence and a congenial, all-purpose character performer who has played both starring and supporting roles in almost two dozen movies since the late 1970s. She was one of a thousand anonymous, struggling unknowns who hailed from rural America and had come to the Big City to find success as an actress when she was discovered by Jack Nicholson in the reception room of Paramount Pictures's New York casting office. He was so impressed with her script reading that he had her flown to Hollywood for a screen test. The result: Steenburgen soon was making her movie debut in a juicy role as the willing heroine opposite Nicholson's grizzled Western outlaw in *Goin' South*.

Steenburgen quickly proved she was no celluloid one-shot with her outstanding performances in *Time after Time* and *Melvin and Howard*. In the former, an underrated combination romantic comedy-thriller-science fiction adventure, she again is the heroine: a twentieth-century woman who becomes the girlfriend of H. G. Wells (Malcolm McDowell), who has traveled in his time machine from Victorian England to the future to pursue Jack the Ripper. *Melvin and Howard* is the story of Melvin Dummar, the likable, anonymous factory worker who claimed he had been left $156 million by the late, eccentric billionaire Howard Hughes. Steenburgen stole the film—and walked off with the Best Supporting Actress Oscar—as Lynda, Dummar's on-again, off-again wife, a woman who is as affectionate as she is dense. Her dialogue, as delivered letter-perfect by Steenburgen, flows like syrup over pancakes. Lynda and Dummar's second wedding ceremony is a garish $39 affair at the Silver Bell Wedding Chapel, the matrimonial equivalent of Burger King. Lynda ever so excitedly gushes, "Oh, Melvin, I'm palpitating," as if she is a blushing, virginal bride; but she clearly is in the very late throes of pregnancy.

After her Oscar, Steenburgen was secure as an A-list actress. She was chosen by Milos Forman and Woody Allen for choice roles in, respectively, *Ragtime* and *A Midsummer Night's Sex Comedy*. As the years passed, she did fine work in a wide variety of films, including *Parenthood*, *One Magic Christmas*, and the television movie *The Attic: The Hiding of Anne Frank*. Lately, Steenburgen's showiest roles have been supporting ones, as older women who have appeared (or will appear) on the turf of the film's young hero. In *What's Eating Gilbert Grape*, she is the lover of Johnny Depp's Gilbert; in *The Grass Harp*, she is a freethinking evangelist who all-too-briefly captures the fancy of a teenager (Edward Furlong).

Mary Steenburgen (right) with Alfre Woodard in *Cross Creek*

Steenburgen has not forgotten her small-town Southern roots and the type of people who were such a part of her early life, a fact that has influenced her selection of roles. She was an appropriate choice as the narrator of *The Long Walk Home*, a consciousness-raising story set in the segregated American South of the mid-1950s. She had one of her best leading roles in *Cross Creek*, playing writer Marjorie Kinnan Rawlings, who abruptly decides to leave her husband and settle in the Florida bayou, where she comes to know the people in her midst and finds inspiration for her work. Nor has Steenburgen's success made her any less cognizant of the very real problems faced by the working folk she left behind when she headed North to pursue her career. She was the executive producer of, and took a small role in, *End of the Line*, a Capraesque tale with a populist plot line. Its heroes are two amiable good old boys (Wilford Brimley and Levon Helm), residents of Clifford, Arkansas (population: 2,506), who have never seen an ocean or heard of Pablo Picasso. They ask nothing of life but salmon pattie dinners, happy evenings around the card table, and a job to wake up to in the morning. Both men have devoted the best years of their lives to the Southland Railroad, but rumors abound that the company intends to convert its operation into an air freight service. When this happens, they promptly pilfer one of Southland's trains and set out for Chicago to confront the company's board chairman.

Also in recent years, Steenburgen has been in the news almost as often for her support of progressive political causes and her friendship with Bill and Hillary Clinton. She will accept a small role in a film because she believes in its artistic quality or political message. Witness her presence in *Philadelphia*, Jonathan Demme's AIDS awareness drama, in which she plays the lawyer hired to malign Andrew Beckett, the Main Line attorney who refuses to die quietly after being dismissed because he is HIV-positive; and in *My Family*, Gregory Nava's multigenerational saga of a Mexican-American family, in which she has the briefest of roles as the sympathetic employer of an illegal immigrant.

—Rob Edelman

STEIGER, Rod

Nationality: American. **Born:** Rodney Stephen Steiger in Westhampton, Long Island, New York, 14 April 1925. **Education:** Attended public schools in Irvington, Bloomfield, and Newark, New

Jersey; studied acting at the New School for Social Research, New York, two years. **Military Service:** U.S. Navy, 1941-45. **Family:** Married 1) the actress Sally Gracie, 1952 (divorced 1958); 2) the actress Claire Bloom, 1959 (divorced 1969), daughter: Anna Justine; 3) Sherry Nelson, 1973 (divorced 1979); 4) Paula Ellis. **Career:** 1947—actor on television, and studied acting at the Dramatic Workshop and the Actors Studio, New York; stage debut in *The Trial of Mary Dugan*; 1951—Broadway debut in *Night Music*; film debut in *Teresa*; 1959—on Broadway in *Rashomon*; 1977—in TV mini-series *Jesus of Nazareth, Hollywood Wives*, 1985, *Passion and Paradise*, 1989, *Sinatra*, 1992, *Armistead Maupin's Tales of the City*, 1994, and *Tom Clancy's Op Center*, 1995. **Awards:** Best Actor, Berlin Festival, Best Foreign Actor, British Academy, for *The Pawnbroker*, 1965; Best Actor Academy Award, Best Actor, New York Film Critics, and Best Foreign Actor, British Academy, for *In the Heat of the Night*, 1967. **Agent:** Gold/Marshak & Associates, 3500 West Olive Avenue, Burbank, CA 91505-5320, U.S.A.

Films as Actor:

1951   *Teresa* (Zinnemann) (as Frank)
1954   **On the Waterfront** (Kazan) (as Charley Malloy)
1955   *The Big Knife* (Aldrich) (as Stanley Hoff); *The Court Martial of Billy Mitchell* (*One-Man Mutiny*) (Preminger) (as Maj. Allan Gullion); *Oklahoma!* (Zinnemann) (as Judd Fry)
1956   *Jubal* (Daves) (as Pinky); *The Harder They Fall* (Robson) (as Nick Benko); *Back from Eternity* (Zinnemann) (as Vasquez)
1957   *Run of the Arrow* (Fuller) (as O'Meara); *Across the Bridge* (Annakin) (as Carl Schaffner); *The Unholy Wife* (Farrow) (as Paul Hochen)
1958   *Cry Terror* (Andrew L. Stone) (as Paul Hoplin)
1959   *Al Capone* (Wilson) (title role)
1960   *Seven Thieves* (Hathaway) (as Paul)
1961   *The Mark* (Guy Green) (as Dr. Edmund McNally); *The World in My Pocket* (*On Friday at Eleven*; *Vendredi 13 Heures*) (Rakoff) (as Frank Morgan)
1962   *Convicts Four* (Kaufman) (as Tiptoes); *The Longest Day* (Annakin, Marton, Wicki, and Oswald) (as destroyer commander); *Thirteen West Street* (Leacock) (as Det. Sgt. Koleski)
1963   *La mani sulla citta* (*Hands over the City*) (Rosi)
1964   *Gli indifferenti* (*A Time of Indifference*) (Maselli) (as Leo)
1965   *The Loved One* (Richardson) (as Mr. Joyboy); *E venne un uomo* (*And There Came a Man*; *A Man Named John*) (Olmi) (as the intermediary); *The Pawnbroker* (Lumet) (as Sol Nazerman); *Doctor Zhivago* (Lean) (as Komarovsky)
1967   *In the Heat of the Night* (Jewison) (as Bill Gillespie); *La ragazza e il generale* (*The Girl and the General*) (Campanile) (as the general)
1968   *The Sergeant* (Flynn) (as Sgt. Albert Callan); *No Way to Treat a Lady* (Smight) (as Christopher Gill)
1969   *The Illustrated Man* (Smight) (as Carl); *Three into Two Won't Go* (Hall) (as Steve Howard)
1970   *Waterloo* (Bondarchuk) (as Napoleon)
1971   *Happy Birthday, Wanda June* (Robson) (as Harold Ryan)
1972   *Giù la testa* (*Duck, You Sucker!*; *A Fistful of Dynamite*) (Leone) (as Juan Miranda)
1973   *The Lolly-Madonna War* (*Lolly Madonna XXX*) (Sarafian) (as Laban Feather); *A proposito Lucky Luciano* (*Re: Lucky Luciano*; *Lucky Luciano*) (Rosi) (as Gene Giannini)
1974   *Mussolini: ultimo atto* (*The Last Four Days*; *Last Days of Mussolini*) (Lizzani) (title role)
1975   *Hennessy* (Sharp) (title role); *Les Innocents aux mains sales* (*Dirty Hands*) (Chabrol) (as Louis)
1976   *W. C. Fields and Me* (Hiller) (as W. C. Fields)

1978   *F.I.S.T.* (Jewison) (as Sen. Madison)
1979   *The Amityville Horror* (Rosenberg) (as Father Delaney); *Love and Bullets* (Rosenberg) (as Joe Bomposa); *Breakthrough* (*Sargent Steiner*) (McLagen) (as Gen. Webster)
1980   *The Lucky Star* (Fischer) (as Col. Gluck); *Klondike Fever* (*Jack London's Klondike Fever*) (Carter) (as Soapy Smith)
1981   *Lion of the Desert* (*Omar Mukhtar*) (Akkad—produced in 1979) (as Mussolini); *Cattle Annie and Little Britches* (Johnson) (as Tilghman)
1982   *The Magic Mountain* (Geissendörfer); *The Chosen* (Kagan) (as Reb Saunders)
1983   *Cook and Peary: The Race to the North Pole* (Day—for TV)
1984   *The Naked Face* (Forbes) (as Lt. McGreavey); *The Glory Boys* (Ferguson—for TV)
1986   *Sword of Gideon* (Anderson—for TV)
1987   *Catch the Heat* (*Feel the Heat*) (Silberg) (as Jason Hannibal); *The Kindred* (Obrow) (as Dr. Philip Lloyd)
1988   *American Gothic* (Hough) (as Pa); *Desperado: Avalanche at Devil's Ridge* (Compton—for TV) (as Silas Slaten)
1989   *Try This One for Size* (Hamilton); *The January Man* (O'Connor) (as Mayor Eamon Flynn); *That Summer of White Roses* (Grlic) (as Martin); *The Exiles* (Kaplan—doc) (as himself); *Passion in Paradise* (Hart—for TV) (as Sir Harry Oakes)
1991   *The Ballad of the Sad Café* (Callow) (as the Reverend Willin); *In the Line of Duty: Manhunt in the Dakotas* (*Midnight Murders*) (Lowry—for TV) (as Gordon Kahl); *Men of Respect* (Reilly) (as Charlie D'Amico)
1992   **The Player** (Altman) (as himself); *Guilty as Charged* (Irvin) (as Ben Kallin); *Lincoln* (Kunhardt—doc for TV) (as voice of Gen. Grant)
1993   *The Neighbor* (Gibbons) (as Myron Hatch); *Earth and the American Dream* (Couturie—doc) (as voice)
1994   *The Last Tattoo* (John Reid) (as Major Gen. Frank); *The Specialist* (Llosa) (as Joe Leon); *Black Water* (*Tennessee Nights*) (Gessner) (as Judge Prescott); *Seven Sundays* (Tacchella) (as Benjamin)
1995   *Columbo: Strange Bedfellows* (for TV) (as Vincenzo Fortelli); *In Pursuit of Honor* (Olin—for TV) (as Col. Owen Stuart); *Choices of the Heart: The Margaret Sanger Story* (Paul Shapiro—for TV) (as Anthony Comstock)
1996   *Mars Attacks!* (Tim Burton) (as Gen. Decker)

Publications

By STEIGER: articles—

"The Year of the Steigers," interview in *Cinema* (Beverly Hills), March 1966.
"Cinema Interviews Steiger," in *Cinema* (Cambridge) December 1968.
"Interview: Rod Steiger," in *Playboy* (Chicago), July 1969.
"Schauspieler II: Rod Steiger's Method-Cowboy," interview with Delmer Daves in *Filmkritik* (Munich), January 1975.
Interview in *Skoop* (Amsterdam), December 1983-January 1984.

On STEIGER: articles—

Current Biography 1965, New York, 1965.
Hall, D. J., "Method Master," in *Films and Filming* (London), December 1970.
Ward, R., "Hollywood's Last Angry Man," in *American Film* (Washington, D.C.), January-February 1982.
Hutchinson, T., "Steiger the Survivor," in *Film Monthly* (Berkhamsted, England), September 1992.

*   *   *

In reexamining Steiger's riveting tour de force as tortured Sol Nazerman in *The Pawnbroker*, one searches for signs of the overstatement and histrionic effluvia that have marred much of Steiger's poststardom work. Catching him as a neo-Nazi posing as a garment district merchant on a *Commish* television movie or dropping one's jaw at his Hispanic crime king in *The Specialist*, one is embarrassed by a personification of Method Acting's worst excesses. Suiting up with various nationalities that never fit comfortably over his stolid Americaness, stocky Steiger now seems like a poor country cousin to world traveler Anthony Quinn, only Quinn wisely uses the same accent no matter what country's spirit he is suppose to be embodying. Steiger tries to sound different but registers as a party bore doing imitations.

Creating a sensation with that semi-improvised taxicab scene from *On the Waterfront*, Steiger fired audiences' imaginations whenever he was linked with forthright directors who brooked no nonsense. Although he won an Oscar for the easier role as a bigoted good old boy who sees the light of brotherhood in *In the Heat of the Night*, his repressed basket case in *The Pawnbroker* was a more daring piece of work. Since these halcyon years (which also brought forth a scene-stealing villain lending sharp menace to the soft-focus *Doctor Zhivago*), Steiger has made curious choices and slipped back into bad habits visible from his pre-stardom days. Huffing and puffing to blow down Jack Palance's career in *The Big Knife*, his amalgam of Louis B. Mayer and Harry Cohn is such a screaming meemie no one could take him seriously, and this is the kind of barnstorming acting that follows his Oscar with few exceptions. Throughout his career, for every occasion of welcome restraint (*Back from Eternity*), there are distracting performances in major studio events such as the homespun *Oklahoma!* in which Steiger is incongruously threatening in a musical that has no ambition to be a rural *Othello*.

It may be instructive that his applauded work in *In the Heat of the Night* is suffused with humor, and that Steiger is splendid as Mr. Joyboy in the hit-and-miss screen version of *The Loved One* and astounding as a one-man screen actor's guild in a film in which he revels in getups while murderously demonstrating the fine art of *No Way to Treat a Lady*. Unfortunately, the blustery versatility so compatible with comedy becomes unbearable when applied with ten times the force to prestige dramas. Recently, and best when sampled in small doses, Steiger is both scary and amusing in the direct-to-video *Black Water* as a classical music-loving judge who releases a prisoner from his hellhole on a whim thanks to the accused's knowledge of the legal dictator's favorite subject. But more often, Steiger has miscast his own eccentricity. In *W. C. Fields and Me*, he misses the point by delivering an accurate caricature but giving no indication of what made that idiosyncratic comic funny.

Dismissing Steiger as a pompous ham is unfair to a talented actor whose erraticness may be unmatched in movie history. For every incisive portrait such as his white supremacist in television's *Midnight Murders*, there are examples of his scenery-chewing egregiousness such as his Southern officer in *In Pursuit of Honor* in which Steiger buttonholes General MacArthur less as a dissenting voice against military policy than as a disgruntled upstager determined to milk his one flashy scene for all it is worth. Considering the critical backlash against Steiger yet refusing to abandon his propensity to sweat and strain on camera, he has become something of a Method Acting joke. If he could jettison that stop-and-start line delivery, the multilingual shtick, and the breast-beating, perhaps firm directors will still steer him toward the basics of Strasberg's acting philosophy—to determine a character's inner core through sense memory, not to flagellate your emotions in order to stop-the-movie-because-you-want-to-get-off-on-yourself.

—Robert Pardi

STEWART, James

Nationality: American. **Born:** James Maitland Stewart in Indiana, Pennsylvania, 20 May 1908. **Education:** Attended Model School; Mercersburg Academy; Princeton University, New Jersey, B.S. in architecture 1932. **Military Service:** U.S. Air Force, 1942-45: colonel (remained in the reserves: brigadier general, 1959). **Family:** Married Gloria Hatrick McLean, 1949 (died 1994), twins: Kelly and Judy. **Career:** 1932—joined Joshua Logan's University Players in West Falmouth, Massachusetts: Broadway debut in the company's production of *Carrie Nation*; 1935—in short *Important News*, then in feature *Murder Man*; contract with MGM; 1947—on Broadway in *Harvey* (reprised in film version, 1951, and on stage later in his career); 1971-72—actor in TV series *The Jimmy Stewart Show*, and in series *Hawkins*, 1973-74; 1986—in TV miniseries *North and South II*; The James Stewart Museum was opened in Indiana, Pennsylvania, in 1995. **Awards:** Best Actor, New York Film Critics, for *Mr. Smith Goes to Washington*, 1939; Best Actor Academy Award, for *The Philadelphia Story*, 1940; Best Actor, New York Film Critics, and Best Actor, Venice Festival, for *Anatomy of a Murder*, 1959; Best Actor, Berlin Festival, for *Mr. Hobbs Takes a Vacation*, 1962; Life Achievement Award, American Film Institute, 1980; Special Academy Award, for "his 50 years of meaningful performances, for his high ideals, both on and off the screen, with the respect and affection of his colleagues," 1984. **Address:** c/o The Prappas Company, 9201 Wilshire Boulevard, Suite 204, Beverly Hills, CA 90210, U.S.A.

Films as Actor:

1934 *This Side of Heaven* (William K. Howard) (as Hal); *Art Trouble* (short)

1935 *Important News* (Lawrence—short); *Murder Man* (Whelan) (as Shorty)

1936 *Rose Marie* (Van Dyke) (as John Flower); *Next Time We Love* (Edward H. Griffith) (as Christopher); *Wife versus Secretary* (Brown) (as Dave); *Small Town Girl* (Wellman) (as Elmer); *Speed* (Marin) (as Terry Martin); *The Gorgeous Hussy* (Brown) (as "Rowdy" Roderick Dow); *Born to Dance* (Del Ruth) (as Ted Barker); *After the Thin Man* (Van Dyke) (as David Graham)

1937 *Seventh Heaven* (Henry King) (as Chico); *The Last Gangster* (Wellman) (as Paul North Sr.); *Navy Blue and Gold* (Wood) (as "Truck" Cross)

1938 *Of Human Hearts* (Brown) (as Jason Wilkins); *Vivacious Lady* (Stevens) (as Peter Morgan); *The Shopworn Angel* (Potter) (as Bill Pettigrew); *You Can't Take It with You* (Capra) (as Tony Kirby)

1939 *Made for Each Other* (Cromwell) (as Johnny Mason); *Ice Follies of 1939* (Schunzel) (as Larry Hall); *It's a Wonderful World* (Van Dyke) (as Guy Johnson); *Mr. Smith Goes to Washington* (Capra) (title role); *Destry Rides Again* (George Marshall) (as Tom Destry)

1940 *The Shop around the Corner* (Lubitsch) (as Alfred Kralik); *The Mortal Storm* (Borzage) (as Martin Brietner); *No Time for Comedy* (Keighley) (as Gaylord Easterbrook); *The Philadelphia Story* (Cukor) (as Mike Connor)

1941 *Come Live with Me* (Brown) (as Bill Smith); *Pot o' Gold* (George Marshall) (as Jimmy Kaskell); *Ziegfeld Girl* (Leonard) (as Gilbert Young)

1942 *Fellow Americans* (short); *Winning Your Wings* (short)

1946 *It's a Wonderful Life* (Capra) (as George Bailey)

1947 *Magic Town* (Wellman) (as Lawrence "Rip" Smith)

1948 *Call Northside 777* (Hathaway) (as McNeal); *10,000 Kids and a Cop* (doc); *On Our Merry Way* (*A Miracle Can Happen*) (King Vidor and Fenton) (as Slim); *Rope* (Hitchcock) (as Rupert Cadell); *You Gotta Stay Happy* (Potter) (as Marvin Payne)

1949 *The Stratton Story* (Wood) (as Monty Stratton); *Malaya* (Thorpe) (as John Royer)

1950 *Winchester '73* (Anthony Mann) (as Lin McAdam); *Broken Arrow* (Daves) (as Tom Jeffords); *Jackpot* (*How Much Do You Owe?*) (Walter Lang) (as Bill Lawrence)

1951 *Harvey* (Koster) (as Elwood Dowd); *No Highway in the Sky* (*No Highway*) (Koster) (as Theodore Honey)

1952 *The Greatest Show on Earth* (Cecil B. DeMille) (as Buttons); *Bend of the River* (Anthony Mann) (as Glyn McLyntock); *Carbine Williams* (Thorpe) (as Marsh Williams)

1953 *The Naked Spur* (Anthony Mann) (as Howard Kemp); *Thunder Bay* (Anthony Mann) (as Steve Martin)

1954 *The Glenn Miller Story* (Anthony Mann) (title role); **Rear Window** (Hitchcock) (as L. B. Jeffries)

1955 *The Far Country* (Anthony Mann) (as Jeff Webster); *Strategic Air Command* (Anthony Mann) (as Lt. Colonel Robert "Dutch" Holland); *The Man from Laramie* (Anthony Mann) (as Will Lockhart)

1956 *The Man Who Knew Too Much* (Hitchcock) (as Ben McKenna)

1957 *The Spirit of St. Louis* (Wilder) (as Charles Lindbergh); *Night Passage* (Neilson) (as Grant McLaine)

1958 **Vertigo** (Hitchcock) (as John "Scottie" Ferguson); *Bell, Book and Candle* (Quine) (as Shepherd Henderson)

1959 **Anatomy of a Murder** (Preminger) (as Paul Biegler); *The FBI Story* (LeRoy) (as Chip Hardesty)

1960 *The Mountain Road* (Daniel Mann) (as Major Baldwin)

1961 *Two Rode Together* (Ford) (as Guthrie McCabe); *X-15* (Richard Donner) (as narrator)

1962 **The Man Who Shot Liberty Valance** (Ford) (as Ranson Stoddard); *Mr. Hobbs Takes a Vacation* (Koster) (title role); *Flashing Spikes* (Ford—for TV) (as Slim Conway)

1963 "The Rivers" ep. of *How the West Was Won* (Hathaway) (as Linus Rawlings); *Take Her, She's Mine* (Koster) (as Frank Michaelson)

1964 *Cheyenne Autumn* (Ford) (as Wyatt Earp)

1965 *Dear Brigitte* (Koster) (as Professor Robert Leaf); *Shenandoah* (McLaglen) (as Charlie); *The Flight of the Phoenix* (Aldrich) (as Frank Towns)

1966 *The Rare Breed* (McLaglen) (as Sam Burnett)

1968 *Firecreek* (McEveety) (as Johnny Cobb); *Bandolero!* (McLaglen) (as Mace Bishop)

1970 *The Cheyenne Social Club* (Kelly) (as John O'Hanlan)

1971 *Fools' Parade* (McLaglen) (as Mattie Appleyard); *Directed by John Ford* (Bogdanovich—doc) (as himself); *The American West of John Ford* (doc—for TV)

1972 *Harvey* (Cook—for TV) (as Elwood P. Dowd)

1973 *Hawkins on Murder* (Taylor—for TV) (as Billy Jim Hawkins)

1974 *That's Entertainment!* (Haley—compilation) (as narrator)

1976 *The Shootist* (Siegel) (as Dr. Hostetler)

1977 *Airport '77* (Jameson) (as Philip Stevens)

1978 *The Magic of Lassie* (Chaffey) (as Clovis Mitchell); *The Big Sleep* (Winner) (as General Sternwood)

1980 *Mr. Krueger's Christmas* (Merrill)

1981 *Afurika Monogatari* (*A Tale of Africa*) (Hani) (as old man)

1983 *Right of Way* (Schaefer—for TV)

1991 *An American Tail 2: Fievel Goes West* (Nibbelink and Wells—animation) (as voice of Wylie Burp)

Publications

By STEWART: book—

Jimmy Stewart and His Poems, New York, 1989.

By STEWART: articles—

"That's Enough for Me," interview in *Films and Filming* (London), April 1966.

Interview with N. P. Hurlez, in *Cahiers du Cinéma* (Paris), April 1984.

Interview with R. Comiskey, in *Cinema Papers* (Melbourne), January 1986.

Interview with David Denicolo, in *Interview* (New York), April 1990.

On STEWART: books—

Jones, Ken D., *The Films of James Stewart*, New York, 1970.

Thompson, Howard, *James Stewart*, New York, 1974.

Parish, James, and Don Stanke, *The All-American*, New Rochelle, New York, 1977.

Eyles, Allen, *James Stewart*, New York, 1984.

Hunter, Allan, *James Stewart*, New York, 1985.

Robbins, Jhan, *Everybody's Man: A Biography of Jimmy Stewart*, New York, 1985.

Le Hanaff, Ronan, *James Stewart*, Paris, 1986.

Thomas, Tony, *A Wonderful Life: The Films and Career of James Stewart*, Secaucus, New Jersey, 1988.

Headine, Doug, *James Stewart*, Paris, 1991.

Molyneaux, Gerard, *James Stewart: A Bio-Bibliography*, Westport, Connecticut, 1992.

Pickard, Roy, *Jimmy Stewart: A Life in Film*, New York, 1993.

Bingham, Dennis, *Acting Male: Masculinities in the Films of James Stewart, Jack Nicholson, and Clint Eastwood*, New Brunswick, New Jersey, 1994.

Coe, Jonathan, *Jimmy Stewart, A Wonderful Life*, New York, 1994.

On STEWART: articles—

Current Biography 1960, New York, 1960.

Sweigart, William R., "James Stewart," in *Films in Review* (New York), December 1964.

Hall, D. J., "Box Office Drawl," and "Portrait of Human Frailty," in *Films and Filming* (London), December 1972, and January/February 1973.

Beaver, Jim, "James Stewart," in *Films in Review* (New York), October 1980.

Sarris, Andrew, "James Stewart," in *The Movie Star*, edited by Elisabeth Weis, New York, 1981.

Cieutat, Michel, "James Stewart ou le bienfondé de l'Amérique," in *Positif* (Paris), October 1984.

Wolfe, C., "The Return of Jimmy Stewart: The Publicity Photograph as Text," in *Wide Angle* (Baltimore, Maryland), vol. 6, no. 4, 1985.

Larvor, M., "Capra et James Stewart: le mariage de l'Europe et du rêve américain," in *Positif* (Paris), July/August 1987.

Baxter, Brian, "James Stewart: A Wonderful Life," in *Films and Filming* (London), June 1988.

Denby, David, "Everybody's All-American," in *Premiere* (New York), February 1990.

Horton, Robert, "Mann & Stewart: Two Rode Together," in *Film Comment* (New York), March/April 1990.

Hendrickson, Paul, "It's Been a Wonderful Life," in *Life* (New York), July 1991.

* * *

James Stewart in *Mr. Smith Goes to Washington*

James Stewart has come a long way since his boyhood days in Pennsylvania. Starting out as an amateur magician and accordionist, he made his acting debut in a Boy Scout play and later performed in shows for the Princeton Triangle Club. He was graduated from Princeton in 1932 with a degree in architecture, but eventually joined the University Players at Falmouth, Massachusetts. It was here he befriended future stars Henry Fonda and Margaret Sullavan. Years later Sullavan would prove to be instrumental to Stewart's career by insisting that he be given parts in her films. In the years since his motion picture debut, James Stewart has earned a place in the hearts of moviegoing audiences as one of Hollywood's best-loved actors. His laconic style and boyish manner seem the embodiment of an uncomplicated honesty that also marked the career of his longtime friend, Henry Fonda (Stewart and Fonda were roommates in New York while working in the theater and also when they first arrived in Hollywood in 1935). Both men came to exemplify a uniquely American style of acting that takes simplicity and directness as its foundation.

Stewart's early screen appearances often found him playing rapidly forgettable callow youths. It was director Frank Capra who first recognized his special blend of bashful humor and underlying strength, and put it to use in several films that cast Stewart as the personification of American idealism. Capra's populist comedies, including *You Can't Take It with You*, *Mr. Smith Goes to Washington*, and *It's a Wonderful*

Life, conveyed the director's belief in the fundamental decency of the common man, and Stewart's skill at combining warmth, humor, and pathos in his performances made him the perfect Capra hero. George Cukor's *The Philadelphia Story* demonstrated his flair for sophisticated comedy alongside Katharine Hepburn and Cary Grant.

Stewart received critical acclaim for *It's a Wonderful Life*, perhaps the quintessential Capra film, in which he gives a moving performance as a man on the verge of suicide whose faith in humanity is restored by a visit from a guardian angel. This movie has since become a holiday staple—being broadcast on television numerous times during the Christmas season. Stewart's air of earnest innocence lent itself naturally to stories of whimsical appeal, as his portrayal of Elwood P. Dowd in *Harvey* confirmed. As the gentle alcoholic who believes himself befriended by an invisible six-foot white rabbit, Stewart displays an easy and engaging charm.

Stewart's work in a number of Westerns, including several with director Anthony Mann, drew on his image as a man of honor and with an unswerving sense of duty. Again, Stewart's deliberate manner and tall, lean form made him an effective presence in this uniquely American film genre. John Ford used Stewart's image to examine the truth behind the Western myth in *The Man Who Shot Liberty Valance*, in which Stewart's character wins fame for an act that his friend, John Wayne, has performed.

Alfred Hitchcock also played on Stewart's familiar persona in four films that reveal a very different side to the actor's talents. In *Rope* he is cast as an intellectual gamesman whose musings on the "perfect crime" lead two young friends to commit a murder. *Rear Window* stars Stewart as a photographer ready to risk his fiancée's safety to satisfy his own voyeuristic curiosity, while in *The Man Who Knew Too Much* he is the desperate father of a kidnapped son. *Vertigo*, one of Hitchcock's finest films, features the actor as an emotionally tormented man obsessed with recreating the image of the woman he has lost. In all four films, there is an underlying edge to Stewart's characters, from his mildly paternalistic treatment of his wife in *The Man Who Knew Too Much* to his overtly disturbed behavior in *Vertigo*. The clash of these qualities with the image of Stewart we have come to expect makes his work for Hitchcock among his most challenging.

Stewart's long career is certainly one of Hollywood's most rewarding, and the actor's occasional interviews and television appearances only strengthen the warm regard in which he is held. With the continuing popularity of many of his best films, he remains a much-loved and much-admired figure in American cinema.

—Janet E. Lorenz, updated by Linda J. Stewart

STONE, Sharon

Nationality: American. **Born:** Meadville, Pennsylvania, 10 March 1958. **Family:** Married the producer Michael Greenburg, 1984 (divorced 1987). **Education:** Attended Edinboro University, Pennsylvania, on a writing scholarship. **Career:** 1977-80—modeled, mostly for TV commercials, in New York, Paris, and Milan; 1980—film debut in *Stardust Memories*; 1983—in TV series *The Bay City Blues*; 1989—in TV mini-series *War and Remembrance*; co-owner of Chaos Productions. **Awards:** Golden Globe, for *Casino*, 1995. **Address:** PMK Public Relations, 1775 Broadway, Suite 701, New York, NY 10019, U.S.A.

Films as Actress:

1981   *Stardust Memories* (Woody Allen) (as dream girl); *Deadly Blessing* (Craven) (as Lana); *Les Uns et les autres (Bolero)* (Lelouch)

1982   *Not Just Another Affair* (Steven Hilliard Stern—for TV) (as Lynette)

1984   *Irreconcilable Differences* (Shyer) (as Blake Chandler); *Calendar Girl Murders* (William A. Graham—for TV) (as Cassie Bascomb); *The Vegas Strip Wars* (Englund—for TV) (as Sarah Shipman)

1985   *King Solomon's Mines* (J. Lee Thompson) (as Jessie Huston)

1987   *Allan Quatermain and the Lost City of Gold* (Gary Nelson and Newt Arnold) (as Jessie Huston); *Cold Steel* (Dorothy Ann Puzo) (as Kathy Connors); *Police Academy 4: Citizens on Patrol* (Jim Drake) (as Claire Mattson)

1988   *Above the Law* (*Nico*) (Andrew Davis) (as Sara Toscani); *Action Jackson* (Baxley) (as Patrice Dellaplane); *Tears in the Rain* (Don Sharp—for TV) (as Casey Cantrell)

1989   *Blood and Sand* (Elorrieta) (as Doña Sol); *Beyond the Stars* (*Personal Choice*) (Saperstein) (as Laurie McCall)

1990   *Total Recall* (Verhoeven) (as Lori Quaid)

1991   *He Said, She Said* (Marisa Silver and Kwapis) (as Linda); *Scissors* (DeFelitta) (as Angie Anderson); *Year of the Gun* (Frankenheimer) (as Alison King)

1992   *Basic Instinct* (Verhoeven) (as Catherine Tramell); *Diary of a Hitman* (London) (as Kiki)

1993   *Last Action Hero* (McTiernan) (cameo as Catherine Tramell); *Sliver* (Noyce) (as Carly Norris); *Where Sleeping Dogs Lie* (Finch) (as Serena Black); *Harlow: The Blond Bombshell* (as narrator)

1994   *The Specialist* (Llosa) (as May Munro); *Intersection* (Rydell) (as Sally Eastman)

1995   *Casino* (Scorsese) (as Ginger McKenna); *Catwalk* (Leacock); *The Quick and the Dead* (Raimi) (as Ellen)

1996   *Last Dance* (Beresford) (as Cindy Liggett); *Diabolique* (Chechik) (as Nicole)

Publications

By STONE: articles—

"Blonde Starlet No Dummy," interview with Susan Morgan, in *Interview* (New York), June 1990.

"Hot Cover," interview with Bill Zehme, in *Rolling Stone* (New York), 14 May 1992.

"The Ultimate Question: Can Sharon Stone Act?," interview with Suzanna Andrews, in *New York Times*, 16 January 1994.

"The Truly Shocking, Unstoppable Sharon Stone," interview with Stephen Rebello, in *Cosmopolitan* (New York), October 1995.

"Holding Her Own with the Big Boys," interview with William Grimes, in *New York Times*, 19 November 1995.

"Sharon's Back in Town," interview with Lloyd Grove, in *Vanity Fair* (New York), March 1996.

Interview with Jess Cagle, in *Advocate* (Los Angeles), 21 May 1996.

On STONE: articles—

Liebovitz, Annie, "Stone Goddess," in *Vanity Fair* (New York), April 1993.

Schruers, Fred, "Stone Free," in *Premiere* (New York), May 1993.

Hirshey, Gerri, "The Diva," in *GQ* (New York), November 1995.

Current Biography 1996, New York, 1996.

*   *   *

Suddenly, with *Casino*, the revelation: Sharon Stone can act! Personally, I never doubted it for a moment (though it did not seem to me her most important attribute). I want first to confront the derision that has been heaped upon her by (mostly male) reviewers over the past few years.

Clearly, the crux is *Basic Instinct*, and specifically the moment when she exposes herself (and her lack of underwear) to a roomful of cops. It is a wonderful moment in a flawed but very interesting film: one of the classic "moments" of modern American cinema, already inscribed in film history. To grasp its significance fully, it is helpful to address an extremely influential article by Peter Baxter, "The Naked Thighs of Miss Dietrich." Baxter analyzes *The Blue Angel* in terms of castration fears and the resulting fetishism: what terrifies men is the woman's "lack," because it arouses their own dread that they might share it. "Miss Dietrich" repeatedly exposes herself "almost, but not quite," thus at once arousing and assuaging castration fears. Stone in *Basic Instinct* goes all the way, exposing her lack of the phallus proudly and defiantly (and in a film in which, according to reports, Michael Douglas adamantly refused to expose his possession of it: we might have seen that, after all, it is just a bit of anatomy). The resentment and anger of our male reviewers, and their escape into facile ridicule, is only explicable in these terms, and seems an admirable vindication of one aspect of Freudian theory.

Yes, Sharon Stone can act, she always could, and did not suddenly begin to because she was directed by Scorsese. But she remains less

Sharon Stone in *Basic Instinct*

striking as an actress than as a *presence*. "Acting" is notoriously difficult to talk about except in the most general terms, but "presence" is even harder. It has something to do with the star's relationship to the camera, but that scarcely takes us very far. It has a lot to do with the eyes—their aliveness or otherwise, the way they look within the image, at other characters, the way they confront the camera. Two contemporary comparisons come to mind: Demi Moore (because, like Stone, she specializes in playing strong women) and Madonna (because she is blond, and is primarily associated with a defiant sexuality). I have the impression that Moore is a capable actress, but after seeing her in about a dozen films I *still* cannot remember what she looks like. As for Madonna, she has neither presence nor acting ability; she has built her career entirely on sheer nerve and a talent for self-promotion.

Reviewers are always impressed by acting (which, like the people who decide the Oscars every year, they usually confuse with certain roles: Stone can be allowed to "act" in *Casino* because her character goes through various stages of degradation, addiction, and near-insanity). They are not very interested in "presence," because it is either there or it is not, it is not the product of really hard work, and the Protestant work ethic is still a potent fact in evaluating performance. Stone has a lot in common with two actresses of earlier generations who equally bore their share of ridicule, but whose performances survive undimmed: Kim Novak and Jean Seberg. Novak in *Vertigo*, Seberg in *Bonjour, Tristesse*: are these not still indelibly stamped in the memory, where so many "great" acting performances have vanished into oblivion? Stone repeatedly reminds me of Novak in particular—perhaps partly because of what Truffaut described as Novak's "carnality," but even more because, whatever character she plays (even, or especially, a bisexual murderess), there is always in her performances an underlying sense of vulnerability. Stone is a Kim Novak for the nineties.

Casino is not the first film in which Stone has shown that she can act, but it is the first she has been in of any great distinction, under one of the great contemporary filmmakers. Aside from that, one can make certain claims for *Basic Instinct*, *The Quick and the Dead*, and *Sliver*, chiefly because of Stone's presence in them. In an attempt to illustrate this "presence" (more precisely, presence-plus-acting), however, I shall draw on a brief scene from a film for which no one is likely to make high claims, *The Specialist*, a very efficient action thriller built upon a strictly formulaic plot (roughly, the pattern long-build-up/big explosion, repeated five times—six if you include the pre-credits sequence). Here, Stone is surrounded by strong actors giving strong performances (notably James Woods and Eric Roberts); the film suffers from an understandable lack of chemistry between Stone and Sylvester Stallone, mitigated by the fact that they do not meet until two-thirds through.

Anyone who wishes to grasp—intuitively, if not intellectually—what is meant by "screen presence" could do no better than examine the brief scene of the second encounter (daytime, in a Miami bar) between Stone and Eric Roberts. (He is one of the three men she watched murder her parents when she was a young child, on whom she has vowed to take revenge). The two-minute scene includes eight full-face shots of Stone as she allows herself to be seduced; they have the effect of close-ups, although the back of Roberts's head is present in most of them, and are intercut with reverse shots as Roberts speaks:

1. The face, looking very vulnerable, expresses nervous tension.

2. A smile, in response: tense, slightly forced.

3. (After he asks to kiss her): the smile becomes more enigmatic and ambiguous as she says "I hardly know you."

4. After his "Wait till you try spending the night," the smile has faded, the lips are tense, the eyes seem to probe; there is a slight look of recoil, almost fear.

5. The smile returns as she glances up at him, then quickly down into her drink.

6, 7, 8. He moves away to help a henchman beat somebody up; she watches in the mirror. The beating evokes (brief flashback) the traumatic night of her parents' murder; her face conveys an extraordinary blend of anger, hatred, and fear.

One might argue that, in such a sequence, the "performance" is constructed in the editing—to which the reply is that nothing can be constructed out of nothing. A suggestion: watch this brief scene on video, then imagine it again with Stone replaced, first by Demi Moore, then by Madonna. The experience should illuminate what is meant by those vague phrases "screen presence" and "star quality."

—Robin Wood

STREEP, Meryl

Nationality: American. **Born:** Mary Louise Streep in Summit, New Jersey, 22 June 1949. **Education:** Attended Bernardsville High School, New Jersey; Vassar College, Poughkeepsie, B.A., 1971; Yale Drama School, M.F.A., 1975. **Family:** Married Don Gummer, 1978, four children. **Career:** 1969—New York stage debut in *The Playboy of Seville*; worked in summer stock with Green Mountain Guild, Vermont; 1975—in Joseph Papp's New York production of *Trelawney of the Wells*; 1977—in TV film *The Deadliest Season*; feature film debut *Julia*; 1978—in TV mini-series *Holocaust*. **Awards:** Best Supporting Actress Academy Award, for *Kramer vs. Kramer*, 1979; Best Supporting Actress, New York Film Critics, for *Kramer vs. Kramer*, and *The Seduction of Joe Tynan*, 1979; Best Actress Academy Award, and Best Actress, New York Film Critics, for *Sophie's Choice*, 1982; Best Actress, New York Film Critics, for *A Cry in the Dark*, 1988. **Agent:** c/o CAA, 9830 Wilshire Boulevard, Beverly Hills, CA 90212, U.S.A.

Films as Actress:

1977 *The Deadliest Season* (Markowitz—for TV); *Julia* (Zinnemann) (as Anne Marie)

1978 *The Deer Hunter* (Cimino) (as Linda)

1979 *Manhattan* (Woody Allen) (as Jill); *The Seduction of Joe Tynan* (Schatzberg) (as Karen Traynor); *Kramer vs. Kramer* (Benton) (as Joanna Kramer); *Uncommon Women . . . and Others* (Mossman and Robman—for TV) (as Leilah)

1981 *The French Lieutenant's Woman* (Reisz) (as Sarah/Anna)

1982 *Sophie's Choice* (Pakula) (title role); *Still of the Night* (Benton) (as Brooke Reynolds)

1983 *Silkwood* (Nichols) (title role)

1984 *Falling in Love* (Grosbard) (as Molly); *In Our Hands* (Richer and Warnow—doc) (appearance)

1985 *Plenty* (Schepisi) (as Susan Traherne); *Out of Africa* (Pollack) (as Karen Blixen)

1986 *Heartburn* (Nichols) (as Rachel)

1987 *Ironweed* (Babenco) (as Helen Archer)

1988 *A Cry in the Dark* (Schepisi) (as Lindy Chamberlain)

1989 *She-Devil* (Seidelman) (as Mary Fisher)

1990 *Postcards from the Edge* (Nichols) (as Suzanne Vale)

1991 *Defending Your Life* (Albert Brooks) (as Julia)

1992 *Death Becomes Her* (Zemeckis) (as Madeline Ashton)

1993 *The House of the Spirits* (August) (as Clara Del Valle Trueba)

1994 *The River Wild* (Hanson) (as Gail Hartman)

1995 *The Bridges of Madison County* (Eastwood) (as Francesca Johnson)

1996 *Before and After* (Schroeder); *Portrait of a Lady* (Campion); *Marvin's Room* (Zaks)

Meryl Streep in *Kramer vs. Kramer*

Publications

By STREEP: articles—

Interview with Thomas Wiener, in *American Film* (Washington, D.C.), December 1983.
"Streeping Beauty," interview with Wendy Wasserstein, in *Saturday Evening Post*, July/August 1989.
"Meryl Streep Comes Calling," interview with Wendy Wasserstein and Brigitte Lacombe, in *Interview* (New York), December 1988.
"Winning Streep," interview with David Handelman, in *Vogue*, April 1992.
"The Perils of Meryl," interview with James Greenberg, in *Entertainment Weekly*, 7 October 1994.

On STREEP: books—

Maychick, Diana, *Meryl Streep: The Reluctant Superstar*, New York, 1984.
Smurthwaite, Nick, *The Meryl Streep Story*, New York, 1984.
Glogger, Helmut-Maria, *Die aktuelle Biographie Meryl Streep: das Portrat eines Weltstars*, Bergisch Gladbach, Germany, 1987.
Pfaff, Eugene E., and Mark Emerson, *Meryl Streep: A Critical Biography*, Jefferson, North Carolina, 1987.

On STREEP: articles—

Silverman, S. M., "Meryl Streep: There's No End to Her Range," in *American Film* (Washington, D.C.), August 1979.
Current Biography 1980, New York, 1980.
Pally, M., "Choice Parts," in *Film Comment* (New York), September/October 1985.
Haskell, Molly, "Meryl Streep: Hiding in the Spotlight," in *Ms. Magazine*, December 1988.
Rayner, Richard, "Esprit de Streep," in *Harper's Bazaar*, March 1994.
Weinraub, Bernard, "Her Peculiar Career," in *New York Times Magazine*, 18 September 1994.

* * *

Meryl Streep is among the contemporary cinema's greatest assets—a star of the first order who, like the Spencer Tracys and Edward G. Robinsons before her, is an exceptional and multifaceted actor. One critic has said that she "manages to make her face an astonishingly clear reflection of her characters' complexities." Indeed, Streep is a master at shaping the intricacies of emotion and bringing them subtly to life through the use of refined and minimalist expression. The result has been an impressive and memorable list of films in which she has appeared, and in which she has offered consistently credible performances playing an astounding variety of roles.

On occasion, Streep has been criticized for taking on so many "accents" in her films. Her characters have been British, Australian, Polish; her "American" roles have ranged from sophisticated New Yorkers to small-town blue collar types, average suburbanites to ravaged alcoholics. One suspects, however, that this disapproval comes from a misguided mistrust of her ability to transform herself with such seeming effortlessness. The fact is that Streep can play—and play brilliantly—just about any character she chooses.

Streep's initial important roles were supporting ones. Her first major part came in *The Deer Hunter*, in which her pale good looks and soft-spoken delivery made a compelling contrast to her male counterparts, small-town Pennsylvania buddies who head off to fight in Vietnam. Her role in the television miniseries *Holocaust* was essentially a reworking of this quietly gentle persona. What is most intriguing about Streep's early career is that she offered award-caliber performances in roles that were not showy, that easily might have been typically bland feminine characters. The year after she made *The Deer Hunter*, Streep appeared in supporting roles in three films: *The Seduction of Joe Tynan* (playing a bright Southern charmer); *Manhattan* (as Woody Allen's estranged spouse); and *Kramer vs. Kramer* (as Dustin Hoffman's confused, insecure estranged wife). Especially in the latter, she fused the quality of introverted shyness that characterized her role in *The Deer Hunter* with a new external effervescence to convey her character's disorientation and instability. As a result, she won an Oscar, and firmly entrenched herself in the minds of moviegoers.

From then on, Streep has had her choice of starring roles in high-prestige features. Her best characterizations have been thoughtfully conceived and complexly drawn; they have been women who are severely troubled, or facing an overwhelming life crisis. Her first starring role came in *The French Lieutenant's Woman*, in which she is cast in a double role, that of an actress and the restrained Victorian woman this character plays in a movie. Here, Streep displays her uncanny ability for understatement and subtle expression as she projects the private madness of the latter character. She was to prove equally brilliant playing a working-class woman under duress in a film that is part drama, part political tract (Karen Silkwood, the ill-fated nuclear parts factory worker, in *Silkwood*); an intellectual in a film that is primarily romantic in tone (Danish writer Karen Blixen, in *Out of Africa*); and an immature, fragile offspring of privileged Hollywood in a cautionary drama whose core is a mother-daughter relationship (the fatigued, drugged-up actress who lives in the shadow of her famous, domineering mother, in *Postcards from the Edge*). On occasion, the torment of Streep's characters directly relates to one of the most personal concerns of any woman: her maternal feelings, coupled with the very survival of her children. In *Sophie's Choice*, she won her second Oscar as the tragic Polish concentration camp survivor, whose "choice" was to decide which of her offspring will live and which will die; in *A Cry in the Dark*, she is an otherwise average Australian woman who experiences the death of her baby and then finds herself charged with murder.

Streep also has accepted roles that are not as psychologically intricate, but which still allow her to display her impressive talent. She can more than effectively play a standard, essentially unglamorous part, such as the average suburban New York commuter who commences an extramarital relationship in *Falling in Love*, and even can add class and intelligence to a generic action-heroine role, as she did in *The River Wild*. And she is capable of playing gentle comedy, witness her likable turn in *Defending Your Life*, and in-your-face farce—her hilarious turns were the sole reasons for seeing *She-Devil* and *Death Becomes Her*.

Most any Streep performance can be examined for its nuances and lauded for its sheer believability. Take *Ironweed*, in which she plays Helen Archer, the longtime companion of street bum Francis Phelan (Jack Nicholson). Archer has, in her time, guzzled too much wine, and her insides are now twisted beyond repair. She raves and rants irrationally, and declares that "everything ails me." At first Streep is almost unrecognizable in the role. Her voice is coarse. Her words sound as if they are emanating from a throat that really has been abused by the constant flow of alcohol. In her best of several exceptional moments, Streep sings a ditty called "He's Me Pal" in a gin mill—and fantasizes that she is doing so in fine voice for high class folk, rather than in a roomful of rummies.

While only at the midpoint of her career, it is without doubt that Streep is the preeminent screen actress of her era. She can play (and has played) just about any role. And, one suspects, she will go on doing so.

—Rob Winning, updated by Rob Edelman

STREISAND, Barbra

Nationality: American. **Born:** Barbara Joan Streisand in Brooklyn, New York, 24 April 1942. **Education:** Attended Erasmus Hall High School. **Family:** Married the actor Elliott Gould, 1963 (divorced 1971), son: Jason Emanuel. **Career:** Singer in New York nightclub; 1961—professional stage debut in *Another Evening with Harry Stoones*; 1963—Broadway debut in *I Can Get It for You Wholesale*; recording star; 1964—phenomenal success in stage play *Funny Girl*, and later in film version, 1968; 1969—co-founder, with Paul Newman and Sidney Poitier, First Artists Productions; 1983—producer and director, as well as actress, *Yentl*. **Awards:** Best Actress Academy Award, David Di Donatello award for Foreign Actress, and Golden Globe award for Best Actress, for *Funny Girl*, 1968; David Di Donatello award for Foreign Actress, *The Way We Were*, 1973; Best Song Academy Award, and Golden Globe award for Best Song, for "Evergreen," in *A Star Is Born*, 1976; Golden Globe award for Best Director, Silver Ribbon (Italy) as Best New Foreign Director, *Yentl*, 1983.

Films as Actress:

1968   *Funny Girl* (Wyler) (as Fanny Brice)
1969   *Hello Dolly!* (Kelly) (as Dolly Levi)
1970   *On a Clear Day You Can See Forever* (Minnelli) (as Daisy Gamble); *The Owl and the Pussycat* (Ross) (as Doris)
1972   *What's Up, Doc?* (Bogdanovich) (as Judy Maxwell); *Up the Sandbox* (Kershner) (as Margaret Reynolds)
1973   *The Way We Were* (Pollack) (as Katie Morosky)
1974   *For Pete's Sake* (Yates) (as Henrietta)
1975   *Funny Lady* (Ross) (as Fanny Brice)
1976   *A Star Is Born* (Pierson) (as Esther Hoffman)
1979   *The Main Event* (Zieff) (as Hillary Kramer)
1981   *All Night Long* (Tramont) (as Cheryl Gibbons)
1987   *Nuts* (Ritt) (as Claudia Draper, + pr, mus)
1990   *Listen Up!: The Lives of Quincy Jones* (doc)

Other Films:

1983   *Yentl* (d, co-pr, sc, title role)
1991   *Prince of Tides* (d, co-pr, ro as Dr. Susan Lowenstein)
1995   *Serving in Silence: The Margarethe Cammermeyer Story* (Bleckner—for TV) (co-exec pr)

Publications

By STREISAND: articles—

"Symbiosis Continued," with William Wyler, in *Action* (Los Angeles), March-April 1968.
"A Star Is Reborn," interview with Michael Shnayerson, in *Vanity Fair*, November 1994.

On STREISAND: books—

Castell, David, *The Films of Barbra Streisand*, London, 1974.
Spada, James, with Christopher Nickens, *Streisand: The Woman and the Legend*, New York, 1981.
Zec, Donald, and Anthony Fowles, *Barbra: A Biography of Barbra Streisand*, 1981.
Considine, Shaun, *Barbra Streisand: The Woman, the Myth, the Music*, London, 1986.

Swenson, Karen, *Barbra: The Second Decade*, Secaucus, New Jersey, 1986.
Gerber, Françoise, *Barbra Streisand*, Paris, 1988.
Kimbrell, James, *Barbra: An Actress Who Sings*, Boston, 1989.
Carrick, Peter, *Barbra Striesand: A Biography*, London, 1991.
Riese, Randall, *Her Name Is Barbra: An Intimate Portrait of the Real Barbra Streisand*, Secaucus, New Jersey, 1993.
Waldman, Allison J., *The Barbra Streisand Scrapbook*, Secaucus, New Jersey, 1994.
Spada, James, *Streisand: Her Life*, New York, 1995.

On STREISAND: articles—

Carnell, R., "Barbra Streisand's Animal Crackers," in *Lumiere* (Melbourne), November 1973.
Stewart, G., "The Woman in the Moon," in *Sight and Sound* (London), Summer 1977.
Maslin, Janet, "Barbra Streisand" in *The Movie Star*, edited by Elisabeth Weis, New York, 1981.
Pally, Marcia, "Kaddish for the Fading Image of Jews in Film," in *Film Comment* (New York), February 1984.
Current Biography 1992, New York, 1992.
Zoglin, Richard, "The Way She Is," in *Time*, 16 May 1994.

*   *   *

Barbra Streisand has become, by sheer force of talent and the strength of her personality, one of the icons of the American cinema and popular culture. Her career has been long, unusual, and incredibly successful, despite the fact that for such a major star, she has a relatively short list of film credits. During the late seventies and eighties when men overwhelmingly dominated the American box office, Streisand was, for the most part, the only woman consistently considered bankable, that is, a performer who could make a project happen. And having directed only two films (with two more underway), she has become one of the most powerful directors in Hollywood as well. In short, Streisand is an industry to herself: a director, a producer, a concert performer, a recording star, and an actress who could secure virtually any part she chooses. She is one of the few performers who has won all four major American entertainment awards: the Emmy for television work, the Grammy for music recording, the Tony for the Broadway stage, and the Academy award for film work. Incredibly, she has even won several awards for composing music. Despite her achievements, criticism of Streisand has always been centered on two fronts: first, charges of egotism and self-centeredness which her defenders reject as actually representing her perfectionism; and second, her choice of projects, many of which have been rather safe vehicles that have not especially stretched her abilities as performer.

Streisand's first screen appearance was in the role she originated on Broadway, Fanny Brice in the film *Funny Girl*. In *Funny Girl* Streisand established the persona which she was to express, with only slight variation, in a series of vehicles over the next several years: an unattractive woman, generally with Jewish vocal inflections, intelligence, ego, and humor, who disarms all about her and is able to transform herself into the successful and morally superior creature who is the romantic object of a Gentile man's affections. In *Funny Girl*, Streisand's energy was overwhelming, indeed threatening. Her slightly crossed eyes and long, crooked nose proved no impediment to her triumphant announcement, in her first film, that "I'm the greatest star...." Along with Dustin Hoffman, Streisand was one of the new generation of Hollywood stars who refused to change their names, get plastic surgery, or conform to the conventional Hollywood stereotypes of attractiveness. That Streisand became a star at all, looking as she did, is itself a sign of her enormous talent: the strong singing voice, the

Barbra Streisand

comic timing, the photogenic face, the considerable on-screen charisma. To say that Streisand forced the Hollywood community and
American moviegoers to reevaluate their concepts of beauty would
not really be an overstatement. For her first film, Hollywood awarded
Streisand an Academy Award, though in a tie with Katharine Hepburn—
a symbol, as it were, of Streisand's uneasy alliance with Hollywood, a
community that fears and respects her, but does not, apparently, love
her with the kind of fevor they reserve for her more conventional
male counterparts.

Funny Girl was followed by two musicals, *On a Clear Day You Can
See Forever*, and the highly underrated *Hello, Dolly!*. Her performance as Dolly Levi was controversial at the time for its tongue-in-
cheek synthesis of Vivien Leigh and Mae West mannerisms. The
film's climax is in a restaurant filled with patrons contemplating
Streisand's beauty (rather than her talent), a concept that would have
been unthinkable only several years earlier. A series of comedies harkening back to the screwball era followed, including *What's Up, Doc?*, in
which Streisand wooed the blond WASP Ryan O'Neal, *For Pete's
Sake*, in which Streisand starred opposite the pretty Michael Sarrazin,
and *The Owl and the Pussycat*, in which Streisand plays opposite
George Segal, and gives what many feel is her most energetic and
inspired comic performance. At least two films in this period indicated untapped wells of dramatic abilities: the commercially unsuccessful feminist comedy *Up the Sandbox*, in which Streisand quietly
and naturalistically plays a mother contemplating another pregnancy,
and *The Way We Were*. The latter, which starred Streisand opposite
blonde WASP superstar Robert Redford, was an incredibly successful
and romantic film. The pairing evoked the kind of chemistry generally associated with the greatest stars of the past, such as Gable and
Crawford. Streisand's persona was fundamentally the same: the awkward, ugly duckling who becomes the romantic object of a handsome
man's affections. When Redford and Streisand divorce at the end of
the film, it is Streisand who is morally righteous.

Streisand followed *The Way We Were* with a series of films attacked
by many for being lazy, self-indulgent, or redundant: another comedy
called *The Main Event*; a sequel to *Funny Girl*, entitled *Funny Lady*, in
which Streisand gets to reject Omar Sharif, reversing the pattern of
the original; and an almost universally reviled but commercially successful remake of *A Star Is Born*. The latter, like *Funny Girl* and
Funny Lady, chronicles the rise to fame by Streisand in a narrative
that also chronicles the decline and moral inferiority of the handsome
man with whom she becomes involved.

Yentl definitely ushered in a new era for Streisand and her career.
The story of a young Jewish woman who masquerades as a man in
order to study Talmud, this quasi musical (in an era when the film
musical had been long considered as extinct as the dinosaur) was directed and produced by Streisand. Although most critics were prepared
to accuse Streisand of total self-centeredness, *Yentl*'s genuine and ostensible quality, for the most part, disarmed them. Certainly Streisand
the director is by no means self-indulgent with Streisand the star:
close-ups of Streisand do not automatically reveal the actress's "good"
(left) side; occasionally, the star will even be photographed out of
focus so the director can emphasize something else within the frame.
The film's cinematography is extraordinary. In *Yentl*, director Streisand
reveals a fetching sensitivity, an interest in androgyny (which would
foreshadow her interest in gay and lesbian issues in the nineties), and
a profoundly lyrical sensuality. Unlike *A Star Is Born*, *Yentl* seems
organically unified, with all facets of production working in harmony
toward one artistic end. For the first time, Streisand's love interest is
as Jewish as she and not morally inferior. Much sympathy (as well as
screen time) is extended to the secondary female lead in the film as
well—another break with the patterns of Streisand's past films.

In 1991, Streisand both directed and acted in *Prince of Tides*, a devi-
ously entertaining love story-cum-melodrama in the style of the classic
women's films of the forties and fifties, updated with subtlety and intelli-

gence to deal head-on with a variety of current issues, most notably
childhood sexual abuse and the socially prescribed gender roles for men
and women. To the surprise of many, including Streisand, the film
turned into a huge event, winning the enthusiastic approbation of an emotionally moved public and significant critical raves. Streisand garnered sensitive performances from her son, Jason Gould, who played her on-screen
son, and particularly from macho Nick Nolte, whose key scene required
him to break down emotionally to childlike vulnerability as he admits to
having been raped as a young boy. The negative backlash to the film was,
unfortunately, muddled in sexism: criticism of Streisand's having photographed herself in a glamorous way (with no criticism of director Streisand
having photographed Nolte similarly), accusations against the genre of
melodrama as inherently unworthy (except to the extent that its focus is
on male characters), and so forth. That the film received seven Academy
award nominations, but again not one for Streisand, its director and star,
became a matter for such public comment that Streisand became the de
facto, acclaimed director of the year.

From 1992, Streisand found herself concentrating on a variety of
other projects: particularly her long-awaited return to headlining live
performance—her first in over twenty-five years—via a triumphantly
successful concert tour. Streisand also became increasingly involved in
feminist issues, AIDS research and AIDS education, and children's
rights. In the process, Streisand, although always socially conscious
and active in the past—particularly through her philanthropic Streisand
Foundation, transformed herself into Hollywood's leading liberal
spokesperson. Incredibly energized by these issues and now the most
visible role model for women directors, women producers, and artists
of all kind engaged in grassroots political action, Streisand continuing
in Hollywood as an actress for hire on others' projects seems difficult
to imagine. After having co-produced, with Glenn Close, a successful
Emmy-award-winning TV movie on homophobia in the military, *Serving in Silence: The Margarethe Cammermeyer Story*, Streisand is in
the process of directing and starring in two major film projects: a love
story, *The Mirror Has Two Faces*; and the long-awaited film version of
Larry Kramer's angry exposé of government inaction during the first
stages of the AIDS epidemic, *The Normal Heart*.

—Charles Derry

SULLAVAN, Margaret

Nationality: American. **Born:** Margaret Brooke Sullavan in Norfolk, Virginia, 16 May 1911. **Education:** Attended Chatham Episcopal Institute; Sullins College, Bristol, Virginia; E. E. Clive Dramatic
School, Boston. **Family:** Married 1) the actor Henry Fonda, 1931
(divorced 1933); 2) the director William Wyler, 1934 (divorced 1936);
3) the agent Leland Hayward, 1936 (divorced 1948); daughter: Brooke;
4) Kenneth Wagg, 1950. **Career:** Late 1920s—joined Joshua Logan's
University Players in West Falmouth, Massachusetts; 1931—Broadway debut in *The Modern Virgin*; 1933—contract with Universal: film
debut in *Only Yesterday*, 1934; 1938—contract with MGM; 1943—on
Broadway in *The Voice of the Turtle*; late 1940s—increasing deafness;
1952—in stage play *Sabrina*. **Awards:** Best Actress, New York Film
Critics, for *Three Comrades*, 1938. **Died:** 1 January 1960.

Films as Actress:

1934   *Only Yesterday* (Stahl) (as Mary Lane); *Little Man, What Now?*
       (Borzage) (as Lammchen Pinneberg)
1935   *The Good Fairy* (Wyler) (as Luisa Ginglebusher); *So Red the
       Rose* (Vidor) (as Vallette Bedford)

Margaret Sullavan (right) with Natalie Wood in *No Sad Songs for Me*

1936   *The Next Time We Love* (Edward Griffith) (as Cicely Tyler);
         The Moon's Our Home (Seiter) (as Cherry Chester)
1938   *Three Comrades* (Borzage) (as Patricia Hollman); *The Shop-
         worn Angel* (Potter) (as Daisy Heath)
1940   *The Shop around the Corner* (Lubitsch) (as Klara Novak); *The
         Mortal Storm* (Borzage) (as Freya Roth)
1941   *So Ends Our Night* (Cromwell) (as Ruth Holland); *Back Street*
         (Stevenson) (as Ray Smith); *Appointment for Love* (Seiter)
         (as Jane Alexander)
1943   *Cry Havoc* (Thorpe) (as Lt. Smith)
1950   *No Sad Songs for Me* (Maté) (as Mary Scott)

Publications

By SULLAVAN: article—

"The Making of a Movie Star," in *American Magazine*, May 1934.

On SULLAVAN: books—

Borrows, Michael, *Patricia Neal and Margaret Sullavan*, St. Austell,
    Cornwall, 1971.

Quirk, Lawrence J., *Margaret Sullavan: Child of Fate*, New York,
    1986.

On SULLAVAN: articles—

Current Biography 1944, New York, 1944.
Obituary in *New York Times*, 2 January 1960.
Jacobs, J., "Margaret Sullavan," in *Films in Review* (New York), April
    1960.
Sarris, Andrew, "Reflections on Margaret Sullavan," in *Film Comment*
    (New York), November-December 1977.

*   *   *

Margaret Sullavan's personal independence characterized her life
on and off screen. Her reluctance to bind herself to a movie star's
contract resulted in a relatively limited number of films. Nevertheless,
she established a strongly identifiable persona of individuality and
courage amid suffering. She used her naturally pensive appearance and
husky, breathless voice as means of characterizing women who were
often doomed but confronted their fate with spirit.

The majority of Sullavan's films were melodramas in which her
characters faced adversity in the form of poverty, sickness, hopeless

romance, political oppression, and, often, death. But even in comedies she projected an air of underlying sadness. When the correspondent never shows up for their first meeting in *The Shop around the Corner*, for example, she wears her disappointment with the same resigned but indomitable acceptance that she does facing serious illness in *Three Comrades* or sitting alone on New Year's Eve waiting for her married lover in *Back Street*.

There was often an otherworldly quality to Sullavan's characters, roles that called for idealism and principle. Her hair was frequently lighted to make it shine, accentuating the angelic way in which her characters accepted their fate. As the mother in *Little Man, What Now?* she makes the birth of her son akin to the Nativity. And those films that call for her character to die seem the fulfillment of her tragic spirit, for the films suggest that her characters are not limited by mortality. In *The Mortal Storm* Freya is killed as she and Martin (James Stewart) are escaping from Nazi Germany, but Stewart nevertheless carries her body to freedom. The memory of her goodness seems to influence her Nazi brother (Robert Stack) to reconsider his commitment to evil. Her final role, in *No Sad Songs for Me*, is perhaps the quintessence of her persona. Told that she is dying, she ingratiates her husband and daughter with another woman, one who can take her place when she is gone.

A sense of self-sacrificing concern was combined with a unique presence, submissive yet strong, smiling but mournful, courageous though doubtful, that made Margaret Sullavan's characters, paradoxically, vulnerable while living—and dying—heroically.

—Jerome Delamater

SUTHERLAND, Donald

Nationality: Canadian. **Born:** Donald McNichol Sutherland in St. John, New Brunswick, Canada, 17 July 1935. **Education:** Attended public schools in Bridgewater, Nova Scotia; University of Toronto, B.A. 1956; London Academy of Music and Dramatic Art, England. **Family:** Married 1) Lois May Hardwick, 1959 (divorced); 2) the actress Shirley Jean Douglas, 1966 (divorced), son: the actor Kiefer, daughter: Rachel; since 1974, has lived with the actress Francine Racette, sons: Roeg, Rossif, and Angus. **Career:** Late 1950s—worked in repertory companies in the United Kingdom; professional debut in London in *The Gimmick*; also acted on television; 1964—film debut in *Castle of the Living Dead*; late 1970s—formed McNichol Picture production company; 1981—New York stage debut in *Lolita*; 1994—in TV mini-series *The Oldest Living Confederate Widow Tells All*. **Awards:** Emmy Award, Golden Globe for Best Supporting Actor, for *Citizen X*, 1995. **Agent:** Creative Artists Agency, 9830 Wilshire Boulevard, Beverly Hills, CA 90212, U.S.A.

Films as Actor:

1964   *Il castello dei morti vivi* (*Castle of the Living Dead*) (Ricci) (as witch/sergeant)

1965   *The Bedford Incident* (James B. Harris) (as Nerny); *Dr. Terror's House of Horrors* (Francis) (as Bob Carroll); *Fanatic* (*Die! Die! My Darling*) (Narizzano) (as Joseph)

1966   *Promise Her Anything* (Hiller)

1967   *The Dirty Dozen* (Aldrich) (as Vernon Pinkley); *Oedipus the King* (Saville) (as chorus leader)

1968   *The Sunshine Patriot* (Sargent—for TV) (as Benedeck); *Interlude* (Billington) (as Lawrence); *Joanna* (Sarne) (as Lord Peter Sanderson); *The Split* (Flemyng) (as Dave Negli); *Mr. Sebastian* (*Sebastian*) (David Greene) (as American)

1970   *Start the Revolution without Me* (Yorkin) (as Charles/Pierre); *Acte du Coeur* (*Act of the Heart*) (Almond) (as Father Michael Ferrier); *M*A*S*H* (Altman) (as Capt. Benjamin Franklin "Hawkeye" Pierce); *Kelly's Heroes* (*The Warriors*) (Hutton) (as Oddball); *Alex in Wonderland* (Mazursky) (title role)

1971   *Johnny Got His Gun* (Trumbo) (as "Christ"); *Little Murders* (Arkin) (as the Minister); ***Klute*** (Pakula) (title role)

1972   *The FTA Show* (*F.T.A.*; *Foxtrot Tango Alpha*; *Free the Army*; *Fuck the Army*) (Francine Parker—doc) (+ co-pr, sc)

1973   *Steelyard Blues* (Myerson) (as Veldini); *Lady Ice* (Gries) (as Andy Hammond); ***Don't Look Now*** (Roeg) (as John Baxter)

1974   *S*P*Y*S* (Kershner) (as Brulard)

1975   *Der Richter und sein Henker* (*End of the Game*; *Murder on the Bridge*; *Getting Away with Murder*) (Schell) (as corpse); *The Day of the Locust* (Schlesinger) (as Homer Simpson); *Alien Thunder* (*Dan Candy's Law*) (Fournier)

1976   ***1900*** (*Novecento*) (Bertolucci) (as Attila); *Casanova* (*Fellini's Casanova*) (Fellini) (title role); *The Eagle Has Landed* (John Sturges) (as Liam Devlin)

1977   *The Kentucky Fried Movie* (Landis) (as waiter); *The Cinema According to Bertolucci* (Bertolucci—doc); *Les Liens de sang* (*Blood Relatives*) (Chabrol) (as Carella); *The Disappearance* (Cooper) (as Jay Mallory)

1978   *National Lampoon's Animal House* (Landis) (as Dave Jennings); *Invasion of the Body Snatchers* (Kaufman) (as Matthew Bennel); *The Great Train Robbery* (*The First Great Train Robbery*) (Michael Crichton) (as Agar)

1979   *Murder by Decree* (Clark) (as Robert Lees); *A Very Big Withdrawal* (*A Man, a Woman, and a Bank*) (Black) (as Reese Halperin); *Bear Island* (Sharp) (as Frank Lansing)

1980   *Ordinary People* (Redford) (as Calvin); *Nothing Personal* (Bloomfield) (as Professor Roger Kelly)

1981   *Gas* (Rose) (as Nick the Noz); *Eye of the Needle* (Marquand) (as Henry Faber); *Threshold* (Pearce) (as Dr. Thomas Vrain)

1983   *Max Dugan Returns* (Ross) (as Brian Costello); *The Winter of Our Discontent* (Hussein—for TV); *Nothing Personal* (Bloomfield)

1984   *Crackers* (Malle) (as Weslake); *Ordeal by Innocence* (Desmond Davis) (as Dr. Arthur Calgary)

1985   *Heaven Help Us* (*Catholic Boys*) (Dinner) (as Brother Thadeus); *Revolution* (Hudson) (as Sgt. Maj. Peasy)

1986   *The Wolf at the Door* (*Oviri*) (Carlsen) (as Paul Gauguin)

1987   *The Rosary Murders* (Walton) (as Father Bob Koesler); *The Trouble with Spies* (Kennedy) (as Appleton Porter)

1988   *Apprentice to Murder* (Thomas) (as John Reese)

1989   *A Dry White Season* (Palcy) (as Ben du Toit); *Lock Up* (Flynn) (as Warden Drumgoole); *Lost Angels* (*The Road Home*) (Hudson) (as Dr. Charles Loftis)

1990   *Bethune: The Making of a Hero* (*Dr. Bethune*) (Borsos—released in U.S. in 1993) (title role); *Buster's Bedroom* (Horn); *Schrei aus Stein* (*Scream of Stone*) (Herzog) (as Ivan)

1991   *Eminent Domain* (Irvin) (as Jozef Burski); *Backdraft* (Ron Howard) (as Ronald Bartel); *JFK* (Oliver Stone) (as Colonel "X")

1992   *Buffy the Vampire Slayer* (Kuzui) (as Merrick); *The Railway Station Man* (Whyte—for TV) (as Roger Hawthorne); *Quicksand: No Escape* (Pressman—for TV)

1993   *Benefit of the Doubt* (Heap) (as Frank); *Shadow of the Wolf* (*Agaguk*) (Dorfmann) (as Henderson); *Six Degrees of Separation* (Schepisi) (as Flan Kittredge); *Younger and Younger* (Adlon) (as Jonathan Younger)

1994   *Disclosure* (Levinson) (as Bob Garvin); *The Puppet Masters* (Orme) (as Andrew Nivens); *Punch* (Birkinshaw and Fluetsch); *The Lifeforce Experiment* (*The Breakthrough*) (Haggard—for TV) (as Dr. "MAC" MacLean)

Donald Sutherland in *Don't Look Now*

1995   *Outbreak* (Petersen) (as Gen. Donnie McClintock); *Citizen X*
          (Gerolmo—for TV) (as Fetisov)
1996   *The Shadow Conspiracy* (*The Shadow Program*) (Cosmatos);
          Hollow Point; *A Time to Kill* (Schumacher) (as Lucien Wilbanks)

Publications

By SUTHERLAND: articles—

Interview, in *Show* (New York), April 1971.
"Recréer l'univers magique de Fellini," interview with G. Morin, in
   Cinéma Québec (Montreal), vol. 5, no. 6, 1977.
Interview with R. Schar, in *Cinema Papers* (Melbourne), April 1977.
Interview with J. Craven, in *Films and Filming* (London), June 1978.
Interview with B. Lewis, in *Films and Filming* (London), March 1987.

On SUTHERLAND: articles—

Eyles, Allen, "Donald Sutherland," in *Focus on Film* (London), Autumn
   1973.

Films and Filming (London), January 1979.
Current Biography 1981, New York, 1981.
Graustark, Barbara, "Donald Sutherland's Seventh-Inning Stretch," in
   American Film (Washington, D.C.), April 1984.
Alion, Yves, "Le magnétisme du regard," in *Revue du Cinéma* (Paris),
   December 1989.

*   *   *

Donald Sutherland continues a long and distinguished, although eclectic, career in North American and European cinema. He has proven himself adept in a wide variety of roles and acting styles, from broad work in action thrillers to subtle, self-deferential characterizations in domestic dramas, as well as conceptual interpretations in European art films.

Sutherland achieved stardom in Robert Altman's *M*A*S*H* as Hawkeye Pierce in 1970, but he had been acting (in Europe and Canada) in a variety of character parts during the 1960s. In an earlier era, the tall, gawky-looking Sutherland might not have achieved the stardom that followed *M*A*S*H*, but Hollywood in the early seventies was open for male stars with unconventional looks. He was hired for the title roles in Paul Mazursky's *Alex in Wonderland* and Alan Pakula's *Klute*, yielding attention in the latter to Jane Fonda's riveting prostitute, Bree Daniels. Sutherland was known to have had antagonistic relationships with some of his early directors (it is an oft-reported story that Sutherland and Elliott Gould attempted to get the studio to fire Altman from *M*A*S*H*), but by the mid-seventies he had rethought his role in the collaborative process. "What I was trying to do all the time was impose my thinking," Sutherland later remarked. "Now I contribute. I offer, I don't put my foot down."

As his career continued, Sutherland would offer his services to many of the brightest directors of the age—John Schlesinger, Bernardo Bertolucci, Federico Fellini, Claude Chabrol, and Louis Malle, among others—but he would have the misfortune of doing so as those directors embarked on some of their more problematic films.

Sutherland's commitment to a director's vision would, however, serve him well in Nicolas Roeg's brilliant *Don't Look Now*, where his willingness to become the object of Julie Christie and Roeg's erotic gaze was unique even in that era's tradition of frontal male nudity. *Don't Look Now*'s John Baxter provided Sutherland with a role that balanced his ability to display subtle nuance through a generally repressed character who could, occasionally, display great depths of emotion. Later, continuing to work in Europe with Bertolucci on *1900* and on *Fellini's Casanova*, Sutherland would take heroic dives off the artistic cliffs his directors put in front of him. While his work as the monstrous fascist Attila in the former would eventually win him respect and even a certain amount of awe (and surely contribute to casting directors' willingness to give him larger-than-life roles in the future), it was considered an embarrassing misstep at the time. Fellini's conception of Casanova would, however, effectively turn Sutherland into a life-sized marionette in one of the Italian auteur's worst pictures.

If Sutherland's allegiance to some directors would backfire in the direction of "overacting," his commitment to Robert Redford in *Ordinary People* (1980) and Fred Schepisi in *Six Degrees of Separation* (1993) would require him to defer attention to the films' other cast members. Surely Sutherland's work in Redford's film equaled Mary Tyler Moore's and Timothy Hutton's, but as a gentle man trying to hold his family together, it was not the kind of performance that impressed casual viewers or won awards. In Schepisi's adaptation of John Guare's dazzling play, Sutherland was given the script's one underconceived part—art speculator Flan Kittredge who is locked into a life by rote while his wife Ouisa has the epiphanies. Still, Sutherland was able to suggest a certain sorrow over a life of unconsummated possibilities.

Perhaps Sutherland's work as a villain, or at least a character prone to malevolence, in numerous films such as *Eye of the Needle*, *Lock Up*, *Backdraft*, and *Disclosure*, used him to most impressive effect in the eighties and nineties. *Eye of the Needle*'s Nazi spy Henry Faber was a complex and bone-chilling characterization; Sutherland's Warden Drumgoole in the Stallone film *Lock Up* evoked his Attila; and in *Disclosure*, as Michael Douglas's corporate boss, Sutherland was able to use his flashing eyes, curling upper lip, and imposingly large frame to subtly convey malevolent intent without any direct acknowledgment within the script. Sutherland did give at least one completely stunning performance in this period as a sympathetic Paul Gauguin in the 1986 film *The Wolf at the Door*, but few saw that French-Danish co-production.

Still, one wishes for more opportunities for this risk-taking actor, one of the most talented of his generation. In the late nineties, Sutherland would be heard doing voice-overs for Volvo commercials and turning in still more villainous performances in such films as *Outbreak*, where boredom seems finally to be creeping into his performances. Considering the quality of the scripts, it is hard to entirely fault him for this.

—Daniel I. Humphrey

SWANSON, Gloria

Nationality: American. **Born:** Gloria May Josephine Svensson in Chicago, Illinois, 27 March 1899. **Education:** Attended public schools in Chicago; Key West, Florida; San Juan, Puerto Rico; and elsewhere. **Family:** Married 1) the actor Wallace Beery, 1916 (divorced 1918); 2) William Somborn, 1919 (divorced), daughter: Gloria, adopted son: Joseph; 3) Marquis Henri de la Falaise, 1924 (divorced 1930); 4) Michael Farmer, 1931 (divorced 1934), daughter: Michelle; 5) William Davey, 1945 (divorced 1948); 6) the writer William Dufty, 1975 (divorced 1981). **Career:** 1915—film debut as extra in *The Fable of Elvira and Farina and the Meal Ticket*, made in Chicago; 1916—leading roles in comedies for Keystone company; 1918—in dramatic roles for Triangle; 1919—contract with Cecil B. DeMille; 1926—formed Gloria Swanson Productions, with backing of producer Joseph Kennedy; 1938—formed Multiprises; 1940s—on stage in *Reflected Glory*, *Let Us Be Gay*, and *A Goose for a Gander*; 1951—on stage in *Twentieth Century*; also clothes designer and artist; founder, Essence of Nature Cosmetics. **Died:** In New York, 4 April 1983.

Films as Actress:

1915   *The Fable of Elvira and Farina and the Meal Ticket* (Baker); *Sweedie Goes to College* (Baker); *The Romance of an American Duchess*; *The Broken Pledge*; *At the End of a Perfect Day* (as extra, hands bouquet to Holmes); *The Ambition of the Baron*; *His New Job* (*Charlie's New Job*) (Chaplin) (as extra, stenographer)

1916   *A Dash of Courage* (Chase); *Hearts and Sparks* (Parrott); *A Social Club* (Badger); *The Danger Girl*; *Love on Skates*; *Haystacks and Steeples* (Badger); *The Nick of Time Baby* (*Whose Baby?*) (Badger)

1917   *Teddy at the Throttle* (Badger); *Baseball Madness* (Mason); *Dangers of a Bride*; *The Sultan's Wife*; *A Pullman Bride* (Badger)

1918   *Society for Sale* (*The Honorable Billy*) (Borzage) (as Phyllis Cline); *Her Decision* (Conway) (as Phyllis Dunbar); *You Can't Believe Everything* (Conway) (as Patricia Reynolds); *Everywoman's Husband* (Hamilton) (as Edith Emerson); *Shifting Sands* (Albert Parker) (as Marcia Grey); *Station Content* (Hoyt); *Secret Code* (Albert Parker) (as Sally Carter Rand); *Wife or Country* (E. Mason Hopper) (as Sylvia Hamilton)

1919   *Don't Change Your Husband* (Cecil B. DeMille) (as Leila Porter); *For Better, for Worse* (Cecil B. DeMille) (as Sylvia Norcross); *Male and Female* (Cecil B. DeMille) (as Lady Mary Lasenby)

1920   *Why Change Your Wife?* (Cecil B. DeMille) (as Beth Gordon); *Something to Think About* (Cecil B. DeMille) (as Ruth Anderson); *The Great Moment* (Wood) (as Nada Pelham)

1921   *The Affairs of Anatole* (Cecil B. DeMille) (as Vivian Spencer); *Under the Lash* (Wood) (as Deborah Krillet); *Don't Tell Everything* (Wood) (as Marion Westover)

1922   *Her Husband's Trademark* (Wood) (as Lois Miller); *Beyond the Rocks* (Wood) (as Theodora Fitzgerald); *Her Gilded Cage* (Wood) (as Suzanne Ornoff); *The Impossible Mrs. Bellew* (Wood) (title role)

1923   *My American Wife* (Wood) (as Natalie Chester); *Prodigal Daughters* (Wood) (as Elinor "Swiftie" Forbes); *Bluebeard's Eighth Wife* (Wood) (as Mona de Briac); *Zaza* (Dwan) (title role); *Hollywood* (*Joligud*) (Cruze and Vacariello) (guest appearance)

1924　*The Humming Bird* (Olcott) (as Toinette); *A Society Scandal* (Dwan) (as Marjorie Colbert); *Manhandled* (Dwan) (as Tessie McGuire); *Her Love Story* (Dwan) (as Princess Maria); *Wages of Virtue* (Dwan) (as Carmelita)

1925　*Madame Sans-Gêne* (Perret) (as Catherine Hubscher); *The Coast of Folly* (Dwan) (as Nadine/Joyce Gathway); *Stage Struck* (Dwan) (as Jennie Hagen)

1926　*Untamed Lady* (Tuttle) (as St. Clair Van Tassel); *Fine Manners* (Rosson) (as Orchid Murphy)

1927　*The Love of Sunya* (Albert Parker) (title role, + pr)

1928　*Sadie Thompson* (Walsh) (title role, + pr); *Queen Kelly* (von Stroheim) (title role, + pr)

1929　*The Trespasser* (Goulding) (as Marion Donnell)

1930　*What a Widow!* (Dwan) (as Tamarind Brooks, + pr)

1931　*Indiscreet* (McCarey) (as Geraldine "Jerry" Trent); *Tonight or Never* (LeRoy) (as Nella Vago)

1933　*Perfect Understanding* (Gardner) (as Judy Rogers, + pr)

1934　*Music in the Air* (Joe May) (as Frieda Hertefeld)

1941　*Father Takes a Wife* (Hively) (as Leslie Collier)

1949　*Down Memory Lane* (Karlson—compilation)

1950　***Sunset Boulevard*** (Wilder) (as Norma Desmond)

1952　*Three for Bedroom C* (Bren) (as Ann Haven)

1956　*Mio figlio Nerone* (*Nero's Mistress*; *Nero's Weekend*) (Steno) (as Agrippina)

1960　*When Comedy Was King* (Youngson—compilation) (as herself)

1972　*Chaplinesque, My Life and Hard Times* (Hurwitz—doc) (as narrator)

1974　*The Killer Bees* (Harrington—for TV) (as Mme. Von Bohlen); *Airport 1975* (Smight) (as herself)

Publications

By SWANSON: book—

Swanson on Swanson, New York, 1980.

By SWANSON: articles—

"Why I Am Going Back to the Screen," interview with Frederick Smith, in *Motion Picture Classic* (Brooklyn), February 1920.

"What Is Love?," in *Photoplay* (New York), November 1924.

"There Is No Formula for Success," in *Photoplay* (New York), April 1926.

"My Most Wonderful Experience," in *Photoplay* (New York), February 1951.

"I Am Not Going to Write My Memoirs," interview with Rui Nogueira, in *Sight and Sound* (London), Spring 1969.

"Gloria! Miss Swanson in Excelsis," interview with Andy Warhol and John Kobal, in *Inter/View* (New York), September 1972.

"Gloria Swanson: 'Les Films d'aujourd'hui sont trop pornographiques ...,'" interview with D. Rabourdin, in *Cinéma* (Paris), May 1974.

On SWANSON: books—

Hudson, Richard M., and Raymond Lee, *Gloria Swanson*, New York, 1970.

Rosen, Marjorie, *Popcorn Venus*, New York, 1973.

Quirk, Lawrence J., *The Films of Gloria Swanson*, Secaucus, New Jersey, 1984.

Madsen, Axel, *Gloria and Joe*, New York, 1988.

On SWANSON: articles—

Smith, Frederick, "The Silken Gloria," in *Motion Picture Classic* (Brooklyn), February 1920.

St. Johns, Adela Rogers, "Gloria! An Impression," in *Photoplay* (New York), September 1923.

Harriman, H. C., "Gloria Swanson," in *New Yorker*, 18 January 1930.

Parsons, Louella, "The Loves of Gloria Swanson," in *Pictures and Picturegoer*, 26 March-16 April 1932.

Current Biography 1950, New York, 1950.

"Forever Gloria," in *Life* (New York), 5 June 1950.

Brownlow, Kevin, "Gloria Swanson," in *Film* (London), Autumn 1964.

Bodeen, DeWitt, "Gloria Swanson," in *Films in Review* (New York), April 1965.

Taylor, John, "Swanson," in *Sight and Sound* (London), Autumn 1968.

Drew, Bernard, "Gloria Swanson," in *The Movie Star*, edited by Elisabeth Weis, New York, 1981.

Braun, Eric, "Swanson: A Star for All Seasons," in *Films* (London), June 1981.

Obituary in *New York Times*, 5 April 1983.

Rodrig, A., and E. Decaux, obituary in *Cinématographe* (Paris), May 1983.

Oderman, Stuart, "Gloria Swanson," in *Films in Review* (New York), March 1988.

*　　*　　*

To a generation of filmgoers, Gloria Swanson will only be the half-mad movie queen of *Sunset Boulevard* who traps screenwriter William Holden in a bizarre world behind the walls of her 1920s mansion. But there is much more to Swanson's career than just this image indelibly etched in film history.

Swanson was one of the biggest stars of the silent era. No personality was more vital, more visible, more passionately alive in Hollywood. Cecil B. DeMille changed her from a routine Mack Sennett comedienne into an elegant, vivacious, and narcissistic clotheshorse. He seldom required his teenage star to act, merely pose, flirt, tyrannize servants, and discreetly reveal portions of her slim, perfectly proportioned body. She became noted for the bathing rituals DeMille incessantly constructed for her. Precisely reflecting the Paramount taste for European manners, lush lighting, and sexual innuendo, DeMille created, in his drawing room sex comedies such as *Don't Change Your Husband*, *Why Change Your Wife?*, and *The Affairs of Anatol*, a style that persisted into Swanson's life outside the studio; her best performances were usually for the papers.

Swanson capitalized on her provocative glance and perpetual slouch to epitomize the emancipated female predator. She collected only the most prestigious male trophies who guaranteed her continued presence in the headlines. Her third husband, an impoverished French marquis, made her one of Hollywood's first legitimate aristocrats. In the mid-1920s she snared as a lover and financier Joseph P. Kennedy, father of John F. Kennedy. Kennedy backed her in the doomed production of Eric von Stroheim's *Queen Kelly*. Ironically, she watches a scene from *Queen Kelly* projected by her butler played by von Stroheim in *Sunset Boulevard*.

Swanson was only 30 years old when sound came. She had no stage training, but a clear, almost piercing voice that suited the primitive systems of the time. She even learned to sing for the 1934 musical *Music in the Air*. But nobody was making films in her intense, sultry style. Clutching at William Holden the way her creator, Gloria Swanson, dug her manicured nails into her stardom, *Sunset Boulevard*'s Norma Desmond was as deluded in her quest for immortality as Swanson was practical in hers. If operettas could not revive her luster in the 1930s, then maybe a screwball comedy such as *Father Takes a Wife* would do the trick in the 1940s. Ultimately, Swanson realized that her legend was not genre or trend dependent. The designer clothes diva remained a media magnet for decades because Swanson elegantly embodied the entire bygone era of the silent cinema; her gift for adaptability prevented her from becoming a dinosaur like Norma Desmond.

Gloria Swanson

Still, it could not have been easy for a grandiloquent symbol to find roles in keeping with her eminence. Incredibly, her follow-up to *Sunset Boulevard*—the greatest comeback of all time—was a tepid farce, *Three for Bedroom C*. In addition to triumphing on Broadway in a revival of *Twentieth Century*, Swanson toured with comedic élan in such plays as *Butterflies Are Free*. That she acted her roles to the hilt seemed of less consequence than her providing living proof of one of *Sunset Boulevard*'s most famous lines: "Stars are ageless. No one ever leaves a star." Her fans never did.

Whether she slummed in the gimmicky horror of a literal B movie, *The Killer Bees*, or sashayed haughtily through the all-star peril of *Airport 1975* in variations of her aristocratic screen image, she remained Swanson: Hallowed Defeater of Crow's Feet and Nutritional Warrior against Junk Food. She defeated Time. However confining it must have been to never sink her teeth into another juicy role, it must have been comforting to know that the public did not make the same demands of her that they did of other silent-era survivors such as Crawford and Gish. As always, her private life was her most effective performance. Even in a silly guest spot on *The Beverly Hillbillies*, Swanson maintained her dignity so thoroughly that even the Clampetts behaved with propriety. Whereas other stars curried admiration, Swanson commanded respect without really trying.

—John Baxter, updated by Robert Pardi

SWEET, Blanche

Nationality: American. **Born:** Sarah Blanche Sweet in Chicago, Illinois, 18 June 1896. **Family:** Married 1) the director Marshall Neilan, 1922 (divorced 1929); 2) the actor Raymond Hackett, 1936 (died). **Career:** On stage from 18 months, then billed as "Baby Blanche" and "Little Blanche"; dancing lessons with Ruth St. Denis; 1909—film debut in *A Man with Three Wives* in New York; 1911—joined the Griffith film group in California, and made a long series of shorts for him; 1914—starred in *Judith of Bethulia*; then contract with Jesse Lasky, and starred in a group of dramas; 1919—contract with Jesse Hampton Productions; 1924-25—made several films in England with Marshall Neilan; 1930—film career ended; toured in vaudeville act *Sweet and Lovely*, and appeared on stage in *The Party's Over* and *The Petrified Forest*; also had a radio program in 1930s; 1950s—clerk in a New York department store. **Died:** In New York City, 6 September 1986.

Films as Actress:

1909 *A Man with Three Wives*; *A Corner in Wheat* (Griffith); *The Day After* (Griffith)
1910 *All on Account of the Milk* (Powell)
1911 *Country Lovers* (Sennett); *Was He a Coward?* (Griffith); *The Lonedale Operator* (Griffith); *How She Triumphed* (Griffith); *The White Rose of the Wild* (Griffith); *A Smile of a Child* (Griffith); *The Last Drop of Water* (Griffith); *Out from the Shadow* (Griffith); *The Blind Princess and the Poet* (Griffith); *The Making of a Man* (Griffith); *The Long Road* (Griffith); *Love in the Hills* (Griffith); *The Battle* (Griffith); *Through Darkened Vales* (Griffith); *A Woman Scorned* (*Woman of Sin*) (Griffith)
1912 *The Eternal Mother* (Griffith); *For His Son* (Griffith); *The Transformation of Mike* (Griffith); *Under Burning Skies* (Griffith); *The Goddess of Sagebrush Gulch* (Griffith); *The Punishment* (Griffith); *One Is Business, The Other Crime* (Griffith); *The Lesser Evil* (Griffith); *The Outcast among Outcasts* (Griffith); *A Temporary Truce* (Griffith); *The Spirit Awakened* (Griffith); *Man's Lust for Gold* (Griffith); *The Painted Lady* (Griffith); *With the Enemy's Help* (Griffith); *A Change of Spirit* (Griffith); *Blind Love* (Griffith); *The Chief's Blanket* (Griffith); *A Sailor's Heart* (Griffith); *The God Within* (Griffith)
1913 *Three Friends* (Griffith); *Pirate Gold*; *Oil and Water* (Griffith); *A Chance Deception* (Cabanne); *Broken Ways* (Griffith); *The Hero of Little Italy* (Griffith); *The Stolen Bride* (Griffith); *Classmates* (Griffith); *Love in an Apartment Hotel* (Griffith); *If We Only Knew* (Griffith); *Death's Marathon* (Griffith); *The Coming of Angelo* (Griffith); *The Mistake* (Griffith); *Two Men on the Desert* (Griffith); *The House of Discord* (Kirkwood); *Her Wedding Bell*
1914 *The Sentimental Sister*; *The Massacre* (Griffith); *Strongheart* (Kirkwood); *Men and Women* (Kirkwood); *Ashes of the Past* (Kirkwood); *The Soul of Honor* (Kirkwood); *The Painted Lady* (Griffith); *The Second Mrs. Roebuck* (O'Brien); *For Those Unborn* (Cabanne); *Her Awakening* (Cabanne); *For Her Father's Sins* (O'Brien); *The Tear That Burned* (O'Brien); *The Odalisque* (Griffith); *The Little Country Mouse* (Griffith); *The Old Maid* (O'Brien); *Judith of Bethulia* (*Her Condoned Sin*) (Griffith) (title role); *The Escape* (Griffith); "The Marriage of Roses and Lilies" ep. of *Home Sweet Home* (Griffith); *The Avenging Conscience* (Griffith) (as Annabel)
1915 *The Warrens of Virginia* (Cecil B. DeMille); *The Captive* (Cecil B. DeMille); *Stolen Goods* (Melford); *The Clue* (Neill); *The Secret Orchard* (Reicher); *The Case of Becky* (Reicher) (title role); *The Secret Sin* (Reicher) (as twin sisters)
1916 *The Ragamuffin* (William DeMille); *Blacklist* (William DeMille); *The Sowers* (William DeMille); *The Thousand Dollar Husband* (Young); *The Dupe* (Reicher); *Public Opinion* (Reicher); *The Storm* (Reicher); *Unprotected* (Young)
1917 *The Evil Eye* (Melford); *Those without Sin* (Neilan); *The Tides of Barnegat* (Neilan); *The Silent Partner* (Neilan)
1919 *The Unpardonable Sin* (Neilan) (as Alice Parcot/Dimmy Parcot); *The Hushed Hour* (Mortimer); *A Woman of Pleasure* (Worsley); *Fighting Cressy* (Thornby) (title role)
1920 *The Deadlier Sex* (Thornby); *Simple Souls* (Thornby); *The Girl in the Web* (Thornby); *Help Wanted—Male* (*Object Matrimony*) (King); *Her Unwilling Husband* (Scardon)
1921 *That Girl Montana* (Thornby)
1922 *Quincy Adams Sawyer* (Badger)
1923 *The Meanest Man in the World* (Cline); *Anna Christie* (Wray) (title role); *In the Palace of the King* (Flynn)
1924 *Those Who Dance* (Hillyer); *Tess of the D'Urbervilles* (Neilan) (title role)
1925 *The Sporting Venus* (Neilan); *His Supreme Moment* (Fitzmaurice); *Why Women Love* (Carewe); *The New Commandment* (Higgin)
1926 *Bluebeard's Seven Wives* (Santell); *The Far Cry* (Balboni); *The Lady from Hell* (Paton) (as Lady Margaret); *Diplomacy* (Neilan)
1927 *Singed* (Wray)
1929 *The Woman in White* (Wilcox) (dual role); *Always Faithful* (Middleton)
1930 *The Woman Racket* (Ober and Kelley); *Showgirl in Hollywood* (LeRoy); *The Silver Horde* (Archainbaud)
1982 *Before the Nickelodeon: The Early Cinema of Edwin S. Porter* (Musser) (as narrator)

Blanche Sweet

Publications

By SWEET: articles—

"Conrad Nagel," in *Photoplay* (New York), June 1924.
"Keep Your Public Guessing," in *Motion Picture Director* (Hollywood), August 1926.
"*Judith of Bethulia*," in *Sight and Sound* (London), Winter 1969-70.
"Blanche Sweet and Marshall Neilan," interview with K. Lewis in *Films in Review* (New York), June-July 1981.

On SWEET: books—

Slide, Anthony, *The Griffith Actresses*, South Brunswick, New Jersey, 1973.
Drew, William M., *Speaking of Silents: First Ladies of the Screen*, Vestal, New York, 1989.

On SWEET: articles—

Owen, K., "The Girl on the Cover," in *Photoplay* (New York), April 1915.
Carr, Harry, "Waiting for Tomorrow," in *Photoplay* (New York), May 1918.
Smith, Frederick, "The New Blanche Sweet," in *Motion Picture Classic* (Brooklyn), November 1918.
St. Johns, Adela Rogers, "An Impression of Blanche Sweet," in *Photoplay* (New York), September 1924.
Bodeen, DeWitt, "Blanche Sweet," in *Films in Review* (New York), November 1965.
Slide, Anthony, "Blanche Sweet and *Anna Christie*," in *Silent Picture* (London), Spring 1972.
Lewis, K., "Happy Birthday Blanche Sweet," in *Films in Review* (New York), March 1986.
Obituary in *Variety* (New York), 10 September 1986.

*   *   *

A pioneering actress, Blanche Sweet had a curious career replete with highlights, falls from favor, and inexplicable absences from the screen. She was one of D. W. Griffith's first stars at Biograph, the actress chosen to head the cast of his first feature-length production, *Judith of Bethulia*, and the star of Griffith's subsequent features. She was set to play the role of Elsie Stoneman in *The Birth of a Nation* when Griffith gave the part to Lillian Gish. Sweet continued to star in films that did little to enhance her career. Then came *Anna Christie*, the first filming of the Eugene O'Neill play and a major dramatic success for its star. Another group of features followed, all minor, except for *Tess of the D'Urbervilles* with a fine performance from Sweet. She had no difficulty adapting to sound film production. She was a delight as the fading silent star in *Showgirl in Hollywood*, playing a suicide scene with consummate skill. Within two years, however, she had disappeared from the screen never to appear again.

Unlike her contemporary Lillian Gish, Blanche Sweet did not handle her professional life successfully. An unhappy marriage to director Marshall Neilan, too many program features, and too few major productions cut short a promising career. It is unfortunate because she was capable of fine and subtle emotional performances. Her range of characterizations was quite extraordinary, from biblical figures to drug addicts and prostitutes. She was a major silent star who deserved better from her career and deserves more recognition today.

—Anthony Slide

———

SYDOW, Max von. *See* **VON SYDOW, Max.**

———

TAKAMINE, Hideko

Nationality: Japanese. **Born:** Hideko Hirayama in Hakodate City, 27 March 1924. **Education:** Attended Bunka Gakuin High School to 1939. **Family:** Married the director Zenzo Matsuyama, 1955. **Career:** Child actress: made film debut at age five in *Haha* for Shochike studio; 1932—first stage appearance; worked for P.C.L. (later Toho) studio until 1946, and Shin-Toho studio, 1947-50; then freelance; popular singer from 1949; also a writer and painter; worked on television from 1968. **Awards:** Japan Mainichi Eiga Concourse, 1954, 1955, 1957 and 1961; Japan Kirema Jumpo Award for Best Actress, for *Floating Clouds*, 1955. **Address:** 1 Azabu Nagasaka-cho, Minato-ku, Tokyo, Japan.

Films as Actress:

1929   *Haha* (Nomura) (as Haruko)
1930   *Dai-Tokyo no ikkaku* (*A Corner of Great Tokyo*) (Gosho); *Reijin* (Shimazu); *Chichi*
1931   *Watashi no papa-san mamaga suki*; *Uruhashiki ai*; *Ai yojinrui to tomo ni are* (Shimazu); *Bofuu no bara*; *Onna wa itsuno you nimo*; *Shimai*; *I chitaro yaai* (Nomura); *Tokyo no gassho* (*Tokyo's Chorus*) (Ozu) (as the daughter); *Reijin no bisho*
1932   *Jonetsu*; *Nanatsu no umi: Teiso-hen*; *Edo gonomi: Ryogoku-zoshi* (Inoue); *Yokin ajo-san*; *Tengoku ni musubu koi*; *Hototogisu* (*A Cuckoo*) (Gosho); *Nezumi-kozo Jirokichi: Kaiketsu-hen* (Akiyama)
1933   *Jukyu-sai no haru*; *Yotamono to kyakusen-bi*; *Hoho o yosureba* (Shimazu); *Riso no otto*; *Rappa to musume* (Shimazu); *Hatsukoi no haru*
1934   *Onna to umareta karanya*; *Toyo no haha*; *Nukiashi sashiashi*; *Nihon josei no uta*; *Sonoyo no onna* (Shimazu)
1935   *Haha no ai* (Ikeda); *Ramuru eteruneru*
1936   *Shindo: Akemi no maki, Ryota no maki*
1937   *Hanayome karuta* (Gosho); *Hanakago no uta* (*Song of the Flower Basket*) (Gosho) (as Hamako); *Otto no teiso: Haru kitareba, Aki futatabi* (Yamamoto) (as Mutsuko); *Edokko Kenchan*; *Misemono okoku*; *Ojo-san*; *Nampu no oka*; *Kaminari oyaji*
1938   *Hanataba no yume*; *Shinryu-ro*; *Tsuzurikata kyoshitsu* (Yamamoto) (as Masako); *Niji tatsu oka* (Otani); *Chokoreito to heitai* (Sato)
1939   *Uruhashiki shuppatsu* (Yamamoto); *Hojiro sensei* (Abe); *Chushingura*; *Higuchi Ichiyo* (Namiki); *Wareraga kyokan* (*Our Teacher*) (Imai)
1940   *Hideko no oendancho* (Chiba); *Shinpen Tange Sazen: Koiguruma no maki*; *Soyokaze chichi to tomoni* (Yamamoto); *Ane no shussei* (Kondo); *Tsurigane-so* (Ishida); *Songoku*
1941   *Sakujitsu kieta otoko* (Makino) (as Okyo); *Uma* (*Horse*) (Yamamoto) (as Ine); *Awa no odoriko* (Makino); *Jogakusei-ki*; *Hideko no shasho-san* (*Hideko the Bus Conductor*) (Naruse)

1942   *Musashibo Benkei*; *Kobo no seishun*; *Matteita oyoko* (Makino); *Minami kara kaetta hito*; *Fukei-zu* (Makino) (as Taeho); *Suiko-den* (as Taeho); *Zohu fuhei-zu* (Makino) (as Taeho)
1943   *Ahen senso* (Makino); *Ai no sekai* (Aoyagi); *Yamaneko Tomi no hanashi*; *Hanako-sen*; *Hyoroku yume monogatari*; *Wakiki hi no yorokobi*
1944   *Obaasan*; *Sanjaku Sagohei*; *Yottsu no kekkon*
1945   *Shori no himade*
1946   *Urashima Taro no koei* (*The Descendants of Taro Urashima*) (Naruse); *Aru yo no tonosama* (*Lord for a Night*) (Kinugasa) (as Taeho); *Toho shoboto*; *Kita no san-nin* (Saeki); *Yoki no onna* (Saeki)
1947   *Toho sen-ichi-ya* (*1001 Nights with Toho*) (Ichikawa); *Oedo no oni* (Hagiwara); *Ai yo hoshi to tomoni* (Abe); *Kofuku he no shotai* (Chiba)
1948   *Aijo shindansho*; *"Machiko" yori: Hana hiraku* (*A Flower Blooms*) (Ichikawa); *Sanbyaku-rokujugo-ya:* (*365 Nights in Tokyo*); *Tokyo-hen* (Ichikawa); *Sanbyaku-rokujugo-ya* (*365 Nights in Osaka*) (Ichikawa); *Niji o idaku shojo*
1949   *Haru no tawamure* (Yamamoto); *Guddobai* (Shima); *Ginza kankan musume* (Shima)
1950   *Shojo-dakara* (Shima); *Sasameyuki* (Abe) (as Taeho); *Munekata Shimai* (*The Munekata Sisters*) (Ozu) (as Mariko); *Senka o koete*; *Sasaki Kojiro*
1951   *Onna no mizukakami*; *Karumen Kokyo ni kaeru* (*Carmen Comes Home*) (Kinoshita) (title role); *Zoku Sasaki Kojiro*; *Karumen Junjo su* (*Carmen's Pure Love*) (Kinoshita) (title role); *Wagaya wa tanoshi* (Nakamura)
1952   *Asa no hamon* (*Trouble in the Morning*; *Morning Conflicts*) (Gosho) (as Atsuko Takimoto); *Tokyo no ekubo*; *Inazuma* (*Lightning*) (Naruse); *Onna to iu shiro: Mari no maki*; *Onna to iu shiro: Yuko no maki*
1953   **Entotsu no mieru basho** (*Four Chimneys*; *Where Chimneys Are Seen*) (Gosho) (as Senko Azuma); *Asu wa docchi da*; *Gan* (*Wild Geese*) (Toyoda) (as Otama)
1954   *Dai-ni no seppun*; *Onna no sono* (*The Garden of Women*) (Kinoshita) (as Yoshie Deishi); *Kono hiroi sora no dokokani*; *Nijushi no hitomi* (*Twenty-Four Eyes*) (Kinoshita) (as Miss Hisako Oishi)
1955   *Ukigumo* (*Floating Clouds*) (Naruse) (as Yukiko Koda); *Wataridori itsukaeru* (Hisamatsu); *Tooi kumo* (*Distant Clouds*) (Kinoshita); *Kuchizuke*; *Onna doshi*
1956   *Shin Heike monogatari Yoshinaka o meguru san-nin no onna* (*Three Women around Yoshinaka*) (Kinugasa) (as Fuyuhime); *Kodomo no me* (Kawazu); *Tsuma no kokoro* (*A Wife's Heart*) (Naruse); *Nagareru* (*Flowing*) (Naruse)
1957   *Kumo no bohyo yori: Sora yukaba*; *Arakure* (*Untamed*) (Naruse) (as Oshima); *Yorokobi mo Kanashimi mo ikutoshitsuki* (*The Lighthouse*) (Kinoshita); *Fuzen no tomoshibi* (*A Candle in the Wind*; *Danger Stalks Near*) (Kinoshita)
1958   *Harikomi* (Nomura); *Muhomatsu no issho* (*The Rickshaw Man*) (Inagaki) (as Mrs. Yoshiko Yoshioka)

Hideko Takamine

1960　*Onna ga kaidan o agaru toki* (*When a Woman Ascends the Stairs*) (Naruse) (as Keiko Yashiro); *Musume tsuma haha* (*Daughters, Wives, and a Mother*) (Naruse); *Fuefuki-gawa* (*The River Fuefuki*) (Kinoshita)

1961　*Namonaku mazushiku utsukushiku* (*Happiness of Us Alone*) (Kinoshita) (as Akiko Katayama); ***Ningen no joken III*** (*A Soldier's Prayer*; *The Human Condition*) (Kobayashi) (as woman in settler's village); *Tsuma to shite haha to shite* (*As a Wife*; *As a Woman*; *The Other Woman*) (Naruse); *Eien no hito* (*The Bitter Spirit*; *Immortal Love*) (Kinoshita)

1962　*Onna no za* (*The Wiser Age*; *Woman's Status*) (Naruse); *Futari de aruita ikutoshitsuki* (*The Seasons We Walked Together*) (Kinoshita); *Horoki* (*A Wanderer's Notebook*; *Lonely Lane*) (Naruse) (as Fumiko Hayashi); *Burari burabura monogatari* (*My Hobo*) (Matsuyama) (as Komako)

1963　*Onna no rekishi* (*A Woman's Life*; *A Woman's Story*) (Naruse) (as Nobuko)

1964　*Midareru* (*Yearning*) (Naruse) (as Reiko Morita)

1965　*Ware hitotsubu no mugi naredo* (*Could I but Live*) (Matsuyama); *Rokujo yukiyama tsumugi* (*Dark the Mountain Snow*) (Matsuyama) (as Ine Rokujo)

1966　*Hikinige* (*Moment of Terror*) (Naruse) (as the mother)

1967　*Zoku namo naku mazushiku utsukushiku* (Matsuyama); *Chichi to ko* (*Our Silent Love*) (Matsuyama); *Hanaoko Seishu no tsuma* (*The Wife of Seishu Hanaoka*) (Masumura) (as Ojaku)

1969　*Oni no sumu yakata* (*Devil's Temple*) (Misumi) (as Kaede)

1973　*Kokotsu no hito* (Toyoda)

1976　*Suri Lanka no ai to wakare* (*Love and Separation in Sri Lanka*) (Kinoshita); *Futari no Iida*

1979　*Shodo satsujin: Musuko yo* (*Oh My Son!*) (Kinoshita) (as the mother)

Publications

By TAKAMINE: books—

Pari hitori-aruki, Tokyo, 1953.
Maimai tsuburo, Tokyo, 1955.
Watashi no interview, Tokyo, 1958.
Watashi no tosei nikki [My Professional Diary], 2 vols., Tokyo, 1976.
Iomono mitsuketa, Tokyo, 1979.
Tabi wa michizure Gandala, with Zenzo Matsuyama, Tokyo, 1979.
Daidokoro no okestra, Tokyo, 1982.
Ninjo banashi matsutaro, Tokyo, 1985.
Watashi no umehara ryuzaburo, Tokyo, 1988.

On TAKAMINE: article—

Birnbaum, P., "The Odor of Pickled Radishes," in *New Yorker*, 5 November 1990.

*　　*　　*

From her first screen appearance at age five, Hideko Takamine was for decades one of the most beloved Japanese screen stars. At the Shochiku Studio, she appeared in films of Gosho, Shimazu, Hotei Nomura, and others, mostly in the family-film genre. Her recognition increased after she moved to the Toho Studio and began to work under the producer Fujimoto and the director Kajiro Yamamoto. In *Tsuzurikata kyoshitsu*, based on a best-selling autobiography, she played an impoverished 13-year-old girl struggling to live a decent life. In *Uma* she played a village girl who raises a horse for the army, and her affection for the horse is delicately accented by the naturalistic direction of the film. In these two films, Takamine won critical acclaim, in addition to her popular fame.

After the Toho labor union's strike of 1946, she left for a new studio, Shin-Toho, and became the main actress there. Her most representative work at this studio was in Ozu's *The Munekata Sisters*, to which she brought her light, comic flair to the serious and tragic tone of the film. After becoming freelance, she began to choose more meaningful roles. Among her various postwar roles, her collaborations with Naruse, Kinoshita, and her husband, Matsuyama, are most important.

Takamine became the indispensable heroine in 12 Naruse films, in which she created the archetype of the strong-willed, hardworking woman unrewarded at the bottom of society or subjugated by the family system. Among these excellent portrayals, her roles in *Floating Clouds* was outstanding, bringing her and the film all the major awards of 1955. Playing a character living in the confusion of postwar Japan, she gave a passionate performance as a woman who cannot help clinging to an unfaithful man, leading to her own destruction.

While Naruse's heroines tend to be caught in tense conflicts with men, which eventually are resolved by the woman's spiritual victory, the heroines of Kinoshita and his student Matsuyama are more melodramatic. Takamine impressively played humanistic heroines who survive their unfortunate environment by good-natured sincere efforts. She moved audiences to tears with her performance in Kinoshita's *Twenty-Four Eyes* and *The Lighthouse* and in Matsuyama's *Zoku namo naku mazushiku utsukushiku*. She also showed her comedic talent as a half-witted stripper in Kinoshito's light satires *Carmen Comes Home* and *Carmen's Pure Love*, which reflected the optimistic mood of the immediately postwar democracy. As Takamine gradually undertook more serious roles, however, she had little subsequent opportunity to demonstrate her comic flair.

—Kyoko Hirano

TALMADGE, Norma

Nationality: American. **Born:** Jersey City, New Jersey, 26 May 1897; sister of the actress Constance Talmadge. **Family:** Married 1) the producer Joseph M. Schenck, 1916 (divorced 1934); 2) the entertainer George Jessel, 1934 (divorced 1939); 3) Carvel James, 1946. **Career:** Model; actress for Vitagraph in New York at age 13; 1911—contract with Vitagraph: made many short films in the period 1910-15; 1913—first billing as Norma Talmadge; 1915—contract with National Pictures, then with D. W. Griffith; 1916—Norma Talmadge Film Company set up by Joseph Schenck: first film for the company, *Panthea*, 1917; 1930—retired from films. **Died:** 24 December 1957.

Films as Actress:

(between 1910-15, Talmadge appeared in numerous Vitagraph shorts including:)

1910   *The Household Pest*; *The Dixie Mother*; *Love of Chrysanthemum*; *A Broken Spell*; *Uncle Tom's Cabin*

1911   *Paola and Francesca*; *In Neighboring Kingdoms*; *Mrs. 'Enery 'Awkins*; *A Tale of Two Cities* (Blackton) (as a midinette); *The Sky Pilot*; *The General's Daughter*; *The Thumb Print*; *Her Hero*; *The Child Crusoes*

1912   *The First Violin* (Brooke); *The Troublesome Stepdaughters*; *Mr. Butler Buttles*; *Fortunes of a Composer*; *Omens and Oracles*; *The Midget's Revenge*; *The Lovesick Maidens of Cuddleton*; *Captain Barnacle's Messmate*; *O'Hara—Squatter and Philosopher*; *Casey at the Bat*

1913   *Just Show People*; *Extremities*; *His Official Appointment*; *Under the Daisies* (Brooke); *The Doctor's Secret* (Brooke); *Father's Husband* (Brooke); *Fanny's Conspiracy* (Brooke); *His Silver Bachelorhood* (Brooke); *'Arriet's Baby*; *An Old Man's Love Story*; *Solitaires*; *The Other Woman*; *The Blue Rose*; *An Elopement at Home* (Brooke); *The Honorable Algernon* (Brooke); *His Little Page* (Brooke); *Officer John Donovan* (Brooke); *The Sacrifice of Kathleen* (Brooke); *Counsel for the Defense*; *The Silver Cigarette Case*

1914   *Sawdust and Salome* (Brooke); *The Vavasour Ball*; *The Helpful Sisterhood* (Brooke); *Cupid versus Money*; *The Right of Way* (Brooke); *John Rance—Gentleman* (Brooke); *Under False Colors* (Brooke); *Goodbye Summer* (Brooke); *The Curing of Myra May*; *Sunshine and Shadow* (Brooke); *A Daughter of Israel* (Brooke); *Miser Murphy's Wedding Present* (Brooke); *Old Reliable* (Brooke); *The Hex on Fogg's Millions* (Thomson); *The Hidden Letters* (Brooke); *Memories and Men's Souls* (Brooke); *Politics and the Press* (Brooke); *The Mill of Life*; *A Loan Shark King* (Brooke); *The Peacemaker* (Brooke)

1915   *A Daughter's Strange Inheritance*; *Janet of the Chorus*; *The Pillar of Flame*; *The Barrier of Faith*; *The Criminal*; *The Battle Cry of Peace* (North); *The Crown Prince's Double* (Brooke); *The Captivating Mary Carstairs* (Mitchell)

1916   *The Missing Links* (Ingraham); *Martha's Vindication* (S. and C. Franklin); *The Children in the House* (S. and C. Franklin); *Going Straight* (*Corruption*) (S. and C. Franklin); *The Devil's Needle* (Withey); *The Social Secretary* (Emerson); *Fifty-Fifty* (Dwan)

1917   *Panthea* (Dwan); *The Law of Compensation* (Styger and Goulden); *Poppy* (Jose); *The Moth* (Jose); *The Secret of the Storm Country* (Miller)

1918   *Ghosts of Yesterday* (Miller); *By Right of Purchase* (Miller); *Deluxe Annie* (West); *The Safety Curtain* (Franklin); *Her Only Way* (Franklin); *The Forbidden City* (Franklin); *The Heart of Wetona* (Franklin)

1919   *Prohibition Wife* (Franklin); *The New Moon* (Withey); *The Way of a Woman* (Leonard); *Isle of Conquest* (Jose)

1920   *She Loves and Lies* (Withey); *A Daughter of Two Worlds* (Young); *The Woman Gives* (Neill); *Yes or No?* (Neill); *The Branded Woman* (Parker); *Passion Flower* (*Love or Hate*) (Brenon); *The Sign on the Door* (Brenon); *The Wonderful Thing* (Brenon); *Love's Redemption* (Parker)

1922   *Smilin' Through* (Franklin); *The Eternal Flame* (Lloyd)

1923   *The Voice from the Minaret* (Lloyd); *Within the Law* (Lloyd); *Ashes of Vengeance* (Lloyd); *Song of Love* (*Dust of Desire*) (Marion and Franklin)

1924   *Secrets* (Borzage); *The Only Woman* (Olcott)

1925   *The Lady* (Borzage); *Graustark* (Buchowetzki)

1926   *Kiki* (Brown)

1927   *Camille* (Niblo) (title role)

1928   *The Dove* (West); *The Woman Disputed* (King and Taylor)

1929   *New York Nights* (Milestone)

1930   *DuBarry: Woman of Passion* (Taylor) (title role)

Publications

By TALMADGE: articles—

"How Men Strike Me," in *Photo-Play Journal*, March 1919.
"The Amazing Interview," with Faith Service in *Motion Picture Classic* (Brooklyn), January 1920.
"What 'Fashion' Really Means," in *Photoplay* (New York), June 1920.
"Eugene O'Brien," in *Photoplay* (New York), June 1924.
"My Lucky Break," in *Pictures and Picturegoer*, July 1928.

On TALMADGE: books—

Talmadge, Mrs. Margaret L., *The Talmadge Sisters*, Philadelphia, 1924.
Loos, Anita, *The Talmadge Girls: A Memoir*, New York, 1978.

On TALMADGE: articles—

Vance, Elsie, "Norma Talmadge—The Adorable," in *Photoplay* (New York), February 1915.
Hornblow, Arthur, "Norma Talmadge," in *Photoplay* (New York), August 1915.
Livingstone, Beulah, "Norma Talmadge—Queen of Versatility," in *Photo-Play Journal*, March 1919.
O'Brien, Eugene, "Norma Talmadge," in *Photoplay* (New York), July 1924.
St. Johns, Adela Rogers, "Our One and Only Great Actress," in *Photoplay* (New York), February 1926.
Spears, J., "Norma Talmadge," in *Films in Review* (New York), January 1967.

*   *   *

Norma Talmadge

Theatrical families were nothing new in Hollywood, but the offspring of Peg Talmadge secured a permanent place in film history. They may not have received the accolades of revival accorded to other players, but their contribution to the cinema was nevertheless considerable.

The eldest of the three Talmadge girls, Norma began her film career with Vitagraph in New York. She made several short films before attracting attention with her small role as the little midinette who accompanied Maurice Costello (Sidney Carton) on his way to the guillotine in the 1911 *Tale of Two Cities*. She eventually blossomed under the direction of Van Dyke Brooks and played frequently with Antonio Moreno as her leading man. In 1915 she made her last appearance with Vitagraph in the propaganda-laden *Battle Cry of Peace*.

A move to the National Picture Corporation with a more gratifying contract did not meet with success. She then joined D. W. Griffith's Fine Arts Company, for whom she made seven films—none, however, directed by Griffith. Having made no less than 250 films for Vitagraph, Talmadge had by now developed a gallery of threatened and misunderstood heroines which appealed to her fans. Her great beauty was to remain a permanent asset. *The Social Secretary*, a comedy written by Anita Loos and directed by John Emerson, gave her an opportunity to disguise that beauty as a girl trying to avoid the unwelcome attentions of her male employers.

Her marriage to Joseph M. Schenck in 1916 was all-important. Under his aegis, and the banner of The Norma Talmadge Film Company, she almost challenged the popularity of Mary Pickford. Her first film for the company was *Panthea*, directed by Allan Dwan. She made many films opposite Eugene O'Brien, a sophisticated and polished actor who provided a perfect foil to her beauty. Her roles included Chinese maidens, Indian half-breeds, and Russian noblewomen. A series of films for First National included those directed by Herbert Brenon, whose version of Benevente's *Passion Flower* allowed her to play a proud Spanish girl caught up in the toils of love and murder. Sidney Franklin's *Smilin' Through* was one of her most popular films—a sentimental story that has earned several remakes. *The Eternal Flame*, based on Balzac's *La Duchesse de Langeais*, was a costume picture, as was *Ashes of Vengeance*, set in the time of the Medicis in France. Bayard Veiller's *Within the Law* presented her as a wrongly imprisoned girl driven to seek revenge through blackmail, but eventually redeemed by love and cleared of her supposed crime. In contrast, the sentimental *Secrets*, directed by Frank Borzage, shows her as an old lady at her sick husband's bedside, dreaming of the past episodes of her life. Inevitably she attempted the role of the Lady of the Camellias in *Camille*, directed by Frank Niblo. Her leading man was the attractive Gilbert Roland, with whom she was to have an affair for some years. The film was elaborately staged, and Talmadge's performance was good, but Niblo never brought the story to life. It is interesting to note that Armand's father was played by her old Vitagraph colleague Maurice Costello.

By now Talmadge was installed in Hollywood and part of the film establishment. Schenck and she remained together until 1927, but he continued to advise her on business matters after the divorce. She acted with Roland in a Mexican story, *The Dove*, and her last silent film was the unhappy *The Woman Disputed*, directed by Henry King, and mangled by front office politics. It was loosely based on de Maupassant's *Boule de Suif*.

Her entry into talking pictures was not auspicious. *New York Nights* and *DuBarry: Woman of Passion* failed (in spite of the elaborate sets by William Cameron Menzies), and her retirement was immediate.

—Liam O'Leary

TANAKA, Kinuyo

Nationality: Japanese. **Born:** Shinomoseki City, 29 December 1909. **Education:** Attended Tennoji Elementary School, Osaka to 1919; studied the musical instrument the chikuzen-biwa, licence 1919. **Family:** Married the director Hiroshi Shimizu, 1929 (divorced 1929). **Career:** 1920-23—member of the Biwa Shojo Kageki girls revue, Osaka; 1924—film debut in *Genroku onna*; 1925—joined Shochiku Kamata Studio, Tokyo, and over the next 15 years became their leading star; 1953—directed her first film, *Koibumi*; appeared on television from the late 1960s. **Awards:** Japan Mainichi Eiga Concourse, 1947, 1948, 1957, 1960, 1974; Japan Kinema Jumpo Awards for Best Actress, for *Ballad of Narayama*, 1958, and *Sandakan, House No. 8*, 1974. Best Actress, Berlin Festival, for *Sandakan, House No.8*, 1975. **Died:** Of a brain tumor, 21 March 1977.

Films as Actress:

1924   *Genroku onna* (Nomura) (as a maid); *Mura no bokujo* (Shimizu) (as Oharu)

1925   *Chiisaki tabigeinin* (Shimizu); *Gekitsu no sakebi* (Shimizu); *Yukan naru koi* (Shimazu); *Shizen wa sabaku* (Shimazu); *Isshinji no hyakunin-giri* (Shimizu); *Koi no torinawa* (Shimizu); *Ochimusha* (Shimizu); *Goiken Gomuyo*

1926   *Nayamashiki koro* (Shimizu); *Machi no hitobito* (*People in the Town*; *Town People*) (Gosho); *Honryu* (*A Torrent*) (Gosho); *Ara nonkida ne*; *Obocchan* (Shimazu); *Uragirareta mono* (Shimizu); *Koi no ikuji*; *Yoto* (Shimizu); *Karabotan* (Nomura); *Shimizu no Jirocho Zen-den: Kohen Ashura fukushu no maki* (Kamata); *Kanojo* (*She*; *Girl Friend*) (Gosho); *Hirameku yaiba*

1927   *Kurayami*; *Chikashitsu*; *Yakko no Koman*; *Tennoji no harakiri*; *Tkada-no-baba*; *Hazukashiiyume* (*Shameful Dream*; *Intimate Dream*) (Gosho); *Kokkyo no uta*; *Mado*; *Shinju fujin*; *Byakko-tai*; *Higan sen-nin giri*; *Musasabi no Sankichi*; *Yoru no kyoja*; *Kisoshinju*

1928   *Kindai musha shugyo* (Ushihara); *Kaikoku-ki* (*Tales from a Country by the Sea*) (Kinugasa); *Moshimo kanojo ga*; *Haha yo kimi no na o kegasu nakare* (*Mother, Do Not Shame Your Name*) (Gosho); *Mura na hanayome* (*The Village Bride*) (Gosho); *Kangeki jidai* (Ushihara); *Fumetsu so ai*; *Eien no kokoro*; *Tetsu no shojo*; *Appare binanshi*

1929   *Hito no yo no sugata* (*The Situation of the Human World*; *Man's Worldly Appearance*) (Gosho); *Kare to denen* (Ushihara); *Gokurosama*; *Riku no ooja* (Ushihara); *Kagayaku Showa*; *Seishun kokyogaku*; *Mura no kajiya*; *Echigo-jishi*; *Kare to jinsei* (Ushihara); *Hinarai naku sato*; *Daitokai: Bakuhatsu-hen* (Ushihara); *Shin josei-kagami*; *Yokina uta Daigaku wa detakeredo* (*I Graduated, But . . .*) (Ozu) (as Machiko); *Yama no gaika* (Ushihara)

1930   *Hohoemu jinsei* (*A Smiling Life*) (Gosho); *Onna wa doko he iku*; *Daitokai: Bakuhatsu-hen* (Ushihara); *Kinuyo monogatari* (*The Kinuyo Story*) (Gosho); *Aiyoku no ki*; *Wakamono yo naze naku ka* (Ushihara); *Ojosan* (*Young Miss*) (Ozu); *Seishun-fu*; *Shingun* (Ushihara); *Tekken seisai*

1931   *Rakudai wa shitakeredo* (*I Flunked, But . . .*) (Ozu) (as Sayoko); *Ai yo jinrui to tomo ni are* (Shimizu); *Hogaraka no nake*; *Shimai* (Shimazu); *Madamu to nyobo* (*The Neighbor's Wife and Mine*) (Gosho) (as the wife); *Runpen to sono musume*; *Shima no ratai-jiken*; *Seikatsusen ABC: Fujie nomaki* (Shimazu) (as Fujie); *Seikatsusen ABC: Zenpen* (Shimazu) (as Kieko)

1932   *Konjiki-yasha* (Nomura) (as Omiya); *Shohai*; *Niisan no baka (You Are Stupid; My Stupid Brother)* (Gosho); *Ginza no yanagi (Willows of Ginza; A Willow Tree in the Ginza)* (Gosho); *Taiyo wa higashi yori*; *Satsueijo remansu: Renai annai*; *Kagayake nihon no josei*; *Koi no Tokyo*; *Seishun no yume ima izuko (Where Now Are the Dreams of Youth?)* (Ozu) (as Oshige); *Chushingura (The Loyal 47 Ronin; The Vengeance of the 47 Ronin)* (Kinugasa) (as Yae)

1933   *Hanayome no negoto (Sleeping Words of the Bride; The Bride Talks in Her Sleep)* (Gosho) (as Haruko); *Izu no odoriko (Dancing Girls of Izu)* (Gosho) (as Kaoru); *Tokyo no onna (A Tokyo Woman)* (Ozu) (as Harue); *Oen-dancho no koi*; *Hijosen no onna (Dragnet Girl)* (Ozu) (as Tokiko); *Seidon*; *Kekkonkaido*; *Yomeiri mae*; *Chinchoge* (Nomura); *Futamabatu*

1934   *Toyo no haha*; *Fukei-zu* (Nomura); *Sakura onda*; *Chijo no seiza: Chijo-hen, Seizahen* (Nomura); *Shinkon-ryoko* (Nomura); *Machi no bofu* (Nomura); *Osaya koisugata* (Shimazu); *Sono yo no onna* (Shimazu); *Watashi no niisan* (Shimazu)

1935   *Hakoiri musume (An Innocent Maid)* (Ozu); *Shunkin-sho: Okoto to Sasuke* (Shimazu) (as Okoto); *Yume Utsutsu*; *Eikyu no ai*; *Semete koyoi o*; *Jinsei ni onimotsu (Burden of Life)* (Gosho) (as Ituko); *Hanayome kurabe*

1936   *Naniwa ereji (Osaka Elegy)* (Mizoguchi) (as Ochika); *Onatsu Seijuro* (Onozuka); *Dansei tai josei*; *Shindo: Akemi no make, Ryota no maki (New Way)* (Gosho); *Waga haha no sho*; *Hanakago no uta (Song of the Flower Basket)* (Gosho) (as Yoko Mori); *Joi Kinuyo sensei* (Nomura); *Otoko no tsugunai* (Nomura)

1937   *Bancho sarayashiki* (Fuyushima); *Akatsuki wa tokedo*

1938   *Hanauta ojosan*; *Shuppatsu*; *Haha to ko* (Shibuya); *Aizen katsura* (Nomura) (as Katsue Takaishi); *Haha no uta*; *Shinshaku: Tojin Okichi, Funshin hen*

1939   *Okayo no kakugo*; *Minamikaze* (Shibuya); *Shunrai*; *Zoku aizen katsura* (Nomura) (as Katsue Takaishi); *Hana aru zasso* (Shimizu); *Kuwa no mi wa akai* (Shimizu); *Aizen katsura: Kanketsu-hen* (Nomura) (as Katsue Takaishi)

1940   *Aizen tsubaki*; *Watashi niwa otto ga aru*; *Kinuyo no hatsukoi* (Nomura); *Akatsuki ni inoru*; *Josei no kakugo*; *Butai sugata*; *Okinu to banto* (Nomura)

1941   *Toka kan no jinsei*; *Genki de ikauyo* (Nomura); *Hana (Flower)* (Yoshimura); *Kanzashi* (Shimizu); *Joi no Kiroku* (Shimizu)

1942   *Kazoku* (Shibuya); *Nihon no haha*; *Aru Onna* (Shibuya)

1943   *Kaisen no zenya*; *Tekki kushu (Enemy Air Attack)* (Yoshimura, Shibuya, and Nomura); *Bocchan dohyo-iri*

1944   *Danjuro sandai (Three Generations of Danjuro)* (Mizoguchi) (as Okano); *Kaettekita otoko*; *Rikugun (The Army)* (Kinoshita) (as the mother); *Miyamoto Musashi (Musashi Miyamoto)* (Mizoguchi) (as Shinobu); *Hissho-ka*; *Sanjusangen-do toshi ya monogatari (A Tale of Archery at the Sanjusangendo)* (Naruse)

1946   *Nikoniko taikai: Uata no hanakago* (Nomura); *Kanojo no hatsugen* (Nomura); *Josei no shori (The Victory of Women)* (Mizoguchi) (as Hiroko); *Utamaro o mehuru go-nin no onna (Utamaro and Five Women)* (Mizoguchi) (as Okita)

1947   *Kekkon (Marriage)* (Kinoshita); *Joyu Sumako no koi (Love of Sumako)* (Mizoguchi) (as Sumako Matsui); *Fujicho (Phoenix)* (Kinoshita)

1948   *Yoru no onna tachi (Women of the Night)* (Mizoguchi) (as Fusako); *Kaze no naka no mendori (A Hen in the Wind)* (Ozu) (as Tokiko Amamiya)

1949   *Waga koi wa moenu (My Love Has Been Burning)* (Mizoguchi) (as Eiko Hirayama); *Yotsuya kaidan (The Yotsuya Ghost Story)* (Kinoshita) (as Oiwa/Osode); *Mahiru no enbukyoku (Waltz at Noon)* (Yoshimura)

1950   *Engeiji ringu (Konyaku yubiwa; Engagement Ring)* (Kinoshita); *Munekata shimai (The Munekata Sisters)* (Ozu) (as Setsuko); *Okusama ni goyojin*

1951   *Oboro kago* (Ito); *Ginza gesho (Ginza Cosmetics)* (Naruse); *Oyu-sama (Miss Oyu)* (Mizoguchi) (title role); *Yoru no mibojin*; *Musashino fujin (Lady Musashino)* (Mizoguchi) (as Michiko Akiyama); *Aizen-bashi*; *Inazuma-zoshi*

1952   *Nishijin no shimai (Sisters of Ninshijin)* (Yoshimura); **Saikaku inchidai onna** *(Life of Oharu)* (Mizoguchi) (as Oharu); *Atake-ke no hitobito* (Hisamatsu); *Okasan (Mother)* (Naruse) (title role); *Himitsu* (Hisamatsu)

1953   *Magokoro*; **Entotsu no mieru basho** *(Four Chimneys)* (Gosho) (as Hiroko Ogata); **Ugetsu monogatari** *(Ugetsu)* (Mizoguchi) (as Miyaki); *Shinsho Taiheiki: Ruten Hiyoshimura* (Hagiwara); *Shishi no za* (Ito) (as Hisa)

1954   **Sansho dayu** *(Sansho: The Bailiff)* (Mizoguchi) (as Tamaki); *Onna no koyomi*; *Uwasa no onna (The Woman of Rumor)* (Mizoguchi) (as Hatsuko Mabuchi)

1955   *Wataridori itsu kaeru*; *Shonen shikei-shu*; *Tsukiyo no kasa* (Hisamatsu); *Osho ichidai* (Ito) (as Koharu)

1956   *Iro-zange*; *Byosai monogatari: Aya ni kanashiki*; *Joshu to tomoni* (Hisamatsu); *Arashi*; *Nagareru (Flowing)* (Naruse)

1957   *Kiiroi karasu (Yellow Crow; Behold Thy Son)* (Gosho) (as Yokiko Matumoto); *Ibo-kyodai* (Ieki); *Dayu san yori: Jotai wa kanashiku* (Inagaki); *Chijo (On the Earth)* (Yoshimura)

1958   *Kanashimi wa onna dakeni (Sorrow Is Only for Women)* (Shindo); *Narayamabushi-ko (Ballad of Narayama)* (Kinoshita) (as Orin); **Higanbana** *(Equinox Flower)* (Ozu) (as Kiyoko Hirayama); *Kono ten no niji*

1959   *Hahako-gusa*; *Subarashiki musumetachi*; *Taiyo ni somuku mono*; *Naniwa ni koi no monogatari*; *Nihon tanjo* (Inagaki)

1960   *Ototo (Her Brother)* (Ichikawa) (as stepmother)

1961   *Wakaret ikiru toki mo (Eternity of Love)* (Horikawa)

1962   *Horo-ki (Lonely Lane)* (Naruse); *Tateshi Danpei*; *Kaasan nagaiki shite ne*

1963   *Kekkon-shiki kekkon shiki* (Nakamura); *Shito no densetsu (Legend of a Duel to the Death; A Legend, Or Was It?)* (Kinoshita); *Taiheiyo hitoribocchi (Alone in the Pacific; My Enemy the Sea)* (Ichikawa); *Hikaru umi* (Nakahira)

1964   *Koge (The Scent of Incense)* (Kinoshita); *Kono sora no aru kagiri*

1965   *Haha no saigetsu*; *Akahige (Red Beard)* (Kurosawa) (as Yasumoto's mother)

1966   *Eriki no wakadaisho (Campus a Go-Go)* (Iwaschi); *Arupusu no wakadaisho (It Started in the Alps)* (Furusawa)

1972   *Otoko wa tsuraiyo: Torajiro yume-makura* (Yamada)

1974   *Sanba* (Nakamura); *Sandakan hachi-ban shokan: Bokyo (Sandakan, House No. 8)* (Kumai) (as Osaki)

1975   *Aru eiga kantoku no shogai: Mizoguchi Kenji no kiroku (Life of a Film Director: Record of Kenji Mizoguchi)* (Shindo—doc)

1976   *Kita no misaki* (Kumai); *Daichi no komori-uta* (Masumura)

Films as Director:

1953   *Koibumi* (+ ro)

1955   *Tsuki wa noborinu* (+ ro); *Nyubo yo eien nare* (+ ro)

1960   *Ruten no oohi* (+ ro); *O-gin Sama (Love under the Crucifix)*

Publications

On TANAKA: book—

Shindo, Kaneto, *Shoestu Tanaka Kinuyo*, Tokyo, 1983.

On TANAKA: article—

Johnson, William, "In Search of a Star: Kinuyo Tanaka," in *Film Comment* (New York), January/February 1994.

* * *

Kinuyo Tanaka's half-century of film stardom began in the 1920s at the Shochiku Studio, leading her to become one of the few Japanese woman directors (producing six films between 1953-62).

She started appearing in contemporary and period melodramas by Hotei Nomura, Shimazu, and Gosho—specializing in cute and naive girl's roles. Through her casting opposite popular stars such as Denmei Suzuki (for director Ushihara) and Chojiro Hayashi (for director Kinugasa), she gradually established her stardom. After she appeared in the first Japanese talkie, Gosho's *Madame and Wife*, her soft voice, with a colloquial accent, attracted more fans. Her attractive, light, and familiar character brought a rush of popularity, making her one of the most commercially successful stars in the early 1930s. Her legendary roles include the heroines of *Konjiki-yasha* and *Zoku aizen katsura*.

Her real critical recognition came when she played the blind Koto player in Shimazu's *Okoto to Sasuke*. Not only did she master the difficult role as a blind woman: she enriched her acting style by successfully conveying the complicated psychology of a strong-willed, wealthy girl, after tremendous effort and training.

The work for Mizoguchi finally awakened Tanaka as an actress. From 1936 (*Osaka Elegy*) she collaborated with this perfectionist director until 1954 (*The Woman of Rumor*). They later parted when she decided to become a director herself. Mizoguchi demanded that she study the role thoroughly, including its background, and her hard work successfully met Mizoguchi's extremely high artistic standards. She became his indispensable partner, creating his ideal woman type in various roles, usually exploited by men, yet in the end "saving" them by warmly supporting them without thought of reward. As Oharu in *Life of Oharu*, she portrayed a woman's terrible fate at the hands of men and the social system. Particularly memorable was her performance as the lowest-class street walker, in which she dared to show the ultimate ugliness and misery of aged and weary womanhood. Contrasting with this dramatic portrayal, her performance as a warm wife who welcomes her unfaithful potter husband in *Ugetsu monogatari* was rather static, yet equally impressive, and elicited equally sensational acclaim from the critics and public.

Tanaka also did fine work collaborating with Naruse (*Ginza Cosmetics* and *Mother*) and Gosho (*Four Chimneys*), playing ordinary, hard-working women with her strong screen presence and convincingly realistic acting style.

—Kyoko Hirano

TATI, Jacques

Nationality: French. **Born:** Jacques Tatischeff in Le Pecq, France, 9 October 1908. **Education:** Attended Lycée de St. Germain-en-Laye; sent to trade school to learn picture framing and conservation in England; left after one year; attended college of arts and engineering, 1924. **Family:** Married Micheline Winter, 1944, children: Sophie and Pierre. **Career:** 1924—apprenticed to Spiller's, a British picture-framer, in London; 1925-30—worked as professional rugby player in Paris; 1931—worked as amateur entertainer, performing sports-related pantomimes in London; 1931—returned to France and became professional cabaret and music hall entertainer; 1932—experimented as filmmaker: writing, directing, and starring in short, *Oscar, cham-*

pion de tennis; 1934—major recognition on stage at the Ritz on bill with Maurice Chevalier; 1935-39—toured European music halls and circuses; 1939-45—served in French Army; 1946—directorial debut in film short *L'Ecole des facteurs*; 1949—directed and starred in first feature film *Jour de fête*; 1961—created play, *Jour de fête a Olympia*, based on *Jour de fête*; 1971—after failure of *Trafic* creditors seized his assets, impounding all his previous feature films; 1973—directed *Parade* for Swedish TV; 1977—Paris distributor paid off Tati's debt and re-released impounded features. **Awards:** Best Script, Venice Film Festival, and Grand Prix du Cinema Francais, for *Jour de fête*, 1949; International Critics Prize, Cannes Film Festival, and Prix Louis Delluc, for *Les Vacances de Monsieur Hulot*, 1953; Special Prize, Cannes Film Festival, Academy Award for Best Foreign Film, New York Film Critics Circle Award, Best Foreign Film, and Prix Melies Best Foreign Film, for *Mon Oncle*, 1958; Grand Prix National des Arts et des Lettres in Cinema, 1979; Commandeur des Arts et des Lettres. **Died:** Near Paris, 5 November 1982.

Films as Actor:

1934   *On demande une brute* (Barrois—short) (+ co-sc)
1935   *Gai Dimanche* (Berry—short) (+ co-sc)
1936   *Soigné ton gauche* (Clement) (+ sc)
1938   *Retour à la terre* (short) (+ pr, sc)
1945   *Sylvie et le fantôme* (*Sylvia and the Phantom*; *Sylvia and the Ghost*) (Autant-Lara) (as Alain de Francigny)
1946   *Le Diable au corps* (*The Devil in the Flesh*) (Autant-Lara—short) (as Soldier in Blue)

Films as Actor, Director, and Screenwriter:

1932   *Oscar, champion de tennis* (short)
1947   *L'Ecole des facteurs*
1949   *Jour de fête* (*The Big Day*) (as François, the postman, co-sc)
1953   ***Les Vacances de Monsieur Hulot*** (*Mr. Hulot's Vacation*; *Mr. Hulot's Holiday*; *Monsieur Hulot's Holiday*) (title role, co-sc, + co-pr)
1958   *Mon Oncle* (*My Uncle*; *My Uncle, Mr. Hulot*) (as M. Hulot, co-sc, + pr)
1967   *Playtime* (as M. Hulot, co-sc)
1971   *Trafic* (*Traffic*) (as M. Hulot, co-sc, + co-ed)
1973   *Parade* (for TV) (as M. Loyal)

Publications

By TATI: articles—

"Tati Speaks," with Harold Woodside, in *Take One* (Montreal), no. 6, 1969.
Interview with E. Burcksen, in *Cinématographe* (Paris), May 1977.
Interview with M. Makeieff, in *Cinématographe* (Paris), January 1985.

On TATI: books—

Carriere, Jean Claude, *Monsieur Hulot's Holiday*, New York, 1959.
Cauliez, Armand, *Jacques Tati*, Paris, 1968.
Gilliatt, Penelope, *Jacques Tati*, London, 1976.
Maddock, Brent, *The Films of Jacques Tati*, Metuchen, New Jersey, 1977.
Fischer, Lucy, *Jacques Tati: A Guide to References and Sources*, Boston, 1983.
Harding, James, *Jacques Tati: Frame by Frame*, London, 1984.

Jacques Tati with Alain Decour at Cannes, 1958

Chion, Michel, *Jacques Tati*, Paris, 1987.
Dondey, Marc, *Tati*, Paris, 1989.

On TATI: articles—

Queval, Jean, "*Jour de fête*," in *Sight and Sound* (London), June 1950.
Knight, Arthur, "One Man's Movie," in *Saturday Review*, 19 June 1954.
Mayer, A. C., "The Art of Jacques Tati," in *Quarterly of Film, Radio, and Television* (Berkeley), Fall 1955.
Simon, John, "Hulot: Or the Common Man as Observer and Critic," in *Yale French Review* (New Haven), no. 23, 1959.
Houston, Penelope, "Conscience and Comedy," in *Sight and Sound* (London), Summer/Autumn 1959.
Current Biography 1961, New York, 1961.
Armes, Roy, "The Comic Art of Jacques Tati," in *Screen* (London), February 1970.
Dale, R. C., "*Playtime* and *Traffic*: Two New Tati's," in *Film Quarterly* (Berkeley), no. 2, 1972-73.
Monaco, James, "Oldies but Goodies, Materialist Farce: Jacques Tati's *Traffic* and *Playtime*," in *Take One* (Montreal), III, no. 11, September 1972.
Gilliatt, Penelope, "Profiles," in *New Yorker*, 27 January 1973.
Rosenbaum, Jonathan, "Tati's Democracy," in *Film Comment* (New York), May/June 1973.
Thompson, Kristin, "Parameters of the Open Film: *Les Vacances de Monsieur Hulot*," in *Wide Angle* (Athens, Ohio), vol. 1, no. 4, 1977.
Thompson, Kristin, "*Playtime*: Comedy on the Edge of Perception," in *Wide Angle* (Athens, Ohio), vol. 3, no. 2, 1979.
"Tati" issue of *Cahiers du Cinéma* (Paris), September 1979.
Fisher, Lucy, "*Playtime*: The Comic Film as Game," in *West Virginia University Philological Papers*, no. 26, August 1980.
"Homage to Jacques Tati," in *Cahiers du Cinéma* (Paris), May 1981.
Obituary in *New York Times*, 11 November 1982.
Fischer, Lucy, "*Jour de fête*: Americans in Paris," in *Film Criticism* (Meadville, Pennsylvania), Winter 1983.
"Jacques Tati" issue of *Cahiers du Cinéma* (Paris), January 1983.
Rosenbaum, Jonathan, "The Death of Hulot," in *Sight and Sound* (London), Spring 1983.
Carriere, Jean-Claude, "Comedie à la Française," in *American Film* (New York), December 1985.
Thompson, Kristin, "Parade," in *The Velvet Light Trap* (Madison, Wisconsin), no. 22, 1986.
Fawell, J., "Sound and Silence: Image and Invisibility in Jacques Tati's *Mon Oncle*," in *Film/Literature Quarterly* (Salisbury, Maryland), vol. XVIII, no. 4, 1990.

*   *   *

Jacques Tati created complex filmic comic structures, in which the recurring figure is Monsieur Hulot played by the director himself. A blank-faced comic cipher garbed in a crumbled raincoat and ill-fitting trousers, with an ever-present pipe muffling any words he may say, and an umbrella clutched in indecisive hands, Hulot determinedly strode across Tati's expansive cinematic canvases. On the basis of a mere four features over two decades, Tati as director and actor managed to reshape the comic genre and create works as complex and as lauded as any in film history.

The Hulot persona all began off screen. In the late 1920s Tati began performing in French music halls and cafés as a pantomimist and impersonator. In the 1930s he began to film comic shorts based on his stage routines. His promising career, like most French of his generation, was then interrupted by World War II and so he would make his first feature film, *Jour de fête*, at the advanced age of 40 years old. Tati played a postman in *Jour de fête*, but unhappy with this François character, he sought a persona with a more universal appeal.

He found him in Monsieur Hulot, a character that would become his cosmic archetype: a nerd (in late twentieth-century parlance) who constantly creates comic anarchy in his wake.

In *Les Vacances de Monsieur Hulot*, Tati introduced himself as Mr. Hulot, on a vacation ever filled with misadventures. Next came *Mon Oncle* dealing with the tension created by Hulot's traditional sensibilities trapped in a world of modern mechanization and consumerism. Both were highly praised in the art cinema world of the 1950s. Tati's masterwork, *Playtime*, is a 70mm, stereophonic sound tour de force which examines the disappearance of humanity within the mazelike confines of postindustrial society, again centered on the figure of Mr. Hulot. Less successful was *Trafic*, less centered as Hulot is caught in the anthropomorphism of automobiles and the mechanization of human beings.

Hulot is the key figure in all four films, yet is never the center of what would be traditionally thought of as a gag sequence. Indeed Hulot frequently disappears from the loosely constructed narratives so that in one sequence in *Playtime* we literally only see him as a reflection in a glass window. Tati the filmmaker uses himself as an actor as Hulot to play against traditional comic figures. But in no way does Tati the director allow us in the audience to identify with Hulot. A Tati film is best thought of as a tangled texture (especially on his densely packed soundtracks) that requires many viewings to unravel.

But while *Playtime* is now recognized as one of the central films of the first century of filmmaking, as an economic product it was a dismal failure and crippled Tati's career. His follow-up, *Trafic*, was also a financial failure and so with his final effort, *Parade*, a low-budget video celebration of pantomime, Tati abandoned Hulot for Monsieur Loyal. A comic era ended.

Hulot was a strange creation, always in the end inscrutable to the audience, even with his comic gags. He had a stubborn independence that reflected his creator. Hulot has a bent bumbling sort of walk, a quiet determination to see things through with a silly little hat, a crumpled raincoat, trousers that are too short, striped socks, a rolled up umbrella, and an omnipresent pipe. Hulot is a chameleon figure, seeming to turn up everywhere and anywhere. He leans forward as he moves, springing on tiptoe. When a great decision is to be made, Hulot arranges his body with care, points himself in the proper direction, and lopes off determined not to fail. He is dignified and restrained.

Although Tati influenced filmmakers as diverse as Jerry Lewis and Robert Altman, his career seems unique—both a beginning and end of a strain of comedy. His structural experiments are nothing short of breathtaking; his acting sublime. But he left little room for anyone to follow, and as the twentieth century ended, no one yet has.

—Douglas Gomery

TAYLOR, Elizabeth

Nationality: British. **Born:** Elizabeth Rosemond Taylor in London of American parents, 27 February 1932. **Education:** Attended the Hawthorne School, Beverly Hills, California; MGM studio school; University High School, Hollywood, graduated 1950. **Family:** Married 1) Nicky Hilton, 1950 (divorced 1951); 2) the actor Michael Wilding, 1952 (divorced 1957), sons: Michael and Christopher; 3) the producer Michael Todd, 1957 (died 1958), daughter: Elizabeth Frances; 4) the singer Eddie Fisher, 1959 (divorced 1964); 5) the actor Richard Burton, 1964 (divorced 1974; remarried 1975, divorced 1976), adopted daughter: Maria; 6) the politician John Warner, 1976 (divorced); 7) Larry Fortensky, 1991 (separated). **Career:** Evacuated to California at outbreak of World War II; 1942—film debut as child in *There's One*

Born Every Minute; 1943—contract with MGM: series of successful films as child, adolescent, and adult over the next ten years; 1981—on Broadway in *The Little Foxes*; 1985-present—founder and National Chairman of American Foundation for AIDS Research; in TV mini-series *North and South*; 1987—launched own perfume line. **Awards:** Best Actress Academy Award for *Butterfield 8*, 1960; Best Actress Academy Award, Best Actress, New York Film Critics, and Best Actress, British Academy, for *Who's Afraid of Virginia Woolf?*, 1966; Best Actress, Berlin Festival, for *Hammersmith Is Out*, 1972; French Légion d'honneur, 1987; Life Achievement Award, American Film Institute, 1993. **Agent:** Chén Sam, 506 E 74th Street, New York, NY 10021, U.S.A.

Films as Actress:

1942   *There's One Born Every Minute* (Young) (as Gloria)
1943   *Lassie Come Home* (Wilcox) (as Priscilla)
1944   *Jane Eyre* (Stevenson) (as Helen Burns); *The White Cliffs of Dover* (Brown) (as Betsy, age 10); *National Velvet* (Brown) (as Velvet Brown)
1946   *Courage of Lassie* (Wilcox) (as Kathie Merrick)
1947   *Cynthia* (Leonard) (title role); *Life with Father* (Curtiz) (as Mary Skinner)
1948   *A Date with Judy* (Thorpe) (as Carol Foster); *Julia Misbehaves* (Conway) (as Susan Packett)
1949   *Little Women* (LeRoy) (as Amy)
1950   *Conspirator* (Saville) (as Melinda Greyton); *The Big Hangover* (Krasna) (as Mary Belney); *Father of the Bride* (Minnelli) (as Kay Banks)
1951   *Father's Little Dividend* (Minnelli) (as Kay Dunston); *A Place in the Sun* (Stevens) (as Angela Vickers); *Quo Vadis* (LeRoy) (cameo role); *Callaway Went Thataway* (Panama) (as herself)
1952   *Love Is Better Than Ever* (Donen) (as Anastacia Macaboy); *Ivanhoe* (Thorpe) (as Rebecca)
1953   *The Girl Who Had Everything* (Thorpe) (as Jean Latimer)
1954   *Rhapsody* (Charles Vidor) (as Louise Durant); *Elephant Walk* (Dieterle) (as Ruth Wiley); *Beau Brummel* (Bernhardt) (as Lady Patricia); *The Last Time I Saw Paris* (Richard Brooks) (as Helen Ellswirth)
1956   *Giant* (Stevens) (as Leslie Lynnton Benedict)
1957   *Raintree County* (Dmytryk) (as Susanna Drake)
1958   *Cat on a Hot Tin Roof* (Richard Brooks) (as Maggie Pollitt)
1959   *Suddenly, Last Summer* (Mankiewicz) (as Catherine Holly)
1960   *Scent of Mystery* (Cardiff) (as Sally Kennedy); *Butterfield 8* (Daniel Mann) (as Gloria Wandrous)
1963   *Cleopatra* (Mankiewicz) (title role); *The V.I.Ps* (Asquith) (as Frances Andros)
1965   *The Sandpiper* (Minnelli) (as Laura Reynolds)
1966   *Who's Afraid of Virginia Woolf?* (Nichols) (as Martha)
1967   *The Taming of the Shrew* (Zeffirelli) (as Katharina, + pr); *Reflections in a Golden Eye* (Huston) (as Leonora Penderton); *The Comedians* (Glenville) (as Martha Pineda); *Doctor Faustus* (Burton) (as Helen of Troy)
1968   *Boom!* (Losey) (as Flora "Sissy" Goforth); *Secret Ceremony* (Losey) (as Leonora)
1970   *The Only Game in Town* (Stevens) (as Fran Walker)
1972   *X, Y, & Zee* (Hutton) (as Zee Blakeley); *Hammersmith Is Out* (Ustinov) (as Jimmie Jean Jackson)
1973   *Under Milk Wood* (Sinclair) (as Rosie Probert); *Night Watch* (Hutton) (as Ellen Wheeler); *Divorce: His/Divorce: Hers* (Hussein—for TV) (as Jane Reynolds); *Ash Wednesday* (Peerce) (as Barbara Sawyer)
1974   *That's Entertainment!* (Haley—compilation) (as narrator)
1975   *The Driver's Seat* (*Identikit*) (Patroni-Griffi) (as Lise)

1976   *The Blue Bird* (Cukor) (as Mother/Witch/Light/Maternal Love)
1977   *A Little Night Music* (Prince) (as Desiree Armfeldt); *Victory at Entebbe* (Chomsky—for TV) (as Edra Vilnosky); *Winter Kills* (Richert) (as Lola Comante)
1978   *Return Engagement* (Hardy—for TV)
1980   *The Mirror Crack'd* (Hamilton) (as Marina Rudd); *Genocide* (Schwartzman—doc) (as narrator)
1982   *Between Friends* (Antonio—for TV) (as Deborah Shapiro)
1985   *Malice in Wonderland* (Trikonis—for TV) (Louella Parsons)
1986   *There Must Be a Pony* (Sargent—for TV) (as Marguerite Sydney)
1987   *Poker Alice* (Seidelman—for TV) (as Alice Moffit)
1988   *Giovane Toscanini* (*Young Toscanini*) (Zeffirelli) (as Nadina Bulicioff); *Who Gets the Friends?* (Lila Garrett—for TV)
1989   *Sweet Bird of Youth* (Roeg—for TV)
1994   *The Flintstones* (Levant) (as Pearl Slaghoople)

Publications

By TAYLOR: books—

Elizabeth Taylor—Her Own Story, New York, 1965.
Elizabeth Takes Off on Self-Esteem and Self-Image, New York, 1988.

On TAYLOR: books—

Waterbury, Ruth, *Elizabeth Taylor*, New York, 1964.
Hirsch, Foster, *Elizabeth Taylor*, New York, 1973.
Rosen, Marjorie, *Popcorn Venus*, New York, 1973.
D'Arcy, Susan, *The Films of Elizabeth Taylor*, London, 1974.
Wallis, Hal, and Charles Higham, *Starmaker*, New York, 1980.
Kelley, Kitty, *Elizabeth Taylor: The Last Star*, London, 1981.
Moore, Dick, *Twinkle, Twinkle, Little Star*, New York, 1984.
Wickens, Christopher, *Elizabeth Taylor: A Biography in Photographs*, New York, 1984.
Morley, Sheridan, *Elizabeth Taylor: A Celebration*, London, 1988.
Tani, Marianne Robin, *The New Elizabeth*, New York, 1988.
Walker, Alexander, *Elizabeth*, London, 1990.
Latham, Caroline, *All about Elizabeth: Elizabeth Taylor, Public and Private*, New York, 1991.
Heymann, C. David, *Liz: An Intimate Biography of Elizabeth Taylor*, New York, 1995.
Spoto, Donald, *A Passion for Life: The Biography of Elizabeth Taylor*, New York, 1995.

On TAYLOR: articles—

Israel, Lee, "Rise and Fall of Elizabeth Taylor," in *Esquire* (New York), March 1967.
Essoe, Gabe, "Elizabeth Taylor," in *Films in Review* (New York), August-September 1970.
Schickel, Richard, "Elizabeth Taylor" in *The Movie Star*, edited by Elisabeth Weis, New York, 1981.
McGilligan, P., "Letter from Hollywood—Elizabeth Taylor," in *Films and Filming* (London), January 1982.
Current Biography 1985, New York, 1985.
Pendleton, Austin, "Elizabeth," in *Film Comment* (New York), May/June 1986.
Bibby, Bruce, "Taylor Made," in *Premiere* (New York), October 1992.

On TAYLOR: mini-series—

Liz: The Elizabeth Taylor Story, directed by Kevin Connor, 1995.

*   *   *

Elizabeth Taylor in *The Taming of the Shrew*

Elizabeth Taylor's star image always has overshadowed her capabilities as a performer. Public and media attention has fallen not on her achievements as an actress, but on the sensational aspects of her private life. Her passage from youth to maturity has been studded with highly publicized marriages and divorces and Lazarus-like recoveries from serious illness, all of which have sustained her reputation as one of the most celebrated products of Hollywood.

Interest in her acting skills has been further diverted by a widespread preoccupation with her appearance. When she was young, her lavender eyes and all-around beauty enthralled audiences and clouded the critical faculties of the press. Decades later, persistent weight problems attracted negative comment from all quarters. Few screen personalities have been so consistently evaluated in terms of physical criteria. Considerations of looks and celebrity aside, however, Taylor emerges as an actress of definite ability whose talents—despite several worthy screen roles in the 1950s and 1960s—have too often been exaggerated or underused.

In the early 1940s, child stars were major revenue earners at the box office. Taylor's uncommon beauty, even at the age of nine, had much to do with her being selected for stardom by MGM, but it was the warmth and freshness of her screen presence which ensured success. The luminous charm that she projected in her earliest films, especially *National Velvet*, struck a chord with the moviegoing public. Unlike many child actors, she made a smooth transition to adult parts, although the path was strewn with weak scripts and undemanding roles. MGM, to which she was under contract for 18 years, was apt to use her as decoration in frothy comedies or typecast her as a poor little rich girl. She received good notices for Minnelli's *Father of the Bride*, and provided solid evidence of acting talent in George Stevens's *A Place in the Sun*. Stevens, who acted as midwife to another memorable Taylor performance in *Giant*, induced her to display considerable emotional range and an unforgettable sensuality. Most of the films she made in the early 1950s, however, were lacking in distinction.

The years from the mid-1950s to mid-1960s represent the zenith of Taylor's career. During this period she created various portraits of women wrestling with adversity, usually of a psychological nature. As Maggie in *Cat on a Hot Tin Roof*, she suffered intense emotional and sexual frustration at the hands of a morose, self-absorbed husband. In *Raintree County* and *Suddenly, Last Summer*, both Oscar-nominated performances, the battle was with the imminent threat of mental disintegration. As Katharina in Zeffirelli's *The Taming of the Shrew*, she was a fury who vigorously warded off the role of obedient wife. In *Who's Afraid of Virginia Woolf?* (for which she won her second Best Actress Oscar, after *Butterfield Eight*), she was a raucous harridan using drink to anaesthetize life's disappointments and verbal aggression to provide the illusion of control.

Taylor has been at her best when playing brash, shrewish women. Few actresses have better demonstrated the power of sarcasm as a weapon against the male ego. After the mid-1960s, however, she seemed increasingly unable to make effective use of her abilities. Even as regal *Cleopatra*, she drew critical fire for being excessively shrill in voice. For many years, too much faith was placed in her drawing power at the box office, and too little thought given to the selection of appropriate parts. Since she never attempted a transition from leading lady to character actress, the onset of middle age accelerated the decline of her film career.

In response to the dearth of suitable movie roles, she has recently diversified into theater and television. Most of these ventures have done little more than capitalize on her star status. A notable exception was *Between Friends*, a television movie in which she and Carol Burnett help each other confront the problems of lonely middle-aged existence in a youth-oriented society. Taylor gives a sensitive, multi-dimensional performance, distinguished by its responsiveness to her fellow actors.

Yet public attention to this day remains directed towards Taylor the legend, rather than Taylor the actress. She continues to be the quintessential star, providing a focus for the fantasies of successive generations. In recent years she has experienced more frequent hospitalizations for hip replacement surgery, yet she also has managed to be at the forefront of the movie industry's campaign to raise awareness of the devastation of AIDS.

—Fiona Valentine, updated by Audrey E. Kupferberg

TAYLOR, Robert

Nationality: American. **Born:** Spangler Arlington Brugh in Filley, Nebraska, 5 August 1911. **Education:** Attended Beatrice High School, Nebraska, graduated 1929; Doane College, Crete, Nebraska; Pomona College, California, B.A. 1933; Neely Dixon Dramatic School, Hollywood. **Family:** Married 1) the actress Barbara Stanwyck, 1939 (divorced 1951); 2) the actress Ursula Thiess, 1954, two children. **Career:** 1934—film debut in *Handy Andy*; 1934-58—contract with MGM; 1943-46—flying instructor in Naval Air Corps, and also directed training films: Lieutenant; 1958—formed Robert Taylor Productions; 1959-62—star of TV series *The Detectives*; 1966-68—host (and occasional actor), TV series *Death Valley Days*. **Died:** 8 June 1969.

Films as Actor:

1934 *Handy Andy* (Butler) (as Lloyd Burmeister); *There's Always Tomorrow* (Sloman) (as Arthur); *A Wicked Woman* (Brabin) (as Bill Renton)

1935 *Buried Loot* (Seitz) (as Al Douglas); *Society Doctor* (Seitz) (as Dr. Ellis); *Times Square Lady* (Seitz) (as Steve); *West Point in the Air* (Rossen) (as Jaskerelli); *Murder in the Fleet* (Sedgwick) (as Lt. Tom Randolph); *Broadway Melody of 1936* (Del Ruth) (as Bob Gordon); *Magnificent Obsession* (Stahl) (as Bobby Merrick)

1936 *Small Town Girl* (Wellman) (as Bob Dakin); *Private Number* (Del Ruth) (as Richard Winfield); *His Brother's Wife* (Van Dyke) (as Chris); *The Gorgeous Hussy* (Brown) (as Bow Timberlake)

1937 *Camille* (Cukor) (as Armand Dural); *Personal Property* (Van Dyke) (as Raymond Dabney); *This Is My Affair* (Seiter) (as Lt. Richard Perry); *Broadway Melody of 1938* (Del Ruth) (as Steve); *Lest We Forget* (Whitbeck—doc) (as himself)

1938 *A Yank at Oxford* (Conway) (as Lee Sheridan); *Three Comrades* (Borzage) (as Erich Lokcamp); *The Crowd Roars* (Thorpe) (as Tommy McCoy)

1939 *Stand Up and Fight* (Van Dyke) (as Blake Cantrell); *Lucky Night* (Taurog) (as Bill Overton); *Lady of the Tropics* (Conway) (as Bill Carey); *Remember?* (McLeod) (as Jeff Holland)

1940 *Flight Command* (Borzage) (as Ensign Alan Drake); *Waterloo Bridge* (LeRoy) (as Roy Cronin); *Escape* (LeRoy) (as Mark Preiping)

1941 *Billy the Kid* (Miller) (as Billy Bonney); *When Ladies Meet* (Leonard) (as Jimmy Lee)

1942 *Johnny Eager* (LeRoy) (title role); *Her Cardboard Lover* (Cukor) (as Terry Trindale)

1943 *Stand by for Action* (Leonard) (as Lt. Gregg Masterson); *Bataan* (Garnett) (as Sgt. Bill Dane); *The Youngest Profession* (Buzzell) (as himself)

1944   *Song of Russia* (Ratoff) (as John Meredith)
1945   *The Fighting Lady* (de Rochemont—doc) (as narrator)
1946   *Undercurrent* (Minnelli) (as Alan Garroway)
1947   *The High Wall* (Bernhardt) (as Steven Kenet)
1948   *The Secret Land* (Dull—doc) (as narrator)
1949   *The Bribe* (Leonard) (as Rigby)
1950   *Ambush* (Wood) (as Ward Kinsman); *Conspirator* (Saville) (as Major Michael Curragh); *The Devil's Doorway* (Anthony Mann) (as Lance Poole)
1951   *Quo Vadis* (LeRoy) (as Marcus Vinicius); *Westward the Women* (Wellman) (as Buck)
1952   *Ivanhoe* (Thorpe) (title role)
1953   *Above and Beyond* (Frank and Panama) (as Colonel Paul Tibbets); *I Love Melvin* (Weis) (as himself); *Ride Vaquero!* (Farrow) (as Rio); *All the Brothers Were Valiant* (Thorpe) (as Joel Shore)
1954   *Knights of the Round Table* (Thorpe) (as Sir Lancelot); *Valley of the Kings* (Pirosh) (as Mark Brandon); *Rogue Cop* (Rowland) (as Christopher Kelvaney)
1955   *Many Rivers to Cross* (Rowland) (as Bushrod Gebtry); *Quentin Durward* (Thorpe) (title role)
1956   *The Last Hunt* (Brooks) (as Charles Gilson); *D-Day, the Sixth of June* (Koster) (as Brad Parker)
1957   *Tip on a Dead Jockey* (Thorpe) (as Lloyd Fredman)
1958   *Saddle the Wind* (Parrish) (as Steve Sinclair); *The Law and Jake Wade* (Sturges) (title role); *Party Girl* (Ray) (as Thomas Farrell)
1959   *The Hangman* (Curtiz) (as Mackenzie Bovard); *The House of the Seven Hawks* (Thorpe) (as John Nordley)
1960   *Killers of Kilimanjaro* (Thorpe) (as Adamson)
1963   *Miracle of the White Stallions* (Hiller) (as Colonel Podhajsky); *Cattle King* (Garnett) (as Sam Brassfield)
1964   *A House Is Not a Home* (Rouse) (as Frank Costigan)
1965   *The Night Walker* (Castle) (as Barry Morland)
1966   *Johnny Tiger* (Wendkos) (as George Dean)
1967   *Savage Pampas* (*Prade's Comet*) (Fregonese) (as Captain Martin); *Return of the Gunfighter* (Nielson—for TV)
1968   *La esfinge de cristal* (*The Glass Sphinx*) (Scattini and Sheikh) (as Prof. Karl Nichols); *Where Angels Go—Trouble Follows* (Nielson) (as Mr. Farriday); *The Day the Hotline Got Hot* (Perier) (as Anderson)

Publications

On TAYLOR: books—

Quirk, Lawrence J., *The Films of Robert Taylor*, Secaucus, New Jersey, 1975.
Wayne, Jane Ellen, *Robert Taylor*, New York, 1989.
Madsen, Axel, *Stanwyck*, New York, 1994.

On TAYLOR: articles—

Current Biography 1952, New York, 1952.
Bowers, Ronald, "Robert Taylor," in *Films in Review* (New York), January 1967.
Obituary in *New York Times*, 9 June 1969.

*   *   *

There seem almost to have been two Robert Taylors. The first was a callow youth, stiff and unformed as an actor, but so very handsome that his stock soared for over a decade after his film debut in the mid-1930s. This young Taylor was earnest in *Magnificent Obsession*, snide and shallow in *Small Town Girl*, the epitome of the naive dream lover in *Camille*. MGM, where Taylor spent most of his career, was a glamour factory and he was groomed to be the perfect leading man: smooth, charming, boyishly sincere.

The other Taylor was less a studio creation than the inevitable assertion of the actor's capabilities and nature. Early in the 1940s, a hard, cold aspect of his personality began to emerge: in *Johnny Eager* he is an unsympathetic racketeer, in *Undercurrent* an unscrupulous, dangerous husband, in *The Bribe* a tough federal agent. Taylor's increasingly craggy countenance made him a natural for Westerns; the Pretty-Boy played the title role in the glamorized *Billy the Kid* but the tougher, more humorless Taylor took things firmly in hand in *Ambush*, *Westward the Women*, *Devil's Doorway*, and *Ride Vaquero!*

His willingness to take on harsh characters, as in *The High Wall*, *Rogue Cop*, and *The Last Hunt*, exhibits his desire to transform himself into a player of greater versatility. Unfortunately, either he did not have it in him or MGM never gave him the chance to stretch. That he had a way with comedy is evidenced by his witty cameo in *I Love Melvin* and some boisterous scenes in *Westward the Women*, but his comedic talents went otherwise unexplored.

Taylor's only respite from the hard, often villainous roles of his later career came in splashy costume dramas—*Ivanhoe*, *Knights of the Round Table*, *Quo Vadis*—in which his dash could be displayed in technicolor opposite such leading ladies as Elizabeth Taylor, Ava Gardner, and Deborah Kerr.

His last decade in films was spent treading water, but *Party Girl*, *The House of the Seven Hawks*, and *Cattle King* are indications of what he could accomplish with a good director and an offbeat setting. He and his ex-wife, Barbara Stanwyck, even accomplished that rarity of rarities in *The Night Walker*: they make it a pretty good William Castle film.

—Frank Thompson

TEMPLE, Shirley

Nationality: American. **Born:** Shirley Jane Temple in Santa Monica, California, 23 April 1928. **Education:** Attended Westlake School for Girls. **Family:** Married 1) the actor John Agar Jr., 1945 (divorced 1949), daughter: Linda Susan; 2) Charles Alden Black, 1950, son: Charles, daughter: Lori. **Career:** Child actress from age four in series of shorts for Educational Pictures; 1934—contract with Fox: series of popular films in the 1930s made her the most popular Hollywood star for the years 1935-38; 1940s—declining popularity; made films for various studios; 1958-60—host, and occasional actor, *The Shirley Temple Storybook* TV series; 1968—appointed U.S. Representative to the United Nations; 1974-76—U.S. Ambassador to Ghana; 1976-77—U.S. Chief of Protocol; 1989-92—U.S. Ambassador to Czechoslovakia. **Awards:** Special Academy Award, "in grateful recognition of her outstanding contribution to screen entertainment during the year 1934." **Address:** 115 Lakeview Drive, Woodside, CA 94062, U.S.A.

Films as Actress:

1932   *War Babies* (Lamont—short) (as Charmaine); *The Runt Page* (La Verne—short) (as Lulu Parsnips); *Pie Covered Wagon* (Lamont—short) (as captive); *Glad Rags to Riches* (Lamont—short) (as La Belle Diaperina); *The Red-Haired Alibi* (Cabanne) (as Gloria)

Shirley Temple

1933 *Kid's Last Fight* (Lamont—short) (as girlfriend); *Kid 'n' Hollywood* (Lamont—short) (as Morelegs Sweet Trick); *Poolytix in Washington* (Lamont—short) (as gold digger); *Kid 'n' Africa* (Lamont—short) (as Madame Cradlebait); *Merrily Yours* (Lamont—short) (as Mary Lou Rogers); *Dora's Dunkin' Doughnuts* (Edwards—short) (as pupil); *To the Last Man* (Hathaway) (as Mary Standing); *Out All Night* (Sam Taylor) (as child)

1934 *Pardon My Pups* (Lamont—short) (as Mary Lou); *Managed Money* (Lamont—short) (as Mary Lou); *New Deal Money* (short); *Carolina* (*The House of Connelly*) (Henry King) (as girl); *Mandalay* (Curtiz) (as Betty Shaw); *Stand Up and Cheer* (McFadden) (as Shirley Dugan); *Now I'll Tell* (*While New York Sleeps*) (Burke) (as Mary Golden); *Change of Heart* (Blystone) (as Shirley, girl on airplane); *Little Miss Marker* (Hall) (title role); *Baby, Take a Bow* (Lachman) (as Shirley); *Now and Forever* (Hathaway) (as Penelope Day); *Bright Eyes* (David Butler) (as Shirley Blake)

1935 *The Little Colonel* (David Butler) (as Lloyd Sherman, the Little Colonel); *Our Little Girl* (Robertson) (as Molly Middleton); *Curly Top* (Cummings) (as Betsy Blair); *The Littlest Rebel* (David Butler) (as Virginia Houston Cary)

1936 *Captain January* (David Butler) (as Star); *Poor Little Rich Girl* (Cummings) (as Barbara Barry); *Dimples* (Seiter) (as Sylvia Dolores); *Stowaway* (Seiter) (as Ching-Ching)

1937 *Wee Willie Winkie* (Ford) (as Priscilla Williams); *Heidi* (Dwan) (title role)

1938 *Rebecca of Sunnybrook Farm* (Dwan) (title role); *Little Miss Broadway* (Cummings) (as Betsy Brown); *Just around the Corner* (Cummings) (as Penny Hale)

1939 *The Little Princess* (Walter Lang) (as Sara Crewe); *Susannah of the Mounties* (Seiter) (title role)

1940 *The Blue Bird* (Walter Lang) (as Mytyl); *Young People* (Dwan) (as Wendy)

1941 *Kathleen* (Bucquet) (title role)

1942 *Miss Annie Rooney* (Marin) (title role)

1944 *Since You Went Away* (Cromwell) (as Bridget Hilton); *I'll Be Seeing You* (Dieterle) (as Barbara Marshall)

1945 *Kiss and Tell* (Wallace) (as Corliss Archer)

1947 *Honeymoon* (*Two Men and a Girl*) (Keighley) (as Barbara Olmstead); *The Bachelor and the Bobby-Soxer* (*Bachelor Knight*) (Reis) (as Susan); *That Hagen Girl* (Godfrey) (title role)

1948 *Fort Apache* (Ford) (as Philadelphia Thursday)

1949   *Mr. Belvedere Goes to College* (Nugent) (as Ellen Baker);
       Adventure in Baltimore (*Bachelor Bait*) (Wallace) (as Dinah
       Sheldon); *The Story of Seabiscuit* (David Butler) (as Marga-
       ret O'Hara); *A Kiss for Corliss* (Wallace) (as Corliss Archer)
1986   *Going Hollywood: The War Years* (doc—archival)
1991   *Why Havel?*

Publications

By TEMPLE: books—

My Young Life, with the editors of *Look*, Garden City, New York, 1945.
Child Star, New York, 1988.

By TEMPLE: article—

"Tomorrow I'll Be Thirty," in *Good Housekeeping*, November 1957.

On TEMPLE: books—

Beatty, Jerome, *Shirley Temple*, Akron, Ohio, 1935.
Eby, Lois, *Shirley Temple: The Amazing Story of the Child Actress Who
   Grew Up to Be America's Fairy Princess*, Derby, Connecticut, 1962.
Kennedy-Minott, Rodney, *The Sinking of the Lollipop; Shirley Temple
   vs. Pete McCloskey*, San Francisco, 1968.
Rosen, Marjorie, *Popcorn Venus*, New York, 1973.
Basinger, Jeanine, *Shirley Temple*, New York, 1975.
Burdick, Loraine, *The Shirley Temple Scrapbook*, Middle Village, New
   York, 1975.
Bowers, Ronald, *The Selznick Players*, South Brunswick, New Jersey, 1976.
Windeler, Robert, *The Films of Shirley Temple*, Secaucus, New Jersey,
   1978.
David, Lester, and Irene David, *The Shirley Temple Story*, New York, 1983.
Moore, Dick, *Twinkle, Twinkle, Little Star*, New York, 1984.
Edwards, Anne, *Shirley Temple: American Princess*, New York, 1988.
Sinclair, Marianne, *Hollywood Lolita: The Nymphet Syndrome in the
   Movies*, London, 1988.

On TEMPLE: articles—

Temple, Gertrude, "Bringing Up Shirley," in *American*, February 1935.
Current Biography 1970, New York, 1970.
Eckert, C., "Shirley Temple and the House of Rockefeller," in *Jump
   Cut* (Chicago), July/August 1974.
Cassa, A., "Shirley Temple Black: America's Foremost Childstar, Who
   Almost Was Dorothy!," in *Hollywood Studio*, no. 3, 1984.
Quinlan, D., "The Way They Were," in *Photoplay*, March 1987.
Bishop, K., "Shirley Temple: Celebrity or Generic Term?," in *New York
   Times*, 29 October 1988.
Ward, G. C., "America's Baby," in *American Heritage*, March 1989.
Yorkshire, H., "Shirley Temple Black Sets the Record Straight," in
   McCall's, March 1989.
"A Salute to Shirley Temple!," in *Hollywood Studio*, no. 3, 1989.
Ryan, Michael, "As Ambassador to Prague, Shirley Temple Black
   Watches a Rebirth of Freedom," in *People Weekly* (New York), 8
   January 1990.
Cadden, V., "Return to Prague," in *McCall's*, April 1990.
Bassan, R., "Nostalgie," in *Revue du Cinéma*, December 1990.
Early, G. L., "Black Like ... Shirley Temple?," in *Harper's* (New York),
   February 1992.
Buckley, M., "Shirley Temple Black," in *Films in Review* (New York),
   May/June 1993.

*   *   *

Shirley Temple was the darling of the Great Depression. She was the
biggest box-office attraction during one of the bleakest periods of
American history. As she sang and danced her way into the hearts of
millions of Americans, Temple became an institution. There were
Shirley Temple dolls, toys, and clothes (including a line of bathing
suits), and her curly hair (which evoked the celebrated curls of America's
first "Little Sweetheart"—Mary Pickford) was imitated eagerly by
countless little girls. Why was Shirley Temple so beloved? Although
her films were formulaic and generally dismissed by critics, she redeemed them with her overwhelming charisma and spirited performances. Indeed, there has been no other child star before or since who
has been as popular or who demonstrated her extraordinary talents as
a singer, dancer, or actress.

Shirley played bit parts in several short films during the early 1930s,
but her star soared with *Stand Up and Cheer* in which she sang "Baby,
Take a Bow." Although she played a minor role, she stole the show
with her cute, dimpled face and irresistible charm, and the film proved
to be a smash hit. Temple's success continued in movies such as *Little
Miss Marker*, *Baby, Take a Bow*, and *Bright Eyes*—in which she delivered her memorable song-and-dance rendition of "On the Good Ship
Lollipop." Despite their youth and innocence, it seemed there was no
challenge too large for Temple's characters. During the mid-1930s,
Temple played an orphan at least nine times, a matchmaker at least
twice, and she reunited her own broken family at least four times. Her
screen characters had even loftier goals as well: she brings peace to
India in *Wee Willie Winkie* and personally asks President Lincoln to
pardon her imprisoned Confederate father in *The Littlest Rebel*. Also
compelling is that Temple's characters display no overt racial or class
biases (although the same cannot be said about her films in general).
On several occasions, she performs with black characters; and when
her characters were wealthy, they typically cavorted with less fortunate characters. Indeed, one of her most engaging performances occurs in *The Little Colonel* when she dances with the legendary Bill
"Bojangles" Robinson. Accordingly, it seems, wrapped up in this little
girl were many of the ideals that Americans cherished but rarely practiced.

Despite that she provided an antidote of sorts to Mae West's scan-
dalously aggressive screen sexuality, the Temple persona evokes an
unmistakable sexual quality that was visible in both her screen
characterizations and her publicity photographs. Indeed, even in
her earliest screen roles she played the leads in a series of one-reel
films titled "Baby Burlesks," that lampooned popular movies and
movie stars, including the sultry Marlene Dietrich. And, in her
subsequent leading roles, she was invariably paired with attentive
older men with whom she expressed a distinct and rather demonstrative affection.

Between 1934 and 1939 Temple was enormously popular, but in
her early teens her popularity started to decline. Her audience was
accustomed to seeing her play enchanting little girls, and was apparently unwilling to accept her on-screen maturity. As a result, in
the early 1940s she played mostly supporting roles as a teenager,
though she did enjoy a brief comeback that started with her appearance in the wartime epic *Since You Went Away*, and continued with
I'll Be Seeing You, and *Kiss and Tell*. Soon however, her star started
to sink once again, and when she was only 21, Temple retired from
movies. Then, after her experience in two short-lived television
shows in the late 1950s and early 1960s, Temple permanently left
acting behind. In the late 1960s, she tried her hand at politics, and
she has been successful in this realm ever since. Her résumé includes her service as a United Nations representative, the U.S.
Chief of Protocol, and as ambassador to both Ghana and Czechoslovakia.

—Maryann Oshana, updated by Cynthia Felando

TERRY-THOMAS

Nationality: British. **Born:** Thomas Terry Hoar Stevens in London, 14 July 1911. **Education:** Attended Ardingly College. **Family:** Married 1) the dancer Ida Patlanskey, 1938 (divorced 1962); 2) Belinda Cunningham, 1963, sons: Tiger and Cushan. **Career:** 1930s—transport clerk, Smithfield Meat Market; also dancer, and ukelele player in band, The Rhythm Maniacs; cabaret work led to film debut as extra, 1936, and radio debut, 1938; 1941-46—served in Army, Signal Corps (won four military service medals); also Entertainments National Service Association; 1946—West End debut in *Piccadilly Hayride*; from 1951—TV performer; shows include *How Do You View?*, and *Strictly T-T*; 1970s—worked in Italy, then forced to stop work through ilness. **Died:** In Godalming, Surrey, of Parkinson's disease, 8 January 1990.

Films as Actor:

1936   *It's Love Again* (Saville) (as extra); *Rhythm in the Air* (Woods); *This'll Make You Whistle* (Wilcox)
1937   *Rhythm Racketeer* (Seymour)
1940   *For Freedom* (Elvey); *Under Your Hat* (Elvey)
1948   *A Date with a Dream* (Leeman) (as Terry); *The Brass Monkey* (*Lucky Mascot*) (Freeland)
1949   *Helter Skelter* (Thomas) (as announcer); *Melody Club* (Berman) (as Freddy Forrester)
1951   *Cookery Nook* (short); *The Queen Steps Out* (Henryson—short)
1956   *Private's Progress* (Boulting) (as Major Hitchcock); *The Green Man* (Day) (as Boughtflower)
1957   *The Brothers in Law* (Boulting) (as Alfred Green); *Lucky Jim* (Boulting) (as Bertrand Welch); *Blue Murder at St. Trinian's* (Launder) (as Captain Romney Carlton-Ricketts); *The Naked Truth* (*Your Past Is Showing*) (Zampi) (as Lord Mayley)
1958   *Happy Is the Bride* (Boulting) (as PC); *Tom Thumb* (Pal) (as Ivan)
1959   *Too Many Crooks* (Zampi) (as Billy Gordon); *Carlton-Browne of the F.O.* (*Man in a Cocked Hat*) (Boulting and Dell) (as Cadogan deVere Carlton-Browne); *I'm All Right, Jack* (Boulting) (as Major Hitchcock)
1960   *School for Scoundrels* (Hamer) (as Raymond Delauney); *Make Mine Mink* (Asher) (as Major Albert Rayne)
1961   *His and Hers* (Hurst) (as Reggie Blake); *A Matter of Who* (Chaffey) (as Archibald Bannister)
1962   *Operation Snatch* (Day) (as Lt. Piggy Wigg); *Bachelor Flat* (Tashlin) (as Professor Bruce); *Kill or Cure* (Pollock) (as J. Barker-Rynde); *The Wonderful World of the Brothers Grimm* (Levin and Pal) (as Ludwig)
1963   *The Mouse on the Moon* (Lester) (as Spender); *It's a Mad, Mad, Mad, Mad World* (Kramer) (as J. Algernon Hawthorne); *The Wild Affair* (Krish) (as Godfrey Deane)
1964   *Strange Bedfellows* (Frank) (as Assistant Mortician); *How to Murder Your Wife* (Quine) (as Charles)
1965   *Those Magnificent Men in Their Flying Machines; or, How I Flew from London to Paris in 25 Hrs and 11 Minutes* (Annakin) (as Sir Percy Ware-Armitage); *You Must Be Joking!* (Winner) (as Major Foskett)
1966   *The Daydreamer* (Bass) (as voice only); *Our Man in Marrakesh* (*Bang, Bang, You're Dead*) (Sharp) (as El Caid); *The Sandwich Man* (Hartford-Davis) (as Scoutmaster); *Munster, Go Home* (Bellamy) (as Freddie Munster); *Kiss the Girls and Make Them Die* (*Se tutte le donne del mondo*) (Levin and Maiuri) (as Lord Aldric/James); *Don't Look Now, We're Being Shot At* (*La Grande Vadrouille*) (Oury) (as Reginald)

1967   *Jules Verne's Rocket to the Moon* (*Those Fantastic Flying Fools*) (Sharp) (as Sir Harry Washington-Smythe); *A Guide for the Married Man* (Kelly) (as Technical Adviser); *Arabella* (Bolognini) (as the Hotel Manager/the General/the Duke); *Arriva Dorellik* (de Steno); *The Karate Killers* (Shear) (as Constable); *The Perils of Pauline* (Leonard) (as Sten Martin); *Top Crack* (Russo); *Diabolik* (*Danger: Diabolik*) (Bava) (as Minister of Finance)
1968   *Don't Raise the Bridge, Lower the River* (Paris) (as H. William Homer); *Uno scacco tutto matto* (Fiz); *Seven Times Seven* (Lupo); *How Sweet It Is* (Paris) (as Gilbert Tilly); *Where Were You When the Lights Went Out?* (Averback) (as Ladislau Walicheck)
1969   *Arthur, Arthur* (Gallu); *2000 Years After* (Tenzer) (as Charles Goodwyn); *Monte Carlo or Bust!* (*Those Daring Young Men in Their Jaunty Jalopies*) (Annakin) (as Sir Cuthbert Ware-Armitage); *Twelve Plus One* (*Thirteen*; *Una su tredici*) (Gessner) (as Albert)
1970   *Le Mur de l'Atlantique* (Camus); *The Cherry Picker* (Curran)
1971   *The Abominable Dr. Phibes* (Fuest) (as Dr. Longstreet)
1972   *Gli eroi* (*The Heroes*) (Tessari); *Dr. Phibes Rises Again* (Fuest) (as Lombardo)
1973   *The Vault of Horror* (*Tales from the Crypt II*) (Baker) (as Critchit); *Robin Hood* (Reitherman) (voice only)
1975   *Side by Side* (Beresford); *The Bawdy Adventures of Tom Jones* (Owen); *Spanish Fly* (Kellett)
1976   *The Mysterious House of Dr. C* (Kneeland) (voice only)
1977   *The Hound of the Baskervilles* (Morrissey) (as Dr. Mortimer); *The Last Remake of Beau Geste* (Feldman) (as Prison Governor)
1981   *Happy Birthday Harry!* (Mattei)

Publications

By TERRY-THOMAS: books—

Filling the Gap, London, 1959.
Terry-Thomas Tells Tales, with Terry Daum, London, 1990.

By TERRY-THOMAS: article—

Interview in *Films Illustrated* (London), September 1976.

On TERRY-THOMAS: articles—

Current Biography 1961, New York, 1961.
Films and Filming (London), February 1985.
Ciné Revue (Paris), June 1989.
TV Times (London), 28 October 1989.
Obituary in *New York Times*, 9 January 1990
Obituary in *Variety* (New York), 17 January 1990.

*   *   *

Terry-Thomas began his 1990 autobiography with some of the descriptions offered by critics through his career: "Terry-Thomas with his permanent air of caddish disdain . . . bounder . . . aristocratic rogue . . . upper-class English twit . . . genuine English eccentric . . . one of the last real gentlemen . . . wet, genteel Englishman . . . highbred idiot . . . cheeky blighter . . . camel-haired cad . . . amiable buffoon . . . pompous Englishman . . . twentieth-century dandy . . . stinker . . . king of the cads . . . ." Such phrases instantly conjure up one of the most easily recognizable of film stars, whose gap-toothed smile, military moustache, florid accent and dapper dress sense cropped up in (and too often propped up) so many films in the 1950s and 1960s.

Yet Terry-Thomas, while invariably playing himself, managed to create a persona whose appeal to film audiences in the 1950s was based on more than just his well-polished comic ability. In those dour days, with its rationing and its collapsing empire, Britain welcomed the fruity humor of Terry-Thomas, with his loud waistcoats, exaggerated vowels, and overfamiliar manner. He was the comic incarnation of the sort of ex-minor-public-schoolboys whose shady dealings were such a feature of postwar British culture.

Though sometimes seen as aristocratic, Terry-Thomas, as British audiences (rather than American ones) may have suspected, was not quite the genuine article. To his own disgust, he was born and raised in Finchley, a suburb of London which was, at most, respectable. As he himself said, "I've cashed in on playing the lower-middle-class pretending to be upper-class." Though educated privately, he was unable subsequently to join the British Army, despite being his school's star cadet officer, since an officer at that time needed an independent income. Instead he took a rather less glamorous job as a transport clerk at Smithfield Meat Market. Though he remained there six years, he made a mark less with his abilities as a clerk than with his regular attire of a buttonhole, a silver-topped Malacca cane and slip-on suede shoes.

He developed his show-business career in the early 1930s through organizing and playing the ukelele with a band called The Rhythm Maniacs, through dancing as a professional at the Cricklewood Palais,

and by impersonating well-known singers on the cabaret circuit. In World War II he served in the army, rising to the rank of sergeant. His success in ENSA, the Forces Entertainment wing, ensured that, like many of his colleagues, he then went on to the London stage. His popularity with British audiences was consolidated by radio work and by his own television show, *How Do You View?*, in 1951.

It is for his film appearances that Terry-Thomas will be remembered, as new generations, seeing his work reshown on television, relish his improbably plummy drawl, and his inevitable catch-phrases. As Major Hitchcock in the Boulting brothers' *Private's Progress*, he described his troops, memorably, as "a shower! An absolute *shower!*" Similarly, the lecherous charm underlying the apparently innocent enquiry, "How do you do?" delighted audiences then and now. Yet his film work in the late 1950s, from his pseudointellectual in *Lucky Jim* to his crooked personnel manager in *I'm All Right, Jack*, and from his bumbling diplomat in *Carleton-Browne of the F.O.* to the hilariously bumptious cad in *School for Scoundrels*, showed Terry-Thomas carrying off subtly different, yet similarly priceless studies of fraudulent Englishmen, with a talent whose depth was perhaps never fully tapped.

By 1960, he was a genuine star, if only as a cameo performer, and inevitably Hollywood beckoned. By happy coincidence, a shift in English culture was occurring which threatened to make his brand of humour an anachronism. Some excellent work (opposite Jack Lemmon

Terry-Thomas (right) in *Private's Progress*

in *How to Murder Your Wife*, for example), was almost overshadowed by a series of cameo roles in less-than-challenging, though financially rewarding, projects. Struck by the amount of money available merely for reproducing what Americans saw as an archetypal Britisher on film, Terry-Thomas was able to finance an extravagant lifestyle without ever extending or developing his considerable comic talents. Although he was never less than watchable, the projects became more obscure and his career waned.

His unusual name was the result of several experiments. Disliking his given name, Tom Stevens, he decided to spell it backwards. But Mot Snevets gave way to Thomas Terry, until confusion with the Terry acting family prompted the adoption of Terry Thomas. The subsequent hyphen, he would often point out, matched the trademark gap between his front teeth. Later, he was delighted when his name was adopted by the field of orthopedic surgery, to describe the gap produced by a disruption of the ligaments in the carpal bones of the wrist.

In the mid-1970s he was diagnosed as having Parkinson's disease, and spent the later years of his life struggling to pay for medical treatment. In the late 1980s, a picture in the British press, showing this once immaculately turned out bon vivant huddled in a blanket, almost unrecognizable and all too clearly stricken by his illness, prompted a charity show from fellow British entertainers. It is to be hoped that he was, at the last, aware of the tremendous affection in which he was held.

—Nicholas Thomas

THOMPSON, Emma

Nationality: British. **Born:** London, England, 15 April 1959; daughter of the stage and TV director Eric Thompson and the actress Phyllida Law; sister of the actress Sophie Thompson. **Family:** Married the actor Kenneth Branagh, 1989 (separated 1995). **Education:** Studied English literature at Cambridge University. **Career:** Late 1970s—began acting while at Cambridge with the comedy troupe Footlights, and wrote and performed in an all-woman program of comedy routines; 1980s—performed as a stand-up comic, then worked on the stage and in British TV; 1987—appeared on the BBC miniseries *Tutti Frutti* and *Fortunes of War*; 1988—created her own six-part TV comedy series, *Thompson*, co-starring her sister and mother; 1988—began performing with Kenneth Branagh's Renaissance Theatre Company; 1989—first appeared on-screen with Branagh in *Henry V*; 1995—became member of board of advisers, FAHRENHEIT Theatre Company, Cincinnati, Ohio. **Awards:** Variety Club Newcomer of the Year, 1987; British Academy Award, Best Actress, for *Tutti Frutti* and *Fortunes of War*, 1987; Best Actress, New York Film Critics Circle, Best Actress, Los Angeles Film Critics Association, Best Actress, National Board of Review, and Academy Award, Best Actress, for *Howards End*, 1992; Golden Globe Award and Academy Award, Best Adapted Screenplay, for *Sense and Sensibility*, 1995. **Agents:** Lorraine Hamilton Management, 19 Denmark Street, London WC2H 8NA, England; and William Morris, 151 El Camino Drive, Beverly Hills, CA 90212, U.S.A.

Emma Thompson (left) with Helena Bonham-Carter in *Howards End*

Films as Actress:

1988 *The Winslow Boy* (for TV) (as Catherine)
1989 *The Tall Guy* (Mel Smith) (as Kate Lemon); *Henry V* (Branagh) (as Katherine of France); *Look Back in Anger* (Dench—for TV) (as Alison Porter)
1991 *Impromptu* (Lapine) (as Duchesse d'Antan); *Dead Again* (Branagh) (as Grace/Margaret Strauss)
1992 *Howards End* (Ivory) (as Margaret Schlegel); *Peter's Friends* (Branagh) (as Maggie)
1993 *Much Ado about Nothing* (Branagh) (as Beatrice); *The Remains of the Day* (Ivory) (as Miss Kenton); *In the Name of the Father* (Sheridan) (as Gareth Peirce)
1994 *My Father, the Hero* (*Daddy Cool*) (Miner) (unbilled cameo as Isabelle); *Junior* (Reitman) (as Dr. Diana Reddin); *The Blue Boy* (Murton—for TV) (as Marie)
1995 *Carrington* (Hampton) (as Dora Carrington); *Sense and Sensibility* (Ang Lee) (as Elinor Dashwood, + sc)
1996 *The Well of Loneliness*

Publications

By THOMPSON: book—

The Sense and Sensibility *Diaries and Screenplay: The Making of the Film Based on the Jane Austen Novel*, New York, 1995.

By THOMPSON: articles—

Interview with Rachel Abramowitz, in *Premiere* (New York), April 1992.
"Inheriting the Crown," interview with Jack Kroll, in *Newsweek* (New York), 4 January 1993.
Interview with Caryn James, in *New York Times*, 28 March 1993.
"Emma's a Gem," interview with Richard Corliss, in *Time* (New York), 29 March 1993.
Interview with Robbie Coltrane, in *Interview* (New York), May 1993.

On THOMPSON: book—

Shuttleworth, Ian, *Ken & Em: A Biography of Kenneth Branagh and Emma Thompson*, New York, 1995.

On THOMPSON: articles—

Jameson, Richard, "The 1989 Movie Revue, II: New Faces of '89," in *Film Comment* (New York), January 1990.
Miller, Russell, "Emma Thompson's Family Business," in *New York Times Magazine*, 28 March 1993.
Goodman, Mark, and Sue Carswell, "Much Ado about Emma," in *People Weekly* (New York), 17 May 1993.
"Emma Thompson: A Close Reading," in *New Yorker*, 15 November 1993.
Current Biography 1995, New York, 1995.
Sessums, Keven, "Never Look Back," in *Vanity Fair* (New York), February 1996.
"Emma Thompson," in *Film Review* (London), March 1996.

*　　*　　*

Emma Thompson's versatility seems boundless. With roots in the British theater and an early inclination towards comedy, she also has a gift for developing full-blooded period characters and has performed adroitly in Shakespearean parts, as well. Her acting education began during childhood as the daughter of television and stage director Eric Thompson and actress Phyllida Law. She studied English literature at Cambridge University, where she performed with a troupe called Footlights, which specialized in comedy. After graduation, she appeared as a stand-up comic and did television work before obtaining a starring role in the hit musical comedy revival *Me and My Girl*. So it is appropriate for Thompson's screen debut to have come in a comedy. She co-starred in *The Tall Guy*, an underrated farce in which she is the love interest of an American actor in London (Jeff Goldblum) who finds himself cast in a musical version of *The Elephant Man* (which, when you think about it, is as silly a vehicle for song and dance as *Les Misérables*).

While working on *Fortunes of War* for the BBC, she met actor-director Kenneth Branagh, who cast her as Katherine of France in his screen version of *Henry V*. They married shortly after the release of *Henry V*, and Branagh cast her in several very different roles in three of his subsequent films. In *Dead Again*, she gives a bravura performance in the dual role of a dazed woman tormented by memories of another woman's murder, and a concert pianist (in flashbacks to the 1940s). In the ensemble film *Peter's Friends*, Thompson has the plum role of Maggie, a spinsterish flake who leaves photos around her apartment so her cat will not forget her. She brings a guileless quality to the role, making it one of the film's stand-out performances. Finally, in *Much Ado about Nothing*, she stars as Beatrice to Branagh's Benedick. As the real-life husband wife team traded sex-based jibes in the Bard's poetic format, they brought an energy to the film that touched a broad-based audience. In 1995, Thompson and Branagh announced they were separating, probably putting an end to a dynamic professional partnership.

It was *Howards End*, not a Branagh project, that propelled Thompson into the upper ranks of screen personalities. She won an Academy Award for her work in this Merchant-Ivory production of an E. M. Forster tale of the social classes in 1910 England. Thompson portrays a self-reliant woman of no economic means who marries a prosperous man (Anthony Hopkins) whose pleasant veneer hides a heartless nature. Thompson and Hopkins are brilliant together, with both characters storing wells of emotion under the constraints of Edwardian British custom.

She was splendidly reteamed with Hopkins in another Merchant-Ivory film, *The Remains of the Day*, set between the two World Wars. Thompson is cast as Miss Kenton, the new housekeeper in the castle of a British lord. Miss Kenton just might be a potential romantic partner to the world's most perfect servant: Stevens (Hopkins), a reserved British butler who is single-mindedly dedicated to his employer. *The Remains of the Day* essentially is a character study of Stevens, who is steadfastly absorbed in his professional role to the exclusion of all else. Thompson brings intelligence and intensity to a role which might have been little more than a plain-Jane housekeeper in another actress's hands. Her layered interpretation of Miss Kenton helps to give dimension to Stevens's character and brings the film to a disturbing and extraordinary ending.

After earning more critical acclaim as a lawyer defending an accused IRA bomber (Daniel Day Lewis) in the U.S.-Irish production *In the Name of the Father*, Thompson surprised moviegoers who only were familiar with her Shakespearean and somber characterizations. Sharing the screen with "pregnant" Arnold Schwarzenegger, Thompson garnered laughs as an eminent British cryogenicist in the Hollywood farce *Junior*. In good spirited fun, she was given an opportunity to spoof the prim image she has gained during her screen career.

She returned to period filmmaking in *Carrington*, a film with lofty ambitions that is more interesting for what it attempts than what it achieves. It is a based-on-fact story, set in the early twentieth century, that charts the evolution of the deep love between a homosexual British writer, Lytton Strachey (Jonathan Pryce), and a little-known painter, Dora Carrington (Thompson). This is fascinating material, but the film often is too slow-moving and unevenly paced. Still, Thompson (along with Pryce) offers an effectively subtle performance.

During her relatively brief film career, Thompson has proven her ability to play all sorts of roles. She can take a character from the pages of literature and make that personality live on-screen, or she can breathe life into broad comedy parts. She has shown audiences many of her talents in just six years.

—Audrey E. Kupferberg

THE THREE STOOGES

SHEMP HOWARD. Nationality: American. **Born:** Samuel Horwitz in Brooklyn, New York, 17 March 1895. **Family:** Married Gertrude Frank, 1925, one son. **Military Service:** U.S. Army during World War I. **Career:** Worked as comic in vaudeville; 1922—worked with Ted Healy; 1938-49—made a number of solo films. **Died:** 23 November 1955.

MOE HOWARD. Nationality: American. **Born:** Moses Horwitz in Bensonhurst, New York, 19 June 1897. **Family:** Married Helen Schonberger, 1925, two children. **Career:** In show business from age 12: ran errands at Vitagraph studios; worked in various comic and singing acts with Ted Healy. **Died:** 4 May 1975.

LARRY FINE. Nationality: American. **Born:** Louis Feinberg in Philadelphia, Pennsylvania, 5 October 1902. **Family:** Married Mabel Haney (died 1967), two children. **Died:** 24 January 1975.

CURLY HORWITZ. Nationality: American. **Born:** Jerome Lester Horwitz in Brooklyn, New York, 22 October 1903. **Family:** Married 1) unknown marriage (annulled); 2) Elaine Ackerman, 1937 (divorced 1940), one daughter; 3) Marion Buxbaum, 1945 (divorced 1946); 4) Valerie Neman, 1947, one daughter. **Died:** 18 January 1952.

Moe, Larry, and Shemp teamed with Ted Healy in mid-1920s for early Stooges act; 1930—film debut in *Soup to Nuts*; 1932—Shemp replaced by Curly in the act, and Healy dropped: long series of shorts and features, for MGM, 1933, and Columbia, 1934-57; 1946—Curly retired from the act for health reasons, and was replaced by Shemp; 1955—Joe Besser joined the act after Shemp's death; 1959—Curly Joe DeRita replaced Joe Besser in the act; 1965—made a series of five-minute TV cartoons.

Films as Actors (all shorts unless noted):

(Larry, Moe, Shemp, and Ted Healy)

1930   *Soup to Nuts* (Stoloff—feature)
1933   *Turn Back the Clock* (Selwyn—feature); *Meet the Baron* (Walter Lang—feature); *Dancing Lady* (Leonard—feature); *Beer and Pretzels* (Cummings), *Hello Pop* (Cummings); *Plane Nuts* (Cummings); *Myrt and Marge* (*Laughter in the Air*) (Boasberg—feature) (as Mullins's helpers); *Nertsery Rhymes* (Cummings); *Hollywood on Parade*; *Screen Snapshots* (Staub)
1934   *Fugitive Lovers* (Boleslawski—feature); *Hollywood Party* (Boleslawski, Dwan, and Rowland—feature); *The Big Idea* (Crowley)

(Larry, Moe, and Curly)

1934   *Woman Haters* (Gottler); *Punch Drunk* (Breslow); *Men in Black* (McCarey); *Three Little Pigskins* (McCarey); *The Captain Hates the Sea* (Milestone—feature); *Crazy People* (Hiscott—feature)
1935   *Screen Snapshots Number Six* (Staub); *Horses Collars* (Buckman); *Restless Knights* (Lamont); *Pop Goes the Easel* (Del Lord); *Uncivil Warriors* (Del Lord); *Pardon My Scotch* (Del Lord); *Hoi Polloi* (Del Lord); *Three Little Beers* (Del Lord)
1936   *Ants in the Pantry* (Black); *Movie Maniacs* (Del Lord); *Half-shot Shooters* (Black); *Disorder in the Court* (Black); *A Pain in the Pullman* (Black); *False Alarms* (Del Lord); *Whoops I'm an Indian* (Del Lord); *Slippery Silks* (Black)
1937   *Grips, Grunts, and Groans* (Black); *Dizzy Doctors* (Del Lord); *Three Dumb Clucks* (Del Lord); *Back to the Woods* (Black); *Goofs and Saddles* (Del Lord); *Cash and Carry* (Del Lord); *Playing the Ponies* (Lamont); *The Sitter-Downers* (Del Lord); *Start Cheering* (Rogell—feature)
1938   *Termites of 1938* (Del Lord); *Wee Wee Monsieur* (Del Lord); *Tassels in the Air* (Chase); *Flat Foot Stooges* (Chase); *Healthy, Wealthy, and Dumb* (Del Lord); *Violent Is the Word for Curly* (Chase); *Three Missing Links* (White); *Mutts to You* (Chase)
1939   *Screen Snapshots Number Nine* (Staub); *Three Little Sew and Sews* (Del Lord); *We Want Our Mummy* (Del Lord); *A-Ducking They Did Go* (Del Lord); *Yes, We Have No Bonanza* (Del Lord); *Saved by the Belle* (Chase); *Calling All Curs* (White); *Oily to Bed, Oily to Rise* (White); *Three Sappy People* (White)
1940   *You Nazty Spy* (White); *Rockin' through the Rockies* (White); *A-Plumbing We Will Go* (Del Lord); *Nutty but Nice* (White); *How High Is Up?* (Del Lord); *From Nurse to Worse* (White); *No Census, No Feelings* (White); *Cockoo Cavaliers* (White); *Boobs in Arms* (White)
1941   *So Long, Mr. Chumps* (White); *Dutiful but Dumb* (Del Lord); *All the World's a Stooge* (Del Lord); *I'll Never Heil Again* (White); *Time Out for Rhythm* (Salkow—feature); *An Ache in Every Stake* (Del Lord); *In the Sweet Pie and Pie* (White); *Some More of Samoa* (Del Lord)
1942   *Loco Boy Makes Good* (White); *Cactus Makes Perfect* (Del Lord); *What's the Matador?* (White); *Matri-Phony* (Edwards); *Three Smart Saps* (White); *Even as I.O.U.* (Del Lord); *My Sister Eileen* (Hall—feature) (as workmen); *Sock-a-Bye Baby* (White)
1943   *The Stooge to Conga* (Del Lord); *Dizzy Detectives* (White); *Back from the Front* (White); *Spook Louder* (Del Lord); *Three Little Twerps* (Edwards); *Higher Than a Kite* (Del Lord); *I Can Hardly Wait* (White); *Dizzy Pilots* (White); *Phony Express* (Del Lord); *A Gem of a Jam* (Del Lord)
1944   *Crash Goes the Hash* (White); *Busy Buddies* (Del Lord); *The Yoke's on Me* (White); *Idle Roomers* (Del Lord); *Gents without Cents* (White); *No Dough, Boys* (White)
1945   *Three Pests in a Mess* (Del Lord); *Booby Dupes* (Del Lord); *Idiots Deluxe* (White); *Rockin' in the Rockies* (Keays—feature); *If a Body Meets a Body* (White); *Micro-Phonies* (Bernds)
1946   *Beer Barrel Polecats* (White); *Swing Parade of 1946* (Karlson—feature); *A Bird in the Head* (Bernds); *Uncivil Warbirds* (White); *Three Troubledoers* (Bernds); *Monkey Businessmen* (Bernds); *Three Loan Wolves* (White); *G.I. Wanna Go Home* (White); *Rhythm and Weep* (White); *Three Little Pirates* (Bernds)
1947   *Half-Wit's Holiday* (White)

The Three Stooges

(Larry, Moe, Curly, and Shemp)

1947   *Hold That Lion* (White)
1986   *Stoogemania* (Workman)

(Larry, Moe, and Shemp)

1947   *Fright Night* (Bernds); *Out West* (Bernds); *Brideless Grooms* (Bernds); *Sing a Song of Six Pants* (White); *All Gummed Up* (White)
1948   *Shivering Sherlocks* (Del Lord); *Pardon My Clutch* (Bernds); *Squareheads of the Round Table* (Bernds); *Fiddlers Three* (White); *Hot Scots* (Bernds); *Heavenly Daze* (White); *I'm a Monkey's Uncle* (White); *Mummy's Dummies* (Bernds); *Crime on Their Hands* (Bernds)
1949   *The Ghost Talks* (White); *Who Done It?* (Bernds); *Hocus Pocus* (White); *Fuelin' Around* (Bernds); *Malice in the Palace* (White); *Vagabond Loafers* (Bernds); *Dunked in the Deep* (White)
1950   *Punchy Cowpunchers* (Bernds); *Hugs and Mugs* (White); *Dopey Dicks* (Bernds); *Love at First Bite* (White); *Self-Made Maids* (McCollum); *Three Hams on Rye* (White); *Studio Stoops* (White); *Slap-Happy Sleuths* (McCollum); *A Snitch in Time* (White)
1951   *Three Arabian Nuts* (Bernds); *Baby Sitters' Jitters* (White); *Don't Throw That Knife* (White); *Scrambled Brains* (White); *Merry Mavericks* (Bernds); *The Tooth Will Out* (Bernds); *Gold Raiders* (Bernds—feature); *Hula La La* (McCollum); *The Pest Man Wins* (White)
1952   *A Missed Fortune* (White); *Listen, Judge* (Bernds); *Corny Casanovas* (White); *He Cooked His Goose* (White); *Gents in a Jam* (Bernds); *Three Dark Horses* (White); *Cuckoo in a Choo Choo* (White)
1953   *Up in Daisy's Penthouse* (White); *Booty and the Beast* (White); *Loose Loot* (White); *Tricky Dicks* (White); *Spooks* (White); *Pardon My Backfire* (White); *Rip, Sew, and Stitch* (White); *Bubble Trouble* (White); *Goof on the Roof* (White)
1954   *Income Tax Sappy* (White); *Musty Musketeers* (White); *Pals and Gals* (White); *Knutzy Knights* (White); *Shot in the Frontier* (White); *Scotched in Scotland* (White)
1955   *Fling in the Ring* (White); *Of Cash and Hash* (White); *Gypped in the Penthouse* (White); *Bedlam in Paradise* (White); *Stone Age Romeos* (White); *Wham Bam Slam* (White); *Hot Ice* (White); *Blunder Boys* (White)
1956   *Husbands Beware* (White); *Creeps* (White); *Flagpole Jitters* (White); *For Crimin' Out Loud* (White); *Rumpus in the Harem* (White); *Hot Stuff* (White); *Scheming Schemers* (White); *Commotion on the Ocean* (White)

(Larry, Moe, and Joe Besser)

1957   *Hoofs and Goofs* (White); *Muscle Up a Little Closer* (White); *A Merry Mix-Up* (White); *Space Ship Sappy* (White); *Guns A-Poppin'* (White); *Horsing Around* (White); *Rusty Romeos* (White); *Outer Space Jitters* (White)

1958   *Quiz Whiz* (White); *Fifi Blows Her Top* (White); *Pies and Guys* (White); *Flying Saucer Daffy* (White); *Oil's Well That Ends Well* (White); *Triple Crossed* (White); *Sappy Bullfighters* (White); *Sweet and Hot* (White)

(Larry, Moe, and Curly Joe DeRita)

1959   *Have Rocket, Will Travel* (Lowell—feature)
1960   *Three Stooges Scrapbook* (Maurer—feature)
1961   *Snow White and the Three Stooges* (*Snow White and the Three Clowns*) (Walter Lang—feature)
1962   *The Three Stooges Meet Hercules* (Bernds—feature); *The Three Stooges in Orbit* (Bernds—feature)
1963   *The Three Stooges Go around the World in a Daze* (Maurer—feature); *It's a Mad, Mad, Mad, Mad World* (Kramer—feature) (as firemen); *Four for Texas* (Aldrich—feature)
1965   *The Outlaws IS Coming!* (*Three Stooges Meet the Gunslinger*) (Maurer—feature)
1968   *Star Spangled Salesman* (Maurer—feature)

Films of Moe Howard (features):

1958   *Space Master X-7* (*Mutiny in Outer Space*) (Bernds) (as cab driver)
1959   *Senior Prom* (Rich)
1966   *Don't Worry, We'll Think of a Title* (Harmon Jones) (as Mr. Raines)
1973   *Doctor Death: Seeker of Souls* (Saeta) (as volunteer)

Films of Shemp Howard (features unless noted):

1934-7 as Knobby Walsh in *Joe Palooka* shorts for Vitaphone
1935   *Convention Girl* (Luther Reed) (as Dan)
1937   *Headin' East* (Ewing Scott) (as Windy)
1938   *Hollywood Roundup* (Ewing Scott) (as Oscar)
1939   *Another Thin Man* (Van Dyke) (as Wacky)
1940   *Millionaires in Prison* (Ray McCarey) (as Professor); *The Leather-Pushers* (Rawlins) (as sailor); *Give Us Wings* (Lamont) (Whitey); *The Bank Dick* (*The Bank Detective*) (Cline) (Joe Guelpe); *Murder over New York* (Lachman) (as Fakir)
1941   *Meet the Chump* (Cline) (as Stinky Fink); *Buck Privates* (*Rookies*) (Lubin) (as Chef); *The Invisible Woman* (A. Edward Sutherland) (as Frankie); *Six Lessons from Madame La Zonga* (Rawlins) (as Gabby); *Mr. Dynamite* (Rawlins) (as Abdullah); *In the Navy* (*Abbott and Costello in the Navy*) (Lubin) (as Dizzy); *Tight Shoes* (Rogell) (as Okay); *San Antonio Rose* (Lamont) (as Benny the Bounce); *Hold That Ghost* (*Oh, Charlie*) (Lubin) (as soda jerk); *Hit the Road* (Joe May) (as Dingbat); *Too Many Blondes* (Freeland) (as hotel manager); *Hellzapoppin'* (Potter) (as Louie); *The Flame of New Orleans* (Clair) (as waiter); *Cracked Nuts* (Cline) (as Robot)
1942   *The Strange Case of Dr. Rx* (Nigh) (as Sgt. Sweeney); *Butch Minds the Baby* (Rogell) (as Squinty Sweeney); *Mississippi Gambler* (Maté) (as Milton Davis); *Private Buckaroo* (Cline) (as Sgt. "Muggsy" Shavel); *Pittsburgh* (Seiler) (as Shorty); *Arabian Nights* (Rawlins) (as Sinbad); *Who Done It?* (Kenton) (as Goof)
1943   *Keep 'em Slugging* (Cabanne) (as Binky); *It Ain't Hay* (*Money for Jam*) (Kenton) (as Umbrella Sam); *How's About It?* (Fenton) (as Alf); *Strictly in the Groove* (Keays) (as Pops); *Crazy House* (Cline) (as Mumbo)

1944   *Moonlight and Cactus* (Cline) (as Punchy); *Strange Affair* (Alfred E. Green) (as laundry truck driver); *Three of a Kind* (Lederman); *Crazy Knights* (*Ghost Crazy*) (Beaudine)
1946   *Blondie Knows Best* (Berlin) (as Jim Gray); *Dangerous Business* (Lederman); *The Gentleman Misbehaves* (Sherman); *One Exciting Week* (Beaudine) (as Marvin)
1949   *Africa Screams* (Barton) (as Gunner)

Publications

By THE THREE STOOGES: books—

Howard, Moe, *Moe Howard and the Three Stooges*, Secaucus, New Jersey, 1977.
Besser, Joe, with Jeff and Greg Lenburg, *Not Just a Stooge*, Orange, California, 1984.
The Three Stooges Book of Scripts, edited by Joan Howard Maurer, Secaucus, New Jersey, 1984.
The Three Stooges Book of Scripts, Volume 2, edited by Joan Howard Maurer and Norman Maurer, Secaucus, New Jersey, 1987.

On THE THREE STOOGES: books—

Forrester, Jeffrey, *The Stoogephile Trivia Book*, Chicago, 1982.
Lenburg, Jeff, Joan Howard Maurer, and Greg Lenburg, *The Three Stooges Scrapbook*, Secaucus, New Jersey, 1982.
Feinberg, Morris ("Moe"), *My Brother Larry: The Stooge in the Middle*, San Francisco, 1984.
Hansen, Tom, with Jeffrey Forrester, *Stoogemania*, Chicago, 1984.
Maurer, Joan Howard, *Curly: An Illustrated Biography of the Superstooge*, Secaucus, New Jersey, 1985.
Flanagan, Bill, *Last of the Moe Haircuts*, Chicago, 1986.
Scordato, Mark, *The Three Stooges*, New York, 1995.

On THE THREE STOOGES: articles—

Bowles, S. E., "The Three Stooges: A Brief Pathology," in *Films in Review* (New York), August/September 1975.
"Re-Stooges," in *American Film* (Washington, D.C.), July/August 1982.
Everson, William K., "Souls of Wit: The Short Films of the Three Stooges," in *Video Movies* (Skokie, Illinois), May 1984.
Neibaur, J., "Interview with Emil Nitka," in *Films in Review* (New York), June/July 1990.

*   *   *

The quality of the comedy films created by the Three Stooges will always be an arguable controversy because critics and fans of the group will never agree on what is good taste. If the talents of this comedy team are compared with other teams—Laurel and Hardy, the Marx Brothers, or even Wheeler and Woolsey and the Ritz Brothers—the ability to create a wide range of humor will balance out in favor of these other groups. Fans will, of course, not care—they like the simple, unpretentious directness of Three Stooges comedy. Over three decades the team created almost 200 shorts, appeared in or starred in some 20 features, and evidently lasted longer than any other team of comedians. In the popular cinema Moe, Larry, and Curly have made a contribution that cannot be dismissed.

The Three Stooges are actually a latter-day version of the wacky slapstick tradition developed by Mack Sennett in the 1920s—a type of unsophisticated comedy that springs from the verbal and physical altercations of circus clowns and vaudeville comedians. All of the kings of silent and sound screen comedy—Charles Chaplin, Harold Lloyd, Buster Keaton, Harry Langdon, W. C. Fields, Laurel and Hardy, and the Marx Brothers—used many scenes with physical abuse (slapstick) and verbal invective. If the Three Stooges can be faulted for the use of such material, it lies mostly in the thin motivation for face slapping and eye poking. A minor disagreement in their films causes Moe to slap Curly or Larry and an exchange of blows develops that seems unnecessary or even silly. Such exchanges, however, are well divorced from reality. As fans know, these are childlike men who will soon be working as a trio to solve, in a bungling way, the problem that confronts them.

Many of the shorts created by the Three Stooges show the basic materials used by other comedians in the 1920s and 1930s. To create a basic situation that was different, the group would take up a variety of occupations: they were waiters, plumbers, salesmen, detectives, soldiers, physicians, and businessmen. And in any of these endeavors, they would botch up the job. Moe, Larry, and Curly also had a relationship that was similar to that used by other comedy teams. Moe Howard, the most durable Stooge over the years, was a leader of sorts—a lowbrow version of Groucho Marx. He also believed he knew more than the others in much the same way Oliver Hardy thought he knew more than Stan Laurel, but Moe had about the same brain power as his comrades. Larry and Curly sometimes served as foils for Moe; they were not merely detractors, they were threats to his assumed leadership. In this sense they worked on a rudimentary level as Chico and Harpo did in their relationship with Groucho. While these relationships are not as clear-cut and consistent as those that existed in the major comedy teams, they indicate the Three Stooges were working on common ground in a way that would appeal to less sophisticated audiences.

While the revival of interest in the Three Stooges was prompted by the 1958 release of many of their shorts to television, it should be realized that theatrical releases of the group's shorts lasted into the late 1950s, ten years after most two-reel comedies had faded from the movie program. The immediate success of the television releases did promote one of their first features in years, the 1959 *Have Rocket, Will Travel*. The features that followed in the 1960s, such as *The Three Stooges Meet Hercules* and *The Three Stooges in Orbit*, were starring vehicles, whereas the features of the 1930s and 1940s were light comedies and musicals that used the group as a minor part in the total films.

The box-office success of the Three Stooges probably assisted in a revival of interest in slapstick comedy such as the high-budget features *It's a Mad, Mad, Mad, Mad World* (1963), *The Great Race* (1965), and *Those Magnificent Men in Their Flying Machines* (1965).

Many of the works of the Marx Brothers, W. C. Fields, Mae West, Laurel and Hardy, and the silent films of Charles Chaplin, Harold Lloyd, and Buster Keaton were revived in the 1960s. As humble as the humor of the Three Stooges might be, they obviously had a part in a comedy tradition that refused to die.

—Donald McCaffrey

THULIN, Ingrid

Nationality: Swedish. **Born:** Solleftea, 27 January 1929. **Education:** Studied ballet: then studied at the Royal Dramatic Theater, Stockholm. **Family:** Married 1) Claes Sylwander, 1951; 2) Harry Schein, 1956. **Career:** Stage actress at theaters in Stockholm, Malmö, and other Swedish cities; 1948—film debut in *Känn dej som Hemma*; 1957—first of several films for Ingmar Bergman, *Wild Strawberries*; 1965—first film directed, *Hängivelse*. **Awards:** Best Actress (collectively awarded), Cannes Festival, for *Brink of Life*, 1958; Swedish Golden Bug for Best Actress, for *The Silence*, 1963. **Address:** Kevingestrand 7B, 18231 Danderyd, Sweden.

Films as Actress:

1948 *Känn dej som Hemma* (Holmsen); *Dit Vindarna Bär* (Ohberg)
1949 *Havets Son* (Husberg); *Kärleken segrar* (*Love Will Conquer*) (Molander)
1950 *Hjärter Knekt* (Ekman); *Nar Kärleken kom till byn* (Mattsson)
1951 *Leva pa hoppet* (Gentele) (as Yvonne)
1952 *Möte med Livet* (Werner); *Kalle Karlsson fran Jularbo* (Johansson)
1953 *En Skärgardsnatt* (Logardt); *Goingehovdingen* (Ohberg)
1954 *Två Sköna Juveler* (Huberg); *I Rök och Dans* (Gamlin and Blomgren)
1955 *Hoppsan!* (Olin); *Danssalongen* (Larsson)
1956 *Foreign Intrigue* (Sheldon Reynolds) (as Brita)
1957 *Aldrig i livet* (Ragneborn); ***Smultronstället*** (*Wild Strawberries*) (Bergman) (as Marianne Borg)
1958 *Nära livet* (*Brink of Life*; *So Close to Life*) (Bergman) (as Cecilia Ellius); *Ansiktet* (*The Face*; *The Magician*) (Bergman) (as Manda Vogler/Aman)
1960 *Domaren* (Sjöberg)
1962 *The Four Horsemen of the Apocalypse* (Minnelli) (as Marguerite Laurier); *Agostino* (Bolognini) (as the mother)
1963 *Nattvardsgästerna* (*Winter Light*) (Bergman) (as Märta Lundberg); ***Tystnaden*** (*The Silence*) (Bergman) (as Ester); *Sekstet* (*Sextet*) (Hovmand)
1964 *Die Lady* (*Games of Desire*; *Frustration*) (Albin and Berneis) (as Nadine Anderson); *Der Film den Niemand sieht* (Triyandafilidis)
1965 *Return from the Ashes* (J. Lee Thompson) (as Dr. Michele Wolf)
1966 *Nattlek* (*Night Games*) (Zetterling) (as Irene); *La Guerre est finie* (*The War Is Over*; *Krigetar Slut*) (Resnais) (as Marianne)
1967 *Domani non siamo più qui* (Rondi)
1968 *Vargtimmen* (*Hour of the Wolf*) (Bergman) (as Veronica Vogler); *Badarna* (*I, a Virgin*) (Gamlin) (as the cook); *Adelaide* (*Fino a farti male*; *The Depraved*) (Simon) (as Elisabeth Hermann); *Cuore di mamma* (*Mother's Heart*) (Benelli) (as Eloisa)
1969 *Riten* (*The Rite*; *The Ritual*) (Bergman—for TV) (as Thea Winkelmann); ***La caduta degli dei*** (*The Damned*) (Visconti) (as Baroness Sophie von Essenbeck); *Un diablo bajo la Almohada* (Forque)
1970 *It Rained All Night the Day I Left* (Gessner)
1971 *N. P.* (*N.P.—The Secret*) (Agosti) (as the wife); *Malastrana* (*Corta notte delle bambole di vetro*) (Lado)
1972 ***Viskningar och rop*** (*Cries and Whispers*) (Bergman) (as Karin); *La Sainte famille* (Marchon)
1973 *En handfull kärlek* (*A Handful of Love*) (Sjoman)
1975 *Mose* (*Moses*; *The Lawgiver*) (de Bosio—for TV) (as Miriam); *Monismanien 1995* (*Monismania 1995*) (Fant); *La Cage* (Granier-Deferre) (as Hélène); *Il viaggio nella vertigini* (De Gregorio)
1976 *Salon Kitty* (*Madame Kitty*) (Brass) (title role)
1977 *The Cassandra Crossing* (Cosmatos) (as Elena Stradner)
1983 *Le Corsaire* (Giraldi—for TV)
1984 *Efter Repetitioner* (*After the Rehearsal*) (Bergman) (as Rakel Egerman)
1985 *Freibuter* (Giraldi—for TV)
1987 *Il giorno prima* (*Control*) (Montaldo) (as Mrs. Havemeyer); *Orn*
1988 *La Casa del sorriso* (*House of Smiles*) (Ferreri)
1990 *Faccia di lepre*

Films as Director:

1965 *Hängivelse* (short)

1978   *En och en* (*One and One*) (co-d with Josephson and Nykvist,
          + ro as Ylva)
1982   *Brusten Himmel* (*Broken Sky*)

Publications

By THULIN: book—

Nagon jag kande [Somebody I Knew], Stockholm, 1992.

By THULIN: article—

"Ingrid Thulin Comments on Visconti," in *Dialogue on Film* (Washington, D.C.), no. 3, 1972.

On THULIN: articles—

Sorenson, E., in *Chaplin* (Stockholm), vol. 33, no. 4, 1991.
Aristarco, G., "Due casi esemplari di modello, persona, attrice," in
   Cinema Nuovo (Rome), March/April 1992.

*   *   *

Of all the actresses brought to prominence through the films of
Ingmar Bergman, Ingrid Thulin perhaps best exemplifies the cool,
blond Swedish beauty who combines sensuality and suffering with Nordic intensity. She first worked with Bergman, who was the artistic
director of the Malmö Municipal Theater, after she had trained at the
Royal Dramatic Theater in Stockholm in the late 1940s. In the film
Wild Strawberries, however, playing the sister-in-law, she made her
mark in Swedish cinema and began her long and fruitful career in
Bergman's films. She appeared in a variety of roles in his films from
1958 in *Brink of Life*, for which she received an award at Cannes along
with Bibi Andersson, to 1972 when she starred with Harriet Andersson
and Liv Ullmann in *Cries and Whispers*. Often cast as a mistress
(*Winter Light*, *Hour of the Wolf*, *The Rite*), Thulin capitalized on the
enigmatic quality of her stunning beauty and her tragic face which
conveys a unique combination of pain and pleasure. Her career in
Swedish cinema has not been restricted to the films of Bergman, however,
and she also has been active in the movies of many other Swedish filmmakers—among them Alf Sjöberg and Mai Zetterling. Particularly noteworthy was her appearance in the latter's *Night Games*.

Ingrid Thulin's international career ranks her among the three
great Swedish actresses with Ingrid Bergman and Greta Garbo. While
the films in which she has appeared outside Sweden have made uneven
use of her talents, her performances in Luchino Visconti's *The Damned*
and Alan Resnais's *La Guerre est finie* were marked by brilliance.
Especially memorable, because it so movingly captured her unique
style, was her portrayal of Yves Montand's loving and long-suffering
wife in the Resnais film. She has acted, but not always very effectively,
in a wide variety of other international films—among them a number
of Italian productions, as well as Vincente Minnelli's remake of *The
Four Horsemen of the Apocalypse*. She has directed the short film
Hängivelse and the feature *Brusten Himmel*, and co-directed *One on
One* with Erland Josephson and Sven Nykvist.

—Charles L. P. Silet

THURMAN, Uma

Nationality: American. **Born:** Uma Karuna Thurman in Boston, Massachusetts, 29 April 1970. **Family:** Married the actor Gary Oldman,
1990 (divorced 1992). **Education:** Attended the Professional

Children's School, New York. **Career:** Mid-1980s—began modeling
while in high school; 1987—began screen career at age 17 in independent production *Kiss Daddy Goodnight*; 1988—made first notable
screen appearance in *Dangerous Liaisons*. **Address:** 9057 Nemo Street,
#A, Los Angeles, CA 90069, U.S.A.

Films as Actress:

1987   *Kiss Daddy Goodnight* (Huemer) (as Laura)
1988   *Johnny Be Good* (Bud Smith) (as Georgia Elkans); *Dangerous
          Liaisons* (Frears) (as Cecile de Volanges)
1989   *The Adventures of Baron Munchausen* (Gilliam) (as Venus/Rose)
1990   *Henry & June* (Kaufman) (as June Miller); *Where the Heart Is*
          (Boorman) (as Daphne)
1991   *Robin Hood* (Irvin—for TV) (as Maid Marian)
1992   *Final Analysis* (Joanau) (as Diana Baylor); *Jennifer Eight*
          (Robinson) (as Helena Robertson)
1993   *Mad Dog and Glory* (McNaughton) (as Glory)
1994   *Even Cowgirls Get the Blues* (Van Sant) (as Sissy Hankshaw);
          Pulp Fiction (Tarantino) (as Mia)
1995   *A Month by the Lake* (Irvin) (as Miss Beaumont)
1996   *Beautiful Girls* (Ted Demme) (as Andrea); *The Truth about
          Cats and Dogs* (Michael Lehmann) (as Noelle Slusarsky)

Publications

By THURMAN: articles—

Interview in *Interview* (New York), July 1987.
Interview with I. Sischy and G. Fuller, in *Interview* (New York), Octo-
   ber 1992.
"Numero Uma," interview with Alex Shoumatoff, in *Vanity Fair* (New
   York), January 1996.

On THURMAN: articles—

Schiff, Stephen, "The Seduction Game," in *Vanity Fair* (New York),
   October 1988.
Blau, E., "Uma Thurman, Prospects in *Liaisons* Were Awesome at
   First," in *New York Times*, 30 December 1988.
Schiff, Stephen, "Sense of Uma," in *Vanity Fair* (New York), March 1989.
Bertram, B., "Uma Thurman," in *Premiere* (New York), April 1989.
Yagoda, Ben, "Uma Thurman: Whatever You Do, Don't Ask This
   Brainy Bombshell for Her Phone Number," in *Rolling Stone* (New
   York), 18 May 1989.
Klinger, J., "*Henry and June*," in *American Film* (Hollywood), Septem-
   ber 1990.
Cott, Jonathan, "Drugstore Cowgirl," in *Rolling Stone* (New York), 11
   November 1993.
Kaylin, Lucy, "Uma in Bloom," in *GQ* (New York), February 1995.
Demarchelier, Patrick, "Uma!," in *Harper's Bazaar* (New York), June
   1995.

*   *   *

Uma Thurman is a lanky, thoroughly beguiling leading lady who is
fast becoming one of the most important American actresses of the
1990s. After making her screen debut in an obscure independent film
(*Kiss Daddy Goodnight*) and appearing to little effect in an atrocious
comedy throwaway (*Johnny Be Good*), Thurman proved she was an
actress to be reckoned with in her first important film: Stephen Frears's
savagely witty *Dangerous Liaisons*, made when she was all of 18, in
which she plays the seduced virgin Cecile de Volanges. Thurman more

Uma Thurman (right) with Maria de Medeiros in *Henry & June*

than held her own playing opposite a well-seasoned cast (including John Malkovich, Glenn Close, and Michelle Pfeiffer). Indeed, in her subsequent roles she has specialized in playing defenseless innocents. She was especially good in this capacity in *Jennifer Eight*, in which she has the difficult role of a young blind woman who just may be the next victim of a serial killer. In one scene, as her character is left alone at a noisy party, Thurman's face subtly and effectively expresses just the right amount of fear, confusion, and anxiety.

Her characters ooze vulnerability even when they are sexually experienced. In *Mad Dog and Glory*, her role in essence is that of a gift, presented to a reserved crime scene photographer (Robert De Niro) who has saved the life of a mobster (Bill Murray). While the focus of *Henry & June* is on the erotic relationship between the writers Henry Miller (Fred Ward) and Anais Nin (Maria de Medeiros) in early 1930s Paris, Thurman's June Miller is very much a part of the scenario as she becomes the final link in a three-cornered love affair. In both these films, Thurman is an exhilarating presence, with her characters at once sexually alluring and deeply human. In *Mad Dog and Glory*, she is especially impressive as she interacts with De Niro.

Perhaps Thurman's most disappointing screen appearance came in Gus Van Sant's disastrous *Even Cowgirls Get the Blues*. She plays a young woman named Sissy Hankshaw, who is "somewhat of a medical oddity" in that she was born with abnormally large thumbs. For years, Sissy has been fulfilling her calling by hitchhiking across America. The crux of the story details her experiences as she encounters a band of lesbian-feminist cowgirls-revolutionaries in a western spa-resort. The film was screened to standing-room-only crowds at the 1993 Toronto Film Festival. Van Sant was not happy with audience reaction, so he took his work back to the editing room. Despite his alterations, critics and audiences remained unenthralled.

Fortunately for Thurman, she escaped unscathed. Her follow-up was the most talked-about film of 1994, Quentin Tarantino's *Pulp Fiction*. Here, she exchanges vulnerability for outright kookiness in her role as Mia, the sexy, flaky wife of a crimelord, who spends an eventful evening in the company of hired gun Vincent Vega (John Travolta). Mia is a character straight out of 1940s film noir, and Thurman gives a deliciously watchable performance, full of clever and outrageous mannerisms. As a result, she earned reams of publicity, and a Best Supporting Actress Oscar nomination. And in the far more conventional *A Month by the Lake*, set in a totally different time and place, her performance is almost as equally over-the-top. Here she plays Miss Beaumont, a nanny who flirts with a dapper older man (Edward Fox) in a Lake Como, Italy, resort immediately prior to the start of World War II.

—Rob Edelman

TIERNEY, Gene

Nationality: American. **Born:** Gene Eliza Tierney in Brooklyn, New York, 19 November 1920. **Education:** Attended Chateau Brilliantmont, Switzerland; Miss Porter's School, Farmington, Connecticut.

Family: Married 1) the designer Oleg Cassini, 1941 (divorced 1947; remarried, divorced 1952), two daughters; 2) W. Howard Lee, 1960. **Career:** 1939—Broadway debut in *Mrs. O'Brien Entertains*; 1940—successful role in Broadway play *The Male Animal*; contract with 20th Century-Fox: film debut in *The Return of Frank James*; mid-1950s—voluntarily entered the Institute of Living for depression, and later at the Menninger Clinic; 1960s—made films and appeared on television; 1980—in TV mini-series *Scruples*. **Died:** 6 October 1991.

Films as Actress:

1940   *The Return of Frank James* (Fritz Lang) (as Eleanor Stone); *Hudson's Bay* (Pichel) (as Barbara)

1941   *Tobacco Road* (Ford) (as Ellie May); *Belle Starr* (Cummings) (title role); *Sundown* (Hathaway) (as Zia)

1942   *The Shanghai Gesture* (von Sternberg) (as Poppy Charteris); *Son of Fury* (Cromwell) (as Eve); *Rings on Her Fingers* (Mamoulian) (as Susan Miller/Linda Worthington); *Thunder Birds* (Wellman) (as Kay Saunders); *China Girl* (Hathaway) (as Miss Young)

1943   *Heaven Can Wait* (Lubitsch) (as Martha)

1944   *Laura* (Preminger and Mamoulian) (title role)

1945   *A Bell for Adano* (King) (as Tina); *Leave Her to Heaven* (Stahl) (as Ellen Berent)

1946   *Dragonwyck* (Lubitsch and Mankiewicz) (as Miranda); *The Razor's Edge* (Goulding) (as Isabel Bradley)

1947   *The Ghost and Mrs. Muir* (Mankiewicz) (as Lucy)

1948   *The Iron Curtain* (Wellman) (as Anna Gouzenko); *That Wonderful Urge* (Sinclair) (as Sara Farley)

1949   *Whirlpool* (Preminger) (as Ann Sutton)

1950   *Night and the City* (Dassin) (as Mary Bristol); *Where the Sidewalk Ends* (Preminger) (as Morgan Taylor)

1951   *The Mating Season* (Leisen) (as Maggie Carleton); *On the Riviera* (Walter Lang) (as Lilli); *The Secret of Convict Lake* (Gordon) (as Marcia Stoddard); *Close to My Heart* (Keighley) (as Midge Sheridan)

1952   *Way of a Gaucho* (Tourneur) (as Teresa); *Plymouth Adventure* (Brown) (as Dorothy Bradford)

1953   *Never Let Me Go* (Daves) (as Marya Lamarkina)

1954   *Personal Affair* (Pelissier) (as Kay Barlow); *Black Widow* (Johnson) (as Iris); *The Egyptian* (Curtiz) (as Baketamon)

1955   *The Left Hand of God* (Dmytryk) (as Ann Scott)

1962   *Advise and Consent* (Preminger) (as Dolly Harrison)

Gene Tierney

1963 *Toys in the Attic* (Hill) (as Albertine Prine)
1964 *The Pleasure Seekers* (Negulesco)
1969 *Daughter of the Mind* (Grauman—for TV)

Publications

By TIERNEY: book—

Self-Portrait, with Mickey Herskowitz, New York, 1974.

On TIERNEY: books—

Devillers, Marcel, *Gene Tierney*, Paris, 1987.
Mérigeau, Pascal, *Gene Tierney*, Paris, 1987.

On TIERNEY: articles—

Shields, Jonathan, "Gene Tierney," in *Films in Review* (New York), November 1971.
Modiano, P., "Gene Tierney," in *Lumière du Cinéma* (Paris), February 1977.
Eyquem, O., "Pour saluer Gene Tierney," in *Avant-Scène du Cinéma* (Paris), 1 December 1979.
Legrand, G., in *Positif* (Paris), May 1984.
Mille, A., "Gene Tierney: star à posteriori," in *Positif* (Paris), June 1985.
Obituary in *Variety* (New York), 11 November 1991.
"Haunted Beauty," in *People Weekly*, 25 November 1991.

* * *

Gene Tierney's exquisitely modeled features graced more than 30 feature films over a period of 25 years. As a contract player for Twentieth Century-Fox she was best cast in roles that combined her qualities as a fresh-faced ingenue with elements that hinted at a more enigmatic, possibly sinister exoticism, as in *Laura* or *Leave Her to Heaven*. Tierney seemed least effective when saddled with parts that utilized only one of these traits; unfortunately, this was most often the case. She was fortunate enough to work with the finest directors Fox had under contract: Lang, Ford, Mamoulian, Wellman, Lubitsch, King, Stahl, Mankiewicz. Otto Preminger directed her in four films, including the role with which she is most often identified, *Laura*. In *Laura* Preminger contrasted her persona as an obscure object of desire in an emblematic painting with the radiantly beautiful, yet more conventional woman she proves to be in real life. Earlier, her country slattern in Ford's *Tobacco Road*, South Seas maiden in *Son of Fury*, and corrupted innocent in von Sternberg's *The Shanghai Gesture* (where she was cast as a Eurasian) displayed her more sultry elements, to her disadvantage.

John Stahl's refined melodrama *Leave Her to Heaven* gave Tierney her most complex role and she rose to the occasion, achieving the only Academy Award nomination of her career. As a jealous, possessive woman who destroys anything that comes between her and her husband's attentions, Tierney's placid beauty contrasts with the methodical working out of her psychosis, which involves drowning, miscarriage, and eventual suicide. Though she was touching in *The Ghost and Mrs. Muir* and remarkably warm in *Night and the City*, her subsequent "starring" roles were often in support of the male leads, as in *The Iron Curtain* and *Where the Sidewalk Ends*. Only in Preminger's *Whirlpool* was her masklike calm used to best advantage. Her 1950s and 1960s work is negligible, but she registers as a sympathetic Washington matron in *Advise and Consent*.

—Lee Tsiantis

TOPOL

Nationality: Israeli. **Born:** Chaim Topol in Tel Aviv, 9 September 1935. **Military Service:** With entertainment unit, 1953. **Family:** Married Galia Finkelstein, 1956, one son and two daughters. **Career:** 1956—founder, The Spring Onion satirical theater, and later founder of the Municipal Theatre of Haifa, 1959; in London stage production of the musical *Fiddler on the Roof*, and in film version, 1971; 1983— in TV mini-series *The Winds of War*, *Queenie*, 1987, and *War and Remembrance*, 1988; 1988—in *Ziegfeld*, London. **Address:** c/o Rosenberg, 8428 Melrose Place, Suite C, Los Angeles, CA 90069, U.S.A.

Films as Actor:

1963 *I Like Mike* (Fry); *El Dorado* (Golan) (as Benny Sherman)
1964 *Sallah* (*Sallah Shabati*) (Kishon) (title role)
1966 *Cast a Giant Shadow* (Shavelson) (as Abou Ibn Kader)
1968 *Every Bastard a King* (Zohar)
1969 *Before Winter Comes* (J. Lee Thompson) (as Janovic); *A Talent for Loving* (*Gun Crazy*) (Quine)
1971 *Hatarnegol* (Zohar) (as Gadi); *The Rooster*; *Fiddler on the Roof* (Jewison) (as Tevye); *The Going Up of David Lev* (Collier—for TV)
1972 *Follow Me* (*The Public Eye*) (Reed) (as Julian Christoforou)
1974 *Ervinka* (Kishon) (title role)
1975 *Galileo* (Losey) (title role)
1979 *The House on Garibaldi Street* (Collinson—for TV)
1980 *Flash Gordon* (Hodges) (as Dr. Hans Zarkov)
1981 *For Your Eyes Only* (Glen) (as Columbo)
1985 *Roman Behemshechim* (Kotler) (as Effi Avidor)
1987 *Queenie* (Peerce—for TV) (as Dimitri Goldner)

Publications

By TOPOL: books—

Topol by Topol, London, 1981.
To Life, 1994.

* * *

Born in Tel Aviv, Topol is Israel's most famous actor. He dropped his first name, Chaim, when he discovered in England that it confused the Anglo-Saxons. His amiable and charismatic screen persona has won audience affection around the world. Like many Israeli actors, Topol began his career in an army entertainment troupe (HaNachal) and since then his work on stage and cinema has included not only comic but also more serious roles from Shakespeare and Brecht.

Topol made his first appearance in Israeli film productions—notably Peter Fry's *I Like Mike* and Menachem Golan's *El Dorado*. But it was the success of the satiric comedy *Sallah* (1964), directed by Ephraim Kishon, that made Topol a kind of national hero and established his international reputation. Topol was already familiar as "Sallah" in HaNachal and in the extremely successful revue *Batzal Yarok* (Spring Onion) in the late 1950s. He played with tremendous energy the role of an oriental Jew (Sephardi) who immigrates to Israel only to face ethnic discrimination and bureaucratic inefficiency by the corrupt Ashkenazi-dominated parties. Topol's portrayal of Sallah as contrastingly warm, amiable, and commonsensical indirectly criticizes the Israeli establishment. Topol himself became popular among Israelis through identification with Sallah, the "Mediterranean

Schweik," in Topol's own words. Although a sabra of European background, Topol used accent and gestures convincingly to portray an oriental Jew 20 years older than himself, a feat subsequently repeated in such films as Melville Shavelson's *Cast a Giant Shadow*, where he played the role of an old Arab sheik, and in Norman Jewison's *Fiddler on the Roof*.

Based on a story by the Jewish writer Sholom Aleichem, the musical *Fiddler on the Roof* catapulted Topol into truly international fame. Topol had already played Tevye on stage in Israel as well as in London. He mentions the influence of the Israeli actor Shmuel Rodensky and his admiration for Zero Mostel, who, in Topol's own words, "created the role for all the rest of us." Topol's familiarity with eastern European culture undoubtedly contributed to his authentic depiction of Tevye. He demonstrated a remarkable capacity to synthesize comic and tragic elements into a character who embodies the polarities of the Jewish experience.

Topol's most internationally noteworthy films since *Fiddler* have been Carol Reed's *Public Eye* and Joseph Losey's *Galileo*. In the romantic comedy *Public Eye*, based on Peter Shaffer's play, Topol played a charming private eye hired by a suspicious jealous husband to follow his innocent wife, whom he subsequently falls in love with. In *Galileo* (based on the Brecht play) Topol forcefully portrayed the Italian astronomer and physicist struggling against the Catholic Church. Though Topol's autobiography expresses reservations about Brecht's political positions, it also speaks of fascination with the down-to-earth skepticism of Brechtian characters.

—Ella Shochat

TRACY, Spencer

Nationality: American. **Born:** Milwaukee, Wisconsin, 5 April 1900. **Education:** Attended St. Rosa's Parochial School and West Side High School, Milwaukee; Marquette Academy, Milwaukee; Northwestern Military Academy, Lake Geneva, Wisconsin; Ripon College, Wisconsin, for three semesters; American Academy of Dramatic Arts, New York, graduated 1923. **Family:** Married Louise Treadwell, 1923, son: John, daughter: Susan. **Career:** 1922—stage debut in Theatre Guild's production of *R.U.R.* in New York; on stage in stock in Grand Rapids and Trenton, also in plays on Broadway, including *Yellow*, 1926, *Baby Cyclone*, 1927, and *The Last Mile*, 1930; 1930—feature film debut in *Up the River*; contract with Fox; 1935-55—contract with MGM; 1942—first of a series of films with Katharine Hepburn, *Woman of the Year*; 1945—on Broadway in *The Rugged Path*. **Awards:** Best Actor Academy Award, for *Captains Courageous*, 1937; Best Actor Academy Award for *Boys' Town*, 1938; Best Actor, Cannes Festival, for *Bad Day at Black Rock*, 1955; Best Actor, British Academy, for *Guess Who's Coming to Dinner?*, 1968. **Died:** 10 June 1967.

Films as Actor:

1930 *Taxi Talks* (short) (as a gunman); *The Hard Guy* (Hurley—short) (as World War I veteran); *Up the River* (Ford) (as St. Louis)

1931 *Quick Millions* (Brown) (as "Bugs" Raymond); *Six Cylinder Love* (Freeland) (as William Dontoy); *Goldie* (Stoloff) (as Bill)

1932 *She Wanted a Millionaire* (Blystone) (as William Kelly); *Sky Devils* (Sutherland) (as Wilkie); *Disorderly Conduct* (Considine) (as Dick Fay); *Young America* (Borzage) (as Jack Doray); *Society Girl* (Lanfield) (as Briscoe); *The Painted Woman* (Blystone) (as Tom Brian); *Me and My Gal* (Walsh) (as Don Dolan)

1933 *Twenty Thousand Years in Sing Sing* (Curtiz) (as Tom Connors); *The Face in the Sky* (Lachman) (as Joe Buck); *The Power and the Glory* (William K. Howard) (as Tom Garner); *Shanghai Madness* (Blystone) (as Pat Jackson); *The Mad Game* (Cummings) (as Edward Carson); *Man's Castle* (Borzage) (as Bill)

1934 *The Show-Off* (Riesner) (as Aubrey Piper); *Bottoms Up* (Butler) (as Smoothie King); *Looking for Trouble* (Wellman) (as Joe Graham); *Now I'll Tell* (Burke) (as Murray Golden); *Marie Galante* (Henry King) (as Crawbett)

1935 *It's a Small World* (Cummings) (as Bill Shevlin); *Dante's Inferno* (Lachman) (as Jim Carter); *The Murder Man* (Whelan) (as Steve Gray); *Whipsaw* (Wood) (as Ross McBride)

1936 *Riffraff* (Leonard) (as Dutch); **Fury** (Fritz Lang) (as Joe Wheeler); *San Francisco* (Van Dyke) (as Father Mullin); *Libeled Lady* (Conway) (as Haggerty)

1937 *They Gave Him a Gun* (Van Dyke) (as Fred); *Captains Courageous* (Fleming) (as Manuel); *The Big City* (Borzage) (as Joe)

1938 *Mannequin* (Borzage) (as John L. Hennessey); *Test Pilot* (Fleming) (as Gunner Sloane); *Boys' Town* (Taurog) (as Father Flanagan)

1939 *Stanley and Livingston* (Henry King) (as Henry Stanley)

1940 *I Take This Woman* (Van Dyke) (as Karl Decker); *Northwest Passage* (King Vidor) (as Major Rogers); *Edison, the Man* (Brown) (title role); *Boom Town* (Conway) (as Square John Sand)

1941 *Men of Boys' Town* (Taurog) (as Father Flanagan); *Dr. Jekyll and Mr. Hyde* (Fleming) (title role)

1942 *Ring of Steel* (Kanin—short) (as narrator); *Woman of the Year* (Stevens) (as Sam Craig); *Tortilla Flat* (Fleming) (as Pilon)

1943 *Keeper of the Flame* (Cukor) (as Steven O'Malley); *A Guy Named Joe* (Fleming) (as Pete Sandidge)

1944 *Battle Stations* (Kanin—short) (as narrator); *The Seventh Cross* (Zinnemann) (as George Heisler); *Thirty Seconds over Tokyo* (LeRoy) (as Lt. Col. James Doolittle)

1945 *Without Love* (Bucquet) (as Pat Jamieson)

1947 *The Sea of Grass* (Kazan) (as Jim Brewton); *Cass Timberlane* (Sidney) (title role)

1948 *State of the Union* (Capra) (as Grant Matthews)

1949 *Edward, My Son* (Cukor) (as Arnold Boult); **Adam's Rib** (Cukor) (as Adam Bonner)

1950 *Malaya* (Thorpe) (as Carnahan); *Father of the Bride* (Minnelli) (as Stanley Banks)

1951 *Father's Little Dividend* (Minnelli) (as Stanley Banks); *The People against O'Hara* (John Sturges) (as James Curtayne)

1952 *Pat and Mike* (Cukor) (as Mike Conovan); *The Plymouth Adventure* (Brown) (as Captain Christopher Jones)

1953 *The Actress* (Cukor) (as Clinton Jones)

1954 *Broken Lance* (Dmytryk) (as Matt Deveraux); *Bad Day at Black Rock* (John Sturges) (as John McReedy)

1956 *The Mountain* (Dmytryk) (as Zachary Teller)

1957 *The Desk Set* (Walter Lang) (as Richard)

1958 *The Old Man and the Sea* (John Sturges) (title role); *The Last Hurrah* (Ford) (as Frank Skeffington)

1960 *Inherit the Wind* (Kramer) (as Henry Drummond)

1961 *The Devil at Four O'Clock* (LeRoy) (as Father Matthew Doonan); *Judgment at Nuremberg* (Kramer) (as Judge Dan Haywood)

1963 *How the West Was Won* (Hathaway, Ford, and Marshall) (as narrator); *It's a Mad, Mad, Mad, Mad World* (Kramer) (as Captain C. G. Culpeper)

1967 *Guess Who's Coming to Dinner?* (Kramer) (as Matt Drayton)

Spencer Tracy with Katharine Hepburn

Publications

By TRACY: article—

Interview in *Film Weekly* (London), 29 August 1936.

On TRACY: books—

Newquist, Roy, *A Special Kind of Magic*, New York, 1967.
Deschner, Donald, *The Films of Spencer Tracy*, New York, 1968; as *The Complete Films of Spencer Tracy*, Secaucus, New Jersey, 1993.
Swindell, Larry, *Spencer Tracy: A Biography*, New York, 1969.
Kanin, Garson, *Tracy and Hepburn*, New York, 1971.
Tozzi, Romano, *Spencer Tracy*, New York, 1973.
Britton, Andrew, *Katharine Hepburn: The Thirties and After*, Newcastle-Upon-Tyne, 1984.
Davidson, Bill, *Spencer Tracy: Tragic Idol*, London, 1987.
Fisher, James, *Spencer Tracy: A Bio-Bibliography*, Westport, Connecticut, 1994.
Leaming, Barbara, *Katharine Hepburn*, New York, 1995.

On TRACY: articles—

Current Biography 1943, New York, 1943.
Cowie, Peter, "Spencer Tracy," in *Films and Filming* (London), June 1961.
Tozzi, Romano, "Spencer Tracy," in *Films in Review* (New York), December 1966.
Obituary in *New York Times*, 11 June 1967.
Gilliatt, Penelope, "The Most Amicable Combatants," in *New Yorker*, 23 September 1972.
Buckley, Michael, "Spencer Tracy Remembered," in *Films in Review* (New York), August/September 1986.
Kenny, Glenn, "Spencer Tracy: This Actor Courageous and Father Figure Won Two in a Row," in *Entertainment Wekly*, March 1995.

* * *

Few actors on the American screen have enjoyed a stardom as sustained and respected as Spencer Tracy's. His roles were wide ranging, the films that contained them generically diverse. He appeared in gangster films, screwball comedies, Westerns, biographies, and romantic adventures. He played seamen, airmen, journalists, lawyers, judges, politicians, and priests. His characters included society's victims and, occasionally, its victimizers—sometimes both at the same time, as in *Dr. Jekyll and Mr. Hyde*. But even when he portrayed ruthless conniving men, Tracy exuded a rugged self-confidence that seemed to etch facets central to the American spirit. He had no airs, on-screen or off. Perhaps because his average looks and chunky frame denied him the romantic casting opportunities available to his more urbane contemporaries, William Powell and Clark Gable, he remained a character actor masquerading as a star.

Tracy's most vivid roles suggest a pragmatic if accidental blending of James Stewart's all-American affability and basic decency with the roguish Irish pugnacity of James Cagney. Although his more mean-spirited characters generally come to their moral senses before the final fadeout, Tracy's delight in depicting comic chicanery (*Libeled Lady*, *Adam's Rib*, *The Last Hurrah*, and *It's a Mad . . . World*) and savage revenge (*Murder Man*, *Sea of Grass*, and, notably, *Fury*) contradict the notion that he was primarily a player of paragons, such as Father Flanagan in *Boys' Town* and *Edison the Man*.

Arguably Tracy's most atypical role was the aforementioned *Dr. Jekyll and Mr. Hyde*. In contrast to John Barrymore and Fredric March, who had played the dual roles in previous versions, Tracy donned little makeup for his Hyde. His was a more psychological approach. For many, including the critics, the subtlety of it all did not work. Reportedly author Somerset Maugham once visited the set and commented, "Which is he now? Jekyll or Hyde." At the height of his fame, and his alcoholism, the always-insecure Tracy would often disappear from the set for days, have to be tracked and persuaded to come back. He remained ashamed of his performance in the film to the end of his life. While perhaps not ranking with the best of his career, it was polished and professional and has worn quite well over the years. One suspects that the hostility with which it was greeted at the time had much to do with critic and audience expectations, and with Tracy's having been cast so firmly against type, a problem that does not seem to arise for viewers today.

Most enduringly of all, however, Tracy will be remembered for his legendary partnership with Katharine Hepburn, with whom he maintained an offscreen relationship for 25 years and co-starred in seven MGM films. Three of them (*Keeper of the Flame* and, memorably, *Adam's Rib* and *Pat and Mike*) were directed by George Cukor, who once characterized their improbable alliance: "They were a very amusing combination. She says that he helped her very much and he didn't spare her, you know. If he thought she was grandiose, he could be terribly funny about her. She talked in a certain elegant way and there was nothing la-di-da about him so, chemically, they were very amusing together." Those personality contrasts provided ore for their best film pairings. In *Woman of the Year*, *Adam's Rib*, and *Pat and Mike* a progressive battle of the sexes is fought to a sparkling standoff as Tracy's plain dealing, cynical men defend their turf against Hepburn's competitive incursions. Together, they Americanized the Restoration comedy of manners.

—Mark W. Estrin, updated by John McCarty

TRAVOLTA, John

Nationality: American. **Born:** Englewood, New Jersey, 18 February 1954. **Education:** Attended Dwight Morrow High School. **Family:** Married Kelly Preston, 1989, son Jett. **Career:** 1966—in Actors Studio workshop production of *Who'll Save the Plowboy?*; as teenager, appeared in summer stock, supper club productions, and commercials; 1973—off-Broadway debut in *Rain*; on tour with the musical *Grease*; 1974—Broadway debut in musical *Over Here!*; 1975—film

debut in *The Devil's Rain*; 1975-77—in TV series *Welcome Back, Kotter*; contract with film producer Robert Stigman. **Awards:** Golden Globe for Best Actor, Musical or Comedy, for *Get Shorty*, 1995. **Address:** 12522 Moorpark Street, #109, Studio City, CA 91604, U.S.A.

Films as Actor:

1975   *The Devil's Rain* (Fuest)
1976   *Carrie* (De Palma) (as Billy Nolan); *The Boy in the Plastic Bubble* (Kleiser—for TV) (title role)
1977   *Saturday Night Fever* (Badham) (as Tony Manero)
1978   *Moment by Moment* (Wagner) (as Strip); *Grease* (Kleiser) (as Danny Zuko)
1980   *Urban Cowboy* (Bridges) (as Bud)
1981   *Blow Out* (De Palma) (as Jack)
1983   *Staying Alive* (Stallone) (as Tony Manero); *Two of a Kind* (Herzfeld) (as Zack)
1985   *Perfect* (Bridges) (as Adam)
1987   *The Dumb Waiter* (Altman); *The Room* (Basements) (Altman and Sino—for TV) (as Ben)
1989   *The Experts* (Thomas) (as Travis); *Look Who's Talking* (Heckerling) (as James); *Twist of Fate* (Ian Sharp—for TV)
1990   *Look Who's Talking Too* (Heckerling) (as James); *Midnight Rider* (Hornaday)
1991   *Shout* (Hornaday) (as Jack Cabe); *Chains of Gold* (Holcomb—for TV, produced 1989) (as Scott Barnes)
1992   *Boris and Natasha* (Simoneau and Charles Martin Smith—for TV) (as himself)
1993   *Look Who's Talking Now* (Ropelewski) (as James Ubriacco); *Eyes of an Angel* (Robert Harmon—produced in 1990)
1994   *Pulp Fiction* (Tarantino) (as Vincent Vega)
1995   *Get Shorty* (Sonnenfeld) (as Chili Palmer); *White Man's Burden* (Nakano) (as Louis Pinnock)
1996   *Broken Arrow* (Woo) (as Vic Deakins); *Phenomenon* (Turteltaub)

Publications

By TRAVOLTA: articles—

"Travolta and De Palma Discuss *Blow Out*," interview with C. Amata, in *Films and Filming* (London), December 1981.
"From an Actor's Notebook," in *Rolling Stone* (Boulder, Colorado), July-August 1985.
"Look Who's Talking," interview with Rosanna Arquette, in *Interview* (New York), August 1994.

On TRAVOLTA: book—

Reeves, Michael, *Travolta: A Photo Bio*, New York, 1978.

On TRAVOLTA: articles—

Current Biography 1978, New York, 1978.
Yakir, Dan, "Vinnie and Wenner," in *Film Comment* (New York), July/August 1985.
Squire, Susan, "Look Who's Talking . . . Back," in *Premiere* (New York), March 1990.
Merrick, H., "Le Syndrome du Phénix," in *Revue du Cinéma* (Paris), May 1990.
Amis, Martin, "Travolta's Second Act," in *New Yorker*, 20 & 27 February 1995.

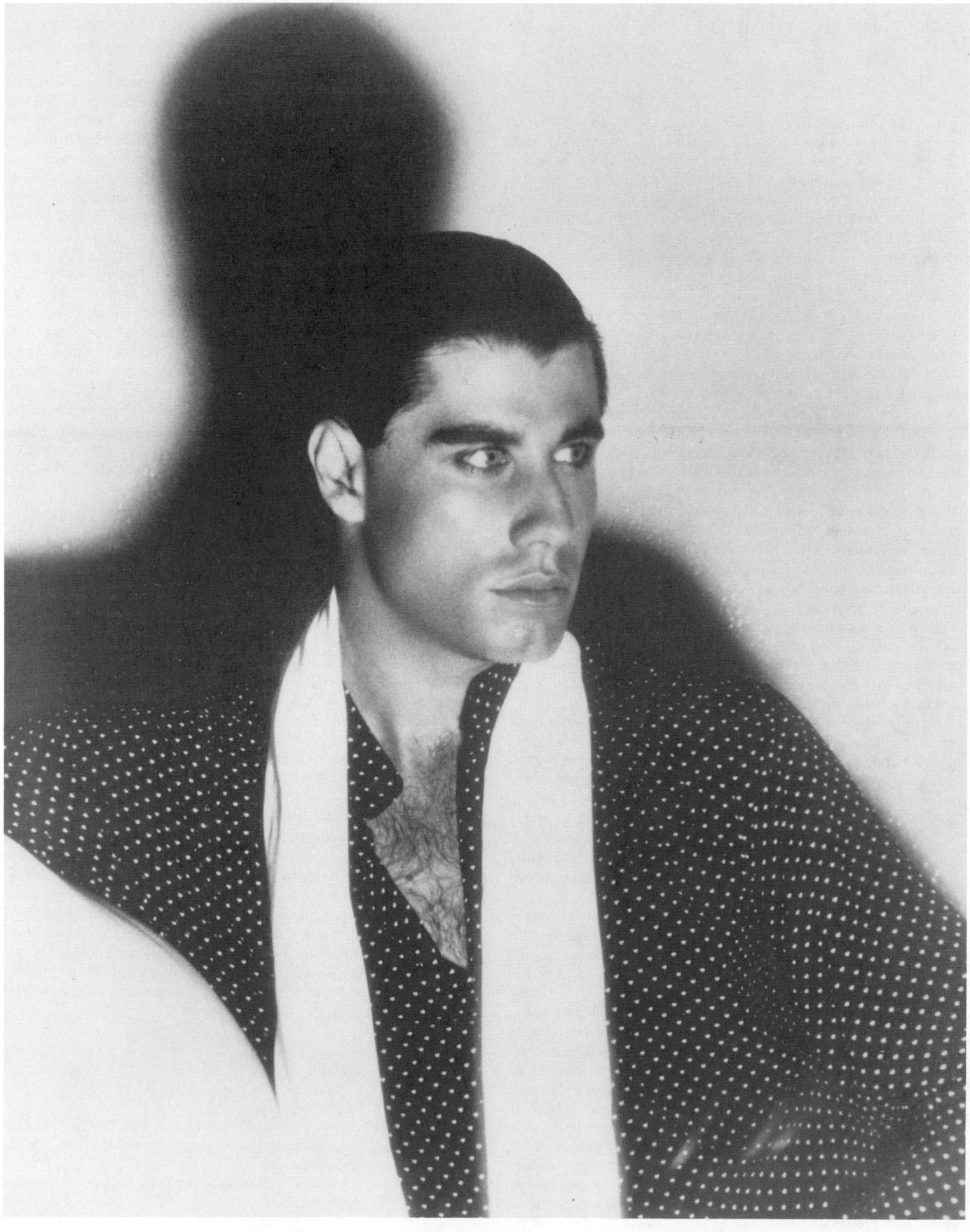

John Travolta

Junod, Tom, "John Travolta Is a Big Being," in *GQ*, October 1995.

Schickel, Richard, "Travolta Fever," in *Time* (New York), 16 October 1995.

* * *

It might be argued that no other actor in the history of motion pictures enjoyed the kind of career renaissance experienced by John Travolta in 1994. Back in the late 1970s and early 1980s, he was a red-hot commodity in Hollywood, as the star of the enormously popular *Saturday Night Fever* and *Grease*. Over the years, however, his career had faltered; before being cast in Quentin Tarantino's *Pulp Fiction*, he was considered a has-been. Despite his appearance in the popular comedy *Look Who's Talking* and its two sequels, Travolta could not buy a prestige part. In fact, a number of his films were even released directly to video, quite an embarrassment for a star of his stature. But *Pulp Fiction*, one of the most talked-about movies of 1994, jump-started his career. For a second time, Travolta found himself atop the A-list of Hollywood stars.

Travolta earned his initial mainstream stardom as Vinnie Barbarino on the television situation comedy *Welcome Back, Kotter*. Teen girls swooned over him, he became a hot new sex symbol—and he was destined to be spared the fate of innumerable other television phenoms who eventually fade into oblivion. Actors who come to stardom in television series often are unable to surmount the public's perception of them in their series role. For this reason, they cannot find work once their shows leave the air. Fortunately for Travolta, he was able to play an extension of Barbarino in his role as disco dancing Tony Manero in *Saturday Night Fever*, the film that earned him an Oscar nomination and won him his big-screen fame. The actor's Brooklyn Italian-American street-boy attitude further endeared him to (mostly female) moviegoers, and his fancy moves on the dance floor almost single-handedly helped popularize the disco craze of the late 1970s. In fact, Travolta-as-Tony Manero became one of the icons of 1970s pop culture. He is as representative of the era as Bogie's Sam Spade and Philip Marlowe are mirrors of the film noirish 1940s, or as Dustin Hoffman's Benjamin Braddock reflects the late 1960s.

Travolta followed *Saturday Night Fever* with another tailor-made screen role: Danny Zuko in *Grease*. The popular musical, a nostalgia piece which fondly looks back on 1950s rock 'n' roll culture, was an ideal property for Travolta, allowing him to dance as impressively as in *Saturday Night Fever* and play yet another Barbarino clone. He also gave impressive performances in two other films: *Urban Cowboy* (which unfortunately failed at the box office), cast as a mechanical bull-riding hard hat; and *Blow Out*, Brian De Palma's variation of Antonioni's *Blow-Up*, playing a sound-effects man who inadvertently becomes involved in a murder scenario.

But Travolta's celluloid successes were destined to be outweighed by his misfires. In 1978, one year after *Saturday Night Fever* and the same year as *Grease*, he co-starred with Lily Tomlin in the dreadful *Moment by Moment*. Through the potentially interesting pairing of Travolta and Tomlin, the film confronts a number of social taboos: the older woman/younger man syndrome; the relationship between a rich woman and poor man; and, above all else, gender reversal. But the film proved a shallow, forced attempt at a feminist declaration. Even if *Moment by Moment* had been artistically successful, it would not have advanced Travolta's career. In *Saturday Night Fever* and *Grease*, he is the macho male, the focus of attention. In *Moment by Moment*, he plays the passive leading role, that of Strip, a drifter-beach bum. Tomlin is the dominant partner, with Travolta the object of desire, and he expresses markedly "feminine" characteristics such as vulnerability, sensitivity, and passivity. Travolta's army of fans had no desire to watch him playing such a role. To add to his misfortune, all of his mid-1980s films—*Staying Alive* (in which he reprises Tony Manero), *Two of a Kind*, and *Perfect*—were downright disasters. By the end of the decade, he was considered a faded star, a view which remained unaltered despite his appearance in *Look Who's Talking*.

In *Pulp Fiction*, the new John Travolta rose like a phoenix from its ashes. In the film, he at once redesigned his on-screen personality and revived his career. Travolta plays ultracool hitman Vincent Vega, who converses memorably with his criminal cohort (Samuel L. Jackson) and his employer's wife (Uma Thurman). In *Pulp Fiction*, Travolta was one of an ensemble; his role as Vega was as important to the story as any one of a half-dozen other characters, and his Oscar nomination as Best Actor easily might have been in the Supporting Actor category. But in his follow-up, *Get Shorty*, he most decidedly was the star of the show. He plays Chili Palmer, another hip thug, a loan shark who loves old movies and ends up hustling his way into the film industry. In *Get Shorty*, Travolta solidified the fame he had rewon in *Pulp Fiction*.

He next appeared as unlucky, inarticulate factory worker Louis Pinnock in *White Man's Burden*, a provocative morality tale set in a society in which African Americans are ensconced in the upper classes while whites inhabit the lower economic wrung. While far more artistically successful than *Moment by Moment*, both films are linked as radical departures at pivotal points in Travolta's career. If Tony Manero and Danny Zuko are macho and Strip is feminized, Vincent Vega and Chili Palmer are empowered and Louis Pinnock is helpless and victimized.

Nevertheless, if Travolta is able to secure enough roles in films similar in quality and popularity to *Pulp Fiction* and *Get Shorty*, he should not reexperience his post-*Saturday Night Fever/Grease* career doldrums.

—Robin Wood, updated by Rob Edelman

TREVOR, Claire

Nationality: American. **Born:** Claire Wemlinger in Bensonhurst, Long Island, New York, 8 March 1909 (some sources say 1912). **Education:** Attended high school in Mamaroneck, Long Island; Columbia University, New York; American Academy of Dramatic Arts, New York, for six months. **Family:** Married 1) the producer Clark Andrews, 1938 (divorced 1942); 2) Cylos William Dunsmoore, 1943 (divorced 1947), son: Charles Cylos; 3) the producer Milton Bren, 1948. **Career:** 1929—professional stage debut with Robert Henderson's Repertory Players in Ann Arbor, Michigan; 1930—with Warner Brothers stock company in St. Louis; 1931—summer stock with Hampton Players in Southampton, Long Island; 1932—Broadway debut in *Whistling in the Dark*; 1933-37—contract with Fox: feature film debut in *Life in the Raw*; 1937-40—in radio series *Big Town* with Edward G. Robinson; 1938-43—contract with Warner Brothers; 1947—on Broadway in *The Big Two*; on television from mid-1950s. **Awards:** Best Supporting Actress Academy Award, for *Key Largo*, 1948. **Address:** Hotel Pierre, 2 East 61st Street, New York, NY 10022, U.S.A.

Films as Actress:

1929   two Vitaphone shorts

1933   *Life in the Raw* (Louis King); *The Last Trail* (Tinling); *The Mad Game* (Cummings) (as Jane Lee); *Jimmy and Sally* (Tinling) (as Sally Johnson)

1934   *Hold That Girl* (MacFadden) (as Tony Bellamy); *Wild Gold* (George Marshall) (as Jerry Jordan); *Baby, Take a Bow* (Lachman) (as Kay Ellison); *Elinor Norton* (MacFadden) (title role)

1935   *Spring Tonic* (Bruckman) (as Betty Ingals); *Black Sheep* (Dwan)
       (as Janette Foster); *Dante's Inferno* (Lachman) (as Betty
       McWade); *Beauty's Daughter* (Dwan)
1936   *My Marriage* (Archainbaud) (as Carol Barton); *The Song and
       Dance Man* (Dwan) (as Julia Carroll); *Human Cargo* (Dwan)
       (as Bonnie Brewster); *To Mary—With Love* (Cromwell) (as
       Kitty Brant); *Star for a Night* (Seiler) (as Nina Lind); *15
       Maiden Lane* (Dwan) (as Jane Martin); *Career Woman*
       (Seiler) (as Carroll Aiken); *Navy Wife* (Dwan) (as Vicky Blake)
1937   *Time Out for Romance* (St. Clair) (as Barbara Blanchard); *King
       of Gamblers* (Florey) (as Dixie); *One Mile from Heaven*
       (Dwan) (as Lucy "Tex" Warren); *Dead End* (Wyler) (as
       Francie); *Second Honeymoon* (Walter Lang) (as Marcia);
       Big Town Girl (Werker) (as Fay Loring)
1938   *Walking Down Broadway* (Norman Foster) (as Joan Bradley);
       The Amazing Dr. Clitterhouse (Litvak) (as Jo Keller); *Valley
       of the Giants* (Keighley) (as Lee Roberts); *Five of a Kind*
       (Leeds) (as Christine Nelson)
1939   *Stagecoach* (Ford) (as Dallas); *I Stole a Million* (Tuttle) (as
       Laura Benson); *Allegheny Uprising* (Seiter) (as Janie)
1940   *Dark Command* (Walsh) (as Mary McCloud)
1941   *Texas* (George Marshall) (as "Mike" King); *Honky Tonk*
       (Conway) (as "Gold Dust" Nelson)
1942   *Crossroads* (Conway) (as Michelle Allain); *Street of Chance*
       (Hively) (as Ruth Dillon); *The Adventures of Martin Eden*
       (Salkow) (as Connie Dawson)
1943   *The Desperadoes* (Carson) (as Countess Maletta); *Good Luck,
       Mr. Yates* (Enright) (as Ruth Yates); *The Woman of the Town*
       (Archainbaud) (as Dora Hand)
1944   *Murder, My Sweet* (*Farewell, My Lovely*) (Dmytryk) (as Mrs. Grayle)
1945   *Johnny Angel* (Marin) (as Lilah)
1946   *Crack-Up* (Reis) (as Terry Cordeau); *The Bachelor's Daugh-
       ters* (*Bachelor Girls*) (Andrew L. Stone) (as Cynthia)
1947   *Born to Kill* (*Lady of Deceit*) (Wise) (as Helen Trent)
1948   *Raw Deal* (Anthony Mann) (as Pat); *Key Largo* (Huston) (as
       Gaye Dawn); *The Velvet Touch* (Gage) (as Marion Webster);
       The Babe Ruth Story (Del Ruth) (as Claire Hodgson)
1949   *The Lucky Stiff* (Lewis R. Foster) (as Marguerite Seaton)
1950   *Borderline* (Seiter) (as Madeleine Haley)
1951   *Best of the Badmen* (William D. Russell) (as Lily Fowler);
       Hard, Fast, and Beautiful (Lupino) (as Milly Farley)
1952   *Hoodlum Empire* (Kane) (as Connie Williams); *My Man and
       I* (Wellman) (as Mrs. Ansel Ames); *Stop, You're Killing Me*
       (Del Ruth) (as Nora Marko)
1953   *The Stranger Wore a Gun* (De Toth) (as Josie Sullivan)
1954   *The High and the Mighty* (Wellman) (as May Hoist)
1955   *Man without a Star* (King Vidor) (as Idonee); *Lucy Gallant*
       (*Oil Town*) (Parrish) (as Lady MacBeth)
1956   *The Mountain* (Dmytryk) (as Marie)
1958   *Marjorie Morningstar* (Rapper) (as Rose Morgenstern)
1962   *Two Weeks in Another Town* (Minnelli) (as Clara Kruger)
1963   *The Stripper* (Schaffner) (as Helen Baird)
1965   *How to Murder Your Wife* (Quine) (as Edna)
1967   *Capetown Affair* (Webb)
1982   *Kiss Me Goodbye* (Mulligan) (as Charlotte Banning)
1988   *Breaking Home Ties* (John Wilder—for TV) (as Grace)

Publications

By TREVOR: articles—

"The Company Remembers *Stagecoach*," in *Action* (Los Angeles),
Ocotber 1971.
Interview with John Gallagher, in *Films in Review* (New York), November 1983.

On TREVOR: articles—

Hagen, Ray, "Claire Trevor," in *Films in Review* (New York), Novem-
ber 1963.
Rainey, Buck, "Claire Trevor: A Provocative Femme Fatale," in *Clas-
sic Images* (Muscatine, Iowa), November 1989 and December 1989.
Pulleine, T., "Stardust Memories," in *Films and Filming* (London),
January 1990.

*   *   *

In the early 1930s, Claire Trevor was one of the "Broadway Imports" to the film colony in the rush to find actors who were capable
of performing in talking pictures. She studied at the American Academy of Dramatic Arts, worked briefly on Broadway, and appeared in
Vitaphone shorts before being signed to a contract with Twentieth
Century-Fox. Unfortunately, her stay there was not marked by any
great distinction, and she found herself typecast as assorted bad girls in
a slew of unmemorable B films. Her presence in *Dead End* (made on
loan to Samuel Goldwyn), with Sylvia Sidney, Joel McCrea, Humphrey
Bogart, and the Dead End Kids, was the exception, rather than rule, of
her early career.

Trevor was destined never to become a star. Indeed, in a 1983 *Films
in Review* interview, she explained that she was unwilling to deal with
the pressures that stardom demanded, and was content to acquit herself in subsidiary roles. In the late 1930s and early 1940s, the quality
of her films increased, and she was never better than when playing
hard-bitten women on the periphery of society. Perhaps her two
greatest roles are the no-nonsense yet understanding prostitute opposite John Wayne's Ringo Kid in John Ford's *Stagecoach*, and the tough
mistress of Edward G. Robinson in John Huston's *Key Largo*. She also
appeared with Wayne in *Allegheny Uprising*, *Dark Command*, and
The High and the Mighty, and had showy roles in *Street of Chance*,
Murder, My Sweet, and *Hard, Fast, and Beautiful*. Her career continued apace until the mid-1950s, at which point she semiretired.

From then on, Trevor only appeared sporadically on screen. Her
last theatrical film to date, a Sally Field/James Caan vehicle called *Kiss
Me Goodbye*, received bad reviews, yet she—ever so typically—won
enthusiastic personal notices.

—Joseph Arkins, updated by Rob Edelman

TRINTIGNANT, Jean-Louis

Nationality: French. **Born:** Port-St. Esprit, 11 December 1930.
Education: Studied law to age 20; studied acting with Charles Dullin
and Tatania Balacgova. **Family:** Married 1) the actress Stéphane
Audran, 1954 (divorced); 2) Nadine Marquand (i.e., the director Nadine
Trintignant), 1960, one son and two daughters (one deceased), includ-
ing the actress Marie Trintignant. **Career:** 1951—stage debut; 1955—
film debut in *Si tous les gars du monde*; 1956-59—military service;
1966—"rediscovered" after role in *Un Homme et une femme*; 1972—
directed the film *Une Journée bien remplie*. **Awards:** Best Actor,
Berlin Festival, for *L'Homme qui ment*, 1968; Best Actor, Cannes
Festival, for *Z*, 1969. **Agent:** c/o Artmédia, 10 av George V, 75008
Paris, France.

Films as Actor:

1955   *Si tous les gars du monde* (*If All the Guys in the World*; *Race
       for Life*) (Christian-Jaque) (as Jean-Louis)

1956 *Et Dieu créa la femme* (*And God Created Woman*) (Vadim) (as Michel); *La Loi des rues* (Habib); *Club de femmes* (Habib)

1959 *Estate violenta* (*Violent Summer*) (Zurlini) (as Carlo); *Les Liaisons dangereuses* (Vadim) (as Danceny)

1960 *Austerlitz* (Gance and Richebé); *Le Coeur battant* (*The French Game*) (Doniol-Valcroze) (as François); *La Millième Fenêtre* (Menegoz) (as Georges)

1961 *Pleins feux sur l'assassin* (Franju) (as Jean-Marie); *Le Combat dans l'île* (*Fire and Ice*) (Cavalier) (as Clement); *Le Jeu de la vérité* (Hossein) (as Guy); *L'Antinea* (*L'Atlantide*; *Journey beneath the Desert*; *The Lost Kingdom*) (Ulmer and Masini) (as Pierre)

1962 "La Luxure" ep. of *Les Septs Péchés capitaux* (*The Seven Capital Sins*) (Demy) (as Paul); *Il sorpasso* (*The Easy Life*) (Risi) (as Roberto Mariani); *Horace '62* (Versini) (as Joseph)

1963 *Il successo* (Morassi) (as Sergio); *Château en Suède* (*Nutty Naughty Chateau*) (Vadim) (as Eric)

1964 *Mata-Hari, Agent H21* (Richard) (as Capt. François Lassalle); *Les Pas perdus* (Robin) (as Georges); *Merveilleuse Angélique* (Borderie) (as the poet)

1965 *Compartiment tueurs* (*The Sleeping Car Murders*) (Costa-Gavras) (as Eric); *La Bonne Occase* (Drach); *Un Jour à Paris* (short); *Fragilité, ton nom est femme* (short); "La donna che vive va sola" ep. of *Io uccido, tu uccidi* (Puccini)

1966 *Le Dix-septième Ciel* (Korber) (as François); *La Longue Marche* (Astruc) (as Philippe); *Paris brûle-t-il?* (*Is Paris Burning?*) (Clément) (as Serge); *Un Homme et une femme* (*A Man and a Woman*) (Lelouch) (as Jean-Louis Duroc); *Safari diamants* (Drach) (as Raphael)

1967 *Col cuore in gola* (*With Baited Breath*; *Deadly Sweet*) (Brass) (as Bernard); *Trans-Europ Express* (Robbe-Grillet) (as Elias/himself); *Un Homme à abattre* (*A Man to Kill*) (Condroyer) (as Raphael); *La morte, la fatto, l'uovo* (*Plucked*; *A Curious Way to Love*) (Questi) (as Marco); *Mon amour, mon amour* (Nadine Trintignant) (as Vincent)

1968 *Les Biches* (*The Does*) (Chabrol) (as Paul Thomas); **Z** (Costa-Gavras) (as the magistrate)

1969 *Le Voleur de crimes* (Nadine Trintignant) (as Jean); *Metti, una sera a cena* (*The Love Circle*; *One Night at Dinner*) (Griffi) (as Michele); *Ma nuit chez Maud* (*My Night at Maud's*) (Rohmer) (as Jean-Louis); *La matriarca* (*The Libertine*) (Campanile) (as Dr. De Marchi); *L'Homme qui ment* (*Shock Troops*; *The Man Who Lies*) (Robbe-Grillet) (as Boris Varissa); *Il grande silenzio* (Corbucci); *L'Opium et le bâton* (Rachedi); *Cosi dolce cosi perversa* (Lenzi)

1970 *L'Américain* (Bozzuffi) (as Bruno); *Le Voyou* (*The Crook*) (Lelouch) (as Simon); **Il conformista** (*The Conformist*) (Bertolucci) (as Marcello)

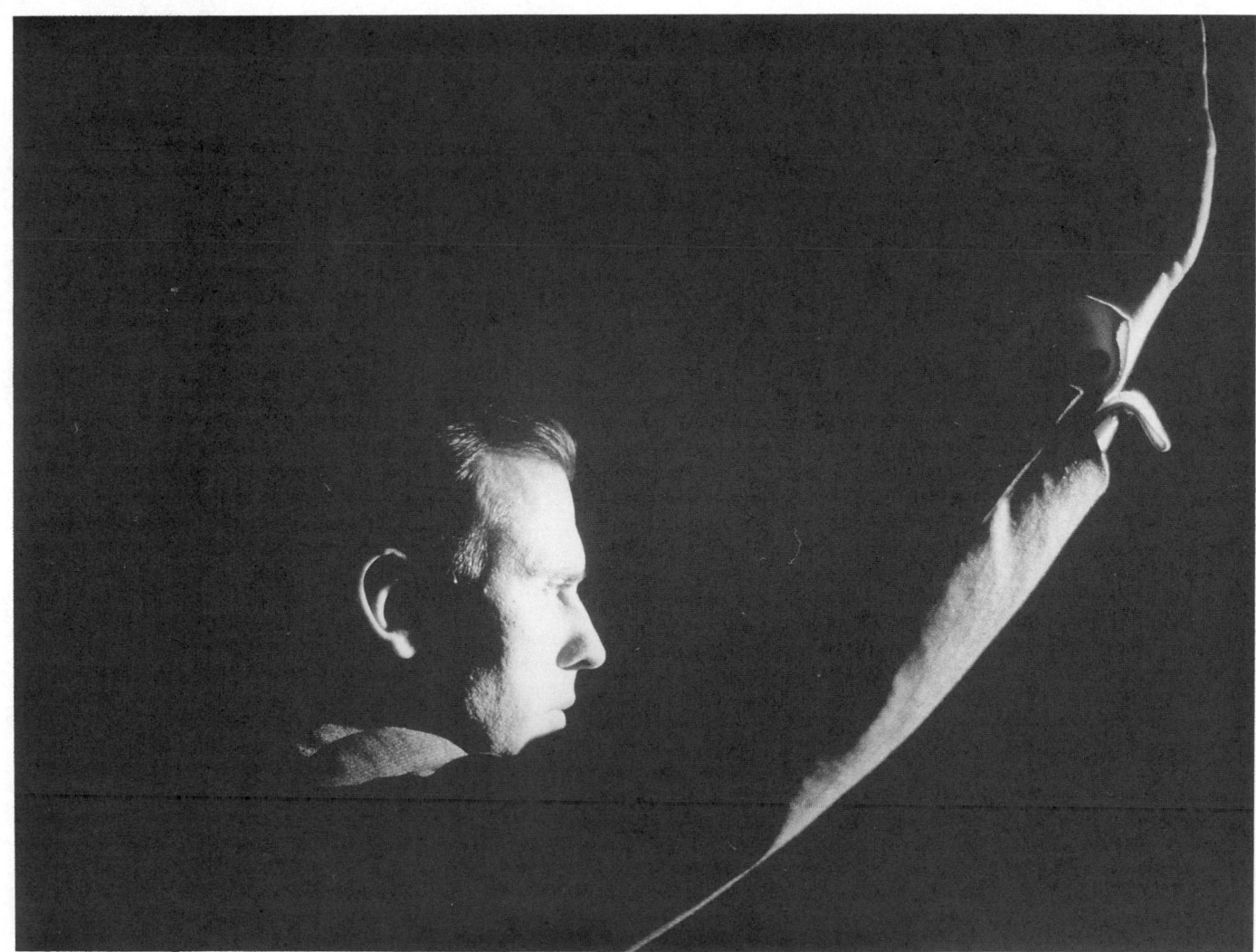

Jean-Louis Trintignant in *Il conformista*

1971 *L'Homme au cerveau greffé* (Doniol-Valcroze); *La Course du lièvre à travers les champs* (*And Hope to Die*) (Clément) (as Froggy); *Sans mobile apparent* (*Without Apparent Motive*) (Labro) (as Detective Carella)

1972 *L'Attentat* (*Plot*; *The French Conspiracy*) (Boisset) (as Darien)

1973 *Un Homme est mort* (*The Outside Man*) (Deray) (as Lucien); *Defense de savoir* (*Forbidden to Know*) (Nadine Trintignant) (as Laubre); *Le Train* (Granier-Deferre) (as Meyereu)

1974 *Les Violons du bal* (Drach) (as Michel); *Le Secret* (*The Secret*) (Enrico) (as David); *Le Mouton enragé* (*Love at the Top*) (Deville) (as Nicholas); *L'Escapade* (Soutter) (as Ferdinand); *Le Jeu avec le feu* (*Playing with Fire*) (Robbe-Grillet) (as Frantz)

1975 *Le Voyage de noces* (Nadine Trintignant) (as Paul); *L'Agression* (*Act of Aggression*) (Pirès) (as Paul Varlin); *Flic Story* (Deray) (as Buisson); *Il pleut sur Santiago* (Soto) (as the Senator); *La donna della domenica* (*The Sunday Woman*) (Comencini) (as Massimo)

1976 *Les Passagers* (Leroy) (as Alex)

1977 *Il deserto dei Tartari* (*The Desert of the Tartars*) (Zurlini) (as the doctor)

1978 *L'Argent des autres* (*Other People's Money*) (du Chalonge) (as Rainier); *Repérages* (*Faces of Love*) (Soutter) (as Victor)

1980 *La Banquière* (Girod) (as Horance Vannister); *Je vous aime* (*I Love All of You*) (Berri)

1981 *Malevil* (du Chalonge) (as Rulbert); *Passion d'amore* (*Passion of Love*) (Scola) (as the doctor); *Eaux profondes* (Deville) (as Victor)

1982 *Colpa al cuore* (*Blow to the Heart*) (Amelio—for TV); *Boulevard des assassins* (Tioulang); *Le Grand Pardon* (Arcady)

1983 *Le Bon Plaisir* (Girod) (as the president); *Under Fire* (Spottiswoode) (as Jazy); *La Nuit de Varennes* (Scola) (as Monsieur Sauce); *Vivement dimanche!* (*Confidentially Yours*; *Finally, Sunday*) (Truffaut) (as Julien Vercel); *La Crime* (*Cover-Up*) (Labro) (as Christian Lacassagne)

1984 *Viva la vie!* (Lelouch) (as François Gaucher); *Partir, revenir* (*Going and Coming Back*) (Lelouch) (as Roland Rivière); *Femmes de personne* (Frank) (as Gilquin)

1985 *L'Été prochaine* (*Next Summer*) (Nadine Trintignant) (as Paul); *L'Homme aux yeux d'argent* (Granier-Deferre) (as Inspector Mayene); *Rendez-vous* (Téchiné) (as Scrutzler); *Sortuz egy fekete bivalyert* (Laszlo Szabo) (as Fodo the Teacher)

1986 *La Femme de ma vie* (Wargnier) (as Pierre); *Un Homme et une femme: vingt ans déjà* (*A Man and a Woman: 20 Years Later*) (Lelouch) (as Jean-Louis Duroc); *Quinzième août* (Garcia)

1987 *Le Moustachu* (Chaussois) (as the general); *La Vallée fantôme* (Tanner) (as Paul)

1989 *Bunker Palace Hotel* (Bilal) (as Holm); *Pour un oui ou pour un non* (Doillon)

1991 *Merci la vie* (*Thanks for Life*) (Blier) (as S.S. officer)

1993 *L'Instinct de l'Ange* (as the colonel)

1994 *Regarde les hommes tomber* (*See How They Fall*) (Audiard) (as Marx); *Trois Couleurs: Rouge* (*Three Colours: Red*) (Kieślowski) (as Judge Joseph Kern); *Ernesto Che Chuevara: Das bolivianische Tagebuch* (Dindo—doc) (as narrator of French version)

1995 *Fiesta* (Pierre Boutron) (as Masagual); *La Cite des Enfants Perdus* (*The City of Lost Children*) (Jeunet and Caro) (as voice of Irvin)

1996 *Les Bidochons* (Serge Korber)

Films as Director:

1972 *Une Journée bien remplie* (*A Well-Filled Day*)

1979 *Le Maître nageur*

Publications

By TRINTIGNANT: book—

Un homme a sa fenêtre/Jean-Louis Trintignant, with Michel Boujut, Paris 1977.

By TRINTIGNANT: articles—

"Two Actors," interview in *Films and Filming* (London), October 1960.
"Jean-Louis Trintignant," interview with Molly Haskell, in *Show* (Hollywood), 20 August 1970.
"L'Acteur témoin de son temps," in *Cinéma* (Paris), February 1972.
Interview with D. Maillet, in *Image et Son* (Paris), March 1973.
Interview with C. Barthelemy, in *Cinématographe* (Paris), July 1985.

On TRINTIGNANT: articles—

Current Biography 1988, New York, 1988.
Veenstra, T., "L'homme qui ment," in *Skrien*, April/May 1993.

* * *

After training in Paris under Charles Dullin, Jean-Louis Trintignant appeared in theatrical repertory before making his film debut in a maritime drama, *Si tous les gars du monde*. In a career closely associated with the French New Wave and with Italian productions, he has achieved distinction in romantic, comic, and dramatic parts but especially in his portrayal of psychologically disturbed characters.

Slight in build with limpid eyes and pale complexion, he projected a romantic image defined by gentleness, diffidence, and vulnerability. In *Et Dieu créa la femme*, he established himself as the kind, unassertive deceived husband, and roles as the vulnerable, inexperienced male followed. In *Estate violenta*, he played the innocent youth seduced by a knowing female, in *Les Liaisons dangereuses* a too-trusting Danceny, in *La Matriarca* a shy doctor initiated into eroticism by a widowed patient, and in *Les Biches* a compliant male for two lesbians. His wittiest exploration of the insecure, morally confused male character came in *Ma nuit chez Maud* as an upright Catholic offered, but not recognizing, sexual opportunity.

Romantic comedy roles came in *Le Coeur battant* and *Le Dix-Septième Ciel*, and in two Italian productions: *Metti, una sera a cena*, as the seductive playwright, and *Passion d'amore*, as the doctor counseling lovesick patients. For Franju he was the romantic lead in *Pleins Feux sur l'assassin*, for Vadim he appeared in *Château en Suède*, and for Lelouch in *Le Voyou* and *Viva la vie*. More serious studies of romantic involvement are found in *Le Train*, where against the setting of the Nazi occupation he falls in love with a fleeing Jewess, played by Romy Schneider, and in Nadine Trintignant's study of an affair in *Mon amour, mon amour*. His most memorable romantic part, however, came in *Un Homme et une femme*, where, partnered with Anouk Aimée, he gave a sensitive but unsentimental performance as the widowed racing driver learning to love again. The two actors were reunited by Lelouch for an unusually late and unmemorable sequel, *Un Homme et une Femme: vingt ans déjà*.

Trintignant's taut and impassively cryptic acting style has suited films dealing with crime, political intrigue, war, or espionage. After an engaging performance as a juvenile criminal in *La Loi des rues*, he was the fascist thug of *Le Combat dans l'île*, the murderer's accomplice in *Compartiment tueurs*, the Frenchman Froggy in Clément's thriller *La Course du lièvre à travers les champs*, and the bored parachutist choosing crime in *Safari-Diamants*. Variations within the detective genre brought roles as Inspector Carella in *Sans mobile apparent*, the disquieting investigator in *Glissements progressifs du plaisir*, and a detective remorselessly pursuing his colleague's killers in *L'Homme aux yeux d'argent*, while as Paul Varlin in *Agression* and Julien Vercel in *Vivement Dimanche!* he turns investigator to establish his innocence.

Roles in war films have included that of Captain François Lassalle in the spy drama *Mata-Hari*, Serge in the liberation spectacle *Paris brûle-t-il?*, the resolute but fallible Resistance leader Philippe in *La Longue Marche*, and, in his first American film, the French spy Jazy working for the CIA in *Under Fire*. In political thrillers he has been a venal left-wing journalist duped by the authorities in *L'Attentat*, the infamous dictator Rulbert in *Malevil*, and the left-wing intellectual implicated in terrorism in *Colpe al cuore*. It was in *Z*, however, that he had his most commanding role as the principled examining magistrate who refuses to bow to political pressures.

In roles as persecuted individuals he was impressive in *Les Violons du bal* as the Jew recalling his boyhood in Nazi France and *Les Passagers* as the increasingly distraught man pursued by a murderous rival, and, in another psychological thriller, *Un Homme est mort*, as a frightened amateur killer tangling with ruthless professionals.

Trintignant's particular strength, however, is depicting the inadequate, sexually depraved, actively or passively aggressive male. In *Trans-Europ Express*, he exteriorized sadistic fantasies with a prostitute; in *La morte, la fatto, l'uovo*, he acted out Jack the Ripper obsessions at a brothel; in *L'Homme qui ment*, he was a pathological liar; and in *Le Voleur de crimes*, directed by his wife Nadine, he was a fantasist claiming homicidal responsibility for a suicide. More actively vicious roles came in *Le Mouton enragé*, as the timid bank clerk turned cynical womanizer. In *Le Secret*, he was a murderous paranoiac; in *Flic Story*, a psychopathic killer; in *La Banquière*, he displayed a chilling Machiavellianism; in *Eaux profondes*, he was the viciously perverse husband; while in *Rendez-vous* and *L'Eté prochaine* he was unscrupulously manipulative. His finest portrayal of an essentially immature and inadequate individual came in *Il conformista* as Marcello Clerici, the guilt-ridden sycophantic homosexual fascist, masterfully depicted with his self-consciously studied movements and his thin, self-absorbed smile.

Recent films have confirmed a growing diversity in Trintignant's roles. In *La Vallée fantôme*, he is seen as a filmmaker seeking inspiration and reflecting on his art; in the black comedy *Le Moustachu*, he appears as a grotesque secret service chief investigating infiltration; in the cartoon-styled science-fiction *Bunker Palace Hotel*, he appeared as the disconcerting, shaven-headed Holm; while in *La Femme de ma vie*, he gave a critically acclaimed performance as a reformed alcoholic helping a fellow victim.

Trintignant's most widely seen later-career performance came in *Red*, the final installment in Krzysztof Kieślowski's *Trois Couleurs* trilogy, playing an embittered, reclusive retired judge, a man on the edge of old age. On occasion, the judge peeps in on his neighbors through the window. More often, via the wonders of modern technology, he listens in on their telephone conversations. The judge, ultimately, is grappling with the moral implications that have deeply rattled his soul. How have his many guilty-or-innocent verdicts affected the lives of those he was empowered to judge? How have his own prejudices and moods affected his ability to judge impartially? Trintignant convincingly peels away the layers of this character, as he reveals himself to the young woman with whom he has come in contact.

Trintignant's spare, undemonstrative acting style has lent itself well to comic understatement, to seeming diffidence or innocence in romantic roles, but most powerfully to the depiction of repressed or dangerously unbalanced individuals given to private fantasies. The interiority of these characters is conveyed through noted idiosyncrasy and telling mannerisms so that they are gradually established as powerful screen presences.

—R. F. Cousins, updated by Rob Edelman

TSUKASA, Yoko

Nationality: Japanese. **Born:** Yoko Shoji in Sakai-minato City, 20 August 1934. **Education:** Studied home economics at the Kyoritsu Women's Junior College, was graduated in 1954. **Family:** Married Eisuke Aizawa, 1969. **Career:** 1954—secretary for Shin-Nihon Broadcast Company, Osaka; also a model; 1954—film debut in *Kimi shinitamoukoto nakare*; then worked for Toho Studio; acted on television from the mid-1960s, and on stage from the mid-1970s. **Awards:** Japan Mainichi Eiga Concourse, Kinema Juappo Award, and Tokyo Blue Ribbon, all 1966. **Address:** 7-10-3 Seijo, Setagaya-ku, Tokyo, Japan.

Films as Actress:

1954 *Kimi shinitamoukoto nakare* (Maruyama) (as Kumiko)
1955 *Tenka taihei*; *Yuki no honoo*; *Fumetsu no nekkyu* (Suzuki); *33-go-sha oto nashi* (Taniguchi); *Oensan*; *Hatsukoi san-nin masuko* (Aoyagi); *Ai no rekishi*; *Meoto zenzai* (Toyoda); *Kuchizuke: Ni-wa, kaettekita wakadanna* (Aoyogi)
1956 *Hesokuri shacho* (Chiba); *Hanayome kaigi* (Aoyogi); *Chiemi no hatsukoi chaccha musume* (Aoyogi); *Mogotona musume* (Mizuho); *Zoku hesokuri shacho* (Chiba); *Aoi me* (Suzuki); *Konyaku samba-garasu* (Sugie); *Gendai no yokubo*; *Harikiri shacho* (Watanabe); *Aru to sono no baai* (Mizuho); *Ani to sono imoto* (Matsubayashi); *Nisshoku no natsu* (Horikawa)
1957 *Bibo no miyako* (Matsubayashi); *Bokyaku no hanabira: Kanketsu-hen*; *Kiken na eiyu* (Suzuki); *Sono yo no himegoto* (Kimura); *Daigaku no samuri-tachi* (Aoyogi); *Aoi sanmyaku: enpen* (Matsubayashi); *Zoku aoi sanmyaku* (Matsubayashi)
1958 *Aijo no miyako* (Sugie); *Shacho sandai-ki* (Matsubayashi); *Zoku shacho sandai-ki* (Matsubayashi); *Tokyo no Kyujitsu*; *Hana no bojo* (Suzuki); *Furyu onsen nikki* (Matsubayashi); *Iwashigumo* (*Herringbone Clouds*) (Naruse); *Mimizuku seppo* (Hisamatsu)
1959 *Suzukake no sampo-michi* (Horikawa); *Hananoren* (Toyoda); *Aisai-ki* (Hisamatsu); *Daigaku no oneichan* (Sugie); *Aru kengo no shogai* (*Samurai Saga*) (Inagaki) (as Chive Hime); *Daigaku no nijuhachi-nin shu*; *Sengoku gunto-den* (*Saga of the Vagabonds*) (Sugie) (as Tazu); *Wakai koibito-tachi*; *Nippon tanjo* (Inagaki)
1960 *Ankokugai no taiketsu* (*The Last Gunfight*) (Okamoto); *Hijo-toshi* (Suzuki); *Aoi yaju* (*The Blue Beast*) (Horikawa) (as Ayaka Eto); *Yoru no nagare* (Kawashima); *Shin onna daigaku* (Hisamatsu); *Chino hate ni ikiru mono* (*The Angry Sea*) (Hisamatsu); *Akibiyori* (*Late Autumn*) (Ozu) (as Ayako, the daughter); *Sarariiman Chushingura* (Matsubayashi)
1961 *Zoku sarariiman Chushingura* (Matsubayashi); *Wakarete ikiru toki mo* (*Eternity of Love*) (Horikawa) (as Michi); *Yojimbo* (*The Bodyguard*) (Kurosawa) (as Nui); *"Chosen" yoi: Ali to honoo to* (*Challenge to Live*) (Sugawa) (as Saeko Sawada); *Honkon no yoru* (*A Night in Hong Kong*) (Chiba) (as Keiko Kimura); *Kohayagawa-ke no aki* (*The End of Summer*; *Early Autumn*; *Last of Summer*) (Ozu) (as Noriko)
1962 *Sarariiman Shimizu minato* (Matsubayashi); *Onna no za* (*The Wiser Age*; *Woman's Status*) (Naruse); *Horoki* (*Lonely Lane*) (Naruse); *Sonoobasho no onna arite*; *Zoku sarariiman Shimizu minato* (Matsubayashi); *Yoru no keisha* (Uchikawa); *Ekimae onsen*; *Chushingura* (*Loyal 47 Ronin*; *47 Samurai*) (Inagaki) (as Yozenin); *Furyu onsen: banto nikki*
1963 *Onna no tsuyokunaru kufu no kazukazu* (Chiba); *Tsuma to iu na no onnatachi*; *Domburi-ike*; *Warera sarariiman*

1964 *Shacho shinshiroku* (Matsubayashi); *Zoku shacho shinshiroku* (Matsubayashi); *Tadaima shinsatsu-chu*; *Tensai sagishi monogatari: Tanuki no hanamichi*; *Nishi no taisho higashi no taisho* (Furusawa); *Gendai shinshi yaro*; *Danchi nanatsu-no taizai* (Chiba and Kakehi)

1965 *Shacho ninpo-cho* (*Five Gents' Trick Book*) (Matsubayashi) (as Kyoko Ishikawa); *Daikon to ninjin* (*Twilight Path*) (as Haruko); *Zoku shacho ninpo-cho* (Matsubayashi); *Urakaidan*; *Kokokara hajimaru* (Tsuboshima)

1966 *Shacho gyojo-ki* (Matsubayashi); *Zoku shacho gyogo-ki* (*Five Gents on the Spot*) (Matsubayashi); *Hikinige* (*Moment of Terror*) (Naruse); *Kinokawa: Hana-no maki, Fumio-no maki* (*The River Ki*) (Nakamura) (as Mayaka); *Jinchoge* (*The Daphne*) (Chiba) (as the second daughter)

1967 *Shacho sen-ichiya* (Matsubayashi); *Sasaki Kojiro* (*Kojiro*) (Inagaki) (as Okinawa Princess); *Joi-uchi* (*Rebellion*; *Hairyozuma shimatsu-ki*) (Kobayashi) (as Ichi Sasahara); *Zoku shacho sen-ichiya* (Matsubayashi); *Midaregumo* (*Two in the Shadow*; *Scattered Clouds*) (Naruse) (as Yumiko)

1968 *Haru ranman* (Chiba); *Shacho hanjo-ki* (Matsubayashi); *Zoku shacho hanjo-ki* (Matsubayashi); *Yamamoto Isoroku* (*Admiral Yamamoto*) (Maruyama)

1969 *Shacho enma-cho* (Matsubayashi); *Nippon-kai dai-kaisen* (*Battle of the Japan Sea*) (Maruyama); *Zoku shacho enma-cho* (Matsubayashi); *Goyokin* (Gosha) (as Shino)

1970 *Shinsen-gumi* (*Band of Assassins*) (Sawashima); *Shacho-gaku ABC* (Matsubayashi); *Zoku shacho-gaku ABC* (Matsubayashi); *Nihon ichi no yakuza otoko*

1971 *Yomigaeru daichi*; *Tochan no po ga kikoeru*

1974 *Nagare no fu: Doran, Yoake* (Sadanaga); *Nostoradamusu no daiyogen* (*Prophecies of Nostradamus*; *Castrophe 1999*) (Masuda)

1977 *Gokumon-to* (*The Devil's Island*; *Island of Horrors*) (Ichikawa) (as the mother)

1978 *Joobachi* (Ichikawa) (as the maid); *Zansho*

1980 *Harukanaru soro*

* * *

Yoko Tsukasa began her career as an actress specializing in the role of the beautiful and sympathetic bourgeois girl so common in the Toho Studio's productions. Cast opposite such popular stars as Ryo Ikebe, Akira Takarada, and Koji Tsuruta, she soon became the most popular Toho melodrama actress of the late 1950s. She projected an air of refined upper-class beauty so successfully that it resulted in her being typecast; nevertheless, she gradually became more ambitious and tried to expand her ability.

She attracted some attention with her enthusiastic performances as the wife of a poor novelist in Hisamatsu's *Aisai-ki* and as the wealthy daughter who is used by the ambitious hero in Horikawa's *The Blue Beast*. Finally, her roles as kindhearted daughters in Ozu's two films, *Late Autumn* and *The End of Summer* brought her real recognition. In both films Tsukasa's soft and natural personality matched Ozu's sensitive portrayal of the serenity of bourgeois family life. A critic pointed out that her character was unusually believable in contrast to the overly dramatized feeling projected by many other actors of that period.

Aside from her contribution to the countless studio comedy series and melodramas through the 1960s, Tsukasa's next important step was the collaboration with Naruse. In *Moment of Terror* she played the dramatic role of a company president's wife who causes a car accident, and in *Two in the Shadow*, by contrast, she played the wife of a car accident victim. Her sensitive performance in the latter, a psychologically complex role in which she is gradually attracted to the man who caused the accident, won her much acclaim.

Although she was also called upon by other directors, such as Kurosawa, Kobayashi, and Ichikawa, her most famous role was as the heroine in Nakamura's *The River Ki*. Here, she gave perhaps her most powerful, yet restrained performance, as she portrayed the life of a woman in a traditional local family.

—Kyoko Hirano

TURNER, Kathleen

Nationality: American. **Born:** Springfield, Missouri, 19 June 1954. **Education:** Attended Southwest Missouri State University, Springfield; University of Maryland, M.F.A., 1977; trained for the stage at Central School of Speech and Drama, London. **Family:** Married Jay Weiss, 1983, daughter: Rachel. **Career:** Acted with the Manitoba Theatre Company, Baltimore Arena Players, and in New York off-off-Broadway; 1976—on Broadway in *Gemini*; 1977-78—in the daytime TV soap opera *The Doctors*; 1981—film debut in *Body Heat*; 1994—directed TV special *Leslie's Folly*. **Awards:** Best Actress, Los Angeles Film Critics, for *Romancing the Stone*, 1984. **Agent:** c/o Phil Gersh, The Gersh Agency, 222 N. Canon Drive, Suite 202, Beverly Hills, CA 90210, U.S.A.

Films as Actress:

1981 *Body Heat* (Kasdan) (as Matty Walker)

1983 *The Man with Two Brains* (Carl Reiner) (as Mrs. Hfuhruhurr)

1984 *Romancing the Stone* (Zemeckis) (as Joan Wilder); *A Breed Apart* (Mora) (as Stella Clayton); *Crimes of Passion* (Russell) (as China Blue/Joanna)

1985 *Prizzi's Honor* (Huston) (as Irene Walker); *The Jewel of the Nile* (Teague) (as Joan Wilder)

1986 *Peggy Sue Got Married* (Coppola) (as Peggy Sue)

1987 *Giulia e Giulia* (*Julia and Julia*) (Del Monte) (as Julia); *Switching Channels* (Kotcheff) (as Christy Colleran)

1988 *Who Framed Roger Rabbit?* (Zemeckis) (as voice of Jessica Rabbit); *The Accidental Tourist* (Kasdan) (as Sarah Leary)

1989 *The War of the Roses* (DeVito) (as Barbara Rose); *Tummy Trouble* (Minkoff—short) (as voice)

1990 *Rollercoaster Rabbit* (short) (as voice of Jessica Rabbit)

1991 *V. I. Warshawski* (Kanew) (title role)

1993 *Trail Mix-Up* (short) (as voice of Jessica Rabbit); *House of Cards* (Lessac) (as Ruth Matthews); *Undercover Blues* (Ross) (as Jane Blue)

1994 *Serial Mom* (Waters) (Mom/Beverly Sutphin); *Naked in New York* (Algrant) (as Dana Coles)

1995 *Friends at Last* (for TV) (as Fanny Conlon, + pr); *Moonlight and Valentino* (Anspaugh) (as Alberta Russell)

Publications

By TURNER: articles—

Interview with N. Mills, in *Stills* (London), March 1986.
Interview with A. Crystal, in *Films and Filming* (London), April 1986.
Interview with Graham Fuller, in *Interview*, August 1995.

On TURNER: book—

Stefoff, Rebecca, *Kathleen Turner*, New York, 1987.

Kathleen Turner in *Prizzi's Honor*

On TURNER: articles—

Doudna, C., "Her Brilliant Career," in *American Film* (Washington, D.C.), November 1984.

Hibbin, S., "Kathleen Turner," in *Films and Filming* (London), October 1985.

Current Biography 1986, New York, 1986.

MacPherson, Malcolm, "Kathleen Turner: The Single-Minded Cinderella," in *Premiere*, November 1989.

Schruers, Fred, "The Sum of Her Parts," in *Premiere*, August 1991.

DeNicolo, David, "Watched Sexpots Still Simmer," in *New York Times*, 10 April 1994.

*   *   *

With her Tallulah voice and sensuous pout, Turner created a sensation by out-fataling the femme fatales of Hollywood's Golden Age in *Body Heat*. This rather academic film noir about instant divorce could have been retitled *Lethal Weapon* with Kathleen unleashed in the title role, but Turner has gone from thinking man's sexpot to character actress with only a brief stopover as major star. While many of her projects outgrossed those of more prestigious contemporaries, she found herself too often pigeonholed vis-à-vis male box-office attractions, with only two hits, *Romancing the Stone* and *Peggy Sue Got Married* (replacing Debra Winger) weighted in her favor. A risk-taker, she shrewdly balanced her steamy debut with a Steve Martin lark, *The Man with Two Brains*, in which she burlesqued her own bitch goddess image. Then, she followed her sensationally popular feminization of *Raiders of the Lost Ark*, *Romancing the Stone*, with a bravura performance as a woman fogged by a sexual identity crisis. Whereas Turner's two-faced characters often camouflaged their amoral purpose, *Crimes of Passion* cleverly split the scheming Turner persona into two aspects of the same personality: Joanna, a repressed 9-to-5 careerist and her after-hours alter ego, a whore named China Blue who indulges Joanna's fantasies. Somehow, her talent flowered in the hothouse atmosphere of Ken Russell's camera flourishes and Barry Sandler's memorably florid dialogue. What lent Turner's work variety was her method of shading a good girl role such as Peggy Sue with a subversive edge while endowing her terminatrix in the corrosively funny *Prizzi's Honor* with a nesting instinct; Irene Walker just happens to kill for a living. Whether victor (*Body Heat*) or victim (*Prizzi's Honor*) in the battle of the sexes, Turner's formidable women never surrender; the impact of her provocative accessibility and killer instinct can be devastating.

After succumbing to sequeldom in *Jewel of the Nile* and rising above the sloppily fashioned but fetching time travel of *Peggy Sue Got Married*, Turner's instincts failed her. Although the leaden black comedy *War of the Roses* drew crowds to its screaming matches, Turner miscalculated by repaying her discoverer, Lawrence Kasdan, by accepting a matronly mourner role in *Accidental Tourist*. More damaging than the Euro-nonsense of *Julia and Julia* or the thuddingly inept remake of *The Front Page*, *Switching Channels*, Turner's drab ancillary turn in *Accidental Tourist* evaporated her sexy demeanor and created the false perception that she was no longer big time. Despite kudos on Broadway for *Cat on a Hot Tin Roof* and *Indiscretions*, Turner slid through muddy problem dramas (*House of Cards*) and inane commercial misfires (*V. I. Warshawski*, *Undercover Blues*) into a slump where her come-hither look now seemed like ancient history. While Turner still flexes the talent to back up her characteristic arrogance, the erosion of youthful allure has limited her career options.

A volatile presence, Turner naughtily parodied sitcom motherhood in John Waters's tame media lampoon *Serial Mom* without erasing memories of Divine and outdazzled her co-stars as a control freak in *Moonlight and Valentino*. No longer a bankable Lorelei, Kathleen has lost none of her pizzazz or outspokenness on or off the screen. It is possible that her manic energy and caustic bite will impressively resurface without further recourse to camp, even though *Serial Mom* revealed that when Turner goes over the top, no one can touch her.

—Robert Pardi

TURNER, Lana

Nationality: American. **Born:** Julia Jean Mildred Frances Turner in Wallace, Idaho, 8 February 1920. **Education:** Attended Hollywood High School. **Family:** Married 1) the musician Artie Shaw, 1940 (divorced 1940); 2) Joseph Stephen Crane, 1942 (divorced 1944), daughter: Cheryl Christine; 3) Henry J. Topping, 1948 (divorced 1952); 4) the actor Lex Barker, 1953 (divorced 1957); 5) Fred May, 1960 (divorced 1962); 6) Robert Eaton, 1965 (divorced 1969); 7) Ronald Dante, 1969 (divorced 1972). **Career:** 1937—film debut in *A Star Is Born*; contract with the director Mervyn LeRoy; role in *They Won't Forget* led to publicity as "Sweater Girl"; 1938-56—contract with MGM; 1958—formed Lanturn Productions; 1966—formed Eltee Productions; 1969—in TV series *The Survivors*; 1971—on stage in *40 Carats*; 1983—in TV series *Falcon Crest*. **Died:** Of throat cancer, in Century City, California, 29 June 1995.

Films as Actress:

1937   *A Star Is Born* (Wellman) (as extra); *They Won't Forget* (LeRoy) (as Mary Clay); *The Great Garrick* (Whale) (as Auber)

1938   *The Adventures of Marco Polo* (Mayo) (as Nazama's maid); *Love Finds Andy Hardy* (Seitz) (as Cynthia Potter); *The Chaser* (Marin) (as Miss Rutherford); *Rich Man, Poor Girl* (Schunzel) (as Helen Thayer); *Dramatic School* (Sinclair) (as Mado); *Four's a Crowd* (Curtiz)

1939   *Calling Dr. Kildare* (Bucquet) (as Rosalie); *These Glamour Girls* (Simon) (as Jane Thomas); *Dancing Co-Ed* (*Every Other Inch a Lady*) (Simon) (as Patty Morgan)

1940   *Two Girls on Broadway* (*Choose Your Partner*) (Simon) (as Pat Mahoney); *We Who Are Young* (Bucquet) (as Margy Brooks)

1941   *Ziegfeld Girl* (Leonard) (as Sheila Regan); *Dr. Jekyll and Mr. Hyde* (Fleming) (as Beatrix Emery); *Honky Tonk* (Conway) (as Elizabeth Cotton)

1942   *Johnny Eager* (LeRoy) (as Lisbeth Bard); *Somewhere I'll Find You* (Ruggles) (as Paula Lane)

1943   *Slightly Dangerous* (Ruggles) (as Peggy Evans/Carol Burden); *The Youngest Profession* (Buzzell) (as herself); *DuBarry Was a Lady* (Del Ruth) (as herself)

1944   *Marriage Is a Private Affair* (Leonard) (as Theo Scofield West)

1945   *Keep Your Powder Dry* (Buzzell) (as Valerie Parks); *Weekend at the Waldorf* (Leonard) (as Bunny Smith)

1946   *The Postman Always Rings Twice* (Garnett) (as Cora Smith)

1947   *Green Dolphin Street* (Saville) (as Marianne Patourel); *Cass Timberlane* (Sidney) (as Virginia Marshland)

1948   *Homecoming* (LeRoy) (as Lt. Jane "Snapshot" McCall); *The Three Musketeers* (Sidney) (as Milady Countess Charlotte de Winter)

1950   *A Life of Her Own* (Cukor) (as Lily Brannel James)

1951   *Mr. Imperium* (*You Belong to My Heart*) (Hartman) (as Fredda Barlo)

Lana Turner

1952	*The Merry Widow* (Bernhardt) (as Crystal Radek); *The Bad and the Beautiful* (Minnelli) (as Georgia Lorrison)
1953	*Latin Lovers* (LeRoy) (as Nora Taylor)
1954	*The Flame and the Flesh* (Thorpe) (as Madeline); *Betrayed* (*The True and the Brave*) (Reinhardt) (as Carla Van Owen)
1955	*The Prodigal* (Thorpe) (as Samarra); *The Sea Chase* (Farrow) (as Elsa Keller); *The Rains of Ranchipur* (Negulesco) (as Edwina Esketh); *Diane* (David Miller) (title role)
1957	*Peyton Place* (Robson) (as Constance MacKenzie)
1958	*The Lady Takes a Flyer* (Arnold) (as Maggie Colby); *Another Time, Another Place* (Lewis Allen) (as Sara Scott)
1959	*Imitation of Life* (Sirk) (as Lora Meredith)
1960	*Portrait in Black* (Michael Gordon) (as Sheila Cabot)
1961	*By Love Possessed* (John Sturges) (as Marjorie Penrose); *Bachelor in Paradise* (Arnold) (as Rosemary Howard)
1962	*Who's Got the Action?* (Daniel Mann) (as Melanie Flood)
1965	*Love Has Many Faces* (Singer) (as Kit Jordan)
1966	*Madame X* (Rich) (as Holly Anderson)
1969	*The Big Cube* (Tito Davison) (as Adriana Roman)
1971	*The Last of the Powerseekers* (Doniger, Leytes, and Henreid—for TV) (as Tracy Carlyle Hastings)
1974	*Persecution* (*Terror of Sheba*; *The Graveyard*) (Chaffey) (as Carrie Masters)
1976	*Bittersweet Love* (David Miller) (as Claire)
1978	*Witches' Brew* (Shorr)

Publications

By TURNER: book—

Lana: The Lady, the Legend, the Truth, New York, 1982.

On TURNER: books—

Wright, Jacqueline, *The Life and Loves of Lana Turner*, New York, 1960.
Morella, Joe, *Lana: The Public and Private Lives of Miss Turner*, New York, 1971.
Rosen, Marjorie, *Popcorn Venus*, New York, 1973.
Basinger, Jeanine, *Lana Turner*, New York, 1976.
Valentino, Lou, *The Films of Lana Turner*, Secaucus, New Jersey, 1976.
Paris, James, *The Hollywood Beauties*, New Rochelle, New York, 1978.
Pero, Taylor, *Always, Lana*, New York, 1982.

Crane, Cheryl, with Cliff Jahr, *Detour: A Hollywood Story*, New York, 1988.

Wayne, Jane Ellen, *Lana: The Life and Loves of Lana Turner*, New York, 1995.

On TURNER: articles—

Current Biography 1943, New York, 1943.

Valentino, Lon, "For Love of Lana," in *Show* (Hollywood), January 1970.

Raborn, G., "Lana Turner," in *Films in Review* (New York), October 1972.

Dyer, Richard, "Four Films of Lana Turner," in *Movie* (London), Winter 1977-78.

"Legendary Lady," in *Harper's Bazaar* (New York), September 1982.

Thomson, David, "A Life of Imitation," in *Film Comment* (New York), May/June 1988.

Obituary in *New York Times*, 1 July 1995.

Obituary in *Variety* (New York), 10 July 1995.

Updike, John, "Legendary Lana," in *New Yorker*, 12 February 1996.

* * *

Lana Turner has come to epitomize the concept of the classical Hollywood movie star. She is identified with glamour, artifice, and excess. The last is not only associated with her on-screen image but also with her offscreen identity. In fact, numerous critics have suggested that Turner's offscreen activities are her primary claim to fame. Aside from the many marriages, the most spectacular instance of her notoriety was the 1958 killing of Turner's gangster lover by her teenaged daughter. The incident catapulted Turner into the realm of celebrity status and it is this distinction that gives her star image a strong contemporary edge. The situation, in deed and coverage, has been only recently surpassed by the media's responses to O. J. Simpson and the double murder. That the scandal has become incorporated into the culture was evidenced by Woody Allen's *September* which features a famous actress and her daughter, who, as a teenager, allegedly killed the mother's lover.

If scandal is an aspect of Turner's contemporary identity, another is a very specific filmic image. The image, Turner dressed in white shorts and halter and wearing a turban, is taken from *The Postman Always Rings Twice* which, in addition to connecting Turner to an illicit lover and murder, presents the actress at her most sexual. It is fitting that she is summed up in a static image since Turner's identity is not associated strongly with performing or a distinctive personality. Martin Scorsese's *Raging Bull* underscores this point in its fleeting but unmistakable reference to the actress—Cathy Moriarty appears, in a poolside scene, in a facsimile of the above-mentioned sunsuit, and, significantly, the context is a nonverbal sequence.

Turner's image as a celebrity is probably reinforced by her films which, on the whole, are not distinguished. Nevertheless, it would be inaccurate to claim that her film career is negligible. Turner, in addition to having an ability to project sexual desire, cultivated a very feminine identity, to the extent that her presence, in terms of grooming and gesture suggested artifice. But Turner is not a passive on-screen presence. Rather, she tends to play women who struggle and refuse to settle for less than what can be had. These characterizations suggest a woman who is desperate and, therefore, reckless; yet, Turner's behavior is often constrained and she, unlike actresses such as Joan Crawford, seems incapable of fully challenging or overriding gender and, in numerous instances, class dictates. Arguably, this happens because she is too fully aligned to femininity, hence a socially controlled identity. Turner's skill resides in her ability to articulate her situation and the insecurities it produces; beneath the somewhat glacial and carefully constructed exterior image, there is a person who is anxious,

fearful, and needs help. It is perhaps this tension which contributes to her appeal as it foregrounds the conflicting responses women experience under patriarchy.

Turner's star image is tightly bound to her sexuality. Such films as *The Prodigal* and *Diane*, in which Turner is paired with weak male co-stars and virtually carries the films herself, suggest that it is her sexual desire that makes her an exciting and transgressive figure. This on-screen emphasis on sex was mirrored offscreen through the marriages and the affairs; yet Turner's offscreen identity was mediated by an emphasis on her as a woman who wanted a lasting marriage, who was a good mother and who was serious about her career. The many contradictions in her identity exploded with the real-life stabbing of her lover and these same contradictions are skillfully utilized by Douglas Sirk in *Imitation of Life*.

Although Turner continued to work into the late 1970s, her film career effectively ends with *Madame X*. From the 1980s onward, Turner shied away from public exposure and the decision to avoid the limelight invested her latter-day image with a degree of dignity. While Turner never fully gained critical acceptance as a performer, she proved herself to be an extremely professional and hard-working woman; and she managed to make an indelible mark on the Hollywood cinema through her presence and star image.

—Richard Lippe

TURTURRO, John

Nationality: American. **Born:** Brooklyn, New York, 28 February 1957; brother of the actor Nicholas Turturro. **Family:** Married the actress Katherine Borowitz, son: Amadeo. **Education:** Was graduated from the State University of New York at New Paltz; earned an M.F.A. in Drama at the Yale Drama School. **Career:** 1980—made screen debut in bit role in *Raging Bull*; 1980s—acted in regional and off-Broadway plays; 1984—made Broadway debut in *Death of a Salesman*; 1988—in TV mini-series *Mario Puzo's The Fortunate Pilgrim*; 1989—first appeared in a Spike Lee-directed film in *Do the Right Thing*; 1992—made screen directing debut with *Mac*. **Awards:** Obie Award, for *Danny and the Deep Blue Sea*, 1985; Best Actor, Cannes Festival, and Independent Feature Project Gotham Award, for *Barton Fink*, 1991; Camera d'Or, Cannes Festival, for *Mac*, 1992. **Address:** 16 North Oak Street, #2B, Ventura, CA 93001, U.S.A.

Films as Actor:

1980   *Raging Bull* (Scorsese)

1984   *Exterminator II* (Buntzman and Sachs) (as Guy No. 1); *The Flamingo Kid* (Garry Marshall) (as Ted from Pinky's)

1985   *Desperately Seeking Susan* (Susan Seidelman) (as Ray); *To Live and Die in L.A.* (Friedkin) (as Carl Cody)

1986   *The Color of Money* (Scorsese) (as Julian); *Gung Ho* (*Working Class Man*) (Ron Howard) (as Willie); *Hannah and Her Sisters* (Woody Allen) (as Writer); *Off Beat* (Dinner) (as Neil Pepper)

1987   *The Sicilian* (Cimino) (as Aspanu Pisciotta)

1989   *Five Corners* (Bill) (as Heinz Sabantino); *Do the Right Thing* (Spike Lee) (as Pino); *Backtrack* (*Catchfire*) (Dennis Hopper—released in U.S. in 1991) (as Pinella)

1990   *Mo' Better Blues* (Spike Lee) (as Moe Flatbush); *Miller's Crossing* (Coen) (as Bernie Bernbaum); *State of Grace* (Joanou) (as Nick)

1991   *Men of Respect* (Reilly) (as Mike Battaglia); ***Barton Fink*** (Coen) (title role); *Jungle Fever* (Spike Lee) (as Paulie Carbone)

John Turturro in *Mac*

1992   *Brain Donors* (Dugan) (as Roland T. Flakfizer)
1993   *Fearless* (Weir) (as Bill Perlman)
1994   *Quiz Show* (Redford) (as Herbert Stempel); *Being Human*
        (Forsyth) (as Lucinnius)
1995   *Clockers* (Spike Lee) (as Larry Mazilli); *Unstrung Heroes*
        (Diane Keaton) (as Sid Lidz); *Search and Destroy* (Salle) (as
        Ron)
1996   *Girl 6* (Spike Lee) (as Murray, the agent)

Films as Director:

1992   *Mac* (+ title role, co-sc)

Publications

By TURTURRO: articles—

"Yale Drama School, John Turturro & Katherine Borowitz," interview
    with Tama Janowitz, in *Interview* (New York), September 1985.
"John Turturro Finks Twice," interview with G. Smith, in *Interview*
    (New York), September 1990.
"Getting Down to the Bone," interview with Marlaine Glicksman, in
    Film Comment (New York), September/October 1990.
"Une irresistible ascension," interview with Michel Ciment and H.
    Niogret, in *Positif* (Paris), September 1991.
"Une histoire universelle," interview with Michel Ciment and H.
    Niogret, in *Positif* (Paris), November 1992.
"John Turturro, Katherine Borowitz," interview with Veronica Cham-
    bers, in *Premiere* (New York), February 1993.
Turturro, John, "Big Mack," in *Village Voice* (New York), 23 February
    1993.
"John Turturro," interview with Manola Dargis, in *Interview* (New
    York), March 1993.

On TURTURRO: articles—

Tyre, P., "Fast Track: John Turturro's Bad-Guy Blues," in *New York*, 5
    October 1987.
Diamond, Jamie, "John Turturro," in *Premiere* (New York), Septem-
    ber 1989.
Dieckmann, K., "John Turturro's Character Building," in *Rolling Stone*
    (New York), 17 May 1990.
Minx, P., "Big Bad John," in *Village Voice* (New York), 19 June 1990.
Weber, B., "Born into a Cast of Characters, What Can One Do but
    Act," in *New York Times*, 5 May 1991.
Solomon, A., "Do the Wrong Thing," in *Village Voice* (New York), 7
    May 1991.
Saada, N., "John Turturro," in *Cahiers du Cinéma* (Paris), June
    1991.
Hoban, Phoebe, "Honest John," in *New York*, 12 August 1991.
Miller, M., "Brooklyn's Common Man," in *Newsweek* (New York), 26
    August 1991.
Carter, Z. F., "Not Just Another Face," in *Premiere* (New York), Sep-
    tember 1991.
Chanko, Kenneth M., "John Turturro," in *Films in Review* (New York),
    September/October 1991.
Wayne, H., "That's Italian," in *Playboy* (Chicago), March 1993.
Webster, A., filmography in *Premiere* (New York), September 1994.

*   *   *

John Turturro is an actor in the mold of Robert De Niro, Al Pacino,
and Harvey Keitel: intense and multitalented, New York City-born

and very much the New York performer. After knocking around films
for several years, this Yale Drama School grad first earned notice in
Five Corners, set in the Bronx, in which he offers a hair-raising performance as Heinz Sabantino, a creep who is sexually obsessed with
pet store worker Linda (Jodie Foster).

Turturro's primary strength is that he is a master at playing a range
of attitudes. He can portray racists who are either upfront in their bias
(Pino, the epithet-spewing pizza man, in Spike Lee's *Do the Right
Thing*) or more subtle and cunning (Moe Flatbush, the greedy jazz club
owner—a character who is an anti-Semitic caricature—in Lee's *Mo'
Better Blues*). On the other hand, he just as effectively can play a child
of the working class who is a gentle soul, one who is put off by the
racial prejudices of others and even is open to a relationship with a
black woman (Paulie Carbone, the sensitive luncheonette operator, in
Lee's *Jungle Fever*).

Turturro can play a thug with a devilishly comic flair (Bernie
Bernbaum, the manic lowlife who earns his keep as an informer and
double-crosser, in *Miller's Crossing*). He can play a reckless, neurotic
nebbish (sore-loser *Twenty-One* contestant Herbert Stempel, in *Quiz
Show*). He can play a sweetly eccentric husband and father (Sid Lidz,
who is faced with the terminal illness of his wife, in *Unstrung Heroes*).
Or he can play an intellectual (the title character in the Hollywood
satire *Barton Fink*, a dedicated New York playwright who heads for
Hollywood in 1941 and whose primary concern is the plight of the
"Common Man"; but he finds himself assigned to pen a wrestling
picture for Wallace Beery—and promptly develops a severe case of
writer's block).

Turturro made his directorial debut with *Mac*, a heartfelt comedy-
drama about one man's determination to realize his American Dream.
The film is set in the mid-1950s and tells the story of three Italian-
American brothers, sons of an immigrant tradesman who has just died.
The story focuses on the title character, Niccolo "Mac" Vitelli, played
by Turturro. The eldest of the trio, Mac is a carpenter like his dad, and
he labors for a bullheaded, penny-pinching contractor who offends his
sense of professionalism; he decides to start his own construction
company, satisfied he can erect better houses and be a more humane
employer. *Mac*, which Turturro co-scripted (with Brandon Cole),
clearly is a film from his heart. It is dedicated to his own carpenter
father, and inspired by the senior Turturro's life. The result is a refreshingly sincere depiction of the lives and struggles of average,
working-class Americans, a subject rarely explored in mainstream
Hollywood movies. But more than anything else, *Mac* is a film about
the dignity of work. "You know what I think happiness is?" Mac asks
at one point. "To love your job. Not many people know this—that's
why they take vacations—but it's the truth. If you hate your work,
you hate your life. I love my work."

Clearly, Turturro loves his work. And if he permits scenes in *Mac* to
run a tad too long, one suspects it is because his respect for the acting
craft obscured his good judgment as a director-storyteller. Nonetheless, one hopes that in the future Turturro will not just confine his
career to acting.

—Rob Edelman

TYSZKIEWICZ, Beata

Nationality: Polish. **Born:** Warsaw, 14 August 1938. **Education:**
Attended Warsaw Theatre School, was graduated in 1959. **Family:**
Married 1) the director Andrzej Wajda, daughter: Karolina; 2) the
director Witold Orzechowski. **Career:** 1957—film debut in *Zemsta*;
1961—first of several films for Wajda, *Samson*; much work on television.

Films as Actress:

1958 *Zemsta* (*Vengeance*; *The Revenge*) (Bohdziewicz)
1959 *Wspólny pokój* (*One-Room Tenants*; *Roomers*) (Has)
1960 *Szklana góra* (*The Glass Mountain*) (Komorowski)
1961 *Odwiedziny prezydenta* (*The President's Visit*; *Visit of a President*) (Batory); *Samson* (Wajda); *Zaduszki* (*Halloween*) (Konwicki) (as Katarzyna); *Dzis w nocy umrze miastro* (*A Town Will Die Tonight*; *Tonight a Town Dies*) (Rybkowsky)
1962 *Spóźnieni przechodnie* (*Those Who Are Late*) (Wohl and Rybkowski); *Czarne skrzydla* (*Black Wings*) (Petelscy)
1963 *Naprawde wczoraj* (*Yesterday in Fact*) (Rybkowski) (as Ewa); *Yokmok* (Mozdzenski); *Skapani w ogniu* (*Christened by Fire*) (Passendorfer)
1964 *Spotkanie ze szpiegem* (*Encounter with a Spy*) (Batory); *Pierwszy dzień wolności* (*The First Day of Freedom*) (Alexander Ford)
1965 *Rekopis znaleziony w Saragossie* (*The Saragossa Manuscript*; *Manuscript Found in Saragossa*) (Has) (as Rebeka Uzeda); *Popioły* (*Ashes*) (Wajda) (as Princess Elzbieta)
1966 *Marysia i Napoleon* (*Maria and Napoleon*) (Buczkowski) (as Maria Walewska); *De man die zijn haar kort liet knippen* (*The Man Who Had His Hair Cut Short*)
1967 *Alexandre i Chanakya*
1968 *Wszystko na sprzedaź* (*Everything for Sale*) (Wajda) (as Beata); *Lalka* (*The Doll*) (Has) (as Izabela Lecka); *L'Homme au crâne rasé* (Delvaux)
1969 *Dvoryanskoye gnezdo* (*A Nest of Gentlefolk*) (Mikhalkov and Konchalovsky) (as Varvara Pavlovna); *Egy örült éjszaka* (*A Mad Night*) (Kardos); *Az idö ablakai* (*The Windows of Time*) (Feher) (as Eva)
1970 *Szep magyar komedia* (*Lovely Hungarian Comedy*)
1977 *Ta Inczacy Tastrzab* (*The Dancing Hawk*) (Krolikiewicz)
1979 *Utközben* (*En cours de route*) (Mészáros) (as wife); *Niewdzieczno is ic* (Kaminski)
1980 *Acht und Siebzig* (*Don Juan, Karl-Liebeknecht-Strasse 78*) (Kuhn); *Sowizdrzal swietokrzyski* (Kluba)
1981 *Mniejsze Wiebo* (*Smaller Sky*) (Morgenstern); *Kontrakt* (*The Contract*) (Zanussi)
1983 *Edith et Marcel* (*Edith and Marcel*) (Lelouch) (as Margot's mother)
1984 *1944* (Konic); *Przypieszenie* (Rebzda); *W Starym Dworku* (Kotkwski) (as Anastasia); *Sexmisja* (*Sex Mission*) (Machulski) (as Berna)
1985 *Megfelelo ember kenyes feladatra* (Kovacsi) (as the Lady in the Hat)
1986 *Komediantka* (Sztwiertnia) (as Cabinska)
1988 *Usmev diabla* (Zeman); *Bernadette* (Delannoy) (as Mrs. Pailhasson)
1989 *Deux* (*Two*) (Zidi) (as Mrs. Muller)
1993 *Dotkniecie reki* (*The Silent Touch*) (Zanussi) (as Gelda); *Dwa ksiezyce* (*Two Moons*) (Baranski)

Publications

By TYSZKIEWICZ: article—

"Good Day, pani Beata!," interview with A. Zimina, in *Soviet Film* (Moscow), no. 11, 1984.

On TYSZKIEWICZ: articles—

Elley, D., "Beata Tyszkiewicz," in *Focus on Film* (London), Autumn 1973.
Tabecki, J., in *Iluzjon* (Warsaw), January/March and April/June 1989.

* * *

Beata Tyszkiewicz is the only leading Polish actress not associated with the theater but who has devoted her talents entirely to film. Without any previous dramatic training, she had her debut at the age of 19 in a film version of the classic play *Vengeance*. Only then did she catch up on her training, and since that time she has almost always had the same kind of role. Tyszkiewicz is the Polish embodiment of the aristocrat by birth. Her stately beauty, coupled with a serene temperament, predestines her for the noble, refined heroines who confront and control their fate with dignity.

To begin with, she played the parts of young contemporary women, and even had the part of the partisan leader Katarzyna in *Halloween*, succeeding in conveying the inborn subtlety of the character despite her strict lifestyle and vigorous principles. A sequence of historical figures followed: Polish countesses who have played a significant role in the country's history and literature and in the national consciousness—Princess Elzbieta in *Ashes*, Maria Walewska in *Maria and Napoleon*, Ewelina Hanska in *The Love of Balzac*, and Izabela Lecka in *The Doll*. In contrast to many actresses who interpret historical personalities with a clearly contemporary flair and in relation to the present day, Tyszkiewicz endows her legendary Polish ladies with a certain splendor that corresponds to the idealized image of them entertained by the modern woman. Ancestry has a particular importance in the Polish consciousness, and Tyszkiewicz satisfies the modern Pole's nostalgic longing to know about his or her ancestors.

Tyszkiewicz has also played other types of roles. The most interesting, in *Everything for Sale* by Andrzej Wajda, is Beata, a thoroughly modern, self-confident, and successful artist. In this film Tyszkiewicz creates a loftier, more serene impression than the other two female characters; she has an inner integrity which none of the other characters in the film possess. Tyszkiewicz has acted for several foreign directors, but never with the same success as in her Polish films.

—Maria Racheva

U-V

ULLMANN, Liv

Nationality: Norwegian. **Born:** Liv Johanne Ullmann in Tokyo, Japan, to Norwegian parents, 16 December 1939. **Education:** Attended schools in Trondheim, Norway; studied acting in London for eight months. **Family:** Married 1) Gappe Stang, 1960 (divorced 1965); 2) Donald Saunders, 1985; one daughter by the director Ingmar Bergman. **Career:** Late 1950s—acted with a repertory company in Stavanger for three years; 1957—film debut in *Fjols til Fjells*; 1960—acted with the National Theatre and the Norwegian Theatre, both in Oslo; 1966—first of a series of films for Bergman. **Awards:** Swedish Gold Bug for Best Actress, for *Skammen*, 1969; Best Actress, New York Film Critics, for *Cries and Whispers* and *The Emigrants*, 1972; Best Actress, New York Film Critics, for *Scenes from a Marriage*, 1974; Best Actress, New York Film Critics, for *Face to Face*, 1976. **Address:** 15 West 81st Street, New York, NY 10024, U.S.A.

Films as Actress:

1957   *Fjols til Fjells* (*Fools in the Mountains*) (Carlmar)

1959   *Ung flukt* (*Young Escape*) (Carlmar)

1962   *Kort är Sommaren* (*Summer Is Short*) (Henning-Jensen) (as Eva)

1965   *De kalte ham Skarven* (*They Call Him Skarven*) (Gustavson) (as Ragna)

1966   *Persona* (Bergman) (as Elisabeth Vogler)

1968   *Vargtimmen* (*Hour of the Wolf*) (Bergman) (as Alma); *An-Magritt* (Skouen) (title role); *Skammen* (*The Shame*) (Bergman) (as Eva Rosenberg)

1969   *En Passion* (*A Passion*; *The Passion of Anna*) (Bergman) (as Anna Fromm)

1971   *The Night Visitor* (Benedek) (as Esther Jenks)

1972   *Pope Joan* (Anderson) (title role); ***Viskningar och rop*** (*Cries and Whispers*) (Bergman) (as a sister); *Utvandrarna* (*The Emigrants*) (Troell) (as Kristina)

1973   *Nybyggarna* (*The New Land*) (Troell) (as Kristina); *Lost Horizon* (Jarrott) (as Catherine); *40 Carats* (Katselar) (as Ann Stanley); *Scener ur ett äktenskap* (*Scenes from a Marriage*) (Bergman—for TV) (as Marianne)

1974   *Zandy's Bride* (Troell) (as Hannah Land); *The Abdication* (Harvey) (as Queen Christina); *L'uomo dalle due ombre* (*De la part des copains*; *Cold Sweat*) (Young) (as Fabienne); *Léonor* (Juan Buñuel) (title role)

1976   *Ansikte mot ansikte* (*Face to Face*) (Bergman—for TV) (as Jenny)

1977   *A Bridge Too Far* (Attenborough) (as Kate ter Horst); *The Serpent's Egg* (*Das Schlangenei*; *Örmens ägg*) (Bergman) (as Manuela Rosenberg)

1978   *Herbstsonate* (*Autumn Sonata*) (Bergman) (as Eva); *Couleur chair* (Wyergans)

1979   *A Look at Liv* (Kaplan—doc) (as herself)

1980   *The Gates of the Forest*

1981   *Richard's Things* (Harvey) (as Kate)

1983   *Children in the Holocaust* (Eisner—doc) (as narrator); *Jacobo Timerman* (*Prisoner without a Name, Cell without a Number*) (Greene—for TV)

1984   *Jenny* (Bronken—for TV); *The Wild Duck* (Safran) (as Gina); *La Diagonale du fou* (*Dangerous Moves*) (Dembo) (as Marina Fromm)

1985   *The Bay Boy* (Petrie) (as Jennie Campbell); *Ingrid* (Annakin, Crabtree, and French)

1986   *Speriamo che sia femmina* (*Let's Hope It's a Girl*) (Monicelli) (as Elena)

1987   *Gaby: A True Story* (Mandoki) (as Sari Brimmer); *Mosca Addio* (*Moscow Goodbye*) (Bolognini) (as Ida Nudel)

1988   *La amiga* (Meerapfel) (as Maria)

1989   *The Rose Garden* (Rademakers) (as Gabriele Schlueter-Freund)

1991   *Mindwalk* (Bernt Capra) (as Sonia Hoffman); *The Ox* (Nykvist) (as Maria)

1992   *The Long Shadow* (Zsigmond) (as Katherine)

1994   *Dromspel* (*Dreamplay*) (Unni Straume) (as ticket seller); *Zorn* (as Gunnar Hallström) (as Emma Zorn)

Films as Director:

1982   *Love* (co-d)

1992   *Sofie* (+ sc)

1995   *Kristin Lavransdatter* (+ sc)

Publications

By ULLMANN: books—

Changing, London, 1977.
Choices, New York, 1984.

By ULLMANN: articles—

Interview with A. Leroux, in *Séquences* (Montreal), July 1975.
"Jouer avec Bergman," interview with M. Ciment, in *Positif* (Paris), March 1978.
Interview with Virginia Wexman, in *Cinema Journal* (Evanston, Illinois), Fall 1980.
"We Are Good - Deep Down; But We Do So Little about It," in *Glamour*, January 1990.
"A New Career for Liv Ullmann," interview in *New York Times*, 4 October 1993.

On ULLMANN: books—

Olsen, Bjorn Gunnar, *Jens Bjorneboe, Liv Ullmann og 16 andge intervjuet*, Oslo, 1976.
Outerbridge, David, *Without Makeup: Liv Ullmann: A Photo-Biography*, New York, 1979.

Liv Ullmann in *Viskningar och rop* © 1973 Cinematograph AB

On ULLMANN: articles—

Current Biography 1973, New York, 1973.
"Liv Ullmann," in *Focus on Film* (London), Spring 1973.
"Scénes de vie conjugale," in *Avant-Scène du Cinéma* (Paris), October 1975.
Raphaelson, S., "For the Love of Liv," in *American Film* (Washington, D.C.), May 1977.
Ecran (Paris), March 1978.
Lally, K., "Ullmann Turns to Directing with Period Saga of *Sofie*," in *Film Journal*, May 1993.

* * *

From the mid-1960s, Liv Ullmann represented to American audiences a sensual and sophisticated screen presence that did not exist within Hollywood. Her earthy beauty was best utilized in a series of provocative films directed by her mentor, Ingmar Bergman.

Her film credits were few and minor—she had appeared in several little-known Norwegian features—when Ullmann first met Bergman in Stockholm. He offered her the principal role of the mute Elisabeth Vogler in the psychologically complicated and exacting study *Persona*. There followed not only an artistic collaboration between the director and actress, but for a time, a deep personal and emotional relationship. *Persona* gave Ullmann a great acting opportunity, and was both an artistic and personal success for her. "It was difficult," says Ullmann. "I prepared myself so that I read the script several times and I tried to divide it into certain sections. Bergman helped me a lot. He differs very much from what the majority of people think of him. People say that he is a demon, but it is not true at all. He simply knows whom to engage. He listens and then he tries to get the maximum from an actor."

Under Bergman's influence, Ullmann became an internationally recognized actress. In the films *Persona*, *Hour of the Wolf*, *Shame*, *Cries and Whispers*, *Scenes from a Marriage*, and *Face to Face*, she creates immensely complicated portraits of contemporary women. Able to communicate an entire range of emotions through minute details of action, she relies neither on sharp mimicry nor intensified vocal intonation in her portrayals. Nevertheless, she is capable of expressing urgency, sensitivity, and agitation by the slightest movement of her eyes. Ullmann interprets the feelings and inner actions of her heroines by suggestion. Although trained in the theater, her experience there is not evident, except perhaps in some long Bergmanesque dialogue passages in which, through her ardor, she is able to draw the audience into her own inner conflict. Ullmann's mastery of the dramatic consists precisely of the simplicity and realism of her expression.

While Ullmann is best known for her work with Bergman, she has performed equally exacting roles while working with other directors. In particular, her portrayal of the rural woman, Kristina, in *The Emigrants* and *The New Land*, Jan Troell's two-part film of immigrant life in 19th-century America, merits extraordinary attention. She also acted under Troell's direction in the psychological drama *Zandy's Bride*.

After the successes of these films, Ullmann accepted several American offers. Her appearances in such films as the musical version of *Lost Horizon*, *40 Carats*, *The Abdication*, and *A Bridge Too Far* are tremendous disappointments to the art-house audiences who had followed her rise to stardom with Bergman.

Between films, Ullmann returns to the stage. "I think that one should not go from one film to another. It is no good. If I do not shoot, I write and meet friends. I make about two films per year and one theatrical play. This is a good working program." Ullmann has performed successfully on the stage in Norway, London, and other cities, in addition to her highly praised literary efforts. Most recently, she has worked behind the camera, having directed and scripted two well-received, similar-themed features: *Sofie*, the tale of a young woman in nineteenth-century Copenhagen who is unable to sever her constricting family ties; and *Kristin Lavransdatter*, set in the Middle Ages, in which a well-born young woman, betrothed to another from her class, disgraces her family upon falling in love with a knight.

These multiple achievements rank Ullmann on a high level of accomplishment—along with such actresses as Ingrid Thulin, Bibi and Harriet Andersson, and Gunnel Lindblom, she has made a remarkable contribution to Scandinavian film art.

—Vaclàv Merhaut, updated by Audrey E. Kupferberg

USTINOV, (Sir) Peter

Nationality: British. **Born:** Peter Alexander Ustinov in London, England, 16 April 1921. **Education:** Attended Westminster School, London, 1934-37; studied for the stage under Michel St. Denis at the London Theatre Studio, 1937-39. **Military Service:** British Army Ordnance Corps, Royal Sussex Regiment, 1942-46; Army film unit, 1943. **Family:** Married 1) Isolde Denham, 1940 (divorced 1950), daughter: Tamara; 2) Suzanne Cloutier, 1954 (divorced 1971), son: Igor, daughters: Pavla and Andrea; 3) Hélène du Lau d'Allemans, 1972. **Career:** 1938—stage debut in a theater in Shere, Surrey; 1939—London stage debut in revue sketch; acted with Aylesbury Repertory Company; 1941—film debut in *Hullo Fame*; 1946—directed first film, *School for Secrets*; playwright and director: appeared in his own plays *The Love of Three Oranges*, 1951, *Romanoff and Juliet*, 1956 (and in film version, 1961), *Photo Finish*, 1962, *The Unknown Soldier and His Wife*, 1968, and *Beethoven's Tenth*, 1983; 1962—directed an opera triple bill at Covent Garden, London; also directed operas in Hamburg and Berlin; 1968-73—Rector, Dundee University; in TV mini-series *Jesus of Nazareth*, 1977, *Around the World in 80 Days*, 1989, and *The Old Curiosity Shop*, 1995; also made recordings of monologues and sketches. **Awards:** Emmy Award, for *The Life of Samuel Johnson*, 1957; Best Supporting Actor Academy Award, for *Spartacus*, 1960; Best Supporting Actor Academy Award, for *Topkapi*, 1964; Emmy Award, for *Barefoot in Athens*, 1966; Emmy Award, for *A Storm in Summer*, 1970; Special Prize, Berlin Festival, 1972; Commander, Order of the British Empire, 1975; knighted, 1990; several honorary degrees. **Agent:** William Morris Agency, 31-32 Soho Square, London W1V 5DG, England.

Films as Actor:

1941 *Hullo Fame* (Buchanan); *Mein Kampf—My Crimes* (Lee)
1942 *Let My People Sing* (Baxter); *The Goose Steps Out* (Dearden and Hay) (as Krauss); *One of Our Aircraft Is Missing* (Powell and Pressburger) (as priest)
1943 *The New Lot* (Reed—doc)
1944 *The Immortal Battalion* (*The Way Ahead*) (Reed) (as Rispoli, + co-sc)
1945 *The True Glory* (Reed and Kanin)
1950 *Odette* (Wilcox) (as Arnaud)
1951 *Quo Vadis* (LeRoy) (as Nero); *Hotel Sahara* (Annakin) (as Emad); *The Magic Box* (John Boulting) (as film distributor); "The Mask," "The Model," and "The House of Madame Tellier" eps. of *Le Plaisir* (*House of Pleasure*) (Max Ophüls) (as narrator of English-language version)
1954 *Beau Brummel* (Bernhardt) (as Prince of Wales); *The Egyptian* (Curtiz) (as Kaptah)
1955 *We're No Angels* (Curtiz) (as Jules); **Lola Montès** (*The Sins of Lola Montès*; *The Fall of Lola Montès*) (Max Ophüls) (as ringmaster)
1956 *I girovaghi* (*The Wanderers*) (Fregonese) (as Don Alfonso)
1957 *Un angel pasò por Brooklyn* (*An Angel over Brooklyn*; *The Man Who Wagged His Tail*) (Vajda) (as Mr. Bossi); *Les Espions* (*The Spies*) (Clouzot) (as Michael Kiminsky)
1959 *The Adventures of Mr. Wonderful* (Grimault) (as voice)
1960 *Spartacus* (Kubrick) (as Lentulus Batiatus); *The Sundowners* (Zinnemann) (as Rupert Venneker)
1963 *La donna del mondo* (*Women of the World*) (Jacopetti) (as narrator); *Alleman* (*Everyman*; *The Human Dutch*) (Haanstra—doc) (as English-language narrator)
1964 *The Peaches* (Gill—short) (as narrator); *Topkapi* (Dassin) (as Arthur Simpson); *John Goldfarb, Please Come Home* (Lee Thompson) (as King Fawz)
1967 *The Comedians* (Glenville) (as Ambassador Pineda)
1968 *Blackbeard's Ghost* (Stevenson) (as Capt. Blackbeard); *Hot Millions* (Till) (as Marcus Pendleton, + co-sc)
1969 *Viva Max!* (Paris) (as Gen. Maximilian Rodrigues de Santos)
1973 *Robin Hood* (Reitherman—animation) (as voice of Prince John)
1975 *One of Our Dinosaurs Is Missing* (Stevenson) (as Hnup Wan)
1976 *Treasure of Matecumbe* (McEveety) (as Dr. Ewing T. Snodgrass); *Logan's Run* (Michael Anderson) (as Old Man)
1977 *Un Taxi mauve* (*The Purple Taxi*) (Boisset) (as Taubelman); *The Last Remake of Beau Geste* (Feldman) (as Sgt. Markov); *The Mouse and His Child* (Wolf and Swenson—animation) (as voice of Manny the Rat)
1978 *Doppio delitto* (*Double Murders*) (Steno) (as Harry Hellman); *Death on the Nile* (Guillermin) (as Hercule Poirot); *Tarka the Otter* (Cobham) (as narrator); *Winds of Change* (Tokashi) (as narrator); *The Thief of Bagdad* (Clive Donner—for TV) (as the Caliph)
1979 *Ashanti* (Fleischer) (as Suleiman); *Nous maigrirons ensemble* (*We'll Grow Thin Together*) (Vocoret) (as Victor)
1981 *Charlie Chan and the Curse of the Dragon Queen* (Clive Donner) (as Charlie Chan); *The Great Muppet Caper* (Henson) (cameo as truck driver); *Grendel, Grendel, Grendel* (Stitt—animation) (as voice of Grendel)
1982 *Evil under the Sun* (Hamilton) (as Hercule Poirot)
1984 *Abgehört* (Rolf Von Sydow—for TV)

1985   *Thirteen at Dinner* (Antonio—for TV) (as Hercule Poirot)
1986   *Dead Man's Folly* (Clive Donner—for TV) (as Hercule Poirot);
          Ferdinand (Behle) (as narrator)
1987   *Three Act Tragedy* (*Murder in Three Acts*) (Gary Nelson—for
          TV) (as Hercule Poirot)
1988   *Appointment with Death* (Winner) (as Hercule Poirot); *Peep
          and Big Wide World* (short); *Kinderen van Ghana*
          (Haanstra—doc, short) (as narrator)
1989   *La Revolution Française* (*The French Revolution*) (Enrico)
          (as Mirabeau); *Grandpa* (Jackson) (as voice)
1990   *C'era un Castello con 40 Cani*
1992   *Lorenzo's Oil* (George Miller) (as Professor Nikolais)

Films as Director and Scriptwriter:

1946   *School for Secrets* (*Secret Flight*) (d only, + co-pr)
1947   *Vice Versa* (+ ro, co-pr)
1949   *Private Angelo* (co-d with Michael Anderson, co-sc, + title
          role, pr)
1961   *Romanoff and Juliet* (*Dig That Juliet*) (+ ro as the general, pr)
1962   *Billy Budd* (co-sc, + ro as Capt. Edward Fairfax Vere, pr)
1965   *Lady L* (+ ro as Prince Otto of Bavaria)
1972   *Hammersmith Is Out* (d only, + ro as the doctor)
1984   *Memed My Hawk* (*The Lion and the Hawk*) (+ ro)

Publications

By USTINOV: books—

House of Regrets (play), London, 1943.
Beyond (play), London, 1944.
The Banbury Nose (play), London, 1945.
Plays about People, London, 1950.
The Love of Four Colonels (play), London, 1951.
The Moment of Truth (play), London, 1953.
Romanoff and Juliet (play), London, 1957.
Add a Dash of Pity (stories), London, 1959.
The Loser (novel), London, 1961.
Ustinov's Diplomats: A Book of Photographs, New York, 1961.
We Were Only Humans (caricatures), London, 1961.
Photo Finish (play), London, 1962.
Five Plays, London, 1965.
The Frontiers of the Sea (stories), London, 1966.
The Unknown Soldier and His Wife (play), New York, 1967.
Halfway Up the Tree (play), New York, 1968.
The Wit of Peter Ustinov, edited by Dick Richards, London, 1969.
Krumnagel (novel), London, 1971.
Dear Me (autobiography), London, 1977.
My Russia, London, 1983.
Beethovan's Tenth: A Comedy in Two Acts (play), New York, 1985.
Ustinov in Russia, London, 1987.
The Disinformer (stories), London, 1989.
The Old Man and Mr. Smith: A Fable (novel), New York, 1991.
Ustinov at Large, London, 1991.
Ustinov Still at Large, London, 1993.
Quotable Ustinov, London, 1995.

By USTINOV: articles—

"Max Ophüls," in *Sight and Sound* (London), Summer 1957.
"Doing It All at Once," in *Films and Filming* (London), May
    1960.
Interview with Gideon Bachmann, in *Film* (London), Winter 1961.

Interview with D. N. Mount, in *Publishers Weekly* (New York), 25
    October 1971.
Interview with Brian McFarlane, in *Cinema Papers* (Melbourne), April
    1982.
Interview with Allan Hunter, in *Films and Filming* (London), Septem-
    ber 1983.
Interview with V. Lacombe, in *Cinéma* (Paris), 27 April 1988.

On USTINOV: books—

Willans, Geoffrey, *Peter Ustinov*, London, 1957.
Thomas, Tony, *Ustinov in Focus*, London, 1971.
Stewart, V. Lorne, *Peter Ustinov and His World: An Authorized Bio-
    graphical Sketch*, Nashville, Tennessee, 1988.
Warwick, Christopher, *The Universal Ustinov*, London, 1990.

On USTINOV: articles—

Current Biography 1955, New York, 1955.
"Peter the Great," in *Variety* (New York), 27 July 1992.
Coali, G., and I. Jachini, "Ustinov in Vaticano," in *Rivista del
    Cinematografo* (Rome), May 1993.
"The Greatest Living Raconteur," in *Forbes* (New York), 22 Novem-
    ber 1993.

                *   *   *

Juggling as many careers as the multitalented Peter Ustinov does—
screen and stage actor, film and stage director, playwright, novelist,
screenwriter, and raconteur—he has never had the inclination to channel
his enormous creative energies into screen acting. Nor does he possess
the pure acting ability to warrant such a career decision. Still, despite
a casualness about his acting that makes him seem a begrudging on-
screen performer (a stance happily appropriate to the playing of
comedy), he has nevertheless accomplished much as a movie actor
with a predisposition toward the humorous.

Born in London, of French and Russian descent, Ustinov attended
the London Theatre Studio as an aspiring actor, debuted on stage at
age 17, and appeared in his first film—*Hullo Fame*—three years later.
The film that first brought him substantial recognition was Mervyn
LeRoy's spectacle, *Quo Vadis*, in which he portrays ancient Rome's
reigning Emperor Nero. His prominent roles thereafter include:
Michael Curtiz's *We're No Angels* as a fellow convict who has escaped
Devil's Island with Humphrey Bogart; Max Ophüls' *Lola Montès* as
the circus ringmaster exhibiting Martine Carol's titular courtesan;
Stanley Kubrick's *Spartacus* as an avaricious slave dealer, a performance that won him the Best Supporting Actor Oscar; *Romanoff and
Juliet*, which he also wrote and directed, as the ruler of a mythical
country; his own film version of Herman Melville's *Billy Budd* as
Captain Vere; Jules Dassin's *Topkapi* as a comic con man (and his
second Oscar); Eric Till's *Hot Millions* as a computer-aided embezzler;
and Jerry Paris's *Viva Max!* as a contemporary Mexican general reclaiming the Alamo.

After a quiet decade or so, during which time his film career
remained a virtual afterthought, the character actor was cast in
1978 as the idiosyncratic, indomitable Belgian supersleuth, Hercule
Poirot, in John Guillermin's *Death on the Nile*, an Agatha Christie
mystery with a star-studded cast. In this bit of fluff, Ustinov's
effortless expertise at dialectal and physical comedy is smoothly
integrated and brightly highlighted, a reminder of how winning this
one-man creative conglomerate's acting franchise can be in the
right comic role.

In the 1980s, he reprised the Poirot role in several subsequent
television movies and two additional theatrical films, *Evil under the
Sun* and *Appointment with Death*. After playing a rather soft-pedaled

version of Mirabeau in the somewhat disappointing big-budget international co-production *The French Revolution* in 1989, Ustinov entered another period of scant screen appearances in the 1990s. He had a nice turn, however, in the disease thriller *Lorenzo's Oil* as a sympathetic yet cautious doctor representative of a risk-averse medical profession.

—Bill Wine, updated by David E. Salamie

VALENTINO, Rudolph

Born: Rodolpho Alfonzo Raffaelo di Valentina d'Antonguolla in Castellaneta, Italy, 6 May 1895. **Education:** Attended a military academy; Royal Academy of Agriculture. **Family:** Married 1) Jean Acker, 1919 (divorced 1922); 2) Natasha Rambova, 1922 (separated 1925). **Career:** Left home for Paris, 1912, and emigrated to the United States, 1913; worked at odd jobs, then a dancer in dance halls, clubs and musicals; worked as extra in films on the east coast, and then in Hollywood; 1921—enormous hit in film *The Four Horsemen of the Apocalypse*, then *The Sheik.* **Died:** Of peritonitis in New York, 23 August 1926.

Films as Actor:

1914   *My Official Wife* (Young)
1916   *Patricia* (L. and T. Wharton—serial)
1918   *Alimony* (Flynn); *A Society Sensation* (Powell); *All Night* (Powell)
1919   *The Delicious Little Devil* (Leonard); *A Rogue's Romance* (Young); *The Homebreaker* (Schertzinger); *Virtuous Sinners* (Flynn); *The Big Little Person* (Leonard); *Out of Luck* (Clifton); *Eyes of Youth* (Parker)
1920   *The Married Virgin* (*Frivolous Wives*) (Maxwell); *An Adventuress* (Balshofer); *The Cheater* (Otto); *Passion's Playground* (Barry); *Once to Every Woman* (Holubar); *Stolen Moments* (Vincent); *The Wonderful Chance* (Archainbaud)
1921   ***The Four Horsemen of the Apocalypse*** (Ingram) (as Julio Desnoyers); *Uncharted Seas* (Ruggles) (as Frank Underwood); *Camille* (Smallwood) (as Armand); *The Conquering Power* (Ingram) (as Charles Grandet); *The Sheik* (Melford) (as Sheik Ahmed Ben Hassan)
1922   *Moran of the Lady Letty* (Melford) (as Ramon Laredo); *Beyond the Rocks* (Wood) (as Lord Bracondale); *Blood and Sand* (Niblo) (as Juan Gallardo); *The Young Rajah* (Rosen) (as Amos Judd)
1924   *Monsieur Beaucaire* (Olcott) (title role); *A Sainted Devil* (Henabery) (as Don Alonzo de Castro)
1925   *Cobra* (Henabery) (as Count Torriani); *The Eagle* (Brown) (as Vladimir Dubrovsky)
1926   *Son of the Sheik* (Fitzmaurice) (as Ahmed)

Publications

By VALENTINO: books—

How You Can Keep Fit, New York, 1923.
Day Dreams (verse), New York, 1923.
My Private Diary, Chicago, 1929.
The Intimate Journal of Rudolph Valentino, New York, 1931.

By VALENTINO: articles—

"Woman and Love," in *Photoplay* (New York), March 1922.
"An Open Letter from Valentino to the American Public," in *Photoplay* (New York), January 1923.
"My Life Story," in *Photoplay* (New York), February-April 1923.
"My Trip Abroad," in *Pictures and Picturegoer*, July 1924-October 1925.
"What Is Love?" in *Photoplay* (New York), February 1925.

On VALENTINO: books—

Newman, Ben-Allah, *Rudolph Valentino*, Hollywood, 1926.
Rambova, Natasha, *Rudy: An Intimate Portrait*, London, 1926.
Ullman, George, *Valentino as I Knew Him*, New York, 1927.
Peterson, Roger, *Valentino, The Unforgotten*, Los Angeles, 1937.
Arnold, Alan, *Valentino*, London, 1952.
Oberfirst, Robert, *Rudolph Valentino: The Man behind the Myth*, New York, 1962.
Shulman, Irving, *Valentino*, New York, 1967.
Predal, René, and Robert Florey, *Rudolph Valentino*, Paris, 1969.
Lahue, Kalton C., *Gentlemen to the Rescue: The Heroes of the Silent Screen*, New York, 1972.
MacKenzie, Norman, *The Magic of Rudolph Valentino*, London, 1974.
Botram, Noel, and Peter Donnelly, *Valentino, The Love God*, London, 1976.
Walker, Alexander, *Rudolph Valentino*, London, 1976.
Hansen, Miriam, *Babel and Babylon: Spectatorship in American Silent Film*, Cambridge, Massachusetts, 1991.

On VALENTINO: articles—

Naldi, Nita, "Rudolph Valentino," in *Photoplay* (New York), June 1924.
Tully, Jim, "Rudolph Valentino," in *Vanity Fair*, October 1926.
Smith, Frederick, "Does Rudy Speak from the Beyond?" in *Photoplay* (New York), February 1927.
Lambert, Gavin, "Fairbanks and Valentino: The Last Heroes," in *Sequence* (London), Summer 1949.
Huff, Theodore, "The Career of Rudolph Valentino," in *Films in Review* (New York), April 1952.
Card, J., "Rudolph Valentino," in *Image* (Rochester, New York), May 1958.
Mencken, H. L., "On Hollywood—and Valentino," in *Cinema Journal* (Evanston, Illinois), Spring 1970.
Schickel, Richard, "Rudolph Valentino," in *The Movie Star*, edited by Elisabeth Weis, New York, 1981.
Slide, Anthony, "Ivano and Valentino: A Unique Partnership," in *American Cinematographer* (Hollywood), August 1985.
Studlar, Gaylyn, "Discourses of Gender and Ethnicity: The Construction and De(con)struction of Rudolph Valentino as Other," in *Film Criticism* (Meadville, Pennsylvania), vol. 13, no. 2, 1989.

On VALENTINO: films—

Valentino, directed by Lewis Allen, 1951.
Legend of Valentino, television movie directed by Melville Shavelson, 1975.
Valentino, directed by Ken Russell, 1977.
The Legend of Valentino, documentary, 1983.

*   *   *

To sustain an image as the world's greatest lover is not an easy task in life; to continue that image after death is even harder. Yet Rudolph Valentino contrived to be a legend in his lifetime and, thanks to the

Rudolph Valentino in *Monsieur Beaucaire*

ministrations of his fans and a life that was both contradictory and confused, he continues as one of the few immediately recognizable giants of the silent screen more than 50 years after his death.

Because Valentino's performances are not major artistic achievements, his career can only be discussed in relation to his private life, a stormy one which certainly helped keep him in the public eye. As a great lover, the star's personal life presents a number of problems, including a first marriage to a lesbian who left her husband on their wedding night for another woman. His second marriage was to the domineering Natasha Rambova who engineered her husband's interest

in spiritualism and influenced Valentino's screen performances. Valentino took an almost masochistic pleasure in conforming to her every whim. *Blood and Sand* at times mirrors the actor's real life, as Nita Naldi (who looks as tempestuous and as Continental as Rambova) seduces the young bullfighter (Valentino), while very much in command of the lovemaking process. It was Rambova who selected *Monsieur Beaucaire* for Valentino, a role which demanded that the star be overly made-up to the point of looking effeminate, and so dandified in his attire that the clothing symbolizes his almost slavelike place in her household.

Through it all, Valentino remained remarkably docile and unaffected; only when a journalist accused him of being effeminate and sporting a slave bracelet did the actor respond with anger. He seemed happy to give his fans whatever he felt they would enjoy. He would strip to the waist in *Monsieur Beaucaire*, offer a little sadistic pleasure in *Son of the Sheik* through being viciously whipped, appear in only the briefest of shorts in *The Young Rajah*. In one promotional short he titillates the audience by sitting in his car and beginning to disrobe, until at a crucial moment in the proceedings he recognizes the presence of the camera and discreetly draws the blinds.

Valentino was not a great actor. Only in the two features directed by Rex Ingram, *The Four Horsemen of the Apocalypse* and *The Conquering Power*, does he display any real ability to lose his identity in the characters he is portraying. In only one other feature, *Moran of the Lady Letty*, does Valentino emerge as a masculine hero, strong and virile. Otherwise the actor is strictly a personality; indeed in *Blood and Sand* and *Monsieur Beaucaire* he is little more than a clothes-horse. Certainly his performances are not without their moments of fun; his forceful seduction of Agnes Ayres in *The Sheik* is memorable, as is his tongue-in-cheek playing throughout *Son of the Sheik*. A great on-screen lover Valentino is certainly not—not by today's standards and almost certainly not by the standards of his day. There is, however, one exception, a memorable moment in *Monsieur Beaucaire* in which he makes love to Doris Kenyon. The emotional intensity between these two is so extraordinary that after 60 years it is still an erotic experience.

By a curious quirk of fate, Valentino's most entertaining film, *Son of the Sheik* was also his last. Had he survived into sound he would certainly not have attained legend status; through his death he became immortal. As one of his leading ladies, Alice Terry, aptly remarked, "The biggest thing Valentino ever did was to die."

—Anthony Slide

VALLI, Alida

Nationality: Italian. **Born:** Alida Maria Altenburger in Pola, 31 May 1921; often billed as Valli in non-Italian films. **Education:** Attended the Centro Sperimentale di Cinematografia, Rome. **Family:** Married the pianist Oscar de Mejo, 1944 (divorced), two sons. **Career:** 1935—film debut in *Il capello a tre punte*; 1947—contract with David O. Selznick: U.S. film debut in *The Paradine Case*; 1949—role in *The Third Man* brought international recognition; international films followed; 1956—founded her own theater company. **Awards:** Nastro d'Argento, 1946-47; David Di Donatello, 1981-82.

Films as Actress:

1935   *Il capello a tre punte*
1936   *I due sargenti* (Guazzoni)
1937   *Sono stato io!* (Matarazzo); *Il feroce Saladino* (Bonnard)
1938   *L'ultima nemica* (Barbaro); *Ma l'amore mio non muore* (Amato); *La casa del peccato* (Neufeld); *Mille lire al mese* (Neufeld); (as Magda)
1939   *Assenza ingiustificata* (Neufeld) (as Vera); *L'ha fatto una signora* (Mattòli); *Ballo al castello* (*Ball at the Castle*) (Neufeld) (as Greta Larsen); *Taverna rossa* (Neufeld)
1940   *La prima donna che passa* (Neufeld) (as Gabriele de Verneine); *Otre l'amore* (Gallone); *Manon Lescaut* (Gallone) (title role)
1941   *Piccolo mondo antico* (*Little Old World*) (Soldati) (as Lucia); *Ore nove lezione di chimica* (*Schoolgirl Diary*) (Mattòli)

(as Anna); *L'amante segreta* (Gallone) (as Renata Kreuze); *Luce nelle tenebre* (Mattòli)

1942   *Catene invisibili* (Mattòli); *Stasera niente di nuovo* (Mattòli); *Noi vivi—addio Kira* (*We the Living*) (Alessandrini) (as Kira Argounova); *Le due orfanelle* (*The Two Orphans*) (Gallone) (as Henrietta)
1943   *I pagliacci* (*Laugh Pagliacci*) (Fatigati) (as Julia); *T'amero sempre* (Camerini)
1944   *Apparizione* (De Limur) (as Andreina); *Circo equestre Za-Bum* (*The Za-Bum Circus*) (Mattòli)
1945   *Il canto della vita* (Gallone); *La vita recominicia* (*Life Begins Anew*; *The Sin of Patricia*) (Mattòli) (as Patrizia)
1946   *Eugenia Grandet* (Soldati) (title role)
1947   *The Paradine Case* (Hitchcock) (as Maddalena Anna Paradine)
1948   *The Miracle of the Bells* (Pichel) (as Olga Treskovna)
1949   ***The Third Man*** (Reed) (as Anna Schmidt)
1950   *Walk Softly, Stranger* (Stevenson) (as Elaine Corelli); *The White Tower* (Tetzlaff) (as Carla Alton)
1951   *Les Miracles n'ont lieu q'une fois* (Yves Allégret) (as Claudia); *Ultimo incontro* (Franciolini) (as Lina)
1953   *Les Amants de Tolède* (*The Lovers of Toledo*) (Decoin) (as Inez); "Siam Donne" ep. of *Il mondo le condanna* (Franciolini); *La mano dello straniero* (*The Stranger's Hand*) (Soldati) (as Roberta)
1954   *Senso* (*The Wanton Countess*) (Visconti) (as Countess Livia Serpieri)
1957   *Il grido* (*The Outcry*) (Antonioni) (as Irma); *Les Bijoutiers du clair de lune* (*The Night Heaven Fell*; *Heaven Fell That Night*) (Vadim) (as Florentine); *La grande strada azzura* (Pontecorvo) (as the wife)
1958   *Barrage contre le Pacifique* (*This Angry Age*; *The Sea Wall*; *La Diga sul Pacifico*) (Clément) (as Claude); *L'uomo dai calzoni corti, o L'amore piu grande* (Pellegrini)
1959   *Arsène Lupin et la toison d'or* (Robert)
1960   *Les Dialogues des Carmelites* (Agostini and Bruckberger) (as Mother Therese); *Le Gigolo* (Deray); ***Les Yeux sans visage*** (*Eyes without a Face*; *The Horror Chamber of Dr. Faustus*) (Franju) (as Louise); *La Fille du torrent* (Herwig)
1961   *Il peccato degli anni verdi, o L'assegno* (Trieste); *Une Aussi Longue Absence* (*The Long Absence*) (Colpi) (as Therese Langlois)
1962   *Il disordine* (*Le desorde*; *Disorder*) (Brusati) (as the mother); *Furto su misura*; *The Happy Thieves* (*Once a Thief*) (George Marshall) (as Duchess Blanca); *Ophélia* (Chabrol) (as Claudia Lesurf); *Homenaje a la hora de la siesta* (*Homage at Siesta Time*) (Nilsson) (as Constance); *Al otro lado de la ciudad*
1963   *El valle de las espadas* (*The Castillian*; *Valley of the Swords*) (Setó) (as Queen Teresa)
1964   *L'Autre Femme* (Villiers)
1965   *Humour noir* (*La muerta viaje demasiado*; *Death Travels Too Much*) (Autant-Lara)
1967   *Edipo Re* (*Oedipus Rex*) (Pasolini) (as Merope)
1969   *Le Champignon* (Simenon) (as Linda); *La strategia del ragno* (*The Spider's Strategem*) (Bertolucci) (as Draifa)
1970   *Concerto per pistola solista* (*The Weekend Murders*) (Lupo); *L'occhio nel labirinto* (*Blood*) (Caiano—for TV)
1972   *La prima notte di quiete* (Zurlini) (as mother); *Lisa e il diavolo* (*Lisa and the Devil*; *The House of Exorcism*; *La Casa dell'exorcismo*) (Bava) (as countess); *Diario di un italiano* (*Diary of an Italian*) (Capogna) (as Olga)
1973   *No es nada mama, solo un juego* (*It's Nothing, Only a Game*) (Forque)
1974   *La Grande Trouille* (Grunstein) (as Heloise); *La Chair de l'orchidée* (*Flesh and the Orchid*; *Flesh of the Orchid*) (Chereau) (as woman); *L'anticristo* (*The Antichrist*; *The*

Tempter) (De Martino) (as Irene); *Tendre Dracula* (*La Grande Trouille*; *Tender Dracula*) (Grunstein) (as Eloise)

1975   *Cher Victor* (Robin Davis) (as Anna); *Il caso Raoul* (Ponzi)

1976   **1900** (*Novecento*) (Bertolucci) (as Signora Pioppi); *Le Jeu de solitaire* (Adam) (as friend); *Indagine su un delitto perfetto* (Leviathan)

1977   *Suspiria* (Argento) (as Miss Tanner); *Berlinguer ti voglio bene* (Bertolucci); *The Cassandra Crossing* (Cosmatos) (as Mrs. Chadwick); *The Cinema According to Bertolucci* (G. Bertolucci—doc); *Un cuore Semplice* (Ferrara)

1978   *Zoo Zero* (Fleischer); *Suor omicidi* (*Killer Nun*) (Berruti); *Porco mundo* (*Porno*) (Bergonzelli); *Un cuore semplice* (Ferrara)

1979   *La Luna* (*Luna*) (Bertolucci) (as Giuseppe's mother)

1980   *Aquella casa en las afueras* (*That House in the Outskirts*) (Martin) (as Isabel); *Puppenspiel mit toten Augen*; *Inferno* (Argento) (as Carol)

1981   *Sezona mira u parizu* (Golubovic); *La caduta degli angeli ribelli* (*The Fall of the Rebel Angels*) (Giordana)

1982   *Sogni mostruosamente proibiti* (Parenti)

1983   *Aspern* (de Gregorio)

1985   *Segreti, segreti* (*Secrets, Secrets*) (Giuseppe Bertolucci)

1987   *A Notre Regrettable Epoux* (Korber) (as Catarina); *Le Jupon rouge* (*Manuela's Loves*) (Lefèbvre) (as Bacha)

1991   *La Bocca* (as The Countess); *Zitti e Mosca* (*The Party's Over*) (Benvenuti) (as Clara)

1993   *Il Lungo Silenzio* (*The Long Silence*) (von Trotta) (as Carla's mother)

1995   *A Month by the Lake* (Irvin) (as Signora Fascioli)

Publications

By VALLI: article—

Interview, in *Cinématographe* (Paris), February 1985.

On VALLI: books—

Bowers, Ronald, *The Selznick Papers*, New York, 1976.
Pellizzari, Lorenzo, *Il romanzo di Alida Valli: storie, film e altre apparizoni della signora del cinema italiano*, Milan, 1995.

On VALLI: article—

Télérama (Paris), 1 August, 1989.

*   *   *

Born of an Austrian father and an Italian mother, Alida Valli was one of the first students to enroll in the acting program of the Rome film school, the Centro Sperimentale di Cinematografia. Debuting in films when she was only 14, she scored an immediate success due to her physical grace and striking looks. She starred in many costume dramas—the most lavish productions in Italy both during and after the war. Especially noteworthy was her performance as the grief-stricken mother in Soldati's screen version of Fogazzaro's novel *Piccolo mondo antico*, and her portrayal of Balzac's Eugenia Grandet. These were romantic dramas in which Valli's grace enabled her to make a more convincing impression in hoop skirts, bonnets, and powdered wigs than did her colleagues.

After the war, David O. Selznick offered her a Hollywood contract but Valli did not make a favorable impression on American audiences. Instead, she went to Britain where she did achieve acclaim, especially in Carol Reed's *The Third Man*, in which she plays a much-suffering refugee in postwar Vienna. In *The Third Man*, as in many of her foreign films, she was billed simply as Valli.

Valli's finest performance was in *Senso*, where she plays an Italian countess during the Austrian occupation of Venice. An aging beauty, she is torn between admiration of her cousin, an Italian army official, her patriotic duty to aid partisan activities, and her passion for a younger, handsome, but degenerate Austrian officer. She also gave a powerful performance as Irma, a poor woman, in Antonioni's *Il grido*.

In 1956 she founded a theater company and appeared on stage occasionally for the following 15 years. She participated in many productions in the United States, Spain, Italy, and France in the 1960s and 1970s. Her services have been called upon to play strong, sometimes eccentric, character roles; among the best of these films are Bertolucci's *1900* and, most particularly, *La strategia del ragno*.

—Elaine Mancini

VAN CLEEF, Lee

Nationality: American. **Born:** Somerville, New Jersey, 9 January 1925. **Family:** Married 1) Ruth Ann (Van Cleef) (divorced); 2) Joan (Van Cleef) (divorced), two sons and one daughter; 3) Barbara Hevelone, 1976. **Career:** World War II—served in the U.S. Navy; then farmhand, factory worker, and accountant; amateur actor; 1950—in road company of play *Mister Roberts*; 1952—film debut in *High Noon*; followed by a series of minor roles as villains; 1954—television debut; 1966—role in *For a Few Dollars More* brought international attention; subsequently a star in his own right, especially in Italy. **Died:** Of a heart attack in Oxnard, California, 16 December 1989.

Films as Actor:

1952   **High Noon** (Zinnemann) (as Jack Colby); *Untamed Frontier* (Fregonese) (as Dave Chittun); *Kansas City Confidential* (Karlson) (as Tony Romano)

1953   *The Lawless Breed* (Walsh) (as Dick Hanley); *Tumbleweed* (Juran) (as Marv); *Arena* (Fleischer) (as Smitty); *Jack Slade* (Schuster) (as Toby MacKay); *The Beast from 20,000 Fathoms* (Lourie) (as Corporal Stone); *White Lightning* (Bernds) (as Brutus); *Vice Squad* (Laven) (as Pete); *The Nebraskan* (Sears) (as Reno); *Private Eyes* (Bernds)

1954   *Rails into Laramie* (Hibbs) (as Ace Winton); *The Bandits of Corsica* (Nazarro) (as Nerva); *The Desperado* (Carr) (as Buck/Paul Creyton); *Gypsy Colt* (Marton) (as Hank); *Arrow in the Dust* (Selander) (as crew boss); *The Yellow Tomahawk* (Selander) (as Fireknife); *Dawn at Socorro* (Sherman) (as Earl Ferris); *Princess of the Nile* (Jones) (as Hakar)

1955   *The Big Combo* (Lewis) (as Fante); *The Road to Denver* (Kane) (as Pecos Larry); *A Man Alone* (Milland) (as Clantin); *The Vanishing American* (Kane) (as Jay Lord); *Treasure of Ruby Hills* (McDonald) (as Emmett); *Ten Wanted Men* (Humberstone) (as Al Drucker); *I Cover the Underworld* (Springsteen) (as Flash Logan); *Man without a Star* (Vidor); *The Naked Street* (Shane); *The Kentuckian* (Lancaster)

1956   *The Conqueror* (Powell) (as Chepei); *It Conquered the World* (Corman) (as Tom Anderson); *Tribute to a Bad Man* (Wise) (as Fat Jones); *Backlash* (John Sturges); *Red Sundown* (Arnold); *Pardners* (Taurog) (as Gus)

1957   *Accused of Murder* (Kane) (as Sgt. Lackey); *The Quiet Gun* (Claxton) (as Sadler); *The Badge of Marshal Brennan* (Gannaway) (as Shad Donaphin); *The Last Stagecoach West* (Kane); *The Lonely Man* (Levin) (as Faro); *Joe Dakota* (Bertlett) (as Adam Grant); *Gunfight at the O.K. Corral*

Lee Van Cleef

(John Sturges) (as Ed Bailey); *Gun Battle at Monterey* (Hittleman) (as Kirby); *China Gate* (Fuller) (as Major Cham); *The Tin Star* (Mann) (as Ed McGaffey); *Raiders of Old California* (Gannaway)

1958   *Day of the Badman* (Keller) (as Jake Hayes); *The Bravados* (King) (as Alfonso Parral); *The Young Lions* (Dmytryk) (as Sgt. Rickett); *Machete* (Neumann) (as Miguel)

1959   *Ride Lonesome* (Boetticher) (as Frank); *Guns, Girls, and Gangsters* (Cahn) (as the husband)

1960   *The Guns of Zangara*

1961   *Posse from Hell* (Coleman) (as Leo)

1962   **The Man Who Shot Liberty Valance** (Ford) (as Reese)

1963   *How the West Was Won* (Ford and others) (as Marty)

1966   *Per qualche dollari in più* (*For a Few Dollars More*) (Leone) (as Colonel Douglas Mortimer); *Call to Glory*; **Il buono, il bruto, il cattivo** (*The Good, The Bad, and the Ugly*) (Leone) (as Setenza)

1967   *Da uomo a uoma* (*Death Rides a Horse*) (Petroni) (as Ryan); *La resa dei conti* (*The Big Gundown*) (Sollima) (as Jonathon Corbett); *I giorno dell'ira* (*Der Tod ritt Dienstags*; *Day of Anger*) (Valerii) (as Frank Tolby)

1968   *Commandos* (Crispino); *L'uomo che viene de lontano* (*The Man from Far Away*); *Al di là della legge* (*Beyond the Law*) (Stegani)

1969   *Bite the Dust*; *Ehi, amico . . . c'e Sabata, hai chiuso?* (*Sabata*) (Kramer) (title role); *Creed of Violence*

1970   *Barquero* (Douglas) (as Travis); *El Condor* (Guillermin) (as Jaroo)

1971   *. . . e continuavano a fregarsi il millione di dollari* (Martin); *Captain Apache* (Singer) (title role)

1972   *E tornato Sabata . . . hai chiuso* (*Return of Sabata*) (Kramer) (title role); *El gran duelo* (*The Grand Duel*) (Santi); *The Magnificent Seven Ride!* (McGowan) (as Chris)

1973   *Johnny le Fligueur* (*Mean Frank and Crazy Tony*); *Dio, sei proprio un padreterno* (*Il suo nome faceva tremare . . . Interpol in allarme!*; *Gangster Story*; *The Gun*) (Lupo)

1974   *Moneda sangrienta* (*Blood Money*) (Dawson)

1975   *Take a Hard Ride* (Dawson) (as Kiefer)

1976   *The Stranger and the Gunfighter* (Dawson); *God's Gun* (Kramer)

1977   *Kid Vengeance* (Manduke); *Verano sangrieto* (*Killers*) (Sirko); *Nowhere to Hide* (Starrett—for TV)

1978   *Controrapina* (*The Squeeze*; *The Big Ripoff*) (Dawson)

1979 *The Hard Way* (Dryhurst—for TV)
1980 *Trieste File*; *The Octagon* (Karson) (as McCarn)
1981 *Escape from New York* (Carpenter) (as Bon Hauk)
1983 *The Killing Machine* (Loma) (as Maitre Julot)
1984 *Codename Wildgeese* (Dawson); *Goma 2* (Loma)
1985 *The Master* (Hessler—for TV); *Jungle Raiders* (*Captain Yankee*;
      La legenda del rudio malese) (Dawson) (as Inspector Warren)
1986 *Armed Response* (Olen Ray) (as Burt Roth)
1988 *Commander* (Dawson)
1989 *Speed Zone* (Drake) (as Grandfather)

Publications

On VAN CLEEF: books—

Horner, William R., *Bad at the Bijou*, Jefferson, North Carolina, 1982.
Buscombe, Ed, editor, *The BFI Companion to the Western*, London, 1989.

On VAN CLEEF: articles—

Simsolo, Noël, "Lee Van Cleef," in *Image et Son* (Paris), September 1973.
Ciné Revue (Paris), 19 May 1983.
Obituary in *Variety*, 20 December 1989.

*   *   *

Lee Van Cleef entered films after a brief and unspectacular stage career. For a while he was a member of a small amateur dramatics group, after which he appeared in Joshua Logan's stage production of *Mister Roberts*. He was then spotted by Stanley Kramer in his starring role in *Heaven Can Wait*. Eventually, he won the part of one of the desperadoes stalking Gary Cooper in *High Noon*, in which Van Cleef was first typecast as a baddie.

Over the years, Van Cleef perfected his screen persona as a ruthless villain. His athletic frame, steely-eyed stare, hooked nose, demonic smile, and imposing presence all contributed to his success as an anti-hero. Inevitably portraying a lone, proficient killer, Van Cleef concealed a gentility beneath his tough exterior that gained the sympathy of the audience; although brutal, his actions could usually be traced to a justifiable grievance.

Van Cleef's flagging film career suddenly picked up in the mid-1960s when he appeared opposite Clint Eastwood in Sergio Leone's spaghetti Westerns *Per qualche dollaro in più* and *Il buono, il bruto, il cattivo*. Unlike Eastwood, who returned to Hollywood to further his career, Van Cleef stayed in Europe, where he successfully rode the spaghetti and paella trail, playing his invincible gunfighter in a succession of European-made Westerns.

By the early 1970s, he was one of the ten most popular box-office stars on the Continent, and had established himself as a cult figure. With well over 800 television and film appearances to his credit, Van Cleef endeared himself to cinemagoers as a man they love to hate. Although typecast from the outset of his Hollywood career, unlike many other actors in his position, he used this obstacle to his advantage by creating a memorable and immensely popular cinema character.

—Curtis Hutchinson

VAN DAMME, Jean-Claude

Nationality: Belgian. **Born:** Jean-Claude Van Varenberg in Brussels, Belgium, 18 October 1960. **Family:** Married: (third marriage) Gladys

Portugues (divorced 1992), children: Kristopher, Bianca; (fourth marriage) Darcy LaPier, 1994. **Career:** 1984—U.S. film debut, *Monaco Forever*; former European karate champion, and winner middleweight championship, European Karate Association.

Films as Actor:

1984 *Monaco Forever* (William A. Levey) (as gay karate man,
      billed as Jean Claude Vandam)
1986 *Rue Barbar*; *No Retreat, No Surrender* (Yuen) (as Ivan the
      Russian)
1987 *Bloodsport* (Arnold) (as Frank Dux)
1988 *Black Eagle* (Karson) (as Andrei)
1989 *Cyborg* (Yuen) (as Gibson Rickenbacker); *Kickboxer* (DiSalle
      and Worth) (as Kurt Sloane)
1990 *Death Warrant* (Sarafian) (as Louis Burke)
1991 *Double Impact* (Lettich) (as Chad/Alex, + co-pr, co-sc);
      Lionheart (*A.W.O.L.*) (Lettich) (as Lyon, + co-sc)
1992 *Universal Soldier* (Emmerich) (as Luke Devreux)
1993 *Nowhere to Run* (Harmon) (as Sam Gillen); *Hard Target* (Woo)
      (as Chance Boudreaux); *Last Action Hero* (McTiernan)
      (cameo, as himself)
1994 *Timecop* (Hyams) (as Max Walker); *Street Fighter* (de Souza)
      (as Col. Guile)
1995 *Sudden Death* (Hyams) (as Darren McCord)

Film as Director:

1996 *The Quest* (+ ro)

Publications

By VAN DAMME: articles—

"The Trigeminal-Nerve-Activating, Tiger-Clawed, Snake-Fingered, Iron-Footed, Shadow-Kicking, Grand-Ultimate Grace of Jean-Claude Van Damme," interview with Susan Morgan and Bruce Weber, in *Interview* (New York), March 1991.
"Van Damme," interview with Nell Scovell, in *Vanity Fair* (New York), July 1993.
Interview with Lawrence Grobel, in *Playboy* (Chicago), January 1995.

On VAN DAMME: articles—

Barth, Jack, "J. C., Superstar," in *Premiere* (New York), July 1992.
Lipton, Michael A., "Muscles from Brussels," in *People Weekly*, August 1992.
Richman, Alan, "Four Weddings and a Front Kick," in *GQ* (New York), August 1995.

*   *   *

Jean-Claude Van Damme is one of the top tier of contemporary action movie stars along with Steven Seagal, Arnold Schwarzenegger, and Chuck Norris. Unlike those other strongmen/athletes who have followed in the footsteps of the iconographic Bruce Lee, however, Van Damme gets the least respect from the press, which tends to dismiss him as the "muscles from Brussels," the Rodney Dangerfield of the martial arts & mayhem movie.

Yet of the top tier, this former European kickboxing champion turned actor is, perhaps, the most lithe and graceful performer. He is also the least pretentious about his work and the image he projects on

Jean-Claude Van Damme in *Hard Target*

screen: that of the nonviolent Mr. Nice Guy with a secret kick that gets used only when he is leaned on too heavily by bad guys. He is also the least intractable about this image, having played a villain once in the 1988 *Black Eagle*, which cast him as a Russian killer on the trail of good guy superspy Sho Kosugi.

After paying his dues in a series of mostly low-budget, straight-to-video action programmers such as the 1987 *Bloodsport*, inspired by the true story of American ninja Frank Dux; *Cyborg* and *Kickboxer* (both 1989); and 1990's *Death Warrant* (as a Mountie who predictably gets his man), Van Damme attempted a career makeover in the Joe Eszterhas-scripted *Nowhere to Run* (1993). The film was designed to humanize Van Damme's screen image of superhero indestructibility, show that he could act, and propel him to the action big leagues. A sort of Shane in rusty armor, he played a self-doubting ex-con who comes to the defense of a put-upon widow (Rosanna Arquette) and her boy. Critic Leonard Maltin termed the resultant mixture of sentimentality and groin kicks "embarrassingly awful." And it was left to Van Damme's next film, *Hard Target*, to achieve the sought-after breakthrough.

An umpteenth variation on the Richard Connell adventure classic *The Most Dangerous Game* with Van Damme as the wily prey hunted by vicious entrepreneur Lance Henriksen, *Hard Target* was hailed by *Entertainment Weekly* critic Owen Gleiberman as "an incendiary action orgy, as joyously excessive as the grand finale in a fireworks show." Nevertheless, most of the kudos were lavished upon the kinetic style of the film's director, Hong Kong action movie maestro John Woo (making his American movie debut) rather than Van Damme.

Hard Target may have been Van Damme's best film up to that time, but it must also be said that he was at his best in it. Woo may have been the catalyst for the breakthrough, but Van Damme has justifiably reaped some of the rewards with bigger budgets, more publicity, and wider spread theatrical release for his subsequent films (*Time Cop, Street Fighter, Sudden Death*). Even the press has begun paying attention, and may finally be on the verge of showing him respect.

—John McCarty

VANEL, Charles

Nationality: French. **Born:** Rennes, 21 August 1892. **Career:** On stage in Paris from age 16; 1912—film debut in *Jim Crow*; followed by some 200 films; 1929—directed the film *Dans la nuit*. **Awards:** Best Actor, Cannes Festival, for *The Wages of Fear*, 1953; special César award, 1978. **Died:** In Cannes, 15 April 1989.

Films as Actor:

1912   *Jim Crow* (Péguy)
1921   *Crépuscule d'epouvante*; *L'Enfant du carnaval*

1922	*L'Atre* (Boudrioz); *La Nuit de la revanche* (Etievant); *Les 50 Ans de Don Juan* (Etievant); *Du Crépuscule à l'aube* (de Feraudy)
1923	*Tempêtes* (Boudrioz); *Miarka, la fille à l'ourse* (Mercanton); *La Maison du mystère* (Volkoff); *Le Vol* (Péguy); *Valvaire d'Amour* (Tourjansky); *Phroso* (Mercanton)
1924	*La Flambée des rêves* (de Baroncelli); *Pêcheur d'Islande* (de Baroncelli); *La Mendiante de Saint-Sulpice* (Burguet); *Martyre* (Burguet); *L'Autre aile* (Andreani)
1925	*Barocco* (Burguet); *Le Réveil* (de Baroncelli); *Ame d'artiste* (Dulac); *La Flamme* (Hervil)
1926	*La Proie du vent* (Clair); *Nitchevo* (de Baroncelli); *600,000 Francs par mois* (Péguy and Koline); *L'Orphelin du cirque* (Lannes); *Feu!* (de Baroncelli)
1927	*L'Esclave blanche* (Genina); *Charité*; *La Femme rêvée* (Durand); *Paname n'est pas Paris* (Malikoff); *Maquillage* (Basch)
1928	*Le Passager* (de Baroncelli); *La Plongée tragique* (Heinz); *Feux Follets* (Waschneck)
1929	*Waterloo* (Grüne); *Les Fourchambault* (Monca)
1930	*Chiqué* (Colombier); *Accusée levez-vous!* (Tourneur); *La Maison jaune de Rio* (Grune and Péguy); *Le Capitaine jaune* (Sandberg); *L'Arlésienne* (de Baroncelli)
1931	*Maison de danses* (Tourneur); *Au nom de la Loi* (Tourneur); *Dainah la métisse* (Gremillon); *Faubourg Montmartre* (Bernard); *Les Croix de bois* (Bernard)
1932	*Gitanes* (de Baroncelli)
1933	*Les Misérables* (Bernard); *Au bout du monde* (Flücht-Linge) (Ucicky and Chomette)
1934	*Le Grand Jeu* (Feyder); *Roi de Canargue* (de Baroncelli); *Obsession* (Tourneur—short)
1935	*L'Impossible aveu* (Glavany); *Le Domino vert* (Selpin and Decoin); *L'Equipage* (*Flight into Darkness*) (Litavak); *Michel Strogoff* (de Baroncelli)
1936	*Les Bateliers de la Volga* (Strijewsky); *Port Arthur* (*I Give My Life*) (Farkas); *Jenny* (Carné); *La Belle equipe* (*They Were Five*) (Duvivier); *Les Grands* (Gandera and Bibal); *L'Assaut* (Ducis); *La Flamme* (Berthomieu); *Courier Sud* (Billon); *Vertige d'un soir* (*La Peur*) (Tourjansky)
1937	*Abus de confiance* (*Abused Confidence*) (Decoin); *Troika sur la piste blanche* (Dréville); *Police mondaine* (Bernheim and Chamborant); *La Femme du bout du monde* (Epstein)
1938	*L'Occident* (Fescourt); *Les Pirates du rail* (Christian-Jaque); *Légions d'honneur* (Gleize); *S.O.S. Sahara* (de Baroncelli); *Bar du Sud* (Fescourt)
1939	*Carrefour* (*Crossroads*) (Bernhardt); *L'Or du Cristobal* (Stelli and Becker); *La Brigade sauvage* (*Savage Brigade*) (Dréville and L'Herbier); *Yamile sous le Cèdres* (d'Espinay)
1940	*La Loi du nord* (*La Piste du nord*) (Feyder); *Le Diamant noir* (Delannoy); *La Nuit merveilleuse* (Paulin)
1941	*Le Soleil a toujours raison* (Billon)
1942	*Promesse à l'inconnue* (Berthomieu)
1943	*Les Affaires sont les affaires* (Dréville); *Le Ciel est à vous* (Gremillon); *Les Roquevillard* (Dréville)
1944	*Haut-le-Vent* (de Baroncelli); *L'Enquête sur le 58* (Tedesco—short)
1945	*La Ferme du pendu* (Dréville)
1946	*La Bateau à soupe* (Gleize); *La Cabane aux souvenirs* (Stelli); *Gringalet* (Berthomieu)
1947	*Le Diable souffle* (Gréville)
1948	*Vertigine d'Amore* (Capuano)
1949	*Mafia* (*Il nome della legge*) (Germi); *La Femme que j'ai assassinée* (Daniel-Norman)
1950	*Il Bivio* (Cerchio); *Malaire* (Perla); *Cuori sul mar* (Bianchi)
1951	*Gli Inesorabili* (Mastrocinque); *Son dernier verdict* (*Ultima Sentenza*) (Bonnard); *Incantesimo Tragico* (Mastrocinque)
1952	*Tempête sur les Mauvents* (Dupé); ***Le Salaire de la peur*** (*The Wages of Fear*) (Clouzot)
1953	*Si Versailles m'était conté* (*Royal Affairs in Versailles*) (Guitry); *L'Affaire Mauritzius* (*On Trial*) (Duvivier)
1954	***Les Diaboliques*** (*Diabolique*) (Clouzot); *Maddalena* (Genina); *Tam Tam* (Napolitano); *To Catch a Thief* (Hitchcock) (as Bertani); *Rafles sur la ville* (*Sinners of Paris*) (Chenal)
1956	*La Mort en ce jardin* (*Gina*; *Evil Eden*) (Buñuel)
1957	*Le Feu aux poudres* (Decoin); *Les Suspects* (Dréville)
1958	*Le Gorille vous salue bien* (Borderie); *Le Piège* (*No Escape*) (Brabant); *Pêcheur d'Islande* (Schlöndorffer)
1959	*Les Naufrageurs* (Brabant); *Les Bateliers de la Volga* (Tourjansky); *La Valse du gorille* (Borderie)
1960	*La Vérité* (*The Truth*) (Clouzot)
1961	*Tintin et le mystère de la Toison d'Or* (Vierne); *L'Aîné des Ferchaux* (Melville); *Maria, matricula de Bilbao* (Vajda); *Symphonie pour un massacre* (*Symphony for a Massacre*) (Deray); *La steppa* (*The Steppe*) (Lattuada)
1962	*Lo Sogarro* (Siano); *Rififi à Tokyo* (*Rififi in Tokyo*) (Deray)
1963	*Un Roi sans divertissement* (*La Poursuite*) (Leterrier)
1964	*Le Chant du monde* (Camus)
1967	*Un Homme de trop* (*Shock Troops*) (Costa-Gavras)
1969	*Ballade pour un chien* (Vergez); *La Nuit bulgare* (Mitrani)
1970	*Ils* (Simon); *Comptes à rebours* (Pigaut)
1972	*Camorra* (Squietieri); *La più bella sereta della mia vita* (Scola) (as Judge)
1973	*Les Martiens* (Ciampi—short); *Le Sang des autres* (Simenon)
1975	*Sept morts sur ordonnance* (Rouffio); *Cadaveri eccelenti* (*Illustrious Corpses*) (Rosi) (as Procura)
1976	*Nuit d'or* (Moatti); *Comme un boomerang* (Giovanni); *Alice, ou la dernière fugue* (Chabrol) (as Vergennes)
1977	*A l'ombre d'un été* (Van Belle); *Ne pleure pas* (Ertaud)
1979	*Le Chemin perdu* (Moraz)
1980	*La Puce et le Privé* (Kay); *Tre fratelli* (*Three Brothers*) (Rosi) (as Donato Giuranna)
1987	*Si le soleil ne revenait pas* (Goretta) (as Anzevui)
1988	*Les Saisons du plaisir* (Mocky) (as Charles)

Films as Director:

1929	*Dans la nuit* (+ ro)
1932	*Au joli coin* (+ ro)

Publications

By VANEL: articles—

"Une Carrière exemplaire: Charles Vanel," interview with R. Predal in *Cinéma aujourd'hui* (Paris), no. 10, 1976.
"Charles Vanel par Charles Vanel," dossier in *Avant-Scene du Cinéma* (Paris), 15 November 1981.
Interview with F. Gévaudan, in *Cinéma* (Paris), January 1982.

On VANEL: books—

Ford, Charles, *Charles Vanel: Un Comedien Exemplaire*, Paris, 1986.
Cartier, Jacqueline, *Monsieur Vanel: Un Siecle de Souvenirs*, Paris, 1989.

On VANEL: articles—

Niogret, Hubert, and Yann Tobin, "Charles Vanel," in *Positif* (Paris), February 1982.

Charles Vanel with Lilian Hall Davis in *Proie du vent*

Sellier, G., "Charles Vanel, un 'non-séducteur' du cinéma français," in *Cinéma* (Paris), October 1983.

*   *   *

Charles Vanel, the grand old man of French cinema, was born in 1892 at Rennes. He was educated for a career at sea, but his poor sight put an end to this ambition. Possessing a very fine voice, he decided to become an actor and went to Paris where, encouraged by Firmin Gemier, he played at the Theatre Antoine and the Gymnase. After four years of the theater, he entered films in 1912, playing in Robert Péguy's *Jim Crow*. He played with Rejane in Mercanton's *Miarka, la fille à l'ourse*, but had his first big success in Robert Boudrioz's remarkable *L'Atre* in 1922. This marked the beginning of a prolific silent film career for Vanel. He acted with Mozhukin in *L'Enfant du carnaval*, *Tenpêtes*, and *La Maison du mystère*, and appeared in many films by Jacques de Baroncelli, particularly in the Pierre Loti story *Pêcheur d'Islande*, filmed in his native Brittany. He played in Germaine Dulac's *Ame d'artiste* and Rene Clair's *Proie du vent* (with Sandra Milowanoff, who had played in the Loti film). Vanel worked for German and Italian directors, and played Napoleon in Karl Grüne's *Waterloo*. In 1929 he directed Sandra Milowanoff in *Dans la nuit*, a film now restored by the Cinémathèque Française which allows us to see a very talented director indeed. This story of rural love and jealousy set among quarry workers has a documentary realism, but as a film it was overshadowed by the coming of sound.

With the arrival of sound, Vanel spent two years in Germany on French versions of German films, and on his return to France became a familiar figure on the cinema screen. He played opposite Harry Baur in Raymond Bernard's two-part versions of *Les Misérables* in 1933 and also appeared in Bernard's *Faubourg Montmarte* and *Les Croix de bois*. He was in Feyder's *Le Grand Jeu* and *La Loi du nord*. For Gustav Ucicky he played in *Flüchtlinge* (*Au bout du monde*), and he was in Marcel Carné's *Jenny*. He was Yves Montand's cowardly partner in Clouzot's *Le Salaire de la peur* (for which he received the Cannes best actor award). He worked for Hitchcock (*To Catch a Thief*), Buñuel (*Le Mort en ce jardin*), and Jean Pierre Melville (*L'Aîné des Ferchaux*). In 1958 he again played in *Pêcheur d'Islande* (Schlöndorffer), and he was in both the Strijewsky and Tourjansky versions of *Les Bateliers de la Volga*. In 1978 Vanel was honored with a special César award, and continued to appear in films in his last years. He had a prolific output of 80 films during a distinguished career covering more than 70 years.

—Liam O'Leary

VEIDT, Conrad

Nationality: German/British. **Born:** Berlin, 22 January 1893; became British citizen, 1939. **Family:** Married 1) Gussy Hall (divorced);

2) Felicitas Radke, one daughter; married third wife. **Career:** Studied with Max Reinhardt, and acted in his company in Berlin, before 1914 and after 1916; 1914-16—served in the German Army; illness permitted him to be assigned to Berlin after 1916; 1917—film debut in *Der Spion*; 1919—controversy over his portrayal of a homosexual in the film *Anders als die Andern*; formed own production company; directed first film, *Wahnsinn*; 1920—role in *Das Kabinett des Dr. Caligari* and other expressionist films in the early 1920s brought him international attention; late 1920s—made some films in Hollywood; 1934—after being detained briefly in Nazi Germany because his third wife was half-Jewish, emigrated to England; 1940-43—worked in the United States. **Died:** 3 April 1943.

Films as Actor:

1917   *Wenn Tote sprechen* (Reinert); *Die Claudia von Geiserhof* (Biebrach); *Der Spion* (Heiland); *Der Weg des Todes* (Reinert) (as Rolf); *Furcht* (Wiene) (as the Indian); *Das Ratsel von Bangalor* (Antalffy) (as Count Dinja)

1918   *Die Serenyi* (Halm); *Das Tagebuch einer Verlorenen* (*The Diary of a Lost Woman*) (Oswald) (as Dr. Julius); *Dida Ibsens Geschichte* (Oswald) (as Erik Knorrensen); *Des Dreimäderlhaus* (Oswald) (as Baron Schober); *Colomba* (von Wieder) (as Henrik van Rhyn); *Jettchen Geberts Geschichte* (Oswald) (as Dr. Köstling); *Henriette Jacoby* (Oswald) (as Dr. Köstling); *Sundige Mutter* (Oswald) (as Herr Kramer); *Opfer der Gesellschaft* (Grunwald) (as Staatsanwalt); *Nocturno der Liebe* (Boese) (as Frederic Chopin); *Die Japanerin* (Dupont) (as the Secretary)

1919   *Gewitter im Mai* (Beck); *Die Reise um die Erde in 80 Tagen* (*Around the World in Eighty Days*) (Oswald) (as Phileas Fogg); *Peer Gynt* (Barnowsky) (as the Button Maker); *Anders als die Andern* (Oswald) (as Paul Körner); *Die Prostitution* (Oswald) (as Alfred Werner); *Die Mexicanerin* (Bonn) (as the Seducer); *Die Prostitution II* (Oswald) (as Editor Hofer); *Die Okarina* (Kraft) (as Jaap); *Prinz Kukuck* (*Prince Cuckoo*) (Leni) (as Karl Kraker); "Prologue and Epilogue" (as Death), "Die Ercheinung" (as the Stranger), "Die Hand" (as the Assassin), "Die schwarze Katze" (as the Traveller), "Der Klub der Selbstmörder" (as Club President), and "Der Spuk" (as the Husband), eps. of *Unheimliche Geschichten* (Oswald); *Nachtgestalten* (Oswald) (as the Comedian); Episode 1 (as the Hermit from Elu/Lucifer), Episode 2 (as Gubetta/Lucifer), and Episode 3 (as Grodski/Lucifer) of *Satanas* (Murnau)

1920   ***Das Kabinett des Dr. Caligari*** (*The Cabinet of Dr. Caligari*) (Wiene) (as Cesare); *Der Reigen* (*Ein Werdegang*) (Oswald) (as Peter Karvan); *Patience* (Leni) (as Sir Percy Parker); *Der Januskopf* (*Janus-Faced*) (Murnau) (as Dr. Warren/Mr. O'Connor); *Liebestaumel* (Hartwig) (as Jalenko); *Die Augen der Welt* (Wilhelm) (as Juliane von Derp's lover); *Kurfürstendamm* (*Ein Höllenspuk in 6 Akten*) (Oswald) (as the Devil); *Moriturus* (Hagen) (as Wilmos); *Abend-Nacht-Morgen* (*The Memoirs of Manolescu*) (Dreier) (as Brilburn); *Kunsterlaunen* (Otto) (as Arpad); *Sehnsucht* (Murnau) (as the student); *Der Gang in die Nacht* (Murnau) (as the blind painter); *Christian Wahnschaffe* (Gade) (title role); *Der Graf von Cagliostro* (Schünzel) (as the Minister); *Das Geheimnis von Bombay* (Holz) (as Tossi), *Menshen im Rausch* (Geisendörfer) (as the composer)

1921   *Die Liebschaften des Hektor Dalmore* (Oswald) (title role); *Der Leidensweg der Inge Kraft* (Dinesen) (as Hendryk Overland); *Landstrasse und Grosstadt* (Wilhelm) (as Raphael Strate); *Lady Hamilton* (Oswald) (as Lord Nelson); *Das Indische Grabmal* (*Mysteries of India; Above All Law; The Indian Tomb*) (May) (as Ayan, the Maharajah)

1922   *Lucrezia Borgia* (Oswald) (as Cesare Borgia)

1923   *Paganini* (Goldberg) (title role); *Wilhelm Tell* (Dworsky) (as Gessler); *Glanz gegen Gluck* (Trotz) (as the Count)

1924   *Carlos und Elisabeth* (Oswald) (as Karl V/Don Carlos); *Das Wachsfigurenkabinett* (*Waxworks*) (Leni) (as Ivan the Terrible); *Orlacs Hande* (*The Hands of Orlac*) (Wiene) (as Paul Orlac); *Nju* (*Husbands or Lovers*) (Czinner) (as the Poet); *Schicksal* (Basch) (as Count Wranna)

1925   *Le Comte Kostia* (Robert) (title role); *Ingmarsarvet* (*In Dalarna and Jerusalem*) (Molander) (as Helgum); *Liebe macht Blind* (*Love Is Blind*) (Mendes) (as Dr. Lamare)

1926   *Der Geiger von Florenz* (Czinner) (as the father); *Die Bruder Schellenberg* (*The Two Brothers*) (Grune) (title roles); *Dürfen wir Schweigen?* (Oswald) (as Paul Hartwig); *Kreuzzug des Weibes* (Berger) (as the Prosecutor); *Der Student von Prag* (*The Student of Prague*) (Berger) (as Balduin); *Die Flucht in die Nacht* (*The Flight in the Night*) (Palermi) (as Count Heinrich di Favari)

1927   *The Beloved Rogue* (Crosland) (as Louis XI); *A Man's Past* (Melford) (as Paul La Roche)

1928   *The Man Who Laughs* (Leni) (as Gwynplaine); *The Last Performance* (*Eric the Great*) (Fejos) (as Erik the Great)

1929   *Das Land Ohne Frauen* (*Bride 68*) (Gallone) (as Dick Ashton)

1930   *Die Letste Kompagnie* (*The Last Company; Thirteen Men and a Girl*) (Bernhardt) (as Hauptmann Burk); *Die Grosse Sehnsucht* (Zselkely) (as himself); *Menschen in Kafig* (Dupont) (as Gordon Kingsley)

1931   *Der Mann, der den Mord beging* (*The Man Who Committed Murder*) (Bernhardt) (as Oberst Sevigne); *Die Nacht der Entscheidung* (Buckowetski) (as General Gregori Paltoff); *Der Kongress tanzt* (*Congress Dances*) (Charell) (as Count Mctternich); *Die Andere Seite* (Paul) (as Captain Denis Stanhope); *Rasputin* (Trotz) (title role)

1932   *Der schwarze Husar* (*The Black Hussar*) (Lamprecht) (as Rittmeister Hansgeorg von Hochberg); *F.P.I.* (Hartl) (as Elissen)

1933   *Ich und die Kaiserin* (Hollaender) (as the Marquis); *Rome Express* (Forde) (as Zurta); *The Wandering Jew* (Elvey) (as Mathias); *I Was a Spy* (Saville) (as Commandant Obersertz)

1934   *Jew Suss* (Power) (Mendes) (as Joseph Oppenheimer); *Wilhelm Tell* (*The Legend of William Tell*) (Paul) (as Gessler); *Bella Donna* (Milton) (as Mahmous Baroudi)

1935   *The Passing of the Third Floor Back* (Viertel) (as the Stranger)

1936   *King of the Damned* (Forde) (as Convict 83)

1937   *Under the Red Robe* (Sjöstrom) (as Gil de Berault); *Dark Journey* (Saville) (as Baron Karl von Marwitz)

1938   *Tempête sur L'Asie* (Oswald) (as Erich Keith); *Le Joueur d'échecs* (*The Chess Player; The Devil Is an Empress*) (Dréville) (as Baron Kempelen)

1939   *The Spy in Black* (*U-Boat 29*) (Powell) (as Captain Hardt)

1940   *Contraband* (*Blackout*) (Powell) (as Captain Anderson); *The Thief of Bagdad* (Berger) (as Jaffar, the Grand Vizier); *Escape* (LeRoy) (as General Kurt von Kalb)

1941   *A Woman's Face* (Cukor) (as Torsten Barring); *Whistling in the Dark* (Sylvan) (as Joseph Jones); *The Men in Her Life* (Ratoff) (as Stanislas Rosing)

1942   *Nazi Agent* (Dassin) (as Otto Becker/Baron Hugo von Detner); *All through the Night* (Sherman) (as Ebbing)

1943   ***Casablanca*** (Curtiz) (as Major Strassner); *Above Suspicion* (Thorpe) (as Hussert Seidel)

Films as Director:

1919   *Wahnsinn* (+ ro as Lorenzen)

1920   *Die Nacht auf Goldenhall* (+ roles as Lord Harald/the nephew)

1922   *Lord Byron* (+ co-pr, sc, title role)

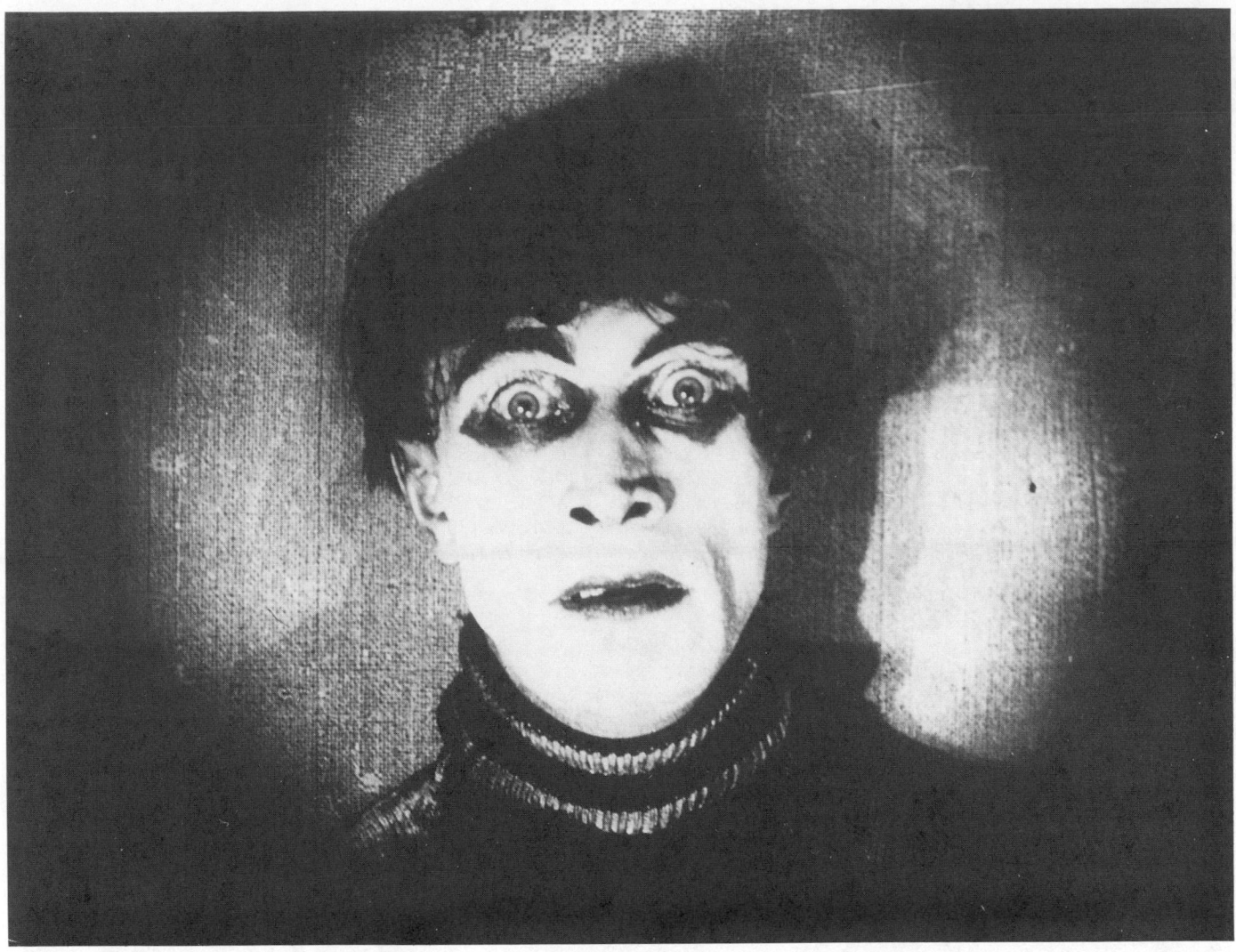

Conrad Veidt in *Das Kabinett des Dr. Caligari*

Publications

By VEIDT: article—

"Conrad Veidt," an interview with R. Herring in *Close-Up* (London), October 1930.

On VEIDT: books—

Kracauer, Siegfried, *From Caligari to Hitler: A Psychological History of the German Film*, Princeton, New Jersey, 1947.
Allen, J. C., *Conrad Veidt: From Caligari to Casablanca*, Pacific Grove, California, 1987.
Jacobsen, Wolfgang, editor, *Conrad Veidt: Lebensbilder: ausgewahlte Fotos und Texte*, Berlin, 1993.

On VEIDT: articles—

Gebauer, D., "Conrad Veidt—Dämon, Teufel, Held, Genie—Ein Magier der Leinwand," in *Information* (Wiesbaden), May 1975.
Holba, Herbert, "From Caligari to Hollywood: Conrad Veidt," in *Focus on Film* (London), Summer 1975.

Nau, P., "Notizen zu drei Stummfilmen mit Conrad Veidt," in *Filmkritik* (Munich), October 1975.

*   *   *

Like many of the prominent stars of the great period of pre-Nazi German cinema, Conrad Veidt received his basic training and stage experience from Max Reinhardt, and appeared at the age of 20—just before World War I—at Reinhardt's Deutsches Theater in Berlin. His career in German film began in 1917. Before making his name internationally, in *Das Kabinett des Dr. Caligari*, he had already been seen in 15 films, two of which, *Wahnsinn* and *Die Nacht auf Goldenhall*, he had directed.

Veidt's impressive height, handsomely gaunt face, and high cheekbones made him natural casting for sinister or symbolistic roles. He had already played the Button Maker in a film version of *Peer Gynt* and Death in *Unheimliche Geschichten*, as well as Phileas Fogg in the silent German film version of *Die Reise um die Erde in 80 Tage*, before achieving his beautifully mimed and choreographed performance as Cesare, the somnambulist murderer in Wiene's *Dr. Caligari*, which had originally been intended as a subject for the developing talents of Fritz Lang. Made on the most modest of postwar budgets, this film, with its expressionist-styled sets and theme of insanity, won an international reputation before its proper recognition in Germany itself. It confirmed Veidt as one of the more sinister personalities of German film. He went on to appear (before going to Hollywood in 1927) as Lucifer in *Satanas*, Dr. Jekyll and Mr. Hyde in *Der Januskopf* (the characters renamed Warren and O'Connor), Lord Nelson in *Lady Hamilton*, Cesare Borgia in *Lucretia Borgia*, and the title roles in *Richard III* and *Lord Byron*. Even more prominent from the international point of view, were his performances as Ivan the Terrible in Paul Leni's *Die Wachsfigurenkabinett*, the lover in Paul Czinner's *Nju*, in the title role in Wiene's *Orlacs Hande*, and the lead in Henryk Galeen's *Der Student von Prag*. He had also extended his range as producer and director as well, with *Lord Byron*.

His initial career in Hollywood, 1927-29, was relatively undistinguished, and he returned to Germany with the coming of sound. Here he was best cast as Count Metternich in *Der Kongress tanzt*, and in the title role of *Rasputin*. With the rise of Hitler he took refuge with his Jewish wife in England and eventually took British citizenship. His natural casting was now that of the sinister German, and he appeared in several of the better British dramas and melodramas in the 1930s—Walter Forde's *Rome Express* and Victor Saville's *I Was a Spy*, Lothar Mendes's *Jew Suss*, Berthold Viertel's *The Passing of the Third Floor Back*, Forde's *King of the Damned*, and Saville's *Dark Journey*. In France he made *Le Joueur d'échecs* before leaving once again for Hollywood. In the short time

before he died prematurely of a heart attack in 1943, he appeared in eight films in his usual German roles, most notably in Michael Curtiz's *Casablanca*. He dropped dead while playing golf at the age of only 50.

—Roger Manvell

VILLAGRA, Nelson

Nationality: Chilean. **Born:** Chillán, 9 August 1937. **Education:** Attended the University of Chile Theatre School, Santiago, graduated 1958. **Career:** 1958-65—worked with the university theater group, Concepción; 1967—film debut in *Regreso al silencio*; 1973—emigrated to Cuba.

Films as Actor:

1967   *Regreso al silencio* (Kramarenko)
1968   *Los testigos* (Elsesser); *Tres tristes tigres* (*Three Sad Tigers*) (Ruiz);
        El Chacal de Nahueltoro (*The Jackal of Nahueltoro*) (Littin)
1970   *Nadie dijo nada* (*Nobody Said Nothing*) (Ruiz)
1971   *La colonia penal* (*The Penal Colony*) (Ruiz)

Nelson Villagra in *El recurso del método*

1972   *La tierra prometida* (*The Promised Land*) (Littin) (as José Duran)
1975   *La cantata de Chile* (Solás)
1976   *La última cena* (*The Last Supper*) (Gutíerrez Alea) (as the Count); *Rio Negro* (Pérez)
1977   *El recurso del método* (*Viva el Presidente*; *Reasons of State*) (Littin)
1978   *Prisioneros desparecidos* (Castilla)
1979   *La viuda de Montiel* (*Montiel's Widow*) (Littin)
1980   *Leyenda* (Paris)
1981   *Polvo rojo* (Diaz); *La rosa de los vientos* (*Rose of the Winds*) (Guzmán)
1982   *Cecilia Valdés* (Solás)
1985   *El corazón sobre la tierra* (Diejo)
1988   *Viento de Colera* (De La Sota)
1990   *Cargo* (Girard) (as Capitaine)
1994   *Amnesia* (Justiniano) (as Capt. Mandiola)

Publications

By VILLAGRA: article—

"Un actor y su trabajo," in *Cine Cubano* (Havana), no. 96, 1980.

On VILLAGRA: book—

Burton, Julianne, editor, *Cinema and Social Change in Latin America: Conversations with Filmmakers*, Austin, Texas, 1986.

*   *   *

The Chilean-born actor Nelson Villagra is one of the most versatile and accomplished of Spanish-American actors. After working in Chilean theater, Villagra then joined the Chilean radical film movement that reached its zenith immediately before and during Marxist-socialist Salvador Allende's presidency (1970-73). Villagra had major roles in some of the movement's key films, which were directed by leading filmmakers: *Tres tristes tigres* directed by Raúl Ruiz, and *El Chacal de Nahueltoro* and *La tierra prometida* both directed by Miguel Littin.

Villagra, a leftist, has lived in exile since the right-wing military coup toppled the Allende government in 1973. The actor has now become associated with Cuba's state-controlled movie industry, and since the mid-1970s he has played important roles in several major films produced or co-produced in Cuba. In these films, Villagra has worked with prominent Cuban directors (e.g., Tomás Gutiérrez Alea, *La última cena*) as well as exiled Chilean directors (e.g., Miguel Littin, *El recurso del método*). In these Cuban films Villagra has often played characters who represent the forces of domination and repression in Latin America: a military officer in charge of a torture center in *Prisioneros desparecidos*, a repressive Latin American dictator in *El recurso del método*, a counter-revolutionary guerrilla leader in *Rio Negro*. Villagra has had many different types of roles throughout his career, however, and his versatility is one of his principal strengths as an actor. He is widely recognized as one of the greatest stars of the sociopolitically oriented cinema of Latin America known as El Nuevo Cine Latinoamericano.

—Dennis West

VITTI, Monica

Nationality: Italian. **Born:** Maria Luisa Ceciarelli in Rome, 3 November 1931. **Education:** Attended Pittman's College and Academy of Dramatic Art, both in Rome. **Career:** Stage actress in Rome;

1955—film debut in *Ridere, ridere, ridere*; 1959—first of several films for Antonioni, *L'avventura*, brought international attention. **Awards:** Three Nastro d'Argento Awards, nine David Di Donatello Awards, and four Italian Golden Grails.

Films as Actress:

1955   *Ridere, ridere, ridere* (Anton); *Adriana Lecouvreur* (Salvani)
1956   *Una pelliccia di visone* (Pellegrini)
1958   *Le dritte* (*Smart Girls*) (Amendola)
1959   *L'avventura* (Antonioni) (as Claudia)
1961   *La notte* (*The Night*) (Antonioni) (as Valentina Gherardini)
1962   *L'eclisse* (*The Eclipse*) (Antonioni) (as Vittoria); "Le Lievre et la tortue" ("The Tortoise and the Hare") ep. of *Les Quatres Vérités* (*Three Fables of Love*) (Blasetti) (as Madeleine)
1963   *Château en Suède* (*Nutty Naughty Chateau*) (Vadim) (as Eleanore Falsen); *Dragées au poivre* (*Sweet and Sour*) (Baratier) (as Elle)
1964   "La sospirosa" ("The Singing Woman" or "The Victim") ep. of *Alta infedeltà* (*High Infidelity*) (Salce) (as Gloria); *Il deserto rosso* (*The Red Desert*) (Antonioni) (as Giuliana); "La ministra" ("The Soup") ep. of *Le bambole* (*Four Kinds of Love*; *The Dolls*) (Rossi) (as Giovanna)
1965   *Il disco volante* (*The Flying Saucer*) (Brass) (as Mercedes); *Fai in fretta ad ucidermi . . . ho Freddo!* (Maselli) (as Giovanna)
1966   *Modesty Blaise* (Losey) (title role); "Fata Sabina" ("Queen Sabina") ep. of *Le fate* (*The Queens*; *Sex Quartet*) (Salce) (title role); *Le piacevoli notti*
1967   *Ti ho sposato per allegria* (*I Married You for Fun*) (Salce) (as Giuliana)
1968   *La ragazza con la pistola* (*The Girl with the Pistol*) (Monicelli) (as Assunta Borello); *La Femme écarlate* (*The Scarlet Woman*) (Valere) (as Lucie)
1969   *La cintura di Castità* (*The Chastity Belt*; *On My Way to the Crusades, I Met a Girl Who . . .*) (Campanile) (as Boccadora); *Vedo nudo* (Risi); *Amore mio, aiutami* (Sordi) (as Raffaella)
1970   *Nini Tirabuscio, la donna che incento la mossa* (Fondato) (as Maria Sarta); *Dramma della gelosia—tutti i particolari in cronaca* (*The Pizza Triangle*; *A Drama of Jealousy*; *The Motive Was Jealousy*) (Scola) (as Adelaide)
1971   *La pacifista* (*Smetti di piovere*; *The Pacifist*) (Jancsó) (as the Journalist); "The Refrigerator" and "The Lion" eps. of *Le coppie* (Monicelli and De Sica); *La supertestimone* (Giraldi)
1972   *Teresa la ladra* (*Teresa the Thief*) (Di Palma); *Gli ordini sono ordini*; *Noi donne siamo fatte cosi* (Rosi) (twelve roles)
1973   *Tosca* (Magni); *Polvere di stelle* (Sordi) (as Dea Adami)
1974   *La Fantôme de la liberté* (*The Phantom of Liberty*; *The Specter of Freedom*) (Buñuel) (as Mrs. Fouca)
1975   *A mezzanotte va la ronda del piacere* (*The Immortal Bachelor*; *Midnight Pleasures*; *Qui comincia l'avventura*) (Fondato) (as Tina Candela); *L'Anatra all'orancia* (*Duck in Orange Sauce*) (Salce) (as Lisa)
1978   *La Raison d'état* (Cayatte) (as Angela)
1979   *An Almost Perfect Affair* (Ritchie) (as Maria); *Letti selvaggi* (Zampa)
1980   *Non ti conasco più amore* (Corbucci)
1981   *Il mistero di Oberwald* (*The Mystery of Oberwald*) (Antonioni) (as the Queen); *Camera d'albergo* (Monicelli); *Tango della gelosia* (*Tigers in Lipstick*) (Steno)
1982   *Io so che tu sai che io so* (*I Know that You Know that I Know*) (Sordi); *Scusa se e poco* (Vicario)
1983   *Flirt* (Russo) (as Laura); *Trenta minuti d'amore* (Vicario)
1986   *Francesco e mia* (Russo) (+ co-sc, story)

Monica Vitti

Film as Actress, Director, and Co-Scriptwriter:

1989 *Scandalo segreto (Secret Scandal)*

Publications

By VITTI: book—

Sette sottane, Milan, 1993.

By VITTI: articles—

Interview with A. Remond, in *Cinéma* (Paris), November 1973.
Interview with E. Decaux and Bruno Villien, in *Cinématographe* (Paris), December 1982.

On VITTI: book—

Delli Colli, Laura, *Monica Vitti*, Rome, 1987.

On VITTI: articles—

Lucas, C., "Monica Vitti," in *Show* (Hollywood), October 1961.
"Le donne del cinema contro questo cinema," edited by Bellumori, in *Bianco e nero* (Rome), January/February 1972.

* * *

Monica Vitti is best known for her representation of the macho Italian version of woman in many of director Antonioni's films, but it must be said that he manipulated her performances with a callow disregard for human integrity. In the director's great trilogy, Vitti appears as the molded woman, not only in the cinematography but also in the narrative. In *L'avventura* she replaces the first woman of Sandro, the male lead. For all his intellectual Weltschmerz, Sandro has the same attitude toward women as that of any *bravo* hanging out in the square of any Italian village. *He*, not *she*, has the luxury of promiscuity and its subsequent guilt. In the last scene, the Vitti persona forgives the repentant lover like some Florentine Madonna—wistful and melancholy, yet always accepting.

L'eclisse is hardly better: in it Vitti plays a sexually exploited woman. To underscore her position she dresses up, applies blackface, and performs a dance for the entertainment of a colonial from Kenya. It may be said that this scene demonstrates a certain sympathy for her situation, but such acceptance of male sympathy is cheap.

In *La notte* she plays the passive observer, the writer manqué. In Antonioni's world, while women can represent symbolically creative apperception, it is only the male poet or director who can actually "make." Finally, in *Il deserto rosso*, her baffled gestures and her wistful smile à la Watteau are excruciatingly painful. This role seems the ultimate degradation that Antonioni could effect upon the Vitti persona.

Probably her finest role, at least as a fully cognizant human being, is that of the title character in Joseph Losey's *Modesty Blaise*. Admittedly, at the time of its appearance, it was a role little appreciated by the critics sharing the same sexual malaise as Antonioni. The film gained a cult following, however, in the radicalized college campuses of the 1960s. Here, Vitti's husky voice is heard to best advantage. But of even greater significance is the film's translation of the refined woman into an active, female James Bond. Here, then, lies the sublime irony of Losey's film: this actress, whom Antonioni had made out to be the helpless and indecisive neurotic, now becomes the ever-competent agent—more competent than her male assistant, played by Terence Stamp. Losey,

in his desire to set the secret-agent genre on its head, could not have found a better actress to represent Modesty Blaise.

—Rodney Farnsworth

VOGLER, Rüdiger

Nationality: German. **Born:** Warthausen, 1942. **Education:** Studied theater at Heidelberg University. **Career:** 1960s—associated with the Frankfurt Theater am Turm: roles in comic and serious plays, especially those by Peter Handke; 1971—first of several films by Wim Wenders, *Die Angst des Tormanns beim Elfmeter*; 1995—in TV mini-series *Der Clan der Anna Voss*.

Films as Actor:

1971 *Die Angst des Tormanns beim Elfmeter (The Goalkeeper's Fear of the Penalty; The Goalie's Anxiety at the Penalty Kick)* (Wenders) (as village idiot)
1973 *Der scharlachrote Buchstabe (The Scarlet Letter)* (Wenders) (as the sailor); *Die Grafin von Rathenow* (Beauvais—for TV)
1974 *Alice in den Städten (Alice in the Cities)* (Wenders) (as Phillip); *Falsche Bewegung (Wrong Movement; The Wrong Move)* (Wenders) (as Wilhelm Meister)
1976 ***Im Lauf der Zeit (Kings of the Road)*** (Wenders) (as Bruno Winter)
1977 *Kreutzer* (Emmerich) (as Andreas Kreutzer); *Fleuchtweg nach Marseille* (Engstrom); *Die Linkshändige Frau (The Left-Handed Woman)* (Handke) (as the actor)
1978 *Alzire oder der Neue Kontinent* (Koerfer); *L'Etat sauvage (The Savage State)* (Girod) (as Tristan)
1979 *Letzte Liebe* (Engstrom)
1980 *Henry Angst* (Kratisch)
1981 *Beate und Mareile* (Gies—for TV)
1982 *Die Bleiere Zeit (The German Sisters; Marianne and Juliane)* (von Trotta) (as Wolfgang); *Logik des Gefühls* (Kratisch) (as George)
1983 *Heller Wahn* (von Trotta); *L'Hôpital de Leningrad* (Maldoror); *Melzer* (Heinz Butler); *Wanda* (Noever)
1984 *Un caso d'incoscienza* (Greco); *Der Havarist* (Buhler); *Machinations* (Gantillon—for TV); *La Nuit de Carrefour* (Bertin); *Praxis der Liebe* (Export)
1985 *Fratelli* (Dordi)
1986 *Tarot* (Thome) (as Otto)
1987 *Lucky Ravi* (Lombard); *Madrid* (Patino) (as Hans); *Das Treibhaus* (Goedel) (as narrator)
1989 *Erdenschwer* (Herbrich) (as Dr. Frank)
1990 *Il sole anche di notte (Night Sun)* (Tavianis) (as King Charles)
1991 *Bis ans Ende der Welt (Until the End of the World)* (Wenders) (as Phillip Winter); *Anna Göldin: letzte Hexe (Anna Goldin, the Last Witch)* (Pinkus) (as Dr. Tsuchidi); *Transit* (Allio) (as the doctor); *Reiche Kunden killt man nicht* (Gutke—for TV)
1992 *Tatort—Bienzle und der Biedermann* (Peter Adam—for TV) (as Paul Stricker); *Schöne Feindin* (Keglevic—for TV) (as Dr. Egon Wirtz); *Das Lange Gespräch mit dem Vogel* (Zanussi—for TV) (as Dr. Halbritter)
1993 *Faraway, So Close! (In Weiter Ferne, So Nah!)* (Wenders) (as Phillip Winter); *Bommels Billigflüge* (Rohne—for TV) (as Volker)

1994   *Het Verdriet Van Belgie* (as Lausengier); *Tod in Miami* (Rola—
       for TV) (as Kai Vogt); *Saubere Aktien* (Mittermayr—for
       TV) (as Brehm); *Hasenjagd—Vor lauter Feigheit gibt es
       kein Erbarmen* (*The Quality of Mercy*; *The Rabbit Hunt*)
       (Gruber) (as Gendarm Birker); *De sueur et du sang*
       (*Wonderboy*) (Vecchiali)
1995   *Viagem a Lisboa* (*Lisbon Story*) (Wenders) (as Phillip Winter)
1996   *Peanuts—Die Bank zahlt alles* (Rola)

Publications

By VOGLER: articles—

Interview, in *Cinéma* (Paris), December 1976.
Interview, in *Cinématographe* (Paris), February 1981.

*   *   *

Although Rüdiger Vogler is associated ineradicably with Wim Wenders
for his starring roles in *Alice in the Cities*, *Kings of the Road*, and the
relatively neglected *Wrong Movement* (not forgetting his smaller parts
in *The Goalkeeper's Fear of the Penalty* and *The Scarlet Letter*, and
roles in Wenders's 1990s films, *Until the End of the World*, *Faraway,
So Close!*, and *Lisbon Story*), his earliest associations were in fact with
Peter Handke. After studying drama at Heidelberg University Vogler
worked at Frankfurt's Theater am Turm from 1966, where he appeared in all of Handke's plays, including the epochal 1968 production *Publikumsbeschimpfung*. He also appeared in Handke's television film *Die Chronik der Laufenden Ereignisse* and, much later, in
the writer's debut as a feature director, *The Left Handed Woman*.

In one of his few published interviews Vogler once said that "just as
a film is something of an image of a reality, so an actor is also the
image of a real man," and in many respects it is extremely tempting to
regard his Wenders films not simply as at-one-remove portraits of
their director but, moreover, as documentaries about the actor himself. Certainly it is very difficult to make the usual distinction between
actor and character, and the continuities from film to film—the tenderness, the poignancy, the fear of "normal" settled-down life, the
need for movement along with a certain unfulfilled desire for some
kind of stability—give his three main films for Wenders the quality of
a trilogy, a quality that stems as much from Vogler's remarkable presence as Wenders's writing and direction.

Vogler's importance, however, goes beyond his roles in early
Wenders, and his gentle, troubled persona has become a key ingredient
in what Thomas Elsaesser has aptly referred to as the "collective
associations and cross-references" that distinguish the New German
Cinema. As he puts it, "what gave the use of actors in the German
cinema the dimension of a star system was their appearance in the
films of different directors, which complemented their roles in the
different films by the same director. One might, for instance, construct for the New German Cinema a recognizable identity and an
existence as a national cinema entirely on the basis of the different
roles and personae that less than a dozen actors and actresses embodied in 40 or 50 films," actors who "helped establish an intertextuality
sufficiently stable to give the impression of a coherent fictional universe, although sufficiently variable to inhibit typecasting." Fassbinder
springs immediately to mind here, as does Herzog's use of Klaus Kinski
and Bruno S., along, of course, with Wenders/Vogler.

Thus when Vogler crops up in von Trotta's *The German Sisters* he
brings to the role all sorts of associations that would not be present
were the character being played by a different actor; indeed, as Elsaesser
notes, he plays a role "which is not so much that of a character within
the fiction as that of a Wenders persona in a von Trotta film, and thus
answering for the spectator the question of what Wenders' attitude

might be to left-wing politics, terrorism and the women's movement."
Directors who have exploited the introspective side of his "Wenders"
persona include Ingemo Engstrom (*Letzte Liebe*) and Ingo Kratisch
(*Logik des Gefühls*) while the restless, rootless aspect (*Alice, Kings*) is
more to the fore in Handke's *The Left-Handed Woman* and Klaus
Emmerich's *Kreutzer*.

—Julian Petley

VOIGHT, Jon

Nationality: American. **Born:** Yonkers, New York, 29 December 1938.
Education: Attended Archbishop Stepinac High School, White Plains,
New York; Catholic University, Washington, D.C.; studied acting at the
Neighborhood Playhouse under Sanford Meisner, 1960-64. **Family:**
Married 1) Lauri Peters, 1962 (divorced 1967); 2) Marcheline Bertrand,
1971 (divorced), children: James, Angelina. **Career:** Early 1960s—
Broadway debut in replacement role in *The Sound of Music*; 1965—
major role in off-Broadway production of *A View from the Bridge*; acted
in the San Diego Shakespeare Festival; 1967—on Broadway with Irene
Papas in *That Summer—That Fall*; film debut in *Fearless Frank*; 1993—
in TV mini-series *Return to Lonesome Dove*; 1995—directing debut with
TV movie *Tin Soldier*. **Awards:** Best Actor, New York Film Critics, for
Midnight Cowboy, 1969; Best Actor Academy Award, Best Actor, Cannes
Festival, and Best Actor, New York Film Critics, for *Coming Home*,
1978. **Agent:** Creative Artists Agency, 9830 Wilshire Boulevard, Beverly
Hills, CA 90210 U.S.A.

Films as Actor:

1967   *Fearless Frank* (*Frank's Greatest Adventure*) (Kaufman) (title
       role); *Hour of the Gun* (John Sturges) (as Curly Bill Brocius)
1969   ***Midnight Cowboy*** (Schlesinger) (as Joe Buck); *Out of It* (Wil-
       liams) (as Russ)
1970   *The Revolutionary* (Williams) (as A); *Catch-22* (Mike Nichols)
       (as Milo Minderbinder)
1972   ***Deliverance*** (Boorman) (as Ed Gentry)
1973   *The All-American Boy* (Eastman) (as Vic Bealer)
1974   *Conrack* (Ritt) (as Pat Conroy); *The Odessa File* (Neame) (as
       Peter Miller)
1975   *Der Richter und sein Henker* (*End of the Game*; *Murder on the
       Bridge*; *Getting Away with Murder*) (Schell) (as Walter Tschanz)
1978   *Coming Home* (Ashby) (as Luke Martin)
1979   *The Champ* (Zeffirelli) (as Billy Flynn)
1982   *Lookin' to Get Out* (Ashby) (as Alex Kovac, + co-sc)
1983   *Table for Five* (Lieberman) (as J. P. Tannen)
1985   *Runaway Train* (Konchalovsky) (as Manny)
1986   *Desert Bloom* (Corr) (as Jack Chismore)
1990   *Eternity* (Paul) (as James/Edward, + sc)
1991   *Chernobyl: The Final Warning* (Page—for TV) (as Dr. Robert Gale)
1992   *The Last of His Tribe* (Hook—for TV) (as Prof. Alfred Kroeber)
1994   *The Rainbow Warrior* (Tuchner) (as Peter Willcox)
1995   *Convict Cowboy* (Holcomb—for TV) (as Ry Weston); *Heat*
       (Michael Mann) (as Nate)
1996   *Mission Impossible* (De Palma) (as Jim Phelps); *Rosewood*
       (Singleton)

Film as Actor and Director:

1995   *Tin Soldier* (for TV) (as Yarik)

Publications

By VOIGHT: article—

"Jon Voight: To Act or Not to Act," interview with S. Miles, in *Interview* (New York), October 1974.

On VOIGHT: articles—

McGillivray, David, "Jon Voight," in *Focus on Film* (London), Autumn 1972.
Current Biography 1974, New York, 1974.
Jerome, Jim, "For Single Father Jon Voight, *Table for Five* Is a Story Close to His Own Painful Experience," in *People Weekly* (New York), 11 April 1983.
Stark, Jon, "Jon Voight Thanks God for Putting Him Back on the Oscar Track with a Rousing Return in *Runaway Train*," in *People Weekly* (New York), 24 March 1986.
Gorkachov, V., "Jon Voight: To Russia with Love," in *Soviet Film* (Moscow), December 1988.

* * *

Jon Voight is a multitalented (but too-little-used) actor whose career is a study in schizophrenia. In the role that solidified his stardom, he played a boyishly naive, inexperienced character who is constantly victimized; as he reached middle-age, his best parts came as grizzled, all-too-experienced heavies, intimidating outlaws one would cross the street to avoid. In between came his most likable character: an Everyman war survivor whose time in battle has at once crippled his body but sharpened his mind, and his sensitivities.

Voight won his initial celebrity in *Midnight Cowboy*, one of the defining films of the late-1960s-early 1970s, playing the ingenuous Texas stud Joe Buck, opposite Dustin Hoffman's Ratso Rizzo. Joe Buck comes to New York thinking he effortlessly will earn wads of money selling himself to wealthy middle-aged ladies who will be taken by his cowboy charm. Instead, he ends up befriending the tubercular Ratso, with whom he shares a frosty room in a condemned building. His sexual contacts are just as often with men and boys as women. As a hustler, Joe Buck is an abysmal failure. At the finale, Ratso—who is his lone friend—dies, and Joe Buck's future remains uncertain. More recently, Voight's most vividly etched roles have been characters totally unlike Joe Buck: heavies who either are psychotic to a spine-rattling degree (the prison escapee in *Runaway Train*, in which he offers an electrifying performance), or simply intimidating (Robert De Niro's criminal contact in *Heat*).

The role that links these two celluloid personalities is the one for which Voight won an Oscar: Luke Martin, the sensitive, perceptive, paraplegic Vietnam veteran in *Coming Home*. Luke is a young American who went off to a war his country had no business fighting. For his trouble, he will be spending the rest of his days in a wheelchair. But harsh real-life experience has not hardened him. Unlike too many other celluloid Vietnam veterans, he is neither psycho criminal nor ne'er-do-well. Despite his plight, Luke Martin demands no pity—and he has become an eloquent antiwar activist. His reward: Jane Fonda, whom he wins from gung-ho marine officer Bruce Dern. Voight's knowing, sympathetic performance makes Luke the kind of guy with whom one might want to share a beer, or pass the hours deep in conversation.

Voight has had several other solid roles in noteworthy films (one of the unfortunates who sets out on what will be a harrowing backwoods canoe trip, in *Deliverance*; the common-sense teacher fighting racism and ignorance in the backwards black school, in *Conrack*). Still, his celluloid output has been spotty; since his screen debut in 1967, he has appeared in less than two dozen films and made-for-television fea-

tures. For this reason alone, Voight's career cannot be considered at the level of Dustin Hoffman, Al Pacino, Richard Dreyfuss, Jack Nicholson, Gene Hackman, or Robert De Niro, his fellow Oscar-winners who also won renown in the late 1960s and early 1970s.

—Rob Edelman

VOLONTÉ, Gian Maria

Nationality: Italian. **Born:** Milan, 9 April 1933. **Education:** Attended Academy of Dramatic Art, Rome. **Family:** Daughter with the actress Carla Gravina: Giovanna. **Career:** 1950s—stage actor for theater companies all over Italy; appeared in TV adaptations of Dostoyevski's *Idiot*, Chekhov's *Uncle Vanya*, and Vittorio Alfieri's *Saul*; 1960—film debut in *Sotto dieci bandiere*; 1964—directed controversial production of Hochhuth's stage play *The Representative*; 1971—arrested during strike in Italy; increasingly took on roles that meshed with his militant leftist politics. **Awards:** Nastro d'Argento Award for Best Actor, for *Oeuvre au noir*, 1988; special jury prize, Felix awards, for *Porte aperte*, 1990; Golden Lion, Venice Film Festival, for career achievement, 1991. **Died:** Of heart attack, in Florina, Greece, 6 December 1994.

Films as Actor:

1960　*Sotto dieci bandiere* (*Under Ten Flags*) (Coletti) (as Braun)
1961　*La ragazza con la valigia* (*Girl with a Suitcase*; *Pleasure Girl*) (Zurlini) (as Piero); *L'Antinea* (*L'Atlantide*; *Journey beneath the Desert*; *The Lost Kingdom*) (Ulmer and Masini) (as Tarath); *Ercole alla conquista di Atlantide* (*Hercules and the Captive Women*) (Cottafavi); *A cavallo della tigre* (Comencini)
1962　*Un uomo da bruciare* (*A Man for Burning*) (Orsini and Taviani) (as Salvatore); *Le quattro giornate de Napoli* (*The Four Days of Naples*) (Loy) (as Stimolo); *Il terrorista* (de Bosio)
1963　*Il peccato* (Grau)
1964　*Per un pugno di dollari* (*A Fistful of Dollars*) (Leone) (as Ramon Rojo, credited as John Wells); *Il magnifico cornuto* (*The Magnificent Cuckold*) (Pietrangeli) (as assessor)
1966　*Per qualche dollari in più* (*For a Few Dollars More*) (Leone) (as Indio, credited as John Wells); *Svegliati e uccidi* (*Lutring . . . reveille-toi et meurs*; *Wake Up and Die*; *Too Soon to Die*) (Lizzani) (as Inspector Moroni); *L'armata Brancaleone* (Monicelli) (title role); *La strega in amore* (*The Witch*; *Aura*) (Damiani) (as Fabrizio)
1967　*Het Gangstermeisje* (*A Gangstergirl*) (Weisz) (as Jascha); *A ciascuno il suo* (*We Still Kill the Old Way*) (Petri) (as Prof. Paolo Laurana); *Faccia a faccia* (*Cara a Cara*; *Face to Face*) (Sollima) (as Prof. Brad Fletcher); *Quien sabe?* (*A Bullet for the General*) (Damiani) (as El Chuncho); *I sette fratelli Cervi* (Puccini)
1968　*Banditi a Milano* (*The Violent Four*) (Lizzani) (as Cavallero); *Summit* (Bontempi) (as Paolo)
1969　*L'amanti di Gramigna* (Lizzani) (title role); *Sotto il segno dello scorpione* (*Under the Sign of Scorpio*) (Taviani) (as Renno)
1970　*Le Vent d'est* (*Wind from the East*; *East Wind*) (Godard) (as soldier); *Indagine su un cittadino al di sopra di ogni sospetto* (*Investigation of a Citizen above Suspicion*) (Petri) (as police inspector); *Le Cercle rouge* (Melville) (as Vogel); *Uomini contro* (Rosi) (as Lt. Ottolenghi)

Gian Maria Volonté in *La classe operaia va in paradiso*

1971   *Sacco e Vanzetti* (*Sacco and Vanzetti*) (Montaldo) (as
        Bartolomeo Vanzetti); *La classe operaia va in paradiso*
        (*The Working Class Goes to Heaven*; *Lulu the Tool*) (Petri)
        (as Lulu Massa); *12 Dicembre* (Zurlini and others—doc); *Il
        caso Mattei* (*The Mattei Affair*) (Rosi) (as Enrico Mattei)

1972   *L'Attentat* (*Plot*; *The French Conspiracy*) (Boisset) (as Sadiel);
        Sbatti il mostro in prima pagina (Bellocchio) (as Bizanti)

1973   *A proposito Lucky Luciano* (*Re: Lucky Luciano*; *Lucky
        Luciano*) (Rosi) (title role); *Giordano Bruno* (Montaldo)
        (title role)

1975   *Il sospetto* (Maselli) (as Emile)

1976   *Todo modo* (Petri) (as the President)

1977   *Io ho paura* (Damiani)

1979   **Cristo si è fermato a Eboli** (*Christ Stopped at Eboli*; *Eboli*)
        (Rosi) (as Carlo Levi)

1980   *Stark System* (Balducci)

1981   *La Dame aux camélias* (*The True Story of Camille*; *La Vera
        storia della signora delle camelie*; *Die Kameliendame*)
        (Bolognini and Festa Campanile)

1982   *The Secret Policeman's Other Ball* (Temple and Gräf—filmed
        concert)

1983   *Scherzo del destinoin aqquato dietro l'angolo come un
        brigante di strada* (*A Joke of Destiny, Lying in Wait around
        the Corner Like a Street Bandit*) (Wertmüller)

1984   *La Mort de Mario Ricci* (*The Death of Mario Ricci*) (Goretta)
        (as Bernard Fontana)

1985   *Actas de Marusia* (*Letters from Marusia*) (Littin)

1986   *Il caso Moro* (*The Moro Affair*) (Ferrara) (as Aldo Moro)

1987   *Cronaca di una morte annunciato* (*Chronicle of a Death Fore-
        told*) (Rosi) (as Dr. Cristo Bedoya); *Un ragazzo di Calabria*
        (Comencini) (as Felice)

1988   *Oeuvre au noir* (*The Abyss*) (Delvaux) (as Prior); *Pestalozzos
        Berg* (Von Gunten) (as Pestalozzi)

1990   *Porte aperte* (*Open Doors*) (Amelio) (as Judge Vito Di
        Francesco); *Tre colone in cronaca* (Vanzina)

1991   *Une Storia Semplice* (*A Simple Story*) (Greco)

1993   *Funes, un gran amor* (*Funes, a Great Love*) (De La
        Torre)

1994   *Tirano Banderas* (*Banderas, the Tyrant*) (García Sánchez)

1995   *Un Eroe Borghese* (Placido); *To Vlemma tou Odyssea* (*Ulysses'
        Gaze*; *The Gaze of Odysseus*; *Le Regarde d'Ulysse*)
        (Angelopoulos)

Publications

By VOLONTÉ: articles—

"Gian Maria Volonté Talks about Cinema and Politics," interview with
    Guy Braucourt, in *Cineaste* (New York), Fall 1975.
Interview in *Cine Cubano* (Havana), no. 115, 1986.
Interview in *Avant-Scène du Cinéma* (Paris), May 1988.

On VOLONTÉ: book—

Daniel, Ferenc, *Gian Maria Volonté*, Budapest, 1978.

On VOLONTÉ: articles—

Simsolo, Noël, "Gian Maria Volonté," in *Image et Son* (Paris), September 1973.
Viktorova, E., "Das Phänomen Volonté," in *Film und Fernsehen* (Berlin), January and February 1980.
Obituary in *New York Times*, 7 December 1994.
Obituary in *Variety* (New York), 12 December 1994.

*   *   *

The leading political actor of the 1960s and 1970s, Gian Maria Volonté shaped the look and style of Italian political filmmaking as much as have the great directors with whom he collaborated: Francesco Rosi, Elio Petri, and Marco Bellocchio. Volonté established a strong reputation on stage and television before he entered cinema; even after he became the leading political spokesman on screen he continued to appear in socially committed theater productions.

Volonté's first roles in films solidified one aspect of his persona: the bad guy. In half a dozen Italian Westerns, including *Per un pugno di dollari* and *Per qualche dollari in più* (in both of which he appeared under the pseudonym John Wells), and *Quien sabe?*, he personified the psychotic villain—powerful, frightening, and nasty. These traits would be combined with a political purpose in his masterful portrayal of the chief police inspector in *Indagine su un cittadino al di sopra di ogni sospetto*. The inspector, a symbol of the patriarchal state with fascist tendencies, cold-bloodedly murders his mistress in order to prove that his position and reputation will place him above suspicion despite volumes of evidence that he is the killer. He played a similar role in Petri's *Todo modo*, a political intrigue that involves state and religious leaders on retreat who kill each other one by one.

Although Volonté was suitably terrifying as power-hungry civil officials, he could also play sympathetic roles. Two of the most notable examples of his positive characters are Lulu Massa, the Milanese factory worker in *La classe operaia va in paradiso*, who achieves political consciousness after his hand is mangled by a machine thereby cutting his productivity, and as the doctor in *Cristo si è fermato a Eboli*, who because of his antifascist activities in 1930s Italy is exiled to a backward village in southern Italy and thus learns of the tremendous difference between himself and the peasants of Calabria.

Throughout the last two decades of his career, Volonté chose his roles carefully, appearing primarily in films that espoused a social commitment similar to his. Two of his better late-career performances were in Rosi's *Cronaca di una morte annunciato* and Gianni Amelio's *Porte aperte*, both of which deal with the dispensing of justice. In the former, based on the novel by Gabriel García Márquez, Volonté returns to his hometown after a 20-year absence seeking the truth about the senseless murder of his boyhood best friend. In the latter, Volonté again confronts murder—this time a brutal triple-homicide committed by an unrepentant killer—as the only member of a multijudge tribunal handling the resulting case who opposes capital punishment. Volonté gives a perfectly restrained performance, conveying dignity and grace in his crusade to save the murderer's life, a quest initially successful, but ultimately doomed to failure.

In his 36th year as an actor, Volonté died in 1994 after having nearly completed work on acclaimed Greek director Theodoros Angelopoulos's *To Vlemma tou Odyssea*, in which he portrays the head of the Sarajevo cinematheque. In addition to leaving a rich assortment of memorable roles, Volonté also left for the acting profession a rare example of an aesthetically successful mixture of private convictions and public performance.

—Elaine Mancini, updated by David E. Salamie

VON SYDOW, Max

Nationality: Swedish. **Born:** Carl Adolf von Sydow in Lund, 10 April 1929. **Education:** Attended Cathedral School of Lund; Royal Academy (now Royal Dramatic Theatre School), Stockholm, graduated 1951. **Family:** Married the actress Kerstin Olin, 1951, sons: Clas and Henrik. **Career:** 1949—film debut in *Bara en Mor*; actor for Norrköping-Linköping Municipal Theatre, 1951-53, Municipal Theatre of Hälsingborg, 1953-55, and Municipal Theatre of Malmö, 1955-60; directed on stage at Malmö by Ingmar Bergman in *Cat on a Hot Tin Roof*, *Peer Gynt*, *Le Misanthrope*, and *Faust*; 1957—first of several films by Bergman, *The Seventh Seal*; 1960—joined the Royal Dramatic Theatre, Stockholm; 1965—role of Christ in first U.S. film, *The Greatest Story Ever Told*; 1977—Broadway debut in *The Night of the Tribades*; 1981—in stage play *Duet for One*; 1988—directed first film, *Katinka*; on stage in *The Tempest* at the Old Vic, London; 1994— in TV mini-series *Radetzkymarsch* (*Radetzky March*), and *Enskilda Samtal*, 1996. **Awards:** Sweden Gold Bug Awards for Best Actor, 1987 and 1988; European Felix Award for Best Actor, for *Pelle the Conqueror*, 1987. **Address:** c/o Filmuset, Box 27126, 102 52 Stockholm 27, Sweden.

Films as Actor:

1949   *Bara en Mor* (*Only a Mother*) (Sjöberg) (as Nils)
1951   ***Froken Julie*** (*Miss Julie*) (Sjöberg) (as Hand)
1953   *Ingens Mans Kvinna* (*No Man's Woman*) (Kjellgren)
1956   *Rätten att Älska* (*The Right to Love*) (Pollack)
1957   ***Det sjunde inseglet*** (*The Seventh Seal*) (Bergman) (as Antonius Block); *Prästen i Uddarbo* (Fant); ***Smultronstället*** (*Wild Strawberries*) (Bergman) (as Akerman)
1958   *Nära livet* (*Brink of Life*; *So Close to Life*) (Bergman) (as Harry Andersson); *Spion 503* (Jeppesen); *Ansiktet* (*The Face*; *The Magician*) (Bergman) (as Albert Emanuel Vogler)
1960   *Jungfrukällen* (*The Virgin Spring*) (Bergman) (as Herr Tore); *Bröllopsdagen* (*The Wedding Day*) (Fant) (as Anders Frost)
1961   *Sasom i em Spegel* (*Through a Glass Darkly*) (Bergman) (as Martin)
1962   *Nils Holgerssons Underbara Resa* (*Adventures of Nils Holgersson*); *Älskarinnan* (*The Swedish Mistress*) (Sjöman) (as married man)
1963   *Nattvardsgästerna* (*Winter Light*) (Bergman) (as Jonas Persson)
1965   *4 x 4* (*Uppehall i Myrlandet*); *The Greatest Story Ever Told* (Stevens) (as Jesus); *The Reward* (Bourguignon) (as Scott Swanson)
1966   *Hawaii* (George Roy Hill) (as Abner Hale); *The Quiller Memorandum* (Anderson) (as Oktober); *Här har du ditt liv* (*Here's Your Life*; *This Is Your Life*) (Troell) (as Smalands-Pelle)
1967   *Svarta palmkroner* (*The Black Palm Trees*) (Lindgren)
1968   *Vargtimmen* (*Hour of the Wolf*) (Bergman) (as Johan Borg); *Skammen* (*Shame*) (Bergman) (as Jan Rosenberg); *Made in Sweden* (Bergenstrahle)
1969   *En Passion* (*A Passion*; *The Passion of Anna*) (Bergman) (as Andreas Winkelman)
1970   *The Kremlin Letter* (Huston) (as Col. Vladimir Kosnov)

1971   *The Night Visitor* (Benedek) (as Salem); *Beröringen* (*The Touch*) (Bergman) (as Andreas Vergerus); *Appelkriget* (*The Apple War*) (Danielsson) (as Roy Lindberg); *I havsbandet* (Lagerkvist—for TV)

1972   *Utvandrarna* (*The Emigrants*) (Troell) (as Karl Oskar); *Embassy* (Hessler) (as Gorenko)

1973   *Nybyggarna* (*The New Land*) (Troell) (as Karl Oskar); *The Exorcist* (Friedkin) (title role)

1974   *Steppenwolf* (Haines) (as Harry Haller); *Agget är löst* (*Egg! Egg! A Hardboiled Story*)

1975   *Foxtrot* (*The Other Side of Paradise*) (Ripstein) (as Larsen); *Three Days of the Condor* (Pollack) (as Joubert); *The Ultimate Warrior* (Clouse) (as the Baron); *Cuore di cane* (Lattuada); *Il contesto* (Rosi)

1976   *Cadaveri eccelenti* (*Illustrious Corpses*) (Rosi) (as Chief Justice); *Voyage of the Damned* (Wanamaker) (as Capt. Schroeder); *Le désert des Tartares* (*Il deserto dei Tartari*; *The Desert of the Tartars*) (Zurlini) (as Hortiz)

1977   *Exorcist II: The Heretic* (Boorman) (as Father Merrin); *March or Die* (Richards) (as François Marneau); *La signora della orroro* (*Black Journal*)

1978   *Brass Target* (Hough) (as Shelley/Weber); *Gran bollito* (Bolognini)

1979   *Hurricane* (Troell) (as Dr. Bascomb); *A Look at Liv* (*Norway's Liv Ullmann*; *Liv Ullmann's Norway*) (Kaplan—doc); *Le Mort en direct* (*Deathwatch*) (Tavernier) (as Gerald Mortenhoe)

1980   *Flash Gordon* (Hodges) (as Emperor Ming); *She Dances Alone* (Dornhelm) (as voice of Nijinsky); *Bugie bianchi* (Rolla)

1981   *Victory* (*Escape to Victory*) (Huston) (as Maj. Karl von Steiner); *Ingenjör Andrees luftfärd* (*Flight of the Eagle*) (Troell) (as Salomon August Andree)

1982   *Conan the Barbarian* (Milius) (as King Osric)

1983   *Strange Brew* (Thomas and Morani) (as Brewmeister Smith); *Never Say Never Again* (Kershner) (as Ernst Stavro Blofeld); *Cercel des passions* (D'Anna)

1984   *Dreamscape* (Ruben) (as Dr. Novotny); *Samson and Delilah* (Philips—for TV); *Letzte Zivlist* (Heynemann—for TV); *Target Eagle* (Loma) (as Col. O'Donnell); *Dune* (Lynch) (as Liet Kynes); *George Stevens: A Filmmaker's Journey* (Stevens Jr.—doc) (as himself); *The Ice Pirates* (Raffill—for TV)

1985   *Kojak: The Belarush File* (Markowitz—for TV); *Code Name: Emerald* (Sanger) (as Jurgen Brausch); *The Last Place on Earth* (Fairfax—for TV); *Il pentito* (Squitteri) (as Spinola); *Quo Vadis* (Rossi—for TV); *Cristoforo Colombo* (*Christopher Columbus*) (Lattuada—for TV) (as King John of Portugal)

1986   *Hannah and Her Sisters* (Woody Allen) (as Frederick); *Duet for One* (Konchalovsky) (as Dr. Louis Feldman); *Second Victory* (Thomas) (as Dr. Huber); *The Wolf at the Door* (*Oviri*) (Carlsen) (as August Strindberg)

1987   *Pelle Erovraren* (*Pelle the Conqueror*) (August) (as Papa Lasse Karlsson)

1989   *Red King, White Knight* (Murphy—for TV) (as Szaz)

1990   *Hiroshima: Out of the Ashes* (Werner—for TV) (as Father Siemes); *Mio caro Dottor Graesler* (*Dr. Graesler, The Bachelor*) (Faenza) (as Von Schleiheim); *Father* (Power) (as Joseph Mueller); *Una Vita Scellerata* (*Violent Life*) (Battiato) (as Pope Clement VII); *Awakenings* (Penny Marshall) (as Dr. Peter Ingham)

1991   *A Kiss before Dying* (Dearden) (as Thor Carlsson); *The Ox* (*Oxen*) (Nykvist) (as the vicar); *Bis ans Ende der Welt* (*Until the End of the World*) (Wenders) (as Henry Farber)

1992   *Zentropa* (*Europa*) (von Trier) (as narrator); *Den Goda Viljan* (*The Best Intentions*) (August) (as Johan Akerblom)

1993   *Dotkniecie reki* (*The Silent Touch*) (Zanussi) (as Henry Kesdi); *Needful Things* (Fraser Heston) (as Leland Gaunt)

1994   *Time Is Money* (Paolo Barzman) (as Joe Kaufman)

1995   *Atlanten* (Enquist, Kristian Petri, and Roed) (as narrator); *Judge Dredd* (Cannon) (as Judge Fargo); *Citizen X* (Gerolmo—for TV) (as Dr. Aleksandr Bukhanovsky)

1996   *Jerusalem* (August); *Hamsun* (Troell) (as Knut Hamsun)

Film as Director:

1988   *Vid vejen* (*Katinka*)

Publications

By VON SYDOW: articles—

"Working with Bergman," interview in *Films and Filming* (London), August 1960.

"Max von Sydow on Ingmar Bergman," interview with J. Gallagher, in *Films in Review* (New York), May 1988.

"Bergman and the Actors," interview with F. J. Marker and L.-L. Marker, in *Theater*, vol. 21, no.1/2, 1990.

On VON SYDOW: books—

Cowie, Peter, *Ingmar Bergman: A Critical Biography*, New York, 1982.

Cowie, Peter, *Max von Sydow: From "The Seventh Seal" to "Pelle the Conqueror,"* Stockholm, 1989.

On VON SYDOW: articles—

Current Biography 1967, New York, 1967.

Ecran (Paris), May 1978.

Kauffmann, Stanley, "An End and a Beginning," in *New Republic* (New York), 23 January 1989.

*   *   *

When you think of Scandinavian movie stars, the first name that comes to mind is Max von Sydow. Since his screen debut in 1949 in Alf Sjoberg's *Only a Mother*, he has appeared in more than six dozen films, including titles as diverse as *Hannah and Her Sisters* and *Conan the Barbarian*, *The Emigrants* and *The Exorcist*, *Pelle the Conqueror* and *Judge Dredd*. The actor is easily recognized by his gaunt appearance: he is tall, with a long, lean face and sharp features. These physical characteristics have been an asset in both aspects of his screen career, comprised of the character roles he has played in English-language films and his status as a principal on-screen interpreter of Ingmar Bergman.

In the United States, von Sydow enjoys the reputation of a serious actor, due to the roles he plays—character ones, rather than leading men or traditional star parts—and his past association with Bergman. His roles have ranged from intellectuals (the painter who is Barbara Hershey's live-in lover in *Hannah and Her Sisters*) to ministers and priests (in *Hawaii* and *The Exorcist*) to stock heavies (a sadistic Nazi in *The Quiller Memorandum*, cold-blooded assassins in *Three Days of the Condor* and *Brass Target*). He was the title character in *The Exorcist*; he also has played Christ, in *The Greatest Story Ever Told*, and the Devil, in *Needful Things*. And he has appeared in as many forgettable, if not outright disastrous, American films (*Dune*, *Judge Dredd*, and *Hurricane* are but a few) as he has in first-rate, Oscar-caliber titles (*Hannah and Her Sisters*, *The Exorcist*, *Awakenings*).

Max Von Sydow in *Det sjunde inseglet* © 1957 **AB Svensk Filmindustri**

Von Sydow has co-starred in a number of European productions by prominent directors, including Mauro Bolognini, Bertrand Tavernier, Jan Troell and, most recently, Bille August. But it is his work with Bergman for which he will be best-remembered. He earned his initial international acclaim in Bergman-directed films, particularly *The Seventh Seal* (as the tormented knight who rides through the plague-ridden countryside in search of a good deed he might perform before the figure of Death takes him away) and *The Virgin Spring* (as the father who avenges the rape-murder of his young daughter). Indeed, in his best roles for Bergman (in which he has, more often than not, played husbands and artists), von Sydow has embodied the anguished soul who suffers as a result of his desires, or guilt, or the guilt he feels because of his desires. Throughout his career, he has remained active on the stage, often working with Bergman on the latter's theatrical undertakings; in fact, he began his collaboration with Bergman in the 1950s when he joined the Municipal Theatre of Malmö, where Bergman was the principal director. More than 35 years later, he capped his association with the filmmaker by taking a supporting role in the Bergman-scripted, Bille August-directed *The Best Intentions*, playing Johan Akerblom, Bergman's maternal grandfather.

Perhaps von Sydow's finest late career role is the aging, illiterate old widower Lasse Karlsson in *Pelle the Conqueror*, also directed by August. Lasse and his young son Pelle are impoverished Swedish immigrants in Denmark: simple folk with modest dreams, who must valiantly struggle for survival in a world rife with everyday cruelty and injustice. Von Sydow eloquently captures his character in voice and mannerism; he plays Lasse brilliantly, with much grace, humor, and understanding, and he went on to earn his first (and, to date, only) Best Actor Academy Award nomination. Finally, nearing age 60, he extended the boundaries of his career by directing his first feature: *Katinka*, a romantic story based on a novel by Herman Bang.

—Rob Edelman

WALBROOK, Anton

Nationality: Austrian/British. **Born:** Adolf Wohlbrück in Vienna, Austria, 19 November 1896; became British citizen, 1947. **Education:** Studied acting at the Max Reinhardt theater school. **Career:** Appeared on German-language stage; 1922—film debut in *Mater Dolorosa*, but made few films until the sound period, when his voice made him a popular leading man; from 1937—made films in England; also appeared in the stage in England. **Awards:** Deutscher Filmpreis (as Adolf Wohlbrück), 1967. **Died:** In Munich, 9 August 1967.

Films as Actor:

1922 *Mater Dolorosa* (von Bovary)
1925 *Das Geheimnis auf Schloss Almshoh (Der Fluch der Bosen Tat)* (Obal)
1931 *Der Stolz der 3 Kompagnie* (Sauer); *Salto Mortale (Trapeze)* (Dupont) (as Robbie); *Cinq gentilshommes maudits* (Duvivier)
1932 *Drei von der Stempelstelle* (Thiele); *Baby* (Lamac)
1933 *Walzerkrieg (Waltz Time in Vienna)* (Berger); *Keine Angst vor Liebe* (Steinhoff); *Viktor and Viktoria* (Schunzel)

Anton Walbrook with Moira Shearer in *The Red Shoes* courtesy of The Rank Organisation Plc

1934 *Der vertauschte Brant* (Lamac); *Maskerade* (*Masquerade in Vienna*) (Forst) (as Heidinick); *Eine Frau, die weiss was sie will* (Janson); *Die englische Heirat* (Schunzel) (as Robert); *Regine* (Waschneck) (as Frank Reynold)

1935 *Zigeuner-baron* (Harth); *Der Student von Prag* (Robison) (as Balduin); *Ich war Jack Mortimer* (Froelich)

1936 *Allotria* (Forst); *Michael Strogoff* (*Der Kurier des Zaren*) (Eichberg) (title role); *The Soldier and the Lady* (*Michael Strogoff*) (Nicholls) (as Strogoff); *I Give My Life* (*Port Arthur*; *Orders from Tokyo*) (Farkas) (as Boris)

1937 *Victoria the Great* (Wilcox) (as Prince Albert); *The Rat* (Raymond) (as Jean Boucheron, title role)

1938 *Sixty Glorious Years* (*Queen Victoria*; *Queen of Destiny*) (Wilcox) (as Prince Albert)

1940 *Gaslight* (*Angel Street*) (Dickinson) (as Paul Mallen)

1941 *49th Parallel* (*The Invaders*) (Powell and Pressburger) (as Peter); *Dangerous Moonlight* (*Suicide Squadron*) (Hurst) (as Stefan Radetzky)

1943 ***The Life and Death of Colonel Blimp*** (*Colonel Blimp*) (Powell and Pressburger) (as Theo Kretschmar-Schuldorff)

1944 *The Man from Morocco* (Max Greene and Greenbaum) (as Karel Langer)

1948 ***The Red Shoes*** (Powell and Pressburger) (as Boris Lermontov); *The Queen of Spades* (Dickinson) (as Herman Suvotin)

1950 ***La Ronde*** (*Circle of Love*) (Max Ophüls) (as Master of Ceremonies); *König für eine Nacht* (May)

1951 *Wien tantz* (*Vienna Waltzes*; *Wiener Walzer*) (Reinert) (as Johann Strauss); *Le Plaisir* (*House of Pleasure*) (Max Ophüls) (as narrator of German version)

1954 *L'Affaire Maurizius* (Duvivier) (as Warenne)

1955 *Oh, Rosalinda!* (*Fledermaus '55*) (Powell and Pressburger) (as Dr. Falke); ***Lola Montès*** (*The Sins of Lola Montès*; *The Fall of Lola Montès*) (Max Ophüls) (as King Ludwig I of Bavaria)

1957 *Saint Joan* (Preminger) (as Cauchon); *I Accuse!* (Ferrer) (as Maj. Esterhazy)

1962 *Laura* (Franz Josef Wild—for TV)

Publications

By WALBROOK: articles—

Interviews, in *Picturegoer* (London), 25 September 1937 and 27 April 1940.

On WALBROOK: articles—

Film Weekly, 25 December 1937.
Obituary, in *Times* (London), 10 August 1967.
Films in Review (New York), December 1967.
Ciné Revue (Paris), 2 February 1978.
Films and Filming (London), March 1978.

*   *   *

For most filmgoers, Anton Walbrook is associated, more than any other role, with the ballet impresario Boris Lermontov in *The Red Shoes*. A slim, straight Diaghilev, Lermontov views ballet as his "religion." He reserves the roles of the virgin consort for Moira Shearer, who, no less dedicated, dances herself literally to death for him and her art. The expressionless Walbrook, whether watching Shearer dance *Swan Lake* to records in a London church hall or summoning her to an overgrown Riviera chateau to reveal her elevation to stardom, defined a vision of the aesthete/saint for whom art is all, and more than enough.

Queen Victoria's consort Prince Albert established the image of the refined and cultured Continental gentleman in the British popular consciousness. Walbrook, who played Albert twice on screen, sustained and explored it. His Polish bomber pilot/pianist in *Dangerous Moonlight* made him the star he had never been in Austria. Richard Addinsell's thundering Warsaw Concerto on the soundtrack expressed the passion and sensitivity of the tortured émigré in a way that instantly captivated audiences.

Powell and Pressburger soon incorporated Walbrook into their stock company. In *49th Parallel* he led a Mennonite community in Canada with Christlike self-effacement. In *The Life and Death of Colonel Blimp* he played Theo Kretschmar-Schuldorff, the classic "good German"—aristocratic, English-speaking, polite, anti-Nazi, Beethoven-loving—to Roger Livesey's equally stylized Briton. In Thorold Dickinson's *The Queen of Spades* and Powell's *Oh, Rosalinda!* based on *Die Fledermaus*, he was no less well-bred.

In 1950 Walbrook capped a career as observer of the vagaries of emotion by playing the weary *meneur de jeu* of Ophüls's *La Ronde*, cynically overseeing the interlocking romances of Schnitzler's lovers. Walbrook is buried in a shady corner of north London's tiny Hampstead Cemetery, fitting interment for an actor who personified European style and good manners for the British.

—John Baxter

WALKEN, Christopher

Nationality: American. **Born:** Ronald Walken, Queens, New York, 31 March 1943. **Education:** Attended Professional Children's School, Manhattan; Hofstra University, New York. **Family:** Married the actress Georgianne Thon. **Career:** Worked as a model starting at age three; early 1950s—appeared in countless live television productions mostly in walk-ons; 1960—Broadway debut in *J. B.* (billed as Ronny Walken); early to mid-1960s—stage performances, mostly in the chorus, include *Best Foot Forward*, *High Spirits*, *Baker Street*, and *West Side Story*; first dramatic stage role in 1966, in *The Lion in Winter*; 1969—film debut in *Me and My Brother*. **Awards:** Best Supporting Actor Academy Award, and Best Supporting Actor, New York Film Critics, for *The Deer Hunter*, 1978. **Address:** 142 Cedar Road, Wilton, CT 06897, U.S.A.

Films as Actor:

1969 *Me and My Brother* (Robert Frank) (bit role)

1971 *The Mind Snatchers* (*The Happiness Cage*) (Girard) (as Pvt. James Reese)

1975 *Valley Forge* (Cook—for TV) (as the Hessian)

1976 *Next Stop, Greenwich Village* (Mazursky) (as Robert)

1977 *The Sentinel* (Winner) (as Rizzo); ***Annie Hall*** (Woody Allen) (as Duane Hall); *Roseland* (Ivory) (as Russel)

1978 ***The Deer Hunter*** (Cimino) (as Nick)

1979 *Last Embrace* (Jonathan Demme) (as Eckart)

1980 ***Heaven's Gate*** (Cimino) (as Nathan D. Champion); *The Dogs of War* (Irvin) (as Jamie Shelton)

1981 *Shoot the Sun Down* (Leeds); *Pennies from Heaven* (Ross) (as Tom)

1982 *Who Am I This Time?* (Jonathan Demme—for TV) (as Harry Nash)

1983 *Brainstorm* (Trumbull) (as Michael Anthony Brace); *The Dead Zone* (Cronenberg) (as Johnny Smith); *Barefoot in Athens* (Schaefer) (as Lamprocles)

Christopher Walken in *The Comfort of Strangers*

1985　*A View to a Kill* (Glen) (as Max Zorin)

1986　*At Close Range* (Foley) (as Brad Whitewood Sr.)

1987　*Deadline* (Gutman) (as Don Stevens)

1988　*Biloxi Blues* (Mike Nichols) (as Sgt. Merwin J. Toomey); *The Milagro Beanfield War* (Redford) (as Kyril Montana); *Puss in Boots* (Marner)

1989　*Homeboy* (Seresin) (as Wesley Pendergrass); *Communion* (Mora) (as Whitley Strieber)

1990　*King of New York* (Ferrara) (as Frank White); *Sarah, Plain and Tall* (Glenn Jordan—for TV) (as Jacob Wittig)

1991　*The Comfort of Strangers* (Schrader) (as Robert); *McBain* (Glickenhaus) (title role)

1992　*All-American Murder* (Anson Williams) (as P. J. Decker); *Batman Returns* (Burton) (as Max Shreck); *Mistress* (Primus) (as Warren Zell)

1993　*True Romance* (Tony Scott) (as Vincenzo Coccotti); *Wayne's World 2* (Surjik) (as Bobby Cahn); *Skylark* (Sargent—for TV) (as Jacob Wittig); *Scam* (Flynn—for TV); *Le Grand Pardon II* (*Day of Atonement*) (Arcady) (as Pasco Meisner)

1995　***Pulp Fiction*** (Tarantino) (as Capt. Koons); *The Addiction* (Ferrara) (as Peina); *A Business Affair* (Brandstrom) (as Vanni Corso); *Nick of Time* (Badham) (as Mr. Smith); *Search and Destroy* (Salle) (as Kim Ulander); *Things to Do in Denver When You're Dead* (Fleder) (as the Man with the Plan); *The Wild Side* (Cammell) (as Bruno)

1996　*The Prophecy* (*God's Army*) (Widen) (as Angel Gabriel); *Last Man Standing* (Walter Hill); *The Funeral* (Ferrara); *Excess Baggage* (Brambilla); *Basquiat* (*Build a Fort, Set It on Fire*) (Schnabel)

Publications

By WALKEN: articles—

"Off the Wall with Walken," interview with Tinkerbelle, in *Interview* (New York), August 1977.

"Talkin' with Walken," interview with V. Visser, in *Interview* (New York), February 1979.

"Introducing Christopher Walken," interview with M. Whitman, in *Films Illustrated* (London), March 1979.

"Out There on a Visit," interview with Gavin Smith, in *Film Comment* (New York), July/August 1992.

Interview with Kurt Markus, in *Interview* (New York), July 1993.

"Interview with the Antichrist," interview with M. Frankel, in *Movieline* (Escondido, California), December 1993.

On WALKEN: articles—

Maslin, Janet, "Movies 'Discover' Christopher Walken," in *New York Times*, 26 December 1978.

Fox, T. C., "Christopher Walken: The Shy and Evil WASP," in *Village Voice* (New York), 15 January 1979.

Hodenfield, C., "Point-Blank: *The Deer Hunter*'s Christopher Walken," in *Rolling Stone* (New York), 8 March 1979.

Chase, D., and J. Coencas, "*Deer Hunter* Vets Step Out: Walken Embraces Acclaim," in *Feature*, April 1979.

Kornbluth, J., "Christopher Walken: The Oscar Winner Nobody Knows," in *Mademoiselle* (New York), December 1980.

Haller, Scot, "I *Am* the Malevolent WASP," in *Esquire* (New York), January 1981.

Wolf, W., "The Walken Enigma," in *New York*, 15 June 1981.

Norman, N., "Walken Tall," in *Photoplay* (London), July 1985.

Gaillac-Morgue, "Christopher Walken," in *Cinéma* (Paris), 18-24 September 1985.

Guerif, F., "Christopher Walken," in *Revue Belge du Cinema* (Brussels), May 1989.

Katsahnias, I., "Christopher Walken," *Cahiers du Cinéma* (Paris), June 1990.

Weinraub, Bernard, "A New York Actor Takes Stardom with a Grain of Salt," in *New York Times*, 24 June 1992.

* * *

Christopher Walken started acting as a child when he appeared in countless television and stage productions. Then, as an adult he enjoyed several years of popularity and critical acclaim on the Broadway stage. In the 1970s, he started working in film, and during the early years of his screen career Walken distinguished himself in several compelling supporting roles, including his amusing performance as Diane Keaton's strangely neurotic younger brother in *Annie Hall*, and as a cunning and comfortably kept gigolo in *Roseland*. Most notably, he appeared as *The Deer Hunter*'s Nick, a naive young man with romantic ideas about the adventures and heroism of war, who becomes emotionally broken, then embittered and suicidally detached as a result of his experience in Vietnam. After this still-memorable award-winning performance secured his formidable film reputation, his first leading screen role (and the first time he received top billing) was in *The Dogs of War* in 1980, the same year he appeared in the epic but commercially disastrous Western *Heaven's Gate*.

One of America's most skillful and unique actors, Walken has amassed a huge list of screen credits and has carved a compelling and singular niche for himself in cinematic history. He has worked with both mainstream directors, such as Tim Burton, Mike Nichols, and Robert Redford, and with more unconventional directors, such as Abel Ferrara, Paul Schrader, and Quentin Tarantino. As deft at comedic as at dramatic performance, Walken is a strikingly complex film presence: supremely confident yet accessible, menacing yet vulnerable, and eccentric yet serious. His characters convey unmistakably askew, and occasionally deeply disturbed, psyches. Tall, thin, and almost-handsome, Walken has one of the most singular visages in contemporary American cinema. Moreover, his talent is multifaceted: along with his nimble physical style (the result of his many years as a stage dancer) which enables him to convey a delicacy and subtlety of bodily expression, Walken has an extraordinary command of his voice—including an unexpected emphasis on certain words and a rich repertoire of rhythms.

His wide-ranging talents have been revealed in several remarkable roles, including *At Close Range* in which he offers a chilling performance as a sociopathic Midwestern hood who commands a gang of thieves and recruits his adrift teenaged sons—among his countless other criminal and moral offenses. In the thriller *The Comfort of Strangers*, he conveys a deep understanding of the powerful combination of scary and funny; his performance as a monstrous and crazed European stranger in murderous pursuit of a vacationing British couple is disturbing and intense, yet also immensely funny.

As his film career has evolved over the years, Walken has altered his acting style, especially in terms of his emotional expressivity, in noteworthy ways. In his early film appearances, including *The Deer Hunter* and *The Dead Zone*, his performances were more overtly emotional. In his more recent roles, Walken's performances have tended to be less revealing and more stoic, thus lending an additional layer of complexity to his characterizations. In *The Milagro Beanfield War*, for example, he appears in only a few scenes as a taciturn troubleshooter working for a group of unethical businessmen and government officials. In a particularly compelling scene, Walken visits the office of a small-town lawyer and community activist where he calmly listens to the man's emotional tirade which is meant to be intimidating. Remaining calm, Walken responds by raising his eyebrow, muttering "mmmmm," and leaving—otherwise keeping his specific thoughts to himself, and thereby withholding the means by which to clearly interpret his interior state.

Recently, Walken redeemed the otherwise weak film *The Prophecy*, in which he appears as the evil, manipulative, yet strangely amusing archangel Gabriel. Also, with a willingness to accept smaller film roles, Walken has an uncanny ability to deliver quite memorable performance. In *Pennies from Heaven*, for example Walken makes a brief appearance as a seamy but seductive and dancing pimp. More recently, as a military buddy of Bruce Willis's dead father in *Pulp Fiction* Walken is riveting—sober and commanding, even as the content of his monologue shifts from noble to amusingly outrageous.

Walken has quite aptly described his screen persona: "I am the malevolent WASP." Indeed, he has achieved the American dream by playing an assortment of offbeat characters who typically represent a distortion of America's puritan ideals.

—Cynthia Felando

WALKER, Robert

Nationality: American. **Born:** Salt Lake City, Utah, 13 October 1918. **Education:** Attended San Diego Army and Naval Institute, Carlsbad-by-the-Sea; American Academy of Dramatic Arts, New York, 1938. **Family:** Married 1) the actress Jennifer Jones, 1939 (divorced 1945), sons: the actors Robert Jr., and Michael; 2) Barbara Ford, 1948. **Career:** Actor in New York; 1938—radio actor, with Jennifer Jones, for the Mutual station, Tulsa; 1939—film debut in *Winter Carnival*; 1940-42—radio actor on *Yesterday's Children, John's Other Wife, Against the Storm*, and *Myrt and Marge* series; 1942—contract with MGM; 1948-49—hospitalized in the Meninger Clinic, Topeka, Kansas. **Died:** In Pacific Palisades, California, 28 August 1951.

Films as Actor:

1939 *Winter Carnival* (Riesner) (as undergraduate); *These Glamour Girls* (Simon) (as undergraduate); *Dancing Co-Ed* (Simon) (bit role)

1943 *Bataan* (Garnett) (as soldier); *Madame Curie* (LeRoy) (as a young scientist)

1944 *See Here, Private Hargrove* (Ruggles) (title role); *Since You Went Away* (Cromwell); *Thirty Seconds over Tokyo* (LeRoy)

1945 *The Clock* (Minnelli); *The Sailor Takes a Wife* (Whorf); *Her Highness and the Bellboy* (Thorpe); *What Next, Corporal Hargrove?* (Thorpe) (title role)

1946 *Till the Clouds Roll By* (Whorf) (as Jerome Kern); *The Sea of Grass* (Kazan)

Robert Walker

1947 *The Beginning of the End* (Taurog); *Song of Love* (Brown) (as Johannes Brahms)
1948 *One Touch of Venus* (Seiter)
1950 *Please Believe Me* (Taurog); *The Skipper Surprised His Wife* (Nugent)
1951 **Strangers on a Train** (Hitchcock) (as Bruno Anthony); *Vengeance Valley* (Thorpe)
1952 *My Son John* (McCarey) (title role)

Publications

On WALKER: books—

Memo from: David O. Selznick, edited by Rudy Behlmer, New York, 1972.
Linet, Beverly, *Star-Crossed: The Story of Robert Walker and Jennifer Jones*, New York, 1986.

On WALKER: articles—

Obituary in *New York Times*, 29 August 1951.
Zucker, Phyllis, "Robert Walker," in *Films in Review* (New York), March 1970.
Newman, D., "People We Like: Robert Walker," in *Film Comment* (New York), May-June 1974.

*   *   *

Robert Walker's skillful, mesmerizing performance as a psychopathic villain in Alfred Hitchcock's suspense thriller *Strangers on a Train* suggested a fruitful career change away from his previously established reputation as a modestly effective, boyish leading man. But it proved to be his penultimate film, as his death the following year ended a short-lived career that was plagued throughout by personal problems.

After attending the Academy of Dramatic Arts in New York, marrying actress Jennifer Jones, snaring a few bit parts in movies, and appearing regularly on network radios, Walker signed a contract with MGM. His first substantial supporting film role was in Tay Garnett's World War II drama, *Bataan*, playing a soldier—as he would many times in the early years of his movie career.

Typecast as sincere and likable, he worked in support of Mervyn LeRoy's biographical epic *Madame Curie* and John Cromwell's World War II melodrama *Since You Went Away*, before ascending to the military lead in Wesley Ruggles's episodic film version of the best seller *See Here, Private Hargrove*. He then co-starred with Van Johnson in LeRoy's *Thirty Seconds over Tokyo*, played the shy, soldierly male lead opposite Judy Garland in Vincente Minnelli's nonmusical romance *The Clock*, starred as the apex of a romantic triangle involving Hedy Lamarr and June Allyson in Richard Thorpe's *Her Highness and the Bellboy*, and reprised his first starring role in Thorpe's sequel, *What Next, Corporal Hargrove?* He further starred as the songwriter Jerome Kern in Richard Whorf's *Till the Clouds Roll By*, and supported Spencer Tracy and Katharine Hepburn, playing their son in Elia Kazan's unsuccessful Western *The Sea of Grass*.

Several more also-ran films, a second broken marriage (to director John Ford's daughter), a drinking problem, and a nervous breakdown all but gutted his ailing career. In *Strangers on a Train*, however, he temporarily resuscitated his reputation with a splendid performance as Bruno Anthony, one of Hitchcock's most colorful, memorable, and effective villains. As the pivotal character, he plays a fey, manipulative, murderous, yet mysteriously appealing and even ultimately sympathetic, antagonist. Casting him against type, Hitchcock had tapped the complex emotional undercurrents of Walker's life.

The following year, the actor took a second step toward the dramatic modification and revitalization of his movie persona. In Leo McCarey's Cold War melodrama *My Son John* he played a son suspected of being a Communist by his reactionary parents. However, footage from the final sequence in *Strangers* had to be borrowed for a second consecutive final-reel death scene—this one posthumous.

—Bill Wine

WALLACH, Eli

Nationality: American. **Born:** Brooklyn, New York, 7 December 1915. **Education:** Attended Erasmus High School; University of Texas, Austin, B.A. 1936; City College of New York, M.Sc. in education 1938; studied acting at the Neighborhood Playhouse school, New York, two years. **Military Service:** U.S. Army Medical Corps, during World War II. **Family:** Married the actress Anne Jackson, 1948, son: Peter David, daughters: Roberta and Katherine. **Career:** 1945—professional stage debut in *Skydrift*; later roles in Eva Le Gallienne's American Repertory Theatre, 1946-47, *Mister Roberts*, 1949-51, *The Rose Tattoo*, 1951, *Camino Real*, 1953, *Major Barbara*, 1956, and *The Chairs*, 1958; 1956—film debut in *Baby Doll*; also acted on television from 1958; 1977—in TV mini-series *Seventh Avenue*; 1977-78—guest artist, with Anne Jackson, at Arena Stage, Washington, D.C.; 1985-86—in TV series *Our Family Honor*; 1992—voices in TV mini-series *Lincoln*, and *Baseball*, 1994; 1995—in TV mini-series *Vendetta II: The New Mafia*; occasional teacher at Actors Studio, New York.

Films as Actor:

1956 *Baby Doll* (Kazan) (as Silva Vacarro)
1958 *The Line-Up* (Siegel) (as Dancer)
1960 *Seven Thieves* (Hathaway) (as Pancho); *The Magnificent Seven* (John Sturges) (as Calvera)
1961 **The Misfits** (Huston) (as Guido)
1962 *Hemingway's Adventures of a Young Man* (*Adventures of a Young Man*) (Ritt) (as John)
1963 "The Outlaws" ep. of *How the West Was Won* (Hathaway) (as Charlie Gant); *The Victors* (Foreman) (as Sergeant Craig); *Act One* (Schary) (as Warren Stone)
1964 *Kisses for My President* (Bernhardt) (as Rodriguez Valdez); *The Moon-Spinners* (Neilson) (as Stratos)
1965 *Genghis Khan* (Levin) (as Shah of Khwarezm); *Lord Jim* (Richard Brooks) (as the General)
1966 *How to Steal a Million* (Wyler) (as David Leland); **Il buono, il brutto, il cattivo** (*The Good, the Bad, and the Ugly*) (Leone) (as Tuco); *The Poppy Is Also a Flower* (Terence Young) (as Locarno)
1967 *The Tiger Makes Out* (Hiller) (as Ben Harris)
1968 *How to Save a Marriage—and Ruin Your Life* (Cook) (as Harry Hunter); *New York City—The Most* (Pitt—doc) (as cabdriver); *A Lovely Way to Die* (Rich) (as Tennessee Fredericks); *Mackenna's Gold* (J. Lee Thompson) (as Ben Baker); *Il quattro dell'ave Maria* (*Ace High*; *Revenge at El Paso*) (Colizzi) (as Cacopoulos)
1969 *Le Cerveau* (*The Brain*) (Oury) (as Scannapieco)
1970 *Zigzag* (*False Witness*) (Colla) (as Mario Gambretti); *The People Next Door* (David Greene) (as Arthur Mason); *The Angel Levine* (Kadar) (as a clerk); *The Adventures of Gerard* (Skolimowski) (as Napoleon)

Eli Wallach in *The Line-Up*

1971   *Romance of a Horsethief* (Polonsky)
1972   *Viva la muerte . . . tua!* (*Don't Turn the Other Cheek*; *The Killer from Yuma*) (Tessari)
1973   *L'Ultima chance* (*Last Chance Motel*; *Stateline Motel*) (Lucidi); *Cinderella Liberty* (Rydell) (as Lynn Forshay); *A Cold Night's Death* (Freedman—for TV) (as Frank Enari)
1974   *Crazy Joe* (Lizzani) (as Don Vittorio); *Indict and Convict* (Sagal—for TV); *L'Chaim—To Life!* (Mayer) (as narrator)
1975   *Il bianco, il giallo, il nero* (*Samurai*) (Corbucci) (as the sheriff); *Attenti al buffone!* (*Eye of the Cat*) (Bevilaqua)
1976   *E tanta paura* (Cavara) (as the detective); *Independence* (Huston—short) (as Benjamin Franklin); *Twenty Shades of Pink* (Stanley); *Nasty Habits* (*The Abbess*) (Lindsay-Hogg) (as the Monsignor)
1977   *The Sentinel* (Winner) (as Gatz); *The Deep* (Yates) (as Adam Coffin); *The Domino Principle* (*The Domino Killings*) (Kramer) (as General Tom Rezer)
1978   *Girlfriends* (Weill) (as Rabbi Gold); "Baxter's Beauties of 1933" (as Pop), and "Dynamite Hands" (as Vince Marlowe), eps. of *Movie Movie* (Donen); *The Pirate* (Annakin—for TV) (as Ben Ezra); *Squadra antimafia* (*Little Italy*) (Corbucci)
1979   *Winter Kills* (Richert) (as Joe Diamond); *Circle of Iron* (*The Silent Flute*) (Richard Moore) (as man in oil); *Firepower* (Winner) (as Sal Hyman)
1980   *The Hunter* (Kulik) (as Ritchie Blumenthal); *Fugitive Family* (Krasny—for TV) (as Olan Vacio)
1981   *The Salamander* (Zinner) (as Leporello); *Acting: Lee Strasberg and the Actors Studio* (doc); *The Pride of Jesse Hallam* (Nelson—for TV) (as Sal Galucci); *Skokie* (Wise—for TV) (as Bert Silverman)
1982   *The Wall* (Markowitz—for TV); *The Executioner's Song* (Schiller—for TV) (as Uncle Vern Damico)
1983   *Anatomy of an Illness* (Heffron—for TV) (as Dr. William Hitzig)
1984   *Sam's Son* (Landon) (as Sam Orowitz)
1985   *Christopher Columbus* (Lattuada—for TV) (as Hernando DeTalavera); *Embassy* (Robert Michael Lewis—for TV); *Murder: By Reason of Insanity* (Page—for TV) (as Dr. Huffman)
1986   *Tough Guys* (Kanew) (as Leo B. Little); *Rocket to the Moon* (Jacobs—for TV) (as Mr. Prince); *Something in Common* (Glenn Jordan—for TV) (as Norman Voss)
1987   *Nuts* (Ritt) (as Dr. Herbert A. Morrison); *Hello Actors Studio* (doc); *Worlds Beyond: The Black Tomb* (Jacobs—for TV); *The Impossible Spy* (Goddard—for TV)
1988   *Funny* (Ferren)
1989   *Rosengarten* (*The Rose Garden*) (Rademakers); *Terezin Diary* (Weissman and Justman)
1990   *The Godfather, Part III* (Francis Ford Coppola) (as Don Altobello); *The Two Jakes* (Nicholson) (as Cotton Weinberger)
1991   *Vendetta: Secrets of a Mafia Bride* (*Bride of Violence*; *A Family Matter*) (Margolin—for TV) (as Frank Latella)
1992   *Night and the City* (Irwin Winkler) (as Peck); *Legacy of Lies* (Meshover-Iorg—for TV) (as Moses Zelnick); *Mistress* (Primus) (as George Lieberhoff); *Article 99* (Deutsch) (as Sam Abrams); *Teamster Boss: The Jackie Presser Story* (Reid—for TV) (as Bill Presser)
1995   *Smoke* (Rissi)
1996   *Two Much* (Trueba) (as Sheldon); *James Dean: A Portrait* (Legon—doc) (as himself)

Publications

By WALLACH: articles—

"My Strange Dilemma," in *Films and Filming* (London), August 1961.
"In All Directions," interview in *Films and Filming* (London), May 1964.

On WALLACH: articles—

Current Biography 1959, New York, 1959.
Marill, Alvin H., in *Films in Review* (New York), August-September 1983.
Catsos, G. J. M., "Eli Wallach," in *Filmfax*, February/March 1991.

*   *   *

Eli Wallach started in the theater, returned to it frequently, but achieved his principal identification through film. Wallach began his film career as the sinister sneering con-man lover in the controversial Elia Kazan/Tennessee Williams film *Baby Doll*. Except for comic presentations later, such as *The Tiger Makes Out*, Wallach never returned to leading man roles.

His second film, Don Siegel's *The Line-Up*, set the mold for Wallach. As the nervous psychotic killer Dancer, Wallach moved with grace, decision, and violence. He became a dancer, a choreographer of death, a man who could not understand why fate kept hitting him in the face. Whether comic or serious, Wallach has continually returned to this image and character, the none-too-bright killer who simply does not have the moral depth to understand why the world wants to destroy him. Whether his identity (and Eastern urban accent) is masked as a Latin bandit, as in *The Magnificent Seven*, or as an urban Italian soldier in *The Victors*, Wallach has become the epitome of the incredulous colorful villain. He had one of his best roles in this vein in the epic Sergio Leone spaghetti Western *The Good, the Bad, and the Ugly*, where he played the final adjective in the title.

Villainy, however, is but one facet of the actor. Occasionally, in a film such as John Huston's *The Misfits*, Wallach has portrayed not a killer of men but a man with a potentially dead soul. The pain behind the unloved eyes can be both contemptuous and pitiful. Unfortunately, it is a portrayal of depth that Wallach was seldom allowed to bring to the screen after *The Misfits*. In more recent films, Wallach's talents and the character type he has evolved have been limited to a decidedly secondary role, often forcing him to rely on the mannerisms which suggest his past portrayals. In the final Steve McQueen film *The Hunter*, for example, Wallach played a somewhat sympathetic Jewish bailbondsman on the thin edge of emotionalism, a polished but surface role at best.

Wallach, fortunately, is a character actor whom age will not diminish, nor, it seems, slow down. He appears in almost as many movies now as he did in his heyday. Among the most visible recent examples: as a mafioso in *The Godfather, Part III*, the final installment of Francis Ford Coppola's Corleone saga; *The Two Jakes*, Jack Nicholson's ill-fated (and ill-advised) sequel to the classic *Chinatown*; and Irwin Winkler's updated remake of the forties noir thriller *Night in the City*. Wallach also joined aging contemporaries Kirk Douglas and Burt Lancaster for the enjoyable septuagenarian caper comedy *Tough Guys*.

—Stuart M. Kaminsky, updated by John McCarty

WASHINGTON, Denzel

Nationality: American. **Born:** Mount Vernon, New York, 28 December 1954. **Education:** Graduated from Fordham University with degrees in drama and journalism; studied one year at the American Conservatory Theater, San Francisco. **Family:** Married the actress and singer Pauletta Pearson, 1982, four children. **Career:** Performed with the New York Shakespeare Festival and the American Place Theater; 1981—off-Broadway in *A Soldier's Play* and as Malcolm X in *When the Chickens Come Home to Roost*; theatrical

Denzel Washington in *Devil in a Blue Dress*

film debut in *Carbon Copy*; 1982-88—as Dr. Phillip Chandler in TV series *St. Elsewhere*; 1988—on Broadway in *Checkmates*; has own production company Mundy Lane Entertainment. **Awards:** Obie Award, for *A Soldier's Play*, 1982; Academy Award, Best Supporting Actor, Golden Globe, for *Glory*, 1989. **Address:** PMK Public Relations, 955 South Carillo Drive, Suite 200, Los Angeles, CA 90048, U.S.A. **Agent:** ICM, 8942 Wilshire Boulevard, Los Angeles, CA 90211, U.S.A.

Films as Actor:

1977   *Wilma* (Greenspan—for TV)
1979   *Flesh & Blood* (Jud Taylor—for TV)
1981   *Carbon Copy* (Schultz) (as Roger Porter)
1984   *A Soldier's Story* (Jewison) (as Pfc. Melvin Peterson); *License to Kill* (Jud Taylor—for TV) (as Martin Sawyer)
1986   *Power* (Lumet) (as Arnold Billings); *The George Mckenna Story* (Laneuville—for TV) (title role)
1987   *Cry Freedom* (Attenborough) (as Stephen Biko)
1988   *Reunion* (short)
1989   *For Queen and Country* (Stellman) (as Reuben James); *Glory* (Zwick) (as Trip); *The Mighty Quinn* (Schenkel) (as Xavier Quinn)
1990   *Heart Condition* (Parriott) (as Napoleon Stone); *Mo' Better Blues* (Spike Lee) (as Bleek Gilliam)

1991   *Ricochet* (Mulcahy) (as Nick Styles)
1992   ***Malcolm X*** (Spike Lee) (title role); *Mississippi Masala* (Nair) (as Demetrius)
1993   *Much Ado about Nothing* (Branagh) (as Don Pedro); *The Pelican Brief* (Pakula) (as Gray Grantham); ***Philadelphia*** (Jonathan Demme) (as Joe Miller)
1995   *Virtuosity* (Brett Leonard) (as Parker Barnes); *Devil in a Blue Dress* (Carl Franklin) (as Easy Rawlins); *Crimson Tide* (Tony Scott) (as Lt. Cmdr. Hunter)
1996   *Courage under Fire* (Zwick) (as Lt. Col. Nathaniel Serling); *The Preacher's Wife* (Penny Marshall) (as Dudley)

Publications

By WASHINGTON: articles—

Interview with Veronica Webb, and photographer Herb Ritts, in *Interview* (New York), July 1990.
"Denzel on Malcolm," interview with Joe Wood, in *Rolling Stone* (New York), 26 November 1992.
"Brothers," interview with Brendan Lemon, in *Interview* (New York), December 1993.
"A League of His Own," interview with Lloyd Grove, in *Vanity Fair* (New York), October 1995.

On WASHINGTON: articles—

Current Biography 1992, New York, 1992.
Clark, John, filmography in *Premiere* (New York), November 1992.
Norment, Lynn, "Denzel Washington Opens Up about Stardom, Family and Sex Appeal," in *Ebony* (Chicago), October 1995.

* * *

Denzel Washington has insisted in interviews that he wants to be thought of as an *actor*, not a *black* actor. In one sense (which is presumably the sense he intends) this is perfectly understandable: as a star he has everything going for him, he is a gifted and intelligent actor, he has a very strong screen presence, and he is one of the handsomest men in contemporary cinema. This eminence as an actor requires no qualification. In another sense, however, in a less than ideal world still riddled with racism, it is inevitable that his blackness would be an important signifying presence in every film in which he appears.

Consider, for example, one of his less interesting films, *Crimson Tide*. Take away his blackness and we are left with a perfectly banal, oft-repeated plot formula: intelligent and pragmatic subordinate clashes with his older, die-hard, commanding officer, who does everything by the book and according to the rules, even risking precipitating World War III and universal nuclear devastation. The sole source of dramatic tension is that here a *black* subordinate defies a *white* commanding officer—this despite the fact that there is no explicit allusion to Washington's color. Or take the case of another, even less interesting, film, *The Pelican Brief*. With a white actor as a leading man, we might find it a refreshing change that hero and heroine do *not* end up as a couple. With Washington in the lead, their failure to unite in a love relationship must inevitably be attributed to issues of race and the still not uncommon fear of miscegenation, ridiculous, in this day and age, to be sure, but still apparently a matter of box-office concern to conservative and unimaginative producers.

Washington's presence alone illuminates these films, which give him little to do except go through the paces of a conventionally conceived and written "hero" role. The films in which Washington gives his strongest performances—which also happen to be the best in which he has appeared—all foreground in one way or another the issue of race: *Malcolm X*, obviously, but also *Mississippi Masala*, *Philadelphia*, and *Devil in a Blue Dress*.

Though ultimately unsatisfying (it degenerates into contrivance and predictability), *Mississippi Masala* is one of the very few Hollywood films to deal in a completely frank, open, and detailed way with an interracial love relationship—though rendered "safe" for white audiences by dramatizing a relationship between an African-American and an Indian woman. Although the action is contained within only a brief time period, we watch Washington mature in the course of the film. At that time (1992) he could still look boyish, exuding an innocent charm, and the scene in the Leopard Lounge when he first dances with Mina (Sarita Choudhury) exhibits his ability to portray subtle shifts of feeling. Using Mina first merely to arouse the jealousy of an old flame who, having "made it big," has treated him with condescension, he experiences a growing attraction to her, until the old flame is forgotten. A delightful chemistry develops between Washington and Choudhury, and the crucial scene by a lake when they first kiss is played by both with marvelous delicacy. Then, when the relationship is threatened and seemingly destroyed by racial tensions, Washington visibly sheds the boyishness, seeming to age into full manhood before our eyes.

This ability not merely to delineate but to develop a character is perhaps at its most striking in *Malcolm X*: Washington convincingly shows us Malcolm's growth from irresponsibility to complete emotional and political maturity. If the film as a whole is somewhat disappointingly conventional—Spike Lee allows himself to slip too easily into the conventions and manner of the worthy but finally unexciting biopic—this is no fault of Washington's: he carries the film securely, and is largely responsible for its limited distinction.

Washington's two finest films are, arguably, *Philadelphia* and *Devil in a Blue Dress*. The relative commercial failure of the latter is a great disappointment: it deserved large audiences, and the studio was apparently planning to follow it with a series of adaptations of the splendid "Easy Rawlins" novels of Walter Mosley, a series which now may never materialize. The film is directed with great intelligence by Carl Franklin, and Washington's performance as an unusually fallible and vulnerable involuntary "private eye" (we are worlds removed here from Philip Marlowe) is a marvel of integrity and insight.

Tom Hanks got most of the attention (and the Best Actor Oscar) for *Philadelphia*—understandably, as his character, a gay man dying of AIDS, is the more showy—but Washington's performance equals his in intelligence and subtlety. Again, Washington traces with surety the character's emotional and psychological development. Initially hostile to the idea of taking on a gay client, a prey to a casual and unthinking homophobia, he comes to understand the parallels between racial prejudice and antigay prejudice, systematically casting off his homophobia intellectually (if never entirely on the emotional level). We see him, in fact, *learning* from the Tom Hanks character, whom he originally rejected: learning especially, in the famous "Maria Callas" scene, the value of the individual life, the essential human creativity expressed in the striving to *live*, not merely exist or survive.

One of the finest Hollywood stars of his generation by any standards, Washington has already made an invaluable contribution to the black presence in America, to the undermining of absurd and long-discredited prejudice.

—Robin Wood

WAYNE, John

Nationality: American. **Born:** Marion Michael Morrison in Winterset, Iowa, 26 May 1907. **Education:** Attended Glendale High School, California; University of Southern California, Los Angeles, 1925-27. **Family:** Married 1) Josephine Saenz, 1933 (divorced 1945), sons: the producer Michael Wayne and the actor Patrick Wayne, two daughters; 2) Esperanza Bauer, 1946 (divorced 1954); 3) Pilar Palette, 1954, son: the actor John Ethan, daughters: Aissa, Marisa. **Career:** 1926—prop man for Fox studio: film debut as extra in *Brown of Harvard*; in early films billed as Duke Morrison; 1930—role in *Men without Women* directed by John Ford, who directed many of Wayne's later films; later worked for Columbia and other studios; 1939—role in Ford's *Stagecoach* made Wayne a leading man; 1942-43—in radio series *Three Sheets to the Wind*; 1944—co-founder, Motion Picture Alliance for the Preservation of American Ideals; 1947—film producer: formed Wayne-Fellows Productions and Batjac production company; 1960—directed the film *The Alamo*. **Awards:** Best Actor Academy Award, for *True Grit*, 1969. **Died:** In Los Angeles, 11 June 1979.

Films as Actor:

(uncredited)

1926 *Brown of Harvard* (Conway)
1927 *The Drop Kick* (*Glitter*) (Webb)
1928 *Mother Machree* (Ford); *Hangman's House* (Ford) (as spectator at horse race)
1929 *Salute* (Ford and David Butler) (as football player)

(as Duke Morrison)

1929　*Words and Music* (Tinling) (as Pete Donahue)
1930　*Men without Women* (Ford) (bit role); *A Rough Romance* (Erickson) (bit role); *Cheer Up and Smile* (Lanfield) (bit role)

(as John Wayne)

1931　*The Big Trail* (Walsh) (as Breck Coleman); *Girls Demand Excitement* (Felix) (as Peter Brooks); *Three Girls Lost* (Lanfield) (as Gordon Wales); *Men Are Like That (Arizona)* (Seitz) (as Lt. Bob Denton); *Range Feud* (Lederman) (as Clint Turner); *Maker of Men* (Sedgwick) (as Dusty); *The Deceiver* (King) (as a corpse)
1932　*Haunted Gold* (Wright) (as John Mason); *Shadow of the Eagle* (Beebe—serial) (as Craig McCoy); *The Hurricane Express* (Schaefer and McGowan—serial) (as Larry Baker); *Texas Cyclone* (Lederman) (as Steve Pickett); *Lady and Gent (The Challenger)* (Roberts) (as Buzz Kinney); *Two-Fisted Law* (Lederman) (as Duke); *Ride Him Cowboy (The Hawk)* (Fred Allen) (as John Drury); *The Voice of Hollywood No. 13* (D'Agostino—short) (as narrator); *The Big Stampede* (Wright) (as John Steele); *The Hollywood Handicap* (Lamont—short) (as himself); *Station S-T-A-R* (short)
1933　*The Telegraph Trail* (Wright) (as John Trent); *Central Airport* (Wellman) (bit role); *His Private Secretary* (Whitman) (as Dick Wallace); *Somewhere in Sonora* (Wright) (as John Bishop); *The Life of Jimmy Dolan (The Kid's Last Fight)* (Mayo) (as Smith); *The Three Musketeers* (Schaefer and Clark—serial) (as Tom Wayne); *Baby Face* (Alfred E. Green) (as Jimmy McCoy); *The Man from Monterey* (Wright) (as Captain John Holmes); *Riders of Destiny* (Bradbury) (as Sandy Saunders); *College Coach (Football Coach)* (Wellman) (as Kim); *Sagebrush Trail* (Schaefer) (as John Brant)
1934　*West of the Divide* (Bradbury) (as Ted Hayden); *The Lucky Texan* (Bradbury) (as Jerry Mason); *Blue Steel* (Bradbury) (as John Carruthers); *The Man from Utah* (Bradbury) (as John Weston); *Randy Rides Alone* (Fraser) (title role); *The Star Packer* (Bradbury) (as John Travers); *The Trail Beyond* (Bradbury) (as Rod Drew); *'Neath the Arizona Skies* (Fraser) (as Chris Morrell); *The Lawless Frontier* (Bradbury) (as John Tobin)
1935　*Texas Terror* (Bradbury) (as John Higgins); *Rainbow Valley* (Bradbury) (as John Martin); *Paradise Canyon* (Pierson) (as John Wyatt); *The Dawn Rider* (Bradbury) (as John Mason); *Westward Ho* (Bradbury) (as John Wyatt); *The Desert Trail* (Lewis) (as John Scott); *The New Frontier* (Pierson) (as John Dawson); *The Lawless Range* (Bradbury) (as John Middleton)
1936　*The Lawless Nineties* (Kane) (as John Tipton); *King of the Pecos* (Kane) (as John Clayborn); *The Oregon Trail* (Pembroke) (as Captain John Delmont); *Winds of the Wasteland* (Wright) (as John Blair); *The Sea Spoilers* (Strayer) (as Bob Randall); *The Lonely Trail* (Kane) (as John); *Conflict* (David Howard) (as Pat)
1937　*California Straight Ahead* (Lubin) (as Biff Smith); *I Cover the War* (Lubin) (as Bob Adams); *Idol of the Crowds* (Lubin) (as Johnny Hanson); *Adventure's End* (Lubin) (as Duke Slade)
1938　*Born to the West (Hell Town)* (Barton) (as Dare Rudd); *Pals of the Saddle* (Sherman) (as Stony Brooke); *Overland Stage Raiders* (Sherman) (as Stony Brooke); *Santa Fe Stampede* (Sherman) (as Stony Brooke); *Red River Range* (Sherman) (as Stony Brooke)

1939　*Stagecoach* (Ford) (as the Ringo Kid); *The Night Raiders* (Sherman) (as Stony Brooke); *Three Texas Steers (Danger Rides the Range)* (Sherman) (as Stony Brooke); *Wyoming Outlaw* (Sherman) (as Stony Brooke); *New Frontier (Frontier Horizon)* (Sherman) (as Stony Brooke); *Allegheny Uprising (The First Rebel)* (Seiter) (as Jim Smith)
1940　*The Dark Command* (Walsh) (as Bob Seton); *Three Faces West (The Refugee)* (Vorhaus) (as John Phillips); *The Long Voyage Home* (Ford) (as Ole Oleson); *Seven Sinners* (Garnett) (as Lt. Dan Brent); *Melody Ranch* (Santley)
1941　*A Man Betrayed (Citadel of Crime; Wheel of Fortune)* (Auer) (as Lynn Hollister); *Lady from Louisiana* (Vorhaus) (as John Reynolds); *The Shepherd of the Hills* (Hathaway) (as Young Matt Mathews); *Lady for a Night* (Jason) (as Jack Morgan)
1942　*Reap the Wild Wind* (Cecil B. DeMille) (as Captain Jack Stewart); *The Spoilers* (Enright) (as Roy Glennister); *In Old California* (McGann) (as Tom Craig); *Flying Tigers* (Miller) (as Jim Gordon); *Reunion in France (Reunion; Mademoiselle France)* (Dassin) (as Pat Talbot); *Pittsburgh* (Seiler) (as Charles "Pittsburgh" Markham)
1943　*A Lady Takes a Chance (The Cowboy and the Girl)* (Seiter) (as Duke Hudkins); *In Old Oklahoma (War of the Wildcats)* (Rogell) (as Dan Somers)
1944　*The Fighting Seabees* (Ludwig) (as Wedge Donovan); *Tall in the Saddle* (Marin) (as Rocklin)
1945　*Flame of the Barbary Coast* (Kane) (as Duke Fergus); *Back to Bataan* (Dmytryk) (as Colonel Joseph Madden); *Dakota* (Kane) (as John Devlin); *They Were Expendable* (Ford) (as Lt. Rusty Ryan)
1946　*Without Reservations* (LeRoy) (as Rusty Thomas)
1947　*Angel and the Badman* (James Edward Grant) (as Quirt Evans); *Tycoon* (Wallace) (as Johnny Munroe)
1948　*Fort Apache* (Ford) (as Captain Kirby York); **Red River** (Hawks) (as Tom Dunson); *Three Grandfathers* (Ford) (as Robert Marmaduke Hightower); *Wake of the Red Witch* (Ludwig) (as Captain Ralls)
1949　**She Wore a Yellow Ribbon** (Ford) (as Captain Nathan Brittles); *Fighting Kentuckian* (Waggner) (as John Breen); *Sands of Iwo Jima* (Dwan) (as Sgt. John Stryker); *Hollywood Rodeo* (short)
1950　*Rio Grande* (Ford) (as Lt. Colonel Kirby York)
1951　*Operation Pacific* (Waggner) (as Duke Gifford); *Flying Leathernecks* (Nicholas Ray) (as Major Dan Kirby)
1952　**The Quiet Man** (Ford) (as Sean Thornton); *Big Jim McLain* (Ludwig) (title role)
1953　*Trouble along the Way* (Curtiz) (as Steve Williams); *Island in the Sky* (Wellman) (as Captain Dooley); *Hondo* (Farrow) (title role)
1954　*The High and the Mighty* (Wellman) (as Dan Roman)
1955　*The Sea Chase* (Farrow) (as Captain Karl Ehrlich); *Rookie of the Year* (Ford—for TV); *Blood Alley* (Wellman) (as Wilder)
1956　*The Conqueror* (Powell) (as Temujin); **The Searchers** (Ford) (as Ethan Edwards)
1957　*The Wings of Eagles* (Ford) (as Frank "Spig" Wead); *Jet Pilot* (von Sternberg) (as Colonel Shannon); *Legend of the Lost* (Hathaway) (as Joe January)
1958　*I Married a Woman* (Kantor) (as himself); *The Barbarian and the Geisha* (Huston) (as Townsend Harris)
1959　*The Horse Soldiers* (Ford) (as Colonel John Marlowe); **Rio Bravo** (Hawks) (as John T. Chance)
1960　*North to Alaska* (Hathaway) (as Sam McCord)
1961　*The Commancheros* (Curtiz) (as Jake Cutter)
1962　**The Man Who Shot Liberty Valance** (Ford) (as Tom Doniphon); *Flashing Spikes* (Ford—for TV); *Hatari!* (Hawks) (as Sean Mercer); *The Longest Day* (Annakin, Marton, Wicki, and Oswald) (as Lt. Colonel Benjamin Vandervoort)

John Wayne

1963 "The Civil War" ep. of *How the West Was Won* (Ford) (as Gen. William Sherman); *Donovan's Reef* (Ford) (as Michael Donovan); *McLintock* (McLaglen) (title role)

1964 *Circus World* (*The Magnificent Showman*) (Hathaway) (as Matt Masters)

1965 *The Greatest Story Ever Told* (Stevens) (as the Centurion); *In Harm's Way* (Preminger) (as Captain Rockwell Torrey); *The Sons of Katie Elder* (Hathaway) (as John Elder)

1966 *Cast a Giant Shadow* (Shavelson) (as General Mike Randolph)

1967 *The War Wagon* (Kennedy) (as Law Jackson); *El Dorado* (Hawks) (as Cole Thorton)

1968 *The Hellfighters* (McLaglen) (as Chance Buckman)

1969 *True Grit* (Hathaway) (as "Rooster" Cogburn); *The Undefeated* (McLaglen) (as Colonel John Thomas)

1970 *Chisum* (McLaglen) (title role); *Rio Lobo* (Hawks) (as Cord McNally); *Chesty: A Tribute to a Legend* (Ford—doc) (as narrator)

1971 *Big Jake* (Sherman) (as Jacob McCandles); *Directed by John Ford* (Bogdanovich—doc)

1972 *The Cowboys* (Rydell) (as Will Anderson); *Cancel My Reservation* (Bogart) (as himself)

1973 *The Train Robbers* (Kennedy) (as Lane); *Cahill, United States Marshal* (*Cahill*) (McLaglen) (title role)

1974 *McQ* (John Sturges) (title role)

1975 *Brannigan* (Hickox) (title role); *Rooster Cogburn* (*Rooster Cogburn and the Lady*) (Miller) (title role)

1976 *The Shootist* (Siegel) (as John Books)

Films as Actor and Director:

1960 *The Alamo* (as Colonel David Crockett)
1968 *The Green Berets* (as Colonel Mike Kirby, co-d)

Publications

By WAYNE: articles—

"Why I Turned Producer and Director," in *Journal of Screen Producers Guild* (Hollywood), September 1960.

"John Wayne Talks Tough," by Joe McInery, in *Film Comment* (New York), September 1972.

"Looking Back," interview with Scott Eyman, in *Focus on Film* (London), Spring 1975.

On WAYNE: books—

Fenin, George, and William K. Everson, *The Western, from Silents to Cinerama*, New York, 1962.

Ricci, Mark, Boris Zmijewsky, and Steve Zmijewsky, *The Films of John Wayne*, New York, 1970.

Tomkies, Mike, *The Big Man: The John Wayne Story*, London, 1971; as *Duke*, Chicago, 1971.

Barbour, Alan, *John Wayne*, New York, 1974.

Zolotow, Maurice, *Shooting Star: A Biography of John Wayne*, New York, 1974.

Campbell, George Jr., *The John Wayne Story*, New Rochelle, New York, 1979.

Eyles, Allen, *John Wayne*, South Brunswick, New Jersey, 1979.

Pascal, François, *John Wayne: Le Dernier Géant*, Paris, 1979.

Scheldeman, Ivan, *De films van John Wayne*, Borgerhout, Belgium, 1979.

Kieskalt, Charles John, *The Official John Wayne Reference Book*, Secaucus, New Jersey, 1985; rev. ed., 1993.

Shepherd, Donald, and others, *Duke: The Life and Times of John Wayne*, London, 1985.

Lepper, David, *John Wayne*, London, 1987.

McDonald, Archie P., editor, *Shooting Stars: Heroes and Heroines of Western Film*, Bloomington, Indiana, 1987.

Levy, Emanuel, *John Wayne: Prophet of the American Way of Life*, Metuchen, New Jersey, 1988.

Leguege, Eric, *John Wayne, le cow-boy et la mort*, Paris, 1989.

Neibaur, James L., *Tough Guy: The American Movie Macho*, Jefferson, North Carolina, 1989.

Wayne, Pilar, with Alex Thorleifson, *John Wayne: My Life with the Duke*, New York, 1989.

Wayne, Aissa, *John Wayne, My Father*, New York, 1991.

Minshall, Bert, *On Board with the Duke: John Wayne and the Wild Goose*, Washington, D.C., 1992.

Riggin, Judith M., *John Wayne: A Bio-Bibliography*, New York, 1992.

Nardo, Don, *John Wayne*, New York, 1994.

Marill, Alvin H., *The Great John Wayne Trivia Book*, Secaucus, New Jersey, 1995.

Roberts, Randy, *John Wayne: American*, New York, 1995.

On WAYNE: articles—

Gray, M., "No-Contract Star," in *Films and Filming* (London), March 1957.

Didion, Joan, "John Wayne," in *The Saturday Evening Post* (Philadelphia), 14 August 1965.

Hall, D. J., "Tall in the Saddle," in *Films and Filming* (London), October 1969.

Current Biography 1972, New York, 1972.

Bentley, Eric, "The Political Theatre of John Wayne," in *Film Society Review* (New York), March/May 1972.

Special issue of *Film Heritage* (New York), Summer 1975.

Suid, L., "The Making of *The Green Berets*," in *Journal of Popular Film* (Bowling Green, Ohio), v. 6, no. 2, 1977.

Beaver, J., "John Wayne," in *Films in Review* (New York), May 1977, see also issue for August/September 1977 and February 1978.

Obituary in *New York Times*, 12 June 1979.

Kroll, Jack, "John Wayne," in *The Movie Star*, edited by Elisabeth Weis, New York, 1981.

Norman, Barry, in *The Film Greats*, London, 1985.

Villien, Bruno, "John Wayne: la force tranquille d'Amérique," in *Cinématographe* (Paris), February 1986.

Edgerton, G., "A Reappraisal of John Wayne," in *Films in Review* (New York), May 1986.

McGhee, R. D., "John Wayne: Hero with a Thousand Faces," in *Literature/Film Quarterly* (Salisbury, Maryland), January 1988.

Barzman, Ben, "The Duke and Me," in *Los Angeles Magazine*, January 1989.

Bell, Joseph N., "True Wayne," in *American Film*, January/February 1992.

*   *   *

During his last years John Wayne's image hardened and became simplified: the movie star became either a national institution or an object of ridicule and vilification (depending upon one's political viewpoint). Wayne himself clearly encouraged this transformation, the potential for which was always there in his image, at least from the 1950s on. His decision to direct and star in *The Green Berets* marks a crucial point of transition, confirmed by his subsequent political pronouncements and the tendency to choose self-mythologizing roles. This development has had the unfortunate effect of obscuring for many people the complexities of the Wayne persona and the extremely interesting uses to which it was put by two of Hollywood's greatest directors, John Ford and Howard Hawks.

Ford is reported as saying, after seeing *Red River*, that he had never realized that Wayne could act. The operative criterion of acting here appears to be the hackneyed one of versatility, the ability to "become" different characters. If a limited actor, Wayne was always, from his first major role in *Stagecoach*, an extremely capable performer: the scenes that develop his relationship with Claire Trevor are played with considerable delicacy and sensitivity. Though the components of the Wayne persona were already clearly present there in *The Long Voyage Home*, Ford did not make full use of them until after World War II, when the dominant tone of his work modulated from idealism (associated with Henry Fonda) to disillusionment and retreat into stoicism. Through the three films of the "cavalry trilogy" (*Fort Apache*, *She Wore a Yellow Ribbon*, and *Rio Grande*) the Wayne persona reaches full expression. The makings of the later "national institution" are all there—conservatism, militarism, adherence to tradition, emphasis on patriotic duty—but they are held within a complex thematic network in which the sustaining of faith in American civilization becomes increasingly problematic, giving way to stoical resignation. Significantly, Ford also used Wayne centrally in films in which he abandons American civilization altogether, for a retreat either into the Irish past (*The Quiet Man*) or to a South Seas never-never land (*Donovan's Reef*). Ford's ultimate use of Wayne, however, was as the incarnation of the lost values of a mythical Old West, rendered obsolete by the civilization it helped build, in T*he Man Who Shot Liberty Valance*.

Hawks never showed much interest in the established social order except as something to escape from, and Wayne is less central to his work than he is to Ford's. *Red River*, while in many ways impressive, suffers from Hawks's insufficient grasp of the material's moral and political implications, to which Wayne's Thomas Dunson is central. Interestingly, in relation to Wayne's later career, the character develops marked connotations of fascism which the film tries to cope with but finally evades. Hawks's finest use of Wayne is undoubtedly in *Rio Bravo*: here the stoicism, self-reliance, and assumption of moral infallibility at once achieve their most complete expression and are subjected to a subtle criticism that defines their limitations. The infallible Wayne is alternately juxtaposed with the all-too-fallible Dean Martin and confronted with the amorous but ironic Angie Dickinson. Both relationships are being used by Hawks to probe, question, and affectionately satirize the Wayne image, exposing its human deficiencies while reaffirming its strength.

It is with Hawks also—in *El Dorado* and *Rio Lobo*—that Wayne enters the last phase of his career, where the central concern becomes age and failing powers. *The Cowboys* was not, as some asserted, the first film in which Wayne died (they forget, for example, *Reap the Wild Wind*, *Sands of Iwo Jima*, and, far more reprehensibly, *Liberty Valance*), but it is the first of his major roles in which he was killed face-to-face by the bad guy. Even more pertinent is *The Shootist*, in which he plays an aging gunfighter who is dying of cancer, the disease against which he himself struggled throughout this late period. If *The Cowboys* (in which Wayne explicitly becomes a role model for the young of America) celebrates the "national institution," even at this stage of his career where the image is at its most petrified it still carries connotations—pain, loss, failure, stoical endurance—which makes it less simple than the popular view of "hawk" patriarch suggests.

Perhaps due to Wayne's larger-than-life iconography as the quintessential American hero, he is as popular with audiences today as he was during his lifetime. His films are never off the television screen and remain among the fastest sellers in video stores. His directorial debut, *The Alamo*, a personal project in which he also starred, has been restored to its original director's cut length after 30 years during which only the abbreviated version released to theaters by United Artists was available—and reissued on tape and laser disc to the lucrative collector's market in a format that retained the film's wide-screen grandeur. In the wake of its commercial success, two of Wayne's rowdiest and most popular non-Ford and non-Hawks Westerns, *McLintock* and *Hondo,* have finally found their way to television and video stores after many years of hibernation, as well.

—Robin Wood, updated by John McCarty

WEAVER, Sigourney

Nationality: American. **Born:** Susan Alexander Weaver in New York, 8 October 1949; daughter of the former president of NBC Sylvester "Pat" Weaver. **Education:** Attended Stanford University, B.A.; Yale University School of Drama, M.A. **Family:** Married the theater director Jim Simpson, 1984, one daughter: Charlotte. **Career:** 1974—stage debut on Broadway in *The Constant Wife*; continues as stage performer; 1976—featured film debut in *Madman*; 1977—walk-on part in *Annie Hall*. **Agent:** Sam Cohn, ICM, 40 West 57th Street, New York, NY 10019, U.S.A.

Films as Actress:

1976 *Madman* (Cohen)
1977 *Annie Hall* (Woody Allen) (as Alvy's date outside theater)
1979 *Alien* (Ridley Scott) (as Ripley)
1981 *Eyewitness* (*The Janitor*) (Yates) (as Tony Sokolow)
1982 *The Year of Living Dangerously* (Weir) (as Jill Bryant)
1983 *Deal of the Century* (Friedkin) (as Mrs. De Voto)
1984 *Ghostbusters* (Reitman) (as Dana Barrett/The Gate Keeper)
1985 *Une Femme ou deux* (*One Woman or Two*) (Vigne) (as Jessica Fitzgerald)
1986 *Aliens* (Cameron) (as Ripley); *Half Moon Street* (Swaim) (as Lauren Slaughter)
1988 *Working Girl* (Mike Nichols) (as Katharine Parker); *Gorillas in the Mist* (Apted) (as Dian Fossey)
1989 *Ghostbusters II* (Reitman) (as Dana Barrett); *Helmut Newton: Frames from the Edge* (doc)
1992 *Alien 3* (Fincher) (as Ripley, + co-pr); *1492: The Conquest of Paradise* (Ridley Scott) (as Queen Isabella)
1993 *Dave* (Reitman) (as Ellen Mitchell)
1994 *Death and the Maiden* (Polanski) (as Paulina Escobar)
1995 *Jeffrey* (Ashley) (as Debra Moorhouse); *Copycat* (Amiel) (as Helen Hudson)
1996 *Snow White in the Black Forest*
1997 *Alien Resurrection*

Publications

By WEAVER: articles—

Interview in *Photoplay* (London), December 1979.
Interview in *Films and Filming* (London), November 1981.
Interview in *Première* (Paris), November 1985.
Interview with M. Pally, in *Film Comment* (New York), November/December 1986.
Interview in *Time Out* (London), 4 January 1989.
"You've Heard of Watergate—This Is Surrogate" (telephone conversation with actor Kevin Kline), in *Interview* (NewYork), May 1993.

On WEAVER: books—

Maguffee, T. D., *Sigourney Weaver*, New York, 1989.
Sellers, Robert, *Sigourney Weaver*, London, 1992.

Sigourney Weaver in *Gorillas in the Mist*

On WEAVER: articles—

Levine, R. M., "Is This Face Funny?," in *American Film* (Washington, D.C.), October 1983.
Films in Review (New York), December 1985.
Kennedy, Harlan, "Weaver, the Woman," in *Film Comment* (New York), July/August 1986.
Current Biography 1989, New York, 1989.
Murphy, Kathleen, "The Last Temptation of Sigourney Weaver," in *Film Comment* (New York), July/August 1992.

*   *   *

Sigourney Weaver has become a feminist icon in the eighties and nineties largely because of the coherence of her determined and tremendously self-reliant screen persona. Although she was memorably paired with Mel Gibson in a sultry turn in *The Year of Living Dangerously,* and has been variously partnered on the screen with Bill Murray, Michael Caine, Bryan Brown, and Charles Dance, Weaver has retained an air of independence about her in even her romantic roles. She is most usually seen on her own, struggling against tremendous threats to her own life and to those under her protection (often animals or small children). Strikingly, however, Weaver has resisted being typecast as watchful mothers or as heroic career women; indeed, she has had a screen career of remarkable variety, although recently she has not often had the most felicitous roles.

Weaver's strong screen persona owes much to her striking physical appearance. Her great height and striking beauty, coupled with her forceful jawline, have lent her a tremendously regal air. This air is itself perhaps intensified by Weaver's background. Like the earlier Hollywood star she most evokes, Katharine Hepburn, Weaver enjoyed an especially patrician upbringing: the daughter of former NBC president Sylvester "Pat" Weaver, she attended Stanford for her undergraduate degree and the Yale Drama School for her M.F.A. Weaver's air of hauteur has often led her to be cast in somewhat aristocratic parts, including those of an American First Lady in *Dave* and of Queen Isabella in *1492: The Conquest of Paradise*. The latter role was practically a cameo; yet so entertaining were Weaver's subtly arch and bemused reactions to Gérard Depardieu's wranglings for patronage that she almost took one's mind off the endless torchlight processions and overwrought debates over navigation in the film's opening half.

Yet the greatest asset to Weaver's persona has been her sheer physicality on the screen. Almost alone among actresses in the last 25 years, Weaver has enjoyed a partial career as an eminently bankable action-adventure hero. In Ridley Scott's *Alien,* Weaver's Second Officer Ripley, her first sizable role in a major film, seized control not only of the space frigate *Nostromo* but also of the audience's attention by sheer dint of her physical authority. The relative interchangeability of the *Nostromo*'s crew roster at the film's beginning (thanks to the script's emphasis on atmosphere rather than character) made the rise of Weaver's Ripley seem all the more astonishing. As the film progresses, the director effectively counterpoints Weaver's levelheadedness with Veronica Cartwright's mounting hysteria, and her humane compassion with Ian Holm's lethal coldness. As a role, Ripley in the first *Alien* film might seem to be on paper scarcely more interesting than a stalked teenager in a run-of-the-mill horror film; yet Weaver so effectively allowed her audience to empathize with her that the role made her a star. When the franchise for the *Alien* films expanded in the eighties, their success owed much to Weaver's presence in them. She stood alone among other action stars of the decade, such as Schwarzenegger, Stallone, and Willis, not only because of her gender but because of her disciplined training and emotional range. Weaver could not only seem effective discharging a flamethrower or uttering wry wisecracks but could also memorably evoke pathos, loneliness, and empathy. James Cameron capitalized on this to tremendous effect in *Aliens,* the second film in the series, by emphasizing Weaver's more maternal aspects, giving her a young child to protect as well as an evil counterpart in the queen alien.

Aside from Ripley and Dr. Helen Hudson in *Copycat* Weaver has not been cast to date in any other true action roles—due in large part, one suspects, to the misogynistic unwillingness of producers and studio executives to recognize her bankability as an adventure heroine. Yet many of her best screen moments have allowed her to display her physical talents. Weaver is never better on the screen than when she is in motion: shoving a car off a cliff in *Death and the Maiden* or roughhousing with one of the title animals in *Gorillas in the Mist,* she is nothing less than magnetic. One of her most remarkable moments in her screen career occurs in the precredits chase sequence to the otherwise negligible *Ghostbusters II.* Weaver watches in horror as poltergeists send her infant son's carriage madly careering through busy Manhattan traffic, and frantically chases after it. Her almost palpable sense of desperation as she races between cars—and then of relief when she at last clasps her child safe against her body—are so powerfully evoked as to overshadow the rest of the film.

Weaver began her stage career out of drama school in the seventies performing in the frenzied comedies of her friend and Yale ex-classmate Christopher Durang. Although the eighties and nineties have not been the most fortuitous period in film history for women's comic roles, Weaver has made the most of those that have come her way. The best of these was in *Working Girl,* where Weaver took her trademark authority and determination to maniacal extremes for hilarious effect. Whether barking orders at Melanie Griffith or schussing down ski slopes with berserk self-confidence, Weaver so thoroughly dominates the film that it seems almost incredible today that *Working Girl* could have made Melanie Griffith a star.

In recent years, Weaver has worked to extend her range by accepting roles that have accentuated her vulnerabilities rather than her strengths. Many of these—such as in *Gorillas in the Mist* and *Death and the Maiden*—have turned in large part upon the kind of vocal histrionics that have never been Weaver's strong suit. Besides being simply no fun in these overemotive roles more typically portrayed by a Jessica Lange or a Glenn Close, Weaver is also simply unconvincing in hysterical parts—perhaps in large part because of the singular coherence of her strong screen persona. The recent *Copycat* sums up Weaver at both her worst and her best. When her Dr. Helen Hudson collapses or hyperventilates into a bag due to her crippling agoraphobia, Weaver seems preposterous; when she is struggling for her life in a women's room against a serial killer, and can use her body to full effect, she is not only convincing but compellingly so. As Sigourney Weaver settles into middle age, one can only hope that she is more fortuitous in the roles that come her way. It would be delightful to see her, for instance, in more heroic parts, or in literate roles (such as of a mature Edith Wharton or Henry James heroine) that would allow her to dominate scenes by dint of her natural authority and strength, rather than through histrionic excess.

—Jay Dickson

WEBB, Clifton

Nationality: American. **Born:** Webb Parmalee Hollenbeck in Indianapolis, Indiana, 19 November 1891. **Education:** Attended Public School No. 87, New York; joined Palmer Cox's Lyceum's Children's Theatre at age 8; studied painting with Robert Henri and singing with Victor Maurel. **Career:** Child actor: debut at age 9 in *The Brownies*; member of the Aborn Opera Company: debut in *Mignon*; 1913—Broadway debut as dancer in *The Purple Road*; 1914—teamed with Mae Murray for engagement at Palace Theatre, then a succession of successful plays in New York as dancer and actor, including *Sunny,* 1925, *As Thousands Cheer,* 1933, *The Man Who Came to Dinner* on tour, 1931, and *Blithe Spirit,* 1941; 1920—film debut in *Polly with a Past*; 1921—London stage debut in *Fun at the Fayre*; 1923—performed with the Dolly Sisters in Paris; 1948—first of several films featuring the character Mr. Belvedere, *Sitting Pretty.* **Died:** 13 October 1966.

Films as Actor:

1920   *Polly with a Past* (de Cordova)
1924   *Let No Man Put Asunder* (Blackton)
1925   *The Heart of a Siren* (Rosen) (as Maxim); *New Toys* (Robertson)
1930   *The Still Alarm* (short)
1944   ***Laura*** (Preminger and Mamoulian) (as Waldo Lydecker)
1946   *The Dark Corner* (Hathaway) (as Hardy Cathcart); *The Razor's Edge* (Goulding) (as Elliott Templeton)
1948   *Sitting Pretty* (Walter Lang) (as Lynn Belvedere)
1949   *Mr. Belvedere Goes to College* (Nugent) (title role)
1950   *Cheaper by the Dozen* (Walter Lang) (as Frank Gilbert); *For Heaven's Sake* (Seaton) (as Charles)
1951   *Mr. Belvedere Rings the Bell* (Koster) (title role); *Elopement* (Koster) (as Howard Osborne)
1952   *Dreamboat* (Binyon) (as Thirton Sayre); *Stars and Stripes Forever* (Koster) (as John Philip Sousa)
1953   *Titanic* (Negulesco) (as Robert Sturges); *Mister Scoutmaster* (Levin) (as Robert Jordan)
1954   *Three Coins in the Fountain* (Negulesco) (as Shadwell); *Woman's World* (Negulesco) (as Gifford)
1956   *The Man Who Never Was* (Neame) (as Commander Ewen Montagu)
1957   *Boy on a Dolphin* (Negulesco) (as Victor Parmalee)
1959   *The Remarkable Mr. Pennypacker* (Levin) (title role); *Holiday for Lovers* (Levin) (as Robert Dean)
1962   *Satan Never Sleeps* (*The Devil Never Sleeps*; *Flight from Terror*) (McCarey) (as Father Bovard)

Publications

On WEBB: book—

Parish, James Robert, and William T. Leonard, *The Funsters*, New Rochelle, New York, 1979.

On WEBB: articles—

Current Biography 1943, New York, 1943.
Obituary in *New York Times*, 14 October 1966.
"Clifton Webb," in *Films in Review* (New York), January 1970.
Holland, L. L., "Clifton Webb," in *Films in Review* (New York), April 1981.

*   *   *

Clifton Webb's career of rather secondary parts in motion pictures obscures his brilliant Broadway career as a singer and dancer. But that was long before his cinema debut and he was never featured as a musical comedy personality in films.

Hollywood found him most useful, however, in bitchy, acerbic roles, most notably that of the columnist Waldo Lydecker in Otto Preminger's *Laura*. His screen career was hardly distinguished, but it was a steady one, and he had occasional strong roles such as the automobile executive in *Woman's World* where he played an excellent foil to the ambitious wives of candidates for an automobile company's vice presidency. But it was the character he played in *Laura* that typecast him, and that gave birth to such pictures as *Sitting Pretty* and the Mr. Belvedere series, which capitalized on his role in it.

Webb's film career, coming as it did on the heels of a long stage career, was diminished only by old age. His last film was in Leo McCarey's film, *Satan Never Sleeps*.

—Joseph Arkins

Paul Wegener in *Der Student von Prag*

WEGENER, Paul

Nationality: German. **Born:** Bischdorf, East Prussia, 11 December 1874. **Education:** Attended high school in Königsberg; studied law in Freiburg and Leipzig. **Family:** Married five times, including marriage to the actress Lyda Salmonova. **Career:** 1895—stage debut in theater in Rostock; 1906-20—member of Max Reinhardt's Deutsches Theater, Berlin: acclaimed role in Reinhardt's version of *Oedipus Rex*, 1917; 1913—film debut in *Der Student von Prag*; often directed or co-directed his subsequent films; made propaganda films during the Nazi era; 1937—named Actor of the State; 1946—on stage in *Nathan the Wise* in Berlin and New York. **Died:** In Berlin, 1948.

Films as Actor:

1913   *Der Student von Prag* (Rye) (as Balduin, + co-sc)
1914   *Die Verfuhrte* (*Geheimnisse des Blutes*) (Rye); *Die Rache des Blutes*
1915   *Peter Schlemihl* (+ co-sc)
1918   *Dornroschen* (Leni); *Welt ohne Waffen* (doc); *Der Galeerensträfling* (Gliese) (+ sc)
1919   *Nachtgestalten*
1920   *Medea* (Lubitsch); *Steuermann Holck* (Wolff); *Die Geliebte Roswolskys* (Basch); *Sumurun* (*One Arabian Night*) (Lubitsch) (as the Sheik)
1921   *Der verlorene Schatten* (*The Lost Shadow*) (Gliese) (as the magician, + sc) ; *Flammende Völker* (Reinert)
1922   *Das Liebensnest* (Dworsky and Walther-Fein); *Lukrezia Borgia* (Oswald); *Monna Vanna* (Eichberg) (as Guido Gurlino); *Sterbende Völker* (*Popoli Morituri*) (Reinert); *Das Weib des Pharao* (*Loves of a Pharaoh*) (Lubitsch) (as King of the Ethiopians)
1923   *Vanina, oder die Galgenhochzeit* (von Gerlach) (as the father); *SOS: Die Insel des Tränen* (Mendes)
1924   *Der Schatz der Gesine Jakobsen* (Walther-Fein)
1925   *Der Mann aus dem Jenseits* (Noa)
1926   *Dagfin* (May)
1927   *Alraune* (*Unholy Love*) (Galeen); *Arme Kleine Sif* (Bergen); *Glanz und Elend der Kurtisanen* (*Survival*) (Noa) (as Collin); *Ramper, der Tiermensch* (*The Strange Case of Captain Ramper*) (Reichmann) (title role); *Svengali* (Grund and Righelli) (title role); *Die Weber* (*The Weavers*) (Zelnik); *Le Magicien* (*The Magician*) (Ingram) (as Dr. Haddo)

1930   *Fundvogel* (Hoffman-Harnisch)
1932   *Marschall Vorwärts* (Paul); *Das Geheimnis um Johann Orth* (Wolff); *Unheimliche Geschichten* (*The Living Dead*) (Oswald) (as the mad inventor)
1933   *Inge und die Millionen* (Engel); *Hans Westmar* (*Horst Wessel*) (Wenzler) (as Russian Commissar)
1935   *Der Mann mir der Pranke* (van der Noss); *. . . nur ein Komödiant* (Engel)
1936   *Ein Liebesroman im Hause Hapsburg* (Wolff) (as Russian Ambassador)
1938   *In geheimer Mission* (von Alten); *Stärker al die Liebe* (*Stranger Than Love*) (Stöchel)
1939   *Das Recht auf Liebe* (*The Right to Love*) (Stöchel); *Das unsterbliche Herz* (Harlan)
1940   *Zwielicht* (van der Noss); *Das Mädchen von Fanö* (Schweikart); *Mein Leben für Irland* (Kimmich)
1942   *Diesel* (Lamprecht); *Der grosse König* (Harlan); *Hochzeit auf Bärenhof* (Froelich)
1943   *Wenn die Sonne wieder scheint* (Barlog)
1944   *Zwischen Nacht und Morgen* (*Augen der Liebe*) (Braun); *Seinerzeit zu meiner Zeit* (Barlog); *Der Fall Molander* (Pabst)
1945   *Dr. Phil Döderlein* (Klinger); *Tierarzt Dr. Vlimmen* (Barlog); *Kohlberg* (Harlan)
1949   *Der grosse Mandarin* (Stroux)

Films as Director and Scriptwriter:

1914   *Die Augen des Ole Brandis* (co-d, + ro); *Evintrude: Die Geschichte eines Abenteurers* (co-d, + ro); *Der Golem* (co-d, + title role)

1916   *Rübezahls Hochzeit* (+ ro); *Der Rattenfänger von Hamlen* (+ ro); *Der Yoghi* (+ ro)
1917   *Der Golem und die Tänzerin* (+ title role); *Hans Trutz in Schlaraffenland* (+ title role)
1918   *Der fremde Furst* (+ ro)
1920   *Der Golem, wie er in die Welt kam* (+ title role)
1922   *Herzog Ferrantes Ende* (+ title role)
1923   *Lebende Buddha* (+ pr, ro)
1934   *Die Freundin eines grossen Mannes*; *Ein Mann will nach Deutschland*
1936   *August der Starke*; *Die Stunde der Versuchung*; *Moskau-Shanghai*
1937   *Krach und Glück um Künnemann*; *Unter Ausschluss der Öffentlichkeit*

Publications

On WEGENER: books—

Möller, Kai, *Paul Wegener*, Hamburg, 1954.
Staehlin Saavedra, Carlos Maria, *Wegener, el doble y el golem*, Valladolid, 1978.

On WEGENER: article—

Obituary in *New York Times*, 14 September 1948.

*   *   *

"The essence of this strongly built, muscle-hard fellow is a straddling permanent manliness. Such a chap, who lives and lets live; in no way tender, yet basically good-natured; hot-tempered, yet also sly, a part Odyseus, but also a part Achilles—in short, a complete fellow." This description by Paul Wegener's contemporary Julius Bab captures a man whose physical presence is as commanding on the screen as it must have been on stage. Wegener's highly successful stage acting career spanned over 50 years; his work in film spanned 35 years and many roles as authority figures or characters with an abnormal bent. Although he never directed on the stage, Wegener's involvement in cinema went well beyond acting to include directing and writing. He explained his attraction to film as such: "I did not go into film as an actor; the problem of this new art form interested me in general. The mysterious possibilities of the camera kindled my fantasies. I conceived the fable *Der Student von Prag* because here was the possibility of acting opposite myself."

On the stage Wegener was known for playing complex characters (Mephisto, Danton, Nathan der Weise); he then realized how filmic devices could be used to further the development of multifaceted characters, or in transforming characters. Wegener's first film, *Der Student von Prag*, suggests the essence of the great actor's contribution to film history: his fascination with the supernatural and the doppelgänger (the evil double of oneself), and the potential inherent in film to exploit both. *Der Student von Prag* is the story of a poor student who makes a Faustian pact with a Satanic magician. The devil figure takes on the student's mirror reflection as his part of the deal—an image that would become familiar as the Doppelgänger in many films to follow. The use of special effects combined with Wegener playing both roles created a haunting depiction of the evil lurking within one—a Romantic vision that Wegener brought forcefully to the screen.

Wegener was responsible for carrying on the German tradition of adult fairy tales, as perfected in E. T. A. Hoffmann's novellas, by transposing them to film. Wegener created and acted in a series of fairy-tale films early in his film career, including *Der Student von*

Prag, *Rübezahls Hochzeit*, *Der Yoghi* (in which he once again played two roles), and *Der Rattenfänger von Hamlen*. Wegener also directed two versions of *Der Golem*. In the second, *Der Golem, wie er in die Welt kam*, Wegener plays a clay giant brought to life, who is capable of unleashing powerful violence or gentle kindness. The role of the Golem offered Wegener the perfect opportunity to demonstrate his style of "discreet acting." He exercised restraint in physical movement, letting his face be the tool of expression. One of Wegener's favorite films was *Lebende Buddha*, in which he plays the role of Buddha. Indeed, Wegener's demeanor was not unlike that of the god's eternal smile; Wegener's face was an embodiment of expressiveness kept in check.

Wegener continued to act until early 1948, although his passion and greatest creative output occured in the early films. His commanding presence extended to the total conception and production of these early films, and was not confined to the dramatic interpretation of his roles.

—Virginia Keller

WEISSMULLER, Johnny

Nationality: American. **Born:** Peter John Weissmuller in Windber, Pennsylvania, 2 July 1904; grew up in Chicago. **Education:** Attended St. Michael's Parochial School, 1908-15, and Menier Public School, 1915-17, both in Chicago. **Family:** Married 1) Camille Louier (divorced); 2) Robbe Arnst (divorced); 3) the actress Lupe Velez, 1933 (divorced 1939); 4) Beryl Scott, 1939 (divorced 1948), three children; 5) Allene Gates, 1948 (divorced 1962); 6) Maria Brock, 1963. **Career:** Champion swimmer as a teenager; member of the Athletic Club of Chicago; holder of numerous national and world records; won five gold medals at the Olympic Games, 1924 and 1928; 1929— appeared in several swimming documentaries; 1932—film debut in first of 12 Tarzan films, *Tarzan, The Ape Man*; 1948—first of series of Jungle Jim Films. **Died:** In Acapulco, Mexico, 20 January 1984.

Films as Actor:

1932   *Tarzan, The Ape Man* (*Tarzan of the Apes*) (Van Dyke) (title role)
1934   *Tarzan and His Mate* (Gibbons) (title role)
1936   *Tarzan Escapes* (Thorpe) (title role)
1939   *Tarzan Finds a Son* (Thorpe) (title role)
1941   *Tarzan's Secret Treasure* (Thorpe) (title role)
1942   *Tarzan's New York Adventure* (Thorpe) (title role)
1943   *Stage Door Canteen* (Borzage) (as himself); *Tarzan Triumphs* (Thiele) (title role); *Tarzan's Desert Mystery* (Thiele) (title role)
1945   *Tarzan and the Amazons* (Neumann) (title role)
1946   *Tarzan and the Leopard Woman* (Neumann) (title role); *Swamp Fire* (Pine) (as Johnny Duval)
1947   *Tarzan and the Huntress* (Neumann) (title role)
1948   *Tarzan and the Mermaids* (Florey) (title role); *Jungle Jim* (Berke) (title role)
1949   *The Lost Tribe* (Berke) (as Jim)
1950   *The Mark of the Gorilla* (Berke) (as Jim); *Captive Girl* (Berke) (as Jim)
1951   *Pygmy Island* (Berke) (as Jim); *Fury of Congo* (Berke) (as Jim); *Jungle Manhunt* (Landers) (as Jim)
1952   *Jungle Jim in the Forbidden Land* (Landers) (title role); *Voodoo Tiger* (Bennett) (as Jim)

Johnny Weissmuller with Maureen O'Sullivan

1953   *Savage Mutiny* (Berke) (as Jim); *Valley of Head Hunters* (Berke)
        (as Jim); *Killer Ape* (Bennett) (as Jim)
1954   *Cannibal Attack* (Sholem) (as himself)
1955   *Jungle Moon-Men* (Gould) (as himself); *Devil Goddess*
        (Bennett) (as himself)
1970   *The Phynx* (Katzin)
1976   *Won Ton Ton, the Dog Who Saved Hollywood* (Winner) (as himself)

Publications

By WEISSMULLER: book—

Swimming the American Crawl, with Clarence A. Bush, 1930.

On WEISSMULLER: books—

Onyx, Narda, *Water, World, and Weissmuller*, Los Angeles, 1964.
Essoe, Gabe, *Tarzan of the Movies*, New York, 1968.
Harmon, Jim, and Donald Glut, *The Great Movie Serials: Their Sound
    and Fury*, New York, 1972.

On WEISSMULLER: article—

Obituary, in *Revue du Cinéma* (Paris), March 1984.

*   *   *

In 1932, after nine years of undefeated swimming competition including five Olympic gold medals, Johnny Weissmuller was signed by MGM to
portray the jungle hero Tarzan. This action was due in part to the studio's
success with the jungle adventure *Trader Horn* a year before, the abundance of jungle stock footage from that project, Weissmuller's status as a
sports celebrity, and the popularity of the jungle figure Tarzan himself.
Tarzan of the Apes was both a critical and popular success and was the first
of a series of Weissmuller vehicles that would last into the late 1940s.

Weissmuller brought to the role a natural athletic grace and manner.
Standing 6' 3", lean but muscular, Weissmuller looked the part of the
man raised by apes and living in a jungle. His outstanding swimming
ability was often highlighted in the films. MGM understood very well
the sex appeal of the young Weissmuller and employed it in the
publicity surrounding the early films. Some of the costumes for
Weissmuller and his most frequent Jane, Maureen O'Sullivan, were
scanty and very revealing. Although the original Tarzan from the
Edgar Rice Burroughs books is an articulate cultured English Lord,
Weissmuller's screen Tarzan is reduced to an animal man of few words
and broken sentences. Weissmuller used to joke that his secret of
success was his ability to grunt.

Weissmuller's popularity as Tarzan typecast him as a jungle actor, and
he played the role in 12 films. An attempt as a "straight role" in *Swamp
Fire* (1946), late in his Tarzan career, did not break the typecasting. Once
age prevented him from donning the loin cloth, Weissmuller played the
character "Jungle Jim" (accurately described as Tarzan in white hunter
clothes) and found continued success in a series of feature films.

—Ray Narducy

WELCH, Raquel

Nationality: American. **Born:** Raquel Tejada in Chicago, Illinois, 5
September 1940. **Education:** Attended La Jolla High School, California; studied ballet with Irene Clark; studied acting at San Diego State

College, one year. **Family:** Married 1) James Westley Welch, 1959
(divorced 1964), son: Damon, daughter: the actress Tahnee Welch; 2)
Patrick Curtis (divorced 1971), two adopted children; 3) André
Weinfeld, 1980 (divorced). **Career:** Worked as weather girl for a
television station in San Diego, model at Neiman-Marcus, Dallas, and
cocktail waitress; 1964—film debut in *A House Is Not a Home*; co-
founder, with Patrick Curtis, Curtwel Productions; 1966—contract
with 20th Century-Fox; 1966-67—roles in *Fantastic Voyage* and *One
Million Years B.C.*, along with publicity blitz, brought international
attention; 1982—appeared on Broadway in *Woman of the Year*; 1996—
in TV series *Central Park West*. **Address:**, c/o Hurwitz, 427 N. Canon
Dr., Suite 215, Beverly Hills CA, 90210, U.S.A.

Films as Actress:

1964   *A House Is Not a Home* (Rouse) (as one of Polly's girls);
        Roustabout (Rich)
1965   *Do Not Disturb* (Levy); *A Swingin' Summer* (Sparr) (as Jeri)
1966   *Fantastic Voyage* (Fleischer) (as Cora Peterson); *Spara forte,
        più forte . . . non capisco* (*Shoot Loud, Louder . . . I Don't
        Understand*) (De Filippo) (as Tania Mottini); "Queen Elena"
        ep. of *Le Fate* (*The Queens*) (Bolognini) (as Elena)
1967   *Bedazzled* (Donen) (as Lilian Lust); *Fathom* (Medak) (as
        Fathom Harvill); *One Million Years B.C.* (Chaffey) (as
        Loana); "La Belle Epoque" ("The Gay Nineties") ep. of *Le
        Plus Vieux Métier du Monde* (*The Oldest Profession*)
        (Pfleghar) (as Nini)
1968   *Bandolero!* (McLaglen) (as Maria); *The Biggest Bundle of
        Them All* (Annakin) (as Juliana); *Lady in Cement* (Douglas)
        (as Kit Forrest)
1969   *Flareup* (Neilson) (as Michele); *100 Rifles* (Gries) (as Sarita)
1970   *The Magic Christian* (McGrath) (as Slave Driver); *Myra
        Breckenridge* (Sarne) (title role)
1971   *Hannie Caulder* (Kennedy) (title role)
1972   *Bluebeard* (Dmytryk) (as Magdalena); *Fuzz* (Colla) (as Eileen
        Marquette); *Kansas City Bomber* (Freedman) (as K. C. Carr)
1973   *The Last of Sheila* (Ross) (as Alice)
1974   *The Three Musketeers* (*The Queen's Diamonds*) (Lester) (as
        Constance)
1975   *The Four Musketeers* (*The Revenge of Milady*) (Lester) (as
        Constance); *The Wild Party* (Ivory) (as Queenie)
1976   *Mother, Jugs and Speed* (Yates) (as Jugs)
1977   *L'Animal* (*Stuntwoman*) (Zidi) (as Jane)
1978   *Crossed Swords* (*The Prince and the Pauper*) (Fleischer) (as
        Lady Edith); *Restless* (*The Beloved*) (Cosmatos) (as Elena)
1979   *You and Me Together*
1982   *The Legend of Walks Far Woman* (Damski—for TV) (title role)
1987   *Right to Die* (Wendkos—for TV)
1988   *Scandal in a Small Town* (Page—for TV); *Trouble in Para-
        dise* (Drew—for TV) (as Rachel Baxely)
1990   *Hero for Hire* (Wynorski)
1993   *Hollyrock-a-Bye Baby* (for TV) (as voice of Shelly Milstone);
        Torch Song (for TV) (as Paula Eastman); *Tainted Blood*
        (Patrick—for TV) (as Elizabeth Kane)
1994   *Naked Gun 33 1/3: The Final Insult* (Segal) (as herself)

Publications

By WELCH: articles—

Interview in *Playboy* (Chicago), January 1970.
"Raquel," interview with Andy Warhol, in *Inter/View* (New York), January 1975.

Raquel Welch in *One Million Years B.C.*

"Still La Belle Raque," interview with Lisa Schwarzbaum, in *Entertainment Weekly*, 21 May 1993.

"The Welch Women: Raquel and Tahnee," interview with Kara Young and Ingrid Sischy, in *Interview*, September 1993.

On WELCH: book—

Haining, Peter, *Raquel Welch: Sex Symbol to Superstar*, London, 1984.

On WELCH: article—

Current Biography 1971, New York, 1971.

* * *

Raquel Welch began her career on a wave of publicity. Newly discovered by the Italian moguls who were anxious to exploit her, she was packaged as the newest model of the American sex symbol. She burst onto American film screens in *One Million Years B.C.*, as a cavewoman whose most noteworthy asset was her very skimpy costume. A series of undistinguished films followed, including *Fantastic Voyage*, *The Biggest Bundle of Them All*, and *100 Rifles*—which brought Welch's cheesecake together with former running back Jim Brown's beefcake. Although Welch's physical attributes secured a place for her in a long tradition of Hollywood sex symbols, from Marilyn Monroe to Jayne Mansfield, Welch represented a contemporary variation—she was not dumb. Indeed, as often as not, her on-screen (as well as offscreen) persona revealed an intelligent woman, competent and in control. Even when dinosaurs were ripping at her clothes, Welch performed with a straight-faced spunkiness that was somehow endearing.

Apparently weary of her sex-symbol image and determined to break out of the critical disrepute her typecasting had brought her, Welch took the role of *Myra Breckenridge*, based on the intellectual and risqué novel by Gore Vidal. Critics received the film and all performances therein (including those of Mae West and Rex Reed) as total fiascos; for a multimillion dollar film to have such a completely camp sensibility proved stultifyingly incredible. In any case, *Myra Breckenridge* did not especially tarnish Welch's reputation. If she was still not quite considered an actress, she was at least finally considered sincere in her attempt to be regarded as one.

In the revenge Western *Hannie Caulder*, Welch at last had a meatier role that required more of her than simply parading her physical assets. A subsequent breakthrough took place with *Kansas City Bomber*, in which Welch took the role of an emotionally troubled roller-derby skater. She gave a performance of considerable vulnerability that finally made critics admit that she might have some genuine acting ability. In her supporting performance in *The Last of Sheila*, Welch's vulnerability and softness were, as in *Kansas City Bomber*, again emphasized; even her physical beauty seemed to be presented somewhat differently than before. If the early Welch was a 1960s sexpot, intelligent if somewhat mechanical and distancing, the 1970s Welch was a more mature beauty, sensitive and vulnerable, less of a Playboy cartoon. In Richard Lester's *The Three Musketeers*, which exploited Welch's physical attributes nevertheless, she demonstrated a fine sense of style and comedy in a much-acclaimed performance.

Unfortunately, it appears that the flowering of Welch's own abilities coincided with a rather difficult period in Hollywood for all actresses except for the most popular superstars. Welch was particularly eschewed by the Hollywood establishment after she was fired in 1982 from *Cannery Row*, replaced by the younger Debra Winger. Although she successfully and with much publicity sued its producing studio in the name of all aging actresses treated unfairly, she may have lost the war, for major feature films did not follow. As a result, Welch's often-predicted career breakthrough never quite materialized, and her lurching movie career has been stalled for two decades now.

Still, ever the self-promoter, Welch has managed rather skillfully to carve out several new niches for herself. She has begun appearing in television films, sometimes producing her own projects. Indeed, as good women's roles have greatly disappeared in the eighties and nineties, many actresses in their forties and above (Sally Field, Marlo Thomas, Ann-Margret, Jane Fonda) have found television to be a salvation. Welch's surprising role as an Indian through many decades in *The Legend of Walks Far Woman* (a kind of female *Little Big Man*, including Welch in heavy makeup as a 102 year old) received some good notices, but was hurt by the network's decision to severely edit the film to fit in a shorter time slot. Other films dealt with social issues: In *Right to Die*, Welch movingly played a woman fighting Lou Gehrig's disease; in the thriller *Scandal in a Small Town*, Welch played a cocktail waitress confronting anti-Semitism; and in *Trouble in Paradise*, a variation on Lina Wertmüller's *Swept Away*, Welch played a woman marooned on a tropical island in a comedy dealing with issues of class and gender. Although all were entertaining, none strongly added to the Welch mystique or provided career breakthrough or significant industry respect.

Welch's other niche, potentially more lucrative for her, was as a primary role model for the eighties' narcissistic focus on the body and on self-actualization. A stunningly beautiful woman, far more striking now than in her pinup days, Welch has starred in several extremely successful exercise videos. Like Jane Fonda, who periodically reinvents herself, Welch has successfully positioned herself as role model for aging yuppies, who look upon her own early career as bikini-clad beauty stalked by dinosaurs as the most comforting nostalgia and thus view her beauty and fitness tips with great credibility.

—Charles Derry

WELD, Tuesday

Nationality: American. **Born:** Susan Ker Weld in New York City, 27 August 1943. **Education:** Attended public school in Fort Lauderdale, two years, and at various schools in New York, including the Professional Children's School. **Family:** Married 1) Claude Harz, 1965 (divorced 1971), daughter: Natasha; 2) the actor Dudley Moore, 1975 (divorced 1980), son: Patrick; 3) the musician Pinchas Zuckerman,

1985. **Career:** Fashion and catalog model from age three; also television actress; 1956—film debut in *Rock, Rock, Rock*, followed by a series of teenage films; 1959-60—in TV series *The Many Loves of Dobie Gillis*. **Address:** P.O. Box 367, Valley Stream, NY 11582, U.S.A.

Films as Actress:

1956	*Rock, Rock, Rock* (Price) (as Dori); *The Wrong Man* (Hitchcock) (as giggly girl)
1958	*Rally 'round the Flag, Boys!* (McCarey) (as Comfort Goodpasture)
1959	*The Five Pennies* (Shavelson) (as Dorothy Nichols, age 12 to 14)
1960	*Because They're Young* (Wendkos) (as Anne); *High Time* (Edwards) (as Joy Elder); *Sex Kittens Go to College* (*Beauty and the Robot*) (Zugsmith) (as Jody)
1961	*The Private Lives of Adam and Eve* (Zugsmith and Rooney) (as Vangie Harper); *Return to Peyton Place* (Ferrer) (as Selena Cross); *Wild in the Country* (Dunne) (as Noreen); *Bachelor Flat* (Tashlin) (as Libby Bushmill)
1963	*Soldier in the Rain* (Ralph Nelson) (as Bobby Jo Pepperdine)
1965	*The Cincinnati Kid* (Jewison) (as Christian); *I'll Take Sweden* (de Cordova) (as JoJo Holcomb)
1966	*Lord Love a Duck* (Axelrod) (as Barbara Ann Greene)
1968	*Pretty Poison* (Black) (as Sue Ann Stepanek)
1970	*I Walk the Line* (Frankenheimer) (as Alma McCain)
1971	*A Safe Place* (Jaglom) (as Susan/Noah)
1972	*Play It as It Lays* (Perry) (as Maria Wyeth)
1974	*Reflections of Murder* (Badham—for TV) (as Vicky)
1976	*F. Scott Fitzgerald in Hollywood* (Page—for TV)
1977	*Looking for Mr. Goodbar* (Richard Brooks) (as Katherine Dunn)
1978	*Who'll Stop the Rain* (*The Dog Soldiers*) (Reisz) (as Marge Converse); *A Question of Guilt* (Robert Butler—for TV)
1980	*Mother and Daughter: The Loving War* (Brinckerhoff—for TV); *Serial* (Persky) (as Kate)
1981	*Madame X* (Miller—for TV) (title role/Holly Richardson); *Thief* (*Violent Streets*) (Michael Mann) (as Jessie)
1982	*Author! Author!* (Hiller) (as Gloria); *The Rainmaker* (for TV) (as Lizzie)
1983	*The Winter of Our Discontent* (Hussein—for TV)
1984	***Once upon a Time in America*** (Leone) (as Carol); *Scorned and Swindled* (Wendkos—for TV)
1986	*Circle of Violence: A Family Drama* (David Greene—for TV) (as Georgia Benfield); *Something in Common* (Glenn Jordan—for TV) (as Shelly Grant)
1988	*Heartbreak Hotel* (Columbus) (as Marie Wolfe)
1993	*Falling Down* (Schumacher) (as Mrs. Prendergast)
1996	*Feeling Minnesota* (Baigleman) (as Norma Clayton)

Publications

By WELD: articles—

"Stormy Tuesday," interview with Lucy Saroyan, in *Interview* (New York), October 1988.

Interview with Henry Cabot Beck, in *Interview* (New York), March 1993.

On WELD: books—

Sinclair, Marianne, *Hollywood Lolita: The Nymphet Syndrome in the Movies*, London, 1988.

Tuesday Weld

Conner, Floyd, *Pretty Poison: The Tuesday Weld Story*, New York, 1995.

On WELD: articles—

Current Biography 1974, New York, 1974.
Druesne, M., "Tuesday Weld," in *Films in Review* (New York), February 1986.
Barra, Allen, "Tuesday Weld," in *American Film* (New York), January/February 1989.

*   *   *

Forty years into her career, Tuesday Weld still percolates through American pop culture. A 1995 biography is devoted to her, and a worldwide web site; she will soon appear in the off-mainstream *Feeling Minnesota*, her first movie since 1993's *Falling Down* (reportedly her first commercially successful film). Weld's uncredited picture adorns the cover of rock musician Matthew Sweet's 1991 *Girlfriend* album, epitomizing her continued if obscure relevance—but also suggesting that her signature star qualities of self-determining sexuality, insolence, and nearly self-destructive wastefulness (philosophically grounded in antimaterialism as it may be) fit the rock 'n' roll era's patterns more than classical Hollywood's.

As a post-studio system actress, Weld is sadly Hollywood-typical in that her talents have far outmatched her opportunities. Trash- and sex-associated, she distinguishes (and attracts cult status to) herself with the rock-star-like air of profligacy she assumes: "Do you think I want a success?... I like the particular position I've been in all these years, with people wanting to save me from the awful films I've been in." There is an abstractedness, always a lot left missing, in her characterizations, that in one way reflects the submerged place where new Hollywood fixed females, especially in the 1970s—but in another way fights against it, by revealing the eeriness and lostness of women unable to make their desires real, heard, or even clear to themselves. A chillingly transposed example occurs at the end of *I Walk the Line* when Gregory Peck takes on Weld's characteristic wide-eyed, blank but brimming expression after she has (probably) mortally wounded him, having (maybe) misled him about her true motivations for their affair. Interestingly, in this as in many of Weld's films, rock music gets used to fill in some of the gaps her physical choices (and the situations and dialogue given to her) leave.

Weld began her film career at 13, a former child model driven to alcohol and nearly suicide. For five years she played "sex kitten" variations: in movies, on television (with dozens of episodes throughout the 1960s), and in the press, for which she refused to either dress or comment politely while dating publicly and prolifically. In the mid-1960s she found meatier film roles, usually as someone's beautiful but jumbled girlfriend; by the early 1970s, she went deeper into such cracked-surface glamour girls with leads in *Play It as It Lays* and *Reflections of Murder*. Many of her feature and television films from 1977 to 1984 ground her "neurotic" type (quite literally) deadly in its feminist-influenced historical context. Weld's acting, however, insistently animates the subjectivities of her narratively unbalanced and decentered women: in her Oscar-nominated work in *Looking for Mr. Goodbar* and in *Thief* especially, she dramatically modulates her vocal pitch and volume and catches her characters' flickering meanings simply by tilting her head or turning her upper body. She thereby demonstrates that, in the principles of modern screen acting, she is highly skilled if—characteristically—proudly unschooled (she reports that the Actors Studio was too conventional for her; other sources claim that her application was rejected because she was too young).

—Susan Knobloch

WELLES, Orson

Nationality: American. **Born:** George Orson Welles in Kenosha, Wisconsin, 6 May 1915. **Education:** Attended Todd School for Boys, Woodstock, Illinois, 1926-31. **Family:** Married 1) Virginia Nicholson, 1934 (divorced 1939), daughter: Christopher; 2) the actress Rita Hayworth, 1943 (divorced 1947), daughter: Rebecca; 3) the actress Paola Mori, 1955, daughter: Beatrice. **Career:** 1931—professional acting debut at the Gate Theatre in Dublin; 1934—Broadway debut with Katherine Cornell, performed in his own film short, played McGafferty at the Phoenix Theatre, and began his radio career, e.g., as "The Shadow"; 1937—played title role in Mercury Production of *Julius Caesar*; 1938—broadcast "The War of the Worlds"; 1939—RKO contract to act in and produce *The Green Goddess* for the RKO Vaudeville Circuit; 1941—played title role in and directed *Citizen Kane*; 1940s—returned to radio and theater, toured military bases with his magic show, "Mercury Wonder Show," continued to star in his own productions, and began appearing in films directed by others; 1949—moved to Europe; 1955—two series for BBC TV, *The Orson Welles Sketchbook* and *The World with Orson Welles*; 1950s and 1960s—starred in his own films, appeared in films directed by others, appeared on TV and in the theater; 1970—moved back to America; 1970s and 1980s—appeared in films, on TV, and in commercials, including role as narrator for TV mini-series *Shogun*, 1980, and occasional role as voice of Robin Masters in TV series *Magnum P.I.*, 1981-85. **Awards:** Academy Award, Best Screenplay, for *Citizen Kane*, 1941; 20th Anniversary Tribute, Cannes Film Festival, 1966; Honorary Oscar, for "superlative and distinguished service in the making of motion pictures," 1970; inducted into the French Legion of Honor, 1972; Life Achievement Award, American Film Institute, 1975; Los Angeles Film Critics Career Achievement Award, 1978; inducted into the Radio Hall of Fame, 1979; Fellowship of the British Film Institute, 1983; D. W. Griffith Award, Directors Guild of America, 1984. **Died:** Of heart attack, in Hollywood, 10 October 1985.

Films as Actor:

1943   *Jane Eyre* (Stevenson) (as Edward Rochester)
1944   *Follow the Boys* (Sutherland) (revue appearance)
1945   *Tomorrow Is Forever* (Pichel) (as John McDonald)
1949   **The Third Man** (Reed) (as Harry Lime); *Black Magic* (Ratoff) (as Cagliostro); *Prince of Foxes* (Henry King) (as Cesare Borgia)
1950   **The Black Rose** (Hathaway) (as General Bayan)
1951   *Return to Glennascaul* (Edwards) (as himself)
1953   *Trent's Last Case* (Wilcox) (as Sigsbee Manderson); *Si Versailles m'était conté* (*Affairs in Versailles; Royal Affairs in Versailles*) (Guitry) (as Benjamin Franklin); *L'Uomo la Bestia e la Virtù* (*Man Beast and Virtue*) (Vanzina) (as the beast); *King Lear* (Brook—for TV) (title role)
1954   *Napoleon* (Guitry) (as Gen. Hudson Lowe); *Trouble in the Glen* (Wilcox) (as Samin Cejador y Mengues)
1955   "Lord Mountdrago" ep. of *Three Cases of Murder* (O'Ferrall) (as Lord Mountdrago)
1956   *Moby Dick* (Huston) (as Father Mapple)
1957   *Man in the Shadow* (*Pay the Devil*) (Arnold) (as Virgil Renckler)
1958   *The Long Hot Summer* (Ritt) (as Will Varner); *The Roots of Heaven* (Huston) (as Cy Sedgwick)
1959   *David e Golia* (*David and Goliath*) (Pottier and Baldi) (as King Saul); *Compulsion* (Fleischer) (as Jonathan Wilk); *Ferry to Hong Kong* (Lewis Gilbert) (as Captain Hart)
1960   *Austerlitz* (*Battle of Austerlitz*) (Gance) (as Robert Fulton); *Crack in the Mirror* (Fleischer) (as Hagolin/Lamorciere); *I Tartari* (*The Tartars*) (Thorpe) (as Barundai)

1961 *Lafayette* (Dreville) (as Benjamin Franklin); *Desordre* (short)

1963 *The V.I.P.s* (Asquith) (as Max Buda); "La Ricotta" ep. of *Rogopag* (*Laviamoci il Cervello*; *Let's Have a Brainwash*) (Pasolini) (as the film director)

1964 *La Fabuleuse Aventure de Marco Polo* (*Marco the Magnificent*) (de la Patelliere and Noel Howard) (as Ackermann)

1965 *The Island of Treasure* (Franco)

1966 *A Man for All Seasons* (Zinnemann) (as Cardinal Wolsey); *Paris brûle-t-il?* (*Is Paris Burning?*) (Clément)

1967 *Casino Royale* (McGrath and Huston) (as Le Chiffre); *The Sailor from Gibraltor* (Richardson) (as Louis Mozambique); *I'll Never Forget What's 'is Name* (Winner) (as Jonathan Lute); *Oedipus the King* (Saville) (as Tiresias)

1968 *House of Cards* (Guillermin) (as Claude Leschenhaut); *Kampf um Rom* (*Fight for Rome*) (Siodmak) (as Emperor Justinian)

1969 *Michael the Brave* (Nicolaescu); *L'Etoile de Sud* (*The Southern Star*) (Hayers) (as Plankett); *Tepepa* (Petroni); *Twelve Plus One* (Gessner) (as Markau); *Mihai Viteazu* (Nicolaescu); *Kampf um Rom II* (*Fight for Rome II*); *Una su 13*

1970 *Catch-22* (Mike Nichols) (as General Dreedle); *The Battle of Neretva* (Bulajic) (as Senator); *Waterloo* (Bondarchuk) (as King Louis XVIII); *Upon This Rock* (Rasky); *The Kremlin Letter* (Huston) (as Aleksei Bresnavitch)

1971 *A Safe Place* (Jaglom) (as the Magician); *The Toy Factory* (Gordon); *I Racconti di Canterbury* (*The Canterbury Tales*) (Pasolini); *To Kill a Stranger* (Collinson)

1972 *Get to Know Your Rabbit* (De Palma) (as Mr. Delasandro); *La Décade prodigieuse* (*Ten Days' Wonder*) (Chabrol) (as Theo Van Horn); *Sutjeska* (Delic); *Malpertuis* (Kumel) (as Cassavius); *Treasure Island* (Hough and Bianchi) (as Long John Silver, + sc); *Necromancy* (*The Witching*) (Gordon) (as Mr. Cato); *The Man Who Came to Dinner* (Kilik) (as Sheridan Whiteside—for TV)

1975 *And Then There Were None* (Collinson) (as voice of himself)

1976 *Voyage of the Damned* (Rosenberg) (as Estedes)

1977 *It Happened One Christmas* (Thomas—for TV)

1978 *Hot Tomorrows* (Brest) (as voice of Parklawn Mortuary)

1979 *Never Trust an Honest Thief* (McCowan); *Tajna Nikole Tesle* (*The Secret of Nicola Tesla*; *Tesla*) (Papic) (as J. P. Morgan); *The Muppet Movie* (Frawley) (as Lord Lew)

1982 *Butterfly* (Cimber) (as Judge Rauch); *The Muppets Take Manhattan* (Oz)

1983 *Where Is Parsifal?* (Helman) (as Klingsor); *In Our Hands* (Richer and Warnow)

1984 *Slapstick of Another Kind* (Paul) (as voice of Alien Father)

1986 *The Transformers: The Movie* (Shin and Morishita) (as voice of Planet Unicron)

1987 *Someone to Love* (Jaglom) (as Danny's friend)

Films as Narrator:

1937 **The Spanish Earth** (Ivens—doc)

1940 *Swiss Family Robinson* (Ludwig)

1946 *Duel in the Sun* (King Vidor)

1955 *Out of Darkness* (doc)

1958 *Les Seigneurs de la Forêt* (*Masters of the Congo Jungle*) (Sielman and Brandt); *The Vikings* (Fleischer)

1959 *High Journey* (Baylis); *South Sea Adventure* (Dudley)

1961 *King of Kings* (Nicholas Ray)

1962 *Der grosse Atlantik* (doc)

1964 *The Finest Hours* (Baylis—doc)

1967 *A King's Story* (Booth—doc)

1969 *Barbed Water* (doc)

1970 *To Build a Fire* (Cobham); *A Horse Called Nijinsky*; *Start the Revolution without Me* (Yorkin)

1971 *Directed by John Ford* (Bogdanovich—doc); *Sentinels of Silence* (Amram—doc); *Happiness in Twenty Years*

1972 *The Crucifixion* (Guenette)

1975 *Bugs Bunny Superstar* (Larry E. Jackson)

1976 *Challenge of Greatness* (*The Challenge*) (Kline)

1978 *A Woman Called Moses* (Wendkos—for TV)

1979 *The Late Great Planet Earth* (Amram—doc); *The Double McGuffin* (Camp)

1981 *Genocide* (Schwartzman); *The Man Who Saw Tomorrow* (Guenette)

1982 *History of the World, Part One* (Mel Brooks)

1983 *Almonds and Raisins* (Karel)

Films as Director:

1934 *The Hearts of Age* (16mm short) (co-d with Vance, + ro)

1938 *Too Much Johnson* (16mm short) (+ sc, co-pr) (unreleased)

1941 **Citizen Kane** (+ ro as Charles Foster Kane, pr, co-sc)

1942 **The Magnificent Ambersons** (+ ro as narrator, pr, sc); *It's All True* (semi-doc) (co-d with Norman Foster, + co-sc, pr) (not completed—released in 1993 with added footage)

1943 *Journey into Fear* (co-d [uncredited] with Norman Foster, + ro as Colonel Haki, pr, co-sc)

1946 *The Stranger* (+ ro as Franz Kindler/Professor Charles Rankin, co-sc [uncredited])

1948 **The Lady from Shanghai** (+ ro as Michael O'Hara, sc); *Macbeth* (+ title role, pr, sc)

1952 *Othello* (+ title role, pr, sc)

1955 *Mr. Arkadin* (*Confidential Report*) (+ ro as Gregory Arkadin, story, sc, art d, cost); *Don Quixote* (+ ro as himself, co-pr, sc) (not completed)

1956 *Fountain of Youth* (TV pilot) (+ ro as the host)

1958 **Touch of Evil** (+ ro as Hank Quinlan, sc)

1962 **Le Procès** (*The Trial*) (+ ro as Advocate Hastler, sc)

1966 **Campanadas a Medianoche** (*Chimes at Midnight*; *Falstaff*) (+ ro as Sir John Falstaff, sc, cost)

1968 *Une Histoire immortelle* (*The Immortal Story*) (for TV) (+ ro as Mr. Clay, sc)

1969 *The Deep* (+ ro as Russ Brewer, sc) (unreleased)

1970 *The Other Side of the Wind* (+ sc) (not completed)

1975 *F for Fake* (*Vérités et mengsonges*; *About Fakes*; *Nothing but the Truth*) (+ ro as himself, sc) (add'l footage by Reichenbach)

Publications

By WELLES: books—

Everybody's Shakespeare, New York, 1933; revised as *The Mercury Shakespeare*, 1939.

The Trial (script), New York, 1970.

This Is Orson Welles, with Peter Bogdanovich, New York, 1972.

Touch of Evil, edited by Terry Comito, New Brunswick, New Jersey, 1985.

Chimes at Midnight, New Brunswick, New Jersey, 1988.

By WELLES: articles—

The Director in the Theatre Today, Theatre Education League, 1939.

Interview with Francis Koval, in *Sight and Sound* (London), December 1950.

Orson Welles

"The Third Audience," in *Sight and Sound* (London), January/March 1954.

Interviews with Andre Bazin and Charles Bitsch, in *Cahiers du Cinéma* (Paris), June and September 1958.

"Conversation at Oxford," with Derrick Griggs, in *Sight and Sound* (London), Spring 1960.

Interview with Everett Sloane, in *Film* (London), no. 37, 1965.

"A Trip to Don Quixoteland: Conversations with Orson Welles," with Juan Cobos and others, in *Cahiers du Cinema in English* (New York), June 1966.

"Welles and Falstaff," interview with Juan Cobos and others, in *Sight and Sound* (London), Autumn 1966.

"Welles on Falstaff," *Cahiers du Cinéma* (Paris), Summer 1967.

"Heart of Darkness," in *Film Comment* (New York), December 1972.

On WELLES: books—

Fowler, Roy, *Orson Welles: A First Biography*, London, 1946.

MacLiammoir, Micheal, *Put Money in Thy Purse*, London, 1952.

Noble, Peter, *The Fabulous Orson Welles*, London, 1956.

Houseman, John, *Run-Through: A Memoir*, New York, 1972.

France, Richard, *The Theater of Orson Welles*, Lewisburg, Pennsylvania, 1977.

McBride, Joseph, *Orson Welles, Actor and Director*, New York, 1977.

Bazin, Andre, *Orson Welles: A Critical View*, translated by Jonathan Rosenbaum, New York, 1978.

Naremore, James, *The Magic World of Orson Welles*, New York, 1979; rev. ed., Dallas, Texas, 1989.

Carringer, Robert, *The Making of Citizen Kane*, Los Angeles, 1985.

Leaming, Barbara, *Orson Welles: A Biography*, New York, 1985.

Brady, Frank, *Citizen Welles*, New York, 1989.

France, Richard, editor, *Orson Welles: On Shakespeare*, New York, 1990.

Wood, Bret, *Orson Welles: A Bio-Bibliography*, Westport, Connecticut, 1990.

Howard, James, *The Complete Films of Orson Welles*, Secaucus, New Jersey, 1991.

Beja, Morris, editor, *Perspectives on Orson Welles*, New York, 1995.

Callow, Simon, *Orson Welles: The Road to Xanadu*, London, 1995.

Thomson, David, *Rosebud: The Story of Orson Welles*, New York, 1996.

On WELLES: articles—

Lindley, D., "He Has the Stage," in *Colliers* (New York), 29 January 1938.

Maloney, Russell, "Orson Welles," in *New Yorker*, 5 October 1938.

Johnson, Alva, and Fred Smith, "How to Raise a Child," in *Saturday Evening Post* (New York), no. 212, 20 January 1940, 27 January 1940, and 3 February 1940.

"Orson at War," in *Time* (New York), 30 November 1942.

"Actor Turns Columnist," in *Time* (New York), 29 January 1945.

"Welles: Young Man of 1,000 Faces," in *Cue*, 29 June 1946.

Hamburger, P., "Television: Omnibus Presentation of *King Lear*," in *New Yorker*, 31 October 1953.

MacLiammoir, Micheal, "Orson Welles," in *Sight and Sound* (London), July/September 1954.

Harvey, E., "TV Imports," in *Colliers* (New York), 14 October 1955.

"Orson Welles's Lear," in *Newsweek* (New York), 23 January 1956.

Lewis, T., "Theatre: Welles as King Lear," in *America* (New York), 28 January 1956.

Adams, Val, "News of TV and Radio," in *New York Times*, 15 December 1957.

Tynan, Kenneth, "Orson Welles," in *Show* (London), October 1961 and November 1961.

Current Biography 1965, New York, 1965.

Archer, Eugene, "Orson Welles: Boy Genius Turns 50," in *New York Times*, 18 April 1965.

Morgenstern, J., and R. Sokolov, "Falstaff as Orson Welles," in *Newsweek* (New York), 27 March 1967.

Rosenbaum, Jonathan, "The Invisible World of Orson Welles: A First Inventory," in *Sight and Sound* (London), Summer 1968.

McBride, Joseph, "Welles' *Chimes at Midnight*," in *Film Quarterly* (Berkeley), Fall 1969.

McBride, Joseph, "Welles before *Kane*," in *Film Quarterly* (Berkeley), Spring 1970.

Wilson, Richard, "It's Not Quite True," in *Sight and Sound* (London), Autumn 1970.

McBride, Joseph, "First Person Singular," in *Sight and Sound* (London), Winter 1970/71.

Wilson, Richard, "Reply to Higham's It's All True," in *Sight and Sound* (London), Winter 1970/71.

"The Cinema of Orson Welles," program by the National Film Theatre (London), 1972.

Smith, Cecil, "Orson Welles: The Perpetual Who Came to Dinner," in *Los Angeles Times,* 28 November 1972.

Gilling, Ted, interview with George Coulouris, in *Sight and Sound* (London), Summer 1973.

"Orson Welles," Life Award Ceremony Program, American Film Institute, 1975.

"Welles" issue of *Positif* (Paris), March 1975.

McBride, Joseph, "The Other Side of Orson Welles," in *American Film* (Washington, D.C.), July-August 1976.

Smith, Cecil, "Orson Welles on Early TV: Pilot Tried before Its Time," in *Los Angeles Times,* Calendar, 9 August 1981.

McLean, A. M., "Orson Welles and Shakespeare: History and Consciousness in *Chimes at Midnight*," in *Literature/Film Quarterly* (Salisbury, Maryland), no. 3, 1983.

Pells, Richard, "The Radical Stage and the Hollywood Film in the 1930s," in *Radical Visions and American Dreams*, Middletown, Connecticut, 1984.

Belcher, Jerry, obituary in *Los Angeles Times*, 11 October 1985.

McCarthy, Todd, obituary in *Daily Variety* (New York), 11 October 1985.

Obituary in *New York Times*, 11 October 1985.

O'Brien, Geoffrey, "A Touch of Ego," in *The Village Voice* (New York), 15 October 1985.

"Orson Welles's Revolution Is Still in Progress," in *New York Times*, 20 October 1985.

Kauffman, Stanley, obituary in *New Republic* (New York), 11 November 1985.

Rodman, Howard, "The Last Days of Orson Welles," in *American Film* (Washington, D.C.), June 1987.

France, Richard, "Orson Welles' First Film," in *Films in Review* (New York), August/September 1987.

Perlmutter, Ruth, "Working with Welles: An Interview with Henry Jaglom," in *Film Quarterly* (Berkeley), Spring 1988.

Simon, William, editor, Special "Welles" issue of *Persistence of Vision* (New York), no. 7, 1989.

Naremore, James, "The Trial: The FBI vs. Orson Welles," in *Film Comment* (New York), January-February 1991.

McBride, Joseph, "The Lost Kingdom of Orson Welles," in *New York Review of Books*, 13 May 1993.

Combs, Richard, "Burning Masterworks: From *Kane* to *F for Fake*," in *Film Comment* (New York), January-February 1994.

Ross, Alex, "A Dark Genius Haunts the Hollywood He Taunted," in *New York Times*, 21 January 1996.

On WELLES: films—

The Filming of Othello, documentary for television, 1978.

Orson Welles à la Cinemateque (documentary, 1982.

Hollywood Mavericks, documentary, 1990.
The Battle over Citizen Kane, television documentary directed by
　Thomas Lennon and Michael Epstein, 1995.

*　　*　　*

Orson Welles's reputation as a director has overshadowed his work
as an actor. When reviewers do consider Welles's film performances,
their assessments are mixed. Some see Welles as a master of bravura
performances. Others argue that his work consists of behavioristic
clichés that pass for decent acting because of Welles's mellifluous
voice and striking physical presence. Welles's performances are not
always flawless, but what his critics miss is that often Welles does not
aim for naturalism, but instead draws on melodramatic tradition that
uses excess and theatricality to illustrate a film's ethical implications.

Welles's best work is in *Citizen Kane, Jane Eyre, Touch of Evil*, and
Chimes at Midnight, along with *The Third Man* and *Compulsion*,
where his performances dominant the films even though he appears in
only a few scenes. Films such as *Moby Dick* and *A Man for All Seasons*
reveal Welles's unique ability to convey the texts' ethical dilemmas,
for with his naturally dramatic voice and imposing presence, his cameo
performances become pivotal moments in the narrative.

A veteran of the Todd Troupers and weekly unofficial productions
under his directorial control, Welles made his professional acting debut at age 16, and his Broadway debut at age 19. That same year, 1934,
he directed and starred in his first film, played a Kane-like figure in a
piece of agit-prop theater, and began starring in radio programs (e.g.,
The Shadow and *First Person Singular*). In 1937, he played Brutus in
his Mercury production of *Julius Caesar*; the next year he broadcast
the infamous "War of the Worlds."

In 1941, Welles played the title role in *Citizen Kane*. Welles's
carefully designed performance does not aim for psychological realism, but instead conveys the different narrators' conflicting views of
Charles Foster Kane. In Thatcher's sequence, Welles's quick-rhythmed
speech and studied innocence express Thatcher's view that Kane is a
young madman headed for a Faustian bargain. In the Bernstein sequence, Welles's exacting diction and flamboyant gestures convey
Bernstein's fraternal image of Charlie-the-Great. In the next segment, Welles's performance reflects Leland's view that his friend
becomes Kane-the-demagogue: Welles deepens his voice to deliver
Kane's political speech, his stance echoes the image on the poster
that hangs behind him, and as the segment ends, Welles's body is as
immobile as a statue, his voice the booming voice of pitiless authority.
In the concluding sequences, Welles's increasingly expressionistic performance shows us that Kane becomes the hollow shell of his ambition, literally puffed-up with self-importance, Kane is an untethered
dirigible crashing about, then finally an orator reduced to a whisper. In
the films that would follow, Welles revealed his abiding interest in
stylized and highly codified characterizations: he consistently played
strong characters with his left, three-quarter profile to camera, and
weak characters, or strong characters in weak moments, right profile
to camera.

Welles was active on stage, screen, and radio throughout the 1940s.
Jane Eyre was Welles's first film acting assignment for another director, and his dramatic performance enhanced the mood of Brontë's
gothic melodrama. In his own *The Lady from Shanghai*, Welles played
O'Hara with a phony brogue that underscored the film's exploration
of deceit, illusion, and artifice. In his last directorial assignment in
Hollywood for a decade, Welles played the title role in his expressionistic *Macbeth*.

The conventional wisdom is that to secure financing for his own
films, Welles spent the next three decades hamming-it-up in other
people's bad pictures. Yet a review of his performances shows that is
not quite the case. Welles gives a brilliant performance in *The Third*
Man, his careful underplaying effectively conveying Harry Lime's
sinister character. In the mid-fifties, Welles created notable performances for television; for example, in 1953, his performance in the
title role of *King Lear* was a major success.

Some of Welles's best work was to come. His characterizations in
The Long Hot Summer and *Compulsion* are the work of an accomplished actor. His performance in his own *Touch of Evil* is disturbing
and masterful. Welles's performance as Falstaff in *Chimes at Midnight*
is, quite arguably, the best performance of his career. Drawing on his
lifelong study of Faustian figures, Welles gives us a Falstaff who is an
endearing but detestable fool. And like his portrayals of other charming but flawed characters, Welles's performance is enriched by the
conflicting aspects of his own image: egotist, visionary, wastrel, martyr.

An international celebrity from the time he was a young man,
Welles continually subjected his public image to scrutiny: in the
1970s, he appeared regularly on late-night variety shows, in commercials, and in films such as *Catch-22* that present us with caricatures of Welles's celebrity personae. *F for Fake* allowed Welles to
reprise one of his signature roles: the entertaining charlatan. *Someone to Love*, Welles's final appearance on film, provided an apt
conclusion to his unique acting career, for it ends with Welles's on-
camera call to "cut."

—Cynthia Baron

WERNER, Oskar

Nationality: Austrian. **Born:** Oskar Joseph Bschliessmayer in
Vienna, 13 November 1922. **Education:** Attended Realschule,
Vienna. **Family:** Married 1) the actress Elisabeth Kallina, 1946
(divorced 1950), daughter: Eleanore; 2) Anne Power, 1954 (divorced), one son. **Career:** 1940—joined the Burgtheater, Vienna;
1941-45—drafted into the German army, but managed to continue
acting until 1944, then wounded; 1945—resumed acting career at
the Burgtheater: roles in *Le Misanthrope, El mayor encanto amor*,
and *Egmont*; also director; 1947—began regular appearances at the
Salzburg Festival; 1948—film debut in *Der Engel mit der Posaune*;
1951—U.S. film debut in *Decision before Dawn*; stage roles in
Hamlet in Frankfurt, and *Don Carlos, Beckett*, and *Candida* in
Vienna; 1959—founded the Theater Ensemble Oskar Werner;
1961—producer and director at the Innsbruck Festival. **Awards:**
Best Actor, New York Film Critics, for *Ship of Fools*, 1965. **Died:**
In Marburg, Germany, 23 October 1984.

Films as Actor:

1948　*Der Engel mit der Posaune* (Hartl)
1949　*Eroica* (Kolm-Veltée and Hartl) (as Karl)
1950　*Un Sourire dans la tempête* (Chanas)
1951　*Decision before Dawn* (Litvak) (as Happy); *The Angel with*
　　　　the Trumpet (Bushell); *Das gestohlene Jahr* (Fross); *Ruf aus*
　　　　dem Äther (Klaren); *Wunder unserer Tage* (The Wonder Kid;
　　　　Wonder Boy) (Hartl) (as Rudi)
1955　*Der letzte Akt* (Ten Days to Die; The Last Ten Days) (Pabst) (as
　　　　Captain Wuest); *Lola Montès* (Ophüls) (as the Student);
　　　　Spionage (Antel); *Mozart* (The Life and Loves of Mozart)
　　　　(Hartl) (title role)
1961　*Jules et Jim* (Truffaut) (as Jules)
1965　*Ship of Fools* (Kramer) (as Dr. Schumann); *The Spy Who Came*
　　　　In from the Cold (Ritt) (as Fiedler)

Oskar Werner (center) in *Jules et Jim*

1966   *Farenheit 451* (Truffaut) (as Montog)
1968   *Interlude* (Billington) (as Stefan Zelter); *The Shoes of the Fisherman* (Anderson) (as Father David Telemond)
1976   *Voyage of the Damned* (Rosenberg) (as Dr. Kreisler)

Publications

By WERNER: article—

"Mistress Cinema," interview in *Films and Filming* (London), November 1966.

On WERNER: books—

Mazura, Margarethe, *Oskar Werner: Maske, Mythos, Mensch*, Vienna, 1986.
Dachs, Robert, *Oskar Werner: Ein Nachklang*, Munich, 1988.

On WERNER: articles—

Current Biography 1966, New York, 1966.
Obituary in *New York Times*, 24 October 1984.
Obituary in *Revue du Cinéma* (Paris), January 1985.

*   *   *

Oskar Werner once stated that "I don't like films, I only do it for the money. I'm married to the theater, films are only my mistress," so it is not surprising that theater played a considerably larger role in his life than cinema. At 18 he joined the Burgtheater in Vienna, the Austrian equivalent of Britain's Old Vic, and soon made a considerable mark, playing in over 50 productions before being drafted into the army in 1941. After the war he became something of a German stage idol, and also turned his attention to films.

His first major screen role, in *Angel with a Trumpet*, brought him to the notice of Anatole Litvak, and he was hired by Twentieth Century-Fox to play in *Decision before Dawn* as a conscience-stricken, anti-Nazi German prisoner of war who volunteers to spy for the Allies behind enemy lines. But, Hollywood had nothing of interest to offer him after this and he returned to Europe. His *Hamlet* in Frankfurt in 1953 was regarded as one of the great interpretations of the time, and assured Werner a key position in the postwar German theater pantheon. He was sometimes referred to as the Laurence Olivier of the continent, and in 1959 he founded his own theatrical troupe, the Theater Ensemble Oskar Werner.

In 1955 he appeared in, among other films, Ophüls' *Lola Montès* and Pabst's *The Last Ten Days*, but it was not until 1961 that he made the first of the films for which he is best known. This was *Jules et Jim*, which introduced Werner's incredibly boyish good looks and characteristic sense of melancholy to burgeoning "art house" audiences everywhere. Another sensitive, soulful role followed, this time in a Hollywood context, in Stanley Kramer's *Ship of Fools*, where he played a romantically world-weary doctor opposite Simone Signoret. Perhaps concerned at being typecast in sensitive, troubled parts he then took on the role of a hard-line East German Communist in *The Spy Who Came In from the Cold*, in which he was surprisingly convincing. The same year, however, he returned both to Truffaut and to another quietly agonised role as a book-burning fireman who has a change of heart in *Fahrenheit 451*. (Curiously, Truffaut and Werner died within two days of each other.)

Having achieved the status of an international film star, Werner nevertheless made only a few more films—*Interlude*, *The Shoes of the Fisherman*, and *Voyage of the Damned*—none of them especially interesting or really worthy of his talents. He also appeared in an episode of *Columbo*. He is reputed to have turned down more than 200 film parts. The increasing rarity of his film (and, for that matter, theater) performances can perhaps partly be ascribed to his frequent quarrels with film and stage directors, and to the fact that in the last ten years of his life, plagued by alcoholism, he lived the life of a virtual recluse.

—Julian Petley

WEST, Mae

Nationality: American. **Born:** Brooklyn, New York, 17 August 1892. **Education:** Attended Brooklyn public schools to age 13. **Family:** Married the entertainer Frank Wallace, 1911 (divorced 1942). **Career:** Child entertainer: joined Hal Clarendon's stock company, Brooklyn, at age eight; toured with Frank Wallace; 1911—Broadway debut in the revue *A la Broadway and Hello, Paris*; then returned to vaudeville tour with star billing; early 1920s—toured in nightclub act with Harry Richman; 1926—on Broadway in her own play *Sex* (later plays produced include *The Drag*, 1926, *The Wicked Age*, 1927, *Diamond Lil*, 1928 and several revivals, *The Pleasure Man*, 1928, *The Constant Sinner*, 1931, and *Catherine Was Great*, 1944); 1932—film debut in *Night After Night*; contract with Paramount; then a series of popular films in the 1930s for which she often wrote the screenplay; 1954-56—toured with nightclub act; 1955—first of several albums of her songs, *The Fabulous Mae West*. **Died:** In Los Angeles, 22 November 1980.

Films as Actress:

1932 *Night After Night* (Mayo) (as Maudie Triplett)
1933 ***She Done Him Wrong*** (Sherman) (as Lady Lou)
1943 *The Heat's On* (*Tropicana*) (Ratoff) (as Fay Lawrence)
1970 *Myra Breckenridge* (Sarne) (as Leticia Van Allen)
1978 *Sextette* (Ken Hughes) (as Marlo Manners)

Films as Actress and Scriptwriter:

1933 *I'm No Angel* (Ruggles) (as Tira)
1934 *Belle of the Nineties* (McCarey) (as Ruby Carter)
1935 *Goin' to Town* (Alexander Hall) (as Cleo Borden)
1936 *Klondike Annie* (Walsh) (as the Frisco Doll/Rose Carlton); *Go West, Young Man* (Hathaway) (as Mavis Arden)
1938 *Every Day's a Holiday* (A. Edward Sutherland) (as Peaches O'Day/Mademoiselle Fifi)
1940 *My Little Chickadee* (Cline) (as Flower Belle Lee, co-sc)

Publications

By WEST: books—

Babe Gordon (novel), New York, 1930; as *The Constant Sinner*, New York, 1931.
Diamond Lil (novel), New York, 1932; as *She Done Him Wrong*, New York, 1932.
Goodness Had Nothing to Do with It, New York, 1959; rev. ed., New York, 1970.
The Wit and Wisdom of Mae West, edited by Joseph Weintraub, New York, 1967.
On Sex, Health, and ESP, New York, 1975.

By WEST: articles—

"Mae West," interview with W. S. Eyman, in *Take One* (Montreal), January 1974.
"Mae West: The Queen at Home in Hollywood," interview with A. Huston and P. Lester, in *Interview* (New York), December 1974.

On WEST: books—

Rosen, Marjorie, *Popcorn Venus*, New York, 1973.
Tuska, Jon, *The Films of Mae West*, Secaucus, New Jersey, 1973; rev. ed., as *The Complete Films of Mae West*, 1992.
Parish, James Robert, and William T. Leonard, *The Funsters*, New Rochelle, New York, 1979.
Cashin, Fergus, *Mae West: A Biography*, London, 1981.
Eells, George, and Stanley Musgrove, *Mae West*, New York, 1982.
Chandler, Charlotte, *The Ultimate Seduction*, New York, 1984.
Bergman, Carol, *Mae West*, New York, 1988.
Ward, Carol Marie, *Mae West: A Bio-Bibliography*, New York, 1989.
Leonard, Maurice, *Mae West: Empress of Sex*, London, 1991.
Sochen, June, *Mae West: She Who Laughs, Lasts*, Arlington Heights, Illinois, 1992.
Baxt, George, *The Mae West Murder Case* (novel), New York, 1993.
Malachosky, Tim, and James Greene, *Mae West*, California, 1993.
Curry, Ramona, *Too Much of a Good Thing: Mae West as Cultural Icon*, Minneapolis, 1995.
Hamilton, Marybeth, *"When I'm Bad, I'm Better": Mae West, Sex, and American Entertainment*, New York, 1995.
Robertson, Pamela, *Guilty Pleasures: Feminist Camp from Mae West to Madonna*, Durham, North Carolina, 1996.

On WEST: articles—

Troy, William, "Mae West and the Classic Tradition," in *Nation* (New York), 8 November 1933.
Arbus, Diane, "Mae West: Emotion in Motion," in *Show* (Hollywood), January 1965.
Current Biography 1967, New York, 1967.
Christie, George, "Mae West Raps," in *Cosmopolitan* (New York), May 1970.
Braun, Eric, "Doing What Comes Naturally," and "One for the Boys," in *Films and Filming* (London), October and November 1970.
Passek, J.-L., "Hommage: Mae West: Sex transit gloria mundi," in *Cinéma* (Paris), November 1973.
Adair, G., "Go West, Old Mae," in *Film Comment* (New York), May/June 1980.
Obituary in *New York Times*, 23 November 1980.
McCourt, James, obituary in *Film Comment* (New York), January/February 1981.
Kobal, John, "Mae West," in *Films and Filming* (London), September 1983.

*   *   *

Mae West

The strongest breakthrough for sophisticated sexual comedy was made by Mae West. The unabashed woman who takes pleasure in her sexuality and ability to control men with her physical charms was delectably burlesqued in her 1933 work *She Done Him Wrong* and *I'm No Angel*. In these movies she played the gaudy kept woman who enjoyed her position in society. Derived from the stage play *Diamond Lil*, which West wrote for herself in 1928, *She Done Him Wrong* was the weaker of the two films. Nevertheless, the movie had much to offer. West's dialogue was sprinkled with double entendres, usually linked with sex. When asked if she had ever found a man who could make her happy, she replied with her famous drawl, a clenched jaw, and a smile: "Sure. Lots of times." And there were the now well-known maxims, such as, "When women go wrong, men go right after them." As in some of her later films, the total work did not have a strong comic design. An old-fashioned, serious love triangle held every story together. Sprinkled into the melodramas, two songs, "I Wonder Where My Easy Rider's Gone" and "I Like a Man Who Takes His Time," gave West the chance to make further sexual comments and display her talents with the torch song and the blues.

I'm No Angel not only displayed a definite improvement over the *Diamond Lil* adaptation, but also was West's most distinguished contribution to the sophisticated comedy film. Her link with the underworld in *I'm No Angel* was rather melodramatic, but her bed-hopping in high society created a comic framework for the total work. Her characterization of Tira, a carnival dancer, shows a woman who is engaged in the put-down with the relish, if not the zip, of a Groucho Marx. When her boss, played by the daddy of all big deals, Edward Arnold, made a conciliatory gesture by stating, "Tira, I've changed my mind," West cracked, "Does it work any better?" With an aggressiveness seldom exhibited in a woman at that time, she took over her own defense in a trial. *I'm No Angel* was also a showcase for still more of the famous West lines. To her servant she drawled: "Beulah, peel me a grape." To a man, fluttering her eyelashes, she observed, "When I'm good, I'm very good, but when I'm bad [very long pause] I'm better." As a gilded, tainted sage she uttered, "It's not the men in your life that count—it's the life in your men." Most remembered and most often repeated (with variations) was the line: "And don't forget—come up and see me sometime."

In her early 1930s movies, however, West's humor was not merely verbal. It consisted of a provocative walk, a toss of the head or hip, or a glint in the eye. She was a personality comedienne with a particular style of her own. Actually, she never possessed strong acting skills: her delivery was, in fact, monotonous. Yet her slender talent and ample body made her a legend in her time and the height of camp in the 1960s.

Since West's sexual wit was nearly eliminated by the Hays Office in 1934, her subsequent films remain a pale shadow of those early works—especially in the wealth of innuendo. Nevertheless, she still portrayed the shady lady in the 1936 *Klondike Annie*, escaping the law by assuming the role of a religious leader in a booming, bawdy frontier community. Her high-handed tactics to "win souls" remain fresh today because they lampoon a type of religious leader who still exists. Ironically, West would not be able to use her sexual humor again until she appeared in *Myra Breckinridge*. At 78, West was still the femme fatale, uttering bawdier lines than she had been allowed to deliver in the 1930s.

—Donald McCaffrey

WHITAKER, Forest

Nationality: American. **Born:** Longview, Texas, 15 July 1961. **Education:** Attended Pomona College; studied voice and theater at the University of Southern California; attended the Drama School in Ber-

keley, California. **Career:** Early 1980s—acted on the stage in the United States and England; 1982—made screen debut in *Fast Times at Ridgemont High*; 1985—in TV mini-series *North and South*; 1986—in TV mini-series *North and South II*; 1988—had first notable starring role in *Bird*; 1993—made directorial debut with *Strapped*. **Awards:** Best Actor, Cannes Festival, for *Bird*, 1988. **Address:** 6409 Flagmore Place, Los Angeles, CA 90068, U.S.A.

Films as Actor:

1982   *Fast Times at Ridgemont High* (Heckerling) (as Charles Jefferson); *Tag: The Assassination Game* (Castle) (as Gowdy's bodyguard)
1985   *Vision Quest* (Becker) (as Bulldozer)
1986   *Platoon* (Oliver Stone) (as Big Harold); *The Color of Money* (Scorsese) (as Amos)
1987   *Stakeout* (Badham) (as Jack Pismo); *Good Morning, Vietnam* (Levinson) (as Edward Garlick): *Hands of a Stranger* (Elikann—for TV) (as Sergeant Delaney); *Bloodsport* (Arnold) (as Rawlins)
1988   *Bird* (Eastwood) (as Charlie Parker)
1989   *Johnny Handsome* (Walter Hill) (as Dr. Steven Fisher)
1990   *Downtown* (Richard Benjamin) (as Dennis Curren); *Criminal Justice* (Wolk—for TV) (as Jessie Williams)
1991   *A Rage in Harlem* (Duke) (as Jackson)
1992   *Article 99* (Deutch) (as Dr. Sid Handleman); *Consenting Adults* (Pakula) (as David Duttonville); ***The Crying Game*** (Neil Jordan) (as Jody); *Diary of a Hit Man* (London) (as Dekker)
1993   *Bank Robber* (Mead) (as Officer Battle); *Lush Life* (Elias) (as Buddy Chester); *Last Light* (Kiefer Sutherland—for TV) (as Fred Whitmore); *Body Snatchers* (Ferrara) (as Major Collins)
1994   *Blown Away* (Stephen Hopkins) (as Anthony Franklin); *Jason's Lyric* (McHenry) (as Maddog); *Ready to Wear* (*Prêt-a-Porter*) (Altman) (as Cy Bianco); *The Enemy Within* (Darby—for TV) (as Col. Mac Casey)
1995   *Smoke* (Wang) (as Cyrus Cole); *Species* (Donaldson) (as Dan Smithson)
1996   *Phenomenon* (Turteltaub)

Films as Director:

1993   *Strapped* (for TV)
1995   *Waiting to Exhale*

Publications

By WHITAKER: article—

Interview with K. Cook, in *Playboy* (Chicago), March 1992.

On WHITAKER: articles—

Lindsay, Robert, "Living the Part: Young Man with a Sax," in *New York Times Magazine*, 11 September 1988.
Wheaton, Robert, and Martha Southgate, "About People: Forest Whitaker," in *Essence* (New York), October 1988.
"Forest Fire," in *Vanity Fair* (New York), November 1988.
McKinney, Rhoda E., "Forest Whitaker: *Bird* Reborn," in *Ebony* (Chicago), November 1988.
"Films and Jazz: Black Notes," in *Nation* (New York), 12 November 1988

Forest Whitaker in *Bird*

Benedetti, S., "Forest Whitaker," in *Revue du Cinéma* (Paris), November 1991.

Grant, James, "One Quiet Man, One Booming Career," in *Los Angeles Times*, 30 June 1994.

Chambers, Veronica, "The Camera Has 2 Sides," in *New York Times*, 16 August 1995.

"Cinema: His Brilliant Career," in *Advocate* (Los Angeles), 12 December 1995.

*   *   *

Because of his looks—he is round-faced, and on the chubby side—Forest Whitaker never will be mistaken for Denzel Washington or Wesley Snipes, and never will be a leading man. But he is an outstanding character actor, always interesting to watch, and he brings appropriate energy and vitality to all of his films. From the earliest stages of his career, he proved he could more than hold his own opposite strong, charismatic performers. This is exemplified by his appearance with Robin Williams in *Good Morning, Vietnam*. Williams, playing the smart-mouthed, delightfully profane military disc jockey Adrian Cronauer, could have been the entire show. But Whitaker, cast as Cronauer's sidekick, has enough of a presence not to be completely wiped off the screen.

The actor earned major stardom playing jazz legend Charlie Parker in the Clint Eastwood-directed biopic, *Bird*. Whitaker's performance blends seamlessly into Eastwood's story of the legendary, innovative bebop saxophonist Charlie "Yardbird" Parker. His bulky build and wide smile allowed him to physically resemble his subject, and his generous performance added immeasurably to Eastwood's compassionate, lovingly detailed portrait of Parker. Whitaker was to go on to play another jazz musician in *Lush Life*: a trumpeter named Buddy Chester who, unlike Parker, is an obscure session man, and who discovers he has a fatal brain tumor.

Whitaker has played both leading and supporting roles, characters running the gamut from hero to heavy, sweet and soft-spoken to vicious and hard-bitten. He has been a solitary, melancholy cop who has seen too much of the streets (in *Downtown*); an ingenuous mamma's boy who foolishly perceives of himself as the defender of a beautiful woman (in *A Rage in Harlem*); a flamingly gay fashion designer (in *Ready to Wear*); and a hired killer, on his last assignment before retirement, whose victim persuades him to pardon her (in *Diary of a Hitman*). He has played embittered men who are violent and ill-fated (the Vietnam veteran in *Jason's Lyric*), and embittered men who have come to accept their lives and fates (the one-armed gas station owner/guilty father in *Smoke*). In the latter film, Whitaker is at his best in a monologue in which his character reveals how he came to lose his arm. He crashed his car while "filled with spirits," resulting in the death of his beloved. He survived, but not with his body completely intact—a fact which serves as an everyday reminder of what a "mean bastard" he really is.

One of Whitaker's most overlooked performances came in *The Crying Game*, in which he is cast as Jody, a British soldier kidnapped by Irish Republican Army terrorists. Fellow cast-members Stephen Rea, Miranda Richardson, and Jaye Davidson may have earned the headlines, but Whitaker—playing a character who is murdered scant minutes into the story—makes Jody deeply human, effectively conveying the man's innermost fears as he barters for his life.

In 1993, Whitaker made his directorial debut with the made-for-television feature *Strapped*, the devastating account of Diquan (Bokeem Woodbine), an otherwise thoughtful black teen who has grown up in a Brooklyn housing project. He deeply loves his pregnant girlfriend, and is willing to take on the responsibilities of fatherhood. But how can he support a family on the $4.35 an hour he earns as a bicycle messenger? When the pressures of the ghetto begin to close in on him, Diquan feels he must do whatever is necessary to support his family, even if it means marketing illegal firearms and becoming a police stoolie. *Strapped* is an uncompromising portrait of urban decay. Primarily, it works as an exacting example of how government bureaucracy and varying state laws make guns as easy to acquire in America as bubble gum at a corner candy store.

Strapped is a film with which Whitaker should forever be proud. And it was not his sole directorial effort. In 1995, he helmed his first theatrical feature, *Waiting to Exhale*, also a narrative about the African-American experience. Based on the best-selling novel by Terry McMillan, it is the story of four black women who establish a camaraderie while seeking love, esteem, and harmony in their lives.

—Rob Edelman

WHITE, Pearl

Nationality: American. **Born:** Greenridge, Illinois, 4 March 1889. **Family:** Married 1) the actor Victor C. Sutherland, 1907 (divorced 1914); 2) the actor Wallace McCutcheon Jr., 1919 (divorced 1921). **Career:** Stage debut at age of 6 as Little Eva in *Uncle Tom's Cabin*; toured with parents in midwest stock companies; 1902-09—performed with equestrian circus act; 1909—serious riding injury, then secretary at Powers Pictures; 1910—film debut in role requiring horseback riding in *The Life of Buffalo Bill*; then made Westerns under director James Young Deer (total of about 100 one- and two-reelers); 1911—joined Lubin company, making about 20 films; 1912-13—in Universal comedies directed by Joseph Golden; 1913—toured Europe for two months; on return signed by Charles Pathé; 1914—release of first serial, *The Perils of Pauline*; 1915—extraordinary success of *The Exploits of Elaine* established international reputation; 1920—contract with Fox; 1922—appeared at Casino de Paris in acrobatic sketch; suffered injury; attempt to resume making serials: *Plunder* poorly received; retired to France; 1924—last film appearance in 1924 serial made in France. **Died:** At French estate, 4 August 1938.

Films as Actress:

(in one- and two-reelers directed by Joseph Golden—partial listing)

1910 *The Life of Buffalo Bill* (three reels); *The New Magdalene*; *The Maid of Niagara*; *The Yankee Girl*; *Sunshine in Poverty Row*

1910-11 *Tommy Gets His Sister Married*; *Her Photograph*; *The Motor Friend*; *A Summer Flirtation*; *The Hoodoo*; *How Rastus Gets His Turkey*; *Home, Sweet Home*; *His Birthday*; *The Stepsisters*; *The Dressmaker's Bill*; *The Girl Next Room*; *Oh! Such a Night*; *Love's Renunciation*; *Her Little Slipper*; *Mayblossom*

(directed by Donald Mackenzie)

1911 *The Lost Necklace*; *The Unforeseen Complication*; *Angel Out of the Slums*; *For Honor of the Name*; *Helping Him Out*; *Locked Out*; *The Quarrel*

(Westerns directed by James Young Deer)

1911 *The Coward*; *Honoring a Hero*; *Winonah's Vengeance*; *The Flaming Arrow*; *Message of the Arrow*; *For Massa's Sake*; *Love Molds Labor*; *A Daughter of the South*; *The Rival Brother's Patriotism*; *Gun o' Gunga Din*; *Prisoner of the Mohican*; *The Compact*; *The Governor's Double*

1912 (series of about 20 films for Lubin Company, under direction of Joseph Smiley, John Ince, or Wilbert Melville)

(directed by Joseph Golden)

1912-13 *The Chorus Girl*; *A Tangled Marriage*; *The Mind Cure*; *His Wife's Stratagem*; *The Visitor*; *Belle's Beau*; *Heroic Harold*; *Her Kid Sister*; *Pearl's Admirers*; *With Her Rival's Help*; *Accident Insurance*; *Strictly Business*; *That Other Girl*; *A Night in Town*; *Knights and Ladies*; *Who Was the Goat?*; *Lovers Three*; *The Drummer's Notebook*; *Pearl as a Clairvoyant*; *Her Twin Brother*; *The Veiled Lady*; *Our Parents-in-Law*; *Two Lunatics*; *Pearl as a Detective*; *When Love Is Young*; *His Awful Daughter*; *Where Charity Begins*; *Mary's Romance*; *The New Typist*; *A Call from Home*; *Will Power*; *The Girl Reporter*; *Who Is in the Box?*; *An Hour of Terror*; *True Chivalry*; *Muchly Engaged*; *Pearl's Dilemma*; *College Chums*; *The Hallroom Girls*; *The Broken Spell*; *What Papa Got*; *Oh! You Scotch Lassie!*; *A Child Influence*; *Starving for Love*; *Pearl and the Tramp*; *Caught in the Act*; *A Greater Influence*; *His Aunt Emma*; *That Crying Baby*; *Pearl's Hero*; *The Convict's Daughter*; *A Woman's Revenge*; *Girls Will Be Boys*; *The Cabaret Singer*; *Her Secretary*; *Oh! You Pearl!*; *His Rich Uncle*; *Robert's Lesson*; *Willie's Great Scheme*; *Pearl and the Poet*; *Pearl's Mistake*; *The Ring*; *Oh! You Puppy!*; *A Father's Devotion*; *A Grateful Outcast*; *Getting Reuben Back*; *Mr. Sweeney's Masterpiece*; *Lizzie and the Iceman*; *Willie's Disguise*; *Oh! You Mummy!*; *Going Some*; *Her New Hat*; *Pearl and the Burglars*; *Easy Money*; *A Telephone Engagement*; *The Bunch That Failed*; *Cops Is a Business*; *What Pearl's Pearl Did*; *A Lady in Distress*; *The Dancing Craze*; *Her Necklace*; *The Book Agents*; *Some Collectors*; *The Maniac's Desire*; *East Lynne in Bugville*; *The Lady Doctor*; *The Tell Tale Brother*; *The Masher*; *A Girl in Pants*; *Shadowed*

(directed by Donald Mackenzie)

1914 *The Perils of Pauline* (serial); *Detective Swift*; *Ticket of Leave Man*; *The Stolen Birthright*; *The Warning*; *The Phantom Thief*; *The Hand of Destiny*; *The House of Mystery*; *Detective Craig's Coup*; *A Pearl of the Punjab*

1915 *The Exploits of Elaine* (serial); *The New Exploits of Elaine* (serial); *The Romance of Elaine* (serial)

Pearl White

1916 *The Iron Claw* (José and Seitz—serial); *The King's Game* (Seitz); *Annabel's Romance* (Gasnier); *Hazel Kirke* (Gasnier); *Pearl of the Army* (José—serial)
1917 *The Fatal Ring* (Seitz—serial)
1918 *The House of Hate* (Seitz—serial); *The Lightning Raider* (Seitz—serial)
1919 *Black Secret* (Seitz—serial)
1920 *The White Moll* (Millarde); *The Dark Mirror* (Giblyn); *Black Is White* (Giblyn); *The Thief* (Giblyn); *A Virgin Paradise* (Dawley)
1921 *The Mountain Woman* (Giblyn); *Tiger's Cub* (Giblyn and Millarde); *Know Your Men* (Giblyn); *Singing River* (Giblyn)
1922 *Plunder* (Seitz—serial)
1924 *Terreur* (José—serial)

Publications

By WHITE: book—

Just Me (autobiography), New York, 1930.

By WHITE: articles—

"Putting It Over," in *Motion Picture Magazine*, February 1917.
"Why I Like to Work for Uncle Sam," in *Pictures and Picturegoer*, 5 October 1918.

On WHITE: books—

Lahue, Kalton, *Continued Next Week*, Oklahoma, 1964.
Weltmann, Manuel, and Raymond Lee, *Pearl White: The Peerless, Fearless Girl*, South Brunswick, New Jersey, 1969.
Mitry, Jean, *Pearl White*, Paris, 1969.
Barbour, Alan G., *Days of Thrills and Adventures*, New York, 1970.
Stedman, Raymond, *The Serials: Suspense and Drama by Installment*, Norman, Oklahoma, 1971.
Harmon, Jim, and Donald Glut, *The Great Movie Serials: Their Sound and Fury*, New York, 1972.
Barbour, Alan, *Cliffhangers: A Pictorial History of the Motion Picture Serial*, New York, 1977.

On WHITE: articles—

Condon, Mabel, "The Real Perils of Pauline," in *Photoplay* (New York), October 1914.
Eyck, John Ten, "Speaking about Pearls," in *Photoplay* (New York), September 1917.
Smith, Frederick, "A Pearl in the Rough," in *Motion Picture Classic* (Brooklyn), January 1919.
Howe, Herbert, "A Star in Search of Her Soul," in *Photoplay* (New York), June 1923.
Stainton, Walter, "Pearl White in Ithaca," in *Films in Review* (New York), May 1951.
Davies, W. E., "Truth about Pearl White," in *Films in Review* (New York), November 1959, also letter from F. L. Smith in issue for December 1959.
Smith, Frank, "Pearl White and Ruth Roland," in *Films in Review* (New York), December 1960.
Lacassin, Francis, "Les Périls de Justine," and "Pour l'amour d'Elaine," by Robert Florey, in *Cinéma* (Paris), no. 79, 1963.

* * *

No one is more closely associated with the serial genre than Pearl White, and few actresses of the silent era are as well known today. Yet

White was not the first to star in serials, and she was barely adequate as an actress. Rather, White starred in two of the most famous of all serials, *The Perils of Pauline* and *The Exploits of Elaine*, which stand up better in memory than on viewing, and she had such an infectious personality, so full of fun, so lacking in temperament, that audiences could easily relate to her. Certainly her initial popularity owed much to the sponsorship of her serials by the Hearst newspaper chain and to the songs, notably "Poor Pauline," that her serials inspired.

Like all major personalities, she invented much about her life, particularly in her autobiography *Just Me*, creating an image to which the public could relate. It was as a comedienne that White first made her mark on screen, looking rather buxom and saucy, and it was a comic element that lay just under the surface in many of her serials. Unlike her two major competitors, Ruth Roland and Kathlyn Williams, she was both trim and attractive. Although apparently wearing a wig, White's blonde hair added to what today might be described as her sex appeal.

From serials White tried unsuccessfully to move on to features with the William Fox Company, but she was hampered by poor scripts and lackluster direction. She went to live in France, but ill health and added weight put an end to her career. It is worth noting that, despite her fame, she never set foot in California, making virtually all of her films in the New York area.

—Anthony Slide

WIDMARK, Richard

Nationality: American. **Born:** Sunrise, Minnesota, 26 December 1914. **Education:** Attended Princeton High School, Illinois, graduated 1932; Lake Forest College, Illinois, B.A., 1936. **Family:** Married Jean Hazlewood, 1942, daughter: Ann. **Career:** 1936-38—drama instructor, Lake Forest College; 1938—began period of radio acting; entertained servicemen under the auspices of the American Theatre Wing during World War II; 1943—Broadway debut in *Kiss and Tell*, followed by other Broadway plays; 1947—film debut in *Kiss of Death*; contract with 20th Century-Fox; formed production company Heath Productions: produced the film *Time Limit*, 1957; 1972-73—starred in TV series *Madigan*; and in the miniseries *Mr. Horn*, 1979. **Agent:** ICM, 8899 Beverly Boulevard, Los Angeles, CA 90048, U.S.A.

Films as Actor:

1947 *Kiss of Death* (Hathaway) (as Tommy Udo)
1948 *Road House* (Negulesco) (as Jefty Robbins); *The Street with No Name* (Keighley) (as Alec Stiles)
1949 *Yellow Sky* (Wellman) (as Dude); *Down to the Sea in Ships* (Hathaway) (as Dan Lanceford); *Slattery's Hurricane* (De Toth) (title role)
1950 *Night and the City* (Dassin) (as Harry Fabian); *Panic in the Streets* (Kazan) (as Clinton Reed); *No Way Out* (Mankiewicz) (as Ray Biddle)
1951 *The Halls of Montezuma* (Milestone) (as Lt. Anderson); *The Frogmen* (Bacon) (as Lt. Commander John Lawrence)
1952 "The Clarion Calls" ep. of *O. Henry's Full House* (Hathaway) (as Johnny Kernan); *Don't Bother to Knock* (Baker) (as Jed Towers); *Red Skies of Montana* (Newman) (as Cliff Mason); *My Pal Gus* (Parrish) (as Dave Jennings)

1953 *Take the High Ground* (Brooks) (as Sgt. Thomas Ryan); *Destination Gobi* (Wise) (as CPO Sam McHale); *Pickup on South Street* (Fuller) (as Skip McCoy)

1954 *Hell or High Water* (Fuller) (as Adam Jones); *Garden of Evil* (Hathaway) (as Fiske); *Broken Lance* (Dmytryk) (as Ben Devereaux)

1955 *The Cobweb* (Minnelli) (as Dr. McInver); *A Prize of Gold* (Robson) (as Joe Lawrence)

1956 *Backlash* (Sturges) (as Jil Slater); *The Last Wagon* (Daves) (as Todd); *Run for the Sun* (Boulting) (as Mike Latimer)

1957 *Saint Joan* (Preminger) (as Dauphin)

1958 *The Law and Jake Wade* (Sturges) (as Clint Hollister); *The Tunnel of Love* (Kelly) (as Angie Poole)

1959 *The Trap* (*The Baited Trap*) (Panama) (as Ralph Anderson); *Warlock* (Dmytryk) (as Gannon)

1960 *The Alamo* (Wayne) (as Jim Bowie)

1961 *Two Rode Together* (Ford) (as Lt. Jim Gary); *Judgment at Nuremberg* (Kramer) (as Colonel Tad Lawson)

1963 *How the West Was Won* (Ford and others) (as Mike King)

1964 *Cheyenne Autumn* (Ford) (as Captain Thomas Archer); *Flight from Ashiya* (Anderson) (as Colonel Glenn Stevenson); *The Long Ships* (Cardiff) (as Rolfe)

1965 *The Bedford Incident* (Harris) (as Captain Eric Finlander)

1966 *Alvarez Kelly* (Dmytryk) (as Colonel Tom Rossiter)

1967 *The Way West* (McLagen) (as Lije Evans)

1968 *Madigan* (Siegel) (title role); *A Talent for Loving* (Quine)

1969 *Death of a Gunfighter* (Siegel and Totten) (as Marshal Frank Patch)

1970 *The Moonshine War* (Quine) (as Dr. Taulbee)

1971 *Vanished* (Kulik—for TV) (as President Roudebush)

1972 *When the Legends Die* (Miller) (as Red Dillon)

1973 *Madigan: Park Avenue Beat* (March—for TV) (title role); *Brock's Last Case* (Rich—for TV) (as Madigan); *Madigan: The Lisbon Beat* (Sagal—for TV) (title role); *Madigan: The Naples Beat* (Sagal—for TV) (title role)

1974 *Murder on the Orient Express* (Lumet) (as Ratchett)

1975 *The Last Day* (McEveety—for TV)

1976 *To the Devil a Daughter* (Sykes) (as John Verney); *The Sell Out* (Collinson) (as Sam Lucas)

1977 *The Domino Principle* (Kramer) (as Tagge); *Rollercoaster* (Goldstone) (as Hoyt); *Twilight's Last Gleaming* (Aldrich) (as Martin MacKenzie)

1978 *Coma* (Crichton) (as Dr. Harris); *The Swarm* (Irwin Allen) (as General Slater); *Dinero Maldito* (*Il braccio violento della mala*) (Pacheco)

1979 *Bear Island* (Sharp) (as Otto Gerran); *Mr. Horn* (Starrett—for TV)

1980 *All God's Children* (Thorpe—for TV)

1981 *A Whale for the Killing* (Heffron—for TV)

1982 *Hanky Panky* (Poitier) (as Ransom); *National Lampoon's Movie Madness* (Giraldi and Jaglom); *The Final Option* (*Who Dares Wins*) (Sharp) (as U.S. Secretary of State)

1984 *Against All Odds* (Hackford) (as Ben Caxton)

1985 *Blackout* (Hickox)

1986 *The Leopards of Kora* (as narrator)

1987 *A Gathering of Old Men* (Schlöndorff—for TV) (as Mapes)

1988 *Once upon a Texas Train* (*Texas Guns*) (Kennedy—for TV) (as Capt. Oren Hayes)

1989 *Cold Sassy Tree* (Tewkesbury—for TV) (as E. Rucker Blakeslee)

1991 *True Colors* (Ross) (as Sen. James B. Stiles)

Films as Producer:

1957 *Time Limit* (Malden) (+ ro as Colonel William Edwards)

1961 *The Secret Ways* (Karlson) (+ ro as Michael Reynolds)

Publications

By WIDMARK: article—

"Creating without Compromise," in *Films and Filming* (London), October 1961.

On WIDMARK: books—

Hunter, Allen, *Richard Widmark: The Man and His Movies*, New York, 1985.
Holston, Kim, *Richard Widmark: A Bio-Bibliography*, Westport, Connecticut, 1990.

On WIDMARK: articles—

Current Biography 1963, New York, 1963.
Buckley, Michael, in *Films in Review* (New York), April, May, and June/July 1986; see also issue for May 1990.
"Richard Widmark," in *Stars*, March 1992.

*   *   *

Richard Widmark never became a major star, but through the middle part of the twentieth century regularly turned in convincing, workmanlike performances. A genuine product of the American midwest, Widmark strove for a career in show business. He worked at the local Princeton, Illinois, movie house as a high school student so he could see all the films free. At Lake Forest College, outside Chicago, he majored in drama, and after graduation made his way to New York to join a radio drama company. Throughout the late 1930s and the early 1940s Widmark was a fixture on radio, acting in hundreds of programs including *Big Sister*, *Stella Dallas*, *Front Page Farrell*, and *March of Time*. He also regularly took parts on Broadway, but always made no secret of his desire to go to Hollywood.

His chance came at an age (33) when most movie actors had long built up a list of credits. Even so Widmark was able to make a memorable impression in a small part in his very first film. His portrayal as a giggling psychopath in Henry Hathaway's *Kiss of Death* earned him his only nomination for an Academy Award. Widmark then signed a standard seven-year contract with Twentieth Century-Fox, and went on to do his best film work during the 1950s and 1960s. He should best be remembered as a sentimental hoodlum in Sam Fuller's *Pickup on South Street*, and as the tender and understanding hero in John Ford's *Two Rode Together* and *Cheyenne Autumn*.

By the 1970s Widmark had turned his considerable talents to television. For a two-part television movie, *Vanished*, he was nominated for an Emmy, but lost. His lone prime-time series, *Madigan*, based on his film role, did better, lasting two seasons. He ended his career with frequent appearances in television movies and mini-series.

—Douglas Gomery

WIEST, Dianne

Nationality: American. **Born:** Kansas City, Missouri, 28 March 1948. **Education:** Attended University of Maryland; sutdied at the American Ballet, New York City. **Family:** Two adopted daughters: Emily and Lily. **Career:** 1977—on stage in *Ashes*; performed with the New York Shakespeare Festival; toured with the American Shakespeare Company; 1978—on stage directed *Dusa, Fish, Stas and VI*, and *Not about Heroes*, 1985; 1980—theatrical film debut in *It's My Turn*;

1985—first of numerous appearances in Woody Allen movies, in *The Purple Rose of Cairo*. **Awards:** Obie Award, 1983; Academy Awards, Best Supporting Actress, for *Hannah and Her Sisters*, 1986, and *Bullets over Broadway*, 1994. **Agent:** Sam Cohn, ICM, 40 West 57th Street, New York, NY, 10019, U.S.A.

Films as Actress:

1975   *Zalman* (for TV)
1978   *In Our Father's House* (for TV)
1980   *It's My Turn* (Weill) (as Gail)
1982   *The Wall* (Markowitz—for TV); *I'm Dancing as Fast as I Can* (Hofsiss) (as Julie Addison)
1983   *Face of Rage* (Wrye—for TV); *Independence Day* (*Follow Your Dreams*) (Mandel) (as Nancy Morgan)
1984   *Falling in Love* (Grosbard) (as Isabelle); *Footloose* (Ross) (as Vi Moore)
1985   *The Purple Rose of Cairo* (Woody Allen) (as Emma)
1986   *Hannah and Her Sisters* (Woody Allen) (as Holly)
1987   *Bigfoot* (Danny Huston—for TV); *The Lost Boys* (Schumacher) (as Lucy); *Radio Days* (Woody Allen) (as Aunt Bea); *September* (Woody Allen) (as Stephanie)
1988   *Bright Lights, Big City* (Bridges) (as Mother)
1989   *Cookie* (Susan Seidelman) (as Lenore); *Parenthood* (Ron Howard) (as Helen)
1990   *Edward Scissorhands* (Burton) (as Peg Boggs)
1991   *Little Man Tate* (Jodie Foster) (as Dr. Jane Grierson)
1994   *Bullets over Broadway* (Woody Allen) (as Helen Sinclair); *The Scout* (Ritchie) (as Dr. H. Aaron); *Cops and Robbersons* (Ritchie) (as Helen Robberson)
1995   *Drunks* (Peter Cohn)
1996   *Birdcage* (Mike Nichols) (as Louise Keeley)

Publications

By WIEST: article—

"Hannah's Neurotic Sister? That Was Ages Ago," interview with Ellen Pall, in *New York Times*, 9 October 1994.

On WIEST: articles—

Lundgren, H., "Portraet: Dianne Wiest," in *Kosmorama* (Copenhagen), Winter 1986.
Privet, G., in *Images* (Dayton, Ohio), January/February 1991.

*   *   *

"He said I was too off-beat looking"—Holly (Dianne Wiest) after an audition in *Hannah and Her Sisters*.

"You look so beautiful"—Mickey (Woody Allen) to Holly later in the same film.

That Dianne Wiest has never achieved stardom and is constantly relegated to supporting roles reflects not on her but on the limitations of Hollywood cinema: she lacks the credentials required for the female star—credentials not invariably restricted to conventional notions of glamour, but Wiest's idiosyncratic presence is not among them—in a cinema that has always maintained a rigid distinction between "leading" and "character" actors. In Europe, things might well have been different: anyone who saw her in *Independence Day* can readily imagine her playing central roles in, for example, the films of Ingmar

Bergman. Which makes it appropriate that in recent years she has been taken up by Woody Allen, whose films have repeatedly foregrounded his sense of affinity with Bergman, including the desire to develop his own "stock company" of sympathetic, dedicated, and talented actors.

Unfortunately, *Independence Day* continues to represent the peak of her achievement in American cinema. It seems safe to say that the (relatively) few people who have seen that film will never forget her performance, which haunts one long after the film itself has faded: a film in which the subplot, to which Wiest is central, completely overshadows the main plot. There are four crucial scenes, within the progress of which Wiest creates and develops the character of a psychologically and physically abused wife whose background and upbringing have trained her for a life of submission to men:

1. Her abusive husband Les (Cliff de Young), after taunting her with (completely unfounded) allegations of what she will get up to while he is away, plays the "game" ("She likes it") of flicking lighted matches at her. Wiest makes us share Nancy's terror and helplessness; when her brother Jack (David Keith) attempts to intervene, she tells him, at her husband's order, to "mind his own business."

2. Jack visits her in the psychiatric ward of the local hospital, after a suicide attempt. Within a few minutes Wiest traverses a whole emotional gamut, passing from delight in seeing her brother through an initial refusal to discuss her situation, the revelation that she is pregnant again (she already has three children), the desolating expression of a desire never to leave the hospital, to hysterics when Jack tries to reconcile her to the idea of another child.

3. Mary Ann (Kathleen Quinlan), the "liberated" heroine of the film's main plot, visits Nancy (in whom she has become interested) at home while Les is at work. Nancy confides her favorite fantasy: to go to a bar and order a "grasshopper." Mary Ann mixes them, and we watch Nancy begin to thaw and blossom. Les comes home to find his wife slightly tipsy, very happy, and his dinner not prepared; he orders Mary Ann from the house and locks the door on her. As she walks away, Mary Ann sees him, through a window, knock Nancy to the floor and begin to beat her.

4. Jack has beaten Les up in a bar; Les, planning retaliation, forces Nancy, under threat of strangulation and further beating, to phone Jack and invite him round at a certain time. She is then to go to her parents' house and stay there. Instead, Nancy returns home to await his return. She orders vodka and crème de menthe delivered from a local store, then locks the windows, seals the cracks, blows out the jets on the stove, turns the gas on full. As the kitchen fills with gas she mixes herself a grasshopper, and Wiest shows us, heartbreakingly, that she feels at peace for the first time. When Les arrives home, opens the door, sniffs the gas, she smiles at him and strikes a match.

I can think of no other Hollywood actress capable of communicating Nancy's predicament and evolution with such inwardness and intensity. In its subtlety, depth, and commitment the performance is worthy to stand with Ingrid Thulin's finest work for Bergman. There is no higher praise.

Were it not for Woody Allen, Wiest's subsequent career would be the story of largely unrewarding roles in second-rate movies, on which, nevertheless, her presence confers a certain distinction: her anxious, lonely single mother in Ron Howard's glib and simplistic *Parenthood*, for example. *Little Man Tate* (Jodie Foster's debut-film as director) is a particular disappointment, built on a simple-minded opposition between intuitive, uneducated motherhood and the intervention of a highly trained, objective and intelligent, but childless, child specialist: the old "instinct vs. intellect" distinction in fact. The film comes down heavily in favor of the former (embodied by Foster herself) at the expense of the latter, represented by Wiest, who can do little to give her character any complexity, which would complicate Foster's project.

Dianne Wiest (right) with Mia Farrow in *September*

Undoubtedly, being taken up by Woody Allen and firmly installed within his shifting but semipermanent company of collaborators is, within the Hollywood context, the best thing that could have happened to Wiest. Allen has given her, in the five films in which she has so far appeared, not only her best roles since *Independence Day* but roles that extend her range, from the trapped, unfulfilled, and desperate Stephanie of *September* to the hilarious and overwhelming theatrical diva of *Bullets over Broadway*. It is necessary, however, to stress the limitations within which Allen's cinema operates, as they consistently limit what is possible for his actors. He has repeatedly invited comparison with Bergman, a number of his films being clearly modeled on Bergman originals (aside from the more obvious examples, *Another Woman* derives from *Wild Strawberries*, *September* in part from *Autumn Sonata*). The comparison is instructive but never works in Allen's favor: it highlights in fact the essentially neurotic inhibition of his art, for all its distinction—the inability to stretch himself, hence stretch his actors, beyond a certain point, so that *September*, for example, relates as much to the New York theater as to a Bergman film. Part-flourishing but also part-trapped within the Allen universe, Wiest will never become the American Harriet Andersson or Ingrid Thulin.

The achievement, however, is there, and one must be grateful for it. It was deservedly honored with the Best Supporting Actress Oscar for *Hannah and Her Sisters*, though her performance in *September* (generally an inferior work) is the one that most stands out as the most detailed, complex, and touching characterization in the film.

And *Bullets over Broadway*—one of Allen's most perfect and satisfying works because it is content to be a charming and funny *divertissement*—establishes her as a superb comedienne in a role as far removed from that in *Independence Day* as it is possible to imagine.

—Robin Wood

WILDE, Cornel

Nationality: American. **Born:** Cornelius Louis Wilde in New York City, 13 October 1915. **Education:** Attended Townsend Harris High School, New York; studied art in Budapest; attended Columbia University, New York, briefly; College of the City of New York, premed degree; studied acting with Lee Strasberg. **Family:** Married 1) the actress Patricia Knight, 1938 (divorced 1951), one daughter; 2) the actress Jean Wallace, 1951 (divorced 1980), one son. **Career:** 1940—member of the U.S. Olympic training squad in saber; on stage in New York: debut in *Moon over Mulberry Street*, and in Olivier and Leigh's *Romeo and Juliet* on Broadway; film debut in *The Lady with Red Hair*: short contract with Warner Brothers; then contract with 20th Century-Fox; 1945—role in *A Song to Remember* brought national popularity and leading man status; 1955—formed Theodora Productions; first film directed was *Storm Fear*, 1956. **Died:** Of leukemia, in Los Angeles, 16 October 1989.

Cornel Wilde

Films as Actor:

1940   *The Lady with Red Hair* (Bernhardt) (bit role)
1941   **High Sierra** (Walsh); *Kisses for Breakfast* (Seiler) (as Chet Oakley); *The Perfect Snob* (McCarey) (as Mike Lord)
1942   *Right to the Heart* (*Knockout*) (Clemens); *Life Begins at 8:30* (Pichel) (as Robert); *Manila Calling* (Leeds) (as Jeff Bailey)
1943   *Guest in the House* (Brahm); *Wintertime* (Brahm) (as Freddie Austin)
1945   *A Thousand and One Nights* (Green) (as Aladdin); *A Song to Remember* (Vidor) (as Chopin); *Leave Her to Heaven* (Stahl) (as Richard Harland)
1946   *The Bandit of Sherwood Forest* (Sherman) (as Robin Hood); *Centennial Summer* (Preminger) (as Philippe Lascalles)
1947   *Forever Amber* (Preminger) (as Bruce Carlton); *It Had to Be You* (Maté and Hartman) (as George/Johnny Blaine); *Stairway for a Star* (as Jimmy Banks); *The Homestretch* (Humberstone) (as Jock Wallace)
1948   *Road House* (Negulesco) (as Pete Morgan); *The Walls of Jericho* (Stahl) (as Dave Connors)
1949   *Four Days Leave* (Lindtberg) (as Stanley Robin); *Shockproof* (Sirk) (as Griff Marat)
1950   *Two Flags West* (Wise) (as Captain Mark Bradford)
1952   *At Sword's Point* (*Sons of the Musketeers*) (Allen) (as D'Artagnan); *The Greatest Show on Earth* (DeMille) (as Sebastian); *Operation Secret* (Seiler) (as Peter Forrester); *California Conquest* (Landers) (as Don Arturo Bordega)
1953   *Saadia* (Lewin) (as Si Lahssen); *Treasure of the Golden Condor* (Daves) (as Jean-Paul); *Main Street to Broadway* (Garnett) (as himself); *Star of India* (Lewin) (as Pierre St. Laurent)
1954   *Passion* (Dwan) (as Jean Obregon); *Woman's World* (Negulesco) (as Bill Baxter)
1955   *The Scarlet Coat* (Sturges) (as Major John Bolton)
1956   *Hot Blood* (Ray) (as Stephen Torino)
1957   *Omar Khayyam* (Dieterle) (title role); *Beyond Mombasa* (Marshall) (as Matt Campbell)
1959   *Edge of Eternity* (Siegel) (as Lee Martin)
1962   *Constantine the Great* (*Constantine and the Cross*) (De Felice) (title role)
1969   *The Comic* (Reiner and Ruben) (as Frank Powers)
1971   *Gargoyles* (Norton—for TV) (as Mercer Boley)
1978   *The Norseman* (Pierce) (as Raynar)
1979   *The Fifth Musketeer* (Annakin) (as D'Artagnan, + co-sc)
1985   *Flesh and Bullets* (Tobalina)

Films as Producer:

1955   *The Big Combo* (Lewis) (+ ro as Diamond)
1970   *No Blade of Grass* (+ d, ro as narrator)
1975   *Shark's Treasure* (+ d, sc, ro as Jim)

Films as Director:

1956   *Storm Fear* (+ ro as Charlie); *The Devil's Hairpin* (+ ro as Nick Jargin)
1958   *Maracaibo* (+ ro as Bic Scott)
1963   *Lancelot and Guinevere* (*Sword of Lancelot*) (+ ro as Lancelot)
1966   *The Naked Prey* (+ title role)
1967   *Beach Red* (+ ro as Captain MacDonald)

Publications

By WILDE: articles—

"Survival!," interview in *Films and Filming* (London), October 1970.
Interview in *Film Reader* (Evanston, Illinois), no. 2, January 1977.

On WILDE: books—

Parish, James Robert, and Don E. Stanke, *The Swashbucklers*, New Rochelle, New York, 1976.
Richards, Jeffrey, *Swordsmen of the Screen: From Douglas Fairbanks to Michael York*, London, 1977.

On WILDE: articles—

Coen, John, "Producer-Director Cornel Wilde," in *Film Comment* (New York), spring 1970.
Photoplay (London), February 1981.
Obituary in *Variety* (New York), 18 October 1989.
Krohn, B., "Cornel Wilde, cinéaste," in *Cahiers du Cinéma* (Paris), December 1989.

*   *   *

In spite of an early Academy Award nomination for best actor in *A Song to Remember*, Cornel Wilde has been remembered as a reliable masculine presence in a series of half-remembered films. Occasionally, as in DeMille's *The Greatest Show on Earth*, Wilde stood out. His vain trapeze artist who sees the light was a commentary on some of his earlier swashbuckling roles.

As an actor-director-producer, however, Cornel Wilde deserves a vote as the most neglected creator in film of the last quarter of a century. Wilde directed eight films, starring in all but one. He began his career as an independent producer with *The Big Combo* in 1955. In all of the films he controlled, Wilde's character had to face extreme natural and physical danger, and prove himself equal to them or be destroyed. As director and actor Wilde always chose to shoot on location, to experience the danger himself. On more than one occasion, Wilde, a former collegiate fencer, risked death to get a shot.

Wilde's commitment was so complete that *Shark's Treasure* may rank as one of the most dangerous movies ever made. During the filming, on a small island in the Caribbean, Wilde and his crew actually battled sharks in single takes with no help from the magic of editing. In another sequence, the cast has to make its way through surf which can best be described as terrifying. As in his other films, Wilde clearly tests himself and his cast as he does his fictional characters.

In *The Naked Prey* Wilde's concept of individuality, survival, and loyalty is clearly evident. The film contains only a few lines of English dialogue. It is virtually a silent tour de force for Wilde. The tactile element in *Naked Prey* is, perhaps, one of the most singular features. Death and torture are graphic, nightmarishly so. The natives—initially seen as loathesomely barbaric—club, bake, stab, and torment their victims. Wilde, running naked through the jungle, tastes a plant, eats a snake, tumbles down a rocky waterfall, dances wildly in a brush fire. One by one, his pursuers catch him, and fall in individual and personal combat. As they pursue and die, mourn and argue, fight and weep, they become personalized and human for the viewer. The question, "What is a villain?," is made uncertain, as it is when dealing with the Japanese in *Beach Red*, the murderous young man in *No Blade of Grass*, and Lobo in *Shark's Treasure*.

—Stuart M. Kaminsky

WILDER, Gene

Nationality: American. **Born:** Jerome Silberman in Milwaukee, Wisconsin, 11 June 1935. **Education:** Attended Black-Foxe Military Institute, Los Angeles; Washington High School, Milwaukee, graduated 1951; studied acting with Herman Gottlieb in Milwaukee; University of Iowa, Iowa City, B.A. 1955; Bristol Old Vic Theatre School, England 1955; Herbert Berghof Studio, New York; Actors Studio, New York, 1961. **Military Service:** Served in the U.S. Army at the neuropsychiatric ward of the Valley Forge Hospital, Pennsylvania, 1956-58. **Family:** Married 1) the actress Mary Mercier, 1960 (divorced), adopted daughter: Katharine Anastasia; 2) Mary Joan Schutz, 1967 (divorced 1974); 3) the actress Gilda Radner, 1984 (died 1989); 4) Karen Boyer, 1991. **Career:** 1961—stage debut in *Roots*, New York: later roles in *Mother Courage and Her Children*, 1963, *One Flew over the Cuckoo's Nest*, 1963, and *Luv*, 1966; 1967—film debut in *Bonnie and Clyde*; 1975—directed first film, *The Adventures of Sherlock Holmes' Smarter Brother*; 1994-95—in TV series *Something Wilder*. **Address:** c/o Pal-Mel Productions, 1511 Sawtelle Boulevard, Suite 155, Los Angeles, CA 90025, U.S.A.

Films as Actor:

1967   *Bonnie and Clyde* (Arthur Penn) (as Eugene Grizzard, undertaker)
1968   *The Producers* (Mel Brooks) (as Leo Bloom)
1970   *Quackser Fortune Has a Cousin in the Bronx* (Hussein) (title role); *Start the Revolution without Me* (Yorkin) (as Claude/Philippe)
1971   *Willy Wonka and the Chocolate Factory* (Stuart) (title role)
1972   *Everything You Always Wanted to Know about Sex but Were Afraid to Ask* (Woody Allen) (as Dr. Ross); *Scarecrow* (Schatzberg)
1974   *Thursday's Games* (Moore—for TV, produced in 1971); *Blazing Saddles* (Mel Brooks) (as Jim: The Waco Kid); *The Little Prince* (Donen) (as the Fox); *Rhinoceros* (O'Horgan) (as Stanley); *Young Frankenstein* (Mel Brooks) (title role, + co-sc)
1976   *Silver Streak* (Hiller) (as George Caldwell)
1979   *The Frisco Kid* (Aldrich) (as Avram)
1980   *Stir Crazy* (Poitier) (as Skip Donahue)
1982   *Hanky Panky* (Poitier) (as Michael Jordon)
1989   *See No Evil, Hear No Evil* (Hiller) (as Dave Lyons, + co-sc)
1990   *Funny about Love* (Nimoy) (as Duffy Bergman)
1991   *Another You* (Phillips) (as George/Abe Fielding)

Films as Actor, Director, and Scriptwriter:

1975   *The Adventures of Sherlock Holmes' Smarter Brother* (as Sigerson Holmes)
1977   *The World's Greatest Lover* (as Rudolph Valentino)
1981   "Skippy" ep. of *Sunday Lovers* (*Les Seducteurs*) (title role)
1984   *The Woman in Red* (as Teddy Pierce)
1986   *Haunted Honeymoon* (as Larry Abbot)

Publications

By WILDER: articles—

Interview with R. Appelbaum, in *Films* (London), July 1981.
"Why Did Gilda Die?," in *People Weekly* (New York), 3 June 1991.

On WILDER: articles—

Current Biography 1978, New York, 1978.
Swertlow, Frank, "Gene & Gilda," in *TV Guide* (Radnor, Pennsylvania), 4 September 1993.

* * *

Both the modest success and the larger failure of Gene Wilder's film career must be traced to the contradictory images of masculinity which the American public has demanded of its movie industry in the last 20 years. On the one hand, Wilder's unthreatening sensitivity, his lack of strong sex appeal and charisma suit a public taste for more androgynous (or perhaps prepubescent) masculine figures. On the other hand, generally organized around idealized romantic fantasy, film narratives only with difficulty find a place for sensitized, androgynous males (unless of course, such a protagonist, such as Arnold Schwarzenegger in *Twins*, can embody a humorously unstable mixture of power and harmlessness).

Wilder's ordinary looks, unmanageable hair, and underdeveloped body make such impersonations impossible for him. This inability is ironically most evident in a film Wilder not only starred in but directed: *The Woman in Red*. The production belongs to a subgenre that attained a good deal of popularity in the 1970s and 1980s: the male midlife crisis romance/comedy. Though a partial critical success, the film was a commercial failure for a number of reasons, including its inability to combine humorous and serious approaches to infidelity and marital dissatisfaction. More important, however, Wilder could not project the sexual energy and despair needed to motor the plot; his character's obsession lacks a romantic intensity that can be sustained.

Woody Allen makes better use of Wilder's limitations in a minor role: that of the general practitioner who falls in love with a sheep in *Everything You Always Wanted to Know about Sex but Were Afraid to Ask*. Here Wilder's ordinariness and desire for comfortable routine make the joke work: the doctor's sodomy is hopelessly absurd. Successful characterizations for Mel Brooks depend on similar ironic contrasts. As the Waco Kid in *Blazing Saddles*, Wilder is the antithesis of the coolly masculine gunslinger; his draw is so fast no human eye can follow it (and that is because he does not really draw at all). *Young Frankenstein* and *The Adventures of Sherlock Holmes' Smarter Brother* both offer Wilder as a junior, hungrier version of a more famous and accomplished relative: the first film works better than the second because its ensemble cast prevents a focus on Wilder's one-dimensional protagonist (*Sherlock*, though a Brooks-inspired parody/pastiche, was directed by Wilder himself).

Sharing the narrative accounts for Wilder's success in two films where he co-starred with Richard Pryor, *Stir Crazy* and *See No Evil, Hear No Evil*. In the former of these, Wilder's Skip Donahue is a restless idealist whose best friend (Pryor) is more streetwise. Sent to prison by mistake, Pryor convinces Wilder that he must "be bad" in order to survive, but Wilder defeats the conventionality of this wisdom by finding other conversions, the sensitive songster inside a huge fellow inmate, former terror of the institution. In the latter film Wilder's deaf character becomes allied with Pryor's blind man: at first full of self-pity, alienated from others, Wilder's character becomes sensitized and benevolent. The commercially successful *Silver Streak* is much the same, featuring a conversion to action and engagement, though this thriller lacks the romantic intensity of its obvious model, Hitchcock's *North by Northwest*.

Wilder's androgynous character suits him well for *Willy Wonka and the Chocolate Factory*; he does an interesting and similar turn as the Fox in *The Little Prince*. Given a religious and political inflection, however, this persona can be put to unusually effective use. In contrast to his other roles (with the exception of the highly anxious and hysterical Leo Bloom in *The Producers*), which do not utilize his Jewishness, Wilder's Avram in *The Frisco Kid* is a rabbi, fresh from yeshiva in Poland, who emigrates to San Francisco to pastor a new congregation. Surviving a series of catastrophes, Avram meets up with a good/bad cowboy (played by Harrison Ford), from whom he learns about the gentile world. Avram falls into secularity, abandoning for a time the black coat and hat of the shtetl, though he is eventually reclaimed for an assimilationist form of Judaism. This extraordinary, if somewhat Capraesque film brings out the philosophical idealism implicit in the sensitivity and friendliness of the Wilder persona. The more recent *Funny about Love* elicits these qualities from the Wilder character's relationship with a young child.

Perhaps his most affecting performance, however, works yet another variation on androgyny: the genuine naïf, the mental defective whose goodness is reflexive, unalloyed, and presexual. As the title character in *Quackser Fortune Has a Cousin in the Bronx*, Wilder plays a man who takes continuing joy in the only job life has made available to him: collecting horse manure from the streets of Dublin. Like Avram, Quackser accepts the world as he finds it and loves other people for what he finds in them. Other people, however, do not measure up to his standards of loving kindness. In the larger context of the contemporary American cinema, however, these roles offer exceptional (and thus not widely appealing) versions of masculine strength and virtue. His undoubted success in them therefore could not make Wilder a star.

—R. Barton Palmer, updated by Linda J. Stewart

WILLIAMS, Esther

Nationality: American. **Born:** Esther Jane Williams in Inglewood, California, 8 August 1923. **Education:** Attended public schools in Los Angeles; Los Angeles City College, University of Southern California, Los Angeles. **Family:** Married 1) Leonard Kovner, 1940 (divorced 1944); 2) the entertainer Ben Gage, 1945 (divorced 1959), sons: Benjamin and Kimball, daughter: Susan; 3) the actor Fernando Lamas, 1967 (died 1982). **Career:** Member of the Los Angeles Athletic Club: set U.S. swimming records in 1939, and on Olympic training team; worked as a model at I. Magnin's department store, Los Angeles; 1940—starred with Johnny Weissmuller in Billy Rose's Aquacade, San Francisco; 1942—contract with MGM: film debut in *Andy Hardy's Double Life*; 1944—starring role in *Bathing Beauty*; then a series of swimming musicals until the mid-1950s; 1984—returned from 22-year retirement to host synchronized swimming events at Olympic Games; made instructional videotape on infant water safety; 1987—christened the Grand Hotel Pool at the Grand Hotel on Mackinac Island, Michigan, in honor of their 100th Anniversary and to acknowledge *This Time for Keeps* (1947) which was shot there on location.

Films as Actress:

1942   *Andy Hardy's Double Life* (Seitz) (as Sheila Brooks)
1943   *A Guy Named Joe* (Fleming) (as Ellen Bright)
1944   *Bathing Beauty* (Sidney) (as Caroline Brooks)
1945   *Thrill of a Romance* (Thorpe) (as Cynthia Glenn)
1946   *Ziegfeld Follies* (Minnelli) (as herself); *The Hoodlum Saint* (Taurog) (as Kay Lorrison); *Easy to Wed* (Buzzell) (as Connie Allenbury); *Till the Clouds Roll By* (Whorf) (as herself)
1947   *Fiesta* (Thorpe) (as Maria Morales); *This Time for Keeps* (Thorpe) (as Nora Cambaretti)
1948   *On an Island with You* (Thorpe) (as Rosalind Reynolds)
1949   *Take Me Out to the Ball Game* (Berkeley) (as K. C. Higgins); *Neptune's Daughter* (Buzzell) (as Eve Barrett)
1950   *Duchess of Idaho* (Leonard) (as Christine Riverton Duncan); *Pagan Love Song* (Alton) (as Mimi Bennett)
1951   *Texas Carnival* (Walters) (as Debbie Telford); *Callaway Went Thataway* (*The Star Said No*) (Panama and Frank) (as herself)
1952   *Skirts Ahoy!* (Lanfield) (as Whitney Young); *Million Dollar Mermaid* (Le Roy) (as Annette Kellerman, older)
1953   *Dangerous When Wet* (Walters) (as Katy Higgins); *Easy to Love* (Walters) (as Julie Hallerton)
1955   *Jupiter's Darling* (Sidney) (as Amytis)
1956   *The Unguarded Moment* (Keller) (as Lois Canway)
1958   *Raw Wind in Eden* (Richard Wilson) (as Laura)
1961   *The Big Show* (James B. Clark) (as Hillary Allen); *La Fuente magica* (*The Magic Fountain*) (Lamas)
1994   *That's Entertainment! III* (Friedgen and Sheridan—compilation) (as host)

Publications

By WILLIAMS: book—

Get in the Swim with Esther Williams, New York, 1957.

On WILLIAMS: book—

Parish, James Robert, and Don E. Stanke, *The Forties Gals*, Westport, Connecticut, 1980.

On WILLIAMS: articles—

Current Biography 1955, New York, 1955.
Ecran (Paris), May 1978.

*   *   *

Esther Williams's rise as a star at MGM was neither unique nor surprising, but carefully orchestrated. A number of factors set the stage for her enormous popularity. A bona fide AAU swimming champion, she was to represent the United States at the 1940 Summer Olympic Games in Helsinki, but World War II canceled the games. Elaborately staged aquatic shows were in vogue during the late 1930s and early 1940s. The cover of *Variety* (19 July 1944) featured an audition call for swimmers claiming a "mermaid shortage." Billy Rose staged two of his Aquacades back to back, one at the New York World's Fair in 1939 and another at San Francisco's Golden Gate International Exposition in 1940. Williams began her professional career in Rose's San Francisco Aquacade, swimming with Johnny Weissmuller and Gertrude Ederle. Annette Kellerman, the Australian swimmer and "pioneer" of the one-piece bathing suit, made a number of films in Hollywood in the 1910s. Eleanor Holm, three-time member of the U.S. Olympic Swim Team and gold-medal winner, signed a contract with Warner Brothers in 1932. Twentieth Century-Fox demonstrated with Sonja Henie that a studio could transform an athletically talented woman into a box-office phenomenon. With such precedents established, MGM assumed it could easily transform Williams into a star.

The beginning of her tenure at MGM slowly developed Williams's image. She first appeared in *Andy Hardy's Double Life*, one of the series of films known as debut showcases for contract starlets. She became a popular GI pin-up and played a USO hostess in one scene in *A Guy Named Joe*. A year later, Williams starred in her first vehicle, *Bathing Beauty*. Essentially structured as a revue or variety show, it featured a plethora of well-known and very popular entertainers of the 1940s (including Red Skelton, Xavier Cugat, Harry James, Helen Forrest, and Ethel Smith) as insurance for the large-scale testing of her persona on the public. The film's climax featured an elaborate water ballet with Williams swimming amidst water fountains, columns of fire, and a troupe of swimmers. She became a sensation—earning approximately $80-90 million for MGM between 1944-55; appearing

Esther Williams

on 15 fan-magazine covers a year (more than any other star); being ranked in 1949 as the number eight moneymaker in Hollywood and the biggest female star after Betty Grable; and winning such appellations as "Queen of the Surf," "Hollywood's Mermaid," "Water Queen of the World," and most curiously, a "prima swimeuse." Each MGM film functioned as a showcase for her swimming prowess; and each film outdid the previous in opulence, especially when Busby Berkeley directed her performance sequences. In *Million Dollar Mermaid*, Williams introduces the finale by leading a phalanx of swimmers through the red smoke of a volcano on white swings. In *Easy to Love*, she leads a battery of water skiers through their paces at Cypress Gardens. In *Dangerous When Wet*, she swims with Hanna/Barbera's animated Tom & Jerry.

Swimming obviously served as the focal point of Williams's films, but it was not always the central or only feature. Her single water performances in *Fiesta*, *Take Me Out to the Ball Game*, *Pagan Love Song*, and *Texas Carnival* seemed included only to fulfill audience expectations. Yet if Williams did not swim at all, as she tried in the dramatic roles near the end of her career, audiences failed to respond favorably. Consequently, her films for MGM adhered to the musical genre's dictates of romantic comedy and blurred through

similarity. Even the titles become hard to differentiate: *Easy to Wed* or *Easy to Love*, *Neptune's Daughter* or *Jupiter's Darling*. (To complicate matters even more, Williams portrayed Annette Kellerman in *Million Dollar Mermaid* and both starred in a film entitled *Neptune's Daughter*.) She most frequently portrayed a strong woman of determination and independent means who ultimately capitulates to the wishes of the man she loves. The most perverse example of this formula occurs in *Million Dollar Mermaid*, when her dominant position must be undercut by an accident that paralyzes her before the male lead can propose marriage. Williams retired from Hollywood after her marriage to Fernando Lamas; she returned to the public after his death. The parallel between her private life and her film roles strikes a curious note of resemblance.

Like Carmen Miranda, Williams seems enshrined as an icon of the Golden Days of Hollywood. Like Miranda, her image centers around a novel performance style. Like Miranda, Williams never fully broke the mold the studio system constructed for her.

—Greg S. Faller

WILLIAMS, Robin

Nationality: American. **Born:** Chicago, Illinois, 21 July 1952. **Education:** Attended Marin College; Claremont Men's College; Juilliard School of Music and Drama. **Family:** Married 1) Valerie Velardi, 1978 (divorced), son: Zachary; 2) Marsha Garces, 1989, children: Cody and Zelda. **Career:** 1970s—cabaret performer in San Francisco and Los Angeles; 1978-82—in TV series *Mork and Mindy*; 1980—film debut in *Popeye*; 1986—recorded stage show in *Robin Williams at the Met.* **Agent:** Carol Bodie, c/o Creative Artists Agency, 9830 Wilshire Boulevard, Beverly Hills, CA 90212, U.S.A.

Films as Actor:

1980   *Popeye* (Altman) (title role)
1982   *The World According to Garp* (George Roy Hill) (as Garp)
1983   *The Survivors* (Ritchie) (as Donald Quinelle)
1984   *Moscow on the Hudson* (Mazursky) (as Vladimir Ivanoff)
1986   *The Best of Times* (Spottiswoode) (as Jack Dundee); *Club Paradise* (Ramis) (as Jack Minoker); *Seize the Day* (Cook—for TV) (as Tommy Wilhelm)
1987   *Good Morning, Vietnam* (Levinson) (as Adrian Cronauer); *Dear America: Letters Home from Vietnam* (Couturie—doc for TV)
1989   *Dead Poets Society* (Weir) (as John Keating); *The Adventures of Baron Munchausen* (Gilliam) (as King of the Moon)
1990   *Cadillac Man* (Donaldson) (as Joey O'Brien); *Awakenings* (Penny Marshall) (as Dr. Malcolm Sayer)
1991   *Dead Again* (Branagh) (as Dr. Cozy Carlisle); *The Fisher King* (Gilliam) (as Parry); *Hook* (Spielberg) (as Peter Pan)
1992   *Toys* (Levinson) (as Leslie Zevo); *Shakes the Clown* (Goldthwait) (as Mime Jerry); *FernGully: The Last Rainforest* (Kroyer—animation) (as voice of Batty Koda); *Aladdin* (Musker and Clements—animation) (as voice of Genie)
1993   *Mrs. Doubtfire* (Columbus) (as Daniel Hillard/Mrs. Iphegenia Doubtfire, + co-pr)
1994   *Being Human* (Forsyth) (as Hector); *The Road to Wellville* (Alan Parker); *In Search of Dr. Seuss* (Paterson) (as the Father)
1995   *Jumanji* (Johnston) (as Alan Parrish); *Nine Months* (Columbus) (as Dr. Kosevich); *To Wong Foo, Thanks for Everything! Julie Newmar* (Kidron) (as John Jacob Jingleheimer Schmidt)
1996   *The Birdcage* (Mike Nichols) (as Armand Goldman); *Jack* (Coppola) (title role); *Hamlet* (Branagh) (as Osric); *The Secret Agent* (Hampton) (as the Professor)

Publications

By WILLIAMS: articles—

Interview in *Interview* (New York), August 1986.
Interview with B. Lewis, in *Films and Filming* (London), September 1988.
Interview with Lisa Grunwald, in *Esquire* (New York), June 1989.
"The Hairiest Man in Hollywood," interview with Frank Sanello, in *Empire* (London), December 1991.
Interview in *Playboy* (Chicago), January 1992.

On WILLIAMS: books—

Moore, Mary Ellen, *Robin Williams*, New York, 1979.
Allen, Steve, *Funny People*, New York, 1981.
Robin-Tani, Marianne, *Robin Williams*, New York, 1988.

On WILLIAMS: articles—

Current Biography 1979, New York, 1979.
Ansen, David, "King of Comedy," in *Newsweek* (New York), 7 July 1986.
Time Out (London), 17 August 1988.
"Actor: On the Job with Robin Williams," in *Life* (New York), Spring 1989.
Chevallier, J., "Protéiforme Robin Williams," in *Revue du Cinéma* (Paris), January 1990.
Lurie, Rod, "Motor Mouth," in *Empire* (London), October 1990.
Morgenstern, Joe, "Robin Williams: More than a Shtick Figure," in *New York Times Magazine*, 11 November 1990.
Giles, Jeff, and Mark Seliger, "Robin Williams: Fears of a Clown," in *Rolling Stone* (New York), 21 February 1991.
Ross, Lillian, "Mr. and Mrs. Williams," in *New Yorker*, 20 September 1993.
Kornbluth, Jesse, "Robin Williams's Change of Life," in *New York*, 22 November 1993.

*   *   *

Buried under makeup as *Popeye* or dragging the literary fantasy apparatus of *The World According to Garp*, Robin Williams failed to make his mark in his first two movies. It took Michael Ritchie's messy contemporary comedy *The Survivors* to set loose the manic power of his stand-up persona. Williams's ability to create a character as it disintegrates makes his Donald, a man who tries to prepare for urban chaos by joining a survivalist camp, a wild original. Williams can assert his star personality and stay in character even while functioning as the most free-swinging element in very knockabout farce. The outlandishly thin-skinned Donald shows Williams in his most antic mode. This is also how he played Jack Dundee in *The Best of Times*, a man who cannot live down having blown his small-town high school football team's final game. Manipulating the old team into replaying the game enables him to get past it—he has to get much crazier before he can calm down. Similarly, as Parry in Terry Gilliam's *Fisher King* we first see Williams talking to "the little people" in conversational switches so fast he seems as much tic as man, and then learn how he became homeless and admittedly, cheerfully psychotic, and how he thinks he can recover. He sends co-star Jeff Bridges—as a burnt-out talk show DJ inadvertently responsible for the death of Williams's wife—on a quest for the Holy Grail which manages to reintegrate them both. If *Fisher King* is not cloying that is largely because of the extended conversations among the four leads. Williams pairs off with an equally whacked-out Amanda Plummer, and romantic comedy never threw screwier balls. These three performances of Williams's cohere wonderfully but are not for people hung up on gradual transitions.

But he can do shading, too. He remains himself while acting in a naturalistic vein in Paul Mazursky's *Moscow on the Hudson*, playing a Russian saxophonist who defects in Bloomingdale's, and in *Dead Poets Society* as a prep-school teacher receiving students in his cramped quarters. Williams can be precious, but he is almost always earthy, with an amazingly unforced broadness of spirit. And he is gone bare-assed in his movies surprisingly often, unthinkable in someone like Danny Kaye. Williams is both freakier and warmer than most big comedy stars—freakier *because* he fires from a solidly realistic launching pad.

The other side of his performance in *Dead Poets Society* is, of course, the stand-up, which he first played as the DJ in *Good Morning, Vietnam*. These pictures give him audiences for his motormouth outbursts within the stories, and then attach our feelings for Williams the entertainer to paltry melodramas in which his characters try to save young boys. Williams as cutup, as opposed to Williams's characters who are cutups, comes across best in *Aladdin* in which he improvised as the voice of the Genie, leaving the animators to keep up. He made

Robin Williams in *Good Morning Vietnam*

the comedy play at five times the speed of any other Disney cartoon feature.

Probably because of Williams's unthreatening directness, several of his pictures function as baby-sitters—*Hook, Toys, Mrs. Doubtfire, Jumanji.* Even as a negligent father or a bitter man, as in *Hook* and *Jumanji,* the scripts make him unpleasant only to redeem him. And Williams is not someone who needs help being likable. *Mrs. Doubtfire* is the most successful of these vehicles because we can see that Daniel, who loses his wife and custody of their children because he cannot assume adult responsibility, really *is* the loose cannon his ex-wife complains of. Even the way he thwarts her, by getting himself hired in

drag as his children's nanny, seems more crazy than touching. This is hilariously clear whenever Williams as *Mrs. Doubtfire* cannot hold "her" tongue around the ex-wife's new boyfriend. In the climactic restaurant scene Daniel sprints from a table where he is supposed to be in drag, to one where he is not, but has so many drinks he loses track. When Daniel in drag snickers that "she" has "to piss like a racehorse," Williams adds burlesque pungency for the adults of all ages in the helpless audience.

As a middle-ground variation Williams can play the relative straight man—superbly to Tim Robbins's deranged husband holding Williams's philandering car salesman hostage in *Cadillac Man,* and less effectively to Nathan Lane as his drag queen "wife" in *The Birdcage*, a remake of *La Cage aux folles*. *The Birdcage* feels like something left onshore by a receding tide, but Williams plays it honest, unself-consciously adopting gay mannerisms. As a comedian Williams is commercial in the best sense and neither cynical or lazy. He has taken on a wide range of projects and varied his approach, letting co-star Bonnie Hunt in *Jumanji* provide the laugh-getting commentary on the action that we expect from Williams, or taking the less flamboyant role in *The Birdcage* in order to avoid simply repeating the formula of *Mrs. Doubtfire*. He challenges himself in a way that allows the audience to keep pace with him. And when he is sparking we feel juiced for life.

—Alan Dale

WILLIS, Bruce

Nationality: American. **Born:** West Germany, 19 March 1955. **Education:** Attended public school in Penn's Grove, New Jersey; Montclair State College, New Jersey—left in 1977 before graduating; studied acting briefly with Stella Adler. **Family:** Married the actress Demi Moore, 1987, daughters: Rumer Glenn, Scout LaRue, and Tallulah Belle. **Career:** 1977—stage debut, off-Broadway in *Heaven and Earth*; member of Barbara Contardi's First Amendment Comedy Theatre; 1980—film debut, *The First Deadly Sin*; 1984-85—worked on TV: guest starred in *Miami Vice* ("No Exit"), *Twilight Zone* ("Shatterday"); 1985-89—starred in TV series *Moonlighting* (as David Addison); 1987—wrote, produced, starred in an HBO special, *The Return of Bruno* (as Bruno); 1987—first starring film role, *Blind Date*; also has performed and recorded as a R & B singer; has done advertisements for Levi's jeans, Seagram's Wine Coolers (1987), Sears (1995). **Awards:** Best Actor Emmy Award, for *Moonlighting*, 1987. **Agent:** Arnold Rifkin, William Morris Agency, 151 El Camino Drive, Beverly Hills, CA 90210, U.S.A.

Films as Actor:

1980 *The First Deadly Sin* (Hutton) (as extra, uncredited)
1982 *The Verdict* (Lumet) (as a courtroom observer, uncredited)
1987 *Blind Date* (Edwards) (as Walter Davis)
1988 *Die Hard* (McTiernan) (as John McClane); *Sunset* (Edwards) (as Tom Mix, + co-exec pr)
1989 *In Country* (Jewison) (as Emmeth Smith); *Look Who's Talking* (Heckerling) (as voice of Mikey); *That's Adequate* (Hurwitz)
1990 *Bonfire of the Vanities* (DePalma) (as Peter Fallow); *Die Hard 2: Die Harder* (*Die Harder*) (Harlin) (as John McClane); *Look Who's Talking Too* (Heckerling) (as voice of Mikey)
1991 *Billy Bathgate* (Benton) (as Bo Weinberg); *Hudson Hawk* (Lehmann) (as Hudson Hawk; + co-story); *The Last Boy Scout* (Tony Scott) (as Joe Hallenbeck); *Mortal Thoughts* (Rudolph) (as James Urbanski)
1992 *Death Becomes Her* (Zemeckis) (as Ernest Menville); *The Player* (Altman) (as himself)
1993 *National Lampoon's Loaded Weapon 1* (Quintano) (as Wrong Mobile Home Owner, uncredited); *Striking Distance* (Herrington) (as Tom Hardy)
1994 *Color of Night* (Rush) (as Dr. Bill Capa); *Nobody's Fool* (Benton) (as Carl Roebuck); *North* (Rob Reiner) (as narrator); *Pulp Fiction* (Tarantino) (as Butch Coolidge)
1995 *Die Hard: With a Vengeance* (*Die Hard 3*) (McTiernan) (as John McClane); "The Man from Hollywood" ep. of *Four Rooms* (Tarantino) (as Leo, uncredited); *12 Monkeys* (Gilliam) (as James Cole)

1996 *Breakfast for Champions* (Rudolph); *Le Cinquieme element* (*The Fifth Element*) (Besson); *Combat!* (Hill); *Firestorm* (Andrew Davis); *Last Man Standing* (Walter Hill)

Publications

By WILLIS: articles—

Interview with Lawrence Grobel, in *Playboy* (Chicago), November 1988.
"Bruce Willis Looks for the Man within the Icon," interview with Kenneth Turan, in *New York Times*, 1 July 1990.
"From the Top of the Heap, a View of the End of the Line," interview with Bernard Weinraub, in *New York Times*, 30 September 1991.
"Mr. Misunderstood? Willis Makes Himself Clear," interview with Bernard Weinraub, in *New York Times*, 21 September 1993.
"Finally, Bruce Willis Gets Invited to the Ball," interview with Jill Gerston, in *New York Times*, 2 October 1994.
"Bruce Willis in the Hot Zone," interview with Jay McInerney, in *Esquire* (New York), May 1995.
"Bruce Willis: Extreme Close-up," interview with Garry Jenkins, in *Cosmopolitan*, June 1995.
Interview with David Sheff, in *Playboy* (Chicago), February 1996.

On WILLIS: book—

Siegel, Barbara, and Scott Siegel, *Cybill & Bruce: Moonlighting Magic*, New York, 1987.

On WILLIS: articles—

Williams, J. P., "The Mystique of *Moonlighting*: 'When You Care Enough to Watch the Very Best,'" in *Journal of Popular Film and Television* (Washington, D.C.), Fall 1988.
Powers, John, "Look upon a Star," in *Sight and Sound* (London), July 1991.
Bart, Peter, "An Artful Gesture," in *Variety* (New York), 4 March 1996.

* * *

Bruce Willis has pioneered a character type that might be called the postmodern proletarian. When his seven years on-stage in New York led to television stardom with *Moonlighting*, all the elements of his arsenal were already on display. Like the show itself, Willis's David Addison was at once a generic staple and a parody. Sturdy physically but stunted emotionally, private-eye Addison is a working man's man as beleaguered as attracted by his nouvelle poor feminist boss (Cybill Shepherd). And yet Addison is also a self-aware, verbally hyperagile ironist—indeed, often a self-conscious media construct.

It is not surprising, given the loaded, conflicted range of emotions called forth from Willis by *Moonlighting*, that he has subsequently forged a multifaceted film persona: as an action hero, a comic foil, and a dramatic artist, a megastar and a supporting player. His pursuit of these many genres and modes of performance has resulted in some strikingly huge hits, and some flops of similar size. *Blind Date*, his first big-screen starring vehicle, faltered in its would-be comic reliance upon the smooth-talking, uneasily romantic side of Willis. (*Sunset* similarly did not translate his comic appeal for movie audiences.) *Die Hard* also deployed his mastery of flippancy, but sparingly, accentuating instead his aura of besieged masculinity. The displaced cop John McClane is, like most of Willis's characters, a battling underdog. McClane, however, does not fight either against or beside a woman; with McClane, the class-edged wars waged by Willis's characters begin to play out centrally not "between the sexes" but upon Willis's ever more bruised, sweating (and even aging) body itself.

Bruce Willis in *Die Hard: With a Vengeance*

Having established himself as a bona fide box-office draw with *Die Hard* (thereby starting a franchise which went on to yield two lucrative sequels), Willis played a wrecked Vietnam veteran in the well-reviewed but little-seen drama, *In Country*. This sort of creative daring underpins the strain of slightly off-mainstream dramas which has combined with supremely mainstream action adventures and comedies to make up the three-pronged thrust of his post-*Die Hard* movie career. In *Look Who's Talking*, Willis brought his comic timing alone to bear on yet a second multiple sequel-spawning franchise, as the voice of a toddler. *North* five years later is of the same genre, although it does allow Willis on-screen in a bunny suit. From 1989 to 1994, Willis had only uneven box-office and critical success, with *Hudson Hawk*, *The Last Boy Scout*, and *Striking Distance* (all in the *Die Hard* mode, all flops), and *Bonfire of the Vanities*, *Billy Bathgate*, *Mortal Thoughts*, *Death Becomes Her*, and *Color of Night* (all stretches—in all but the last Willis sacrifices top billing for artistic satisfaction—but none hits).

In 1994, however, Willis's embrace of working acting and not just stardom paid handsome dividends in the capital of hip. As Butch Coolidge, doomed but unbowed boxer in wunderkind Quentin Tarantino's *Pulp Fiction*, Willis is a perfect match for Tarantino's characteristic man-to-man battering, and bantering. By 1996, *Variety* would publish a column praising Willis's willingness to accept little money to do low-budget but high-quality projects; such publicity around films such as *Pulp* and *Nobody's Fool* countermanded the rash of earlier articles that had decried the "excess" of Willis's multimillion dollar per picture salaries.

His thinning hair shaved to the nub, Willis was not first-billed in *Pulp*; but his performance in it surely helped win him the similarly coifed lead role of James Cole in Terry Gilliam's 1995 remake of the Chris Marker landmark *La Jetée*, *12 Monkeys*. Cole allows all of Willis's talents to shine, in a way that not one of his projects has since *Moonlighting*. A man under attack from unknown quarters, very possibly from the very social forces that command him, Cole fights through abuse and confusion—at first against, then towards, and finally alongside a psychiatrist played by Madeleine Stowe. The moment when Cole hears a pop song on the doctor's car radio epitomizes what Willis brings to the film, and to film in general. Stress draining from his face, Cole's unwillingly assumed armor drops away for an instant as he connects to something of the best in human creation, trivial as it may seem to the unenlightened. Willis knows how to depict not only the fight but what the fight is for, and it is this that has made him one of the modern screen's most prominent artists of the ordinary man.

—Susan Knobloch

WINGER, Debra

Nationality: American. **Born:** Mary Debra Winger in Cleveland, Ohio, 16 May 1955. **Family:** Married the actor Timothy Hutton, 1986 (divorced 1990), son: Emanuel Noah. **Education:** Attended California State University, Northridge; studied acting with Michael V. Gazzo. **Career:** Appeared in Los Angeles area theater workshops; played Drusilla the Wonder Girl in the TV series *Wonder Woman*. **Awards:** Best Actress, National Society of Film Critics, for *Terms of Endearment*, 1983. **Agent:** Rick Nicita, Creative Artists Agency, 9830 Wilshire Boulevard, Beverly Hills, CA 90212, U.S.A.

Films as Actress:

1977   *Slumber Party '57* (William A. Levey) (as Debbie)
1978   *Thank God It's Friday* (Klane) (as Jennifer); *Special Olympics* (*A Special Kind of Love*) (Philips—for TV)

1979   *French Postcards* (Huyck) (as Melanie)
1980   *Urban Cowboy* (James Bridges) (as Sissy)
1982   *Cannery Row* (David S. Ward) (as Suzy De Soto); *E. T.—The Extraterrestrial* (Spielberg) (as E. T.'s voice only, unbilled); *An Officer and a Gentleman* (Hackford) (as Paula Pokrifki)
1983   *Terms of Endearment* (James L. Brooks) (as Emma Greenway Horton)
1984   *Mike's Murder* (James Bridges) (as Betty Ann Parish)
1986   *Legal Eagles* (Reitman) (as Laura J. Kelly)
1987   *Black Widow* (Rafelson) (as Alexandra Barnes/Jessica Bates); *Made in Heaven* (Alan Rudolph) (as Emmett Humbird, unbilled)
1988   *Betrayed* (Costa-Gavras) (as Katie Phillips/Cathy Weaver)
1990   *Everybody Wins* (Reisz) (as Angela Crispini); *The Sheltering Sky* (Bernardo Bertolucci) (as Kit Moresby)
1992   *Leap of Faith* (Richard Pearce) (as Jane)
1993   *Wilder Napalm* (Caron) (as Vida Foudroyant); *A Dangerous Woman* (Gyllenhaal) (as Martha Horgan); *Shadowlands* (Attenborough) (as Joy Gresham)
1995   *Forget Paris* (Crystal) (as Ellen Andrews)

Publications

By WINGER: articles—

"Straight Shooting Star," interview with Lynn Hirschberg, in *American Film* (New York), July-August 1988.
"Confessions of a Reluctant Sex Goddess," interview with Tom Robbins, in *Esquire* (New York), February 1993.
"Debra Winger, Caught on a Winter Afternoon," interview with Jan Hoffman, in *New York Times*, 9 January 1994.

On WINGER: book—

Cahill, M. J., *Debra Winger: Hollywood's Wild Child*, New York, 1984.

On WINGER: articles—

Thomson, David, "Dean, Clift, Brando . . . Winger!" in *California Magazine*, February 1983.
Current Biography 1984, New York, 1984.
Lubow, Arthur, "Debra Wings It," in *Vanity Fair* (New York), February 1987.
Collins, Nancy, "Winger on the Wild Side," in *Vanity Fair* (New York), October 1990.
Clark, John, "Debra Winger," in *Premiere* (New York), December 1990.
Corliss, Richard, "Debra Winger: Dangerous Woman," in *Time* (New York), 24 January 1994.

*   *   *

In *Urban Cowboy* Debra Winger as Travolta's trailer-park wife Sissy was not shellacked with the big-star gloss that froze Travolta, and so nothing lessened the heat and immediacy of her performance. She fully embodied Sissy's avidity for experience, rocking forward on her toes in anticipation of something new even though she was not sure she could handle it. (Likewise, the rough-velvet nap of her voice seemed eager rather than knowing, as it might have in a 1940s movie.) Sissy put herself out there and we saw her take it on the chin more than once; Winger's virtues start from a resilient chin. She is the most tomboyish of top-flight female stars and this allows her to play women who take plunges, and get in over their heads, without asking the audience to admire (i.e., patronize) them for their bravery.

Debra Winger with Richard Gere in *An Officer and a Gentleman*

Her impact in *Urban Cowboy* led to starring roles in *An Officer and a Gentleman*, which expanded on Sissy, and in *Terms of Endearment* in which she brought her undisguised divisions, lack of coyness, and full-length immersion in character to an upper-middle-class character. Winger provided a much-needed realistic core for that composite of sitcoms and disease-of-the-week television movies. It could not have been such a hit without Winger to provide the texture that Shirley MacLaine's more processed performance lacked.

Winger has managed to remain a star despite a decade in which she has not appeared in any popular successes; she has, however, given several astounding performances. In *Mike's Murder* she plays a bank teller who investigates the death of a young tennis instructor she had dated sporadically. It is not a showy role, but it requires us to watch Winger like a monitor as she uncovers and comprehends the undoing of an attractive young man in the cocaine and hustling subculture attached to the L.A. entertainment industry. The script is frank yet tactful; Winger's Betty never overreacts, nothing is overstated. Betty takes the mess in and manages to absorb what happened without emerging into another world, as a heroine of high tragedy would. She continues at the bank having internalized more of the world's complications than is needful for her life—her curiosity rounds out her basic sanity.

As Angela Crispini in the Arthur Miller-scripted *Everybody Wins*, Winger's naturalism as a Marilyn Monroe type disintegrating in the middle of a murder mystery is flamboyant without being actressy. Again, you could see how Angela had got herself beyond the breakers

in a sea of corruption; but for Angela there is no way back because her bad choices are compounded by fundamental instability. Winger's Angela is a lost woman and we watch helplessly through Nick Nolte's eyes as she looms large and then recedes; it is actually anguishing. Winger also gives a stylized performance as Martha, a mentally handicapped woman in *A Dangerous Woman*. Winger audaciously gives her research re-creation of Martha's physical and emotional idiosyncracies a slapstick kick. Winger, drawing on memories of teenage awkwardness, had the wit to see Martha's handicaps as a way to identify with her without condescension. Martha can unironically be called dangerous because her honesty and her eroticism are single-mindedly passionate—she can not lower her expectations. Martha is slow, but like the rest of us, she is a victim of her own emotions, and Winger never angles to make her more conventionally appealing for the sake of her own vanity.

Winger has been dull in standard fare such as *Legal Eagles* as well as in the pretentious, too-damn-pictorial *Sheltering Sky*, though you cannot blame her for wanting to work with Bertolucci. But she has never treated herself as a brand-name product, and had the good grace to appear in the lively, tent-revival picture *Leap of Faith* without trying to grab scenes from the picture's star Steve Martin. Even in *Shadowlands*, a tidy piece of Oscarbait, Winger has her signature sense of emotional adventure and defiance. She does not hide anything or force anything; she has the rough perfection of a crystal-as-found-in-nature. Ingmar Bergman has been able to get the same kind of naturalness from his repertory actresses, but Winger does it minus the chilly, high-toned deliberateness of Bergman's artistic intentions. Winger just lives her roles—she plays ordinary women so thoroughly they are both absolutely believable in context and more vivid than life.

—Alan Dale

WINKLER, Angela

Nationality: German. **Career:** Stage actress from the 1960s, and member of the Berlin Schaubühne from the 1970s; 1969—film debut in *The Hunters Are the Hunted*; 1975—role in the first of several films by Volker Schlöndorff, *The Lost Honor of Katharina Blum.*

Films as Actress:

1969 *Jagdszenden aus Niederbayern* (*The Hunters Are the Hunted*; *Hunting Scenes in Bavaria*) (Fleischmann) (as Hannelore)
1975 *Die verlorene Ehre der Katharina Blum* (*The Lost Honor of Katharina Blum*) (Schlöndorff) (title role)
1977 *Die Linkshändige Frau* (*The Left-Handed Woman*) (Handke) (as Franziska)
1978 *Die Blechtrommel* (*The Tin Drum*) (Schlöndorff) (as Agnes Matzerath); *Deutschland im Herbst* (*Germany in Autumn*) (Schlöndorff and others); *Messer im Kopf* (*Knife in the Head*) (Hauff) (as Ann Hoffmann)
1979 *Letzte Liebe* (Engstrom)
1980 *La Provinciale* (*The Girl from Lorraine*) (Goretta) (as Claire)
1982 *Heller Wahn* (*L'Amie*; *Sheer Madness*; *Friends and Husbands*) (von Trotta) (as Ruth); *Danton* (Wajda) (as Lucile Desmoulins)
1983 *Krieg und Frieden* (*War and Peace*) (Schlöndorff and others) (as Margot); *Edithes Tagebuch* (*Edith's Diary*) (Geissendörfer) (as Edith Baumeister)
1984 *De Grens* (de Winter) (as Rosa Clement)
1987 *Un Altare per la Madre*
1991 *Bronsteins Kinder* (*Bronstein's Children*) (Kawalerowicz) (as Elle Bronstein)
1992 *Benny's Video* (Haneke) (as Mother)
1994 *Ein Letzer Wille* (Wessel—for TV) (as Susanne Elling)
1995 *Der Kopf des Mohren* (*The Moor's Head*) (Manker) (as Anna)

Publications

By WINKLER: article—

Interview, in *Filmecho/Woche* (Wiesbaden), 2 September 1983.

On WINKLER: articles—

Films and Filming (London), September 1983.
Slodowski, J., "Blaszany bebenek," in *Filmowy Serwis Prasowy* (Warsaw), Bol. 38, no. 8/9, 1992.

*   *   *

One of the most talented actresses of the new German cinema, Angela Winkler began acting in the theater in the 1960s. In the 1970s she became a member of the great Berlin Schaubühne, the theatrical ensemble directed by Peter Stein. Her filmic presence is, however,

extremely restrained for a theater-trained actor. Winkler often plays an innocent victim or obsessed neurotic, projecting a vulnerable, brooding quality not unlike an awkward Irene Papas. She is often the embodiment of repression, which either feeds her obsessive behavior or erupts into violence.

In some films she is only passive. She plays down her role as the unassuming wife of Bruno Ganz's powerful protagonist in Reinhard Hauff's *Knife in the Head*. In Schlöndorff's segment of the collective film *Germany in Autumn* she has her most passive role as a blank-faced Antigone performing several different versions of the play for German television executives. This passivity cannot be contained in the other films she made for Schlöndorff-von Trotta. In *The Lost Honor of Katharina Blum* she portrays a dull, orderly working girl who, after being slandered by a yellow press journalist, calmly murders him. She plays an acquiescent, schizophrenic woman who impulsively kills her chauvinistic husband at the end of von Trotta's *Sheer Madness*. In Schlöndorff's *The Tin Drum* she plays the boy Oskar's mother, who bursts through the constraints of conventional bourgeois behavior. She begins a passionate affair with her cousin in backstreet hotels in Gdansk. She dies after obsessively stuffing raw fish down her throat in a fit of ennui. By the time Schlöndorff directed Winkler in the Böll-scripted segment of the collective film *War and Peace* her character lacks passivity; she is a frantic survivor of nuclear holocaust pleading for entry into a fallout shelter.

—Howard Feinstein

WINTERS, Shelley

Nationality: American. **Born:** Shirley Schrift in East St. Louis, Illinois, 18 August 1922. **Education:** Attended Thomas Jefferson High School, Brooklyn; studied acting at the New Theatre School, New York, and with Charles Laughton. **Family:** Married 1) Mack Paul Mayer, 1943 (divorced 1947); 2) the actor Vittorio Gassman, 1952 (divorced 1955), daughter: Vittoria Gina; 3) the actor Anthony Franciosa, 1957 (divorced 1960). **Career:** Worked as dress model in New York, then in the chorus at La Conga nightclub and in summer stock: small roles in New York, and supporting role in *Rosalinda*, 1942; 1943—film debut in *What a Woman!* and contract with Columbia; 1948—contract with Universal; 1951—began studying at The Actors Studio, New York; continued stage work: roles in *Born Yesterday*, 1950, *A Hatful of Rain*, 1955, *The Night of the Iguana*, 1963, *Cages*, 1963, and *Under the Weather*, 1966; 1971—her play *One Night Stands of a Noisy Passenger* produced in New York. **Awards:** Special Jury Prize for Ensemble Acting, Venice Festival, for *Executive Suite*, 1954; Best Supporting Actress Academy Award, for *The Diary of Anne Frank*, 1959; Best Supporting Actress Academy Award, for *A Patch of Blue*, 1965. **Agent:** ICM, 8899 Beverly Boulevard, Los Angeles, CA 90048, U.S.A.

Films as Actress:

1943 *What a Woman!* (Cummings) (as secretary)
1944 *Knickerbocker Holiday* (Brown) (as Ulda Tienhoven); *She's a Soldier Too* (Castle) (as "Silver" Rankin); *Sailor's Holiday* (Berke) (as Gloria); *Together Again* (Charles Vidor) (as girl); *Cover Girl* (Charles Vidor) (as girl)
1945 *Tonight and Every Night* (Saville) (as Bubbles); *A Thousand and One Nights* (Green) (as handmaiden)
1946 *Two Smart People* (Dassin) (as Princess)

1947   *The Gangster* (Wiles) (as Hazel); *A Double Life* (Cukor) (as Pat Kroll); *Living in a Big Way* (La Cava); *New Orleans* (Lubin) (as secretary)

1948   *Cry of the City* (Siodmak) (as Brenda); *Larceny* (Sherman) (as Tory); **Red River** (Hawks) (as dance-hall girl)

1949   *The Great Gatsby* (Nugent) (as Myrtle Wilson); *Take One False Step* (Erskine) (as Catherine Sykes); *Johnny Stool Pigeon* (Castle) (as Terry)

1950   *South Sea Sinner* (*East of Java*) (Humberstone) (as Coral); *Winchester '73* (Anthony Mann) (as Lola Manners); *Frenchie* (Louis King) (title role)

1951   **A Place in the Sun** (Stevens) (as Alice Tripp); *He Ran All the Way* (Berry) (as Peg); *Behave Yourself!* (Beck) (as Kate); *The Raging Tide* (Sherman) (as Connie Thatcher); *Meet Danny Wilson* (Pevney) (as Joy Carroll)

1952   *Phone Call from a Stranger* (Negulesco) (as Binky Gay); *My Man and I* (Wellman) (as Nancy); *Untamed Frontier* (Fregonese) (as Jane Stevens)

1954   *Saskatchewan* (*O'Rourke of the Royal Mounted*) (Walsh) (as Grace Markey); *Executive Suite* (Wise) (as Eva Bardeman); *Playgirl* (Pevney) (as Fran); *Tennessee Champ* (Wilcox) (as Sarah Wurble)

1955   *Mambo* (Rossen) (as Toni Salerno); **The Night of the Hunter** (Laughton) (as Willa Harper); *I Am a Camera* (Cornelius) (as Natalia Landauer); *The Big Knife* (Aldrich) (as Dixie Evans); *The Treasure of Pancho Villa* (Sherman) (as Ruth Harris); *I Died a Thousand Times* (Heisler) (as Marie)

1956   *To Dorothy, a Son* (*Cash on Delivery*) (Box) (as Myrtle La Mar)

1959   *The Diary of Anne Frank* (Stevens) (as Mrs. Van Daan); *Odds against Tomorrow* (Wise) (as Lorry); *Let No Man Write My Epitaph* (Leacock) (as Nellie)

1961   *The Young Savages* (Frankenheimer) (as Mary Di Pace)

1962   **Lolita** (Kubrick) (as Charlotte Haze); *The Chapman Report* (Cukor) (as Sarah Garnell)

1963   *The Balcony* (Strick) (as Madame Irma); *Wives and Lovers* (Rich) (as Fran Cabrell)

1964   *A House Is Not a Home* (Rouse) (as Polly Adler); *Gli Indifferenti* (*A Time of Indifference*) (Maselli) (as Lisa)

1965   *The Greatest Story Ever Told* (Stevens) (as woman of no name); *A Patch of Blue* (Green) (as Rose-Ann D'Arcy)

1966   *Harper* (*The Moving Target*) (Smight) (as Fay Estabrook); *Alfie* (Gilbert) (as Ruby)

1967   *Enter Laughing* (Carl Reiner) (as Mrs. Kolowitz)

1968   *The Scalphunters* (Pollock) (as Kate); *Wild in the Streets* (Shear) (as Mrs. Flatow); *Buona Sera, Mrs. Campbell* (Frank) (as Shirley Newman); *The Mad Room* (Girard) (as Mrs. Armstrong)

1969   *Arthur! Arthur?* (Gallu)

1970   *Bloody Mama* (Corman) (as Ma Barker); *How Do I Love Thee* (Gordon) (as Lena Mervin); *Flap* (*The Last Warrior*) (Reed)

1971   *What's the Matter with Helen?* (Harrington) (title role); *Who Slew Auntie Roo?* (Harrington) (as Rosie Forrest); *Revenge!* (Taylor—for TV) (as Amanda Hilton); *A Death of Innocence* (Wendkos—for TV)

1972   *Something to Hide* (Reid) (as Gabriella); *The Poseidon Adventure* (Neame) (as Belle Rosen); *The Adventures of Nick Carter* (Krasny—for TV)

1973   *Blume in Love* (Mazursky) (as Mrs. Carmer); *Cleopatra Jones* (Starrett) (as Mommy); *The Devil's Daughter* (Szwarc—for TV) (as Lilith Malone)

1974   *Double Indemnity* (Smith—for TV); *The Sex Symbol* (Rich—for TV); *Big Rose* (Krasny—for TV); *Journey into Fear* (Daniel Mann) (as Mrs. Mathews)

1975   *That Lucky Touch* (Miles) (as Diane Steedman)

1976   *Next Stop, Greenwich Village* (Mazursky) (as Mrs. Lapinsky); *Diamonds* (Golan) (as Zelda Shapiro); *The Tenant* (Polanski) (as the concierge)

1977   *Tentacles* (Hellman) (as Tillie Turner); *Pete's Dragon* (Chaffey) (as Lena Gogan); *The Three Sisters* (Bogart) (as Natalya); *Un borghese piccolo piccolo* (*An Average Man*) (Monicelli)

1978   *King of the Gypsies* (Pierson) (as Queen Rachel); *The Initiation of Sarah* (Day—for TV) (as Miss Erica); *Elvis* (Carpenter) (as Elvis's mother)

1979   *Redneck Country* (Robinson); *City on Fire* (Bakoff) (as Nurse Andrea Harper); *The Magician of Lublin* (Golan) (as Elzbieta)

1980   *Il visitatore* (*The Visitor*) (Paradisei) (as Jane Phillips)

1981   *S.O.B.* (Edwards) (as Eva Brown); *Looping* (Bockmayer); *My Mother, My Daughter* (Werba)

1983   *Fanny Hill* (O'Hara)

1984   *Ellie* (Wittman) (as Cora); *Over the Brooklyn Bridge* (Golan) (as Becky Sherman)

1985   *Déjà Vu* (Richmond) (as Olga Nabokov)

1986   *Witchfire* (Privitera) (as Lydia); *The Delta Force* (Golan) (as Eddie Kaplan); *Very Close Quarters* (Rif) (as Galina)

1987   *Marilyn Monroe: Beyond the Legend* (Feldman—TV doc)

1988   *The Purple People Eater* (Shayne) (as Rita)

1989   *An Unremarkable Life* (Chaudri) (as Evelyn McEllany)

1990   *Helena* (Vuille); *Touch of a Stranger* (Brad Gilbert) (as Lily)

1991   *The Linguini Incident* (Shepherd); *Stepping Out* (Lewis Gilbert) (as Mrs. Fraser); *Superstar: The Life and Times of Andy Warhol* (Workman—doc)

1992   *Weep No More, My Lady* (Andrieu—for TV) (as Vi)

1993   *The Pickle* (Mazursky) (as Yetta)

1994   *Il Silenzio dei Prosciutti* (*The Silence of the Hams*) (Greggio)

1995   *Jury Duty* (Fortenberry) (as Mrs. Collins); *Heavy* (Mangold) (as Dolly); *Backfire* (A. Dean Bell) (as Lieut. Shithouse)

Publications

By WINTERS: books—

Shelley, also Known as Shirley, New York, 1980.
Shelley II: The Middle of My Century, New York, 1989.

By WINTERS: articles—

Actors Talk about Acting, edited by Lewis Funke and John E. Booth, New York, 1961.
Interview in *Photoplay* (London), December 1971.
Interview with Jim Haspiel, in *Films in Review* (New York), June-July 1980.
"Shelley Winters: Idol Chatter," interview with Christine Spines, in *Premiere* (New York), January 1995.

On WINTERS: articles—

Current Biography 1952, New York, 1952.
Buckley, Michael, "Shelley Winters," in *Films in Review* (New York), March 1970.

*   *   *

Despite performances that generally rise above them, the films of Shelley Winters are overwhelmingly mediocre or forgettable. From them emerge key stock figures who, for better or worse, epitomize the role to which she became progressively typed: blond, imitation-Harlow bombshells; vulgar but vulnerable victims; slatterns; mistresses;

Shelley Winters

whorehouse madames; and Jewish mothers in caftans. The offscreen image of a brassy, high-flying sexpot—fostered by Universal-International's publicity department—and reports of tantrums thrown on and off the set heightened the public's early association of the actress with the parts she played and evolved in due course into the television talk show blabbermouth regaling Johnny, Merv, Jay, and Dave.

But Shelley Winters's extensive stage and screen credits, spanning four decades, are dotted with surprises. In her aspirations and, occasionally, her achievements, she has revealed herself to be an actress of deceptive complexity. Nurtured by directors George Cukor (*A Double Life*, *The Chapman Report*) and, especially, George Stevens (*A Place in the Sun*, *The Diary of Anne Frank*, *The Greatest Story Ever Told*), she intuitively began to explore her roles with Method creatively before she or they fully grasped its theoretical base.

Intent on stretching her acting range beyond the level offered by most of her Hollywood assignments, Winters commuted regularly to New York, where for six years she observed Elia Kazan and Lee Strasberg in action during the formative years of the Actors Studio. Upon expiration of her Universal contract, she risked a return to Broadway (where in the 1940s she had replaced Celeste Holm as Ado Annie in Rodgers and Hammerstein's musical *Oklahoma!*) to star, triumphantly, as a drug addict's wife in Michael Gazzo's play *A Hatful of Rain*. Officially admitted to Actors Studio membership, she continued to appear through this period, arguably the richest of her career, in important dramatic roles on Broadway, in repertory, on national tours, and on television. Until then, she once told an interviewer, "I never really believed I was an actress. It didn't matter what they said to me about *A Place in the Sun*. I thought it was a fluke, that it was the publicity jazz and the blonde hair and bosoms.... I thought it was an accident."

But *A Place in the Sun* was no accident. She fought aggressively for the role and, as Alice Tripp in George Stevens's adaptation of Theodore Dreiser's *An American Tragedy*, drew the definitive Winters screen characterization. The brash Universal late-1940s blonde, on loan to Paramount, was transformed into Dreiser's mousy, whiny mill girl in an early 1950s performance of remarkable subtlety and depth. Though she received co-star billing (and was nominated for a Best Actress Oscar), Winters's film career has been essentially fulfilled as a character actress in unsympathetic roles, as her two Best Supporting Actress Academy Awards—for grasping Mrs. Van Daan in *Diary of Anne Frank* and the monstrous Rose-Ann D'Arcy in *A Patch of Blue*—attest.

George Cukor's *A Double Life*, the film that triggered her rise to fame, Charles Laughton's *Night of the Hunter* (from James Agee's script), and Stanley Kubrick's *Lolita* (from Vladimir Nabokov's novel) also endure as landmark Winters films. In all three, she meets characteristically premature, violent—and memorable—ends. Winters's performance style and her persona, particularly as a psychotic, deluded, aging hag, has led to a cult status of sorts, particularly around several of her lesser, trashier films. Note *Something to Hide*, in which she plays the nagging, pathetic wife of Peter Finch (again meeting a memorable end). Also *Heartbreak Motel*, in which she plays the insane, possessive wife of the motel's owner. In 1971 alone she played a murderous psycho addicted to religious radio broadcasts in *What's the Matter with Helen?*, and the deranged maternal figure with a fetish for orphans in *Who Slew Auntie Roo?* Both are excellent examples of Winters's unique ability to turn even the most dismal scripts into over-the-top camp hilarity.

Like so many actors and—especially—actresses of a certain age, Winters is now rarely cast in major motion pictures. She continues to work, however, usually appearing in minimally reviewed films. Invariably, she performs competently, sometimes (as in so many of her earlier screen appearances) rising well above her material. Note her nice turn as Mrs. Fraser, the grouchy pianist in *Stepping Out*, adapted to the screen from the popular English stage comedy as a vehicle for Liza Minnelli.

—Mark W. Estrin, updated by Matthew Hays

WISDOM, Norman

Nationality: British. **Born:** Marylebone, London, 4 February 1925. **Family:** Married Freda Simpson, 1948, two children. **Military Service:** Joined the army as musician, also won Army boxing awards. **Career:** Worked as pageboy, waiter and cabin boy, before joining the army; 1946—debut in Music Hall; formed double act with Jerry Desmonde; 1948—debut on television, also film debut in *A Date with a Dream*; 1952—signed long-term contract with Rank; 1986—subject of TV documentary *Just Wisdom*. **Awards:** British Academy Award for Best Newcomer, for *Trouble in Store*, 1953. **Address:** c/o Eric Glass Ltd., 28 Berkeley Square, London W1X 6HD, England.

Films as Actor:

1948   *A Date with a Dream* (Leeman)
1953   *Trouble in Store* (Carstairs) (as Norman)
1954   *One Good Turn* (Carstairs) (as Norman)
1955   *Man of the Moment* (Carstairs) (as Norman)
1956   *Up in the World* (Carstairs) (as Norman)
1957   *Just My Luck* (Carstairs) (as Norman Hackett); *As Long as They're Happy* (J. Lee Thompson) (uncredited)
1958   *The Square Peg* (Carstairs) (as Norman Pitkin/Gen. Schreiber)
1959   *Follow a Star* (Asher) (as Norman Truscott)
1960   *There Was a Crooked Man* (Burge) (as Davy Cooper); *The Bulldog Breed* (Asher) (as Norman Puckle, + co-sc)
1961   *The Girl on the Boat* (Kaplan) (as Sam)
1962   *On the Beat* (Asher) (as Norman Pitkin/Guilio Napolitani, + co-sc)
1963   *A Stitch in Time* (Asher) (as Norman Pitkin, + co-sc)
1965   *The Early Bird* (Asher) (as Norman Pitkin, + co-sc)
1966   *The Sandwich Man* (Hartford-Davis) (as Father O'Malley); *Press for Time* (Asher) (as Norman Shields/Sir Wilfred Shields/Emily, + co-sc)
1968   *The Night They Raided Minsky's* (*The Night They Invented Striptease*) (Friedkin) (as Chick Williams)
1969   *What's Good for the Goose* (*Girl Trouble*) (Golan) (as Timothy Bartlett)
1977   *To See Such Fun* (Scofield—compilation)
1981   *Going Gently* (Frears—for TV)
1992   *Double X: The Name of the Game* (*Double X*; *Run Rabbit Run*) (Grewal) (as Arthur Clutten/Maurice Rigby)

Publications

By WISDOM: book—

Don't Laugh at Me (autobiography), with William Hall, n.p., 1992.

By WISDOM: articles—

Interview, in *Photoplay* (London), June 1976.
Interview, in *TV Times* (London), 20 October 1977.
Interview, in *Radio Times* (London), 30 May 1981.
Interview, in *Time Out* (London), 17 December 1986.

On WISDOM: books—

Murphy, Robert, *Realism and Tinsel*, London, 1989.
Dacre, Richard, *Trouble in Store: Norman Wisdom: A Career in Comedy*, Dumfries, Scotland, 1991.

Norman Wisdom in *Follow a Star* **courtesy of The Rank Organisation Plc**

On WISDOM: articles—

Sight and Sound (London), April 1954.
Marks, Louis, "Top Billing," in *Films and Filming* (London), December 1954.
Article on TV career, in *Primetime*, October/December 1983.

*   *   *

Unlike his contemporary Peter Sellers, who created a whole gallery of comic monsters, Norman Wisdom confined his ingenuity, like Charlie Chaplin, George Formby, and most of the early film comedians, to variations on a single character: the bullied, good-hearted, disaster-prone little man he called "the Gump." Film critics never had had much time for low-brow British film comedy, and Wisdom, sentimental without being vulgar, was a particular target for critical contempt, but his endearingly gentle form of slapstick brought him worldwide popularity.

John Paddy Carstairs, the director assigned to several of Wisdom's first films, was a colorful, multitalented character and *Trouble in Store*, *Up in the World*, and *The Square Peg* at least, are well organized and effective comedies. At the end of the 1950s he was succeeded by Robert Asher (the brother of cameraman Jack Asher) who was more susceptible than the worldly, hard-boiled Carstairs to Norman's insistence on the importance of pathos. This was not in itself a disadvantage. In *Follow a Star* the fact that his girlfriend is crippled works very well, tying in usefully with Norman's castrating dependence both on her and the Machiavellian crooner (Jerry Desmonde) who "steals" his voice. And in *The Bulldog Breed* the pathos surrounding Norman's little man, such a washout with women that he joins the navy as the only alternative to suicide, at least avoids the strains on credulity of a standard film comedy romance. But there is a tendency in the Asher directed films for maudlin sentimentality to creep in.

In 1960 Wisdom, eager to expand his repertoire, broke free of the Rank Organisation to make two films for United Artists, *There Was a Crooked Man* and *The Girl on the Boat*. *There Was a Crooked Man*, ably directed by Stuart Burge, retains the traditional Wisdom-film format of an innocent falling among thieves and scoundrels but eventually escaping unscathed to win the girl and bring happiness to those who deserve it. But Burge takes it all rather more seriously than Carstairs and Asher, and what the film loses in inspired slapstick it gains in better characterization and plausibility of plot. *The Girl on the Boat*, directed by Henry Kaplan, is based on a novel by P. G. Wodehouse and has Norman strangely cast as an upper-class dilettante. He struggles gamely with the part but fails to rid himself entirely of his cloth-cap image and though the film has its moments, it only briefly takes off into that frenzy of manic confusion which both Wisdom and Wodehouse are capable of at their best.

Changes to the Wisdom persona did not go down well at the box office and the two United Artists films were much less successful than their predecessors. Norman returned to Rank for two more films—*On the Beat* and *A Stitch in Time*—that restored his box-office popularity. But he found it difficult to break out from the confines of the British film industry and the expectations of his audience. *The Early Bird* holds few surprises and *Press for Time* is poorly scripted and directed, redeemed only by one brilliant sequence where Norman, fearing his bicycle will be stolen, insists on bringing it into the luxurious home of the mayor and ends up with it suspended from the chandelier. Despite playing a major role in William Friedkin's *The Night They Raided Minsky's* he failed to establish himself in Hollywood and returned to Britain to star as a timid bank clerk who falls for a promiscuous young swinger (Sally Geeson) in Menahem Golan's irredeemably tacky *What's Good for the Goose*. He has since taken on very infrequent assignments, including a magnificent straight performance in 1981 as a dying cancer patient in *Going Gently*, a television film directed by Stephen Frears. The early 1990s have seen his take on a dual role in *Double X: The Name of the Game*, as well as the publication of a biography and his autobiography, *Don't Laugh at Me*.

—Robert Murphy

WITHERS, Googie

Nationality: British. **Born:** Georgette Lizette Withers in Karachi, India (now Pakistan), 12 March 1917; to a British father and a Dutch mother. **Education:** Attended convent school in England, also at Italia Conti Stage School. **Family:** Married the actor John McCallum, 1948, daughter: the actress Joanna McCallum. **Career:** 1929—stage debut in *The Windmill Man*; 1931—appeared in cabaret; 1934—film debut in *The Girl in the Crowd*; 1950s—moved to Australia; 1970s—as Governor Faye Boswell in *Within These Walls*, for TV.

Films as Actress:

1934   *The Girl in the Crowd* (Powell) (as Sally)
1935   *The Love Test* (Powell) (as Minnie); *Windfall* (George King) (as Dodie); *Her Last Affaire* (Powell) (as Effie); *All at Sea* (Kimmins) (as Daphne Tomkins); *Dark World* (Vorhaus) (as Annie)
1936   *Crown versus Stevens* (Powell) (as Ella); *King of Hearts* (*Little Gel*) (Mitchell and Tennyson) (as Elaine); *She Knew What She Wanted* (Bentley) (as Dora); *Accused* (Freeland) (as Ninette); *Crime over London* (Zeisler) (as Miss Dupres)
1937   *Pearls Bring Tears* (Haynes) (as Doreen); *Action for Slander* (Whelan) (as Mary); *The Green Cockatoo* (*Four Dark Hours*) (Menzies); *Paradise for Two* (*The Gaiety Girls*) (Freeland) (as Miki)
1938   *Paid in Error* (Rogers) (as Jean Mason); *If I Were Boss* (Rogers) (as Pat); *Kate Plus Ten* (*Queen of Crime*) (Denham) (as Lady Moya); *Strange Boarders* (Mason) (as Elsie); *Convict 99* (Varnel) (as Lottie); *The Lady Vanishes* (Hitchcock) (as Blanche); *You're the Doctor* (Lockwood) (as Helen Firmstone)

1939   *Murder in Soho* (*Murder in the Night*) (Norman Lee) (as Lola Matthews); *Trouble Brewing* (Kimmins) (as Mary Brown); *The Gang's All Here* (*The Amazing Mr. Forrest*) (Freeland) (as Alice Forrest); *She Couldn't Say No* (Grayson) (as Dora); *Dead Men Are Dangerous* (French)
1940   *Bulldog Sees It Through* (Huth) (as Toots); *Busman's Honeymoon* (*Haunted Honeymoon*) (Woods) (as Polly)
1941   *Jeannie* (*Girl in Distress*) (French) (as Laundress)
1942   *One of Our Aircraft Is Missing* (Powell and Pressburger) (as Jo de Vries); *Back-Room Boy* (Mason) (as Bobbie)
1943   *The Silver Fleet* (Wellesley and Sewell) (as Helene van Leyden)
1944   *On Approval* (Clive Brook) (as Helen Hale); *They Came to a City* (Dearden) (as Alice)
1945   "Haunted Mirror" ep. of **Dead of Night** (Hamer) (as Joan Courtland); *Pink String and Sealing Wax* (Hamer) (as Pearl Bond)
1947   *The Loves of Joanna Godden* (Frend) (title role); *It Always Rains on Sunday* (*Whitechapel*) (Hamer) (as Rose Sandigate)
1948   *Miranda* (Annakin) (as Clare Marten); *Once upon a Dream* (Thomas) (as Carol Gilbert)
1949   *Traveller's Joy* (Thomas) (as Bumble Pelham)
1950   *Night and the City* (Dassin) (as Helen Nosseross)
1951   *White Corridors* (Jackson) (as Dr. Sophie Dean); *The Magic Box* (John Boulting) (as sitter in Bath studio); *Lady Godiva Rides Again* (Launder)
1952   *Derby Day* (*Four against Fate*) (Wilcox) (as Betty Molloy)
1954   *Devil on Horseback* (Frankel) (as Jane Cadell)
1956   *Port of Escape* (Tony Young) (as Anne Stirling)
1970   *The Nickel Queen* (McCallum) (as Meg Blake)
1985   *Time after Time* (Hays) (as Leda Klein)
1986   *Northanger Abbey* (Giles Foster—for TV) (as Mrs. Allen); *Hotel du Lac* (Giles Foster—for TV) (as Mrs. Pusey)
1995   *Country Life* (Blakemore) (as Hannah)
1996   *Shine* (as Katherine Pritchard)

Publications

By WITHERS: articles—

Interview, in *Picturegoer* (London), 13 April 1946.
Interview, in *Photoplay Film Monthly* (London), January 1976.

On WITHERS: books—

McCallum, John, *Life with Googie*, London, 1979.
Murphy, Robert, *Realism and Tinsel*, London, 1989.

On WITHERS: article—

Picturegoer (London), 17 January 1948.

*   *   *

Only for a regrettably short time—ten years or so—was Googie Withers a leading screen actress. During that period, though, she succeeded in creating a lasting image as a strong, passionate woman, classically dark and, when the occasion demanded, ruthless.

Given such a marked screen persona, it is hard to credit that she could ever have played dumb blonds. But there she is, fluffy and giggling, in a whole string of dire British prewar comedies, the recipient of half-hearted passes from the likes of George Formby. Now and again, by way of a change, she played bad girls, but the material was hardly an improvement.

Googie Withers with John McCallum in *It Always Rains on Sunday*

She was rescued by the war, and by Michael Powell, who remembered her from small roles in his early quota quickies and had noticed that "her beauty had an erotic quality, strange and provocative." Although she had never played serious drama, Powell cast her as a Dutch resistance leader in *One of Our Aircraft Is Missing*. It was perceptive casting, and not only because Withers was half-Dutch. For the first time she was allowed to play, literally, to her strengths, as a resourceful, self-reliant woman who could keep her cool under pressure. She graduated to female lead as another Dutchwoman, Ralph Richardson's wife, in *Silver Fleet* (produced though not directed by Powell-Pressburger). In both, she amply vindicated Powell's instinct that drama was her forte.

Withers had a gift for high comedy, too, though the cinema seldom offered her much scope. An exception was Clive Brook's sole directorial venture, the stylish and unduly neglected *On Approval*, which found her delectably holding her own against the formidable competition of Beatrice Lillie. But the finest roles of her screen career were all dramatic, in the three films she made with Robert Hamer.

For Hamer, Withers is invariably linked with dark, dangerous passions that threaten to disrupt a tamely respectable world. In the "Haunted Mirror" episode of *Dead of Night*, the mirror she gives her bland young fiancé sucks him into a past of sexual violence. As the

publican's wife, reigning over a glittering demimonde in *Pink String and Sealing Wax*, she lures another insipid young man, son of a local pillar of Victorian rectitude, into a maelstrom of drink, lust, and murder. So vital is her presence that with her death the whole film falls limply apart.

"The definitive Googie Withers role," in Charles Barr's estimation, is in *It Always Rains on Sunday*. Again she plays a woman trapped in a stultifying relationship, tempted by an alluring but destructive past. After the intensity of her brief fling with her escaped-convict ex-lover, the film's closing moment of renunciation, as she resigns herself to her poky terraced house and her decent, dull husband, conveys a poignant sense of loss.

She had another strong though more conventional role, as a staunchly self-sufficient farmer in turn-of-the-century Kent, in *The Loves of Joanna Godden*, partly directed by Hamer when Charles Frend fell ill. But after Hamer's departure from Ealing the studio could find no more use for her. Nor, on the whole, could the British cinema of the 1950s, where independent, sensual women were little in demand. Her last good film until 1970 was Dassin's London-based noir, *Night and the City*, presiding over a sleazy nightclub and avidly playing off gross husband (Francis Sullivan) against her lover, a hustler (Richard Widmark). As written, it was routine hard-bitch stuff, but Withers

ACTORS AND ACTRESSES

found depth and warmth in the character, investing her with the urgency of a woman desperate to escape her stifling, dead-end milieu.

For all her undoubted screen aptitude, Withers never seemed too concerned about building a conventional movie career, brushing aside studio requests that she change her name to something more euphonious ("Googie" is Bengali for "crazy," a nickname dating from her Indian childhood). She often neglected films in favor of the theater, and eventually turned her back on Britain and the cinema altogether. She had married her co-star from *It Always Rains on Sunday*, the Australian actor-impresario John McCallum, and in the late 1950s settled with him in Australia.

Subsequently, her film appearances have been rare but always welcome. In 1970's *The Nickel Queen*, directed by McCallum, Withers was charming as a pub owner in the Australian outback facing and adapting to changes brought on by the discovery of nickel in the area. Unfortunately, the film received scant distribution outside Australia (it was also noteworthy, however, as the film debut of Joanna McCallum, Withers and John McCallum's daughter, playing, of course, Withers's daughter).

Withers also made several welcome appearances on British television in the mid-1980s, but her most widely seen part in three decades came in 1995 with *Country Life*, Michael Blakemore's successful translation of Chekhov's *Uncle Vanya* to the Australian outback. Her small but lively role as Hannah, an acerbic Irish housekeeper who likes to serve mutton, showed that Withers had lost none of her talent for acting or for comedy as she approached her 80th birthday.

—Philip Kemp, updated by David E. Salamie

WONG, Anna May

Nationality: American. **Born:** Wong Liu Tsong in Los Angeles, California, 3 January 1905. **Education:** Attended California Street School, Chinese Mission School, a Chinese school, and Los Angeles High School. **Career:** 1919—film debut at age 14 in *The Red Lantern*; 1921—first credited role in *Bits of Life*; 1922—first starring role in *The Toll of the Sea*; 1928—made her first film in Germany, *Song*; 1929—stage debut in *The Circle of Chalk* with Laurence Olivier in London; made first film in England, *Piccadilly*; 1930—New York stage debut in *On the Spot*; on tour in Brooklyn, Chicago, Pittsburgh, and Los Angeles; on stage in Vienna in *Tschun Tschi* (*Springtime*), which she also produced; 1933—special one-week appearance in Blackpool, England, on stage in *Variety Fair*; 1934—on stage in Italy, Switzerland, and the British Isles; 1935—on stage in Denmark, Norway, and Sweden; 1937—stars in *Princess Turandot* at the Westchester Playhouse, Mount Kisco, NY, and Westport, Connecticut; 1939—on stage in Melbourne, Australia; 1951—TV debut starring in *The Gallery of Mme. Liu-Tsong*. **Died:** In Santa Monica, California, 3 February 1961.

Films as Actress:

1919   *The Red Lantern* (Capellani) (uncredited bit as lantern bearer)
1920   *Dinty* (Neilan and MacDermott) (uncredited bit)
1921   *The First Born* (Campbell) (uncredited bit as servant); *Outside the Law* (Browning) (uncredited bit as Chinese girl); *Bits of Life* (Neilan) (as Toy Sing); *Shame* (Flynn) (as Lotus Blossom)
1922   *The Toll of the Sea* (Franklin) (as Lotus Flower)

1923   *Mary of the Movies* (McDermott) (as herself); *Drifting* (Browning) (as Rose Li); *Thundering Dawn* (Garson) (as honky-tonk girl)
1924   *The Alaskan* (Brenon) (as Keok); *The Thief of Bagdad* (Walsh) (as the Mongol slave); *The Fortieth Door* (Seitz—serial) (as Zira); *Peter Pan* (Brenon) (as Tiger Lily)
1925   *Forty Winks* (Urson and Iribe) (as Annabelle Wu); *His Supreme Moment* (Fitzmaurice) (as harem girl in play); *Screen Snapshots No. 3* (short) (as herself)
1926   *Fifth Avenue* (Vignola) (as Nan Lo); *A Trip to Chinatown* (Kerr) (as Ohtai); *The Silk Bouquet* (as Dragon Horse); *The Desert's Toll* (Smith) (as Oneta)
1927   *Driven from Home* (Young); *Mr. Wu* (Nigh) (as Loo Song); *The Honorable Mr. Buggs* (Jackman—short) (as Baroness Stoloff); *Old San Francisco* (Crosland) (as Chinese girl); *The Chinese Parrot* (Leni) (as Nautch dancer); *The Devil Dancer* (Niblo and Rebich. Shores) (as Sada); *Streets of Shanghai* (Gasnier) (as Su Quan)
1928   *Across to Singapore* (Nigh) (as Bailarina); *The Crimson City* (Mayo) (as Su); *Chinatown Charlie* (Hines) (as the Mandarin's sweetheart); *Song* (Eichberg) (title role)
1929   *Großstadtschmetterling* (*The City Butterfly*) (Eichberg) (as Mah); *Piccadilly* (Dupont) (as Sho-Sho)
1930   *The Road to Dishonour* (as Hai-Tang) (Eichberg) (as Hai-Tang); *Hai-Tang* (German version of *The Road to Dishonour*) (title role); *L'Amour Maître Des Choses* (French version of *The Road to Dishonour*) (Kemm) (as Hai-Tang); *Elstree Calling* (Brunel and Hitchcock) (as herself); *The Flame of Love* (Eichberg) (as Hai-Tang); *Wasted Love* (Eichberg)
1931   *Daughter of the Dragon* (Corrigan) (as Princess Ling Moy)
1932   *Shanghai Express* (von Sternberg) (as Hue Fei)
1933   *A Study in Scarlet* (Marin) (as Mrs. Pyke); *Tiger Bay* (Wills) (as Liu Chang)
1934   *Chu Chin Chow* (Forde) (as Zahrat); *Limehouse Blues* (Hall) (as Tu Tuan)
1935   *Java Head* (Ruben) (as Taou Yen)
1937   *Daughter of Shanghai* (Florey) (as Lan Ying Lin); *Hollywood Party* (Rowland—short) (as herself)
1938   *Dangerous to Know* (Florey) (as Mme. Lan Ying); *When Were You Born?* (McGann) (as Mei Lee Ling)
1939   *Island of Lost Men* (Neumann) (as Kim Ling); *King of Chinatown* (Grinde) (as Dr. Mary Ling)
1940   *Chinese Garden Festival* (short) (as herself)
1941   *Ellery Queen's Penthouse Mystery* (Hogan) (as Lois Ling)
1942   *Bombs over Burma* (Lewis) (as Lin Ying); *Lady from Chungking* (Nigh) (as Mme. Kwan Mei)
1949   *Impact* (Lubin) (as Su Lin)
1960   *Portrait in Black* (Gordon) (as Tani)

Publications

By WONG: article—

"The True Life Story of a Chinese Girl," in *Pictures*, August 1926 and September 1926.

On WONG: book—

Parish, James Robert, and William T. Leonard, *Hollywood Players: The Thirties*, New Rochelle, New York, 1976.

On WONG: articles—

"Anna May Wong: Combination of East and West," in *New York Herald Tribune*, 9 November 1930.

Anna May Wong

Davis, Mac, "Fled from Fame for 5 Years," in *New York Enquirer*, 18 February 1957.

Obituary in *New York Times*, 4 February 1961.

Leibfried, Philip, "Anna May Wong," in *Films in Review* (New York), March 1987 and November 1987; see also issues for October 1987, and January, February, and April 1988.

Sakamoto, Edward, "Anna May Wong and the Dragon-Lady Syndrome," in *Los Angeles Times*, calendar section, 12 July 1987.

Okrent, Neil, "Right Place, Wong Time: Why Hollywood's First Asian Star, Anna May Wong, Died a Thousand Movie Deaths," in *Los Angeles Magazine*, May 1990.

Leibfried, Philip, "Anna May Wong's Silent Film Career," in *Silent Film Monthly* (New York), February 1995.

*   *   *

Anna May Wong is chiefly remembered as the first actress of Asian extraction to achieve stardom and as the epitome of the "Oriental temptress," so much a fixture of melodramas in the late 1920s and 1930s. She began at Metro in 1919 at the age of 14 with a bit part in a Nazimova vehicle, *The Red Lantern*, and continued in such roles until receiving her initial screen credit in the first anthology film, *Bits of Life*. Although she starred in the first true Technicolor feature made in Hollywood, *Toll of the Sea*, and had an important role in Douglas Fairbanks's classic fantasy, *The Thief of Bagdad*, most of the remainder of her Hollywood films in the 1920s saw her as either an exotic dancer or a temptress.

Fed up with that stereotype, she fled to more tolerant Europe in 1928, where she became a true star in German and British films. She also appeared on stage in London, Vienna, Oslo, Copenhagen, Goteborg, Switzerland, Italy, and throughout the British Isles, with periodic returns to New York and Hollywood up until 1935. In 1936 she visited China for the only time, where she purchased costumes that she later used in films and on stage. The following year she was back in Hollywood under contract at Paramount, for whom she made four thrillers in three years, as well as a loan-out to Warner Brothers, none of which aided her flagging film career. She traveled to Australia in 1939, where she appeared on stage in Melbourne to raise funds for Chinese War Relief, to which she devoted her energies up until the end of World War II, appearing only in two Poverty Row productions during the war, after which she was in virtual retirement form the screen. She appeared in one film in 1949, and two years later tackled television in her own series on the Dumont network, which lasted only 11 episodes. She appeared on a number of television programs throughout the 1950s before her final film appearance in *Portrait in Black* in 1960.

—Philip Leibfried

WOOD, Natalie

Nationality: American. **Born:** Natasha Virapaeff, later Gurdin in San Francisco, California, 20 July 1938. **Education:** Attended studio schools and public schools. **Family:** Married 1) the actor Robert Wagner, 1957 (divorced 1962), one daughter; 2) the producer Richard Gregson, 1969 (divorced 1972), daughter: Natasha; 3) remarried Robert Wagner, 1972, son: Courtney. **Career:** 1943—film debut at age five in *Happy Land*; 1953-54—in TV series *The Pride of the Family*; 1979—in TV mini-series *From Here to Eternity*. **Died:** Drowned, off Santa Catalina Island, California, 29 November 1981.

Films as Actress:

1943   *Happy Land* (Pichel)
1946   *Tomorrow Is Forever* (Pichel); *The Bride Wore Boots* (Pichel)
1947   *Miracle on 34th Street* (*The Big Heart*) (Seaton) (as Susan Walker); *Driftwood* (Dwan); *The Ghost and Mrs. Muir* (Mankiewicz) (as Anna)
1948   *Scudda-Hoo! Scudda-Hay!*(Herbert) (as Bean McGill)
1949   *Chicken Every Sunday* (Seaton); *Father Was a Fullback* (Stahl); *The Green Promise* (Russell)
1950   *No Sad Songs for Me* (Maté); *The Jackpot* (Walter Lang); *Our Very Own* (Miller); *Never a Dull Moment* (Marshall)
1951   *Dear Brat* (Seiter); *The Blue Veil* (Bernhardt)
1952   *Just for You* (Nugent); *The Rose Bowl Story* (Beaudine)
1953   *The Star* (Heisler)
1954   *The Silver Chalice* (Saville)
1955   *One Desire* (Hopper); **Rebel without a Cause** (Ray) (as Judy)
1956   *A Cry in the Night* (Tuttle); **The Searchers** (Ford); *The Burning Hills* (Heisler); *The Girl He Left Behind* (Butler)
1957   *Bombers B-52* (Douglas); *Marjorie Morningstar* (Rapper); *No Sleep till Dawn* (Douglas)
1958   *Kings Go Forth* (Daves)
1959   *Cash McCall* (Pevney)
1960   *All the Fine Young Cannibals* (Anderson)
1961   *West Side Story* (Wise and Robbins) (as Maria); *Splendor in the Grass* (Kazan) (as Wilma Dean Loomis)
1962   *Gypsy* (LeRoy) (title role)
1963   *Love with the Proper Stranger* (Mulligan) (as Angie Ronnini)
1964   *Sex and the Single Girl* (Quine) (as Helen Gurley Brown)
1965   *The Great Race* (Edwards) (as Maggie DuBois)
1966   *Penelope* (Hiller) (title role); *This Property Is Condemned* (Pollack) (as Alva Starr); *Inside Daisy Clover* (Mulligan) (title role)
1969   *Bob and Carol and Ted and Alice* (Mazursky) (as Carol Sanders)
1972   *The Candidate* (Ritchie); *I'm a Stranger Here Myself* (Helpern—doc) (as herself)
1973   *The Affair* (Cates—for TV)
1975   *Peeper* (Hyams) (as Ellen Prendergast)
1976   *Cat on a Hot Tin Roof* (Moore—for TV) (as Maggie)
1979   *Meteor* (Neame) (as Tatiana); *The Cracker Factory* (Brinckerhoff—for TV)
1980   *The Last Married Couple in America* (Cates) (as Mari Thompson); *Willie and Phil* (Mazursky)
1981   *Brainstorm* (Trumbull) (as Karen Brace)

Publications

On WOOD: books—

Wood, Lana, *Natalie: A Memoir by Her Sister*, New York, 1984.
Nickens, Christopher, *Natalie Wood: A Biography in Pictures*, New York, 1986.
Crivello, Kirk, *Fallen Angels: The Lives and Untimely Deaths of 14 Hollywood Beauties*, Secaucus, New Jersey, 1988.
Harris, Warren G., *Natalie and R. J.: Hollywood's Star-Crossed Lovers*, New York, 1988.
Parker, John, *Five for Hollywood*, Secaucus, New Jersey 1991.

On WOOD: articles—

Current Biography 1962, New York, 1962.
Kempton, Murray, "Natalie Wood: Mother, Men and the Muse," in *Show* (Hollywood), March 1962.
Obituary in *New York Times*, 30 November 1981.
Fieschi, J., obituary, in *Cinématographe* (Paris), December 1981.
Obituary in *Films and Filming* (London), February 1982.
Lewis, K., "Natalie Wood," in *Films in Review* (New York), December 1986.

*   *   *

Natalie Wood's death in 1981 at the age of 43 brought to an abrupt end one of the most enduring careers in cinema history. Often referred to as "Hollywood's youngest veteran," she had worked in films almost continuously since her first screen appearance at the age of five in *Happy Land*. With apparent ease, she negotiated the occupational minefields which for most of her contemporaries had spelled disaster. She made a fluent transition from child actress to teenage star, survived the studio system, and achieved a metamorphosis from lightweight starlet into serious actress. Since she was never considered a great actress—in fact, it was customary among industry observers to poke fun at her limitations—her staying power poses an intriguing conundrum.

As a child, Wood tended to play minor roles in films featuring established stars. Although she was pretty and pert, she was seldom, if ever, expected to outshine the chief luminaries. Sometimes she served merely as a foil; at other times, as in *Miracle on 34th Street*, she was pivotal to the plot but not required to carry films on her own merits. This early career as a scene-stealer rather than as a star may have eased her transition to older parts. The public grew accustomed to her face but it did not learn to idolize her or to expect too much. Her transition to older roles was also facilitated by a change in her screen persona. As a child, she could be bratty or sweet, but she was always lively and confident. As a teenager and young adult, she was tentative, insecure, and vulnerable. In this way, Wood offered audiences a new screen identity and it was one with which female audiences of her own age group could readily identify. In *Rebel without a Cause*, a watershed in her career development, she, along with James Dean, perfectly captured the unfocused restlessness of a generation.

After an undistinguished phase as Warner's resident love interest, Wood's star status gained immeasurably from the popular success of *West Side Story*. It was *Splendor in the Grass*, however, which first earned her respect as an adult actress. As a young woman whose sexual impulses are constrained by society's moral imperatives, she struck a recognizable chord with the moviegoing public. The part earned Wood her second Academy Award nomination (the first was for *Rebel without a Cause*). *Love with the Proper Stranger* (her third Oscar nomination) was her finest achievement. Her performance was notable for its dramatic range and for the depth of feeling conveyed by nonverbal technique. It was also another film which probed a contemporary moral dilemma—the choice between a precarious independence and marriage for convenience's sake.

Her screen image as a vulnerable, put-upon female endured in films such as *Inside Daisy Clover* and *This Property Is Condemned*, but it found decreasing popular and critical favor. At the height of her fame, seemingly aware of the need to diversify, Wood branched out into comedy. In this new incarnation, however, she was only intermit-

Natalie Wood

tently successful. Her best comedy performance was in *Bob and Carol and Ted and Alice*, a brilliant satire on the 1960s obsession with self-discovery and sexual freedom. Unfortunately, her comedic talent was never again harnessed to good effect. During the 1970s her film appearances were infrequent and unexceptional, and she turned increasingly to television. In this medium, as in cinema, her record was uneven. Although she was widely lambasted for her performance in *Cat on a Hot Tin Roof*, she drew critical praise for her portrait of a manic-depressive housewife in *The Cracker Factory*. At the time of her death, she was planning to make her stage debut in a production of *Anastasia*.

Throughout her career, Wood seemed more at ease when she was one step removed from the limelight. In *Inside Daisy Clover*, the only film in which she was the principal focus of attention, she seemed uncomfortable with her responsibilities. In the much underrated *Gypsy*, she was more convincing as the mousy daughter sitting on the sideline than as the brassy burlesque artist occupying center stage. Her ability to survive in an industry notorious for its casualties owed something to this capacity for self-effacement. All her life, she seemed content to support rather than to compete with her fellow actors. Equally important to her longevity as a film actress was her willingness to diversify. She was also helped by the perennial youthfulness of her looks. If Natalie Wood often failed to shine, she nevertheless brightened many moments in cinema history. Her legacy is a memorable series of portraits which threw penetrating light on the changing mores of her generation.

—Fiona Valentine

WOODS, James

Nationality: American. **Born:** James Howard Woods in Vernal, Utah, 18 April 1947. **Education:** Attended Massachusetts Institute of Technology, 1966-69. **Family:** Married 1) Kathryn Greko, 1980 (divorced 1983); 2) Sarah Owen, 1989 (divorced 1990). **Career:** 1970—Broadway debut in *The Borstal Boy*; 1971—TV movie debut in *All the Way Home*; 1972—feature film debut in *The Visitors*; 1978—in TV miniseries *Holocaust*; 1993—in TV series *Fallen Angels*. **Awards:** Obie, Derwent, and Theatre World awards, for *Saved*, 1971; Emmy Award, for *Promise*, 1986. **Agent:** Toni Howard, ICM, 8942 Wilshire Boulevard, Beverly Hills, CA 90211, U.S.A.

Films as Actor:

1971   *All the Way Home* (Coe—for TV) (as Andrew)

1972   *The Visitors* (Kazan) (as Bill Schmidt); *Hickey and Boggs* (Culp) (as Lt. Wyatt); *Footsteps* (*Nice Guys Finish Last*) (Wendkos—for TV) (as reporter); *A Great American Tragedy* (J. Lee Thompson—for TV) (as Rick)

1973   *The Way We Were* (Pollack) (as Frankie McVeigh)

1974   *The Gambler* (Reisz) (as bank officer)

1975   *Distance* (Lover) (as Larry); *Night Moves* (Arthur Penn) (as Quentin); *Foster and Laurie* (Moxey—for TV) (as the addict)

1976   *Alex and the Gypsy* (*Love and Other Crimes*) (Korty) (as Crainpool); *F. Scott Fitzgerald in Hollywood* (Anthony Page—for TV) (as Lenny Schoenfeld); *The Disappearance of Aimee* (Anthony Harvey—for TV) (as Joseph Ryan)

1977   *The Choirboys* (Aldrich) (as Harold Bloomgard); *Raid on Entebbe* (Kershner—for TV) (as Capt. Sammy Berg)

1978   *The Gift of Love* (Chaffey—for TV) (as Alfred Browning)

1979   *The Onion Field* (Becker) (as Gregory Powell); *And Your Name Is Jonah* (Richard Michaels—for TV) (as Danny Corelli); *The Incredible Journey of Doctor Meg Laurel* (Guy Green—for TV) (as the Sin Eater)

1980   *The Black Marble* (Becker) (as Fiddler)

1981   *Eyewitness* (*The Janitor*) (Yates) (as Aldo Mercer)

1982   *Fast-Walking* (James B. Harris) (as Fast-Walking Miniver); *Split Image* (Kotcheff) (as Charles Pratt)

1983   *Videodrome* (Cronenberg) (as Max Renn)

1984   *Against All Odds* (Hackford) (as Jake Wise); **Once upon a Time in America** (Leone) (as Max)

1985   *Cat's Eye* (Teague) (as Morrison); *Joshua Then and Now* (Kotcheff) (as Joshua Shapiro); *Badge of the Assassin* (Damski—for TV) (as Robert K. Tannenbaum)

1986   *Salvador* (Oliver Stone) (as Richard Boyle); *Promise* (Glenn Jordan—for TV) (as D. J.)

1987   *Best Seller* (John Flynn) (as Cleve); *In Love and War* (Paul Aaron—for TV) (as Jim Stockdale)

1988   *Cop* (James B. Harris) (as Lloyd Hopkins, + co-pr); *The Boost* (Becker) (as Lenny Brown)

1989   *True Believer* (Ruben) (as Eddie Dodd); *Immediate Family* (*Parental Guidance*) (Kaplan) (as Michael Spector); *My Name Is Bill W.* (Petrie—for TV) (as Bill Wilson)

1990   *Women and Men: Stories of Seduction* (Tony Richardson—for TV) (as Robert)

1991   *The Hard Way* (Badham) (as John Moss); *The Boys* (Glenn Jordan—for TV) (as Walter Farmer)

1992   *Straight Talk* (Kellman) (as Jack Russell); *Diggstown* (*Midnight Sting*) (Ritchie) (as Gabriel Caine); *Chaplin* (Attenborough) (as Lawyer Scott); *Citizen Cohn* (Pierson—for TV) (title role)

1994   *The Getaway* (Donaldson) (as Jack Benyon); *The Specialist* (Llosa) (as Ned Trent); *Jane's House* (Glenn Jordan—for TV) (as Paul Clark); *Next Door* (Tony Bill—for TV) (as Matt Coler)

1995   *Casino* (Scorcese) (as Lester Diamond); *Nixon* (Oliver Stone) (as H. R. "Bob" Haldeman); *Indictment: The McMartin Trial* (Mick Jackson—for TV) (as Daniel Davis); *Curse of the Starving Class* (McClary—for TV) (as Weston Tate)

1996   *For Better or Worse* (Jason Alexander) (as James); *The Killer* (Metcalfe)

Publications

By WOODS: articles—

Interview with C. Dreifus, in *Playboy* (Chicago), April 1982.

Interview in *CineFantastique* (Oak Park, Illinois), 1983-84.

"On Woods' Edge," interview with Kenneth Turan and Aaron Rapoport, in *Interview* (New York), February 1989.

"Guilty Pleasures," in *Film Comment* (New York), April-May 1991.

Interview with Michael Musto, in *Interview* (New York), August 1992.

On WOODS: articles—

Meley, D., "The Voice of Experience," in *Screen Actor* (Los Angeles), 1981.

Bauer, J., "James Woods," in *Ciné Revue* (Brussels), 11 August 1983.

Seberechts, K., "*Once upon a Time in America*," in *Film en Televisie* (Brussels), September 1984.

McGillivray, D., "James Woods: Bio-Filmography," in *Films and Filming* (London), February 1985.

Danvers, L., "James Woods," in *Visions* (Brussels), Summer 1985.

Shewey, Don, *Caught in the Act: New York Actors Face to Face*, New York, 1986.

James Woods in *Once upon a Time in America*

Farber, S., "James Woods: More Than a Villain," in *New York Times*, 7 December 1986.

Crawley, T., "Weasels and Scumbags," in *Photoplay: Movies & Video* (London), February 1987.

Babitz, E., "Out of the Woods," in *American Film* (Farmingdale, New York), May 1987.

Denby, D., "Rear Window: James Woods Demands More," in *Premiere* (New York), November 1987.

Immergut, S. J., filmography in *Premiere* (New York), November 1987.

Mayer, M., "James Woods," in *Film und Fernsehen* (Pottsdam, Germany), 1988.

"James Woods ou les regards de L'indicible," in *Revue du Cinéma* (Paris), September 1988.

Current Biography 1989, New York, 1989.

Borns, Betsy, "Arresting Appeal: Partners vs. Crime," in *Harper's Bazaar* (New York), February 1989.

Woodward, Richard B., "Fighting His Way to the Top," in *New York Times*, 20 April 1989.

Muse, V., "Wild Woods," in *Life* (New York), December 1989.

"James Woods: He's Brash, Always Unpredictable, but He's Not Psychotic. Is He?," in *American Film* (Los Angeles), May 1990.

Seberechts, K., "Woods in Mineur," in *Film en Televisie* (Brussels), April 1991.

Maude, C., "Hard Woods," in *Time Out* (London), 1 May 1991.

"Open Challenge to Woods," in *Movieline* (Escondido, California), September 1991.

Parish, James Robert, and Don Stanke, *Hollywood Baby Boomers*, New York, 1992.

Szymanski, Michael, "James Woods Is Roy Cohn," in *Advocate* (Los Angeles), 8 September 1992.

*   *   *

Hyper live-wire James Woods understandably grew weary of being typecast as the scum of the earth. What is less comprehensible is his professed desire to be perceived as a conventional leading man when bland emoting in a high-toned soaper such as *Immediate Family* or a fizzless comedy such as *Straight Talk* reveals this actor at his most forgettable. (Did Jack Nicholson ever lose any sleep wishing that he could be George Peppard?) If the movies have never treated the unhandsome Woods like a star, television has proven liberating for the outspoken actor who varies backup work in high-profile prestige such as *Casino* and *Nixon* with superb delineations of more complex roles in television fare such as *Indictment: The McMartin Trial, Citizen Cohn,* and *The Boys.*

Leaving academic pursuits behind (after an injury to his right arm ended his dream of a career in medicine), Woods threw himself into the hard-knocks school of theatrical ventures. By the time he was taking bows off and on Broadway (even fooling the producers of *The Borstal Boy* into believing he was actually from Liverpool), the edgy actor felt frustrated by his opportunities and began concertedly studying film acting, self-taught by viewing movies. Putting his research to work with a master, Elia Kazan, in that veteran's little-seen independent film, *The Visitors,* Woods worked his way up the television movie ranks, always drawing the discerning viewer's eye no matter how small or narrowly conceived the role. After standing out in the glittering ensemble of the mini-series *Holocaust* (as a Jewish victim married to shiksa Meryl Streep), Woods nailed down his big screen breakthrough in *The Onion Field.* As a coldblooded cop killer who torments his surviving victim by turning jailhouse lawyer, Woods made audiences' skin crawl. Not since Richard Widmark pushed that wheelchair-bound old lady down the stairs in *Kiss of Death* had a villain caused such a sensation; Woods's portrayal of evil incarnate could have been lifted from a documentary on an actual avocational murderer.

Frustrated when *The Onion Field* did not open Hollywood's eyes to his unconventional screen power, Woods drifted back into supporting roles that he seemed to color with his own inner rage. What set his rogues gallery apart from the lowlifes of previous eras was boundless enterprise and brain power. Not descendants from Crimeland's primordial slime, Woods's bad boys celebrate their outmaneuvering of the gullible with arias of vitriol. No matter how full of self-loathing his wheeler-dealers in *Against All Odds* or *Once upon a Time in America* may be, the full force of their venom is reserved for others. Offscreen, Woods never concerned himself with campaigns to win friends and influence people, but filmmakers found his presence so violently original that he continued chalking up triumphs despite his knack for overassertiveness. In the underappreciated Faustian black comedy thriller, *Best Seller,* Woods was sublimely unrepentant as a cocky criminal in the mood for memoirs. An unexpected bid for a best actor Oscar for *Salvador* was both a tribute to his performance and to his reputation as an actor's actor. After this staggeringly acute interpretation of a nihilist redeemed in spite of himself, Woods started getting antihero roles informed by character flaws rather than working malice. If *Salvador* did not propel him to the front rank of film stars, it not only may be due to the limitations of an offbeat persona but also be the result of a risk-taking approach that sometimes sends him so far over the top he parodies himself. If *The Hard Way* is merely a misguided star vehicle ambushed by Woods's pushiness, his unleavened intensity transforms the anticocaine diatribe, *The Boost,* into a *Reefer Madness* for the 1980s.

Surviving the bad press hovering around his post-*Boost* personal life (a real life "fatal attraction" affair with co-star Sean Young), Woods has found his metier in television even if he yearns for the heady air breathed by De Niro and Pacino on the silver screen. (Actually, Woods's television work has been more perceptive and fully realized than anything those two icons have done since their heyday.) Whether crystallizing the terrifying self-awareness of a schizophrenic in *Promise* or chronicling the self-destructive binges of the co-founder of Alcoholics Anonymous in *My Name Is Bill W.,* Woods never distances himself from imperfections in the characters he tackles. Imposing that trademark Woodsian fury on his roles, he still differentiates between a tortured prisoner of war in *In Love and War* and a cynical lawyer-for-sale who reclaims his soul by fearlessly defending the McMartin family on trumped-up child molestation charges in *Indictment.*

As with other character actors turned stars by force of talent (Robert Duvall, Gene Hackman), Woods feeds off a gift for quickly penetrating details, a craft one can only refine through years of labor in the salt mines of small roles. His towering achievement as the tarnished legal savior in *Indictment* is matched if not surpassed by his spin on the sleazebag role of a lifetime, *Citizen Cohn*'s Roy Cohn, a legendary opportunist whose closeted sexuality and hypocritical backstabbing assume Shakespearean dimensions in Woods's hands. Tellingly, this dynamic actor makes Cohn's diabolical evil not comprehensible but believable. Just as his monster-men never reveal their true faces until they are at their victims' throats, Woods's antiheroes often get the better of their antagonists with ass-kissing trickery and guile, only this time in the service of a good cause. Having been cinema's specialist in criminal behavior, Woods is now an expert in suggesting how conflicted characters struggle to patch up the fault lines in their personalities. If he continues working at his present level of excellence, Woods will end up being acknowledged as an acting genius.

—Robert Pardi

WOODWARD, Joanne

Nationality: American. **Born:** Thomasville, Georgia, 27 February 1930. **Education:** Attended high school in Greenville, South Carolina; Louisiana State University, Baton Rouge, for two years; studied acting with Sanford Meisner at the Neighborhood Playhouse School of the Theatre, New York. **Family:** Married the actor Paul Newman, 1958, three daughters. **Career:** Joined the Little Theatre Group in Greenville, then played in summer stock in Chatham, Massachusetts; then television work in New York, and understudy role in Broadway production of *Picnic*; 1955—contract with 20th Century-Fox; film debut in *Count Three and Pray*; 1956—on Broadway in *The Lovers*; 1968—directed by Newman in *Rachel, Rachel*; has made several TV movies. **Awards:** Best Actress Academy Award, for *The Three Faces of Eve*, 1957; Best Actress, New York Film Critics, for *Rachel, Rachel*, 1968; Best Actress, Cannes Festival, for *The Effect of Gamma Rays on Man-in-the-Moon Marigolds*, 1973; Best Actress, New York Film Critics, 1973, and Best Actress, British Academy, 1974, for *Summer Wishes, Winter Dreams*; Best Actress, New York Film Critics, for *Mr. and Mrs. Bridge*, 1990. **Address:** 1120 5th Avenue #1C, New York, NY 10128, U.S.A.

Films as Actress:

1955 *Count Three and Pray* (Sherman) (as Lissy)
1956 *A Kiss before Dying* (Oswald) (as Dorothy Kingship)
1957 *The Three Faces of Eve* (Johnson) (title role); *No Down Payment* (Ritt) (as Leola Boone)
1958 *The Long, Hot Summer* (Ritt) (as Clara Varner); *Rally 'round the Flag, Boys!* (McCarey) (as Grace Bannerman)
1959 *The Sound and the Fury* (Ritt) (as Quentin Compson)
1960 *The Fugitive Kind* (Lumet) (as Carol Cutrere); *From the Terrace* (Robson) (as Mary St. John)
1961 *Paris Blues* (Ritt) (as Lillian Corning)
1963 *The Stripper* (*Woman of Summer*) (Schaffner) (as Lila Green); *A New Kind of Love* (Shavelson) (as Samantha Blake)
1965 *Signpost to Murder* (Englund) (as Molly Thomas)
1966 *A Fine Madness* (Kershner) (as Rhoda Shillitoe); *A Big Hand for the Little Lady* (*Big Deal at Dodge City*) (Cook) (as Mary)
1968 *Rachel, Rachel* (Newman) (title role)
1969 *Winning* (Goldstone) (as Elora)
1970 *WUSA* (Rosenberg) (as Geraldine); *King: A Filmed Record... Montgomery to Memphis* (Lumet and Mankiewicz—doc)
1971 *They Might Be Giants* (Harvey) (as Dr. Mildred Watson)
1972 *The Effect of Gamma Rays on Man-in-the-Moon Marigolds* (Newman) (as Beatrice)
1973 *Summer Wishes, Winter Dreams* (Cates) (as Rita Walden)
1975 *The Drowning Pool* (Rosenberg) (as Iris Devereaux)
1976 *Sybil* (Petrie—for TV) (as Dr. Wilbur)
1977 *Come Back, Little Sheba* (Narizzano—for TV)
1978 *The End* (Burt Reynolds) (as Jessica); *See How She Runs* (Heffron—for TV) (as Betty Quinn); *A Christmas to Remember* (Englund—for TV) (as Mildred McCloud)
1979 *The Streets of L.A.* (Freedman—for TV)
1980 *The Shadow Box* (Newman—for TV); *Angel Dust* (doc—for TV) (as narrator)
1981 *Crisis at Central High* (Johnson—for TV)
1984 *Harry and Son* (Newman) (as Lilly); *Passions* (Stern—for TV) (as Catherine Kennerly)
1985 *Do You Remember Love* (Bleckner—for TV) (as Barbara Wyatt-Hollis)
1987 *The Glass Menagerie* (Newman) (as Amanda)
1990 *Mr. and Mrs. Bridge* (Ivory) (as India Bridge)
1993 *Blind Spot* (Michael Toshiyuki Uno—for TV) (as Congresswoman Nell, + co-pr); *Foreign Affairs* (O'Brien—for TV) (as Vinnie Miner); *Philadelphia* (Jonathan Demme) (as Sarah Beckett); *Age of Innocence* (Scorsese) (as narrator)

1994 *Breathing Lessons* (Erman—for TV) (as Maggie Moran)
1995 *Remembering the Kindertransports* (as narrator)
1995 *James Dean: A Portrait* (Legon—doc for TV) (as herself)

Films as Director:

1982 *Come along with Me* (for TV)
1984 *The Hump Back Angel*

Publications

By WOODWARD: article—

"Mr. and Mrs. Bridge," interview with Graham Fuller, in *Interview* (New York), November 1990.

On WOODWARD: books—

Morella, Joe, and Edward Z. Epstein, *Paul and Joanne: A Biography of Paul Newman and Joanne Woodward*, New York, 1988.
Netter, Susan, *Paul Newman and Joanne Woodward*, London, 1989.
Stern, Stewart, *No Tricks in My Pocket: Paul Newman Directs*, New York, 1989.

On WOODWARD: articles—

Current Biography 1958, New York, 1958.
Ecran (Paris), December 1979.
McGillivray, David, "Joanne Woodward," in *Films and Filming* (London), October 1984.
Dowd, Maureen, "Paul Newman and Joanne Woodward: A Lifetime of Shared Passions," in *McCall's*, January 1991.
Vineberg, Steve, "Joanne Woodward: From *The Stripper* to *Mrs. Bridge*, a Master Manipulator of Mood," in *American Film* (Washington, D.C.), November-December 1991.

*   *   *

While not as prolific a film actor as her illustrious husband, Paul Newman, Joanne Woodward nonetheless has etched some memorable celluloid characterizations. Outstanding in her early film career is her portrayal of the title role in *The Three Faces of Eve*, in which she plays a mentally disturbed young woman who has three distinct personalities: a dull Southern housewife, a sex kitten, and a well-balanced and reasonable woman. What makes this film work is the fascination and credibility of Woodward's triple-personality character, right down to the details of voices, gestures, and body movements which she adjusted for each of the women inside Eve's mind. Although this was only her third appearance in films, the tour-de-force performance established her as a star and earned her an Academy Award (a feat she accomplished a full three decades prior to Newman).

From the very start of her career, Woodward displayed versatility. She could play a suburbanite (*No Down Payment* and *Rally 'round the Flag, Boys!*), a dissatisfied Southern belle (*The Long, Hot Summer*), a spinster (*Rachel, Rachel*), or the title role in *The Stripper* (which originally was meant for Marilyn Monroe). What gives unity to her portrayals is the spirit and spunk with which she endows the characters. It should be noted that Woodward started acting in movies at a time when it was fashionable for female characters to be glamorous and almost altogether helpless. Woodward, a pretty blond who never really bespoke glamour, usually was cast as women who were discontent, "causey" or more seriously rebellious, or were fated to cope with the unfortunate lot they had been dealt.

Joanne Woodward

In her very first appearance in *Count Three and Pray*, she is a feisty, unwashed teenaged backwoods girl who eventually becomes civilized—without relinquishing all of her spiritedness—when she encounters a willful, handsome parson (Van Heflin). She acts the part with great strength of purpose, and displays a gamin quality which she subsequently carried over into several comedy roles. This especially was the case in *A New Kind of Love*, in which she plays an American plain-Jane in Paris who obtains a fashion makeover and in so doing attracts the attention of a playboy journalist, played by Paul Newman. The more serious and earthy rebel character came out in her role as a sex-hungry urchin who craves Marlon Brando in *The Fugitive Kind*.

After *The Three Faces of Eve*, Woodward's best screen roles came either opposite Newman or in films directed by her husband. Their first effective pairing occurred in *The Long, Hot Summer*, and they are said to have fallen in love on the set. Indeed, they were married the same year. One can feel the heat between the two characters, he a handsome and clever but low-class drifter who strives for a more advantageous position in life, and she, the daughter of wealth, who passionately desires this beautiful stranger but fights against being manipulated by her father into marriage. Since then, Woodward and Newman have appeared together in comedies (*Rally 'round the Flag, Boys!* and *A New Kind of Love*), a glossy Hollywood soap opera (*From the Terrace*), and a string of dramas, including the very fine *Paris Blues*, an offbeat Paris-based romance of two jazz musicians and the two female tourists they befriend. In more recent years, they teamed for *Mr. and Mrs. Bridge*, based on two Evan S. O'Connell novels, which chronicles two decades in the life of a staid Kansas City couple.

With Newman as her director, Woodward presented several outstanding, multitiered characterizations at a time when Hollywood actresses were complaining of the sparsity of solid screen roles. She most often was cast as middle-aged women who were quietly leading unfulfilled lives, and who experience emotional crises. Possibly the finest is the drama *Rachel, Rachel*, in which she portrays a sexually naive old maid schoolteacher who is frustrated by the lack of meaning in her life. Another memorable performance is in the film version of Paul Zindel's Pulitzer Prize-winning play *The Effect of Gamma Rays on Man-in-the-Moon Marigolds*, where she plays an eccentric, alienated mother of two daughters. *Summer Wishes, Winter Dreams* places her in the role of an unhappy, frigid woman who is caught in an unfulfilled upper-middle-class marriage. She is at odds with her son, who is gay, and has just experienced the sudden demise of her elderly mother.

Over the years, Woodward has been a vigorous crusader for various liberal social and political causes. Her dedication to these causes has been reflected in her choice of parts, particularly her decision to play a college professor who falls victim to Alzheimer's disease in a highly praised, television movie *Do You Remember Love*. This particular disease is spoken of mainly in hushed tones or not discussed at all by many families of its victims, so it was quite a bold—and instructive—move for Woodward to portray the sufferings of this character. She won an Emmy for her efforts, but the greater reward came in making known some of the more confounding facts of the illness. Also along that line is her role on the big screen as the mother of a gay man (Tom Hanks) who is battling AIDS in *Philadelphia*. Another interesting recent role came opposite James Garner in the television movie *Breathing Lessons*, a sensitive comedy-drama of a longtime married couple in which she once more portrayed an offbeat, troubled middle-aged wife struggling to live a meaningful life.

Over and over, from the beginning of her career, Woodward has created fascinating, full-blooded screen characters whose personalities have shed light on the cobwebbed corners of intimate and disturbed minds, or given joy through their offbeat and comical bent. For her offscreen social issue work and her on-screen accomplishments, she has won the respect of her industry colleagues and the public.

—Audrey E. Kupferberg

WRAY, Fay

Nationality: American. **Born:** Vina Fay Wray near Cardston, Alberta, Canada, 15 September 1907; became U.S. citizen, 1935. **Education:** Attended Hollywood High School. **Family:** Married 1) the writer John Monk Saunders, 1928 (divorced 1939), daughter: Susan; 2) the writer Robert Riskin, 1942 (died 1955), daughter: Vicki, son: Robert Jr.; 3) Sanford Rothenberg, 1971. **Career:** 1923—film debut in short *Gasoline Love*; 1928—in von Stroheim's *The Wedding March*; 1931—stage debut in Saunders's play *Nikki on Broadway*; 1935-36—made several films in England; later stage work includes roles in *The Night of January 16th* and *The Petrified Forest*, 1938, in her own and Sinclair Lewis's play *Angela Is Twenty-Two* in Detroit and Chicago, 1939, *Golden Wings on Broadway*, 1941, and *Mr. Big*, 1941; 1953-55—in TV series *The Pride of the Family*. **Address:** 2160 Century Park East #1901, Los Angeles, CA 90067, U.S.A.

Films as Actress:

1923 *Gasoline Love* (short)

1925 *The Coast Patrol* (Barsky) (as Beth Slocum); *A Cinch for the Gander*

1926 *The Man in the Saddle* (Reynolds or Smith) (as Pauline Stewart); *The Wild Horse Stampede* (Rogell) (as Jessie Hayden); *Lazy Lightning* (Wyler) (as Lila Rogers)

1927 *Loco Luck* (Smith) (as Molly Vernon); *A One Man Game* (Laemmle) (as Roberts); *Spurs and Saddles* (Smith) (as Mildred Orth)

1928 *Legion of the Condemned* (Wellman) (as Christine Charteris); *Street of Sin* (Stiller) (as Elizabeth); *The First Kiss* (Lee) (as Anna Lee); *The Wedding March* (von Stroheim) (as Mitzi Schrammell)

1929 *The Four Feathers* (Cooper, Schoedsack, and Mendes) (as Ethne Eustace); *Thunderbolt* (von Sternberg) (as Ritzy); *Pointed Heels* (Sutherland) (as Laura Nixon)

1930 *Behind the Makeup* (Milton) (as Marie); "Dream Girl" technicolor segment of *Paramount on Parade*; *The Texan* (Cromwell) (as Consuelo); *The Border Legion* (Brower and Knopf) (as Joan Randall); *The Sea God* (Abbott) (as Daisy)

1931 *The Finger Points* (Dillon) (as Marcia Collins); *Not Exactly Gentlemen*; *The Conquering Horde* (Sloman) (as Taisie Lockhart); *Three Rogues* (Stoloff) (as Lee Carleton); *Dirigible* (Capra) (as Helen); *Captain Thunder* (Crosland) (as Ynez Dominguez); *The Honeymoon* (von Stroheim) (as Mitzi Schrammell); *The Lawyer's Secret* (Gasnier and Marcin) (as Kay Roberts); *The Unholy Garden* (Fitzmaurice) (as Camille)

1932 *Stowaway* (Whitman); *Doctor X* (Curtiz) (as Joan Xavier); *The Most Dangerous Game* (Schoedsack and Pichel) (as Eve Trowbridge)

1933 *The Vampire Bat* (Strayer) (as Ruth Bertin); *Mystery of the Wax Museum* (Curtiz) (as Charlotte Duncan); *King Kong* (Cooper and Schoedsack) (as Ann Darrow); *Below the Sea* (Rogell) (as Diane Templeton); *Ann Carver's Profession* (Buzzell) (title role); *The Woman I Stole* (Cummings) (as Vida Carew); *The Big Brain* (Archainbaud) (as Cynthia Glennon); *One Sunday Afternoon* (Roberts) (as Virginia Brush); *Shanghai Madness* (Blystone) (as Wildeth Christie); *The Bowery* (Walsh) (as Lucy Calhoun); *Master of Men* (Hillyer) (as Kay Walling)

1934 *Madame Spy* (Freund) (as Maria); *Once to Every Woman* (Hillyer) (as Mary Fanshawe); *Cheating Cheaters* (Thorpe) (as Nan Brockton); *Woman in the Dark* (Rosen); *White Lies* (Bulgakov); *The Countess of Monte Cristo* (Freund) (as Janet

Fay Wray in *King Kong*

Kreuger); *Viva Villa!* (Conway) (as Teresa); *Black Moon* (Neill) (as Gail); *The Affairs of Cellini* (La Cava) (as Angela); *The Richest Girl in the World* (Seiter) (as Sylvia Vernon)

1935 *The Clairvoyant* (*The Evil Mind*) (Elvey) (as Renee); *Come Out of the Pantry* (Raymond) (as Hilda Beach-Howard); *Alias Bulldog Drummond* (*Bulldog Jack*) (Forde) (as Ann Manders); *Mills of the Gods* (Neill)

1936 *When Knights Were Bold* (Raymond) (as Lady Rowena); *Roaming Lady* (Rogell) (as Joyce); *They Met in a Taxi* (Green) (as Mary)

1937 *It Happened in Hollywood* (*Once a Hero*) (Lachman) (as Gloria Gay); *Murder in Greenwich Village* (Rogell) (as Kay Cabot)

1938 *Smashing the Spy Ring* (Cabanne) (as Eleanor Dunlap); *The Jury's Secret* (Sloman) (as Linda Ware)

1939 *Navy Secrets* (Bretherton) (as Carol)

1940 *Wildcat Bus* (Woodruff) (as daughter of bus-line owner)

1941 *Adam Had Four Sons* (Ratoff) (as Molly); *Melody for Three* (Kenton) (as the mother)

1942 *Not a Ladies' Man* (Landers)

1944 *This Is the Life* (Feist) (+ sc)

1953 *Small Town Girl* (Kardos) (as Mrs. Kimbell); *Treasure of the Golden Condor* (Daves) (as Marquise)

1955 *The Cobweb* (Minnelli) (as Edna Devanel); *Queen Bee* (MacDougall) (as Sue McKinnon)

1956 *Hell on Frisco Bay* (Tuttle) (as Kay Stanley); *In Times Like These* (Seiter)

1957 *Crime of Passion* (Oswald) (as Alice Pope); *Tammy and the Bachelor* (Pevny) (as Mrs. Brent); *Rock, Pretty Baby* (Bartlett) (as Beth Daley)

1958 *Summer Love* (Haas) (as Beth Daley); *Dragstrip Riot* (*The Reckless Age*) (Bradley)

1980 *Gideon's Trumpet* (Collins—for TV) (as Edna Curtis)

Publications

By WRAY: book—

On the Other Hand: A Life Story, New York, 1989.

By WRAY: articles—

Interview with Roy Kinnard, in *Films in Review* (New York), April 1990.
"The Gorilla I Left Behind," in *Premiere* (New York), Winter 1994.

On WRAY: book—

Parish, James Robert, and William T. Leonard, *Hollywood Players: The Thirties*, New York, 1976.

On WRAY: articles—

Kinnard, Roy, "Fay Wray," in *Films in Review* (New York), February 1987.

Harmetz, Aljean, "Kong and Wray: 60 Years of Love," in *New York Times*, 28 February 1993.

*   *   *

If Fay Wray had made only one film in her career—*King Kong*—she would have earned her spot in the annals of screen history. When she co-starred as the classic damsel-in-distress opposite moviedom's most famous ape, she already was an established actress who had worked in major silent and sound Hollywood productions. Her sometimes stiff, sometimes exaggerated performance in *King Kong* has been misread by film enthusiasts who have not had the awareness of her earlier career.

Five years before *King Kong*, von Stroheim realized Wray's potential for expressive acting when he cast her in *The Wedding March* as Mitzi, an ill-fated commoner who becomes the love object of a prince. But *The Wedding March* was a Hollywood oddity, an extravagant art film and a commercial failure, so Wray was unable to sustain her career playing in similar films. Instead, she was destined to be cast as conventional leads, with the exception coming when her association with *King Kong* directors Merian C. Cooper and Ernest B. Schoedsack led to her all-too-brief reign in horror films. She became the genre's first sex symbol in *King Kong*, as well as in *Mystery of the Wax Museum*, *Dr. X*, *Vampire Bat*, and others, with her wholesome good looks and innocent demeanor effectively presented in contrast to the "monsters."

Wray is remembered for these few horror films, and it is disappointing that she did not appear in additional ones. As she aged, she might have been an asset to the 1940s horror cycle and 1950s science-fiction films.

—Anthony Ambrogio, updated by Audrey E. Kupferberg

WYMAN, Jane

Nationality: American. **Born:** Sarah Jane Fulks in St. Joseph, Missouri, 4 January 1914. **Education:** Attended Los Angeles High School; University of Missouri, Columbia, 1935. **Family:** Married 1) Myron Futterman, 1937 (divorced 1939); 2) the actor Ronald Reagan, 1940 (divorced 1948), daughter: Maureen, adopted son: Michael; 3) Freddie Karger, 1952 (divorced 1955). **Career:** 1932—film debut (as Sarah Jane Fulks) in *The Kid from Spain*; had a few small parts in other films, then enrolled at the University of Missouri; radio singer (as Jane Durrell); 1936-49—contract with Warner Brothers; 1955-58—host and actress on TV series *The Jane Wyman Theater*; 1981-90—starring role in TV series *Falcon Crest*. **Awards:** Best Actress Academy Award, for *Johnny Belinda*, 1948. **Address:** 3970 Overland Avenue, Culver City, CA 90230, U.S.A.

Films as Actress:

(as Sarah Jane Fulks)

1932   *The Kid from Spain* (McCarey) (as a Goldwyn Girl)
1933   *Elmer the Great* (LeRoy) (bit role)
1934   *College Rhythm* (Taurog) (bit role)
1935   *Rumba* (Gering) (as chorus girl); *All the King's Horses* (Tuttle) (bit role); *Stolen Harmony* (Werker) (bit role as girl)

1936   *King of Burlesque* (Lanfield) (bit role as girl); *Anything Goes* (*Tops Is the Limit*) (Milestone) (bit role); *My Man Godfrey* (La Cava) (as party-goer)

(as Jane Wyman)

1936   *Stage Struck* (Berkeley) (as Bessie Fuffnick); *Cain and Mabel* (Lloyd Bacon) (bit role); *Polo Joe* (McGann) (as polo spectator); *Smart Blonde* (McDonald) (as Dixie)
1937   "Love and War" production number of *Gold Diggers of 1937* (Lloyd Bacon) (as chorus girl); *Ready, Willing and Able* (Enright) (as Dot); *The King and the Chorus Girl* (LeRoy) (as Babette); *Slim* (Enright) (as Stumpy's girl friend); *The Singing Marine* (Enright) (as Joan); *Mr. Dodd Takes the Air* (Alfred E. Green) (as Marjorie Day); *Public Wedding* (Grinde) (as Flip Lane)
1938   *The Spy Ring* (Joseph H. Lewis) (as Elaine Burdette); *Fools for Scandal* (LeRoy) (bit role); *He Couldn't Say No* (Seiler); *Wide Open Faces* (Neumann) (as Betty Martin); *The Crowd Roars* (Thorpe) (as Vivian); *Brother Rat* (Keighley) (as Claire Adams)
1939   *Tail Spin* (Del Ruth) (as Alabama); *Private Detective* (Noel Smith) (as Myrna Winslow); *The Kid from Kokomo* (Seiler) (as Miss Bronson); *Torchy Plays with Dynamite* (Noel Smith) (as Torchy Blane); *Kid Nightingale* (Amy) (as Judy Craig)
1940   *Brother Rat and a Baby* (Enright) (as Claire Ramm); *An Angel from Texas* (Enright) (as Marge Allen); *Flight Angels* (Seiler) (as Nan Hudson); *My Love Came Back* (Bernhardt) (as Joy O'Keefe); *Tugboat Annie Sails Again* (Seiler) (as Peggy Armstrong); *Gambling on the High Seas* (Amy) (as Laurie Ogden)
1941   *Honeymoon for Three* (Lloyd Bacon) (as Elizabeth Clochessy); *Bad Men of Missouri* (Enright) (as Mary Hathaway); *You're in the Army Now* (Seiler) (as Bliss Dobson); *The Body Disappears* (Lederman) (as Lynn Shotesbury)
1942   *Larceny, Inc.* (Lloyd Bacon) (as Denny Costello); *My Favorite Spy* (Garnett) (as Connie); *Footlight Serenade* (Ratoff) (as Flo La Verne)
1943   *Princess O'Rourke* (Krasna) (as Jean)
1944   *Make Your Own Bed* (Godfrey) (as Susan Courtney); *Crime by Night* (Clemens) (as Robbie Vance); *The Doughgirls* (Kern) (as Vivian); *Hollywood Canteen* (Daves) (as herself)
1945   ***The Lost Weekend*** (Wilder) (as Helen St. James)
1946   *One More Tomorrow* (Godfrey) (as Fran Connors); *Night and Day* (Curtiz) (as Gracie Harris); *The Yearling* (Brown) (as Ma Baxter)
1947   *Cheyenne* (Walsh) (as Ann Kincaid); *Magic Town* (Wellman) (as Mary Peterman)
1948   *Johnny Belinda* (Negulesco) (as Belinda McDonald)
1949   *A Kiss in the Dark* (Daves) (as Polly Haines); *The Lady Takes a Sailor* (Curtiz) (as Jennifer Smith); *It's a Great Feeling* (David Butler) (as herself)
1950   *Stage Fright* (Hitchcock) (as Eve Gill); *The Glass Menagerie* (Rapper) (as Laura Wingfield)
1951   *Three Guys Named Mike* (Walters) (as Marcy Lewis); *Here Comes the Groom* (Capra) (as Emmadel Jones); *The Blue Veil* (Bernhardt) (as Louise Mason); *Starlift* (Del Ruth) (as herself)
1952   *The Story of Will Rogers* (Curtiz) (as Betty Rogers); *Just for You* (Nugent) (as Carolina Hill)
1953   *Let's Do It Again* (Hall) (as Constance Stuart); *So Big* (Wise) (as Selina Dejong)
1954   *Magnificent Obsession* (Sirk) (as Helen Phillips)
1955   *Lucy Gallant* (Parrish) (title role); ***All that Heaven Allows*** (Sirk) (as Cary Scott)

Jane Wyman

1956   *Miracle in the Rain* (Maté) (as Ruth Wood)
1959   *Holiday for Lovers* (Levin) (as Mary Dean)
1960   *Pollyanna* (Swift) (as Aunt Polly)
1962   *Bon Voyage!* (Neilson) (as Katie Willard)
1969   *How to Commit Marriage* (Lilley) (as Elaine Benson)
1971   *The Failing of Raymond* (Sagal—for TV) (as Mary Bloomquist)
1978   *The Outlanders* (Green)
1979   *The Incredible Journey of Dr. Meg Laurel* (Guy Green—for TV) (as Granny Arrowroot)

Publications

On WYMAN: books—

Parish, James Robert, and Don E. Stanke, *The Forties Gals*, Westport, Connecticut, 1980.
Morella, Joe, and Edward Z. Epstein, *Jane Wyman*, New York, 1985.
Quirk, Lawrence J., *Jane Wyman: The Actress and the Woman*, New York, 1986.

On WYMAN: articles—

Current Biography 1949, New York, 1949.
Bawden, J., "Jane Wyman: American Star Par Excellence," in *Films in Review* (New York), April 1975.
Briggs, C., "Jane Wyman," in *Hollywood: Then and Now*, vol. 23, no. 11, 1990.

*   *   *

Decades before she was to become the star of the prime-time television soap opera *Falcon Crest*, Jane Wyman was just another "cute" Hollywood blond with a turned-up nose who populated dozens of B films, usually playing a wisecracking friend of the star or a gold-digging chorus girl. Wyman provided some light, enjoyable moments in a wide variety of 1930s comedies such as *Brother Rat* and *The Kid from Kokomo*. As the war years dawned, she began to get increasingly better parts, mostly in Warner Brothers features such as *Larceny, Inc.* and *The Doughgirls*.

In 1945 Wyman's career changed sharply for the better when she began to dye her hair brown and appeared in several well-received straight dramatic roles. Beginning with the critically acclaimed *The Lost Weekend*, Wyman showed a dramatic depth to her acting which the public had not seen. During the late 1940s and early 1950s she received several Academy Award nominations and received an Oscar for Best Actress for her touching performance as the deaf-mute heroine of *Johnny Belinda*.

Wisely varying her genres once she attained major stardom, Wyman often highlighted a chin-quivering vulnerability while playing down the verve she displayed as the longest-running starlet in B-movie history. Despite being outclassed in terms of theatrical training and despite being too old for the tricky role, her halting Laura is the most memorable performance in *The Glass Menagerie*. Although she radiates movie-star assuredness in all her 1950s soap operas (*So Big, Lucy Gallant, Magnificent Obsession*) she is most incandescent in *All that Heaven Allows*, the most caustic slap at suburban America's snobbism and agism that has ever slipped past a major studio head's attention span. If she had sobbed at the victim well once too often by the time she experienced her *Miracle in the Rain*, she also brought new meaning to the word "vivacious" in some minor musicals (*Just for You, Here Comes the Groom, Let's Do It Again*) that should have made MGM sit up and take notice.

Although her screen appearances grew sparse, particularly after the rise and fall of her heralded television anthology, *The Jane Wyman Show*, she always could be counted on to enliven the proceedings even in vanilla-flavored Disney ventures. Still, none of her joie de vivre prepared Wyman groupies for her steely stint in *Falcon Crest*, in which she huffed and puffed hammily, reportedly ran the set with an iron glove borrowed from the character she played, and locked horns with such formidable guest-starring divas as Kim Novak, Gina Lollobrigida, and Lana Turner. If her Angela Channing, the Wicked Witch of the Wine Country, cannot be considered fine acting on a par with her most masterful big-screen legacy, *The Yearling*, it is just as unforgettable in its own shameless, scenery-chewing way. Popping up infrequently since her vintage soap series was canceled, Wyman can regard her kaleidoscopic career as a testament to the resilience, clear-sightedness, and good humor her fans have always responded to, whether Wyman happened to be casting herself as fluffy contract player, song-and-dance gal, drama doyenne, or television matriarch from Hell.

—Patricia King Hanson, updated by Robert Pardi

YAMADA, Isuzu

Nationality: Japanese. **Born:** Mitsu Yamada in Osaka, 5 February 1917; daughter of the actor Kusuo Yamada. **Education:** Began studying dance, singing (*samisen*), and narration (*kiyomoto*) in 1922, license in *kiyomoto*, 1927. **Family:** Married 1) the actor Ichiro Tsukida, 1935 (divorced 1942), daughter: the actress Michiko Saga; 2) the producer Kazuo Takimura, 1942 (divorced); 3) the actor Shotaro Hanayagi, 1943 (divorced); 4) the director Teinosuke Kinugasa (divorced); 5) the actor Yoshi Kato, 1950 (divorced 1954); one additional marriage. **Career:** 1930—joined the Nikkatsu Studio, and studied with the director Kunio Watanabe; film debut in *Tsurugi o koete*; established her reputation as an actress during the next decade with films from the Nikkatsu Studio, the Daiichi Company, 1934-36, Shinko Kinema, 1936-38, Toho studio, 1938-46, and Shin-Toho studio, 1947; 1931—stage debut; 1951—joined the leftist Mingei theater group, and later co-founded the Gendai Haiyu Kyokai theater group with Kato; 1957—international recognition for role in Kurosawa's *Throne of Blood*; active in television after 1957, and concentrated on stage work after 1964. **Awards:** Many Japanese prizes for both film and stage acting.

Films as Actress:

1930   *Tsurugi o koete* (Watanabe) (as Okayo); *Dai-Chushingura* (Ikeda) (as Hinagiku); *Fuun tenman-zoshi*; *Suronin Chuya* (Ito) (as Yae); *Udeippon* (Watanabe); *Kyoen koigassen* (Watanabe); *Koiguruma* (Watanabe); *Koi moyo*; *Sakanaka ronin*; *Nigeyuku Kodenji* (Itami); *Kobo Shinsen-gumi: Zenshi, Ko-shi* (Ito); *Sarutobi Sasuke*; *Tadanao-kyo gyojo-ki* (as Matsue)

1931   *Edo bishonen-roku*; *Onai goju-ryo*; *Edokko ichiba*; *Mabuta no haha* (Inagaki) (as Otoyo); *Tabi no hito*; *Araki Mataemon*; *Ohitsu oharetsu Somekawa Shohachi*; *Nippon niju-roku seijin*; *Zoku Ooka seidan: Mazo kaiketsu-hen* (Ito) (as Osuzu); *Fuyuki shinju* (Tsuji) (as Okiku); *Adauchi senshu* (Uchida) (as Oshizu)

1932   *Kokushi muso* (Itami) (as Yae); *Yatoro-gasa: Kyorai no maki, Dokuho no maki* (Inagaki) (as Oyuki); *Yamiuchi tosei* (Itami) (as Oshizu); *Ai wa dokomaremo* (Uchida); *Kinno inakazamurai* (as Kishimatsu); *Byakuya no kyoen* (Makino) (as Oichi)

1933   *Iniwa Hachiro*; *Shinju fujin*; *Koya no ka*; *Tsukigata Hanpeita* (Ito) (as Umematsu); *Tange Sazen* (Ito) (as Hagino); *Konjikiyasha* (as Omiya); *Nyonin Mandara* (Ito) (as Yukiyo); *Dansai Hyoe issho-tabi*

1934   *Nyonin Mandara, Part II* (Ito) (as Yokimo); *Jinya no Shotaro*; *Budo kagami* (Itami) (as Otae); *Furyu katsujin-ken* (Yamanaka) (as Okyo); *Chirimen kuyo*; *Tange Sazen: Kenteki-hen*; *Ureshii koro*; *Chushingura: Ninjo-hen, Fukushu-hen* (as Yozenin); *Aizo-toge* (*The Mountain Pass of Love and Hate*) (Mizoguchi) (as Utakichi); *Sado jowa*; *Kensetsu no hitobito* (Ito)

1935   *Orizuru Osen* (*The Downfall of Osen*) (Mizoguchi) (as Osen); *Oroku kanzashi*; *Maria no Oyuki* (*Oyuki the Madonna*) (Mizoguchi) (title role); *Ojo Okichi*; *Chichi kaeru haha no kokoro*; *Shinno Tsuruchiyo* (Ito) (as Kikuhime and Himegiku)

1936   *Naniwa ereji* (*Osaka Elegy*) (Mizoguchi) (as Ayako Murai); *Shiju-hachi-nin me* (Ito); *Gion no shimai* (*Sisters of Gion*) (Mizoguchi) (as Umekichi); *Kutsukake Tokijiro* (Kinugasa) (as Okinu); *Aozora roshi* (as Fujio-hime)

1937   *Kinno inaka-zamurai*; *Then kurote-gume*; *Yoshia goten* (Nobuchi); *Nangoku satsuma-uta*; *Kekkon he no michi* (Tanaka); *Osaka natsu no jin* (*The Summer Battle of Osaka*) (Minugasa) (as Sen-hime)

1938   *Shizuka gozen*; *Uta-kichi andon*; *Tsuruhachi tsurijiro* (Naruse) (as Tsuruhachi); *Budo sen-ichi-ya*; *Shinpen Tange Sazen: Yoto no maki, Futate no maki* (Watanabe)

1939   *Chushingura, Part II* (as Okaru); *Higuchi Ichiyo* (title role); *Kenka-tobi* (Ishida); *Sono Zenya*; *Shinpen Tange Sazen: Sogan no maki, Koiguruma no maki* (Watanabe)

1940   *Keshoyuki*; *Hebihime-sama* (*The Snake Princess*) (Jinugasa) (as Oshima); *Niizuma kagami* (Watanabe); *Arashi nisakuhana*; *Mozu*; *Sakujitsu kieta oto* (as Kotomi)

1941   *Ani no hanayome*; *Shinpen bocchan*; *Kaiketsu*; *Shanhai no tsuki* (*Shanghai Moon*) (Naruse); *Yukiko to Natsuko*; *Jogakusei-ki*; *Kawanakajima gassen* (*The Battle of Kawanakajima*) (Jinugasa) (as Oshino)

1942   *Musashibo Benkei*; *Matteita otoko* (Makino); *Fukei-zu* (Makino) (as Otsuta); *Zoku Fukei-zu* (Makino) (as Otsuta)

1943   *Ina no Kantaro* (Takizawa) (as Oshin); *Uta-andon* (*The Song Lantern*) (Naruse) (as Osode), *Meijin Chojiro-bori* (Hagiwara) (as Outa); *Himetaru kakugo*

1944   *Shibaido* (*The Way of Drama*) (Naruse); *Yottsu no kekkon*

1946   *Hinoki butai* (Toyoda); *Aru yo no tonosama* (*Lord for a Night*) (Kinugasa) (as Omitsu)

1947   *Toho senichiya* (*1001 Nights with Toho*) (Ichikawa); *Joyu* (*Actress*) (Kinugasa) (as Sumako Matsui)

1948   *Koban-zame: Aizo-hen* (Kinugasa); *Koi okami-bi* (Suda) (as Kiyoshi Kusuda)

1949   *Hana no tsukihi*; *Koga yashiki* (*Koga Mansion*) (Kinugasa); *Hebihime dochu* (Kimura)

1950   *Koku Hebihime dochu* (Kimura); *Kageboshi*; *Zoku Kageboshi*; *Haruka nari haha no kuni* (Ito); *Otomi to Tosaburo* (Fuyushima) (as Otomi); *Bojo*; *Tateshi Danpei* (Makino); *Fuun Konpira-san*; *Amagi kara kita otoko*; *Midareboshi Aragami-yama* (Hagiwara)

1951   *Oboro-kago*; *Otsuya goroshi* (Makino); *Wagaya wa tanoshi* (Nakamura); *Kurama-tengu: Kakubei-jishi*; *Natsumaturi sando-gasa*; *Orizuru-gasa* (Fuyushima); *Umi no hanabi*; *Oedo gonin otoko*; *Satsuma hikyaku*

1952   *Haha nareba onna nareba* (Kamei); *Shusse tohi*; *Hanahagi sensei to Santa*; *Hakone fuun-roku* (Yamamoro, Kusuda, and Kosaka) (as Ritsu); *Ako-jo* (Hagiwara); *Tsukigata Hanpeita*; *Zoku Ako-jo* (Hagiwara); *Mazo*; *Itoshigo to taete yukamu* (Nakagawa); *Gendaijin* (Shibuya); *Mangetsu sanju-koku-sen* (Murune)

Isuzu Yamada

1953   *Edo iroha matsuri; Kaga-sodo* (Saeki); *Onna hitori daichi
       o yuku* (Kamei); *Shukuzu (Epitome)* (Shindo); *Kumo
       nagareru hate ni* (Ieki); *Abare-jishi; Miseraretaru
       tamashii; Hiroshima* (Sekigawa); *Onna Kanja hibun: Ako-
       roshi* (Sasaki)

1954   *Tojin Okichi; Mama no shinkon-ryoko; Kinsei Meishobu
       monogatari: Ogongai no hosha; Ooka seidan: Yogiden:
       Hakuro no kamen, Jigokudani no taiketsu; Mittsu no ai;
       Chushingura (47 Loyal Ronin)* (Ohsone) (as Riku); *Hirate
       Miki; Karatachi no hana; Okuman-choja (A Billionaire)*
       (Ichikawa)

1955   *Aisureba koso; Tokyo no sora no shita niwa; Ai no onimotsu*
       (Kawashima); *Banba no Chutaro; Yataro-gasa; Furisode
       kenpo; Minamoto Yoritsune; Takekurabe (Comparison of
       Heights; Growing Up; Daughters of Yoshiwara)* (Gosho) (as
       Oyoshi); *Hana hiraku; Araki Mataemon; Seido no Kirisuto*
       (Shibuya); *Jinsei tohbo-gaeri; Ishi-gassen* (Wakasugi) (as
       the mother); *Wakaki ushio*

1956   *Oatari otoko ichidai; Namida no hanamichi; Zoku
       Minamoto Toshitsune; Yuyake-gume (Clouds at Twilight)*
       (Kinoshita); *Hahako-zo* (Saeki); *Byosai monogatari; Aya
       ni kanashiki; Kyoraku yonin otoko; Neko to Shozo to
       futari no onna (A Man, a Cat and Two Women)* (Toyoda)
       (as Shinako); *Nagareru (Flowing)* (Naruse) (as Tsuta-
       yakko); *Oshidori no aida*

1957   *Kumonosu-jo (Throne of Blood; Cobweb Castle; The Castle
       of the Spider's Web; Macbeth)* (Kurosawa) (as Lady
       Washizu); *Onna dake no machi; Abarenbo kaido*
       (Uchida); *Tokyo boshoku (Tokyo Twilight)* (Ozu) (as
       Kikuko Soma); *Hikage no musume; Ikiteiru ningyo; Dai
       Chushingura; Donzoko (The Lower Depths)* (Kurosawa)
       (as Osugi, the landlady); *Kuroi kawa* (Kobayashi);
       Shitamachi (Downtown) (Chiba) (as Orio); *Samurai
       Nippon*

1958   *Haha san-nin; Shiki no aiyoku; Noren* (Kawashima); *Taiko-ki;
       Dai-Tokyo tanjo: Oedo no kane; Nemuri Kyoshiro burai
       hikae: Majin jigoku; Akujo no kisetsu* (Shibuya)

1959   *Fubuki to tomo ni kieyukinu; Shura-zakura; Aijo-fudo; Banjun
       no santo-kocho; Hime-yasha gyojo-ki; Todoke haha no
       sakebi; Hana no Banzui-in; Wakare; Furai monogatari:
       Ninkyo-hen; Onatsu torimono-cho: Tsukiyo ni kieta onna;
       Painappuru butai*

1960   *Sen-hime goten; Nurekami kenka tabi; Yokaren monogatari:
       Konpeki no sora toku; Hiho; Bonchi* (Ichikawa); *Tenpo
       rokkasen: Jigokuno hanamichi; Kusama no Hanjiro: Kiri
       no naka no wataridori; Ruten; Yoru no nagare; Onatsu
       torimono-cho: Torima; Furyu Fukagawa-uta; Furai
       monogatari: Abare Hisha; Tenka gomen; Robo no ishi (The
       Wayside Pebble)* (Hisamatsu)

1961   *Osaka-jo monogatari (Daredevil in the Castle; Devil in the
       Castle)* (Inagaki) (as Yodogimi); *Mozu* (Shibuya); **Yojimbo**
       (The Bodyguard) (Kurosawa) (as Orin); *Anju to Zushio-
       maru* (animation) (as voice); *Hitorine; Shaka (Buddha)*
       (Misumi) (as Kalidevi)

1962   *Sanroku; Yama no sanka: Moyuru wakamono-tachi (Glory
       on the Summit; Burning Youth)* (Shinoda) (as Taka Hirooka);
       Sanbyaku-rokuju-go-ya; Shin no shikotei (The Great Wall)
       (Tanaka) (as dowager empress)

1963   *Sakiko-san chotto; Ratai (The Body)* (Narusawa)

1967   *Ooku maruhi monogatari*

1970   *Onna kumicho*

1978   *Yagyu ichizoku no inbo (Shogun's Samurai)* (Fukasaku) (as
       Sugenin Oeyo)

Publications

By YAMADA: article—

"Memories of Mizoguchi," in *Cinema* (Beverly Hills), Spring 1971.

*   *   *

Still a teenager, but an actor's daughter, Isuzu Yamada began her
career as a period film star at the Nikkatsu Studio in 1930. She studied
with director Kunio Watanabe, and, through working with excellent
period film directors such as Ito, Itami, Uchida, Inagaki, Makino, and
Yamanaka, and playing opposite such stars as Denjiro Okochi and
Chiezo Kataoko, she gradually established herself as the most popular
actress at Nikkatsu.

She did not gain critical acclaim, however, until her two films for
Mizoguchi in 1936: *Osaka Elegy* and *Sisters of Gion*. In both films she
played strong-willed "modern girls" (*moga*) who rebel against their
environments, using their beauty and youth to take advantage of
exploitative men, although they are finally vanquished by them.
Yamada achieved powerful performances, even utilizing the Osaka
and Kyoto dialects to project a heightened realism. In the famous last
shot of *Osaka Elegy*, which is the film's only close-up, Yamada stares
defiantly at the camera, directly implicating the audience in her
character's downfall.

During the war she established the theater group Shin Engi-za with
actor Kazuo Hasegawa and continued her stage activities. Her postwar
film work began with her collaboration with Kinugasa, producing fine
results such as *Lord for a Night*, in which she lightly played the role of
a pure-hearted inn maid, and *Actress*, in which she passionately portrayed the innovative actress Sumako Matsui.

After her private relationship with Kinugasa (her fourth of six
husbands) ended and she began a new relationship with leftist actor
Yoshi Kato, Yamada started to participate in the leftist independent
film movement. One of the representative works that brought her
recognition was her performance as the wife in the feudal period piece
Hakone fuun-roku.

Although Yamada, in a prolific professional career, played various
roles for many directors including Ichikawa, Kobayashi, Kawashima,
Shibuya and Shinoda, her most memorable postwar roles are those of
the ex-wife in Toyoda's comedy, *A Man, a Cat and Two Women*, and
of the weary brothel owner in Naruse's *Flowing*. For Kurosawa, she
played Lady Washizu (Macbeth) in *Throne of Blood*, employing the
Noh play-style of acting with horrifying effectiveness; the role brought
her international acclaim. She also starred as the greedy landlord's
wife in *The Lower Depths* and the nagging wife of the head of a
competing sect in *Yojimbo*. Her intensity was well-suited to Kurosawa's
powerful direction. She excelled at powerful portrayals of strong-
willed women as well as the more delicate characterizations of women
who are aging and showing the suffering of life.

Her achievements were acknowledged many times during her long
stage and screen career. The consistent high quality of her best-known
performances makes one wish her many other films were more widely
available.

—Kyoko Hirano, updated by Corey K. Creekmur

YAMAMURA, So

Nationality: Japanese. **Born:** Yoshisda Koga in Tenri City, 24 February 1910. **Education:** Studied German literature at Imperial University, Tokyo, was graduated in 1935. **Military Service:** 1944-45.

Career: Actor and director with the Taiyo-za theater; joined the Shochiku studio's Kansai Shimpa group; 1936—co-founder of the Inoue Engeki Dojo theater group, and formed the Bunka-za theater group, 1942; 1946—film debut in *Inochi aru kagiri*; 1952-54—founding member of Gendai Production Company; 1953—directed his first film, *Kani-ko sen*; 1954-65—director of the Ginza Production Company; active in television since the mid-1960s. **Awards:** Several Japanese prizes for acting and directing.

Films as Actor:

1946 *Inochi aru kagiri* (Kusada)
1947 *Chikagai no nijuyo-jikan*; *Joyu Sumako no koi* (Mizoguchi) (as Hogetsu Shimamura)
1948 *Dai-ni no jinsei* (Sekigawa); *Otoko o sabaku onna* (Sasaki); *Taifu-ken no onna* (as gangster boss); *Midori naki shima*; *Yukyo no mure* (Osone)
1949 *Onna no tatakai*; *Kirare no Senta*; *Utsukushiki batsu* (Oba); *Ryusei* (Abe); *Umi no yaju*; *Daitokai no kao* (Abe); *Maboroshi fujin*; *Hana no sugao*
1950 *Shojo-dakara* (Shima); *Kageboshi*; *Hakuchu no ketto* (Saeiki); *Haha-tsubaki*; *Tokyo mushuku* (Chiba); *Josei tai dansei* (Saburi); *Ai no sanga*; *Dokuga* (Sunohara); *Shiroi yaju*; *Nankai no joka*; *Munekata-shima* (*The Munekata Sisters*) (Ozu) (as Kyosuke Mimura); *Senka o koete* (Sekigawa); *Yuki-fujin ezu* (*Madame Yuki*) (Mizoguchi) (as Tatsuoka); *Gunkan sudeni kemuri nashi* (Sekigawa); *Otone no yogiri* (Hirade); *Kikyo* (Oba); *Jonetsu no rumuba*
1951 *Eriko to tomoni* (Toyoda) (as Eriko's father); *Zemma* (*The Good Fairy*) (Kinoshita); *Nessa no byakuran* (Kimura); *Jiyu gakko* (Yoshimura); *Sonohito no na wa ienai* (Sugie); *Dare ga watashi o sabakunoka* (Taniguchi); *Sekirei no kyoku* (Toyoda); *Maihime*; *Musashino fujin* (*Lady Musashino*) (Mizoguchi) (as Eiji Ono); *Hirate Miki* (Namiki) (title role); *Hibari no komori-uta*; *Honoo no hada*
1952 *Meshi* (*Repast*) (Naruse); *Kenju jigoku*; *Keian hi-cho*; *Gunro no machi*; *Seishun kaigi*; *Kaze futatabi* (Toyoda); *Uogashi shunjitsu*; *Okuni to Gohei*; *Shinrun dorobo*; *Atakake no hitobito* (Hisamatsu); *Konna watashi ja nakattani*; *Onna no inochi*; *Asakusa yonin shimai*; *Gendaijin* (Shibuya); *Choito neesan omoide yanagi*; *Ashi ni sawatta onna* (*The Woman Who Touched Legs*) (Ichikawa); *Oka wa hanazakari* (Chiba); *Ringo-en no shojo*; *Joka* (Oba)
1953 *Fukeyo harukaza* (Taniguchi); *Mura hachibu* (Imaizumi); *Shukuzu* (*Epitome*) (Shindo); *Ganpeki* (Nakamura); *Ochiba nikki*; *Tokyo monogatari* (*Tokyo Story*) (Ozu) (as Koichi); *Nigorie* (*Muddy Water*) (Imai)
1954 *Yama no oto* (*Sounds from the Mountains*; *Sound of the Mountain*) (Naruse); *Moeru Shanhai*; *Shinjitsu ichiro*; *Rakei kazoku*; *Kaze tachinu*; *Mama no shinkon-ryoko*; *Kakute yume ari*; *Dobu* (*Gutter*) (Shindo); *Nippon yaburezu*; *Karatachi no hana*; *Otsukisama niwa waruikedo*
1955 *Hitokiri Hikosai*; *Aisureba koso*; *Sugata Sanshiro*; *Ikitoshi ikeru mono*; *Sengoku hibun*; *Bocchan kisha*; *Ai no inomotsu*; *Mori Ranmaru*; *Yuki no honoo*; *Jukyu no hanayome*; *Seishun kaidan*; *Yokihi* (*Princess Yang Kwei-fei*) (Mizoguchi) (as Anrokuzan); *Ashita kuru hito*; *Fukushu no shichikamen*
1956 *Soshun* (*Early Spring*) (Ozu) (as Yutaka Kawai); *Ma no kisetsu: Haru no mizuumi*; *Mahiru no ankoku* (*Darkness at Noon*) (Imai); *Shu to midori* (Nakamura); *Wasureenu bojo* (Champi); *Tsuruhachi Tsurujiro*; *Nisshoku no natsu* (Horikawa); *Tsukigata Hanpeita: Hana no maki, Arashi no maki* (Kinugasa) (as Kogoro Katsura); *Yonjuhachi-sai no teiko* (*48-Year-Old Rebel*; *Protest at 48 Years Old*)

(Yoshimura); *Hana futatabi*; *Typhon sur Nagasaki* (*Typhoon over Nagasaki*) (Ciampi)
1957 *Kyofu no kuchu satsujin*; *Hakuji no hito*; *Fujinka-i no kokuhaku*; *Tokyo boshoku* (*Tokyo Twilight*) (Ozu) (as Tsumoru Sekiguchi); *Doshaburi* (Nakamura); *Jigokubana*; *Chieko-sho* (Kumagai) (as Kotaro Takamura); *Yoruno cho* (*Night Butterflies*) (Yoshimura); *Bakuon to daichi* (Sekigawa); *Ana* (*The Pit*; *The Hole*) (Ichikawa)
1958 *Anzukko* (Naruse); *Gendai mushuku*; *Yatsu no hajiki wa jigoku daze*; *Oban: Kanketsu-hen* (Chiba); *Hibari no hanagata tantei gassen*; *Kibo no otome*; *Murasaki zukin*; *Musume no naka no musume*; *The Barbarian and the Geisha* (Huston) (as Tamura)
1959 *Chushingura* (as Hyobu Chisaka); **Ningen no joken** (*The Human Condition*; *No Greater Love*) (Kobayashi) (as Okishima); *Muhomachi no yarodomo*; *Yoru no haiyaku*; *Kurobune*; *Itazura* (Nakamura); *Tatsumaki bugyo*; *Jigoku no soko made tsukiauze*; *Jyan Arima no shugeki*; *Shizukanaru kyodan*; *Shingo jubanshobu, Part II*; *Yami o yokogire*
1960 *Hibari no zoku beranmee geisha*; *Hatamoto to Banshiin: Otoko no Taiketsu*; *Orekara ikuzo*; *Shori to haiboku*; *Keishicho monogatari: Kikikomi*; *Fundoshi isha* (*The Country Doctor*; *Life of a Country Doctor*) (Inagaki) (as Dr. Meikai Ikeda); *Sabaku o wataru taiyo*; *Furyo shojo*
1961 *Berammee geisha makaridoru*; *Ore ga jigoku no tejina-shi da*; *Are ga minato no tomoshibi da* (*That Is the Port Light*) (Imai); *Hanjo* (Nakamura); *Hatamoto kenka-daka*; *Gonin no totsugekitai*; *Waga koi no tabiji*; *Hayabusa daimyo*; *Anju to Zushio-maru* (animation) (as voice); *Kako* (Nakamura); *Haitoku no mesu* (Nomura); *Netsuaisha*; *Happyakuman-goku ni idomu otoko*; *Sekai daisenso* (Matsubayashi); *Aijo no keifu* (*Record of Love*; *Love's Family Tree*) (Gosho) (as Shuzo sugi)
1962 *Katei no jijo*; *Senkyaku banrai* (Nakamura); *Yume de aritai*; *Yopparai tengoku*; *Karami-ai* (*The Inheritance*) (Kobayashi) (as clerk); *Musume to watashi* (*My Daughter and I*) (Horikawa) (as the father); *Taiheiyo senso to himeyurri butai*; *Ano kumo no hate ni hoshi wa matataku*; *Akitsu onsen* (Yoshida); *Honkon no hoshi* (*Star of Hong Kong*) (Chiba); *Yama no sanka: Moyuru wakamonotachi* (*Glory on the Summit*; *Burning Youth*) (Shinoda) (as Eijo Hirooka); *Gishi shimatu-ki*; *Namidao Shishi no tategami no* (*Tears on the Lion's Mane*) (Shinoda); *Kanshaku rojin nikki* (Kimura); *Kawano hotoride* (*Born in Sin*)
1963 *Ano hashi no tamoto de, Part III: Ano hito was ima* (Nomura); *Staatanjo*; *Hana no saku ie*; *Zoku shinobi no mono* (*Return of Ninja*) (Yamamoto) (as Mitsuhide Akechi); *Gyangu chushingura*; *Oni-kenji*; *Akatsuki no gassho*
1964 *Kizudarake no sanga* (Yamamoto) (as Katsuhei Arima)
1965 *Nikutai no gakko* (*School for Sex*; *School of Love*) (Kinoshita); *Ane to imouto*; *Utsukishisa to kanashimi to* (*With Beauty and Sorrow*) (Shinoda) (as Toshio Ooki); *Taiheiyo kiseki no sakusen: Kisuka*
1967 *Nippon no ichiban nagai hi* (*The Emperor and a General*) (Okamoto) (as Navy Minister)
1970 *Gekido no Showa-shi: Gunbatsu* (Horikawa); *Tora! Tora! Tora!* (Flcischer) (as Adm. Isoroku Yamamoto)
1972 *Kozure ookami: Oya no kokoro ko no kokoro*
1973 *Hissatsu shikake-nin*; *Hissatsu shikaki-nin: Baiko ari-jigoku*
1974 *Hissatsu shikake-nin: Shinsetsu shikake-bari*; *Nostoradamusu no daiyogen* (*Prophecies of Nostradamus*; *Catastrophe 1999*) (Masuda)
1975 *Domyaku retto* (Masumura)
1978 *Inubue* (Nakajima)

So Yamamura (right) with Kuniko Miyake in _Tokyo monogatari_

1983   _Nankyoku monogatari (Antarctica)_ (Kurahara)
1986   _Gung Ho (Working Class Man)_ (Ron Howard) (as Mr. Sakamoto)

Films as Actor and Director:

1953   _Kani-ko sen (The Crab-Canning Ship)_ (ro as Matsuki, + sc)
1954   _Kuroi ushio (Black Tide)_ (as Hayami)
1955   _Sara no hanano toge_
1959   _Hahakogusa_; _Kashimanada no onna (The Maidens of Yashima Sea)_
1960   _Furyu Fukagawa uta (The Song of Fukagawa)_

Publications

On YAMAMURA: article—

Buehrer, Beverley Bare, in _Japanese Films: A Filmography and Commentary, 1921-1989_, Jefferson, North Carolina, 1990.

*   *   *

So Yamamura began his career as a stage actor, shifting to film after World War II. Perhaps because of his origins, he always studies the screenplay before accepting a role. His acting style is as careful as his attitude.

Yamamura's greatest recognition in his early period was the result of his portrayal of the stagnant husband in Ozu's _The Munekata Sisters_. He depicted this lonely man's frustration so effectively that he made the character seem sympathetic as well as depressing. His vivid performance seemed to symbolize the bleak family relationships of the postwar period. Among Yamamura's contributions to Ozu's other films, his controlled performance as the eldest son in _Tokyo Story_ is especially memorable.

In addition to his work with Ozu, Yamamura played several important roles of the films of Mizoguchi. Eventually, however, he established a leftist independent film company, Gendai Productions, and actively involved himself in the independent film movement. He produced and directed several films that were politically controversial and were not accepted by the major studios, but that demonstrated his ability to give realistic performances and to create dynamic and carefully constructed films. Examples of these include _Kani-ko sen_, which depicts the exploitation of a crab ship's workers (based on a proletarian literary classic), and _Kuroi ushio_, which tells the story of a reporter who challenges authority, only to be ultimately defeated by it.

Perhaps Yamamura's most remarkable characteristic is his versatility. Some of his most moving performances have been in the role of an older man in love with a younger woman, as in the sensitive film adaptations of Kawabata's novels, _Sound of the Mountain_ and _With Beauty and Sorrow_. Perhaps the most outstanding creation of Yamamura's film career, however, is the business mogul in Satsuo Yamamoto's _Kizudarake no sanga_, which has become the archetype of the lonely villain who is also a victim of his own boundless ambition. Yamamura's versatility as an actor is ample proof that his talent is equal to his integrity and devotion to his craft.

—Kyoko Hirano

YANKOVSKY, Oleg

Pseudonym: Oleg Jankowski. **Nationality:** Russian. **Born:** 23 February1944. **Education:** Studied acting at the Solonov Actors Studio, Saratov, was graduated 1965. **Family:** Married Lyudmila Zorina, one son. **Career:** Stage actor with the Saratov Drama Theatre, and since 1977 at the Lenin Komsomol Theatre, Moscow: roles in Russian and foreign classics; 1968—film debut in *Shchit i mech*; also a television actor. **Address:** Komsomolsky Prospekt 41, Apt. 10, 119270 Moscow, Russia.

Films as Actor:

1968 *Shchit i mech* (*Shield and Sword*) (Basov) (as Heinrich Schwartzkopf); *Sluzhili dva tovarishcha* (*Two Comrades Served*) (Karelov) (as Nekrasov)

1969 *Beloe solntse pustiny* (*The White Sun of the Wilderness*) (Motyl); *Zhdi menya, Ana* (*Wait for Me, Ana*) (Vinogradov) (as Sergei Novikov); *Daleko ot voiny* (*Far from War*)

1970 *Ya, Frantsisk skorina* (Stepanov) (title role); *Rasplata* (*Payment*) (Filippov) (as Alexei Platov); *Sokhranivshie ogon* (Karelov) (as Semion)

1971 *O lyubvi* (*About Love*)

1972 *Gonshchiki* (*The Racers*) (Maslennikov) (as Sergachev)

1974 *Ghev* (Gibu and Proskurov) (as Leonte Chebotaru); *Pod kamennym nebom* (*Beneath a Stony Sky*) (Anderson and Maslennikov) (as Iashka); *Premiya* (*The Prize*) (Mikaelyan) (as Sololakhin)

1975 *Zerkalo* (*The Mirror*) (Tarkovsky) (as Otets); *Chuzhie pisma* (*Other People's Letters*) (Averbakh) (as Priakhin); *Zvezda plenitelnogo schastya* (*The Star of Captivating Happiness*) (Motyl) (as Ryleev)

1976 *Dlinnoe, dlinnoe delo* (*A Long, Long Affair*) (Aronov and Shredel) (as Vorontsov); *Doverie* (*Trust*) (Tregubovich) (as Piatakov); *Polkovnik v otstavke* (*The Retired Colonel*) (Sheshukov) (as Alexei); *72 gradusa nizhe nulia* (*72 Degrees below Zero*) (Danilin and Tatarskii) (as Sergei Popov); *Sladkaya zhenzhchina* (*A Sweet Woman*) (Fetin) (as Tikhon); *Slovo dlya zashchity* (*A Word for the Defense*) (Abrashitov) (as Ruslan); *Sentimentalnyi roman* (Maslennikov) (as Ilya Gorodnitskii)

1977 *Obratnaya svyaz* (*Feedback*) (Tregubovich) (as Sakulin); *The Shooting Party* (Lotyanu)

1978 *Moi laskovyi i nezhnyi zver* (*My Tender Loving Beast*) (Lotyanu) (as Kamyshev); *Povorot* (*The Turning Point*) (Abrashitov) (as Viktor Vedeneev); *Obuknovennoe utro* (Zakharov) (as Khoziain)

1979 *Tot samyi Myunkhauzen* (*Munchhausen Himself*) (Zakharov) (title role); *Otkrytaya kniga* (*An Open Book*) (Fetin) (as Raevskii)

1980 *My, nizhepodpisavshiesya...* (*We, the Undersigned*) (Lioznova) (as Semenov)

1981 *Shlyapa* (*The Hat*) (Kvinikhidze) (as Lenisov); *Sobaka Baskervilei* (Maslennikov—for TV) (as Stepelton)

1982 *Vlublen po sobstvennomu zelanij* (*Voluntarily in Love*) (Mikaelyan) (as Igor); *Polioty vo sne naiavou* (*Dream Flights*) (Balayan) (as Sergei Makarov); *Dom, kotoryi postroil svift* (Zakharov—for TV)

1983 *Nostalghia* (*Nostalgia*) (Tarkovsky) (as Gortchkov)

1986 *Khrani menio, moi talisman* (Balayan) (as Liosha Dmitriev)

1987 *Kreutzerova Sonata* (Shveytizer) (as Vasili Pozdynshev)

1988 *Filer* (Balayan)

1989 *Ubit Drakona* (Zakharov); *Az en XX. Szazadom* (*My 20th Century*) (Enyedi) (as Z)

1990 *Mado, Poste Restante* (as Jean-Marie Zerlini)

1991 *Tsareubiitsa* (*Assassin of the Tsar*) (Shakhnazarov) (as Dr. Smirnov/Tsar Nicholas II)

1993 *Moi Ivan, Toi Abraham* (*Ivan and Abraham*; *Me Ivan, You Abraham*) (Zauberman)

1995 *Mute Witness* (Waller) (as Larsen)

Publications

By YANKOVSKY: articles—

Isskustvo Kino (Moscow), November 1973.
Interviews in *Soviet Film* (Moscow), no. 11, 1976, and no. 10, 1978.
Interview with Clare Kitson, in the *Guardian* (London), 20 April 1989.

On YANKOVSKY: articles—

"Actors and Roles: Oleg Yankovsky," in *Soviet Film* (Moscow), no. 242, 1977.
Lyndina, E., "Strong, Manly, Tender," in *Soviet Film* (Moscow), no. 12, 1981.
Soviet Film (Moscow), no. 10, 1984, and no. 1, 1987.

*   *   *

Oleg Yankovsky's film career was launched by a chance meeting with the Soviet film director Vladimir Basov in a cafe in Lvov. Basov invited the young actor, a graduate of the Solonov Actors Studio in Saratov, to play the antagonist in his next film, *Shchit i mech*.

Since that auspicious debut, Yankovsky's career has been closely tied to the new artistic tendencies in Soviet cinema, particularly when it comes to portraying new conceptions of traditional figures. In the 1960s and early 1970s, Yankovsky's roles were predominantly patterned around this theme—several directors found his boyish figure, intelligently ironic features, and sardonic smile ideally suited to their unconventional approaches to historical characters. The most notable example of Yankovsky's work from this period is his Nekrasov in *Sluzhili dva tovarishcha*, a student in St. Petersburg who joins the Red Army, taking part in the Revolution not only with his gun, but with his camera. The director, Karelov, had originally intended Yankovsky for the part of the antagonist Brusnetzov (played by Vladimir Visodsky), but gambled successfully on Yankovsky's ability to play heroic roles without resorting to larger-than-life mannerisms. Instead, Yankovsky's special ability appears to be his talent for making historic figures seem familiar and understandable to contemporary audiences, an attribute also evident in his performance in the title role of *Ya, Frantsisk skorina* as an enlightened 14th-century humanitarian.

Yankovsky's realistic talent made him a natural candidate for roles in contemporary Soviet films that focused on the complex moral and social issues confronting a socialist economic system. His ability to express the inner emotions of his characters lifted his portrayals of Communist Party leaders (in *Premiya* and *Obratnaya svyaz*) far above the popular film stereotypes.

Oleg Yankovsky in *Zerkalo*

Perhaps the most consistent feature of Yankovsky's film career has been his constant diversification of roles. This tendency became very evident in the 1970s, when Yankovsky's creative restlessness propelled him through a large group of varied roles, not all of them major (some were small and even episodic). Throughout this diversity, a unifying theme remained in the actor's continued exploration of complex, often contradictory characters, who frequently undergo violent emotional turmoil. An especially interesting example is Yankovsky's performance in Emil Lotyanu's *Moi laskovyi i nezhnyi zver*. In this adaptation of Chekhov's *Hunting Drama*, Yankovsky's character is Kamyshev, a bright and gifted man whose personality is dramatically crushed by the mediocre pettiness and false morality of a small provincial Russian town. Yankovsky gives one of his best performances as he expresses the gradual deterioration of Kamyshev's character, which ultimately transforms him into a murderer.

Character transformation is also a central theme of the musical *Shlyapa*, in which Yankovsky played an egocentric trumpeter who survives a deep emotional crisis, affecting both his private life and his career. Similarly, Yankovsky has played Igor, an alcoholic who reforms, in *Vlublen po sobstvennomu zelanij*.

Yankovsky is also known for his collaboration with the director Andrey Tarkovsky in *Nostalghia* and *Zerkalo*. In addition to his active film career, Yankovsky also continues to act on the stage, maintaining his status as one of the most popular Russian actors.

—Christina Stoyanova

YORK, Susannah

Nationality: British. **Born:** Susannah Yolande Fletcher in London, England, 9 January 1941. **Education:** Attended Marr College, Troon, Scotland; Royal Academy of Dramatic Art, London, 1956-58. **Family:** Married Michael Wells, 1960 (divorced 1976), children: Sasha, Orlando. **Career:** On stage with provincial repertory companies; 1960—film debut in *Tunes of Glory*; 1964—on stage in *Wings of the Dove*; later roles in *The Maids*, 1974, *Peter Pan*, 1977, *Hedda Gabler*, 1981, and *Agnes of God*, 1983; 1982—in TV series *We'll Meet Again*; also *Trainer* and *Devices and Desires*, 1991; 1985—in TV mini-series

Tender Is the Night. **Awards:** Best Supporting Actress, British Academy, for *They Shoot Horses, Don't They?*, 1969; Best Actress, Cannes Festival, for *Images*, 1972.

Films as Actress:

1960   *Tunes of Glory* (Neame) (as Morag Sinclair); *There Was a Crooked Man* (Burge) (as Ellen)

1961   *The Greengage Summer* (*Loss of Innocence*) (Lewis Gilbert) (as Joss Grey)

1962   *Freud* (*Freud: The Secret Passion*) (Huston) (as Cecily Koertner)

1963   **Tom Jones** (Richardson) (as Sophie Western)

1964   *The Seventh Dawn* (Lewis Gilbert) (as Candace Trumpey); *Scene Nun, Take One* (Hatton) (as the actress)

1965   *Scruggs* (Hart) (as Susan); *Sands of the Kalahari* (Endfield) (as Grace Monckton)

1966   *Kaleidoscope* (*The Bank Breaker*) (Smight) (as Angel McGinnis); *A Man for All Seasons* (Zinnemann) (as Margaret More)

1968   *Mr. Sebastian* (*Sebastian*) (David Greene) (as Becky Howard); *Duffy* (Parrish) (as Segolene); *The Killing of Sister George* (Aldrich) (as Alice "Childie" McNaught)

1969   *Lock Up Your Daughters* (Coe) (as Hilaret); *Oh! What a Lovely War* (Attenborough) (as Eleanor); *Battle of Britain* (Hamilton) (as Section Officer Maggie Harvey); *They Shoot Horses, Don't They?* (Pollack) (as Alice LeBlanc); *Country Dance* (*Brotherly Love*) (J. Lee Thompson) (as Hilary Dow)

1971   *Zee and Company* (*X, Y, and Zee*) (Hutton) (as Stella); *Jane Eyre* (Delbert Mann—for TV) (title role); *Happy Birthday, Wanda June* (Robson) (as Penelope Ryan); *Second Chance* (Tewksbury—for TV)

1972   *Images* (Altman) (as Cathryn, + story)

1974   *Gold* (Hunt) (as Terry Steyner)

1975   *Conduct Unbecoming* (Anderson) (as Mrs. Marjorie Scarlett); *The Maids* (Miles) (as Claire); *That Lucky Touch* (Miles) (as Julia Richardson)

1976   *Sky Riders* (Hickox) (as Ellen Bracken); *Eliza Fraser* (Burstall) (title role)

1978   *Superman* (Richard Donner) (as Lara); *The Shout* (Skolimowski) (as Rachel)

1979   *The Silent Partner* (Duke) (as Julie Carver); *The Golden Gate Murders* (*Phantom of the Golden Gate*; *Specter on the Bridge*) (Grauman—for TV) (as Sister Venecia)

1980   *The Awakening* (Newell) (as Jane Turner); *Superman II* (Lester) (as Lara); *Long Shot* (Hatton) (as herself); *Falling in Love Again* (*In Love*) (Paul) (as Sue Lewis, + co-sc); *Loophole* (*Break In*) (Quested) (as Dinah Booker)

1982   *We'll Meet Again* (Wharmby—for TV)

1983   *Yellowbeard* (Damski) (as Lady Churchill); *Nelly's Version* (Hatton) (as narrator)

1984   *A Christmas Carol* (Clive Donner—for TV) (as Mrs. Cratchit); *Macho* (Gessner—for TV)

1985   *A Month in the Country* (Lawrence); *Star Quality* (Dosser—for TV) (as Lorraine Barry)

1986   *Alice* (Gruza); *Daemon* (Finbow); *Thriller* (Gessner—for TV); *Walkie Talkie* (Perkins)

1987   *Prettykill* (Kaczender) (as Toni); *Barbablu Barbablu* (Carpi); *Mio, moy mio* (Grammatikov) (as The Weaver Woman); *Superman IV: The Quest for Peace* (Furie) (as voice of Lara)

1988   *Just Ask for a Diamond* (*Diamond's Edge*) (Bayly) (as Lauren Bacardi); *A Summer Story* (Haggard) (as Mrs. Narracombe); *American Roulette* (Hatton—for TV)

1989   *Melancholia* (Engel) (as Catherine Lanham Franck); *En Handfull Tid* (*A Handful of Time*) (Asphaug)

1990   *Fate* (Paul); *The Man from the Pru* (Rohrer—for TV) (as Amy Wallace)

1992   *Illusions* (Kulle) (as Dr. Sanders)

1993   *Piccolo Grande Amore* (*Pretty Princess*) (Vanzina) (as Queen Christina)

Publications

By YORK: books—

In Search of Unicorns, London, 1973.
Lark's Castle, London, 1974.
The Big One, edited by York, London, 1984.

By YORK: articles—

"Experiences," interview with D. Elley, in *Focus on Film* (London), Spring 1972.
"House of York," interview with J. Williams, in *Films Illustrated* (London), 25 November 1972.
Interview with J. Calendo, in *Interview* (New York), January 1973.
"Susannah York: Realization and Relationships," interview in *Films* (London), April 1981.

On YORK: articles—

Lawrenson, H., "Susannah York," in *Show* (Hollywood), January 1962.
Elley, D., "Wistfulness and Dry Hankies: Susannah York," in *Focus on Film* (London), Summer 1972.
"Susannah!," in *Harper's Bazaar* (New York), September 1981.

*   *   *

When Susannah York started her career, one might have been tempted to think of her merely as the thinking man's bimbo with her blond, engaging loveliness and ingenuous blue eyes. She has, however, tackled a wide variety of roles in her film career and given the lie to this crass assumption.

After her first film role, as Alec Guinness's daughter in *Tunes of Glory*, Guinness called her "the best thing in films since Audrey Hepburn." York also played a sweet young thing in the Norman Wisdom comedy *There Was a Crooked Man*, and a lovesick schoolgirl in *The Greengage Summer* with Kenneth More, then appeared opposite Montgomery Clift in John Huston's *Freud*. The role that made her name, however, was as the captivating, innocent, and sensuous Sophie Western opposite Albert Finney in *Tom Jones*. After three fairly dire American films, she departed from her usual parts to play Sir Thomas More's grave and intellectual daughter in *A Man for All Seasons* and the passive and childlike lesbian roommate of Beryl Reid in *The Killing of Sister George* amidst all the publicity attendant upon her love scene with Coral Browne. In 1969 she won an Oscar for her performance as a blond flapper/movie aspirant in *They Shoot Horses, Don't They?* She also made *Sky Riders* with James Coburn, starred with Elizabeth Taylor and Michael Caine in *Zee and Company*, and appeared in a television film of *Jane Eyre* with George C. Scott.

While her roles in the 1960s and 1970s made her an international name, superstardom eluded her. One of her most interesting films of this period was Robert Altman's dreamlike psycho-thriller *Images* in which she played an author of children's books, which she subsequently became in real life.

Her most recent role in a major film was as Christopher Reeve's birth mother on the planet Krypton in the first two *Superman* films;

Susannah York

her voice alone returned for the final installment in the series, *Superman IV: The Quest for Peace*. She continues to remain active in films for British and American television—among the most interesting recent examples of which was *The Man from the Pru*, a fictional recounting of Britain's notorious Wallace murder case (the same case that inspired the play and film *Dial M for Murder*), co-starring Jonathan Pryce.

—Sylvia Paskin, updated by John McCarty

YOUNG, Loretta

Nationality: American. **Born:** Gretchen Michaela Young in Salt Lake City, 6 January 1913; grew up in Hollywood. **Education:** Attended the Ramona Convent, Alhambra, California. **Family:** Married 1) Grant Withers, 1930 (divorced 1931), adopted daughter: Judy; 2) Thomas H. A. Lewis, 1940, sons: Christopher Paul and Peter; 3) costume designer Jean Louis, 1993. **Career:** Film debut as extra at age five in *The Only Way*; late 1920s—contract with First National, and with 20th Century-Fox, 1933-40; 1953-61—host and occasionally actress in *The Loretta Young Show* (anthology program), and actress in the drama series *The New Loretta Young Show*, 1962-63. **Awards:** Best Actress Academy Award for *The Farmer's Daughter*, 1947.

Films as Actress:

1919　*The Only Way* (Melford) (as child on the operating table); *Sirens of the Sea* (bit role)
1921　*The Son of the Sheik* (Melford) (as Arab child)
1927　*Naughty but Nice* (Webb)
1928　*Her Wild Oat* (Neilan); *The Whip Woman* (Boyle); *Laugh, Clown, Laugh* (Bernon); *The Magnificent Flirt* (D'Arrast); *The Head Man* (Cline); *Scarlett Seas* (Dillon)
1929　*The Squall* (Korda) (as Irma); *The Girl in the Glass Cage* (Dawson) (as Gladys Cosgrove); *Fast Life* (Dillon); *The Careless Age* (Wray) (as Muriel); *The Show of Shows* (Adolfi); *The Forward Pass* (Cline) (as Patricia Carlyle)
1930　*The Man from Blankley's* (Green) (as Margery Seaton); *The Second-Story Murder* (Del Ruth) (as Marian Ferguson); *Loose Ankles* (Wilde) (as Ann Harper Berry); *Road to Paradise* (Beaudine) (as Margaret Waring/Mary Brennan); *Kismet* (Dillon) (as Marsinah); *The Truth about Youth* (Seiter) (as Phyllis Ericson); *The Devil to Pay* (Fitzmaurice) (as Dorothy Hope)
1931　*Beau Ideal* (Brenon) (as Isobel Brandon); *The Right of Way* (Lloyd) (as Rosalie Evantural); *Three Girls Lost* (Lanfield) (as Noreen McMann); *Too Young to Marry* (Leroy) (as Elaine Bumpstead); *Big Business Girl* (Seiter) (as Claire McIntyre); *I Like Your Nerve* (McGann) (as Diane); *Platinum Blonde* (Capra) (as Gallagher); *The Ruling Voice* (Lee) (as Gloria Bannister)
1932　*Taxi!* (Del Ruth) (as Sue Riley); *The Hatchet Man* (Wellman) (as Toya San); *Play Girl* (*Love on a Budget*) (Enright) (as Buster); *Weekend Marriage* (Freeland) (as Lola Davis); *Life Begins* (Flood and Nugent) (as Grace Sutton); *They Call It Sin* (Freeland) (as Marion Cullen)
1933　*Employee's Entrance* (Del Ruth) (as Madeline); *Grand Slam* (Dieterle) (as Marcia Stanislavsky); *Zoo in Budapest* (Lee) (as Eve); *The Life of Jimmy Dolan* (*The Sucker*) (Mayo) (as Peggy); *Midnight Mary* (*Lady of the Night*) (Wellman) (as Mary Martin); *Heros for Sale* (*Breadline*) (Wellman) (as

Ruth Loring); *The Devil's in Love* (Dieterle) (as Margot); *She Had to Say Yes* (Berkeley and Amy) (as Florence Denny); *A Man's Castle* (Borzage) (as Trina)
1934　*The House of Rothschild* (Werker) (as Julie); *Born to Be Bad* (Sherman) (as Letty Strong); *Bulldog Drummond Strikes Back* (Del Ruth) (as Lola Field); *Caravan* (Charell) (as Countess Wilma); *The White Parade* (Cummings) (as June Arden)
1935　*Clive of India* (Boleslawski) (as Margaret Maskelyne Clive); *Shanghai* (Flood) (as Barbara Howard); *Call of the Wild* (Wellman) (as Claire Blake); *The Crusades* (DeMille) (as Berengaria)
1936　*The Unguarded Hour* (Wood) (as Lady Helen Dearden); *Private Number* (Del Ruth) (as Ellen Neal); *Ramona* (King) (title role); *Ladies in Love* (Edward Griffith) (as Susie Schmidt)
1937　*Love Is News* (Garnett) (as Tony Gateson); *Café Metropole* (Edward Griffith) (as Laura Ridgeway); *Love under Fire* (Marshall) (as Myra Cooper); *Wife, Doctor, and Nurse* (Walter Lang) (as Ina); *Second Honeymoon* (Walter Lang) (as Vickie)
1938　*Four Men and a Prayer* (Ford) (as Lynn Cherrington); *Three Blind Mice* (Seiter) (as Pamela Charters); *Suez* (Dwan) (as Empress Eugenie); *Kentucky* (Butler) (as Sally Goodwin)
1939　*Wife, Husband, Friend* (Ratoff) (as Doris Blair Borland); *The Story of Alexander Graham Bell* (Cummings) (as Mrs. Bell); *Eternally Yours* (Garnett) (as Anita Halstead)
1940　*The Doctor Takes a Wife* (Hall) (as June Cameron); *He Stayed for Breakfast* (Hall) (as Marianne Duval)
1941　*The Lady from Cheyenne* (Lloyd) (as Annie); *The Men in Her Life* (Ratoff) (as Lina Varsavina)
1942　*Bedtime Story* (Hall) (as Jane Drake)
1943　*A Night to Remember* (Wallace) (as Nancy Troy); *China* (Farrow) (as Carolyn Grant)
1944　*Ladies Courageous* (Rawlins) (as Roberta Harper); *And Now Tomorrow* (Pichel) (as Emily Blair)
1945　*Along Came Jones* (Heisler) (as Cherry de Longpre)
1946　*The Stranger* (Welles) (as Mary Longstreet)
1947　*The Perfect Marriage* (Lewis Allen) (as Maggie Williams); *The Farmer's Daughter* (Potter) (as Katrin Holstrom); *The Bishop's Wife* (Koster) (as Julia Brougham)
1948　*Rachel and the Stranger* (Foster) (as Rachel)
1949　*The Accused* (Dieterle) (as Wilma Tuttle); *Mother Is a Freshman* (Bacon) (as Abigail Fortitude Abbott); *Come to the Stable* (Koster) (as Sister Margaret)
1950　*Key to the City* (Sidney) (as Clarissa Standish)
1951　*Cause for Alarm* (Garnett) (as Ellen Jones); *Half Angel* (Sale) (as Nora)
1952　*Paula* (Maté) (title role); *Because of You* (Pevney) (as Christine Carroll)
1953　*It Happens Every Thursday* (Pevney) (as Jane MacAvoy)
1986　*Christmas Eve* (Cooper—for TV) (as Amanda Kingsley); *Going Hollywood: The War Years* (doc—archival)
1989　*Lady in the Corner* (Levin—for TV) (as Grace Guthrie)

Publications

By YOUNG: book—

The Things I Had to Learn, as told to Helen Ferguson, New York, 1961.

On YOUNG: books—

Eells, George, *Ginger, Loretta, and Irene Who?*, New York, 1976.
Morella, Joe, and Edward Z. Epstein, *Loretta Young: An Extraordinary Life*, New York, 1986.
Lewis, Judy, *Uncommon Knowledge*, New York, 1994.

Loretta Young

On YOUNG: articles—

Current Biography 1948, New York, 1948.
Bowers, Ronald L., "Loretta Young," in *Films in Review* (New York),
    April 1969.
Films in Review (New York), November 1987.
Williams, Lena, "For Loretta Young, at 82, Life Still Waltzes On," in
    New York Times, 30 March 1995.

*   *   *

Loretta Young's career is perhaps the archetype of those stars of the 1930s who prolonged careers by living an image rather than merely performing in films. Laughable as some of the side-effects of that effort may have been, it was also a way of enhancing one's professional durability—Young managed to work a very long time.

Indeed, she was practically a child performer when she made her first featured film appearance in a Colleen Moore vehicle, *Naughty but Nice*. Her performance in that film gained her a contract with First National Pictures, and she was soon playing opposite Lon Chaney in *Laugh, Clown, Laugh*. She survived the transition to talkies, and entered into a busy career of B picture assignments. Most of these roles were of the sweet ingenue variety, and it was only in the occa-

sional film, such as *Born to Be Bad*, that she got a dramatically challenging part. This was due to her hesitancy at essaying unsympathetic roles, a mistake that ultimately made her film career less distinctive than it might have been, since she could be a moving and effective actress when the occasion demanded. A concrete example of her ironclad public image of upstanding Catholicism was given by Leonard Spiegelgass (in an interview with George Eells). Spiegelgass, a scriptwriter on her film *The Perfect Marriage*, noted that: "we had all kinds of problems because she didn't want to mention the word 'divorce' . . . the whole play was about a divorce she never got. That's why she agreed to do it. She'd say 'separation' but not 'divorce'." This counterproductive attitude, and a marriage that put her into semiretirement, brought her career to an ebb in the mid-1940s. At the urging of MGM's Dore Schary, she made a stunning comeback in *The Farmer's Daughter*, for which she received an Academy Award.

Despite this success, Young's career did not return to its prewar heights. Her well-established screen persona of virginal womanhood was perhaps less appealing to moviegoers in the postwar era. There was a new trend toward pictures that depicted life in greater complexity, without clear-cut happy endings. While her lighter, wholesome roles were waning, Young was used to advantage in several films noir, including *The Accused, Cause for Alarm*, and *The Stranger*. In the latter film she plays the fiancée of director Orson Welles's character;

he is an escaped Nazi posing as a New England college professor. In this film Young's rosy beauty and innocence exemplify the superficial, naive realm in which ugliness and evil sometimes flourish.

Young's image of wholesome, unsullied femininity was a "natural" for television, however, and she made a smooth transition to that medium in the early 1950s. She produced a pilot show for television that later became *The Loretta Young Show*, a series that won several Emmy Awards as well as a special prize at the Cannes Film Festival. After several years of success in that medium, the show was canceled, and she has been in semiretirement since.

Whatever her public image of yielding femininity might be, there is no denying that she was a forceful and commanding personality as a businesswoman, and it was this tenacity that ensured her lasting success in the entertainment field.

—Joseph Arkins, updated by Frank Uhle

YOUNG, Robert

Nationality: American. **Born:** Robert George Young in Chicago, Illinois, 22 February 1907. **Education:** Attended Lincoln High School, Los Angeles. **Family:** Married Elizabeth Louise Henderson, 1933, daughters: Carol Anne, Barbara Queen, Elizabeth Louise, and Kathleen Joy. **Career:** Worked as clerk, salesman, reporter, and loan company collector while studying and acting with the Pasadena Playhouse; 1931—toured with a stock company's production of *The Ship*; 1931-45—contract with MGM: film debut in *The Black Camel*; 1938—on radio program *Good News of 1938*, and on *Maxwell House Coffee Time*, 1944; 1947—founder, with Eugene Rodney, Cavalier Productions; 1949-54—star of the radio series *Father Knows Best*, and then transferred to the TV version, 1954-61; also in the TV series *The Window on Main Street*, 1961-62, *Marcus Welby, M.D.*, 1969-76, and *Little Women*, 1979.

Films as Actor:

1931   *The Black Camel* (MacFadden) (as Jimmy Bradshaw); *The Sin of Madelon Claudet* (Selwyn) (as Dr. Claudet); *The Guilty Generation* (Rowland V. Lee) (as Marco Ricca); *Hell Divers* (George Hill) (as young officer)

1932   *The Wet Parade* (Fleming) (as young officer); *New Morals for Old* (Brabin) (as Ralph Thomas); *Unashamed* (Beaumont) (as Dick Ogden); *Strange Interlude* (Leonard) (as Gordon); *The Kid from Spain* (McCarey) (as Ricardo)

1933   *Men Must Fight* (Selwyn) (as Geoffrey); *Today We Live* (Hawks) (as Claude); *Hell Below* (Conway) (as Lt. Brick Walters); *Tugboat Annie* (LeRoy) (as Alec Brennan); *Saturday's Millions* (Sedgwick) (as Jim Fowler); *The Right to Romance* (Santell) (as Bob Preble); *La ciudad de carton* (*Cardboard City*) (King) (as himself)

1934   *Carolina* (*The House of Connelly*) (Henry King) (as Will Connelly); *Spitfire* (Cromwell) (as John Stafford); *The House of Rothschild* (Werker) (as Captain Fitzroy); *Lazy River* (Seitz) (as Bill Drexel); *Hollywood Party* (Rowland and others) (as himself); *Whom the Gods Destroy* (Walter Lang) (as Jack Forrester); *Paris Interlude* (Marin) (as Pat Wells); *Death on the Diamond* (Sedgwick) (as Larry Kelly); *The Band Plays On* (Mack) (as Tony Ferrera)

1935   *West Point of the Air* (Rosson) (as Little Mike); *Vagabond Lady* (Sam Taylor) (as Tony Spear); *Calm Yourself* (Seitz) (as Pat); *Red Salute* (*Her Enlisted Man*; *Runaway Daugh-*

ter; *Arms and the Girl*) (Lanfield) (as Jeff); *Remember Last Night?* (Whale) (as Tony Milburn); *The Bride Comes Home* (Ruggles) (as Jack Bristow)

1936   *Three Wise Guys* (Seitz) (as Joe); *It's Love Again* (Saville) (as Peter Carlton); *The Bride Walks Out* (Jason) (as Hugh MacKenzie); *Secret Agent* (Hitchcock) (as Marvin); *Sworn Enemy* (Marin) (as Hank Sherman); *The Longest Night* (Taggart) (as Charley Phelps); *Stowaway* (Seiter) (as Tommy Randall)

1937   *Dangerous Number* (Thorpe) (as Hank Medhill); *I Met Him in Paris* (Ruggles) (as Gene Anders); *Married before Breakfast* (Marin) (as Tom Wakefield); *The Emperor's Candlesticks* (Fitzmaurice) (as Grand Duke Peter); *The Bride Wore Red* (Arzner) (as Rudi Pal); *Navy Blue and Gold* (Wood) (as Roger Ash)

1938   *Paradise for Three* (Buzzell) (as Fritz Hagedorn); *Josette* (Dwan) (as Pierre Brossard); *The Toy Wife* (Thorpe) (as Andre Vallaire); *Three Comrades* (Borzage) (as Gottfried Lenz); *Rich Man, Poor Girl* (Schunzel) (as Bill Harrison); *The Shining Hour* (Borzage) (as David Linden)

1939   *Honolulu* (Buzzell) (as Brooks Mason/George Smith); *Bridal Suite* (Thiele) (as Neil McGill); *Miracles for Sale* (Browning) (as Michael Morgan); *Maisie* (Marin) (as Slim Martin)

1940   *Northwest Passage* (Conway and King Vidor) (as Langdon Towne); *Florian* (Marin) (as Anton); *The Mortal Storm* (Borzage) (as Fritz Marberg); *Sporting Blood* (Simon) (as Myles Vanders); *Dr. Kildare's Crisis* (Bucquet) (as Douglas Lamont)

1941   *The Trial of Mary Dugan* (McLeod) (as Jimmy Blake); *Western Union* (Fritz Lang) (as Richard Blake); *Lady Be Good* (McLeod) (as Eddie Crane); *Married Bachelor* (Buzzell) (as Randolph Haven); *H.M. Pulham, Esq.* (King Vidor) (title role)

1942   *Joe Smith, American* (*Highway to Freedom*) (Thorpe) (title role); *Cairo* (Van Dyke) (as Homer Smith); *Journey for Margaret* (Van Dyke) (as John Davis)

1943   *Slightly Dangerous* (Ruggles) (as Bob Stuart); *Claudia* (Goulding) (as David Naughton); *Sweet Rosie O'Grady* (Cummings) (as Sam Mackeever)

1944   *The Canterville Ghost* (Dassin) (as Cuffy Williams)

1945   *The Enchanted Cottage* (Cromwell) (as Oliver); *Those Endearing Young Charms* (Lewis Allen) (as Hank)

1946   *Lady Luck* (Marin) (as Scott); *The Searching Wind* (Dieterle) (as Alex Hazen); *Claudia and David* (Walter Lang) (as David Naughton)

1947   *They Won't Believe Me* (Pichel) (as Larry Ballantine); *Crossfire* (Dmytryk) (as Captain Finlay)

1948   *Relentless* (Sherman) (as Nick Buckley); *Sitting Pretty* (Walter Lang) (as Harry)

1949   *Adventure in Baltimore* (Wallace) (as Dr. Sheldon); *Bride for Sale* (William D. Russell) (as Steve Adams); *That Forsyte Woman* (*The Forsyte Saga*) (Bennett) (as Philip Bosinney); *And Baby Makes Three* (Levin) (as Vernon Walsh)

1951   *The Second Woman* (Kern) (as Jeff Cohalan); *Goodbye, My Fancy* (Sherman) (as James Merrill)

1952   *The Half-Breed* (Gilmore) (as Dan Craig)

1954   *Secret of the Incas* (Jerry Hopper) (as Dr. Stanley Moorehead)

1969   *Marcus Welby, M.D.* (*A Matter of Humanities*) (Rich—for TV) (title role)

1971   *Vanished* (Kulik—for TV) (as Senator Earl Gannon)

1972   *All My Darling Daughters* (Rich—for TV) (as Judge Charles Raleigh)

1973   *My Darling Daughters' Anniversary* (Pevney) (as Judge Charles Raleigh)

1978   *Little Women* (Rich—for TV) (as James Laurence)
1984   *The Return of Marcus Welby, M.D.* (Singer—for TV) (title role)
1987   *Mercy or Murder?* (Gethers—for TV) (as Roswell Gilbert); *Conspiracy of Love* (Black—for TV) (as Grampa Joe Woldarski)
1988   *Marcus Welby, M.D.—A Holiday Affair* (Singer—for TV) (title role)

Publications

By YOUNG: article—

"How I Won the War of the Sexes by Losing Every Battle," in *Good Housekeeping*, January 1962.

On YOUNG: book—

Parish, James Robert, and Gregory W. Mank, *The Hollywood Reliables*, Westport, Connecticut, 1980.

On YOUNG: article—

Current Biography 1950, New York, 1950.

       *   *   *

After a long screen career that was noteworthy primarily for his survival while other, more flamboyant actors burned brightly and then disappeared, Robert Young achieved his greatest success at an age when most actors begin to think of retirement. Exuding a screen personality that conveyed a carefree yet honest and sympathetic air, he made a career of playing light romantic leads in predominately B pictures. When he grew too old to play such roles convincingly, he made a smooth transition to character parts. His stock in trade was that, while conveying a strength that was sufficient to win the heroine, he did not exhibit a fiery passion that would make her feel threatened.

Young's strongest screen work came in the immediate postwar period: *The Searching Wind* (playing a deluded U.S. ambassador in prewar Europe); *They Won't Believe Me* (as a deceitful husband); and *Crossfire* (as a weary but determined cop attempting to solve a murder). His best screen performance, however, that of Oliver in *The Enchanted Cottage*, demonstrated Young's considerable range. The film, intended to raise the morale of disfigured soldiers returning from the war, required the actor to play a G.I. who returns from combat with severe scars and nerve damage, afraid to face his former fiancée. Playing opposite Dorothy Maguire, who acted the role of a similar social outcast, he created an unforgettable character that, while rooted in the quiet reality one expects from a Young portrayal, soared briefly in the enchantment of his own self-deception. In the end, the actor merged both aspects of the character to create a man, who, although physically deformed, could look upon himself as miraculously whole in the aspects of life that are the most meaningful.

Perhaps it was this image of self-acceptance and quiet strength that somehow transformed him into the prototypical patriarch of the universal American family on television in the 1950s. In the new medium, he enjoyed an even stronger success than he had known on the large screen. The long-running *Father Knows Best* rejuvenated his career and propelled him into an equally popular series that began in 1969, *Marcus Welby, M.D.*

          —Stephen L. Hanson, updated by Audrey E. Kupferberg

ZETTERLING, Mai (Elisabeth)

Nationality: Swedish. **Born:** Västeras, 24 May 1925. **Education:** Attended Ordtuery Theatre School, 1941; Royal Dramatic Theatre, Stockholm, 1942. **Family:** Married 1) the ballet dancer Tutte Lemkow (divorced), two sons: Etienne and Louis; 2) the writer David Hughes (divorced). **Career:** 1942-44—in repertory with the Royal Dramatic Theatre; 1944—film debut in Alf Sjöberg's *Frenzy*; 1947—English-language film debut in Basil Dearden's *Frieda*; 1948—London stage debut in Ibsen's *Wild Duck;* 1954—Hollywood film debut in Norman Panama's *Knock on Wood*; 1960—turned director with the BBC documentary *The Polite Invasion*. **Awards:** Best Short Film Award, Venice Film Festival, for *The War Game*, 1963. **Died:** Of cancer, in London, England, 15 March 1994.

Films as Actress:

1941   *Lasse-Maja* (Olsson)
1943   *Jag drapte* (Molander)
1944   *Hets* (*Torment*; *Frenzy*) (Sjöberg) (as Bertha Olsson); *Prins Gustaf* (Bauman)
1946   *Iris och Lojtnantshjarta* (*Iris and the Lieutenant*) (Sjöberg) (as Iris); *Driver dagg faller Regn* (*Sunshine Follows Rain*)
1947   *Frieda* (Dearden) (title role)
1948   *Musik i moerker* (*Music in Darkness*; *Night Is My Future*) (Bergman) (as Ingrid); *The Bad Lord Byron* (Macdonald) (as Teresa Guiccioli); *The Girl in the Painting* (*Portrait from Life*) (Fisher) (as Hildegarde)
1949   *Quartet* (Annakin and others) (as Jeanne); *The Romantic Age* (*Naughty Arlette*) (Greville) (as Arlette)
1950   *Blackmailed* (Marc Allégret) (as Carol Edwards); *The Lost People* (Knowles) (as Lili)
1951   *Hell Is Sold Out* (Anderson) (as Valerie Martin)
1952   *The Tall Headlines* (*The Frightened Bride*) (Young) (as Doris Richardson); *The Ringer* (*The Gaunt Stranger*) (Hamilton) (as Lisa)
1953   *Desperate Moment* (Bennett) (as Anna de Burgh)
1954   *Dance Little Lady* (Guest) (as Nina Gordon); *Knock on Wood* (Panama) (as Ilse Nordstrom)
1955   *A Prize of Gold* (Robson) (as Maria)
1957   *Abandon Ship!* (*Seven Waves Away*) (Sale) (as Julie)
1958   *The Truth about Women* (Box) (as Julie); *Lek pa regnbagen* (Kjellgren)
1959   *Jet Storm* (Endfield) (as Carol Tilley)
1960   *Faces in the Dark* (Eady) (as Christiane Hammond); *Piccadilly Third Stop* (Rilla) (as Christine Pready)
1961   *Offbeat* (Owen) (as Ruth Lombard)
1962   *The Man Who Finally Died* (Lawrence) (as Lisa); *Only Two Can Play* (Gilliat) (as Elizabeth Gruffydd Williams); *The Main Attraction* (Petrie) (as Gina)
1963   *The Bay of St. Michael* (Ainsworth) (as Helene Bretton)
1965   *The Vine Bridge* (Nykvist)
1988   *Calling the Shots* (Cole—doc) (appearance)
1990   *The Witches* (Roeg) (as Helga); *Hidden Agenda* (Loach) (as Moa)
1993   *Morfars Resa* (*Grandfather's Journey*) (Staffan Lamm) (as Elin Fromm)

Films as Director:

1960   *The Polite Invasion* (doc—for TV)
1961   *Lords of Little Egypt* (doc—for TV); *The War Game* (short) (+ pr)
1962   *The Prosperity Race* (doc—for TV)

Mai Zetterling

1963   *The Do-It-Yourself Democracy* (doc—for TV)
1964   *Alskande par* (*Loving Couples*) (co-d with David Hughes, + co-sc)
1966   *Nattlek* (*Night Games*) (+ co-sc)
1967   *Doktor Glas* (co-d with David Hughes)
1968   *Flickorna* (*The Girls*) (co-d with David Hughes)
1971   *Vincent the Dutchman* (doc) (co-d with David Hughes, + pr)
1973   "The Strongest" ep. of *Visions of Eight* (co-d with David Hughes)
1976   *We har manje namn* (*We Have Many Names*) (+ ro, sc, ed)
1977   *Stockholm* (for TV) (+ ro)
1978   *The Rain's Hat* (for TV) (+ ed)
1982   *Love* (for TV) (co-d, + co-sc)
1983   *Scrubbers* (+ co-sc)
1986   *Amorosa* (+ sc, co-ed)
1990   *Sunday Pursuit*

Publications

By ZETTERLING: books—

Shadow of the Sun (short stories), New York, 1975.
Bird of Passage (novel), New York, 1976.

Ice Island (novel), New York, 1979.
Rain's Hat (children's book), New York, 1979.
All Those Tomorrows (autobiography), London, 1985.

By ZETTERLING: articles—

"Some Notes on Acting," in *Sight and Sound* (London), October/
    December 1951.
Interview in *Cahiers du Cinéma* (Paris), April 1966.
"Mai Zetterling at the Olympic Games," interview in *American Cin-
    ematographer* (Los Angeles), November 1972.

On ZETTERLING: books—

Bjorkman, Stig, *Film in Sweden, the New Directors*, London, 1979.
Heck-Rabi, Louise, *Women Filmmakers: A Critical Reception*,
    Metuchen, New Jersey, 1984.

On ZETTERLING: articles—

"Meeting with Mai Zetterling," in *Cahiers du Cinéma in English* (New
    York), December 1966.

Pyros, J., "Notes on Women Directors," in *Take One* (Montreal), November/December 1970.

McGregor, C., "Mai Is behind the Camera Now," in *New York Times*, 30 April 1972.

Elley, Derek, "Hiding It under a Bushel: Free Fall," in *Films and Filming* (London), April 1974.

Obituary in *New York Times*, 19 March 1994.

* * *

This Swedish actress turned controversial filmmaker combined the earthy sexiness of Ingrid Bergman with, as one critic noted, "a Dietrich-like suggestion of a steel vertebrae."

Zetterling was 19 when she made her screen debut as a prostitute in the international hit *Frenzy*, respectively directed and written by two of her country's major talents, Alf Sjöberg and Ingmar Bergman, the latter just beginning his long and distinguished career. She later appeared for Bergman himself in his 1948 film *Night Is My Future*, playing a Lolita-ish maid, though by this time she possessed greater international renown than he did, having made her English-language film debut as a German war bride in the British drama *Frieda* and her theatrical debut on London's West End in a revival of Ibsen's *Wild Duck*.

Following in the footsteps of two other Swedish expatriates, Greta Garbo, then in retirement, and Ingrid Bergman, then persona non grata due to her scandalous relationship with Roberto Rossellini, Zetterling was lured to Hollywood to take their place. After making her American film debut as the love interest of star Danny Kaye in the 1954 espionage spoof *Knock on Wood*, however, she abruptly turned her back on Hollywood and left, never to return. In her autobiography, she writes that she was always too serious about her craft ever to do jobs just for the money. "For that I had a reputation as a freak in Hollywood, but I can't say I ever regretted [never going back]."

Settling in London, she remained active in the British cinema for the next decade, and appeared in two more American films as well, Mark Robson's crime caper *A Prize of Gold* and Richard Sale's taut tale of survival at sea, *Abandon Ship!*, based on a true story and starring Tyrone Power. The former was shot in Germany, the latter on a British soundstage. Subsequently, she appeared opposite a miscast Pat Boone in the lust and sawdust circus drama *The Main Attraction* and in the thriller *The Man Who Finally Died*, both made in Britain in 1962. She had one of her best roles the same year as a high society dame romanced by Peter Sellers in the comedy *Only Two Can Play*, based on a satiric novel by Kingsley Amis.

Disheartened by the quality of most of the films she was being offered, Zetterling turned her back on acting after the routine action thriller *The Bay of St. Michael* and became a director, starting with several documentaries made for the BBC and the award-winning 1963 short *The War Game* (not to be confused with the 1967 Peter Watkins "ban the bomb" film of the same name). Returning to Sweden, she launched her feature directing career with *Loving Couples*, which was heavily censored in the United States and elsewhere due to its sexual explicitness. She directed her one of her last films, *Amorosa*, in 1986, having turned her attention to writing short stories and novels, as well as a frank autobiography called *All Those Tomorrows*.

—John McCarty

ZHAO DAN

Nationality: Chinese. **Born:** Zhao Fengao in Yangzhao, 1914. **Education:** Attended Technical College of Art, Shanghai, 1931-34.

Family: Married twice, children from both marriages, and two adopted sons. **Career:** 1925—first film appearance at age 11 in *Young Master Feng*; also wrote stories and plays for left-wing magazine; publication censored by Kuomintang government; Zhao changed name to Dan ("Red") as political gesture; 1934—by time of graduation, acting regularly on stage and in films; 1937—reputation established by appearances in the films *Street Angel* and *Crossroads*; when Shanghai fell to Japanese, joined touring company performing anti-Japanese plays; 1939—captured by Kuomintang warlord, imprisoned for four years; 1943—returned to stage following release from prison; 1947—film directing debut; 1965—made last film, *Red Crag*; at outbreak of Cultural Revolution, arrested and imprisoned for five-and-a-half years; 1973—released; 1976—rejoined Shanghai Film Studio, as teacher; also stage director. **Died:** Of cancer, in Peking, 19 October 1980.

Films as Actor:

1925   *Young Master Feng*
1932   *Spring Sorrow of the Pipa*
1933   *Twenty-Four Hours of Shanghai*; *Children of the Century*
1934   *Homesick for a Mountain Village*; *To the North-West*; *Bible for Girls*
1935   *Passionate, Faithful Spirit*
1936   *The Qingming Festival*; *Xiao Lingzi*
1937   *Shizi jietou* (*Crossroads*) (as an unemployed graduate); *Malu tianshi* (*Street Angel*)
1939   *Children of China*
1947   *Faraway Love*; *Rhapsody of Happiness*
1948   *Irrepressible Brightness of Spring*; *Wuya yu Maque* (*Crows and Sparrows*) (as the peddler, + co-sc)
1949   *The Story of a Girl*
1950   *The Life of Wu Xun*
1951   *A Couple*
1956   *Li Shizhen, The Great Pharmacologist* (title role); *For Peace*
1957   *Hai hun* (*Soul of the Sea*) (as the sailor)
1959   *Lin zexu* (*The Opium War*) (as the nobleman); *Nie er*
1960   *Contemporary Heroes*
1965   *Lie Huozhong yongsheng* (*Red Crag*) (as the Communist leader)

Films as Director:

1947   *The Dress Returns to Glory*
1953   *Bless the Children*
1958   *An Evergreen Tree*; *Precious Green Mountains* (+ ro)

Publications

On ZHAO DAN: books—

Berry, Chris, editor, *Perspectives on Chinese Cinema*, New York, 1985; rev. ed., London, 1991.

Clark, Paul, *Chinese Cinema: Culture and Politics since 1949*, Cambridge, 1987.

On ZHAO DAN: articles—

The Annual Obituary 1980, New York, 1981.

Blank, M., "Le testament de Zhao Dan," in *Cahiers du Cinéma* (Paris), February 1981.

Zhao Dan (right) in *Li Shizhen*

Chevillard, P.-B., in *Positif* (Paris), September 1981.
Nacache, J., in *Cinéma*, October 1981.

*   *   *

The riches of Chinese cinema still remain largely unknown to the West—otherwise, Zhao Dan would probably rank among the greatest screen actors. In Chinese terms, he might be considered roughly the equivalent of Humphrey Bogart or Gary Cooper, though far more versatile than either. Gravel-voiced, energetic, warmly likable, Zhao could play comedy without heavy mugging, and serious roles without being ponderous. In his later films he attained an unpretentious nobility, completely removed from the posturing heroics favored during the Cultural Revolution.

Zhao's stage experience included Shakespeare and Ibsen, and he made nearly 30 films before the two which brought him to stardom. Both—not unlike Warner films of the period—blended romantic comedy with sharp-edged social comment. As the unemployed graduate of *Crossroads*, Zhao was cheerfully optimistic in the face of adversity;

for the more somber-toned *Street Angel* his performance darkened, a note of manic violence creeping into his energy.

Unpopular with both the Japanese and the Kuomintang government for his left-wing beliefs, Zhao was imprisoned by the latter during the war. After his release he continued, undeterred, to make anti-KMT movies, most notably the teeming, exhilaratingly vital *Crows and Sparrows*, which he also co-scripted. His richly subtle performance as the opportunistic peddler meshed with inspired ensemble playing from the whole cast. Around this time he also started directing, making four competent but unremarkable films.

Increasingly, Zhao was cast as humanely heroic figures: the title role of *Li Shizhen*, father of Chinese herbal medicine; the sailor disgusted by his superiors' brutality in *Soul of the Sea*; patriotically resisting British imperialism in *The Opium War*; the imprisoned, tortured Communist leader of *Red Crag*. This, tragically prophetic, was his last film. Arrested by order of Jiang Qing—Mao's wife, who had acted with Zhao in the thirties—he was imprisoned again for more than five years. Broken in health, he never acted again.

—Philip Kemp

NATIONALITY INDEX

AMERICAN
Bud Abbott
Danny Aiello
Woody Allen
Don Ameche
Dana Andrews
Ann-Margret
Roscoe ("Fatty") Arbuckle
Alan Arkin
Jean Arthur
Fred Astaire
Mary Astor
Gene Autry
Lew Ayres
Lauren Bacall
Kevin Bacon
Lucille Ball
Anne Bancroft
Vilma Banky
Theda Bara
Ellen Barkin
Ethel Barrymore
John Barrymore
Lionel Barrymore
Richard Barthelmess
Kim Basinger
Angela Bassett
Kathy Bates
Anne Baxter
Warren Beatty
Wallace Beery
Ralph Bellamy
John Belushi
Joan Bennett
Joan Blondell
Humphrey Bogart
Ward Bond
Ernest Borgnine
Clara Bow
Charles Boyer
Marlon Brando
Walter Brennan
Jeff Bridges
Charles Bronson
Louise Brooks
Mel Brooks
Joe E. Brown
Ellen Burstyn
James Caan
Nicolas Cage
James Cagney
Louis Calhern
Eddie Cantor
Harry Carey
John Carradine
Madeleine Carroll
Lon Chaney
Geraldine Chaplin
Cyd Charisse
Cher
Montgomery Clift
Glenn Close

Lee J. Cobb
Charles Coburn
James Coburn
Claudette Colbert
Eddie Constantine
Gary Cooper
Jackie Cooper
Lou Costello
Kevin Costner
Joseph Cotten
Broderick Crawford
Joan Crawford
Bing Crosby
Tom Cruise
Jamie Lee Curtis
Tony Curtis
Willem Dafoe
Linda Darnell
Marion Davies
Bette Davis
Geena Davis
Doris Day
Olivia de Havilland
Robert De Niro
James Dean
Johnny Depp
Bruce Dern
Danny DeVito
Angie Dickinson
Marlene Dietrich
Matt Dillon
Kirk Douglas
Melvyn Douglas
Michael Douglas
Richard Dreyfuss
Margaret Dumont
Faye Dunaway
Irene Dunne
Jimmy Durante
Deanna Durbin
Dan Duryea
Robert Duvall
Clint Eastwood
Nelson Eddy
Douglas Fairbanks
Peter Falk
Frances Farmer
Mia Farrow
Alice Faye
José Ferrer
Sally Field
W. C. Fields
Laurence Fishburne
Errol Flynn
Henry Fonda
Jane Fonda
Joan Fontaine
Glenn Ford
Harrison Ford
Jodie Foster
Kay Francis
Morgan Freeman

Clark Gable
Greta Garbo
Andy García
Ava Gardner
John Garfield
Judy Garland
James Garner
Greer Garson
Janet Gaynor
Richard Gere
Mel Gibson
John Gilbert
Lillian Gish
Paulette Goddard
Whoopi Goldberg
Ruth Gordon
Elliott Gould
Betty Grable
Stewart Granger
Cary Grant
Lee Grant
Sydney Greenstreet
Melanie Griffith
Gene Hackman
Tom Hanks
Oliver Hardy
Jean Harlow
Ed Harris
William S. Hart
Goldie Hawn
Sterling Hayden
Susan Hayward
Rita Hayworth
Sonja Henie
Paul Henreid
Katharine Hepburn
Barbara Hershey
Charlton Heston
Dustin Hoffman
William Holden
Judy Holliday
Bob Hope
Miriam Hopkins
Dennis Hopper
Edward Everett Horton
Rock Hudson
Holly Hunter
William Hurt
Anjelica Huston
John Huston
Walter Huston
Samuel L. Jackson
Sam Jaffe
Al Jolson
James Earl Jones
Jennifer Jones
Tommy Lee Jones
Raul Julia
Danny Kaye
Buster Keaton
Diane Keaton

Michael Keaton
Ruby Keeler
Harvey Keitel
Gene Kelly
Grace Kelly
Arthur Kennedy
Kevin Kline
Alan Ladd
Veronica Lake
Hedy Lamarr
Dorothy Lamour
Burt Lancaster
Elsa Lanchester
Martin Landau
Harry Langdon
Jessica Lange
Angela Lansbury
Charles Laughton
Stan Laurel
Bruce Lee
Spike Lee
Janet Leigh
Jennifer Jason Leigh
Jack Lemmon
Jerry Lewis
Juliette Lewis
Harold Lloyd
Carole Lombard
Myrna Loy
Ida Lupino
Jeanette MacDonald
Shirley MacLaine
Fred MacMurray
Karl Malden
John Malkovich
Dorothy Malone
Jayne Mansfield
Fredric March
Mae Marsh
Dean Martin
Steve Martin
Lee Marvin
The Marx Brothers
Raymond Massey
Walter Matthau
Victor Mature
Joel McCrea
Hattie McDaniel
Steve McQueen
Adolphe Menjou
Burgess Meredith
Bette Midler
Ann Miller
Sal Mineo
Liza Minnelli
Robert Mitchum
Tom Mix
Marilyn Monroe
Robert Montgomery
Demi Moore
Agnes Moorehead

Paul Muni
Eddie Murphy
Bill Murray
Alla Nazimova
Patricia Neal
Pola Negri
Paul Newman
Jack Nicholson
Nick Nolte
Mabel Normand
Kim Novak
Warren Oates
Edmond O'Brien
Margaret O'Brien
Donald O'Connor
Maureen O'Hara
Edward James Olmos
Al Pacino
Geraldine Page
Jack Palance
Gregory Peck
Sean Penn
Anthony Perkins
Joe Pesci
Michelle Pfeiffer
Walter Pidgeon
Brad Pitt
Sidney Poitier
Dick Powell
Eleanor Powell
William Powell
Tyrone Power
Elvis Presley
Robert Preston
Vincent Price
Richard Pryor
Edna Purviance
Dennis Quaid
Anthony Quinn
George Raft
Claude Rains
Ronald Reagan
Robert Redford
Keanu Reeves
Lee Remick
Burt Reynolds
Debbie Reynolds
Thelma Ritter
Jason Robards
Tim Robbins
Julia Roberts
Cliff Robertson
Paul Robeson
Bill ("Bojangles") Robinson
Edward G. Robinson
Ginger Rogers
Roy Rogers
Will Rogers
Mickey Rooney
Mickey Rourke
Gena Rowlands

Jane Russell
Rosalind Russell
Meg Ryan
Robert Ryan
Winona Ryder
Eva Marie Saint
Susan Sarandon
Roy Scheider
Arnold Schwarzenegger
George C. Scott
Randolph Scott
Jean Seberg
George Segal
Norma Shearer
Martin Sheen
Sam Shepard
Sylvia Sidney
Jean Simmons
Frank Sinatra
Everett Sloane
Wesley Snipes
Sissy Spacek
Sylvester Stallone
Harry Dean Stanton
Barbara Stanwyck
Mary Steenburgen
Rod Steiger
James Stewart
Sharon Stone
Meryl Streep
Barbra Streisand
Margaret Sullavan
Gloria Swanson
Blanche Sweet
Norma Talmadge
Robert Taylor
Shirley Temple
The Three Stooges
Uma Thurman
Gene Tierney
Spencer Tracy
John Travolta
Claire Trevor
Kathleen Turner
Lana Turner
John Turturro
Lee Van Cleef
Jon Voight
Christopher Walken
Robert Walker
Eli Wallach
Denzel Washington
John Wayne
Sigourney Weaver
Clifton Webb
Johnny Weissmuller
Raquel Welch
Tuesday Weld
Orson Welles
Mae West
Forest Whitaker

Pearl White
Richard Widmark
Dianne Wiest
Cornel Wilde
Gene Wilder
Esther Williams
Robin Williams
Bruce Willis
Debra Winger
Shelley Winters
Anna May Wong
Natalie Wood
James Woods
Joanne Woodward
Fay Wray
Jane Wyman
Robert Young
Loretta Young

AUSTRALIAN
Judy Davis

AUSTRIAN
Klaus Maria Brandauer
Oscar Homolka
Emil Jannings
Werner Krauss
Romy Schneider
Arnold Schwarzenegger
Anton Walbrook
Oskar Werner

BELGIAN
Jean-Claude Van Damme

BRAZILIAN
Sonia Braga
Carmen Miranda

BRITISH
Julie Andrews
Richard Attenborough
Stanley Baker
Alan Bates
Elisabeth Bergner
Claire Bloom
Dirk Bogarde
Helena Bonham-Carter
Kenneth Branagh
Jack Buchanan
Richard Burton
Michael Caine
Madeleine Carroll
Charles Chaplin
Julie Christie
John Cleese
Ronald Colman
Sean Connery
Donald Crisp
Peter Cushing
Daniel Day-Lewis

Robert Donat
Diana Dors
Denholm Elliott
Edith Evans
Gracie Fields
Ralph Fiennes
Peter Finch
Albert Finney
John Gielgud
Hugh Grant
Joan Greenwood
Alec Guinness
Rex Harrison
Jack Hawkins
Audrey Hepburn
Anthony Hopkins
Bob Hoskins
Leslie Howard
Trevor Howard
John Hurt
Jeremy Irons
Glenda Jackson
Celia Johnson
Boris Karloff
Kay Kendall
Deborah Kerr
Ben Kingsley
Stan Laurel
Christopher Lee
Vivien Leigh
Margaret Lockwood
Herbert Marshall
James Mason
Malcolm McDowell
John Mills
Helen Mirren
Dudley Moore
Anna Neagle
David Niven
Ivor Novello
Gary Oldman
Laurence Olivier
Donald Pleasence
Anthony Quayle
Michael Redgrave
Vanessa Redgrave
Oliver Reed
Miranda Richardson
Ralph Richardson
Rachel Roberts
Margaret Rutherford
George Sanders
Greta Scacchi
Peter Sellers
Robert Shaw
Jean Simmons
Maggie Smith
Terence Stamp
Elizabeth Taylor
Terry-Thomas
Emma Thompson

Peter Ustinov
Conrad Veidt
Anton Walbrook
Norman Wisdom
Googie Withers
Susannah York

CANADIAN
Geneviève Bujold
John Candy
Marie Dressler
Kate Nelligan
Keanu Reeves
Donald Sutherland

CHILEAN
Nelson Villagra

CHINESE
Jackie Chan
Gong Li
Zhao Dan

CZECH
Vlastimil Brodský
Herbert Lom

DANISH
Anna Karina
Harald Madsen
Asta Nielsen
Carl Schenstrøm

DUTCH
Lil Dagover

EGYPTIAN
Omar Sharif

FRENCH
Isabelle Adjani
Anouk Aimée
Arletty
Antonin Artaud
Stéphane Audran
Brigitte Bardot
Jean-Louis Barrault
Nathalie Baye
Jean-Paul Belmondo
Jules Berry
Juliette Binoche
Bernard Blier
Charles Boyer
Pierre Brasseur
Leslie Caron
Jean-Pierre Cassel
Maurice Chevalier
Eddie Constantine
Alain Cuny
Marcel Dalio
Danielle Darrieux

Alain Delon
Cathérine Deneuve
Gérard Depardieu
Fernandel
Edwige Feuillère
Jean Gabin
Daniel Gélin
Annie Girardot
Isabelle Huppert
Louis Jourdan
Louis Jouvet
Jean-Pierre Léaud
Max Linder
Jean Marais
Gaston Modot
Yves Montand
Jeanne Moreau
Michèle Morgan
Philippe Noiret
Gérard Philipe
Michel Piccoli
Micheline Presle
Raimu
Françoise Rosay
Dominique Sanda
Delphine Seyrig
Simone Signoret
Simone Simon
Jacques Tati
Jean-Louis Trintignant
Charles Vanel

GERMAN
Gustav Fröhlich
Nastassja Kinski
Armin Mueller-Stahl
Fritz Rasp
Hanna Schygulla
Conrad Veidt
Rüdiger Vogler
Paul Wegener
Angela Winkler

GREEK
Melina Mercouri
Irene Papas

HUNGARIAN
Vilma Banky

INDIAN
Dev Anand
Shabana Azmi
Soumitra Chatterjee
Dilip Kumar
Smita Patil

IRISH
Cyril Cusack
Barry Fitzgerald
Richard Harris

John Huston
Liam Neeson
Sam Neill
Peter O'Toole

ISRAELI
Topol

ITALIAN
Roberto Benigni
Francesca Bertini
Rossano Brazzi
Claudia Cardinale
Gino Cervi
Aldo Fabrizi
Vittorio Gassman
Giancarlo Giannini
Gina Lollobrigida
Sophia Loren
Anna Magnani
Silvana Mangano
Giulietta Masina
Marcello Mastroianni
Isabella Rossellini
Greta Scacchi
Alberto Sordi
Alida Valli
Monica Vitti
Gian Maria Volonté

JAPANESE
Setsuko Hara
Kazuo Hasegawa
Sessue Hayakawa
Kyoko Kagawa
Machiko Kyo
Toshiro Mifune
Masayuki Mori
Eiji Okada
Chishu Ryu
Takashi Shimura
Hideko Takamine
Kinuyo Tanaka
Yoko Tsukasa
Isuzu Yamada
So Yamamura

MEXICAN
Pedro Armendáriz
Cantinflas

Dolores del Rio
María Félix
Pedro Infante

MONÉGASQUE
Grace Kelly

NEW ZEALANDER
Sam Neill

NORWEGIAN
Liv Ullmann

POLISH
Tadeusz Łomnicki
Jan Nowicki
Daniel Olbrychski
Beata Tyszkiewicz

RUSSIAN
Sergei Bondarchuk
Nikolai Cherkassov
Vera Maretskaya
Ivan Mozhukin
Oleg Yankovsky

SPANISH
Victoria Abril
Antonio Banderas
Carmen Maura
Fernando Rey

SWEDISH
Bibi Andersson
Harriet Andersson
Ingrid Bergman
Gunnar Björnstrand
Eva Dahlbeck
Erland Josephson
Lena Olin
Ingrid Thulin
Max Von Sydow
Mai Zetterling

SWISS
Yul Brynner
Bruno Ganz
Maria Schell
Maximilian Schell
Michel Simon

FILM TITLE INDEX

The following list of titles cites all films included in the *Actors and Actresses* volume of this series, including cross-references for alternative or English-language titles. The name(s) in parentheses following the title and date refer the reader to the appropriate entry or entries where full information is given. Titles appearing in bold are covered in the *Films* volume.

$, 1971 (Beatty; Hawn)
009 Mission to Hong Kong. *See* Geheimnis der drei Dschunken, 1965
1, 2, 3, Soleil, 1993 (Mastroianni)
1, 2, 3, Sun. *See* 1, 2, 3, Soleil, 1993
2 Août 1914, 1914 (Linder)
2-Buldi-2, 1929 (Maretskaya)
2 Days in the Valley, 1996 (Aiello)
2 x Forsyth (No Comebacks): A Careful Man, 1984 (Cusack)
3:10 to Yuma, 1957 (Ford, G.)
4 x 4, 1965 (Von Sydow)
5% de risque, 1979 (Cassel; Ganz)
6 in Paris. *See* Paris vu par ..., 1965
7 Morts sur ordonnance, 1975 (Depardieu)
8½, 1963 (Aimée; Cardinale)
8 Million Ways to Die, 1986 (Curtis, J.; Bridges; García)
9½ Weeks, 1986 (Basinger; Rourke)
9/30/55, 1977 (Quaid)
10, 1979 (Andrews, J.; Dudley Moore)
10 Rillington Place, 1971 (Attenborough; Hurt, J.)
10:30 P.M. Summer, 1966 (Finch; Mercouri; Schneider)
10 to Midnight, 1982 (Bronson)
11 Harrow House, 1974 (Gielgud; Mason)
12 Dicembre, 1971 (Volonté)
12 Monkeys, 1995 (Pitt)
12 Monkeys, 1995 (Willis)
12:01, 1993 (Landau)
13 at Dinner, 1985 (Dunaway)
13 Rue Madeleine, 1946 (Cagney; Jaffe; Malden)
15 from Rome. *See* I mostri, 1963
15 Maiden Lane, 1936 (Trevor)
17e ciel, 1966 (Dalio)
$20 a Week, 1924 (Colman)
20 Juli, 1955 (Maximilian Schell)
20 Mule Team, 1940 (Baxter; Beery)
21 Carat Snatch. *See* Popsy Pop, 1970
21 Days, 1937 (Leigh, V.; Olivier)
21 Hours at Munich, 1976 (Holden)
23½ Hours Leave, 1937 (Bond)
24 Hours in a Woman's Life. *See* Vingt-quatre heures de la vie d'une femme, 1968
24 Hours of the Rebel. *See* 9/30/55, 1977
25e Heure, 1967 (Dalio; Quinn; Reggiani; Rosay)
25th Hour. *See* 25e Heure, 1967
27 Horas, 1986 (Banderas)
27 Hours. *See* 27 Horas, 1986
27, Rue de la Paix, 1936 (Berry)
29th Street, 1991 (Aiello)
30 Foot Bride of Candy Rock, 1959 (Abbott)
30 Is a Dangerous Age, Cynthia, 1968 (Dudley Moore)
30 Years of Fun, 1963 (Hardy)
33-go-sha oto nashi, 1955 (Tsukasa)
36 Fillette, 1988 (Léaud)
36 Hours, 1965 (Garner; Saint)
36 Wooden Men. *See* Shaolin Wooden Men, 1976
40 Carats, 1973 (Ullmann)
42nd Street, 1933 (Keeler; Powell, D.; Rogers, G.)
45 Minutes from Hollywood, 1926 (Hardy)
47 Loyal Ronin. *See* Chushingura, 1954
47 Samurai. *See* Chushingura, 1962
48 Hrs., 1982 (Murphy; Nolte)
48-Year-Old Rebel. *See* Yonjuhachi-sai no teiko, 1956
49th Parallel, 1941 (Howard, L.; Massey; Olivier; Walbrook)
50 Ans de Don Juan, 1922 (Vanel)
52 Pick-Up, 1986 (Ann-Margret; Scheider)
55 Days at Peking, 1962 (Heston; Gardner; Niven)
72 Degrees below Zero. *See* 72 gradusa nizhe nulia, 1976

72 gradusa nizhe nulia, 1976 (Yankovsky)
84 Charing Cross Road, 1986 (Bancroft; Brooks, M.; Hopkins, A.)
99, 1918 (Lugosi)
99 and 44/100 Per Cent Dead, 1974 (Harris, R.; O'Brien, E.)
99 mujeres, 1968 (Lom; Schell, Maria)
99 Women. *See* 99 mujeres, 1968
100 Men and a Girl, 1937 (Durbin; Menjou)
100% Pure. *See* Girl from Missouri, 1934
100 Rifles, 1969 (Reynolds, B.; Welch)
101 Dalmations, 1996 (Close)
102 Boulevard Haussmann, 1990 (Bates, A.)
300 Spartans, 1961 (Richardson, R.)
365 Nights in Hollywood, 1934 (Faye)
365 Nights in Osaka. *See* Sanbyaku-rokujugo-ya, 1948
365 Nights in Tokyo. *See* Sanbyaku-rokujugo-ya, 1948
400 Blows. *See* **Quatre Cents Coups**, 1959
588 Rue Paradis, 1992 (Cardinale; Sharif)
633 Squadron, 1964 (Robertson)
711 Ocean Drive, 1950 (O'Brien, E.)
800 Leguas por el Amazona, 1960 (Armendáriz)
1000 Carat Diamond. *See* Supercolpo da 7 miliard, 1966
$1,000 a Touchdown, 1939 (Brown)
1001 Nights with Toho. *See* Toho senichiya, 1947
1492: The Conquest of Paradise, 1992 (Depardieu; Rey; Weaver)
1776, or The Hessian Renegades, 1909 (Pickford)
1877: The Grand Army of Starvation, 1985 (Jones, James Earl)
1900, 1976 (Bertini; Depardieu; Hayden; Lancaster; Sanda; Sutherland; Valli)
1914, die letzten Tage vor dem Weltbrand, 1931 (Homolka)
1919, 1985 (Schell, Maria)
1931: Once upon a Time in New York. *See* Piazza Pulita, 1972
1941, 1979 (Belushi; Candy; Lee, C.; Mifune; Oates; Rourke)
1944, 1984 (Tyszkiewicz)
1969, 1988 (Dern; Ryder)
1984, 1956 (O'Brien, E.; Pleasence; Redgrave, M.)
1984, 1984 (Burton; Cusack; Hurt, J.)
2000 Years After, 1969 (Terry-Thomas)
2010, 1984 (Mirren; Scheider)
3000 Scenarios contre un virus, 1994 (Gélin)
3,000 Scenarios to Combat a Virus. *See* 3000 Scenarios contre un virus, 1994
10,000 Kids and a Cop, 1948 (Stewart)
20,000 Leagues under the Sea, 1954 (Lukas; Mason)
20,000 Years in Sing Sing, 1933 (Calhern; Davis, B.)
80,000 Suspects, 1963 (Bloom; Cusack)
600,000 Francs par mois, 1926 (Vanel)

A belles dents, 1966 (Gélin)
A bout de souffle, 1959 (Belmondo; Seberg)
A cavallo della tigre, 1961 (Volonté)
A chacun son enfer, 1976 (Girardot)
A ciascuno il sou, 1967 (Papas; Volonté)
A coeur joie, 1967 (Bardot)
A couteaux tirés, 1962 (Dalio)
A csoda vege, 1983 (Brodský)
A da veni ... Don Calogero. *See* Filo d'erba, 1952
A Dama do Lotacdao, 1978 (Braga)
A donde van nuestros hijos, 1958 (Del Rio)
A doppia faccia. *See* Double Face, 1969
A Doppia mandata. *See* Double tour, 1959
A-Ducking They Did Go, 1939 (Three Stooges)
A gaiwak, 1983 (Chan)
A gaiwatsuktsap, 1987 (Chan)
A-Haunting We Will Go, 1942 (Laurel and Hardy)
A Hecc, 1989 (Mueller-Stahl)
A Hercegnoe es a Kobold, 1993 (Bloom)
A L'Horizon du Sud, 1924 (Modot)
A L'Italienne. *See* Made in Italy, 1965

Achena Mukh, 1984 (Chatterjee)
Acht und Siebzig, 1980 (Tyszkiewicz)
Achtung! Bandit!, 1951 (Lollobrigida)
Acque di primavera, 1942 (Cervi)
Acque di primavera, 1989 (Kinski)
Acquitted for Having Committed the Deed. *See* Assolto per aver commesso il
    Fatto, 1992
Acrobate, 1940 (Fernandel)
Across 110th Street, 1972 (Quinn)
Across the Border. *See* Special Inspector, 1939
Across the Bridge, 1957 (Steiger)
Across the Lake, 1988 (Hopkins, A.)
Across the Line, 1931 (Carey)
Across the Moon, 1994 (Meredith)
Across the Pacific, 1926 (Loy)
Across the Pacific, 1942 (Astor; Bogart; Greenstreet; Huston, J.)
Across the Tracks, 1991 (Pitt)
Across the Wide Missouri, 1951 (Gable; Menjou)
Across to Singapore, 1928 (Crawford, J.; Novarro; Wong)
Act of Aggression. *See* Agression, 1975
Act of Betrayal. *See* Scandalo segreto, 1990
Act of Contrition, 1991 (Cardinale)
Act of Deceit. *See* French Kiss, 1981
Act of Love, 1953 (Bardot; Douglas, K.; Reggiani)
Act of Love, 1980 (Rourke)
Act of Love, 1981 (Bogarde; Jackson, G.)
Act of Murder, 1948 (March; O'Brien, E.)
Act of the Heart. *See* Acte du coeur, 1970
Act of Vengeance ... A True Story, 1989 (Burstyn; Bronson)
Act of Vengeance, 1986 (Barkin; Bronson; Reeves)
Act of Violence, 1948 (Ryan, R.; Astor; Leigh, Janet)
Act One, 1963 (Robards; Segal; Wallach)
Actas de Marusia, 1985 (Volonté)
Acte d'amour. *See* Act of Love, 1953
Acte du coeur, 1970 (Bujold; Sutherland)
Acting: Lee Strasberg and the Actors Studio, 1981 (Wallach)
Action for Slander, 1937 (Withers)
Action in Arabia, 1944 (Dalio; Sanders)
Action in the North Atlantic, 1943 (Bogart; Gordon; Massey)
Action Jackson, 1988 (Stone)
Action Man. *See* Soleil des voyous, 1967
Action of the Tiger, 1957 (Connery; Lom)
Actor, 1989 (Piccoli; Quinn)
Actor Finney's Finish, 1914 (Beery)
Actor's Revenge. *See* Yokino-jo henge, 1963
Actors and Sin, 1952 (Robinson, E.)
Actress, 1928 (Shearer)
Actress, 1953 (Gordon; Perkins; Tracy)
Actress. *See* Szinèszno, 1920
Actress. *See* Joyu, 1947
Ad ogni costo, 1968 (Kinski; Robinson, E.; Leigh, Janet)
Ada, 1961 (Hayward; Martin, D.)
Ada dans la jungle, 1988 (Blier; Abril)
Adam and Eva, 1922 (Davies)
Adam and Evelyne, 1949 (Granger)
Adam at 6 A.M., 1970 (Douglas, Michael)
Adam Had Four Sons, 1941 (Bergman; Hayward; Wray)
Adam und Eva, 1923 (Krauss)
Adam's Rib, 1949 (Gordon; Hepburn, K.; Holliday; Sidney; Tracy)
Adam's Woman, 1970 (Mills)
Adauchi goyomi, 1940 (Hasegawa)
Adauchi kokyogaku, 1940 (Shimura)
Adauchi kyodai kagami, 1933 (Hasegawa)
Adauchi senshu, 1931 (Yamada)
Addams Family, 1991 (Huston, A.; Julia)
Addams Family Values, 1993 (Huston, A.; Julia)
Addiction, 1995 (Walken)
Addio mia bella signora, 1953 (Cervi)
Addition, 1984 (Abril)
Addition, 1985 (Abril)
Address Unknown, 1944 (Lukas)

Adelaide, 1968 (Thulin)
Adelita, 1937 (Armendáriz)
Adéma i aviateur, 1933 (Fernandel)
Adharm, 1992 (Azmi)
Adhémar, 1951 (Fernandel)
Adieu Blaireau, 1985 (Girardot)
Adieu Bonaparte, 1984 (Piccoli)
Adieu Chérie, 1945 (Darrieux)
Adieu l'ami, 1968 (Bronson; Delon)
Adieu Léonard, 1943 (Brasseur)
Adios. *See* Lash, 1930
Adios Amigo, 1975 (Pryor)
Adios companeros. *See* Per una bara piena di dollari, 1970
Adios Sabata. *See* Indio Black, sai che ti dico: sei un gran figlio di ..., 1970
Adjudant des Zaren, 1929 (Mozhukin)
Admi, 1968 (Kumar)
Admiral Ushakov, 1953 (Bondarchuk)
Admiral Was a Lady, 1950 (O'Brien, E.)
Admiral Yamamoto. *See* Yamamoto Isoroku, 1968
Adolescente, 1979 (Moreau)
Adolescents. *See* Fleur de l'age, 1964
Adolphe, ou l'âge tendre, 1968 (Noiret)
Adoption, 1978 (Chaplin, G.)
Adorable, 1933 (Gaynor)
Adorable Idiot. *See* Ravissante idiote, 1964
Adorable Julia, 1962 (Boyer)
Adorables créatures, 1952 (Darrieux; Gélin; Feuillère)
Adriana Lecouvreur, 1955 (Vitti)
Adrien, 1943 (Fernandel)
Adrienne Lecouvreur, 1938 (Fresnay)
Adua e la compagne, 1960 (Mastroianni)
Advance to the Rear, 1964 (Blondell; Douglas, Melvyn; Ford, G.)
Adventuras del Marques de Bradomin. *See* Sonatas, 1959
Adventure, 1925 (Beery)
Adventure, 1945 (Blondell; Gable; Garson)
Adventure à Paris, 1936 (Berry)
Adventure for Two. *See* Demi-Paradise, 1943
Adventure for Two. *See* Á Nous deux, 1979
Adventure in Algiers, 1952 (Raft)
Adventure in Baltimore, 1949 (Temple; Young, R.)
Adventure in Manhattan, 1936 (Arthur; McCrea)
Adventure in the Autumn Woods, 1912 (Carey; Barrymore, L.)
Adventure Starts Here. *See* Här börjar äventyret, 1965
Adventurer, 1917 (Chaplin, C.; Purviance)
Adventurer. *See* Äventyrare, 1942
Adventurers, 1950 (Hawkins)
Adventurers, 1970 (Borgnine; Brazzi; De Havilland; Rey)
Adventure's End, 1937 (Wayne)
Adventures in Washington, 1941 (Marshall)
Adventures of a Private Eye, 1977 (Dors)
Adventures of a Young Man. *See* Hemingway's Adventures of a Young Man,
    1962
Adventures of Baron Munchausen, 1989 (Thurman; Williams, R.; Reed)
Adventures of Billy, 1911 (Crisp)
Adventures of Buckaroo Banzai across the Eighth Dimension, 1984 (Barkin;
    Curtis, J.)
Adventures of Bullwhip Griffin, 1967 (Malden; McDowall)
Adventures of Captain Fabian, 1951 (Flynn; Moorehead; Presle; Price)
Adventures of Don Juan, 1949 (Flynn)
Adventures of Don Quixote, 1973 (Harrison)
Adventures of Gerard, 1970 (Cardinale; Hawkins; Wallach)
Adventures of Huck Finn, 1993 (Robards)
Adventures of Huckleberry Finn, 1939 (Rooney)
Adventures of Huckleberry Finn, 1960 (Carradine; Keaton, B.)
Adventures of Huckleberry Finn, 1986 (Gish)
Adventures of Ichabod and Mr. Toad, 1949 (Crosby)
Adventures of Marco Polo, 1938 (Constantine; Rathbone; Turner, L.)
Adventures of Mark Twain, 1944 (Carradine; Crisp; March)
Adventures of Martin Eden, 1942 (Ford, G.; Trevor)
Adventures of Milo and Otis, 1989 (Moore, Dudley)
Adventures of Mr. Wonderful, 1959 (Ustinov)

Adventures of Nick Carter, 1972 (Winters; Crawford, B.)
Adventures of Nils Holgersson. *See* Nils Holgerssons Underbara Resa, 1962
Adventures of Picasso. *See* Picassos aeventyr, 1978
Adventures of Pinocchio, 1996 (Landau)
Adventures of Priscilla, Queen of the Desert, 1993 (Stamp)
Adventures of Quentin Durward, 1955 (Kendall)
Adventures of Rabbi Jacob. *See* Aventures de Rabbi Jacob, 1973
Adventures of Robin Hood, 1938 (De Havilland; Flynn; Rains; Rathbone)
Adventures of Sherlock Holmes, 1939 (Lupino; Rathbone)
Adventures of Sherlock Holmes' Smarter Brother, 1975 (Finney; Wilder)
Adventures of Takla Makan. *See* Kiganjo no boken, 1966
Adventures of Tartu, 1943 (Donat)
Adventures of the Queen, 1975 (Bellamy)
Adventures of Tom Sawyer, 1938 (Brennan)
Adventuress, 1920 (Valentino)
Adventuress. *See* I See a Dark Stranger, 1946
Adventurous Sex, 1925 (Bow)
Advise and Consent, 1962 (Ayres; Fonda, H.; Laughton; Meredith; Pidgeon; Tierney)
Aerial Antics. *See* Hog Wild, 1930
Aerial Gunner, 1943 (Mitchum; Gable)
Aeriel Joyride, 1916 (Laurel and Hardy)
Aeropuerto, 1953 (Rey)
Affair, 1973 (Wood)
Affair in Havana, 1957 (Armendáriz)
Affair in Monte Carlo. *See* Twenty-Four Hours in a Woman's Life, 1952
Affair in Trinidad, 1952 (Ford, G.; Hayworth)
Affair Lafont. *See* Conflit, 1938
Affair of the Skin, 1963 (Grant, L.)
Affair to Remember, 1957 (Grant, C.; Kerr)
Affair with a Stranger, 1953 (Mature)
Affaire Clémenceau, 1918 (Bertini)
Affaire de la Rue de Lourcine, 1923 (Chevalier)
Affaire des femmes, 1989 (Huppert)
Affaire des poisons?, 1955 (Darrieux)
Affaire Dominici, 1972 (Depardieu; Gabin)
Affaire d'une nuit, 1960 (Bardot)
Affaire Lafarge, 1937 (Dalio)
Affaire Mauritzius, 1953 (Vanel; Gélin; Walbrook)
Affaires publiques, 1934 (Dalio)
Affaires sont les affaires, 1943 (Vanel)
Affairs in Versailles. *See* Si Versailles m'était conté, 1953
Affairs of a Gentleman, 1934 (Lukas)
Affairs of Anatole, 1921 (Swanson)
Affairs of Annabel, 1938 (Ball)
Affairs of Cappy Ricks, 1937 (Brennan)
Affairs of Cellini, 1934 (Ball; Calhern; March; Wray)
Affairs of Dobie Gillis, 1953 (Reynolds, D.)
Affairs of Dr. Holl. *See* Angelika, 1951
Affairs of Messalina. *See* Messalina, 1951
Affairs of Susan, 1945 (Fontaine)
Affectionately Yours, 1941 (Bellamy; Hayworth; McDaniel; Oberon)
Affinita elettive, 1996 (Huppert)
Affirmative Action, 1996 (De Niro)
Affondamento della Valiant. *See* Valiant, 1962
Affreux, 1959 (Fresnay)
Afghanistan porquoi, 1983 (Papas)
Afgrunden, 1910 (Nielsen)
Afirma Pereira. *See* Sostiene Pereira, 1996
Afraid to Talk, 1932 (Calhern)
Africa Express, 1975 (Palance)
Africa Screams, 1949 (Abbott and Costello; Three Stooges)
Africa—Texas Style!, 1967 (Mills)
Africa: The Serengeti, 1994 (Jones, James Earl)
Africain, 1983 (Deneuve; Noiret)
African. *See* Africain, 1983
African. *See* Africain, 1983
African Queen, 1951 (Hepburn, K.; Huston, J.; Bogart)
African Queen, 1977 (Oates)
Afsar, 1950 (Anand)
Afskedens timme, 1973 (Andersson, B.)

After Dark, My Sweet, 1990 (Dern)
After Darkness, 1985 (Abril; Hurt, J.)
After Five, 1915 (Hayakawa)
After Midnight, 1927 (Shearer)
After Midnight. *See* Captain Carey U.S.A., 1950
After Office Hours, 1935 (Gable)
After Pilkington, 1987 (Richardson, M.)
After the Fall, 1974 (Dunaway)
After the Fox. *See* Caccia alla volpe, 1966
After the Rehearsal. *See* Efter Repetitionen, 1984
After the Thin Man, 1936 (Loy; Powell, W.; Stewart)
After Your Own Heart, 1921 (Mix)
Aftermath. *See* Mädchen ohne Heimat, 1926
Afurika monogatari, 1981 (Stewart)
Again a Love Story. *See* Homme qui me plait, 1969
Against All Flags, 1952 (Flynn; O'Hara; Quinn)
Against All Odds, 1984 (Bridges; Widmark; Woods)
Against Her Will: An Incident in Baltimore, 1992 (Matthau)
Against Oblivion. *See* Contre l'oubli, 1991
Against the Law, 1934 (Bond)
Against the Wall, 1994 (Jackson, S.; Stanton)
Against the Wind. *See* Contra el Viento, 1990
Agakuk. *See* Shadow of the Wolf, 1993
Agaman, 1988 (Chatterjee)
Agantuk, 1991 (Depardieu)
Agatha, 1977 (Redgrave, V.)
Agatha, 1979 (Gilbert; Hoffman)
Age d'or, 1930 (Modot)
Age ingrat, 1964 (Fernandel)
Age of Consent, 1969 (Mason; Mirren)
Age of Curiosity, 1963 (Farrow)
Age of Discretion. *See* Prima di Natale, 1990
Age of Indiscretion, 1935 (Lukas)
Age of Innocence, 1934 (Dunne)
Age of Innocence, 1993 (Bloom; Chaplin, G.; Day-Lewis; Pfeiffer; Ryder; Woodward)
Age of Love, 1931 (Horton)
Age vermeil, 1984 (Darrieux)
Âge ingrat, 1964 (Gabin)
Agee, 1980 (Huston, J.)
Agence Cacahuete, 1912-14 (Raimu)
Agence matrimoniale, 1951 (Noiret; Blier)
Agency, 1981 (Mitchum)
Agent 38-24-36. *See* Ravissante idiote, 1964
Agent 8 3/4. *See* Hot Enough for June, 1963
Agent Orange: Policy of Poison, 1987 (Christie)
Agent Trouble, 1987 (Deneuve)
Agget är löst, 1974 (Von Sydow)
Agguato a Tangeri, 1958 (Cantinflas; Cervi)
Agnes of God, 1985 (Bancroft; Fonda, J.)
Agni Bhraman, 1973 (Chatterjee)
Agni Sanket, 1988 (Chatterjee)
Agonies of Agnes, 1918 (Dressler)
Agonizing Adventure. *See* Angoissante Aventure, 1919
Agony and the Ecstasy, 1965 (Harrison; Heston)
Agony of Love. *See* Lowat el Hub, 1960
Agostino, 1962 (Thulin)
Agradani, 1982 (Chatterjee)
Agression, 1975 (Deneuve)
Aguila o sol, 1937 (Cantinflas)
Aguirre, der Zorn Göttes, 1973 (Kinski)
Agun, 1962 (Chatterjee)
Agun, 1988 (Chatterjee)
Ah, Wilderness, 1935 (Barrymore, L.; Rooney; Beery)
Ahen senso, 1943 (Takamine)
Ahí viene Martin Corona, 1951 (Infante)
Ahí está el detalle, 1940 (Cantinflas)
Ahora soy rico, 1952 (Infante)
Ai Margini della Metropoli, 1953 (Masina)
Ai Midori no nakama, 1954 (Mori)
Ai no inomotsu, 1955 (Yamamura)

Ai no kane, 1959 (Kagawa)
Ai no onimotsu, 1955 (Yamada)
Ai no rekishi, 1955 (Tsukasa)
Ai no sanga, 1950 (Yamamura)
Ai no sekai, 1943 (Takamine)
Ai to honoho to, 1961 (Shimura; Mori)
Ai to nikushimi no kaneta e, 1951 (Mifune)
Ai wa dokomaremo, 1932 (Yamada)
Ai wa furu hoshi no kanata ni, 1956 (Mori)
Ai yo hoshi to tomoni, 1947 (Takamine)
Ai yo jinrui to tomo ni are, 1931 (Tanaka; Takamine)
Aida, 1953 (Loren)
Aigle à deux têtes, 1947 (Feuillère; Marais)
Aijo fudo, 1959 (Kagawa; Yamada)
Aijo no keifu, 1961 (Yamamura)
Aijo no kessan, 1956 (Mifune)
Aijo no miyako, 1958 (Tsukasa)
Aijo shindansho, 1948 (Takamine)
Aile ou la cuisse, 1976 (Dalio)
Ailes de la Colombe, 1981 (Huppert; Sanda)
Aimez-vous Brahms? See Goodbye Again, 1961
Aimez-vous les femmes?, 1964 (Feuillère)
Ain't It the Truth, 1915 (Beery)
Aîné des Ferchaux, 1962 (Belmondo; Vanel)
Air America, 1990 (Gibson)
Air Cadet, 1951 (Hudson)
Air de Paris, 1954 (Arletty; Gabin)
Air Force, 1943 (Carey; Garfield; Kennedy)
Air Force One, 1997 (Ford, H.)
Air Hawks, 1935 (Bellamy)
Air Mail, 1932 (Bellamy)
Air Raid Wardens, 1943 (Laurel and Hardy)
Air Tonic, 1933 (Grable)
Air Up There, 1994 (Bacon)
Aire de un crimen, 1988 (Rey)
Airman's Letter to His Mother, 1941 (Gielgud)
Airport, 1970 (Lancaster; Martin, D.; Seberg)
Airport 1975, 1974 (Andrews, D.; Heston; Loy; Swanson)
Airport '77, 1977 (Cotten; De Havilland; Grant, L.; Lee, C.; Lemmon; Stewart)
Airport '80—The Concorde. See Concorde—Airport '79, 1979
Aisai-ki, 1959 (Tsukasa)
Aisureba koso, 1955 (Kagawa; Yamada; Yamamura)
Aiyoku no ki, 1930 (Tanaka)
Aiyoku no sabaki, 1953 (Kagawa)
Aizen-bashi, 1951 (Tanaka)
Aizen katsura, 1938 (Tanaka)
Aizen katsura, 1954 (Kyo)
Aizen tsubaki, 1940 (Tanaka)
Aizo-toge, 1934 (Yamada)
Aizome-gasa, 1956 (Hasegawa)
Ajana Shapath, 1967 (Chatterjee)
Ajos vandados, 1978 (Chaplin, G.)
Akademik Ivan Pavlov, 1949 (Cherkassov)
Akage, 1969 (Mifune)
Akahige, 1965 (Kagawa; Mifune; Ryu; Shimura; Tanaka)
Akai jinbaori, 1958 (Kagawa)
Akanishi Kakita, 1936 (Shimura)
Akarshan, 1988 (Patil)
Akasen chitai, 1956 (Kyo)
Akasen no hi wa kiezu, 1958 (Kyo)
Akash Kusum, 1965 (Chatterjee)
Akatsuki ni inoru, 1940 (Tanaka)
Akatsuki no gassho, 1963 (Yamamura)
Akatsuki, no Gassho, 1955 (Kagawa)
Akatsuki no yushi, 1927 (Hasegawa)
Akatsuki wa tokedo, 1937 (Tanaka)
Akibiyori, 1960 (Hara; Ryu; Tsukasa)
Akira Kurosawa's Dreams, 1990 (Ryu)
Akitsu onsen, 1962 (Yamamura)
Ako-jo, 1952 (Yamada)

Akrosh, 1980 (Patil)
Aktenskapabrottaren, 1964 (Björnstrand)
Aku no tanoshisa, 1954 (Mori)
Akujo no kisetsu, 1958 (Yamada)
Al caer de la tarde, 1948 (Armendáriz)
Al Capone, 1959 (Steiger)
Al di la delle nuvole. See Par dela les nuages, 1995
Al di la della legge, 1968 (Van Cleef)
Al Jennings of Oklahoma, 1951 (Duryea)
Al Mas à la Al Kubra. See Great Question, 1983
Al Moaten Al Myssri, 1991 (Sharif)
Al Mohager, 1994 (Piccoli)
Al otro lado de la ciudad, 1962 (Valli)
Al otro lado del Túnel, 1993 (Rey)
Al-Risalah. See Message, 1976
Aladdin, 1992 (Williams, R.)
Aladdin and His Wonderful Lamp, 1984 (Jones, James Earl)
Alambrista!, 1977 (Olmos)
Alamo, 1960 (Wayne; Widmark)
Alamo Bay, 1985 (Harris, E.)
Alamo: Thirteen Days to Glory, 1987 (Julia)
Alarcosbal, 1918 (Lugosi)
Alarm, 1914 (Arbuckle; Normand)
Alarm, 1941 (Rasp)
Alarm auf Gleis B. See Gleisdreieck, 1936
Alarm aus Station III, 1939 (Fröhlich)
Alarm in Peking, 1937 (Fröhlich)
Alas and Alack, 1915 (Chaney)
Alas! Poor Yorick, 1913 (Arbuckle)
Alaska, 1944 (Carradine)
Alaska, 1996 (Heston)
Alaska Seas, 1954 (Ryan, R.)
Alaskafüchse, 1964 (Mueller-Stahl)
Alaskan, 1924 (Wong)
Alba, 1917 (Bertini)
Albert Pinto ko gussa kyon aata hai, 1980 (Azmi; Patil)
Albert Savarus, 1992 (Sanda)
Albert Schweitzer, 1955 (March; Meredith)
Alberto Express, 1990 (Moreau)
Albino Alligator, 1996 (Dillon)
Albuquerque, 1948 (Scott, R.)
Albur de amor, 1947 (Armendáriz)
Alcalde de Zalamea, 1953 (Rey)
Alcohol Abuse: The Early Warning Signs, 1977 (Fonda, H.)
Aldebaran, 1935 (Cervi)
Aldila della nuvole. See Par dela les nuages, 1995
Aldrig i livet, 1957 (Thulin)
Alerte en Méditerranée, 1938 (Fresnay)
Alex and the Gypsy, 1976 (Bujold; Lemmon; Woods)
Alex in Wonderland, 1970 (Burstyn; Moreau; Sutherland)
Alexander den store, 1917 (Madsen and Schenstrøm)
Alexander Nevsky, 1938 (Cherkassov)
Alexander Popov, 1949 (Cherkassov)
Alexander the Great, 1955 (Burton; March; Baker; Bloom; Cushing; Darrieux)
Alexander the Great. See Alexander den store, 1917
Alexander's Ragtime Band, 1938 (Ameche; Carradine; Faye; Power)
Alexandre i Chanakya, 1967 (Tyszkiewicz)
Alexandre le bienheureux, 1968 (Noiret)
Aleyar Alo, 1970 (Chatterjee)
Alf's Button, 1930 (Oberon)
Alf's Carpet. See Rocket Bus, 1929
Alfie, 1966 (Caine; Elliott; Winters)
Alfredo Alfredo, 1972 (Hoffman)
Algiers, 1938 (Boyer; Lamarr)
Algol, 1920 (Jannings)
Ali Baba et les quarante voleurs, 1953 (Fernandel)
Ali Baba Goes to Town, 1937 (Cantor; Carradine; Cobb; Del Rio)
Alía en el bajia, 1941 (Armendáriz)
Alias a Gentleman, 1948 (Beery)
Alias Bulldog Drummond, 1935 (Richardson, R.; Wray)
Alias Jesse James, 1959 (Autry; Bond; Constantine; Crosby; Hope; Rogers, R.)

Alias Jimmy Valentine, 1929 (Barrymore, L.)
Alias John Preston, 1956 (Lee, C.)
Alias Mary Dow, 1935 (Carradine; Milland)
Alias Nick Beale, 1949 (Milland)
Alias the Deacon. *See* Half a Sinner, 1934
Alias the Doctor, 1932 (Barthelmess; Karloff)
Alibi, 1937 (Jouvet; Dalio)
Alibi, 1942 (Lockwood; Mason)
Alibi, 1969 (Gassman)
Alibi Ike, 1935 (Brown; De Havilland)
Alice. *See* Alicja, 1979
Alice, 1986 (York)
Alice, 1990 (Allen; Davis, J.; Farrow; Hurt, W.)
Alice Adams, 1935 (Hepburn, K.; MacMurray; McDaniel)
Alice Doesn't Live Here Anymore, 1974 (Burstyn; Foster; Keitel)
Alice in den Städten, 1974 (Vogler)
Alice in the Cities. *See* Alice in den Städten, 1974
Alice in Wonderland, 1933 (Constantine; Fields, W. C.; Grant, C.; Horton;
    Marsh; Borgnine)
Alice in Wonderland, 1985 (Malden; O'Connor)
Alice, ou la dernière fugue, 1976 (Vanel)
Alice through the Looking Glass, 1966 (Durante; Moorehead)
Alice's Adventures in Wonderland, 1972 (Moore, Dudley; Richardson, R.;
    Sellers)
Alicja, 1979 (Cassel)
Alien, 1979 (Hurt, J.; Stanton; Weaver)
Alien 3, 1992 (Weaver)
Alien Encounter, 1976 (Lee, C.)
Alien Nation, 1988 (Caan; Stamp)
Alien Orders. *See* Malaya, 1950
Alien Resurrection, 1997 (Ryder; Weaver)
Alien Souls, 1916 (Hayakawa)
Alien Thunder, 1975 (Sutherland)
Alien Within, 1995 (McDowall)
Alien's Return. *See* Return, 1980
Aliens, 1986 (Weaver)
Aliens Are Coming, 1980 (Harris, E.)
Alimony, 1918 (Valentino)
Aline, 1950 (Lollobrigida)
Alistair MacLean's Death Train, 1993 (Lee, C.)
Alive, 1993 (Malkovich)
Alive and Kicking, 1958 (Harris, R.)
Alive by Night. *See* Evil Spawn, 1987
All Aboard, 1917 (Lloyd)
All about Eve, 1950 (Baxter; Davis, B.; Monroe; Ritter; Sanders)
All about People, 1967 (Fonda, H.; Heston; Lancaster)
All-American, 1932 (Brennan)
All-American, 1953 (Curtis, T.)
All-American Boy, 1973 (Voight)
All-American Co-ed, 1941 (Langdon)
All Ashore, 1953 (Rooney)
All at Sea, 1935 (Harrison; Withers)
All at Sea. *See* Barnacle Bill, 1957
All Benigni. *See* Tuttobenigni, 1985
All Creatures Great and Small, 1974 (Hopkins, A.)
All Dogs Go to Heaven, 1989 (Reynolds, B.)
All Fall Down, 1962 (Beatty; Lansbury; Malden; Saint)
All Fired Up. *See* Tout feu tout flamme, 1982
All for a Girl, 1916 (Laurel and Hardy)
All for a Woman. *See* Danton, 1920
All for Peggy, 1915 (Chaney)
All God's Children, 1980 (Widmark)
All Gummed Up, 1947 (Three Stooges)
All Hands, 1940 (Mills)
All I Desire, 1953 (O'Sullivan; Stanwyck)
All I Want for Christmas, 1991 (Bacall)
All in a Night's Work, 1961 (MacLaine; Martin, D.; Robertson)
All Is Confusion. *See* Riding on Air, 1937
All Is Well. *See* Tenka taihai, 1955
All Mine to Give, 1957 (Jaffe)
All Mixed Up. *See* Sac de noeuds, 1985

All My Darling Daughters, 1972 (Massey; Young, R.)
All My Good Countrymen. *See* Vsichni dobri rodaci, 1968
All My Sons, 1948 (Lancaster; Robinson, E.)
All Night, 1918 (Valentino)
All Night Long, 1924 (Langdon)
All Night Long, 1961 (Attenborough; Girardot)
All Night Long, 1981 (Hackman; Quaid; Streisand)
All of Me, 1934 (Raft; Hopkins, M.; March)
All of Me, 1984 (Martin, S.)
All of Me, 1991 (Łomnicki)
All on Account of the Milk, 1910 (Pickford; Sweet)
All over the Town, 1949 (Baker; Cusack)
All over Town, 1937 (Ladd)
All Quiet on the Western Front, 1930 (Ayres)
All Quiet on the Western Front, 1979 (Neal; Pleasence)
All-Star Bond Rally, 1945 (Crosby; Darnell; Grable; Hope; Sidney)
All-Star Production of Patriotic Episodes for the Second Liberty Loan, 1917
    (Hart)
All that Heaven Allows, 1955 (Moorehead; Wyman; Hudson)
All That Jazz, 1979 (Lange; Scheider)
All That Money Can Buy, 1941 (Huston, W.)
All the Brothers Were Valiant, 1923 (Chaney)
All the Brothers Were Valiant, 1953 (Granger; Taylor, R.)
All the Fine Young Cannibals, 1960 (Wood)
All the Gold in the World. *See* Tout l'or du monde, 1961
All the King's Horses, 1935 (Horton; Wyman)
All the King's Men, 1949 (Crawford, B.)
...All the Marbles, 1981 (Falk)
All the Mornings of the World. *See* Tous les matins du monde, 1992
All the President's Men, 1976 (Gilbert; Hoffman; Redford; Robards)
All the Right Moves, 1983 (Cruise)
All the Way, Boys. *See* Piu forte ragazzi!, 1972
All the Way Home, 1963 (Preston)
All the Way Home, 1971 (Woods)
All the Winners, 1934 (Niven)
All the World's a Stooge, 1941 (Three Stooges)
All the Young Men, 1960 (Ladd; Poitier)
All These Women. *See* För att inte tala om alla dessa kvinnor, 1964
All This and Glamour Too. *See* Vogues of 1938, 1937
All This and Heaven Too, 1940 (Boyer; Davis, B.)
All This and Money Too. *See* Love Is a Ball, 1963
All through the Night, 1942 (Bogart; Lorre; Veidt)
All Tied Up, 1987 (Gould)
All Weekend Lovers. *See* Jeu de massacre, 1967
All Women, 1918 (Marsh)
All Women Have Secrets, 1939 (Lake)
All You Need Is Cash, 1978 (Belushi; Murray)
All's Fair, 1988 (Segal)
All-American Murder, 1992 (Walken)
Allan Quatermain and the Lost City of Gold, 1987 (Jones, James Earl; Stone)
Alle man på post, 1940 (Björnstrand)
Allegheny Uprising, 1939 (Sanders; Trevor; Wayne)
Allegro squadrone, 1954 (Gélin; Sordi)
Allemagne annee 90 neuf zero, 1991 (Constantine)
Alleman, 1963 (Ustinov)
Aller simple, 1971 (Giannini)
Alles für Geld, 1923 (Jannings)
Alles Schwindel, 1940 (Fröhlich)
Allez France, 1966 (Dors)
Allez Oop, 1934 (Keaton, B.)
Alliance, 1970 (Karina)
Alligator Named Daisy, 1955 (Dors; Rutherford)
Allonsanfan, 1974 (Mastroianni)
Allotment Wives, 1945 (Francis)
Allotria, 1936 (Walbrook)
Allskande par, 1964 (Björnstrand)
Allvarsamma leken, 1945 (Dahlbeck)
Allvarsamma leken, 1977 (Josephson)
Alma de bronce, 1944 (Armendáriz)
Almería Case. *See* Caso Almería, 1984
Almonds and Raisins, 1983 (Welles)

Almost a Bride. *See* Kiss for Corliss, 1949
Almost a Husband, 1919 (Rogers, W.)
Almost an Actress, 1913 (Chaney)
Almost an Angel, 1990 (Heston)
Almost Human. *See* Shock Waves, 1975
Almost Married, 1932 (Bellamy)
Almost Perfect Affair, 1979 (Vitti)
Alô, alô, Brasil!, 1935 (Miranda)
Alô, alô carnaval!, 1936 (Miranda)
Aloha, bobby and rose, 1975 (Olmos)
Aloha ou Le Chant des îles, 1937 (Arletty)
Aloise, 1974 (Huppert; Seyrig)
Aloma of the South Seas, 1926 (Powell, W.)
Aloma of the South Seas, 1941 (Lamour)
Alone in the Dark, 1982 (Landau; Palance; Pleasence)
Alone in the Neon Jungle, 1988 (Aiello)
Alone in the Pacific. *See* Taiheiyo hitoribocchi, 1963
Along Came Auntie, 1926 (Laurel and Hardy)
Along Came Jones, 1945 (Constantine; Duryea; Young, L.)
Along the Border, 1916 (Mix)
Along the Great Divide, 1951 (Brennan; Douglas, K.)
Along the Navajo Trail, 1945 (Rogers, R.)
Alouette, je te plumerai, 1988 (Presle)
Alpagueur, 1976 (Belmondo)
Alpentragödie, 1927 (Kortner)
Alpha Beta, 1972 (Finney; Roberts, R.)
Alpha Caper, 1973 (Fonda, H.)
Alphabet Murders, 1965 (Rutherford)
Alphaville, 1965 (Constantine; Karina; Léaud)
Alraune, 1927 (Wegener)
Älskande par, 1964 (Andersson, H.; Dahlbeck; Zetterling)
Älskarinnan, 1962 (Andersson, B.; Von Sydow)
Also es war so, 1976 (Karina)
Also es war so, 1980 (Karina)
Alt-Heidelberg, 1923 (Krauss)
Alta infedeltà, 1964 (Blier; Cassel; Vitti; Bloom)
Altar Stairs, 1922 (Karloff)
Altare per la Madre, 1987 (Winkler)
Altars of the East, 1955 (Ayres)
Altars of the World, 1976 (Ayres)
Alte Gesetz, 1923 (Krauss)
Alte Lied, 1930 (Dagover)
Alte und der junge König, 1935 (Jannings)
Altered States, 1979 (Hurt, W.)
Altes Herz wird wieder jung, 1943 (Jannings)
Altitude 3200, 1937 (Barrault; Blier)
Altri tempi, 1952 (Fabrizi; Lollobrigida)
Alvarez Kelly, 1966 (Holden; Widmark)
Always, 1989 (Dreyfuss; Hepburn, A.; Hunter)
Always Faithful, 1929 (Sweet)
Always Goodbye, 1938 (Marshall; Stanwyck)
Always in My Heart, 1942 (Francis; Huston, W.)
Always Together, 1947 (Bogart; Flynn)
Alzire oder der Neue Kontinent, 1978 (Vogler)
Am Meer, 1924 (Nielsen)
Am Rande der Gross-stadt, 1922 (Kortner)
Am roten Kliff, 1921 (Kortner)
Ama a tu prójimo, 1958 (Cantinflas)
Amagi kara kita otoko, 1950 (Yamada)
Amai shiru, 1964 (Kyo)
Aman Ke Farishte, 1990 (Anand)
Amant. *See* Lover, 1992
Amant de Bornéo, 1942 (Arletty)
Amant de cinq jours, 1960 (Presle; Seberg; Cassel)
Amant de Lady Chatterley, 1955 (Darrieux)
Amante di Paride. *See* Eterna femmina, 1954
Amante italiana. *See* Sultans, 1966
Amante segreta, 1941 (Valli)
Amantes, 1990 (Abril)
Amanti, 1968 (Dunaway; Mastroianni)
Amanti del deserto, 1956 (Cervi)

Amanti del mostro, 1974 (Kinski)
Amanti di Gramigna, 1969 (Volonté)
Amantia Pestilens, 1963 (Bujold)
Amants, 1958 (Cuny; Modot; Moreau)
Amants de demain, 1957 (Brasseur)
Amants de la Villa Borghese, 1954 (Philipe)
Amants de Tolède, 1953 (Armendáriz; Valli)
Amants de Vérone, 1948 (Aimée; Brasseur; Dalio; Reggiani)
Amants de villa Borghese. *See* Villa Borghese, 1953
Amants du Pont Neuf, 1991 (Binoche)
Amants du Tage, 1955 (Armendáriz; Dalio; Gélin; Howard, T.)
Amants et voleurs, 1935 (Arletty)
Amapola del Camino, 1937 (Armendáriz)
Amar, 1954 (Kumar)
Amar Akbar Anthony, 1977 (Azmi)
Amar deep, 1979 (Azmi; Anand)
Amar Geeti, 1983 (Chatterjee)
Amar Shapath, 1989 (Chatterjee)
Amarilly of Clothes-Line Alley, 1918 (Pickford)
Amateur, 1994 (Huppert)
Amateur Gentleman, 1926 (Barthelmess)
Amateur Gentleman, 1936 (Lockwood)
Amateur Night at the Dixie Bar and Grill, 1979 (Quaid)
Amazing Adventure. *See* Amazing Quest of Ernest Bliss, 1936
Amazing Captain Nemo, 1978 (Ferrer; Meredith)
Amazing Dobermans, 1976 (Astaire)
Amazing Dr. Clitterhouse, 1938 (Bogart; Bond; Crisp; Hayward; Huston, J.;
   Robinson, E.; Trevor)
Amazing Dr. G, 1965 (Rey)
Amazing Grace and Chuck, 1987 (Curtis, J.; Peck)
Amazing Howard Hughes, 1977 (Harris, E.; Jones, T.)
Amazing Monsieur Fabre. *See* Monsieur Fabre, 1951
Amazing Mr. Blunden, 1972 (Dors)
Amazing Mr. Forrest. *See* Gang's All Here, 1939
Amazing Mr. Williams, 1939 (Blondell; Douglas, Melvyn)
Amazing Mrs. Holliday, 1943 (Durbin; Fitzgerald; O'Brien, E.)
Amazing Quest of Ernest Bliss, 1936 (Grant, C.)
Amazon Women on the Moon, 1987 (Bellamy; Pfeiffer)
Amazons, 1917 (Menjou)
Amazons of Rome. *See* Vergine di Roma, 1961
Amazzone mascherata, 1914 (Bertini)
Amba, 1990 (Azmi)
Ambassador, 1984 (Burstyn; Hudson; Mitchum; Pleasence)
Ambassador at Large, 1964 (Homolka)
Ambassador Bill, 1931 (Milland; Rogers, W.)
Ambassadors, 1977 (Remick)
Ambassador's Daughter, 1956 (De Havilland; Loy; Menjou)
Ambassador's Envoy, 1914 (Hayakawa)
Ambiciosos. *See* Fièvre monte à El Pao, 1960
Ambitieuse, 1959 (O'Brien, E.)
Ambition of the Baron, 1915 (Swanson)
Ambitious. *See* Bakumatsu, 1970
Ambitious Butler, 1912 (Normand)
Ambitious Ethel, 1916 (Laurel and Hardy)
Ambulance, 1990 (Jones, James Earl)
Ambush, 1939 (Crawford, B.)
Ambush, 1950 (Taylor, R.)
Ambush. *See* Machibuse, 1970
Ambush at Cimarron Pass, 1957 (Eastwood)
Ambush Bay, 1966 (Rooney)
Ambush of Ghosts, 1993 (Bujold)
Ambushers, 1967 (Martin, D.)
Ame d'artiste, 1925 (Vanel)
Ame de clown, 1933 (Fresnay)
Ame de Pierre, 1912 (Modot)
Amelia Earhart: The Final Flight, 1994 (Dern; Keaton, D.)
Amère victoire, 1957 (Burton)
America, 1924 (Barrymore, L.)
America and Lewis Hine, 1984 (Robards)
America at the Movies, 1976 (Heston; Delon)
America Can Give It, 1942 (Huston, W.)

America's Sweetheart: The Mary Pickford Story, 1978 (Fonda, H.)
American Aristocracy, 1916 (Fairbanks)
American Buffalo, 1996 (Hoffman)
American Cinema, 1995 (Keitel)
American Citizen, 1914 (Barrymore, J.)
American Creed, 1946 (Jones, Jennifer)
American Dream, 1966 (Leigh, Janet)
American Dream, 1981 (Malkovich)
American Dreamer, 1984 (Giannini)
American Film, 1967 (Heston)
American Flyers, 1984 (Costner)
American Friend. See **Amerikanische Freund**, 1977
American Gigolo, 1980 (Gere)
American Girls, 1978 (Andrews, D.)
American Gothic, 1988 (Steiger)
American Graffiti, 1973 (Dreyfuss; Ford, H.)
American Guerilla in the Philippines, 1950 (Power; Presle)
American Heart, 1993 (Bridges)
American in Paris, 1951 (Caron; Kelly, Gene)
American Madness, 1932 (Huston, W.)
American Me, 1992 (Olmos)
American People, 1945 (Huston, W.)
American Portrait, 1949 (Ladd)
American President, 1995 (Douglas, Michael; Dreyfuss; Redford; Sheen)
American Prisoner, 1929 (Carroll)
American Raspberry. See Prime Time, 1977
American Rickshaw, 1991 (Pleasence)
American Roulette, 1988 (García; York)
American Success Company, 1980 (Bridges)
American Tail 2: Fievel Goes West, 1991 (Cleese; Stewart)
American Tragedy, 1931 (Sidney)
American Venus, 1926 (Brooks, L.)
American Way, 1986 (Hopper)
American West of John Ford, 1971 (Stewart)
American Widow, 1917 (Barrymore, E.)
American Wife. See Sposa Americana, 1986
Americana, 1981 (Hershey)
Americanization of Emily, 1964 (Andrews, J.; Coburn, J.; Douglas, Melvyn; Garner)
Americano, 1916 (Fairbanks)
Americano, 1955 (Ford, G.)
Americano a Roma, 1954 (Sordi)
Amerikanische Freund, 1977 (Ganz)
Amerique en otage. See Iran: Days of Crisis, 1991
Ametralladora, 1943 (Infante)
Ami de Vincent, 1981 (Karina)
Ami Retrouvé, 1988 (Robards; Washington)
Ami viendra ce soir, 1945 (Gélin)
Amici di Nick Nezard, 1976 (Cobb)
Amici miei, 1975 (Blier; Noiret)
Amici miei, atto due, 1982 (Noiret)
Amici miei atto III, 1985 (Blier)
Amie. See Heller Wahn, 1982
Amiga, 1988 (Ullmann)
Amir Garib, 1974 (Anand)
Amityville 3-D, 1983 (Ryan, M.)
Amityville Horror, 1979 (Steiger)
Amityville II: The Possession, 1982 (Aiello)
Amnesia, 1994 (Villagra)
Amo non amo, 1979 (Stamp; Schell, Maximilian)
Amoire volante, 1948 (Modot)
Amok, 1944 (Félix)
Among the Living, 1941 (Carey; Farmer; Hayward)
Among the Mourners, 1915 (Arbuckle)
Among Those Present, 1921 (Lloyd)
Among Vultures. See Unter Geiern, 1964
Amor de Don Juan, 1956 (Rey)
Amor e Dedinhos de Pe, 1990 (Cassel)
Amor en el aire, 1967 (Rey)
Amor Indio. See Tizoc, 1956
Amor non ho ... pero ... pero, 1951 (Lollobrigida)

Amor y deditos del pie. See Amor e Dedinhos de Pe, 1990
Amor y sexo, 1963 (Félix)
Amore, 1935 (Cervi; Feuillère)
Amore, 1947 (Magnani)
Amore, 1965 (Brazzi)
Amore!, 1993 (Gould)
Amore difficile, 1962 (Gassman)
Amore e chiacchiere, 1957 (Cervi)
Amore e guai, 1958 (Mastroianni)
Amore mio, aiutami, 1969 (Sordi; Vitti)
Amore, piombo, e furore, 1978 (Oates)
Amore primitivo, 1964 (Mansfield)
Amore vince amore, 1921 (Bertini)
Amori di Ercole, 1960 (Mansfield)
Amori di mezzo secolo, 1954 (Sordi)
Amorosa, 1986 (Josephson)
Amorosa, 1986 (Zetterling)
Amorous Adventures of Moll Flanders, 1965 (Lansbury; Novak; Sanders)
Amorous General. See Waltz of the Toreadors, 1962
Amorous Prawn, 1962 (Greenwood)
Amos & Andrew, 1993 (Cage; Jackson, S.)
Amos, 1985 (Douglas, K.)
Amour à la mer, 1964 (Delon)
Amour à vingt ans, 1962 (Léaud)
Amour autour de la maison, 1946 (Brasseur)
Amour c'est gai, l'amour c'est triste, 1968 (Dalio)
Amour d'une femme, 1953 (Presle)
Amour de Jeanne Ney. See Liebe der Jeanne Ney, 1927
Amour de pluie, 1974 (Schneider)
Amour de poche, 1957 (Marais)
Amour de Swann. See Swann in Love, 1984
Amour en Allemagne. See Eine Liebe im Deutschland, 1983
Amour en fuite, 1979 (Léaud)
Amour en question, 1978 (Andersson, B.; Girardot)
Amour est en jeu, 1957 (Girardot)
Amour interdit, 1984 (Rey)
Amour, madame ..., 1951 (Arletty)
Amour maître des choses, 1930 (Wong)
Amour necessario, 1991 (Kingsley)
Amour par terre, 1984 (Chaplin, G.)
Amour tenace, 1912 (Linder)
Amoureux sont seuls au monde, 1948 (Jouvet)
Amours célèbre, 1961 (Brasseur; Bardot; Belmondo; Delon; Feuillère; Girardot; Noiret)
Amours de Casanova, 1933 (Mozhukin)
Ampélopède, 1973 (Huppert)
Amsterdam Kill, 1977 (Mitchum)
Amy, 1981 (O'Brien, M.)
Amy and the Angel, 1981 (Jones, James Earl; Ryan, M.)
An-Magritt, 1968 (Ullmann)
An quarante, 1940 (Berry)
Ana, 1957 (Kyo; Yamamura)
Aña y los lobos, 1973 (Chaplin, G.)
Analfabeto, 1960 (Cantinflas)
Anam, 1956 (Sharif)
Anand Aur Anand, 1984 (Anand; Patil)
Anarchistes ou la Bande à Bonnot, 1967 (Girardot)
Anastasia, 1956 (Bergman; Brynner)
Anastasia mio fratello, 1973 (Sordi)
Anastasia: The Mystery of Anna, 1986 (Bloom; De Havilland; Harrison; Sharif)
Anata to watashi no ai-kotoba: Sayonara, konnichiwa, 1959 (Kyo)
Anatomy of a Murder, 1959 (Remick; Scott, G.; Stewart)
Anatomy of an Illness, 1983 (Wallach)
Anatomy of Love. See Tempi nostri, 1953
Anatomy of Love, 1972 (Nowicki)
Anatra all'orancia, 1975 (Vitti)
Anchors Aweigh, 1945 (Kelly, Gene; Sidney)
Anciens de Saint-Loup, 1950 (Blier; Reggiani)
Ancient Mariner, 1926 (Bow)
And Baby Makes Six, 1979 (Oates)

And Baby Makes Three, 1949 (Young, R.)
And Comes the Dawn...but Colored Red. See Nella stretta morsa del ragno, 1971
And...God Created Woman. See Et...Dieu créa la femme, 1956
And God Said to Cain. See E Dio disse a Caino ..., 1969
And Happiness Will Be Possible. See Shchastiya bylo tak vozmotzno, 1916
...And Hope to Die. See Course, du lièvre a travers les champs, 1972
...And Justice for All, 1979 (Pacino)
And No One Could Save Her, 1973 (Remick)
...And Nobody Was Ashamed. See und keiner schämte sich, 1960
And Nothing but the Truth, 1984 (Jackson, G.)
And Now for Something Completely Different, 1971 (Cleese)
And Now the Screaming Starts, 1973 (Cushing; Lom)
And Now Tomorrow, 1944 (Hayward; Ladd; Young, L.)
And So They Were Married, 1936 (Astor; Douglas, Melvyn)
And Sudden Death, 1936 (Scott, R.)
...And Suddenly It's Murder. See Crimen, 1960
And Surely Set Us Free Lord. See Y Del Seguro, Libranos Señor, 1982
And the Angels Sing, 1943 (Lamour; MacMurray)
And the Band Played On, 1993 (Baye; Gere; Huston, A.; Martin, S.)
And the Dance Goes On, 1990 (Bujold)
And the Wild, Wild Women. See Nella città l'inferno, 1958
And Then There Were None, 1945 (Fitzgerald; Huston, W.)
And Then There Were None, 1974 (Audran; Lom; Attenborough; Welles)
And There Came a Man. See E venne un uomo, 1965
And Your Name Is Jonah, 1979 (Woods)
Andaz, 1949 (Kumar)
Andere, 1930 (Kortner)
Andere Blick, 1991 (Presle)
Andere Ich, 1918 (Kortner)
Andere Seite, 1931 (Veidt)
Anders als die Andern, 1919 (Veidt)
Anderson Tapes, 1971 (Connery)
Andersonville Trial, 1970 (Scott, G.; Sheen)
Anderssonskans Kalle, 1950 (Andersson, H.)
Ando volando bajo, 1957 (Armendáriz)
Andrei Kozhukhov, 1917 (Mozhukin)
Andreina, 1917 (Bertini)
Andremo in città, 1966 (Chaplin, G.)
Andrina, 1981 (Cusack)
Androcles and the Lion, 1952 (Lanchester; Mature)
Android, 1982 (Kinski)
Andy Hardy Comes Home, 1958 (Rooney)
Andy Hardy Gets Spring Fever, 1939 (Rooney)
Andy Hardy Meets Debutante, 1940 (Garland; Rooney)
Andy Hardy Steps Out. See Andy Hardy's Double Life, 1942
Andy Hardy's Blonde Trouble, 1944 (Marshall; Rooney)
Andy Hardy's Double Life, 1942 (Rooney; Williams, E.)
Andy Hardy's Private Secretary, 1941 (Rooney)
Ane jaloux. See Max et son âne, 1911
Ane no shussei, 1940 (Takamine)
Ane to imouto, 1965 (Yamamura)
Ange de la nuit, 1943 (Barrault)
Ange noir, 1994 (Piccoli)
Angeklagt nach Paragraph 218, 1966 (Łomnicki)
Angel, 1937 (Dietrich; Douglas, Melvyn; Horton; Marshall)
Angel 4: Undercover, 1994 (McDowall)
Angel and Sinner. See Boule de suif, 1945
Angel and the Badman, 1947 (Carey; Wayne)
Angel, Angel, Down We Go, 1969 (Jones, Jennifer; McDowall)
Angel Baby, 1961 (Blondell; Reynolds, B.)
Angel City, 1980 (Leigh, Jennifer Jason)
Angel Dust, 1980 (Woodward)
Angel Face, 1952 (Mitchum; Marshall)
Angel from Texas, 1940 (Reagan; Wyman)
Angel Heart, 1987 (De Niro; Rourke)
Angel Levine, 1970 (Wallach)
Angel of Contention, 1914 (Gish)
Angel of Death. See Egy Barany, 1970
Angel on Earth. See Engel auf Erden, 1959
Angel on Earth. See Mademoiselle Ange, 1959

Angel on My Shoulder, 1946 (Baxter; Muni; Rains)
Angel on My Shoulder, 1980 (Hershey)
Angel Out of the Slums, 1911 (White)
Angel over Brooklyn, 1957 (Ustinov)
Angel with the Trumpet, 1951 (Schell, Maria; Werner)
Angel Wore Red, 1960 (Bogarde; Cotten; Gardner)
Angela, 1955 (Brazzi)
Angela. See Tarots, 1972
Angela, 1977 (Huston, J.; Loren)
Angela. See Love Comes Quietly, 1975
Angelas Krig, 1984 (Josephson)
Angèle, 1934 (Fernandel)
Angelic Attitude, 1916 (Mix)
Angelika, 1951 (Schell, Maria)
Angelina. See Onorevole Angelina, 1947
Angelitos negros, 1948 (Infante)
Angelo e il diavolo, 1947 (Cervi)
Angelo, My Love, 1983 (Duvall)
Angels Brigade, 1979 (Palance)
Angels in the Outfield, 1951 (Crosby; Leigh, Janet)
Angels of Darkness. See Donne proibite, 1953
Angels of Mercy, 1942 (Crosby)
Angels One Five, 1951 (Hawkins)
Angels over Broadway, 1940 (Hayworth)
Angels Wash Their Faces, 1939 (Reagan)
Angels with Dirty Faces, 1938 (Bogart; Cagney)
Angelus, 1922 (Astor)
Anger in His Eyes. See Con la rabbia agli occhi, 1976
Anges Gardiens, 1996 (Depardieu)
Angie, 1994 (Davis, G.)
Anglais tel que Max le parle, 1914 (Linder)
Angoissante Aventure, 1919 (Mozhukin)
Angora Love, 1929 (Laurel and Hardy)
Angriff der Gegenwart aud die Ubrige Zeit, 1985 (Mueller-Stahl)
Angry Age. See Diga sul Pacifico, 1958
Angry Harvest. See Bittere Ernte, 1986
Angry Hills, 1959 (Baker; Mitchum)
Angry Man. See Homme en colère, 1979
Angry Sea. See Chino hate ni ikiru mono, 1960
Angry Silence, 1960 (Attenborough; Reed)
Angst, 1928 (Fröhlich)
Angst, 1955 (Bergman)
Angst des Tormanns beim Elfmeter, 1971 (Vogler)
Angus, 1995 (Bates, K.; Scott, G.)
Ani imoto, 1953 (Kyo; Mori)
Ani no hanayome, 1941 (Yamada)
Ani to sono imoto, 1956 (Tsukasa)
Anima allegra, 1918 (Bertini)
Anima del demi-monde, 1913 (Bertini)
Anima Nera, 1962 (Gassman)
Anima persa, 1976 (Deneuve; Gassman)
Anima redenta, 1917 (Bertini)
Anima selvaggia, 1920 (Bertini)
Animal, 1977 (Belmondo; Welch)
Animal Behavior, 1989 (Hunter)
Animal Crackers, 1930 (Dumont; Marx Brothers)
Animal Kingdom, 1932 (Howard, L.; Loy)
Animals Film, 1981 (Christie)
Animas Trujano, 1961 (Mifune)
Anita Garibaldi. See Camicie rosse, 1951
Anjali, 1988 (Chatterjee)
Anjoke no butokai, 1947 (Mori; Hara)
Anju to Zushio-maru, 1961 (Yamada; Yamamura)
Anjuman, 1986 (Azmi)
Ankoku-gai, 1956 (Mifune)
Ankoku-gai no taiketsu, 1960 (Mifune; Tsukasa)
Ankur, 1973 (Azmi)
Ann Carver's Profession, 1933 (Wray)
Ann Vickers, 1933 (Dunne; Huston, W.)
Anna, 1951 (Gassman; Loren; Mangano)
Anna, 1965 (Karina)

Anna, 1970 (Andersson, H.)
Anna, 1986 (Karina)
Anna and the King of Siam, 1946 (Cobb; Darnell; Dunne; Harrison)
Anna Boleyn, 1920 (Jannings)
Anna Christie, 1923 (Sweet)
Anna Christie, 1930 (Dressler; Garbo)
Anna di Brooklyn, 1958 (Lollobrigida)
Anna Göldin: letzte Hexe, 1991 (Vogler)
Anna Karamazoff, 1991 (Moreau)
Anna Karenina. *See* Love, 1927
Anna Karenina, 1935 (Garbo; March; O'Sullivan; Rathbone)
Anna Karenina, 1948 (Cervi; Leigh, V.; Richardson, R.)
Anna Lucasta, 1949 (Crawford, B.; Goddard; Homolka)
Anna of Brooklyn. *See* Anna di Brooklyn, 1958
Anna the Adventuress, 1920 (Colman)
Annabel Takes a Tour, 1939 (Ball)
Annabel's Romance, 1916 (White)
Annabelle Lee, 1972 (O'Brien, M.)
Annabelle's Affairs, 1931 (MacDonald; McLaglen)
Annapolis Salute, 1937 (Carey)
Anne against the World, 1929 (Karloff)
Anne and Muriel. *See* Deux Anglaises et le continent, 1971
Anne Frank Remembered, 1995 (Branagh)
Anne of the Indies, 1951 (Jourdan; Marshall)
Anne of the Thousand Days, 1969 (Bujold; Burton; Papas; Quayle)
Anneaux d'or, 1956 (Cardinale)
Année dernière à Marienbad, 1961 (Seyrig)
Année prochaine si tout va bien, 1981 (Adjani)
Année sainte, 1975 (Gabin; Darrieux)
Années lumières. *See* Light Years Away, 1981
Annelie, 1941 (Krauss)
Anni ruggenti, 1962 (Cervi)
Annibale, 1960 (Mature)
Annie, 1982 (Finney; Huston, J.)
Annie Get Your Gun, 1950 (Calhern)
Annie Hall, 1977 (Allen; Keaton, D.; Walken; Weaver)
Annie Laurie, 1927 (Gish)
Annie Oakley, 1935 (Douglas, Melvyn; Stanwyck)
Annie Oakley, 1985 (Curtis, J.)
Anniversary, 1963 (Pidgeon)
Anniversary, 1968 (Davis, B.)
Announce faite a Mariei, 1991 (Cuny)
Ano hashi no tamoto de, Part III: Ano hito was ima, 1963 (Yamamura)
Ano kumo no hate ni hoshi wa matataku, 1962 (Yamamura)
Anokha bandhan, 1982 (Azmi)
Anokha Milan, 1972 (Kumar)
Anokha Pyar, 1948 (Kumar)
Anonymous Queen. *See* Reina Anonima, 1992
Anote konote, 1952 (Mori)
Another 48 Hrs., 1990 (Nolte; Murphy)
Another Dawn, 1937 (Flynn; Francis)
Another Face, 1935 (McDaniel)
Another Fine Mess, 1930 (Laurel and Hardy)
Another Language, 1933 (Montgomery)
Another Man, Another Chance. *See* Autre homme, une autre chance, 1977
Another Man's Poison, 1952 (Davis, B.)
Another Man's Wife, 1924 (Beery)
Another Part of the Forest, 1948 (Duryea; March)
Another Part of the Forest, 1948 (O'Brien, E.)
Another Stakeout, 1993 (Dreyfuss)
Another Thin Man, 1939 (Loy; Powell, W.; Three Stooges)
Another Time, Another Place, 1958 (Connery; Turner, L.)
Another Woman, 1988 (Allen; Farrow; Hackman; Rowlands)
Another You, 1991 (Pryor; Wilder)
Ansatsu, 1964 (Okada)
Ansichten eines Clowns, 1975 (Schygulla)
Ansiedad, 1952 (Infante)
Ansikte mot ansikte, 1976 (Björnstrand; Ullmann; Josephson; Olin)
Ansiktet, 1958 (Andersson, B.; Björnstrand; Josephson; Thulin; Von Sydow)
Antagonists, 1982 (O'Toole)
Anthony Adverse, 1936 (De Havilland; March; Rains)

Anthony of Padua. *See* Antonio di Padova, 1949
Anticristo, 1974 (Kennedy; Valli)
Antigone, 1960 (Papas)
Antinea, 1961 (Trintignant; Volonté)
Antoine et Antoinette, 1946 (Modot)
Antonieta, 1982 (Adjani; Schygulla)
Antonio di Padova, 1949 (Fabrizi)
Antonito, 1961 (Finch)
Antony and Cleopatra, 1973 (Heston; Rey)
Ants in His Pants, 1939 (Finch)
Ants in the Pantry, 1936 (Three Stooges)
Ants! *See* It Happened at Lakewood Manor, 1977
Anugraham, 1978 (Patil)
Anwalt des Herzens, 1927 (Dagover)
Any Man's Death, 1990 (Borgnine)
Any Number Can Play, 1949 (Astor; Gable)
Any Number Can Play. *See* Mélodie en sous-sol, 1962
Any Old Port, 1932 (Laurel and Hardy)
Any Second Now, 1969 (Granger)
Any Wednesday, 1966 (Fonda, J.; Robards)
Any Which Way You Can, 1980 (Eastwood; Gordon)
Anya és leánya, 1981 (Nowicki)
Anybody's Goat, 1932 (Arbuckle)
Anybody's Woman, 1930 (Lukas)
Anyone Can Kill Me. *See* Tous peuvent me tuer, 1957
Anyone Can Play. *See* Dolci signore, 1967
Anything Can Happen, 1951 (Ferrer)
Anything Goes, 1936 (Carradine; Crosby; Dumont; Lupino; Wyman)
Anything Goes, 1956 (Crosby; O'Connor)
Anything Once, 1917 (Chaney)
Anything Once, 1927 (Normand)
Anzio. *See* Lo sbarco di Anzio, 1968
Anzukko, 1958 (Kagawa; Yamamura)
Aobajo no oni, 1962 (Hasegawa)
Aogashima no kodomotachi: Onnakyoshi no kiroku, 1955 (Kagawa)
Aoi me, 1956 (Tsukasa)
Aoi sanmyaku, 1949 (Hara)
Aoi sanmyaku: enpen, 1957 (Tsukasa)
Aoi yaju, 1960 (Tsukasa)
Aozora roshi, 1936 (Yamada)
Apache, 1954 (Bronson; Lancaster)
Apache Country, 1952 (Autry)
Apache Rose, 1947 (Rogers, R.)
Apache's Gratitude, 1913 (Mix)
Aparichita, 1969 (Chatterjee)
Apartment, 1960 (Lemmon; MacLaine; MacMurray)
Apartment for Peggy, 1948 (Holden)
Ape, 1940 (Karloff)
Ape Man, 1943 (Lugosi)
Ape Woman. *See* Donna scimmia, 1963
Apne paraye, 1980 (Azmi)
Apocalypse Now, 1979 (Brando; Duvall; Fishburne; Ford, H.; Hopper; Sheen)
Apollo 13, 1995 (Bacon; Hanks; Harris, E.)
Apon Amar Apon, 1990 (Chatterjee)
Apostasy. *See* Hakai, 1948
Apostle of Vengeance, 1916 (Gilbert; Hart)
Appaloosa, 1966 (Brando)
Appare binanshi, 1928 (Tanaka)
Apparizione, 1944 (Valli)
Appassionata, 1944 (Björnstrand)
Appearances, 1921 (Crisp)
Appearances, 1990 (Borgnine)
Appel du sang, 1920 (Novello)
Appelez-moi Mathilde, 1968 (Blier)
Appelkriget, 1971 (Von Sydow)
Apple War. *See* Appelkriget, 1971
Appointment, 1969 (Aimée; Sharif)
Appointment for Love, 1941 (Boyer; Sullavan)
Appointment in Berlin, 1943 (Sanders)
Appointment in Honduras, 1953 (Ford, G.)
Appointment in London, 1953 (Bogarde)

Appointment with a Shadow. *See* Midnight Story, 1957
Appointment with Crime, 1946 (Lom)
Appointment with Danger, 1951 (Ladd)
Appointment with Death, 1988 (Bacall; Gielgud; Ustinov)
Appointment with Venus, 1951 (Niven)
Apprentice to Murder, 1988 (Sutherland)
Apprenticeship of Duddy Kravitz, 1974 (Dreyfuss; Elliott)
Apprentis sorciers, 1977 (Hopper)
Appuntamento col disonore, 1970 (Kinski; Sanders)
Appuntamento per le spie, 1966 (Andrews, D.)
Après après-demain, 1990 (Presle)
Après l'amour, 1992 (Huppert)
Après l'orage, 1942 (Berry)
April Folly, 1920 (Davies)
April Fools, 1969 (Boyer; Deneuve; Lemmon; Loy)
April in Paris, 1952 (Day)
April in Portugal, 1954 (Howard, T.)
April Morning, 1988 (Jones, T.)
April Showers, 1926 (Jolson)
Apur Sansar, 1959 (Chatterjee)
Aquarians, 1970 (Ferrer)
Aquella casa en las afueras, 1980 (Valli; Maura)
Aqui d'el Rei!, 1991 (Cassel)
Aquila nera, 1946 (Cervi; Brazzi; Lollobrigida)
Ara nonkida ne, 1926 (Tanaka)
Arab, 1924 (Novarro)
Arabella, 1916 (Negri)
Arabella, 1924 (Marsh)
Arabella, 1967 (Giannini; Marsh; Rutherford; Terry-Thomas)
Arabella, der Roman eines Pferdes, 1924 (Rasp)
Arabesque, 1966 (Loren; Peck)
Arabian Adventure, 1979 (Cushing; Lee, C.; Rooney)
Arabian Knight, 1920 (Hayakawa)
Arabian Love, 1922 (Gilbert)
Arabian Nights, 1942 (Three Stooges)
Arakawa no Sakichi, 1936 (Hasegawa)
Araki Mataemon, 1931 (Yamada)
Araki Mataemon, 1955 (Yamada)
Arakure, 1957 (Mori; Takamine)
Arakure daimyo, 1960 (Kagawa)
Aranyar din Ratri, 1970 (Chatterjee)
Arashi, 1956 (Tanaka)
Arashi nisakuhana, 1940 (Yamada)
Arashi no maki, 1956 (Yamamura)
Arashi no naka no haha, 1952 (Kagawa)
Arashi no naka no otoko, 1957 (Kagawa; Mifune)
Arcadian Maid, 1910 (Pickford)
Arcagelo, 1969 (Gassman)
Arcata Promise, 1974 (Nelligan)
Arch of Triumph, 1948 (Bergman; Boyer; Calhern; Laughton)
Arch of Triumph, 1985 (Hopkins, A.; Pleasence)
Arche de Noë, 1946 (Brasseur)
Archimède le clochard, 1958 (Gabin; Blier)
Archipel des amours, 1983 (Presle)
Archipelago, 1992 (Piccoli)
Architect Athfield, 1977 (Neill)
Architecture, art de l'espace, 1961 (Barrault)
Architecture of Doom, 1991 (Ganz; Moreau)
Architecture of Frank Lloyd Wright, 1983 (Baxter)
Arcidiavolo. *See* Diavolo innamorato, 1966
Ard el Salam, 1955 (Sharif)
Ardh Satya, 1983 (Patil)
Are Crooks Dishonest?, 1918 (Lloyd)
Are ga minato no tomoshibi da, 1961 (Yamamura)
Are Husbands Necessary?, 1942 (Milland)
Are Parents People?, 1925 (Menjou)
Are Women to Blame?, 1928 (Negri)
Are You a Mason?, 1915 (Barrymore, J.)
Are You in the House Alone?, 1978 (Quaid)
Are You with It?, 1948 (O'Connor)
Aren't We All, 1932 (Oberon)

Arena, 1953 (Van Cleef)
Argent, 1928 (Berry; Artaud)
Argent des autres, 1978 (Deneuve)
Argine, 1937 (Cervi)
Aria, 1987 (Hurt, J.)
Ariane, 1931 (Bergner)
Arise My Love, 1940 (Colbert; Milland)
Aristocats, 1970 (Chevalier)
Aristocrates, 1955 (Fresnay)
Arizona, 1919 (Fairbanks)
Arizona, 1940 (Arthur; Holden)
Arizona. *See* Men Are Like That, 1931
Arizona Bound, 1927 (Constantine)
Arizona Bushwhackers, 1968 (Cagney)
Arizona Dream, 1992 (Depp; Dunaway; Lewis, Jerry)
Arizona Kid, 1930 (Lombard)
Arizona Kid, 1939 (Rogers, R.)
Arizona Mission. *See* Gun the Man Down, 1956
Arizona to Broadway, 1933 (Bennett)
Arizona Wildcat, 1927 (Mix)
Arizona Wooing, 1915 (Mix)
Arizonian, 1935 (Calhern)
Arkansas Judge, 1941 (Rogers, R.)
Arlésienne, 1930 (Vanel)
Arlésienne, 1942 (Jourdan; Raimu)
Arlette et ses papas, 1933 (Berry)
Arma, 1978 (Cardinale)
Arma de dos filos. *See* Shark, 1970
Arma dei vigliacchi, 1913 (Bertini)
Armaan, 1953 (Anand)
Armageddon, 1977 (Delon)
Armata assura, 1932 (Cervi)
Armata Brancaleone, 1966 (Gassman; Volonté)
Arme Jenny, 1912 (Nielsen)
Arme Kleine Sif, 1927 (Wegener)
Arme Sünderin, 1923 (Kortner)
Arme Violetta, 1921 (Negri)
Armed and Dangerous, 1986 (Candy; Ryan, M.)
Armed Response, 1986 (Van Cleef)
Armée des ombres, 1969 (Cassel; Reggiani)
Armes kleines Mädchen, 1924 (Kortner)
Armoire volante, 1948 (Fernandel; Reynolds, B.)
Armored Attack. *See* North Star, 1943
Armour of God. *See* Lunghing fudai, 1986
Armour of God II: Operation Condor. *See* Lunghing fudai tsuktsap, 1990
Arms and the Girl. *See* Red Salute, 1935
Arms and the Woman. *See* Mr. Winkle Goes to War, 1944
Army. *See* Rikugun, 1944
Army, 1991 (Reed)
Army Intelligence. *See* Renaissance Man, 1994
Army of One, 1994 (Segal)
Arnold, 1973 (McDowall; Lanchester)
Around the World in 80 Minutes, 1931 (Fairbanks)
Around the World in Eighty Days, 1956 (Boyer; Brown; Cantinflas; Carradine; Coburn, C.; Colman; Dietrich; Fernandel; Gardner; Gielgud; Howard, T.; Keaton, B.; Lorre; MacLaine; McLaglen; Mills; Niven; Raft; Sidney)
Around the World in Eighty Days. *See* Reise um die Erde in 80 Tagen, 1919
Around the World with Orson Welles, 1956 (Constantine)
Arouse and Beware. *See* Man from Dakota, 1940
Arrangement, 1969 (Douglas, K.; Dunaway; Kerr)
Arrêtez les tambours, 1961 (Blier)
Arriba las mujeres, 1943 (Infante)
'Arriet's Baby, 1913 (Talmadge)
Arriva Dorellik, 1967 (Terry-Thomas)
Arrivani i titani, 1961 (Armendáriz)
Arrivano i dollari!, 1957 (Sordi)
Arrivano Joe e Margherito, 1974 (Cusack)
Arrivederce e Grazie, 1989 (Aimée)
Arrivederci, Baby, 1966 (Curtis, T.)
Arriving Tuesday, 1986 (Grant, L.)
Arrivista, 1913 (Bertini)

Astro-Zombies, 1968 (Carradine)
Astronaut, 1972 (Cooper)
Asu aru kagiri, 1962 (Kagawa)
Asu o tsukuru hitobito, 1946 (Mori)
Asu wa docchi da, 1953 (Kagawa; Takamine)
Aswa medher ghora, 1981 (Patil)
Asylum, 1972 (Cushing; Lom)
Asylum Erotica. See Bestia uccide a sangue freddo, 1971
At a Quarter to Two, 1911 (Pickford)
At Close Range, 1986 (Penn; Walken)
At Dawn We Die. See Tomorrow We Live, 1942
At First Sight. See Coup de foudre, 1983
At Gunpoint, 1955 (MacMurray; Malone; Brennan)
At It Again, 1912 (Normand)
At Long Last Love, 1975 (Reynolds, B.)
At Midnight in the Tomb. See V polnotch na kladbische, 1914
At Play in the Fields of the Lord, 1991 (Bates, K.)
At Sword's Point, 1952 (O'Hara; Wilde)
At the Cinema Palace—Liam O'Leary, 1984 (Cusack)
At the Circus, 1939 (Dumont; Marx Brothers)
At the Duke's Command, 1911 (Pickford)
At the Earth's Core, 1976 (Cushing)
At the End of a Perfect Day, 1915 (Swanson)
At the Grey House. See Zur Chronik von Grieshuus, 1925
At the Old Maid's Ball, 1913 (Beery)
At the Old Stage Door, 1919 (Lloyd)
At the Other End of the Tunnel. See Al Otro Lado del Túnel, 1993
At War with the Army, 1950 (Lewis, Jerry; Martin, D.)
At ziji duchove, 1976 (Brodský)
Atakake no hitobito, 1952 (Tanaka; Yamamura)
Atal Jaler Ahwan, 1962 (Chatterjee)
Atame!, 1990 (Abril; Banderas)
Atanka, 1987 (Chatterjee)
Atarashiki tsuchi, 1937 (Hara)
Atentat u Sarajevu. See Days that Shook the World, 1975
Athena, 1954 (Calhern; Reynolds, D.)
Athleten, 1925 (Nielsen)
Athletic Ambitions, 1915 (Mix)
Atithee, 1978 (Azmi)
Atlanta Child Murders, 1985 (Freeman; Jones, James Earl; Robards; Sheen)
Atlanten, 1995 (Von Sydow)
Atlantic, 1929 (Carroll)
Atlantic Adventure, 1935 (Langdon)
Atlantic City, 1981 (Lancaster; Piccoli; Sarandon)
Atlantic Episode. See Catch as Catch Can, 1937
Atlantic Ferry, 1941 (Redgrave, M.)
Atlantide. See Antinea, 1961
Atlantik, 1929 (Kortner)
Ato ni tsuzuku o shinzu, 1945 (Hasegawa)
Atoll K, 1951 (Laurel and Hardy)
Atomic Fireman. See Bombero atómico, 1950
Atomic Kid, 1954 (Rooney)
Atonement of Gösta Berling. See **Gösta Berlings Saga**, 1924
Atre, 1922 (Vanel)
Att älska, 1964 (Andersson, H.)
Atta Boy, 1926 (Laurel and Hardy)
Attack!, 1956 (Marvin; Palance)
Attack and Retreat. See Italiani brava gente, 1964
Attack Force Z, 1980 (Gibson; Neill)
Attack from the Sea. See Ships Are Storming the Bastions, 1953
Attack of the Robots. See Cartes sur table, 1965
Attack Squadron. See Taiheiyo no tsubasa, 1963
Attaque nocturne, 1931 (Fernandel)
Attendat, 1973 (Scheider)
Attendenti, 1961 (Cervi)
Attentat, 1972 (Noiret; Piccoli; Seberg; Volonté)
Attenti al buffone!, 1975 (Wallach)
Attention, les enfants regardent, 1977 (Delon)
Attic, 1980 (Milland)
Attic: The Hiding of Anne Frank, 1988 (Steenburgen)
Attica, 1980 (Freeman)

Attila. See Attila flagello di dio, 1954
Attila flagello di dio, 1954 (Quinn)
Attila the Hun. See Attila flagello di dio, 1954
Atto di accusa, 1951 (Mastroianni)
Atto di dolore, 1990 (Cardinale)
Au bout du monde, 1933 (Vanel)
Au-delà du bien et du mal. See Oltre il bene e il male, 1977
Au-delà des grilles, 1949 (Gabin)
Au-delà de la Mort, 1922 (Modot)
Au deuil du Harem, 1922 (Modot)
Au grand balcon, 1949 (Fresnay)
Au joli coin, 1932 (Vanel)
Au nom de la Loi, 1931 (Vanel)
Au petit bonheur, 1946 (Darrieux)
Au petit Marguery, 1995 (Audran)
Au rendez-vous de la mort joyeuse, 1972 (Depardieu)
Au Royaume des cieux, 1947 (Reggiani)
Au secours!, 1923 (Linder)
Au service du Tsar. See Adjudant des Zaren, 1929
Auberge du Petit-Dragon, 1934 (Modot)
Auberge rouge, 1951 (Fernandel; Rosay)
Auction Sale of Run-Down Ranch, 1915 (Mix)
Audace colpo dei soliti ignoti, 1959 (Cardinale; Gassman)
Audacious Mr. Squire, 1923 (Buchanan)
Audience. See Udienza, 1972
Audition, 1996 (Lewis, Juliette)
Audrey Rose, 1977 (Hopkins, A.)
Auf den Tag genau, 1986 (Mueller-Stahl)
Aufruhr in Indien. See Mistero del tempio indiano, 1963
Auge des Buddha, 1919 (Kortner)
Auge des Toten, 1922 (Banky)
Augen der Liebe. See Zwischen Nacht und Morgen, 1944
Augen der Mumie Ma, 1918 (Jannings; Negri)
Augen der Welt, 1920 (Veidt)
Augen des Ole Brandis, 1914 (Wegener)
August, 1995 (Hopkins, A.)
August der Starke, 1936 (Dagover; Wegener)
Augustina de Aragón, 1950 (Rey)
Aujourd'hui peut-etre ..., 1991 (Masina)
Auld Lang Syne, 1917 (Buchanan)
Aunt Bill, 1916 (Laurel and Hardy)
Aunt Clara, 1954 (Rutherford)
Aunt Julia and the Scriptwriter. See Tune in Tomorrow, 1990
Auntie Mame, 1958 (Dumont; Russell, R.)
Aura. See Strega in amore, 1966
Aurora, 1984 (Noiret)
Aurora. See Qualcosa di biondo, 1985
Aus dem Schwarzbuch eines Polizeikommissars, 1921 (Kortner)
Aus Mangel an Beweisen, 1916 (Jannings)
Ausgerechnet Bananen, 1980 (Karina)
Ausgestossen, 1982 (Mueller-Stahl)
Ausgestossenen, 1927 (Kortner)
Aussagen nach einer Verhaftung, 1978 (Schygulla)
Aussi loin que l'amour, 1971 (Audran; Dalio)
Aussi longue absence, 1961 (Valli)
Austerlitz, 1960 (Caron; Brazzi; Cardinale; Gélin; Marais; Palance; Trintignant; Welles)
Australia, 1989 (Irons)
Author! Author!, 1982 (Pacino; Weld)
Autopsia de un fantasma, 1968 (Carradine)
Autopsie d'un monstre. See Chacun son enfer, 1976
Autopsy of a Ghost, 1967 (Rathbone)
Autopsy on a Ghost. See Autopsia de un fantasma, 1968
Autour de l'arbre, 1982 (Moreau)
Autour de minuit. See **'Round Midnight**, 1986
Autour d'une enquête, 1931 (Modot)
Autre aile, 1924 (Vanel)
Autre femme, 1964 (Girardot; Valli)
Autre homme, une autre chance, 1977 (Bujold; Caan)
Autumn Afternoon. See **Samma no aji**, 1962
Autumn Child. See Reflection of Fear, 1973

Autumn Crocus, 1934 (Hawkins; Novello)
Autumn Leaves, 1956 (Crawford, J.; Robertson)
Autumn Sonata. *See* Herbstsonate, 1978
Aux Petits Bonheurs, 1993 (Schygulla)
Aux yeux du souvenir, 1948 (Morgan; Marais)
Availing Prayer, 1914 (Crisp)
Avalanche, 1978 (Farrow; Hudson)
Avalanche Express, 1979 (Marvin; Schell, Maximilian; Shaw)
Avalon, 1990 (Mueller-Stahl)
Avant la musique, 1962 (Cervi; Fernandel)
Avant le déluge, 1954 (Blier)
Avanti!, 1972 (Lemmon)
Avanti c'è posto, 1942 (Fabrizi)
Avanti la musica. *See* Avant la musique, 1962
Avanzi di galera, 1955 (Constantine)
Avaro, 1990 (Lee, C.; Sordi)
Ave Maria, 1984 (Karina)
Avec amour et avec rage. *See* Costanza della ragione, 1964
Avec André Gide, 1950 (Philipe)
Avec Claude Monet, 1966 (Gélin)
Avec le sourire, 1936 (Chevalier)
Avenger. *See* Rächer, 1960
Avengers. *See* Day Will Dawn, 1942
Avenging Angel, 1995 (Coburn, J.; Heston)
Avenging Angels. *See* Messenger of Death, 1988
Avenging Bill, 1915 (Laurel and Hardy)
Avenging Conscience, 1914 (Crisp; Marsh; Sweet)
Avenging Waters, 1936 (Bond)
Aventura de Gil Blas, 1956 (Rey)
Aventuras de Juan Lucas, 1949 (Rey)
Aventure à Paris, 1936 (Arletty)
Aventure à Pigalle, 1949 (Dalio)
Aventure de Billy le Kid, 1973 (Léaud)
Aventure de Cabassou, 1946 (Fernandel)
Aventure de Catherine C., 1990 (Schygulla)
Aventures de Rabbi Jacob, 1973 (Dalio)
Aventures de Till L'Espiègle, 1956 (Philipe)
Aventures du Roi Pausole, 1933 (Feuillère)
Aventures extraordinaires de Cervantes. *See* Avventure e gli amori di Miguel Cervantes, 1968
Aventuriers, 1967 (Delon; Reggiani)
Äventyrare, 1942 (Björnstrand)
Average Man. *See* Borghese piccolo piccolo, 1977
Aveu, 1970 (Montand)
Aveux les plus doux, 1971 (Noiret)
Aviator, 1929 (Horton)
Avignon, bastion de la provence, 1951 (Philipe)
Avion de minuit, 1938 (Berry)
Avocate D'amour, 1938 (Darrieux)
Avtaar, 1983 (Azmi)
Avventura, 1959 (Vitti)
Avventura di Annabella, 1943 (Magnani)
Avventura di Salvator Rosa, 1940 (Cervi)
Avventure di Pinocchio, 1947 (Gassman)
Avventure di Pinocchio, 1971 (Lollobrigida)
Avventure e gli amori di Miguel Cervantes, 1968 (Ferrer; Jourdan; Lollobrigida; Rey)
Avventuriero. *See* Rover, 1967
Avventurosa fuga. *See* Ultimi angeli, 1977
Avvoltoio nero, 1913 (Bertini)
Awa no odoriko, 1941 (Hasegawa; Takamine)
Awakening, 1909 (Pickford)
Awakening, 1928 (Banky)
Awakening, 1980 (Heston; York)
Awakening of Helen Ritchie, 1916 (Barrymore, E.)
Awakenings, 1990 (De Niro; Von Sydow; Williams, R.)
Awful Truth, 1937 (Bellamy; Dunne; Grant, C.)
Awfully Big Adventure, 1995 (Grant, H.)
Awwal Number, 1990 (Anand)
Axiliad. *See* Siekierezada, 1986
Ay, Carmela!, 1990 (Maura)

Aya ni kanashiki, 1956 (Yamada)
Ayamna el Hilwa, 1954 (Sharif)
Ayananta, 1964 (Chatterjee)
Az azredes, 1917 (Lugosi)
Az de corazon, 1974 (Rooney)
Az elet kiralya, 1918 (Lugosi)
Az en XX. Szazadom, 1989 (Yankovsky)
Az idő ablakai, 1969 (Tyszkiewicz)
Až přijde kocour, 1963 (Brodský)
Azad, 1955 (Kumar)
B. F.'s Daughter, 1948 (Coburn, C.; Stanwyck)
B. J. Lang Presents, 1971 (Rooney)
B. Must Die. *See* Hay que matar a B., 1973
Ba Wang Bie Ji, 1993 (Gong Li)
Baadbaan, 1954 (Anand)
Baal, 1969 (Schygulla)
Baal, 1970 (Schygulla)
Baarish, 1957 (Anand)
Baat Ek Raat Ki, 1962 (Anand)
Baazi, 1951 (Anand)
Babbitt, 1934 (McDaniel)
Babe Ruth Story, 1948 (Trevor)
Babel Yemen, 1977 (Howard, T.)
Babenberger in Oesterreich, 1976 (Brandauer)
Babes in Arms, 1939 (Garland; Rooney)
Babes in Bagdad, 1952 (Goddard; Lee, C.)
Babes in Toyland, 1934 (Laurel and Hardy; Reeves)
Babes on Broadway, 1941 (Garland; O'Brien, M.; Rooney)
Babe's School Days, 1915 (Laurel and Hardy)
Babette s'en va-t-en guerre, 1959 (Bardot)
Babette's Feast. *See* Babette's Gastebud, 1987
Babette's Gastebud, 1987 (Andersson, B.; Audran)
Babies for Sale, 1940 (Ford, G.)
Babies Having Babies, 1986 (Sheen)
Bab's Burglar, 1917 (Barthelmess)
Bab's Diary, 1917 (Barthelmess)
Babu Moshai, 1977 (Chatterjee)
Babul, 1950 (Kumar)
Baby, 1915 (Laurel and Hardy)
Baby, 1932 (Walbrook)
Baby. *See* Bebek, 1973
Baby and the Battleship, 1956 (Attenborough; Mills)
Baby Blue Marine, 1976 (Gere)
Baby Boom, 1987 (Keaton, D.; Shepard)
Baby Day, 1913 (Normand)
Baby Doll, 1916 (Laurel and Hardy)
Baby Doll, 1956 (Malden; Wallach)
Baby Face, 1933 (Brennan; Stanwyck; Wayne)
Baby Face Harrington. *See* Baby Face, 1933
Baby Face Nelson, 1957 (Rooney)
Baby l'indiavolate. *See* My Little Baby, 1916
Baby Love, 1968 (Dors)
Baby Maker, 1970 (Hershey)
Baby of Macon, 1993 (Fiennes)
Baby, Take a Bow, 1934 (Temple; Trevor)
Baby the Rain Must Fall, 1964 (McQueen; Remick)
Babysitter, 1995 (Segal)
Babysitter's Club, 1995 (Burstyn)
Babysitters' Jitters, 1951 (Three Stooges)
Baccara, 1935 (Berry)
Bacciamo le mani, 1973 (Kennedy)
Bachelor. *See* Mio caro Dottor Graesler, 1990
Bachelor and the Bobby-Soxer, 1947 (Grant, C.; Loy; Temple)
Bachelor Apartment, 1931 (Dunne)
Bachelor Bait. *See* Adventure in Baltimore, 1949
Bachelor Daddy, 1941 (Horton)
Bachelor Father, 1931 (Davies; Milland)
Bachelor Flat, 1961 (Terry-Thomas; Weld)
Bachelor Girls. *See* Bachelor's Daughters, 1946
Bachelor in Paradise, 1961 (Hope; Moorehead; Turner, L.)
Bachelor Mother, 1939 (Coburn, C.; Niven; Rogers, G.)

Bachelor of Arts, 1934 (Marsh)
Bachelor Party, 1984 (Hanks)
Bachelor's Affairs, 1932 (Menjou)
Bachelor's Daughters, 1946 (Menjou; Trevor)
Bachelor's Folly. See Calendar, 1931
Back Door to Hell, 1964 (Nicholson)
Back from Eternity, 1956 (Ryan, R.; Steiger)
Back from the Front, 1943 (Three Stooges)
Back in Circulation, 1937 (Blondell)
Back in the Saddle, 1941 (Autry)
Back Page, 1931 (Arbuckle)
Back Roads, 1981 (Field; Jones, T.)
Back Stage, 1919 (Laurel and Hardy; Arbuckle; Keaton, B.)
Back Street, 1932 (Dunne)
Back Street, 1941 (Boyer; Sullavan)
Back Street, 1961 (Hayward)
Back to Bataan, 1945 (Quinn; Wayne)
Back to God's Country, 1953 (Hudson)
Back to Life, 1913 (Chaney)
Back to Shanghai, 1991 (Gong Li)
Back to the Farm, 1914 (Laurel and Hardy)
Back to the Future, Part III, 1990 (Steenburgen)
Back to the Primitive, 1911 (Mix)
Back to the Soil, 1911 (Pickford)
Back to the Streets of San Francisco, 1992 (Malden)
Back to the Wall. See Dos au mur, 1958
Back to the Woods, 1918 (Normand; Lloyd)
Back to the Woods, 1937 (Three Stooges)
Back Yard, 1920 (Laurel and Hardy)
Backdraft, 1991 (De Niro; Leigh, Jennifer Jason; Sutherland)
Backfire, 1950 (O'Brien, E.)
Backfire, 1995 (Mitchum; Winters)
Backfire. See Echappement libre, 1964
Background to Danger, 1943 (Greenstreet; Lorre; Raft)
Backlash, 1956 (Van Cleef; Widmark)
Back-Room Boy, 1942 (Withers)
Backstairs. See Hintertreppe, 1921
Backstreet of Paris, 1948 (Rosay)
Backtrack, 1969 (Lupino)
Backtrack, 1989 (Foster; Hopper; Pesci; Price; Turturro)
Backyard. See Två trappor över gården, 1950
Bacon Grabbers, 1929 (Laurel and Hardy; Harlow)
Bad and the Beautiful, 1952 (Calhern; Douglas, K.; Grahame; Pidgeon; Powell, D.; Turner, L.)
Bad Bascomb, 1946 (Beery; O'Brien, M.)
Bad Blood. See Mauvaise graine, 1934
Bad Blood. See First Offence, 1936
Bad Blood. See Blood Feud, 1983
Bad Blood. See Mauvais sang, 1986
Bad Boy, 1935 (Carradine)
Bad Boys, 1983 (Penn)
"Bad Buck" of Santa Ynez, 1915 (Hart)
Bad Charleston Charlie, 1973 (Carradine)
Bad Company, 1931 (Carey)
Bad Company. See Mauvaises fréquentations, 1967
Bad Company, 1972 (Bridges)
Bad Company, 1995 (Barkin; Fishburne)
Bad Day at Black Rock, 1954 (Brennan; Marvin; Ryan, R.; Tracy; Borgnine)
Bad Eggs. See Rötägg, 1946
Bad for Each Other, 1953 (Heston)
Bad Lands, 1925 (Carey)
Bad Lieutenant, 1992 (Keitel)
Bad Lord Byron, 1948 (Zetterling; Greenwood)
Bad Man, 1929 (Huston, W.)
Bad Man, 1941 (Barrymore, L.; Beery; Reagan)
Bad Man Bobbs, 1915 (Mix)
Bad Man of Brimstone, 1938 (Beery)
Bad Man of Deadwood, 1941 (Rogers, R.)
Bad Man of Wyoming. See Wyoming, 1940
Bad Man's River, 1972 (Lollobrigida)
Bad Man's River, 1972 (Mason)

Bad Medicine, 1985 (Arkin)
Bad Men of Missouri, 1941 (Kennedy; Wyman)
Bad Men of Tombstone, 1948 (Crawford, B.)
Bad News Bears, 1976 (Matthau)
Bad News Bears Go to Japan, 1978 (Curtis, T.)
Bad One, 1930 (Del Rio; Karloff)
Bad Sister, 1931 (Bogart; Davis, B.)
Bad Sister. See White Unicorn, 1947
Bad Sleep Well. See Warui yatsu hodo yoku nemuru, 1960
Bad Timing, 1980 (Elliott; Keitel)
Badarna, 1968 (Thulin)
Badge 373, 1973 (Duvall)
Badge of Marshal Brennan, 1957 (Van Cleef)
Badge of the Assassin, 1985 (Woods)
Badlanders, 1958 (Borgnine; Ladd)
Badlands, 1973 (Oates; Spacek; Sheen)
Badlands of Dakota, 1941 (Crawford, B.; Farmer)
Badman's Territory, 1946 (Scott, R.)
Baffled!, 1973 (Roberts, R.)
Bagdad, 1949 (O'Hara; Price)
Bagdad Cafe, 1987 (Palance)
Baggage Smasher, 1914 (Arbuckle)
Baghini, 1968 (Chatterjee)
Bagnosträfling, 1949 (Fröhlich)
Bagula bhagat, 1979 (Azmi)
Bahama Passage, 1941 (Carroll; Hayden)
Baia di Napoli. See It Started in Naples, 1960
Baie des anges, 1962 (Moreau)
Baikunther Will, 1985 (Chatterjee)
Bailiff. See **Sansho dayu**, 1954
Baîllonnée, 1922 (Fresnay)
Bairaag, 1976 (Kumar)
Baisers volés, 1968 (Léaud; Seyrig)
Baited Trap. See Trap, 1959
Baja Oklahoma, 1988 (Roberts, J.)
Bajarse al Moro, 1988 (Banderas)
Baker's Wife. See **Femme du boulanger**, 1938
Bakom Jalusin, 1984 (Josephson)
Baksha Badal, 1965 (Chatterjee)
Bakui ichidai, 1951 (Shimura)
Bakumatsu, 1970 (Mifune)
Bakuon to daichi, 1957 (Yamamura)
Bakuro ich-dai, 1951 (Mifune)
Bakushu, 1951 (Hara; Ryu)
Bakuto ichidai, 1951 (Kyo)
Bal, 1931 (Darrieux)
Bal des casse-pieds, 1992 (Piccoli)
Bal des espions, 1960 (Piccoli)
Bal du Comte d'Orgel, 1969 (Presle)
Balalaika, 1939 (Eddy)
Balance, 1982 (Baye)
Balbao, 1986 (Curtis, T.)
Balboa, 1982 (Curtis, T.)
Balcony, 1962 (Grant, L.; Falk; Winters)
Ball at the Anjo House. See Anjoke no butokai, 1947
Ball at the Castle. See Ballo al castello, 1939
Ball der Nationen, 1954 (Fröhlich)
Ball of Fire, 1941 (Andrews, D.; Constantine; Duryea; Homolka; Stanwyck)
Ball of the Anjo Family. See Anjoke no butokai, 1947
Ball-Trap on the Cote Sauvage, 1989 (Richardson, M.)
Ballad. See Sorvanetch, 1914
Ballad for the Kid, 1974 (Seberg)
Ballad in Blue, 1964 (Henreid)
Ballad of Andy Crocker, 1969 (Moorehead)
Ballad of Cable Hogue, 1970 (Robards)
Ballad of Gregorio Cortez, 1982 (Olmos)
Ballad of Josie, 1967 (Day)
Ballad of Narayama. See Narayamabushi-ko, 1958
Ballad of Smokey the Bear, 1966 (Cagney)
Ballad of the Sad Café, 1991 (Redgrave, V.; Steiger)
Ballade de Mamlouk, 1982 (Papas)

Baroni, 1974 (Fabrizi)
Baroud, 1932 (Henreid)
Barquero, 1970 (Oates; Van Cleef)
Barrage contre le Pacifique, 1958 (Magnano; Perkins; Valli)
Barrel Full of Dollars. *See* Per una bara piena di dollari, 1970
Barrendero, 1981 (Cantinflas)
Barretts of Wimpole Street, 1934 (Laughton; March; O'Sullivan; Shearer)
Barretts of Wimpole Street, 1957 (Gielgud; Jones, Jennifer)
Barricade, 1939 (Faye)
Barricade, 1950 (Massey)
Barricade du point du jour, 1978 (Noiret)
Barrier, 1926 (Barrymore, L.)
Barrier. *See* Bariera, 1966
Barrier of Faith, 1915 (Talmadge)
Barriera delle legge, 1953 (Brazzi)
Barrings, 1955 (Dagover)
Barrios Altos, 1987 (Abril)
Barry, 1948 (Fresnay)
Barry Mackenzie Holds His Own, 1974 (Pleasence)
Barton Fink, 1991 (Davis, J.; Turturro)
Baruffe chiozzotte, 1943 (Brazzi)
Bas-fonds, 1936 (Gabin; Jouvet)
Basanta Bilap, 1972 (Chatterjee)
Baseball Madness, 1917 (Swanson)
Basements. *See* Room, 1987
Bashful, 1917 (Lloyd)
Bashful Suitor, 1921 (Astor)
Basic Instinct, 1992 (Douglas, Michael; Malone; Stone)
Basileus Quartet, 1984 (Cuny)
Basketball Diaries, 1995 (Lewis, Juliette)
Basquiat, 1995 (Hopper; Oldman; Dafoe; Walken)
Bastard, 1995 (Olbrychski)
Bastardi, 1969 (Kinski)
Bastardi, I gatti. *See* Sons of Satan, 1971
Bat, 1959 (Moorehead; Price)
Bat 21, 1988 (Hackman)
Bata no zeni: Ogon oni ranbu no maki, 1931 (Hasegawa)
Bataan, 1943 (Taylor, R.; Walker)
Bataille, 1923 (Hayakawa)
Bataille, 1933 (Boyer)
Bataille de San Sébastian, 1967 (Bronson)
Bataille des trois rois, 1989 (Bondarchuk; Cardinale; Keitel; Rey)
Bataille silencieuse, 1937 (Fresnay)
Bataillon du ciel, 1946 (Dalio)
Batalla de los Tres Reyes, 1990 (Papas)
Batard, 1983 (Abril)
Bateau à soupe, 1946 (Vanel)
Bateau d'Emile, 1961 (Brasseur; Girardot)
Bateau de verre, 1928 (Rosay)
Bateau ivre, 1949 (Barrault)
Bateau sur l'herbe, 1971 (Cassel)
Bateliers de la Volga, 1936 (Vanel)
Bateliers de la Volga, 1959 (Vanel)
Bath House Beauty, 1914 (Arbuckle)
Bathhouse Scandal, 1918 (Beery)
Bathing Beauty, 1944 (Dumont; Rathbone; Williams, E.)
Batman, 1966 (Meredith)
Batman, 1989 (Basinger; Keaton, M.; Nicholson; Palance)
Batman Forever, 1995 (Jones, T.)
Batman Returns, 1992 (DeVito; Keaton, M.; Pfeiffer; Walken)
Bato no zeni: Kesho-bosatsu no maki, 1931 (Hasegawa)
Baton Rouge, 1988 (Abril; Banderas; Maura)
Battaglia di Mareth. *See* Grande attacco, 1977
Battant, 1982 (Delon)
Battements de coeur, 1939 (Darrieux)
Battered, 1978 (Blondell)
Battered! *See* Intimate Strangers, 1977
Battle, 1911 (Barrymore, L.; Crisp; Sweet)
Battle, 1934 (Boyer; Oberon)
Battle at Elderbush Gulch, 1913 (Gish)
Battle beyond the Stars, 1980 (Jaffe)

Battle Circus, 1953 (Bogart)
Battle Cry, 1955 (Malone; Massey)
Battle Cry of Peace, 1915 (Talmadge)
Battle Flag. *See* Standarte, 1977
Battle for Anzio. *See* Lo sbarco di Anzio, 1968
Battle for Britain, 1957 (Hawkins)
Battle for the Planet of the Apes, 1973 (Ayres; Huston, J.; McDowall)
Battle Force. *See* Grande Attacco, 1977
Battle Hymn, 1957 (Duryea; Hudson)
Battle of Austerlitz. *See* Austerlitz, 1960
Battle of Britain, 1943 (Huston, W.)
Battle of Britain, 1969 (Caine; Howard, T.; Olivier; Richardson, R.; Shaw; York)
Battle of Broadway, 1937 (McLaglen; McDaniel)
Battle of Elderbush Gulch, 1914 (Barrymore, L.; Marsh)
Battle of Kawanakajima. *See* Kawanakajima gassen, 1941
Battle of Mareth. *See* Grande Attacco, 1977
Battle of Midway, 1942 (Crisp)
Battle of Neretva, 1970 (Welles)
Battle of San Pietro, 1944 (Huston, J.)
Battle of Stalingrad. *See* Stalingradskaya bitva, 1949
Battle of the Bulge, 1965 (Andrews, D.; Bronson; Fonda, H.; Ryan, R.; Shaw)
Battle of the Century, 1927 (Laurel and Hardy)
Battle of the Coral Sea, 1959 (Robertson)
Battle of the Japan Sea. *See* Nihonkai daikaisen, 1969
Battle of the River Plate, 1956 (Finch; Lee, C.)
Battle of the River Plate, 1956 (Quayle)
Battle of the Sexes, 1914 (Crisp; Gish)
Battle of the Sexes, 1959 (Pleasence; Sellers)
Battle of the V 1, 1958 (Lee, C.)
Battle of the Villa Fiorita, 1965 (Brazzi; O'Hara)
Battle of the Worlds. *See* Il planet degli uomini spenti, 1960
Battle of Three Kings. *See* Bataille des trois rois, 1989
Battle of Who Ran, 1913 (Normand)
Battle Royal, 1916 (Laurel and Hardy)
Battle Stations, 1944 (Cagney; Rogers, G.; Tracy)
Battle Taxi, 1954 (Hayden)
Battleship Gallactica, 1978 (Astaire)
Battleshock. *See* Woman's Devotion, 1956
Battlestar Galactica, 1978 (Milland; Ayres)
Battling Butler, 1926 (Keaton, B.)
Battling Charlie. *See* Champion, 1915
Battling for Baby, 1992 (Reynolds, D.)
Bauer von Babylon, 1983 (Moreau)
Baule-les-pins, 1990 (Baye)
Bavu, 1923 (Beery)
Bawdy Adventures of Tom Jones, 1975 (Howard, T.; Terry-Thomas)
Baxter, 1973 (Cassel; Neal)
Baxter—Vera Baxter, 1976 (Depardieu; Seyrig)
Bay Boy, 1984 (Audran; Ullmann)
Bay of Angels. *See* Baie des anges, 1962
Bay of St. Michael, 1963 (Zetterling)
Baza ludzi umarłlych, 1959 (Łomnicki)
Bazaar, 1982 (Patil)
Bazoku geisha, 1954 (Kyo)
Be Big, 1931 (Laurel and Hardy)
Be Careful!, 1944 (Gable)
Be Happy These Two Lovers. *See* Kono futari ni sachi are, 1957
Be My Wife, 1919 (Lloyd; Linder)
Be Your Age, 1923 (Laurel and Hardy)
Be Your Age, 1926 (Laurel and Hardy)
Beach Blanket Bingo, 1965 (Keaton, B.)
Beach Club, 1928 (Lombard)
Beach House. *See* Casotto, 1977
Beach Hut. *See* Casotto, 1977
Beach Nut, 1919 (Beery)
Beach Pajamas, 1931 (Arbuckle)
Beach Party, 1963 (Malone; Price)
Beach Red, 1967 (Wilde)
Beachcomber, 1954 (Pleasence)
Beachcomber. *See* Vessel of Wrath, 1937

Beaches, 1988 (Hershey; Midler)

Beachhead, 1954 (Curtis, T.)

Bear, 1984 (Stanton)

Bear and the Doll. *See* Ours et la poupée, 1969

Bear Island, 1980 (Lee, C.; Redgrave, V.; Sutherland; Widmark)

Bear of a Story, 1916 (Mix)

Bearer of the Golden Star. *See* Knight of the Gold Star, 1950

Bearn o la Sala de Munecas, 1983 (Rey)

Bears and Bad Men, 1918 (Laurel and Hardy)

Beast. *See* Bête, 1974

Beast at Bay, 1912 (Pickford)

Beast from 20,000 Fathoms, 1953 (Van Cleef)

Beast Must Die, 1974 (Cushing)

Beast of the City, 1932 (Harlow; Huston, W.; Rooney)

Beast with Five Fingers, 1946 (Lorre)

Beasts of Berlin. *See* Hitler, Beast of Berlin, 1939

Beat Girl, 1960 (Lee, C.; Reed)

Beat It, 1918 (Lloyd)

Beat the Devil, 1953 (Bogart; Huston, J.; Jones, Jennifer; Lollobrigida; Lorre)

Beate und Mareile, 1981 (Vogler)

Beatnik et le minet, 1965 (Depardieu)

Beatrice, 1919 (Bertini)

Beatrice Cenci, 1956 (Cervi; Presle)

Beatrice devant le désir, 1944 (Berry)

Beau Brummell, 1924 (Astor; Barrymore, J.)

Beau Brummell, 1954 (Granger; Taylor, E.; Ustinov)

Beau Geste, 1926 (Colman; McLaglen; Powell, W.)

Beau Geste, 1939 (Constantine; Crawford, B.; Hayward; Milland; O'Connor; Preston)

Beau Hunks, 1931 (Laurel and Hardy)

Beau Ideal, 1931 (Young, L.)

Beau James, 1957 (Durante; Hope)

Beau jour de noces, 1932 (Fernandel)

Beau Monde. *See* Andaz, 1949

Beau-Père, 1981 (Baye)

Beau Sabreur, 1928 (Constantine; Powell, W.)

Beau temps, mais orageux en fin de journée, 1986 (Presle)

Beaumarchais, l'insolent, 1996 (Piccoli)

Beauté du Diable, 1949 (Modot; Philipe)

Beauties of the Night. *See* Belles de nuit, 1952

Beautiful Blond from Bashful Bend, 1949 (Grable)

Beautiful but Dangerous. *See* Donna più bella del mondo, 1955

Beautiful but Dangerous. *See* She Couldn't Say No, 1954

Beautiful City, 1925 (Barthelmess; Powell, W.)

Beautiful Girls, 1996 (Dillon; Thurman)

Beautiful Rebel. *See* Janice Meredith, 1924

Beautiful Stranger, 1953 (Ferrer; Baker; Lom)

Beautiful Stranger. *See* Twist of Fate, 1954

Beautiful Swindlers. *See* Plus Belles Escroqueries du monde, 1964

Beautiful Troublemaker. *See* Belle Noiseuse, 1990

Beauty. *See* Reijin, 1946

Beauty and the Barge, 1937 (Hawkins; Rutherford; Scott, G.)

Beauty and the Beast. **See Belle et la bête, 1946**

Beauty and the Beast, 1983 (Kinski)

Beauty and the Beast, 1991 (Lansbury)

Beauty and the Bullfighter. *See* Sang et lumières, 1953

Beauty and the Devil. *See* Beauté du Diable, 1949

Beauty and the Robot. *See* Sex Kittens Go to College, 1960

Beauty for the Asking, 1939 (Ball)

Beauty Prize. *See* Prix de beauté, 1930

Beauty Shop. *See* Schönheit-spflästerchen, 1937

Beauty's Daughter, 1935 (Bellamy; Trevor)

Beauty's Worth, 1922 (Davies)

Beaux Jours, 1935 (Barrault)

Bébé de l'escadron, 1935 (Brasseur)

Bebek, 1973 (Andersson, H.)

Bebo's Girl. *See* Ragazza di Bube, 1963

Because of Him, 1946 (Durbin; Laughton)

Because of You, 1952 (Young, L.)

Because They're Young, 1960 (Weld)

Becket, 1964 (Burton; Cervi; Gielgud; O'Toole)

Becky Sharp, 1935 (Hopkins, M.)

Becoming Colette, 1991 (Huppert; Brandauer)

Bed. *See* Secrets d'alcôve, 1953

Bed and Board. *See* Domicile conjugal, 1970

Bed of Roses, 1933 (McCrea)

Bed Sitting Room, 1969 (Moore, Dudley; Richardson, R.)

Bedazzled, 1967 (Moore, Dudley; Welch)

Bedelia, 1946 (Lockwood)

Bedevilled, 1955 (Baxter)

Bedford Incident, 1965 (Poitier; Sutherland; Widmark)

Bedknobs and Broomsticks, 1971 (Jaffe; Lansbury; McDowall)

Bedlam, 1946 (Karloff)

Bedlam in Paradise, 1955 (Three Stooges)

Bedroom Window, 1987 (Huppert)

Bedtime for Bonzo, 1951 (Reagan)

Bedtime Story, 1933 (Chevalier; Horton)

Bedtime Story, 1941 (March; Young, L.)

Bedtime Story, 1963 (Dern; Brando; Niven)

Bedtime with Rosie, 1974 (Dors)

Bee Keeper. *See* O Melissokomos, 1986

Beef and the Banana. *See* Biffen och Bananen, 1951

Beehive. *See* Colmena, 1982

Beekeeper. *See* O Melissokomos, 1986

Beekeeper Dies—The Other Tale. *See* Melissokomos Patheni—O Alles Mythos, 1986

Been Down So Long It Looks Like Up to Me, 1971 (Julia)

Beer and Pretzels, 1933 (Three Stooges)

Beer Barrel Polecats, 1946 (Three Stooges)

Bees, 1978 (Carradine)

Bees in His Bonnet, 1918 (Lloyd)

Beethoven, 1927 (Kortner)

Beethoven, le voleur de femmes. *See* Grand Amour de Beethoven, 1936

Beethoven's Nephew. *See* Neveu de Beethoven, 1985

Beetlejuice, 1988 (Davis, G.; Keaton, M.)

Beetlejuice, 1988 (Ryder)

Before and After, 1996 (Neeson; Streep)

Before Breakfast, 1919 (Lloyd)

Before Him All Rome Trembled. *See* Devanti a lui tremava tutta Roma, 1946

Before I Hang, 1940 (Karloff)

Before Midnight, 1934 (Bellamy)

Before the Nickelodeon: The Early Cinema of Edwin S. Porter, 1982 (Sweet)

Before Winter Comes, 1969 (Hurt, J.; Karina; Niven; Quayle; Topol)

Before Xmas. *See* Prima di Natale, 1990

Beggar. *See* Tainstvennie nekto, 1914

Beggar Maid, 1921 (Astor)

Beggar on Horseback, 1925 (Horton)

Beggar Prince, 1920 (Hayakawa)

Beggar's Opera, 1953 (Olivier)

Beggarman, Thief, 1979 (Ford, G.)

Beggars of Life, 1928 (Beery; Brooks, L.)

Beginning and End. *See* Bidaya wa Nihaya, 1960

Beginning of the End, 1947 (Walker)

Beguiled, 1971 (Eastwood; Page)

Behave Yourself!, 1951 (Winters)

Behind Closed Shutters. *See* Persiane chiuse, 1951

Behind Office Doors, 1931 (Astor)

Behind That Curtain, 1929 (Karloff)

Behind the Counter, 1927 (Horton)

Behind the Door, 1919 (Beery)

Behind the Door. *See* Man with Nine Lives, 1940

Behind the Front, 1926 (Beery)

Behind the Iron Mask, 1977 (De Havilland; Harrison)

Behind the Iron Mask. *See* Fifth Musketeer, 1979

Behind the Make Up, 1930 (Francis; Lukas; Powell, W.; Wray)

Behind the Mask, 1932 (Karloff)

Behind the Mask, 1958 (Redgrave, M.; Redgrave, V.)

Behind the Mask, 1991 (Redgrave, V.)

Behind the Rising Sun, 1943 (Ryan, R.)

Behind the Scenes, 1914 (Pickford)

Behind the Scenes: A Portrait of Pierre Guffroy. *See* Envers du Decor: Portrait de Pierre Guffroy, 1992

Behind the Screen, 1916 (Chaplin, C.; Purviance)
Behind the Screen. *See* Kulissi ekrana, 1916
Behind the Shutters. *See* Bakom Jalusin, 1984
Behind the Shutters. *See* Corrupción de Chris Miller, 1973
Behold a Pale Horse, 1964 (Peck; Quinn; Sharif)
Behold My Wife, 1935 (Sidney)
Behold Thy Son. *See* Kiiroi karasu, 1957
Behold We Live. *See* If I Were Free, 1933
Beichte einer Toten, 1920 (Krauss)
Being, 1983 (Malone; Ferrer; Landau)
Being Human, 1994 (Turturro; Williams, R.)
Being There, 1979 (Douglas, Melvyn; MacLaine; Sellers)
Bekenntnisse des Hochstaplers Felix Krull, 1957 (Dagover)
Bekenntnisse des Hochstaplers Felix Krull, 1982 (Rey)
Bela Lugosi Meets a Brooklyn Gorilla, 1952 (Lugosi)
Believe Me Xant(h)ippe, 1918 (Crisp)
Believed Violent. *See* Presumé dangereux, 1990
Believers, 1987 (Sheen)
Belizaire the Cajun, 1986 (Duvall)
Bell, Book, and Candle, 1958 (Lanchester; Lemmon; Novak; Stewart)
Bell Boy, 1918 (Arbuckle; Keaton, B.)
Bell for Adano, 1945 (Dalio; Tierney)
Bell'Antonio, 1960 (Brasseur; Cardinale; Mastroianni)
Bella di Roma, 1955 (Sordi)
Bella Donna, 1923 (Menjou; Negri)
Bella Donna, 1934 (Veidt)
Bella Donna, 1982 (Josephson)
Bella mugnaia, 1955 (Loren)
Bella Otéro. *See* Belle Otéro, 1954
Bellboy, 1960 (Lewis, Jerry)
Belle Aventure, 1942 (Jourdan; Presle)
Belle Aventure. *See* Schöne Abenteuer, 1932
Belle de jour, 1967 (Deneuve; Piccoli)
Belle de Paris. *See* Under My Skin, 1950
Belle dell'aria, 1958 (Cervi)
Belle della notte. *See* Belles de nuit, 1952
Belle equipe, 1936 (Vanel; Gabin)
Belle et la bête, 1946 (Marais)
Belle famiglie, 1964 (Girardot)
Belle Marinière, 1932 (Gabin)
Belle mugnaia, 1955 (Mastroianni)
Belle Noiseuse, 1990 (Piccoli)
Belle of New York, 1919 (Davies)
Belle of New York, 1952 (Astaire)
Belle of the Nineties, 1934 (West)
Belle of the Yukon, 1944 (Scott, R.)
Belle Otéro, 1954 (Félix)
Belle que voilà, 1950 (Morgan)
Belle Russe, 1919 (Bara)
Belle Starr, 1941 (Andrews, D.; Scott, R.; Tierney)
Belle's Beau, 1912-13 (White)
Belles de nuit, 1952 (Lollobrigida; Philipe)
Belles on Their Toes, 1952 (Loy)
Bellissima, 1951 (Magnani)
Bellissimo novembre, 1968 (Lollobrigida)
Bello mia belleza mia, 1982 (Giannini)
Bello, onesto, emigrato Australia sposerebbe compaesana illibata, 1971 (Cardinale)
Bells, 1926 (Barrymore, L.; Karloff)
Bells Are Ringing, 1960 (Holliday; Martin, D.)
Bells Go Down, 1943 (Mason)
Bells of Capistrano, 1942 (Autry)
Bells of Colorado, 1950 (Rogers, R.)
Bells of Rosarita, 1945 (Rogers, R.)
Bells of San Angelo, 1947 (Rogers, R.)
Bells of St. Mary's, 1945 (Bergman; Crosby)
Beloe solntse pustiny, 1969 (Yankovsky)
Beloved, 1934 (Rooney)
Beloved, 1971 (Hawkins)
Beloved. *See* Restless, 1978
Beloved Bachelor, 1931 (Lukas)

Beloved Brat, 1938 (Crisp)
Beloved Brute, 1924 (McLaglen)
Beloved Enemy, 1936 (Oberon; Crisp; Niven)
Beloved Infidel, 1959 (Kerr; Peck)
Beloved Jim, 1917 (Carey)
Beloved Rogue, 1927 (Barrymore, J.; Veidt)
Beloved Traitor, 1918 (Marsh)
Beloved Vagabond, 1936 (Chevalier; Lockwood)
Below the Sea, 1933 (Bellamy; Wray)
Below Zero, 1930 (Laurel and Hardy)
Belstone Fox, 1973 (Roberts, R.)
Beltenebros, 1991 (Stamp)
Belva, 1970 (Kinski)
Ben-Hur, 1926 (Loy; Novarro)
Ben-Hur, 1959 (Hawkins; Heston; Jaffe)
Ben Webster: The Brute and the Beautiful, 1989 (Cardinale)
Ben's Kid, 1909 (Arbuckle)
Bend of the River, 1952 (Hudson; Kennedy; Stewart)
Beneath a Stony Sky. *See* Pod kamennym nebom, 1974
Beneath the Planet of the Apes, 1969 (Heston)
Benefit of the Doubt, 1965 (Jackson, G.)
Benefit of the Doubt, 1993 (Sutherland)
Bengal Brigade, 1954 (Hudson)
Bengali Night. *See* Nuit Bengali, 1988
Bengazi, 1955 (McLaglen)
Beni-komori, 1950 (Hasegawa)
Benjamin ou Les mémoires d'un puceau, 1968 (Deneuve; Morgan; Piccoli)
Benjy, 1951 (Fonda, H.)
Benny & Joon, 1993 (Depp)
Benny's Video, 1992 (Winkler)
Benson Murder Case, 1930 (Lukas; Powell, W.)
Benten-kozo, 1928 (Hasegawa)
Benvenuta, 1983 (Gassman)
Benvenuto reverendo!, 1950 (Fabrizi)
Bequest to the Nation, 1973 (Finch; Jackson, G.; Quayle)
Berammee geisha makaridoru, 1961 (Yamamura)
Berceau de cristal, 1976 (Sanda)
Beretta's Island, 1994 (Schwarzenegger)
Bergère et le ramoneur, 1952 (Aimée; Brasseur; Reggiani)
Berget på månens baksida, 1982 (Andersson, B.)
Bergkatze, 1921 (Negri)
Berkeley Square, 1933 (Barrymore, L.; Howard, L.)
Berlin Alexanderplatz, 1980 (Schygulla)
Berlin Correspondent, 1942 (Andrews, D.)
Berlin Express, 1948 (Kortner; Lukas; Oberon; Ryan, R.)
Berlin Tunnel Twenty-One, 1981 (Ferrer)
Berlingot et Cie, 1939 (Fernandel)
Berlinguer ti voglio bene, 1977 (Valli; Benigni)
Bermuda Triangle. *See* Triangulo diabolico de la Bermudas, 1978
Bermuda: la fossa maledetta, 1978 (Kennedy)
Bernadette, 1988 (Tyszkiewicz)
Bernard Shaw's Village, 1951 (Kaye)
Bernardine, 1957 (Gaynor)
Beröringen, 1971 (Andersson, B.; Gould; Von Sydow)
Berserk!, 1967 (Dors; Crawford, J.)
Bert Rigby, You're a Fool, 1989 (Bancroft)
Berth Marks, 1929 (Goddard; Laurel and Hardy)
Bertoldo, Bertoldino e Cacasenno, 1984 (Sordi)
Bertolucci secondo il cinema, 1975 (Depardieu; Hayden)
Beryl Markham: A Shadow on the Sun, 1988 (Bloom)
Beside the Bonnie Brier Bush, 1921 (Crisp)
Best Bad Man, 1925 (Mix; Bow)
Best Defense, 1984 (Moore, Dudley; Murphy)
Best Foot Forward, 1943 (Ball)
Best Friends, 1982 (Hawn; Reynolds, B.)
Best House in London, 1968 (Cleese; Sanders)
Best Intentions. *See* Goda Viljan, 1992
Best Little Girl in the World, 1981 (Lange; Leigh, Jennifer Jason; Saint)
Best Little Whorehouse in Texas, 1982 (Reynolds, B.)
Best Man, 1928 (Lombard)
Best Man, 1964 (Fonda, H.; Robertson)

Best Man Wins, 1913 (Crisp)
Best Man Wins, 1935 (Lugosi)
Best of Enemies. *See* I due nemici, 1961
Best of Everything, 1959 (Crawford, J.; Jourdan)
Best of Everything, 1983 (Hoffman)
Best of Friends, 1994 (Gielgud)
Best of the Badmen, 1951 (Brennan; Preston; Ryan, R.; Trevor)
Best of the Best, 1989 (Jones, James Earl)
Best of the Blues Brothers, 1993 (Belushi)
Best of the Martial Arts Films, 1990 (Lee, B.)
Best of Times, 1981 (Cage)
Best of Times, 1986 (Williams, R.)
Best Seller, 1987 (Woods)
Best Shot. *See* Hoosiers, 1986
Best Things in Life Are Free, 1956 (Borgnine)
Best Years of Our Lives, 1946 (Andrews, D.; Loy; March)
Bestellt—Geklaut—Geliefert, 1979 (Constantine)
Bestia, 1915 (Negri)
Bestia uccide a sangue freddo, 1971 (Kinski)
Bestiare d'amour, 1964 (Reggiani)
Bestione, 1974 (Giannini)
Besuch, 1964 (Bergman; Quinn)
Besuch der alten Dame, 1982 (Schell, Maria)
Bête, 1974 (Dalio)
Bête à l'affût, 1959 (Piccoli)
Bête aux sept manteaux, 1936 (Berry)
Bête de scène, 1994 (Piccoli)
Bête humaine, 1938 (Gabin)
Bête noire, 1983 (Constantine)
Bethsabée, 1947 (Darrieux)
Bethune: The Making of a Hero, 1990 (Aimée; Mirren; Nelligan; Sutherland)
Betrayal, 1929 (Constantine; Jannings)
Betrayal, 1983 (Irons; Kingsley)
Betrayal. *See* Foerraederi, 1994
Betrayed, 1954 (Calhern; Gable; Mature; Turner, L.)
Betrayed, 1988 (Winger)
Betsy, 1978 (Duvall; Jones, T.; Olivier)
Betsy's Wedding, 1990 (Jackson, S.; Pesci)
Better Halves, 1916 (Laurel and Hardy)
Better Late than Never, 1982 (Niven; Pleasence; Smith)
Better to Be Pretty and Rich. *See* Jobb Szepnek es Gazdagnak Lenni, 1993
Better Way, 1911 (Pickford)
Bettlerin von St. Marien, 1916 (Jannings)
Betty, 1993 (Audran)
Betty Becomes a Maid, 1911 (Normand)
Betty Ford Story, 1987 (Rowlands)
Betty in the Lions' Den, 1913 (Normand)
Between Friends, 1982 (Taylor, E.)
Between Heaven and Earth. *See* Entre el cielo y la tierre, 1993
Between Heaven and Earth. *See* Mezi nebem a zemi, 1958
Between Heaven and Hell, 1956 (Crawford, B.)
Between Men, 1916 (Hart)
Between Midnight and Dawn, 1950 (O'Brien, E.)
Between Showers, 1914 (Chaplin, C.)
Between Two Women, 1937 (O'Sullivan)
Between Two Women, 1944 (Barrymore, L.)
Between Two Worlds, 1944 (Garfield; Greenstreet; Henreid)
Between Two Worlds. *See* Müde Tod, 1921
Between Us Girls, 1942 (Francis)
Between Us Thieves. *See* Oss tjuvar emellan eller En burk ananas, 1945
Beute der Erinnyen, 1921 (Krauss)
Beverly Hills Brats, 1989 (Goldberg; Keeler; Sheen)
Beverly Hills Cop, 1984 (Murphy)
Beverly Hills Cop II, 1987 (Murphy)
Beverly Hills Cop III, 1994 (Murphy)
Beverly Hills Madam, 1986 (Dunaway; Jourdan)
Beverly of Graustark, 1926 (Davies)
Beware, My Lovely, 1952 (Lupino; Ryan, R.)
Beware of a Holy Whore. *See* Warnung vor einer heiligen Nutte, 1971
Beware of Married Men, 1928 (Loy)
Beware Spooks!, 1939 (Brown)

Beyond a Reasonable Doubt, 1956 (Andrews, D.; Fontaine)
Beyond All Limits. *See* Flor de mayo, 1957
Beyond Glory, 1948 (Ladd)
Beyond Good and Evil. *See* Oltre il bene e il male, 1977
Beyond Justice, 1992 (Gould; Sharif)
Beyond Love and Hate. *See* Ai to nikushimi no kaneta e, 1951
Beyond Mombasa, 1956 (Lee, C.; Wilde)
Beyond the Bermuda Triangle, 1975 (MacMurray)
Beyond the Blue Horizon, 1941 (Lamour)
Beyond the Border, 1925 (Carey)
Beyond the Clouds. *See* Par dela les nuages, 1995
Beyond the Door. *See* Oltre la porta, 1982
Beyond the Forest, 1949 (Cotten; Davis, B.)
Beyond the Last Frontier, 1943 (Mitchum)
Beyond the Law. *See* Al di là della legge, 1968
Beyond the Limit, 1983 (Gere)
Beyond the Limit. *See* Honorary Consul, 1983
Beyond the Mountains. *See* Más allá de las montañas, 1967
Beyond the Poseidon Adventure, 1979 (Caine; Field; Malden)
Beyond the Purple Hills, 1950 (Autry)
Beyond the Rainbow, 1922 (Bow)
Beyond the Rocks, 1922 (Swanson; Valentino)
Beyond the Sky. *See* Hoyere enn Himmelen, 1993
Beyond the Stars, 1989 (Sheen; Stone)
Beyond the Wall. *See* Müde Tod, 1921
Beyond Therapy, 1987 (Jackson, G.)
Beyond Tomorrow, 1940 (Carey)
Bhavna, 1984 (Azmi)
Bhavni bhavai, 1981 (Patil)
Bhowani Junction, 1955 (Gardner; Granger)
Bhumika, 1977 (Patil)
Biala Wizytowka, 1986 (Nowicki)
Bianchi cavalli d'Agosto, 1975 (Seberg)
Bianco, il giallo, il nero, 1975 (Wallach)
Bianco, rosso e ..., 1971 (Loren; Rey)
Bibbia, 1966 (Gardner; Harris, R.; Huston, J.; O'Toole; Scott, G.)
Bible. *See* Bibbia, 1966
Bible for Girls, 1934 (Zhao Dan)
Bibo no miyako, 1957 (Tsukasa)
Bibo no umi, 1950 (Kyo)
Bice skoro propast sveta, 1968 (Girardot)
Biches, 1968 (Audran)
Bicicletas son para el verano, 1983 (Abril)
Bicycle Flirt, 1928 (Lombard)
Bicycles Are for the Summer. *See* Bicicletas son para el verano, 1983
Bidaya wa Nihaya, 1960 (Sharif)
Bidochons, 1996 (Girardot; Trintignant)
Bidochoun, 1996 (Gélin)
Bidone, 1955 (Crawford, B.; Masina)
Bien-aimée, 1967 (Morgan)
Bienfaiteur, 1941 (Raimu)
Bienvenido a Veraz, 1991 (Douglas, K.)
Bienvenido, Mr. Marshall!, 1952 (Rey)
Biff Bang Buddy, 1924 (Arthur)
Biffen och Bananen, 1951 (Andersson, H.)
Big, 1988 (Hanks)
Big and the Bad. *See* Si puo fare ... amigo, 1971
Big Bad Mama, 1974 (Dickinson)
Big Bad Momma II, 1987 (Dickinson)
Big Bankroll. *See* King of the Roaring Twenties, 1961
Big Barrier. *See* Schloss Hubertus: Der Fischer von Heiligensee, 1955
Big Blockade, 1942 (Mills; Redgrave, M.)
Big Boodle, 1957 (Armendáriz; Flynn)
Big Boss. *See* Ankokugai no kaoyaku, 1959
Big Boss. *See* Fists of Fury, 1971
Big Bounce, 1969 (Grant, L.)
Big Boy, 1930 (Jolson)
Big Brain, 1933 (Wray)
Big Brawl, 1980 (Chan; Ferrer)
Big Broadcast, 1932 (Crosby)
Big Broadcast of 1936, 1935 (Crosby; Robinson, B.; Milland)

Big Broadcast of 1938, 1938 (Fields, W. C.; Hope; Lamour)

Big Brown Eyes, 1936 (Bennett; Grant, C.; Pidgeon)

Big Bus, 1976 (Ferrer; Gordon)

Big Business, 1929 (Laurel and Hardy)

Big Business, 1988 (Midler)

Big Business Girl, 1931 (Blondell; Young, L.)

Big Cage, 1933 (Rooney)

Big Carnival, 1951 (Douglas, K.)

Big Chance, 1933 (Rooney)

Big Chief. *See* Grand chef, 1959

Big Chill, 1983 (Close; Costner; Hurt, W.; Kline)

Big Circus, 1959 (Lorre; Mature; Price)

Big City, 1928 (Chaney)

Big City, 1937 (Rainer; Tracy)

Big City, 1948 (O'Brien, M.; Preston)

Big City Blues, 1932 (Blondell; Bogart)

Big Clock, 1948 (Lanchester; Laughton; Milland; O'Sullivan)

Big Combo, 1955 (Van Cleef; Wilde)

Big Country, 1958 (Heston; Peck)

Big Cube, 1969 (Turner, L.)

Big Day, 1960 (Pleasence)

Big Day. *See* Jour de fête, 1949

Big Deal at Dodge City. *See* Big Hand for the Little Lady, 1966

Big Deal on Madonna Street ... Twenty Years Later. *See* I soliti ignoti vent' anni dopo, 1985

Big Delirium. *See* Grand Délire, 1974

Big Diamond, 1929 (Mix)

Big Easy, 1987 (Barkin; Quaid)

Big Feast. *See* Grande Bouffe, 1973

Big Fella, 1937 (Robeson; Rutherford)

Big Fisherman, 1959 (Lom)

Big Fix, 1978 (Dreyfuss)

Big Flash, 1932 (Langdon)

Big Game, 1972 (Milland)

Big Game. *See* Grand Jeu, 1954

Big Grab. *See* Mélodie en sous-sol, 1962

Big Gundown. *See* Resa dei conti, 1967

Big Guns, 1972 (Delon)

Big Guy, 1939 (Cooper; McLaglen)

Big Hand for the Little Lady, 1966 (Fonda, H.; Meredith; Robards; Woodward)

Big Hangover, 1950 (Taylor, E.)

Big Heat, 1953 (Ford, G.; Grahame; Marvin)

Big House, 1930 (Beery; Montgomery)

Big House, U.S.A., 1955 (Bronson; Crawford, B.)

Big Idea, 1918 (Lloyd)

Big Idea, 1934 (Three Stooges)

Big Jack, 1949 (Beery)

Big Jake, 1971 (O'Hara; Wayne)

Big Jim McLain, 1952 (Wayne)

Big Kick, 1930 (Langdon)

Big Killing, 1928 (Beery)

Big Knife, 1955 (Lupino; Palance; Sloane; Steiger; Winters)

Big Land, 1957 (Ladd; O'Brien, E.)

Big Leaguer, 1953 (Robinson, E.)

Big Lift, 1950 (Clift)

Big Little Person, 1919 (Valentino)

Big Man, 1991 (Grant, H.; Neeson)

Big Moments from Little Pictures, 1924 (Rogers, W.)

Big Mouth, 1967 (Lewis, Jerry)

Big News, 1929 (Ayres; Lombard)

Big Night, 1996 (Rossellini)

Big Noise, 1944 (Laurel and Hardy)

Big Operator, 1959 (Rooney)

Big Parade, 1925 (Gilbert)

Big Picture, 1989 (Bacon; Cleese; Gould; Leigh, Jennifer Jason; McDowall)

Big Pond, 1930 (Chevalier; Colbert)

Big Red, 1962 (Pidgeon)

Big Red One, 1978 (Marvin; Audran)

Big Rip-Off, 1975 (Curtis, T.)

Big Ripoff. *See* Controrapina, 1978

Big Risk. *See* Classe tous risques, 1958

Big Rose, 1974 (Winters)

Big Sam. *See* Great Scout and Cathouse Thursday, 1976

Big Scam. *See* Nightingale Sang in Berkeley Square, 1979

Big Shakedown, 1934 (Davis, B.)

Big Shot, 1931 (O'Sullivan)

Big Shot, 1942 (Bogart)

Big Shot. *See* Doughboys, 1930

Big Show, 1936 (Autry; Rogers, R.)

Big Show, 1961 (Robertson; Williams, E.)

Big Sky, 1952 (Douglas, K.)

Big Sleep, 1946 (Bacall; Bogart; Malone)

Big Sleep, 1978 (Mills; Mitchum; Reed; Stewart)

Big Snatch. *See* Mélodie en sous-sol, 1962

Big Sombrero, 1949 (Autry)

Big Stampede, 1932 (Wayne)

Big Steal, 1949 (Mitchum; Novarro)

Big Store, 1941 (Dumont; Marx Brothers)

Big Street, 1942 (Ball; Fonda, H.; Moorehead)

Big Timber, 1950 (McDowall)

Big Time Vaudeville Reels, 1936 (McDaniel)

Big Toe, 1964 (Cusack)

Big Town, 1987 (Dern; Dillon; Grant, L.; Jones, T.)

Big Town Girl, 1937 (Trevor)

Big Town Round-up, 1921 (Mix)

Big Trail, 1930 (Bond; Wayne)

Big Trees, 1952 (Douglas, K.)

Big Trouble, 1985 (Arkin; Falk)

Big Wave, 1962 (Hayakawa)

Big Wheel, 1949 (McDaniel; Rooney)

Big Yellow Schooner to Byzantium, 1978 (Fonda, H.)

Bigamist, 1953 (Fontaine; Lupino; O'Brien, E.)

Bigamist. *See* Bigamo, 1956

Bigamo, 1956 (Mastroianni)

Bigfoot, 1973 (Carradine)

Bigfoot, 1987 (Wiest)

Bigger and Better Blondes, 1927 (Arthur)

Bigger than Life, 1956 (Mason; Matthau)

Biggest Bank Robbery. *See* Nightingale Sang in Berkeley Square, 1980

Biggest Battle. *See* Grande Attacco, 1977

Biggest Bundle of Them All, 1968 (Welch)

Biggles: Adventures in Time, 1985 (Cushing)

Bijo no tokudane, 1952 (Kyo)

Bijo to tozoku, 1952 (Kyo; Mori)

Bijo to yaju, 1952 (Shimura)

Bijobu Sakyo, 1931 (Hasegawa)

Bijoutiers au clair de lune, 1957 (Rey; Bardot; Cantinflas; Valli)

Bikini Beach, 1964 (Karloff)

Biko Inquest, 1984 (Finney)

Bildnis, 1925 (Banky)

Bilet Pherat, 1972 (Chatterjee)

Biljett till paradiset, 1962 (Dahlbeck)

Bill & Ted's Bogus Journey, 1991 (Reeves)

Bill & Ted's Excellent Adventure, 1989 (Reeves)

Bill, 1981 (Quaid; Rooney)

Bill. *See* Addition, 1985

Bill Haywood, Producer, 1915 (Mix)

Bill of Divorcement, 1932 (Barrymore, J.; Hepburn, K.; Marshall; Menjou)

Bill of Divorcement, 1940 (O'Hara)

Bill Sharkley's Last Game, 1909 (Carey)

Bill: On His Own, 1983 (Quaid; Rooney)

Billboard Girl, 1932 (Crosby)

Bille en tête, 1989 (Darrieux)

Billet de mille, 1935 (Rosay)

Billion Dollar Brain, 1967 (Caine; Homolka; Malden)

Billion Dollar Threat, 1979 (Bellamy)

Billion for Boris, 1984 (Grant, L.)

Billionaire. *See* Okuman-choja, 1954

Billions, 1920 (Nazimova)

Billions. *See* Miliardi, 1990

Billy Bathgate, 1991 (Hoffman)

Billy Blazes, Esq, 1919 (Lloyd)
Billy Budd, 1962 (Douglas, Melvyn; Ryan, R.; Stamp; Ustinov)
Billy Galvin, 1986 (Malden)
Billy Liar, 1963 (Christie)
Billy Rose's Diamond Horseshoe, 1945 (Dumont)
Billy Rose's Jumbo. See Jumbo, 1962
Billy the Kid, 1930 (Beery; Hart)
Billy the Kid, 1941 (Taylor, R.)
Billy the Kid Returns, 1938 (Rogers, R.)
Billy the Kid vs. Dracula, 1966 (Carradine)
Billy Two Hats, 1973 (Peck)
Biloxi Blues, 1988 (Walken)
Bing Crosby's Washington State, 1968 (Crosby)
Bing Presents Oreste, 1955 (Crosby)
Bingo Long Traveling All-Stars and Motor Kings, 1976 (Jones, James Earl; Pryor)
Biography of a Bachelor Girl, 1935 (Horton; Montgomery)
Bionda, 1992 (Kinski)
Birch-wood. See Brzezina, 1970
Bird, 1988 (Eastwood; Whitaker)
Bird in the Head, 1946 (Three Stooges)
Bird of Paradise, 1932 (Del Rio; McCrea)
Bird of Paradise, 1951 (Jourdan; Sloane)
Bird of Prey. See Epervier, 1933
Bird on a Wire, 1990 (Gibson; Hawn)
Bird's Singing. See Para recibir el canto de los pajaros, 1995
Birdcage, 1996 (Hackman; Wiest; Williams, R.)
Birdcall. See Lockfågeln, 1971
Birdman of Alcatraz, 1962 (Lancaster; Malden; O'Brien, E.; Ritter)
Birds and the Bees, 1956 (Niven)
Birds Come to Die in Peru. See Oiseaux vont mourir au Pérou, 1968
Birds Do It. See Oiseaux vont mourir au Pérou, 1968
Birds in Peru. See Oiseaux vont mourir aux Pérou, 1968
Birds of a Feather, 1917 (Lloyd)
Birds of Prey, 1930 (Hawkins)
Birdy, 1984 (Cage)
Birgitt Haas Must Be Killed. See Faut tuer Birgitt Haas, 1981
Birha Ki Raat, 1950 (Anand)
Birth of a Nation, 1915 (Crisp; Gish; Marsh)
Birth of a Star, 1944 (Kaye)
Birth of Love. See Naissance de l'amour, 1993
Birth of Mankind, 1946 (Lee, B.)
Birth of the Blues, 1941 (Crosby)
Birthday Party, 1968 (Shaw)
Bis ans Ende der Welt, 1991 (Hurt, W.; Mitchum; Moreau; Neill; Ryu; Vogler; Von Sydow)
Bis wir uns Wiedersehen, 1953 (Schell, Maria)
Bisbetica Domata. See Taming of the Shrew, 1967
Biscuit Eater, 1972 (Ayres)
Bishop Misbehaves, 1935 (O'Sullivan)
Bishop Murder Case, 1930 (Rathbone)
Bishop's Candlesticks, 1929 (Huston, W.)
Bishop's Wife, 1947 (Grant, C.; Lanchester; Niven; Young, L.)
Bismarck, 1940 (Dagover)
Bitch. See Garce, 1989
Bite and Run. See Mordi e fuggi, 1972
Bite the Bullet, 1975 (Coburn, J.; Hackman)
Bite the Dust, 1969 (Van Cleef)
Bitka na Neretvi, 1969 (Bondarchuk; Brynner)
Bits of Life, 1921 (Chaney; Wong)
Bitter Apples, 1927 (Loy)
Bitter Grass. See Zeugin aus der Hölle, 1965
Bitter Moon. See Lunes de Fiel, 1992
Bitter Rice. See Riso amaro, 1948
Bitter Spirit. See Eien no hito, 1961
Bitter Sweet, 1933 (Neagle)
Bitter Sweet, 1940 (Eddy; MacDonald; Sanders)
Bitter Tea of General Yen, 1933 (Stanwyck)
Bitter Tears of Petra von Kant. See Bitteren Tranen der Petra von Kant, 1972
Bitter Victory, 1957 (Lee, C.)
Bitter Victory. See Amère victoire, 1957

Bittere Ernte, 1986 (Mueller-Stahl)
Bitteren Tranen der Petra von Kant, 1972 (Schygulla)
Bittersweet Love, 1976 (Turner, L.)
Bivio, 1950 (Vanel)
Bizarre Bizarre. See Drôle de drame, 1937
Black Abbot. See Schwarze Abt, 1963
Black Adder's Christmas Carol, 1988 (Richardson, M.)
Black and White Like Day and Night. See Schwarz und Weiss wie Tage und Nächte, 1978
Black Angel, 1946 (Crawford, B.; Duryea)
Black Angel, 1946 (Lorre)
Black Angel. See Ange noir, 1994
Black Angel. See Paroxismus, 1969
Black Arrow, 1985 (Rey)
Black Bart, 1948 (Duryea)
Black Belly of the Tarantula. See Tarantol dal ventre nero, 1971
Black Bird, 1975 (Audran; Segal)
Black Buccaneer. See Gordon, il Pirato Nero, 1961
Black Camel, 1931 (Lugosi; Young, R.)
Black Castle, 1952 (Karloff)
Black Cat, 1934 (Carradine; Karloff; Lugosi)
Black Cat, 1941 (Crawford, B.; Ladd; Lugosi; Rathbone)
Black Cauldron, 1985 (Hurt, J.; Huston, J.)
Black Crows. See Svarte fugler, 1983
Black Dragon. See Keitsik, 1989
Black Dragons, 1942 (Lugosi)
Black Eagle, 1988 (Van Damme)
Black Eagle. See Aquila Nera, 1946
Black Fox, 1962 (Dietrich)
Black Friday, 1940 (Karloff; Lugosi)
Black Fury, 1935 (Bond; Marsh; Muni)
Black Fury. See Mitsuyu-sen, 1954
Black Gold, 1947 (Quinn)
Black Gunn, 1972 (Landau)
Black Hand, 1950 (Kelly, Gene)
Black Hole, 1979 (Borgnine; Perkins; Schell, Maximilian)
Black Horse Canyon, 1954 (McCrea)
Black Hussar. See Schwarze Husar, 1932
Black Hut. See Chernyi barak, 1933
Black Is White, 1920 (White)
Black Jack, 1950 (Marshall)
Black Jack, 1980 (Cushing)
Black Jack. See Captain Blackjack, 1949
Black Journal. See Signora della orroro, 1977
Black Killer, 1971 (Kinski)
Black Knight, 1954 (Cushing; Ladd)
Black Leather Jacket, 1990 (Hopper)
Black Legion, 1937 (Bogart)
Black Lightning, 1924 (Bow)
Black Limelight, 1939 (Massey)
Black Lizard. See Kurotokage, 1962
Black Magic, 1949 (Welles)
Black Marble, 1980 (Stanton; Woods)
Black Midnight, 1949 (McDowall)
Black Milan. See Milan noir, 1989
Black Moon, 1934 (Wray)
Black Moon Rising, 1986 (Jones, T.)
Black Narcissus, 1947 (Kerr)
Black Noon, 1971 (Grahame; Milland)
Black Orchid, 1959 (Loren; Quinn)
Black Oxen, 1924 (Bow)
Black Palm Trees. See Svarta palmkroner, 1967
Black Parachute, 1944 (Carradine)
Black Pirate, 1926 (Crisp; Fairbanks)
Black Rain, 1989 (Douglas, Michael; García)
Black Rainbow, 1989 (Robards)
Black Room, 1935 (Karloff)
Black Rose, 1950 (Hawkins; Lom; Power; Welles)
Black Roses, 1921 (Hayakawa)
Black Roses. See Svarta rosor, 1945
Black Sabbath, 1964 (Karloff)

Black Sea Fighters, 1942 (March)
Black Secret, 1919 (White)
Black Sheep, 1935 (Trevor)
Black Sheep, 1956 (Carradine)
Black Sheep of Whitehall, 1941 (Mills)
Black Shield of Falworth, 1954 (Curtis, T.; Leigh, Janet; Marshall)
Black Sleep, 1956 (Lugosi; Rathbone)
Black Spider, 1920 (Colman)
Black Spurs, 1964 (Darnell)
Black Stallion, 1979 (Rooney)
Black Stallion Returns, 1982 (Rooney)
Black Sun. See Soleil noir, 1966
Black Sunday, 1977 (Dern; Shaw)
Black Swan, 1942 (O'Hara; Power; Quinn; Sanders)
Black Tent, 1956 (Pleasence)
Black Tide. See Kuroi ushio, 1954
Black Tights. See Collants noirs, 1960
Black Tights. See Un, deux, trois, quatre?, 1960
Black Tuesday, 1954 (Robinson, E.)
Black Tulip. See Tulipe noire, 1963
Black Veil for Lisa. See Morte non ha sesso, 1969
Black Watch, 1929 (Loy; McLaglen; Scott, R.)
Black Water, 1994 (Steiger)
Black Whip, 1956 (Dickinson)
Black Widow, 1954 (Raft; Rogers, G.; Tierney)
Black Widow, 1987 (Hopper; Winger)
Black Windmill, 1974 (Caine; Pleasence; Seyrig)
Black Wings. See Czarne skrzydla, 1962
Blackbeard the Pirate, 1952 (Darnell)
Blackbeard's Ghost, 1968 (Lanchester; Ustinov)
Blackbird, 1926 (Chaney)
Blackboard Jungle, 1955 (Calhern; Ford, G.; Poitier)
Blacklist, 1916 (Sweet)
Blacklist. See Liste noire, 1985
Blackmail, 1939 (Robinson, E.)
Blackmailed, 1950 (Zetterling; Bogarde)
Blackout. See Contraband, 1940
Blackout, 1977 (Milland)
Blackout, 1985 (Widmark)
Blacksmith, 1922 (Keaton, B.)
Blackwell's Island, 1939 (Garfield)
Blade on the Feather, 1980 (Elliott)
Blade Runner, 1982 (Ford, H.; Olmos)
Blague dans le coin, 1963 (Fernandel)
Blame It on Father, 1953 (Lee, B.)
Blame It on Love, 1940 (Ladd)
Blame It on Rio, 1984 (Caine; Moore, Demi)
Blame It on the Bellboy, 1991 (Moore, Dudley)
Blame the Woman, 1932 (Menjou)
Blanc. See Trzy Kolory: Czerwony, 1993
Blanc de chine, 1988 (Piccoli)
Blanc et le noir, 1930 (Fernandel; Raimu)
Blanca Paloma, 1989 (Banderas)
Blanche Fury, 1947 (Granger)
Blandt byens børn, 1922 (Madsen and Schenstrøm)
Blankt Vapen, 1990 (Andersson, H.)
Blast of Life. See Botta di vita, 1989
Blaubart, 1952 (Kortner)
Blaue Diamant, 1993 (Borgnine)
Blaue Engel, 1930 (Dietrich; Jannings)
Blaue Hand, 1967 (Kinski)
Blaze, 1989 (Newman)
Blaze of Noon, 1947 (Baxter; Hayden; Holden)
Blazing Forest, 1952 (Moorehead)
Blazing Magnums. See Tony Saitta, 1976
Blazing Saddles, 1974 (Brooks, M.; Pryor; Wilder)
Blazing Sun, 1950 (Autry)
Blé en herbe, 1953 (Feuillère)
Blé en liasses, 1969 (Dalio)
Blechtrommel, 1978 (Olbrychski; Winkler)
Bleiere Zeit, 1982 (Vogler)

Bleka Greven, 1937 (Madsen and Schenstrøm)
Bless the Children, 1953 (Zhao Dan)
Blessed Event, 1932 (Powell, D.)
Blessure, 1921 (Bertini)
Bleu. See Trzy Kolory: Niebieski, 1993
Bleus de la marine, 1934 (Fernandel)
Blind Adventure, 1933 (Bellamy)
Blind Alley, 1939 (Bellamy)
Blind Bargain, 1922 (Chaney)
Blind Chance. See Przypadek, 1982
Blind Date, 1934 (Rooney)
Blind Date, 1959 (Baker; Presle)
Blind Date, 1987 (Basinger; Willis)
Blind Desire. See Part de l'ombre, 1945
Blind Director. See Angriff der Gegenwart aud die Ubrige Zeit, 1985
Blind Goddess, 1948 (Bloom)
Blind Husbands, 1919 (Carey)
Blind Justice, 1934 (Mills)
Blind Love, 1912 (Sweet)
Blind Man. See Dritte, 1972
Blind Man's Bluff, 1936 (Mason)
Blind Man's Bluff, 1967 (Karloff)
Blind Passion. See V boynoi slepote strastei, 1916
Blind Princess and the Poet, 1911 (Sweet)
Blind Spot, 1958 (Caine)
Blind Spot, 1993 (Woodward)
Blind Spot. See Flüsternde Tod, 1975
Blind Terror, 1971 (Farrow)
Blinde Passagerer. See Blinde Passagiere, 1936
Blinde Passagiere, 1936 (Madsen and Schenstrøm)
Blindfold, 1966 (Cardinale)
Blindfold, 1966 (Hudson)
Blindside, 1987 (Keitel)
Bliss, 1917 (Lloyd)
Bliss of Mrs. Blossom, 1968 (Attenborough; Cleese; MacLaine)
Blithe Spirit, 1945 (Harrison; Rutherford)
Blithe Spirit, 1966 (Bogarde)
Blitz on the Fritz, 1943 (Langdon)
Blizzard, 1921 (Laurel and Hardy)
Blob, 1958 (McQueen)
Block Busters, 1944 (Langdon)
Block-Heads, 1938 (Laurel and Hardy; Langdon)
Block-Notes di un regista, 1969 (Mastroianni)
Block Signal, 1926 (Arthur)
Blockade, 1938 (Carroll; Fonda, H.)
Blockhouse, 1973 (Sellers)
Blond Cheat, 1938 (Fontaine)
Blonde. See Bionda, 1992
Blonde and Groom, 1943 (Langdon)
Blonde Bombshell. See Bombshell, 1933
Blonde Crazy, 1931 (Blondell; Cagney; Calhern; Milland)
Blonde de Pekin, 1968 (Robinson, E.)
Blonde Dynamite. See She's Dangerous, 1937
Blonde Fever, 1944 (Astor; Gardner; Grahame)
Blonde for Danger. See Sois belle et tais-toi, 1958
Blonde from Peking. See Blonde de Pekin, 1968
Blonde in Black Leather, 1977 (Cardinale)
Blonde or Brunette, 1927 (Menjou)
Blonde Sinner. See Yield to the Night, 1956
Blonde Venus, 1932 (Dietrich; Grant, C.; Marshall; McDaniel)
Blondie Johnson, 1933 (Blondell)
Blondie Knows Best, 1946 (Three Stooges)
Blondie of the Follies, 1932 (Davies; Durante; Montgomery)
Blondie on a Budget, 1940 (Hayworth)
Blondie Plays Cupid, 1940 (Ford, G.)
Blondy, 1975 (Andersson, B.)
Blood. See Occhio nel labirinto, 1970
Blood Alley, 1955 (Bacall; Wayne)
Blood and Lace, 1970 (Grahame)
Blood and Sand, 1922 (Valentino)
Blood and Sand, 1941 (Carradine; Darnell; Hayworth; Nazimova; Power;

Quinn)
Blood and Sand, 1989 (Stone)
Blood Beast Terror, 1968 (Cushing)
Blood Brother. *See* Rodnoi brat, 1929
Blood Brothers. *See* I guappi, 1973
Blood Demon. *See* Schlangengrube und das Pendel, 1967
Blood Feud. *See* Fatto di sangue fra due uomini per causa di una vedova, 1978
Blood Feud. *See* Revenge, 1979
Blood Feud, 1983 (Aiello; Borgnine; Ferrer)
Blood Fiend. *See* Theatre of Death, 1967
Blood in the Streets, 1976 (Reed)
Blood Kin, 1969 (Coburn, J.)
Blood Money, 1933 (Ball)
Blood Money. *See* Moneda sangrienta, 1974
Blood Money. *See* Clinton and Nadine, 1988
Blood Need Not Be Spilled. *See* Ni nado kruvi, 1917
Blood of Dracula's Castle, 1969 (Carradine)
Blood of Frankenstein. *See* Dracula vs. Frankenstein, 1969
Blood of Fu Manchu, 1968 (Lee, C.)
Blood of Ghastly Horror, 1972 (Carradine)
Blood of Others. *See* Sang des autres, 1984
Blood of the Iron Maiden, 1970 (Carradine)
Blood of the Man Devil. *See* House of the Black Death, 1965
Blood on My Hands. *See* Kiss the Blood off My Hands, 1948
Blood on the Badge, 1992 (Sheen)
Blood on the Moon, 1948 (Brennan; Mitchum; Preston)
Blood on the Sun, 1945 (Cagney; Sidney)
Blood Red, 1988 (Hopper; Roberts, J.)
Blood Red, 1990 (Giannini)
Blood Relatives. *See* Liens de sang, 1977
Blood Seekers. *See* Dracula vs. Frankenstein, 1969
Blood Suckers. *See* Dr. Terror's Gallery of Horrors, 1967
Blood, Sweat and Fear. *See* Mark il poliziotta, 1975
Blood Tide, 1982 (Ferrer; Jones, James Earl)
Bloodbath at the House of Death, 1983 (Price)
Bloodbrothers, 1978 (Aiello; Gere)
Bloodhounds of Broadway, 1952 (Bronson)
Bloodhounds of Broadway, 1989 (Dillon)
Bloodhounds of the North, 1913 (Chaney)
Bloodlaw, 1990 (Curtis, T.)
Bloodline, 1979 (Hepburn, A.; Papas; Schneider; Sharif)
Bloodsport, 1987 (Van Damme; Whitaker)
Bloodsuckers. *See* Incense for the Damned, 1970
Bloody Birthday, 1986 (Ferrer)
Bloody Brood, 1959 (Falk)
Bloody Chamber, 1983 (Stamp)
Bloody Hands of the Law. *See* Lo mano spietata della legge, 1976
Bloody Hands of the Law. *See* Mano spietat della legge, 1973
Bloody Judge. *See* Processo de las brujas, 1970
Bloody Mama, 1970 (De Niro; Dern; Winters)
Bloomfield, 1969 (Harris, R.; Schneider)
Blossoms in the Dust, 1941 (Garson; Pidgeon)
Blot, 1921 (Calhern)
Blotto, 1930 (Laurel and Hardy)
Blow Out, 1981 (Travolta)
Blow-Out. *See* **Grande Bouffe**, 1973
Blow! The Spring Breeze. *See* Fukeyo harukaze, 1953
Blow-Up, 1966 (Redgrave, V.)
Blowing Hot and Cold, 1984 (Giannini)
Blowing Wild, 1953 (Bond; Constantine; Quinn; Stanwyck)
Blown Away, 1994 (Bridges; Jones, T.; Whitaker)
Blu Elettrico, 1988 (Cardinale)
Blue, 1968 (Malden; Stamp)
Blue. *See* Trzy Kolory: Niebieski, 1993
Blue Angel. *See* **Blaue Engel**, 1930
Blue Beast. *See* Aoi yaju, 1960
Blue Bird, 1940 (Temple)
Blue Bird, 1976 (Taylor, E.)
Blue Blazes, 1936 (Keaton, B.)
Blue Blazes Rawden, 1918 (Hart)
Blue Blood, 1973 (Reed)

Blue Boy, 1994 (Thompson)
Blue Canadian Rockies, 1952 (Autry)
Blue Chips, 1994 (Nolte)
Blue Collar, 1978 (Keitel; Pryor)
Blue Dahlia, 1946 (Ladd; Lake)
Blue Eagle, 1926 (Gaynor)
Blue Envelope Mystery, 1916 (Menjou)
Blue Exile. *See* Mavi Surgun, 1993
Blue Gardenia, 1953 (Baxter)
Blue Hawaii, 1961 (Lansbury; Presley)
Blue Helmet. *See* Casque Bleu, 1994
Blue Ice, 1992 (Caine; Hoskins)
Blue in the Face, 1995 (Keitel)
Blue Knight, 1973 (Holden)
Blue Lagoon, 1949 (Cusack)
Blue Lamp, 1950 (Bogarde)
Blue Max, 1966 (Mason)
Blue Montana Skies, 1939 (Autry)
Blue Mountains. *See* Aoi sanmyaku, 1949
Blue Murder at St. Trinian's, 1957 (Terry-Thomas)
Blue Notte, 1990 (Caron)
Blue of the Night, 1933 (Crosby)
Blue or the Gray, 1913 (Gish)
Blue Remembered Hills, 1979 (Mirren)
Blue Rose, 1913 (Talmadge)
Blue Skies, 1946 (Astaire; Crosby)
Blue Skies Again, 1983 (García)
Blue Sky, 1994 (Jones, T.; Lange)
Blue Steel, 1934 (Wayne)
Blue Steel, 1990 (Curtis, J.)
Blue Streak McCoy, 1920 (Carey)
Blue Thunder, 1983 (McDowell; Oates; Scheider)
Blue Tiger, 1994 (Stanton)
Blue Veil, 1951 (Blondell; Cusack; Laughton; Moorehead; Sloane; Wood; Wyman)
Blue Velvet, 1986 (Hopper; Rossellini)
Blue Water, 1924 (Shearer)
Blue, White, and Perfect, 1941 (Marsh)
Bluebeard, 1944 (Carradine)
Bluebeard. *See* Barbe-Bleue, 1951
Bluebeard. *See* Barbe-Bleue, 1972
Bluebeard. *See* Landru, 1963
Bluebeard, Bluebeard. *See* Barbablu, Barbablu, 1987
Bluebeard's Eighth Wife, 1923 (Swanson)
Bluebeard's Eighth Wife, 1938 (Colbert; Constantine; Horton; Niven)
Bluebeard's Seven Wives, 1926 (Sweet)
Bluebeard's Six Wives. *See* Sei mogli di Barbablu', 1950
Bluebeard's Ten Honeymoons, 1960 (Sanders)
Bluebird, 1976 (Fonda, J.; Gardner)
Bluebottles, 1928 (Lanchester; Laughton)
Bluegrass, 1987 (Rooney)
Blueprint for Murder, 1953 (Cotten; Marsh)
Blues Brothers, 1980 (Belushi; Candy)
Blues for Lovers. *See* Ballad in Blue, 1964
Bluff, 1976 (Quinn)
Blume in Love, 1973 (Segal; Winters)
Blumenfrau von Lindenau, 1931 (Lamarr)
Blunder Boys, 1955 (Three Stooges)
Blundering Boob. *See* New Janitor, 1914
Blunt, 1986 (Hopkins, A.)
Blut der Ahnen, 1920 (Dagover)
Bo no Kanashimi, 1994 (Okada)
Boarding School. *See* Passion Flower Hotel, 1978
Boardwalk, 1979 (Gordon; Leigh, Janet)
Boat, 1921 (Keaton, B.)
Boatniks, 1970 (Ameche)
Bob & Carol & Ted & Alice, 1969 (Gould; Wood)
Bob Hope Reports to the Nation, 1947 (Kaye)
Bob Mathias Story, 1954 (Bond)
Bob Roberts, 1992 (Robbins; Sarandon)
Bobbie of the Ballet, 1916 (Chaney)

Bobby Deerfield, 1977 (Pacino)
Bobo, 1967 (Brazzi; Sellers)
Bobo Jacco, 1979 (Girardot)
Bobosse, 1958 (Presle)
Boca, 1994 (Sheen)
Bocca, 1991 (Valli)
Boccaccio, 1972 (Blier)
Boccaccio '70, 1961 (Loren; Schneider)
Bocchan dohyo-iri, 1943 (Tanaka)
Bocchan kisha, 1955 (Yamamura)
Bodas de Fuego, 1949 (Armendáriz)
Bodas de sangre, 1976 (Papas)
Body. See Ratai, 1963
Body and Soul, 1925 (Robeson)
Body and Soul, 1927 (Barrymore, L.)
Body and Soul, 1931 (Bogart; Loy)
Body and Soul, 1947 (Garfield)
Body Disappears, 1941 (Wyman; Horton)
Body Double, 1984 (Griffith)
Body Heat, 1981 (Hurt, W.; Rourke; Turner, K.)
Body of Evidence, 1993 (Dafoe)
Body Snatcher, 1945 (Karloff; Lugosi)
Body Snatchers, 1993 (Whitaker)
Body Stealers, 1969 (Sanders)
Bodyguard, 1992 (Costner; Reynolds, D.)
Bodyguard. See Yojimbo, 1961
Boeing-Boeing, 1965 (Curtis, T.; Lewis, Jerry; Ritter)
Bofuu no bara, 1931 (Takamine)
Bogus, 1996 (Depardieu; Goldberg)
Bohème, 1926 (Horton; Gilbert; Gish)
Bohemian Girl, 1922 (Novello)
Bohemian Girl, 1936 (Goddard; Laurel and Hardy)
Bohemian Life. See Vie de Boheme, 1993
Boia di Lilla, 1952 (Brazzi)
Boiling Point, 1993 (Hopper; Snipes)
Bois des amants, 1960 (Rosay)
Bois sacré, 1939 (Dalio)
Boîte aux rêves, 1944 (Philipe)
Bojo, 1950 (Yamada)
Bojo no hito, 1961 (Hara)
Bokser, 1966 (Olbrychski)
Boku wa san-nin mae, 1958 (Kagawa)
Bokyaku no hanabira: Kanketsu-hen, 1957 (Tsukasa)
Bold and the Brave, 1956 (Rooney)
Bolero, 1933 (Raft; Lombard; Milland)
Bolero. See Uns et les autres, 1981
Boléro, 1941 (Arletty)
Bolero de Raquel, 1956 (Cantinflas)
Bolivar 63-29, 1963 (Gélin)
Bolivia, 1946 (Ferrer)
Bom the Flyer. See Flyg-Bom, 1952
Bomb for a Dictator. See Fanatiques, 1957
Bombardier, 1943 (Ryan, R.; Scott, R.)
Bombardment of Monte Carlo. See Bomben auf Monte Carlo, 1931
Bombe, 1909 (Linder)
Bomben auf Monte Carlo, 1931 (Lorre)
Bomben auf Monte Carlo, 1960 (Constantine)
Bombero atómico, 1950 (Cantinflas)
Bombers B-52, 1957 (Malden; Wood)
Bombs and Banknotes, 1916 (Beery)
Bombs over Burma, 1942 (Wong)
Bombs over London. See Midnight Menace, 1936
Bombshell, 1933 (Harlow)
Bombsight Stolen. See Cottage to Let, 1941
Bommels Billigflüge, 1993 (Vogler)
Bon baisers de Hong Kong, 1975 (Rooney)
Bon Dieu sans confession, 1953 (Darrieux)
Bon et les méchants, 1976 (Reggiani)
Bon Plaisir, 1983 (Deneuve)
Bon Roi Dagobert, 1963 (Cervi; Fernandel)
Bon Voyage, 1962 (MacMurray; Wyman)

Bonchi, 1960 (Kyo; Yamada)
Bond, 1918 (Chaplin, C.; Purviance)
Bond Between, 1917 (Crisp)
Bond Boy, 1922 (Barthelmess)
Bondage, 1917 (Chaney)
Bondage of Barbara, 1919 (Marsh)
Bonds of Honor, 1919 (Hayakawa)
Bonfire of the Vanities, 1990 (Freeman; Griffith; Hanks; Willis)
Bonheur, 1933 (Boyer; Marais)
Boniface somnambule, 1950 (Fernandel)
Bonjour, Monsieur Lewis, 1982 (Martin, D.)
Bonjour New York!, 1928 (Chevalier)
Bonjour Tristesse, 1958 (Kerr; Niven; Seberg)
Bonne Chance, Charlie, 1962 (Constantine)
Bonne Étoile, 1942 (Fernandel)
Bonne Occase, 1965 (Trintignant)
Bonne pour monsieur, un domestique pour madame, 1910 (Linder)
Bonne Soupe, 1963 (Gélin; Blier)
Bonne Soupe, 1964 (Girardot)
Bonne Tisane, 1957 (Blier)
Bonnes à tuer, 1954 (Darrieux)
Bonnes Causes, 1963 (Brasseur)
Bonnes Femmes, 1960 (Audran)
Bonnie and Clyde, 1967 (Beatty; Dunaway; Hackman; Wilder)
Bonnie Brier Bush. See Beside the Bonnie Brier Bush, 1921
Bonnie Prince Charlie, 1923 (Novello)
Bonnie Prince Charlie, 1948 (Hawkins; Niven)
Bonnie Scotland, 1935 (Laurel and Hardy)
Bons baisers à lundi, 1974 (Blier)
Bons Vivants, 1965 (Blier)
Bonsoir Paris, bonjour l'amour, 1956 (Gélin)
Bonzo Goes to College, 1952 (O'Sullivan)
Boob, 1926 (Crawford, J.)
Boobs in Arms, 1940 (Three Stooges)
Boobs in the Wood, 1925 (Langdon)
Booby Dupes, 1945 (Three Stooges)
Boogey Man, 1980 (Carradine)
Boogie Man Will Get You, 1942 (Karloff; Lorre)
Book Agents, 1912-13 (White)
Bookworms, 1920 (Howard, L.)
Boom, 1963 (Sordi)
Boom!, 1968 (Burton; Taylor, E.)
Boom in the Moon. See Moderno Barba Azul, 1946
Boom Town, 1940 (Colbert; Lamarr; Tracy)
Boomerang, 1947 (Andrews, D.; Cobb; Kennedy; Malden)
Boomerang, 1992 (Murphy)
Boomerang Bill, 1922 (Barrymore, L.)
Boomtown, 1940 (Gable)
Boon. See Anugraham, 1978
Boost, 1988 (Woods)
Bootlegger, 1922 (Laurel and Hardy)
Bootleggers, 1922 (Shearer)
Boots, 1919 (Barthelmess)
Boots and Saddles, 1937 (Autry)
Boots Malone, 1952 (Holden)
Booty and the Beast, 1953 (Three Stooges)
Bopha!, 1993 (Freeman; McDowell)
Boquetière des Innocents, 1922 (Modot)
Boran—Zeit zum zielen, 1987 (Léaud)
Border, 1981 (Nicholson; Keitel; Oates)
Border Cafe, 1937 (Carey)
Border Devils, 1932 (Carey)
Border Flight, 1936 (Farmer)
Border Legion, 1930 (Wray)
Border Legion, 1940 (Rogers, R.)
Border Patrol, 1928 (Carey)
Border Patrol, 1943 (Mitchum)
Border River, 1954 (Armendáriz; McCrea)
Border Shootout, 1990 (Ford, G.)
Border Wireless, 1918 (Hart)
Borderline, 1925 (Robeson)

Borderline, 1950 (MacMurray; Trevor)
Borderline, 1980 (Bronson; Harris, E.)
Bordertown, 1935 (Armendáriz; Davis, B.; Muni)
Borges Tales Part I. See Cuentos de Borges I, 1991
Borghese piccolo piccolo, 1977 (Sordi; Winters)
Boris and Natasha, 1991 (Candy; Travolta)
Boris Godunov, 1986 (Bondarchuk)
Born Again, 1978 (Andrews, D.)
Born for Glory. See Brown on Resolution, 1935
Born in Sin. See Kawano hotoride, 1962
Born Losers, 1967 (Russell, J.)
Born Natturunna, 1991 (Ganz)
Born on the Fourth of July, 1989 (Cruise; Dafoe)
Born Reckless, 1930 (Bond; Brown)
Born Reckless, 1937 (Carey)
Born to Battle, 1926 (Arthur)
Born to Be Bad, 1934 (Grant, C.; Young, L.)
Born to Be Bad, 1950 (Fontaine; Ryan, R.)
Born to Be Wild, 1938 (Bond)
Born to Buck, 1968 (Fonda, H.)
Born to Dance, 1936 (Powell, E.; Stewart)
Born to Kill, 1947 (Trevor)
Born to Love, 1931 (McCrea)
Born to Sing, 1942 (Dumont)
Born to the West, 1938 (Wayne)
Born to Win, 1971 (De Niro; Segal)
Born Yesterday, 1950 (Crawford, B.; Holden; Holliday)
Born Yesterday, 1993 (Griffith)
Boro no kesshitai, 1942 (Hara)
Borrasca humana, 1939 (Armendáriz)
Borsalino, 1970 (Belmondo; Delon)
Borsalino & Co., 1974 (Delon)
Börsenkönigin, 1917 (Nielsen)
Bosambo. See Sanders of the River, 1935
Bosque encantado, 1987 (Rey)
Boss Tweed, 1933 (Coburn, C.)
Bossu, 1944 (Modot)
Bossu de Rome. See Gobbo, 1960
Boston Strangler, 1968 (Curtis, T.; Fonda, H.)
Bostonians, 1984 (Redgrave, V.)
Botany Bay, 1953 (Ladd; Mason)
Botta di vita, 1989 (Blier; Sordi)
Botta e risposta, 1949 (Fernandel)
Bottle Imp, 1917 (Hayakawa)
Bottle Rocket, 1996 (Caan)
Bottleneck. See Ingorgo, 1979
Bottom of the Bottle, 1956 (Cotten)
Bottoms Up, 1934 (Ball; Tracy)
Boucher, 1970 (Audran)
Boucher, la star, et l'orpheline. See Evlalie quitte les champs, 1973
Bought, 1931 (Milland)
Boulanger de Valorgue, 1952 (Fernandel)
Boule de suif, 1945 (Presle)
Boulevard des assassins, 1982 (Audran)
Boulevard du rhum, 1971 (Bardot)
Bound in Morocco, 1918 (Fairbanks)
Bound on the Wheel, 1915 (Chaney)
Bounty, 1984 (Day-Lewis; Gibson; Hopkins, A.; Neeson; Olivier)
Bounty Hunter, 1954 (Borgnine; Scott, R.)
Bounty Hunters. See Indio Black, sai che ti dico: sei un gran figlio di ..., 1970
Bounty Killer, 1965 (Duryea)
Bouquet, 1915 (Beery)
Bourne Identity, 1988 (Elliott; Quayle)
Bourse et la vie, 1965 (Fernandel)
Bout-de-chou, 1935 (Brasseur)
Boutique de l'orfever, 1989 (Olbrychski)
Bowery, 1933 (Ball; Beery; Cooper; Raft; Wray)
Bowery at Midnight, 1942 (Lugosi)
Bowery Boys, 1914 (Arbuckle)
Bowery to Broadway, 1944 (O'Connor)
Bowling Match, 1913 (Normand)

Boxcar Bertha, 1972 (Carradine; Hershey)
Boxer. See Bokser, 1966
Boxer. See Uomo dalla pelle dura, 1971
Boxing Gloves, 1929 (Cooper)
Boxoffice, 1982 (Constantine)
Boy, a Girl and a Bike, 1949 (Dors)
Boy and a Bike, 1951 (Buchanan)
Boy and His Dog, 1975 (Robards)
Boy and the Fog. See Nino y la niebla, 1953
Boy Called Hate, 1995 (Caan; Gould)
Boy, Did I Get a Wrong Number, 1966 (Hope)
Boy Friend, 1971 (Jackson, G.)
Boy from Barnado's. See Lord Jeff, 1938
Boy in Blue, 1986 (Cage)
Boy in the Plastic Bubble, 1976 (Bellamy; Travolta)
Boy Meets Girl, 1938 (Bellamy; Cagney; Reagan)
Boy of the Streets, 1937 (Cooper)
Boy on a Dolphin, 1957 (Ladd; Loren; Webb)
Boy Ten Feet Tall, 1965 (Robinson, E.)
Boy Trouble, 1939 (O'Connor)
Boy with Green Hair, 1948 (Ryan, R.)
Boycotted Baby, 1917 (Laurel and Hardy)
Boykott, 1930 (Dagover)
Boys, 1991 (Woods)
Boys, 1996 (Ryder)
Boys from Brazil, 1978 (Elliott; Ganz; Mason; Olivier; Peck)
Boys from Brooklyn. See Bela Lugosi Meets a Brooklyn Gorilla, 1952
Boys in Brown, 1949 (Attenborough; Bogarde)
Boys' Night Out, 1962 (Garner; Homolka; Novak)
Boys on the Side, 1995 (Goldberg)
Boys Town, 1938 (Rooney; Tracy)
Boys Will Be Boys, 1921 (Rogers, W.)
Boyz N the Hood, 1991 (Bassett; Fishburne)
Braccio violento della mala. See Dinero Maldito, 1978
Brain. See Cerveau, 1969
Brain Donors, 1992 (Turturro)
Brainstorm, 1965 (Andrews, D.)
Brainstorm, 1983 (Robertson; Walken; Wood)
Brainwashed. See Schachnovelle, 1960
Brainwashed. See Droit d'aimer, 1972
Brainwaves, 1982 (Curtis, T.)
Bram Stoker's Dracula, 1992 (Hopkins, A.; Oldman; Reeves; Ryder)
Bramble Bush, 1960 (Burton; Dickinson)
Brancaleone alle Crociate, 1970 (Gassman)
Branches of the Tree. See Shakha Proshakha, 1990
Brand in der Oper, 1930 (Fröhlich)
Brand New Hero, 1914 (Arbuckle)
Brand of Cowardice, 1916 (Barrymore, L.)
Brand of Lopez, 1920 (Hayakawa)
Brand X, 1970 (Shepard)
Branded, 1951 (Ladd)
Branded Woman, 1920 (Talmadge)
Branding Broadway, 1918 (Hart)
Brandnacht, 1992 (Ganz)
Brandy Ashore. See Green Grow the Rushes, 1951
Brannigan, 1975 (Attenborough; Wayne)
Brannigar, 1935 (Bergman)
Braqueuses, 1994 (Girardot)
Bras de la nuit, 1961 (Darrieux)
Brasher Doubloon, 1947 (Kortner)
Brasier ardent, 1923 (Mozhukin)
Brass Monkey, 1948 (Lom; Terry-Thomas)
Brass Target, 1978 (Loren; Von Sydow)
Brat, 1919 (Nazimova)
Brats, 1930 (Laurel and Hardy)
Bratya, 1912 (Mozhukin)
Bratya razbotchniki, 1912 (Mozhukin)
Bräutigan, die Komödiantin, und der Zuhalter, 1968 (Schygulla)
Bravados, 1958 (Peck; Van Cleef)
Brave Bulls, 1951 (Quinn)
Brave Deserve the Fair, 1915 (Mix)

Brave Hunter, 1912 (Normand)
Brave Ones, 1916 (Laurel and Hardy)
Brave Rifles, 1966 (Kennedy)
Brave Sünder, 1931 (Kortner)
Braveheart, 1995 (Gibson)
Bravest Way, 1918 (Hayakawa)
Bravissimo, 1955 (Sordi)
Bravo di Venezia, 1941 (Brazzi)
Bravo Ready, 1996 (Scacchi)
Brazen Bell, 1962 (Cobb)
Brazil, 1944 (Horton; Rogers, R.)
Brazil, 1985 (De Niro; Hoskins)
Bread and Chocolate. *See* Pane e cioccolata, 1973
Bread, Love and Dreams. *See* Pane, amore, e fantasia, 1953
Break, 1995 (Sheen)
Break In. *See* Loophole, 1980
Break of Hearts, 1935 (Boyer; Hepburn, K.)
Break the News, 1937 (Buchanan; Chevalier)
Break Up. *See* Rupture, 1970
Breakdown. *See* Si j'étais un espion, 1967
Breakfast at Sunrise, 1927 (Dressler)
Breakfast at Tiffany's, 1961 (Hepburn, A.; Neal; Rooney)
Breakfast for Champions, 1996 (Willis)
Breakfast for Two, 1937 (Marshall; Stanwyck)
Breakheart Pass, 1975 (Bronson)
Breaking Away, 1979 (Quaid)
Breaking Home Ties, 1988 (Robards; Saint; Trevor)
Breaking In, 1989 (Reynolds, B.)
Breaking Point, 1950 (Garfield; Neal)
Breaking the Sound Barrier. *See* Sound Barrier, 1952
Breaking Up, 1978 (Remick)
Breakout, 1975 (Bronson; Duvall; Huston, J.)
Breakout. *See* Danger Within, 1959
Breakthrough, 1979 (Burton; Mitchum; Steiger)
Breakthrough. *See* Lifeforce Experiment, 1994
Breakup. *See* Rupture, 1970
Breath of Life, 1990 (Redgrave, V.; Rey)
Breath of Life. *See* Diceria dell'untore, 1990
Breath of Scandal, 1960 (Chevalier; Lansbury; Loren)
Breathing Lessons, 1994 (Garner; Woodward)
Breathless. *See* **A Bout de souffle**, 1960
Breathless, 1983 (Gere)
Bred in the Bone, 1915 (Crisp)
Breed Apart, 1984 (Pleasence; Turner, K.)
Breed of Men, 1919 (Hart)
Breezy, 1973 (Eastwood; Holden)
Bremen Freedom. *See* Bremer Freiheit, 1972
Bremer Freiheit, 1972 (Schygulla)
Brennende Acker, 1922 (Krauss)
Brennende Grenze, 1926 (Homolka)
Brennende Herz, 1929 (Fröhlich)
Brennendes Herz, 1995 (Sanda)
Brevi amori a Palma di Majorca, 1959 (Cervi; Sordi)
Brewster's Millions, 1921 (Arbuckle)
Brewster's Millions, 1935 (Buchanan)
Brewster's Millions, 1985 (Candy; Pryor)
Brian's Song, 1970 (Caan)
Bribe, 1949 (Gardner; Laughton; Price; Taylor, R.)
Bric-a-Brac, 1935 (Brennan)
Bric a Brac et Cie, 1931 (Fernandel)
Bridal Suite, 1939 (Young, R.)
Bride, 1985 (Page)
Bride 68. *See* Land Ohne Frauen, 1929
Bride and Gloom, 1918 (Lloyd)
Bride by Mistake, 1944 (Langdon)
Bride Came C.O.D., 1941 (Cagney; Davis, B.)
Bride Came through the Ceiling. *See* Bruden kom genom taket, 1947
Bride Comes Home, 1935 (Colbert; MacMurray; Young, R.)
Bride for Sale, 1949 (Colbert; Young, R.)
Bride Is Much Too Beautiful. *See* Mariée est trop belle, 1956
Bride of Frankenstein, 1935 (Brennan; Carradine; Karloff; Lanchester)

Bride of the Monster, 1955 (Lugosi)
Bride of the Regiment, 1930 (Loy; Pidgeon)
Bride of Vengeance, 1949 (Goddard)
Bride of Violence. *See* Vendetta: Secrets of a Mafia Bride, 1991
Bride sur le cou, 1961 (Bardot)
Bride Talks in Her Sleep. *See* Hanayome no negoto, 1933
Bride to Be. *See* Petita Jimenez, 1976
Bride Walks Out, 1936 (Bond; McDaniel; Stanwyck; Young, R.)
Bride Wore Black. *See* Mariée etait en noir, 1968
Bride Wore Boots, 1946 (Stanwyck; Wood)
Bride Wore Red, 1937 (Crawford, J.; Young, R.)
Bride's Play, 1922 (Davies)
Bridegroom, the Comedienne, and the Pimp. *See* Bräutigan, die Komödiantin, und der Zuhalter, 1968
Brideless Grooms, 1947 (Three Stooges)
Brides of Dracula, 1960 (Cushing)
Brides of Fu Manchu, 1966 (Lee, C.)
Bridge at Remagen, 1969 (Segal)
Bridge in the Jungle, 1971 (Huston, J.)
Bridge of San Luis Rey, 1944 (Calhern; Nazimova)
Bridge on the River Kwai, 1957 (Guinness; Hawkins; Hayakawa; Holden)
Bridge to Silence, 1989 (Remick)
Bridge Too Far, 1977 (Attenborough; Bogarde; Caan; Caine; Connery; Elliott; Gould; Hackman; Hopkins, A.; Olivier; Redford; Schell, Maximilian; Ullmann)
Bridge Wives, 1932 (Arbuckle)
Bridger, 1976 (Field)
Bridges at Toko-Ri, 1954 (Kelly, Grace; March; Holden; Rooney)
Bridges of Madison County, 1995 (Eastwood; Streep)
Brief Ecstasy, 1937 (Lukas)
Brief einer Toten, 1917 (Kortner)
Brief Encounter, 1945 (Howard, T.; Johnson)
Brief Encounter, 1974 (Burton; Loren)
Brief Moment, 1933 (Lombard)
Brigade mondaine, vaudou aux Caraïbes, 1980 (Dalio)
Brigade sauvage, 1939 (Vanel)
Brigadier Gerard. *See* Fighting Eagle, 1927
Brigadoon, 1954 (Charisse; Kelly, Gene)
Brigand, 1952 (Quinn)
Brigand of Kandahar, 1965 (Reed)
Brigante Musolino, 1950 (Mangano)
Briganti italiani, 1961 (Blier; Borgnine; Gassman; Presle)
Brigaten Rache, 1920 (Nielsen)
Brigham Young—Frontiersman, 1940 (Astor; Carradine; Darnell; Power; Price)
Bright and Early, 1918 (Laurel and Hardy)
Bright Angel, 1991 (Shepard)
Bright Day, 1994 (Ganz)
Bright Eyes, 1934 (Temple)
Bright Leaf, 1950 (Bacall; Constantine; Crisp; Neal)
Bright Lights, 1916 (Arbuckle; Normand)
Bright Lights, 1931 (Carradine)
Bright Lights, 1935 (Brown)
Bright Lights, Big City, 1988 (Robards; Wiest)
Bright Shawl, 1923 (Astor; Barthelmess; Powell, W.; Robinson, E.)
Bright Victory, 1951 (Hudson; Kennedy)
Brighton Rock, 1947 (Attenborough)
Brighty of the Grand Canyon, 1967 (Cotten)
Brimstone, 1949 (Brennan)
Brimstone and Treacle, 1982 (Elliott)
Bring Me the Head of Alfredo Garcia, 1974 (Oates)
Bring on the Girls, 1945 (Lake)
Bringin' Home the Bacon, 1924 (Arthur)
Bringing Up Baby, 1938 (Fitzgerald; Grant, C.; Hepburn, K.)
Bringing Up Father, 1928 (Dressler)
Brink of Life. *See* Nära livet, 1958
Brink's Job, 1978 (Falk; Oates; Rowlands)
Briseur de chaînes, 1941 (Fresnay)
Brita i grosshandlarhuset, 1946 (Dahlbeck)
Brita in the Wholesaler's House. *See* Brita i grosshandlarhuset, 1946
Britannia Hospital, 1981 (Bates, A.; McDowell)

Britannia of Billingsgate, 1933 (Mills)
British Agent, 1934 (Francis; Howard, L.)
British Intelligence, 1940 (Karloff)
British—Are They Artistic?, 1947 (Donat)
Briton and Boer, 1910 (Mix)
Broad Minded, 1931 (Brown; Lugosi)
Broadcast News, 1987 (Hunter; Hurt, W.; Nicholson)
Broadside: Taking on the Bomb, 1984 (Christie)
Broadway, 1942 (Crawford, B.; Raft)
Broadway after Dark, 1924 (Menjou)
Broadway after Dark, 1924 (Shearer)
Broadway Bad, 1933 (Blondell; Crisp)
Broadway Bad, 1933 (Rogers, G.)
Broadway Bill, 1934 (Ball; Bond; Loy)
Broadway Bound, 1992 (Bancroft)
Broadway Danny Rose, 1984 (Allen; Farrow)
Broadway Gondolier, 1935 (Blondell; Menjou; Powell, D.)
Broadway Limited, 1941 (McLaglen)
Broadway Love, 1918 (Chaney)
Broadway Melody of 1936, 1935 (Powell, E.; Taylor, R.)
Broadway Melody of 1938, 1937 (Garland; Powell, E.; Taylor, R.)
Broadway Melody of 1940, 1940 (Astaire; Powell, E.)
Broadway Nights, 1927 (Sidney; Stanwyck)
Broadway Scandal, 1918 (Chaney)
Broadway Serenade, 1939 (Ayres; MacDonald)
Broadway Singer. See Torch Singer, 1933
Broadway thru a Keyhole, 1933 (Ball)
Broadway to Hollywood, 1933 (Cooper; Durante; Eddy; Rooney)
Broadway's Like That, 1930 (Blondell; Bogart)
Brock's Last Case, 1973 (Widmark)
Broken Arrow, 1950 (Stewart)
Broken Arrow, 1996 (Travolta)
Broken Barriers, 1924 (Menjou; Shearer)
Broken Blossoms, 1919 (Barthelmess; Crisp; Gish)
Broken Dreams, 1933 (Scott, R.)
Broken Gate, 1927 (Arthur)
Broken Journey. See Uttoran, 1994
Broken Lance, 1954 (Tracy; Widmark)
Broken Land, 1961 (Nicholson)
Broken Locket, 1909 (Pickford)
Broken Lullaby, 1932 (Barrymore, L.)
Broken Melody, 1934 (Oberon)
Broken Pledge, 1915 (Beery; Swanson)
Broken Rainbow, 1985 (Sheen)
Broken Sabre, 1966 (Carradine)
Broken Sky. See Brusten Himmel, 1982
Broken Spell, 1910 (Talmadge)
Broken Spell, 1912-13 (White)
Broken Vows, 1987 (Jones, T.)
Broken Ways, 1913 (Carey; Sweet)
Broken Wing, 1932 (Douglas, Melvyn)
Brölloppsnatt. See Noc Poslubna, 1959
Bröllopsdagen, 1960 (Andersson, B.; Von Sydow)
Broncho Twister, 1927 (Mix)
Bronco Billy, 1980 (Eastwood)
Bronco Bullfrog, 1969 (Shepard)
Bronco Busters. See Gone with the West, 1975
Bronsteins Kinder, 1991 (Mueller-Stahl; Winkler)
Brontë Sisters. See Soeurs Brontë, 1979
Bronx Tale, 1993 (De Niro; Pesci)
Brood, 1979 (Reed)
Brooding Eyes, 1926 (Barrymore, L.)
Brooklyn Laundry, 1991 (Close)
Broth of a Boy, 1959 (Fitzgerald)
Brother Brigands. See Bratya razbotchniki, 1912
Brother, Can You Spare a Dime?, 1975 (Cagney)
Brother John, 1971 (Poitier)
Brother of the Bear, 1921 (Astor)
Brother Orchid, 1940 (Bellamy; Bogart; Crisp; Robinson, E.)
Brother Rat, 1938 (Reagan; Wyman)
Brother Rat and a Baby, 1940 (Ladd; Reagan; Wyman)

Brother Sun, Sister Moon. See Fratello Sole, Sorella Luna, 1972
Brother's Keeper, 1939 (McDowall)
Brotherhood, 1968 (Papas; Douglas, K.)
Brotherhood of Justice, 1986 (Reeves)
Brotherhood of the Bell, 1970 (Ford, G.)
Brotherhood of the Rose, 1989 (Mitchum)
Brotherhood of the Yakuza. See Yakuza, 1975
Brotherly Love, 1928 (Arthur)
Brotherly Love. See Country Dance, 1969
Brothers, 1912 (Carey)
Brothers. See Bratya, 1912
Brothers and Sisters of the Toda Family. See Todake no kyodai, 1941
Brothers in Law, 1957 (Attenborough; Terry-Thomas)
Brothers Karamazov. See Brüder Karamasoff, 1920
Brothers Karamazov, 1958 (Bloom; Brynner; Cobb; Schell, Maria)
Brothers under the Chin, 1924 (Laurel and Hardy)
Brott i paradiset, 1959 (Björnstrand; Andersson, H.)
Brown Bread Sandwiches, 1989 (Giannini)
Brown of Harvard, 1926 (Wayne)
Brown on Resolution, 1935 (Mills)
Brown's Seance, 1912 (Normand)
Brownie. See Daring Young Man, 1942
Browning Version, 1951 (Redgrave, M.)
Browning Version, 1994 (Finney; Scacchi)
Brubaker, 1980 (Freeman; Redford)
Bruden kom genom taket, 1947 (Björnstrand)
Brüder Karamasoff, 1920 (Jannings; Kortner; Krauss)
Brüder Schellenberg, 1926 (Dagover; Veidt)
Bruegel, 1967 (Gélin)
Brune piquante, 1932 (Fernandel)
Brushfire, 1962 (Sloane)
Brusten Himmel, 1982 (Thulin)
Brutal Justice. See Roma a mano armato, 1976
Brutality, 1912 (Barrymore, L.)
Brute Force, 1912 (Marsh)
Brute Force, 1914 (Barrymore, L.)
Brute Force, 1947 (Lancaster)
Bruto, 1952 (Armendáriz)
Brzezina, 1970 (Olbrychski)
Bubble Trouble, 1953 (Three Stooges)
Buccaneer, 1938 (Brennan; March; Quinn)
Buccaneer, 1958 (Bloom; Boyer; Brynner; Heston; Quinn)
Buccaneer's Girl, 1950 (Lanchester)
Buchanan Rides Alone, 1958 (Scott, R.)
Büchse der Pandora, 1927 (Kortner; Brooks, L.)
Buck and the Preacher, 1972 (Poitier)
Buck Benny Rides Again, 1940 (Bond)
Buck Privates, 1941 (Abbott and Costello; Three Stooges)
Buck Privates Come Home, 1947 (Abbott and Costello)
Buck Rogers in the 25th Century, 1979 (Palance)
Bucking Broadway, 1917 (Carey)
Bucklige und die Tänzerin, 1920 (Krauss)
Buckskin Frontier, 1943 (Cobb)
Budd Doble Comes Back, 1913 (Mix)
Buddenbrooks, 1959 (Dagover)
Buddenbrooks, 1984 (Gielgud)
Buddha. See Shaka, 1961
Buddy Buddy, 1981 (Kinski; Lemmon; Matthau)
Buddy System, 1983 (Dreyfuss; Sarandon)
Budo kagami, 1934 (Yamada)
Budo sen-ichi-ya, 1938 (Yamada)
Bufera, 1913 (Bertini)
Bufere, 1952 (Gabin; Reggiani)
Buffalo Bill, 1944 (Darnell; McCrea; O'Hara; Quinn)
Buffalo Bill and the Indians, or Sitting Bull's History Lesson, 1976 (Chaplin, G.; Keitel; Lancaster; Newman)
Buffalo Hunting, 1914 (Mix)
Buffet froid, 1979 (Blier; Depardieu)
Buffy the Vampire Slayer, 1992 (Sutherland)
Bugambilia, 1944 (Armendáriz; Del Rio)
Bughouse Bellhops, 1915 (Lloyd)

Bugiarda, 1989 (Olbrychski)
Bugie bianchi, 1980 (Von Sydow)
Bugle Sounds, 1942 (Beery)
Bugles in the Afternoon, 1952 (Milland)
Bugs Bunny Superstar, 1975 (Welles)
Bugsy, 1991 (Beatty; Gould; Keitel; Kingsley)
Bugsy Malone, 1976 (Foster)
Build a Fort, Set It on Fire. See Basquiat, 1996
Build Me a World, 1979 (Jackson, G.)
Build Thy House, 1920 (Rains)
Bull Durham, 1988 (Costner; Robbins; Sarandon)
Bulldog Breed, 1960 (Caine; Reed; Wisdom)
Bulldog Drummond, 1929 (Ball; Bennett; Colman)
Bulldog Drummond Comes Back, 1937 (Barrymore, J.)
Bulldog Drummond Escapes, 1937 (Milland)
Bulldog Drummond in Africa, 1938 (Quinn)
Bulldog Drummond Strikes Back, 1934 (Ball; Colman; Young, L.)
Bulldog Drummond's Peril, 1938 (Barrymore, J.)
Bulldog Drummond's Revenge, 1937 (Barrymore, J.)
Bulldog Drummond's Third Round, 1925 (Buchanan)
Bulldog Jack. See Alias Bulldog Drummond, 1935
Bulldog Sees It Through, 1940 (Buchanan; Withers)
Bulle und das Mädchen, 1985 (Olbrychski)
Bullet, 1976 (Anand)
Bullet for Berlin, 1918 (Hart)
Bullet for Joey, 1955 (Raft; Robinson, E.)
Bullet for Sandoval. See Desperados, 1970
Bullet for Stefano. See Passatore, 1947
Bullet for the General. See Quien sabe?, 1967
Bullet Proof, 1920 (Carey)
Bullet Wound. See Dankon, 1969
Bulletproof, 1996 (Caan)
Bullets and Brown Eyes, 1916 (Gilbert)
Bullets for O'Hara, 1941 (Quinn)
Bullets or Ballots, 1921 (Astor)
Bullets or Ballots, 1936 (Blondell; Bogart; Robinson, E.)
Bullets over Broadway, 1994 (Allen; Wiest)
Bullfighter. See Matador, 1986
Bullfighters, 1945 (Laurel and Hardy)
Bullitt, 1968 (Duvall; McQueen)
Bullseye!, 1990 (Caine; Cleese)
Bump, 1920 (Howard, L.)
Bumping into Broadway, 1919 (Lloyd)
Bunch That Failed, 1912-13 (White)
Bundle of Joy, 1956 (Reynolds, D.)
Bungles Enforces the Law, 1916 (Laurel and Hardy)
Bungles Lands a Job, 1916 (Laurel and Hardy)
Bungles' Elopement, 1916 (Laurel and Hardy)
Bungles' Rainy Day, 1916 (Laurel and Hardy)
Bungs and Bunglers, 1919 (Laurel and Hardy)
Bunker, 1981 (Hopkins, A.)
Bunker Bean, 1936 (Ball)
Bunker Palace Hotel, 1989 (Léaud)
Bunny Lake Is Missing, 1965 (Olivier)
Bunny O'Hare, 1972 (Borgnine; Davis, B.)
Buona Sera, Mrs. Campbell, 1968 (Grant, L.; Lollobrigida; Winters)
Buonanotte ... avvocato!, 1955 (Sordi)
Buono, il bruto, il cattivo, 1966 (Eastwood; Van Cleef; Wallach)
Burari burabura monogatari, 1962 (Takamine)
'Burbs, 1988 (Dern; Hanks)
Burden of Dreams, 1982 (Cardinale; Kinski; Robards)
Burden of Life. See Jinsei ni onimotsu, 1935
Burden of Proof, 1917 (Davies)
Bureau of Missing Persons, 1933 (Davis, B.)
Burglar, 1957 (Duryea; Mansfield; Goldberg)
Burglars. See Casse, 1971
Burglar's Dilemma, 1912 (Barrymore, L.; Gish)
Burgtheater, 1936 (Krauss)
Buried Alive, 1990 (Leigh, Jennifer Jason; Pleasence)
Buried Loot, 1935 (Taylor, R.)
Buried Treasure, 1921 (Davies)

Burke & Wills, 1985 (Scacchi)
Burlesque, 1928 (Brown)
Burlesque on Carmen, 1915 (Purviance)
Burn!, 1969 (Brando)
Burn 'em Up O'Connor, 1939 (Carey)
Burn Witch Burn. See Mark of the Devil, 1970
Burning, 1981 (Hunter)
Burning Bridges, 1928 (Carey)
Burning Heart. See Brennende Herz, 1929
Burning Heart. See Brennendes Herz, 1995
Burning Hills, 1956 (Wood)
Burning Season, 1994 (Braga; Julia; Olmos; Brandauer)
Burning Secret, 1988 (Dunaway)
Burning Soil. See Brennende Acker, 1922
Burning the Wind, 1929 (Karloff)
Burning Youth. See Yama no sanka: Moyuru wakamono-tachi, 1962
Burnt Offering. See Passport to Hell, 1932
Burnt Offerings, 1976 (Davis, B.; Meredith; Reed)
Bus Riley's Back in Town, 1965 (Ann-Margret)
Bus Stop, 1956 (Monroe)
Busher, 1919 (Gilbert)
Bushido Blade, 1978 (Jones, James Earl; Mifune)
Bushido zankoku monogatari, 1963 (Mori)
Business Affair, 1995 (Walken)
Business and Pleasure, 1931 (Karloff; McCrea; Rogers, W.)
Business as Usual, 1987 (Jackson, G.)
Business Is a Pleasure, 1934 (Grable)
Business of Love, 1925 (Horton)
Busman's Honeymoon, 1940 (Withers)
Busted Hearts, 1916 (Laurel and Hardy)
Busted Hearts. See Those Love Pangs, 1914
Busted Johnny. See Making a Living, 1914
Buster, 1988 (Quayle)
Buster Keaton Story, 1957 (Lorre; O'Connor)
Buster se marie, 1929 (Rosay)
Buster's Bedroom, 1990 (Chaplin, G.; Sutherland)
Buster's Last Stand. See His Ex Marks the Spot, 1940
Bustin' Loose, 1981 (Pryor)
Busting, 1974 (Gould)
Busy Bodies, 1933 (Laurel and Hardy)
Busy Body, 1967 (Baxter; Pryor; Ryan, R.)
Busy Buddies, 1944 (Three Stooges)
Busy Day, 1914 (Chaplin, C.)
But Not for Me, 1959 (Cobb; Gable)
But the Flesh Is Weak, 1932 (Horton; Montgomery)
Butai sugata, 1940 (Tanaka)
Butch Cassidy and the Sundance Kid, 1969 (Newman; Redford)
Butch Minds the Baby, 1942 (Crawford, B.; Three Stooges)
Butcher. See **Boucher**, 1970
Butcher Boy, 1917 (Arbuckle)
Butcher Boy, 1917 (Keaton, B.)
Butcher's Wife, 1991 (Moore, Demi; Steenburgen)
Butley, 1974 (Bates, A.)
Butterfield 8, 1960 (Taylor, E.)
Butterflies Are Free, 1972 (Hawn)
Butterfly, 1982 (Welles)
Butterfly Affair. See Popsy Pop, 1971
Butterfly Ball, 1976 (Price)
Butterfly's Dream. See Sogno della farfalla, 1994
Buy & Cell, 1988 (McDowell)
Buzzin' Around, 1933 (Arbuckle)
By Candlelight, 1934 (Lukas)
By Dawn's Early Light, 1990 (Jones, James Earl; Landau)
By Hook or by Crook. See I Dood It, 1943
By Indian Post, 1919 (Carey)
By Love Possessed, 1961 (Robards; Sloane; Turner, L.)
By Right of Purchase, 1918 (Talmadge)
By the Light of the Silvery Moon, 1953 (Day)
By the Sad Sea Waves, 1917 (Lloyd)
By the Sea, 1915 (Chaplin, C.; Purviance)
By the Sun's Rays, 1914 (Chaney)

By Your Leave, 1934 (Grable)
Byakko-tai, 1927 (Tanaka)
Byakuran no uta, 1939 (Hasegawa)
Byakuya no kyoen, 1932 (Yamada)
Bye-Bye Birdie, 1963 (Leigh, Janet; Ann-Margret)
Bye-Bye Braverman, 1968 (Segal)
Bye-Bye Monkey. *See* Ciao maschio, 1978
Bye-Bye Red Riding Hood. *See* Piroska és a farkas, 1988
Byosai monogatari: Aya ni kanashiki, 1956 (Tanaka; Yamada)
C-Man, 1949 (Carradine)
C.A.S.H. *See* Whiffs, 1975
C.A.S.H.: A Political Fairy Tale. *See* Märchen der Gebruder Nimm
    Schweinegold, 1989
C.C. and Company, 1970 (Ann-Margret)
C.I.D., 1956 (Anand)
Ça aussi c'est Paris, 1930 (Fresnay)
Ça colle, 1933 (Fernandel)
Ça n'arrive qu'a moi, 1985 (Blier)
Ça n'arrive qu'aux autres, 1971 (Deneuve; Mastroianni)
Ça va barder!, 1955 (Constantine)
Ça va etre ta fête, 1961 (Constantine)
Caballero a la medida, 1953 (Cantinflas)
Caballero del dragon, 1985 (Keitel; Kinski; Rey)
Cabane aux souvenirs, 1946 (Vanel)
Cabaret, 1953 (Rey)
Cabaret, 1972 (Minnelli)
Cabaret du grand large, 1946 (Hayakawa)
Cabaret Singer, 1912-13 (White)
Cabin in the Cotton, 1932 (Barthelmess; Davis, B.)
Cabinet of Dr. Caligari. *See* **Kabinett des Dr. Caligari**, 1920
Cabiria. *See* Notti di Cabiria, 1956
Cable Car Murders. *See* Cross Current, 1971
Caboblanco, 1979 (Bronson; Rey; Robards; Sanda)
Caccia alla volpe, 1966 (Mature; Sellers)
Cachao ... como su ritmo no hay dos, 1993 (Duvall; García)
Cache. *See* Battant, 1982
Cactus, 1986 (Huppert)
Cactus Flower, 1969 (Bergman; Hawn; Matthau)
Cactus Jack. *See* Villain, 1979
Cactus Jack Heartbreaker, 1914 (Mix)
Cactus Jim's Shopgirl, 1915 (Mix)
Cactus Makes Perfect, 1942 (Three Stooges)
Cactus Nell, 1917 (Beery)
Cadaveri eccelenti, 1975 (Cuny; Rey; Vanel; Von Sydow)
Caddy, 1953 (Lewis, Jerry; Martin, D.)
Caddy's Dream, 1911 (Pickford)
Caddyshack, 1980 (Murray)
Cadeau, 1982 (Cardinale)
Cadence, 1989 (Fishburne; Sheen)
Cadet Girl, 1941 (Ladd)
Cadets de l'océan, 1941 (Gélin)
Cadillac Man, 1990 (Robbins; Williams, R.)
Caduta degli angeli ribelli, 1981 (Valli)
Caduta degli dei, 1969 (Bogarde; Thulin)
Caesar and Cleopatra, 1946 (Granger; Kendall; Leigh, V.; Rains)
Caf' Conc 1954, 1954 (Chevalier)
Cafe au lait. *See* Metisse, 1993
Café Colón de la Cerna, 1958 (Armendáriz; Felix)
Café de Paris, 1938 (Berry; Brasseur)
Café du Cadran, 1946 (Blier)
Café Electric, 1927 (Dietrich)
Café Metropole, 1937 (Menjou; Power; Young, L.)
Cafc Socicty, 1939 (Carroll; MacMurray)
Café tabac, 1965 (Piccoli)
Cage, 1975 (Thulin)
Cage aux Folles 3: The Wedding, 1985 (Audran)
Cage of Gold, 1950 (Lom)
Caged, 1950 (Moorehead)
Cagliostro, 1949 (Mangano)
Cagna, 1972 (Deneuve; Mastroianni; Piccoli)
Cahill, United States Marshal, 1973 (Wayne)

Caïd, 1960 (Fernandel)
Caïds, 1972 (Reggiani)
Caimano del Piave, 1950 (Cervi)
Cain and Mabel, 1936 (Davies; Gable; Wyman)
Cain's Cutthroats, 1970 (Carradine)
Cain's Way. *See* Cain's Cutthroats, 1970
Caine Mutiny, 1954 (Bogart; Ferrer; MacMurray; Marvin)
Cairo, 1942 (Young, R.; MacDonald)
Cairo, 1963 (Sanders)
Caissière du Grand Cafe, 1946 (Fernandel)
Cake Eater, 1924 (Rogers, W.)
Cal, 1984 (Mirren)
Calamity Jane, 1953 (Day)
Calaveras del terror, Guadalajara, 1943 (Armendáriz)
Calcutta, 1947 (Ladd)
Calendar, 1931 (Marshall)
Calendar, 1948 (Dors)
Calendar Girl, 1947 (McLaglen)
Calendar Girl Murders, 1984 (Stone)
Calibre 44, 1959 (Armendáriz)
Califfa, 1971 (Schneider)
California, 1946 (Fitzgerald; Milland; Quinn; Stanwyck)
California Conquest, 1952 (Wilde)
California Dolls. *See* ...All the Marbles, 1981
California Kid, 1974 (Nolte; Sheen)
California Romance, 1922 (Gilbert)
California Split, 1974 (Gould; Segal)
California Straight Ahead, 1937 (Wayne)
California Suite, 1978 (Caine; Fonda, J.; Matthau; Pryor; Smith)
Caligula, 1980 (Gielgud; McDowell; Mirren; O'Toole)
Call from Home, 1912-13 (White)
Call from Space, 1989 (Coburn, J.)
Call Harry Crown. *See* 99 and 44/100 Per Cent Dead, 1974
Call Her Mom, 1971 (Charisse)
Call Her Savage, 1932 (Bow)
Call Him Mr. Shatter, 1975 (Cushing)
Call It a Day, 1937 (De Havilland)
Call Me Anna, 1990 (Malden)
Call Me Bwana, 1963 (Hope)
Call Me Genius. *See* Rebel, 1960
Call Me Madam, 1953 (O'Connor; Sanders)
Call Me Mister, 1951 (Grable)
Call Northside 777, 1948 (Cobb; Ritter; Stewart)
Call of Her People, 1917 (Barrymore, E.)
Call of the Blood. *See* Appel du sang, 1920
Call of the Canyon, 1942 (Autry)
Call of the Cuckoos, 1927 (Laurel and Hardy)
Call of the East, 1917 (Hayakawa)
Call of the Flesh, 1930 (Dressler; Novarro)
Call of the Road, 1920 (McLaglen)
Call of the Song, 1911 (Pickford)
Call of the Wild, 1935 (Gable; Young, L.)
Call of the Wild, 1972 (Heston)
Call Out the Marines, 1942 (McLaglen)
Call the Cops! *See* Find the Lady, 1976
Call to Arms, 1910 (Pickford)
Call to Glory, 1966 (Van Cleef)
Callahans and the Murphys, 1927 (Dressler)
Callaway Went Thataway, 1951 (Gable; MacMurray; Taylor, E.; Williams, E.)
Caller, 1989 (McDowell)
Callie & Son, 1981 (Pfeiffer)
Calling All Curs, 1939 (Three Stooges)
Calling All Tars, 1936 (Hope)
Calling Bulldog Drummond, 1951 (Pidgeon)
Calling Dr. Gillespie, 1942 (Barrymore, L.; Gardner)
Calling Dr. Kildare, 1939 (Ayres; Barrymore, L.; Turner, L.)
Calling the Shots, 1988 (Moreau; Zetterling)
Calm Yourself, 1935 (Young, R.)
Calmos, 1975 (Blier)
Calvert's Folly. *See* Calvert's Valley, 1922
Calvert's Valley, 1922 (Gilbert)

Calypso Joe, 1957 (Dickinson)
Camarades. *See* I compagni, 1963
Cambiale, 1959 (Gassman)
Cambio de Sexo, 1976 (Abril)
Cambio della guardia, 1962 (Cervi)
Camelia, 1953 (Félix)
Camelot, 1967 (Harris, R.; Redgrave, V.)
Cameo Kirby, 1923 (Arthur; Gilbert; Loy)
Camera d'albergo, 1980 (Gassman; Vitti)
Cameraman, 1928 (Keaton, B.)
Cameriera bella presenza offrersi, 1951 (Cervi; Masina; Fabrizi; Sordi)
Camicie rosse, 1951 (Cuny; Reggiani; Magnani)
Camille, 1915 (Gordon)
Camille, 1917 (Bara)
Camille, 1919 (Negri)
Camille, 1921 (Nazimova; Valentino)
Camille, 1927 (Talmadge)
Camille, 1937 (Barrymore, L.; Garbo; Taylor, R.)
Camille, 1984 (Elliott; Gielgud; Kingsley: Scacchi)
Camille. *See* Dame aux camélias, 1934
Camille Claudel, 1988 (Adjani; Cuny; Depardieu)
Camille without Camelias. *See* Signora senza camelie, 1953
Camino de infierno, 1950 (Armendáriz)
Camion, 1977 (Depardieu)
Camion blanc, 1943 (Berry)
Camorra, 1972 (Seberg; Vanel)
Camorra, 1986 (Keitel)
Camp Nowhere, 1994 (Meredith)
Campagne electorale, 1909 (Linder)
Campana de mi pueblo, 1944 (Armendáriz)
Campanadas a medianoche. *See* **Chimes at Midnight**, 1966
Campane a martello, 1949 (Lollobrigida)
Campbell's Kingdom, 1957 (Baker; Bogarde)
Camping, 1919 (Arbuckle)
Campo dei fiori, 1943 (Fabrizi; Magnani)
Campus a Go-Go. *See* Eriki no wakadaisho, 1966
Campus Carmen, 1928 (Lombard)
Campus Cinderella, 1938 (Hayward)
Campus Confession, 1938 (Grable)
Campus Sweethearts, 1930 (Rogers, G.)
Can This Be Dixie?, 1936 (McDaniel)
Canadian Bacon, 1994 (Candy)
Canadian Conspiracy, 1986 (Candy)
Canadian Pacific, 1949 (Scott, R.)
Canadians, 1961 (Ryan, R.)
Canary Murder Case, 1929 (Arthur; Brooks, L.; Powell, W.)
Canasta de cuentos mexicanos, 1956 (Armendáriz; Félix)
Canby Hill Outlaws, 1916 (Mix)
Can-Can, 1960 (Chevalier; Dalio; Jourdan; MacLaine; Sidney)
Cancel My Reservation, 1972 (Bellamy; Crosby)
Cancel My Reservation, 1972 (Hope; Saint; Wayne)
Candidat, 1991 (Gélin)
Candidate, 1972 (Crawford, B.; Douglas, Melvyn; Redford; Wood)
Candidate for a Killing. *See* Candidato per un assassino, 1969
Candidato per un assassino, 1969 (Rey)
Candide, 1960 (Brasseur; Cassel)
Candle in the Wind. *See* Fuzen no tomoshibi, 1957
Candlelight in Algeria, 1943 (Mason)
Candles in the Dark, 1993 (Schell, Maximilian)
Candleshoe, 1977 (Foster; Niven)
Candy, 1968 (Brando; Burton; Coburn, J.; Huston, J.; Matthau)
Candy Kid, 1917 (Laurel and Hardy)
Candy Man, 1969 (Sanders)
Candy Trail, 1916 (Laurel and Hardy)
Canicule, 1983 (Marvin)
Cannery Row, 1982 (Huston, J.; Nolte; Winger)
Cannibal Attack, 1954 (Weissmuller)
Cannibal King, 1915 (Laurel and Hardy)
Cannonball, 1976 (Stallone)
Cannonball Fever. *See* Speed Zone!, 1989
Cannonball Run, 1981 (Chan; Martin, D.; Reynolds, B.)

Cannonball Run II, 1984 (Chan; MacLaine; Martin, D.; Reynolds, B.; Sidney)
Can't Help Singing, 1944 (Durbin)
Cantata de Chile, 1975 (Villagra)
Canterbury Tales. *See* I Racconti di Canterbury, 1971
Canterville Ghost, 1944 (Gielgud; Laughton; O'Brien, M.; Young, R.)
Cantiflas boxeador, 1940 (Cantinflas)
Cantiflas ruletero, 1940 (Cantinflas)
Cantiflas y su prima, 1940 (Cantinflas)
Canto a mi tierra, 1938 (Armendáriz)
Canto della vita, 1945 (Valli)
Canyon of Light, 1926 (Mix)
Canyon of the Fools, 1923 (Carey)
Canyon Pass. *See* Raton Pass, 1951
Canyon Passage, 1946 (Andrews, D.; Bond; Hayward)
Canzone di Werner, 1914 (Bertini)
Canzoni, canzoni, canzoni, 1953 (Sordi)
Cap de l'Espérance, 1951 (Feuillère)
Capable Lady Cook, 1916 (Beery)
Cape Fear, 1962 (Mitchum; Peck)
Cape Fear, 1991 (De Niro; Lange; Lewis, Juliette; Mitchum; Nolte; Peck)
Capello a tre punte, 1935 (Valli)
Capestro degli Asburgo, 1915 (Bertini)
Capetown Affair, 1967 (Trevor)
Capitaine Corsaire. *See* Mollenard, 1938
Capitaine Fracassé, 1927 (Boyer)
Capitaine Fracasse, 1961 (Marais; Noiret)
Capitaine jaune, 1930 (Vanel)
Capitaine Mollenard. *See* Mollenard, 1938
Capital Punishment, 1925 (Bow)
Capitan Malacara, 1944 (Armendáriz)
Capone, 1975 (Stallone)
Caporal épinglé, 1962 (Cassel)
Cappucetto rosso, Cenerentola ... et voi ci credete, 1972 (Brazzi)
Capriccio all'italiana, 1968 (Mangano)
Caprice, 1913 (Pickford)
Caprice, 1967 (Day; Harris, R.)
Caprices, 1941 (Blier; Darrieux)
Caprices de Marie, 1970 (Noiret)
Capricious Summer. *See* Rozmarné léto, 1968
Capricorn One, 1978 (Gould)
Captain Apache, 1971 (Van Cleef)
Captain Bandeira vs. Dr. Moura, 1970 (Braga)
Captain Barnacle's Messmate, 1912 (Talmadge)
Captain Blackjack, 1949 (Dalio; Moorehead; Sanders)
Captain Blood, 1935 (De Havilland; Flynn; Rathbone)
Captain Boycott, 1947 (Donat; Granger)
Captain Carey U.S.A., 1950 (Ladd)
Captain Caution, 1940 (Ladd; Mature)
Captain Clegg, 1962 (Cushing; Reed)
Captain Eddie, 1945 (MacMurray)
Captain Eo, 1986 (Huston, A.)
Captain from Castile, 1947 (Cobb; Power)
Captain Fury, 1939 (Carradine; Lukas; McLaglen)
Captain Grant's Children. *See* Deti kapitana Granta, 1936
Captain Hates the Sea, 1934 (Gilbert; McLaglen; Three Stooges)
Captain Horatio Hornblower, 1951 (Baker; Lee, C.; Peck)
Captain Is a Lady, 1940 (Coburn, C.)
Captain James Cook, 1988 (Rey)
Captain January, 1936 (Carradine; Temple)
Captain Kate, 1911 (Mix)
Captain Kidd, 1945 (Carradine; Laughton; Scott, R.)
Captain Kidd, Jr., 1919 (Pickford)
Captain Kidd's Kids, 1919 (Lloyd)
Captain Lash, 1929 (McLaglen)
Captain Lightfoot, 1955 (Hudson)
Captain Macklin, 1915 (Gish)
Captain Nemo and the Underwater City, 1970 (Ryan, R.)
Captain Newman, M.D., 1963 (Curtis, T.; Dickinson; Duvall; Peck)
Captain Sinbad, 1963 (Armendáriz)
Captain Thunder, 1931 (Wray)
Captain Yankee. *See* Jungle Raiders, 1985

Captain's Paradise, 1953 (Guinness; Johnson)
Captains Courageous, 1937 (Barrymore, L.; Carradine; Douglas, Melvyn; Rooney; Tracy)
Captains Courageous, 1977 (Malden)
Captains of the Clouds, 1942 (Cagney)
Captiva Island, 1995 (Borgnine)
Captivating Enemy. See Incantevole nemica, 1952
Captivating Mary Carstairs, 1915 (Talmadge)
Captive, 1915 (Sweet)
Captive, 1986 (Reed)
Captive City. See Citta prigioniera, 1962
Captive Girl, 1950 (Weissmuller)
Captive God, 1916 (Hart)
Captive Heart, 1946 (Redgrave, M.)
Captive Heart: The James Mink Story, 1996 (Nelligan)
Captive Rage, 1988 (Reed)
Captive Wild Woman, 1943 (Carradine)
Capture, 1950 (Ayres)
Captured!, 1933 (Howard, L.; Lukas)
Car Ninety-Nine, 1935 (MacMurray)
Car of Dreams, 1935 (Mills)
Car Wash, 1976 (DeVito; Pryor)
Cara a Cara. See Faccia a faccia, 1967
Cara del terror, 1962 (Rey)
Carambolages, 1962 (Delon)
Caravan, 1934 (Boyer; Young, L.)
Caravan, 1946 (Granger)
Caravane, 1934 (Brasseur)
Caravans, 1978 (Cotten; Lee, C.; Quinn)
Carbine Williams, 1952 (Stewart)
Carbon Copy, 1981 (Segal; Washington)
Cárcel de Cananca, 1960 (Armendáriz)
Card, 1952 (Guinness)
Cardboard Cavalier, 1949 (Lockwood)
Cardboard City. See Ciudad de carton, 1933
Cardigan's Last Case. See State's Attorney, 1932
Cardinal, 1963 (Huston, J.; Meredith; Schneider)
Cardinal Richelieu, 1935 (Carradine; O'Sullivan)
Cardinal's Conspiracy, 1909 (Pickford)
Cardinale Lambertini, 1955 (Cervi)
Cards on the Table. See Cartas boca arriba, 1965
Care Bears Movie, 1985 (Rooney; Stanton)
Career, 1959 (MacLaine; Martin, D.)
Career Opportunities, 1991 (Candy)
Career Woman, 1936 (Trevor)
Carefree, 1938 (Astaire; Bellamy; Rogers, G.)
Careless Age, 1929 (Young, L.)
Careless Lady, 1932 (Bennett)
Careless Love. See Bonne Soupe, 1963
Caretaker, 1963 (Bates, A.; Pleasence; Shaw)
Caretakers, 1963 (Crawford, J.; Marshall)
Carey Treatment, 1972 (Coburn, J.)
Cargaison blanche, 1936 (Berry; Dalio)
Cargo, 1990 (Villagra)
Cargo of Innocents. See Stand by for Action, 1942
Cargo to Capetown, 1950 (Crawford, B.)
Cariboo Trail, 1950 (Scott, R.)
Carlito's Way, 1993 (Pacino; Penn)
Carlos, 1971 (Chaplin, G.; Karina)
Carlos und Elisabeth, 1924 (Veidt)
Carlton-Browne of the F.O., 1958 (Sellers; Terry-Thomas)
Carmen, 1915 (Bara)
Carmen, 1916 (Chaplin, C.)
Carmen, 1918 (Negri)
Carmen, 1926 (Modot)
Carmen, 1943 (Marais)
Carmen, Baby, 1967 (Kinski)
Carmen Comes Home. See Karemen Kyoko ni kaeru, 1951
Carmen Miranda: Bananas Is My Business, 1994 (Faye)
Carmen von St. Pauli, 1928 (Rasp)
Carmen's Pure Love. See Karumen Junjo su, 1951

Carmilla, 1990 (McDowall)
Carnal Knowledge, 1971 (Ann-Margret; Nicholson)
Carnaval, 1953 (Fernandel)
Carne de horca, 1954 (Brazzi)
Carne de presidio, 1952 (Armendáriz)
Carnet de bal, 1937 (Fernandel; Jouvet; Raimu; Rosay)
Carnival, 1921 (McLaglen; Novello)
Carnival, 1935 (Ball; Durante)
Carnival. See Karneval, 1961
Carnival Boat, 1932 (Rogers, G.)
Carnival in Costa Rica, 1947 (Cobb)
Carnival Man, 1929 (Huston, W.)
Carnival of Killers. See Spie contro il mondo, 1966
Carnival of Sinners. See Main du diable, 1942
Carnival Story, 1954 (Baxter)
Carny, 1980 (Foster)
Caro Gorbaciov, 1988 (Keitel)
Caro Michele, 1976 (Seyrig)
Caro papà, 1979 (Gassman)
Carol for Another Christmas, 1964 (Hayden; Saint; Shaw)
Carola, 1975 (Caron)
Carolina, 1934 (Barrymore, L.; Gaynor; Temple; Young, R.)
Carolina Blues, 1944 (Miller)
Carolina Moon, 1940 (Autry)
Carolina Skeletons, 1991 (Dern)
Caroline?, 1990 (Neal)
Caroline chérie, 1967 (Blier)
Caronna nera. See Corona negra, 1952
Carosella napolitano, 1953 (Loren)
Carosello di varietà, 1955 (Fabrizi)
Carpenter, 1922 (Laurel and Hardy)
Carpetbaggers, 1963 (Ayres; Ladd)
Carpool, 1983 (Borgnine)
Carquake. See Cannonball, 1976
Carradines in Concert, 1980 (Carradine)
Carrefour, 1938 (Berry; Vanel)
Carrefour de passion. See Uomini sono nemici, 1948
Carrefour des enfants perdus, 1943 (Reggiani)
Carrie, 1951 (Hopkins, M.; Jones, Jennifer; Olivier)
Carrie, 1976 (Spacek; Travolta)
Carried Away, 1996 (Hopper)
Carrington, 1995 (Thompson)
Carrington, V.C., 1954 (Niven)
Carrosse d'or, 1953 (Magnani)
Carry Harry, 1942 (Langdon)
Carson City, 1952 (Massey; Scott, R.)
Carson City Kid, 1940 (Rogers, R.)
Cartagine in fiamme, 1959 (Brasseur; Cervi; Gélin)
Cartas boca arriba, 1965 (Rey)
Cartas marcadas, 1947 (Infante)
Carte du Tendre. See **Map of the Human Heart**, 1993
Carter's Army, 1970 (Pryor)
Cartes sur table, 1965 (Constantine; Rey)
Carthage in Flames. See Cartagine in fiamme, 1960
Cartouche, 1962 (Belmondo; Cardinale; Dalio)
Carve Her Name with Pride, 1958 (Aimée; Caine)
Cas de conscience, 1939 (Berry)
Cas de malheur, 1958 (Bardot; Feuillère; Gabin)
Cas du docteur Laurent, 1956 (Gabin)
Casa chica, 1950 (Del Rio)
Casa colorado, 1947 (Armendáriz)
Casa de mujeres, 1966 (Del Rio)
Casa del peccato, 1938 (Valli)
Casa del sorriso, 1988 (Thulin)
Casa del tappeto giallo, 1983 (Josephson)
Casa dell'exorcismo. See Lisa e il diavolo, 1972
Casa Ricordi, 1954 (Mastroianni; Presle)
Casa sin fronteras, 1972 (Chaplin, G.)
Casablanca, 1942 (Bergman; Bogart; Dalio; Greenstreet; Henreid; Lorre; Rains; Veidt)
Casablanca, Casablanca, 1984 (Olbrychski)

Casablanca Express, 1989 (Ford, G.)
Casanova, 1927 (Mozhukin)
Casanova, 1976 (Sutherland; Cassel)
Casanova, 1987 (Dunaway; Schygulla)
Casanova '70, 1965 (Mastroianni)
Casanova & Co., 1977 (Curtis, T.)
Casanova Brown, 1944 (Constantine)
Casanova farebbe cosi, 1942 (Sordi)
Casanova in Burlesque, 1944 (Brown)
Casanova's Bad Night, 1954 (Rathbone)
Casanova's Big Night, 1954 (Carradine; Fontaine; Hope; Price)
Casanova's Return. See Retour de Casanova, 1992
Casanove wider willen, 1931 (Rosay)
Casbah, 1948 (Lorre)
Case against Ferro, 1980 (Montand)
Case against Mrs. Ames, 1936 (Carroll)
Case de malheur, 1958 (Cassel)
Case Dismissed, 1924 (Arthur)
Case of Becky, 1915 (Sweet)
Case of Colonel Redl. See Fall des Generalstabsoberst Redl, 1931
Case of Gabriel Perry, 1935 (Lockwood)
Case of Irresponsibility. See Caso di incoscienza, 1984
Case of the Curious Bride, 1935 (Flynn)
Case of the Howling Dog, 1934 (Astor)
Case of the Mukkinese Battlehorn, 1955 (Sellers)
Casey at the Bat, 1912 (Talmadge)
Casey at the Bat, 1927 (Beery)
Casey's Shadow, 1978 (Matthau)
Cash, 1933 (Donat)
Cash and Carry, 1937 (Three Stooges)
Cash McCall, 1959 (Garner; Wood)
Cash on Delivery. See To Dorothy, a Son, 1956
Cash on Demand, 1961 (Cushing)
Cash Parrish's Pal, 1915 (Hart)
Casimir, 1950 (Fernandel)
Casino, 1980 (Cotten)
Casino, 1995 (De Niro; Pesci; Stone; Woods)
Casino de Paree. See Go into Your Dance, 1935
Casino Murder Case, 1935 (Lukas; Russell, R.)
Casino Royale, 1966 (Raft; Allen; Belmondo; Boyer; Holden; Huston, J.; Kerr; Niven; O'Toole; Sellers; Welles)
Caso Almería, 1984 (Banderas)
Caso Cerrado, 1985 (Banderas)
Caso d'incoscienza, 1984 (Josephson; Vogler)
Caso Mattei, 1971 (Volonté)
Caso Moro, 1986 (Volonté)
Caso Raoul, 1975 (Valli)
Casotto, 1977 (Deneuve; Foster)
Casper, 1995 (Eastwood; Gibson)
Casque Bleu, 1994 (Abril; Cassel; Presle)
Casque d'or, 1951 (Modot; Reggiani)
Cass Timberlane, 1947 (Astor; Pidgeon; Tracy; Turner, L.)
Cassandra Crossing, 1977 (Gardner; Harris, R.; Lancaster; Loren; Sheen; Thulin; Valli)
Casse, 1971 (Belmondo; Sharif)
Casse-pieds, 1948 (Blier)
Cast a Dark Shadow, 1955 (Bogarde; Lockwood)
Cast a Giant Shadow, 1966 (Brynner; Dickinson; Douglas, K.; Douglas, Michael; Sidney; Topol; Wayne)
Cast Iron. See Virtuous Sin, 1929
Cast the First Stone, 1989 (Ayres)
Casta e pura, 1981 (Rey)
Castaway, 1986 (Reed)
Castaway Cowboys, 1974 (Garner)
Castello dei morti viva, 1964 (Lee, C.; Sutherland)
Castello delle donne maledotti. See House of Freaks, 1973
Castello di paura, 1972 (Brazzi)
Castiglione, 1954 (Brazzi)
Castilian, 1962 (Crawford, B.)
Castilian. See Valle de las espadas, 1963
Castle, 1991 (Jackson, G.; Sharif)

Castle. See Schloss, 1968
Castle in the Air, 1952 (Rutherford)
Castle Keep, 1969 (Dern; Falk; Lancaster)
Castle of Fu Manchu, 1970 (Lee, C.)
Castle of Terror. See Vergine de Norimberga, 1964
Castle of the Living Dead. See Castello dei morti vivi, 1964
Castle of the Spider's Web. See Kumonosu-jo, 1957
Castle on the Hudson, 1940 (Garfield; Meredith)
Castle without a Name, 1920 (Lukas)
Castrophe 1999. See Nostoradamusu no daiyogen, 1974
Casualties of War, 1989 (Penn)
Cat. See Chatte, 1958
Cat and Mouse. See Chat et la souris, 1975
Cat and Mouse. See Mousey, 1974
Cat and the Canary, 1939 (Goddard; Hope)
Cat and the Fiddle, 1934 (MacDonald; Novarro)
Cat Ballou, 1965 (Fonda, J.; Marvin)
Cat Creature, 1973 (Carradine)
Cat from Outer Space, 1978 (McDowall; McDowell)
Cat o' Nine Tails. See Gatto a nove code, 1969
Cat on a Hot Tin Roof, 1958 (Newman; Taylor, E.; Olivier; Wood)
Cat on a Hot Tin Roof, 1984 (Jones, T.; Lange)
Cat People, 1982 (Kinski; McDowell)
Cat, Shozo, and the Two Women. See Neko to Shozo to futaru no onna, 1956
Catacombs, 1965 (Andrews, D.)
Catastrophe 1999. See Nostoradamusu no daiyogen, 1974
Catch-22, 1970 (Arkin; Dalio; Perkins; Sheen; Voight; Welles)
Catch as Catch Can, 1937 (Mason; Rutherford)
Catch as Catch Can. See Lo scatenato, 1967
Catch Me a Spy, 1971 (Blier; Douglas, K.; Howard, T.)
Catch My Smoke, 1922 (Mix)
Catch the Heat, 1987 (Steiger)
Catcher, 1972 (Baxter)
Catchfire. See Backtrack, 1989
Catene invisibili, 1942 (Valli)
Catered Affair, 1956 (Borgnine; Davis, B.; Fitzgerald; Reynolds, D.)
Catherine and I. See Io e Caterina, 1981
Catherine the Great. See Katherina die Grosse, 1920
Catherine the Great, 1934 (Bergner)
Catholic Boys. See Heaven Help Us, 1985
Catholics, 1973 (Cusack; Howard, T.; Sheen)
Catlow, 1971 (Brynner)
Cats. See Kattorna, 1965
Cats. See I bastardi, 1969
Cats. See Sons of Satan, 1971
Cat's Eye, 1985 (Woods)
Cat's Meow, 1924 (Langdon)
Cat's Paw, 1934 (Lloyd)
Cattiva, 1991 (Josephson)
Cattle Annie and Little Britches, 1979 (Lancaster; Steiger)
Cattle Drive, 1951 (McCrea)
Cattle Empire, 1958 (McCrea)
Cattle King, 1963 (Taylor, R.)
Cattle Queen of Montana, 1954 (Reagan; Stanwyck)
Cattle Thief, 1936 (Bond)
Catwalk, 1995 (Stone)
Cauchemar de Max, 1910 (Linder)
Caught, 1949 (Mason; Ryan, R.)
Caught, 1996 (Olmos)
Caught in a Cabaret, 1914 (Chaplin, C.; Normand)
Caught in a Flue, 1914 (Arbuckle)
Caught in the Act, 1912-13 (White)
Caught in the Draft, 1941 (Hope; Lamour)
Caught in the Rain, 1914 (Chaplin, C.)
Caught Short, 1930 (Dressler)
Cauldron of Blood. See Blind Man's Bluff, 1967
Cause Celebre, 1987 (Mirren)
Cause for Alarm, 1951 (Young, L.)
Cause for Concern, 1974 (Howard, T.)
Cause toujours ... tu m'intéresses!, 1979 (Girardot)
Cause toujours, mon lapin, 1961 (Constantine)

Cavalcade, 1933 (Grable)
Cavalcade des heures, 1943 (Fernandel)
Cavalcade of Academy Awards, 1940 (Jolson)
Cavalcade of Stars, 1938 (Buchanan)
Cavalcade of the Academy Awards, 1941 (Barrymore, L.)
Cavale des Fous, 1993 (Piccoli)
Cavaleur, 1978 (Darrieux; Girardot)
Cavalier Lafleur, 1934 (Fernandel)
Cavalier of the West, 1931 (Carey)
Cavaliere Costante Nicosia indemontiato ovvero Dracula in Brianza, 1975
    (Brazzi)
Cavaliere misterioso, 1948 (Gassman)
Cavaliers on the Road. See Motorkavalierer, 1950
Cavalleria, 1936 (Magnani)
Cavalleria Rusticana, 1953 (Quinn)
Cavallina storna, 1953 (Cervi)
Cave Girl, 1921 (Karloff)
Cave In!, 1979 (Milland)
Cave Man, 1926 (Loy)
Cave of Sharks. See Bermuda: la fossa maledetta, 1978
Cave se rebiffe, 1961 (Blier; Gabin; Rosay)
Caveman, 1981 (Quaid)
Caveman. See His Prehistoric Past, 1914
Caves of Steel, 1967 (Cushing)
Cayenne-Palace, 1987 (Karina)
Ce cher Victor, 1975 (Blier)
Ce coquin d'Anatole, 1951 (Modot)
Ce corps tant désiré, 1957 (Gélin)
Ce qu'on dit, ce qu'on pense, 1930 (Brasseur)
Ce siècle a cinquante ans, 1950 (Fresnay)
Ce soir ou jamais, 1961 (Karina)
Cecilia of the Pink Roses, 1917 (Davies)
Cecilia Valdés, 1982 (Villagra)
Ceiling Zero, 1935 (Cagney)
Cela s'appelle l'aurore, 1955 (Modot)
Celebrity Art Portfolio, 1974 (Novak)
Cell Block Girls. See Thunder County, 1974
Celluloid, 1995 (Giannini)
Celluloid Closet, 1994 (Curtis, T.; Goldberg; Hanks; MacLaine)
Celui qui doit mourir, 1957 (Mercouri)
Cemetery Club, 1993 (Aiello; Burstyn)
Cent Dollars mort ou vif, 1909 (Modot)
Cent et une nuits, 1995 (Aimée; Belmondo; Delon; Deneuve; De Niro;
    Depardieu; Ford, H.; Léaud; Lollobrigida; Mastroianni; Moreau; Piccoli;
    Schygulla; Sheen; Stanton)
Cent mille dollars au soleil, 1963 (Belmondo; Blier)
Centennial Summer, 1946 (Brennan; Darnell; Wilde)
Center of the Web, 1992 (Curtis, T.)
Cento anni d'amore, 1953 (Chevalier; Fabrizi; Masina)
Central Airport, 1933 (Barthelmess; Wayne)
Central Park, 1932 (Blondell)
Century, 1993 (Richardson, M.)
C'era un Castello con 40 Cani, 1990 (Ustinov)
C'era una volta, 1967 (Del Rio; Loren; Sharif)
C'era una volta Angelo Musco, 1953 (Brazzi)
C'era una volta il West, 1968 (Bronson; Cardinale; Fonda, H.; Robards)
C'eravamo tanti amati, 1974 (Fabrizi; Gassman; Mastroianni)
Cercasi Gesu, 1982 (Rey)
Cercel des passions, 1983 (Von Sydow)
Cercle rouge, 1969 (Delon; Montand; Volonté)
Ceremonie, 1995 (Cassel; Huppert)
Ceremony, 1963 (Rey)
Certain Desire. See Flagrant Desire, 1985
Certain Smile, 1958 (Brazzi; Fontaine)
Certain, Very Certain, as a Matter of Fact ... Probable. See Certo, certissimo
    ... anzi probabile, 1970
Certain Young Man, 1928 (Novarro)
Certaine Charme, 1990 (Bujold)
Certaines nouvelles, 1976 (Presle)
Certo, certissimo ... anzi probabile, 1970 (Cardinale)
Cervantes. See Avventure e gli amori di Miguel Cervantes, 1968

Cerveau, 1969 (Belmondo; Niven; Wallach)
Ces dames preferent le Mambo, 1958 (Constantine)
Ces dames s'en melent, 1965 (Constantine)
Ces messieurs de la santé, 1933 (Feuillère; Raimu)
César, 1936 (Fresnay; Raimu)
César et Rosalie, 1972 (Huppert; Montand; Piccoli; Schneider)
C'est dur pour tout le monde, 1975 (Blier)
C'est la vie. See Baule-les-pins, 1990
C'est pas parce qu'on a rien à dire qu'il fermer sa gueule, 1974 (Blier)
Cet homme est dangereux, 1953 (Constantine)
Cet obscur objet de désir, 1977 (Rey)
Cette sacrée gamine, 1955 (Bardot)
Ceux du deuxième bureau. See Homme à abattre, 1937
Chacal de Nahueltoro, 1968 (Villagra)
Chacun sa chance, 1931 (Gabin)
Chad Hanna, 1940 (Carradine; Darnell; Fonda, H.; Lamour)
Chadwick Family, 1974 (MacMurray)
Chagall, 1963 (Price)
Chagrin et la pitié, 1971 (Chevalier)
Chaim—To Life!, 1974 (Wallach)
Chain Lightning, 1950 (Bogart; Massey)
Chain of Desire, 1993 (McDowell)
Chain Reaction, 1996 (Freeman; Reeves)
Chained, 1934 (Crawford, J.; Gable; Rooney)
Chaines d'or. See Anneaux d'or, 1956
Chains of Gold, 1991 (Travolta)
Chair de l'orchidée, 1974 (Feuillère; Valli)
Chair et le diable. See Fuco nelle vene, 1953
Chairman. See Most Dangerous Man in the World, 1969
Chairs, 1962 (Cusack)
Chakkari fujin to ukkari fujin, 1952 (Kagawa)
Chakra, 1980 (Patil)
Chaleur du sein, 1938 (Arletty)
Chalk Garden, 1964 (Evans; Kerr; Mills)
Challenge, 1960 (Quayle)
Challenge. See It Takes a Thief, 1961
Challenge. See Fireball, 1950
Challenge, 1970 (Crawford, B.; Lukas)
Challenge. See Challenge of Greatness, 1976
Challenge, 1982 (Mifune)
Challenge of Greatness, 1976 (Welles)
Challenge—Science against Cancer, 1950 (Massey)
Challenge to Lassie, 1949 (Crisp)
Challenger. See Lady and Gent, 1932
Challenger, 1990 (Bassett)
Challengers, 1970 (Baxter; Mineo)
Chamade, 1968 (Deneuve; Piccoli)
Chamber of Horrors, 1966 (Curtis, T.)
Chambre en ville, 1982 (Darrieux; Piccoli; Sanda)
Chambre verte, 1978 (Baye)
Chameleons, 1989 (Granger)
Champ, 1931 (Beery; Cooper)
Champ, 1979 (Blondell; Dunaway; Voight)
Champ of the Champs Elysées. See Roi des Champs Elysées, 1934
Champagne amer, 1985 (Christie)
Champagne Charlie, 1944 (Kendall)
Champagne Charlie, 1989 (Audran; Grant, H.)
Champagne Charlie. See Night Out, 1915
Champagne for Caesar, 1950 (Colman; Hayworth; Price)
Champagne Murders. See Scandale, 1967
Champagne Waltz, 1937 (MacMurray)
Champignon, 1969 (Valli)
Champion, 1913 (Normand)
Champion, 1915 (Chaplin, C.; Purviance)
Champion, 1949 (Douglas, K.; Kennedy)
Champions, 1983 (Hurt, J.)
Chamsin, 1972 (Schell, Maria)
Chanayaka Chandragupta, 1980 (Kumar)
Chance, 1931 (Rosay)
Chance at Heaven, 1933 (McCrea; Rogers, G.)
Chance Deception, 1913 (Sweet)

Chance et l'amour, 1964 (Blier; Chevalier; Piccoli)
Chance Meeting. *See* Blind Date, 1959
Chance to Live, 1990 (Hepburn, A.)
Chandler, 1971 (Caron; Grahame; Oates)
Chandu, the Magician, 1932 (Lugosi)
Chanel solitaire, 1981 (Caron)
Change, 1974 (Schell, Maria)
Change of Habit, 1969 (Presley)
Change of Heart, 1934 (Gaynor; Rogers, G.; Temple)
Change of Seasons, 1980 (Hopkins, A.; MacLaine)
Change of Spirit, 1912 (Sweet)
Changeling, 1979 (Douglas, Melvyn; Scott, G.)
Changeling, 1994 (Grant, H.; Hoskins)
Channachara, 1988 (Chatterjee)
Channing of the Northwest, 1922 (Shearer)
Chanson d'une nuit, 1932 (Brasseur)
Chanson de Roland, 1978 (Cuny; Kinski; Sanda)
Chant du départ. *See* Desert Song, 1943
Chant du monde, 1965 (Deneuve; Vanel)
Chantelouve, 1921 (Boyer)
Chanteur de Seville, 1930 (Novarro)
Chapeau-Claqué, 1909 (Linder)
Chapeau de Max, 1913 (Linder)
Chapeau de paille d'Italie, 1940 (Fernandel)
Chaplin, 1992 (Attenborough; Chaplin, G.; Hopkins, A.; Kline; Woods)
Chaplinesque, My Life and Hard Times, 1972 (Swanson)
Chapman Report, 1962 (Bloom; Fonda, J.; Winters)
Chappaqua, 1966 (Barrault)
Chapter Two, 1979 (Caan)
Charade, 1953 (Mason)
Charade, 1963 (Coburn, J.; Grant, C.; Hepburn, A.; Matthau)
Charge Is Murder. *See* Twilight of Honor, 1963
Charge of the Lancers, 1953 (Goddard)
Charge of the Light Brigade, 1936 (Crisp; De Havilland; Flynn; Niven)
Charge of the Light Brigade, 1968 (Gielgud; Howard, T.; Redgrave, V.)
Charing Cross Road, 1935 (Mills)
Chariots of Fire, 1981 (Gielgud)
Charité, 1927 (Vanel)
Charlemagne, 1933 (Raimu)
Charles and Diana: A Royal Love Story, 1982 (Lee, C.)
Charleston, 1977 (Lom)
Charley and the Angel, 1973 (MacMurray)
Charley's American Aunt. *See* Charley's Aunt, 1941
Charley's Aunt, 1915 (Laurel and Hardy)
Charley's Aunt, 1941 (Baxter; Francis)
Charley's Tante, 1934 (Rasp)
Charlie and the Sausage. *See* Mabel's Busy Day, 1914
Charlie and the Umbrella. *See* Between Showers, 1914
Charlie at the Races. *See* Gentlemen of Nerve, 1914
Charlie at the Studio. *See* Film Johnnie, 1914
Charlie Bubbles, 1967 (Finney; Minnelli)
Charlie Chan and the Curse of the Dragon Queen, 1981 (Dickinson; Grant, L.; Hayden; McDowall; Pfeiffer; Roberts, R.; Ustinov)
Charlie Chan in Egypt, 1935 (Hayworth)
Charlie Chan in London, 1934 (Milland)
Charlie Chaplin's Burlesque on Carmen. *See* Carmen, 1916
Charlie Cobb: Nice Night for a Hanging, 1977 (Bellamy)
Charlie McCarthy, Detective, 1939 (Calhern)
Charlie on the Ocean. *See* Shanghaied, 1915
Charlie on the Spree. *See* In the Park, 1915
Charlie the Burglar. *See* Police!, 1916
Charlie the Hobo. *See* Tramp, 1915
Charlie the Sailor. *See* Shanghaied, 1915
Charlie Varrick, 1973 (Matthau)
Charlie's Angels, 1976 (Jones, T.)
Charlie's Day Out. *See* By the Sea, 1915
Charlie's New Job. *See* His New Job, 1915
Charlie's Recreation. *See* Tango Tangles, 1914
Charlotte et son Jules, 1958 (Belmondo)
Charlotte's Web, 1972 (Moorehead; Reynolds, D.)
Charly, 1968 (Bloom; Robertson)

Charm of Life, 1953 (Harrison)
Charm School. *See* Collegiate, 1936
Charmants garçons, 1957 (Gélin)
Charme discret de la bourgeoisie, 1972 (Audran; Cassel; Piccoli; Rey; Seyrig)
Charmer, 1925 (Negri)
Charming Sinners, 1929 (Powell, W.)
Charrette fantôme, 1939 (Fresnay; Jouvet)
Charro!, 1969 (Presley)
Charro negro, 1940 (Armendáriz)
Chartreuse de Parme, 1948 (Philipe)
Charulata, 1964 (Chatterjee)
Chase, 1946 (Lorre; Morgan)
Chase, 1966 (Brando; Dickinson; Duvall; Fonda, J.; Hopkins, M.; Redford)
Chase a Crooked Shadow, 1958 (Baxter; Lom)
Chaser, 1928 (Langdon)
Chaser, 1938 (Turner, L.)
Chasers. *See* Dragueurs, 1959
Chasers, 1994 (Hopper)
Chasing Dreams, 1981 (Costner)
Chasing Rainbows, 1930 (Dressler)
Chasing the Moon, 1922 (Mix)
Chasse à l'homme, 1964 (Belmondo; Blier; Deneuve; Presle)
Chaste Suzanne, 1937 (Raimu)
Chastity, 1969 (Cher)
Chastity Belt. *See* Cintura di castita, 1967
Chat, 1971 (Gabin)
Chat et la souris, 1975 (Morgan; Reggiani)
Chatarra, 1991 (Maura)
Château au soleil, 1987 (Feuillère)
Château de rêve, 1933 (Darrieux)
Château de verre, 1950 (Marais; Morgan)
Château des amants maudits. *See* Beatrice Cenci, 1956
Château en Suède, 1963 (Trintignant; Vitti)
Châteaux en Espagne, 1953 (Darrieux)
Châtelaine du Liban, 1926 (Modot)
Chato's Land, 1971 (Bronson; Palance)
Chatpatee, 1983 (Patil)
Chattahoochee, 1989 (Hopper; Oldman)
Chatte, 1958 (Blier)
Chatte sur un doigt brûlant, 1974 (Dalio)
Chatterbox, 1936 (Ball)
Chatterbox, 1943 (Brown)
Chausette surprise, 1978 (Dalio; Karina)
Che!, 1969 (Palance; Sharif)
Che?, 1972 (Mastroianni)
Che c'entriamo noi con la rivoluzione?, 1972 (Gassman)
Che distinta famiglia, 1943 (Cervi)
Che gioia vivere, 1961 (Cervi; Delon)
Che ora e?, 1990 (Mastroianni)
Che Tempi!, 1948 (Sordi)
Cheap Detective, 1978 (Ann-Margret; Falk)
Cheaper by the Dozen, 1950 (Loy; Webb)
Cheat, 1915 (Hayakawa)
Cheat, 1923 (Negri)
Cheat. *See* Manèges, 1950
Cheated Hearts, 1921 (Karloff)
Cheater, 1920 (Valentino)
Cheaters. *See* Tricheurs, 1958
Cheating Cheaters, 1934 (Wray)
Check and Double Check, 1930 (Crosby)
Checkered Flag or Crash, 1978 (Sarandon)
Checkpoint, 1956 (Baker)
Cheer Up and Smile, 1930 (Wayne)
Cheering a Husband, 1914 (Beery)
Chef. *See* On the Fire, 1919
Chef at Circle G, 1915 (Mix)
Chef de famille, 1981 (Feuillère)
Chef schickt seinen besten Mann. *See* Requiem per un agent segreto, 1967
Chelovek, drama nachidnya, 1912 (Mozhukin)
Chelovek s drugoi storoni, 1972 (Andersson, B.)

Chelovek s ruzhyom, 1938 (Cherkassov)
Chemin de l'honneur, 1939 (Brasseur)
Chemin de Rio. *See* Cargaison blanche, 1936
Chemin des écoliers, 1959 (Delon)
Chemin perdu, 1979 (Vanel; Seyrig)
Chemist, 1936 (Keaton, B.)
Chena Achena, 1969 (Chatterjee)
Chena Achena, 1983 (Chatterjee)
Cher Inconnu, 1980 (Seyrig)
Cher Victor, 1975 (Valli)
Chère Louise, 1972 (Moreau)
Cheri de sa concierge, 1934 (Fernandel)
Chéri, 1984 (Morgan)
Chéri-Bibi, 1937 (Dalio; Fresnay)
Chernobyl: The Final Warning, 1991 (Robards; Voight)
Chernyi barak, 1933 (Maretskaya)
Cherry 2000, 1985 (Griffith)
Cherry 2000, 1988 (Fishburne)
Cherry Picker, 1970 (Terry-Thomas)
Chess Game, 1983 (Stamp)
Chess Game. *See* Partie d'echecs, 1994
Chess Player. *See* Joueur d'échecs, 1938
Chess Players. *See* Shatranj Ke Khilari, 1978
Chesty: A Tribute to a Legend, 1970 (Wayne)
Chetyre vizity Samuelya Vulfa, 1934 (Maretskaya)
Chevalier de Gaby, 1920 (Modot)
Chevalier de Ménilmontant, 1953 (Chevalier)
Chevelure, 1961 (Piccoli)
Chèvre, 1981 (Depardieu)
Cheyenne, 1947 (Kennedy; Wyman)
Cheyenne Autumn, 1964 (Carradine; Del Rio; Kennedy; Malden; Marsh;
    Mineo; Robinson, E.; Stewart; Widmark)
Cheyenne Social Club, 1970 (Fonda, H.; Kelly, Gene; Stewart)
Chhupa Rustom, 1973 (Anand)
Chhutir Phande, 1974 (Chatterjee)
Chi dice donna dice ... donna, 1975 (Audran)
Chi è senza peccato, 1952 (Rosay)
Chi l'ha visto?, 1945 (Sordi)
Chi ni somuku mono, 1929 (Hasegawa)
Chi to suna, 1965 (Mifune)
Chi Trova, un Amico, Trova un Tesoro, 1983 (Maura)
Chica del Lunes, 1966 (Kennedy; Page)
Chicago Calling, 1951 (Duryea)
Chicago Deadline, 1949 (Kennedy; Ladd)
Chicago-Digest, 1950 (Gélin)
Chicago Digest, 1952 (Piccoli)
Chicas de club, 1972 (Rey)
Chichi, 1930 (Takamine)
Chichi ariki, 1942 (Ryu)
Chichi kaeru haha no kokoro, 1935 (Yamada)
Chichi to ko, 1967 (Takamine)
Chicken Chaser, 1914 (Arbuckle)
Chicken Every Sunday, 1949 (Wood)
Chickens, 1916 (Laurel and Hardy)
Chickens Come Home, 1931 (Laurel and Hardy)
Chidambaram, 1985 (Patil)
Chiedo asilo, 1979 (Benigni)
Chief, 1933 (Rooney)
Chief Cook, 1917 (Laurel and Hardy)
Chief Crazy Horse, 1955 (Mature)
Chief from Göinge. *See* Göingehövdingen, 1953
Chief's Blanket, 1912 (Barrymore, L.)
Chief's Blanket, 1912 (Sweet)
Chief's Predicament, 1913 (Normand)
Chieko-sho, 1957 (Hara; Yamamura)
Chieko-sho, 1967 (Okada)
Chiemi no hatsukoi chaccha musume, 1956 (Tsukasa)
Chien, 1984 (Presle)
Chien de pique, 1960 (Constantine)
Chien qui rapporte, 1909 (Linder)
Chien qui rapporte, 1931 (Arletty)

Chiens, 1978 (Depardieu)
Chiens perdus sans collier, 1955 (Gabin)
Chigo no kenpo, 1927 (Hasegawa)
Chiisai tobosha, 1966 (Kyo)
Chiisaki tabigeinin, 1925 (Tanaka)
Chijin no ai, 1949 (Kyo; Mori)
Chijo, 1957 (Kagawa; Tanaka)
Chijo no seiza: Chijo-hen, Seizahen, 1934 (Tanaka)
Chika-gai no dankon, 1949 (Kyo)
Chikagai no nijuyo-jikan, 1947 (Yamamura)
Chikamatsu monogatari, 1954 (Hasegawa; Kagawa)
Chikashitsu, 1927 (Tanaka)
Chikita, 1961 (Ganz)
Child, 1954 (Mason)
Child Crusoes, 1911 (Talmadge)
Child in the House, 1956 (Baker)
Child Influence, 1912-13 (White)
Child Is Waiting, 1963 (Garland; Lancaster; Rowlands)
Child of Manhattan, 1933 (Grable)
Child of the Night. *See* Enfant de la nuit, 1996
Child of the Paris Streets, 1916 (Marsh)
Child of the Prairie, 1915 (Mix)
Child, the Dog, and the Villain, 1915 (Mix)
Child's Impulse, 1910 (Pickford)
Child's Play, 1972 (Mason; Preston)
Children, 1990 (Chaplin, G.; Kingsley; Novak)
Children. *See* Enfants, 1985
Children in the Holocaust, 1983 (Ullmann)
Children in the House, 1916 (Talmadge)
Children Nobody Wanted, 1981 (Pfeiffer)
Children of a Lesser God, 1986 (Hurt, W.)
Children of Chance. *See* Campane a martello, 1949
Children of Chaos. *See* Carrefour des enfants perdus, 1943
Children of China, 1939 (Zhao Dan)
Children of Divorce, 1927 (Bow; Constantine)
Children of Mata Hari. *See* Peau de Torpédo, 1969
Children of Paradise. *See* **Enfants du paradis**, 1945
Children of Rage, 1975 (Cusack)
Children of Sanchez, 1978 (Davis, B.; Del Rio; Quinn)
Children of the Century, 1933 (Zhao Dan)
Children of the City. *See* Ditya bolchogo goroda, 1914
Children of the Dust, 1991 (Poitier)
Children of the Night. *See* Nattbarn, 1956
Children of the Revolution, 1996 (Davis, J.)
Children of the Whirlwind, 1925 (Barrymore, L.)
Children of Theatre Street, 1977 (Kelly, Grace)
Children Pay, 1916 (Gish)
Children Remember the Holocaust, 1995 (Reeves)
Children Thief. *See* Ladron del Ninos, 1991
Children Thief. *See* Voleur d'enfants, 1991
Children's Hour, 1961 (Garner; Hepburn, A.; Hopkins, M.; MacLaine)
Chilly Scenes of Winter. *See* Head over Heels, 1979
Chimes at Midnight, 1966 (Gielgud; Moreau; Rey; Rutherford; Welles)
Chimney's Secret, 1915 (Chaney)
Chimp, 1932 (Laurel and Hardy)
China, 1943 (Ladd; Young, L.)
China 9, Liberty 37. *See* Amore, piombo, e furore, 1978
China Blue. *See* Crimes of Passion, 1984
China Clipper, 1936 (Bogart)
China Corsair, 1951 (Borgnine)
China Doll, 1958 (Bond; Mature)
China Gate, 1957 (Dalio; Dickinson; Van Cleef)
China Girl, 1942 (McLaglen; Tierney)
China hilaria, 1939 (Armendáriz)
China Moon, 1994 (Harris, E.)
China poblana, 1943 (Félix)
China Rose, 1983 (Scott, G.)
China Seas, 1935 (Beery; Gable; Harlow; McDaniel; Russell, R.)
China Sky, 1945 (Quinn; Scott, R.)
China Syndrome, 1979 (Douglas, Michael; Fonda, J.; Lemmon)
China Venture, 1953 (O'Brien, E.)

China's 400,000,000, 1939 (March)
China's Little Devils, 1945 (Carey)
Chinatown, 1974 (Dunaway; Huston, J.; Nicholson)
Chinatown Charlie, 1928 (Wong)
Chinatown Mystery, 1915 (Hayakawa)
Chinatown Nights, 1929 (Beery)
Chinchoge, 1933 (Tanaka)
Chinese Adventures in China. *See* Tribulations d'un chinois en Chine, 1965
Chinese Bungalow, 1931 (Neagle)
Chinese Bungalow, 1941 (Lukas)
Chinese Connection, 1972 (Lee, B.)
Chinese Den. *See* Chinese Bungalow, 1941
Chinese Garden Festival, 1940 (Wong)
Chinese Parrot, 1927 (Wong)
Chinese Roulette. *See* Chinesisches Roulette, 1976
Chinesisches Roulette, 1976 (Karina)
Chino. *See* Valdez il mezzosanque, 1973
Chino hate ni ikiru mono, 1960 (Tsukasa)
Chinois à Paris, 1974 (Blier)
Chinoise, 1967 (Léaud)
Chip of the Flying U, 1914 (Mix)
Chip Off the Old Block, 1944 (O'Connor)
Chips Are Down. *See* Jeux sont faits, 1947
Chiqué, 1930 (Vanel)
Chirimen kuyo, 1934 (Yamada)
Chisum, 1970 (Wayne)
Chiyoda no ninjo, 1930 (Hasegawa)
Chlen pravitelstva, 1939 (Maretskaya)
Chobotnice Z II. Patra, 1987 (Brodský)
Choc, 1982 (Audran; Delon; Deneuve)
Chocolate Soldier, 1941 (Eddy)
Choice of a Goal, 1975 (Bondarchuk)
Choice of Arms. *See* Choix des armes, 1981
Choice of Weapons. *See* Dirty Knight's Work, 1976
Choices, 1981 (Moore, Demi)
Choices, 1986 (Scott, G.)
Choices of the Heart, 1983 (Sheen)
Choices of the Heart: The Margaret Sanger Story, 1995 (Steiger)
Choirboys, 1977 (Woods)
Choito neesan omoide yanagi, 1952 (Yamamura)
Choix des armes, 1981 (Depardieu; Montand; Deneuve)
Chokon yasha, 1928 (Hasegawa)
Chokoreito to heitai, 1938 (Takamine)
Chômeur de Clochemerle, 1957 (Fernandel)
Choose Me, 1984 (Bujold)
Choose Your Partner. *See* Two Girls on Broadway, 1940
Chop Suey and Co., 1919 (Lloyd)
Chor Sipahi, 1977 (Azmi)
Chorus Girl, 1912-13 (White)
Chorus Line, 1985 (Attenborough; Douglas, Michael)
Chorus of Disapproval, 1989 (Hopkins, A.; Irons)
Chosen, 1978 (Douglas, K.; Quayle)
Chosen, 1982 (Schell, Maximilian; Steiger)
Chosen Survivors, 1974 (Cooper)
"Chosen" yoi: Ali to honoo to, 1961 (Tsukasa)
Choses de la vie, 1970 (Piccoli; Schneider)
Chouans, 1947 (Marais)
Chouans, 1988 (Cassel; Noiret)
Christ Stopped at Eboli. *See* **Cristo si è fermato a Eboli**, 1979
Christa, 1970 (Gélin)
Christened by Fire. *See* Skapani w ogniu, 1963
Christian Wahnschaffe, 1920 (Veidt; Krauss)
Christina, 1929 (Gaynor)
Christine, 1958 (Delon; Presle)
Christine, 1959 (Schneider)
Christine, 1963 (Mueller-Stahl)
Christine, 1983 (Stanton)
Christmas at the Brothel. *See* Natale in Casa di Appuntamento, 1976
Christmas Box, 1995 (O'Hara)
Christmas Carol, 1965 (Depardieu)
Christmas Carol, 1984 (Scott, G.; York)

Christmas Coal Mine Miracle, 1977 (Carradine)
Christmas Eve. *See* Notch pered Rozdestvom, 1913
Christmas Eve, 1947 (Raft; Scott, R.)
Christmas Eve, 1986 (Howard, T.; Young, L.)
Christmas Holiday, 1944 (Durbin; Kelly, Gene)
Christmas in Connecticut, 1945 (Greenstreet; Stanwyck; Curtis, T.)
Christmas in Connecticut, 1992 (Schwarzenegger)
Christmas in July, 1940 (Powell, D.)
Christmas Lilies of the Field, 1979 (Schell, Maria)
Christmas Party, 1931 (Davies; Dressler; Gable; Shearer)
Christmas Reunion, 1994 (Coburn, J.)
Christmas that Almost Wasn't. *See* Natale che quasi non fu, 1966
Christmas to Remember, 1978 (Robards; Saint; Woodward)
Christmas Tree, 1969 (Holden)
Christmas Vacation '91. *See* Vacanze di Natale '91, 1992
Christmas Wife, 1988 (Robards)
Christopher Bean, 1933 (Barrymore, L.; Dressler)
Christopher Columbus, 1949 (Cusack; March)
Christopher Columbus. *See* Cristoforo Colombo, 1985
Christopher Columbus: The Discovery, 1992 (Brando)
Christopher Strong, 1933 (Hepburn, K.)
Christus, 1919 (Krauss)
Chrome Hearts. *See* C.C. and Company, 1970
Chronicle of a Death Foretold. *See* Cronaca di una morte annunciata, 1987
Chronicle of a Love Affair. *See* Kronika wypadkow milosnych, 1986
Chronicle of Flaming Years. *See* Povest plamennykh, 1961
Chronicles of the Grey House. *See* Zur Chronik von Grieshuus, 1925
Chrysanthemums. *See* Krisantemi, 1914
Chu Chin Chow, 1934 (Kortner; Wong)
Chu Chu and the Philly Flash, 1981 (Aiello; Arkin)
Chuji uridasu, 1935 (Shimura)
Chuka, 1967 (Borgnine; Mills)
Chump at Oxford, 1940 (Cushing; Laurel and Hardy; Langdon)
Churchill and the Generals, 1979 (Cotten)
Churetsu nikudan sanyushi, 1936 (Shimura)
Churning. *See* Manthan, 1977
Chushingura, 1932 (Hasegawa; Tanaka)
Chushingura, 1939 (Hasegawa; Takamine)
Chushingura, 1954 (Yamada)
Chushingura, 1958 (Hasegawa; Kyo; Shimura; Yamamura)
Chushingura, 1962 (Hara; Mifune; Tsukasa)
Chushingura, Part II, 1939 (Yamada)
Chushingura: Ninjo-hen, Fukushu-hen, 1934 (Yamada)
Chusingura, 1962 (Shimura)
Chute d'un corps, 1973 (Rey)
Chute dans le bonheur. *See* Chacun sa chance, 1931
Chuzhie pisma, 1975 (Yankovsky)
Ci troviamo in galleria, 1953 (Sordi; Loren)
Ciao maschio, 1978 (Depardieu; Mastroianni)
Ciclon, 1977 (Kennedy)
Cid, 1961 (Heston; Lom; Loren)
Cieca di Sorrento, 1934 (Magnani)
Ciel est à vous, 1943 (Vanel)
Cielo è rosso, 1950 (Cervi)
Cielo negro, 1951 (Rey)
Cimarron, 1930 (Dunne)
Cimarron, 1960 (Baxter; Ford, G.; Schell, Maria)
Cinch for the Gander, 1925 (Wray)
Cincinnati Kid, 1965 (Ann-Margret; Blondell; Malden; McQueen; Robinson, E.; Weld)
Cinderella, 1914 (Pickford)
Cinderella, 1965 (Rogers, G.)
Cinderella, Italian Style. *See* C'era una volta, 1967
Cinderella Jones, 1946 (Horton)
Cinderella Liberty, 1973 (Caan; Wallach)
Cinderella Man, 1917 (Marsh)
Cinderfella, 1960 (Lewis, Jerry)
Cindy Eller: A Modern Fairy Tale, 1985 (Grant, L.)
Cinéma, 1988 (Feuillère)
Cinema According to Bertolucci, 1977 (Sutherland; Valli)
Cinema Murder, 1919 (Davies)

Cinema of Unease, 1996 (Neill)
Cinema Paradiso, 1988 (Noiret)
Cinema secondo Bertolucci. *See* Bertolucci secondo il cinema, 1975
Cinerama's Russian Adventure, 1965 (Crosby)
Cinq gentilshommes maudits, 1931 (Walbrook)
Cinq jours en juin, 1989 (Girardot)
Cinq sous de Lavarède, 1938 (Fernandel)
Cinque ore in contanti, 1961 (Sanders)
Cinque per l'inferno, 1968 (Kinski)
Cinque pistole di violenca. *See* Mio nome è Shanghai Joe, 1973
Cinque poveri in automobile, 1952 (Fabrizi)
Cinquieme element, 1996 (Willis)
Cintura di Castità, 1969 (Curtis, T.; Vitti)
Ciociara, 1961 (Belmondo)
Cipola Colt, 1975 (Hayden)
Circle, 1925 (Crawford, J.)
Circle, 1957 (Mills)
Circle, 1976 (Hayworth)
Circle of Children, 1977 (Roberts, R.)
Circle of Danger, 1951 (Milland)
Circle of Deceit. *See* Fälschung, 1981
Circle of Iron, 1979 (Coburn, J.; Lee, B.; McDowall; Wallach)
Circle of Love. *See* **Ronde**, 1950
Circle of Love. *See* Ronde, 1965
Circle of Two, 1980 (Burton)
Circle of Violence: A Family Drama, 1986 (Weld)
Circo, 1942 (Cantinflas)
Circo equestre Za-Bum, 1944 (Fabrizi; Sordi; Valli)
Circonstances atténuantes, 1939 (Arletty)
Circulez!, 1931 (Brasseur)
Circus, 1928 (Chaplin, C.)
Circus Ace, 1927 (Mix)
Circus Clown, 1934 (Brown)
Circus Hoodoo, 1934 (Langdon)
Circus Kid, 1928 (Brown)
Circus King. *See* Zirkuskönig, 1924
Circus of Fear, 1967 (Kinski; Lee, C.)
Circus of Horrors, 1960 (Pleasence)
Circus Queen Murder, 1933 (Menjou)
Circus Shadow. *See* Shadow, 1937
Circus World, 1964 (Cardinale; Hayworth; Wayne)
Cisaruv Slavik. *See* Emperor's Nightingale, 1951
Cisco Kid and the Lady, 1940 (Bond)
Cisco Pike, 1972 (Hackman; Stanton)
Citadel, 1938 (Donat; Harrison; Richardson, R.; Russell, R.)
Citadel of Crime. *See* Man Betrayed, 1941
Cité de l'indiciblepeur. *See* Grande frousse, 1964
Cité de la peur: une comédie familiale, 1993 (Gélin)
Cité des Enfants Perdus, 1995 (Trintignant)
Citizen Cohn, 1992 (Grant, L.; Woods)
Citizen Kane, 1941 (Cotten; Ladd; Moorehead; Sloane; Welles)
Citizen X, 1995 (Sutherland; Von Sydow)
Città delle donne, 1979 (Mastroianni)
Città prigioniera, 1962 (Niven)
Città si difende, 1951 (Lollobrigida)
Città violenta, 1970 (Bronson)
City, 1971 (Quinn)
City across the River, 1949 (Curtis, T.; Ritter)
City beneath the Sea, 1953 (Quinn; Ryan, R.)
City beneath the Sea, 1970 (Cotten)
City Butterfly. *See* Großstadtschmetterling, 1929
City for Conquest, 1940 (Cagney; Crisp; Kennedy; Quinn)
City Girl, 1930 (Brown)
City Gone Wild, 1927 (Brooks, L.)
City Hall, 1996 (Aiello; Landau; Pacino)
City Heat, 1984 (Eastwood; Reynolds, B.)
City Hunter, 1992 (Chan)
City in Fear, 1980 (Rourke)
City in the Night, 1956 (O'Brien, E.)
City Is Dark. *See* Crime Wave, 1954
City Jungle. *See* Young Philadelphians, 1959

City Lights, 1931 (Chaplin, C.; Harlow)
City Limits, 1985 (Jones, James Earl)
City of Dim Faces, 1918 (Hayakawa)
City of Dreams. *See* Dharavi, 1991
City of Hope, 1991 (Bassett)
City of Industry, 1996 (Keitel)
City of Joy, 1992 (Azmi)
City of Lost Children. *See* Cite des Enfants Perdus, 1995
City of Secrets. *See* Stadt ist voller Geheimnisse, 1955
City of Shadows, 1955 (McLaglen)
City of the Dead, 1960 (Lee, C.)
City of Women. *See* Città delle donne, 1979
City on Fire, 1979 (Fonda, H.; Gardner; Winters)
City Slicker, 1918 (Lloyd)
City Slickers, 1991 (Palance)
City Slickers II: The Legend of Curly's Gold, 1994 (Palance)
City Story, 1954 (Ford, G.)
City Streets, 1931 (Constantine; Goddard; Lukas; Sidney)
City under the Sea, 1965 (Price)
City without Men, 1943 (Darnell)
Ciudad de carton, 1933 (Barrymore, L.; Gaynor; Young, R.)
Clair de femme, 1979 (Benigni; Montand; Schneider)
Clair de terre, 1969 (Presle; Feuillère; Girardot)
Clairvoyant, 1935 (Rains; Wray)
Clambake, 1967 (Presley)
Clan de los immorales, 1973 (Ferrer)
Clan des Siciliens, 1968 (Delon; Gabin)
Claque, 1932 (Fernandel)
Clara et les chics types, 1980 (Adjani)
Clara's Heart, 1988 (Goldberg)
Clarence, 1922 (Menjou)
Claretta, 1984 (Cardinale)
Claretta and Ben. *See* Permettete che ami vostre figlia?, 1974
Clarissa, 1941 (Fröhlich)
Clash by Night, 1952 (Monroe; Ryan, R.; Stanwyck)
Clash of the Titans, 1981 (Bloom; Meredith; Olivier; Smith)
Class, 1983 (Robertson)
Class Action, 1991 (Fishburne; Hackman)
Class of '44, 1973 (Candy)
Class of 1984, 1983 (McDowall)
Class of 1999, 1990 (McDowell)
Class of Miss MacMichael, 1979 (Jackson, G.; Reed)
Classe operaia va in paradiso, 1971 (Volonté)
Classe tous risques, 1958 (Belmondo; Dalio)
Classmates, 1913 (Barrymore, L.; Sweet)
Classmates, 1924 (Barthelmess)
Claudelle Inglish, 1961 (Kennedy)
Claudia, 1943 (Young, R.)
Claudia and David, 1946 (Astor; Young, R.)
Claudia von Geiserhof, 1917 (Veidt)
Claudine, 1974 (Jones, James Earl)
Claudine à l'école, 1938 (Brasseur)
Clay Pigeon, 1971 (Meredith)
Clé sur la porte, 1978 (Girardot)
Clean and Sober, 1988 (Freeman; Keaton, M.)
Clean Slate, 1994 (Jones, James Earl)
Clean Slate. *See* Coup de torchon, 1981
Cleaner. *See* Leon, 1994
Cleaning Time, 1915 (Laurel and Hardy)
Cleaning Up, 1926 (Arbuckle)
Clear All Wires, 1933 (Marshall)
Clear and Present Danger, 1994 (Dafoe; Ford, H.; Jones, James Earl)
Clearing, 1991 (Segal)
Clemenceau Case, 1915 (Bara)
Clémentine Chérie, 1963 (Noiret)
Cléo de cinq à sept, 1962 (Constantine; Karina)
Cleopatra, 1917 (Bara)
Cleopatra, 1934 (Carradine; Colbert)
Cleopatra, 1963 (Burton; Harrison; Landau; McDowall; Taylor, E.)
Cleopatra Jones, 1973 (Winters)
Clérambard, 1969 (Noiret)

Clever Dummy, 1917 (Beery)
Clever Mrs. Carfax, 1917 (Crisp)
Client, 1994 (Jones, T.; Sarandon)
Cliente seductor, 1931 (Chevalier)
Cliffhanger, 1993 (Stallone)
Clifford, 1994 (Steenburgen)
Climats, 1962 (Piccoli)
Climax, 1944 (Karloff)
Climbers, 1927 (Loy)
Climbers. *See* Ambitieuse, 1959
Climbing High, 1939 (Redgrave, M.)
Clinic. *See* Sanitarium, 1910
Clinton and Nadine, 1988 (Barkin; Freeman; García)
Clive of India, 1935 (Ameche; Carradine; Colman; Young, L.)
Cloak and Dagger, 1946 (Constantine)
Clochmerle, 1972 (Cusack)
Clock, 1945 (Garland; Walker)
Clockers, 1995 (Keitel; Lee, S.; Turturro)
Clockmaker. *See* Horloger de Saint-Paul, 1974
Clockwise, 1986 (Cleese)
Clockwork Orange, 1971 (McDowell)
Clodoche, 1938 (Berry)
Clone Master, 1978 (Bellamy)
Cloportes, 1966 (Rosay)
Close Call, 1916 (Mix)
Close Encounters of the Third Kind, 1977 (Dreyfuss)
Close Harmony, 1929 (Harlow)
Close Relations, 1933 (Arbuckle)
Close to My Heart, 1951 (Milland)
Close to My Heart, 1951 (Tierney)
Closed Case. *See* Caso Cerrado, 1985
Closed Circuit. *See* System ohne Schatten, 1983
Closely Watched Trains. *See* **Ostře sledované vlaky**, 1966
Closer, 1991 (Aiello)
Clothes Make the Man, 1915 (Laurel and Hardy)
Clothes Make the Woman, 1928 (Pidgeon)
Cloudburst, 1951 (Baker; Preston)
Clouded Name, 1923 (Shearer)
Clouded Yellow, 1950 (Howard, T.)
Clouds at Twilight. *See* Yuyake-gume, 1956
Clouds over Europe. *See* Q Planes, 1939
Clown, 1953 (Bronson)
Clown. *See* Ansichten eines Clowns, 1975
Clown bux, 1935 (Modot)
Clown Murders, 1976 (Candy)
Club de femmes, 1936 (Darrieux; Trintignant)
Club des aristocrates, 1937 (Berry)
Club des soupirants, 1941 (Fernandel)
Club Extinction, 1989 (Bates, A.)
Club Life, 1987 (Curtis, T.)
Club Paradise, 1986 (O'Toole; Williams, R.)
Clubs Are Trump, 1917 (Lloyd)
Clue, 1915 (Hayakawa; Sweet)
Clue of the New Pin, 1929 (Gielgud)
Cluny Brown, 1946 (Boyer; Jones, Jennifer)
Coal Miner's Daughter, 1980 (Jones, T.; Spacek)
Coartada en disco rojo, 1970 (Rey)
Coast Guard, 1939 (Bellamy; Scott, R.)
Coast of Folly, 1925 (Swanson)
Coast of Skeletons. *See* Skeleton Coast, 1987
Coast Patrol, 1925 (Wray)
Cobb, 1994 (Jones, T.)
Cobra, 1925 (Valentino)
Cobra, 1967 (Andrews, D.)
Cobra, 1986 (Stallone)
Cobra Mission, 1986 (Pleasence)
Cobra Verde, 1987 (Kinski)
Cobweb, 1955 (Bacall; Boyer; Gish; Grahame; Widmark; Wray)
Cobweb Castle. *See* Kumonosu-jo, 1957
Coca-Cola Kid, 1985 (Scacchi)
Cocagne, 1960 (Fernandel)

Cocaine Cowboys, 1979 (Palance)
Cock o' the Walk, 1930 (Loy)
Cockeyed Cowboys of Calico County, 1970 (Rooney)
Cock-Eyed World, 1929 (Brown; McLaglen)
Cockfighter, 1974 (Oates; Stanton)
Cockleshell Heroes, 1955 (Ferrer; Howard, T.; Lee, C.)
Cockoo Cavaliers, 1940 (Three Stooges)
Cocktail, 1988 (Cruise)
Cocktail Hour, 1933 (Scott, R.)
Cocktails, 1927 (Madsen and Schenstrøm)
Cocktails for Three, 1978 (Cardinale)
Cocktails in the Kitchen. *See* For Better, for Worse, 1954
Cocoanuts, 1929 (Dumont; Francis; Marx Brothers)
Coconut Grove, 1938 (MacMurray)
Cocoon, 1985 (Ameche)
Cocoon: The Return, 1988 (Ameche)
Cocu magnifique, 1946 (Barrault)
Code Name Alpha, 1987 (Granger)
Code Name: Emerald, 1985 (Harris, E.; Von Sydow)
Code Name Heraclitus, 1967 (Baker)
Code of Scotland Yard. *See* Shop at Sly Corner, 1946
Code of Silence, 1960 (Cushing)
Code of the Secret Service, 1939 (Reagan)
Code of the Streets, 1938 (Carey)
Codename Wildgeese, 1984 (Borgnine; Kinski; Van Cleef)
Codename: Kyril, 1988 (Elliott)
Codename: The Soldier. *See* Soldier, 1982
Coeur à l'envers, 1980 (Girardot)
Coeur battant, 1960 (Trintignant)
Coeur de coq, 1946 (Fernandel)
Coeur de Lilas, 1931 (Fernandel; Gabin)
Coeur de Tzigane, 1909 (Modot)
Coeur gros comme ça, 1962 (Morgan)
Coeur joyeux, 1931 (Gabin)
Coffee House. *See* Kaffeehaus, 1970
Coffret de laque, 1932 (Darrieux)
Cohen and Tate, 1988 (Scheider)
Cohen at Coney Island, 1912 (Normand)
Cohen Saves the Flag, 1913 (Normand)
Cohens and Kellys in Hollywood, 1932 (Ayres; Karloff)
Cohens and the Kellys in Trouble, 1933 (O'Sullivan)
Coiffeur pour dames, 1952 (Fernandel)
Coïncidences, 1946 (Reggiani)
Colbys, 1985 (Heston)
Cold-Blooded Beast. *See* Bestia uccide a sangue freddo, 1971
Cold Comfort, 1957 (Sellers)
Cold Deck, 1917 (Hart)
Cold Feet, 1990 (Bridges)
Cold Front, 1989 (Sheen)
Cold Night's Death, 1973 (Wallach)
Cold Room, 1984 (Segal)
Cold Sassy Tree, 1989 (Dunaway; Widmark)
Cold Steel, 1987 (Stone)
Cold Sweat. *See* Uomo dalle due ombre, 1971
Cold Turkey, 1940 (Langdon)
Cold Turkey, 1971 (Horton)
Colditz Story, 1955 (Mills)
Cólera del viente, 1971 (Rey)
Colette. *See* Becoming Colette, 1992
Colinot. *See* Histoire très bonne et très joyeuse de Colinot Trousse-Chemise, 1973
Collants noirs, 1960 (Charisse)
Collars and Cuffs, 1923 (Laurel and Hardy)
Collection, 1978 (Mirren)
Collector, 1965 (Stamp)
Colleen, 1936 (Blondell; Keeler)
Colleen, 1936 (Powell, D.)
College, 1927 (Keaton, B.)
College Boob, 1926 (Arthur)
College Chums, 1912-13 (White)
College Coach, 1933 (Powell, D.; Wayne)

College Confidential, 1960 (Marshall)
College Days, 1926 (Montgomery)
College Humor, 1933 (Crosby)
College Is a Nice Place. *See* Daigaku yoitoko, 1936
College Rhythm, 1934 (Wyman)
College Swing, 1938 (Grable; Hope; Horton)
College Widow, 1927 (Ryan, R.)
Collegians, 1926 (Gable)
Collegiate, 1936 (Grable)
Collégiennes, 1956 (Deneuve)
Collier vivant, 1909 (Modot)
Collision Course, 1975 (Fonda, H.)
Colmena, 1982 (Abril)
Colomba, 1918 (Veidt)
Colomba, 1933 (Modot)
Colombine, 1920 (Jannings)
Colonel. *See* Az azredes, 1917
Colonel Chabert, 1943 (Raimu)
Colonel Chabert, 1995 (Depardieu)
Colonel Effingham's Raid, 1945 (Bennett; Coburn, C.)
Colonel March Investigates, 1953 (Karloff)
Colonel Redl. *See* Redl Ezredes, 1985
Colonel Wolodyjowski. *See* Pan Wołodyjowski, 1969
Colonia penal, 1971 (Villagra)
Colonna di ferro, 1940 (Mastroianni)
Color of Evening, 1990 (Burstyn; McDowall)
Color of Evening, 1992 (Landau)
Color of Money, 1986 (Cruise; Newman; Turturro; Whitaker)
Color of Night, 1994 (Willis)
Color Purple, 1985 (Fishburne; Goldberg)
Colorado, 1940 (Rogers, R.)
Colorado Sunset, 1939 (Autry)
Colorado Territory, 1949 (Malone; McCrea)
Colored Villainy, 1915 (Arbuckle)
Colors, 1988 (Duvall; Hopper; Penn)
Colosseum and Juicy Lucy, 1970 (Baker)
Colpa altrui, 1914 (Bertini)
Colpo di vento, 1936 (Berry)
Colt 45, 1950 (Scott, R.)
Colt Comrades, 1943 (Mitchum)
Columbo: A Bird in the Hand, 1992 (Falk)
Columbo and the Murder of a Rock Star, 1991 (Falk)
Columbo: Butterflies in Shades of Grey, 1994 (Falk)
Columbo Goes to College, 1990 (Falk)
Columbo Goes to the Guillotine, 1989 (Falk)
Columbo: Grand Deception, 1990 (Falk)
Columbo: It's All in the Game, 1993 (Dunaway; Falk)
Columbo: Murder Can Be Hazardous to Your Health, 1991 (Falk)
Columbo: Strange Bedfellows, 1995 (Falk; Steiger)
Columbo: Undercover, 1994 (Falk)
Coma, 1978 (Bujold; Douglas, Michael; Harris, E.; Widmark)
Comanche, 1956 (Andrews, D.)
Comanche Station, 1960 (Scott, R.)
Comanche Territory, 1950 (O'Hara)
Comancheros, 1961 (Marvin)
Comancho blanco, 1967 (Cotten)
Combat!, 1996 (Willis)
Combat America, 1944 (Gable)
Combat dans l'île, 1961 (Schneider; Trintignant)
Combourg, visage de pierre, 1948 (Fresnay)
Come along with Me, 1982 (Woodward)
Come and Get It, 1936 (Brennan; Farmer; McCrea)
Come Back, Little Sheba, 1953 (Lancaster; Olivier; Woodward)
Come Back to Me. *See* Doll Face, 1946
Come Back to the 5 and Dime, Jimmy Dean, Jimmy Dean, 1982 (Bates, K.; Cher)
Come Blow Your Horn, 1963 (Cobb; Martin, D.; Sidney)
Come Clean, 1931 (Laurel and Hardy)
Come Dance with Me. *See* Voulez-vous danser avec moi?, 1959
Come due Coccodrilli, 1994 (Giannini)
Come Fill the Cup, 1951 (Cagney; Massey)

Come Fly with Me, 1963 (Malden)
Come Live with Me, 1941 (Lamarr; Stewart)
Come Next Spring, 1956 (Brennan)
Come on Leathernecks, 1938 (Ladd)
Come on, Marines!, 1934 (Lupino)
Come-On, 1956 (Baxter)
Come-On, 1956 (Hayden)
Come On, Rangers, 1938 (Rogers, R.)
Come Out of the Pantry, 1935 (Buchanan; Wray)
Come See the Paradise, 1990 (Quaid)
Come September, 1961 (Hudson; Lollobrigida)
Come to the Stable, 1949 (Lanchester; Young, L.)
Come un bambino, 1990 (Gassman; Sanda)
Come una rosa al naso, 1976 (Gassman)
Comeback, 1970 (Hopkins, M.)
Comedians. *See* Cómicos, 1952
Comédians, 1964 (Brasseur)
Comedians, 1967 (Burton; Gish; Guinness; Jones, James Earl; Taylor, E.; Ustinov)
Comedians in Africa, 1967 (Burton; Gish; Guinness)
Comedie d'amour, 1989 (Girardot)
Comédie du bonheur, 1940 (Jourdan; Novarro; Presle)
Comediens ambulants, 1946 (Fernandel)
Comédiens ambulants, 1950 (Jouvet)
Comedy of Death. *See* Komedia smerti, 1915
Comedy of Errors, 1983 (Cusack)
Comedy of Terrors, 1963 (Brown; Karloff; Lorre; Price; Rathbone)
Comes a Horseman, 1978 (Caan; Fonda, J.)
Comes a Horseman, 1978 (Robards)
Comet over Broadway, 1938 (Crisp; Francis; Hayward)
Comets, 1930 (Lanchester)
Comfort of Strangers, 1991 (Mirren; Walken)
Comic, 1969 (Rooney; Wilde)
Cómicos, 1952 (Rey)
Comin' at Ya!, 1981 (Abril)
Comin' Round the Mountain, 1936 (Autry)
Comin' Round the Mountain, 1951 (Abbott and Costello)
Coming Home, 1978 (Dern; Fonda, J.; Voight)
Coming of Angelo, 1913 (Sweet)
Coming of the Law, 1919 (Mix)
Coming through, 1925 (Beery; Branagh)
Coming through, 1985 (Mirren)
Coming to America, 1988 (Ameche; Bellamy; Jackson, S.; Jones, James Earl; Murphy)
Commancheros, 1961 (Wayne)
Command Decision, 1948 (Gable; Pidgeon)
Command in Hell. *See* Alone in the Neon Jungle, 1988
Commander, 1988 (Pleasence; Van Cleef)
Commander of the Navy. *See* Flottans överman, 1958
Commanding Officer, 1915 (Crisp)
Commando. *See* Marcia o crepa, 1963
Commando, 1985 (Schwarzenegger)
Commando Attack. *See* I leopardi di Churchill, 1970
Commando Leopard. *See* Kommando Leopard, 1985
Commandos, 1968 (Van Cleef)
Commandos Strike at Dawn, 1942 (Gish; Muni)
Comme Icarus, 1979 (Montand)
Comme s'il en pleuvait, 1963 (Constantine)
Comme un boomerang, 1976 (Delon; Vanel)
Comme un poisson dans l'eau, 1962 (Noiret)
Comme une carpe, 1932 (Fernandel)
Comment Max fait le tour du monde, 1913 (Linder)
Comment qu'elle est!, 1960 (Constantine)
Comment reussir dans la vie quand on est con et pleurnichard, 1974 (Audran)
Commissario, 1962 (Sordi)
Common Clay, 1930 (Ayres)
Common Ground, 1990 (Jackson, S.)
Common Heritage, 1940 (Howard, L.)
Common Law, 1931 (McCrea)
Common Sense of Modesty. *See* Commune senso del pudore, 1976
Common Threads, 1989 (Hoffman)

Commotion on the Ocean, 1956 (Three Stooges)

Commune senso del pudore, 1976 (Noiret)

Communion, 1989 (Walken)

Communion solennelle, 1976 (Dalio; Baye)

Communists Are Comfortable, 1985 (Dafoe)

Communo senso del pudore, 1976 (Cardinale)

Como ser mujer y no morir en el intento, 1991 (Maura)

Como ser infeliz y disfrutarlo, 1994 (Maura)

Compact, 1911 (White)

Compagna di viaggio, 1996 (Piccoli)

Compagni, 1963 (Blier; Girardot; Mastroianni)

Compagno Don Camillo, 1965 (Cervi; Fernandel)

Companions in Nightmare, 1968 (Baxter; Douglas, Melvyn)

Company Business, 1991 (Hackman)

Company of Cowards? *See* Advance to the Rear, 1964

Company of Killers, 1970 (Milland)

Company of Wolves, 1984 (Lansbury; Stamp)

Company She Keeps, 1951 (Bridges)

Company: Inigo and His Jesuits, 1991 (Cusack)

Compañeros. *See* Vamos a matar, compañeros!, 1970

Comparison of Heights. *See* Takekurabe, 1955

Compartiment tueurs, 1965 (Gélin; Montand; Piccoli; Reggiani; Trintignant)

Compères, 1983 (Depardieu)

Competition, 1980 (Dreyfuss; Remick)

Compleat Beatles, 1982 (McDowell)

Complessi, 1965 (Sordi)

Complicato intrigo di donne, vicoli e delitti. *See* Camorra, 1986

Compliments of Mister Flow. *See* Mister Flow, 1936

Compromis, 1978 (Blier)

Compromising Positions, 1985 (Julia; Sarandon)

Comptes à rebours, 1970 (Moreau; Reggiani; Vanel)

Comptesse Doddy, 1919 (Negri)

Compulsion, 1959 (Welles)

Comrade X, 1940 (Gable; Homolka; Lamarr)

Comrades, 1986 (Redgrave, V.)

Comte de Monte-Cristo, 1914 (Modot)

Comte de Monte-Cristo, 1953 (Marais)

Comte de Monte Cristo, 1961 (Jourdan)

Comte Kostia, 1925 (Veidt)

Con Artists, 1981 (Quinn)

Con la rabbia agli occhi, 1976 (Brynner)

Con los dorados de Pancho Villa, 1939 (Armendáriz)

Con Men. *See* Te deum, 1973

Conan the Barbarian, 1982 (Jones, James Earl; Schwarzenegger; Von Sydow)

Conan the Destroyer, 1984 (Schwarzenegger)

Concerto per pistola solista, 1970 (Valli)

Concorde affaire, 1979 (Cotten)

Concorde—Airport '79, 1979 (Andersson, B.; Delon)

Concrete Cowboys, 1979 (Penn)

Concrete Jungle. *See* Criminal, 1960

Condamnés, 1947 (Fresnay)

Conde Dracula, 1971 (Kinski; Lee, C.)

Condemned!, 1929 (Colman)

Condemned of Altona. *See* Sequestri di Altona, 1962

Condominium, 1979 (Bellamy; Malone)

Condor, 1970 (Van Cleef)

Condorman, 1981 (Reed)

Conduct Report on Professor Ishinaka. *See* Ishinaka-sensei gyojoki datsugoko, 1950

Conduct Unbecoming, 1975 (Attenborough; Howard, T.; York)

Conductor, 1979 (Gielgud)

Cone of Silence, 1961 (Sanders)

Coney Island, 1917 (Keaton, B.)

Coney Island, 1943 (Grable)

Confession, 1929 (Barrymore, L.)

Confession, 1937 (Crisp; Francis; Rathbone)

Confession, 1964 (Gould; Milland; Rogers, G.)

Confession. *See* Aveu, 1970

Confessional, 1989 (Quayle)

Confessions from the David Galaxy Affair, 1979 (Dors)

Confessions of a Co-ed, 1931 (Crosby; Sidney)

Confessions of a Driving Instructor, 1975 (Dors)

Confessions of a Nazi Spy, 1939 (Lukas; Robinson, E.; Sanders)

Confessions of a Newlywed. *See* Vous n'avez rien a déclarer?, 1937

Confessions of an Opium Eater, 1962 (Price)

Confessions of Felix Krull. *See* Bekenntnisse des Hochstaplers Felix Krull, 1957

Confessions: Two Faces of Evil, 1994 (Jones, James Earl)

Confetti, 1927 (Buchanan)

Confidences a un inconnu, 1995 (Hurt, W.)

Confident de ces dames, 1959 (Fernandel)

Confidential Agent, 1945 (Bacall; Boyer; Lorre)

Confidential Report, 1955 (Redgrave, M.)

Confidential Report. *See* Mr. Arkadin, 1955

Confidentially Connie, 1953 (Calhern; Leigh, Janet)

Confirm or Deny, 1941 (Ameche; Bennett; McDowall)

Conflict, 1936 (Bond; Wayne)

Conflict, 1943 (Greenstreet)

Conflict, 1945 (Bogart)

Conflit, 1938 (Dalio; Reggiani)

Conformista, 1970 (Sanda)

Confrontation, 1970 (Hackman)

Congiuntura, 1964 (Gassman)

Congiura dei dieci. *See* Lo spadaccino di Sienna, 1963

Congo Crossing, 1956 (Lorre)

Congo Vivo, 1962 (Seberg)

Congress Dances. *See* Kongress tanzt, 1931

Connecticut Yankee in King Arthur's Court, 1931 (Loy; O'Sullivan; Rogers, W.; Crosby)

Connecting Rooms, 1971 (Davis, B.; Redgrave, M.)

Conquérants solitaires, 1952 (Cuny)

Conquered City. *See* Citta prigioniera, 1962

Conquering Horde, 1931 (Wray)

Conquering Power, 1921 (Valentino)

Conqueror, 1956 (Armendáriz; Hayward; Moorehead; Powell, D.; Van Cleef; Wayne)

Conqueror Worm. *See* **Witchfinder General**, 1968

Conquest, 1937 (Boyer; Garbo)

Conquest of the Air, 1936 (Olivier)

Conquest of the Planet of the Apes, 1972 (McDowall)

Conquête, 1908 (Linder)

Conquêtes du froid, 1951 (Aimée)

Conrack, 1974 (Voight)

Conscience of Hassan Bey, 1913 (Gish)

Consenting Adult, 1985 (Sheen)

Consenting Adults, 1992 (Kline; Whitaker)

Consigna: Tanger 67. *See* Requiem per un agent segreto, 1967

Consolation Marriage, 1931 (Dunne; Loy)

Consortium, 1968 (Constantine)

Conspiracy of Love, 1987 (Young, R.)

Conspiracy: The Trial of the Chicago 8, 1987 (Sheen; Gould)

Conspirator, 1950 (Taylor, E.; Taylor, R.)

Conspirators, 1944 (Dalio; Greenstreet; Henreid; Lamarr; Lorre)

Constance aux enfers, 1964 (Morgan)

Constant Husband, 1954 (Harrison; Kendall)

Constant Nymph, 1928 (Lanchester; Novello)

Constant Nymph, 1943 (Boyer; Coburn, C.; Dalio; Fontaine; Lorre)

Constantine the Great, 1962 (Wilde)

Consuelita, 1922 (Bertini)

Consul. *See* Daimler-Benz Limuzyna, 1982

Consuming Passions, 1988 (Redgrave, V.)

Contact, 1992 (Pitt)

Contact, 1996 (Foster)

Contact: The Yahomani Indians of Brazil, 1991 (Scheider)

Conte Max, 1957 (Sordi)

Contemporary Heroes, 1960 (Zhao Dan)

Contempt. *See* Mépris, 1963

Contessa di Challant, 1911 (Bertini)

Contessa Sarah, 1919 (Bertini)

Contestazione generale, 1970 (Gassman; Sordi)

Contesto, 1975 (Cuny; Rey; Von Sydow)

Continental Divide, 1981 (Belushi)

Continental Express. *See* Silent Battle, 1939
Contra el Viento, 1990 (Banderas)
Contra la corrienta, 1936 (Novarro)
Contraband, 1940 (Veidt)
Contraband Spain, 1955 (Aimée)
Contrabbandieri del mare, 1948 (Brazzi)
Contract, 1978 (Caron)
Contract. *See* Kontrakt, 1981
Contract on Cherry Street, 1977 (Sidney)
Contre l'oubli, 1992 (Deneuve; Huppert; Noiret; Piccoli)
Contrebandiers, 1906 (Linder)
Contribution. *See* Kontrybucja, 1967
Contro la legge, 1950 (Mastroianni)
Control, 1987 (Josephson; Lancaster; Nelligan)
Control. *See* Giorno prima, 1987
Contrôleur des wagon-lits, 1935 (Darrieux)
Controrapina, 1978 (Van Cleef)
Convent. *See* O Convento, 1995
Convention City, 1933 (Astor; Blondell; Menjou; Powell, D.)
Convention Girl, 1935 (Three Stooges)
Conversation, 1974 (Duvall; Ford, H.; Hackman)
Conversation Piece. *See* Gruppo di famiglia in un interno, 1974
Conversion of Frosty Blake, 1915 (Hart)
Conversion of Smiling Tom, 1915 (Mix)
Convict 13, 1920 (Keaton, B.)
Convict 99, 1938 (McDowall; Withers)
Convict Cowboy, 1995 (Voight)
Convict Women. *See* Thunder County, 1974
Convict's Daughter, 1912-13 (White)
Convicted, 1938 (Hayworth)
Convicted, 1950 (Crawford, B.; Ford, G.; Malone)
Convicted Woman, 1940 (Ford, G.)
Convicts, 1988 (Duvall)
Convicts, 1991 (Duvall; Jones, James Earl)
Convicts Four, 1962 (Crawford, B.; Price; Steiger)
Convoy, 1940 (Granger)
Convoy, 1978 (Borgnine; Coburn, J.)
Coogan's Bluff, 1968 (Cobb; Eastwood)
Cook. *See* Dough and Dynamite, 1914
Cook, 1918 (Arbuckle; Keaton, B.)
Cook and Peary: The Race to the North Pole, 1983 (Steiger)
Cook of Canyon Camp, 1917 (Crisp)
Cook, the Thief, His Wife & Her Lover, 1989 (Mirren)
Cooked Trails, 1916 (Mix)
Cookery Nook, 1951 (Terry-Thomas)
Cookie, 1989 (Falk; Lewis, Jerry; Wiest)
Cool Blue, 1988 (Penn)
Cool Hand Luke, 1967 (Hopper; Newman; Stanton)
Cool Ones, 1967 (McDowall)
Cool Runnings, 1993 (Candy)
Cool World, 1992 (Basinger; Pitt)
Cooperstown, 1993 (Arkin)
Cop, 1928 (Crisp)
Cop, 1988 (Woods)
Cop. *See* Flic, 1972
Cop. *See* Ripoux, 1984
Cop and a Half, 1993 (Reynolds, B.)
Cop and the Girl. *See* Bulle und das Mädchen, 1985
Cop au Vin. *See* Poulet au vinaigre, 1985
Cop Killer. *See* Corrupt, 1983
Copacabana, 1947 (Marx Brothers; Miranda)
Copain suavé sa peau, 1967 (Blier)
Copains, 1964 (Noiret)
Copains du dimanche, 1956 (Belmondo; Piccoli)
Copie conforme, 1946 (Jouvet)
Coplan sauve sa peau, 1967 (Kinski)
Cop-Out. *See* Stranger in the House, 1967
Copper Canyon, 1950 (Lamarr; Milland)
Copperhead, 1920 (Barrymore, L.)
Coppia tranquilla. *See* Ruba al prossimo tuo, 1969
Coppie, 1970 (Sordi; Vitti)

Cops & Robbersons, 1994 (Palance)
Cops, 1922 (Keaton, B.)
Cops and Robbers. *See* Guardie e ladri, 1951
Cops and Robbersons, 1994 (Wiest)
Cops and Robin, 1978 (Borgnine)
Cops and Watches. *See* Twenty Minutes of Love, 1914
Cops Is a Business, 1912-13 (White)
Cop's Sunday. *See* Dimanche de flics, 1982
Copycat, 1995 (Hunter; Weaver)
Coq du regiment, 1933 (Fernandel)
Coquecigrole, 1932 (Darrieux)
Coquette, 1929 (Pickford)
Coquille et le clergyman, 1927 (Artaud)
Coraggio, 1955 (Cervi)
Coralie et Cie, 1935 (Rosay)
Corazón sobre la tierra, 1985 (Villagra)
Corbeau, 1943 (Fresnay)
Cordial Gorbatschev. *See* Caro Gorbaciov, 1988
Cordon-bleu, 1931 (Feuillère)
Corinna, Corinna, 1994 (Ameche; Goldberg)
Corinthian Jack, 1921 (McLaglen)
Corky, 1971 (McDowall)
Corleone, 1978 (Cardinale)
Cormorant, 1993 (Fiennes)
Corn Is Green, 1945 (Davis, B.)
Corn Is Green, 1978 (Hepburn, K.)
Cornbread, Earl and Me, 1975 (Fishburne)
Corner in Water, 1916 (Mix)
Corner in Wheat, 1909 (Sweet)
Corner of Great Tokyo. *See* Dai-Tokyo no ikkaku, 1930
Cornered, 1945 (Powell, D.)
Cornet, 1955 (Rasp)
Corny Casanovas, 1952 (Three Stooges)
Corona di ferro, 1940 (Cervi)
Corona negra, 1950 (Brazzi; Félix)
Corona negra, 1952 (Gassman)
Coroner Creek, 1948 (Scott, R.)
Corps de Diane, 1969 (Moreau)
Corps de mon ennemi, 1976 (Belmondo; Blier)
Corps et bien, 1986 (Sanda; Darrieux; Léaud)
Corps źa Corps, 1987 (Audran)
Corpse Came C.O.D., 1947 (Blondell)
Corpse Vanished. *See* Revenge of the Zombies, 1944
Corpse Vanishes, 1942 (Lugosi)
Corridor of Mirrors, 1948 (Lee, C.)
Corridors of Blood, 1958 (Lee, C.)
Corridors of Blood, 1963 (Karloff)
Corriere del re, 1947 (Brazzi)
Corrupción de Chris Miller, 1973 (Seberg)
Corrupt, 1983 (Keitel)
Corruption, 1968 (Cushing)
Corruption. *See* Going Straight, 1916
Corruption. *See* Corruzione, 1963
Corruption of Chris Miller. *See* Corrupción de Chris Miller, 1973
Corruzione, 1963 (Cuny)
Corruzione al palazzo di giustizia, 1974 (Rey)
Corsa in Discesa, 1987 (Keitel)
Corsaire, 1939 (Dalio; Jourdan)
Corsaire, 1983 (Thulin)
Corsario negro, 1944 (Armendáriz)
Corsican Brothers, 1985 (Chaplin, G.; Pleasence)
Corsican Brothers. *See* Frères corses, 1939
Corta notte delle bambole di vetro. *See* Malastrana, 1971
Corte de Faraon, 1985 (Banderas)
Corvette K-225, 1943 (Fitzgerald; Mitchum; Scott, R.; Robertson)
Cose da pazzi, 1953 (Fabrizi)
Cose di Cosa Nostra, 1971 (Fabrizi)
Cosi come sei, 1978 (Kinski; Mastroianni)
Cosmic Man, 1959 (Carradine)
Cossacks, 1928 (Gilbert)
Costa azzurra, 1959 (Sordi)

Cosa Nostra: An Arch Enemy of the FBI, 1967 (Duvall; Pidgeon)
Costanza della ragione, 1964 (Deneuve)
Coster Bill of Paris. See Crainquebille, 1933
Cottage to Let, 1941 (Mills)
Cotton Club, 1984 (Cage; Fishburne; Gere; Hoskins)
Coub de jeune, 1992 (Cassel)
Couch in New York. See Divan a New York, 1996
Couch Trip, 1988 (Matthau)
Couer gros comme ca, 1962 (Belmondo)
Could I but Live. See Ware hitotsubu no mugi naredo, 1965
Couleur chair, 1978 (Hopper; Ullmann)
Couleur de temps. See Démons de midi, 1978
Counsel for Romance. See Avocate D'amour, 1938
Counsel for the Defense, 1913 (Talmadge)
Counsel on De Fence, 1934 (Langdon)
Counsellor-at-Law, 1933 (Barrymore, J.; Douglas, Melvyn)
Count, 1916 (Chaplin, C.; Purviance)
Count Dracula, 1970 (Lom)
Count Dracula. See Conde Dracula, 1971
Count Dracula and His Vampire Brides. See Satanic Rites of Dracula, 1973
Count of Monk's Bridge. See Munkbrogreven, 1934
Count of Monte Cristo, 1934 (Calhern; Donat)
Count of Monte Cristo, 1974 (Curtis, T.; Howard, T.; Jourdan; Nelligan; Pleasence)
Count of Monte Cristo. See Comte de Monte Cristo, 1961
Count of Monte Cristo. See Comte de Monte-Cristo, 1953
Count the Votes, 1919 (Lloyd)
Count Three and Pray, 1955 (Woodward)
Count Your Blessings, 1959 (Brazzi; Chevalier; Kerr)
Count Your Change, 1919 (Lloyd)
Countdown, 1968 (Caan; Duvall)
Countdown in Kung Fu, 1975 (Chan)
Counted Out. See Knockout, 1914
Counter-Attack, 1945 (Muni)
Counter Jumper, 1922 (Laurel and Hardy)
Counterfeit Constable. See Allez France, 1966
Counterfeit Lady, 1937 (Bellamy)
Counterfeit Traitor, 1962 (Dahlbeck; Holden; Kinski)
Counterfeiters of Paris. See Cave se rebiffe, 1961
Counterforce, 1988 (Jourdan)
Counterpoint, 1967 (Heston; Schell, Maximilian)
Countess Charming, 1917 (Crisp)
Countess from Hong Kong, 1967 (Brando; Chaplin, C.; Chaplin, G.; Loren; Rutherford)
Countess of Monte Cristo, 1934 (Lukas; Wray)
Countess of Monte Cristo, 1948 (Henie)
Countess Sweedie, 1914 (Beery)
Countless Families, 1953 (Lee, B.)
Country, 1984 (Greenwood; Lange; Shepard)
Country Dance, 1969 (Cusack; O'Toole; York)
Country Doctor, 1909 (Pickford)
Country Doctor. See Fundoshi isha, 1960
Country Girl, 1954 (Crosby; Holden; Kelly, Grace)
Country Girls, 1983 (Neill)
Country Hero, 1917 (Arbuckle; Keaton, B.)
Country Life, 1994 (Scacchi; Withers)
Country Lovers, 1911 (Sweet)
Country Music U.S.A.. See Vegas Hillbillies, 1966
Country of Bells. See Paese dei campanelli, 1953
County Chairman, 1935 (Rooney)
County Hospital, 1932 (Laurel and Hardy)
Coup de bambou, 1963 (Presle)
Coup de foudre, 1976 (Deneuve; Huppert; Noiret)
Coup de grâce, 1965 (Darrieux; Piccoli)
Coup de jeune, 1992 (Gélin)
Coup de torchon, 1981 (Audran; Huppert; Noiret)
Coupe de Ville, 1990 (Arkin)
Coupe franche, 1989 (Reggiani)
Couple, 1951 (Zhao Dan)
Couple. See O Casal, 1974
Couple Takes a Wife, 1972 (Loy)

Couple témoin, 1977 (Constantine)
Couples. See Coppie, 1970
Coups de feu à l'aube, 1932 (Artaud; Modot)
Courage, 1921 (Menjou)
Courage, 1986 (Loren)
Courage for Everyday. See Každý den odvahu, 1964
Courage, fuyons, 1980 (Deneuve)
Courage Mountain, 1989 (Caron)
Courage of Kavik, the Wolf Dog, 1980 (Candy)
Courage of Lassie, 1946 (Taylor, E.)
Courage of Marge O'Doone, 1919 (Karloff)
Courage under Fire, 1996 (Ryan, M.; Washington)
Courageous Coward, 1919 (Hayakawa)
Courageous Mr. Penn. See Penn of Pennsylvania, 1942
Courier Sud, 1936 (Vanel)
Courier to the Tsar. See Strogoff, 1968
Cours après moi que je t'attrape, 1976 (Girardot)
Cours de route. See Utközben, 1979
Course, du lièvre a travers les champs, 1972 (Ryan, R.)
Court Jester, 1956 (Carradine; Kaye; Lansbury; Rathbone)
Court Martial. See Carrington, V.C., 1954
Court Martial of Billy Mitchell, 1955 (Bellamy; Constantine; Steiger)
Court-Martial of Jackie Robinson, 1990 (Dern)
Court of the Pharaoh. See Corte de Faraon, 1985
Courtes Jambes, 1938 (Dalio)
Courthouse Crooks, 1915 (Lloyd)
Courting of Mary, 1911 (Pickford)
Courtneys of Curzon Street, 1947 (Neagle)
Courtship of Andy Hardy, 1942 (Rooney)
Courtship of Eddie's Father, 1963 (Ford, G.)
Courtship of O'Sann. See O Mimi san, 1914
Cousin Pons, 1923 (Modot)
Cousins, 1959 (Audran)
Cousins, 1989 (Rossellini)
Couteau dans la plaie, 1962 (Loren)
Couturier de ces dames, 1956 (Fernandel)
Couvent. See O Convento, 1995
Covenant with Death, 1967 (Hackman)
Cover Girl, 1944 (Hayworth; Kelly, Gene; Winters)
Cover Up, 1984 (Jourdan)
Covert Action. See Sono stato un'agente CIA, 1978
Covert Assassin, 1994 (Scheider)
Cow and I. See Vache et le prisonnier, 1959
Cow Country, 1953 (O'Brien, E.)
Cow Town, 1950 (Autry)
Coward, 1911 (White)
Coward and the Holy Man. See Kapurush-o-Mahapurush, 1965
Cowboy, 1958 (Ford, G.; Lemmon)
Cowboy and the Ballerina, 1984 (Huston, A.)
Cowboy and the Girl. See Lady Takes a Chance, 1943
Cowboy and the Indians, 1949 (Autry; Brennan; Constantine)
Cowboy and the Lady, 1938 (Oberon)
Cowboy and the Senorita, 1944 (Rogers, R.)
Cowboy Commandos, 1943 (Bond)
Cowboy Cop, 1926 (Arthur)
Cowboy from Brooklyn, 1938 (Powell, D.; Reagan)
Cowboy Serenade, 1942 (Autry)
Cowboy Sheik, 1924 (Rogers, W.)
Cowboys, 1971 (Dern; Wayne)
Cowboys Cry for It, 1923 (Laurel and Hardy)
Cowgirls, 1986 (Dunaway)
Cowpuncher's Peril, 1916 (Mix)
Crab-Canning Ship. See Kani-ko sen, 1953
Crack in the Mirror, 1960 (Welles)
Crack in the Mirror, 1989 (Aiello)
Crack in the World, 1965 (Andrews, D.)
Crack Your Heels, 1919 (Lloyd)
Cracked Nuts, 1931 (Karloff)
Cracker Factory, 1979 (Wood)
Crackerjack, 1994 (Kinski)
Crackers, 1984 (Penn; Sutherland)

Cracking Up, 1983 (Lewis, Jerry)
Cracksman, 1963 (Sanders)
Crack-Up, 1937 (Lorre)
Crack-Up, 1946 (Marshall; Trevor)
Cradle of Courage, 1920 (Hart; Hayakawa)
Cradle of Genius, 1958 (Cusack; Fitzgerald)
Crag of the Spirits. See Peñon de las ánimas, 1942
Craig's Wife, 1936 (Russell, R.)
Crainquebille, 1922 (Rosay)
Crainquebille, 1933 (Modot)
Cran d' Arret, 1970 (Karina)
Crash, 1976 (Carradine)
Crash, 1977 (Ferrer)
Crash, 1996 (Hunter)
Crash Dive, 1943 (Andrews, D.; Baxter; Power)
Crash Donovan, 1936 (Bond)
Crash Goes the Hash, 1944 (Three Stooges)
Crash Landing: The Rescue of Flight 232, 1992 (Heston; Coburn, J.)
Crash of Silence. See Mandy, 1952
Crashing Hollywood, 1931 (Arbuckle; Grable)
Crashout, 1955 (Kennedy)
Crawlspace, 1971 (Kennedy)
Crawlspace, 1986 (Kinski)
Craze, 1973 (Dors; Evans; Howard, T.; Palance)
Crazy for Love. See Trou normand, 1952
Crazy House, 1943 (Rathbone; Three Stooges)
Crazy House. See House in Nightmare Park, 1973
Crazy in Love, 1992 (Hunter; Rowlands)
Crazy Joe, 1974 (Wallach)
Crazy Knights, 1944 (Three Stooges)
Crazy Like a Fox, 1926 (Laurel and Hardy)
Crazy Mama, 1975 (Quaid)
Crazy People, 1934 (Three Stooges)
Crazy People, 1990 (Moore, Dudley)
Crazy Quilt, 1966 (Meredith)
Crazy Streets. See Forever, Lulu, 1986
Crazy That Way, 1930 (Bennett)
Crazy to Act, 1926 (Laurel and Hardy)
Crazy to Kill. See Dr. Gillespie's Criminal Case, 1943
Crazy to Marry, 1921 (Arbuckle)
Crazy World of Julius Vrooder, 1974 (Hershey)
Crazy World of Laurel and Hardy, 1966 (Laurel and Hardy)
Cream Puff Romance, 1916 (Arbuckle)
Created to Kill. See Embryo, 1976
Creator, 1985 (O'Toole)
Creature. See Titan Find, 1984
Creature, 1985 (Kinski)
Creature with the Blue Hand. See Blaue Hand, 1967
Créatures, 1966 (Dahlbeck; Deneuve; Piccoli)
Creditors. See Fordringsagare, 1989
Creed of Violence, 1969 (Van Cleef)
Creepers. See Phenomena, 1985
Creeping Flesh, 1972 (Cushing; Lee, C.)
Creeps, 1956 (Three Stooges)
Creepshow, 1982 (Harris, E.)
Creepshow II, 1987 (Lamour)
Crépuscule d'epouvante, 1921 (Vanel)
Crest of the Wave, 1954 (Kelly, Gene)
Cresus, 1960 (Fernandel)
Crew. See Załoga, 1952
Cri de coeur, 1974 (Seyrig; Audran)
Cri du cormoran le soir au-dessus des jonques, 1970 (Blier; Depardieu)
Cria Cuervos, 1976 (Chaplin, G.)
Cricca dorata, 1913 (Bertini)
Cries and Whispers. See **Viskningar och rop**, 1972
Crime, 1992 (Delon)
Crime and Passion, 1975 (Sharif)
Crime and Punishment, 1935 (Lorre)
Crime and Punishment, 1993 (Redgrave, V.)
Crime by Night, 1944 (Wyman)
Crime Club, 1973 (Sheen)

Crime de Monsieur Lange, 1936 (Berry)
Crime de Monsieur Pégotte, 1935 (Berry)
Crime Doctor, 1934 (Crisp)
Crime Does Not Pay. See Crime ne paie pas, 1962
Crime et châtiment, 1956 (Blier; Gabin)
Crime in a Night Club. See Zločin v šantánu, 1968
Crime in Paradise. See Brott i paradiset, 1959
Crime in the Street, 1956 (Mineo)
Crime ne paie pas, 1962 (Brasseur; Cervi; Darrieux; Feuillère; Girardot; Morgan; Noiret)
Crime Nobody Saw, 1937 (Ayres; McDaniel)
Crime of Dr. Hallet, 1938 (Bellamy)
Crime of Helen Stanley, 1934 (Bellamy; Bond)
Crime of Passion, 1956 (Hayden; Stanwyck; Wray)
Crime on a Summer Morning. See Par un beau matin d'été, 1965
Crime on Their Hands, 1948 (Three Stooges)
Crime over London, 1936 (Withers)
Crime School, 1938 (Bogart)
Crime Story, 1993 (Chan)
Crime Wave, 1954 (Bronson; Hayden)
Crime without Passion, 1934 (Rains)
Crimebusters, 1961 (Dern)
Crimen, 1960 (Blier; Gassman; Mangano; Sordi)
Crimen de Cuenca, 1980 (Rey)
Crimes and Misdemeanors, 1989 (Allen; Bloom; Farrow; Huston, A.; Landau)
Crimes de l'amour. See Rideau cramoisi, 1952
Crime's End. See My Son Is Guilty, 1939
Crimes et Jardin, 1991 (Gélin)
Crimes of Passion, 1984 (Perkins; Turner, K.)
Crimes of the Heart, 1986 (Keaton, D.; Lange; Shepard; Spacek)
Criminal, 1915 (Talmadge)
Criminal, 1960 (Baker)
Criminal Affair, 1967 (Ann-Margret)
Criminal Code, 1929 (Huston, W.)
Criminal Code, 1931 (Karloff)
Criminal Justice, 1990 (Whitaker)
Criminal Law, 1989 (Bacon; Oldman)
Criminal Symphony. See Sette uomini e un Cervello, 1968
Criminals. See Once upon a Crime, 1992
Criminals at Large. See Liberty, 1929
Criminals of the Air, 1937 (Hayworth)
Crimson City, 1928 (Loy; Wong)
Crimson Cult, 1970 (Karloff)
Crimson Cult. See Curse of the Crimson Altar, 1968
Crimson Curtain. See Rideau cramoisi, 1952
Crimson Pirate, 1952 (Lancaster; Lee, C.)
Crimson Tide, 1995 (Hackman; Washington)
Crimson Trail, 1935 (Bond)
Cripta de l'incubo, 1963 (Lee, C.)
Crise est finie, 1934 (Darrieux)
Crisis, 1950 (Ferrer; Grant, C.; Novarro)
Crisis at Central High, 1981 (Woodward)
Criss Cross, 1948 (Curtis, T.; Duryea; Lancaster)
Crisscross, 1992 (Hawn)
Cristo proibito, 1951 (Cervi; Cuny)
Cristo si e fermato a Eboli, 1979 (Papas; Cuny; Volonté)
Cristoforo Colombo, 1985 (Brazzi; Dunaway; Von Sydow)
Critic, 1963 (Brooks, M.)
Critical Condition, 1987 (Pryor)
Critical Condition, 1987 (Snipes)
Critical List. See Terminal Choice, 1985
Critics Choice, 1963 (Ball; Hope)
Critters 4, 1992 (Bassett)
Croisée des chemins, 1942 (Brasseur)
Croisière pour l'inconnu, 1947 (Brasseur)
Croix de bois, 1931 (Artaud; Vanel)
Croix de vivants, 1962 (Cuny)
Cromwell, 1911 (Berry)
Cromwell, 1970 (Guinness; Harris, R.)
Cronaca di una morte annunciata, 1987 (Cuny; Papas; Volonté)
Cronaca familiare, 1962 (Mastroianni)

Cronaca nera, 1947 (Cervi)
Cronache di poveri amanti, 1954 (Mastroianni)
Crooked Billet, 1929 (Carroll)
Crooked Hearts, 1972 (O'Sullivan; Russell, R.)
Crooked Hearts, 1991 (Leigh, Jennifer Jason; Lewis, Juliette)
Crooked Road, 1964 (Granger; Ryan, R.)
Crooklyn, 1994 (Lee, S.)
Crooks and Coronets, 1969 (Evans; Oates)
Crooks Anonymous, 1962 (Christie)
Crooks Can't Win, 1928 (Brown)
Crooks in Clover. See Penthouse, 1933
Cross-Country Cruise, 1934 (Ayres)
Cross-Country Original, 1909 (Linder)
Cross-Country Romance, 1940 (Ladd)
Cross Creek, 1983 (McDowell; Steenburgen)
Cross Current, 1971 (Ferrer)
Cross of Iron, 1977 (Coburn, J.; Schell, Maximilian)
Cross of Lorraine, 1943 (Kelly, Gene; Lorre)
Cross of the Living. See Croix de vivants, 1962
Cross Red Nurse, 1918 (Dressler)
Cross Shot, 1976 (Cobb)
Crossbeams. See Tvärbalk, 1967
Crossed Swords, 1978 (Harrison; Reed; Scott, G.; Welch)
Crossed Swords. See Maestro di Don Giovanni, 1953
Crossed Swords. See Prince and the Pauper, 1977
Crossfire, 1947 (Grahame; Mitchum; Ryan, R.; Young, R.)
Crossing Guard, 1995 (Dickinson; Huston, A.; Nicholson; Penn)
Crossing the Line. See Big Man, 1991
Crossing to Freedom. See Pied Piper, 1990
Crossroads. See Shizi jietou, 1937
Crossroads. See Carrefour, 1939
Crossroads, 1942 (Lamarr; Powell, W.; Rathbone; Trevor)
Crossroads, 1955 (Lee, C.)
Crouching Beast, 1935 (Kortner)
Crowd Roars, 1932 (Blondell; Cagney)
Crowd Roars, 1938 (O'Sullivan; Taylor, R.; Wyman)
Crowded Day, 1954 (Roberts, R.)
Crowded Sky, 1960 (Andrews, D.)
Crowhaven Farm, 1970 (Carradine)
Crown of Lies, 1926 (Negri)
Crown of Thorns. See I.N.R.I., 1923
Crown Prince's Double, 1915 (Talmadge)
Crown versus Stevens, 1936 (Withers)
Crows and Sparrows. See Wuya yu Maque, 1948
Crucial Test, 1916 (Menjou)
Crucible, 1996 (Day-Lewis; Ryder)
Crucible. See Sorcières de Salem, 1956
Crucifer of Blood, 1991 (Heston)
Crucifixion, 1972 (Welles)
Crudeli, 1967 (Cotten)
Cruel, Cruel Love, 1914 (Chaplin, C.)
Cruel Sea, 1952 (Baker; Elliott; Hawkins)
Cruise into Terror, 1978 (Milland)
Cruise Missile. See Teheran Incident, 1979
Cruise of the Zaca, 1952 (Flynn)
Cruising, 1980 (Pacino)
Crusade, 1996 (Schwarzenegger)
Crusades, 1935 (Carradine; Young, L.)
Crush Proof, 1971 (Hopper)
Crushin' Thru, 1923 (Carey)
Cruz diablo, 1934 (Hayworth)
Cry-Baby, 1990 (Dafoe; Depp)
Cry Baby Killer, 1958 (Nicholson)
Cry Blood, Apache, 1970 (McCrea)
Cry Danger, 1951 (Powell, D.)
Cry for Happy, 1960 (Ford, G.; O'Connor)
Cry for Help, 1912 (Barrymore, L.; Carey; Gish)
Cry Freedom, 1987 (Attenborough; Kline; Washington)
Cry Havoc, 1943 (Blondell; Sullavan)
Cry Havoc!, 1943 (Mitchum)
Cry in the Dark, 1988 (Neill; Streep)

Cry in the Night, 1956 (Ladd; Wood)
Cry in the Night, 1993 (Girardot)
Cry of the Banshee, 1970 (Bergner; Price)
Cry of the City, 1948 (Mature; Winters)
Cry of the Hunted, 1953 (Gassman)
Cry of the Innocent, 1978 (Cusack)
Cry of the Innocent, 1980 (Cusack)
Cry of the Penguins. See Mr. Forbush and the Penguins, 1971
Cry of Triumph. See Hempas bar, 1977
Cry Onion. See Cipola Colt, 1975
Cry Terror, 1958 (Dickinson; Marsh; Mason; Steiger)
Cry, the Beloved Country, 1952 (Poitier)
Cry, the Beloved Country, 1995 (Harris, R.; Jones, James Earl)
Cry Wolf, 1947 (Flynn; Stanwyck)
Crying Game, 1992 (Richardson, M.; Whitaker)
Crystal and Fox, 1975 (Cusack)
Crystal Ball, 1943 (Goddard; Milland)
Crystal Eye, 1988 (Lom)
Crystal or Ash, Fire or Wind, as Long as It's Love, 1989 (Sanda)
Csak egy mozi, 1985 (Léaud)
Cuando habla el corazón, 1943 (Infante)
Cuando viva villa es la muerte, 1958 (Armendáriz)
Cuandolloran los valientes, 1945 (Infante)
Cuatro milpas, 1937 (Armendáriz)
Cuatro Robinsones, 1940 (Rey)
Cuba, 1979 (Connery; Elliott)
Cuban Love Song, 1931 (Durante)
Cuban Rebel Girls, 1959 (Flynn)
Cucaracha, 1958 (Armendáriz; Del Rio; Félix)
Cuckoo. See Hototogisu, 1932
Cuckoo in a Choo Choo, 1952 (Three Stooges)
Cuentos de Borges I, 1991 (Banderas)
Cueva de los tiburones. See Bermuda: la fossa maledetta, 1978
Cuidado con el amor, 1954 (Infante)
Cuisine au beurre, 1963 (Fernandel)
Culastrice nobile veneziano, 1976 (Mastroianni)
Cul-de-Sac, 1966 (Pleasence)
Culpables, 1958 (Rey)
Cult of the Damned. See Angel, Angel, Down We Go, 1969
Cunegonde, 1932 (Fernandel)
Cuore di cane, 1975 (Von Sydow)
Cuore di mamma, 1968 (Thulin)
Cuore semplice, 1978 (Valli)
Cuori nella tormenta, 1940 (Sordi)
Cuori senza fontiere, 1950 (Lollobrigida)
Cuori sul mare, 1950 (Loren; Mastroianni; Vanel)
Cup of Life and Death. See Kubok zhizhni i smerti, 1912
Cupboard Was Bare. See Armoire volante, 1948
Cupid Takes a Holiday, 1938 (Kaye)
Cupid the Cowpuncher, 1920 (Rogers, W.)
Cupid versus Money, 1914 (Talmadge)
Cupid's Rival, 1917 (Laurel and Hardy)
Cupid's Roundup, 1918 (Mix)
Cupid's Target, 1915 (Laurel and Hardy)
Curacao, 1993 (Scott, G.)
Cure, 1917 (Chaplin, C.; Purviance)
Cure for Love, 1949 (Donat)
Cure for Timidity. See Timidité vaincue, 1909
Cure That Failed, 1913 (Normand)
Curée, 1966 (Fonda, J.; Piccoli)
Curing a Husband, 1914 (Beery)
Curing of Myra May, 1914 (Talmadge)
Curious Conduct of Judge Legarde, 1915 (Barrymore, L.)
Curious Way to Love. See Morte la fatto, l'uovo, 1967
Curly Top, 1935 (Temple)
Curse III: Blood Sacrifice, 1991 (Lee, C.)
Curse of Frankenstein, 1957 (Cushing; Lee, C.)
Curse of King Tut's Tomb, 1980 (Saint)
Curse of the Crimson Affair. See Crimson Cult, 1970
Curse of the Crimson Altar, 1968 (Lee, C.)
Curse of the Demon. See Night of the Demon, 1957

Dancer, 1988 (Rainer)
Dancer, 1993 (Josephson)
Dancers in the Dark, 1932 (Hopkins, M.; Raft)
Dances with Wolves, 1990 (Costner)
Danchi nanatsu-no taizai, 1964 (Tsukasa)
Dancin' Days, 1978 (Braga)
Dancing Co-Ed, 1939 (Turner, L.; Walker)
Dancing Craze, 1912-13 (White)
Dancing Dynamite, 1931 (Brennan)
Dancing Girls of Izu. *See* Izu no odoriko, 1933
Dancing Hawk. *See* Ta Inczacy Tastrzab, 1977
Dancing in the Dark, 1949 (Menjou; Powell, W.)
Dancing Instructor, 1929 (Brown)
Dancing Lady, 1933 (Astaire; Crawford, J.; Eddy; Gable; Three Stooges)
Dancing Machine, 1990 (Delon)
Dancing Masters, 1943 (Dumont; Laurel and Hardy; Mitchum)
Dancing Mothers, 1926 (Bow)
Dancing with Crime, 1947 (Attenborough; Bogarde; Dors)
Dandin, 1988 (Gélin)
Dandy in Aspic, 1968 (Farrow)
Danger: Diabolik, 1968 (Piccoli)
Danger Girl, 1916 (Swanson)
Danger—Go Slow, 1918 (Chaney)
Danger Grows Wild. *See* Poppy Is Also a Flower, 1966
Danger in the Skies. *See* Pilot, 1981
Danger Island, 1939 (Lorre)
Danger Lights, 1930 (Arthur)
Danger Line. *See* Bataille, 1923
Danger—Love at Work, 1937 (Carradine; Horton)
Danger on the Air, 1938 (Cobb)
Danger Patrol, 1937 (Carey)
Danger Rides the Range. *See* Three Texas Steers, 1939
Danger Route, 1967 (Dors)
Danger Stalks Near. *See* Fuzen no tomoshibi, 1957
Danger Within, 1959 (Attenborough; Caine)
Dangerous, 1936 (Davis, B.)
Dangerous, 1995 (Gould)
Dangerous Age. *See* Beloved Brat, 1938
Dangerous Business, 1946 (Three Stooges)
Dangerous Cargo. *See* Forbidden Cargo, 1925
Dangerous Comment, 1940 (Mills)
Dangerous Corner, 1934 (Douglas, Melvyn)
Dangerous Curves, 1929 (Bow; Francis)
Dangerous Exile, 1958 (Jourdan)
Dangerous Females, 1929 (Dressler)
Dangerous Game, 1993 (Keitel)
Dangerous Hero. *See* Kiken no eiyu, 1957
Dangerous Indiscretion, 1995 (McDowell)
Dangerous Intrigue, 1936 (Bellamy)
Dangerous Liaisons, 1988 (Close; Malkovich; Pfeiffer; Reeves; Thurman)
Dangerous Love, 1988 (Gould)
Dangerous Man: Lawrence after Arabia, 1991 (Fiennes)
Dangerous Minds, 1995 (Pfeiffer)
Dangerous Mission, 1954 (Mature; Price)
Dangerous Money, 1924 (Powell, W.)
Dangerous Moonlight, 1941 (Walbrook)
Dangerous Moves. *See* Diagonale du fou, 1984
Dangerous Number, 1937 (Young, R.)
Dangerous Profession, 1949 (Raft)
Dangerous Secrets, 1938 (Lukas)
Dangerous to Know, 1938 (Quinn; Wong)
Dangerous When Wet, 1953 (Williams, E.)
Dangerous Woman, 1993 (Hershey; Winger)
Dangerous Years, 1948 (Monroe)
Dangerous Years of Kiowa Jones, 1966 (Mineo)
Dangerously They Live, 1941 (Garfield; Massey)
Dangers of a Bride, 1917 (Swanson)
Daniel, 1983 (Barkin)
Daniel and the Devil. *See* All That Money Can Buy, 1941
Daniel Boone, 1936 (Carradine)
Daniele Cortis, 1946 (Cervi; Gassman)

Danjuro sandai, 1944 (Kyo; Tanaka)
Dankon, 1969 (Okada)
Danny Kaye Story. *See* Birth of a Star, 1944
Danny, the Champion of the World, 1989 (Cusack; Irons)
Dans la nuit, 1929 (Vanel)
Dans la poussière du soleil, 1971 (Schell, Maria)
Dans la vie tout s'arrange, 1950 (Henreid)
Dans la Ville Blanche, 1983 (Ganz)
Dansa min docka, 1953 (Björnstrand)
Dansai Hyoe issho-tabi, 1933 (Yamada)
Danse Macabre. *See* Tanyets smerti, 1916
Dansei No. 1, 1955 (Mifune)
Dansei tai josei, 1936 (Tanaka)
Danseuse voilée, 1916 (Modot)
Danssalongen, 1955 (Thulin)
Dante's Inferno, 1935 (Hayworth; Tracy; Trevor)
Dante's Inferno. *See* Jacob's Ladder, 1990
Dante's Inferno: The Life of Dante Gabriel Rossetti, 1967 (Reed)
Danton, 1920 (Jannings; Kortner; Krauss)
Danton, 1932 (Kortner)
Danton, 1982 (Depardieu; Winkler)
Daphne. *See* Jinchoge, 1966
Daphne and the Pirate, 1916 (Gish)
Daphne, the Virgin of the Golden Laurels, 1951 (Barrymore, E.)
Darby O'Gill and the Little People, 1959 (Connery)
Darby's Rangers, 1958 (Garner)
Dard ka rishta, 1983 (Patil)
Dare ga watashi o sabakunoka, 1951 (Yamamura)
Daredevil, 1920 (Mix)
Daredevil in the Castle. *See* Osaka-jo monogatari, 1961
Daredevil Jack, 1920 (Chaney)
Daredevil's Reward, 1928 (Mix)
Dåres förvarstal, 1976 (Andersson, B.)
Darf ich mitspielen?, 1976 (Brandauer)
Daring Years, 1923 (Bow)
Daring Young Man, 1942 (Brown)
Dark Angel, 1925 (Banky; Colman; March)
Dark Angel, 1935 (Marshall; Oberon)
Dark Angel, 1989 (O'Toole)
Dark at Noon, or Eyes and Lies. *See* Oeil qui ment, 1992
Dark at the Top of the Stairs, 1960 (Preston; Lansbury)
Dark Avenger, 1955 (Finch; Flynn)
Dark Avengers, 1955 (Lee, C.)
Dark Backward, 1991 (Caan)
Dark City, 1950 (Heston)
Dark Command, 1940 (Pidgeon; Rogers, R.; Trevor; Wayne)
Dark Corner, 1946 (Ball; Webb)
Dark Delusion, 1947 (Barrymore, L.)
Dark Eyes. *See* Oci ciornie, 1987
Dark Eyes of London. *See* Human Monster, 1939
Dark Eyes of London. *See* Toten Augen von London, 1961
Dark Hazard, 1934 (Robinson, E.)
Dark Holiday, 1989 (Remick)
Dark Horse, 1932 (Davis, B.)
Dark House, 1923 (Laurel and Hardy)
Dark Journey, 1937 (Leigh, V.; Veidt)
Dark Mansions, 1986 (Fontaine)
Dark Mirror, 1920 (White)
Dark Mirror, 1946 (Ayres; De Havilland)
Dark Page. *See* Scandal Sheet, 1952
Dark Passage, 1947 (Bacall; Bogart; Moorehead)
Dark Past, 1949 (Cobb; Holden)
Dark Places, 1973 (Lee, C.; Lom)
Dark Purpose, 1964 (Brazzi; Presle; Sanders)
Dark Sands. *See* Jericho, 1937
Dark Secret of Harvest Home, 1978 (Davis, B.; Pleasence)
Dark Side of Love. *See* My Kidnapper, My Love, 1980
Dark Star, 1919 (Davies)
Dark Sun. *See* Sole buio, 1990
Dark the Mountain Snow. *See* Rokujo yukiyama tsumugi, 1965
Dark Tower, 1943 (Lom)

Dark Venture, 1956 (Carradine)
Dark Victory, 1939 (Bogart; Davis, B.; Reagan)
Dark Victory, 1976 (Hopkins, A.)
Dark Waters, 1944 (Oberon)
Dark Wind, 1991 (Redford)
Dark World, 1935 (Withers)
Dark-Adapted Eye, 1994 (Bonham-Carter)
Darkening Trail, 1915 (Hart)
Darker Side of Terror, 1979 (Milland)
Darker than Amber, 1970 (Russell, J.)
Darkest Hour. See Hell on Frisco Bay, 1955
Darkman, 1990 (Neeson)
Darkness at Noon. See Mahiru no ankoku, 1956
Darling, 1965 (Bogarde; Christie)
Darling Darling, 1977 (Anand)
Darling, How Could You!, 1951 (Fontaine)
Darling Lili, 1970 (Andrews, J.; Hudson)
Darling of Paris, 1917 (Bara)
Darling of the Gods. See Liebling der Götter, 1930
Darpachurna, 1980 (Chatterjee)
Dårskab, dyd og driverter, 1923 (Madsen and Schenstrøm)
Dårskapens hus, 1951 (Andersson, H.)
Dash of Courage, 1916 (Beery; Swanson)
Dash through the Clouds, 1911 (Normand)
Dastaan, 1972 (Kumar)
Date with a Dream, 1948 (Terry-Thomas; Wisdom)
Date with a Lonely Girl. See T. R. Baskin, 1971
Date with an Unknown. See Mouid maa el Maghoul, 1958
Date with Destiny. See Return of October, 1948
Date with Judy, 1948 (Beery; Miranda; Taylor, E.)
Date with the Falcon, 1941 (Sanders)
Datsugoku, 1950 (Mifune)
Datta, 1976 (Chatterjee)
Daughter-in-Law. See Snotchak, 1912
Daughter of Darkness, 1990 (Perkins)
Daughter of Eve, 1919 (Colman)
Daughter of Israel, 1914 (Talmadge)
Daughter of Israel. See Dots Izrila, 1917
Daughter of Luxury. See Five and Ten, 1931
Daughter of Rosie O'Grady, 1950 (Reynolds, D.)
Daughter of Shanghai, 1937 (Quinn; Wong)
Daughter of the Dragon, 1931 (Hayakawa; Wong)
Daughter of the Mind, 1969 (Carradine; Miland; Tierney)
Daughter of the Night. See Tanz auf dem Vulkan, 1921
Daughter of the South, 1911 (White)
Daughter of Two Worlds, 1920 (Talmadge)
Daughters Courageous, 1939 (Crisp; Garfield; Rains)
Daughters of Darkness. See Rouge aux lèvres, 1971
Daughters of Destiny. See Destinées, 1954
Daughters of Pleasure, 1924 (Bow)
Daughters of Yoshiwara. See Takekurabe, 1955
Daughter's Strange Inheritance, 1915 (Talmadge)
Daughters Who Pay, 1925 (Lugosi)
Daughters, Wives, and a Mother. See Musume tsuma haha, 1960
Dave, 1993 (Kingsley; Kline; Schwarzenegger; Weaver)
David, 1996 (Pitt)
David and Bathsheba, 1951 (Hayward; Massey; Peck)
David and Goliath. See David e Golia, 1959
David Copperfield, 1935 (Barrymore, L.; Fields, W. C.; Lanchester; O'Sullivan; Rathbone)
David Copperfield, 1970 (Attenborough; Cusack; Evans; Olivier; Redgrave, M.; Richardson, R.)
David e Golia, 1959 (Welles)
David Harum, 1934 (Rogers, W.)
Dawn, 1914 (Crisp)
Dawn, 1928 (Marshall)
Dawn, 1991 (Kinski)
Dawn at Socorro, 1954 (Van Cleef)
Dawn Maker, 1916 (Hart)
Dawn of Tomorrow, 1915 (Pickford)
Dawn of Understanding, 1918 (Gilbert)

Dawn Patrol, 1930 (Barthelmess)
Dawn Patrol, 1938 (Crisp; Fitzgerald; Flynn; Niven; Rathbone)
Dawn Rider, 1935 (Wayne)
Dawning, 1988 (Grant, H.; Hopkins, A.; Howard, T.)
Day. See Antonito, 1961
Day After, 1909 (Sweet)
Day After, 1983 (Robards; De Havilland)
Day at School, 1916 (Laurel and Hardy)
Day at the Beach, 1970 (Sellers)
Day at the Races, 1937 (Dumont; Marx Brothers)
Day at the Races, 1937 (O'Sullivan)
Day Before. See Giorno prima, 1987
Day by Day, 1913 (Beery)
Day for Night. See Nuit américaine, 1973
Day in Court. See Giorno in pretura, 1954
Day in the Death of Joe Egg, 1971 (Bates, A.)
Day in the Life of Wood Newton, 1990 (Reynolds, B.)
Day of a Man of Affairs, 1929 (Rogers, G.)
Day of Anger. See I giorno dell'ira, 1967
Day of Atonement. See Grand Pardon II, 1993
Day of the Assassin, 1981 (Ford, G.)
Day of the Badman, 1958 (MacMurray; Van Cleef)
Day of the Dolphin, 1973 (Scott, G.)
Day of the Evil Gun, 1968 (Ford, G.; Kennedy; Stanton)
Day of the Jackal, 1973 (Cusack; Seyrig)
Day of the Landgrabbers. See Land Raiders, 1970
Day of the Locust, 1975 (Meredith; Page; Sutherland)
Day of the Outlaw, 1959 (Ryan, R.)
Day of the Owl. See Giorno della civetta, 1968
Day of Triumph, 1954 (Cobb)
Day the Bookies Wept, 1939 (Grable)
Day the Clown Cried, 1972 (Lewis, Jerry)
Day the Earth Caught Fire, 1961 (Caine)
Day the Earth Moved, 1974 (Cooper)
Day the Earth Stood Still, 1951 (Jaffe; Neal)
Day the Hotline Got Hot, 1969 (Boyer; Taylor, R.)
Day the Sun Rose. See Gion matsuri, 1968
Day They Robbed the Bank of England, 1960 (O'Toole)
Day Time Ended, 1980 (Malone)
Day to Remember. See Aujourd'Hui Peut-Etre ..., 1991
Day to Remember. See Two Bits, 1995
Day Will Come. See Es kommt ein Tag, 1950
Day Will Dawn, 1942 (Kerr; Richardson, R.)
Day's Pleasure, 1919 (Chaplin, C.; Purviance)
Daybreak, 1931 (Novarro)
Daybreak. See Jour se lève, 1939
Daydreamer, 1962 (Hayakawa)
Daydreamer, 1966 (Karloff; Terry-Thomas)
Daydreams, 1922 (Keaton, B.)
Daydreams, 1928 (Lanchester; Laughton)
Daylight, 1996 (Stallone)
Daylight Burglar, 1913 (Crisp)
Days and Nights in the Forest. See Aranyar din Ratri, 1970
Days of Fury. See Giorno del furore, 1973
Days of Fury, 1978 (Price)
Days of Glory, 1943 (Peck)
Days of Heaven, 1978 (Gere; Shepard)
Days of Jesse James, 1939 (Rogers, R.)
Days of Thrills and Laughter, 1963 (Laurel and Hardy)
Days of Thunder, 1990 (Cruise; Duvall)
Days of Wilfred Owen, 1965 (Burton)
Days of Wine and Roses, 1962 (Lemmon; Remick)
Days of Youth. See Wakaki hi, 1929
Days that Shook the World, 1975 (Schell, Maximilian)
Daytime Wife, 1939 (Darnell; Power)
Dayu san yori: Jotai wa kanashiku, 1957 (Tanaka)
D-Day, the Sixth of June, 1956 (O'Brien, E.; Taylor, R.)
De aire y fuego, 1972 (Brazzi)
De Drapeau noir flotte sur le marmite, 1971 (Gabin)
De Flyngande Djavlarna. See Flying Devils, 1985
De force avec d'autres, 1993 (Gélin; Léaud; Reggiani)

De Grens, 1984 (Winkler)
De haut à bas, 1933 (Lorre)
De Ijsallon, 1985 (Ganz)
De kalte ham Skarven, 1965 (Ullmann)
De keder sig pålandet. *See* Et sommereventyr, 1919
De la Légion, 1936 (Fernandel)
De l'amour, 1964 (Karina; Piccoli)
De la part des copains. *See* Uomo dalle due ombre, 1971
De la part des copains. *See* Uomo dalle due ombre, 1974
De la poudre et des balles. *See* Bonne Chance, Charlie, 1962
De man die zijn haar kort liet knippen, 1966 (Tyszkiewicz)
De Mayerling à Sarajevo, 1940 (Feuillère)
De Renoir à Picasso, 1950 (Brasseur)
De Sade, 1969 (Huston, J.)
De sista stegen, 1961 (Dahlbeck)
De sueur et du sang, 1994 (Vogler)
De Två Saliga, 1985 (Andersson, H.)
Dea del mare, 1907 (Bertini)
Deacon's Trouble, 1912 (Normand)
Dead, 1987 (Huston, A.; Huston, J.)
Dead Again, 1991 (Branagh; García; Schygulla; Thompson; Williams, R.)
Dead and Alive: The Race for Gus Farace, 1991 (Jackson, S.)
Dead Calm, 1989 (Neill)
Dead City. *See* Nekri Politeia, 1951
Dead Don't Die, 1975 (Milland)
Dead Don't Scream, 1975 (Blondell)
Dead End, 1937 (Bogart; Bond; McCrea; Sidney; Trevor)
Dead Eyes of London. *See* Toten Augen von London, 1961
Dead Heat, 1988 (Price)
Dead Heat on a Merry-Go-Round, 1966 (Coburn, J.; Ford, H.)
Dead Image. *See* Dead Ringer, 1964
Dead Letter, 1915 (Laurel and Hardy)
Dead Line. *See* Gray Horizon, 1919
Dead Man, 1996 (Depp; Hurt, J.; Mitchum)
Dead Man Out, 1989 (Jackson, S.)
Dead Man Walking, 1995 (Penn; Robbins; Sarandon)
Dead Man's Folly, 1986 (Ustinov)
Dead Man's Revenge, 1994 (Dern)
Dead Men Are Dangerous, 1939 (Withers)
Dead Men Don't Die, 1991 (Gould)
Dead Men Don't Wear Plaid, 1982 (Martin, S.)
Dead Men's Shoes, 1939 (McDowall)
Dead of Night, 1945 (Redgrave, M.; Withers)
Dead of Summer. *See* Ondata di calore, 1970
Dead of Winter, 1987 (McDowall; Steenburgen)
Dead on Arrival, 1979 (Palance)
Dead on Course. *See* Wings of Danger, 1952
Dead or Alive. *See* Escondido, 1968
Dead or Alive. *See* Minuto per pregare, un instante per morire, 1968
Dead Pigeon on Beethoven Street, 1972 (Audran)
Dead Poets Society, 1989 (Williams, R.)
Dead Pool, 1988 (Eastwood; Neeson)
Dead Presidents, 1995 (Sheen)
Dead Reckoning, 1947 (Bogart)
Dead Reckoning, 1990 (Robertson)
Dead Ringer, 1964 (Davis, B.; Henreid; Malden)
Dead Ringers, 1988 (Bujold; Irons)
Dead Tired. *See* Grosse Fatigue, 1994
Dead Zone, 1983 (Lom; Sheen; Walken)
Deadfall, 1968 (Caine)
Deadfall, 1993 (Cage; Coburn, J.)
Deadhead Miles, 1972 (Arkin; Lupino; Raft)
Deadlier Sex, 1919 (Karloff; Sweet)
Deadliest Art: The Best of the Martial Arts Films, 1990 (Chan)
Deadliest Season, 1977 (Streep)
Deadline, 1987 (Hurt, J.; Walken)
Deadline—U.S.A., 1952 (Barrymore, E.; Bogart)
Deadline at Dawn, 1946 (Hayward; Lukas)
Deadly Advice, 1994 (Mills)
Deadly Affair, 1966 (Andersson, H.; Mason; Schell, Maximilian)
Deadly Blessing, 1981 (Borgnine; Stone)

Deadly Business, 1986 (Arkin)
Deadly Circuit. *See* Mortelle randonnée, 1983
Deadly Companions, 1961 (O'Hara)
Deadly Decision. *See* Dadah Is Death, 1988
Deadly Desire. *See* Maybe I'll Come Home in the Spring, 1971
Deadly Dreams, 1971 (Leigh, Janet)
Deadly Game, 1982 (Howard, T.)
Deadly Game, 1991 (McDowall)
Deadly Hero, 1976 (DeVito; Jones, James Earl)
Deadly Pursuit. *See* Shoot to Kill, 1988
Deadly Roulette. *See* How I Spent My Summer Vacation, 1967
Deadly Sting. *See* Evil Spawn, 1987
Deadly Strangers, 1974 (Hayden)
Deadly Thief. *See* Shalimar, 1978
Deadly Three. *See* Enter the Dragon, 1973
Deadly Trackers, 1973 (Harris, R.)
Deadly Trap. *See* Maison sous les arbres, 1971
Deadwood Coach, 1924 (Mix)
Deaf Smith and Johnny Ears, 1973 (Quinn)
Deal of the Century, 1983 (Weaver)
Dealing for Daisy. *See* Mr. "Silent" Haskins, 1915
Dealing: Or the Berkeley-to-Boston Forty-Brick Lost-Bag Blues, 1972 (Hershey)
Dear America: Letters Home from Vietnam, 1987 (Burstyn; Dafoe; De Niro; Dillon; Keitel; Penn; Williams, R.)
Dear Brat, 1951 (Wood)
Dear Brigitte, 1965 (Bardot; Stewart)
Dear, Dead Delilah, 1972 (Moorehead)
Dear Detective. *See* Tendre poulet, 1978
Dear Gorbachev. *See* Caro Gorbaciov, 1988
Dear Heart, 1964 (Ford, G.; Lansbury; Page)
Dear Inspector. *See* Tendre poulet, 1978
Dear Mr. Prohack, 1949 (Bogarde; Elliott)
Dear Mr. Wonderful, 1982 (Pesci)
Dear Octopus, 1943 (Johnson; Lockwood)
Dear Ruth, 1947 (Holden)
Dear Wife, 1949 (Holden)
Death among Friends, 1975 (Henreid)
Death and the Maiden, 1994 (Kingsley; Weaver)
Death at 45 RPM. *See* Meurtre en 45 tours, 1960
Death at Broadcasting House, 1934 (Hawkins)
Death at Love House, 1976 (Blondell; Carradine; Lamour)
Death Becomes Her, 1992 (Caine; Hawn; Rossellini; Streep; Willis)
Death Bite, 1982 (Reed)
Death Blow, 1987 (Landau)
Death Collector, 1975 (Pesci)
Death Corps. *See* Shock Waves, 1975
Death Drives Through, 1935 (Huston, J.)
Death Flight. *See* SST—Death Flight, 1977
Death Game, 1977 (Spacek)
Death Hits the Jackpot, 1991 (Falk)
Death Hunt, 1981 (Bronson; Dickinson; Marvin)
Death in a French Garden. *See* Péril en la demeure, 1984
Death in Brunswick, 1991 (Neill)
Death in the Garden. *See* Mort en ce jardin, 1956
Death in the Sun. *See* Flüsternde Tod, 1975
Death in the Vatican. *See* Morte in Vaticano, 1982
Death in Venice. *See* **Morte a Venezia**, 1971
Death, Japanese Style. *See* Ososhiki, 1984
Death Kiss, 1933 (Lugosi)
Death Line, 1972 (Lee, C.)
Death List. *See* Terminal Choice, 1985
Death Live, 1972 (Pleasence)
Death of a Centerfold: The Dorothy Stratten Story, 1981 (Curtis, J.)
Death of a Champion, 1939 (O'Connor)
Death of a Gunfighter, 1969 (Widmark)
Death of a Prophet, 1981 (Freeman)
Death of a Salesman, 1951 (March)
Death of a Salesman, 1957 (Sellers)
Death of a Salesman, 1985 (Hoffman)
Death of a Salesman, 1986 (Malkovich)

Death of a Scoundrel, 1956 (Sanders)
Death of a Soldier, 1986 (Coburn, J.)
Death of a Tea Master. *See* Sen no Rikyu, 1989
Death of an Expert Witness, 1983 (Cusack)
Death of Innocence, 1971 (Kennedy; Winters)
Death of Mario Ricci. *See* Mort de Mario Ricci, 1984
Death of Ocean View Park, 1979 (Landau)
Death of the Heart, 1985 (Richardson, M.)
Death on Safari. *See* Ten Little Indians, 1989
Death on the Diamond, 1934 (Rooney; Young, R.)
Death on the Mountain. *See* Aru sonan, 1961
Death on the Nile, 1978 (Davis, B.; Farrow; Lansbury; Niven; Smith; Ustinov)
Death Race 2000, 1975 (Stallone)
Death Rage. *See* Con la rabbia agli occhi, 1976
Death Ride to Osaka. *See* Girls of the White Orchid, 1983
Death Rides a Horse. *See* Da uomo a uoma, 1967
Death Scream, 1975 (Julia)
Death Sentence, 1974 (Nolte)
Death Squad, 1974 (Douglas, Melvyn)
Death Takes a Holiday, 1934 (March)
Death Takes a Holiday, 1971 (Douglas, Melvyn; Loy)
Death Travels Too Much. *See* Humour noir, 1965
Death Warrant, 1990 (Van Damme)
Death Wheelers. *See* Living Dead, 1972
Death, Where Is Thy Victory? *See* Mort, où est ta victoire?, 1964
Death Wish, 1974 (Bronson)
Death Wish II, 1981 (Bronson; Fishburne)
Death Wish III, 1985 (Bronson)
Death Wish IV: The Crackdown, 1987 (Bronson)
Death Wish V: The Face of Death, 1994 (Bronson)
Death Woman. *See* Senora Muerte, 1967
Deathbed. *See* Terminal Choice, 1985
Deathmask, 1984 (Aiello)
Death's Marathon, 1913 (Barrymore, L.; Sweet)
Deathtrap, 1982 (Caine)
Deathwatch, 1982 (Stanton)
Deathwatch. *See* Mort en Direct, 1979
Debibaran, 1988 (Chatterjee)
Debshishu, 1986 (Patil)
Debt. *See* His Debt, 1919
Débuts au cinématographe. *See* Débuts de Max au cinéma, 1910
Débuts de Max au cinéma, 1910 (Linder)
Débuts d'un aviateur. *See* Max dans les airs, 1914
Débuts d'un patineur, 1908 (Linder)
Débuts d'un yachtman, 1909 (Linder)
Décade prodigieuse, 1972 (Perkins; Piccoli; Welles)
Decameron. *See* Decamerone, 1971
Decameron Nights, 1924 (Barrymore, L.)
Decameron Nights, 1953 (Fontaine; Jourdan)
Decameron Nights. *See* Dekameron-Nächte, 1924
Decamerone, 1971 (Mangano)
Deceived, 1991 (Hawn)
Deceiver, 1931 (Wayne)
December 7th, 1943 (Andrews, D.; Huston, W.)
December Evening, 1973 (Azmi)
Deception, 1946 (Davis, B.; Henreid; Rains)
Deception, 1956 (Howard, T.)
Deception. *See* Richter und sein Henker, 1975
Deception, 1992 (Neeson)
Deception against Time. *See* Man in the Sky, 1957
Deceptions, 1985 (Lollobrigida; McDowall)
Decima vittima, 1965 (Mastroianni)
Decimals of Love. *See* Kärlekens decimaler, 1960
Decimo clandestino, 1989 (Sanda)
Decision against Time. *See* Man in the Sky, 1956
Decision at Sundown, 1957 (Scott, R.)
Decision before Dawn, 1951 (Kinski; Malden; Werner)
Decisions! Decisions!, 1972 (Carradine)
Decks Ran Red, 1958 (Crawford, B.; Mason)
Declassée, 1925 (Gable)
Declic et des claques, 1965 (Girardot)

Decoration Day, 1990 (Fishburne; Garner)
Decorator, 1920 (Laurel and Hardy)
Decree of Destiny, 1911 (Pickford)
Dédé la tendresse, 1972 (Dalio)
Dédée, 1934 (Darrieux)
Dédée d'Anvers, 1948 (Blier; Dalio)
Deedar, 1951 (Kumar)
Deep, 1969 (Welles)
Deep, 1977 (Nolte; Shaw; Wallach)
Deep Blue Sea, 1955 (Leigh, V.)
Deep Cover. *See* Blade on the Feather, 1980
Deep Cover, 1992 (Fishburne)
Deep Down, 1994 (Segal)
Deep End, 1970 (Dors)
Deep in My Heart, 1954 (Astaire; Charisse; Ferrer; Henreid; Kelly, Gene; Miller; Oberon; Pidgeon)
Deep River, 1995 (Kagawa; Mifune)
Deep Sea Fishing, 1952 (Flynn)
Deep Six, 1958 (Ladd)
Deep Valley, 1947 (Lupino)
Deep Water. *See* Eaux profondes, 1981
Deep Waters, 1920 (Gilbert)
Dccp Waters, 1948 (Andrews, D.; Marsh)
Deer Hunter, 1977 (De Niro; Streep; Walken)
Deerslayer. *See* Lederstrumpf, 1920
Def by Temptation, 1990 (Jackson, S.)
Defection of Simas Kurdirka, 1978 (Arkin; Pleasence)
Defective Detectives, 1944 (Langdon)
Defector, 1966 (Clift; McDowall)
Defence of the Realm, 1985 (Elliott; Scacchi)
Defend My Love. *See* Difendo il mio amore, 1956
Defending Your Life, 1991 (Grant, L.; MacLaine; Streep)
Defense of Sebastopol. *See* Oborono Sevastopolya, 1911
Defense Rests, 1934 (Arthur; Bond)
Defenseless, 1991 (Hershey; Shepard)
Defiance, 1980 (Aiello)
Defiance. *See* Trots, 1952
Defiant Ones, 1958 (Curtis, T.; Poitier)
Défroqué, 1953 (Fresnay)
Degourdis de la onzième, 1937 (Fernandel)
Deidre, 1956 (Cusack)
Déjà Vu, 1985 (Bloom; Winters)
Déjeuner de soleil, 1937 (Berry)
Dekalog 3, 1988 (Olbrychski)
Dekalog 8, 1988 (Łomnicki)
Dekameron-Nächte, 1924 (Krauss)
Dekigokoro, 1933 (Ryu)
Del odio nace el amor, 1950 (Armendáriz; Goddard)
Del ranco a la capital, 1941 (Armendáriz)
Delfini, 1960 (Cardinale)
Délibábok országa, 1983 (Nowicki)
Delicate Balance, 1973 (Cotten; Hepburn, K.; Remick)
Delicate Delinquent, 1957 (Lewis, Jerry)
Delicious, 1931 (Gaynor)
Delicious Little Devil, 1919 (Valentino)
Delightfully Dangerous, 1945 (Bellamy)
Delirious, 1991 (Candy)
Delitto, 1984 (Gélin)
Delitto di Giovanni Episcopo, 1947 (Fabrizi; Lollobrigida; Mangano; Sordi)
Delitto quasi perfetto, 1966 (Blier)
Deliverance, 1972 (Reynolds, B.; Voight)
Deliverance. *See* Sadgati, 1981
Della, 1965 (Crawford, J.)
Delo Artamonovykh, 1941 (Maretskaya)
Delta Fever, 1987 (Landau)
Delta Force, 1986 (Marvin; Schygulla; Winters)
Deluge. *See* Potop, 1915
Deluge. *See* Potop, 1974
Delusion, 1984 (Cotten)
Delusions of Grandeur. *See* Folie des grandeurs, 1971
Deluxe Annie, 1918 (Talmadge)

Demain, 1992 (Moreau)
Demasiado Corazon, 1992 (Abril)
Demaskierung. *See* Nacht der Verwandlung, 1935
Demetrius and the Gladiators, 1954 (Bancroft; Borgnine; Burton; Hayward; Mature)
Demi-Bride, 1927 (Shearer)
Demi-Paradise, 1943 (Olivier; Rutherford)
Demi-Gods and Semi-Devils, 1993 (Gong Li)
Demoiselles de Rochefort, 1967 (Darrieux; Deneuve; Piccoli)
Demoiselles ont eu 25 Ans, 1993 (Deneuve)
Demolition Man, 1993 (Snipes; Stallone)
Demon in My View. *See* Mann nebenan, 1991
Demon Murder Case, 1983 (Bacon)
Demon Seed, 1977 (Christie)
Demoniaque. *See* Louves, 1957
Démons de midi, 1978 (Presle)
Démons de minuit, 1961 (Boyer)
Demütiger und die Sängerin, 1925 (Dagover)
Dendai inchiki monogatari: Dotanuki, 1963 (Kyo)
Denen Kokyogaku, 1938 (Hara)
Dengeki Shutsudo, 1944 (Mori)
Dennis the Menace, 1993 (Matthau)
Dentellière, 1977 (Huppert)
Dentist. *See* Laughing Gas, 1914
Dentist, 1932 (Fields, W. C.)
Dents longues, 1952 (Bardot; Gélin)
Denver and Rio Grande, 1951 (Hayden; O'Brien, E.)
Départ, 1966 (Léaud)
Depraved. *See* Adelaide, 1968
Deputat Baltiki, 1936 (Cherkassov)
Derby Day, 1952 (Neagle; Withers)
Derek and Clive Get the Horn, 1978 (Moore, Dudley)
Derelitta, 1981 (Olbrychski)
Dernier amant romantique, 1979 (Rey)
Dernier amour, 1948 (Moreau)
Dernier Atout, 1942 (Modot)
Dernier baiser, 1977 (Girardot)
Dernier des six, 1941 (Fresnay)
Dernier été à Tanger, 1987 (Karina)
Dernier Métro, 1980 (Deneuve; Depardieu)
Dernier mot, 1991 (Schell, Maria)
Dernier refuge, 1947 (Modot)
Dernier soir, 1964 (Chaplin, G.)
Dernière attaque. *See* Guerra continua, 1962
Dernière chanson, 1986 (Karina)
Dernière femme. *See* Ultimata donna, 1976
Dernière jeunesse, 1939 (Brasseur; Raimu)
Derniers jours de Pompéi, 1948 (Presle)
Derrière la façade, 1939 (Berry)
Des Dreimäderlhaus, 1918 (Veidt)
Des enfants gâtés, 1977 (Huppert; Piccoli)
Des feux mal éteints, 1994 (Gélin)
Des frissons partout, 1964 (Constantine)
Des gens sans importance, 1955 (Gabin)
Des jeunes filles dans la nuit, 1943 (Berry)
Des Pardes, 1978 (Anand)
Des Teufels Advokat, 1977 (Audran)
Des verlorene Gesicht, 1948 (Fröhlich)
Desarraigados, 1958 (Armendáriz)
Desarroi, 1946 (Berry)
Descanse en piezas, 1986 (Malone)
Descendants of Taro Urashima. *See* Urashima Taro no koei, 1946
Descending Angel, 1990 (Scott, G.)
Deseada, 1951 (Del Rio)
Desert Attack. *See* Ice Cold in Alex, 1958
Desert Bloom, 1986 (Barkin; Voight)
Desert Breed, 1915 (Chaney)
Desert Calls Its Own, 1916 (Mix)
Désert de Pigalle, 1957 (Girardot)
Désert des Tartares, 1976 (Gassman; Noiret; Rey; Von Sydow)
Desert Driven, 1923 (Carey)

Desert Fox, 1951 (Mason; Sloane)
Desert Fury, 1947 (Astor; Lancaster)
Desert Gold, 1926 (Powell, W.)
Desert Hawk, 1950 (Hudson)
Desert Hero, 1919 (Arbuckle; Keaton, B.)
Desert Legion, 1953 (Ladd)
Desert Love, 1920 (Mix)
Desert Man, 1917 (Hart)
Desert Nights, 1929 (Gilbert)
Desert of the Tartars. *See* Désert des Tartares, 1976
Desert Patrol. *See* Sea of Sand, 1958
Desert Rats, 1953 (Burton; Mason)
Desert Sands, 1955 (Carradine)
Desert Song, 1929 (Loy)
Desert Song, 1943 (Dalio)
Desert Song, 1953 (Massey)
Desert Trail, 1935 (Wayne)
Desert Warrior. *See* Amanti del deserto, 1956
Deserter, 1971 (Huston, J.)
Deserter. *See* Disertore, 1983

Deserto dei Tartari. *See* Désert des Tartares, 1976
Deserto rosso, 1964 (Harris, R.; Vitti)
Desert's Toll, 1926 (Wong)
Design for Living, 1933 (Constantine; Hopkins, M.; Horton; March)
Design for Scandal, 1941 (Pidgeon; Russell, R.)
Designing Woman, 1957 (Bacall; Peck)
Desir, 1983 (Cassel)
Desirable, 1934 (Brennan)
Desire, 1936 (Constantine; Dietrich; Belmondo)
Desire. *See* Salt on Our Skin, 1992
Desire in the Dust, 1960 (Bennett)
Desire Me, 1947 (Garson; Mitchum)
Desire under the Elms, 1958 (Loren; Perkins)
Désiré, 1937 (Arletty)
Desirée, 1954 (Brando; Blondell; Oberon)
Desk Set, 1957 (Hepburn, K.; Tracy)
Desorde. *See* Disordine, 1962
Désordre et la nuit, 1958 (Cassel; Darrieux; Gabin)
Despair. *See* Eine Reise ins Licht, 1977
Desperado, 1954 (Van Cleef)
Desperado, 1995 (Banderas)
Desperado: Avalanche at Devil's Ridge, 1988 (Steiger)
Desperado Outpost. *See* Dokuritsu gurenta, 1959
Desperadoes, 1943 (Ford, G.; Scott, R.; Trevor)
Desperados, 1969 (Borgnine; Palance)
Desperate Adventure, 1938 (Novarro)
Desperate Case, 1981 (Lee, C.)
Desperate Chance. *See* "Bad Buck" of Santa Ynez, 1915
Desperate Characters, 1971 (MacLaine)
Desperate Hours, 1955 (Bogart; Kennedy; March)
Desperate Hours, 1990 (Hopkins, A.; Rourke)
Desperate Journey, 1942 (Flynn; Kennedy; Massey; Reagan)
Desperate Lover, 1912 (Normand)
Desperate Moment, 1953 (Bogarde; Zetterling)
Desperate Moves, 1986 (Lee, C.)
Desperate Ones. *See* Más allá de las montañas, 1967
Desperate Trails, 1921 (Carey)
Desperately Seeking Susan, 1985 (Turturro)
Dessous des cartes, 1947 (Reggiani)
Destin fabuleux de Desirée Clary, 1941 (Barrault)
Destination Fury. *See* Pleine bagarre, 1961
Destination Gobi, 1953 (Widmark)
Destination Milan, 1954 (Cusack)
Destination Moonbase Alpha, 1973 (Landau)
Destination Tokyo, 1944 (Garfield; Grant, C.)
Destination Unknown, 1933 (Bellamy)
Destinées, 1952 (Piccoli)
Destinées, 1954 (Colbert; Morgan)
Destiny. *See* Müde Tod, 1921
Destiny of a Man. *See* Sudba cheloveka, 1959

Destiny of a Spy, 1969 (Quayle; Roberts, R.)
Destroy, She Said. *See* Détruite, dit-elle, 1969
Destroyer, 1943 (Ford, G.; Robinson, E.)
Destroyer, 1988 (Perkins)
Destruction, 1916 (Bara)
Destruction of Sakura-Jima. *See* Wrath of the Gods, 1914
Destructors. *See* Marseilles Contract, 1974
Destry Rides Again, 1932 (Mix)
Destry Rides Again, 1939 (Dietrich; Stewart)
Det är aldrig för sent, 1956 (Björnstrand)
Det regnar på vår kärlek, 1946 (Björnstrand)
Det svänger på slottet, 1959 (Björnstrand)
Detained, 1924 (Laurel and Hardy)
Detained While Waiting for Justice, Why? *See* Detenuto in attesa di giudizio, 1971
Detective. *See* Father Brown, 1954
Detective, 1968 (Duvall; Remick; Sidney)
Détective, 1985 (Baye; Cuny; Léaud)
Detective Clive, Bart. *See* Scotland Yard, 1930
Detective Craig's Coup, 1914 (White)
Detective Story, 1951 (Douglas, K.; Grant, L.)
Detective Swift, 1914 (White)
Detenuto in attesa di giudizio, 1971 (Sordi)
Deti kapitana Granta, 1936 (Cherkassov)
Deti Vanyousina, 1915 (Mozhukin)
Detour, 1978 (Cushing)
Detras de esa puerta, 1972 (Brazzi)
Détruite, dit-elle, 1969 (Gélin)
Deutschland im Herbst, 1978 (Winkler)
Deutschmeister, 1955 (Schneider)
Deux, 1989 (Depardieu; Tyszkiewicz)
Deux anglaises et le continent, 1971 (Léaud)
Deux combinards, 1937 (Berry)
Deux grandes filles dans un pyjama, 1974 (Presle)
Deux heures à tuer, 1965 (Brasseur)
Deux hommes dans la ville, 1973 (Delon; Depardieu; Gabin)
Deux timides, 1928 (Rosay)
Deux timides, 1942 (Brasseur)
Deuxième Procès d'Artur London, 1969 (Montand)
Devanti a lui tremava tutta Roma, 1946 (Magnani)
Devata, 1978 (Azmi)
Devdas, 1955 (Kumar)
Devdas, 1979 (Chatterjee)
Devi, 1960 (Chatterjee)
Devil. *See* Diavolo, 1963
Devil and Daniel Webster. *See* All That Money Can Buy, 1941
Devil and Max Devlin, 1981 (Gould)
Devil and Miss Jones, 1941 (Arthur; Coburn, C.)
Devil and the Deep, 1932 (Constantine; Grant, C.; Laughton)
Devil and the Six Commandments. *See* Diable et les dix commandments, 1962
Devil at Four O'Clock, 1961 (Dalio; Sidney; Tracy)
Devil at His Elbow, 1916 (Menjou)
Devil Bat, 1941 (Lugosi)
Devil by the Tail. *See* Diable par la queue, 1968
Devil Commands, 1941 (Karloff)
Devil Dancer, 1927 (Wong)
Devil Dodger, 1917 (Gilbert)
Devil Dogs of the Air, 1935 (Bond; Cagney)
Devil Doll, 1936 (Barrymore, L.; O'Sullivan)
Devil Goddess, 1955 (Weissmuller)
Devil Horse, 1932 (Carey)
Devil in a Blue Dress, 1995 (Washington)
Devil in Love. *See* Diavolo innamorato, 1966
Devil in the Castle. *See* Osaka-jo monogatari, 1961
Devil in the Flesh. *See* **Diable au corps**, 1946
Devil Is a Sissy, 1936 (Cooper; Rooney)
Devil Is a Woman, 1935 (Dietrich; Horton)
Devil Is a Woman. *See* Soriso del grande tentatore, 1973
Devil Is an Empress. *See* Joueur d'échecs, 1938
Devil Makes Three, 1952 (Kelly, Gene)
Devil-May-Care, 1930 (Novarro)

Devil Never Sleeps. *See* Satan Never Sleeps, 1962
Devil of a Fellow. *See* Teufelskerl, 1935
Devil of the Desert. *See* Shaitan el Sahara, 1954
Devil on Horseback, 1936 (Miller)
Devil on Horseback, 1954 (Withers)
Devil Rides Out, 1968 (Lee, C.)
Devil Takes the Count. *See* Devil Is a Sissy, 1936
Devil to Pay, 1930 (Colman; Loy; Young, L.)
Devil to Pay, 1960 (Keaton, B.)
Devil with Women, 1930 (Bogart; McLaglen)
Devil within Her. *See* I Don't Want to Be Born, 1975
Devilish Honeymoon. *See* Kam čert nemuže, 1970
Devils, 1971 (Redgrave, V.; Reed)
Devil's Advocate, 1977 (Mills)
Devil's Advocate. *See* Des Teufels Advokat, 1977
Devil's Agent, 1961 (Cushing; Lee, C.)
Devil's Bride. *See* Devil Rides Out, 1968
Devil's Brigade, 1968 (Andrews, D.; Holden; Robertson)
Devil's Brother. *See* Fra Diavolo, 1933
Devil's Cargo, 1925 (Beery)
Devil's Chaplain, 1929 (Karloff)
Devil's Circus, 1926 (Shearer)
Devil's Claim, 1920 (Hayakawa)
Devil's Cross. *See* Cruz diablo, 1934
Devil's Daffodil, 1962 (Lee, C.)
Devil's Daffodil. *See* Geheimnis der gelben Narzissen, 1961
Devil's Daughter, 1915 (Bara)
Devil's Daughter, 1972 (Cotten; Winters)
Devil's Daughter. *See* Fille du diable, 1945
Devil's Daughter. *See* Setta, 1991
Devil's Disciple, 1959 (Douglas, K.; Lancaster; Olivier)
Devil's Doorway, 1950 (Calhern; Taylor, R.)
Devil's Double, 1916 (Hart)
Devil's Envoys. *See* Visiteurs du soir, 1942
Devil's Eye. *See* Djävulens öga, 1960
Devil's Garden, 1920 (Barrymore, L.)
Devil's Garden. *See* Coplan sauve sa peau, 1967
Devil's Hairpin, 1956 (Astor; Wilde)
Devil-Ship Pirates, 1964 (Lee, C.)
Devil's Holiday, 1930 (Lukas)
Devil's Imposter. *See* Pope Joan, 1972
Devil's in Love, 1933 (Lugosi; Young, L.)
Devil's Island, 1940 (Karloff)
Devil's Island. *See* Gokumon-to, 1977
Devil's Lottery, 1932 (McLaglen)
Devil's Men, 1976 (Cushing; Pleasence)
Devil's Needle, 1916 (Talmadge)
Devil's Own. *See* Witches, 1966
Devil's Own, 1996 (Ford, H.; Pitt)
Devil's Own Envoy. *See* Visiteurs du soir, 1942
Devil's Partner, 1923 (Shearer)
Devil's Party, 1938 (McLaglen)
Devil's Playground, 1937 (Bond; Del Rio)
Devil's Rain, 1975 (Borgnine; Lupino; Travolta)
Devil's Tail. *See* Mal d'aimer, 1986
Devil's Temple. *See* Oni no sumu yakata, 1969
Devil's Triangle, 1974 (Price)
Devil's Widow. *See* Tam Lin, 1971
Devonsville Terror, 1983 (Pleasence)
Devoradora, 1946 (Félix)
Devotion, 1931 (Howard, L.)
Devotion, 1946 (De Havilland; Greenstreet; Henreid; Kennedy; Lupino)
Devourer. *See* Devoradora, 1946
Dharam Adhikari, 1986 (Kumar)
Dharavi, 1991 (Azmi)
D'homme à hommes, 1948 (Barrault; Blier)
Di padre in figlio, 1982 (Gassman)
Di quelle, 1953 (Fabrizi)
Día con el diablo, 1945 (Cantinflas)
Diable au corps, 1946 (Presle; Philipe; Tati)
Diable dans la boîte, 1976 (Presle)

Diable et les dix commandements, 1962 (Dalio; Darrieux; Delon; Fernandel; Modot; Presle)

Diable par la queue, 1968 (Montand; Schell, Maria)

Diable souffle, 1947 (Vanel)

Diablo bajo la Almohada, 1969 (Thulin)

Diablo del desierto, 1954 (Armendáriz)

Diabolical Wedding, 1971 (O'Brien, M.)

Diabolically Yours. *See* Diaboliquement vôtre, 1967

Diabolik, 1967 (Terry-Thomas)

Diabolique, 1996 (Adjani; Bates, K.; Stone)

Diaboliquement vôtre, 1967 (Delon)

Diaboliques, 1954 (Vanel)

Diadalmas elet, 1923 (Lukas)

Diadiouskina kvartira, 1913 (Mozhukin)

Diagnosis: Murder, 1975 (Lee, C.)

Diagonale du fou, 1984 (Caron; Olbrychski; Piccoli; Ullmann)

Dial M for Murder, 1954 (Kelly, Grace; Milland)

Dial M for Murder, 1967 (Cusack)

Dial M for Murder, 1981 (Dickinson)

Dialog, 1968 (Léaud)

Dialogo de exilados. *See* Dialogue d'exilés, 1974

Dialogue d'exilés, 1974 (Gélin)

Dialogue des Carmélites, 1960 (Barrault; Brasseur; Moreau; Valli)

Diamant noir, 1922 (Fresnay)

Diamant noir, 1940 (Vanel)

Diamanti che nessuno voleva rubare, 1968 (Andrews, D.)

Diamond City, 1949 (Dors)

Diamond Cut Diamond. *See* Blame the Woman, 1932

Diamond Earrings. *See* **Madame de ...**, 1953

Diamond Fleece, 1992 (Nelligan)

Diamond Frontier, 1940 (McLaglen)

Diamond Head, 1962 (Heston)

Diamond Horseshoe. *See* Billy Rose's Diamond Horseshoe, 1945

Diamond Jim, 1935 (Arthur)

Diamond Mercenaries. *See* Killer Force, 1975

Diamond's Edge. *See* Just Ask for a Diamond, 1988

Diamonds, 1975 (Hershey; Shaw; Winters)

Diamonds Are Brittle. *See* Millard un billard, 1965

Diamonds Are Forever, 1971 (Connery)

Diamonds for Breakfast, 1968 (Mastroianni)

Diana l'affascinatrice, 1915 (Bertini)

Diane, 1955 (Turner, L.)

Diane, 1956 (Armendáriz)

Diane of the Follies, 1916 (Gish)

Diane's Body. *See* Corps de Diane, 1969

Diario de invierno, 1988 (Rey)

Diario di un italiano, 1972 (Valli)

Diary for My Children. *See* Napló gyermekeimnek, 1982

Diary for My Father and Mother. *See* Napló apamanak, anyammnak, 1990

Diary for My Loves. *See* Napló szerelmeimnek, 1987

Diary for Timothy, 1945 (Gielgud; Redgrave, M.)

Diary of a Chambermaid, 1946 (Goddard; Meredith)

Diary of a Chambermaid. *See* Journal d'une femme de chambre, 1964

Diary of a Hitman, 1992 (Whitaker; Stone)

Diary of a Lost Girl. *See* Tagebuch einer Verlorenen, 1929

Diary of a Lost Woman. *See* Tagebuch einer Verlorenen, 1918

Diary of a Lover. *See* Tagebuch einer Verliebten, 1953

Diary of a Madman, 1963 (Price)

Diary of a Madman. *See* Para gnedych, 1915

Diary of an Innocent Boy. *See* Benjamin ou Les mémoires d'un puceau, 1968

Diary of an Italian. *See* Diario di un italiano, 1972

Diary of Anne Frank, 1959 (Winters)

Diary of Anne Frank, 1980 (Schell, Maximilian)

Diary of Forbidden Dreams. *See* Che?, 1972

Diary of Major Thompson. *See* French They Are a Funny Race, 1956

Diary of Oharu. *See* **Saikaku ichidai onna**, 1952

Diavolo, 1963 (Sordi)

Diavolo bianco, 1947 (Brazzi)

Diavolo innamorato, 1966 (Gassman; Rooney)

Diavolo nel Cervello, 1971 (Presle)

Dicen que soy mujeriego, 1948 (Infante)

Diceria dell'untore, 1990 (Redgrave, V.; Rey)

Dick Tracy, 1990 (Bates, K.; Beatty; Caan; Hoffman; Pacino)

Dick Tracy Meets Gruesome, 1947 (Karloff)

Dick Tracy's G-Men, 1939 (Jones, Jennifer)

Dick Turpin, 1925 (Lombard; Mix)

Dick Turpin, 1933 (McLaglen)

Dick Turpin, 1981 (Dors)

Dictator, 1935 (Carroll)

Dida Ibsens Geschichte, 1918 (Veidt)

Die! Die! My Darling. *See* Fanatic, 1965

Die Hard, 1988 (Willis)

Die Hard 2: Die Harder, 1990 (Willis)

Die Hard: With a Vengeance, 1995 (Irons; Jackson, S.; Willis)

Die Lady, 1964 (Thulin)

Die Laughing, 1980 (Lanchester)

Die, Monster, Die!, 1965 (Karloff)

Dieci commandamenti, 1945 (Brazzi)

Dieci italiani per un Tedesco, 1962 (Cervi)

Dien Bien phu, 1991 (Pleasence)

Diese Mann gehört mir, 1950 (Fröhlich)

Diese Nacht vergess' ich nie, 1949 (Fröhlich)

Diesel, 1942 (Wegener)

Dieses Leid bliebt bei dir. *See* Kabarett, 1954

Dieu a besoin des hommes, 1950 (Fresnay; Gélin)

Dieu a choisi Paris, 1969 (Belmondo)

Difendo il mio amore, 1956 (Gassman)

Different Man, 1914 (Crisp)

Different Sons. *See* Futari no musuko, 1962

Difficult Years, 1950 (Garfield)

Dig That Juliet. *See* Romanoff and Juliet, 1961

Diga sul Pacifico. *See* Barrage contre le Pacifique, 1958

Diggstown, 1992 (Dern; Woods)

Digital Dreams, 1983 (Coburn, J.)

Dil Diya Dard Liya, 1966 (Kumar)

Dil e Nadaan, 1982 (Patil)

Dillinger, 1973 (Dreyfuss; Oates; Stanton)

Dillinger and Capone, 1995 (Sheen)

Dillinger è morto, 1968 (Girardot; Piccoli)

Dilruba, 1950 (Anand)

Dimanche de flics, 1982 (Mueller-Stahl)

Dimanche de la vie, 1965 (Darrieux)

Dimanche nous volerons, 1956 (Belmondo)

Dime a Dance, 1937 (Kaye)

Dimenticare Palermo, 1991 (Gassman; Noiret)

Dimenticare Venezia, 1979 (Josephson)

Dimples, 1936 (Carradine; Robinson, B.; Temple)

Dina chez les lois, 1967 (Arletty)

Diner, 1982 (Bacon; Barkin; Rourke)

Dinero Maldito, 1978 (Widmark)

Ding Dong, 1995 (Hoskins)

Dingaka, 1965 (Baker)

Dinky, 1935 (Astor; Cooper)

Dinner at Eight, 1933 (Barrymore, J.; Barrymore, L.; Beery; Dressler; Harlow)

Dinner at Eight, 1989 (Bacall)

Dinner at the Ritz, 1937 (Lukas; Niven)

Dino, 1957 (Mineo)

Dinty, 1920 (Wong)

Dio, sei proprio un padreterno, 1973 (Van Cleef)

Dios eligió sus viajeros, 1963 (Rey)

Diosa arrodillada, 1947 (Félix)

Diplomacy, 1926 (Sweet)

Diplomaniacs, 1933 (Calhern)

Diplomatic Courier, 1952 (Bronson; Malden; Marvin; Neal; Power)

Dir Tür mit den sieben Schlössern, 1962 (Kinski)

Direct Hit, 1994 (Segal)

Directed by Andrei Tarkovsky, 1989 (Josephson)

Directed by John Ford, 1971 (Fonda, H.; Stewart; Wayne; Welles)

Directed by William Wyler, 1986 (Davis, B.; Garson; Hepburn, K.; Heston; Huston, J.; Olivier; Peck; Stamp)

Director, 1915 (Barrymore, J.)

Director of the Cinema. *See* Luke's Movie Muddle, 1916

Doctor at Large, 1957 (Bogarde)
Doctor at Sea, 1955 (Bardot; Bogarde)
Doctor Bull, 1933 (Rogers, W.)
Dr. Cook's Garden, 1971 (Crosby)
Dr. Crippen, 1962 (Pleasence)
Doctor Death: Seeker of Souls, 1973 (Three Stooges)
Doctor Dolittle, 1967 (Attenborough; Harrison)
Dr. Ehrlich's Magic Bullet, 1940 (Robinson, E.)
Doctor Faustus, 1967 (Burton; Taylor, E.)
Dr. Fischer of Geneva, 1984 (Bates, A.; Cusack; Mason; Scacchi)
Dr. Gillespie's Criminal Case, 1943 (Barrymore, L.; O'Brien, M.)
Dr. Gillespie's New Assistant, 1942 (Barrymore, L.)
Dr. Goldfoot and the Bikini Machine, 1965 (Price)
Dr. Goldfoot and the Girl Bombs, 1966 (Price)
Dr. Graesler. See Mio caro Dottor Graesler, 1990
Dr. Heckyl and Mr. Hype, 1980 (Reed)
Dr. Holl. See Angelika, 1951
Doctor in Distress, 1963 (Bogarde)
Doctor in the House, 1954 (Bogarde; Kendall)
Dr. Jack, 1922 (Lloyd)
Dr. Jekyll and Mr. Hyde. See Januskopf, 1920
Dr. Jekyll and Mr. Hyde, 1920 (Barrymore, J.)
Dr. Jekyll and Mr. Hyde, 1932 (Hopkins, M.; March)
Dr. Jekyll and Mr. Hyde, 1941 (Bergman; Crisp; Tracy; Turner, L.)
Dr. Jekyll and Mr. Hyde, 1972 (Palance)
Dr. Jekyll and Mr. Hyde. See Edge of Sanity, 1989
Dr. Kildare Goes Home, 1940 (Ayres; Barrymore, L.)
Dr. Kildare's Crisis, 1940 (Ayres; Barrymore, L.; Young, R.)
Dr. Kildare's Strange Case, 1940 (Ayres; Barrymore, L.)
Dr. Kildare's Victory, 1941 (Ayres; Barrymore, L.)
Dr. Kildare's Wedding Day, 1941 (Ayres; Barrymore, L.)
Dr. M. See Club Extinction, 1989
Dr. Mabuse, der Spieler, 1922 (Dagover)
Dr. Max, 1974 (Cobb)
Dr. Med. Hiob Preaetorius, 1965 (Rasp)
Dr. Monica, 1934 (Francis)
Dr. No, 1962 (Connery)
Doctor of Seven Dials. See Corridors of Blood, 1963
Dr. Phibes Rises Again, 1972 (Cushing; Price; Terry-Thomas)
Dr. Phil Döderlein, 1945 (Wegener)
Dr. Pickle and Mr. Pryde, 1925 (Laurel and Hardy)
Doctor Rhythm, 1938 (Crosby)
Doctor Says. See Angeklagt nach Paragraph 218, 1966
Dr. Socrates, 1935 (Muni)
Dr. Strange, 1978 (Mills)
Dr. Strangelove: Or, How I Learned to Stop Worrying and Love the Bomb, 1964 (Hayden; Jones, James Earl; Scott, G.; Sellers)
Dr. Syn, 1937 (Lockwood)
Doctor Takes a Wife, 1940 (Milland; Young, L.)
Dr. Terror's Gallery of Horrors, 1967 (Carradine)
Dr. Terror's House of Horrors, 1964 (Cushing; Lee, C.; Sutherland)
Dr. Who and the Daleks, 1965 (Cushing)
Dr. Wislizenus, 1924 (Kortner)
Doctor X, 1932 (Wray)
Doctor Zhivago, 1965 (Chaplin, G.; Christie; Guinness; Kinski; Richardson, R.; Sharif; Steiger)
Doctored Affair, 1913 (Normand)
Doctors. See Hommes en blanc, 1955
Doctor's Dilemma, 1958 (Bogarde; Caron)
Doctors Don't Tell, 1941 (Bond)
Doctor's Orders, 1934 (Mills)
Doctor's Secret, 1913 (Talmadge)
Doctors' Wives, 1931 (Bennett)
Doctors' Wives, 1971 (Bellamy; Hackman; Roberts, R.)
Dodge City, 1939 (Bond; De Havilland; Flynn)
Dodging a Million, 1918 (Normand)
Dødsbokseren, 1926 (Madsen and Schenstrøm)
Dodsworth, 1936 (Astor; Huston, W.; Lukas; Niven)
Does. See Biches, 1968
Dog and Cat, 1977 (Basinger)
Dog Day. See Canicule, 1983

Dog Day Afternoon, 1975 (Pacino)
Dog Eat Dog. See Einer frisst den anderem, 1964
Dog It Was That Died, 1988 (Bates, A.)
Dog of Flanders, 1959 (Crisp)
Dog Soldiers. See Who'll Stop the Rain, 1978
Doggone Mixup, 1938 (Langdon)
Dogo no kishi, 1932 (Hasegawa)
Dog's Life, 1918 (Chaplin, C.; Purviance)
Dog's Life. See Vita da cani, 1950
Dogs of War, 1923 (Lloyd)
Dogs of War, 1980 (Walken)
Doin' Time on Planet Earth, 1988 (McDowall)
Doing Her Bit, 1917 (Gilbert)
Doing His Best. See Making a Living, 1914
Doktor Eva, 1970 (Nowicki)
Doktor Glas, 1967 (Zetterling)
Doku azami, 1927 (Hasegawa)
Dokuga, 1950 (Yamamura)
Dokuritsu bijin-tai, 1963 (Kagawa)
Dokuritsu gurenta, 1959 (Mifune)
Dolce cinema, 1983 (Hayden)
Dolce vita, 1960 (Aimée; Cuny; Mastroianni)
Dolci signore, 1967 (Cassel)
Doll. See Lalka, 1968
Doll Face, 1946 (Miranda)
Doll that Took the Town. See Donna del giorno, 1957
Doll's House, 1916 (Chaney)
Doll's House, 1922 (Nazimova)
Doll's House, 1973 (Bloom; Elliott; Evans; Fonda, J.; Hopkins, A.; Howard, T.; Richardson, R.; Seyrig)
Dollar, 1938 (Bergman)
Dollar-a-Year Man, 1921 (Arbuckle)
Dollaro a testa, 1967 (Rey; Reynolds, B.)
Dollaro per 7 vigliacchi, 1970 (Hoffman)
Dollmaker, 1982 (Fonda, J.)
Dollmaker, 1984 (Hanks; Page)
Dolls. See Bambole, 1964
Dolly Sisters, 1945 (Grable)
Dolly's Scoop, 1916 (Chaney)
Dolores Claiborne, 1995 (Bates, K.; Leigh, Jennifer Jason)
Dolwyn. See Last Days of Dolwyn, 1948
Dom, kotoryi postroil svift, 1982 (Yankovsky)
Dom na Trubnoi, 1928 (Maretskaya)
Dom Wariatow, 1984 (Łomnicki)
Domani non siamo più qui, 1967 (Thulin)
Domaren, 1960 (Thulin)
Domburi-ike, 1963 (Tsukasa)
Domenica d'agosto, 1950 (Mastroianni)
Domenica della buona gente, 1953 (Loren)
Domenica e sempre domenica, 1958 (Sordi)
Domicile conjugal, 1970 (Léaud)
Domik v Kolomna, 1913 (Mozhukin)
Dominick and Eugene, 1988 (Curtis, J.)
Dominique, 1978 (Robertson)
Domino, 1943 (Blier)
Domino Principle, 1976 (Hackman; Rooney; Wallach; Widmark)
Domino vert, 1935 (Darrieux; Vanel)
Domyaku retto, 1975 (Yamamura)
Don Camillo, 1983 (Ayres; Cusack)
Don Camillo à Moscou. See Compagno Don Camillo, 1965
Don Camillo e i giovani d'oggi, 1972 (Cervi)
Don Camillo e l'onorevole Peppone, 1955 (Cervi; Fernandel)
Don Camillo en Russie. See Compagno Don Camillo, 1965
Don Camillo, monsignore ... ma non troppo, 1961 (Cervi; Fernandel)
Don Cesare di Bazan, 1942 (Cervi)
Don Is Dead, 1973 (Quinn)
Don Juan, 1926 (Astor; Barrymore, J.; Loy)
Don Juan, 1955 (Fernandel)
Don Juan 1973 ou Si Don Juan était une femme, 1973 (Bardot)
Don Juan DeMarco, 1995 (Brando; Depp; Dunaway)
Don Juan in Hell, 1962 (Cusack)

Don Juan, Karl-Liebeknecht-Strasse 78. *See* Acht und Siebzig, 1980
Don Juan, or if Don Juan Were a Woman. *See* Don Juan 1973 ou Si Don Juan était une femme, 1973
Don Juan Quilligan, 1945 (Blondell)
Don Kikhot, 1957 (Cherkassov)
Don Lucio y el harmano pio, 1960 (Rey)
Don Pietro Caruso, 1917 (Bertini)
Don Q, Son of Zorro, 1925 (Astor; Crisp; Fairbanks)
Don Quijote cabalga de nuevo, 1972 (Cantinflas)
Don Quijote sin mancha, 1969 (Cantinflas)
Don Quixote, 1926 (Madsen and Schenstrøm)
Don Quixote, 1955 (Welles)
Don Quixote. *See* Don Kikhot, 1957
Don Quixote, 1966 (Rey)
Don Quixote de la Mancha, 1947 (Rey)
Dona Juana, 1927 (Bergner)
Donatella, 1956 (Fabrizi)
Donato and Daughter, 1993 (Bronson)
Done in Wax, 1915 (Beery)
Donkey Skin. *See* Peau d'âne, 1970
Donna alla frontiera. *See* Frauen, die durch die Hölle gehen, 1966
Donna Brasco, 1996 (Pacino)
Donna che inventà l'amore, 1952 (Brazzi)
Donna del fiume, 1954 (Loren)
Donna del giorno, 1957 (Reggiani)
Donna del mondo, 1963 (Ustinov)
Donna della domenica, 1976 (Mastroianni)
Donna della luna, 1988 (Scacchi)
Donna delle meraviglie, 1985 (Cardinale)
Donna di una notte, 1930 (Bertini)
Donna di vita. *See* Lola, 1961
Donna è una cosa meravigliosa, 1964 (Fabrizi)
Donna, il diavolo, il tempo, 1921 (Bertini)
Donna libera, 1953 (Cervi)
Donna nuda, 1918 (Bertini)
Donna più bella del mondo, 1955 (Gassman; Lollobrigida)
Donna scimmia, 1963 (Girardot)
Donna spezzata, 1988 (Josephson)
Donna!, 1914 (Bertini)
Donne proibite, 1953 (Darnell; Masina; Quinn)
Donne senza nome, 1949 (Cervi; Rosay)
Donnie Brasco, 1996 (Depp)
Donovan's Brain, 1953 (Ayres)
Donovan's Kid, 1979 (Rooney)
Donovan's Reef, 1962 (Dalio; Lamour; Marvin; Marsh; Wayne)
Don't Be Blue. *See* Tout peut arriver, 1969
Don't Be Jealous, 1928 (Brown)
Don't Bet on Blondes, 1935 (Flynn)
Don't Bet on Love, 1933 (Ayres; Rogers, G.)
Don't Bet on Women, 1931 (MacDonald)
Don't Bother to Knock, 1952 (Bancroft; Monroe; Widmark)
Don't Change Your Husband, 1919 (Swanson)
Don't Deceive Yourself, My Heart. *See* No te engañes corazón, 1936
Don't Drink the Water, 1969 (Allen)
Don't Drink the Water, 1994 (Allen)
Don't Fence Me In, 1945 (Rogers, R.)
Don't Give Up the Ship, 1959 (Lewis, Jerry)
Don't Go in the House, 1980 (Pesci)
Don't Go Near the Water, 1957 (Ford, G.)
Don't Go to Sleep, 1982 (Gordon)
Don't Hook Now, 1938 (Crosby; Hope)
Don't Look Now, 1973 (Christie; Sutherland)
Don't Look Now, We're Being Shot At, 1966 (Terry-Thomas)
Don't Make Waves, 1967 (Cardinale; Curtis, T.)
Don't Open the Window. *See* Fin de semana para los muertos, 1974
Don't Park There, 1924 (Rogers, W.)
Don't Pave Main Street: Carmel's Heritage, 1994 (Eastwood)
Don't Play with Love. *See* Man spielt nicht mit der Liebe, 1926
Don't Raise the Bridge, Lower the River, 1968 (Terry-Thomas; Lewis, Jerry)
Don't Shove, 1919 (Lloyd)
Don't Tease the Mosquito. *See* Non stuzzicate la zanzara, 1967

Don't Tell Everything, 1921 (Swanson)
Don't Tell the Wife, 1937 (Ball; McDaniel)
Don't Tempt the Devil. *See* Bonnes Causes, 1963
Don't Throw That Knife, 1951 (Three Stooges)
Don't Torture the Duckling. *See* Non si servizia un paperino, 1972
Don't Touch the Loot. *See* Touchez pas au grisbi, 1953
Don't Touch White Women. *See* Touche pas à la femme blanche, 1974
Don't Trust Your Husband, 1948 (Carroll; MacMurray)
Don't Turn 'em Loose, 1936 (Grable)
Don't Turn the Other Cheek. *See* Viva la muerte ... tua!, 1972
Don't Worry, We'll Think of a Title, 1966 (Three Stooges)
Donzoko, 1957 (Kagawa; Mifune; Yamada)
Doña Barbara, 1943 (Félix)
Doña Diabla, 1949 (Félix)
Doña Flor e Seus Dois Maridos, 1977 (Braga)
Doña Perfecta, 1951 (Del Rio)
Doña Perfecta, 1977 (Abril)
Doolins of Oklahoma, 1949 (Scott, R.)
Doombeach, 1990 (Jackson, G.)
Doomed. *See* **Ikiru**, 1952
Doomed to Die, 1940 (Karloff)
Doomsday, 1928 (Constantine)
Doomsday Flight, 1966 (O'Brien, E.)
Doomsday Gun, 1994 (Arkin)
Doomsday Voyage, 1972 (Cotten)
Doomwatch, 1972 (Sanders)
Doors, 1991 (Ryan, M.)
Doors Slam. *See* Portes claquent, 1960
Doorway to Hell, 1930 (Ayres; Cagney)
Doosri Doolhan, 1983 (Azmi)
Dopey Dicks, 1950 (Three Stooges)
Doppelganger, 1969 (Lom)
Doppelgängerin, 1925 (Dagover)
Doppia taglia per Monnesota Stinky, 1972 (Kinski)
Doppio delitto, 1978 (Mastroianni; Ustinov)
Dora, 1943 (Bertini)
Dora Brandes, 1916 (Nielsen)
Dora Thorne, 1915 (Barrymore, L.)
Dora's Dunkin' Doughnuts, 1933 (Temple)
Dorian Gray, 1970 (Lom)
Dorian Gray im Spiegel der Boulevardpresse, 1984 (Constantine; Seyrig)
Dorian's Divorce, 1916 (Barrymore, L.)
Dornroschen, 1918 (Wegener)
Dorothée cherche l'amour, 1945 (Berry)
Dorothy Vernon of Haddon Hall, 1924 (Pickford)
Dortoir des grandes, 1953 (Marais; Moreau)
Dos au mur, 1958 (Moreau)
Dos de la Mafia. *See* Due mafiosi contre Goldginger, 1965
Dos hijos desobedientes, 1960 (Armendáriz)
Dos mundos y un amor, 1954 (Armendáriz)
Dos tipos de cuidado, 1952 (Infante)
Dos y media y venuno, 1959 (Rey)
Doshaburi, 1957 (Yamamura)
Dossier noir, 1955 (Blier)
Dotanba, 1957 (Shimura)
Dotkniecie reki, 1993 (Tyszkiewicz; Von Sydow)
Doto ichi man kairi, 1966 (Mifune)
Dots Izrila, 1917 (Mozhukin)
Double Confession, 1953 (Lorre)
Double Crime sur la Ligne Maginot, 1938 (Blier)
Double Crossbones, 1951 (O'Connor)
Double Crossed. *See* Cash Parrish's Pal, 1915
Double Daring, 1926 (Arthur)
Double Deal, 1984 (Jourdan)
Double Dynamite, 1951 (Marx Brothers; Russell, J.; Sidney)
Double Edge, 1992 (Dunaway)
Double Exposure, 1935 (Hope)
Double Face, 1969 (Kinski)
Double Harness, 1933 (Powell, W.)
Double Impact, 1991 (Van Damme)
Double Indemnity, 1944 (MacMurray; Robinson, E.; Stanwyck)

Double Indemnity, 1974 (Cobb; Winters)
Double Life, 1947 (Colman; Gordon; O'Brien, E.; Winters)
Double Man, 1967 (Brynner)
Double McGuffin, 1979 (Borgnine; Welles)
Double Murders. See Doppio delitto, 1978
Double Negative, 1980 (Candy; Perkins)
Double or Nothing, 1937 (Crosby)
Double Sixes, 1931 (Carey)
Double tour, 1959 (Belmondo)
Double Trouble, 1915 (Fairbanks)
Double Trouble, 1941 (Langdon)
Double Trouble, 1967 (Presley)
Double Trouble, 1992 (McDowall)
Double Vision, 1992 (Lee, C.)
Double Wedding, 1937 (Loy; Powell, W.)
Double Whoopee, 1929 (Laurel and Hardy; Harlow)
Double X: The Name of the Game, 1992 (Wisdom)
Doublecross, 1956 (Shaw)
Doublecrossed, 1991 (Hopper)
Doubletake, 1985 (Bassett)
Doubling for Romeo, 1921 (Rogers, W.)
Doubting Thomas, 1935 (Rogers, W.)
Doucement les basses!, 1971 (Delon)
Douceur d'aimer, 1930 (Arletty)
Dough and Dynamite, 1914 (Chaplin, C.)
Dough-Nuts, 1917 (Laurel and Hardy)
Doughboys, 1930 (Keaton, B.)
Doughboys in Ireland, 1943 (Mitchum)
Doughgirls, 1944 (Wyman)
Doughnut Designer. See Dough and Dynamite, 1914
Doulos, 1963 (Belmondo; Piccoli)
Doulos, 1963 (Reggiani)
Doulos—The Fingerman. See Doulos, 1963
Dourman, 1912 (Mozhukin)
Dove, 1928 (Talmadge)
Dove, 1974 (Peck)
Dove scenda il sole. See Unter Geiern, 1964
Dove vai in vacanza?, 1978 (Sordi)
Dove vai tutta nuda?, 1969 (Gassman)
Doverie, 1976 (Yankovsky)
Down among the Sheltering Palms, 1951 (Marvin)
Down among the Z Men, 1952 (Sellers)
Down and Out in America, 1985 (Grant, L.)
Down and Out in Beverly Hills, 1986 (Dreyfuss; Midler; Nolte)
Down Argentina Way, 1940 (Ameche; Grable; Miranda)
Down by Law, 1986 (Barkin; Benigni)
Down Came a Blackbird, 1995 (Julia; Redgrave, V.)
Down Dakota Way, 1949 (Rogers, R.)
Down Memory Lane, 1949 (Fields, W. C.; Normand; Swanson)
Down Mexico Way, 1941 (Autry)
Down Missouri Way, 1946 (Carradine)
Down Periscope, 1996 (Dern; Stanton)
Down River, 1931 (Laughton)
Down the Ancient Stairs. See Per le antiche scale, 1975
Down the Hill to Creditville, 1914 (Crisp)
Down the Stretch, 1936 (Rooney)
Down Three Dark Streets, 1954 (Crawford, B.)
Down to Earth, 1917 (Fairbanks)
Down to Earth, 1932 (Rogers, W.)
Down to Earth, 1947 (Hayworth; Horton)
Down to the Sea in Ships, 1923 (Bow)
Down to the Sea in Ships, 1949 (Barrymore, L.; Widmark)
Down Where the Buffalo Go, 1988 (Keitel)
Downfall of Osen. See Orizuru Osen, 1935
Downhill, 1927 (Novello)
Downhill Racer, 1969 (Hackman; Redford)
Downstairs, 1932 (Gilbert; Lukas)
Downtown, 1990 (Whitaker)
Downtown. See Shitamachi, 1957
Dowry. See Wiano, 1964
Dracula, 1931 (Lugosi)

Dracula, 1958 (Cushing; Lee, C.)
Dracula, 1974 (Palance)
Dracula, 1979 (Nelligan; Olivier; Pleasence)
Dracula A.D. 1972, 1972 (Cushing; Lee, C.)
Dracula: Dead and Loving It, 1995 (Brooks, M.)
Dracula Has Risen from the Grave, 1968 (Lee, C.)
Dracula im Schloss des Schreckens. See Nella stretta morsa del ragno, 1971
Dracula in the Provinces. See Cavaliere Costante Nicosia indemontiato ovvero Dracula in Brianza, 1975
Dracula, père et fils. See Dracula's Son, 1975
Dracula—Prince of Darkness, 1966 (Lee, C.)
Dracula vs. Frankenstein, 1969 (Carradine)
Dracula's Dog. See Zoltan ... Hound of Dracula, 1977
Dracula's Son, 1975 (Lee, C.)
Drag, 1929 (Barthelmess)
Dragée haute, 1959 (Piccoli)
Dragées au poivre, 1963 (Belmondo; Karina; Vitti)
Dragnet, 1928 (Powell, W.)
Dragnet, 1987 (Hanks)
Dragnet Girl. See Hijosen no onna, 1933
Dragon Lord. See Lung siuye, 1982
Dragon Painter, 1919 (Hayakawa)
Dragon Seed, 1944 (Barrymore, L.; Hepburn, K.; Huston, W.; Moorehead)
Dragonard, 1988 (Lom; Reed)
Dragonfly. See One Summer Love, 1976
Dragonheart, 1996 (Christie; Connery; Quaid)
Dragons Forever, 1987 (Chan)
Dragonslayer, 1981 (Richardson, R.)
Dragonwyck, 1946 (Huston, W.; Price; Tierney)
Dragstrip Riot, 1958 (Wray)
Dragueurs, 1959 (Aimée)
Drama della gelosia, 1970 (Mastroianni)
Drama of Jealousy. See Dramma della gelosia—Tutti i particolari in cronaca, 1970
Drama of the Rich. See Fatti di gente per bene, 1974
Dramatic School, 1938 (Dumont; Goddard; Rainer; Turner, L.)
Drame de Shanghaî, 1938 (Jouvet)
Dramma della Casbah, 1953 (Papas)
Dramma della gelosia—tutti i particolari in cronaca, 1970 (Vitti; Giannini)
Drango, 1957 (Crisp)
Draw!, 1984 (Coburn, J.; Douglas, K.)
Dream, 1911 (Pickford)
Dream. See His Prehistoric Past, 1914
Dream a Little Dream, 1989 (Robards; Stanton)
Dream Flights. See Polioty vo sne naiavou, 1982
Dream House, 1932 (Crosby)
Dream of Happiness. See Lyckodrömmen, 1963
Dream of Kings, 1969 (Papas; Quinn)
Dream of Love, 1928 (Crawford, J.)
Dream of Passion, 1978 (Burstyn; Mercouri)
Dream of Zorro. See Sogno di Zorro, 1951
Dream On, 1981 (Harris, E.)
Dream One, 1984 (Keitel)
Dream Team, 1989 (Keaton, M.)
Dream to Believe, 1986 (Reeves)
Dream Wife, 1953 (Grant, C.; Kerr; Pidgeon)
Dreamboat, 1952 (Lanchester; Rogers, G.; Webb)
Dreaming, 1944 (Kendall)
Dreaming Lips, 1937 (Bergner; Massey)
Dreaming Lips. See Traumende Mund, 1953
Dreamplay. See Dromspel, 1994
Dreams, 1940 (Cushing)
Dreams. See Kvinnodröm, 1955
Dreams. See Akira Kurosawa's Dreams, 1990
Dreams of Glass, 1969 (DeVito)
Dreams of Gold: The Mel Fisher Story, 1986 (Robertson)
Dreamscape, 1984 (Quaid; Von Sydow)
Dreamy Knights, 1916 (Laurel and Hardy)
Drei um Edith, 1929 (Rasp)
Drei von der Stempelstelle, 1932 (Walbrook)
Dreigroschenoper, 1931 (Artaud; Rasp)

Dreiklang, 1938 (Dagover)
Dress. See Klänningen, 1964
Dress Parade, 1927 (Crisp)
Dress Returns to Glory, 1947 (Zhao Dan)
Dressed to Kill, 1928 (Astor; Brown)
Dressed to Kill, 1946 (Rathbone)
Dressed to Kill, 1980 (Caine; Dickinson)
Dresser, 1983 (Finney)
Dressmaker's Bill, 1910-11 (White)
Dreyfus, 1930 (Homolka; Kortner; Rasp)
Dreyfus Case. See Dreyfus, 1930
Drifter, 1929 (Mix)
Driftin' Thru, 1926 (Carey)
Drifting, 1923 (Beery; Wong)
Drifting Weeds. See Ukigusa, 1959
Driftwood, 1947 (Brennan; Wood)
Drink's Lure, 1913 (Crisp)
Dritte, 1958 (Vitti)
Dritte, 1972 (Mueller-Stahl)
Dritte Generation, 1979 (Constantine; Schygulla)
Drive a Crooked Road, 1954 (Rooney)
Drive, He Said, 1970 (Dern; Nicholson)
Driven from Home, 1927 (Wong)
Driver, 1978 (Adjani; Dern)
Driver dagg faller Regn, 1946 (Zetterling)
Driver's Seat, 1975 (Taylor, E.)
Driving Miss Daisy, 1989 (Freeman)
Droit d'aimer, 1972 (Sharif)
Drole d'endroit pour une rencontre, 1988 (Deneuve; Depardieu)
Drôle de dimanche, 1958 (Arletty; Belmondo; Darrieux)
Drôle de drame, 1937 (Barrault; Jouvet; Rosay)
Dromspel, 1994 (Andersson, B.; Josephson; Ullmann)
Drop Dead, Darling. See Arrivederci, Baby, 1966
Drop Kick, 1927 (Wayne)
Drop Squad, 1994 (Lee, S.)
Drop Zone, 1994 (Snipes)
Dropkick, 1927 (Barthelmess)
Dropout. See Vacanza, 1969
Drowning Pool, 1975 (Griffith; Newman; Woodward)
Drugstore Cowboy, 1925 (Arthur)
Drugstore Cowboy, 1989 (Dillon)
Drum, 1938 (Massey)
Drum, 1976 (Oates)
Drum Beat, 1954 (Bronson; Ladd)
Drummer of Vengeance, 1974 (Brazzi)
Drummer's Notebook, 1912-13 (White)
Drums. See Drum, 1938
Drums across the River, 1954 (Brennan)
Drums along the Mohawk, 1939 (Bond; Carradine; Colbert; Fonda, H.)
Drums for a Queen, 1961 (Quayle)
Drums of Fire, 1991 (Papas)
Drums of Fire. See Bataille des trois rois, 1989
Drums of Jeopardy, 1923 (Beery)
Drums of Love, 1928 (Barrymore, L.)
Drunken Angel. See Yoidore Tenshi, 1948
Drunken Master, 1979 (Chan)
Drunken Master II. See Tsui Kun II, 1994
Drunken Monkey in a Tiger's Eye. See Drunken Master, 1979
Drunkenness and Its Consequences. See Pianstvo i yevo pozledstvia, 1913
Drunks, 1995 (Wiest)
Druzya, 1938 (Cherkassov)
Dry Martini, 1928 (Astor)
Dry White Season, 1989 (Brando; Sarandon; Sutherland)
Du är mitt äventyr, 1958 (Andersson, B.; Björnstrand)
Du Crépuscule à l'aube, 1922 (Vanel)
Du grabuge chez les veuves, 1963 (Darrieux)
Du mou dans la gachette, 1966 (Blier)
Du Rififi à Paname, 1965 (Gabin; Raft)
Du Rififi chez les femmes, 1959 (Constantine; Rosay)
Du sang dans la sciure. See Chicago-Digest, 1950
Dual Alibi, 1947 (Lom)

Duba, 1972 (Rey)
DuBarry Was a Lady, 1943 (Ball; Gardner; Kelly, Gene; Turner, L.)
DuBarry: Woman of Passion, 1930 (Talmadge)
Duchess and the Dirtwater Fox, 1976 (Hawn; Segal)
Duchess of Idaho, 1950 (Powell, E.; Williams, E.)
Duchesse de Langeais, 1941 (Feuillère)
Duck in Orange Sauce. See Anatra all'orancia, 1975
Duck Soup, 1927 (Laurel and Hardy)
Duck Soup, 1933 (Calhern; Dumont; Marx Brothers)
Duck, You Sucker! See Giù la testa, 1972
Duckweed Story. See Ukigusa, 1959
Due colonelli, 1962 (Pidgeon)
Due compari, 1955 (Fabrizi)
Due Foscari, 1942 (Brazzi)
Due mafiosi contre Goldginger, 1965 (Rey)
Due Marines e un Generale, 1967 (Keaton, B.)
Due nemici, 1961 (Niven; Sordi)
Due notti con Cleopatra, 1953 (Loren; Sordi)
Due occhi diabolici, 1990 (Keitel)
Due orfanelle, 1942 (Valli)
Due pezzi di pane, 1978 (Noiret; Gassman)
Due sargenti, 1936 (Valli; Cervi)
Due vita di Mattia Pascal, 1985 (Blier; Mastroianni)
Due volte Giuda, 1968 (Kinski)
Due volti della paura. See Coartada en disco rojo, 1970
Duel, 1912 (Normand)
Duel, 1939 (Fresnay)
Duel, 1941 (Raimu)
Duel à Mort, 1950 (Keaton, B.)
Duel at Diablo, 1966 (Andersson, B.; Garner; Poitier)
Duel at Ichijoji Temple. See Zoko Miyamoto Musashi, 1955
Duel at Silver Creek, 1951 (Marvin)
Duel de Max, 1913 (Linder)
Duel de Monsieur Myope, 1908 (Linder)
Duel in the Forest. See Schinderhannes, 1958
Duel in the Jungle, 1954 (Andrews, D.)
Duel in the Sun, 1946 (Barrymore, L.; Carey; Cotten; Gish; Huston, W.; Jones, Jennifer; Marshall; Peck; Welles)
Duel of Champions. See Orazi e Curiazi, 1961
Duel of Hearts, 1990 (Chaplin, G.)
Duellists, 1977 (Finney; Keitel)
Duello nel mundo, 1966 (Blier)
Dueños del silencio, 1987 (Andersson, B.; Falk)
Duet for One, 1986 (Andrews, J.; Bates, A.; Neeson; Von Sydow)
Duffy, 1968 (Coburn, J.; Mason; York)
Duffy of San Quentin, 1954 (O'Sullivan)
Duffy's Tavern, 1945 (Crosby; Fitzgerald; Goddard; Ladd; Lake; Lamour)
Duke of West Point, 1938 (Fontaine)
Duke Steps Out, 1929 (Crawford, J.)
Dulce Piel de Mujer, 1978 (Rey)
Dulcima, 1971 (Mills)
Dulcimer Street. See London Belongs to Me, 1948
Dulcinea del Toboso, 1966 (Rey)
Dulcy. See Not So Dumb, 1930
Dum Bom, 1953 (Andersson, B.)
Dumb Girl of Portici, 1916 (Karloff)
Dumb Waiter, 1987 (Travolta)
Dummy, 1928 (March)
Dummy, 1962 (Cusack)
Dune, 1984 (Ferrer; Mangano; Von Sydow)
Dunera Boys, 1985 (Hoskins)
Duniya, 1968 (Anand)
Duniya, 1984 (Kumar)
Dunked in the Deep, 1949 (Three Stooges)
Dunkirk, 1958 (Attenborough; Mills)
Dunston Checks In, 1996 (Dunaway)
Dunwich Horror, 1970 (Jaffe)
Dupe, 1916 (Sweet)
Dupont Lajoie, 1974 (Huppert)
Durand of the Bad Lands, 1917 (Mix)
Durand of the Badlands, 1925 (Lombard)

Dürfen wir schweigen, 1926 (Kortner; Veidt)
During the Round Up, 1913 (Gish)
Durs à cuire, 1964 (Audran)
Dushman, 1957 (Anand)
Dust, 1985 (Howard, T.)
Dust Be My Destiny, 1939 (Bond; Garfield)
Dust of Desire. See Song of Love, 1923
Dusty Ermine, 1936 (Rutherford)
Dutch at the Double. See Nederland in 7 Lessen, 1948
Dutiful but Dumb, 1941 (Three Stooges)
Dutiful Dub, 1919 (Lloyd)
Dvoryanskoye gnezdo, 1969 (Tyszkiewicz)
Dwa ksiezyce, 1993 (Tyszkiewicz)
Dwie brygady, 1948 (Łomnicki)
Dyadya Vanya, 1970 (Bondarchuk)
Dying Young, 1991 (Burstyn; Field; Roberts, J.)
Dylan Thomas, 1961 (Burton)
Dylan Thomas: Return Journey, 1990 (Hopkins, A.)
Dynamite, 1929 (Lombard; McCrea; Scott, R.)
Dynamite Chicken, 1971 (Pryor)
Dynamite Dan, 1924 (Karloff)
Dynamite Jack, 1960 (Fernandel)
Dynamite Man from Glory Jail. See Fools' Parade, 1971
Dynamite Smith, 1924 (Beery)
Dynasty, 1976 (Ford, H.)
Dzis w nocy umrze miastro, 1961 (Tyszkiewicz)
Dziura w ziemi, 1969 (Nowicki)
E. T.—The Extraterrestrial, 1982 (Winger)
E arrivato l'accordatore, 1952 (Loren; Sordi)
È caduta una donna, 1940 (Brazzi)
...E continuavano a fregarsi il millione di dollari, 1971 (Van Cleef; Lollobrigida)
E Dio disse a Caino ..., 1969 (Kinski)
E' Lollipop, 1975 (Ferrer)
E più facile che un cammello ..., 1950 (Gabin)
E ropeya del camino, 1941 (Armendáriz)
E tanta paura, 1976 (Wallach)
E tornato Sabata ... hai chiuso, 1972 (Van Cleef)
E venne l'ora della vendetta, 1970 (Cotten)
E venne un uomo, 1965 (Steiger)
Each Dawn I Die, 1939 (Cagney; Raft)
Each Dawn I Die, 1940 (Holden)
Each to His Kind, 1917 (Hayakawa)
Each to His Own Way. See Var sin väg, 1948
Eadie Was a Lady, 1945 (Miller)
Eagle, 1925 (Banky; Valentino)
Eagle and the Hawk, 1933 (Grant, C.; Lombard; March)
Eagle Has Landed, 1976 (Caine; Duvall; Quayle; Pleasence; Sutherland)
Eagle in a Cage, 1970 (Gielgud; Richardson, R.)
Eagle of the Pacific. See Taiheiyo no washi, 1953
Eagle of the Sea, 1926 (Karloff)
Eagle with Two Heads. See Aigle à deux têtes, 1947
Eagle's Mate, 1914 (Pickford)
Eagles of the Fleet. See Flat Top, 1952
Eagle's Shadow, 1984 (Chan)
Eagle's Shadow. See Snake in the Eagle's Shadow, 1978
Eagle's Wing, 1978 (Audran; Keitel; Sheen)
Earl Carroll's Sketch Book, 1946 (Horton)
Earl of Chicago, 1940 (Montgomery)
Early Autumn. See Kohayagawa-ke no aki, 1961
Early Bird, 1965 (Wisdom)
Early Days, 1981 (Richardson, R.)
Early Frost, 1985 (Rowlands)
Early Spring. See Shoshun, 1956
Early Summer. See Bakushu, 1951
Early to Bed, 1928 (Laurel and Hardy)
Earrings of Madame De. See **Madame de ...**, 1953
Earth and the American Dream, 1993 (Caan; Ford, H.; Gibson; Grant, L.; Hackman; Hoffman; Hopkins, A.; Irons; Keaton, M.; Lemmon; Malden; Midler; Steenburgen; Steiger)
Earth Angel, 1991 (McDowall)

Earth Girls Are Easy, 1989 (Davis, G.)
Earth II, 1971 (Ayres)
Earthling, 1980 (Holden)
Earthquake, 1974 (Bujold; Gardner; Heston; Matthau)
Earth's Final Fury. See When Time Ran Out, 1980
Earthworm Tractors, 1936 (Brown)
Easiest Profession. See Chômeur de Clochemerle, 1957
Easiest Way, 1931 (Gable; Menjou; Montgomery)
East Is East, 1916 (Evans)
East Is West, 1930 (Ayres; Robinson, E.)
East Lynne, 1916 (Bara)
East Lynne in Bugville, 1912-13 (White)
East of Eden, 1955 (Dean; Massey)
East of Elephant Rock, 1976 (Hurt, J.)
East of Java. See South Sea Sinner, 1950
East of Sudan, 1964 (Quayle)
East of Suez, 1925 (Negri)
East of Sumatra, 1953 (Quinn)
East of the Rising Sun. See Malaya, 1950
East of the River, 1940 (Garfield)
East Side of Heaven, 1939 (Blondell; Crosby)
East Side, West Side, 1949 (Charisse; Gardner; Mason; Stanwyck)
East Wind. See Vent d'est, 1970
East Wind. See Vend d'est, 1993
Easter Bunny Is Comin' to Town, 1977 (Astaire)
Easter Parade, 1948 (Astaire; Garland; Miller)
Easter Sunday. See Being, 1983
Eastern Westerner, 1920 (Lloyd)
Easy Come, Easy Go, 1928 (Arthur)
Easy Come, Easy Go, 1947 (Fitzgerald)
Easy Come, Easy Go, 1967 (Lanchester; Presley)
Easy Go. See Free and Easy, 1930
Easy Life. See Legkaya zhizn, 1964
Easy Life. See Sorpasso, 1962
Easy Living, 1937 (Arthur; Milland)
Easy Living, 1949 (Ball; Mature)
Easy Money, 1912-13 (White)
Easy Money, 1983 (Leigh, Jennifer Jason; Pesci)
Easy Rider, 1969 (Hopper; Nicholson)
Easy Street, 1917 (Chaplin, C.; Purviance)
Easy to Love, 1934 (Astor; Horton; Menjou)
Easy to Love, 1953 (Charisse; Williams, E.)
Easy to Wed, 1946 (Ball; Williams, E.)
Easy Way. See Room for One More, 1951
Eat the Rich, 1987 (Richardson, M.)
Eaux profondes, 1981 (Huppert)
Eaux vives, eaux mortes, 1966 (Gélin)
Ebb Tide, 1932 (Oberon)
Ebb Tide, 1937 (Farmer; Fitzgerald; Homolka; Milland)
Ebberöds Bank, 1926 (Madsen and Schenstrøm)
Ebony Tower, 1984 (Olivier; Scacchi)
Ebreo errante, 1947 (Gassman)
Ecce homo, 1966 (Fresnay)
Ecce Homo, 1968 (Papas)
Ecco, 1963 (Sanders)
Echappement libre, 1964 (Belmondo; Rey; Seberg)
Echec au porteur, 1957 (Moreau; Reggiani)
Echec au roi, o Le Roi s'ennui, 1931 (Rosay)
Echigo-jishi, 1929 (Tanaka)
Echigo-jishi matsuri, 1939 (Hasegawa)
Echo, 1985 (Reggiani)
Echoes of a Summer, 1976 (Foster; Harris, R.)
Echos de plateau, 1952 (Gabin; Gélin)
Eclisse, 1962 (Delon; Vitti)
Ecole buissonière, 1949 (Blier; Modot)
Ecole des cocottes, 1958 (Blier)
Ecole des facteurs, 1947 (Tati)
Ecole des femmes, 1972 (Adjani)
Ecole des cocottes, 1935 (Raimu)
Ecoute voir ..., 1978 (Deneuve)
Ecrire contre l'oubli. See Contre l'oubli, 1991

Ecstasy. *See* Symphonie der Liebe, 1933
Ed Murrow: This Reporter, 1990 (Bacall)
Ed Wood, 1994 (Depp; Landau; Murray)
Eddie, 1996 (Goldberg)
Eddie and the Cruisers, 1983 (Barkin)
Eddie Cantor Story, 1953 (Cantor)
Eddie Duchin Story, 1956 (Power)
Eddie Macon's Run, 1983 (Douglas, K.)
Eddie Murphy Raw, 1987 (Jackson, S.; Murphy)
Eddy Duchin Story, 1956 (Novak)
Edge of Darkness, 1943 (Flynn; Gordon; Huston, W.)
Edge of Doom, 1950 (Andrews, D.)
Edge of Eternity, 1959 (Wilde)
Edge of Sanity, 1989 (Perkins)
Edge of the City, 1957 (Poitier)
Edge of the Wind, 1985 (Mills; Sharif)
Edipo Re, 1967 (Mangano; Valli)
Edison Bugg's Invention, 1916 (Laurel and Hardy)
Edison the Man, 1940 (Coburn, C.; Tracy)
Edith et Marcel, 1983 (Tyszkiewicz)
Edith's Diary. *See* Edithes Tagebuch, 1983
Edithes Tagebuch, 1983 (Winkler)
Edmund Kean—Prince among Lovers. *See* Kean, 1924
Edo bishonen-roku, 1931 (Yamada)
Edo gonomi Ryogoku-zoshi, 1932 (Hasegawa; Takamine)
Edo iroha matsuri, 1953 (Yamada)
Edo mujo, 1963 (Hasegawa)
Edo saigo no hi, 1941 (Shimura)
Edo sodachi, 1928 (Hasegawa)
Edo wa utsuru, 1934 (Hasegawa)
Edokko ichiba, 1931 (Yamada)
Edokko Kenchan, 1937 (Takamine)
Edokko matsuri, 1958 (Hasegawa)
Edouard et Caroline, 1951 (Gélin)
Educating Rita, 1983 (Caine)
Education, 1915 (Beery)
Education de prince, 1926 (Purviance)
Education de prince, 1938 (Jouvet)
Education sentimentale, 1985 (Léaud)
Edward and Caroline. *See* Edouard et Caroline, 1951
Edward, My Son, 1949 (Kerr; Tracy)
Edward Scissorhands, 1990 (Arkin; Depp; Price; Ryder; Wiest)
Edwin, 1984 (Guinness)
Effect of Gamma Rays on Man-in-the-Moon Marigolds, 1972 (Woodward; Newman)
Effeuillant la marguerite, 1956 (Bardot; Gélin)
Effi Briest. *See* Fontane: Effi Briest, 1974
E-Flat Man, 1935 (Keaton, B.)
Efter Repetitioner, 1984 (Josephson; Olin; Thulin)
Egen ingång, 1956 (Andersson, B.)
Egg, 1922 (Laurel and Hardy)
Egg and I, 1947 (Colbert; MacMurray)
Egg! Egg! A Hardboiled Story. *See* Agget är löst, 1974
Ego prevoskhoditelstvo, 1927 (Cherkassov)
Ego zovut Sukhe-Bator, 1942 (Cherkassov)
Egy Barany, 1970 (Olbrychski)
Egy fiunak a fele, 1923 (Lukas)
Egy örült éjszaka, 1969 (Tyszkiewicz)
Egypt by Three, 1953 (Constantine; Cotten)
Egyptian, 1954 (Carradine; Mature; Tierney; Ustinov)
Egyptologists, 1965 (Heston)
Ehe, 1929 (Dagover)
Ehe der Luise Rohrbach, 1917 (Jannings)
Ehe der Maria Braun, 1978 (Schygulla)
Ehe des Dr. Med. Danwitz, 1956 (Schell, Maximilian)
Ehe für eine Nacht, 1953 (Fröhlich)
Ehi, amico ... c'e Sabata, hai chiuso?, 1969 (Van Cleef)
Ehne el Talamza, 1959 (Sharif)
Ehrengard, 1982 (Cassel)
Ehrengard, 1986 (Cassel)
Ei gerochsky podvig, 1914 (Mozhukin)

Eien no hito, 1961 (Takamine)
Eien no kokoro, 1928 (Tanaka)
Eifersucht, 1925 (Krauss)
Eiger Sanction, 1975 (Eastwood)
Eight Bells, 1935 (Bellamy)
Eight Cylinder Bull, 1926 (Arthur)
Eight Iron Men, 1952 (Marvin)
Eight O'Clock Walk, 1953 (Attenborough)
Eight on the Lam, 1967 (Hope)
Eighth Day of the Week. *See* Ósmy dzień tygodnia, 1958
Eight-Thirteen, 1920 (Beery)
Eighty Steps to Jonah, 1969 (Mineo; Rooney)
Eiko eno 5000 kiro, 1969 (Mifune)
Eiko eno kurohyo, 1969 (Ryu)
Eikyu no ai, 1935 (Tanaka)
Eine alltägliche Geschichte, 1944 (Fröhlich)
Eine DuBarry von Heute, 1926 (Dietrich)
Eine Frau, die weiss was sie will, 1934 (Walbrook)
Eine Insel wird entdeckt, 1937 (Madsen and Schenstrøm)
Eine Liebe im Deutschland, 1983 (Mueller-Stahl; Schygulla)
Eine Liebe in Deutschland, 1985 (Olbrychski)
Eine Mann mit Herz, 1932 (Fröhlich)
Eine Nacht der Liebe. *See* Liebesnächte, 1929
Eine Reise ins Licht, 1977 (Bogarde)
Eine Rose für Jane, 1970 (Constantine)
Eine Versunkene Welt, 1922 (Lukas)
Einer Frau, die weiss, was sie will, 1934 (Dagover)
Einer frisst den anderern, 1964 (Mansfield)
Einmal werd'ich Dir gefallende, 1937 (Rasp)
Einsichten eines Clowns, 1976 (Schell, Maximilian)
Eisenbahnkönig, 1921 (Kortner)
Ek baar kaho, 1980 (Azmi)
Ek Din Achanak, 1988 (Azmi)
Ek Doctor Ki Maut, 1990 (Azmi)
Ek hi bhool, 1981 (Azmi)
Ek hi rasta, 1977 (Azmi)
Ek Ke Baad Ek, 1960 (Anand)
Ek Pal, 1986 (Azmi)
Ek Tuku Basa, 1965 (Chatterjee)
Ekhane Amar Swarga, 1990 (Chatterjee)
Eki Ange Eto Rup, 1965 (Chatterjee)
Ekimae onsen, 1962 (Tsukasa)
Ekti Jiban, 1988 (Chatterjee)
El Dorado, 1963 (Topol)
El Dorado, 1967 (Caan; Mitchum; Wayne)
Elakoon Itsemurhaaja, 1984 (Olbrychski)
Elanprostekt nr. 4, 1986 (Constantine)
Eleanora Duse, 1947 (Brazzi)
Elective Affinities. *See* Affinita elettive, 1996
Electra, 1962 (Papas)
Electric Blue. *See* Blu Elettrico, 1988
Electric Horseman, 1979 (Fonda, J.; Redford)
Electric House, 1922 (Keaton, B.)
Elegant John and His Ladies. *See* Great Smokey Roadblock, 1978
Elegy. *See* Ereji, 1951
Elena and Her Men. *See* Élena et les hommes, 1956
Elena et les hommes, 1957 (Bergman; Marais; Modot)
Eleni, 1985 (Malkovich; Nelligan)
Elephant. *See* Barnförbjudet, 1979
Elephant Games, 1986 (Meredith)
Elephant God. *See* Joi Baba Felunath, 1978
Elephant Man, 1980 (Bancroft; Brooks, M.; Gielgud; Hopkins, A.; Hurt, J.)
Elephant Walk, 1954 (Andrews, D.; Finch; Leigh, V.; Taylor, E.)
Elephant Walk. *See* Barnförbjudet, 1979
Elephants Never Forget. *See* Zenobia, 1939
Elevator, 1974 (McDowall)
Elevator, 1975 (Loy)
Elevator to the Gallows. *See* Ascenseur pour l'échafaud, 1958
Eleven Harrowhouse, 1974 (Howard, T.)
Elf Teufel, 1927 (Fröhlich)
Eliminator. *See* Teheran Incident, 1979

Elinor Norton, 1934 (Trevor)
Elisa, 1956 (Reggiani)
Elisa, 1994 (Depardieu)
Elisa, My Life. *See* Elisa, vida mía, 1977
Elisa, vida mía, 1977 (Chaplin, G.; Rey)
Elisabeth von Osterreich, 1931 (Dagover)
Elisir d'amore, 1947 (Lollobrigida; Mangano)
Eliza Fraser, 1976 (Howard, T.; York)
Eliza's Horiscope, 1970 (Jones, T.)
Elizabeth of Austria. *See* Elisabeth von Osterreich, 1931
Elizabeth of Ladymead, 1949 (Neagle)
Ella Cinders, 1926 (Langdon)
Elle, 1918 (Modot)
Elle boit pas, elle fume pas, elle drague pas ... mais elle cause, 1970 (Girardot; Blier)
Elle cause plus ... elle flingue, 1972 (Girardot; Blier)
Elle disait non, 1932 (Fernandel)
Ellery Queen, 1975 (Milland)
Ellery Queen and the Murder Ring, 1941 (Bellamy)
Ellery Queen and the Perfect Crime, 1941 (Bellamy)
Ellery Queen, Master Detective, 1940 (Bellamy)
Ellery Queen's Penthouse Mystery, 1941 (Bellamy; Wong)
Elles étaient 12 femmes, 1940 (Presle; Rosay)
Elles ne pensent qu'a ca, 1994 (Cardinale)
Ellie, 1984 (Winters)
Ellis Island, 1984 (Dunaway; Greenwood)
Elly y yo, 1951 (Armendáriz)
Elmer Gantry, 1960 (Kennedy; Lancaster)
Elmer the Great, 1933 (Brown; Wyman)
Elogia della pazzia di desiderio erasmo, 1984 (Rey)
Elopement, 1916 (Dressler)
Elopement, 1951 (Webb)
Elopement at Home, 1913 (Talmadge)
Else von Erlenhof, 1919 (Kortner)
Elstree Calling, 1930 (Wong)
Elus de la mer, 1925 (Modot)
Elusive Corporal. *See* Caporal épinglé, 1962
Elusive Pimpernel, 1950 (Cusack; Hawkins; Niven)
Elvis, 1978 (Winters)
Elvis on Tour, 1972 (Presley)
Elvis: That's the Way It Was, 1970 (Grant, C.; Presley)
Embarkation at Midnight. *See* Imbarco a mezzanotte, 1952
Embassy, 1972 (Crawford, B.; Milland; Von Sydow)
Embassy, 1985 (Wallach)
Embers. *See* Glut, 1983
Embezzler, 1914 (Chaney)
Embryo, 1976 (Hudson; McDowall)
Embuscade, 1941 (Berry)
Emergency Squad, 1940 (Quinn)
Emigrant. *See* Al Mohager, 1994
Émigrante, 1939 (Feuillère)
Emigrantes, 1949 (Fabrizi)
Emigrants. *See* Utvandrarna, 1972
Emil und die Detektive, 1931 (Rasp)
Emile des Roses, 1991 (Reggiani)
Emile des Roses, 1993 (Sanda)
Emile et les détectives. *See* Emil und die Detektive, 1931
Emile l'africain, 1947 (Fernandel)
Eminent Domain, 1991 (Sutherland)
Emma, 1932 (Dressler; Loy; Rooney)
Emma Hamilton. *See* Lady Hamilton, 1969
Emma's War, 1986 (Remick)
Emmanuelle, 1974 (Cuny)
Emmanuelle on Taboo Island. *See* Spiaggia del desiderio, 1976
Empereur de Perou, 1981 (Rooney)
Emperor and a General. *See* Nippon no ichiban nagai hi, 1967
Emperor Jones, 1933 (Robeson)
Emperor of Peru. *See* Empereur de Perou, 1981
Emperor of the North Pole, 1972 (Marvin; Borgnine)
Emperor Waltz, 1948 (Crosby; Fontaine)
Emperor's Candlesticks, 1937 (O'Sullivan; Powell, W.; Rainer; Young, R.)

Emperor's New Clothes, 1966 (Carradine)
Emperor's Nightingale, 1951 (Karloff)
Empire de la nuit, 1962 (Constantine)
Empire of the Sun, 1987 (Malkovich; Richardson, M.)
Empire State, 1987 (Landau)
Empire Strikes Back, 1980 (Ford, H.; Guinness; Jones, James Earl)
Employee's Entrance, 1933 (Young, L.)
Empreinte des géants, 1980 (Reggiani)
Empress, 1917 (Barrymore, J.)
Empress Dowager, 1989 (Gong Li)
Empty Canvas. *See* Noia, 1964
Empty Gun, 1917 (Chaney)
Empty Hands, 1924 (Shearer)
Empty Hearts, 1924 (Bow)
Empty Saddles, 1936 (Brooks, L.)
Empty Star. *See* Estrella vacia, 1958
Enamorada, 1946 (Armendáriz; Félix)
Enamorado, 1951 (Infante)
Enchanted, 1959 (Cusack)
Enchanted April, 1992 (Richardson, M.)
Enchanted Cottage, 1924 (Barthelmess)
Enchanted Cottage, 1945 (Marshall; Young, R.)
Enchanted Forest. *See* Bosque encantado, 1987
Enchanted Island, 1958 (Andrews, D.)
Enchantment, 1921 (Davies)
Enchantment, 1948 (Niven)
Encontra a Mallorca, 1962 (Dors)
Encounter. *See* Imbarco a mezzanotte, 1952
Encounter with a Spy. *See* Spotkanie ze szpiegem, 1964
End, 1978 (Field; Loy; Reynolds, B.; Woodward)
End of a Day. *See* Fin du jour, 1938
End of a Priest. *See* Faráťuv konec, 1968
End of Desire. *See* Vie, 1958
End of Summer. *See* Kohayagawa-ke no aki, 1961
End of the Affair, 1955 (Cushing; Kerr)
End of the Affair, 1955 (Mills)
End of the Feud, 1914 (Chaney)
End of the Game. *See* Richter und sein Henker, 1975
End of the Line, 1988 (Bacon; Hunter; Steenburgen)
End of the Rainbow. *See* Northwest Outpost, 1947
End of the Road, 1970 (Jones, James Earl)
End of the Tour, 1917 (Barrymore, L.)
End of the World, 1978 (Ayres; Lee, C.)
End of the World in Our Usual Bed in a Night Full of Rain, 1977 (Giannini)
Enda natt, 1939 (Bergman)
Ende von Liede, 1919 (Nielsen)
Ending Up, 1990 (Mills)
Endless Game, 1989 (Finney; Quayle; Segal)
Endless Love, 1981 (Cruise)
Endless Night, 1971 (Sanders)
Enemies, a Love Story, 1989 (Huston, A.; Olin)
Enemies of Women, 1923 (Barrymore, L.; Bow)
Enemy, 1927 (Gish; McCrea)
Enemy Agent. *See* British Intelligence, 1940
Enemy Air Attack. *See* Tekki kushu, 1943
Enemy Below, 1957 (Mitchum; Powell, D.)
Enemy Mine, 1985 (Quaid)
Enemy of the People, 1978 (Andersson, B.; McQueen)
Enemy of the People. *See* Ganashatru, 1989
Enemy Within, 1994 (Robards; Whitaker)
Enesorabilia, 1950 (Brazzi)
Enfant de la nuit, 1996 (Deneuve)
Enfant de la tourmente. *See* Retour au bonheur, 1939
Enfant de ma soeur, 1932 (Artaud)
Enfant du carnaval, 1921 (Mozhukin; Vanel)
Enfant du carnaval, 1934 (Mozhukin)
Enfants, 1985 (Gélin)
Enfants de salaud, 1996 (Baye)
Enfants du Naufrageur, 1992 (Marais)
Enfants du paradis, 1945 (Brasseur; Modot)
Enfer, 1994 (Cassel)

Enfer de Dien Bien Phu. *See* Jump into Hell, 1955
Enfer des anges, 1939 (Blier)
Enforcer, 1951 (Bogart; Sloane)
Enforcer, 1976 (Eastwood)
Engagement Italiano. *See* Ragazza in prestito, 1965
Engagement Ring. *See* Engeiji ringu, 1950
Engagement Ring. *See* Konyaku yubiwa, 1950
Engeiji ringu, 1950 (Tanaka)
Engel auf Erden, 1959 (Schneider)
Engel mit der Posaune, 1948 (Schell, Maria; Werner)
Engelein, 1913 (Nielsen)
Engeleins Hochzeit, 1914 (Nielsen)
England Made Me, 1973 (Finch)
Englische Heirat, 1934 (Walbrook)
English Patient, 1995 (Dafoe; Binoche; Fiennes)
English without Tears, 1944 (Rutherford)
Englishman Abroad, 1985 (Bates, A.)
Englishman and the Girl, 1910 (Pickford)
Englishman Who Went Up a Hill but Came Down a Mountain, 1995 (Grant, H.)
Englishman's Home, 1939 (Henreid)
Enigma, 1982 (Neill; Sheen)
Enigmatique Monsieur Parkes, 1930 (Colbert; Menjou)
Enlèvement en hydroplane, 1913 (Linder)
Enlevez-moi, 1932 (Arletty)
Ennemi public No. 1, 1953 (Fernandel)
Ennemis, 1960 (Brasseur)
Enoch Arden, 1915 (Gish)
Enormous Changes at the Last Minute, 1983 (Bacon)
Enormous Changes at the Last Minute, 1985 (Barkin)
Enough to Do, 1925 (Laurel and Hardy)
Enquête de l'inspecteur Morgan. *See* Blind Date, 1959
Enquête sur le 58, 1944 (Gélin; Vanel)
Enrico Caruso, leggenda di una voce, 1951 (Lollobrigida)
Enrico IV, 1984 (Cardinale; Mastroianni)
Ensign Pulver, 1964 (Matthau; Nicholson)
Entebbe: Operation Thunderbolt, 1977 (Kinski)
Enter Laughing, 1966 (Ferrer; Winters)
Enter Madame, 1935 (Grant, C.)
Enter the Dragon, 1973 (Chan; Lee, B.)
Entertainer, 1960 (Bates, A.; Finney; Olivier)
Entertainer, 1976 (Lemmon)
Entertaining the Troops, 1988 (Lamarr; Lamour; Sidney)
Entführung, 1936 (Fröhlich)
Enticement, 1925 (Astor)
Entity, 1983 (Hershey)
Entlassung, 1942 (Jannings; Krauss)
Entotsu no mieru basho, 1953 (Takamine; Tanaka)
Entraîneuse, 1940 (Morgan)
Entre el cielo y la tierra, 1993 (Maura; Cassel)
Entre Hermanos, 1944 (Armendáriz)
Entre la mer et l'eau douce, 1967 (Bujold)
Entre Nous. *See* Coup de foudre, 1983
Entre onze heures et minuit, 1948 (Jouvet)
Entre Tinieblas, 1983 (Maura)
Entrée des artistes, 1938 (Blier; Dalio; Jouvet)
Entrega immediata, 1963 (Cantinflas)
Envers du Decor: Portrait de Pierre Guffroy, 1992 (Ford, H.; Kinski)
Epar Opar, 1973 (Chatterjee)
Epervier, 1933 (Boyer; Marais)
Epic that Never Was, 1963 (Bogarde)
Epidemic, 1914 (Beery)
Epilog, 1950 (Kortner)
Epitome. *See* Shukuzu, 1953
Epoque Formidable, 1991 (Abril)
Equilibriste, 1991 (Piccoli)
Equilibrium. *See* Story of Three Loves, 1953
Equinox Flower. *See* **Higanbana**, 1958
Equipage, 1935 (Vanel)
Equus, 1977 (Burton)
Er oder Dich. *See* Seine grösster Bluff, 1927

Era du venerdi 17, 1956 (Sordi)
Era lui, si! si!, 1951 (Loren)
Era notte a Roma, 1960 (Bondarchuk)
Eran trecento, 1952 (Brazzi)
Eraser, 1996 (Caan; Coburn, J.; Schwarzenegger)
Ercole al centro della terra, 1961 (Lee, C.)
Ercole alla conquista di Atlantide, 1961 (Volonté)
Erdenschwer, 1989 (Vogler)
Erdgeist, 1923 (Nielsen)
Eredità Ferramonti, 1976 (Quinn; Sanda)
Ereji, 1951 (Mifune)
Erendira, 1982 (Papas)
Erfinder, 1980 (Ganz)
Erfolg, 1991 (Ganz)
Eric, 1975 (Neal)
Eric the Great. *See* Last Performance, 1928
Erik the Viking, 1989 (Cleese; Robbins; Rooney)
Eriki no wakadaishō, 1966 (Tanaka)
Eriko to tomoni, 1951 (Yamamura)
Ernani, 1911 (Bertini)
Ernest le rebelle, 1938 (Fernandel)
Ernesto Che Chuevara: Das bolivianische Tagebuch, 1965 (Trintignant)
Ernst Thälman Führer seiner Klasse, 1955 (Piccoli)
Eroe Borghese, 1995 (Volonté)
Eroe dei nostri tempi, 1955 (Sordi)
Eroi, 1972 (Terry-Thomas)
Eroi della domenica, 1952 (Mastroianni)
Eroica, 1949 (Werner)
Eroica, 1958 (Łomnicki)
Eroismo d'amore, 1914 (Bertini)
Erotissimo, 1968 (Girardot)
Errand Boy, 1961 (Lewis, Jerry)
Erreur judiciaire, 1947 (Dalio)
Erste Frühlingstag, 1956 (Fröhlich)
Erste Liebe, 1970 (Sanda; Schell, Maximilian)
Erste Polka, 1979 (Josephson; Schell, Maria)
Ervinka, 1974 (Topol)
Es Dach überem Chopf, 1962 (Ganz)
Es flüstert die liebe, 1935 (Fröhlich; Dagover)
Es gibt eine Frau, die Dich niemals vergisst, 1930 (Dagover)
Es Hat Mich Sehr Gefreut, 1987 (Novak)
Es kommt ein Tag, 1950 (Dagover; Schell, Maria)
Es war eine rauschende Ballnacht, 1939 (Rasp)
Es werde Licht, 1918 (Krauss)
Esa pareja feliz, 1951 (Rey)
Escale au soleil, 1947 (Fernandel)
Escalier de service, 1954 (Darrieux)
Escalier sans fin, 1943 (Fresnay)
Escándalo de estrellas, 1944 (Infante)
Escapade, 1935 (Powell, W.; Rainer)
Escapade. *See* Atoll K, 1951
Escapade, 1955 (Mills)
Escapade, 1957 (Jourdan)
Escapade in Japan, 1957 (Eastwood)
Escape, 1914 (Crisp; Gish; Marsh; Sweet)
Escape, 1930 (Carroll)
Escape, 1940 (Nazimova; Shearer; Taylor, R.; Veidt)
Escape, 1948 (Cusack; Harrison)
Escape, 1971 (Grahame)
Escape Artist, 1982 (Julia)
Escape by Night, 1937 (Bond)
Escape from Alcatraz, 1978 (Eastwood)
Escape from Fort Bravo, 1953 (Holden)
Escape from L.A., 1996 (Robertson)
Escape from New York, 1981 (Borgnine; Curtis, J.; Pleasence; Stanton; Van Cleef)
Escape from Prison. *See* Datsugoku, 1950
Escape from Sobibor, 1987 (Arkin)
Escape from the Planet of the Apes, 1971 (McDowall; Mineo)
Escape from Yesterday. *See* Bandera, 1935
Escape from Zahrain, 1961 (Brynner; Mason; Mineo)

Escape into Dreams. *See* Natale al campo 119, 1948
Escape Me Never, 1935 (Bergner)
Escape Me Never, 1947 (Flynn; Lupino)
Escape of Jim Dolan, 1913 (Mix)
Escape to Athena, 1979 (Cardinale; Gould; Niven)
Escape to Burma, 1955 (Ryan, R.; Stanwyck)
Escape to Happiness. *See* Intermezzo: A Love Story, 1939
Escape to the North. *See* Flucht in den Norden, 1986
Escape to the Sun. *See* Habrichka el hashemersh, 1972
Escape to Victory. *See* Victory, 1981
Escape to Witch Mountain, 1975 (Milland; Pleasence)
Escapes, 1987 (Price)
Escarpins de Max, 1913 (Linder)
Esclave, 1923 (Boyer)
Esclave, 1953 (Gélin)
Esclave blanche, 1927 (Vanel)
Esclave blanche, 1939 (Dalio)
Escondida, 1955 (Armendáriz; Félix)
Escondido, 1968 (Ryan, R.)
Escort West, 1959 (Mature)
Escuadró de la muerte, 1966 (Crawford, B.)
Escuadron. *See* Counterforce, 1988
Escuela de música, 1955 (Infante)
Escuela de rateros, 1956 (Infante)
Escuela de vagabundos, 1954 (Infante)
Esfinge de cristal, 1968 (Taylor, R.)
Eshaet Hub, 1960 (Sharif)
Eskimo-Baby, 1917 (Nielsen)
Esmeralda Bay, 1988 (Rey)
Esmerelda, 1915 (Pickford)
España insolita, 1965 (Rey)
Especially on Sunday, 1993 (Ganz)
Especially on Sunday. *See* Specialmente la domenica, 1991
Espion. *See* Defector, 1966
Espion, lève toi, 1981 (Piccoli)
Espionage, 1937 (Lukas)
Espionage Agent, 1939 (McCrea)
Espions. *See* Spione, 1928
Espions, 1957 (Jaffe; Ustinov)
Espontánes, 1963 (Rey)
Essence. *See* Susman, 1986
Essor, 1920 (Fresnay)
Estacion de paso, 1992 (Andersson, B.)
Estambul 65, 1965 (Kinski)
Estate in quattro, 1969 (Andersson, B.; Björnstrand)
Estate violenta, 1959 (Trintignant)
Esther Waters, 1948 (Bogarde; Cusack)
Estouffade à la Carabei, 1967 (Seberg)
Estrangeira, 1982 (Rey)
Estrella vacia, 1958 (Félix)
Estudantes, 1935 (Miranda)
Et ... Dieu créa la femme, 1956 (Bardot; Trintignant)
Et l'autre, 1967 (Noiret)
Et moi j'te dis qu'elle t'a fait de l'oeil, 1935 (Berry)
...Et Satan conduit le bal, 1962 (Deneuve)
Et si on faisait l'amour? *See* Scusi, facciamo l'amore, 1968
Et sommereventyr, 1919 (Madsen and Schenstrøm)
Et ta soeur, 1958 (Arletty; Cassel; Fresnay)
Età dell'amore, 1953 (Fabrizi)
Etat de siège, 1973 (Montand)
Etat sauvage, 1978 (Piccoli; Vogler)
Eté meurtrier, 1983 (Adjani)
Eté prochain, 1985 (Noiret; Cardinale)
Eterna femmina, 1954 (Lamarr)
Eternal. *See* Amar, 1954
Eternal City, 1923 (Barrymore, L.; Bennett; Colman)
Eternal Flame, 1922 (Menjou; Talmadge)
Eternal Grind, 1916 (Pickford)
Eternal Husband. *See* Homme au chapeau rond, 1946
Eternal Love, 1929 (Barrymore, J.)
Eternal Melodies. *See* Melodie eterne, 1940

Eternal Mother, 1911 (Normand)
Eternal Mother, 1912 (Sweet)
Eternal Mother, 1917 (Barrymore, E.)
Eternal Retour, 1943 (Marais)
Eternal Sappho, 1916 (Bara)
Eternal Sea, 1955 (Hayden)
Eternal Sin, 1917 (Barthelmess)
Eternal Struggle, 1923 (Beery)
Eternal Woman. *See* Eterna femmina, 1954
Eternally Yours, 1939 (Crawford, B.; Niven; Young, L.)
Eternel Conflit, 1947 (Modot)
Êternelle Jeunesse, 1988 (Reggiani)
Eternity, 1990 (Voight)
Eternity of Love. *See* Wakarete ikiru toki mo, 1961
Ethan Frome, 1993 (Neeson)
Ethel's Romeos, 1915 (Laurel and Hardy)
Etienne of the Glad Heart, 1914 (Mix)
Etoile de mer, 1926 (Artaud)
Etoile de Sud, 1969 (Welles; Segal)
Etoile du nord, 1982 (Noiret)
Etoile filant, 1930 (Brasseur)
Etoile sans lumière, 1945 (Berry; Montand; Reggiani)
Etoiles ne meurent jamais, 1957 (Raimu)
Etrange Affaire, 1981 (Baye; Piccoli)
Etrange Madame X, 1951 (Morgan)
Etrange Mr. Steve, 1957 (Moreau)
Etrange Monsieur Victor, 1938 (Raimu)
Etranger. *See* Lo straniero, 1967
Etroit mousquetaire. *See* Three Must-Get-Theres, 1922
Ettaro di cielo, 1958 (Mastroianni)
Ettore Fieramosca, 1937 (Cervi)
Ettore lo fusto, 1971 (Giannini)
Etwas wird sichtbar, 1981 (Ganz)
Eu Te Amo, 1981 (Braga)
Eugene Onegin, 1996 (Fiennes)
Eugenia de Montijo, 1944 (Rey)
Eugenia Grandet, 1946 (Valli)
Eugenie—The Story of Her Journey into Perversion, 1970 (Lee, C.)
Eulogy to 5.02, 1965 (Burton)
Eureka, 1984 (Hackman; Pesci; Rourke)
Eureka Stockade, 1949 (Finch)
Europa '51, 1951 (Bergman; Masina)
Europa. *See* Zentropa, 1992
Europa Abends, 1989 (Constantine)
Europeans, 1979 (Remick)
Eusebe depute, 1938 (Berry)
Eva, 1935 (Henreid)
Eva, 1948 (Dahlbeck)
Eva, 1962 (Baker; Moreau)
Eva and the Grasshopper. *See* Jugendrausch, 1927
Evadés, 1954 (Fresnay)
Evangelimann, 1923 (Bergner)
Evangeline, 1929 (Del Rio)
Eve. *See* Eva, 1962
Eve. *See* Face of Eve, 1968
Eve Knew Her Apples, 1945 (Miller)
Eve of St. Mark, 1944 (Baxter; Price)
Eve's Love Letters, 1926 (Laurel and Hardy)
Eve's Lover, 1925 (Bow)
Evelyn Prentice, 1934 (Loy; Powell, W.; Russell, R.)
Even as I.O.U., 1942 (Three Stooges)
Even Break, 1917 (Menjou)
Even Cowgirls Get the Blues, 1994 (Dickinson; Hurt, J.; Reeves; Thurman)
Evénement le plus important depuis que l'homme a marché sur la lune, 1973 (Deneuve; Mastroianni; Presle)
Evening Clothes, 1927 (Brooks, L.; Menjou)
Evening Star, 1996 (Lewis, Juliette; MacLaine; Nicholson; Richardson, M.)
Evenings for Sale, 1932 (Marshall)
Evensong, 1934 (Guinness; Kortner)
Eventful Evening, 1916 (Mix)
Ever in My Heart, 1933 (Bellamy; Stanwyck)

F. Scott Fitzgerald in Hollywood, 1976 (Weld; Woods)
F.I.S.T., 1978 (Stallone; Steiger)
F.P. 1 antwortet nicht, 1932 (Lorre; Boyer; Brasseur; Veidt)
FTA Show, 1972 (Sutherland)
F/X, 1986 (Bassett)
Fabiola, 1948 (Morgan)
Fabiola, 1949 (Cervi)
Fabiola, 1960 (Rey)
Fable of Elvira and Farina and the Meal Ticket, 1915 (Swanson)
Fable of Napoleon and the Bumpkin, 1914 (Beery)
Fable of the Brash Drummer and the Nectarine, 1914 (Beery)
Fable of the Bushleague Lover Who Failed to Qualify, 1914 (Beery)
Fable of the Business Boy and the Droppers-in, 1914 (Beery)
Fable of the Coming Champion Who Was Delayed, 1914 (Beery)
Fable of the Roystering Blades, 1915 (Beery)
Fabuleuse Aventure de Marco Polo, 1964 (Welles; Quinn; Sharif)
Fabulous Baker Boys, 1989 (Bridges; Pfeiffer)
Faccia a faccia, 1967 (Volonté)
Faccia di lepre, 1990 (Thulin)
Facciamo paradiso, 1995 (Noiret)
Face. See Ansiktet, 1958
Face at the Window, 1915 (Mix)
Face at the Window, 1932 (Massey)
Face au destin, 1941 (Berry)
Face behind the Mask, 1941 (Lorre)
Face in the Crowd, 1957 (Matthau; Neal; Remick)
Face in the Dark, 1918 (Marsh)
Face in the Fog, 1922 (Barrymore, L.)
Face in the Sky, 1933 (Tracy)
Face of a Fugitive, 1959 (Coburn, J.; MacMurray)
Face of a Stranger, 1991 (Rowlands)
Face of Another. See Tanin no kao, 1966
Face of Eve, 1968 (Lee, C.; Lom)
Face of Fear. See Cara del terror, 1962
Face of Fu Manchu, 1965 (Lee, C.)
Face of Marble, 1946 (Carradine)
Face of Rage, 1983 (Wiest)
Face of Terror. See Cara del terror, 1962
Face on the Bar-Room Floor, 1914 (Chaplin, C.)
Face that Launched a Thousand Ships. See Eterna femmina, 1954
Face to face. See Ansikte mot ansikte, 1976
Face to Face, 1952 (Mason; Preston)
Face to Face. See Faccia a faccia, 1967
Face-Off, 1971 (Candy)
Faces, 1968 (Rowlands)
Faces in the Dark, 1960 (Zetterling)
Faces of Love. See Repérages, 1977
Facts of Life, 1960 (Ball; Hope)
Facts of Murder. See Maledetto imbroglio, 1959
Fade to Black, 1980 (Rourke)
Fade-In, 1968 (Reynolds, B.)
Faded Lilies, 1909 (Pickford)
Fahrendes Volk, 1938 (Rosay)
Fahrenheit 451, 1966 (Christie; Cusack)
Fai in fretta ad ucidermi ... ho Freddo!, 1965 (Vitti)
Faibles femmes, 1959 (Delon)
Fail Safe, 1964 (Fonda, H.; Matthau)
Failing of Raymond, 1971 (Henreid; Wyman)
Faille, 1974 (Piccoli)
Failure, 1911 (Crisp)
Faim de loup, 1932 (Brasseur)
Faint Perfume, 1925 (Powell, W.)
Fair Co-ed, 1927 (Davies; McCrea)
Fair Dentist, 1911 (Pickford)
Fair Exchange. See Getting Acquainted, 1914
Fair Wind to Java, 1953 (MacMurray; McLaglen)
Faisons le point sur les Spoutniks, 1957 (Gélin)
Faisons un rêve, 1935 (Raimu; Arletty)
Faites vos jeux, mesdames. See Feu à volonte, 1965
Faith Healer, 1921 (Menjou)
Faith, Hope and Hogan, 1953 (Crosby)

Faithful, 1996 (Cher)
Faithful Heart, 1932 (Marshall)
Faithful Narrative of the Capture, Sufferings, and Miraculous Escape of Eliza Fraser. See Eliza Fraser, 1976
Faithfully in My Fashion, 1946 (Horton)
Faithless, 1932 (Montgomery)
Faits divers, 1923 (Artaud)
Fakers. See Hell's Bloody Devils, 1970
Faking with Society. See Caught in a Cabaret, 1914
Fakira, 1976 (Azmi)
Falbalas, 1944 (Presle)
Falchivi koupon, 1912 (Mozhukin)
Falcon and the Co-Eds, 1943 (Malone)
Falcon and the Snowman, 1985 (Penn)
Falcon Takes Over, 1942 (Bond; Sanders)
Falcon's Brother, 1942 (Sanders)
Fall des Generalstabsoberst Redl, 1931 (Dagover)
Fall Franza, 1986 (Mueller-Stahl)
Fall Guy, 1921 (Laurel and Hardy)
Fall Guy, 1965 (Keaton, B.)
Fall Lucona, 1993 (Sanda)
Fall Molander, 1944 (Wegener)
Fall of Italy. See Pad Italje, 1985
Fall of Lola Montès. See **Lola Montès**, 1955
Fall of the House of Usher. See House of Usher, 1960
Fall of the House of Usher, 1982 (Landau)
Fall of the Rebel Angels. See Caduta degli angeli ribelli, 1981
Fall of the Roman Empire, 1964 (Quayle; Guinness; Loren; Mason; Sharif)
Fall Sylvester matuska, 1982 (Mueller-Stahl)
Fall Time, 1995 (Rourke)
Fallen Angel, 1944 (Darnell; Andrews, D.; Carradine; Faye)
Fallen Idol, 1948 (Hawkins; Morgan; Richardson, R.)
Fallen Sparrow, 1943 (Garfield; O'Hara)
Fallende Stern, 1950 (Krauss)
Falling Down, 1993 (Douglas, Michael; Duvall; Hershey; Weld)
Falling for You, 1995 (Beatty)
Falling in Love, 1984 (De Niro; Keitel; Streep; Wiest)
Falling in Love Again, 1980 (Gould; Pfeiffer; York)
Falsche Bewegung, 1974 (Kinski; Schygulla; Vogler)
Fälschung, 1981 (Ganz; Schygulla)
False Alarms, 1936 (Three Stooges)
False Colors, 1943 (Mitchum)
False Eyelashes. See Pestañas Postizas, 1982
False Faces, 1919 (Chaney)
False Identity, 1990 (Bujold)
False Madonna, 1932 (Francis)
False Millionaire. See Pour mon coeur et ses millions, 1931
False Note. See Falchivi koupon, 1912
False Witness. See Transient Lady, 1935
False Witness. See Zigzag, 1970
False Witness. See Fälschung, 1981
Falstaff, 1913 (Rosay)
Fama, 1921 (Bertini)
Fame and Fortune, 1918 (Mix)
Fame Is the Name of the Game, 1966 (Duvall)
Famiglia, 1987 (Gassman; Noiret)
Famiglia Passaguai, 1951 (Fabrizi)
Famiglia Passaguai fa fortuna, 1952 (Fabrizi)
Familie Buchholz, 1944 (Fröhlich)
Famille duraton, 1939 (Berry)
Family. See Città violenta, 1970
Family. See Kareinaru Ichizoku, 1974
Family. See Famiglia, 1987
Family Affair, 1937 (Barrymore, L.; Rooney)
Family Business, 1989 (Connery; Hoffman)
Family Diary. See Cronaca familiare, 1962
Family Divided, 1995 (Dunaway)
Family Doctor. See Medico della mutua, 1968
Family Enforcer. See Death Collector, 1975
Family for Joe, 1990 (Mitchum)
Family Home. See His Trysting Place, 1914

Family Honeymoon, 1948 (Colbert; MacMurray; McDaniel)
Family Jewels, 1965 (Baxter; Lewis, Jerry)
Family Life. *See* Vie de famille, 1985
Family Life. *See* Życie rodzinne, 1971
Family Matter. *See* Vendetta: Secrets of a Mafia Bride, 1991
Family of Spies, 1990 (Bassett)
Family Pictures, 1993 (Huston, A.; Neill)
Family Plot, 1976 (Dern)
Family Reunion. *See* Daughters Courageous, 1939
Family Reunion, 1981 (Davis, B.)
Family Rico, 1972 (Mineo)
Family Secret, 1951 (Cobb)
Family Secrets, 1979 (Blondell)
Family Swedenhielms. *See* Swedenhielms, 1935
Family Thing, 1996 (Duvall; Jones, James Earl)
Family Upside Down, 1978 (Astaire)
Family Way, 1967 (Mills)
Famine, 1915 (Hayakawa)
Famous Ferguson Case, 1932 (Blondell)
Fan, 1949 (Carroll; Sanders)
Fan, 1981 (Bacall; Garner)
Fan, 1996 (Barkin; De Niro; Snipes)
Fanatic, 1965 (Sutherland)
Fanatiques, 1957 (Fresnay)
Fanatisme, 1934 (Negri)
Fanchon, the Cricket, 1915 (Pickford)
Fanciulla di Amalfi, 1921 (Bertini)
Fancy Answers, 1941 (Gardner)
Fancy Baggage, 1929 (Loy)
Fancy Pants, 1950 (Ball; Hope)
Fandango, 1985 (Costner)
Fanfan, 1993 (Presle)
Fanfan la Tulipe, 1951 (Lollobrigida; Philipe)
Fango sulla metropoli, 1965 (Giannini)
Fanny, 1932 (Fresnay; Raimu)
Fanny, 1960 (Caron; Boyer; Chevalier)
Fanny and Alexander. *See* **Fanny och Alexander**, 1982
Fanny by Gaslight, 1944 (Granger; Mason)
Fanny Hill, 1964 (Hopkins, M.)
Fanny Hill, 1983 (Reed; Winters)
Fanny och Alexander, 1982 (Andersson, H.; Björnstrand; Josephson; Olin)
Fanny's Conspiracy, 1913 (Talmadge)
Fan's Notes, 1972 (Meredith)
Fantasia chez les ploucs, 1971 (Delon)
Fantasma d'amore, 1980 (Mastroianni; Schneider)
Fantasmi a Roma, 1960 (Gassman; Mastroianni)
Fantastic Night. *See* Nuit fantastique, 1942
Fantastic Voyage, 1966 (Kennedy; O'Brien, E.; Pleasence; Welch)
Fantastica, 1980 (Reggiani)
Fanteuil 47, 1937 (Rosay)
Fantômas, 1931 (Modot)
Fantômas, 1964 (Marais)
Fantômas contre Scotland Yard, 1967 (Marais)
Fantômas se déchaine, 1965 (Marais)
Fantômas Strikes Back. *See* Fantômas se déchaine, 1965
Fantôme avec chauffeur, 1996 (Gélin; Noiret)
Fantôme de bonheur, 1929 (Modot)
Fantôme de la liberté, 1974 (Piccoli; Vitti)
Far and Away, 1992 (Cruise; Cusack)
Far Call, 1929 (Scott, R.)
Far Country, 1955 (Brennan; Stewart)
Far Cry, 1926 (Sweet)
Far Cry, 1959 (Finch)
Far from Berlin, 1992 (Mueller-Stahl)
Far from Dallas, 1972 (Gélin)
Far from the Madding Crowd, 1967 (Bates, A.; Christie; Finch; Stamp)
Far from War. *See* Daleko ot voiny, 1969
Far Frontier, 1948 (Rogers, R.)
Far Horizons, 1954 (Heston; MacMurray)
Far North, 1988 (Lange; Shepard)
Far Off Place, 1993 (Schell, Maximilian)

Far Pavilions, 1984 (Brazzi; Gielgud; Lee, C.; Sharif)
Faraar, 1955 (Anand)
Farandolle, 1944 (Blier)
Faráľuv konec, 1968 (Brodský)
Faraway Love, 1947 (Zhao Dan)
Faraway, So Close, 1993 (Dafoe; Ganz; Kinski; Vogler)
Farceur, 1961 (Aimée; Cassel)
Farenheit 451, 1966 (Werner)
Farewell Friend. *See* Adieu l'ami, 1968
Farewell My Concubine. *See* **Ba Wang Bie Ji**, 1993
Farewell, My Lovely. *See* Murder, My Sweet, 1944
Farewell, My Lovely, 1975 (Mitchum; Stallone; Stanton)
Farewell Sweet War. *See* Uova di Garofano, 1992
Farewell to Arms, 1932 (Constantine; Menjou)
Farewell to Arms, 1957 (Homolka; Hudson; Huston, J.; Jones, Jennifer; Sordi)
Farewell to the King, 1989 (Nolte)
Farina del diavolo, 1975 (Brazzi)
Farinet oder das falsche Geld, 1939 (Barrault)
Farinet ou l'or dans la montagne. *See* Farinet oder das falsche Geld, 1939
Farm of the Year. *See* Miles from Home, 1988
Farmer in the Dell, 1936 (Ball)
Farmer Takes a Wife, 1935 (Fonda, H.; Gaynor)
Farmer Takes a Wife, 1953 (Grable; Ritter)
Farmer's Daughter, 1947 (Barrymore, E.; Cotten; Young, L.)
Faró da padre, 1974 (Papas)
Far-West, 1973 (Piccoli)
Fascinating Youth, 1926 (Menjou)
Fascination, 1931 (Carroll; Oberon)
Fascination of the Fleur de Lis, 1915 (Chaney)
Fashions in Love, 1929 (Menjou)
Fashions of 1934, 1934 (Davis, B.; Powell, W.)
Faslah, 1974 (Azmi)
Fast and Fearless, 1924 (Arthur)
Fast and Loose, 1930 (Hopkins, M.; Lombard)
Fast and Loose, 1939 (Montgomery; Russell, R.)
Fast and Loose, 1954 (Kendall)
Fast and Sexy. *See* Anna di Brooklyn, 1958
Fast Break, 1979 (Fishburne)
Fast Companions, 1932 (O'Sullivan; Rooney)
Fast Company, 1918 (Chaney)
Fast Company, 1938 (Calhern; Douglas, Melvyn)
Fast Drive in the Country: The Heydays of Le Mans, 1976 (Coburn, J.)
Fast Forward, 1985 (Poitier)
Fast Lady, 1963 (Christie)
Fast Life, 1929 (Young, L.)
Fast Mail, 1922 (Menjou)
Fast Play. *See* Campus Confession, 1938
Fast Set, 1924 (Menjou)
Fast Times at Ridgemont High, 1982 (Cage; Leigh, Jennifer Jason; Penn; Whitaker)
Fast Workers, 1933 (Gilbert)
Fastest Gun Alive, 1956 (Crawford, B.; Ford, G.)
Fästman i taget, 1952 (Björnstrand)
Fästmö uthyres, 1950 (Björnstrand; Dahlbeck)
Fast-Walking, 1982 (Woods)
Fat and Fickle, 1917 (Laurel and Hardy)
Fat City, 1972 (Bridges; Huston, J.)
Fat Man, 1951 (Hudson)
Fat Man and Little Boy, 1989 (Newman)
Fat Spy, 1966 (Mansfield)
Fatal Attraction. *See* Head On, 1980
Fatal Attraction, 1987 (Close; Douglas, Michael)
Fatal Beauty, 1988 (Goldberg)
Fatal Chocolates, 1912 (Normand)
Fatal Deception: Mrs. Lee Harvey Oswald, 1993 (Bonham-Carter)
Fatal Desire. *See* Cavalleria Rusticana, 1953
Fatal Glass of Beer, 1933 (Fields, W. C.)
Fatal Hour, 1940 (Karloff)
Fatal Image, 1990 (Cassel)
Fatal Instinct, 1993 (Nelligan)
Fatal Lady, 1936 (Pidgeon)

Female Cop, 1914 (Laurel and Hardy)
Female Impersonator. *See* Masquerader, 1914
Female Instinct. *See* Snoop Sisters, 1972
Female Jungle, 1956 (Carradine; Mansfield)
Female of the Species, 1912 (Pickford)
Female on the Beach, 1955 (Crawford, J.)
Female Prisoner. *See* Prisonnière, 1968
Feminine Touch, 1941 (Ameche; Francis)
Feminine Touch, 1994 (Gould; Segal)
Femme à sa fenêtre, 1976 (Noiret; Schneider)
Femme aux bottes rouges, 1974 (Deneuve; Rey)
Femme chipée, 1934 (Berry)
Femme d'à côte, 1981 (Depardieu)
Femme d'un nuit, 1931 (Artaud; Bertini)
Femme de mon pote, 1982 (Huppert)
Femme de papier, 1989 (Léaud)
Femme disparait, 1941 (Rosay)
Femme douce, 1969 (Sanda)
Femme du boulanger, 1938 (Raimu)
Femme du bout du monde, 1937 (Vanel)
Femme du Ganges, 1973 (Depardieu)
Femme écarlate, 1968 (Vitti)
Femme en bleu, 1972 (Piccoli)
Femme en homme, 1931 (Rosay)
Femme en rouge, 1946 (Gélin)
Femme enfant, 1982 (Kinski)
Femme est passée. *See* Nunca pasa nada, 1963
Femme est une femme, 1961 (Belmondo; Karina; Moreau)
Femme et le pantin, 1958 (Bardot)
Femme fardée, 1989 (Moreau)
Femme fatale, 1945 (Brasseur)
Femme Fatale, 1994 (Pleasence)
Femme infidèle, 1969 (Audran)
Femme mariée, 1964 (Léaud)
Femme Nikita, 1990 (Moreau)
Femme ou deux, 1985 (Depardieu; Sanda; Weaver)
Femme que j'ai assassinée, 1949 (Vanel)
Femme que j'ai le plus aimée, 1942 (Arletty; Blier)
Femme qui se partage, 1936 (Brasseur)
Femme rêvée, 1927 (Vanel)
Femme secrète, 1986 (Noiret)
Femme sur la lune. *See* Frau im Mond, 1929
Femmes, 1969 (Bardot)
Femmes d'abord, 1963 (Constantine)
Femmes d'un été. *See* Racconti d'estate, 1958
Femmes fatales. *See* Calmos, 1975
Femmes s'en balancent, 1954 (Constantine)
Femmes sont marrantes, 1957 (Presle)
Femmine di lusso, 1960 (Cervi)
Ferdinand, 1986 (Ustinov)
Ferdinand le noceur, 1935 (Fernandel)
Ferdinando I, re di Napoli, 1959 (Mastroianni)
Feri, 1954 (Anand)
Feria de las flores, 1942 (Infante)
Ferita, 1921 (Bertini)
Fermata Etna, 1981 (Ganz)
Ferme du pendu, 1945 (Vanel)
Fernandel the Dressmaker. *See* Couturier de ces dames, 1956
Fernando I, re di Napoli, 1959 (Fabrizi)
FernGully: The Last Rainforest, 1992 (Williams, R.)
Feroce Saladino, 1937 (Valli)
Ferrente. *See* Bacciamo le mani, 1973
Ferréol, 1916 (Bertini)
Ferry to Hong Kong, 1959 (Welles)
Ferryman. *See* Passatore, 1947
Festa di maggio, 1957 (Fabrizi)
Festin des mots, 1965 (Cuny)
Festival Game, 1969 (Heston; Hopper)
Fête des pères. *See* Mords pas, on t'aime, 1975
Fête des pères, 1989 (Presle)
Fête espagnole, 1919 (Modot)

Fêtes galantes, 1965 (Cassel)
Fetus. *See* Magzat, 1993
Feu!, 1926 (Vanel)
Feu!, 1928 (Brasseur)
Feu!, 1937 (Feuillère)
Feu à volonte, 1965 (Constantine)
Feu aux poudres, 1957 (Vanel)
Feu follet, 1962 (Moreau)
Feu la mère de madame, 1936 (Arletty)
Feu Mathias Pascal, 1925 (Mozhukin)
Feu sacré, 1920 (Linder)
Feud, 1919 (Mix)
Feud in the Kentucky Hills, 1912 (Pickford)
Feudin', Fussin', and A-Fightin', 1948 (O'Connor)
Feuer, 1914 (Nielsen)
Feuerwerk, 1954 (Schneider)
Feux de la chandeleur, 1971 (Girardot)
Feux Follets, 1928 (Vanel)
Fever, 1991 (Neill)
Fever in the Blood, 1961 (Ameche; Dickinson)
Fever in the Blood, 1961 (Marshall)
Fever Pitch, 1985 (Giannini)
Few Days with Me. *See* Quelques jours avec moi, 1987
Few Good Men, 1992 (Bacon; Cruise; Moore, Demi; Nicholson)
Ffolkes, 1980 (Mason; Perkins)
Fi Baitina Rajul, 1961 (Sharif)
Fiamma che no si spegne, 1949 (Cervi)
Fiancée for Hire. *See* Fästmö uthyres, 1951
Fiancés du Pont Macdonald, 1961 (Karina)
Fiasco in Milan. *See* Audace colpo dei soliti ignoti, 1959
Fickleness of Sweedie, 1914 (Beery)
Fiddler on the Roof, 1971 (Topol)
Fiddlers Three, 1944 (Kendall)
Fiddlers Three, 1948 (Three Stooges)
Fiddlesticks, 1927 (Langdon)
Fidele Bauer, 1927 (Krauss)
Fidele Gefängnis, 1917 (Jannings)
Field, 1990 (Harris, R.; Hurt, J.)
Field of Dreams, 1989 (Costner; Jones, James Earl; Lancaster)
Fields of Honour, 1918 (Marsh)
Fiend with the Electronic Brain. *See* Blood of Ghastly Horror, 1972
Fiendish Ghouls. *See* Flesh and the Fiends, 1960
Fiendish Plot of Dr. Fu Manchu, 1980 (Mirren; Sellers)
Fierce Creatures, 1996 (Cleese; Curtis, J.; Kline)
Fiercest Heart, 1961 (Massey)
Fiesta, 1926 (Hayworth)
Fiesta, 1947 (Astor; Charisse; Williams, E.)
Fiesta, 1995 (Trintignant)
Fiesta de Santa Barbara, 1935 (Keaton, B.; Garland; Constantine)
Fièvre, 1921 (Modot)
Fièvre monte à El Pao, 1960 (Félix; Philipe)
Fifi Blows Her Top, 1958 (Three Stooges)
Fifteen Wives, 1935 (Dumont)
Fifth Avenue, 1926 (Wong)
Fifth Avenue Girl, 1939 (Calhern; Rogers, G.)
Fifth Chair. *See* It's in the Bag, 1945
Fifth Element. *See* Cinquieme element, 1996
Fifth Man, 1914 (Mix)
Fifth Monkey, 1990 (Kingsley)
Fifth Musketeer. *See* Behind the Iron Mask, 1977
Fifth Musketeer, 1979 (Ferrer; Wilde)
Fifth Offensive. *See* Sutjeska, 1972
Fifty-Fifty, 1916 (Talmadge)
Fifty-Fifty, 1925 (Barrymore, L.)
Fifty-Five Days at Peking, 1963 (Lukas)
Fifty Million Frenchmen, 1931 (Lugosi)
Fifty Roads to Town, 1937 (Ameche)
Fight for Life, 1987 (Freeman; Lewis, Jerry)
Fight for Love, 1919 (Carey)
Fight for Rome. *See* Kampf um Rom, 1968
Fight for Rome II. *See* Kampf um Rom II, 1969

Fireman, 1916 (Purviance)
Fireman, Save My Child, 1918 (Lloyd)
Fireman, Save My Child, 1927 (Beery)
Fireman, Save My Child, 1932 (Brown)
Firepower, 1979 (Coburn, J.; Loren; Mature)
Firepower, 1979 (Wallach)
Fires of Rebellion, 1916 (Chaney)
Fires of Youth. *See* Up for Murder, 1931
Fires Within, 1991 (Scacchi)
Firestarter, 1984 (Scott, G.; Sheen)
Firestorm, 1996 (Stallone; Willis)
Firm, 1988 (Oldman)
Firm, 1993 (Cruise; Hackman; Harris, E.; Hunter)
First 100 Years, 1938 (Montgomery)
First and the Last. *See* 21 Days, 1937
First Baby, 1936 (McDaniel)
First Blood, 1982 (Stallone)
First Born, 1921 (Hayakawa; Wong)
First Born, 1928 (Carroll)
First Comes Courage, 1943 (Oberon)
First Day of Freedom. *See* Pierwszy dzień wolności, 1964
First Deadly Sin, 1980 (Dunaway; Sidney; Willis)
First Great Train Robbery. *See* Great Train Robbery, 1978
First Hundred Years, 1924 (Langdon)
First Kiss, 1928 (Constantine; Wray)
First Knight, 1995 (Connery; Gere; Gielgud)
First Lady, 1937 (Francis)
First Legion, 1951 (Boyer)
First Love, 1939 (Durbin)
First Love. *See* Erste Liebe, 1970
First Love. *See* Pervaya lyubov, 1933
First Men in the Moon, 1964 (Finch)
First Mission, 1985 (Chan)
First Mission. *See* Heart of the Dragon, 1986
First Misunderstanding, 1911 (Pickford)
First Monday in October, 1981 (Matthau)
First of the Few, 1942 (Howard, L.; Niven)
First Offence, 1936 (Mills)
First Polka. *See* Erste Polka, 1979
First Rebel. *See* Allegheny Uprising, 1939
First Texan, 1956 (McCrea)
First Time, 1982 (Leigh, Jennifer Jason)
First to Fight, 1967 (Hackman)
First Traveling Saleslady, 1956 (Eastwood; Rogers, G.)
First Violin, 1912 (Talmadge)
First Wives Club, 1996 (Hawn; Keaton, D.; Midler; Smith)
First Year, 1932 (Gaynor)
First, You Cry, 1978 (Perkins)
Fish Called Wanda, 1988 (Cleese; Curtis, J.; Kline)
Fish Soup. *See* Zuppa Di Pesce, 1992
Fisher King, 1991 (Bridges; Williams, R.)
Fisher-maid, 1911 (Pickford)
Fist of Death, 1987 (Chan)
Fist of Fury. *See* Chinese Connection, 1972
Fist of the North Star, 1995 (McDowell)
Fistful of Dollars. *See* Per un pugno di dollari, 1964
Fistful of Dynamite. *See* Giù la testa, 1972
Fists and Fodder, 1920 (Laurel and Hardy)
Fists of Fury, 1971 (Lee, B.)
Fit for a King, 1937 (Brown)
Fitzcarraldo, 1982 (Cardinale; Kinski)
Fitzwilly, 1967 (Evans)
Fiume di dollari, 1966 (Duryea)
Five against the House, 1955 (Novak)
Five and Ten, 1931 (Davies; Howard, L.)
Five Angles on Murder. *See* Woman in Question, 1950
Five Bloody Graves, 1970 (Carradine)
Five Boys of Barska Street. *See* Piątka z ulicy Barskiej, 1954
Five Branded Women, 1959 (Moreau)
Five Branded Women. *See* Jovanda e le altre, 1960
Five Came Back, 1939 (Ball; Carradine)

Five Card Stud, 1968 (Martin, D.; McDowall; Mitchum)
Five Cities of June, 1963 (Heston)
Five Corners, 1988 (Foster; Robbins; Turturro)
Five Days One Summer, 1982 (Connery)
Five Days to Live, 1922 (Hayakawa)
Five Easy Pieces, 1970 (Nicholson)
Five Finger Exercise, 1962 (Hawkins; Russell, R.; Schell, Maximilian)
Five Fingers, 1952 (Darrieux; Mason)
Five Gents on the Spot. *See* Zoku shacho gyogo-ki, 1966
Five Gents' Trick Book. *See* Shacho ninpo-cho, 1965
Five Golden Dragons, 1967 (Duryea; Kinski; Lee, C.; Raft)
Five Golden Hours, 1961 (Charisse)
Five Graves to Cairo, 1943 (Baxter)
Five Guns West, 1955 (Malone)
Five into Hell. *See* Cinque per l'inferno, 1968
Five Miles to Midnight, 1962 (Perkins)
Five O'Clock Girl, 1929 (Davies)
Five of a Kind, 1938 (Trevor)
Five of the Jazzband. *See* Fünf von der Jazzband, 1932
Five Pennies, 1959 (Hope; Kaye; Weld)
Five Pound Reward, 1920 (Howard, L.)
Five Star Final, 1931 (Karloff; Robinson, E.)
Five Steps to Danger, 1956 (Hayden)
Five Thousand Elopement, 1916 (Mix)
Five Weeks in a Balloon, 1962 (Lorre; Marshall)
Five-Day Lover. *See* Amant de cinq jours, 1961
Five-Leaf Clover. *See* Trèfle à cinq feuilles, 1972
Fixed Bayonets, 1951 (Dean)
Fixer, 1968 (Bates, A.; Bogarde)
Fixer-Uppers, 1935 (Laurel and Hardy)
Fjols til Fjells, 1957 (Ullmann)
Flag Lieutenant, 1933 (Neagle)
Flagpole Jitters, 1956 (Three Stooges)
Flagrant Desire, 1985 (Aimée)
Flambée des rêves, 1924 (Vanel)
Flame, 1947 (Crawford, B.)
Flame, 1948 (McDaniel)
Flame and the Arrow, 1950 (Lancaster)
Flame and the Flesh, 1954 (Turner, L.)
Flame in the Streets, 1962 (Mills)
Flame of Araby, 1951 (O'Hara)
Flame of Life, 1923 (Beery)
Flame of Love, 1930 (Wong)
Flame of New Orleans, 1941 (Dietrich)
Flame of the Barbary Coast, 1945 (Wayne)
Flame over India, 1959 (Bacall; Lom)
Flame Within, 1935 (Marshall; O'Sullivan)
Flames, 1926 (Karloff)
Flames of Passion, 1922 (Marsh)
Flaming Arrow, 1911 (White)
Flaming Feather, 1951 (Hayden)
Flaming Forties, 1924 (Carey)
Flaming Frontier, 1965 (Granger)
Flaming Fury, 1926 (Karloff)
Flaming Guns, 1932 (Mix)
Flaming Star, 1960 (Del Rio; Presley)
Flaming Sword, 1915 (Barrymore, L.)
Flaming Torch. *See* Bob Mathias Story, 1954
Flaming Years. *See* Povest plamennykh, 1961
Flamingo Kid, 1984 (Dillon; Turturro)
Flamingo Road, 1949 (Crawford, J.; Greenstreet)
Flamme, 1922 (Negri)
Flamme, 1925 (Vanel)
Flamme, 1936 (Vanel)
Flammende Völker, 1921 (Wegener)
Flanagan, 1985 (Page)
Flap, 1970 (Quinn; Winters)
Flapper, 1920 (Shearer)
Flapper Wives, 1924 (Horton)
Flareup, 1969 (Welch)
Flash Back, 1975 (Huppert)

Flash Gordon, 1980 (Topol; Von Sydow)
Flash of Green, 1984 (Harris, E.)
Flashback, 1989 (Hopper)
Flashes Festivals, 1965 (Harrison)
Flashing Spikes, 1962 (Stewart; Wayne)
Flashlight Girl, 1916 (Chaney)
Flat Foot Stooges, 1938 (Three Stooges)
Flat Top, 1952 (Hayden)
Flatbed Annie and Sweetiepie: Lady Truckers, 1979 (Stanton)
Flatliners, 1990 (Bacon; Douglas, Michael; Roberts, J.)
Flavor of Green Tea over Rice. See Ochazuke no aji, 1952
Flea in Her Ear, 1968 (Harrison; Jourdan; Roberts, R.)
Fled, 1996 (Fishburne)
Fledermaus '55. See Oh, Rosalinda!, 1955
Fleet's In, 1928 (Bow)
Fleet's In, 1941 (Lamour)
Fleet's In, 1942 (Holden)
Flesh, 1932 (Beery)
Flesh and Blood, 1922 (Chaney)
Flesh and Blood, 1951 (Greenwood)
Flesh and Blood, 1979 (Washington)
Flesh and Blood, 1985 (Leigh, Jennifer Jason)
Flesh and Bone, 1993 (Caan; Quaid; Ryan, M.)
Flesh and Bullets, 1985 (Wilde)
Flesh and Desire. See Fuco nelle vene, 1953
Flesh and Fantasy, 1943 (Boyer; Dalio; Robinson, E.; Stanwyck)
Flesh and Fury, 1951 (Curtis, T.)
Flesh and the Devil, 1926 (Garbo; Gilbert)
Flesh and the Fiends, 1960 (Cushing; Pleasence)
Flesh and the Woman. See Grand Jeu, 1954
Flesh Creatures. See Horror of the Blood Monsters, 1970
Flesh Feast, 1973 (Lake)
Flesh of the Orchid. See Chair de l'orchidée, 1974
Flesh Will Surrender. See Delitto di Giovanni Episcopo, 1947
Fletch, 1985 (Davis, G.)
Fleuchtweg nach Marseille, 1977 (Vogler)
Fleur au fusil, 1959 (Rosay)
Fleur de l'age, 1947 (Reggiani)
Fleur de l'age, 1964 (Bujold)
Fleur de l'âge, 1947 (Aimée)
Fleur de Rubis, 1990 (Adjani; Belmondo)
Fleur de Rubis, 1990 (Deneuve)
Fleurs du soleil. See I girasoli, 1969
Fleuve Dieu, 1956 (Fresnay)
Flic, 1972 (Delon; Deneuve)
Flic ou voyou, 1979 (Belmondo)
Flic Story, 1975 (Delon)
Flickan från fjällbyn, 1948 (Dahlbeck)
Flickan från tredje raden, 1949 (Björnstrand)
Flickan i regnet, 1955 (Andersson, B.)
Flickorna, 1968 (Andersson, B.; Andersson, H.; Björnstrand; Josephson)
Flickorna, 1968 (Zetterling)
Flight. See Flucht, 1977
Flight Angels, 1940 (Bellamy; Wyman)
Flight Command, 1940 (Pidgeon; Taylor, R.)
Flight for Freedom, 1943 (MacMurray; Marshall; Russell, R.)
Flight from Ashiya, 1964 (Brynner; Widmark)
Flight from Pomerania. See Flucht aus Pommern, 1982
Flight from Terror. See Satan Never Sleeps, 1962
Flight in the Night. See Flucht in die Nacht, 1926
Flight into Darkness. See Equipage, 1935
Flight into Nowhere, 1938 (Bond)
Flight Lieutenant, 1942 (Dalio; Ford, G.)
Flight of the Eagle. See Ingenjör Andrees luftfård, 1981
Flight of the Intruder, 1991 (Dafoe)
Flight of the Phoenix, 1965 (Attenborough; Borgnine; Duryea; Finch; Stewart)
Flight to Berlin. See Fluchtpunkt Berlin, 1984
Flight to Fury, 1966 (Nicholson)
Flight to Tangier, 1953 (Dalio; Fontaine; Palance)
Flim-Flam Man, 1967 (Scott, G.)
Fling in the Ring, 1955 (Three Stooges)

Flintstones, 1994 (Taylor, E.)
Flip Out. See Get Crazy, 1983
Flips and Flops, 1919 (Laurel and Hardy)
Flirt, 1917 (Lloyd)
Flirt, 1983 (Vitti)
Flirt's Mistake, 1914 (Arbuckle)
Flirtation Walk, 1934 (Keeler; Powell, D.; Power)
Flirting Husband, 1912 (Normand)
Flirting Scholar, 1993 (Gong Li)
Flirting Widow, 1930 (Rathbone)
Flirting with Disaster, 1996 (Segal)
Flirting with Fate, 1916 (Gish)
Flirting with Fate, 1938 (Brown)
Flirts. See Between Showers, 1914
Flirty Sleepwalker, 1932 (Grable)
Floating Clouds. See Ukigumo, 1955
Floating Outfit: Trigger Fast, 1994 (Sheen)
Floating Weeds. See Ukigusa, 1959
Flood. See Johnstown Flood, 1926
Flood, 1976 (Hershey; McDowall)
Flood. See Inondation, 1993
Floods of Fear, 1959 (Cusack)
Floor Below, 1918 (Normand)
Floorwalker, 1916 (Chaplin, C.; Purviance)
Flor de mayo, 1957 (Armendáriz; Félix; Palance)
Flor Silvestre, 1943 (Armendáriz; Del Rio)
Floradora Girl, 1930 (Davies)
Florence Nightingale, 1985 (Bloom)
Florian, 1940 (Coburn, C.; Young, R.)
Florida Straights, 1986 (Julia)
Flottans glada gossar, 1954 (Björnstrand)
Flottans överman, 1958 (Andersson, H.)
Flower. See Hana, 1941
Flower Blooms. See "Machiko" yori: Hana hiraku, 1948
Flower of Faith, 1914 (Mix)
Flower of Night, 1925 (Negri)
Flower Woman of Lindenau. See Blumenfrau von Lindenau, 1931
Flowers of St. Francis. See Francesco—giullare di Dio, 1950
Flowing. See Nagareru, 1956
Flowing Gold, 1939 (Garfield; Farmer)
Fluch der Bosen Tat. See Geheimnis auf Schloss Almshoh, 1925
Fluch der Menschheit, 1920 (Lugosi)
Flucht, 1977 (Mueller-Stahl)
Flucht aus Pommern, 1982 (Mueller-Stahl)
Flucht in den Norden, 1986 (Olin)
Flucht in die Nacht, 1926 (Veidt)
Flüchtling aus Chikago, 1934 (Dagover; Fröhlich)
Fluchtpunkt Berlin, 1984 (Constantine)
Fluga gör ingen sommar, 1947 (Björnstrand)
Flügel der Nacht, 1982 (Mueller-Stahl)
Fluke, 1995 (Jackson, S.)
Flüsternde Tod, 1975 (Howard, T.)
Flûte merveilleuse, 1910 (Linder)
Fluttering Hearts, 1927 (Laurel and Hardy)
Fly, 1958 (Marshall; Price)
Fly, 1986 (Brooks, M.; Davis, G.)
Fly Cop, 1917 (Laurel and Hardy)
Fly Cop, 1921 (Laurel and Hardy)
Flyg-Bom, 1952 (Björnstrand)
Flying. See Dream to Believe, 1986
Flying Deuces, 1939 (Laurel and Hardy; Langdon)
Flying Devils, 1933 (Bellamy)
Flying Devils, 1985 (Josephson)
Flying Down to Rio, 1933 (Astaire; Del Rio; Rogers, G.)
Flying Elephants, 1928 (Laurel and Hardy)
Flying Fleet, 1929 (Novarro)
Flying Leathernecks, 1951 (Ryan, R.; Wayne)
Flying Luck, 1927 (Arthur)
Flying Missile, 1950 (Ford, G.)
Flying Saucer. See Disco Volante, 1965
Flying Saucer Daffy, 1958 (Three Stooges)

Flying Saucers Coming! *See* Talíre nad Velkym Malikovem, 1977
Flying Saucers over Our Town. *See* Talíre nad Velkym Malikovem, 1977
Flying Scotsman, 1929 (Milland)
Flying Skyscraper, 1949 (Mills)
Flying Sneaker, 1992 (Brodský)
Flying Squad, 1940 (Hawkins)
Flying Tigers, 1942 (Wayne)
Foerraederi, 1994 (Hurt, J.)
Fog, 1980 (Curtis, J.; Leigh, Janet)
Fog over Frisco, 1934 (Davis, B.)
Foghorn. *See* Muteki, 1952
Folchetto di Narbonne, 1911 (Bertini)
Folie des grandeurs, 1971 (Montand)
Folies Bergère, 1935 (Chevalier; Oberon)
Folies-Bergère, 1957 (Constantine)
Folies bourgeoises, 1976 (Ann-Margret; Audran; Cassel; Dern; Schell, Maria)
Folk Tale. *See* Bhavni bhavai, 1981
Folket i Simlångsdalen, 1947 (Dahlbeck)
Folks!, 1992 (Ameche)
Follie per l'opera, 1948 (Lollobrigida)
Follies, 1927 (Cantor)
Follow a Star, 1959 (Wisdom)
Follow Me, 1972 (Farrow; Topol)
Follow Me, Boys!, 1966 (Gish; MacMurray)
Follow That Dream, 1962 (Presley)
Follow the Band, 1943 (Mitchum)
Follow the Boys, 1944 (Dietrich; Fields, W. C.; MacDonald; O'Connor; Raft; Welles)
Follow the Crowd, 1918 (Lloyd)
Follow the Fleet, 1936 (Astaire; Ball; Grable; Rogers, G.; Scott, R.)
Follow the Leader, 1930 (Rogers, G.)
Follow the River, 1995 (Burstyn)
Follow the Sun, 1951 (Baxter; Ford, G.)
Follow Your Dreams. *See* Independence Day, 1983
Following Her Heart, 1994 (Ann-Margret; Grant, L.; Segal)
Following the Fuhrer. *See* Mitläufer, 1984
Folly of Anne, 1914 (Gish)
Fontane: Effi Briest, 1974 (Schygulla)
Food of the Gods, 1976 (Lupino)
Fool, 1990 (Cusack)
Fool for Love, 1985 (Basinger; Shepard; Stanton)
Fool Killer, 1965 (Perkins)
Fool There Was, 1915 (Bara)
Fool's Luck, 1926 (Arbuckle)
Foolish Heart, 1996 (Dafoe; Kinski)
Foolish Husbands. *See* Historie de rire, 1941
Fools, 1970 (Robards)
Fools for Luck, 1928 (Fields, W. C.)
Fools for Scandal, 1938 (Bellamy; Lombard; Wyman)
Fools in the Mountains. *See* Fjols til Fjells, 1957
Fools of Fortune, 1990 (Christie)
Fools' Parade, 1971 (Baxter; Stewart)
Foot of Romance, 1914 (Beery)
Football Coach. *See* College Coach, 1933
Footlight Parade, 1933 (Blondell; Cagney; Garfield; Keeler; Powell, D.)
Footlight Serenade, 1942 (Grable; Mature; Wyman)
Footlights. *See* Sunny Side Up, 1926
Footlights and Fools, 1929 (March)
Footloose, 1984 (Bacon; Wiest)
Footpath, 1953 (Kumar)
Footprints. *See* Orme, 1974
Footsteps, 1972 (Woods)
Footsteps in the Dark, 1941 (Bellamy; Flynn)
Footsteps in the Fog, 1955 (Granger)
Footsteps in the Snow, 1966 (Lake)
For a Cop's Hide. *See* Pour la peau d'un flic, 1970
For a Few Dollars More. *See* Per qualche dollaro in più, 1966
För att inte tala om alla dessa kvinnor, 1964 (Andersson, B.; Andersson, H.; Josephson; Dahlbeck)
For Auld Lang Syne, 1938 (Cagney)
For Beauty's Sake, 1941 (Dumont)

For Better and for Worse. *See* Terror Stalks the Class Reunion, 1992
For Better, for Worse, 1919 (Swanson)
For Better, for Worse, 1954 (Bogarde)
For Better or Worse, 1996 (Woods)
For Better or Worse. *See* That Little Band of Gold, 1915
For Big Stakes, 1922 (Mix)
For Cash, 1915 (Chaney)
For Crimin' Out Loud, 1956 (Three Stooges)
For Freedom, 1940 (Terry-Thomas)
For Friendship. *See* För vänskaps skull, 1965
For fuld Fart. *See* Cocktails, 1927
For God and Country, 1943 (Huston, W.)
For Heaven's Sake, 1926 (Lloyd)
For Heaven's Sake, 1950 (Bennett; Blondell; Webb)
For Her Brother's Sake, 1911 (Pickford)
For Her Father's Sins, 1914 (Sweet)
For His Son, 1912 (Sweet)
For Honor of the Name, 1911 (White)
For Ladies Only, 1981 (Grant, L.)
For Lizzie's Sake, 1913 (Normand)
For Love ... For Magic. *See* Per amore ... per magia, 1966
For Love Alone, 1985 (Neill)
For Love of a Queen. *See* Dictator, 1935
For Love of Ivy, 1968 (Poitier)
For Love or Money, 1963 (Douglas, K.; Ritter)
For Love or Money. *See* Cash, 1933
For Massa's Sake, 1911 (White)
For Me and My Gal, 1942 (Garland; Kelly, Gene)
For Men Only, 1951 (Henreid)
For Peace, 1956 (Zhao Dan)
For Pete's Sake, 1974 (Streisand)
For Queen and Country, 1989 (Washington)
For Richer, for Poorer, 1992 (Lemmon)
For Sale, 1924 (Menjou)
For the Boys, 1991 (Caan; Midler; Segal)
For the Defense, 1930 (Francis; Powell, W.)
For the Love of Mabel, 1913 (Arbuckle; Normand)
For the Love of Mary, 1948 (Durbin; O'Brien, E.)
For the Love of Mike, 1927 (Colbert)
For the Love of Mike, 1932 (Oberon)
For the Queen's Honor, 1911 (Pickford)
For the Sake of a Woman. *See* Min Ajl Imraa, 1958
For the Soviet Homeland. *See* Ka sovetskuyu rodinu, 1937
For Those Unborn, 1914 (Sweet)
For Those We Love, 1921 (Chaney)
For Those Who Dare. *See* Lust for Gold, 1949
For Those Who Think Young, 1964 (Burstyn; Raft)
For Us, the Living, 1983 (Fishburne)
For Valour, 1917 (Barthelmess)
För vänskaps skull, 1965 (Andersson, H.)
For Whom the Bell Tolls, 1943 (Bergman; Constantine)
For You Alone. *See* When You're in Love, 1937
For Your Eyes Only, 1981 (Topol)
For Your Love Only. *See* Reifezeugnis, 1976
Forbid Them Not, 1961 (Ferrer)
Forbidden, 1932 (Bellamy; Menjou; Stanwyck)
Forbidden, 1953 (Curtis, T.)
Forbidden Cargo, 1925 (Karloff)
Forbidden Christ. *See* Cristo proibito, 1951
Forbidden City, 1918 (Talmadge)
Forbidden Fruit. *See* Fruit défendu, 1952
Forbidden Fruit, 1995 (Josephson)
Forbidden Hours, 1928 (Novarro)
Forbidden Music. *See* Land without Music, 1936
Forbidden Paradise, 1924 (Gable; Menjou; Negri)
Forbidden Path, 1918 (Bara)
Forbidden Paths, 1917 (Hayakawa)
Forbidden Planet, 1956 (Pidgeon)
Forbidden Room, 1914 (Chaney)
Forbidden Room. *See* Anima persa, 1976
Forbidden Street, 1949 (Andrews, D.; O'Hara)

Forbidden Women. *See* Donne Proibite, 1953
Force majeure, 1989 (Bates, A.)
Force of Arms, 1951 (Holden)
Force of Evil, 1948 (Garfield)
Force Ten from Navarone, 1978 (Ford, H.; Shaw)
Forced to Be with Others. *See* De force avec d'autres, 1993
Ford: The Man and the Machine, 1987 (Robertson)
Fordringsagare, 1989 (Andersson, B.)
Foreign Affair, 1948 (Arthur; Dietrich)
Foreign Affairs, 1993 (Woodward)
Foreign Body, 1986 (Howard, T.)
Foreign Correspondent, 1940 (Marshall; McCrea; Sanders)
Foreign Field, 1993 (Bacall; Chaplin, G.; Guinness; Moreau)
Foreign Intrigue, 1956 (Mitchum; Thulin)
Foreman of Bar Z Ranch, 1915 (Mix)
Foreman's Choice, 1915 (Mix)
Forest Rangers, 1942 (Goddard; Hayward; MacMurray)
Forêt sacrée, 1950 (Philipe)
Forever After, 1926 (Astor)
Forever Amber, 1947 (Darnell; Sanders; Wilde)
Forever and a Day, 1943 (Crisp; Horton; Keaton, B.; Lanchester; Laughton; Lupino; Marshall; Milland; Neagle; Oberon; Rains)
Forever, Darling, 1956 (Ball; Calhern; Mason)
Forever England. *See* Brown on Resolution, 1935
Forever Female, 1953 (Holden; Rogers, G.)
Forever in Love. *See* Pride of the Marines, 1945
Forever, Lulu, 1986 (Schygulla)
Forever My Heart, 1954 (Aimée)
Forever Young, 1992 (Curtis, J.; Gibson)
Forever Young, Forever Free. *See* E' Lollipop, 1975
Forfaiture, 1937 (Hayakawa; Jouvet)
Forgery and the Use of Forgeries. *See* Faux et l'usage de Faux, 1990
Forget Mozart! *See* Zabudnite na Mozarta, 1985
Forget Paris, 1995 (Winger)
Forgiven Sinner. *See* Léon Morin, prêtre, 1961
Forgotten Commandments, 1932 (Carradine)
Forgotten Faces, 1928 (Powell, W.)
Forgotten Faces, 1936 (Marshall)
Forgotten Village, 1941 (Meredith)
Forked Trails, 1915 (Mix)
Formula, 1980 (Brando; Gielgud; Scott, G.)
Formula for Murder, 1985 (Brazzi)
Formula I, febbre della velocità, 1978 (Hackman)
Fornaretto di Venezia, 1964 (Morgan)
Forrest Gump, 1994 (Field; Hanks)
Forsaking All Others, 1934 (Montgomery; Russell, R.; Crawford, J.; Gable)
Forsyte Saga. *See* That Forsyte Woman, 1949
Fort Apache, 1948 (Armendáriz; Bond; Fonda, H.; McLaglen; Temple; Wayne)
Fort Apache, the Bronx, 1981 (Aiello; Newman)
Fort Graveyard. *See* Chi to suna, 1965
Fort Massacre, 1958 (McCrea)
Fort Saganne, 1983 (Deneuve; Depardieu; Noiret)
Fort Worth, 1951 (Scott, R.)
Fortieth Door, 1924 (Wong)
Fortuna di essere donna, 1955 (Loren; Mastroianni; Boyer)
Fortuna viene dal cielo, 1943 (Magnani)
Fortunat, 1960 (Morgan)
Fortunate Pilgrim, 1988 (Loren)
Fortune, 1974 (Nicholson)
Fortune, 1975 (Beatty)
Fortune Cookie, 1966 (Lemmon; Matthau)
Fortune Hunter. *See* Lyckoriddare, 1921
Fortune Is a Woman, 1957 (Hawkins; Lee, C.)
Fortune's Fool. *See* Alles für Geld, 1923
Fortune's Mask, 1922 (Laurel and Hardy)
Fortunella, 1958 (Masina; Sordi)
Fortunes of a Composer, 1912 (Talmadge)
Fortunes of War, 1994 (Sheen)
Forty Carats, 1973 (Kelly, Gene)
Forty Deuce, 1982 (Bacon)

Forty Guns, 1957 (Stanwyck)
Forty Little Mothers. *See* Mioche, 1936
Forty Little Mothers, 1940 (Cantor; Lake)
Forty Pounds of Trouble, 1962 (Curtis, T.)
Forty Winks, 1925 (Wong)
Forty-Five Fathers, 1937 (McDaniel)
Forward March! *See* Doughboys, 1930
Forward Pass, 1929 (Young, L.)
Forza bruta, 1940 (Brazzi)
Foster and Laurie, 1975 (Woods)
Fou de Labo 4, 1967 (Brasseur; Blier)
Foul Play, 1978 (Hawn; Meredith; Moore, Dudley; Roberts, R.)
Foule hurle, 1932 (Gabin)
Foundling, 1915 (Crisp; Pickford)
Fountain, 1934 (Lukas)
Fountain of Youth, 1956 (Welles)
Fountainhead, 1948 (Constantine; Massey; Neal)
Four against Fate. *See* Derby Day, 1952
Four Bags Full. *See* Traversée de Paris, 1956
Four Chimneys. *See* **Entotsu no mieru basho**, 1953
Four Clowns, 1970 (Laurel and Hardy)
Four Companions. *See* Vier gesellen, 1938
Four Dark Hours. *See* Green Cockatoo, 1937
Four Daughters, 1938 (Garfield; Rains)
Four Days Leave, 1949 (Wilde)
Four Days of Naples. *See* Quattro giornate de Napoli, 1962
Four Deuces, 1975 (Palance)
Four Devils, 1928 (Gaynor)
Four Faces West, 1948 (McCrea)
Four Feathers, 1929 (Powell, W.; Wray; Richardson, R.)
Four Flights to Love. *See* Paradis perdu, 1940
Four for Texas, 1963 (Bronson; Martin, D.; Sidney; Three Stooges)
Four Frightened People, 1934 (Colbert; Marshall)
Four Girls in Town, 1956 (Hudson)
Four Guns to the Border, 1954 (Brennan)
Four Horsemen of the Apocalypse, 1921 (Beery; Novarro; Valentino)
Four Horsemen of the Apocalypse, 1961 (Boyer; Cobb; Ford, G.; Henreid; Lansbury; Lukas; Thulin)
Four Hours to Kill, 1935 (Barthelmess; Milland)
Four Jills in a Jeep, 1944 (Faye; Francis; Grable; Miranda)
Four Kinds of Love. *See* Bambole, 1964
Four Men and a Girl. *See* Kentucky Moonshine, 1938
Four Men and a Prayer, 1938 (Carradine; Fitzgerald; Niven; Sanders; Young, L.)
Four Minutes Late, 1914 (Mix)
Four Mothers, 1941 (Rains)
Four Musketeers, 1974 (Cassel; Chaplin, G.; Dunaway; Heston; Lee, C.; Reed; Welch)
Four Poster, 1952 (Harrison)
Four Robinsons. *See* Cuatro Robinsones, 1940
Four Rooms, 1995 (Banderas; Willis)
Four Shorts on Architecture, 1975 (Neill)
Four Sons, 1940 (Ameche)
Four Steps in the Clouds. *See* Quattro passi fra le nuvole, 1942
Four Thirds Off. *See* Taming of the Snood, 1940
Four Visits of Samuel Wolf. *See* Chetyre vizity Samuelya Vulfa, 1934
Four Walls, 1928 (Crawford, J.; Gilbert)
Four Ways Out. *See* Città si difende, 1951
Four Weddings and a Funeral, 1994 (Grant, H.)
Four Wives, 1939 (Garfield; Rains)
Fourchambault, 1929 (Vanel)
Four's a Crowd, 1938 (De Havilland; Flynn; Russell, R.; Turner, L.)
Fourteen Hours, 1951 (Kelly, Grace; Moorehead)
Fourth Horseman, 1932 (Mix)
Fourth Power. *See* Quatrième Pouvoir, 1985
Fourth Protocol, 1987 (Caine)
Fourth War, 1990 (Scheider; Stanton)
Fourth Wise Man, 1985 (Arkin; Bellamy; Sheen)
Fox, 1921 (Carey)
Fox and the Hound, 1981 (Rooney)
Fox Movietone Follies of 1929, 1929 (Cooper)

Frenchy, 1914 (Crisp)
Frenesia dell'estate, 1963 (Gassman)
Frenzied Finance, 1916 (Laurel and Hardy)
Frenzy. *See* Hets, 1944
Fréquence meurtre, 1988 (Deneuve)
Frères corses, 1939 (Brasseur)
Frères d'Afrique, 1939 (Brasseur)
Frères Karamazov. *See* Mörder Dimitri Karamasoff, 1931
Fresh, 1994 (Jackson, S.)
Fresh from the Farm, 1915 (Lloyd)
Freshman, 1925 (Lloyd)
Freshman, 1990 (Brando; Schell, Maximilian)
Freshman Year, 1938 (Ladd)
Freud, 1962 (Clift; Huston, J.; York)
Freud: The Secret Passion. *See* Freud, 1962
Freudlose Gasse, 1925 (Dietrich; Garbo; Krauss; Nielsen)
Freundin eines grossen Mannes, 1934 (Wegener)
Fric-Frac, 1939 (Arletty; Fernandel)
Friday the 13th, 1980 (Bacon; Depp)
Friday the Thirteenth, 1933 (Richardson, R.)
Fridericus, 1936 (Dagover)
Fridericus Rex, 1923 (Krauss)
Fried Green Tomatoes, 1991 (Bates, K.)
Frieda, 1947 (Zetterling)
Friedensreiter, 1917 (Krauss)
Friedrich Schiller, 1940 (Dagover)
Friend of the Family, 1949 (Mills)
Friend of the Family. *See* Patate, 1964
Friend of Vincent. *See* Ami de Vincent, 1983
Friend Will Come Tonight. *See* Ami viendra ce soir, 1945
Friendly Persuasion, 1956 (Constantine; Perkins)
Friends, 1912 (Barrymore, L.; Carey; Pickford)
Friends. *See* Druzya, 1938
Friends and Husbands. *See* Heller Wahn, 1982
Friends and Lovers, 1931 (Menjou; Olivier)
Friends at Last, 1995 (Turner, K.)
Friends of Eddie Coyle, 1973 (Mitchum)
Friesenblut, 1925 (Fröhlich)
Fright Night, 1947 (Three Stooges)
Fright Night, 1985 (McDowall)
Fright Night Part 2, 1989 (McDowall)
Frightened Bride. *See* Tall Headlines, 1952
Frightened City, 1961 (Connery; Lom)
Frios ojos miedo, 1970 (Rey)
Frisco Jenny, 1933 (Calhern)
Frisco Kid, 1935 (Cagney)
Frisco Kid, 1979 (Ford, H.; Wilder)
Frisky, 1955 (Lollobrigida)
Frivolous Wives. *See* Married Virgin, 1920
Frog, 1937 (Hawkins)
Frog. *See* Living Dead, 1972
Frogmen, 1951 (Andrews, D.; Widmark)
Frogs, 1972 (Milland; Gould)
Fröken April, 1958 (Björnstrand)
Froken Julie, 1951 (Von Sydow)
From a Far Country: Pope John Paul II. *See* Z dalekiego kraju, 1981
From a Whisper to a Scream, 1986 (Price)
From beyond the Grave, 1973 (Dors; Pleasence; Cushing)
From Blitzkrieg to the Bomb, 1985 (Sheen)
From Dusk Till Dawn, 1996 (Keitel; Lewis, Juliette)
From Earth to the Moon, 1958 (Sanders)
From Hand to Mouth, 1919 (Lloyd)
From Headquarters, 1933 (Brennan)
From Hell to Heaven, 1933 (Lombard)
From Hell to Texas, 1958 (Hopper)
From Hell to Victory. *See* Da Dunkerque all vittoria, 1979
From Here to Eternity, 1953 (Borgnine; Clift; Kerr; Lancaster; Sidney)
From Italy's Shores, 1915 (Lloyd)
From Noon Till Three, 1976 (Bronson)
From Nurse to Worse, 1940 (Three Stooges)
From Russia with Love, 1963 (Armendáriz; Connery; Shaw)

From Soup to Nuts, 1928 (Laurel and Hardy)
From the Bottom of the Sea, 1911 (Pickford)
From the Earth to the Moon, 1958 (Cotten)
From the Four Corners, 1941 (Howard, L.)
From the Hip, 1987 (Hurt, J.)
From the Mixed-Up Files of Mrs. Basil E. Frankweiler, 1973 (Bergman)
From the Mixed-Up Files of Mrs. Basil E. Frankweiler, 1995 (Bacall)
From the Police, with Thanks. *See* Polizia ringrazia, 1972
From the Terrace, 1960 (Loy; Newman; Woodward)
From This Day Forward, 1946 (Fontaine)
From Time to Time, 1992 (Irons; Piccoli)
From Whom Cometh My Help, 1949 (Poitier)
Fromme Lüge, 1938 (Negri)
Front, 1976 (Aiello; Allen)
Front Page, 1931 (Horton; Menjou)
Front Page, 1974 (Lemmon; Matthau; Sarandon)
Front Page Story, 1922 (Horton)
Front Page Story, 1953 (Hawkins)
Front Page Woman, 1935 (Davis, B.)
Frontier Hellcat. *See* Unter Geiern, 1964
Frontier Horizon. *See* New Frontier, 1939
Frontier Marshal, 1934 (Bond)
Frontier Marshal, 1939 (Bond; Carradine; Scott, R.)
Frontier Pony Express, 1939 (Rogers, R.)
Frontier Rangers, 1959 (Dickinson)
Frontier Trail, 1926 (Carey)
Frontiere, 1934 (Cervi)
Frosch mit der Maske, 1959 (Rasp)
Frou Frou, 1918 (Bertini)
Frou frou, 1955 (Cervi)
Frozen Dead, 1967 (Andrews, D.)
Frozen Hearts, 1923 (Laurel and Hardy)
Frozen North, 1922 (Keaton, B.)
Fruehlings Erwachen, 1929 (Rasp)
Fruhlingssinfonie, 1985 (Kinski)
Fruit défendu, 1952 (Fernandel)
Fruitful Vine, 1921 (Rathbone)
Fruits de l'été, 1954 (Feuillère)
Fruits of Passion, 1982 (Kinski)
Fruits of the Faith, 1922 (Rogers, W.)
Frullo del passero, 1988 (Noiret)
Frusta e il corpo, 1963 (Lee; C.)
Frustration. *See* Lady, 1964
Fubuki ni sakebu ookami, 1931 (Hasegawa)
Fubuki to tomo ni keiyukinu, 1959 (Mori; Yamada)
Fubuki-toge, 1929 (Hasegawa)
Fuck the Army. *See* FTA Show, 1972
Fuco nelle vene, 1953 (Brazzi)
Fuefuki-gawa, 1960 (Takamine)
Fuelin' Around, 1949 (Three Stooges)
Fuente magica, 1961 (Williams, E.)
Fuentovejuna, 1947 (Rey)
Fuga, 1964 (Aimée)
Fuggitiva, 1941 (Magnani)
Fugitifs, 1986 (Depardieu)
Fugitive. *See* Taking of Luke McVane, 1915
Fugitive. *See* Return of Draw Egan, 1916
Fugitive, 1947 (Armendáriz; Bond; Del Rio; Fonda, H.)
Fugitive, 1993 (Ford, H.; Jones, T.)
Fugitive Family, 1980 (Wallach)
Fugitive from Chicago. *See* Flüchtling aus Chicago, 1934
Fugitive in 6B. *See* Brigante Musolino, 1950
Fugitive Kind, 1960 (Brando; Magnani; Woodward)
Fugitive Lady, 1934 (Ball)
Fugitive Lovers, 1933 (Montgomery)
Fugitive Lovers, 1934 (Three Stooges)
Fugitives, 1929 (Harlow)
Fugue de Jim Baxter. *See* Son Oncle de Normandie, 1939
Fuite de gaz, 1912 (Linder)
Fujicho, 1947 (Tanaka)
Fujinkai no kokuhaku, 1957 (Yamamura)

Fujinkai no himitsu, 1959 (Hara)
Fukei-zu, 1934 (Tanaka)
Fukei-zu, 1942 (Hasegawa; Takamine; Yamada)
Fukei-zu, 1949 (Hasegawa)
Fukeyo harukaza, 1953 (Yamamura; Mifune)
Fukkatsu, 1950 (Kyo)
Fukkatsu no hi, 1980 (Ford, G.; Olmos)
Fukushu no shichikamen, 1955 (Yamamura)
Full Circle, 1976 (Farrow)
Full Confession, 1939 (Fitzgerald; McLaglen)
Full Fathom Five, 1934 (Gielgud)
Full House. See O. Henry's Full House, 1952
Full Moon in Blue Water, 1988 (Hackman; Meredith)
Full of Life, 1956 (Holliday)
Full Treatment, 1961 (Rosay)
Fuller Brush Girl, 1950 (Ball)
Fumée, histoire et fantaisie, 1962 (Piccoli)
Fumetsu no nekkyu, 1955 (Tsukasa)
Fumetsu so ai, 1928 (Tanaka)
Fumo di Londra, 1966 (Sordi)
Fun in Acapulco, 1963 (Lukas; Presley)
Fun of Your Life, 1975 (Heston)
Fun with Dick and Jane, 1977 (Fonda, J.; Segal)
Fundoshi isha, 1960 (Hara; Yamamura)
Fundvogel, 1930 (Wegener)
Funeral, 1996 (Rossellini; Walken)
Funeral. See Ososhiki, 1984
Funeral in Berlin, 1966 (Caine; Homolka)
Funeral Rites. See Ososhiki, 1984
Funerale a Los Angeles. See Homme est morte, 1973
Funes, un gran amor, 1993 (Volonté)
Fünf Patronenhülsen, 1960 (Mueller-Stahl)
Fünf von der Jazzband, 1932 (Lorre)
Funkzauber, 1927 (Krauss)
Funny, 1986 (Pryor)
Funny, 1988 (Wallach)
Funny about Love, 1990 (Wilder)
Funny Bones, 1995 (Caron; Lewis, Jerry; Reed)
Funny Face, 1957 (Astaire; Hepburn, A.)
Funny Girl, 1968 (Pidgeon; Sharif; Streisand)
Funny Lady, 1975 (Caan; McDowall; Sharif; Streisand)
Funny Man, 1994 (Lee, C.)
Funny Thing Happened on the Way to the Crusades. See Cintura di castita, 1967
Funny Thing Happened on the Way to the Forum, 1966 (Keaton, B.)
Funny, You Don't Look 200, 1987 (Dreyfuss)
Funtoosh, 1956 (Anand)
Fuorilegge, 1949 (Gassman)
Fuorilegge del matrimonio, 1963 (Girardot)
Furai monogatari: Abare Hisha, 1960 (Hasegawa; Yamada)
Furai monogatari: Ninkyo-hen, 1959 (Hasegawa; Yamada)
Furankenshutain tai Baragon, 1966 (Shimura)
Furcht, 1917 (Veidt)
Furia, 1947 (Brazzi; Cervi)
Furie des S.S.. See Dieci italiani per un Tedesco, 1962
Furies, 1950 (Huston, W.; Stanwyck)
Furin kaza, 1969 (Mifune; Shimura)
Furisode kenpo, 1955 (Yamada)
Furisode kyojo, 1952 (Hasegawa)
Fürst oder Clown, 1927 (Homolka)
Further Perils of Laurel and Hardy, 1967 (Laurel and Hardy)
Furto e l'anima del commercio, 1971 (Blier)
Furto su misura, 1962 (Valli)
Fury, 1922 (Barthelmess)
Fury, 1936 (Brennan; Sidney; Tracy)
Fury, 1978 (Douglas, K.)
Fury at Furnace Creek, 1948 (Mature)
Fury at Smuggler's Bay, 1961 (Cushing)
Fury of Congo, 1951 (Weissmuller)
Furyo shojo, 1960 (Yamamura)
Furyu Fukagawa-uta, 1960 (Yamada; Yamamura)

Furyu katsujin-ken, 1934 (Yamada)
Furyu onsen nikki, 1958 (Tsukasa)
Furyu onsen: banto nikki, 1962 (Tsukasa)
Fusen, 1956 (Mori)
Fusetsu ni ju-nen, 1951 (Okada)
Fussgänger, 1974 (Bergner; Dagover; Rosay; Schell, Maximilian)
Futamabatu, 1933 (Tanaka)
Futari de aruita ikutoshitsuki, 1962 (Takamine)
Futari no Iida, 1976 (Takamine)
Futari no Musashi, 1960 (Hasegawa)
Futari no musuko, 1962 (Shimura)
Futatsu dore, 1933 (Hasegawa)
Future Is Woman. See Futuro e donna, 1984
Future Schlock, 1984 (Guinness)
Future Women. See Rio '70, 1970
Futures vedettes, 1954 (Bardot; Marais)
Futureworld, 1976 (Brynner)
Futuro e donna, 1984 (Schygulla)
Fuun Konpira-san, 1950 (Yamada)
Fuun senryo-bune, 1952 (Hasegawa)
Fuun tenman-zoshi, 1930 (Yamada)
Fuunji: Oda Nobunaga, 1959 (Kagawa)
Fuunjo-shi, 1928 (Hasegawa)
Fuyuki shinju, 1930 (Hasegawa)
Fuyuki shinju, 1931 (Yamada)
Fuzen no tomoshibi, 1957 (Takamine)
Fuzz, 1972 (Brynner; Reynolds, B.; Welch)
Fuzzy Pink Nightgown, 1956 (Menjou; Russell, J.)
Fy og Bi i Kantonnement, 1931 (Madsen and Schenstrøm)
Fy og Bi i Paradis. See Eine Insel wird entdeckt, 1937
Fy og Bi Prøvefilm, 1930 (Madsen and Schenstrøm)
G.I. Jane. See Undisclosed, 1996
G.I. Blues, 1960 (Presley)
G.I. Joe. See Story of G.I. Joe, 1945
G.I. Wanna Go Home, 1946 (Three Stooges)
Ga, Ga—chwala bohaterom. See O-bi, O-bi—Koniec cywilizacji, 1985
Gabriel over the White House, 1933 (Huston, W.)
Gabriela, 1983 (Braga; Mastroianni)
Gabriele ein, zwei, drei, 1937 (Fröhlich)
Gabrielle, 1954 (Björnstrand)
Gaby, 1956 (Caron)
Gaby: A True Story, 1987 (Ullmann)
Gadfly. See Poprigunya, 1955
Gagnant, 1979 (Audran)
Gai Dimanche, 1935 (Tati)
Gai Savoir, 1968 (Léaud)
Gaiety Girls. See Paradise for Two, 1937
Gaily, Gaily, 1969 (Mercouri)
Gaités de l'escadron, 1932 (Fernandel; Gabin; Raimu)
Gaités de la finance, 1935 (Fernandel)
Gal Who Took the West, 1949 (Coburn, C.)
Galathea, 1921 (Banky)
Galaxies Are Colliding, 1992 (Mills)
Galeerensträfling, 1918 (Wegener)
Galileo, 1968 (Cusack)
Galileo, 1974 (Gielgud)
Galileo, 1975 (Topol)
Galiyon Ka Badshah, 1989 (Patil)
Gallant Defender, 1935 (Rogers, R.)
Gallant Hours, 1960 (Cagney; Montgomery)
Gallant Hussar, 1928 (Novello)
Gallant Journey, 1946 (Ford, G.)
Gallant Ladies. See Dames Galantes, 1991
Gallant Sons, 1940 (Cooper)
Gallery of Horror. See Dr. Terror's Gallery of Horrors, 1967
Galley Slave, 1915 (Bara)
Gallipoli, 1981 (Gibson)
Galloping Ghosts, 1927 (Laurel and Hardy)
Gaman, 1978 (Patil)
Gamberge, 1961 (Arletty; Cassel)
Gambit, 1966 (Caine; Lom; MacLaine)

Gambler, 1971 (Anand)
Gambler, 1974 (Caan; Woods)
Gambler Returns: Luck of the Draw, 1991 (Rooney)
Gamblers Sometimes Win. *See* March Hare, 1956
Gambling Hell. *See* Macao, L'Enfer du jeu, 1939
Gambling House, 1950 (Mature)
Gambling Lady, 1934 (McCrea; Stanwyck)
Gambling on the High Seas, 1940 (Wyman)
Gambling Samurai. *See* Kunisada Chuji, 1960
Gambling Ship, 1933 (Grant, C.)
Game for Vultures, 1979 (Elliott; Milland; Harris, R.)
Game Is Over. *See* Curée, 1966
Game of Chance. *See* Baazi, 1951
Game of Death, 1979 (Lee, B.)
Game of Love. *See* Blé en herbe, 1953
Game That Kills, 1937 (Hayworth)
Games, 1967 (Caan)
Games, 1969 (Baker)
Games of Desire. *See* Lady, 1964
Games of Love and Loneliness. *See* Allvarsamma Leken, 1977
Gametsui yatsu, 1960 (Mori)
Gan, 1953 (Takamine)
Ganadevata, 1978 (Chatterjee)
Ganashatru, 1989 (Chatterjee)
Gandahar, 1987 (Close)
Gandhi, 1982 (Attenborough; Day-Lewis; Gielgud; Howard, T.; Kingsley; Mills; Sheen)
Gang, 1976 (Delon)
Gang Buster, 1931 (Arthur)
Gang des tractions-arrière, 1950 (Berry)
Gang in die Nacht, 1920 (Veidt)
Gang That Couldn't Shoot Straight, 1971 (De Niro)
Gang War, 1958 (Bronson)
Gang's All Here, 1939 (Buchanan; Horton; Withers)
Gang's All Here, 1943 (Faye; Horton; Miranda)
Ganga Jumna, 1961 (Kumar)
Gangs Inc.. *See* Paper Bullets, 1941
Gangs of Chicago, 1940 (Ladd)
Gangster, 1947 (Winters)
Gangster '70, 1968 (Cotten)
Gangster in London. *See* Rätsel der roten Orchidee, 1961
Gangster malgré lui, 1935 (Rosay)
Gangster Story, 1960 (Matthau)
Gangster Story. *See* Dio, sei proprio un padreterno, 1973
Gangstergirl. *See* Het Gangstermeisje, 1967
Gangsters, 1913 (Arbuckle)
Gangster's Boy, 1938 (Cooper)
Gangvaa, 1984 (Azmi)
Gangway for Tomorrow, 1943 (Ryan, R.; Carradine)
Ganpeki, 1953 (Yamamura)
Gantelet vert. *See* Green Glove, 1951
Gaol Birds. *See* Pardon Us, 1931
Garage, 1919 (Arbuckle)
Garage, 1920 (Keaton, B.)
Garbage. *See* Sal Gordo, 1983
Garbo Talks, 1984 (Bancroft)
Garce, 1989 (Huppert)
Garçon!, 1983 (Montand)
Garçonne, 1936 (Arletty)
Garcu, 1994 (Depardieu)
Garde à Vue, 1980 (Schneider)
Garden of Allah, 1936 (Boyer; Carradine; Dietrich; Rathbone)
Garden of Evil, 1954 (Constantine; Hayward; Widmark)
Garden of the Finzi-Continis. *See* Giardino dei Finzi Contini, 1970
Garden of Women. *See* Onna no sono, 1954
Gardener, 1922 (Laurel and Hardy)
Gardens of Stone, 1987 (Caan; Fishburne; Huston, A.; Jones, James Earl)
Gargoyles, 1971 (Wilde)
Garibaldi—The General, 1986 (Josephson)
Garment Jungle, 1957 (Cobb)
Garnison amoureuse, 1933 (Fernandel; Brasseur)

Garou-Garou, le passe-muraille, 1950 (Greenwood)
Garrison's Finish, 1914 (Mix)
Garrison's Finish, 1923 (Pickford)
Garten, 1985 (Bergner)
Gartenlaube, 1982 (Mueller-Stahl)
Gas, 1981 (Hayden; Sutherland)
Gas and Air, 1923 (Laurel and Hardy)
Gas-oil, 1955 (Gabin; Moreau)
Gaslight, 1940 (Walbrook)
Gaslight, 1944 (Bergman; Boyer; Cotten; Lansbury)
Gasoline Engagement, 1911 (Pickford)
Gasoline Gus, 1921 (Arbuckle)
Gasoline Love, 1923 (Wray)
Gasoline Wedding, 1918 (Lloyd)
Gaspard de Besse, 1935 (Raimu)
Gaspards, 1973 (Depardieu; Noiret)
Gasthaus an der Themse. *See* Dir Tür mit den sieben Schlössern, 1962
Gastone, 1960 (Sordi)
Gate of Hell. *See* **Jigokumon**, 1953
Gates of Paris. *See* Porte de Lilas, 1957
Gates of the Forest, 1980 (Ullmann)
Gates of the Night. *See* Portes de la nuit, 1946
Gateway, 1938 (Ameche; Carey; Carradine)
Gateway of the Moon, 1928 (Del Rio; Pidgeon)
Gateway to Glory. *See* Aa, kaigun, 1969
Gathering of Eagles, 1963 (Hudson)
Gathering of Old Men, 1987 (Hunter; Widmark)
Gathering Storm, 1974 (Burton)
Gatling Gun, 1973 (Carradine)
Gator, 1976 (Reynolds, B.)
Gatti. *See* I bastardi, 1969
Gatto a nove code, 1969 (Malden)
Gattopardo, 1963 (Cardinale; Delon; Lancaster; Reggiani)
Gaucho, 1928 (Fairbanks)
Gaucho, 1964 (Gassman)
Gaucho Serenade, 1940 (Autry)
Gaulois, 1996 (Depardieu)
Gauloises bleues, 1968 (Girardot)
Gauner im Paradies, 1986 (Mueller-Stahl)
Gaunt Stranger. *See* Ringer, 1952
Gaunt Woman. *See* Destiny of a Spy, 1969
Gauntlet, 1977 (Eastwood)
Gavilán pollero, 1950 (Infante)
Gavilanes, 1954 (Infante)
Gay Adventure. *See* Golden Arrow, 1953
Gay Bride, 1935 (Lombard)
Gay Caballero, 1932 (McLaglen)
Gay Corinthian, 1925 (McLaglen)
Gay Desperado, 1936 (Lupino)
Gay Divorcee, 1934 (Astaire; Grable; Horton; Rogers, G.)
Gay Duellist. *See* Meet Me at Dawn, 1947
Gay Falcon, 1941 (Sanders)
Gay Lady. *See* Trottie True, 1949
Gay Mrs. Trexel. *See* Susan and God, 1940
Gay Nineties. *See* Floradora Girl, 1930
Gay Purr-ee, 1962 (Garland)
Gay Ranchero, 1948 (Rogers, R.)
Gay Sisters, 1942 (Crisp; Stanwyck)
Gaze of Odysseus. *See* To Vlemma tou Odyssea, 1995
Gazebo, 1959 (Landau; Reynolds, D.; Ford, G.)
Gazon Maudit, 1995 (Abril)
Gedächtnis: Ein Film für Curt Bois und Bernhard Minetti, 1982 (Ganz)
Gee Whiz, Genevieve, 1924 (Rogers, W.)
Gefahren der Brautzeit. *See* Liebesnächte, 1929
Gefährliche Alter, 1927 (Nielsen)
Gefährliches Abenteuer, 1953 (Fröhlich)
Geheimaktion schwarze Kapelle, 1961 (Cervi)
Geheime Kurier, 1926 (Dagover)
Geheime Kurier, 1928 (Mozhukin)
Geheimnis auf Schloss Almshoh, 1925 (Walbrook)
Geheimnis der chinesischen Nelke, 1964 (Kinski)

Geheimnis der drei Dschunken, 1965 (Granger)
Geheimnis der gelben Mönche, 1966 (Granger; Kinski)
Geheimnis der gelben Narzissen, 1961 (Kinski)
Geheimnis der schwarzen Witwe, 1963 (Kinski)
Geheimnis des 13. Wagen, 1993 (Cassel)
Geheimnis des Carlo Cavelli. *See* Hohe Schule, 1934
Geheimnis des indischen Tempels. *See* Mistero del tempio indiano, 1963
Geheimnis um Johann Orth, 1932 (Wegener)
Geheimnis von Bergsee, 1950 (Dagover)
Geheimnis von Bombay, 1920 (Dagover; Veidt)
Geheimnis von London. *See* Toten Augen von London, 1961
Geheimnisse des Blutes. *See* Verfuhrte, 1914
Geheimnisse einer Seele, 1926 (Krauss)
Geheimnisvolle Spiegel, 1928 (Rasp)
Gehetzte Frauen, 1927 (Fröhlich; Nielsen)
Geiger von Florenz, 1926 (Bergner; Veidt)
Geisha, 1914 (Hayakawa)
Geisha Boy, 1958 (Hayakawa; Lewis, Jerry)
Geisha Konatsu, 1955 (Shimura)
Gekido no Showa-shi: Gunbatsu, 1970 (Yamamura)
Gekiryu, 1952 (Mifune)
Gekitsu no sakebi, 1925 (Tanaka)
Gekka no kyoba, 1927 (Hasegawa)
Gekka no wakamusha, 1938 (Hasegawa)
Gelbe Schein, 1918 (Negri)
Geld auf der Strasse, 1930 (Lamarr)
Geliebte Corinna, 1956 (Kinski)
Geliebte des Gouverneurs, 1927 (Kortner)
Geliebte Roswolskys, 1920 (Wegener; Nielsen)
Gem of a Jam, 1943 (Three Stooges)
Gen to fudo-myoh, 1961 (Ryu; Mifune)
Gendai mushuku, 1958 (Yamamura)
Gendai no yokubo, 1956 (Tsukasa)
Gendai shinshi yaro, 1964 (Tsukasa)
Gendaijin, 1952 (Yamada; Yamamura)
Gendarme desconocido, 1941 (Cantinflas)
Gene Autry and the Mounties, 1951 (Autry)
Gene Krupa Story, 1959 (Mineo)
General, 1926 (Keaton, B.)
General Crack, 1929 (Barrymore, J.)
Général de l'armée morte, 1982 (Aimée; Mastroianni; Piccoli)
General Died at Dawn, 1936 (Carroll; Constantine)
General Nuisance, 1941 (Keaton, B.)
General von Döbeln, 1942 (Björnstrand)
General's Daughter, 1911 (Talmadge)
Generala, 1970 (Félix)
Generation. *See* Pokolenie, 1955
Generation of Conquerors. *See* Pokolenie pobeditelei, 1936
Genesis, 1968 (Carradine; Azmi)
Genevieve, 1953 (Kendall)
Genghis Khan, 1965 (Mason; Sharif; Wallach)
Genio, due compari, un pollo, 1975 (Kinski)
Genius, 1917 (Laurel and Hardy)
Genius, 1993 (Caron)
Genius. *See* Genio, due compari, un pollo, 1975
Genius at Work, 1946 (Lugosi)
Genius in the Family. *See* So Goes My Love, 1946
Genji monogatari, 1951 (Hasegawa; Kyo)
Genji monogatari: Ukifune, 1957 (Hasegawa)
Genki de ikauyo, 1941 (Tanaka)
Genocide, 1980 (Taylor, E.; Welles)
Genroku bushido, 1940 (Shimura)
Genroku onna, 1924 (Tanaka)
Gens du voyage, 1938 (Rosay)
Gente dell'aria, 1942 (Cervi)
Gentile Alouette, 1985 (Chaplin, G.)
Gentle Art of Murder. *See* Crime ne paie pas, 1962
Gentle Art of Seduction. *See* Chasse à l'homme, 1964
Gentle Creature. *See* Femme douce, 1969
Gentle Cyclone, 1926 (Laurel and Hardy)
Gentle Gunman, 1952 (Bogarde; Mills)

Gentle Julia, 1936 (McDaniel)
Gentle Sex, 1943 (Greenwood; Howard, L.)
Gentleman after Dark, 1942 (Hopkins, M.)
Gentleman d'Epsom, 1962 (Gabin)
Gentleman de Cocody, 1965 (Marais)
Gentleman from America, 1923 (Karloff)
Gentleman Jim, 1942 (Bond; Flynn)
Gentleman Misbehaves, 1946 (Three Stooges)
Gentleman of Paris, 1927 (Menjou)
Gentleman Tramp, 1975 (Harrison; Matthau)
Gentleman's Agreement, 1935 (Leigh, V.)
Gentleman's Agreement, 1947 (Garfield; Jaffe; Peck)
Gentleman's Fate, 1931 (Gilbert)
Gentlemen from Blue Gulch. *See* Roughneck, 1915
Gentlemen Marry Brunettes, 1955 (Russell, J.)
Gentlemen of Nerve, 1914 (Chaplin, C.; Normand)
Gentlemen of the Press, 1929 (Francis; Huston, W.)
Gentlemen Prefer Blondes, 1953 (Coburn, C.; Dalio; Monroe; Russell, J.)
Gentlemen Tramp, 1975 (Chaplin, G.)
Gents in a Jam, 1952 (Three Stooges)
Gents without Cents, 1944 (Three Stooges)
Genuine Risk, 1990 (Stamp)
Genzaburo ihen: Hissatsuken oni no maki, 1934 (Hasegawa)
Genzaburo ihen: Shokuran renbo no maki, 1934 (Hasegawa)
Georg Elser—Einer aus Deutschland, 1990 (Brandauer)
George Balanchine's The Nutcracker, 1993 (Kline)
George Mckenna Story, 1986 (Washington)
George Raft Story, 1961 (Mansfield)
George Stevens: A Filmmaker's Journey, 1984 (Astaire; Hepburn, K.; Rogers, G.; Von Sydow; Huston, J.)
George Washington, 1984 (Ferrer; Howard, T.)
George Washington Slept Here, 1942 (Coburn, C.; McDaniel)
George White's Scandals, 1934 (Durante; Faye)
George White's Scandals, 1935 (Faye; Powell, E.)
Georgia, 1987 (Davis, J.)
Georgia, 1995 (Leigh, Jennifer Jason)
Georgy Girl, 1966 (Bates, A.; Mason)
Gerarchi si muore, 1962 (Fabrizi)
Gerechtigkeit, 1920 (Kortner)
German Sisters. *See* Bleiere Zeit, 1982
Germany in Autumn. *See* Deutschland im Herbst, 1978
Germany Year 90 Nine Zero. *See* Allemagne annee 90 neuf zero, 1991
Germicide. *See* Blondy, 1975
Germinal, 1963 (Blier)
Germinal, 1993 (Depardieu)
Gern hab' ich die Frau'n gekillt. *See* Spie contro il mondo, 1966
Geronimo: An American Legend, 1993 (Duvall; Hackman)
Gervaise, 1955 (Schell, Maria)
Geschäft, 1917 (Jannings)
Geschäft nit Amerika. *See* Yes Mr. Brown, 1932
Geschichte einer Liebe, 1981 (Ganz)
Geschichte eines Lebens. *See* Annelie, 1941
Geschichten aus dem Wienerwald, 1981 (Schell, Maximilian)
Geschichten aus den Wienerwald, 1979 (Dagover)
Geschlossene Gesellschaft, 1978 (Mueller-Stahl)
Geschlossene Kette, 1920 (Negri)
Gesicht im Dunkeln. *See* Double Face, 1969
Gestohlene Jahr, 1951 (Werner)
Gesunkenen, 1924 (Nielsen)
Get Carter, 1970 (Caine)
Get Crazy, 1983 (McDowell)
Get 'em Young, 1926 (Laurel and Hardy)
Get Hep to Love, 1942 (O'Connor)
Get Off My Back. *See* Synanon, 1965
Get Out and Get Under, 1920 (Lloyd)
Get Out Your Handkerchiefs. *See* Préparez vos mouchoirs, 1977
Get-Rich-Quick Wallingford. *See* New Adventures of Get-Rich-Quick Wallingford, 1931
Get Shorty, 1995 (DeVito; DeVito; Hackman; Keitel; Midler; Travolta)
Get That Venus, 1933 (Arthur)
Get to Know Your Rabbit, 1972 (Welles)

Get Your Man, 1927 (Bow)
Get Your Man, 1934 (Harrison)
Getaway, 1972 (McQueen)
Getaway, 1994 (Basinger; Woods)
Getting a Start in Life, 1915 (Mix)
Getting a Ticket, 1929 (Cantor)
Getting Acquainted, 1914 (Chaplin, C.; Normand)
Getting an Eyeful, 1938 (Kaye)
Getting Away from It All, 1972 (Meredith)
Getting Away with Murder, 1995 (Lemmon)
Getting Away with Murder. See Richter und sein Henker, 1975
Getting Even, 1909 (Pickford)
Getting Gotti, 1994 (Burstyn)
Getting His Goat. See Property Man, 1914
Getting It Right, 1989 (Bonham-Carter; Gielgud)
Getting Mary Married, 1919 (Davies)
Getting Out, 1994 (Burstyn)
Getting Reuben Back, 1912-13 (White)
Getting Straight, 1970 (Ford, H.; Gould)
Gettysburg, 1993 (Nolte; Sheen)
Gewitter im Mai, 1919 (Veidt)
Ghaltit Habibi, 1957 (Sharif)
Ghar Ki Izzat, 1948 (Kumar)
Ghar Number 44. See Makan no. 44, 1955
Gharam el Asyad, 1960 (Sharif)
Ghare Baire, 1984 (Chatterjee)
Gharer Baire Ghar, 1980 (Chatterjee)
Ghev, 1974 (Yankovsky)
Ghidrah. See Sandai kaiju chikyu saidai no kessen, 1965
Ghost, 1990 (Goldberg; Moore, Demi)
Ghost and Mrs. Muir, 1947 (Harrison; Sanders; Tierney; Wood)
Ghost and the Darkness, 1996 (Douglas, Michael)
Ghost Breakers, 1940 (Goddard; Lukas; Quinn; Ryan, R.)
Ghost Brigade. See Killing Box, 1993
Ghost Camera, 1933 (Lupino; Mills)
Ghost Crazy. See Crazy Knights, 1944
Ghost Dad, 1990 (Poitier)
Ghost Downstairs, 1982 (Cusack)
Ghost Goes West, 1936 (Donat; Lanchester)
Ghost Goes Wild, 1947 (Horton)
Ghost in Monte Carlo, 1989 (Reed)
Ghost in the Invisible Bikini, 1966 (Karloff; Rathbone)
Ghost in the Noonday Sun, 1974 (Sellers)
Ghost of Flight 401, 1978 (Basinger)
Ghost of Frankenstein, 1942 (Bellamy; Lugosi)
Ghost of Love. See Fantasma d'amore, 1981
Ghost Steps Out, 1946 (Abbott and Costello)
Ghost Story, 1981 (Astaire; Douglas, Melvyn; Neal)
Ghost Talks, 1929 (Brown)
Ghost Talks, 1949 (Three Stooges)
Ghost Town, 1937 (Carey)
Ghost Writer, 1984 (Bloom)
Ghostbreakers, 1940 (Hope)
Ghostbusters, 1984 (Murray; Weaver)
Ghostbusters II, 1989 (Murray; Weaver)
Ghosts, 1986 (Branagh)
Ghosts Can't Do It, 1990 (Quinn)
Ghosts in the Night. See Ghosts on the Loose, 1943
Ghosts, Italian Style. See Questi fantasmi, 1967
Ghosts of Rome. See Fantasmi a Roma, 1961
Ghosts of Yesterday, 1918 (Talmadge)
Ghosts on the Loose, 1943 (Gardner; Lugosi)
Ghosts—Italian Style. See Questi fantasmi, 1967
Ghoul, 1933 (Karloff; Richardson, R.)
Ghoul, 1975 (Cushing; Hurt, J.)
Ghungroo, 1983 (Patil)
Giallo napoletano, 1979 (Mastroianni; Piccoli)
Giant, 1956 (Dean; Hopper; Hudson; Mineo; Taylor, E.)
Giarabub, 1942 (Sordi)
Giardino dei Finzi Contini, 1970 (Sanda)
Gibier de potence, 1951 (Arletty)

Gibson Goddess, 1909 (Pickford)
Gideon and Sampson. See I Grande condottieri, 1968
Gideon of Scotland Yard. See Gideon's Day, 1958
Gideon's Day, 1958 (Hawkins; Cusack)
Gideon's Trumpet, 1980 (Fonda, H.; Wray)
Gidget, 1959 (Robertson)
Gidget Gets Married, 1972 (Bennett)
Gifle, 1974 (Adjani; Baye; Girardot)
Gift, 1979 (Bacon; Ford, G.)
Gift. See Cadeau, 1982
Gift Horse, 1951 (Howard, T.; Attenborough)
Gift of Gab, 1934 (Karloff; Lugosi; Lukas)
Gift of Love, 1958 (Bacall; Woods)
Gift of Love: A Christmas Story, 1983 (Lansbury; Remick)
Gift Supreme, 1920 (Chaney)
Giftgas, 1929 (Kortner)
Gigi, 1948 (Noiret)
Gigi, 1958 (Caron; Chevalier; Jourdan)
Gigolette, 1935 (Bellamy)
Gigolette, 1937 (Morgan)
Gigolettes, 1932 (Arbuckle)
Gigolo, 1960 (Valli)
Gigot, 1962 (Kelly, Gene)
Gil angeli dalle mani bendate, 1975 (Brazzi)
Gilbert and Sullivan. See Story of Gilbert and Sullivan, 1953
Gilda, 1946 (Ford, G.; Hayworth)
Gilded Highway, 1926 (Loy)
Gilded Lily, 1935 (Colbert; MacMurray; Milland)
Gilded Spider, 1916 (Chaney)
Gina. See Mort en ce jardin, 1956
Ginecologo della mutua, 1977 (Fabrizi)
Gingchat gusi, 1985 (Chan)
Gingchat gusi tsuktsap, 1988 (Chan; Masina)
Ginger e Fred, 1986 (Mastroianni)
Ginger in the Morning, 1973 (Spacek)
Ginrei no hate, 1947 (Mifune; Shimura)
Ginza Cosmetics. See Ginza gesho, 1951
Ginza gesho, 1951 (Kagawa; Tanaka)
Ginza kankan musume, 1949 (Takamine)
Ginza no yanagi, 1932 (Tanaka)
Giochi particolari, 1970 (Mastroianni)
Gioco al massacra, 1989 (Gould; Baye)
Gion matsuri, 1968 (Mifune; Shimura)
Gion no shimai, 1936 (Yamada)
Giordano Bruno, 1973 (Volonté)
Giornata speciale, 1977 (Loren; Mastroianni)
Giorni d'amore, 1954 (Mastroianni)
Giorni di fuoco. See Winnetou: II Teil, 1964
Giorno del furore, 1973 (Cardinale; Reed)
Giorno del guidizio, 1971 (Brazzi)
Giorno dell'ira, 1967 (Van Cleef)
Giorno della civetta, 1968 (Cardinale; Cobb; Reggiani)
Giorno in pretura, 1954 (Loren; Sordi; Aimée; Belmondo; Girardot; Granger;
      Mastroianni; Niven)
Giorno prima, 1987 (Josephson; Lancaster; Thulin)
Giovane leone, 1959 (Sordi)
Giovane Toscanini, 1988 (Taylor, E.)
Giovanna d'Arco al rogo, 1954 (Bergman)
Giovanni delle Bande Nere, 1956 (Gassman)
Giovanni Senzapensieri, 1986 (Fabrizi)
Giovinezza, 1952 (Sordi)
Giovinezza del diavolo, 1921 (Bertini)
Girara, 1967 (Okada)
Girasoli, 1969 (Loren; Mastroianni)
Girl, 1987 (Lee, C.)
Girl, a Guy, and a Gob, 1941 (Ball; Lloyd; O'Brien, E.)
Girl and the Legend. See Robinson soll nicht sterben, 1957
Girl and the General. See Ragazza e il generale, 1967
Girl and the Mail Bag, 1915 (Mix)
Girl and the Shoes. See Pigen og skoene, 1959
Girl Can't Help It, 1956 (Mansfield; O'Brien, E.)

Girl Crazy, 1943 (Garland; Rooney)
Girl Friend. *See* Kanojo, 1926
Girl Friends. *See* Podrugi, 1935
Girl from Chicago, 1927 (Loy)
Girl from Everywhere, 1927 (Lombard)
Girl from Flanders. *See* Mädchen aus Flandern, 1956
Girl from Hamburg. *See* Fille de Hambourg, 1957
Girl from Jones Beach, 1949 (Reagan)
Girl from Lorraine. *See* Provinciale, 1980
Girl from Manhattan, 1948 (Lamour; Laughton)
Girl from Mexico, 1939 (Bond)
Girl from Missouri, 1934 (Barrymore, L.; Harlow)
Girl from Nowhere, 1928 (Lombard)
Girl from Petrovka, 1974 (Hawn; Hopkins, A.)
Girl from Rio, 1927 (Pidgeon)
Girl from State Street. *See* State Street Sadie, 1928
Girl from Tenth Avenue, 1935 (Davis, B.)
Girl from the Moon. *See* Spadla s měsíce, 1966
Girl from the Mountain Village. *See* Flickan från fjällbyn, 1948
Girl from the Third Row. *See* Flickan från tredje raden, 1949
Girl Getters. *See* System, 1964
Girl Grief, 1932 (Goddard)
Girl Habit, 1931 (Goddard; Dumont)
Girl Happy, 1965 (Presley)
Girl He Left Behind. *See* Gang's All Here, 1943
Girl He Left Behind, 1956 (Garner; Wood)
Girl I Loved. *See* Waga koiseshi otome, 1946
Girl I Made. *See* Made on Broadway, 1933
Girl in a Million, 1946 (Greenwood)
Girl in Black Stockings, 1956 (Bancroft)
Girl in Danger, 1934 (Bellamy; Bond)
Girl in Distress. *See* Jeannie, 1941
Girl in Every Port, 1928 (Brooks, L.; McLaglen)
Girl in Every Port, 1952 (Marx Brothers)
Girl in His Pocket. *See* Amour de poche, 1957
Girl in Pants, 1912-13 (White)
Girl in Room 17. *See* Vice Squad, 1953
Girl in Room 43. *See* Passport to Shame, 1959
Girl in the Bikini. *See* Manina, la fille sans voiles, 1952
Girl in the Checkered Coat, 1916 (Chaney)
Girl in the Crowd, 1934 (Withers)
Girl in the Glass Cage, 1929 (Young, L.)
Girl in the Limousine, 1924 (Laurel and Hardy)
Girl in the News, 1940 (Lockwood)
Girl in the Painting, 1948 (Lom; Zetterling)
Girl in the Rain. *See* Flickan i regnet, 1955
Girl in the Red Velvet Swing, 1955 (Milland)
Girl in the Web, 1920 (Sweet)
Girl in the Yellow Pajamas. *See* Ragazza in Pigiamo Giallo, 1978
Girl in White, 1952 (Kennedy)
Girl Most Likely, 1957 (Robertson)
Girl Must Live, 1939 (Lockwood)
Girl Named Sooner, 1975 (Remick)
Girl Next Room, 1910-11 (White)
Girl No. 6, 1996 (Lee, S.; Turturro)
Girl of Gold Gulch, 1916 (Mix)
Girl of My Dreams. *See* Sweetheart of Sigma Chi, 1933
Girl of the Golden West, 1938 (Eddy; MacDonald; Pidgeon)
Girl of the Night, 1915 (Chaney)
Girl of the Rio, 1932 (Del Rio)
Girl of Vaniousine. *See* Deti Vanyousina, 1915
Girl of Yesterday, 1915 (Crisp; Pickford)
Girl on a Motorcycle, 1968 (Delon)
Girl on Approval, 1962 (Roberts, R.)
Girl on the Boat, 1961 (Wisdom)
Girl on the Late Late Show, 1974 (Grahame; Pidgeon)
Girl Overboard, 1936 (Pidgeon)
Girl Reporter, 1912-13 (White)
Girl Rush, 1944 (Mitchum)
Girl Rush, 1955 (Russell, R.)
Girl Said No, 1930 (Dressler)

Girl Shy, 1924 (Lloyd)
Girl Stroke Boy, 1971 (Greenwood)
Girl Trouble, 1942 (Ameche; Bennett)
Girl Trouble. *See* What's Good for the Goose, 1969
Girl Who Couldn't Say No. *See* Suo modo di fare, 1968
Girl Who Had Everything, 1953 (Powell, W.; Taylor, E.)
Girl Who Stayed at Home, 1919 (Barthelmess)
Girl Who Wouldn't Work, 1925 (Barrymore, L.)
Girl with a Suitcase. *See* Ragazza con la valigia, 1961
Girl with Green Eyes, 1963 (Finch)
Girl with Ideas, 1937 (Pidgeon)
Girl with the Golden Panties, 1980 (Abril)
Girl with the Pistol. *See* Ragazza con la pistola, 1968
Girlfriends. *See* Biches, 1968
Girlfriends, 1978 (Wallach)
Girls, 1957 (Kelly, Gene; Kendall)
Girls. *See* Flickorna, 1968
Girls about Town, 1931 (Francis; McCrea)
Girls Can Play, 1937 (Hayworth)
Girls Demand Excitement, 1931 (Wayne)
Girls' Dormitory, 1936 (Marshall; Power)
Girls! Girls! Girls!, 1962 (Presley)
Girls Gone Wild, 1929 (MacMurray)
Girls He Left Behind. *See* Gang's All Here, 1943
Girls in Prison, 1956 (Marsh)
Girls of Huntingdon House, 1973 (Spacek)
Girls of Pleasure Island, 1953 (Lanchester)
Girls of Summer. *See* Satisfaction, 1988
Girls of the White Orchid, 1983 (Leigh, Jennifer Jason; Hayward)
Girls on Probation, 1938 (Reagan)
Girls on the Loose, 1958 (Henreid)
Girls' School, 1938 (Bellamy)
Girl's Stratagem, 1913 (Barrymore, L.; Marsh)
Girl's Way, 1923 (Lukas)
Girls Will Be Boys, 1912-13 (White)
Girls with Guns. *See* Braqueuses, 1994
Giro City, 1982 (Jackson, G.)
Girovaghi, 1956 (Ustinov)
Gisants, 1949 (Fresnay)
Giselle, 1952 (Buchanan)
Gishi shimatu-ki, 1962 (Yamamura)
Git along Little Dogies, 1937 (Autry)
Gitan, 1975 (Delon; Girardot)
Gitana tenias que ser, 1953 (Infante)
Gitane, 1986 (Audran)
Gitanes, 1932 (Vanel)
Gitanilla, 1940 (Rey)
Gitta entdeckt ihr Herz, 1932 (Fröhlich)
Giù la testa, 1972 (Coburn, J.; Steiger)
Giù le mani ... carogna, 1970 (Kinski)
Giudizio universale, 1961 (Aimée; Durante; Fernandel; Gassman; Mercouri; Sordi)
Giulia e Giulia, 1987 (Turner, K.)
Giulietta degli spiriti, 1965 (Masina)
Giulietta e Romeo. *See* Romeo and Juliet, 1954
Giuseppe Verdi, 1938 (Brasseur)
Giustiziere sfida la citta, 1975 (Cotten)
Give a Girl a Break, 1953 (Reynolds, D.)
Give Her a Ring, 1934 (Granger)
Give Her the Moon. *See* Caprices de Marie, 1970
Give Me a Sailor, 1938 (Grable; Hope)
Give Me Your Heart, 1936 (Francis)
Give My Regards to Broad Street, 1984 (Richardson, R.)
Give Out Sisters, 1942 (O'Connor)
Give Us the Moon, 1944 (Lockwood)
Give Us Wings, 1940 (Three Stooges)
Giving Them Fits, 1915 (Lloyd)
Givoi troup, 1912 (Mozhukin)
Glad Rags to Riches, 1932 (Temple)
Glade Gøglere. *See* Lumpenkavaliere, 1932
Gladiator, 1938 (Brown)

Glaive et la balance, 1963 (Perkins)
Glamorous Hollywood, 1958 (Niven)
Glamour, 1934 (Lukas)
Glamour Boy, 1941 (Cooper)
Glanz gegen Gluck, 1923 (Veidt)
Glanz und Elend der Kurtisanen, 1927 (Wegener)
Glasberget, 1953 (Björnstrand)
Glass Bottom Boat, 1966 (Day)
Glass Key, 1935 (Milland; Raft)
Glass Key, 1942 (Ladd; Lake)
Glass Menagerie, 1950 (Douglas, K.; Kennedy; Wyman)
Glass Menagerie, 1973 (Hepburn, K.; Malkovich)
Glass Menagerie, 1987 (Newman; Woodward)
Glass Mountain. See Szklana góra, 1960
Glass Shield, 1994 (Gould)
Glass Slipper, 1955 (Caron; Lanchester; Pidgeon)
Glass Sphinx. See Esfinge de cristal, 1968
Glass Wall, 1953 (Gassman; Grahame)
Glass Web, 1953 (Robinson, E.)
Glaubt Gott nicht mehr, 1981 (Mueller-Stahl)
Glaubt Gott nicht mehr, 1982 (Mueller-Stahl)
Glaubt Gott nicht mehr, 1985 (Mueller-Stahl)
Gleam O'Dawn, 1922 (Gilbert)
Glee Quartette, 1930 (Buchanan)
Gleisdreieck, 1936 (Fröhlich)
Glen or Glenda?, 1952 (Lugosi)
Glengarry Glen Ross, 1992 (Arkin; Harris, E.; Lemmon; Pacino)
Glenn Miller Story, 1954 (Stewart)
Glimpse of Los Angeles, 1914 (Normand)
Glissements progressifs du plaisir, 1974 (Huppert)
Glitter. See Drop Kick, 1927
Glitter, 1984 (Neal)
Glitter Dome, 1985 (Garner)
Global Affair, 1964 (Hope)
Globalny Pressing, 1987 (Mastroianni)
Gloria, 1913 (Bertini)
Gloria, 1931 (Fröhlich; Gabin)
Gloria, 1980 (Rowlands)
Gloria's Romance, 1916 (Barthelmess)
Glorifying the American Girl, 1929 (Cantor)
Glorious Adventure, 1918 (Marsh)
Glorious Adventure, 1922 (McLaglen)
Glorious Days. See Lilacs in the Spring, 1955
Glorious Life, 1923 (Lukas)
Glory, 1956 (Brennan; O'Brien, M.)
Glory, 1989 (Freeman; Washington)
Glory Alley, 1952 (Caron)
Glory at Sea. See Gift Horse, 1952
Glory Boy. See My Old Man's Place, 1971
Glory Boys, 1984 (Perkins; Steiger)
Glory Brigade, 1952 (Marvin; Mature)
Glory Guys, 1965 (Caan)
Glory of Love. See While Paris Sleeps, 1923
Glory on the Summit. See Yama no sanka: Moyuru wakamonotachi, 1962
Glory Stompers, 1967 (Hopper)
Glory to Me, Death to the Enemy! See Slava nam, smert vragam!, 1914
Glove, 1978 (Blondell)
Gluck auf der Alm, 1958 (Schell, Maximilian)
Glückliche Mutter, 1928 (Dietrich)
Glücklichen Jahre der Thorwalds, 1962 (Bergner)
Glut, 1983 (Mueller-Stahl)
Glut im Herzen. See Glut, 1983
G-Men, 1935 (Cagney)
Gnome-Mobile, 1967 (Brennan)
Go-Between, 1971 (Bates, A.; Christie; Redgrave, M.)
Go Chase Yourself, 1938 (Ball)
Go into Your Dance, 1935 (Jolson; Keeler)
Go, Man, Go!, 1954 (Poitier)
Go Naked in the World, 1961 (Borgnine; Lollobrigida)
Go Tell the Spartans, 1978 (Lancaster)
Go to Blazes, 1962 (Smith)

Go West, 1925 (Arbuckle; Keaton, B.)
Go West, 1940 (Marx Brothers)
Go West, Young Lady, 1941 (Ford, G.; Miller)
Go West, Young Man, 1936 (Scott, R.; West)
Goalie's Anxiety at the Penalty Kick. See Angst des Tormanns beim Elfmeter, 1971
Goat, 1917 (Laurel and Hardy)
Goat, 1918 (Crisp; Novarro)
Goat, 1921 (Keaton, B.)
Goat. See Chèvre, 1981
Gobbo, 1960 (Blier)
Goben no tsubaki, 1965 (Okada)
GoBots: Battle of the Rock Lords, 1986 (McDowall)
God afton, Herr Wallenberg, 1990 (Josephson)
God Bless the Child, 1988 (Leigh, Jennifer Jason)
God Doesn't Believe in Us Anymore. See Uns glaubt Gott nicht mehr, 1985
God Game. See Magus, 1968
God Is My Co-Pilot, 1945 (Massey)
God Is My Partner, 1957 (Brennan)
God Needs Men. See Dieu a besoin des hommes, 1950
God Rot Tunbridge Wells, 1985 (Howard, T.)
God Within, 1912 (Barrymore, L.; Sweet)
Goda Viljan, 1992 (Von Sydow)
Godchild, 1974 (Palance)
Goddess. See Devi, 1960
Goddess of Sagebrush Gulch, 1912 (Sweet)
Godelureaux, 1961 (Audran)
Godfather, 1972 (Brando; Caan; Duvall; Hayden; Keaton, D.; Pacino)
Godfather, Part II, 1974 (Aiello; Caan; De Niro; Duvall; Keaton, D.; Pacino; Stanton)
Godfather, Part III, 1990 (García; Keaton, D.; Pacino; Wallach)
Godmother, 1972 (Aiello)
Godmothers, 1973 (Rooney)
God's Army. See Prophecy, 1996
God's Country, 1946 (Keaton, B.)
God's Gift to Women, 1931 (Blondell; Brooks, L.)
God's Gun, 1976 (Van Cleef)
God's Gun, 1978 (Palance)
God's Little Acre, 1958 (Ryan, R.)
Gods of the Plague. See Gotter der Pest, 1969
Godson. See **Samourai**, 1967
Godson. See Cose di Cosa Nostra, 1971
Godzilla, King of the Monsters. See Gojira, 1954
Godzilla vs. the Thing. See Mosura, 1961
Gog, 1954 (Marshall)
Goha, 1957 (Cardinale; Sharif)
Goiken Gomuyo, 1925 (Tanaka)
Goin' South, 1978 (Belushi; DeVito; Nicholson; Steenburgen)
Goin' to Town, 1935 (West)
Going and Coming Back. See Partir, revenir, 1985
Going Ape!, 1981 (DeVito)
Going Bananas, 1988 (Lom)
Going Berserk, 1983 (Candy)
Going Bye-Bye!, 1934 (Laurel and Hardy)
Going Gently, 1981 (Wisdom)
Going! Going! Gone!, 1919 (Lloyd)
Going Highbrow, 1935 (Horton)
Going Hollywood, 1933 (Crosby; Davies)
Going Hollywood: The War Years, 1986 (Temple; Young, L.; Lamarr)
Going Home, 1971 (Mitchum)
Going My Way, 1944 (Crosby; Fitzgerald)
Going of the White Swan, 1914 (Mix)
Going Places, 1938 (Powell, D.; Reagan)
Going Places. See Valseuses, 1974
Going Some, 1912-13 (White)
Going South Shopping. See Bajarse al Moro, 1988
Going Spanish, 1934 (Hope)
Going Straight, 1916 (Talmadge)
Going to Congress, 1924 (Rogers, W.)
Going Under, 1991 (McDowall)
Going Up of David Lev, 1971 (Bloom; Topol)

Going West to Make Good, 1916 (Mix)
Going Wild, 1931 (Brown; Pidgeon)
Göingehövdingen, 1953 (Dahlbeck; Thulin)
Gojira, 1954 (Shimura)
Goju man-nin no isan, 1963 (Mifune)
Gokumon-to, 1977 (Tsukasa)
Gokumoncho, 1955 (Kagawa)
Gokurosama, 1929 (Tanaka)
Gold, 1974 (Gielgud; Milland; York)
Gold and Glitter, 1912 (Barrymore, L.; Gish)
Gold and the Girl, 1925 (Lombard)
Gold and the Woman, 1916 (Bara)
Gold Diggers, 1970 (Ford, G.)
Gold Diggers, 1984 (Christie)
Gold Diggers of 1933, 1933 (Blondell; Keeler; Powell, D.; Rogers, G.)
Gold Diggers of 1935, 1935 (Menjou; Powell, D.)
Gold Diggers of 1937, 1936 (Blondell; Powell, D.; Wyman)
Gold Dust and the Squaw, 1915 (Mix)
Gold Ghost, 1934 (Keaton, B.)
Gold Is Where You Find It, 1938 (De Havilland; Rains)
Gold Mine in the Sky, 1938 (Autry)
Gold Necklace, 1910 (Pickford)
Gold of Naples. *See* Oro di Napoli, 1955
Gold of the Amazon Women, 1979 (Pleasence)
Gold Raiders, 1951 (Three Stooges)
Gold Rimmed Glasses. *See* Occhiali d'oro, 1987
Gold Rush, 1925 (Chaplin, C.)
Gold von Sam Cooper. *See* Ognuno per se, 1968
Golden Age of Comedy, 1957 (Laurel and Hardy)
Golden Arrow, 1936 (Davis, B.)
Golden Arrow, 1953 (Meredith)
Golden Blade, 1953 (Hudson)
Golden Boy, 1939 (Cobb; Holden; Menjou; Stanwyck)
Golden Child, 1986 (Murphy)
Golden Coach. *See* **Carrosse d'or**, 1953
Golden Earrings, 1947 (Dietrich; Milland)
Golden Eighties, 1986 (Seyrig)
Golden Flame, 1967 (Fonda, H.)
Golden Fleecing, 1940 (Ayres)
Golden Follies, 1938 (Menjou)
Golden Fortress. *See* Sonar Kella, 1974
Golden Gate, 1981 (Griffith)
Golden Gate, 1994 (Dillon)
Golden Gate Murders, 1979 (York)
Golden Gloves, 1940 (Ryan, R.)
Golden Hawk, 1952 (Hayden)
Golden Head, 1964 (Sanders)
Golden Helmet. *See* **Casque d'or**, 1951
Golden Hour, 1996 (Olin)
Golden Hour. *See* Pot o' Gold, 1941
Golden Marie. *See* **Casque d'or**, 1951
Golden Moment: An Olympic Love Story, 1980 (Jones, James Earl)
Golden Needles, 1974 (Meredith)
Golden Rendezvous, 1977 (Carradine; Harris, R.; Malone; Meredith)
Golden River. *See* Rio del oro, 1986
Golden Rule Kate, 1917 (Gilbert)
Golden Salamander, 1949 (Aimée; Howard, T.; Lom)
Golden Snare, 1921 (Beery)
Golden Stallion, 1949 (Rogers, R.)
Golden Thought, 1916 (Mix)
Golden Vampire, 1974 (Cushing)
Golden Virgin, 1957 (Crawford, J.)
Golden Web, 1926 (Karloff)
Golden West, 1932 (McDaniel)
Goldengirl, 1979 (Caron; Coburn, J.)
Goldenrod, 1977 (Pleasence)
Goldfinger, 1964 (Connery)
Goldie, 1931 (Harlow; Tracy)
Goldpuppen. *See* Pleasure Girls, 1965
Goldtown Ghost Raiders, 1953 (Autry)
Goldwyn Follies, 1938 (Ladd)

Golem, 1914 (Wegener)
Golem, 1980 (Nowicki)
Golem, l'Esprit de l'Exil, 1992 (Schygulla)
Golem und die Tänzerin, 1917 (Wegener)
Golem, wie er in die Welt kam, 1920 (Wegener)
Golf, 1922 (Laurel and Hardy)
Golf Link Champion "Chick" Evans Links with Sweedie, 1914 (Beery)
Golf Specialist, 1930 (Fields, W. C.)
Golf's Golden Years, 1970 (Crosby)
Golgotha, 1935 (Feuillère; Gabin)
Goliat contra los gigantes, 1961 (Rey)
Goliath against the Giants. *See* Goliat contra los gigantes, 1961
Goliath and the Dragon. *See* Vendetta di Ercole, 1960
Goma 2, 1984 (Van Cleef)
Gone to Earth, 1950 (Cusack; Jones, Jennifer)
Gone to Earth, 1952 (Cotten)
Gone with the West, 1975 (Caan)
Gone with the Wind, 1939 (Bond; De Havilland; Gable; Howard, L.; Leigh, V.; McDaniel)
Gonin no totsugekitai, 1961 (Yamamura)
Gonshchiki, 1972 (Yankovsky)
Gonzague, 1923 (Chevalier)
Good and Faithful Servant, 1974 (Cusack)
Good and Naughty, 1926 (Negri)
Good Bad Girl. *See* Inez from Hollywood, 1924
Good Bad Man, 1916 (Fairbanks)
Good Companions, 1933 (Gielgud; Hawkins)
Good Companions, 1957 (Johnson; Roberts, R.)
Good Dame, 1934 (Brennan; March; Sidney)
Good Day for a Hanging, 1958 (MacMurray)
Good Day for Fighting. *See* Custer of the West, 1968
Good Die Young, 1954 (Baker; Grahame)
Good Doctor: The Paul Fleiss Story, 1996 (Segal)
Good Earth, 1937 (Muni; Rainer)
Good Evening, Mr. Wallenberg. *See* God afton, Herr Wallenberg, 1990
Good Fairy, 1935 (Marshall; Sullavan)
Good Fairy. *See* Zemma, 1951
Good Father, 1986 (Hopkins, A.)
Good Girls Go to Paris, 1939 (Blondell; Douglas, Melvyn)
Good Guys Always Win. *See* Outfit, 1973
Good Guys and the Bad Guys, 1969 (Carradine; Mitchum)
Good Guys Wear Black, 1977 (Andrews, D.)
Good Idea! *See* It Seemed Like a Good Idea at the Time, 1975
Good Indian, 1913 (Mix)
Good King Wenceslas, 1994 (Fontaine)
Good Little Devil, 1914 (Pickford)
Good Luck, Miss Wyckoff, 1979 (Malone; Pleasence)
Good Luck, Mr. Yates, 1943 (Trevor)
Good Man in Africa, 1994 (Connery)
Good Medicine, 1929 (Horton)
Good Men and True, 1922 (Carey)
Good Morning. *See* Ohayo, 1959
Good Morning, Babilonia, 1987 (Scacchi)
Good Morning Doctor. *See* You Belong to Me, 1941
Good Morning, Miss Dove, 1955 (Jones, Jennifer)
Good Morning, Vietnam, 1987 (Whitaker; Williams, R.)
Good Mother, 1988 (Bellamy; Keaton, D.; Neeson; Robards)
Good Neighbor Sam, 1964 (Lemmon; Robinson, E.; Schneider)
Good Night, Nurse!, 1918 (Arbuckle; Keaton, B.)
Good Old Boy, 1988 (O'Sullivan)
Good Old Boys, 1995 (Jones, T.; Spacek)
Good Old School Days. *See* Those Were the Days, 1940
Good Old Soak, 1937 (Beery)
Good People's Sunday. *See* Domenica della buona gente, 1953
Good Sam, 1948 (Constantine)
Good Soup. *See* Bonne Soupe, 1964
Good Sport, 1984 (Remick)
Good, The Bad, and the Ugly. *See* **Buono, il bruto, il cattivo**, 1966
Good Time Girl, 1948 (Dors; Lom)
Good Times, 1967 (Cher; Sanders)
Good to Go, 1986 (Huston, A.)

Good Wife, 1986 (Neill)
Good-for-Nothing. *See* His New Profession, 1914
Goodbye Again, 1933 (Blondell)
Goodbye Again, 1961 (Bergman; Brynner; Montand; Perkins)
Goodbye and Amen. *See* Goodbye e Amen, 1977
Goodbye Charlie, 1964 (Burstyn; Curtis, T.; Matthau; Reynolds, D.)
Goodbye, Columbus, 1969 (Midler)
Goodbye e Amen, 1977 (Cardinale)
Goodbye Gemini, 1970 (Redgrave, M.)
Goodbye Girl, 1977 (Dreyfuss)
Goodbye, Hello. *See* Anata to watashi no ai-kotoba: Sayonara, konnichiwa, 1959
Goodbye, Mr. Chips, 1939 (Donat; Garson; Henreid; Mills)
Goodbye, Mr. Chips, 1969 (O'Toole; Redgrave, M.)
Goodbye, My Fancy, 1951 (Crawford, J.; Young, R.)
Goodbye, My Lady, 1956 (Brennan; Poitier)
Goodbye Raggedy Ann, 1971 (Farrow; Sheen)
Goodbye Summer, 1914 (Talmadge)
Goodfellas, 1990 (De Niro; Jackson, S.; Pesci)
Goodnight Vienna, 1932 (Buchanan; Neagle)
Goof on the Roof, 1953 (Three Stooges)
Goofs and Saddles, 1937 (Three Stooges)
Goose Alone in the World, 1961 (Lee, B.)
Goose and the Gander, 1935 (Francis)
Goose de riche, 1938 (Brasseur)
Goose Step. *See* Hitler, Beast of Berlin, 1939
Goose Steps Out, 1942 (Ustinov)
Gopi, 1970 (Kumar)
Gor, 1988 (Palance; Reed)
Gorath. *See* Yosei Gorath, 1962
Gordon, il Pirato Nero, 1961 (Price)
Gorge Trave. *See* Zeugin aus der Hölle, 1965
Gorgeous Hussy, 1936 (Barrymore, L.; Calhern; Crawford, J.; Stewart; Taylor, R.)
Gorgon, 1964 (Cushing; Lee, C.)
Gorgona, 1942 (Brazzi)
Gorilla, 1927 (Pidgeon)
Gorilla, 1931 (Pidgeon)
Gorilla, 1939 (Lugosi)
Gorilla, 1988 (Mueller-Stahl)
Gorilla at Large, 1954 (Bancroft; Cobb; Marvin)
Gorillas in the Mist, 1988 (Weaver)
Gorille vous salue bien, 1958 (Vanel)
Gorky Park, 1982 (Marvin; Hurt, W.)
Gorp, 1980 (Quaid)
Gorre Sarri, 1913 (Mozhukin)
Goryachie dyenechki, 1935 (Cherkassov)
Gospa, 1995 (Sheen)
Gospel According to Vic, 1985 (Mirren)
Gospodjica doktor—Spijunka bez imena. *See* Fräulein Doktor, 1968
Gösta Berlings Saga, 1924 (Garbo)
Gösta Berlings Saga, 1986 (Andersson, H.)
Gotham, 1988 (Jones, T.)
Goto, île d'amour, 1968 (Brasseur)
Gotter der Pest, 1969 (Schygulla)
Göttin der Rache. *See* Kali-Yug, la dea della vendetta, 1963
Götz von Berlichigen, 1925 (Rasp)
Government Girl, 1943 (De Havilland; Moorehead)
Governor's Double, 1911 (White)
Goyokin, 1969 (Tsukasa)
Goyosen, 1927 (Hasegawa)
Gozonji asumaotoko, 1939 (Hasegawa)
Grace Quigley. *See* Ultimate Solution of Grace Quigley, 1984
Graduate, 1967 (Bancroft; Dreyfuss; Hoffman)
Graduation, 1973 (Lancaster)
Graf Sylvains Rache, 1919 (Nielsen)
Graf von Cagliostro, 1920 (Veidt)
Graf von Essex, 1922 (Kortner; Krauss)
Grafin von Rathenow, 1973 (Vogler)
Graft, 1915 (Carey)
Graft, 1931 (Karloff)

Grain de sable, 1964 (Brasseur)
Grain de sable, 1983 (Seyrig)
Gran bollito, 1978 (Von Sydow)
Gran duelo, 1972 (Van Cleef)
Gran Fiesta, 1987 (Julia)
Gran hotel, 1944 (Cantinflas)
Gran varietà, 1954 (Sordi)
Gran vita. *See* Grande Vie, 1960
Grand Amour de Beethoven, 1936 (Barrault; Dalio)
Grand Blond avec une chaussure noire, 1972 (Blier)
Grand Bluff, 1957 (Constantine)
Grand Canyon, 1991 (Kline; Martin, S.)
Grand Canyon Trial, 1948 (Rogers, R.)
Grand chef, 1959 (Cervi; Fernandel)
Grand Combat, 1942 (Berry)
Grand Délire, 1974 (Huppert)
Grand Départ, 1971 (Hayden)
Grand Duchess and the Waiter, 1926 (Menjou)
Grand Duel. *See* Gran duelo, 1972
Grand Escogriffe, 1976 (Montand)
Grand Escroc, 1963 (Seberg)
Grand Frère, 1982 (Depardieu)
Grand Hotel, 1932 (Barrymore, J.; Barrymore, L.; Beery; Crawford, J.; Garbo)
Grand Hotel. *See* Menschen im Hotel, 1960
Grand Illusion. *See* **Grande Illusion**, 1937
Grand Isle, 1992 (Burstyn)
Grand Jeu, 1934 (Rosay; Vanel)
Grand Jeu, 1954 (Arletty; Lollobrigida)
Grand Larceny, 1988 (Jourdan; Sharif)
Grand Maneuver. *See* Grandes Manoeuvres, 1955
Grand nord. *See* Tashunga, 1995
Grand Old Girl, 1935 (MacMurray)
Grand Pardon II, 1993 (Walken)
Grand Passion, 1918 (Chaney)
Grand Passion. *See* Grande Passion, 1929
Grand Patron, 1951 (Fresnay)
Grand Prix, 1966 (Garner; Mifune; Montand; Saint)
Grand Restaurant, 1966 (Blier)
Grand Silence. *See* Grande silenzio, 1968
Grand Slam, 1933 (Lukas; Young, L.)
Grand Slam. *See* Ad Ogni Costo, 1968
Grand Slam Opera, 1936 (Keaton, B.)
Granddaughter of Dracula. *See* Nocturna, 1979
Grande Attacco, 1977 (Huston, J.; Fonda, H.)
Grande aurora, 1946 (Brazzi)
Grande avventura, 1953 (Cervi)
Grande Bagarre de Don Camillo. *See* Don Camillo e l'onorevole Peppone, 1955
Grande Bouffe, 1973 (Mastroianni; Noiret; Piccoli)
Grande Bourgeoise. *See* Fatti di gente perbene, 1974
Grande Carnaval, 1983 (Noiret)
Grande condottieri, 1968 (Rey)
Grande Délire, 1975 (Seberg)
Grande Fausto, 1994 (Ganz)
Grande frousse, 1964 (Barrault)
Grande giuoco. *See* Grand Jeu, 1954
Grande guerra, 1959 (Gassman; Mangano; Sordi)
Grande Guerre. *See* Grande querra, 1959
Grande Illusion, 1937 (Dalio; Fresnay; Gabin; Modot)
Grande Mare, 1930 (Chevalier; Colbert)
Grande Passion, 1929 (Dagover)
Grande querra, 1959 (Blier)
Grande ritorno di Django, 1987 (Pleasence)
Grande scrofa nera, 1972 (Cuny)
Grande silenzio, 1968 (Kinski)
Grande Strada Azzura. *See* Lunga strada azzura, 1958
Grande Trouille, 1974 (Cushing; Valli)
Grande Vadrouille. *See* Don't Look Now, We're Being Shot At, 1966
Grande Vie, 1960 (Masina)
Grandes Familles, 1958 (Blier; Brasseur; Gabin)
Grandes Manoeuvres, 1955 (Bardot; Morgan; Philipe)

Grandes Personnes, 1961 (Presle; Seberg)
Grandeur et Decadence d'un petit commerce du cinéma, 1986 (Léaud)
Grandeur nature, 1973 (Piccoli)
Grandfather's Journey. *See* Morfars Resa, 1993
Grandi Cacciatori, 1990 (Keitel)
Grandma's Boy, 1922 (Lloyd)
Grandpa, 1989 (Ustinov)
Grands, 1936 (Vanel)
Grands Chemins, 1962 (Aimée)
Grands ducs, 1996 (Noiret)
Grands Seigneurs. *See* Gentleman d'Epsom, 1962
Grandview, U.S.A., 1984 (Curtis, J.; Leigh, Jennifer Jason)
Granges brûlées, 1973 (Delon)
Granica, 1977 (Łomnicki)
Granitsa, 1935 (Cherkassov)
Grant Wood, 1950 (Fonda, H.)
Grapes of Wrath, 1940 (Bond; Carradine; Fonda, H.; Marsh)
Grasp of Greed, 1916 (Chaney)
Grass Country Goes Dry, 1914 (Beery)
Grass Harp, 1995 (Lemmon; Matthau; Spacek; Steenburgen)
Grass Is Greener, 1960 (Grant, C.; Kerr; Mitchum)
Grasshopper. *See* Poprigunya, 1955
Grasshopper, 1970 (Cotten)
Grateful Outcast, 1912-13 (White)
Grausame Freundin, 1932 (Rasp)
Grausige Nächte, 1921 (Krauss)
Graustark, 1925 (Talmadge)
Grave Robbers from Outer Space. *See* Plan Nine from Outer Space, 1959
Graveside Story. *See* Comedy of Terrors, 1964
Graveyard. *See* Persecution, 1974
Gray Horizon, 1919 (Hayakawa)
Gray Lady Down, 1978 (Heston)
Graziella, 1925 (Artaud)
Grease, 1978 (Blondell; Travolta)
Grease II, 1982 (Pfeiffer)
Greased Lightning, 1977 (Pryor)
Great! *See* Troppo forte, 1986
Great Adventure, 1921 (Barrymore, L.)
Great Adventure, 1976 (Palance)
Great Adventure. *See* Adventurers, 1950
Great American Beauty Contest, 1973 (Jourdan)
Great American Broadcast, 1941 (Faye)
Great American Cowboy, 1974 (McCrea)
Great American Fourth of July and Other Disasters, 1982 (Dillon)
Great American Pastime, 1956 (Miller)
Great American Tragedy, 1972 (Woods)
Great Balloon Adventure. *See* Olly, Olly, Oxen Free, 1977
Great Balls of Fire!, 1989 (Quaid; Ryder)
Great Bank Hoax. *See* Great Georgia Bank Hoax, 1977
Great Bank Robbery, 1969 (Jaffe; Novak)
Great Battle. *See* Grande attaco, 1977
Great Catherine, 1967 (Hawkins; Moreau; O'Toole)
Great Chase, 1963 (Gish)
Great Conqueror's Concubine. *See* Xi chu bawang, 1994
Great Dan Patch, 1949 (Brennan)
Great Dawn. *See* Grande aurora, 1946
Great Deception, 1926 (Rathbone)
Great Dictator, 1940 (Chaplin, C.; Goddard)
Great Divide, 1925 (Beery)
Great Divide, 1930 (Loy)
Great Escape, 1963 (Attenborough; Bronson; Coburn, J.; Garner; McQueen; Pleasence)
Great Escape II: The Untold Story, 1988 (Pleasence)
Great Expectations, 1946 (Guinness; Mills)
Great Expectations, 1974 (Quayle; Mason; Roberts, R.)
Great Flamarion, 1945 (Duryea)
Great Flirtation, 1934 (Menjou)
Great Frenzy. *See* Grande Délire, 1975
Great Game, 1930 (Harrison)
Great Game, 1952 (Dors)
Great Garrick, 1937 (De Havilland; Horton; Turner, L.)

Great Gatsby, 1926 (Powell, W.)
Great Gatsby, 1949 (Ladd; Winters)
Great Gatsby, 1974 (Dern; Farrow; Redford)
Great Georgia Bank Hoax, 1977 (Meredith)
Great Gilbert and Sullivan. *See* Story of Gilbert and Sullivan, 1953
Great Guns, 1941 (Laurel and Hardy; Ladd; Marsh)
Great Guy, 1936 (Cagney)
Great Hotel Murder, 1935 (McLaglen)
Great Houdinis, 1976 (Cushing; Gordon; O'Sullivan)
Great Hunter. *See* Grandi Cacciatori, 1990
Great Ice Ripoff, 1974 (Cobb)
Great Impersonation, 1942 (Bellamy)
Great Imposter, 1960 (Curtis, T.; Malden; Massey; O'Brien, E.)
Great John L., 1944 (Darnell)
Great K & A Train Robbery, 1926 (Mix)
Great Kankinsky, 1995 (Harris, R.)
Great Leap, 1914 (Crisp)
Great Lie, 1941 (Astor; Davis, B.; McDaniel)
Great Love, 1918 (Gish)
Great Lover, 1931 (Dunne; Menjou)
Great Lover, 1949 (Hope)
Great Man, 1956 (Ferrer)
Great Man Votes, 1939 (Barrymore, J.)
Great Man's Lady, 1942 (McCrea; Stanwyck)
Great Manhunt. *See* State Secret, 1950
Great McGonagall, 1974 (Sellers)
Great Missouri Raid, 1950 (Bond)
Great Moment, 1920 (Swanson)
Great Moment, 1945 (Carey; McCrea)
Great Moments in Aviation, 1993 (Hurt, J.; Redgrave, V.)
Great Mouse Detective, 1986 (Price)
Great Muppet Caper, 1981 (Bacall; Cleese; Falk; Ustinov)
Great Northfield, Minnesota Raid, 1972 (Duvall; Robertson)
Great O'Malley, 1937 (Bogart; Crisp)
Great Outdoors, 1988 (Candy)
Great Post Office Robbery, 1993 (Nowicki)
Great Prince Shan, 1924 (Hayakawa)
Great Question, 1983 (Reed)
Great Race, 1965 (Curtis, T.; Falk; Lemmon; Wood)
Great Redeemer, 1920 (Gilbert)
Great Rupert, 1950 (Durante)
Great St. Louis Bank Robbery, 1958 (McQueen)
Great Santini, 1979 (Duvall)
Great Schnozzle. *See* Palooka, 1934
Great Scout and Cathouse Thursday, 1976 (Marvin; Reed)
Great Sinner, 1949 (Barrymore, E.; Douglas, Melvyn; Gardner; Huston, W.; Moorehead; Peck)
Great Sioux Massacre, 1965 (Cotten)
Great Smokey Roadblock, 1978 (Fonda, H.; Sarandon)
Great Spy Chase. *See* Barbouzes, 1964
Great Spy Mission. *See* Operation Crossbow, 1965
Great Szu. *See* Wielki Szu, 1983
Great Train Robbery, 1978 (Connery; Sutherland)
Great Waldo Pepper, 1975 (Redford; Sarandon)
Great Wall. *See* Shin no shi-kotei, 1962
Great Waltz, 1938 (Rainer)
Great Waltz, 1972 (Brazzi)
Great War. *See* Grande querra, 1959
Great While It Lasted, 1915 (Lloyd)
Great White Hope, 1970 (Dalio; Jones, James Earl)
Great White Hype, 1996 (Jackson, S.)
Great Wind Cometh, 1984 (Minnelli)
Great Ziegfeld, 1936 (Loy; Powell, W.; Rainer)
Greater Glory, 1926 (Karloff)
Greater Influence, 1912-13 (White)
Greatest, 1977 (Borgnine; Duvall; Jones, James Earl)
Greatest Gift, 1974 (Ford, G.)
Greatest Love. *See* Europa '51, 1951
Greatest Power, 1917 (Barrymore, E.)
Greatest Question, 1919 (Gish)

Greatest Show on Earth, 1952 (Crosby; Grahame; Heston; Hope; Lamour; O'Brien, E.; Stewart; Wilde)

Greatest Story Ever Told, 1965 (Ferrer; Heston; Landau; Lansbury; McDowall; Mineo; Pleasence; Poitier; Rains; Von Sydow; Wayne; Winters)

Greatest Thing in Life, 1918 (Gish)

Greatest Thing that Almost Happened, 1977 (Jones, James Earl)

Greco, 1966 (Rey)

Greed in the Sun. See Cent Mille Dollars au Soleil, 1963

Greedy, 1994 (Douglas, K.)

Greek Tycoon, 1978 (Quinn)

Greeks Had a Word for It, 1932 (Blondell; Grable)

Green Berets, 1968 (Pryor; Wayne)

Green Card, 1990 (Depardieu)

Green Carnation. See Trials of Oscar Wilde, 1960

Green Cockatoo, 1937 (Mills; Withers)

Green Dolphin Street, 1947 (Turner, L.)

Green Fire, 1954 (Granger)

Green Fire, 1954 (Kelly, Grace)

Green for Danger, 1946 (Howard, T.)

Green Ghost. See Unholy Night, 1929

Green Glove, 1951 (Ford, G.)

Green Grass of Wyoming, 1948 (Coburn, C.; McDowall)

Green Grow the Rushes, 1951 (Burton)

Green Hell, 1940 (Bennett; Price; Sanders)

Green Henry. See Grüne Heinrich, 1993

Green Hornet, 1939 (Ladd)

Green Ice, 1981 (Sharif)

Green Journey. See Love She Sought, 1990

Green Light, 1937 (Flynn)

Green Man, 1956 (Terry-Thomas)

Green Man, 1991 (Finney)

Green Mansions, 1959 (Cobb; Hayakawa; Hepburn, A.; Perkins)

Green Murder Case, 1929 (Powell, W.)

Green Native Country. See Midorino furusato, 1946

Green Promise, 1949 (Brennan; Wood)

Green Room. See Chambre verte, 1978

Green Scarf, 1954 (Redgrave, M.)

Green Serpent. See Zelenyi Zmii, 1926

Green Years, 1946 (Coburn, C.)

Greene Murder Case, 1929 (Arthur)

Green-Eyed Devil, 1914 (Gish)

Greengage Summer, 1961 (Darrieux; York)

Greenwich Village, 1944 (Ameche; Holliday; Miranda)

Greetings, 1969 (De Niro)

Gregor Marold, 1918 (Kortner)

Grekh, 1916-17 (Mozhukin)

Gremlins II: The New Batch, 1990 (Lee, C.)

Grendel, Grendel, Grendel, 1981 (Ustinov)

Grenzfeuer, 1934 (Rasp)

Greyfriar's Bobby, 1961 (Crisp)

Greyhounds, 1994 (Coburn, J.)

Greystoke: The Legend of Tarzan, Lord of the Apes, 1984 (Close; Richardson, R.)

Gribiche, 1925 (Rosay)

Gribouille, 1937 (Blier; Dalio; Morgan; Raimu)

Gridiron Flash, 1935 (Dumont)

Grido, 1957 (Valli)

Griffin and Phoenix: A Love Story, 1976 (Falk)

Grifters, 1990 (Huston, A.)

Grillon du foyer, 1923 (Boyer)

Grim Prairie Tales, 1990 (Jones, James Earl)

Grind, 1915 (Chaney)

Gringalet, 1946 (Vanel)

Grip of Fear. See Experiment in Terror, 1962

Grip of Jealousy, 1916 (Chaney)

Grip of the Strangler. See Haunted Strangler, 1958

Grips, Grunts, and Groans, 1937 (Three Stooges)

Grisbi. See Touchez pas au grisbi, 1953

Grisou, 1938 (Blier; Brasseur)

Grit, 1924 (Bow)

Grizzly Gulch Chariot Race, 1915 (Mix)

Grocery Clerk's Romance, 1912 (Normand)

Grønkøbings glade gavtyve, 1925 (Madsen and Schenstrøm)

Groom Wore Spurs, 1951 (Rogers, G.)

Groove Room, 1974 (Dors)

Gros Lot, 1933 (Fernandel)

Grosse Atlantik, 1962 (Welles)

Grosse Fall, 1944 (Fröhlich)

Grosse Fatigue, 1994 (Noiret)

Grosse Gafahr, 1915 (Kortner)

Grosse König, 1942 (Fröhlich; Wegener)

Grosse Licht, 1920 (Jannings)

Grosse Mandarin, 1949 (Wegener)

Grosse Sehnsucht, 1930 (Dagover; Kortner; Rasp; Veidt)

Grosse Tête, 1962 (Constantine)

Großtadtschmetterling, 1929 (Wong)

Grotesque, 1995 (Bates, A.)

Ground Zero, 1987 (Pleasence)

Groundhog Day, 1993 (Murray)

Groundhogs. See Marmottes, 1993

Group Picture with Lady. See Gruppenbild mit Dame, 1977

Growing Up. See Faustine et le bel été, 1971

Growing Up. See Takekurabe, 1955

Growing Years, 1951 (Fonda, H.)

Grudge, 1915 (Hart)

Gruft mit dem Räselschloss, 1964 (Kinski)

Grumpier Old Men, 1995 (Ann-Margret; Lemmon; Loren; Matthau; Meredith)

Grumpy, 1930 (Lukas)

Grumpy Old Men, 1993 (Ann-Margret; Lemmon; Matthau; Meredith)

Grüne Heinrich, 1993 (Sanda)

Gruppenbild mit Dame, 1977 (Schneider)

Gruppo di famiglia in un interno, 1974 (Cardinale; Lancaster; Sanda; Mangano)

Guadalcanal Diary, 1943 (Quinn)

Guappi, 1973 (Cardinale)

Guard That Girl, 1935 (Bond)

Guardia, guardia scelta, brigadiere e maresciallo, 1956 (Cervi; Fabrizi; Sordi)

Guardian, 1984 (Sheen)

Guardie e ladri, 1951 (Fabrizi)

Guarding Tess, 1994 (Cage; MacLaine)

Gubijinso, 1984 (Ryu)

Guddobai, 1949 (Mori; Takamine)

Guerillas. See American Guerilla in the Philippines, 1950

Guérillera, 1982 (Cassel)

Guerilleros. See I briganti italiani, 1961

Guérisseur, 1954 (Marais)

Guerra continua, 1962 (Palance; Reggiani)

Guerra de los pasteles, 1943 (Armendáriz)

Guerra e pace. See War and Peace, 1956

Guerra segreta. See Guerre secrète, 1966

Guerre des karts. See Grosse Tête, 1962

Guerre des valses. See Walzerkrieg, 1933

Guerre est finie, 1966 (Bujold; Montand; Piccoli; Thulin)

Guerre la plus glorieuse, 1989 (Huppert; Josephson)

Guerre Lasse, 1988 (Baye)

Guerre secrète, 1966 (Fonda, H.; Gassman; Girardot; Kinski; Ryan, R.)

Guerriers et captives, 1989 (Caron; Sanda)

Guerrilleros. See I briganti italiani, 1961

Guess Who's Coming to Dinner, 1967 (Poitier; Hepburn, K.; Tracy)

Guest. See Caretaker, 1963

Guest in the House, 1944 (Baxter; Bellamy; Wilde)

Guest Wife, 1945 (Ameche; Colbert)

Guests of the Nation, 1935 (Cusack)

Gueule d'amour, 1937 (Gabin)

Gueule de l'emploi, 1973 (Gélin; Presle)

Gueule ouverte, 1974 (Baye)

Gueux au paradis, 1945 (Fernandel; Raimu)

Guglielmo Tell, 1949 (Cervi)

Guide, 1965 (Anand)

Guide for the Married Man, 1967 (Ball; Jaffe; Kelly, Gene; Mansfield; Matthau; Terry-Thomas)

Guidizio universale, 1961 (Mangano; Palance)

Guignol, marionnette de France, 1943 (Fernandel)
Guignolo, 1980 (Belmondo)
Guile of Women, 1921 (Rogers, W.)
Guilietta e Romeo, 1911 (Bertini)
Guilt Is Not Mine. *See* Ingiusta condanna, 1952
Guilt of Janet Ames, 1947 (Douglas, Melvyn; Russell, R.)
Guilty as Charged, 1932 (McLaglen)
Guilty as Charged, 1992 (Steiger)
Guilty by Suspicion, 1991 (De Niro)
Guilty Conscience, 1985 (Hopkins, A.)
Guilty Generation, 1931 (Karloff; Young, R.)
Guilty Hands, 1931 (Barrymore, L.; Francis)
Guilty Ones, 1916 (Laurel and Hardy)
Guilty until Proven Innocent, 1991 (Sheen)
Guinea Pig, 1948 (Attenborough)
Gulag, 1985 (McDowell)
Gulliver's Travels, 1977 (Harris, R.)
Gulliver's Travels, 1996 (Chaplin, G.; Gielgud; O'Toole; Sharif; Steenburgen)
Gumball Rally, 1976 (Julia)
Gumshoe, 1971 (Finney)
Gun. *See* Dio, sei proprio un padreterno, 1973
Gun. *See* Arma, 1978
Gun Battle at Monterey, 1957 (Van Cleef; Hayden)
Gun Crazy. *See* Talent for Loving, 1969
Gun Fighter, 1917 (Hart)
Gun Fightin' Gentleman, 1919 (Carey)
Gun for a Coward, 1957 (MacMurray)
Gun Fury, 1953 (Marvin)
Gun Glory, 1957 (Granger)
Gun Law, 1919 (Carey)
Gun Law, 1938 (Bond)
Gun Moll. *See* Jigsaw, 1949
Gun Moll. *See* Poopsie, 1974
Gun o' Gunga Din, 1911 (White)
Gun Packer, 1919 (Carey)
Gun Pusher. *See* Gun Packer, 1919
Gun Riders. *See* Five Bloody Graves, 1970
Gun Runner. *See* Santiago, 1956
Gun Runners, 1958 (Sloane)
Gun the Man Down, 1956 (Dickinson)
Gunbatsu, 1970 (Mifune; Shimura)
Gunfight, 1971 (Douglas, K.)
Gunfight at Dodge City, 1959 (McCrea)
Gunfight at Sandoval, 1959 (Duryea; Douglas, K.; Hopper; Lancaster; Van Cleef)
Gunfighter, 1950 (Malden; Marsh; Peck)
Gunfighters, 1947 (Scott, R.)
Gung Ho, 1986 (Keaton, M.; Turturro; Yamamura)
Gung Ho!, 1943 (Mitchum; Scott, R.)
Gunga Din, 1939 (Fontaine; Grant, C.; Jaffe; McLaglen)
Gunkan sudeni kemuri nashi, 1950 (Yamamura)
Gunpoint! *See* At Gunpoint!, 1955
Gunro no machi, 1952 (Yamamura)
Gunrunner, 1989 (Costner)
Guns A-Poppin', 1957 (Three Stooges)
Guns A' Blazing. *See* Law and Order, 1932
Guns and Guitars, 1936 (Autry)
Guns at Batasi, 1964 (Attenborough; Farrow; Hawkins)
Guns for San Sebastian, 1968 (Jaffe; Quinn)
Guns, Girls, and Gangsters, 1959 (Van Cleef)
Guns in the Afternoon. *See* **Ride the High Country**, 1961
Guns of Darkness, 1962 (Caron; Niven)
Guns of Diablo, 1964 (Bronson)
Guns of Honor. *See* Floating Outfit: Trigger Fast, 1994
Guns of Loos, 1928 (Carroll)
Guns of Navarone, 1961 (Baker; Harris, R.; Niven; Papas; Peck; Quayle; Quinn)
Guns of the Magnificent Seven, 1969 (Rey)
Guns of the Timberland, 1960 (Ladd)
Guns of Zangara, 1960 (Van Cleef)
Gunsight Ridge, 1957 (McCrea)

Günstling von Schönbrunn, 1929 (Dagover)
Gus and the Anarchists, 1915 (Laurel and Hardy)
Gusanos no Llevan Bufanda, 1991 (McDowall; Perkins)
Gusher, 1913 (Normand)
Gutter. *See* Dobu, 1954
Guy de Maupassant, 1978 (Gélin)
Guy Named Joe, 1943 (Barrymore, L.; Bond; Dunne; Tracy; Williams, E.)
Guy Who Came Back, 1951 (Bennett; Darnell)
Guyana Tragedy: The Story of Jim Jones, 1980 (Jones, James Earl)
Guyana: Cult of the Damned, 1980 (Cotten)
Guys and Dolls, 1955 (Brando; Sidney)
Gyangu chushingura, 1963 (Yamamura)
Gycklarnas afton, 1953 (Andersson, H.; Björnstrand)
Gypped in the Penthouse, 1955 (Three Stooges)
Gypsy, 1962 (Malden; Russell, R.; Wood)
Gypsy, 1993 (Midler)
Gypsy and the Gentleman, 1958 (Mercouri)
Gypsy Blood. *See* Zügelloses Blut, 1917
Gypsy Colt, 1954 (Bond; Van Cleef)
Gypsy Girl. *See* Sky West and Crooked, 1966
Gypsy Moths, 1969 (Hackman; Kerr; Lancaster)
Gypsy Queen, 1913 (Arbuckle; Normand)
H + 2, 1971 (Lancaster)
H. M. Pulham, Esq., 1941 (Lamarr; Coburn, C.; Gardner; Young, R.)
H.M.S. Defiant, 1962 (Bogarde; Guinness)
Ha fatto una signora, 1939 (Valli)
Haadsaa, 1983 (Patil)
Hääyö. *See* Noc Poslubna, 1959
Habeus Corpus, 1928 (Laurel and Hardy)
Habit of Happiness, 1916 (Fairbanks; Menjou)
Habit vert, 1937 (Berry; Blier)
Habitantes de la casa deshabitada, 1958 (Rey)
Habitation of Dragons, 1992 (O'Sullivan)
Habrichka el hashemersh, 1972 (Hawkins)
Haghard and Signe. *See* Rode kappe, 1967
Haha, 1929 (Takamine)
Haha, 1958 (Kyo)
Haha nareba onna nareba, 1952 (Yamada)
Haha no ai, 1935 (Hasegawa; Takamine)
Haha no chizu, 1942 (Mori)
Haha no hatsukoi, 1954 (Kagawa)
Haha no saigetsu, 1965 (Tanaka)
Haha no uta, 1938 (Tanaka)
Haha san-nin, 1958 (Yamada)
Haha to ko, 1938 (Tanaka)
Haha-tsubaki, 1950 (Yamamura)
Haha yo kimi no na o kegasu nakare, 1928 (Tanaka)
Hahako-gusa, 1959 (Tanaka; Yamamura)
Hahako-zo, 1956 (Yamada)
Hai hun, 1957 (Zhao Dan)
Hail Caesar, 1994 (Jackson, S.)
Hail Hero, 1969 (Kennedy)
Hail, Hero!, 1969 (Douglas, Michael)
Hail, Mafia. *See* Je vous salue, Mafia, 1965
Hail Mary. *See* Je vous salue, Marie, 1985
Haine, 1979 (Kinski)
Hairy Ape, 1944 (Hayward)
Hairyozuma shimatsu-ki. *See* Joi-uchi, 1967
Hai-Tang, 1930 (Wong)
Haitoku no mesu, 1961 (Yamamura)
Haka o kowazuya, 1934 (Ryu)
Hakai, 1948 (Mori)
Hakoiri musume, 1935 (Tanaka)
Hakone fuun-roku, 1952 (Yamada)
Hakuchi, 1951 (Hara; Mifune; Mori; Shimura)
Hakuchu no ketto, 1950 (Yamamura)
Hakugy, 1953 (Hara)
Hakuji no hito, 1957 (Yamamura)
Halbzart, 1959 (Schneider)
Half a Bride, 1928 (Constantine; Lombard)
Half a Loaf of Kung Fu, 1980 (Chan)

Half a Man, 1925 (Laurel and Hardy)
Half a Sinner, 1934 (Brennan; McCrea; Rooney)
Half Angel, 1936 (Carradine)
Half Angel, 1951 (Cotten; Young, L.)
Half Breed, 1916 (Fairbanks)
Half Human, 1957 (Carradine)
Half Moon Street, 1986 (Caine; Weaver)
Half Way to Heaven, 1929 (Arthur; Lukas)
Half-Breed, 1952 (Young, R.)
Half-Nelson, 1985 (Martin, D.)
Half-shot Shooters, 1936 (Three Stooges)
Halfway House, 1944 (Rosay)
Half-Wit's Holiday, 1947 (Three Stooges)
Hallelujah, 1993 (Jones, James Earl)
Hallelujah, I'm a Bum, 1933 (Jolson; Langdon)
Hallelujah Trail, 1965 (Lancaster; Landau; Pleasence; Remick)
Halliday Brand, 1957 (Bond; Cotten)
Hallo, Afrika forude, 1929 (Madsen and Schenstrøm)
Halloween, 1978 (Curtis, J.; Pleasence)
Halloween. See Zaduszki, 1961
Halloween II, 1981 (Curtis, J.; Pleasence)
Halloween IV: The Return of Michael Myers, 1988 (Pleasence)
Halloween V: The Revenge of Michael Myers, 1989 (Pleasence)
Halloween VI: The Curse of Michael Myers, 1995 (Pleasence)
Hallroom Girls, 1912-13 (White)
Halls of Anger, 1970 (Bridges)
Halls of Montezuma, 1950 (Malden; Palance; Widmark)
Hallucinations sadiques, 1969 (Gélin)
Hallucinators. See Naked Zoo, 1971
Ham and Eggs at the Front, 1927 (Loy)
Ham Artist. See Face on the Bar-Room Floor, 1914
Hambone and Hillie, 1984 (Gish)
Hamlet, 1920 (Nielsen)
Hamlet, 1939 (Gielgud; Hawkins)
Hamlet, 1948 (Cushing; Gielgud; Lee, C.; Olivier; Quayle)
Hamlet, 1960 (Schell, Maximilian)
Hamlet, 1964 (Burton; Gielgud)
Hamlet, 1969 (Hopkins, A.; Huston, A.)
Hamlet, 1976 (Mirren)
Hamlet, 1990 (Bates, A.; Bonham-Carter; Close; Gibson; Kline)
Hamlet, 1996 (Branagh; Christie; Depardieu; Gielgud; Heston; Lemmon; Mills; Williams, R.)
Hamlet, Prince of Denmark, 1980 (Bloom)
Hammerhead, 1968 (Dors)
Hammersmith Is Out, 1972 (Burton; Raft; Taylor, E.; Ustinov)
Hamsun, 1996 (Von Sydow)
Han, Hun og Hamlet, 1922 (Madsen and Schenstrøm)
Han, Hun og Hamlet, 1932 (Madsen and Schenstrøm)
Hana, 1941 (Tanaka)
Hana aru zasso, 1939 (Tanaka)
Hana futatabi, 1956 (Yamamura)
Hana hiraku, 1955 (Yamada)
Hana no Banzui-in, 1959 (Yamada)
Hana no bojo, 1958 (Tsukasa)
Hana no kenka-jo, 1953 (Hasegawa)
Hana no Kodo-kan, 1953 (Hasegawa)
Hana no nagawakizashi, 1954 (Hasegawa)
Hana no saku ie, 1963 (Yamamura)
Hana no sugao, 1949 (Okada; Yamamura)
Hana no tsukihi, 1949 (Yamada)
Hana no wataridori, 1956 (Hasegawa)
Hana no yukyo-den, 1958 (Hasegawa)
Hanahagi sensei to Santa, 1952 (Yamada)
Hanakago no uta, 1936 (Tanaka; Takamine)
Hanako-sen, 1943 (Takamine)
Hanakurabe tanuki-goten, 1949 (Kyo)
Hanano sandogasa, 1954 (Hasegawa)
Hananoren, 1959 (Tsukasa)
Hanaoko Seishu no tsuma, 1967 (Takamine)
Hanataba no yume, 1938 (Takamine)
Hanauta ojosan, 1938 (Tanaka)

Hanayome kaigi, 1956 (Tsukasa)
Hanayome karuta, 1937 (Takamine)
Hanayome kurabe, 1935 (Tanaka)
Hanayome no negoto, 1933 (Tanaka)
Hanayome no negoto, 1935 (Hasegawa)
Hand, 1981 (Caine)
Hand in Glove, 1994 (Gielgud)
Hand of Death. See Countdown in Kung Fu, 1975
Hand of Destiny, 1914 (White)
Handcuffs or Kisses?, 1921 (Colman)
Handful of Clouds. See Doorway to Hell, 1930
Handful of Dust, 1988 (Guinness; Huston, A.)
Handful of Love. See Handfull kärlek, 1973
Handful of Time. See Handfull Tid, 1989
Handfull kärlek, 1973 (Thulin)
Handfull Tid, 1989 (York)
Handle With Care, 1965 (Lancaster)
Händler der vier Jahreszeiten, 1971 (Schygulla)
Handmaid's Tale, 1990 (Dunaway; Duvall)
Hands across the Border, 1943 (Rogers, R.)
Hands across the Table, 1935 (Bellamy; Lombard; MacMurray)
Hands of a Stranger, 1987 (Whitaker)
Hands of Cormac Joyce, 1972 (Cusack)
Hands of Orlac, 1960 (Lee, C.; Pleasence)
Hands of Orlac. See Orlacs Hände, 1925
Hands Off, 1921 (Mix)
Hands over the City. See Mani sulla citta, 1963
Hands Up! See Rece do gory, 1967
Handsome Gigolo, Poor Gigolo, 1930 (Barrymore, J.)
Handy Andy, 1934 (Rogers, W.; Taylor, R.)
Handy Man, 1918 (Laurel and Hardy)
Handy Man, 1923 (Laurel and Hardy)
Hang 'em High, 1967 (Dern; Eastwood; Hopper)
Hanged Man, 1965 (O'Brien, E.)
Hanging Tree, 1959 (Constantine; Malden; Schell, Maria; Scott, G.)
Hängivelse, 1965 (Thulin)
Hangman, 1959 (Taylor, R.)
Hangman's House, 1928 (McLaglen; Wayne)
Hangman's Knot, 1952 (Marvin; Scott, R.)
Hangmen Also Die, 1943 (Brennan)
Hangover. See Female Jungle, 1956
Hangover Square, 1944 (Darnell; McDowall; Sanders)
Hanjo, 1961 (Yamamura)
Hanky Panky, 1982 (Poitier; Widmark; Wilder)
Hanna's War, 1988 (Burstyn; Elliott; Pleasence)
Hannah and Her Sisters, 1985 (Allen; Caine; Farrow; Hershey; O'Sullivan; Turturro; Von Sydow; Wiest)
Hannibal. See Annibale, 1960
Hannibal Brooks, 1969 (Reed)
Hannie Caulder, 1971 (Borgnine; Dors; Lee, C.; Welch)
Hanno rubato un tram, 1955 (Fabrizi)
Hanover Street, 1979 (Ford, H.)
Hanran, 1954 (Kagawa)
Hans Christian Andersen, 1952 (Kaye)
Hans Christian Andersen's Thumbelina, 1994 (Hurt, J.)
Hans engelska fru, 1926 (Dagover)
Hans le Marin, 1948 (Dalio)
Hans the Sailor. See Hans le Marin, 1948
Hans Trutz im Schlaraffenland, 1917 (Rasp; Wegener)
Hans Westmar, 1933 (Wegener)
Hansom Cabman, 1924 (Langdon)
Hanussen, 1955 (Kinski)
Hanussen, 1989 (Brandauer; Josephson)
Hanya: Portrait of a Dance Legend, 1984 (Andrews, J.)
Haomen Yeyan, 1991 (Gong Li)
Happening, 1966 (Dunaway; Homolka; Quinn)
Happidrome, 1943 (Buchanan)
Happiest Days of Your Life, 1950 (Rutherford)
Happiest Millionaire, 1967 (Garson; MacMurray; Page)
Happily Ever After. See C'era una volta, 1967
Happily Ever After, 1985 (DeVito)

Happily Ever After, 1990 (McDowell)
Happiness, 1917 (Gilbert)
Happiness. *See* Schastye, 1932
Happiness Ahead, 1934 (Powell, D.)
Happiness Cage. *See* Mind Snatchers, 1971
Happiness in Twenty Years, 1971 (Welles)
Happiness of Us Alone. *See* Namonaku mazushiku utsukushiku, 1961
Happy Alexander. *See* Alexandre le bienheureux, 1968
Happy and Joyous Story of Colinot, the Man Who Pulls Up Skirts. *See*
    Histoire très bonne et très joyeuse de Colinot Trousse-Chemise, 1973
Happy Anniversary, 1959 (Niven)
Happy as the Grass Was Green, 1973 (Page)
Happy Birthday. *See* Forever My Heart, 1954
Happy Birthday Harry!, 1981 (Terry-Thomas)
Happy Birthday to Me, 1981 (Ford, G.)
Happy Birthday, Wanda June, 1971 (Steiger; York)
Happy Days, 1929 (Rogers, W.; Gaynor; Grable)
Happy Easter. *See* Joyeuses Pâques, 1984
Happy Ending, 1924 (Buchanan)
Happy Ending, 1969 (Rowlands)
Happy Ever After, 1954 (Fitzgerald; Niven)
Happy Go Lovely, 1951 (Niven)
Happy Go Lucky, 1942 (Powell, D.)
Happy Is the Bride, 1958 (Terry-Thomas)
Happy Lads of the Fleet. *See* Flottans glada gossar, 1954
Happy Land, 1943 (Ameche; Carey; Wood)
Happy Landing, 1938 (Ameche; Henie)
Happy Mother's Day—Love George, 1973 (Neal)
Happy New Year, 1987 (Falk)
Happy Road, 1956 (Cassel; Chevalier; Redgrave, M.)
Happy Thieves, 1962 (Harrison; Hayworth; Valli)
Happy Time, 1952 (Boyer; Dalio; Jourdan)
Happy Together, 1989 (Pitt)
Happy Warrior, 1917 (Howard, L.)
Happyakuman-goku ni idomu otoko, 1961 (Yamamura)
Här börjar äventyret, 1965 (Andersson, H.)
Här har du ditt liv, 1966 (Björnstrand; Von Sydow)
Här kommer vi, 1947 (Björnstrand)
Harakiri, 1919 (Dagover)
Harakiri. *See* Battle, 1934
Hard-Boiled, 1926 (Mix)
Hard Contract, 1969 (Coburn, J.; Hayden; Meredith; Remick)
Hard Country, 1981 (Basinger)
Hard, Fast, and Beautiful, 1951 (Lupino; Trevor)
Hard Guy, 1930 (Tracy)
Hard Luck, 1921 (Keaton, B.)
Hard Promises, 1992 (Spacek)
Hard Target, 1993 (Van Damme)
Hard Times, 1975 (Bronson; Coburn, J.)
Hard Times, 1994 (Bates, A.)
Hard Times for Vampires. *See* Tempi duri per vampiri, 1959
Hard to Get, 1938 (De Havilland; Powell, D.)
Hard to Handle, 1933 (Cagney)
Hard Way, 1942 (Lupino)
Hard Way, 1979 (Van Cleef)
Hard Way, 1991 (Woods)
Hardboiled Rose, 1929 (Loy)
Hardcore, 1979 (Scott, G.)
Hardcore, 1982 (McDowell)
Hardcore Life. *See* Hardcore, 1979
Harder They Fall, 1956 (Bogart; Steiger)
Hardly Working, 1981 (Lewis, Jerry)
Hardys Ride High, 1939 (Rooney)
Hare-kosode, 1961 (Hasegawa)
Hare Rama Hare Krishna, 1971 (Anand)
Harem, 1985 (Gardner; Kingsley; Kinski; Sharif)
Harikiri shacho, 1956 (Tsukasa)
Harikomi, 1958 (Takamine)
Harlem, 1993 (Snipes)
Harlem Globetrotters on Gilligan's Island, 1981 (Landau)
Harlem in Heaven, 1938 (Robinson, B.)

Harlem Nights, 1989 (Aiello; Murphy; Pryor)
Harlequin, 1980 (Crawford, B.)
Harley Davidson and the Marlboro Man, 1991 (Rourke)
Harlow, 1965 (Lansbury; Rogers, G.)
Harlow: The Blond Bombshell, 1993 (Stone)
Harmony Parade. *See* Pigskin Parade, 1936
Harnessing Peacocks, 1993 (Mills)
Harold and Maude, 1971 (Cusack; Gordon)
Harold Lloyd's Funny Side of Life, 1966 (Lloyd)
Harold Lloyd's World of Comedy, 1962 (Lloyd)
Harold's Bad Man, 1915 (Mix)
Harper, 1966 (Bacall; Leigh, Janet; Newman; Winters)
Harrad Experiment, 1973 (Griffith)
Harriet Craig, 1950 (Crawford, J.)
Harry and Son, 1984 (Barkin; Freeman; Newman; Woodward)
Harry and the Hendersons, 1987 (Ameche)
Harry and Tonto, 1974 (Burstyn)
Harry and Walter Go to New York, 1976 (Caan; Caine; Gould; Keaton, D.)
Harry Black, 1958 (Granger)
Harry in Your Pocket, 1973 (Coburn, J.; Pidgeon)
Harry Tracy, 1982 (Dern)
Harry's War, 1981 (Page)
Hart to Hart, 1979 (McDowall)
Hart to Hart: Crimes of the Hart, 1994 (Ayres)
Hart to Hart: Home Is Where the Hart Is, 1994 (McDowall; O'Sullivan)
Haru no tawamure, 1949 (Takamine)
Haru no uzumaki, 1954 (Kyo)
Haru No Kane, 1986 (Okada)
Haru ramman, 1966 (Mori)
Haru ranman, 1968 (Tsukasa)
Haruka nari haha no kuni, 1950 (Yamada)
Harukana Jidai No Daidan O, 1995 (Okada)
Harukanari haha no kuni, 1950 (Kyo)
Harukanaru soro, 1980 (Tsukasa)
Harukoma no Uta, 1986 (Kagawa)
Harum Scarum, 1965 (Presley)
Harusugata gonin-otoko, 1936 (Hasegawa)
Harvest. *See* Regain, 1937
Harvey, 1951 (Stewart)
Harvey, 1972 (Stewart)
Harvey Girls, 1946 (Charisse; Garland; Lansbury)
Has Anybody Seen My Gal?, 1952 (Coburn, C.; Dean; Hudson)
Hasard et l'amour, 1913 (Linder)
Hasard et la violence, 1974 (Montand)
Hasegawa Roppa no Iemitsu to Hikosa, 1941 (Hasegawa)
Hasenjagd—Vor lauter Feigheit gibt es kein Erbarmen, 1994 (Vogler)
Hash-House Hero. *See* Star Boarder, 1914
Hasimura Togo, 1917 (Hayakawa)
Hasshu kyokakujin, 1936 (Shimura)
Hasty Heart, 1950 (Neal; Reagan)
Hat, 1964 (Moore, Dudley)
Hat. *See* Shlyapa, 1981
Hat Check Girl, 1932 (Rogers, G.)
Hatamoto kenka-daka, 1961 (Yamamura)
Hatamoto to Banshiin: Otoko no Taiketsu, 1960 (Yamamura)
Hatari!, 1962 (Wayne)
Hatarnegol, 1971 (Topol)
Hatchet Man, 1932 (Robinson, E.; Young, L.)
Hateful Dead, 1989 (McDowell)
Hater of Men, 1917 (Gilbert)
Haters. *See* Grudge, 1915
Hatfields and the McCoys, 1975 (Palance)
Hatful of Rain, 1957 (Saint)
Hathat Dekha, 1967 (Chatterjee)
Hatred. *See* Mollenard, 1938
Hats Off, 1927 (Laurel and Hardy)
Hatsugaro-ondo, 1936 (Shimura)
Hatsukoi no haru, 1933 (Takamine)
Hatsukoi san-nin masuko, 1955 (Tsukasa)
Hatter's Castle, 1941 (Mason; Kerr)
Hauen Sie ab mit Heldentum. *See* Kinder, Mütter, und ein General, 1954

Haunted Gold, 1932 (Wayne)
Haunted Hat, 1915 (Laurel and Hardy)
Haunted Honeymoon, 1940 (Montgomery)
Haunted Honeymoon, 1986 (Wilder)
Haunted Honeymoon. See Busman's Honeymoon, 1940
Haunted House, 1921 (Keaton, B.)
Haunted Palace, 1964 (Price)
Haunted Spooks, 1920 (Lloyd)
Haunted Strangler, 1958 (Karloff)
Haunted World. See Ercole al centro della terra, 1961
Haunting, 1963 (Bloom)
Haunting of Julia, 1981 (Farrow)
Haunting of Rosalind, 1973 (Sarandon)
Haus am Meer, 1971 (Schygulla)
Haus der Lüge, 1925 (Krauss)
Haus der tausend Freuden, 1967 (Price)
Haus des Lebens, 1952 (Fröhlich; Rasp)
Haus zum Mond, 1920 (Kortner)
Haut bas fragile, 1995 (Karina)
Haut des marches, 1983 (Darrieux; Presle)
Haut-le-Vent, 1944 (Vanel)
Haut les mains! See Pleine bagarre, 1961
Hautes solitudes, 1974 (Seberg)
Hautnah, 1986 (Mueller-Stahl)
Havana, 1990 (Arkin; Julia; Olin; Redford)
Havana Widows, 1933 (Blondell)
Havarist, 1984 (Vogler)
Have Rocket, Will Travel, 1959 (Three Stooges)
Have You Nothing to Declare? See Vous n'avez rien a déclarer?, 1937
Havets Son, 1949 (Thulin)
Having Babies III, 1978 (Cooper)
Having Wonderful Time, 1938 (Ball; Miller; Rogers, G.)
Havsbandet, 1971 (Andersson, H.; Von Sydow)
Hawaii, 1966 (Andrews, J.; Hackman; Harris, R.; Midler; Von Sydow)
Hawaii Calls, 1938 (Bond)
Hawaii Five-O, 1968 (Ayres)
Hawaiians, 1970 (Chaplin, G.; Heston)
Hawk, 1993 (Mirren)
Hawk. See Ride Him Cowboy, 1932
Hawk the Slayer, 1980 (Palance)
Hawkins on Murder, 1973 (Stewart)
Hay que matar a B., 1973 (Audran; Meredith; Neal)
Hay Wire. See Hog Wild, 1930
Hayabusa daimyo, 1961 (Yamamura)
Hayseed, 1919 (Arbuckle; Keaton, B.)
Hayseed Romance, 1935 (Keaton, B.)
Haystacks and Steeples, 1916 (Swanson)
Haywire, 1980 (Remick; Robards)
Hazard, 1948 (Goddard)
Hazard of Hearts, 1987 (Bonham-Carter; Granger)
Hazel Kirke, 1916 (White)
Hazel's People. See Happy as the Grass Was Green, 1973
Hazukashiiyume, 1927 (Tanaka)
He, 1933 (Rosay)
He. See Rosier de Madame Husson, 1932
He Ain't Heavy. See Road Home, 1995
He Comes Up Smiling, 1918 (Fairbanks)
He Cooked His Goose, 1952 (Three Stooges)
He Couldn't Say No, 1938 (Wyman)
He Did and He Didn't, 1916 (Arbuckle; Normand)
He Found a Star, 1941 (Greenwood)
He Knows You're Alone, 1980 (Hanks)
He Laughs Last, 1920 (Laurel and Hardy)
He Leads, Others Follow, 1919 (Lloyd)
He Loved an Actress, 1938 (Langdon)
He Loved Her So. See Twenty Minutes of Love, 1914
He Married His Wife, 1940 (McCrea)
He Ran All the Way, 1951 (Garfield; Winters)
He Rides Tall, 1963 (Duryea)
He Said, She Said, 1991 (Bacon; Stone)
He Stayed for Breakfast, 1940 (Douglas, Melvyn; Young, L.)

He Was Her Man, 1934 (Blondell; Cagney)
He Who Gets Slapped, 1924 (Chaney; Shearer)
He Who Must Die. See Celui qui doit mourir, 1957
He Winked and Won, 1917 (Laurel and Hardy)
He Would a Hunting Go, 1913 (Arbuckle)
Head, 1968 (Hopper; Mature; Nicholson)
Head above Water, 1996 (Costner; Keitel)
Head Guy, 1930 (Langdon)
Head Man, 1928 (Young, L.)
Head of the Family. See Padre di famiglia, 1967
Head Office, 1986 (DeVito)
Head On, 1980 (Huston, J.)
Head over Heels, 1922 (Menjou; Normand)
Head over Heels, 1979 (Grahame)
Headin' East, 1937 (Three Stooges)
Headin' South, 1918 (Fairbanks)
Heading Home, 1990 (Oldman)
Headless Horseman, 1922 (Rogers, W.)
Headline Shooter, 1933 (Bellamy)
Headline Woman, 1935 (Bond)
Headlines of Destruction. See Je suis un sentimental, 1955
Heads, 1994 (McDowall)
Heads or Tails. See Pile ou face, 1980
Heads Up, Charly. See Kopf hoch, Charly!, 1926
Headstrong. See Bille en tête, 1989
Healer, 1935 (Bellamy; Rooney)
Health, 1979 (Garner; Keitel)
Health, 1980 (Bacall; Jackson, G.)
Health for the Nation, 1940 (Richardson, R.)
Healthy and Happy, 1919 (Laurel and Hardy)
Healthy, Wealthy, and Dumb, 1938 (Three Stooges)
Heap Big Chief, 1919 (Lloyd)
Hear 'em Rave, 1918 (Lloyd)
Hear No Evil, 1993 (Sheen)
Hearse, 1980 (Cotten)
Hearst and Davies Affair, 1985 (Mitchum)
Heart and Soul, 1917 (Bara)
Heart Beat, 1980 (Nolte; Spacek)
Heart Buster, 1924 (Mix)
Heart Condition, 1990 (Hoskins; Washington)
Heart in Pawn, 1919 (Hayakawa)
Heart Is a Lonely Hunter, 1968 (Arkin)
Heart o' the Hills, 1919 (Gilbert; Pickford)
Heart of a Child, 1920 (Nazimova)
Heart of a Child, 1958 (Pleasence)
Heart of a Man, 1959 (Neagle)
Heart of a Nation. See Untel Père et fils, 1943
Heart of a Siren, 1925 (Webb)
Heart of Darkness, 1994 (Malkovich)
Heart of Justice, 1993 (Hopper; Price)
Heart of Maryland, 1927 (Loy)
Heart of Midnight, 1988 (Leigh, Jennifer Jason)
Heart of Paris. See Gribouille, 1937
Heart of Salome, 1926 (Pidgeon)
Heart of Show Business, 1957 (Chevalier; Crosby; Lancaster)
Heart of Texas Ryan, 1917 (Mix)
Heart of the Dragon, 1986 (Chan)
Heart of the Golden West, 1942 (Rogers, R.)
Heart of the Matter, 1953 (Elliott; Finch; Howard, T.; Schell, Maria)
Heart of the Rio Grande, 1942 (Autry)
Heart of the Rockies, 1951 (Rogers, R.)
Heart of the Sheriff, 1915 (Mix)
Heart of the West, 1975 (Pleasence)
Heart of Variety, 1969 (Heston)
Heart of Wetona, 1918 (Talmadge)
Heart to Heart, 1928 (Astor)
Heart Trouble, 1928 (Langdon)
Heart's Desire, 1915 (Mix)
Heartbeat. See Schpountz, 1937
Heartbeat, 1946 (Menjou; Rathbone; Rogers, G.)
Heartbreak Hotel, 1988 (Weld)

Heartbreak House, 1986 (Harrison)
Heartbreak Ridge, 1986 (Eastwood)
Heartburn, 1986 (Nicholson; Streep)
Heartland, 1985 (Hopkins, A.)
Hearts Adrift, 1914 (Pickford)
Hearts and Masks, 1914 (Mix)
Hearts and Minds. *See* Uomo da rispettare, 1974
Hearts and Saddles, 1917 (Mix)
Hearts and Sparks, 1916 (Swanson)
Hearts and Spurs, 1925 (Lombard)
Hearts Divided, 1936 (Davies; Horton; McDaniel; Powell, D.; Rains)
Hearts in Bondage, 1936 (Ayres)
Hearts in Springtime. *See* Glamour Boy, 1941
Hearts of Age, 1934 (Welles)
Hearts of Darkness: A Filmmaker's Apocalypse, 1991 (Fishburne)
Hearts of Steel. *See* Stalowe serca, 1947
Hearts of the Jungle, 1915 (Mix)
Hearts of the West, 1975 (Arkin; Bridges)
Hearts of the World, 1918 (Gish)
Hearts Up, 1921 (Carey)
Hearts upon the Sea. *See* Cuori su mare, 1950
Heartsounds, 1984 (Garner)
Heat, 1987 (Reynolds, B.)
Heat, 1995 (De Niro; Pacino; Voight)
Heat and Dust, 1983 (Christie; Scacchi)
Heat of Anger, 1971 (Cobb; Hayward)
Heat of Desire. *See* Plein sud, 1980
Heat Wave!, 1974 (Ayres)
Heat Wave, 1990 (Jones, James Earl)
Heathers, 1989 (Ryder)
Heat's On, 1943 (West)
Heatwave, 1983 (Davis, J.)
Heaven, 1987 (Keaton, D.)
Heaven and Earth, 1993 (Jones, T.; Reynolds, D.)
Heaven and Hell. *See* Tengoku to-jigoku, 1963
Heaven and Pancakes. *See* Himmel och pannkaka, 1959
Heaven Can Wait, 1943 (Ameche; Calhern; Coburn, C.; Tierney)
Heaven Can Wait, 1978 (Beatty; Christie; Mason)
Heaven Fell That Night. *See* Bijoutiers du clair de lune, 1957
Heaven Help Us, 1985 (Sutherland)
Heaven Knows, Mr. Allison, 1957 (Huston, J.; Kerr; Mitchum)
Heaven on Earth, 1931 (Ayres; Carradine)
Heaven with a Barbed Wire Fence, 1939 (Bond; Ford, G.)
Heaven with a Gun, 1969 (Ford, G.; Hershey)
Heaven's Gate, 1980 (Bridges; Cotten; Dafoe; Huppert; Hurt, J.; Rourke; Walken)
Heavenly Body, 1943 (Lamarr; Powell, W.)
Heavenly Daze, 1948 (Three Stooges)
Heavenly Pursuits. *See* Gospel According to Vic, 1985
Heavenly Sin. *See* Tengoku No Taizai, 1992
Heavens Above, 1963 (Sellers)
Heavy, 1995 (Winters)
Heavy Metal, 1981 (Candy)
Hebihime dochu, 1949 (Hasegawa; Kyo; Yamada)
Hebihime-sama, 1940 (Hasegawa; Yamada)
Hebihime-sama, 1951 (Hasegawa)
Hechizo tragico. *See* Incantesimo tragico, 1951
Hectic Days. *See* Goryachie dyenechki, 1935
Hedda, 1975 (Jackson, G.)
Hedda Gabler, 1924 (Nielsen)
Hedda Hopper's Hollywood No. 6, 1942 (Bennett; Colbert)
Heera Panna, 1973 (Anand)
Heidi, 1937 (Temple)
Heidi, 1968 (Redgrave, M.; Schell, Maximilian)
Heidi, 1993 (Neal; Robards)
Heidi Chronicles, 1995 (Curtis, J.)
Height of Glory. *See* Na viershina slavy, 1916
Heiji happy-aku-ya-cho, 1949 (Hasegawa)
Heilige Flamme, 1931 (Fröhlich)
Heilige Lüge, 1927 (Homolka)
Heimkehr, 1928 (Fröhlich)

Heimkehr des alten Herrn, 1977 (Schygulla)
Heimlich nach St. Pauli, 1964 (Mansfield)
Heimliche Ehen, 1956 (Mueller-Stahl)
Heinze's Resurrection, 1913 (Normand)
Heiratsvermittlerin, 1975 (Schell, Maria)
Heiress, 1949 (Clift; De Havilland; Hopkins, M.; Richardson, R.)
Heiresses. *See* Orökseg, 1980
Heirs. *See* Herederos, 1969
Heissen Blut, 1910 (Nielsen)
Heist. *See* $, 1971
Hélas pour moi, 1993 (Depardieu)
Held by the Enemy, 1920 (Crisp)
Heldorado, 1946 (Rogers, R.)
Helen Keller: The Miracle Continues, 1984 (Cushing)
Helen Morgan Story, 1957 (Newman)
Helen of Troy. *See* Sköna Helena, 1951
Helen of Troy, 1955 (Baker; Bardot)
Helen's Babies, 1924 (Bow; Horton)
Helena, 1990 (Winters)
Hélène, 1936 (Barrault)
Helicon, 1991 (Coburn, J.)
Helicopter Spies, 1968 (Carradine)
Hell. *See* Enfer, 1994
Hell Below, 1933 (Durante; Huston, W.; Montgomery; Young, R.)
Hell below Zero, 1954 (Baker; Ladd)
Hell Bent, 1918 (Carey)
Hell Bent for Glory. *See* Lafayette Escadrille, 1957
Hell Divers, 1931 (Beery; Gable; Young, R.)
Hell Drivers, 1957 (Baker; Connery; Lom)
Hell Hound of Alaska. *See* Darkening Trail, 1915
Hell Hunters, 1988 (Granger)
Hell in Korea. *See* Hill in Korea, 1956
Hell in the City. *See* Nella città l'inferno, 1958
Hell in the Pacific, 1968 (Marvin; Mifune)
Hell Is a City, 1960 (Baker; Pleasence)
Hell Is for Heroes, 1962 (Coburn, J.; McQueen)
Hell Is Sold Out, 1951 (Attenborough; Lom; Zetterling)
Hell Morgan's Girl, 1916 (Chaney)
Hell on Frisco Bay, 1955 (Mansfield; Ladd; Robinson, E.; Wray)
Hell or High Water, 1954 (Widmark)
Hell-Roarin' Reform, 1919 (Mix)
Hell Ship Mutiny, 1957 (Carradine; Lorre)
Hell to Eternity, 1960 (Hayakawa)
Hell Town. *See* Born to the West, 1938
Hell with Heroes, 1968 (Cardinale)
Hellas, 1960 (Schell, Maria)
Hellbenders. *See* I crudeli, 1967
Hellcats of the Navy, 1957 (Reagan)
Helldorado, 1935 (Bellamy)
Heller in Pink Tights, 1960 (Loren; Novarro; O'Brien, M.; Quinn)
Heller Wahn, 1982 (Schygulla; Winkler; Vogler)
Hellfighters, 1968 (Wayne)
Hellfire Club, 1961 (Cushing)
Hellgate, 1952 (Bond; Hayden)
Hellinger's Law, 1981 (Penn)
Hellion, 1924 (Karloff)
Hello Actors Studio, 1987 (Burstyn; Newman; Wallach)
Hello Cheyenne, 1928 (Mix)
Hello, Dolly!, 1969 (Kelly, Gene; Matthau; Streisand)
Hello Down There, 1968 (Dreyfuss; Leigh, Janet; McDowall)
Hello Everybody!, 1933 (Scott, R.)
Hello Frisco, Hello, 1943 (Bond; Faye)
Hello God, 1958 (Flynn)
Hello Lafayette, 1926 (Arthur)
Hello London, 1958 (Henie)
Hello, Mabel!, 1914 (Normand)
Hello Pop, 1933 (Three Stooges)
Hello Trouble, 1913 (Beery)
Hello, Trouble, 1932 (Bond)
Hell's Angels, 1930 (Harlow)
Hell's Angels on Wheels, 1967 (Nicholson)

Hell's Bloody Devils, 1970 (Carradine; Crawford, B.)
Hell's Devils. *See* Hitler, Beast of Berlin, 1939
Hell's Half Acre, 1954 (Lanchester)
Hell's Heroes, 1930 (Huston, J.)
Hell's Hinges, 1916 (Gilbert; Hart)
Hell's House, 1932 (Davis, B.)
Hell's Kitchen, 1939 (Reagan)
Hellzapoppin', 1941 (Three Stooges)
Helmut Newton: Frames from the Edge, 1989 (Deneuve; Weaver)
Help! Help!, Hydrophobia!, 1913 (Arbuckle)
Help Wanted—Male, 1920 (Sweet)
Helpful Sisterhood, 1914 (Talmadge)
Helping Him Out, 1911 (White)
Helping Himself. *See* His New Profession, 1914
Helpmates, 1932 (Laurel and Hardy)
Helsinki Napoli: All Night Long, 1987 (Constantine)
Helter Skelter, 1949 (Terry-Thomas)
Hemingway's Adventures of a Young Man, 1962 (Kennedy; Newman; Wallach)
Hempas bar, 1977 (Andersson, H.)
Hen in the Wind. *See* Kaze no naka no mendori, 1948
Hennes melodi, 1940 (Björnstrand)
Hennessy, 1975 (Howard, T.; Remick; Steiger)
Henri Langlois, 1970 (Bergman; Deneuve; Gish)
Henriette Jacoby, 1918 (Veidt)
Henry & June, 1990 (Thurman)
Henry Angst, 1980 (Vogler)
Henry IV. *See* Enrico IV, 1984
Henry V, 1945 (Olivier)
Henry V, 1989 (Branagh; Thompson)
Henry VIII and His Six Wives, 1972 (Pleasence)
Her Awakening, 1911 (Normand)
Her Awakening, 1914 (Sweet)
Her Birthday Present, 1914 (Crisp)
Her Bounty, 1914 (Chaney)
Her Boy Friend, 1924 (Laurel and Hardy)
Her Brother. *See* Ototo, 1960
Her Cardboard Lover, 1928 (Davies)
Her Cardboard Lover, 1942 (Sanders; Shearer; Taylor, R.)
Her Choice, 1915 (Laurel and Hardy)
Her Condoned Sin. *See* Judith of Bethulia, 1914
Her Darkest Hour, 1911 (Pickford)
Her Deceitful Lover. *See* Mabel's Awful Mistake, 1913
Her Decision, 1918 (Swanson)
Her Dilemma. *See* Confessions of a Co-ed, 1931
Her Double Life, 1916 (Bara)
Her Dramatic Debut. *See* Mabel's Dramatic Career, 1913
Her Enlisted Man. *See* Red Salute, 1935
Her Escape, 1914 (Chaney)
Her Father's Silent Partner, 1913 (Barrymore, L.; Crisp)
Her Favourite Husband, 1950 (Rutherford)
Her First Affair. *See* Premier rendez-vous, 1941
Her First Affaire, 1932 (Lupino)
Her First Beau, 1941 (Cooper)
Her First Biscuits, 1909 (Pickford)
Her First Romance, 1940 (Ladd)
Her First Romance, 1951 (O'Brien, M.)
Her Friend the Bandit, 1914 (Chaplin, C.; Normand)
Her Gilded Cage, 1922 (Swanson)
Her Grave Mistake, 1914 (Chaney)
Her Greatest Love, 1917 (Bara)
Her Heritage, 1919 (Buchanan)
Her Hero, 1911 (Talmadge)
Her Highness and the Bellboy, 1945 (Lamarr; Moorehead; Walker)
Her Honor, the Governor, 1926 (Karloff)
Her Husband Lies, 1937 (Calhern)
Her Husband's Affair, 1947 (Horton; Ball)
Her Husband's Trademark, 1922 (Swanson)
Her Jungle Love, 1938 (Lamour; Milland)
Her Kid Sister, 1912-13 (White)
Her Last Affaire, 1935 (Withers)

Her Life's Story, 1914 (Chaney)
Her Little Slipper, 1910-11 (White)
Her Love Story, 1924 (Swanson)
Her Majesty Love, 1931 (Fields, W. C.)
Her Man Gilbey. *See* English without Tears, 1944
Her Melody. *See* Hennes melodi, 1940
Her Mother's Necklace, 1914 (Crisp)
Her Necklace, 1912-13 (White)
Her New Hat, 1912-13 (White)
Her Night of Romance, 1925 (Colman)
Her Only Way, 1918 (Talmadge)
Her Panelled Door. *See* Woman with No Name, 1950
Her Photograph, 1910-11 (White)
Her Primitive Man, 1944 (Horton)
Her Private Life, 1929 (Pidgeon)
Her Reputation. *See* Broadway Bad, 1933
Her Secretary, 1912-13 (White)
Her Sister from Paris, 1925 (Colman)
Her Slight Mistake, 1915 (Mix)
Her Strange Desire. *See* Potiphar's Wife, 1931
Her Sweetheart. *See* Christopher Bean, 1933
Her Twelve Men, 1954 (Garson; Ryan, R.)
Her Twin Brother, 1912-13 (White)
Her Unwilling Husband, 1920 (Sweet)
Her Wedding Bell, 1913 (Sweet)
Her Wedding Night, 1930 (Bow)
Her Wild Oat, 1928 (Young, L.)
Herbe rouge, 1985 (Léaud)
Herbstsonate, 1978 (Bergman; Björnstrand; Josephson; Ullmann)
Hercule, 1938 (Berry; Fernandel)
Hercule ou l'incorruptible, 1938 (Brasseur)
Hercules and the Amazon Women, 1994 (Quinn)
Hercules and the Captive Women. *See* Ercole alla conquista di Atlantide, 1961
Hercules and the Circle of Fire, 1994 (Quinn)
Hercules and the Lost Kingdom, 1994 (Quinn)
Hercules at the Center of the Earth. *See* Ercole al centro della terra, 1961
Hercules in New York, 1970 (Schwarzenegger)
Hercules in the Maze of the Minotaur, 1994 (Quinn)
Hercules in the Underworld, 1994 (Quinn)
Here Come the Co-eds, 1945 (Abbott and Costello)
Here Come the Girls, 1918 (Lloyd)
Here Come the Girls, 1953 (Hope)
Here Come the Nelsons, 1952 (Hudson)
Here Come the Waves, 1944 (Crosby)
Here Comes Mr. Jordan, 1941 (Horton; Montgomery; Rains)
Here Comes Mr. Zerk, 1943 (Langdon)
Here Comes the Bride, 1919 (Barrymore, J.)
Here Comes the Groom, 1934 (Bond)
Here Comes the Groom, 1951 (Crosby; Lamour; Wyman)
Here Comes the Huggetts, 1948 (Dors)
Here Comes the Navy, 1934 (Cagney)
Here Is a Fountain. *See* Koko ni izuni ari, 1955
Here Is a Man. *See* All That Money Can Buy, 1941
Here Is My Heart, 1934 (Crosby)
Here Is Your Life. *See* Här har du ditt liv, 1966
Here We Come. *See* Här kommer vi, 1947
Here We Go 'Round the Mulberry Bush, 1967 (Elliott)
Herederos, 1969 (Léaud)
Heredity, 1912 (Carey)
Here's Las Vegas. *See* Spree, 1967
Here's Looking at You, Warner Bros., 1991 (Davis, B.; Hawn)
Here's the Point. *See* Ahí está el detalle, 1940
Here's to the Girls. *See* Ojosan kampai, 1949
Here's Your Life. *See* Här har du ditt liv, 1966
Heritage of the Desert, 1933 (Scott, R.)
Héritier, 1973 (Belmondo; Berry)
Héritier des Mondésir, 1939 (Fernandel)
Héritières. *See* Örökseg, 1980
Hermann und Dorothea von heute. *See* Liebesleute, 1935
Hermanos del hierro, 1963 (Armendáriz)
Hero, 1917 (Laurel and Hardy)

Hero, 1992 (Davis, G.; García; Hoffman)
Hero. *See* Bloomfield, 1971
Hero at Large, 1980 (Bacon)
Hero for Hire, 1990 (Welch)
Hero of Little Italy, 1913 (Carey; Sweet)
Hero of Our Time, 1991 (Hopper)
Hero's Island, 1961 (Oates; Mason; Stanton)
Heroes, 1916 (Laurel and Hardy)
Heroes. *See* Eroi, 1972
Heroes, 1977 (Field; Ford, H.)
Heroes and Sinners. *See* Héros sont fatigués, 1955
Heroes for Sale, 1933 (Barthelmess; Bond; Young, L.)
Heroes in Yellow and Blue. *See* Hjältar i gult och blått, 1940
Heroes of Desert Storm, 1992 (Bassett)
Heroes of Telemark, 1965 (Douglas, K.; Douglas, Michael; Harris, R.;
    Redgrave, M.)
Heroic Harold, 1912-13 (White)
Heroine of Mons, 1914 (Howard, L.)
Héroique Monsieur Boniface, 1949 (Fernandel)
Heros sont fatigués, 1955 (Montand)
Héros de la Marne, 1938 (Raimu)
Héros sont fatigués, 1955 (Félix)
Herostratus, 1967 (Mirren)
Herr Arnes penningar, 1954 (Andersson, B.)
Herr och fru Stockholm, 1921 (Garbo)
Herr Tartuff. *See* Tartuff, 1925
Herr über Leben und Tod, 1955 (Schell, Maria)
Herrin der Welt, 1959 (Presle; Cervi)
Herringbone Clouds. *See* Iwashigumo, 1958
Herrscher, 1937 (Jannings)
Hers to Hold, 1943 (Cotten; Durbin)
Herz geht vor Anker, 1940 (Fröhlich)
Herz kehrt Heim, 1956 (Schell, Maximilian)
Herz modern möbliert, 1940 (Fröhlich)
Herzbube, 1972 (Lollobrigida)
Herzog Ferrantes Ende, 1922 (Wegener)
He's a Cockeyed Wonder, 1950 (Rooney)
He's Not Your Son, 1984 (Malone)
Hesokuri shacho, 1956 (Tsukasa)
Het Gangstermeisje, 1967 (Volonté)
Het Verdriet Van Belgie, 1994 (Vogler)
Hets, 1944 (Björnstrand; Zetterling)
Hetszàzeves szerelem, 1921 (Lukas)
Heure de rêve, 1930 (Brasseur)
Heure exquise. *See* Nuit de Décembre, 1939
Heureux qui comme Ulysse, 1969 (Fernandel)
Heut' kommt's drauf an, 1933 (Rainer)
Hex, 1973 (Carradine)
Hex on Fogg's Millions, 1914 (Talmadge)
Hexen bis aufs Blutgeqvält. *See* Mark of the Devil, 1970
Hexer, 1932 (Rasp)
Hey! Hey! USA!, 1938 (McDowall)
Hey, Let's Twist, 1961 (Pesci)
Hey, Pop!, 1932 (Arbuckle)
Hey Rookie, 1944 (Miller)
Hey Stranger, 1994 (Schygulla)
Hey There!, 1918 (Lloyd)
Hi, Beautiful, 1944 (McDaniel)
Hi Diddle Diddle, 1943 (Menjou; Negri)
Hi mo tsuki, 1969 (Mori)
Hi, Mom!, 1970 (De Niro)
Hi, Nellie!, 1934 (Muni)
Hi no tori, 1950 (Hasegawa; Kyo)
Hi-sen-ryo, 1960 (Hasegawa; Kagawa)
Hibari no hanagata tantei gassen, 1958 (Yamamura)
Hibari no komori-uta, 1951 (Yamamura)
Hibari no zoku beranmee geisha, 1960 (Yamamura)
Hickey and Boggs, 1972 (Woods)
Hickory Hiram, 1918 (Laurel and Hardy)
Hidden Agenda, 1990 (Zetterling)
Hidden Fires, 1918 (Marsh)

Hidden Fortress. *See* Kakushi toride no san-akunin, 1958
Hidden Gold, 1933 (Mix)
Hidden Guns, 1956 (Carradine; Dickinson)
Hidden Letters, 1914 (Talmadge)
Hidden Master, 1940 (Cushing)
Hidden Pearls, 1918 (Hayakawa)
Hidden Power. *See* Sabotage, 1937
Hidden River. *See* Rio escondido, 1947
Hidden Room. *See* Obsession, 1948
Hidden Woman. *See* Escondida, 1955
Hide in Plain Sight, 1979 (Caan; Aiello)
Hide-Out, 1934 (Montgomery; O'Sullivan; Rooney)
Hideko no oendancho, 1940 (Takamine)
Hideko no shasho-san, 1941 (Takamine)
Hideko the Bus Conductor. *See* Hideko no shasho-san, 1941
Hideous Mutant Freekz. *See* Freaked, 1993
Hideout in the Alps. *See* Dusty Ermine, 1936
Hifazaat. *See* In Custody, 1994
Higan sen-nin giri, 1927 (Tanaka)
Higanbana, 1958 (Ryu; Tanaka)
Higegi no shogun Yamashita Yasubumi, 1953 (Hayakawa)
High and Dizzy, 1920 (Lloyd)
High and Low. *See* Tengoku to-jigoku, 1963
High and the Mighty, 1954 (Trevor; Wayne)
High Anxiety, 1977 (Brooks, M.)
High Bright Sun, 1964 (Bogarde; Elliott)
High Brow Stuff, 1924 (Rogers, W.)
High Cost of Loving, 1958 (Ferrer; Rowlands)
High Crime. *See* Polizia incrimina, la legge assolve, 1973
High Finance, 1933 (Lupino)
High Flight, 1956 (Milland)
High Flyers, 1938 (Dumont)
High Fury. *See* White Cradle Inn, 1947
High Heels. *See* Docteur Popaul, 1972
High Heels. *See* Tacones Lejanos, 1991
High Infidelity. *See* Alta infideltà, 1964
High Journey, 1959 (Welles)
High Noon, 1952 (Constantine; Kelly, Grace; Van Cleef)
High Plains Drifter, 1973 (Eastwood)
High Pressure, 1932 (Powell, W.)
High Risk, 1981 (Borgnine; Coburn, J.; Quinn)
High Rollers. *See* Bluff, 1976
High Rolling, 1977 (Davis, J.)
High Season, 1987 (Branagh; Papas)
High Sierra, 1941 (Bogart; Huston, J.; Kennedy; Lupino; Wilde)
High Sign, 1921 (Keaton, B.)
High Society, 1956 (Calhern; Crosby; Kelly, Grace; Sidney)
High Society Blues, 1930 (Gaynor)
High Speed, 1932 (Bond; Rooney)
High Spirits, 1988 (Neeson; O'Toole)
High Stakes, 1989 (Bates, K.)
High Steppers, 1926 (Astor; Del Rio)
High Tension, 1936 (McDaniel)
High Tide, 1987 (Davis, J.)
High Time, 1960 (Crosby; Weld)
High Treason, 1951 (Quinn)
High Treason. *See* Hochverrat, 1929
High Vermilion. *See* Silver City, 1951
High Voltage, 1929 (Lombard)
High Wall, 1947 (Taylor, R.; Marshall)
High, Wide, and Handsome, 1937 (Dunne; Lamour; Scott, R.)
High Wind in Jamaica, 1965 (Coburn, J.; Quinn)
Higher and Higher, 1943 (Morgan)
Higher Learning, 1995 (Fishburne)
Higher Than a Kite, 1943 (Three Stooges)
Highland Fling, 1948 (Cusack)
Highlander, 1986 (Connery)
Highlander II, 1991 (Connery)
Highly Dangerous, 1950 (Lockwood)
Highpoint, 1984 (Harris, R.)
Highway Dragnet, 1954 (Bennett)

Highway to Freedom. *See* Joe Smith, American, 1942
Highway West, 1941 (Kennedy)
Highwayman, 1951 (Coburn, C.)
Higuchi Ichiyo, 1939 (Takamine; Yamada)
Hiho, 1960 (Yamada)
Hijacking of the Achille Lauro, 1989 (Grant, L.; Malden)
Hijo del Pistolero, 1966 (Rey)
Hijo-toshi, 1960 (Tsukasa)
Hijos de Maria Morales, 1952 (Infante)
Hijosen no onna, 1933 (Ryu; Tanaka)
Hikage no musume, 1957 (Kagawa; Yamada)
Hikarigoke, 1991 (Okada; Ryu)
Hikaritokage, 1946 (Hara)
Hikaru umi, 1963 (Mori; Tanaka)
Hiking through Holland with Will Rogers, 1927 (Rogers, W.)
Hikinige, 1966 (Takamine; Tsukasa)
Hill, 1965 (Connery; Redgrave, M.)
Hill in Korea, 1956 (Baker; Caine; Shaw)
Hillbillys in a Haunted House, 1967 (Carradine; Rathbone)
Hills of Home, 1948 (Crisp; Leigh, Janet)
Hills of Utah, 1951 (Autry)
Hills Run Red. *See* Fiume di dollari, 1966
Himawari-musume, 1953 (Mifune)
Hime-yasha gyojo-ki, 1959 (Yamada)
Himegimi to ronin, 1953 (Kagawa)
Himetaru kakugo, 1943 (Hasegawa; Yamada)
Himeyuri Lily Tower. *See* Himeyuri ro to, 1953
Himeyuri ro to, 1953 (Kagawa; Okada)
Himitsu, 1952 (Tanaka)
Himmel och pannkaka, 1959 (Björnstrand)
Himmel og Helvede, 1988 (Andersson, H.)
Himmel über Berlin, 1987 (Falk; Ganz)
Hinarai naku sato, 1929 (Tanaka)
Hindenberg, 1975 (Scott, G.; Bancroft; Meredith)
Hindu, 1953 (Karloff)
Hindustan Hamara, 1950 (Anand)
Hinok butai, 1946 (Hasegawa; Yamada)
Hinrichtung, 1975 (Robards)
Hintertreppe, 1921 (Kortner)
Hip Action, 1933 (Fields, W. C.)
Hips, Hips, Hooray!, 1934 (Grable)
Hira aur Patthar, 1977 (Azmi)
Hirak Rajar Deshe, 1980 (Chatterjee)
Hirameku yaiba, 1926 (Tanaka)
Hirate Miki, 1951 (Yamamura)
Hirate Miki, 1954 (Yamada)
Hired and Fired, 1916 (Laurel and Hardy)
Hired Hand, 1971 (Oates)
Hired to Kill, 1989 (Ferrer)
Hired to Kill, 1991 (Reed)
Hired Wife, 1940 (Russell, R.)
Hireling, 1973 (Shaw)
Hiren hikui-zuka, 1931 (Hasegawa)
Hiroshima, 1953 (Yamada)
Hiroshima, mon amour, 1959 (Okada)
Hiroshima: Out of the Ashes, 1990 (Von Sydow)
His Affair. *See* This Is My Affair, 1937
His Alibi, 1916 (Arbuckle)
His and Hers, 1961 (Reed; Terry-Thomas)
His Athletic Wife, 1913 (Beery)
His Aunt Emma, 1912-13 (White)
His Awful Daughter, 1912-13 (White)
His Birth Right, 1918 (Hayakawa)
His Birthday, 1910-11 (White)
His Bridal Sweet, 1935 (Langdon)
His Brother's Wife, 1936 (Stanwyck; Taylor, R.)
His Butler's Sister, 1943 (Durbin)
His Daredevil Queen. *See* Mabel at the Wheel, 1914
His Day Out, 1918 (Laurel and Hardy)
His Debt, 1919 (Hayakawa)
His Diving Beauty. *See* Sea Nymphs, 1914

His Double Life, 1933 (Gish)
His Dress Shirt, 1911 (Pickford)
His Duty. *See* Man from Nowhere, 1915
His English Wife. *See* Hans engelska fru, 1926
His Ex Marks the Spot, 1940 (Keaton, B.)
His Excellency. *See* Ego prevoskhoditelstvo, 1927
His Father's Deputy, 1913 (Mix)
His Father's Son, 1917 (Barrymore, L.)
His Favorite Pastime, 1914 (Arbuckle; Chaplin, C.)
His Fight, 1914 (Mix)
His First Flame, 1927 (Langdon; Bellamy; Grant, C.)
His Girl Friday, 1940 (Russell, R.)
His Glorious Night, 1929 (Barrymore, L.; Gilbert)
His Greatest Bluff. *See* Seine grösster Bluff, 1927
His Heroic Action. *See* Ei gerochsky podvig, 1914
His Hour of Manhood, 1914 (Hart)
His Inspiration, 1913 (Barrymore, L.)
His Jonah Day, 1920 (Laurel and Hardy)
His Kind of Woman, 1951 (Mitchum; Price; Russell, J.)
His Lady. *See* When a Man Loves, 1927
His Lesson, 1914 (Crisp; Gish)
His Little Page, 1913 (Talmadge)
His Lordship's Dilemma, 1915 (Fields, W. C.)
His Lost Love, 1909 (Pickford)
His Majesty Bunker Bean. *See* Bunker Bean, 1936
His Majesty, King Ballyhoo. *See* Man braucht kein Geld, 1931
His Majesty O'Keefe, 1954 (Lancaster)
His Majesty, the American, 1919 (Fairbanks; Karloff)
His Marriage Mixup, 1935 (Langdon)
His Marriage Wow, 1925 (Langdon)
His Master's Voice, 1936 (Horton)
His Mother's Trust, 1914 (Crisp)
His Musical Career, 1914 (Chaplin, C.)
His Name Is Sukhe-Bator. *See* Ego zovut Sukhe-Bator, 1942
His New Job, 1915 (Chaplin, C.; Swanson)
His New Mama, 1924 (Langdon)
His New Profession, 1914 (Chaplin, C.)
His Night Out, 1915 (Purviance)
His Night Out, 1934 (Bond; Horton)
His Official Appointment, 1913 (Talmadge)
His Only Father, 1919 (Lloyd)
His Picture in the Papers, 1916 (Fairbanks)
His Prehistoric Past, 1914 (Chaplin, C.)
His Private Life, 1926 (Arbuckle)
His Private Life, 1928 (Menjou)
His Private Secretary, 1933 (Wayne)
His Reckless Fling. *See* His Favorite Pastime, 1914
His Regeneration, 1914 (Chaplin, C.)
His Rich Uncle, 1912-13 (White)
His Royal Flush. *See* Mr. "Silent" Haskins, 1915
His Royal Slyness, 1920 (Lloyd)
His Secretary, 1925 (Shearer)
His Silver Bachelorhood, 1913 (Talmadge)
His Sister's Kids, 1913 (Arbuckle)
His Supreme Moment, 1925 (Colman; Sweet; Wong)
His Sweetheart, 1917 (Crisp)
His Tiger Wife, 1928 (Menjou)
His Trysting Place, 1914 (Chaplin, C.; Normand)
His Unlucky Night, 1928 (Lombard)
His Wedding Night, 1917 (Arbuckle; Keaton, B.)
His Wife's Mistake, 1916 (Arbuckle)
His Wife's Stratagem, 1912-13 (White)
His Wife's Visitor, 1909 (Pickford)
His Woman, 1931 (Colbert; Constantine)
His Young Wife. *See* Miserie del signor Travet, 1946
Hissatsu shikake-nin, 1973 (Yamamura)
Hissatsu shikake-nin: Shinsetsu shikake-bari, 1974 (Yamamura)
Hissatsu shikaki-nin: Baiko ari-jigoku, 1973 (Yamamura)
Hissho-ka, 1944 (Tanaka)
Histoira de una traición, 1970 (Rey)
Histoire comique. *See* Félicie Nanteuil, 1942

Hollywood in Uniform, 1943 (Ford, G.; Gable)
Hollywood Knights, 1980 (Pfeiffer)
Hollywood Lights, 1932 (Arbuckle; Grable)
Hollywood Luck, 1932 (Arbuckle; Grable)
Hollywood Mavericks, 1990 (Hopper)
Hollywood on Parade, 1933 (Cagney; Keaton, B.; Rogers, G.; Three Stooges)
Hollywood on Parade Nos. 3-4, 1932 (Mix)
Hollywood on Parade No. 8, 1933 (Brown)
Hollywood on Parade, No. 9, 1933 (Rogers, G.)
Hollywood on Parade, No. 13, 1934 (Del Rio; Dressler)
Hollywood on Trial, 1977 (Huston, J.)
Hollywood or Bust, 1956 (Lewis, Jerry; Martin, D.)
Hollywood Park, 1946 (Grable)
Hollywood Party, 1934 (Durante; Laurel and Hardy; Three Stooges; Young, R.)
Hollywood Party, 1937 (Wong)
Hollywood Revue of 1929, 1929 (Barrymore, L.; Crawford, J.; Davies; Dressler; Gilbert; Laurel and Hardy; Keaton, B.; Shearer)
Hollywood Rodeo, 1949 (Wayne)
Hollywood Roundup, 1938 (Three Stooges)
Hollywood Story, 1951 (McCrea)
Hollywood Today Number Four, 1928 (Mix)
Hollywood Victory Caravan, 1945 (Crosby; Hope; Ladd)
Holy Matrimony, 1943 (Fields, G.)
Holy Matrimony, 1994 (Mueller-Stahl)
Holy Terror, 1931 (Bogart)
Homage at Siesta Time. See Homenaje a la hora de la siesta, 1962
Hombre, 1966 (March; Newman)
Hombre nuestro de Cada Dia, 1959 (Armendáriz)
Home Alone, 1990 (Candy; Pesci)
Home Alone 2: Lost in New York, 1992 (Pesci)
Home and the World. See Ghare Baire, 1984
Home at Seven, 1952 (Hawkins; Richardson, R.)
Home Cured, 1926 (Arbuckle)
Home Folks, 1912 (Barrymore, L.; Pickford)
Home for Christmas, 1990 (Rooney)
Home for the Holidays, 1972 (Brennan; Field)
Home for the Holidays, 1995 (Bancroft; Chaplin, G.; Foster; Hunter)
Home from the Hill, 1960 (Mitchum; Sloane)
Home Girl, 1928 (Hopkins, M.)
Home in Indiana, 1943 (Brennan; Bond)
Home in Oklahoma, 1946 (Rogers, R.)
Home in Wyomin', 1942 (Autry)
Home Is the Hero, 1959 (Kennedy)
Home Is Where the Heart Is. See Square Dance, 1987
Home Movies, 1980 (Douglas, K.)
Home of Our Own, 1993 (Bates, K.)
Home of the Hopeless, 1950 (Fonda, H.)
Home on the Prairie, 1939 (Autry)
Home on the Range, 1935 (Scott, R.)
Home, Sweet Home, 1910-11 (White)
Home, Sweet Home, 1914 (Crisp; Gish; Marsh; Sweet)
Home Sweet Homicide, 1946 (Scott, R.)
Home to Danger, 1951 (Baker)
Home to Stay, 1978 (Fonda, H.)
Home Town Story, 1951 (Crisp; Monroe)
Homeboy, 1989 (Rourke; Walken)
Homebreaker, 1919 (Valentino)
Homecoming. See Heimkehr, 1928
Homecoming, 1947 (Gable)
Homecoming, 1948 (Baxter; Turner, L.)
Homecoming, 1973 (Cusack)
Homecoming, 1994 (Papas)
Homecoming: A Christmas Story, 1971 (Neal)
Homeless, 1989 (Grant, L.)
Homenaje a la hora de la siesta, 1962 (Valli)
Homer and Eddie, 1989 (Goldberg)
Homes of Tipperary. See Knocknagow, 1918
Homesick for a Mountain Village, 1934 (Zhao Dan)
Homestretch, 1947 (O'Hara; Wilde)
Homeward Bound II: Lost in San Francisco, 1996 (Field)

Homeward Bound: The Incredible Journey, 1993 (Ameche; Field)
Homicide Bureau, 1938 (Hayworth)
Hommage irrespectueux comme tous les hommages, 1974 (Dalio)
Homme à abattre, 1937 (Berry; Dalio)
Homme à femmes, 1960 (Darrieux)
Homme à femmes, 1960 (Deneuve)
Homme à l'imperméable, 1957 (Blier; Fernandel)
Homme à la Buick, 1967 (Darrieux; Fernandel)
Homme à la cagoule noire. See Bête aux sept manteaux, 1936
Homme amoreux, 1987 (Cardinale; Curtis, J.; Scacchi)
Homme au chapeau rond, 1946 (Raimu)
Homme au crâne rasé, 1968 (Tyszkiewicz)
Homme aux clefs d'or, 1956 (Fresnay; Girardot)
Homme blesse, 1983 (Mueller-Stahl)
Homme de la Jamaique, 1950 (Brasseur)
Homme de Londres, 1943 (Berry; Modot)
Homme de ma vie, 1951 (Moreau)
Homme de Rio, 1964 (Belmondo)
Homme de trop, 1967 (Piccoli; Vanel)
Homme d'Istanbul. See Estambul 65, 1965
Homme du jour, 1936 (Chevalier)
Homme du Large, 1920 (Boyer)
Homme en colère, 1979 (Dickinson; Pleasence)
Homme est Mort, 1973 (Ann-Margret; Dickinson; Scheider)
Homme et l'enfant, 1956 (Constantine)
Homme et une femme, 1966 (Aimée)
Homme et une femme: vingt ans déjà, 1986 (Aimée; Morgan)
Homme nu, 1912-14 (Raimu)
Homme presse, 1977 (Delon)
Homme qui aimait les femmes, 1977 (Baye; Caron)
Homme qui cherche la verité, 1939 (Raimu)
Homme qui me plait, 1969 (Belmondo; Girardot)
Homme sans nom, 1932 (Fernandel)
Homme voilé, 1987 (Piccoli)
Hommes de Las Vegas. See Vegas 500 milliones, 1968
Hommes en blanc, 1955 (Moreau)
Homo eroticus, 1971 (Blier)
Homo Faber. See Voyager, 1991
Hondo, 1953 (Bond; Page; Wayne)
Honest, Decent and True, 1985 (Oldman)
Honest Hutch, 1920 (Rogers, W.)
Honey. See Dulce Piel de Mujer, 1978
Honey Pot, 1967 (Harrison; Hayward; Robertson; Smith)
Honeycomb. See Madriguera, 1969
Honeymoon, 1931 (Wray)
Honeymoon, 1947 (Temple)
Honeymoon. See Lune di miel, 1985
Honeymoon Academy, 1990 (Lee, C.)
Honeymoon for Three, 1915 (Evans)
Honeymoon for Three, 1941 (Wyman)
Honeymoon Hotel, 1964 (Lanchester)
Honeymoon in Bali, 1939 (Carroll; MacMurray)
Honeymoon in Vegas, 1992 (Bancroft; Caan; Cage)
Honeymoon Machine, 1961 (McQueen)
Honeymoon Trio, 1931 (Arbuckle)
Honeymoon with a Stranger, 1969 (Leigh, Janet)
Honeymoons. See Voyage des noces, 1975
Hong Faan Kui, 1995 (Chan)
Hong gaoliang, 1987 (Gong Li)
Hong Kong, 1951 (Reagan)
Honkers, 1972 (Coburn, J.)
Honkon no hoshi, 1962 (Yamamura)
Honkon no yoru, 1961 (Tsukasa)
Honky Tonk, 1941 (Gable; Trevor; Turner, L.)
Honky Tonk Freeway, 1981 (Page)
Honkytonk Man, 1982 (Eastwood)
Honolulu, 1939 (Powell, E.; Young, R.)
Honoo no hada, 1951 (Yamamura)
Honor among Lovers, 1931 (Colbert; March; Rogers, G.)
Honor among Thieves. See Adieu l'ami, 1968
Honor First, 1922 (Gilbert)

Honor of His House, 1918 (Hayakawa)
Honor of the Mounted, 1914 (Chaney)
Honor of the Nation. See Ei gerochsky podvig, 1914
Honor Thy Father, 1912 (Pickford)
Honorable Algernon, 1913 (Talmadge)
Honorable Billy. See Society for Sale, 1918
Honorable Catherine, 1941 (Feuillère)
Honorable Friend, 1916 (Hayakawa)
Honorable Mr. Buggs, 1927 (Laurel and Hardy; Wong)
Honorable Société, 1978 (Dalio; Gélin)
Honorary Consul, 1983 (Caine; Gere; Hoskins)
Honoré de Marseilles, 1956 (Fernandel)
Honoring a Hero, 1911 (White)
Honour Redeemed. See Victoria Cross, 1917
Honours Easy, 1935 (Lockwood)
Honryu, 1926 (Tanaka)
Hooch, 1976 (Aiello)
Hoodlum, 1919 (Pickford)
Hoodlum Empire, 1952 (Trevor)
Hoodlum Saint, 1946 (Lansbury; Powell, W.; Williams, E.)
Hoodoo, 1910-11 (White)
Hoodoo Ann, 1916 (Marsh)
Hoodwink, 1981 (Davis, J.)
Hoofs and Goofs, 1957 (Three Stooges)
Hook, 1963 (Douglas, K.)
Hook, 1991 (Close; Hoffman; Hoskins; Roberts, J.; Smith; Williams, R.)
Hook, Line and Sinker, 1969 (Lewis, Jerry)
Hookibi, 1928 (Hasegawa)
Hooks and Jabs, 1933 (Langdon)
Hoop Dreams, 1994 (Lee, S.)
Hooper, 1978 (Field; Reynolds, B.)
Hoopla, 1933 (Bow)
Hooray for Love, 1935 (Robinson, B.)
Hoose-Gow, 1929 (Laurel and Hardy)
Hoosier Schoolboy, 1937 (Rooney)
Hoosiers, 1986 (Hackman; Hershey; Hopper)
Hoot Mon, 1919 (Laurel and Hardy)
Hop the Bell-Hop, 1919 (Laurel and Hardy)
Hop to It, 1925 (Laurel and Hardy)
Hope, 1922 (Astor)
Hope Chest, 1918 (Barthelmess)
Hope Diamond Mystery, 1921 (Karloff)
Hope of Blue Sky. See Kibo no aozora, 1960
Hôpital de Leningrad, 1983 (Vogler)
Hoppla, jetzt kommt Eddie!, 1958 (Constantine)
Hoppsan!, 1955 (Andersson, H.; Thulin)
Hoppy Serves a Writ, 1943 (Mitchum)
Hopscotch, 1980 (Jackson, G.; Lom; Matthau)
Hora Bruja, 1985 (Abril)
Horace '62, 1962 (Trintignant)
Horace Greeley, Jr., 1925 (Langdon)
Horizons West, 1952 (Hudson; Ryan, R.)
Horloger de Saint-Paul, 1974 (Noiret)
Horn Blows at Midnight, 1945 (Dumont)
Hornet's Nest, 1970 (Hudson)
Horns and Hoofs. See Pinto Ben, 1915
Horo-ki, 1962 (Tanaka)
Horoki, 1954 (Okada)
Horoki, 1962 (Takamine; Tsukasa)
Horror Castle. See Vergine de Norimberga, 1964
Horror Chamber of Dr. Faustus. See **Yeux sans visage**, 1960
Horror Express, 1974 (Lee, C.)
Horror Express. See Panico en el Transiberiano, 1972
Horror Motel. See City of the Dead, 1960
Horror of Dracula. See **Dracula**, 1958
Horror of the Blood Monsters, 1970 (Carradine)
Horror Show, 1979 (Perkins)
Hors Saison. See Zwischensaison, 1992
Horse, 1970 (Gabin)
Horse. See Uma, 1941
Horse Called Nijinsky, 1970 (Welles)

Horse Feathers, 1932 (Marx Brothers)
Horse Hoofs, 1931 (Carey)
Horse on Holiday, 1959 (Greenwood)
Horse Shoes, 1927 (Arthur)
Horse Soldiers, 1959 (Holden; Wayne)
Horse without a Head, 1963 (Lom)
Horseman of the Plains, 1928 (Mix)
Horseman on the Roof. See Hussard sur le toit, 1995
Horsemasters, 1961 (Pleasence)
Horsemen, 1971 (Palance; Sharif)
Horsemen of the Wind. See Vsadniki vetra, 1930
Horses Collars, 1935 (Three Stooges)
Horse's Mouth, 1958 (Guinness)
Horsing Around, 1957 (Three Stooges)
Horst Wessel. See Hans Westmar, 1933
Hose, 1927 (Krauss)
Hosen des Ritters von Bredow, 1973 (Mueller-Stahl)
Hospital, 1971 (Scott, G.)
Hostage, 1917 (Novarro)
Hostage, 1966 (Stanton)
Hostage, 1967 (Carradine)
Hostage, 1992 (Neill)
Hostage for a Day, 1994 (Candy)
Hostage Tower, 1980 (Johnson; Roberts, R.)
Hostages, 1943 (Homolka; Lukas; Rainer)
Hostages, 1993 (Bates, K.; Stanton)
Hostile Witness, 1967 (Milland)
Höstsonaten. See Herbstsonate, 1978
Hot Blood, 1956 (Russell, J.; Wilde)
Hot Dogs. See Mabel's Busy Day, 1914
Hot Enough for June, 1963 (Bogarde)
Hot Finish. See Mabel at the Wheel, 1914
Hot for Paris, 1929 (McLaglen)
Hot Heiress, 1931 (Pidgeon)
Hot Ice, 1955 (Three Stooges)
Hot Lead. See Run of the Arrow, 1957
Hot Millions, 1968 (Malden; Smith; Ustinov)
Hot Money Girls. See Treasure of San Teresa, 1959
Hot News, 1928 (Lukas)
Hot Pepper, 1933 (McLaglen)
Hot Rhythm, 1944 (Langdon)
Hot Rock, 1972 (Redford; Segal)
Hot Rods to Hell, 1967 (Andrews, D.)
Hot Saturday, 1932 (Grant, C.; Scott, R.)
Hot Scots, 1948 (Three Stooges)
Hot Shots!, Part Deux, 1993 (Sheen)
Hot Spell, 1958 (MacLaine; Quinn)
Hot Spot, 1941 (Grable; Mature)
Hot Spot, 1990 (Hopper)
Hot Stuff, 1956 (Three Stooges)
Hot Stuff. See Paura in città, 1976
Hot to Trot, 1988 (Candy; Meredith)
Hot Tomorrows, 1978 (Welles)
Hot Water, 1924 (Lloyd)
Hot Wind. See Neppu, 1943
Hotel, 1967 (Douglas, Melvyn; Malden; Oberon)
Hotel Berlin, 1945 (Lorre; Massey)
Hotel Colonial, 1987 (Duvall)
Hotel des Amériques, 1982 (Deneuve)
Hotel du Lac, 1986 (Elliott; Withers)
Hotel du paradis, 1986 (Rey)
Hotel for Women, 1939 (Darnell)
Hotel Imperial, 1927 (Negri)
Hotel Imperial, 1939 (Milland)
Hotel Mixup. See Mabel's Strange Predicament, 1914
Hotel New Hampshire, 1984 (Foster; Kinski)
Hotel of the Americas. See Hotel des Amériques, 1982
Hotel Paradise. See Man Who Bought Paradise, 1965
Hotel Paradiso, 1966 (Guinness; Lollobrigida)
Hotel Paradiso, 1966 (Guinness; Lollobrigida)
Hotel Potemkin, 1924 (Banky)
Hotel Reserve, 1944 (Lom; Mason)

Hotel Room, 1993 (Stanton)
Hotel Sahara, 1951 (Ustinov)
Hotel Terminus, 1987 (Moreau)
Hôtel du libre échange, 1934 (Fernandel)
Hôtel du Nord, 1938 (Arletty; Blier; Jouvet)
Hotori musuko, 1936 (Ryu)
Hototogisu, 1932 (Hasegawa; Takamine)
Hottentot, 1929 (Horton)
Hotter than Hot, 1929 (Langdon)
Houdini, 1953 (Curtis, T.; Leigh, Janet)
Hound of the Baskervilles, 1939 (Carradine; Rathbone; Cushing)
Hound of the Baskervilles, 1959 (Lee, C.)
Hound of the Baskervilles, 1969 (Granger)
Hound of the Baskervilles, 1977 (Elliott; Greenwood; Moore, Dudley; Terry-Thomas)
Hound of the Baskervilles, 1983 (Elliott)
Hour after Hour, 1974 (Nowicki)
Hour before the Dawn, 1944 (Lake)
Hour of Glory. See Small Back Room, 1949
Hour of Parting. See Afskedens timme, 1973
Hour of Terror, 1912-13 (White)
Hour of the Gun, 1967 (Garner; Robards; Ryan, R.; Voight)
Hour of the Pig, 1994 (Pleasence)
Hour of the Wolf. See Vargtimmen, 1968
Hour-Glass Sanatorium. See Sanatorium pod klepsydra, 1972
Hours Between. See Twenty-Four Hours, 1931
House across the Bay, 1940 (Bennett; Pidgeon; Raft)
House Arrest, 1996 (Curtis, J.)
House at the End of the World. See Die, Monster, Die!, 1965
House Built upon Sand, 1917 (Gish)
House by the Sea. See Haus am Meer, 1971
House Calls, 1978 (Jackson, G.; Matthau)
House Divided, 1931 (Huston, J.; Huston, W.)
House I Live In, 1945 (Sidney)
House in Nightmare Park, 1973 (Milland)
House Is Not a Home, 1964 (Crawford, B.; Taylor, R.; Welch; Winters)
House No. 44. See Makan no. 44, 1955
House of a Thousand Dolls. See Haus der tausend Freuden, 1967
House of Bamboo, 1955 (Hayakawa; Ryan, R.)
House of Bernarda Alba, 1991 (Jackson, G.)
House of Cards, 1968 (Welles)
House of Cards, 1993 (Jones, T.; Turner, K.)
House of Connelly. See Carolina, 1934
House of Crazies. See Asylum, 1972
House of Dark Shadows, 1970 (Bennett)
House of Darkness, 1913 (Barrymore, L.; Gish)
House of Death. See Smerti doma, 1915
House of Discord, 1913 (Barrymore, L.; Sweet)
House of Doom. See Black Cat, 1934
House of Dracula, 1945 (Carradine)
House of Dracula's Daughter, 1972 (Crawford, B.; Carradine)
House of Errors, 1942 (Langdon)
House of Evil, 1972 (Karloff)
House of Exorcism. See Lisa e il diavolo, 1972
House of Fate. See Muss 'em Up, 1936
House of Fear, 1945 (Rathbone)
House of Folly. See Dårskapens hus, 1951
House of Frankenstein, 1944 (Carradine; Karloff)
House of Freaks, 1973 (Brazzi)
House of Fright. See Two Faces of Dr. Jekyll, 1960
House of Hate, 1918 (White)
House of Long Shadows, 1983 (Carradine)
House of Lovers. See Pot-Bouille, 1957
House of Mystery, 1914 (White)
House of Numbers, 1957 (Palance)
House of Pleasure. See Plaisir, 1951
House of Ricordi. See Casa Ricordi, 1954
House of Rothschild, 1934 (Karloff; Young, L.)
House of Rothschild, 1934 (Young, R.)
House of Settlement. See Mr. Soft Touch, 1949
House of Seven Gables, 1940 (Price; Sanders)

House of Silence, 1918 (Crisp)
House of Smiles. See Casa del sorriso, 1988
House of Strangers, 1949 (Hayward)
House of the Arrow, 1953 (Homolka)
House of the Black Death, 1965 (Carradine)
House of the Long Shadows, 1982 (Cushing; Lee, C.; Price)
House of the Seven Corpses, 1974 (Carradine)
House of the Seven Hawks, 1959 (Taylor, R.)
House of the Spirits, 1993 (Banderas; Close; Irons; Mueller-Stahl; Redgrave, V.; Ryder; Streep)
House of the Yellow Carpet. See Casa del tappetto giallo, 1983
House of Usher, 1960 (Price)
House of Usher, 1988 (Pleasence; Reed)
House of Wax, 1953 (Bronson; Price)
House of Women. See Kvinnohuset, 1953
House on Fifty-Sixth Street, 1933 (Francis)
House on Garibaldi Street, 1979 (Topol)
House on Green Apple Road, 1970 (Leigh, Janet; Pidgeon)
House on Haunted Hill, 1959 (Price)
House on Trubnaya Street. See Dom na Trubnoi, 1928
House Party 2, 1991 (Goldberg)
House That Dripped Blood, 1970 (Cushing; Elliott; Lee, C.)
House That Wouldn't Die, 1970 (Stanwyck)
House Where Death Lives. See Delusion, 1984
House with Seven Locks. See Dir Tür mit den sieben Schlössern, 1962
House without a Christmas Tree, 1972 (Robards)
Houseboat, 1958 (Grant, C.; Loren)
Household Pest, 1910 (Talmadge)
Housekeeper's Daughter, 1939 (Bennett; Mature; Menjou)
Housesitter, 1992 (Hawn; Martin, S.)
Housewife, 1934 (Brennan; Davis, B.)
How Awful about Allan, 1970 (Perkins)
How Could You, Jean?, 1918 (Pickford)
How Did a Nice Girl Like You Get into This Business? See Wie dommt ein so reizendes Mädchen zu diesem Gewerbe?, 1970
How Do I Love Thee?, 1970 (O'Hara; Winters)
How Funny Can Sex Be? See Sesso matto, 1973
How Green Was My Valley, 1941 (Crisp; Fitzgerald; McDowall; O'Hara; Pidgeon)
How Hazel Got Even, 1915 (Crisp)
How High Is Up?, 1940 (Three Stooges)
How Hiram Won Out, 1914 (Arbuckle)
How I Play Golf, 1931 (Cagney)
How I Play Golf No. 7: The Spoon, 1933 (Huston, W.)
How I Spent My Summer Vacation, 1967 (Pidgeon)
How It Happened, 1913 (Mix)
How Max Went around the World. See Comment Max fait le tour du monde, 1913
How Much Do You Owe? See Jackpot, 1950
How Nerves Are Made, 1914 (Normand)
How Not to Dress. See Herr och fru Stockholm, 1921
How Rastus Gets His Turkey, 1910-11 (White)
How She Triumphed, 1911 (Sweet)
How Sweet It Is, 1968 (Garner; Terry-Thomas; Dalio; Reynolds, D.)
How the West Was Won, 1963 (Brennan; Cobb; Fonda, H.; Malden; Massey; Moorehead; Peck; Preston; Reynolds, D.; Ritter; Stewart; Tracy; Van Cleef; Wallach; Wayne; Widmark)
How to Be a Woman and Not Die Trying. See Como ser Mujer y no morir en el intento, 1991
How to Be Miserable and Enjoy It. See Como Ser Infeliz y Disfrutarlo, 1994
How to Be Very, Very Popular, 1955 (Coburn, C.; Grable)
How to Beat the High Co$t of Living, 1980 (Lange)
How to Commit Marriage, 1969 (Hope; Wyman)
How to Destroy the Reputation of the Greatest Secret Agent .... See Magnifique, 1974
How to Handle Women, 1928 (Lugosi)
How to Make an American Quilt, 1995 (Bancroft; Burstyn; Nelligan; Ryder)
How to Marry a Millionaire, 1953 (Bacall; Grable; Monroe; Powell, W.)
How to Murder a Rich Uncle, 1957 (Caine; Coburn, C.)
How to Murder Your Wife, 1965 (Lemmon; Terry-Thomas; Trevor)
How to Rob a Bank. See Nice Little Bank that Should Be Robbed, 1958

How to Save a Marriage—and Ruin Your Life, 1968 (Martin, D.; Wallach)
How to Score a Movie, 1978 (Howard, T.)
How to Steal a Million, 1966 (Boyer; Dalio; Hepburn, A.; O'Toole; Wallach)
How to Steal an Airplane, 1971 (Mineo)
How to Stuff a Wild Bikini, 1965 (Keaton, B.; Rooney)
How Weary Went Wooing, 1915 (Mix)
How's About It?, 1943 (Three Stooges)
How've You Been?, 1933 (Arbuckle)
Howard the Duck, 1986 (Robbins)
Howards End, 1992 (Bonham-Carter; Hopkins, A.; Redgrave, V.; Thompson)
Howards of Virginia, 1940 (Grant, C.; Ladd)
Howling, 1980 (Carradine)
Howling II: Your Sister Is a Werewolf, 1985 (Lee, C.)
Hoyere enn Himmelen, 1993 (Andersson, H.)
Hoyo, 1953 (Mifune)
Hr. Tell og Søn, 1929 (Madsen and Schenstrøm)
Hrabina Cosel, 1968 (Olbrychski)
Hu Man, 1974 (Moreau; Stamp)
Hua Hun. See Peintre, 1994
Hubbi el Wahid, 1960 (Sharif)
Hubby's Job, 1913 (Normand)
Huckleberry Finn. See Adventures of Huckleberry Finn, 1960
Hucksters, 1947 (Gable; Gardner; Greenstreet; Kerr; Menjou)
Hud, 1963 (Douglas, Melvyn; Neal; Newman; Stamp)
Huddle, 1932 (Novarro)
Hudson Hawk, 1991 (Aiello; Coburn, J.; Willis)
Hudson's Bay, 1940 (Muni; Tierney; Price)
Hudsucker Proxy, 1994 (Leigh, Jennifer Jason; Newman; Robbins)
Hugh Hefner: Once upon a Time, 1992 (Coburn, J.)
Hugs and Mugs, 1950 (Three Stooges)
Huis clos, 1954 (Arletty)
Hula, 1927 (Bow)
Hula from Hollywood, 1954 (Kaye)
Hula La La, 1951 (Three Stooges)
Hulchul, 1951 (Kumar)
Hulda from Holland, 1916 (Pickford)
Hullo Everybody. See Getting Acquainted, 1914
Hullo Fame, 1941 (Ustinov)
Hulyeseg nem Akadaly, 1985 (Nowicki)
Hum Bhi Insaan Hain, 1948 (Anand)
Hum Dono, 1961 (Anand)
Hum Ek Hain, 1946 (Anand)
Hum Farishte Nahin, 1988 (Patil)
Hum Naujawan, 1985 (Anand)
Hum paanch, 1980 (Azmi)
Hum Rahe Na Hum, 1984 (Azmi)
Human Cargo, 1936 (Hayworth; Trevor)
Human Comedy, 1943 (Mitchum; Rooney)
Human Condition. See **Ningen no joken III**, 1961
Human Desire, 1954 (Crawford, B.; Ford, G.; Grahame)
Human Dutch. See Alleman, 1963
Human Factor, 1979 (Attenborough; Gielgud; Mills)
Human Highway, 1982 (Hopper)
Human Hounds, 1916 (Laurel and Hardy)
Human Monster, 1939 (Lugosi)
Human Side, 1934 (Bond; Menjou)
Human Stuff, 1920 (Carey)
Humanity. See Insaniyat, 1955
Humanoid. See Unanoide, 1979
Humeur vagabonde, 1971 (Moreau)
Humming Bird, 1924 (Swanson)
Humoresque, 1946 (Crawford, J.; Garfield)
Humour noir, 1964 (Brasseur; Valli)
Hump Back Angel, 1984 (Woodward)
Humsafar, 1953 (Anand)
Hunchback, 1914 (Gish)
Hunchback of Notre Dame, 1923 (Chaney; Laughton; O'Brien, E.; O'Hara)
Hunchback of Notre Dame, 1981 (Gielgud)
Hunchback of Notre Dame, 1983 (Hopkins, A.)
Hunchback of Notre Dame, 1996 (Kline; Moore, Demi)
Hunchback of Notre Dame. See Notre Dame de Paris, 1956

Hunchback of Rome. See Gobbo, 1960
Hund von Baskerville, 1929 (Rasp)
Hund von Baskerville, 1936 (Rasp)
Hundert Tage, 1935 (Krauss)
Hundred and One Nights. See Cent et une Nuits, 1995
Hundred Pound Window, 1943 (Attenborough)
Hungarian Nights. See Es flüstert die Nacht, 1929
Hungarian Rhapsody. See Ungarische Rhapsodie, 1928
Hunger, 1984 (Dafoe; Deneuve; Sarandon)
Hungry Hearts, 1916 (Laurel and Hardy)
Hungry Hill, 1947 (Lockwood)
Huns and Hyphens, 1918 (Laurel and Hardy)
Hunt for Red October, 1990 (Connery; Jones, James Earl; Neill)
Hunt to Kill. See White Buffalo, 1977
Hunted, 1952 (Bogarde)
Hunted. See Touch Me Not, 1973
Hunted Men, 1938 (Quinn)
Hunter, 1980 (Belmondo; McQueen; Wallach)
Hunters, 1958 (Mitchum; Powell, D.)
Hunters Are for Killing, 1970 (Douglas, Melvyn; Reynolds, B.)
Hunters Are the Hunted. See Jagdszenden aus Niederbayern, 1969
Hunting Flies. See Polowanie na muchy, 1969
Hunting for Germans in Berlin with Will Rogers, 1927 (Rogers, W.)
Hunting Party, 1971 (Hackman; Reed)
Hunting Scenes in Bavaria. See Jagdszenden aus Niederbayern, 1969
Hurrah! Ich lebe!, 1928 (Fröhlich)
Hurricane, 1937 (Astor; Carradine; Lamour; Massey)
Hurricane, 1979 (Farrow; Howard, T.; Robards; Von Sydow)
Hurricane Express, 1932 (Wayne)
Hurricane Horseman, 1925 (Arthur)
Hurricane Rider, 1931 (Carey)
Hurricane's Girl, 1922 (Beery)
Hurry Sundown, 1966 (Caine; Dunaway; Fonda, J.; Meredith)
Hurry Up, or I'll Be 30, 1973 (DeVito)
Husband Hunters, 1927 (Arthur)
Husbands, 1970 (Falk)
Husbands and Wives, 1992 (Allen; Davis, J.; Farrow; Lewis, Juliette; Neeson)
Husbands Beware, 1956 (Three Stooges)
Husbands or Lovers. See Nju, 1924
Husbands or Lovers. See Honeymoon in Bali, 1939
Hush ... Hush, Sweet Charlotte, 1964 (Astor; Cotten; Davis, B.; De Havilland; Dern; Moorehead)
Hush Money, 1931 (Bennett; Loy; Raft)
Hushed Hour, 1919 (Sweet)
Husmenna, 1986 (Andersson, B.)
Hussard sur le toit, 1995 (Binoche)
Hussards, 1955 (Blier)
Hussy, 1980 (Mirren)
Hustle, 1975 (Borgnine; Deneuve; Reynolds, B.)
Hustler, 1961 (Newman; Scott, G.)
Hustlin' Hawk, 1923 (Rogers, W.)
Hustling, 1975 (Remick)
Hustling for Health, 1919 (Laurel and Hardy)
Hymn of Nations, 1946 (Meredith)
Hyoroku yume monogatari, 1943 (Takamine)
Hypnotized, 1932 (McDaniel)
Hypochondriac. See Malato imaginario, 1979
I.N.R.I., 1923 (Krauss)
I.Q., 1994 (Matthau; Robbins; Ryan, M.)
I, a Virgin. See Badarna, 1968
I Accuse, 1957 (Ferrer; Lom; Walbrook)
I Aim at the Stars, 1960 (Lom)
I Am a Camera, 1955 (Winters)
I Am a Fugitive from a Chain Gang, 1932 (Muni)
I Am a Thief, 1935 (Astor)
I Am Pierre Rivière. See Je suis Pierre Rivière, 1975
I Am the Law, 1922 (Beery)
I Am the Law, 1938 (Robinson, E.)
I Am the Man, 1924 (Barrymore, L.)
I as in Icarus. See I comme Icarus, 1979
I Became a Criminal. See They Made Me a Criminal, 1947

Ichiban utsukushiku, 1944 (Shimura)
Ichijoji no ketto, 1955 (Mifune)
I'd Climb the Highest Mountain, 1951 (Hayward)
I'd Rather be Rich, 1964 (Chevalier)
Idaho, 1943 (Rogers, R.)
Idaten kaido, 1944 (Hasegawa)
Idaten kisha, 1953 (Kagawa)
Ideal Husband, 1947 (Goddard)
Idée fixe, 1968 (Fresnay)
Idée folle, 1932 (Arletty)
Identikit. See Driver's Seat, 1975
Idillio tragico, 1912 (Bertini)
Idiot, 1914 (Crisp)
Idiot, 1946 (Feuillère; Philipe)
Idiot à Paris, 1966 (Blier)
Idiot. See Hakuchi, 1951
Idiot qui se croit Max, 1910 (Linder)
Idiot's Delight, 1939 (Coburn, C.; Gable; Meredith; Shearer)
Idiots Deluxe, 1945 (Three Stooges)
Idle Class, 1921 (Chaplin, C.; Purviance)
Idle Roomers, 1931 (Arbuckle)
Idle Roomers, 1944 (Three Stooges)
Ido zero daisakusen, 1970 (Cotten)
Idoire, 1932 (Fernandel)
Idol, 1966 (Jones, Jennifer)
Idol. See Dots Izrila, 1917
Idol. See Idole, 1948
Idol Dancer, 1920 (Barthelmess)
Idol of the Crowds, 1937 (Wayne)
Idole, 1948 (Montand)
Idolo infranto, 1913 (Bertini)
Idyll of the Hills, 1915 (Chaney)
Idylle à la ferme, 1912 (Linder)
Ieri, oggi, domani, 1963 (Loren; Mastroianni)
If ..., 1968 (McDowell)
If a Body Meets a Body, 1945 (Three Stooges)
If a Man Answers, 1962 (Presle)
If All the Guys in the World. See Si tous les gars du monde, 1955
If I Had a Million, 1932 (Constantine; Fields, W. C.; Laughton; Raft)
If I Had My Way, 1940 (Crosby)
If I Had to Do It All over Again. See Si c'était à refaire, 1976
If I Were a Spy. See Si j'étais un espion, 1967
If I Were Boss, 1938 (Withers)
If I Were Free, 1933 (Dunne)
If I Were King, 1938 (Colman; Rathbone)
If I Were Single, 1927 (Loy)
If I Were Young Again, 1914 (Mix)
If I'm Lucky, 1946 (Miranda)
If It Were Raining. See Comme s'il en pleuvait, 1963
If My Country Should Call, 1916 (Chaney)
"If Only" Jim, 1921 (Carey)
If Paris Were Told to Us. See Si Paris nous était conté, 1955
If These Walls Could Talk, 1996 (Moore, Demi)
If They Tell You That I Fell. See Si Te Dicen Que Caí, 1989
If This Be Sin. See That Dangerous Age, 1950
If Tomorrow Comes, 1971 (Baxter)
If We Only Knew, 1913 (Sweet)
If Winter Comes, 1947 (Lansbury; Leigh, Janet; Pidgeon; Kerr)
If You Could Only Cook, 1935 (Arthur; Marshall)
If You Feel Like Singing. See Summer Stock, 1950
If You Knew Susie, 1948 (Cantor)
Igano minatsuki, 1958 (Hasegawa)
Ignace, 1937 (Fernandel)
Ihr grosse Fall. See Grosse Fall, 1944
Ihr Privatsekretär, 1940 (Fröhlich)
Il giorno più corto, 1963 (Pidgeon)
Il giudizio universale, 1961 (Borgnine)
Il planet degli uomini spenti, 1960 (Rains)
Ikimono no kiroku, 1955 (Shimura; Mifune)
Ikiru, 1952 (Shimura)
Ikiteiru ningyo, 1957 (Yamada)

Ikitoshi ikeru mono, 1955 (Yamamura)
Il est minuit, Docteur Schweitzer, 1952 (Fresnay; Moreau)
Il était une fois un flic, 1972 (Delon)
Il faut tuer Birgitt Haas, 1981 (Noiret)
Il faut vivre dangereusement, 1975 (Girardot)
Il n'y a pas de fumée sans feu, 1972 (Girardot)
Il y a des jours ... et des lunes, 1990 (Girardot; Reggiani)
I'll Be Home for Christmas, 1988 (Saint)
I'll Be Seeing You, 1944 (Cotten; Rogers, G.; Temple)
I'll Be Your Sweetheart, 1945 (Lockwood)
I'll Be Yours, 1947 (Durbin; Menjou)
I'll Cry Tomorrow, 1955 (Hayward)
I'll Defend You My Love. See Difendo il mio amore, 1956
I'll Dig Your Grave. See Sono Sartana, il vostro bechino, 1969
I'll Do Anything, 1994 (Nolte)
I'll Get By, 1950 (Mature; Ritter)
I'll Get Him Yet, 1919 (Barthelmess)
I'll Get You, 1951 (Raft)
I'll Give a Million, 1938 (Carradine; Lorre)
I'll Give My Life, 1959 (Dickinson)
Ill Met by Moonlight, 1957 (Bogarde; Cusack; Lee, C.)
I'll Never Forget What's 'is Name, 1967 (Reed; Welles)
I'll Never Forget You, 1951 (Power)
I'll Never Heil Again, 1941 (Three Stooges)
I'll See You in My Dreams, 1951 (Day)
I'll Take Romance, 1937 (Douglas, Melvyn)
I'll Take Romance, 1990 (Close)
I'll Take Sweden, 1965 (Hope; Weld)
Illegal, 1955 (Mansfield)
Illegal Traffic, 1938 (Preston)
Illicit, 1931 (Blondell; Stanwyck)
Illusion, 1929 (Francis; Lukas)
Illusions, 1992 (York)
Illustrated Man, 1969 (Bloom; Steiger)
Illustrious Corpses. See Cadaveri eccelenti, 1975
Illustrious Prince, 1919 (Hayakawa)
Ils, 1970 (Vanel)
Ils sont grands ces petits, 1979 (Deneuve)
I'm a Monkey's Uncle, 1948 (Three Stooges)
I'm a Paranormal Phenomenon. See Sono un fenomeno paranormale, 1985
I'm a Stranger Here Myself, 1972 (Wood)
I'm All Right, Jack, 1959 (Attenborough; Rutherford; Sellers; Terry-Thomas)
Im Angesicht des Toten, 1916 (Jannings)
Im Banne der Vergangenheit, 1915 (Kortner)
Im Brunnen der Traeume, 1996 (Lee, C.)
I'm Dancing as Fast as I Can, 1982 (Pesci; Page; Wiest)
I'm Dangerous Tonight, 1990 (Perkins)
Im Geheimdienst, 1931 (Homolka)
Im grossen Augenblick, 1910 (Nielsen)
Im Lauf der Zeit, 1976 (Vogler)
Im letzten Augenblick, 1920 (Banky)
I'm No Angel, 1933 (Grant, C.; McDaniel; West)
I'm on My Way, 1919 (Lloyd)
Im Schützengraben, 1914 (Jannings)
Image. See Bildnis, 1925
Image, 1989 (Pitt)
Image, 1990 (Finney)
Images, 1972 (York)
Imaginary Baron. See Juxbaron, 1927
Imaginary Crimes, 1994 (Keitel)
Imaginary Invalid. See Malato Imaginario, 1979
Imaginary Sweetheart. See Professional Sweetheart, 1933
Imagine, 1973 (Astaire)
Imagining America, 1989 (Keitel)
Imbarco a mezzanotte, 1952 (Muni)
Imitation General, 1958 (Ford, G.)
Imitation of Life, 1934 (Colbert; McDaniel)
Imitation of Life, 1959 (Turner, L.)
Immaculate Conception, 1991 (Azmi)
Immediate Disaster. See Stranger from Venus, 1954
Immediate Family, 1989 (Close; Woods)

Immigrant, 1917 (Chaplin, C.; Purviance)
Immobilien, 1973 (Schell, Maria)
Immortal, 1969 (Bellamy)
Immortal Bachelor. See Mezzanotte va la ronda del piacere, 1975
Immortal Battalion, 1944 (Ustinov)
Immortal Beloved, 1994 (Oldman; Rossellini)
Immortal Land, 1958 (Gielgud; Redgrave, M.)
Immortal Love. See Eien no hito, 1961
Immortal Sergeant, 1943 (Fonda, H.; O'Hara)
Immortal Story. See Histoire immortelle, 1968
Immortal Vagabond. See Unsterbliche Lump, 1930
Immortals, 1995 (Curtis, T.)
Immortel Amour. See Miracle in the Rain, 1956
Impact, 1949 (Coburn, C.; Marsh; Wong)
Impasse, 1969 (Reynolds, B.)
Impatient Maiden, 1932 (Ayres)
Impatient Years, 1944 (Arthur; Coburn, C.)
Imperative, 1982 (Caron)
Imperativo categorio: control il crimine con rabbia, 1973 (Kinski)
Imperfect Lady, 1947 (Milland; Quinn)
Imperial Venus. See Venere imperiale, 1962
Impersonation of Tom, 1915 (Mix)
Impetuous Youth. See Geiger von Florenz, 1926
Importance of Being Earnest, 1952 (Evans; Greenwood; Redgrave, M.; Rutherford)
Important c'est d'aimer, 1975 (Kinski; Schneider)
Important Man. See Animas Trujano, 1961
Important News, 1935 (Stewart)
Impossible aveu, 1935 (Vanel)
Impossible Mrs. Bellew, 1922 (Swanson)
Impossible objet, 1973 (Bates, A.; Sanda)
Impossible Spy, 1987 (Wallach)
Impossible Years, 1968 (Niven)
Imposter, 1944 (Gabin)
Impostor, 1956 (Armendáriz)
Imprécateur, 1977 (Piccoli)
Impression of John Steinbeck—Writer, 1969 (Fonda, H.)
Impressionable Years, 1952 (Fonda, H.)
Imprévisto, 1961 (Aimée)
Imprint of Giants. See Empreinte des géants, 1980
Impromptu, 1990 (Davis, J.; Grant, H.; Thompson)
Improper Channels, 1981 (Arkin)
Impulse, 1954 (Kennedy)
Impures, 1954 (Presle)
In a Lonely Place, 1950 (Bogart; Grahame)
In Again, Out Again, 1917 (Fairbanks)
In and Out, 1914 (Beery)
In Broad Daylight. See W. Bialy dzie in, 1980
In Caliente, 1935 (Del Rio; Horton)
In Camera Mia, 1992 (Kinski)
In Case of Adversity. See Cas de malheur, 1958
In Celebration, 1975 (Bates, A.)
In Country, 1989 (Willis)
In Custody, 1994 (Azmi)
In Dalarna and Jerusalem. See Ingmarsarvet, 1925
In Defiance of the Law, 1914 (Mix)
In Eagle Dragon Fist. See Dragon Fist, 1979
In faccia al destino, 1913 (Bertini)
In from the Cold, 1988 (Bacall)
In Gay Madrid, 1930 (Novarro)
In geheimer Mission, 1938 (Fröhlich; Wegener)
In God We Trust, 1980 (Pryor)
In Harm's Way, 1965 (Andrews, D.; Douglas, K.; Fonda, H.; Meredith; Neal; Wayne)
In Heaven as on Earth. See Entre el cielo y la tierre, 1993
In-Laws, 1979 (Arkin; Falk)
In Like Flint, 1967 (Cobb; Coburn, J.)
In Love. See Falling in Love Again, 1980
In Love and War, 1987 (Woods)
In Love and War, 1996 (Attenborough)
In Memoriam, 1977 (Chaplin, G.)

In My Daughter's Name, 1992 (Grant, L.)
In Name Only, 1939 (Coburn, C.; Francis; Grant, C.; Lombard)
In Name Only, 1969 (Lancaster)
In Neighboring Kingdoms, 1911 (Talmadge)
In nome del popolo sovrano, 1990 (Sordi)
In Old Amarillo, 1951 (Rogers, R.)
In Old Arizona, 1929 (Brown)
In Old Caliente, 1939 (Rogers, R.)
In Old California, 1942 (Wayne)
In Old California When the Gringos Came, 1911 (Mix)
In Old Cheyenne, 1941 (Rogers, R.)
In Old Chicago, 1938 (Ameche; Faye; Power)
In Old Kentucky, 1909 (Pickford)
In Old Kentucky, 1935 (Robinson, B.; Rogers, W.)
In Old Madrid, 1911 (Pickford)
In Old Missouri, 1940 (Ladd)
In Old Monterey, 1939 (Autry)
In Old Oklahoma, 1943 (Wayne)
In Old Santa Fe, 1934 (Autry)
In Olden Days. See Altri tempi, 1952
In Our Father's House, 1978 (Wiest)
In Our Hands, 1983 (Welles)
In Our Hands, 1984 (Streep)
In Our Time, 1944 (Henreid; Lupino; Nazimova)
In Person, 1935 (Rogers, G.)
In Pursuit of Honor, 1995 (Steiger)
In Saigon, Some May Live. See Some May Live, 1967
In Search of America, 1970 (Bridges; Mineo)
In Search of Dr. Seuss, 1994 (Williams, R.)
In Search of Dracula, 1971 (Lee, C.)
In Search of Gregory, 1970 (Christie; Hurt, J.)
In Search of the Castaways, 1962 (Chevalier; Sanders)
In Society, 1944 (Abbott and Costello)
In the Aisles of the Wild, 1912 (Carey; Gish)
In the Best Interest of the Child, 1990 (Bassett)
In the Bishop's Carriage, 1913 (Pickford)
In the Bleak Midwinter. See Midwinter's Tale, 1995
In the Blood, 1923 (McLaglen)
In the Clutches of the Gang, 1914 (Arbuckle; Normand)
In the Cool of the Day, 1963 (Finch; Fonda, J.; Lansbury)
In the Custody of Strangers, 1982 (Sheen)
In the Days of Daring, 1916 (Mix)
In the Days of Gold, 1911 (Mix)
In the Days of the Thundering Herd, 1914 (Mix)
In the Deep Woods, 1992 (Perkins)
In the Dough, 1933 (Arbuckle)
In the Employ of the Secret Service. See Im Geheimdienst, 1931
In the Face of Demolition, 1954 (Lee, B.)
In the French Style, 1962 (Baker; Seberg)
In the Glitter Palace, 1977 (Hershey)
In the Good Old Summertime, 1949 (Garland; Keaton, B.; Minnelli)
In the Hands of a Pitiless Destiny. See V roukatch bespotchadnogo roka, 1914
In the Heat of the Night, 1967 (Grant, L.; Oates; Poitier; Steiger)
In the Heat of the Night: A Matter of Justice, 1994 (Scott, G.)
In the King of Prussia, 1983 (Sheen)
In the Line of Duty: Manhunt in the Dakotas, 1991 (Steiger)
In the Line of Fire, 1993 (Eastwood; Malkovich)
In the Maiden's Room. See Diadiouskina kvartira, 1913
In the Mouth of Madness, 1995 (Heston; Neill)
In the Name of Life. See Vo imya zhizni, 1946
In the Name of Love, 1925 (Beery)
In the Name of the Father, 1993 (Day-Lewis; Thompson)
In the Name of the People, 1985 (Sheen)
In the Name of the Sovereign People. See In nome del popolo sovrano, 1990
In the Navy, 1941 (Abbott and Costello; Powell, D.; Three Stooges)
In the Palace of the King, 1923 (Sweet)
In the Park, 1915 (Chaplin, C.; Purviance)
In the Pope's Eye. See Pap'Occhio, 1981
In the Rose Garden. See Prima di Natale, 1990
In the Sage Brush Country, 1914 (Hart)
In the Season of Buds, 1910 (Pickford)

In the Spirit, 1990 (Falk; Griffith)
In the Sultan's Garden, 1911 (Pickford)
In the Sweet Pie and Pie, 1941 (Three Stooges)
In the Train, 1963 (Cusack)
In the Wake of the Bounty, 1933 (Flynn)
In the Watches of the Night, 1909 (Pickford)
In the White City. *See* Dans la Ville Blanche, 1983
In the Woods. *See* **Rashomon**, 1950
In This Our Life, 1942 (Astor; Bogart; Bond; Coburn, C.; Davis, B.; De
      Havilland; Huston, J.; Huston, W.; McDaniel)
In Times Like These, 1956 (Wray)
In una notta di chiaro di luna, 1989 (O'Toole; Sanda)
In una notte piena di Pioggia, 1977 (Giannini)
In viaggio con papa, 1982 (Sordi)
In Weiter Ferne, So Nah!, 1993 (Falk)
In Weiter Ferne, So Nah! *See* Faraway, So Close, 1993
In Which We Serve, 1942 (Attenborough; Howard, L.; Johnson; Mills)
In Wrong. *See* Between Showers, 1914
Ina no Kantaro, 1943 (Hasegawa; Yamada)
Inadmissible Evidence, 1968 (Moore, Dudley)
Inazuma, 1952 (Kagawa; Takamine)
Inazuma-zoshi, 1951 (Tanaka)
Incantesimo tragico, 1951 (Brazzi; Félix; Vanel)
Incantevole nemica, 1952 (Keaton, B.; Sordi)
Incendiary Blonde, 1945 (Fitzgerald)
Incense for the Damned, 1970 (Cushing)
Inchiesta, 1987 (Keitel)
Inchon, 1981 (Mifune; Olivier; Sharif)
Incident, 1967 (Ritter; Sheen)
Incident, 1990 (Matthau)
Incident at Blood Pass. *See* Machibuse, 1970
Incident at Oglala, 1992 (Redford)
Incident at Phantom Hill, 1965 (Duryea)
Incident in a Small Town, 1994 (Matthau)
Incognito, 1933 (Brasseur)
Incognito, 1958 (Constantine)
Income Tax Sappy, 1954 (Three Stooges)
Incompetent Hero, 1914 (Arbuckle)
Incompreso, 1967 (Quayle)
Inconnu dans al Maison, 1992 (Belmondo)
Inconnue de Monte-Carlo, 1938 (Berry)
Inconnus dans la maison, 1941 (Fresnay)
Inconnus dans la maison, 1949 (Raimu)
Incorrigible, 1975 (Belmondo; Bujold)
Incorrigible. *See* Incorrigible, 1975
Incorrigible Dukane, 1915 (Barrymore, J.)
Incorruptible. *See* Hercule, 1937
Incredible Invasion, 1971 (Karloff)
Incredible Journey of Doctor Meg Laurel, 1979 (Woods)
Incredible Journey of Dr. Meg Laurel, 1979 (Wyman)
Incredible Petrified World, 1960 (Carradine)
Incredible Sarah, 1976 (Jackson, G.)
Incredible Two-Headed Transplant, 1970 (Dern)
Indagine su un cittadino al di sopra di ogni sospetto, 1970 (Volonté)
Indagine su un delitto perfetto, 1976 (Valli)
Indecent Proposal, 1993 (Moore, Demi; Redford)
Indée d'apache, 1907 (Linder)
Independence, 1976 (Huston, J.; Wallach)
Independence Day, 1983 (Wiest)
India Song, 1975 (Seyrig)
Indian Fighter, 1955 (Douglas, K.; Matthau)
Indian Love Call. *See* Rose Marie, 1936
Indian Runner, 1991 (Bronson; Hopper; Penn)
Indian Runner's Romance, 1909 (Pickford)
Indian Summer, 1912 (Pickford)
Indian Summer, 1978 (Delon; Giannini)
Indian Summer, 1993 (Arkin)
Indian Territory, 1950 (Autry)
Indian Tomb. *See* Indische Grabmal, 1921
Indian Wife's Devotion, 1910 (Mix)
Indian's Loyalty, 1913 (Gish)

Indiana Jones and the Last Crusade, 1989 (Connery; Elliott; Ford, H.)
Indiana Jones and the Temple of Doom, 1984 (Ford, H.)
Indians Are Still Far Away. *See* Indiens sont encore loin, 1977
Indict and Convict, 1974 (Loy; Wallach)
Indictment: The McMartin Trial, 1995 (Woods)
Indiens sont encore loin, 1977 (Huppert)
Indifferenti, 1964 (Cardinale; Goddard; Steiger; Winters)
Indio, 1939 (Armendáriz)
Indio Black, sai che ti dico: sei un gran figlio di ..., 1970 (Brynner)
Indira, 1983 (Chatterjee)
Indische Grabmal, 1921 (Veidt)
Indische Tuch, 1963 (Kinski)
Indiscreet, 1931 (Swanson)
Indiscreet, 1958 (Bergman; Grant, C.)
Indiscretion, 1982 (Sanda)
Indiscretion of an American Wife. *See* Stazioni termini, 1953
Indochine, 1992 (Deneuve)
Indomitable Teddy Roosevelt, 1985 (Scott, G.)
Indonesia Calling, 1946 (Finch)
Induito, 1960 (Armendáriz)
Industrial Symphony No. 1: The Dream of the Broken Hearted, 1990 (Cage)
Inesorabili, 1951 (Vanel)
Incz from Hollywood, 1924 (Astor)
Infancy, 1951 (Lee, B.)
Infedeli, 1953 (Lollobrigida)
Infernal Idol. *See* Craze, 1974
Infernal Trio. *See* Trio infernal, 1973
Inferno, 1953 (Ryan, R.)
Inferno, 1980 (Valli)
Infidel, 1922 (Karloff)
Infideli, 1953 (Papas)
Infidelity. *See* Altri tempi, 1952
Infidelity. *See* Amant de cinq jours, 1960
Information Kid. *See* Fast Companions, 1932
Information Please, 1940 (Gordon)
Information Please, 1942 (Carradine)
Information Please Number Eight, 1941 (Karloff)
Information Please Number Twelve, 1941 (Karloff)
Informer, 1912 (Barrymore, L.; Carey; Pickford)
Informer, 1929 (Milland)
Informer, 1935 (Bond; McLaglen)
Inge und die Millionen, 1933 (Wegener)
Ingen dans på rosor. *See* I Never Promised You a Rose Garden, 1977
Ingénieux Attendat, 1909 (Linder)
Ingenjör Andrees luftfärd, 1981 (Von Sydow)
Ingens Mans Kvinna, 1953 (Von Sydow)
Ingiusta condanna, 1952 (Brazzi)
Ingmar Bergman, 1971 (Andersson, B.; Gould)
Ingmarsarvet, 1925 (Veidt)
Ingorgo, 1979 (Cardinale; Depardieu; Girardot; Mastroianni; Rey; Sordi)
Ingrid, 1984 (Gielgud; Lansbury; Quinn; Ullmann)
Inherit the Wind, 1960 (Kelly, Gene; March; Tracy)
Inherit the Wind, 1988 (Douglas, K.; Robards)
Inheritance. *See* Karami-ai, 1962
Inheritance, 1963 (Burton; Ryan, R.)
Inheritance. *See* Eredità Ferramonti, 1976
Inheritor. *See* Héritier, 1973
Initiation of Sarah, 1978 (Winters)
Iniwa Hachiro, 1933 (Yamada)
Inkognito, 1936 (Fröhlich)
Inmates: A Love Story, 1981 (Curtis, T.)
Inn in Tokyo. *See* Tokyo no yado, 1935
Inn of the Damned, 1974 (Bennett)
Inn of the Sixth Happiness, 1958 (Bergman; Donat)
Innamorati, 1955 (Cervi)
Inner Circle, 1912 (Pickford)
Inner Circle, 1991 (Hoskins)
Innerspace, 1987 (Quaid; Ryan, M.)
Innocence Is Bliss. *See* Miss Grant Takes Richmond, 1949
Innocent, 1921 (Rathbone)
Innocent. *See* Innocente, 1976

Innocent. *See* Masoom, 1982
Innocent, 1984 (Neeson; Richardson, M.)
...Innocent. *See* Und der Himmel steht still, 1993
Innocent Affair. *See* Don't Trust Your Husband, 1948
Innocent Blood, 1992 (Bassett)
Innocent Bystanders, 1972 (Andrews, D.; Baker; Chaplin, G.; Pleasence)
Innocent Casimiro. *See* Innocente Casimiro, 1945
Innocent Magdalene, 1916 (Gish)
Innocent Maid. *See* Hakoiri musume, 1935
Innocent Moves. *See* Searching for Bobby Fisher, 1993
Innocent Sorcerers. *See* Niewinni czarodzieje, 1960
Innocent Victims. *See* Tree of Hands, 1990
Innocente, 1976 (Giannini)
Innocente Casimiro, 1945 (Sordi)
Innocents, 1961 (Kerr; Redgrave, M.)
Innocents aux mains sales, 1975 (Schneider; Steiger)
Innocents in Paris, 1953 (Bloom; Lee, C.; Rutherford)
Innocents of Paris, 1929 (Chevalier)
Inocente, 1955 (Infante)
Inochi aru kagiri, 1946 (Yamamura)
Inochi no minato, 1944 (Hasegawa)
Inochi o kakeru otoko, 1958 (Hasegawa)
Inondation, 1993 (Huppert)
Inquest. *See* Voruntersuchung, 1931
Inquiry. *See* Inchiesta, 1987
INRI, 1923 (Nielsen)
Insaniyat, 1955 (Anand; Kumar)
Insaziabili, 1969 (Malone)
Insel, 1934 (Rosay)
Inserts, 1975 (Dreyfuss; Hoskins)
Insh' Allah, 1965 (Bates, A.)
Inside a Girls' Dormitory. *See* Dortoir des grandes, 1953
Inside Daisy Clover, 1965 (Gordon; McDowall; Redford; Wood)
Inside Information, 1939 (Carey)
Inside Job. *See* Alpha Caper, 1973
Inside Man, 1984 (Hopper)
Inside Out, 1986 (Gould)
Inside the Third Reich, 1981 (Gielgud; Schell, Maria)
Insignificance, 1985 (Curtis, T.)
Insomnia Is Good for You, 1957 (Sellers)
Insoumis, 1964 (Delon)
Inspecteur La Bavure, 1980 (Depardieu)
Inspection of the Crime Scene 1901. *See* Wizja lokalna 1901, 1980
Inspector, 1961 (Pleasence)
Inspector Clouseau, 1968 (Arkin)
Inspector General, 1949 (Kaye; Lanchester)
Inspector Hornleigh Goes to It, 1941 (Cusack)
Inspector Maigret. *See* Maigret tend un piège, 1957
Inspiration, 1931 (Garbo; Montgomery)
Instant Karma, 1991 (Lamarr)
Insult, 1932 (Gielgud)
Insulted and the Injured, 1991 (Kinski)
Insurance, 1930 (Cantor)
Insurance Man, 1985 (Day-Lewis)
Intelligence Service. *See* Ill Met by Moonlight, 1957
Intent to Kill, 1958 (Lom)
Interdit de séjour, 1953 (Piccoli)
Interference, 1929 (Powell, W.)
Interiors, 1978 (Allen; Keaton, D.; Page)
Interlude, 1957 (Brazzi; Rosay)
Interlude, 1968 (Cleese; Sutherland; Werner)
Intermezzo, 1936 (Bergman)
Intermezzo, 1939 (Bergman; Howard, L.)
Intermezzo einer Ehe in sieben Tagen. *See* Soll man heiraten?, 1925
Internal Affairs, 1990 (García; Gere)
International House, 1933 (Fields, W. C.; Lugosi)
International Lady, 1941 (Rathbone)
International Settlement, 1938 (Carradine; Del Rio; Sanders)
International Squadron, 1941 (Reagan)
International Velvet, 1978 (Hopkins, A.)
Internecine Project, 1974 (Coburn, J.; Grant, L.)

Interns, 1962 (Robertson)
Interns Can't Take Money, 1937 (McCrea; Stanwyck)
Interpol, 1957 (Howard, T.; Mature)
Interrupted Melody, 1955 (Ford, G.)
Intersection, 1994 (Gere; Landau; Stone)
Interval, 1973 (Oberon)
Interview. *See* Intervista, 1987
Interview with the Vampire, 1994 (Banderas; Cruise; Pitt)
Intervista, 1987 (Kinski; Mastroianni)
Intimate Contact, 1987 (Bloom)
Intimate Dream. *See* Hazukashiiyume, 1927
Intimate Interview, 1930 (Cagney)
Intimate Relations. *See* Parents terribles, 1948
Intimate Strangers, 1977 (Douglas, Melvyn)
Intimita proibite di una giovane sposa, 1970 (Brazzi)
Into the Badlands, 1991 (Dern)
Into the Dark. *See* Entre Tinieblas, 1983
Into the Deep, 1994 (Nelligan)
Into the Night, 1985 (Papas; Pfeiffer)
Into the West, 1993 (Barkin)
Into Thin Air, 1985 (Burstyn)
Intoccabili, 1968 (Falk; Rowlands)
Intolerance, 1916 (Crisp; Fairbanks; Gish; Marsh)
Intriguantes, 1953 (Moreau)
Intrigue, 1948 (Raft)
Intrigue. *See* Dark Purpose, 1964
Introducing Audrey Hepburn, 1953 (Hepburn, A.)
Introduction to English Poetry, 1384-Present, 1984 (Cusack)
Introduction to the Enemy, 1974 (Fonda, J.)
Intruder. *See* Invader, 1936
Intruder, 1953 (Hawkins)
Intruder. *See* Moon 44, 1990
Intruder. *See* Intruso, 1993
Intruders, 1970 (Ford, H.; O'Brien, E.)
Intruso, 1993 (Abril)
Inubue, 1978 (Yamamura)
Invader, 1936 (Keaton, B.)
Invaders. *See* 49th Parallel, 1941
Invasion, 1970 (Piccoli)
Invasion of the Animal People, 1962 (Carradine)
Invasion of the Body Snatchers, 1978 (Duvall; Sutherland)
Invasion of the Body Stealers. *See* Body Stealers, 1969
Inventiamo l'amore, 1938 (Cervi)
Inventor. *See* Erfinder, 1980
Invenzione di Morel, 1974 (Karina)
Investigation. *See* Inchiesta, 1987
Investigation of a Citizen above Suspicion. *See* Indagine su un cittadino al di sopra di ogni sospetto, 1970
Investigation of Murder. *See* Laughing Policeman, 1974
Investigation: Inside a Terrorist Bombing. *See* Who Bombed Birmingham?, 1990
Invincible Mr. Disraeli, 1963 (Garson)
Invisible Agent, 1942 (Lorre)
Invisible Enemy, 1931 (Buchanan)
Invisible Ghost, 1941 (Lugosi)
Invisible Invaders, 1959 (Carradine)
Invisible Man, 1933 (Carradine; Rains)
Invisible Man, 1975 (Cooper)
Invisible Man Returns, 1940 (Price)
Invisible Man's Revenge, 1944 (Carradine)
Invisible Menace, 1938 (Karloff)
Invisible Opponent. *See* Unsichtbare Gegner, 1933
Invisible Ray, 1936 (Lugosi)
Invisible Stripes, 1940 (Bogart; Holden; Raft)
Invisible Woman, 1941 (Barrymore, J.; Homolka; Three Stooges)
Invitata, 1969 (Piccoli)
Invitation, 1952 (Calhern)
Invitation to a Gunfighter, 1964 (Brynner; Segal)
Invitation to Happiness, 1939 (Dunne; MacMurray)
Invitation to Monte Carlo, 1959 (Sidney)
Invitation to the Dance, 1957 (Charisse; Kelly, Gene)

It Happens Every Spring, 1949 (Milland)
It Happens Every Thursday, 1953 (Young, L.)
It Hurts Only When I Laugh. *See* Only When I Laugh, 1981
It Is Raining on Santiago. *See* Pleut sur Santjago, 1975
It Lives Again, 1978 (Constantine)
It Might Be You, 1947 (Cushing)
It Mustn't Be Forgotten, 1954 (Bondarchuk)
It Only Happens to Others. *See* Ça n'arrive qu'aux autres, 1971
It Pays to Advertise, 1919 (Crisp)
It Pays to Advertise, 1931 (Brooks, L.; Lombard)
It Rained All Night the Day I Left, 1979 (Curtis, T.; Thulin)
It Rains in My Village. *See* Bice skoro propast sveta, 1968
It Rains on Our Love. *See* Det regnar på vår kärlek, 1946
It Runs in the Family, 1994 (Steenburgen)
It Seemed Like a Good Idea at the Time, 1975 (Candy)
It Should Happen to You, 1954 (Holliday; Lemmon)
It Snows in the Everglades. *See* Thunder County, 1974
It Started in Naples, 1960 (Gable; Loren)
It Started in Paradise, 1952 (Kendall)
It Started in the Alps. *See* Arupusu no wakadaisho, 1966
It Started with a Kiss, 1959 (Ford, G.; Reynolds, D.)
It Started with Eve, 1941 (Durbin; Laughton)
It Takes a Thief. *See* Challenge, 1960
It Takes a Thief, 1961 (Mansfield)
It Was a Wonderful Life, 1993 (Foster)
It Was Night in Rome. *See* Era notte a Roma, 1960
Italia vive, 1983 (Giannini)
Italian Barber, 1911 (Pickford)
Italian Connection. *See* "mala" ordina, 1973
Italian Job, 1969 (Baker; Brazzi; Caine)
Italian Stallion, 1970 (Stallone)
Italian Straw Hat. *See* Chapeau de paille d'Italie, 1940
Italiani brava gente, 1964 (Falk; Kennedy)
Italiano brava gente. *See* Italiani brava gente, 1964
Italiano in America, 1966 (Sordi)
Itaro jishi, 1955 (Hasegawa)
Itawari Asataro, 1927 (Hasegawa)
Itazura, 1959 (Yamamura)
Itihaas, 1984 (Azmi)
Itihaas, 1987 (Azmi)
Itinéraire d'un enfant gâté, 1987 (Belmondo; Gélin)
Itinerary of a Spoiled Child. *See* Itinéraire d'un enfant gâté, 1987
Itohan monogatari, 1957 (Kyo)
Itoshigo to taete yukamu, 1952 (Yamada)
It's a 2' 6" above the Ground World, 1972 (Cleese)
It's a Big Country, 1951 (Barrymore, E.; Calhern; Constantine; Leigh, Janet; Powell, W.; Kelly, Gene; March)
It's a Boy, 1933 (Horton)
It's a Cinch, 1932 (Arbuckle)
It's a Date, 1940 (Durbin; Francis; Pidgeon)
It's a Dog's Life. *See* Vita di cani, 1950
It's a Gift, 1934 (Fields, W. C.)
It's a Grand Life, 1953 (Dors)
It's a Great Feeling, 1949 (Constantine; Crawford, J.; Day; Flynn; Greenstreet; Kaye; Neal; Reagan; Robinson, E.; Wyman)
It's a Mad, Mad, Mad, Mad World, 1963 (Keaton, B.; Brown; Falk; Horton; Durante; Lewis, Jerry; Rooney; Terry-Thomas; Three Stooges; Tracy)
It's a Pleasure, 1945 (Henie)
It's a Shame to Say It. *See* Stydno skazat, 1930
It's a Small World, 1935 (Tracy)
It's a Wild Life, 1918 (Lloyd)
It's a Wise Child, 1931 (Davies)
It's a Wonderful Life, 1946 (Barrymore, L.; Bond; Stewart; Grahame)
It's a Wonderful World, 1939 (Colbert; Stewart)
It's Alive II. *See* It Lives Again, 1978
It's All True, 1942 (Welles)
It's All Yours, 1937 (Carroll)
It's Always Fair Weather, 1955 (Charisse; Kelly, Gene)
It's Great to Be Crazy, 1918 (Laurel and Hardy)
It's Great to Be Young, 1956 (Mills)
It's Him, Yes! Yes! *See* Era lui, sì! sì!, 1951

It's Hot in Hell. *See* Singe en hiver, 1962
It's in the Bag, 1945 (Ameche; Carradine)
It's Love Again, 1936 (Terry-Thomas)
It's Love Again, 1936 (Young, R.)
It's Love I'm After, 1937 (Davis, B.; De Havilland; Howard, L.)
It's My Life. *See* **Vivre sa vie**, 1962
It's My Party, 1996 (Grant, L.; McDowall; Segal)
It's My Turn, 1980 (Douglas, Michael; Wiest)
It's Never Too Late. *See* Det är aldrig för sent, 1956
It's Not Cricket, 1949 (Dors)
It's Not the Size That Counts. *See* Percy's Progress, 1974
It's Nothing, Only a Game. *See* No es nada mama, solo un juego, 1973
It's Nothing Personal, 1993 (Bloom; Dern)
It'$ Only Money, 1962 (Lewis, Jerry)
It's the Old Army Game, 1926 (Brooks, L.; Fields, W. C.)
It's Your Birthday. *See* Ca va etre ta fête, 1961
Itsuwareru seiso, 1950 (Kyo)
Ivan and Abraham, 1993 (Olbrychski)
Ivan Franko, 1956 (Bondarchuk)
Ivan Groznyi, 1944 (Cherkassov)
Ivan Groznyi II: Boyarsky zagovor, 1958 (Cherkassov)
Ivan the Terrible. *See* **Ivan Groznyi**, 1944
Ivan the Terrible, Part II: The Boyars' Plot. *See* **Ivan Groznyi II: Boyarsky zagovor**, 1958
Ivanhoe, 1952 (Fontaine; Sanders; Taylor, E.; Taylor, R.)
Ivanhoe, 1982 (Mason; Neill)
I've Got Your Number, 1934 (Blondell)
Ivonne, 1915 (Bertini)
Ivory Ape, 1980 (Palance)
Ivory Hunters, 1990 (Jones, James Earl; Rossellini)
Ivy, 1947 (Fontaine; Marshall)
Iwashigumo, 1958 (Tsukasa)
Izu no odoriko, 1933 (Tanaka)
Izzatdar, 1990 (Kumar)
Izzy and Moe, 1985 (Cooper)
J.F.K., 1991 (Bacon)
J. Edgar Hoover. *See* Private Files of J. Edgar Hoover, 1977
J. W. Coop, 1971 (Page; Robertson)
Ja, der Himmel über Wien, 1930 (Rainer)
Ja und Nein, 1981 (Mueller-Stahl)
Jaal, 1952 (Anand; Lom)
Jaali Note, 1960 (Anand)
Jaaneman, 1976 (Anand)
Jab Pyar Kisise Hota Hai, 1961 (Anand)
Jack, 1996 (Williams, R.)
Jack and the Beanstalk, 1952 (Abbott and Costello)
Jack L. Warner: The Last Mogul, 1993 (Reynolds, D.)
Jack London, 1943 (Hayward)
Jack London's Klondike Fever. *See* Klondike Fever, 1980
Jack of Diamonds, 1967 (Cotten)
Jack of Hearts. *See* Hjärter Knekt, 1950
Jack Slade, 1953 (Malone; Van Cleef)
Jack the Bear, 1993 (DeVito)
Jack the Ripper, 1976 (Kinski)
Jack the Ripper, 1988 (Caine)
Jack's Pals, 1915 (Mix)
Jackal of Nahueltoro. *See* **Chacal de Nahueltoro**, 1968
Jackals, 1967 (Price)
Jackass Mail, 1942 (Beery)
Jackie Chan's Police Force. *See* Gingchat gusi, 1985
Jackie Cooper's Christmas. *See* Christmas Party, 1931
Jacknife, 1988 (De Niro; Harris, E.)
Jacko and Lise. *See* Bobo Jacco, 1979
Jackoman and Tetsu. *See* Jaokman to Tetsu, 1949
Jackpot, 1950 (Stewart; Wood)
Jackpot, 1992 (Lee, C.)
Jackson County Jail, 1976 (Jones, T.)
Jacob, 1994 (Giannini; Papas)
Jacob the Liar. *See* Jakob der Lügner, 1975
Jacob's Ladder, 1990 (Aiello; Robbins)
Jacobo Timerman: Prisoner without a Name, Cell without a Number, 1983

(Scheider; Ullmann)
Jacqueline, 1956 (Cusack)
Jacqueline Kennedy's Asian Journey, 1962 (Massey)
Jacqueline Susann's Valley of the Dolls, 1981 (Coburn, J.; Dreyfuss)
Jacques Cousteau—The First 75 Years, 1985 (Ferrer)
Jade Elephants. *See* Man from Downing Street, 1922
Jadi Jantem, 1974 (Chatterjee)
Jag älskar, du älskar, 1968 (Andersson, H.)
Jag dräpte, 1943 (Björnstrand; Zetterling)
Jag rödnar, 1981 (Andersson, B.)
Jagd nach dem Tode, 1920 (Dagover)
Jagdszenden aus Niederbayern, 1969 (Winkler; Schygulla)
Jagged Edge, 1985 (Bridges; Close)
Jaguar Lives!, 1979 (Huston, J.; Lee, C.; Pleasence)
Jaguar's Claws, 1917 (Hayakawa; Novarro)
Jahrmarkt des Lebens, 1927 (Fröhlich)
J'ai bien l'honneur, 1984 (Constantine)
J'ai engagé un tueur, 1991 (Léaud; Reggiani)
J'ai espouse une ombre, 1982 (Abril; Baye)
J'ai quelque chose à vous dire, 1930 (Fernandel)
J'ai tué!, 1924 (Hayakawa)
J'ai tué Raspoutine, 1967 (Chaplin, G.)
J'ai un idée, 1934 (Raimu)
Jail Bait, 1937 (Keaton, B.)
Jail Bait. *See* Wildwechsel, 1972
Jailbirds. *See* Pardon Us, 1931
Jailhouse Rock, 1957 (Presley)
J'aime toutes les femmes, 1935 (Darrieux)
Jake Spanner, Private Eye, 1988 (Borgnine; Mitchum)
Jake Speed, 1986 (Hurt, J.)
Jako yashiki, 1955 (Hasegawa)
Jakob der Lügner, 1975 (Brodský; Mueller-Stahl)
Jakob von Günten, 1971 (Schygulla)
Jalisco nunca pierde, 1937 (Armendáriz)
Jallianwala Bagh, 1987 (Azmi)
Jalousie, 1975 (Baye)
Jam Session, 1944 (Miller)
Jamaica Inn, 1939 (Laughton; O'Hara)
Jamaica Rum, 1953 (Milland)
Jambon d'Ardenne, 1977 (Girardot)
James and the Giant Peach, 1996 (Dreyfuss; Sarandon)
James Dean: A Portrait, 1995 (Hopper; Wallach; Woodward)
James Dean: The First American Teenager, 1975 (Caron; Hopper)
James Wong Howe, 1974 (Lancaster)
Jan Knukke's Wedding. *See* Zhenitba Jana Knukke, 1934
Jane Austen in Manhattan, 1980 (Baxter)
Jane B. par Agnès V, 1988 (Léaud)
Jane Doe, 1983 (Saint)
Jane Eyre, 1944 (Fontaine; Marsh; Moorehead; O'Brien, M.; Taylor, E.; Welles)
Jane Eyre, 1971 (Hawkins; Scott, G.; York)
Jane Eyre, 1996 (Chaplin, G.; Hurt, W.)
Jane's House, 1994 (Woods)
Janet of the Chorus, 1915 (Talmadge)
Janice Meredith, 1924 (Davies; Fields, W. C.)
Janie, 1944 (McDaniel)
Janie Gets Married, 1946 (Malone; McDaniel)
Janitor, 1916 (Beery)
Janitor. *See* Eyewitness, 1981
Janitor's Joyful Job, 1915 (Laurel and Hardy)
Janitor's Vacation, 1916 (Beery)
Jankar, 1989 (Chatterjee)
January Man, 1989 (Aiello; Keitel; Kline; Sarandon; Steiger)
Janus-Faced. *See* Januskopf, 1920
Januskopf, 1920 (Lugosi; Veidt)
Januskopf, 1972 (Mueller-Stahl)
Jaokman to Tetsu, 1949 (Mifune)
Japanerin, 1918 (Veidt)
Jardin de las delicias, 1970 (Chaplin, G.)
Jardin qui bascule, 1974 (Moreau; Seyrig)
Jardinier, 1973 (Fresnay)

Jardinier d'Argenteuil, 1966 (Gabin)
Jardins du diable. *See* Coplan sauve sa peau, 1967
Jarret, 1973 (Ford, G.; Quayle)
Jason's Lyric, 1994 (Whitaker)
Jassy, 1947 (Lockwood)
Jatszani Kell. *See* Lily in Love, 1985
Java Head, 1933 (Richardson, R.; Wong)
J'avais sept filles, 1955 (Chevalier)
Jaws, 1975 (Dreyfuss; Scheider; Shaw)
Jaws II, 1978 (Scheider)
Jaws 3-D, 1983 (Quaid)
Jaws—the Revenge, 1987 (Caine)
Jayne Mansfield Story, 1981 (Schwarzenegger)
Jazz Age, 1929 (McCrea)
Jazz Cinderella, 1930 (Loy)
Jazz Singer, 1927 (Jolson; Loy)
Jazz Singer, 1980 (Olivier)
Jazz Waiter. *See* Caught in a Cabaret, 1914
Jazzed Honeymoon, 1919 (Lloyd)
Je bridge au plafond, 1909 (Linder)
Je chante, 1938 (Presle)
Je hais les acteurs, 1986 (Blier; Depardieu)
Je l'ai été trois fois, 1952 (Blier)
Je m'appelle Victor, 1993 (Moreau; Presle)
Je reviendrai à Kandara, 1956 (Gélin)
Je sais rien, mais je dirai tout, 1973 (Blier)
Je suis avec toi, 1943 (Blier; Fresnay)
Je suis de la revue. *See* Botta e risposta, 1949
Je suis Pierre Rivière, 1975 (Huppert)
Je suis un as, 1930 (Brasseur)
Je suis un sentimental, 1955 (Constantine)
Je t'aime, 1973 (Moreau)
Je t'aime, moi non plus, 1975 (Depardieu)
Je t'aime, tu danses, 1975 (Seyrig)
Jc tc confie ma femme, 1933 (Arletty)
Je te tiens, tu me tiens par la barbichette, 1978 (Presle)
Je tire chemin, 1968 (Barrault)
Je vais craquer, 1979 (Baye)
Je veux rentrer à la maison, 1989 (Chaplin, G.; Depardieu; Presle)
Je voudrais un enfant, 1909 (Linder)
Je vous aime, 1980 (Deneuve; Depardieu)
Je vous salue, Mafia, 1965 (Constantine; Presle)
Je vous salue, Marie, 1985 (Binoche)
Jealousy, 1929 (March)
Jealousy, 1934 (Ball)
Jealousy, 1984 (Dickinson)
Jealousy. *See* Eifersucht, 1925
Jealousy. *See* Enfer, 1994
Jealousy. *See* Revnost, 1914
Jean de Florette, 1986 (Depardieu; Montand)
Jean de Florette 2. *See* **Manon des sources**, 1986
Jean de la lune, 1948 (Darrieux)
Jean-Louis Barrault—Man of the Theatre, 1984 (Moreau)
Jean Renoir, 1993 (Caron; Meredith)
Jeanne Dielman, 23 Quai du Commerce, 1080 Bruxelles, 1975 (Seyrig)
Jeanne Eagels, 1957 (Moorehead; Novak)
Jeannie, 1941 (Redgrave, M.; Withers)
Jedem sein Hölle. *See* Chacun son enfer, 1976
Jeena yahan, 1979 (Azmi)
Jeepers Creepers, 1939 (Rogers, R.)
Jeet, 1949 (Anand)
Jefe maximo, 1940 (Armendáriz)
Jeff, 1969 (Delon)
Jefferson in Paris, 1995 (Jones, James Earl; Nolte; Scacchi)
Jeffrey, 1995 (Weaver)
Jego Ostatni Czyn, 1916 (Negri)
Jekyll & Hyde, 1990 (Caine)
J'embrasse pas, 1991 (Léaud; Noiret)
Jengibre contra dinamita, 1939 (Cantinflas)
Jennie. *See* Portrait of Jennie, 1948
Jennie Gerhardt, 1933 (Astor; Sidney)

Jennifer, 1953 (Lupino)
Jennifer Eight, 1992 (García; Malkovich; Thurman)
Jennifer on My Mind, 1971 (De Niro)
Jenny, 1936 (Barrault; Rosay; Vanel)
Jenny, 1984 (Ullmann)
Jenny Is a Good Thing, 1969 (Lancaster)
Jenny Lind, 1931 (Rosay)
Jenny's War, 1985 (Grant, H.)
Jeopardy, 1953 (Stanwyck)
Jeremiah Johnson, 1972 (Redford)
Jericho, 1937 (Robeson)
Jéricho, 1946 (Brasseur)
Jerk, 1979 (Martin, S.)
Jerky Boys, 1994 (Arkin)
Jerrico, the Wonder Clown. *See* Three Ring Circus, 1954
Jerry Lewis Live, 1984 (Lewis, Jerry)
Jerry Maguire, 1997 (Cruise)
Jerusalem, 1996 (Von Sydow)
Jerusalem File, 1972 (Pleasence)
Jesse, 1988 (Remick)
Jesse James, 1939 (Barrymore, J.; Carradine; Fonda, H.; Power; Scott, R.)
Jesse James at Bay, 1941 (Rogers, R.)
Jessica, 1962 (Chevalier; Dalio; Dickinson; Moorehead)
Jesus of Nazareth, 1979 (Bancroft)
Jesusita en Chihuahua, 1942 (Infante)
Jet over the Atlantic, 1959 (Raft)
Jet Pilot, 1957 (Leigh, Janet; Wayne)
Jet Storm, 1959 (Attenborough; Baker; Zetterling)
J'étais une aventurière, 1938 (Feuillère)
Jettchen Geberts Geschichte, 1918 (Veidt)
Jeu avec le feu, 1975 (Noiret)
Jeu de la vérité, 1961 (Trintignant)
Jeu de massacre, 1967 (Cassel)
Jeu de solitaire, 1976 (Valli)
Jeune fille romanesque, 1909 (Linder)
Jeunes filles en détresse, 1939 (Presle)
Jeunes filles à marier, 1935 (Berry)
Jeunesse d'abord, 1935 (Brasseur)
Jeux d'adultes. *See* Padre di famiglia, 1967
Jeux de l'amour, 1959 (Cassel)
Jeux de la comtesse, 1980 (Cuny)
Jeux sont faits, 1947 (Presle)
Jew Suss, 1934 (Veidt)
Jewel, 1933 (Hawkins)
Jewel of the Nile, 1985 (DeVito; Douglas, Michael; Turner, K.)
Jewel Robbery, 1932 (Francis; Powell, W.)
Jewel Thief, 1967 (Anand)
Jeweller's Shop, 1987 (Lancaster)
Jewels in Our Hearts. *See* Tokyo no koibito, 1952
Jezebel, 1938 (Crisp; Davis, B.; Fonda, H.; Huston, J.)
Jezebel's Kiss, 1990 (McDowell)
JFK, 1991 (Candy; Costner; Jones, T.; Lemmon; Matthau; Oldman; Pesci; Sheen; Spacek; Sutherland)
Jhinder Bandi, 1961 (Chatterjee)
Jhoothi Shaan, 1992 (Azmi)
Jhoothi Sharm, 1989 (Azmi)
Jiban Saikate, 1972 (Chatterjee)
Jigoku-bana, 1957 (Kyo)
Jigoku kaido, 1929 (Hasegawa)
Jigoku no mon, 1952 (Hasegawa)
Jigoku no mushi, 1938 (Shimura)
Jigoku no soko made tsukiauze, 1959 (Yamamura)
Jigokubana, 1957 (Yamamura)
Jigokumon, 1953 (Hasegawa; Kyo)
Jigsaw, 1949 (Dietrich; Fonda, H.; Garfield; Meredith)
Jigsaw, 1972 (O'Brien, E.)
Jigsaw. *See* Homme en colère, 1979
Jigsaw Man, 1984 (Caine; Olivier)
Jihishincho, 1954 (Kagawa)
Jikizamurai, 1930 (Hasegawa)
Jilting of Granny Weatherall, 1980 (Fonda, H.)

Jim, 1914 (Mix)
Jim Bougne, boxeur, 1923 (Chevalier)
Jim Cameron's Wife, 1914 (Hart)
Jim Crow, 1912 (Vanel)
Jim la houlette, 1935 (Fernandel)
Jim the Penman, 1921 (Barrymore, L.)
Jim Thorpe: All American, 1951 (Lancaster)
Jimmy and Sally, 1933 (Trevor)
Jimmy Hayes and Muriel, 1914 (Mix)
Jimmy Hollywood, 1994 (Abril; Ford, H.; Pesci)
Jimmy the Gent, 1934 (Cagney; Davis, B.)
Jimmy the Kid, 1983 (Gordon)
Jinchoge, 1966 (Kyo; Tsukasa)
Jinpinin, 1928 (Hasegawa)
Jinsei gekijo seishun-hen, 1958 (Mifune)
Jinsei ni onimotsu, 1935 (Tanaka)
Jinsei tohbo-gaeri, 1955 (Yamada)
Jinx, 1919 (Normand)
Jinxed!, 1982 (Midler)
Jinya no Shotaro, 1934 (Yamada)
Jirocho Fuji, 1959 (Hasegawa; Kyo)
Jirokichi goshi, 1952 (Hasegawa)
Jisei wa utsuru, 1930 (Hasegawa)
Jitney Elopement, 1915 (Chaplin, C.; Purviance)
Jitterbugs, 1943 (Laurel and Hardy)
Jiyu-gakko, 1951 (Kyo; Yamamura)
Jo, 1971 (Blier)
Jo Jo Dancer, Your Life Is Calling, 1986 (Pryor)
Joan at the Stake. *See* Giovanna d'Arco al rogo, 1954
Joan of Arc, 1948 (Bergman; Bond; Ferrer)
Joan of Ozark, 1942 (Brown)
Joan of Paris, 1942 (Dalio; Henreid; Ladd; Morgan)
Joan of Plattsburg, 1918 (Normand)
Joan of the Cattle Country. *See* Straight Shooting, 1917
Joan the Woman, 1915 (Crisp; Novarro)
Joanna, 1925 (Del Rio)
Joanna, 1968 (Sutherland)
Joanna Francesca, 1973 (Moreau)
Joaquin Murieta, 1964 (Kennedy)
Job Charnaker Bibi, 1978 (Chatterjee)
Jobb Szepnek es Gazdagnak Lenni, 1993 (Olbrychski)
Jocks, 1987 (Lee, C.)
Joe, 1970 (Sarandon)
Joe and Ethel Turp Call on the President, 1939 (Brennan)
Joe Battle. *See* Brannigan, 1975
Joe Butterfly, 1957 (Meredith)
Joe Dakota, 1957 (Van Cleef)
Joe Kidd, 1972 (Duvall; Eastwood)
Joe Palooka, 1934-7 (Three Stooges)
Joe Palooka. *See* Palooka, 1934
Joe Smith, American, 1942 (Gardner; Young, R.)
Joe Valachi: I segretti di Cosa Nostra. *See* Valachi Papers, 1972
Joe versus the Volcano, 1990 (Hanks; Ryan, M.)
Joe y Margherito. *See* Arrivano Joe e Margherito, 1974
Joe's Bed-Stuy Barbershop: We Cut Heads, 1983 (Lee, S.)
Joen no hatoba, 1951 (Kyo)
Jofusei, 1927 (Hasegawa)
Jogakusei-ki, 1941 (Takamine; Yamada)
Jogan, 1950 (Kumar)
Jogashima no ame, 1950 (Hasegawa)
Johann Hopkins der Dritte, 1921 (Lugosi)
Johann Strauss, K und I. Hofballmusikdirektor. *See* Kaiserwalzer, 1932
Johanna D'Arc of Mongolia, 1988 (Marais; Seyrig)
Johanna Enlists, 1918 (Beery; Pickford)
Johannes Goth, 1920 (Krauss)
Johannisnacht, 1933 (Dagover)
John and Julie, 1955 (Sellers)
John and Mary, 1969 (Farrow; Hoffman)
John F. Kennedy: Years of Lightning, Day of Drums, 1966 (Peck; Schell, Maximilian)
John Goldfarb, Please Come Home, 1964 (MacLaine; Ustinov)

John Halifax, Gentleman, 1938 (McDowall)
John Huston: A War Remembered, 1981 (Huston, J.)
John Huston: The Man, the Movies, the Maverick, 1988 (Mitchum)
John Huston's Dublin, 1980 (Huston, J.)
John Loves Mary, 1949 (Neal; Reagan)
John Paul Jones, 1959 (Coburn, C.; Cushing; Davis, B.; Farrow)
John Petticoats, 1919 (Hart)
John Rance—Gentleman, 1914 (Talmadge)
John Smith, 1922 (Astor)
John Smith Wakes Up, 1940 (Greenwood)
Johnny Allegro, 1949 (Raft)
Johnny Angel, 1945 (Trevor)
Johnny Angelo, 1945 (Raft)
Johnny Apollo, 1940 (Lamour; Power)
Johnny Be Good, 1988 (Thurman)
Johnny Belinda, 1948 (Ayres; Moorehead; Wyman)
Johnny Belinda, 1967 (Farrow)
Johnny Belinda, 1982 (Quaid)
Johnny Bull, 1986 (Bates, K.; Robards)
Johnny Come Lately, 1943 (Cagney; McDaniel)
Johnny Concho, 1956 (Sidney)
Johnny Dangerously, 1984 (DeVito; Keaton, M.)
Johnny Dark, 1954 (Curtis, T.)
Johnny Doesn't Live Here Anymore, 1944 (Mitchum)
Johnny Eager, 1942 (Taylor, R.; Turner, L.)
Johnny Frenchman, 1945 (Rosay)
Johnny Get Your Gun, 1919 (Crisp)
Johnny Got His Gun, 1971 (Robards; Sutherland)
Johnny Guitar, 1954 (Bond; Borgnine; Carradine; Crawford, J.; Hayden; Hopper)
Johnny Handsome, 1989 (Freeman; Rourke; Whitaker; Barkin)
Johnny haute-couture, 1934 (Brasseur)
Johnny in the Clouds. See Way to the Stars, 1945
Johnny le Fligueur, 1973 (Van Cleef)
Johnny Mera Naam, 1970 (Anand)
Johnny Mnemonic, 1995 (Reeves)
Johnny Nobody, 1960 (Cusack)
Johnny O'Clock, 1947 (Cobb; Powell, D.)
Johnny Reno, 1966 (Andrews, D.; Russell, J.)
Johnny Stecchino, 1991 (Benigni)
Johnny Stool Pigeon, 1949 (Curtis, T.; Duryea; Winters)
Johnny Suede, 1992 (Jackson, S.; Pitt)
Johnny Tiger, 1966 (Taylor, R.)
Johnny Toothpick. See Johnny Stecchino, 1991
Johnny Trouble, 1957 (Barrymore, E.)
Johnny Vagabond. See Johnny Come Lately, 1943
Johnny, We Hardly Knew Ye, 1977 (Meredith)
Johnstown Flood, 1926 (Gable; Gaynor)
Joi Baba Felunath, 1978 (Chatterjee)
Joi Kinuyo sensei, 1936 (Tanaka)
Joi no Kiroku, 1941 (Tanaka)
Joi-uchi, 1967 (Mifune; Tsukasa)
Joka, 1952 (Yamamura)
Joke of Destiny, Lying in Wait around the Corner Like a Street Bandit. See Scherzo del destinoin aqquato dietro l'angolo come un brigante di strada, 1983
Jokei, 1960 (Kyo)
Jokei kazoku, 1963 (Kyo)
Joker, 1987 (Mueller-Stahl)
Joker. See Farceur, 1961
Joker. See Lethal Obsession, 1988
Joker Is Wild, 1957 (Sidney)
Jokers, 1966 (Reed)
Joli Mai, 1962 (Karina; Montand)
Joligud. See Hollywood, 1923
Jolson Sings Again, 1949 (Jolson)
Jolson Story, 1946 (Jolson)
Jonan no Yoemon, 1931 (Hasegawa)
Jonas in the Desert, 1993 (Pacino)
Jonathan Swift, 1967 (Cusack)
Jones Family in Hollywood, 1939 (Keaton, B.)

Jones Family in Quick Millions, 1939 (Keaton, B.)
Jonetsu, 1932 (Takamine)
Jonetsu no rumuba, 1950 (Yamamura)
Jons und Erdme, 1959 (Masina)
Joobachi, 1952 (Mori)
Joobachi, 1978 (Tsukasa)
Joradighir Choudhury Paribar, 1966 (Chatterjee)
Josef und seine Brüder, 1922 (Krauss)
Josei no kakugo, 1940 (Tanaka)
Josei no shori, 1946 (Tanaka)
Josei tai dansei, 1950 (Yamamura)
Joseph, 1995 (Kingsley; Landau)
Joseph Andrews, 1976 (Ann-Margret: Gielgud)
Josephine and Men, 1955 (Buchanan; Finch)
Josette, 1936 (Fernandel)
Josette, 1938 (Ameche; Young, R.)
Joshila, 1973 (Anand)
Joshu to tomoni, 1957 (Hara; Kagawa; Tanaka)
Joshua Then and Now, 1985 (Arkin; Woods)
Jotai, 1969 (Okada)
Jouens le jeu, 1952 (Brasseur)
Jouet Criminel, 1970 (Marais)
Jouet de la fatalité. See Adhémar, 1951
Joueur, 1948 (Rosay)
Joueur, 1958 (Blier; Philipe)
Joueur d'echecs, 1938 (Modot; Rosay; Veidt)
Jouons le jeu ... L'Avarice, 1952 (Chevalier)
Jour à Paris, 1965 (Trintignant)
Jour de fête, 1949 (Tati)
Jour de fête, 1974 (Baye)
Jour de tournage, 1969 (Montand)
Jour des Rois, 1991 (Darrieux)
Jour et l'heure, 1963 (Piccoli)
Jour peut-être à San Pedro ou ailleurs, 1977 (Cardinale)
Jour se lève, 1939 (Arletty; Berry; Blier; Gabin; Reggiani)
Journal d'un combat, 1964 (Delon)
Journal d'un suicide, 1972 (Seyrig)
Journal d'une femme de chambre. See Diary of a Chambermaid, 1946
Journal d'une femme de chambre, 1964 (Moreau; Piccoli)
Journal du Seducteur, 1995 (Presle)
Journal of a Crime, 1934 (Menjou; Pidgeon)
Journal tombe à cing heures, 1942 (Blier; Fresnay)
Journalist. See Zhurnalist, 1966
Journalist, 1979 (Neill)
Journée bien remplie, 1972 (Trintignant)
Journey, 1959 (Aimée; Brynner; Kerr; Robards)
Journey, 1972 (Bujold)
Journey. See Viaggio, 1973
Journey. See Viaje, 1992
Journey, 1995 (Robards)
Journey Back to Oz, 1974 (Minnelli; Rooney)
Journey beneath the Desert. See Antinea, 1961
Journey for Margaret, 1942 (O'Brien, M.; Young, R.)
Journey into Autumn. See Kvinnodröm, 1955
Journey into Fear, 1942 (Cotten; Del Rio; Moorehead; Sloane; Welles)
Journey into Fear, 1974 (Pleasence; Price; Winters)
Journey into Light, 1951 (Hayden)
Journey into the Beyond, 1977 (Carradine)
Journey of Honor, 1992 (Lee, C.)
Journey of Honor. See Shogun Mayeda, 1991
Journey of Love. See Viaggio d'Amore, 1990
Journey to Italy. See **Viaggio in Italia**, 1953
Journey to Shiloh, 1968 (Caan; Ford, H.)
Journey to the Center of the Earth, 1959 (Mason)
Journey to the Far Side of the Sun. See Doppelganger, 1969
Journey Together, 1945 (Attenborough; Harrison)
Journey Together, 1946 (Robinson, E.)
Journey with Papa. See In viaggio con papa, 1982
Jours tranquilles à Clichy, 1990 (Audran)
Jovanda e le altre, 1960 (Mangano)
Jowita, 1967 (Olbrychski)

Joy Girl, 1927 (Dressler)
Joy House. *See* Félins, 1964
Joy in the Morning, 1965 (Homolka; Kennedy)
Joy of Learning. *See* Gai Savoir, 1968
Joy of Living, 1938 (Ball; Dunne)
Joyeuses Pâques, 1984 (Belmondo)
Joyless Streets. *See* Freudlose Gasse, 1925
Joyride, 1977 (Griffith)
Joyu, 1947 (Yamada)
Joyu Sumako no koi, 1947 (Tanaka; Yamamura)
Ju Dou, 1990 (Gong Li)
Juan Charrasqueado, 1947 (Armendáriz)
Juana Gallo, 1959 (Félix)
Juarez, 1939 (Calhern; Crisp; Davis, B.; Garfield; Huston, J.; Muni; Rains)
Jubal, 1956 (Borgnine; Bronson; Ford, G.; Steiger)
Jubilo, 1920 (Rogers, W.)
Jubilo, Jr., 1924 (Rogers, W.)
Jubilo. *See* Too Busy to Work, 1932
Jud Süss, 1940 (Krauss)
Judas von Tirol, 1932 (Rasp)
Judge and His Hangman. *See* Richter und sein Henker, 1975
Judge and Jake Wyler, 1972 (Davis, B.)
Judge and the Assassin. *See* Juge et l'assassin, 1976
Judge Dredd, 1995 (Stallone; Von Sydow)
Judge Hardy and Son, 1939 (Rooney)
Judge Hardy's Children, 1938 (Rooney)
Judge Priest, 1934 (McDaniel; Rogers, W.)
Judgment at Nuremberg, 1961 (Clift; Dietrich; Garland; Lancaster; Schell, Maximilian; Tracy; Widmark)
Judgment in Berlin, 1988 (Penn; Sheen)
Judgment in Stone. *See* Ceremonie, 1995
Judith, 1965 (Finch; Hawkins; Loren)
Judith of Bethulia, 1914 (Barrymore, L.; Carey; Gish; Marsh; Sweet)
Judo Saga. *See* Sugata Sanshiro, 1965
Judo Saga, Part II. *See* Zoku Sugata Sanshiro, 1945
Jueces de la Biblia, 1966 (Rey)
Juego Mas Divertido, 1987 (Abril)
Juge et l'assassin, 1976 (Huppert; Noiret)
Jugement de minuit, 1932 (Fernandel)
Jugend, 1922 (Rasp)
Jugend und Tollheit, 1912 (Nielsen)
Jugendrausch, 1927 (Fröhlich)
Juggernaut, 1974 (Cusack; Harris, R.; Hopkins, A.; Sharif)
Juggler, 1953 (Douglas, K.)
Juggler of Our Lady, 1957 (Karloff)
Juggling with Fate, 1913 (Mix)
Jugnu, 1947 (Kumar)
Juice, 1992 (Jackson, S.)
Juif errant, 1926 (Artaud)
Jujin Yukiotoko. *See* Half Human, 1957
Juke Girl, 1942 (Reagan)
Jukyu no hanayome, 1955 (Yamamura)
Jukyu-sai no haru, 1933 (Takamine)
Jules et Jim, 1962 (Moreau; Werner)
Jules of the Strong Heart, 1918 (Crisp)
Jules Verne's Rocket to the Moon, 1967 (Terry-Thomas)
Julia, 1977 (Fonda, J.; Redgrave, V.; Robards; Schell, Maximilian; Streep)
Julia and Julia. *See* Giulia e Giulia, 1987
Julia Has Two Lovers, 1991 (Hershey)
Julia Misbehaves, 1948 (Garson; Pidgeon; Taylor, E.)
Julie, 1956 (Day; Jourdan; Marsh)
Julie de Carneilhan, 1950 (Brasseur; Feuillère)
Julie la Rousse, 1959 (Gélin)
Julie the Redhead. *See* Julie la Rousse, 1959
Juliet of the Spirits. *See* Giulietta degli spiriti, 1965
Julietta, 1953 (Marais; Moreau)
Juliette et Juliette, 1973 (Girardot)
Juliette ou la clef des songes, 1951 (Philipe)
Julius Caesar, 1950 (Heston)
Julius Caesar, 1953 (Brando; Calhern; Garson; Gielgud; Kerr; Mason; O'Brien, E.)

Julius Caesar, 1970 (Gielgud; Heston; Lee, C.; Robards)
July 14th. *See* Quatorze Juillet, 1933
Jumanji, 1995 (Williams, R.)
Jumbo, 1962 (Day; Durante)
Jumeaux de Brighton, 1936 (Raimu)
Jump into Hell, 1955 (Dalio)
Jumpin' at the Boneyard, 1992 (Jackson, S.)
Jumpin' Jack Flash, 1986 (Goldberg)
Jumping Jacks, 1952 (Lewis, Jerry; Martin, D.)
June Bride, 1948 (Davis, B.; Montgomery; Reynolds, D.)
June Night. *See* Juninatt, 1965
Jungfrukällen, 1960 (Von Sydow)
Jungle Book, 1968 (Sanders)
Jungle Book. *See* Rudyard Kipling's the Jungle Book, 1994
Jungle Fever, 1991 (Jackson, S.; Lee, S.; Quinn; Robbins; Snipes; Turturro)
Jungle Fighters. *See* Long and the Short and the Tall, 1961
Jungle Jim, 1948 (Weissmuller)
Jungle Jim in the Forbidden Land, 1952 (Weissmuller)
Jungle Manhunt, 1951 (Weissmuller)
Jungle Mission. *See* Unser Mann im Dschungel, 1986
Jungle Moon-Men, 1955 (Weissmuller)
Jungle Patrol, 1944 (Finch)
Jungle Princess, 1936 (Lamour; Milland)
Jungle Raiders, 1985 (Van Cleef)
Juninatt, 1965 (Andersson, B.)
Juninatten, 1940 (Bergman; Björnstrand)
Junior, 1994 (DeVito; Schwarzenegger; Thompson)
Junior Bonner, 1972 (Lupino; McQueen; Preston)
Juno and the Paycock, 1929 (Fitzgerald)
Junoon, 1978 (Azmi)
Junpaku no yoru, 1951 (Mori)
Jupiter's Darling, 1954 (Sanders; Williams, E.)
Jupiter's Thigh. *See* On a volé la cuisse de Jupiter, 1980
Jupon rouge, 1987 (Valli)
Jurassic Park, 1993 (Attenborough; Jackson, S.; Neill)
Jurokuya seishin, 1931 (Hasegawa)
Juror, 1996 (Moore, Demi)
Jury Duty, 1995 (Winters)
Jury of One. *See* Testament, 1974
Jury's Evidence, 1936 (Lockwood)
Jury's Secret, 1938 (Wray)
Jus' Passin' Through, 1923 (Rogers, W.)
Jusqu-au dernier, 1956 (Moreau)
Just a Few Little Things, 1916 (Beery)
Just a Gigolo, 1931 (Milland)
Just a Gigolo. *See* Schöner Gigolo—armer Gigolo, 1979
Just a Little Inconvenience, 1977 (Hershey)
Just a Song at Twilight, 1922 (Barthelmess)
Just an Echo, 1934 (Crosby)
Just Another Blonde, 1926 (Brooks, L.)
Just Another Pretty Face. *See* Sois belle et tais-toi, 1958
Just around the Corner, 1938 (Robinson, B.; Temple)
Just Ask for a Diamond, 1988 (York)
Just before Nightfall. *See* Juste avant la nuit, 1971
Just Brown's Luck, 1913 (Normand)
Just Call Me Jim, 1920 (Rogers, W.)
Just Cause, 1995 (Connery; Fishburne)
Just Cause, 1995 (Harris, E.)
Just Dropped In, 1919 (Lloyd)
Just for Kicks. *See* Hecc, 1989
Just for You, 1952 (Barrymore, E.; Crosby; Wood; Wyman)
Just Gold, 1913 (Barrymore, L.; Gish)
Just Great. *See* **Tout va bien**, 1973
Just Imagine, 1930 (O'Sullivan)
Just Kids, 1913 (Gish)
Just Like a Woman, 1912 (Pickford)
Just Like at Home. *See* Olyan, mint otthon, 1978
Just Like Friends. *See* För vänskaps skull, 1965
Just Me. *See* Ma Pomme, 1950
Just My Luck, 1957 (Rutherford; Wisdom)
Just Neighbors, 1919 (Lloyd)

Katherine, 1975 (Spacek)
Kathleen, 1941 (Marshall; Temple)
Kathleen Mavourneen, 1919 (Bara)
Kathy O', 1957 (Duryea)
Katia, 1938 (Darrieux)
Katia, 1960 (Schneider)
Katie: Portrait of a Centerfold, 1978 (Basinger; Malone)
Katinka. See Vid vejen, 1988
Kato and the Green Hornet, 1974 (Lee, B.)
Kattorna, 1965 (Dahlbeck)
Katug nogenkai, 1948 (Hara)
Katzelmacher, 1969 (Schygulla)
Kaufmann von Venedig, 1923 (Krauss)
Kauft Mariett-Aktien, 1922 (Banky)
Kavik, the Wolf Dog. See Courage of Kavik, the Wolf Dog, 1980
Kawanakajima gassen, 1941 (Hasegawa; Yamada)
Kawano hotoride, 1962 (Yamamura)
Kazan-myaku, 1950 (Mori)
Každý den odvahu, 1964 (Brodský)
Kaze futatabi, 1952 (Yamamura)
Kaze no naka no mendori, 1948 (Ryu; Tanaka)
Kaze tachinu, 1954 (Yamamura)
Kazoku, 1942 (Tanaka)
Kean, 1924 (Mozhukin)
Kean, 1940 (Brazzi)
Kean, 1956 (Gassman)
Kean, 1978 (Hopkins, A.)
Keene, 1969 (Cotten)
Keep 'em Rolling, 1934 (Huston, W.)
Keep 'em Slugging, 1943 (Three Stooges)
Keep 'em Flying, 1941 (Abbott and Costello)
Keep It Up Downstairs, 1976 (Dors)
Keep Laughing, 1932 (Arbuckle)
Keep Smiling, 1938 (Fields, G.)
Keep the Change, 1992 (Palance)
Keep Your Powder Dry, 1945 (Moorehead; Turner, L.)
Keeper, 1983 (Lee, C.)
Keeper of the Bees, 1925 (Bow)
Keeper of the Flame, 1943 (Hepburn, K.; Tracy)
Keepers. See Tête contre les murs, 1958
Keeping Fit, 1942 (Crawford, B.)
Keian hi-cho, 1952 (Yamamura)
Keimendes Leben, 1918-19 (Jannings)
Keine Angst vor Liebe, 1933 (Walbrook)
Keine zufällige Geschichte, 1984 (Mercouri)
Keishicho monogatari:, 1960 (Yamamura)
Keitsik, 1989 (Chan)
Kekkon, 1947 (Tanaka)
Kekkon he no michi, 1937 (Yamada)
Kekkonkaido, 1933 (Tanaka)
Kekkonshiki kekkonshiki, 1963 (Tanaka)
Kelly's Heroes, 1970 (Eastwood; Stanton; Sutherland)
Ken Murray's Hollywood, 1965 (Grant, C.)
Ken to hana, 1972 (Mori)
Kenju jigoku, 1952 (Yamamura)
Kenka-tobi, 1939 (Hasegawa; Yamada)
Kennel Murder Case, 1933 (Astor; Powell, W.)
Keno Bates, Liar, 1915 (Hart)
Kensetsu no hitobito, 1934 (Yamada)
Kent State, 1981 (Barkin)
Kentuckian, 1955 (Carradine; Lancaster; Matthau; Van Cleef)
Kentucky, 1938 (Brennan; Young, L.)
Kentucky Fried Movie, 1977 (Sutherland)
Kentucky Kernels, 1934 (Dumont)
Kentucky Moonshine, 1938 (Carradine)
Kept Husbands, 1931 (McCrea)
Kermesse héroïque, 1935 (Jouvet; Rosay)
Kesho, 1985 (Kyo)
Keshoyuki, 1940 (Yamada)
Kessen no ozura e, 1943 (Hara)
Kettevalt Mennyezet, 1982 (Nowicki)

Ketto ganryu-jima, 1956 (Mifune; Shimura)
Ketto kagiya no tsuji, 1952 (Mifune; Shimura)
Keufs, 1987 (Léaud)
Key, 1934 (Crisp; Powell, W.)
Key, 1953 (Lancaster)
Key, 1958 (Caine; Holden; Homolka; Howard, T.; Loren)
Key and the Ring. See Nyckeln och ringen, 1947
Key Exchange, 1985 (Aiello)
Key Largo, 1948 (Bacall; Barrymore, L.; Bogart; Huston, J.; Robinson, E.; Trevor)
Key Man, 1954 (Lansbury)
Key to Rebecca, 1985 (Quayle; Robertson)
Key to the City, 1950 (Gable; Young, L.)
Key Witness, 1958 (Hopper)
Keyhole, 1933 (Brennan; Francis)
Keys of the Kingdom, 1944 (McDowall; Peck; Price)
Keys to Freedom, 1988 (Elliott; Sharif)
Khamosh, 1985 (Azmi)
Khandahar, 1983 (Azmi)
Khartoum, 1966 (Heston; Olivier; Richardson, R.)
Khel, 1950 (Anand)
Khel Khiladi ka, 1977 (Azmi)
Khelar Putul, 1981 (Chatterjee)
Khoon ki pukar, 1978 (Azmi)
Khrani menio, moi talisman, 1986 (Yankovsky)
Khunje Berai, 1971 (Chatterjee)
Kibo no aozora, 1960 (Hara)
Kibo no otome, 1958 (Yamamura)
Kick Back, 1922 (Carey)
Kick In, 1931 (Bow; Crisp)
Kickboxer, 1989 (Van Damme)
Kicked Out, 1918 (Lloyd)
Kicking and Screaming, 1996 (Gould)
Kicking the Germ out of Germany, 1918 (Lloyd)
Kicking the Moon Around, 1938 (O'Hara)
Kid, 1921 (Chaplin, C.; Purviance)
Kid 'n' Africa, 1933 (Temple)
Kid 'n' Hollywood, 1933 (Temple)
Kid Auto Races at Venice, 1914 (Chaplin, C.)
Kid Blue, 1973 (Hopper; Oates)
Kid Boots, 1926 (Bow; Cantor)
Kid Brother, 1927 (Lloyd)
Kid Cheung, 1949 (Lee, B.)
Kid for Two Farthings, 1955 (Dors; Johnson)
Kid from Brooklyn, 1946 (Kaye)
Kid from Kokomo, 1939 (Blondell; Bond; Wyman)
Kid from Left Field, 1953 (Bancroft)
Kid from Spain, 1932 (Cantor; Goddard; Grable; Wyman; Young, R.)
Kid Galahad, 1937 (Bogart; Carey; Davis, B.; Robinson, E.)
Kid Galahad, 1962 (Bronson; Presley)
Kid Glove Killer, 1942 (Gardner)
Kid Gloves. See Split Decisions, 1988
Kid Millions, 1934 (Ball; Bond; Cantor; Goddard)
Kid Nightingale, 1939 (Wyman)
Kid Rodelo, 1965 (Crawford, B.; Leigh, Janet)
Kid Speed, 1924 (Laurel and Hardy)
Kid Vengeance, 1977 (Van Cleef)
Kid Who Loved Christmas, 1990 (Murphy)
Kid's Last Fight, 1933 (Temple)
Kidnapped, 1938 (Carradine)
Kidnapped, 1948 (McDowall)
Kidnapped, 1960 (Finch; O'Toole)
Kidnapped, 1971 (Caine; Hawkins; Howard, T.; Pleasence)
Kidnappers, 1964 (Meredith)
Kidnapping of the President, 1980 (Gardner)
Kids Are Alright, 1978 (Martin, S.)
Kids of the Round Table, 1995 (McDowell)
Kiganjo no boken, 1966 (Mifune)
Kiiroi karasu, 1957 (Tanaka)
Kika, 1994 (Abril)
Kiken na eiyu, 1957 (Mifune; Tsukasa)

Kiki, 1926 (Colman; Talmadge)
Kiki, 1931 (Grable; Pickford)
Kikikomi, 1960 (Yamamura)
Kikugoro goshi, 1932 (Hasegawa; Hasegawa)
Kikyo, 1950 (Yamamura)
Kikyo, 1964 (Mori)
Kilenc hónap, 1976 (Nowicki)
Kill!, 1971 (Seberg)
Kill a Dragon, 1967 (Palance)
Kill or Cure, 1923 (Laurel and Hardy)
Kill or Cure, 1962 (Terry-Thomas)
Killer, 1996 (Woods)
Killer Ape, 1953 (Weissmuller)
Killer aus Florida, 1983 (Ganz)
Killer Bees, 1974 (Swanson)
Killer Cop. See Polizia ha le mani legate, 1974
Killer Elite, 1975 (Caan; Duvall)
Killer Force, 1975 (Lee, C.)
Killer from Yuma. See Viva la muerte ... tua!, 1972
Killer in the Family, 1983 (Mitchum)
Killer Inside Me, 1976 (Carradine)
Killer Is Loose, 1956 (Cotten)
Killer McCoy, 1947 (Rooney)
Killer Meteors, 1976 (Chan)
Killer Nun. See Suor omicidi, 1978
Killer on a Horse. See Welcome to Hard Times, 1967
Killer Shark, 1950 (McDowall)
Killer That Stalked New York, 1950 (Malone)
Killers, 1946 (Gardner; Huston, J.; Lancaster; O'Brien, E.)
Killers, 1963 (Dickinson; Marvin; Reagan)
Killers. See Verano sangrieto, 1977
Killers Carnival. See Spie contro il mondo, 1966
Killers of Kilimanjaro, 1959 (Pleasence; Taylor, R.)
Killing, 1956 (Hayden)
Killing 'em Softly. See Man in 5A, 1983
Killing Beach. See Turtle Beach, 1992
Killing Blue. See Midnight Cop, 1989
Killing Box, 1993 (Sheen)
Killing Cars, 1986 (Gélin)
Killing Dad, 1989 (Elliott)
Killing Fields, 1984 (Malkovich)
Killing Game. See Jeu de massacre, 1967
Killing Horace, 1914 (Arbuckle)
Killing in a Small Town, 1990 (Hershey)
Killing in Monte Carlo. See Crimen, 1960
Killing Machine, 1983 (Van Cleef)
Killing of Randy Webster, 1981 (Leigh, Jennifer Jason; Penn)
Killing of Sister George, 1968 (York)
Killjoy, 1981 (Basinger)
Kilroy on Deck. See French Leave, 1948
Kilroy Was Here, 1947 (Cooper)
Kim, 1950 (Flynn; Lukas)
Kim, 1984 (O'Toole)
Kimi shinitamoukoto nakare, 1954 (Tsukasa)
Kimi to yuku amerika-kogo, 1950 (Kagawa)
Kin no tamago, 1952 (Kagawa)
Kinare Kinare, 1963 (Anand)
Kind Hearts and Coronets, 1949 (Greenwood; Guinness)
Kind Lady, 1935 (Rathbone)
Kind Lady, 1951 (Barrymore, E.; Lansbury)
Kind of Loving, 1962 (Bates, A.)
Kind ruft, 1914 (Nielsen)
Kindai musha shugyo, 1928 (Tanaka)
Kinder des Generals, 1912 (Nielsen)
Kinder in Gottes Hand, 1952 (Dahlbeck)
Kinder, Mütter, und ein General, 1954 (Kinski; Schell, Maximilian)
Kinderen van Ghana, 1988 (Ustinov)
Kindergarten, 1984 (Brandauer)
Kindergarten Cop, 1990 (Bassett; Schwarzenegger)
Kinderseelen klagen euch an, 1927 (Rasp)
Kindred, 1987 (Steiger)

Kinema no tenchi, 1986 (Ryu)
King, 1930 (Langdon)
King. See Roi, 1949
King: A Filmed Record ... Montgomery to Memphis, 1970 (Heston; Jones, James Earl; Lancaster; Quinn; Woodward)
King and Country, 1964 (Bogarde)
King and Four Queens, 1956 (Gable)
King and I, 1956 (Brynner; Kerr)
King and the Chorus Girl, 1937 (Blondell; Horton; Wyman)
King Charlie. See His Prehistoric Past, 1914
King Cowboy, 1928 (Mix)
King Creole, 1958 (Matthau; Presley)
King David, 1985 (Gere)
King Gun. See Gatling Gun, 1973
King in New York, 1957 (Chaplin, C.)
King Kong, 1933 (Wray)
King Kong, 1976 (Bridges; Lange)
King Lear, 1953 (Welles)
King Lear, 1971 (Cusack)
King Lear, 1983 (Hurt, J.; Olivier)
King Lear, 1987 (Allen; Meredith)
King of Africa. See One Step to Hell, 1968
King of Alcatraz, 1938 (Carey; Preston; Quinn)
King of Burlesque, 1936 (Faye; Wyman)
King of Chinatown, 1939 (Quinn; Wong)
King of Comedy, 1982 (De Niro; Lewis, Jerry; Minnelli)
King of Gamblers, 1937 (Brooks, L.; Trevor)
King of Hearts, 1936 (Withers)
King of Hearts, 1966 (Bates, A.; Brasseur; Bujold; Presle)
King of Jazz, 1930 (Brennan; Crosby)
King of Kings, 1961 (Ryan, R.; Welles)
King of Life. See Az elet kiralya, 1918
King of Marvin Gardens, 1972 (Burstyn; Dern; Nicholson)
King of New York, 1990 (Fishburne; Snipes; Walken)
King of Paris, 1934 (Richardson, R.)
King of Paris. See Roi de Paris, 1995
King of Soho. See Street of Sin, 1928
King of the Circus. See Zirkuskönig, 1924
King of the Cowboys, 1943 (Rogers, R.)
King of the Damned, 1936 (Veidt)
King of the Gypsies, 1978 (Hayden; Sarandon; Winters)
King of the Hill, 1993 (Redford)
King of the Khyber Rifles. See Black Watch, 1929
King of the Mountain, 1981 (Hopper)
King of the Newsboys, 1938 (Ayres)
King of the Pecos, 1936 (Wayne)
King of the River, 1995 (Maura)
King of the Roaring Twenties, 1961 (Dors; Rooney)
King of the Turf, 1939 (Menjou)
King of the Underworld, 1939 (Bogart; Francis)
King of the Wild, 1931 (Karloff)
King of the Wind, 1989 (Harris, R.; Jackson, G.; Quayle)
King on Main Street, 1925 (Menjou)
King, Queen, Knave, 1972 (Niven)
King Ralph, 1991 (Hurt, J.; O'Toole)
King Rat, 1965 (Elliott; Mills; Segal)
King Richard and the Crusaders, 1954 (Harrison; Sanders)
King Richard the Lion-Hearted, 1923 (Beery)
King Solomon, 1918 (Laurel and Hardy)
King Solomon's Mines, 1937 (Robeson)
King Solomon's Mines, 1950 (Granger; Kerr)
King Solomon's Mines, 1985 (Lom; Stone)
Kingdom of Diamonds. See Hirak Rajar Deshe, 1980
Kingfisher, 1983 (Cusack; Harrison)
Kingpin, 1996 (Murray)
King's Dancer. See Tänzerin von Sanssouci, 1933
King's Game, 1916 (White)
Kings Go Forth, 1958 (Curtis, T.; Sidney; Wood)
King's Jester. See Re si diverte, 1941
Kings of the Road. See **Im Lauf der Zeit**, 1976
Kings of the Sun, 1963 (Brynner)

King's Rhapsody, 1955 (Flynn; Neagle)
Kings Row, 1941 (Coburn, C.; Rains; Reagan)
King's Story, 1967 (Welles)
King's Thief, 1955 (Niven; Sanders)
King's Vacation, 1933 (Powell, D.)
Kinjite: Forbidden Subjects, 1989 (Bronson)
Kinkan-shoku, 1975 (Kyo)
Kinno inakazamurai, 1932 (Yamada)
Kinno inakazamurai, 1937 (Yamada)
Kinno jidai, 1927 (Hasegawa)
Kinoerzaehler, 1993 (Mueller-Stahl)
Kinokawa: Hana-no maki, Fumio-no maki, 1966 (Tsukasa)
Kinsei Meishobu monogatari: Ogongai no hosha, 1954 (Yamada)
Kinu Goyalar Gali, 1964 (Chatterjee)
Kinuyo monogatari, 1930 (Tanaka)
Kinuyo no hatsukoi, 1940 (Tanaka)
Kipps, 1941 (Redgrave, M.)
Kirare no Senta, 1949 (Yamamura)
Kirare Yosa, 1928 (Hasegawa)
Kiri no minato no akai hana, 1962 (Kagawa)
Kiri no yobanashi, 1946 (Hasegawa)
Kismet, 1931 (Fröhlich; Young, L.)
Kismet, 1944 (Colman; Dietrich)
Kisoji no tabigasa, 1937 (Shimura)
Kisoshinju, 1927 (Tanaka)
Kiss, 1916 (Menjou)
Kiss, 1929 (Ayres; Garbo)
Kiss and Kill. See Blood of Fu Manchu, 1968
Kiss and Make Up, 1934 (Grant, C.; Horton)
Kiss and Tell, 1945 (Temple)
Kiss before Dying, 1956 (Astor; Woodward)
Kiss before Dying, 1991 (Dillon; Von Sydow)
Kiss before the Mirror, 1933 (Lukas; Pidgeon)
Kiss Daddy Goodnight, 1987 (Thurman)
Kiss for Corliss, 1949 (Niven; Temple)
Kiss in the Dark, 1925 (Menjou)
Kiss in the Dark, 1949 (Crawford, B.; Niven; Wyman)
Kiss Me Again, 1925 (Bow)
Kiss Me Again, 1931 (Horton; Pidgeon)
Kiss Me Goodbye, 1982 (Bridges; Caan; Field; Trevor)
Kiss Me Kate, 1953 (Miller)
Kiss Me, Stupid, 1964 (Martin, D.; Novak)
Kiss My Hand. See Bacciamo le mani, 1973
Kiss of a Killer, 1993 (Saint)
Kiss of Death, 1995 (Cage; Jackson, S.)
Kiss of Fire, 1995 (Palance)
Kiss of Fire. See Naples au baiser de feu, 1937
Kiss of Hate, 1916 (Barrymore, E.)
Kiss of the Spider Woman, 1985 (Braga; Hurt, W.; Julia)
Kiss on the Cruise. See Kyssen på kryssen, 1950
Kiss Shot, 1989 (Goldberg)
Kiss the Blood off My Hands, 1948 (Fontaine; Lancaster)
Kiss the Boys Goodbye, 1941 (Ameche)
Kiss the Girls and Make Them Die, 1966 (Terry-Thomas)
Kiss Them for Me, 1957 (Grant, C.; Mansfield)
Kiss Tomorrow Goodbye, 1950 (Bond; Cagney)
Kissa Kursi Ka, 1977 (Azmi)
Kisses for Breakfast, 1941 (Wilde)
Kisses for My President, 1964 (MacMurray; Wallach)
Kissin' Cousins, 1964 (Presley)
Kissing Bandit, 1948 (Charisse; Miller; Sidney)
Kissing Cup's Race, 1930 (Carroll)
Kit & Co.—Lockruf des Goldes, 1974 (Mueller-Stahl)
Kit Carson, 1940 (Andrews, D.; Bond)
Kit Carson's Wooing, 1911 (Mix)
Kita no misaki, 1976 (Tanaka)
Kita no san-nin, 1946 (Takamine)
Kite. See Patang, 1994
Kitten with a Whip, 1964 (Ann-Margret)
Kitty, 1945 (Goddard; Milland)
Kitty Foyle, 1940 (Rogers, G.)

Kitty und die grosse Welt, 1956 (Schneider)
Kizoku no kaidan, 1959 (Mori)
Kizudarake no otoko, 1950 (Hasegawa)
Kizudarake no sanga, 1964 (Yamamura)
Klänningen, 1964 (Björnstrand)
Klansman, 1974 (Burton; Marvin)
Klein Dorrit, 1934 (Rasp)
Kleine Napoleon. See So sind die Männer, 1922
Kleine Residenz, 1942 (Dagover)
Kleine Stadt will schlafen gehen, 1954 (Fröhlich)
Kleine und die grosse Liebe, 1938 (Fröhlich)
Kleinstadtsunder, 1927 (Nielsen)
Klondike Annie, 1936 (McLaglen; West)
Klondike Fever, 1980 (Dickinson; Steiger)
Klown aus Liebe. See Zirkuskönig, 1925
Klub nravstvennosti, 1915 (Mozhukin)
Klute, 1971 (Fonda, J.; Scheider; Sutherland)
Knave of Hearts, 1954 (Greenwood; Philipe)
Knickerbocker Buckaroo, 1919 (Fairbanks)
Knickerbocker Holiday, 1944 (Coburn, C.; Eddy; Huston, W.; Winters)
Knife in the Head. See Messer im Kopf, 1978
Knight Duty, 1933 (Langdon)
Knight of the Dragon. See Caballero del Dragon, 1985
Knight of the Gold Star, 1950 (Bondarchuk)
Knight of the Plains, 1939 (Laurel and Hardy)
Knight of the Trails, 1915 (Hart)
Knight without Armor, 1937 (Dietrich; Donat)
Knightriders, 1981 (Harris, E.)
Knights and Ladies, 1912-13 (White)
Knights of the Round Table, 1953 (Baker; Gardner; Taylor, R.)
Knock on Any Door, 1949 (Bogart)
Knock on Wood, 1954 (Kaye; Zetterling)
Knock ou Le Triomphe de la médecine, 1950 (Jouvet)
Knocknagow, 1918 (Cusack)
Knockout, 1914 (Arbuckle; Chaplin, C.)
Knockout, 1941 (Kennedy; Quinn)
Knockout. See Right to the Heart, 1942
Know Your Enemy: Japan, 1943 (Huston, W.)
Know Your Enemy: Japan, 1945 (Andrews, D.)
Know Your Men, 1921 (White)
Knox und die lustigen Vagabunden, 1935 (Madsen and Schenstrøm)
Knute Rockne—All American, 1940 (Crisp; Reagan)
Knutzy Knights, 1954 (Three Stooges)
Koban-zame: Aizo-hen, 1948 (Hasegawa; Yamada)
Koban-zame: Aizo-hen, 1949 (Hasegawa)
Kobo no seishun, 1942 (Takamine)
Kobo Shinsen-gumi: Zen-shi, Ko-shi, 1930 (Yamada)
Kodachi o tsukau onna, 1961 (Kyo)
Kodomo no me, 1956 (Takamine)
Koenig Drosselbart, 1984 (Schell, Maria)
Koenigsmark, 1935 (Artaud; Fresnay)
Koffer des Herrn O.F., 1931 (Lamarr; Lorre)
Kofuku he no shotai, 1947 (Takamine)
Kofuku no isu, 1948 (Mori)
Koga Mansion. See Koga yashiki, 1949
Koga-yashiki, 1949 (Hasegawa; Yamada)
Koge, 1964 (Tanaka)
Kogen no eki yo sayounara, 1951 (Kagawa)
Kohayagawa-ke no aki, 1961 (Hara; Ryu; Tsukasa)
Kohinoor, 1960 (Kumar)
Kohlberg, 1945 (Wegener)
Kohlhiesels Töchter, 1920 (Jannings)
Koi moyo, 1930 (Yamada)
Koi no ikuji, 1926 (Tanaka)
Koi no Oranda-zaka, 1951 (Kyo)
Koi no Tokyo, 1932 (Tanaka)
Koi no torinawa, 1925 (Tanaka)
Koi okami-bi, 1948 (Yamada)
Koibumi, 1953 (Kagawa; Mori; Tanaka)
Koiguruma, 1930 (Yamada)
Koina no Ginpei, 1933 (Hasegawa)

Kyo no inochi, 1957 (Mori)
Kyo ware ren-ai su, 1949 (Mori)
Kyoen koigassen, 1930 (Yamada)
Kyofu no kuchu satsujin, 1957 (Yamamura)
Kyokaku harusame-gasa, 1933 (Hasegawa)
Kyokaku harusame-gasa, 1960 (Hasegawa)
Kyoraku hicho, 1928 (Hasegawa)
Kyokaku Soga, 1934 (Hasegawa)
Kyoraku yonin otoko, 1956 (Yamada)
Kyrelor, bandit par amour, 1909 (Linder)
Kys, Klap og Kommers, 1929 (Madsen and Schenstrøm)
Kyssen på kryssen, 1950 (Björnstrand)
Kyujo hiroba, 1951 (Mori)
L.A. Story, 1991 (Martin, S.)
La hacienda de la flor, 1948 (Armendáriz)
Laberinto de Pasiones, 1982 (Banderas)
Labor of Love. See Heller Wahn, 1982
Labyrinth. See Reflection of Fear, 1973
Labyrinth, 1992 (Brodský; Schell, Maximilian)
Labyrinth of Passion. See Laberinto de Pasiones, 1982
Labyrinthe, 1977 (Dickinson)
Lace, 1984 (Quayle)
Lacemaker. See **Dentellière**, 1977
Lachende Grauen, 1920 (Krauss)
Lachte man gerne, 1920 (Rasp)
Lackey and the Lady, 1919 (Howard, L.)
Lacrimae rerum, 1917 (Bertini)
Ladder Jinx, 1922 (Horton)
Laddie, 1935 (Crisp)
Laddie, 1940 (Cushing)
Ladies, 1984 (Cooper)
Ladies Courageous, 1944 (Young, L.)
Ladies Doctor. See Ginecologo della mutua, 1977
Ladies in Love, 1936 (Ameche; Gaynor; Lukas; Power; Young, L.)
Ladies in Retirement, 1941 (Lanchester; Lupino)
Ladies Love Brutes, 1930 (Astor; March)
Ladies Man, 1931 (Francis; Lombard; Powell, W.)
Ladies Man, 1961 (Lewis, Jerry; Raft)
Ladies Must Live, 1921 (Gilbert)
Ladies of Leisure, 1930 (Stanwyck)
Ladies of the Big House, 1932 (Sidney)
Ladies of the Chorus, 1948 (Monroe)
Ladies of the Mob, 1928 (Bow)
Ladies of the Night. See Onna dake no yuro, 1947
Ladies of Washington, 1944 (Quinn)
Ladies Should Listen, 1934 (Grant, C.; Horton)
Ladies They Talk About, 1933 (Stanwyck)
Ladies to Board, 1924 (Mix)
Ladro lui, ladra lei, 1958 (Sordi)
Ladron de Ninos, 1993 (Mastroianni)
Ladron del Ninos, 1991 (Piccoli)
Lady, 1925 (Talmadge)
Lady and Gent, 1932 (Wayne)
Lady and the Highwayman, 1989 (Bloom; Grant, H.; Mills)
Lady and the Lynchings, 1977 (Carradine)
Lady and the Mob, 1939 (Lupino)
Lady and the Mouse, 1913 (Barrymore, L.; Gish)
Lady Audley's Secret, 1915 (Bara)
Lady Be Careful, 1936 (Ayres)
Lady Be Good, 1941 (Barrymore, L.; Powell, E.; Young, R.)
Lady Beware. See Thirteenth Guest, 1932
Lady by Choice, 1934 (Lombard)
Lady Caroline Lamb, 1972 (Mills; Olivier; Richardson, R.)
Lady Charlie. See Busy Day, 1914
Lady Chatterley's Lover. See Amant de Lady Chatterley, 1955
Lady Consents, 1936 (Marshall)
Lady Dances. See Merry Widow, 1934
Lady Doctor, 1912-13 (White)
Lady Escapes, 1937 (Sanders)
Lady Eve, 1941 (Coburn, C.; Fonda, H.; Stanwyck)
Lady for a Night, 1941 (Blondell; Wayne)

Lady Frankenstein. See Figlia di Frankenstein, 1971
Lady from Boston. See Pardon My French, 1950
Lady from Cheyenne, 1941 (Preston; Young, L.)
Lady from Chungking, 1942 (Wong)
Lady from Frisco. See Rebellion, 1936
Lady from Hell, 1926 (Sweet)
Lady from Louisiana, 1941 (Wayne)
Lady from Nowhere, 1936 (Astor)
Lady from Paris. See Schöne Abenteuer, 1924
Lady from Shanghai, 1948 (Hayworth; Sloane; Welles)
Lady from the Sea, 1929 (Milland)
Lady Gambles, 1949 (Curtis, T.; Preston; Stanwyck)
Lady Godiva, 1955 (Eastwood; McLaglen; O'Hara)
Lady Godiva Rides Again, 1951 (Dors; Howard, T.; Kendall; Withers)
Lady Hamilton, 1921 (Krauss; Veidt)
Lady Hamilton. See That Hamilton Woman, 1941
Lady Hamilton, 1969 (Mills)
Lady Has Plans, 1942 (Goddard; Milland)
Lady Ice, 1973 (Duvall; Sutherland)
Lady in a Cage, 1964 (Caan; De Havilland)
Lady in a Jam, 1942 (Bellamy; Dunne)
Lady in Cement, 1968 (Sidney; Welch)
Lady in Distress, 1912-13 (White)
Lady in Distress, 1939 (Lukas)
Lady in Grey, 1922 (Lukas)
Lady in Question, 1940 (Ford, G.; Hayworth)
Lady in the Car with Glasses and a Gun. See Dame dans l'auto avec des lunettes et un fusil, 1970
Lady in the Corner, 1989 (Young, L.)
Lady in the Dark, 1944 (Milland; Rogers, G.)
Lady in the Lake, 1946 (Montgomery)
Lady Is a Square, 1959 (Neagle)
Lady Is Willing, 1934 (Howard, L.)
Lady Is Willing, 1942 (Dietrich; MacMurray)
Lady Jane, 1986 (Bonham-Carter)
Lady Jane Grey. See Tudor Rose, 1936
Lady Killer, 1933 (Cagney)
Lady Killer of Rome. See Assassino, 1961
Lady L, 1965 (Dalio; Loren; Newman; Niven; Noiret; Piccoli; Ustinov)
Lady Liberty. See Mortadella, 1972
Lady Lies, 1929 (Colbert; Huston, W.)
Lady Luck, 1946 (Young, R.)
Lady Musashino. See Musashino fujin, 1951
Lady o' the Pines, 1921 (Astor)
Lady of Burlesque, 1943 (Stanwyck)
Lady of Chance, 1928 (Shearer)
Lady of Deceit. See Born to Kill, 1947
Lady of Scandal, 1930 (Rathbone)
Lady of the Night, 1925 (Crawford, J.; Shearer)
Lady of the Night. See Midnight Mary, 1933
Lady of the Rose. See Bride of the Regiment, 1930
Lady of the Tropics, 1939 (Lamarr; Taylor, R.)
Lady on a Train, 1945 (Bellamy; Durbin; Duryea; Horton)
Lady on the Bus. See Dama do Lotacdao, 1978
Lady Paname, 1949 (Jouvet)
Lady Pays Off, 1951 (Darnell)
Lady! Please!, 1932 (Grable)
Lady Possessed, 1952 (Mason)
Lady Robin Hood, 1925 (Karloff)
Lady Says No!, 1951 (Niven)
Lady Sings the Blues, 1972 (Pryor)
Lady Surrenders, 1930 (Rathbone)
Lady Surrenders. See Love Story, 1944
Lady Takes a Chance, 1943 (Arthur; Wayne)
Lady Takes a Flyer, 1958 (Turner, L.)
Lady Takes a Sailor, 1949 (Wyman)
Lady to Love, 1930 (Banky; Robinson, E.)
Lady Tubbs, 1935 (Brennan)
Lady Vanishes, 1938 (Lockwood; Lukas; Redgrave, M.; Withers)
Lady Vanishes, 1979 (Gould; Lansbury; Lom)
Lady Violette, 1922 (Lukas)

Last Mile, 1959 (Rooney)
Last Mohican, 1963 (Arkin)
Last Moment, 1923 (Calhern)
Last Moment, 1954 (Cusack)
Last Moments. *See* Venditore di palloncini, 1974
Last Movie, 1971 (Hopper)
Last Movie. *See* Splendor, 1989
Last Night. *See* Revolutions-hochzeit, 1927
Last of His Tribe, 1992 (Voight)
Last of Mrs. Cheyney, 1929 (Rathbone; Shearer)
Last of Mrs. Cheyney, 1937 (Crawford, J.; Montgomery; Powell, W.)
Last of Philip Banter, 1986 (Curtis, T.)
Last of Sheila, 1973 (Coburn, J.; Mason; Perkins; Welch)
Last of Summer. *See* Kohayagawa-ke no aki, 1961
Last of the Buccaneers, 1950 (Henreid)
Last of the Clintons, 1935 (Carey)
Last of the Comanches, 1952 (Crawford, B.)
Last of the Cowboys. *See* Great Smokey Roadblock, 1978
Last of the Dogmen, 1995 (Hershey)
Last of the Duanes, 1924 (Mix)
Last of the Duanes, 1930 (Loy)
Last of the Line, 1914 (Hayakawa)
Last of the Mobile Hot-Shots. *See* Blood Kin, 1969
Last of the Mohicans, 1920 (Beery; Karloff)
Last of the Mohicans, 1932 (Carey)
Last of the Mohicans, 1936 (Scott, R.)
Last of the Mohicans, 1992 (Day-Lewis)
Last of the Outlaws. *See* Last Outlaw, 1936
Last of the Pony Riders, 1953 (Autry)
Last of the Powerseekers, 1971 (Turner, L.)
Last of the Red Hot Lovers, 1972 (Arkin)
Last of the Renegades. *See* Winnetou: II Teil, 1964
Last Outlaw, 1919 (Carey)
Last Outlaw, 1927 (Constantine)
Last Outlaw, 1936 (Carey)
Last Outlaw, 1993 (Rourke)
Last Outpost, 1935 (Grant, C.; Rains)
Last Outpost, 1951 (Reagan)
Last P.O.W.? The Bobby Garwood Story, 1993 (Sheen)
Last Page, 1952 (Dors)
Last Pair Out. *See* Sista paret ut, 1956
Last Parade, 1931 (Karloff)
Last Party, 1993 (Lee, S.; Penn)
Last Performance, 1928 (Veidt)
Last Picture Show, 1971 (Bridges; Burstyn)
Last Place on Earth, 1985 (Von Sydow)
Last Polka, 1984 (Candy)
Last Posse, 1953 (Crawford, B.)
Last Prostitute, 1991 (Braga)
Last Remake of Beau Geste, 1977 (Ann-Margret; Howard, T.; Jones, James Earl; Terry-Thomas; Ustinov)
Last Ride, 1994 (Rourke)
Last Ride of the Dalton Gang, 1979 (Palance)
Last Romantic Lover. *See* Dernier amant romantique, 1979
Last Round-Up, 1934 (Scott, R.)
Last Roundup, 1947 (Autry)
Last Run, 1971 (Huston, J.; Scott, G.)
Last Safari, 1967 (Granger)
Last Seance, 1986 (Moreau)
Last Song. *See* Dernière chanson, 1986
Last Squadron, 1932 (McCrea)
Last Stage to Santa Cruz. *See* Letzte Ritt nach Santa Cruz, 1964
Last Stagecoach West, 1957 (Van Cleef)
Last Starfighter, 1984 (Preston)
Last Straw, 1991 (Mills)
Last Summer, 1969 (Hershey)
Last Summer. *See* Sista leken, 1984
Last Summer at Tangiers. *See* Dernier été à Tanger, 1987
Last Summer in the Hamptons, 1995 (McDowall)
Last Sunset, 1961 (Cotten; Douglas, K.; Hudson; Malone)
Last Supper. *See* Última cena, 1976

Last Survivors, 1975 (Sheen)
Last Tango in Paris. *See* **Ultimo tango a Parigi**, 1972
Last Target, 1972 (Redgrave, M.)
Last Tattoo, 1994 (Steiger)
Last Temptation of Christ, 1988 (Dafoe; Hershey; Keitel; Stanton)
Last Ten Days. *See* Letzte Akt, 1955
Last Tenant, 1978 (Aiello)
Last Time I Saw Archie, 1961 (Mitchum)
Last Time I Saw Paris, 1954 (Pidgeon; Taylor, E.)
Last Trail, 1921 (Beery)
Last Trail, 1927 (Mix)
Last Trail, 1933 (Trevor)
Last Train from Gun Hill, 1959 (Douglas, K.; Quinn)
Last Train from Madrid, 1937 (Ayres; Ladd; Lamour; Quinn)
Last Tycoon, 1976 (Andrews, D.; Carradine; Curtis, T.; De Niro; Huston, A.; Milland; Mitchum; Moreau; Nicholson; Pleasence)
Last Unicorn, 1981 (Bridges; Arkin; Farrow; Lansbury; Lee, C.)
Last Valley, 1970 (Caine; Sharif)
Last Voyage, 1960 (Malone; O'Brien, E.; Sanders)
Last Wagon, 1956 (Widmark)
Last Warrior. *See* Flap, 1970
Last Will and Testament of Tom Smith, 1943 (Brennan; Barrymore, L.)
Last Witness, 1993 (Josephson)
Last Woman. *See* Ultima donna, 1976
Last Word, 1979 (Harris, R.; Landau)
Last Word, 1995 (Dreyfuss)
Last Year at Marienbad. *See* **Année dernière à Marienbad**, 1961
Laster den Menschheit, 1927 (Nielsen; Krauss)
Late Autumn. *See* Akibiyori, 1960
Late Extra, 1935 (Cusack; Mason)
Late George Apley, 1946 (Marsh; Colman)
Late Great Planet Earth, 1979 (Welles)
Late Liz, 1971 (Baxter)
Late Mathias Pascal. *See* **Feu Mathias Pascal**, 1925
Late Shift, 1996 (Bates, K.)
Late Spring. *See* **Banshun**, 1949
Latest from Paris, 1928 (Shearer)
Latest from Paris. *See* Lettera da Parigi, 1992
Latin Lovers, 1953 (Calhern; Turner, L.)
Latin Quarter, 1945 (Greenwood)
Latitude Zero. *See* Ido zero daisakusen, 1970
Laugh and the World Laughs. *See* Habit of Happiness, 1916
Laugh, Clown, Laugh, 1928 (Chaney; Young, L.)
Laugh Pagliacci. *See* I pagliacci, 1943
Laughing Anne, 1953 (Lockwood)
Laughing at Life, 1933 (McLaglen)
Laughing at Trouble, 1936 (Carradine)
Laughing Bill Hyde, 1918 (Rogers, W.)
Laughing Boy, 1934 (Novarro)
Laughing Gas, 1914 (Chaplin, C.)
Laughing Gravy, 1931 (Laurel and Hardy)
Laughing Policeman, 1973 (Dern; Matthau)
Laughing Sinners, 1931 (Crawford, J.; Gable)
Laughter, 1930 (March)
Laughter in Paradise, 1951 (Hepburn, A.)
Laughter in the Air. *See* Myrt and Marge, 1933
Laughter in the Dark, 1969 (Karina)
Laundress, 1914 (Beery)
Laura, 1944 (Andrews, D.; Price; Tierney; Webb)
Laura, 1962 (Walbrook)
Laura Lansing Slept Here, 1988 (Hepburn, K.)
Laurel and Hardy in Toyland. *See* Babes in Toyland, 1934
Laurel and Hardy Murder Case, 1930 (Laurel and Hardy)
Laurel and Hardy's Laughing Twenties, 1965 (Laurel and Hardy)
Lautlose Waffen. *See* Defector, 1966
Lavender Hill Mob, 1951 (Guinness; Hepburn, A.; Shaw)
Laviamoci il Cervello. *See* Rogopag, 1963
Law. *See* Loi, 1959
Law and Disorder, 1958 (Redgrave, M.)
Law and Disorder, 1974 (Borgnine)
Law and Jake Wade, 1958 (Taylor, R.; Widmark)

Law and Order, 1932 (Brennan; Carey; Huston, J.; Huston, W.)
Law and Order, 1950 (Malone)
Law and Order, 1953 (Reagan)
Law and the Lady, 1951 (Garson)
Law and the Outlaw, 1913 (Mix)
Law and Tombstone. See Hour of the Gun, 1967
Law beyond the Range, 1935 (Brennan)
Law Enforcers. See Polizia ringrazia, 1972
Law Is the Law. See Loi, c'est la loi, 1957
Law of Compensation, 1917 (Talmadge)
Law of Desire. See Ley del Deseo, 1987
Law of the Range, 1928 (Crawford, J.)
Law West of Tombstone, 1938 (Bond; Carey)
Lawa, 1989 (Łomnicki; Nowicki)
Lawful Cheaters, 1925 (Bow)
Lawgiver. See Mose, 1975
Lawless Breed, 1952 (Hudson; Van Cleef)
Lawless Frontier, 1934 (Wayne)
Lawless Nineties, 1936 (Wayne)
Lawless Range, 1935 (Wayne)
Lawless Street, 1955 (Lansbury; Scott, R.)
Lawman, 1971 (Cobb; Duvall; Lancaster; Ryan, R.)
Lawrence of Arabia, 1962 (Ferrer; Guinness; Hawkins; Kennedy; O'Toole; Quayle; Quinn; Rains; Sharif)
Lawyer Man, 1932 (Blondell; Powell, W.)
Lawyer's Secret, 1931 (Arthur; Wray)
Lawyers, 1987 (Darrieux)
Lazy Bones. See Hallelujah, I'm a Bum, 1933
Lazy Lightning, 1926 (Wray)
Lazy River, 1934 (Young, R.)
Leader, 1964 (Kumar)
Leading Lizzie Astray, 1914 (Arbuckle)
League of Gentlemen, 1959 (Attenborough; Hawkins; Reed)
League of Their Own, 1992 (Davis, G.; Hanks)
Lean on Me, 1989 (Freeman)
Leap in the Dark. See Salto nel vuoto, 1979
Leap into the Void. See Salto nel vuoto, 1979
Leap of Faith, 1988 (Neill)
Leap of Faith, 1992 (Martin, S.; Neeson; Winger)
Leap Year, 1922 (Arbuckle)
Lease of Life, 1954 (Donat; Elliott)
Leather Boys, 1963 (Elliott)
Leather Burners, 1943 (Mitchum)
Leather Necker, 1935 (Langdon)
Leather Pushers, 1922 (Shearer)
Leather-Pushers, 1940 (Three Stooges)
Leathernecking, 1930 (Dunne)
Leathernecks Have Landed, 1936 (Ayres; Bond)
Leave 'em Laughing, 1928 (Laurel and Hardy)
Leave 'em Laughing, 1981 (Cooper; Rooney)
Leave All Fair, 1985 (Gielgud)
Leave Her to Heaven, 1945 (Price; Tierney; Wilde)
Leave It to Blanche, 1934 (Harrison)
Leave It to Dad, 1933 (Langdon)
Leaving Las Vegas, 1995 (Cage)
Leb' wohl Christina, 1945 (Fröhlich)
Lebbra bianca, 1951 (Loren)
Lebende Buddha, 1923 (Wegener)
Leda. See Double tour, 1959
Lederstrumpf, 1920 (Lugosi)
Left Hand of God, 1955 (Bogart; Cobb; Moorehead; Tierney)
Left-Handed Gun, 1958 (Newman)
Left-Handed Man, 1913 (Carey; Gish)
Left-Handed Woman. See Linkshändige Frau, 1977
Legacy. See Vse ostaetsia lyudyam, 1963
Legacy of Blood, 1973 (Carradine)
Legacy of Lies, 1992 (Landau; Wallach)
Legacy of the 500,000. See Goju man-nin no isan, 1963
Legacy of the Hollywood Blacklist, 1987 (Lancaster)
Legal Advice, 1916 (Mix)
Legal Eagles, 1986 (Redford; Stamp; Winger)

Legal Light, 1915 (Mix)
Legend, 1985 (Cruise)
Legend, Or Was It? See Shito no densetsu, 1963
Legend in Leotards. See Return of Captain Invincible, 1983
Legend of a Duel to the Death. See Shito no densetsu, 1963
Legend of Earl Durand, 1975 (Sheen)
Legend of Frenchie King. See Pétroleuses, 1971
Legend of Hell House, 1973 (McDowall)
Legend of Lylah Clare, 1968 (Borgnine; Finch; Novak)
Legend of O. B. Taggart, 1995 (Rooney; Borgnine)
Legend of Sleepy Hollow, 1972 (Carradine)
Legend of the Holy Drinker. See Leggenda del santo bevitore, 1988
Legend of the Lone Ranger, 1981 (Robards)
Legend of the Lost, 1957 (Brazzi; Loren; Wayne)
Legend of the Seven Golden Vampires. See Golden Vampire, 1974
Legend of the Werewolf, 1974 (Cushing)
Legend of Walks Far Woman, 1982 (Welch)
Legend of William Tell. See Wilhelm Tell, 1934
Legend of Wolf Mountain, 1992 (Rooney)
Legenda del rudio malese. See Jungle Raiders, 1985
Légende de Polichinelle, 1907 (Linder)
Legends of the Fall, 1994 (Hopkins, A.)
Legends of the Fall, 1994 (Pitt)
Legge. See Loi, 1959
Legge dei gangsters, 1969 (Kinski)
Legge violenta della squadra anticrimine. See Cross Shot, 1976
Leggenda de Genoffeffa, 1951 (Brazzi)
Leggenda del santo bevitore, 1988 (Quayle)
Legion of Terror, 1936 (Bond)
Legion of the Condemned, 1928 (Constantine; Wray)
Legion's Last Patrol. See Marcia o crepa, 1963
Légions d'honneur, 1938 (Vanel)
Légitime défense, 1958 (Blier)
Legkaya zhizn, 1964 (Maretskaya)
Leibeigenen, 1927 (Homolka)
Leichte Isabell, 1927 (Fröhlich)
Leidenschaft, 1940 (Rasp)
Leidenschaftliche Bluemchen. See Passion Flower Hotel, 1978
Leidensweg der Inge Kraft, 1921 (Veidt)
Lek pa regnbagen, 1958 (Zetterling)
Lektion i kärlek, 1954 (Andersson, H.; Björnstrand; Dahlbeck)
Le Mans, 1971 (McQueen)
Lemmy pour les dames, 1962 (Constantine)
Lemon Drop Kid, 1951 (Hope)
Lemon Sisters, 1990 (Gould; Keaton, D.)
Lemon Sky, 1987 (Bacon)
Len Deighton's Bullet to Beijing, 1995 (Caine)
Lena and the Geese, 1912 (Pickford)
Lenin i 1918 godu, 1939 (Cherkassov)
Lenny, 1974 (Hoffman)
Leo the Last, 1970 (Mastroianni)
Leon, 1994 (Aiello; Oldman)
Léon Morin, prêtre, 1961 (Belmondo)
Leonard Part 6, 1987 (Fonda, J.)
Leone di Amalfi, 1950 (Gassman)
Leone have sept cabecas, 1970 (Léaud)
Léonor, 1974 (Piccoli; Ullmann)
Leopard, 1917 (Lugosi)
Leopard. See **Gattopardo**, 1963
Leopard's Foundling, 1914 (Mix)
Leopardi di Churchill, 1970 (Kinski)
Leopards of Kora, 1986 (Widmark)
Lepke, 1974 (Curtis, T.)
Less than Zero, 1987 (Pitt)
Less Than Dust, 1916 (Pickford)
Less Than Kin, 1918 (Crisp)
Lesser Evil, 1912 (Marsh; Sweet)
Lesson in Love. See Lektion i kärlek, 1954
Lest We Forget, 1937 (Constantine; Taylor, R.)
Let Freedom Ring, 1939 (Barrymore, L.; Eddy; McLaglen)
Let It Be Me, 1995 (Caron; Gould)

Let It Rain, 1927 (Karloff)
Let It Ride, 1989 (Dreyfuss)
Let Joy Reign Supreme. *See* Que la fête commence, 1975
Let My People Sing, 1942 (Ustinov)
Let No Man Put Asunder, 1924 (Webb)
Let No Man Write My Epitaph, 1959 (Seberg; Winters)
Let There Be Light, 1946 (Huston, J.; Huston, W.)
Let Us Be Gay, 1930 (Dressler; Shearer)
Let Us Live, 1939 (Bellamy; Fonda, H.; O'Sullivan)
Let Women Alone, 1925 (Beery)
Lethal Attraction. *See* Heathers, 1989
Lethal Obsession. *See* Joker, 1987
Lethal Obsession, 1988 (Gould)
Lethal Weapon, 1987 (Gibson)
Lethal Weapon 2, 1989 (Gibson; Pesci)
Lethal Weapon 3, 1992 (Gibson; Pesci)
Let's Be Ritzy, 1934 (Ayres)
Let's Dance, 1950 (Astaire)
Let's Do It Again, 1953 (Milland; Wyman)
Let's Do It Again, 1975 (Poitier)
Let's Face It, 1943 (Hope)
Let's Get Harry, 1987 (Duvall)
Let's Get Married, 1937 (Bellamy; Lupino)
Let's Go, 1918 (Lloyd)
Let's Go Crazy, 1951 (Sellers)
Let's Go Native, 1930 (Francis; MacDonald)
Let's Go Places, 1929 (Grable)
Let's Have a Brainwash. *See* Rogopag, 1963
Let's Hope It's a Girl. *See* Speriamo che sia femmina, 1985
Let's Live a Little, 1948 (Lamarr)
Let's Make a Million, 1937 (Horton)
Let's Make It Legal, 1951 (Colbert; Monroe)
Let's Make Love, 1960 (Crosby; Kelly, Gene; Monroe; Montand)
Let's Make Up. *See* Lilacs in the Spring, 1955
Let's Talk about Women. *See* Se permettete parliamo di donne, 1964
Letste Kompagnie, 1930 (Veidt)
Letter, 1929 (Marshall)
Letter, 1940 (Davis, B.; Marshall)
Letter, 1982 (Remick)
Letter from a Novice. *See* Lettere di una novizia, 1960
Letter from an Unknown Woman, 1948 (Fontaine; Jourdan)
Letter from Bataan, 1942 (Hayward)
Letter from Home, 1941 (Johnson)
Letter of Introduction, 1938 (Menjou)
Letter to Three Wives, 1949 (Darnell; Douglas, K.; Marsh; Ritter)
Lettera da Parigi, 1992 (Papas)
Lettere di una novizia, 1960 (Belmondo)
Letters, 1973 (Lupino; Stanwyck)
Letters from a Friend, 1943 (Ladd)
Letters from Frank, 1979 (Ayres)
Letters from Marusia. *See* Actas de Marusia, 1985
Letters from Three Lovers, 1973 (Sheen)
Letters Home, 1986 (Seyrig)
Letters Home from Vietnam. *See* Dear America, 1987
Letti selvaggi, 1979 (Vitti)
Letto. *See* Secrets d'alcôve, 1954
Letty Lynton, 1932 (Crawford, J.; Montgomery)
Letzen vier von St. Paul, 1936 (Rosay)
Letzer Wille, 1994 (Winkler)
Letzte Akt, 1955 (Werner)
Letzte Brücke, 1954 (Schell, Maria)
Letzte Illusion, 1932 (Dagover)
Letzte Liebe, 1979 (Vogler; Winkler)
Letzte Mann, 1924 (Jannings)
Letzte Mann, 1955 (Schneider)
Letzte Nacht, 1949 (Schell, Maria)
Letzte Ritt nach Santa Cruz, 1964 (Kinski)
Letzte Schrei, 1977 (Seyrig)
Letzte Stunde. *See* Hotel Potemkin, 1924
Letzte Walzer, 1927 (Rasp)
Letzte Zivlist, 1984 (Von Sydow)

Letzten werden die Ersten sein, 1957 (Schell, Maximilian)
Leuchter des Kaisers, 1936 (Rasp)
Leuchtturm des Chaos, 1983 (Hayden)
Leur Dernière Nuit, 1953 (Gabin)
Lev farlight, 1944 (Björnstrand)
Leva pa hoppet, 1951 (Thulin)
Leviathan, 1960 (Jourdan)
Ley del Deseo, 1987 (Banderas; Maura)
Leyenda, 1980 (Villagra)
Li Shizhen, The Great Pharmacologist, 1956 (Zhao Dan)
Li Ting Lang, 1920 (Hayakawa)
Liaisons dangereuses, 1959 (Moreau; Philipe; Trintignant)
Lianbron, 1965 (Andersson, H.)
Liar, Liar, 1993 (Nelligan)
Liar's Moon, 1982 (Crawford, B.; Dillon)
Liars. *See* Menteurs, 1961
Libaas, 1984 (Azmi)
Libaas, 1989 (Azmi)
Libel, 1959 (Bogarde; De Havilland; Shaw)
Libeled Lady, 1936 (Harlow; Loy; McDaniel; Powell, W.; Tracy)
Libera, amore mio, 1973 (Cardinale)
Liberation, 1971 (Olbrychski)
Liberation, 1994 (Goldberg; Kingsley)
Liberation of L. B. Jones, 1970 (Cobb; Hershey)
Libertarias, 1996 (Abril)
Liberté enchaînée, 1929 (Modot)
Liberty, 1929 (Harlow; Laurel and Hardy)
Liberty, 1986 (Bloom; Cassel)
Liberty Belle, 1983 (Binoche)
Libido, 1967 (Giannini)
Libro del buen amor, 1969 (Rey)
License to Kill. *See* Nick Carter va tout casser, 1964
License to Kill, 1984 (Washington)
Licking Hitler, 1977 (Nelligan)
Lidé z maringotek, 1966 (Brodský)
Lie, 1914 (Chaney)
Lie, 1970 (Segal)
Lie. *See* Mensonge, 1992
Lie Huozhong yongsheng, 1965 (Zhao Dan)
Liebe, 1926 (Bergner)
Liebe, 1956 (Schell, Maria)
Liebe bleibt nicht ohne Schmerzen, 1980 (Schell, Maria)
Liebe der Jeanne Ney, 1927 (Rasp)
Liebe der Mitzu. *See* Atarashiki tsuchi, 1937
Liebe der Mitzu. *See* Tochter des Samurai, 1937
Liebe des Dalai Lama. *See* Verbotene Land, 1924
Liebe ist kalter als der Tod, 1969 (Schygulla)
Liebe Lust und Lied, 1926 (Rasp)
Liebe macht Blind, 1925 (Dagover; Jannings; Veidt)
Liebe und Trompetenklang. *See* Abenteuer eines jungen Herrn in Polen, 1934
Liebende Buddhas, 1924 (Nielsen)
Liebensnest, 1922 (Wegener)
Lieber Karl, 1984 (Olbrychski)
Lieberman in Love, 1995 (Aiello)
Liebes A.B.C., 1916 (Nielsen)
Liebesbriefe. *See* Liebesnächte, 1929
Liebeskarussell, 1965 (Deneuve)
Liebeskommando, 1931 (Fröhlich)
Liebesleute, 1935 (Fröhlich)
Liebeslied, 1931 (Fröhlich)
Liebesnächte, 1929 (Dietrich)
Liebesroman im Hause Hapsburg, 1936 (Wegener)
Liebestaumel, 1920 (Veidt)
Liebestraum, 1991 (Novak)
Liebling der Götter, 1930 (Jannings)
Lieblingsfrau des Maharadscha, 1920 (Kortner)
Liebschaften des Hektor Dalmore, 1921 (Veidt)
Lied der Ströme, 1954 (Robeson)
Lied, ein Kuss, ein Mädel, 1932 (Fröhlich)
Lien de Parenté, 1986 (Marais)
Liens du sang, 1978 (Audran; Pleasence; Sutherland)

Lies of the Twins, 1991 (Rossellini)
Lieu du crime, 1986 (Darrieux; Deneuve)
Lieutenant Schuster's Wife, 1972 (Grant, L.)
Lieutenant souriant. *See* Smiling Lieutenant, 1931
Life and Death of Colonel Blimp, 1943 (Kerr; Walbrook)
Life and Loves of Beethoven. *See* Grand Amour de Beethoven, 1936
Life and Loves of Mozart. *See* Mozart, 1955
Life and Nothing But. *See* Vie et rien d'autre, 1989
Life and Times of Judge Roy Bean, 1972 (Huston, J.; Gardner; Perkins; Newman; McDowall)
Life as a Couple. *See* Vie à deux, 1958
Life at Stake. *See* Key Man, 1954
Life Begins, 1932 (Young, L.)
Life Begins Again. *See* Życie raz jeszcze, 1965
Life Begins Anew. *See* Vita recominicia, 1945
Life Begins at 8:30, 1942 (Lupino; Wilde)
Life Begins at Forty, 1935 (Rogers, W.)
Life Begins for Andy Hardy, 1941 (Garland; Rooney)
Life behind a Mask. *See* Vsyou zhizn pod maskoi, 1915
Life Dances on, Christine. *See* Carnet de bal, 1937
Life for the Czar. *See* Zhizn na Tzarya, 1911
Life in Death. *See* Zhizn na smerti, 1914
Life in Hollywood Number Four, 1927 (Mix)
Life in Sometown, U.S.A., 1938 (Keaton, B.)
Life in the Balance, 1954 (Bancroft; Marvin)
Life in the Raw, 1933 (Trevor)
Life in the Theater, 1993 (Lemmon)
Life in Your Hands, 1975 (Lancaster)
Life Is a Bed of Roses. *See* Vie est un roman, 1984
Life Is a Long Quiet River. *See* Vie est un long fleuve tranquille, 1988
Life Is Short but Art Is Eternal. *See* Zhizn mig iskusstvo vetchno, 1916
Life Life, 1919 (Beery)
Life Love Death. *See* Vie, l'amour, la mort, 1968
Life, Loves and Adventures of Omar Khayyam. *See* Omar Khayyam, 1957
Life of a Country Doctor. *See* Fundoshi isha, 1960
Life of a Film Director: Record of Kenji Mizoguchi. *See* Aru eiga kantoku no shogai: Mizoguchi Kenji no kiroku, 1975
Life of a Horse-Trader. *See* Bakuro ich-dai, 1951
Life of Beethoven. *See* Beethoven, 1927
Life of Brian. *See* Monty Python's Life of Brian, 1979
Life of Buffalo Bill, 1910 (White)
Life of Emile Zola, 1937 (Calhern; Crisp; Muni)
Life of Her Own, 1950 (Calhern; Milland; Turner, L.)
Life of Jimmy Dolan, 1933 (Rooney; Wayne; Young, L.)
Life of Oharu. *See* **Saikaku inchidai onna**, 1952
Life of Simon Bolivar, 1943 (Armendáriz)
Life of Sin, 1992 (Julia)
Life of the Party, 1920 (Arbuckle)
Life of the Party, 1937 (Miller)
Life of the Party, 1938 (Dumont)
Life of Vergie Winters, 1934 (Crisp)
Life of Wu Xun, 1950 (Zhao Dan)
Life on the Edge. *See* Meet the Hollowheads, 1989
Life Savers, 1916 (Laurel and Hardy)
Life Size. *See* Grandeur nature, 1973
Life Stinks!, 1991 (Brooks, M.)
Life Study, 1973 (Jones, T.)
Life Timer, 1913 (Mix)
Life with Father, 1947 (Dunne; Powell, W.; Taylor, E.)
Life with Henry, 1941 (Cooper)
Lifeforce Experiment, 1994 (Sutherland)
Life's Little Treasures. *See* Aux Petits Bonheurs, 1993
Life's Whirlpool, 1917 (Barrymore, E.; Barrymore, L.)
Lifesavers. *See* Mixed Nuts, 1994
Lifespan, 1975 (Kinski)
Lifted Veil, 1917 (Barrymore, E.)
Light, 1919 (Bara)
Light. *See* Lumière, 1976
Light across the Street. *See* Lumière d'en face, 1955
Light and Shadow. *See* Hikaritokage, 1946
Light at the Edge of the World. *See* Luz del fin del mondo, 1971

Light in the Dark, 1922 (Chaney)
Light in the Jungle, 1991 (McDowell)
Light in the Piazza, 1962 (Brazzi; De Havilland)
Light of Day, 1987 (Rowlands)
Light of Heart. *See* Life Begins at 8:30, 1942
Light of Western Stars, 1940 (Ladd)
Light Sleeper, 1992 (Dafoe; Sarandon)
Light That Came, 1909 (Pickford)
Light that Failed, 1939 (Colman; Huston, W.; Lupino)
Light Touch, 1951 (Granger; Sanders)
Light Touch. *See* Touch and Go, 1955
Light Years. *See* Gandahar, 1987
Light Years Away, 1981 (Howard, T.)
Lighter that Failed, 1927 (Laurel and Hardy)
Lighthouse. *See* Yorokobi mo Kanashimi mo ikutoshitsuki, 1957
Lighthouse Keeper, 1911 (Pickford)
Lighthouse Keeper's Daughter. *See* Manina, la fille sans voiles, 1952
Lightnin', 1930 (McCrea; Rogers, W.)
Lightnin' Wins, 1926 (Constantine)
Lightning. *See* Inazuma, 1952
Lightning Bill, 1926 (Arthur)
Lightning Raider, 1918 (Karloff; White)
Lightning Rider, 1924 (Carey)
Lightning—The White Stallion, 1986 (Rooney)
Lights! Camera! Annie!, 1982 (Huston, J.)
Lights and Shadows, 1914 (Chaney)
Lights of Old Broadway, 1925 (Davies)
Lights of Old Santa Fe, 1944 (Rogers, R.)
Lights of Variety. *See* Luci del varietà, 1951
Lights Out. *See* Bright Victory, 1951
Lights Out in Europe, 1939 (March)
Lightship, 1986 (Brandauer; Duvall)
Ligne de demarcation, 1966 (Seberg; Audran; Gélin)
Like a Rolling Stone. *See* Bo no Kanashimi, 1994
Like Father, Like Son, 1987 (Moore, Dudley)
Like His Rhythm There Is No Other. *See* Cachao ... como su ritmo no hay dos, 1993
Like Two Crocodiles. *See* Come due Coccodrilli, 1994
Li'l Abner, 1940 (Keaton, B.)
Lilac Time, 1928 (Constantine)
Lilacs in the Spring, 1955 (Connery; Flynn; Neagle)
Lili, 1918 (Lugosi)
Lili, 1953 (Caron)
Lili Lamont, 1983 (Presle)
Lili Marleen, 1981 (Giannini; Schygulla)
Lilies of the Field, 1963 (Poitier)
Liliom, 1934 (Artaud; Boyer)
Lilith, 1964 (Beatty; Hackman; Seberg)
Lilla Märta kommer tilbaka, 1948 (Björnstrand)
Lille Lise Letpåtå, 1924 (Madsen and Schenstrøm)
Lilli Marlene, 1950 (Baker)
Lillian Gish, 1984 (Moreau)
Lillian Russell, 1940 (Ameche; Faye; Fonda, H.)
Lilly Turner, 1933 (Brennan)
Lily and the Rose, 1915 (Gish)
Lily Dale, 1996 (Shepard)
Lily in Love, 1985 (Smith)
Lily of the Dust, 1924 (Negri)
Limehouse Blues, 1934 (Raft; Wong)
Limelight, 1936 (Buchanan; Neagle)
Limelight, 1952 (Bloom; Chaplin, C.; Chaplin, G.; Keaton, B.; Purviance)
Limping Man, 1953 (Roberts, R.)
Lin zexu, 1959 (Zhao Dan)
Lina Braake, 1976 (Rasp)
Linceul n'a pas de poches, 1974 (Gélin)
Lincoln, 1992 (Close; Dreyfuss; Jones, James Earl; Meredith; Schwarzenegger; Steiger)
Lincoln's Gettysburg Address, 1973 (Heston)
Lindbergh Kidnapping Case, 1976 (Cotten; Hopkins, A.; Pidgeon)
Line of Demarcation. *See* Ligne de demarcation, 1966
Line of Fire: The Morris Dees Story, 1991 (Bassett)

Line, the Cross, and the Curve, 1993 (Richardson, M.)
Line-Up, 1958 (Wallach)
Linea del fiume, 1976 (Hurt, J.)
Linguini Incident, 1991 (Winters)
Link, 1986 (Stamp)
Linkshändige Frau, 1977 (Depardieu; Ganz; Vogler; Winkler)
Linus. *See* Linus eller Tegelhusets hemlighet, 1979
Linus eller Tegelhusets hemlighet, 1979 (Andersson, H.)
Liola, 1964 (Aimée; Brasseur)
Liola. *See* Stagione del nostro amore, 1965
Lion, 1962 (Holden; Howard, T.)
Lion and the Hawk. *See* Memed, My Hawk, 1983
Lion and the Mouse, 1928 (Barrymore, L.)
Lion des Mogols, 1924 (Mozhukin)
Lion Has Seven Heads. *See* Leone have sept cabecas, 1970
Lion Has Wings, 1939 (Oberon; Richardson, R.)
Lion in the Desert, 1990 (Sharif)
Lion in the Streets. *See* Lion Is in the Streets, 1953
Lion in Winter, 1968 (Hepburn, K.; Hopkins, A.; O'Toole)
Lion Is in the Streets, 1953 (Cagney)
Lion King, 1994 (Goldberg; Irons; Jones, James Earl)
Lion of the Desert, 1981 (Gielgud; Papas; Quinn; Reed; Steiger)
Lion, The Lamb, The Man, 1914 (Chaney)
Lionheart, 1991 (Van Damme)
Lions and Ladies, 1919 (Laurel and Hardy)
Lion's Love, 1969 (Constantine)
Lions sont lachés, 1961 (Morgan; Cardinale; Darrieux)
Lipstick, 1976 (Bancroft)
Liquidators, 1965 (Howard, T.)
Lisa. *See* Inspector, 1961
Lisa, Bright and Dark, 1973 (Baxter)
Lisa e il diavolo, 1972 (Valli)
Lisbon, 1956 (Milland; O'Hara; Rains)
Lisbon Story. *See* Viagem a Lisboa, 1995
Lise Fleron, 1919 (Bertini)
List of Adrian Messenger, 1963 (Curtis, T.; Dalio; Douglas, K.; Huston, J.;
    Lancaster; Marshall; Mitchum; Scott, G.; Sidney)
Liste noire, 1985 (Girardot)
Listen, Darling, 1938 (Astor; Garland; Pidgeon)
Listen, Judge, 1952 (Three Stooges)
Listen, Let's Make Love. *See* Scusi, facciamo l'amore, 1968
Listen to Me, 1989 (Scheider)
Listen Up!: The Lives of Quincy Jones, 1990 (Sidney; Streisand)
Lit à Colonne, 1942 (Marais)
Lite Trap. *See* Wessten leuchtet, 1981
Little American, 1917 (Beery; Novarro)
Little Annie Rooney, 1925 (Pickford)
Little Big League, 1994 (Robards)
Little Big Man, 1970 (Dunaway; Hoffman)
Little Big Shot, 1935 (Bond; Horton)
Little Boy Lost, 1953 (Crosby)
Little Brunette. *See* Moreninha, 1970
Little Buddha, 1993 (Reeves)
Little Caesar, 1931 (Robinson, E.)
Little Colonel, 1935 (Barrymore, L.; McDaniel; Robinson, B.; Temple)
Little Country Mouse, 1914 (Sweet)
Little Damozel, 1933 (Neagle)
Little Darling, 1909 (Pickford)
Little Darlings, 1980 (Dillon)
Little Devil. *See* Piccolo diavolo, 1988
Little Dorrit, 1987 (Cusack; Greenwood; Guinness)
Little Drummer Boy, 1969 (Ferrer; Garson)
Little Drummer Boy Book II, 1968 (Garson)
Little Drummer Girl, 1984 (Keaton, D.; Kinski)
Little Fauss and Big Halsy, 1970 (Redford)
Little Fox, 1920 (Lukas)
Little Foxes, 1941 (Davis, B.; Duryea; Marshall)
Little 'fraid Lady, 1920 (Marsh)
Little Gel. *See* King of Hearts, 1936
Little Giant, 1933 (Astor; Robinson, E.)
Little Giant, 1946 (Abbott and Costello; Dumont)

Little Girl in Blue Velvet. *See* Petite fille en velours bleu, 1978
Little Girl Who Lives down the Lane, 1977 (Foster; Sheen)
Little Gloria ... Happy at Last, 1982 (Davis, B.; Lansbury)
Little Hero, 1913 (Normand)
Little House in Kolomn. *See* Domik v Kolomna, 1913
Little Hut, 1956 (Gardner; Granger; Niven)
Little Italy. *See* Squadra antimafia, 1978
Little Journey, 1927 (Carey)
Little Kidnappers, 1990 (Heston)
Little King, 1932 (Keaton, B.)
Little Ladies of the Night, 1977 (Malone)
Little Liar, 1916 (Marsh)
Little Lord Fauntleroy, 1921 (Pickford)
Little Lord Fauntleroy, 1936 (Rooney)
Little Lord Fauntleroy, 1980 (Guinness)
Little Malcolm and His Struggle against the Eunuchs, 1974 (Hurt, J.)
Little Man Tate, 1991 (Foster; Wiest)
Little Man, What Now?, 1934 (Marsh; Sullavan)
Little Marcel. *See* Petit Marcel, 1975
Little Märta Returns. *See* Lilla Märta kommer tilbaka, 1948
Little Men, 1934 (McDaniel)
Little Men, 1940 (Francis)
Little Mermaid, 1984 (Mirren)
Little Minister, 1934 (Crisp; Hepburn, K.)
Little Miss Broadway, 1938 (Durante; Temple)
Little Miss Marker, 1934 (Menjou; Temple)
Little Miss Marker, 1980 (Andrews, J.; Curtis, T.; Grant, L.; Matthau)
Little Miss Nobody, 1936 (Carey)
Little Mo, 1978 (Baxter)
Little Moon and Jud McGraw. *See* Gone with the West, 1975
Little Moon of Alban, 1965 (Bogarde)
Little Murders, 1971 (Arkin; Gould; Sutherland)
Little Napoleon. *See* So sind die Männer, 1922
Little Nellie Kelly, 1940 (Garland)
Little Nemo: Adventures in Slumberland, 1992 (Rooney)
Little Night Music, 1977 (Taylor, E.)
Little Nikita, 1988 (Poitier)
Little Odessa, 1994 (Redgrave, V.; Schell, Maximilian)
Little Old New York, 1923 (Davies)
Little Old New York, 1940 (Bond; Faye; MacMurray)
Little Old World. *See* Piccolo mondo antico, 1941
Little Pal, 1915 (Pickford)
Little Pal. *See* Healer, 1935
Little Piece of Sunshine, 1990 (Bacall)
Little Prince, 1974 (Wilder)
Little Princess, 1917 (Pickford)
Little Princess, 1939 (Temple)
Little Rascals, 1994 (Brooks, M.; Goldberg)
Little Red Riding Hood, 1911 (Pickford)
Little Riders, 1996 (McDowell)
Little Romance, 1979 (Crawford, B.; Olivier)
Little Shepherd of Kingdom Come, 1928 (Barthelmess)
Little Shop of Horrors, 1960 (Nicholson)
Little Shop of Horrors, 1986 (Candy; Martin, S.; Murray)
Little Sister, 1914 (Mix)
Little Soldier. *See* Petit Soldat, 1960
Little Spies, 1986 (Rooney)
Little Sweetheart, 1988 (Hurt, J.)
Little Teacher, 1909 (Pickford)
Little Teacher, 1915 (Arbuckle; Normand)
Little Theater of Jean Renoir. *See* Petit théâtre de Jean Renoir, 1969
Little Tiger from Canton, 1971 (Chan)
Little Tough Guys in Society, 1938 (Horton)
Little Treasure, 1985 (Lancaster)
Little Troll Prince, 1987 (Price)
Little Wild Girl, 1928 (Karloff)
Little Wildcat, 1922 (Laurel and Hardy)
Little Women, 1933 (Bennett; Hepburn, K.; Lukas)
Little Women, 1949 (Astor; Brazzi; Leigh, Janet; O'Brien, M.; Taylor, E.)
Little Women, 1978 (Garson; Young, R.)
Little Women, 1994 (Ryder; Sarandon)

Little World of Don Camillo. *See* Petit Monde de Don Camillo, 1952
Littlest Outlaw, 1955 (Armendáriz)
Littlest Rebel, 1935 (Robinson, B.; Temple)
Liv Ullmann's Norway. *See* Look at Liv, 1979
Live a Little, Love a Little, 1968 (Presley)
Live Again, Die Again, 1974 (Page; Pidgeon)
Live Dangerously. *See* Lev farlight, 1944
Live Fast, Die Young, 1958 (Henreid)
Live for Life. *See* Vivre pour vivre, 1967
Live Ghost, 1934 (Laurel and Hardy)
Live, Love, and Learn, 1937 (Montgomery; Rooney; Russell, R.)
Live Today for Tomorrow. *See* Act of Murder, 1948
Live Wire, 1917 (Colman)
Lives of a Bengal Lancer, 1935 (Constantine)
Livid Flame, 1914 (Mix)
Living Corpse. *See* Givoi troup, 1912
Living Corpse. *See* Zhivoi trup, 1929
Living Dead. *See* Unheimliche Geschichten, 1932
Living Dead, 1972 (Sanders)
Living Dead at the Manchester Morgue. *See* Fin de semana para los muertos, 1974
Living Dead Man. *See* **Feu Mathias Pascal**, 1925
Living in a Big Way, 1947 (Kelly, Gene; Winters)
Living It Up, 1954 (Lewis, Jerry; Leigh, Janet; Martin, D.)
Living on Velvet, 1935 (Francis)
Liza. *See* Cagna, 1972
Lizard with a Woman's Skin. *See* Lucertola con la pelle di donna, 1971
Lizzie, 1957 (Blondell)
Lizzie and the Iceman, 1912-13 (White)
Lloyd's of London, 1936 (Power; Sanders; Carroll)
Lo chiamavano King ..., 1971 (Kinski)
Lo ciociara, 1961 (Loren)
Lo mano spietata della legge, 1976 (Cusack)
Lo otra, 1946 (Del Rio)
Lo sbaglio di essere vivo, 1945 (Cervi)
Lo sbarco di Anzio, 1968 (Falk; Giannini; Kennedy; Mitchum; Ryan, R.)
Lo scandalo, 1966 (Aimée)
Lo scapolo, 1956 (Sordi)
Lo scatenato, 1967 (Gassman)
Lo sceicco bianco, 1952 (Masina; Sordi)
Lo Scocciatore. *See* Via Padova 46, 1954
Lo sconosciuto, 1979 (Schneider)
Lo scopone scientifico, 1972 (Cotten; Davis, B.; Mangano; Sordi)
Lo smania addosso, 1963 (Gassman)
Lo Sogarro, 1962 (Vanel)
Lo spadaccino di Sienna, 1963 (Granger)
Lo sparviero del Nilo, 1949 (Gassman)
Lo straniero, 1967 (Blier; Karina)
Lo zio indegno, 1989 (Gassman; Giannini)
Loaded Pistols, 1949 (Autry)
Loan Shark, 1952 (Raft)
Loan Shark King, 1914 (Talmadge)
Lobster Man from Mars, 1989 (Curtis, T.)
Local Boy Makes Good, 1931 (Brown)
Local Color, 1913 (Mix)
Local Color, 1916 (Mix)
Local Hero, 1983 (Lancaster)
Locandiera, 1943 (Cervi)
Locataire, 1976 (Adjani)
Lock, Stock, and Barrel, 1971 (Meredith)
Lock Up, 1989 (Stallone; Sutherland)
Lock Up Your Daughters, 1969 (York)
Locked Door, 1929 (Goddard; Stanwyck)
Locked Out, 1911 (White)
Locked Up: A Mother's Rage, 1992 (Bassett)
Locket, 1946 (Mitchum)
Lockfågeln, 1971 (Björnstrand)
Lockspitzel Asew, 1935 (Rasp)
Lockvogel, 1934 (Rasp)
Loco Boy Makes Good, 1942 (Three Stooges)
Loco Luck, 1927 (Wray)

Locura de amor, 1948 (Rey)
Lodger, 1926 (Novello)
Lodger, 1932 (Hawkins; Novello)
Lodger, 1944 (Oberon; Sanders)
Lodging for the Night, 1912 (Pickford)
Log kya kahenge, 1982 (Azmi)
Log of the Black Pearl, 1974 (Bellamy)
Loga de la casa, 1950 (Armendáriz)
Logan's Run, 1976 (Ustinov)
Logik des Gefühls, 1982 (Ganz; Vogler)
Loi, 1959 (Brasseur; Lollobrigida; Mastroianni; Mercouri; Montand)
Loi, c'est la loi, 1957 (Fernandel)
Loi des hommes, 1962 (Arletty; Dalio; Presle)
Loi des rues, 1956 (Trintignant)
Loi du nord, 1940 (Vanel)
Loi du nord, 1942 (Morgan)
Loi du 21 juin 1907, 1942 (Arletty)
Lola, 1961 (Aimée)
Lola. *See* Twinky, 1969
Lola, 1981 (Mueller-Stahl)
Lola Montès, 1955 (Ustinov; Walbrook; Werner)
Lolas de Lola, 1976 (Léaud)
Lolita, 1962 (Mason; Sellers; Winters)
Lolita, 1996 (Griffith; Irons)
Lolly-Madonna War, 1973 (Bridges; Steiger; Ryan, R.)
Lon of the Lone Mountain, 1915 (Chaney)
London after Midnight, 1927 (Chaney)
London Belongs to Me, 1948 (Attenborough)
London Calling. *See* Hello London, 1958
London Entertains, 1951 (Sellers)
London Melody, 1937 (Neagle)
London Nobody Knows, 1967 (Mason)
London Town, 1946 (Kendall)
Lone Cowboy, 1934 (Cooper)
Lone Hand, 1953 (McCrea)
Lone Star, 1952 (Barrymore, L.; Crawford, B.; Gable; Gardner)
Lone Star Ranger, 1923 (Mix)
Lone Star Trail, 1943 (Mitchum)
Lone Wolf Returns, 1935 (Douglas, Melvyn)
Lone Wolf Spy Hunt, 1939 (Hayworth; Lupino)
Lone Wolf's Daughter. *See* Lone Wolf Spy Hunt, 1939
Lonedale Operator, 1911 (Sweet)
Loneliness of the Long-Distance Runner, 1962 (Redgrave, M.)
Loneliness of the Long-Distance Singer. *See* Solitude du chanteur de fond, 1974
Lonely Are the Brave, 1962 (Douglas, K.; Douglas, Michael; Matthau; Rowlands)
Lonely Guy, 1984 (Martin, S.)
Lonely in America, 1991 (Lee, S.)
Lonely Lane. *See* Horo-ki, 1962
Lonely Man, 1957 (Palance; Perkins; Van Cleef)
Lonely Man. *See* Five Bloody Graves, 1970
Lonely Passion of Judith Hearne, 1987 (Hoskins; Smith)
Lonely Profession, 1969 (Cotten)
Lonely Trail, 1936 (Wayne)
Lonely Villa, 1909 (Pickford)
Lonely Wife. *See* **Charulata**, 1964
Lonely Wives, 1931 (Horton)
Lonely Woman. *See* Roses rouges et piments verts, 1975
Lonely Woman. *See* **Viaggio in Italia**, 1954
Lonelyhearts, 1958 (Clift; Ryan, R.)
Loners, 1972 (Grahame)
Lonesome Luke, 1915 (Lloyd)
Lonesome Luke, Circus King, 1916 (Lloyd)
Lonesome Luke from London to Laramie, 1917 (Lloyd)
Lonesome Luke, Lawyer, 1917 (Lloyd)
Lonesome Luke Lolls in Luxury, 1916 (Lloyd)
Lonesome Luke Loses Patients, 1917 (Lloyd)
Lonesome Luke, Mechanic, 1917 (Lloyd)
Lonesome Luke, Messenger, 1917 (Lloyd)
Lonesome Luke on Tin Can Alley, 1917 (Lloyd)

Lonesome Luke, Plumber, 1917 (Lloyd)
Lonesome Luke, Social Gangster, 1915 (Lloyd)
Lonesome Luke's Honeymoon, 1917 (Lloyd)
Lonesome Luke's Lively Life, 1917 (Lloyd)
Lonesome Luke's Wild Women, 1917 (Lloyd)
Lonesome Trail, 1914 (Mix)
Long Absence. See Aussi Longue Absence, 1961
Long Ago Tomorrow. See Raging Moon, 1971
Long and the Short and the Tall, 1961 (Harris, R.)
Long Arm, 1956 (Hawkins)
Long Dark Hall, 1951 (Harrison)
Long Day's Journey into Night, 1962 (Hepburn, K.; Richardson, R.; Robards)
Long Day's Journey into Night, 1973 (Olivier)
Long Day's Journey into Night, 1987 (Lemmon)
Long des trottoirs, 1956 (Rosay)
Long Duel, 1967 (Brynner; Howard, T.)
Long Good Friday, 1980 (Constantine; Hoskins; Mirren)
Long Goodbye, 1973 (Gould; Hayden; Schwarzenegger)
Long Gray Line, 1955 (Bond; Crisp; O'Hara; Power)
Long Haul, 1957 (Dors; Mature)
Long Hot Summer, 1958 (Lansbury; Newman; Remick; Welles; Woodward)
Long Hot Summer, 1985 (Gardner; Robards)
Long Live the King, 1926 (Laurel and Hardy)
Long, Long Affair. See Dlinnoe, dlinnoe delo, 1976
Long, Long Trailer, 1954 (Ball)
Long Lost Father, 1934 (Barrymore, J.)
Long Memory, 1953 (Mills)
Long Night, 1947 (Fonda, H.; Price)
Long Pants, 1927 (Langdon)
Long Ride Home. See Time for Killing, 1967
Long Riders, 1980 (Quaid)
Long Road, 1911 (Sweet)
Long Road Home, 1996 (Aiello)
Long Shadow, 1992 (Ullmann)
Long Ships, 1964 (Homolka; Poitier; Widmark)
Long Shot, 1980 (York)
Long Silence. See Lungo Silenzio, 1993
Long Summer of George Adams, 1982 (Garner)
Long Trail, 1910 (Mix)
Long Trail, 1929 (Brennan)
Long Voyage Home, 1940 (Bond; Fitzgerald; Wayne)
Long Wait, 1954 (Coburn, C.; Quinn)
Long Walk Home, 1990 (Goldberg; Spacek; Steenburgen)
Long Winter. See Largo Invierno, 1992
Longest Day, 1962 (Arletty; Barrault; Burton; Connery; Fonda, H.; Gélin; McDowall; Mineo; Mitchum; O'Brien, E.; Rosay; Ryan, R.; Segal; Steiger; Wayne)
Longest Night, 1936 (Young, R.)
Longest Yard, 1974 (Reynolds, B.)
Look at Liv, 1979 (Andersson, B.; Finch; Hackman; Josephson; Ullmann; Von Sydow)
Look Away, 1987 (Burstyn)
Look Back in Anger, 1959 (Bloom; Burton; Evans; Pleasence)
Look Back in Anger, 1980 (McDowell)
Look Back in Anger, 1989 (Branagh; Thompson)
Look before You Love, 1948 (Lockwood)
Look Out Below, 1919 (Lloyd)
Look Pleasant, Please, 1918 (Lloyd)
Look See .... See Ecoute voir ..., 1978
Look Up and Laugh, 1935 (Fields, G.; Leigh, V.)
Look What's Happened to Rosemary's Baby, 1976 (Crawford, B.; Gordon; Milland)
Look Who's Laughing, 1941 (Ball)
Look Who's Talking, 1989 (Segal; Travolta; Willis)
Look Who's Talking Now, 1993 (DeVito; Keaton, D.; Segal; Travolta)
Look Who's Talking Too, 1990 (Brooks, M.; Pryor; Travolta; Willis)
Looker, 1981 (Coburn, J.; Finney)
Looker, 1986 (Finney)
Lookin' Good. See Corky, 1971
Lookin' to Get Out, 1982 (Ann-Margret; Voight)
Looking for Mr. Goodbar, 1977 (Gere; Keaton, D.; Weld)

Looking for Richard, 1996 (Gielgud; Jones, James Earl; Pacino; Ryder)
Looking for Trouble, 1914 (Beery)
Looking for Trouble. See Tip-Off, 1931
Looking for Trouble, 1934 (Tracy)
Looking Forward, 1933 (Barrymore, L.)
Looking Glass War, 1969 (Hopkins, A.; Richardson, R.)
Looking on the Bright Side, 1932 (Fields, G.)
Loonies at Large. See Cavale des Fous, 1993
Loophole, 1954 (Malone)
Loophole, 1980 (Finney; Sheen; York)
Looping, 1981 (Winters)
Looping the Loop, 1928 (Krauss)
Loose Ankles, 1930 (Young, L.)
Loose Cannons, 1989 (Hackman)
Loose Loot, 1953 (Three Stooges)
Loose Shoes, 1980 (Murray)
Loot, 1970 (Attenborough; Remick)
Looters. See Estouffade à la Carabei, 1967
Lootmaar, 1980 (Anand)
Lord am Alexander-Platz, 1967 (Mueller-Stahl)
Lord Byron, 1922 (Veidt)
Lord Chumley, 1914 (Gish)
Lord Elgin and Some Stones of No Value, 1987 (Grant, H.)
Lord for a Night. See Aru yo no tonosama, 1946
Lord Jeff, 1938 (Coburn, C.; Rooney)
Lord Jim, 1965 (Hawkins; Lukas; Mason; O'Toole; Reggiani; Wallach)
Lord Love a Duck, 1966 (Gordon; McDowall; Weld)
Lord of the Rings, 1978 (Hurt, J.)
Lords of Flatbush, 1974 (Stallone)
Lords of Little Egypt, 1961 (Zetterling)
Lorenzo il Magnifico, 1911 (Bertini)
Lorenzo's Oil, 1992 (Nolte; Sarandon; Ustinov)
Lorie, 1984 (Azmi)
Lorna Doone, 1935 (Lockwood)
Loser Takes All, 1956 (Brazzi)
Losin' It, 1983 (Cruise)
Losing Chase, 1996 (Bacon; Mirren)
Losing Fight, 1914 (Mix)
Losing Isaiah, 1995 (Jackson, S.; Lange)
Loss of Innocence. See Greengage Summer, 1961
Lost—A Wife, 1925 (Menjou)
Lost and Found, 1979 (Candy; Jackson, G.; Segal)
Lost Angel, 1944 (Gardner; O'Brien, M.)
Lost Angels, 1989 (Sutherland)
Lost Boys, 1987 (Wiest)
Lost Bridegroom, 1916 (Barrymore, J.)
Lost Bridge. See Zerwany most, 1963
Lost Chord, 1933 (Hawkins)
Lost Command, 1966 (Cardinale; Delon; Morgan; Quinn; Segal)
Lost Elephant. See Ivory Hunters, 1990
Lost Empires, 1986 (Olivier)
Lost Face. See Ztracena tvar, 1965
Lost Highway, 1996 (Pryor)
Lost Honor of Katharina Blum. See Verlorene Ehre der Katharina Blum, 1975
Lost Horizon, 1937 (Colman; Horton; Jaffe; Gielgud)
Lost Horizon, 1973 (Boyer; Finch; Ullmann)
Lost House, 1915 (Gish)
Lost Idol, 1990 (Aiello)
Lost Illusion. See Fallen Idol, 1948
Lost in a Harem, 1944 (Abbott and Costello)
Lost in Alaska, 1952 (Abbott and Costello)
Lost in the Arctic, 1911 (Mix)
Lost in the Garden of the World, 1923 (Gilbert)
Lost in the Garden of the World, 1975 (Hoffman)
Lost in the Jungle, 1911 (Mix)
Lost in the Stratosphere, 1934 (McDaniel)
Lost in Transit, 1917 (Crisp)
Lost in Yonkers, 1993 (Dreyfuss)
Lost Jools. See Stolen Jools, 1931
Lost Jungle, 1934 (Rooney)
Lost Kingdom. See Antinea, 1961

Lost Lady, 1934 (Stanwyck)
Lost Man, 1969 (Poitier)
Lost Moment, 1947 (Hayward; Moorehead)
Lost Necklace, 1911 (White)
Lost One. *See* Verlorene, 1951
Lost Patrol, 1934 (Karloff; McLaglen)
Lost People, 1950 (Attenborough; Lom; Zetterling)
Lost Shadow. *See* Verlorene Schatten, 1921
Lost Soul. *See* Anima persa, 1976
Lost Squadron, 1932 (Astor)
Lost Tribe, 1949 (Weissmuller)
Lost Weekend, 1945 (Milland; Wyman)
Lost Weekend. *See* Puente, 1976
Lost World, 1925 (Beery)
Lost World, 1960 (Rains)
Lost World of Sinbad. *See* Daitozuku, 1964
Lottery Bride, 1930 (Brown; MacDonald)
Lottery Lover, 1935 (Ayres)
Lotus Eater, 1921 (Barrymore, J.)
Lotus Eater, 1962 (Cusack)
Loudest Whisper. *See* These Three, 1936
Loudest Whisper. *See* Children's Hour, 1961
Louis, L'enfant du roi, 1993 (Maura)
Louisa, 1950 (Coburn, C.; Reagan)
Louisiana Purchase, 1941 (Hope)
Loulou, 1980 (Depardieu; Huppert)
Loups entre eux, 1936 (Berry)
Louves, 1957 (Moreau; Presle)
Lovable Cheat, 1949 (Keaton, B.)
Love, 1919 (Arbuckle)
Love, 1927 (Garbo; Gilbert)
Love, 1928 (Barrymore, L.)
Love. *See* Liebe, 1956
Love. *See* Karlekan, 1980
Love, 1982 (Ullmann; Zetterling)
Love à la Carte. *See* Adua e la compagne, 1960
Love Affair, 1932 (Bogart)
Love Affair, 1939 (Boyer; Dunne)
Love Affair, 1994 (Beatty; Hepburn, K.)
Love Affair: The Eleanor and Lou Gehrig Story, 1978 (Neal)
Love Affair of the Dictator. *See* Dictator, 1935
Love after Love. *See* Apres l'Amour, 1992
Love among the Millionaires, 1930 (Bow)
Love among the Roses, 1910 (Pickford)
Love among the Ruins, 1975 (Hepburn, K.; Olivier)
Love among Thieves, 1987 (Hepburn, A.)
Love and Anarchy. *See* **Film d'amore e d'anarchia**, 1973
Love and Bullets, 1914 (Arbuckle)
Love and Bullets, 1978 (Bronson; Steiger)
Love and Courage, 1913 (Arbuckle)
Love and Death, 1975 (Allen; Keaton, D.)
Love and Death of Ogin. *See* Oginsawa, 1979
Love and Downhill Skiing. *See* Kärlek och störtlopp, 1946
Love and Duty, 1916 (Laurel and Hardy)
Love and Faith of Ogin. *See* Ogin Sama, 1982
Love and Fascination. *See* Bojo no hito, 1961
Love and Fear. *See* Paura e amore, 1988
Love and Hate. *See* Lyubov i nenavist, 1935
Love and Hate: A Marriage Made in Hell. *See* Love and Hate: The Story of Colin and JoAnn Thatcher, 1990
Love and Hate: The Story of Colin and JoAnn Thatcher, 1990 (Nelligan)
Love and Larceny. *See* Mattatore, 1960
Love and Lobsters. *See* He Did and He Didn't, 1916
Love and Lunch. *See* Mabel's Busy Day, 1914
Love and Money, 1982 (Kinski)
Love and Other Crimes. *See* Alex and the Gypsy, 1976
Love and Pain and the Whole Damn Thing, 1972 (Smith)
Love and Sacrifice. *See* America, 1924
Love and Separation in Sri Lanka. *See* Suri Lanka no ai to wakare, 1976
Love and Soda, 1914 (Beery)
Love and the Frenchwoman. *See* Française et l'amour, 1960

Love and Trouble, 1915 (Beery)
Love at First Bite, 1950 (Three Stooges)
Love at the Top. *See* Mouton enragé, 1974
Love at Twenty. *See* Amour à vingt ans, 1962
Love Ban. *See* It's a 2' 6" above the Ground World, 1972
Love before Breakfast, 1936 (Lombard)
Love Birds, 1934 (Rooney)
Love Boat: The Christmas Cruise, 1986 (Lollobrigida)
Love Bugs, 1917 (Laurel and Hardy)
Love Burglar, 1919 (Beery)
Love Cage. *See* Félins, 1964
Love Comes Quietly, 1975 (Hershey)
Love Crazy, 1941 (Loy; Powell, W.)
Love Detectives, 1934 (Grable)
Love Doll. *See* Grandeur nature, 1973
Love 'em and Feed 'em, 1927 (Laurel and Hardy)
Love 'em and Leave 'em, 1926 (Brooks, L.)
Love 'em and Weep, 1927 (Laurel and Hardy)
Love Field, 1992 (Pfeiffer)
Love Finds Andy Hardy, 1938 (Garland; Rooney; Turner, L.)
Love Flower, 1920 (Barthelmess)
Love from a Stranger, 1937 (Rathbone)
Love Gambler, 1922 (Gilbert)
Love Game. *See* Jeux de l'amour, 1959
Love Game. *See* Kära leken, 1959
Love God?, 1969 (O'Brien, E.)
Love Habit, 1931 (Lanchester)
Love Happy, 1949 (Marx Brothers; Monroe)
Love Has Many Faces, 1965 (Robertson; Turner, L.)
Love Heeds Not the Showers, 1911 (Pickford)
Love in a Hot Climate. *See* Sang et lumières, 1953
Love in a Teacup. *See* Himawari-musume, 1953
Love in an Apartment Hotel, 1912 (Barrymore, L.; Carey; Marsh; Sweet)
Love in Armor, 1915 (Arbuckle)
Love in Germany. *See* Eine Liebe im Deutschland, 1983
Love in Morocco. *See* Baroud, 1932
Love in the Afternoon, 1957 (Chevalier; Constantine; Hepburn, A.)
Love in the Hills, 1911 (Sweet)
Love in the Rough, 1930 (Montgomery)
Love Insurance, 1919 (Crisp)
Love Is a Ball, 1963 (Boyer; Ford, G.)
Love Is a Funny Thing. *See* Homme qui me plait, 1969
Love Is a Headache, 1938 (Rooney)
Love Is a Many Splendored Thing, 1923 (Gilbert)
Love Is a Many Splendored Thing, 1955 (Holden; Jones, Jennifer)
Love Is a Racket, 1932 (Raft)
Love Is Better Than Ever, 1952 (Taylor, E.)
Love Is Blind. *See* Liebe macht Blind, 1925
Love Is Colder than Death. *See* Liebe ist kalter als der Tod, 1969
Love Is Like That. *See* Jazz Cinderella, 1930
Love Is My Profession. *See* Cas de malheur, 1958
Love Is News, 1937 (Ameche; Power; Sanders; Young, L.)
Love Is on the Air, 1937 (Reagan)
Love, Laughs, and Lather, 1917 (Lloyd)
Love Laughs at Andy Hardy, 1946 (Rooney)
Love Leads the Way, 1984 (Borgnine; Neal; Saint)
Love Letters. *See* Liebesnächte, 1929
Love Letters, 1945 (Cotten; Jones, Jennifer)
Love Letters, 1983 (Curtis, J.)
Love, Life, and Laughter, 1934 (Fields, G.)
Love Light, 1921 (Pickford)
Love, Loot and Crash, 1915 (Lloyd)
Love Lottery, 1953 (Bogart; Lom; Niven)
Love Machine, 1971 (Cooper; Ryan, R.)
Love Makers. *See* Viaccia, 1961
Love Makes Us Blind. *See* Liebe macht Blind, 1923
Love Maniac. *See* Blood of Ghastly Horror, 1972
Love Marriage, 1959 (Anand)
Love Mart, 1927 (Karloff)
Love Mates. *See* Madly, 1969
Love Me or Leave Me, 1955 (Cagney; Day)

Love Me Tender, 1956 (Presley)
Love Me Tonight, 1932 (Chevalier; Loy; MacDonald)
Love Molds Labor, 1911 (White)
Love Nest, 1923 (Keaton, B.)
Love Nest, 1951 (Monroe)
Love Nest on Wheels, 1937 (Keaton, B.)
Love of Chrysanthemum, 1910 (Talmadge)
Love of Sumako. *See* Joyu Sumako no koi, 1947
Love of Sunya, 1927 (Swanson)
Love of the Eighteenth Century, 1921 (Lukas)
Love on a Budget. *See* Play Girl, 1932
Love on a Pillow. *See* Repos du guerrier, 1962
Love on Skates, 1916 (Swanson)
Love on the Dole, 1941 (Kerr)
Love on the Ground. *See* Amour par terre, 1984
Love on the Riviera. *See* Racconti d'estate, 1958
Love on the Run, 1936 (Crawford, J.; Gable)
Love on the Run. *See* Amour en fuite, 1979
Love or Hate. *See* Passion Flower, 1920
Love Parade, 1930 (Barrymore, L.; Chevalier; Harlow; MacDonald)
Love Play. *See* Recreation, 1960
Love Potion No. 9, 1992 (Bancroft)
Love Route, 1915 (Crisp)
Love Rumor. *See* Eshaet Hub, 1960
Love She Sought, 1990 (Elliott; Lansbury)
Love Sickness at Sea, 1913 (Normand)
Love, Soldiers and Women. *See* Destinées, 1954
Love Song. *See* Valencia, 1926
Love Songs. *See* Paroles et musique, 1984
Love Specialist. *See* Ragazza del palio, 1957
Love Spell, 1979 (Burton; Cusack)
Love Storm. *See* Menschen in Käfig, 1930
Love Story. *See* Intermezzo, 1939
Love Story, 1944 (Granger; Lockwood)
Love Story, 1970 (Jones, T.; Milland)
Love Streams, 1984 (Rowlands)
Love Test, 1935 (Withers)
Love the Italian Way. *See* Femmine di lusso, 1960
Love Thief. *See* Rounder, 1914
Love under Fire, 1937 (Ameche; Carradine; Young, L.)
Love under the Crucifix. *See* O-gin Sama, 1960
Love War, 1970 (Dickinson)
Love Will Conquer. *See* Kärleken segrar, 1949
Love with the Proper Stranger, 1963 (McQueen; Wood)
Love without a Person, 1995 (Okada)
Loved, 1996 (Hurt, W.)
Loved One, 1965 (Andrews, D.; Coburn, J.; Gielgud; McDowall; Steiger)
Lovejoy: The Lost Colony, 1994 (Gielgud)
Loveless, 1982 (Dafoe)
Lovely Hungarian Comedy. *See* Szep magyar komedia, 1970
Lovely to Look At, 1952 (Dalio; Miller)
Lovely Way to Die, 1968 (Douglas, K.; Wallach)
Lover, 1992 (Moreau)
Lover Boy. *See* Knave of Hearts, 1954
Lover Come Back, 1946 (Ball)
Lover Come Back, 1961 (Day; Hudson)
Lovers. *See* Amants, 1958
Lovers?, 1927 (Novarro)
Lovers: A True Story. *See* Amantes, 1990
Lovers and Liars. *See* Viaggio con Anita, 1979
Lovers and Other Strangers, 1970 (Keaton, D.)
Lovers Courageous, 1932 (Montgomery)
Lovers, Happy Lovers. *See* Knave of Hearts, 1954
Lovers Like Us. *See* Sauvage, 1975
Lover's Luck, 1914 (Arbuckle)
Lovers Must Learn. *See* Rome Adventure, 1962
Lover's Net. *See* Amants du Tage, 1955
Lover's Oath, 1925 (Novarro)
Lovers of Lisbon. *See* Amants du Tage, 1955
Lovers of Montparnasse. *See* Montparnasse 19, 1957
Lovers of Toledo. *See* Amants de Tolède, 1953

Lovers of Verona. *See* Amants de Vérone, 1948
Lovers on the Pont-Neuf. *See* Amants du Pont Neuf, 1991
Lover's Post Office, 1914 (Arbuckle; Normand)
Lovers Three, 1912-13 (White)
Love's Command. *See* Liebeskommando, 1931
Love's Family Tree. *See* Aijo no keifu, 1961
Love's Greatest Mistake, 1927 (Powell, W.)
Loves of a Dictator. *See* Dictator, 1935
Loves of a Pharaoh. *See* Weib des Pharao, 1922
Loves of an Actress, 1928 (Lukas; Negri)
Loves of Ariane. *See* Ariane, 1931
Loves of Carmen, 1927 (Del Rio; McLaglen)
Loves of Carmen, 1948 (Ford, G.; Hayworth)
Loves of Edgar Allan Poe, 1942 (Darnell)
Loves of Hercules. *See* Amori di Ercole, 1960
Loves of Isadora. *See* Isadora, 1968
Loves of Joanna Godden, 1947 (Withers)
Loves of Pharaoh. *See* Weib des Pharao, 1921
Loves of Three Queens. *See* Eterna femmina, 1954
Love's Redemption, 1920 (Talmadge)
Love's Renunciation, 1910-11 (White)
Lovesick, 1983 (Guinness; Huston, J.; Moore, Dudley)
Lovesick Maidens of Cuddleton, 1912 (Talmadge)
Lovey: A Circle of Children, Part II, 1978 (Aiello)
Lovin' Molly, 1974 (Perkins; Sarandon)
Loving, 1970 (Hayden; Saint; Scheider; Segal)
Loving Couples. *See* Allskande par, 1964
Loving Couples, 1980 (Coburn, J.; MacLaine; Sarandon)
Loving in the Rain. *See* Amour de pluie, 1974
Loving You, 1957 (Presley)
Lowat el Hub, 1960 (Sharif)
Lower Depths. *See* Donzoko, 1957
Loyal 47 Ronin. *See* Chushingura, 1962
Loyalties, 1933 (Rathbone)
L-Shaped Room, 1962 (Attenborough; Caron)
Lucas, 1986 (Ryder)
Luce nelle tenebre, 1941 (Valli)
Lucertola con la pelle di donna, 1971 (Baker)
Luci del varietà, 1950 (Loren; Masina)
Lucia di Lammermoor, 1946 (Lollobrigida)
Lucie Aubrac, 1996 (Binoche)
Lucien chez les barbares, 1981 (Moreau)
Lucinda Brayford, 1980 (Neill)
Luck of Ginger Coffey, 1964 (Shaw)
Luck of the Foolish, 1924 (Langdon)
Luck of the Game. *See* Gridiron Flash, 1935
Luck of the Irish, 1948 (Baxter; Cobb; Power)
Luck That Jealousy Brought, 1917 (Mix)
Lucky Boy, 1929 (Jolson)
Lucky Cisco Kid, 1940 (Andrews, D.)
Lucky Deal, 1915 (Mix)
Lucky Dog, 1917 (Laurel and Hardy)
Lucky Five. *See* Cinque poveri in automobile, 1952
Lucky Horseshoe, 1925 (Mix)
Lucky Jim, 1957 (Terry-Thomas)
Lucky Jo, 1964 (Constantine)
Lucky Joe, 1964 (Brasseur)
Lucky Jordan, 1943 (Ladd)
Lucky Lady, 1926 (Barrymore, L.)
Lucky Lady, 1975 (Hackman; Minnelli; Reynolds, B.)
Lucky Luciano. *See* Proposito Lucky Luciano, 1973
Lucky Mascot. *See* Brass Monkey, 1948
Lucky Me, 1954 (Dalio; Day; Dickinson)
Lucky Nick Cain, 1951 (Raft)
Lucky Night, 1939 (Loy; Taylor, R.)
Lucky Partners, 1940 (Colman; Rogers, G.)
Lucky Ravi, 1987 (Vogler)
Lucky Star, 1929 (Gaynor)
Lucky Star, 1980 (Steiger)
Lucky Stars, 1925 (Langdon)
Lucky Stiff, 1948 (Lamour; Trevor)

Lucky Stiff, 1988 (Perkins)
Lucky Strike, 1915 (Laurel and Hardy)
Lucky Texan, 1934 (Wayne)
Lucky to Be a Woman. *See* Fortuna di essere donna, 1955
Lucky Toothache, 1910 (Pickford)
Lucona Affair. *See* Fall Lucona, 1993
Lucrèce, 1943 (Feuillère)
Lucrèce Borgia, 1935 (Artaud; Feuillère; Modot)
Lucrèce Borgia, 1953 (Armendáriz)
Lucretia Lombard, 1923 (Shearer)
Lucrezia Borgia, 1922 (Veidt)
Lucy Gallant, 1955 (Heston; Ritter; Trevor; Wyman)
Ludwig, 1972 (Howard, T.; Mangano; Schneider)
Ludwig II, 1954 (Kinski)
Luffar-Petter, 1922 (Garbo)
Lüge, 1950 (Fröhlich)
Luise Millerin, 1922 (Dagover; Kortner; Krauss)
Luke and the Bang-Tails, 1916 (Lloyd)
Luke and the Bomb Throwers, 1916 (Lloyd)
Luke and the Mermaids, 1916 (Lloyd)
Luke and the Rural Roughnecks, 1916 (Lloyd)
Luke—Crystal Gazer, 1916 (Lloyd)
Luke Does the Midway, 1916 (Lloyd)
Luke Foils the Villain, 1916 (Lloyd)
Luke Joins the Navy, 1916 (Lloyd)
Luke Laughs Last, 1916 (Lloyd)
Luke Leans to the Literary, 1916 (Lloyd)
Luke Locates the Loot, 1916 (Lloyd)
Luke Lugs Luggage, 1916 (Lloyd)
Luke, Patient Provider, 1916 (Lloyd)
Luke Pipes the Pippins, 1916 (Lloyd)
Luke Rides Roughshod, 1916 (Lloyd)
Luke the Candy Cut-Up, 1916 (Lloyd)
Luke, the Chauffeur, 1916 (Lloyd)
Luke, the Gladiator, 1916 (Lloyd)
Luke Wins Ye Ladye Faire, 1917 (Lloyd)
Luke's Busy Days, 1917 (Lloyd)
Luke's Double, 1916 (Lloyd)
Luke's Fatal Flivver, 1916 (Lloyd)
Luke's Fireworks Fizzle, 1916 (Lloyd)
Luke's Late Lunches, 1916 (Lloyd)
Luke's Lost Lamb, 1916 (Lloyd)
Luke's Lost Liberty, 1917 (Lloyd)
Luke's Model Movie. *See* Luke's Movie Muddle, 1916
Luke's Movie Muddle, 1916 (Lloyd)
Luke's Newsie Knockout, 1916 (Lloyd)
Luke's Preparedness Preparations, 1916 (Lloyd)
Luke's Shattered Sleep, 1916 (Lloyd)
Luke's Society Mix-Up, 1916 (Lloyd)
Luke's Speedy Club Life, 1916 (Lloyd)
Luke's Trolley Trouble, 1917 (Lloyd)
Luke's Washful Waiting, 1916 (Lloyd)
Lukrezia Borgia, 1922 (Wegener)
Lullaby of Broadway, 1951 (Day)
Lulu, 1917 (Jannings)
Lulu, 1953 (Mastroianni)
Lulu Belle, 1947 (Lamour)
Lulu the Tool. *See* Classe operaia va in paradiso, 1971
Lumière, 1976 (Ganz; Moreau)
Lumière d'en face, 1955 (Bardot)
Lumière d'été, 1943 (Barrault; Brasseur)
Lumière du lac, 1988 (Barrault)
Luminous Moss. *See* Hikarigoke, 1992
Lumpenkavaliere, 1932 (Madsen and Schenstrøm)
Luna, 1979 (Benigni; Valli)
Luna sleva, 1928 (Cherkassov)
Lune dans le caniveau, 1983 (Depardieu; Kinski; Abril)
Lune di miel, 1985 (Baye)
Lunes de Fiel, 1992 (Grant, H.)
Lunettes d'or. *See* Occhiali d'oro, 1987
Lung siuye, 1982 (Chan)

Lung Ta: Les cavaliers du vent, 1990 (Adjani)
Lunga notte del '43, 1960 (Cervi)
Lunga strada azzurra, 1958 (Montand)
Lunghing fudai, 1986 (Chan)
Lunghing fudai tsuktsap, 1990 (Chan)
Lungo Silenzio, 1993 (Valli)
Lupo della Sila, 1949 (Gassman; Mangano)
Lure of Ambition, 1919 (Bara)
Lure of Broadway. *See* Bright Lights, 1916
Lure of Hollywood, 1931 (Arbuckle)
Lure of the Sila. *See* Lupo della Sila, 1950
Lure of the Wilderness, 1952 (Brennan)
Lure of the Windigo, 1914 (Mix)
Lured, 1947 (Ball; Coburn, C.; Karloff; Sanders)
Lush Life, 1993 (Whitaker)
Lust for Evil. *See* Plein soleil, 1959
Lust for Gold, 1949 (Ford, G.; Lupino)
Lust for Life, 1956 (Douglas, K.; Quinn; Sloane)
Lust in the Sun. *See* Dans la poussière du soleil, 1971
Lustgården, 1961 (Andersson, B.; Björnstrand)
Lusty Men, 1952 (Hayward; Kennedy; Mitchum)
Lute: Camina o Revienta, 1987 (Abril)
Lutring ... reveille-toi et meurs. *See* Svegliati e uccidi, 1966
Luv, 1967 (Falk; Ford, H.; Lemmon)
Luz del fin del mondo, 1971 (Douglas, K.; Rey; Brynner)
Luz del Fin del Mundo, 1981 (Douglas, K.)
Lyckodrömmen, 1963 (Andersson, H.; Björnstrand)
Lyckoriddare, 1921 (Garbo)
Lydia, 1941 (Cotten; Oberon)
Lykkehjulet, 1926 (Madsen and Schenstrøm)
Lysistrata. *See* Destinées, 1954
Lyubliu tebya?, 1934 (Cherkassov)
Lyubov i nenavist, 1935 (Maretskaya)
Lyubov silna na strastyou potseluya, 1916 (Mozhukin)
M, 1931 (Lorre)
M-G-M Story, 1951 (Barrymore, L.)
M. Butterfly, 1993 (Irons)
M. Scrupule, gangster, 1953 (Dalio)
Ma femme, mon gosse, et moi. *See* Amour est en jeu, 1957
Ma l'amore mio non muore, 1938 (Valli)
Ma no kisetsu: Haru no mizuumi, 1956 (Yamamura)
Ma no ogon, 1950 (Mori)
Ma Pomme, 1950 (Chevalier)
Ma Saison Préférée, 1993 (Deneuve)
Mabel and Fatty Viewing the World's Fair at San Francisco, California, 1915 (Arbuckle; Normand)
Mabel and Fatty's Married Life, 1915 (Arbuckle; Normand)
Mabel and Fatty's Simple Life, 1915 (Arbuckle; Normand)
Mabel and Fatty's Wash Day, 1915 (Arbuckle; Normand)
Mabel at the Wheel, 1914 (Chaplin, C.; Normand)
Mabel, Fatty, and the Law, 1915 (Arbuckle; Normand)
Mabel Lost and Won, 1915 (Normand)
Mabel's Adventures, 1912 (Normand)
Mabel's Awful Mistake, 1913 (Normand)
Mabel's Bear Escape, 1914 (Normand)
Mabel's Blunder, 1914 (Normand)
Mabel's Busy Day, 1914 (Chaplin, C.; Normand)
Mabel's Dramatic Career, 1913 (Arbuckle; Normand)
Mabel's Flirtation. *See* Her Friend the Bandit, 1914
Mabel's Heroes, 1913 (Normand)
Mabel's Latest Prank, 1914 (Normand)
Mabel's Lovers, 1912 (Normand)
Mabel's Married Life, 1914 (Chaplin, C.; Normand)
Mabel's Nerve, 1914 (Normand)
Mabel's New Hero, 1913 (Arbuckle; Normand)
Mabel's New Job, 1914 (Normand)
Mabel's Stormy Love Affair, 1914 (Normand)
Mabel's Strange Predicament, 1914 (Chaplin, C.; Normand)
Mabel's Strategem, 1912 (Normand)
Mabel's Wilful Way, 1915 (Arbuckle; Normand)
Maboroshi fujin, 1949 (Yamamura)

Maboroshi-jo, 1940 (Shimura)
Mabuta no haha, 1931 (Yamada)
Mabuta no haha, 1938 (Hasegawa)
Mac, 1992 (Barkin; Turturro)
Macadam, 1946 (Rosay)
Macahans, 1976 (Saint)
Macao, 1952 (Grahame; Mitchum; Russell, J.)
Macao, L'Enfer du jeu, 1939 (Hayakawa)
Macaroni. See Maccheroni, 1985
Macaroni Blues. See Elanprostekt nr. 4, 1986
MacArthur, 1977 (Peck)
Macbeth, 1948 (McDowall; Welles)
Macbeth. See Kumonosu-jo, 1957
Maccheroni, 1985 (Lemon; Mastroianni)
Macchia rosa, 1969 (Giannini)
Macédoine, 1970 (Brasseur)
Macheath, 1987 (Hurt, J.)
Machete, 1958 (Van Cleef)
Machi no bofu, 1934 (Tanaka)
Machi no hitobito, 1926 (Tanaka)
Machibuse, 1970 (Mifune)
"Machiko" yori: Hana hiraku, 1948 (Takamine)
Machinations, 1984 (Vogler)
Machine, 1994 (Baye; Depardieu)
Machine Gun Kelly, 1958 (Bronson)
Machine Gun McCain. See Intoccabili, 1968
Macho, 1984 (York)
Macho Callahan, 1970 (Cobb; Seberg)
Macht der Versuchung, 1922 (Dagover)
Mack, 1973 (Pryor)
Mack and His Pack. See Mack, 1973
Mack at It Again, 1914 (Normand)
Mack the Knife, 1989 (Harris, R.; Julia)
Mackendrick, 1986 (Coburn, J.)
MacKenna's Gold, 1968 (Cobb; Massey; Meredith; Peck; Quayle; Robinson, E.; Sharif; Wallach)
Mackintosh and T. J., 1975 (Rogers, R.; Huston, J.; Mason; Newman; Sanda)
Maclovia, 1948 (Armendáriz; Félix)
Macomber Affair, 1947 (Bennett; Peck; Preston)
Mad about Men, 1954 (Rutherford)
Mad about Money. See He Loved an Actress, 1938
Mad about Music, 1938 (Durbin; Marshall)
Mad Adventures of Rabbi Jacob. See Aventures de Rabbi Jacob, 1973
Mad Atlantic. See Doto ichi man kairi, 1966
Mad Checkmate. See Uno scacco tutto matto, 1968
Mad Doctor, 1941 (Rathbone)
Mad Dog. See Mad Dog Morgan, 1976
Mad Dog and Glory, 1993 (De Niro; Murray; Thurman)
Mad Dog Coll, 1961 (Hackman)
Mad Dog Morgan, 1976 (Hopper)
Mad Dogs and Englishmen, 1995 (Bloom)
Mad Game, 1933 (Tracy; Trevor)
Mad Genius, 1931 (Barrymore, J.; Karloff)
Mad Love. See Mania, 1918
Mad Love, 1935 (Lorre)
Mad Magician, 1954 (Price)
Mad Masquerade. See Washington Masquerade, 1932
Mad Max, 1979 (Gibson)
Mad Max 2. See Road Warrior, 1982
Mad Max 3. See Mad Max: Beyond Thunderdome, 1985
Mad Max: Beyond Thunderdome, 1985 (Gibson)
Mad Miss Manton, 1938 (Fonda, H.; McDaniel; Stanwyck)
Mad Monkey. See Sueno del Mono Loco, 1989
Mad Monster Party, 1967 (Karloff)
Mad Night. See Egy örült éjszaka, 1969
Mad Queen. See Locura de amor, 1948
Mad Racer, 1926 (Arthur)
Mad Room, 1968 (Winters)
Mad Wednesday, 1947 (Lloyd)
Madadayo, 1993 (Kagawa)
Madam, Permit Me to Love Your Daughter. See Permettete che ami vostre

figlia?, 1974
Madame. See Madame Sans-Gêne, 1961
Madame Bäurin, 1993 (Schygulla)
Madame Bovary, 1937 (Negri)
Madame Bovary, 1949 (Jones, Jennifer; Jourdan; Mason)
Madame Bovary, 1991 (Huppert)
Madame Butterfly, 1915 (Pickford)
Madame Butterfly, 1932 (Grant, C.; Sidney)
Madame Claude, 1976 (Dalio; Kinski)
Madame Curie, 1943 (Garson; O'Brien, M.; Pidgeon; Walker)
Madame de ..., 1953 (Boyer; Darrieux)
Madame Double X, 1914 (Beery)
Madame DuBarry, 1919 (Bara; Jannings; Negri)
Madame DuBarry, 1934 (Del Rio)
Madame Guillotine, 1931 (Carroll)
Madame Kitty. See Salon Kitty, 1976
Madame Mystery, 1926 (Bara; Laurel and Hardy)
Madame Peacock, 1920 (Nazimova)
Madame Pimpernel. See Paris Underground, 1945
Madame Racketeer, 1932 (Raft)
Madame Récamier, 1928 (Rosay)
Madame Sans-Gêne, 1925 (Brasseur; Swanson)
Madame Sans-Gêne, 1941 (Arletty)
Madame Sans-Gêne, 1943 (Cuny)
Madame Sans-Gêne, 1961 (Loren)
Madame Sin, 1972 (Davis, B.; Elliott)
Madame Sourdis, 1984 (Baye)
Madame Sousatzka, 1988 (Azmi; MacLaine)
Madame Spy, 1934 (Wray)
Madame Wants No Children. See Madame wünscht keine Kinder, 1926
Madame wünscht keine Kinder, 1926 (Dietrich)
Madame X, 1929 (Barrymore, L.)
Madame X, 1966 (Meredith; Turner, L.)
Madame X, 1981 (Weld)
Madame Yuki. See Yuki-fujin ezu, 1950
Madamu to nyobo, 1931 (Tanaka)
Mädchen aus Flandern, 1956 (Schell, Maximilian)
Mädchen in Uniform, 1958 (Schneider)
Mädchen Irene, 1936 (Dagover)
Mädchen ohne Heimat, 1926 (Homolka)
Mädchen ohne Vaterland, 1912 (Nielsen)
Mädchen und die Männer, 1919 (Krauss)
Mädchen von Fanö, 1940 (Wegener)
Mädchenjahre einer Königin, 1954 (Schneider)
Mädchenräuber, 1936 (Madsen and Schenstrøm)
Maddalena, 1953 (Cervi; Vanel)
Maddalena Ferat, 1921 (Bertini)
Maddening, 1995 (Dickinson; Reynolds, B.)
Made a Coward, 1913 (Mix)
Made for Each Other, 1939 (Bond; Coburn, C.; Lombard; Stewart)
Made in America, 1993 (Douglas, Michael; Goldberg)
Made in Heaven, 1987 (Barkin; Winger)
Made in Italy, 1965 (Fabrizi; Magnani; Sordi)
Made in Paris, 1966 (Dalio; Ann-Margret; Jourdan)
Made in Sweden, 1968 (Von Sydow)
Made in U.S.A., 1966 (Karina; Léaud)
Made on Broadway, 1933 (Montgomery)
Mademoiselle, 1966 (Moreau)
Mademoiselle Ange, 1959 (Belmondo)
Mademoiselle Docteur, 1937 (Barrault; Fresnay; Jouvet; Modot)
Mademoiselle France. See Reunion in France, 1942
Mademoiselle ma mère, 1937 (Brasseur; Darrieux)
Mademoiselle Mozart, 1936 (Darrieux; Morgan)
Mademoiselle Porte-bonheur. See Lucky Me, 1954
Madhouse, 1974 (Cushing; Price)
Madhubala, 1950 (Anand)
Madhumati, 1958 (Kumar)
Madigan, 1968 (Fonda, H.; Widmark)
Madigan: Park Avenue Beat, 1973 (Widmark)
Madigan: The Lisbon Beat, 1973 (Widmark)
Madigan: The Naples Beat, 1973 (Widmark)

Madigan's Millions. *See* Dollaro per 7 vigliacchi, 1970
Madison Avenue, 1962 (Andrews, D.)
Madly, 1969 (Delon)
Madman, 1976 (Weaver)
Madman's Defence. *See* Dåres försvarstal, 1976
Madmen of Europe. *See* Englishman's Home, 1939
Madness of King George, 1994 (Mirren)
Madness of the Heart, 1949 (Lockwood)
Madness of Youth, 1923 (Gilbert)
Mado, 1927 (Tanaka)
Mado, 1976 (Baye; Piccoli)
Mado, 1978 (Schneider)
Mado kara tobidase, 1950 (Kagawa)
Mado, Poste Restante, 1990 (Yankovsky)
Madonna in the Gaucho, 1927 (Pickford)
Madonna of the Seven Moons, 1944 (Granger)
Madonna of the Storm, 1913 (Gish)
Madonna of the Streets, 1924 (Beery; Nazimova)
Madre, 1913 (Bertini)
Madregilda, 1993 (Rey)
Madrid, 1987 (Vogler)
Madriguera, 1969 (Chaplin, G.)
Madron, 1970 (Caron)
Madwoman of Chaillot, 1969 (Boyer; Brynner; Evans; Henreid; Hepburn, K.;
    Homolka; Kaye; Masina; Pleasence)
Mae West, 1982 (McDowall)
Maestrina, 1913 (Bertini)
Maestro, 1958 (Fabrizi)
Maestro, 1979 (Cassel)
Maestro, 1989 (McDowell)
Maestro d'amore, 1977 (Brazzi)
Maestro di Don Giovanni, 1953 (Flynn; Lollobrigida)
Maestro di Vigevano, 1963 (Bloom; Sordi)
Maestro i Margarita, 1972 (Cuny)
Maffia fait la loi. *See* Giorno della civetta, 1968
Mafia, 1949 (Vanel)
Mafia. *See* Giorno della civetta, 1968
Mafia Princess, 1986 (Curtis, T.)
Mafia War. *See* Bacciamo le mani, 1973
Mafioso, 1962 (Sordi)
Mafu Cage, 1978 (Grant, L.)
Magdalene, 1988 (Kinski; Quayle)
Maggie, 1986 (Gardner)
Maggie's First False Step, 1917 (Beery)
Magic, 1978 (Ann-Margret; Attenborough; Hopkins, A.; Meredith)
Magic Bow, 1946 (Granger)
Magic Box, 1951 (Attenborough; Donat; Olivier; Rutherford; Schell, Maria;
    Ustinov; Withers)
Magic Carpet, 1951 (Ball)
Magic Christian, 1970 (Attenborough; Brynner; Cleese; Lee, C.; Sellers;
    Welch)
Magic Donkey. *See* Peau d'âne, 1970
Magic Fire, 1956 (Cushing; Rasp)
Magic Flame, 1927 (Banky; Colman)
Magic Fountain. *See* Fuente magica, 1961
Magic Mountain, 1982 (Steiger)
Magic Night. *See* Goodnight Vienna, 1932
Magic of Lassie, 1978 (Faye; Rooney; Stewart)
Magic Shoes, 1935 (Finch)
Magic Sword, 1962 (Rathbone)
Magic Town, 1947 (Stewart; Wyman)
Magic Voyage, 1992 (Rooney)
Magical World of Chuck Jones, 1992 (Goldberg; McDowall)
Magician. *See* Magicien, 1927
Magician. *See* Ansiktet, 1958
Magician in Spite of Himself, 1951 (Loren)
Magician of Lublin, 1979 (Arkin; Winters)
Magicien, 1927 (Wegener)
Magistrato, 1959 (Cardinale)
Magliari, 1959 (Sordi)
Magnat, 1987 (Nowicki)

Magnate, 1973 (Cassel)
Magnet of Doom. *See* Aîné des Ferchaux, 1962
Magnificent Ambersons, 1942 (Baxter; Cotten; Moorehead; Welles)
Magnificent Bodyguards, 1978 (Chan)
Magnificent Brute, 1936 (McLaglen)
Magnificent Cuckold. *See* Magnifico cornuto, 1964
Magnificent Doll, 1946 (Meredith; Niven; Rogers, G.)
Magnificent Dope, 1942 (Ameche; Fonda, H.; Horton)
Magnificent Flirt, 1928 (Young, L.)
Magnificent Lie, 1931 (Bellamy; Boyer; Rosay)
Magnificent Matador, 1955 (O'Hara; Quinn)
Magnificent Obsession, 1935 (Dunne; Taylor, R.)
Magnificent Obsession, 1954 (Hudson; Moorehead; Wyman)
Magnificent One. *See* Magnifique, 1974
Magnificent Roughnecks, 1956 (Rooney)
Magnificent Seven, 1960 (Bronson; Brynner; Coburn, J.; McQueen; Wallach)
Magnificent Seven Ride!, 1972 (Van Cleef)
Magnificent Showman. *See* Circus World, 1964
Magnificent Sinner. *See* Katia, 1960
Magnificent Tramp. *See* Archimède, le clochard, 1959
Magnificent Yankee, 1950 (Calhern)
Magnifico avventuriero, 1963 (Blier)
Magnifico cornuto, 1964 (Blier; Cardinale; Volonté)
Magnifique, 1974 (Belmondo)
Magnum Force, 1973 (Eastwood)
Mago, 1949 (Cantinflas)
Magokoro, 1953 (Tanaka)
Magot de Joséfa, 1964 (Brasseur; Magnani)
Magus, 1968 (Caine; Karina; Quinn)
Magzat, 1993 (Nowicki)
Mahal, 1969 (Anand)
Mahaprithivi, 1992 (Chatterjee)
Maharlika, 1970 (Crawford, B.)
Mahashweta, 1967 (Chatterjee)
Mahiru no ankoku, 1956 (Yamamura)
Mahiru no enbukyoku, 1949 (Tanaka)
Mahogany, 1975 (Perkins)
Maid, 1992 (Cassel; Sheen)
Maid and the Martian. *See* Pajama Party, 1964
Maid for Murder, 1961 (Karina)
Maid in Paris. *See* Paris canaille, 1955
Maid of Niagara, 1910 (White)
Maid of Salem, 1937 (Colbert; MacMurray)
Maid of the Mist, 1915 (Chaney)
Maid of War, 1914 (Beery)
Maid or Man, 1911 (Pickford)
Maid to Order, 1916 (Laurel and Hardy)
Maiden for a Prince. *See* Vergine per il principe, 1965
Maiden for the Prince. *See* Vergine per il principe, 1965
Maidens of Yashima Sea. *See* Kashimanada no onna, 1959
Maids, 1974 (Jackson, G.; York)
Maids and Muslin, 1920 (Laurel and Hardy)
Maid's Night Out, 1911 (Normand)
Maid's Night Out, 1938 (Fontaine)
Maigret, 1988 (Harris, R.)
Maigret a Pigalle, 1967 (Cervi)
Maigret et l'affaire Saint-Fiacre, 1958 (Gabin)
Maigret Lays a Trap. *See* Maigret tend un piège, 1957
Maigret tend un piège, 1957 (Gabin; Girardot)
Maigret voit rouge, 1963 (Gabin)
Maihime, 1951 (Yamamura)
Mail Order Bride, 1963 (Oates)
Mail Train. *See* Inspector Hornleigh Goes to It, 1941
...La main à couper, 1974 (Blier)
Main Attraction, 1962 (Zetterling)
Main Azaad Hoon, 1989 (Azmi)
Main du diable, 1942 (Fresnay)
Main Event, 1979 (Murray; Streisand)
Main Street after Dark, 1944 (Duryea)
Main Street to Broadway, 1953 (Barrymore, E.; Barrymore, L.; Calhern;
    Harrison; Moorehead; Wilde)

Main Thing Is to Love. *See* Important c'est d'aimer, 1975
Mains d'Orlac. *See* Hands of Orlac, 1960
Mains sales, 1951 (Brasseur; Gélin)
Mais n'te promène donc pas toute nue, 1936 (Arletty)
Mais où et donc ornicar?, 1978 (Chaplin, G.)
Maisen, 1936 (Shimura)
Maisie, 1939 (Young, R.)
Maisie Goes to Reno, 1944 (Gardner)
Maisie Was a Lady, 1941 (Ayres; Gardner; O'Sullivan)
Maison Bonnadieu, 1951 (Blier; Darrieux)
Maison de campagne, 1969 (Darrieux)
Maison de danses, 1931 (Vanel)
Maison du Maltais, 1938 (Dalio; Jouvet)
Maison du mystère, 1922 (Mozhukin; Vanel)
Maison du silence, 1952 (Gélin)
Maison du souvenir. *See* Casa Ricordi, 1954
Maison jaune de Rio, 1930 (Vanel)
Maison sous la mer, 1946 (Aimée)
Maison sous les arbres, 1971 (Dunaway)
Maître après Dieu, 1950 (Brasseur)
Maître nageur, 1979 (Trintignant)
Maîtres-Nageurs, 1950 (Berry)
Maîtresse, 1975 (Depardieu)
Maja desnuda, 1958 (Cervi; Gardner)
Maja zwischen zwei Ehen, 1938 (Dagover)
Major and the Minor, 1942 (Milland; Rogers, G.)
Major Barbara, 1941 (Harrison; Kerr)
Major Dundee, 1965 (Coburn, J.; Harris, R.; Heston; Oates)
Major League, 1989 (Snipes)
Major que no tuvo infancia, 1956 (Armendáriz)
Majority of One, 1961 (Guinness; Russell, R.)
Makan no. 44, 1955 (Anand)
Make a Wish, 1937 (Rathbone)
Make It Real, 1948 (Ford, G.)
Make Me a Star, 1932 (Blondell; Chevalier; Colbert; Constantine; March; Sidney)
Make Me an Offer!, 1954 (Finch)
Make Mine Mink, 1960 (Terry-Thomas)
Make Mine Music, 1946 (Eddy)
Make Up. *See* Kesho, 1985
Make Way for a Lady, 1936 (Marshall)
Make Your Own Bed, 1944 (Wyman)
Maker of Men, 1931 (Wayne)
Making a Living, 1914 (Chaplin, C.)
Making It Pleasant for Him, 1909 (Arbuckle)
Making Mr. Right, 1987 (Malkovich)
Making of a "Local Hero," 1983 (Lancaster)
Making of a Lady. *See* Lady Hamilton, 1969
Making of a Man, 1911 (Sweet)
Making of Do the Right Thing, 1989 (Aiello)
Making of Superman: The Movie, 1980 (Hackman)
Mal. *See* Rage, 1966
Mal d'aimer, 1986 (Josephson)
Mal de mer, 1912 (Linder)
"Mala" ordina, 1973 (Cusack)
Malade imaginaire. *See* Malato imaginario, 1979
Maladie d'amour, 1987 (Kinski; Piccoli)
Malady of Love. *See* Mal d'aimer, 1986
Malady of Love. *See* Maladie d'amour, 1987
Malaga, 1954 (O'Hara)
Malaga. *See* Moment of Danger, 1960
Malahierra, 1940 (Armendáriz)
Malaire, 1950 (Vanel)
Malaria, 1941 (Hayakawa)
Målarpirater, 1959 (Björnstrand)
Malastrana, 1971 (Thulin)
Malatesta, 1970 (Constantine)
Malato imaginario, 1979 (Blier; Sordi)
Malaya, 1949 (Barrymore, L.; Greenstreet; Stewart; Tracy)
Malayadaan, 1971 (Chatterjee)
Malcolm X, 1972 (Jones, James Earl)

Malcolm X, 1992 (Bassett; Dillon; Lee, S.; Washington)
Male and Female, 1919 (Swanson)
Male Animal, 1942 (De Havilland; Fonda, H.; McDaniel)
Male Companion. *See* Monsieur de compagnie, 1964
Male Hunt. *See* Chasse à l'homme, 1964
Male oscuro, 1990 (Giannini)
Maledetto imbroglio, 1959 (Cardinale)
Malia, 1918 (Bertini)
Malia, 1945 (Brazzi; Cervi)
Malibu, 1983 (Coburn, J.; Novak; Saint)
Malice, 1993 (Bancroft; Scott, G.)
Malice in the Palace, 1949 (Three Stooges)
Malice in Wonderland, 1985 (Robbins; Taylor, E.)
Malina, 1990 (Huppert)
Malle au mariage, 1912 (Linder)
Malmaison, 1963 (Fresnay)
Malone, 1987 (Reynolds, B.; Robertson)
Malpertuis, 1972 (Cassel; Welles)
Malquerida, 1949 (Del Rio)
Malta Story, 1953 (Guinness; Hawkins)
Maltese Falcon, 1941 (Astor; Bogart; Bond; Greenstreet; Huston, J.; Huston, W.; Lorre)
Malu tianshi, 1937 (Zhao Dan)
Małżeństwo z rozsądki, 1967 (Olbrychski)
Mama cumple cien años, 1979 (Chaplin, G.)
Mama no shinkon-ryoko, 1954 (Yamada; Yamamura)
Mama Turns 100. *See* Mama cumple cien años, 1979
Mama's Dirty Girls, 1974 (Grahame)
Maman et la putain, 1973 (Léaud)
Mambo, 1954 (Gassman; Mangano; Winters)
Mambo Kings, 1992 (Banderas)
Mame, 1974 (Ball; Preston)
Mamma mia, che impressione, 1951 (Sordi)
Mamma Roma, 1962 (Magnani)
Mamma's Boy's, 1916 (Laurel and Hardy)
Mammy, 1930 (Jolson)
Mamouret. *See* Briseur de chaînes, 1941
Mam'selle Striptease. *See* Effeuillant la marguerite, 1956
Mam'zell Pigalle. *See* Cette Sacrée gamine, 1955
Mam'zelle Bonaparte, 1941 (Feuillère)
Mam'zelle Cricri. *See* Deutschmeister, 1955
Mam'zelle Nitouche, 1931 (Raimu)
Mam'zelle Nitouche, 1953 (Fernandel)
Man, 1972 (Ayres; Jones, James Earl; Meredith)
Man, a Cat and Two Women. *See* Neko to Shozo to futari no onna, 1956
Man: A Modern Drama. *See* Chelovek, drama nachidnya, 1912
Man, a Woman, and a Bank. *See* Very Big Withdrawal, 1979
Man about the House. *See* Vendetta nel sole, 1947
Man about Town, 1923 (Laurel and Hardy)
Man about Town, 1939 (Grable; Lamour)
Man about Town. *See* Silence est d'or, 1947
Man against Man. *See* Mr. "Silent" Haskins, 1915
Man against Man. *See* Otoko tai otoko, 1960
Man Alive, 1945 (Menjou)
Man Alone, 1955 (Bond; Milland; Van Cleef)
Man among Men. *See* Dansei No. 1, 1955
Man and a Woman. *See* Homme et une femme, 1966
Man and a Woman: 20 Years Later. *See* Homme et une femme: vingt ans déjà, 1986
Man and His Mate. *See* One Million B.C., 1940
Man and Wife, 1923 (Shearer)
Man Bait, 1926 (Crisp)
Man Beast and Virtue. *See* Uomo la Bestia e la Virtù, 1953
Man behind the Door, 1914 (Menjou)
Man Behind the Gun, 1952 (Scott, R.)
Man behind the Mask, 1936 (Carey)
Man Beneath, 1919 (Hayakawa)
Man Betrayed, 1941 (Bond; Wayne)
Man Between, 1953 (Bloom; Mason)
Man braucht kein Geld, 1931 (Lamarr)
Man by the Roadside. *See* Mensch am Wege, 1923

Man Called Horse, 1970 (Harris, R.)
Man Called Sledge, 1971 (Garner)
Man Called Sullivan. *See* Great John L., 1944
Man Could Get Killed, 1966 (Garner; Mercouri)
Man for All Seasons, 1966 (Hurt, J.; Redgrave, V.; Shaw; Welles; York)
Man for All Seasons, 1988 (Gielgud; Heston; Redgrave, V.)
Man for Burning. *See* Uomo da bruciare, 1962
Man Friday, 1975 (O'Toole)
Man from Blankley's, 1930 (Barrymore, J.; Young, L.)
Man from Cairo, 1953 (Papas; Raft)
Man from Cheyenne, 1942 (Rogers, R.)
Man from Cocody. *See* Gentleman de Cocody, 1965
Man from Colorado, 1948 (Ford, G.; Holden)
Man from Dakota, 1940 (Beery; Del Rio)
Man from Del Rio, 1956 (Quinn)
Man from Down Under, 1943 (Laughton)
Man from Downing Street, 1922 (Karloff)
Man from Far Away. *See* Uomo che viene de lontano, 1968
Man from Frisco, 1944 (Duryea)
Man from Galveston, 1963 (Coburn, J.)
Man from Hell's River, 1922 (Beery)
Man from Laramie, 1955 (Crisp; Kennedy; Stewart)
Man from Left Field, 1993 (Reynolds, B.)
Man from Mexico, 1914 (Barrymore, J.)
Man from Monterey, 1933 (Wayne)
Man from Morocco, 1944 (Walbrook)
Man from Music Mountain, 1938 (Autry)
Man from Music Mountain, 1943 (Rogers, R.)
Man from Nowhere, 1915 (Hart)
Man from Oklahoma, 1945 (Rogers, R.)
Man from Painted Post, 1917 (Fairbanks)
Man from Red Gulch, 1925 (Carey)
Man from Snowy River, 1982 (Douglas, K.)
Man from Texas, 1915 (Mix)
Man from Texas, 1924 (Carey)
Man from the Alamo, 1953 (Ford, G.)
Man from the Diner's Club, 1963 (Kaye; Sloane; Stanton)
Man from the East, 1914 (Mix)
Man from the Folies Bergère. *See* Folies Bergère, 1935
Man from the Other Side. *See* Chelovek s drugoi storoni, 1972
Man from the Pru, 1990 (York)
Man from Utah, 1934 (Wayne)
Man from Wyoming, 1930 (Constantine)
Man from Yesterday, 1932 (Boyer; Colbert)
Man Hunt, 1941 (Bennett; Carradine; McDowall; Pidgeon; Sanders)
Man I Killed. *See* Broken Lullaby, 1932
Man I Love, 1946 (Lupino)
Man I Married, 1940 (Bennett)
Man in 5A, 1983 (Segal)
Man in a Cocked Hat. *See* Carlton-Browne of the F.O., 1958
Man in Demand, 1955 (Lee, C.)
Man in Grey, 1943 (Granger; Lockwood; Mason)
Man in Hiding. *See* Mantrap, 1953
Man in Love. *See* Homme amoureux, 1987
Man in Our House. *See* Fi Baitina Rajul, 1961
Man in Possession, 1931 (Montgomery)
Man in the Attic, 1953 (Palance)
Man in the Dark, 1953 (O'Brien, E.)
Man in the Glass Booth, 1975 (Schell, Maximilian)
Man in the Gray Flannel Suit, 1956 (Cobb; Jones, Jennifer; March; Peck)
Man in the Iron Mask, 1939 (Bennett; Cushing)
Man in the Iron Mask, 1977 (Jourdan; Richardson, R.)
Man in the Middle, 1964 (Howard, T.; Mitchum)
Man in the Mirror, 1936 (Horton)
Man in the Net, 1959 (Ladd)
Man in the Raincoat. *See* Homme à l'imperméable, 1957
Man in the Road, 1956 (Cusack)
Man in the Saddle, 1926 (Karloff; Wray)
Man in the Saddle, 1951 (Scott, R.)
Man in the Santa Claus Suit, 1979 (Astaire)
Man in the Shadow, 1957 (Welles)

Man in the Sky, 1956 (Hawkins; Pleasence)
Man in the Storm. *See* Arashi no naka no otoko, 1957
Man in the White Suit, 1951 (Greenwood; Guinness)
Man in the Wilderness, 1971 (Harris, R.; Huston, J.)
Man Inside, 1958 (Palance; Pleasence)
Man Inside, 1990 (Baye)
Man Is to Man ..., 1962 (Brynner)
Man-Made Famine, 1986 (Jackson, G.)
Man Named John. *See* E venne un uomo, 1965
Man of a Thousand Faces, 1957 (Cagney; Malone)
Man of Action, 1933 (Brennan)
Man of Bronze. *See* Jim Thorpe: All American, 1951
Man of Conquest, 1939 (Fontaine)
Man of Destiny, 1981 (Seyrig)
Man of Evil. *See* Fanny by Gaslight, 1944
Man of Iron. *See* Iron Road, 1925
Man of Iron, 1935 (Astor)
Man of La Mancha, 1972 (Loren; O'Toole)
Man of Marble. *See* **Człowiek z marmaru**, 1978
Man of Mayfair, 1931 (Buchanan)
Man of Nerve, 1925 (Arthur)
Man of No Importance, 1994 (Finney)
Man of Passion, 1989 (Quinn)
Man of the Earth, 1915 (Lukas)
Man of the Family. *See* Top Man, 1943
Man of the Forest, 1933 (Carey; Scott, R.)
Man of the Hour. *See* Homme du jour, 1936
Man of the Hour. *See* Colonel Effingham's Raid, 1945
Man of the Moment, 1935 (Lockwood)
Man of the Moment, 1955 (Wisdom)
Man of the West, 1958 (Cobb; Constantine)
Man of the World, 1931 (Lombard; Powell, W.)
Man of the Year. *See* Homo eroticus, 1971
Man on a Bus, 1955 (Crawford, B.)
Man on a Flying Trapeze, 1935 (Brennan)
Man on a String, 1960 (Borgnine)
Man on a Swing, 1974 (Robertson)
Man on a Tightrope, 1953 (Grahame; March; Menjou)
Man on America's Conscience. *See* Tennessee Johnson, 1942
Man on Fire, 1957 (Crosby)
Man on Fire, 1987 (Aiello; Pesci)
Man on the Eiffel Tower, 1949 (Laughton; Meredith)
Man on the Flying Trapeze, 1935 (Fields, W. C.)
Man on the Move. *See* Jigsaw, 1972
Man on the Run. *See* Kidnappers, 1964
Man Pasand, 1980 (Anand)
Man, Pride, and Vengeance. *See* Uomo, l'orgoglio, la vendetta, 1967
Man-Proof, 1938 (Loy; Pidgeon; Russell, R.)
Man spielt nicht mit der Liebe, 1926 (Krauss)
Man spielt nicht mit der Liebe, 1949 (Dagover)
Man That Corrupted Hadleyburg, 1980 (Preston)
Man They Could Not Hang, 1939 (Karloff)
Man to Man, 1922 (Carey)
Man to Men. *See* D'homme à hommes, 1948
Man to Respect. *See* Uomo da rispettare, 1974
Man Trouble, 1992 (Barkin; Nicholson; Stanton)
Man under Suspicion. *See* Morgen in Alabama, 1984
Man Upstairs, 1958 (Attenborough)
Man Upstairs, 1993 (Hepburn, K.)
Man Wanted, 1932 (Francis)
Man Who Bought Paradise, 1965 (Keaton, B.)
Man Who Broke 1,000 Chains, 1988 (Braga)
Man Who Broke the Bank at Monte Carlo, 1935 (Bennett; Colman; Carradine)
Man Who Came Back, 1930 (Gaynor)
Man Who Came Back. *See* Swamp Water, 1941
Man Who Came to Dinner, 1941 (Durante; Davis, B.)
Man Who Came to Dinner, 1972 (Welles)
Man Who Came to the Port. *See* Minato e kita otoko, 1952
Man Who Captured Eichmann, 1996 (Duvall)
Man Who Cheated Himself, 1950 (Cobb)
Man Who Cheated Life. *See* Student von Prag, 1926

Man Who Committed Murder. *See* Mann, der den Mord beging, 1931
Man Who Could Cheat Death, 1959 (Lee, C.)
Man Who Could Work Miracles, 1936 (Richardson, R.; Sanders)
Man Who Fights Alone, 1924 (Horton)
Man Who Finally Died, 1962 (Baker; Cushing; Zetterling)
Man Who Found Himself, 1937 (Fontaine)
Man Who Had His Hair Cut Short. *See* De man die zijn haar kort liet knippen, 1966
Man Who Knew Too Much, 1934 (Fresnay; Lorre)
Man Who Knew Too Much, 1956 (Day; Gélin; Stewart)
Man Who Laughed Last, 1929 (Hayakawa)
Man Who Laughs, 1928 (Veidt)
Man Who Lived Twice, 1936 (Bellamy; Bond)
Man Who Lost Himself, 1941 (Francis)
Man Who Lost His Way. *See* Crossroads, 1942
Man Who Loved Cat Dancing, 1973 (Cobb; Reynolds, B.)
Man Who Loved the Redheads, 1954 (Elliott)
Man Who Loved Women. *See* Homme qui aimait les femmes, 1977
Man Who Loved Women, 1983 (Andrews, J.; Basinger; Reynolds, B.)
Man Who Never Was, 1955 (Grahame; Sellers; Cusack; Webb)
Man Who Paid, 1922 (Shearer)
Man Who Played God, 1922 (Astor)
Man Who Played God, 1932 (Davis, B.; Milland)
Man Who Reclaimed His Head, 1935 (Bennett; Rains)
Man Who Saw Tomorrow, 1981 (Welles)
Man Who Seeks the Truth. *See* Homme qui cherche la verité, 1939
Man Who Shot Liberty Valance, 1962 (Carradine; Marvin; O'Brien, E.; Stewart; Van Cleef; Wayne)
Man Who Talked Too Much, 1940 (Barthelmess)
Man Who Understood Women, 1959 (Caron; Dalio; Fonda, H.)
Man Who Wagged His Tail. *See* Angel pasò por Brooklyn, 1957
Man Who Wanted to Be Guilty. *See* Manden, der ville vaere Skyldig, 1990
Man Who Watched Trains Go By. *See* Paris Express, 1953
Man Who Would Be King, 1975 (Caine; Connery; Huston, J.; Malone)
Man Who Wouldn't Die, 1995 (McDowell)
Man Who Wouldn't Talk, 1940 (Marsh)
Man Who Wouldn't Talk, 1958 (Neagle; Quayle)
Man with a Cloak, 1951 (Calhern; Caron; Cotten; Stanwyck)
Man with a Gun. *See* Chelovek s ruzhyom, 1938
Man with a Million. *See* Million Pound Note, 1955
Man with an Umbrella. *See* Det regnar på vår kärlek, 1946
Man with Bogart's Face, 1978 (Raft; Lom)
Man with Nine Lives, 1940 (Karloff)
Man with One Red Shoe, 1985 (Hanks)
Man with the Deadly Lens. *See* Wrong Is Right, 1982
Man with the Electric Voice. *See* Fifteen Wives, 1935
Man with the Golden Arm, 1955 (Novak; Sidney)
Man with the Golden Gun, 1974 (Lee, C.)
Man with the Green Carnation. *See* Trials of Oscar Wilde, 1960
Man with the Gun, 1955 (Dickinson; Mitchum)
Man with the Synthetic Brain. *See* Blood of Ghastly Horror, 1972
Man with the X-Ray Eyes, 1963 (Milland)
Man with Thirty Sons. *See* Magnificent Yankee, 1950
Man with Three Wives, 1909 (Sweet)
Man with Two Brains, 1983 (Martin, S.; Spacek; Turner, K.)
Man with Two Faces, 1934 (Astor; Calhern; Robinson, E.)
Man Within, 1916 (Mix)
Man Within, 1947 (Attenborough; Greenwood; Redgrave, M.)
Man without a Country, 1973 (Robertson; Ryan, R.)
Man without a Face, 1935 (Cusack)
Man without a Face. *See* Who?, 1974
Man without a Face, 1993 (Gibson)
Man without a Gun. *See* Man with the Gun, 1955
Man without a Name. *See* Mann ohne Namen, 1920
Man without a Name. *See* Mensch ohne Namen, 1932
Man without a Soul. *See* Man without Desire, 1923
Man without a Star, 1955 (Douglas, K.; Trevor; Van Cleef)
Man without Desire, 1923 (Novello)
Man without Mercy. *See* Gone with the West, 1975
Man, Woman, and Child, 1983 (Sheen)
Man, Woman, and Sin, 1927 (Gilbert)

Managed Money, 1934 (Temple)
Manasi, 1990 (Chatterjee)
Manbait. *See* Last Page, 1952
Manchurian Candidate, 1962 (Lansbury; Leigh, Janet; Sidney)
Mandalay, 1934 (Francis; Temple)
Mandarin Mix-Up, 1924 (Laurel and Hardy)
Mandarine, 1972 (Girardot; Noiret)
Mandate of Heaven, 1979 (Carradine)
Manden, der ville vaere Skyldig, 1990 (Karina)
Mandi, 1983 (Azmi; Patil)
Mandingo, 1975 (Mason)
Mandy, 1952 (Hawkins)
Maneater. *See* Shark, 1970
Manèges, 1950 (Blier)
Mangeclous, 1988 (Blier; Cassel)
Mangetsu sanju-koku-sen, 1952 (Yamada)
Manhandled, 1924 (Swanson)
Manhandled, 1949 (Duryea; Hayden; Lamour)
Manhattan, 1979 (Allen; Keaton, D.; Streep)
Manhattan Cocktail, 1928 (Lukas)
Manhattan Madness, 1916 (Fairbanks; Menjou)
Manhattan Madness. *See* Woman Wanted, 1935
Manhattan Madness. *See* Adventure in Manhattan, 1936
Manhattan Melodrama, 1934 (Gable; Loy; Powell, W.; Rooney)
Manhattan Merry-Go-Round, 1937 (Autry)
Manhattan Murder Mystery, 1993 (Allen; Huston, A.; Keaton, D.)
Manhunt. *See* From Hell to Texas, 1958
Manhunt. *See* "mala" ordina, 1973
Manhunt, 1986 (Borgnine)
Manhunt in Milan. *See* "mala" ordina, 1973
Mani sporche, 1978 (Mastroianni)
Mani sulla citta, 1963 (Steiger)
Mania, 1918 (Negri)
Mania. *See* Flesh and the Fiends, 1960
Maniac, 1978 (Reed)
Maniac's Desire, 1912-13 (White)
Maniacs on Wheels. *See* Once a Jolly Swagman, 1948
Manihar, 1966 (Chatterjee)
Manika, une vie plus tard, 1988 (Audran)
Manila Calling, 1942 (Wilde)
Manina, la fille sans voiles, 1952 (Bardot)
Manitou, 1977 (Curtis, T.; Meredith)
Manly Man, 1911 (Pickford)
Mann aus dem Jenseits, 1925 (Wegener)
Mann, der den Mord beging, 1931 (Veidt)
Mann der Tat, 1919 (Jannings)
Mann mir der Pranke, 1935 (Wegener)
Mann nebenan, 1991 (Perkins)
Mann ohne Namen, 1920 (Krauss)
Mann will nach Deutschland, 1934 (Wegener)
Mannequin, 1926 (Pidgeon)
Mannequin, 1937 (Crawford, J.; Tracy)
Mannequin assassiné, 1947 (Gélin)
Männeskor mötas och ljuv musik uppstår i hjärtat. *See* Mënniskor modes og sod musik opstår i hjertet, 1967
Mano che nutre la morte, 1973 (Kinski)
Mano dello straniero, 1953 (Howard, T.; Valli)
Mano nascosta di Dio, 1971 (Kinski)
Mano spietat della legge, 1973 (Kinski)
Manolesco, roi des voleurs. *See* Manolescu, 1929
Manolescu, 1929 (Mozhukin)
Manon, 1947 (Reggiani)
Manon 70, 1968 (Deneuve)
Manon des sources, 1986 (Montand)
Manon Lescaut, 1926 (Dietrich)
Manon Lescaut, 1940 (Valli)
Manon of the Spring. *See* **Manon des sources**, 1986
Manpower, 1941 (Bond; Dietrich; Raft; Robinson, E.)
Man's Castle, 1933 (Tracy; Young, L.)
Man's Country, 1919 (Chaney)
Man's Enemy, 1914 (Gish)

Man's Favorite Sport?, 1964 (Hudson)
Man's Game, 1934 (Bond)
Man's Genesis, 1912 (Marsh)
Man's Heritage. *See* Spirit of Culver, 1939
Man's Lust for Gold, 1912 (Sweet)
Man's Man, 1929 (Garbo; Gilbert)
Man's Past, 1927 (Veidt)
Man's Worldly Appearance. *See* Hito no yo no sugata, 1929
Mansarda, 1963 (Łomnicki)
Mansion of the Doomed, 1975 (Grahame)
Manslaughter, 1930 (Colbert; March)
Manthan, 1977 (Patil)
Mantramugdha, 1977 (Chatterjee)
Mantrap, 1926 (Bow)
Mantrap, 1953 (Henreid; Kendall)
Mantrap, 1960 (O'Brien, E.)
Manuela, 1957 (Armendáriz; Howard, T.; Pleasence)
Manuela's Loves. *See* Jupon rouge, 1987
Manuscript Found in Saragossa. *See* Rekopis znaleziony w Saragossie, 1965
Many a Slip, 1931 (Ayres; Bennett)
Many Happy Returns, 1934 (Milland)
Many Happy Returns, 1986 (Segal)
Many Rivers to Cross, 1955 (McLaglen; Taylor, R.)
Many Voices, 1956 (Heston)
Manya, die Türkin, 1915 (Kortner)
Manzil, 1960 (Anand)
Map of the Human Heart, 1993 (Mifune; Moreau)
Maquillage, 1927 (Vanel)
Maquillage, 1932 (Feuillère)
Mara Maru, 1952 (Flynn)
Maracaibo, 1958 (Wilde)
Marat/Sade, 1967 (Jackson, G.)
Marathon, 1919 (Lloyd)
Marathon, 1980 (Cooper)
Marathon Man, 1976 (Gilbert; Hoffman; Olivier; Scheider)
Marauders, 1955 (Duryea)
Marcelino, 1956 (Rey)
Marcelino, pan y vino, 1954 (Rey)
Marcellini Millions, 1917 (Crisp)
March Hare, 1956 (Cusack)
March of Dimes, 1942 (Gable)
March of the Wooden Soldiers. *See* Babes in Toyland, 1934
March of Time, 1931 (Keaton, B.)
March of Time. *See* Show Business at War, 1943
March or Die, 1977 (Deneuve; Hackman; Von Sydow)
March to Aldermaston, 1958 (Burton)
Marchand d'amour, 1935 (Rosay)
Marche ou crève, 1959 (Blier)
Märchen der Gebruder Nimm Schweinegold, 1989 (Mueller-Stahl)
Marchesa d'Arminiani, 1920 (Negri)
Marchese del Grillo, 1982 (Sordi)
Marcia o crepa, 1963 (Granger)
Marcia su Roma, 1962 (Gassman)
Marco the Magnificent. *See* Fabuleuse Aventure de Marco Polo, 1965
Marcus-Nelson Murders, 1973 (Ferrer)
Marcus Welby, M.D., 1969 (Ayres; Baxter; Young, R.)
Marcus Welby, M.D.—A Holiday Affair, 1988 (Young, R.)
Mardon Wali Baat, 1988 (Azmi)
Mare matto, 1963 (Belmondo; Lollobrigida)
Mare Nostrum, 1948 (Félix)
Mare Nostrum, 1950 (Rey)
Maresi, 1948 (Schell, Maria)
Marez-moi ce soir. *See* Love Me Tonight, 1932
Margaret's Museum, 1995 (Bonham-Carter; Nelligan)
Margie, 1946 (McDaniel)
Margin for Error, 1943 (Bennett)
Marginal, 1983 (Belmondo)
Marguerite de la nuit, 1956 (Montand; Morgan)
Mari à prix fixe, 1963 (Karina)
Mari en laisse. *See* If a Man Answers, 1962
Mari rêve, 1936 (Arletty; Brasseur)

Maria and Napoleon. *See* Marysia i Napoleon, 1966
Maria Antonieta Rivas Mercado. *See* Antonieta, 1982
María Candelaria, 1943 (Armendáriz; Del Rio)
Maria Chapdelaine, 1934 (Gabin)
Maria Chapdelaine, 1950 (Morgan)
Maria Elena, 1935 (Armendáriz)
María Eugenia, 1942 (Félix)
Maria, matricula de Bilbao, 1961 (Vanel)
Maria no Oyuki, 1935 (Yamada)
Maria Stuart, 1927 (Kortner)
Maria's Lovers, 1984 (Kinski; Mitchum)
Maria's Story, 1990 (Olmos)
Mariachi 2. *See* Desperado, 1995
Mariage à l'américaine, 1909 (Linder)
Mariage à la mode, 1974 (Chaplin, G.)
Mariage au puzzle, 1909 (Linder)
Mariage au téléphone, 1912 (Linder)
Mariage blanc, 1985 (Olbrychski)
Mariage d'amour, 1907 (Linder)
Mariage de chiffon, 1942 (Blier)
Mariage de Max. *See* Max se marie, 1910
Mariage forcé, 1909 (Linder)
Mariage imprévu, 1913 (Linder)
Marianne, 1929 (Davies)
Marianne and Juliane. *See* Bleiere Zeit, 1982
Marido de ida y vuelta, 1955 (Rey)
Marie, 1974 (Schell, Maria)
Marie, 1985 (Freeman; Spacek)
Marie Antoinette, 1938 (Barrymore, J.; Fitzgerald; Power; Shearer)
Marie-Antoinette, 1956 (Morgan; Piccoli)
Marie Chantal against Dr. Kha. *See* Marie-Chantal contre le docteur Kha, 1965
Marie-Chantal contre le docteur Kha, 1965 (Audran; Reggiani)
Marie Chapdelaine, 1950 (Rosay)
Marie-Christine, 1970 (Bujold)
Marie des Angoisses, 1935 (Rosay)
Marie du port, 1949 (Gabin)
Marie Galante, 1934 (Tracy)
Marie, Marie, 1984 (Darrieux)
Marie-Martine, 1943 (Berry; Blier)
Marie-Octobre, 1959 (Blier; Darrieux; Reggiani)
Marie qui se fait attendre, 1910 (Chevalier)
Marie Soleil, 1964 (Bardot; Piccoli)
Marie Walewska. *See* Conquest, 1937
Mariée est trop belle, 1956 (Bardot; Jourdan; Presle)
Mariée etait en noir, 1968 (Moreau)
Mariée recalcitrante, 1911 (Chevalier)
Mariés de l'an II, 1971 (Belmondo; Brasseur)
Marie's Millions. *See* Tillie's Punctured Romance, 1914
Marie's Millions. *See* Tillie's Punctured Romance, 1928
Mariette in Ecstasy, 1995 (Saint)
Marilyn, 1963 (Hudson)
Marilyn Monroe: Beyond the Legend, 1987 (Winters)
Marina's Story. *See* Fatal Deception: Mrs. Lee Harvey Oswald, 1993
Marine Raiders, 1944 (Ryan, R.)
Marines Fly High, 1940 (Ball)
Marines Have Landed. *See* Leathernecks Have Landed, 1936
Mario and the Magician. *See* Mario und der Zauberer, 1994
Mario und der Zauberer, 1994 (Brandauer)
Marion, 1921 (Bertini)
Marionette, 1938 (Mastroianni)
Marito, 1958 (Sordi)
Marius, 1931 (Fresnay; Raimu)
Mariute, 1918 (Bertini)
Marjorie Morningstar, 1958 (Kelly, Gene; Sloane; Trevor; Wood)
Mark, 1961 (Schell, Maria; Steiger)
Mark il poliziotta, 1975 (Cobb)
Mark of Cain, 1916 (Chaney)
Mark of the Devil, 1970 (Lom)
Mark of the Gorilla, 1950 (Weissmuller)
Mark of the Hawk, 1958 (Poitier)
Mark of the Renegade, 1951 (Charisse)

Mark of the Vampire, 1935 (Barrymore, L.; Lugosi)
Mark of Zorro, 1920 (Fairbanks)
Mark of Zorro, 1940 (Darnell; Power; Rathbone)
Mark Twain and Me, 1991 (Robards)
Marked Deck. *See* Mr. "Silent" Haskins, 1915
Marked Man, 1917 (Carey)
Marked Men, 1919 (Carey)
Marked Woman, 1937 (Bogart; Davis, B.)
Market Place. *See* Mandi, 1983
Markurells i Wadköping, 1968 (Dahlbeck)
Marlene, 1984 (Schell, Maximilian)
Marlowe, 1969 (Garner; Lee, B.)
Marmalade Revolution. *See* Marmeladupproret, 1980
Marmeladupproret, 1980 (Andersson, B.; Josephson)
Marmottes, 1993 (Aimée; Gélin)
Marnie, 1964 (Connery; Dern)
Maroc 7, 1967 (Charisse; Elliott)
Marooned, 1969 (Grant, L.; Hackman; Peck)
Marquis de Sade: Justine, 1968 (Kinski; Palance)
Marquis Preferred, 1929 (Menjou)
Marquise of O. *See* Marquise von O, 1975
Marquise von O, 1975 (Ganz)
Marquise von Pompadour, 1922 (Krauss)
Marraine de Charley, 1959 (Cassel)
Marrana, 1992 (Rey)
Marriage. *See* Svadba, 1944
Marriage. *See* Kekkon, 1947
Marriage Cheat, 1924 (Menjou)
Marriage Circle, 1924 (Menjou)
Marriage-Go-Round, 1960 (Hayward; Mason)
Marriage Humor, 1933 (Langdon)
Marriage in Transit, 1925 (Lombard)
Marriage Is a Private Affair, 1944 (Turner, L.)
Marriage Italian Style. *See* Matrimonio all 'italiana, 1964
Marriage License, 1926 (Pidgeon)
Marriage Maker, 1923 (Astor)
Marriage of Maria Braun. *See* **Ehe der Maria Braun**, 1978
Marriage of Molly O, 1916 (Marsh)
Marriage on the Rocks, 1965 (Kerr; Martin, D.; Sidney)
Marriage Playground, 1929 (Francis; March)
Marriage Rows, 1931 (Arbuckle)
Marriage Wrestler. *See* Aktenskapabrottaren, 1964
Marriage: Year One, 1970 (Field; Moorehead)
Married Bachelor, 1941 (Young, R.)
Married before Breakfast, 1937 (Young, R.)
Married but Single. *See* This Thing Called Love, 1941
Married by the Stork. *See* Storch hat uns getraut, 1933
Married Flirts, 1924 (Shearer)
Married in Haste. *See* Jitney Elopement, 1915
Married in Haste. *See* Consolation Marriage, 1931
Married Man, 1984 (Hopkins, A.)
Married to the Mob, 1988 (Pfeiffer)
Married Virgin, 1920 (Valentino)
Married Woman. *See* Femme mariée, 1964
Marry Me, 1925 (Horton)
Marrying Kind, 1952 (Bronson; Gordon; Holliday)
Marrying Man, 1991 (Basinger)
Mars Attacks!, 1996 (Close; Nicholson; Steiger)
Marschall Vorwärts, 1932 (Wegener)
Marseillaise, 1937 (Jouvet; Modot)
Marseilles Contract, 1974 (Caine; Mason; Quinn)
Marshal's Capture, 1913 (Mix)
Martha und Ich, 1990 (Piccoli)
Martha's Vindication, 1916 (Talmadge)
Marthe Richard au service de la France, 1937 (Dalio; Feuillère)
Marthe Richard, l'espionne au service de la France. *See* Marthe Richard au
     service de la France, 1937
Martian Chronicles, 1979 (McDowall)
Martiens, 1973 (Vanel)
Martin Roumagnac, 1946 (Dietrich; Gabin; Gélin)
Martin Scorsese Directs, 1990 (Keitel)

Martin's Day, 1985 (Coburn, J.; Harris, R.)
Marty, 1955 (Borgnine)
Martyre, 1924 (Vanel)
Martyrium, 1920 (Negri)
Maruche, 1932 (Fernandel)
Marusa no Onna II, 1988 (Ryu)
Marva Collins Story, 1981 (Freeman)
Marvin's Room, 1996 (De Niro; Keaton, D.; Streep)
Mary Burns, Fugitive, 1935 (Douglas, Melvyn; Sidney)
Mary from Beijing. *See* Mungding sifan, 1992
Mary, Mary, 1963 (Reynolds, D.)
Mary, Mary, Bloody Mary, 1975 (Carradine)
Mary Names the Day. *See* Dr. Kildare's Wedding Day, 1941
Mary of Scotland, 1936 (Carradine; Crisp; Hepburn, K.; March)
Mary of the Movies, 1923 (Wong)
Mary Poppins, 1964 (Andrews, J.; Lanchester)
Mary, Queen of Scots, 1971 (Howard, T.; Jackson, G.; Redgrave, V.)
Mary Reilly, 1996 (Close; Malkovich; Roberts, J.)
Mary Shelley's Frankenstein, 1994 (Bonham-Carter; Branagh; Cleese; De
     Niro)
Mary Stevens, M.D., 1933 (Francis)
Maryada, 1989 (Chatterjee)
Maryland, 1940 (Brennan; McDaniel)
Mary's Romance, 1912-13 (White)
Marysia i Napoleon, 1966 (Tyszkiewicz)
Más allá de las montañas, 1967 (Papas; Rey; Schell, Maximilian)
Ma's Girls, 1915 (Mix)
Masamod, 1920 (Lukas)
Maschera, 1988 (Bonham-Carter)
Masculin-féminin, 1966 (Bardot; Léaud)
M*A*S*H, 1970 (Duvall; Gould; Sutherland)
Mashaal, 1984 (Kumar)
Masher, 1910 (Pickford)
Masher, 1912-13 (White)
Mask, 1918 (Gilbert)
Mask, 1985 (Cher)
Mask. *See* Maschera, 1988
Mask of Dimitrios, 1944 (Greenstreet; Lorre)
Mask of Fu Manchu, 1932 (Karloff; Loy)
Mask of Love, 1916 (Chaney)
Mask of Riches. *See* Mask, 1918
Mask of Sheba, 1969 (Pidgeon)
Mask of the Avenger, 1951 (Quinn)
Masked Ball. *See* Alarcosbal, 1918
Masked Bride, 1925 (Rathbone)
Masked Bride, 1978 (Chaplin, G.)
Masked Menace, 1927 (Arthur)
Masked Raider, 1919 (Karloff)
Masken, 1929 (Homolka)
Maskerade, 1934 (Walbrook)
Masks. *See* **Persona**, 1966
Masks of Death. *See* Sherlock Holmes and the Masks of Death, 1984
Masks of the Devil, 1928 (Gilbert)
Masoom, 1982 (Azmi)
Masque de fer, 1962 (Marais)
Masque of the Red Death, 1964 (Price)
Masque of the Red Death, 1989 (Lom)
Masquerada, 1949 (Armendáriz)
Masquerade. *See* Masquerader, 1914
Masquerade. *See* Escapade, 1935
Masquerade, 1965 (Hawkins; Piccoli; Robertson)
Masquerade in Mexico, 1945 (Lamour)
Masquerade in Vienna. *See* Maskerade, 1934
Masquerader, 1914 (Arbuckle; Chaplin, C.)
Masquerader, 1933 (Colman)
Masques, 1986 (Noiret)
Mass Appeal, 1985 (Lemmon)
Massacre, 1914 (Barrymore, L.; Sweet)
Massacre, 1934 (Barthelmess)
Massacre at Fort Holman. *See* Ragione per vivere e una per morire, 1973
Massacre Hill. *See* Eureka Stockade, 1949

Max et les ferrailleurs, 1970 (Piccoli; Schneider)
Max et l'espion, 1915 (Linder)
Max et l'inauguration de la statue, 1910 (Linder)
Max et sa belle-mère, 1910 (Linder)
Max et ses trois mariages, 1910 (Linder)
Max et son âne, 1911 (Linder)
Max et son chien Dick, 1911 (Linder)
Max et son rival, 1910 (Linder)
Max et son taxi. *See* Max in a Taxi, 1917
Max et son voisin. *See* Voisin ... voisin, 1911
Max fait au ski, 1910 (Linder)
Max fait de la photo, 1910 (Linder)
Max fait des conquêtes, 1913 (Linder)
Max fait du patinage à roulette, 1910 (Linder)
Max Goes Skiing. *See* Max fait au ski, 1910
Max Has the Boxing Fever. *See* Max champion de boxe, 1910
Max hypnotisé, 1910 (Linder)
Max illusioniste, 1914 (Linder)
Max in a Taxi, 1917 (Linder)
Max in America. *See* Max Comes Across, 1917
Max Is Absent-Minded. *See* Max est distrait, 1911
Max Is Almost Married. *See* Max manque un riche mariage, 1910
Max jaloux. *See* Max et le mari jaloux, 1914
Max jockey par amour, 1912 (Linder)
Max joue le drame, 1910 (Linder)
Max lance la mode, 1911 (Linder)
Max Linder contre Nick Winter, 1912 (Linder)
Max maître d'hôtel, 1914 (Linder)
Max maîtresse de piano, 1910 (Linder)
Max manque un riche mariage, 1910 (Linder)
Max médicin malgré lui, 1914 (Linder)
Max Mon Amour, 1986 (Abril)
Max My Love. *See* Max Mon Amour, 1986
Max n'aime pas les chats, 1913 (Linder)
Max ne se mariera pas, 1910 (Linder)
Max part en Amérique. *See* Max Comes Across, 1917
Max part en vacances, 1913 (Linder)
Max pédicure, 1914 (Linder)
Max peintre par amour, 1912 (Linder)
Max pratique tous les sports, 1912 (Linder)
Max prend un bain, 1910 (Linder)
Max professeur de tango, 1912 (Linder)
Max reprend sa liberté, 1911 (Linder)
Max sauveteur, 1914 (Linder)
Max se marie, 1910 (Linder)
Max se trompe d'etage, 1910 (Linder)
Max Tango Teacher. *See* Max professeur de tango, 1912
Max toréador, 1912 (Linder)
Max veut divorcer. *See* Max Wants a Divorce, 1917
Max veut faire du théâtre, 1911 (Linder)
Max veut grandir, 1912 (Linder)
Max victime de la main qui etreint. *See* Max et la main qui etreint, 1916
Max victime du Quinquina, 1911 (Linder)
Max virtuose, 1913 (Linder)
Max Wants a Divorce, 1917 (Linder)
Maxie, 1985 (Close; Gordon)
Maxime, 1958 (Arletty; Boyer; Morgan)
Maximum Force, 1992 (Rooney)
Max's Divorce Case. *See* Max Wants a Divorce, 1917
Max's Feet Are Pinched. *See* Soulier trop petit, 1909
May and December, 1910 (Pickford)
May Blossom, 1915 (Crisp)
May Fools. *See* Milou en mai, 1990
May We Borrow Your Husband?, 1986 (Bogarde)
Maya, 1949 (Dalio)
Maya, 1961 (Anand)
Maybe I'll Come Home in the Spring, 1971 (Cooper; Field)
Maybe It's Love, 1930 (Bennett; Brown)
Mayblossom, 1910-11 (White)
Mayday at 40,000 Feet, 1976 (Crawford, B.; Milland)
Mayerling, 1936 (Boyer; Darrieux)

Mayerling, 1957 (Hepburn, K.; Massey)
Mayerling, 1968 (Deneuve; Gardner; Mason; Sharif)
Mayerling to Sarajevo. *See* De Mayerling à Sarajevo, 1940
Mayfair Bank Caper. *See* Nightingale Sang in Berkeley Square, 1979
Mayflower: The Pilgrim's Adventure, 1979 (Hopkins, A.)
Mayor of Forty-Fourth St., 1942 (Barthelmess)
Mayor of Hell, 1933 (Cagney)
Mayrig, 1991 (Cardinale; Sharif)
Maytime, 1923 (Bow)
Maytime, 1937 (Barrymore, J.; Eddy; MacDonald)
Maytime in Mayfair, 1949 (Neagle)
Mazdoor, 1983 (Kumar)
Mazes and Monsters, 1982 (Hanks)
Mazo, 1952 (Yamada)
Mazurka, 1935 (Negri)
Mazzabubu ... quante come stanno quaggiu?, 1971 (Giannini)
McBain, 1991 (Walken)
McCabe and Mrs. Miller, 1971 (Beatty; Christie)
McCloud: Who Killed Miss U.S.A.?, 1970 (Julia)
McConnell Story, 1955 (Ladd)
McGuire Go Home! *See* High Bright Sun, 1964
McHale's Navy, 1964 (Borgnine)
McLintock!, 1963 (O'Hara; Wayne)
McMasters, 1970 (Carradine; Palance)
McNaughton's Daughter, 1976 (Bellamy)
McQ, 1974 (Wayne)
McVeagh of the South Seas, 1914 (Carey)
Me an' Bill, 1914 (Mix)
Me and My Brother, 1968 (Shepard; Walken)
Me and My Gal, 1932 (Bennett; Tracy)
Me and My Pal, 1933 (Laurel and Hardy)
Me and the Colonel, 1958 (Kaye; Rosay)
Me and the Kid, 1993 (Aiello)
Me faire ca à moi!, 1961 (Constantine)
Me, Gangster, 1928 (Brown; Lombard)
Me Ivan, You Abraham. *See* Moi Ivan, Toi Abraham, 1993
Me, Myself & I, 1992 (Segal)
Me Natalie, 1969 (Lanchester; Pacino)
Meadow. *See* Prato, 1979
Meals on Wheels, 1984 (Chan)
Mean Frank and Crazy Tony. *See* Johnny le Fligueur, 1973
Mean Johnny Barrows, 1976 (Gould; McDowall)
Mean Season, 1985 (García)
Mean Streets, 1973 (De Niro; Keitel)
Meanest Gal in Town, 1934 (Carradine)
Meanest Man in the World, 1923 (Sweet)
Meanest Men in the West, 1962 (Bronson)
Meantime, 1984 (Oldman)
Measure for Measure, 1978 (Nelligan)
Measure of a Man, 1915 (Chaney)
Meat and Romance, 1940 (Ladd)
Meatballs, 1979 (Murray)
Meatcleaver Massacre, 1977 (Lee, C.)
Mechanic, 1972 (Bronson)
Med fuld musik, 1933 (Madsen and Schenstrøm)
Médaille de sauvetage. *See* Max sauveteur, 1914
Medal for Benny, 1944 (Lamour)
Medan porten var stängd, 1946 (Björnstrand)
Medan staden sover, 1950 (Andersson, H.)
Meddling Women, 1924 (Barrymore, L.)
Medea, 1920 (Negri; Wegener)
Medea, 1969 (Mangano)
Médcin de service, 1933 (Brasseur)
Media tono. *See* Donde van nuestros hijos, 1958
Mediante de Saint-Sulpice, 1923 (Modot)
Medic. *See* Toubib, 1979
Medical Story, 1975 (Ferrer)
Medicine Man, 1992 (Connery)
Medico della mutua, 1968 (Sordi)
Medico e lo stregone, 1957 (Mastroianni; Sordi)
Mediterranean Holiday, 1964 (Kelly, Grace)

Medium, 1921 (Dagover; Krauss)
Medusa Touch, 1978 (Burton; Remick)
Meet Danny Wilson, 1951 (Sidney; Winters)
Meet John Doe, 1941 (Brennan; Constantine; Stanwyck)
Meet Me after the Show, 1951 (Grable)
Meet Me at Dawn, 1947 (Rutherford)
Meet Me in Las Vegas, 1956 (Charisse; Henreid; Lorre; Moorehead; Reynolds, D.; Sidney)
Meet Me in St. Louis, 1944 (Astor; Garland; O'Brien, M.)
Meet Mr. Lucifer, 1953 (Kendall)
Meet Nero Wolfe, 1936 (Hayworth)
Meet the Baron, 1933 (Durante; Three Stooges)
Meet the Chump, 1941 (Three Stooges)
Meet the Hollowheads, 1989 (Lewis, Juliette)
Meet the Missus, 1940 (Ladd)
Meet the Nelsons. See Here Come the Nelsons, 1952
Meet the People, 1944 (Ball; Powell, D.)
Meet the Stars No. 4, 1941 (Abbott and Costello)
Meet the Stewarts, 1942 (Holden)
Meet the Wildcat, 1940 (Bellamy)
Meeting in the Night. See Möte i natten, 1946
Meeting of the Ghost of Après Guerre. See Sengo-ha obake taikai, 1951
Meeting Venus, 1991 (Close; Josephson)
Meetings with Remarkable Men, 1979 (Stamp)
Méfiez-vous, mesdames!, 1963 (Darrieux; Morgan)
Megfelelo ember kenyes feladatra, 1985 (Tyszkiewicz)
Meglin Kiddie Revue, 1929 (Garland)
Megumi ni kenka, 1935 (Hasegawa)
Meigetsu somato, 1951 (Hasegawa)
Meijin Choji-bori, 1943 (Hasegawa)
Meijin Chojiro-bori, 1943 (Yamada)
Meilleure Bobonne, 1930 (Fernandel)
Meilleure part, 1955 (Philipe)
Mein Kampf—My Crimes, 1941 (Lom, Ustinov)
Mein Leben für das Deine, 1927 (Kortner)
Mein Leben fur das deine. See Odette, 1928
Mein Leben für Irland, 1940 (Wegener)
Mein Leopold, 1931 (Fröhlich)
Mein Sohn, der Herr Minister, 1937 (Rosay)
Meine 16 Söhne, 1955 (Dagover)
Meistersinger of Nuremberg. See Miester von Nürnberg, 1927
Mejor alcalde, el Rey, 1973 (Rey)
Mela, 1948 (Kumar)
Melancholia, 1989 (York)
Melanie Rose. See High Stakes, 1989
Melba, 1988 (Greenwood)
Melbourne—Olympic City, 1955 (Finch)
Melissokomos Patheni—O Alles Mythos, 1986 (Mastroianni)
Mellem muntre musikanter, 1922 (Madsen and Schenstrøm)
Melodie des Herzens, 1929 (Dagover)
Melodie eterne, 1940 (Cervi)
Mélodie en sous-sol, 1962 (Delon; Gabin)
Melody and Romance, 1937 (Lockwood)
Melody Club, 1949 (Terry-Thomas)
Melody Cruise, 1933 (Grable)
Melody for Three, 1941 (Wray)
Melody for Two, 1937 (O'Connor)
Melody of Life. See Symphony of Six Million, 1932
Melody of Love, 1928 (Pidgeon)
Melody of the Heart. See Melodie des Herzens, 1929
Melody of Youth. See They Shall Have Music, 1939
Melody Ranch, 1940 (Autry; Durante; Miller; Wayne)
Melody Time, 1948 (Rogers, R.)
Melody Trail, 1935 (Autry)
Melvin and Howard, 1980 (Grahame; Robards; Steenburgen)
Melzer, 1983 (Vogler)
Member of the Government. See Chlen pravitelstva, 1939
Memed My Hawk, 1984 (Lom, Ustinov)
Memento Mori, 1992 (Cusack; Smith)
Memo for Joe, 1944 (Constantine)
Mémoire Tatouée, 1988 (Christie)

Mémoire courte, 1978 (Baye)
Mémoire tranquee, 1992 (Hurt, J.)
Memoirs of a Survivor, 1981 (Christie)
Memoirs of an Invisible Man, 1992 (Neill)
Memoirs of Manolescu. See Abend-Nacht-Morgen, 1920
Memories and Men's Souls, 1914 (Talmadge)
Memories of Famous Hollywood Comedians, 1952 (Brown)
Memories of Me, 1988 (Connery)
Memories of Monet, 1984 (Bloom)
Memory Expert. See Man on a Flying Trapeze, 1935
Memory of Eva Ryker, 1980 (Bellamy; McDowall)
Men, 1924 (Negri)
Men, 1950 (Brando; Sloane)
Men and Wolves. See Uomini e lupi, 1956
Men and Women, 1914 (Barrymore, L.; Sweet)
Men Are Children Twice. See Valley of Song, 1952
Men Are Like That, 1931 (Wayne)
Men Are Like This. See So sind die Männer, 1922
Men Are Not Gods, 1936 (Harrison; Hopkins, M.)
Men Are Such Fools, 1938 (Bogart)
Men behind Bars. See Duffy of San Quentin, 1954
Men Call It Love, 1931 (Menjou)
Men Don't Leave, 1990 (Bates, K.; Lange)
Men in Black, 1934 (Three Stooges)
Men in Black, 1996 (Jones, T.)
Men in Her Life, 1941 (Veidt; Young, L.)
Men in War, 1957 (Ryan, R.)
Men in White, 1934 (Gable; Loy)
Men Must Fight, 1933 (Young, R.)
Men of Boys Town, 1941 (Cobb; Rooney; Tracy)
Men of Chance, 1931 (Astor)
Men of Destiny. See Men of Texas, 1942
Men of Respect, 1991 (Steiger; Turturro)
Men of Steel, 1926 (McLaglen)
Men of Texas, 1942 (Bellamy; Cooper; Crawford, B.)
Men of the Fighting Lady, 1954 (Calhern; Pidgeon)
Men of the Night, 1934 (Ball; Bond)
Men of the Sea. See Midshipman Easy, 1935
Men of Tomorrow, 1932 (Donat; Oberon)
Men of War, 1929 (Laurel and Hardy)
Men Who Tread on the Tiger's Tail. See Tota no o o fumu otokotachi, 1945
Men with Wings, 1938 (MacMurray; Milland; O'Connor)
Men without Names, 1935 (MacMurray)
Men without Souls, 1940 (Ford, G.)
Men without Women, 1930 (Wayne)
Men's Club, 1986 (Keitel; Leigh, Jennifer Jason; Scheider)
Menace, 1932 (Davis, B.)
Menace, 1934 (Milland)
Menace, 1977 (Montand)
Menace II Society, 1993 (Jackson, S.)
Menace de mort, 1949 (Dalio)
Menace on the Mountain, 1970 (Foster)
Menace to Carlotta, 1914 (Chaney)
Menace Unseen, 1988 (Cusack)
Menage. See Tenue de soirée, 1986
Ménage à Trois. See Better Late than Never, 1982
Mender of Nets, 1912 (Normand; Pickford)
Mendiante de Saint-Sulpice, 1924 (Vanel)
Mendiants, 1987 (Sanda)
Menendez: A Killing in Beverly Hills, 1993 (Olmos)
Mënniskor modes og sod musik opstår i hjertet, 1967 (Andersson, H.; Dahlbeck)
Mensch am Wege, 1923 (Dietrich; Rasp)
Mensch ohne Namen, 1932 (Krauss)
Menschen am Meer, 1925 (Rasp)
Menschen im Hotel, 1960 (Morgan)
Menschen in Käfig, 1930 (Kortner; Veidt)
Menschenfeind, 1923 (Krauss)
Menshen im Rausch, 1920 (Veidt)
Mensonge, 1992 (Baye)
Menteurs, 1961 (Modot)

Meoto zenzai, 1955 (Tsukasa)
Mephisto, 1931 (Gabin)
Mephisto, 1981 (Brandauer)
Mépris, 1963 (Bardot; Palance; Piccoli)
Meraviglie di Aladino, 1961 (Fabrizi; O'Connor)
Mercante di Venezia, 1912 (Bertini)
Mercenario, 1969 (Palance)
Mercenary. See Mercenario, 1969
Merchant of Four Seasons. See Händler der vier Jahreszeiten, 1971
Merchant of Venice, 1973 (Olivier)
Merci la vie, 1991 (Depardieu; Girardot)
Mercy or Murder?, 1987 (Young, R.)
Merely Mary Ann, 1931 (Gaynor)
Merlin, 1995 (Pleasence)
Merlin and the Sword. See Arthur the King, 1985
Mermaids, 1990 (Cher; Hoskins; Ryder)
Merrily We Go to Hell, 1932 (Grant, C.; March; Sidney)
Merrily Yours, 1933 (Temple)
Merry Andrew, 1958 (Kaye)
Merry Chase. See Resa di Titi, 1945
Merry Mavericks, 1951 (Three Stooges)
Merry Mix-Up, 1957 (Three Stooges)
Merry Monahans, 1944 (O'Connor)
Merry Monarch. See Abenteur des Königs Pausole, 1933
Merry Widow, 1925 (Gable; Gilbert)
Merry Widow, 1934 (Chevalier; Horton; MacDonald)
Merry Widow, 1952 (Dalio; Turner, L.)
Merry Widower, 1926 (Laurel and Hardy)
Merry Wives of Gotham. See Lights of Old Broadway, 1925
Merry Wives of Windsor, 1982 (Davis, J.; Kingsley)
Merton of the Movies, 1947 (Grahame)
Merveilleuse Angélique, 1964 (Trintignant)
Merveilleuse Vie de Jeanne d'Arc, 1928 (Modot)
Merveilleux Parfum d'oseille, 1969 (Rosay)
Mes tantes et moi, 1936 (Morgan)
Mes voisins me font danser, 1909 (Linder)
Meshi, 1951 (Hara; Yamamura)
Mesmerized, 1986 (Foster)
Message, 1976 (Papas; Quinn)
Message in the Bottle, 1911 (Pickford)
Message of the Arrow, 1911 (White)
Message to Garcia, 1936 (Beery; Carradine; Hayworth; Stanwyck)
Message to My Daughter, 1973 (Sheen)
Messager, 1937 (Blier; Gabin)
Messages, 1996 (Loren)
Messalina, 1951 (Félix)
Messenger, 1918 (Laurel and Hardy)
Messenger of Death, 1988 (Bronson)
Messer im Kopf, 1978 (Ganz; Winkler)
Messieurs les ronds-de-cuir, 1959 (Brasseur)
Messieurs Ludovic, 1946 (Berry; Blier)
Mestice: A Escrava Indomavel, 1973 (Braga)
Mestiza, the Indomitable Slave. See Mestice: A Escrava Indomavel, 1973
Mesu-inu, 1951 (Shimura)
Mesuinu, 1951 (Kyo)
Métamorphose des cloportes, 1965 (Brasseur)
Metamorphosis of a Melody, 1993 (Schygulla)
Meteor, 1979 (Connery; Fonda, H.; Howard, T.; Landau; Malden; Wood)
Meteor Man, 1993 (Jackson, S.; Jones, James Earl)
Metisse, 1993 (Cassel)
Metro, 1996 (Murphy)
Metropolis, 1926 (Fröhlich; Rasp)
Metropolitan, 1935 (Brennan)
Metti, una sera a cena, 1969 (Girardot)
Meurtes, 1950 (Moreau)
Meurtre en 45 tours, 1960 (Darrieux)
Meurtre est un meurtre, 1972 (Audran)
Mexicali Rose, 1929 (Stanwyck)
Mexicali Rose, 1939 (Autry)
Mexican, 1914 (Mix)
Mexican Affair. See Flor de mayo, 1957

Mexican Hayride, 1948 (Abbott and Costello)
Mexican Sweethearts, 1909 (Pickford)
Mexicanerin, 1919 (Veidt)
Mexicanos al grito de guerra, 1943 (Infante)
Mexico ... Estamos Contigo, 1985 (Cantinflas)
Mexico in Flames, 1982 (Bondarchuk)
Mezi nebem a zemi, 1958 (Brodský)
Mezzogiorno di fuoco par Lin-Hao. See Mio nome è Shanghai Joe, 1973
Mi candidato, 1938 (Armendáriz)
Mi Familia. See My Family, 1995
Mi General, 1986 (Rey)
Mi manda piccone, 1984 (Giannini)
Mi permette babbo!, 1956 (Fabrizi; Sordi)
Mia signora, 1964 (Mangano; Sordi)
Miai-kekkon, 1958 (Kagawa)
Miami Blues, 1990 (Leigh, Jennifer Jason)
Miami Exposé, 1956 (Cobb)
Miami Rhapsody, 1995 (Banderas; Farrow)
Miarka, Daughter of the Bear. See Miarka, fille l'ours, 1920
Miarka, fille l'ours, 1920 (Novello)
Miarka la fille à l'ours, 1937 (Dalio)
Miarka, la fille à l'ourse, 1923 (Vanel)
Michael, 1996 (Hurt, W.)
Michael and Mary, 1931 (Marshall)
Michael Carmichael, 1972 (Cushing)
Michael Collins, 1996 (Neeson; Roberts, J.)
Michael Jackson's Thriller, 1984 (Price)
Michael Kohlhaas—Der Rebell, 1969 (Karina)
Michael the Brave, 1969 (Welles)
Michel Strogoff, 1926 (Mozhukin)
Michel Strogoff, 1935 (Vanel; Walbrook)
Michelangelo and Me, 1989 (Sharif)
Michurin, 1948 (Bondarchuk)
Mickey, 1918 (Normand)
Mickey, 1948 (McDaniel)
Mickey One, 1965 (Beatty)
Mickey Rooney, Then and Now, 1953 (Rooney)
Mickey's Ape Man, 1933 (Rooney)
Mickey's Champs, 1930 (Rooney)
Mickey's Circus, 1927 (Rooney)
Mickey's Great Idea, 1929 (Rooney)
Mickey's Minstrels, 1934 (Rooney)
Mickey's Parade, 1928 (Rooney)
Mickey's Stampede, 1931 (Rooney)
Mickey's Travels, 1932 (Rooney)
Micki and Maude, 1984 (Moore, Dudley)
Micro-Phonies, 1945 (Three Stooges)
Midareboshi Aragami-yama, 1950 (Yamada)
Midaregumo, 1967 (Mori; Tsukasa)
Midareru, 1964 (Takamine)
Midas Run, 1969 (Astaire; McDowall; Richardson, R.)
Middle Age Crazy, 1980 (Ann-Margret; Dern)
Middle of the Night, 1959 (Grant, L.; March; Novak)
Middle Watch, 1939 (Buchanan)
Middlin' Stranger, 1927 (Karloff)
Midget's Revenge, 1912 (Talmadge)
Midnight, 1934 (Bogart)
Midnight, 1939 (Ameche; Astor; Barrymore, J.; Colbert)
Midnight, 1989 (Curtis, T.)
Midnight Adventure, 1909 (Pickford)
Midnight Alibi, 1934 (Barthelmess)
Midnight Angel. See Pacific Blackout, 1942
Midnight Club, 1933 (Raft)
Midnight Cop, 1989 (Mueller-Stahl)
Midnight Cowboy, 1969 (Hoffman; Voight)
Midnight Crossing, 1987 (Dunaway)
Midnight Elopement, 1912 (Normand)
Midnight Express, 1978 (Hurt, J.)
Midnight Girl, 1925 (Lugosi)
Midnight in Paris. See Monsieur la Souris, 1941
Midnight Kiss, 1926 (Gaynor)

Midnight Lace, 1960 (Day; Harrison; Loy; Marshall; McDowall)
Midnight Man, 1974 (Lancaster)
Midnight Mary, 1933 (Young, L.)
Midnight Menace, 1936 (Kortner)
Midnight Murders. *See* In the Line of Duty: Manhunt in the Dakotas, 1991
Midnight Patrol, 1933 (Laurel and Hardy)
Midnight Pleasures. *See* Mezzanotte va la ronda del piacere, 1975
Midnight Ride, 1993 (Mitchum)
Midnight Rider, 1990 (Travolta)
Midnight Run, 1988 (De Niro)
Midnight Sting. *See* Diggstown, 1992
Midnight Story, 1957 (Curtis, T.)
Midnight Taxi, 1928 (Loy)
Midori naki shima, 1948 (Yamamura)
Midorino furusato, 1946 (Hara)
Midshipmaid, 1932 (Mills)
Midshipmaid Gob. *See* Midshipmaid, 1932
Midshipman, 1925 (Novarro)
Midshipman Easy, 1935 (Lockwood)
Midsummer Night's Dream. *See* Sommernachtstraum, 1924
Midsummer Night's Dream, 1935 (Brown; Cagney; De Havilland; Powell, D.; Rooney)
Midsummer Night's Dream, 1961 (Burton)
Midsummer Night's Dream, 1968 (Mirren)
Midsummer Night's Dream, 1981 (Mirren)
Midsummer Night's Sex Comedy, 1982 (Allen; Farrow; Ferrer; Steenburgen)
Midt i byens hjerte, 1938 (Madsen and Schenstrøm)
Midvinterblot, 1946 (Björnstrand)
Midway, 1976 (Coburn, J.; Fonda, H.; Ford, G.; Heston; Mifune; Mitchum; Robertson)
Midwinter Blood. *See* Midvinterblot, 1946
Midwinter's Tale, 1995 (Branagh)
Miei primi 40 anni, 1987 (Gould)
Miércoles de ceniza, 1958 (Félix)
Miester von Nürnberg, 1927 (Fröhlich)
Mighty Aphrodite, 1995 (Allen; Bloom; Bonham-Carter)
Mighty Barnum, 1934 (Beery; Menjou)
Mighty Lak a Goat, 1942 (Gardner)
Mighty McGurk, 1947 (Beery)
Mighty Quinn, 1989 (Washington)
Migrants, 1974 (Spacek)
Migrations. *See* Guerre la plus glorieuse, 1989
Mihai Viteazu, 1969 (Welles)
Mike's Murder, 1984 (Winger)
Mikey and Nicky, 1976 (Falk)
Mikis Theodorakis: A Profile of Greatness, 1974 (Bates, A.)
Mil amores, 1954 (Infante)
Milagro Beanfield War, 1988 (Braga; Griffith; Redford; Walken)
Milan, 1946 (Kumar)
Milan noir, 1989 (Huppert)
Milana the Millionairess. *See* Milano miliardaria, 1951
Milano miliardaria, 1951 (Loren)
Milap, 1955 (Anand)
Mildred Pierce, 1945 (Crawford, J.)
Mile-a-Minute Romeo, 1923 (Mix)
Miles from Home, 1988 (Gere; Malkovich)
Miliardi, 1990 (Pleasence)
Militant School Ma'am, 1914 (Mix)
Militant Suffragette. *See* Busy Day, 1914
Militare e mezzo, 1960 (Fabrizi)
Militarists. *See* Gunbatsu, 1970
Military Policemen. *See* Off Limits, 1952
Milk Money, 1994 (Griffith; Harris, E.; McDowell)
Milkfed Boy, 1914 (Crisp)
Milkman, 1950 (Durante; Lewis, Jerry; O'Connor)
Milky Life. *See* Vida Lactea, 1991
Milky Way, 1936 (Lloyd; Menjou; Quinn)
Milky Way. *See* Voie lactée, 1968
Mill of Life, 1914 (Talmadge)
Mill on the Floss, 1937 (Mason)
Millard un billard, 1965 (Seberg)

Mille et Deuxième Nuits, 1932 (Modot; Mozhukin)
Mille et une nuits, 1922 (Modot)
Mille et une nuits. *See* Meraviglie di Aladino, 1961
Mille et une nuits, 1990 (Gassman)
Mille et une recettes du cuisinier a moureux, 1996 (Darrieux)
Mille lire al mese, 1938 (Valli)
Mille milliards de dollars, 1981 (Moreau)
Miller's Beautiful Wife. *See* Belle mugnaia, 1955
Miller's Crossing, 1990 (Finney; Turturro)
Miller's Wife. *See* Bella mugnaia, 1955
Milles, 1994 (Noiret)
Millie, 1931 (Blondell)
Millième Fenêtre, 1960 (Fresnay; Trintignant)
Milliner. *See* Masamod, 1920
Million Dollar Baby, 1941 (Reagan)
Million Dollar Face, 1981 (Curtis, T.; Grant, L.)
Million Dollar Job. *See* Film Johnnie, 1914
Million Dollar Legs, 1932 (Fields, W. C.)
Million Dollar Legs, 1939 (Grable; Holden; O'Connor)
Million Dollar Mermaid, 1952 (Mature; Pidgeon; Williams, E.)
Million Eyes of Su-muru. *See* Su-muru, 1967
Million Pound Note, 1955 (Peck)
Million to Juan, 1993 (Olmos)
Million to One, 1938 (Fontaine)
Million to One. *See* Million to Juan, 1993
Millionaire, 1917 (Laurel and Hardy)
Millionaire, 1931 (Cagney)
Millionaire. *See* Let's Make Love, 1960
Millionaire, 1978 (Bellamy)
Millionaire Cowboy, 1910 (Mix)
Millionaire for Christy, 1951 (Crosby; MacMurray)
Millionaire Merry-Go-Round. *See* Kicking the Moon Around, 1938
Millionaire Paupers, 1915 (Chaney)
Millionaire Playboy. *See* Park Avenue Logger, 1937
Millionaire Vagrant, 1917 (Gilbert)
Millionaire's Double, 1917 (Barrymore, L.)
Millionaires in Prison, 1940 (Three Stooges)
Millionairess, 1960 (Loren; Sellers)
Millionnaires d'un jour, 1949 (Brasseur)
Millón de Madigan. *See* Dollaro per 7 vigliacchi, 1970
Millones de Chafian, 1938 (Armendáriz)
Mills of the Gods, 1935 (Wray)
Milou en mai, 1990 (Piccoli)
Mimi metallurgico ferito nell'onore, 1972 (Giannini)
Mimi the Metalworker. *See* Mimi metallurgico ferito nell'onore, 1972
Mimizuku seppo, 1958 (Tsukasa)
Min Ajl Imraa, 1958 (Sharif)
Min and Bill, 1930 (Beery; Dressler)
Min kära är en ros, 1963 (Björnstrand)
Min syster och jag, 1950 (Björnstrand)
Minami kara kaetta hito, 1942 (Takamine)
Minami ni kaze, 1942 (Ryu)
Minamikaze, 1939 (Tanaka)
Minamoto Yoritsune, 1955 (Yamada)
Minato e kita otoko, 1952 (Mifune)
Mind Benders, 1962 (Bogarde)
Mind Cure, 1912-13 (White)
Mind of Mr. Soames, 1970 (Stamp)
Mind Snatchers, 1971 (Walken)
Mindwalk, 1991 (Ullmann)
Mine Own Executioner, 1948 (Meredith)
Miner, 1922 (Laurel and Hardy)
Miner's Romance, 1914 (Chaney)
Minestrone, 1980 (Benigni)
Minesweeper, 1943 (Mitchum)
Mini-Skirt Mob, 1968 (Stanton)
Ministro y Yo, 1976 (Cantinflas)
Ministry of Fear, 1943 (Duryea)
Ministry of Fear, 1944 (Milland)
Miniver Story, 1950 (Finch; Garson)
Miniver Story, 1950 (Pidgeon)

Minnelli on Minnelli: Liza Remembers Vincente, 1987 (Minnelli)
Minnie and Moskowitz, 1971 (Rowlands)
Minor Love and the Real Thing. *See* Kleine und die grosse Liebe, 1938
Minor Miracle, 1983 (Huston, J.)
Minuit, Place Pigalle, 1935 (Raimu)
Minute de vérité, 1952 (Gabin; Gélin; Morgan)
Minuto per pregare, un instante per morire, 1968 (Kennedy)
Mio caro Dottor Graesler, 1990 (Von Sydow)
Mio Caro Dr. Graessler, 1991 (Richardson, M.)
Mio figlio Nerone, 1956 (Bardot; Sordi; Swanson)
Mio figlio professore, 1946 (Fabrizi)
Mio in the Land of Faraway. *See* Mio, moy Mio, 1987
Mio, moy mio, 1987 (York; Lee, C.)
Mio nome e nessuno, 1974 (Fonda, H.)
Mio nome è Shanghai Joe, 1973 (Kinski)
Mio Padre Monsignore, 1971 (Giannini)
Mioche, 1936 (Morgan)
Miquette. *See* Miquette et sa mère, 1940
Miquette et sa mère, 1940 (Gélin)
Miquette et sa mère, 1949 (Jouvet)
Mir hat es immer Spass gemacht. *See* Wie dommt ein so reizendes Mädchen zu diesem Gewerbe?, 1970
Miracle, 1959 (Gassman)
Miracle, 1988 (Quayle)
Miracle. *See* Keitsik, 1989
Miracle Baby, 1923 (Carey)
Miracle Can Happen, 1946 (Huston, J.)
Miracle Can Happen. *See* On Our Merry Way, 1948
Miracle des loups, 1924 (Modot)
Miracle des loups, 1961 (Barrault)
Miracle in Soho, 1957 (Cusack)
Miracle in the Rain, 1956 (Dalio; Wyman)
Miracle Man, 1919 (Chaney)
Miracle Man, 1932 (Karloff; Sidney)
Miracle of Hickory, 1944 (Garson)
Miracle of Marcelino. *See* Marcelino, pan y vino, 1954
Miracle of Sound, 1940 (Lamarr)
Miracle of the Bells, 1948 (Cobb; MacMurray; Sidney; Valli)
Miracle of the White Stallions, 1963 (Taylor, R.)
Miracle of the Wolves. *See* Miracle des loups, 1924
Miracle on 34th Street, 1947 (O'Hara; Ritter; Wood)
Miracle on 34th Street, 1974 (McDowall)
Miracle on 34th Street, 1994 (Attenborough)
Miracle on 44th Street: A Portrait of the Actor's Studio, 1991 (Keitel)
Miracle on Ice, 1981 (Malden)
Miracle Rider, 1933 (Mix)
Miracle Woman, 1931 (Stanwyck)
Miracle Worker, 1962 (Bancroft)
Miracles for Sale, 1939 (Young, R.)
Miracles n'ont lieu q'une fois, 1951 (Marais; Valli)
Miracles: The Canton Godfather. *See* Keitsik, 1989
Miraculé, 1987 (Moreau)
Mirage, 1965 (Matthau; Peck)
Mirage, 1995 (Olmos)
Mirages, 1937 (Barrault)
Mirages. *See* Si tu m'aimes, 1937
Miranda, 1948 (Rutherford; Withers)
Mirch Masala, 1986 (Patil)
Mirele Efros, 1912 (Mozhukin)
Miroir, 1947 (Gabin; Gélin)
Miroir à deux faces, 1958 (Morgan)
Miroir aux alouettes, 1934 (Brasseur; Feuillère)
Mirror, 1911 (Pickford)
Mirror. *See* **Zerkalo**, 1975
Mirror Crack'd, 1980 (Chaplin, G.; Curtis, T.; Hudson; Lansbury; Novak; Taylor, E.)
Mirror Crack'd from Side to Side. *See* Miss Marple: The Mirror Crack'd, 1993
Mirror Has Two Faces. *See* Miroir à deux faces, 1958
Mirror Has Two Faces, 1996 (Moore, Dudley)
Mirror, Mirror, 1980 (Leigh, Janet)
Mirror Mirror 2: Raven Dance, 1994 (McDowall)

Mirth and Melody. *See* Let's Go Places, 1929
Misadventures of Buster Keaton, 1951 (Keaton, B.)
Misbehaving Husbands, 1940 (Langdon)
Misemono okoku, 1937 (Takamine)
Miser. *See* Avaro, 1990
Miser Murphy's Wedding Present, 1914 (Talmadge)
Miserabili, 1947 (Cervi; Mastroianni)
Misérables, 1933 (Vanel)
Misérables, 1935 (Carradine; Laughton; March)
Miserables. *See* I miserabili, 1948
Misérables, 1950 (Hayakawa)
Misérables, 1952 (Lanchester)
Misérables, 1957 (Gabin; Reggiani)
Misérables, 1958 (Blier)
Misérables, 1978 (Cusack; Gielgud; Johnson; Perkins)
Misérables, 1995 (Belmondo; Girardot; Marais; Presle)
Miseraretaru tamashii, 1953 (Yamada)
Miseria e nobiltà, 1954 (Loren)
Miserie del signor Travet, 1945 (Cervi; Sordi)
Misery, 1990 (Bacall; Bates, K.; Caan)
Misfits, 1961 (Clift; Gable; Huston, J.; Monroe; Ritter; Wallach)
Mishima, 1985 (Scheider)
Misión blanca, 1945 (Rey)
Misión Lisboa, 1965 (Rey)
Misleading Lady, 1932 (Colbert)
Misplaced Foot, 1914 (Arbuckle; Normand)
Miss Annie Rooney, 1942 (Temple)
Miss April. *See* Fröken April, 1958
Miss Arizona, 1988 (Mastroianni; Schygulla)
Miss Bracebirdle Does Her Duty, 1936 (Lanchester)
Miss Else. *See* Fräulein Else, 1929
Miss Europe. *See* Prix de beauté, 1930
Miss Fatty's Seaside Lovers, 1915 (Arbuckle; Lloyd)
Miss Firecracker, 1989 (Hunter; Robbins; Steenburgen)
Miss Grant Takes Richmond, 1949 (Ball; Holden)
Miss Hobbs, 1920 (Crisp)
Miss Italy, 1950 (Lollobrigida)
Miss Julie. *See* **Fröken Julie**, 1951
Miss Julie, 1972 (Mirren)
Miss Lonelyhearts. *See* Lonelyhearts, 1958
Miss Marple: The Mirror Crack'd, 1993 (Bloom)
Miss Mary, 1986 (Christie)
Miss Nobody, 1926 (Pidgeon)
Miss Oyu. *See* Oyu-sama, 1951
Miss Pacific Fleet, 1935 (Blondell)
Miss Pinkerton, 1932 (Blondell)
Miss Robin Hood, 1952 (Rutherford)
Miss Rose White, 1992 (Schell, Maximilian)
Miss Sadie Thompson, 1953 (Bronson; Ferrer; Hayworth)
Miss Susie Slagle's, 1946 (Gish; Lake)
Miss Tatlock's Millions, 1948 (Fitzgerald; Milland)
Miss Tulip Stays the Night, 1955 (Dors)
Missä on Musette?, 1992 (Léaud)
Missed Fortune, 1952 (Three Stooges)
Missile X. *See* Teheran Incident, 1979
Missing, 1982 (Lemmon; Spacek)
Missing Are Deadly, 1975 (Ferrer)
Missing, Believed Married, 1937 (Rutherford)
Missing Link: Ruby Cairo. *See* Deception, 1992
Missing Links, 1916 (Talmadge)
Missing Ten Days. *See* Ten Days in Paris, 1939
Mission, 1986 (De Niro; Irons; Neeson)
Mission Impossible, 1996 (Cruise; Redgrave, V.; Voight)
Mission over Korea, 1953 (O'Sullivan)
Mission to Moscow, 1943 (Charisse; Homolka; Huston, W.)
Mission to No Man's Land, 1959 (Brynner)
Missionary, 1982 (Elliott; Howard, T.; Smith)
Mississippi, 1935 (Bennett; Crosby; Fields, W. C.)
Mississippi Burning, 1988 (Dafoe; Hackman)
Mississippi Gambler, 1929 (Bennett)
Mississippi Gambler, 1942 (Three Stooges)

Mississippi Gambler, 1953 (Power)
Mississippi Masala, 1992 (Washington)
Mississippi Mermaid. *See* Sirène du Mississippi, 1969
Missouri Breaks, 1976 (Brando; Nicholson; Stanton)
Missouri Traveler, 1957 (Marvin)
Mistake, 1913 (Sweet)
Mistake in Rustlers, 1916 (Mix)
Mistaken Masher, 1913 (Normand)
Mistakes Will Happen, 1916 (Mix)
Mister 880, 1950 (Lancaster)
Mr. Ace, 1946 (Raft)
Mr. and Mrs. Bridge, 1990 (Newman; Woodward)
Mr. and Mrs. Smith, 1941 (Lombard; Montgomery)
Mr. and Mrs. Stockholm. *See* Herr och fru Stockholm, 1921
Mr. Arkadin, 1955 (Welles)
Mr. Ashton Was Indiscreet. *See* Senator Was Indiscreet, 1947
Mr. Barnes of New York, 1922 (Novarro)
Mr. Belvedere Goes to College, 1949 (Temple; Webb)
Mr. Belvedere Rings the Bell, 1951 (Webb)
Mister Big, 1943 (O'Connor)
Mr. Blandings Builds His Dream House, 1948 (Douglas, Melvyn; Grant, C.; Loy; McDaniel)
Mister Buddwing, 1966 (Garner; Lansbury)
Mr. Butler Buttles, 1912 (Talmadge)
Mr. Canton and Lady Rose. *See* Keitsik, 1989
Mr. Chedworth Steps Out, 1939 (Finch)
Mr. Corbett's Ghost, 1987 (Meredith)
Mister Cory, 1957 (Curtis, T.)
Mr. Deeds Goes to Town, 1936 (Arthur; Constantine)
Mr. Denning Drives North, 1951 (Lom; Mills)
Mr. Destiny, 1990 (Caine)
Mr. Dippy Dipped, 1913 (Beery)
Mr. District Attorney, 1941 (Lorre)
Mr. Dodd Takes the Air, 1937 (Wyman)
Mr. Dodek. *See* Pan Dodek, 1971
Mr. Dynamite, 1941 (Three Stooges)
Mr. Fix-It, 1912 (Normand)
Mr. Fix-It, 1918 (Fairbanks)
Mister Flow, 1936 (Feuillère; Jouvet)
Mr. Forbush and the Penguins, 1971 (Hurt, J.)
Mister Freedom, 1969 (Montand; Noiret; Pleasence; Seyrig)
Mister Frost, 1990 (Bates, A.; Cassel; Gélin)
Mr. Galindez. *See* Señor Galindez, 1983
Mister Halpren and Mister Johnson, 1983 (Olivier)
Mr. Hobbs Takes a Vacation, 1962 (O'Hara; Stewart)
Mr. Holland's Opus, 1996 (Dreyfuss)
Mr. Horn, 1979 (Widmark)
Mr. Hulot's Holiday. *See* **Vacances de Monsieur Hulot**, 1953
Mr. Hulot's Vacation. *See* **Vacances de Monsieur Hulot**, 1953
Mr. Imperium, 1951 (Reynolds, D.; Turner, L.)
Mister Jefferson Green, 1913 (Barrymore, L.)
Mister Jericho, 1969 (Lom)
Mr. Jones, 1993 (Bancroft; Gere; Olin)
Mr. Kingstreet's War, 1971 (Brazzi)
Mr. Kinky. *See* Profeta, 1967
Mr. Klein, 1976 (Delon; Moreau)
Mr. Krueger's Christmas, 1980 (Stewart)
Mr. Lemon of Orange, 1931 (Cantor)
Mr. Logan, U.S.A., 1918 (Mix)
Mr. Lucky, 1943 (Grant, C.)
Mr. Majestyk, 1974 (Bronson)
Mr. Mike's Mondo Video, 1979 (Murray)
Mr. Mom, 1983 (Keaton, M.)
Mr. Moses, 1965 (Mitchum)
Mr. Moto in Danger Island, 1939 (Bond)
Mr. Moto Takes a Chance, 1938 (Lorre)
Mr. Moto Takes a Vacation, 1939 (Lorre)
Mr. Moto's Gamble, 1938 (Bond; Lorre)
Mr. Moto's Last Warning, 1939 (Carradine; Lorre; Sanders)
Mr. Music, 1950 (Coburn, C.; Crosby; Marx Brothers)
Mr. Nobody. *See* In the Sage Brush Country, 1914

Mr. North, 1988 (Bacall; Huston, A.; Huston, J.; Mitchum; Stanton)
Mr. Patman, 1980 (Coburn, J.; Nelligan)
Mr. Peabody and the Mermaid, 1948 (Powell, W.)
Mr. Peek-a-boo. *See* Garou-Garou, le passe-muraille, 1950
Mr. Potts Goes to Moscow. *See* Top Secret, 1952
Mr. Ricco, 1975 (Martin, D.)
Mr. Roberts, 1955 (Bond; Cagney; Fonda, H.; Lemmon; Powell, W.)
Mr. Robinson Crusoe, 1932 (Fairbanks)
Mr. Sardonicus, 1961 (Homolka)
Mr. Saturday Night, 1992 (Lewis, Jerry)
Mr. Scarface. *See* I padroni della città, 1977
Mister Scoutmaster, 1953 (Webb)
Mr. Sebastian, 1968 (Bogarde; Gielgud; Sutherland; York)
Mr. "Silent" Haskins, 1915 (Hart)
Mr. Skeffington, 1944 (Davis, B.; Rains)
Mr. Skitch, 1933 (Rogers, W.)
Mr. Smith Goes to Washington, 1939 (Arthur; Carey; Rains; Stewart)
Mr. Smith Wakes Up, 1929 (Lanchester)
Mr. Soft Touch, 1949 (Ford, G.)
Mr. Sweeney's Masterpiece, 1912-13 (White)
Mr. Sycamore, 1975 (Robards)
Mr. Topaze, 1961 (Lom; Sellers)
Mister Will Shakespeare, 1936 (Shearer)
Mr. Winkle Goes to War, 1944 (Mitchum; Robinson, E.)
Mr. Wonderful, 1993 (Dillon; Hurt, W.)
Mr. Wong, Detective, 1938 (Karloff)
Mr. Wong at Headquarters. *See* Fatal Hour, 1940
Mr. Wong in Chinatown, 1939 (Karloff)
Mr. Wu, 1927 (Chaney; Wong)
Mr. X, 1984 (Azmi)
Mister Zehn Prozent—Miezen und Moneten, 1967 (Kinski)
Misterio en la isla de los monstruos, 1980 (Cushing; Stamp)
Mistero del tempio indiano, 1963 (Kinski)
Mistero di Oberwald, 1981 (Vitti)
Mistress, 1992 (Aiello; Borgnine; De Niro; Landau; Walken; Wallach)
Mrs. 'Arris Goes to Paris, 1992 (Lansbury; Sharif)
Mrs. 'Enery 'Awkins, 1911 (Talmadge)
Mrs. Andersson's Charlie. *See* Anderssonskans Kalle, 1950
Mrs. Cage, 1992 (Bancroft)
Mrs. Death. *See* Senora Muerte, 1967
Mrs. Delafield Wants to Marry, 1986 (Elliott; Hepburn, K.)
Mrs. Doubtfire, 1993 (Field; Williams, R.)
Mistress for the Summer. *See* Fille pour l'été, 1959
Mrs. Gibbons' Boys, 1962 (Dors)
Mrs. Jones' Birthday, 1909 (Arbuckle)
Mrs. Lambert Remembers Love, 1991 (Burstyn; Matthau)
Mrs. Manley's Baby, 1914 (Beery)
Mrs. Mike, 1949 (Powell, D.)
Mrs. Miniver, 1942 (Garson; Pidgeon)
Mrs. Murphy's Cooks, 1915 (Mix)
Mistress Nell, 1915 (Pickford)
Mistress of Paradise, 1978 (Bujold)
Mistress of the World. *See* Herrin der Welt, 1959
Mrs. Parker and the Vicious Circle, 1994 (Leigh, Jennifer Jason)
Mrs. Parkington, 1944 (Duryea; Moorehead; Pidgeon; Garson)
Mrs. Pollifax—Spy, 1971 (Russell, R.)
Mrs. R.—Death among Friends. *See* Death among Friends, 1975
Mrs. Soffel, 1984 (Gibson; Keaton, D.)
Mrs. Wiggs of the Cabbage Patch, 1934 (Fields, W. C.)
Mrs. Winterbourne, 1996 (MacLaine)
Misunderstood. *See* Incompreso, 1967
Misunderstood, 1984 (Hackman)
Misunderstood Boy, 1913 (Barrymore, L.; Gish)
Mit den Augen einer Frau, 1942 (Fröhlich)
Mit Django kam der Tod. *See* Uomo, l'orgoglio, la vendetta, 1967
Mitico Gianluca, 1988 (Mastroianni)
Mitläufer, 1984 (Mueller-Stahl)
Mito Komon umi o wataru, 1961 (Hasegawa)
Mitsu no shinju, 1949 (Kyo)
Mitsuyu-sen, 1954 (Mifune)
Mitt folk är icke ditt, 1944 (Björnstrand)

Mittsu no ai, 1954 (Yamada)
Mix Me a Person, 1962 (Baxter)
Mix-Up in Movies, 1916 (Mix)
Mixed Flats, 1915 (Laurel and Hardy)
Mixed Magic, 1936 (Keaton, B.)
Mixed Nuts, 1919 (Laurel and Hardy)
Mixed Nuts, 1994 (Lewis, Juliette; Martin, S.)
Mixup for Mazie, 1915 (Lloyd)
Mixup in Hearts, 1917 (Laurel and Hardy)
Miyamoto Musashi, 1944 (Tanaka)
Miyamoto Musashi, 1954 (Holden; Mifune)
Miyamoto Musashi: Ichijo-ji no ketto, 1941 (Shimura)
M'Liss, 1918 (Pickford)
M'Lord of the White Road, 1923 (McLaglen)
Mniejsze Wiebo, 1981 (Tyszkiewicz)
Mo' Better Blues, 1990 (Jackson, S.; Lee, S.; Snipes; Turturro; Washington)
Mob, 1951 (Borgnine; Bronson; Crawford, B.)
Mob Justice, 1995 (Jackson, S.)
Mobsters, 1991 (Quinn)
Moby Dick, 1930 (Barrymore, J.; Bennett)
Moby Dick, 1956 (Huston, J.; Lee, C.; Peck; Welles)
Mockery, 1927 (Chaney)
Mod Lyset, 1918 (Madsen and Schenstrøm; Nielsen)
Model and the Marriage Broker, 1951 (Ritter)
Model Shop, 1969 (Aimée)
Model Wife, 1941 (Blondell; Powell, D.)
Moderato cantabile, 1960 (Belmondo; Moreau)
Modern Bluebeard. See Moderno Barba Azul, 1946
Modern DuBarry. See Eine DuBarry von Heute, 1926
Modern Hero, 1934 (Barthelmess)
Modern Love, 1990 (Reynolds, B.)
Modern Magdalen, 1915 (Barrymore, L.)
Modern Miracle. See Story of Alexander Graham Bell, 1939
Modern Musketeer, 1918 (Fairbanks)
Modern Times, 1936 (Chaplin, C.; Goddard)
Moderne Ehen, 1924 (Kortner)
Moderner Don Juan, 1927 (Dagover)
Moderno Barba Azul, 1946 (Keaton, B.)
Moderns, 1988 (Bujold; Chaplin, G.)
Modest Hero, 1913 (Gish)
Modesty Blaise, 1966 (Bogarde; Stamp; Vitti)
Modigliani of Montparnasse. See Montparnasse 19, 1957
Modiste, 1917 (Laurel and Hardy)
Moeru Shanhai, 1954 (Mori; Yamamura)
Mogambo, 1953 (Gable; Gardner; Kelly, Grace)
Mogliamante, 1977 (Mastroianni)
Moglie del prete, 1971 (Loren; Mastroianni)
Moglie e buoi ..., 1956 (Cervi)
Moglie per una notte, 1952 (Cervi; Lollobrigida)
Mogotona musume, 1956 (Tsukasa)
Mohammad, Messenger of God. See Message, 1976
Mohan, 1947 (Anand)
Moi et l'impératrice, 1933 (Boyer; Brasseur)
Moi, Fleur Bleue, 1978 (Foster)
Moi Ivan, Toi Abraham, 1993 (Yankovsky)
Moi laskovyi i nezhnyi zver, 1978 (Yankovsky)
Moi syn, 1928 (Cherkassov)
Moi y'en a vouloir des sous, 1973 (Blier)
Mois le plus beau, 1968 (Gélin)
Mojave Moon, 1996 (Aiello)
Molchaniye Doktoraivens, 1973 (Bondarchuk)
Molière, 1955 (Belmondo)
Moll Flanders, 1996 (Freeman)
Mollenard, 1938 (Dalio)
Molly and Me, 1929 (Brown)
Molly and Me, 1945 (Fields, G.; McDowall)
Molly McGuires, 1969 (Connery; Harris, R.)
Molly O', 1921 (Normand)
Mollycoddle, 1920 (Beery; Fairbanks)
Moloch, 1978 (Nowicki)
Molti sogni per le strade, 1947 (Magnani)

Môme vert-de-gris, 1953 (Constantine; Modot)
Moment by Moment, 1978 (Travolta)
Moment of Danger, 1960 (Howard, T.)
Moment of Terror. See Hikinige, 1966
Moment of Truth. See Minute de vérité, 1952
Moment to Moment, 1965 (Seberg)
Momento più bello, 1957 (Mastroianni)
Mommie Dearest, 1981 (Dunaway)
Mommy Market. See Trading Mom, 1994
Momo, 1986 (Mueller-Stahl)
Mon ami Victor, 1932 (Brasseur)
Mon Ami Max, 1994 (Bujold)
Mon amour, mon amour, 1967 (Piccoli)
Mon Beau-frère a tué ma soeur, 1986 (Binoche; Piccoli)
Mon Chapeau, 1933 (Dalio)
Mon Chien rapporte. See Chien qui rapporte, 1909
Mon Coeur et ses millions, 1931 (Berry)
Mon Coeur t'appelle, 1934 (Darrieux)
Mon Faust, 1969 (Fresnay)
Mon gosse de père, 1930 (Menjou)
Mon homme, 1996 (Léaud)
Mon Oncle, 1958 (Tati)
Mon Oncle Benjamin, 1969 (Blier)
Mon Oncle d'Amerique, 1980 (Depardieu)
Mon Père le heros, 1991 (Depardieu)
Mon Père et mon papa, 1938 (Berry)
Mon Premier Amour, 1978 (Aimée; Baye)
Mona Lisa, 1986 (Caine; Hoskins)
Monaca di Monza, 1947 (Brazzi)
Monaca di Monza, 1962 (Cervi)
Monaco Forever, 1984 (Van Damme)
Monastero, 1990 (Lee, C.)
Monastery. See Monastero, 1990
Monday's Child. See Chica del Lunes, 1966
Monde desert, 1985 (Olbrychski)
Mondo balordo, 1967 (Karloff)
Mondo di notte. See Ecco, 1963
Mondo le condanna, 1952 (Reggiani; Valli)
Mondo nuovo, 1966 (Brasseur)
Moneda sangrienta, 1974 (Van Cleef)
Money, 1975 (DeVito)
Money, 1990 (Cardinale; Douglas, K.)
Money—a Tragicomedy. See Pengar—en tragikomisk saga, 1946
Money Corral, 1919 (Hart)
Money for Jam. See It Ain't Hay, 1943
Money for Speed, 1933 (Lupino)
Money from Home, 1953 (Lewis, J.; Martin, D.)
Money Mad, 1918 (Marsh)
Money, Money, Money. See Cave se rebiffe, 1961
Money on the Side, 1982 (Curtis, J.)
Money on the Street. See Geld auf der Strasse, 1930
Money on Your Life, 1938 (Kaye)
Money Pit, 1986 (Hanks)
Money Plays, 1996 (Braga)
Money Train, 1995 (Snipes)
Money Trap, 1966 (Cotten; Ford, G.; Hayworth)
Mongo's Back in Town, 1971 (Field; Sheen)
Mongoli, 1961 (Palance)
Mongols. See I mongoli, 1961
Monismania 1995. See Monismanien 1995, 1975
Monismanien 1995, 1975 (Andersson, H.; Josephson; Thulin)
Monitors, 1969 (Arkin)
Monja alférez, 1944 (Félix)
Monje blanco, 1945 (Félix)
Monk, 1969 (Leigh, Janet)
Monkey Business, 1931 (Marx Brothers)
Monkey Business, 1952 (Coburn, C.; Grant, C.; Monroe; Rogers, G.)
Monkey Businessmen, 1946 (Three Stooges)
Monkey in Winter. See Singe en hiver, 1962
Monkey People, 1989 (Sarandon)
Monkey Trouble, 1994 (Keitel)

Monkeys, Go Home!, 1967 (Chevalier)
Monna Vanna, 1922 (Wegener)
Monocle noir, 1961 (Blier)
Monocle rit Jaune, 1964 (Dalio)
Monocle vert, 1929 (Modot)
Monolith, 1993 (Hurt, J.)
Monpti, 1957 (Schneider)
Monseigneur, 1949 (Blier)
Monsieur, 1964 (Gabin; Noiret)
Monsieur Albert, 1932 (Feuillère)
Monsieur Albert, 1976 (Noiret)
Monsieur Alibi. See Copie conforme, 1946
Monsieur Beaucaire, 1924 (Valentino)
Monsieur Beaucaire, 1946 (Crosby; Hope)
Monsieur Bébé. See Bedtime Story, 1933
Monsieur Brotonneau, 1939 (Raimu)
Monsieur Cognac. See Wild and Wonderful, 1964
Monsieur de compagnie, 1964 (Cassel; Dalio; Deneuve; Girardot)
Monsieur Don't-Care, 1924 (Laurel and Hardy)
Monsieur Fabre, 1951 (Fresnay)
Monsieur Gregoire s'évadé, 1945 (Berry; Blier)
Monsieur Hector, 1940 (Fernandel)
Monsieur Hulot's Holiday. See **Vacances de Monsieur Hulot**, 1953
Monsieur la Souris, 1941 (Raimu)
Monsieur Papa, 1977 (Baye)
Monsieur Personne, 1935 (Berry)
Monsieur Ripois. See Knave of Hearts, 1954
Monsieur Verdoux, 1947 (Chaplin, C.; Purviance)
Monsieur Vincent, 1947 (Fresnay)
Monsignor, 1982 (Bujold; Rey)
Monsignor Quixote, 1985 (Guinness)
Monster, 1925 (Chaney)
Monster, 1979 (Carradine)
Monster. See Mostro, 1994
Monster: The Legend That Became a Terror. See Monster, 1979
Monster and the Girl, 1941 (Lukas)
Monster Club, 1980 (Carradine; Pleasence; Price)
Monster in the Closet, 1987 (Carradine)
Monster Island. See Misterio en la isla de los monstruos, 1980
Monster Maker, 1989 (Stanton)
Monster Meets the Gorilla. See Bela Lugosi Meets a Brooklyn Gorilla, 1952
Monster of Terror. See Die, Monster, Die!, 1965
Monster of the Island, 1953 (Karloff)
Montana, 1950 (Flynn)
Montana, 1990 (Rowlands)
Montana Belle, 1952 (Russell, J.)
Montana Moon, 1930 (Crawford, J.)
Monte Carlo, 1928 (Bertini)
Monte Carlo, 1930 (Buchanan; MacDonald)
Monte Carlo, 1986 (McDowell)
Monte Carlo Baby, 1951 (Hepburn, A.)
Monte Carlo Madness. See Bomben auf Monte Carlo, 1931
Monte Carlo or Bust!, 1969 (Hawkins; Moore, Dudley; Terry-Thomas)
Monte Carlo or Bust! See Quei temerari sulle loro pazze, scatenate, scalcinate carriole, 1969
Monte Carlo Story, 1957 (Dietrich)
Monte Cristo, 1922 (Gilbert)
Monte Cristo, 1928 (Dagover; Modot)
Monte Walsh, 1969 (Marvin; Moreau; Palance)
Montenegro, 1981 (Josephson)
Montenruba no yo wa hukete, 1952 (Kagawa)
Montgomery Clift, 1983 (Remick)
Month by the Lake, 1995 (Redgrave, V.; Thurman; Valli)
Month in the Country, 1985 (York)
Month in the Country, 1987 (Branagh)
Montiel's Widow. See Viuda de Montiel, 1979
Montmartre. See Flamme, 1922
Montmartre-sur-Seine, 1941 (Barrault)
Montparnasse 19, 1957 (Aimée; Philipe)
Montreur d'ombre. See **Schatten**, 1923
Monty Python and the Holy Grail, 1975 (Cleese)

Monty Python Live at the Hollywood Bowl, 1982 (Cleese)
Monty Python's Life of Brian, 1979 (Cleese)
Monty Python's the Meaning of Life, 1983 (Cleese)
Monzaburo no Hide, 1931 (Hasegawa)
Mooching through Georgia, 1939 (Keaton, B.)
Moon 44, 1990 (McDowell)
Moon and Sixpence, 1942 (Marshall; Sanders)
Moon and Sixpence, 1957 (Cusack)
Moon for the Misbegotten, 1975 (Robards)
Moon in the Gutter. See Lune dans le caniveau, 1983
Moon Is Blue, 1953 (Holden; Niven)
Moon Is Down, 1943 (Cobb)
Moon Is to the Left. See Luna sleva, 1928
Moon over Burma, 1940 (Lamour; Preston)
Moon over Miami, 1941 (Ameche; Grable)
Moon over Parador, 1988 (Braga; Dreyfuss; Julia; Rey)
Moon Pilot, 1962 (O'Brien, E.)
Moon-Spinners, 1964 (Greenwood; Negri; Papas; Wallach)
Moonchild, 1974 (Carradine)
Mooncussers, 1962 (Homolka)
Moonfleet, 1955 (Granger; Greenwood; Sanders)
Moonlight and Cactus, 1932 (Arbuckle)
Moonlight and Cactus, 1944 (Three Stooges)
Moonlight and Noses, 1925 (Laurel and Hardy)
Moonlight and Valentino, 1995 (Goldberg; Turner, K.)
Moonlighter, 1953 (Bond; MacMurray; Stanwyck)
Moonlighting, 1982 (Irons)
Moonrise, 1948 (Barrymore, E.)
Moon's Our Home, 1936 (Brennan; Fonda, H.; Sullavan)
Moonshine, 1918 (Arbuckle; Keaton, B.)
Moonshine War, 1970 (Widmark)
Moonshiners, 1916 (Arbuckle)
Moonshot. See Countdown, 1968
Moonstruck, 1987 (Aiello; Cage; Cher)
Moontide, 1942 (Gabin; Lupino; Rains)
Moor's Head. See Kopf des Mohren, 1995
Mopey Dope, 1944 (Langdon)
Mor Curé chez les pauvres, 1956 (Arletty)
Moral, 1979 (Schell, Maria)
Moral Code, 1917 (Barthelmess)
Moral der Gasse, 1925 (Krauss)
Moral und Liebe, 1933 (Homolka)
Moralist. See Moralista, 1959
Moralista, 1959 (Sordi)
Moran of the Lady Letty, 1922 (Valentino)
Moran of the Marines, 1928 (Harlow)
Morbidone, 1965 (Aimée)
Mörder Dimitri Karamasoff, 1931 (Kortner; Rasp)
Mordi e fuggi, 1972 (Mastroianni; Reed)
Mords pas, on t'aime, 1975 (Presle)
More American Graffiti, 1979 (Ford, H.)
More Dead Than Alive, 1968 (Price)
More Than a Miracle. See C'era una volta, 1967
More Than a Secretary, 1936 (Arthur)
More the Merrier, 1943 (Arthur; Coburn, C.; McCrea)
More Trouble, 1918 (Gilbert)
Morfalous, 1983 (Belmondo)
Morfars Resa, 1993 (Zetterling)
Morgan! A Suitable Case for Treatment, 1966 (Redgrave, V.)
Morgen in Alabama, 1984 (Schell, Maximilian)
Mori Ranmaru, 1955 (Yamamura)
Mori to mizuumi no matsuri, 1958 (Kagawa)
Morianerna, 1965 (Dahlbeck)
Morianna. See Morianerna, 1965
Moriarty. See Sherlock Holmes, 1922
Morishaige yo doko e iku, 1956 (Kagawa)
Morituri, 1948 (Kinski)
Morituri. See Saboteur—Code Name Morituri, 1965
Moriturus, 1920 (Veidt)
Morning. See Subah, 1983
Morning After, 1986 (Bates, K.; Bridges; Julia; Fonda, J.)

Morning Conflicts. *See* Asa no hamon, 1952

Morning Departure, 1950 (Attenborough; Mills)

Morning Glory, 1933 (Hepburn, K.; Menjou)

Moro Affair. *See* Caso Moro, 1986

Morocco, 1930 (Constantine; Dietrich; Menjou)

Mors aux dents, 1979 (Piccoli)

Mort d'un pourri, 1977 (Audran; Delon; Kinski)

Mort d'un toréador, 1907 (Linder)

Mort de Mario Ricci, 1984 (Volonté)

Mort en ce jardin, 1956 (Piccoli; Vanel)

Mort en direct, 1979 (Keitel; Noiret; Schneider; Von Sydow)

Mort en fuite, 1936 (Berry)

Mort en fuite. *See* Break the News, 1938

Mort en sautoir, 1980 (Darrieux)

Mort ne reçoit plus, 1944 (Berry)

Mort, où est ta victoire?, 1964 (Noiret)

Mortacci. *See* Hateful Dead, 1989

Mortadella, 1972 (DeVito; Loren; Sarandon)

Mortal Storm, 1940 (Bond; Stewart; Sullavan; Young, R.)

Mortal Thoughts, 1991 (Keitel; Moore, Demi; Willis)

Morte a Venezia, 1971 (Bogarde; Mangano)

Morte civile, 1912 (Bertini)

Morte en fraude, 1956 (Gélin)

Morte in Vaticano, 1982 (Stamp)

Morte la fatto, l'uovo, 1967 (Lollobrigida)

Morte non ha sesso, 1969 (Mills)

Morte-saison des amours, 1961 (Gélin)

Morte sorride all'assassino, 1973 (Kinski)

Mortelle randonnée, 1983 (Adjani)

Mosca addio, 1987 (Olbrychski; Ullmann)

Moscow Goodbye. *See* Mosca Addio, 1987

Moscow Nights, 1935 (Olivier; Quayle)

Moscow on the Hudson, 1984 (Williams, R.)

Mose, 1972 (Lancaster)

Mose, 1975 (Papas; Thulin; Quayle)

Moses. *See* Mose, 1972

Moses. *See* Mose, 1975

Moshimo kanojo ga, 1928 (Tanaka)

Moskau-Shanghai, 1936 (Negri; Wegener)

Mosquito Coast, 1986 (Ford, H.; Mirren)

Moss Rose, 1947 (Barrymore, E.; Mature; Price)

Most Beautiful. *See* Ichiban utsukushiku, 1944

Most Beautiful Night. *See* Noche Mas Hermosa, 1984

Most Dangerous Game, 1932 (McCrea; Wray)

Most Dangerous Man in the World, 1969 (Peck)

Most Dangerous Sin. *See* Crime et châtiment, 1956

Most Immoral Lady, 1929 (Pidgeon)

Most Important Thing Is Love. *See* Important c'est d'aimer, 1975

Most Precious Thing in Life, 1934 (Arthur; Bond)

Most Wanted Man. *See* Ennemi public No. 1, 1953

Most Wonderful Evening of My Life. *See* Più bella serata della mia vita, 1972

Most Wonderful Moment. *See* Momento più bello, 1957

Mostri, 1963 (Gassman)

Mostro, 1994 (Benigni)

Mostro dell'isola. *See* Monster of the Island, 1953

Mosura, 1961 (Kagawa; Shimura)

Mot nya tider, 1939 (Björnstrand)

Möte i natten, 1946 (Dahlbeck)

Möte med Livet, 1952 (Thulin)

Möten i skymningen, 1957 (Dahlbeck)

Moth, 1917 (Menjou; Talmadge)

Mother. *See* Okasan, 1952

Mother. *See* Mat, 1955

Mother. *See* 588 Rue Paradis, 1992

Mother, 1996 (Reynolds, D.)

Mother and Daughter. *See* Sredi dobrykh lyudei, 1962

Mother and Daughter. *See* Anya és leánya, 1981

Mother and Daughter: The Loving War, 1980 (Weld)

Mother and the Law, 1919 (Marsh)

Mother and the Whore. *See* Maman et la putain, 1973

Mother Carey's Chickens, 1938 (Brennan; Keeler)

Mother, Do Not Shame Your Name. *See* Haha yo kimi no na o kegasu nakare, 1928

Mother Instinct, 1917 (Gilbert)

Mother Is a Freshman, 1949 (Young, L.)

Mother, Jugs and Speed, 1976 (Keitel; Welch)

Mother Lode, 1982 (Basinger; Heston)

Mother Machree, 1928 (McLaglen; Wayne)

Mother—Sir! *See* Navy Wife, 1956

Mother Should Be Loved. *See* Haka o kowazuya, 1934

Mother Teresa, 1986 (Attenborough)

Mother Wore Tights, 1947 (Baxter; Grable)

Mothering Heart, 1913 (Gish)

Mother's Atonement, 1915 (Chaney)

Mother's Boy, 1913 (Arbuckle)

Mother's Boys, 1994 (Curtis, J.; Redgrave, V.)

Mother's Child, 1916 (Laurel and Hardy)

Mother's Cry, 1930 (Karloff)

Mother's Heart. *See* Cuore di mamma, 1968

Mother's Holiday, 1932 (Arbuckle)

Mother's Joy, 1923 (Laurel and Hardy)

Mother's Prayer, 1995 (Dern; Nelligan)

Mother's Right: The Elizabeth Morgan Story, 1992 (Neal)

Mother's Tears, 1953 (Lee, B.)

Mothra. *See* Mosura, 1961

Mothra tai Godzilla. *See* Mosura, 1961

Motion and Emotion, 1990 (Falk; Hopper; Stanton)

Motive Was Jealousy. *See* Dramma della gelosia—tutti i particolari in cronaca, 1970

Motor Friend, 1910-11 (White)

Motorcyclette. *See* Girl on a Motorcycle, 1968

Motorkavalierer, 1950 (Andersson, H.)

Mouid maa el Maghoul, 1958 (Sharif)

Moulin Rouge, 1934 (Ball)

Moulin Rouge, 1952 (Cushing; Ferrer; Huston, J.; Lee, C.)

Mountain, 1956 (Tracy; Trevor)

Mountain Justice, 1915 (Chaney)

Mountain Men, 1980 (Heston)

Mountain Pass of Love and Hate. *See* Aizo-toge, 1934

Mountain Rat, 1914 (Crisp)

Mountain Rhythm, 1939 (Autry)

Mountain Road, 1960 (Stewart)

Mountain Woman, 1921 (White)

Mountaineer's Honor, 1909 (Pickford)

Mountains of the Moon, 1990 (Sharif)

Mourir d'aimer, 1970 (Girardot)

Mourning Becomes Electra, 1947 (Douglas, K.; Massey; Redgrave, M.; Russell, R.)

Mouse, a Mystery and Me, 1987 (O'Connor)

Mouse and His Child, 1977 (Ustinov)

Mouse on the Moon, 1963 (Rutherford; Terry-Thomas)

Mouse That Roared, 1959 (Seberg; Sellers)

Mousey, 1974 (Douglas, K.; Seberg)

Mouth Agape. *See* Gueule ouverte, 1974

Mouthpiece, 1932 (Goddard)

Mouton à cinq pattes, 1953 (Fernandel)

Mouton enragé, 1974 (Cassel; Schneider)

Move, 1970 (Gould)

Move On, 1917 (Lloyd)

Move Over, Darling, 1963 (Day; Garner; Ritter)

Movers and Shakers, 1985 (Martin, S.; Matthau)

Movie Crazy, 1932 (Lloyd)

Movie Experience: A Matter of Choice, 1968 (Heston)

Movie Life of George, 1989 (Caine)

Movie Maniacs, 1936 (Three Stooges)

Movie Movie, 1978 (Scott, G.; Wallach)

Movie Murderer, 1970 (Kennedy; Oates)

Movie Nut. *See* Film Johnnie, 1914

Movie Teller. *See* Kinoerzaehler, 1993

Movies, 1925 (Arbuckle)

Movies Murderer, 1980 (Kennedy)

Moving, 1988 (Pryor)

Moving Picture Cowboy, 1914 (Mix)
Moving Target. *See* Harper, 1966
Moving Target, 1990 (Borgnine)
Moviola: The Scarlett O'Hara War, 1980 (Curtis, T.)
Moyuru daichi, 1940 (Hasegawa)
Mozart, 1955 (Werner)
Mozu, 1940 (Yamada)
Mozu, 1961 (Yamada)
Ms. Don Juan. *See* Don Juan 1973 ou Si Don Juan était une femme, 1973
M'sieur la caille, 1955 (Moreau)
Much Ado about Nothing, 1993 (Branagh; Keaton, M.; Reeves; Thompson; Washington)
Muchly Engaged, 1912-13 (White)
Mud and Sand, 1922 (Laurel and Hardy)
Muddle in Horse Thieves , 1913 (Mix)
Muddy Water. *See* Nigorie, 1953
Müde Tod, 1921 (Dagover)
Mudlark, 1950 (Dunne; Guinness)
Muerta viaje demasiado. *See* Humour noir, 1965
Muerte de un presidente, 1970 (Rey)
Muertres, 1950 (Fernandel)
Muggsy Becomes a Hero, 1910 (Pickford)
Muggsy's First Sweetheart, 1910 (Pickford)
Mughal-e-Azam, 1960 (Kumar)
Mugsy's Girls, 1984 (Gordon)
Mühle im Schwarzwäldertal, 1952 (Rasp)
Muhomachi no yarodomo, 1959 (Yamamura)
Muhomatsu no issho, 1958 (Mifune; Ryu; Takamine)
Mujer Bajo la Lluvia, 1992 (Banderas)
Mujer cualquiera, 1949 (Félix)
Mujer de todos, 1945 (Félix)
Mujer que yo perdí, 1949 (Infante)
Mujer sin alma, 1943 (Félix)
Mujeres al borde de un ataque de nervios, 1988 (Banderas; Maura)
Mujers de mi general, 1950 (Infante)
Mulata, 1953 (Armendáriz)
Mule Train, 1950 (Autry)
Mules and Mortgages, 1919 (Laurel and Hardy)
Mulholland Falls, 1996 (Griffith; Malkovich; Nolte)
Multiplicity, 1996 (Keaton, M.)
Mummy, 1932 (Karloff)
Mummy, 1959 (Cushing; Lee, C.)
Mummy Lives, 1994 (Curtis, T.)
Mummy's Dummies, 1948 (Three Stooges)
Mummy's Ghost, 1944 (Carradine)
Mummy's Shroud, 1967 (Cushing)
Mumsie, 1927 (Marshall)
Mumyo-yumyo, 1939 (Shimura)
Munchhausen Himself. *See* Tot samyi Myunkhauzen, 1979
Munekata-shima, 1950 (Yamamura)
Munekata shimai, 1950 (Ryu; Tanaka; Takamine)
Munekata Sisters. *See* Munekata shimai, 1950
Mungding sifan, 1992 (Gong Li)
Municipal Bandwagon, 1931 (Astaire)
Munimji, 1955 (Anand)
Munkbrogreven, 1934 (Bergman)
Munshiji, 1973 (Azmi)
Munster, Go Home!, 1966 (Carradine; Terry-Thomas)
Muppet Christmas Carol, 1992 (Caine)
Muppet Movie, 1979 (Brooks, M.; Coburn, J.; Gould; Hope; Martin, S.; Pryor; Welles)
Muppets Take Manhattan, 1982 (Welles; Gould; Minnelli)
Muqaddar Ka Badshah, 1990 (Azmi)
Mur de l'Atlantique, 1970 (Terry-Thomas)
Mura di Malapaga. *See* Au-delà des grilles, 1949
Mura hachibu, 1953 (Yamamura)
Mura na hanayome, 1928 (Tanaka)
Mura no bokujo, 1924 (Tanaka)
Mura no kajiya, 1929 (Tanaka)
Murasaki zukin, 1958 (Yamamura)
Murder, 1930 (Marshall)

Murder: By Reason of Insanity, 1985 (Wallach)
Murder à la Carte. *See* Voici le temps des assassins, 1955
Murder Ahoy, 1964 (Rutherford)
Murder at 45 RPM. *See* Meurtre en 45 tours, 1960
Murder at Monte Carlo, 1935 (Flynn)
Murder at the Gallop, 1963 (Rutherford)
Murder at the Vanities, 1934 (McLaglen)
Murder at the World Series, 1977 (Leigh, Janet)
Murder by Death, 1976 (Falk; Guinness; Lanchester; Niven; Sellers; Smith)
Murder by Decree, 1978 (Gielgud; Bujold; Mason; Quayle; Sutherland)
Murder by Mail. *See* Schizoid, 1980
Murder by Television, 1935 (Lugosi)
Murder for Sale. *See* Temporary Widow, 1930
Murder, He Says, 1945 (MacMurray)
Murder in Greenwich Village, 1937 (Wray)
Murder in Peyton Place, 1977 (Malone)
Murder in Soho, 1939 (Withers)
Murder in the Air, 1940 (Reagan)
Murder in the Cathedral, 1964 (Cusack)
Murder in the Central Committee. *See* Asesinato en el Comite Central, 1982
Murder in the Family, 1938 (McDowall)
Murder in the First, 1995 (Bacon; Oldman)
Murder in the Fleet, 1935 (Bond; Taylor, R.)
Murder in the Night. *See* Murder in Soho, 1939
Murder in Thornton Square. *See* Gaslight, 1944
Murder in Three Acts. *See* Three Act Tragedy, 1987
Murder, Inc., 1960 (Falk)
Murder Is Easy, 1982 (De Havilland)
Murder Man, 1935 (Stewart; Tracy)
Murder Men, 1962 (Coburn, J.)
Murder Most Foul, 1964 (Rutherford)
Murder, My Sweet, 1944 (Powell, D.; Trevor)
Murder of Dr. Harrigan, 1936 (Astor)
Murder of Mary Phagan, 1988 (Lemmon)
Murder of Quality, 1991 (Elliott; Jackson, G.)
Murder of Sherlock Holmes, 1985 (Lansbury)
Murder on Flight 502, 1975 (Bellamy; Pidgeon)
Murder on Monday. *See* Home at Seven, 1952
Murder on the Bayou. *See* Gathering of Old Men, 1987
Murder on the Bridge. *See* Richter und sein Henker, 1975
Murder on the Orient Express, 1974 (Bacall; Bergman; Cassel; Connery; Finney; Gielgud; Perkins; Redgrave, V.; Roberts, R.; Widmark)
Murder or Mercy, 1974 (Douglas, Melvyn)
Murder Ordained, 1987 (Bates, K.)
Murder over New York, 1940 (Three Stooges)
Murder She Said, 1961 (Kennedy; Rutherford)
Murder Story, 1989 (Lee, C.)
Murder That Wouldn't Die, 1980 (Ferrer)
Murder Will Out, 1939 (Hawkins; McDowall)
Murder with Mirrors, 1985 (Davis, B.; Mills)
Murder with Pictures, 1936 (Ayres)
Murderer Dimitri Karamazov. *See* Mörder Dmitri Karamasoff, 1931
Murderer Lives at Number 21. *See* Assassin habite au 21, 1942
Murderer Made in Italy. *See* Segreto del vestito rosso, 1963
Murderers among Us: The Simon Wiesenthal Story, 1989 (Kingsley)
Murderers' Row, 1966 (Ann-Margret; Martin, D.; Malden)
Murders in the Rue Morgue, 1932 (Huston, J.; Lugosi)
Murders in the Rue Morgue, 1971 (Lom; Robards)
Murders in the Rue Morgue, 1986 (Scott, G.)
Murders in the Zoo, 1933 (Scott, R.)
Murdoch's Gang, 1973 (Leigh, Janet)
Muriel, 1963 (Seyrig)
Murmur of the Heart. *See* **Souffle au coeur**, 1971
Muro de Silencio, 1993 (Redgrave, V.)
Murphy's Law, 1986 (Bronson)
Murphy's Romance, 1985 (Field; Garner)
Murphy's War, 1971 (Noiret; O'Toole)
Murri Affair. *See* Fatti di gente per bene, 1974
Musafir, 1957 (Kumar)
Musasabi no Sankichi, 1927 (Tanaka)
Musashi and Kojiro. *See* Ketto ganryu-jima, 1956

Musashi Miyamoto. *See* Miyamoto Musashi, 1944
Musashibo Benkei, 1942 (Takamine; Yamada)
Musashino fujin, 1951 (Mori; Tanaka; Yamamura)
Muscle Beach Party, 1964 (Lorre)
Muscle Up a Little Closer, 1957 (Three Stooges)
Music Blasters. *See* You're Darn Tootin', 1928
Music Box, 1932 (Laurel and Hardy)
Music Box, 1989 (Lange; Mueller-Stahl)
Music for Madame, 1937 (Fontaine)
Music for Millions, 1944 (Durante; Gardner; O'Brien, M.)
Music Hall. *See* Tango Tangles, 1914
Music Hall, 1985 (Olbrychski)
Music in Darkness. *See* Musik i mörker, 1948
Music in My Heart, 1939 (Hayworth)
Music in the Air, 1934 (Swanson)
Music Is Magic, 1935 (Faye; McDaniel)
Music Lovers, 1971 (Jackson, G.)
Music Man, 1962 (Preston)
Musica, 1966 (Seyrig)
Musical Tramps. *See* His Musical Career, 1914
Musiciens du ciel, 1940 (Morgan)
Musik i mörker, 1948 (Björnstrand; Zetterling)
Musik in Salzburg, 1944 (Dagover)
Musketeers of Pig Alley, 1912 (Barrymore, L.; Carey; Gish)
Muss 'em Up, 1936 (Bond)
Mussolini and I. *See* Io e il duce, 1985
Mussolini—ultimo atto, 1974 (Fonda, H.; Steiger)
Mussorgsky, 1950 (Cherkassov)
Mustang: The Hidden Kingdom, 1994 (Ford, H.)
Mustang Country, 1977 (McCrea)
Musty Musketeers, 1954 (Three Stooges)
Musume no boken, 1958 (Kyo)
Musume no naka no musume, 1958 (Yamamura)
Musume to watashi, 1962 (Hara; Yamamura)
Musume tsuma haha, 1960 (Hara; Mori; Takamine)
Muta di Portici, 1954 (Mastroianni)
Mutations, 1974 (Pleasence)
Mute Witness, 1995 (Guinness; Yankovsky)
Muteki, 1952 (Mifune; Shimura)
Mutiny, 1952 (Lansbury)
Mutiny at Fort Sharp. *See* Escuadró de la muerte, 1966
Mutiny in Outer Space. *See* Space Master X-7, 1958
Mutiny on the Bounty, 1935 (Cagney; Crisp; Gable; Laughton; Niven)
Mutiny on the Bounty, 1962 (Brando; Harris, R.; Howard, T.)
Mutiny on the Elsinore, 1938 (Lukas)
Mutiny on the Seas. *See* Outside the 3-Mile Limit, 1940
Mutts to You, 1938 (Three Stooges)
My African Adventure. *See* Going Bananas, 1988
My American Wife, 1923 (Swanson)
My Antonia, 1995 (Robards; Saint)
My Apple. *See* Ma Pomme, 1950
My Baby, 1912 (Barrymore, L.; Gish; Pickford)
My Beautiful Laundrette, 1985 (Day-Lewis)
My Best Friend's Girl. *See* Femme de mon pote, 1982
My Best Girl, 1927 (Pickford)
My Bill, 1938 (Francis)
My Blue Heaven, 1950 (Grable)
My Blue Heaven, 1990 (Hawn; Martin, S.)
My Body, My Child, 1982 (Redgrave, V.)
My Bodyguard, 1980 (Dillon; Gordon)
My Boys Are Good Boys, 1978 (Lupino)
My Brilliant Career, 1979 (Davis, J.; Neill)
My Brother, the Outlaw. *See* My Outlaw Brother, 1951
My Brother's Keeper, 1948 (Lee, C.)
My Brother's Keeper, 1995 (Burstyn)
My Brother-in-Law Has Killed My Sister. *See* Mon Beau-frère a tué ma soeur, 1986
My Cousin Rachel, 1952 (Burton; De Havilland)
My Cousin Vinny, 1992 (Pesci)
My Darling Clementine, 1946 (Bond; Brennan; Darnell; Fonda, H.; Marsh; Mature)

My Darling Daughters' Anniversary, 1973 (Massey; Young, R.)
My Daughter and I. *See* Musume to watashi, 1962
My Daughter Joy, 1950 (Robinson, E.)
My Dear Miss Aldrich, 1937 (O'Sullivan; Pidgeon)
My Dear Secretary, 1948 (Douglas, K.)
My Dog Stupid, 1991 (Falk)
My Dream Is Yours, 1949 (Day; Menjou)
My Enemy the Sea. *See* Taiheiyo hitoribocchi, 1963
My Fair Lady, 1964 (Harrison; Hepburn, A.)
My Family, 1995 (Olmos; Steenburgen)
My Father, My Son, 1988 (Malden)
My Father, the Hero, 1993 (Depardieu; Thompson)
My Father's House, 1975 (Preston; Robertson)
My Favorite Blonde, 1942 (Carroll; Crosby; Hope)
My Favorite Brunette, 1947 (Crosby; Hope; Ladd; Lamour; Lorre)
My Favorite Spy, 1942 (Lloyd; Wyman)
My Favorite Spy, 1951 (Hope; Lamarr)
My Favorite Wife, 1940 (Dunne; Grant, C.; Scott, R.)
My Favorite Year, 1982 (O'Toole)
My First 40 Years. *See* I miei primi 40 anni, 1987
My First Love. *See* Mon Premier Amour, 1978
My Foolish Heart, 1949 (Andrews, D.; Hayward)
My Forbidden Past, 1951 (Douglas, Melvyn; Gardner; Mitchum)
My Friend Flicka, 1943 (McDowall)
My Friend Irma, 1949 (Lewis, Jerry; Martin, D.)
My Friend Irma Goes West, 1950 (Lewis, Jerry; Martin, D.)
My Friend Max. *See* Mon Ami Max, 1994
My Friend Nicholas, 1961 (Brynner)
My Friends. *See* Amici miei, 1975
My Gal Sal, 1942 (Hayworth; Mature)
My Geisha, 1962 (MacLaine; Montand; Robinson, E.)
My General. *See* Mi General, 1986
My Girl, 1991 (Curtis, J.)
My Girl 2, 1994 (Curtis, J.)
My Handsome My Beautiful. *See* Bello mia belleza mia, 1982
My Hero, 1912 (Barrymore, L.; Carey)
My Heroes Have Always Been Cowboys, 1991 (Rooney)
My Hobo. *See* Burari burabura monogatari, 1962
My Home, My Prison, 1992 (Sheen)
My Husband, His Mistress and I. *See* Rivale, 1974
My Irish Molly, 1939 (O'Hara)
My Kidnapper, My Love, 1980 (Rooney)
My Kingdom for a Cook, 1943 (Coburn, C.)
My Lady of Whims, 1926 (Bow)
My Lady's Lips, 1925 (Bow; Powell, W.)
My Lady's Past, 1929 (Brown)
My Left Foot, 1989 (Cusack; Day-Lewis)
My Life, 1993 (Keaton, M.)
My Life Is Yours. *See* People vs. Dr. Kildare, 1941
My Life to Live. *See* **Vivre sa vie**, 1962
My Life with Caroline, 1941 (Colman)
My Little Baby, 1916 (Bertini)
My Little Chickadee, 1940 (Fields, W. C.; West)
My Little Field. *See* Polyushko-pole, 1956
My Little Girl, 1986 (Jones, James Earl; Page)
My Little Pony, 1986 (DeVito)
My Love Came Back, 1940 (De Havilland; Wyman)
My Love Has Been Burning. *See* Waga koi wa moenu, 1949
My Love Is Like a Rose. *See* Min kära är en ros, 1963
My Love Letters. *See* Love Letters, 1983
My Lover, My Son, 1970 (Schneider)
My Lover's Mistake. *See* Ghaltit Habibi, 1957
My Lucky Star, 1938 (Henie)
My Lucky Stars, 1985 (Chan)
My Man and I, 1952 (Trevor; Winters)
My Man Godfrey, 1936 (Lombard; Powell, W.; Wyman)
My Man Godfrey, 1957 (Niven)
My Marriage, 1936 (Trevor)
My Mother, My Daughter, 1981 (Winters)
My Name Is Bill W., 1989 (Garner; Woods)
My Name Is Nobody. *See* Mio nome e nessuno, 1974

My Name Is Puck. *See* Puck heter jag, 1951
My Name Is Victor. *See* Je m'appelle Victor, 1993
My New Partner. *See* Ripoux, 1984
My New Partner II. *See* Ripoux contre ripoux, 1990
My, nizhepodpisavshiesya ..., 1980 (Yankovsky)
My Official Wife, 1914 (Valentino)
My Old Man, 1979 (Oates)
My Old Man's Place, 1971 (Kennedy)
My Only Love. *See* Hubbi el Wahid, 1960
My Outlaw Brother, 1951 (Preston; Rooney)
My Own Pal, 1926 (Mix)
My Own Private Idaho, 1991 (Reeves)
My Own True Love, 1948 (Douglas, Melvyn)
My Pal Gus, 1952 (Widmark)
My Pal, the King, 1932 (Mix; Rooney)
My Pal Trigger, 1946 (Rogers, R.)
My Past, 1931 (Blondell)
My People Are Not Yours. *See* Mitt folk är icke ditt, 1944
My Perfect Season. *See* Ma Saison Préférée, 1993
My Reputation, 1946 (Stanwyck)
My Science Project, 1985 (Hopper)
My Seven Little Sins. *See* J'avais sept filles, 1955
My Sin, 1930 (March)
My Sister and I, 1948 (Dors)
My Sister and I. *See* Min syster och jag, 1950
My Sister Eileen, 1942 (Russcll, R.; Three Stooges)
My Sister Eileen, 1955 (Leigh, Janet; Lemmon)
My Sister, My Love. *See* Mafu Cage, 1978
My Sister, My Love. *See* Syskonbädd 1782, 1965
My Six Convicts, 1952 (Bronson)
My Six Loves, 1963 (Reynolds, D.; Robertson)
My Son, 1925 (Nazimova)
My Son. *See* Moi syn, 1928
My Son A-Chen, 1948 (Lee, B.)
My Son Is Guilty, 1939 (Carey; Ford, G.)
My Son John, 1952 (Walker)
My Son, My Son!, 1940 (Carroll)
My Son, the Hero. *See* Hermanos del hierro, 1963
My Son, The Vampire. *See* Old Mother Riley Meets the Vampire, 1952
My Stars, 1926 (Arbuckle)
My Stepmother Is an Alien, 1988 (Basinger; Lewis, Juliette)
My Stupid Brother. *See* Niisan no baka, 1932
My Summer Story. *See* It Runs in the Family, 1994
My Teenage Daughter, 1956 (Neagle)
My Tender Loving Beast. *See* Moi laskovyi i nezhnyi zver, 1978
My True Story, 1951 (Rooney)
My 20th Century. *See* Az en XX. Szazadom, 1989
My Uncle. *See* Mon Oncle, 1958
My Uncle, Mr. Hulot. *See* Mon Oncle, 1958
My Valet, 1915 (Normand)
My Weakness, 1933 (Ayres; Langdon)
My Wicked, Wicked Ways ... The Legend of Errol Flynn, 1985 (Hershey)
My Widow and I. *See* Lo sbaglio di essere vivo, 1945
My Wife's Best Friend, 1952 (Baxter)
My Wife's Enemy. *See* Nemico di mia moglie, 1959
My Wife's Family, 1941 (Greenwood)
My Wife's Husband. *See* Cuisine au beurre, 1963
My Wife's Lodger, 1952 (Dors)
My Wife's Relation, 1922 (Keaton, B.)
My Wonderful Yellow Car. *See* Fukeyo harukaze, 1953
Myohoin Kanpachi, 1939 (Shimura)
Myoreki meikenshi, 1934 (Hasegawa)
Myra Breckenridge, 1970 (Carradine; Huston, J.; Welch; West)
Myriad Homes. *See* Countless Families, 1953
Myrt and Marge, 1933 (Three Stooges)
Mystère, 1949 (Rosay)
Mystère de la chambre jaune, 1948 (Modot; Reggiani)
Mystère Imberger, 1934 (Modot)
Mystère Saint-Val, 1945 (Fernandel)
Mystères de Paris, 1922 (Fresnay; Modot)
Mysteries of India. *See* Indische Grabmal, 1921

Mysteries of New York. *See* Reggie Mixes In, 1916
Mysteries of the Novgorod Fair. *See* Taina niegorodskoi yamarki, 1915
Mysterious Avenger, 1936 (Rogers, R.)
Mysterious Dr. Fu Manchu, 1929 (Arthur)
Mysterious House of Dr. C, 1976 (Terry-Thomas)
Mysterious Island, 1929 (Barrymore, L.)
Mysterious Island, 1961 (Lom; Greenwood)
Mysterious Island of Captain Nemo. *See* Isola misteriosa e il capitano Nemo, 1973
Mysterious Lady, 1928 (Garbo)
Mysterious Mr. Moto, 1938 (Lorre)
Mysterious Mr. Wong, 1935 (Lugosi)
Mysterious Shot, 1914 (Crisp)
Mystery Castle in the Carpathians. *See* Tajemny hrad v Karpatech, 1981
Mystery Mountain, 1934 (Autry)
Mystery of Blood. *See* Tajemství krve, 1953
Mystery of Edwin Drood, 1935 (Rains)
Mystery of Henry Moore, 1985 (Nelligan)
Mystery of Monster Island. *See* Misterio en la isla de los monstruos, 1980
Mystery of Mr. Wong, 1939 (Karloff)
Mystery of Mr. X, 1934 (Montgomery)
Mystery of Oberwald. *See* Mistero di Oberwald, 1981
Mystery of the Leaping Fish, 1916 (Fairbanks)
Mystery of the Marie Celeste. *See* Phantom Ship, 1935
Mystery of the Wax Museum, 1933 (Wray)
Mystery of Wentworth Castle. *See* Doomed to Die, 1940
Mystery Street, 1950 (Lanchester)
Mystic Pizza, 1988 (Roberts, J.)
Myth of Fingerprints, 1996 (Scheider)
N.P., 1971 (Papas; Thulin)
Na viershina slavy, 1916 (Mozhukin)
Nach dem Gesetz, 1919 (Nielsen)
Nach dem Sturm, 1950 (Schell, Maria)
Nach zwanzig Jahren, 1918 (Jannings)
Nacht auf Goldenhall, 1920 (Veidt)
Nacht der Entscheidung, 1931 (Veidt)
Nacht der Entscheidung, 1938 (Negri)
Nacht der grossen Liebe, 1933 (Fröhlich)
Nacht der Königin Isabeau, 1920 (Kortner)
Nacht der Medici, 1922 (Krauss)
Nacht der Regisseure, 1995 (Schygulla)
Nacht der Verwandlung, 1935 (Fröhlich)
Nacht des Grauens, 1916 (Krauss)
Nacht des Schreckens, 1929 (Kortner)
Nächte des Grauens, 1916 (Jannings)
Nächte von Port Said, 1931 (Homolka)
Nachtfalter, 1910 (Nielsen)
Nachtgestalten, 1919 (Veidt; Wegener)
Nachtkolonne, 1931 (Homolka)
Nacido para la música, 1959 (Rey)
Nackt unter Wölfen, 1963 (Mueller-Stahl)
Nadaan, 1951 (Anand)
Nadi Theke Sagare, 1978 (Chatterjee)
Nadie dijo nada, 1970 (Villagra)
Nadie Hablara de Nosotras Cuando Hayamos Muerto, 1995 (Abril)
Nadine, 1987 (Basinger; Bridges)
Nadiya Ke Paar, 1948 (Kumar)
Nagana, 1933 (Douglas, Melvyn)
Nagare no fu: Doran, Yoake, 1974 (Tsukasa)
Nagareru, 1956 (Takamine; Tanaka; Yamada)
Nagasaki no uta wa wasureji, 1952 (Kyo)
Nagasaki no yuro, 1955 (Hasegawa)
Nagaya Shinshiroku, 1947 (Ryu)
Nagebushi Yasuke: Edo no maki, 1931 (Hasegawa)
Nagebushi Yasuke: Michinoku no maki, 1931 (Hasegawa)
Nagrody i odznaczenia, 1974 (Łomnicki)
Nahr el Hub, 1960 (Sharif)
Nails, 1992 (Hopper)
Nairobi Affair, 1980 (Heston)
Naïs, 1945 (Fernandel)
Naissance de l'amour, 1993 (Léaud)

Naissance du jour, 1981 (Sanda)
Nakayoshi-ondo: Nippon ichi dayo, 1962 (Hasegawa; Kyo)
Naked Alibi, 1954 (Grahame; Hayden)
Naked among the Wolves. *See* Nackt unter Wölfen, 1963
Naked and the Dead, 1958 (Massey; Robertson)
Naked City, 1948 (Fitzgerald)
Naked Dawn, 1955 (Kennedy)
Naked Edge, 1961 (Constantine; Cushing; Kerr)
Naked Eye, 1957 (Massey)
Naked Face, 1984 (Gould; Steiger)
Naked Gun 33 1/3: The Final Insult, 1994 (Gould; Jones, James Earl; Welch)
Naked Heart. *See* Marie Chapdelaine, 1950
Naked in New York, 1994 (Curtis, T.; Goldberg; Turner, K.)
Naked Jungle, 1953 (Heston)
Naked Lovers. *See* Naked Zoo, 1971
Naked Lunch, 1991 (Davis, J.; Scheider)
Naked Maja. *See* Maja desnuda, 1958
Naked Night. *See* **Gycklarnas afton**, 1953
Naked Passion. *See* Pasión desnuda, 1953
Naked Prey, 1966 (Wilde)
Naked Runner, 1967 (Sidney)
Naked Spur, 1953 (Leigh, Janet; Ryan, R.; Stewart)
Naked Street, 1955 (Bancroft; Quinn; Van Cleef)
Naked Tango, 1990 (Rey)
Naked Target. *See* Gusanos no Llevan Bufanda, 1991
Naked Terror, 1961 (Price)
Naked Truth, 1958 (Sellers; Terry-Thomas)
Naked under Leather. *See* Girl on a Motorcycle, 1968
Naked Zoo, 1971 (Hayworth)
Nakia, 1974 (Kennedy)
Namak halal, 1982 (Patil)
Name of the Rose, 1986 (Connery)
Namida no hanamichi, 1956 (Yamada)
Namidao Shishi no tategami no, 1962 (Yamamura)
Namkeen, 1982 (Azmi)
Namonaku mazushiku utsukushiku, 1961 (Takamine)
Nampu no oka, 1937 (Takamine)
Namuna, 1949 (Anand)
Nana, 1926 (Krauss)
Nana, 1934 (Ball)
Nana, 1954 (Boyer)
Nanas, 1984 (Binoche)
Nanatsu no kao no Ginji, 1955 (Hasegawa; Kagawa)
Nanatsu no umi: Teiso-hen, 1932 (Takamine)
Nancy Comes Home, 1918 (Gilbert)
Nancy Goes to Rio, 1950 (Calhern; Miranda)
Nancy Steele Is Missing, 1937 (Carradine; Lorre; McLaglen)
Nandita, 1976 (Chatterjee)
Nangoku satsuma-uta, 1937 (Yamada)
Naniwa ereji, 1936 (Shimura; Tanaka; Yamada)
Naniwa hina, 1930 (Hasegawa)
Naniwa ni koi no monogatari, 1959 (Tanaka)
Nankai no joka, 1950 (Yamamura)
Nankyoku monogatari, 1983 (Okada; Yamamura)
Nanny, 1965 (Davis, B.)
Nanny Dear. *See* Tata Mia, 1986
Nanou, 1986 (Day-Lewis)
Nanu, sie kennen Korff noch nicht?, 1938 (Rasp)
Naples au baiser de feu, 1928 (Modot)
Naples au baiser de feu, 1937 (Dalio)
Naples Connection. *See* Camorra, 1986
Napló apamanak, anyammnak, 1990 (Nowicki)
Napló gyermekeimnek, 1982 (Nowicki)
Napló szerelmeimnek, 1987 (Nowicki)
Napoleon, 1954 (Welles)
Napoleon and Samantha, 1972 (Douglas, Michael; Foster)
Napoleon auf St. Helena, 1929 (Krauss)
Napoléon, 1927 (Artaud)
Napoléon, 1954 (Cervi; Darrieux; Gabin; Gélin; Marais; Montand; Presle; Reggiani; Schell, Maria)
Napoléon, 1955 (Brasseur; Morgan)

Napoléon II, l'aiglon, 1961 (Cassel)
Napoleons kleiner Brüder. *See* So sind die Männer, 1922
Napoleon's Little Brother. *See* So sind die Männer, 1922
Naprawde wczoraj, 1963 (Tyszkiewicz)
Nar Kärleken kom till byn, 1950 (Thulin)
Nära livet, 1958 (Andersson, B.; Dahlbeck; Josephson; Thulin; Von Sydow)
Narayamabushi-ko, 1958 (Tanaka)
Narazumono, 1956 (Mifune)
Nark. *See* Balance, 1982
Narrow Corner, 1933 (Bellamy)
Narrow Margin, 1990 (Hackman)
Narrow Road, 1912 (Pickford)
Narrow Trail, 1917 (Hart)
Naruto hicho, 1957 (Hasegawa)
Nashville, 1975 (Chaplin, G.; Christie; Gould)
Nasihat, 1986 (Azmi)
Nasilje na trgu, 1961 (Andersson, B.; Crawford, B.)
Nasty Habits, 1976 (Evans; Jackson, G.; Mercouri; Page; Wallach)
Naszdal, 1918 (Lugosi)
Nat Pinkerton, 1921 (Lugosi)
Natale al campo 119, 1948 (Fabrizi)
Natale che quasi non fu, 1966 (Brazzi)
Natale in Casa di Appuntamento, 1976 (Borgnine)
Natasha Rostova, 1915 (Mozhukin)
Nate and Hayes, 1983 (Jones, T.)
Nathalie, 1957 (Piccoli)
Nathalie Granger, 1972 (Depardieu; Moreau)
Nathan der Weise, 1922 (Krauss)
National Health, 1973 (Hoskins)
National Lampoon's Animal House, 1978 (Bacon; Belushi; Sutherland)
National Lampoon's Christmas Vacation, 1989 (Lewis, Juliette)
National Lampoon's Loaded Weapon 1, 1993 (Goldberg; Jackson, S.; Willis)
National Lampoon's Movie Madness, 1982 (Widmark)
National Lampoon's Vacation, 1983 (Candy)
National Velvet, 1944 (Crisp; Lansbury; Rooney; Taylor, E.)
Native Drums. *See* Tam Tam Mayumba, 1955
Native Earth, 1946 (Finch)
Native Land, 1942 (Robeson)
Native Son, 1986 (Dillon; Page)
Natsumaturi sando-gasa, 1951 (Yamada)
Natt ihamn, 1943 (Björnstrand)
Natt på Glimmingehus, 1954 (Andersson, B.)
Nattbarn, 1956 (Andersson, H.)
Natten ljus, 1957 (Björnstrand)
Nattlek, 1966 (Thulin; Zetterling)
Nattvardsgästerna, 1963 (Björnstrand; Thulin; Von Sydow)
Natun Diner Alo, 1972 (Chatterjee)
Natural, 1984 (Basinger; Close; Duvall; Hershey; Redford)
Natural Born Killers, 1994 (Jones, T.; Lewis, Juliette)
Natural Born Salesman. *See* Earthworm Tractors, 1936
Natural Enemies, 1979 (Ferrer)
Nature retrouvée, 1968 (Gélin)
Nau Do Gyarah, 1957 (Anand)
Naufrageurs, 1959 (Vanel)
Naught Flirt, 1931 (Loy)
Naughty Arlette. *See* Romantic Age, 1949
Naughty but Nice, 1927 (Young, L.)
Naughty but Nice, 1939 (Powell, D.; Reagan)
Naughty Marietta, 1935 (Eddy; Lanchester; MacDonald)
Naughty Nineties, 1945 (Abbott and Costello)
Nauka Dubi. *See* Milan, 1946
Nauka Dubi, 1979 (Chatterjee)
Navajo Joe. *See* Dollaro a testa, 1967
Navigator, 1924 (Crisp; Keaton, B.)
Navire des hommes perdus. *See* Schiff der verlorenen Menschen, 1929
Navire Night, 1978 (Sanda)
Navy Blue and Gold, 1937 (Barrymore, L.; Stewart; Young, R.)
Navy Blue Days, 1925 (Laurel and Hardy)
Navy Comes Through, 1942 (Cooper)
Navy Gravy, 1925 (Laurel and Hardy)
Navy Secrets, 1939 (Wray)

Navy Steps Out. *See* Girl, a Guy, and a Gob, 1941
Navy Wife. *See* Beauty's Daughter, 1935
Navy Wife, 1936 (Trevor)
Navy Wife, 1956 (Bennett)
Naxalitees, 1980 (Patil)
Naya Daur, 1957 (Kumar)
Nayamashiki koro, 1926 (Tanaka)
Naze kanojo wa sonatta ka, 1956 (Kagawa)
Nazi Agent, 1942 (Veidt)
Nazi Hunter: The Beate Klarsfield Story, 1986 (Page)
Nazrana, 1987 (Patil)
Ne le criez pas sur les toits, 1942 (Fernandel)
Ne pleure pas, 1977 (Vanel)
Ne réveillez pas un flic qui dort, 1988 (Delon; Reggiani)
Né pour la musique. *See* Nacido para la música, 1959
Nea, 1976 (Presle)
Neapolitan Carousel. *See* Carosella napolitano, 1953
Neapolitan Thriller. *See* Giallo napoletano, 1979
Near Dublin, 1924 (Laurel and Hardy)
Near to Earth, 1913 (Barrymore, L.)
Nearly a King, 1916 (Barrymore, J.; Menjou)
Nearly Married, 1917 (Barthelmess)
'Neath the Arizona Skies, 1934 (Wayne)
Nebraskan, 1953 (Van Cleef)
Necesito dinero, 1951 (Infante)
Necessary Love. *See* Amour necessario, 1991
Necessary Parties, 1987 (Arkin)
Neck and Neck, 1931 (Brennan)
Necklace, 1909 (Pickford)
Necromancy, 1972 (Welles)
Ned McCobb's Daughter, 1929 (Lombard)
Nederland in 7 Lessen, 1948 (Hepburn, A.)
Needful Things, 1993 (Harris, E.; Von Sydow)
Neel Kamal, 1947 (Kumar)
Nefertite—Regina del Nilo, 1961 (Price)
Negatives, 1968 (Jackson, G.)
Neige était sale, 1953 (Gélin)
Neighbor, 1993 (Steiger)
Neighbors, 1920 (Keaton, B.)
Neighbors, 1981 (Belushi)
Neighbor's Wife and Mine. *See* Madamu to nyobo, 1931
Neighbour Downstairs. *See* Ghost Downstairs, 1982
Neigungsehe. *See* Familie Buchholz, 1944
Neither Blood Nor Sand. *See* Ni sangre ni arena, 1941
Neither by Day nor Night, 1973 (Robinson, E.)
Neko to shozo to futari no onna, 1956 (Kagawa; Yamada)
Nekri Politeia, 1951 (Papas)
Nel giardino delle rose. *See* Prima di Natale, 1990
Nel gorgo della vita. *See* Lacrimae rerum, 1917
Nel segno di Roma, 1959 (Cervi)
Nelken in Aspik, 1976 (Mueller-Stahl)
Nell, 1994 (Foster; Neeson)
Nell Gwyn, 1935 (Neagle)
Nella città l'inferno, 1958 (Magnani; Masina; Sordi)
Nella fornace, 1915 (Bertini)
Nella stretta morsa del ragno, 1971 (Kinski)
Nell'anno del signore, 1969 (Cardinale; Magnani)
Nelly la gigolette, 1914 (Bertini)
Nelly's Version, 1983 (York)
Nelson Affair. *See* Bequest to the Nation, 1973
N'embrassez pas votre bonne, 1909 (Linder)
N'embrassez pas votre bonne, 1914 (Linder)
Nemico di mia moglie, 1959 (Mastroianni)
Nemo. *See* Dream One, 1984
Nemrod et Compagnie, 1911 (Modot)
Nemuri Kyoshiro burai hikae: Majin jigoku, 1958 (Yamada)
Nene, 1924 (Modot)
Neni Sirotek Jako Sirotek, 1986 (Brodský)
Neokonchennaya povest, 1955 (Bondarchuk)
Neon Bible, 1994 (Rowlands)
Neon Ceiling, 1971 (Grant, L.)

Neppu, 1943 (Hara)
Neptune Disaster. *See* Neptune Factor, 1973
Neptune Factor, 1973 (Borgnine; Pidgeon)
Neptune's Daughter, 1949 (Williams, E.)
Nero Wolfe, 1979 (Baxter)
Nero's Mistress. *See* Mio figlio Nerone, 1956
Nero's Weekend. *See* Mio figlio Nerone, 1956
Nerone a Messalina, 1953 (Cervi)
Nertsery Rhymes, 1933 (Three Stooges)
Nerve and Gasoline, 1916 (Laurel and Hardy)
Nessa no byakuran, 1951 (Yamamura)
Nessa no chikai, 1940 (Hasegawa)
Nessuno torna indietro, 1943 (Cervi)
Nest of Gentlefolk. *See* Dvoryanskoye gnezdo, 1969
Nesting. *See* Phobia, 1979
Nesting, 1981 (Grahame)
Nestor's Last Trip. *See* Nestore l'Ultima Corsa, 1994
Nestore l'Ultima Corsa, 1994 (Sordi)
Net. *See* Jaal, 1952
Netchaïev est de retour, 1990 (Montand)
Netchaïev Is Back. *See* Netchaïev est de retour, 1990
Netsuaisha, 1961 (Yamamura)
Network, 1976 (Dunaway; Duvall; Finch; Holden)
Netz, 1975 (Kinski)
Neues vom Hexer, 1965 (Kinski)
Neutron Bomb Incident. *See* Teheran Incident, 1979
Nevada, 1927 (Constantine; Powell, W.)
Nevada, 1944 (Mitchum)
Nevada City, 1941 (Rogers, R.)
Nevada Kid. *See* Per una bara piena di dollari, 1970
Nevada Smith, 1966 (Kennedy; Landau; Malden; McQueen)
Nevadan, 1950 (Malone; Scott, R.)
Never a Dull Moment, 1950 (Dunne; MacMurray; Wood)
Never a Dull Moment, 1968 (Robinson, E.)
Never Again!, 1910 (Pickford)
Never Again, 1915 (Mix)
Never Again, 1916 (Laurel and Hardy)
Never Cry Devil. *See* Night Visitor, 1989
Never Fear, 1950 (Lupino)
Never Give a Sucker an Even Break, 1941 (Fields, W. C.; Dumont)
Never Give an Inch. *See* Sometimes a Great Notion, 1971
Never Let Go, 1961 (Sellers)
Never Let Me Go, 1953 (Gable; Tierney)
Never Love a Stranger, 1957 (McQueen)
Never on Sunday. *See* Pote tin kryiaki, 1960
Never on Tuesday, 1988 (Cage)
Never Say Die, 1939 (Hope)
Never Say Goodbye, 1946 (Flynn; McDaniel)
Never Say Goodbye, 1956 (Eastwood; Hudson; Sanders)
Never Say Never Again, 1983 (Basinger; Brandauer; Connery; Von Sydow)
Never So Few, 1959 (Bronson; Henreid; Lollobrigida; McQueen; Sidney)
Never Steal Anything Small, 1959 (Cagney)
Never Strike a Woman with a Flower. *See* Spadla s měsíce, 1966
Never Talk to Strangers, 1995 (Banderas; Stanton)
Never the Twain Shall Meet, 1925 (Karloff)
Never the Twain Shall Meet, 1931 (Howard, L.)
Never Too Late, 1965 (O'Sullivan)
Never Too Old, 1926 (Laurel and Hardy)
Never Touched Me, 1919 (Lloyd)
Never Trouble Trouble, 1931 (Oberon)
Never Trust an Honest Thief, 1979 (Welles)
Never Wave at a WAC, 1952 (Russell, R.)
Never Weaken, 1921 (Lloyd)
Neveu de Beethoven, 1985 (Baye)
Neveu de Rameau, 1968 (Fresnay)
Nevtelen vàr, 1920 (Lukas)
New Adventures of Get-Rich-Quick Wallingford, 1931 (Durante)
New Adventures of J. Rufus Wallingford, 1915 (Laurel and Hardy)
New Age, 1994 (Davis, J.; Jackson, S.)
New Age of Fools. *See* Shin baka jidai, 1946
New Butler, 1915 (Laurel and Hardy)

New Centurions, 1972 (Scott, G.)
New Commandment, 1925 (Sweet)
New Deal. *See* Looking Forward, 1933
New Deal Money, 1934 (Temple)
New Earth. *See* Atarashiki tsuchi, 1937
New Exploits of Elaine, 1915 (White)
New Faces of 1937, 1937 (Miller)
New Fist of Fury. *See* Xin Ching-Wu Men, 1976
New Frontier, 1935 (Wayne)
New Frontier, 1939 (Jones, Jennifer; Wayne)
New House. *See* Novyi dom, 1947
New Interns, 1964 (Segal)
New Jack City, 1991 (Snipes)
New Janitor, 1914 (Chaplin, C.)
New Jersey Drive, 1995 (Lee, S.)
New Kind of Love, 1963 (Chevalier; Newman; Ritter; Woodward)
New Land. *See* Nybyggarna, 1973
New Land. *See* Terra Nova, 1991
New Leaf, 1971 (Matthau)
New Life. *See* Suicide's Wife, 1979
New Life, 1988 (Ann-Margret)
New Lot, 1943 (Ustinov)
New Magdalene, 1910 (White)
New Maverick, 1978 (Garner)
New Mexico, 1951 (Ayres)
New Monsters. *See* I nuovi mostri, 1977
New Moon, 1919 (Talmadge)
New Moon, 1930 (Menjou)
New Moon, 1940 (Eddy; Keaton, B.; MacDonald)
New Morals for Old, 1932 (Loy; Young, R.)
New Movietone Follies of 1930. *See* Fox Movietone Follies of 1930, 1930
New Neighbor, 1912 (Normand)
New Order at Sjögårda. *See* Nyordning på Sjögårda, 1944
New Orleans, 1947 (Winters)
New Orleans Adventure. *See* Adventures of Captain Fabian, 1951
New Teacher, 1915 (Beery)
New Teacher, 1941 (Cushing)
New Toys, 1925 (Barthelmess; Webb)
New Typist, 1912-13 (White)
New Way. *See* Shindo: Akemi no make, Ryota no maki, 1936
New World. *See* Nuit de Varennes, 1981
New Year's Eve, 1929 (Astor)
New York, 1927 (Powell, W.)
New York. *See* Hallelujah, I'm a Bum, 1933
New York City—The Most, 1968 (Wallach)
New York Confidential, 1954 (Bancroft; Crawford, B.)
New York Crossing, 1996 (Giannini)
New York expresz kabel, 1921 (Lukas)
New York Hat, 1912 (Barrymore, L.; Gish; Marsh; Pickford)
New York, New York, 1977 (De Niro; Minnelli)
New York Nights, 1929 (Harlow; Jolson; Talmadge)
New York Nights, 1984 (Dafoe)
New York Stories, 1989 (Allen; Farrow; Giannini; Nolte)
New York Town, 1941 (MacMurray; Preston)
Newer Woman, 1914 (Crisp)
Newlyweds, 1910 (Pickford)
News at Eleven, 1986 (Sheen)
Newsboys' Home, 1938 (Cooper)
Newsies, 1992 (Ann-Margret; Duvall)
Next Aisle Over, 1919 (Lloyd)
Next Corner, 1924 (Chaney)
Next Door, 1994 (Woods)
Next Man, 1976 (Connery)
Next of Kin, 1942 (Hawkins)
Next of Kin. *See* Lien de Parenté, 1986
Next of Kin, 1989 (Neeson)
Next Stop, Greenwich Village, 1976 (Walken; Winters)
Next Summer. *See* Été prochain, 1985
Next Time I Marry, 1938 (Ball)
Next Time We Love, 1936 (McDaniel; Milland; Stewart; Sullavan)
Next Year If All Goes Well. *See* Année prochaine si tout va bien, 1981

Nez de cuir, 1952 (Marais)
Nezumi-kozo Jirokichi, 1932 (Hasegawa; Takamine)
Nezumi-kozo Kirokichi: Kaiketsu-hen, 1932 (Hasegawa)
Nezumi-kozo shinobikomi-hikae, 1956 (Hasegawa; Kagawa)
Nezumi-kozo shinobikomi-hikae: Ne-no-koku sanjo, 1957 (Hasegawa)
Ni nado kruvi, 1917 (Mozhukin)
Ni sangre ni arena, 1941 (Armendáriz; Cantinflas)
Niagara, 1953 (Cotten; Monroe)
Niagara Falls, 1932 (Arbuckle)
Nibelungen, 1966 (Lom)
Nibelungen II, 1967 (Lom)
Nice and Friendly, 1922 (Chaplin, C.)
Nice Girl?, 1941 (Brennan; Durbin)
Nice Guys Finish Last. *See* Footsteps, 1972
Nice Little Bank that Should Be Robbed, 1958 (Rooney)
Nicherin to Moko daishurai, 1958 (Hasegawa)
Nicholas and Alexandra, 1971 (Hawkins; Olivier; Redgrave, M.)
Nicht lange täuschte mich das Glück, 1917 (Negri)
Nick Carter, Master Detective, 1939 (Pidgeon)
Nick Carter casse tout. *See* Nick Carter va tout casser, 1964
Nick Carter et le trefle rouge, 1965 (Constantine)
Nick Carter va tout casser, 1964 (Constantine)
Nick of Time, 1995 (Depp; Walken)
Nick of Time Baby, 1916 (Swanson)
Nick the Sting. *See* I Amici di Nick Nezard, 1976
Nickcl Hoppcr, 1926 (Karloff; Laurcl and Hardy; Normand)
Nickel Queen, 1970 (Withers)
Nickelodeon, 1976 (Reynolds, B.)
Nico. *See* Above the Law, 1988
Nicole, 1972 (Caron)
Nid d'espions. *See* Mademoiselle Docteur, 1936
Nido de viudas. *See* Widow's Nest, 1977
Nie er, 1959 (Zhao Dan)
Niet! *See* Habrichka el hashemersh, 1972
Niewdzieczno is ic, 1979 (Tyszkiewicz)
Niewinni czarodzieje, 1960 (Łomnicki)
Niewolnica Zmyslow, 1914 (Negri)
Nigeyuku Kodenji, 1930 (Yamada)
Night. *See* **Notte**, 1961
Night Affair. *See* Désordre et la nuit, 1958
Night after Night, 1932 (Calhern; Raft; West)
Night Ambush. *See* Ill Met by Moonlight, 1957
Night and Day, 1946 (Grant, C.; Malone; Wyman)
Night and the City, 1950 (Kendall; Lom; Tierney; Widmark; Withers)
Night and the City, 1992 (De Niro; Lange; Wallach)
Night and the Moment, 1994 (Dafoe; Olin; Richardson, M.)
Night Angel, 1930 (March)
Night at Glimminge Castle. *See* Natt på Glimmingehus, 1954
Night at the Biltmore Bowl, 1935 (Grable)
Night at the Opera, 1935 (Dumont; Marx Brothers)
Night Before, 1988 (Reeves)
Night Boat to Dublin, 1945 (Lom)
Night Butterflies. *See* Yoruno cho, 1957
Night Caller. *See* Peur sur la ville, 1975
Night Club Lady, 1932 (Menjou)
Night Club Scandal, 1937 (Barrymore, J.)
Night Court, 1932 (Huston, W.; Raft)
Night Creature, 1977 (Pleasence)
Night Creatures. *See* Captain Clegg, 1962
Night Crossing, 1982 (Hurt, J.)
Night Digger. *See* Road Builder, 1971
Night Falls on Manhattan, 1996 (Dreyfuss; García; Olin)
Night Fighters, 1960 (Mitchum)
Night Fighters. *See* Terrible Beauty, 1960
Night Flight, 1933 (Barrymore, J.; Barrymore, L.; Gable; Loy; Montgomery)
Night Flight. *See* Vol de nuit, 1978
Night Flight from Moscow. *See* Serpent, 1973
Night Freight, 1955 (Sanders)
Night Full of Rain. *See* End of the World in Our Usual Bed in a Night Full of Rain, 1977
Night Gallery, 1969 (Crawford, J.; Jaffe; McDowall)

Nine Hours to Rama, 1962 (Ferrer)
Nine Lives Are Not Enough, 1941 (Reagan)
Nine Months. *See* Kilenc hónap, 1976
Nine Months, 1995 (Grant, H.; Williams, R.)
Nine to Five, 1980 (Fonda, J.; Hayden)
Ninety-Two in the Shade, 1975 (Meredith; Oates; Stanton)
Ningen gyorai shutsugeki su, 1956 (Mori)
Ningen no joken, 1959 (Yamamura)
Ningen no joken III, 1961 (Ryu; Takamine)
Ningen no kabe, 1959 (Kagawa)
Ningen no shomei, 1977 (Crawford, B.; Mifune)
Ningyo bushi, 1928 (Hasegawa)
Ningyo Girai, 1982 (Okada)
Nini Tirabuscio, la donna che incento la mossa, 1970 (Vitti)
Ninja Thunderbolt, 1985 (Chan)
Ninjo misui, 1957 (Hasegawa)
Ninjutsu. *See* Soryu hiken, 1958
Ninjutsu Sarutobi Sasuke, 1976 (Shimura)
Nino terno-secco. *See* Ternosecco, 1986
Nino y la niebla, 1953 (Del Rio)
Ninotchka, 1939 (Douglas, Melvyn; Garbo; Lugosi)
Niño y el muro, 1964 (Gélin)
Nippon-kai dai-kaisen, 1969 (Mifune; Tsukasa)
Nippon niju-roku seijin, 1931 (Yamada)
Nippon no ichiban nagai hi, 1967 (Mifune; Ryu; Shimura; Yamamura)
Nippon tanjo, 1959 (Kagawa; Mifune; Tsukasa)
Nippon yaburezu, 1954 (Yamamura)
Nirala, 1950 (Anand)
Nishant, 1975 (Azmi; Patil)
Nishi Kanya, 1973 (Chatterjee)
Nishi Mrigaya, 1975 (Chatterjee)
Nishi no taisho higashi no taisho, 1964 (Tsukasa)
Nishijin no shimai, 1952 (Tanaka)
Nisshoku no natsu, 1956 (Tsukasa; Yamamura)
Nitchevo, 1926 (Vanel)
Nitchevo, 1936 (Mozhukin)
Nitwits, 1935 (Grable)
Nixon, 1995 (Harris, E.; Hopkins, A.; Hoskins; Steenburgen; Woods)
Nju, 1924 (Bergner; Jannings; Veidt)
No Blade of Grass, 1970 (Wilde)
No Census, No Feelings, 1940 (Three Stooges)
No Country for Old Men, 1981 (Cusack)
No Deposit, No Return, 1976 (Niven)
No desearás la mujer de tu hijo, 1949 (Infante)
No Diamonds for Ursula. *See* I diamanti che nessuno voleva rubare, 1968
No Dough, Boys, 1944 (Three Stooges)
No Down Payment, 1957 (Woodward)
No Drums, No Bugles, 1971 (Sheen)
No encontre rosas para mi madre, 1972 (Darrieux)
No es nada mama, solo un juego, 1973 (Valli)
No Escape. *See* I Escaped from the Gestapo, 1943
No Escape, 1953 (Ayres)
No Escape. *See* Piège, 1958
No Exit. *See* Huis clos, 1954
No Funny Business, 1933 (Olivier)
No Greater Love. *See* Ona zashchishchaet Rodinu, 1943
No Greater Love. *See* **Ningen no joken**, 1959
No Highway in the Sky, 1951 (Dietrich; Hawkins; Stewart)
No Justice, 1989 (Sharif)
No Limit, 1931 (Bow)
No Love for Johnnie, 1961 (Finch; Pleasence; Reed)
No Man of Her Own, 1932 (Gable; Lombard)
No Man of Her Own, 1950 (Stanwyck)
No Man's Gold, 1926 (Mix)
No Man's Land, 1978 (Richardson, R.)
No Man's Law, 1927 (Laurel and Hardy)
No Man's Road, 1957 (Hopper)
No Man's Woman. *See* Ingens Mans Kvinna, 1953
No Means No, 1988 (Sheen)
No Mercy, 1986 (Basinger; Gere)
No Minor Vices, 1948 (Andrews, D.)

No Minor Voices, 1948 (Jourdan)
No More God, No More Love, 1985 (Mifune)
No More Ladies, 1935 (Crawford, J.; Fontaine; Montgomery)
No More Orchids, 1932 (Lombard)
No More Women, 1934 (McLaglen)
No, My Darling Daughter, 1961 (Redgrave, M.)
No, No, Nanette, 1941 (Mature; Neagle)
No One Man, 1932 (Lombard; Lukas)
No Other Woman, 1928 (Del Rio)
No Other Woman, 1933 (Dunne)
No Place Like Home, 1989 (Bates, K.; Grant, L.)
No Place Like Jail, 1919 (Laurel and Hardy)
No Place to Go, 1927 (Astor)
No Place to Hide, 1974 (Stallone)
No Place to Hide, 1983 (Sheen)
No Place to Hide, 1993 (Landau)
No Pockets in a Shroud. *See* Linceul n'a pas de poches, 1974
No Publicity, 1927 (Horton)
No Regrets for My Youth. *See* Waga seishun ni kui nashi, 1946
No Resting Place, 1952 (O'Sullivan)
No Retreat, No Surrender, 1986 (Van Damme)
No Road Back, 1956 (Connery)
No Room for the Groom, 1952 (Curtis, T.)
No Sad Songs for Me, 1950 (Sullavan; Wood)
No Sleep. *See* Anam, 1956
No Sleep on the Deep, 1934 (Langdon)
No Sleep till Dawn. *See* Bombers B-52, 1957
No Small Affair, 1984 (Moore, Demi; Robbins)
No te engañes corazón, 1936 (Cantinflas)
No-Tell Hotel, 1994 (Lee, C.)
No Time for Breakfast. *See* Docteur Françoise Gailland, 1975
No Time for Comedy, 1940 (Russell, R.; Stewart)
No Time for Love, 1943 (Colbert)
No Time for Tears. *See* Otoko arite, 1955
No Time for Tears, 1957 (Neagle; Quayle)
No Time to Die, 1958 (Mature)
No Time to Die, 1992 (Falk)
No Time to Marry, 1938 (Astor)
No Trees in the Street, 1959 (Lom)
No Way Back. *See* Herr über Leben und Tod, 1955
No Way Out, 1950 (Darnell; Poitier; Widmark)
No Way Out. *See* Big Guns, 1972
No Way Out, 1987 (Costner; Hackman)
No Way to Treat a Lady, 1968 (Remick; Segal; Steiger)
Noah's Ark, 1928 (Loy)
Noah's Ark. *See* Arche de Noë, 1946
Nob Hill, 1945 (Bennett; Raft)
Nobody Lives Forever, 1946 (Brennan; Garfield)
Nobody Loves Me. *See* Personne ne m'aime, 1994
Nobody Runs Away, 1956 (Cotten)
Nobody Said Nothing. *See* Nadie dijo nada, 1970
Nobody Will Talk about Us When We're Dead. *See* Nadie Hablara de Nosotras Cuando Hayamos Muerto, 1995
Nobody's Child, 1986 (Grant, L.)
Nobody's Children, 1994 (Ann-Margret; Sanda)
Nobody's Darling, 1943 (Calhern)
Nobody's Fault. *See* Little Dorrit, 1987
Nobody's Fool, 1936 (Horton)
Nobody's Fool, 1994 (Griffith; Newman; Willis)
Nobody's Kid, 1921 (Marsh)
Nobody's Widow, 1927 (Crisp)
Noc Poslubna, 1959 (Andersson, H.)
Noces de papier, 1989 (Bujold)
Noces rouges, 1973 (Audran; Piccoli)
Noche avanza, 1951 (Armendáriz)
Noche de Reyes, 1947 (Rey)
Noche de sabado, 1950 (Félix)
Noche de tormenta, 1951 (Aimée)
Noche mas hermosa, 1984 (Abril)
Nocturna, 1979 (Carradine)
Nocturne, 1946 (Raft)

Nocturno der Liebe, 1918 (Veidt)
Nogitsune Sanji, 1930 (Hasegawa)
Noi donne siamo fatte cosi, 1972 (Vitti)
Noi gangsters, 1959 (Cervi)
Noi vivi—addio Kira, 1942 (Brazzi; Valli)
Noia, 1964 (Davis, B.)
Noir au citron, 1992 (Cassel)
Noise from the Deep, 1913 (Arbuckle; Normand)
Noises Off, 1991 (Caine; Elliott)
Noisy Six, 1913 (Mix)
Nomads of the North, 1920 (Chaney)
Nome della legge. See Mafia, 1949
Nome delle popolo italiano, 1971 (Gassman)
Nommé La Rocca, 1961 (Belmondo)
Non c'è amore piu grande, 1955 (Cervi)
Non ci resta che piangere, 1984 (Benigni)
Non e mai troppe tardi, 1953 (Mastroianni)
Non si servizia un paperino, 1972 (Papas)
Non-Stop Kid, 1918 (Lloyd)
Non stuzzicate la zanzara, 1967 (Giannini; Masina)
Non ti conasco più amore, 1980 (Vitti)
Non toccate la donna bianca, 1973 (Fabrizi)
None but the Brave. See Storm over the Nile, 1955
None but the Brave, 1965 (Sidney)
None but the Lonely Heart, 1944 (Barrymore, E.; Duryea; Grant, C.; Fitzgerald)
Nonki saiban, 1955 (Kagawa)
Noon Whistle, 1923 (Laurel and Hardy)
Noose, 1928 (Barthelmess)
Noose Hangs High, 1948 (Abbott and Costello)
Nora, 1923 (Kortner)
Nora-inu, 1949 (Shimura)
Nora oder Ein Puppenheim, 1965 (Schell, Maria)
Norainu, 1949 (Mifune)
Noren, 1958 (Yamada)
Norliss Tapes, 1973 (Dickinson)
Norma Rae, 1979 (Field)
Norman Conquests in the Bayeux Tapestry, 1967 (Evans)
Norman Rockwell's Breaking Home Ties. See Breaking Home Ties, 1988
Noroît, 1976 (Chaplin, G.)
Norseman, 1978 (Wilde)
North, 1994 (Arkin; Bates, K.; Willis)
North by Northwest, 1959 (Grant, C.; Landau; Mason; Saint)
North Dallas Forty, 1978 (Nolte)
North of Hudson Bay, 1923 (Mix)
North of the Great Divide, 1950 (Rogers, R.)
North of the Rio Grande, 1937 (Cobb)
North Sea Hijack. See Ffolkes, 1980
North Star, 1925 (Gable)
North Star, 1943 (Andrews, D.; Baxter; Brennan; Huston, W.)
North Star. See Étoile du nord, 1982
North to Alaska, 1960 (Granger; Wayne)
North to the Klondike, 1942 (Crawford, B.)
Northanger Abbey, 1986 (Withers)
Northern Frontier, 1935 (Brennan)
Northern Pursuit, 1943 (Flynn)
Northwest Frontier. See Flame over India, 1959
Northwest Mounted Police, 1940 (Carroll; Constantine; Goddard; Preston; Ryan, R.)
Northwest Outpost, 1947 (Eddy; Lanchester)
Northwest Passage, 1940 (Brennan; Tracy; Young, R.)
Northwest Rangers, 1942 (Carradine)
Northwest U.S.A.. See Pacific Northwest, 1944
Norway's Liv Ullmann. See Look at Liv, 1979
Nos Veremos en el cielo, 1950 (Armendáriz)
Nosferatu a Venezia: Il ritorno di Nosferatu, 1988 (Kinski)
Nosferatu—Phantom der Nacht, 1979 (Adjani; Ganz; Kinski)
Nosotros los pobres, 1947 (Infante)
Nostalghia, 1983 (Josephson; Yankovsky)
Nostalgia. See Nostalghia, 1983
Nostoradamusu no daiyogen, 1974 (Tsukasa; Yamamura)

Nostri mariti, 1966 (Sordi)
Not a Ladies' Man, 1942 (Wray)
Not as a Stranger, 1955 (Crawford, B.; De Havilland; Grahame; Marvin; Mitchum; Sidney)
Not by Coincidence. See Keine zufällige Geschichte, 1984
Not Exactly Gentlemen, 1931 (Wray)
Not for Children. See Barnförbjudet, 1979
Not for Honor and Glory. See Lost Command, 1966
Not Just Another Affair, 1982 (Stone)
Not My Kid, 1985 (Segal)
Not So Dumb, 1930 (Davies)
Not to Be Trusted, 1926 (Rooney)
Not Wanted, 1949 (Lupino)
Not with My Wife, You Don't, 1966 (Curtis, T.; Scott, G.)
Not without My Daughter, 1990 (Field)
Not Yet. See Madadayo, 1993
Notater om Korlighedon, 1989 (Nowicki)
Notch pered Rozdestvom, 1913 (Mozhukin)
Nothing but Pleasure, 1940 (Keaton, B.)
Nothing but the Best, 1963 (Bates, A.; Elliott)
Nothing but the Night, 1972 (Cushing; Dors; Lee, C.)
Nothing but the Truth, 1941 (Goddard; Hope)
Nothing but the Truth. See F for Fake, 1975
Nothing but Trouble, 1918 (Lloyd)
Nothing but Trouble, 1945 (Laurel and Hardy)
Nothing but Trouble, 1991 (Candy; Moore, Demi)
Nothing in Common, 1986 (Hanks; Saint)
Nothing Lasts Forever, 1980 (Jaffe)
Nothing Lasts Forever, 1984 (Murray)
Nothing Personal, 1980 (Sutherland)
Nothing Personal, 1983 (Sutherland)
Nothing Sacred, 1937 (Lombard; March; McDaniel)
Nothing to Lose. See Death in Brunswick, 1991
Nothing Underneath. See Sotto il vestito niente, 1985
Notorious, 1946 (Bergman; Calhern; Grant, C.; Rains)
Notorious, 1992 (Cassel)
Notorious Affair, 1930 (Francis; Rathbone)
Notorious Gentleman. See Rake's Progress, 1945
Notorious Landlady, 1962 (Astaire; Lemmon; Novak)
Notre Dame de Paris, 1956 (Cuny; Lollobrigida; Quinn)
Notre histoire, 1985 (Baye; Delon)
Notre Regrettable Epoux, 1987 (Valli)
Notte, 1961 (Mastroianni; Moreau; Vitti)
Notte dei fiori, 1972 (Sanda)
Notte del nozze. See Tradita, 1954
Notte delle beffe, 1940 (Sordi)
Notti bianche, 1957 (Marais; Schell, Maria; Mastroianni)
Notti di Cabiria, 1956 (Masina)
Notturno, 1988 (Olbrychski)
Nous Deux, 1992 (Noiret)
Nous irons à Deauville, 1962 (Constantine)
Nous irons à Monte Carlo, 1951 (Dalio; Hepburn, A.)
Nous irons à Paris, 1949 (Raft)
Nous irons tous au paradis, 1977 (Gélin)
Nous le Gosses, 1941 (Modot)
Nous les jeunes, 1938 (Barrault)
Nous maigrirons ensemble, 1979 (Ustinov)
Nouveaux riches, 1938 (Raimu)
Nouvelle brigades du tigre, 1987 (Constantine)
Nouvelle Vague, 1990 (Delon)
Nove ospiti per un delitto, 1976 (Kennedy)
Novecento. See **1900**, 1976
November Plan, 1976 (Malone)
Novices, 1970 (Bardot; Girardot)
Novyi dom, 1947 (Cherkassov)
Now, Voyager, 1942 (Davis, B.; Henreid; Rains)
Now about All These Women. See För att inte tala om alla dessa kvinnor, 1964
Now and Forever, 1934 (Constantine; Lombard; Temple)
Now and Then, 1995 (Griffith; Moore, Demi)
Now Barabbas Was a Robber ..., 1949 (Burton)

Now I'll Tell, 1934 (Faye; Temple; Tracy)
Now I'll Tell One, 1926 (Laurel and Hardy)
Now or Never, 1921 (Lloyd)
Now We're in the Air, 1927 (Beery; Brooks, L.)
Now You're Talking, 1940 (Mills)
Nowhere to Go, 1958 (Smith)
Nowhere to Hide, 1977 (Van Cleef)
Nowhere to Run, 1993 (Van Damme)
Noyade interdite, 1987 (Noiret)
Nuage entre les dents, 1974 (Noiret)
Nude Bomb, 1980 (Gassman)
Nude in His Pocket. *See* Amour de poche, 1957
Nudo di donna, 1983 (Cassel)
Nuestra Natacha, 1936 (Rey)
Nueva cenicienta, 1964 (Rey)
Nuisance, 1921 (Laurel and Hardy)
Nuit à l'hôtel, 1934 (Dalio)
Nuit agitée, 1912 (Linder)
Nuit américaine, 1973 (Baye; Léaud)
Nuit Bengali, 1988 (Azmi; Chatterjee; Grant, H.; Hurt, J.)
Nuit blanche, 1948 (Brasseur)
Nuit bulgare, 1969 (Vanel)
Nuit d'or, 1976 (Blier; Vanel; Kinski)
Nuit d'orage. *See* Noche de tormenta, 1951
Nuit de Carrefour, 1984 (Vogler)
Nuit de Décembre, 1939 (Blier)
Nuit de folies, 1934 (Fernandel)
Nuit de generaux. *See* Night of the Generals, 1967
Nuit de l'ocean, 1988 (Moreau)
Nuit de la revanche, 1922 (Vanel)
Nuit de Sybille, 1946 (Gélin)
Nuit de Varennes, 1981 (Barrault; Gélin; Keitel; Mastroianni; Piccoli; Schygulla)
Nuit des adieux, 1965 (Cherkassov)
Nuit du 11 Septembre, 1919 (Mozhukin)
Nuit est mon royaume, 1951 (Gabin)
Nuit et le Moment. *See* Night and the Moment, 1994
Nuit fantastique, 1942 (Blier; Presle)
Nuit merveilleuse, 1940 (Fernandel; Vanel)
Nuit tous les chats sont gris, 1977 (Depardieu)
Nuits de décembre, 1939 (Reggiani)
Nukiashi sashiashi, 1934 (Takamine)
Number One, 1969 (Dern; Heston)
Number, Please, 1920 (Lloyd)
Numbered Woman, 1938 (Bond)
Nun. *See* Religieuse, 1965
Nun's Story, 1959 (Evans; Finch; Hepburn, K.)
Nunca pasa nada, 1963 (Cassel)
Nuovi mostri, 1977 (Gassman; Sordi)
Nuovo Cinema Paradiso. *See* Cinema Paradiso, 1988
...Nur ein Komödiant, 1935 (Henreid; Wegener)
Nuregame Botan, 1961 (Kyo)
Nurekami kenka tabi, 1960 (Yamada)
Nurse Edith Cavell, 1939 (Neagle; Sanders)
Nusumareta koi, 1951 (Mori)
Nut, 1921 (Chaplin, C.; Fairbanks)
Nut-Cracker, 1926 (Horton)
Nutcracker Fantasy, 1979 (Lee, C.; McDowall)
Nutcracker Prince, 1990 (O'Toole)
Nuts, 1987 (Dreyfuss; Malden; Streisand; Wallach)
Nuts in May, 1917 (Laurel and Hardy)
Nutty but Nice, 1940 (Three Stooges)
Nutty Naughty Chateau. *See* Château en Suède, 1963
Nutty Professor, 1963 (Lewis, Jerry)
Nutty Professor, 1996 (Murphy)
Nyay Adhikar, 1987 (Chatterjee)
Nyay Anyay, 1981 (Chatterjee)
Nybyggarna, 1973 (Ullmann; Von Sydow)
Nyckeln och ringen, 1947 (Dahlbeck)
Nyobo gakko, 1961 (Mori)
Nyonin Mandara, 1933 (Yamada)

Nyonin Mandara, Part II, 1934 (Yamada)
Nyordning på Sjögårda, 1944 (Björnstrand)
Nyubo yo, eien nare, 1955 (Mori; Tanaka)
O Beijo Da Mulher Aranha. *See* Kiss of the Spider Woman, 1985
O Casal, 1974 (Braga)
O Convento, 1995 (Deneuve; Malkovich)
O Lucky Man!, 1973 (McDowell; Mirren; Richardson, R.; Roberts, R.)
O lyubvi, 1971 (Yankovsky)
O Melissokomos, 1986 (Mastroianni; Reggiani)
O Mimi san, 1914 (Hayakawa)
O Pioneers!, 1992 (Lange)
O Samba, 1988 (Mastroianni)
O. C. and Stiggs, 1985 (Hopper)
O. Henry's Full House, 1952 (Baxter; Laughton; Monroe; Widmark)
O.H.M.S., 1937 (Mills)
O.K. Nerone, 1951 (Cervi)
O.S.S., 1946 (Ladd)
Oasis, 1955 (Morgan)
Oatari otoko ichidai, 1956 (Yamada)
Obaasan, 1944 (Takamine)
Oban: Kanketsu-hen, 1958 (Yamamura)
Oberdan, 1916 (Bertini)
Oberst Redl. *See* Redl Ezredes, 1985
Oberwachtmeister Schwenek, 1935 (Fröhlich)
Obey the Law, 1933 (Bond)
O-bi, O-bi—Koniec cywilizacji, 1985 (Nowicki; Olbrychski)
Object Matrimony. *See* Help Wanted—Male, 1920
Object of Beauty, 1991 (Malkovich)
Objection, 1986 (Olbrychski)
Objective, Burma!, 1945 (Flynn)
Obliging Young Lady, 1941 (O'Brien, E.)
Oblong Box, 1969 (Lee, C.; Price)
Obo Kissa, 1929 (Hasegawa)
Obocchan, 1926 (Tanaka)
Oboro kago, 1951 (Tanaka; Yamada)
Oborono Sevastopolya, 1911 (Mozhukin)
Obratnaya svyaz, 1977 (Yankovsky)
Obryv, 1913 (Mozhukin)
Obscure Illness. *See* Male oscuro, 1990
Obsession, 1934 (Vanel)
Obsession, 1948 (Baker)
Obsession, 1954 (Morgan)
Obsession, 1976 (Abril; Bujold; Robertson)
Obsession. *See* Junoon, 1978
Obuknovennoe utro, 1978 (Yankovsky)
Occhi, la bocca, 1982 (Piccoli)
Occhiali d'oro, 1987 (Noiret)
Occhio del ragno, 1971 (Kinski)
Occhio nel labarinto, 1970 (Valli)
Occident, 1938 (Berry; Vanel)
Occupe-toi d'Amélie, 1949 (Darrieux)
Ocean Breakers. *See* Brannigar, 1935
Ocean's Eleven, 1960 (Dickinson; MacLaine; Martin, D.; Raft; Sidney)
Och en, 1978 (Josephson; Thulin)
Ochazuke no aji, 1952 (Ryu)
Ochiba nikki, 1953 (Yamamura)
Ochimusha, 1925 (Tanaka)
Oci ciornie, 1987 (Mastroianni; Mangano)
Oci pro plac, 1984 (Brodský)
Ociano, 1989 (Borgnine; Papas)
Octagon, 1980 (Van Cleef)
October, 1982 (Bondarchuk)
October Man, 1947 (Greenwood; Mills)
October Revolution, 1967 (Gielgud)
Octopussy, 1983 (Jourdan)
Od zitrka necaruji, 1979 (Brodský)
Odalisque, 1914 (Sweet)
Odd Couple, 1968 (Lemmon; Matthau)
Odd Man Out, 1947 (Cusack; Mason)
Odd Obsession. *See* Kagi, 1959
Oddball Hall, 1991 (Ameche; Meredith)

Old Boyfriends, 1979 (Belushi)
Old Clothes, 1925 (Crawford, J.)
Old Cobbler, 1914 (Chaney)
Old Corral, 1936 (Autry; Rogers, R.)
Old Dark House, 1932 (Douglas, Melvyn; Karloff; Laughton; Massey)
Old Dracula. *See* Vampira, 1974
Old Dudino. *See* Granitsa, 1935
Old Enough, 1984 (Aiello)
Old Explorers, 1990 (Ferrer)
Old Fashioned Girl, 1915 (Crisp)
Old Fashioned Way, 1934 (Fields, W. C.)
Old Greatheart. *See* Way Back Home, 1932
Old Grey Manor, 1935 (Hope)
Old Gringo, 1989 (Fonda, J.; Peck)
Old Gun. *See* Vieux Fusil, 1975
Old Homestead, 1935 (Rogers, R.)
Old Hutch, 1936 (Beery)
Old Ironsides, 1926 (Beery; Karloff)
Old Lady Who Walked in the Sea. *See* Vielle qui marchait dans le mer, 1992
Old Louisianna, 1937 (Hayworth)
Old Loves and New, 1926 (Pidgeon)
Old Maid, 1914 (Sweet)
Old Maid, 1939 (Crisp; Davis, B.; Hopkins, M.)
Old Man and the Sea, 1958 (Tracy)
Old Man and the Sea, 1990 (Quinn)
Old Man Rhythm, 1935 (Ball; Grable)
Old Man Who Cried Wolf, 1970 (Jaffe; Robinson, E.)
Old Man's Love Story, 1913 (Talmadge)
Old Monk's Tale, 1913 (Lloyd)
Old Mother Riley Meets the Vampire, 1952 (Lugosi)
Old Reliable, 1914 (Talmadge)
Old San Francisco, 1927 (Wong)
Old Spanish Custom. *See* Invader, 1936
Old Times, 1990 (Malkovich)
Old Times, 1993 (Nelligan; Richardson, M.)
Old West, 1952 (Autry)
Old Wyoming Trail, 1937 (Rogers, R.)
Older Brother, Younger Sister. *See* Ani imoto, 1953
Oldest Living Graduate, 1980 (Fonda, H.)
Oldest Profession. *See* Plus Vieux Métier du monde, 1967
Ole Opfinders offer, 1924 (Madsen and Schenstrøm)
Olga e i suoi figli, 1985 (Gélin; Girardot)
Olimpiadi dei mariti, 1960 (Cervi)
Oliva. *See* Incantesimo tragico, 1951
Oliver!, 1968 (Reed)
Oliver & Company, 1988 (Midler)
Oliver the Eighth, 1934 (Laurel and Hardy)
Oliver Twist, 1922 (Chaney)
Oliver Twist, 1948 (Dors; Guinness)
Oliver Twist, 1982 (Scott, G.)
Oliver's Story, 1978 (Milland)
Olivia, 1950 (Feuillère; Noiret)
Olly, Olly, Oxen Free, 1977 (Hepburn, K.)
Ölprinz, 1965 (Granger)
Oltre il bene e il male, 1977 (Josephson; Sanda)
Oltre la porta, 1982 (Mastroianni; Piccoli)
Oltre le legge, 1919 (Bertini)
Olvidados de dios, 1940 (Armendáriz)
Olyan, mint otthon, 1978 (Karina; Nowicki)
Olympia, 1931 (Rosay)
Olympia. *See* Breath of Scandal, 1960
O'Malley, 1982 (Rooney)
O'Malley of the Mounted, 1921 (Hart)
Omar Khayyam, 1957 (Massey; Wilde)
Omar Mukhtar. *See* Lion of the Desert, 1981
Omar the Tentmaker, 1922 (Karloff)
Omatsuri Hanjiro, 1953 (Hasegawa)
Ombra, 1919 (Bertini)
Ombra nell' ombra, 1977 (Papas)
Ombre Bianche. *See* Savage Innocents, 1960
Ombre des châteaux, 1976 (Dalio)

Ombre et secrets, 1982 (Marais)
Ombre rouge, 1981 (Baye)
Ombres qui passent, 1924 (Mozhukin)
Omega Man, 1971 (Heston)
Omen, 1976 (Peck; Remick)
Omen III: The Final Conflict. *See* Final Conflict, 1981
Omens and Oracles, 1912 (Talmadge)
Omokage, 1929 (Hasegawa)
Omokage no machi, 1942 (Hasegawa)
Ön, 1964 (Andersson, B.)
On a Clear Day You Can See Forever, 1970 (Nicholson; Montand; Streisand)
On a Moonlit Night. *See* In una notta di chiaro di luna, 1989
On a volé la cuisse de Jupiter, 1980 (Girardot; Noiret)
On an Island with You, 1948 (Charisse; Durante; Williams, E.)
On Any Sunday, 1971 (McQueen)
On Approval, 1944 (Withers)
On Borrowed Time, 1939 (Barrymore, L.)
On Dangerous Ground, 1951 (Bond; Lupino; Ryan, R.)
On Deadly Ground, 1994 (Caine)
On demande une brute, 1934 (Tati)
On demande un assassin, 1949 (Fernandel)
On efface tout, 1978 (Presle)
On Friday at Eleven. *See* World in My Pocket, 1961
On Golden Pond, 1981 (Fonda, H.; Fonda, J.; Hepburn, K.)
On Ice, 1933 (Langdon)
On Moonlight Bay, 1951 (Day)
On My Own, 1992 (Davis, J.)
On My Way to the Crusades, I Met a Girl Who .... *See* Cintura di Castità, 1969
On n'aime qu'une fois, 1950 (Rosay)
On Our Merry Way. *See* Miracle Can Happen, 1946
On Our Merry Way, 1948 (Fonda, H.; Goddard; Lamour; Laughton; MacMurray; Meredith; Stewart)
On Our Way, 1985 (Leigh, Janet)
On purge bébé, 1931 (Fernandel)
On the Archipelago Boundary. *See* I havsbandet, 1971
On the Avenue, 1937 (Carroll; Faye; Powell, D.)
On the Beach, 1959 (Astaire; Gardner; Peck; Perkins)
On the Beat, 1962 (Wisdom)
On the Carpet. *See* Little Giant, 1946
On the Double, 1961 (Dors; Kaye; Rutherford)
On the Eagle Trail, 1915 (Mix)
On the Earth. *See* Chijo, 1957
On the Edge, 1985 (Dern)
On the Edge of Reality, 1977 (Lancaster)
On the Fiddle, 1961 (Connery)
On the Fire, 1919 (Lloyd)
On the Front Page, 1926 (Laurel and Hardy; Hardy)
On the Harmfulness of Tobacco, 1959 (Newman)
On the Jump, 1918 (Lloyd)
On the Level, 1930 (McLaglen)
On the Line. *See* Rio Abajo, 1984
On the Little Big Horn, 1910 (Mix)
On the Loose, 1931 (Laurel and Hardy)
On the Loose, 1951 (Douglas, Melvyn)
On the Move. *See* Útkösben, 1979
On the Night of the Fire, 1940 (Richardson, R.)
On the Night Stage, 1915 (Hart)
On the Old Spanish Trail, 1947 (Rogers, R.)
On the Quiet, 1918 (Barrymore, J.)
On the Riviera, 1951 (Dalio; Kaye; Tierney)
On the Road with Red Mole, 1977 (Neill)
On the Sunny Side. *See* Pa solsidan, 1936
On the Sunny Side, 1942 (McDowall)
On the Town, 1949 (Kelly, Gene; Miller; Sidney)
On the Waterfront, 1954 (Brando; Cobb; Malden; Saint; Steiger)
On the Wrong Trek, 1936 (Laurel and Hardy)
On Top of Old Smoky, 1953 (Autry)
On Trial. *See* Affaire Mauritzius, 1953
On with the Show, 1929 (Brown)
On Your Toes, 1939 (O'Connor)

Ona zashchishchaet Rodinu, 1943 (Maretskaya)
Onai goju-ryo, 1931 (Yamada)
Onatsu Seijuro, 1936 (Hasegawa; Tanaka)
Onatsu torimono-cho: Torima, 1960 (Yamada)
Onatsu torimono-cho: Tsukiyo ni kieta onna, 1959 (Yamada)
Once ..., 1990 (Price; Quayle)
Once a Cop. *See* Police Story 4: Project S, 1993
Once a Crook, 1941 (Cusack)
Once a Gentleman, 1930 (Horton)
Once a Hero, 1931 (Arbuckle)
Once a Hero. *See* It Happened in Hollywood, 1937
Once a Jolly Swagman, 1948 (Bogarde; Cusack)
Once a Lady, 1931 (Novello)
Once a Sinner, 1931 (McCrea)
Once a Thief. *See* Happy Thieves, 1962
Once a Thief, 1965 (Ann-Margret; Delon)
Once a Thief. *See* Tueurs de San Francisco, 1965
Once a Year, Every Year. *See* Tutti Gli anni una volta l'anno, 1994
Once Around, 1991 (Aiello; Dreyfuss; Hunter; Rowlands)
Once Every Ten Minutes, 1915 (Lloyd)
Once in a Lifetime, 1932 (Ladd)
Once Is Not Enough, 1975 (Douglas, K.; Mercouri)
Once More, My Darling, 1949 (Montgomery)
Once More, with Feeling!, 1960 (Brynner; Kendall)
Once to Every Woman, 1920 (Valentino)
Once to Every Woman, 1934 (Bellamy; Wray)
Once upon a Crime, 1992 (Candy; Giannini)
Once Upon a Dead Man, 1971 (Hudson)
Once upon a Dream, 1948 (Withers)
Once upon a Honeymoon, 1942 (Grant, C.; Rogers, G.)
Once upon a Spy, 1980 (Lee, C.)
Once upon a Texas Train, 1988 (Dickinson; Widmark)
Once upon a Time, 1944 (Grant, C.)
Once upon a Time in America, 1984 (Aiello; De Niro; Pesci; Weld; Woods)
Once upon a Time in the West. *See* **C'era una volta il West**, 1968
Once upon a Time ... Is Now, 1977 (Grant, L.; Grant, C.)
Once upon a Tram, 1960 (Cusack)
Oncle de Pekin, 1933 (Brasseur)
Ondata di calore, 1970 (Seberg)
One A.M., 1916 (Chaplin, C.)
One against the Wind, 1991 (Davis, J.; Elliott; Neill)
One and One. *See* Och en, 1978
One and Only Genuine Original Family Band, 1968 (Brennan; Hawn)
One Arabian Night. *See* Sumurun, 1920
One Body Too Many, 1944 (Lugosi)
One Born Every Minute. *See* Flim-Flam Man, 1967
One Christmas, 1994 (Hepburn, K.)
One Crazy Summer, 1986 (Moore, Demi)
One Deadly Summer. *See* Été meurtrier, 1983
One Desire, 1955 (Baxter; Hudson; Wood)
One Exciting Week, 1946 (Three Stooges)
One-Eyed Jacks, 1961 (Brando; Malden)
One Fiancé at a Time. *See* Fästman i taget, 1952
One Flew over the Cuckoo's Nest, 1975 (DeVito; Douglas, Michael; Nicholson)
One Foot in Heaven, 1941 (March)
One Foot in Hell, 1960 (Ladd)
One from the Heart, 1982 (Julia; Kinski; Stanton)
One Glorious Day, 1922 (Rogers, W.)
One Good Cop, 1991 (Keaton, M.)
One Good Turn, 1931 (Laurel and Hardy)
One Good Turn, 1954 (Wisdom)
One Hot Summer. *See* That Night, 1993
One Hour Late, 1935 (Milland)
One Hour Married, 1926 (Normand)
One Hour to Doomsday. *See* City beneath the Sea, 1970
One Hour with You, 1932 (Chevalier; MacDonald)
One Hundred Percent American, 1918 (Pickford)
One Hundred Percent Pure. *See* Girl from Missouri, 1934
One Hundred Twenty Thousand a Year. *See* Sto dvadtsat tysyach v god, 1929
One Hysterical Night, 1929 (Brennan)

One in a Million, 1937 (Ameche; Henie; Menjou)
One Is a Lonely Number, 1972 (Douglas, Melvyn; Leigh, Janet)
One Is Business, The Other Crime, 1912 (Sweet)
One Is Guilty, 1934 (Bellamy)
One Life. *See* Vie, 1958
One Little Indian, 1973 (Foster; Garner)
One Magic Christmas, 1985 (Stanton; Steenburgen)
One-Man Game, 1927 (Wray)
One-Man Jury, 1978 (Palance)
One-Man Mutiny. *See* Court Martial of Billy Mitchell, 1955
One Man's Journey, 1933 (Barrymore, L.; McCrea)
One Man's War, 1990 (Hopkins, A.)
One Mile from Heaven, 1937 (Robinson, B.; Trevor)
One Million A.D., 1973 (Carradine)
One Million B.C., 1940 (Mature)
One Million Dollars. *See* Congiuntura, 1964
One Million Years B.C., 1967 (Welch)
One Minute to Zero, 1952 (Mitchum)
One More American, 1918 (Crisp)
One More Chance, 1931 (Crosby)
One More Spring, 1935 (Gaynor)
One More Time, 1970 (Cushing; Lewis, Jerry; Lee, C.)
One More Tomorrow, 1946 (Wyman)
One Mysterious Night, 1944 (Malone)
One Night, a Train. *See* Soir, un train, 1968
One Night in Lisbon, 1941 (Carroll; Dalio; MacMurray)
One Night in the Tropics, 1940 (Abbott and Costello)
One Night with You, 1948 (Lee, C.)
One of Her Own, 1994 (Sheen)
One of Our Aircraft Is Missing, 1942 (Ustinov; Withers)
One of Our Dinosaurs Is Missing, 1975 (Ustinov)
One of Our Own, 1975 (Homolka)
One of Ourselves, 1983 (Cusack)
One of the Best, 1927 (Lanchester)
One of the Blood. *See* His Majesty, the American, 1919
One of the Boys, 1982 (Rooney)
One of Them Is Named Brett, 1965 (Baker)
One on One, 1977 (Griffith)
One-Piece Bathing Suit. *See* Million Dollar Mermaid, 1952
One Precious Year, 1933 (Rathbone)
One Quiet Night, 1931 (Arbuckle)
One Rainy Afternoon, 1936 (Lupino)
One Romantic Night, 1930 (Dressler; Gish)
One-Room Tenants. *See* Wspólny pokój, 1959
One-Run Elmer, 1935 (Keaton, B.)
One Russian Summer. *See* Giorno del furore, 1973
One She Loved, 1912 (Barrymore, L.; Gish; Pickford)
One Shoe Makes It Murder, 1982 (Dickinson; Mitchum)
One Special Victory, 1991 (Bassett)
One Spy Too Many. *See* Where the Spies Are, 1965
One Spy Too Many. *See* Spy in the Green Hat, 1966
One Step to Eternity. *See* Affaire des poisons?, 1955
One Step to Hell, 1968 (Brazzi; Sanders)
One Stolen Night, 1922 (Laurel and Hardy)
One Summer Love, 1976 (Sarandon)
One Sunday Afternoon, 1933 (Constantine; Wray)
One Sunday Afternoon, 1948 (Malone)
One Sunday Morning, 1926 (Arbuckle)
One Swallow Doesn't Make a Summer. *See* Fluga gör ingen sommar, 1947
One, Take Two, 1978 (Howard, T.)
...One Third of a Nation, 1939 (Sidney)
One Thousand Dollars a Touchdown, 1939 (Hayward)
One Too Many, 1916 (Laurel and Hardy)
One Touch of Venus, 1948 (Gardner; Walker)
One-Two-Three, 1914 (Beery)
One, Two, Three, 1961 (Cagney)
One Way. *See* Senso unico, 1973
One Way Out. *See* Convicted, 1950
One Way Passage, 1932 (Francis; Powell, W.)
One Way Street, 1950 (Duryea; Hudson; Mason)
One Week, 1920 (Keaton, B.)

One Wild Night. *See* Career Opportunities, 1991
One Wild Oat, 1951 (Hepburn, A.)
One Woman Idea, 1929 (Rosay)
One Woman or Two. *See* Femme ou deux, 1985
One Woman's Story. *See* Passionate Friends, 1949
One Year Later, 1933 (Brennan)
Onesta che uccide, 1914 (Bertini)
Ongaku dai-shingun, 1943 (Hasegawa)
Oni azami, 1950 (Hasegawa)
Oni-kenji, 1963 (Yamamura)
Oni no sumu yakata, 1969 (Takamine)
Oni srazhalis za rodinu, 1975 (Bondarchuk)
Oni znali Mayakovsky, 1955 (Cherkassov)
Onion Field, 1979 (Woods)
Onionhead, 1958 (Matthau)
Onkel Bräsig, 1936 (Rasp)
Only a Dancing Girl. *See* Bara en danserska, 1927
Only a Janitor, 1919 (Beery)
Only a Mother. *See* Bara en mor, 1949
Only a Shop Girl, 1922 (Beery)
Only a Woman. *See* Ich bin auch nur eine Frau, 1962
Only Angels Have Wings, 1939 (Arthur; Barthelmess; Grant, C.; Hayworth)
Only Count the Happy Moments. *See* Räkna de lyckliga stunderna blott, 1944
Only Game in Town, 1969 (Beatty; Taylor, E.)
Only Girl, 1933 (Boyer)
Only One Night. *See* Enda natt, 1939
Only Son. *See* Hotori musuko, 1936
Only the Brave, 1930 (Constantine)
Only the French Can. *See* French Cancan, 1955
Only the Lonely, 1991 (Candy; O'Hara; Quinn)
Only the Valiant, 1951 (Bond; Peck)
Only Two Can Play, 1962 (Attenborough; Sellers; Zetterling)
Only Way, 1919 (Young, L.)
Only When I Larf, 1968 (Attenborough)
Only When I Laugh, 1981 (Bacon)
Only Woman, 1924 (Talmadge)
Only Yesterday, 1934 (Sullavan)
Onna bakari no yoru, 1961 (Kagawa)
Onna dake no machi, 1957 (Yamada)
Onna dake no yuro, 1947 (Hara)
Onna de arukoto, 1958 (Kagawa; Mori)
Onna doshi, 1955 (Takamine)
Onna ga kaidan o agaru toki, 1960 (Takamine)
Onna ga kaidan o noboru toku, 1960 (Mori)
Onna-gokoro, 1959 (Mori)
Onna-gokoro dare ga shiru, 1951 (Kagawa; Mifune)
Onna Goroshi abura jigoku, 1957 (Kagawa)
Onna hitori daichi o yuku, 1953 (Yamada)
Onna Kanja hibun: Ako-roshi, 1953 (Yamada)
Onna kumicho, 1970 (Yamada)
Onna no hada, 1957 (Kyo)
Onna no inochi, 1952 (Yamamura)
Onna no issho, 1962 (Kyo)
Onna no koyomi, 1954 (Kagawa; Tanaka)
Onna no kunsho, 1961 (Kyo; Mori)
Onna no mizukakami, 1951 (Takamine)
Onna no rekishi, 1963 (Takamine)
Onna no sono, 1954 (Takamine)
Onna no tatakai, 1949 (Yamamura)
Onna no tsuyokunaru kufu no kazukazu, 1963 (Tsukasa)
Onna no za, 1962 (Ryu; Takamine; Tsukasa)
Onna to iu shiro: Mari no maki, 1952 (Takamine)
Onna to iu shiro: Yuko no maki, 1952 (Takamine)
Onna to kaizoku, 1959 (Kyo)
Onna to umareta karanya, 1934 (Takamine)
Onna tokaizoku, 1959 (Hasegawa)
Onna wa doko he iku, 1930 (Tanaka)
Onna wa itsuno you nimo, 1931 (Takamine)
Onna wa yoru kesho-suru, 1961 (Mori)
Onna-gokoru, 1959 (Hara)
Onnade arukoto, 1958 (Hara)

Onorevole Angelina, 1947 (Magnani)
Onorevoli, 1963 (Cervi)
Ooka seidan: Yogiden: Hakuro no kamen, Jigokudani no taiketsu, 1954 (Yamada)
Ooku maruhi monogatari, 1967 (Yamada)
Oonch Neech Beech, 1989 (Azmi; Patil)
Oopsie Poopsie, 1980 (Loren; Mastroianni)
Oosho ichidai, 1955 (Kagawa)
Oozora no chikai, 1952 (Kagawa)
Open All Night, 1924 (Menjou)
Open Book. *See* Otkrytaya kniga, 1979
Open City. *See* **Roma, città aperta**, 1945
Open Doors. *See* Porte aperte, 1990
Open Season, 1974 (Holden)
Open Space: Death on Delivery, 1990 (Jackson, G.)
Opening Night, 1977 (Blondell; Falk; Rowlands)
Opéra de quat' sous. *See* **Dreigroschenoper**, 1931
Operación Istanbul. *See* Estambul 65, 1965
Operación Relámpage, 1959 (Rey)
Operation Amsterdam, 1959 (Finch)
Operation C.I.A., 1965 (Reynolds, B.)
Operation Cicero. *See* Five Fingers, 1952
Operation Cougar. *See* Daihao Meizhoubao, 1989
Operation Crossbow, 1965 (Henreid; Howard, T.; Loren; Mills; Quayle)
Operation Disaster. *See* Morning Departure, 1950
Operation Head Start, 1965 (Lancaster)
Operation Heartbeat. *See* U.M.C., 1969
Operation Leontine. *See* Faut pas prendre les enfants du bon dieu pour des canards sauvages, 1968
Operation M. *See* Hell's Bloody Devils, 1970
Operation Mad Ball, 1957 (Lemmon; Rooney)
Operation Pacific, 1951 (Bond; Neal; Wayne)
Operation Petticoat, 1959 (Curtis, T.; Grant, C.; Cooper)
Operation St. Peter's, 1968 (Robinson, E.)
Operation Secret, 1952 (Malden; Wilde)
Operation Snafu. *See* On the Fiddle, 1961
Operation Snafu, 1970 (Falk; Landau; Robards)
Operation Snatch, 1962 (Sanders; Terry-Thomas)
Operation Undercover. *See* Report to the Commissioner, 1975
Operation X. *See* My Daughter Joy, 1950
Operation Zebracka, 1991 (Irons)
Operator Thirteen, 1934 (Constantine; Davies; McDaniel)
Operazione Crossbow. *See* Operation Crossbow, 1965
Opfer der Gesellschaft, 1918 (Veidt)
Ophélia, 1962 (Valli)
Opiate '67. *See* I mostri, 1963
Opinione pubblica, 1953 (Gélin)
Opium, 1918 (Krauss)
Opium War. *See* Lin zexu, 1959
Oppåt med gröna hissen, 1952 (Björnstrand)
Opponent, 1990 (Borgnine)
Opposite Sex, 1956 (Blondell; Miller; Moorehead)
Optimist. *See* Big Shot, 1931
Optimist, 1973 (Sellers)
Optimist of Nine Elms. *See* Optimist, 1973
Or, 1936 (Dalio)
Or dans la rue, 1934 (Darrieux)
Or du Cristobal, 1939 (Vanel)
Or du duc, 1965 (Brasseur; Darrieux; Girardot)
Orage, 1938 (Barrault; Boyer; Morgan)
Oranges and Lemons, 1920 (Laurel and Hardy)
Orazi e Curiazi, 1962 (Fabrizi; Ladd)
Orca, 1977 (Harris, R.)
Orchestre rouge, 1989 (Olbrychski)
Orchids and Ermine, 1927 (Rooney)
Orchids to You, 1935 (Dumont)
Ordeal by Innocence, 1984 (Sutherland)
Order of Death. *See* Corrupt, 1983
Order to Kill. *See* Clan de los immorales, 1973
Orderly, 1918 (Laurel and Hardy)
Orderly. *See* Ordonnance, 1933

Orders Are Orders, 1954 (Pleasence; Sellers)
Orders from Tokyo. *See* I Give My Life, 1936
Orders Is Orders, 1933 (Milland)
Orders to Kill, 1958 (Gish)
Ordinary People, 1980 (Redford; Sutherland)
Ordini sono ordini, 1972 (Vitti)
Ordonnance, 1933 (Fernandel)
Ordonnance malgré lui, 1932 (Fernandel)
Ordre et la sécurité du monde, 1978 (Cotten; Hopper; Pleasence)
Ore, 1989 (Giannini)
Ore ga jigoku no tejina-shi da, 1961 (Yamamura)
Ore nove lezione di chimica, 1941 (Valli)
Ore was Tokichiro, 1955 (Hasegawa)
Oregon Trail, 1936 (Wayne)
Oregon Trail, 1959 (Carradine; MacMurray)
Orekara ikuzo, 1960 (Yamamura)
Organization, 1971 (Julia; Poitier)
Organizer. *See* I compagni, 1963
Orgueilleux, 1953 (Morgan; Philipe)
Orient-Express, 1927 (Dagover)
Oriental Dream. *See* Kismet, 1944
Original Intent, 1992 (Sheen)
Original Sin, 1989 (Heston)
Orizuru-gasa, 1951 (Hasegawa; Yamada)
Orizuru Osen, 1935 (Yamada)
Orizushichi nana-henge, 1941 (Hasegawa)
Orlacs Hände, 1925 (Kortner; Veidt)
Orme, 1974 (Kinski)
Ormen, 1966 (Andersson, H.)
Örmens ägg. *See* Serpent's Egg, 1977
Orn, 1987 (Thulin)
Oro di Napoli, 1954 (Loren; Mangano)
Orökseg, 1980 (Huppert; Nowicki)
Oroku kanzashi, 1935 (Yamada)
O'Rourke of the Royal Mounted. *See* Saskatchewan, 1954
Orphan, 1958 (Lee, B.)
Orphan of the Ring. *See* Kid from Kokomo, 1939
Orphan Train, 1979 (Close)
Orphan's Song, 1955 (Lee, B.)
Orphan's Tragedy, 1955 (Lee, B.)
Orphans, 1987 (Finney)
Orphans of the Storm, 1921 (Gish)
Orphée, 1950 (Marais)
Orphelin du cirque, 1926 (Vanel)
Orpheus. *See* **Orphée**, 1950
Orpheus Descending, 1990 (Redgrave, V.)
Orrori del castello di Norimberga, 1972 (Cotten)
Orzowei, 1975 (Baker)
Osaka Elegy. *See* **Naniwa ereji**, 1936
Osaka-jo monogatari, 1961 (Kagawa; Mifune; Shimura; Yamada)
Osaka monogatari, 1957 (Kagawa)
Osaka natsu no jin, 1937 (Yamada)
Osaka no onna, 1958 (Kyo)
Osaya koisugata, 1934 (Tanaka)
Oscar, 1966 (Borgnine; Brennan; Cotten; Crawford, B.; Hope; Oberon; Sidney)
Oscar, 1991 (Ameche; Douglas, K.; Stallone)
Oscar, champion de tennis, 1932 (Tati)
Oscar Wilde, 1960 (Richardson, R.)
Ose Hangoro, 1928 (Hasegawa)
O'Shaughnessy's Boy, 1935 (Beery; Cooper)
Oshidori no aida, 1956 (Yamada)
Osho ichidai, 1955 (Tanaka)
Ósmy dzień tygodnia, 1958 (Łomnicki)
Ososhiki, 1984 (Ryu)
Oss tjuvar emellan eller En burk ananas, 1945 (Dahlbeck)
Osseg Oder die Warheit uber Hansel und Gretel, 1987 (Léaud)
Osterman Weekend, 1982 (Hopper; Hurt, J.; Lancaster)
Ostře sledované vlaky, 1966 (Brodský)
Ostrich Has Two Eggs. *See* Oeufs de l'autruche, 1957
Ostrov sokrovishch, 1937 (Cherkassov)

Osvobojdienie, 1971 (Olbrychski)
Otets i syn, 1917 (Mozhukin)
Otets Sergii, 1917 (Mozhukin)
Othello, 1922 (Jannings; Krauss)
Othello, 1952 (Cotten; Fontaine; Welles)
Othello, 1956 (Bondarchuk; Olivier; Smith)
Othello, 1981 (Hopkins, A.; Hoskins)
Othello, 1996 (Branagh; Fishburne)
Othello—The Black Commando, 1982 (Curtis, T.)
Other Eye. *See* Andere Blick, 1991
Other Girl, 1917 (Laurel and Hardy)
Other Half, 1947 (Stanwyck)
Other Half of the Sky: A China Memoir, 1974 (MacLaine)
Other Love. *See* Vot vspynulo utro, 1915
Other Love, 1947 (Niven)
Other Man, 1916 (Arbuckle)
Other Men's Women, 1931 (Blondell; Cagney)
Other One. *See* Et l'autre, 1967
Other People's Letters. *See* Chuzhie pisma, 1975
Other People's Money, 1991 (DeVito; Peck)
Other Side of Midnight, 1977 (Sarandon)
Other Side of Paradise. *See* Foxtrot, 1975
Other Side of the Tunnel. *See* Al Otro Lado del Túncl, 1993
Other Side of the Wind, 1970 (Huston, J.; Welles)
Other Woman, 1913 (Talmadge)
Other Woman. *See* Tsuma to shitc haha to shite, 1961
Otkrytaya kniga, 1979 (Yankovsky)
Otley, 1968 (Schneider)
Otoko arite, 1955 (Mifune; Shimura)
Otoko-girai, 1964 (Mori)
Otoko no hanamichi, 1941 (Hasegawa)
Otoko no tsugunai, 1936 (Tanaka)
Otoko o sabaku onna, 1948 (Yamamura)
Otoko tai otoko, 1960 (Mifune; Shimura)
Otoko wa Tsuraiyo, 1985 (Ryu)
Otoko wa tsuraiyo: Shiretoko bojo, 1987 (Mifune)
Otoko wa tsuraiyo: Torajiro Haru no yume, 1979 (Kagawa)
Otoko wa tsuraiyo: Torajiro junjo-shishu, 1976 (Kyo)
Otoko wa tsuraiyo: Torajiro yume-makura, 1972 (Tanaka)
Otoko wa Tsuraiyo: Toraijiro kokoro no tabiji, 1989 (Ryu)
Otoko wa Tsuraiyo: Torajiro Salada kinenbi, 1988 (Ryu)
Otokowa tsuraiyo: Torajiro koiuta, 1971 (Shimura)
Otomi to Tosaburo, 1950 (Yamada; Hasegawa)
Otone no yogiri, 1950 (Yamamura)
Ototo, 1960 (Tanaka)
Otouto, 1960 (Mori)
Otra Mujer. *See* Autre Femme, 1964
Otre l'amore, 1940 (Valli)
Otsukisama niwa waruikedo, 1954 (Yamamura)
Otsuya goroshi, 1951 (Yamada)
Otto e mezzo, 1963 (Mastroianni)
Otto no teiso: Haru kitareba, Aki futatabi, 1937 (Takamine)
Our Active Earth, 1972 (Heston)
Our Blushing Brides, 1930 (Crawford, J.; Montgomery)
Our Congressman, 1924 (Rogers, W.)
Our Country Cousin, 1914 (Arbuckle)
Our Daily Bread, 1921 (Garbo)
Our Dancing Daughters, 1928 (Crawford, J.)
Our Father. *See* Padre Nuestro, 1984
Our Happy Days. *See* Ayamna el Hilwa, 1954
Our Hollywood Education, 1992 (Ford, G.)
Our Hospitality, 1923 (Keaton, B.)
Our Husbands. *See* I nostri mariti, 1966
Our Leading Citizen, 1939 (Hayward)
Our Little Girl, 1935 (McCrea; Temple)
Our Man Flint, 1966 (Cobb; Coburn, J.)
Our Man in Havana, 1959 (Guinness; O'Hara; Richardson, R.)
Our Man in Marrakesh, 1966 (Kinski; Lom; Terry-Thomas)
Our Mrs. McChesney, 1918 (Barrymore, E.)
Our Modern Maidens, 1929 (Crawford, J.)
Our Mother's House, 1967 (Bogarde)

Our Parents-in-Law, 1912-13 (White)
Our Relations, 1936 (Laurel and Hardy)
Our Russian Front, 1941 (Huston, W.)
Our Silent Love. See Chichi to ko, 1967
Our Sons, 1991 (Andrews, J.; Ann-Margret; Grant, H.)
Our Story. See Notre histoire, 1985
Our Teacher. See Wareraga kyokan, 1939
Our Time. See Tempi nostri, 1953
Our Town, 1940 (Holden)
Our Very Own, 1950 (Wood)
Our Vines Have Tender Grapes, 1945 (Moorehead; O'Brien, M.; Robinson, E.)
Our Wife, 1931 (Laurel and Hardy)
Our Wife, 1941 (Coburn, C.; Douglas, Melvyn)
Our Winning Season, 1978 (Quaid)
Ours, 1919 (Modot)
Ours en Peluche, 1993 (Delon)
Ours et la poupée, 1969 (Bardot; Cassel)
Out All Night, 1933 (Temple)
Out California Way, 1946 (Rogers, R.)
Out from the Shadow, 1911 (Crisp; Sweet)
Out of Africa, 1985 (Brandauer; Redford; Streep)
Out of Darkness, 1955 (Welles)
Out of Ireland, 1994 (Neeson)
Out of It, 1969 (Voight)
Out of Luck, 1919 (Valentino)
Out of Petticoat Lane, 1914 (Mix)
Out of Rosenheim. See Bagdad Cafe, 1987
Out of Season, 1975 (Redgrave, V.; Robertson)
Out of the Blue, 1980 (Hopper)
Out of the Darkness, 1985 (Sheen)
Out of the Fog, 1919 (Nazimova)
Out of the Fog, 1941 (Garfield; Lupino)
Out of the Night, 1947 (Page)
Out of the Past, 1947 (Douglas, K.; Mitchum)
Out of the Ruins, 1928 (Barthelmess)
Out of this World, 1945 (Crosby; Lake)
Out-of-Towners, 1970 (Lemmon)
Out on a Limb, 1987 (MacLaine)
Out One—Out Two. See Spectre, 1973
Out West, 1918 (Arbuckle; Keaton, B.)
Out West, 1947 (Three Stooges)
Out West with the Hardys, 1938 (Rooney)
Outbreak, 1995 (Freeman; Hoffman; Sutherland)
Outcast, 1922 (Powell, W.)
Outcast among Outcasts, 1912 (Sweet)
Outcast Lasy, 1934 (Marshall)
Outcast of the Islands, 1951 (Howard, T.; Richardson, R.)
Outcasts of Poker Flat, 1919 (Carey)
Outcasts of Poker Flat, 1952 (Baxter; Hopkins, M.)
Outcry. See Grido, 1957
Outer Heat. See Alien Nation, 1988
Outer Limit of Solitude. See Hautes solitudes, 1974
Outer Space Jitters, 1957 (Three Stooges)
Outfit, 1973 (Duvall; Ryan, R.)
Outland, 1981 (Connery)
Outlanders, 1978 (Wyman)
Outlaw, 1943 (Huston, W.; Russell, J.)
Outlaw and the Lady, 1949 (Armendáriz)
Outlaw Josey Wales, 1976 (Eastwood)
Outlaw of Gor, 1989 (Palance)
Outlaw Reward, 1911 (Mix)
Outlaw's Bride, 1915 (Mix)
Outlawed, 1929 (Mix)
Outlaws of Red River, 1927 (Mix)
Outlaws IS Coming!, 1965 (Three Stooges)
Outpost in Malaya. See Planter's Wife, 1952
Outpost in Morocco, 1949 (Raft)
Outrage, 1950 (Lupino)
Outrage, 1964 (Bloom; Newman; Robinson, E.)
Outrage!, 1986 (Meredith; Preston)
Outrage. See Dispara!, 1993

Outrageous Fortune, 1987 (Midler)
Outriders, 1950 (McCrea; Novarro)
Outside Man. See Homme est morte, 1973
Outside the 3-Mile Limit, 1940 (Carey)
Outside the Gates, 1915 (Chaney)
Outside the Law, 1921 (Chaney; Wong)
Outside the Law, 1930 (Robinson, E.)
Outsider, 1926 (Pidgeon)
Outsider, 1940 (McDowall; Sanders)
Outsider. See Guinea Pig, 1948
Outsider, 1961 (Curtis, T.)
Outsider, 1967 (O'Brien, E.)
Outsider, 1979 (Hayden)
Outsider. See Marginal, 1983
Outsiders. See Band à part, 1964
Outsiders, 1983 (Cruise; Dillon)
Outskirts. See Extramuros, 1991
Outward Bound, 1930 (Howard, L.)
Outwitting Dad, 1914 (Laurel and Hardy)
Oveja negra, 1949 (Infante)
Over the Bouncing Blue with Will Rogers, 1928 (Rogers, W.)
Over the Brooklyn Bridge, 1983 (Gould; Winters)
Over the Counter, 1932 (Grable)
Over the Edge, 1979 (Dillon)
Over the Fence, 1917 (Lloyd)
Over the Garden Wall, 1910 (Normand)
Over the Goal, 1937 (McDaniel)
Over the Hill, 1931 (Marsh)
Over-the-Hill Gang, 1969 (Brennan)
Over-the-Hill Gang Rides Again, 1970 (Astaire; Brennan)
Over the Moon, 1937 (Harrison; Oberon)
Over the Top, 1986 (Stallone)
Over the Wall, 1938 (Bond)
Over 21, 1945 (Coburn, C.; Dunne)
Overboard, 1978 (Dickinson; Robertson)
Overboard, 1987 (Hawn; McDowall)
Overdrawn at the Memory Bank, 1985 (Julia)
Overgreppet. See Viol, 1967
Overindulgence, 1987 (Elliott)
Overland Red, 1920 (Carey)
Overland Stage Raiders, 1938 (Brooks, L.; Wayne)
Overnight. See That Night in London, 1933
Overtaxed. See I tartassati, 1959
Oviri. See Wolf at the Door, 1986
Owd Bob, 1938 (Lockwood)
Owen Marshall, Counselor at Law, 1981 (Sarandon)
Owl and the Pussycat, 1970 (Segal; Streisand)
Ox, 1991 (Josephson; Ullmann; Von Sydow)
Ox-Bow Incident, 1942 (Andrews, D.; Fonda, H.; Quinn)
Oxen. See Ox, 1991
Oyashiki-zame, 1959 (Hasegawa)
Oyster Dredger, 1915 (Chaney)
Oyu-sama, 1951 (Tanaka)
Oyuki the Madonna. See Maria no Oyuki, 1935
Ozark Romance, 1918 (Lloyd)
Pa Liv Och Dod, 1986 (Olin)
Pa Says, 1913 (Barrymore, L.)
Pa solsidan, 1936 (Bergman)
Paamenento bruu: Manatsu no koi, 1976 (Okada)
Paar, 1984 (Azmi)
Pablo Picasso Pintor, 1982 (Rey)
Pablo y Carolina, 1955 (Infante)
Pace That Thrills, 1925 (Astor)
Pacemakers, 1925 (Gable)
Pacha, 1967 (Gabin)
Pacific Blackout, 1942 (Preston)
Pacific Destiny, 1956 (Elliott)
Pacific Heights, 1990 (Griffith; Keaton, M.)
Pacific Liner, 1939 (Fitzgerald; McLaglen)
Pacific Northwest, 1944 (Huston, W.)
Pacifist. See Pacifista, 1971

Pacifista, 1970 (Olbrychski; Vitti)
Pack of Lies, 1987 (Bates, A.; Burstyn)
Pack Train, 1953 (Autry)
Pack Up Your Troubles, 1932 (Goddard; Laurel and Hardy)
Package, 1989 (Hackman; Jones, T.)
Paco, 1975 (Ferrer)
Pact with the Devil. See Pacto diabolico, 1968
Pacto diabolico, 1968 (Carradine)
Pad Italje, 1985 (Olbrychski)
Paddy O'Day, 1935 (Hayworth)
Paddy the Next Best Thing, 1923 (Marsh)
Paddy the Next Best Thing, 1933 (Gaynor)
Padmagolap, 1970 (Chatterjee)
Padre di famiglia, 1967 (Caron)
Padre Nuestro, 1984 (Abril; Rey)
Padrecito, 1964 (Cantinflas)
Padroni della città, 1977 (Palance)
Paese dei campanelli, 1953 (Loren)
Pagan, 1929 (Crisp; Novarro)
Pagan Love Song, 1950 (Williams, E.)
Paganini, 1923 (Veidt)
Paganini, 1989 (Blier; Kinski)
Paganini Horror, 1988 (Pleasence)
Page d'amour, 1977 (Chaplin, G.; Dalio; Aimée)
Page Miss Glory, 1935 (Astor; Davies; Powell, D.)
Pagemaster, 1994 (Goldberg)
Pages from the Story, 1957 (Bondarchuk)
Pagliacci, 1943 (Valli)
Pagliacci, 1948 (Lollobrigida)
Pagode, 1914 (Krauss)
Paid, 1930 (Crawford, J.)
Paid in Advance, 1919 (Chaney)
Paid in Error, 1938 (Withers)
Paid to Dance, 1937 (Hayworth)
Paid to Love, 1927 (Powell, W.)
Paigham, 1959 (Kumar)
Pain in the Pullman, 1936 (Three Stooges)
Painappuru butai, 1959 (Yamada)
Paint It Black, 1989 (Landau)
Paint Your Wagon, 1968 (Marvin; Eastwood; Seberg)
Painted Desert, 1931 (Gable)
Painted Faces, 1929 (Brown)
Painted Lady, 1912 (Sweet)
Painted Lady, 1914 (Sweet)
Painted Post, 1928 (Mix)
Painted Veil, 1934 (Brennan; Garbo; Marshall)
Painted Woman, 1932 (Tracy)
Paisà, 1946 (Masina)
Paisan. See **Paisà**, 1946
Paix sur le Rhin, 1938 (Rosay)
Pajama Game, 1957 (Day)
Pajama Party, 1964 (Keaton, B.; Lamour; Lanchester)
Pakten, 1995 (Josephson; Mitchum; Robertson; Schygulla)
Pal Joey, 1957 (Hayworth; Novak; Sidney)
Palamino, 1991 (Saint)
Pale Rider, 1985 (Eastwood)
Paleface, 1922 (Keaton, B.)
Paleface, 1948 (Hope; Russell, J.)
Palermo Connection. See Dimenticare Palermo, 1991
Palestinian, 1977 (Redgrave, V.)
Pallbearer, 1996 (Hershey)
Palm Beach Story, 1942 (Astor; Colbert; McCrea)
Palm Springs, 1936 (Niven)
Palmares des chansons, 1968 (Fernandel)
Palmy Days, 1931 (Cantor; Grable; Raft)
Paloma Cojo, 1995 (Maura)
Palomas, 1964 (Rey)
Palooka, 1934 (Durante)
Palooka from Paducah, 1935 (Keaton, B.)
Pals, 1987 (Ameche; Scott, G.)
Pals and Gals, 1954 (Three Stooges)

Pals and Pugs, 1920 (Laurel and Hardy)
Pals First, 1926 (Del Rio)
Pals in Blue, 1915 (Mix)
Pals of the Golden West, 1951 (Rogers, R.)
Pals of the Saddle, 1938 (Wayne)
Paltoquet, 1986 (Moreau; Piccoli)
Pan. See Kort är sommaren, 1962
Pan Dodek, 1971 (Łomnicki)
Pan Wołodyjowski, 1969 (Łomnicki; Nowicki; Olbrychski)
Panama Lady, 1939 (Ball)
Panama Sugar and the Dog Thief, 1990 (Reed)
Paname n'est pas Paris, 1927 (Vanel)
Pancho Villa, 1949 (Armendáriz)
Pancho Villa y la valentina, 1958 (Armendáriz)
Pandemonium, 1982 (O'Connor)
Pandilla del soborno, 1957 (Armendáriz)
Pandora and the Flying Dutchman, 1951 (Gardner; Mason)
Pandora's Box. See **Büchse der Pandora**, 1927
Pandora's Box, 1985 (Andrews, J.)
Pane, amore, e ..., 1955 (Loren)
Pane, amore, e fantasia, 1953 (Lollobrigida)
Pane, amore, e gelosia, 1954 (Lollobrigida)
Pane e cioccolata, 1973 (Karina)
Panic. See Panik, 1939
Panic at Lakewood Manor. See It Happened at Lakewood Manor, 1977
Panic Button, 1964 (Chevalier; Mansfield)
Panic in Needle Park, 1971 (Julia; Pacino)
Panic in the City, 1967 (Hopper)
Panic in the Streets, 1950 (Palance; Widmark)
Panic in Year Zero, 1962 (Milland)
Panic on the Air, 1936 (Ayres)
Panico en el Transiberiano, 1972 (Cushing)
Panik, 1939 (Björnstrand)
Panische Zeiten, 1980 (Constantine)
Pankhiraj, 1980 (Chatterjee)
Panny z Wilka, 1978 (Olbrychski)
Pano Kato Ke Plagios, 1993 (Papas)
Pantaloons. See Don Juan, 1955
Pantaloons, 1956 (Rey)
Panthea, 1917 (Talmadge)
Panther, 1995 (Bassett)
Panurge, 1932 (Darrieux)
Paola and Francesca, 1911 (Talmadge)
Paolo il caldo, 1973 (Giannini)
Pap'occhio, 1981 (Benigni; Rossellini)
Papa diventa Mamma, 1952 (Fabrizi)
Papa les petits bateaux, 1971 (Dalio)
Papa sans le savoir, 1931 (Brasseur; Rosay)
Papal Audience. See Udienza, 1971
Paparazzi, 1964 (Bardot)
Papas de Francine, 1909 (Modot)
Paper, 1994 (Close; Duvall; Keaton, M.; Robards)
Paper Bullets, 1941 (Ladd)
Paper Hanger. See Work, 1915
Paper Hearts, 1991 (Sheen)
Paper Lion, 1968 (Scheider)
Paper Tiger, 1974 (Mifune; Niven)
Paper Tigers. See Tigres de Papel, 1977
Paper Wedding. See Noces de papier, 1989
Paperhanger's Helper, 1915 (Laurel and Hardy)
Papillon, 1973 (Hoffman; McQueen)
Pappa Bom, 1949 (Björnstrand)
Pappa sökes, 1947 (Björnstrand)
Pappa, varför är du arg? Du gjorde likadant själv när du var ung, 1969 (Björnstrand)
Pappagalli, 1956 (Fabrizi; Sordi)
Pappagallo della zia Berta, 1912 (Bertini)
Par dela les nuages, 1995 (Malkovich; Mastroianni; Moreau)
Par habitude, 1914 (Chevalier)
Par habitude, 1923 (Chevalier)
Par habitude, 1932 (Fernandel)

Par le sang des autres, 1973 (Blier)
Par original, 1912 (Linder)
Par out'es Rentre? On t'a pas vue sortir, 1984 (Lewis, Jerry)
Par un beau matin d'été, 1964 (Belmondo; Chaplin, G.)
Para gnedych, 1915 (Mozhukin)
Para recibir el canto de los pajaros, 1995 (Chaplin, G.)
Paracelsus, 1943 (Krauss; Rasp)
Parachute Battalion, 1941 (Carey; O'Brien, E.; Preston)
Parachute Jumper, 1933 (Brennan; Davis, B.)
Parade, 1973 (Tati)
Parade, 1984 (Page)
Parade en sept nuits, 1941 (Barrault; Berry; Jourdan; Presle; Raimu)
Paradigma. *See* Pouvoir du mal, 1985
Paradine Case, 1947 (Barrymore, E.; Coburn, C.; Jourdan; Laughton; Peck; Valli)
Paradis des pilotes perdus, 1948 (Gélin)
Paradis des riches, 1977 (Dalio)
Paradis perdu, 1940 (Presle)
Paradis pour tous, 1982 (Audran)
Paradise. *See* Captain's Paradise, 1953
Paradise. *See* Paradiset, 1955
Paradise, 1991 (Griffith)
Paradise Alley, 1978 (Stallone)
Paradise Calling. *See* Pyramides bleue, 1988
Paradise Canyon, 1935 (Wayne)
Paradise for Buster, 1952 (Keaton, B.)
Paradise for Three, 1938 (Astor; Young, R.)
Paradise for Two, 1937 (Withers)
Paradise, Hawaiian Style, 1966 (Presley)
Paradiset, 1955 (Dahlbeck)
Parallax Garden, 1993 (Bacall)
Parallax View, 1974 (Beatty)
Parallel Lives, 1994 (Minnelli; Moore, Dudley; Rowlands)
Paramount on Parade, 1930 (Arthur; Bow; Chevalier; Constantine; Francis; March; Powell, W.; Wray)
Paranoiac, 1963 (Reed)
Parapluies de Cherbourg, 1964 (Deneuve)
Pararazzi, 1964 (Piccoli)
Parasite, 1982 (Moore, Demi)
Paratrooper. *See* Red Beret, 1953
Pardners, 1956 (Lewis, Jerry; Martin, D.; Moorehead; Van Cleef)
Pardon My Backfire, 1953 (Three Stooges)
Pardon My Berth Marks, 1940 (Keaton, B.)
Pardon My Clutch, 1948 (Three Stooges)
Pardon My French, 1950 (Henreid; Oberon)
Pardon My Past, 1946 (MacMurray)
Pardon My Pups, 1934 (Temple)
Pardon My Sarong, 1942 (Abbott and Costello)
Pardon My Scotch, 1935 (Three Stooges)
Pardon Us, 1931 (Laurel and Hardy; Karloff)
Paree, Paree, 1934 (Hope)
Pareja de Tres, 1995 (Maura)
Parent Trap, 1961 (O'Hara)
Parental Claim. *See* Lien de Parenté, 1986
Parental Guidance. *See* Immediate Family, 1989
Parenthood, 1989 (Martin, S.; Reeves; Robards; Steenburgen; Wiest)
Parents terribles, 1948 (Marais)
Parents Terribles, 1980 (Marais)
Parfum de la dame en noir, 1949 (Modot; Piccoli; Reggiani)
Pari, 1966 (Kumar)
Pari e figli, 1957 (Mastroianni)
Paria, 1968 (Marais)
Parigi e sempre Parigi, 1951 (Mastroianni; Montand; Fabrizi)
Parigina a Roma, 1954 (Sordi)
Parinay, 1974 (Azmi)
Parineeta, 1969 (Chatterjee)
Paris, 1926 (Crawford, J.)
Paris, 1929 (Buchanan)
Paris after Dark, 1943 (Dalio; Sanders)
Paris at Dawn. *See* Paris s'eveille, 1991
Paris at Midnight, 1926 (Barrymore, L.)

Paris Awakens. *See* Paris s'eveille, 1991
Paris-béguin, 1931 (Fernandel; Gabin)
Paris Blues, 1961 (Newman; Poitier; Reggiani; Woodward)
Paris Bound, 1929 (March)
Paris brûle-t-il?, 1966 (Belmondo; Brynner; Caron; Cassel; Delon; Douglas, K.; Ford, G.; Gélin; McDowall; Montand; Perkins; Piccoli; Boyer; Welles)
Paris by Night, 1989 (Oldman)
Paris Calling, 1941 (Bergner; Cobb; Rathbone; Scott, R.)
Paris canaille, 1955 (Gélin)
Paris chante toujours, 1950 (Montand)
Paris Commune. *See* Zori Parizha, 1936
Paris coquin. *See* Paris canaille, 1955
Paris Does Strange Things. *See* Elena et les hommes, 1957
Paris Express, 1952 (Aimée; Lom; Rains)
Paris Frills. *See* Falbalas, 1944
Paris Holiday, 1958 (Hope)
Paris Honeymoon, 1939 (Crosby; Horton)
Paris in Spring, 1935 (Lupino)
Paris Interlude, 1934 (Young, R.)
Paris la belle, 1959 (Arletty)
Paris Match. *See* French Kiss, 1995
Paris Model, 1953 (Goddard)
Paris—New York, 1939 (Berry)
Paris-Palace Hôtel, 1956 (Boyer)
Paris s'eveille, 1991 (Léaud)
Paris, Texas, 1984 (Kinski; Shepard); Stanton
Paris tous les deux, 1957 (Fernandel)
Paris Trout, 1991 (Harris, E.; Hershey; Hopper)
Paris Underground, 1945 (Fields, G.)
Paris vu par ..., 1965 (Audran)
Paris vu par ... 20 ans après, 1984 (Léaud)
Paris Waltz. *See* Valse de Paris, 1949
Paris Was Made for Lovers. *See* Time for Loving, 1971
Paris When It Sizzles, 1964 (Astaire; Curtis, T.; Dietrich; Hepburn, K.; Holden; Sidney)
Parishodh, 1968 (Chatterjee)
Parisian Love, 1925 (Bow)
Parisian Nights, 1925 (Karloff)
Parisian Romance, 1916 (Menjou)
Parisienne, 1957 (Bardot; Boyer)
Parisiennes, 1961 (Deneuve)
Park Avenue Logger, 1937 (Bond)
Park Is Mine, 1985 (Jones, T.)
Parking, 1985 (Marais)
Parlementaire, 1916 (Mozhukin)
Parlor, Bedroom, and Bath, 1931 (Keaton, B.)
Parnell, 1937 (Crisp; Gable; Loy)
Parole, 1936 (Quinn)
Parole, 1982 (Barkin)
Parole de flic, 1985 (Delon)
Parole Fixer, 1940 (Quinn)
Parole Girl, 1933 (Bellamy)
Paroles et musique, 1984 (Deneuve)
Paroxismus, 1969 (Kinski)
Parque de Madrid, 1958 (Rey)
Parrish, 1961 (Colbert; Malden)
Parson Who Fled West, 1915 (Mix)
Part de l'ombre, 1945 (Barrault; Feuillère)
Part du feu, 1977 (Cardinale; Piccoli)
Partie d'echecs, 1994 (Deneuve)
Partir, revenir, 1985 (Girardot; Piccoli)
Partisan Mission/Answer to Violence. *See* Zamach, 1959
Partners, 1976 (Elliott)
Partners, 1982 (Hurt, J.)
Partners in Crime, 1928 (Beery; Powell, W.)
Partners in Crime, 1937 (Quinn)
Partners in Crime, 1973 (Grant, L.)
Party, 1968 (Sellers)
Party at Kitty and Studs. *See* Italian Stallion, 1970
Party Crashers, 1958 (Farmer)
Party Girl, 1958 (Charisse; Cobb; Taylor, R.)

Party Wire, 1935 (Arthur)
Party's Over, 1963 (Reed)
Party's Over, 1966 (Hawkins)
Party's Over. See Zitti e Mosca, 1991
Parvarish, 1977 (Azmi)
Pas de caviar pour tante Olga, 1965 (Brasseur)
Pas de panique, 1965 (Brasseur)
Pas de week-end pour notre amour, 1950 (Berry)
Pas på Pigerne, 1930 (Madsen and Schenstrøm)
Pas perdus, 1964 (Morgan; Trintignant)
Pas si méchant que ça, 1974 (Depardieu)
Pas Suspendu de la Cigogne. See To Meteoro Vima tou Pelargou, 1991
Pas tres Catholique, 1994 (Presle)
Pas un mot à ma femme, 1931 (Fernandel)
Pascali's Island, 1988 (Kingsley; Mirren)
Pascsagier—Welcome to Germany, 1988 (Curtis, T.)
Pasha's Wives. See Esclave blanche, 1939
Pasion de hombre. See Man of Passion, 1989
Pasión desnuda, 1953 (Félix)
Paso, 1949 (Hayden)
Pasodoble, 1988 (Rey)
Pasqualino Settebelleze, 1975 (Giannini; Rey)
Passage, 1979 (Lee, C.; Mason; McDowell; Neal, Quinn)
Passage, 1986 (Delon)
Passage Home, 1955 (Cusack; Finch)
Passage Interdit, 1935 (Modot)
Passage of Love. See I Was Happy Here, 1965
Passage to Algiers, 1945 (Rathbone)
Passage to India, 1965 (Cusack)
Passage to India, 1984 (Davis, J.; Guinness)
Passage to Marseilles, 1944 (Bogart; Dalio; Greenstreet; Lorre; Morgan; Rains)
Passager, 1928 (Vanel)
Passager clandestin, 1957 (Arletty; Reggiani)
Passager de la pluie, 1969 (Bronson)
Passante du Sans-Souci, 1981 (Piccoli; Schell, Maria; Schneider)
Passaporto per l'Oriente, 1951 (Lollobrigida)
Passatore, 1947 (Brazzi; Sordi)
Passe-Muraille. See Garou-Garou, le passe-muraille, 1950
Passé à vendre, 1936 (Brasseur)
Passed Away, 1992 (Hoskins)
Passenger. See **Professione: Reporter**, 1975
Passenger 57, 1992 (Snipes)
Passing Fancy. See Dekigokoro, 1933
Passing of Pete, 1916 (Mix)
Passing of the Third Floor Back, 1935 (Veidt)
Passing of Two-Gun Hicks, 1914 (Hart)
Passing Through. See Good Bad Man, 1916
Passion. See Madame DuBarry, 1919
Passion, 1954 (Wilde)
Passion, 1969 (Andersson, B.; Josephson; Ullmann; Von Sydow)
Passion, 1982 (Huppert; Piccoli; Schygulla)
Passion de Jeanne d'Arc, 1928 (Artaud)
Passion Fish, 1992 (Bassett)
Passion Flower, 1920 (Talmadge)
Passion Flower, 1930 (Francis; Milland)
Passion Flower, 1985 (Hershey)
Passion Flower Hotel, 1978 (Kinski)
Passion for Life. See Ecole buissonnière, 1948
Passion in Paradise, 1989 (Steiger)
Passion Island. See Isla de la pasion, 1941
Passion of Anna. See Passion, 1969
Passion, travail et amour. See Passion, 1982
Passion's Playground, 1920 (Valentino)
Passionate, Faithful Spirit, 1935 (Zhao Dan)
Passionate Friends, 1949 (Howard, T.; Rains)
Passionate Plumber, 1932 (Durante; Keaton, B.)
Passionate Stranger, 1956 (Richardson, R.)
Passionate Thief. See Risate di Gioia, 1960
Passione d'amore, 1981 (Blier)
Passione secondo San Matteo, 1949 (Cervi)
Passionels Tagebuch, 1916 (Jannings)

Passions, 1984 (Woodward)
Passions, He Had Three, 1913 (Arbuckle)
Passover Plot, 1976 (Pleasence)
Passport to Destiny, 1944 (Lanchester)
Passport to Fame. See Whole Town's Talking, 1935
Passport to Hell, 1932 (Crisp; Lukas)
Passport to Oblivion. See Where the Spies Are, 1965
Passport to Pimlico, 1948 (Rutherford)
Passport to Shame, 1959 (Caine; Constantine; Dors; Lom)
Passport to Terror. See Dark Holiday, 1989
Password Is Courage, 1962 (Bogarde)
Password: Korn, 1967 (Nowicki)
Past Caring, 1985 (Elliott)
Past of Mary Holmes, 1933 (Arthur)
Pastoral Symphony. See Denen Kokyogaku, 1938
Pat and Mike, 1952 (Bronson; Gordon; Hepburn, K.; Tracy)
Pat Garrett and Billy the Kid, 1973 (Coburn, J.; Robards; Stanton)
Pat und Patachon im Paradies. See Eine Insel wird entdeckt, 1937
Patang, 1994 (Azmi)
Patate, 1964 (Darrieux; Marais)
Patch of Blue, 1965 (Poitier; Winters)
Patchwork Girl of Oz, 1914 (Lloyd)
Patent Leather Kid, 1927 (Barthelmess)
Paternity, 1981 (Reynolds, B.)
Path of Glory, 1949 (Bondarchuk)
Paths of Glory, 1957 (Douglas, K.; Menjou)
Pathways of Life, 1916 (Gish)
Patience, 1920 (Veidt)
Patient Vanishes. See This Man Is Dangerous, 1941
Patita, 1953 (Anand)
Patria, 1917 (Beery)
Patricia, 1916 (Valentino)
Patricia Neal Story. See Act of Love, 1981
Patrick the Great, 1945 (O'Connor)
Patriot, 1916 (Hart)
Patriot, 1928 (Jannings)
Patriot Games, 1992 (Ford, H.; Harris, R.; Jackson, S.; Jones, James Earl)
Patrol Car 777. See Patrullero 777, 1978
Patrouille Blanche, 1941 (Hayakawa)
Patrouille des sables, 1954 (Dalio)
Patrullero 777, 1978 (Cantinflas)
Patsy, 1928 (Davies; Dressler)
Patsy, 1964 (Carradine; Lewis, Jerry; Lorre; Raft; Sloane)
Pattern of Morality. See Owen Marshall, Counselor at Law, 1981
Pattern of Roses, 1983 (Bonham-Carter)
Patters, 1956 (Sloane)
Pattes de mouche, 1936 (Brasseur)
Patton, 1970 (Malden; Scott, G.)
Paul Chevrolet en de ultieme hallucinatie, 1985 (Constantine)
Paul Claudel, 1951 (Barrault)
Paul Robeson, 1978 (Jones, James Earl)
Paul Temple Returns, 1952 (Lee, C.)
Paula. See Framed, 1947
Paula, 1952 (Young, L.)
Paulina 1880, 1972 (Schell, Maximilian)
Pauline Cushman, the Federal Spy, 1913 (Mix)
Paura. See Angst, 1955
Paura e amore, 1988 (Scacchi)
Paura in città, 1976 (Cusack)
Pavillon brûle, 1941 (Blier; Marais)
Pawn Shop. See Stampen, 1955
Pawnbroker, 1965 (Freeman; Steiger)
Pawnshop, 1916 (Chaplin, C.; Purviance)
Pay as You Enter, 1928 (Loy)
Pay Day, 1922 (Chaplin, C.; Purviance)
Pay Me, 1916 (Chaney)
Pay or Die, 1960 (Borgnine)
Pay the Devil. See Man in the Shadow, 1957
Pay Your Dues, 1919 (Lloyd)
Paying Guest, 1957 (Anand)
Payment. See Rasplata, 1970

Payment Deferred, 1932 (Laughton; Milland; O'Sullivan)
Payment on Demand, 1951 (Davis, B.)
Payoff, 1991 (Stanton)
Pays sans étoiles, 1945 (Brasseur; Philipe)
Peaceful Oscar, 1927 (Arbuckle)
Peacemaker, 1914 (Talmadge)
Peacemaker. *See* Ambassador, 1984
Peach Basket Hat, 1909 (Pickford)
Peaches, 1964 (Ustinov)
Peaks of Zelengore, 1976 (Bondarchuk)
Peanuts—Die Bank zahlt alles, 1996 (Vogler)
Pearl. *See* Perla, 1945
Pearl and the Burglars, 1912-13 (White)
Pearl and the Poet, 1912-13 (White)
Pearl and the Tramp, 1912-13 (White)
Pearl as a Clairvoyant, 1912-13 (White)
Pearl as a Detective, 1912-13 (White)
Pearl of Death, 1944 (Rathbone)
Pearl of the Army, 1916 (White)
Pearl of the Punjab, 1914 (White)
Pearl's Admirers, 1912-13 (White)
Pearls Bring Tears, 1937 (Withers)
Pearl's Dilemma, 1912-13 (White)
Pearl's Hero, 1912-13 (White)
Pearl's Mistake, 1912-13 (White)
Pearls of the Crown. *See* Perles de la couronne, 1937
Peasant's Fate. *See* Krestyanskaya dolia, 1912
Peat and Repeat, 1931 (Arbuckle)
Peau d'âne, 1970 (Deneuve; Marais; Presle; Seyrig)
Peau d'espion, 1967 (Blier; Jourdan; O'Brien, E.)
Peau de banane, 1964 (Belmondo; Cuny; Moreau)
Peau de l'ours, 1957 (Cassel)
Peau de torpédo, 1969 (Audran; Kinski)
Peau douce, 1964 (Léaud)
Pecado de una madre, 1960 (Del Rio)
Peccato, 1963 (Volonté)
Peccato che sia una canaglia, 1954 (Loren; Mastroianni)
Peccato degli anni verdi, o L'assegno, 1961 (Valli)
Peccato mortale, 1972 (Lollobrigida)
Peccatrice, 1940 (Cervi)
Pêcheur d'Islande, 1924 (Vanel)
Pêcheur d'Islande, 1958 (Vanel)
Peck's Bad Boy, 1934 (Cooper)
Peck's Bad Girl, 1918 (Normand)
Pecora nera, 1969 (Gassman)
Peculiar Patients' Pranks, 1915 (Lloyd)
Peddlar and the Lady. *See* Campo dei fiori, 1943
Peddler, 1914 (Arbuckle)
Pedestrian. *See* Fussgänger, 1974
Pedro's Dilemma, 1912 (Normand)
Peeks at Hollywood, 1945 (Flynn)
Peep and Big Wide World, 1988 (Ustinov)
Peeper, 1975 (Caine; Wood)
Peeping Pete, 1913 (Arbuckle)
Peer Gynt, 1919 (Veidt)
Peer Gynt, 1945 (Heston)
Peer Gynt, 1965 (Heston)
Peg o' My Heart, 1933 (Davies)
Peg of Old Drury, 1935 (Hawkins; Neagle)
Peggy, 1949 (Coburn, C.; Hudson)
Peggy on a Spree. *See* Peggy på vift, 1946
Peggy på vift, 1946 (Björnstrand)
Peggy Sue Got Married, 1986 (Cage; Carradine; O'Sullivan; Turner, K.)
Pehavy Max a Strasilda, 1988 (Constantine)
Peintre, 1994 (Gong Li)
Peking Express, 1951 (Cotten)
Peking Remembered, 1966 (Henreid)
Pèlerin de la beauce, 1950 (Fresnay)
Pelican Brief, 1993 (Roberts, J.; Shepard; Washington)
Pelle, 1981 (Cardinale; Lancaster; Mastroianni)
Pelle Erovraren, 1987 (Von Sydow)

Pellegrini d'amore, 1953 (Loren)
Pelliccia di visone, 1956 (Vitti)
Pena de muerte, 1973 (Rey)
Penal Colony. *See* Colonia penal, 1971
Penalty, 1920 (Chaney)
Penalty, 1941 (Barrymore, L.)
Penalty of Fame. *See* Okay America, 1932
Pendler, 1986 (Ganz)
Pendu, 1906 (Linder)
Pendulum, 1969 (Seberg)
Penelope, 1966 (Falk; Wood)
Pengar—en tragikomisk saga, 1946 (Dahlbeck)
Penitent, 1988 (Julia)
Penn of Pennsylvania, 1942 (Kerr)
Penne nere, 1952 (Mastroianni)
Pennies from Heaven, 1936 (Crosby)
Pennies from Heaven, 1981 (Martin, S.; Walken)
Penny and the Pownall Case, 1948 (Dors; Lee, C.)
Penny Points to Paradise, 1951 (Sellers)
Penny Princess, 1951 (Bogarde)
Penny Serenade, 1941 (Dunne; Grant, C.)
Pension Mimosas, 1935 (Arletty; Rosay)
Pension sonnenschein, 1990 (Łomnicki)
Pentecost Outing. *See* Pfingstausflug, 1978
Penthouse, 1933 (Loy)
Pentito, 1985 (Von Sydow)
Peñon de las ánimas, 1942 (Félix)
People against O'Hara, 1951 (Bronson; Tracy)
People in the Town. *See* Machi no hitobito, 1926
People Meet and Sweet Music Fills the Air. *See* Mënniskor modes og sod musik opstår i hjertet, 1967
People Next Door, 1970 (Wallach)
People of the Forest: The Chimps of Gombe, 1991 (Mirren)
People of the Simlången Valley. *See* Folket i Simlångsdalen, 1947
People on Wheels. *See* Lidé z maringotek, 1966
People's Enemy, 1935 (Coburn, C.; Douglas, Melvyn)
People Soup, 1969 (Arkin)
People vs. Dr. Kildare, 1941 (Ayres; Barrymore, L.)
People Will Talk, 1951 (Grant, C.)
Pepe, 1960 (Cantinflas; Chevalier; Coburn, C.; Crosby; Curtis, T.; Durante; Garland; Garson; Leigh, Janet; Lemmon; Martin, D.; Novak; Reynolds, D.; Robinson, E.; Sidney)
Pepe El Toro, 1952 (Infante)
Pépé le Moko, 1936 (Dalio; Gabin; Modot)
Pepi, Luci, Bom y otras chicas del montón, 1980 (Maura)
Peppermint frappé, 1967 (Chaplin, G.)
Peppy Polly, 1919 (Barthelmess)
Pequeno proscrito, 1955 (Armendáriz)
Pequeno salvaje, 1959 (Armendáriz)
Per amore ... per magia, 1966 (Brazzi)
Per il blasone, 1914 (Bertini)
Per la sua gioia, 1913 (Bertini)
Per le antiche scale, 1975 (Mastroianni)
Per qualche dollari in più, 1966 (Eastwood; Van Cleef; Volonté; Kinski)
Per un dollaro di gloria. *See* Escuadró de la muerte, 1966
Per un pugno di dollari, 1964 (Eastwood; Volonté)
Per una bara piena di dollari, 1970 (Kinski)
Percy, 1971 (Elliott)
Percy and Thunder, 1993 (Jones, James Earl)
Percy's Progress, 1974 (Elliott; Price)
Père, 1971 (Fresnay)
Père de mademoiselle, 1953 (Arletty)
Père et l'enfant, 1959 (Montand)
Père Lebonnard, 1939 (Brasseur)
Père Noel et fils, 1983 (Girardot)
Pereira Declares. *See* Sostiene Pereira, 1996
Perez Family, 1995 (Huston, A.)
Perfect, 1985 (Curtis, J.; Travolta)
Perfect Alibi. *See* Birds of Prey, 1930
Perfect Clown, 1924 (Laurel and Hardy)
Perfect Crime, 1921 (Lombard)

Perfect Day, 1929 (Laurel and Hardy)
Perfect Friday, 1970 (Baker)
Perfect Furlough, 1958 (Curtis, T.; Dalio; Leigh, Janet)
Perfect Gentlemen, 1978 (Bacall; Cooper; Gordon)
Perfect Lady, 1915 (Purviance)
Perfect Marriage, 1946 (Niven; Young, L.)
Perfect Snob, 1941 (Quinn; Wilde)
Perfect Specimen, 1937 (Blondell; Flynn; Horton)
Perfect Strangers, 1945 (Kerr; Donat)
Perfect Strangers, 1950 (Ritter; Rogers, G.)
Perfect Thirty-Six, 1918 (Normand)
Perfect Tribute, 1991 (Robards)
Perfect Understanding, 1933 (Olivier; Swanson)
Perfect Weekend. See St. Louis Kid, 1934
Perfect World, 1993 (Costner; Eastwood)
Perfectionist. See Grand Patron, 1951
Perfidy of Mary, 1913 (Barrymore, L.)
Peril. See Péril en la demeure, 1984
Péril en la demeure, 1984 (Piccoli)
Perilous Voyage, 1976 (Grant, L.)
Perils of Pauline, 1914 (White)
Perils of Pauline, 1967 (Horton; Terry-Thomas)
Perils of the Wind, 1925 (Karloff)
Perinbaba, 1985 (Masina)
Period of Adjustment, 1962 (Fonda, J.)
Perla, 1945 (Armendáriz)
Perla del cinema, 1916 (Bertini)
Perle, 1932 (Feuillère)
Perles de la couronne, 1937 (Arletty; Barrault; Dalio; Raimu)
Permanent Record, 1988 (Reeves)
Permette? Rocco Papaleo, 1971 (Mastroianni)
Permettete che ami vostre figlia?, 1974 (Fabrizi)
Permission to Kill, 1975 (Bogarde; Gardner)
Perry Mason: The Case of the Grimacing Governor, 1994 (Curtis, T.)
Perry Mason: The Case of the Musical Murder, 1989 (Reynolds, D.)
Perry Mason: The Case of the Silenced Singer, 1990 (Bassett)
Persecution, 1974 (Howard, T.; Turner, L.)
Persiane chiuse, 1951 (Masina)
Persona, 1966 (Andersson, B.; Björnstrand; Ullmann)
Personal Affair, 1954 (Tierney)
Personal Choice. See Beyond the Stars, 1989
Personal Column. See Pièges, 1939
Personal Column. See Lured, 1947
Personal Journey by Sam Neill. See Cinema of Unease, 1996
Personal Property, 1937 (Harlow; Taylor, R.)
Personne ne m'aime, 1994 (Léaud)
Persons Unknown. See I soliti ignoti, 1958
Pervaya lyubov, 1933 (Cherkassov)
Pest, 1917 (Laurel and Hardy)
Pest, 1919 (Normand)
Pest, 1922 (Laurel and Hardy)
Pest from the West, 1939 (Keaton, B.)
Pest Man Wins, 1951 (Three Stooges)
Pestalozzidorf, 1953 (Dahlbeck)
Pestalozzos Berg, 1988 (Volonté)
Pestañas Postizas, 1982 (Banderas)
Peste. See Plague, 1992
Pestka, 1995 (Olbrychski)
Pestonjee, 1987 (Azmi)
Pet. See Monkey Trouble, 1994
Pet Pyar nur Paap, 1984 (Patil)
Pět z milionů, 1959 (Brodský)
Petain, 1992 (Cassel)
Pete Kelly's Blues, 1955 (Leigh, Janet; Mansfield; Marvin; O'Brien, E.)
Pete 'n' Tillie, 1972 (Matthau; Page)
Pete, Pearl and the Pole. See Piazza Pulita, 1972
Pete's Dragon, 1977 (Rooney; Winters)
Peter and Paul, 1981 (Hopkins, A.)
Peter der Grosse, 1922 (Jannings; Kortner)
Peter Ibbetson, 1935 (Constantine; Lupino)
Peter Pan, 1924 (Wong)

Peter Pan, 1976 (Farrow)
Peter Schlemihl, 1915 (Wegener)
Peter the Crazy. See Pierrot le fou, 1965
Peter the Great. See Peter der Grosse, 1922
Peter the Great. See Piotr Pervyi, 1937-9
Peter the Great, 1986 (Howard, T.)
Peter the Tramp. See Luffar-Petter, 1922
Peter's Friends, 1992 (Branagh; Thompson)
Petersburgskiya trushchobi, 1915 (Mozhukin)
Petit Bougnat, 1969 (Adjani)
Petit Café, 1919 (Linder)
Petit Café, 1930 (Chevalier; Rosay)
Petit Chose, 1938 (Arletty)
Petit Garcon de l'ascenseur, 1961 (Dalio)
Petit garçon, 1993 (Reggiani)
Petit Hotel à louer, 1923 (Modot)
Petit Jacques, 1922 (Fresnay)
Petit Jeune Homme, 1909 (Linder)
Petit jour, 1964 (Karina)
Petit Marcel, 1975 (Huppert)
Petit monde de Don Camillo, 1952 (Fernandel; Cervi)
Petit riens, 1941 (Berry)
Petit Soldat, 1960 (Karina)
Petit théâtre de Jean Renoir, 1969 (Moreau)
Petit Trou pas cher, 1934 (Berry)
Petita Jimenez, 1976 (Baker)
Petite Chocolatière, 1932 (Raimu)
Petite Femme dans le train, 1932 (Feuillère)
Petite fille en velours bleu, 1978 (Cardinale; Piccoli)
Petite peste, 1938 (Presle)
Petite Republique, 1946 (Carroll)
Petite Rosse, 1909 (Linder)
Petite Vertu, 1967 (Brasseur)
Petites du quai aux Fleurs, 1943 (Blier; Gélin; Jourdan; Philipe)
Petits Chats, 1959 (Deneuve)
Petits heures du matin, 1994 (Deneuve)
Petits Matins, 1961 (Arletty; Blier; Brasseur; Gélin)
Petits Riens, 1941 (Fernandel; Raimu)
Petrified Forest, 1936 (Bogart; Davis, B.; Howard, L.)
Petrified Garden, 1993 (Schygulla)
Pétrole, pétrole, 1981 (Blier)
Pétroleuses, 1971 (Bardot; Cardinale; Presle)
Petronella, 1927 (Homolka)
Petrus, 1946 (Dalio; Brasseur; Fernandel)
Petticoat Fever, 1936 (Loy; Montgomery)
Petticoat Politics, 1941 (Ladd)
Petting Preferred, 1934 (Langdon)
Petulia, 1968 (Christie; Cotten; Scott, G.)
Peu de soleil dans l'eau froide, 1971 (Depardieu)
Peur. See Vertige d'un soir, 1936
Peur de l'eau. See Max a peur de l'eau, 1913
Peur sur la ville, 1975 (Belmondo)
Peyton Place, 1957 (Kennedy; Turner, L.)
Peyton Place—The Next Generation, 1985 (Malone)
Pfarrhauskomödie, 1972 (Schell, Maria)
Pfingstausflug, 1978 (Bergner)
Pflicht zu schweigen, 1927 (Fröhlich)
Phaedra, 1962 (Mercouri; Perkins)
Phantom, 1916 (Gilbert)
Phantom, 1922 (Dagover)
Phantom Baron. See Baron fantôme, 1943
Phantom Buster, 1927 (Karloff)
Phantom Creeps, 1939 (Cobb; Lugosi)
Phantom Empire, 1935 (Autry)
Phantom Fiend. See Lodger, 1932
Phantom of Death, 1988 (Pleasence)
Phantom of Hollywood, 1974 (Crawford, B.)
Phantom of Liberty. See Fantôme de la liberté, 1974
Phantom of Paris, 1931 (Gilbert)
Phantom of the Golden Gate. See Golden Gate Murders, 1979
Phantom of the North, 1929 (Karloff)

Phantom of the Opera, 1924 (Chaney)
Phantom of the Opera, 1943 (Eddy; Rains)
Phantom of the Opera, 1962 (Lom)
Phantom of the Opera, 1983 (Schell, Maximilian)
Phantom of the Opera, 1990 (Cassel; Lancaster)
Phantom of the Rue Morgue, 1954 (Malden)
Phantom President, 1932 (Colbert; Durante)
Phantom Raiders, 1940 (Pidgeon)
Phantom Riders, 1918 (Carey)
Phantom Ship, 1935 (Lugosi)
Phantom Thief, 1914 (White)
Pharmacist, 1933 (Fields, W. C.)
Phenomena, 1985 (Pleasence)
Phenomenon, 1996 (Duvall; Trayolta; Whitaker)
Phffft!, 1954 (Holliday; Lemmon; Novak)
Philadelphia, 1993 (Banderas; Hanks; Robards; Steenburgen; Washington; Woodward)
Philadelphia Story, 1940 (Grant, C.; Hepburn, K.; Stewart)
Philosophy of the Boudoir. *See* Eugenie—The Story of Her Journey into Perversion, 1970
Phir Kabb Milogi, 1974 (Kumar)
Phobia, 1980 (Carradine; Huston, J.)
Phoenix. *See* Fujicho, 1947
Phone Call from a Stranger, 1952 (Davis, B.; Winters)
Phoney Photos, 1918 (Laurel and Hardy)
Phony Express, 1943 (Three Stooges)
Phroso, 1923 (Vanel)
Phynx, 1970 (Blondell; Keeler; O'Sullivan; Pryor; Weissmuller)
Physical Evidence, 1989 (Reynolds, B.)
Pia De' Tolomei, 1911 (Bertini)
Piacevoli notti, 1966 (Gassman; Lollobrigida; Vitti)
Piano, 1993 (Hunter; Keitel; Neill)
Piano for Mrs. Cimino, 1982 (Davis, B.)
Piano Mooner, 1942 (Langdon)
Piano Movers. *See* His Musical Career, 1914
Piano Tuner Has Arrived. *See* E'arrivato l'accordatore, 1951
Pianos mécaniques, 1965 (Mason; Mercouri)
Pianstvo i yevo pozledstvia, 1913 (Mozhukin)
Piątka z ulicy Barskiej, 1954 (Łomnicki)
Piatto piange, 1974 (Blier)
Piazza Pulita, 1972 (Papas)
Picari, 1987 (Blier; Gassman; Giannini)
Picaros. *See* I picari, 1987
Picasso Summer, 1972 (Brynner; Finney)
Picassos aeventyr, 1978 (Olin)
Piccadilly, 1929 (Laughton; Wong)
Piccadilly Incident, 1946 (Neagle)
Piccadilly Jim, 1936 (Montgomery)
Piccadilly null Uhr swölf, 1963 (Kinski)
Piccadilly Third Stop, 1960 (Zetterling)
Picciola, 1911 (Normand)
Piccioni di Piazza San Marco, 1980 (Belmondo)
Piccolo diavolo, 1988 (Benigni; Matthau)
Piccolo Fonte, 1918 (Bertini)
Piccolo Grande Amore, 1993 (York)
Piccolo mondo antico, 1941 (Valli)
Piccolo posta, 1955 (Sordi)
Pick a Star, 1937 (Laurel and Hardy)
Pick and Shovel, 1923 (Laurel and Hardy)
Pick-Up, 1933 (Raft; Sidney)
Pick-Up Artist, 1987 (Aiello; Beatty; Hopper; Keitel)
Picking Peaches, 1924 (Langdon)
Pickle, 1993 (Aiello; Moore, Dudley; Rossellini; Winters)
Pickup Alley. *See* Interpol, 1957
Pickup on 101, 1972 (Sheen)
Pickup on South Street, 1953 (Ritter; Widmark)
Picnic, 1955 (Holden; Novak; Robertson; Russell, R.)
Picnic, 1990 (Azmi)
Picnic at Hanging Rock, 1976 (Roberts, R.)
Pictura, 1952 (Fonda, H.; Peck; Price)
Picture Bride, 1994 (Mifune)

Picture Mommy Dead, 1966 (Ameche)
Picture of Dorian Gray, 1945 (Lansbury; Sanders)
Picture Snatcher, 1933 (Bellamy; Cagney)
Pie Covered Wagon, 1932 (Temple)
Pie-Eyed, 1925 (Laurel and Hardy)
Pie in the Sky. *See* Terror in the City, 1963
Piece of the Action, 1977 (Jones, James Earl; Poitier)
Pied Piper, 1942 (Baxter; Dalio; McDowall)
Pied Piper, 1971 (Dors; Hurt, J.; Kaye; Pleasence)
Pied Piper, 1990 (O'Toole)
Pied Piper of Hamelin, 1961 (Rains)
Pieds nickelés, 1964 (Presle)
Piège, 1958 (Vanel)
Pièges, 1939 (Chevalier)
Pier 13. *See* Me and My Gal, 1932
Piernas de seda, 1935 (Hayworth)
Piero Gherardi, 1967 (Cardinale)
Pierre dans la bouche, 1983 (Keitel)
Pierrot le fou, 1965 (Belmondo; Karina; Léaud)
Pierwszy dzień wolności, 1964 (Łomnicki; Tyszkiewicz)
Pies and Guys, 1958 (Three Stooges)
Pigalle-Saint-Germain-des-Prés, 1950 (Cassel; Moreau)
Pigen og skoene, 1959 (Karina)
Pigeon, 1969 (Malone)
Pigeon That Took Rome, 1962 (Heston)
Pigpen. *See* Porcile, 1969
Pigskin Parade, 1936 (Garland; Grable; Ladd)
Pigsty. *See* Porcile, 1969
Pikovaya dama, 1916 (Mozhukin)
Pilatus und andere—ein Film für Karfreitag, 1975 (Olbrychski)
Pile Driver. *See* Fatal Mallet, 1914
Pile ou face, 1980 (Noiret)
Pilgrim, 1923 (Chaplin, C.; Purviance)
Pilgrim of Love. *See* Pellegrini d'amore, 1953
Pill of Death. *See* Peau de Torpédo, 1969
Pillar of Flame, 1915 (Talmadge)
Pillars of the Sky, 1956 (Bond; Malone; Marvin)
Pillow Talk, 1959 (Dalio; Day; Hudson; Ritter)
Pillow to Post, 1945 (Greenstreet; Lupino)
Pilot, 1979 (Robertson)
Pilot, 1981 (Andrews, D.)
Pilot No. 5, 1943 (Gardner; Kelly, Gene)
Pilote de la morte. *See* Flight Lieutenant, 1942
Pimpernel Smith, 1941 (Howard, L.)
Pin-Up Girl, 1944 (Brown; Dalio; Grable)
Pinched, 1917 (Lloyd)
Pine's Revenge, 1915 (Chaney)
Pink Cadillac, 1989 (Eastwood)
Pink Floyd—The Wall, 1982 (Hoskins)
Pink Gods, 1922 (Menjou)
Pink Jungle, 1968 (Garner)
Pink Panther, 1964 (Cardinale; Niven; Sellers)
Pink Panther Strikes Again, 1976 (Cardinale; Cooper; Lom; Sellers; Sharif)
Pink String and Sealing Wax, 1945 (Withers)
Pinky, 1949 (Barrymore, E.)
Pinocchio, 1995 (Bujold)
Pinocchio and the Emperor of the Night, 1987 (Jones, James Earl; Minnelli)
Pins Are Lucky, 1914 (Laurel and Hardy)
Pinto, 1920 (Normand)
Pinto Ben, 1915 (Hart)
Pionere in Ingolstadt, 1970 (Schygulla)
Piotr Pervyi, 1937-9 (Cherkassov)
Piovra, 1918 (Bertini)
Pipe Dreams, 1916 (Laurel and Hardy)
Pipe the Whiskers, 1918 (Lloyd)
Piper's Price, 1916 (Chaney)
Pipes of Pan, 1914 (Chaney)
Pirate, 1948 (Garland; Kelly, Gene)
Pirate, 1978 (Lee, C.; Wallach)
Pirate Gold, 1913 (Sweet)
Pirate Party on Catalina Island, 1936 (Davies; Flynn; Grant, C.)

Pirates. *See* Kaizoki-sen, 1950
Pirates, 1986 (Matthau)
Pirates du rail, 1938 (Dalio; Vanel)
Pirates of Blood River, 1962 (Lee, C.; Reed)
Pirates of Penzance, 1983 (Kline; Lansbury)
Pirates of Tripoli, 1954 (Henreid)
Pirates on the Malaren. *See* Mälarpirater, 1959
Pirogov, 1947 (Cherkassov)
Piroska és a farkas, 1988 (Nowicki)
Piscine, 1968 (Delon; Schneider)
Piste du nord. *See* Loi du nord, 1940
Piste du Sud, 1938 (Barrault)
Pistol Packin' Nitwits, 1945 (Langdon)
Pistolen, 1973 (Björnstrand)
Pistolero of Red River. *See* Last Challenge, 1967
Pistols for Breakfast, 1919 (Lloyd)
Pit. *See* Ana, 1957
Pit and the Pendulum, 1961 (Price)
Pit and the Pendulum, 1991 (Reed)
Pit Stop, 1969 (Burstyn)
Pitfalls, 1948 (Powell, D.)
Pittsburgh, 1942 (Dietrich; Scott, R.; Three Stooges; Wayne)
Piu fortc ragazzi!, 1972 (Cusack)
Più bella serata della mia vita, 1972 (Brasseur; Sordi; Vanel)
Pizza Triangle. *See* Dramma della gelosia—Tutti i particolari in cronaca, 1970
Place beyond the Winds, 1916 (Chaney)
Place de la Concorde, 1938 (Blier)
Place for Annie, 1994 (Spacek)
Place for Lovers. *See* Amanti, 1968
Place in the Sun, 1951 (Clift; Taylor, E.; Winters)
Place of One's Own, 1945 (Lockwood; Mason)
Place of Skulls, 1989 (Coburn, J.)
Place Vendome, 1996 (Deneuve)
Placer de Matar, 1987 (Abril; Banderas)
Places in the Heart, 1984 (Field; Harris, E.; Malkovich)
Plague, 1992 (Duvall; Hurt, W.; Julia)
Plague Dogs, 1982 (Hurt, J.)
Plague Sowers. *See* Diceria dell'untore, 1990
Plain Clothes, 1925 (Langdon)
Plain Song, 1910 (Pickford)
Plainsman, 1936 (Arthur; Constantine; Quinn)
Plaisir, 1951 (Brasseur; Darrieux; Gabin; Gélin; Ustinov; Walbrook)
Plan Nine from Outer Space, 1959 (Lugosi)
Plane Fear. *See* Revenge of the Red Baron, 1994
Plane Nuts, 1933 (Three Stooges)
Planes, Trains and Automobiles, 1987 (Bacon; Candy; Martin, S.)
Planet of Blood. *See* Queen of Blood, 1966
Planet of the Apes, 1968 (Heston; McDowall)
Planter's Wife, 1952 (Colbert; Hawkins)
Plastic Age, 1925 (Bow; Gable)
Plates, 1990 (Falk)
Platinum Blonde, 1931 (Harlow; Young, L.)
Platinum High School, 1960 (Duryea; Rooney)
Platoon, 1986 (Dafoe; Depp; Whitaker)
Play Dirty, 1968 (Caine)
Play Girl, 1932 (Young, L.)
Play Girl, 1940 (Francis)
Play It Again, Sam, 1972 (Allen; Keaton, D.)
Play It as It Lays, 1972 (Perkins; Weld)
Play Misty for Me, 1971 (Eastwood)
Playboy. *See* Kicking the Moon Around, 1938
Playboy of Paris, 1930 (Chevalier)
Playboys, 1992 (Finney)
Player, 1992 (Cher; Coburn, J.; Falk; Goldberg; Gould; Huston, A.; Lemmon; McDowell; Nolte; Reynolds, B.; Robbins; Roberts, J.; Sarandon; Scacchi; Steiger; Willis)
Players, 1979 (Schell, Maximilian)
Playgirl, 1954 (Winters)
Playgirl after Dark. *See* Too Hot to Handle, 1960
Playgirl and the War Minister. *See* Amorous Prawn, 1962
Playhouse, 1922 (Keaton, B.)

Playing for Time, 1980 (Redgrave, V.)
Playing the Ponies, 1937 (Three Stooges)
Playing Truant. *See* Skola skolen, 1949
Playing with Souls, 1925 (Astor)
Playmates, 1918 (Laurel and Hardy)
Playmates, 1941 (Barrymore, J.)
Plaything, 1929 (Milland)
Playtime. *See* Recreation, 1960
Playtime, 1967 (Tati)
Playtime in Hollywood, 1956 (Lancaster)
Plaza Suite, 1971 (Grant, L.; Matthau)
Please, 1933 (Crosby)
Please Believe Me, 1950 (Kerr; Walker)
Please Don't Eat the Daisies, 1960 (Day; Niven)
Please, Mr. Balzac. *See* Effeuillant la marguerite, 1956
Please Murder Me, 1956 (Lansbury)
Please, Not Now! *See* Bride sur le cou, 1961
Pleasure Garden. *See* Lustgården, 1961
Pleasure Girl. *See* Ragazza con la valigia, 1961
Pleasure Girls, 1965 (Kinski)
Pleasure Mad, 1923 (Shearer)
Pleasure of His Company, 1961 (Astaire; Reynolds, D.)
Pleasure of Killing. *See* Placer de Matar, 1987
Pleasure Palace, 1980 (Ferrer; Sharif)
Pleasure Seekers, 1964 (Ann-Margret; Tierney)
Plein aux As, 1939 (Modot)
Plein de super, 1976 (Baye)
Plein Fer, 1990 (Reggiani)
Plein soleil, 1959 (Delon; Schneider)
Plein sud, 1980 (Moreau)
Pleine bagarre, 1961 (Constantine)
Pleins feux sur l'assassin, 1961 (Brasseur; Trintignant)
Plenty, 1985 (Gielgud; Neill; Streep)
Pleut sur Santiago, 1975 (Andersson, B.; Girardot)
Plongée tragique, 1928 (Vanel)
Plot. *See* Attentat, 1972
Plouffe, 1985 (Audran)
Plough and the Stars, 1936 (Stanwyck; Fitzgerald)
Plough and the Stars, 1982 (Cusack)
Pluck of the Irish. *See* Great Guy, 1936
Plucked. *See* Morte la fatto, l'uovo, 1967
Plumber. *See* Work, 1915
Plunder, 1922 (White)
Plunder of the Sun, 1953 (Ford, G.)
Plus Belles Escroqueries du monde, 1964 (Cassel; Deneuve)
Plus Grande Musée, 1985 (Huppert; Moreau)
Plus Vieux Métier du monde, 1967 (Dalio; Karina; Léaud; Moreau; Welch)
Plutocrat, 1931 (Rogers, W.)
Plymouth Adventure, 1952 (Tierney; Tracy)
Po' di cielo, 1956 (Fabrizi)
Pobre diablo, 1940 (Armendáriz)
Pobre Mariposa, 1986 (Andersson, B.)
Pocahontas, 1995 (Gibson)
Pocharde, 1952 (Brasseur)
Pocitani ovecek, 1982 (Brodský)
Pocket Money, 1972 (Marvin; Newman)
Pocketful of Miracles, 1961 (Ann-Margret; Davis, B.; Falk; Ford, G.; Horton)
Pocketmaar, 1956 (Anand)
Pod kamennym nebom, 1974 (Yankovsky)
Podrugi, 1935 (Cherkassov)
Poet i tsar, 1927 (Cherkassov)
Poet Iv Montan, 1957 (Montand)
Poie pour l'ombre, 1960 (Gélin)
Poil de carotte, 1973 (Noiret)
Poilus de la Neuvieme, 1910 (Modot)
Point Blank, 1967 (Dickinson; Marvin)
Point Break, 1991 (Reeves)
Point de mire, 1977 (Girardot)
Point du jour, 1949 (Modot; Piccoli)
Point of No Return, 1993 (Bancroft; Keitel)
Pointe courte, 1955 (Noiret)

Pointed Heels, 1929 (Powell, W.; Wray)
Poison, 1906 (Linder)
Poison Candy. *See* Little Sweetheart, 1988
Poison Ivy. *See* Môme vert-de-gris, 1953
Poison Pen, 1939 (McDowall)
Poisoned Paradise, 1924 (Bow)
Poitin, 1979 (Cusack)
Poker Alice, 1987 (Taylor, E.)
Poker Faces, 1926 (Horton)
Pokoj no. 13, 1915 (Negri)
Pokolenie, 1955 (Łomnicki)
Pokolenie pobeditelei, 1936 (Maretskaya)
Polenta, 1980 (Ganz)
Policarpo, ufficiale di scrittura, 1959 (Sordi)
Police, 1915 (Purviance)
Police!, 1916 (Chaplin, C.)
Police, 1985 (Depardieu)
Police Academy 4: Citizens on Patrol, 1987 (Stone)
Police Academy 7: Mission to Moscow, 1994 (Lee, C.)
Police Can't Move. *See* Polizia ha le mani legate, 1974
Police Car Seventeen, 1933 (Bond)
Police Force. *See* Gingchat gusi, 1985
Police mondaine, 1937 (Barrault; Vanel)
Police Nr. 1111, 1915 (Kortner)
Police Python 357, 1976 (Montand)
Police Story 4: Project S, 1993 (Chan)
Police Story. *See* Gingchat gusi, 1985
Police Story Part II. *See* Gingchat gusi tsuktsap, 1988
Police Story: The Freeway Killings, 1987 (Dickinson)
Polio and Communicable Diseases Hospital Trailer, 1949 (Grant, C.)
Polioty vo sne naiavou, 1982 (Yankovsky)
Polis Paulus' Påskasmäll, 1925 (Madsen and Schenstrøm)
Polite Invasion, 1960 (Zetterling)
Politic Flapper. *See* Patsy, 1928
Political Asylum. *See* Detras de esa puerta, 1972
Political Party, 1934 (Mills)
Politics, 1931 (Dressler)
Politics and the Press, 1914 (Talmadge)
Politics Film, 1972 (Falk)
Polizia è al servizio del cittadino, 1973 (Gélin)
Polizia ha le mani legate, 1974 (Kennedy)
Polizia incrimina, la legge assolve, 1973 (Rey)
Polizia ringrazia, 1972 (Cusack)
Polizia sta a guardare, 1973 (Cobb)
Polkovnik v otstavke, 1976 (Yankovsky)
Polly Fulton. *See* B. F.'s Daughter, 1948
Polly of the Circus, 1917 (Marsh)
Polly of the Circus, 1932 (Davies; Gable; Milland)
Polly with a Past, 1920 (Webb)
Pollyanna, 1920 (Pickford)
Pollyanna, 1960 (Crisp; Malden; Menjou; Moorehead; Wyman)
Polo Joe, 1936 (Brown; Wyman)
Polowanie na muchy, 1969 (Olbrychski)
Polvere di stelle, 1973 (Sordi; Vitti)
Polvo rojo, 1981 (Villagra)
Polyushko-pole, 1956 (Maretskaya)
Pompeii. *See* Warrior Queen, 1987
Ponjola, 1923 (Crisp)
Pontiac Moon, 1994 (Steenburgen)
Pontius Pilate, 1964 (Rathbone)
Pontius Pilate. *See* Ponzio Pilato, 1962
Ponto di Vetro, 1940 (Brazzi)
Pony Express, 1925 (Beery)
Pony Express, 1952 (Heston)
Pony Express Rider, 1916 (Mix)
Pony Soldier, 1952 (Power)
Ponzio Pilato, 1962 (Marais)
Pookie. *See* Sterile Cuckoo, 1969
Pool Sharks, 1915 (Fields, W. C.)
Pooly-tix in Washington, 1933 (Temple)
Poopsie, 1974 (Loren; Mastroianni)

Poor Boob, 1919 (Crisp)
Poor Butterfly. *See* Pobre Mariposa, 1986
Poor Cow, 1967 (McDowell; Stamp)
Poor Devil, 1973 (Lee, C.)
Poor Jake's Demise, 1913 (Chaney)
Poor Little Peppina, 1916 (Pickford)
Poor Little Rich Girl, 1917 (Pickford)
Poor Little Rich Girl, 1936 (Faye; Temple)
Poor Little Rich Girl: The Barbara Hutton Story, 1987 (Audran)
Poor Nut, 1927 (Arthur)
Poor Relation, 1921 (Rogers, W.)
Poor Rich, 1931 (Horton)
Poor Rich, 1934 (Bond)
Poorly Extinguished Fires. *See* Des Feux mal éteints, 1994
Pop Goes the Easel, 1935 (Three Stooges)
Pop's Pal, 1933 (Langdon)
Pope Joan, 1972 (De Havilland; Howard, T.; Schell, Maximilian; Ullmann)
Pope John Paul II, 1984 (Finney)
Pope Must Die, 1991 (Lom)
Pope of Greenwich Village, 1984 (Page; Rourke)
Popeye, 1980 (Williams, R.)
Popi, 1969 (Arkin)
Popioł, 1965 (Nowicki)
Popioly, 1965 (Tyszkiewicz; Olbrychski)
Poplach v oblacich, 1979 (Brodský)
Popoli Morituri. *See* Sterbende Völker, 1922
Poppy, 1917 (Talmadge)
Poppy, 1936 (Fields, W. C.)
Poppy Girl's Husband, 1919 (Hart)
Poppy Is Also a Flower, 1966 (Brynner; Dickinson; Hawkins; Hayworth; Howard, T.; Mastroianni; Quayle; Sharif; Wallach)
Poprigunya, 1955 (Bondarchuk)
Popsy Pop, 1971 (Baker; Cardinale)
Por ellas aunque mal paguen, 1952 (Infante)
Por mis pistolas, 1968 (Cantinflas)
Por querer a una mujer, 1951 (Armendáriz)
Porcile, 1969 (Léaud)
Porco mondo, 1978 (Kennedy; Valli)
Porgy and Bess, 1959 (Poitier)
Pork Chop Hill, 1959 (Landau; Peck)
Porno. *See* Porco mondo, 1978
Port Afrique, 1956 (Lee, C.)
Port Arthur, 1936 (Darrieux; Vanel)
Port de la tentation. *See* Temptation Harbour, 1947
Port du désir, 1954 (Gabin)
Port of Desire. *See* Fille de Hambourg, 1957
Port of Escape, 1956 (Withers)
Port of Missing Girls, 1938 (Carey)
Port of New York, 1949 (Brynner)
Port of Seven Seas, 1938 (Beery; O'Sullivan)
Port of Shadows. *See* **Quai des brumes**, 1938
Port of Shame. *See* Amants du Tage, 1955
Porte aperte, 1990 (Volonté)
Porte d'Orient, 1950 (Dalio)
Porte de Lilas, 1957 (Brasseur)
Porter. *See* New Janitor, 1914
Portes claquent, 1960 (Deneuve)
Portes de la nuit, 1946 (Brasseur; Montand; Reggiani)
Porteuse de pain, 1934 (Fernandel)
Porteuse de pain, 1963 (Noiret)
Portnoy's Complaint, 1972 (Carradine; Grant, L.)
Portrait, 1993 (Bacall; Peck)
Portrait d'un assassin, 1949 (Arletty; Berry; Brasseur; Dalio)
Portrait de son père, 1953 (Bardot)
Portrait from Life. *See* Girl in the Painting, 1948
Portrait in Black, 1960 (Quinn; Turner, L.; Wong)
Portrait of a Hit Man, 1977 (Palance)
Portrait of a 60% Perfect Man, 1980 (Matthau)
Portrait of a Lady, 1996 (Hershey; Malkovich; Streep)
Portrait of a Library, 1976 (Cusack)
Portrait of a Showgirl, 1982 (Curtis, T.)

President Vanishes, 1934 (Russell, R.)
President's Analyst, 1967 (Coburn, J.)
President's Lady, 1953 (Hayward; Heston)
President's Plane Is Missing, 1971 (Kennedy; Massey)
President's Visit. *See* Odwiedziny prezydenta, 1961
Presidio, 1988 (Connery; Ryan, M.)
Press for Time, 1966 (Wisdom)
Pressing His Suit, 1915 (Lloyd)
Pressure Point, 1962 (Falk; Poitier)
Prestige, 1932 (Douglas, Melvyn; Menjou)
Preston Sturges: The Rise and Fall of an American Dreamer, 1990 (McCrea)
Presumé dangereux, 1990 (Mitchum)
Presumed Innocent, 1990 (Ford, H.; Julia; Scacchi)
Prêt-a-Porter. *See* Ready to Wear, 1994
Prête-moi ta femme, 1936 (Brasseur)
Pretty Baby, 1978 (Sarandon)
Pretty Boy Floyd, 1960 (Falk)
Pretty Girl, 1950 (Lanchester)
Pretty in Pink, 1986 (Stanton)
Pretty Ladies, 1925 (Crawford, J.; Loy; Shearer)
Pretty Maids All in a Row, 1971 (Dickinson; Hudson; McDowall)
Pretty Poison, 1968 (Perkins; Weld)
Pretty Polly, 1967 (Howard, T.)
Pretty Princess. *See* Piccolo Grande Amore, 1993
Pretty Woman, 1990 (Bellamy; Gere; Roberts, J.)
Prettykill, 1987 (York)
Prevailing Craze, 1914 (Beery)
Preyasi, 1982 (Chatterjee)
Prezzo del potere, 1969 (Rey)
Price of a Party, 1924 (Astor)
Price of Death. *See* Venditore di morte, 1972
Price of Fear, 1956 (Oberon)
Price of Happiness, 1916 (Menjou)
Price of Power. *See* Prezzo del potere, 1969
Price of Silence, 1916 (Chaney)
Prick Up Your Ears, 1987 (Oldman; Redgrave, V.)
Pride. *See* Aan, 1952
Pride and Prejudice, 1940 (Garson; O'Sullivan; Olivier)
Pride and the Passion, 1957 (Grant, C.; Loren; Sidney)
Pride of Jesse Hallam, 1981 (Wallach)
Pride of Race. *See* Last of the Line, 1914
Pride of the Clan, 1917 (Pickford)
Pride of the Marines, 1936 (Bond)
Pride of the Marines, 1945 (Garfield)
Pride of the Range, 1910 (Mix)
Pride of the Yankees, 1942 (Brennan; Constantine; Duryea)
Priest of Love, 1981 (Gardner; Gielgud; Mirren)
Priest's Wife. *See* Moglie del prete, 1971
Prigionera della torre dell cuoco, 1952 (Brazzi)
Prigioniera. *See* Prisonnière, 1968
Prigionieri del male, 1956 (Blier)
Prima comunione, 1950 (Fabrizi)
Prima di Natale, 1990 (Giannini)
Prima donna che passa, 1940 (Valli)
Prima notte, 1958 (Cardinale)
Prima notte di quiete, 1972 (Delon; Giannini; Valli)
Primal Call, 1911 (Crisp)
Primal Fear, 1996 (Gere)
Primal Lure, 1916 (Hart)
Primanerehe. *See* Boykott, 1930
Primanerliebe, 1927 (Kortner)
Prime Cut, 1972 (Hackman; Marvin; Spacek)
Prime Minister, 1941 (Gielgud)
Prime of Miss Jean Brodie, 1969 (Johnson; Smith)
Prime Suspect: Inner Circles, 1996 (Mirren)
Prime Suspect: The Lost Child, 1995 (Mirren)
Prime Target, 1989 (Dickinson)
Prime Target, 1991 (Curtis, T.)
Prime Time, 1977 (Oates)
Primitifs du XIIIe, 1960 (Arletty)
Primitive Love. *See* Amore primitivo, 1964

Primitive Peoples: Australian Aborigines, 1949 (Finch)
Primrose Path, 1925 (Bow)
Primrose Path, 1940 (McCrea; Rogers, G.)
Prince and Betty, 1919 (Karloff)
Prince and the Pauper, 1937 (Flynn; Rains)
Prince and the Pauper, 1977 (Borgnine; Heston)
Prince and the Pauper. *See* Crossed Swords, 1978
Prince and the Showgirl, 1957 (Monroe; Olivier)
Prince Babby, 1929 (Horton)
Prince Cuckoo. *See* Prinz Kukuck, 1919
Prince Jack, 1984 (Andrews, D.)
Prince of Arcadia, 1933 (Lupino)
Prince of Central Park, 1977 (Gordon)
Prince of Darkness, 1987 (Pleasence)
Prince of Foxes, 1949 (Power; Sloane; Welles)
Prince of Jutland, 1994 (Mirren)
Prince of Pennsylvania, 1988 (Reeves)
Prince of Players, 1955 (Burton; Marsh; Massey)
Prince of Rogues. *See* Schinderhannes, 1927
Prince of Shadows. *See* Beltenebros, 1991
Prince of Tides, 1991 (Nelligan; Nolte; Streisand)
Prince Philip, 1953 (Hawkins)
Prince Valiant, 1954 (Crisp; Hayden; Leigh, Janet; Mason; McLaglen)
Prince Who Was a Thief, 1951 (Curtis, T.; Sloane)
Princesa de los Ursinos, 1947 (Rey)
Princess and the Goblin. *See* Herccgnoe es a Kobold, 1993
Princess and the Pirate, 1944 (Brennan; Crosby; Hope; McLaglen)
Princess and the Plumber, 1930 (O'Sullivan)
Princess Bride, 1987 (Falk)
Princess Caraboo, 1994 (Kline)
Princess Comes Across, 1936 (Lombard; MacMurray)
Princess Daisy, 1983 (Cardinale)
Princess from Hoboken, 1927 (Karloff)
Princess from the Moon. *See* Taketori monogatari, 1987
Princess O'Rourke, 1943 (Coburn, C.; De Havilland; Wyman)
Princess of New York, 1921 (Crisp)
Princess of the Dark, 1917 (Gilbert)
Princess of the Nile, 1954 (Van Cleef)
Princess Olala. *See* Prinzessin Olala, 1928
Princess Tarahanova. *See* Principessa Tarahanova, 1938
Princess Yang Kwei-fei. *See* Yokihi, 1955
Princesse de Clèves, 1961 (Marais)
Principessa delle Canarie, 1954 (Mastroianni)
Principessa Giorgio, 1919 (Bertini)
Principessa straniera, 1914 (Bertini)
Principessa Tarahanova, 1938 (Sordi)
Prins Gustaf, 1944 (Zetterling)
Printemps, l'automne et l'amour, 1953 (Fernandel)
Prinz Kukuck, 1919 (Veidt)
Prinzessin Olala, 1928 (Dietrich)
Prinzessin Sawarin, 1923 (Dagover)
Priorities on Parade, 1942 (Miller)
Prisioneros desparecidos, 1978 (Villagra)
Prison Break, 1938 (Bond; O'Brien, E.)
Prison Breaker, 1936 (Mason)
Prison Farm, 1938 (Holden)
Prison Ship. *See* Star Slammer, 1988
Prisoner, 1923 (Karloff)
Prisoner, 1955 (Guinness; Hawkins)
Prisoner. *See* Island on Fire, 1990
Prisoner of Cabanas, 1913 (Mix)
Prisoner of Honor, 1991 (Dreyfuss; Reed)
Prisoner of Second Avenue, 1975 (Bancroft; Lemmon; Stallone)
Prisoner of Shark Island, 1936 (Carey; Carradine)
Prisoner of the Mohican, 1911 (White)
Prisoner of War, 1954 (Homolka; Reagan)
Prisoner of Zenda, 1922 (Novarro)
Prisoner of Zenda, 1937 (Astor; Carroll; Colman; Massey; Niven)
Prisoner of Zenda, 1952 (Calhern; Granger; Kerr; Mason)
Prisoner of Zenda, 1979 (Sellers)
Prisoner without a Name, Cell without a Number. *See* Jacobo Timerman, 1983

Prisoners, 1929 (Lugosi)
Prisoners of the Casbah, 1953 (Grahame)
Prisonnière, 1968 (Piccoli)
Prisonnières, 1988 (Girardot)
Private Affair, 1959 (Mineo)
Private Affairs of Bel Ami, 1947 (Carradine; Lansbury; Sanders)
Private Angelo, 1949 (Ustinov)
Private Benjamin, 1980 (Hawn; Stanton)
Private Bom. See Soldat Bom, 1948
Private Buckaroo, 1942 (O'Connor; Three Stooges)
Private Conversations, 1985 (Hoffman)
Private Detective, 1939 (Wyman)
Private Detective 62, 1933 (Powell, W.)
Private Entrance. See Egen ingång, 1956
Private Eyes, 1953 (Van Cleef)
Private Files of J. Edgar Hoover, 1977 (Crawford, B.; Ferrer)
Private Function, 1985 (Elliott; Smith)
Private General. See General Nuisance, 1941
Private Hell 36, 1954 (Lupino; Malone)
Private Life of Don Juan, 1934 (Fairbanks; Oberon)
Private Life of Henry VIII, 1933 (Donat; Lanchester; Laughton; Oberon)
Private Life of Oliver the Eighth. See Oliver the Eighth, 1934
Private Life of Sherlock Holmes, 1970 (Lee, C.)
Private Lives, 1931 (Montgomery; Shearer)
Private Lives of Adam and Eve, 1961 (Rooney; Weld)
Private Lives of Elizabeth and Essex, 1939 (Crisp; Davis, B.; De Havilland; Flynn; Price)
Private Matter, 1992 (Spacek)
Private Navy of Sgt. O'Farrell, 1968 (Hope; Lollobrigida)
Private Number, 1936 (Rathbone; Taylor, R.; Young, L.)
Private Property, 1959 (Oates)
Private Resort, 1985 (Depp)
Private Screening. See Visioni Privati, 1990
Private Secretary, 1935 (Horton)
Private War of Major Benson, 1955 (Heston; Mineo)
Private Worlds, 1935 (Bennett; Boyer; Colbert; McCrea)
Privates on Parade, 1982 (Cleese)
Private's Progress, 1955 (Attenborough; Lee, C.; Terry-Thomas)
Privileged, 1982 (Grant, H.)
Prix de beauté, 1930 (Brooks, L.)
Prix de la survie. See Preiss für Überleben, 1979
Prix du danger, 1982 (Piccoli)
Prize, 1963 (Newman; Presle; Robinson, E.)
Prize. See Premiya, 1974
Prize Baby, 1915 (Laurel and Hardy)
Prize of Arms, 1962 (Baker)
Prize of Gold, 1955 (Widmark; Zetterling)
Prize Winners, 1916 (Laurel and Hardy)
Prizefighter and the Lady, 1933 (Huston, W.; Loy)
Prizzi's Honor, 1985 (Huston, A.; Huston, J.; Nicholson; Turner, K.)
Pro. See Number One, 1969
Probation, 1932 (Grable)
Probe, 1972 (Gielgud; Meredith)
Procès, 1962 (Perkins; Moreau; Schneider; Welles)
Procès de Mary Dugan, 1929 (Boyer; Rosay)
Processo a Verona, 1963 (Mangano)
Processo de las brujas, 1970 (Lee, C.; Schell, Maria)
Processo per direttissima, 1974 (Blier)
Pródiga, 1946 (Rey)
Prodigal, 1955 (Calhern; Turner, L.)
Prodigal Daughters, 1923 (Swanson)
Prodigal Son. See Onna Goroshi abura jigoku, 1957
Producers, 1968 (Brooks, M.; Wilder)
Profe, 1970 (Cantinflas)
Professeur. See Prima notte di quiete, 1972
Professional. See Leon, 1994
Professional Gun. See Mercenario, 1969
Professional Soldier, 1936 (McLaglen)
Professional Sweetheart, 1933 (Rogers, G.)
Professionals, 1966 (Bellamy; Cardinale; Lancaster; Marvin; Palance; Ryan, R.)

Professione: Reporter, 1975 (Nicholson)
Professionnel, 1981 (Belmondo)
Professor Bean's Removal, 1913 (Arbuckle; Normand)
Professor Beware, 1938 (Bond; Lloyd)
Professor My Son. See Mio figlio professore, 1946
Professor Petersens plejebørn, 1924 (Madsen and Schenstrøm)
Professor's Daughter, 1913 (Normand)
Profeta, 1967 (Ann-Margret; Gassman)
Profile of a Miracle, 1960 (Brynner)
Profumo di donna, 1974 (Gassman)
Program, 1993 (Caan)
Progress for Freedom, 1962 (Ferrer)
Prohibition Wife, 1919 (Talmadge)
Proie du vent, 1926 (Vanel)
Project A. See Gaiwak, 1983
Project A: Part II. See Gaiwatsuktsap, 1987
Project ALF, 1996 (Sheen)
Project M7. See Net, 1952
Project S. See Police Story 4: Project S, 1993
Prokliatiye millioni, 1917 (Mozhukin)
Prokuror, 1917 (Mozhukin)
Prom, 1992 (Leigh, Jennifer Jason)
Prom Night, 1980 (Curtis, J.)
Promesse à l'inconnue, 1942 (Brasseur; Vanel)
Promesse de l'aube, 1970 (Mercouri)
Promessi sposi, 1941 (Cervi)
Promise, 1986 (Garner; Woods)
Promise at Dawn. See Promesse de l'aube, 1970
Promise Her Anything, 1966 (Beatty; Caron; Sutherland)
Promised Land. See Tierra prometida, 1972
Promised Land. See Ziema obiecana, 1975
Promised Land, 1988 (Redford; Ryan, M.)
Promises! Promises!, 1963 (Mansfield)
Promises to Keep, 1985 (Bloom; Mitchum)
Promoter. See Card, 1952
Pronoy Pasha, 1978 (Chatterjee)
Proof of the Man. See Ningen no shomei, 1977
Property Man, 1914 (Chaplin, C.)
Prophecies of Nostradamus. See Nostoradamusu no daiyogen, 1974
Prophecy, 1996 (Walken)
Prophet. See Profeta, 1967
Prospector, 1917 (Laurel and Hardy)
Prosperity, 1932 (Dressler)
Prosperity Race, 1962 (Zetterling)
Prospero's Books, 1991 (Gielgud; Josephson)
Prosperous Times, 1980 (Andersson, B.)
Prosseneti, 1975 (Cuny)
Prostituta al servizio del pubblico e in regol con le leggi dello stato, 1971 (Giannini)
Prostitution, 1919 (Krauss; Veidt)
Prostitution II, 1919 (Veidt)
Prostye serdtsa, 1928 (Maretskaya)
Protection, 1929 (Brown)
Protector, 1985 (Aiello; Chan)
Protest at 48 Years Old. See Yonjuhachi-sai no teiko, 1956
Protocol, 1984 (Hawn)
Proud and Profane, 1956 (Holden; Kerr; Ritter)
Proud and the Beautiful. See Orgueilleux, 1953
Proud Flesh, 1925 (Crawford, J.)
Proud Men, 1987 (Heston)
Proud Ones, 1956 (Brennan; Ryan, R.)
Proud Rebel, 1958 (Carradine; De Havilland; Ladd)
Proud Valley, 1940 (Robeson)
Provesso e morte di Socrate, 1940 (Brazzi)
Providence, 1977 (Bogarde; Burstyn; Gielgud)
Provinciale, 1953 (Lollobrigida)
Provinciale, 1980 (Baye; Ganz; Winkler)
Provocation, 1970 (Marais; Schell, Maria)
Prowlers of the Plains. See Knight of the Trails, 1915
Prowling around France with Will Rogers, 1927 (Rogers, W.)
Prozess der Kitty Kellermann. See Hokuspokus, 1930

Prudence and the Pill, 1968 (Evans; Kerr; Niven)
Przgody pana Michala, 1982 (Łomnicki; Olbrychski)
Przypadek, 1982 (Łomnicki)
Przypieszenie, 1984 (Tyszkiewicz)
Psych-Out, 1968 (Dern; Nicholson)
Psyche '59, 1964 (Neal)
Psycho, 1960 (Leigh, Janet; Perkins)
Psycho II, 1983 (Perkins)
Psycho III, 1986 (Perkins)
Psycho IV: The Beginning, 1990 (Perkins)
Psycho a Go-Go! *See* Blood of Ghastly Horror, 1972
Psycho-Circus. *See* Circus of Fear, 1967
Psycho Killers. *See* Flesh and the Fiends, 1960
Psychomania. *See* Living Dead, 1972
Psychout for Murder. *See* Salvare la faccia, 1969
PT 109, 1963 (Robertson)
Public Be Hanged. *See* World Gone Mad, 1933
Public Cowboy Number One, 1937 (Autry)
Public Deb Number One, 1940 (Bellamy)
Public Defender, 1931 (Karloff)
Public Enemy, 1931 (Blondell; Cagney; Harlow)
Public Eye. *See* Follow Me, 1972
Public Eye, 1992 (Hershey; Pesci)
Public Hero Number One, 1935 (Arthur; Barrymore, L.)
Public Menace, 1935 (Arthur)
Public Opinion, 1916 (Sweet)
Public Prosecutor. *See* Prokuror, 1917
Public Prosecutor. *See* Justice d'abord, 1919
Public Wedding, 1937 (Wyman)
Puce et le Privé, 1980 (Vanel)
Puck heter jag, 1951 (Andersson, H.)
Pueblo, canto, y esperanza, 1954 (Infante)
Pueblo Legend, 1912 (Pickford)
Puente, 1976 (Abril)
Puerta ... joven, 1949 (Cantinflas)
Puerta falsa, 1950 (Armendáriz)
Pugilist. *See* Knockout, 1914
Puits aux trois vérités, 1961 (Morgan)
Pull My Daisy, 1958 (Seyrig)
Pullman Bride, 1917 (Swanson)
Pullman Porter, 1919 (Arbuckle)
Pulp, 1972 (Caine; Rooney)
Pulp Fiction, 1994 (DeVito; Jackson, S.; Keitel; Thurman; Travolta; Walken; Willis)
Pumping Iron, 1977 (Schwarzenegger)
Pumpkin Eater, 1963 (Bancroft; Finch; Mason; Smith)
Punashcha, 1961 (Chatterjee)
Punch, 1994 (Sutherland)
Punch and Jody, 1974 (Ford, G.)
Punch Drunk, 1934 (Three Stooges)
Punchline, 1988 (Field; Hanks)
Punchy Cowpunchers, 1950 (Three Stooges)
Punctured Life. *See* Vie crevee, 1992
Punishment, 1912 (Sweet)
Punition, 1973 (Dalio)
Puny Soul of Peter Rand, 1915 (Mix)
Pupa del gangster, 1975 (Mastroianni)
Puppe vom Lunapark, 1925 (Rasp)
Puppenmacher von Kiang-Ning, 1923 (Krauss)
Puppenspiel mit toten Augen, 1980 (Valli)
Puppet Masters, 1994 (Sutherland)
Purchase Price, 1932 (Stanwyck)
Pure as a Rose. *See* Come una rosa al naso, 1976
Pure Formalité, 1994 (Depardieu)
Puritain, 1937 (Barrault; Fresnay)
Puritaine, 1986 (Piccoli)
Puritan Passions, 1923 (Astor)
Purple Heart, 1944 (Andrews, D.; Baxter)
Purple Mask, 1955 (Curtis, T.; Lansbury)
Purple Night, 1972 (Caron)
Purple Noon. *See* Plein soleil, 1959

Purple People Eater, 1988 (Winters)
Purple Plain, 1955 (Peck)
Purple Rose of Cairo, 1985 (Aiello; Allen; Farrow; Wiest)
Purple Taxi. *See* Taxi mauve, 1977
Pursued, 1947 (Mitchum)
Pursuit, 1972 (Sheen)
Pursuit of D. B. Cooper, 1981 (Duvall)
Pursuit of Happiness, 1934 (Bennett)
Pursuit of Happiness, 1971 (Hershey)
Pursuit of the Graf Spee. *See* Battle of the River Plate, 1956
Pushing the Limits, 1994 (Gélin)
Pushover, 1954 (MacMurray; Malone; Novak)
Puss in Boots, 1988 (Walken)
Put 'Em All in Jail. *See* Tutti dentro, 1984
Putney Swope, 1969 (Brooks, M.)
Putter, 1932 (Brown)
Puttin' on the Ritz, 1930 (Bennett)
Putting It Over, 1919 (Crisp)
Putting One Over. *See* Masquerader, 1914
Putting Pants on Philip, 1927 (Laurel and Hardy)
Puzzle, 1986 (Banderas)
Puzzle of a Downfall Child, 1970 (Dunaway; Scheider)
Puzzle of horrors. *See* Double Face, 1969
Puzzle of the Red Orchid. *See* Rätsel der röten Orchidee, 1961
Pyaasi Aankhen, 1983 (Azmi)
Pyar Ka Tarana, 1992 (Anand)
Pyar Mohabbat, 1966 (Anand)
Pygmalion, 1938 (Howard, L.; Quayle)
Pygmalion, 1983 (O'Toole)
Pygmy Island, 1951 (Weissmuller)
Pyramides bleue, 1988 (Sharif)
Pyrates, 1991 (Bacon)
Pyromaniac's Love Story, 1995 (Mueller-Stahl)
Q & A, 1990 (Nolte)
Q Planes, 1939 (Olivier; Richardson, R.)
Qayamat, 1983 (Patil)
Qin Yong, 1989 (Gong Li)
Qingming Festival, 1936 (Zhao Dan)
Qiu Ju Da Guansi, 1992 (Gong Li)
Quack. *See* Kurpfuscherin, 1974
Quackser Fortune Has a Cousin in the Bronx, 1970 (Wilder)
Quadrille d'amour, 1934 (Brasseur)
Quaeta specie d'amore, 1972 (Seberg)
Quai des brumes, 1938 (Brasseur; Gabin; Morgan)
Quai des Orfèvres, 1947 (Blier; Jouvet)
Quai Notre Dame, 1961 (Aimée)
Qualcosa di biondo, 1985 (Loren; Noiret)
Qualen der Nacht, 1926 (Rasp)
Quality of Mercy. *See* Hasenjagd—Vor lauter Feigheit gibt es kein Erbarmen, 1994
Quality Street, 1927 (Davies)
Quality Street, 1937 (Fontaine; Hepburn, K.)
Quand la femme s'en mêle, 1957 (Blier; Delon; Feuillère)
Quand la vie était belle. *See* Bébé de l'escadron, 1935
Quand même, 1916 (Fresnay)
Quand minuit sonnera, 1936 (Dalio)
Quand on est belle, 1931 (Rosay)
Quand passent les faisans, 1965 (Blier)
Quand tu nous tiens, amour, 1932 (Fernandel)
Quando eravmo repressi, 1992 (Gassman)
Quantez, 1957 (MacMurray; Malone)
Quarantièmes Rugissants, 1982 (Christie)
Quarantined, 1970 (Jaffe)
Quarrel, 1911 (White)
Quarta pagina, 1942 (Cervi)
Quarta parete, 1971 (Blier)
Quarter Time, 1990 (Bridges)
Quarterback Princess, 1983 (Robbins)
Quartermaine's Terms, 1987 (Gielgud)
Quartet, 1948 (Bogarde; Rosay; Zetterling)
Quartet, 1981 (Adjani; Bates, A.; Smith)

Rachel, Rachel, 1968 (Newman; Woodward)
Rachel and the Stranger, 1948 (Holden; Mitchum; Young, L.)
Rachel Cade. *See* Sins of Rachel Cade, 1960
Rachel's Man, 1975 (Rooney)
Rächer, 1960 (Kinski)
Racing Lady, 1937 (Carey; McDaniel)
Racing Luck. *See* Red Hot Tires, 1935
Racing Strain, 1918 (Marsh)
Racing with the Moon, 1984 (Cage; Penn)
Rack, 1956 (Marvin; Newman; O'Brien, E.; Pidgeon)
Racket, 1951 (Mitchum; Ryan, R.)
Racket Busters, 1938 (Bogart)
Racketeer, 1929 (Lombard)
Rackety Rax, 1932 (Bond; McLaglen)
Radio City Revels, 1938 (Miller)
Radio Days, 1987 (Aiello; Allen; Farrow; Keaton, D.; Wiest)
Radio Flyer, 1992 (Douglas, Michael; Hanks)
Radio Star—Die AFN-Story, 1994 (Rooney)
Radishes and Carrots. *See* Daikon to ninjin, 1964
Rafferty and the Gold Dust Twins, 1975 (Arkin; Stanton)
Raffles, 1930 (Colman; Francis)
Raffles, 1940 (De Havilland; Niven)
Raffles, the Amateur Cracksman, 1917 (Barrymore, J.)
Rafles sur la ville, 1954 (Vanel)
Rafles sur la ville, 1958 (Piccoli)
Rafter Romance, 1934 (Rogers, G.)
Ragamuffin, 1916 (Sweet)
Ragazza con la pistola, 1968 (Baker; Vitti)
Ragazza con la valigia, 1961 (Cardinale; Volonté)
Ragazza del palio, 1957 (Dors; Gassman)
Ragazza della Salina, 1957 (Mastroianni)
Ragazza di Bube, 1963 (Cardinale)
Ragazza e il generale, 1967 (Steiger)
Ragazza in Pigiamo Giallo, 1978 (Milland)
Ragazza in prestito, 1965 (Brazzi; Girardot)
Ragazze d'oggi, 1955 (Rosay)
Ragazze delle nuvole, 1957 (Cervi)
Ragazze di Piazza di Spagna, 1952 (Mastroianni)
Ragazzo del bersagliere, 1966 (Brazzi)
Ragazzo di Calabria, 1987 (Volonté)
Rage, 1966 (Ford, G.)
Rage, 1972 (Scott, G.; Sheen)
Rage at Dawn, 1955 (Scott, R.)
Rage in Harlem, 1991 (Whitaker)
Rage in Heaven, 1941 (Bergman; Homolka; Montgomery; Sanders)
Rage of Paris, 1938 (Darrieux)
Rage of the Buccaneer. *See* Gordon, il Pirato Nero, 1961
Rage to Kill, 1989 (Reed)
Ragged Girl of Oz. *See* Patchwork Girl of Oz, 1914
Raggedy Man, 1981 (Shepard; Spacek)
Raggedy Rawney, 1990 (Hoskins)
Raggedy Rose, 1926 (Laurel and Hardy; Normand)
Raging Bull, 1980 (De Niro; Pesci; Turturro)
Raging Moon, 1971 (McDowell)
Raging Tide, 1951 (Winters)
Raging Waters. *See* Green Promise, 1949
Ragione per vivere e una per morire, 1973 (Coburn, J.)
Rags, 1915 (Pickford)
Ragtime, 1981 (Cagney; Jackson, S.; O'Connor; Steenburgen)
Ragtime Snap Shots, 1915 (Lloyd)
Rahi, 1952 (Anand)
Rahi Badal Gaye, 1985 (Azmi)
Raid, 1954 (Bancroft; Marvin)
Raid on Entebbe, 1977 (Bronson; Constantine; Finch; Woods)
Raid on Rommel, 1971 (Burton)
Raiders, 1916 (Mix)
Raiders of Old California, 1957 (Van Cleef)
Raiders of the Lost Ark, 1981 (Elliott; Ford, H.)
Railrodder, 1965 (Keaton, B.)
Rails into Laramie, 1954 (Duryea; Van Cleef)
Railway Station Man, 1992 (Christie; Sutherland)

Rain, 1932 (Crawford, J.; Huston, W.)
Rain for a Dusty Summer, 1971 (Borgnine)
Rain Man, 1988 (Cruise; Hoffman)
Rain People, 1969 (Caan; Duvall)
Rainbow, 1978 (Cooper)
Rainbow, 1989 (Jackson, G.)
Rainbow, 1994 (Hoskins)
Rainbow Island, 1917 (Lloyd)
Rainbow Island, 1943 (Lamour)
Rainbow over Texas, 1946 (Rogers, R.)
Rainbow Professional. *See* Cobra Mission, 1986
Rainbow Thief, 1990 (Lee, C.; O'Toole; Sharif)
Rainbow Trail, 1925 (Mix)
Rainbow Valley, 1935 (Wayne)
Rainbow Warrior, 1994 (Neill; Voight)
Rainmaker, 1956 (Hepburn, K.; Lancaster)
Rainmaker, 1982 (Jones, T.; Weld)
Rains Came, 1939 (Loy; Power)
Rain's Hat, 1978 (Zetterling)
Rains of Ranchipur, 1955 (Burton; MacMurray; Turner, L.)
Raintree County, 1956 (Marvin; Clift; Moorehead; Saint; Taylor, E.)
Rainy Day Women, 1984 (Cusack)
Rainy Night Duel. *See* Kuroobi sangokushi, 1956
Raise Ravens. *See* **Cria Cuervos**, 1976
Raise the Red Lantern. *See* **Dahong Denglong Gaogao Guo**, 1991
Raise the Titanic, 1980 (Guinness; Robards)
Raisin in the Sun, 1961 (Poitier)
Raising Arizona, 1987 (Cage; Hunter)
Raison d'état, 1978 (Vitti)
Raj Kanya, 1965 (Chatterjee)
Raj Purush, 1987 (Chatterjee)
Rajah, 1919 (Lloyd)
Rake's Progress, 1945 (Harrison)
Rakei kazoku, 1954 (Yamamura)
Raketbussen. *See* Rocket Bus, 1929
Rakhwala, 1989 (Azmi)
Räkna de lyckliga stunderna blott, 1944 (Dahlbeck)
Rakoczy-Marsch, 1933 (Fröhlich)
Rakudai wa shitakeredo, 1930 (Ryu; Tanaka)
Rally 'round the Flag, Boys!, 1958 (Newman; Weld; Woodward)
Rally, 1980 (Lee, C.)
Ram Aur Shyam, 1967 (Kumar)
Ram Tera Desh, 1984 (Azmi)
Rambling Rose, 1991 (Duvall)
Rambo III, 1988 (Stallone)
Rambo: First Blood, Part II, 1985 (Stallone)
Ramona, 1916 (Crisp)
Ramona, 1928 (Del Rio)
Ramona, 1936 (Ameche; Carradine; Young, L.)
Rampage, 1963 (Hawkins; Mitchum)
Rampage at Apache Wells. *See* Ölprinz, 1965
Ramper, der Tiermensch, 1927 (Wegener)
Ramrod, 1947 (Crisp; Lake; McCrea)
Ramuntcho, 1938 (Jouvet; Rosay)
Ramuru eteruneru, 1935 (Takamine)
Ranch Life in the Great Southwest, 1910 (Mix)
Ranch Romance, 1914 (Chaney)
Rancher's Revenge, 1913 (Barrymore, L.)
Ranchero's Revenge, 1913 (Carey)
Rancho Deluxe, 1974 (Bridges; Stanton)
Rancho Grande, 1940 (Autry)
Rancho Notorious, 1952 (Dietrich; Kennedy)
Rande des Schreckens, 1960 (Rasp)
Randolph Family. *See* Dear Octopus, 1943
Random Harvest, 1942 (Colman; Garson)
Randy Rides Alone, 1934 (Wayne)
Range Feud, 1931 (Wayne)
Range Girl and the Cowboy, 1915 (Mix)
Range Law, 1913 (Mix)
Range Rider, 1910 (Mix)
Ranger and the Lady, 1940 (Rogers, R.)

Reckless Age. *See* Dragstrip Riot, 1958
Reckless Hour, 1931 (Blondell)
Reckless Moment, 1949 (Bennett; Mason)
Reckless Romeo. *See* Cream Puff Romance, 1916
Reckless Romeo, 1917 (Keaton, B.)
Reckoning, 1970 (Roberts, R.)
Reconstructed Rebel, 1912 (Mix)
Record of a Living Being. *See* Ikimono no kiroku, 1955
Record of a Tenement Gentleman. *See* Nagaya Shinshiroku, 1947
Record of Love. *See* Aijo no keifu, 1961
Recreation, 1914 (Chaplin, C.)
Recreation, 1960 (Seberg)
Recruits in Ingolstadt. *See* Pionere in Ingolstadt, 1970
Recurso del metedo, 1975 (Cuny)
Recurso del método, 1977 (Villagra)
Red. *See* Trzy Kolory: Bialy, 1994
Red and Blue, 1967 (Redgrave, V.)
Red and the Black. *See* Geheime Kurier, 1926
Red and the Black. *See* Rouge et le noir, 1954
Red Badge of Courage, 1951 (Huston, J.)
Red Ball Express, 1952 (Poitier)
Red Beard. *See* Akahige, 1965
Red Bells: I've Seen the Birth of the New World, 1983 (Bondarchuk)
Red Beret, 1953 (Baker; Ladd)
Red Circle. *See* Cercle rouge, 1970
Red Crag. *See* Lie Huozhong yongsheng, 1965
Red Dance, 1928 (Del Rio)
Red Danube, 1949 (Barrymore, E.; Calhern; Lansbury; Leigh, Janet; Pidgeon)
Red Dawn, 1984 (Stanton)
Red Desert. *See* **Deserto rosso**, 1964
Red Dragon. *See* Geheimnis der drei Dschunken, 1965
Red Dust, 1932 (Astor; Crisp; Gable; Harlow)
Red Earth, White Earth, 1989 (Bujold)
Red Hair, 1928 (Bow)
Red-Haired Alibi, 1932 (Temple)
Red Headed Woman, 1932 (Boyer; Harlow)
Red Heat, 1988 (Fishburne; Schwarzenegger)
Red, Hot, and Blue, 1949 (Mature)
Red Hot Romance, 1913 (Normand)
Red Hot Tires, 1935 (Astor)
Red House, 1947 (Robinson, E.)
Red Inn. *See* Auberge rouge, 1951
Red King, White Knight, 1989 (Von Sydow)
Red Kitchen Murder. *See* House on Greenapple Road, 1970
Red Knight, White Knight, 1989 (Mirren)
Red Lantern, 1919 (Nazimova; Wong)
Red Light, 1949 (Raft)
Red Lily, 1924 (Beery; Novarro)
Red Line 7000, 1965 (Caan)
Red Lion. *See* Akage, 1969
Red Mantle. *See* Rode kappe, 1967
Red Margaret-Moonshiner, 1913 (Chaney)
Red Mill, 1927 (Arbuckle; Davies)
Red Mountain, 1951 (Kennedy; Ladd)
Red Peacock. *See* Camille, 1919
Red Pony, 1949 (Calhern; Loy; Mitchum)
Red Pony, 1973 (Fonda, H.; O'Hara)
Red Riding Hood, 1987 (Rossellini)
Red River, 1948 (Brennan; Carey; Clift; Wayne; Winters)
Red River Range, 1938 (Wayne)
Red River Valley, 1936 (Autry)
Red River Valley, 1941 (Rogers, R.)
Red Rock West, 1993 (Cage; Hopper)
Red Roses for the Führer. *See* Rose rosse per il Fuhrer, 1968
Red Salute, 1935 (Stanwyck; Young, R.)
Red Shirts. *See* Camicie rosse, 1951
Red Shoes, 1948 (Walbrook)
Red Skies of Montana, 1952 (Bronson; Widmark)
Red Sky at Morning, 1945 (Finch)
Red Sky at Morning, 1971 (Bloom)
Red Sonja, 1985 (Schwarzenegger)

Red Sorghum. *See* Hong gaoliang, 1987
Red Sun. *See* Soleil rouge, 1971
Red Sundown, 1956 (Van Cleef)
Red Tent. *See* Tenda rossa, 1969
Red Thorns, 1976 (Nowicki)
Red Tomahawk, 1967 (Crawford, B.)
Red Viper, 1919 (Gilbert)
Red Wedding. *See* Noces rouges, 1973
Red Widow, 1916 (Barrymore, J.)
Redeeming Sin, 1925 (Nazimova)
Redemption, 1930 (Gilbert)
Redhead and the Cowboy, 1950 (Ford, G.; O'Brien, E.)
Redhead from Wyoming, 1953 (O'Hara)
Redl Ezredes, 1985 (Brandauer; Mueller-Stahl)
Redneck Country, 1979 (Winters)
Redoubtable Deceased. *See* Strasnia pokoynik, 1912
Reds, 1981 (Beatty; Hackman; Keaton, D.; Nicholson)
Reducing, 1931 (Dressler)
Reeling down the Rhine with Will Rogers, 1927 (Rogers, W.)
Ref, 1994 (Davis, J.)
Reflection of Fear, 1973 (Shaw)
Reflections in a Golden Eye, 1967 (Brando; Huston, J.; Taylor, E.)
Reflections of Murder, 1974 (Weld)
Reformatory, 1938 (Bond)
Reformed Outlaw. *See* Scourge of the Desert, 1915
Reformer and the Redhead, 1950 (Powell, D.)
Reformers, 1916 (Laurel and Hardy)
Refugee. *See* Three Faces West, 1940
Regain, 1937 (Fernandel)
Regal Cavalcade. *See* Royal Cavalcade, 1935
Regarde d'Ulysse. *See* To Vlemma tou Odyssea, 1995
Regarding Henry, 1991 (Ford, H.)
Reggie Mixes In, 1916 (Fairbanks)
Regina, 1982 (Gardner; Quinn)
Regina di Navarra, 1941 (Cervi)
Regina di Saba, 1952 (Cervi)
Regine, 1934 (Walbrook)
Regine, die Tragödie einer Frau, 1927 (Homolka)
Règle du jeu, 1939 (Dalio; Modot)
Règlements de comptes, 1962 (Gélin)
Regreso al silencio, 1967 (Villagra)
Rehearsal for Murder, 1982 (Preston)
Reiche Kunden killt man nicht, 1991 (Vogler)
Reifende Jugend, 1955 (Schell, Maximilian)
Reifezeugnis, 1976 (Kinski)
Reigen, 1920 (Nielsen; Veidt)
Reijin, 1930 (Takamine)
Reijin, 1946 (Hara)
Reijin no bisho, 1931 (Takamine)
Reimei hachigatsu jugo-nichi, 1952 (Kagawa)
Reimei izen, 1931 (Hasegawa)
Reina Anonima, 1992 (Maura)
Reina del Rio, 1940 (Armendáriz)
Reina Santa, 1947 (Rey)
Reine Blanche, 1991 (Deneuve)
Reine des resquilleuses, 1936 (Brasseur)
Reine Margot, 1953 (Moreau; Rosay)
Reine Margot, 1994 (Adjani)
Reise um die Erde in 80 Tagen, 1919 (Veidt)
Reisenrad, 1961 (Schell, Maria)
Reivers, 1969 (McQueen; Meredith)
Rejected Woman, 1924 (Lugosi)
Rejedor de Milagros, 1961 (Armendáriz)
Rekopis znaleziony w Saragossie, 1965 (Tyszkiewicz)
Relaxe-toi, cheri, 1964 (Fernandel)
Relazioni Pericolose. *See* Liaisons dangereuses, 1959
Relentless, 1948 (Young, R.)
Relic of Old Japan, 1915 (Hayakawa)
Religieuse, 1965 (Karina; Presle)
Religion and Gun Practice, 1913 (Mix)
Reluctant Debutante, 1958 (Harrison; Kendall; Lansbury)

Reluctant Dragon, 1941 (Ladd)
Reluctant Heroes, 1971 (Oates)
Reluctant Saint, 1962 (Schell, Maximilian)
Remains of the Day, 1993 (Grant, H.; Hopkins, A.; Thompson)
Remains to Be Seen, 1953 (Calhern; Lansbury)
Remando al Viento, 1988 (Andersson, B.; Grant, H.)
Remarkable Andrew, 1942 (Holden)
Remarkable Mr. Pennypacker, 1959 (Coburn, C.; Webb)
Rembrandt, 1936 (Lanchester; Laughton)
Remember?, 1939 (Ayres; Garson; Taylor, R.)
Remember Last Night?, 1935 (Young, R.)
Remember Mary Magdalene, 1914 (Chaney)
Remember My Name, 1978 (Chaplin, G.; Perkins)
Remember That Face. See Mob, 1951
Remember the Day, 1941 (Colbert)
Remember the Night, 1940 (MacMurray; Stanwyck)
Remember When?, 1925 (Langdon)
Remembering the Kindertransports, 1995 (Woodward)
Remembrance, 1982 (Oldman)
Remembrance of Love, 1982 (Douglas, K.)
Re-mizeraburu, 1950 (Mori)
Remodeling Her Husband, 1920 (Gish)
Remorques, 1941 (Cuny; Gabin; Morgan)
Remueménage, 1981 (Presle)
Renacida, 1981 (Hopper)
Renaissance Man, 1994 (DeVito; Robertson)
Renaldo and Clara, 1978 (Shepard; Stanton)
Renate im Quartett, 1939 (Fröhlich)
Rencontre imprévue, 1908 (Linder)
Rencontres, 1961 (Brasseur; Morgan)
Rendezvous, 1935 (Dumont; Powell, W.; Russell, R.)
Rendezvous. See Darling, How Could You!, 1951
Rendez-vous, 1961 (Girardot; Noiret; Piccoli; Sanders)
Rendez-vous, 1985 (Binoche)
Rendez-vous à Bray, 1971 (Karina)
Rendezvous at Midnight, 1935 (Bellamy)
Rendez-vous aux Champs-Elysées, 1937 (Berry)
Rendez-vous avec Maurice Chevalier, 1957 (Chevalier)
Rendez-vous d'Anna, 1978 (Cassel)
Rendez-vous de Juillet, 1948 (Gélin; Modot)
Rendezvous de Max, 1913 (Linder)
Rendez-vous de Nöel, 1961 (Piccoli)
Rendezvous in Trieste. See Zwei Whisky und ein Sofa, 1963
Rendezvous with Dishonor. See Appuntamento col disonore, 1970
Rendezvous with Dishonor. See Appuntamento col disonore, 1970
René la Canne, 1976 (Depardieu; Piccoli)
Renegade Ranger, 1938 (Hayworth)
Renegades, 1930 (Loy; Lugosi)
Renoir, les portraits de la beauté, 1987 (Moreau)
Renous, 1935 (Rosay)
Rent-a-Cop, 1988 (Minnelli; Reynolds, B.)
Rent Collector, 1921 (Laurel and Hardy)
Rentadick, 1972 (Cleese)
Renunciation, 1909 (Pickford)
Repast. See Meshi, 1951
Repérages, 1977 (Seyrig)
Répétition chez Jean-Louis Barrault, 1964 (Barrault)
Repo Man, 1983 (Stanton)
Report from Miss Greer Garson, 1943 (Garson)
Report from the Aleutians, 1943 (Huston, J.)
Report on China, 1963 (Massey)
Report to the Commissioner, 1975 (Gere)
Reportaje, 1953 (Armendáriz; Del Rio; Félix; Infante)
Reporters, 1981 (Deneuve; Gere; Kelly, Gene)
Repos du guerrier, 1962 (Bardot)
Représentation au cinéma, 1905 (Linder)
Reprieve. See Convicts Four, 1962
Reproduction interdite, 1956 (Girardot)
Réprouvés, 1936 (Modot)
Republic of Sin. See Fièvre monte à El Pao, 1960
Repulsion, 1964 (Deneuve)

Requiem for a Heavyweight, 1962 (Quinn; Rooney)
Requiem for a Snake. See Coplan sauve sa peau, 1967
Requiem per un agent segreto, 1967 (Granger)
Réquiem por un Campsino Español, 1985 (Banderas)
Resa dei conti, 1967 (Van Cleef)
Resa di Titi, 1945 (Brazzi)
Resa i natten, 1955 (Dahlbeck)
Rescue, 1916 (Chaney)
Rescue, 1929 (Colman)
Rescued by Her Lions, 1911 (Mix)
Rescuers, 1977 (Page)
Rescuers Down Under, 1990 (Candy; Scott, G.)
Reserved for Ladies. See Service for the Ladies, 1932
Reservoir Dogs, 1992 (Keitel)
Residencia para espias, 1967 (Constantine)
Resident Alien, 1991 (Hurt, J.)
Resistance, 1976 (Burton)
Rest in Pieces. See Descanse en piezas, 1986
Rest Is Silence. See Potem nastąpi cisza, 1966
Restez diner, 1933 (Fernandel)
Resting Place, 1986 (Freeman)
Restless. See Beloved, 1971
Restless, 1978 (Welch)
Restless Breed, 1956 (Bancroft)
Restless Knights, 1935 (Brennan; Three Stooges)
Restless Sex, 1920 (Davies; Shearer)
Restoration, 1909 (Pickford)
Restoration, 1996 (Grant, H.; Neill; Ryan, M.)
Restoration and Augustan Poetry, 1984 (Cusack)
Resurrection. See Vozrozhdennia, 1915
Resurrection, 1927 (Del Rio)
Resurrection, 1980 (Burstyn; Shepard)
Resurrection of Zachary Wheeler, 1971 (Dickinson)
Retenez moi ... ou je Fais un Malheur!, 1984 (Lewis, Jerry)
Retired Colonel. See Polkovnik v otstavke, 1976
Retour à l'aube, 1938 (Darrieux)
Retour à la bien aimée, 1978 (Ganz; Huppert)
Retour à la terre, 1938 (Tati)
Retour à la vie, 1949 (Blier; Jouvet)
Retour au bonheur, 1939 (Berry)
Retour de Casanova, 1992 (Cuny; Delon)
Retour de Don Camillo, 1953 (Cervi; Fernandel)
Retour de Manivelle, 1957 (Blier; Gélin; Morgan)
Retour de Martin Guerre, 1981 (Baye; Depardieu)
Retreat from Kiska. See Taiheyo kiseki no sakusen Kiska, 1965
Return, 1980 (Landau)
Return Engagement, 1978 (Taylor, E.)
Return from the Ashes, 1965 (Lom; Schell, Maximilian; Thulin)
Return from the Past. See Dr. Terror's Gallery of Horrors, 1967
Return from the River Kwai, 1988 (Elliott)
Return from Witch Mountain, 1978 (Davis, B.)
Return of a Man Called Horse, 1976 (Harris, R.)
Return of Bulldog Drummond, 1934 (Richardson, R.)
Return of Captain Invincible, 1983 (Arkin; Lee, C.)
Return of Chandu, 1934 (Lugosi)
Return of Dr. Fu Manchu, 1930 (Arthur)
Return of Doctor X, 1939 (Bogart)
Return of Draw Egan, 1916 (Hart)
Return of Frank James, 1940 (Carradine; Cooper; Fonda, H.; Tierney)
Return of Jack Slade, 1955 (Dickinson)
Return of Marcus Welby, M.D., 1984 (Young, R.)
Return of Mickey Spillane's Mike Hammer, 1986 (Rooney)
Return of Ninja. See Zoku shinobi no mono, 1963
Return of October, 1948 (Ford, G.)
Return of Peter Grimm, 1926 (Gaynor)
Return of Peter Grimm, 1935 (Barrymore, L.)
Return of Sabata. See E tornato Sabata ... hai chiuso, 1972
Return of Sherlock Holmes, 1929 (Crisp)
Return of Sophie Lang, 1936 (Milland)
Return of Superfly, 1990 (Jackson, S.)
Return of Swamp Thing, 1989 (Jourdan)

Return of the Ape Man, 1944 (Carradine; Lugosi)
Return of the Badmen, 1948 (Ryan, R.; Scott, R.)
Return of the Black Eagle. *See* Aquila Nera, 1946
Return of the Boomerang. *See* Adam's Woman, 1970
Return of the Cisco Kid, 1939 (Bond)
Return of the Dragon, 1973 (Lee, B.)
Return of the Fly, 1959 (Price)
Return of the Golem. *See* It!, 1967
Return of the Gunfighter, 1967 (Taylor, R.)
Return of the Jedi, 1983 (Ford, H.; Guinness; Jones, James Earl)
Return of the Musketeers, 1989 (Cassel; Chaplin, G.; Lee, C.; Noiret; Reed)
Return of the Pink Panther, 1974 (Lom; Sellers; Sharif)
Return of the Rat, 1928 (Novello)
Return of the Scarlet Pimpernel, 1937 (Mason)
Return of the Seven, 1966 (Brynner; Oates; Rey)
Return of the Six-Million-Dollar Man and the Bionic Woman, 1987 (Landau)
Return of the Soldier, 1982 (Ann-Margret; Bates, A.; Christie; Jackson, G.)
Return of the Terror, 1934 (Astor)
Return of the Texan, 1952 (Brennan)
Return of the Vampire, 1944 (Lugosi)
Return to Earth, 1976 (Bellamy; Robertson)
Return to Fantasy Island, 1978 (Cotten)
Return to Glennascaul, 1951 (Welles)
Return to Macon County, 1975 (Nolte)
Return to Paradise, 1953 (Constantine)
Return to Peyton Place, 1961 (Astor; Ferrer; Weld)
Return to the Beloved. *See* Retour à la bien aimée, 1978
Return to Witch Mountain, 1978 (Lee, C.)
Reunion, 1936 (McDaniel)
Reunion, 1973 (Cusack)
Reunion, 1980 (Ayres)
Reunion. *See* Ami Retrouvé, 1988
Reunion, 1994 (Grant, L.)
Reunion at Fairborough, 1985 (Kerr)
Reunion at Fairborough, 1985 (Mitchum)
Reunion in France, 1942 (Carradine; Crawford, J.; Gardner; Wayne)
Reunion in Vienna, 1933 (Barrymore, J.)
Reve de Singe. *See* Ciao maschio, 1978
Rêve blond, 1931 (Brasseur)
Réveil, 1925 (Vanel)
Reveille, das grosse Wecken, 1925 (Krauss)
Reveille-toi, chérie, 1960 (Gélin)
Reveille with Beverly, 1943 (Miller)
Revelation, 1918 (Nazimova)
Reveler, 1914 (Mix)
Revenant, 1946 (Jouvet)
Revenge, 1928 (Del Rio)
Revenge. *See* Uomo ritorna, 1946
Revenge. *See* Zemsta, 1958
Revenge!, 1971 (Winters)
Revenge. *See* Fatto di sangue fra due uomini per causa di una vedova, 1978
Revenge, 1979 (Loren)
Revenge, 1986 (Carradine)
Revenge, 1990 (Costner; Quinn)
Revenge at El Paso. *See* Quattro dell'ave Maria, 1968
Revenge Is Sweet. *See* Babes in Toyland, 1934
Revenge of Hercules. *See* Vendetta di Ercole, 1960
Revenge of Milady. *See* Four Musketeers, 1974
Revenge of the Creature, 1955 (Eastwood)
Revenge of the Dead, 1975 (Lee, C.)
Revenge of the Pink Panther, 1978 (Lom; Sellers)
Revenge of the Red Baron, 1994 (Rooney)
Revenge of the Stolen Stars, 1985 (Kinski)
Revenge of the Zombies, 1944 (Carradine)
Revengers, 1972 (Borgnine; Hayward; Holden)
Reversal of Fortune, 1990 (Close; Irons)
Rêves d'amour, 1947 (Berry)
Revnost, 1914 (Mozhukin)
Revolt of Mamie Stover, 1956 (Moorehead; Russell, J.)
Revolt of the Slaves. *See* Rivolta degli schiavi, 1960
Revolte dans la prison, 1930 (Boyer)

Revolte des confitures. *See* Marmeladupproret, 1980
Revolte im Erziehungshaus, 1929 (Homolka)
Revolution, 1985 (Kinski; Pacino; Sutherland)
Révolution Française, 1989 (Brandauer; Cardinale; Neill; Ustinov)
Revolutionary, 1970 (Duvall; Voight)
Revolutions-hochzeit, 1927 (Kortner)
Revolver. *See* Blood in the Streets, 1976
Revolver Bill. *See* "Bad Buck" of Santa Ynez, 1915
Reward, 1965 (Von Sydow)
Reward of Patience, 1916 (Menjou)
Rex, King of the Wild Horses, 1923 (Laurel and Hardy)
Rey de Africa. *See* One Step to Hell, 1968
Rey que rabió, 1944 (Rey)
Rhapsodie in Blei. *See* Treasure of San Teresa, 1959
Rhapsody, 1954 (Calhern; Gassman; Taylor, R.)
Rhapsody in August, 1991 (Gere)
Rhapsody in Blue, 1945 (Cantor; Coburn, C.; Jolson)
Rhapsody of Happiness, 1947 (Zhao Dan)
Rhinemann Exchange, 1977 (Huston, J.)
Rhinestone, 1984 (Stallone)
Rhinoceros, 1974 (Wilder)
Rhode Island Murders. *See* Demon Murder Case, 1983
Rhodes of Africa, 1936 (Homolka; Huston, W.)
Rhythm and Weep, 1946 (Three Stooges)
Rhythm in the Air, 1936 (Terry-Thomas)
Rhythm of the Saddle, 1938 (Autry)
Rhythm on the Range, 1936 (Crosby; Farmer; Rogers, R.)
Rhythm on the River, 1940 (Crosby; Rathbone)
Rhythm Parade, 1943 (Dumont)
Rhythm Racketeer, 1937 (Terry-Thomas)
Rhythm Romance. *See* Some Like It Hot, 1939
Ricco, 1973 (Kennedy)
Rich and Famous, 1981 (Ryan, M.)
Rich and Respectable. *See* Ab Morgen sind wir reich und ehrlich, 1977
Rich Are Always with Us, 1932 (Davis, B.)
Rich, Full Life. *See* Cynthia, 1947
Rich in Love, 1993 (Finney)
Rich Man, Poor Girl, 1938 (Ayres; Turner, L.; Young, R.)
Rich Man, Poor Man, 1918 (Barthelmess)
Rich Revenge, 1910 (Pickford)
Rich, Young, and Deadly. *See* Platinum High School, 1959
Rich, Young, and Pretty, 1951 (Dalio; Darrieux)
Richard, 1972 (Carradine; Rooney)
Richard III, 1955 (Baker; Bloom; Gielgud; Olivier; Richardson, R.)
Richard III, 1996 (Smith)
Richard Pryor Here and Now, 1983 (Pryor)
Richard Pryor Is Back Live in Concert, 1979 (Pryor)
Richard Pryor, Live and Smokin', 1981 (Pryor)
Richard Pryor Live in Concert, 1978 (Pryor)
Richard Pryor Live on the Sunset Strip, 1982 (Pryor)
Richard's Things, 1981 (Ullmann)
Richelieu, 1914 (Chaney)
Richest Girl in the World, 1934 (Hopkins, M.; McCrea; Wray)
Richter und sein Henker, 1975 (Dagover; Schell, Maximilian; Shaw; Sutherland; Voight)
Richter von Zalamea, 1921 (Dagover)
Rickshaw Man. *See* Muhomatsu no issho, 1958
Ricochet, 1991 (Washington)
Rid i natt, 1942 (Dahlbeck)
Riddle Gawne, 1918 (Chaney; Hart)
Ride 'Em Cowboy, 1942 (Abbott and Costello)
Ride a Crooked Mile, 1938 (Farmer)
Ride a Crooked Trail, 1958 (Matthau)
Ride Back, 1957 (Quinn)
Ride beyond Vengeance, 1966 (Blondell; Grahame)
Ride Clear of Diablo, 1953 (Duryea)
Ride for a Bride, 1913 (Arbuckle)
Ride Him Cowboy, 1932 (Wayne)
Ride Lonesome, 1959 (Coburn, J.; Scott, R.; Van Cleef)
Ride Out for Revenge, 1957 (Grahame)
Ride, Ranger, Ride, 1936 (Autry)

Ride, Tenderfoot, Ride, 1940 (Autry)
Ride the High Country, 1962 (McCrea; Oates; Scott, R.)
Ride the Pink Horse, 1947 (Montgomery)
Ride the Whirlwind, 1966 (Nicholson)
Ride Tonight! *See* Rid i natt, 1942
Ride Vaquero!, 1953 (Gardner; Quinn; Taylor, R.)
Rideau carmoisi, 1952 (Cuny; Aimée)
Rideau rouge, 1952 (Brasseur)
Rider of Death Valley, 1932 (Mix)
Rider of the Law, 1919 (Carey)
Rider on the Rain. *See* Passager de la pluie, 1969
Ridere, ridere, ridere, 1955 (Vitti)
Riders in the Sky, 1949 (Autry)
Riders of Destiny, 1933 (Wayne)
Riders of the Deadline, 1943 (Mitchum)
Riders of the Plains, 1924 (Karloff)
Riders of the Purple Sage, 1925 (Mix)
Riders of the Storm. *See* American Way, 1986
Riders of the Whistling Pines, 1949 (Autry)
Riders of Vengeance, 1919 (Carey)
Riders to the Stars, 1954 (Marshall)
Ridin' a Rainbow, 1941 (Autry)
Ridin' Down the Canyon, 1942 (Rogers, R.)
Ridin' Romeo, 1921 (Mix)
Ridin' Rowdy, 1927 (Brennan)
Riding de Trail, 1911 (Carey)
Riding for a Fall. *See* Manèges, 1950
Riding High, 1943 (Lamour; Powell, D.)
Riding High, 1950 (Bond; Crosby; Laurel and Hardy)
Riding on Air, 1937 (Brown)
Riding Shotgun, 1954 (Bronson; Scott, R.)
Rien ne va plus, 1979 (Presle)
Riff Raff Girls. *See* Du Rififi chez les femmes, 1959
Riffraff, 1935 (Harlow; Rooney; Tracy)
Rififi à Tokyo, 1962 (Vanel)
Rififi in Paris. *See* Du Rififi à Paname, 1966
Right Bank, Left Bank. *See* Rive droit, rive gauche, 1984
Right Bed, 1929 (Horton)
Right Cross, 1950 (Barrymore, L.; Monroe; Powell, D.)
Right of Way, 1914 (Talmadge)
Right of Way, 1931 (Young, L.)
Right of Way, 1983 (Davis, B.; Stewart)
Right Sort. *See* Ugolok, 1916
Right Stuff, 1983 (Harris, E.; Hershey; Quaid; Shepard)
Right to Die, 1987 (Welch)
Right to Love, 1930 (Lukas)
Right to Love. *See* Recht auf Liebe, 1939
Right to Love. *See* Rätten att Älska, 1956
Right to Love. *See* Droit d'aimer, 1972
Right to Romance, 1933 (Young, R.)
Right to the Heart, 1942 (Wilde)
Rights for the Dead. *See* Antigone, 1960
Rigolboche, 1936 (Berry)
Rikigun daikoshin, 1932 (Hasegawa)
Riku no ooja, 1929 (Tanaka)
Rikugun, 1944 (Tanaka)
Rim of the Canyon, 1949 (Autry)
Rime of the Ancient Mariner, 1968 (Burton)
Rimrock Jones, 1918 (Crisp)
Rimsky-Korsakov, 1952 (Cherkassov)
Rincón cerca del cielo, 1952 (Infante)
Ring, 1912-13 (White)
Ring der Giuditta Foscari, 1917 (Jannings)
Ring of Steel, 1942 (Tracy)
Ring Up the Curtain, 1919 (Lloyd)
Ring Up the Curtain. *See* Broadway to Hollywood, 1933
Ringer, 1952 (Elliott; Lom; Zetterling)
Ringo-en no shojo, 1952 (Yamamura)
Rings around the World, 1966 (Ameche)
Rings on Her Fingers, 1942 (Fonda, H.; Tierney)
Rink, 1916 (Chaplin, C.; Purviance)

Rinzo shusse-tabi, 1934 (Hasegawa)
Rio, 1939 (McLaglen; Rathbone)
Rio Abajo, 1984 (Abril)
Rio Blanco, 1967 (Del Rio)
Rio Bravo, 1959 (Bond; Brennan; Dickinson; Martin, D.; Wayne)
Rio Conchos, 1964 (O'Brien, E.)
Rio das mortes, 1970 (Schygulla)
Rio del oro, 1986 (Ganz)
Rio escondido, 1947 (Félix)
Rio Grande, 1950 (McLaglen; O'Hara; Wayne)
Rio Hondo. *See* Comancho blanco, 1967
Rio Lobo, 1970 (Wayne)
Rio Negro, 1976 (Villagra)
Rio Rita, 1942 (Abbott and Costello)
Rio '70, 1970 (Sanders)
Riot, 1913 (Arbuckle)
Riot, 1968 (Hackman)
Rip, Sew, and Stitch, 1953 (Three Stooges)
Riposo del guerriero. *See* Repos du guerrier, 1962
Ripoux, 1984 (Noiret)
Ripoux contre ripoux, 1990 (Noiret)
Ripped-Off. *See* Uomo dalla pelle dura, 1971
Ripper. *See* Fear City, 1984
Ripstitch the Tailor, 1930 (Crosby)
Riptide, 1934 (Brennan; Marshall; Montgomery; Shearer)
Risate di Gioia, 1960 (Magnani)
Rise against the Sword. *See* Abare Goemon, 1966
Rise and Fall of Legs Diamond, 1959 (Oates)
Rise and Rise of Casanova. *See* Casanova & Co., 1977
Rise and Rise of Michael Rimmer, 1970 (Cleese; Elliott)
Rise and Shine, 1941 (Brennan; Darnell)
Rise of Helga. *See* Susan Lenox, Her Fall and Rise, 1931
Rise of the Johnsons, 1914 (Laurel and Hardy)
Rising Damp, 1980 (Elliott)
Rising of the Moon, 1957 (Cusack)
Rising Sun, 1993 (Connery; Keitel; Snipes)
Risk. *See* Suspect, 1960
Risky Business, 1983 (Cruise)
Riso amaro, 1948 (Gassman; Mangano)
Riso no otto, 1933 (Takamine)
Rita. *See* Lettere di una novizia, 1960
Rita la zanzara, 1966 (Giannini)
Rita Ritter, 1984 (Mueller-Stahl)
Rita the Mosquito. *See* Rita la zanzara, 1966
Riten, 1969 (Björnstrand; Thulin)
Rites of Summer. *See* White Water Summer, 1987
Ritorno, 1940 (Brazzi)
Ritorno di Clint il solitario, 1972 (Kinski)
Ritratto dell'amata, 1912 (Bertini)
Ritual. *See* Riten, 1969
Ritual of Evil, 1970 (Baxter; Jourdan)
Riusciranno i nostri eroi a ritrovare l'amico misteriosamente scomparso in Africa?, 1968 (Sordi)
Riusciranno i nostri eroi a trovare il loro amico misteriosamente scomparso in Africa?, 1968 (Blier)
Rival. *See* Rivale, 1974
Rival Brother's Patriotism, 1911 (White)
Rival Demon. *See* Rural Dream, 1914
Rival Mashers. *See* Those Love Pangs, 1914
Rival Stage Lines, 1914 (Mix)
Rival Suitors. *See* Fatal Mallet, 1914
Rivale, 1974 (Andersson, B.)
Rivalité de Max, 1913 (Linder)
Rivalry and War, 1914 (Beery)
Rivals, 1912 (Normand)
Rive droit, rive gauche, 1984 (Baye; Depardieu)
Rivelazione, 1956 (Blier)
River, 1984 (Gibson; Spacek)
River Fuefuki. *See* Fuefuki-gawa, 1960
River Ki. *See* Kinokawa: Hana-no maki, Fumio-no maki, 1966
River Lady, 1948 (Duryea)

River Niger, 1976 (Jones, James Earl)
River of Death, 1989 (Lom; Pleasence)
River of Gold, 1971 (Milland)
River of Love. *See* Nahr el Hub, 1960
River of Mystery, 1969 (O'Brien, E.)
River of No Return, 1954 (Mitchum; Monroe)
River of Romance, 1929 (Beery)
River Pirate, 1928 (Crisp; McLaglen)
River Rat, 1984 (Jones, T.)
River Runs through It, 1992 (Pitt; Redford)
River Wild, 1994 (Bacon; Streep)
River Wolves, 1934 (Mills)
River Woman, 1928 (Barrymore, L.)
River's Edge, 1957 (Milland; Quinn)
River's Edge, 1987 (Hopper; Reeves)
Rivolta degli schiavi, 1960 (Cervi; Rey)
Road. *See* **Strada**, 1954
Road Builder, 1971 (Neal)
Road Demon, 1921 (Mix)
Road Demon, 1938 (Robinson, B.)
Road Games, 1981 (Curtis, J.)
Road Home. *See* Lost Angels, 1989
Road Home, 1995 (Aiello)
Road House, 1928 (Brown)
Road House, 1948 (Lupino; Widmark; Wilde)
Road Show. *See* Chasing Rainbows, 1930
Road Show, 1941 (Langdon; Menjou)
Road to Bali, 1952 (Bogart; Hope; Lewis, Jerry; Lamour; Martin, D.; Russell, J.)
Road to Corinth. *See* Route de Corinthe, 1967
Road to Denver, 1955 (Cobb; Van Cleef)
Road to Dishonour, 1930 (Wong)
Road to Frisco. *See* They Drive By Night, 1940
Road to Glory, 1926 (Lombard)
Road to Glory, 1936 (Barrymore, L.; March)
Road to Hollywood, 1946 (Crosby)
Road to Hong Kong, 1962 (Crosby; Hope; Lamour; Martin, D.; Niven; Sellers; Sidney)
Road to Hope, 1951 (Ladd)
Road to Mandalay, 1926 (Chaney)
Road to Mecca, 1991 (Bates, K.)
Road to Morocco, 1942 (Crosby; Hope; Lamour; Quinn)
Road to Paradise, 1930 (Young, L.)
Road to Peace, 1949 (Crosby)
Road to Reno, 1938 (Scott, R.)
Road to Rio, 1947 (Crosby; Hope; Lamour)
Road to Romance, 1927 (Novarro)
Road to Salina, 1971 (Hayworth)
Road to Singapore, 1931 (Calhern; Powell, W.; Lamour)
Road to Singapore, 1940 (Coburn, C.; Crosby; Hope; Quinn)
Road to the Wall, 1962 (Cagney)
Road to Utopia, 1945 (Crosby; Hope; Lamour)
Road to Victory, 1944 (Crosby; Grant, C.; Sidney)
Road to Wellville, 1994 (Hopkins, A.; Williams, R.)
Road to Zanzibar, 1941 (Crosby; Hope; Lamour)
Road Warrior, 1982 (Gibson)
Road West. *See* This Savage Land, 1966
Roadhouse Nights, 1929 (Durante)
Roadhouse 66, 1984 (Dafoe)
Roads to the South. *See* Routes du sud, 1978
Roadside Impressario, 1917 (Crisp)
Roaming Lady, 1936 (Bellamy; Wray)
Roaming Romeo, 1933 (Langdon)
Roaming the Emerald Isle with Will Rogers, 1927 (Rogers, W.)
Roar, 1981 (Griffith)
Roar of the Dragon, 1932 (Horton)
Roaring Rails, 1924 (Carey)
Roaring Twenties, 1939 (Bogart; Cagney)
Rob Roy, 1995 (Hurt, J.; Lange; Neeson)
Robber Symphony, 1935 (Rosay)
Robber's Roost, 1933 (O'Sullivan)

Robbery, 1967 (Baker)
Robbery under Arms, 1957 (Finch)
Robbery under Arms, 1984 (Neill)
Robe, 1953 (Burton; Mature)
Robe noire pour un tueur, 1980 (Girardot)
Robert et Robert, 1978 (Morgan)
Robert Koch, 1939 (Jannings; Krauss)
Robert's Lesson, 1912-13 (White)
Roberta, 1935 (Astaire; Ball; Dunne; Rogers, G.; Scott, R.)
Robin and Marian, 1976 (Abril; Connery; Elliott; Harris, R.; Hepburn, A.; Shaw)
Robin and the Seven Hoods, 1964 (Crosby; Falk; Martin, D.; Robinson, E.; Sidney)
Robin Hood, 1922 (Beery; Fairbanks)
Robin Hood, 1973 (Terry-Thomas; Ustinov)
Robin Hood, 1991 (Thurman)
Robin Hood: Men in Tights, 1993 (Brooks, M.)
Robin Hood: Prince of Thieves, 1991 (Connery; Costner; Freeman)
Robin Hood of Texas, 1947 (Autry)
Robin Hood of the Pecos, 1941 (Rogers, R.)
Robinson Crusoeland. *See* Atoll K, 1951
Robinson soll nicht sterben, 1957 (Schneider)
Robo de diamantes, 1967 (Rey)
Robo no ishi, 1960 (Hara; Yamada)
Robust Romeo, 1914 (Arbuckle)
Rocambole, 1946 (Brasseur)
Rocco e i suoi fratelli, 1960 (Cardinale; Delon)
Rocco Papaleo. *See* Permette? Rocco Papaleo, 1971
Rocinante, 1986 (Hurt, J.)
Rock, 1996 (Cage; Connery; Harris, E.)
Rock Pretty Baby, 1956 (Mineo; Wray)
Rock, Rock, Rock, 1956 (Weld)
Rock-a-Bye-Baby, 1958 (Lewis, Jerry)
Rockabye, 1932 (Lukas; McCrea; Pidgeon)
Rocket Bus, 1929 (Madsen and Schenstrøm)
Rocket Gibraltar, 1988 (Lancaster)
Rocket Man, 1954 (Coburn, C.)
Rocket to the Moon, 1986 (Davis, J.; Malkovich; Wallach)
Rocketeer, 1990 (Arkin)
Rockford Files, 1974 (Garner)
Rockford Files: A Blessing in Disguise, 1995 (Garner)
Rockford Files: Friends and Foul Play, 1996 (Garner)
Rockford Files: Godfather Knows Best, 1996 (Garner)
Rockford Files: I Still Love L.A., 1994 (Garner)
Rockford Files: If the Frame Fits ..., 1996 (Garner)
Rockin' in the Rockies, 1945 (Three Stooges)
Rockin' through the Rockies, 1940 (Three Stooges)
Rocking-Horse Winner, 1950 (Mills)
Rocky, 1948 (McDowall)
Rocky, 1976 (Meredith; Stallone)
Rocky II, 1979 (Meredith; Stallone)
Rocky III, 1982 (Meredith; Stallone)
Rocky IV, 1985 (Stallone)
Rocky V, 1990 (Meredith; Stallone)
Rocky Horror Picture Show, 1975 (Sarandon)
Rocky Mountain, 1950 (Flynn)
Rocky Mountain Mystery, 1935 (Scott, R.)
Rocky Road to Dublin, 1968 (Huston, J.)
Rod Laver's Wimbledon, 1969 (Heston)
Rode kappe, 1967 (Björnstrand; Dahlbeck)
Rodeo Girl, 1980 (Cooper)
Rodnoi brat, 1929 (Cherkassov)
Roe vs. Wade, 1989 (Bates, K.; Hunter)
Rogelia, 1962 (Rey)
Roger la Honte, 1966 (Papas)
Roger Touhy, Gangster, 1944 (McLaglen; Quinn)
Rogopag, 1963 (Welles)
Rogue, 1918 (Laurel and Hardy)
Rogue Cop, 1954 (Leigh, Janet; Raft; Taylor, R.)
Rogue Male, 1975 (O'Toole)
Rogue of the Rio Grande, 1930 (Loy)

Rogue Song, 1930 (Barrymore, L.; Laurel and Hardy)
Rogue's Regiment, 1948 (Powell, D.; Price)
Rogue's Romance, 1919 (Valentino)
Roi, 1936 (Raimu)
Roi, 1949 (Chevalier)
Roi de Canargue, 1934 (Vanel)
Roi de coeur. See King of Hearts, 1966
Roi de Paris, 1995 (Noiret)
Roi de tiercé. See Gentleman d'Epsom, 1962
Roi des Champs Elysées, 1934 (Keaton, B.)
Roi des palaces, 1932 (Berry)
Roi du cirque. See Zirkuskönig, 1924
Roi sans divertissement, 1963 (Vanel)
Rois des aulnes. See Unhold, 1996
Rois du sport, 1937 (Berry; Fernandel; Raimu)
Rokujo yukiyama tsumugi, 1965 (Takamine)
Role. See Bhumika, 1977
Roll of Thunder, Hear My Cry, 1978 (Freeman)
Roll on Texas Moon, 1946 (Rogers, R.)
Rolled Stockings, 1927 (Brooks, L.)
Rollerball, 1975 (Caan; Richardson, R.)
Rollercoaster, 1977 (Fonda, H.; Segal; Widmark)
Rollercoaster Rabbit, 1990 (Turner, K.)
Rollerna tre, 1996 (Andersson, B.; Andersson, H.)
Rollicking Adventures of Eliza Fraser. See Eliza Fraser, 1976
Rolling Man, 1972 (Moorehead)
Rolling Sea. See Bärande hav, 1951
Rolling Thunder, 1977 (Jones, T.)
Rollover, 1981 (Fonda, J.)
Roma, 1972 (Magnani; Sordi)
Roma. See Regina, 1982
Roma a mano armato, 1976 (Kennedy)
Roma Bene, 1971 (Papas)
Roma, città aperta, 1945 (Fabrizi; Magnani; Mastroianni)
Roma rivuole Cesare, 1973 (Olbrychski)
Roman Behemshechim, 1985 (Topol)
Roman Cowboy, 1917 (Mix)
Roman d'un jeune homme pauvre, 1935 (Fresnay)
Roman de Max, 1912 (Linder)
Roman der Christine von Herre, 1921 (Krauss)
Roman Holiday, 1953 (Hepburn, A.; Peck)
Roman Scandals, 1933 (Ball; Cantor; Goddard)
Roman Spring of Mrs. Stone, 1961 (Beatty; Leigh, V.)
Romana, 1954 (Gélin; Lollobrigida)
Romance, 1930 (Garbo)
Romance à trois, 1942 (Blier)
Romance and Rhythm. See Cowboy from Brooklyn, 1938
Romance and Riches. See Amazing Quest of Ernest Bliss, 1936
Romance for Three. See Paradise for Three, 1938
Romance in Manhattan, 1934 (Rogers, G.)
Romance in the Dark, 1938 (Barrymore, J.)
Romance in the Jugular Vein, 1980 (Price)
Romance Land, 1923 (Mix)
Romance of a Horsethief, 1971 (Brynner; Wallach)
Romance of an American Duchess, 1915 (Swanson)
Romance of Elaine, 1915 (Barrymore, L.; White)
Romance of Happy Valley, 1918 (Gish)
Romance of Old Bagdad, 1922 (McLaglen)
Romance of Rosy Ridge, 1947 (Leigh, Janet)
Romance of the Hope Diamond. See Hope Diamond Mystery, 1921
Romance of the Redwoods, 1917 (Pickford)
Romance of the Rio Grande, 1911 (Mix)
Romance of the Underworld, 1928 (Astor)
Romance of the Western Hills, 1910 (Pickford)
Romance on the High Seas, 1948 (Day)
Romance on the Orient Express, 1985 (Gielgud)
Romance on the Range, 1942 (Rogers, R.)
Romance with a Double Bass, 1974 (Cleese)
Romancing the Stone, 1984 (DeVito; Douglas, Michael; Turner, K.)
Romanoff and Juliet, 1961 (Ustinov)
Romantic Age, 1949 (Zetterling)

Romantic Comedy, 1983 (Moore, Dudley; Steenburgen)
Romantic Englishwoman, 1975 (Caine; Jackson, G.; Nelligan)
Romantic Young Lady. See Jeune Fille romanesque, 1909
Romantica avventura, 1940 (Cervi)
Romany, 1923 (McLaglen)
Romanza d'amore, 1950 (Brazzi; Darrieux)
Rome Adventure, 1962 (Brazzi; Dickinson)
Rome Armed to the Teeth. See Roma a mano armato, 1976
Rome Express, 1933 (Veidt)
Rome, Open City. See **Roma, città aperta**, 1945
Rome Wants Another Caesar. See Roma rivuole Cesare, 1973
Romeo and Juliet, 1916 (Bara; Menjou)
Romeo and Juliet, 1936 (Barrymore, J.; Howard, L.; Rathbone; Shearer)
Romeo and Juliet, 1954 (Gielgud)
Romeo and Juliet, 1968 (Olivier)
Romeo Is Bleeding, 1993 (Oldman; Olin; Scheider; Lewis, Juliette)
Romeo-Juliet, 1990 (Hurt, J.; Kingsley; Redgrave, V.; Smith)
Romero, 1989 (Julia)
Romola, 1924 (Colman; Gish; Powell, W.)
Romona, 1910 (Pickford)
Ronde, 1950 (Barrault; Darrieux; Gélin; Philipe; Reggiani; Walbrook)
Ronde, 1965 (Fonda, J.; Karina)
Ronde infernale, 1928 (Boyer)
Ronin fubuki, 1939 (Hasegawa)
Ronintabi sassho bosatsu, 1935 (Hasegawa)
Rooftree. See Tvärbalk, 1967
Rookie, 1990 (Braga; Eastwood; Julia)
Rookie of the Year, 1955 (Wayne)
Rookie of the Year, 1973 (Foster)
Rookie of the Year, 1993 (Candy)
Rookie's Return, 1921 (Beery)
Rookies. See Buck Privates, 1941
Rookies Come Home. See Buck Privates Come Home, 1947
Room, 1989 (Pleasence; Travolta)
Room 43. See Passport to Shame, 1959
Room for One More, 1951 (Grant, C.)
Room in Town. See Chambre en ville, 1982
Room Service, 1938 (Ball; Marx Brothers; Miller)
Room Upstairs. See Martin Roumagnac, 1946
Room with a View, 1986 (Bonham-Carter; Day-Lewis; Elliott; Smith)
Roomers. See Wspólny pokój, 1959
Roommates, 1995 (Burstyn; Falk)
Rooney, 1958 (Fitzgerald)
Roop Ki Rani Choron Ka Raja, 1961 (Anand)
Rooster, 1971 (Topol)
Rooster Cogburn, 1975 (Hepburn, K.; Wayne)
Roosters, 1993 (Braga; Olmos)
Rootin' Tootin' Rhythm, 1937 (Autry)
Roots in a Parched Ground, 1988 (Duvall)
Roots of Heaven, 1958 (Flynn; Howard, T.; Huston, J.; Lom; Lukas; Welles)
Rope, 1948 (Stewart)
Rope of Sand, 1949 (Henreid; Jaffe; Lancaster; Lorre; Rains)
Ropin' Fool, 1922 (Rogers, W.)
Roping a Bride, 1915 (Mix)
Roping a Sweetheart, 1916 (Mix)
Roquevillard, 1943 (Vanel)
Rosa de los vientos, 1981 (Villagra)
Rosa dei nomi. See Name of the Rose, 1986
Rosa di Tebe, 1912 (Bertini)
Rosa Luxemburg, 1986 (Olbrychski)
Rosa per tutti, 1966 (Cardinale)
Rosa rossa, 1973 (Cuny)
Rosalie, 1937 (Eddy; Powell, E.)
Rosario, 1935 (Armendáriz)
Rosary, 1922 (Beery)
Rosary Murders, 1987 (Sutherland)
Rosauro Castro, 1950 (Armendáriz)
Rose, 1979 (Bates, A.; Midler; Stanton)
Rose and the Sword. See Flesh + Blood, 1985
Rose Bernd, 1919 (Krauss)
Rose Bernd, 1957 (Schell, Maria)

Rose Bowl Story, 1952 (Wood)

Rose der Wildnes, 1917 (Nielsen)

Rose e spine, 1914 (Bertini)

Rose et le réséda, 1947 (Barrault)

Rose for Everyone. See Rosa per tutti, 1966

Rose Garden, 1989 (Schell, Maximilian; Ullmann; Wallach)

Rose in the Mud. See Warui yatsu hodo yoku nemuru, 1960

Rose-Marie, 1928 (Crawford, J.)

Rose Marie, 1936 (Eddy; MacDonald; Niven; Stewart)

Rose of Blood, 1917 (Bara)

Rose of the Golden West, 1927 (Astor)

Rose of the Winds. See Rosa de los vientos, 1981

Rose of Washington Square, 1939 (Faye; Jolson; Power)

Rose rosse per il Fuhrer, 1968 (Milland)

Rose Tattoo, 1955 (Lancaster; Magnani)

Rose's Story, 1911 (Pickford)

Roseanna McCoy, 1949 (Massey)

Rosebud, 1975 (Attenborough; Huppert; O'Toole)

Rosebud Beach Hotel, 1984 (Lee, C.)

Roseland, 1977 (Chaplin, G.; Walken)

Rosemary's Baby, 1968 (Bellamy; Curtis, T.; Farrow; Gordon)

Rosemary's Baby II. See Look What's Happened to Rosemary's Baby, 1976

Rosemunda e Alboino, 1961 (Palance)

Rosen, die der Sturm entblättert, 1917 (Negri)

Rosen aus dem Süden, 1954 (Fröhlich)

Rosen im Herbst, 1955 (Dagover)

Rosencrantz and Guildenstern Are Dead, 1991 (Dreyfuss; Oldman)

Roses Are for the Rich, 1987 (Dern)

Roses rouges et piments verts. See No encontre rosas para mi madre, 1972

Roses rouges et piments verts, 1975 (Lollobrigida)

Rosewood, 1996 (Voight)

Rosie: The Rosemary Clooney Story, 1982 (Cooper)

Rosie!, 1968 (Russell, R.)

Rosier de Madame Husson, 1932 (Fernandel; Rosay)

Rosita, 1923 (Pickford)

Rosolino paternò, soldato .... See Operation Snafu, 1970

Rossini, Rossini, 1991 (Noiret)

Rossiter Case, 1951 (Baker)

Roswell, 1994 (Sheen)

Rötägg, 1946 (Björnstrand)

Rote Kreis, 1960 (Rasp)

Rote Liebe, 1982 (Constantine)

Rote Rausch, 1962 (Kinski)

Rote Rosen, rote Lippen, roter Wein, 1953 (Dagover)

Rothausgasse, 1928 (Fröhlich; Homolka)

Rouge. See Trzy Kolory: Bialy, 1994

Rouge aux lèvres, 1971 (Seyrig)

Rouge est mis, 1957 (Gabin; Girardot)

Rouge et le noir. See Geheime Kurier, 1928

Rouge et le noir, 1954 (Darrieux; Philipe; Sordi)

Rouge Gorge, 1985 (Abril)

Rough Company. See Violent Men, 1954

Rough Cut, 1980 (Niven; Reynolds, B.)

Rough Day for the Queen. See Rude journée pour la reine, 1973

Rough Diamond, 1921 (Mix)

Rough House, 1917 (Arbuckle; Keaton, B.)

Rough House Rosie, 1927 (Bow)

Rough Justice, 1987 (Kinski)

Rough Night in Jericho, 1967 (Martin, D.)

Rough Riders, 1927 (Astor)

Rough Riders' Roundup, 1939 (Rogers, R.)

Rough-Riding Romance, 1919 (Mix)

Rough Romance, 1930 (Wayne)

Rough Shoot. See Shoot First, 1953

Rough, Tough, and Ready, 1945 (McLaglen)

Roughest Africa, 1923 (Laurel and Hardy)

Roughly Speaking, 1945 (Russell, R.)

Roughneck, 1915 (Hart)

Roughshod, 1949 (Grahame)

Roullez jeunesse, 1993 (Gélin)

'Round Midnight, 1986 (Noiret)

Round-Up, 1920 (Arbuckle)

Round-Up Time in Texas, 1937 (Autry)

Roundabout. See Tour de manège, 1989

Rounders, 1914 (Arbuckle; Chaplin, C.)

Rounders, 1965 (Fonda, H.; Ford, G.; Oates)

Roundup, 1920 (Beery)

Roustabout. See Property Man, 1914

Roustabout, 1964 (Presley; Stanwyck; Welch)

Route d'un homme, 1967 (Barrault; Feuillère)

Route de Corinthe, 1967 (Seberg)

Route de Salina. See Road to Salina, 1971

Route heureuse, 1935 (Feuillère)

Route Napoléon, 1953 (Fresnay)

Routes du sud, 1978 (Montand)

Rover, 1967 (Hayworth; Quinn)

Rovin' Tumbleweeds, 1939 (Autry)

Rowan and Martin at the Movies, 1969 (Heston)

Rowboat Romance, 1914 (Arbuckle)

Rowing with the Wind. See Remando al Viento, 1988

Rowlandson's England, 1955 (Guinness)

Roxanne, 1987 (Martin, S.)

Roxie Hart, 1942 (Menjou; Rogers, G.)

Royal Affair. See Roi, 1949

Royal Affairs in Versailles. See Si Versailles m'était conté, 1953

Royal Bed, 1930 (Astor)

Royal Blood, 1916 (Laurel and Hardy)

Royal Cavalcade, 1935 (Mills)

Royal Divorce, 1938 (Hawkins)

Royal Family of Broadway, 1930 (March)

Royal Flash, 1975 (McDowell; Reed; Bates, A.; Hoskins)

Royal Flush. See Two Guys from Milwaukee, 1946

Royal Game. See Schachnovelle, 1960

Royal Hunt of the Sun, 1969 (Shaw)

Royal Romance of Charles and Diana, 1982 (De Havilland; Granger; Milland)

Royal Scandal. See Hose, 1927

Royal Scandal, 1945 (Baxter; Coburn, C.; Price)

Royal Tour of New South Wales, 1956 (Finch)

Royal Wedding, 1947 (Neagle)

Royal Wedding, 1951 (Astaire)

Roza, 1982 (Olbrychski)

Różaniec z granatow, 1969 (Olbrychski)

Rozdennie polzat utat ne mozet, 1914 (Mozhukin)

Rozmarné léto, 1968 (Brodský)

Ruba al prossimo tuo, 1969 (Cardinale; RubaHudson)

Rube and the Baron, 1913 (Normand)

Rübezahls Hochzeit, 1916 (Wegener)

Ruby, 1992 (Aiello)

Ruby Cairo. See Deception, 1992

Ruby Gentry, 1952 (Heston; Jones, Jennifer; Malden)

Ruby Keeler, 1928 (Keeler)

Ruby's Dream. See Dear Mr. Wonderful, 1982

Rudd Family Goes to Town. See Dad and Dave Come to Town, 1938

Rude Awakening, 1989 (Elliott)

Rude journée pour la reine, 1973 (Depardieu)

Rudolph Valentino, 1938 (Negri)

Rudyard Kipling's the Jungle Book, 1994 (Cleese; Neill)

Rue Barbar, 1986 (Van Damme)

Rue de l'Estrapade, 1953 (Gélin; Jourdan)

Rue des prairies, 1959 (Gabin)

Rue du Bac, 1991 (Bujold)

Rue du départ, 1986 (Depardieu)

Rue Fontaine, 1984 (Léaud)

Ruf, 1949 (Kortner)

Ruf aus dem Äther, 1951 (Werner)

Ruf des Schicksals, 1922 (Kortner)

Ruffian, 1983 (Cardinale)

Rugged Water, 1925 (Beery)

Ruggles of Red Gap, 1923 (Horton)

Ruggles of Red Gap, 1935 (Laughton)

Ruhe sanft, Bruno, 1983 (Mueller-Stahl)

Ruins. See Khandahar, 1983

Ruisseau, 1938 (Rosay)
Rulers of the City. *See* I padroni della città, 1977
Rulers of the Sea, 1939 (Ladd; Lockwood)
Rules of the Game. *See* **Règle du jeu**, 1939
Ruling Class, 1972 (O'Toole)
Ruling Voice, 1931 (Huston, W.; Young, L.)
Rum and Wallpaper, 1915 (Arbuckle)
Rum Runner. *See* Boulevard du rhum, 1971
Rumba, 1935 (Lombard; Raft; Wyman)
Rumba, 1987 (Piccoli)
Rumble Fish, 1983 (Cage; Dillon; Fishburne; Hopper; Rourke)
Rumble in the Bronx. *See* Hong Faan Kui, 1995
Rumor Mill. *See* Malice in Wonderland, 1985
Rumor of War, 1980 (Fishburne)
Rumpus in the Harem, 1956 (Three Stooges)
Run a Crooked Mile, 1969 (Jourdan)
Run for Cover, 1955 (Borgnine; Cagney)
Run for the Sun, 1956 (Howard, T.; Widmark)
Run for Your Money, 1949 (Guinness)
Run, Girl, Run, 1928 (Lombard)
Run If You Can, 1987 (Landau)
Run Like a Thief. *See* Robo de diamantes, 1967
Run of the Arrow, 1957 (Bronson; Dickinson; Steiger)
Run of the Country, 1995 (Finney)
Run on Gold. *See* Midas Run, 1969
Run Rabbit Run. *See* Double X: The Name of the Game, 1992
Run, Run, Joe. *See* Arrivano Joe e Margherito, 1974
Run Silent, Run Deep, 1958 (Gable; Lancaster)
Run, Simon, Run, 1970 (Reynolds, B.)
Run, Stranger, Run. *See* Happy Mother's Day—Love George, 1973
Run Wild, Run Free, 1969 (Mills)
Runaround, 1946 (Crawford, B.)
Runaway, 1926 (Bow; Powell, W.)
Runaway Barge, 1975 (Nolte)
Runaway Bride, 1930 (Astor; Crisp)
Runaway Bus, 1954 (Rutherford)
Runaway Daughter. *See* Red Salute, 1935
Runaway Romany, 1917 (Davies)
Runaway Train, 1985 (Voight)
Rund um eine Million, 1933 (Fröhlich)
Runnin' Kind, 1989 (Lewis, Juliette)
Running, 1979 (Douglas, Michael)
Running, Jumping, and Standing Still Film, 1960 (Sellers)
Running Man, 1963 (Bates, A.; Remick; Rey)
Running Man, 1987 (Schwarzenegger)
Running Mates, 1992 (Harris, E.; Keaton, D.)
Running Out of Luck, 1986 (Hopper)
Running Wild, 1927 (Fields, W. C.)
Running Wild, 1994 (Sheen)
Runpen to sono musume, 1931 (Tanaka)
Runt Page, 1932 (Temple)
Rupert of Cole-Slaw, 1924 (Laurel and Hardy)
Rupert of Hentzau, 1923 (Menjou)
Rupture, 1970 (Audran; Cassel)
Ruptures, 1993 (Aimée; Piccoli)
Rural Dream, 1914 (Arbuckle)
Ruse, 1915 (Hart)
Ruse de Max, 1913 (Linder)
Ruses du Diable, 1965 (Piccoli)
Ruses, Rhymes and Roughnecks, 1915 (Lloyd)
Rush, 1991 (Leigh, Jennifer Jason)
Rusk. *See* Skorpan, 1957
Ruslan i Ludmila, 1915 (Mozhukin)
Russia House, 1990 (Brandauer; Connery; Pfeiffer; Scheider)
Russian Roulette, 1975 (Elliott; Segal)
Russians Are Coming, the Russians Are Coming, 1966 (Arkin; Saint)
Russicum, 1987 (Aiello; Brazzi)
Rustlers, 1919 (Carey)
Rustler's Rhapsody, 1985 (Rey)
Rustler's Roundup, 1933 (Mix)
Rustler's Valley, 1937 (Cobb)

Rustlers' Paradise, 1935 (Carey)
Rusty Romeos, 1957 (Three Stooges)
Ruten, 1956 (Kagawa)
Ruten no oohi, 1960 (Kyo; Tanaka; Yamada)
Ruthless, 1948 (Greenstreet)
Ruthless Four. *See* Ognuno per se, 1968
Ruthless People, 1986 (DeVito; Midler)
Rutles. *See* All You Need Is Cash, 1978
Ruy Blas, 1947 (Darrieux; Marais)
Ryan White Story, 1989 (Scott, G.)
Ryan's Daughter, 1970 (Howard, T.; Mills; Mitchum)
Ryuko sokitai, 1937 (Shimura)
Ryusei, 1949 (Yamamura)
S.1., 1913 (Nielsen)
S*H*E, 1980 (Sharif)
S.O.B., 1981 (Andrews, J.; Holden; Preston; Winters)
S.O.S. Coastguard, 1937 (Lugosi)
S.O.S. Concorde. *See* Concorde affaire, 1979
S.O.S. Noronha, 1956 (Marais)
S.O.S. Pacific, 1959 (Attenborough; Constantine)
S.O.S. Sahara, 1938 (Vanel)
S.O.S. Titanic, 1979 (Mirren)
S*P*Y*S, 1974 (Gould; Sutherland)
SST—Death Flight, 1977 (Meredith)
Saadia, 1954 (Cusack; Wilde)
Saat Pake Bandha, 1963 (Chatterjee)
Sabaka. *See* Hindu, 1953
Sabakareru Echizen no kami, 1962 (Hasegawa)
Sabaku o wataru taiyo, 1960 (Yamamura)
Sabata. *See* Ehi, amico ... c'e Sabata, hai chiuso?, 1969
Sabina, 1979 (Andersson, H.)
Sabotage, 1936 (Homolka; Sidney)
Sabotage, 1952 (Andersson, H.; Dahlbeck)
Saboteur—Code Name Morituri, 1965 (Brando; Brynner; Howard, T.)
Sabre and the Arrow. *See* Last of the Comanches, 1952
Sabrina, 1954 (Bogart; Dalio; Dickinson; Hepburn, A.; Holden)
Sabrina, 1995 (Ford, H.)
Sabrina Fair. *See* Sabrina, 1954
Sac de noeuds, 1985 (Huppert)
Sacco and Vanzetti. *See* Sacco e Vanzetti, 1971
Sacco e Vanzetti, 1971 (Cusack; Volonté)
Sachche Ka Bol Bala, 1989 (Anand)
Sacketts, 1979 (Ford, G.)
Sacrée jeunesse, 1958 (Cassel)
Sacrifice. *See* **Offret**, 1986
Sacrifice of Kathleen, 1913 (Talmadge)
Sacrificial Horse. *See* Aswa medher ghora, 1981
Sad Sack, 1957 (Lewis, Jerry; Lorre)
Saddle Girth, 1917 (Mix)
Saddle Pals, 1947 (Autry)
Saddle the Wind, 1958 (Crisp; Taylor, R.)
Saddle Tramp, 1950 (McCrea)
Sadgati, 1981 (Patil)
Sadhu Aur Shaitan, 1968 (Kumar)
Sadie and Jon, 1987 (Reynolds, D.)
Sadie McKee, 1934 (Crawford, J.)
Sadie Thompson, 1928 (Barrymore, L.; Swanson)
Sadist. *See* Träfracken, 1966
Sado jowa, 1934 (Yamada)
Safari, 1940 (Carroll)
Safari, 1956 (Leigh, Janet; Mature)
Safari 3000. *See* Rally, 1980
Safari 5000. *See* Eiko eno 5000 kiro, 1969
Safe Passage, 1994 (Sarandon; Shepard)
Safe Place, 1971 (Nicholson; Weld; Welles)
Safecracker, 1958 (Milland)
Safeguarding Military Information, 1941 (Huston, W.; Rogers, G.)
Safety Curtain, 1918 (Talmadge)
Safety First, 1941 (Cushing)
Safety in Numbers, 1930 (Lombard)
Safety Last, 1923 (Lloyd)

Safety Worst, 1915 (Laurel and Hardy)
Såg det med blommer, 1952 (Björnstrand)
Sag' die Wahrheit, 1946 (Fröhlich)
Saga of Death Valley, 1939 (Rogers, R.)
Saga of the Vagabonds. *See* Sengoki gunto-den, 1959
Sage-femme, le curé et le bon dieu. *See* Jessica, 1962
Sagebrush Tom, 1915 (Mix)
Sagebrush Trail, 1922 (Beery; Wayne)
Sagebrush Troubadour, 1935 (Autry)
Sagina, 1974 (Kumar)
Sagina Mahato, 1970 (Kumar)
Saginaw Trail, 1953 (Autry)
Sagnarelle, 1907 (Linder)
Sahara, 1943 (Bogart; Duryea)
Sahara, 1983 (Mills)
Saheb Bahadur, 1977 (Anand)
Saigo ni warau otoko, 1949 (Kyo)
Saigon, 1948 (Ladd; Lake)
Saigon. *See* Off Limits, 1988
Saigon Baby, 1995 (Hurt, J.)
Saikai, 1953 (Mori)
Saikaku ichidai onna, 1952 (Mifune; Shimura; Tanaka)
Sailor Beware, 1951 (Lewis, Jerry; Martin, D.)
Sailor, Beware!, 1952 (Dean)
Sailor from Gibraltar, 1967 (Hurt, J.; Moreau; Redgrave, V.; Welles)
Sailor-Made Man, 1921 (Lloyd)
Sailor Takes a Wife, 1945 (Walker)
Sailors Beware!, 1927 (Laurel and Hardy)
Sailor's Heart, 1912 (Sweet)
Sailor's Holiday, 1944 (Winters)
Sailor's Lady, 1940 (Andrews, D.)
Sailor's Sweetheart, 1927 (Loy)
Sailors' Wives, 1928 (Astor)
St. Elmo, 1923 (Gilbert)
St. Elmo's Fire, 1985 (Moore, Demi)
Saint in London, 1939 (Sanders)
Saint in Palm Springs, 1941 (Sanders)
St. Ives, 1976 (Bronson; Schell, Maximilian)
Saint Jack, 1979 (Elliott)
Saint Joan, 1957 (Gielgud; Seberg; Walbrook; Widmark)
St. Louis Blues, 1938 (Lamour)
St. Louis Kid, 1934 (Cagney)
Saint-Louis ou l'ange de la paix, 1950 (Philipe)
St. Martin's Lane, 1938 (Harrison; Leigh, V.; Laughton)
Saint of Fort Washington, 1993 (Dillon)
Saint prend l'affût, 1966 (Marais)
Saint Strikes Back, 1939 (Fitzgerald; Sanders)
Saint Takes Over, 1940 (Sanders)
Saint-Tropez Blues, 1960 (Audran)
Saint-Tropez, devoir de vacances, 1952 (Brasseur; Gélin; Piccoli)
St. Valentine's Day Massacre, 1967 (Dern; Robards; Segal)
Sainte famille, 1972 (Thulin)
Sainted Devil, 1924 (Valentino)
Sainted Sisters, 1948 (Fitzgerald; Lake)
Saintes Nitouches, 1962 (Blier)
Saint's Double Trouble, 1940 (Lugosi; Sanders)
Sais seule que j'aime, 1938 (Presle)
Saisons du plaisir, 1988 (Audran; Vanel)
Sakanaka ronin, 1930 (Yamada)
Sakharov, 1984 (Jackson, G.; Robards)
Sakiko-san chotto, 1963 (Yamada)
Sakujitsu kieta oto, 1940 (Yamada)
Sakujitsu kieta otoko, 1941 (Hasegawa; Takamine)
Sakura onda, 1934 (Tanaka)
Sakura-ondo: Kyo wa odotte, 1947 (Hasegawa)
Sakurada-mon, 1961 (Hasegawa)
Sal Gordo, 1983 (Maura)
Salaire de la peur, 1953 (Vanel; Montand)
Salaire du péché, 1956 (Darrieux; Moreau)
Salamander, 1980 (Lee, C.)
Salamander, 1981 (Cardinale; Quinn; Reggiani; Wallach)

Salem's Lot, 1979 (Ayres; Mason)
Sallah, 1964 (Topol)
Sallah Shabati. *See* Sallah, 1964
Sallie's Sure Short, 1913 (Mix)
Sally, 1929 (Brown)
Sally in Our Alley, 1931 (Fields, G.)
Sally, Irene, and Mary, 1925 (Crawford, J.; Durante; Faye)
Sally of the Sawdust, 1925 (Fields, W. C.)
Salmonberries, 1992 (Palance)
Salome, 1913 (Bertini)
Salome, 1918 (Bara)
Salome, 1923 (Nazimova)
Salome, 1953 (Granger; Hayworth; Laughton)
Salome's Last Dance, 1988 (Jackson, G.)
Salomy Jane. *See* Wild Girl, 1932
Salon Kitty, 1976 (Thulin)
Salonique. *See* Mademoiselle Docteur, 1936
Salonique, nid d'espions. *See* Mademoiselle Docteu, 1937
Saloon Bar, 1940 (McDowall)
Salt in the Wound. *See* Dito nell piaga, 1969
Salt of This Black Earth. *See* Sól ziemi czarnej, 1970
Salt on Our Skin, 1992 (Scacchi)
Salto Mortale, 1931 (Walbrook)
Salto nel vuoto, 1979 (Aimée; Noiret; Piccoli)
Salty O'Rourke, 1945 (Ladd)
Salut l'artiste, 1973 (Mastroianni)
Salute, 1929 (Bond; Wayne)
Salute to France, 1944 (Meredith)
Salute to Romance. *See* Annapolis Salute, 1937
Salute to the Marines, 1943 (Beery)
Salute to the Theatres, 1955 (Gish)
Salvador, 1986 (Woods)
Salvare la faccia, 1969 (Brazzi)
Salzburg Connection, 1972 (Brandauer; Karina)
Sam Cooper's Gold. *See* Ognuno per se, 1968
Sam Hill: Who Killed the Mysterious Mr. Foster?, 1971 (Dern; Jaffe)
Sam Marlow, Private Eye. *See* Man with Bogart's Face, 1979
Sam Whiskey, 1969 (Dickinson; Reynolds, B.)
Sam's Son, 1984 (Wallach)
Samaritan: The Mitch Snyder Story, 1986 (Sheen)
Samay Ki Dhara, 1986 (Azmi)
Same Time Next Year, 1978 (Burstyn)
Sameera, 1981 (Azmi)
Samma no aji, 1962 (Ryu)
Sammy and Rosie Get Laid, 1987 (Bloom)
Sammy in Siberia, 1919 (Lloyd)
Samourai, 1967 (Delon)
Samson, 1914 (Lloyd)
Samson, 1961 (Tyszkiewicz)
Samson and Delilah, 1949 (Lamarr; Lansbury; Mature; Sanders)
Samson and Delilah, 1984 (Ferrer; Mature; Schell, Maria; Von Sydow)
Samson und Delilah, 1922 (Lukas)
Samuel Beckett Is Coming Soon, 1993 (Arkin)
Samurai, 1964 (Shimura; Mifune)
Samurai. *See* Bianco, il giallo, il nero, 1975
Samurai. *See* Miyamoto Musashi, 1954
Samurai Assassin. *See* Samurai, 1965
Samurai Banners. *See* Furin kaza, 1969
Samurai Daughter. *See* Kodachi o tsukau onna, 1961
Samurai Nippon, 1957 (Yamada)
Samurai, Part II. *See* Ichijoji no ketto, 1955
Samurai, Part III. *See* Ketto ganryu-jima, 1956
Samurai Pirate. *See* Daitozuku, 1964
Samurai Saga. *See* Aru kengo no shogai, 1959
San Antonio, 1945 (Flynn)
San Antonio Rose, 1941 (Three Stooges)
San Diego, I Love You, 1944 (Horton; Keaton, B.)
San Fernando Valley, 1944 (Rogers, R.)
San Francisco, 1936 (Gable; MacDonald; Tracy)
San Francisco Docks, 1941 (Fitzgerald; Meredith)
San Francisco Story, 1952 (McCrea)

San-kyodai no ketto, 1960 (Hasegawa)
San-nin no kaoyaku, 1960 (Hasegawa; Kyo)
San Quentin, 1937 (Bogart)
Sanam, 1951 (Anand)
Sanatorium pod klepsydra, 1972 (Nowicki)
Sanba, 1974 (Tanaka)
Sanbyaku-rokuju-go-ya, 1962 (Yamada)
Sanbyaku-rokujugo-ya, 1948 (Takamine)
Sanctuary, 1961 (Montand; Remick)
Sand, 1920 (Hart)
Sand Pebbles, 1966 (Attenborough; McQueen)
Sandai kaiju chikyu saidai no kessen, 1965 (Okada; Shimura)
Sandakan hachi-ban shokan: Bokyo, 1974 (Tanaka)
Sandakan, House No. 8. *See* Sandakan hachi-ban shokan: Bokyo, 1974
Sanders of the River, 1935 (Robeson)
Sandhya Pradeep, 1985 (Chatterjee)
Sandino, 1990 (Abril)
Sandlot, 1993 (Jones, James Earl)
Sandpiper, 1965 (Bronson; Burton; O'Toole; Saint; Taylor, E.)
Sandra. *See* Vaghe stelle dell'Orsa, 1965
Sands of Dee, 1912 (Marsh)
Sands of Fate, 1914 (Crisp)
Sands of Iwo Jima, 1949 (Wayne)
Sands of the Kalahari, 1965 (Baker; York)
Sandwich Man, 1966 (Dors; Terry-Thomas; Wisdom)
Sandy Steps Out, 1941 (Horton)
Sanford Meisner: The Theatre's Best Kept Secret, 1984 (Falk)
Sanfte Lauf, 1967 (Ganz)
Sang à la tête, 1955 (Gabin)
Sang d'Allah, 1922 (Modot)
Sang des autres, 1973 (Vanel)
Sang des autres, 1983 (Audran; Foster; Neill; Presle)
Sang et lumières, 1953 (Gélin)
Sanga Moyu, 1984 (Mifune)
Sangdil, 1952 (Kumar)
Sangharsh, 1968 (Kumar)
Sangini, 1974 (Chatterjee)
Sangue bleu, 1914 (Bertini)
Sanitarium, 1910 (Arbuckle)
Sanjaku Sagohei, 1944 (Takamine)
Sanju-san-gen-do toshi-ya monogatari, 1945 (Hasegawa; Tanaka)
Sanjuro. *See* Tsubaki Sanjuro, 1962
Sanroku, 1962 (Yamada)
Sans famille, 1958 (Blier; Brasseur; Cervi)
Sans laisser d'adresse, 1950 (Blier; Piccoli)
Sans lendemain, 1940 (Feuillère)
Sans mobile apparent, 1971 (Audran; Sanda)
Sans Peur et Sans Reproche, 1988 (Abril)
Sans tambour ni trompette, 1950 (Berry; Rosay)
Sansar, 1971 (Chatterjee)
Sansar Simantey, 1975 (Chatterjee)
Sanshiro Sugata. *See* Zoku Sugata Sanshiro, 1945
Sansho dayu, 1954 (Kagawa; Tanaka)
Sansho: The Bailiff. *See* **Sansho dayu**, 1954
Santa Claus Is Comin' to Town, 1970 (Astaire)
Santa Claus: The Movie, 1985 (Meredith; Moore, Dudley)
Santa Elena piccolo isola, 1942 (Sordi)
Santa Fe, 1951 (Scott, R.)
Santa Fe Stampede, 1938 (Wayne)
Santa Fe Trail, 1940 (Bond; De Havilland; Flynn; Kennedy; Massey; Reagan)
Santee, 1972 (Ford, G.)
Santiago, 1956 (Ladd)
Sanza shigure, 1929 (Hasegawa)
Saotome-ke no musumetachi, 1962 (Kagawa)
Sap, 1929 (Horton)
Sap from Abroad. *See* Sap from Syracuse, 1930
Sap from Syracuse, 1930 (Rogers, G.)
Saphead, 1920 (Keaton, B.)
Sappho, 1921 (Krauss; Negri)
Sappy Bullfighters, 1958 (Three Stooges)
Saps at Sea, 1940 (Laurel and Hardy; Langdon)

Sara no hanano toge, 1955 (Yamamura)
Saraband. *See* Saraband for Dead Lovers, 1948
Saraband for Dead Lovers, 1948 (Granger; Greenwood; Lee, C.; Quayle; Rosay)
Saracinesca, 1918 (Bertini)
Sarafina!, 1992 (Goldberg)
Saragossa Manuscript. *See* Rekopis znaleziony w Saragossie, 1965
Sarah and Son, 1929 (March)
Sarah and the Squirrel, 1984 (Farrow)
Sarah et le cri de la langouste, 1985 (Seyrig)
Sarah, Plain and Tall, 1991 (Close; Walken)
Sarah Siddons, 1938 (McDowall)
Sarajevo, 1955 (Kortner)
Sarajewo, 1955 (Kinski)
Sarariiman Chushingura, 1960 (Tsukasa)
Sarariiman Shimizu minato, 1962 (Tsukasa)
Sarati le terrible, 1937 (Dalio)
Saratoga, 1937 (Barrymore, L.; Gable; McDaniel; Pidgeon)
Saratoga Trunk, 1945 (Bergman; Constantine)
Sarga Arnyèk, 1920 (Lukas)
Sargent Steiner. *See* Breakthrough, 1979
Sarhad, 1960 (Anand)
Sartana, 1968 (Kinski)
Sarutobi Sasuke, 1930 (Yamada)
Sasaki Kojiro, 1950 (Takamine)
Sasaki Kojiro, 1967 (Tsukasa)
Sasameyuki, 1950 (Kagawa; Takamine)
Sasameyuki, 1959 (Kyo)
Sasek a kralovna, 1987 (Brodský)
Saskatchewan, 1954 (Ladd)
Saskatchewan, 1954 (Winters)
Såsom i en spegel, 1961 (Andersson, H.; Björnstrand; Von Sydow)
Satan Bug, 1965 (Andrews, D.)
Satan Leads the Dance. *See* ...Et Satan conduit le bal, 1962
Satan Met a Lady, 1936 (Davis, B.)
Satan Murders, 1974 (Sarandon)
Satan Never Sleeps, 1962 (Holden; Webb)
Satan Town, 1926 (Carey)
Satan Triumphant. *See* Satana likuyushchii, 1917
Satan's Cheerleaders, 1977 (Carradine)
Satan's Triangle, 1975 (Novak)
Satana likuyushchii, 1917 (Mozhukin)
Satanas, 1919 (Kortner; Veidt)
Satanic Rites of Dracula, 1973 (Cushing; Lee, C.)
Sati, 1989 (Azmi)
Satisfaction, 1988 (Neeson; Roberts, J.)
Satsueijo remansu: Renai annai, 1932 (Tanaka)
Satsuma hikyaku, 1951 (Yamada)
Satsunan sodoin, 1930 (Hasegawa)
Saturday Afternoon, 1926 (Langdon)
Saturday Island. *See* Island of Desire, 1952
Saturday Night and Sunday Morning, 1960 (Finney; Roberts, R.)
Saturday Night Fever, 1977 (Travolta)
Saturday Night Kid, 1929 (Arthur; Bow; Harlow)
Saturday, Sunday and Monday. *See* Sobato, Domenica e Lunedi, 1990
Saturday's Children, 1940 (Garfield; Rains)
Saturday's Millions, 1933 (Ladd; Young, R.)
Saturn 3, 1980 (Keitel)
Saturn Three, 1980 (Douglas, K.)
Satyricon. *See* Fellini Satyricon, 1969
Sau Crore, 1991 (Anand)
Saubere Aktien, 1994 (Vogler)
Saucepan Journey. *See* Kastrullresan, 1950
Saudagar, 1991 (Kumar)
Saut de l'ange, 1971 (Hayden)
Sauvage, 1975 (Deneuve; Montand)
Sauve qui peut (la vie), 1980 (Baye; Huppert)
Sauve-toi Lola, 1986 (Moreau)
Savage, 1952 (Heston)
Savage, 1973 (Landau)
Savage. *See* Sauvage, 1975

Savage Brigade. *See* Brigade sauvage, 1939
Savage Guns. *See* Tierra brutal, 1962
Savage Hearts, 1995 (Harris, R.)
Savage Innocents, 1960 (O'Toole; Quinn)
Savage Is Loose, 1974 (Scott, G.)
Savage Messiah, 1972 (Mirren)
Savage Mutiny, 1953 (Weissmuller)
Savage Pampas, 1967 (Taylor, R.)
Savage Princess. *See* Aan, 1952
Savage State. *See* Etat sauvage, 1978
Savant, 1974 (Fresnay)
Save Our Beach. *See* Sunset Cove, 1978
Save the Ship, 1923 (Laurel and Hardy)
Save the Tiger, 1973 (Lemmon)
Saved by a Watch, 1914 (Mix)
Saved by Her Horse, 1915 (Mix)
Saved by the Belle, 1939 (Three Stooges)
Saved by the Pony Express, 1913 (Mix)
Saved from Himself, 1911 (Normand)
Saving Grace, 1986 (Giannini; Josephson; Olmos; Rey)
Saving Mabel's Dad, 1913 (Normand)
Sawdust and Salome, 1914 (Talmadge)
Sawdust and Tinsel. *See* **Gycklarnas afton**, 1953
Sawmill, 1921 (Laurel and Hardy)
Saxon Charm, 1948 (Hayward; Montgomery)
Say Goodbye, Maggie Cole, 1972 (Hayward)
Say It in French, 1938 (Milland)
Say It with Babies, 1926 (Laurel and Hardy)
Say It with Flowers, 1934 (Coburn, C.)
Say It with Flowers. *See* Säg det med blommer, 1952
Say It with Songs, 1929 (Jolson)
Say One for Me, 1959 (Crosby; Reynolds, D.)
Say! Young Fellow, 1918 (Fairbanks)
Sayonara, 1957 (Brando; Garner; Hopper)
Saysons gais, 1930 (Rosay)
Sazaa, 1951 (Anand)
Sbatti il mostro in prima pagina, 1972 (Volonté)
Scalawag, 1973 (DeVito; Douglas, K.)
Scalphunters, 1968 (Lancaster; Winters)
Scam, 1993 (Walken)
Scambio, 1990 (Giannini)
Scamp, 1957 (Attenborough)
Scampolo, 1958 (Schneider)
Scandal, 1989 (Hurt, J.)
Scandal. *See* Shubun, 1950
Scandal. *See* Sukyandaru, 1950
Scandal at Scourie, 1953 (Garson; Moorehead; Pidgeon)
Scandal at Zamalek. *See* Fediha fil Zamalek, 1958
Scandal in a Small Town, 1988 (Welch)
Scandal in Paris, 1946 (Sanders)
Scandal in Paris. *See* Frau auf der Folter, 1927
Scandal in Sorrento. *See* Pane, amore, e ..., 1955
Scandal Sheet, 1931 (Francis)
Scandal Sheet, 1952 (Crawford, B.)
Scandal Sheet, 1985 (Lancaster)
Scandal Street, 1938 (Ayres)
Scandale, 1934 (Marais)
Scandale, 1967 (Audran; Perkins)
Scandalo segreto, 1990 (Gould; Vitti)
Scandalous, 1984 (Gielgud)
Scanian Guerilla. *See* Snapphanar, 1942
Scano boa, 1961 (Cuny)
Scapegoat, 1914 (Mix)
Scapegoat, 1958 (Davis, B.; Guinness)
Scappamento aperto. *See* Echappement libre, 1964
Scappamento Aperto. *See* Chasse à l'homme, 1964
Scar. *See* Hollow Triumph, 1948
Scaramouche, 1923 (Novarro)
Scaramouche, 1952 (Granger; Leigh, Janet)
Scarecrow, 1920 (Keaton, B.)
Scarecrow, 1922 (Astor)

Scarecrow, 1973 (Hackman; Pacino; Wilder)
Scarecrow, 1982 (Carradine)
Scared Stiff, 1953 (Crosby; Hope; Lewis, Jerry; Malone; Martin, D.; Miranda)
Scared Straight: 10 Years Later, 1987 (Goldberg)
Scared to Death, 1947 (Lugosi)
Scarface, 1932 (Karloff; Muni; Raft)
Scarface, 1983 (Pacino; Pfeiffer)
Scarlatine, 1985 (Audran)
Scarlet and the Black, 1983 (Gielgud; Peck)
Scarlet Angel, 1952 (Hudson)
Scarlet Blade, 1963 (Reed)
Scarlet Buccaneer. *See* Swashbuckler, 1976
Scarlet Camellia. *See* Goben no tsubaki, 1965
Scarlet Car, 1917 (Chaney)
Scarlet Claw, 1944 (Rathbone)
Scarlet Coat, 1955 (Sanders; Wilde)
Scarlet Days, 1920 (Barthelmess)
Scarlet Drop, 1918 (Carey)
Scarlet Empress, 1934 (Dietrich; Jaffe)
Scarlet Letter, 1926 (Gish)
Scarlet Letter, 1995 (Duvall; Moore, Demi; Oldman)
Scarlet Letter. *See* Scharlachrote Buchstabe, 1973
Scarlet Pimpernel, 1935 (Howard, L.; Massey; Oberon)
Scarlet River, 1933 (Loy; McCrea)
Scarlet Runner, 1916 (Menjou)
Scarlet Saint, 1925 (Astor)
Scarlet Seas, 1928 (Barthelmess)
Scarlet Street, 1945 (Bennett; Duryea; Robinson, E.)
Scarlet West, 1925 (Bow)
Scarlet Woman. *See* Femme écarlate, 1968
Scarlett Seas, 1928 (Young, L.)
Scars and Stripes, 1919 (Laurel and Hardy)
Scars of Dracula, 1970 (Lee, C.)
Scattered Clouds. *See* Midaregumo, 1967
Scavenger Hunt, 1979 (Gordon; McDowall; Schwarzenegger)
Scélérats, 1960 (Morgan)
Scene Nun, Take One, 1964 (York)
Scene of the Crime. *See* Lieu du crime, 1986
Scener ur ett äktenskap, 1973 (Andersson, B.; Ullmann)
Scenes from a Mall, 1991 (Allen; Midler)
Scenes from a Marriage. *See* Scener ur ett äktenskap, 1973
Scènes de la vie parallèle: 3 Noroît. *See* Noroît, 1976
Scènes de ménage, 1954 (Blier)
Sceno di querra, 1985 (Blier)
Scent of a Woman. *See* Profumo di donna, 1974
Scent of a Woman, 1992 (Pacino)
Scent of Incense. *See* Koge, 1964
Scent of Mystery, 1960 (Dors; Elliott; Lorre; Lukas; Taylor, E.)
Schachnovelle, 1960 (Bloom)
Schädel der Pharaonentochter, 1920 (Jannings; Kortner)
Scharlachrote Buchstabe, 1973 (Vogler)
Scharloachrote Dschunke. *See* Scotland Yard jagt Doktor Mabuse, 1963
Schastlivogo plavaniya, 1949 (Cherkassov)
Schastye, 1932 (Cherkassov)
Schatten, 1923 (Kortner; Rasp)
Schattenkinder des Glücks, 1922 (Banky)
Schatz, 1923 (Krauss)
Schatz der Gesine Jakobsen, 1924 (Wegener)
Schéhérazade, 1962 (Rey)
Schéma d'une identification, 1945 (Philipe)
Schemers, 1916 (Laurel and Hardy)
Scheming Schemers, 1956 (Three Stooges)
Scherben, 1921 (Krauss)
Scherzo del destinoin aqquato dietro l'angolo come un brigante di strada, 1983 (Volonté)
Schiava del paradiso, 1967 (Brazzi)
Schiava di Bagdad. *See* Schéhérazade, 1962
Schicksal, 1924 (Veidt)
Schicksal des Freiherrn von Leisenbohg, 1991 (Aimée; Piccoli)
Schicksal einer schönen Frau, 1932 (Dagover)
Schiff der verlorene Menschen, 1929 (Modot; Dietrich; Kortner)

Schiff in Not, 1925 (Fröhlich)
Schinderhannes, 1927 (Holmolka; Rasp)
Schinderhannes, 1958 (Schell, Maria)
Schindler's List, 1993 (Fiennes; Kingsley; Neeson)
Schizoid. *See* Lucertola con la pelle di donna, 1971
Schizoid, 1980 (Kinski)
Schlagerparade, 1953 (Chevalier)
Schlangenei. *See* Serpent's Egg, 1977
Schlangengrube und das Pendel, 1967 (Lee, C.)
Schloss, 1968 (Schell, Maximilian)
Schloss Hubertus: Der Fischer von Heiligensee, 1955 (Dagover)
Schlussakkord, 1936 (Dagover)
Schmetterlingsschlacht, 1924 (Nielsen)
Schneeweissrosenrot, 1991 (Penn)
Schnüffler, 1983 (Constantine)
Schodami w Gore, Schodami w Dol, 1988 (Nowicki)
Scholar, 1918 (Laurel and Hardy)
Schöne Abenteuer, 1924 (Banky)
Schöne Abenteuer, 1932 (Arletty)
Schöne Feindin, 1992 (Vogler)
Schöne Lügnerin, 1959 (Schneider)
Schöner Gigolo—armer Gigolo, 1979 (Dietrich; Schell, Maria)
Schönheit-spflästerchen, 1937 (Dagover)
School Daze, 1988 (Fishburne; Jackson, S.; Lee, S.)
School for Brides. *See* Two on the Tiles, 1951
School for Husbands, 1937 (Harrison)
School for Scandal, 1923 (Rathbone)
School for Scandal, 1930 (Carroll; Harrison)
School for Scoundrels, 1960 (Terry-Thomas)
School for Secrets, 1946 (Richardson, R.; Ustinov)
School for Secrets. *See* Secret Flight, 1946
School for Sex. *See* Nikutai no gakko, 1965
School of Echoes. *See* Yamabiko gakko, 1952
School of Love. *See* Nikutai no gakko, 1965
School Teacher and the Waif, 1912 (Pickford)
Schoolgirl Diary. *See* Ore nove lezione di chimica, 1941
Schoolmaster of Mariposa, 1911 (Mix)
Schornstein No. 4. *See* Voleuse, 1966
Schpountz, 1937 (Brasseur; Fernandel)
Schrei aus Stein, 1990 (Sutherland)
Schuhpalast Pinkus, 1916 (Rasp)
Schuss am Nebelhorn, 1932 (Rasp)
Schuss im Morgengrauen, 1932 (Lorre)
Schwartze Schaf, 1960 (Rasp)
Schwarz und Weiss wie Tage und Nächte, 1978 (Ganz)
Schwarze Abt, 1963 (Kinski)
Schwarze Husar, 1932 (Veidt)
Schwarze Kobra, 1963 (Kinski)
Schwarze Walfisch, 1934 (Jannings)
Schweigende Mund, 1951 (Homolka)
Schweik's New Adventures, 1943 (Attenborough)
Schweinegold, 1989 (Mueller-Stahl)
Schweitzer. *See* Light in the Jungle, 1991
Schwere Jungens—Leichte Mädchen, 1927 (Fröhlich)
Schwur des Peter Hergatz, 1921 (Jannings)
Science, 1911 (Pickford)
Scientific Cardplayer. *See* Lo scopone scientifico, 1972
Scipione detto anche l'Africano, 1970 (Gassman; Mangano; Mastroianni)
Scissors, 1991 (Stone)
Scolgiera del peccato, 1950 (Cervi)
Sconosciuto di San Marino, 1947 (Magnani)
Scoop, 1987 (Elliott; Lom; Pleasence)
Scorchers, 1992 (Dunaway; Elliott; Jones, James Earl)
Scorching Sands, 1923 (Laurel and Hardy)
Scorned and Swindled, 1984 (Weld)
Scorpio, 1973 (Delon; Lancaster)
Scorpio, Virgo, and Sagittarius. *See* Skorpion, panna, i lucznik, 1972
Scotched in Scotland, 1954 (Three Stooges)
Scotland Yard, 1930 (Bennett; Crisp)
Scotland Yard Hunts Dr. Mabuse. *See* Scotland Yard jagt Doktor Mabuse, 1963

Scotland Yard jagt Doktor Mabuse, 1963 (Kinski)
Scott of the Antarctic, 1948 (Lee, C.; Mills)
Scoumoune, 1972 (Belmondo; Cardinale; Depardieu)
Scoundrel. *See* Mariés de l'an II, 1971
Scoundrel. *See* Narazumono, 1956
Scoundrel in White. *See* Docteur Popaul, 1972
Scourge of the Desert, 1915 (Hart)
Scout, 1994 (Wiest)
Scouts to the Rescue, 1939 (Cooper)
Scram!, 1932 (Laurel and Hardy)
Scrambled Brains, 1951 (Three Stooges)
Scratch as Scratch Can, 1930 (Brennan)
Scream and Scream Again, 1970 (Cushing; Lee, C.; Price)
Scream of Fear. *See* Taste of Fear, 1961
Scream of Stone. *See* Schrei aus Stein, 1990
Scream, Pretty Peggy, 1973 (Davis, B.)
Screamers, 1978 (Cotten)
Screaming Woman, 1972 (Cotten; De Havilland; Pidgeon)
Screen Snapshots, 1932 (Rogers, G.)
Screen Snapshots, 1933 (Three Stooges)
Screen Snapshots No. 1, 1934 (Cagney)
Screen Snapshots No. 5, 1930 (Brown)
Screen Snapshots No. 6, 1935 (Three Stooges)
Screen Snapshots No. 8, 1931 (Brown)
Screen Snapshots No. 9, 1939 (Three Stooges)
Screen Snapshots No. 11, 1934 (Cantor; Karloff)
Screen Snapshots No. 103, 1943 (Dietrich)
Screen Snapshots No. 107, 1942 (Barrymore, J.)
Screen Snapshots No. 206, 1952 (Baxter)
Screen Snapshots No. 225, 1954 (Abbott and Costello)
Scribe, 1966 (Keaton, B.)
Scrim, 1976 (Chaplin, G.)
Scrooge, 1970 (Evans; Finney; Guinness)
Scrooged, 1988 (Mitchum; Murray)
Scrubbers, 1983 (Zetterling)
Scrublady, 1917 (Dressler)
Scruffy, 1938 (McDowall)
Scruggs, 1965 (York)
Scudda Hoo! Scudda Hay!, 1948 (Brennan; Monroe; Wood)
Scusa se e poco, 1982 (Vitti)
Scusi, facciamo l'amore, 1968 (Feuillère)
Scusi, lei è favorevole o contrario, 1966 (Andersson, B.; Mangano; Sordi)
Se incontri Sartana, prega per la tua morte. *See* Sartana, 1968
Se infiel y no mires con quien, 1985 (Maura)
Se permettete parliamo di donne, 1964 (Gassman)
Se tutte le donne del mondo. *See* Kiss the Girls and Make Them Die, 1966
Sea Bat, 1930 (Karloff)
Sea Beast, 1926 (Barrymore, J.)
Sea Chase, 1955 (Turner, L.; Wayne)
Sea Devils, 1937 (Lupino; McLaglen)
Sea Devils, 1953 (Hudson)
Sea Dog's Tale, 1926 (Laurel and Hardy)
Sea Dogs, 1916 (Laurel and Hardy)
Sea Fury, 1958 (Baker; McLaglen; Shaw)
Sea God, 1930 (Wray)
Sea Gull, 1968 (Elliott; Mason; Redgrave, V.)
Sea Gypsies, 1978 (Leigh, Janet)
Sea Hawk, 1924 (Beery)
Sea Hawk, 1940 (Rains; Crisp; Flynn)
Sea Horses, 1926 (Powell, W.)
Sea Nymphs, 1914 (Arbuckle; Normand)
Sea of Grass, 1946 (Walker)
Sea of Grass, 1947 (Carey; Douglas, Melvyn; Hepburn, K.; Tracy)
Sea of Lost Ships, 1953 (Brennan)
Sea of Love, 1989 (Barkin; Jackson, S.; Pacino)
Sea of Sand, 1958 (Attenborough)
Sea Shall Not Have Them, 1955 (Bogarde; Redgrave, M.)
Sea Spoilers, 1936 (Wayne)
Sea Squawk, 1925 (Langdon)
Sea Tiger, 1927 (Astor)
Sea Urchin, 1913 (Chaney)

Sea Wall. *See* Diga sul Pacifico, 1958

Sea Wolf, 1941 (Fitzgerald; Garfield; Lupino; Robinson, E.)

Sea Wolf, 1993 (Bronson)

Sea Wolves, 1980 (Howard, T.; Niven)

Sea Wolves, 1981 (Peck)

Sea Wyf. *See* Sea Wyf and Biscuit, 1957

Sea Wyf and Biscuit, 1957 (Burton)

Sea's Hold. *See* I havsbandet, 1971

Seagull. *See* Kaitchka, 1915

Seagull. *See* Woman of the Sea, 1926

Seagulls over Sorrento. *See* Crest of the Wave, 1954

Sealed Cargo, 1951 (Andrews, D.; Rains)

Sealed Room, 1909 (Pickford)

Sealed Train, 1987 (Caron)

Sealed Verdict, 1948 (Crawford, B.; Milland)

Seance on a Wet Afternoon, 1964 (Attenborough)

Séance de cinématographe, 1909 (Linder)

Seapower, 1965 (Ford, G.)

Search, 1948 (Clift)

Search. *See* Probe, 1972

Search and Destroy, 1995 (Hopper; Turturro; Walken)

Search for Beauty, 1934 (Lupino)

Search for Shaw, 1982 (Cusack)

Search for the Gods, 1975 (Bellamy)

Searchers, 1956 (Bond; Marsh; Wayne; Wood)

Searching for Bobby Fischer, 1993 (Fishburne; Kingsley)

Searching Wind, 1946 (Young, R.)

Seashell and the Clergyman. *See* **Coquille et le clergyman**, 1927

Season for Love. *See* Morte-saison des amours, 1961

Season of Passion, 1961 (Baxter; Borgnine; Lansbury; Mills)

Seasons of the Heart, 1994 (Grant, L.; McDowell; Segal)

Seasons We Walked Together. *See* Futari de aruita ikutoshitsuki, 1962

Seats of the Mighty, 1914 (Barrymore, L.)

Sebastian. *See* Mr. Sebastian, 1968

Sechs Tage Heimaturlaub, 1941 (Fröhlich)

Second Best, 1972 (Bates, A.)

Second Best, 1994 (Hurt, J.; Hurt, W.)

Second Chance, 1953 (Darnell; Mitchum; Palance)

Second Chance, 1971 (York)

Second Chance. *See* Si c'était à refaire, 1976

Second Chance, 1981 (Deneuve)

Second Chances. *See* Probation, 1932

Second Chorus, 1940 (Astaire; Goddard; Meredith)

Second Coming of Suzanne, 1974 (Dreyfuss)

Second Face. *See* Zweite Gesicht, 1982

Second Fiddle, 1923 (Astor)

Second Fiddle, 1939 (Henie; Power)

Second Greatest Story Ever Told, 1993 (McDowell)

Second Hand Wife, 1933 (Bellamy)

Second Honeymoon, 1937 (Power; Trevor; Young, L.)

Second Hundred Years, 1927 (Laurel and Hardy)

Second Mrs. Fenway. *See* Her Honor, the Governor, 1926

Second Mrs. Roebuck, 1914 (Sweet)

Second Serve, 1986 (Redgrave, V.)

Second Sight, 1911 (Pickford)

Second-Story Murder, 1930 (Young, L.)

Second Time Around, 1961 (Reynolds, D.; Ritter)

Second Touch. *See* Twee Vrouwen, 1979

Second Victory, 1986 (Von Sydow)

Second Victory Loan Campaign Fund, 1945 (Davis, B.)

Second Wife, 1936 (Bond)

Second Woman, 1951 (Young, R.)

Seconds, 1966 (Hudson)

Secret, 1974 (Noiret)

Secret. *See* Segreto, 1990

Secret, 1992 (Douglas, K.)

Secret Agent, 1936 (Carroll; Gielgud; Lorre; Young, R.)

Secret Agent, 1996 (Depardieu; Hoskins; Williams, R.)

Secret behind the Door, 1948 (Redgrave, M.)

Secret beyond the Door, 1948 (Bennett)

Secret Bride, 1935 (Stanwyck)

Secret Ceremony, 1968 (Farrow; Mitchum; Taylor, E.)

Secret Code, 1918 (Swanson)

Secret de Mayerling, 1949 (Marais)

Secret de Monte-Cristo, 1948 (Brasseur)

Secret de Polichinelle, 1936 (Raimu; Rosay)

Secret del Sacerdote, 1941 (Armendáriz)

Secret Diary of Sigmund Freud, 1984 (Kinski)

Secret du Chevalier d'Eon, 1960 (Blier)

Secret Flight, 1946 (Attenborough)

Secret Flight. *See* School for Secrets, 1946

Secret Friends, 1992 (Bates, A.)

Secret Fury, 1950 (Colbert; Ryan, R.)

Secret Game, 1917 (Hayakawa)

Secret Garden, 1949 (Lanchester; Marshall; O'Brien, M.)

Secret Garden, 1993 (Smith)

Secret Heart, 1946 (Barrymore, L.; Colbert; Pidgeon)

Secret Hour, 1928 (Negri)

Secret Invasion, 1964 (Granger; Rooney)

Secret Land, 1948 (Montgomery; Taylor, R.)

Secret Life of an American Wife, 1968 (Matthau)

Secret Life of Walter Mitty, 1947 (Karloff; Kaye)

Secret Man, 1917 (Carey)

Secret Marriage. *See* Heimliche Ehen, 1956

Secret Mission, 1942 (Granger; Lom; Mason)

Secret Obsession, 1987 (Christie)

Secret of Anna. *See* **Cria Cuervos**, 1976

Secret of Blood. *See* Tajemství krve, 1953

Secret of Convict Lake, 1951 (Barrymore, E.; Cusack; Ford, G.; Tierney)

Secret of Dorian Gray. *See* Dorian Gray, 1970

Secret of Dr. Kildare, 1939 (Ayres; Barrymore, L.)

Secret of Madame Blanche, 1933 (Dunne)

Secret of Mayerling. *See* Secret de Mayerling, 1949

Secret of Nicola Tesla. *See* Tajna Nikole Tesle, 1979

Secret of NIMH, 1982 (Carradine)

Secret of Santa Vittoria, 1969 (Giannini; Magnani; Quinn)

Secret of Stambov, 1936 (Mason)

Secret of the Black Widow. *See* Geheimnis der schwarzen Witwe, 1963

Secret of the Blue Room, 1933 (Lukas)

Secret of the Casbah. *See* Adventure in Algiers, 1952

Secret of the Chinese Carnation. *See* Geheimnis der chinesischen Nelke, 1964

Secret of the Incas, 1954 (Heston; Young, R.)

Secret of the Purple Reef, 1960 (Falk)

Secret of the Storm Country, 1917 (Talmadge)

Secret Orchard, 1915 (Sweet)

Secret Partner, 1960 (Granger)

Secret People, 1951 (Hepburn, A.; Reggiani)

Secret Places of the Heart, 1989 (Bujold)

Secret Policeman's Ball, 1979 (Cleese)

Secret Policeman's Other Ball, 1982 (Cleese; Volonté)

Secret Policeman's Third Ball, 1987 (Cleese)

Secret Scandal. *See* Scandalo segreto, 1990

Secret Scrolls. *See* Yagyu bugei-cho, 1957

Secret Scrolls, Part II. *See* Soryu hiken, 1958

Secret Service of the Air, 1939 (Reagan)

Secret Sin, 1915 (Hayakawa; Sweet)

Secret Six, 1931 (Beery; Bellamy; Gable; Harlow)

Secret Society, 1991 (Keaton, D.)

Secret War of Harry Frigg, 1968 (Newman)

Secret Ways, 1961 (Widmark)

Secret Weapons, 1985 (Davis, G.)

Secret Wife. *See* Femme secrète, 1986

Secrets, 1924 (Talmadge)

Secrets, 1933 (Howard, L.; Pickford)

Secrets d'alcôve, 1954 (Blier; Moreau)

Secrets of a Secretary, 1931 (Colbert; Marshall)

Secrets of a Soul. *See* Geheimnisse einer Seele, 1926

Secrets of a Soul. *See* Des verlorene Gesicht, 1948

Secrets of an Actress, 1938 (Francis)

Secrets of the City. *See* Stadt ist voller Geheimnisse, 1955

Secrets of the German Ambassador. *See* Taina Germanskovo posolstva, 1914

Secrets of the Orient. *See* Shéhérazade, 1928

Secrets of the Red Bedroom. See Secret Weapons, 1985
Secrets of the Titanic, 1987 (Sheen)
Secrets of Women. See Kvinnors väntan, 1952
Secrets professionnels du Docteur Apfelgluck, 1991 (Gélin)
Secrets, Secrets. See Segreti, segreti, 1985
Secrets Shared with a Stranger. See Confidences a un inconnu, 1995
Sect. See Setta, 1991
Section spéciale, 1975 (Montand)
Seduced, 1985 (Ferrer)
Seduced by Madness: The Diane Borchardt Story, 1996 (Ann-Margret)
Seducer's Diary. See Journal du Seducteur, 1995
Seducers. See Death Game, 1977
Séducteurs. See Sunday Lovers, 1980
Seduction of Joe Tynan, 1979 (Douglas, Melvyn; Streep)
Seduction of Mimi. See Mimi metallurgico ferito nell'onore, 1972
Seduttore, 1954 (Sordi)
See America Thirst, 1930 (Langdon)
See Here, Private Hargrove, 1944 (Walker)
See How She Runs, 1978 (Woodward)
See No Evil. See Blind Terror, 1971
See No Evil, Hear No Evil, 1989 (Pryor; Wilder)
See the Man Run, 1971 (Dickinson)
See You in Hell, Darling. See American Dream, 1966
See You in the Morning, 1988 (Bridges)
Seed, 1931 (Davis, B.)
Seed of Man. See Seme dell'uomo, 1969
Seedling. See Ankur, 1973
Seeing the World, 1927 (Laurel and Hardy)
Seekers, 1954 (Hawkins)
Seekers, 1979 (Carradine; Harris, E.)
Seems Like Old Times, 1980 (Hawn)
Seeschlacht, 1917 (Krauss)
Seger i mörker, 1954 (Björnstrand)
Segno di Venere, 1955 (Loren; Sordi)
Segreti, segreti, 1985 (Valli)
Segreto, 1990 (Kinski)
Segreto del vestito rosso, 1963 (Charisse)
Segreto di Don Giovanni, 1947 (Lollobrigida)
Sehnsucht, 1920 (Veidt)
Sehnsucht, 202, 1932 (Rainer)
Sehnsucht der Veronika Voss, 1982 (Mueller-Stahl)
Sehnsucht jeder Frau, 1930 (Banky)
Sei mogli di Barbablu', 1950 (Loren)
Seidman and Son, 1956 (Cantor)
Seido no Kirisuto, 1955 (Kagawa; Yamada)
Seidon, 1933 (Tanaka)
Seigneurs de la Forêt, 1958 (Welles)
Seikatsusen ABC: Fujie nomaki, 1931 (Tanaka)
Seikatsusen ABC: Zenpen, 1931 (Tanaka)
Seine Frau, die Unbekannte, 1923 (Dagover)
Seine grösster Bluff, 1927 (Dietrich)
Seine Tochter ist der Peter, 1955 (Fröhlich)
Seinerzeit zu meiner Zeit, 1944 (Wegener)
Seins de glace, 1974 (Delon)
Seishun dekameron, 1950 (Kagawa)
Seishun-fu, 1930 (Tanaka)
Seishun gonin otoko, 1937 (Shimura)
Seishun kaidan, 1955 (Yamamura)
Seishun kaigi, 1952 (Yamamura)
Seishun kokyogaku, 1929 (Tanaka)
Seishun no yume ima izuko, 1932 (Ryu; Tanaka)
Seize the Day, 1986 (Williams, R.)
Sekai daisenso, 1961 (Yamamura)
Seki no Yatappe, 1930 (Hasegawa)
Seki no Yatappe, 1959 (Hasegawa)
Sekirei no kyoku, 1951 (Yamamura)
Sekstet, 1963 (Thulin)
Selected Exits, 1993 (Hopkins, A.)
Self-Made Maids, 1950 (Three Stooges)
Selfish Yates, 1918 (Hart)
Selfsame Gräfin, 1961 (Rasp)

Sell Out, 1976 (Reed; Widmark)
Sellout, 1952 (Malden; Pidgeon; Sloane)
Selskaya uchitelnitsa, 1947 (Maretskaya)
Seltsame Gräfin, 1961 (Dagover; Kinski)
Selva de fuego, 1945 (Del Rio)
Semaine de vacances, 1980 (Baye; Noiret)
Seme dell'uomo, 1969 (Girardot)
Semete koyoi o, 1935 (Tanaka)
Semi-Tough, 1977 (Preston; Reynolds, B.)
Seminarista, 1949 (Infante)
Seminole, 1953 (Hudson; Marvin; Quinn)
Semmelweis, 1980 (Cuny)
Sen-hime, 1954 (Kyo)
Sen-hime goten, 1960 (Yamada)
Sen no Rikyu, 1989 (Mifune; Okada)
Sen noci svatojánské, 1961 (Burton)
Sen Yan's Devotion, 1924 (Hayakawa)
Senator Was Indiscreet, 1947 (Loy; Powell, W.)
Senba-zuru, 1953 (Mori)
Senba-zuru, 1969 (Kyo)
Send a Woman When the Devil Fails. See Quand la femme s'en mêle, 1957
Send Me No Flowers, 1964 (Day; Hudson)
Sendung der Lysistrata, 1961 (Kortner; Schneider)
Senechal the Magnificent. See Sénéchal le magnifique, 1957
Sénéchal le magnifique, 1957 (Fernandel)
Sengo-ha obake taikai, 1951 (Mifune)
Sengoki gunto-den, 1959 (Shimura)
Sengoku-burai, 1952 (Mifune)
Sengoku gunto-den, 1959 (Mifune; Tsukasa)
Sengoku hibun, 1955 (Yamamura)
Senilità, 1961 (Cardinale)
Senior Prom, 1959 (Three Stooges)
Senior Trip, 1981 (Rooney)
Seniors, 1978 (Quaid)
Senka no hate, 1950 (Mori)
Senka o koete, 1950 (Takamine; Yamamura)
Senkyaku banrai, 1962 (Yamamura)
Senora Muerte, 1967 (Carradine)
Senorita, 1927 (Powell, W.)
Senoritas Vivanco, 1958 (Armendáriz)
Senryo-hada, 1950 (Hasegawa)
Sensa famiglia, 1944 (Cervi)
Sensations. See Sensations of 1945, 1944
Sensations of 1945, 1944 (Fields, W. C.)
Sensations of 1945, 1945 (Powell, E.)
Sense and Sensibility, 1995 (Grant, H.; Thompson)
Sensible Man, 1949 (Cusack)
Sensitive, Passionate Man, 1977 (Dickinson)
Senso, 1954 (Valli)
Senso unico, 1973 (Rey)
Sensual Man. See Paolo il caldo, 1973
Sensual Obsession. See Bad Timing, 1980
Sensualità, 1952 (Mastroianni)
Sensuous Assassin. See Qui?, 1970
Sensuous Sicilian. See Paolo il caldo, 1973
Sentimental Journey, 1946 (O'Hara)
Sentimental Journey, 1987 (Cassel)
Sentimental Sister, 1914 (Sweet)
Sentimentalnyi roman, 1976 (Yankovsky)
Sentinel, 1977 (Carradine; Ferrer; Gardner; Kennedy; Meredith; Walken; Wallach)
Sentinel Asleep, 1911 (Pickford)
Sentinels of Silence, 1971 (Welles)
Senza pietà, 1948 (Masina)
Senzo famiglia, nullatenenti, cercano affetto ..., 1972 (Gassman)
Señor de la salle, 1964 (Rey)
Señor doctor, 1965 (Cantinflas)
Señor fotógrafo, 1952 (Cantinflas)
Señor Galindez, 1983 (Banderas)
Señora Ama, 1954 (Del Rio)
Señora de Fátima, 1951 (Rey)

Sex Kittens Go to College, 1960 (Carradine; Weld)
Sex Mission. *See* Sexmisja, 1984
Sex Quartet. *See* Fate, 1966
Sex Symbol, 1974 (Winters)
Sexe des Anges. *See* Voci bianche, 1964
Sexe faible, 1933 (Brasseur)
Sexmisja, 1984 (Tyszkiewicz)
Sexpionage. *See* Secret Weapons, 1985
Sextet. *See* Sekstet, 1963
Sextette, 1978 (Curtis, T.; Pidgeon; Raft; West)
Sezona mira u parizu, 1981 (Valli)
Sfinnge, 1919 (Bertini)
Sgt. Bilko, 1996 (Martin, S.)
Shabnam, 1949 (Kumar)
Shacho enma-cho, 1969 (Tsukasa)
Shacho-gaku ABC, 1970 (Tsukasa)
Shacho gyojo-ki, 1966 (Tsukasa)
Shacho hanjo-ki, 1968 (Tsukasa)
Shacho ninpo-cho, 1965 (Tsukasa)
Shacho sandai-ki, 1958 (Tsukasa)
Shacho sen-ichiya, 1967 (Tsukasa)
Shacho shinshiroku, 1964 (Tsukasa)
Shack Out on 101, 1955 (Marvin)
Shackled, 1918 (Gilbert)
Shadow, 1937 (Hayworth)
Shadow. *See* Skuggan, 1953
Shadow Army. *See* Armée des ombres, 1969
Shadow Box, 1980 (Newman; Woodward)
Shadow Conspiracy, 1996 (Sutherland)
Shadow House, 1972 (Carradine)
Shadow in the Streets, 1975 (Andrews, D.)
Shadow Makers. *See* Fat Man and Little Boy, 1989
Shadow of a Doubt, 1943 (Cotten)
Shadow of a Flower. *See* Temptress Moon, 1995
Shadow of Blackmail. *See* Wife Wanted, 1946
Shadow of China, 1991 (Neill)
Shadow of Chinatown, 1936 (Lugosi)
Shadow of the Eagle, 1932 (Wayne)
Shadow of the Glen, 1938 (Cusack)
Shadow of the Law, 1926 (Bow)
Shadow of the Law, 1930 (Powell, W.)
Shadow of the Thin Man, 1941 (Loy; Powell, W.)
Shadow of the Wolf, 1993 (Mifune; Sutherland)
Shadow on the Land, 1968 (Cooper; Hackman)
Shadow on the Sun. *See* Beryl Markham: A Shadow on the Sun, 1988
Shadow Program. *See* Shadow Conspiracy, 1996
Shadowed, 1912-13 (White)
Shadowlands, 1985 (Bloom)
Shadowlands, 1993 (Attenborough; Hopkins, A.; Winger)
Shadows, 1922 (Chaney)
Shadows and Fog, 1992 (Allen; Bates, K.; Farrow; Foster; Malkovich; Nelligan; Pleasence)
Shadows in a Conflict. *See* Sombras en una Batalla, 1993
Shadows of Doubt, 1976 (Hurt, J.)
Shadows of Paris, 1924 (Menjou; Negri)
Shadows Run Black, 1981 (Costner)
Shady Lady, 1945 (Coburn, C.)
Shaggy Dog, 1959 (MacMurray)
Shaheed, 1948 (Kumar)
Shaitan el Sahara, 1954 (Sharif)
Shaka, 1961 (Kyo; Yamada)
Shaka Zulu, 1986 (Howard, T.; Lee, C.)
Shake Hands with the Devil, 1959 (Cagney; Cusack; Harris, R.; Redgrave, M.)
Shake, Rattle and Rock, 1956 (Dumont)
Shakedown, 1929 (Huston, J.)
Shakedown, 1936 (Ayres)
Shakedown, 1960 (Pleasence)
Shaker Run, 1985 (Robertson)
Shakes the Clown, 1992 (Williams, R.)
Shakespeare's Country, 1944 (Gielgud)
Shakespeare's Theater: The Globe Playhouse, 1950 (Colman)

Shakha Proshakha, 1990 (Chatterjee; Depardieu)
Shakma, 1990 (McDowall)
Shakti, 1982 (Kumar; Patil)
Shalako, 1968 (Bardot; Connery; Hawkins)
Shalimar, 1978 (Harrison)
Shall the Children Pay? *See* What Price Innocence?, 1933
Shall We Dance, 1937 (Astaire; Horton; Rogers, G.)
Shama, 1981 (Azmi)
Shame, 1921 (Gilbert; Wong)
Shame. *See* Skammen, 1968
Shame of the Jungle, 1975 (Belushi; Murray)
Shameful Dream. *See* Hazukashiiyume, 1927
Shamisen to otobai, 1961 (Mori)
Shampoo, 1975 (Beatty; Christie; Grant, L.; Hawn)
Shamrock Handicap, 1926 (Gaynor)
Shamus, 1973 (Reynolds, B.)
Shane, 1953 (Arthur; Ladd; Palance)
Shangai 1937, 1996 (Girardot)
Shanghai, 1935 (Boyer; Young, L.)
Shanghai. *See* Shanghai Gesture, 1941
Shanghai Express, 1932 (Dietrich; Wong)
Shanghai Gesture, 1941 (Dalio; Huston, W.; Mature; Tierney)
Shanghai Madness, 1933 (Tracy; Wray)
Shanghai Moon. *See* Shanhai no tsuki, 1941
Shanghai Story, 1954 (O'Brien, E.)
Shanghai Surprise, 1986 (Penn)
Shanghai Triad. *See* Yao ayao yao dao waipo qiao, 1995
Shanghaied, 1915 (Chaplin, C.; Purviance)
Shanghaied Lovers, 1924 (Langdon)
Shanhai gaeri no Riru, 1952 (Kagawa)
Shanhai no tsuki, 1941 (Yamada)
Shannons of Broadway, 1929 (Brennan)
Shaolin Chamber of Death. *See* Shaolin Wooden Men, 1976
Shaolin Wooden Men, 1976 (Chan)
Shape of Things to Come, 1979 (Palance)
Shaque, 1976 (Azmi)
Sharabi, 1964 (Anand)
Shareef Badmash, 1973 (Anand)
Shark, 1970 (Kennedy; Reynolds, B.)
Shark Monroe, 1918 (Hart)
Shark's Treasure, 1975 (Wilde)
Sharkey's Machine, 1981 (Gassman)
Sharkfighters, 1956 (Mature)
Sharks' Cave. *See* Bermuda: la fossa maledetta, 1978
Sharky's Machine, 1982 (Reynolds, B.)
Sharp Shooters, 1928 (Scott, R.)
Shart, 1985 (Azmi)
Shasti, 1962 (Chatterjee)
Shati el Asrar, 1957 (Sharif)
Shatranj Ke Khilari, 1978 (Attenborough; Azmi)
Shatter. *See* Call Him Mr. Shatter, 1975
Shattered. *See* Scherben, 1921
Shattered. *See* Something to Hide, 1972
Shattered, 1991 (Hoskins; Scacchi)
Shattered Silence. *See* When Michael Calls, 1971
Shattered Spirits, 1985 (Sheen)
Shattered Trust: The Shari Karney Story, 1993 (Burstyn; Nelligan)
Shattered Vows, 1984 (Neal)
Shawshank Redemption, 1994 (Freeman; Robbins)
Shaysr, 1949 (Anand)
Shazka o spiatchek, 1914 (Mozhukin)
Shchit i mech, 1968 (Yankovsky)
She, 1935 (Scott, R.)
She, 1965 (Cushing; Lee, C.)
She. *See* Kanojo, 1926
She and He. *See* Kanojo to kare, 1963
She Came to the Valley, 1977 (Jones, Jennifer)
She Couldn't Say No, 1939 (Withers; Mitchum)
She Couldn't Take It, 1935 (Bennett; Raft)
She Dances Alone, 1980 (Von Sydow)
She Defends Her Country. *See* Ona zashchishchaet Rodinu, 1943

She-Devil, 1919 (Bara)
She-Devil, 1989 (Streep)
She Done Him Wrong, 1933 (Grant, C.; West)
She Fell among Thieves, 1978 (McDowell)
She Gets Her Man, 1935 (Bond; Carradine)
She Had to Say Yes, 1933 (Young, L.)
She Knew All the Answers, 1941 (Bennett)
She Knew What She Wanted, 1936 (Withers)
She Landed a Big One, 1914 (Beery)
She Learned about Sailors, 1934 (Ayres; Faye)
She Loves and Lies, 1920 (Talmadge)
She Loves Me Not, 1918 (Lloyd)
She Loves Me Not, 1934 (Crosby; Hopkins, M.)
She Married Her Boss, 1935 (Colbert; Douglas, Melvyn)
She Played with Fire. See Fortune Is a Woman, 1957
She Said No, 1990 (Grant, L.)
She Waits, 1971 (Ayres)
She Wanted a Millionaire, 1932 (Bennett; Tracy)
She Went to the Races, 1945 (Gardner; Keaton, B.)
She Wolves. See Louves, 1957
She Wore a Yellow Ribbon, 1949 (McLaglen; Wayne)
She Wouldn't Say Yes, 1945 (Russell, R.)
Sheba, 1919 (Colman)
Sheep Has Five Legs. See Mouton à cinq pattes, 1953
Sheepman, 1958 (Ford, G.; MacLaine)
Sheer Madness. See Heller Wahn, 1982
Shéhérazade, 1928 (Modot)
Shéhérazade, 1962 (Karina)
Shéhérazade. See Mille et une nuits, 1990
Sheik, 1921 (Menjou; Valentino)
Sheik Steps Out, 1937 (Novarro)
Sheila Levine Is Dead and Living in New York, 1975 (Scheider)
Shell 43, 1916 (Gilbert)
She'll Have to Go. See Maid for Murder, 1961
Shell Seekers, 1989 (Lansbury)
Shelley Duvall's Tall Tales and Legends: Annie Oakley. See Annie Oakley, 1985
Sheltering Sky, 1990 (Malkovich; Winger)
Shenandoah, 1965 (Stewart)
Shenanigans. See Great Georgia Bank Hoax, 1977
Shepherd of the Hills, 1941 (Bond; Carey; Wayne)
Sheriff, 1918 (Arbuckle)
Sheriff and the Rustler, 1913 (Mix)
Sheriff of Fractured Jaw, 1958 (Mansfield)
Sheriff of Tombstone, 1941 (Rogers, R.)
Sheriff of Yawapai County, 1913 (Mix)
Sheriff's Baby, 1913 (Barrymore, L.; Carey)
Sheriff's Blunder, 1916 (Mix)
Sheriff's Duty, 1916 (Mix)
Sheriff's Reward, 1914 (Mix)
Sheriff's Streak of Yellow, 1915 (Hart)
Sherlock and Me. See Without a Clue, 1988
Sherlock Holmes, 1922 (Barrymore, J.; Powell, W.)
Sherlock Holmes and the Baskerville Curse, 1984 (O'Toole)
Sherlock Holmes and the Deadly Necklace. See Sherlock Holmes und das Halsband des Todes, 1962
Sherlock Holmes and the Leading Lady, 1990 (Lee, C.)
Sherlock Holmes and the Masks of Death, 1984 (Cushing; Baxter; Mills)
Sherlock Holmes and the Secret Weapon, 1942 (Rathbone)
Sherlock Holmes and the Voice of Terror, 1942 (Rathbone)
Sherlock Holmes Faces Death, 1943 (Rathbone)
Sherlock Holmes in New York, 1976 (Huston, J.)
Sherlock Holmes in Washington, 1943 (Rathbone)
Sherlock Holmes und das Halsband des Todes, 1962 (Lee, C.)
Sherlock, Jr., 1924 (Arbuckle; Keaton, B.)
She's a Sheik, 1927 (Powell, W.)
She's a Soldier Too, 1944 (Winters)
She's Dangerous, 1937 (Brennan; Pidgeon)
She's Gotta Have It, 1986 (Lee, S.)
She's Having a Baby, 1988 (Bacon; Candy; Keaton, M.; Murray)
She's in the Army Now, 1981 (Curtis, J.; Griffith)

She's Oil Mine, 1941 (Keaton, B.)
She's Working Her Way through College, 1952 (Reagan)
Shesh Prahar, 1963 (Chatterjee)
Shesh Pristhay Dekhun, 1973 (Chatterjee)
Shestdesyat dnei, 1943 (Cherkassov)
Shibai-do, 1944 (Hasegawa; Yamada)
Shichi-nin no keiji: Onn o sagase, 1963 (Kagawa)
Shichi-nin no samurai, 1954 (Mifune; Shimura)
Shield and Sword. See Shchit i mech, 1968
Shield for Murder, 1954 (O'Brien, E.)
Shifting Sands, 1918 (Swanson)
Shigure-gasa, 1928 (Hasegawa)
Shiinomi Gakuen, 1955 (Kagawa)
Shiju-hachi-nin me, 1936 (Yamada)
Shikast, 1953 (Kumar)
Shiki no aiyoku, 1958 (Yamada)
Shikibu monogatari, 1990 (Kagawa)
Shima no ratai-jiken, 1931 (Tanaka)
Shimai, 1931 (Takamine; Tanaka)
Shimizu no Jirocho Zen-den: Kohen Ashura fukushu no maki, 1926 (Tanaka)
Shimmy Lugano e tarantelle e vino, 1979 (Loren; Mastroianni)
Shin baka jidai, 1946 (Mifune)
Shin-Heike monogatari: Shizuka to Yoshitsune, 1956 (Kagawa)
Shin Heike monogatari Yoshinaka o meguru san-nin no onna, 1956 (Kyo; Takamine)
Shin josei-kagami, 1929 (Tanaka)
Shin josei mondo, 1955 (Kyo)
Shin no shi-kotei, 1962 (Hasegawa)
Shin no shikotei, 1962 (Kyo; Yamada)
Shin onna daigaku, 1960 (Tsukasa)
Shina no yoru, 1940 (Hasegawa)
Shinbone Alley, 1971 (Carradine)
Shindo: Akemi no make, Ryota no maki, 1936 (Takamine; Tanaka)
Shine, 1996 (Withers)
Shine On, Harvest Moon, 1938 (Rogers, R.)
Shingo jubanshobu, Part II, 1959 (Yamamura)
Shingun, 1930 (Tanaka)
Shining, 1980 (Nicholson)
Shining Future, 1944 (Crosby; Grant, C.)
Shining Hour, 1938 (Crawford, J.; Douglas, Melvyn; McDaniel; Young, R.)
Shining Star. See That's the Way of the World, 1975
Shining Through, 1992 (Douglas, Michael; Gielgud; Griffith; Neeson)
Shining Victory, 1941 (Crisp; Davis, B.)
Shinjitsu ichiro, 1954 (Yamamura)
Shinju fujin, 1927 (Tanaka)
Shinju fujin, 1933 (Yamada)
Shinkansen diabakuha, 1974 (Shimura)
Shinkon-ryoko, 1934 (Tanaka)
Shinku chitai, 1952 (Okada)
Shinno Tsuruchiyo, 1935 (Yamada)
Shinpen bocchan, 1941 (Yamada)
Shinpen Tange Sazen: Koiguruma no maki, 1940 (Takamine)
Shinpen Tange Sazen: Sogan no maki, Koiguruma no maki, 1939 (Yamada)
Shinpen Tange Sazen: Yoto no maki, Futate no maki, 1938 (Yamada)
Shinrun dorobo, 1952 (Yamamura)
Shinryu-ro, 1938 (Takamine)
Shinsen-gumi, 1969 (Mifune; Tsukasa)
Shinshaku: Tojin Okichi, Funshin hen, 1938 (Tanaka)
Shinsho Taiheiki: Ruten Hiyoshimura, 1953 (Tanaka)
Shiosai, 1954 (Mifune)
Ship Ahoy, 1942 (Powell, E.)
Ship Day, 1948 (Cusack)
Ship of Fools, 1965 (Ferrer; Leigh, V.; Marvin; Segal; Werner)
Ship of Lost Souls. See Schiff der verlorene Menschen, 1929
Ship that Died of Shame, 1955 (Attenborough)
Shipmates, 1931 (Montgomery)
Shipmates Forever, 1935 (Keeler; Powell, D.)
Ships Are Storming the Bastions, 1953 (Bondarchuk)
Shipwrecked Children. See Enfants du Naufrageur, 1992
Shipyard Sally, 1939 (Fields, G.)
Shirai Gonpachi, 1928 (Hasegawa)

Shiralee, 1957 (Finch)
Shirazu no Yataro, 1954 (Hasegawa)
Shiroi akuma, 1958 (Mori)
Shiroi yaju, 1950 (Yamamura)
Shishi no za, 1953 (Hasegawa; Tanaka)
Shitamachi, 1957 (Mifune; Yamada)
Shito no densetsu, 1963 (Tanaka)
Shivering Sherlocks, 1948 (Three Stooges)
Shivers, 1934 (Langdon)
Shizen wa sabaku, 1925 (Tanaka)
Shizi jietou, 1937 (Zhao Dan)
Shizuka gozen, 1938 (Yamada)
Shizukaru ketto, 1949 (Mifune; Shimura)
Shizukaru kyodan, 1959 (Yamamura)
Shkval, 1916 (Mozhukin)
Shli soldaty, 1958 (Bondarchuk)
Shlyapa, 1981 (Yankovsky)
Shobushi ro sono musume, 1959 (Shimura)
Shochiku biggu paredo, 1930 (Hasegawa)
Shock, 1923 (Chaney)
Shock, 1946 (Price)
Shock. See Choc, 1982
Shock to the System, 1990 (Caine; Jackson, S.)
Shock Treatment, 1964 (Bacall; McDowall)
Shock Treatment. See Traitement du choc, 1972
Shock Troop. See Lost Idol, 1990
Shock Troops. See Homme de trop, 1967
Shock Waves, 1975 (Carradine; Cushing)
Shocked. See Mesmerized, 1986
Shocking Miss Pilgrim, 1946 (Grable)
Shockproof, 1949 (Wilde)
Shoddy the Tailor, 1915 (Laurel and Hardy)
Shodo satsujin: Musuko yo, 1979 (Takamine)
Shoes of the Fisherman, 1968 (Gielgud; Olivier; Quinn; Werner)
Shogun Mayeda, 1990 (Lee, C.; Mifune)
Shogun's Samurai. See Yagyu ichizoku no inbo, 1978
Shohai, 1932 (Tanaka)
Shojo-dakara, 1950 (Takamine; Yamamura)
Shonen shikei-shu, 1955 (Tanaka)
Shonen tanteidan, 1956-7 (Okada)
Shoot, 1976 (Borgnine; Robertson)
Shoot First, 1953 (Lom; McCrea)
Shoot Loud, Louder ... I Don't Understand. See Spara forte, più forte ... non capisco, 1966
Shoot-Out at Medicine Bend, 1957 (Dickinson; Garner; Scott, R.)
Shoot the Moon, 1982 (Finney; Keaton, D.)
Shoot the Sun Down, 1981 (Walken)
Shoot to Kill, 1988 (Poitier)
Shoot! See ¡Dispara!, 1993
Shootdown, 1988 (Lansbury)
Shooting, 1966 (Nicholson; Oates)
Shooting High, 1940 (Autry)
Shooting Party, 1977 (Yankovsky; Gielgud; Mason)
Shooting Up the Movies, 1916 (Mix)
Shootist, 1976 (Bacall; Carradine; Stewart; Wayne)
Shootout, 1971 (Peck)
Shootout, 1984 (Poitier)
Shop around the Corner, 1940 (Stewart; Sullavan)
Shop at Sly Corner, 1946 (Dors; Homolka)
Shop Talk, 1936 (Hope)
Shopworn, 1932 (Stanwyck)
Shopworn Angel, 1928 (Constantine; Lukas; McDaniel; Pidgeon; Stewart; Sullavan)
Shore Leave, 1925 (Barthelmess)
Shore of Mystery. See Shati el Asrar, 1957
Shori no himade, 1945 (Takamine)
Shori to haiboku, 1960 (Yamamura)
Short Cut. See Tempo di Uccidere, 1990
Short Cut to Hell, 1957 (Cagney)
Short Cuts, 1993 (Leigh, Jennifer Jason; Lemmon; Robbins)
Short Fuse. See Good to Go, 1986

Short Is the Summer. See Kort är sommaren, 1962
Short Kilts, 1924 (Laurel and Hardy)
Short Memory. See Mémoire courte, 1978
Short Orders, 1923 (Laurel and Hardy)
Short Step, 1991 (Christie)
Shortest Day. See Giorno più corto, 1963
Shoshun, 1956 (Ryu)
Shot at Dawn See Schuss im Morgengrauen, 1932
Shot in the Dark, 1933 (Hawkins)
Shot in the Dark, 1964 (Lom; Sanders; Sellers)
Shot in the Frontier, 1954 (Three Stooges)
Shotgun, 1955 (Hayden)
Shotgun Jones, 1914 (Mix)
Shotgun Man and the Stage Driver, 1913 (Mix)
Shotguns that Kick, 1914 (Arbuckle)
Should a Doctor Tell?, 1931 (Neagle)
Should a Woman Tell?, 1919 (Gilbert)
Should Ladies Behave?, 1933 (Barrymore, L.)
Should Married Men Go Home?, 1928 (Laurel and Hardy)
Should Men Walk Home?, 1926 (Laurel and Hardy; Normand)
Should Sailors Marry?, 1925 (Laurel and Hardy)
Should Tall Men Marry?, 1926 (Laurel and Hardy)
Shoulder Arms, 1918 (Chaplin, C.; Purviance)
Shout, 1978 (Bates, A.; Hurt, J.; York)
Shout, 1991 (Travolta)
Shout at the Devil, 1975 (Marvin)
Show, 1927 (Barrymore, L.; Gilbert)
Show Boat, 1936 (Dunne; Robeson)
Show Boat, 1951 (Brown; Moorehead)
Show Business, 1932 (Goddard)
Show Business, 1944 (Cantor; Malone)
Show Business at War, 1943 (Cagney; Durbin; Fields, W. C.; Hayworth; Lamarr; Loy; Mature; Rogers, G.)
Show Folks, 1928 (Lombard)
Show Girl in Hollywood, 1930 (Pidgeon)
Show Goes On, 1937 (Fields, G.)
Show of Shows, 1929 (Barrymore, J.; Barthelmess; Buchanan; Loy; Young, L.)
Show of Force, 1990 (Duvall; García)
Show-Off, 1926 (Brooks, L.)
Show-Off, 1934 (Tracy)
Show People, 1928 (Chaplin, C.; Davies; Gilbert; Hart)
Showa no inochi, 1968 (Okada)
Showa zankyo-den: Karajishi jingi, 1969 (Shimura)
Showboat, 1951 (Gardner)
Showdown, 1950 (Brennan)
Showdown, 1973 (Hudson; Martin, D.)
Showdown at Boot Hill, 1958 (Bronson; Carradine)
Showdown at Ulcer Gulch, 1958 (Crosby; Hope)
Shower. See Shuu, 1956
Showgirl in Hollywood, 1930 (Jolson; Sweet)
Shriek in the Night, 1933 (Rogers, G.)
Shrike, 1955 (Ferrer)
Shrimp, 1930 (Langdon)
Shrine of Lorna Love. See Death at Love House, 1976
Shrinking Corpse. See Blind Man's Bluff, 1967
Shu to midori, 1956 (Yamamura)
Shubun, 1950 (Mifune)
Shubun. See Sukyandaru, 1950
Shujin-sen, 1956 (Mifune)
Shukuzu, 1953 (Yamada; Yamamura)
Shunju-ittoryu, 1939 (Shimura)
Shunkin monogatari, 1954 (Kyo)
Shunkin-sho: Okoto to Sasuke, 1935 (Tanaka)
Shunrai, 1939 (Tanaka)
Shuppatsu, 1938 (Tanaka)
Shura-jo hibun: Soryu no maki, 1952 (Hasegawa)
Shura yako: Edo no hana-osho, 1936 (Shimura)
Shura-zakura, 1959 (Yamada)
Shusse tohi, 1952 (Yamada)
Shut My Big Mouth, 1942 (Brown)

Shuttered Room, 1967 (Reed)
Shuttlecock, 1990 (Bates, A.)
Shuu, 1956 (Hara; Kagawa)
Shy People, 1987 (Hershey)
Shyam Saheb, 1986 (Chatterjee)
Si c'était à refaire, 1976 (Aimée; Deneuve)
Si ça peut vous faire plaisir, 1948 (Fernandel)
Si j'avais mille ans, 1983 (Olbrychski)
Si j'étais un espion, 1967 (Blier)
Si je suis comme ça, c'est la faute de papa, 1978 (Deneuve)
Si jeunesse savait, 1948 (Berry)
Si jolie petite plage, 1949 (Philipe)
S'il vous plaît ... la mer?, 1978 (Presle)
Si l'empereur savait ca!, 1930 (Rosay)
Si le soleil ne revenait pas, 1987 (Vanel)
Si me han de matar manaña, 1946 (Infante)
Si Paris m'était conté, 1955 (Philipe)
Si Paris nous était conté, 1955 (Darrieux; Marais; Morgan)
Si puo fare ... amigo, 1971 (Palance)
Si salvi chi vuole, 1980 (Cardinale)
Si, Senor, 1919 (Lloyd)
Si Si Senor, 1930 (Arbuckle)
Si te hubieses casado con migo, 1948 (Rey)
Si Te Dicen Que Caí, 1989 (Abril; Banderas)
Si tous les gars du monde, 1955 (Trintignant)
Si tu m'aimes, 1937 (Arletty)
Si Versailles m'était conte, 1953 (Bardot; Barrault; Cervi; Colbert; Gélin; Marais; Philipe; Presle; Vanel; Welles)
Si yo fuera diputado, 1951 (Cantinflas)
Si yo fuera millionario, 1962 (Félix)
Siamo donne, 1953 (Bergman; Magnani)
Siamo tutti im libertà provvisoria, 1972 (Noiret)
Siamo tutti inquilini, 1953 (Fabrizi)
Sic 'em Sam!, 1918 (Fairbanks)
Sic 'em Towser, 1918 (Lloyd)
Sicari di Hitler, 1960 (Cervi)
Sicilian, 1987 (Stamp; Turturro)
Sicilian Clan. See Clan des Siciliens, 1968
Sid and Nancy, 1986 (Oldman)
Sidai cheutma, 1980 (Chan)
Side by Side, 1975 (Terry-Thomas)
Side Show. See Two Flaming Youths, 1927
Sidetracked, 1916 (Laurel and Hardy)
Sidewalks of London. See St. Martin's Lane, 1938
Sidewalks of New York, 1931 (Keaton, B.)
Sidney Sheldon's Bloodline. See Bloodline, 1979
Sidonie Panache, 1934 (Artaud)
Siege of Syracuse. See Assedio di Siracusa, 1960
Siegfried. See Zygfryd, 1986
Siekierezada, 1986 (Olbrychski)
Siempre listo en las tinieblas, 1939 (Cantinflas)
Sierra, 1950 (Curtis, T.)
Sierra Sue, 1941 (Autry)
Siesta, 1987 (Barkin; Foster; Rossellini; Sheen)
Siete machos, 1950 (Cantinflas)
Sigillo rosso, 1950 (Cervi)
Sign of the Cross, 1932 (Carradine; Colbert; Laughton; March)
Sign of the Pagan, 1954 (Palance)
Sign of Venus. See Segno di Venere, 1955
Sign on the Door, 1920 (Talmadge)
Signal Tower, 1924 (Beery)
Signalman, 1976 (Elliott)
Signe de lion, 1959 (Audran)
Signé Charlotte, 1985 (Huppert)
Signed Charlotte. See Signé Charlotte, 1985
Signo de la muerte, 1939 (Cantinflas)
Signora dalle camelie, 1915 (Bertini)
Signora dell'ovest, 1942 (Brazzi)
Signora della camelie, 1948 (Cervi)
Signora della orroro, 1977 (Von Sydow)
Signora senza camelie, 1953 (Cervi; Cuny)

Signore e signori, buonanotte, 1976 (Gassman; Mastroianni)
Signori in carrozzo, 1951 (Fabrizi)
Signorina, 1942 (Sordi)
Signorine della villa accanto, 1941 (Sordi)
Signpost to Murder, 1965 (Woodward)
Signs of Life, 1989 (Bates, K.; Kennedy)
Sigpress contro Scotland Yard. See Mister Zehn Prozent—Miezen und Moneten, 1967
Silas Marner: The Weaver of Raveloe, 1985 (Kingsley)
Silence ... antenne, 1945 (Montand)
Silence. See **Tystnaden**, 1963
Silence d'ailleurs, 1990 (Olbrychski)
Silence est d'or, 1947 (Chevalier; Modot)
Silence Is Golden. See Silence est d'or, 1947
Silence of Dr. Evans. See Molchaniye Doktoraivens, 1973
Silence of the Hams. See Silenzio dei prosciutti, 1994
Silence of the Lambs, 1991 (Foster; Hopkins, A.)
Silence of the North, 1981 (Burstyn)
Silencers, 1966 (Charisse; Martin, D.)
Silent Battle, 1939 (Harrison)
Silent Bell-Ringer, 1915 (Mozhukin)
Silent Command, 1923 (Lugosi)
Silent Cries, 1993 (Rowlands)
Silent Death, 1957 (Karloff)
Silent Duel. See Shizukanaru ketto, 1949
Silent Fall, 1994 (Dreyfuss)
Silent Flute, 1978 (Lee, C.)
Silent Flute. See Circle of Iron, 1979
Silent Man, 1917 (Hart)
Silent Movie, 1976 (Bancroft; Brooks, M.; Caan; Minnelli; Newman; Reynolds, B.)
Silent Night. See Magdalene, 1988
Silent Night, Bloody Night, 1973 (Carradine)
Silent Night, Deadly Night 5: The Toy Maker, 1991 (Rooney)
Silent Night, Lonely Night, 1969 (Bridges)
Silent Partner, 1917 (Sweet)
Silent Partner, 1979 (Candy; Gould; York)
Silent Running, 1971 (Dern)
Silent Sanderson, 1925 (Carey)
Silent Sandy, 1914 (Gish)
Silent Scream, 1984 (Cushing)
Silent Stranger. See Man from Nowhere, 1915
Silent Tongue, 1992 (Bates, A.; Harris, R.; Shepard)
Silent Touch. See Dotkniecie reki, 1993
Silent Voice. See Amazing Grace and Chuck, 1987
Silent Witnesses. See Rozdennie polzat utat ne mozet, 1914
Silenzio dei prosciutti, 1994 (Brooks, M.; Winters)
Silenzio, si gira, 1943 (Brazzi)
Silhouette, 1990 (Dunaway)
Silk Bouquet, 1926 (Wong)
Silk Hat Kid, 1935 (Ayres)
Silk Legs. See Piernas de seda, 1935
Silk Stockings, 1957 (Astaire; Charisse; Lorre)
Silken Affair, 1957 (Niven)
Silks and Saddles, 1928 (Brennan)
Silkwood, 1983 (Cher; Streep)
Silver Bears, 1978 (Audran; Caine; Jourdan)
Silver Canyon, 1951 (Autry)
Silver Chalice, 1954 (Newman; Palance; Wood)
Silver Chord, 1933 (McCrea)
Silver Cigarette Case, 1913 (Talmadge)
Silver City, 1951 (Fitzgerald; O'Brien, E.)
Silver Cord, 1933 (Dunne)
Silver Dollar, 1932 (Robinson, E.)
Silver Fleet, 1943 (Richardson, R.; Withers)
Silver Horde, 1930 (Arthur; McCrea; Sweet)
Silver Lining, 1931 (O'Sullivan)
Silver Lode, 1954 (Duryea)
Silver River, 1948 (Flynn)
Silver Spurs, 1943 (Carradine; Rogers, R.)
Silver Streak, 1976 (Pryor; Wilder)

Silver Valley, 1927 (Mix; Cleese; Costner)
Silverado, 1985 (Kline)
Simanta Raag, 1982 (Chatterjee)
Simba, 1955 (Bogarde)
Simba—Mark of Mau Mau. *See* Simba, 1955
Simon, 1980 (Arkin)
Simon and Laura, 1955 (Finch; Kendall)
Simon Bolivar. *See* Life of Simon Bolivar, 1943
Simon Bolivar, 1969 (Schell, Maximilian)
Simon, Simon, 1970 (Caine; Sellers)
Simp and the Sophomores, 1915 (Laurel and Hardy)
Simple Charity, 1910 (Pickford)
Simple Hearts. *See* Prostye serdtsa, 1928
Simple Justice, 1993 (Jackson, S.)
Simple Sis, 1927 (Loy)
Simple Souls, 1920 (Sweet)
Simple Story. *See* Histoire simple, 1978
Simple Story. *See* Storia Semplice, 1991
Simple Twist of Fate, 1994 (Martin, S.)
Simplet, 1942 (Fernandel)
Sin, 1915 (Bara)
Sin. *See* Grekh, 1916-17
Sin. *See* Beloved, 1971
Sin. *See* Bianco, rosso e ..., 1971
Sin of Harold Diddlebock. *See* Mad Wednesday, 1947
Sin of Madelon Claudet, 1931 (Young, R.)
Sin of Olga Brandt, 1915 (Chaney)
Sin of Patricia. *See* Vita recominicia, 1945
Sin Ship, 1931 (Astor)
Sin Takes a Holiday, 1930 (Rathbone)
Sin Town, 1942 (Bond; Crawford, B.)
Sinatra in Israel, 1962 (Sidney)
Sinatra: 80 Years My Way, 1995 (Peck)
Sinbad the Sailor, 1947 (O'Hara; Quinn)
Since You Went Away, 1944 (Barrymore, L.; Colbert; Cotten; Jones, Jennifer;
    McDaniel; Moorehead; Nazimova; Temple; Walker)
Sincerely Charlotte. *See* Signé Charlotte, 1985
Sinful Davey, 1969 (Hurt, J.; Huston, A.; Huston, J.)
Sing a Song of Six Pants, 1947 (Three Stooges)
Sing and Like It, 1934 (Horton)
Sing as We Go, 1934 (Fields, G.)
Sing, Baby, Sing, 1936 (Faye; Menjou)
Sing, Bing, Sing, 1933 (Crosby)
Sing Boy Sing, 1958 (O'Brien, E.)
Sing, Sinner, Sing, 1933 (Brennan; Lukas)
Sing You Sinners, 1938 (Crosby; MacMurray; O'Connor)
Sing Your Worries Away, 1942 (Dumont)
Singapore, 1947 (Gardner; MacMurray)
Singapore Sue, 1932 (Grant, C.)
Singe en hiver, 1962 (Belmondo; Gabin)
Singed, 1927 (Sweet)
Singed Wings, 1922 (Menjou)
Singer Jim McKee, 1924 (Hart)
Singer Not the Song, 1961 (Bogarde; Mills)
Singin' in the Rain, 1952 (Charisse; Kelly, Gene; O'Connor; Reynolds, D.)
Singing Cowboy, 1936 (Autry)
Singing Fool, 1928 (Jolson)
Singing Guns, 1950 (Bond; Brennan)
Singing Hill, 1941 (Autry)
Singing Kid, 1936 (Horton; Jolson; McDaniel)
Singing Marine, 1937 (Powell, D.; Wyman)
Singing Musketeer. *See* Three Musketeers, 1939
Singing Nun, 1966 (Garson; Moorehead; Reynolds, D.)
Singing Princess, 1967 (Andrews, J.)
Singing River, 1921 (White)
Singing Vagabond, 1935 (Autry)
Single Room Furnished, 1967 (Mansfield)
Single Standard, 1929 (Garbo; McCrea)
Single White Female, 1992 (Leigh, Jennifer Jason)
Singles, 1992 (Dillon)
Sinister Invasion. *See* Incredible Invasion, 1971

Sinking of the Rainbow Warrior. *See* Rainbow Warrior, 1994
Sinner. *See* Sünderin, 1950
Sinner's Holiday, 1930 (Cagney)
Sinner's Holiday. *See* Christmas Eve, 1947
Sinners. *See* Piscine, 1968
Sinners in Silk, 1924 (Menjou)
Sinners in the Sun, 1932 (Grant, C.; Lombard)
Sinners of Paris. *See* Rafles sur la ville, 1954
Sinners' Holiday, 1930 (Blondell)
Sins, 1986 (Kelly, Gene)
Sins of Dorian Gray, 1983 (Perkins)
Sins of Jezebel, 1953 (Goddard)
Sins of Lola Montès. *See* **Lola Montès**, 1955
Sins of Man, 1936 (Ameche)
Sins of Pompeii. *See* Derniers Jours de Pompéi, 1948
Sins of Rachel Cade, 1960 (Dickinson; Finch)
Sins of Rose Bernd. *See* Rose Bernd, 1957
Sins of the Borgias. *See* Lucrèce Borgia, 1953
Sins of the Children, 1930 (Montgomery)
Sins of the Fathers, 1928 (Arthur; Jannings)
Sins of the Father, 1985 (Coburn, J.)
Sins of the Fathers. *See* Vater und Sonhe, 1988
Sin's Pay Day, 1932 (Rooney)
Sioux City Sue, 1946 (Autry)
Sir Arne's Treasure. *See* Herr Arnes penningar, 1954
Sir Henry at Rawlinson End, 1980 (Howard, T.)
Siren of Bagdad, 1953 (Henreid)
Siren's Song, 1919 (Bara)
Sirène du Mississippi, 1969 (Belmondo)
Sirens, 1994 (Grant, H.; Neill)
Sirens of the Sea, 1919 (Young, L.)
Sirocco, 1951 (Bogart; Cobb; Sloane)
Sis Hopkins, 1919 (Normand)
Sis Hopkins, 1941 (Hayward)
Siska, 1962 (Andersson, H.)
Sissi, 1956 (Schneider)
Sissi—die junge Kaiserin, 1957 (Schneider)
Sissi—Schichsalsjahre einer Kaiserin, 1958 (Schneider)
Sista leken, 1984 (Andersson, B.)
Sista paret ut, 1956 (Andersson, B.; Andersson, H.; Dahlbeck)
Sister Act, 1992 (Goldberg; Keitel; Smith)
Sister Act 2: Back in the Habit, 1993 (Coburn, J.; Goldberg; Smith)
Sister Kenny, 1946 (Russell, R.)
Sister, Sister, 1987 (Leigh, Jennifer Jason)
Sisters, 1914 (Crisp; Gish)
Sisters, 1938 (Crisp; Davis, B.; Flynn; Hayward)
Sisters. *See* Some Girls, 1989
Sisters of Darkness. *See* Entre Tinieblas, 1983
Sisters of Gion. *See* Gion no shimai, 1936
Sisters of Ninshijin. *See* Nishijin no shimai, 1952
Sit Tight, 1931 (Brown)
Sitter-Downers, 1937 (Three Stooges)
Sitting Pretty, 1933 (Rogers, G.)
Sitting Pretty, 1948 (O'Hara; Webb; Young, R.)
Sitting Target, 1972 (Reed)
Situation Hopeless, but Not Serious, 1965 (Guinness; Redford)
Situation Normal All Fouled Up. *See* Operation Snafu, 1970
Situation of the Human World. *See* Hito no yo no sugata, 1929
Situm, 1984 (Patil)
Siukun gwaitsiu, 1979 (Chan)
Six Best Cellars, 1920 (Crisp)
Six Black Horses, 1961 (Duryea)
Six Bridges to Cross, 1955 (Curtis, T.; Mineo)
Six Characters in Search of an Author, 1964 (Cusack)
Six Cylinder Love, 1917 (Mix)
Six Cylinder Love, 1931 (Horton; Tracy)
Six Degrees of Separation, 1993 (Sutherland)
Six Lessons from Madame La Zonga, 1941 (Three Stooges)
Six of a Kind, 1934 (Fields, W. C.)
Six Shooter Andy, 1918 (Mix)
Six Thousand Enemies, 1939 (Pidgeon)

Six Weeks, 1982 (Moore, Dudley)
Six-Day Bike Rider, 1934 (Brown)
Sixième étage, 1939 (Brasseur)
Sixth and Main, 1977 (McDowall)
Sixty Days. *See* Shestdesyat dnei, 1943
Sixty Glorious Years, 1938 (Neagle; Walbrook)
Sizzle Beach, 1986 (Costner)
Sjunde himlen, 1956 (Björnstrand)
Sjunde inseglet, 1957 (Andersson, B.; Björnstrand; Von Sydow)
Skag, 1980 (Malden)
Skammen, 1968 (Björnstrand; Ullmann; Von Sydow)
Skandal in der Botschaft, 1950 (Rasp)
Skapani w ogniu, 1963 (Tyszkiewicz)
Skärgardsnatt, 1953 (Thulin)
Skating Bug, 1911 (Pickford)
Skeleton Coast, 1988 (Borgnine; Lom; Reed)
Skidoo, 1968 (Marx Brothers; Meredith; Raft; Rooney)
Skin. *See* Pelle, 1981
Skin Game, 1971 (Garner)
Skipper Next to God. *See* Maître après Dieu, 1950
Skipper Surprised His Wife, 1950 (Walker)
Skippy, 1931 (Cooper)
Skirmish on the Home Front, 1944 (Hayward; Hopkins, M.; Ladd)
Skirt Chaser. *See* Cavaleur, 1978
Skirts Ahoy!, 1952 (Reynolds, D.; Williams, E.)
Sklaven der Sinne, 1921 (Nielsen)
Sklaven Roms. *See* Rivolta degli schiavi, 1960
Skok, 1969 (Olbrychski)
Skokie, 1981 (Kaye; Wallach)
Skola skolen, 1949 (Björnstrand)
Sköna Helena, 1951 (Dahlbeck)
Skorpan, 1957 (Björnstrand)
Skorpion, panna, i lucznik, 1972 (Nowicki)
Skrivanci na niti, 1968 (Brodský)
Skuggan, 1953 (Dahlbeck)
Skull, 1965 (Cushing; Lee, C.)
Skullduggery, 1970 (Reynolds, B.)
Sky Boy, 1929 (Langdon)
Sky Bride, 1932 (Scott, R.)
Sky Commando, 1953 (Duryea)
Sky Devils, 1932 (Tracy)
Sky Giant, 1938 (Carey; Fontaine)
Sky High, 1922 (Mix)
Sky Murder, 1940 (Pidgeon)
Sky Pilot, 1911 (Talmadge)
Sky Pirate, 1914 (Arbuckle)
Sky Riders, 1976 (Coburn, J.; York)
Sky Terror. *See* Skyjacked, 1972
Sky West and Crooked, 1966 (Mills)
Sky's the Limit, 1937 (Buchanan)
Sky's the Limit, 1943 (Astaire; Ryan, R.)
Skyjacked, 1971 (Heston; Pidgeon)
Skylark, 1941 (Colbert; Milland)
Skylark, 1993 (Close; Walken)
Skyline, 1931 (Loy; O'Sullivan)
Skyscraper Souls, 1932 (O'Sullivan)
Skyscraper Wilderness. *See* Big City, 1937
Skyward, 1981 (Davis, B.)
Sladkaya zhenzhchina, 1976 (Yankovsky)
Slalom, 1965 (Gassman)
Slamdance, 1987 (Stanton)
Slap. *See* Gifle, 1974
Slap-Happy Sleuths, 1950 (Three Stooges)
Slapshot, 1977 (Newman)
Slapstick of Another Kind, 1984 (Lewis, Jerry; Welles)
Slattery's Hurricane, 1949 (Darnell; Lake; Widmark)
Slaughter Hotel. *See* Bestia uccide a sangue freddo, 1971
Slaughter on Tenth Avenue, 1957 (Duryea; Matthau)
Slava nam, smert vragam!, 1914 (Mozhukin)
Slave, 1909 (Pickford)
Slave, 1917 (Laurel and Hardy)

Slave Girl, 1947 (Crawford, B.)
Slave of Fashion, 1925 (Shearer)
Slave Ship, 1937 (Beery; Rooney; Sanders)
Slavers, 1977 (Howard, T.; Milland)
Sleazy Uncle. *See* Lo zio indegno, 1989
Sleep, My Love, 1948 (Ameche; Colbert)
Sleeper, 1973 (Allen; Keaton, D.)
Sleeper. *See* Little Nikita, 1988
Sleepers, 1996 (Bacon; De Niro; Hoffman; Pitt)
Sleeping Beauty. *See* Shazka o spiatchek, 1914
Sleeping Car, 1933 (Carroll; Novello)
Sleeping Car Murder. *See* Compartiment tueurs, 1965
Sleeping Dogs, 1977 (Neill; Oates)
Sleeping Tiger, 1954 (Bogarde)
Sleeping with the Enemy, 1991 (Roberts, J.)
Sleeping Words of the Bride. *See* Hanayome no negoto, 1933
Sleepless in Seattle, 1993 (Hanks; Ryan, M.)
Sleeps Six, 1984 (Kingsley)
Slender Thread, 1965 (Bancroft; Poitier)
Sleuth, 1925 (Laurel and Hardy)
Sleuth, 1972 (Caine; Olivier)
Sleuths at the Floral Parade, 1913 (Normand)
Slide, Kelly, Slide, 1927 (Carey)
Slight Case of Larceny, 1953 (Rooney)
Slight Case of Murder, 1938 (Robinson, E.)
Slightly Dangerous, 1943 (Bond; Brennan; Turner, L.; Young, R.)
Slightly French, 1948 (Lamour; Ameche)
Slightly Honorable, 1940 (Crawford, B.)
Slightly Pregnant Man. *See* Evénement le plus important depuis que l'homme
   a marché sur la lune, 1973
Slightly Scarlet, 1930 (Lukas)
Slightly Static, 1935 (Rogers, R.)
Slim, 1937 (Fonda, H.; Wyman)
Slim Higgins, 1915 (Mix)
Slim Princess, 1915 (Beery)
Slim Princess, 1920 (Normand)
Slipper. *See* Tofflan-en lycklig komedi, 1967
Slipper and the Rose, 1976 (Evans; Lockwood)
Slippery Pearls, 1932 (Constantine)
Slippery Pearls. *See* Stolen Jools, 1931
Slippery Silks, 1936 (Three Stooges)
Slipping Wives, 1927 (Laurel and Hardy)
Slipstream, 1989 (Kingsley)
Slither, 1973 (Caan)
Sliver, 1993 (Landau; Stone)
Slogan, 1969 (Gélin)
Slovo dlya zashchity, 1976 (Yankovsky)
Slow Burn, 1986 (Depp)
Slow Motion. *See* Sauve qui peut (la vie), 1980
Slumber Party '57, 1977 (Winger)
Sluzhili dva tovarishcha, 1968 (Yankovsky)
Small Back Room, 1948 (Hawkins; Cusack)
Small Town Bully. *See* Little Teacher, 1915
Small Town Girl, 1936 (Gaynor; Stewart; Taylor, R.)
Small Town Girl, 1953 (Miller; Wray)
Small Town Idol, 1921 (Novarro)
Smaller Sky. *See* Mniejsze Wiebo, 1981
Smallest Show on Earth, 1957 (Rutherford; Sellers)
Smania addosso, 1963 (Cervi)
Smart Blonde, 1936 (Wyman)
Smart Girl, 1935 (Lupino)
Smart Girls. *See* Dritte, 1958
Smart Money, 1931 (Cagney; Karloff; Robinson, E.)
Smart Woman, 1931 (Astor; Horton)
Smart Work, 1931 (Arbuckle)
Smarty, 1934 (Blondell; Horton)
Smash and Grab, 1937 (Buchanan)
Smash-Up: The Story of a Woman, 1947 (Hayward)
Smash-Up on Interstate 5, 1976 (Jones, T.)
Smashing the Crime Syndicate. *See* Hell's Bloody Devils, 1970
Smashing the Money Ring, 1939 (Reagan)

Smashing the Spy Ring, 1939 (Bellamy)
Smerti doma, 1915 (Mozhukin)
Smetti di piovere. *See* Pacifista, 1971
Smich se lepi na paty, 1987 (Brodský)
Smile, 1974 (Dern; Griffith)
Smile Jenny, You're Dead, 1974 (Foster)
Smile of a Child, 1911 (Sweet)
Smile Please, 1924 (Langdon)
Smiles of a Summer Night. *See* **Sommarnattens leende**, 1955
Smiley, 1956 (Richardson, R.)
Smilin' Guns, 1929 (Brennan)
Smilin' Through, 1922 (Talmadge)
Smilin' Through, 1932 (Howard, L.; March; Shearer)
Smilin' Through, 1941 (MacDonald)
Smiling Along. *See* Keep Smiling, 1938
Smiling Lieutenant, 1931 (Chevalier; Colbert; Hopkins, M.)
Smiling Life. *See* Hohoemu jinsei, 1930
Smith, 1939 (Richardson, R.)
Smith!, 1969 (Ford, G.; Oates)
Smith's Pony, 1927 (Lombard)
Smithy, 1924 (Laurel and Hardy)
Smithy's Grandma's Party, 1913 (Beery)
Smog, 1962 (Girardot)
Smoke, 1995 (Hurt, W.; Keitel; Wallach; Whitaker)
Smoke in the Wind, 1971 (Brennan)
Smoke Jumpers. *See* Red Skies of Montana, 1952
Smoke Signal, 1955 (Andrews, D.)
Smoker, 1910 (Pickford)
Smokey and the Bandit, 1977 (Field; Reynolds, B.)
Smokey and the Bandit II, 1980 (Field; Reynolds, B.)
Smokey and the Bandit III, 1983 (Reynolds, B.)
Smokey and the Bandit Ride Again. *See* Smokey and the Bandit II, 1980
Smoky, 1946 (Baxter; MacMurray)
Smorgasbord. *See* Cracking Up, 1983
Smrt nacerno, 1976 (Brodský)
Smuggler's Daughter, 1914 (Laurel and Hardy)
Smugglers. *See* Man Within, 1947
Smultronstället, 1957 (Andersson, B.; Björnstrand; Thulin; Von Sydow)
Snack Bar Budapest, 1988 (Giannini)
Snake and Crane Arts of Shaolin, 1977 (Chan)
Snake Eyes, 1990 (McDowell)
Snake Eyes. *See* Dangerous Game, 1993
Snake Fist Fighter, 1981 (Chan)
Snake in the Eagle's Shadow, 1978 (Chan)
Snake Pit, 1948 (De Havilland; Marsh)
Snake Princess. *See* Hebihime-sama, 1940
Snapphanar, 1942 (Björnstrand)
Sneakers, 1992 (Jones, James Earl; Kingsley; Poitier; Redford)
Sniper, 1952 (Menjou)
Sniper, 1987 (Cardinale)
Snitch in Time, 1950 (Three Stooges)
Snob, 1924 (Shearer)
Snob, 1984 (Brandauer)
Snoop Sisters, 1972 (Goddard)
Snooper Service, 1945 (Langdon)
Snotchak, 1912 (Mozhukin)
Snow Carnival, 1949 (Constantine)
Snow Goose, 1971 (Harris, R.)
Snow Hawk, 1925 (Laurel and Hardy)
Snow in the Desert, 1919 (Colman)
Snow Trail. *See* Ginrei no hate, 1947
Snow Was Black. *See* Neige était sale, 1953
Snow White, 1916 (Barthelmess)
Snow White and the Three Clowns. *See* Snow White and the Three Stooges, 1961
Snow White and the Three Stooges, 1961 (Three Stooges)
Snow White in the Black Forest, 1996 (Weaver)
Snowbound, 1947 (Dalio; Lom)
Snows of Kilimanjaro, 1952 (Dalio; Gardner; Hayward; Peck)
SnowwhiteRosered. *See* Schneeweissrosenrot, 1991
So Big, 1924 (Beery)

So Big, 1932 (Davis, B.; Stanwyck)
So Big, 1953 (Wyman; Hayden)
So Bright the Flame. *See* Girl in White, 1952
So Close to Life. *See* Nära livet, 1958
So Dear to My Heart, 1949 (Carey)
So ein Mädel vergisst man nicht, 1932 (Kortner)
So Ends Our Night, 1940 (March; Ford, G.; Sullavan)
So Evil My Love, 1948 (Milland)
So Goes My Love, 1946 (Ameche; Loy)
So I Married an Axe Murderer, 1993 (Arkin)
So lang noch ein Walzer von Strauss erklingt, 1931 (Fröhlich)
So Little Time, 1952 (Schell, Maria)
So Long at the Fair, 1950 (Bogarde)
So Long, Mr. Chumps, 1941 (Three Stooges)
So Near, Yet So Far, 1912 (Barrymore, L.; Pickford)
So oder so ist das Leben, 1976 (Schell, Maria)
So Proudly We Hail, 1943 (Colbert; Goddard; Lake)
So Red the Rose, 1935 (Scott, R.; Sullavan)
So Runs the Way, 1913 (Barrymore, L.; Gish)
So sind die Männer, 1922 (Dietrich)
So This Is College, 1929 (McCrea; Montgomery)
So This Is London, 1930 (O'Sullivan; Granger; Rogers, W.; Sanders)
So This Is Paris, 1926 (Loy)
So This Is Paris, 1954 (Curtis, T.)
So Well Remembered, 1947 (Howard, T.; Mills)
So You Won't Squawk, 1941 (Keaton, B.)
So You Won't Talk, 1940 (Brown)
So Young, So Bad, 1950 (Henreid)
So's Your Old Man, 1926 (Fields, W. C.)
Soaking the Clothes, 1915 (Lloyd)
Soapdish, 1991 (Field; Goldberg; Kline)
Sobaka Baskervilei, 1981 (Yankovsky)
Sobato, Domenica e Lunedi, 1990 (Loren)
Sobre las olas, 1950 (Infante)
Social Celebrity, 1926 (Brooks, L.; Menjou)
Social Club, 1916 (Swanson)
Social Exile. *See* Declassée, 1925
Social Secretary, 1916 (Talmadge)
Society Doctor, 1935 (Taylor, R.)
Society for Sale, 1918 (Swanson)
Society Girl, 1932 (Tracy)
Society Lawyer, 1939 (Pidgeon)
Society Scandal, 1924 (Swanson)
Society Sensation, 1918 (Valentino)
Sock-a-Bye Baby, 1942 (Three Stooges)
Sodoma e Gomorra, 1962 (Aimée; Baker; Granger)
Soeurs Brontë, 1979 (Adjani; Huppert)
Sofie, 1992 (Josephson; Ullmann)
Soft Beds and Hard Battles, 1973 (Sellers)
Soft-Boiled, 1923 (Mix)
Soft Cushions, 1927 (Karloff)
Soft Money, 1919 (Lloyd)
Soft Shoes, 1925 (Carey)
Soft Skin. *See* Peau douce, 1964
Soft Tenderfoot, 1917 (Mix)
Sogeki, 1968 (Mori)
Sogni mostruosamente proibiti, 1982 (Valli)
Sogno della farfalla, 1994 (Andersson, B.)
Sogno di tutti, 1941 (Cervi)
Sogno di Zorro, 1951 (Gassman; Loren)
Sohn ohne Heimat, 1955 (Krauss)
Söhne des Herrn Gaspary, 1948 (Dagover)
Soigné ton gauche, 1936 (Tati)
Soilers, 1923 (Laurel and Hardy)
Soir ... par hasard, 1964 (Brasseur)
Soir de réveillon, 1933 (Arletty)
Soir, un train, 1968 (Aimée; Montand)
Soirée mondaine, 1917 (Chevalier)
Sois belle et tais-toi, 1958 (Belmondo; Delon)
Sokhranivshie ogon, 1970 (Yankovsky)
Sol Madrid, 1968 (Lukas)

Sol, sommer og studiner, 1922 (Madsen and Schenstrøm)
Sól ziemi czarnej, 1970 (Olbrychski)
Solange du da bist, 1953 (Schell, Maria)
Solar Crisis, 1990 (Heston; Palance)
Solarbabies, 1986 (Brooks, M.)
Solas Contigo, 1990 (Abril)
Sold for Marriage, 1916 (Gish)
Soldat Bom, 1948 (Björnstrand)
Soldatess, 1965 (Karina)
Soldier, 1982 (Kinski)
Soldier and the Lady, 1936 (Walbrook)
Soldier Blue, 1970 (Pleasence)
Soldier in Love. See Fanfan la Tulipe, 1951
Soldier in Love, 1967 (Bloom)
Soldier in the Rain, 1963 (McQueen; Weld)
Soldier Man, 1927 (Langdon)
Soldier Marched. See Shli soldaty, 1958
Soldier of Fortune, 1955 (Gable; Hayward)
Soldier of Fortune. See Laser Mission, 1990
Soldier of Victory. See Żołnierz zwycięstwa, 1953
Soldier's Duties. See Krigsmans erinran, 1947
Soldier's Pay. See Soldier's Plaything, 1930
Soldier's Plaything, 1930 (Langdon)
Soldier's Prayer. See **Ningen no joken III**, 1961
Soldier's Story, 1984 (Washington)
Soldiers of Fortune, 1919 (Beery)
Soldiers of Pancho Villa. See Cucaracha, 1958
Soldiers of the King, 1934 (Horton)
Soldiers Three, 1951 (Cusack; Granger; Niven; Pidgeon)
Sole anche di notte, 1990 (Giannini; Kinski; Vogler)
Sole buio, 1990 (Josephson)
Soleil a toujours raison, 1941 (Brasseur; Presle; Vanel)
Soleil dans l'oeil, 1961 (Karina)
Soleil de minuit, 1941 (Hayakawa; Berry)
Soleil des voyous, 1967 (Gabin)
Soleil en face, 1979 (Audran; Cassel)
Soleil noir, 1966 (Gélin)
Soleil rouge, 1971 (Bronson; Delon; Mifune)
Solid Gold Cadillac, 1956 (Holliday)
Soliloques du pauvre, 1954 (Brasseur)
Solita de Cordoue, 1946 (Cuny)
Solitaire, 1987 (Belmondo)
Solitaire Man, 1933 (Marshall)
Solitaires, 1913 (Talmadge)
Solitary Man, 1979 (Pfeiffer)
Soliti ignoti, 1958 (Cardinale; Gassman; Mastroianni)
Soliti ignoti vent' anni dopo, 1985 (Gassman; Mastroianni)
Solitude du chanteur de fond, 1974 (Montand)
Soll man heiraten?, 1925 (Banky)
Solo for Sparrow, 1962 (Caine)
Solomon and Sheba, 1959 (Brynner; Lollobrigida; Sanders)
Solva Saal, 1958 (Anand)
Som här inträden ..., 1945 (Björnstrand)
Sombras en una Batalla, 1993 (Maura)
Sombre dimanche, 1948 (Dalio)
Sombrero, 1953 (Charisse; Gassman)
Some Baby, 1915 (Lloyd)
Some Call It Loving, 1973 (Pryor)
Some Came Running, 1958 (Kennedy; MacLaine; Martin, D.; Sidney)
Some Collectors, 1912-13 (White)
Some Day, 1935 (Lockwood)
Some Duel, 1916 (Mix)
Some Girls, 1989 (Redford)
Some Kind of a Nut, 1969 (Dickinson)
Some Kind of Hero, 1982 (Pryor)
Some Like It Cool. See Casanova & Co., 1977
Some Like It Hot, 1939 (Hope)
Some Like It Hot, 1959 (Brown; Curtis, T.; Lemmon; Monroe; Raft)
Some Like It Rough, 1944 (Buchanan)
Some May Live, 1967 (Cotten; Cushing)
Some More of Samoa, 1941 (Three Stooges)

Some Nerve. See Gentlemen of Nerve, 1914
Some Nerve, Charlie at the Races. See Gentlemen of Nerve, 1914
Some of the Best, 1949 (Barrymore, L.)
Some of Us May Die. See Journey, 1959
Somebody Has to Shoot the Picture, 1990 (Scheider)
Somebody Killed Her Husband, 1978 (Bridges)
Somebody to Love, 1994 (Keitel; Quinn)
Somebody Up There Likes Me, 1956 (McQueen; Mineo; Newman; Sloane)
Somebody's Daughter, 1992 (Gould)
Someone behind the Door. See Quelqu'un derriére la porte, 1971
Someone to Love, 1987 (Welles)
Something about Amelia, 1984 (Close)
Something Big, 1971 (Martin, D.)
Something Evil, 1972 (Bellamy)
Something Fishy. See Pas tres Catholique, 1994
Something for a Lonely Man, 1968 (Oates)
Something for Everyone, 1970 (Lansbury)
Something for Joey, 1977 (Page)
Something for Mrs. Gibbs, 1965 (Carradine)
Something for the Birds, 1952 (Mature; Neal)
Something for the Boys, 1944 (Holliday; Miranda)
Something in Common, 1986 (Burstyn; Wallach; Weld)
Something in Her Eye, 1915 (Laurel and Hardy)
Something in the Wind, 1947 (Durbin; O'Connor)
Something of Value, 1957 (Hudson; Poitier)
Something Short of Paradise, 1979 (Sarandon)
Something to Do, 1919 (Crisp)
Something to Hide, 1972 (Finch; Winters)
Something to Live For, 1952 (Fontaine; Grant, L.; Marshall; Milland)
Something to Live For: The Alison Gertz Story, 1992 (Landau)
Something to Shout About, 1943 (Ameche; Charisse)
Something to Sing About, 1937 (Cagney)
Something to Talk About, 1995 (Duvall; Hawn; Quaid; Roberts, J.; Rowlands)
Something to Think About, 1920 (Swanson)
Something Wicked This Way Comes, 1983 (Robards)
Something Wild, 1986 (Griffith)
Sometimes a Great Notion, 1971 (Fonda, H.; Newman; Remick)
Somewhere I'll Find You, 1942 (Gable; Turner, L.)
Somewhere in Sonora, 1933 (Wayne)
Somewhere in the Night, 1946 (Kortner)
Somewhere in Turkey, 1918 (Lloyd)
Somewhere in Wrong, 1925 (Laurel and Hardy)
Sommaren med Monika, 1953 (Andersson, H.)
Sommarkvåller på Jorden, 1987 (Andersson, H.)
Sommarnattens leende, 1955 (Andersson, B.; Andersson, H.; Björnstrand; Dahlbeck)
Sommarnöje sökes, 1957 (Andersson, B.; Björnstrand; Dahlbeck)
Sommerfuglene, 1974 (Chaplin, G.)
Sommergäste, 1975 (Ganz)
Sommernachtstraum, 1924 (Krauss; Rasp)
Sommersby, 1993 (Foster; Gere; Jones, James Earl)
Somnambul, 1929 (Kortner)
Son-Daughter, 1932 (Novarro)
Son dernier verdict, 1951 (Vanel)
Son Dernier Rôle, 1946 (Dalio)
Son Is Born, 1946 (Finch)
Son nom de Venise dans Calcutta désert, 1976 (Seyrig)
Son of a Gunfighter. See Hijo del Pistolero, 1966
Son of a Sailor, 1933 (Brown)
Son of Ali Baba, 1952 (Curtis, T.)
Son of David, 1920 (Colman)
Son of Flubber, 1963 (MacMurray)
Son of Frankenstein, 1939 (Karloff; Lugosi; Rathbone)
Son of Fury, 1942 (Carradine; Farmer; Lanchester; McDowall; Power; Sanders; Tierney)
Son of India, 1931 (Novarro)
Son of Lassie, 1945 (Crisp)
Son of Monte Cristo, 1940 (Bennett; Sanders)
Son of Paleface, 1952 (Crosby; Hope)
Son of Paleface, 1952 (Rogers, R.; Russell, J.)
Son of Sinbad, 1955 (Novak; Price)

Son of the Gods, 1930 (Barthelmess)
Son of the Golden West, 1928 (Mix)
Son of the Pink Panther, 1993 (Azmi; Benigni; Cardinale; Lom)
Son of the Sheik, 1921 (Young, L.)
Son of the Sheik, 1926 (Banky; Valentino)
Son Oncle de Normandie, 1939 (Berry)
Sonar Kella, 1974 (Chatterjee)
Sonatas, 1959 (Félix; Rey)
Söndag i september, 1963 (Andersson, H.)
Song, 1928 (Wong)
Song and Dance Man, 1936 (Dumont; Trevor)
Song for David, 1996 (Douglas, K.; Douglas, Michael)
Song for Tomorrow, 1948 (Lee, C.)
Song Is Born, 1947 (Kaye)
Song Lantern. See Uta-andon, 1943
Song o' My Heart, 1930 (O'Sullivan)
Song of Arizona, 1946 (Rogers, R.)
Song of Bernadette, 1943 (Cobb; Dalio; Darnell; Jones, Jennifer; Price)
Song of Freedom, 1936 (Robeson)
Song of Fukagawa. See Furyu Fukagawa uta, 1960
Song of Love, 1923 (Talmadge)
Song of Love, 1947 (Henreid; Hepburn, K.; Walker)
Song of Marriage. See Naszdal, 1918
Song of Nevada, 1944 (Rogers, R.)
Song of Norway, 1970 (Homolka; Robinson, E.)
Song of Russia, 1944 (Taylor, R.)
Song of Songs, 1933 (Dietrich)
Song of Surrender, 1949 (Rains)
Song of Texas, 1943 (Rogers, R.)
Song of the Flower Basket. See Hanakago no uta, 1936
Song of the Heart. See Udvari levego, 1917
Song of the Islands, 1942 (Grable; Mature)
Song of the Open Road, 1944 (Fields, W. C.)
Song of the Rivers. See Lied der Ströme, 1954
Song of the South, 1947 (McDaniel)
Song of the Thin Man, 1947 (Grahame; Loy; Powell, W.)
Song of the West, 1930 (Brown)
Song of the Wildwood Flute, 1910 (Pickford)
Song to Remember, 1944 (Muni; Oberon; Wilde)
Song without End, 1960 (Bogarde; Dalio)
Songoku, 1940 (Takamine)
Songs of Truce, 1913 (Mix)
Sonnenstrahl, 1933 (Fröhlich)
Sonnwendhof, 1918 (Kortner)
Sonny, 1922 (Barthelmess)
Sonny Boy, 1929 (Horton)
Sono fotogenico, 1980 (Gassman)
Sono imoto, 1953 (Kagawa)
Sono Sartana, il vostro bechino, 1969 (Kinski)
Sono stato io, 1973 (Giannini)
Sono stato io!, 1937 (Valli)
Sono stato un'agente CIA, 1978 (Kennedy)
Sono un fenomeno paranormale, 1985 (Sordi)
Sono yo no himegoto, 1957 (Tsukasa)
Sono yo no onna, 1934 (Tanaka)
Sono yo no tsuma, 1930 (Ryu)
Sono Zenya, 1939 (Yamada)
Sonohito no na wa ienai, 1951 (Yamamura)
Sonoobasho no onna arite, 1962 (Tsukasa)
Sonoyo no onna, 1934 (Takamine)
Sons, 1989 (Audran)
Sons and Lovers, 1960 (Howard, T.; Pleasence)
Sons o' Guns, 1936 (Blondell; Brown)
Sons of Katie Elder, 1965 (Hopper; Martin, D.; Wayne)
Sons of Liberty, 1939 (Rains)
Sons of Men, 1918 (Gilbert)
Sons of New Mexico, 1950 (Autry)
Sons of Satan. See I bastardi, 1969
Sons of Satan, 1971 (Hayworth)
Sons of the Desert, 1933 (Laurel and Hardy)
Sons of the Legion. See Sons of the Desert, 1933

Sons of the Legion, 1938 (O'Connor)
Sons of the Musketeers. See At Sword's Point, 1952
Sons of the Pioneers, 1942 (Rogers, R.)
Sons of the Sea. See Old Ironsides, 1926
Sons of Thunder. See Arrivani i titani, 1961
Son's Return, 1909 (Pickford)
Sont morts les bâtisseurs, 1959 (Fresnay)
Sooky, 1931 (Cooper)
Sophia Loren: Her Own Story, 1980 (Loren)
Sophie's Choice, 1982 (Kline; Streep)
Sophie's Place. See Crooks and Coronets, 1969
Sophomore, 1929 (Ayres)
Sorcerer, 1977 (Scheider)
Sorcerer's Village, 1958 (Meredith)
Sorcerers, 1967 (Karloff)
Sorcières de Salem, 1956 (Piccoli; Montand)
Sorekara, 1986 (Ryu)
Sorelle, 1969 (Giannini)
Soriso del grande tentatore, 1973 (Bardot; Jackson, G.)
Sorority House, 1939 (Lake)
Sorpasso, 1962 (Gassman; Trintignant)
Sorprese dell'amore, 1959 (Gassman)
Sorrow and the Pity. See **Chagrin et la pitié**, 1971
Sorrow Is Only for Women. See Kanashimi wa onna dakeni, 1958
Sorrowful Jones, 1949 (Ball; Hope)
Sorrows of Sarah. See Gorre Sarri, 1913
Sorrows of Satan, 1926 (Menjou)
Sorrows of the Unfaithful, 1910 (Pickford)
Sorry, Wrong Number, 1948 (Lancaster; Stanwyck)
Sorte Drom, 1910 (Nielsen)
Sortie de secours, 1970 (Delon)
Sortilèges, 1944 (Piccoli)
Sorvanetch, 1914 (Mozhukin)
Soryu hiken, 1958 (Kagawa; Mifune)
SOS Mediterranean. See Alerte en Méditerranée, 1938
SOS: Die Insel des Tränen, 1923 (Wegener)
Soshun, 1956 (Yamamura)
Sospetto, 1975 (Girardot; Volonté)
Sostiene Pereira, 1996 (Mastroianni)
Sotto dieci bandiere, 1960 (Laughton; Volonté)
Sotto il ristorante cinese, 1987 (Blier)
Sotto il segno dello scorpione, 1969 (Volonté)
Sotto il sole di Roma, 1948 (Sordi)
Sotto il vestito niente, 1985 (Pleasence)
Soubrette and the Simp, 1914 (Laurel and Hardy)
Souffle au coeur, 1971 (Gélin)
Soul Man, 1986 (Jones, James Earl)
Soul Mate, 1914 (Mix)
Soul of a Painter. See Peintre, 1994
Soul of Buddha, 1918 (Bara)
Soul of Honor, 1914 (Sweet)
Soul of Kura-san, 1916 (Hayakawa)
Soul of Magdalen, 1917 (Barthelmess)
Soul of the Sea. See Hai hun, 1957
Soulfire, 1925 (Barthelmess)
Soulier trop petit, 1909 (Linder)
Souls at Sea, 1937 (Carey; Constantine)
Souls at Sea, 1937 (Raft)
Souls for Sale, 1923 (Chaplin, C.)
Souls Triumphant, 1915 (Gish)
Sound and the Fury, 1959 (Brynner; Rosay; Woodward)
Sound Barrier, 1952 (Elliott; Richardson, R.)
Sound of Music, 1965 (Andrews, J.)
Sound of the Mountain. See Yama no oto, 1954
Sound Off, 1952 (Rooney)
Sounds from the Mountains. See Yama no oto, 1954
Soup to Nuts, 1930 (Three Stooges)
Souper, 1992 (Piccoli)
Souricière, 1950 (Blier)
Sourire dans la tempête, 1950 (Werner)
Sous la Griffe, 1912 (Modot)

Sous la signe de Monte-Cristo, 1968 (Brasseur)
Sous le Ceil d'Orient. *See* Shéhérazade, 1928
Sous le ciel de Provence, 1956 (Fernandel)
Sous le signe du taureau, 1969 (Gabin)
Sous le soleil de Satan, 1987 (Depardieu)
Sous les ponts de Paris. *See* Clodoche, 1938
Sous les toits de Paris, 1930 (Modot)
Sous les yeux d'occident, 1936 (Fresnay)
Sous les yeux d'Occident, 1936 (Barrault)
South of Caliente, 1951 (Rogers, R.)
South of Pago-Pago, 1940 (Farmer; McLaglen)
South of Santa Fe, 1942 (Rogers, R.)
South of St. Louis, 1949 (Malone; McCrea)
South of Tahiti, 1941 (Crawford, B.)
South of the Border, 1939 (Autry)
South Pacific, 1958 (Brazzi; Fontaine)
South Riding, 1937 (Richardson, R.)
South Sea Adventure, 1959 (Welles)
South Sea Bubble, 1928 (Novello)
South Sea Sinner, 1950 (Winters)
South Sea Woman, 1953 (Lancaster)
South West Pacific, 1944 (Finch)
South Wind. *See* Minami ni kaze, 1942
Southern Maid, 1933 (Granger)
Southern Star. *See* Etoile de Sud, 1969
Southward Ho, 1939 (Rogers, R.)
Southwest to Sonora. *See* Appaloosa, 1966
Souvenir. *See* Aux yeux du souvenir, 1948
Souvenir d'Italie, 1957 (Sordi)
Souvenir de Gibralter, 1975 (Constantine)
Souvenirs d'en France, 1975 (Moreau)
Souvenirs perdus, 1950 (Blier; Brasseur; Feuillère; Montand; Philipe)
Souvenirs, souvenirs, 1984 (Girardot; Noiret)
Sowers, 1916 (Sweet)
Sowizdrzal swietokrzyski, 1980 (Tyszkiewicz)
Soy charro de Rancho Grande, 1947 (Infante)
Soy puro mexicano, 1942 (Armendáriz)
Soy un prófugo, 1946 (Cantinflas)
Soyez les bienvenus, 1940 (Berry; Gélin)
Soyez ma femme. *See* Be My Wife, 1921
Soylent Green, 1973 (Cotten; Heston; Robinson, E.)
Soyokaze chichi to tomoni, 1940 (Takamine)
Soyons gai, 1931 (Menjou)
Space Jam, 1996 (Murray)
Space Master X-7, 1958 (Three Stooges)
Space Ship Sappy, 1957 (Three Stooges)
Spaceballs, 1987 (Brooks, M.; Candy; Hurt, J.)
Spadla s měsice, 1966 (Brodský)
Spaggia privata, 1986 (Blier)
Spaghetti, 1916 (Laurel and Hardy)
Spaghetti a la Mode, 1915 (Laurel and Hardy)
Spaghetti and Lottery, 1915 (Laurel and Hardy)
Span of Life, 1914 (Barrymore, L.)
Spanish Dancer, 1923 (Beery; Menjou; Negri)
Spanish Dilemma, 1912 (Normand)
Spanish Earth, 1937 (Welles)
Spanish Fly, 1975 (Terry-Thomas)
Spanish Gardener, 1956 (Bogarde; Cusack)
Spanish Love, 1922 (Powell, W.)
Spanish Main, 1945 (Henreid; O'Hara)
Spara forte, piu forte ... non capisco, 1966 (Mastroianni; Welch)
Spara per primo vivrai di più. *See* Consortium, 1968
Spare the Rod, 1961 (Pleasence)
Sparrow. *See* Storia di una Capinera, 1993
Sparrows, 1926 (Pickford)
Sparsh, 1984 (Azmi)
Spartacus, 1960 (Curtis, T.; Douglas, K.; Laughton; Lom; Olivier; Ustinov)
Spasms. *See* Death Bite, 1982
Spassenieto, 1984 (Nowicki)
Spawn of the North, 1938 (Barrymore, J.; Fonda, H.; Lamour; Raft)
Speak Easily, 1932 (Durante; Keaton, B.)

Special Agent, 1935 (Davis, B.)
Special Day. *See* Giornata speciale, 1977
Special Delivery, 1927 (Arbuckle; Cantor; Powell, W.)
Special Delivery, 1955 (Cotten)
Special Inspector, 1939 (Hayworth)
Special Kind of Love. *See* Special Olympics, 1978
Special Olympics, 1978 (Winger)
Special Section. *See* Section spéciale, 1975
Specialist, 1992 (Keitel)
Specialist, 1994 (Stallone; Steiger; Stone; Woods)
Specialmente la domenica, 1991 (Noiret)
Specialmente la domenica. *See* Especially on Sunday, 1993
Species, 1995 (Kingsley; Whitaker)
Speckled Band, 1931 (Massey)
Specter of Freedom. *See* Fantôme de la liberté, 1974
Specter on the Bridge. *See* Golden Gate Murders, 1979
Specters. *See* Spettri, 1987
Spectre, 1973 (Léaud)
Spectre, 1977 (Hurt, J.)
Speechless, 1994 (Davis, G.; Keaton, M.)
Speed, 1936 (Stewart)
Speed, 1994 (Hopper; Reeves)
Speed Fever. *See* Formula I, febbre della velocità, 1978
Speed Hound, 1927 (Cantor)
Speed Kings, 1913 (Arbuckle; Normand)
Speed Maniac, 1919 (Mix)
Speed Queen, 1913 (Normand)
Speed Zone, 1989 (Candy; Van Cleef)
Speedway, 1968 (Presley)
Speedy, 1928 (Lloyd)
Spell, 1977 (Grant, L.)
Spellbound, 1945 (Bergman; Peck)
Spencer Tracy Legacy: A Tribute by Katharine Hepburn, 1986 (Hepburn, K.)
Spencer's Mountain, 1963 (Crisp; Fonda, H.; O'Hara)
Spender, 1919 (Barrymore, E.)
Spending Time with Family, 1993 (Bujold)
Spendthrift, 1936 (Fonda, H.)
Speriamo che sia femmina, 1985 (Blier; Deneuve; Noiret; Ullmann)
Spettri, 1987 (Pleasence)
SPFX 1140, 1982 (Dreyfuss)
Sphinx. *See* Spynx, 1917
Sphinx, 1981 (Gielgud)
Spiaggia del desiderio, 1976 (Kennedy)
Spice of Life. *See* Casse-pieds, 1948
Spices. *See* Mirch Masala, 1986
Spider Woman, 1944 (Rathbone)
Spider's Strategem. *See* Strategia del ragno, 1969
Spider's Web. *See* Spinnennets, 1988
Spiders, Part 1: The Golden Lake. *See* Spinnen, Part 1: Der goldene See, 1919
Spiders, Part 2: The Diamond Ship. *See* Spinnen, Part 2: Das Brillantenschiff, 1920
Spie contro il mondo, 1966 (Granger; Kinski)
Spiel der Verlierer, 1977 (Schell, Maria)
Spielereien einer Kaiserin, 1929 (Dagover)
Spies. *See* Espions, 1957
Spies at Work. *See* Spione am Werk, 1932
Spies Like Us, 1985 (Hope)
Spike of Bensonhurst, 1988 (Borgnine)
Spikes Gang, 1973 (Marvin)
Spilers, 1920 (Laurel and Hardy)
Spin of a Coin. *See* George Raft Story, 1961
Spinnen, Part 1: Der goldene See, 1919 (Dagover)
Spinnen, Part 2: Das Brillantenschiff, 1920 (Dagover)
Spinnennets, 1988 (Brandauer; Mueller-Stahl)
Spinout, 1966 (Presley)
Spinster. *See* Two Loves, 1961
Spion, 1917 (Veidt)
Spion 503, 1958 (Von Sydow)
Spionage, 1955 (Werner)
Spione, 1928 (Rasp)
Spione am Werk, 1932 (Homolka)

Spione unter sich. *See* Guerre secrète, 1966
Spionin, 1921 (Nielsen)
Spiral. *See* Spirála, 1978
Spiral Road, 1962 (Hudson; Rowlands)
Spiral Staircase, 1946 (Barrymore, E.; Lanchester)
Spirála, 1978 (Nowicki)
Spirit and the Flesh. *See* I promessi sposi, 1941
Spirit Awakened, 1912 (Sweet)
Spirit of 1976, 1935 (Grable)
Spirit of Culver, 1939 (Cooper)
Spirit of Notre Dame, 1931 (Ayres)
Spirit of St. Louis, 1957 (Stewart)
Spirit of the People. *See* Abe Lincoln in Illinois, 1940
Spiritismo, 1919 (Bertini)
Spiritismus, 1920 (Dagover)
Spirits of the Dead. *See* Histoires extraordinaires, 1969
Spiritual Kung-Fu, 1978 (Chan)
Spit-Ball Sadie, 1915 (Lloyd)
Spite Marriage, 1929 (Keaton, B.)
Spitfire, 1934 (Bellamy; Hepburn, K.; Young, R.)
Spitfire. *See* First of the Few, 1942
Spitfire Grill, 1996 (Burstyn)
Splash, 1984 (Candy; Hanks)
Splendid Road, 1925 (Barrymore, L.)
Splendor, 1935 (Hopkins, M.; McCrea; Niven)
Splendor, 1989 (Mastroianni)
Splendor in the Grass, 1961 (Beatty; Wood)
Splendor in the Grass, 1981 (Pfeiffer; Saint)
Split, 1968 (Borgnine; Hackman; Oates; Sutherland)
Split Decisions, 1988 (Hackman)
Split Image, 1982 (Woods)
Split Second, 1953 (Powell, D.)
Split Second to an Epitaph, 1968 (Cotten; O'Brien, M.)
Splitting Heirs, 1993 (Cleese; Hershey)
Spoiled Children. *See* Des Enfants gâtés, 1977
Spoilers, 1930 (Constantine)
Spoilers, 1942 (Barthelmess; Carey; Dietrich; Scott, R.; Wayne)
Spoilers, 1955 (Baxter)
Spoilers of the Plains, 1951 (Rogers, R.)
Spoils of War, 1994 (Nelligan)
Spokojne lata, 1981 (Nowicki)
Spook Louder, 1943 (Three Stooges)
Spook Speaks, 1940 (Keaton, B.)
Spooks, 1953 (Three Stooges)
Spooks Run Wild, 1941 (Lugosi)
Sport of a Nation. *See* All-American, 1932
Sport of Kings, 1921 (McLaglen)
Sport Parade, 1932 (McCrea)
Sporting Blood, 1931 (Gable)
Sporting Blood, 1940 (O'Sullivan; Young, R.)
Sporting Oasis, 1952 (Ladd)
Sporting Venus, 1925 (Colman; Sweet)
Sposa Americana, 1986 (Keitel)
Sposa bella, 1959 (Fabrizi)
Sposa bella. *See* Angel Wore Red, 1960
Sposa non puo attendere, 1949 (Cervi; Lollobrigida)
Spotkanie ze szpiegem, 1964 (Tyszkiewicz)
Spotlight Sadie, 1919 (Marsh)
Spotlight Scandals, 1943 (Langdon)
Spotswood. *See* Efficiency Expert, 1992
Spóźnieni przechodnie, 1962 (Tyszkiewicz)
Spree, 1967 (Mansfield)
Spring. *See* Vesna, 1947
Spring and Port Wine, 1970 (Mason)
Spring Fever. *See* Recreation, 1914
Spring Fever, 1919 (Lloyd)
Spring Fever, 1924 (Arthur)
Spring Fever, 1927 (Crawford, J.)
Spring in Park Lane, 1948 (Neagle)
Spring Madness, 1938 (Ayres; Meredith; O'Sullivan)
Spring Meeting, 1941 (Rutherford)

Spring Parade, 1940 (Durbin)
Spring Reunion, 1957 (Andrews, D.)
Spring Song, 1946 (Kendall)
Spring Sorrow of the Pipa, 1932 (Zhao Dan)
Spring Symphony. *See* Fruhlingssinfonie, 1985
Spring Tonic, 1935 (Ayres; Trevor)
Spring Wind on Venaya, 1959 (Bondarchuk)
Springfield Rifle, 1952 (Constantine)
Springtime, 1920 (Laurel and Hardy)
Springtime in the Rockies, 1937 (Autry)
Springtime in the Rockies, 1942 (Grable; Horton; Miranda)
Springtime in the Sierras, 1947 (Rogers, R.)
Spritsmuglerne. *See* Polis Paulus' Påskasmäll, 1925
Sprung ins Leben, 1924 (Dietrich)
Spurs and Saddles, 1927 (Wray)
Spy against the World. *See* Spie contro il mondo, 1966
Spy in Black, 1939 (Veidt)
Spy in the Green Hat, 1966 (Leigh, Janet; Palance)
Spy in the Pantry. *See* Ten Days in Paris, 1939
Spy in White. *See* Secret of Stambov, 1936
Spy in Your Eye. *See* Appuntamento per le spie, 1966
Spy of Napoleon, 1936 (Barthelmess)
Spy Ring, 1938 (Wyman)
Spy Thirteen. *See* Operator Thirteen, 1934
Spy Who Came in from the Cold, 1965 (Cusack; Bloom; Burton; Werner)
Spy with a Cold Nose, 1966 (Elliott)
Spynx, 1917 (Lukas)
Squabs and Squabbles, 1919 (Laurel and Hardy)
Squadra antimafia, 1978 (Wallach)
Squall, 1929 (Loy; Young, L.)
Squall. *See* Shkval, 1916
Square Dance, 1987 (Robards; Ryder)
Square Deal. *See* Ruse, 1915
Square Deal Man. *See* Ruse, 1915
Square Deal Man, 1917 (Hart)
Square Deal Sanderson, 1919 (Hart)
Square Jungle, 1955 (Borgnine; Curtis, T.)
Square Mile, 1953 (Guinness)
Square of Violence. *See* Nasilje na trgu, 1961
Square Peg, 1958 (Wisdom)
Square Ring, 1953 (Kendall)
Squarehead. *See* Mabel's Married Life, 1914
Squareheads of the Round Table, 1948 (Three Stooges)
Squaw's Love, 1911 (Normand)
Squeaker. *See* Zinker, 1963
Squeaks and Squawks, 1920 (Laurel and Hardy)
Squeeze. *See* Controrapina, 1978
Squeeze, 1987 (Keaton, M.)
Sredi dobrykh lyudei, 1962 (Maretskaya)
Staatanjo, 1963 (Yamamura)
Stablemates, 1938 (Beery; Rooney)
Stacey's Knights, 1981 (Costner)
Staden vid vattnen, 1955 (Andersson, B.)
Stadt Anatol, 1936 (Fröhlich)
Stadt ist voller Geheimnisse, 1955 (Kortner)
Stage, 1951 (Anand)
Stage Door, 1937 (Ball; Hepburn, K.; Menjou; Miller; Rogers, G.)
Stage Door Canteen, 1943 (Bellamy; Fields, G.; Hepburn, K.; Jaffe; Muni; Oberon; Raft; Weissmuller)
Stage Fright, 1950 (Dietrich; Wyman)
Stage Hand, 1933 (Langdon)
Stage Irishman, 1968 (Cusack)
Stage Mother, 1933 (O'Sullivan)
Stage Stars Off Screen, 1925 (Buchanan)
Stage Struck, 1925 (Swanson)
Stage Struck, 1936 (Powell, D.; Wyman)
Stage Struck, 1958 (Fonda, H.; Greenwood; Marshall)
Stagecoach, 1939 (Carradine; Trevor; Wayne)
Stagecoach, 1966 (Ann-Margret; Crosby)
Stagecoach Driver and the Girl, 1915 (Mix)
Stagecoach Guard, 1915 (Mix)

Stagecoach to Dancer's Rock, 1962 (Landau)
Stagestruck, 1936 (Blondell)
Stagione all' inferno, 1971 (Stamp)
Stagione del nostro amore, 1965 (Aimée)
Stained Glass at Fairford, 1956 (Donat)
Staircase, 1969 (Burton; Harrison; Moore, Dudley)
Stairs of Sand, 1929 (Arthur; Beery)
Stairway for a Star, 1947 (Wilde)
Stairway to Heaven. *See* **Matter of Life and Death**, 1946
Stajio wa tenya wanya, 1957 (Kyo)
Stake Uncle Sam to Play Your Hand, 1918 (Normand)
Stakeout, 1987 (Dreyfuss; Whitaker)
Staking His Life. *See* Conversion of Frosty Blake, 1915
Stalag 17, 1953 (Holden)
Stalin, 1992 (Duvall; Schell, Maximilian)
Stalin's Funeral, 1991 (Redgrave, V.)
Stalingradskaya bitva, 1949 (Cherkassov)
Stalking Moon, 1968 (Peck; Saint)
Stallion Road, 1947 (Reagan)
Stalowe serca, 1947 (Łomnicki)
Stamboul Quest, 1934 (Brennan; Loy)
Stampede, 1911 (Pickford)
Stampeded. *See* Big Land, 1957
Stampen, 1955 (Björnstrand)
Stand and Deliver, 1928 (Crisp)
Stand and Deliver, 1988 (García; Olmos)
Stand by for Action, 1942 (Brennan; Laughton; Taylor, R.)
Stand by Me, 1986 (Dreyfuss)
Stand-In, 1937 (Blondell; Bogart; Howard, L.)
Stand Up and Be Counted, 1972 (Cooper)
Stand Up and Cheer, 1934 (Temple)
Stand Up and Fight, 1939 (Beery; Taylor, R.)
Standarte, 1977 (Cushing; Dagover)
Standing Room Only, 1944 (Goddard; MacMurray)
Stanley and Iris, 1990 (De Niro; Fonda, J.)
Stanley and Livingstone, 1939 (Brennan; Coburn, C.; Tracy)
Stanno tutti bene, 1990 (Mastroianni; Morgan)
Star, 1952 (Davis, B.; Hayden; Wood)
Star 80, 1983 (Robertson)
Star Boarder, 1914 (Chaplin, C.)
Star Boarder, 1917 (Laurel and Hardy)
Star Chamber, 1983 (Douglas, Michael)
Star Dust, 1940 (Darnell)
Star for a Night, 1936 (McDaniel; Trevor)
Star for Two, 1990 (Bacall; Quinn)
Star in the Dust, 1956 (Eastwood)
Star Is Born, 1937 (Gaynor; March; Menjou; Turner, L.; Bogart)
Star Is Born, 1954 (Garland; Marsh; Mason)
Star Is Born, 1976 (Streisand)
Star Knight. *See* Caballero del dragon, 1985
Star Maker, 1939 (Crosby)
Star Maker, 1981 (Griffith; Hudson)
Star Night at the Cocoanut Grove, 1935 (Crosby; Constantine)
Star of Captivating Happiness. *See* Zvezda plenitelnogo schastya, 1975
Star of Hong Kong. *See* Honkon no hoshi, 1962
Star of India, 1953 (Lom; Wilde)
Star of Midnight, 1935 (Powell, W.; Rogers, G.)
Star of the Sea, 1915 (Chaney)
Star Packer, 1934 (Wayne)
Star Quality, 1985 (York)
Star Said No. *See* Callaway Went Thataway, 1951
Star Slammer, 1988 (Carradine)
Star Spangled Rhythm, 1942 (Crosby; Goddard; Hayward; Hope; Ladd;
    Lamour; MacMurray; Milland; Powell, D.; Preston; Lake)
Star Spangled Salesman, 1968 (Three Stooges)
Star, The Orphan, and the Butcher. *See* Evlalie quitte les champs, 1973
Star Trek Generations, 1994 (Goldberg; McDowell)
Star Wars, 1977 (Cushing; Ford, H.; Guinness; Jones, James Earl)
Star without Light. *See* Étoile sans lumière, 1945
Star Witness, 1931 (Huston, W.)
Star!, 1968 (Andrews, J.; Scheider)

Stardust. *See* Polvere di stelle, 1973
Stardust Memories, 1980 (Allen; Stone)
Stardust on the Sage, 1942 (Autry)
Stark, 1985 (Hopper)
Stark System, 1980 (Volonté)
Stärker al die Liebe, 1938 (Wegener)
Stärkere, 1918 (Kortner)
Starlift, 1951 (Cagney; Constantine; Day; Scott, R.; Wyman)
Starman, 1984 (Bridges; Douglas, Michael)
Staroye Dudino. *See* Granitsa, 1935
Starring in Western Stuff, 1916 (Mix)
Stars and Bars, 1988 (Day-Lewis; Stanton)
Stars and Guitars. *See* Brazil, 1944
Stars and Stripes Forever, 1952 (Webb)
Stars Fell on Henrietta, 1995 (Duvall; Eastwood)
Stars in My Crown, 1950 (McCrea)
Stars Look Down, 1939 (Lockwood; Redgrave, M.)
Stars on Horseback, 1943 (Davis, B.)
Stars' War: The Flight of the Wild Geese, 1978 (Burton)
Starship Invasions. *See* Alien Encounter, 1976
Start Cheering, 1938 (Crawford, B.; Durante; Three Stooges)
Start the Revolution without Me, 1970 (Sutherland; Welles; Wilder)
Starting Over, 1979 (Bacon; Reynolds, B.)
Starving for Love, 1912-13 (White)
Stasera mi butto, 1967 (Giannini)
Stasera mi butto i due bagnani, 1968 (Giannini)
Stasera niente di nuovo, 1942 (Valli)
State Fair, 1933 (Ayres; Gaynor; Rogers, W.)
State Fair, 1945 (Andrews, D.)
State Fair, 1962 (Ann-Margret; Faye; Ferrer)
State of Emergency, 1986 (Sheen)
State of Grace, 1990 (Harris, E.; Meredith; Oldman; Penn; Turturro)
State of Siege. *See* Etat de siège, 1973
State of the Union, 1948 (Hepburn, K.; Lansbury; Menjou; Tracy)
State Secret, 1950 (Hawkins; Lom)
State Street Sadie, 1928 (Loy)
State's Attorney, 1932 (Barrymore, J.)
Stateline Motel. *See* Ultima chance, 1973
Station Content, 1918 (Swanson)
Station Master, 1917 (Laurel and Hardy)
Station S-T-A-R, 1932 (Wayne)
Station Six-Sahara, 1962 (Elliott)
Station West, 1948 (Moorehead; Powell, D.)
Statue, 1970 (Cleese; Niven)
Statue of Liberty, 1986 (Irons)
Stavisky, 1973 (Belmondo; Boyer; Depardieu)
Stay as You Are. *See* Cosi come sei, 1978
Stay Away, Joe, 1968 (Blondell; Meredith; Presley)
Stay Hungry, 1976 (Bridges; Field; Schwarzenegger)
Stay the Night, 1992 (Hershey)
Staying Alive, 1983 (Stallone; Travolta)
Staying on, 1980 (Howard, T.; Johnson)
Staying Together, 1989 (Grant, L.)
Stazione termini, 1953 (Cervi; Clift; Jones, Jennifer)
Steady Company, 1915 (Chaney)
Steal Big, Steal Little, 1995 (Arkin; García)
Stealers, 1920 (Shearer)
Stealing Beauty, 1996 (Irons; Marais)
Stealing Heaven, 1989 (Elliott)
Stealing Home, 1988 (Foster)
Steamboat Bill, Jr., 1928 (Keaton, B.)
Steamboat round the Bend, 1935 (Rogers, W.)
Steaming, 1984 (Dors)
Steaming, 1985 (Redgrave, V.)
Steel Cage, 1954 (O'Sullivan)
Steel Cowboy, 1978 (Griffith)
Steel Fist, 1951 (McDowall)
Steel Highway, 1931 (Astor)
Steel Magnolias, 1989 (Field; MacLaine; Roberts, J.; Shepard)
Steel Trap, 1952 (Cotten)
Steelyard Blues, 1972 (Fonda, J.; Sutherland)

Stein unter Steinen, 1916 (Jannings)
Steinbruch, 1942 (Schell, Maria)
Stella, 1950 (Mature; Mercouri; Midler)
Stella Dallas, 1925 (Colman)
Stella Dallas, 1937 (Stanwyck)
Stella emigranti, 1983 (Lollobrigida)
Stella Maris, 1918 (Pickford)
Stelle emigranti, 1983 (Cardinale)
Step Lively, 1917 (Lloyd)
Step Lively. *See* Count Your Change, 1919
Step Lively, 1944 (Menjou; Sidney)
Step Out of Line, 1970 (Falk)
Steppa, 1961 (Vanel)
Steppe, 1977 (Bondarchuk)
Steppe. *See* Steppa, 1961
Steppenwolf, 1974 (Sanda; Von Sydow)
Steppin' in Society, 1945 (Horton)
Stepping Fast, 1923 (Mix)
Stepping Out, 1991 (Minnelli; Winters)
Steps, 1984 (Papas)
Stepsisters, 1910-11 (White)
Steptoe and Son Ride Again, 1973 (Dors)
Sterbende Völker, 1922 (Kortner; Wegener)
Sterile Cuckoo, 1969 (Minnelli)
Sterling Metal. *See* Sporting Blood, 1940
Steuermann Holk, 1920 (Nielsen; Wegener)
Stevie, 1978 (Howard, T.; Jackson, G.)
Stew in the Caribbean. *See* Estouffade à la Carabei, 1967
Stick, 1985 (Reynolds, B.; Segal)
Stick Around, 1925 (Laurel and Hardy)
Sticky Affair, 1916 (Laurel and Hardy)
Stier von Olivera, 1921 (Jannings)
Stiletto, 1969 (Julia; Scheider)
Still Alarm, 1930 (Webb)
Still of the Night, 1982 (Scheider; Streep)
Stille nacht. *See* Magdalene, 1988
Stillwatch, 1987 (Dickinson)
Stilts. *See* Zancos, 1984
Stimme des Anderen, 1952 (Kortner)
Stimulantia, 1967 (Andersson, H.; Bergman; Björnstrand)
Sting, 1973 (Newman; Redford; Shaw)
Sting II, 1983 (Malden; Reed)
Stingaree, 1934 (Dunne)
Stips, 1951 (Fröhlich)
Stir Crazy, 1980 (Poitier; Pryor; Wilder)
Stitch in Time, 1963 (Wisdom)
Sto dvadtsat tysyach v god, 1929 (Maretskaya)
Stockade. *See* Cadence, 1989
Stockholm, 1977 (Zetterling)
Stolen Birthright, 1914 (White)
Stolen Bride, 1913 (Gish; Sweet)
Stolen Face, 1952 (Henreid)
Stolen Frontier. *See* Uloupená hranice, 1947
Stolen Glory, 1912 (Normand)
Stolen Goods, 1915 (Sweet)
Stolen Harmony, 1935 (Raft; Wyman)
Stolen Heaven, 1931 (Calhern)
Stolen Holiday, 1936 (Francis; Rains)
Stolen Hours, 1963 (Hayward)
Stolen Jools, 1932 (Beery; Brown; Chevalier; Dunne; Laurel and Hardy; Keaton, B.; Shearer)
Stolen Kisses. *See* Baisers volés, 1968
Stolen Life, 1939 (Bergner; Redgrave, M.)
Stolen Life, 1946 (Brennan; Davis, B.; Ford, G.)
Stolen Magic, 1915 (Normand)
Stolen Moccasins, 1913 (Mix)
Stolen Moments, 1920 (Valentino)
Stolen: One Husband, 1990 (Gould)
Stolz der 3 Kompagnie, 1931 (Walbrook)
Stone Age Romeos, 1955 (Three Stooges)
Stone Boy, 1984 (Close; Duvall)

Stone in the Mouth. *See* Pierre dans la bouche, 1983
Stone Killer, 1973 (Bronson)
Stone Pillow, 1985 (Ball)
Stones for Ibarra, 1988 (Close)
Stoning in Fulham County, 1988 (Pitt)
Stooge, 1953 (Lewis, Jerry; Martin, D.)
Stooge to Conga, 1943 (Three Stooges)
Stoogemania, 1986 (Three Stooges)
Stool Pigeon, 1915 (Chaney)
Stop Calling Me Baby! *See* Moi, Fleur Bleue, 1978
Stop, Look, and Listen, 1926 (Laurel and Hardy)
Stop Me before I Kill. *See* Full Treatment, 1961
Stop Polio, 1981 (Jackson, G.)
Stop Train 349. *See* Verspätung in Marienborn, 1963
Stop, You're Killing Me, 1952 (Crawford, B.; Dumont; Trevor)
Stop! Luke! Listen!, 1917 (Lloyd)
Stop! Or My Mom Will Shoot, 1992 (Stallone)
Stopover Tokyo, 1957 (O'Brien, E.)
Stopping the Show, 1932 (Chevalier)
Storch hat uns getraut, 1933 (Dagover)
Store. *See* Floorwalker, 1916
Storia, 1985 (Cardinale)
Storia di Piera, 1982 (Huppert; Mastroianni; Schygulla)
Storia del pugliato degli antichi ad oggi, 1974 (Brazzi)
Storia di una Capinera, 1993 (Redgrave, V.)
Storia di una donna, 1969 (Andersson, B.; Girardot)
Storia Semplice, 1991 (Volonté)
Storie d'amore, 1942 (Mastroianni)
Stork Bites Man, 1947 (Cooper)
Stork Club, 1945 (Fitzgerald)
Storm, 1916 (Sweet)
Storm, 1930 (Huston, J.)
Storm at Daybreak, 1933 (Francis; Huston, W.)
Storm Center, 1956 (Davis, B.)
Storm Fear, 1955 (Duryea; Grant, L.; Wilde)
Storm in a Teacup, 1937 (Harrison; Leigh, V.)
Storm in a Water Glass. *See* Blumenfrau von Lindenau, 1931
Storm over the Nile, 1955 (Lee, C.)
Storm Warning, 1951 (Day; Reagan; Rogers, G.)
Storm Within. *See* Parents terribles, 1948
Storms of Passion. *See* Stürme der Leidenschaft, 1931
Stormswept, 1923 (Beery)
Stormy Era. *See* Showa no inochi, 1968
Stormy Monday, 1988 (Griffith; Jones, T.)
Stormy Waters. *See* Remorques, 1941
Stormy Weather, 1943 (Robinson, B.)
Story from Chikamatsu. *See* Chikamatsu monogatari, 1954
Story in Scarlet, 1973 (Nowicki)
Story of a Girl, 1949 (Zhao Dan)
Story of a Love Story. *See* Impossible Objet, 1973
Story of a Mother. *See* Historien om en moder, 1979
Story of a Real Man, 1948 (Bondarchuk)
Story of a Recluse, 1987 (Granger)
Story of a Woman. *See* Storia di una donna, 1969
Story of a Woman. *See* I miei primi 40 anni, 1987
Story of Adèle H.. *See* Histoire d'Adèle H., 1975
Story of Alexander Graham Bell, 1939 (Ameche; Coburn, C.; Fonda, H.; Young, L.)
Story of Cinderella. *See* Slipper and the Rose, 1976
Story of Colonel Drake, 1955 (Price)
Story of David, 1960 (Pleasence)
Story of Dr. Ehrlich's Magic Bullet, 1939 (Calhern; Crisp; Gordon; Huston, J.)
Story of Dr. Wassell, 1944 (Constantine)
Story of Drunken Master. *See* Drunken Master, 1979
Story of Esther Costello, 1957 (Brazzi; Crawford, J.)
Story of G.I. Joe, 1945 (Meredith; Mitchum)
Story of Gilbert and Sullivan, 1953 (Finch)
Story of Hollywood, 1988 (Reynolds, B.)
Story of Irene and Vernon Castle, 1939 (Brennan)
Story of Jacob and Joseph, 1974 (Bates, A.)

Story of Louis Pasteur, 1935 (Muni)

Story of Mankind, 1957 (Carradine; Coburn, C.; Colman; Hopper; Horton; Lamarr; Lorre; Marx Brothers; Moorehead; Price)

Story of Papworth, 1936 (Carroll)

Story of Piera. See Storia di Piera, 1982

Story of Pretty Boy Floyd, 1974 (Sheen)

Story of Qiu Ju. See **Qiu Ju Da Guansi**, 1992

Story of Robin Hood and His Merrie Men, 1952 (Finch)

Story of Seabiscuit, 1949 (Fitzgerald; Temple)

Story of Temple Drake, 1933 (Carradine; Hopkins, M.; McDaniel)

Story of the Count of Monte Cristo. See Comte de Monte Cristo, 1961

Story of the First Christmas Snow, 1975 (Lansbury)

Story of the Turbulent Years. See Povest plamennykh, 1961

Story of Three Loves, 1953 (Barrymore, E.; Caron; Douglas, K.; Mason; Moorehead)

Story of Tosca. See Tosca, 1940

Story of Vernon and Irene Castle, 1939 (Astaire; Rogers, G.)

Story of Vickie. See Mädchenjahre einer Königen, 1954

Story of Will Rogers, 1952 (Cantor; Wyman)

Story of Women. See Affaire des femmes, 1989

Story on Page One, 1960 (Hayworth)

Storyville, 1992 (Robards)

Stowaway, 1932 (Wray)

Stowaway, 1936 (Faye; Temple; Young, R.)

Stowaway Girl. See Manuela, 1957

Stowaway in the Sky, 1962 (Lemmon)

Stowaway to the Moon, 1975 (Carradine)

Strada, 1954 (Masina; Quinn)

Stradivari, 1935 (Fröhlich)

Stradivarius, 1935 (Feuillère)

Straight and Narrow, 1918 (Laurel and Hardy)

Straight from the Heart, 1935 (Astor)

Straight from the Shoulder, 1921 (Laurel and Hardy)

Straight from the Shoulder, 1936 (Bellamy)

Straight Shooting, 1917 (Carey)

Straight Talk, 1992 (Woods)

Straight Time, 1978 (Bates, K.; Gilbert; Hoffman; Stanton)

Straight to Hell, 1987 (Hopper)

Straightaway, 1934 (Bond)

Strait-Jacket, 1964 (Crawford, J.)

Stranded, 1916 (Laurel and Hardy)

Stranded, 1935 (Francis)

Stranded, 1987 (O'Sullivan)

Stranded in Paris. See Artists and Models Abroad, 1938

Strange Affair, 1944 (Three Stooges)

Strange Affair of Uncle Harry. See Uncle Harry, 1945

Strange Affection. See Scamp, 1957

Strange Alibi, 1941 (Kennedy)

Strange Bedfellows, 1964 (Hudson; Terry-Thomas; Lollobrigida)

Strange Boarder, 1920 (Rogers, W.)

Strange Boarders, 1938 (Withers)

Strange Brew, 1983 (Von Sydow)

Strange Caravan. See Fighting Kentuckian, 1949

Strange Cargo, 1936 (Sanders)

Strange Cargo, 1940 (Crawford, J.; Gable; Lorre; Lukas)

Strange Case of Captain Ramper. See Ramper, der Tiermensch, 1927

Strange Case of Dr. Jekyll and Mr. Hyde, 1989 (Elliott; Homolka)

Strange Case of Dr. Rx, 1942 (Three Stooges)

Strange Case of the End of Civilisation as We Know It, 1977 (Cleese; Elliott)

Strange Confession. See Imposter, 1944

Strange Countess. See Seltsame Gräfin, 1961

Strange Days, 1995 (Bassett; Fiennes; Lewis, Juliette)

Strange Death of Adolf Hitler, 1943 (Kortner)

Strange Deception. See Cristo proibito, 1951

Strange Door, 1951 (Karloff; Laughton)

Strange Holiday, 1945 (Rains)

Strange Incident. See Ox-Bow Incident, 1942

Strange Interlude, 1932 (Gable; O'Sullivan; Young, R.)

Strange Interlude, 1988 (Branagh; Ferrer; Jackson, G.)

Strange Interval. See Strange Interlude, 1932

Strange Intruder, 1956 (Lupino)

Strange Lady in Town, 1955 (Andrews, D.; Garson)

Strange Love of Martha Ivers, 1946 (Douglas, K.; Stanwyck)

Strange Meeting, 1909 (Pickford)

Strange Monster of Strawberry Cove, 1971 (Meredith; Moorehead)

Strange Passion of a Kiss. See Lyubov silna na strastyou potseluya, 1916

Strange People, 1933 (Brennan)

Strange Place to Meet. See Drole d'endroit pour une rencontre, 1988

Strange Shadows in an Empty Room. See Tony Saitta, 1976

Strange Woman, 1946 (Lamarr; Sanders)

Stranger, 1917 (Laurel and Hardy)

Stranger, 1946 (Huston, J.; Robinson, E.; Welles; Young, L.)

Stranger, 1973 (Ayres)

Stranger. See Agantuk, 1991

Stranger. See Lo straniero, 1967

Stranger among Us, 1992 (Griffith)

Stranger and the Gunfighter, 1976 (Van Cleef)

Stranger Came Home, 1954 (Goddard)

Stranger from Venus, 1954 (Neal)

Stranger in Between. See Hunted, 1952

Stranger in My Arms, 1959 (Astor; Coburn, C.)

Stranger in the House, 1967 (Chaplin, G.; Mason)

Stranger in the House, 1990 (Stamp; Stanton)

Stranger in the House. See Inconnu dans al Maison, 1992

Stranger on Horseback, 1955 (Carradine; McCrea)

Stranger on My Land, 1988 (Jones, T.)

Stranger on the Prowl. See Imbarco a mezzanotte, 1952

Stranger on the Run, 1967 (Baxter; Duryea; Fonda, H.; Mineo)

Stranger on the Third Floor, 1940 (Lorre)

Stranger Than Love. See Stärker al die Liebe, 1938

Stranger Wore a Gun, 1953 (Borgnine; Marvin; Scott, R.; Trevor)

Stranger's Hand. See Mano dello straniero, 1953

Stranger's Return, 1933 (Barrymore, L.; Hopkins, M.)

Strangers, 1979 (Davis, B.)

Strangers in 7A, 1972 (Lupino)

Strangers in Love, 1932 (Francis; March)

Strangers in the House. See Inconnus dans la maison, 1949

Strangers May Kiss, 1931 (Montgomery; Shearer)

Strangers on a Train, 1951 (Walker)

Strangers When We Meet, 1960 (Douglas, K.; Matthau; Novak)

Strangers: The Story of a Mother and Daughter, 1979 (Rowlands)

Straniero, 1967 (Mastroianni)

Strapless, 1988 (Ganz)

Strapped, 1993 (Whitaker)

Straschnaia miest, 1913 (Mozhukin)

Strasnia pokoynik, 1912 (Mozhukin)

Strategia del ragno, 1969 (Valli)

Strategic Air Command, 1955 (Stewart)

Stratford Adventure, 1954 (Guinness)

Stratton Story, 1949 (Moorehead; Stewart)

Strauberg ist Da, 1978 (Piccoli)

Straw Dogs, 1971 (Hoffman)

Strawberry Blonde, 1941 (Cagney; De Havilland; Hayworth)

Strawberry Road, 1991 (Mifune)

Strawberry Roan, 1948 (Autry)

Stray Dog. See Nora-inu, 1949

Stream Line. See Linea del fiume, 1976

Streamlined Swing, 1938 (Keaton, B.)

Stree, 1972 (Chatterjee)

Street Angel, 1928 (Gaynor)

Street Angel. See Malu tianshi, 1937

Street Fighter, 1994 (Julia; Van Damme)

Street of Abandoned Children, 1929 (Negri)

Street of Chance, 1930 (Arthur; Francis; Powell, W.)

Street of Chance, 1942 (Meredith; Trevor)

Street of Forgotten Men, 1925 (Brooks, L.)

Street of Missing Men, 1939 (Carey)

Street of Shadows. See Mademoiselle Docteur, 1936

Street of Shadows, 1953 (Kendall)

Street of Shame. See **Akasen chitai**, 1956

Street of Sin, 1928 (Jannings; Wray)

Street of Sorrow. See Freudlose Gasse, 1925

Street of Women, 1932 (Francis)
Street Scene, 1931 (Sidney)
Street Scenes, 1970 (Keitel)
Street Singer, 1937 (Lockwood)
Street Smart, 1987 (Freeman)
Street War. *See* Paura in città, 1976
Street with No Name, 1948 (Widmark)
Streetcar Named Desire, 1951 (Brando; Leigh, V.; Malden)
Streetcar Named Desire, 1984 (Ann-Margret; Lange)
Streetfighter. *See* Hard Times, 1975
Streets of Fire, 1984 (Dafoe)
Streets of Gold, 1986 (Brandauer; Snipes)
Streets of Illusion, 1917 (Barthelmess)
Streets of L.A., 1979 (Woodward)
Streets of Laredo, 1949 (Holden)
Streets of New York, 1939 (Cooper)
Streets of San Francisco, 1972 (Douglas, Michael; Malden)
Streets of Shanghai, 1927 (Wong)
Streets of Sorrow. *See* Freudlose Gasse, 1925
Strega in amore, 1966 (Volonté)
Streghe, 1965 (Eastwood)
Streghe, 1967 (Girardot; Mangano; Sordi)
Streit um den Knaben Jo, 1937 (Dagover)
Stresemann, 1956 (Aimée)
Stress es tres tres, 1968 (Chaplin, G.)
Strictly Business, 1912-13 (White)
Strictly Business, 1991 (Jackson, S.)
Strictly Confidential. *See* Broadway Bill, 1934
Strictly Dishonorable, 1931 (Lukas)
Strictly Dishonorable, 1951 (Leigh, Janet)
Strictly Dynamite, 1934 (Durante)
Strictly for Pleasure. *See* Perfect Furlough, 1958
Strictly in the Groove, 1943 (O'Connor; Three Stooges)
Strictly Personal, 1933 (Calhern)
Strife over the Boy Jo. *See* Streit um den Knaben Jo, 1937
Strike Force, 1975 (Gere)
Strike It Rich, 1990 (Gielgud)
Strike Me Pink, 1936 (Cantor)
Strike Up the Band, 1940 (Garland; Rooney)
Strikers. *See* I compagni, 1963
Striking Distance, 1993 (Willis)
Strip, 1951 (Rooney)
Strip-Tease, 1976 (Rey; Stamp)
Stripes, 1981 (Candy; Murray; Oates)
Stripper, 1963 (Trevor; Woodward)
Striptease, 1996 (Moore, Demi; Reynolds, B.)
Strogoff, 1968 (Bergner)
Stroker Ace, 1983 (Reynolds, B.)
Stromboli, 1950 (Bergman)
Strong Boy, 1929 (McLaglen; Ryan, R.)
Strong Man, 1926 (Langdon)
Strong Medicine, 1979 (Julia)
Strong Medicine, 1986 (Neill)
Strong Revenge, 1913 (Normand)
Stronger, 1976 (Grant, L.)
Stronger Love. *See* 'Tween Two Loves, 1911
Stronger Mind, 1915 (Chaney)
Stronger Sex, 1931 (Lanchester)
Stronger than Desire, 1939 (Pidgeon)
Stronger Than Death, 1915 (Chaney)
Stronger Than Death, 1920 (Nazimova)
Stronger Than Fear. *See* Edge of Doom, 1950
Strongheart, 1914 (Barrymore, L.)
Strongheart, 1914 (Sweet)
Stronghold, 1952 (Lake)
Struggle for Life. *See* Küzdelem a letert, 1918
Struggle in the Nile. *See* Sera's fil Nil, 1959
Struggle in the Pier. *See* Sera'a fil Mina, 1955
Struggle in the Steeple. *See* Tools of Providence, 1915
Struggle in the Valley. *See* Sera's fil Wadi, 1953
Struktura kryształu, 1969 (Olbrychski)

Strumpet City, 1980 (Cusack)
Studenci, 1916 (Negri)
Student of Prague. *See* Student von Prag, 1926
Student Prince. *See* Alt-Heidelberg, 1923
Student Prince, 1927 (Shearer)
Student Prince, 1954 (Calhern)
Student Prince in Old Heidelberg, 1927 (Novarro)
Student Tour, 1934 (Durante; Eddy; Grable)
Student von Prag, 1913 (Wegener)
Student von Prag, 1926 (Krauss; Veidt)
Student von Prag, 1935 (Walbrook)
Studio Murder Mystery, 1928 (March)
Studio Stoops, 1950 (Three Stooges)
Studs Lonigan, 1960 (Nicholson)
Study in Scarlet, 1933 (Wong)
Study in Terror, 1965 (Quayle)
Stuff, 1985 (Aiello)
Stumme, 1975 (Schygulla)
Stunde der Versuchung, 1936 (Fröhlich; Wegener)
Stunt Man, 1980 (Hershey; O'Toole)
Stuntman, 1969 (Lollobrigida)
Stuntwoman. *See* Animal, 1977
Stupid Bom. *See* Dum Bom, 1953
Sturm in Wasserglas. *See* Blumenfrau von Lindenau, 1931
Stürme der Leidenschaft, 1931 (Jannings)
Stürme des lebens, 1918 (Krauss)
Stydno skazat, 1930 (Maretskaya)
Su exelencia, 1966 (Cantinflas)
Su-muru, 1967 (Kinski)
Sub-A-Dub-Dub. *See* Hello Down There, 1968
Subah, 1983 (Patil)
Subarashiki musumetachi, 1959 (Tanaka)
Subduing of Mrs. Nag, 1911 (Normand)
Sube y bajo, 1958 (Cantinflas)
Subject Was Roses, 1968 (Neal; Sheen)
Submarine Command, 1951 (Holden)
Submarine D-1, 1937 (Crawford, B.)
Submarine Patrol, 1938 (Bond; Carradine)
Submarine X-1, 1968 (Caan)
Subterraneans, 1960 (Caron; McDowall)
Subway, 1985 (Adjani)
Succès de la prestidigitation. *See* Que peut-il avoir? Max escamoteur, 1912
Success, 1923 (Astor)
Success, 1991 (Keaton, D.)
Success. *See* American Success Company, 1980
Success at Any Price, 1934 (Horton)
Success Is the Best Revenge, 1984 (Aimée; Hurt, J.; Piccoli)
Successful Calamity, 1932 (Astor; Scott, R.)
Successful Failure, 1913 (Beery)
Successo, 1963 (Aimée; Gassman; Trintignant)
Such a Little Queen, 1914 (Crisp; Pickford)
Such a Pretty Cloud, 1971 (Schell, Maria)
Such Good Friends, 1971 (Meredith)
Such High Mountains, 1974 (Bondarchuk)
Such Is Life, 1915 (Chaney)
Such Men Are Dangerous, 1930 (Lugosi)
Such Men Are Dangerous. *See* Racers, 1955
Sucker. *See* Life of Jimmy Dolan, 1933
Sucre, 1978 (Depardieu; Piccoli)
Sudario a la medida. *See* Candidato per un assassino, 1969
Sudba cheloveka, 1959 (Bondarchuk)
Sudden Death, 1995 (Van Damme)
Sudden Fear, 1952 (Crawford, J.; Grahame; Palance)
Sudden Impact, 1983 (Eastwood)
Sudden Money, 1939 (Crawford, B.)
Suddenly, 1954 (Hayden; Sidney)
Suddenly It's Spring, 1947 (Goddard; MacMurray)
Suddenly Last Summer, 1959 (Clift; Hepburn, K.; Smith; Taylor, E.)
Suddenly, Love, 1978 (Ayres; Bennett)
Suddenly, One Day. *See* Ek Din Achanak, 1988
Suddenly Single, 1971 (Moorehead)

Suds, 1920 (Pickford)
Sudur Niharika, 1975 (Chatterjee)
Sue My Lawyer, 1938 (Langdon)
Sueno del Mono Loco, 1989 (Richardson, M.)
Suez, 1938 (Power; Young, L.)
Suffit d'une fois, 1946 (Feuillère)
Suffrageten, 1913 (Nielsen)
Suffragette Minstrels, 1913 (Barrymore, L.)
Sugar Daddies, 1927 (Laurel and Hardy)
Sugar Hill. See Harlem, 1993
Sugarfoot, 1951 (Massey; Scott, R.)
Sugarland Express, 1974 (Hawn)
Sugata Sanshiro, 1943 (Shimura)
Sugata Sanshiro, 1955 (Yamamura)
Sugata Sanshiro, 1965 (Mifune; Okada)
Suicide Battalion, 1944 (Huston, W.)
Suicide Club. See Klub nravstvennosti, 1915
Suicide Fleet, 1931 (Rogers, G.)
Suicide Run. See Too Late the Hero, 1969
Suicide Squadron. See Dangerous Moonlight, 1941
Suicide Troops of the Watchtower. See Boro no kesshitai, 1942
Suicide's Wife, 1979 (Dickinson)
Suiko-den, 1942 (Takamine)
Suivez cet homme!, 1953 (Blier)
Suivez-moi, jeune homme, 1957 (Gélin)
Suivez Mon Regard, 1986 (Audran)
Sukumar Ray, 1987 (Chatterjee)
Sukyandaru, 1950 (Shimura)
Sul Ponte dei Sospiri, 1952 (Rosay)
Sullivan's Travels, 1941 (Lake; McCrea)
Sullivans, 1944 (Baxter; Bond)
Sultan's Wife, 1917 (Swanson)
Sultane de l'amour, 1919 (Modot)
Sultans, 1965 (Gélin; Jourdan; Lollobrigida; Noiret)
Summer and Smoke, 1961 (Page)
Summer Battle of Osaka. See Osaka natsu no jin, 1937
Summer City, 1977 (Gibson)
Summer Fires. See Mademoiselle, 1966
Summer Flirtation, 1910-11 (White)
Summer Guests. See Sommergäste, 1975
Summer Heat, 1987 (Bates, K.)
Summer Holiday, 1948 (Huston, W.; Moorehead; Rooney)
Summer House, 1993 (Moreau)
Summer Is Short. See Kort är Sommaren, 1962
Summer Lightning. See Scudda Hoo! Scudda Hay!, 1948
Summer Love, 1958 (Wray)
Summer Madness. See Summertime, 1955
Summer Manoeuvres. See Grandes Manoeuvres, 1955
Summer of Miss Forbes. See Verano de la Señorita Forbes, 1988
Summer of Silence. See Sommerfuglene, 1974
Summer of the 17th Doll. See Season of Passion, 1959
Summer Place, 1959 (Kennedy)
Summer Place Wanted. See Sommarnöje sökes, 1957
Summer Rental, 1985 (Candy)
Summer Solstice, 1981 (Fonda, H.)
Summer Solstice, 1983 (Loy)
Summer Stock, 1950 (Garland; Kelly, Gene)
Summer Storm, 1944 (Darnell; Horton; Sanders)
Summer Story, 1988 (York)
Summer Tables. See Racconti d'estate, 1958
Summer to Remember. See Seryozha, 1960
Summer Wishes, Winter Dreams, 1973 (Woodward)
Summer with Monika. See Sommaren med Monika, 1953
Summer's Lease, 1989 (Gielgud)
Summerspell, 1983 (Penn)
Summertime, 1955 (Brazzi; Hepburn, K.)
Summertime Killer, 1973 (Malden)
Summertree, 1971 (Douglas, K.; Douglas, Michael)
Summit, 1968 (Volonté)
Sumurun, 1920 (Negri; Wegener)
Sun Above, Death Below. See Sogeki, 1968

Sun Also Rises, 1957 (Dalio; Flynn; Gardner; Power)
Sun Also Rises, 1984 (Audran)
Sun Comes Up, 1949 (MacDonald)
Sun Never Sets, 1939 (Rathbone)
Sun Shines Bright, 1953 (Marsh)
Sun Valley Serenade, 1940 (Henie)
Suna no onna, 1963 (Okada)
Sunburn, 1979 (Matthau)
Sunday, Bloody Sunday, 1971 (Day-Lewis; Finch; Jackson, G.)
Sunday Dinner for a Soldier, 1944 (Baxter)
Sunday Father, 1973 (Hoffman)
Sunday in New York, 1963 (Fonda, J.; Robertson)
Sunday in September. See Söndag i september, 1963
Sunday in the Country, 1975 (Borgnine)
Sunday Lovers, 1981 (Elliott; Wilder)
Sunday Punch, 1942 (Gardner)
Sunday Pursuit, 1990 (Zetterling)
Sunday Woman. See Donna della domenica, 1976
Sunden der Väter, 1912 (Nielsen)
Sünderin, 1950 (Fröhlich)
Sundige Mutter, 1918 (Veidt)
Sündige Hof, 1932 (Rasp)
Sundown, 1941 (Carey; Sanders; Tierney)
Sundown Rider, 1933 (Bond)
Sundown Slim, 1920 (Carey)
Sundowners, 1950 (Preston)
Sundowners, 1960 (Kerr; Mitchum; Ustinov)
Sunflower. See I girasoli, 1969
Sunflower Girl. See Himawari-musume, 1953
Sunkist Stars at Palm Springs, 1936 (Keaton, B.)
Sunny, 1941 (Horton; Neagle)
Sunny Side Up, 1926 (Crisp)
Sunny Side Up, 1929 (Brown; Cooper; Gaynor)
Sunnyside, 1919 (Chaplin, C.; Purviance)
Sunrise, 1927 (Gaynor)
Sunrise at Campobello, 1960 (Bellamy; Garson)
Sunrise—A Song of Two Humans. See **Sunrise**, 1927
Sunset, 1988 (Garner; McDowell; Willis)
Sunset Boulevard, 1950 (Holden; Keaton, B.; Swanson)
Sunset Boys. See Pakten, 1996
Sunset Cove, 1978 (Carradine)
Sunset Derby, 1927 (Astor)
Sunset Heat, 1992 (Hopper)
Sunset in El Dorado, 1945 (Dumont; Rogers, R.)
Sunset in the West, 1950 (Rogers, R.)
Sunset in Wyoming, 1941 (Autry)
Sunset on the Desert, 1942 (Rogers, R.)
Sunset Pass, 1933 (Carey; Scott, R.)
Sunset Serenade, 1942 (Rogers, R.)
Sunshine Alley, 1917 (Marsh)
Sunshine and Shadow, 1914 (Talmadge)
Sunshine Boys, 1975 (Matthau)
Sunshine Christmas, 1977 (Hershey)
Sunshine Follows Rain. See Driver dagg faller Regn, 1946
Sunshine in Poverty Row, 1910 (White)
Sunshine Nan, 1918 (Barthelmess)
Sunshine Patriots, 1968 (Robertson; Sutherland)
Sunshine Sue, 1910 (Crisp)
Suo modo di fare, 1968 (Segal)
Suo nome faceva tremare ... Interpol in allarme! See Dio, sei proprio un padreterno, 1973
Suonatrice ambulante, 1912 (Bertini)
Suor letizia, 1956 (Magnani)
Suor omicidi, 1978 (Valli)
Super, 1991 (Pesci)
Super Ace. See As des as, 1982
Super Fuzz, 1981 (Borgnine)
Super Mario Bros., 1993 (Hopper; Hoskins)
Super Secret Service, 1953 (Sellers)
Superchick, 1973 (Carradine)
Supercolpo da 7 miliard, 1966 (Andrews, D.)

Supercop: Police Story III, 1992 (Chan)
Supercop 2. *See* Police Story 4: Project S, 1993
Supergirl, 1984 (Dunaway; Farrow; O'Toole)
Superman, 1978 (Brando; Cooper; Ford, G.; Hackman; Howard, T.; Schell, Maria; Stamp; York)
Superman II, 1980 (Cooper; Hackman; Stamp; York)
Superman III, 1983 (Cooper; Hackman; Pryor)
Superman IV: The Quest for Peace, 1987 (Cooper; Hackman; York)
Supernatural, 1933 (Lombard; Scott, R.)
Supersabio, 1948 (Cantinflas)
Supersnooper. *See* Super Fuzz, 1981
Superstar: The Life and Times of Andy Warhol, 1990 (Hopper; Winters)
Supertestimone, 1971 (Vitti)
Supertrain, 1979 (Crawford, B.)
Supper. *See* Souper, 1992
Support Your Local Gunfighter, 1971 (Blondell; Garner)
Support Your Local Sheriff, 1968 (Brennan; Dern; Garner)
Suppose They Gave a War and Nobody Came?, 1970 (Ameche; Borgnine; Curtis, T.)
Sur la terre comme au ciel. *See* Entre el cielo y la tierre, 1993
Sur le Sentier de la guerre, 1909 (Modot)
Sur toute la gamme, 1954 (Chevalier)
Sur un arbre perché, 1971 (Chaplin, G.)
Suraag, 1982 (Azmi)
Surcouf, 1924 (Artaud)
Sure Shot Morgan, 1919 (Carey)
Sure Thing, 1985 (Robbins)
Surf. *See* Brannigar, 1935
Surf. *See* Shiosai, 1954
Suri Lanka no ai to wakare, 1976 (Takamine)
Surmenés, 1957 (Cassel)
Suronin Chuya, 1930 (Yamada)
Surprise Package, 1960 (Brynner)
Surprise Sock. *See* Chaussette surprise, 1978
Surprises de la radio, 1939 (Gélin)
Surrender, 1927 (Mozhukin)
Surrender, 1931 (Bellamy)
Surrender, 1950 (Brennan)
Surrender, 1987 (Caine; Cooper; Field)
Surrounded by Women. *See* Between Two Women, 1937
Survival. *See* Glanz und Elend der Kurtisanen, 1927
Survival. *See* Guide, 1965
Survival Run, 1977 (Milland)
Surviving, 1985 (Burstyn)
Surviving Picasso, 1995 (Hopkins, A.)
Survivor, 1980 (Cotten)
Survivors, 1983 (Matthau; Williams, R.)
Susan and God, 1940 (Crawford, J.; Hayworth; March)
Susan Lenox, Her Fall and Rise, 1931 (Gable; Garbo)
Susan Slept Here, 1954 (Powell, D.; Reynolds, D.)
Susanna Pass, 1949 (Rogers, R.)
Susannah of the Mounties, 1939 (Lockwood; Scott, R.; Temple)
Susie Steps Out, 1946 (Dumont)
Susman, 1986 (Azmi)
Suspect, 1944 (Laughton)
Suspect, 1960 (Cushing; Pleasence)
Suspect, 1987 (Cher; Neeson; Quaid)
Suspects, 1957 (Vanel)
Suspended Ordeal, 1914 (Arbuckle)
Suspended Step of the Stork, 1991 (Moreau)
Suspicion, 1941 (Fontaine; Grant, C.)
Suspiria, 1977 (Bennett; Valli)
Sussie, 1945 (Björnstrand)
Sussurro nel buio, 1976 (Cotten)
Susume dokuritsu-ki, 1943 (Hasegawa; Mori)
Sutjeska, 1972 (Burton; Papas; Welles)
Sutradhar, 1987 (Patil)
Sutter's Gold, 1936 (Carey)
Suzanna, 1922 (Normand)
Suzukake no sampo-michi, 1959 (Tsukasa; Mori)
Suzy, 1936 (Grant, C.; Harlow)

Svadba, 1944 (Maretskaya)
Svart Gryning, 1987 (Andersson, B.)
Svarta palmkroner, 1967 (Andersson, B.; Von Sydow)
Svarta rosor, 1945 (Dahlbeck)
Svarte fugler, 1983 (Andersson, B.)
Svegliati e uccidi, 1966 (Volonté)
Svengali, 1927 (Wegener)
Svengali, 1931 (Barrymore, J.; Crisp)
Svengali, 1983 (Foster; Hunter; O'Toole)
Svensk tiger, 1948 (Björnstrand)
Svigersønnerne. *See* Swiegersöhne, 1926
Svy Dager for Elisabeth, 1927 (Henie)
Swami, 1977 (Azmi)
Swami Dada, 1982 (Anand)
Swamp, 1921 (Hayakawa)
Swamp Fire, 1946 (Weissmuller)
Swamp Thing, 1982 (Jourdan)
Swamp Water, 1941 (Andrews, D.; Baxter; Bond; Brennan; Carradine; Huston, W.)
Swan, 1925 (Menjou)
Swan, 1956 (Guinness; Jourdan; Kelly, Grace; Moorehead)
Swan Princess, 1994 (Cleese; Palance)
Swan Song, 1992 (Branagh; Gielgud)
Swanee River, 1939 (Ameche; Jolson)
Swann in Love, 1984 (Delon; Irons)
Swap, 1980 (De Niro)
Swaralipi, 1961 (Chatterjee)
Swarg narak, 1978 (Azmi)
Swarm, 1978 (Caine; De Havilland; Ferrer; Fonda, H.; Grant, L.; MacMurray; Widmark)
Swashbuckler, 1976 (Bujold; Huston, A.; Jones, James Earl; Shaw)
Swashbuckler, 1984 (Belmondo)
Swastika Savages. *See* Hell's Bloody Devils, 1970
Swat the Crook, 1919 (Lloyd)
Swayambara, 1961 (Chatterjee)
Swedenhielms, 1935 (Bergman)
Swedes in America, 1943 (Bergman)
Swedish Fly Girls. *See* Christa, 1970
Swedish Mistress. *See* Älskarinnan, 1962
Swedish Tiger. *See* Svensk tiger, 1948
Swedish Wildcats. *See* Groove Room, 1974
Sweedie and Her Dog, 1915 (Beery)
Sweedie and the Double Exposure, 1914 (Beery)
Sweedie and the Hypnotist, 1914 (Beery)
Sweedie and the Janitor, 1916 (Beery)
Sweedie and the Lord, 1914 (Beery)
Sweedie and the Sultan's Present, 1915 (Beery)
Sweedie and the Trouble Maker, 1914 (Beery)
Sweedie at the Fair, 1914 (Beery)
Sweedie Collects for Charity, 1915 (Beery)
Sweedie Goes to College, 1915 (Beery; Swanson)
Sweedie in Vaudeville, 1915 (Beery)
Sweedie Learns to Ride, 1915 (Beery)
Sweedie Learns to Swim, 1914 (Beery)
Sweedie Springs a Surprise, 1914 (Beery)
Sweedie, the Swatter, 1914 (Beery)
Sweedie's Clean-Up, 1914 (Beery)
Sweedie's Finish, 1915 (Beery)
Sweedie's Hero, 1915 (Beery)
Sweedie's Hopeless Love, 1915 (Beery)
Sweedie's Skate, 1914 (Beery)
Sweedie's Suicide, 1915 (Beery)
Sweekar kiya maine, 1983 (Azmi)
Sweeney II, 1978 (Elliott)
Sweeney Todd, 1982 (Lansbury)
Sweepings, 1933 (Barrymore, L.)
Sweet Adeline, 1935 (Calhern; Dunne)
Sweet Aloes. *See* Give Me Your Heart, 1936
Sweet and Hot, 1958 (Three Stooges)
Sweet and Lowdown, 1944 (Darnell)
Sweet and Sour. *See* Dragées au poivre, 1963

Sweet and Twenty, 1909 (Pickford)
Sweet as You Are, 1987 (Neeson; Richardson, M.)
Sweet Bird of Youth, 1962 (Newman; Page; Taylor, E.)
Sweet Charity, 1969 (MacLaine)
Sweet Country, 1987 (Papas)
Sweet Devil, 1938 (Buchanan)
Sweet Dreams, 1985 (Harris, E.; Lange)
Sweet Heart's Dance, 1988 (Sarandon)
Sweet Hostage, 1975 (Sheen)
Sweet Hunters, 1969 (Hayden)
Sweet Justice, 1993 (Rooney)
Sweet Kitty Bellairs, 1930 (Pidgeon)
Sweet Liberty, 1986 (Caine; Gish; Hoskins; Pfeiffer)
Sweet Memories of Yesterday, 1911 (Pickford)
Sweet Revenge, 1913 (Beery)
Sweet Revenge, 1987 (Landau)
Sweet Rosie O'Grady, 1943 (Grable; Menjou; Young, R.)
Sweet Sixteen. See Futures vedettes, 1954
Sweet Smell of Success, 1957 (Curtis, T.; Lancaster)
Sweet Sweat. See Amai shiru, 1964
Sweet Woman. See Sladkaya zhenzhchina, 1976
Sweetheart of Sigma Chi, 1933 (Grable)
Sweetheart of the Campus, 1941 (Keeler)
Sweethearts, 1938 (Eddy)
Sweethearts, 1938 (MacDonald)
Swept Away .... See Travolti da un insolito destino nell'azzurro mare d'agosto,
    1974
Swiegersöhne, 1926 (Madsen and Schenstrøm)
Swift Current. See Gekiryu, 1952
Swim Princess, 1928 (Lombard)
Swimmer, 1968 (Lancaster)
Swimming Pool. See Piscine, 1969
Swimsuit, 1989 (Charisse)
Swindle. See Bidone, 1955
Swindlers. See I magliari, 1959
Swing Fever, 1943 (Gardner)
Swing High, Swing Low, 1937 (Lamour; Lombard; MacMurray; Quinn)
Swing Kids, 1992 (Branagh; Hershey)
Swing Parade of 1946, 1946 (Three Stooges)
Swing Shift, 1984 (Harris, E.; Hawn; Hunter)
Swing, Teacher, Swing. See College Swing, 1938
Swing Time, 1936 (Astaire; Rogers, G.)
Swing with Bing, 1940 (Crosby)
Swing Your Lady, 1938 (Bogart; Reagan)
Swing Your Partners, 1918 (Lloyd)
Swinger, 1966 (Ann-Margret)
Swingin' on a Rainbow, 1945 (Langdon)
Swingin' Summer, 1965 (Welch)
Swinging at the Castle. See Det svänger på slottet, 1959
Swiss Conspiracy, 1977 (Milland)
Swiss Family Robinson, 1940 (Welles)
Swiss Family Robinson, 1960 (Hayakawa; Mills)
Swiss Miss, 1938 (Laurel and Hardy)
Switch, 1991 (Barkin)
Switch Tower, 1913 (Barrymore, L.)
Switches and Sweeties, 1919 (Laurel and Hardy)
Switching Channels, 1988 (Reynolds, B.; Turner, K.)
Sword for Hire. See Sengoku-burai, 1952
Sword in the Desert, 1949 (Andrews, D.)
Sword of Doom. See Daibosatsu toge, 1966
Sword of Gideon, 1986 (Steiger)
Sword of Lancelot. See Lancelot and Guinevere, 1963
Sword of Sherwood Forest, 1960 (Cushing; Reed)
Sword of the Conqueror. See Rosemunda e Alboino, 1961
Sword of the Ninja. See Challenge, 1982
Sword of the Valiant: The Legend of Gawain and the Green Knight, 1983
    (Connery; Cushing; Howard, T.)
Swords of Blood. See Cartouche, 1962
Swordsman of Siena. See Lo spadaccino di Sienna, 1963
Sworn Enemy, 1936 (Quinn; Young, R.)
Sworn to Silence, 1987 (Neeson)

S/Y Glaedjen, 1989 (Olin)
S/Y Joy. See S/Y Glaedjen, 1989
Sybil, 1976 (Field; Woodward)
Sydenham Plan, 1949 (Ferrer)
Sylvia, 1965 (O'Brien, E.)
Sylvia and the Ghost. See Sylvie et le fantôme, 1945
Sylvia and the Phantom. See Sylvie et le fantôme, 1945
Sylvia Scarlett, 1935 (Grant, C.; Hepburn, K.)
Sylvie et le fantôme, 1945 (Tati)
Symphonie der Liebe, 1933 (Lamarr)
Symphonie fantastique, 1942 (Barrault; Berry; Blier)
Symphonie pastorale, 1946 (Morgan)
Symphonie pour un massacre, 1961 (Vanel)
Symphony in Two Flats, 1930 (Novello)
Symphony of Love. See Symphonie der Liebe, 1933
Symphony of Love. See Fruhlingssinfonie, 1985
Symphony of Six Million, 1932 (Dunne)
Synanon, 1965 (O'Brien, E.)
Syncopation, 1942 (Cooper; Menjou)
Synnöve Solbakken, 1957 (Andersson, H.)
Syskonbädd 1782, 1965 (Andersson, B.; Björnstrand)
System, 1964 (Reed)
System bouboule. See Deux Combinards, 1937
System ohne Schatten, 1983 (Ganz)
Szep magyar komedia, 1970 (Tyszkiewicz)
Szinèszno, 1920 (Lukas)
Szklana góra, 1960 (Tyszkiewicz)
T. R. Baskin, 1971 (Caan)
T. Rex, 1995 (Goldberg; Mueller-Stahl)
T.G.I.F., 1967 (Arkin)
T'amero sempre, 1943 (Berry; Cervi; Valli)
T'amerò sempre, 1933 (Cervi)
T'es fou, Marcel, 1974 (Montand)
Ta Inczacy Tastrzab, 1977 (Tyszkiewicz)
Täällä Alkaa Seikkilu. See Här börjar äventyret, 1965
Tabarin, 1957 (Piccoli)
Tabi no hito, 1931 (Yamada)
Tabigaeru kokyo no uta, 1932 (Hasegawa)
Table aux crèves, 1951 (Fernandel)
Table for Five, 1983 (Costner; Voight)
Table tournante, 1989 (Aimée)
Taboo. See Tabu, 1977
Taboos of the World. See I tabù, 1965
Tabù, 1965 (Price)
Tabu, 1977 (Björnstrand)
Tacaszi vihar, 1918 (Lugosi)
Tacones Lejanos, 1991 (Abril)
Tadaima shinsatsu-chu, 1964 (Tsukasa)
Tadanao-kyo gyojo-ki, 1930 (Yamada)
Taenk på ett tal, 1969 (Andersson, B.)
Tag till Himlen, 1989 (Coburn, J.)
Tag: The Assassination Game, 1982 (Whitaker)
Tagebuch einer Verliebten, 1953 (Schell, Maria)
Tagebuch einer Verlorenen, 1918 (Krauss; Veidt)
Tagebuch einer Verlorenen, 1929 (Brooks, L.; Rasp)
Tagebuch für einen Mörder, 1988 (Mueller-Stahl)
Taggart, 1964 (Duryea)
Tagori, 1985 (Chatterjee)
Taifu-ken no onna, 1948 (Yamamura)
Taiheiyo hitoribotchi, 1963 (Mori; Tanaka)
Taiheiyo kiseki no sakusen: Kisuka, 1965 (Yamamura)
Taiheiyo no arashi, 1960 (Mifune; Shimura)
Taiheiyo no tsubasa, 1963 (Mifune)
Taiheiyo no washi, 1953 (Mifune)
Taiheiyo senso to himeyurri butai, 1962 (Yamamura)
Taiheyo kiseki no sakusen Kiska, 1965 (Mifune)
Taiko-ki, 1958 (Yamada)
Tail Gunner Joe, 1977 (Carradine; Meredith; Neal)
Tail Spin, 1939 (Faye; Wyman)
Tailor from Torzhok. See Zakroishchik iz Torzhka, 1925
Tailor's Maid. See Pari e figli, 1957

Tarakanowa, 1938 (Magnani)
Tarana, 1951 (Kumar)
Tarang, 1984 (Patil)
Tarantol dal ventre nero, 1971 (Giannini)
Tarantula, 1955 (Eastwood)
Taras Balba, 1962 (Brynner; Curtis, T.)
Taras Shevchenko, 1951 (Bondarchuk)
Tarass Boulba, 1936 (Darrieux)
Target, 1985 (Dillon; Hackman)
Target Eagle, 1984 (Von Sydow)
Target for Killing. See Geheimnis der gelben Mönche, 1966
Target for Scandal. See Washington Story, 1952
Target in the Sun. See Man Who Would Not Die, 1975
Target Zero, 1955 (Bronson)
Targets, 1968 (Karloff)
Tarka the Otter, 1978 (Ustinov)
Tarnish, 1924 (Colman)
Tarnished Angel, 1938 (Miller)
Tarnished Angels, 1957 (Hudson; Malone)
Tarot, 1973 (Rey)
Tarot, 1986 (Vogler)
Tarots, 1972 (Grahame)
Tarps Elin, 1956 (Dahlbeck)
Tars and Stripes, 1935 (Keaton, B.)
Tartari, 1960 (Mature; Welles)
Tartarin de Tarascon, 1934 (Raimu)
Tartars. See I tartari, 1961
Tartassati, 1959 (Fabrizi)
Tartu. See Adventures of Tartu, 1943
Tartüff, 1925 (Dagover; Jannings; Krauss)
Tartuffe, 1984 (Depardieu)
Tarzan and His Mate, 1934 (O'Sullivan; Weissmuller)
Tarzan and Jane Regained ... Sort of, 1963 (Hopper)
Tarzan and the Amazons, 1945 (Weissmuller)
Tarzan and the Golden Lion, 1927 (Karloff)
Tarzan and the Huntress, 1947 (Weissmuller)
Tarzan and the Leopard Woman, 1946 (Weissmuller)
Tarzan and the Mermaids, 1948 (Weissmuller)
Tarzan Escapes, 1936 (O'Sullivan; Weissmuller)
Tarzan Finds a Son, 1939 (O'Sullivan; Weissmuller)
Tarzan in Manhattan, 1990 (Curtis, T.)
Tarzan of the Apes. See Tarzan, The Ape Man, 1932
Tarzan, the Ape Man, 1932 (O'Sullivan)
Tarzan, the Ape Man, 1981 (Harris, R.)
Tarzan the Magnificent, 1960 (Carradine)
Tarzan, The Ape Man, 1932 (Weissmuller)
Tarzan Triumphs, 1943 (Weissmuller)
Tarzan versus I.B.M.. See Alphaville, 1965
Tarzan's Desert Mystery, 1943 (Weissmuller)
Tarzan's Greatest Adventure, 1959 (Connery; Quayle)
Tarzan's New York Adventure, 1942 (O'Sullivan; Weissmuller)
Tarzan's Secret Treasure, 1941 (Fitzgerald; O'Sullivan; Weissmuller)
Tashunga, 1995 (Caan)
Task Force, 1949 (Brennan; Constantine)
Tassels in the Air, 1938 (Three Stooges)
Tassinaro, 1983 (Sordi)
Tassinaro a New York, 1987 (Sordi)
Taste for Women. See Aimez-vous les femmes?, 1964
Taste of Evil, 1971 (McDowall; Stanwyck)
Taste of Fear, 1961 (Lee, C.)
Taste the Blood of Dracula, 1970 (Lee, C.)
Tata Mia, 1986 (Maura)
Tateshi Danpei, 1950 (Yamada)
Tateshi Danpei, 1962 (Tanaka)
Tatort—Bienzle und der Biedermann, 1992 (Vogler)
Tatort—Eine todsichere Falle, 1995 (Cassel)
Tatort—Freiwild, 1984 (Mueller-Stahl)
Tatoué, 1968 (Gabin)
Tatsu. See Toburoku no Tatsu, 1962
Tatsumaki bugyo, 1959 (Yamamura)
Tattered Web, 1971 (Crawford, B.)

Tattoo, 1981 (Dern)
Tausend Augen, 1984 (Mueller-Stahl)
Tausend Worte Deutsch, 1930 (Madsen and Schenstrøm)
Tavaszni szerelem, 1921 (Banky)
Tavern of Tragedy, 1914 (Crisp)
Taverna rossa, 1939 (Valli)
Taverne du poisson couronne, 1947 (Berry)
Taxandria, 1996 (Mueller-Stahl)
Taxi, 1953 (Page)
Taxi Dancer, 1927 (Crawford, J.)
Taxi Driver, 1954 (Anand)
Taxi Driver, 1976 (De Niro; Foster; Keitel)
Taxi Driver. See Tassinaro, 1983
Taxi Driver in New York. See Tassinaro a New York, 1987
Taxi mauve, 1977 (Astaire; Noiret; Ustinov)
Taxi Talks, 1930 (Tracy)
Taxi!, 1932 (Cagney; Raft; Young, L.)
Taxi! Taxi!, 1927 (Horton)
Taxichauffeur Bänz, 1957 (Schell, Maximilian)
Taza, Son of Cochise, 1954 (Hudson)
Tchan, 1979 (Brodský)
Tchaz Boulat, 1913 (Mozhukin)
Tchin-Tchin. See Fine Romance, 1992
Te deum, 1973 (Palance)
Tea and Rice. See Ochazuke no aji, 1952
Tea and Sympathy, 1956 (Kerr)
Tea for Two, 1950 (Day)
Teacher and the Miracle. See Maestro, 1958
Teacher's Pet, 1958 (Day; Gable)
Teachers, 1984 (Freeman; Grant, L.; Nolte)
Teahouse of the August Moon, 1956 (Brando; Ford, G.; Kyo)
Teamster Boss: The Jackie Presser Story, 1992 (Wallach)
Tear that Burned, 1914 (Gish; Sweet)
Tearin' into Trouble, 1927 (Brennan)
Tearin' Loose, 1925 (Arthur)
Tears Are Not Enough, 1985 (Candy)
Tears in the Rain, 1988 (Stone)
Tears on the Lion's Mane. See Namidao Shishi no tategami no, 1962
Ted & Venus, 1991 (Rowlands)
Teddy at the Throttle, 1917 (Beery; Swanson)
Teddy Bear. See Ours en Peluche, 1993
Tee Audience. See Udienza, 1971
Teen Bhubhaner Parey, 1969 (Chatterjee)
Teen Deviyan, 1965 (Anand)
Teen Kanya, 1961 (Chatterjee)
Teenage Rebel, 1956 (Rogers, G.)
Teerosen, 1977 (Schell, Maria)
Teeth, 1924 (Mix)
Teheran 1943. See Teheran Incident, 1979
Teheran Incident, 1979 (Carradine; Delon)
Tekka bugyo, 1954 (Hasegawa; Kagawa)
Tekken seisai, 1930 (Tanaka)
Tekki kushu, 1943 (Tanaka)
Telefon, 1977 (Bronson; Pleasence; Remick)
Telefoni bianchi, 1976 (Brazzi; Gassman)
Teleftaio Stichima, 1987 (Olbrychski)
Telegram from New York. See New York expresz kabel, 1921
Telegraph Trail, 1933 (Wayne)
Telephone, 1956 (Fernandel)
Telephone, 1987 (Goldberg; Gould)
Telephone Engagement, 1912-13 (White)
Telephone Etiquette, 1974 (Neill)
Telephone Girl and the Lady, 1913 (Barrymore, L.; Marsh)
Telethon, 1977 (Leigh, Janet)
Television Spy, 1939 (Quinn)
Tell It to the Judge, 1949 (Russell, R.)
Tell It to the Marines, 1926 (Chaney)
Tell Me a Riddle, 1980 (Douglas, Melvyn; Grant, L.)
Tell Me Lies, 1968 (Jackson, G.)
Tell Me That You Love Me, Junie Moon, 1969 (Minnelli)
Tell No Tales, 1939 (Douglas, Melvyn)

Tell Tale Brother, 1912-13 (White)
Tell-Tale Heart, 1953 (Baker)
Tell Tale Light, 1913 (Arbuckle)
Tell Them Willie Boy Is Here, 1969 (Redford)
Tell Your Children, 1924 (Crisp)
Telltale Knife, 1911 (Mix
Telltale Knife, 1914 (Mix)
Temoin, 1978 (Blier; Noiret; Sordi)
Temp, 1993 (Dunaway)
Temp di Roma, 1962 (Arletty)
Temperamental Husband, 1912 (Normand)
Tempest, 1928 (Barrymore, J.)
Tempest, 1982 (Gassman; Julia; Rowlands; Sarandon)
Tempestà, 1959 (Gassman; Homolka; Mangano; Moorehead)
Tempête, 1940 (Arletty)
Tempête sur l'Asie, 1938 (Hayakawa; Veidt)
Tempête sur les Mauvents, 1952 (Vanel)
Tempête sur Paris, 1940 (Dalio)
Tempêtes, 1921 (Mozhukin; Vanel)
Tempi duri per vampiri, 1959 (Lee, C.)
Tempi nostri, 1953 (Loren; Montand; Sordi)
Temple of Dusk, 1918 (Hayakawa)
Temple of Venus, 1924 (Arthur)
Tempo degli assassino, 1975 (Brazzi)
Tempo di Uccidere, 1990 (Cage; Giannini)
Tempo hiken-roku, 1927 (Hasegawa)
Tempo massimo, 1934 (Magnani)
Temporale Rosy, 1979 (Depardieu)
Temporary Lady, 1920 (Howard, L.)
Temporary Truce, 1912 (Sweet)
Temporary Widow, 1930 (Olivier)
Temps de mourir, 1969 (Karina)
Temptation, 1916 (Hayakawa)
Temptation, 1946 (Lukas; Oberon)
Temptation. See Yuwaku, 1948
Temptation Harbour, 1947 (Dalio)
Tempter. See Anticristo, 1974
Tempter. See Soriso del grande tentatore, 1973
Temptress, 1926 (Barrymore, L.; Garbo)
Temptress Moon, 1995 (Gong Li)
Ten Cents a Dance, 1931 (Barrymore, L.; Stanwyck)
Ten Commandments, 1923 (Loy)
Ten Commandments. See I dieci commandamenti, 1945
Ten Commandments, 1956 (Baxter; Brynner; Carradine; Heston; Price;
    Robinson, E.)
Ten Days in Paris, 1939 (Harrison)
Ten Days to Die. See Letzte Akt, 1955
Ten Days to Tulara, 1958 (Hayden)
Ten Days' Wonder. See Décade prodigieuse, 1972
Ten Dollar Raise, 1935 (Horton)
Ten Gentlemen from West Point, 1942 (Bond; O'Hara)
Ten Girls Ago, 1962 (Keaton, B.)
Ten-ichibo to Iganosuke, 1933 (Hasegawa)
Ten Little Indians, 1975 (Reed)
Ten Little Indians, 1989 (Lom; Pleasence)
Ten Little Indians. See And Then There Were None, 1974
Ten Little Niggers. See And Then There Were None, 1974
Ten Million Dollar Grab. See Supercolpo da 7 miliard, 1966
Ten North Frederick, 1958 (Bronson; Constantine)
Ten Seconds to Hell, 1959 (Palance)
Ten Tall Men, 1951 (Lancaster)
Ten Thousand Bedrooms, 1957 (Dalio; Henreid; Martin, D.)
Ten to sen, 1958 (Shimura)
Ten Wanted Men, 1955 (Scott, R.; Van Cleef)
Tenant, 1976 (Douglas, Melvyn; Winters)
Tenant. See Locataire, 1976
Tenda rossa, 1969 (Cardinale; Connery; Finch)
Tender Comrade, 1943 (Rogers, G.; Ryan, R.)
Tender Dracula. See Tendre Dracula, 1974
Tender-Hearted Boy, 1912 (Barrymore, L.)
Tender Is the Night, 1961 (Fontaine; Jones, Jennifer; Lukas; Robards)

Tender Mercies, 1983 (Barkin; Duvall)
Tender Scoundrel. See Tendre voyou, 1966
Tender Trap, 1955 (Reynolds, D.; Sidney)
Tender Years, 1947 (Brown)
Tenderfoot, 1932 (Brown; Rogers, G.)
Tenderfoot's Triumph, 1915 (Mix)
Tenderly. See Suo modo di fare, 1968
Tendre Dracula, 1974 (Valli)
Tendre poulet, 1978 (Girardot; Noiret)
Tendre voyou, 1966 (Belmondo; Dalio; Noiret)
Tendres requins. See Zärliche Haie, 1966
Tenero Tramonto, 1984 (Cassel)
Tengoku ni musubu koi, 1932 (Takamine)
Tengoku No Taizai, 1992 (Sharif)
Tengoku to-jigoku, 1963 (Kagawa; Mifune; Shimura)
Tengu-daoshi, 1944 (Kyo)
Tenjodaifu, 1956 (Kagawa)
Tenka gomen, 1960 (Yamada)
Tenka taihai, 1955 (Mifune; Tsukasa)
Tennessee Champ, 1954 (Bronson; Winters)
Tennessee Johnson, 1942 (Barrymore, L.)
Tennessee Nights. See Black Water, 1994
Tennessee's Partner, 1955 (Dickinson; Reagan)
Tennoji no harakiri, 1927 (Tanaka)
Tenpo rokkasen: Jigokuno hanamichi, 1960 (Yamada)
Tenpo Yasubei, 1935 (Hasegawa)
Tensai sagishi monogatari: Tanuki no hanamichi, 1964 (Tsukasa)
Tension, 1949 (Charisse)
Tension at Table Rock, 1956 (Dickinson; Malone)
Tentacles, 1977 (Fonda, H.; Huston, J.; Winters)
Tentacoli. See Tentacles, 1977
Tentation de Barbizon, 1945 (Gélin)
Tentazioni proibite, 1963 (Bardot; Sordi)
Tenth Avenue Angel, 1948 (Lansbury; O'Brien, M.)
Tenth Man, 1988 (Cusack; Hopkins, A.)
Tenth Victim. See Decima vittima, 1965
Tenue de soirée, 1986 (Depardieu)
Teodora, Imperatrice di Bisanzio, 1954 (Papas)
Teorema, 1968 (Mangano; Stamp)
Tepepa, 1969 (Welles)
Tequila Sunrise, 1988 (Gibson; Julia; Pfeiffer)
Tercera palabra, 1955 (Infante)
Tere Ghar Ke Saamne, 1963 (Anand)
Tere Mere Sapne, 1971 (Anand)
Teresa, 1951 (Steiger)
Teresa de Jesús, 1960 (Rey)
Teresa la ladra, 1972 (Vitti)
Teresa the Thief. See Teresa la ladra, 1972
Teresa Venerdi, 1941 (Magnani)
Terezin Diary, 1989 (Wallach)
Term of Trial, 1962 (Olivier; Stamp)
Terminal Choice, 1985 (Barkin)
Terminal Man, 1974 (Segal)
Terminal Station. See Stazione termini, 1953
Terminal Velocity, 1994 (Kinski)
Terminator, 1984 (Schwarzenegger)
Terminator 2: Judgment Day, 1991 (Schwarzenegger)
Termites of 1938, 1938 (Three Stooges)
Terms of Endearment, 1983 (DeVito; MacLaine; Nicholson; Winger)
Ternosecco, 1986 (Abril; Giannini)
Terra Nova, 1991 (Banderas)
Terra promessa, 1913 (Bertini)
Terra-Cotta Warrior. See Qin Yong, 1989
Terrazza, 1979 (Gassman; Mastroianni; Reggiani)
Terre du Diable, 1922 (Modot)
Terre étrangère, 1987 (Piccoli)
Terres jaunes, 1989 (Deneuve)
Terreur, 1924 (White)
Terreur de la Pampa, 1932 (Fernandel)
Terreur en Oklahoma, 1951 (Piccoli)
Terrible Beauty, 1960 (Cusack; Harris, R.)

Terrible Beauty. *See* Night Fighters, 1960

Terrible Joe Moran, 1984 (Barkin; Cagney)

Terrible Night. *See* Zlatcha notch, 1914

Terrible Tragedy, 1916 (Laurel and Hardy)

Terrible Vengeance. *See* Straschnaia miest, 1913

Terribly Stuck Up, 1915 (Lloyd)

Terror, 1920 (Mix)

Terror, 1928 (Horton)

Terror, 1963 (Nicholson)

Terror. *See* House of Freaks, 1973

Terror by Night, 1946 (Rathbone)

Terror Castle. *See* House of Freaks, 1973

Terror House. *See* Night Has Eyes, 1941

Terror in a Texas Town, 1958 (Hayden)

Terror in the Aisles, 1985 (Pleasence)

Terror in the City, 1963 (Grant, L.)

Terror in the Crypt. *See* Cripta de l'incubo, 1963

Terror in the Midnight Sun. *See* Invasion of the Animal People, 1962

Terror in the Sky, 1971 (McDowall)

Terror in the Wax Museum, 1973 (Carradine; Crawford, B.; Lanchester; Milland)

Terror of Dr. Chaney. *See* Mansion of the Doomed, 1975

Terror of Sheba. *See* Persecution, 1974

Terror of the Tongs, 1961 (Lee, C.)

Terror on a Train. *See* Time Bomb, 1952

Terror Stalks the Class Reunion, 1992 (Nelligan)

Terror Street. *See* Thirty-Six Hours, 1953

Terror Trail, 1933 (Mix)

Terror Train, 1980 (Curtis, J.)

Terrore dell 'Andalusia. *See* Carne de horca, 1954

Terrorgram, 1991 (Jones, James Earl)

Terrorista, 1963 (Aimée; Volonté)

Terrorists, 1974 (Connery)

Terry Fox Story, 1983 (Duvall)

Tesla. *See* Tajna Nikole Tesle, 1979

Tess, 1980 (Kinski)

Tess of the D'Urbervilles, 1924 (Sweet)

Tess of the Storm Country, 1914 (Pickford)

Tess of the Storm Country, 1922 (Pickford)

Tess of the Storm Country, 1932 (Gaynor)

Test, 1909 (Pickford)

Test of Honor, 1919 (Barrymore, J.)

Test Pilot, 1938 (Barrymore, L.; Gable; Loy; Tracy)

Testament, 1974 (Loren)

Testament, 1983 (Costner)

Testament d'Orphée, 1959 (Bardot; Brynner; Gélin; Léaud; Marais)

Testament d'un poete Juif assassine, 1987 (Josephson)

Testament du Docteur Cordelier, 1959 (Barrault; Modot)

Testament of a Murdered Jewish Poet. *See* Testament d'un poete Juif assassine, 1987

Testament of John, 1984 (Quayle)

Testament of Orpheus. *See* Testament d'Orphée, 1959

Testigos, 1968 (Villagra)

Testimone. *See* Témoin, 1978

Testimony, 1987 (Kingsley)

Testing Block, 1920 (Hart)

Tête blonde, 1950 (Berry)

Tête contre les murs, 1958 (Aimée; Brasseur)

Tête d'horloge, 1969 (Fresnay)

Tête dans la nuages, 1988 (Darrieux; Girardot)

Tetsu no shojo, 1928 (Tanaka)

Teufelsanbeter, 1920 (Lugosi)

Teufelskerl, 1935 (Fröhlich)

Tex, 1982 (Dillon)

Texan, 1920 (Mix)

Texan, 1930 (Constantine; Wray)

Texans, 1938 (Bennett; Brennan; Scott, R.)

Texans Never Cry, 1951 (Autry)

Texas, 1941 (Ford, G.; Holden; Trevor)

Texas across the River, 1966 (Delon; Martin, D.)

Texas Bad Man, 1932 (Mix)

Texas Carnival, 1951 (Miller; Williams, E.)

Texas Chainsaw Massacre Part II, 1986 (Hopper)

Texas Cyclone, 1932 (Brennan; Wayne)

Texas Guns. *See* Once upon a Texas Train, 1988

Texas Lady, 1955 (Colbert)

Texas Rangers, 1936 (MacMurray)

Texas Rangers Ride Again, 1940 (Crawford, B.; Quinn; Ryan, R.)

Texas Rose. *See* Return of Jack Slade, 1955

Texas Steer, 1927 (Rogers, W.)

Texas Terror, 1935 (Wayne)

Texas to Tokyo. *See* We've Never Been Licked, 1943

Texas Trail, 1925 (Carey)

Texasville, 1990 (Bridges)

Texican, 1966 (Crawford, B.)

Thank God It's Friday, 1978 (Winger)

Thank You, Jeeves, 1936 (Niven)

Thank You, Mr. Moto, 1937 (Carradine; Lorre)

Thank Your Lucky Stars, 1943 (Bogart; Cantor; Davis, B.; De Havilland; Flynn; Garfield; Horton; Lupino; McDaniel)

Thanks a Million, 1935 (Powell, D.)

Thanks for Everything, 1938 (Menjou)

Thanks for Life. *See* Merci la vie, 1991

Thanks for the Memory, 1938 (Hope)

Thanksgiving Day, 1990 (Curtis, T.)

Thanksgiving Promise, 1986 (Bridges)

That Cat. *See* Až přijde kocour, 1963

That Certain Age, 1938 (Cooper; Douglas, Melvyn; Durbin)

That Certain Feeling, 1956 (Hope; Saint; Sanders)

That Certain Summer, 1972 (Sheen)

That Certain Woman, 1937 (Crisp; Davis, B.; Fonda, H.)

That Championship Season, 1982 (Dern; Mitchum; Sheen)

That Crying Baby, 1912-13 (White)

That Dangerous Age, 1950 (Loy)

That Darn Cat!, 1965 (Lanchester; McDowall)

That Devil Bateese, 1918 (Chaney)

That Forsyte Woman, 1949 (Flynn; Garson; Leigh, Janet; Pidgeon; Young, R.)

That Funny Feeling, 1965 (O'Connor)

That Girl from College. *See* Sorority House, 1939

That Girl from Paris, 1936 (Ball)

That Girl Montana, 1921 (Sweet)

That Hagen Girl, 1947 (Reagan; Temple)

That Hamilton Woman, 1941 (Leigh, V.; Olivier)

That Happy Pair. *See* Esa pareja feliz, 1951

That House in the Outskirts. *See* Aquella Casa en las Afueras, 1980

That Is the Port Light. *See* Are ga minato no tomoshibi da, 1961

That Kind of Woman, 1959 (Loren; Sanders)

That Lady, 1955 (De Havilland; Lee, C.; Rosay)

That Lady in Ermine, 1948 (Grable)

That Little Band of Gold, 1915 (Arbuckle; Normand)

That Lucky Touch, 1975 (Cobb; Winters; York)

That Man from Rio. *See* Homme de Rio, 1964

That Man in Istanbul. *See* Estambul 65, 1965

That Midnight Kiss, 1949 (Barrymore, E.)

That Minstrel Man, 1914 (Arbuckle)

That Navy Spirit. *See* Hold 'em Navy, 1937

That Night, 1917 (Beery)

That Night, 1993 (Lewis, Juliette)

That Night in London, 1933 (Donat)

That Night in Rio, 1941 (Ameche; Faye; Miranda)

That Night in Varennes. *See* Nuit de Varennes, 1981

That Night with You, 1945 (Keaton, B.)

That Night's Wife. *See* Sono yo no tsuma, 1930

That Obscure Object of Desire. *See* Cet obscur objet de désir, 1977

That Other Girl, 1912-13 (White)

That Other Woman, 1942 (Duryea)

That Party in Person, 1929 (Cantor)

That Royle Girl, 1925 (Fields, W. C.)

That Splendid November. *See* Bellissimo novembre, 1968

That Summer of White Roses, 1989 (Steiger)

That Thing You Do, 1996 (Hanks)

That Touch of Mink, 1962 (Day; Grant, C.)

That Uncertain Feeling, 1941 (Douglas, Melvyn; Meredith; Oberon)
That Was Then ... This Is Now, 1985 (Freeman)
That Way with Women, 1947 (Greenstreet)
That Wonderful Urge, 1948 (Power; Tierney)
That's a Good Girl, 1932 (Buchanan)
That's Adequate, 1989 (Willis)
That's Dancing!, 1985 (Charisse; Kelly, Gene; Minnelli)
That's Entertainment!, 1974 (Astaire; Crosby; Kelly, Gene; Minnelli;
    O'Connor; Reynolds, D.; Rooney; Sidney; Stewart; Taylor, E.)
That's Entertainment, Part 2, 1976 (Astaire; Kelly, Gene)
That's Entertainment! III, 1994 (Caron; Charisse; Day; Jourdan; Kelly, Gene;
    Lamarr; Miller; O'Connor; Reynolds, D.; Rogers, G.; Rooney; Williams,
    E.)
That's Him, 1918 (Lloyd)
That's Life!, 1986 (Andrews, J.; Lemmon)
That's Me, 1962 (Arkin)
That's My Boy, 1932 (Marsh)
That's My Boy, 1951 (Lewis, Jerry; Marsh)
That's My Boy, 1951 (Martin, D.)
That's My Line, 1931 (Arbuckle)
That's My Man, 1947 (Ameche)
That's My Meat, 1931 (Arbuckle)
That's My Wife, 1929 (Laurel and Hardy)
That's Right—You're Wrong, 1939 (Ball; Horton; Menjou)
That's the Spirit, 1945 (Keaton, B.)
That's the Way of the World, 1975 (Keitel)
Theatre of Blood, 1973 (Dors; Hawkins; Price)
Theatre of Death, 1967 (Lee, C.)
Theatre of Life. See Jinsei gekijo seishun-hen, 1958
Théâtre national populaire, 1956 (Philipe)
Theban Plays by Sophocles, 1986 (Gielgud; Quayle)
Theban Plays: Oedipus the King, 1986 (Cusack)
Their Cheap Vacation, 1914 (Beery)
Their First Acquaintance, 1914 (Crisp)
Their First Mistake, 1932 (Laurel and Hardy)
Their Honeymoon, 1916 (Laurel and Hardy)
Their Own Desire, 1929 (Montgomery; Shearer)
Their Purple Moment, 1928 (Laurel and Hardy)
Their Social Splash, 1915 (Lloyd)
Their Ups and Downs, 1914 (Arbuckle)
Their Vacation, 1916 (Laurel and Hardy)
Thelma & Louise, 1991 (Davis, G.; Keitel; Pitt; Sarandon)
Thelonious Monk: Straight No Chaser, 1989 (Eastwood)
Them Thar Hills!, 1934 (Laurel and Hardy)
Them Was the Happy Days!, 1916 (Lloyd)
Themroc, 1973 (Piccoli)
Then Came Bronson, 1969 (Sheen)
Then kurote-gume, 1937 (Yamada)
Theodora Goes Wild, 1936 (Douglas, Melvyn; Dunne)
Theodora, Slave and Empress. See Teodora, Imperatrice di Bisanzio, 1954
Theodore et Cie, 1933 (Raimu)
Theodore Rex. See T. Rex, 1995
Theorum. See Teorema, 1968
There Goes My Heart, 1938 (Langdon; March)
There Goes the Bride, 1932 (Niven)
There Goes the Bride, 1980 (Crawford, B.)
There Goes the Groom, 1937 (Meredith)
There He Goes, 1925 (Langdon)
There Is No Escape, 1952 (Henreid)
There Is the Detail. See Ahí está el detalle, 1940
There Must Be a Pony, 1986 (Rooney; Taylor, E.)
There Was a Crooked Man, 1960 (Wisdom; York)
There Was a Crooked Man, 1970 (Douglas, K.; Fonda, H.; Grant; Meredith;
    Oates)
There Was a Father. See Chichi ariki, 1942
There Were Days and Moons, 1990 (Aimée)
There Were Days and Moons. See Y a des jours ... et des lunes, 1990
There's a Girl in My Soup, 1970 (Dors; Hawn; Sellers)
There's Always a Price Tag. See Retour de manivelle, 1957
There's Always a Woman, 1938 (Astor; Blondell; Douglas, Melvyn;
    Hayworth)

There's Always Tomorrow, 1934 (Taylor, R.)
There's Always Tomorrow, 1956 (Bennett; MacMurray; Stanwyck)
There's No Business Like Show Business, 1954 (Monroe; O'Connor)
There's Nothing Left but Crying. See Non ci resta che piangere, 1984
There's One Born Every Minute, 1942 (Taylor, E.)
There's That Woman Again, 1939 (Douglas, Melvyn)
Thérèse Desqueyroux, 1962 (Noiret)
These Are the Damned. See Damned, 1962
These Blessed Two. See De Två Saliga, 1985
These Dangerous Years, 1957 (Neagle)
These Foolish Things. See Daddy Nostalgie, 1990
These Foolish Times. See Shin baka jidai, 1946
These Glamour Girls, 1939 (Ayres; Turner, L.; Walker)
These Kids Are Grown-ups. See Ils sont grands ces petits, 1979
These Thousand Hills, 1959 (Remick)
These Three, 1936 (Brennan; Hopkins, M.; McCrea; Oberon)
These Wilder Years, 1956 (Cagney; Pidgeon; Stanwyck)
They, 1993 (Redgrave, V.)
They All Kissed the Bride, 1942 (Crawford, J.; Douglas, Melvyn)
They All Laughed, 1981 (Hepburn, A.)
They Also Kill. See Some May Live, 1967
They Call Him Skarven. See De kalte ham Skarven, 1965
They Call It Sin, 1932 (Calhern; Young, L.)
They Call Me Mister Tibbs!, 1970 (Poitier; Landau)
They Came to a City, 1944 (Withers)
They Came to Blow Up America, 1943 (Bond; Sanders)
They Came to Cordura, 1959 (Constantine; Hayworth)
They Came to Rob Las Vegas. See Vegas 500 milliones, 1968
They Dare Not Love, 1941 (Cushing; Lukas)
They Died with Their Boots On, 1941 (De Havilland; Flynn; Greenstreet;
    Kennedy; McDaniel; Quinn)
They Drive by Night, 1940 (Lupino; Raft)
They Drive By Night, 1940 (Bogart)
They Flew Alone, 1942 (Neagle)
They Fought for the Country. See Oni srazhalis za rodinu, 1975
They Gave Him a Gun, 1937 (Tracy)
They Go Boom, 1929 (Laurel and Hardy)
They Got Me Covered, 1942 (Hope; Lamour)
They Had to See Paris, 1927 (Rogers, W.)
They Knew Mayakovsky. See Oni znali Mayakovsky, 1955
They Knew Mr. Knight, 1945 (Greenwood)
They Knew What They Wanted, 1940 (Carey; Laughton; Lombard; Malden)
They Leap into Life. See Sprung ins Leben, 1924
They Made Me a Criminal, 1939 (Bond; Garfield; Rains)
They Made Me a Fugitive, 1947 (Howard, T.)
They Met in a Taxi, 1936 (Bond; Wray)
They Met in Argentina, 1941 (O'Hara)
They Met in Bombay, 1941 (Gable; Lorre; Russell, R.)
They Met in the Dark, 1943 (Mason)
They Might Be Giants, 1971 (Scott, G.; Woodward)
They Only Kill Their Masters, 1972 (Garner; O'Brien, E.)
They Ran for Their Lives, 1968 (Carradine)
They Shall Have Music, 1939 (Brennan; McCrea)
They Shoot Horses, Don't They?, 1969 (Dern; Fonda, J.; York)
They Watch. See They, 1993
They Were Expendable, 1945 (Bond; Montgomery; Wayne)
They Were Five. See Belle equipe, 1936
They Were Not Divided, 1950 (Lee, C.)
They Were Sisters, 1945 (Mason)
They Who Dare, 1954 (Bogarde; Elliott)
They Won't Believe Me, 1947 (Hayward; Young, R.)
They Won't Forget, 1937 (Rains; Turner, L.)
They Would Elope, 1909 (Pickford)
They've Taken Our Children: The Chowchilla Kidnapping, 1993 (Malden)
Thicker than Water, 1935 (Laurel and Hardy)
Thief, 1920 (White)
Thief, 1952 (Milland)
Thief, 1971 (Dickinson)
Thief, 1981 (Caan; Weld)
Thief and the Cobbler, 1981 (Price)
Thief Catcher. See Her Friend the Bandit, 1914

Thief in Paradise, 1925 (Colman)
Thief of Bagdad, 1924 (Fairbanks; Wong)
Thief of Bagdad, 1940 (Veidt)
Thief of Bagdad, 1978 (Stamp; McDowall; Ustinov)
Thief of Damascus, 1952 (Henreid)
Thief of Paris. See Velour, 1967
Thief Who Came to Dinner, 1973 (Oates)
Thieves After Dark, 1983 (Presle)
Thieves Fall Out, 1941 (Quinn)
Thieves' Gold, 1918 (Carey)
Thieves' Highway, 1949 (Cobb)
Thin Air. See Body Stealers, 1969
Thin Ice, 1937 (Henie; Power)
Thin Ice, 1981 (Gish)
Thin Man, 1934 (Loy; O'Sullivan; Powell, W.)
Thin Man Goes Home, 1944 (Loy; Powell, W.)
Thing, 1981 (Pleasence)
Thing with Two Heads, 1972 (Milland)
Things Are Looking Up, 1934 (Leigh, V.)
Things Change, 1988 (Ameche)
Things in Their Season, 1974 (Neal)
Things of Life. See Choses de la Vie, 1970
Things to Come, 1936 (Massey; Richardson, R.; Sanders)
Things to Do in Denver When You're Dead, 1995 (García; Walken)
Things We Did Last Summer, 1977 (Belushi; Murray)
Think Fast, Mr. Moto, 1937 (Lorre)
Think of a Number. See Taenk på ett tal, 1969
Think Twentieth, 1967 (Hayward; Heston)
Third. See Dritte, 1972
Third Day, 1965 (Marshall; McDowall)
Third Eye, 1969 (Meredith)
Third Finger, Left Hand, 1940 (Douglas, Melvyn; Loy)
Third Generation. See Dritte Generation, 1979
Third Girl from the Left, 1973 (Curtis, T.; Novak)
Third Key. See Long Arm, 1956
Third Lover. See Oeil du malin, 1962
Third Man, 1949 (Cotten; Howard, T.; Valli; Welles)
Third Man on the Mountain, 1959 (Lom)
Third Part of the Night, 1971 (Nowicki)
Third Secret, 1964 (Attenborough; Hawkins)
Third Solution. See Russicum, 1987
Third Voice, 1960 (O'Brien, E.)
Thirteen. See Twelve Plus One, 1969
Thirteen at Dinner, 1985 (Ustinov)
Thirteen Hours by Air, 1936 (Bennett; MacMurray)
Thirteen Men and a Girl. See Letste Kompagnie, 1930
Thirteen Trunks of Mr. O.F.. See Koffer des Herrn O.F., 1931
Thirteen West Street, 1962 (Ladd; Steiger)
Thirteen Women, 1932 (Dunne; Loy)
Thirteenth Chair, 1929 (Lugosi)
Thirteenth Guest, 1932 (Rogers, G.)
Thirteenth Hour, 1927 (Barrymore, L.)
Thirteenth Juror, 1927 (Pidgeon)
Thirteenth Letter, 1950 (Boyer; Darnell; Rosay)
Thirty Day Princess, 1934 (Sidney)
Thirty Days, 1916 (Laurel and Hardy)
Thirty Days. See Silver Lining, 1931
Thirty Seconds over Tokyo, 1944 (Mitchum; Tracy; Walker)
Thirty-Day Princess, 1934 (Grant, C.)
Thirty-Nine Steps, 1978 (Mills)
Thirty-Six Hours, 1953 (Duryea)
This above All, 1942 (Fontaine; Power)
This Ancient Law. See Alte Gesetz, 1923
This Angry Age. See Barrage contre le Pacifique, 1958
This Boy's Life, 1993 (Barkin; De Niro)
This Can't Be Love, 1994 (Hepburn, K.; Quinn)
This Day and Age, 1933 (Carradine)
This Earth Is Mine, 1959 (Hudson; Rains)
This England, 1941 (McDowall)
This Girl for Hire, 1983 (Ferrer; McDowall)
This Greedy Old Skin. See Gametsui yatsu, 1960

This Gun for Hire, 1942 (Ladd; Lake; Preston)
This Happy Breed, 1944 (Johnson; Mills)
This Happy Feeling, 1958 (Astor; Reynolds, D.)
This House Possessed, 1981 (Bennett)
This Is Heaven, 1929 (Banky)
This Is Lloyd's, 1962 (Quayle)
This Is London, 1956 (Harrison)
This Is My Affair, 1937 (Carradine; McLaglen; Stanwyck; Taylor, R.)
This Is My Love, 1954 (Darnell; Duryea)
This Is My Street, 1963 (Hurt, J.)
This Is Spinal Tap, 1984 (Huston, A.)
This Is the Army, 1943 (Reagan)
This Is the Life, 1914 (Beery)
This Is the Life, 1933 (Milland)
This Is the Life, 1944 (O'Connor; Wray)
This Is the Night, 1932 (Grant, C.)
This Is the Sea, 1994 (Harris, R.)
This Is Your Life. See Här har du ditt liv, 1966
This Kind of Love. See Quaeta specie d'amore, 1972
This Land Is Mine, 1943 (Laughton; O'Hara; Sanders)
This Lightning Always Strikes Twice, 1985 (Bloom)
This Love of Ours, 1945 (Oberon; Rains)
This Mad World, 1930 (Rathbone)
This Man Is Dangerous, 1941 (Mason)
This Man Is Dangerous, 1952 (Crawford, J.)
This Man Is Mine, 1934 (Bellamy; Dunne)
This Man's Navy, 1945 (Beery)
This Modern Age, 1931 (Crawford, J.)
This Modern Age, Number Sixteen. See British—Are They Artistic?, 1947
This Must Not Be Forgotten. See It Mustn't Be Forgotten, 1954
This Property Is Condemned, 1966 (Bronson; Redford; Wood)
This Rugged Land, 1962 (Bronson)
This Savage Land, 1966 (Scott, G.)
This Side of Heaven, 1934 (Barrymore, J.; Barrymore, L.; Stewart)
This Sporting Life, 1963 (Harris, R.; Jackson, G.; Roberts, R.)
This Sweet Sickness. See Dites-lui que je l'aime, 1977
This Thing Called Love, 1929 (Harlow)
This Thing Called Love, 1941 (Cobb; Douglas, Melvyn; Russell, R.)
This Time for Keeps, 1942 (Gardner)
This Time for Keeps, 1947 (Durante; Williams, E.)
This Transient Life, 1971 (Okada)
This Way Out, 1915 (Laurel and Hardy)
This Way Please, 1937 (Grable)
This Week of Grace, 1933 (Fields, G.)
This Woman, 1924 (Bow)
This Woman Is Mine, 1941 (Brennan)
This'll Make You Whistle, 1936 (Buchanan; Terry-Thomas)
Thodisi bewafai, 1980 (Azmi)
Thomas Crown Affair, 1968 (Dunaway; McQueen)
Thompson's Last Run, 1986 (Mitchum)
Thoroughbred, 1955 (Cusack)
Thoroughbreds. See Silks and Saddles, 1928
Thoroughbreds Don't Cry, 1937 (Garland; Rooney)
Thoroughly Modern Millie, 1967 (Andrews, J.)
Those Calloways, 1965 (Brennan)
Those Country Kids, 1914 (Arbuckle; Normand)
Those Daring Young Men in Their Jaunty Jalopies. See Monte Carlo or Bust!, 1969
Those Daring Young Men in Their Jaunty Jalopies. See Quei temerari sulle loro pazze, scatenate, scalcinate carriole, 1969
Those Endearing Young Charms, 1945 (Young, R.)
Those Fantastic Flying Fools. See Jules Verne's Rocket to the Moon, 1967
Those Good Old Days, 1913 (Normand)
Those Happy Days, 1914 (Arbuckle)
Those Love Pangs, 1914 (Chaplin, C.; Laurel and Hardy)
Those Magnificent Men in Their Flying Machines, 1965 (Cassel; Sordi; Terry-Thomas)
Those Redheads from Seattle, 1953 (Moorehead)
Those We Love, 1932 (Astor)
Those Were the Days, 1934 (Mills)
Those Were the Days, 1940 (Holden; Ladd)

Those Were the Years. *See* C'eravamo tanti amati, 1974
Those Who Are Late. *See* Spóźnieni przechodnie, 1962
Those Who Dance, 1924 (Sweet)
Those Who Make Tomorrow. *See* Asu o tsukuru hitobito, 1946
Those Wise Guys Who Fool Around, 1956 (Lee, B.)
Those without Sin, 1917 (Sweet)
Thou Shalt Not Kill, 1982 (Grant, L.)
Thousand and One Nights, 1945 (Wilde; Winters)
Thousand Clowns, 1965 (Holliday; Robards)
Thousand Cranes. *See* Senba-zuru, 1969
Thousand Dollar Husband, 1916 (Sweet)
Thousand Eyes. *See* Tausend Augen, 1984
Thousand Heroes. *See* Crash Landing: The Rescue of Flight 232, 1992
Thousands Cheer, 1943 (Astor; Ball; Barrymore, L.; Charisse; Garland; Kelly, Gene; O'Brien, M.; Powell, E.; Rooney)
Thread of Destiny, 1910 (Pickford)
Threads of Fate, 1915 (Chaney)
Threat. *See* Menace, 1977
Three Act Tragedy, 1987 (Ustinov)
Three Ages, 1923 (Beery; Keaton, B.; Laurel and Hardy)
Three Amigos, 1986 (Martin, S.)
Three Arabian Nuts, 1951 (Three Stooges)
Three Bad Men in a Hidden Fortress. *See* Kakushi toride no san akunin, 1958
Three Bites of the Apple, 1967 (Fabrizi)
Three Blind Mice, 1938 (McCrea; Niven; Young, L.)
Three Brave Men, 1957 (Borgnine; Milland)
Three Brothers. *See* Tre fratelli, 1980
Three Came Home, 1950 (Colbert; Hayakawa)
Three Came Home, 1986 (Colbert)
Three Cases of Murder, 1955 (Welles)
Three Coins in the Fountain, 1954 (Brazzi; Jourdan; Webb)
Three Colours: Blue. *See* **Trois Couleurs: Bleu,** 1993
Three Colours: Red. *See* **Trois Couleurs: Rouge,** 1994
Three Colours: White. *See* **Trois Couleurs: Blanc,** 1993
Three Comrades, 1938 (Sullavan; Taylor, R.; Young, R.)
Three Daring Daughters, 1948 (MacDonald)
Three Dark Horses, 1952 (Three Stooges)
Three Days of the Condor, 1975 (Dunaway; Redford; Robertson)
Three Days of the Condor, 1975 (Von Sydow)
Three Dumb Clucks, 1937 (Three Stooges)
Three Fables of Love. *See* Quatre Vérités, 1962
Three Faces of a Woman. *See* I tre volti, 1965
Three Faces of Eve, 1957 (Cobb; Woodward)
Three Faces of Sin. *See* Puits aux trois vérités, 1961
Three Faces West, 1940 (Coburn, C.; Wayne)
Three for All, 1974 (Dors)
Three for Bedroom C, 1952 (Dumont; Swanson)
Three for the Show, 1954 (Grable)
Three for the Show, 1955 (Lemmon)
Three Forbidden Stories. *See* Tre storie proibite, 1952
Three Friends, 1912 (Carey)
Three Friends, 1913 (Barrymore, L.; Sweet)
Three Fugitives, 1989 (Jones, James Earl; Nolte)
Three Generations of Danjuro. *See* Danjuro sandai, 1944
Three Ghosts. *See* Questi fantasmi, 1967
Three Girls about Town, 1941 (Blondell)
Three Girls from Rome. *See* Ragazze di Piazza di Spagna, 1952
Three Girls Looking for Husbands. *See* Tre ragazze cercano marito, 1944
Three Girls Lost, 1931 (Wayne; Young, L.)
Three Godfathers, 1936 (Brennan)
Three Godfathers, 1948 (Armendáriz; Bond)
Three Godfathers, 1949 (Marsh)
Three Gold Coins, 1920 (Mix)
Three Grandfathers, 1948 (Wayne)
Three Guys Named Mike, 1951 (Wyman)
Three Hams on Rye, 1950 (Three Stooges)
Three Headed Monster. *See* Sandai kaiju chikyu saidai no kessen, 1965
Three Hearts for Julia, 1943 (Douglas, Melvyn)
Three Hollywood Girls, 1930 (Arbuckle)
Three Hours to Kill, 1954 (Andrews, D.)
Three Hundred Miles for Stephanie, 1981 (Olmos)

Three into Two Won't Go, 1969 (Bloom; Steiger)
Three Is a Family, 1944 (McDaniel)
Three Jumps Ahead, 1923 (Mix)
Three Little Beers, 1935 (Three Stooges)
Three Little Pigskins, 1934 (Three Stooges)
Three Little Pirates, 1946 (Three Stooges)
Three Little Powders, 1914 (Beery)
Three Little Sew and Sews, 1939 (Three Stooges)
Three Little Twerps, 1943 (Three Stooges)
Three Little Words, 1950 (Astaire; Reynolds, D.)
Three Live Ghosts, 1929 (Bennett; Montgomery)
Three Lives, 1953 (Heston)
Three Loan Wolves, 1946 (Three Stooges)
Three Loves. *See* Frau, nach der Mann sich sehnt, 1929
Three Loves Has Nancy, 1938 (Gaynor; Montgomery)
Three Maxims, 1937 (Neagle)
Three Men and a Girl, 1919 (Barthelmess)
Three Men and a Girl. *See* Golden Arrow, 1953
Three Men in White, 1944 (Barrymore, L.; Gardner)
Three Men on a Horse, 1936 (Blondell)
Three Men to Destroy. *See* Trois Hommes à abattre, 1980
Three Mesquiteers, 1936 (Carey)
Three Missing Links, 1938 (Three Stooges)
Three Mounted Men, 1918 (Carey)
Three Moves to Freedom. *See* Schachnovelle, 1960
Three Murderesses. *See* Faibles femmes, 1959
Three Musketeers, 1921 (Fairbanks; Menjou)
Three Musketeers, 1933 (Wayne)
Three Musketeers, 1935 (Ball; Lukas)
Three Musketeers, 1939 (Ameche; Carradine)
Three Musketeers. *See* Tres mosqueteros, 1942
Three Musketeers, 1948 (Kelly, Gene; Lansbury; Price; Turner, L.)
Three Musketeers, 1973 (Cassel; Chaplin, G.; Dunaway; Heston; Lee, C.)
Three Musketeers, 1974 (Reed; Welch)
Three Must-Get-Theres, 1922 (Linder)
Three of a Kind, 1944 (Three Stooges)
Three on a Couch, 1966 (Leigh, Janet; Lewis, Jerry)
Three on a Limb, 1936 (Keaton, B.)
Three on a Match, 1932 (Blondell; Bogart; Davis, B.)
Three on a Weekend. *See* Bank Holiday, 1938
Three Pals, 1926 (Constantine)
Three Pests in a Mess, 1945 (Three Stooges)
Three Pilots. *See* I tre aquilotti, 1942
Three Ring Circus, 1954 (Lanchester; Lewis, Jerry; Martin, D.)
Three-Ring Marriage, 1928 (Astor)
Three Rogues, 1930 (McLaglen; Wray)
Three Sad Tigers. *See* Tres tristes tigres, 1968
Three Sailors and a Girl, 1953 (Lancaster)
Three Sappy People, 1939 (Three Stooges)
Three Seats for the 26th. *See* Trois places pour le 26, 1988
Three Secrets, 1950 (Neal)
Three Sinners, 1928 (Lukas; Negri)
Three Sinners. *See* Muertres, 1950
Three Sisters, 1911 (Pickford)
Three Sisters, 1970 (Bates, A.; Olivier)
Three Sisters, 1977 (Page; Winters)
Three Sisters. *See* Paura e amore, 1988
Three Smart Girls, 1936 (Durbin; Milland)
Three Smart Girls Grow Up, 1939 (Durbin)
Three Smart Saps, 1942 (Three Stooges)
Three Sovereigns for Sarah, 1985 (Redgrave, V.)
Three Steps North. *See* Tre passi a nord, 1951
Three Stooges Go around the World in a Daze, 1963 (Three Stooges)
Three Stooges in Orbit, 1962 (Three Stooges)
Three Stooges Meet Hercules, 1962 (Three Stooges)
Three Stooges Meet the Gunslinger. *See* Outlaws IS Coming!, 1965
Three Stooges Scrapbook, 1960 (Three Stooges)
Three Stories of Love. *See* Story of Three Loves, 1953
Three Strangers, 1946 (Greenstreet; Huston, J.; Lorre)
Three Texas Steers, 1939 (Wayne)
Three Thousand Mile Chase, 1977 (Ford, G.)

Three Treasures. *See* Nippon tanjo, 1959
Three Troubledoers, 1946 (Three Stooges)
Three Violent People, 1956 (Baxter; Heston)
Three Waltzes. *See* Trois Valses, 1938
Three Weekends, 1928 (Bow)
Three Wise Fools, 1946 (Barrymore, L.; Charisse; O'Brien, M.)
Three Wise Girls, 1931 (Harlow)
Three Wise Guys, 1936 (Young, R.)
Three Wishes. *See* Tre önskningar, 1960
Three Women. *See* Trzy koniety, 1957
Three Women, 1977 (Spacek)
Three Women around Yoshinaka. *See* Shin Heike monogatari Yoshinaka o meguru san-nin no onna, 1956
Three Word Brand, 1921 (Hart)
Three X Gordon, 1918 (Gilbert)
Three's a Crowd, 1927 (Langdon)
Three-Cornered Moon, 1933 (Colbert)
Threepenny Opera. *See* **Dreigroschenoper**, 1931
Threepenny Opera. *See* Mack the Knife, 1989
Threshold, 1981 (Sutherland)
Threshold. *See* Subah, 1983
Thrill of a Lifetime, 1937 (Grable; Lamour)
Thrill of a Romance, 1945 (Williams, E.)
Thrill of Brazil, 1946 (Miller)
Thrill of Genius. *See* Hitchcock: il brividio del geno, 1985
Thrill of It All, 1963 (Day; Garner)
Thriller, 1986 (York)
Thrilling, 1965 (Sordi)
Throne of Blood. *See* Kumonosujo, 1957
Throne of Fire. *See* Processo de las brujas, 1970
Thronfolger, 1980 (Schell, Maria)
Through a Glass Darkly. *See* Såsom i en spegel, 1961
Through Darkened Vales, 1911 (Sweet)
Through Days and Months. *See* Hi mo tsuki, 1969
Through Switzerland and Bavaria with Will Rogers, 1927 (Rogers, W.)
Through the Back Door, 1921 (Menjou; Pickford)
Through the Wire, 1990 (Sarandon)
Throw Momma from the Train, 1987 (DeVito)
Thru Different Eyes, 1929 (Sidney)
Thumb Print, 1911 (Talmadge)
Thumb Tripping, 1972 (Dern)
Thumbs Up, 1943 (Lanchester)
Thunder, 1929 (Chaney)
Thunder across the Pacific. *See* Wide Blue Yonder, 1951
Thunder Afloat, 1939 (Beery)
Thunder Bay, 1953 (Duryea; Stewart)
Thunder Below, 1932 (Lukas)
Thunder Birds, 1942 (Tierney)
Thunder County, 1974 (Rooney)
Thunder in the City, 1930 (Robinson, E.; Richardson, R.)
Thunder in the East, 1953 (Boyer; Kerr; Ladd)
Thunder in the East. *See* Battle, 1934
Thunder in the Sun, 1959 (Hayward)
Thunder Island, 1963 (Nicholson)
Thunder of Drums, 1961 (Bronson)
Thunder on the Hill, 1951 (Colbert)
Thunder over the Plains, 1953 (Scott, R.)
Thunder Pass, 1954 (Carradine)
Thunder Road, 1958 (Mitchum)
Thunder Rock, 1942 (Mason; Redgrave, M.)
Thunderball, 1965 (Connery)
Thunderbirds, 1952 (Bond)
Thunderbolt, 1929 (Wray)
Thunderbolt, 1995 (Chan)
Thunderbolt and Lightfoot, 1974 (Bridges; Eastwood)
Thunderhead—Son of Flicka, 1945 (McDowall)
Thunderheart, 1992 (De Niro; Shepard)
Thundering Dawn, 1923 (Wong)
Thundering Fleas, 1926 (Laurel and Hardy)
Thundering Herd, 1933 (Carey; Scott, R.)
Thundering Romance, 1924 (Arthur)

Thundering Through, 1925 (Arthur)
Thunderstorm, 1957 (Lee, B.)
Thursday the 12th. *See* Pandemonium, 1982
Thursday's Child, 1943 (Granger; Rowlands)
Thursday's Children, 1953 (Burton)
Thursday's Game, 1974 (Burstyn; Wilder)
THX-1138, 1971 (Duvall; Pleasence)
Thy Name Is Woman, 1924 (Novarro)
Ti attende una corda ... Ringo. *See* Ritorno di Clint il solitario, 1972
Ti ho sposato per allegria, 1967 (Vitti)
Tiara Tahiti, 1962 (Lom; Mason; Mills)
...Tick...Tick...Tick..., 1969 (March; Łomnicki)
Ticket of Leave Man, 1914 (White)
Ticket to Paradise. *See* Biljett till paradiset, 1962
Ticket to Ride, 1988 (Brazzi)
Ticket to Tomahawk, 1950 (Baxter; Brennan; Monroe)
Tickle Me, 1965 (Presley)
Tides of Barnegat, 1917 (Sweet)
Tides of Passion, 1925 (Marsh)
Tides of War, 1990 (Borgnine)
Tie Me Up! Tie Me Down! *See* ¡Atame!, 1990
Tied for Life, 1933 (Langdon)
Tiefland, 1922 (Dagover)
Tiempo de silencio, 1986 (Rey; Abril)
Tiera sedienta, 1945 (Rey)
Tieraerztin Christine, 1993 (Borgnine)
Tieraerztin Christine II, 1995 (Borgnine)
Tierarzt Dr. Vlimmen, 1945 (Wegener)
Tierra baja, 1950 (Armendáriz)
Tierra brutal, 1962 (Rey)
Tierra de pasiónes, 1944 (Armendáriz)
Tierra prometida, 1972 (Villagra)
Tieta d'agreste, 1981 (Loren)
Tieta de Agreste, 1997 (Braga)
Tiger and the Pussycat. *See* Tigre, 1967
Tiger Bay, 1933 (Wong)
Tiger Bay, 1959 (Mills)
Tiger in the Sky. *See* McConnell Story, 1955
Tiger Loves Fresh Blood. *See* Tigre aime la chair fraîche, 1964
Tiger Makes Out, 1967 (Hoffman; Wallach)
Tiger Man, 1918 (Hart)
Tiger Rose, 1929 (MacMurray)
Tiger Shark, 1932 (Robinson, E.)
Tiger Thompson, 1924 (Carey)
Tiger Town, 1983 (Scheider)
Tiger Woman, 1917 (Bara)
Tiger—Fruhling in Wien, 1985 (Constantine)
Tiger's Cub, 1921 (White)
Tigers Don't Cry, 1976 (Quinn)
Tigers in Lipstick. *See* Tango della gelosia, 1981
Tiger's Tale, 1988 (Ann-Margret)
Tight Little Island. *See* Whisky Galore!, 1949
Tight Shoes, 1941 (Crawford, B.; Three Stooges)
Tight Spot, 1955 (Robinson, E.; Rogers, G.)
Tightrope, 1984 (Bujold; Eastwood)
Tigre, 1967 (Ann-Margret; Gassman)
Tigre aime la chair fraîche, 1964 (Audran)
Tigres de Papel, 1977 (Maura)
'Til We Meet Again, 1940 (Oberon)
Till Death Do Us Part. *See* Buried Alive, 1990
Till the Clouds Roll By, 1946 (Charisse; Garland; Lansbury; Sidney; Walker; Williams, E.)
Till the End of Time, 1946 (Mitchum)
Till Tomorrow Comes. *See* Asu aru kagiri, 1962
Till We Meet Again, 1922 (Marsh)
Till We Meet Again, 1936 (Marshall)
Till We Meet Again, 1944 (Milland)
Till We Meet Again, 1989 (Grant, H.)
Tillie and Gus, 1933 (Fields, W. C.)
Tillie the Toiler, 1927 (Davies)
Tillie Wakes Up, 1915 (Dressler)

Tillie's Day Off, 1916 (Dressler)
Tillie's Divorce Case, 1916 (Dressler)
Tillie's Love Affair, 1916 (Dressler)
Tillie's Nightmare. *See* Tillie's Punctured Romance, 1914
Tillie's Punctured Romance, 1914 (Arbuckle; Chaplin, C.; Dressler; Normand)
Tillie's Punctured Romance, 1928 (Fields, W. C.)
Tillie's Tomato Surprise, 1917 (Dressler)
Tim, 1979 (Gibson)
Timber Tramps, 1975 (Cotten)
Timberjack, 1954 (Hayden; Menjou)
Timbuktu. *See* Legend of the Lost, 1957
Timbuktu, 1959 (Mature)
Time after Time, 1979 (McDowell; Steenburgen)
Time after Time, 1985 (Gielgud; Howard, T.; Withers)
Time Bandits, 1981 (Cleese; Connery; Richardson, R.)
Time Bomb, 1952 (Ford, G.)
Time for Action. *See* Tip on a Dead Jockey, 1957
Time for Killing, 1967 (Ford, G.; Ford, H.; Stanton)
Time for Love, 1927 (Powell, W.)
Time for Loving, 1971 (Noiret)
Time for Miracles, 1980 (Brazzi)
Time for Terror. *See* Flesh Feast, 1973
Time Is Money, 1923 (Rasp)
Time Is Money, 1994 (Landau; Von Sydow)
Time Limit, 1957 (Malden; Widmark)
Time Lock, 1957 (Connery)
Time Lost and Time Remembered. *See* I Was Happy Here, 1965
Time of Destiny, 1988 (Hurt, W.)
Time of Indifference. *See* Indifferenti, 1964
Time of Silence. *See* Tiempo de Silencio, 1986
Time of Their Lives, 1946 (Abbott and Costello)
Time of Your Life, 1948 (Bond; Cagney; Crawford, B.)
Time Out for Love. *See* Grandes Personnes, 1961
Time Out for Rhythm, 1941 (Miller; Three Stooges)
Time Out for Romance, 1937 (Trevor)
Time Past. *See* Czas przeszły, 1961
Time to Die, 1983 (Harrison)
Time to Kill, 1996 (Jackson, S.; Sutherland)
Time to Kill. *See* Tempo di Uccidere, 1990
Time to Live, 1985 (Minnelli)
Time to Love and a Time to Die, 1958 (Kinski)
Time to Remember, 1990 (O'Connor)
Time to Run, 1973 (Hershey)
Time without Pity, 1956 (Cushing; Redgrave, M.)
Timecop, 1994 (Van Damme)
Timely Interception, 1913 (Barrymore, L.; Gish)
Times Gone By. *See* Altri tempi, 1952
Times Square Lady, 1935 (Taylor, R.)
Timestalkers, 1987 (Kinski)
Timid Young Man, 1935 (Keaton, B.)
Timidité vaincue, 1909 (Linder)
Timothy Dobbs, That's Me, 1916 (Beery)
Tin Cup, 1996 (Costner)
Tin Drum. *See* **Blechtrommel**, 1978
Tin Gods, 1926 (Powell, W.)
Tin Men, 1987 (DeVito; Dreyfuss; Hershey)
Tin Pan Alley, 1940 (Faye; Grable)
Tin Soldier, 1995 (Voight)
Tin Star, 1957 (Fonda, H.; Perkins; Van Cleef)
Tingler, 1960 (Price)
Tinkering with Trouble, 1915 (Lloyd)
Tintin et le mystère de la Toison d'Or, 1961 (Vanel)
Tintomara, 1970 (Dahlbeck)
Tip, 1918 (Lloyd)
Tip-Off, 1931 (Rogers, G.)
Tip-Off Girls, 1938 (Quinn)
Tip on a Dead Jockey, 1957 (Dalio; Malone; Taylor, R.)
Tip Toes, 1927 (Rogers, W.)
Tipo chi mi place. *See* Homme qui me plaît, 1969
Tipperary, 1992 (Landau)
Tirano Banderas, 1994 (Volonté)

Tire a part, 1996 (Stamp)
Tire Man, Spare My Tires, 1942 (Langdon)
Tired Feet, 1933 (Langdon)
Tirez s'il vous plait, 1908 (Berry)
Tiro a segno per uccidere. *See* Geheimnis der gelben Mönche, 1966
Tiroir secret, 1986 (Moreau; Morgan)
Tit for Tat, 1935 (Laurel and Hardy)
Titan Find, 1984 (Kinski)
Titan-Michaelangelo, 1949 (March)
Titanic, 1953 (Ritter; Stanwyck; Webb)
Titans. *See* Arrivani i titani, 1961
Title Shot, 1979 (Curtis, T.)
Tizoc, 1956 (Félix; Infante)
Tkada-no-baba, 1927 (Tanaka)
To Be Called For, 1914 (Mix)
To Be or Not to Be, 1942 (Lombard)
To Be or Not to Be, 1983 (Bancroft; Brooks, M.; Ferrer)
To Be the Best, 1992 (Hopkins, A.)
To Bed or Not to Bed. *See* Diavolo, 1963
To Build a Fire, 1970 (Welles)
To Catch a Cop. *See* Retenez moi ... ou je Fais un Malheur!, 1984
To Catch a Thief, 1954 (Grant, C.; Kelly, Grace; Vanel)
To Commit a Murder. *See* Peau d'espion, 1967
To Die For, 1995 (Dillon; Segal)
To Die in Madrid, 1967 (Gielgud)
To Dorothy, a Son, 1956 (Winters)
To Each His Own, 1946 (De Havilland)
To Forget Venice. *See* Dimenticare Venezia, 1979
To Gillian on Her 37th Birthday, 1996 (Pfeiffer)
To Have and Have Not, 1944 (Bacall; Bogart; Brennan; Dalio)
To Heir Is Human, 1944 (Langdon)
To Kill a Mockingbird, 1962 (Duvall; Peck)
To Kill a Priest, 1989 (Harris, E.)
To Kill a Stranger, 1971 (Welles)
To Kill a Stranger, 1982 (Pleasence)
To Kill or to Die. *See* Mio nome è Shanghai Joe, 1973
To Kill with Intrigue, 1978 (Chan)
To Live. *See* **Ikiru**, 1952
To Live, 1994 (Gong Li)
To Live and Die in L.A., 1985 (Dafoe; Turturro)
To Live in Peace. *See* Vivere in pace, 1946
To Love. *See* Att älska, 1964
To Love, Perhaps to Die, 1975 (Sordi)
To Mary—with Love, 1936 (Loy; Trevor)
To Meteoro Vima tou Pelargou, 1991 (Mastroianni)
To Paris with Love, 1954 (Guinness)
To Please a Lady, 1950 (Gable; Menjou; Stanwyck)
To Protect Mother Earth, 1989 (Redford)
To Russia with Elton, 1979 (Moore, Dudley)
To Save Her Soul, 1909 (Pickford)
To See Such Fun, 1977 (Bogarde; Guinness; Wisdom)
To Sir with Love, 1967 (Poitier)
To the Devil a Daughter, 1975 (Elliott; Kinski; Lee, C.; Widmark)
To the Ends of the Earth, 1948 (Powell, D.)
To the Ladies, 1923 (Astor; Horton)
To the Last Man, 1933 (Carradine; Scott, R.; Temple)
To the Lighthouse, 1983 (Branagh)
To the North-West, 1934 (Zhao Dan)
To the Shores of Tripoli, 1942 (O'Hara; Scott, R.)
To the Victor. *See* Owd Bob, 1938
To the Victor, 1948 (Malone)
To the Western World, 1981 (Huston, J.)
To Vlemma tou Odyssea, 1995 (Josephson; Keitel; Volonté)
To Wong Foo, Thanks for Everything! Julie Newmar, 1995 (Snipes; Williams, R.)
Toast of New Orleans, 1950 (Niven)
Toast of New York, 1937 (Farmer; Grant, C.)
Toast of the Legion. *See* Kiss Me Again, 1931
Tobacco Road, 1941 (Andrews, D.; Bond; Tierney)
Tobias Wants Out, 1913 (Mix)
Tobruk, 1966 (Hudson)

Toburoku no Tatsu, 1962 (Mifune)
Tochan no po ga kikoeru, 1971 (Tsukasa)
Tochter der Landstrasse, 1914 (Nielsen)
Tochter des Mehemed, 1919 (Jannings)
Tochter des Samurai, 1937 (Hayakawa)
Tochter des Samurai. *See* Atarashiki tsuchi, 1937
Tod in Miami, 1994 (Vogler)
Tod in Sevilla, 1913 (Nielsen)
Tod ritt Dienstags. *See* I giorno dell'ira, 1967
Todake no kyodai, 1941 (Ryu)
Today Is Forever. *See* Griffin and Phoenix: A Love Story, 1976
Today We Live, 1933 (Constantine; Crawford, J.; Young, R.)
Todd Killings, 1970 (Grahame)
Tödlicher Irrtum, 1970 (Mueller-Stahl)
Todo es posible en Granada, 1954 (Oberon)
Todo modo, 1976 (Mastroianni; Piccoli; Volonté)
Todoke haha no sakebi, 1959 (Yamada)
Tofflan-en lycklig komedi, 1967 (Björnstrand)
Together. *See* Amo non Amo, 1978
Together Again, 1944 (Boyer; Coburn, C.; Dunne; Winters)
Together We Stand, 1986 (Gould)
Togger, 1937 (Rasp)
Tohjin Okichi, 1935 (Hayakawa)
Toho sen-ichi-ya, 1947 (Hasegawa; Takamine; Yamada)
Toho shoboto, 1946 (Takamine)
Toi que j'adore, 1933 (Feuillère)
Toilers, 1919 (Colman)
Tojin Okichi, 1954 (Yamada)
Tojuro no koi, 1938 (Hasegawa)
Tojuro no koi, 1955 (Hasegawa; Kyo)
Toka kan no jinsei, 1941 (Tanaka)
Tokyo boshoku, 1957 (Hara; Ryu; Yamada; Yamamura)
Tokyo-ga, 1985 (Ryu)
Tokyo-hen, 1948 (Takamine)
Tokyo hika, 1951 (Mori)
Tokyo Joe, 1949 (Bogart; Hayakawa)
Tokyo monogatari, 1953 (Hara; Kagawa; Ryu; Yamamura)
Tokyo mushuku, 1950 (Yamamura)
Tokyo no ekubo, 1952 (Takamine)
Tokyo no gassho, 1931 (Takamine)
Tokyo no hiroin, 1950 (Mori)
Tokyo no koibito, 1952 (Mifune)
Tokyo no kyujitsu, 1958 (Hara; Kagawa; Mifune; Tsukasa)
Tokyo no onna, 1933 (Ryu; Tanaka)
Tokyo no sora no shita niwa, 1955 (Yamada)
Tokyo no yado, 1935 (Ryu)
Tokyo Story. *See* **Tokyo monogatari**, 1953
Tokyo Sweetheart. *See* Tokyo no koibito, 1952
Tokyo Twilight. *See* Tokyo boshoku, 1957
Tokyo Woman. *See* Tokyo no onna, 1933
Tokyo's Chorus. *See* Tokyo no gassho, 1931
Tol'able David, 1921 (Barthelmess)
Tol'able David, 1930 (Carradine)
Tolgo il disturbo, 1990 (Gassman; Gould; Sanda)
Toll Gate, 1920 (Hart)
Toll of the Sea, 1922 (Wong)
Tolle Nacht, 1943 (Fröhlich)
Tom & Viv, 1994 (Dafoe; Richardson, M.)
Tom and Jerry Mix, 1917 (Mix)
Tom Brown of Culver, 1932 (Power)
Tom, Dick, and Harry, 1941 (Meredith; Rogers, G.)
Tom Horn, 1980 (McQueen)
Tom Jones, 1963 (Evans; Finney; Greenwood; York)
Tom Mix in Arabia, 1922 (Mix)
Tom Sawyer, 1973 (Foster; Oates)
Tom Sawyer—Detective, 1938 (O'Connor)
Tom Thumb, 1958 (Sellers; Terry-Thomas)
Tom Toms of Mayumba. *See* Tam Tam Mayumba, 1955
Tomahawk, 1951 (Hudson)
Tomalio, 1933 (Arbuckle)
Tomb, 1986 (Carradine)

Tomb of Ligeia, 1965 (Price)
Tombola, paradiso nero, 1947 (Fabrizi)
Tomboy Bessie, 1912 (Normand)
Tombstone, 1993 (Heston; Mitchum)
Tommy, 1975 (Ann-Margret; Nicholson; Reed)
Tommy Gets His Sister Married, 1910-11 (White)
Tomorrow, 1972 (Duvall)
Tomorrow and Tomorrow, 1932 (Lukas)
Tomorrow at Ten, 1963 (Shaw)
Tomorrow Is Forever, 1946 (Colbert; Welles; Wood)
Tomorrow Never Comes, 1978 (Pleasence; Reed)
Tomorrow the World, 1944 (March; Moorehead)
Tomorrow We Live, 1942 (Lom)
Tomoshibi, 1954 (Kagawa)
Tom's Sacrifice, 1916 (Mix)
Tom's Strategy, 1916 (Mix)
Tong Man, 1919 (Hayakawa)
Toni, 1928 (Buchanan)
Tonic, 1928 (Lanchester)
Tonight a Town Dies. *See* Dzis w nocy umrze miastro, 1961
Tonight and Every Night, 1945 (Hayworth; Winters)
Tonight Is Ours, 1933 (Colbert; March)
Tonight Let's All Make Love in London, 1968 (Marvin; Redgrave, V.)
Tonight or Never, 1931 (Douglas, Melvyn; Karloff; Swanson)
Tonight We Raid Calais, 1943 (Cobb; Dalio)
Tonight We Sing, 1953 (Bancroft)
Tonight's the Night. *See* Happy Ever After, 1954
Tonite Let's All Make Love in London, 1967 (Christie)
Tonka, 1958 (Mineo)
Tonnerre de Dieu, 1965 (Gabin)
Tontons flingueurs, 1973 (Blier)
Tony Arzenta. *See* Big Guns, 1972
Tony Rome, 1967 (Rowlands; Sidney)
Tony Runs Wild, 1926 (Mix)
Tony Saitta, 1976 (Landau)
Too Bad She's Bad. *See* Peccato che sia una canaglia, 1955
Too Beautiful for You. *See* Trop belle pour toi, 1989
Too Busy to Work, 1932 (Powell, D.; Rogers, W.)
Too Dangerous to Love. *See* Perfect Strangers, 1950
Too Far to Go, 1979 (Close)
Too Hot to Handle, 1938 (Gable; Loy; Pidgeon)
Too Hot to Handle, 1960 (Lee, C.; Mansfield)
Too Hot to Handle. *See* Marrying Man, 1991
Too Late for Divorce, 1956 (Lee, B.)
Too Late for Tears, 1949 (Duryea; Kennedy)
Too Late the Hero, 1970 (Caine; Elliott; Fonda, H.; Robertson)
Too Late to Talk to Billy, 1982 (Branagh)
Too Little, Too Late. *See* Our Sons, 1991
Too Many Blondes, 1941 (Three Stooges)
Too Many Chefs, 1916 (Mix)
Too Many Chefs. *See* Who Is Killing the Great Chefs of Europe?, 1978
Too Many Cooks, 1920 (Howard, L.)
Too Many Crooks, 1930 (Olivier)
Too Many Crooks, 1959 (Terry-Thomas)
Too Many Girls, 1940 (Ball; Miller)
Too Many Husbands, 1940 (Arthur; Douglas, Melvyn; MacMurray)
Too Many Kisses, 1925 (Marx Brothers; Powell, W.)
Too Many Parents, 1936 (Farmer)
Too Many Suspects. *See* Ellery Queen, 1975
Too Many Thieves, 1966 (Falk)
Too Many Women. *See* God's Gift to Women, 1931
Too Much Business, 1922 (Horton)
Too Much Harmony, 1933 (Crosby)
Too Much Johnson, 1919 (Crisp)
Too Much Johnson, 1938 (Holliday; Welles)
Too Much Mustard. *See* Max professeur de tango, 1912
Too Much Sun, 1990 (Arkin)
Too Much, Too Soon, 1958 (Flynn; Malone)
Too Scared to Scream, 1985 (O'Sullivan)
Too Soon to Die. *See* Svegliati e uccidi, 1966
Too Soon to Love, 1959 (Nicholson)

Too Tough to Kill, 1935 (Bond)
Too Wise Wives, 1921 (Calhern)
Too Young to Die?, 1990 (Lewis, Juliette; Pitt)
Too Young to Know, 1945 (Malone)
Too Young to Marry, 1931 (Young, L.)
Tooi kumo, 1955 (Takamine)
Tools of Providence, 1915 (Hart)
Toote Khilone, 1978 (Azmi)
Tooth Will Out, 1951 (Three Stooges)
Tootsie, 1982 (Davis, G.; Hoffman; Lange; Murray)
Tootsie and Tamales, 1919 (Laurel and Hardy)
Top Crack, 1967 (Terry-Thomas)
Top Gun, 1955 (Hayden)
Top Gun, 1986 (Cruise; Ryan, M.; Robbins)
Top Hat, 1934 (Astaire; Ball; Horton; Rogers, G.)
Top Job. See Ad ogni costo, 1968
Top Man, 1943 (Gish; O'Connor)
Top o' the Morning, 1949 (Crosby; Fitzgerald)
Top Secret, 1952 (Homolka; Lee, C.)
Top Secret Affair, 1957 (Douglas, K.; Hayward)
Top Secret!, 1984 (Cushing; Sharif)
Top Speed, 1930 (Brown)
Topaz, 1969 (Noiret; Piccoli)
Topaze, 1933 (Barrymore, J.; Feuillère; Jouvet; Loy)
Topaze, 1950 (Fernandel)
Topkapi, 1964 (Mercouri; Schell, Maximilian; Ustinov)
Topper, 1937 (Grant, C.)
Topper Returns, 1941 (Blondell)
Tops Is the Limit. See Anything Goes, 1936
Topsy-Turvy Sweedie, 1914 (Beery)
Tora-ko, 1935 (Shimura)
Tora-San Goes North. See Otoko wa tsuraiyo: Shiretoko bojo, 1987
Tora-San Goes to Vienna. See Otoko wa Tsuraiyo: Toraijiro kokoro no tabiji, 1989
Tora-San's Forbidden Love. See Otoko wa Tsuraiyo, 1985
Tora! Tora! Tora!, 1970 (Cotten; Robards; Yamamura)
Tora's Pure Love. See Otoko wa tsuraiyo: Torajiro junjo-shishu, 1976
Tora's Spring Dream. See Otoko wa tsuraiyo: Torajiro Haru no yume, 1979
Torajiro Shinjitsu Ichiro. See Otoko wa Tsuraiyo, 1985
Torch. See Del odio nace el amor, 1950
Torch Singer, 1933 (Colbert)
Torch Song, 1953 (Crawford, J.; Welch)
Torch Song Trilogy, 1988 (Bancroft)
Torchy Plays with Dynamite, 1939 (Wyman)
Torchy's Millions, 1921 (Shearer)
Tordenstenene, 1927 (Madsen and Schenstrøm)
Torero, 1957 (Del Rio)
Torguvi dom Karski, 1917 (Mozhukin)
Toribe-yama shinju, 1928 (Hasegawa)
Toribeyama shinju: Osome Hankuro, 1936 (Hasegawa)
Torii Kyozaemon, 1942 (Shimura)
Torment. See Hets, 1944
Tormented Hearts. See Cuori nella tormenta, 1940
Torn between Two Lovers, 1979 (Remick)
Torn Curtain, 1966 (Andrews, J.; Newman)
Tornavara, 1941 (Hayakawa)
Toro-no-o o fumu otokotachi, 1945 (Mori)
Torpedo Bay. See Finchè dura la tempesta, 1964
Torpedo Raider. See Brown on Resolution, 1935
Torpedo Run, 1958 (Borgnine; Ford, G.)
Torreani, 1951 (Fröhlich)
Torrent, 1926 (Garbo)
Torrent. See Honryu, 1926
Torrents of Spring. See Acque di primavera, 1989
Torrid Zone, 1940 (Cagney)
Torro de falisco, 1940 (Armendáriz)
Torticola contre Frankensberg, 1952 (Brasseur; Gélin; Piccoli)
Tortilla Flat, 1942 (Garfield; Lamarr; Tracy)
Torture Garden, 1967 (Cushing; Meredith; Palance)
Torture par l'espérance, 1928 (Modot)
Tosca, 1918 (Bertini)

Tosca, 1940 (Brazzi)
Tosca, 1973 (Fabrizi; Gassman; Vitti)
Tosca. See Devanti a lui tremava tutta Roma, 1946
Toselli. See Romanzo d'amore, 1950
Toss of the Coin, 1911 (Pickford)
Tot samyi Myunkhauzen, 1979 (Yankovsky)
Tota no o o fumu otokotachi, 1945 (Shimura)
Total Recall, 1990 (Schwarzenegger; Stone)
Total War in Britain, 1945 (Mills)
Totem Mark, 1911 (Mix)
Toten Augen, 1917 (Negri)
Toten Augen von London, 1961 (Kinski)
Toteninsel, 1920 (Dagover)
Totentanz, 1912 (Nielsen)
Totentanz, 1919 (Krauss)
Totò, Fabrizi e i giovani d'oggi, 1960 (Fabrizi)
Totò contro i quattro, 1963 (Fabrizi)
Totò d'Arabia. See Totò de Arabia, 1965
Totò de Arabia, 1965 (Rey)
Totò e i re di Roma, 1952 (Sordi)
Totò e Marcellino, 1958 (Cardinale)
Toubib, 1979 (Delon)
Touch. See Beröringen, 1971
Touch and Die, 1992 (Sheen)
Touch and Go, 1955 (Hawkins)
Touch and Go, 1986 (Keaton, M.)
Touch and Go. See Poudre d'escampette, 1971
Touch Me Not, 1973 (Remick)
Touch of a Stranger, 1990 (Winters)
Touch of Class, 1973 (Jackson, G.; Segal)
Touch of Evil, 1958 (Cotten; Dietrich; Heston; Leigh, Janet; Welles)
Touch of Larceny, 1960 (Mason; Sanders)
Touch of Scandal, 1984 (Dickinson)
Touch of the Sun, 1979 (Cushing)
Touche à tout, 1935 (Berry)
Touche pas à la femme blanche, 1973 (Deneuve; Noiret; Piccoli; Reggiani)
Touche pas la femme blanche, 1974 (Cuny; Mastroianni)
Touchez pas au grisbi, 1953 (Gabin; Moreau)
Tough Enough, 1983 (Oates; Quaid)
Tough Guy, 1935 (Cooper)
Tough Guys, 1986 (Douglas, K.; Lancaster; Wallach)
Tough Guys Don't Dance, 1987 (Rossellini)
Tough Tony. See Tony Saitta, 1976
Toughlove, 1985 (Dern; Remick)
Toujours seuls, 1990 (Girardot)
Tour de manège, 1989 (Binoche)
Tour de Nèsle, 1955 (Brasseur)
Tour Pour rien, 1933 (Rosay)
Tour Rheumatism. See Mabel's Latest Prank, 1914
Tourbillon de Paris, 1928 (Dagover)
Tourelle 3, 1939 (Blier)
Tourist, 1921 (Laurel and Hardy)
Tourist, 1925 (Arbuckle)
Tourists, 1912 (Normand)
Tous les chemins mènent à Rome, 1948 (Philipe; Presle)
Tous les matins du monde, 1992 (Depardieu)
Tous peuvent me tuer, 1957 (Aimée)
Tous vedettes, 1979 (Caron)
Tout ça ne vaut pas l'amour, 1931 (Gabin)
Tout chante autour de moi, 1954 (Piccoli)
Tout dépend des filles, 1979 (Presle)
Tout est à nous, 1979 (Chaplin, G.)
Tout est bien qui finit bien. See Max et son rival, 1910
Tout feu tout flamme, 1982 (Adjani; Montand)
Tout feu, tout flamme. See Ca va etre ta fête, 1961
Tout l'or du monde, 1961 (Noiret)
Tout le monde il est beau, tout le monde il est gentil, 1972 (Blier)
Tout peut arriver, 1969 (Deneuve)
Tout va bien, 1973 (Fonda, J.; Montand)
Toute Innocence, 1987 (Baye)
Toute la ville danse. See Great Waltz, 1938

Toutes les femmes se ressemblent, 1990 (Gélin)
Tovarich, 1937 (Boyer; Colbert; Rathbone)
Toward the Decisive Battle in the Sky. *See* Kessen no ozura e, 1943
Toward the Unknown, 1956 (Garner; Holden)
Towards New Times. *See* Mot nya tider, 1939
Towed in a Hole, 1932 (Laurel and Hardy)
Tower of Lies, 1925 (Chaney; Shearer)
Tower of Lilies. *See* Himeyuri ro to, 1953
Tower of London, 1939 (Karloff; Price; Rathbone)
Tower of London, 1962 (Price)
Towering Inferno, 1974 (Astaire; Dunaway; Holden; Jones, Jennifer;
    McQueen; Newman)
Town by the Sea. *See* Staden vid vattnen, 1955
Town Called Bastard. *See* Town Called Hell, 1971
Town Called Hell, 1971 (Landau; Rey; Shaw)
Town Like Alice, 1956 (Finch)
Town on Trial, 1957 (Coburn, C.; Mills)
Town People. *See* Machi no hitobito, 1926
Town Tamer, 1965 (Andrews, D.)
Town That Cried Terror. *See* Maniac, 1978
Town Went Wild, 1944 (Horton)
Town Will Die Tonight. *See* Dzis w nocy umrze miastro, 1961
Town without Pity, 1961 (Douglas, K.)
Toxic Affair, 1993 (Adjani)
Toy, 1982 (Pryor)
Toy Factory, 1971 (Welles)
Toy Soldiers, 1984 (Robbins)
Toy Soldiers, 1991 (Elliott)
Toy Story, 1995 (Hanks)
Toy Wife, 1938 (Douglas, Melvyn; Rainer; Young, R.)
Toyo no haha, 1934 (Takamine; Tanaka)
Toys, 1992 (O'Connor; Williams, R.)
Toys in the Attic, 1963 (Martin, D.; Page; Tierney)
Toys of Fate, 1918 (Nazimova)
Tra moglie e Mario, 1975 (Sordi)
Track 29, 1988 (Oldman)
Track of the Cat, 1954 (Mitchum)
Trackdown: Finding the Goodbar Killer, 1983 (Segal)
Tracks, 1976 (Hopper)
Trade Winds, 1938 (Bellamy; Bennett; March)
Trader Horn, 1931 (Carey)
Tradimento, 1951 (Gassman)
Trading Hearts, 1987 (Julia)
Trading Mom, 1994 (Spacek)
Trading Places, 1983 (Ameche; Bellamy; Curtis, J.; Elliott; Murphy)
Tradita, 1954 (Bardot)
Tradition de minuit, 1939 (Dalio)
Traffic. *See* Trafic, 1971
Traffic in Souls. *See* Cargaison blanche, 1937
Traffic Jam. *See* Ingorgo, 1979
Trafic, 1971 (Tati)
Träfracken, 1966 (Björnstrand)
Tragala, pervo, 1981 (Rey)
Tragarz puchu. *See* Warszawa Year 5703, 1992
Tragedia di un uomo ridiculo, 1981 (Aimée)
Tragedy of a Ridiculous Man. *See* Tragedia di un uomo ridiculo, 1981
Tragedy of Love. *See* Tragödie der Liebe, 1923
Tragedy of the Orient, 1914 (Hayakawa)
Tragedy of the Street. *See* Dirnentragödie, 1927
Tragedy of Whispering Creek, 1914 (Chaney)
Tragic General. *See* Higegi no shogun Yamashita Yasubumi, 1953
Tragico ritorno, 1952 (Mastroianni)
Tragikomödie, 1922 (Krauss)
Tragödie der Liebe, 1923 (Dietrich; Jannings)
Trail Beyond, 1934 (Wayne)
Trail Mix-Up, 1993 (Turner, K.)
Trail of '98, 1928 (Carey; Del Rio)
Trail of Robin Hood, 1950 (Rogers, R.)
Trail of the Law, 1924 (Shearer)
Trail of the Lonesome Pine, 1936 (Fonda, H.; MacMurray; Sidney)
Trail of the Pink Panther, 1982 (Lom; Niven; Sellers)

Trail of the Vigilantes, 1940 (Crawford, B.)
Trail Street, 1947 (Ryan, R.; Scott, R.)
Trail to San Antone, 1947 (Autry)
Trailin', 1921 (Mix)
Train, 1964 (Lancaster; Moreau)
Train, 1973 (Schneider)
Train, 1987 (Sanda)
Train de 8 h 47, 1934 (Fernandel)
Train de nuit, 1994 (Piccoli)
Train of Events, 1949 (Finch)
Train Robbers, 1973 (Ann-Margret; Wayne)
Traitement de choc, 1972 (Delon; Girardot)
Traitor's Gate. *See* Verratertor, 1965
Traitors, 1957 (Lee, C.)
Tramonte, 1913 (Bertini)
Tramp, 1915 (Chaplin, C.; Purviance)
Tramp, Tramp, Tramp, 1926 (Crawford, J.; Langdon)
Tramplers. *See* Uomini dal passo pesante, 1966
Tramps, 1915 (Laurel and Hardy)
Tranches de vie, 1985 (Cassel)
Tranquillo posto di campagna, 1968 (Redgrave, V.)
Transatlantic, 1931 (Loy)
Transatlantic Tunnel. *See* Tunnel, 1935
Transatlantis, 1995 (Olbrychski)
Transformation of Mike, 1912 (Sweet)
Transformers: The Movie, 1986 (Welles)
Transgression, 1931 (Francis)
Transient Lady, 1935 (Carradine)
Transit, 1991 (Vogler)
Transmutations. *See* Underworld, 1985
Transport from Paradise. *See* Transport z rje, 1963
Transport z rje, 1963 (Brodský)
Transylvania 6-5000, 1985 (Davis, G.)
Trap, 1913 (Chaney)
Trap, 1922 (Chaney)
Trap, 1959 (Cobb; Widmark)
Trap, 1966 (Reed)
Trapeze, 1956 (Curtis, T.; Lancaster; Lollobrigida)
Trapeze. *See* Salto Mortale, 1931
Trapped beneath the Sea, 1974 (Cobb)
Trapped by Fear. *See* Distractions, 1960
Trapped by Television, 1936 (Astor)
Trapped in Paradise, 1994 (Cage)
Trapped in Tangiers. *See* Agguato a Tangeri, 1958
Traquenard. *See* Haine, 1979
Trash, 1970 (Spacek)
Tratta delle bianche, 1952 (Gassman)
Trauma, 1979 (Cotten)
Trauma, 1983 (Mueller-Stahl)
Trauma. *See* Terminal Choice, 1985
Traümende Mund, 1932 (Bergner)
Traumende Mund, 1953 (Schell, Maria)
Traumulus, 1936 (Jannings)
Trauschein, 1983 (Schell, Maria)
Travelin' Fast, 1924 (Arthur)
Travelin' On, 1922 (Hart)
Traveling Saleslady, 1935 (Blondell; McDaniel)
Traveling Salesman, 1921 (Arbuckle)
Traveller. *See* Musafir, 1957
Traveller's Joy, 1949 (Withers)
Travellin' On, 1914 (Carey)
Travels with Anita. *See* Viaggio con Anita, 1979
Travels with My Aunt, 1972 (Smith)
Traversée de Paris, 1956 (Gabin)
Travolti da un insolito destino nell'azzurro mare d'agosto, 1974 (Giannini)
Tre aquilotti, 1942 (Sordi)
Tre colone in cronaca, 1990 (Volonté)
Tre eccetera del colonnello. *See* Trois etc ... du colonel, 1959
Tre fratelli, 1981 (Noiret; Vanel)
Tre önskningar, 1960 (Dahlbeck)
Tre passi a nord, 1951 (Fabrizi)

Tre piger i Paris, 1963 (Gélin)
Tre ragazze cercano marito, 1944 (Sordi)
Tre storie proibite, 1952 (Cervi)
Tre straniere a Roma, 1958 (Cardinale)
Tre volti, 1965 (Harris, R.; Sordi)
Tre volti della paura. *See* Black Sabbath, 1964
Treacherous Crossing, 1992 (Dickinson)
Treachery Within. *See* Double Crime sur la Ligne Maginot, 1938
Tread Softly Stranger, 1958 (Dors)
Treason. *See* Old Louisianna, 1937
Treasure. *See* Schatz, 1923
Treasure Island, 1920 (Chaney)
Treasure Island, 1934 (Barrymore, L.; Beery; Cooper)
Treasure Island. *See* Ostrov sokrovishch, 1937
Treasure Island, 1972 (Welles)
Treasure Island, 1989 (Lee, C.)
Treasure Island, 1990 (Heston; Reed)
Treasure Island, 1991 (Karina; Léaud)
Treasure of Matecumbe, 1976 (Ustinov)
Treasure of Pancho Villa, 1955 (Winters)
Treasure of Ruby Hills, 1955 (Van Cleef)
Treasure of San Teresa, 1959 (Constantine; Lee, C.)
Treasure of Silver Lake, 1962 (Lom)
Treasure of the Amazon, 1985 (Pleasence)
Treasure of the Golden Condor, 1953 (Bancroft; Wilde; Wray)
Treasure of the Lost Canyon, 1951 (Powell, W.)
Treasure of the Sierra Madre, 1948 (Bogart; Huston, J.; Huston, W.)
Treasure of the Yankee Zephyr. *See* Race for the Yankee Zephyr, 1982
Treat 'em Rough, 1919 (Mix)
Tree Grows in Brooklyn, 1945 (Blondell; Marsh)
Tree Grows in Brooklyn, 1974 (Robertson)
Tree in a Test Tube, 1943 (Laurel and Hardy)
Tree of Hands, 1990 (Bacall)
Tree of Liberty. *See* Howards of Virginia, 1940
Trèfle à cinq feuilles, 1972 (Noiret)
Treibhaus, 1987 (Vogler)
Treize à table, 1955 (Girardot; Presle)
Tremors, 1990 (Bacon)
Trenchcoat in Paradise, 1989 (Dern)
Treno crociato, 1942 (Brazzi)
Trent's Last Case, 1929 (Crisp; Lockwood; Welles)
Trenta minuti d'amore, 1983 (Vitti)
Trenta secondi d'amore, 1936 (Magnani)
Trente secondes d'amour. *See* Trenta secondi d'amore, 1936
Tres Desejos, 1996 (Maura)
Tres Garcia, 1946 (Infante)
Tres huastecos, 1948 (Infante)
Tres mosqueteros, 1942 (Cantinflas)
Tres tristes tigres, 1968 (Villagra)
Très Moutarde, 1908 (Linder)
Tresor des montagnes bleues. *See* Winnetou: II Teil, 1964
Trespasser, 1929 (Swanson)
Trêve, 1968 (Gélin)
Trial, 1955 (Ford, G.; Kennedy)
Trial, 1993 (Hopkins, A.; Robards)
Trial. *See* **Procès**, 1962
Trial and Error. *See* Dock Brief, 1962
Trial by Combat, 1976 (Cushing)
Trial by Combat. *See* Dirty Knight's Work, 1976
Trial by Jury, 1994 (Hurt, W.)
Trial of Mary Dugan, 1929 (Shearer)
Trial of Mary Dugan, 1941 (Young, R.)
Trial of the Catonsville Nine, 1972 (Peck)
Trial of Vivienne Ware, 1932 (Bennett)
Trial Run, 1984 (Grant, L.)
Trials of Oscar Wilde, 1960 (Finch; Mason)
Triangulo diabolico de la Bermudas, 1978 (Huston, J.)
Tribulations d'un chinois en Chine, 1965 (Belmondo)
Tribute, 1980 (Lemmon; Remick)
Tribute to a Bad Man, 1956 (Cagney; Papas; Van Cleef)
Tricheurs, 1958 (Belmondo)

Trick of the Eye, 1994 (Burstyn)
Trick That Failed, 1909 (Pickford)
Tricks, 1926 (Constantine)
Tricky Dicks, 1953 (Three Stooges)
Triebmörder. *See* Bestia uccide a sangue freddo, 1971
Trieste File, 1980 (Van Cleef)
Trifling Women, 1922 (Novarro)
Trigger Fast. *See* Floating Outfit: Trigger Fast, 1994
Trigger Happy. *See* Deadly Companions, 1961
Trigger Happy, 1996 (Reynolds, B.)
Trigger, Jr., 1950 (Rogers, R.)
Trilby's Love Disaster, 1916 (Mix)
Trilogy, 1969 (Page)
Trimmed in Furs, 1934 (Langdon)
Trimming of Paradise Gulch, 1910 (Mix)
Trio infernal, 1974 (Piccoli; Schneider)
Trip, 1967 (Dern; Hopper; Nicholson)
Trip through a Hollywood Studio, 1935 (Cagney; Del Rio)
Trip to Bountiful, 1985 (Page)
Trip to Chinatown, 1926 (Wong)
Trip to Terror. *See* Blood of the Iron Maiden, 1970
Triple Cross, 1966 (Brynner; Howard, T.; Schneider)
Triple Crossed, 1958 (Three Stooges)
Triple Echo, 1973 (Jackson, G.; Reed)
Triple Trouble, 1918 (Chaplin, C.; Purviance)
Triple Trouble. *See* Kentucky Kernels, 1934
Tripoli, 1950 (O'Hara)
Tripoli, bel suol d'amore, 1954 (Sordi)
Tristan and Isolde. *See* Tristan et Iseult, 1973
Tristan and Isolt. *See* Love Spell, 1979
Tristan et Iseult, 1973 (Cusack)
Tristana, 1970 (Deneuve; Rey)
Tristano e Isotta, 1911 (Bertini)
Tristi amori, 1943 (Berry; Cervi)
Triumph, 1916 (Chaney)
Triumph eines Genies. *See* Friedrich Schiller, 1940
Triumph of Lester Snapwell, 1963 (Keaton, B.)
Triumph of the Rat, 1926 (Novello)
Triumph of the Spirit, 1989 (Dafoe; Olmos)
Triumph Tiger '57. *See* Hempas bar, 1977
Triumphs of a Man Called Horse, 1982 (Harris, R.)
Trödler von Amsterdam, 1925 (Krauss)
Trog, 1970 (Crawford, J.)
Troika. *See* Vot mchitza troika potchtovaia, 1913
Troîka sur la piste blanche, 1937 (Dalio; Vanel)
Trois Argentines à Montmartre, 1939 (Brasseur)
Trois chambres à Manhattan, 1965 (Girardot)
Trois Couleurs: Blanc, 1993 (Binoche)
Trois Couleurs: Bleu, 1993 (Binoche)
Trois Couleurs: Rouge, 1994 (Binoche; Trintignant)
Trois etc ... du colonel, 1959 (Gélin)
Trois filles à Paris. *See* Tre piger i Paris, 1963
Trois Hommes à abattre, 1980 (Delon)
Trois jours à vivre, 1957 (Gélin; Moreau)
Trois milliards sans ascenseur, 1972 (Reggiani)
Trois Mousquetaires, 1953 (Cervi)
Trois Pages d'un journal. *See* Tagebuch einer Verlorenen, 1929
Trois places pour le 26, 1988 (Montand)
Trois-six-neuf, 1937 (Blier)
Trois soeurs. *See* Paura e amore, 1988
Trois Valses, 1938 (Fresnay)
Trois Vies et Une Seule Mort, 1996 (Abril; Mastroianni)
Troisième Dalle, 1942 (Berry)
Trojan Women, 1971 (Bujold; Hepburn, K.; Papas; Redgrave, V.)
Trompe-l'oeil, 1974 (Presle)
Tron, 1982 (Bridges)
Trooper Hook, 1957 (McCrea; Stanwyck)
Trop aimée, 1909 (Linder)
Trop belle pour toi, 1989 (Depardieu)
Trop c'est trop, 1975 (Dalio; Gélin)
Trop crédules, 1908 (Chevalier)

Tropennächte, 1931 (Rasp)
Tropic Holiday, 1938 (Lamour; Milland)
Tropic of Cancer, 1970 (Burstyn)
Tropic Zone, 1953 (Reagan)
Tropicana. *See* Heat's On, 1943
Troppo forte, 1986 (Sordi)
Trots, 1952 (Andersson, H.; Dahlbeck)
Trotta, 1971 (Schell, Maximilian)
Trottie True, 1949 (Lee, C.)
Trou dans le mur, 1930 (Brasseur)
Trou normand, 1952 (Bardot)
Trouble, 1922 (Beery)
Trouble along the Way, 1953 (Coburn, C.; Wayne)
Trouble Brewing, 1939 (Withers)
Trouble for Two, 1936 (Montgomery; Russell, R.)
Trouble in Mind, 1985 (Bujold)
Trouble in Paradise, 1932 (Francis; Hopkins, M.; Horton; Marshall)
Trouble in Paradise, 1988 (Welch)
Trouble in Store, 1953 (Rutherford; Wisdom)
Trouble in Sundown, 1939 (Bond)
Trouble in Texas, 1937 (Hayworth)
Trouble in the Glen, 1954 (Lockwood; McLaglen; Welles)
Trouble in the Morning. *See* Asa no hamon, 1952
Trouble in the Sky. *See* Code of Silence, 1960
Trouble Shooter, 1924 (Mix)
Trouble Shooter. *See* Man with the Gun, 1955
Trouble with Angels, 1966 (Lupino; Russell, R.)
Trouble with Girls, 1969 (Carradine; Presley; Price)
Trouble with Harry, 1955 (MacLaine)
Trouble with Michael Caine, 1989 (Caine)
Trouble with Spies, 1987 (Sutherland)
Trouble with Women, 1947 (Milland)
Troubled Waters, 1936 (Mason; Rutherford)
Troubles. *See* Making a Living, 1914
Troubles We've Seen: A History of Journalism in Wartime. *See* Veillees d'armes, 1994
Troublesome Secretaries, 1911 (Normand)
Troublesome Stepdaughters, 1912 (Talmadge)
Trouping with Ellen, 1924 (Rathbone)
Trousers. *See* Hose, 1927
Trout. *See* Truite, 1982
Trovatore, 1910 (Bertini)
Truands, 1956 (Constantine; Modot)
True and the Brave. *See* Betrayed, 1954
True Believer, 1989 (Woods)
True Chivalry, 1912-13 (White)
True Colors, 1991 (Widmark)
True Confession, 1937 (Barrymore, J.; Lombard; MacMurray; McDaniel)
True Confessions, 1981 (Cusack; De Niro; Duvall; Meredith)
True Glory, 1945 (Ustinov)
True Grit, 1969 (Duvall; Hopper; Wayne)
True Grit, 1978 (Oates)
True Heart Susie, 1919 (Gish)
True Identity, 1991 (Jones, James Earl)
True Lies, 1994 (Curtis, J.; Heston; Schwarzenegger)
True Life of Antonio H.. *See* Vera Vita di Antonio H., 1994
True Romance, 1993 (Hopper; Jackson, S.; Oldman; Pitt; Walken)
True Story of Camille. *See* Dame aux Camélias, 1980
True Story of Jesse James, 1957 (Carradine; Moorehead)
True Story of the Civil War, 1956 (Massey)
True to Life, 1943 (Powell, D.)
True to the Army, 1941 (Miller)
True to the Navy, 1930 (Bow; March)
True West, 1982 (Malkovich; Shepard)
Truite, 1982 (Cassel; Huppert; Moreau; Olbrychski)
Trumpet Blows, 1934 (Menjou; Raft)
Trumps. *See* Enormous Changes at the Last Minute, 1985
Trunk to Cairo, 1966 (Sanders)
Trunks of Mr. O.F.. *See* Koffer des Herrn O.F., 1931
Trust, 1915 (Chaney)
Trust. *See* Doverie, 1976

Trust Me, 1989 (Landau)
Trusting Wives, 1929 (Horton)
Truth. *See* Vérité, 1960
Truth about Cats and Dogs, 1996 (Thurman)
Truth about Spring, 1965 (Mills)
Truth about Women, 1958 (Lee, C.; Zetterling)
Truth about Youth, 1930 (Loy; Young, L.)
Truth or Dare, 1991 (Banderas; Beatty; Costner)
Truthful Liar, 1924 (Rogers, W.)
Truthful Tulliver, 1917 (Hart)
Truxton King, 1923 (Gilbert)
Truxtonia. *See* Truxton King, 1923
Try and Get It, 1924 (Horton)
Try This One for Size, 1989 (Steiger)
Trygon Factor, 1966 (Granger)
Tryout, 1916 (Laurel and Hardy)
Tryptych, 1963 (Cusack)
Trzy koniety, 1957 (Łomnicki)
Tsareubiitsa, 1991 (McDowell; Yankovsky)
Tsubaki Sanjuro, 1962 (Mifune; Shimura)
Tsubakuro-gasa, 1955 (Hasegawa)
Tsubasa wa kokoro ni tsukete, 1978 (Kagawa)
Tsui Kun II, 1994 (Chan)
Tsuki kara kita otoko, 1951 (Hasegawa)
Tsuki no wataridori, 1951 (Hasegawa)
Tsuki wa noborinu, 1955 (Tanaka)
Tsukigata Hanpeita, 1929 (Hasegawa)
Tsukigata Hanpeita, 1933 (Yamada)
Tsukigata Hanpeita, 1934 (Hasegawa)
Tsukigata Hanpeita, 1952 (Yamada)
Tsukigata Hanpeita, 1956 (Hasegawa; Kyo)
Tsukigata Hanpeita: Hana no maki, 1956 (Yamamura)
Tsukiyo no kasa, 1955 (Tanaka)
Tsuma no kokoro, 1956 (Mifune; Takamine)
Tsuma to iu na no onnatachi, 1963 (Tsukasa)
Tsuma to shite haha to shite, 1961 (Takamine)
Tsuma to shite onnato shite, 1961 (Mori)
Tsurigane-so, 1940 (Takamine)
Tsurugi no ketsuen, 1928 (Hasegawa)
Tsurugi o koete, 1930 (Yamada)
Tsuruhachi Tsurujiro, 1938 (Hasegawa; Yamada; Yamamura)
Tsuzurikata kyodai, 1958 (Kagawa)
Tsuzurikata kyoshitsu, 1938 (Takamine)
Tu m'appartiens, 1929 (Bertini)
Tu m'as sauvé la vie, 1950 (Fernandel)
Tu mi turbi, 1982 (Benigni)
Tua donna, 1954 (Neal)
Tucker, 1988 (Bridges; Landau)
Tucker: The Man and His Dream. *See* Tucker, 1988
Tudor Rose, 1936 (Mills)
Tueur, 1971 (Blier; Depardieu; Gabin)
Tueur triste, 1984 (Feuillère)
Tueurs de San Francisco, 1965 (Palance)
Tugboat Annie, 1933 (Beery; Dressler; O'Sullivan; Young, R.)
Tugboat Annie Sails Again, 1940 (Reagan; Wyman)
Tulipe noire, 1963 (Delon)
Tull-Bom, 1951 (Björnstrand)
Tulsa, 1949 (Armendáriz; Hayward; Preston)
Tumbleweed, 1953 (Van Cleef)
Tumbleweeds, 1925 (Hart)
Tumbling River, 1927 (Mix)
Tumbling Tumbleweeds, 1935 (Autry; Rogers, R.)
Tummy Trouble, 1989 (Turner, K.)
Tumultes, 1931 (Boyer)
Tuna Clipper, 1949 (McDowall)
Tune in Tomorrow ..., 1990 (Falk; Hershey; Reeves)
Tunel, 1988 (Rey)
Tuner Has Arrived. *See* E arrivato l'accordatore, 1952
Tunes of Glory, 1960 (Guinness; Mills; York)
Tuning His Ivories. *See* Laughing Gas, 1914
Tunisian Victory, 1943 (Huston, J.; Meredith)

Tunnel, 1935 (Huston, W.)
Tunnel. *See* Tunel, 1988
Tunnel of Love, 1958 (Day; Kelly, Gene; Widmark)
Tunnel to the Sun. *See* Kurobe no taiyo, 1968
Tunnelvision, 1976 (Candy)
Turandot, princesse de Chine, 1934 (Dalio)
Turn Back the Clock, 1933 (Three Stooges)
Turn Back the Hours, 1928 (Loy; Pidgeon)
Turn of the Screw, 1992 (Audran)
Turnabout, 1940 (Astor; Menjou)
Turnaround, 1989 (Borgnine)
Turner and Hooch, 1989 (Hanks)
Turning Point, 1952 (Holden; O'Brien, E.)
Turning Point, 1977 (Bancroft; MacLaine)
Turning Point. *See* Povorot, 1978
Turno, 1981 (Gassman)
Turtle Beach, 1992 (Scacchi)
Turtle Diary, 1985 (Jackson, G.; Kingsley)
Tuskegee Airmen, 1995 (Fishburne)
Tutti a casa, 1960 (Reggiani; Sordi)
Tutti dentro, 1984 (Pesci; Sordi)
Tutti Gli anni una volta l'anno, 1994 (Gassman)
Tutti innamorati, 1959 (Mastroianni)
Tuttles of Tahiti, 1942 (Laughton)
Tuttobenigni, 1985 (Benigni)
TV Dante, 1990 (Gielgud)
Två kvinnor, 1947 (Andersson, H.; Björnstrand; Dahlbeck)
Två Sköna Juveler, 1954 (Thulin)
Två trappor över gården, 1950 (Andersson, H.)
Tvärbalk, 1967 (Andersson, H.)
Twee frouwen, 1980 (Andersson, B.; Perkins)
'Tween Two Loves, 1911 (Pickford)
Twelfth Night, 1996 (Bonham-Carter; Kingsley)
Twelve Angry Men, 1957 (Cobb; Fonda, H.)
Twelve Chairs, 1970 (Brooks, M.)
Twelve Crowded Hours, 1939 (Ball)
Twelve Miles Out, 1927 (Crawford, J.; Gilbert)
Twelve O'Clock High, 1949 (Peck)
Twelve Plus One, 1969 (Terry-Thomas; Welles)
Twelve Plus One. *See* Su tredici, 1969
Twentieth Century, 1934 (Barrymore, J.; Lombard)
Twenty-Four Hours, 1931 (Francis; Hopkins, M.)
Twenty-Four Hours in a Woman's Life, 1952 (Oberon)
Twenty-Four Hours to Kill, 1965 (Rooney)
Twenty Million Sweethearts, 1934 (Powell, D.; Rogers, G.)
Twenty Minutes at Warner Brothers Studios, 1927 (Barrymore, J.)
Twenty Minutes of Love, 1914 (Chaplin, C.)
Twenty One, 1923 (Barthelmess)
Twenty-One Days Together. *See* 21 Days, 1937
Twenty-One Hours at Munich, 1976 (Quayle)
Twenty Plus Two, 1961 (Moorehead)
Twenty Shades of Pink, 1976 (Wallach)
Twenty Thousand Leagues under the Sea, 1954 (Douglas, K.; Lorre)
Twenty Thousand Men a Year, 1939 (Scott, R.)
Twenty Thousand Years in Sing Sing, 1933 (Tracy)
Twenty-Four Eyes. *See* Nijushi no Hitomi, 1954
Twenty-Four Hours of Shanghai, 1933 (Zhao Dan)
Twice a Woman. *See* Twee frouwen, 1980
Twice Branded, 1936 (Mason)
Twice in a Lifetime, 1985 (Ann-Margret; Burstyn; Hackman)
Twice-Told Tales, 1963 (Price)
Twice Two, 1920 (Howard, L.)
Twice Two, 1933 (Laurel and Hardy)
Twice upon a Time, 1953 (Hawkins)
Twilight. *See* Belle Aventure, 1942
Twilight for the Gods, 1958 (Charisse; Hudson; Kennedy)
Twilight Girls. *See* Collégiennes, 1956
Twilight in the Sierras, 1950 (Rogers, R.)
Twilight in Tokyo. *See* Tokyo boshoku, 1957
Twilight Meetings. *See* Möten i skymningen, 1957
Twilight of Honor, 1963 (Rains)

Twilight on the Rio Grande, 1947 (Autry)
Twilight Path. *See* Daikon to ninjin, 1964
Twilight Time, 1983 (Malden)
Twilight Zone: Rod Serling's Lost Classics, 1994 (Jones, James Earl; Palance)
Twilight Zone—The Movie, 1983 (Meredith)
Twilight's Last Gleaming, 1977 (Cotten; Douglas, Melvyn; Lancaster; Widmark)
Twin Beds, 1942 (Bennett)
Twin Detectives, 1976 (Gish)
Twin Dragons, 1992 (Chan)
Twin Flats, 1916 (Laurel and Hardy)
Twin Peaks: Fire Walk with Me, 1992 (Stanton)
Twin Sisters, 1915 (Laurel and Hardy)
Twinkle in God's Eye, 1955 (Rooney)
Twinkle, Twinkle, Lucky Stars, 1985 (Chan)
Twinky, 1969 (Bronson; Hawkins; Howard, T.)
Twins, 1925 (Laurel and Hardy)
Twins, 1988 (DeVito; Schwarzenegger)
Twins of Evil, 1971 (Cushing)
Twist. *See* Folies bourgeoises, 1976
Twist Again à Moscou, 1986 (Blier; Noiret)
Twist, ninfette e vitelloni, 1962 (Fabrizi)
Twist of Fate, 1954 (Rogers, G.)
Twist of Fate, 1989 (Travolta)
Twist of Fate. *See* Beautiful Stranger, 1953
Twisted Lives. *See* Menteurs, 1961
Twisted Obsession. *See* Sueno del Mono Loco, 1989
Twisted Trail, 1910 (Pickford)
Twisted Trails, 1916 (Mix)
Twisted Triggers, 1926 (Arthur)
Twister, 1988 (Robbins)
Twister, 1989 (Stanton)
Twixt Love and Fire, 1914 (Arbuckle)
Two. *See* Deux, 1989
Two against the City. *See* Deux hommes dans la ville, 1973
Two against the World, 1936 (Bogart)
Two Americans, 1929 (Huston, J.; Huston, W.)
Two Arabian Knights, 1927 (Astor; Karloff)
Two Are Guilty. *See* Glaive et la balance, 1963
Two before Zero, 1962 (Rathbone)
Two Bits, 1995 (Pacino)
Two Bright Boys, 1939 (Cooper)
Two Brothers, 1910 (Pickford)
Two Brothers. *See* Brüder Schellenberg, 1926
Two Can Play, 1926 (Bow)
Two Colonels. *See* I due colonelli, 1962
Two Comrades Served. *See* Sluzhili dva tovarishcha, 1968
Two Daughters. *See* Teen Kanya, 1961
Two Daughters of Eve, 1912 (Gish)
Two Deaths, 1996 (Braga)
Two Dinky Dramas of a Non-Serious Kind, 1914 (Beery)
Two English Girls. *See* Deux Anglaises et le continent, 1971
Two Evil Eyes. *See* Due occhi diabolici, 1990
Two-Faced Woman, 1941 (Douglas, Melvyn; Garbo; Gordon)
Two Faces of Doctor Jekyll, 1960 (Lee, C.; Reed)
Two Fisted Law, 1932 (Brennan; Wayne)
Two Flags West, 1950 (Cotten; Darnell; Wilde)
Two Flaming Youths, 1927 (Fields, W. C.)
Two for the Money, 1971 (Brennan; Dreyfuss)
Two for the Road, 1966 (Finney; Hepburn, A.; Ryan, M.)
Two for the Seesaw, 1962 (MacLaine; Mitchum)
Two for Tonight, 1935 (Bennett; Crosby)
Two from One Housing Block. *See* Two from the Same Block, 1957
Two from the Same Block, 1957 (Bondarchuk)
Two Girls and a Sailor, 1944 (Durante; Gardner; Keaton, B.)
Two Girls on Broadway, 1940 (Blondell; Turner, L.)
Two Girls Wanted, 1927 (Gaynor)
Two-Gun Cupid. *See* Bad Man, 1941
Two-Gun Gussie, 1918 (Lloyd)
Two Guns, 1917 (Carey)
Two Guys Abroad, 1961 (Raft)

Two Guys from Milwaukee, 1946 (Bacall; Bogart)
Two Guys from Texas, 1948 (Malone)
Two-Headed Spy, 1958 (Caine; Hawkins; Pleasence)
Two Hearts that Beat as Ten, 1915 (Beery)
Two in a Crowd, 1936 (Bennett; McCrea)
Two in the Bush. *See* Rally, 1980
Two in the Shadow. *See* Midaregumo, 1967
Two Jakes, 1990 (Dunaway; Keitel; Nicholson; Wallach)
Two Kinds of Women, 1932 (Hopkins, M.)
Two-Lane Blacktop, 1971 (Oates; Stanton)
Two Leaves and a Bud. *See* Rahi, 1952
Two Lives of Mattia Pascal. *See* Due vita di Mattia Pascal, 1985
Two Lovers, 1928 (Banky; Colman; Lukas)
Two Loves, 1961 (Hawkins; MacLaine)
Two Lunatics, 1912-13 (White)
Two Men and a Girl. *See* Honeymoon, 1947
Two Men in Town. *See* Deux hommes dans la ville, 1973
Two Men of the Desert, 1913 (Carey; Crisp; Sweet)
Two Minds for Murder. *See* Quelqu'un derriére la porte, 1971
Two-Minute Warning, 1976 (Heston; Pidgeon; Rowlands)
Two Moons. *See* Dwa ksiezyce, 1993
Two Mrs. Carrolls, 1947 (Bogart; Stanwyck)
Two Much, 1996 (Aiello; Banderas; Griffith; Wallach)
Two Mules for Sister Sara, 1970 (Eastwood; MacLaine)
Two Nights with Cleopatra. *See* Due notti con Cleopatra, 1953
Two Nudes Bathing, 1995 (Hurt, J.)
Two of a Kind. *See* Rounder, 1914
Two of a Kind, 1951 (O'Brien, E.)
Two of a Kind, 1983 (Bates, K.; Reed; Robertson; Travolta)
Two of Them. *See* Ok ketten, 1977
Two of Us. *See* Nous Deux, 1992
Two Old Tars, 1913 (Arbuckle)
Two on the Tiles, 1951 (Lom)
Two Orphans, 1915 (Bara)
Two Orphans. *See* Due orfanelle, 1942
Two Paths, 1911 (Crisp)
Two People, 1972 (Baye)
Two Plus Fours, 1930 (Crosby)
Two Rode Together, 1961 (Marsh; Stewart; Widmark)
Two Scrambled, 1918 (Lloyd)
Two Seconds, 1932 (Robinson, E.)
Two Sisters, 1929 (Karloff)
Two Sisters from Boston, 1946 (Durante)
Two Smart People, 1946 (Ball; Winters)
Two Tars, 1928 (Laurel and Hardy)
Two Thousand Years Later, 1969 (Horton)
Two Tickets to Broadway, 1951 (Leigh, Janet; Miller)
Two Tickets to London, 1943 (Fitzgerald; Morgan)
Two Wagons, Both Covered, 1923 (Rogers, W.)
Two-Way Stretch, 1960 (Sellers)
Two Weeks in Another Town, 1962 (Charisse; Douglas, K.; Robinson, E.; Trevor)
Two Weeks in September. *See* Coeur joie, 1967
Two Weeks with Love, 1950 (Calhern; Reynolds, D.)
Two White Arms, 1932 (Menjou)
Two Women. *See* Två kvinnor, 1947
Two Women. *See* Ciociara, 1961
Two Women. *See* Två Kvinnor, 1975
Two Women. *See* Ok ketten, 1977
Two Women. *See* Twee Vrouwen, 1979
Two Years before the Mast, 1946 (Fitzgerald; Ladd)
Ty pomnis li?, 1914 (Mozhukin)
Tycoon, 1947 (Quinn; Wayne)
Tykho Moon, 1996 (Piccoli)
Type bien, 1990 (Gélin)
Typhon sur Nagasaki, 1956 (Darrieux; Marais; Yamamura)
Typhoon, 1914 (Hayakawa)
Typhoon, 1940 (Preston)
Typhoon over Nagasaki. *See* Typhon sur Nagasaki, 1956
Typical Budget, 1925 (Buchanan)
Tyrant of Toledo. *See* Amants de Tolède, 1953

Tyson, 1995 (Scott, G.)
Tystnaden, 1963 (Thulin)
Tyvepak, 1921 (Madsen and Schenstrøm)
U-Boat 29. *See* Spy in Black, 1939
U-boat 39. *See* Ubåt 39, 1952
U.M.C., 1969 (Robinson, E.)
U.S.S. Teakettle. *See* You're in the Navy Now, 1951
Ubåt 39, 1952 (Andersson, H.; Dahlbeck)
Uberflussige Menschen, 1926 (Krauss; Rasp)
Ubit Drakona, 1989 (Yankovsky)
Uccidere in silenzio, 1972 (Cervi)
Uchiiri zenya, 1941 (Shimura)
Uchveli uzh davno krisantemi v sadu, 1916 (Mozhukin)
Udan Khatola, 1955 (Kumar)
Udeippon, 1930 (Yamada)
Udhaar, 1949 (Anand)
Udienza, 1971 (Cardinale; Cuny; Gassman; Piccoli)
Udvari levego, 1917 (Lukas)
Uemon torimono-cho: Uemon Edo-sugata, 1940 (Shimura)
UFO Incident, 1975 (Jones, James Earl)
Uforia, 1985 (Stanton)
Ugetsu monogatari, 1953 (Kyo; Mori; Tanaka)
Ugly American, 1963 (Brando; Okada)
Ugolok, 1916 (Mozhukin)
Uijin, 1933 (Hasegawa)
Ukigumo, 1955 (Mori; Takamine)
Ukigusa, 1959 (Kyo; Ryu)
Ulisse, 1954 (Douglas, K.; Mangano; Quinn)
Uloupená hranice, 1947 (Brodský)
Ultima carrozella, 1943 (Fabrizi; Magnani)
Ultima chance, 1973 (Wallach)
Ultima cinque minuti, 1955 (Brazzi)
Ultima donna, 1976 (Baye; Depardieu)
Ultima Mazurka, 1986 (Josephson)
Ultima nemica, 1938 (Valli)
Ultima Sentenza. *See* Son dernier verdict, 1951
Última cena, 1976 (Villagra)
Ultimata donna, 1976 (Piccoli)
Ultimate Solution of Grace Quigley, 1983 (Hepburn, K.; Nolte)
Ultimate Warrior, 1975 (Brynner; Von Sydow)
Ultimatum. *See* Ultimatum alla città, 1975
Ultimatum alla città, 1975 (Cobb)
Ultimi angeli, 1977 (Kennedy)
Ultimi cinque minuti, 1955 (Darnell)
Ultimo addio, 1942 (Cervi)
Ultimo incontro, 1951 (Valli)
Ultimo Lord. *See* Femme en homme, 1931
Ultimo Rey de los Incas. *See* Vermachtnis des Inka, 1966
Ultimo sogno, 1921 (Bertini)
Ultimo tango a Parigi, 1972 (Brando; Léaud)
Ultimo uomo della terra, 1964 (Price)
Ultimos dias de Pompeya, 1960 (Rey)
Últimos de Filipinas, 1945 (Rey)
Ulvejaegerne, 1926 (Madsen and Schenstrøm)
Ulysses. *See* Ulisse, 1954
Ulysses' Gaze. *See* To Vlemma tou Odyssea, 1995
Ulzana's Raid, 1972 (Lancaster)
Um Thron und Liebe. *See* Sarajewo, 1955
Uma, 1941 (Takamine)
Umanità, 1946 (Cervi)
Umarete wa mita keredo, 1932 (Ryu)
Umarmungen und andere Sachen, 1976 (Léaud)
Umbartha. *See* Subah, 1983
Umbracle, 1970 (Lee, C.)
Umbrella Woman. *See* Good Wife, 1986
Umbrellas of Cherbourg. *See* Parapluies de Cherbourg, 1964
Umi no hanabi, 1951 (Yamada)
Umi no yaju, 1949 (Yamamura)
Umi o wataru sairei, 1941 (Shimura)
Umon torimonocho: Harebare gojusan-tsugi, 1936 (Shimura)
Umwege zum Glück, 1939 (Dagover)

Un, deux, trois, quatre?, 1960 (Chevalier)
Una su 13, 1969 (Welles)
Una su tredici, 1969 (Gassman)
Unaccustomed as We Are, 1929 (Laurel and Hardy)
Unanoide, 1979 (Kennedy)
Unapproachable. *See* Unerreichbare, 1982
Unashamed, 1932 (Young, R.)
Unbearable Lightness of Being, 1988 (Binoche; Day-Lewis; Josephson; Olbrychski; Olin)
Unbekannte Morgen, 1923 (Krauss; Lukas)
Uncanny, 1977 (Cushing; Greenwood; Milland; Pleasence)
Uncensored Movies, 1923 (Rogers, W.)
Uncertain Glory, 1944 (Flynn; Lukas)
Uncertain Lady, 1934 (Horton)
Unchanging Sea, 1910 (Pickford)
Uncharted Seas, 1921 (Valentino)
Unchastened Woman, 1925 (Bara)
Uncivil Warbirds, 1946 (Three Stooges)
Uncivil Warriors, 1935 (Three Stooges)
Uncle Buck, 1989 (Candy)
Uncle Harry, 1945 (Sanders)
Uncle Tom's Cabin, 1910 (Talmadge)
Uncle Tom's Cabin, 1957 (Massey)
Uncle Tom's Cabin, 1968 (Lom)
Uncle Tom's Cabin, 1987 (Dern)
Uncle Vanya. *See* Dyadya Vanya, 1970
Uncle Was a Vampire. *See* Tempi duri per vampiri, 1959
Uncommon Love, 1983 (Hunter)
Uncommon Valor, 1983 (Hackman)
Uncommon Women ... and Others, 1979 (Streep)
Unconquered, 1947 (Bond; Constantine; Goddard; Karloff)
Uncontrollable Circumstances. *See* Force majeure, 1989
Unconventional Linda. *See* Holiday, 1938
...Und deine Liebe auch, 1962 (Mueller-Stahl)
...Und der Himmel steht still, 1993 (Hopkins, A.; Rossellini)
...Und keiner schämte sich, 1960 (Fröhlich)
Undefeated, 1969 (Hudson; Wayne)
Under a Shadow, 1915 (Chaney)
Under a Texas Moon, 1930 (Loy)
Under Burning Skies, 1912 (Sweet)
Under California Skies, 1948 (Rogers, R.)
Under Capricorn, 1949 (Bergman; Cotten)
Under Cover, 1987 (Leigh, Jennifer Jason)
Under-Cover Man, 1933 (Raft)
Under Cover Rouge. *See* Voci bianche, 1964
Under False Colors, 1914 (Talmadge)
Under Fiesta Stars, 1941 (Autry)
Under Fire, 1926 (Arthur)
Under Fire, 1983 (Hackman; Harris, E.; Nolte)
Under Heat, 1994 (Grant, L.)
Under Milk Wood, 1973 (Burton; O'Toole; Taylor, E.)
Under My Skin, 1950 (Garfield; Presle)
Under Nevada Skies, 1946 (Rogers, R.)
Under Pressure, 1935 (McLaglen)
Under Satan's Sun. *See* Sous le soleil de Satan, 1987
Under Sheriff, 1914 (Arbuckle)
Under Siege, 1986 (Ayres)
Under Siege, 1992 (Jones, T.)
Under Suspicion, 1992 (Neeson)
Under Ten Flags. *See* Sotto dieci bandiere, 1960
Under the Banner of Samurai. *See* Furin kaza, 1969
Under the Clock. *See* Clock, 1945
Under the Daisies, 1913 (Talmadge)
Under the Gaslight, 1914 (Barrymore, L.)
Under the Gun, 1950 (Jaffe)
Under the Influence, 1986 (Reeves)
Under the Lash, 1921 (Swanson)
Under the Pampas Moon, 1935 (Hayworth)
Under the Red Robe, 1924 (Powell, W.)
Under the Red Robe, 1937 (Massey; Veidt)
Under the Roofs of Paris. *See* Sous les toits de Paris, 1930

Under the Sign of Scorpio. *See* Sotto il segno dello scorpione, 1969
Under the Sun of Rome. *See* Sotto il sole di Roma, 1948
Under the Top, 1918 (Crisp)
Under the Volcano, 1984 (Finney; Huston, J.)
Under the Yoke, 1918 (Bara)
Under the Yoke of Sin. *See* Vo vlasti gretcha, 1915
Under the Yum-Yum Tree, 1963 (Lemmon)
Under Two Flags, 1916 (Bara)
Under Two Flags, 1936 (Carradine; Colbert; Colman; McLaglen; Russell, R.)
Under Two Jags, 1923 (Laurel and Hardy)
Under Western Stars, 1938 (Rogers, R.)
Under Your Hat, 1940 (Henreid; Terry-Thomas)
Undercover, 1943 (Baker)
Undercover Blues, 1993 (Quaid; Turner, K.)
Undercover Doctor, 1939 (Crawford, B.)
Undercover Hero. *See* Soft Beds and Hard Battles, 1973
Undercover Man, 1949 (Ford, G.)
Undercurrent, 1946 (Hepburn, K.; Mitchum; Taylor, R.)
Underground. *See* Undercover, 1943
Underground Aces, 1980 (Griffith)
Understanding Heart, 1927 (Crawford, J.)
Undertow, 1949 (Hudson)
Underwater Odyssey. *See* Neptune Factor, 1973
Underwater!, 1954 (Russell, J.)
Underworld, 1985 (Richardson, M.; Elliott)
Underworld. *See* Ankoku-gai, 1956
Underworld Story, 1950 (Duryea; Marshall)
Underworld, U.S.A., 1961 (Robertson)
Undisclosed, 1996 (Moore, Demi)
Unearthly, 1957 (Carradine)
Unerreichbare, 1982 (Caron)
Unexpected Uncle, 1941 (Coburn, C.)
Unfaithful, 1931 (Lukas)
Unfaithful, 1947 (Ayres)
Unfaithful Wife. *See* **Femme infidèle**, 1969
Unfaithfully Yours, 1948 (Darnell; Harrison; Kinski; Moore, Dudley)
Unfaithfuls. *See* Infedeli, 1953
Unfinished Business, 1941 (Dunne; Montgomery)
Unfinished Dance, 1947 (Charisse; O'Brien, M.)
Unfinished Journey, 1943 (Gielgud)
Unfinished Rainbows, 1941 (Ladd)
Unfinished Story. *See* Neokonchennaya povest, 1955
Unfinished Tale. *See* Neokonchennaya povest, 1955
Unforeseen Complication, 1911 (White)
Unforgiven, 1960 (Gish; Hepburn, A.; Huston, J.; Lancaster)
Unforgiven, 1992 (Eastwood; Freeman; Hackman; Harris, R.)
Unfriendly Enemies, 1925 (Laurel and Hardy)
Ung flukt, 1959 (Ullmann)
Ungarische Rhapsodie, 1928 (Dagover)
Ungarn in Flammen, 1957 (Schell, Maria)
Unguarded Hour, 1936 (Young, L.)
Unguarded Moment, 1956 (Russell, R.; Williams, E.)
Unguarded Woman, 1924 (Astor)
Unheilbar, 1916 (Jannings)
Unheimliche Geschichten, 1919 (Veidt)
Unheimliche Geschichten, 1932 (Wegener)
Unhold, 1996 (Malkovich)
Unholy, 1988 (Howard, T.)
Unholy Four. *See* Stranger Came Home, 1954
Unholy Garden, 1931 (Colman; Wray)
Unholy Love. *See* Alraune, 1927
Unholy Night, 1929 (Barrymore, L.; Karloff)
Unholy Partner, 1941 (Robinson, E.)
Unholy Partners, 1941 (Dalio)
Unholy Three, 1925 (Chaney; McLaglen)
Unholy Three, 1930 (Chaney)
Unholy Wife, 1957 (Dors; Steiger)
Unhook the Stars, 1996 (Depardieu; Rowlands)
Unicorn Fist, 1973 (Lee, B.)
Uniformes et grandes manoeuvres, 1950 (Fernandel)
Uninhibited. *See* Pianos mécaniques, 1965

Uninvited, 1944 (Crisp; Milland)
Union Depot, 1932 (Blondell)
Union Pacific, 1939 (McCrea; Preston; Quinn; Stanwyck)
Union Square, 1950 (Fitzgerald)
Union Station, 1950 (Holden)
Universal Soldier, 1992 (Van Damme)
Universe, 1961 (Meredith)
Unkissed Man, 1929 (Harlow)
Unknown, 1927 (Chaney; Crawford, J.)
Unknown Man, 1951 (Pidgeon)
Unknown Valley, 1933 (Bond)
Unlawful Trade, 1914 (Chaney)
Unmarried, 1939 (O'Connor)
Unmarried. See Glasberget, 1953
Unmarried Woman, 1977 (Bates, A.)
Unmögliche Frau, 1936 (Fröhlich)
Unmögliche Liebe, 1932 (Nielsen)
Unnatural Pursuits, 1991 (Bates, A.)
Uno scacco tutto matto, 1968 (Robinson, E.; Terry-Thomas)
Unpardonable Sin, 1919 (Beery; Sweet)
Unprotected, 1916 (Sweet)
Unremarkable Life, 1989 (Neal; Winters)
Uns et les autres, 1981 (Caan; Chaplin, G.; Olbrychski; Stone)
Unseeing Eyes, 1923 (Barrymore, L.)
Unseen, 1945 (Marshall; McCrea)
Unseen Enemy, 1912 (Carey; Gish)
Unseen Hands, 1924 (Beery)
Unseen Heroes. See Battle of the V 1, 1958
Unser Mann im Dschungel, 1986 (Mueller-Stahl)
Unsichtbare Gegner, 1933 (Homolka; Lorre)
Unsinkable Molly Brown, 1964 (Reynolds, D.)
Unsterbliche Herz, 1939 (Wegener)
Unsterbliche Lump, 1930 (Fröhlich)
Unstrung Heroes, 1995 (Keaton, D.; Turturro)
Unsuspected, 1947 (Rains)
Untamed, 1920 (Mix)
Untamed, 1929 (Crawford, J.; Montgomery)
Untamed, 1940 (Milland)
Untamed, 1955 (Hayward; Moorehead; Power)
Untamed. See Arakure, 1957
Untamed Frontier, 1952 (Cotten; Van Cleef; Winters)
Untamed Lady, 1926 (Swanson)
Untel Pere et Fils, 1943 (Jourdan; Jouvet; Morgan; Raimu)
Unter Ausschluss der Offentlichkeit, 1927 (Krauss)
Unter Ausschluss der Öffentlichkeit, 1937 (Wegener)
Unter falscher Flagge, 1932 (Fröhlich)
Unter Geiern, 1964 (Granger)
Unter Palmen am blauen Meer, 1957 (Dagover)
Untergangens Arkitektur. See Architecture of Doom, 1991
Until the Day We Meet Again. See Mata au hi made, 1950
Until the End of the World. See Bis ans Ende der Welt, 1991
Until They Sail, 1957 (Fontaine; Newman)
Until We Meet Again. See Mata au hi made, 1950
Untouchables, 1987 (Connery; Costner; De Niro; García)
Unveiling, 1911 (Normand)
Unwelcome Children. See Kreuzzug des Weibes, 1926
Unwelcome Guest, 1912 (Carey; Gish; Pickford)
Unzipped, 1994 (Gere; Minnelli)
Uogashi shunjitsu, 1952 (Yamamura)
Uomini contro, 1970 (Cuny; Volonté)
Uomini dal passo pesante, 1966 (Cotten)
Uomini e lupi, 1956 (Armendáriz; Mangano; Montand)
Uomini non sono ingrati, 1937 (Cervi)
Uomini sono nemici, 1948 (Mangano)
Uomo che viene de lontano, 1968 (Van Cleef)
Uomo da bruciare, 1962 (Volonté)
Uomo da rispettare, 1974 (Douglas, K.)
Uomo dai calzoni corti, o L'amore piu grande, 1958 (Valli)
Uomo dai cinque palloni, 1965 (Mastroianni)
Uomo dalla pelle dura, 1971 (Borgnine)
Uomo dalle due ombre, 1971 (Bronson; Mason; Ullmann)

Uomo di Corleone, 1977 (Papas)
Uomo, l'orgoglio, la vendetta, 1967 (Kinski)
Uomo la Bestia e la Virtù, 1953 (Welles)
Uomo ritorna, 1946 (Cervi; Magnani)
Uova di Garofano, 1992 (Cuny)
Up a Tree, 1930 (Arbuckle)
Up and Going, 1922 (Mix)
Up Close and Personal, 1996 (Nelligan; Pfeiffer; Redford)
Up, Down and Sideways. See Pano Kato Ke Plagios, 1993
Up for Murder, 1931 (Ayres)
Up from the Beach, 1965 (Crawford, B.; Robertson; Rosay)
Up in Arms, 1944 (Andrews, D.; Calhern; Dumont; Kaye)
Up in Central Park, 1948 (Durbin; Price)
Up in Daisy's Penthouse, 1953 (Three Stooges)
Up in the World, 1956 (Wisdom)
Up Periscope, 1959 (Garner; Oates; O'Brien, E.)
Up Pops the Devil, 1931 (Lombard)
Up Pops the Duke, 1931 (Arbuckle)
Up San Juan Hill, 1910 (Mix)
Up the Creek, 1958 (Sellers)
Up the Front, 1972 (Hoskins; Bogart; Brown)
Up the River, 1930 (Tracy)
Up the River, 1938 (Robinson, B.)
Up the Sandbox, 1972 (Streisand)
Up to Date, 1989 (Dunaway)
Up to His Ears. See Tribulations d'un chinois en Chine, 1965
Up with the Green Lift. See Oppåt med gröna hissen, 1952
Upheaval, 1916 (Barrymore, L.)
Uphill All the Way, 1986 (Reynolds, B.)
Upon This Rock, 1970 (Bogarde; Evans; Welles)
Uppdragnet, 1978 (Rey)
Uppehall i Myrlandet. See 4 x 4, 1965
Upper Crust, 1981 (Crawford, B.)
Upper Hand. See Du Rififi à Paname, 1966
Upperworld, 1934 (Astor; Rogers, G.; Rooney)
Upright Sinner. See Brave Sünder, 1931
Ups and Downs, 1914 (Beery; Laurel and Hardy)
Upstage, 1926 (Shearer)
Upstairs, 1919 (Normand)
Upstairs and Downstairs, 1959 (Cardinale)
Upstairs, Downstairs. See Schodami w Gore, Schodami w Dol, 1988
Uptown Saturday Night, 1974 (Poitier; Pryor)
Upturned Glass, 1947 (Mason)
Uragirareta mono, 1926 (Tanaka)
Urakaidan, 1965 (Tsukasa)
Uranus, 1991 (Depardieu; Noiret)
Urashima Taro no koei, 1946 (Takamine)
Urban Cowboy, 1980 (Travolta; Winger)
Urbashe, 1986 (Chatterjee)
Ureshii koro, 1934 (Yamada)
Urgano sul Po, 1955 (Schell, Maria)
Urge to Kill. See With Intent to Kill, 1984
Ursule et Grelu, 1973 (Dalio; Girardot)
Uruhashiki ai, 1931 (Takamine)
Uruhashiki shuppatsu, 1939 (Takamine)
Used People, 1992 (Bates, K.; MacLaine; Mastroianni)
Users, 1978 (Curtis, T.; Fontaine)
Usmev diabla, 1988 (Tyszkiewicz)
Ustedes los ricos, 1948 (Infante)
Usual Way, 1913 (Beery)
Uta-andon, 1943 (Yamada)
Uta-kichi andon, 1938 (Yamada)
Utah, 1945 (Rogers, R.)
Utah Kid, 1930 (Karloff)
Utamaro and Five Women. See Utamaro o mehuru go-nin no onna, 1946
Utamaro o mehuru go-nin no onna, 1946 (Tanaka)
Utamaro o meguru gonin no onna, 1959 (Hasegawa)
Útkösben, 1979 (Nowicki; Tyszkiewicz)
Utopia, 1978 (Sanda)
Utopia. See Atoll K, 1951
Utsukishisa to kanashimi to, 1965 (Yamamura)

Utsukushii hito, 1954 (Kagawa)
Utsukushiki batsu, 1949 (Yamamura)
Uttarayan, 1985 (Azmi)
Uttoran, 1994 (Chatterjee)
Utvandrarna, 1972 (Ullmann; Von Sydow)
Utz, 1993 (Mueller-Stahl)
Uwasa no onna, 1954 (Tanaka)
V. I. Warshawski, 1991 (Turner, K.)
V.I.P.s, 1963 (Burton; Jourdan; Rutherford; Smith; Taylor, E.; Welles)
V boynoi slepote strastei, 1916 (Mozhukin)
V polnotch na kladbische, 1914 (Mozhukin)
V roukatch bespotchadnogo roka, 1914 (Mozhukin)
Va bangue, 1930 (Dagover)
Va voir maman, papa travaille, 1977 (Presle)
Vacances conjugales, 1933 (Brasseur)
Vacances de Max. See Max part en vacances, 1913
Vacances de Monsieur Hulot, 1953 (Tati)
Vacances explosives, 1956 (Arletty)
Vacances portugaises, 1962 (Deneuve; Gélin)
Vacanza, 1969 (Redgrave, V.)
Vacanza, 1988 (Mastroianni)
Vacanze d'inverno, 1959 (Morgan; Sordi)
Vacanze di Natale '91, 1992 (Sordi)
Vacation. See Vacanza, 1969
Vacation from Marriage. See Perfect Strangers, 1945
Vache et le prisonnier, 1959 (Fernandel)
Vacuum Zone. See Shinku chitai, 1952
Vado a riprendermi il gatto, 1987 (Cassel)
Vaeddeløberen, 1919 (Madsen and Schenstrøm)
Vagabond, 1916 (Chaplin, C.; Purviance)
Vagabond King, 1930 (MacDonald)
Vagabond King, 1956 (Price)
Vagabond Lady, 1935 (Young, R.)
Vagabond Loafers, 1949 (Three Stooges)
Vagabond Lover, 1929 (Dressler)
Vagabond Violinist. See Broken Melody, 1934
Vagabonds du rêve, 1949 (Rosay)
Vaghe stelle dell'Orsa, 1965 (Cardinale)
Vagrant, 1992 (Brooks, M.)
Valachi Papers, 1972 (Bronson)
Valborgsmassoafton, 1935 (Bergman)
Valdez Horses. See Valdez il mezzosanque, 1973
Valdez il mezzosanque, 1973 (Bronson)
Valdez Is Coming, 1971 (Lancaster)
Valdez, the Halfbreed. See Valdez il mezzosanque, 1973
Valencia, 1926 (Karloff)
Valentina, 1965 (Félix)
Valentina, 1983 (Quinn)
Valentine, 1979 (DeVito)
Valentine Girl, 1917 (Barthelmess; Menjou)
Valentino, 1977 (Caron)
Valerie, 1957 (Hayden)
Valiant, 1929 (Muni)
Valiant, 1962 (Mills; Shaw)
Valiant Is the Word for Carrie, 1936 (Carey; McDaniel)
Valientes no mueren, 1961 (Armendáriz)
Valle de las espadas, 1963 (Rey; Valli)
Vallée aux loups, 1966 (Fresnay)
Valley Forge, 1974 (Fonda, H.; Walken)
Valley Girl, 1983 (Cage)
Valley of Decision, 1915 (Bennett)
Valley of Decision, 1945 (Barrymore, L.; Crisp; Duryea; Garson; Peck)
Valley of Fire, 1951 (Autry)
Valley of Fury. See Chief Crazy Horse, 1955
Valley of Head Hunters, 1953 (Weissmuller)
Valley of Night, 1919 (Barrymore, L.)
Valley of Song, 1952 (Roberts, R.)
Valley of the Dolls, 1967 (Dreyfuss; Grant, L.; Hayward)
Valley of the Dolls. See Jacqueline Susann's Valley of the Dolls, 1981
Valley of the Eagles, 1951 (Lee, C.)
Valley of the Giants, 1938 (Crisp; Trevor)

Valley of the Kings, 1954 (Taylor, R.)
Valley of the Sun, 1942 (Ball)
Valley of the Swords. See Valle de las espadas, 1963
Valparaiso, Valparaiso, 1971 (Cuny)
Vals, 1985 (Carradine)
Valse de Paris, 1949 (Fresnay)
Valse du gorille, 1959 (Vanel)
Valse eternelle, 1936 (Brasseur)
Valse renversante, 1914 (Chevalier)
Valseuses, 1973 (Depardieu; Moreau)
Valseuses, 1974 (Huppert)
Value for Money, 1955 (Dors; Pleasence)
Valvaire d'Amour, 1923 (Vanel)
Vamos a matar, compañeros!, 1970 (Palance; Rey)
Vamping Venus. See Property Man, 1914
Vampir, 1969 (Lee, C.)
Vampira, 1974 (Niven)
Vampiras, 1969 (Carradine)
Vampire Bat, 1933 (Douglas, Melvyn; Wray)
Vampire Beast Craves Blood. See Blood Beast Terror, 1968
Vampire Hookers, 1978 (Carradine)
Vampire in Brooklyn, 1995 (Bassett; Murphy)
Vampire Lovers, 1970 (Cushing)
Vampire Men of the Lost Planet. See Horror of the Blood Monsters, 1970
Vampire over London. See Old Mother Riley Meets the Vampire, 1952
Vampire's Kiss, 1989 (Cage)
Vampires. See Vampiras, 1969
Van, 1976 (DeVito)
Vanessa, Her Love Story, 1935 (Crisp; Montgomery)
Vanganza, 1957 (Rey)
Vanina, 1922 (Nielsen)
Vanina, oder die Galgenhochzeit, 1923 (Wegener)
Vanina Vanini. See Vanina, 1922
Vanished, 1971 (Widmark; Young, R.)
Vanishing, 1993 (Bridges)
Vanishing Act, 1986 (Gould)
Vanishing American, 1955 (Van Cleef)
Vanishing Body. See Black Cat, 1934
Vanishing Cornwall, 1958 (Redgrave, M.)
Vanishing Legion, 1931 (Carey)
Vanishing Pioneer, 1928 (Powell, W.)
Vanishing Rider, 1928 (Karloff)
Vanishing Shadow, 1934 (Cobb)
Vanity, 1927 (Crisp)
Vanity Fair, 1932 (Loy)
Var sin väg, 1948 (Björnstrand; Dahlbeck)
Varelserna. See Créatures, 1966
Vargtimmen, 1968 (Josephson; Thulin; Ullmann; Von Sydow)
Variété, 1925 (Jannings)
Variétés, 1935 (Gabin)
Variety Girl, 1947 (Constantine; Crosby; Fitzgerald; Goddard; Hayden; Holden; Hope; Ladd; Lake; Lamour; Lancaster; Milland; Preston; Stanwyck)
Variety Lights. See Luci del varietà, 1950
Variola vera, 1982 (Josephson)
Varsity Girl. See Fair Co-ed, 1927
Varsity Show, 1937 (Powell, D.)
Vas-y maman, 1978 (Girardot)
Vasundhara, 1984 (Chatterjee)
Vater und Sonhe, 1988 (Christie; Ganz)
Vatican Affair. See Qualsiasi prezzo, 1968
Vatican Pimpernel, 1982 (Gielgud)
Vatican Story. See Qualsiasi prezzo, 1968
Vault of Horror, 1973 (Elliott; Terry-Thomas)
Vavasour Ball, 1914 (Talmadge)
Vedo nudo, 1969 (Vitti)
Vedovo, 1959 (Sordi)
Vegas, 1978 (Curtis, T.)
Vegas Strip War, 1984 (Hudson; Jones, James Earl)
Vegas Strip Wars, 1984 (Stone)
Veilchenfresser, 1926 (Dagover)

Veiled Lady, 1912-13 (White)
Veiled Man. *See* Homme voilé, 1987
Veiled Woman, 1928 (Lugosi)
Veille d'Armes, 1926 (Modot)
Veillees d'armes, 1994 (Noiret)
Veils of Bagdad, 1953 (Mature)
Veinard, 1975 (Cassel)
Veine d'Anatole. *See* Gros Lot, 1933
Veleno della parole, 1914 (Bertini)
Velour, 1967 (Bujold)
Velvet Touch, 1948 (Greenstreet; Russell, R.; Trevor)
Vend d'est, 1993 (McDowell)
Vendetta, 1919 (Jannings; Negri)
Vendetta. *See* Joaquin Murieta, 1964
Vendetta, 1995 (Josephson)
Vendetta di Aquila Nera, 1951 (Brazzi)
Vendetta di Ercole, 1960 (Crawford, B.)
Vendetta e un piatto che si serve freddo, 1971 (Kinski)
Vendetta nel sole, 1947 (Lollobrigida)
Vendetta of Samurai. *See* Ketto kagiya no tsuji, 1952
Vendetta: Secrets of a Mafia Bride, 1991 (Wallach)
Venditore di morte, 1972 (Kinski)
Venditore di palloncini, 1974 (Cobb; Cusack)
Vendredi 13 Heures. *See* World in My Pocket, 1961
Venere imperiale, 1962 (Lollobrigida; Presle)
Venetian Affair, 1967 (Karloff)
Venezia, la luna, e tu, 1958 (Sordi)
Vengeance. *See* Vanganza, 1957
Vengeance. *See* Zemsta, 1958
Vengeance. *See* Noroît, 1976
Vengeance d'une femme, 1990 (Huppert)
Vengeance du domestique, 1912 (Linder)
Vengeance Is Mine, 1969 (Borgnine)
Vengeance of Fu Manchu, 1967 (Lee, C.)
Vengeance of Galora, 1913 (Barrymore, L.)
Vengeance of the 47 Ronin. *See* Chushingura, 1932
Vengeance of the West, 1916 (Chaney)
Vengeance Trail. *See* Vendetta e un piatto che si serve freddo, 1971
Vengeance Valley, 1951 (Lancaster; Walker)
Venom, 1982 (Hayden; Kinski; Reed)
Vent d'est, 1970 (Volonté)
Vento del sud, 1959 (Cardinale)
Vento mi ha cantato una canzone, 1948 (Sordi)
Venus in Furs. *See* Paroxismus, 1969
Venus in the East, 1918 (Crisp)
Venus Model, 1918 (Normand)
Vénus impériale. *See* Venere imperiale, 1962
Vera Cruz, 1954 (Borgnine; Bronson; Constantine; Lancaster)
Vera Holgk und ihre Töchter. *See* Unmögliche Liebe, 1932
Vera storia della signora delle Camelie, 1981 (Rey)
Vera Vita di Antonio H., 1994 (Mastroianni)
Verano de la Señorita Forbes, 1988 (Schygulla)
Verano sangrieto, 1977 (Van Cleef)
Verbotene Land, 1924 (Banky)
Verdict, 1946 (Greenstreet; Lorre)
Verdict, 1974 (Gabin)
Verdict. *See* Testament, 1974
Verdict, 1982 (Mason; Newman; Willis)
Verdun, visions d'histoire, 1928 (Artaud)
Verflucht dies Amerika, 1973 (Chaplin, G.)
Verfuhrte, 1914 (Wegener)
Vergesst Mozart. *See* Zabudnite na Mozarta, 1985
Vergine de Norimberga, 1964 (Lee, C.)
Vergine di Roma, 1961 (Jourdan; Piccoli)
Vergine per il principe, 1965 (Gassman)
Vergiss, wenn Du kannst, 1956 (Fröhlich)
Vérité, 1960 (Bardot; Vanel)
Vérité sur Bébé Donge, 1951 (Darrieux; Gabin)
Vérités et mengsonges. *See* F for Fake, 1975
Verliebte Firma, 1932 (Fröhlich)
Verlorene, 1951 (Lorre)

Verlorene Ehre der Katharina Blum, 1975 (Winkler)
Verlorene Schatten, 1921 (Wegener)
Vermachtnis des Inka, 1966 (Rey)
Vermilion Pencil, 1922 (Hayakawa)
Verna—USO Girl, 1978 (Hurt, W.; Spacek)
Vernon Johns Story, 1994 (Jones, James Earl)
Verona Trial. *See* Processo a Verona, 1963
Veronika Voss. *See* Sehnsucht der Veronika Voss, 1982
Verratertor, 1965 (Kinski)
Vers l'abine, 1934 (Rosay)
Verschwörung zu Genua, 1921 (Kortner)
Verso sera, 1990 (Mastroianni)
Verspätung in Marienborn, 1963 (Ferrer)
Vertauschte Braut, 1915 (Krauss)
Vertauschte Braut, 1934 (Walbrook)
Vertige, 1934 (Arletty)
Vertige d'un soir, 1936 (Vanel)
Vertigine d'Amore, 1948 (Vanel)
Vertigo. *See* Dourman, 1912
Vértigo, 1945 (Félix)
Vertigo, 1958 (Novak; Stewart)
Verwegene Musikanten, 1956 (Dagover)
Very Big Withdrawal, 1979 (Sutherland)
Very Close Quarters, 1986 (Winters)
Very Good Young Man, 1919 (Crisp; Brown)
Very Handy Man. *See* Liola, 1964
Very Handy Man. *See* Stagione del nostro amore, 1965
Very Happy Alexander. *See* Alexandre le bienheureux, 1968
Very Honorable Guy, 1934 (Brown)
Very Private Affair. *See* Vie privée, 1962
Very Special Favor, 1965 (Boyer; Caron; Hudson)
Vesna, 1947 (Cherkassov)
Vessel of Wrath, 1937 (Lanchester; Laughton)
Vestervovvov, 1927 (Madsen and Schenstrøm)
Vestire gli ignudi, 1953 (Brasseur)
Veszelyban a pokol, 1921 (Banky)
Veuve Couderc, 1971 (Delon)
Vezelay, 1950 (Fresnay)
Vi som går scenvägen, 1938 (Björnstrand)
Vi tre debutera, 1953 (Björnstrand)
Vi två, 1939 (Björnstrand)
Via lattea. *See* Voie lactée, 1969
Via Montenapoleone, 1987 (Gélin)
Via Padova 46, 1954 (Masina; Sordi)
Viaccia, 1961 (Belmondo; Cardinale)
Viadukt, 1982 (Mueller-Stahl)
Viagem a Lisboa, 1995 (Vogler)
Viager, 1972 (Depardieu)
Viaggio, 1973 (Burton; Loren)
Viaggio con Anita, 1979 (Giannini; Hawn)
Viaggio d'Amore, 1990 (Sharif)
Viaggio de lavoro, 1968 (Mangano)
Viaggio in Italia, 1953 (Sanders; Bergman)
Viaggio nella vertigini, 1975 (Thulin)
Viaje, 1992 (Sanda)
Viale della speranza, 1952 (Mastroianni)
Vibes, 1988 (Falk)
Vice and Virtue. *See* Vice et la vertu, 1962
Vice et la vertu, 1962 (Deneuve; Girardot)
Vice Squad, 1931 (Francis; Lukas)
Vice Squad, 1953 (Goddard; Robinson, E.; Van Cleef)
Vice Versa, 1947 (Ustinov)
Vicious Circle, 1948 (Kortner)
Vicious Circle. *See* Circle, 1957
Vicious Circle. *See* Chakra, 1980
Vicious Circle, 1985 (Moreau; Sharif)
Vicoli e delitti. *See* Camorra, 1986
Vicomte règle ses comptes, 1967 (O'Brien, E.; Rey)
Victim, 1961 (Bogarde)
Victim of Jealousy, 1910 (Pickford)
Victims, 1982 (Nelligan)

Victims of Terror, 1967 (Lee, C.)

Victims of Vesuvius. *See* Victims of Terror, 1967

Victor, 1915 (Beery)

Victor, 1951 (Gabin)

Victor/Victoria, 1982 (Andrews, J.; Garner; Preston)

Victoria Cross, 1917 (Hayakawa)

Victoria the Great, 1937 (Henreid; Neagle; Walbrook)

Victors, 1963 (Finney; Mercouri; Moreau; Schneider; Wallach)

Victory, 1919 (Beery; Chaney)

Victory, 1941 (March)

Victory, 1981 (Caine; Huston, J.; Stallone; Von Sydow)

Victory, 1995 (Dafoe; Neill)

Victory at Entebbe, 1976 (Douglas, K.; Dreyfuss; Hopkins, A.; Lancaster; Taylor, E.)

Victory at Yorktown, 1965 (Hawkins)

Victory in the Dark. *See* Seger i mörker, 1954

Victory of Women. *See* Josei no shori, 1946

Victory Wedding, 1944 (Mills)

Vid vejen, 1988 (Von Sydow)

Vida es magnifica. *See* Voleur du Tibidabo, 1964

Vida Lactea, 1991 (Rey; Rooney)

Vida no vale nada, 1954 (Infante)

Videodrome, 1983 (Woods)

Vidhata, 1982 (Kumar)

Vidya, 1948 (Anand)

Vie, 1958 (Schell, Maria)

Vie à deux, 1958 (Brasseur; Darrieux; Fernandel; Feuillère; Philipe)

Vie. *See* Sauve qui peut, 1980

Vie continue, 1982 (Cassel; Girardot)

Vie crevee, 1992 (Piccoli)

Vie de Bohême, 1942 (Jourdan)

Vie de Boheme, 1993 (Léaud)

Vie de château, 1966 (Brasseur; Deneuve; Noiret)

Vie de chien, 1941 (Fernandel)

Vie de famille, 1985 (Binoche)

Vie de Polichinelle, 1905 (Linder)

Vie de Raimu, 1948 (Raimu)

Vie est à nous, 1936 (Modot)

Vie est un long fleuve tranquille, 1988 (Gélin)

Vie est un roman, 1984 (Chaplin, G.; Gassman)

Vie et rien d'autre, 1989 (Noiret)

Vie, l'amour, la mort, 1968 (Girardot)

Vie parisienne, 1936 (Morgan)

Vie privée, 1962 (Bardot; Mastroianni)

Vieille Fille, 1972 (Girardot; Noiret)

Vielle qui marchait dans la mer, 1992 (Moreau)

Vienna Burgtheater. *See* Burgtheater, 1936

Vienna Waltzes. *See* Wien tantz, 1951

Viennese Nights, 1930 (Lugosi; Pidgeon)

Vient de paraître, 1949 (Fresnay)

Viento de Colera, 1988 (Villagra)

Vier gesellen, 1938 (Bergman)

Vier vom Bob, 1931 (Rasp)

Vierge du Rhin, 1953 (Gabin)

Vierge folle, 1928 (Fresnay)

Vietnam! Vietnam!, 1971 (Heston)

Vietnam War Story 2, 1988 (Snipes)

Vieux de la vieille, 1959 (Gabin; Fresnay)

Vieux Fusil, 1975 (Noiret; Schneider)

View to a Kill, 1985 (Walken)

Vigil, 1914 (Hayakawa)

Vigil in the Night, 1940 (Cushing; Lombard)

Vigile, 1960 (Sordi)

Vigilia di natale, 1913 (Bertini)

Vignes du seigneur, 1958 (Fernandel)

Vigour of Youth. *See* Spirit of Notre Dame, 1931

Viking, 1929 (Crisp)

Vikings, 1958 (Borgnine; Curtis, T.; Douglas, K.; Leigh, Janet; Welles)

Viktor and Viktoria, 1933 (Walbrook)

Villa Borghese, 1953 (Presle)

Villa des mille joies, 1928 (Modot)

Villa Rides, 1968 (Bronson; Brynner; Lom; Mitchum; Rey)

Villa vuelve, 1949 (Armendáriz)

Village. *See* Pestalozzidorf, 1953

Village Bride. *See* Mura na hanayome, 1928

Village of the Damned, 1960 (Sanders)

Village Scandal, 1915 (Arbuckle)

Village School-Teacher. *See* Selskaya uchitelnitsa, 1947

Village Squire, 1935 (Leigh, V.)

Village Tale, 1935 (Scott, R.)

Villain, 1917 (Laurel and Hardy)

Villain, 1971 (Burton)

Villain, 1979 (Ann-Margret; Douglas, K.; Schwarzenegger)

Villain Still Pursued Her, 1940 (Keaton, B.)

Ville de silences, 1979 (Cassel)

Vincent, 1983 (Price)

Vincent. *See* Vincent—The Life and Death of Vincent van Gogh, 1987

Vincent et Theo, 1990 (Cassel)

Vincent, Francois, Paul, et les autres, 1974 (Audran; Depardieu; Montand; Piccoli; Reggiani)

Vincent the Dutchman, 1971 (Zetterling)

Vincent—The Life and Death of Vincent van Gogh, 1987 (Hurt, J.)

Vine Bridge, 1965 (Zetterling)

Vine Garden. *See* Lianbron, 1965

Vingt-cinquième heure. *See* 25e Heure, 1967

Vingt-quatre heures de la vie d'une femme, 1968 (Darrieux)

Vingt-cinquième Heure. *See* 25e Heure, 1967

Vintage, 1957 (Morgan)

Viol, 1967 (Andersson, B.)

Violanta, 1977 (Depardieu)

Violence et Passion. *See* Gruppo di famiglia in un interno, 1974

Violent City. *See* Città violenta, 1970

Violent Four. *See* Banditi a Milano, 1968

Violent Is the Word for Curly, 1938 (Three Stooges)

Violent Life. *See* Vita Scellerata, 1990

Violent Men, 1954 (Ford, G.; Robinson, E.; Stanwyck)

Violent Playground, 1957 (Baker; Cushing)

Violent Saturday, 1955 (Borgnine; Marvin; Mature)

Violent Streets. *See* Thief, 1981

Violent Summer. *See* Estate violenta, 1959

Violets Are Blue, 1986 (Kline; Spacek)

Violette. *See* Violette Nozière, 1978

Violette et François, 1977 (Adjani; Reggiani)

Violette Nozière, 1978 (Audran; Huppert)

Violin Maker, 1915 (Chaney)

Violin Maker of Cremona, 1909 (Pickford)

Violinist of Florence. *See* Geiger von Florenz, 1926

Violins Came with the Americans, 1986 (Ferrer)

Virgen que forjó una Patria, 1942 (Novarro)

Virgin Island, 1958 (Poitier)

Virgin of Stamboul, 1920 (Beery)

Virgin Paradise, 1920 (White)

Virgin Queen, 1955 (Davis, B.; Marshall)

Virgin Spring. *See* Jungfrukällen, 1960

Virginia, 1941 (Carroll; Hayden; MacMurray)

Virginia City, 1940 (Bogart; Bond; Flynn; Hopkins, M.; Scott, R.)

Virginia Hill Story, 1974 (Keitel)

Virginian, 1929 (Constantine; Huston, W.; Scott, R.)

Virginian, 1946 (McCrea)

Viridiana, 1961 (Rey)

Virtue, 1932 (Bond; Lombard)

Virtue Is Its Own Reward, 1914 (Chaney)

Virtuosity, 1995 (Washington)

Virtuous Bigamist. *See* Era du venerdi 17, 1956

Virtuous Bigamist. *See* Sous le ciel de Provence, 1956

Virtuous Husband, 1931 (Arthur)

Virtuous Sin, 1929 (Huston, W.; Francis)

Virtuous Sinners, 1919 (Valentino)

Virtuous Tramps. *See* Fra Diavolo, 1933

Virus. *See* Fukkatsu no hi, 1980

Visages de femmes, 1939 (Brasseur)

Viscount. *See* Vicomte règle ses comptes, 1967

Vishwasghaat, 1976 (Azmi)
Vision, 1987 (Bogarde; Bonham-Carter; Remick)
Vision. *See* Deedar, 1951
Vision Quest, 1985 (Whitaker)
Visioni Privati, 1990 (Charisse)
Visions of Eight, 1973 (Zetterling)
Visit. *See* Besuch, 1964
Visit, 1987 (Arkin)
Visit of a President. *See* Odwiedziny prezydenta, 1961
Visit to a Small Planet, 1960 (Lewis, Jerry)
Visitatore, 1980 (Ford, G.; Huston, J.; Winters)
Visite à Maurice Chevalier, 1954 (Chevalier)
Visiteur, 1946 (Fresnay)
Visiteurs du soir, 1942 (Arletty; Berry; Cuny)
Visiting Hours, 1982 (Grant, L.)
Visitor, 1912-13 (White)
Visitor, 1991 (Matthau)
Visitor. *See* Agantuk, 1991
Visitor. *See* Visitatore, 1980
Visitors, 1972 (Woods)
Viskningar och rop, 1972 (Andersson, H.; Josephson; Thulin; Ullmann)
Vita da cani, 1950 (Lollobrigida; Mastroianni)
Vita di cani, 1950 (Fabrizi)
Vita difficile, 1961 (Gassman; Mangano; Sordi)
Vita è bella, 1943 (Magnani)
Vita katten, 1950 (Björnstrand)
Vita recominicia, 1945 (Valli)
Vita Scellerata, 1990 (Kingsley; Von Sydow)
Vitelloni, 1953 (Sordi)
Vittima dell'ideale, 1916 (Bertini)
Viuda de Montiel, 1979 (Chaplin, G.; Villagra)
Viva el Presidente. *See* Recurso del método, 1977
Viva Gringo. *See* Vermachtnis des Inka, 1966
Viva Italia! *See* I nuovi mostri, 1977
Viva Knievel!, 1977 (Kelly, Gene)
Viva la muerte ... tua!, 1972 (Wallach)
Viva la vie, 1983 (Piccoli)
Viva Las Vegas, 1964 (Ann-Margret; Presley)
Viva Las Vegas. *See* Meet Me in Las Vegas, 1956
Viva Maria, 1965 (Bardot; Moreau)
Viva Max!, 1969 (Ustinov)
Viva mi desgracia, 1943 (Infante)
Viva revolución, 1956 (Armendáriz)
Viva Villa!, 1934 (Beery; Wray)
Viva Zapata!, 1952 (Brando; Quinn)
Vivacious Lady, 1938 (Coburn, C.; Rogers, G.; Stewart)
Vive Henri IV, vive l'amour!, 1961 (Blier; Brasseur; Darrieux; Mercouri)
Vive la classe, 1931 (Fernandel)
Vive la sociale, 1983 (Cassel)
Vive la vie, 1984 (Aimée)
Vivere ancora, 1944 (Cervi)
Vivere in pace, 1946 (Fabrizi)
Vivre Ensemble, 1974 (Karina)
Vivre pour vivre, 1967 (Girardot; Montand)
Vivre sa vie, 1962 (Karina)
Vixen, 1916 (Bara)
Vixen. *See* Jotai, 1969
Vlast tmy, 1915 (Mozhukin)
Vlublen po sobstvennomu zelanij, 1982 (Yankovsky)
Vo imya zhizni, 1946 (Cherkassov)
Vo vlasti gretcha, 1915 (Mozhukin)
Voce, 1982 (Brazzi)
Voce del silenzio, 1952 (Fabrizi; Marais)
Voce della Luna, 1989 (Benigni)
Voce nel tuo cuore, 1949 (Gassman)
Voci bianche, 1964 (Aimée)
Vogelhändler, 1935 (Dagover)
Voglia da morire, 1966 (Girardot)
Voglia di vivere, 1989 (Sanda)
Voglio vivere con Letizia, 1938 (Cervi)
Vogues of 1938, 1937 (Bennett)

Voice from the Minaret, 1923 (Talmadge)
Voice in the Mirror, 1958 (Matthau)
Voice in the Night, 1934 (Bond)
Voice in Your Heart. *See* Voce nel tuo cuore, 1949
Voice of Bugle Ann, 1936 (Barrymore, L.)
Voice of Bugle Ann, 1936 (O'Sullivan)
Voice of Hollywood Nos. 1-2, 1930 (Mix)
Voice of Hollywood No. 10, 1929 (Keaton, B.)
Voice of Hollywood No. 13, 1932 (Wayne)
Voice of Hollywood, 1930 (Dressler)
Voice of Hollywood, 1932 (Constantine)
Voice of La Raza, 1972 (Quinn)
Voice of the Moon. *See* Voce della Luna, 1989
Voice of the Turtle, 1947 (Reagan)
Voices across the Sea, 1928 (Gilbert; Shearer)
Voices in the Garden, 1991 (Aimée)
Voices of the City, 1922 (Chaney)
Voici le temps des assassins, 1955 (Gabin)
Voie lactée, 1969 (Cuny; Piccoli; Seyrig)
Voina i mir, 1912 (Mozhukin)
Voina i mir, 1965-7 (Bondarchuk)
Voisin ... voisin, 1911 (Linder)
Vol, 1923 (Vanel)
Vol de nuit, 1978 (Howard, T.)
Volcano, 1926 (Beery)
Volcano. *See* Vulcano, 1949
Volcano. *See* Krakatoa, East of Java, 1969
Volcano, 1976 (Burton)
Voleur, 1967 (Belmondo)
Voleur d'enfants, 1991 (Mastroianni)
Voleur de Femmes, 1936 (Berry)
Voleur du Tibidabo, 1964 (Karina)
Voleurs de la nuit. *See* Thieves After Dark, 1983
Voleuse, 1966 (Piccoli; Schneider)
Volga en flammes, 1934 (Darrieux)
Volles Herz und leere taschen, 1962 (Cervi; Rosay)
Volpone, 1939 (Jouvet)
Voltati Eugenio, 1980 (Blier)
Voluntarily in Love. *See* Vlublen po sobstvennomu zelanij, 1982
Volunteer, 1944 (Olivier; Richardson, R.)
Volunteers, 1985 (Candy; Hanks)
Vom Freudenhaus in die Ehe. *See* Mädchen ohne Heimat, 1926
Von der Liebe reden wir später, 1953 (Fröhlich)
Von Himmel gefallen. *See* Special Delivery, 1955
Von Ryan's Express, 1965 (Howard, T.; Sidney)
Voodoo Island. *See* Silent Death, 1957
Voodoo Man, 1944 (Carradine; Lugosi)
Voodoo Tiger, 1952 (Weissmuller)
Vordertreppe-Hintertreppe, 1914 (Nielsen)
Vore venners vinter, 1923 (Madsen and Schenstrøm)
Vorn Teufel gejagt, 1950 (Dagover)
Vortex, 1927 (Novello)
Vortex. *See* Blondy, 1975
Vortice, 1953 (Papas)
Voruntersuchung, 1931 (Fröhlich)
Vot mchitza troika potchtovaia, 1913 (Mozhukin)
Vot vspynulo utro, 1915 (Mozhukin)
Vote. *See* Voto, 1950
Vote for Huggett, 1949 (Dors)
Voto, 1950 (Loren)
Votre Devoue, Blake, 1954 (Constantine)
Voulez-vous danser avec moi?, 1959 (Bardot)
Vous n'avez rien a déclarer?, 1937 (Brasseur; Raimu)
Vous pigez?, 1956 (Constantine)
Voyage, 1984 (Abril)
Voyage à Biarritz, 1962 (Arletty; Fernandel)
Voyage. *See* Viaggio, 1973
Voyage. *See* Viaje, 1992
Voyage de Monsieur Perrichon, 1933 (Arletty)
Voyage de noces, 1932 (Brasseur)
Voyage de noces, 1975 (Baye)

Voyage de noces en Espagne, 1912 (Linder)
Voyage du père, 1966 (Fernandel; Noiret)
Voyage en Amérique, 1951 (Fresnay)
Voyage en Amérique, 1975 (Seyrig)
Voyage en douce, 1980 (Chaplin, G.; Sanda)
Voyage of Terror: The Achille Lauro Affair, 1990 (Lancaster; Sanda)
Voyage of the Damned, 1976 (Dunaway; Elliott; Ferrer; Grant, L.; McDowell; Rey; Schell, Maria; Von Sydow; Welles; Werner)
Voyage Round My Father, 1982 (Bates, A.; Olivier)
Voyage sans espoir, 1943 (Marais)
Voyage to a Prehistoric Planet, 1967 (Rathbone)
Voyage to America. See Voyage en Amérique, 1951
Voyage to Italy. See **Viaggio in Italia**, 1953
Voyage to the Bottom of the Sea, 1961 (Fontaine; Lorre; Pidgeon)
Voyager, 1991 (Shepard)
Voyageur de la Toussaint, 1942 (Reggiani; Berry)
Voyageur sans baggage, 1943 (Fresnay)
Vozrozhdennia, 1915 (Mozhukin)
Vrooder's Hooch. See Crazy World of Julius Vrooder, 1974
Vsadniki vetra, 1930 (Cherkassov)
Vse ostaetsia lyudyam, 1963 (Cherkassov)
Vsichni dobri rodaci, 1968 (Brodský)
Vsyou zhizn pod maskoi, 1915 (Mozhukin)
Vuelen los Garcia, 1946 (Infante)
Vulcano, 1949 (Brazzi; Magnani)
Vulture, 1966 (Crawford, B.)
Vultures. See Morfalous, 1983
Vultures of the Sea, 1928 (Karloff)
W. B. Yeats—A Tribute, 1950 (Cusack)
W. C. Fields and Me, 1976 (Steiger)
W. C. Fields: Straight Up, 1986 (Moore, Dudley)
W. W. and the Dixie Dancekings, 1975 (Reynolds, B.)
W Bialy dzie in, 1980 (Nowicki)
"W" Plan, 1930 (Carroll)
W Starym Dworku, 1984 (Tyszkiewicz)
Wabash Avenue, 1950 (Grable; Mature)
Wachsfigurenkabinett, 1923 (Jannings; Krauss; Veidt)
Wackiest Ship in the Army, 1961 (Lemmon)
Wacky World of Mother Goose, 1967 (Rutherford)
Waco, 1966 (Russell, J.)
Wade Brent Pays, 1914 (Mix)
Waga haha no sho, 1936 (Tanaka)
Waga koi no tabiji, 1961 (Yamamura)
Waga koi wa moenu, 1949 (Tanaka)
Waga koiseshi otome, 1946 (Hara)
Waga seishun ni kui nashi, 1946 (Hara; Shimura)
Waga shogai no kagayakeru hi, 1949 (Mori)
Wagaya wa tanoshi, 1951 (Takamine; Yamada)
Wages of Fear. See **Salaire de la peur**, 1952
Wages of Virtue, 1924 (Swanson)
Wagner, 1982 (Burton; Cusack; Gielgud; Greenwood; Olivier; Redgrave, V.; Richardson)
Wagon Team, 1952 (Autry)
Wagon Tracks, 1919 (Hart)
Wagon Trail, 1935 (Carey)
Wagon Wheels, 1934 (Scott, R.)
Wagonmaster, 1950 (Bond)
Wagons East!, 1994 (Candy)
Wagons Roll at Night, 1941 (Bogart; Sidney)
Wahnsinn, 1919 (Veidt)
Waikiki Wedding, 1937 (Crosby; Quinn)
Waise von Lowood, 1926 (Rasp)
Waisenhauskind, 1917 (Nielsen)
Wait for Me, Ana. See Zhdi menya, Ana, 1969
Wait until Dark, 1967 (Arkin; Hepburn, A.)
Wait until Spring, Bandini, 1989 (Dunaway)
Waiter No. 5, 1910 (Pickford)
Waiter! See Garçon!, 1983
Waiters' Ball, 1916 (Arbuckle)
Waiters' Picnic, 1913 (Arbuckle)
Waiting for the Light, 1990 (MacLaine)

Waiting to Exhale, 1995 (Bassett; Snipes; Whitaker)
Waiting Women. See Kvinnors väntan, 1952
Wakai koibito-tachi, 1959 (Tsukasa)
Wakaki hi, 1929 (Ryu)
Wakaki ushio, 1955 (Yamada)
Wakamono yo naze naku ka, 1930 (Tanaka)
Wakare, 1959 (Yamada)
Wakaret ikiru toki mo, 1961 (Tanaka)
Wakasama zamurai torimonocho: Nazo no noh-men yashiki, 1950 (Kagawa)
Wakasama zamurai torimonocho: Noroi no ningyo-shi, 1951 (Kagawa)
Wake Island, 1942 (Preston)
Wake of the Red Witch, 1948 (Wayne)
Wake Up and Die. See Svegliati e uccidi, 1966
Wake Up and Live, 1937 (Faye)
Wakiki hi no yorokobi, 1943 (Takamine)
Waking Up the Town, 1925 (Shearer)
Wald, 1979 (Schell, Maria)
Waldwinter, 1956 (Kinski)
Walk a Tightrope, 1963 (Duryea)
Walk Don't Run, 1966 (Grant, C.)
Walk in the Clouds, 1995 (Giannini; Quinn; Reeves)
Walk in the Spring Rain, 1970 (Bergman; Quinn)
Walk in the Sun, 1945 (Andrews, D.)
Walk on the Wild Side, 1962 (Baxter; Fonda, J.; Stanwyck)
Walk Softly, Stranger, 1950 (Cotten; Valli)
Walk the Proud Land, 1956 (Bancroft)
Walk with Love and Death, 1969 (Huston, A.; Huston, J.)
Walker, 1987 (Harris, E.)
Walkie Talkie, 1986 (York)
Walkin' My Baby Back Home, 1953 (O'Connor)
Walking a Tightrope. See Equilibriste, 1991
Walking after Midnight, 1988 (Coburn, J.; Sheen)
Walking Down Broadway, 1938 (Trevor)
Walking Hills, 1949 (Kennedy; Scott, R.)
Walking My Baby Back Home, 1953 (Leigh, Janet)
Wall, 1982 (Roberts, R.; Wallach; Wiest)
Wall in Jerusalem, 1972 (Burton)
Wall of Silence. See Muro de Silencio, 1993
Wall Street, 1987 (Douglas, Michael; Sheen; Stamp)
Wall Street Cowboy, 1939 (Rogers, R.)
Wallenberg: A Hero's Story, 1985 (Andersson, B.; Olin)
Wallflowers, 1928 (Arthur)
Wallop, 1921 (Carey)
Walls of Jericho, 1948 (Baxter; Darnell; Douglas, K.; Wilde)
Walls of Malapaga. See Au-delà des grilles, 1949
Walpurgis Night. See Valborgsmassoafton, 1935
Walter & Carlo i Amerika, 1989 (Curtis, T.)
Walter Wanger's Vogues of 1938. See Vogues of 1938, 1937
Waltz at Noon. See Mahiru no enbukyoku, 1949
Waltz of the Toreadors, 1962 (Cusack; Sellers)
Waltz Time, 1945 (Kendall)
Waltz Time in Vienna. See Walzerkrieg, 1933
Walzerkrieg, 1933 (Arletty; Walbrook)
Wand, 1995 (Brandauer)
Wanda, 1983 (Vogler)
Wanda la peccatrice, 1952 (Rosay)
Wanda Nevada, 1979 (Fonda, H.)
Wanderer, 1913 (Barrymore, L.)
Wanderer, 1926 (Beery; Carey)
Wanderers. See I girovaghi, 1956
Wanderer's Notebook. See Horoki, 1962
Wandering Jew, 1933 (Veidt)
Wandering Jew. See Ebreo errante, 1947
Wandering Papas, 1925 (Laurel and Hardy)
Waning Sex, 1926 (Shearer)
Wanted—A Bad Man, 1917 (Laurel and Hardy)
Wanted—$5000, 1919 (Lloyd)
Wanted Men. See Wolves, 1930
Wanters, 1923 (Shearer)
Wanton Countess. See Senso, 1954
War, 1994 (Costner)

War and Peace. *See* Voina i mir, 1912

War and Peace, 1956 (Fonda, H.; Gassman; Hepburn, A.; Homolka; Lom; Mills)

War and Peace. *See* **Voina i mir**, 1965-7

War and Peace. *See* Krieg und frieden, 1983

War Arrow, 1954 (O'Hara)

War at Home, 1996 (Bates, K.; Sheen)

War Babies, 1932 (Temple)

War between Men and Women, 1972 (Lemmon; Robards)

War Bonnet. *See* Savage, 1952

War Brides, 1916 (Barthelmess; Nazimova)

War Comes to America, 1945 (Huston, W.)

War Correspondent. *See* Story of G.I. Joe, 1945

War Game, 1961 (Zetterling)

War Games. *See* Suppose They Gave a War and Nobody Came?, 1970

War Gods of the Deep. *See* City under the Sea, 1965

War Hunt, 1962 (Redford)

War in the Land of Egypt. *See* Al Moaten Al Myssri, 1991

War in the Mediterranean, 1943 (Howard, L.)

War Is Over. *See* Guerre est finie, 1966

War, Italian Style. *See* Due Marines e un Generale, 1967

War Lord. *See* West of Shanghai, 1937

War Lord, 1965 (Heston)

War Lover, 1962 (McQueen)

War Nurse, 1930 (Montgomery)

War of the Roses, 1989 (DeVito; Douglas, Michael; Turner, K.)

War of the Wildcats. *See* In Old Oklahoma, 1943

War Relief, 1917 (Fairbanks)

War Requiem, 1989 (Olivier)

War Shock. *See* Woman's Devotion, 1956

War That Never Ends, 1991 (Kingsley)

War Wagon, 1967 (Dern; Douglas, K.; Wayne)

Ware hitotsubu no mugi naredo, 1965 (Takamine)

Ware nakinurete, 1948 (Mori)

Warera sarariiman, 1963 (Tsukasa)

Wareraga kyokan, 1939 (Takamine)

Waris, 1988 (Patil)

Warlock, 1959 (Fonda, H.; Malone; Quinn; Widmark)

Warlords of Atlantis, 1978 (Charisse)

Warm December, 1973 (Poitier)

Warm Reception, 1916 (Laurel and Hardy)

Warm-Blooded Spy. *See* Ravissante idiote, 1964

Warming Up, 1928 (Arthur)

Warning, 1914 (Crisp; White)

Warning Shadows. *See* **Schatten**, 1923

Warning Shot, 1967 (Gish; Pidgeon; Sanders)

Warnung vor einer heiligen Nutte, 1970 (Constantine; Schygulla)

Warpath, 1951 (O'Brien, E.)

Warrant, 1975 (Anand)

Warrens of Virginia, 1915 (Sweet)

Warrior of the Lost Word, 1984 (Pleasence)

Warrior Queen, 1987 (Pleasence)

Warrior Spirits, 1994 (Gélin)

Warriors. *See* Dark Avengers, 1955

Warriors. *See* Kelly's Heroes, 1970

Warrior's Rest. *See* Repos du guerrier, 1962

Warriors and Prisoners. *See* Guerriers et captives, 1989

Warriors Five. *See* Guerra continua, 1962

Wars of the Primal Tribes. *See* McVeagh of the South Seas, 1914

Warsaw—Year 5703. *See* Warszawa Year 5703, 1992

Warszawa Year 5703, 1992 (Schygulla)

Wartezimmer zum Jenseits, 1964 (Kinski)

Warui yatsu hodo yoku nemuru, 1960 (Kagawa; Mifune; Mori; Ryu; Shimura)

Warum lauft Herr R amok?, 1969 (Schygulla)

Was Frauen träumen, 1933 (Fröhlich; Lorre)

Was He a Coward?, 1911 (Sweet)

Washington Cowboy. *See* Rovin' Tumbleweeds, 1939

Washington Masquerade, 1932 (Barrymore, L.; McDaniel)

Washington Story, 1952 (Calhern; Neal)

Wasted Love, 1930 (Wong)

Wasted Night, 1972 (Nowicki)

Wasureenu bojo, 1956 (Yamamura)

Wataridori itsu kaeru, 1955 (Takamine; Tanaka)

Watashi niwa otto ga aru, 1940 (Tanaka)

Watashi no niisan, 1934 (Hasegawa; Tanaka)

Watashi no papa-san mamaga suki, 1931 (Takamine)

Watch on the Rhine, 1943 (Davis, B.; Lukas)

Watch the Birdie, 1935 (Hope; Miller)

Watcher in the Woods, 1980 (Davis, B.)

Watchmaker of Lyon. *See* Horloger de Saint-Paul, 1974

Water, 1985 (Caine)

Water Babies, 1978 (Greenwood)

Water Cure, 1916 (Laurel and Hardy)

Water Dog, 1914 (Arbuckle)

Water Engine, 1992 (Sheen)

Water Nymph, 1912 (Normand)

Water, Water Everywhere, 1920 (Rogers, W.)

Waterdance, 1992 (Snipes)

Waterfront, 1939 (Bond)

Waterfront, 1944 (Carradine)

Waterfront, 1950 (Burton)

Waterfront Lady, 1935 (Bond)

Waterfront Women. *See* Waterfront, 1950

Waterhole Number Three, 1967 (Blondell; Coburn, J; Dern)

Waterland, 1992 (Irons)

Waterloo, 1929 (Vanel)

Waterloo, 1970 (Bondarchuk; Hawkins; Steiger; Welles)

Waterloo Bridge, 1931 (Davis, B.)

Waterloo Bridge, 1940 (Leigh, V.; Taylor, R.)

Waterloo Road, 1944 (Granger; Mills)

Watership Down, 1978 (Elliott; Hurt, J.; Richardson, R.)

Waterworld, 1995 (Costner; Hopper)

Wattstax, 1973 (Pryor)

Waxworks. *See* Wachsfigurenkabinett, 1923

Way ... Way Out, 1966 (Lewis, Jerry)

Way Ahead, 1944 (Howard, T.; Niven)

Way Ahead. *See* Immortal Battalion, 1944

Way Back Home, 1932 (Davis, B.)

Way Down East, 1920 (Barthelmess; Gish; Shearer)

Way Down East, 1935 (Fonda, H.)

Way for a Sailor, 1930 (Beery; Gilbert; Milland)

Way of a Gaucho, 1952 (Sloane; Tierney)

Way of a Man with a Maid, 1918 (Crisp)

Way of a Woman, 1919 (Talmadge)

Way of All Flesh, 1927 (Jannings)

Way of Drama. *See* Shibaido, 1944

Way of Man, 1909 (Pickford)

Way of the Dragon. *See* Return of the Dragon, 1973

Way of the Redman, 1914 (Mix)

Way of the Rem Redman, 1916 (Mix)

Way Out West, 1937 (Laurel and Hardy)

Way They Were. *See* Así Como Habían Sido, 1987

Way to Love, 1933 (Chevalier; Horton)

Way to the Gold, 1957 (Brennan)

Way to the Stars, 1945 (Howard, T.; Mills; Redgrave, M.)

Way Up Thar, 1935 (Rogers, R.)

Way We Were, 1973 (Redford; Streisand; Woods)

Way West, 1967 (Douglas, K.; Field; Mitchum; Widmark)

Wayne's World 2, 1993 (Basinger; Heston; Walken)

Ways of Love. *See* Amore, 1947

Wayside Pebble. *See* Robo no ishi, 1960

Wayward Bus, 1956 (Mansfield)

We All Help, 1941 (Cushing)

We All Loved Each Other So Much. *See* C'eravamo tanti amati, 1974

We Are in the Navy Now, 1962 (Bogarde)

We Are Not Alone, 1939 (Muni)

We Dive at Dawn, 1943 (Mills)

We Faw Down, 1928 (Laurel and Hardy)

We from the Theatre. *See* Vi som går scenvägen, 1938

We har manje namn, 1976 (Zetterling)

We Have Many Names. *See* We har manje namn, 1976

We Have Our Moments, 1937 (Niven)

We Humans. *See* Young America, 1932
We Joined the Navy. *See* We Are in the Navy Now, 1962
We Live Again, 1934 (Jaffe; March)
We Must Have Music, 1941 (Garland)
We Need No Money. *See* Man braucht kein Geld, 1931
We Never Sleep, 1917 (Lloyd)
We Owe It to Our Children, 1955 (Lee, B.)
We Serve, 1941 (Johnson)
We Slip Up. *See* We Faw Down, 1928
We Still Kill the Old Way. *See* Ciascuno il suo, 1967
We Students. *See* Ehne el Talamza, 1959
We, the Undersigned. *See* My, nizhepodpisavshiesya ..., 1980
We, the Women. *See* Siamo donne, 1953
We Think the World of You, 1988 (Bates, A.; Oldman)
We Three Debutantes. *See* Vi tre debutera, 1953
We Two. *See* Vi två, 1939
We Two. *See* Hum Dono, 1961
We Want Our Mummy, 1939 (Three Stooges)
We Were Dancing, 1942 (Douglas, Melvyn; Gardner; Shearer)
We Were Strangers, 1949 (Armendáriz; Garfield; Huston, J.; Jones, Jennifer;
    Novarro)
We Who Are Young, 1940 (Turner, L.)
We Will All Go to Heaven. *See* Nous irons tous au paradis, 1977
Weak and the Wicked, 1953 (Dors; Roberts, R.)
Weak-End Party, 1922 (Laurel and Hardy)
Weapon, 1957 (Marshall)
Weary River, 1929 (Barthelmess)
Weavers. *See* Weber, 1927
Web, 1947 (O'Brien, E.; Price)
Web. *See* Netz, 1975
Web of Fear. *See* Constance aux enfers, 1964
Web of Passion. *See* Double tour, 1959
Web of the Spider. *See* Nella stretta morsa del ragno, 1971
Weber, 1927 (Wegener)
Weda'an Bonapart. *See* Adieu Bonaparte, 1984
Wedding. *See* Svadba, 1944
Wedding. *See* Wesele, 1973
Wedding, 1978 (Chaplin, G.; Farrow; Gassman; Gish)
Wedding Bells. *See* Royal Wedding, 1951
Wedding Breakfast. *See* Catered Affair, 1956
Wedding Day. *See* Bröllopsdagen, 1960
Wedding Dress, 1962 (Cusack)
Wedding in Blood. *See* Noces rouges, 1973
Wedding in Monaco, 1956 (Kelly, Grace)
Wedding in White, 1973 (Pleasence)
Wedding March, 1928 (Wray)
Wedding Night, 1935 (Bellamy; Brennan; Constantine)
Wedding Night. *See* Noc Poslubna, 1959
Wedding of Jack and Jill, 1930 (Garland)
Wedding Party, 1969 (De Niro)
Wedding Present, 1936 (Bennett; Grant, C.)
Wedding Rehearsal, 1932 (Oberon)
Wedlock, 1918 (Gilbert)
Wednesday, 1974 (Lemmon)
Wee Wee Monsieur, 1938 (Three Stooges)
Wee Willie Winkie, 1937 (McLaglen; Temple)
Weeds, 1987 (Nolte)
Week-end, 1967 (Léaud)
Week-End for Three, 1941 (Horton)
Week's Vacation. *See* Semaine de vacances, 1980
Weekend à Zuydcoote, 1964 (Belmondo)
Weekend at Dunkirk. *See* Weekend à Zuydcoote, 1964
Weekend at the Waldorf, 1945 (Pidgeon; Rogers, G.; Turner, L.)
Weekend in Havana, 1941 (Faye; Miranda)
Weekend Marriage, 1932 (Young, L.)
Weekend Murders. *See* Concerto per pistola solista, 1970
Weekend sur deux, 1990 (Baye)
Weekend with Father, 1951 (Neal)
Weekends Only, 1932 (Bennett)
Weep No More, My Lady, 1992 (Winters)

Weg des Todes, 1917 (Veidt)
Weg ins Freie, 1983 (Brandauer)
Wege im Zwielicht, 1948 (Fröhlich)
Wege nach Rio, 1931 (Homolka)
Weib des Pharao, 1921 (Jannings; Wegener)
Weisse Dämon, 1932 (Lorre)
Weisse Rosen, 1914 (Nielsen)
Weisse Teufel, 1929 (Dagover; Mozhukin)
Welcome Danger, 1929 (Lloyd)
Welcome Home, Johnny Bristol, 1972 (Landau; Sheen)
Welcome Home, Roxy Carmichael, 1990 (Ryder)
Welcome Intruder, 1913 (Barrymore, L.)
Welcome, Mr. Marshall! *See* ¡Bienvenido, Mr. Marshall!, 1952
Welcome Stranger, 1947 (Crosby; Fitzgerald)
Welcome to Blood City, 1977 (Palance)
Welcome to Britain, 1943 (Hope; Meredith)
Welcome to Hard Times, 1966 (Fonda, H.; Oates)
Welcome to L.A., 1976 (Chaplin, G.; Keitel; Spacek)
Welcome to Veraz. *See* Bienvenido a Veraz, 1991
Well, 1913 (Barrymore, L.)
Well-Digger's Daughter. *See* Fille du puisatier, 1940
Well-Filled Day. *See* Journée bien remplie, 1972
Well-Groomed Bride, 1946 (De Havilland; Milland)
We'll Grow Thin Together. *See* Nous maigrirons ensemble, 1979
We'll Meet Again, 1982 (York)
We'll Meet in the Gallery. *See* Ci troviamo in Galleria, 1953
Well of Loneliness, 1996 (Thompson)
Well-Digger's Daughter. *See* Fille du puisatier, 1946
Wells Fargo, 1937 (McCrea)
Welsh Singer, 1915 (Evans)
Welt am Draht, 1973 (Constantine)
Welt ohne Waffen, 1918 (Wegener)
Weltbrand, 1920 (Kortner)
Wenn das Herz in Hass erglüht, 1918 (Negri)
Wenn der weisse Flieder wieder blüht, 1953 (Schneider)
Wenn die Maske fällt, 1912 (Nielsen)
Wenn die Schwalben heimwärts ziehn, 1928 (Fröhlich)
Wenn die Sonne wieder scheint, 1943 (Wegener)
Wenn ein Weib den Weg verliert. *See* Café Electric, 1927
Wenn Frauen lieben und hassen, 1917 (Krauss)
Wenn Männer Schlange stehen. *See* Chikita, 1961
Wenn Tote sprechen, 1917 (Veidt)
Wenn vier dasselbe tun, 1917 (Jannings)
Werdegeng. *See* Reigen, 1920
We're Back! A Dinosaur's Story, 1993 (Malkovich)
We're Fighting Back, 1981 (Barkin)
We're Going to Be Rich, 1938 (Fields, G.; McLaglen)
We're in the Money, 1935 (Blondell)
We're in the Navy Now, 1926 (Beery)
We're No Angels, 1955 (Bennett; Bogart; Rathbone; Ustinov)
We're No Angels, 1989 (De Niro; Moore, Demi; Penn)
We're Not Dressing, 1934 (Crosby; Lombard; Milland)
We're Not Married, 1952 (Calhern; Marvin; Monroe; Rogers, G.)
We're Not the Jet Set, 1977 (Duvall)
Wesele, 1973 (Olbrychski)
Wessten leuchtet, 1981 (Mueller-Stahl)
West 11, 1963 (Dors)
West Is West, 1920 (Carey)
West of Broadway, 1931 (Bellamy; Gilbert)
West of Hot Dog, 1924 (Laurel and Hardy)
West of Shanghai, 1937 (Karloff)
West of the Divide, 1934 (Wayne)
West of the Pecos, 1945 (Mitchum)
West of Zanzibar, 1928 (Barrymore, L.; Chaney)
West Point, 1928 (Crawford, J.)
West Point of the Air, 1935 (Beery; O'Sullivan; Russell, R.; Taylor, E.;
    Young, R.)
West Point Story, 1950 (Cagney; Day)
West Side Story, 1961 (Wood)
West Side Waltz, 1995 (MacLaine; Minnelli)
Westbound, 1959 (Scott, R.)

Westerberg High. *See* Heathers, 1989
Western Blood, 1918 (Mix)
Western Courage, 1935 (Bond)
Western Hearts, 1911 (Mix)
Western Jamboree, 1938 (Autry)
Western Masquerade, 1916 (Mix)
Western Union, 1941 (Carradine; Scott, R.; Young, R.)
Westerner, 1940 (Andrews, D.; Brennan; Constantine)
Westward Ho, 1935 (Wayne)
Westward Passage, 1932 (Olivier)
Westward the Women, 1951 (Taylor, R.)
Westward the Wagon. *See* Hitched, 1971
Westworld, 1973 (Brynner)
Wet and Wild Summer, 1993 (Gould)
Wet Gold, 1984 (Meredith)
Wet Parade, 1932 (Durante; Huston, W.; Loy; Young, R.; Redgrave, V.)
We've Never Been Licked, 1943 (Mitchum; Robertson)
Whale for the Killing, 1981 (Widmark)
Whales of August, 1987 (Davis, B.; Gish; Price; Steenburgen)
Wham Bam Slam, 1955 (Three Stooges)
Wharf Angel, 1934 (McLaglen)
Wharf Rat, 1916 (Marsh)
What? *See* Che?, 1972
What a Carve Up!, 1961 (Pleasence)
What a Cinch, 1915 (Laurel and Hardy)
What a Life!, 1939 (Cooper)
What a Man. *See* Never Give a Sucker an Even Break, 1941
What a Way to Go!, 1964 (Dumont; Kelly, Gene; MacLaine; Martin, D.; Mitchum; Newman)
What a Widow!, 1930 (Swanson)
What a Woman!, 1943 (Russell, R.; Winters)
What about Bob?, 1991 (Dreyfuss; Murray)
What Are Best Friends For?, 1973 (Grant, L.)
What Did You Do in the War, Daddy?, 1966 (Coburn, J.)
What Does Dorrie Want?, 1982 (Keaton, D.)
What Ever Happened to Aunt Alice, 1969 (Gordon; Page)
What Ever Happened to Baby Jane?, 1991 (Redgrave, V.)
What Every Woman Knows, 1934 (Crisp)
What Every Woman Knows, 1959 (Cusack)
What Happened to Rosa?, 1920 (Menjou; Normand)
What Have I Done to Deserve This? *See* ¿Qué he hecho yo para merecer esto?, 1984
What He Forgot, 1915 (Laurel and Hardy)
What Makes Lizzy Dizzy?, 1942 (Langdon)
What Money Can Buy, 1928 (Carroll)
What Next, Corporal Hargrove?, 1945 (Walker)
What! No Beer?, 1933 (Durante; Keaton, B.)
What Papa Got, 1912-13 (White)
What Pearl's Pearl Did, 1912-13 (White)
What Price Beauty, 1928 (Loy)
What Price Glory, 1926 (Del Rio; McLaglen)
What Price Glory?, 1952 (Cagney)
What Price Innocence?, 1933 (Grable)
What Sex Am I?, 1985 (Grant, L.)
What Shall We Do with Our Old, 1911 (Crisp)
What the Birds Knew. *See* Ikimono no kiroku, 1955
What the Daisy Said, 1910 (Pickford)
What the Scotch Started, 1933 (Harlow)
What the Swedish Butler Saw. *See* Groove Room, 1974
What Time Is It? *See* Che ora e?, 1990
What Times! *See* Che Tempi!, 1948
What Women Dream. *See* Was Frauen träumen, 1933
Whatever Happened to Baby Jane?, 1962 (Crawford, J.; Davis, B.)
What's a Girl Like You ... ?, 1971 (Price)
What's a Nice Girl Like You ... ?, 1971 (McDowall; O'Brien, E.)
What's Buzzin' Cousin?, 1943 (Miller)
What's Cookin'?, 1942 (O'Connor)
What's Eating Gilbert Grape, 1993 (Depp, Lewis, Juliette; Steenburgen)
What's Good for the Goose, 1969 (Wisdom)
What's Love Got to Do with It, 1993 (Bassett; Fishburne)
What's New, Pussycat?, 1965 (Allen; Burton; O'Toole; Schneider; Sellers)

What's Sauce for the Goose, 1916 (Laurel and Hardy)
What's So Bad about Feeling Good?, 1968 (Ritter)
What's the Matador?, 1942 (Three Stooges)
What's the Matter with Helen?, 1971 (Moorehead; Reynolds, D.; Winters)
What's Up, Doc?, 1972 (Streisand)
What's Up, Tiger Lily?, 1966 (Allen)
What's Worth While?, 1921 (Calhern)
What's Your Hurry, 1909 (Pickford)
Wheel of Fortune. *See* Man Betrayed, 1941
Wheeler Dealers, 1963 (Garner; Remick)
Wheels of Chance, 1928 (Barthelmess)
Wheels of Justice, 1911 (Mix)
Wheels of Terror, 1987 (Reed)
When a Feller Needs a Friend, 1932 (Cooper)
When a Man Loves, 1911 (Pickford)
When a Man Loves, 1927 (Barrymore, J.)
When a Man Loves a Woman, 1994 (Burstyn; García; Ryan, M.)
When a Stranger Calls, 1979 (Roberts, R.)
When a Woman Ascends the Stairs. *See* Onna ga kaidan o agaru toki, 1960
When a Woman Loses Her Way. *See* Café Electric, 1927
When a Woman Sins, 1918 (Bara)
When Bearcat Went Dry, 1919 (Chaney)
When Boys Leave Home. *See* Downhill, 1927
When Comedy Was King, 1960 (Laurel and Hardy; Langdon; Swanson)
When Cupid Slipped, 1916 (Mix)
When Doctors Disagree, 1919 (Normand)
When Dreams Come True, 1913 (Arbuckle)
When Eight Bells Toll, 1971 (Hawkins; Hopkins, A.)
When Harry Met Sally ..., 1989 (Ryan, M.)
When He's Not a Stranger, 1989 (Dillon)
When Hell Broke Loose, 1958 (Bronson)
When Hell Was in Session, 1979 (Saint)
When I Fall in Love. *See* Everybody's All-American, 1988
When I Grow Up, 1951 (Preston)
When I Was a Kid, I Didn't Dare. *See* Si je suis comme ça, c'est la faute de papa, 1978
When Johnny Comes Marching Home, 1943 (O'Connor)
When Kings Were the Law, 1912 (Crisp)
When Knighthood Was in Flower, 1922 (Davies; Powell, W.)
When Knights Were Bold, 1936 (Buchanan; Fitzgerald; Wray)
When Knights Were Cold, 1922 (Laurel and Hardy)
When Ladies Meet, 1933 (Loy; Montgomery)
When Ladies Meet, 1941 (Crawford, J.; Garson; Marshall; Taylor, R.)
When Love Is Young, 1912-13 (White)
When Love Is Young, 1937 (Brennan)
When Love Took Wings, 1915 (Arbuckle)
When Men Desire, 1919 (Bara)
When Michael Calls, 1971 (Douglas, Michael)
When My Baby Smiles at Me, 1948 (Grable)
When Strangers Marry, 1944 (Mitchum)
When Strangers Meet, 1933 (Bond)
When Strangers Meet. *See* Einer frisst den anderern, 1964
When the Bough Breaks, 1994 (Sheen)
When the Chrysanthemums Fade. *See* Uchveli uzh davno krisantemi v sadu, 1916
When the Clouds Roll By, 1919 (Fairbanks)
When the Cook Fell Ill, 1914 (Mix)
When the Daltons Rode, 1940 (Crawford, B.; Francis; Scott, R.)
When the Girls Meet the Boys. *See* Girl Crazy, 1943
When the Gods Played a Badger Game, 1915 (Chaney)
When the Legends Die, 1972 (Widmark)
When the Whales Came, 1989 (Mirren)
When the Wind Blows, 1986 (Mills)
When the Woman Gets Confused. *See* Quand la femme s'en mêle, 1957
When Time Ran Out, 1980 (Borgnine; Holden; Meredith; Newman)
When Tomorrow Comes, 1939 (Boyer; Dunne)
When We Are Old, 1983 (Ryu)
When We Were in Our Teens, 1910 (Pickford)
When We Were Repressed. *See* Quando eravmo repressi, 1992
When Were You Born?, 1938 (Wong)
When Willie Comes Marching Home, 1950 (Marsh)

White Squall, 1996 (Bridges)
White Stallion, 1984 (Borgnine)
White Star, 1985 (Hopper)
White Sun of the Wilderness. *See* Beloe solntse pustiny, 1969
White Telephones. *See* I telefoni bianchi, 1976
White Tie and Tails, 1946 (Duryea)
White Tiger, 1923 (Beery)
White Tower, 1950 (Ford, G.; Homolka; Rains; Valli)
White Unicorn, 1947 (Greenwood; Lockwood)
White Voices. *See* Voci bianche, 1964
White Water Summer, 1987 (Bacon)
White Wing's Bride, 1925 (Langdon)
White Wings, 1922 (Laurel and Hardy)
White Witch Doctor, 1953 (Hayward; Mitchum)
White Woman, 1933 (Laughton; Lombard)
White Zombie, 1932 (Lugosi)
Whitechapel. *See* It Always Rains on Sunday, 1947
Whitsun Outing. *See* Pfingstausflug, 1978
Whity, 1970 (Schygulla)
Who?, 1974 (Gould; Howard, T.)
Who Am I This Time?, 1982 (Sarandon; Walken)
Who Bombed Birmingham?, 1990 (Hurt, J.)
Who Dares Wins. *See* Final Option, 1982
Who Done It?, 1942 (Abbott and Costello; Three Stooges)
Who Done It?, 1949 (Three Stooges)
Who Finds a Friend Finds Treasure. *See* Chi Trova, un Amico, Trova un Tesoro, 1983
Who Framed Roger Rabbit?, 1988 (Hoskins; Sidney; Turner, K.)
Who Gets the Friends?, 1988 (Taylor, E.)
Who Goes Next?, 1938 (Hawkins)
Who Got Stung? *See* Caught in the Rain, 1914
Who Has Seen the Wind?, 1965 (Baker; Schell, Maria)
Who Has Seen the Wind?, 1977 (Ferrer)
Who Is Harry Kellerman and Why Is He Saying Those Terrible Things about Me?, 1971 (Hoffman)
Who Is in the Box?, 1912-13 (White)
Who Is Killing the Great Chefs of Europe?, 1978 (Cassel; Noiret; Segal)
Who Is the Man?, 1924 (Gielgud)
Who Killed Gail Preston?, 1938 (Hayworth)
Who Killed Max? *See* Qui a tué Max?, 1913
Who Killed Santa Claus? *See* Assassinat du Père Noël, 1941
Who Killed Teddy Bear?, 1965 (Mineo)
Who Knows a Woman's Heart? *See* Onna-gokoro dare ga shiru, 1951
Who Murdered Joy Morgan? *See* Killjoy, 1981
Who Pays My Wife's Bill? *See* Be My Wife, 1921
Who Rides with Kane. *See* Young Billy Young, 1969
Who Says I Can't Ride a Rainbow?, 1971 (Freeman)
Who Slew Auntie Roo?, 1971 (Richardson, R.; Winters)
Who Stole the Doggies?, 1915 (Laurel and Hardy)
Who Stole the Shah's Jewels?, 1974 (Kinski)
Who Wants to Sleep? *See* Liebeskarussell, 1965
Who Was Lee Harvey Oswald?, 1993 (Oldman)
Who Was That Lady?, 1960 (Curtis, T.; Leigh, Janet; Martin, D.)
Who Was the Goat?, 1912-13 (White)
Who Will Love My Children?, 1983 (Ann-Margret)
Whole Town's Talking, 1926 (Del Rio; Horton)
Whole Town's Talking, 1935 (Arthur; Ball; Robinson, E.)
Whole Truth, 1923 (Laurel and Hardy)
Whole Truth, 1958 (Granger; Sanders)
Who'll Stop the Rain, 1978 (Nolte; Weld)
Wholly Moses!, 1980 (Moore, Dudley; Pryor)
Whom the Gods Destroy, 1934 (Young, R.)
Whom the Gods Wish to Destroy. *See* Nibelungen, 1966
Whoopee Boys, 1986 (Elliott)
Whoopee!, 1930 (Cantor; Grable)
Whoops Apocalypse, 1987 (Lom)
Whoops I'm an Indian, 1936 (Three Stooges)
Who's Afraid of Virginia Woolf?, 1966 (Burton; Segal; Taylor, E.)
Who's Been Sleeping in My Bed?, 1963 (Martin, D.)
Who's Got the Action, 1962 (Martin, D.; Matthau; Turner, L.)
Who's Got the Black Box? *See* Route de Corinthe, 1967

Who's Harry Crumb?, 1989 (Candy)
Who's Minding the Mint?, 1967 (Brennan)
Who's Minding the Store?, 1963 (Lewis; Jerry; Moorehead)
Who's Seen Him? *See* Chi l'ha visto?, 1945
Who's that Knocking at My Door?, 1968 (Keitel)
Who's That Girl?, 1987 (Mills)
Who's Your Father?, 1918 (Mix)
Who's Your Lady Friend?, 1937 (Lockwood)
Whose Baby? *See* Nick of Time Baby, 1916
Whose Life Is It Anyway?, 1981 (Dreyfuss)
Whose Little Girl Are You? *See* Better Late than Never, 1982
Whose Zoo, 1918 (Laurel and Hardy)
Why Albert Pinto Is Angry. *See* Albert Pinto ko gussa kyon aata hai, 1980
Why Change Your Wife?, 1920 (Swanson)
Why Does Herr R Run Amok? *See* Warum lauft Herr R amok?, 1969
Why Girls Go Back Home, 1926 (Loy)
Why Girls Love Sailors, 1927 (Laurel and Hardy)
Why Girls Say No, 1927 (Laurel and Hardy)
Why Havel?, 1991 (Newman; Temple)
Why Pick on Me?, 1918 (Lloyd)
Why Smith Left Home, 1919 (Crisp)
Why the Sheriff Is a Bachelor, 1914 (Mix)
Why Their News Is Bad News, 1984 (Christie)
Why Women Love, 1925 (Sweet)
Why Worry?, 1923 (Lloyd)
Wiano, 1964 (Łomnicki)
Wicked, 1931 (McLaglen)
Wicked as They Come, 1954 (Marshall)
Wicked City. *See* Hans le Marin, 1948
Wicked Darling, 1919 (Chaney)
Wicked Go to Hell. *See* Salauds vont en enfer, 1955
Wicked Lady, 1945 (Lockwood; Mason)
Wicked Lady, 1983 (Bates, A.; Dunaway; Elliott; Gielgud)
Wicked Stepmother, 1989 (Davis, B.)
Wicked Woman, 1934 (Taylor, R.)
Wicker Man, 1973 (Lee, C.)
Wide Blue Road. *See* Lunga strada azzurra, 1958
Wide Blue Yonder, 1951 (Brennan)
Wide Open, 1930 (Horton)
Wide Open Faces, 1938 (Brown; Wyman)
Wide Open Spaces, 1924 (Laurel and Hardy)
Widerspenstigen Zaehmung, 1974 (Brandauer)
Widow by Proxy, 1919 (Gilbert)
Widow from Chicago, 1930 (Robinson, E.)
Widow from Monte Carlo, 1936 (Del Rio)
Widow's Nest, 1977 (Lollobrigida; Neal)
Widows' Peak, 1994 (Farrow)
Widow's Walk. *See* Noyade interdite, 1987
Wie kommt ein so reizendes Mädchen zu diesem Gewerbe?, 1970 (Crawford, B.; Kinski)
Wie tötet man eine Dame. *See* Geheimnis der gelben Mönche, 1966
Wielki Szu, 1983 (Nowicki)
Wien 1910, 1942 (Dagover)
Wien tantz, 1951 (Walbrook)
Wiener Walzer. *See* Wien tantz, 1951
Wife, 1914 (Gish)
Wife, Doctor, and Nurse, 1937 (Young, L.)
Wife for a Night. *See* Moglie per una notte, 1952
Wife, Husband, Friend, 1939 (Young, L.)
Wife of Monte Cristo, 1946 (Kortner)
Wife of Seishu Hanaoka. *See* Hanaoko Seishu no tsuma, 1967
Wife or Country, 1918 (Swanson)
Wife Savers, 1928 (Beery)
Wife Takes a Flyer, 1942 (Bennett)
Wife Tamers, 1926 (Barrymore, L.)
Wife versus Secretary, 1936 (Gable; Harlow; Loy; Stewart)
Wife Wanted, 1946 (Francis)
Wife's Heart. *See* Tsuma no kokoro, 1956
Wifemistress. *See* Mogliamante, 1977
Wiggs Takes the Rest Cure, 1914 (Mix)
Wilbur Crawfords wundersames Abenteuer. *See* Seine Frau, die Unbekannte,

1923
Wilby Conspiracy, 1975 (Caine; Poitier)
Wild Affair, 1963 (Terry-Thomas)
Wild and the Willing, 1962 (Hurt, J.)
Wild and Wonderful, 1964 (Curtis, T.; Dalio)
Wild and Wooly, 1917 (Fairbanks)
Wild and Wooly, 1937 (Brennan)
Wild Angels, 1966 (Dern)
Wild at Heart, 1990 (Cage; Dafoe; Rossellini; Stanton)
Wild Bill, 1995 (Barkin; Bridges; Hurt, J.)
Wild Bill Hiccup, 1923 (Hart; Laurel and Hardy)
Wild Bill Hickok Rides, 1941 (Bond)
Wild Boys of the Road, 1933 (Bond)
Wild Brian Kent, 1936 (Bellamy)
Wild Bunch, 1969 (Borgnine; Holden; Oates; O'Brien, E.; Ryan, R.)
Wild Company, 1930 (Lugosi)
Wild Duck, 1983 (Irons; Ullmann)
Wild Duck. See Wildente, 1976
Wild for Kicks. See Beat Girl, 1960
Wild Game. See Wildwechsel, 1972
Wild Geese. See Gan, 1953
Wild Geese, 1978 (Burton; Granger; Harris, R.)
Wild Geese II, 1985 (Olivier)
Wild Geese Calling, 1941 (Bennett; Fonda, H.)
Wild Girl, 1932 (Bellamy; Bennett)
Wild Girl of the Sierras, 1916 (Marsh)
Wild Gold, 1934 (Trevor)
Wild Harvest, 1946 (Ladd; Lamour; Preston)
Wild Heart, 1950 (Cusack; Jones, Jennifer)
Wild Heart, 1952 (Cotten)
Wild Hearts Can't Be Broken, 1991 (Robertson)
Wild Heritage, 1958 (O'Sullivan)
Wild Honey, 1922 (Beery)
Wild Horse Mesa, 1933 (Scott, R.)
Wild Horse Rodeo, 1937 (Rogers, R.)
Wild Horse Stampede, 1926 (Wray)
Wild in the Country, 1961 (Presley; Weld)
Wild in the Streets, 1968 (Pryor; Winters)
Wild Is the Wind, 1957 (Magnani; Quinn)
Wild Justice. See Case of Gabriel Perry, 1935
Wild Love. See Innamorati, 1955
Wild Money, 1937 (Horton)
Wild Mustang, 1935 (Carey)
Wild North, 1951 (Charisse; Granger)
Wild One, 1953 (Marvin)
Wild One, 1954 (Brando)
Wild Orchid, 1990 (Rourke)
Wild Orchids, 1929 (Garbo)
Wild Party, 1929 (Bow; March)
Wild Party, 1956 (Quinn)
Wild Party, 1975 (Welch)
Wild Poses, 1932 (Laurel and Hardy)
Wild Ride, 1960 (Nicholson)
Wild River, 1960 (Clift; Dern; Remick)
Wild Roots of Love. See Petits Chats, 1959
Wild Rovers, 1971 (Holden; Malden; Roberts, R.)
Wild Side, 1995 (Walken)
Wild Strawberries. See **Smultronstället**, 1957
Wild Times, 1980 (Hopper)
Wild West, 1987 (Bronson)
Wild Wind of Spring. See Tacaszi vihar, 1918
Wild Women, 1918 (Carey)
Wildcat Bus, 1940 (Ladd; Wray)
Wildcats, 1986 (Hawn; Snipes)
Wildcatter, 1937 (Bond; McDaniel)
Wildcatters, 1980 (Malden)
Wildente, 1976 (Ganz; Seberg)
Wildentes, 1925 (Rasp)
Wilder Napalm, 1993 (Quaid; Winger)
Wilderness Mail, 1914 (Mix)
Wilderness Trail, 1919 (Mix)

Wildfire, 1915 (Barrymore, L.)
Wildflower, 1991 (Keaton, D.)
Wildwechsel, 1972 (Schygulla)
Wilful Peggy, 1910 (Pickford)
Wilhelm Tell, 1923 (Veidt)
Wilhelm Tell, 1934 (Veidt)
Will Get You. See Hunter, 1980
Will Penny, 1967 (Dern; Heston; Pleasence)
Will Power, 1912-13 (White)
Will Success Spoil Rock Hunter?, 1957 (Blondell; Mansfield; Marx Brothers)
Will There Really Be a Morning, 1983 (Grant, L.)
Will Tomorrow Ever Come. See That's My Man, 1947
Willard, 1971 (Borgnine; Lanchester)
Willi eine Zauberposse. See Also es war so ..., 1976
William Tell. See Guglielmo Tell, 1949
Willie and Phil, 1980 (Fishburne; Wood)
Willie's Disguise, 1912-13 (White)
Willie's Great Scheme, 1912-13 (White)
Willow Tree in the Ginza. See Ginza no yanagi, 1932
Willows of Ginza. See Ginza no yanagi, 1932
Willy Wonka and the Chocolate Factory, 1971 (Wilder)
Wilma, 1977 (Washington)
Wilmar 8, 1980 (Grant, L.)
Wilson, 1944 (Coburn, C.; Dalio; Price)
Winchester '73, 1950 (Curtis, T.; Duryea; Hudson; Stewart; Winters)
Winchester '73, 1966 (Blondell; Duryea)
Wind, 1928 (Gish)
Wind, 1992 (Robertson)
Wind across the Everglades, 1958 (Falk)
Wind and the Lion, 1975 (Connery; Huston, J.)
Wind Cannot Read, 1958 (Bogarde; Pleasence)
Wind from the East. See Vent d'est, 1970
Wind of Change, 1961 (Pleasence)
Wind Sang Me a Song. See Vento mi ha cantato una canzone, 1948
Windfall, 1935 (Withers)
Windom's Way, 1957 (Finch)
Window, 1949 (Kennedy)
Window in London, 1940 (Redgrave, M.)
Windows of Time. See Az idö ablakai, 1969
Windprints, 1989 (Hurt, J.)
Winds of Chance, 1925 (McLaglen)
Winds of Change, 1978 (Ustinov)
Winds of the Wasteland, 1936 (Wayne)
Windwalker, 1981 (Howard, T.)
Windy Riley Goes Hollywood, 1931 (Arbuckle; Brooks, L.)
Wine, 1913 (Arbuckle)
Wine, 1924 (Bow)
Wing and a Prayer, 1944 (Ameche; Andrews, D.)
Winged Victory, 1944 (Cobb; Holliday; Malden; O'Brien, E.)
Winging 'round Europe with Will Rogers, 1927 (Rogers, W.)
Wings, 1927 (Bow; Constantine)
Wings in the Dark, 1935 (Grant, C.; Loy)
Wings of a Dove. See Ailes de la colombe, 1981
Wings of Danger, 1952 (Kendall)
Wings of Desire. See Himmel über Berlin, 1987
Wings of Eagles, 1957 (Bond; Marsh; O'Hara; Wayne)
Wings of Fame, 1990 (O'Toole)
Wings of Fire, 1967 (Bellamy)
Wings of Night. See Flügel der Nacht, 1982
Wings of the Morning, 1937 (Fonda, H.)
Wings of the Navy, 1939 (De Havilland)
Wings over Honolulu, 1937 (Milland)
Wings Up, 1944 (Gable)
Winner, 1914 (Beery)
Winner. See Couer gros comme ca, 1962
Winner Take All, 1932 (Cagney)
Winner Take All, 1975 (Blondell)
Winners and Sinners, 1983 (Chan)
Winners of the Wilderness, 1927 (Crawford, J.)
Winnetou: II Teil, 1964 (Kinski)
Winning, 1969 (Newman)

Winning, 1969 (Woodward)
Winning Back His Love, 1910 (Crisp)
Winning of Barbara Worth, 1926 (Banky; Colman; Constantine)
Winning of the West, 1953 (Autry)
Winning Steak. *See* Stacey's Knights, 1981
Winning Team, 1952 (Day; Reagan)
Winning Way. *See* All-American, 1953
Winning Your Wings, 1942 (Stewart)
Winonah's Vengeance, 1911 (White)
Winslow Boy, 1948 (Donat; Thompson)
Winter Carnival, 1939 (Walker)
Winter Kill, 1974 (Nolte)
Winter Kills, 1979 (Bridges; Hayden; Huston, J.; Malone; Mifune; Perkins;
    Taylor, E.; Wallach)
Winter Light. *See* Nattvardsgästerna, 1963
Winter Meeting, 1948 (Davis, B.)
Winter of Our Discontent, 1983 (Sutherland; Weld)
Winter of Our Dreams, 1982 (Davis, J.)
Winterset, 1936 (Ball; Carradine; Meredith)
Wintertime, 1943 (Henie; Wilde)
Wir brauchen kein Geld. *See* Man braucht kein Geld, 1931
Wir um schalten auf Hollywood, 1931 (Menjou)
Wisdom, 1986 (Moore, Demi)
Wise Blood, 1979 (Huston, J.; Stanton)
Wise Girl, 1937 (Dumont; Hopkins, M.; Milland)
Wise Guy, 1926 (Astor)
Wise Guys, 1937 (Langdon)
Wise Guys, 1986 (DeVito; Keitel)
Wise Guys Prefer Brunettes, 1926 (Laurel and Hardy)
Wisecracks, 1992 (Goldberg; Reagan)
Wiser Age. *See* Onna no za, 1962
Wiser Sex, 1932 (Colbert; Douglas, Melvyn)
Wished on Mabel, 1915 (Arbuckle; Normand)
Wistful Widow. *See* Wistful Widow of Wagon Gap, 1947
Witch. *See* Strega in amore, 1966
Witch Hunt, 1994 (Hopper)
Witches. *See* Streghe, 1965
Witches, 1966 (Fontaine)
Witches. *See* Streghe, 1967
Witches, 1990 (Huston, A.; Zetterling)
Witches' Brew, 1978 (Turner, L.)
Witches of Eastwick, 1987 (Cher; Nicholson; Pfeiffer; Sarandon)
Witches of Salem. *See* Sorcières de Salem, 1956
Witchfinder General, 1968 (Price)
Witchfire, 1986 (Winters)
Witching. *See* Necromancy, 1972
Witchita, 1955 (McCrea)
With a Little Help from His Friends. *See* Making of a "Local Hero", 1983
With a Smile. *See* Avec le sourire, 1936
With a Song in My Heart, 1952 (Hayward; Ritter)
With Beauty and Sorrow. *See* Utsukishisa to kanashimi to, 1965
With Her Rival's Help, 1912-13 (White)
With Honors, 1994 (Pesci)
With Intent to Kill, 1984 (Hunter; Malden)
With Love and Hisses, 1927 (Laurel and Hardy)
With Murder in Mind, 1992 (O'Sullivan)
With Savage Intent. *See* With Murder in Mind, 1992
With Six You Get Egg Roll, 1968 (Day; Hershey)
With the Aid of the Law, 1915 (Mix)
With the Enemy's Help, 1912 (Pickford; Sweet)
With Will Rogers in Dublin, 1927 (Rogers, W.)
With Will Rogers in London, 1927 (Rogers, W.)
With Will Rogers in Paris, 1927 (Rogers, W.)
Within Memory. *See* Uns et les autres, 1981
Within the Law, 1923 (Talmadge)
Without a Clue, 1988 (Caine; Kingsley)
Without a Trace, 1983 (Nelligan)
Without Apparent Motive. *See* Sans mobile apparent, 1971
Without Benefit of Clergy, 1921 (Karloff)
Without Fear or Blame. *See* Sans Peur et Sans Reproche, 1988
Without Honor, 1950 (Moorehead)

Without Honors, 1932 (Carey)
Without Love, 1945 (Ball; Grahame; Hepburn, K.; Tracy)
Without Orders, 1936 (Bond)
Without Pity. *See* Senza pietà, 1948
Without Regret, 1935 (Niven)
Without Reservations, 1946 (Colbert; Grant, C.; Wayne)
Without Warning. *See* Invisible Menace, 1938
Without Warning, 1980 (Landau; Palance)
Witness. *See* Témoin, 1978
Witness, 1985 (Ford, H.)
Witness for the Prosecution, 1957 (Dietrich; Lanchester; Laughton)
Witness for the Prosecution, 1958 (Power)
Witness for the Prosecution, 1982 (Kerr; Pleasence; Richardson, R.)
Witness Out of Hell. *See* Zeugin aus der Hölle, 1965
Witness to Murder, 1954 (Sanders; Stanwyck)
Witnesses, 1986 (Mills)
Wives and Lovers, 1963 (Leigh, Janet; Winters)
Wives Beware. *See* Two White Arms, 1932
Wives Never Know, 1936 (Menjou)
Wiz, 1978 (Pryor)
Wizard of Babylon. *See* Bauer von Babylon, 1983
Wizard of Mars, 1965 (Carradine)
Wizard of Oz, 1924 (Laurel and Hardy)
Wizard of Oz, 1939 (Garland)
Wizja lokalna 1901, 1980 (Łomnicki; Olbrychski)
Wo ist Herr Belling?, 1944 (Jannings)
Wolf, 1994 (Nelligan; Nicholson; Pfeiffer)
Wolf at the Door, 1986 (Sutherland; Von Sydow)
Wolf Lowry, 1917 (Hart)
Wolf Man, 1924 (Shearer)
Wolf Man, 1941 (Bellamy; Lugosi; Rains)
Wolf Song, 1929 (Constantine)
Wolfen, 1981 (Finney; Olmos)
Wolves, 1930 (Laughton)
Wolves of the Trail, 1918 (Hart)
Woman, 1915 (Chaplin, C.; Purviance)
Woman. *See* Amore, 1947
Woman Accused, 1933 (Calhern; Grant, C.)
Woman against Woman, 1938 (Astor)
Woman Alone. *See* Sabotage, 1936
Woman and the Puppet. *See* Femme et le pantin, 1958
Woman at Her Window. *See* Femme à sa fenêtre, 1976
Woman Between. *See* Woman I Love, 1937
Woman Called Golda, 1982 (Davis, J.)
Woman Called Moses, 1978 (Welles)
Woman Chases Man, 1937 (Crawford, B.; Hopkins, M.; McCrea)
Woman Commands, 1932 (Negri; Rathbone)
Woman Conquers, 1922 (Karloff)
Woman Destroyed. *See* Donna spezzata, 1988
Woman Disputed, 1928 (Talmadge)
Woman from Hell, 1929 (Astor)
Woman from Mellon's, 1910 (Pickford)
Woman from Monte Carlo, 1932 (Dagover; Huston, W.)
Woman from Moscow, 1928 (Lukas; Negri)
Woman Gives, 1920 (Talmadge)
Woman Hater, 1948 (Feuillère; Granger)
Woman Haters, 1913 (Arbuckle)
Woman Haters, 1934 (Brennan; Three Stooges)
Woman He Loved, 1988 (De Havilland)
Woman He Scorned, 1930 (Negri)
Woman Hunt. *See* Au Royaume des cieux, 1947
Woman I Love, 1937 (Hopkins, M.; Muni)
Woman I Love, 1971 (Dunaway)
Woman I Stole, 1933 (Wray)
Woman in a Dressing Gown, 1957 (Quayle)
Woman in a Leopardskin Coat. *See* Kvinna i leopard, 1958
Woman in Black, 1914 (Barrymore, L.)
Woman in Brown. *See* Vicious Circle, 1948
Woman in Green, 1945 (Rathbone)
Woman in Hiding, 1949 (Lupino)
Woman in Hiding. *See* Mantrap, 1953

Woman in His House. *See* Animal Kingdom, 1932
Woman in Leopardskin. *See* Kvinna i leopard, 1958
Woman in Love. *See* Enamorada, 1946
Woman in Question, 1950 (Bogarde)
Woman in Red, 1935 (Stanwyck)
Woman in Red, 1984 (Wilder)
Woman in Room Thirteen, 1932 (Bellamy; Loy)
Woman in the Case. *See* Allotment Wives, 1945
Woman in the Dark, 1934 (Bellamy; Douglas, Melvyn; Wray)
Woman in the Dunes. *See* **Suna no onna**, 1963
Woman in the Moon. *See* Donna della luna, 1988
Woman in the Rain. *See* Mujer Bajo la Lluvia, 1992
Woman in the Ultimate, 1913 (Gish)
Woman in the Window, 1944 (Bennett; Duryea; Massey; Robinson, E.)
Woman in White, 1929 (Sweet)
Woman in White, 1948 (Greenstreet; Moorehead)
Woman in White. *See* Kvinna i vitt, 1949
Woman Inside, 1981 (Blondell)
Woman Is a Woman. *See* Femme est une femme, 1961
Woman Like Satan. *See* Femme et le pantin, 1958
Woman Next Door. *See* Femme d'à côte, 1981
Woman Obsessed, 1959 (Hayward)
Woman of Affairs, 1928 (Garbo; Gilbert)
Woman of Antwerp. *See* Dédée d'Anvers, 1948
Woman of Darkness. *See* Yngsjömordet, 1966
Woman of Desire, 1993 (Mitchum)
Woman of Distinction, 1950 (Ball; Milland; Russell, R.)
Woman of Paris, 1923 (Chaplin, C.; Menjou; Purviance)
Woman of Pleasure, 1919 (Sweet)
Woman of Rome. *See* Romana, 1954
Woman of Rumor. *See* Uwasa no onna, 1954
Woman of Sin. *See* Woman Scorned, 1911
Woman of Straw, 1964 (Connery; Lollobrigida; Richardson, R.)
Woman of Substance, 1983 (Mills; Richardson, M.)
Woman of Summer. *See* Stripper, 1963
Woman of the River. *See* Donna del fiume, 1954
Woman of the Sea, 1926 (Purviance)
Woman of the Town, 1943 (Trevor)
Woman of the World, 1925 (Negri)
Woman of the Year, 1942 (Hepburn, K.; Tracy)
Woman of Tomorrow. *See* Zhemtshina zavtrastchevo dnia, 1914
Woman of Wonders. *See* Donna delle meraviglie, 1985
Woman on Pier 13, 1949 (Ryan, R.)
Woman on the Beach, 1947 (Bennett; Ryan, R.)
Woman on Trial, 1927 (Negri)
Woman One Longs For. *See* Frau, nach der Man sich sehnt, 1929
Woman or Two. *See* Femme ou deux, 1985
Woman-Proof, 1923 (Astor)
Woman Racket, 1930 (Sweet)
Woman Racket. *See* Cargaison blanche, 1937
Woman Rebels, 1936 (Crisp; Hepburn, K.; Marshall)
Woman Scorned, 1911 (Sweet)
Woman Tamer. *See* She Couldn't Take It, 1935
Woman There Was, 1919 (Bara)
Woman Times Seven, 1967 (Arkin; Brazzi; Caine; Gassman; MacLaine; Noiret; Sellers)
Woman under the Cross. *See* Žena pod křižem, 1937
Woman under the Influence, 1974 (Falk; Rowlands)
Woman, Wake Up!, 1922 (Calhern)
Woman Wanted, 1935 (Calhern; McCrea; O'Sullivan)
Woman Who Cried Murder. *See* Death Scream, 1975
Woman Who Touched Legs. *See* Ashi ni sawatta onna, 1952
Woman Who Wouldn't Die. *See* Catacombs, 1965
Woman Wise, 1928 (Pidgeon)
Woman with a Dagger. *See* Zhenshchina s kinzhalom, 1916
Woman with No Name, 1950 (Burton)
Woman with the Red Boots. *See* Femme aux bottes rouges, 1974
Woman without a Face. *See* Mister Buddwing, 1966
Woman without a Soul. *See* Mujer sin alma, 1943
Womanlight. *See* Clair de femme, 1979
Woman's Devotion, 1956 (Henreid)

Woman's Face, 1941 (Crawford, J.; Douglas, Melvyn; Veidt)
Woman's Face. *See* Kvinnas ansikte, 1938
Woman's Fool, 1918 (Carey)
Woman's Heart. *See* Onna-gokoru, 1959
Woman's Life. *See* Onna no rekishi, 1963
Woman's Revenge, 1912-13 (White)
Woman's Revenge. *See* Vengeance d'une femme, 1990
Woman's Secret, 1924 (Marsh)
Woman's Secret, 1949 (Douglas, Melvyn; Grahame; O'Hara)
Woman's Secret. *See* Fujinkai no himitsu, 1959
Woman's Story. *See* Onna no rekishi, 1963
Woman's Touch. *See* Woman Chases Man, 1937
Woman's Vengeance, 1947 (Boyer)
Woman's World, 1954 (Bacall; MacMurray; Webb; Wilde)
Women & Men II, 1991 (Binoche; Dillon)
Women & Men: In Love There Are No Rules. *See* Women & Men II, 1991
Women, 1939 (Crawford, J.; Dumont; Fontaine; Goddard; Russell, R.; Shearer)
Women. *See* Nanas, 1984
Women against Women, 1938 (Marshall)
Women and Men: Stories of Seduction, 1990 (Griffith; Woods)
Women and War. *See* Arrêtez les tambours, 1961
Women Are Like That, 1938 (Francis)
Women Are Weak. *See* Faibles femmes, 1959
Women Have Only One Thing on Their Minds. *See* Elles ne pensent qu'a ca, 1994
Women in Chains, 1972 (Lupino)
Women in Love, 1969 (Bates, A.; Jackson, G.; Reed; Jackson, G.)
Women in Prison. *See* Joshu to tomoni, 1957
Women in the Wind, 1939 (Francis)
Women in War, 1940 (Cushing)
Women Love Diamonds, 1927 (Barrymore, L.)
Women Love Once, 1931 (Lukas)
Women Make Movies. *See* Gold Diggers, 1984
Women Men Marry, 1931 (Scott, R.)
Women Next Door. *See* Signorine della villa accanto, 1941
Women of All Nations, 1931 (Bogart; Lugosi; McLaglen)
Women of Glamour, 1937 (Douglas, Melvyn)
Women of the Night. *See* Yoru no onna tachi, 1948
Women of the World. *See* Donna del mondo, 1963
Women of Tokyo. *See* Tokyo no onna, 1933
Women of Valor, 1986 (Sarandon)
Women on the Verge of a Nervous Breakdown. *See* **Mujeres al Borde de un Ataque de Nervios**, 1988
Women Unveiled. *See* Onnade arukoto, 1958
Women with the Red Boots. *See* Femme aux bottes rouges, 1974
Women without Men. *See* Dirnentragödie, 1927
Women without Names. *See* Donne senza nome, 1950
Women's Prison, 1955 (Lupino)
Women's Prison Escape. *See* Thunder County, 1974
Women's Room, 1980 (Remick)
Won by a Fish, 1912 (Pickford)
Won by a Neck, 1930 (Arbuckle)
Won in a Closet, 1914 (Normand)
Won Ton Ton, the Dog Who Saved Hollywood, 1976 (Blondell; Borgnine; Carradine; Charisse; Crawford, B.; Dern; Faye; Mature; Miller; Pidgeon; Weissmuller)
Wonder Bar, 1934 (Del Rio; Francis; Jolson; Powell, D.)
Wonder Boy. *See* Wunder unserer Tage, 1951
Wonder Man, 1945 (Kaye)
Wonderboy. *See* De sueur et du sang, 1994
Wonderful Chance, 1920 (Valentino)
Wonderful Country, 1959 (Armendáriz; Mitchum)
Wonderful Crook. *See* Pas si méchant que ça, 1974
Wonderful Thing, 1920 (Talmadge)
Wonderful Things, 1958 (Neagle)
Wonderful Times. *See* Epoque Formidable, 1991
Wonderful World of the Brothers Grimm, 1962 (Bloom; Homolka; Terry-Thomas)
Wonders of Aladdin. *See* Meraviglie di Aladino, 1961
Wooden Horse, 1950 (Finch)

Wooden Soldiers. *See* Babes in Toyland, 1934
Word, 1978 (Huston, J.)
Word for the Defense. *See* Slovo dlya zashchity, 1976
Word of Honor, 1981 (Malden; Malkovich)
Wordless Message, 1913 (Mix)
Words and Music, 1929 (Bond; Wayne)
Words and Music, 1948 (Charisse; Garland; Kelly, Gene; Leigh, Janet;
    Rooney)
Words for Battle, 1941 (Olivier)
Words upon the Window Pane, 1994 (Chaplin, G.)
Work, 1915 (Chaplin, C.; Purviance)
Workers' Quarters. *See* Rabotchaia slobodka, 1912
Workhouse Ward, 1963 (Cusack)
Working Class Goes to Heaven. *See* Classe operaia va in paradiso, 1971
Working Class Man. *See* Gung Ho, 1986
Working Girl, 1988 (Ford, H.; Griffith; Weaver)
Working Girls, 1931 (Lukas)
Working Man, 1933 (Davis, B.)
World According to Garp, 1982 (Close; Williams, R.)
World and the Flesh, 1932 (Hopkins, M.)
World Apart, 1988 (Hershey)
World Changes, 1933 (Astor; Muni; Rooney)
World for Ransom, 1954 (Duryea)
World Gone Mad, 1933 (Calhern)
World Gone Wild, 1988 (Dern)
World in His Arms, 1952 (Peck; Quinn)
World in My Pocket, 1961 (Steiger)
World Moves On, 1934 (Carroll)
World of Abbott and Costello, 1965 (Abbott and Costello)
World of Andrew Wyeth, 1977 (Fonda, H.)
World of Apu. *See* **Apur Sansar**, 1959
World of Henry Orient, 1964 (Lansbury; Sellers)
World of Sport Fishing, 1972 (Crosby)
World of Suzie Wong, 1960 (Holden)
World of Wall Street, 1929 (Lukas)
World Premiere, 1941 (Barrymore, J.; Farmer)
World War II: When Lions Roared, 1994 (Caine; Hoskins)
World War III, 1982 (Hudson)
World Was His Jury, 1958 (O'Brien, E.)
World's Applause, 1923 (Menjou)
World's Greatest Lover, 1977 (DeVito; Wilder)
World's Greatest Swindlers. *See* Plus Belles Escroqueries du monde, 1964
Worlds Beyond: The Black Tomb, 1987 (Wallach)
Worm's Eye View, 1951 (Dors)
Worse You Are, the Better You Sleep. *See* Warui yatsu hodo yoku nemuru,
    1960
Worst Woman in Paris?, 1933 (Menjou)
Wounded in the Forest. *See* Ranny v lesie, 1964
Woyzeck, 1979 (Kinski)
Wrath of God, 1972 (Hayworth; Mitchum)
Wrath of the Gods, 1914 (Hayakawa)
Wreath of Orange Blossoms, 1911 (Crisp)
Wreck of the Mary Deare, 1959 (Constantine; Harris, R.; Heston; Redgrave,
    M.)
Wrecker, 1933 (Bond)
Wrecking Crew, 1968 (Martin, D.)
Wrecking Crew, 1979 (Lee, B.)
Wrestling Ernest Hemingway, 1993 (Duvall; Harris, R.; MacLaine)
Written Law, 1931 (Carroll)
Written on the Wind, 1956 (Bacall; Hudson; Malone)
Wrong Again, 1929 (Laurel and Hardy)
Wrong Arm of the Law, 1962 (Caine; Sellers)
Wrong Box, 1966 (Caine; Mills; Moore, Dudley; Richardson, R.; Sellers)
Wrong Is Right, 1982 (Connery; Leigh, Jennifer Jason)
Wrong Man, 1956 (Fonda, H.; Quayle; Weld)
Wrong Move. *See* Falsche Bewegung, 1974
Wrong Room, 1939 (Lake)
Wrongdoers, 1925 (Barrymore, L.)
Wspólny pokój, 1959 (Tyszkiewicz)
Wszystko na sprzedaż, 1968 (Olbrychski; Tyszkiewicz)
Wunder unserer Tage, 1951 (Werner)

Wunderbaren Sommer. *See* Gluck auf der Alm, 1958
WUSA, 1970 (Newman; Perkins; Woodward)
Wuthering Heights, 1939 (Crisp; Niven; Oberon; Olivier)
Wuthering Heights, 1992 (Binoche; Fiennes)
Wuya yu Maque, 1948 (Zhao Dan)
Wyatt Earp, 1994 (Costner; Hackman; Quaid; Rossellini)
Wyoming, 1940 (Beery)
Wyoming Outlaw, 1939 (Wayne)
X-15, 1961 (Bronson; Stewart)
X from Outer Space. *See* Girara, 1967
X, Y, & Zee, 1972 (Taylor, E.)
Xanadu, 1980 (Kelly, Gene)
Xi chu bawang, 1994 (Gong Li)
Xiao Lingzi, 1936 (Zhao Dan)
Xin Ching-Wu Men, 1976 (Chan)
Xochimilco. *See* **María Candelaria**, 1944
Y Del Seguro, Libranos Señor, 1982 (Banderas)
Y el projimo?, 1973 (Chaplin, G.)
Y'a Bon les blancs, 1988 (Piccoli)
Ya, Frantsisk skorina, 1970 (Yankovsky)
Yaadon K.I. Zanjeer, 1984 (Azmi)
Yabure amigasa, 1927 (Hasegawa)
Yabure-daiko, 1949 (Mori)
Yabure kabure, 1970 (Kyo)
Yagyu bugei-cho, 1957 (Mifune; Kagawa)
Yagyu ichizoku no inbo, 1978 (Yamada)
Yahudi, 1958 (Kumar)
Yaji Kita, 1933 (Hasegawa)
Yaji Kita bijn sodo, 1932 (Hasegawa)
Yakko Kagami-san, 1934 (Hasegawa)
Yakko no Koman, 1927 (Tanaka)
Yakuza, 1975 (Mitchum; Okada)
Yama no gaika, 1929 (Tanaka)
Yama no oto, 1954 (Hara; Yamamura)
Yama no sanka: Moyuru wakamono-tachi, 1962 (Yamada; Yamamura)
Yamabiko gakko, 1952 (Okada)
Yamada Nagamasa Oja no tsurugi, 1959 (Hasegawa)
Yamamoto Isoroku, 1968 (Mifune; Mori; Tsukasa)
Yamaneko Tomi no hanashi, 1943 (Takamine)
Yamashita Yasubumi. *See* Higegi no shogun Yamashita Yasubumi, 1953
Yami o yokogire, 1959 (Yamamura)
Yamile sous le Cèdres, 1939 (Vanel)
Yamiuchi tosei, 1932 (Yamada)
Yangyu. *See* Yagyu bugei-cho, 1957
Yank at Eton, 1942 (Rooney)
Yank at Oxford, 1938 (Barrymore, L.; Leigh, V.; O'Sullivan; Taylor, R.)
Yank Came Back, 1947 (Meredith)
Yank in Dutch. *See* Wife Takes a Flyer, 1942
Yank in London. *See* I Live in Grosvenor Square, 1945
Yank in the R.A.F., 1941 (Grable; Power)
Yankee at King Arthur's Court. *See* Connecticut Yankee, 1931
Yankee Doodle Dandy, 1942 (Cagney; Huston, W.)
Yankee Girl, 1910 (White)
Yankee in King Arthur's Court. *See* Connecticut Yankee, 1949
Yankee Pasha, 1954 (Cobb)
Yankee Senor, 1926 (Mix)
Yanks, 1979 (Gere; Redgrave, V.; Roberts, R.)
Yao ayao yao dao waipo qiao, 1995 (Gong Li)
Yaps and Yokels, 1919 (Laurel and Hardy)
Yaqui Cur, 1913 (Barrymore, L.)
Yari no Gonzo, 1929 (Hasegawa)
Yashu Honno-ji, 1934 (Hasegawa)
Yataro-gasa, 1955 (Yamada)
Yato kaze no naka o hashiru, 1961 (Ryu)
Yatoro-gasa: Kyorai no maki, Dokuho no maki, 1932 (Yamada)
Yatsu no hajiki wa jigoku daze, 1958 (Yamamura)
Year of Living Dangerously, 1982 (Gibson; Weaver)
Year of the Comet, 1992 (Jourdan)
Year of the Dragon, 1985 (Rourke)
Year of the Gun, 1991 (Stone)
Year of the Woman, 1973 (Beatty)

Year without a Santa Claus, 1974 (Rooney)
Yearling, 1946 (Peck; Wyman)
Yearning. *See* Midareru, 1964
Years Between, 1946 (Redgrave, M.)
Years without Days. *See* Castle on the Hudson, 1940
Yeh Gulistan Hamara, 1972 (Anand)
Yeh kaisa insaaf, 1980 (Azmi)
Yeh Nazdeekiyan, 1982 (Azmi)
Yellow Canary, 1943 (Neagle; Rutherford)
Yellow Crow. *See* Kiiroi karasu, 1957
Yellow Headed Summer, 1974 (Pidgeon)
Yellow Jack, 1938 (Coburn, C.; Montgomery)
Yellow Passport. *See* Yellow Ticket, 1931
Yellow Rolls-Royce, 1964 (Bergman; Delon; Harrison; MacLaine; Moreau; Scott, G.; Sharif)
Yellow Rose of Texas, 1944 (Rogers, R.)
Yellow Sands, 1938 (McDowall)
Yellow Sky, 1948 (Baxter; Peck; Widmark)
Yellow Stain, 1922 (Gilbert)
Yellow Streak, 1915 (Barrymore, L.)
Yellow Ticket, 1931 (Barrymore, L.; Karloff; Olivier)
Yellow Ticket. *See* Gelbe Schein, 1918
Yellow Tomahawk, 1954 (Van Cleef)
Yellowbeard, 1983 (Cleese; Mason; York)
Yellowstone Kelly, 1959 (Oates)
Yentl, 1983 (Streisand)
Yes Mr. Brown, 1932 (Buchanan)
Yes or No?, 1920 (Talmadge)
Yes Sir, That's My Baby, 1949 (Coburn, C.; O'Connor)
Yes, Virginia, There Is a Santa Claus, 1991 (Bronson)
Yes, We Have No Bonanza, 1939 (Three Stooges)
Yes, Yes, Nanette, 1925 (Laurel and Hardy)
Yesterday in Fact. *See* Naprawde wczoraj, 1963
Yesterday, Today, and Tomorrow. *See* Ieri, oggi, e domani, 1963
Yesterday's Enemy, 1959 (Baker)
Yeux cernés, 1964 (Morgan)
Yeux de l'amour, 1959 (Blier; Darrieux)
Yeux fermés, 1971 (Dalio)
Yeux sans visage, 1960 (Brasseur; Valli)
Yield to the Night, 1956 (Dors)
Yilmaz Güney: His Life, His Films, 1987 (Christie)
Yin and Yang of Mr. Go, 1970 (Bridges)
Ying and the Yang. *See* Third Eye, 1969
Yngsjömordet, 1966 (Dahlbeck)
Yo, la peor de Todas, 1990 (Sanda)
Yo Pecador, 1959 (Armendáriz)
Yoba, 1976 (Kyo)
Yodelin' Kid from Pine Ridge, 1937 (Autry)
Yoghi, 1916 (Wegener)
Yogiri no ketto, 1959 (Mori)
Yogoreta Eiyu, 1983 (Okada)
Yoidore nito-ryu, 1954 (Hasegawa)
Yoidore tenshi, 1948 (Mifune; Shimura)
Yojimbo, 1961 (Mifune; Shimura; Tsukasa; Yamada)
Yokaren monogatari: Konpeki no sora toku, 1960 (Yamada)
Yoke's on Me, 1944 (Three Stooges)
Yoki no onna, 1946 (Takamine)
Yokihi, 1955 (Kyo; Mori; Yamamura)
Yokin ajo-san, 1932 (Takamine)
Yokina uta Daigaku wa detakeredo, 1929 (Tanaka)
Yokino-jo henge, 1935 (Hasegawa)
Yokino-jo henge, 1963 (Hasegawa)
Yokino-jo henge: Kaiketsu-hen, 1936 (Hasegawa)
Yokmok, 1963 (Tyszkiewicz)
Yolanda, 1924 (Davies)
Yolanda and the Thief, 1945 (Astaire)
Yomeiri mae, 1933 (Tanaka)
Yomigaeru daichi, 1971 (Okada; Tsukasa)
Yonjuhachi-sai no teiko, 1956 (Yamamura)
Yopparai tengoku, 1962 (Yamamura)
Yorck, 1931 (Krauss)

Yorokobi mo Kanashimi mo ikutoshitsuki, 1957 (Takamine)
Yoru no cho, 1957 (Kyo)
Yoru no haiyaku, 1959 (Yamamura)
Yoru no keisha, 1962 (Tsukasa)
Yoru no kyoja, 1927 (Tanaka)
Yoru no mibojin, 1951 (Tanaka)
Yoru no nagare, 1960 (Tsukasa; Yamada)
Yoru no onna tachi, 1948 (Tanaka)
Yoru no sugao, 1958 (Kyo)
Yoru no togyo, 1959 (Kyo)
Yoru no tsuzumi, 1958 (Mori)
Yoruno cho, 1957 (Yamamura)
Yosei Gorath, 1962 (Shimura)
Yosei wa hana no nioi ga suru, 1953 (Mori)
Yosemite: The Fate of Heaven, 1989 (Redford)
Yoshia goten, 1937 (Yamada)
Yoshinaka o meguru san-nin no onna, 1956 (Hasegawa)
Yoshiwara, 1937 (Hayakawa)
Yotamono to kyakusen-bi, 1933 (Takamine)
Yoto, 1926 (Tanaka)
Yotsuya Ghost Story. *See* Yotsuya kaidan, 1949
Yotsuya kaidan, 1949 (Tanaka)
Yotsuya kaidan, 1959 (Hasegawa)
Yottsu no kekkon, 1944 (Takamine; Yamada)
You and Me, 1938 (Carey; Raft; Sidney)
You and Me, 1975 (Hershey)
You and Me Together, 1979 (Welch)
You Are My Adventure. *See* Du är mitt äventyr, 1958
You Are Stupid. *See* Niisan no baka, 1932
You Belong to Me, 1941 (Fonda, H.; Stanwyck)
You Belong to My Heart. *See* Mr. Imperium, 1951
You Can Change the World, 1949 (Crosby)
You Can't Beat Love, 1937 (Fontaine)
You Can't Believe Everything, 1918 (Swanson)
You Can't Cheat an Honest Man, 1939 (Fields, W. C.)
You Can't Do That to Me. *See* Maisie Goes to Reno, 1944
You Can't Fool Your Wife, 1940 (Ball)
You Can't Get Away with Murder, 1939 (Bogart)
You Can't Go Home Again, 1979 (Grant, L.)
You Can't Have Everything, 1937 (Ameche; Faye)
You Can't Run Away from It, 1956 (Lemmon; Powell, D.)
You Can't Sleep Here. *See* I Was a Male War Bride, 1949
You Can't Take It with You, 1938 (Arthur; Barrymore, L.; Miller; Stewart)
You Can't Win 'em All, 1970 (Bronson; Curtis, T.)
You Disturb Me. *See* Tu mi turbi, 1982
You Gotta Stay Happy, 1948 (Fontaine; Stewart)
You, John Jones, 1943 (Cagney)
You Lie So Deep, My Love, 1975 (Pidgeon)
You Must Be Joking!, 1965 (Elliott; Terry-Thomas)
You Nazty Spy, 1940 (Three Stooges)
You Never Can Tell, 1951 (Powell, D.)
You Only Live Once, 1937 (Bond; Fonda, H.; Sidney)
You Only Live Twice, 1967 (Connery; Pleasence)
You Said a Mouthful, 1932 (Brown; Rogers, G.)
You Were Never Lovelier, 1942 (Astaire; Hayworth; Menjou)
You Who Are about to Enter ... . *See* I som här inträden ..., 1945
You Will Remember, 1941 (McDowall)
You'll Find Out, 1940 (Karloff; Lorre; Lugosi)
You'll Never Get Rich, 1941 (Astaire; Hayworth)
Young Again, 1986 (Reeves)
Young America, 1932 (Bellamy; Tracy)
Young Americans, 1993 (Keitel)
Young and Eager. *See* Claudelle Inglish, 1961
Young and the Passionate. *See* **I vitelloni**, 1953
Young and Willing, 1943 (Hayward; Holden)
Young and Willing. *See* Weak and the Wicked, 1953
Young and Willing. *See* Wild and the Willing, 1962
Young April, 1926 (Crisp)
Young as You Feel, 1931 (Rogers, W.)
Young as You Feel, 1940 (Lake)
Young at Heart, 1954 (Barrymore, E.; Day; Malone; Sidney)

Young Bess, 1953 (Granger; Kerr; Laughton)
Young Bill Hickok, 1940 (Rogers, R.)
Young Billy Young, 1969 (Dickinson; Mitchum)
Young Buffalo Bill, 1940 (Rogers, R.)
Young Cassidy, 1965 (Christie; Evans; Redgrave, M.; Smith)
Young Country, 1970 (Brennan)
Young Diana, 1922 (Davies)
Young Doctor Kildare, 1938 (Ayres)
Young Doctors, 1961 (March; Reagan; Segal)
Young Doctors in Love, 1982 (Moore, Demi; Stanton)
Young Don't Cry, 1957 (Mineo)
Young Donovan's Kid, 1931 (Cooper; Karloff)
Young Dr. Kildare, 1938 (Barrymore, L.)
Young Eagles, 1930 (Arthur; Lukas)
Young Escape. See Ung flukt, 1959
Young Frankenstein, 1974 (Brooks, M.; Hackman; Wilder)
Young Giants. See Minor Miracle, 1983
Young Girls of Rochefort, 1968 (Kelly, Gene)
Young Girls Turn 25. See Demoiselles ont eu 25 Ans, 1993
Young Guard, 1948 (Bondarchuk)
Young Guns, 1988 (Palance; Stamp)
Young Guns II, 1990 (Coburn, J.)
Young Have No Morals. See Dragueurs, 1959
Young Hearts. See Promised Land, 1988
Young Ideas, 1943 (Astor; Gardner; Marshall)
Young in Heart, 1938 (Gaynor; Goddard)
Young Indiana Jones Chronicles: Paris, May 1919, 1993 (Cusack)
Young Ironsides, 1932 (Goddard)
Young Ladies from Wilko. See Panny z Wilka, 1978
Young Land, 1957 (Hopper)
Young Lawyers, 1969 (Pryor)
Young Lions, 1958 (Brando; Clift; Martin, D.; Schell, Maximilian; Van Cleef)
Young Lovers. See Never Fear, 1950
Young Man of Manhattan, 1930 (Colbert; Rogers, G.)
Young Man of Music. See Young Man with a Horn, 1950
Young Man with a Horn, 1950 (Bacall; Day; Douglas, K.)
Young Man with Ideas, 1951 (Ford, G.)
Young Master. See Sidai cheutma, 1980
Young Master Feng, 1925 (Zhao Dan)
Young Master in Love. See Lung siuye, 1982
Young Miss. See Ojosan, 1930
Young Mr. Jazz, 1919 (Lloyd)
Young Mr. Lincoln, 1939 (Bond; Fonda, H.)
Young Mr. Pitt, 1942 (Donat; Lom; Mills)
Young Nowheres, 1929 (Barthelmess)
Young Painter, 1922 (Astor)
Young People, 1940 (Marsh; Temple)
Young Philadelphians, 1959 (Newman)
Young Rajah, 1922 (Valentino)
Young Rebel. See Avventure e gliamori di Miguel Cervantes, 1968
Young Runaways, 1968 (Dreyfuss)
Young Savages, 1961 (Lancaster; Winters)
Young Scarface. See Brighton Rock, 1947
Young Tom Edison, 1940 (Rooney)
Young Toscanini. See Giovane Toscanini, 1988
Young Warriors, 1983 (Borgnine)
Young Widow, 1946 (Russell, J.)
Young Winston, 1972 (Attenborough; Bancroft; Hawkins; Hopkins, A.; Mills; Shaw)
Young Wives' Tale, 1951 (Greenwood; Hepburn, A.)
Young Woodley, 1930 (Carroll)
Young World. See Mondo nuovo, 1966
Youngblood, 1986 (Reeves)
Youngblood Hawke, 1964 (Astor)
Younger and Younger, 1993 (Sutherland)
Youngest Profession, 1943 (Garson; Moorehead; Pidgeon; Powell, W.; Taylor, R.; Turner, L.)
Your Girl and Mine, 1914 (Mix)
Your Past Is Showing. See Naked Truth, 1958
Your Ticket Is No Longer Valid, 1980 (Harris, R.; Moreau)
Your Turn, Darling. See Toi de faire, Mignonne, 1963

Your Turn, My Turn. See Va voir maman, papa travaille, 1977
Your Uncle Dudley, 1936 (Horton)
Your Witness, 1950 (Baker; Montgomery)
You're a Big Boy Now, 1966 (Page)
You're a Sweetheart, 1937 (Faye)
You're Darn Tootin', 1928 (Laurel and Hardy)
You're in the Army Now. See O.H.M.S., 1937
You're in the Army Now, 1941 (Durante; Wyman)
You're in the Navy Now, 1951 (Bronson; Constantine; Marvin)
You're My Everything, 1949 (Baxter; Keaton, B.)
You're Never Too Young, 1955 (Lewis, Jerry; Martin, D.)
You're Only Young Once, 1938 (Rooney)
You're Telling Me!, 1934 (Fields, W. C.)
You're the Doctor, 1938 (Withers)
You're the One, 1941 (Horton)
Yours for the Asking, 1936 (Lupino; Raft)
Yours, Mine and Ours, 1968 (Ball; Fonda, H.; Hershey)
Youth and His Amulet. See Gen to Fudo-myoh, 1961
Youth in Revolt. See Altitude 3200, 1938
Youth on Parole, 1938 (Dumont)
Youth Takes a Fling, 1938 (McCrea)
Youthful Sinners. See Tricheurs, 1958
You've Got to Walk It Like You Talk It or You'll Lose That Beat, 1971 (Pryor)
Yugato, 1953 (Kagawa)
Yukan naru koi, 1925 (Tanaka)
Yuki-fujin ezu, 1950 (Yamamura)
Yuki no honoo, 1955 (Tsukasa; Yamamura)
Yuki no wataridori, 1957 (Hasegawa)
Yukiko to Natsuko, 1941 (Yamada)
Yukyo gonin otoko, 1958 (Hasegawa)
Yukyo no mure, 1948 (Hasegawa; Yamamura)
Yume de aritai, 1962 (Yamamura)
Yume Utsutsu, 1935 (Tanaka)
Yurakucho de aimasho, 1958 (Kyo)
Yurei akatsuki ni shisu, 1948 (Hasegawa)
Yurei hanjo-ki, 1960 (Kagawa)
Yuri Nosenko, KGB, 1986 (Jones, T.)
Yushima no shiraume, 1955 (Mori)
Yuwaku, 1948 (Hara)
Yuyake-gume, 1956 (Yamada)
Yves Montand chante en U.S.S.R.. See Poet Iv Montan, 1957
Yves Montand Chante, 1960 (Montand)
Yvonne la nuit, 1949 (Cervi)
Z, 1969 (Montand; Papas)
Z dalekiego kraju, 1981 (Neill)
Z.P.G., 1972 (Chaplin, G.; Reed)
Za-Bum Circus. See Circo equestre Za-Bum, 1944
Zabriskie Point, 1970 (Ford, H.; Shepard)
Zabudnite na Mozarta, 1985 (Mueller-Stahl)
Zaduszki, 1961 (Tyszkiewicz)
Zakroishchik iz Torzhka, 1925 (Maretskaya)
Zalman, 1975 (Wiest)
Załoga, 1952 (Łomnicki)
Zalzala, 1952 (Anand)
Zamach, 1959 (Łomnicki)
Zamanat, 1977 (Azmi)
Zampó y yo, 1965 (Rey)
Zancos, 1984 (Banderas)
Zandalee, 1991 (Cage)
Zander the Great, 1925 (Davies)
Zandy's Bride, 1974 (Hackman; Ullmann)
Zangiku monogatari, 1956 (Hasegawa)
Zanna bianca, 1973 (Rey)
Zansho, 1978 (Tsukasa)
Zany Adventures of Robin Hood, 1984 (McDowall; Segal)
Zapatas Bande, 1914 (Nielsen)
Zarak, 1956 (Mature)
Zarco, 1957 (Armendáriz)
Zardoz, 1973 (Connery)
Zářijové noci, 1957 (Brodský)

Zärliche Haie, 1966 (Karina)
Zatoichi: Abare Himatsuri, 1970 (Mori)
Zatoichi hatashi-jo, 1968 (Shimura)
Zatoichi Meets Yojimbo. *See* Zatoichi to Yojimbo, 1970
Zatoichi to Yojimbo, 1970 (Mifune)
Zatoichi's Conspiracy, 1973 (Okada; Shimura)
Zaza, 1923 (Swanson)
Zaza, 1939 (Colbert; Marshall; Nazimova)
Zazie dans le métro, 1960 (Noiret)
Zazie in the Underground. *See* Zazie dans le métro, 1960
Zdjęcia próbne, 1976 (Olbrychski)
Zeb vs. Paprika, 1924 (Laurel and Hardy)
Zebracka Opera. *See* Operation Zebracka, 1991
Zee and Company, 1971 (Caine; York)
Zehnte Pavillon der Zitadelle, 1916 (Jannings)
Zelenyi Zmii, 1926 (Maretskaya)
Zelig, 1983 (Allen; Farrow)
Zelly and Me, 1988 (Rossellini)
Zemma, 1951 (Mori; Yamamura)
Zemsta, 1958 (Tyszkiewicz)
Žena pod křížem, 1937 (Lom)
Zenigata Heiji, 1951 (Hasegawa)
Zenigata Heiji torimon-hikae, 1952 (Hasegawa)
Zenigata Heiji torimono-hikae: Bijin-gumo, 1960 (Hasegawa)
Zenigata Heiji torimono-hikae: Bijin-zame, 1961 (Hasegawa)
Zenigata Heiji torimono-hikae: Doguro-kago, 1955 (Hasegawa)
Zenigata Heiji torimono-hikae: Hachi-nin no hanayome, 1958 (Hasegawa)
Zenigata Heiji torimono-hikae: Hitohada-gumo, 1956 (Hasegawa)
Zenigata Heiji torimono-hikae: Karakuri yashiki, 1953 (Hasegawa)
Zenigata Heiji torimono-hikae: Koibumi dochu, 1951 (Hasegawa)
Zenigata Heiji torimono-hikae: Konjiki no ookami, 1953 (Hasegawa)
Zenigata Heiji torimono-hikae: Madara-hebi, 1957 (Hasegawa)
Zenigata Heiji torimono-hikae: Megitsune yashiki, 1957 (Hasegawa)
Zenigata Heiji torimono-hikae: Onibi doro, 1958 (Hasegawa; Kagawa)
Zenigata Heiji torimono-hikae: Shibijin-buro, 1956 (Hasegawa)
Zenigata Heiji torimono-hikae: Yoru no emmacho, 1961 (Hasegawa)
Zenigata Heiji torimono-hikae: Yuki-onna no ashiato, 1958 (Hasegawa; Kagawa)
Zenigata Heiji torimono-hikae: Yurei daimyo, 1954 (Hasegawa)
Zenobia, 1939 (Langdon; Laurel and Hardy; McDaniel)
Zentropa, 1992 (Constantine; Von Sydow)
Zerbrochene Krug, 1937 (Jannings)
Zerkalo, 1975 (Yankovsky)
Zero Hour, 1957 (Andrews, D.; Hayden; Darnell)
Zero Population Growth. *See* Z.P.G., 1972
Zerwany most, 1963 (Łomnicki)
Zeugin aus der Hölle, 1965 (Gélin; Papas)
Zevetut na Inkata. *See* Vermachtnis des Inka, 1966
Zhdi menya, Ana, 1969 (Yankovsky)
Zhemtshina zavtrastchevo dnia, 1914 (Mozhukin)
Zhenitba Jana Knukke, 1934 (Cherkassov)
Zhenshchina s kinzhalom, 1916 (Mozhukin)
Zhivoi trup, 1929 (Maretskaya)
Zhizn mig iskusstvo vetchno, 1916 (Mozhukin)
Zhizn na smerti, 1914 (Mozhukin)
Zhizn na Tzarya, 1911 (Mozhukin)
Zhurnalist, 1966 (Girardot)
Ziddi, 1948 (Anand)
Ziegfeld Follies, 1946 (Astaire; Ball; Charisse; Garland; Kelly, Gene; Powell, W.; Rooney; Williams, E.)
Ziegfeld Girl, 1941 (Cooper; Garland; Horton; Lamarr; Stewart; Turner, L.)
Ziema obiecana, 1975 (Olbrychski)
Zigeuner-baron, 1935 (Walbrook)
Zigeunerblut, 1910 (Nielsen)
Zigzag, 1970 (Wallach)
Zigzag, 1974 (Deneuve)
Zinker, 1931 (Rasp)
Zinker, 1963 (Kinski; Rasp)
Zip, the Dodger, 1914 (Arbuckle)
Zirkus des Lebens, 1921 (Krauss)
Zirkus Saran. *See* Knox und die lustigen Vagabunden, 1935

Zirkusblut, 1916 (Krauss)
Zirkuskönig, 1924 (Banky; Linder)
Zitra vstanu a oparim se cajem, 1977 (Brodský)
Zitti e Mosca, 1991 (Valli)
Zizanie, 1978 (Girardot)
Zlatcha notch, 1914 (Mozhukin)
Zločin v šantánu, 1968 (Brodský)
Zoe, 1992 (Papas)
Zohu fuhei-zu, 1942 (Takamine)
Zoko Miyamoto Musashi, 1955 (Mifune)
Zoko Shimizu-minato, 1940 (Shimura)
Zoku aizen katsura, 1939 (Tanaka)
Zoku Ako-jo, 1952 (Yamada)
Zoku aoi sanmyaku, 1957 (Tsukasa)
Zoku Fukei-zu, 1942 (Hasegawa; Yamada)
Zoku Hebi-hime dochu, 1950 (Hasegawa; Kyo)
Zoku Hebihime-sama, 1940 (Hasegawa)
Zoku hesokuri shacho, 1956 (Tsukasa)
Zoku jirocho Fuji, 1960 (Hasegawa)
Zoku Kageboshi, 1950 (Yamada)
Zoku Minamoto Toshitsune, 1956 (Yamada)
Zoku namo naku mazushiku utsukushiku, 1967 (Takamine)
Zoku ningen kakumei, 1976 (Shimura)
Zoku Ooka seidan: Mazo kaiketsu-hen, 1931 (Yamada)
Zoku otoko wa tsuraiyo, 1969 (Shimura)
Zoku sarariiman Chushingura, 1961 (Tsukasa)
Zoku sarariiman Shimizu minato, 1962 (Tsukasa)
Zoku Sasaki Kojiro, 1951 (Takamine)
Zoku shacho enma-cho, 1969 (Tsukasa)
Zoku shacho-gaku ABC, 1970 (Tsukasa)
Zoku shacho gyogo-ki, 1966 (Tsukasa)
Zoku shacho hanjo-ki, 1968 (Tsukasa)
Zoku shacho ninpo-cho, 1965 (Tsukasa)
Zoku shacho sandai-ki, 1958 (Tsukasa)
Zoku shacho sen-ichiya, 1967 (Tsukasa)
Zoku shacho shinshiroku, 1964 (Tsukasa)
Zoku shinobi no mono, 1963 (Yamamura)
Zoku Sugata Sanshiro, 1945 (Mori)
Żołnierz zwycięstwa, 1953 (Łomnicki)
Zoltan ... Hound of Dracula, 1977 (Ferrer)
Zombies on Broadway, 1945 (Lugosi)
Zona, 1916 (Negri)
Zone de la mort, 1917 (Modot)
Zoo in Budapest, 1933 (Young, L.)
Zoo zéro, 1978 (Kinski; Valli)
Zoot Suit, 1981 (Olmos)
Zora. *See* Silent Night, Bloody Night, 1973
Zorba the Greek, 1964 (Bates, A.; Papas; Quinn)
Zori Parizha, 1936 (Maretskaya)
Zorn, 1994 (Ullmann)
Zorro, 1975 (Baker; Delon)
Zorro, 1996 (Banderas)
Zotz!, 1962 (Dumont)
Zouzou, 1934 (Gabin)
Ztracena tvar, 1965 (Brodský)
Zu jedem kommt einmal die Liebe. *See* Alte Lied, 1930
Zügelloses Blut, 1917 (Negri)
Zulu, 1963 (Baker; Burton; Caine; Hawkins)
Zulu Dawn, 1979 (Elliott; Hoskins; Lancaster; Mills; O'Toole)
Zum Tode gehetzt, 1912 (Nielsen)
Zuppa Di Pesce, 1992 (Noiret)
Zur Chronik von Grieshuus, 1925 (Dagover)
Zuzu the Band Leader, 1913 (Normand)
Zvezda plenitelnogo schastya, 1975 (Yankovsky)
Zwei Girls vom roten Stern, 1965 (Gélin)
Zwei Menschen, 1930 (Fröhlich)
Zwei vagabunden in Prater, 1925 (Madsen and Schenstrøm)
Zwei Whisky und ein Sofa, 1963 (Schell, Maria)
Zweite Frühling, 1975 (Constantine)
Zweite Gesicht, 1982 (Scacchi)
Zweite Leben, 1916 (Kortner)

Zwielicht, 1940 (Wegener)
Zwischen Abend und Morgen, 1923 (Krauss; Rasp)
Zwischen Himmel und Erde, 1942 (Krauss)
Zwischen Nacht und Morgen, 1931 (Homolka)
Zwischen Nacht und Morgen, 1944 (Wegener)
Zwischensaison, 1992 (Chaplin, G.)
Życie raz jeszcze, 1965 (Łomnicki)
Życie rodzinne, 1971 (Nowicki; Olbrychski)
Zygfryd, 1986 (Nowicki)

NOTES ON
ADVISERS AND CONTRIBUTORS

ABRAMS, Joanne. Essayist. Freelance writer and film critic, Chicago. **Essay:** Marvin.

AFFRON, Charles. Essayist. Professor of French, New York University, since 1965. Author of *Star Acting: Gish, Garbo, Davis*, 1977, *Cinema and Sentiment*, 1982, *Divine Garbo*, 1985, *Fellini's 8½*, 1987, and *Sets in Motion: Art Direction and Film Narrative*, 1995. General editor of Rutgers Films in Print Series. **Essays:** Boyer; Colman; Durbin; Garson; MacDonald; Rainer.

AMBROGIO, Anthony. Essayist. Formerly film and composition instructor, Wayne State University, Detroit. Contributor to *Film Criticism* and *Pukka Afflatus*. **Essays:** Lugosi; S. Simon; Wray.

ARKINS, Joseph. Essayist. Registrar, exhibitions program, New York Public Library. **Essays:** Carroll; Negri; Trevor; Webb; L. Young.

BARON, Cynthia. Essayist. Assistant lecturer, University of Southern California. Contributor to *The Cinema and the Postmodern, Film and Philosophy,* and *Spectator*. **Essays:** D. Andrews; Astor; Brando; Colman; Preston; Welles.

BASINGER, Jeanine. Adviser and essayist. Corwin-Fuller Professor of Film Studies, Wesleyan University, Middletown, Connecticut; also chair, Film Studies program, and Curator/Founder, Wesleyan Cinema Archives. Trustee, American Film Institute; steering committee, National Center for Film and Video Preservation; and formerly on the Board of Advisers of the AIVF. Author of *Anthony Mann*, 1979, *The World War II Combat Film: Anatomy of a Genre*, 1986, *The It's a Wonderful Life Book*, 1986, *A Woman's View: How Hollywood Spoke to Women, 1930-1960*, 1993, *American Cinema: 100 Years of Filmmaking*, 1994, and numerous articles. **Essays:** Astaire; Colbert; Dunne; Hayworth; Mature; Montgomery; G. Rogers; Rooney; R. Ryan.

BAXTER, John. Essayist. Novelist, screenwriter, television producer, and film historian. Visiting lecturer, Hollins College, Virginia, 1974-75; broadcaster with BBC Radio and Television, 1976-91. Editor of two anthologies of science fiction; author of six novels, various screenplays for documentary films and features, and works of film criticism: *Hollywood in the Thirties*, 1968, *The Australian Cinema*, 1970, *The Gangster Film*, 1970, *Science Fiction in the Cinema*, 1970, *The Cinema of John Ford*, 1971, *The Cinema of Josef von Sternberg*, 1971, *Hollywood in the Sixties*, 1972, *An Appalling Talent: Ken Russell*, 1973, *Sixty Years of Hollywood*, 1973, *Stunt*, 1974, *The Hollywood Exiles*, 1976, *King Vidor*, 1976, *The Video Handbook* (with Brian Norris), 1982, *Filmstruck*, 1989, *Fellini*, 1993, and *Buñuel*, 1994. **Essays:** Bardot; Carey; Cobb; Dalio; B. Davis; Deneuve; Finch; Garbo; Holden; Massey; McQueen; E. O'Brien; Olivier; Pryor; Swanson; Walbrook.

BERENSTEIN, Rhona. Adviser. Associate Professor, Film Studies, University of California, Irvine. Author of *Attack of the Leading Ladies: Gender, Sexuality, and Spectatorship in Classic Horror Cinema*, 1996. Contributor to *Camera Obscura, CineAction!, Film History,* and *GLQ*.

BOWERS, Ronald. Essayist. Financial editor, E. F. Hutton and Company, since 1982. Editor, *Films in Review*, 1979-81. Co-author (with James Robert Parrish) of *The MGM Stock Company*, 1973; author of *The Selznick Players*, 1976. **Essays:** Gélin; Granger; Lukas.

BRITO, Rui Santana. Adviser. Cinemateca Portuguesa, Museu do Cinema. Co-compiler of *Catalogo da Biblioteca Suplemento 1982*, for Cinemateca Portuguesa, 1982.

BROESKE, Pat H. Essayist. Film critic for *L. A. Times, Washington Post,* and others. Co-author (with Peter Harry Brown) of *Howard Hughes: The Untold Story*, 1996. **Essay:** T. Curtis.

BURGOYNE, Robert. Adviser. Associate Professor of English, Wayne State University, Detroit. Editor of *Enclitic,* and contributor to *Cinema*

Journal, Film Quarterly, and *October*. Author of *Bertolucci's 1900: A Narrative and Historical Analysis*, 1991; co-author (with Robert Stam and Sandy Flitterman-Lewis) of *New Vocabularies in Film Semiotics*, 1992.

CIMENT, Michel. Adviser. Associate Professor in American Studies, University of Paris. Member of the Editorial Board of *Positif.* Author of *Erich von Stroheim*, 1967, *Kazan by Kazan*, 1973, *Le Dossier Rosi*, 1976, *Le Livre de Losey*, 1979, *Kubrick*, 1980, *Les Conquérants d'un nouveau monde*, 1981, *Elia Kazan: An Outsider*, 1982, *All about Mankiewicz*, 1983, *Boorman*, 1985, *Francesco Rosi: Chornique d'un film annoncé*, 1987, and *Passport pour Hollywood*, 1987.

CLARK, Constance. Essayist. Director, Speech and Theatre Department, Lehman College, New York. **Essays:** Ferrer; Jaffe.

CLEMENTS, William M. Essayist. Professor of English, Arkansas State University. **Essays:** Bloom; Maximilian Schell.

COFFMAN, Elizabeth. Essayist. Assistant Professor, University of Tampa. Videographer. Currently working on *Women in Motion,* a study of the influence of modern dance on films of the twenties and thirties. **Essay:** Gish.

COHEN, Allen. Essayist. Retired librarian. Head, Cataloging Department and Collection Development Head for Film Studies, University of California, Santa Barbara Library. Co-author of *John Huston, A Guide to References and Resources*, 1997. **Essays:** Aiello; Cusack.

COOK, Samantha. Essayist. Freelance editor, researcher, and writer, London. **Essay:** Bridges.

COUSINS, R. F. Essayist. Lecturer in French, University of Birmingham, England. Author of *Zola's Thérèse Raquin*, 1991, and contributor to *University Vision* and *Literature/Film Quarterly.* Executive Member of British Universities Film and Video Council. **Essays:** Darrieux; Gabin; Girardot; Huppert; Morgan; Noiret; Philipe; Piccoli; Presle; Reggiani; Trintignant.

CREEKMUR, Corey K. Essayist. Assistant Professor, Wayne State University. Co-editor (with Alexander Doty) of *Out in Culture: Gay, Lesbian and Queer Essays on Popular Culture*, 1995. Contributor to *Film Quarterly, Wide Angle,* and *Journal of Film and Video*. **Essays:** Astaire; Dunne; Hara; Keitel; Kyo; Demi Moore; Robeson; Ryu; Yamada.

CURRY, Ramona. Essayist. Film critic and instructor. Program coordinator, Goethe Institute, Chicago, 1978-84. Author of *Too Much of a Good Thing: Mae West as Cultural Icon*, 1996. **Essay:** Schygulla.

DALE, Alan. Essayist. Lecturer, Princeton University. **Essays:** Barkin; Cage; Day-Lewis; Gould; Hoffman; D. Keaton; Murray; Nolte; Penn; Pfeiffer; R. Williams; Winger.

DELAMATER, Jerome. Essayist. Associate Professor, Department of Communication Arts, Hofstra University, Hempstead, New York, since 1978. Author of *Dance in the American Musical*, 1981. **Essays:** Charisse; Hara; Gene Kelly; Miller; O'Connor; B. Robinson; Sinatra; Sullavan.

DERRY, Charles. Essayist. Head of Motion Picture Studies, Wright State University, Dayton, Ohio, since 1978. Author of *Dark Dreams: A Psychological History of the Horror Film*, 1978, and *The Suspense Thriller: Films in the Shadow of Alfred Hitchcock*, 1988; co-author (with Jack Ellis and Sharon Kern) of *The Film Book Bibliography: 1940-1975*, 1979. Writer/director of *Cerebral Accident*, 1986, and *Joan Crawford Died for Your Sins*, 1987; fiction published in *Reclaiming the Heartland: Gay & Lesbian Voices from the Midwest*, 1996. **Essays:** Ann-Margret; Audran; Farrow; G. Jackson; S. Martin; Reagan; Streisand; Welch.

DiBATTISTA, Maria. Essayist. Professor of English and Comparative Literature, Princeton University. Author of forthcoming book on American film comedy of the thirties and forties. **Essays:** Basinger; Kline; Loy; Stanwyck.

DICKSON, Jay. Essayist. Lecturer in English, Princeton University. **Essay:** Weaver.

DOLL, Susan M. Essayist. Instructor in film at Oakton Community College and at the School of the Art Institute of Chicago. Author of *Elvis, a Tribute to His Life*, 1989, *Marilyn: Her Life and Legend*, 1990, and *Elvis, Rock 'n' Roll Legend*, 1994. **Essays:** Armendáriz; Brynner; Cardinale; Murphy.

DURGNAT, Raymond. Essayist. Visiting Professor of Film, Wright State University, Dayton, Ohio. Author of numerous publications on film, including *Durgnat on Film*, 1975, *King Vidor—American*, 1988, and *Michael Powell and the English Genius*, 1991. **Essays:** Caine; Elliott; Matthau; Sellers.

EDELMAN, Rob. Essayist. Writer, reporter, and editor. Author of *Great Baseball Films*, 1994; co-author (with Audrey Kupferberg) of *Angela Lansbury: A Life on Stage and Screen*, 1996. Contributing editor of Leonard Maltin's *Movie and Video Guide* and *Leonard Maltin's Movie Encyclopedia*, 1994. Contributor to *A Political Companion to American Film*. Director of programming, Home Film Festival. **Essays:** Attenborough; Bardot; A. Bates; Belmondo; Belushi; Bonham-Carter; Brandauer; Bridges; Caan; G. Chaplin; Cobb; Costner; J. Curtis; Deneuve; De Niro; Depardieu; Dillon; Michael Douglas; Elliott; Fiennes; Finch; Finney; Fishburne; H. Fonda; Freeman; García; Gardner; Garfield; Goldberg; Gong Li; Hackman; R. Harris; W. Hurt; J. Huston; S. Jackson; James Earl Jones; Julia; Landau; Jennifer Jason Leigh; Lemmon; Malden; Mastroianni; Matthau; Mature; Maura; Olmos; O'Sullivan; Pacino; Palance; Pesci; Rainer; Redford; V. Redgrave; M. Richardson; Robbins; Rossellini; Rourke; Rowlands; Ryder; Scacchi; Seberg; Segal; Sheen; Snipes; Spacek; Stallone; Stamp; Steenburgen; Streep; Thurman; Travolta; Trevor; Trintignant; Turturro; Voight; von Sydow; Whitaker.

ESTRIN, Mark W. Essayist. Professor of English and Director of Film Studies, Rhode Island College, Providence, since 1966. Author of *Lillian Hellman: Plays, Films, Memoirs*, 1980. Contributor to *Literature/Film Quarterly*, *Modern Drama*, and *Journal of Narrative Technique*. **Essays:** Burton; Christie; Gordon; Greenstreet; Irons; Tracy; Winters.

FALK, Quentin. Essayist. Founding editor of *Flicks* magazine, and regular contributor to national newspapers. Formerly editor of *Screen International*, London, and author of books on Graham Greene, Anthony Hopkins, the Rank Organisation, and Albert Finney. **Essays:** Attenborough; A. Hopkins.

FALLER, Greg S. Essayist. Associate Professor in Film, Towson State University, Baltimore, since 1986. Taught at Northwestern University, 1984-86. Assistant/Associate Editor of *The International Dictionary of Films and Filmmakers*, first edition, vols. 3, 4, and 5; and of *Journal of Film and Video*, 1985-87. Editor of *Film Reader 6*, 1985. **Essays:** Close; Faye; Keeler; Midler; Miranda; E. Powell; E. Williams.

FALSETTO, Mario. Essayist. Associate Professor, Concordia University, Montreal. Author of *Stanley Kubrick: A Narrative and Stylistic Analysis*, 1994; editor of *Perspectives on Stanley Kubrick*, 1996. **Essay:** T. Jones.

FARNSWORTII, Rodney. Essayist. Assistant Professor of English, Indiana University-Purdue University, Fort Wayne. **Essays:** Bond; Lemmon; Marais; McLaglen; O'Hara; Seyrig; Vitti.

FEINSTEIN, Howard. Essayist. Film editor, *The Village Voice*, New York. **Essays:** Constantine; Robeson; Winkler.

FELANDO, Cynthia. Essayist. University instructor and freelance writer; recently received doctorate from University of California, Los Angeles,

Department of Film and Television. **Essays:** Arletty; Juliette Lewis; J. Russell; Temple; Walken.

FONSECA, M. S. Essayist. Researcher, Programming Department, Cinemateca Portuguesa, since 1981. Film critic for *Expresso* newspaper, Lisbon, and author of *Pamorama do Cinema Dinamarqués*, 1983, and *Cinema Novo Potugués*, 1985, among others. **Essay:** Nielsen.

FOREMAN, Alexa L. Essayist. Account executive, Video Duplications, Atlanta, since 1986. Formerly theater manager, American Film Institute. Author of *Women in Motion*, 1983. **Essays:** Dressler; Farmer.

GABROSEK, Anita. Essayist. M.F.A. candidate in Film, and teaching assistant, Ohio University. **Essay:** Bassett.

GALLAGHER, John A. Essayist. Writer, filmmaker, and lecturer. Member of National Board of Review of Motion Pictures, since 1982. **Essays:** E. Barrymore; Beery; Power.

GANDHY, Behroze. Essayist. Co-editor, BFI Dossier on Indian Cinema, 1982. **Essays:** Anand; Azmi; Chatterjee; Patil.

GATEWARD, Frances. Essayist. Assistant Professor, American University. Independent film and video maker. **Essay:** G. Rogers.

GEVINSON, Alan. Essayist. Researcher for the American Film Institute Catalog of Feature Films. Associate editor of *Meet Frank Capra*, 1990. **Essay:** Grace Kelly.

GLANCY, H. M. Essayist. Freelance writer and lecturer. **Essay:** Cher.

GOLDMAN, Ilene S. Essayist. Film studies instructor, Chicago. Contributor to *Jump Cut*, *The Independent*, and *Studies in Latin American Popular Culture*. **Essays:** Braga; Félix; A. Hepburn.

GOMERY, Douglas. Adviser and essayist. Professor, College of Journalism, University of Maryland. Author of nine books, including *The Hollywood Studio System*, 1986, and *Shared Pleasures*, 1992; co-editor of *The Future of News*, 1992. Contributor of numerous articles to periodicals such as *Village Voice*, *American Journalism Review*, and *Screen*. **Essays:** Abbott and Costello; Autry; Crosby; Dern; Fox; Grable; Griffith; E. Harris; Hawn; Henie; Hope; Jolson; Kennedy; Lamour; D. Martin; Poitier; D. Powell; R. Rogers; W. Rogers; R. Scott; Shearer; Sloane; Tati; Widmark.

HÁBA, Veroslav. Essayist. Film historian, Prague. **Essay:** Sidney.

HANSON, Patricia King. Essayist. Executive editor, American Film Institute, Los Angeles, since 1983. Film critic, *Screen International*, since 1986. Associate editor, Salem Press, 1978-83. Editor, *American Film Institute Catalog of Feature Films 1911-1920* and *1931-1940*. Co-editor of *Film Review Index*, vols. I and II, 1986-87, and *Sourcebook for the Performing Arts*, 1988; executive editor of *Meet Frank Capra*, 1990. **Essays:** L. Barrymore; Bennett; Brazzi; M. O'Brien; O'Sullivan; Wyman.

HANSON, Stephen L. Essayist. Humanities biographer, University of Southern California, Los Angeles, since 1969. Film critic, *Screen International*, since 1986. Associate editor, Salem Press, 1978-83. Co-editor of *Film Review Index*, vols. I and II, 1986-87, and *Sourcebook for the Performing Arts*, 1988. **Essays:** Flynn; Masina; R. Young.

HAYS, Matthew. Essayist. Freelance writer and editor, Montreal. Editor of *MagNet*, an online film magazine. Film critic for the weekly Montreal *Mirror*. **Essays:** J. Fonda; Hopper; Hunter; Schwarzenegger; Winters.

HENRY, Catherine. Essayist. Director of College Publications, University of Chicago, since 1980. **Essays:** Guinness; L. Howard; Lanchester; Monroe; R. Russell.

HIGGINS, Steven. Essayist. Former senior database editor, Baseline, Inc., New York. Author of *D. W. Griffith and the Biograph Company,* 1985. **Essay:** Gilbert.

HIRANO, Kyoko. Essayist. Film Program Coordinator, Japan Society, New York, since 1986. Author of *Mr. Smith Goes to Tokyo: The Japanese Cinema under the American Occupation, 1945-1952,* 1992. Editor, *Cinéma Gras,* Tokyo, 1977-79, and contributor to *Cineaste* and *Theater Craft.* **Essays:** Hasegawa; Kagawa; Kyo; Mori; Okada; Shimura; Takamine; Tanaka; Tsukasa; Yamada; Yamamura.

HONG, Guo-Juin. Essayist. Instructor, University of California, Santa Cruz, and San Francisco State University. Independent documentary filmmaker; current projects mainly in affiliation with the Gay and Lesbian Historical Society of Northern California, the Oral History Project. **Essays:** Bogart; Clift; Connery; Garbo; C. Grant; Irons; B. Lee; Olivier; J. Roberts.

HUMPHREY, Daniel. Essayist. Teacher, freelance writer, and filmmaker, San Francisco. **Essays:** Bacon; Malkovich; McDowell; M. Ryan; Sutherland.

HUTCHINGS, Peter. Essayist. Lecturer in film studies, Department of Historical and Critical Studies, Newcastle Polytechnic. **Essay:** C. Lee.

HUTCHINSON, Curtis. Essayist. Freelance writer. **Essays:** Lamarr; Lollobrigida; Van Cleef.

KAMINSKY, Stuart M. Essayist. Professor of Film, Northwestern University, Evanston, Illinois. Author of *Don Siegel, Director,* 1973, *Clint Eastwood,* 1974, *American Film Genres,* 1977, *John Huston, Maker of Magic,* 1978, *Coop: The Life and Legend of Gary Cooper,* 1980, *Basic Filmmaking* (co-author), 1981, and *American Television Genres,* 1985; co-author (with Mark Walker) of *Writing for Television,* 1988. Editor of *Ingmar Bergman: Essays in Criticism,* 1975. Also a novelist: works include *Murder on the Yellow Brick Road,* 1978, *He Done Her Wrong,* 1983, *A Cold Red Sunrise,* 1988, *Buried Caesars,* 1989, and *Blood and Rubles,* 1996. **Essays:** G. Cooper; Duryea; Hayden; Heston; Mix; Saint; Wallach; Wilde.

KELLER, Virginia. Essayist. Writer and lecturer, Chicago. **Essay:** Wegener.

KEMP, Philip. Essayist. Freelance writer and film historian; contributor to *Sight and Sound* and *World Film Directors.* Author of *Lethal Innocence: The Cinema of Alexander Mackendrick,* 1991. **Essays:** Adjani; Baye; Connery; H. Fonda; Greenwood; A. Huston; Johnson; Jouvet; Karloff; Kendall; Lorre; Mercouri; Papas; Sanders; Signoret; Withers; Zhao Dan.

KNOBLOCH, Susan. Essayist. Ph.D. candidate in Film and Television Critical Studies, University of California, Los Angeles. Contributor to *Film Quarterly.* **Essays:** De Vito; Monroe; Neal; Pitt; Quaid; Weld; Willis.

KUPFERBERG, Audrey E. Essayist. Film consultant, New York. Co-author (with Rob Edelman) of *Angela Lansbury: A Life on Stage and Screen,* 1996. **Essays:** Ameche; Arkin; Ayres; Bacall; Ball; Banky; E. Barrymore; J. Barrymore; L. Barrymore; K. Bates; Beatty; Branagh; M. Brooks; Charisse; Cher; Colbert; G. Davis; K. Douglas; Gaynor; Henreid; K. Hepburn; Hershey; A. Hopkins; Kaye; M. Keaton; Lupino; Meredith; Miller; Niven; D. Reynolds; Sidney; E. Taylor; Thompson; Ullmann; Woodward; Wray; R. Young.

LEIBFRIED, Philip. Essayist. Freelance writer. Author of forthcoming *Star of India—The Life and Films of Sabu.* Contributor to *Films in Review, The Silent Film Monthly, Filmfax,* and *Hollywood Studio Magazine.* **Essay:** Wong.

LIEBENSON, Donald. Essayist. Freelance writer for *Chicago Reader* and *Chicago Sun-Times.* **Essays:** Borgnine; Stanton.

LIEBMAN, Roy. Essayist. Librarian and film bibliographer, California State University, Los Angeles. Author of *Silent Film Performers,* 1996, as well as several articles on media production. **Essays:** Calhern; Pidgeon.

LIPPE, Richard. Essayist. Lecturer in film at Atkinson College, York University, Ontario. On the editorial board of *CineAction!* **Essays:** de Havilland; Melvyn Douglas; Fontaine; Gardner; Garland; Jennifer Jones; MacLaine; Minnelli; Novak; L. Turner.

LORENZ, Janet E. Essayist. Associate editor and film critic *Z Channel magazine,* since 1984. Assistant supervisor, University of Southern California Cinema Research Library, Los Angeles, 1979-82, and film critic, *SelecTV Magazine,* 1980-84. **Essays:** J. Andrews; G. Chaplin; Clift; C. Grant; K. Kinski; Léaud; Rains; Stewart.

LÖWE, Judah. Essayist. Freelance writer. **Essay:** Brasseur.

MACNAB, G. C. Essayist. Freelance writer, researcher, and filmmaker, London. Author of *J. Arthur Rank and the British Film Industry,* 1993. **Essays:** Josephson; Mills; M. Redgrave.

MALPEZZI, Frances M. Essayist. Associate Professor, Arkansas State University. **Essay:** Goddard.

MANCINI, Elaine. Essayist. Has taught film at the College of Staten Island, and at St. John's University, New York. Author of *The Free Years of the Italian Film Industry, 1930-1935,* 1981, *Struggles of the Italian Film Industry during Fascism, 1930-1935,* 1985, and *Luchino Visconti: A Guide to References and Resources,* 1986. **Essays:** Cervi; Crisp; Fabrizi; Hayakawa; Lancaster; Mangano; Mastroianni; Pickford; Sordi; Valli; Volonté.

MANVELL, Roger. Essayist. Formerly Professor of Film, Boston University. Director, British Film Academy, London, 1947-59, and a Governor and Head of Department of Film History, London Film School, until 1974; Bingham Professor of the Humanities, University of Louisville, 1973. Editor, *Penguin Film Review,* 1946-49, and the Pelican annual *Cinema,* 1950-52; associate editor, *New Humanist,* 1968-75, and director, Rationalist Press, London, from 1966; editor-in-chief, *International Encyclopaedia of Film,* 1972. Author of *Film,* 1944, *The Animated Film,* 1954, *The Film and the Public,* 1955, *On the Air,* 1955, *The Technique of Film Music,* 1957, 1976, *The Living Screen,* 1961, *What Is a Film?,* 1965, *New Cinema in the U.S.A.,* 1968, *New Cinema in Britain,* 1969, *Art in Movement,* 1970, *Shakespeare and the Film,* 1971, *Films and the Second World War,* 1975, *Love Goddesses of the Movies,* 1975, *Theatre and Film,* 1979, *Art and Animation: Halas and Batchelor, 1940-1980,* 1980, and *Ingmar Bergman,* 1980; co-author of *The Technique of Film Animation* (with John Halas), 1959, *Design in Motion* (with John Halas), 1962, *The German Cinema* (with Heinrich Fraenkel), 1971, and *Images of Madness: The Portrayal of Insanity in the Feature Film* (with Michael Fleming), 1985; also novels, biographies of theatrical personalities and of personalities of the Third Reich. Died 1987. **Essays:** Bara; Bogarde; Bogart; Bow; L. Brooks; Cherkassov; Dagover; Donat; Dumont; Gielgud; Harlow; T. Howard; Laughton; V. Leigh; Marshall; Mason; Oberon; Rasp; M. Simon; Veidt.

MARCHETTI, Gina. Adviser and essayist. Associate Professor, University of Maryland, College Park. Author of *Romance and the "Yellow Peril": Race, Sex, and Discursive Strategies in Hollywood Fiction,* 1993. Staff editor of *Jump Cut.* **Essay:** Chan.

McCAFFREY, Donald W. Essayist. Emeritus Professor of English, University of North Dakota. Author of *Four Great Comedians: Chaplin, Lloyd, Keaton, and Langdon,* 1968, *The Golden Age of Sound Comedy: Comic Films and Comedians of the Thirties,* 1973, *Three Classic Silent*

Film Comedies Starring Harold Lloyd, 1976, and *Assault on Society: Satirical Literature to Film,* 1992; editor of *Focus on Chaplin,* 1971. **Essays:** Allen; Arbuckle; Brown; Candy; Cantor; C. Chaplin; Chevalier; Cleese; J. Cooper; Durante; Fernandel; W. C. Fields; B. Keaton; Langdon; Lloyd; Dudley Moore; Normand; Raimu; Three Stooges; West.

McCARTY, John. Essayist. Author and freelance writer. Assistant editor of *Mystery Scene.* Author of *Splatter Movies,* 1984, *The Complete Films of John Huston,* 1987, *The Modern Horror Film,* 1990, *Hollywood Gangland,* 1993, *Movie Psychos and Madmen,* 1993, *The Fearmakers,* 1994, *The Sleaze Merchants,* 1995, and ten other books on film and television history. **Essays:** Adjani; Bloom; Bogarde; Bondarchuk; Borgnine; Bronson; Burton; Caine; J. Coburn; T. Curtis; Cushing; Dean; Falk; Flynn; Fontaine; Gable; Garner; Granger; H. Grant; Guinness; Heston; Hoskins; Hudson; J. Hurt; A. Huston; Jourdan; Karloff; Grace Kelly; Kingsley; Lancaster; C. Lee; Janet Leigh; Jerry Lewis; Lom; Massey; McQueen; Mercouri; Mifune; Mills; Mix; Murphy; Neeson; Nicholson; E. O'Brien; Oldman; Pleasence; Price; Reed; Robards; E. Robinson; Rooney; Maximilian Schell; Sellers; Signoret; Tracy; Van Damme; Wallach; Wayne; York; Zetterling.

McELHANEY, Joe. Essayist. Freelance film critic, New York. **Essays:** McCrea; Ritter.

MEDHURST, Andy. Essayist. Lecturer in Media Studies at the University of Sussex. Contributor to *Sight and Sound.* **Essays:** Evans; V. Redgrave.

MERHAUT, Vacláv. Essayist. Film historian and member of staff, Film Archives of Czechoslovakia, Prague. Author of *Actors and Actresses of the Italian Cinema;* co-author (with Karel Caslavsky) of *Hvezdy Ceskeho Filmu,* 1995. **Essays:** Mifune; Ullmann.

MILICIA, Joseph. Essayist. Professor of English, University of Wisconsin, Sheboygan Center. Contributor to *Multicultural Review, The New York Review of Science Fiction, Contemporary Literature,* among others. Author of articles on science fiction films for Gregg Press. **Essays:** Bujold; Hanks; N. Kinski; S. Lee; Reeves.

MONTY, Ib. Adviser and essayist. Director of Det Danske Filmmuseum, Copenhagen, since 1960. Literary and film critic for the newspaper *Morgenavisen Jyllands-Posten,* since 1958. Editor-in-chief of the film periodical *Kosmorama,* 1960-67. Author of *Leonardo da Vinci,* 1953; co-editor (with Morten Piil) of *Se-det-er film I-iii* (anthology of articles on film), 1964-66; editor of *TV Broadcasts on Films and Filmmakers,* 1972. **Essay:** Madsen and Schenstrøm.

MRAZ, John. Essayist. Researcher, Center for the Study of Contemporary History, University of Puebla, Mexico, since 1984. Distinguished Visiting Professor, Mexican-American Studies, San Diego State University, 1991. Visiting Professor, Art and Latin American Studies, University of Connecticut, 1990. Visiting Professor, History, University of California, Santa Cruz, 1988. Coordinator of Graphic History, Center for the Historical Study of the Mexican Labor Movement, 1981-83. Contributor to *Jump Cut.* **Essays:** Cantinflas; Félix; Infante.

MURPHY, Robert. Essayist. Lecturer in Film Studies at Sheffield City Polytechnic. Author of *Realism and Tinsel,* 1989, and *Sixties British Cinema,* 1992. **Essays:** Dors; Wisdom.

NARDUCY, Ray. Essayist. Film critic and historian, Chicago. **Essays:** J. Coburn; Weissmuller.

NEWMAN, Kim. Essayist. Freelance writer and broadcaster. Author of *Nightmare Movies,* 1988, and *Wild West Movies,* 1990. Contributor to *Sight and Sound, Empire, New Musical Express,* and other periodicals, and film critic for *Box Office* on Channel 4, London. Also a writer of fiction. **Essays:** Garner; R. Harris; Lom; Price.

NOLLETTI, Arthur, Jr. Essayist. Professor of English, Framingham State College, Massachusetts. Contributor to *Film Criticism, Jump Cut,* and *Journal of Popular Film and Television.* **Essays:** Seberg; Stanwyck.

OBALIL, Linda J. Essayist. Assistant, Special Effects Unit, Dreamscape, Bruce Cohn Curtis Productions/Bella productions, since 1983. **Essays:** Carradine; Chaney; Horton; Kaye; McDowall; Muni; Rathbone.

O'BRIEN, Daniel. Essayist. Freelance writer and critic, London. **Essays:** Reed; Stamp.

O'CONNOR, Margaret. Essayist. Freelance writer and lecturer, London. **Essays:** G. Fields; Lockwood; J. Roberts.

OKA, Susan. Adviser. Administrative/Acquisitions Librarian, Margaret Herrick Library, Academy of Motion Picture Arts and Sciences.

O'LEARY, Liam. Essayist. Film viewer, Radio Telefis Eireann, Dublin, 1966-86. Director, Liam O'Leary Film Archives, Dublin, from 1976. Producer, Abbey Theatre, 1944. Director of the Film History Cycle at the National Film Theatre, London, and Acquisitions Officer, National Film Archive, London, 1953-66; co-founder, 1936, and honorary secretary, 1936-44, Irish Film Society. Director of the films, *Our Country,* 1948, *Mr. Careless,* 1950, and *Portrait of Dublin,* 1951. Author of *Invitation to the Film,* 1945, *The Silent Cinema,* 1965, *Rex Ingram, Master of the Silent Cinema,* 1980, and *Cinema Ireland, 1896-1950,* 1990. Died 1992. **Essays:** Artaud; Barthelmess; Bertini; Fröhlich; Jannings; Menjou; Mozhukin; Nazimova; Rosay; Talmadge; Vanel.

OSHANA, Maryann. Essayist. Film historian, Northwestern University, Evanston, Illinois. Author of *Women of Color: A Filmography of Minority and Third World Women,* 1985. **Essays:** C. Coburn; Garfield; Holliday; B. Lee; McDaniel; Temple.

OTTER, Kelly. Essayist. Teacher and administrator, New York University. Doctoral candidate in arts and humanities. **Essays:** B. Andersson; Baxter; Binoche; Garson; Girardot; Karina; Olin; Shepard.

PALMER, R. Barton. Essayist. Professor of English, Clemson University; formerly professor of English, Georgia State University. Author of *Hollywood's Dark Cinema: The American Film Noir,* 1994, and *Perspectives on Film Noir,* 1996. Editor of *Studies in the Literary Imagination.* **Essays:** Ameche; Ball; Hawkins; D. Keaton; MacMurray; Malden; March; Nicholson; Palance; Peck; Quayle; Wilder.

PARDI, Robert. Essayist. M.A. in Film History/Criticism, University of Southern California. Staff writer for *The Motion Picture Guide.* Managing editor/chief reviewer of *Movies on TV* for six editions. Author of *Cable and TV.* Co-author of *Movie Blockbusters* and *The Complete Guide to Videocassette Movies.* Freelance contributor to *Baseline, Delphi Internet, Billboard, Cinemax, Film Journal, Video Business,* and *Cineaste.* **Essays:** Abril; Bancroft; Burstyn; Cagney; Caron; Cotten; J. Crawford; Cruise; Darnell; B. Davis; Day; de Havilland; Dietrich; Dunaway; Duvall; Field; H. Ford; Foster; Garland; Gere; Gibson; Harlow; Holden; Jennifer Jones; Gene Kelly; Kerr; Lange; Lansbury; V. Leigh; Loren; Mansfield; Mitchum; Moorehead; Moreau; Neill; Nelligan; O'Connor; O'Hara; O'Toole; Perkins; Quinn; B. Reynolds; Sarandon; Simmons; Smith; Steiger; Swanson; K. Turner; Woods; Wyman.

PASKIN, Sylvia. Essayist. Freelance film critic, London. **Essays:** R. Roberts; Rutherford; York.

PETLEY, Julian. Essayist. Lecturer in communications at Brunel University. Contributor to *Sight and Sound, Monthly Film Bulletin,* and *Broadcast.* **Essays:** Hoskins; Vogler; Werner.

RACHEVA, Maria. Essayist. Selector of films for the International Film Festival, Munich, since 1983. Teacher of film history, High School for

Cinema, Sofia, Bulgaria, 1974-81. Editor of the cultural review *Westermannns Monatschefte*, Munich, 1981-82. Author of *Presentday Bulgarian Cinema*, 1970, and *Kino: For and Against*, 1986; co-author (with Klaus Eder) of *Andrzej Wajda*, 1980. **Essays:** Mueller-Stahl; Tyszkiewicz.

RICHARDS, Nancy Jane. Essayist. Assistant Professor of Communications, Baker University, Baldwin, Kansas. Author of *James Agee: An Annotated Bibliography of Published Primary and Secondary Sources 1925-1985*, 1986. **Essays.** Modot, Purviance, Maria Schell.

SALAMIE, David E. Essayist. Contributing editor, third edition of the *International Dictionary of Films and Filmmakers, Actors and Actresses* volume. Freelance writer and co-owner of InfoWorks Development Group, a reference publication development and editorial services company. **Essays:** Benigni; Cantinflas; Constantine; Gélin; Giannini; Harrison; Huppert; K. Kinski; Lamarr; Masina; Montand; Mueller-Stahl; Noiret; Okada; Pryor; Remick; Rey; R. Ryan; Saint; Schygulla; Shaw; Ustinov; Volonté; Withers.

SATER, Richard. Essayist. Freelance writer and critic. **Essays:** Darnell; Francis; M. Hopkins; Kerr; Niven; W. Powell.

SCHUTH, H. Wayne. Essayist. Professor of Drama and Communications, University of New Orleans. Author of *Mike Nichols*, 1978. Member, Board of Trustees, University Film and Video Foundation. **Essays:** Del Rio; G. Scott.

SHOCHAT, Ella. Essayist. Freelance writer, New York. **Essay:** Topol.

SHORT, Don M. Essayist. Former instructor of film at York University, Toronto. **Essay:** G. Ford.

SIEGLOHR, Ulrike. Essayist. Film lecturer and writer, London. **Essay:** Schneider.

SILET, Charles L. P. Essayist. Professor of English, Iowa State University, Ames. Author of *Lindsay Anderson: A Guide to References and Resources*, 1979; co-editor of *Images of American Indians on Film: An Annotated Bibliography*, 1985. Contributor to *Quarterly Review of Film, Film Heritage, Journal of Popular Film*, and *Magill's Cinema Annual*. **Essays:** B. Andersson; Arthur; Björnstrand; Hudson; Lombard; Thulin.

SITNEY, P. Adams. Adviser. Lecturer, Princeton University. Formerly Director of Library and Publications, Anthology Film Archives. Author of *Film Culture Reader*, 1970, *Visionary Film*, 1974, *The Avant-Garde Film*, 1978, *Modernist Montage: The Obscurity of Vision in Cinema and Literature*, 1990, and *Visual Crises in Italian Cinema*, 1995.

SLIDE, Anthony. Adviser and essayist. Author and editor of more than 50 books on the history of popular entertainment, including *The Films of D. W. Griffith*, 1975, *The American Film Industry: A Historical Dictionary*, 1986, *Nitrate Won't Wait: A History of Film Preservation in the United States*, 1992, and *The Encyclopedia of Vaudeville*, 1994. Also editor of the Scarecrow Press "Filmmakers Series," and a documentary filmmaker. **Essays:** Astor; Ayres; Banderas; Banky; Buchanan; Fitzgerald; Gaynor; Harrison; Hart; W. Huston; Meredith; Mirren; Neagle; Novarro; Novello; R. Richardson; Sweet; Valentino; White.

SMALL, Edward S. Essayist. Director of Film Studies, University of Missouri, Columbia, since 1983. Executive Vice President, University Film and Video Association, 1983-86. Author of *Direct Theory: Experimental Film/Video as Major Genre*, 1994. **Essay:** Dean.

SPRINGER, Claudia. Essayist. Freelance writer, Chicago. **Essay:** Marx Brothers.

STAFFORD, Jeff. Essayist. Program consultant, Films Inc., Atlanta. **Essays:** B. Crawford; Grahame.

STEWART, Linda J. Essayist. Writer/festival judge, New York City. Writer/director of radio special "Fine Tuning," 1990; writer/reviewer for *Cinebooks Motion Picture Annual*, 1991, 1992, 1993; writer/editor, *Movie Blockbusters;* writer/on-air announcer, *The WNYE Concerthall;* judge, The International Film & Television Festival of New York, since 1988. **Essays:** J. Andrews; Christie; Gielgud; L. Grant; Peck; Scheider; Sharif; Sinatra, Stewart, Wilder.

STOYANOVA, Christina. Essayist. Freelance writer, Bulgaria. **Essays:** Maretskaya; Yankovsky.

TABERY, Karel. Essayist. Film researcher and historian, France. Historian/Archivist, Czechoslovakian Film Archives, Prague, 1974-82. **Essays:** Aimée; Barrault; Belmondo; Bergner; Berry; Blier; Bondarchuk; Cassel; Cuny; Delon; Feuillère; Fresnay; Montand.

THOMAS, Nicholas. Essayist. Editor of the second edition of the *International Dictionary of Films and Filmmakers*. **Essay:** Terry-Thomas.

THOMPSON, Frank. Essayist. Author of *William A. Wellman*, 1983, *Alamo Movies*, 1991, *Robert Wise: A Bio-Bibliography*, 1995, and *Lost Films: Important Movies that Disappeared*, 1996; editor of *Between Action and Cut: Five American Directors*, 1985. **Essays:** Baxter; Bellamy; Blondell; Davies; Ladd; Linder; Milland; Preston; D. Reynolds; E. Robinson; R. Taylor.

TOMLINSON, Doug. Essayist. Associate Professor of Film Studies, Montclair State College, New Jersey. Principal researcher for *Voices of Film Experience*, edited by Jay Leyda, 1977; editor of *Actors on Acting for the Screen*, 1994. Died 1992. **Essays:** Arkin; Beatty; L. Grant; Homolka; Krauss; Page; Presley; Rowlands; Sharif.

TSIANTIS, Lee. Essayist. Publicist for Twentieth Century-Fox, Atlanta, Georgia. Former lecturer in film. **Essays:** Marsh; Tierney.

TUDOR, Andrew. Essayist. Head of the Department of Sociology, University of York. Author of *Theories of Film: Image and Influence*, 1974, and *Monsters and Mad Scientists*, 1989. **Essays:** Eastwood; Newman.

UHLE, Frank. Essayist. Movie projectionist and librarian. Proofreader/researcher, *Psychotronic Video* magazine. **Essays:** Arthur; Chaney; G. Ford; Goddard; Malone; McDowall; Presley; Robertson; Stanton; L. Young.

URGOŠÍKOVÁ, Blažena. Essayist. Film historian. Head of Department of Film History and Cataloguing, Národní filmovýarchiv Praha. Author of *A Famous Era of the Swedish Cinema*, 1969, *Rudolph Valentino*, 1970, *History of Science Fiction Films*, 1973, 1982, *Remakes*, 1977, and *Czech Fiction Films*, 1995. **Essays:** Brodský; Łomnicki; Nowicki; Olbrychski.

VALENTINE, Fiona. Essayist. Member of Faculty, School of Speech, Northwestern University, Evanston, Illinois. **Essays:** Hackman; Redford; E. Taylor; Wood.

VASUDEVAN, Ravi. Essayist. Fellow, Nehru Centre for Contemporary Studies, New Delhi. Formerly film critic of *The Sunday Observer*, Delhi. **Essay:** Kumar.

VENKATACHALLAM, Usha. Essayist. Graduate student of film and video, American University, Washington, D.C. Documentary filmmaker. **Essays:** Anand; Azmi; Chatterjee; Kumar.

WALKER, Mark. Essayist. Teacher and freelance writer, Maryland. Co-author (with Stuart Kaminsky) of *Writing for Television*, 1988; author of *Vietnam Veteran Films*, 1991. **Essays:** Belushi; Costner.

WALSH, George. Essayist. Publisher and freelance writer, Chicago. **Essays:** Day; Kortner.

WEBB, Graham. Essayist. Freelance writer, artist, and researcher, London. Animator on *Yellow Submarine*, 1967. Co-editor of *The Great Movie Cartoon Parade*, 1975, and *The Great Cartoon Stars: A Who's Who*, 1979. **Essay:** J. Barrymore.

WELSH, James M. Essayist. Associate Professor of English, Salisbury State University. Editor, *Literature/Film Quarterly*. Author of *His Majesty the American: The Films of Douglas Fairbanks Sr.*, 1977, *Abel Gance*, 1978, and *Peter Watkins: A Guide to References and Resources*, 1986. **Essays:** A. Bates; Cagney; Fairbanks; J. Fonda; Stallone.

WEST, Dennis. Essayist. Associate Professor, University of Idaho, Moscow, since 1981. Director, Indiana University Film Studies Program, 1976-77. Contributor on Latin American and Spanish cinema to *Latin American Research Review, Cineaste, New Scholar*, and others. **Essay:** Villagra.

WILSON, James D. Essayist. Professor of English, Georgia State University, Atlanta, since 1984. **Essay:** Henreid.

WILSON, Richard. Essayist. Freelance writer. **Essays:** Karina; Mansfield; Raft.

WINE, Bill. Essayist. Assistant Professor of Communications, La Salle College, Philadelphia, since 1981. Film, theater, and television critic, *Camden Courier-Post*, 1974-81. **Essays:** Brennan; K. Douglas; Eddy; Falk; Gassman; Giannini; Lansbury; Pleasence; Robertson; Shaw; Ustinov; Walker.

WINNING, Rob. Essayist. Author and film scholar, Pittsburgh. **Essays:** Brandauer; Bronson; Cushing; Lake; Malone; Oates; Robards; Scheider; Streep.

WOOD, Robin. Adviser and essayist. Professor of Film Study, Department of Fine Arts, Atkinson College, York University, Toronto, 1977-90. Member of the Film Studies Department, Queen's University, Kingston, Ontario, 1969-72, and University of Warwick, England, 1973-77. Author of *Hitchcock's Films*, 1965, *Arthur Penn*, 1968, *Ingmar Bergman*, 1969, *Antonioni* (co-author), 1971, *The Apu Trilogy of Satyajit Ray*, 1971, *Personal Views: Explorations in Film*, 1976, *Howard Hawks*, 1977, *The American Nightmare: Essays on the Horror Film* (co-author), 1979, *Hollywood from Vietnam to Reagan*, 1985, and *Hitchcock's Films Revisited*, 1989. Took early retirement to devote himself to fiction, 1990. Novels: *That Last and Fatal Time*, 1990, and *I Remember . . .*, 1991. **Essays:** H. Andersson; Bergman; Dafoe; Dahlbeck; J. Davis; De Niro; Depp; Dickinson; Hayward; K. Hepburn; J. Hurt; Jourdan; Laurel and Hardy; Janet Leigh; Magnani; Mineo; Moorehead; Neal; Pacino; Perkins; Remick; Rey; J. Russell; Ryu; Sanda; Simmons; Stone; Travolta; Washington; Wayne; Wiest.

YECK, Joanne L. Essayist. Lecturer on humanities and film, Art Center College of Design, Pasadena. Co-author (with Tom McGreevey) of *Movie Westerns*, 1994. **Essays:** Bacall; Gable.

ZUCKER, Carole. Adviser and essayist. Associate Professor, Department of Cinema, Concordia University, Montreal. Author of *The Idea of Image: Josef von Sternberg's Dietrich Films*, 1988, and *Figures of Light: Actors and Directors Illuminate the Art of Film Acting*, 1995; editor of *Making Visible the Invisible: An Anthology of Original Essays on Film Acting*, 1990. Regular contributor to *Film Quarterly*. **Essays:** Dreyfuss; Ganz.